Comics Buyer's Guide

2007

13th Edition

Comic Book Checklist & Price Guide

1961- Present

Maggie Thompson • Brent Frankenhoff

Peter Bickford • John Jackson Miller

Published by

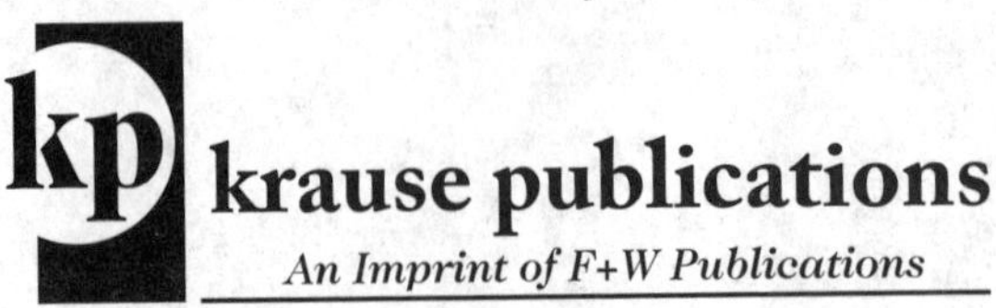

700 East State Street • Iola, WI 54990-0001
715-445-2214 • 888-457-2873

Our toll-free number to place an order or obtain
a free catalog is (800) 258-0929.

Library of Congress Catalog Number: 1082-5649

ISBN 13-digit: 978-0-89689-417-4
ISBN 10-digit: 0-89689-417-7

Designed by Stacy Bloch and Sandi Morrison

Edited by
Brent Frankenhoff
Maggie Thompson
John Jackson Miller

Printed in the United States of America

Contents

Thanks, first to **you**, for buying this book — and also to the many people who helped us put this book together. As ever, there are so many of them to thank that we're bound to miss a few. To anyone who should be thanked but isn't (you know who you are): We're sorry, and you know we couldn't have done this without you.

First and foremost, without the copious contributions of *ComicBase* developer Peter Bickford, this edition simply wouldn't exist. While his research has often paralleled our own, he has also obtained information to which we didn't have access, just as our information has added many titles to his computerized comics database program.

John Jackson Miller has contributed tons of additional data to the database again this year (including all sorts of new data on Harvey and Archie titles).

Ray Sidman has diligently provided a great deal of help in entering new titles and other information.

That brings us to the publishers and individual creators who provided copies of their titles, so that we could maintain a database based on actually published material. We thank them all and encourage others to do the same.

Thanks also to the readers of our previous editions who have been providing additional data on their favorite titles. This year again, special thanks goes to Howard Michaels Jr., Carl Tietz, Perry Parsons, and Harold Crump, who provided an ongoing stream of information to make our compendium of information even more detailed and precise. Thanks as well go to Nick Pope, James Jobe, Byron Glass, and Andrew Rathbun, who helped us compile the most complete listing ever of Marvel and DC Whitman variants.

This is the third time we've had original art on the cover of this work: Thanks go to Marvel Characters Inc. and artist Alex Horley for use of it — and to Marc Patten and Destination Entertainment for helping make it all happen.

Thanks go as well to our own behind-the-scenes people, including: Tammy Kuhnle and Steve Duberstein, computer services; Sandi Morrison and Stacy Bloch in our book production department; and the entire pop culture division at Krause Publications.

Most of all, we acknowledge the work of Don Thompson, who nursed this project through the last 11 years of his life. We miss you, Don.

And, again, we thank you all.

Maggie Thompson
Brent Frankenhoff
John Jackson Miller
Iola, Wisconsin
September 21, 2006

SAVE YOUR COMICS!

We see it all the time: Rare and valuable comics, going for pennies on the dollar in estate sales.

Or rotting away, stuffed in corners in wet basements.

Because most people don't know what they have. Whether their comics are rare and valuable — or whether they're plentiful and worth less (though not worth*less*). And because most people don't know how best to take care of the comics they have.

But you won't have that problem — ***The CBG Comic Book Checklist & Price Guide*** is here to help.

We're the people behind ***Comics Buyer's Guide***, the world's longest-running magazine about comics. Started in 1971, it's been published continuously and recently passed the 1,625-issue mark. We've maintained a price guide since the early 1980s — and in the early 1990s, we published the first edition of this *Checklist* as both a price guide and a collectors' utility for comics published after 1960.

Since then, we've added to the line with the mammoth ***CBG Standard Catalog of Comic Books***, which includes everything that's in this volume plus story titles, circulation figures, and comics from the 1930s, 1940s, and 1950s. Of course, it's a monster of a book — the latest edition is 1,624 pages — so the *Checklist* maintains its value as a quick and handy reference for the comics you're most likely to find. (It's also a lot easier to carry around to conventions and stores!)

So the role of the *Checklist* has evolved somewhat — but it's still intended to function in a number of fashions.

There's more than one way to use it.

You can use it as a "have" list, in which you maintain an inventory of the comics you're collecting. (Make an "X" in the box for each one you have. If you don't use the "X" system, you can use your own symbols indicating what you please, including condition, in the open box. You can then see at a glance what you're still looking for of a title you want to collect.)

You can use it as a guide to show prices you can expect to pay for items, if you look for them in comics shops throughout the country, online, or at conventions. The prices listed are arrived at by surveying comics shops, online sales, convention sales, and mail-order houses.

With that information, our price guide reflects what a smart person with those choices would be willing to pay for a given issue.

You can use it as a guide for value, when you're buying or trading items.

And you can carry it with you in your comics storage box, because it's sized to fit in a comics box.

Condition is vital.

Whether you're buying or selling comic books, one of the most important factors in setting the price is the condition of the material.

A scuffed, torn "reading copy" (that is, one that is suitable for reading but

*Specially sized comics bags — like these, from **Bags Unlimited**, one of several providers of comics storage devices — can slow the deterioration of your comics.*

not for getting high prices at resale) will bring only a fraction of the price of a copy of the same issue which looks as though it has just come off the newsstand.

Picky collectors will even go through all the copies on a newsstand so as to buy the one in best condition. [Even a so-called "newsstand mint" copy of *Fantastic Four* #1 may have what is called "Marvel chipping" (a frayed right edge), since many of those early-'60s issues were badly cut by the printer.]

On the other hand, beat-up copies can provide bargains for collectors whose primary focus is *reading* the comic-book story. The same goes for reprints of comics which would otherwise be hard to find.

In fact, you may find prices on poor-condition copies even lower than the prices in this guide, depending on the attitude of the seller. It's a good time to get into collecting comics for the *fun* of it.

A major change in the comics-collecting world, CGC grading, has meant a huge jump in prices for certain hotly collected issues in almost-perfect condition. The third-party graders of Comics Guaranty LLC evaluate the condition of submitted copies and then encapsulate the graded issue in a labeled container. Because of the independent nature of the process and the reliability of the evaluating team, confidence in buying such items has meant a premium over the standard price in that condition.

For example, at press time, a CGC 9.4 (Near Mint) is bringing at auction *four times* our Near Mint price for non-encapsulated comics. More information on the company can be found in the pages ahead.

Our price guide is constantly evolving.

For comics, maybe the right word is "mutating."

Each year, the most important changes in this guide from previous editions are, of course, the addition of countless chunks of data that we have compiled from consulting physical copies of the issues in question. (Thanks again to the many who helped.) Alone among checklists of Silver Age comics, this book contains original cover data and original pricing information for tens of thousands of comics.

We've also provided more than 2,000 cover photos with enough additional information, we hope, to whet a collector's appetite. We want to provide the most accurate picture of what you, as a customer, can expect to pay for comics when you walk into a shop or comics convention with your want list.

Answers for readers who are NEW TO COMICS...

Readers have been kind enough to ask many questions about our price guide. To help you make the best use of this volume, we're answering many of them here (and we're answering questions you didn't ask, too, in an attempt to provide more information than you can possibly use).

Why do we need a price guide at all?

We've spent 24 years developing a guide so that buyers and sellers of back issues will have help knowing what a consumer with various buying choices can expect to pay, if he's looking — for example — for that issue that will complete his run of the two DC series of *Shade the Changing Man*. The collector will find that even the highest-priced issue in the best condition probably won't cost more than about $4 — and that's the sort of information that can motivate a casual reader to become a collector.

Moreover, we try to provide helpful information to people who purchase it in order to have a (yes) guide to buying comics. Pricing information is just *part* of what we offer. In fact, we are increasingly intrigued by the more detailed information you'll find in this book, including character appearances and publishing anomalies.

Why can't I find a title in your list?

We're working constantly to expand the listings themselves and increase the information on those we already provide. Check out what we have included, and — if you have something we're not listing — please let us know the details!

We need to know the information as given in the indicia of the issue (that's the tiny print, usually on the first few pages, that gives the publishing information): the full title, the number, and the issue month and year — and the U.S. price given on the cover. If you find work by a creator on our abbreviations list that we haven't noted in this guide, please include that information. If there's a significant event (especially as given in the abbreviations list), please include that, too. This is an *annual* volume designed to consolidate our information — but our monthly *Comics Buyer's Guide* runs updated information (with commentary on recent sales activity), and we add to the data constantly — including updates to such market changes as the effects of CGC grading.

Check, too, on whether you're looking up the title as it appears in the indicia. For example, we list *The Vampire Lestat (Anne Rice's)*, not *Anne Rice's The Vampire Lestat*; we list *Mack Bolan: The Executioner (Don Pendleton's)*, not *Don Pendleton's Mack Bolan: The Executioner*. Many Marvel titles have adjectives. *Hulk*, for example, is listed as *Incredible Hulk*.

What's in this book?

This Silver Age and more recent price guide began as a quarterly update of activity in comics published since 1961, as reflected in prices comics shops were likely to charge. Moreover, the focus was pretty much limited to Silver Age super-hero titles — in fact, Silver Age super-hero titles *that were being published when the price guide began*. This meant that such titles as *OMAC*, a Silver Age title that starred a super-hero but was not still being published by 1983, didn't get listed in that earliest edition. It also meant that so-called "funny animal" titles, "war" titles, and the like were not included.

However, once the listings were begun (not by *Comics Buyer's Guide* staff, incidentally; the material was started

for another publication), Don Thompson took over the compilation. From that point, every effort was made to include every issue of every comic book received in the office. However, since the entries were not on a database and had to be compressed to fit the space available, annotation, dates, and original prices were not usually part of the listing. On the other hand (and because of Don's care, once he took over the project), material which was often overlooked by other reference publishers has been listed from the beginning in the *CBG* listings. *Concrete* and *Teenage Mutant Ninja Turtles*, for example, were first listed in *CBG*'s price listings.

And we continue to fill in remaining information whenever we get it. Our cooperative agreement with *ComicBase* has led to the inclusion of hundreds of new titles and issues, as well as a wealth of variant editions.

What is the "Silver Age?"

Comic-book collectors divide the history of comics into the "Golden Age" and the "Silver Age." "Golden Age" indicates the first era of comic-book production — the '30s and '40s. It was a time of incredible creation in the field, when such characters as Superman and Batman first appeared. It's the era *before* material in this price guide was published.

"Silver Age" is used to indicate a period of comic-book production of slightly less (nostalgic?) luster than that of the Golden Age. It is usually considered to have begun with the publication of the first revival of a '40s super-hero: the appearance of The Flash in *Showcase* #4 (Sep-Oct 1956). However, that was a lone appearance at the time, so this price guide concentrates on titles from the time Marvel reentered the superhero field with the publication of *Fantastic Four* #1 (1961). Listings for such long-running titles as *Batman, Superman,* and others have been extended back to mid-1956.

This guide lists #8 and #10. Where's #9?

We haven't seen a copy and can't verify its existence. There was a time when comics collectors could safely assume that issue numbers would run in normal sequence, when no numbers were skipped and when there were no special numbers to confuse completists. That's not the case any more. What we need from those who want to help add to our information is confirmation that an item has *actually been published.*

This guide *does* include information on published material that was not widely distributed. Eternity's *Uncensored Mouse* #2, for example, was pulled from distribution after legal problems with The Walt Disney Company — but copies *do* exist. So few transactions involve it, however, that retailers have not yet established a standard price for the item.

So do you own all these comics?

No, many publishers and collectors have helped us over the years by sending photocopies of indicia, records of publication, annotations, and the like — all of which has permitted us to provide collectors with more information every year. What *ComicBase* and we cannot do — and *do* not do — is pull information from other price guides or from announcements of what is *scheduled* for publication. The former would not be proper; the latter leads to errors — the sort of errors that have been known to become imbedded in some price guides' information files.

This is also why information sometimes seems varied. Every effort has been made to make the notations consistent, but this list has more than 100,000 individual issues coordinated between *ComicBase* and Krause Publications, so this can be an arduous task. Nevertheless, we're whittling away at problems between issues of *Comics Buyer's Guide* and assorted other projects.

Why do some of your listings say (first series), (second series), etc., while others have (Vol. 1), (Vol. 2), and so on? Is there a difference?

Although publishers may begin a series again at #1, they often don't update the volume number in the indicia, which leads to the (first series) and

(second series) notations. If the volume number changes (and it's a clear change, as in the case of Marvel's "Heroes Reborn" and "Heroes Return" title restarts), that is what differentiates the series.

On the other hand, when the volume number changes each year (as was the case with some early Silver Age material) but the series number is ongoing in sequence (Vol. 2, #21), then we don't note that change. Marvel's return to original numbering for *Fantastic Four* and *Amazing Spider-Man* in mid-2003 has caused both titles' later listings, beginning with #500 for each, to revert to the respective title's first volume. To help show where the issues from later volumes of those series fall in sequences, we've added parenthetical notations to the original numbers like this: 1 (442).

I've heard some of my square-bound comics referred to variously as "bookshelf format," "prestige format," and "Dark Knight format." What's the difference?

Various formats — usually reserved for special projects (mini-series and one-shots) — have different names, depending on the publisher. We use the term "prestige format" generically to indicate a fancier package than the average comic book. Marvel refers to some titles in upscale formats as "bookshelf format," whereas DC initially solicited some of its titles in the format of *Batman: The Dark Knight* as "Dark Knight format." Details of fancy formats can be widely varied.

I tried to sell my comics to a retailer, but he wouldn't even offer me 10% of the prices you list. Is he trying to cheat me? Are your prices wrong?

Remember, our prices are based on what an informed collector with some choices is willing to pay for a comic book, not necessarily what a shop is charging or paying for that comic book. A shop has huge overhead and needs to tailor its stock to match the interest shown by its customers. If no one locally is buying comics starring Muggy-Doo, Boy Cat, it doesn't matter that *Muggy-Doo, Boy Cat* is bringing high prices elsewhere in the country.

Comics listed at their original prices may be showing no movement in most comics shops. In such cases, a retailer won't usually be interested in devoting store space to such titles, no matter *how* nice they are or *how* much you're discounting them.

I'm a publisher, and I'd be willing to buy a hundred copies of my first issue at the price you list. I get calls from all over America from would-be buyers who would pay 10 times the price you give here for out-of-print issues of my comics. What's going on?

A publisher like you hears from faithful fans across the nation. A comics shop deals with a market of one community or smaller. You're dealing with a narrow, focused market of aficionados of your product who are looking for the specific issues they're missing. And with more and more online offerings, those fans find it easier to seek you out.

As a result, a publisher who has back issues for sale may get higher prices than readers will find in this checklist.

It doesn't mean you're ripping off fans; it means fans looking to buy that material are competing within a nationwide pool; the Internet may eventually put everyone in the same pool.

Can I just order the back-issue comics I want from Comics Buyer's Guide?

This price guide is just that: a guide to the average back-issue prices comics shops are likely to charge their customers.

We maintain no back-issue stock for sale; we leave that to retailers who specialize in back issues. (Start with your local shops. You'll be able to check out the variety of material available and take a look in advance at what you're buying.)

Comics Buyer's Guide itself is the magazine of the comic-book field. As such, it carries ads from retailers across the country. You can check those advertisements for specific back

issues that you're looking for. You can even take out a "wanted" ad to locate particular items, if that appeals to you. Subscription information can be found at ***www.cbgxtra.com***.

What are "cover variants"?

These occur when publishers try to increase "collectibility" of and interest in a title by releasing an issue with an assortment of covers. This is in hopes that completists will want to buy multiple copies, instead of just one. (The practice even spread to publications like *TV Guide*.) So how are these performing as "rare" back issues? So far: poorly. Prices may rise at the time of release, but they usually fall again relatively quickly.

What's the first thing to do when I find a bunch of old comics?

If you've found a box of old comics in the attic and wonder what to do next, the first thing to do is find out what you've got.

The same goes when you're looking for what you want to buy.

Here are some basics: Look at the copyright dates; if there are multiple dates, look at the *last* date. (If they're before 1950, chances are the comics are considered "Golden Age," and they're not covered in this price guide. Comics from the mid-1950s and later are Silver Age or more recent.)

Almost all comics are collected and identified by title and issue number. Look at the indicia, the fine print on the inside front page or inside front cover. That's what you'll use to find a specific issue in this or any other price guide. You'll want to check the issue title as given there — and the issue number.

What's the second thing to look at when I find a bunch of old comics?

Evaluate the condition of the copies. What does the comic book look like? Check the "condition" pages of our price guide to get a feel for the shape your comics are in.

If they're beaten up, enjoy them for reading but don't expect to get a lot of money for them. For this reason, many beginning collectors focus on exactly such poor issues, getting the pleasure of reading without making a heavy investment.

What's next for comic-book collecting?

The Internet has gained in its importance to collectors, e-mail is connecting collectors around the world, a third-party grading service has led to incredible price variations in some back issues, and computers are permitting collectors, as well as retailers, to monitor what they've got, what condition it's in, and what they want to buy.

One advance we continue to work on is the expansion of the information in our files on as many back issues as possible.

To that end, the assistance of Human Computing's *ComicBase* program has been invaluable. Our combined informational base has grown rapidly, and we look forward to an even greater mutual compilation of data. Collectors who choose to do so will be able to access the information in both electronic and printed form. Both companies have for years been in an aggressive program to improve and increase the data for collectors, and collectors today are already experiencing services not available in the 1900s.

So it'll help my collecting to have a computer?

You bet. If you have a home computer, you'll find it increases your sources for buying and selling. (And *ComicBase* can help in your inventory.)

Some sites of special interest include:

www.cbgxtra.com
(our own official site)

www.ebay.com
www.amazon.com
www.diamondcomics.com

But they're not the only spots comics collectors will find fascinating. Surf the Web to find more!

CONDITION!

Why are comics from the 1940s, 1950s, and 1960s generally considered sound investment material, when comics from last Wednesday aren't?

Part of that is because comics are literally living things — they were once trees, after all — and their natural inclination over the years is to decompose.

So even if the number of copies around to begin with can be determined, there's a mortality factor at work, meaning comics in great shape are going to be harder and harder to find over time. Even if they haven't been loved to death through multiple readings and spine folds, comics are still going to try to turn yellow and brittle.

Collectors can slow that process with **storage devices**, ranging from the very expensive to the makeshift. The most common archival storage solution involves products made from **Mylar**, a transparent chemically inert substance.

Much more common are bags made from plastic, most commonly polypropylene, of varying thicknesses and backing boards with coated surfaces.

In general, the cheaper the method, the less protection it tends to afford.

Communicating the condition of your comics to buyers — and understanding what condition sellers' comics are in — requires knowing a few simple terms.

For the last few decades, back-issue comic books have been sold with a designation indicating their condition.

The eight grades recognized by the **CBG Comic Book Checklist & Price Guide**, *Comics Buyer's Guide*, and *ComicBase* appear on pages 13-17, along with aids to help you see what each condition basically allows.

The names:

Mint
Near Mint
Very Fine
Fine
Very Good
Good
Fair
Poor

The terms seen above have universal acceptance, even if different price guides — and, indeed, individual collectors and dealers — may not fully agree when it comes to what the attributes a comic book in each grade should have.

It's that difference of opinion, in fact, that led to third-party grading, described in detail after our grading and defects guide...

Photo Grading Guide

When comics are compared with the Photo Grading Guide, it's easy to see there are many comics which fall between categories in something of an infinite gradation. For example, a "Fair" condition comic book (which falls between "Good" and "Poor") may have a soiled, slightly damaged cover, a badly rolled spine, cover flaking, corners gone, tears, and the like. It is an issue with multiple problems but it is intact — and some collectors enjoy collecting in this grade for the fun of it. Tape may be present and is always considered a defect.

The condition of a comic book is a vital factor in determining its price.

MINT

(Abbreviated **M, Mt**)

This is a perfect comic book. Its cover has full luster, with edges sharp and pages like new. There are no signs of wear or aging. It is not imperfectly printed or off-center. "Mint" means just what it says.

[The term for this grade is the same one used for CGC's 10.0 grade.]

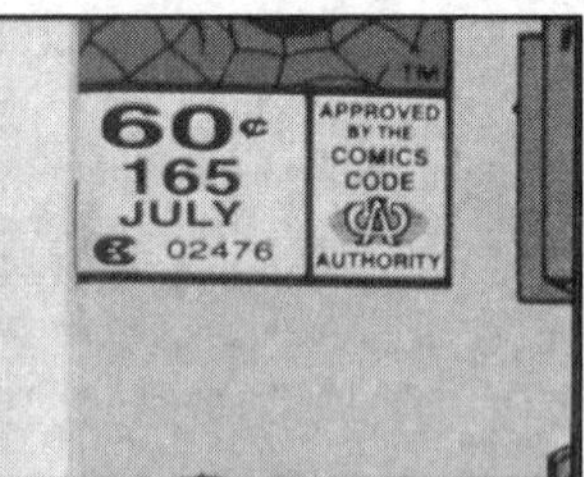

NEAR MINT

(Abbreviated **NM**)

This is a nearly perfect comic book.

Its cover shows barely perceptible signs of wear. Its spine is tight, and its cover has only minor loss of luster and only minor printing defects. Some discoloration is acceptable in older comics — as are signs of aging.

[The term for this grade is the same one used for CGC's 9.4 grade.]

VERY FINE

(Abbreviated **VF**)
This is a nice comic book with beginning signs of wear. There can be slight creases and wrinkles at the staples, but it is a flat, clean issue with definite signs of being read a few times. There is some loss of the original gloss, but it is in general an attractive comic book.
[The term for this grade is the same one used for CGC's 8.0 grade.]

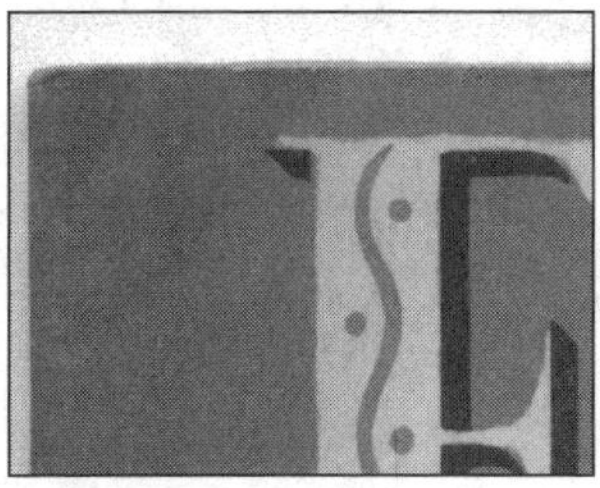

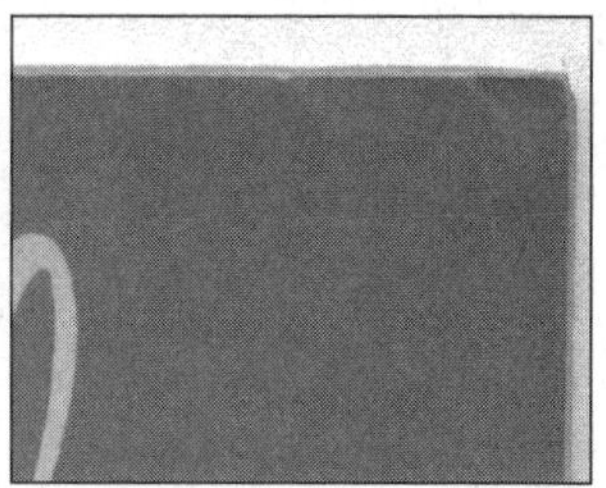

FINE

(Abbreviated **F, Fn**)
This comic book's cover is worn but flat and clean with no defacement. There is usually no cover writing or tape repair. Stress lines around the staples and more rounded corners are permitted. It is a good-looking issue at first glance.
[The term for this grade is the same one used for CGC's 6.0 grade.]

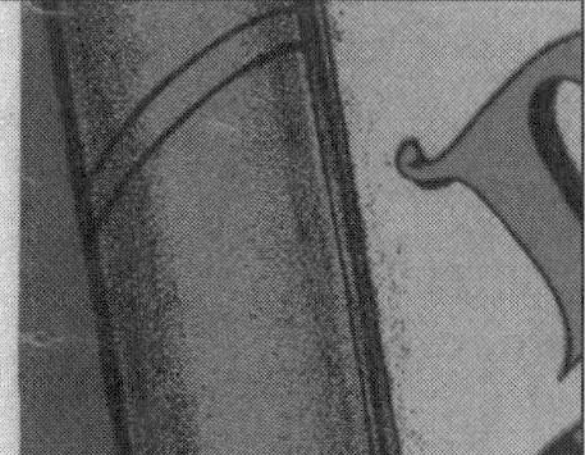

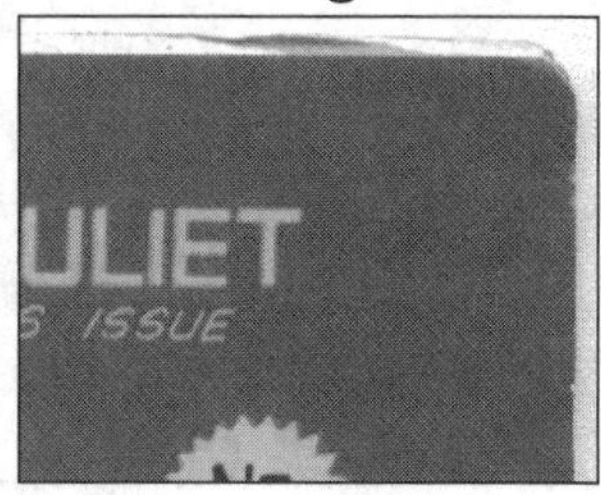

VERY GOOD

(Abbreviated **VG, VGd**)
Most of the original gloss is gone from this well-read issue.
There are minor markings, discoloration, and/or heavier stress lines around the staples and spine. The cover may have minor tears and/or corner creases, and spine-rolling is permissible.
[The term for this grade is the same one used for CGC's 4.0 grade.]

GOOD

(Abbreviated **G, Gd**)
This is a very worn comic book with nothing missing.
Creases, minor tears, rolled spine, and cover flaking are permissible. Older Golden Age comic books often come in this condition.
[The term for this grade is the same one used for CGC's 2.0 grade.]

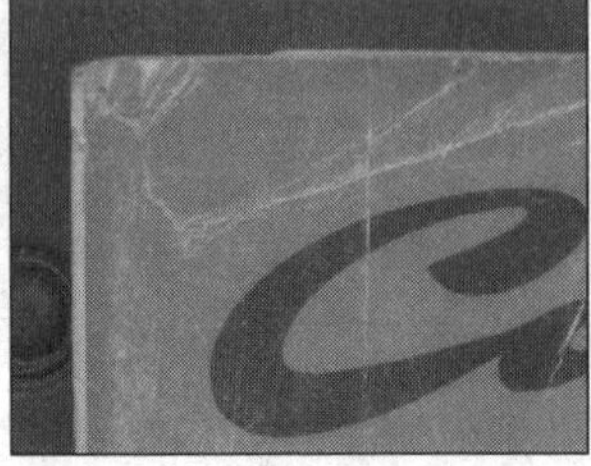
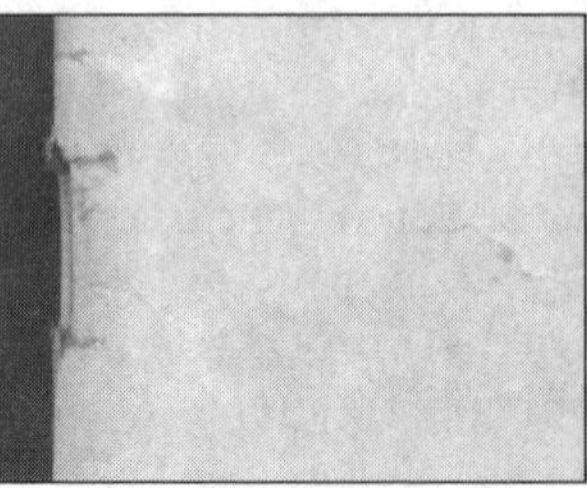

FAIR

(Abbreviated **FA, Fr**)
This comic book has multiple problems but is structurally intact.
Copies may have a soiled, slightly damaged cover, a badly rolled spine, cover flaking, corners gone, and tears. Tape may be present and is always considered a defect.
[The term for this grade is the same one used for CGC's 1.0 grade.]

POOR

(Abbreviated **P, Pr**)
This issue is damaged and generally considered unsuitable for collecting.
While the copy may still contain some readable stories, major defects get in the way. Copies may be in the process of disintegrating and may do so with even light handling.
[The term for this grade is the same one used for CGC's 0.5 grade.]

Guide to Defects

Theoretically, given a set of grading rules, determining the condition of a comic book should be simple. But flaws vary from item to item, and it can be difficult to pin one label on a particular issue — as with a sharp issue with a coupon removed. Another problem lies in grading historically significant vs. run-of-the-mill issues.

The examples shown here represent specific defects listed. These defects need to be taken into account when grading, but should *not* be the sole determinant of a comic's grade.

(For example, the copy with stamped arrival date, off-center staple is *not* in mint condition aside from those defects.)

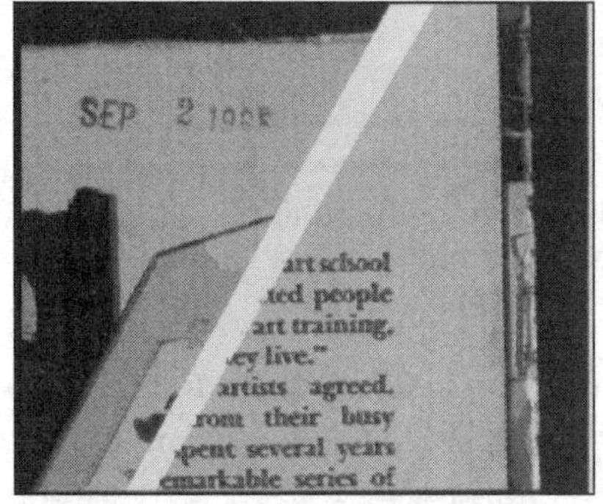

Stamped arrival date and off-center cover and off-center stapling.
Minor defects. Some will not call it "Mint"; some will.

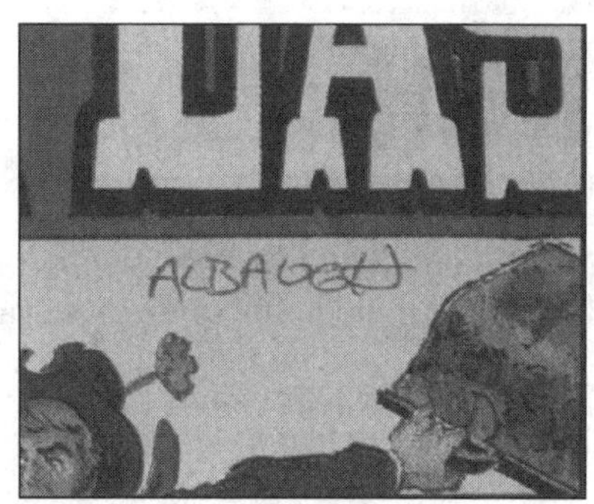

Writing defacing cover.
Marking can include filling in light areas or childish scribbling. Usually no better than "Good."

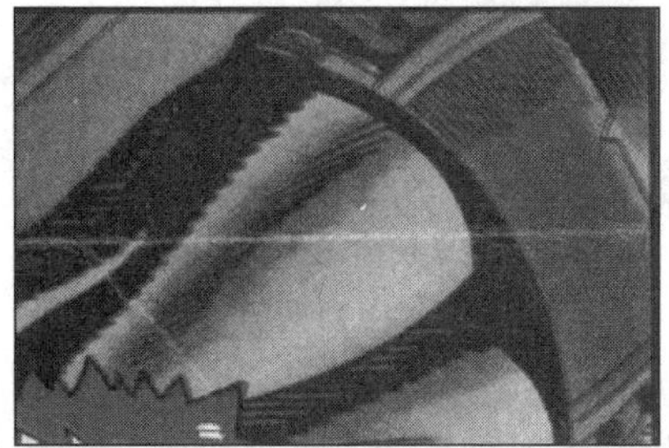

Subscription crease.
Comic books sent by mail were often folded down the middle, leaving a permanent crease. Definitely no better than "Very Good"; probably no better than "Good."

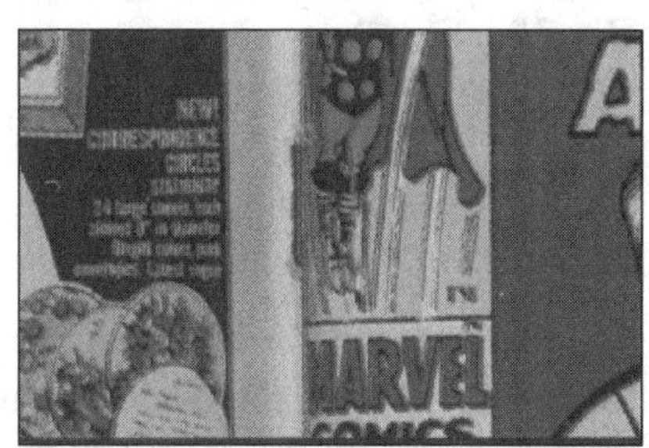

Rusty staple.
Caused by dampness during storage, rust stains around staples may be minor — or more apparent. No better than "Very Good."

Chunk missing.
Sizable piece missing from the cover (front or back).
No better than "Fair."

Water damage.
Varies from simple page-warping to staining shown here on Jimmy's shirt. Less damage than this could be "Very Good"; this is no better than "Good."

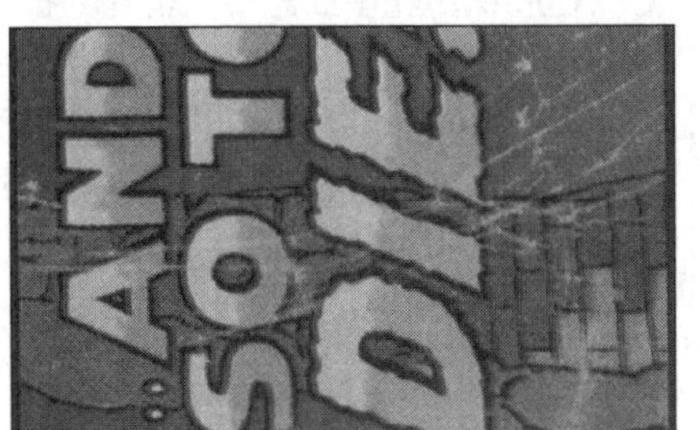

Multiple folds and wrinkles.
No better than "Fair" condition.

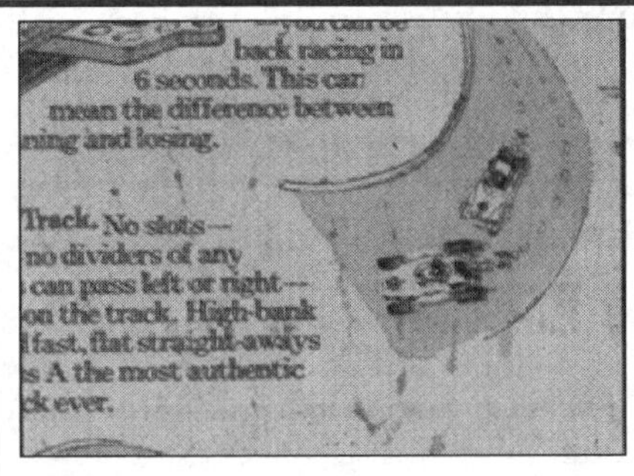

Stains.
Can vary widely, depending on cause. These look like mud — but food, grease, and the like also stain. No better than "Good."

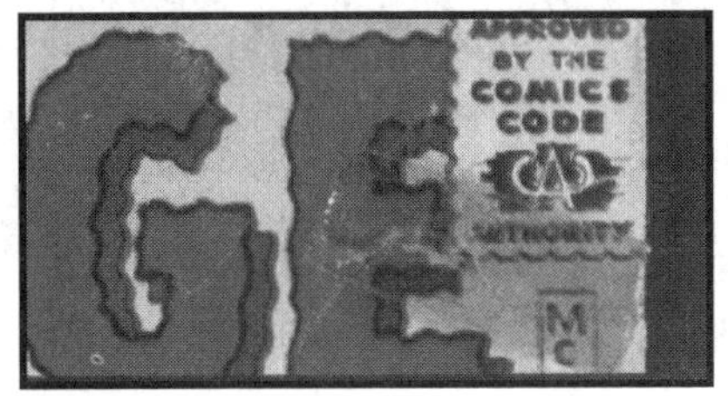

Tape.
This extreme example of tape damage is used to show *why* tape shouldn't be used on a comic book — or *any* book — for repairs. *All* tape (even so-called "magic" tape) ages badly — as does rubber cement. Use of tape usually means "Fair," at best.

Rolled Spine.
Caused by folding back each page while reading — rather than opening the issue flat. Repeated folding permanently bent the spine. *May* be corrected, but the issue is no better than "Very Good."

PRICING!

Traditionally, comics price guides have relied solely on those "in-the-know" — advisors with recent experience in buying or selling comics.

While a method tried by most pricing publications at one time or another over the years, its shortcomings are readily apparent. Advisor information sometimes tended to be anecdotal, speaking in broad terms about entire lines rather than in specifics about particular issues in certain grades. Price guides often received advice in the form of spoken or written reports, rather than spreadsheets or other electronic formats likelier to deal in numerical detail.

And, too often, critics charged, advisors — most of whom were also retailers themselves — provided the prices they would have liked to have sold comics at, rather than the prices that they had actually sold comics at.

Wishful thinking (plus a simple business desire not to devalue their inventory) on behalf of advisors therefore tended to drive pricing in many guides up, up, up — even when prices were clearly falling for thousands of comic books.

The ***Comic Book Checklist and Price Guide*** determines a single Near-Mint price for each comic book through research by parties with no vested interest in seeing prices increase. Additionally, sales of CGC-graded copies are also analyzed, with the current sales ratios for non-encapsulated comics applied to the CGC prices to determine how the market is reacting.

Ungraded-copy price research

This volume includes a Near-Mint price for each of the comic books listed herein. The prices are the result of a combined effort by Human Computing, producers of *ComicBase*, and the staff of *Comics Buyer's Guide*.

Human Computing has set more than 1 million prices for comic books over the years. It's investigated every title at least once, usually multiple times over the years, rechecking whenever a new trend surfaces. Convention sales, mail-order sales, and shop prices throughout the United States are gathered on a continual basis.

Comics Buyer's Guide has used many of the same methods, including making reference to the largest sortable database of actual online transactions ever assembled in comics. Since 2000, the *Comics Buyer's Guide* staff has downloaded hundreds of thousands of completed transactions from the eBay auction service, including every single auction involving comic books graded by CGC.

These transactions are sorted by publisher, title, issue number, and grade, and a range of prices is determined. These transactions have been used to inform, rather than set, the prices for "unslabbed" comics seen herein. One or two transactions, even for a high-profile rare comic book, can't always be solely counted on to estimate the typical going rate everywhere else.

The highest price isn't always right. Our philosophy isn't to publish the highest prices we can find to make people feel better about their collections, but rather to publish the prices that smart collectors shopping at a variety of retail, convention, and online venues are likely to find.

If you're in a remote area with only one shop or the Internet to rely on, the prices you're likely to find will be higher. Likewise, a comic book with some pedigree — having come from a famous collection — may also sell for more.

We've included a handy multiplier bar at the bottom of each page of the price guide to help determine prices in the other grades. The full list of all grades appears at right.

Note that **one size does not necessarily fit all when it comes to these ratios.** Most Very Fine books fetch a third less than their Near Mint equivalents — but some very rare books fetch more, and some newer ones bring less. These figures are provided as a guide.

To find prices for other grades for comic books **not graded by CGC, multiply our listed NM prices by:**	
Mint: 150%	F-: 30%
NM/M:125%	VG/F: 25%
NM+: 110%	VG+: 23%
NM-: 90%	**Very Good: 20%**
VF/NM: 83%	VG-: 17%
VF+: 75%	G+: 14%
Very Fine: 66.6%	**Good: 12.5%**
VF-: 55%	G-: 11%
F/VF: 48%	FR/G: 10%
F+: 40%	**Fair: 8%**
Fine: 33.3%	**Poor: 2%**

CGC-graded prices

Simply toughening grading standards and raising NM prices to reflect the high prices CGC-slabbed comics fetch is not a solution. From our observations, we can say that it is not generally the case that the high CGC prices have exerted upward influence on identical unslabbed copies.

Rather, there seem to be two separate markets developing with two separate sets of valuations.

In general, a Near Mint unslabbed comic book is fetching about what a slabbed VF/VF+ issue is bringing!

You can estimate CGC prices through the ratios we've developed. We've included a handy set of multipliers at the bottom of this page to help determine prices in the other grades.

At press time, the presence of a CGC slab and a Near-Mint (9.4) grade label on a random Near Mint comic book from before 1990 made that comic book tend to fetch **four** times our NM value in online auctions. The comic book on the border between Near Mint and Mint (CGC 9.8), brought **12 times** the NM value.

To find the median price offered on eBay at press time for pre-1990 **CGC-graded comics**, multiply by:	
9.9 (M): **26**	8.5 (VF+): **1.1**
9.8(NM/M): **12**	8.0 (VF): **0.85**
9.6 (NM+): **6**	7.5 (VF-): **0.6**
9.4 (NM): **4**	7.0 (F/VF): **0.5**
9.2 (NM-): **2.3**	6.5 (F+): **0.4**
9.0 (VF/NM): **1.6**	6.0 (F-): **0.33**

These are median prices of all CGC comics auctioned on eBay; prices for individual issues will vary. In some cases above, **actual** online sale prices appear.

"CGC" and "slabbed" comics

CGC became part of the comics collector's lexicon in 2000, when the Certified Collectibles Group of companies began serving the comic-book field. Today, **CGC grading** is widely used by online buyers and sellers to provide a standard on which both can agree.

Info is available on the website, *www.CGCcomics.com*, and by calling (877) NM-COMIC. There are several levels of service.

Graders do not determine a value; they identify defects and place a grade on the comic book. This lets online buyers purchase items evaluated by a common standard — and identifies for buyer and seller such matters as whether issues have been restored.

If you plan to buy a CGC-graded comic book:

First, yes: You *can* remove the comic book from the sealed container. If you retain the container and paperwork with the comic book, CGC even offers a discount on re-encapsulation.

The observed price ratio for
CGC-graded comics published after 1990 is...

1	: 2	: 4	: 10
9.6 NM+	9.8 NM/M	9.9 M	10.0 M

The observed price ratio for
CGC-graded comics published before 1990 is...

1	: 2	: 4	: 10	: 20	: 50
2.0 G	4.0 VG	6.0 F	8.0 VF	9.0 VF/NM	9.4 NM

What's in the *Checklist*

- Most English-language **comic books published and offered for sale in North America since 1961** for which we've been able to confirm existence. (This includes, for example, reprints of Fleetway's British comics that the publisher repackaged for the American market.)
- All DC comic books from the beginning of the Silver Age (Sept. 1956).
- Many English-language **giveaway comic books** published in North America since 1961.
- Many English-language **graphic novels** and **collection of comic book reprints** published in North America, hardcover and softcover, whose existence we've been able to confirm.

What's not in the *Checklist*

- DC comic books published before September, 1956, and most other comics published before 1961. Prices for those comics can be found in the ***Standard Catalog of Comic Books***, also from this publisher.
- Some comic books released close to press time. Updated prices on new comics can be found in ***Comics Buyer's Guide*** magazine.
- Comic books whose existence we have not been able to confirm.
- Comics in languages other than English.
- Comics not published in North America.
- Paperback or hardcover reprints of comic strips not published in the dimensions of a comic book; *e.g.*, Fawcett *Peanuts* reprints.

Finding a title

The real, legal name of any comic book appears in its **indicia**, a block of small print usually found on the first inside page of most comics. **It does not necessarily match what's on the cover**; publishers have been known to relabel a single (or several) issues within a series for a stunt, while never *really* changing the names of their series.

We alphabetize titles as if there were no spaces in their names. Numbers are spelled out.

Drop proper names

Many titles have the name of one of their creators or the owner of a studio in their proper titles, such as *Kurt Busiek's Astro City*. In most cases, we have listed these comics in this manner: ***Astro City (Kurt Busiek's...).***

There are a handful of cases where the series has only ever been identified by the name of a creator or studio, and in those few cases, such as ***Walt Disney's Comics & Stories***, we've left the title alone.

Multiple series, same name

When a publisher has used the same name for a series more than once, such as in the case of ***Amazing Spider-Man Vol. 1*** and ***Amazing Spider-Man Vol. 2***, we list those different titles in order of release with some indicator to differentiate them from each other. We generally, but not always, run them uninterrupted in order of their release.

When two or more publishers have published distinct and unrelated series with the same name, we generally run them in chronological order of release. This is a change from the first edition, which sorted those titles alphabetically by publisher name.

When a series changes publishers but does not interrupt its numbering, we tend to print them as separate listings but in consecutive chronological order.

Abbreviations

Issue details

(a) — Artist (interior)
(c) — Artist (cover)
(w) — Writer
A — Appearance of
D — Death of
DF — Dynamic Forces Edition
Giant — Giant Size
I — Introduction of
J — Joining of
JLA — Justice League of America
JSA — Justice Society of America
L — Leaving of
nn — no number
O — Origin of
rep. — reprint
V — versus
1 — first appearance of
2 — second appearance of

Creator initials

AA — Alfredo Alcala
AAd — Art Adams
AF — Al Feldstein
AM — Al Milgrom
AMo — Alan Moore
AN — Alex Nino
AR — Alex Raymond
AT — Angelo Torres
ATh — Alex Toth
AW — Al Williamson

BA — Brent Anderson
BB — Brian Bolland
BE — Bill Elder
BEv — Bill Everett
BG — Butch Guice
BH — Bob Hall
BK — Bernie Krigstein
BL — Bob Layton
BMc — Bob McLeod
BO — Bob Oksner
BS — Barry Smith
BSz — Bill Sienkiewicz
BT — Bryan Talbot
BW — Basil Wolverton
BWa — Bill Ward
BWi — Bob Wiacek
BWr — Berni Wrightson

CB — Carl Barks
CCB — C.C. Beck
CI — Carmine Infantino
CR — P. Craig Russell
CS — Curt Swan
CV — Charles Vess

DA — Dan Adkins
DC — Dave Cockrum
DD — Dick Dillin
DaG — Dave Gibbons
DG — Dick Giordano
DGr — Dan Green
DGry — Devin Grayson
DH — Don Heck
DN — Don Newton
DP — Don Perlin
DR — Don Rosa
DS — Dan Spiegle
DSt — Dave Stevens

EC — Ernie Colon
EL — Erik Larsen

FB — Frank Brunner
FF — Frank Frazetta
FG — Floyd Gottfredson
FGu — Fred Guardineer
FH — Fred Hembeck
FM — Frank Miller
FMc — Frank McLaughlin
FR — Frank Robbins
FS — Frank Springer
FT — Frank Thorne

The entry for *Incredible Hulk* #119 reads...

HT(c); SL (w); HT (a)

...which means Herb Trimpe was the cover and interior artist and Stan Lee was the writer.

GC — Gene Colan
GD — Gene Day
GE — George Evans
GI — Graham Ingels
GK — Gil Kane
GM — Gray Morrow
GP — George Pérez
GT — George Tuska

HC — Howard Chaykin
HK — Harvey Kurtzman
HT — Herb Trimpe

IN — Irv Novick

JA — Jim Aparo
JAb — Jack Abel
JB — John Buscema
JBy — John Byrne
JCr — Johnny Craig
JD — Jayson Disbrow
JDu — Jan Duursema
JJ — Jeff Jones
JK — Jack Kirby
JKa — Jack Kamen
JKu — Joe Kubert
JL — Jose Luis Garcia Lopez
JLee — Jim Lee
JM — Jim Mooney
JO — Joe Orlando
JOy — Jerry Ordway
JR — John Romita
JR2 — John Romita Jr.
JS — John Stanley
JSa — Joe Staton
JSe — John Severin
JSh — Jim Sherman
JSn — Jim Starlin
JSo — Jim Steranko
JSt — Joe Sinnott

KB — Kurt Busiek
KG — Keith Giffen
KGa — Kerry Gammill
KJ — Klaus Janson
KN — Kevin Nowlan
KP — Keith Pollard
KS — Kurt Schaffenberger

LMc — Luke McDonnell

MA — Murphy Anderson
MB — Matt Baker
MD — Mort Drucker
ME — Mark Evanier
MG — Michael Golden
MGr — Mike Grell
MGu — Mike Gustovich
MK — Mike Kaluta
MM — Mort Meskin
MN — Mike Nasser
MP — Mike Ploog
MR — Marshall Rogers
MW — Matt Wagner
MZ — Mike Zeck

NA — Neal Adams
NC — Nick Cardy
NG — Neil Gaiman
NR — Nestor Redondo

PB — Pat Broderick
PD — Peter David
PG — Paul Gulacy
PM — Pete Morisi
PS — Paul Smith

RA — Ross Andru
RB — Rich Buckler
RBy — Reggie Byers
RCo — Rich Corben
RE — Ric Estrada
RH — Russ Heath
RHo — Richard Howell
RK — Roy Krenkel
RL — Rob Liefeld
RM — Russ Manning
RMo — Ruben Moreira
RT — Romeo Tanghal

SA — Sergio Aragonés
SB — Sal Buscema
SD — Steve Ditko
SL — Stan Lee
SR — Steve Rude
SRB — Steve Rude

TA — Tony DeZuniga
TMc — Todd McFarlane
TP — Tom Palmer
TS — Tom Sutton
TVE — Trevor Von Eeden
TY — Tom Yeates

VM — Val Mayerik

WE — Will Eisner
WH — Wayne Howard
WK — Walt Kelly
WP — Wendy Pini
WS — Walter Simonson
WW — Wally Wood

The entry for *Incredible Hulk* #180 reads...

HT(c); HT, JAb (a); 1: Wolverine (cameo). A: Wendigo. Marvel Value Stamp #67: Cyclops,

...which means Herb Trimpe was the cover artist, he and Jack Abel were interior artists, Wolverine makes his first appearance in a cameo, Wendigo (who's also featured on the cover) makes an appearance, and the issue contains one of the Marvel Value Stamps issued in the mid-1970s, this one featuring Cyclops (who does not make an appearance in this issue).

Aaron Strips

Reprints the early Adventures of Aaron

©Image

Abbott & Costello (Charlton)

Stand-up duo's cartoon incarnations

©Charlton

A.B.C. Warriors

"Atomic, Bacterial, Chemical" fighting robots

©Fleetway-Quality

A. Bizarro

Mini-series for the dimwitted Superman foe

©DC

Abominations

Mini-series based on Hulk: Future Imperfect

©Marvel

N-MINT

A1 TRUE LIFE BIKINI CONFIDENTIAL
ATOMEKA

❑1, b&w ... 6.95

A1 (VOL. 1)
ATOMEKA

❑1 1989, BB (c); AMo, NG (w); DaG, BSz (a) ... 6.00
❑2 1989, AMo, NG (w); MW, DaG, BB (a) ... 10.00
❑3 1990, BB (c); BB, AMo (w); BB (a) ... 6.00
❑4 1990, BB, AMo (w); BSz (a) ... 6.00
❑5 1991, JKu, JJ, NG (w); JKu, JJ (a) ... 8.00
❑6 1992 ... 9.00
❑7 ... 8.00

A1 (VOL. 2)
MARVEL / EPIC

❑1, ca. 1992 FM (w); CR (a) ... 6.00
❑2, ca. 1992 FM (w) ... 6.00
❑3, ca. 1992 ... 6.00
❑4, ca. 1993 ... 6.00

A'
VIZ

❑1, b&w ... 15.95

ÄARDWOLF
AARDWOLF

❑1, Dec 1994 ... 2.95
❑2, Feb 1995 ... 2.95

AARON STRIPS
IMAGE

❑1, Apr 1997 ... 2.95
❑2, Jun 1997 ... 2.95
❑3, Aug 1997 ... 2.95
❑4, Oct 1997; has "Aaron Warner's Year of the Monkey" back-up; goes to Amazing Aaron Productions ... 2.95
❑5, Jan 1999; continued numbering from Image series ... 2.95
❑6, Mar 1999 ... 2.95

ABADAZAD
CROSSGEN

❑1, Feb 2004 ... 5.00
❑1/2nd, Feb 2004 ... 4.00
❑2, Mar 2004 ... 2.95
❑3, Apr 2004 ... 4.00
❑3/2nd, Apr 2004 ... 2.95

ABBOTT & COSTELLO (CHARLTON)
CHARLTON

❑1, Feb 1968 ... 30.00
❑2, Apr 1968 ... 20.00
❑3, Jun 1968 ... 20.00
❑4, Aug 1968 ... 14.00
❑5, Oct 1968 ... 14.00
❑6, Dec 1968 ... 14.00
❑7, Mar 1969 ... 14.00
❑8, Apr 1969 ... 14.00
❑9, Jun 1969 ... 14.00
❑10, Aug 1969 ... 14.00
❑11, Oct 1969 ... 12.00
❑12, Dec 1969, Abbott & Costello, Pie-In-The-Face Maze Page; Hearty Humor (text story); Abbott & Costello Game Page ... 12.00
❑13, Feb 1970 ... 12.00
❑14, Apr 1970 ... 12.00
❑15, Jun 1970, "Crazy Quiz", Joke Page; Ivan Inventorsky The Inventor "Build Your Private Beach" (text story); Maze Page ... 12.00
❑16, Aug 1970 ... 12.00
❑17, Oct 1970, Nutty daisy poster; Haunted House Maze ... 12.00
❑18, Dec 1970 ... 12.00
❑19, Feb 1971 ... 12.00
❑20, Apr 1971 ... 12.00
❑21, Jun 1971 ... 12.00
❑22, Aug 1971 ... 12.00

ABBOTT AND COSTELLO: THE CLASSIC COMICS
ETERNITY

❑Book 1, b&w ... 14.95

ABC: A TO Z - GREYSHIRT AND COBWEB
DC / AMERICA'S BEST COMICS

❑1, Jan 2006 ... 3.99

ABC: A TO Z - TERRA OBSCURA AND SPLASH BRANNIGAN
DC / AMERICA'S BEST COMICS

❑1, Mar 2006 ... 3.99

ABC: A TO Z - TOM STRONG AND JACK B. QUICK
DC / AMERICA'S BEST COMICS

❑1 2005 ... 3.99

ABC: A TO Z - TOP 10 AND TEAMS
DC / AMERICA'S BEST COMICS

❑1, Aug 2006 ... 3.99

A.B.C. WARRIORS
FLEETWAY-QUALITY

❑1 1990 ... 2.00
❑2 1990 ... 2.00
❑3 1990 ... 2.00
❑4 1990 ... 2.00
❑5 1990 ... 2.00
❑6 1990 ... 2.00
❑7 1990 ... 2.00
❑8 1990 ... 2.00

ABC WARRIORS: KHRONICLES OF KHAOS
FLEETWAY-QUALITY

❑1 ... 2.95
❑2 ... 2.95
❑3 ... 2.95
❑4 ... 2.95

ABE SAPIEN DRUMS OF THE DEAD
DARK HORSE

❑1, Mar 1998; Hellboy back-up ... 2.95

A. BIZARRO
DC

❑1, Jul 1999 ... 2.50
❑2, Aug 1999 ... 2.50
❑3, Sep 1999 ... 2.50
❑4, Oct 1999 ... 2.50

A-BOMB
ANTARCTIC / VENUS

❑1, Dec 1993 ... 2.95
❑2, Mar 1994 ... 2.95
❑3, Jun 1994; Barr Girls story ... 2.95
❑4, Sep 1994; Barr Girls story ... 2.95
❑5, Dec 1994 ... 2.95
❑6, Mar 1995 ... 2.95
❑7, Jun 1995 ... 2.95
❑8, Sep 1995 ... 2.95
❑9, Nov 1995 ... 2.95
❑10, Jan 1996 ... 2.95
❑11, Mar 1996; Title page shows Vol. 2 #1 ... 2.95
❑12, May 1996 ... 2.95
❑13, Jul 1996 ... 2.95
❑14, Sep 1996 ... 2.95
❑15, Nov 1996 ... 2.95
❑16, Jan 1997 ... 2.95

ABOMINATIONS
MARVEL

❑1, Dec 1996; follows events in Hulk: Future Imperfect ... 1.50
❑2, Jan 1997 ... 1.50
❑3, Feb 1997 ... 1.50

ABOVE & BELOW: TWO TALES OF THE AMERICAN FRONTIER
DRAWN & QUARTERLY

❑1, Dec 2004 ... 9.95

ABRAHAM STONE (EPIC)
MARVEL / EPIC

❑1, Jul 1995 ... 6.95
❑2, Aug 1995 ... 6.95

ABSOLUTE VERTIGO
DC / VERTIGO

❑1, Win 1995 ... 3.50

ABSOLUTE ZERO
ANTARCTIC

❑1, Feb 1995, b&w ... 3.50
❑2, May 1995, b&w ... 2.95
❑3, Aug 1995, b&w ... 2.95
❑4, Oct 1995, b&w ... 2.95
❑5, Dec 1995, b&w ... 2.95
❑6, Feb 1996, b&w ... 2.95

ABSURD ART OF J.J. GRANDVILLE
TOME

❑1, b&w; no date of publication ... 2.50

ABYSS
DARK HORSE

❑1, Aug 1989 ... 2.50
❑2, Sep 1989 ... 2.50

AC ANNUAL
AC

❑1 ... 3.50
❑2 ... 5.00
❑3 ... 3.50
❑4 ... 3.95

ACCELERATE
DC / VERTIGO

❑1, Aug 2000 ... 2.95
❑2, Sep 2000 ... 2.95
❑3, Oct 2000 ... 2.95
❑4, Nov 2000 ... 2.95

ACCIDENTAL DEATH
FANTAGRAPHICS

❑nn, Dec 1993, b&w ... 3.50

Other grades: Multiply price above by 5/6 for VF/NM • 2/3 for VERY FINE • 1/3 for FINE • 1/5 for VERY GOOD • 1/8 for GOOD

ACCIDENT MAN
DARK HORSE

❑1, ca. 1993 ... 2.50
❑2, ca. 1993 ... 2.50
❑3, ca. 1993 ... 2.50

ACCLAIM ADVENTURE ZONE
ACCLAIM

❑1 1997; Ninjak on cover ... 4.50
❑2 1997; Turok on cover ... 4.50
❑3 1997; Turok and Dinosaur on cover 4.50

ACE
HARRIER

❑1, b&w; no indicia ... 1.95

ACE COMICS PRESENTS
ACE

❑1, May 1987; Daredevil (Golden Age) vs. The Claw; Silver Streak ... 2.00
❑2, Jul 1987; Jack Bradbury ... 2.00
❑3, Sep 1987; The Golden Age of Klaus Nordling ... 2.00
❑4, Nov 1987; Lou Fine ... 2.00

ACE MCCOY
AVALON

❑1, b&w ... 2.95
❑2, b&w ... 2.95
❑3, b&w ... 2.95

ACE OF SPADES
ZUZUPETAL

❑1 ... 2.50

ACES
ECLIPSE

❑1, Apr 1988 ... 3.00
❑2, ca. 1988 ... 3.00
❑3, ca. 1988 ... 3.00
❑4, ca. 1988 ... 3.00
❑5, ca. 1988 ... 3.00

ACES HIGH (RCP)
RCP

❑1, Apr 1999 ... 2.50
❑2, May 1999 ... 2.50
❑3, Jun 1999 ... 2.50
❑4, Jul 1999 ... 2.50
❑5, Aug 1999 ... 2.50
❑Annual 1; Collects Aces High #1-5 ... 13.50

ACG CHRISTMAS SPECIAL
AVALON

❑1, Cover reads "Christmas Horror" ... 2.95

ACG'S CIVIL WAR
AVALON

❑1 1995 ... 2.50

ACG'S HALLOWEEN SPECIAL
AVALON

❑1; Cover reads "Halloween Horror" ... 2.95

ACHILLES STORM: DARK SECRET
BRAINSTORM

❑1 ... 2.95
❑2 ... 2.95

ACHILLES STORM/RAZMATAZ
AJA BLU

❑1, Oct 1990 ... 2.25
❑2, Jan 1991 ... 2.25
❑3, May 1991 ... 2.25
❑4, Nov 1991 ... 2.25

ACID BATH CASE
KITCHEN SINK

❑1 ... 4.95

ACK THE BARBARIAN
INNOVATION

❑1, b&w ... 2.25

ACME
FANDOM HOUSE

❑1 ... 3.00
❑2 ... 3.00
❑3 ... 3.00
❑4 ... 3.00
❑5 ... 3.00
❑6 ... 3.00
❑7 ... 3.00
❑8, Fal 1987 ... 2.00
❑9, Sum 1989 ... 3.00

ACME NOVELTY LIBRARY
FANTAGRAPHICS

❑1, Win 1993 ... 10.00
❑1/2nd, Dec 1995; Jimmy Corrigan ... 3.95
❑2, Sum 1994; Quimby the Mouse ... 7.00
❑2/2nd, Sum 1995; Quimby the Mouse 4.95
❑3, Aut 1994; digest-sized; Blind Man 5.00
❑4, Win 1994; Sparky's Best Comics and Stories ... 5.00
❑4/2nd ... 4.95
❑5 1995; digest-sized; Jimmy Corrigan 3.95
❑6, Fal 1995; digest-sized; Jimmy Corrigan ... 3.95
❑7 1996; Oversized; Book of Jokes ... 6.95
❑8, Win 1996; digest-sized; Jimmy Corrigan ... 4.75
❑9, Win 1997; digest-sized; Jimmy Corrigan ... 4.50
❑10, Spr 1998; digest-sized; Jimmy Corrigan ... 4.95
❑11, Fal 1998; digest-sized; Jimmy Corrigan ... 4.50
❑12, Spr 1999; digest-sized; Jimmy Corrigan ... 4.50
❑16, Jan 2006 ...
❑14, Aut 1999; Jimmy Corrigan ... 10.95

ACOLYTE
MAD MONKEY

❑1, ca. 1993, b&w ... 3.95

ACTION COMICS
DC

❑0, Oct 1994; BG (a); 1: Kenny Braverman. Peer Pressure, Part 4; ▲1994-40 ... 3.00
❑1/2nd, ca. 1976, 2nd printing (giveaway, 1976?) FGu (w); FGu (a); O: Superman. 1: Zatara. 1: Superman. 1: Tex Thomson. 1: Lois Lane ... 18.00
❑1/3rd, ca. 1983, 3rd printing (giveaway, 1983?) FGu (w); FGu (a); O: Superman. 1: Zatara. 1: Superman. 1: Tex Thomson. 1: Lois Lane ... 14.00
❑1/4th, ca. 1987, 4th printing (Nestle Quik 16-page giveaway, 1988) O: Superman ... 6.00
❑1/5th, ca. 1992; FGu (w); FGu (a); O: Superman. 1: Zatara. 1: Superman. 1: Tex Thomson. 1: Lois Lane. 5th printing (1992) ... 5.00
❑221, Oct 1956 ... 240.00
❑222, Nov 1956 ... 240.00
❑223, Dec 1956 ... 240.00
❑224, Jan 1957 ... 240.00
❑225, Feb 1957 ... 240.00
❑226, Mar 1957 ... 240.00
❑227, Apr 1957 ... 240.00
❑228, May 1957 ... 240.00
❑229, Jun 1957 ... 240.00
❑230, Jul 1957 ... 240.00
❑231, Aug 1957 ... 240.00
❑232, Sep 1957, CS (c) ... 240.00
❑233, Oct 1957, CS (c) ... 240.00
❑234, Nov 1957, CS (c) ... 240.00
❑235, Dec 1957, CS (c) ... 240.00
❑236, Jan 1958, CS (c) ... 240.00
❑237, Feb 1958, CS (c) ... 240.00
❑238, Mar 1958, CS (c) ... 240.00
❑239, Apr 1958, CS (c) ... 240.00
❑240, May 1958, CS (c) ... 240.00
❑241, Jun 1958, CS (c); 1: Fortress of Solitude ... 250.00
❑242, Jul 1958, CS (c); O: Brainiac. 1: Kandor. 1: Brainiac ... 1200.00
❑243, Aug 1958, CS (c) ... 185.00
❑244, Sep 1958, CS (c); CS (a) ... 185.00
❑245, Oct 1958, CS (c) ... 185.00
❑246, Nov 1958, CS (c) ... 185.00
❑247, Dec 1958, CS (c) ... 185.00
❑248, Jan 1959, CS (c); 1: Congorilla 185.00
❑249, Feb 1959, CS (c) ... 185.00
❑250, Mar 1959, CS (c) ... 185.00
❑251, Apr 1959, CS (c); Tommy Tomorrow; Legion ... 185.00
❑252, May 1959, CS (c); O: Supergirl. 1: Anti-Kryptonite. 1&O: Supergirl .. 1200.00
❑253, Jun 1959, CS (c); 2: Supergirl . 425.00
❑254, Jul 1959, CS (c); A: Bizarro. 325.00
❑255, Aug 1959, CS (c); 1: Bizarro Lois Lane ... 225.00
❑256, Sep 1959, CS (c) ... 100.00
❑257, Oct 1959, CS (c) ... 100.00
❑258, Nov 1959, CS (c); New Stars for Old Glory (PSA) ... 100.00
❑259, Dec 1959, CS (c); A: Superboy. Congorilla back-up ... 100.00
❑260, Jan 1960, CS (c) ... 100.00
❑261, Feb 1960, CS (c); 1&O: Streaky the Supercat. 1: X-Kryptonite ... 100.00
❑262, Mar 1960, CS (c) ... 90.00
❑263, Apr 1960, CS (c); O: Bizarro World ... 100.00
❑264, May 1960, CS (c) ... 80.00
❑265, Jun 1960, CS (c); CS (a) ... 80.00
❑266, Jul 1960, CS (c); CS (a) ... 80.00
❑267, Aug 1960, CS (c); 1: Chameleon Boy. 1: Colossal Boy. 1: Invisible Kid I (Lyle Norg) ... 550.00
❑268, Sep 1960, CS (c) ... 80.00
❑269, Oct 1960, CS (c) ... 80.00
❑270, Nov 1960, CS (c) ... 80.00
❑271, Dec 1960, CS (c) ... 65.00
❑272, Jan 1961, CS (c) ... 65.00
❑273, Feb 1961, CS (c); V: Mxyzptlk .. 65.00
❑274, Mar 1961, CS (c) ... 65.00
❑275, Apr 1961, CS (c) ... 65.00
❑276, May 1961, CS (c); JM (a); Triplicate Girl, Phantom Girl, Brainiac 5, Shrinking Violet, Bouncing Boy joins team ... 125.00
❑277, Jun 1961, CS (c) ... 60.00
❑278, Jul 1961, CS (c) ... 60.00
❑279, Aug 1961, CS (c) ... 60.00
❑280, Sep 1961, CS (c) ... 60.00
❑281, Oct 1961, CS (c) ... 60.00
❑282, Nov 1961, CS (c) ... 60.00
❑283, Dec 1961, CS (c); Legion of Super-Villains ... 60.00
❑284, Jan 1962, CS (c); Mon-El ... 60.00
❑285, Feb 1962, CS (c); NA (a); A: Legion of Super-Heroes. Supergirl goes public ... 100.00
❑286, Mar 1962, CS (c); Legion of Super-Villains ... 60.00
❑287, Apr 1962, CS (c); JM (a); A: Legion of Super-Heroes ... 60.00
❑288, May 1962, CS (c); Mon-El ... 60.00
❑289, Jun 1962, CS (c); JM (a); A: Legion of Super-Heroes ... 60.00
❑290, Jul 1962, CS, KS (c); CS (a); A: Legion of Super-Heroes ... 60.00
❑291, Aug 1962, CS (c); NA (a) ... 60.00
❑292, Sep 1962, CS (c); A: Superhorse (Comet) ... 60.00
❑293, Oct 1962, CS (c); O: Superhorse (Comet) ... 60.00
❑294, Nov 1962, CS (c); CS (a) ... 60.00
❑295, Dec 1962, CS (c); JM (a) ... 60.00
❑296, Jan 1963, CS (c); CS, JM (a) ... 60.00
❑297, Feb 1963, CS (c); JM (a) ... 60.00
❑298, Mar 1963, CS (c); CS, JM (a) ... 60.00
❑299, Apr 1963, CS (c) ... 60.00
❑300, May 1963, 300th anniversary issue CS (c) ... 50.00
❑301, Jun 1963 ... 50.00
❑302, Jul 1963, CS (a) ... 50.00
❑303, Aug 1963, CS (a) ... 50.00
❑304, Sep 1963, CS, JM (a); 1: Black Flame ... 50.00
❑305, Oct 1963 ... 50.00
❑306, Nov 1963 ... 50.00
❑307, Dec 1963 ... 50.00
❑308, Jan 1964 ... 50.00
❑309, Feb 1964, NA (a); A: Supergirl's parents. Legion ... 50.00
❑310, Mar 1964, 1: Jewel Kryptonite.. 50.00
❑311, Apr 1964 ... 50.00
❑312, May 1964 ... 50.00
❑313, Jun 1964, A: Batman ... 50.00
❑314, Jul 1964, A: Batman ... 50.00
❑315, Aug 1964 ... 50.00
❑316, Sep 1964 ... 50.00
❑317, Oct 1964 ... 40.00
❑318, Nov 1964 ... 40.00
❑319, Dec 1964 ... 40.00
❑320, Jan 1965 ... 40.00
❑321, Feb 1965, CS (a) ... 40.00
❑322, Mar 1965 ... 40.00
❑323, Apr 1965 ... 40.00
❑324, May 1965 ... 40.00
❑325, Jun 1965 ... 40.00

Other grades: Multiply price above by 5/6 for VF/NM • 2/3 for VERY FINE • 1/3 for FINE • 1/5 for VERY GOOD • 1/8 for GOOD

Ace Comics Presents

A tribute series honoring Jack Cole

©Ace

Ace McCoy

Adventures of a stuntman-turned-hero

©Avalon

Aces High (RCP)

Reprints the E.C. "New Direction" title

©RCP

Achilles Storm: Dark Secret

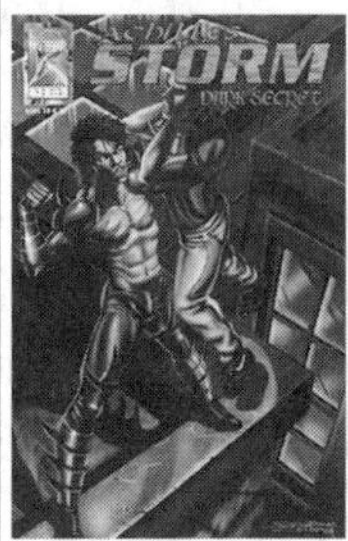

Costumed martial artist takes to the streets

©Brainstorm

Ack the Barbarian

Computer-generated humor comic book

©Innovation

	N-MINT
❑326, Jul 1965	40.00
❑327, Aug 1965, Imaginary Superman story	40.00
❑328, Sep 1965	40.00
❑329, Oct 1965	40.00
❑330, Nov 1965	40.00
❑331, Dec 1965	40.00
❑332, Jan 1966, Imaginary Superwoman Story	40.00
❑333, Feb 1966, Imaginary Superwoman Story	40.00
❑334, Mar 1966; Giant-sized issue; O: Supergirl. aka 80 Page Giant #G-20	60.00
❑335, Mar 1966	40.00
❑336, Apr 1966, O: Akvar	40.00
❑337, May 1966	40.00
❑338, Jun 1966, CS (a)	40.00
❑339, Jul 1966, CS, JM (a)	50.00
❑340, Aug 1966, 1: Parasite	40.00
❑341, Sep 1966, A: Batman	40.00
❑342, Oct 1966	40.00
❑343, Nov 1966	40.00
❑344, Dec 1966, A: Batman	40.00
❑345, Jan 1967, A: Allen Funt	40.00
❑346, Feb 1967	40.00
❑347, Apr 1967; Giant-sized issue; aka 80 Page Giant #G-33; Supergirl; reprints Superman #140 and Action #290 and #293	50.00
❑348, Mar 1967	40.00
❑349, Apr 1967	40.00
❑350, May 1967, JM (a)	40.00
❑351, Jun 1967	40.00
❑352, Jul 1967	40.00
❑353, Aug 1967	40.00
❑354, Sep 1967	40.00
❑355, Oct 1967	40.00
❑356, Nov 1967	40.00
❑357, Dec 1967, CS (a)	40.00
❑358, Jan 1968, CS (a)	40.00
❑359, Feb 1968, CS (a)	40.00
❑360, Mar 1968; Giant-sized issue; aka 80 Page Giant #G-45; Supergirl	40.00
❑361, Apr 1968	40.00
❑362, May 1968	40.00
❑363, Jun 1968	30.00
❑364, Jul 1968, KS (a); D: Superman	30.00
❑365, Aug 1968, D: Superman	30.00
❑366, Sep 1968, D: Superman	30.00
❑367, Oct 1968, CS (a)	30.00
❑368, Nov 1968, CS, JAb (a)	30.00
❑369, Dec 1968, CS, JAb (a)	30.00
❑370, Jan 1969, CS, JAb (a)	30.00
❑371, Feb 1969, CS, JAb (a)	30.00
❑372, Mar 1969, CS, JAb (a)	30.00
❑373, Apr 1969; NA, CS (a); A: Supergirl. aka Giant #G-57; Supergirl stories; Giants drop to 64 pages	30.00
❑374, Mar 1969, CS, JAb (a)	20.00
❑375, Apr 1969, CS, JAb (a); A: Batman	20.00
❑376, May 1969, CS, JAb (a)	20.00
❑377, Jun 1969, CS, JAb (a); Legion; Reprint from Adventure Comics #300	20.00
❑378, Jul 1969, CS, JAb (a); Legion	20.00
❑379, Aug 1969, CS, JAb (a); Legion	20.00
❑380, Sep 1969, CS (a); Legion	20.00
❑381, Oct 1969, CS (a); Legion	20.00
❑382, Nov 1969, CS (a); Legion	20.00
❑383, Dec 1969, CS (a); Legion	20.00
❑384, Jan 1970, CS (a); Legion	20.00
❑385, Feb 1970, CS (a); Legion	20.00
❑386, Mar 1970, CS (a); Legion	20.00
❑387, Apr 1970, CS (a); Legion	20.00
❑388, May 1970, CS (a); Legion; Reprints Legion story from Adventure Comics #302	20.00
❑389, Jun 1970, CS (a); Legion	20.00
❑390, Jul 1970, CS (a); Legion	20.00
❑391, Aug 1970, CS (a); Legion	20.00
❑392, Sep 1970, CS (a); Super-Sons; Last Legion of Super-Heroes	20.00
❑393, Oct 1970, CS (c); CS (a)	20.00
❑394, Nov 1970, CS (a)	20.00
❑395, Dec 1970, CS (a)	20.00
❑396, Jan 1971, MA, CS (a); Tales of the Fortress	20.00
❑397, Feb 1971, CS (a); Tales of the Fortress	20.00
❑398, Mar 1971, CS (a)	20.00
❑399, Apr 1971, CS (a)	20.00
❑400, May 1971, CS (a)	35.00
❑401, Jun 1971, CS (a)	17.00
❑402, Jul 1971, CS (a); Tales of the Fortress	17.00
❑403, Aug 1971; CS (a); Reprints from Adventure #310	17.00
❑404, Sep 1971; CS (a); Aquaman and Atom reprint stories	17.00
❑405, Oct 1971; CS (a); Aquaman and Vigilante reprint stories	17.00
❑406, Nov 1971; CS (c); ATh, CS (a); Atom and Flash story, part 1; reprinted from Brave and the Bold #53	17.00
❑407, Dec 1971; CS (c); ATh, CS (a); Atom and Flash story, part 2; reprinted from Brave and theBold #53	15.00
❑408, Jan 1972; CS (c); GK, CS (a); reprints The Atom #9	15.00
❑409, Feb 1972; CS (a); Teen Titans reprint story	15.00
❑410, Feb 1972; CS (a); Teen Titans reprint story	13.00
❑411, Apr 1972; CS (a); O: Eclipso. Eclipso reprint story	13.00
❑412, May 1972; CS (a); Eclipso reprint story	12.00
❑413, Jun 1972; ATh, CS (a); Eclipso and Metamorpho reprint stories	12.00
❑414, Jul 1972, CS (a)	12.00
❑415, Aug 1972, CS (a)	12.00
❑416, Sep 1972, CS (a)	11.00
❑417, Oct 1972, CS (a)	11.00
❑418, Nov 1972, CS (a)	11.00
❑419, Dec 1972, CS (a); 1: Human Target	14.00
❑420, Jan 1973, CS (a)	11.00
❑421, Feb 1973, CS (a); Green Arrow begins	11.00
❑422, Mar 1973, CS (a)	11.00
❑423, Apr 1973, CS (a)	10.00
❑424, Jun 1973, MA, DG, CS (a); Green Arrow	10.00
❑425, Jul 1973, MA, DG, NA, CS (a)	19.00
❑426, Aug 1973, CS (a)	8.00
❑427, Sep 1973, CS (a)	8.00
❑428, Oct 1973, CS (a)	8.00
❑429, Nov 1973, CS (a)	8.00
❑430, Dec 1973, CS (a); Atom back-up	8.00
❑431, Jan 1974, CS (a); Green Arrow back-up	8.00
❑432, Feb 1974, CS (a)	8.00
❑433, Mar 1974, CS (a)	8.00
❑434, Apr 1974, CS (a)	8.00
❑435, May 1974, CS (a)	8.00
❑436, Jun 1974, CS (a)	8.00
❑437, Jul 1974, Giant-sized issue (100 pages); NC (c); MA, CI, GK, CS, RH, KS (a); Reprints Sea Devils #1, Mystery in Space #85, Western Comics #77, My Greatest Adventure #3, Doll Man #13; Appearance of Flash, Green Arrow, and Green Lantern	29.00
❑438, Aug 1974, CS (a)	8.00
❑439, Sep 1974, CS (a); Atom back-up	8.00
❑440, Oct 1974, MGr, CS (a); 1st Green Arrow by Mike Grell	25.00
❑441, Nov 1974, MGr, CS (a); A: Flash. Green Arrow back-up	12.00
❑442, Dec 1974, CS (a)	8.00
❑443, Jan 1975, NC (c); MA, CI, GK, CS, RH (a); 100-Page Super Spectacular; JLA, Sea Devils, Matt Savage, Adam Strange, Hawkman and Black Pirate; reprints stories from Sea Devils #3, Western Comics #78, Mystery in Space #87 and Sensation Comics #4	26.00
❑444, Feb 1975; CS (a); A: Green Lantern. Green Arrow back-up	7.00
❑445, Mar 1975 CS (a)	7.00
❑446, Apr 1975 CS (a)	7.00
❑447, May 1975 CS (a)	7.00
❑448, Jun 1975 CS (a)	7.00
❑449, Jul 1975, JK, CS (a); Green Arrow giant	7.00
❑450, Aug 1975 CS (a)	7.00
❑451, Sep 1975; CS (a); Green Arrow back-up	7.00
❑452, Oct 1975 CS (a)	7.00
❑453, Nov 1975; CS (a); Atom back-up	7.00
❑454, Dec 1975; CS (a); last Atom back-up	7.00
❑455, Jan 1976 CS (a)	6.00
❑456, Feb 1976; CS (a); Green Arrow/Black Canary back-up	6.00
❑457, Mar 1976, CS (a); Green Arrow/Black Canary back-up; Superman reveals ID to Pete Ross' son	6.00
❑458, Apr 1976, MGr, CS (a); 1: Blackrock. Green Arrow	6.00
❑459, May 1976, CS (a)	6.00
❑460, Jun 1976, CS (a); 1: Karb-Brak. Mxyzptlk back-up	6.00
❑461, Jul 1976, CS (a); V: Karb-Brak. Superman in colonial America; Bicentennial #30	6.00
❑462, Aug 1976, CS (a)	6.00
❑463, Sep 1976, CS (a); Bicentennial story	6.00
❑464, Oct 1976, CS (a)	6.00
❑465, Nov 1976, CS (a)	6.00
❑466, Dec 1976, CS (a)	5.00
❑467, Jan 1977, CS (a)	5.00

Other grades: Multiply price above by 5/6 for VF/NM • 2/3 for VERY FINE • 1/3 for FINE • 1/5 for VERY GOOD • 1/8 for GOOD

❑468, Feb 1977, CS (a)........................ 5.00
❑469, Mar 1977, CS (a)........................ 5.00
❑470, Apr 1977, CS (a)........................ 5.00
❑471, May 1977, CS (a)........................ 5.00
❑472, Jun 1977, CS (a); V: Faora Hu-Ul 5.00
❑473, Jul 1977, CS (a)........................ 5.00
❑474, Aug 1977, CS (a)........................ 5.00
❑475, Sep 1977, CS (a)........................ 5.00
❑476, Oct 1977, CS (a)........................ 5.00
❑477, Nov 1977, CS (a)........................ 5.00
❑478, Dec 1977, CS (a)........................ 5.00
❑479, Jan 1978, CS (a)........................ 5.00
❑480, Feb 1978, CS (a)........................ 5.00
❑481, Mar 1978, CS (a); 1: Supermobile. V: Amazo........................ 5.00
❑481/Whitman, Mar 1978, CS (a); 1: Supermobile. V: Amazo. Whitman variant........................ 10.00
❑482, Apr 1978, CS (a)........................ 5.00
❑482/Whitman, Apr 1978, CS (a); Whitman variant........................ 10.00
❑483, May 1978, CS (a); V: Amazo..... 5.00
❑483/Whitman, May 1978, CS (a); V: Amazo. Whitman variant............ 10.00
❑484, Jun 1978, 40th anniversary; CS (a); Wedding of E-2 Superman and Lois Lane........................ 5.00
❑484/Whitman, Jun 1978, CS (a); Wedding of E-2 Superman and Lois Lane; Whitman variant........... 10.00
❑485, Jul 1978, CS (a)........................ 5.00
❑485/Whitman, Jul 1978, CS (a); Whitman variant........................ 10.00
❑486, Aug 1978, CS (a)........................ 5.00
❑486/Whitman, Aug 1978, CS (a); Whitman variant........................ 10.00
❑487, Sep 1978, CS (a); O: Atom....... 5.00
❑487/Whitman, Sep 1978, CS (a); O: Atom. Whitman variant.............. 10.00
❑488, Oct 1978, CS (a)........................ 5.00
❑488/Whitman, Oct 1978, CS (a); Whitman variant........................ 10.00
❑489, Nov 1978, CS (a); Atom back-up 5.00
❑489/Whitman, Nov 1978, CS (a); Atom back-up; Whitman variant...... 10.00
❑490, Dec 1978, CS (a)........................ 5.00
❑490/Whitman, Dec 1978, CS (a); Whitman variant........................ 10.00
❑491, Jan 1979, CS (a)........................ 5.00
❑491/Whitman, Jan 1979, r; CS (a); Whitman variant........................ 10.00
❑492, Feb 1979, CS (a)........................ 5.00
❑492/Whitman, Feb 1979, CS (a); Whitman variant........................ 10.00
❑493, Mar 1979, CS (a)........................ 5.00
❑493/Whitman, Mar 1979, CS (a); Whitman variant........................ 10.00
❑494, Apr 1979, CS (a)........................ 5.00
❑494/Whitman, Apr 1979, CS (a); Whitman variant........................ 10.00
❑495, May 1979, CS (a); 1: Silver Banshee........................ 5.00
❑495/Whitman, May 1979, CS (a); 1: Silver Banshee. Whitman variant 10.00
❑496, Jun 1979, CS (a)........................ 5.00
❑496/Whitman, Jun 1979, CS (a); Whitman variant........................ 10.00
❑497, Jul 1979, CS (a)........................ 5.00
❑497/Whitman, Jul 1979, CS (a); Whitman variant........................ 10.00
❑498, Aug 1979, CS (a)........................ 5.00
❑498/Whitman, Aug 1979, CS (a); Whitman variant........................ 10.00
❑499, Sep 1979, CS (a)........................ 5.00
❑499/Whitman, Sep 1979, CS (a); Whitman variant........................ 10.00
❑500, Oct 1979; Giant-sized; CS (a); O: Superman. Superman's life......... 5.00
❑500/Whitman, Oct 1979; CS (a); O: Superman. Superman's life; Whitman variant........................ 10.00
❑501, Nov 1979, CS (a)........................ 5.00
❑501/Whitman, Nov 1979, CS (a); Whitman variant........................ 10.00
❑502, Dec 1979, CS (a)........................ 5.00
❑502/Whitman, Dec 1979, CS (a); Whitman variant........................ 10.00
❑503, Jan 1980, CS (a)........................ 5.00
❑503/Whitman, Jan 1980, CS (a); Whitman variant........................ 10.00
❑504, Feb 1980, CS (a)........................ 4.00
❑504/Whitman, Feb 1980, CS (a); Whitman variant........................ 8.00
❑505, Mar 1980, CS (a)........................ 4.00
❑505/Whitman, Mar 1980, CS (a); Whitman variant........................ 8.00
❑506, Apr 1980, CS (a)........................ 4.00
❑506/Whitman, Apr 1980, CS (a); Whitman variant........................ 8.00
❑507, May 1980, CS (a)........................ 4.00
❑507/Whitman, May 1980, CS (a); Whitman variant........................ 8.00
❑508, Jun 1980, CS (a)........................ 4.00
❑508/Whitman, Jun 1980, CS (a); Whitman variant........................ 8.00
❑509, Jul 1980, JSn, CS, JSt (a); Radio Shack promo insert............. 4.00
❑510, Aug 1980, CS (a)........................ 4.00
❑511, Sep 1980, CS (a)........................ 4.00
❑512, Oct 1980, CS (a); Air Wave back-up........................ 4.00
❑513, Nov 1980, CS (a)........................ 4.00
❑514, Dec 1980, CS (a)........................ 4.00
❑515, Jan 1981, CS (a); V: Vandal Savage. Atom back-up.................. 4.00
❑516, Feb 1981, CS (a); V: Vandal Savage. Atom back-up.................. 4.00
❑517, Mar 1981, CS (a)........................ 4.00
❑518, Apr 1981, CS (a); Aquaman back-up........................ 4.00
❑519, May 1981, CS (a)........................ 4.00
❑520, Jun 1981, CS (a)........................ 4.00
❑521, Jul 1981, CS (a); 1: Vixen. Atom, Aquaman back-up........................ 4.00
❑522, Aug 1981, CS (a); Atom back-up 4.00
❑523, Sep 1981, CS (a); Atom back-up 4.00
❑524, Oct 1981, CS (a); Airwave and Atom back-up........................ 4.00
❑525, Nov 1981, CS (a); 1: Neutron... 4.00
❑526, Dec 1981, CS (a)........................ 4.00
❑527, Jan 1982, CS (a); 1: Lord Satanis. Airwave, Aquaman back-up........... 4.00
❑528, Feb 1982, CS (a); A: Brainiac. Aquaman back-up........................ 4.00
❑529, Mar 1982, CS (a)........................ 4.00
❑530, Apr 1982, CS (a)........................ 4.00
❑531, May 1982, CS (a)........................ 4.00
❑532, Jun 1982, CS (a)........................ 4.00
❑533, Jul 1982, CS (a)........................ 4.00
❑534, Aug 1982, CS (a)........................ 4.00
❑535, Sep 1982, CS (a); A: Omega Men 4.00
❑536, Oct 1982, CS (a); A: Omega Men 4.00
❑537, Nov 1982, CS (a); Aquaman back-up; Masters of the Universe preview........................ 4.00
❑538, Dec 1982, CS (a)........................ 4.00
❑539, Jan 1983, GK, CS (a); Flash, Atom........................ 4.00
❑540, Feb 1983, CS (a); Aquaman back-up........................ 4.00
❑541, Mar 1983, CS (a)........................ 4.00
❑542, Apr 1983, CS (a); V: Vandal Savage........................ 4.00
❑543, May 1983, CS (a); V: Neutron.. 4.00
❑544, Jun 1983; 45th anniversary; DG, GK (c); GK, CS (a); O: Brainiac (New). O: Lex Luthor (New). 1: Brainiac (New). 1: Lex Luthor (New). 45th Anniversary issue; New Luthor and Braniac; Joe Shuster pin-up.......... 4.00
❑545, Jul 1983 CS (a); V: New Brainiac 3.00
❑546, Aug 1983, CS (a); A: JLA, Titans 3.00
❑547, Sep 1983 CS (a)........................ 3.00
❑548, Oct 1983 CS (a)........................ 3.00
❑549, Nov 1983 CS (a)........................ 3.00
❑550, Dec 1983 CS (a)........................ 3.00
❑551, Jan 1984 CS (a); 1: Red Star (Starfire)........................ 3.00
❑552, Feb 1984; CS (a); 1: Legion of Forgotten Heroes. A: Animal Man. Cave Carson, Congorilla, Suicide Squad, Animal Man, Rip Hunter, Immortal Man, Sea Devils, Dolphin 3.00
❑553, Mar 1984; CS (a); A: Animal Man. A: Legion of Forgotten Heroes. Cave Carson, Congorilla, Suicide Squad, Animal Man, Rip Hunter, Immortal Man, Sea Devils, Dolphin........... 3.00
❑554, Apr 1984; CS (a); Jerry and Joey create Superman........................ 3.00
❑555, May 1984; CS (a); A: Supergirl. V: Parasite. Anniversary of Supergirl's debut in Action Comics; Continues in Supergirl #20............ 3.00
❑556, Jun 1984; CS (a); V: Vandal Savage. Neutron........................ 3.00
❑557, Jul 1984 CS (a)........................ 3.00
❑558, Aug 1984 CS (a)........................ 3.00
❑559, Sep 1984 CS (a)........................ 3.00
❑560, Oct 1984 CS (a); A: Ambush Bug 3.00
❑561, Nov 1984 CS (a)........................ 3.00
❑562, Dec 1984 CS (a)........................ 3.00
❑563, Jan 1985; CS (a); Ambush Bug vs. Mxyzptlk........................ 3.00
❑564, Feb 1985 CS (a)........................ 3.00
❑565, Mar 1985 CS (a); A: Ambush Bug 3.00
❑566, Apr 1985 CS (a); V: Captain Strong 3.00
❑567, May 1985 CS (a)........................ 2.00
❑568, Jun 1985 CS (a)........................ 2.00
❑569, Jul 1985 CS (a)........................ 2.00
❑570, Aug 1985 CS (a)........................ 2.00
❑571, Sep 1985 CS (a)........................ 2.00
❑572, Oct 1985; MWa (w); CS (a); Mark Waid's first major comics work....... 2.00
❑573, Nov 1985; CS (a); MASK preview 2.00
❑574, Dec 1985 CS (a)........................ 2.00
❑575, Jan 1986 CS (a)........................ 2.00
❑576, Feb 1986 CS (a)........................ 2.00
❑577, Mar 1986 CS (a)........................ 2.00
❑578, Apr 1986 CS (a)........................ 2.00
❑579, May 1986 CS (a)........................ 2.00
❑580, Jun 1986 CS (a)........................ 2.00
❑581, Jul 1986 CS (a)........................ 2.00
❑582, Aug 1986 CS (a)........................ 2.00
❑583, Sep 1986; AMo (w); CS (a); Continued from Superman #423; Last pre-Crisis on Infinite Earths Superman........................ 2.00
❑584, Jan 1987; JBy (w); JBy, DG (a); A: Titans. Post-Crisis Superman begins........................ 2.00
❑585, Feb 1987 JBy, DG (a); A: Phantom Stranger........................ 2.00
❑586, Mar 1987; JBy, DG (a); A: Orion. New Gods; "Legends" Chapter 19... 2.00
❑587, Apr 1987 JBy, DG (a); A: Demon 2.00
❑588, May 1987; JBy, DG (a); A: Hawkman. Shadow War; Continued from Hawkman #10, continues in Hawkman #11 and Action #589......... 2.00
❑589, Jun 1987 JBy, DG (a); A: Green Lantern Corps........................ 2.00
❑590, Jul 1987; JBy, DG (a); A: Metal Men. new Chemo........................ 2.00
❑591, Aug 1987 JBy, DG (a); A: Superboy........................ 2.00
❑592, Sep 1987 JBy, DG (a); A: Big Barda........................ 2.00
❑593, Oct 1987 JBy, DG (a); A: Mr. Miracle........................ 2.00
❑594, Nov 1987; JBy (a); A: Batman. Continues in Booster Gold #23....... 2.00
❑595, Dec 1987; JBy (a); A: Batman. J'onn J'onzz........................ 2.00
❑596, Jan 1988; JBy (a); A: Spectre. "Millennium" Week 4..................... 2.00
❑597, Feb 1988 JBy (a); A: Lois Lane and Lana Lang........................ 2.00
❑598, Mar 1988 JBy (a); 1: Checkmate 4.00
❑599, Apr 1988; JBy, RA (a); A: Metal Men. Bonus Book #1, Jimmy Olsen 2.00
❑600, May 1988; GP, JBy (a); 50th Anniversary, 80-page Giant; Wonder Woman; pin-ups; "Genesis" prequel 5.00
❑601, Aug 1988; Superman, Blackhawk, Green Lantern, Deadman, Wild Dog, Secret Six; Action Comics begins weekly issues........................ 2.00
❑602, Aug 1988; Superman, Blackhawk, Green Lantern, Deadman, Wild Dog, Secret Six........................ 1.75
❑603, Aug 1988; Superman, Blackhawk, Green Lantern, Deadman, Wild Dog, Secret Six........................ 1.75
❑604, Aug 1988; Superman, Blackhawk, Green Lantern, Deadman, Wild Dog, Secret Six........................ 1.75
❑605, Aug 1988; Superman, Blackhawk, Green Lantern, Deadman, Wild Dog, Secret Six........................ 1.75
❑606, Sep 1988; Superman, Blackhawk, Green Lantern, Deadman, Wild Dog, Secret Six...... 1.75
❑607, Sep 1988; Superman, Blackhawk, Green Lantern, Deadman, Wild Dog, Secret Six...... 1.75

Other grades: Multiply price above by 5/6 for VF/NM • 2/3 for VERY FINE • 1/3 for FINE • 1/5 for VERY GOOD • 1/8 for GOOD

Action Comics

The series that gave birth to Superman

©DC

A.C.T.I.O.N. Force (Lightning)

Not related to the Marvel UK series

©Lightning

Action Girl Comics

Springboard series for female cartoonists

©Slave Labor

Action Planet Comics

Anthology series starring Monsterman

©Action Planet

Actions Speak (Sergio Aragonés)

Sergio Aragonés' wordless humor series

©Dark Horse

	N-MINT
❑608, Sep 1988; Superman, Blackhawk, Green Lantern, Deadman, Wild Dog, Secret Six	1.75
❑609, Sep 1988; BB (c); Superman, Black Canary, Green Lantern, Deadman, Wild Dog, Secret Six	1.75
❑610, Sep 1988; PD (w); CS (a); Superman, Phantom Stranger, Black Canary, Green Lantern, Deadman, Secret Six	1.75
❑611, Oct 1988; PD (w); Superman, Catwoman, Black Canary, Green Lantern, Deadman, Secret Six	1.75
❑612, Oct 1988; PG (c); Superman, Catwoman, Black Canary, Green Lantern, Deadman, Secret Six	1.75
❑613, Oct 1988; Superman, Nightwing/Speedy, Phantom Stranger, Catwoman, Black Canary, Green Lantern	1.75
❑614, Oct 1988; Superman, Nightwing/Speedy, Phantom Stranger, Catwoman, Black Canary, Green Lantern	1.75
❑615, Oct 1988; Superman, Wild Dog, Blackhawk, Nightwing/Speedy, Black Canary, Green Lantern	1.75
❑616, Nov 1988; Superman, Wild Dog, Blackhawk, Nightwing/Speedy, Black Canary, Green Lantern	1.75
❑617, Nov 1988; Superman, Phantom Stranger, Wild Dog, Blackhawk, Nightwing/Speedy, Green Lantern	1.75
❑618, Nov 1988; Superman, Deadman, Wild Dog, Blackhawk, Nightwing/Speedy, Green Lantern	1.75
❑619, Nov 1988; Superman, Secret Six, Deadman, Wild Dog, Blackhawk, Green Lantern	1.75
❑620, Dec 1988; Superman, Secret Six, Deadman, Wild Dog, Blackhawk, Green Lantern	1.75
❑621, Dec 1988; Superman, Secret Six, Deadman, Wild Dog, Blackhawk, Green Lantern	1.75
❑622, Dec 1988; Superman, Starman, Secret Six, Wild Dog, Blackhawk, Green Lantern	1.75
❑623, Dec 1988; BA (c); BA (a); Superman, Deadman, Phantom Stranger, Shazam!, Secret Six, Green Lantern	1.75
❑624, Dec 1988; Superman, Black Canary, Deadman, Shazam!, Secret Six, Green Lantern	1.75
❑625, Dec 1988; Superman, Black Canary, Deadman, Shazam!, Secret Six, Green Lantern	1.75
❑626, Nov 1988; Superman, Black Canary, Deadman, Shazam!, Secret Six, Green Lantern	1.75
❑627, Nov 1988; Superman, Nightwing/Speedy, Black Canary, Secret Six, Green Lantern	1.75
❑628, Nov 1988; Superman, Blackhawk, Nightwing/Speedy, Black Canary, Secret Six, Green Lantern	1.75
❑629, Dec 1988; Superman, Blackhawk, Nightwing/Speedy, Black Canary, Secret Six, Green Lantern	1.75
❑630, Dec 1988; Superman, Blackhawk, Nightwing/Speedy, Black Canary, Secret Six, Green Lantern	1.75
❑631, Dec 1988; Superman, Phantom Stranger, Blackhawk, Nightwing/Speedy, Black Canary, Green Lantern	1.75
❑632, Dec 1988; Superman, Phantom Stranger, Blackhawk, Nightwing/Speedy, Black Canary, Green Lantern	1.75
❑633, Jan 1989; Superman, Phantom Stranger, Blackhawk, Nightwing/Speedy, Black Canary, Green Lantern	1.75
❑634, Jan 1989; Superman, Phantom Stranger, Blackhawk, Nightwing/Speedy, Black Canary, Green Lantern	1.75
❑635, Jan 1989; Superman, Blackhawk, Black Canary, Green Lantern; All characters in first story	1.75
❑636, Jan 1989; 1: new Phantom Lady. Superman, Phantom Lady, Wild Dog, Demon, Speedy, Phantom Stranger	1.75
❑637, Jan 1989; 1: Hero Hotline. Superman, Hero Hotline, Phantom Lady, Wild Dog, Demon, Speedy	1.75
❑638, Feb 1989; JK (c); JK, CS, TD (a); 2: Hero Hotline. Superman, Hero Hotline, Phantom Lady, Wild Dog, Demon, Speedy	1.75
❑639, Feb 1989; A: Hero Hotline. Superman, Hero Hotline, Phantom Lady, Wild Dog, Demon, Speedy	1.75
❑640, Feb 1989; A: Hero Hotline. Superman, Hero Hotline, Phantom Lady, Wild Dog, Demon, Speedy	1.75
❑641, Mar 1989; Superman, Phantom Stranger, Human Target, Phantom Lady, Wild Dog, Demon	1.75
❑642, Mar 1989; Superman, Green Lantern, Nightwing, Deadman, Guy Gardner in one story; Last weekly issue	1.75
❑643, Jul 1989; GP (a); Cover swipe from Superman #1; Title returns to Action Comics; Monthly issues begin again	1.75
❑644, Aug 1989 GP (a)	1.75
❑645, Sep 1989; GP (a); 1: Maxima. V: Maxima. Starman	1.75
❑646, Oct 1989 KG, GP (a)	1.75
❑647, Nov 1989; GP (a); O: Brainiac. Braniac Trilogy, Part 1	1.75
❑648, Dec 1989; GP (a); Braniac Trilogy, Part 2	1.75
❑649, Jan 1990; GP (a); Braniac Trilogy, Part 3	1.75
❑650, Feb 1990 JO, GP (a); A: Lobo	1.75
❑651, Mar 1990; V: Maxima. Day of the Krypton Man, Part 3	1.75
❑652, Apr 1990; Day of the Krypton Man, Part 6	1.75
❑653, May 1990	1.75
❑654, Jun 1990; Batman	1.75
❑655, Jul 1990	1.75
❑656, Aug 1990	1.75
❑657, Sep 1990; Toyman	1.75
❑658, Oct 1990 CS (a); A: Sinbad	1.75
❑659, Nov 1990; Krisis of the Krimson Kryptonite, Part 3	1.75
❑660, Dec 1990 D: Lex Luthor (fake death)	2.50
❑661, Jan 1991; Plastic Man; ▲1991-3	1.75
❑662, Feb 1991; Clark Kent reveals Superman identity to Lois Lane ▲1991-6	4.00
❑662/2nd, Feb 1991; Clark Kent reveals Superman identity to Lois Lane; ▲1991-6, 2nd Printing	1.50
❑663, Mar 1991; Superman in 1940s; JSA; ▲1991-9	1.75
❑664, Apr 1991; A: Chronos. Dinosaurs; ▲1991-12	1.75
❑665, May 1991; ▲1991-15	1.75
❑666, Jun 1991; ▲1991-18	1.75
❑667, Jul 1991; ▲1991-22	2.00
❑668, Aug 1991; ▲1991-26	1.75
❑669, Sep 1991; A: Thorn. ▲1991-30	1.75
❑670, Oct 1991; 1: Lex Luthor II. Armageddon; ▲1991-34	1.75
❑671, Nov 1991; Blackout, Part 2; ▲1991-38	1.75
❑672, Dec 1991; BMc (a); ▲1991-42	1.75
❑673, Jan 1992; BMc (a); V: Hellgrammite. ▲1992-4	1.75
❑674, Feb 1992; BMc (a); Panic in the Sky, Prologue; Supergirl; ▲1992-8	1.75
❑675, Mar 1992; BMc (a); Panic in the Sky, Part 4; ▲1992-12	1.75
❑676, Apr 1992; BG (a); ▲1992-16	1.75
❑677, May 1992; BG (a); ▲1992-20	1.75
❑678, Jun 1992; BG (a); O: Luthor. ▲1992-24	2.00
❑679, Jul 1992; BG (a); ▲1992-28	1.75
❑680, Aug 1992; BG (a); Blaze/Satanus War; ▲1992-32	1.75
❑681, Sep 1992; BG (a); V: Rampage. ▲1992-36	1.75
❑682, Oct 1992; V: Hi-Tech. ▲1992-40	1.75
❑683, Nov 1992; BG (a); Doomsday; ▲1992-44	2.50
❑683/2nd, Nov 1992; BG (a); Doomsday; ▲1992-44, 2nd Printing	1.50
❑684, Dec 1992; BG (a); Doomsday; ▲1992-48	2.50
❑684/2nd, Dec 1992; BG (a); Doomsday; ▲1992-48, 2nd Printing	1.50
❑685, Jan 1993; BG (a); Funeral For a Friend, Part 2; ▲1993-4	2.00
❑685/2nd, Jan 1993; BG (a); Funeral For a Friend, Part 2; ▲1993-4, 2nd Printing	1.25
❑685/3rd, Jan 1993; BG (a); Funeral For a Friend, Part 2; ▲1993-4, 3rd Printing	1.25
❑686, Feb 1993; BG (a); Funeral For a Friend, Part 6; ▲1993-8	2.00
❑687, Jun 1993; BG (a); 1: alien Superman. A: ▲1993-12, 1st. Reign of the Supermen; ▲1993-12	1.50
❑687/CS, Jun 1993; BG (a); Reign of the Supermen; Eradicator; ▲1993-12; Die-cut cover	2.50
❑688, Jul 1993; BG (a); Reign of the Supermen; Guy Gardner; ▲1993-16	2.00
❑689, Jul 1993; BG (a); Reign of the Supermen; ▲1993-20	2.00
❑690, Aug 1993; BG (a); Reign of the Supermen; ▲1993-24	2.00
❑691, Sep 1993; BG (a); Reign of the Supermen; ▲1993-28	2.00
❑692, Oct 1993; BG (a); Clark Kent returns; ▲1993-32	2.00
❑693, Nov 1993; BG (a); ▲1993-36	2.00
❑694, Dec 1993; BG (a); V: Hi-Tech. ▲1993-40	1.75

Other grades: Multiply price above by 5/6 for VF/NM • 2/3 for VERY FINE • 1/3 for FINE • 1/5 for VERY GOOD • 1/8 for GOOD

N-MINT

❑695, Jan 1994; BG (a); A: Lobo. ▲1994-4 .... 1.75
❑695/Variant, Jan 1994; BG (a); A: Lobo. enhanced cover; ▲1994-4 .... 2.50
❑696, Feb 1994; BG (a); Return of Doomsday; ▲1994-8 .... 1.75
❑697, Mar 1994; BG (a); Bizarro's World, Part 3; ▲1994-12 .... 1.75
❑698, Apr 1994; BG (a); ▲1994-16 .... 1.75
❑699, May 1994; The Battle for Metropolis; ▲1994-20 .... 1.75
❑700, Jun 1994; Giant-size; BG (a); The Fall Of Metropolis; Wedding of Pete Ross and Lana Lang; Destruction of the Daily Planet building; ▲1994-24 .... 3.25
❑700/Platinum, Jun 1994; Giant-size; BG (a); No cover price; The Fall Of Metropolis; Wedding of Pete Ross and Lana Lang; Destruction of the Daily Planet building; ▲1994-24 .... 5.00
❑701, Jul 1994; BG (a); Fall of Metropolis; ▲1994-28 .... 1.75
❑702, Aug 1994; BG (a); V: Bloodsport. ▲1994-32 .... 1.75
❑703, Sep 1994; BG (a); A: Liri Lee. A: Starro. Zero Hour; ▲1994-36 .... 1.75
❑704, Nov 1994; BG (a); V: Eradictor and The Outsiders. Dead Again; ▲1994-44 .... 1.75
❑705, Dec 1994; BG (a); Dead Again; ▲1994-48 .... 1.75
❑706, Jan 1995; BG (a); Supergirl; ▲1995-4 .... 1.75
❑707, Feb 1995; BG (a); V: Shadowdragon. ▲1995-8 .... 1.75
❑708, Mar 1995; BG (a); A: Mister Miracle. ▲1995-12 .... 1.75
❑709, Apr 1995; V: Guy Gardner. ▲1995-16 .... 1.75
❑710, Jun 1995; Death of Clark Kent; ▲1995-20 .... 1.95
❑711, Jul 1995; BG (a); D: Kenny Braverman (Conduit). Death of Clark Kent; ▲1995-24 .... 1.95
❑712, Aug 1995; ▲1995-29 .... 1.95
❑713, Sep 1995; ▲1995-33 .... 1.95
❑714, Oct 1995; A: Joker. ▲1995-37 .... 1.95
❑715, Nov 1995; V: Parasite. ▲1995-42 .... 1.95
❑716, Dec 1995; Trial of Superman; ▲1995-46 .... 1.95
❑717, Jan 1996; Trial of Superman; ▲1996-1 .... 1.95
❑718, Feb 1996; 1: Demolitia. ▲1996-5 .... 1.95
❑719, Mar 1996; A: Batman. ▲1996-9 .... 1.95
❑720, Apr 1996; Lois Lane breaks off engagement to Clark Kent; ▲1996-14 .... 2.00
❑720/2nd, Apr 1996; Lois Lane breaks off engagement to Clark Kent; ▲1996-14, 2nd Printing 1.95
❑721, May 1996; A: Mxyzptlk. ▲1996-18 .... 1.95
❑722, Jun 1996; ▲1996-22 .... 1.95
❑723, Jul 1996; ▲1996-27 .... 1.95
❑724, Aug 1996; O: Brawl. D: Brawl. ▲1996-31 .... 1.95
❑725, Sep 1996; V: Tolos. The Bottle City, Part 1; ▲1996-35 .... 1.95
❑726, Oct 1996; V: Barrage. ▲1996-40 .... 1.95
❑727, Nov 1996; Final Night; ▲1996-44 .... 1.95
❑728, Dec 1996; Hawaiian Honeymoon; ▲1996-49 .... 1.95
❑729, Jan 1997; A: Mr. Miracle, Big Barda. Power Struggle; ▲1997-3 .... 1.95
❑730, Feb 1997; V: Superman Revenge Squad (Anomaly, Maxima, Misa, Barrage and Riot). ▲1997-8 .... 1.95
❑731, Mar 1997; V: Cauldron. ▲1997-12 .... 1.95
❑732, Apr 1997; V: Atomic Skull. more energy powers manifest; ▲1997-17 .... 1.95
❑733, May 1997; A: Ray. new uniform; ▲1997-21 .... 1.95
❑734, Jun 1997; Scorn vs. Rock; ▲1997-25 .... 1.95
❑735, Jul 1997; V: Saviour. ▲1997-29 .... 1.95
❑736, Aug 1997; ▲1997-33 .... 1.95
❑737, Sep 1997; Jimmy pursued by Intergang; ▲1997-37 .... 1.95
❑738, Oct 1997; 1: Inkling. ▲1997-42 .... 1.95
❑739, Nov 1997; A: Sam Lane. V: Locksmith. Lois captured by Naga; ▲1997-46 .... 1.95
❑740, Dec 1997; V: Ripper. Face cover; ▲1997-50 .... 1.95
❑741, Jan 1998; A: Legion of Super-Heroes. ▲1998-4 .... 1.95

N-MINT

❑742, Mar 1998; Cover forms diptych with Superman: Man of Steel #77; ▲1998-10 .... 1.95
❑743, Apr 1998; Orgin of Inkling; ▲1998-14 .... 1.95
❑744, May 1998; Millennium Giants; ▲1998-18 .... 1.95
❑745, Jun 1998; V: Prankster. Toyman; ▲1998-23 .... 1.95
❑746, Jul 1998; V: Prankster. Toyman; ▲1998-27 .... 1.95
❑747, Aug 1998; A: Dominus. ▲1998-31 .... 1.95
❑748, Sep 1998; A: Waverider. V: Dominus. ▲1998-35 .... 1.95
❑749, Dec 1998; into Kandor; ▲1998-41 .... 2.00
❑750, Jan 1999; Giant-size; 1: Crazytop. ▲1999-1 .... 2.00
❑751, Feb 1999; A: Lex Luthor. A: Geo-Force. A: DEO agents. ▲1999-6 .... 1.99
❑752, Mar 1999; A: Supermen of America. ▲1999-11 .... 1.99
❑753, Apr 1999; A: Justice League of America. A: JLA. ▲1999-15 .... 1.99
❑754, May 1999; V: Dominus. ▲1999-20 .... 1.99
❑755, Jul 1999; ▲1999-25 .... 1.99
❑756, Aug 1999; V: Doomslayers. ▲1999-30 .... 1.99
❑757, Sep 1999; Superman as Hawkman; ▲1999-34 .... 1.99
❑758, Oct 1999; V: Intergang. ▲1999-38 .... 1.99
❑759, Nov 1999; SB (a); A: Strange Visitor. ▲1999-42 .... 1.99
❑760, Dec 1999; ▲1999-49 .... 1.99
❑761, Jan 2000; A: Wonder Woman. ▲2000-4 .... 1.99
❑762, Feb 2000; ▲2000-9 .... 1.99
❑763, Mar 2000; ▲2000-13 .... 1.99
❑764, Apr 2000; ▲2000-17 .... 1.99
❑765, May 2000; Joker, Harley Quinn; ▲2000-21 .... 1.99
❑766, Jun 2000; ▲2000-25 .... 1.99
❑767, Jul 2000; ▲2000-29 .... 1.99
❑768, Aug 2000; A: Captain Marvel Jr.. A: Captain Marvel. A: Mary Marvel. ▲2000-33 .... 1.99
❑769, Sep 2000; ▲2000-37 .... 2.25
❑770, Oct 2000; Giant-size; A: Joker. ▲2000-42 .... 3.50
❑771, Nov 2000; A: Nightwing. ▲2000-46 .... 2.25
❑772, Dec 2000; A: Encantadora. A: Talia. ▲2000-50 .... 2.25
❑773, Jan 2001; ▲2001-5 .... 2.25
❑774, Feb 2001; ▲2001-9 .... 2.25
❑775, Mar 2001; Giant-size; ▲2001-13 .... 5.00
❑775/2nd, Mar 2001; Second Printing 3.75
❑776, Apr 2001; ▲2001-17 .... 2.25
❑777, May 2001; ▲2001-21 .... 2.25
❑778, Jun 2001; ▲2001-25 .... 2.25
❑779, Jul 2001; ▲2001-29 .... 2.25
❑780, Aug 2001; ▲2001-33 .... 2.25
❑781, Sep 2001; ▲2001-37 .... 2.25
❑782, Oct 2001; ▲2001-41 .... 2.25
❑783, Nov 2001; ▲2001-45 .... 2.25
❑784, Dec 2001; ▲2001-49 .... 2.25
❑785, Jan 2002; ▲2002-4 .... 2.25
❑786, Feb 2002 .... 2.25
❑787, Mar 2002 .... 2.25
❑788, Apr 2002 .... 2.25
❑789, May 2002 .... 2.25
❑790, Jun 2002 .... 2.25
❑791, Jul 2002 .... 2.25
❑792, Aug 2002 .... 2.25
❑793, Sep 2002 .... 2.25
❑794, Oct 2002 .... 2.25
❑795, Nov 2002 KN (c) 2.25
❑796, Dec 2002 .... 2.25
❑797, Jan 2003 .... 2.25
❑798, Feb 2003 .... 2.25
❑799, Mar 2003 .... 2.25
❑800, Apr 2003 .... 3.95
❑801, May 2003 .... 2.25
❑802, Jun 2003 .... 2.25
❑803, Jul 2003 .... 2.25
❑804, Jun 2003 .... 2.25
❑805, Jul 2003 .... 2.25
❑806, Aug 2003 .... 2.25
❑807, Sep 2003 .... 2.25
❑808, Oct 2003 .... 2.25
❑809, Jan 2004 .... 2.25

N-MINT

❑810, Feb 2004 .... 2.25
❑811, Mar 2004 .... 5.00
❑812, Apr 2004 .... 8.00
❑812/2nd, Apr 2004 .... 2.25
❑813, May 2004 .... 4.00
❑814, Jun 2004 .... 3.00
❑815, Jul 2004 .... 3.00
❑816, Aug 2004 .... 3.00
❑817, Sep 2004 .... 3.00
❑818, Oct 2004 .... 4.00
❑819, Nov 2004 .... 2.50
❑820, Dec 2004 .... 2.50
❑821, Jan 2005 .... 2.50
❑822, Feb 2005 .... 2.50
❑823, Mar 2005 .... 2.50
❑824, Mar 2005 .... 2.50
❑825, Apr 2005 .... 2.99
❑826, May 2005 .... 5.00
❑827, Jun 2005 .... 2.50
❑828, Jul 2005 .... 2.50
❑829, Aug 2005 .... 6.00
❑829/Variant, Aug 2005 .... 2.50
❑830, Sep 2005 .... 4.00
❑831, Oct 2005 .... 2.99
❑832 .... 2.99
❑833, Jan 2006 .... 2.99
❑834, Feb 2006 .... 2.99
❑835, Mar 2006 .... 2.99
❑836, Apr 2006 .... 2.99
❑837, Jun 2006 .... 2.99
❑838, Jul 2006 .... 2.99
❑839, Aug 2006 .... 2.99
❑840, Sep 2006 .... 2.99
❑1000000, Nov 1998 .... 1.00
❑Annual 1 1987; DG (a); Batman, female vampire 4.00
❑Annual 2 1989; JO, GP, CS (a); 1: The Eradicator. Matrix and Cat Grant bios; pin-up 3.00
❑Annual 3 1991; Armageddon 2001, Part 8 .... 2.50
❑Annual 4 1992; Eclipso: The Darkness Within, Part 10 .... 2.50
❑Annual 5 1993; JPH (w); 1: Loose Cannon. Bloodlines: Earthplague 2.50
❑Annual 6, ca. 1994; JBy (a); Elseworlds 2.95
❑Annual 7, ca. 1995; Year One 3.95
❑Annual 8, ca. 1996; A: Bizarro. Bizarro; Legends of the Dead Earth 2.95
❑Annual 9, ca. 1997; Pulp Heroes #9 .... 3.95

A.C.T.I.O.N. FORCE (LIGHTNING)
LIGHTNING

❑1, Jan 1987 .... 1.75

ACTION GIRL COMICS
SLAVE LABOR

❑1, Oct 1994 .... 3.50
❑1/2nd, Feb 1996 .... 2.75
❑2, Jan 1995 .... 3.00
❑2/2nd, Oct 1995 .... 2.75
❑3, Apr 1995 .... 3.00
❑3/2nd, Feb 1996 .... 2.75
❑4, Jul 1995 .... 3.00
❑4/2nd, Jul 1996 .... 3.00
❑4/3rd 3.00
❑5, Oct 1995 .... 3.00
❑6, Jan 1996 .... 2.75
❑6/2nd 2.75
❑7, May 1996 .... 2.75
❑8, Jul 1996 .... 2.75
❑9 .... 2.75
❑10, Jan 1997 .... 2.75
❑11, May 1997, b&w 2.75
❑12, Jul 1997 .... 2.75
❑13, Oct 1997 .... 2.75
❑14, Jul 1998 .... 2.75

ACTION PLANET COMICS
ACTION PLANET

❑1, b&w 3.95
❑2, Sep 2000, b&w 3.95
❑3, Sep 1997, b&w 3.95
❑Ashcan 1, b&w; preview of series; "Philly Ashcan Ed." 2.00
❑Giant Size 1, Oct 1998 .... 5.95

Other grades: Multiply price above by 5/6 for VF/NM • 2/3 for VERY FINE • 1/3 for FINE • 1/5 for VERY GOOD • 1/8 for GOOD

A.D.A.M.

Scientist discovers the secret to superpowers
©The Toy Man

Adam-12

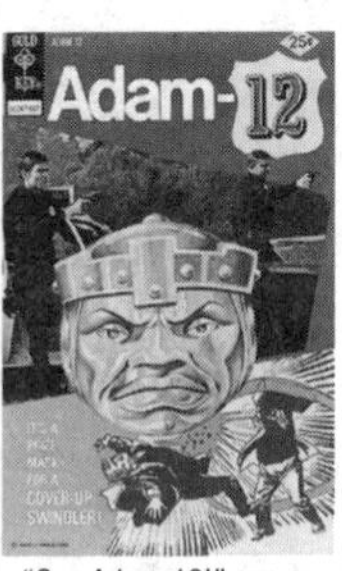

"One Adam-12!" comes to comics from TV
©Gold Key

Adam and Eve A.D.

Science fiction title from the 1980s b&w boom
©Bam

Adam Strange

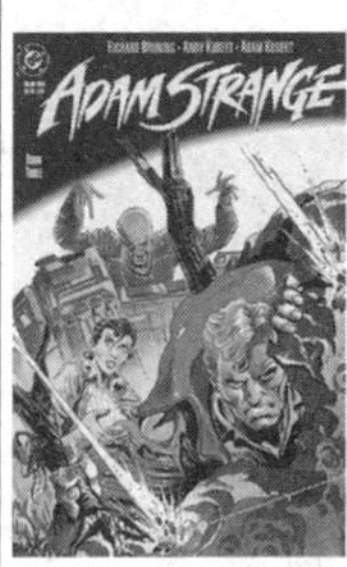

Earthborn space hero gets his own miniseries
©DC

Addam Omega

Post-apocalyptic space series
©Antarctic

N-MINT

ACTIONS SPEAK (SERGIO ARAGONÉS)
Dark Horse
❑1, Jan 2001 2.99
❑2, Feb 2001 2.99
❑3, Mar 2001 2.99
❑4, Apr 2001 2.99
❑5, May 2001 2.99
❑6, Jun 2001 2.99

ADA LEE
NBM
❑1 9.95

A.D.A.M.
The Toy Man
❑1 2.95
❑Ashcan 1; no cover price; preview 1.00

ADAM-12
Gold Key
❑1, Dec 1973 20.00
❑2, Feb 1974 15.00
❑3, May 1974 12.00
❑4, Aug 1974 12.00
❑5, Nov 1974 12.00
❑6, Mar 1975 10.00
❑7, May 1975 10.00
❑8, Aug 1975 10.00
❑9, Nov 1975 10.00
❑10, Feb 1976 10.00

ADAM AND EVE A.D.
Bam
❑1, Sep 1985 1.50
❑2, Nov 1985 1.50
❑3, Jan 1986 1.50
❑4, Mar 1986 1.50
❑5, May 1986 1.50
❑6, Jul 1986 1.50
❑7, Oct 1986 1.50
❑8, Nov 1986 1.50
❑9, Jan 1987 1.50
❑10, Mar 1987 1.50

ADAM BOMB COMICS
Blue Monkey
❑1, Sum 1999, b&w 2.00

ADAM STRANGE
DC
❑1, Mar 1990 3.95
❑2, May 1990 3.95
❑3, Jul 1990 3.95

ADAM STRANGE (2ND SERIES)
DC
❑1, Nov 2004 10.00
❑2, Dec 2004 6.00
❑3, Jan 2005 6.00
❑4, Feb 2005 5.00
❑5, Mar 2005 5.00
❑6, Apr 2005 5.00
❑7, May 2005 7.00
❑8, Jun 2005 8.00

ADDAM OMEGA
Antarctic
❑1, Jan 1997 2.95
❑2, Apr 1997 2.95

N-MINT

❑3, Jun 1997 2.95
❑4, Aug 1997 2.95

ADDAMS FAMILY
Gold Key
❑1, Oct 1974 60.00
❑2, ca. 1975 35.00
❑3, Apr 1975 35.00

ADDAMS FAMILY EPISODE GUIDE
Comic Chronicles
❑1, b&w; illustrated episode guide to original TV series 5.95

ADOLESCENT RADIOACTIVE BLACK BELT HAMSTERS
Eclipse
❑1, b&w 2.00
❑1/Gold 1993; Gold edition; Published by Parody; 500 copies printed 2.95
❑1/2nd 1.50
❑2, Spr 1986 1.50
❑3, Jul 1986 1.50
❑4, Nov 1986 1.50
❑5, Feb 1987 1.50
❑6, May 1987 1.50
❑7, Aug 1987 1.50
❑8, Oct 1987 2.00
❑9, Jan 1988 2.00

ADOLESCENT RADIOACTIVE BLACK BELT HAMSTERS CLASSICS
Parody
❑1, Aug 1992, b&w; Reprints ARBBH in 3-D #1 2.50
❑2, b&w; Reprints ARBBH in 3-D #2 2.50
❑3; Reprints ARBBH (Eclipse) #3 2.50
❑4; Reprints ARBBH: Massacre the Japanese Invasion 2.50
❑5; Reprints ARBBH in 3-D #4; holiday cover 2.50

ADOLESCENT RADIOACTIVE BLACK BELT HAMSTERS IN 3-D
Eclipse
❑1, Jul 1986 2.50
❑2, Sep 1986 2.50
❑3, Nov 1986, aka Eclipse 3-D #13 2.50
❑4, Dec 1986, aka Eclipse 3-D #14 2.50

ADOLESCENT RADIOACTIVE BLACK BELT HAMSTERS: LOST AND ALONE IN NEW YORK
Parody
❑1 2.95

ADOLESCENT RADIOACTIVE BLACK BELT HAMSTERS MASSACRE THE JAPANESE INVASION
Eclipse
❑1, Aug 1989, b&w 2.50

ADOLESCENT RADIOACTIVE BLACK BELT HAMSTERS: THE LOST TREASURES
Parody
❑1, b&w; Reprints portions of ARBBH (Eclipse) #9; cardstock cover 2.95

N-MINT

ADRENALYNN
Image
❑1, Aug 1999 2.50
❑2, Oct 1999 2.50
❑3, Dec 1999; Includes sketchbook pages 2.50
❑4, Feb 2000; Pin-up page 2.50

ADULT ACTION FANTASY FEATURING: TAWNY'S TALES
Louisiana Leisure
❑1 2.50
❑2 2.50

ADULTS ONLY! COMIC MAGAZINE
Inkwell
❑1, Aug 1979 2.50
❑2, Fal 1985 2.50
❑3 2.50

ADVANCED DUNGEONS & DRAGONS
DC
❑1, Dec 1988 2.00
❑2, Jan 1989 1.50
❑3, Feb 1989 1.50
❑4, Mar 1989 1.50
❑5, Apr 1989 1.50
❑6, May 1989 1.50
❑7, Jun 1989 1.50
❑8, Jul 1989 1.50
❑9, Aug 1989 1.50
❑10, Sep 1989 1.50
❑11, Oct 1989 1.50
❑12, Nov 1989 1.50
❑13, Dec 1989 1.50
❑14, Jan 1990 1.50
❑15, Feb 1990 1.50
❑16, Mar 1990 1.50
❑17, Apr 1990 1.50
❑18, May 1990 1.50
❑19, Jun 1990 1.50
❑20, Jul 1990 1.50
❑21, Aug 1990 1.50
❑22, Sep 1990 1.50
❑23, Nov 1990 1.50
❑24, Dec 1990 1.50
❑25, Jan 1991 1.50
❑26, Feb 1991 1.50
❑27, Mar 1991 1.50
❑28, Apr 1991 1.50
❑29, May 1991 1.50
❑30, Jun 1991 1.50
❑31, Jul 1991 1.50
❑32, Aug 1991 1.50
❑33, Sep 1991 1.50
❑34, Oct 1991 1.50
❑35, Nov 1991 1.50
❑36, Dec 1991 1.50
❑Annual 1, ca. 1990 3.00

ADVENTURE COMICS
DC
❑229, Oct 1956, Superboy cover 170.00
❑230, Nov 1956, Superboy cover 170.00
❑231, Dec 1956; Superboy cover; Superbaby story 170.00
❑232, Jan 1957, Superboy cover 170.00

	N-MINT
❑233, Feb 1957, Superboy cover	170.00
❑234, Mar 1957, Superboy cover	170.00
❑235, Apr 1957, Superboy cover	170.00
❑236, May 1957, Superboy cover; Pa Kent regains superpowers	170.00
❑237, Jun 1957, Superboy cover	170.00
❑238, Jul 1957, Superboy cover	170.00
❑239, Aug 1957; CS (c); Superboy cover	170.00
❑240, Sep 1957, Superboy cover	170.00
❑241, Oct 1957, Superboy cover	170.00
❑242, Nov 1957, Superboy cover	170.00
❑243, Dec 1957, Superboy cover	170.00
❑244, Jan 1958; Superboy cover	170.00
❑245, Feb 1958, Superboy cover	170.00
❑246, Mar 1958, Superboy cover	170.00
❑247, Apr 1958, 1&O: Legion of Super-Heroes, Cosmic Boy, Saturn Girl, Lightning Lad. Superboy joins Legion of Super-Heroes	4400.00
❑248, May 1958, Superboy cover	130.00
❑249, Jun 1958, Superboy cover	130.00
❑250, Jul 1958, Superboy cover	130.00
❑251, Aug 1958, Superboy cover	130.00
❑252, Sep 1958; Superboy cover	130.00
❑253, Oct 1958, Superboy cover; Robin meets Superboy	130.00
❑254, Nov 1958, Superboy cover	130.00
❑255, Dec 1958, 1: Red Kryptonite. Superboy cover; Clark and Superboy separated by alien	130.00
❑256, Jan 1959, JK (a); O: Green Arrow. Superboy cover	525.00
❑257, Feb 1959; Superboy cover	125.00
❑258, Mar 1959, Superboy cover; Young Oliver Queen visits Smallville	125.00
❑259, Apr 1959; Superboy cover	125.00
❑260, May 1959, O: Aquaman. Superboy cover	500.00
❑261, Jun 1959, Superboy cover; Lois Lane meets Superboy	80.00
❑262, Jul 1959, O: Speedy. Superboy cover; Krypto gets super-sized	80.00
❑263, Aug 1959, Superboy cover	80.00
❑264, Sep 1959, Superboy cover	80.00
❑265, Oct 1959, A: Superman. Superboy cover; Superboy builds first Superman robot	80.00
❑266, Nov 1959, A: Superman. Superboy cover	80.00
❑267, Dec 1959, JM (a); 2: Legion of Super-Heroes. Superboy cover	740.00
❑268, Jan 1960, Superboy cover	80.00
❑269, Feb 1960, 1: Aqualad. Superboy cover	225.00
❑270, Mar 1960, A: Congorilla. Superboy cover	80.00
❑271, Apr 1960, O: Lex Luthor. A: Congorilla. Superboy cover	225.00
❑272, May 1960; A: Congorilla. Superboy cover	65.00
❑273, Jun 1960, A: Congorilla. Superboy cover	65.00
❑274, Jul 1960; A: Congorilla. Superboy cover	65.00
❑275, Aug 1960, O: Superman/Batman Team-up. A: Congorilla. Superboy cover	145.00
❑276, Sep 1960, 1: Sun Boy. A: Congorilla. Superboy cover	65.00
❑277, Oct 1960, A: Congorilla. Superboy cover	65.00
❑278, Nov 1960, A: Supergirl. A: Congorilla. Superboy cover	65.00
❑279, Dec 1960, CS (a); 1: White Kryptonite. A: Congorilla. Superboy cover	65.00
❑280, Jan 1961, A: Lori Lemaris. A: Congorilla. Superboy meets Lori Lemaris	65.00
❑281, Feb 1961, A: Congorilla. Congo Bill	60.00
❑282, Mar 1961, O: Starboy. 1: Starboy. A: Congorilla. Superboy cover	95.00
❑283, Apr 1961; 1: Phantom Zone. A: Congorilla. Superboy cover	100.00
❑284, May 1961, Superboy cover	60.00
❑285, Jun 1961, 1: Bizarro World. Tales of the Bizarro World	110.00
❑286, Jul 1961, 1: Bizarro Mxyzptlk. Tales of the Bizarro World	110.00
❑287, Aug 1961, Superboy cover	60.00

	N-MINT
❑288, Sep 1961, 1: Dev-Em. Superboy cover	60.00
❑289, Oct 1961; Superboy cover	60.00
❑290, Nov 1961, O: Sun Boy. A: Legion of Super-Heroes. Sun Boy joins Legion of Super-Heroes	100.00
❑291, Dec 1961, Superboy cover	45.00
❑292, Jan 1962, Superboy cover	45.00
❑293, Feb 1962, CS (a); O: Mon-El. 1: Mon-El in Legion. 1: Legion of Super-Pets. Bizarro Luthor	100.00
❑294, Mar 1962, 1: Bizarro Marilyn Monroe. Superboy cover	90.00
❑295, Apr 1962, Superboy cover	45.00
❑296, May 1962, Superboy cover	45.00
❑297, Jun 1962, Superboy cover	45.00
❑298, Jul 1962, Superboy cover	45.00
❑299, Aug 1962, 1: Gold Kryptonite. Superboy; Bizarro world story	55.00
❑300, Sep 1962, 300th anniversary issue; Legion cover; Mon-El joins team; Legion of Super-Heroes begins as a regular back-up feature	200.00
❑301, Oct 1962, O: Bouncing Boy	70.00
❑302, Nov 1962, Legion	55.00
❑303, Dec 1962, 1: Matter-Eater Lad. Matter-Eater Lad joins team; Legion	55.00
❑304, Jan 1963, D: Lightning Lad. Legion	55.00
❑305, Feb 1963, Legion	55.00
❑306, Mar 1963, 1: Legion of Substitute Heroes. "Teen-age" Mxyzptlk	45.00
❑307, Apr 1963, 1: Element Lad. 1: Roxxas. Element Lad joins team; Legion	45.00
❑308, May 1963, 1: Lightning Lass. 1: Proty. Legion; Lightning Lass joins team	45.00
❑309, Jun 1963, Legion	45.00
❑310, Jul 1963, Legion	45.00
❑311, Aug 1963, 1: Legion of Super-Heroes Headquarters. A: Legion of Substitute Heroes. Legion	45.00
❑312, Sep 1963, D: Proty. Legion; Return of Lightning Lad	45.00
❑313, Oct 1963, CS (a); Legion	45.00
❑314, Nov 1963, Legion	45.00
❑315, Dec 1963, Legion	45.00
❑316, Jan 1964, CS (a); profile pages; Legion	45.00
❑317, Feb 1964, 1: Dream Girl. Dream Girl joins team; Legion	45.00
❑318, Mar 1964, Legion	45.00
❑319, Apr 1964, Legion	45.00
❑320, May 1964, Legion	45.00
❑321, Jun 1964, 1: Time Trapper. Legion	45.00
❑322, Jul 1964, Legion	45.00
❑323, Aug 1964, Legion	45.00
❑324, Sep 1964, 1: Duplicate Boy. 1: Heroes of Lallor (later Wanderers). Legion	40.00
❑325, Oct 1964, Legion	40.00
❑326, Nov 1964, Legion	40.00
❑327, Dec 1964, 1: Timber Wolf. Timber Wolf joins team	40.00
❑328, Jan 1965, Legion	40.00
❑329, Feb 1965, JM (a); 1: Bizarro Legion of Super-Heroes. Legion	40.00
❑330, Mar 1965, JM (a); Dynamo Boy joins team; Legion	40.00
❑331, Apr 1965, JM (a); 1: Saturn Queen. Legion	40.00
❑332, May 1965, Legion	40.00
❑333, Jun 1965, Legion	40.00
❑334, Jul 1965, Legion	40.00
❑335, Aug 1965, 1: Magnetic Kid. 1: Starfinger. Legion	40.00
❑336, Sep 1965, Legion	40.00
❑337, Oct 1965, Legion; Wedding of Lightning Lad and Saturn Girl, Mon-El and Phantom Girl (fake weddings)	40.00
❑338, Nov 1965, 1: Glorith. V: Time-Trapper, Glorith	40.00
❑339, Dec 1965, Legion	40.00
❑340, Jan 1966, CS (a); 1: Computo. D: one of Triplicate Girl's bodies. Legion	40.00
❑341, Feb 1966, CS (a); Legion	40.00
❑342, Mar 1966, CS (a); 1: Kid. Legion	40.00
❑343, Apr 1966, CS (a); Legion; reprints story from Superboy #90	40.00
❑344, May 1966, CS (a); Legion	40.00

	N-MINT
❑345, Jun 1966, CS (a); 1: Khunds. D: Blockade Boy, Weight Wizard. Legion	40.00
❑346, Jul 1966, 1: Karate Kid, Princess Projectra, Ferro Lad. Karate Kid, Princess Projecta, Ferro Lad joins team	40.00
❑347, Aug 1966, CS (a); Legion	40.00
❑348, Sep 1966, O: Sunboy. 1: Doctor Regulus. V: Doctor Regulus. Legion	40.00
❑349, Oct 1966, 1: Rond Vidar	40.00
❑350, Nov 1966, CS (a); 1: Mysa Nal. 1: Prince Evillo. Legion	40.00
❑351, Dec 1966, CS (a); 1: White Witch	50.00
❑352, Jan 1967, CS (a); 1: The Fatal Five. Legion	35.00
❑353, Feb 1967, CS (a); D: Ferro Lad	35.00
❑354, Mar 1967, CS (a); Legion	35.00
❑355, Apr 1967, CS (a); Adult Legion story	35.00
❑356, May 1967, CS (a); Legion	30.00
❑357, Jun 1967, CS (a); 1: Controllers. Legion	30.00
❑358, Jul 1967, Legion	30.00
❑359, Aug 1967, CS (a); Legion	30.00
❑360, Sep 1967, CS (a); Legion	30.00
❑361, Oct 1967, JM (a); A: Dominators. V: Unkillables. Legion	30.00
❑362, Nov 1967, V: Mantis Morlo. Legion	30.00
❑363, Dec 1967, V: Mantis Morlo. Legion	30.00
❑364, Jan 1968, CS (a); Legion	30.00
❑365, Feb 1968, NA, CS (a); 1: Shadow Lass	30.00
❑366, Mar 1968, NA (c); NA, CS (a); V: Validus. Legion; Shadow Lass joins Legion	30.00
❑367, Apr 1968, NA (c); CS (a); 1: The Dark Circle. Legion	25.00
❑368, May 1968, Legion	25.00
❑369, Jun 1968, 1: Mordru. Legion in Smallville	25.00
❑370, Jul 1968, Legion	25.00
❑371, Aug 1968, NA (a); 1: Chemical King. 1: Legion Academy. Legion; Colossal Boy leaves team	25.00
❑372, Sep 1968, NA (a); Legion; Chemical King joins Legion; Timber Wolf joins Legion	25.00
❑373, Oct 1968, Legion	22.00
❑374, Nov 1968, Legion	22.00
❑375, Dec 1968, NA (a); 1: Wanderers. 1: Quantum Queen. Legion	22.00
❑376, Jan 1969, Legion	22.00
❑377, Feb 1969, NA (c); NA (a); Legion	22.00
❑378, Mar 1969, NA (c); NA (a); Legion	22.00
❑379, Apr 1969, NA (c); NA (a); Legion	22.00
❑380, Apr 1969, CS (c); CS (a); Legion; Legion of Super-Heroes stories end	22.00
❑381, Jun 1969, Supergirl stories begin	58.00
❑382, Jul 1969, Supergirl	22.00
❑383, Aug 1969, Supergirl	22.00
❑384, Sep 1969, CS (c); Supergirl	22.00
❑385, Oct 1969, Supergirl	22.00
❑386, Nov 1969, A: Mxyzptlk. Supergirl	22.00
❑387, Dec 1969, V: Lex Luthor. Supergirl	22.00
❑388, Jan 1970, V: Lex Luthor. Supergirl	22.00
❑389, Feb 1970, Supergirl	22.00
❑390, Apr 1970, aka Giant #G-69; All-Romance issue	22.00
❑391, Mar 1970, Supergirl	22.00
❑392, Apr 1970, Supergirl	22.00
❑393, May 1970, Supergirl	22.00
❑394, Jun 1970, Supergirl	22.00
❑395, Jul 1970, Supergirl	22.00
❑396, Aug 1970, Supergirl	22.00
❑397, Sep 1970, Supergirl	22.00
❑398, Oct 1970, Supergirl	22.00
❑399, Nov 1970, Supergirl; previously unpublished Black Canary story	22.00
❑400, Dec 1970, 35th anniversary; Supergirl	22.00
❑401, Jan 1971, Supergirl	21.00
❑402, Feb 1971, Supergirl loses powers	21.00
❑403, Apr 1971, CS (c); aka Giant #G-81; Death and rebirth of Lightning Lad (reprints from Adventure Comics #302, #305, #308, and #312; G-81	30.00

Other grades: Multiply price above by 5/6 for VF/NM • 2/3 for VERY FINE • 1/3 for FINE • 1/5 for VERY GOOD • 1/8 for GOOD

Adolescent Radioactive Black Belt Hamsters

Best-remembered of the Turtles knockoffs

©Eclipse

AD Police

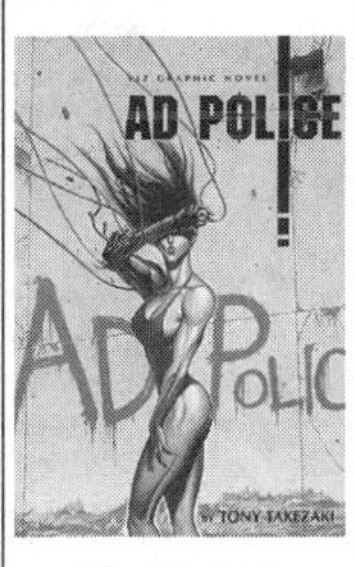

Spinoff from the Bubblegum Crisis series

©Viz

Adrenalynn

A sweet little girl with built-in firepower

©Image

Advanced Dungeons & Dragons

Role-playing game comes to comics

©DC

Adventure Comics

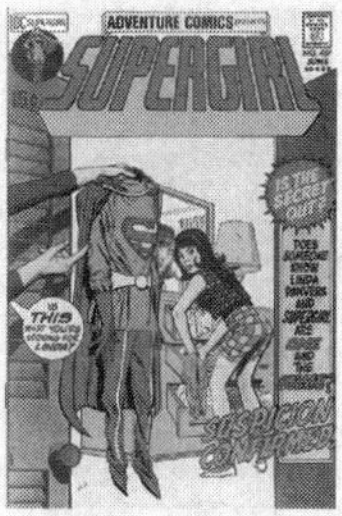

Legion, Superboy all starred in this classic title

©DC

N-MINT

❑404, Mar 1971, Supergirl gets exo-skeleton ... 20.00
❑405, Apr 1971 ... 20.00
❑406, May 1971, Linda graduates from college, takes job at TV station ... 20.00
❑407, Jun 1971, Supergirl gets new costume ... 20.00
❑408, Jul 1971 ... 20.00
❑409, Aug 1971; reprints Legion story from Adventure #313; Supergirl gets new costume ... 20.00
❑410, Sep 1971 ... 20.00
❑411, Oct 1971, BO (a); reprints Legion story from Adventure #337 ... 20.00
❑412, Nov 1971, BO (a); 1: Animal Man. Animal Man reprint; reprints Strange Adventures #180 ... 20.00
❑413, Dec 1971 BO (a) ... 20.00
❑414, Jan 1972 BO (a); A: Animal Man ... 20.00
❑415, Feb 1972; BO (a); Animal Man reprint ... 20.00
❑416, Mar 1972, a.k.a. DC 100-Page Super Spectacular #DC-10; all-women issue; wrap-around cover; reprints stories from Flash Comics #86, Wonder Woman #28, Police Comics #17, Star Spangled Comics #90, and Action Comics #324 ... 18.00
❑417, Mar 1972, BO, FF (a); reprints Frazetta Shining Knight story; reprints Enchantress origin ... 13.00
❑418, Apr 1972, BO (a); Contains previously unpublished Golden Age Doctor Mid-Nite story ... 13.00
❑419, May 1972, BO (a) ... 13.00
❑420, Jun 1972, CS (a); Animal Man reprint ... 13.00
❑421, Jul 1972, Animal Man reprint ... 13.00
❑422, Aug 1972, BO, GM (a) ... 13.00
❑423, Sep 1972 ... 13.00
❑424, Oct 1972 ... 13.00
❑425, Jan 1973, ATh (a); O: Captain Fear. 1: Captain Fear ... 13.00
❑426, Mar 1973 ... 13.00
❑427, May 1973 ... 13.00
❑428, Aug 1973, 1: Black Orchid ... 28.00
❑429, Oct 1973, A: Black Orchid ... 15.00
❑430, Dec 1973, A: Black Orchid ... 15.00
❑431, Feb 1974, ATh, JA (a); A: Spectre. Spectre stories begin ... 28.00
❑432, Apr 1974 ... 15.00
❑433, Jun 1974, JA (a); A: Spectre ... 15.00
❑434, Aug 1974 ... 12.00
❑435, Oct 1974, JA (a); A: Spectre. Aquaman back-up ... 12.00
❑436, Dec 1974, JA (a); A: Spectre. Aquaman back-up ... 10.00
❑437, Feb 1975; Previously unpublished Seven Soldiers of Victory back-up; Aquaman ... 10.00
❑438, Apr 1975; Previously unpublished Seven Soldiers of Victory back-up; Aquaman ... 10.00
❑439, Jun 1975; Previously unpublished Seven Soldiers of Victory back-up; Aquaman ... 8.00
❑440, Aug 1975, O: Spectre-New. Previously unpublished Seven Soldiers of Victory back-up; Aquaman ... 8.00

N-MINT

❑441, Oct 1975, Previously unpublished Seven Soldiers of Victory back-up; Aquaman ... 8.00
❑442, Dec 1975, Previously unpublished Seven Soldiers of Victory back-up; Aquaman ... 6.00
❑443, Feb 1976, Previously unpublished Seven Soldiers of Victory back-up; Aquaman ... 6.00
❑444, Apr 1976, Aquaman ... 6.00
❑445, Jun 1976 ... 6.00
❑446, Aug 1976, Bicentennial #31 ... 6.00
❑447, Oct 1976 ... 6.00
❑448, Nov 1976 ... 5.00
❑449, Jan 1977 ... 5.00
❑450, Mar 1977 ... 5.00
❑451, May 1977 ... 5.00
❑452, Jul 1977, Aquaman stories end ... 5.00
❑453, Sep 1977, A: Barbara Gordon. Superboy stories begin ... 5.00
❑454, Nov 1977 ... 5.00
❑455, Jan 1978 ... 5.00
❑456, Mar 1978 ... 5.00
❑457, May 1978 ... 5.00
❑458, Jul 1978 ... 5.00
❑459, Sep 1978; DN, JSa, JA (a); no ads; expands contents and raises price to $1 ... 3.50
❑460, Nov 1978 DN, SA, JSa (a) ... 3.50
❑461, Jan 1979, Giant-size issue; DN, JSa, JA (a); incorporates JSA story from unpublished All-Star Comics #75 ... 6.00
❑462, Mar 1979, Giant-size issue DG, JSa, JL (a); D: E-2 Batman ... 7.00
❑463, May 1979, FMc, DH, JSa, JL (a) ... 3.50
❑464, Jul 1979; contains previously unpublished Deadman story from Showcase #105 ... 3.50
❑465, Sep 1979 ... 3.50
❑466, Nov 1979, final JSA case before group retired in the '50s; final $1 issue ... 3.50
❑467, Jan 1980 ... 3.50
❑468, Feb 1980 ... 3.50
❑469, Mar 1980, 1&O: Starman III (Prince Gavyn) ... 3.50
❑470, Apr 1980, O: Starman III (Prince Gavyn) ... 3.50
❑471, May 1980 ... 3.50
❑472, Jun 1980 ... 3.50
❑473, Jul 1980 ... 3.50
❑474, Aug 1980 ... 3.50
❑475, Sep 1980 ... 3.50
❑476, Oct 1980 ... 3.50
❑477, Nov 1980 ... 3.50
❑478, Dec 1980 ... 3.50
❑479, Mar 1981, 1: Victoria Grant. 1: Christopher King. Dial "H" For Hero ... 3.50
❑480, Apr 1981, Dial "H" For Hero ... 3.00
❑481, May 1981, Dial "H" For Hero ... 3.00
❑482, Jun 1981, Dial "H" For Hero ... 3.00
❑483, Jul 1981, Dial "H" For Hero ... 3.00
❑484, Aug 1981, Dial "H" For Hero ... 3.00
❑485, Sep 1981, Dial "H" For Hero ... 3.00
❑486, Oct 1981, Dial "H" For Hero ... 3.00
❑487, Nov 1981, Dial "H" For Hero ... 3.00

N-MINT

❑488, Dec 1981, Dial "H" For Hero ... 3.00
❑489, Jan 1982, Dial "H" For Hero ... 3.00
❑490, Feb 1982, Dial "H" For Hero; series goes on hiatus ... 3.00
❑491, Sep 1982, digest size begins; Returns from hiatus; digests begin; reprints Black Canary story from Adventure #418 ... 3.00
❑492, Oct 1982; reprints Black Canary story from Adventure #419 ... 3.00
❑493, Nov 1982, A: Challengers of the Unknown ... 3.00
❑494, Dec 1982, A: Challengers of the Unknown ... 3.00
❑495, Jan 1983, A: Challengers of the Unknown ... 3.00
❑496, Feb 1983, A: Challengers of the Unknown ... 3.00
❑497, Mar 1983, A: Challengers of the Unknown ... 3.00
❑498, Apr 1983 ... 3.00
❑499, May 1983 ... 3.00
❑500, Jun 1983 ... 3.00
❑501, Jul 1983 ... 3.00
❑502, Aug 1983 ... 3.00
❑503, Sep 1983 ... 3.00

ADVENTURE COMICS (2ND SERIES)
DC

❑1, May 1999 ... 1.99
❑Giant Size 1, Oct 1998; Giant size; Wonder Woman, Captain Marvel, Superboy, Green Arrow, Legion, Supergirl, Bizarro ... 4.95

ADVENTURE OF THE COPPER BEECHES
TOME

❑1; Reprints Cases of Sherlock Holmes #9 ... 2.50

ADVENTURERS (AIRCEL)
AIRCEL

❑1; regular cover ... 2.00
❑1/Ltd.; skeleton cover; Limited ed ... 2.00
❑2 ... 2.00

ADVENTURERS (BOOK 1)
ADVENTURE

❑0, ca. 1986 ... 1.50
❑1, Aug 1986 ... 1.50
❑1/2nd, Aug 1986; published by Adventure ... 1.50
❑2, ca. 1986 ... 1.50
❑3, ca. 1986; no indicia ... 1.50
❑4, ca. 1986 ... 1.50
❑5, ca. 1986 ... 1.50
❑6, Jun 1987 ... 1.50
❑7, Jul 1987 ... 1.50
❑8, Sep 1987 ... 1.50
❑9, Oct 1987 ... 1.75
❑10, Nov 1987 ... 1.75

ADVENTURERS (BOOK 2)
ADVENTURE

❑0, Jul 1988, b&w ... 1.95
❑1, Dec 1987; regular cover ... 1.50
❑1/Ltd., Dec 1987; Limited edition cover; Limited edition cover ... 1.50
❑2, Mar 1988 ... 1.50
❑3, Apr 1988 ... 1.50
❑4, Jun 1988 ... 1.50

- ❑5, Aug 1988 1.50
- ❑6, Nov 1988 1.50
- ❑7, Mar 1989, b&w 1.50
- ❑8, ca. 1989 1.50
- ❑9, ca. 1989 1.50
- ❑10, ca. 1989 1.50

ADVENTURERS (BOOK 3)
ADVENTURE

- ❑1, Oct 1989; regular cover 2.25
- ❑1/Ltd., Oct 1989; Limited edition cover; Limited edition cover 2.25
- ❑2, Nov 1989 2.25
- ❑3, Dec 1989 2.25
- ❑4, Jan 1990 2.25
- ❑5, Feb 1990 2.25
- ❑6, Mar 1990 2.25

ADVENTURES OF BIO BOY
SPEAKEASY COMICS

- ❑1, Oct 2005 2.99

ADVENTURES @ EBAY
EBAY

- ❑1, ca. 2000; eBay employee premium 1.00

ADVENTURES IN READING STARRING: THE AMAZING SPIDER-MAN
MARVEL

- ❑1, Sep 1990; Giveaway to promote literacy 1.00

ADVENTURES IN THE DC UNIVERSE
DC

- ❑1, Apr 1997, JLA 2.50
- ❑2, May 1997, O: The Flash III (Wally West) 2.00
- ❑3, Jun 1997; Batman vs. Poison Ivy; Wonder Woman vs. Cheetah 2.00
- ❑4, Jul 1997, Mr. Miracle; Green Lantern 2.00
- ❑5, Aug 1997, A: Ultra the Multi-Alien. Martian Manhunter 2.00
- ❑6, Sep 1997, Power Girl; Aquaman 2.00
- ❑7, Oct 1997, A: Clark Kent. A: Lois Lane. Marvel Family 2.00
- ❑8, Nov 1997; Question; Blue Beetle; Booster Gold 2.00
- ❑9, Dec 1997, Flash vs. Gorilla Grodd 2.00
- ❑10, Jan 1998, Legion of Super-Heroes 2.00
- ❑11, Feb 1998, Wonder Woman, Green Lantern 2.00
- ❑12, Mar 1998; JLA vs. Cipher 2.00
- ❑13, Apr 1998, Green Arrow; Impulse, Martian Manhunter 1.95
- ❑14, May 1998, Nightwing; Superboy, Flash 1.95
- ❑15, Jun 1998; Aquaman; Captain Marvel 1.95
- ❑16, Jul 1998; Green Arrow; Green Lantern 1.95
- ❑17, Aug 1998, Creeper; Batman 1.95
- ❑18, Sep 1998, JLA vs. Amazo 1.95
- ❑19, Oct 1998; Wonder Woman, Catwoman 1.99
- ❑Annual 1, Oct 1998; DG (a); Doctor Fate, Impulse, Superboy, Thorn, Mr. Miracle; events crossover with Superman Adventures Annual #1 and Batman & Robin Adventures Annual #2 3.95

ADVENTURES IN THE MYSTWOOD
BLACKTHORNE

- ❑1, Aug 1986 2.00

ADVENTURES IN THE RIFLE BRIGADE
DC / VERTIGO

- ❑1, Oct 2000 2.50
- ❑2, Nov 2000 2.50
- ❑3, Dec 2000 2.50

ADVENTURES IN THE RIFLE BRIGADE: OPERATION BOLLOCK
DC / VERTIGO

- ❑1, Oct 2001 2.50
- ❑2, Nov 2001 2.50
- ❑3, Dec 2001 2.50

ADVENTURES INTO THE UNKNOWN (A+)
A-PLUS

- ❑1, ca. 1991, b&w; Reprints 2.50
- ❑2, ca. 1990, Reprints 2.50
- ❑3, Reprints 2.50
- ❑4, Reprints 2.50

ADVENTURES MADE IN AMERICA
RIP OFF

- ❑0; Preview 2.75
- ❑1 2.75
- ❑2 2.75
- ❑3 2.75
- ❑4 2.75
- ❑5 2.75
- ❑6 2.75

ADVENTURES OF AARON
CHIASMUS

- ❑1 2.50
- ❑2, Jul 1995 2.50

ADVENTURES OF AARON (2ND SERIES)
IMAGE

- ❑1, Mar 1997 2.95
- ❑2, May 1997 2.95
- ❑3, Sep 1997, "Adventures of Dad" back-up 2.95
- ❑100, Jul 1997 2.95

ADVENTURES OF ADAM & BRYON
AMERICAN MULE

- ❑1, May 1998 2.50

ADVENTURES OF A LESBIAN COLLEGE SCHOOL GIRL
NBM

- ❑1 8.95

ADVENTURES OF BAGBOY AND CHECKOUT GIRL
ACETELYNE

- ❑Ashcan 1, Apr 2002 1.00

ADVENTURES OF BARON MUNCHAUSEN
NOW

- ❑1, Jul 1989 2.00
- ❑2, Aug 1989 2.00
- ❑3, Sep 1989 2.00
- ❑4, Oct 1989 2.00

ADVENTURES OF BARRY WEEN, BOY GENIUS
IMAGE

- ❑1, Mar 1999, b&w 2.95
- ❑2, Apr 1999, b&w; Jeremy turned into dinosaur 2.95
- ❑3, May 1999, b&w; at museum 2.95

ADVENTURES OF BARRY WEEN, BOY GENIUS 2.0
ONI

- ❑1, Feb 2000, b&w 2.95
- ❑2, Mar 2000, b&w; in the old West 2.95
- ❑3, Apr 2000, b&w 2.95

ADVENTURES OF BARRY WEEN, BOY GENIUS 3: MONKEY TALES
ONI

- ❑1, Feb 2001, b&w 2.95
- ❑2, Apr 2001, b&w 2.95
- ❑3, Jun 2001, b&w 2.95
- ❑4, Aug 2001, b&w 2.95
- ❑5, Oct 2001, b&w 2.95
- ❑6, Feb 2002, b&w 2.95

ADVENTURES OF BAYOU BILLY
ARCHIE

- ❑1, Sep 1989, Archie, Jughead, Betty, and Veronica public service announcement inside back cover 1.00
- ❑2, Nov 1989 1.00
- ❑3, Jan 1990 1.00
- ❑4, Apr 1990 1.00
- ❑5, Jun 1990 1.00

ADVENTURES OF BOB HOPE
DC

- ❑41, Oct 1956 55.00
- ❑42, Dec 1956 55.00
- ❑43, Feb 1957 55.00
- ❑44, Apr 1957 55.00
- ❑45, Jun 1957 55.00
- ❑46, Aug 1957 55.00
- ❑47, Oct 1957 55.00
- ❑48, Dec 1957 55.00
- ❑49, Feb 1958 55.00
- ❑50, Apr 1958 55.00
- ❑51, Jun 1958 40.00
- ❑52, Aug 1958 40.00
- ❑53, Oct 1958 40.00
- ❑54, Dec 1958 40.00
- ❑55, Feb 1959 40.00
- ❑56, Apr 1959 40.00
- ❑57, Jun 1959 40.00
- ❑58, Aug 1959 40.00
- ❑59, Oct 1959 40.00
- ❑60, Dec 1959 40.00
- ❑61, Feb 1960 35.00
- ❑62, Apr 1960 35.00
- ❑63, Jun 1960 35.00
- ❑64, Aug 1960 35.00
- ❑65, Oct 1960 35.00
- ❑66, Dec 1960 35.00
- ❑67, Feb 1961 35.00
- ❑68, Apr 1961 35.00
- ❑69, Jun 1961 35.00
- ❑70, Aug 1961 35.00
- ❑71, Oct 1961 30.00
- ❑72, Dec 1961 30.00
- ❑73, Feb 1962 30.00
- ❑74, Apr 1962, MD (a) 30.00
- ❑75, Jun 1962, MD (a) 30.00
- ❑76, Aug 1962, MD (a) 30.00
- ❑77, Oct 1962 30.00
- ❑78, Dec 1962 30.00
- ❑79, Feb 1963 30.00
- ❑80, Apr 1963 30.00
- ❑81, Jun 1963 25.00
- ❑82, Aug 1963, MD (a) 25.00
- ❑83, Oct 1963 25.00
- ❑84, Dec 1963 25.00
- ❑85, Feb 1964, MD (a) 25.00
- ❑86, Apr 1964 25.00
- ❑87, Jun 1964, MD (a) 25.00
- ❑88, Aug 1964 25.00
- ❑89, Oct 1964, MD (a) 25.00
- ❑90, Dec 1964, MD (a) 25.00
- ❑91, Feb 1965, MD (a) 15.00
- ❑92, Apr 1965 15.00
- ❑93, Jun 1965 15.00
- ❑94, Aug 1965, A: Aquaman 15.00
- ❑95, Oct 1965, 1: Super-Hip and monster faculty 15.00
- ❑96, Dec 1965 15.00
- ❑97, Feb 1966 15.00
- ❑98, Apr 1966 15.00
- ❑99, Jun 1966 15.00
- ❑100, Aug 1966, Super-Hip as President 15.00
- ❑101, Oct 1966 15.00
- ❑102, Dec 1966 15.00
- ❑103, Feb 1967, A: Batman, Nancy, Ringo Starr, Frank Sinatra, Stanley and his Monster 15.00
- ❑104, May 1967 15.00
- ❑105, Jun 1967, A: David Janssen, Dan Blocker, Ed Sullivan, Don Adams 15.00
- ❑106, Aug 1967, NA (c); NA (a) 25.00
- ❑107, Oct 1967, NA (c); NA (a) 25.00
- ❑108, Dec 1967, NA (c); NA (a) 25.00
- ❑109, Feb 1968, NA (c); NA (a) 25.00

ADVENTURES OF B.O.C.
INVASION

- ❑1, Nov 1986 1.50
- ❑2, Jan 1987 1.50
- ❑3, Mar 1987 1.50

ADVENTURES OF BROWSER & SEQUOIA
SABERCAT

- ❑1, Aug 1999 2.95

ADVENTURES OF CAPTAIN AMERICA
MARVEL

- ❑1, Sep 1991 4.95
- ❑2, Nov 1991 4.95
- ❑3, Dec 1991 4.95
- ❑4, Jan 1992 4.95

ADVENTURES OF CAPTAIN JACK
FANTAGRAPHICS

- ❑1, Jun 1986 2.00
- ❑2, Sep 1986 2.00
- ❑3, Oct 1986 2.00
- ❑4, Nov 1986 2.00
- ❑5, Dec 1986; no indicia 2.00
- ❑6, Jan 1987 2.00
- ❑7, Mar 1987 2.00

Adventurers (Book 1)

Well-done sword and sorcery title

©Adventure

Adventures in the DC Universe

DC heroes get Batman Adventures treatment

©DC

Adventures of Bob Hope

Film, stand-up, and TV star conquers comics

©DC

Adventures of Captain Jack

Funny-animal science fiction series

©Fantagraphics

Adventures of Jerry Lewis

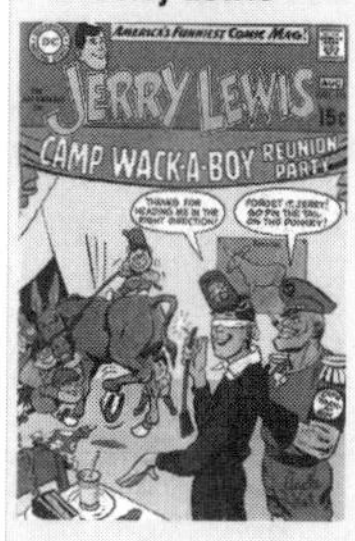

Series changed names after Martin/Lewis split

©DC

N-MINT

❑8, Jul 1987 .... 2.00
❑9, Oct 1987 .... 2.00
❑10, May 1988 .... 2.00
❑11, Nov 1988 .... 2.00
❑12, Jan 1989 .... 2.00
❑Book 1, Nov 1995, b&w; collects stories from Critters #2 and Adventures of Captain Jack #1-3 .... 12.95

ADVENTURES OF CAPTAIN NEMO
RIP OFF

❑1, b&w 2.50

ADVENTURES OF CHRISSIE CLAUS
HERO

❑1, Spr 1991 .... 2.95
❑2, Jan 1994, w/ trading card 2.95

ADVENTURES OF CHUK THE BARBARIC
WHITE WOLF

❑1, Jul 1987 .... 1.50
❑2, Aug 1987, becomes Chuk the Barbaric 1.50

ADVENTURES OF CYCLOPS AND PHOENIX
MARVEL

❑1, May 1994 .... 2.95
❑2, Jun 1994 .... 2.95
❑3, Jul 1994 .... 2.95
❑4, Aug 1994 .... 2.95
❑Book 1, Collects The Adventures of Cyclops and Phoenix #1-4 .... 14.95

ADVENTURES OF DEAN MARTIN & JERRY LEWIS
DC

❑32, Oct 1956 .... 55.00
❑33, Nov 1956 .... 55.00
❑34, Jan 1957 .... 55.00
❑35, Feb 1957 .... 55.00
❑36, Apr 1957 .... 55.00
❑37, May 1957 .... 55.00
❑38, Jul 1957 .... 55.00
❑39, Aug 1957 .... 55.00
❑40, Oct 1957, Series continues as The Adventures of Jerry Lewis 55.00

ADVENTURES OF DR. GRAVES
A-PLUS

❑1, b&w; Reprints 2.50

ADVENTURES OF DOLO ROMY
DÔLO BLUE

❑1 .... 2.95

ADVENTURES OF DORIS NELSON, ATOMIC HOUSEWIFE
JAKE COMICS

❑1, Aug 1996, b&w; reprints Doris Nelson, Atomic Housewife 2.95

ADVENTURES OF EDGAR MUDD AND ELAINE
WET EARTH

❑1 .... 3.50

ADVENTURES OF EVIL & MALICE
IMAGE

❑1, Jun 1999 .... 3.50
❑2, Aug 1999 .... 3.50
❑3, Nov 1999; cover says Oct, indicia says Nov 3.50

N-MINT

ADVENTURES OF FELIX THE CAT
HARVEY

❑1 .... 1.50

ADVENTURES OF FORD FAIRLANE
DC

❑1, May 1990 .... 1.50
❑2, Jun 1990 .... 1.50
❑3, Jul 1990 .... 1.50
❑4, Aug 1990 .... 1.50

ADVENTURES OF JERRY LEWIS
DC

❑41, Nov 1957, Series continued from Adventures of Dean Martin & Jerry Lewis 40.00
❑42, Jan 1958 .... 36.00
❑43, Feb 1958 .... 36.00
❑44, Apr 1958 .... 36.00
❑45, May 1958 .... 36.00
❑46, Jul 1958 .... 36.00
❑47, Aug 1958 .... 36.00
❑48, Oct 1958 .... 36.00
❑49, Nov 1958 .... 36.00
❑50, Jan 1959 .... 36.00
❑51, Mar 1959 .... 34.00
❑52, May 1959 .... 34.00
❑53, Jul 1959 .... 34.00
❑54, Sep 1959 .... 34.00
❑55, Nov 1959 .... 34.00
❑56, Jan 1960 .... 34.00
❑57, Mar 1960 .... 34.00
❑58, May 1960 .... 34.00
❑59, Jul 1960 .... 34.00
❑60, Sep 1960 .... 34.00
❑61, Nov 1960 .... 28.00
❑62, Jan 1961 .... 28.00
❑63, Mar 1961 .... 28.00
❑64, May 1961 .... 28.00
❑65, Jul 1961 .... 28.00
❑66, Sep 1961 .... 28.00
❑67, Nov 1961 .... 28.00
❑68, Jan 1962 .... 28.00
❑69, Mar 1962 .... 28.00
❑70, May 1962 .... 28.00
❑71, Jul 1962 .... 28.00
❑72, Sep 1962, MD (a) 28.00
❑73, Nov 1962 .... 28.00
❑74, Jan 1963, adapts It's Only Money 28.00
❑75, Mar 1963 .... 28.00
❑76, May 1963 .... 28.00
❑77, Jul 1963 .... 28.00
❑78, Sep 1963 .... 28.00
❑79, Nov 1963, 1: Mr. Yes 28.00
❑80, Jan 1964 .... 28.00
❑81, Mar 1964 .... 25.00
❑82, May 1964 .... 25.00
❑83, Jul 1964, Frankenstein, Dracula, Werewolf 25.00
❑84, Sep 1964, Jerry becomes The Fearless Tarantula 25.00
❑85, Nov 1964, 1: Renfrew 25.00
❑86, Jan 1965, BO (a) 25.00
❑87, Mar 1965, BO (a); A: Renfrew 25.00
❑88, May 1965, 1: Witch Kraft 25.00
❑89, Jul 1965 .... 25.00

N-MINT

❑90, Sep 1965 .... 25.00
❑91, Nov 1965 .... 25.00
❑92, Jan 1966, A: Superman 30.00
❑93, Mar 1966 .... 25.00
❑94, May 1966 .... 25.00
❑95, Jul 1966 .... 25.00
❑96, Sep 1966 .... 25.00
❑97, Nov 1966, A: Batman, Robin, Penguin, Riddler, Joker 35.00
❑98, Jan 1967, A: Ringo Starr, Ilya Kurakin (on stamps) 25.00
❑99, Mar 1967 .... 25.00
❑100, May 1967, 1: Jerry Mess-terpiece pin-up 25.00
❑101, Jul 1967, NA (c); NA (a) 32.00
❑102, Sep 1967, NA (c); NA (a); A: The Beatles 55.00
❑103, Nov 1967, NA (c); NA (a) 32.00
❑104, Jan 1968, NA (c); NA (a) 32.00
❑105, Mar 1968, A: Superman, Lex Luthor 32.00
❑106, May 1968 .... 14.00
❑107, Jul 1968 .... 14.00
❑108, Sep 1968 .... 14.00
❑109, Nov 1968 .... 14.00
❑110, Jan 1969 .... 14.00
❑111, Mar 1969 .... 14.00
❑112, May 1969, A: Flash 14.00
❑113, Jul 1969 .... 14.00
❑114, Sep 1969 .... 14.00
❑115, Nov 1969 .... 14.00
❑116, Jan 1970 .... 14.00
❑117, Mar 1970, A: Wonder Woman .. 20.00
❑118, May 1970 .... 14.00
❑119, Jul 1970 .... 14.00
❑120, Sep 1970 .... 12.00
❑121, Nov 1970 .... 12.00
❑122, Jan 1971 .... 12.00
❑123, Mar 1971 .... 12.00
❑124, May 1971 .... 12.00

ADVENTURES OF KELLY BELLE: PERIL ON THE HIGH SEAS
ATLANTIS

❑1 1996, b&w 2.95

ADVENTURES OF KOOL-AID MAN
MARVEL

❑1, ca. 1983, giveaway; JR (c); DDC (a); 60 cent value on cover 1.00
❑5 .... 1.00

ADVENTURES OF LIBERAL MAN
POLITICAL

❑1 .... 2.95
❑2 .... 2.95
❑3 .... 2.95
❑4, Jul 1996 .... 2.95
❑5, Sep 1996 .... 2.95
❑6, Oct 1996 .... 2.95
❑7, Nov 1996 .... 2.95

ADVENTURES OF LUTHER ARKWRIGHT (VALKYRIE)
VALKYRIE

❑1, Oct 1987 BT (w); BT (a) 2.50
❑2, Dec 1987 BT (w); BT (a) 2.50
❑3, Feb 1988 BT (w); BT (a) 2.50

Other grades: Multiply price above by 5/6 for VF/NM • 2/3 for VERY FINE • 1/3 for FINE • 1/5 for VERY GOOD • 1/8 for GOOD

N-MINT

❑4, Apr 1988 BT (w); BT (a) 2.50
❑5, Jun 1988 BT (w); BT (a) 2.50
❑6, Aug 1988 BT (w); BT (a).............. 2.50
❑7, Oct 1988 BT (w); BT (a) 2.50
❑8, Dec 1988 BT (w); BT (a).............. 2.50
❑9, Feb 1989 BT (w); BT (a) 2.50
❑10, Apr 1989; BT (w); BT (a); Essays 2.50

ADVENTURES OF LUTHER ARKWRIGHT (DARK HORSE)

DARK HORSE

❑1, Mar 1990; BT (w); BT (a); Reprints Adventures of Luther Arkwright (Valkyrie) #1 .... 2.50
❑2, Apr 1990; BT (w); BT (a); Reprints Adventures of Luther Arkwright (Valkyrie) #2 .... 2.00
❑3, May 1990; BT (w); BT (a); Reprints Adventures of Luther Arkwright (Valkyrie) #3 .... 2.00
❑4, Jun 1990; BT (w); BT (a); Reprints Adventures of Luther Arkwright (Valkyrie) #4 .... 2.00
❑5, Jul 1990; BT (w); BT (a); Reprints Adventures of Luther Arkwright (Valkyrie) #5 .... 2.00
❑6, Aug 1990; BT (w); BT (a); Reprints Adventures of Luther Arkwright (Valkyrie) #6 .... 2.00
❑7, Nov 1990; BT (w); BT (a); Reprints Adventures of Luther Arkwright (Valkyrie) #7 .... 2.00
❑8, Nov 1990; BT (w); BT (a); Reprints Adventures of Luther Arkwright (Valkyrie) #8 .... 2.00
❑9, Feb 1990; BT (w); BT (a); trading cards; Reprints Adventures of Luther Arkwright (Valkyrie) #9 .... 2.00

ADVENTURES OF MARK TYME

JOHN SPENCER & CO.

❑1 .... 2.00
❑2 .... 2.00

ADVENTURES OF MIGHTY MOUSE (GOLD KEY)

GOLD KEY

❑166, Mar 1979, Has Spider-Man in Hostess Ad: "...Meets June Jitsui!". 4.00
❑167, May 1979 .... 4.00
❑168, Jul 1979 .... 4.00
❑169, Sep 1979 .... 4.00
❑170, Oct 1979 .... 4.00
❑171, Nov 1979 .... 4.00
❑172, Jan 1980 .... 4.00

ADVENTURES OF MR. PYRIDINE

FANTAGRAPHICS

❑1, b&w 2.50

ADVENTURES OF MISTY

FORBIDDEN FRUIT

❑1, Apr 1991 .... 2.95
❑2, May 1991 .... 2.95
❑3, Jun 1991 .... 2.95
❑4, Jul 1991 .... 2.95
❑5, Aug 1991 .... 2.95
❑6, Oct 1991 .... 2.95
❑7, Dec 1991 .... 2.95
❑8, Feb 1992 .... 2.95
❑9, Apr 1992 .... 2.95
❑10, Jun 1992 .... 2.95
❑11, Aug 1992 .... 2.95
❑12, Oct 1992 .... 2.95

ADVENTURES OF MONKEY

WOMP

❑1, Jul 1995 .... 2.00
❑2, Jun 1996 .... 2.00
❑3, Jun 1997 .... 2.00
❑4, Jun 1998; Freshmen back-up 2.00

ADVENTURES OF QUIK BUNNY

MARVEL

❑1 1984, giveaway; A: Spider-Man. 60 cent value on cover 3.00

ADVENTURES OF RHEUMY PEEPERS & CHUNKY HIGHLIGHTS

ONI

❑1, Feb 1999 .... 2.95

ADVENTURES OF RICK RAYGUN

STOP DRAGON

❑1, Sep 1986 .... 2.00
❑2, Oct 1986 .... 2.00
❑3, Fal 1986 .... 2.00
❑4, Nov 1986 .... 2.00
❑5, Jan 1987 .... 2.00

ADVENTURES OF ROBIN HOOD

GOLD KEY

❑1, Mar 1974 .... 8.00
❑2, May 1974 .... 5.00
❑3, Jul 1974 .... 4.00
❑4, Aug 1974 .... 4.00
❑5, Sep 1974 .... 4.00
❑6, Nov 1974 .... 4.00
❑7, Jan 1975 .... 4.00

ADVENTURES OF ROMA

FORBIDDEN FRUIT

❑1, Jan 1993, b&w 3.50

ADVENTURES OF SNAKE PLISSKEN

MARVEL

❑1, Jan 1997 .... 2.50

ADVENTURES OF SPENCER SPOOK

ACE

❑1, Oct 1986; reprints stories from Giggle Comics #77 and Spencer Spook #102 .... 2.00
❑2, Dec 1986 .... 2.00
❑3, Jan 1987 .... 2.00
❑4, Mar 1987 .... 2.00
❑5 .... 2.00
❑6 .... 2.00

ADVENTURES OF SPIDER-MAN

MARVEL

❑1, Apr 1996; A: Punisher. animated series adaptations 2.00
❑2, May 1996 V: Hammerhead 1.50
❑3, Jun 1996 A: X-Men. V: Mr. Sinister 1.50
❑4, Jul 1996 .... 1.50
❑5, Aug 1996 V: Rhino 1.50
❑6, Sep 1996; A: Thing. Human Torch 1.50
❑7, Oct 1996 V: Enforcers 1.50
❑8, Nov 1996 V: Kingpin 1.50
❑9, Dec 1996 .... 1.50
❑10, Jan 1997 V: Beetle 1.50
❑11, Feb 1997 A: Venom. V: Doctor Octopus and Venom 1.50
❑12, Mar 1997 A: Venom. V: Doctor Octopus and Venom 1.50

ADVENTURES OF STICKBOY

STINKY ARMADILLO

❑1 .... 0.50

ADVENTURES OF SUPERBOY

DC

❑19, Sep 1991; Series continued from Superboy (2nd Series) #18 .... 1.50
❑20, Oct 1991 JM (a); O: Knickknack. 1.50
❑21, Nov 1991 .... 1.50
❑22, Dec 1991 CS (a) 1.50

ADVENTURES OF SUPERMAN

DC

❑0, Oct 1994; ▲1994-39 .... 2.50
❑424, Jan 1987 JOy (a) 2.50
❑425, Feb 1987 JOy (a) 4.00
❑426, Mar 1987; JOy (a); 1: Bibbo. Legends 3.00
❑427, Apr 1987 JOy (a) 2.00
❑428, May 1987 JOy (a) 2.00
❑429, Jun 1987 JOy (a) 2.00
❑430, Jul 1987 JOy (a) 2.00
❑431, Aug 1987 JOy (a) 2.00
❑432, Sep 1987 JOy (a); 1: Jose Delgado (Gangbuster) 2.00
❑433, Oct 1987 JOy (a) 2.00
❑434, Nov 1987 JOy (a); 1: Gangbuster 2.00
❑435, Dec 1987 JOy (a) 2.00
❑436, Jan 1988; JOy (a); Millennium. 2.00
❑437, Feb 1988; JOy (a); V: Gangbuster. Millennium 2.00
❑438, Mar 1988 JOy (a); O: Brainiac II (Milton Moses Fine). 1: Brainiac II (Milton Moses Fine) 2.00
❑439, Apr 1988 JOy (a) 2.00
❑440, May 1988 JOy (a) 2.00
❑441, Jun 1988 JOy (a); V: Mxyzptlk. 2.00
❑442, Jul 1988 JOy, JBy (a) 2.00
❑443, Aug 1988 JOy (a) 2.00
❑444, Sep 1988; JOy (a); Supergirl.... 2.00
❑445, Oct 1988 JOy (a) 2.00
❑446, Nov 1988 JOy (a); A: Gangbuster 2.00
❑447, Dec 1988 JOy (a) 2.00
❑448, Dec 1988 JOy (a) 2.00
❑449, Jan 1989; Invasion! 2.00
❑450, Jan 1989; Invasion! 2.00
❑451, Feb 1989 .... 2.00
❑452, Mar 1989 .... 2.00
❑453, Apr 1989 .... 2.00
❑454, May 1989 1: Draaga 2.00
❑455, Jun 1989 .... 2.00
❑456, Jul 1989 .... 2.00
❑457, Aug 1989 .... 2.00
❑458, Sep 1989; Jimmy as Elastic Lad 2.00
❑459, Oct 1989; Eradicator buried in Antarctic 2.00
❑460, Nov 1989 1: Fortress of Solitude 2.00
❑461, Dec 1989 .... 2.00
❑462, Jan 1990 .... 2.00
❑463, Feb 1990; A: Flash. Superman/ Flash race 3.00
❑464, Mar 1990; V: Lobo. Krypton Man 2.00
❑465, Apr 1990; Krypton Man 2.00
❑466, May 1990 1: Hank Henshaw (becomes cyborg Superman) 3.00
❑467, Jun 1990; Batman 2.00
❑468, Jul 1990 .... 2.00
❑469, Aug 1990 1: Blaze 2.00
❑470, Sep 1990 .... 2.00
❑471, Oct 1990 A: Sinbad 2.00
❑472, Nov 1990 .... 2.00
❑473, Dec 1990; A: Green Lantern. Guy Gardner 2.00
❑474, Jan 1991 .... 2.00
❑475, Feb 1991; Wonder Woman; Batman, Flash 2.00
❑476, Mar 1991 1: The Linear Men. V: Linear Man 2.00
❑477, Apr 1991 A: Legion 2.00
❑478, May 1991 V: Dev-Em 2.00
❑479, Jun 1991 .... 2.00
❑480, Jul 1991; Giant-size 2.50
❑481, Aug 1991 .... 2.00
❑482, Sep 1991 V: Parasite 2.00
❑483, Oct 1991 1: Atomic Skull 2.00
❑484, Nov 1991; Blackout 2.00
❑485, Dec 1991; Blackout 2.00
❑486, Jan 1992 .... 2.00
❑487, Feb 1992 .... 2.00
❑488, Mar 1992 .... 2.00
❑489, Apr 1992 .... 2.00
❑490, May 1992 .... 2.00
❑491, Jun 1992 V: Metallo 2.00
❑492, Jul 1992; JOy (w); V: Agent Liberty. ▲1992-27 .... 2.00
❑493, Aug 1992 1: Lord Satanus. V: Blaze 2.00
❑494, Sep 1992 1: Kismet 2.00
❑495, Oct 1992 A: Forever People 2.00
❑496, Nov 1992; Mxyzptlk 3.00
❑496/2nd, Nov 1992 .... 2.00
❑497, Dec 1992; JOy (w); Doomsday; ▲1992-47 .... 3.00
❑497/2nd, Dec 1992; JOy (w); 2nd printing, ▲1992-47 .... 2.00
❑498, Jan 1993; JOy (w); ▲1993-3 ... 3.00
❑498/2nd, Jan 1993; JOy (w); ▲1993-3 .... 2.00
❑499, Feb 1993; JOy (w); ▲1993-7 ... 2.50
❑500, Jun 1993; JOy (w); begins return from dead 3.00
❑500/CS, Jun 1993; JOy (w); translucent cover; trading card; begins return from dead 3.50
❑500/Silver, Jun 1993; silver edition JOy (w) 20.00
❑501, Jun 1993; 1: Superboy (clone). ▲1993-15 .... 2.00
❑501/Variant, Jun 1993; 1: Superboy (clone). Die-cut cover; ▲1993-15 .. 2.00
❑502, Jul 1993; A: Supergirl. ▲1993-19 .... 1.75
❑503, Aug 1993; Superboy vs. Cyborg 1.75
❑504, Sep 1993 .... 1.75
❑505, Oct 1993; ▲1993-31 .... 1.75
❑505/Variant, Oct 1993; ▲1993-31, Special (prism) cover edition; ▲1993-31; Special (prism) cover edition 2.50
❑506, Nov 1993 .... 1.50
❑507, Dec 1993 V: Bloodsport 1.50
❑508, Jan 1994; Challengers 1.50

Adventures of Kool-Aid Man

Commercial icon spawned Archie giveaway
©Marvel

Adventures of Liberal Man

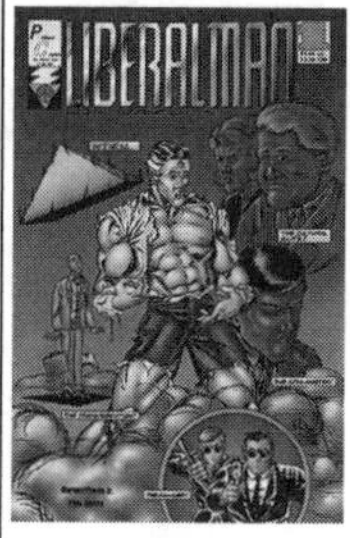

Democratic hero serves his political party
©Political

Adventures of Rick Raygun

Police officer fights crime in outer space
©Stop Dragon

Adventures of Robin Hood

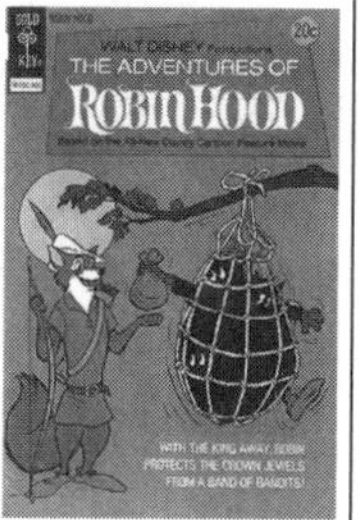

Based on animated Disney adventure
©Gold Key

Adventures of Snake Plissken

He "Escaped from New York" into comics
©Marvel

	N-MINT
❑509, Feb 1994 A: Auron	1.50
❑510, Mar 1994; Bizarro	1.50
❑511, Apr 1994 A: Guardian	1.50
❑512, May 1994 A: Guardian. V: Parasite	1.50
❑513, Jun 1994; ▲1994-23	1.50
❑514, Jul 1994	1.50
❑515, Aug 1994 V: Massacre	1.50
❑516, Sep 1994; A: Alpha Centurion. "Zero Hour"	1.50
❑517, Nov 1994	1.50
❑518, Dec 1994 A: Darkseid	1.50
❑519, Jan 1995; V: Brainiac. Dead Again; ▲1995-3	1.50
❑520, Feb 1995 A: Thorn	1.50
❑521, Mar 1995 A: Thorn	1.50
❑522, Apr 1995; Return of Metropolis	1.50
❑523, May 1995	1.50
❑524, Jun 1995	2.00
❑525, Jul 1995	2.00
❑526, Aug 1995; Bloodsport vs. Bloodsport	2.00
❑527, Sep 1995; Alpha-Centurion returns	2.00
❑528, Oct 1995	2.00
❑529, Nov 1995	2.00
❑530, Dec 1995; SCU vs. Hellgrammite; "Trial of Superman/Underworld Unleashed"	2.00
❑531, Jan 1996; Cyborg Superman sentenced to a black hole; ▲1996-4	2.00
❑532, Feb 1996; Return of Lori Lemaris; ▲1996-8	2.00
❑533, Mar 1996; A: Impulse. ▲1996-12	2.00
❑534, May 1996	2.00
❑535, Jun 1996	2.00
❑536, Jul 1996; Brainiac takes over Superman's body	2.00
❑537, Aug 1996	2.00
❑538, Sep 1996; Clark Kent named acting managing editor; Perry White has cancer	2.00
❑539, Oct 1996 JOy (w); O: Anomaly. 1: Anomaly	2.00
❑540, Nov 1996; JOy (w); 1: Ferro. "Final Night"; ▲1996-43	2.00
❑541, Dec 1996; A: Superboy. Clark shot by terrorists	2.00
❑542, Jan 1997	2.00
❑543, Feb 1997 V: Superman Revenge Squad	2.00
❑544, Mar 1997; return of Intergang; ▲1997-11	2.00
❑545, Apr 1997; V: Metallo. energy powers begin	2.00
❑546, May 1997; V: Metallo. new uniform	2.00
❑547, Jun 1997 A: Atom	2.00
❑548, Jul 1997 A: Phantom Stranger	2.00
❑549, Aug 1997 A: Newsboy Legion, Dingbats of Danger Street	2.00
❑550, Sep 1997; Giant-size; Jimmy's special airs	3.50
❑551, Oct 1997 V: Cyborg Superman	1.95
❑552, Nov 1997; V: Parasite. ▲1997-45	1.95
❑553, Dec 1997; Face cover	1.95
❑554, Dec 1997 V: Ripper	1.95
❑555, Feb 1998; Superman Red vs. Superman Blue	1.95
❑556, Apr 1998; V: Millennium Guard. ▲1998-13	1.95
❑557, May 1998; Millennium Giants	1.95
❑558, Jun 1998; set in Silver Age	1.95
❑559, Jul 1998; set in Silver Age	1.95
❑560, Aug 1998; A: Kismet. set in Silver Age	1.95
❑561, Sep 1998 V: Dominus	2.00
❑562, Oct 1998; D: Machine Gunn, Torcher. D: "Machine" Gunn, Torcher. Daily Planet closed	2.00
❑563, Dec 1998; V: Cyborg. in Kandor	2.00
❑564, Feb 1999 JOy (w); A: Geo-Force	2.00
❑565, Mar 1999 JOy (w); A: D.E.O. agents. A: Justice League of America. A: Captain Boomerang. A: Metropolis Special Crimes Unit. A: Captain Cold	2.00
❑566, Apr 1999 JOy (w); A: Lex Luthor	2.00
❑567, May 1999; JOy (w); Lois' robot guardian returns; ▲1999-19	2.00
❑568, Jun 1999; ▲1999-24	2.00
❑569, Jul 1999; SCU forms meta-unit; ▲1999-28	2.00
❑570, Sep 1999; Superman as protector of Rann	2.00
❑571, Oct 1999 V: Atomic Skull	2.00
❑572, Nov 1999; SB (a); A: Strange Visitor. V: War. ▲1999-41	2.00
❑573, Dec 1999; ▲1999-47	2.00
❑574, Jan 2000; ▲2000-2	2.00
❑575, Feb 2000; ▲2000-6	2.00
❑576, Mar 2000	2.00
❑577, Apr 2000	2.00
❑578, May 2000; ▲2000-19	2.00
❑579, Jun 2000; ▲2000-23	2.00
❑580, Jul 2000; ▲2000-27	2.00
❑581, Aug 2000; V: Adversary. ▲2000-31; Lex Luthor announces candidacy for President	2.00
❑582, Sep 2000; ▲2000-35	2.00
❑583, Oct 2000; ▲2000-40	2.25
❑584, Nov 2000; 1: Devouris the Conqueror. A: Lord Satanus. ▲2000-44	2.25
❑585, Dec 2000; A: Rampage. A: Adversary. A: Thorn. A: Prankster. ▲2000-48	2.25
❑586, Jan 2001; ▲2000-52	2.25
❑587, Feb 2001; ▲2001-7	2.25
❑588, Mar 2001; ▲2001-11	2.25
❑589, Apr 2001; ▲2001-15	2.25
❑590, May 2001; ▲2001-19	2.25
❑591, Jun 2001; ▲2001-23	2.25
❑592, Jul 2001	2.25
❑593, Aug 2001	2.25
❑594, Sep 2001	2.25
❑595, Oct 2001; ▲2001-39	2.25
❑596, Nov 2001; ▲2001-43	2.25
❑597, Dec 2001; ▲2001-47	2.25
❑598, Jan 2002; ▲2002-6	2.25
❑599, Feb 2002	2.25
❑600, Mar 2002; Giant-size	3.95
❑601, Apr 2002	2.25
❑602, May 2002	2.25
❑603, Jun 2002 A: Super-Baby	2.25
❑604, Jul 2002	2.25
❑605, Aug 2002	2.25
❑606, Sep 2002	2.25
❑607, Oct 2002	2.25
❑608, Nov 2002	2.25
❑609, Dec 2002	2.25
❑610, Jan 2003	2.25
❑611, Feb 2003	2.25
❑612, Mar 2003	2.25
❑613, Apr 2003	2.25
❑614, May 2003	2.25
❑615, Jun 2003	2.25
❑616, Jul 2003	2.25
❑617, Aug 2003	2.25
❑618, Sep 2003	2.25
❑619, Oct 2003	2.25
❑620, Nov 2003	2.25
❑621, Dec 2003	2.25
❑622, Jan 2004	2.25
❑623, Feb 2004	2.25
❑624, Mar 2004	5.00
❑625, Apr 2004	4.00
❑625/2nd, Apr 2004	3.00
❑626, May 2004	2.25
❑627, Jun 2004	2.50
❑628, Jul 2004	2.50
❑629, Aug 2004	2.50
❑630, Sep 2004	2.50
❑631, Oct 2004	2.50
❑632, Nov 2004	2.50
❑633, Dec 2004	2.50
❑634, Jan 2005	2.50
❑635, Feb 2005	2.50
❑636, Mar 2005	5.00
❑637, Apr 2005	4.00
❑638, May 2005	2.50
❑639, Jun 2005	5.00
❑640, Jul 2005	4.00
❑641, Aug 2005	4.00
❑642, Sep 2005	6.00
❑643, Oct 2005	2.99
❑643/2nd, Oct 2005	2.99
❑644, Nov 2005	2.99
❑645, Dec 2005	2.99
❑646, Jan 2006	2.99
❑647, Feb 2006	2.99
❑648, Mar 2006	2.99
❑649, May 2006	2.99
❑1000000, Nov 1998 A: Resurrection Man	2.00
❑Annual 1, Sep 1987	4.00
❑Annual 2, Aug 1990; JBy (a); A: Lobo. L.E.G.I.O.N. '90	3.00
❑Annual 3, Oct 1991	3.00
❑Annual 4, ca. 1992	3.00
❑Annual 5, ca. 1993 1: Sparx	3.00
❑Annual 6, ca. 1994; concludes in Superboy Annual #1 (1994); Elseworlds	2.95
❑Annual 7, ca. 1995; V: Kalibak. Year One	3.95
❑Annual 8, ca. 1996; Elseworlds; Legends of the Dead Earth	2.95
❑Annual 9, Sep 1997; Pulp Heroes	3.95

Other grades: Multiply price above by 5/6 for VF/NM • 2/3 for VERY FINE • 1/3 for FINE • 1/5 for VERY GOOD • 1/8 for GOOD

ADVENTURES OF TAD MARTIN

CALIBER

	N-MINT
❑1	2.50

ADVENTURES OF THE BIG BOY

WEBS GROUP

	N-MINT
❑1, ca. 1956, BEv (c); SL (w); BEv (a); No "free" label	750.00
❑1/East, ca. 1956, BEv (c); SL (w); BEv (a); Blond eastern variant	750.00
❑2, ca. 1956, BEv (c); BEv (a); Ice skating cover	295.00
❑2/East, ca. 1956, BEv (c); BEv (a); Blond eastern variant	295.00
❑3, ca. 1956, Contest cover	125.00
❑3/East, ca. 1956, Blond eastern variant; contest cover	125.00
❑4, ca. 1956	90.00
❑4/East, ca. 1956, Blond eastern variant	90.00
❑5, ca. 1956	75.00
❑5/East, ca. 1956, Blond eastern variant	75.00
❑6, ca. 1956	50.00
❑7, ca. 1956, DDC (c); DDC (a); Name the Puppy contest	50.00
❑8, ca. 1956, DDC (c); DDC (a); Dinosaur cover	45.00
❑8/East, ca. 1956, DDC (c); DDC (a); Dinosaur cover	45.00
❑9, ca. 1956, DDC (c); DDC (a)	45.00
❑9/East, ca. 1956, DDC (c); DDC (a); Blond eastern variant	45.00
❑10, ca. 1957, DDC (c); DDC (a); Rip Van Winkle cover	45.00
❑10/East, ca. 1957, DDC (c); DDC (a); Rip Van Winkle cover	45.00
❑11, ca. 1957, DDC (c); DDC (a)	30.00
❑12, ca. 1957, DDC (c); DDC (a)	30.00
❑13, ca. 1957, DDC (c); DDC (a); Ice fishing cover	30.00
❑13/East, ca. 1957, DDC (c); DDC (a); Blond eastern variant; ice fishing cover	30.00
❑14, ca. 1957	30.00
❑15, ca. 1957	30.00
❑16, ca. 1957	24.00
❑17, ca. 1957	24.00
❑18, ca. 1957	24.00
❑18/East, ca. 1957, Blond eastern variant	24.00
❑19, ca. 1957, "Washington Monument Stolen"	24.00
❑19/East, ca. 1957, "Washington Monument Stolen"	24.00
❑20, ca. 1958, Statue of Liberty cover	24.00
❑21, ca. 1958	16.00
❑22, ca. 1958	16.00
❑23, ca. 1958, Happy New Year cover	16.00
❑24, ca. 1958	16.00
❑25, ca. 1958, Science fiction cover	16.00
❑26, ca. 1958, Hook the Crook cover	12.00
❑27, ca. 1958	12.00
❑28, ca. 1958, African native cover	12.00
❑29, ca. 1959	12.00
❑30, ca. 1959, Dragon cover	12.00
❑30/East, ca. 1959, Blond Eastern variant	12.00
❑31, ca. 1959	10.00
❑31/East, ca. 1959, Blond eastern variant	10.00
❑32, ca. 1959	10.00
❑33, ca. 1959	10.00
❑34, ca. 1959, No creator credits listed	10.00
❑35, ca. 1959	10.00
❑36, ca. 1959, Samson cover	10.00
❑37, ca. 1959, Roller coaster cover	10.00
❑37/East, ca. 1959, Blond eastern variant	10.00
❑38, ca. 1959, Invisible Man cover	10.00
❑38/East, ca. 1959, Invisible Man cover; blond eastern variant	10.00
❑39, ca. 1960, Whale cover	10.00
❑39/East, ca. 1960, Blond eastern variant	10.00
❑40, ca. 1960	10.00
❑41, ca. 1960, 1960/1961 Club Membership offer	6.00
❑42, ca. 1960	6.00
❑43, ca. 1960	6.00
❑44, ca. 1960	6.00
❑44/East, ca. 1960, Blond eastern variant	6.00
❑45, ca. 1960	6.00
❑45/East, ca. 1960, Blond eastern variant	6.00
❑46, ca. 1960, Football cover	6.00
❑46/East, ca. 1960, Blond eastern variant	6.00
❑47, ca. 1960, Santa Claus cover	6.00
❑48, Jan 1961, Giant robot cover	6.00
❑48/East, Jan 1961, Blond eastern variant	6.00
❑49, ca. 1961	6.00
❑50, ca. 1961	6.00
❑50/East, ca. 1961, Blond eastern variant	6.00
❑51, ca. 1961, Giant Nugget cover	5.00
❑52, ca. 1961, "3-D" cover	8.00
❑53, ca. 1961	5.00
❑54, ca. 1961, TV quiz show story	5.00
❑54/East, ca. 1961, Blond eastern variant; TV quiz show story	5.00
❑55, ca. 1961	5.00
❑56, ca. 1961	5.00
❑57, Jan 1962	5.00
❑58, Feb 1962	5.00
❑59, Mar 1962	5.00
❑60, Apr 1962	5.00
❑61, May 1962	5.00
❑62, Jun 1962, Magic Mirror cover	5.00
❑62/East, Jun 1962, Blonde eastern variant	5.00
❑63, Jul 1962	5.00
❑64, Aug 1962	5.00
❑65, Sep 1962, Cowboys and Indians cover	5.00
❑66, Oct 1962	5.00
❑67, Nov 1962, Genie cover	5.00
❑68, Dec 1962	5.00
❑68/East, Dec 1962	5.00
❑69/East, Jan 1963, Infinity cover; blond eastern variant	5.00
❑69, Jan 1963, Infinity cover	5.00
❑70, Feb 1963	5.00
❑71, Mar 1963, Abominable snowman story	5.00
❑71/East, Mar 1963, Abominable snowman story; blond eastern variant	5.00
❑72, Apr 1963, 1963 club application ad on front	5.00
❑72/East, Apr 1963, 1963 club application ad on front	5.00
❑73, May 1963	5.00
❑74, Jun 1963	5.00
❑75, Jul 1963, Sherlock Holmes cover	5.00
❑76, Aug 1963	5.00
❑77, Sep 1963, Reprinted as #165	5.00
❑77/East, Sep 1963, Blond eastern variant	5.00
❑78, Jul 1963, Caveman cover	5.00
❑78/East, Jul 1963, Caveman cover; blond eastern variant	5.00
❑79, Nov 1963	5.00
❑80, Dec 1963	5.00
❑81/East, Jan 1964, Undersea cover/ blond eastern variant	5.00
❑81, Jan 1964, Undersea cover	5.00
❑82, Feb 1964, Big Boy fans cover	5.00
❑82/East, Feb 1964, Big Boy fans cover; blond eastern variant	
❑83, Mar 1964	5.00
❑84, Apr 1964	5.00
❑85, May 1964	5.00
❑86, Jun 1964	5.00
❑87, Jul 1964	5.00
❑88, Aug 1964	5.00
❑89, Sep 1964, Knight cover	5.00
❑90, Oct 1964, Robot cover	5.00
❑91, Nov 1964	5.00
❑92, Dec 1964	5.00
❑93, Jan 1965, Time machine cover	5.00
❑94, Feb 1965, Jack and the Beanstalk cover	5.00
❑94/East, Feb 1965, Blond eastern variant; Jack and the Beanstalk cover	5.00
❑95, Mar 1965	5.00
❑96, Apr 1965	5.00
❑97, May 1965, Two Big Boys on cover	5.00
❑98, Jun 1965, Detective cover	5.00
❑99, Jul 1965	5.00
❑100, Aug 1965, Castle cover	5.00
❑101, Sep 1965, False alarms story	4.00
❑101/East, Sep 1965, Blond eastern variant	4.00
❑102, Oct 1965	4.00
❑103, Nov 1965	4.00
❑104, Dec 1965	4.00
❑105, Jan 1966	4.00
❑106, Feb 1966, Cover reused for #186	4.00
❑107, Mar 1966, Skiing cover	4.00
❑108, Apr 1966	4.00
❑109, May 1966	4.00
❑110, Jun 1966	4.00
❑111, Jul 1966, Fireman cover	4.00
❑112, Aug 1966	4.00
❑113, Sep 1966, Sea monster cover	4.00
❑113/East, Sep 1966, Blond eastern variant	4.00
❑114, Oct 1966, Falling tree cover	4.00
❑115, Nov 1966, Fireman cover	4.00
❑116, Dec 1966, Big Boy mistaken for sun god; rare continued story	4.00
❑116/East, Dec 1966, Blond eastern variant	4.00
❑117, Jan 1967, Rare continued story	4.00
❑117/East, Jan 1967, Blond eastern variant	4.00
❑118, Feb 1967, Seasons Greetings cover	4.00
❑119, Mar 1967, Giant on cover	4.00
❑119/East, Mar 1967, Blond eastern variant	4.00
❑120, Apr 1967, Tower cover	4.00
❑121, May 1967	4.00
❑122, Jun 1967, Hamlet cover	4.00
❑122/East, Jun 1967, Blond eastern variant; Hamlet cover	4.00
❑123/East, Jul 1967, Blond eastern variant; mermaid cover	4.00
❑123, Jul 1967, Mermaid cover	4.00
❑124, Aug 1967, Skydiving cover	4.00
❑125, Sep 1967	4.00
❑126, Oct 1967, Monster-tracking cover	4.00
❑126/East, Oct 1967, Blond eastern variant; monster-tracking cover	4.00
❑127, Nov 1967, Execution cover (!)	4.00
❑128, Dec 1967, Volcano cover	4.00
❑129, Jan 1968, Robot cover	4.00
❑130, Feb 1968, Holiday cover	4.00
❑131, Mar 1968	4.00
❑132, Apr 1968, Jack and the Beanstalk cover; cover reused from #94	4.00
❑133, May 1968	4.00
❑133/East, May 1968, Blond eastern variant	4.00
❑134, Jun 1968, Train robbery cover	4.00
❑135, Jul 1968	4.00
❑136, Aug 1968, Robin Hood cover	4.00
❑137, Sep 1968	4.00
❑138, Oct 1968	4.00
❑139, Nov 1968	4.00
❑140, Dec 1968	4.00
❑141, Jan 1969, Aliens cover	4.00
❑142, Feb 1969	4.00
❑143, Mar 1969	4.00
❑144, Apr 1969	4.00
❑145, May 1969, Scuba cover	4.00
❑145/East, May 1969, Blond eastern variant; scuba cover	4.00
❑146, Jun 1969, Jungle cover	4.00
❑146/East, Jun 1969, Blond eastern variant	4.00
❑147, Jul 1969	4.00
❑148, Aug 1969	4.00
❑148/East, Aug 1969, Blond eastern variant	4.00
❑149, Sep 1969, Hypnotism cover	4.00
❑150, Oct 1969, Skiing cover	4.00
❑150/East, Oct 1969, Skiing cover; blond eastern variant	4.00
❑151, Nov 1969	3.00
❑152, Dec 1969, Christmas cover	3.00
❑152/East, Dec 1969, Blond eastern variant	3.00
❑153, Jan 1970	3.00
❑154, Feb 1970, Airplane cover	3.00
❑155, Mar 1970	3.00
❑156, Apr 1970, Smoke signal cover	3.00
❑157, May 1970, Medieval cover	3.00
❑158, Jun 1970	3.00
❑159, Jul 1970, Statue of Liberty cover; art swipe (not a reprint) from #20	3.00

Adventures of Spencer Spook

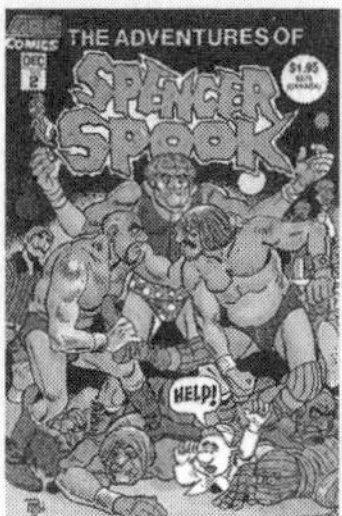

This ghost wasn't as successful as Casper

©Ace

Adventures of Spider-Man

Companion comic book to animated series

©Marvel

Adventures of Superboy

The final four issues of Superboy (2nd Series)

©DC

Adventures of Superman

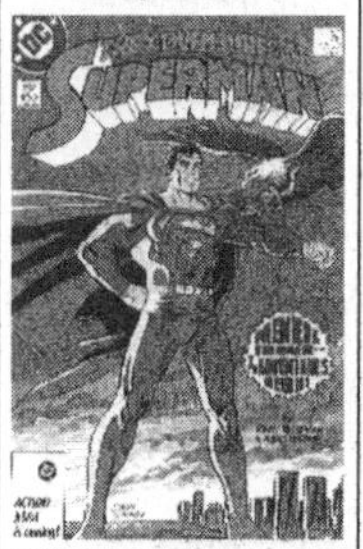

Picked up where Superman (1st Series) left off

©DC

Adventures of the Big Boy

Long-running restaurant chain freebie

©WEBS Group

	N-MINT
❑160, Aug 1970	3.00
❑161, Sep 1970	3.00
❑162, Oct 1970, Flower-picking cover	3.00
❑163, Nov 1970	3.00
❑164, Dec 1970	3.00
❑165, Jan 1971, Reprints #77 (Western cover)	3.00
❑166, Feb 1971	3.00
❑167, Mar 1971	3.00
❑168, Apr 1971	3.00
❑169, May 1971	3.00
❑170, Jun 1971, Tiger cover	3.00
❑171, Jul 1971, Centerfold has "Big Boy's Great Mythology Puzzle"	3.00
❑172, Aug 1971, Airplane motor cover	3.00
❑173, Sep 1971, Art contest; cover gag reused in #234	3.00
❑174, Oct 1971, Has art contest	3.00
❑175, Nov 1971	3.00
❑176, Dec 1971	3.00
❑177, Jan 1972	3.00
❑178, Feb 1972	3.00
❑179, Mar 1972, Electrocution cover	3.00
❑180, Apr 1972	3.00
❑181, May 1972	3.00
❑182, Jun 1972	3.00
❑183, Jul 1972	3.00
❑184, Aug 1972, Win a Bike contest cover	3.00
❑185, Sep 1972	3.00
❑186, Oct 1972, Reprints and reuses cover from #106 (West Coast)	3.00
❑187, Nov 1972	3.00
❑188, Dec 1972, Poster in centerfold	3.00
❑189, Jan 1973, Big Boy as animal trainer	3.00
❑190, Feb 1973	3.00
❑191, Mar 1973, Salute to North Carolina	3.00
❑192, Apr 1973	3.00
❑193, May 1973, Time machine story	3.00
❑194, Jun 1973	3.00
❑195, Jul 1973, Igloo cover	3.00
❑196, Aug 1973	3.00
❑197, Sep 1973	3.00
❑198, Oct 1973	3.00
❑199, Nov 1973	3.00
❑200, Dec 1973	3.00
❑201, Jan 1974	2.50
❑202, Feb 1974	2.50
❑203, Mar 1974, Reuses cover from #140	2.50
❑204, Apr 1974, (w); (a); 50 States Puzzle	2.50
❑205, May 1974	2.50
❑206, Jun 1974, Art gallery cover	2.50
❑207, Jul 1974	2.50
❑208, Aug 1974	2.50
❑209, Sep 1974	2.50
❑210, Oct 1974	2.50
❑211, Nov 1974, Salute to Arizona; no creator credits listed	2.50
❑212, Dec 1974, African savages cover	2.50
❑213, Jan 1975, Violence joke cover	2.50
❑214, Feb 1975	2.50
❑215, Mar 1975	2.50
❑216, Apr 1975, Roman columns cover	2.50
❑217, May 1975	2.50
❑218, Jun 1975, Slingshot cover	2.50
❑219, Jul 1975, American flag cover	2.50
❑220, Aug 1975	2.50
❑221, Sep 1975	2.50
❑222, Oct 1975	2.50
❑223, Nov 1975	2.50
❑224, Dec 1975	2.50
❑225, Jan 1976	2.50
❑226, Feb 1976, Has special Bicentennial page	2.50
❑227, Mar 1976	2.50
❑228, Apr 1976	2.50
❑229, May 1976	2.50
❑230, Jun 1976	2.50
❑231, Jul 1976	2.50
❑232, Aug 1976	2.50
❑233, Sep 1976, Revolutionary War cover	2.50
❑234, Oct 1976, Reuses magnet cover gag from #173	2.50
❑235, Nov 1976	2.50
❑236, Dec 1976, Christmas cover	2.50
❑237, Jan 1977	2.50
❑238, Feb 1977, Valentine cover	2.50
❑239, Mar 1977, Wizard of Oz cover promoting CBS broadcast	2.50
❑240, Apr 1977	2.50
❑241, May 1977, Mother's Day cover	2.50
❑242, Jun 1977	2.50
❑243, Jul 1977	2.50
❑244, Aug 1977	2.50
❑245, Sep 1977	2.50
❑246, Oct 1977	2.50
❑247, Nov 1977	2.50
❑248, Dec 1977	2.50
❑249, Jan 1978	2.50
❑250, Feb 1978, King Tut cover	2.50
❑251, Mar 1978	2.50
❑252, Apr 1978	2.50
❑253, May 1978, Airplane races	2.50
❑254, Jun 1978, Donny and Marie Osmond interview	2.50
❑255, Jul 1978, In King Arthur's Court	2.50
❑256, Aug 1978, Baseball cover	2.50
❑257, Sep 1978, Versus Teacher's Helper	2.50
❑258, Oct 1978	2.50
❑259, Nov 1978, UFO cover	2.50
❑260, Dec 1978, "Good Wishes" cover	2.50
❑261, Jan 1979, Annie musical crossover	2.50
❑262, Feb 1979, Battlestar Galactica interview	2.50
❑263, Mar 1979	2.50
❑264, Apr 1979, Roots of Rock contest; Donny and Marie Osmond feature	2.50
❑265, May 1979	2.50
❑266, Jun 1979, A: Superman. Superman movie crossover	2.50
❑267, Jul 1979, Battlestar Galactica contest and story	2.50
❑268, Aug 1979, Bad News Bears movie crossover	2.50
❑269, Sep 1979	2.50
❑270, Oct 1979	2.50
❑271, Nov 1979	2.50
❑272, Dec 1979	2.50
❑273, Jan 1980	2.50
❑274, Feb 1980	2.50
❑275, Mar 1980	2.50
❑276, Apr 1980	2.50
❑277, May 1980	2.50
❑278, Jun 1980	2.50
❑279, Jul 1980	2.50
❑280, Aug 1980	2.50
❑281, Sep 1980	2.50
❑282, Oct 1980	2.50
❑283, Nov 1980	2.50
❑284, Dec 1980	2.50
❑285, Jan 1981, New Year's Cover	2.50
❑286, Feb 1981	2.50
❑287, Mar 1981	2.50
❑288, Apr 1981	2.50
❑289, May 1981	2.50
❑290, Jun 1981	2.50
❑291, Jul 1981	2.50
❑292, Aug 1981	2.50
❑293, Sep 1981	2.50
❑294, Oct 1981	2.50
❑295, Nov 1981	2.50
❑296, Dec 1981, Christmas cover	2.50
❑297, Jan 1982	2.50
❑298, Feb 1982	2.50
❑299, Mar 1982	2.50
❑300, Apr 1982, Anniversary cover; Burt Reynolds hidden in cover scene	2.50
❑301, May 1982, Nostalgia reprint included	2.00
❑302, Jun 1982	2.00
❑303, Jul 1982	2.00
❑304, Aug 1982	2.00
❑305, Sep 1982	2.00
❑306, Oct 1982	2.00
❑307, Nov 1982	2.00
❑308, Dec 1982	2.00
❑309, Jan 1983, New Year's Cover	2.00
❑310, Feb 1983	2.00
❑311, Mar 1983, Has Dolly's Art Gallery #3	2.00
❑312, Apr 1983	2.00
❑313, May 1983	2.00
❑314, Jun 1983	2.00
❑315, Jul 1983, Protest cover	2.00
❑316, Aug 1983	2.00
❑317, Sep 1983	2.00
❑318, Oct 1983, Dolly's Art Gallery #4	2.00
❑319, Nov 1983	2.00
❑320, Dec 1983, Christmas cover	2.00
❑321, Jan 1984, Happy New Year cover	2.00
❑322, Feb 1984	2.00
❑323, Mar 1984	2.00
❑324, Apr 1984	2.00
❑325, May 1984	2.00
❑326, Jun 1984	2.00
❑327, Jul 1984	2.00
❑328, Aug 1984	2.00
❑329, Sep 1984	2.00
❑330, Oct 1984	2.00
❑331, Nov 1984	2.00

Other grades: Multiply price above by 5/6 for VF/NM • 2/3 for VERY FINE • 1/3 for FINE • 1/5 for VERY GOOD • 1/8 for GOOD

❑332, Dec 1984, Christmas "Good Wishes" cover; essentially reprints #260's cover 2.00
❑333, Jan 1985, Happy New Year cover 2.00
❑334, Feb 1985, Valentine's Day cover 2.00
❑335, Mar 1985 .... 2.00
❑336, Apr 1985 .... 2.00
❑337, May 1985, Dolly elected queen. 2.00
❑338, Jun 1985, Astronaut cover; collectors page on foreign cars....... 2.00
❑339, Jul 1985, Independence Day cover 2.00
❑340, Aug 1985 .... 2.00
❑341, Sep 1985 .... 2.00
❑342, Oct 1985 .... 2.00
❑343, Nov 1985 .... 2.00
❑344, Dec 1985 .... 2.00
❑345, Jan 1986 .... 2.00
❑346, Feb 1986, Valentine's Day cover 2.00
❑347, Mar 1986, Leprechaun cover.... 2.00
❑348, Apr 1986 .... 2.00
❑349, May 1986 .... 2.00
❑350, Jun 1986 .... 2.00
❑351, Jul 1986 .... 2.00
❑352, Aug 1986 .... 2.00
❑353, Sep 1986, Mermaid cover 2.00
❑354, Oct 1986 .... 2.00
❑355, Nov 1986 .... 2.00
❑356, Dec 1986 .... 2.00
❑357, Jan 1987 .... 2.00
❑358, Feb 1987 .... 2.00
❑359, Mar 1987, rare continued story 2.00
❑360, Apr 1987, Some copies have Bob's Big Boy die-cut 30th Anniversary false cover.......... 2.00
❑361, May 1987, Some copies have Bob's Big Boy die-cut 30th Anniversary false cover.......... 2.00
❑362, Jun 1987, Some copies have Bob's Big Boy die-cut 30th Anniversary false cover.......... 2.00
❑363, Jul 1987, Some copies have Bob's Big Boy die-cut 30th Anniversary false cover.......... 2.00
❑364, Aug 1987, Some copies have Bob's Big Boy die-cut 30th Anniversary false cover.......... 2.00
❑365, Sep 1987, Some copies have Bob's Big Boy die-cut 30th Anniversary false cover.......... 2.00
❑366, Oct 1987 .... 2.00
❑367, ca. 1987 .... 2.00
❑368, ca. 1987 .... 2.00
❑369, ca. 1988 .... 2.00
❑370, ca. 1988 .... 2.00
❑371, ca. 1988 .... 2.00
❑372 1988 .... 2.00
❑373 1988 .... 2.00
❑374 1988 .... 2.00
❑375 1988 .... 2.00
❑376 1988 .... 2.00
❑377 1988 .... 2.00
❑378 1988 .... 2.00
❑379 1988 .... 2.00
❑380 1989 .... 2.00
❑381, ca. 1989 .... 2.00
❑382, ca. 1989 .... 2.00
❑383, ca. 1989 .... 2.00
❑384, ca. 1989 .... 2.00
❑385, ca. 1989 .... 2.00
❑386, ca. 1989 .... 2.00
❑387, ca. 1989 .... 2.00
❑388, ca. 1989 .... 2.00
❑389, ca. 1989 .... 2.00
❑390 1989 .... 2.00
❑391 1990 .... 2.00
❑392 1990 .... 2.00
❑393, ca. 1990 .... 2.00
❑394, ca. 1990 .... 2.00
❑395, ca. 1990 .... 2.00
❑396 1990 .... 2.00
❑397 1990 .... 2.00
❑398 1990 .... 2.00
❑399 1990 .... 2.00
❑400, ca. 1991, Pirate story 2.00
❑401, ca. 1991 .... 2.00
❑402, ca. 1991 .... 2.00
❑403, ca. 1991, Animal shelter story.. 2.00
❑404 1991 .... 2.00
❑405 1991 .... 2.00
❑406 1991 .... 2.00
❑407 1991 .... 2.00
❑408 1991 .... 2.00
❑409 1991 .... 2.00
❑410 1991 .... 2.00
❑411 1991 .... 2.00
❑412 1991 .... 2.00
❑413 1992 .... 2.00
❑414 1992 .... 2.00
❑415 1992 .... 2.00
❑416 1992 .... 2.00
❑417 1992 .... 2.00
❑418 1992 .... 2.00
❑419 1992 .... 2.00
❑420 1992 .... 2.00
❑421 1992 .... 2.00
❑422 1992 .... 2.00
❑423 1992 .... 2.00
❑424 1992 .... 2.00
❑425 1992 .... 2.00
❑426 1993 .... 2.00
❑427 1993 .... 2.00
❑428 1993 .... 2.00
❑429 1993 .... 2.00
❑430 1993 .... 2.00
❑431 1993 .... 2.00
❑432 1993 .... 2.00
❑433 1993 .... 2.00
❑434 1993 .... 2.00
❑435 1993 .... 2.00
❑436 1993 .... 2.00
❑437 1993, Protest cover 2.00
❑438 1994 .... 2.00
❑439 1994 .... 2.00
❑440 1994 .... 2.00
❑441 1994 .... 2.00
❑442 1994 .... 2.00
❑443 1994 .... 2.00
❑444 1994 .... 2.00
❑445, Nov 1994, Stamp collecting story 2.00
❑446, Dec 1994 .... 2.00
❑447, Jan 1995 .... 2.00
❑448, Feb 1995 .... 2.00
❑449, Mar 1995 .... 2.00
❑450, Apr 1995 .... 2.00
❑451, May 1995 .... 1.50
❑452, Jun 1995 .... 1.50
❑453, Jul 1995 .... 1.50
❑454, Aug 1995 .... 1.50
❑455, Sep 1995 .... 1.50
❑456, Oct 1995, Buffalo credits; supports release of comics postage stamps; Yellow Kid, Katzenjammer Kids, Little Nemo, Buster Brown, Little Orphan Annie, Skeezix appearance 1.50
❑457, Nov 1995 .... 1.50
❑458, Dec 1995 .... 1.50
❑459, Jan 1996 .... 1.50
❑460, Feb 1996 .... 1.50
❑461, Mar 1996 .... 1.50
❑462, Apr 1996 .... 1.50
❑463, ca. 1996 .... 1.50
❑464, ca. 1996 .... 1.50
❑465, ca. 1996, Rare serialized story. 1.50
❑466, ca. 1996, Last WEBS issue 1.50
❑467, ca. 1996, First Yoe Studios issue; Weinerville; title changes to Big Boy Magazine 1.50
❑468, ca. 1996 .... 1.50
❑469, ca. 1996 .... 1.50
❑470, ca. 1996, Space Ghost interview 1.50
❑471, ca. 1996 .... 1.50
❑472, ca. 1996, Adam West interview and cover 1.50
❑473, ca. 1996 .... 1.50
❑474, ca. 1996, Interview with "Kenan & Kel" 1.50
❑475, ca. 1997 .... 1.50
❑476, ca. 1997, Lisa Simpson "interview" and cover 1.50
❑477, ca. 1997 .... 1.50
❑478, ca. 1997 .... 1.50
❑479, ca. 1997, Larisa Oleynik (Alex mack) photo cover 1.50
❑480, ca. 1997 .... 1.50
❑481, ca. 1998 .... 1.50
❑482, ca. 1998, Superman "interview" and cover 1.50
❑483, ca. 1998 .... 1.50
❑484, ca. 1998 .... 1.50
❑485, ca. 1998 .... 1.50
❑486, ca. 1998, 40th Anniversary issue 1.50
❑487, ca. 1999 .... 1.50
❑488, ca. 1999, N'Sync interview and photo cover 1.50
❑489, ca. 1999 .... 1.50
❑490, ca. 1999 .... 1.50
❑491, ca. 1999 .... 1.50
❑492, ca. 1999 .... 1.50
❑493, ca. 2000 .... 1.50
❑494, ca. 2000 .... 1.50
❑495, ca. 2000 .... 1.50
❑496, ca. 2000 .... 1.50
❑497, ca. 2000 .... 1.50
❑498, ca. 2000 .... 1.50
❑499, ca. 2001 .... 1.50
❑500, ca. 2001 .... 1.50
❑501, ca. 2001 .... 1.00
❑502, ca. 2001, (c); LMc (a) 1.00
❑503, ca. 2001 .... 1.00
❑504, ca. 2001 .... 1.00
❑505, ca. 2001 .... 1.00
❑506, ca. 2002 .... 1.00
❑507, ca. 2002 .... 1.00
❑508, ca. 2002 .... 1.00
❑509, ca. 2002, Adventures of Jimmy Neutron cover and "interview" 1.00
❑510, ca. 2003 .... 1.00
❑511, ca. 2003 .... 1.00
❑512, ca. 2003 .... 1.00
❑513, ca. 2003 .... 1.00
❑514, ca. 2004 .... 1.00
❑515, ca. 2004 .... 1.00
❑516, ca. 2004 .... 1.00
❑517, ca. 2004 .... 1.00
❑518, ca. 2005 .... 1.00
❑519, ca. 2005 .... 1.00
❑520, ca. 2005 .... 1.00
❑521, ca. 2005 .... 1.00

ADVENTURES OF THE BIG BOY (PARAGON)

Paragon

❑1, ca. 1976 .... 2.00
❑2, ca. 1976 .... 2.00
❑3, ca. 1976 .... 2.00
❑4, ca. 1976, Circus Cover 2.00
❑5, ca. 1976 .... 2.00
❑6, ca. 1976 .... 2.00
❑7, ca. 1976 .... 2.00
❑8, ca. 1977, Contains outside advertising 2.00
❑9, ca. 1977, Football cover 2.00
❑10, ca. 1977 .... 2.00
❑11, ca. 1977 .... 2.00
❑12, ca. 1977 .... 2.00
❑13, ca. 1977 .... 2.00
❑14, ca. 1977 .... 2.00
❑15, ca. 1977 .... 2.00
❑16, ca. 1977 .... 2.00
❑17, ca. 1977 .... 2.00
❑18, ca. 1978 .... 2.00
❑19, ca. 1978, Ham radio story 2.00
❑20, ca. 1978 .... 2.00
❑21, ca. 1978 .... 2.00
❑22, ca. 1978, Santa Claus cover 2.00
❑23, ca. 1978, Happy New Year cover 2.00
❑24, ca. 1979 .... 2.00
❑25, ca. 1979 .... 2.00
❑26, ca. 1979, 1: Vac II 2.00
❑27, ca. 1979 .... 2.00
❑28, ca. 1979 .... 2.00
❑29, ca. 1979, Liberty Bell story......... 2.00
❑30, ca. 1979, Skydiving story 2.00
❑31, ca. 1979 .... 2.00
❑32, ca. 1979 .... 2.00
❑33, ca. 1979 .... 2.00
❑34, ca. 1979 .... 2.00
❑35, Jan 1980, Happy New Year 1980 cover 1.00
❑36, Feb 1980 .... 1.00
❑37, Mar 1980 .... 1.00
❑38, Apr 1980 .... 1.00
❑39, May 1980 .... 1.00

Adventures of the Fly

Archie dusted off its own hero for the Silver Age
©Archie

Adventures of the Jaguar

Veterinarian takes on an alter ego
©Archie

Adventures of the Little Green Dinosaur

Funny-animal underground title from the 1970s
©Last Gasp

Adventures of the Mask

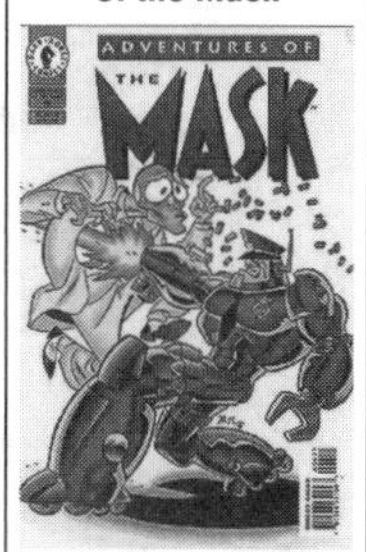

Mask's adventures continued after the movie
©Dark Horse

Adventures of the Outsiders

Continuation of series, without Batman
©DC

N-MINT

❑40, Jun 1980 .... 1.00
❑41, Jul 1980, Independence Day cover 1.00
❑42, Aug 1980 .... 1.00
❑43, Sep 1980 .... 1.00
❑44, Oct 1980 .... 1.00
❑45, Nov 1980, Thanksgiving cover ... 1.00
❑46, Dec 1980 .... 1.00
❑47 1981 .... 1.00
❑48 1981 .... 1.00
❑49 1981 .... 1.00
❑50 1981 .... 1.00
❑51 1981 .... 1.00
❑52 1981 .... 1.00
❑53 1981 .... 1.00
❑54 1981 .... 1.00
❑55 1981 .... 1.00
❑56 1981 .... 1.00
❑57 1981 .... 1.00
❑58 1981 .... 1.00
❑59 1982 .... 1.00
❑60 1982 .... 1.00
❑61 1982 .... 1.00
❑62 1982 .... 1.00
❑63 1982, Disco story 1.00
❑64, ca. 1982 .... 1.00
❑65, ca. 1982 .... 1.00
❑66, ca. 1982 .... 1.00
❑67, ca. 1982, A: Vac II. World's Fair issue, featuring the 1982 Knoxville World's fair 1.00
❑68, ca. 1982, V: Doctor Maybe 1.00
❑69, Nov 1982, A: Vac II. Thanksgiving cover 1.00
❑70, Dec 1983, A: Santa Claus. Christmas cover 1.00
❑71, Jan 1983, V: Doctor Maybe 1.00
❑72, Feb 1983 .... 1.00
❑73, Mar 1983, A: Vac II 1.00
❑74, Apr 1983 .... 1.00
❑75, May 1983, V: Doctor Maybe 1.00

ADVENTURES OF THE FLY
ARCHIE / RADIO

❑1, Aug 1959, JK (w); JS, JK (a); O: Fly 220.00
❑2, Sep 1959, AW, JK (a); Private Strong 140.00
❑3, Nov 1959 .... 100.00
❑4, Jan 1960 .... 80.00
❑5, Mar 1960 .... 80.00
❑6, May 1960 .... 70.00
❑7, Jul 1960 .... 70.00
❑8, Sep 1960 .... 70.00
❑9, Nov 1960 .... 70.00
❑10, Jan 1961 .... 70.00
❑11, Mar 1961 .... 70.00
❑12, May 1961 .... 70.00
❑13, Jul 1961 .... 70.00
❑14, Sep 1961 .... 70.00
❑15, Oct 1961 .... 70.00
❑16, Nov 1961 .... 70.00
❑17, Jan 1962 .... 70.00
❑18, Mar 1962 .... 40.00
❑19, May 1962 .... 40.00
❑20, Jul 1962 .... 40.00
❑21, Sep 1962 .... 40.00

N-MINT

❑22, Oct 1962 .... 40.00
❑23, Nov 1962 .... 40.00
❑24, Feb 1963 .... 40.00
❑25, Apr 1963 .... 40.00
❑26, Jun 1963 .... 40.00
❑27, Aug 1963 .... 30.00
❑28, Oct 1963 .... 30.00
❑29, Jan 1964 .... 30.00
❑30, Oct 1964 .... 30.00
❑31, May 1965, Later issues published as Fly Man 30.00

ADVENTURES OF THE JAGUAR
ARCHIE / RADIO

❑1, Sep 1961 .... 125.00
❑2, Oct 1961 .... 75.00
❑3, Nov 1961 .... 50.00
❑4, Jan 1962 .... 40.00
❑5, Mar 1962 .... 40.00
❑6, May 1962 .... 30.00
❑7, Jul 1962 .... 30.00
❑8, Aug 1962 .... 30.00
❑9, Sep 1962 .... 30.00
❑10, Nov 1962 .... 30.00
❑11, Mar 1963 .... 22.00
❑12, May 1963 .... 22.00
❑13, Aug 1963 .... 22.00
❑14, Oct 1963 .... 22.00
❑15, Nov 1963 .... 22.00

ADVENTURES OF THE LITTLE GREEN DINOSAUR
LAST GASP

❑1, b&w 5.00
❑2, b&w 5.00

ADVENTURES OF THE MAD HUNDA DAY DAY
THAUMATURGE

❑1, Win 1995, b&w 2.00

ADVENTURES OF THE MASK
DARK HORSE

❑1, Jan 1996 .... 2.50
❑2, Feb 1996 V: Walter 2.50
❑3, Mar 1996 .... 2.50
❑4, Apr 1996 1: Bombshell 2.50
❑5, May 1996 .... 2.50
❑6, Jun 1996 .... 2.50
❑7, Jul 1996 .... 2.50
❑8, Aug 1996; Milo dons the mask 2.50
❑9, Sep 1996; James Bond parody 2.50
❑10, Oct 1996 V: Walter 2.50
❑11, Nov 1996; Mask as Santa 2.50
❑12, Dec 1996 .... 2.50
❑Special 1, Oct 1996; Toys R Us Special Ed. Giveaway; newsprint cover 1.00

ADVENTURES OF THE OUTSIDERS
DC

❑33, May 1986; Continued from Batman and the Outsiders #32 .... 1.00
❑34, Jun 1986 V: Masters of Disaster 1.00
❑35, Jul 1986 .... 1.00
❑36, Aug 1986 .... 1.00
❑37, Sep 1986 .... 1.00
❑38, Oct 1986 .... 1.00
❑39, Nov 1986 V: Nuclear Family 1.00

N-MINT

❑40, Dec 1986 JA (a); V: Nuclear Family 1.00
❑41, Jan 1987 JA (a); V: Force of July 1.00
❑42, Feb 1987 .... 1.00
❑43, Mar 1987 .... 1.00
❑44, Apr 1987 V: Duke of Oil 1.00
❑45, May 1987 V: Duke of Oil 1.00
❑46, Jun 1987 .... 1.00

ADVENTURES OF THEOWN
PYRAMID

❑1 1986 .... 2.00
❑2 1986 .... 2.00
❑3 1986 .... 2.00

ADVENTURES OF THE SCREAMER BROTHERS
SUPERSTAR

❑1, Dec 1990 .... 1.50
❑2, Mar 1991 .... 1.50
❑3, Jun 1991 .... 1.50

ADVENTURES OF THE SCREAMER BROTHERS (VOL. 2)
SUPERSTAR

❑1, Aug 1991 .... 1.95
❑2 .... 1.95
❑3, Dec 1991 .... 1.95

ADVENTURES OF THE SUPER MARIO BROS.
VALIANT

❑1, Feb 1991 .... 4.00
❑2, Mar 1991, swimsuit issue 3.00
❑3, Apr 1991 .... 3.00
❑4, May 1991 .... 3.00
❑5, Jun 1991 .... 3.00
❑6, Jul 1991 .... 2.50
❑7, Aug 1991 .... 2.50
❑8, Sep 1991 .... 2.50
❑9, Oct 1991 .... 2.50

ADVENTURES OF THE THING
MARVEL

❑1, Apr 1992; JBy (w); JBy, JSt (a); Reprints Marvel Two-In-One #50; Thing vs. Thing 1.50
❑2, May 1992 .... 1.50
❑3, Jun 1992 FM (a) 1.50
❑4, Jul 1992; A: Man-Thing. Reprints Marvel Two-In-One #77 .... 1.50

ADVENTURES OF THE VITAL-MAN
BUDGIE

❑1, Jun 1991, b&w 2.00
❑2 .... 2.00
❑3 .... 2.00
❑4 .... 2.00

ADVENTURES OF THE X-MEN
MARVEL

❑1, Apr 1996; Wolverine vs. Hulk 2.00
❑2, May 1996 .... 1.50
❑3, Jun 1996 A: Spider-Man. V: Mr. Sinister 1.50
❑4, Jul 1996 .... 1.50
❑5, Aug 1996 V: Magneto 1.50
❑6, Sep 1996; Magneto vs. Apocalypse 1.25
❑7, Oct 1996 .... 1.25
❑8, Nov 1996 .... 1.25
❑9, Dec 1996 V: Vanisher 1.25

Other grades: Multiply price above by 5/6 for VF/NM • 2/3 for VERY FINE • 1/3 for FINE • 1/5 for VERY GOOD • 1/8 for GOOD

N-MINT

❑10, Jan 1997 V: Mojo ... 1.25
❑11, Feb 1997 A: Man-Thing ... 1.25
❑12, Mar 1997 ... 1.25

ADVENTURES ON SPACE STATION FREEDOM
TADCORPS

❑1, educational giveaway on International Space Station ... 2.50

ADVENTURES ON THE FRINGE
FANTAGRAPHICS

❑1, Mar 1992 ... 2.25
❑2, May 1992 ... 2.25
❑3, Jul 1992 ... 2.25
❑4, Oct 1992 ... 2.25
❑5, Feb 1993 ... 2.25

ADVENTURES ON THE PLANET OF THE APES
MARVEL

❑1, Oct 1975; JSn (c); JSn (a); Adapts movie ... 9.00
❑2, Nov 1975; Adapts movie ... 4.00
❑3 1976; Adapts movie ... 4.00
❑4 1976 ... 3.50
❑5, Apr 1976 ... 3.50
❑5/30 cent, Apr 1976, 30 cent price variant ... 20.00
❑6, Jun 1976 ... 4.00
❑6/30 cent, Jun 1976, 30 cent price variant ... 20.00
❑7, Aug 1976 ... 4.00
❑7/30 cent, Aug 1976, 30 cent price variant ... 20.00
❑8, Sep 1976 ... 4.00
❑9, Oct 1976; Adapts Beneath the Planet of the Apes ... 4.00
❑10, Nov 1976; AA (a); Adapts Beneath the Planet of the Apes ... 4.00
❑11, Dec 1976; AA (a); Adapts Beneath the Planet of the Apes; Destruction of Earth ... 4.00

ADVENTURE STRIP DIGEST
WCG

❑1, Aug 1994 ... 2.50
❑2, Apr 1995 ... 2.50
❑3 ... 2.50
❑4, Jun 1996 ... 2.50

ADVENTUROUS UNCLE SCROOGE MCDUCK, (WALT DISNEY'S...)
GLADSTONE

❑1, Jan 1998, CB (w); CB (a); reprints Barks' "The Twenty-Four Carat Moon" ... 2.50
❑2, Mar 1998, 50th anniversary of Uncle Scrooge ... 2.50

AEON FLUX
DARK HORSE

❑1, Sep 2005 ... 2.99
❑2, Oct 2005 ... 2.99
❑3, Nov 2005 ... 2.99
❑4, Dec 2006 ... 2.99

AEON FOCUS
AEON

❑1, Mar 1994; Justin Hampton's Twitch ... 2.95
❑2, Jun 1994; Colin Upton's Other Other Even Bigger Than Slightly Smaller That Got Bigger Big Thing.. 2.95
❑3, Oct 1994; Filthy Habits ... 2.95
❑4, Nov 1994; Ward Sutton's Ink Blot ... 2.95
❑5, ca. 1997 ... 2.95

AERTIMISAN: WAR OF SOULS
ALMAGEST

❑1, Nov 1997 ... 2.75
❑2, Jan 1998 ... 2.75

AESOP'S DESECRATED MORALS
MAGNECOM

❑1, b&w ... 2.95

AESOP'S FABLES
FANTAGRAPHICS

❑1, Spr 1991 ... 2.50
❑2, Fal 1991 ... 2.50
❑3, Win 1991 ... 2.50

AETERNUS
BRICK

❑1, Jun 1997 ... 2.95

N-MINT

AETOS THE EAGLE
ORPHAN UNDERGROUND

❑1, Sep 1994, b&w ... 2.50
❑2, Oct 1995, b&w ... 2.50

AETOS THE EAGLE (VOL. 2)
GROUND ZERO

❑1, Aug 1997 ... 3.00
❑2 ... 3.00
❑3 ... 3.00

AFFABLE TALES FOR YOUR IMAGINATON
LEE ROY BROWN

❑1, Jan 1987, b&w ... 3.00

AFTER APOCALYPSE
PARAGRAPHICS

❑1, May 1987 ... 1.95

AFTER DARK
MILLENNIUM

❑1 ... 2.95

AFTERMATH
PINNACLE

❑1, ca. 1986, b&w; sequel to Messiah ... 1.50

AFTERMATH (CHAOS)
CHAOS

❑1, ca. 2000 ... 2.95

AFTER/SHOCK: BULLETINS FROM GROUND ZERO
LAST GASP

❑1, b&w ... 2.00

AGAINST BLACKSHARD: 3-D: THE SAGA OF SKETCH, THE ROYAL ARTIST
SIRIUS

❑1 ... 2.25

AGENCY
IMAGE

❑Ashcan 1/Gold; Ashcan preview ... 5.00
❑Ashcan 1; Ashcan preview ... 5.00
❑1/A, Aug 2001; Several figures standing on cover ... 2.50
❑1/B, Aug 2001; Woman sitting on cover ... 2.50
❑1/C, Aug 2001; Woman leaning on gun on cover ... 2.50
❑2, ca. 2001 ... 2.50
❑3, ca. 2001 ... 2.95
❑4, ca. 2001 ... 2.95
❑5, Feb 2002 ... 2.95
❑6, Mar 2002; Giant-size ... 4.95

AGENT
MARVEL

❑1 ... 9.95

AGENT "00" SOUL
TWIST RECORDS

❑1; no price ... 5.00

AGENT AMERICA
AWESOME

❑Ashcan 1; Preview edition; 1: Coven. Series preempted by Marvel lawsuit ... 5.00

AGENT LIBERTY SPECIAL
DC

❑1 1991 ... 2.00

AGENTS
IMAGE

❑1, Apr 2003 ... 2.95
❑2, May 2003 ... 2.95
❑3, Jul 2003 ... 2.95
❑4, Aug 2003 ... 2.95
❑5, Sep 2003 ... 2.95
❑6, Oct 2003 ... 2.95

AGENTS OF LAW
DARK HORSE

❑1, Mar 1995 ... 2.50
❑2 1995 ... 2.50
❑3 1995 ... 2.50
❑4 1995 ... 2.50
❑5 1995 ... 2.50
❑6, Sep 1995 ... 2.50

AGENT 13: THE MIDNIGHT AVENGER
TSR

❑1 ... 7.95

N-MINT

AGENT THREE ZERO
GALAXINOVELS

❑1; Galaxinovels w/ Trading Card and Poster ... 3.95

AGENT THREE ZERO: THE BLUE SULTAN'S QUEST/BLUE SULTAN- GALAXI FACT FILES
GALAXINOVELS

❑1; Flip-book; poster; trading card ... 2.95
❑1/Platinum; Platinum edition ... 2.95
❑2 ... 2.95
❑3 ... 2.95
❑4 ... 2.95

AGENT UNKNOWN
RENEGADE

❑1, Oct 1987 ... 2.00
❑2, Jan 1988 ... 2.00
❑3, Apr 1988 ... 2.00

AGENT X
MARVEL

❑1, Sep 2002 ... 2.25
❑2, Oct 2002 ... 2.25
❑3, Nov 2002 ... 2.25
❑4, Dec 2002 ... 2.25
❑5, Jan 2003 ... 2.25
❑6, Feb 2003 ... 2.25
❑7, Mar 2003 ... 2.99
❑8, Apr 2003 ... 2.99
❑9, May 2003 ... 2.99
❑10, Jun 2003 ... 2.99
❑11, Jul 2003 ... 2.99
❑12, Aug 2003 ... 2.99
❑13, Nov 2003 ... 2.99
❑14, Dec 2003 ... 2.99
❑15, Dec 2003 ... 2.99

AGE OF APOCALYPSE: THE CHOSEN
MARVEL

❑1 ... 2.50

AGE OF BRONZE
IMAGE

❑1, Nov 1998 ... 3.50
❑2, Jan 1999 ... 3.00
❑3, Mar 1999 ... 3.00
❑4, May 1999 ... 3.00
❑5, Oct 1999 ... 3.00
❑6, Jan 2000; cover says Dec, indicia says Jan ... 3.00
❑7, Mar 2000; cover says Apr, indicia says Mar ... 3.00
❑8, Aug 2000, b&w ... 3.50
❑9, Dec 2000; cover says Nov, indicia says Dec ... 3.50
❑10, Feb 2001 ... 3.50
❑11, Mar 2001 ... 3.50
❑12, Apr 2001 ... 3.50
❑13, May 2001 ... 3.50
❑14, Aug 2002 ... 3.50
❑15, Nov 2002, Indicia says Nov, cover says Oct ... 3.50
❑16, Feb 2003 ... 3.50
❑17, Jul 2003 ... 3.50
❑18, Oct 2003 ... 3.50
❑19, Apr 2004 ... 3.50
❑20 2005 ... 3.50
❑21 2005 ... 3.50
❑22, Jan 2006 ... 3.50
❑23, Jul 2006 ... 3.50
❑Special 1, Jul 1999; cover says Jun, indicia says Jul ... 2.95
❑Special 2, May 2002; Behind the Scenes ... 3.50

AGE OF HEROES
HALLOWEEN

❑1 1996, b&w ... 2.95
❑2 1996, b&w ... 2.95
❑3, Mar 1997, b&w ... 2.95
❑4, May 1997, b&w ... 2.95
❑5, ca. 1999, b&w ... 3.50
❑Special 1; reprints Age of Heroes #1 and 2 (Halloween) ... 4.95
❑Special 2 ... 6.95

AGE OF HEROES, THE: WEX
IMAGE

❑1, Nov 1998, b&w ... 2.95

Other grades: Multiply price above by 5/6 for VF/NM • 2/3 for VERY FINE • 1/3 for FINE • 1/5 for VERY GOOD • 1/8 for GOOD

Adventures of the X-Men

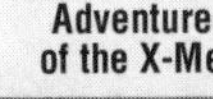

Adapts the fourth season of the cartoon

©Marvel

Adventures On the Planet of the Apes

Marvel adaptation of the movie series

©Marvel

Age of Bronze

Eric Shanower retells the Trojan War

©Image

Age of Heroes

Wonders in the land of Xera

©Halloween

Airboy

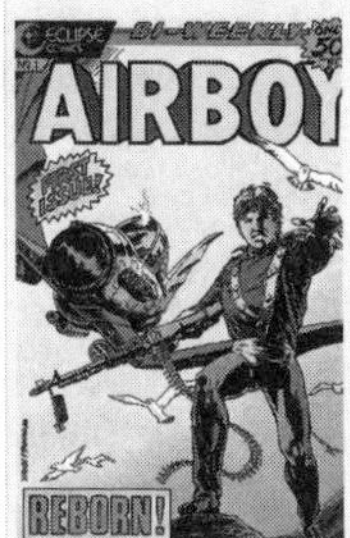

Revival of Golden Age aerial hero

©Eclipse

N-MINT

AGE OF INNOCENCE: THE REBIRTH OF IRON MAN
MARVEL
❑1 — 2.50

AGE OF REPTILES
DARK HORSE
❑1, Nov 1993 — 2.50
❑2, Dec 1993 — 2.50
❑3, Jan 1994 — 2.50
❑4, Feb 1994 — 2.50

AGE OF REPTILES: THE HUNT
DARK HORSE
❑1, May 1996 — 2.95
❑2, Jun 1996 — 2.95
❑3, Jul 1996 — 2.95
❑4, Aug 1996 — 2.95
❑5, Sep 1996 — 2.95

AGONY ACRES
AA2
❑1, May 1995 — 2.95
❑1/Ashcan 1996 — 2.50
❑2 1996 — 2.95
❑3 1996, b&w — 2.95
❑4 1996 — 2.95
❑5 1996 — 2.95

AHLEA
RADIO
❑1, Aug 1997 — 2.95
❑2, Oct 1997 — 2.95

AIDA-ZEE
NATE BUTLER
❑1 — 1.50

AIDEN MCKAIN CHRONICLES: BATTLE FOR EARTH
DIGITAL WEBBING
❑1, Sep 2005 — 2.99
❑1/Incentive, Sep 2005 — 10.00

AIDS AWARENESS
CHAOS CITY
❑1, ca. 1993, b&w — 3.00

AIM (VOL. 2)
CRYPTIC
❑1 — 1.95

AIRBOY
ECLIPSE
❑1, Jul 1986, O: Airboy II (modern). 1: Airboy II (modern). D: Airboy I (Golden Age) — 2.00
❑2, Jul 1986, 1: Skywolf (Golden Age, in modern era). 1: Marisa — 1.50
❑3, Aug 1986, A: The Heap — 1.50
❑4, Aug 1986 — 1.50
❑5, Sep 1986, DSt (a); Return of Valkyrie — 1.50
❑6, Sep 1986, 1: Iron Ace (in modern age) — 1.50
❑7, Oct 1986, PG (c) — 1.50
❑8, Oct 1986 — 1.50
❑9, Nov 1986; Full-size issues begin O: Airboy (Golden Age). 1: Flying Fool (in modern age) — 1.50
❑10, Nov 1986 1: Manic — 1.25
❑11, Dec 1986; O: Airboy (Golden Age). O: Birdie. 1: Ito. Skywolf back-up — 1.25
❑12, Dec 1986; 1: Kip Thorne. Iron Ace's identity revealed — 1.25
❑13, Jan 1987; 1: Bald Eagle (in modern age). Airfighters back-up — 1.25
❑14, Jan 1987 — 1.25
❑15, Feb 1987 — 1.25
❑16, Feb 1987 D: Manic — 1.25
❑17, Mar 1987 1: Lacey Lyle. A: Harry Truman — 1.25
❑18, Mar 1987 1: Black Angel (in modern age) — 1.25
❑19, Apr 1987 V: Rats — 1.25
❑20, Apr 1987 PG (c); 1: The Rats (in modern age). V: Rats — 1.25
❑21, May 1987 GE (a); 1: Rat Mother — 1.25
❑22, May 1987; 1: Lester Mansfield. 1: El Lobo Alado (Skywolf's father). Skywolf back-up story — 1.25
❑23, Jun 1987 — 1.25
❑24, Jun 1987 A: Heap — 1.25
❑25, Jul 1987 O: Manure Man. 1: Manure Man. A: Heap — 1.25
❑26, Jul 1987 1: Flying Dutchman (in modern age). 1: Road Rats — 1.25
❑27, Aug 1987 — 1.25
❑28, Aug 1987 1: Black Axis — 1.25
❑29, Sep 1987 — 1.25
❑30, Sep 1987 — 1.25
❑31, Oct 1987 — 1.25
❑32, Oct 1987 — 1.25
❑33, Nov 1987 — 1.75
❑34, Dec 1987 DS (a) — 1.75
❑35, Jan 1988 — 1.75
❑36, Feb 1988 — 1.75
❑37, Mar 1988 — 1.75
❑38, Apr 1988 — 1.75
❑39, May 1988 — 1.75
❑40, Jun 1988 — 1.75
❑41, Jul 1988 — 1.75
❑42, Aug 1988 — 1.95
❑43, Sep 1988 — 1.95
❑44, Oct 1988 — 1.95
❑45, Nov 1988 — 1.95
❑46, Jan 1989; Airboy Diary — 1.95
❑47, Mar 1989; Airboy Diary — 1.95
❑48, Apr 1989; Airboy Diary — 1.95
❑49, Jun 1989; Airboy Diary — 1.95
❑50, Oct 1989; Giant-size JKu (a) — 4.95

AIRBOY MEETS THE PROWLER
ECLIPSE
❑1, Dec 1987 — 1.95

AIRBOY-MR. MONSTER SPECIAL
ECLIPSE
❑1, Aug 1987 — 1.75

AIRBOY VERSUS THE AIRMAIDENS
ECLIPSE
❑1, Jul 1988 — 1.95

AIR FIGHTERS CLASSICS
ECLIPSE
❑1, Nov 1987; squarebound; cardstock cover; Reprints Air Fighters Comics #1 — 3.95
❑2, Jan 1988; Reprints Air Fighters Comics #2 — 3.95
❑3, Mar 1988; Reprints Air Fighters Comics #3 — 3.95
❑4; Reprints Air Fighters Comics #4 — 3.95
❑5 1989; Reprints Air Fighters Comics #5 — 3.95
❑6; Reprints Air Fighters Comics #6 — 3.95
❑7; Reprints Air Fighters Comics #7 — 3.95

AIRFIGHTERS MEET SGT. STRIKE SPECIAL
ECLIPSE
❑1, Jan 1988 — 1.95

AIRLOCK
ECLECTUS
❑1, Jun 1990, b&w — 2.50
❑2, Jul 1991 — 2.50
❑3, Oct 1991 — 2.50

AIRMAIDENS SPECIAL
ECLIPSE
❑1, Aug 1987 — 1.75

AIRMAN
MALIBU
❑1 — 1.95

AIRMEN
MANSION
❑1, Feb 1995, b&w — 2.50

AIR RAIDERS
MARVEL / STAR
❑1, Nov 1987 — 1.00
❑2, Dec 1987 — 1.00
❑3, Jan 1988 — 1.00
❑4, Feb 1988 — 1.00
❑5, Mar 1988 — 1.00

AIRTIGHT GARAGE
MARVEL / EPIC
❑1, Jul 1993 — 2.50
❑2, Aug 1993 — 2.50
❑3, Sep 1993 — 2.50
❑4, Oct 1993 — 2.50

AIR WAR STORIES
DELL
❑1, Nov 1964 — 22.00
❑2, Feb 1965 — 14.00
❑3, May 1965 — 14.00
❑4, Aug 1965 — 14.00
❑5, Nov 1965 — 14.00
❑6, Feb 1966 — 14.00
❑7, May 1966 — 14.00
❑8, Aug 1966; Final issue? — 14.00

AIRWAVES
CALIBER
❑1, Feb 1991 — 2.50
❑2 1991 — 2.50
❑3 1991 — 2.50
❑4 1991 — 2.50

AI YORI AOSHI
TOKYOPOP
❑1, Jan 2004 — 9.95
❑2, Mar 2004 — 9.95
❑3, May 2004 — 9.95
❑4, Jul 2004 — 9.95
❑5, Sep 2004 — 9.95
❑6, Nov 2004 — 9.95
❑7, Jan 2005 — 9.95
❑8, Mar 2005 — 9.95

Other grades: Multiply price above by 5/6 for VF/NM • 2/3 for VERY FINE • 1/3 for FINE • 1/5 for VERY GOOD • 1/8 for GOOD

N-MINT

❑9, Jun 2005 9.95
❑10, Sep 2005 9.95
❑11, Dec 2005 9.95

A.K.A. GOLDFISH
Caliber

❑1, Joker 3.50
❑2, Ace 3.95
❑3, ca. 1995, Jack 3.95
❑4, ca. 1995, Queen 2.95
❑5, Mar 1996, King; cardstock cover 3.95
❑Book 1, collects mini-series 17.95
❑Book 1/2nd, Reprints 16.95

AKIKO
Sirius

❑1, Mar 1996 6.00
❑2, Apr 1996 4.50
❑3, May 1996 4.00
❑4, Jun 1996 4.00
❑5 1996; no indicia 4.00
❑6, Aug 1996 3.50
❑7, Sep 1996 3.50
❑8, Oct 1996 3.50
❑9, Dec 1996 3.50
❑10, Jan 1997 3.50
❑11, Feb 1997 2.50
❑12, Mar 1997 2.50
❑13, Apr 1997 2.50
❑14, May 1997 2.50
❑15, Jul 1997 2.50
❑16, Aug 1997 2.50
❑17, Aug 1997; indicia says "Aug" 2.50
❑18, Sep 1997 2.50
❑19, Oct 1997; Beeba's story 2.50
❑20, Nov 1997; Beeba's story 2.50
❑21, Dec 1997 2.50
❑22, Jan 1998 2.50
❑23, Feb 1998 2.50
❑24, Mar 1998 2.50
❑25, May 1998 2.50
❑26, Jul 1998 2.50
❑27, Aug 1998 2.50
❑28, Oct 1998 2.50
❑29, Nov 1998 2.50
❑30, Dec 1998 2.50
❑31, Feb 1998 2.50
❑32, Mar 1998 2.50
❑33, May 1998 2.50
❑34, Jun 1999 2.50
❑35, Sep 1999, b&w 2.50
❑36, Oct 1999, b&w 2.50
❑37, Dec 1999, b&w 2.50
❑38, Feb 2000, b&w 2.50
❑39, May 2000, b&w 2.50
❑40, Aug 2000, b&w 2.95
❑41, Oct 2000, b&w 2.95
❑42 2001 0.00
❑43 2001 0.00
❑44 2001 0.00
❑45 2001 0.00
❑46 2001 0.00
❑47 2002 0.00
❑48 2002 0.00
❑49 2002 2.95
❑50, Jun 2003 3.50
❑51, Nov 2003 2.95

AKIKO ON THE PLANET SMOO
Sirius

❑1, Dec 1995, b&w; Fold-out cover 5.00
❑1/2nd, May 1998, b&w; cardstock cover 4.00
❑Fan ed. 1/A; free promotional giveaway 3.00

AKIKO ON THE PLANET SMOO: THE COLOR EDITION
Sirius

❑1, Feb 2000, cardstock cover 4.95

AKIRA
Marvel / Epic

❑1, Sep 1988 8.00
❑1/2nd 1988 4.00
❑2, Oct 1988 5.00
❑2/2nd 1988 4.00
❑3, Nov 1988 5.00
❑4, Dec 1988 4.00
❑5, Jan 1989 4.00
❑6, ca. 1989 4.00
❑7, ca. 1989 4.00
❑8, ca. 1989 4.00
❑9, ca. 1989 4.00
❑10, ca. 1989 4.00
❑11, ca. 1989 4.00
❑12, ca. 1989 4.00
❑13, ca. 1989 4.00
❑14, ca. 1989 4.00
❑15, ca. 1989 4.00
❑16, ca. 1989 4.00
❑17, ca. 1990 4.00
❑18, ca. 1990 4.00
❑19, ca. 1990 4.00
❑20, ca. 1990 4.00
❑21, ca. 1990 4.00
❑22, ca. 1990 4.00
❑23, ca. 1990 4.00
❑24, ca. 1990 4.00
❑25, ca. 1990 4.00
❑26, ca. 1990 4.00
❑27, ca. 1991 4.00
❑28, ca. 1991 4.00
❑29, ca. 1991 4.00
❑30, ca. 1991 4.00
❑31, ca. 1991 4.00
❑32, ca. 1992 4.00
❑33, ca. 1992 4.00
❑34, ca. 1994 4.00
❑35, ca. 1995 4.00
❑36 1995 A: Lady Miyako 4.00
❑37, ca. 1995 4.00
❑38, ca. 1995 4.00
❑Book 1; Collects Akira #1-3 13.95
❑Book 2 14.95
❑Book 3 14.95
❑Book 4 14.95
❑Book 5 14.95
❑Book 6 14.95
❑Book 7; Collects Akira #19-21 16.95
❑Book 8; Collects Akira #22-24 16.95
❑Book 9 16.95
❑Book 10 17.95

A*K*Q*J
Fantagraphics

❑1, Mar 1991, b&w; Captain Jack 2.75

ALADDIN (CONQUEST)
Conquest

❑0, Feb 1993, b&w 2.95

ALADDIN (DISNEY'S...)
Marvel

❑1, Oct 1994 1.50
❑2, Nov 1994 1.50
❑3, Dec 1994 1.50
❑4, Jan 1995 1.50
❑5, Feb 1995 1.50
❑6, Mar 1995 1.50
❑7, Apr 1995 1.50
❑8, May 1995 1.50
❑9, Jun 1995 1.50
❑10, Jul 1995 1.50
❑11, Aug 1995 1.50

ALAMO
Antarctic

❑1, Apr 2004 4.95

ALARMING ADVENTURES
Harvey

❑1, Oct 1962 40.00
❑2, Dec 1962 25.00
❑3, Feb 1963 20.00

ALBEDO (1ST SERIES)
Thoughts & Images

❑0, ca. 1986; Blue cover; 500 printed 8.00
❑0/A, ca. 1986; Only 50 copies printed; White cover (yellow table) 30.00
❑0/B, ca. 1986; Less than 500 copies printed; White cover (no yellow) 15.00
❑0/2nd, ca. 1986; Blue cover 5.00
❑0/3rd, ca. 1986, b&w; Blue cover 3.00
❑0/4th, Dec 1986; Yellow cover front, blue cover back 2.50
❑1, ca. 1984; Dark red cover 14.00
❑1/A, ca. 1984; Bright red cover 10.00
❑1/2nd, ca. 1984; Bright red cover 10.00
❑2, Nov 1984 1: Usagi Yojimbo 250.00
❑3, Apr 1985; Usagi Yojimbo back-up 5.00
❑4, Jul 1985; Usagi Yojimbo back-up 4.00
❑5, Oct 1985 4.00
❑6, Jan 1986 3.00
❑7, Mar 1986 3.00
❑8, Jul 1986 3.00
❑9, May 1987 2.00
❑10, Sep 1987; cardstock cover 2.00
❑11, Dec 1987 2.00
❑12, Mar 1988 2.00
❑13, Jun 1988 2.00
❑14, Spr 1989 2.00

ALBEDO (2ND SERIES)
Antarctic

❑1, Jun 1991 4.00
❑2, Sep 1991 3.00
❑3, Dec 1991 3.00
❑4, Mar 1992 3.00
❑5, Jun 1992 2.50
❑6, Sep 1992 2.50
❑7, Dec 1992 2.50
❑8, Mar 1993 2.50
❑9, Jun 1993 2.50
❑10, Oct 1993 2.75
❑Special 1, Jul 1993 4.00

ALBEDO (3RD SERIES)
Antarctic

❑1, Feb 1994 2.95
❑2, Oct 1994 2.95
❑3, Feb 1995 2.95
❑4, Jan 1996 2.95

ALBEDO (4TH SERIES)
Antarctic

❑1, Dec 1996 2.95
❑2, Jan 1999 2.99

ALBEDO (5TH SERIES)
Antarctic

❑1, ca. 2002 2.99

ALBINO SPIDER OF DAJETTE
Verotik

❑1, ca. 1997 2.95
❑2, Jun 1997 2.95
❑0, ca. 1998 2.95

ALBION
DC/WildStorm

❑1, Aug 2005 2.99
❑2, Sep 2005 2.99
❑3 2005 2.99
❑4, Jun 2006 2.99
❑5, Jul 2006 2.99

AL CAPP'S LI'L ABNER: THE FRAZETTA YEARS
Dark Horse

❑1, ca. 2003 18.95
❑2, ca. 2003 18.95
❑3, ca. 2004 18.95
❑4, ca. 2004 18.95

ALEC DEAR
Mediocre Concepts

❑1 1996, b&w; magazine-sized comic book with cardstock cover; no cover price 2.00

ALEC: LOVE AND BEERGLASSES
Escape

❑1 3.50

ALEISTER ARCANE
Idea & Design Works

❑1, Apr 2004 3.99
❑2, May 2004 3.99
❑3, Jul 2004 3.99

ALEX
Fantagraphics

❑1 2.95
❑2, Apr 1994 2.95
❑3, Jul 1994 2.95
❑4, Oct 1994 2.95
❑5, Nov 1994 2.95
❑6, Jan 1995, b&w 2.95

ALEXIS (VOL. 2)
Fantagraphics / Eros

❑1 1995 2.95
❑2, Jul 1995 2.95
❑3 1995 2.95

Other grades: Multiply price above by 5/6 for VF/NM • 2/3 for VERY FINE • 1/3 for FINE • 1/5 for VERY GOOD • 1/8 for GOOD

Akiko

Charming series follows fourth-grader in space

©Sirius

Akira

Marvel import from before manga was hot

©Marvel

Albedo (1st Series)

Funny animal space epic from Steve Gallacci

©Thoughts & Images

Alf

Alien Life Form from NBC cracks comics jokes

©Marvel

Alias (Marvel)

Bendis takes on ex-Avenger private eye

©Marvel

	N-MINT
❑4 1995	2.95
❑5, Mar 1996	2.95

ALF
MARVEL

	N-MINT
❑1, Mar 1988	2.00
❑2, Apr 1988	1.25
❑3, May 1988	1.25
❑4, Jun 1988	1.25
❑5, Jul 1988	1.25
❑6, Aug 1988	1.00
❑7, Sep 1988	1.00
❑8, Oct 1988	1.00
❑9, Nov 1988	1.00
❑10, Dec 1988	1.00
❑11, Jan 1989	1.00
❑12, Feb 1989	1.00
❑13, Mar 1989	1.00
❑14, Apr 1989	1.00
❑15, May 1989	1.00
❑16, Jun 1989	1.00
❑17, Jul 1989	1.00
❑18, Aug 1989	1.00
❑19, Sep 1989	1.00
❑20, Oct 1989	1.00
❑21, Nov 1989	1.00
❑22, Nov 1989; X-Men parody	1.00
❑23, Dec 1989	1.00
❑24, Dec 1989	1.00
❑25, Jan 1990	1.00
❑26, Feb 1990	1.00
❑27, Mar 1990	1.00
❑28, Apr 1990	1.00
❑29, May 1990; "3-D" cover	1.00
❑30, Jun 1990	1.00
❑31, Jul 1990	1.00
❑32, Aug 1990	1.00
❑33, Sep 1990	1.00
❑34, Oct 1990	1.00
❑35, Nov 1990	1.00
❑36, Dec 1990	1.00
❑37, Jan 1991	1.00
❑38, Feb 1991	1.00
❑39, Mar 1991	1.00
❑40, Apr 1991	1.00
❑41, May 1991	1.00
❑42, Jun 1991	1.00
❑43, Jul 1991	1.00
❑44, Aug 1991; X-Men parody	1.00
❑45, Sep 1991	1.00
❑46, Oct 1991	1.00
❑47, Nov 1991	1.00
❑48, Dec 1991	1.00
❑49, Jan 1992	1.00
❑50, Feb 1992; Giant-size	1.50
❑Annual 1, ca. 1988; Dynamic Forces edition	1.50
❑Annual 2, ca. 1989	1.50
❑Annual 3, ca. 1990; TMNT parody	1.50
❑Holiday 1, Hol 1988; magazine-sized comic book with cardstock cover; Holiday Special #1; magazine-sized comic book with cardstock cover	1.50
❑Holiday 2, Hol 1989; Dynamic Forces edition; Holiday Special #2	1.50
❑Spring 1	1.75

ALF COMICS MAGAZINE
MARVEL

	N-MINT
❑1, Nov 1988; digest	2.00
❑2, Jan 1989; digest	2.00

ALIAS:
NOW

	N-MINT
❑1, Jul 1990	1.75
❑2, Aug 1990	1.75
❑3, Sep 1990	1.75
❑4, Oct 1990	1.75
❑5, Nov 1990	1.75

ALIAS (MARVEL)
MARVEL / MAX

	N-MINT
❑1, Nov 2001 BMB (w)	3.50
❑2, Dec 2001 BMB (w)	3.00
❑3, Jan 2002 BMB (w)	3.00
❑4, Feb 2002 BMB (w)	3.00
❑5, Mar 2002 BMB (w)	3.00
❑6, Apr 2002 BMB (w)	3.00
❑7, May 2002 BMB (w)	3.00
❑8, Jun 2002 BMB (w)	3.00
❑9, Jul 2002 BMB (w)	3.00
❑10, Aug 2002 BMB (w)	3.00
❑11, Sep 2002 BMB (w)	2.99
❑12, Sep 2002 BMB (w)	2.99
❑13, Oct 2002 BMB (w)	2.99
❑14, Nov 2002 BMB (w)	2.99
❑15, Dec 2002 BMB (w)	2.99
❑16, Jan 2003 BMB (w)	2.99
❑17, Feb 2003 BMB (w)	2.99
❑18, Mar 2003 BMB (w)	2.99
❑19, Apr 2003 BMB (w)	2.99
❑20, May 2003 BMB (w)	2.99
❑21, May 2003 BMB (w)	2.99
❑22, Jul 2003 BMB (w); O: Jessica Jones	2.99
❑23, Aug 2003 BMB (w); O: Jessica Jones	2.99
❑24, Sep 2003, BMB (w)	2.99
❑25, Oct 2003, BMB (w)	2.99
❑26, Nov 2003, BMB (w)	2.99
❑27, Dec 2003, BMB (w)	2.99
❑28, Jan 2004, BMB (w)	2.99

ALI-BABA: SCOURGE OF THE DESERT
GAUNTLET

	N-MINT
❑1	3.50

ALICE IN LOST WORLD
RADIO

	N-MINT
❑1	2.95
❑2, ca. 2001	2.95
❑3, ca. 2001	2.95
❑4, ca. 2001	2.95

ALIEN 3
DARK HORSE

	N-MINT
❑1, Jun 1992	2.50
❑2, Jun 1992	2.50
❑3, Jun 1992	2.50

ALIEN DUCKLINGS
BLACKTHORNE

	N-MINT
❑1, Oct 1986	2.00
❑2, Dec 1986	2.00
❑3, Feb 1987	2.00
❑4, Apr 1987	2.00

ALIEN ENCOUNTERS (FANTACO)
FANTACO

	N-MINT
❑1 1980	1.50

ALIEN ENCOUNTERS (ECLIPSE)
ECLIPSE

	N-MINT
❑1, Jun 1985 MGu (a)	2.00
❑2, Aug 1965	2.00
❑3, Oct 1985	2.00
❑4, Dec 1985	2.00
❑5, Feb 1986	2.00
❑6, Apr 1986; Story "Nada" used as basis for movie "They Live"	2.00
❑7, Jun 1986 RHo (a)	2.00
❑8, Aug 1986	2.00
❑9, Oct 1986	2.00
❑10, Dec 1986 TS, GM (a)	2.00
❑11, Feb 1987	2.00
❑12, Apr 1987	2.00
❑13, Jun 1987	2.00
❑14, Aug 1987	2.00

ALIEN FIRE
KITCHEN SINK

	N-MINT
❑1, Jan 1987	2.00
❑2, May 1987	2.00
❑3, May 1987	2.00

ALIEN FIRE: PASS IN THUNDER
KITCHEN SINK

	N-MINT
❑1, May 1995, b&w; squarebound	6.95

ALIEN HERO
ZEN

	N-MINT
❑1, Feb 1999; illustrated novella featuring Zen	8.95

ALIEN LEGION (VOL. 1)
MARVEL / EPIC

	N-MINT
❑1, Apr 1984; Giant-size	2.00
❑2, Jun 1984	1.50
❑3, Aug 1984	1.50
❑4, Oct 1984	1.50
❑5, Dec 1984	1.50
❑6, Feb 1985	1.50
❑7, Apr 1985	1.50
❑8, Jun 1985	1.50
❑9, Aug 1985	1.50
❑10, Oct 1985	1.50
❑11, Dec 1985	1.50
❑12, Feb 1986	1.50
❑13, Apr 1986	1.50
❑14, Jun 1986	1.50
❑15, Aug 1986	1.50
❑16, Oct 1986	1.50
❑17, Dec 1986	1.50
❑18, Feb 1987	1.50
❑19, Apr 1987	1.50
❑20, Jun 1987	1.50

Other grades: Multiply price above by 5/6 for VF/NM • 2/3 for VERY FINE • 1/3 for FINE • 1/5 for VERY GOOD • 1/8 for GOOD

N-MINT | N-MINT | N-MINT

ALIEN LEGION (VOL. 2)
MARVEL / EPIC
❑1, Oct 1987 .... 1.50
❑2, Dec 1987 .... 1.50
❑3, Feb 1988 .... 1.50
❑4, Apr 1988 .... 1.50
❑5, Jun 1988 .... 1.50
❑6, Aug 1988 .... 1.50
❑7, Oct 1988 .... 1.50
❑8, Dec 1988 .... 1.50
❑9, Feb 1989 .... 1.50
❑10, Apr 1989 .... 1.50
❑11, Jun 1989 .... 1.50
❑12, Aug 1989 .... 1.50
❑13, Oct 1989 .... 1.50
❑14, Dec 1989 .... 1.50
❑15, Feb 1990 .... 1.50
❑16, Apr 1990 .... 1.50
❑17, Jun 1990 .... 1.50
❑18, Aug 1990 .... 1.50

ALIEN LEGION: A GREY DAY TO DIE
MARVEL
❑1 .... 5.95

ALIEN LEGION: BINARY DEEP
MARVEL / EPIC
❑1, Sep 1993 .... 3.50

ALIEN LEGION: JUGGER GRIMROD
MARVEL / EPIC
❑1, Aug 1992 .... 5.95

ALIEN LEGION: ONE PLANET AT A TIME
MARVEL / EPIC
❑1, ca. 1993 .... 4.95
❑2, ca. 1993 .... 4.95
❑3, ca. 1993 .... 4.95

ALIEN LEGION: ON THE EDGE
MARVEL / EPIC
❑1, Nov 1990 .... 4.50
❑2, Dec 1990 .... 4.50
❑3, Jan 1991 .... 4.50

ALIEN LEGION: TENANTS OF HELL
MARVEL / EPIC
❑1, ca. 1991; cardstock cover 4.50
❑2, ca. 1991; cardstock cover 4.50

ALIEN NATION
DC
❑1, Dec 1988 .... 3.00

ALIEN NATION: A BREED APART
ADVENTURE
❑1, Nov 1990 .... 2.50
❑2, Dec 1990 .... 2.50
❑3, Jan 1991 .... 2.50
❑4, Mar 1991 .... 2.50

ALIEN NATION: THE FIRSTCOMERS
ADVENTURE
❑1, May 1991 .... 2.50
❑2, Jun 1991 .... 2.50
❑3, Jul 1991 .... 2.50
❑4, Aug 1991 .... 2.50

ALIEN NATION: THE LOST EPISODE
MALIBU
❑1 1992, b&w; squarebound; adapts second season opener 4.95

ALIEN NATION: THE PUBLIC ENEMY
ADVENTURE
❑1, Dec 1991 .... 2.50
❑2, Jan 1992 .... 2.50
❑3, Feb 1992 .... 2.50
❑4, Mar 1992 .... 2.50

ALIEN NATION: THE SKIN TRADE
ADVENTURE
❑1, Mar 1991 .... 2.50
❑2, Apr 1991 .... 2.50
❑3, May 1991 .... 2.50
❑4, Jun 1991 .... 2.50

ALIEN NATION: THE SPARTANS
ADVENTURE
❑1, Mar 1990; Yellow 2.50
❑1/A, Mar 1990; Green 2.50
❑1/B, Mar 1990; Blue 2.50
❑1/C, Mar 1990; Red 2.50
❑1/Ltd., Mar 1990 .... 3.00
❑2 1990 .... 2.50
❑3 1990 .... 2.50
❑4 1990 .... 2.50
❑Book 1 .... 9.95

ALIEN RESURRECTION
DARK HORSE
❑1, Oct 1997 .... 2.50
❑2, Nov 1997 .... 2.50

ALIENS
GOLD KEY
❑1 .... 12.00
❑2 1982 .... 5.00

ALIENS (VOL. 1)
DARK HORSE
❑1, May 1988 .... 4.50
❑1/2nd 2.50
❑1/3rd 2.00
❑1/4th 2.00
❑1/5th 2.00
❑1/6th 2.00
❑2, Sep 1988 .... 3.50
❑2/2nd 2.50
❑2/3rd 2.00
❑2/4th, Jul 1989 .... 2.00
❑3, Jan 1989 .... 2.50
❑3/3rd, Sep 1989 .... 2.00
❑3/2nd 2.00
❑4, Mar 1989 .... 2.50
❑4/2nd 2.00
❑5, Jun 1989 .... 2.50
❑5/2nd, Jun 1989 .... 2.00
❑6, Jul 1989 .... 2.50
❑6/2nd 2.00

ALIENS (VOL. 2)
DARK HORSE
❑1, Aug 1989 .... 3.00
❑2, Dec 1989 .... 2.50
❑3, Mar 1990 .... 2.50
❑4, May 1990 .... 2.50

ALIENS: ALCHEMY
DARK HORSE
❑1, Oct 1997 .... 2.95
❑2, Nov 1997 .... 2.95
❑3, Nov 1997 .... 2.95

ALIENS: APOCALYPSE: THE DESTROYING ANGELS
DARK HORSE
❑1, Jan 1999 .... 2.95
❑2, Feb 1999 .... 2.95
❑3, Mar 1999 .... 2.95
❑4, Apr 1999 .... 2.95

ALIENS: BERSERKER
DARK HORSE
❑1, Jan 1995 .... 2.50
❑2, Feb 1995 .... 2.50
❑3, Mar 1995 .... 2.50
❑4, Apr 1995 .... 2.50

ALIENS: COLONIAL MARINES
DARK HORSE
❑1, Jan 1993 .... 2.50
❑2, Feb 1993 .... 2.50
❑3, Mar 1993 .... 2.50
❑4, Apr 1993 .... 2.50
❑5, May 1993 .... 2.50
❑6, Jun 1993 .... 2.50
❑7, Jul 1993 .... 2.50
❑8, Aug 1993 .... 2.50
❑9, Sep 1993 .... 2.50
❑10, Oct 1993 .... 2.50

ALIENS: EARTH ANGEL
DARK HORSE
❑1, Aug 1994 .... 2.95

ALIENS: EARTH WAR
DARK HORSE
❑1, Jun 1990 .... 3.00
❑1/2nd 2.50
❑2, Jul 1990 .... 2.50
❑3, Sep 1990 .... 2.50
❑4, Oct 1990 .... 2.50

ALIEN SEX/MONSTER LUST
FANTAGRAPHICS / EROS
❑1, Apr 1992, b&w 2.50

ALIENS: GENOCIDE
DARK HORSE
❑1, Nov 1991 .... 2.50
❑2, Dec 1991 .... 2.50
❑3, Jan 1992 .... 2.50
❑4, Feb 1992 .... 2.50

ALIENS: GLASS CORRIDOR
DARK HORSE
❑1, Jun 1998 .... 2.95

ALIENS: HAVOC
DARK HORSE
❑1, Jun 1997 .... 2.95
❑2, Jul 1997 SA, CR (a) 3.95

ALIENS: HIVE
DARK HORSE
❑1, Feb 1992 .... 2.50
❑2, Mar 1992 .... 2.50
❑3, Apr 1992 .... 2.50
❑4, May 1992 .... 2.50

ALIENS: KIDNAPPED
DARK HORSE
❑1, Dec 1997 .... 2.50
❑2, Jan 1998 .... 2.50
❑3, Feb 1998 .... 2.50

ALIENS: LABYRINTH
DARK HORSE
❑1, Sep 1993 .... 2.50
❑2, Oct 1993 .... 2.50
❑3, Nov 1993 .... 2.50
❑4, Dec 1993 .... 2.50

ALIENS: LOVESICK
DARK HORSE
❑1, Dec 1996 .... 2.95

ALIENS: MONDO HEAT
DARK HORSE
❑1, Feb 1996 .... 2.50

ALIENS: MONDO PEST
DARK HORSE
❑1 .... 2.95

ALIENS: MUSIC OF THE SPEARS
DARK HORSE
❑1, Jan 1994 .... 2.50
❑2, Feb 1994 .... 2.50
❑3, Mar 1994 .... 2.50
❑4, Apr 1994 .... 2.50

ALIENS: NEWT'S TALE
DARK HORSE
❑1, Jun 1992 .... 4.95
❑2, Aug 1992 .... 4.95

ALIENS: PIG
DARK HORSE
❑1, Mar 1997 .... 2.95

ALIENS/PREDATOR: THE DEADLIEST OF THE SPECIES
DARK HORSE
❑1, Jul 1993 .... 2.50
❑1/Ltd., Jul 1993; no cover price 4.00
❑2, Sep 1993 .... 2.50
❑3, Nov 1993 .... 2.50
❑4, Jan 1994 .... 2.50
❑5, Mar 1994 .... 2.50
❑6, May 1994 .... 2.50
❑7, Aug 1994 .... 2.50
❑8, Oct 1994 .... 2.50
❑9, Dec 1994 .... 2.50
❑10, Feb 1995 .... 2.50
❑11, May 1995 .... 2.50
❑12, Aug 1995 .... 2.50

ALIENS: PURGE
DARK HORSE
❑1, Aug 1997 .... 2.95

ALIENS: ROGUE
DARK HORSE
❑1, Apr 1993 .... 2.50
❑2, May 1993 .... 2.50
❑3, Jun 1993 .... 2.50
❑4, Jul 1993 .... 2.50

ALIENS: SACRIFICE
DARK HORSE
❑1, ca. 1993 .... 4.95

Other grades: Multiply price above by 5/6 for VF/NM • 2/3 for VERY FINE • 1/3 for FINE • 1/5 for VERY GOOD • 1/8 for GOOD

Alien Legion (Vol. 1)

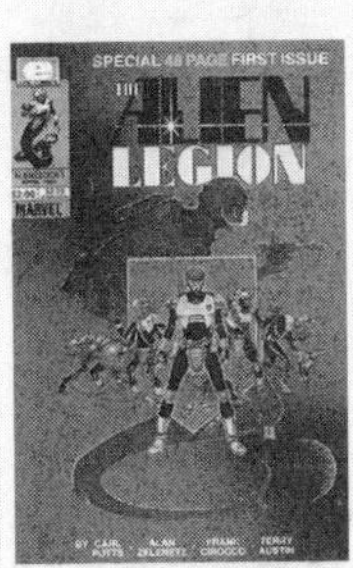
Interplanetary police force from Epic
©Marvel

Alien Nation

Adapts movie that spawned at TV series
©DC

Aliens

First issue reprinted back-up story from Magnus
©Gold Key

Aliens (Vol. 1)

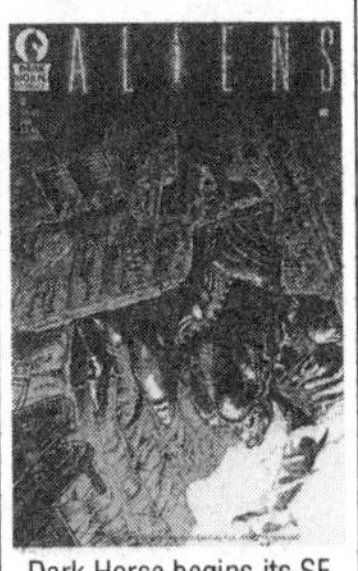
Dark Horse begins its SF adaptation mastery
©Dark Horse

Aliens vs. Predator

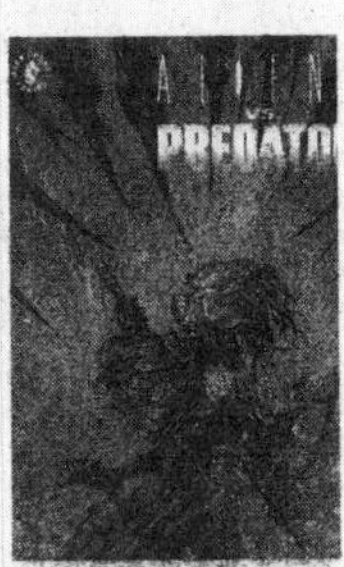
Movies spawned comic, which spawned movie
©Dark Horse

N-MINT

ALIENS: SALVATION
DARK HORSE
❑1, ca. 1993 .... 4.95

ALIENS: SALVATION AND SACRIFICE
DARK HORSE
❑1, Mar 2001 .... 12.95

ALIENS: SPECIAL
DARK HORSE
❑1, Jun 1997 .... 2.50

ALIENS: STALKER
DARK HORSE
❑1, Jun 1998 .... 2.50

ALIENS: STRONGHOLD
DARK HORSE
❑1, May 1994 .... 2.50
❑2, Jun 1994 .... 2.50
❑3, Jul 1994 .... 2.50
❑4, Sep 1994 .... 2.50

ALIENS: SURVIVAL
DARK HORSE
❑1, Feb 1998 .... 2.95
❑2, Mar 1998 .... 2.95
❑3, Apr 1998 .... 2.95

ALIENS VS. PREDATOR
DARK HORSE
❑0, Jul 1990, b&w; reprints story from Dark Horse Presents #34-36 .... 4.00
❑1, Jun 1990 .... 4.00
❑1/2nd, ca. 1990 .... 2.50
❑2, Aug 1990 .... 3.50
❑2/2nd, ca. 1990 .... 2.50
❑3, Oct 1990 .... 3.00
❑3/2nd, ca. 1990 .... 2.50
❑4, Dec 1990 .... 3.00
❑4/2nd, ca. 1990 .... 2.50
❑Annual 1, Jul 1999 .... 4.95

ALIENS VS. PREDATOR: BOOTY
DARK HORSE
❑1, Jan 1996 .... 2.50

ALIENS VS. PREDATOR: DUEL
DARK HORSE
❑1, Mar 1995 .... 2.50
❑2, Apr 1995 .... 2.50

ALIENS VS. PREDATOR: ETERNAL
DARK HORSE
❑1, Jun 1998 .... 2.50
❑2, Jul 1998 .... 2.50
❑3, Aug 1998 .... 2.50
❑4, Sep 1998 .... 2.50

ALIENS VS. PREDATOR VS. THE TERMINATOR
DARK HORSE
❑1, Apr 2000 .... 2.95
❑2, May 2000 .... 2.95
❑3, Jun 2000 .... 2.95
❑4, Jul 2000 .... 2.95

ALIENS VS. PREDATOR: WAR
DARK HORSE
❑0 1995 .... 2.50
❑1 1995 .... 2.50
❑2, Jun 1995 .... 2.50

N-MINT

❑3, Jul 1995 .... 2.50
❑4, Aug 1995 .... 2.50

ALIENS VS. PREDATOR: XENOGENESIS
DARK HORSE
❑1, Dec 1999 .... 2.95
❑2, Jan 2000 .... 2.95
❑3, Feb 2000 .... 2.95
❑4, Mar 2000 .... 2.95

ALIENS: WRAITH
DARK HORSE
❑1, Jul 1998 .... 2.95

ALIENS: XENOGENESIS
DARK HORSE
❑1, Aug 1999 .... 2.95
❑2, Sep 1999 .... 2.95
❑3, Oct 1999 .... 2.95
❑4, Nov 1999 .... 2.95

ALIEN: THE ILLUSTRATED STORY
HM COMMUNICATIONS
❑1 .... 5.00

ALIEN WORLDS
PACIFIC
❑1, Dec 1982 AW, NR, VM (a) 2.50
❑2, May 1983 DSt (w); DSt (a) 2.00
❑3, Jul 1983 TY (a) 2.00
❑4, Sep 1983 AW, JJ, DSt (a) 2.00
❑5, Dec 1983 TY (a) 2.00
❑6, Feb 1984 FB (a) 2.00
❑7, ca. 1984 GM, GP, BA (a) 2.00
❑8, Nov 1984; AW (a); Eclipse Comics begins as publisher 2.00
❑9, Jan 1985 FB (a) 2.00
❑3D 1, Jul 1984; Full-size issues begin DSt (a) 2.00

ALIEN WORLDS (BLACKTHORNE)
BLACKTHORNE
❑1, b&w 5.95

ALISON DARE, LITTLE MISS ADVENTURES
ONI
❑1, Sep 2000, b&w 4.50

ALISTER THE SLAYER
MIDNIGHT
❑1, Oct 1995 .... 2.50

ALIZARIN'S JOURNAL
AVATAR
❑1, Mar 1999, b&w 3.50

ALLAGASH INCIDENT
TUNDRA
❑1, Jul 1993 .... 2.95

ALL-AMERICAN COMICS (2ND SERIES)
DC
❑1, May 1999 A: Johnny Thunder. A: Green Lantern 2.00

ALLEGRA
IMAGE
❑1, Aug 1996 .... 2.50
❑1/Variant, Aug 1996; foil cover 2.50
❑2, Sep 1996 .... 2.50

N-MINT

❑3, Nov 1996 .... 2.50
❑4, Dec 1996 .... 2.50

ALLEY CAT
IMAGE
❑1, Jul 1999 .... 2.50
❑1/A, Jul 1999; Another Universe Edition; school girl cover 3.00
❑1/B, Jul 1999; Wizard World Edition; reclining with claws extended 2.50
❑2, Aug 1999 .... 2.50
❑2/A, Aug 1999; Monster Mart Edition; in red dress with stake in hand 2.50
❑3, Sep 1999; in front of grave 2.50
❑3/A, Sep 1999 .... 2.50
❑4, Oct 1999 .... 2.50
❑5, Dec 1999 .... 2.50
❑6, Feb 2000; with headdress 2.95
❑Ashcan 1, May 1999; Limited Preview Edition on cover; holding arms over head 2.95
❑Ashcan 1/A, May 1999; Dynamic Forces edition 3.00
❑Ashcan 1/B, May 1999; Dynamic Forces edition; front shot; Wizard World logo at bottom right 3.00
❑Ashcan 1/C, May 1999; Dynamic Forces edition; sketch cover 3.00
❑Ashcan 1/D, May 1999; Dynamic Forces edition; drawn color cover; kneeling on rooftop 3.00
❑Ashcan 1/E; Cover depicts claw outstretched, green background ....

ALLEY CAT LINGERIE EDITION
IMAGE
❑1, Oct 1999; photos and pin-ups; cardstock cover 4.95

ALLEY CAT VS. LADY PENDRAGON
IMAGE
❑1 2000 .... 3.00
❑1/A 2000; Wizard Mall variant; flipbook with Alley Cat Con Exclusive Preview 3.00

ALLEY OOP (DRAGON LADY)
DRAGON LADY
❑1 .... 5.95
❑2; time machine 6.95
❑3; Hercules 7.95

ALLEY OOP ADVENTURES
ANTARCTIC
❑1, Aug 1998 .... 2.95
❑2, Oct 1998 .... 2.95
❑3, Dec 1998 .... 2.95

ALLEY OOP QUARTERLY
ANTARCTIC
❑1, Sep 1999 .... 2.50
❑2, Dec 1999 .... 2.95
❑3, Mar 2000 .... 2.95

ALL GIRLS SCHOOL MEETS ALL BOYS SCHOOL
ANGEL
❑1 .... 3.00

ALL HALLOW'S EVE
INNOVATION
❑1 .... 4.95

Other grades: Multiply price above by 5/6 for VF/NM • 2/3 for VERY FINE • 1/3 for FINE • 1/5 for VERY GOOD • 1/8 for GOOD

ALLIANCE
IMAGE

❑1, Aug 1995 ... 2.50
❑1/A, Aug 1995; variant cover ... 2.50
❑2, Sep 1995 ... 2.50
❑2/A, Sep 1995; variant cover ... 2.50
❑3, Nov 1995 ... 2.50
❑3/A, Nov 1995; variant cover ... 2.50

ALL NEW ADVENTURES OF THE MIGHTY CRUSADERS
ARCHIE / RED CIRCLE

❑1, Mar 1983 ... 1.00
❑2, May 1983 ... 1.00
❑3, Jul 1983, b&w; Title becomes Mighty Crusaders with #4 ... 1.00

ALL NEW COLLECTORS' EDITION
DC

❑C-53, Dec 1977 ... 26.00
❑C-54, Jan 1978 ... 12.00
❑C-55, Feb 1978; MGr (a); Legion; Wedding of Lightning Lad and Saturn Girl ... 15.00
❑C-56, Apr 1978 NA (w); NA (a) ... 40.00
❑C-56/Whitman, Apr 1978; Whitman variant ... 35.00
❑C-58, Jun 1978; RB, DG (a); Superman vs. Shazam ... 12.00
❑C-60, ca. 1978 ... 20.00
❑C-62, Mar 1979 ... 12.00

ALL NEW EXILES
MALIBU / ULTRAVERSE

❑0, Sep 1995; "Black September"; Number infinity ... 1.50
❑0/Variant, Sep 1995; alternate cover; "Black September"; Number infinity ... 1.50
❑1, Oct 1995 ... 1.50
❑2, Nov 1995 ... 1.50
❑3, Dec 1995 ... 1.50
❑4, Jan 1996 ... 1.50
❑5, Feb 1996 ... 2.50
❑6, Mar 1996 ... 1.50
❑7, Apr 1996 ... 1.50
❑8, May 1996 ... 1.50
❑9, Jun 1996 ... 1.50
❑10, Jul 1996, alternate cover ... 1.50
❑11, Aug 1996, continues in UltraForce #12 ... 1.50

ALL NEW OFFICIAL HANDBOOK OF THE MARVEL UNIVERSE A TO Z
MARVEL

❑1, Mar 2006 ... 3.99
❑2, May 2006 ... 3.99
❑3, Jun 2006 ... 3.99
❑4, Jul 2006 ... 3.99
❑5, Aug 2006 ... 3.99
❑6, Sep 2006 ... 3.99

ALL-NEW TENCHI MUYO PART 1
VIZ

❑1, May 2002 ... 2.95
❑2, Jun 2002 ... 2.95
❑3, Jul 2002 ... 2.95
❑4, Aug 2002 ... 2.95
❑5, Sep 2002 ... 2.95
❑Book 1 2003 ... 15.95

ALL-NEW TENCHI MUYO PART 2
VIZ

❑1, Oct 2002 ... 2.95
❑2, Nov 2002 ... 2.95
❑3, Dec 2002 ... 2.95
❑4, Jan 2003 ... 2.95
❑5, Feb 2003 ... 2.95

ALL NEW UNDERGROUND COMIX
LAST GASP

❑1, b&w ... 5.00
❑2, b&w ... 3.00
❑3, b&w ... 3.00
❑4, b&w ... 3.00
❑5, b&w; Two-Fisted Zombies ... 3.00

ALL-OUT WAR
DC

❑1, Oct 1979, JKu (c); GE, RT (a); O: Viking Commando ... 3.00
❑2, Dec 1979 ... 2.50
❑3, Feb 1980, JKu (c) ... 2.50
❑4, Apr 1980, JKu (c) ... 2.50
❑5, Jun 1980, JKu (c) ... 2.50
❑6, Aug 1980 ... 2.50

ALLOY
PHENOMINAL CHILI

❑Ashcan 1; White Ashcan edition 1: Alloy ... 0.50
❑Ashcan 1/A; Green ashcan edition 1: Alloy ... 0.50

ALL SHOOK UP
RIP OFF

❑1, Jun 1990, b&w; earthquake ... 3.50

ALL STAR BATMAN AND ROBIN, THE BOY WONDER
DC

❑1/Batman, Aug 2005 ... 6.00
❑1/Robin, Aug 2005 ... 5.00
❑1/Special, Jan 2006 ... 5.00
❑1/RRP, Aug 2005 ... 50.00
❑2/Miller, Sept 2005 ... 4.00
❑2/Lee, Sept 2005 ... 4.00
❑3, Feb 2006 ... 4.00

ALL-STAR COMICS
DC

❑58, Feb 1976; WW, RE (a); 1: Power Girl. Power Girl joins team; regrouping of JSA; Series begins again after hiatus (1976) ... 12.00
❑59, Apr 1976 V: Brainwave, Per Degaton ... 6.00
❑60, Jun 1976, KG, WW (a); V: Vulcan ... 6.00
❑61, Aug 1976, KG, WW (a); V: Vulcan. Bicentennial #17 ... 6.00
❑62, Oct 1976, KG, WW (a); A: E-2 Superman. V: Zanadu ... 6.00
❑63, Dec 1976, KG, WW (a); V: Injustice Gang, Solomon Grundy ... 6.00
❑64, Feb 1977, WW (a); A: Shining Knight. V: Vandal Savage ... 6.00
❑65, Apr 1977, WW (a); V: Vandal Savage ... 6.00
❑66, Jun 1977, BL, JSa (a); V: Icicle, Wizard, Thinker ... 8.00
❑67, Aug 1977, BL, JSa (a) ... 6.00
❑68, Oct 1977, BL, JSa (a); V: Psycho Pirate ... 6.00
❑69, Dec 1977, BL, JSa (a); 1: The Huntress II (Helena Wayne). Original JSA vs. New JSA ... 6.00
❑70, Feb 1978, BL, JSa (a); Huntress ... 6.00
❑71, Apr 1978, BL, JSa (a) ... 6.00
❑72, Jun 1978, V: Thorn, Sportsmaster, original Huntress ... 6.00
❑73, Aug 1978, JSa (a); V: Thorn, Sportsmaster, original Huntress ... 6.00
❑74, Oct 1978, JSa (a); V: Master Summoner ... 8.00

ALL STAR COMICS (2ND SERIES)
DC

❑1, May 1999 ... 2.95
❑2, May 1999 ... 2.95
❑Giant Size 1, Sep 1999 ... 4.95

ALL-STAR INDEX
ECLIPSE / INDEPENDENT

❑1, Feb 1987; background on members of the JSA and first four issues of All-Star Comics (1st series) and DC Special #29 ... 2.00

ALL-STAR SQUADRON
DC

❑1, Sep 1981, RB, JOy (a); 1: Danette Reilly (later Firebrand II) ... 4.00
❑2, Oct 1981, RB, JOy (a) ... 2.00
❑3, Nov 1981, RB, JOy (a) ... 2.00
❑4, Dec 1981, RB, JOy (a); 1: Dragon King ... 1.50
❑5, Jan 1982, RB, JOy (a); 1: Firebrand II (Danette Reilly) ... 1.50
❑6, Feb 1982 ... 1.50
❑7, Mar 1982, JKu (a) ... 1.50
❑8, Apr 1982, O: Steel. V: Kung ... 1.50
❑9, May 1982, JKu (a); O: Baron Blitzkrieg ... 1.50
❑10, Jun 1982, JKu (a) ... 1.50
❑11, Jul 1982, JKu (a) ... 1.25
❑12, Aug 1982, JKu (a); V: Hastor ... 1.25
❑13, Sep 1982, JKu (a) ... 1.25
❑14, Oct 1982, JKu (a) ... 1.25
❑15, Nov 1982, JKu (a) ... 1.25
❑16, Dec 1982, JKu (a); V: Nuclear ... 1.25
❑17, Jan 1983, JKu (a); Trial of Robotman ... 1.25
❑18, Feb 1983, JKu (a); V: Villain from Valhalla ... 1.25
❑19, Mar 1983, V: Brainwave ... 1.25
❑20, Apr 1983, V: Brainwave ... 1.25
❑21, May 1983, 1: Deathbolt. 1: Cyclotron. V: Cyclotron ... 1.25
❑22, Jun 1983 ... 1.25
❑23, Jul 1983, 1: Amazing Man ... 1.25
❑24, Aug 1983, 1: Infinity Inc.. 1: Brainwave Jr. ... 1.25
❑25, Sep 1983, 1: Infinity Inc. ... 1.25
❑26, Oct 1983, O: Infinity Inc.. 2: of Infinity Inc.. 2: of Jade. A: Infinity Inc. ... 1.00
❑27, Nov 1983, A: Spectre ... 1.00
❑28, Dec 1983 A: Spectre ... 1.00
❑29, Jan 1984 A: Seven Soldiers of Victory ... 1.00
❑30, Feb 1984 V: Black Dragon Society ... 1.00
❑31, Mar 1984 A: Uncle Sam ... 1.00
❑32, Apr 1984 ... 1.00
❑33, May 1984 O: Freedom Fighters ... 1.00
❑34, Jun 1984 V: Tsunami ... 1.00
❑35, Jul 1984; D: Red Bee. Hourman vs. Baron Blitzkrieg ... 1.00
❑36, Aug 1984 A: Captain Marvel ... 1.00
❑37, Sep 1984 A: Marvel Family ... 1.00
❑38, Oct 1984 A: Amazing Man ... 1.00
❑39, Nov 1984; A: Amazing Man. Junior JSA kit repro ... 1.00
❑40, Dec 1984; A: Monitor. Amazing Man vs. Real American ... 1.00
❑41, Jan 1985 O: Starman ... 1.00
❑42, Feb 1985 ... 1.00
❑43, Mar 1985 ... 1.00
❑44, Apr 1985 V: Night and Fog ... 1.00
❑45, May 1985 1: Zyklon ... 1.00
❑46, Jun 1985; Liberty Belle gets new powers ... 1.00
❑47, Jul 1985 TMc (a); O: Doctor Fate ... 3.00
❑48, Aug 1985; A: Shining Knight. Blackhawk ... 1.00
❑49, Sep 1985 A: Doctor Occult ... 1.00
❑50, Oct 1985; Double-size issue; A: Harbinger. Mr. Mind to Earth-2; Crisis; Uncle Sam and others to Earth-X; Steel to Earth-1 ... 1.25
❑51, Nov 1985 V: Monster Society of Evil (Oom, Mr. Who, Ramulus, Nyola, Mr. Mind) ... 1.00
❑52, Dec 1985; A: Captain Marvel. Crisis ... 1.00
❑53, Jan 1986; Superman vs. Monster Society; Crisis ... 1.00
❑54, Feb 1986; V: Monster Society. Crisis ... 1.00
❑55, Mar 1986; V: Ultra-Humanite in 1980s. Crisis ... 1.00
❑56, Apr 1986; A: Seven Soldiers of Victory. Crisis ... 1.00
❑57, May 1986; Crisis ... 1.00
❑58, Jun 1986 A: Mekanique ... 1.00
❑59, Jul 1986 1: Aquaman in All-Star Squadron ... 1.00
❑60, Aug 1986; events of Crisis catch up with All-Star Squadron ... 1.00
❑61, Sep 1986 O: Liberty Belle ... 1.00
❑62, Oct 1986 O: Shining Knight ... 1.00
❑63, Nov 1986 O: Robotman ... 1.00
❑64, Dec 1986; retells Golden Age Superman story post-Crisis ... 1.00
❑65, Jan 1987 O: Johnny Quick ... 1.00
❑66, Feb 1987 O: Tarantula ... 1.00
❑67, Mar 1987; final issue: JSA's first case ... 1.00
❑Annual 1, Nov 1982 JOy (a); O: Atom, Wildcat, Guardian ... 2.00
❑Annual 2, Nov 1983 JOy (a); A: Infinity Inc.. D: Cyclotron ... 1.25
❑Annual 3, Sep 1984 DN, KG, JOy, GP (a); V: Ian Karkull ... 1.25

ALL-STAR SUPERMAN
DC

❑1, Jan 2006 ... 5.00
❑2, Mar 2006 ... 4.00
❑3, Jun 2006 ... 3.00
❑4, Sep 2006 ... 3.00

ALL-STAR WESTERN (2ND SERIES)
DC

❑1, Sep 1970, (c); CI (a); A: Pow-Wow Smith ... 30.00
❑2, Nov 1970, NA (c); GM (a) ... 15.00
❑3, Jan 1971, NA (c); GM, GK (a); O: El Diablo ... 15.00

Other grades: Multiply price above by 5/6 for VF/NM • 2/3 for VERY FINE • 1/3 for FINE • 1/5 for VERY GOOD • 1/8 for GOOD

Alley Cat

Image gives a Playboy model a comic book

©Image

All-Star Comics

1970s revival of classic Golden Age DC series

©DC

All-Star Squadron

Roy Thomas does World War II

©DC

All-Star Western (2nd Series)

Showcase for darker-themed Western tales

©DC

Alpha Flight (1st Series)

Canada's answer to The Avengers

©Marvel

N-MINT

❑4, Mar 1971, NA (c); GM, GK (a) 14.00
❑5, May 1971, NA (c); DG, JA (a) 14.00
❑6, Jul 1971, GK (w); GK (a) 9.00
❑7, Sep 1971; DG, JKu (a); expands to 48 pages 9.00
❑8, Nov 1971 CI, JKu, GK (a) 9.00
❑9, Jan 1972 SA (w); CI, FF, JKu, NC (a) 9.00
❑10, Mar 1972 SA (w); GM, NC (a); 1: Jonah Hex 260.00
❑11, May 1972; Giant-size; NR (c); SA (w); GM, CI, NC (a); 2: Jonah Hex. Series continues as Weird Western Tales 70.00

ALL SUSPENSE
AVALON

❑1 1998, b&w; reprints Nemesis and Mark Midnight stories 2.95

ALL THE RULES HAVE CHANGED
RIP OFF

❑1 9.95

ALL THE WRONG PLACES
LASZLO / ACG

❑1 2.95

ALL-THRILL COMICS
MANSION

❑845; Actually #1 2.95

ALLY
ALLY-WINSOR

❑1, Fal 1995, b&w 2.95
❑2 2.95
❑3, Flip-book 2.95

ALMURIC
DARK HORSE

❑1, Feb 1991 10.95

ALONE IN THE DARK
IMAGE

❑1, Jul 2002 4.95
❑2, Mar 2003 4.95

ALONE IN THE SHADE SPECIAL
ALCHEMY

❑1, b&w 2.00

ALPHABET
DARK VISIONS

❑1, Dec 1993; Pages denoted by letters rather than numbers 2.50

ALPHA CENTURION SPECIAL
DC

❑1 2.95

ALPHA FLIGHT (1ST SERIES)
MARVEL

❑1, Aug 1983 JBy (c); JBy (w); JBy (a); 1: Wildheart (not identified)\. 1: Diamond Lil (not identified). 1: Puck, Marina 5.00
❑2, Sep 1983, JBy (w); JBy (a); O: Marina. O: Alpha Flight. 1: The Master. 1: Guardian I (James Hudson). Vindicator becomes Guardian I 4.00
❑3, Oct 1983, JBy (w); JBy (a); O: Marina. O: The Master. O: Alpha Flight 4.00
❑4, Nov 1983, JBy (w); JBy (a); O: Marina 4.00
❑5, Dec 1983, JBy (w); JBy (a); O: Elizabeth Twoyoungmen. 1: Elizabeth Twoyoungmen 4.00

N-MINT

❑6, Jan 1984, JBy (w); JBy (a); O: Shaman. all-white issue 4.00
❑7, Feb 1984, JBy (w); JBy (a); O: Snowbird 4.00
❑8, Mar 1984, JBy (w); JBy (a) 4.00
❑9, Apr 1984, JBy (w); JBy (a); O: Aurora. A: Thing 4.00
❑10, May 1984, JBy (w); JBy (a); O: Northstar. O: Sasquatch 4.00
❑11, Jun 1984, JBy (w); JBy (a); O: Sasquatch. 1: Wild Child. 1: Diamond Lil (identified) 3.00
❑12, Jul 1984, Double-size JBy (w); JBy (a); D: Guardian 3.00
❑13, Aug 1984, JBy (w); JBy (a); A: Wolverine 3.00
❑14, Sep 1984, JBy (w); JBy (a) 3.00
❑15, Oct 1984, JBy (w); JBy (a); A: Sub-Mariner 3.00
❑16, Nov 1984, JBy (w); JBy (a); A: Sub-Mariner. Wolverine cameo 3.00
❑17, Dec 1984, JBy (w); JBy (a); X-Men crossover; Wolverine cameo 3.00
❑18, Jan 1985, JBy (w); JBy (a) 3.00
❑19, Feb 1985, JBy (w); JBy (a); O: Talisman II (Elizabeth Twoyoungmen). 1: Talisman II (Elizabeth Twoyoungmen) 3.00
❑20, Mar 1985, JBy (w); JBy (a); New headquarters 1.50
❑21, Apr 1985, JBy (w); JBy (a); O: Diablo. V: Diablo 2.00
❑22, May 1985, JBy (w); JBy (a) 2.00
❑23, Jun 1985, JBy (w); JBy (a) 2.00
❑24, Jul 1985; Double-size JBy (w); JBy (a) 1.50
❑25, Aug 1985, JBy (w); JBy (a) 1.00
❑26, Sep 1985, JBy (w); JBy (a) 1.00
❑27, Oct 1985, JBy (w); JBy (a) 1.00
❑28, Nov 1985, JBy (w); JBy (a); Secret Wars II; Last Byrne issue 3.00
❑29, Dec 1985, A: Hulk 2.00
❑30, Jan 1986 2.00
❑31, Feb 1986 2.00
❑32, Mar 1986 2.00
❑33, Apr 1986; SB (a); A: X-Men. Wolverine 2.00
❑34, May 1986; SB (a); O: Wolverine. Wolverine 2.50
❑35, Jun 1986; SB (a); Wolverine 1.50
❑36, Jul 1986; SB (a); Wolverine 1.50
❑37, Aug 1986; Wolverine 1.50
❑38, Sep 1986; Wolverine 1.50
❑39, Oct 1986; Wolverine 1.50
❑40, Nov 1986; Wolverine 1.50
❑41, Dec 1986; Wolverine 1.50
❑42, Jan 1987; Wolverine 1.50
❑43, Feb 1987; Wolverine 1.50
❑44, Mar 1987; D: Snowbird. Wolverine 1.50
❑45, Apr 1987; Wolverine 1.50
❑46, May 1987; Wolverine 3.00
❑47, Jun 1987; Wolverine 4.00
❑48, Jul 1987; Wolverine 1.50
❑49, Aug 1987; Wolverine 1.50
❑50, Sep 1987 2.00
❑51, Oct 1987; JLee, JL (a); A: Wolverine. 1st Jim Lee work at Marvel 2.00
❑52, Nov 1987 A: Wolverine 2.00

N-MINT

❑53, Dec 1987 1: Laura Dean. A: Wolverine 2.00
❑54, Jan 1988 O: Laura Dean 3.00
❑55, Feb 1988 JLee (a) 2.00
❑56, Mar 1988 JLee (a); 1: The Dreamqueen 2.00
❑57, Apr 1988 JLee (a) 1.00
❑58, May 1988 JLee (a) 1.00
❑59, Jun 1988 JLee (a) 1.00
❑60, Jul 1988 JLee (a) 1.25
❑61, Aug 1988 JLee (a) 1.25
❑62, Sep 1988 JLee (a) 1.25
❑63, Oct 1988 1.25
❑64, Nov 1988 1.25
❑65, Dec 1988 1.25
❑66, Jan 1989 1.25
❑67, Feb 1989 O: The Dream Queen 1.25
❑68, Mar 1989 1.25
❑69, Apr 1989 1.25
❑70, May 1989 1.25
❑71, Jun 1989 1: Llan the Sorcerer 1.25
❑72, Jul 1989 1.25
❑73, Aug 1989 1.25
❑74, Sep 1989 1.25
❑75, Oct 1989; Double-size 2.00
❑76, Nov 1989 1.50
❑77, Nov 1989 1.50
❑78, Dec 1989 1.50
❑79, Dec 1989; Acts of Vengeance 1.50
❑80, Jan 1990; Acts of Vengeance 1.50
❑81, Feb 1990 1.50
❑82, Mar 1990 1.50
❑83, Apr 1990 O: Talisman II (Elizabeth Twoyoungmen) 1.50
❑84, May 1990 1.50
❑85, Jun 1990 1.50
❑86, Jul 1990 1.50
❑87, Aug 1990; JLee (c); JLee (a); 1: Windshear. Wolverine 2.00
❑88, Sep 1990; JLee (c); JLee (a); Wolverine; Guardian I reappears as cyborg 2.00
❑89, Oct 1990; JLee (c); JLee (a); Wolverine; Guardian returns 2.00
❑90, Nov 1990 JLee (c); JLee (a) 2.00
❑91, Dec 1990; Doctor Doom 1.75
❑92, Jan 1991 1.75
❑93, Feb 1991 1.75
❑94, Mar 1991; Fantastic 4 1.75
❑95, Apr 1991 1.75
❑96, May 1991 1.75
❑97, Jun 1991 1.75
❑98, Jul 1991 1.75
❑99, Aug 1991 1.75
❑100, Sep 1991 A: Galactus. A: Avengers 1.75
❑101, Oct 1991 1.75
❑102, Nov 1991 1: Weapon Omega 1.75
❑103, Dec 1991 1.75
❑104, Jan 1992 1.75
❑105, Feb 1992 1.75
❑106, Mar 1992; Northstar admits he's gay 3.00
❑106/2nd, Mar 1992; Northstar admits he's gay 2.00
❑107, Apr 1992 A: X-Factor 1.75

Other grades: Multiply price above by 5/6 for VF/NM • 2/3 for VERY FINE • 1/3 for FINE • 1/5 for VERY GOOD • 1/8 for GOOD

❑108, May 1992 1.75
❑109, Jun 1992 1.75
❑110, Jul 1992 1.75
❑111, Aug 1992 PB (a) 1.75
❑112, Sep 1992 1.75
❑113, Oct 1992 1.75
❑114, Nov 1992 PB (a) 1.75
❑115, Dec 1992 1: Wyre 1.75
❑116, Jan 1993 PB (a) 1.75
❑117, Feb 1993 PB (a) 1.75
❑118, Mar 1993 PB (a); O: Wildheart. 1: Wildheart 1.75
❑119, Apr 1993 PB (a); V: Wrecking Crew 1.75
❑120, May 1993; PB (a); with poster 2.25
❑121, Jun 1993 A: Spider-Man 1.75
❑122, Jul 1993 PB (a) 1.75
❑123, Aug 1993 PB (a) 1.75
❑124, Sep 1993; PB (a); Infinity Crusade 1.75
❑125, Oct 1993 1.75
❑126, Nov 1993 1.75
❑127, Dec 1993 1.75
❑128, Jan 1994 1.75
❑129, Feb 1994 1.75
❑130, Mar 1994 2.25
❑Annual 1, Sep 1986 4.00
❑Annual 2, Dec 1987 1.25
❑Special 1, Jun 1992; 1992 Special Edition (Vol. 2); A: Wolverine. No number on cover 2.50

ALPHA FLIGHT (2ND SERIES)
MARVEL

❑1, Aug 1997; gatefold summary; wraparound cover 3.00
❑2, Sep 1997; gatefold summary; "Presenting: The Master of Chaos" on cover 2.00
❑2/A, Sep 1997; gatefold summary; alternate cover 2.00
❑3, Oct 1997; gatefold summary 2.00
❑4, Nov 1997; gatefold summary 2.00
❑5, Dec 1997; gatefold summary 2.00
❑6, Jan 1998; gatefold summary 1.99
❑7, Feb 1998; gatefold summary 1.99
❑8, Mar 1998; gatefold summary 1.99
❑9, Apr 1998; gatefold summary 1.99
❑10, May 1998; gatefold summary 1.99
❑11, Jun 1998; gatefold summary 1.99
❑12, Jul 1998; gatefold summary 1.99
❑13, Aug 1998; gatefold summary 1.99
❑14, Sep 1998; gatefold summary 1.99
❑15, Oct 1998; gatefold summary 1.99
❑16, Nov 1998; gatefold summary 1.99
❑17, Dec 1998; gatefold summary 1.99
❑18, Jan 1999; gatefold summary 1.99
❑19, Feb 1999 1.99
❑20, Mar 1999 1.99
❑Annual 1998, ca. 1998; Alpha Flight/ Inhumans '98; wraparound cover 3.50

ALPHA FLIGHT (3RD SERIES)
MARVEL

❑1, May 2004 2.99
❑2, Jun 2004 2.99
❑3, Jul 2004 2.99
❑4, Aug 2004 2.99
❑5, Sep 2004 2.99
❑6, Oct 2004 2.99
❑7, Nov 2004 2.99
❑8, Dec 2004 2.99
❑9, Jan 2005 2.99
❑10, Feb 2005 2.99
❑11, Mar 2005 2.99
❑12, Apr 2005 2.99

ALPHA FLIGHT: IN THE BEGINNING
MARVEL

❑-1, Jul 1997, Wedding of James Hudson and Heather McNeil; "Flashback" 2.00

ALPHA FLIGHT SPECIAL
MARVEL

❑1, Jul 1991; Reprints Alpha Flight #97 2.00
❑2, Aug 1991; Reprints Alpha Flight #98 2.00
❑3, Sep 1991; Reprints Alpha Flight #99 2.00
❑4, Oct 1991; Reprints Alpha Flight #100 2.00

ALPHA ILLUSTRATED
ALPHA PRODUCTIONS

❑0, Apr 1994, b&w; free; Preview 1.00
❑1, b&w 3.50

ALPHA KORPS
DIVERSITY

❑1, Sep 1996 2.50
❑Ashcan 1; Preview issue 1.00

ALPHA TEAM OMEGA
FANTASY GRAPHICS

❑1, ca. 1983, b&w 0.50

ALPHA TRACK
FANTASY GENERAL

❑1, Feb 1985 1.75
❑2 1.75

ALPHA WAVE
DARKLINE

❑1 1.75

ALTERED IMAGE
IMAGE

❑1, Apr 1998 2.50
❑2, Jun 1998 2.50
❑3, Oct 1998; cover says "Sep"; indicia says "Oct" 2.50
❑Book 1 9.95

ALTERED REALITIES
ALTERED REALITY

❑1 2.00

ALTER EGO
FIRST

❑1, May 1986, 1: Alter Ego 1.50
❑2, Jul 1986 1.50
❑3, Sep 1986 1.50
❑4, Nov 1986 1.50

ALTERNATE EXISTANCE
DRAGONMASTER

❑1, May 1982 1.25
❑2, ca 1982 1.25

ALTERNATE HEROES
PRELUDE

❑1 1.95

ALTERNATING CRIMES
ALTERNATING CRIMES

❑1, Fal 1996 2.95
❑2, Fal 1997 3.25

ALTERNATION
IMAGE

❑1, Mar 2004 2.95
❑2, Mar 2004 2.95
❑3, Apr 2004 2.95
❑4, Aug 2004 2.95

ALTERNATIVE COMICS
REVOLUTIONARY

❑1, Jan 1994; Pearl Jam/Cure/REM 2.50

ALTERNITY
NAVIGATOR

❑1, May 1992 2.50

ALVAR MAYOR: DEATH AND SILVER
4WINDS

❑1, b&w 8.98

ALVIN
DELL

❑1, Oct 1962, 12-021-212 25.00
❑2, Jan 1963, 12-021-303 18.00
❑3, Apr 1963, 12-021-306 15.00
❑4, Jul 1963, 12-021-309 15.00
❑5, Oct 1963, 12-021-312 15.00
❑6, Jan 1964, 12-021-403 15.00
❑7, Apr 1964, 12-021-406 15.00
❑8, Jul 1964, 12-021-409 15.00
❑9, Oct 1964, 12-021-412 15.00
❑10, Jan 1965 15.00
❑11, Apr 1965 12.00
❑12, Jul 1965 12.00
❑13 1965 12.00
❑14 1966 12.00
❑15, Jun 1966 12.00
❑16, Sep 1966 12.00
❑17, Dec 1966 12.00
❑18, Mar 1967 12.00
❑19, ca. 1968 12.00
❑20, Oct 1969 12.00
❑21, Oct 1970 8.00
❑22, Oct 1971 8.00
❑23, Jan 1972, 01-021-201 8.00
❑24, Apr 1972, 01-021-204 8.00
❑25, Jul 1972 8.00
❑26, Oct 1972 8.00
❑27, Jul 1973 8.00
❑28, Oct 1973 8.00

ALVIN AND THE CHIPMUNKS
HARVEY

❑1 2.00
❑2 1.50
❑3 1.50
❑4 1.50
❑5 1.50

AMANDA AND GUNN
IMAGE

❑1, Apr 1997, b&w 2.95
❑2, Jun 1997, b&w 2.95
❑3, Aug 1997, b&w 2.95
❑4, Oct 1997, b&w 2.95

AMAZING ADULT FANTASY
MARVEL

❑7, Dec 1961, SL (w); SD (a); Series continued from Amazing Adventures #6 600.00
❑8, Jan 1962, SL (w); SD (a) 475.00
❑9, Feb 1962, SL (w); SD (a) 425.00
❑10, Mar 1962, SL (w); SD (a) 425.00
❑11, Apr 1962, SL (w); SD (a) 425.00
❑12, May 1962, SL (w); SD (a) 425.00
❑13, Jun 1962, SL (w); SD (a) 425.00
❑13/2nd, SL (w); SD (a) 2.50
❑14, Jul 1962, SD (a); Professor X prototype; Series continued in Amazing Fantasy #15 525.00

AMAZING ADVENTURE
MARVEL

❑1, Jul 1988; squarebound 4.95

AMAZING ADVENTURES (2ND SERIES)
MARVEL

❑1, Jun 1961, SL (w); SD (a); O: Doctor Droom. A: Doctor Droom. 1st appearance/origin Dr. Droom (first Marvel Silver Age superhero) 900.00
❑2, Jul 1961, SL (w); SD (a); A: Doctor Droom. Dr. Droom 525.00
❑3, Aug 1961, SL (w); SD (a); A: Doctor Droom. Dr. Droom 425.00
❑4, Sep 1961, SL (w); SD (a); A: Doctor Droom 425.00
❑5, Oct 1961, SL (w); SD (a); A: Doctor Droom 425.00
❑6, Nov 1961, SL (w); SD (a); A: Doctor Droom. Series continues as Amazing Adult Fantasy #7 425.00

AMAZING ADVENTURES (3RD SERIES)
MARVEL

❑1, Aug 1970, JK (w); JB, JK (a); Inhumans 30.00
❑2, Sep 1970, Inhumans 20.00
❑3, Nov 1970, BEv (a); Black Widow; Inhumans 20.00
❑4, Jan 1971, BEv (a); Black Widow; Inhumans 14.00
❑5, Mar 1971, GC, BEv, NA (a) 14.00
❑6, May 1971, SB, DH, NA (a); Inhumans, Black Widow 20.00
❑7, Jul 1971, BEv, NA (a); Inhumans, Black Widow 14.00
❑8, Sep 1971, BEv, DH, NA (a); Inhumans, Black Widow 22.00
❑9, Nov 1971, BEv (a); A: Black Bolt 20.00
❑10, Jan 1972, Inhumans; Reprinted from Thor #146 20.00
❑11, Mar 1972, O: Beast (in furry form). 1: Beast (in furry form). Beast 140.00
❑12, May 1972, A: Beast. Beast; Iron Man 20.00
❑13, Jul 1972, 1: Robert Buzz Baxter. 1: Robert "Buzz" Baxter. Beast 20.00
❑14, Sep 1972, Beast 20.00
❑15, Nov 1972, O: Griffin. 1: Griffin. Beast 20.00
❑16, Jan 1973, Beast; Rutland, Vermont story 20.00
❑17, Mar 1973, Beast; reprinted, with changes, from X-Men (1st series) 49-53 20.00

Alpha Flight (2nd Series)

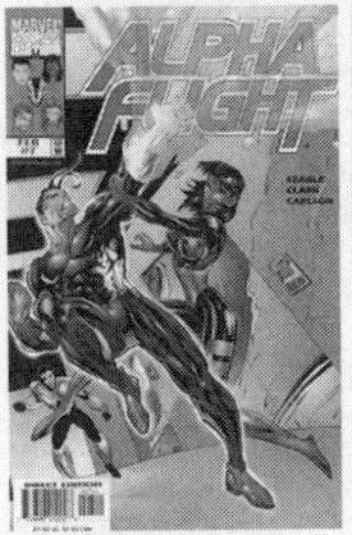

Revival of 1980s hit didn't last as long

©Marvel

Alpha Flight (3rd Series)

Second revival in seven years for Canadians

©Marvel

Alvin

Annoying chipmunk and annoying friends

©Dell

Amazing Adult Fantasy

"Middle phase" of Amazing Fantasy title

©Marvel

Amazing Adventures (3rd Series)

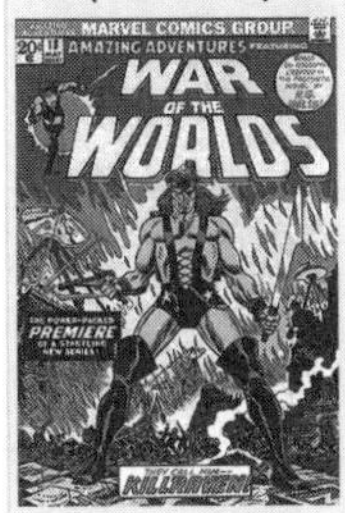

Notable for turning The Beast blue

©Marvel

N-MINT

❑18, May 1973, HC, NA (a); O: Killraven. 1: Killraven 14.00
❑19, Jul 1973, Killraven 5.00
❑20, Sep 1973, HT (a); Killraven 5.00
❑21, Nov 1973, Killraven 5.00
❑22, Jan 1974, Killraven 5.00
❑23, Mar 1974, Killraven; Marvel Value Stamp #13: Dr. Strange 5.00
❑24, May 1974, HT (a); V: High Overlord. Killraven; Marvel Value Stamp #58: The Mandarin 5.00
❑25, Jul 1974, V: Skar. Killraven 5.00
❑26, Sep 1974, GC (a); Killraven: Marvel Value Stamp #96: Dr. Octopus 4.00
❑27, Nov 1974, JSn, CR, JSt (a); O: Killraven. Marvel Value Stamp #22: Man-Thing 4.00
❑28, Jan 1975, CR (a); O: Volcana. Killraven 4.00
❑29, Mar 1975, CR (a); Killraven 4.00
❑30, May 1975, CR (a); Killraven 3.00
❑31, Jul 1975, CR (a); Killraven 3.00
❑32, Sep 1975, CR (a); Killraven 3.00
❑33, Nov 1975, HT, CR (a); Killraven; Marvel Value Stamp #52: Quicksilver 3.00
❑34, Jan 1976, CR (a); D: Hawk. D: Grok. Killraven; Marvel Value Stamp B/10 .... 3.00
❑35, Mar 1976, KG, CR, JAb (a); Killraven 3.00
❑36, May 1976, CR (a); Killraven 3.00
❑36/30 cent, May 1976, 30 cent regional price variant 20.00
❑37, Jul 1976, CR (a); O: Old Skull 3.00
❑37/30 cent, Jul 1976, CR (a); O: Old Skull. 30 cent regional price variant 20.00
❑38, Sep 1976, KG, CR (a); Killraven 3.00
❑39, Nov 1976, CR (a); Killraven 3.00

AMAZING ADVENTURES (4TH SERIES)
MARVEL

❑1, Dec 1979; SL (w); JK (a); 1: the X-Men. Reprints first part of X-Men (1st Series) #1; 2nd story reprinted from X-Men (1st series) #38 .... 3.00
❑2, Jan 1980; SL (w); JK (a); O: Cyclops. Reprints second half of X-Men (1st Series) #1; 2nd story reprinted from X-Men (1st Series) #39 .... 2.00
❑3, Feb 1980; Reprinted from X-Men (first series) #2; 2nd story reprinted from X-Men (1st Series) #40 .... 2.00
❑4, Mar 1980; Reprinted from X-Men (first series) #2, retitled from "No One Can Stop the Vanisher"; 2nd story reprinted from X-Men (1st Series) #41 .... 2.00
❑5, Apr 1980; Reprinted from X-Men (first series) #3; 2nd story reprinted from X-Men (1st Series) #42 .... 2.00
❑6, May 1980; Reprinted from X-Men (first series) #3, retitled from "Beware, the Blob"; 2nd story reprinted from X-Men (1st Series) #43 .... 2.00
❑7, Jun 1980; Reprinted from X-Men (first series) #4; 2nd story reprinted from X-Men (1st Series) #44 .... 2.00
❑8, Jul 1980; Reprinted from X-Men (first series) #4, retitled from "The Brotherhood of Evil Mutants"; 2nd story reprinted from X-Men (1st Series) #45 .... 2.00

N-MINT

❑9, Aug 1980; Reprinted from X-Men (first series) #5, retitled from "Trapped: One X-Man"; 2nd story reprinted from X-Men (1st Series) #46 .... 2.00
❑10, Sep 1980; Reprinted from X-Men (first series) #5; 2nd story reprinted from X-Men (1st Series) #47 .... 2.00
❑11, Oct 1980, Reprinted from X-Men (first series) #6; 2nd story reprinted from X-Men (1st Series) #48 .... 2.00
❑12, Nov 1980, Reprinted from X-Men (first series) #6, retitled from "Search for the Sub-Mariner"; 2nd story reprinted from Strange Tales #168 .... 2.00
❑13, Dec 1980, Reprinted from X-Men (first series) #7 .... 2.00
❑14, Jan 1981, Reprinted from X-Men (first series) #8 .... 2.00

AMAZING ADVENTURES OF ACE INTERNATIONAL
STARHEAD

❑1, Nov 1993, b&w 2.95

AMAZING ADVENTURES OF FRANK AND JOLLY (ALAN GROENING'S...)
PRESS THIS

❑1 .... 1.75
❑2 .... 1.75
❑3 .... 1.75
❑4 .... 1.75
❑5 .... 1.75
❑6 .... 1.75
❑7 .... 1.75
❑8 .... 1.75
❑9 .... 1.75

AMAZING ADVENTURES OF PROFESSOR JONES
ANTARCTIC

❑1, Nov 1996 .... 2.95
❑2, Dec 1996 .... 2.95
❑3 .... 2.95
❑4 .... 2.95

AMAZING ADVENTURES OF THE ESCAPIST (MICHAEL CHABON PRESENTS THE)
DARK HORSE

❑1, Feb 2004, JSn, HC (w); JSn, HC (a); A: The Escapist. based on Chabon's book The Amazing Adventures of Kavalier and Clay 8.95
❑2, Apr 2004 .... 8.95
❑3, Jun 2004 .... 8.95
❑4, Jul 2004 .... 8.95
❑5, Jan 2005 .... 8.95
❑6, Apr 2005 .... 8.95
❑7, May 2005 .... 10.00
❑8, Nov 2005 .... 8.95
❑Book 1, ca. 2004 .... 17.95

AMAZING CHAN AND THE CHAN CLAN
GOLD KEY

❑1, May 1973, ME (w); Mark Evanier's first story published in U.S. 14.00
❑2, Aug 1973 .... 9.00
❑3, Nov 1973 .... 9.00
❑4, Feb 1974 .... 9.00

N-MINT

AMAZING COMICS PREMIERES
AMAZING

❑1 1987 .... 1.95
❑2 1987 .... 1.95
❑3 1987 .... 1.95
❑4, Jul 1987 .... 1.95
❑5 1987; Stargrazers 1.95

AMAZING CYNICALMAN
ECLIPSE

❑1, b&w 2.50

AMAZING FANTASY
MARVEL

❑15, Aug 1962, JK (c); SL (w); SD (a); O: Spider-Man. 1: Spider-Man 32000.00
❑15/2nd, Aug 2002; Reprint packaged with Spider-Man movie DVD 5.00
❑16, Dec 1995; KB (w); cardstock cover; fills in gaps between Amazing Fantasy #15 and Amazing Spider-Man #1 .... 4.50
❑17, Jan 1996; KB (w); cardstock cover 4.50
❑18, Mar 1996; KB (w); cardstock cover 4.50

AMAZING FANTASY (2ND SERIES)
MARVEL

❑1, Aug 2004 .... 4.00
❑2, Sep 2004 .... 2.99
❑3, Oct 2004 .... 2.99
❑4, Nov 2004 .... 2.99
❑5, Dec 2004 .... 2.99
❑6, Jan 2005 .... 2.99
❑7, Feb 2005 .... 2.99
❑8, Mar 2005 .... 2.99
❑9, Jun 2005 .... 2.99
❑10, Jul 2005 .... 2.99
❑11, Aug 2005 .... 2.99
❑12, Sep 2005 .... 2.99
❑13, Oct 2005 .... 2.99
❑14 .... 2.99
❑15, Dec 2005 .... 2.99
❑16, Feb 2006 .... 2.99
❑17, Mar 2006 .... 2.99
❑18, May 2006 .... 2.99
❑19, Jun 2006 .... 2.99
❑20, Jul 2006 .... 2.99

AMAZING HEROES SWIMSUIT SPECIAL
FANTAGRAPHICS

❑Annual 1990, Jun 1990, b&w 6.00
❑Annual 1991, Jun 1991 .... 8.00
❑Annual 1992, Jun 1992 .... 10.00
❑4, Mar 1993; published by Spoof Comics 3.95
❑5, Aug 1993; published by Spoof Comics 4.95

AMAZING HIGH ADVENTURE
MARVEL

❑1, Aug 1984 JSe (a) 2.50
❑2, Sep 1985 PS (a) 2.50
❑3, Oct 1986 .... 2.50
❑4, Nov 1986 .... 2.50
❑5, Dec 1986 .... 2.50

AMAZING JOY BUZZARDS
IMAGE

❑1, Feb 2005 ... 2.95
❑2, Mar 2005 ... 2.95
❑3, Apr 2005 ... 2.95
❑4, May 2005 ... 2.95

AMAZING JOY BUZZARDS (VOLUME 2)
IMAGE

❑1, Nov 2005 ... 2.95
❑2, Dec 2005 ... 2.95
❑3, Jan 2006 ... 2.95
❑4, Feb 2006 ... 2.95

AMAZING SCARLET SPIDER
MARVEL

❑1, Nov 1995 ... 1.95
❑2, Dec 1995 A: Joystick. A: Green Goblin IV ... 1.95
❑2/Direct ed., Dec 1995; Direct Edition 1.95

AMAZING SCREW-ON HEAD
DARK HORSE

❑1, May 2002 ... 2.99
❑1/2nd, Feb 2004 ... 2.99

AMAZING SPIDER-MAN
MARVEL

❑-1, Jul 1997, Flashback ... 2.50
❑1, Mar 1963, SD (c); SL (w); SD, JK (a); O: Spider-Man. 1: John Jameson. 1: J. Jonah Jameson. 1: Chameleon. A: Fantastic Four ... 27000.00
❑1/Golden Record, ca. 1966, SL (w); SD (a); O: Spider-Man. 1: J. Jonah Jameson. 1: Chameleon. A: Fantastic Four. Golden Records reprint ... 200.00
❑2, May 1963, SD (c); SL (w); SD (a); 1: Mysterio (as alien). 1: Mysterio (as "alien"). 1: Tinkerer. 1: Vulture .. 3400.00
❑3, Jul 1963, SD (c); SL (w); SD (a); O: Doctor Octopus. 1: Doctor Octopus 4600.00
❑4, Sep 1963, SD (c); SL (w); SD (a); O: Sandman (Marvel). 1: Betty Brant. 1: Sandman (Marvel) ... 2300.00
❑5, Oct 1963, SD (c); SL (w); SD (a); V: Doctor Doom ... 2500.00
❑6, Nov 1963, SD (c); SL (w); SD (a); O: The Lizard. 1: The Lizard ... 1650.00
❑7, Dec 1963, SD (c); SL (w); SD (a); 2: The Vulture. V: Vulture ... 1100.00
❑8, Jan 1964, SD (c); SL (w); SD (a); A: Human Torch. V: Flash Thompson. V: Living Brain ... 800.00
❑9, Feb 1964, SD (c); SL (w); SD (a); O: Electro. 1: Doctor Bromwell. 1: Electro ... 1025.00
❑10, Mar 1964, SD (c); SL (w); SD, JK (a); 1: Fancy Dan. 1: Big Man. 1: Montana. 1: Enforcers. 1: Ox ... 990.00
❑11, Apr 1964, SD (c); SL (w); SD (a); 2: Doctor Octopus. V: Doctor Octopus ... 1900.00
❑12, May 1964, SD (c); SL (w); SD (a); V: Doctor Octopus. Spider-Man unmasked ... 825.00
❑13, Jun 1964, SD (c); SL (w); SD (a); O: Mysterio. 1: Mysterio ... 1200.00
❑14, Jul 1964, SD (c); SL (w); SD (a); 1: Green Goblin I (Norman Osborn). A: Hulk. A: Enforcers ... 2050.00
❑15, Aug 1964, SD (c); SL (w); SD (a); O: Kraven the Hunter. 1: Anna May Watson. 1: Kraven the Hunter. 1: Mary Jane Watson (name mentioned). A: Chameleon ... 1800.00
❑16, Sep 1964, SD (c); SL (w); SD (a); 1: The Great Gambonnos. 1: Princess Python. A: Daredevil. V: Ringmaster and Circus of Crime ... 790.00
❑17, Oct 1964, SD (c); SL (w); SD (a); 2: Green Goblin I (Norman Osborn). A: Torch. V: Green Goblin I (Norman Osborn) ... 775.00
❑18, Nov 1964, SD (c); SL (w); SD (a); V: Sandman (Marvel) ... 510.00
❑19, Dec 1964, SD (c); SL (w); SD (a); 1: MacDonald Mac Gargan [later becomes the Scorpion]. 1: Rock Gimpy. 1: MacDonald "Mac" Gargan [later becomes the Scorpion]. V: Sandman (Marvel). V: Enforcers ... 460.00
❑20, Jan 1965, SD (c); SL (w); SD (a); O: The Scorpion. 1: The Scorpion ... 510.00
❑21, Feb 1965, SD (c); SL (w); SD (a); 2: The Beetle. A: Torch. V: Beetle ... 510.00
❑22, Mar 1965, SD (c); SL (w); SD (a); V: Ringmaster and Circus of Crime. 425.00
❑23, Apr 1965, SD (c); SL (w); SD (a); A: Green Goblin I (Norman Osborn). V: Green Goblin I (Norman Osborn) 510.00
❑24, May 1965, SD (c); SL (w); SD (a); V: Mysterio ... 500.00
❑25, Jun 1965, SD (c); SL (w); SD (a); 1: Spencer Smythe. 1: Spider-Slayers. 1: Mary Jane Watson (cameo-face not shown) ... 500.00
❑26, Jul 1965, SD (c); SD, SL (w); SD (a); 1: Crime-Master. 1: Patch. A: Green Goblin I (Norman Osborn) ... 550.00
❑27, Aug 1965, SD (c); SD, SL (w); SD (a); A: Green Goblin I (Norman Osborn). D: Crime-Master ... 500.00
❑28, Sep 1965, SD (c); SD, SL (w); SD (a); O: Molten Man. 1: Molten Man. 2: Spencer Smythe. Peter Parker graduates from high school ... 325.00
❑29, Oct 1965, SD (c); SD, SL (w); SD (a); 2: The Scorpion. V: The Scorpion 240.00
❑30, Nov 1965, SD (c); SD, SL (w); SD (a); V: Cat Burglar ... 240.00
❑31, Dec 1965, SD (c); SD, SL (w); SD (a); 1: Professor Warren. 1: Gwen Stacy. 1: Harry Osborn ... 325.00
❑32, Jan 1966, SD (c); SD, SL (w); SD (a); Master Planner revealed as Doctor Octopus ... 175.00
❑33, Feb 1966, SD (c); SD, SL (w); SD (a); V: Doctor Octopus (as Master Planner) ... 140.00
❑34, Mar 1966, SD (c); SD, SL (w); SD (a); A: Green Goblin I (Norman Osborn). V: Kraven the Hunter ... 240.00
❑35, Apr 1966, SD (c); SD, SL (w); SD (a); 1: Spider Tracer. V: Molten Man 225.00
❑36, May 1966, SD (c); SD, SL (w); SD (a); 1: Looter (later Meteor Man in Marvel Team-Up #33) ... 225.00
❑37, Jun 1966, SD (c); SD, SL (w); SD (a); 1: Norman Osborn. A: Patch. V: Professor Mendel Stromm ... 195.00
❑38, Jul 1966, SD (c); SD, SL (w); SD (a); 2: Mary Jane Watson (cameo). 195.00
❑39, Aug 1966, JR (c); SL (w); JR (a); V: Green Goblin I (Norman Osborn). Green Goblin revealed as Norman Osborn ... 350.00
❑40, Sep 1966, JR (c); SL (w); JR (a); O: Green Goblin I (Norman Osborn) 325.00
❑41, Oct 1966, JR (c); SL (w); JR (a); 1: Rhino ... 300.00
❑42, Nov 1966, JR (c); SL (w); JR (a); A: Mary Jane Watson (first time her face is shown). A: Rhino ... 185.00
❑43, Dec 1966, JR (c); SL (w); JR (a); O: Rhino. V: Rhino ... 120.00
❑44, Jan 1967, JR (c); SL (w); JR (a); V: Lizard ... 175.00
❑45, Feb 1967, JR (c); SL (w); JR (a); V: Lizard ... 115.00
❑46, Mar 1967, JR (c); SL (w); JR (a); O: Shocker. 1: Shocker ... 200.00
❑47, Apr 1967, JR (c); SL (w); JR (a); V: Kraven the Hunter ... 105.00
❑48, May 1967, JR (c); SL (w); JR (a); V: second Vulture ... 120.00
❑49, Jun 1967, JR (c); SL (w); JR (a); V: Kraven the Hunter. V: Vulture ... 125.00
❑50, Jul 1967, JR (c); SL (w); JR (a); 1: Kingpin ... 625.00
❑51, Aug 1967, JR (c); SL (w); JR (a); O: Mysterio. 1: Robbie Robertson. 2: Kingpin. V: Kingpin ... 175.00
❑52, Sep 1967, JR (c); SL (w); JR (a); 1: Joe Robertson. D: Big Man (Frederick Foswell). V: Kingpin ... 150.00
❑53, Oct 1967, JR (c); SL (w); JR (a); V: Doctor Octopus ... 105.00
❑54, Nov 1967, JR (c); SL (w); JR (a); V: Doctor Octopus ... 110.00
❑55, Dec 1967, JR (c); SL (w); JR (a); V: Doctor Octopus ... 110.00
❑56, Jan 1968, JR (c); SL (w); JR (a); 1: Captain Stacy. V: Doctor Octopus 90.00
❑57, Feb 1968, JR (c); SL (w); JR (a); A: Ka-Zar and Zabu ... 75.00
❑58, Mar 1968, JR (c); SL (w); JR (a); A: Ka-Zar and Zabu. V: Spencer Smythe. V: J. Jonah Jameson ... 80.00
❑59, Apr 1968, JR (c); SL (w); JR (a); 1: Doctor Winkler. 1: Slade. V: Kingpin (as Brainwasher) ... 70.00
❑60, May 1968, JR (c); SL (w); DH, JR (a); 2: Doctor Winkler. 2: Slade. V: Kingpin ... 105.00
❑61, Jun 1968, JR (c); SL (w); DH, JR (a); V: Kingpin ... 72.00
❑62, Jul 1968, JR (c); SL (w); DH, JR (a); A: Medusa ... 75.00
❑63, Aug 1968, JR (c); SL (w); DH, JR (a); V: both Vultures ... 160.00
❑64, Sep 1968, JR (c); SL (w); DH, JR (a); V: Vulture ... 60.00
❑65, Oct 1968, JR (c); SL (w); JR, JM (a) 55.00
❑66, Nov 1968, JR (c); SL (w); DH, JR (a); A: Mysterio. V: Mysterio ... 80.00
❑67, Dec 1968, JR (c); SL (w); JR, JM (a); 1: Randy Robertson. V: Mysterio 60.00
❑68, Jan 1969, JR (c); SL (w); JR, JM (a); 1: Louis Wilson. V: Kingpin ... 60.00
❑69, Feb 1969, JR (c); SL (w); JR, JM (a); V: Kingpin ... 75.00
❑70, Mar 1969, JR (c); SL (w); JR, JM (a); 1: Vanessa Fisk (Kingpin's wife-face not shown). V: Kingpin ... 70.00
❑71, Apr 1969, JR (c); SL (w); JR, JM (a); A: Quicksilver ... 70.00
❑72, May 1969, JR (c); SL (w); JB, JR, JM (a); V: Shocker ... 85.00
❑73, Jun 1969, JR (c); SL (w); JB, JR, JM (a); 1: Man-Mountain Marko. 1: Caesar Cicero. 1: Silvermane ... 50.00
❑74, Jul 1969, JR (c); SL (w); JB, JM (a); V: Man-Mountain Marko. V: Caesar Cicero. V: Silvermane ... 80.00
❑75, Aug 1969, JR (c); SL (w); JB, JM (a); V: Man-Mountain Marko. V: Caesar Cicero. V: Silvermane ... 65.00
❑76, Sep 1969, JR (c); SL (w); JB, JM (a); A: Human Torch. V: Lizard ... 65.00
❑77, Oct 1969, JR (c); JR, SL (w); JB, JM (a); A: Human Torch. V: Lizard .. 60.00
❑78, Nov 1969, JR (c); JB, SL (w); JB, JM (a); 1: The Prowler ... 70.00
❑79, Dec 1969, JB (c); SL (w); JB, JM (a); 2: The Prowler. V: The Prowler. V: Prowler ... 60.00
❑80, Jan 1970, JR (c); SL (w); JB, JR, JM (a); V: Chameleon ... 60.00
❑81, Feb 1970, JR (c); SL (w); JR, JM (a); O: The Kangaroo. 1: The Kangaroo ... 55.00
❑82, Mar 1970, SL (w); JR, JM (a); O: Electro. V: Electro ... 50.00
❑83, Apr 1970, JR (c); SL (w); JR (a); 1: Richard Fisk (The Schemer). 1: Richard Fisk ("The Schemer"). 1: Vanessa Fisk (Full-Kingpin's wife). V: Kingpin. V: Schemer ... 50.00
❑84, May 1970, JR (c); SL (w); JR, JM (a); V: Kingpin. V: Schemer ... 55.00
❑85, Jun 1970, JR (c); SL (w); JR, JM (a); V: Kingpin. V: Schemer ... 55.00
❑86, Jul 1970, JR (c); SL (w); JR, JM (a); O: Black Widow ... 50.00
❑87, Aug 1970, JR (c); SL (w); JR, JM (a); Peter reveals his secret identity 75.00
❑88, Sep 1970, JR (c); SL (w); JR, JM (a); A: Doctor Octopus. V: Doctor Octopus ... 60.00
❑89, Oct 1970, JR (c); SL (w); GK, JR (a); A: Doctor Octopus. V: Doctor Octopus ... 70.00
❑90, Nov 1970, GK, JR (c); SL (w); GK, JR (a); A: Doctor Octopus. D: Captain Stacy ... 75.00
❑91, Dec 1970, JR (c); SL (w); GK, JR (a); 1: Sam Bullit ... 50.00
❑92, Jan 1971, JR (c); SL (w); GK, JR (a); A: Sam Bullit. A: Iceman ... 62.00
❑93, Feb 1971, JR (c); SL (w); JR (a); A: Prowler ... 50.00
❑94, Mar 1971, JR (c); SL (w); SB, JR (a); O: Spider-Man. A: Beetle. Spider-Man's Origin retold ... 65.00
❑95, Apr 1971, JR (c); SL (w); SB, JR (a); Spider-Man goes to London ... 52.00
❑96, May 1971, GK (c); SL (w); GK, JR (a); A: Green Goblin I (Norman Osborn). Drug topics not approved by CCA ... 85.00
❑97, Jun 1971, JR (c); SL (w); GK (a); A: Green Goblin I (Norman Osborn). Drug topics not approved by CCA ... 72.00
❑98, Jul 1971, GK (c); SL (w); GK (a); A: Green Goblin I (Norman Osborn). Drug topics not approved by CCA ... 80.00

Amazing Chan and the Chan Clan

Hanna-Barbera series had Evanier's first work

©Gold Key

Amazing Comics Premieres

Showcase title for Amazing's new talent

©Amazing

Amazing Cynicalman

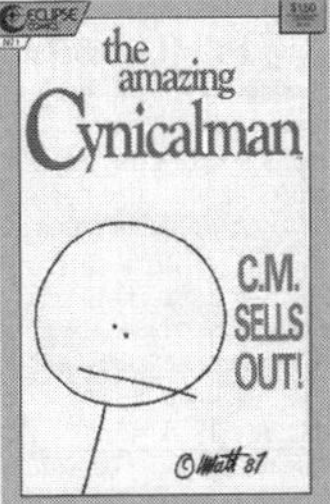

Stick-figure fun from Matt Feazell

©Eclipse

Amazing Fantasy

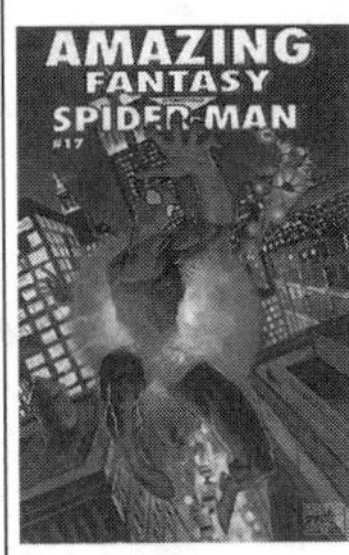

The series that spawned Spider-Man

©Marvel

Amazing Fantasy (2nd Series)

Revisiting the "unpublished" Fantasy issues

©Marvel

	N-MINT
❑99, Aug 1971, GK (c); SL (w); GK (a); A: Johnny Carson	60.00
❑100, Sep 1971, 100th anniversary issue; JR (c); SL (w); GK (a); A: Green Goblin I (Norman Osborn). Peter grows four extra arms	100.00
❑101, Oct 1971, GK (c); GK (a); 1: Morbius	130.00
❑101/2nd; GK (a); 1: Morbius. Metallic ink cover	2.50
❑102, Nov 1971, Giant-sized GK (c); GK (a); O: Morbius. A: Lizard. A: Morbius	105.00
❑103, Dec 1971, GK (c); GK (a); 1: Gog. V: Kraven the Hunter	45.00
❑104, Jan 1972, GK (c); GK (a); 2: Gog. V: Kraven the Hunter	90.00
❑105, Feb 1972, GK (c); SL (w); GK (a); V: Spider Slayer. V: Spencer Smythe. vs. Spider-Slayer	25.00
❑106, Mar 1972, JR (c); SL (w); JR (a); V: Spider Slayer. V: Spencer Smythe	32.00
❑107, Apr 1972, JR (c); SL (w); JR (a); V: Spider Slayer. V: Spencer Smythe	27.00
❑108, May 1972, JR (c); SL (w); JR (a); 1: Sha Shan. A: Flash Thompson	27.00
❑109, Jun 1972, JR (c); SL (w); JR (a); A: Doctor Strange	30.00
❑110, Jul 1972, JR (c); SL (w); JR (a); O: The Gibbon. 1: The Gibbon	30.00
❑111, Aug 1972, JR (c); JR (a); V: The Gibbon, Kraven the Hunter	34.00
❑112, Sep 1972, JR (c); JR (a); A: The Gibbon. V: Doctor Octopus	30.00
❑113, Oct 1972, JR (c); JSn, JR (a); 1: Hammerhead. V: Doctor Octopus	33.00
❑114, Nov 1972, JR (c); JSn, JR (a); O: Hammerhead. 1: Doctor Jonas Harrow	40.00
❑115, Dec 1972, JR (c); JR (a); V: Hammerhead, Doctor Octopus	33.00
❑116, Jan 1973, JR (c); SL (w); JR, JM (a); 1: Smasher (was Man Monster). V: Richard Raleigh. Reprints Spectacular Spider-Man #1 ("Lo, This Monster") with some new art and dialogue; Man Monster renamed Smasher	22.00
❑117, Feb 1973, reprints story from Spectacular Spider-Man (magazine) #1 with updates; JR (c); SL (w); JR, JM (a); 1: Disruptor. Reprints Spectacular Spider-Man #1 ("Lo, This Monster") with some new art and dialogue; Man Monster renamed Smasher	25.00
❑118, Mar 1973, JR (c); JR, JM (a); V: Disruptor, Smasher. Reprints Spectacular Spider-Man #1 ("Lo, This Monster") with some new art and dialogue; Man Monster renamed Smasher	22.00
❑119, Apr 1973, JR (c); JR (a); A: Incredible Hulk. V: Hulk in Canada	50.00
❑120, May 1973, GK (c); GK, JR (a); A: Incredible Hulk. V: Hulk	47.00
❑121, Jun 1973, GK (c); GK, JR (a); D: Gwen Stacy. V: Green Goblin I (Norman Osborn)	150.00
❑122, Jul 1973, GK (c); GK, JR (a); D: Green Goblin I (Norman Osborn)	130.00
❑123, Aug 1973, GK (c); GK, JR (a); A: Luke Cage	35.00
❑124, Sep 1973, GK (c); GK, JR (a); 1: Man-Wolf	42.00

	N-MINT
❑125, Oct 1973, RA (c); JR, RA (a); O: Man-Wolf	30.00
❑126, Nov 1973, RA (c); RA, JM (a); A: Doctor Jonas Harrow. A: Human Torch. D: Kangaroo. Harry Osborn becomes Green Goblin	18.00
❑127, Dec 1973, RA (c); RA (a); V: third Vulture	25.00
❑128, Jan 1974, RA (c); RA (a); O: third Vulture	20.00
❑129, Feb 1974, RA (c); RA (a); 1: The Punisher. 1: Jackal	225.00
❑129/Ace, Apr 2002, Wizard Ace Edition	6.00
❑130, Mar 1974, RA (c); RA (a); 1: Spider-Mobile. V: Doctor Octopus. V: Hammerhead. V: Jackal. Marvel Value Stamp #2: Hulk	16.00
❑131, Apr 1974, RA (c); RA (a); V: Doctor Octopus. V: Hammerhead. Dr. Octopus, Hammerhead; Marvel Value Stamp #34: Mr. Fantastic	25.00
❑132, May 1974, JR (c); JR (a); V: Molten Man. Marvel Value Stamp #6: Thor	22.00
❑133, Jun 1974, RA (c); RA (a); V: Molten Man. Molten Man's relationship to Liz Allan revealed; Marvel Value Stamp #66: General Ross	16.00
❑134, Jul 1974, RA (c); RA (a); 1: Tarantula I (Anton Rodriguez). A: Punisher. Marvel Value Stamp #3: Conan	28.00
❑135, Aug 1974, RA (c); RA (a); O: Tarantula I (Anton Rodriguez). A: Punisher. Marvel Value Stamp #4: Thing	45.00
❑136, Sep 1974, RA (c); RA (a); 1: Green Goblin II (Harry Osborn). Marvel Value Stamp #95: Mole-Man	50.00
❑137, Oct 1974, RA (c); RA (a); 2: Green Goblin II (Harry Osborn). V: Green Goblin II (Harry Osborn). Marvel Value Stamp #99: Sandman	25.00
❑138, Nov 1974, RA (c); RA (a); O: The Mindworm. 1: The Mindworm. Peter moves in with Flash Thompson; Marvel Value Stamp #41: Gladiator	12.00
❑139, Dec 1974, RA (c); RA (a); 1: Grizzly. A: Jackal. Marvel Value Stamp #42: Man-Wolf	19.00
❑140, Jan 1975, GK (c); RA (a); O: Grizzly. 1: Gloria Grant. V: Jackal. Marvel Value Stamp #75: Morbius	17.00
❑141, Feb 1975, JR (c); RA (a); V: second Mysterio. Spider-Mobile sinks in Hudson; Marvel Value Stamp #35: Killraven	12.00
❑142, Mar 1975, JR (c); RA (a); V: second Mysterio	18.00
❑143, Apr 1975, GK, JR (c); RA (a); 1: Cyclone	14.00
❑144, May 1975, GK, JR (c); RA (a); O: Cyclone. 1: Gwen Stacy clone. V: Cyclone. Marvel Value Stamp #17: Black Bolt	17.00
❑145, Jun 1975, GK, JR (c); RA (a); A: Scorpion. V: Scorpion. Marvel Value Stamp #100: Galactus	15.00
❑146, Jul 1975, JR (c); JR2, RA (a); A: Scorpion. V: Jackal, Scorpion. Marvel Value Stamp #67: Cyclops	15.00
❑147, Aug 1975, JR (c); RA (a); V: Jackal, Tarantula. Marvel Value Stamp #42: Man-Wolf	14.00

	N-MINT
❑148, Sep 1975, GK, JR (c); RA (a); V: Jackal, Tarantula. Professor Warren revealed as Jackal	25.00
❑149, Oct 1975, GK, JR (c); RA (a); 1: Ben Reilly. D: Jackal. D: Spider-clone (faked death)	27.00
❑150, Nov 1975, GK (c); GK (a); A: Ben Reilly. Spider-Man attempts to determine if he is the clone or the original	16.00
❑151, Dec 1975, JR (c); JR, RA (a); A: Ben Reilly. V: Shocker. Spider-Man disposes of clone's body (faked)	24.00
❑152, Jan 1976, GK, JR (c); RA (a); V: Shocker	11.00
❑153, Feb 1976GK, JR (c); RA (a)	10.00
❑154, Mar 1976, JR (c); SB (a); V: Sandman (Marvel)	10.00
❑155, Apr 1976, JR (c); SB (a)	12.00
❑155/30 cent, Apr 1976, JR (c); SB (a); 30 cent regional price variant	20.00
❑156, May 1976, JR (c); RA (a); O: Mirage I (Desmond Charne). 1: Mirage I (Desmond Charne)	12.00
❑156/30 cent, May 1976, JR (c); RA (a); 30 cent regional price variant	20.00
❑157, Jun 1976, JR (c); RA (a); return of Doctor Octopus	12.00
❑157/30 cent, Jun 1976, JR (c); RA (a); 30 cent regional price variant; return of Doctor Octopus	20.00
❑158, Jul 1976, GK, JR (c); RA (a); V: Doctor Octopus. Hammerhead regains physical form	10.00
❑158/30 cent, Jul 1976, GK, JR (c); RA (a); 30 cent regional price variant; Hammerhead regains physical form	20.00
❑159, Aug 1976, GK (c); RA (a); 2: The Tinkerer. V: Doctor Octopus, Hammerhead	11.00
❑159/30 cent, Aug 1976, GK (c); RA (a); 30 cent regional price variant	20.00
❑160, Sep 1976, GK, JR (c); RA (a); V: Tinkerer. return of Spider-Mobile	9.00
❑161, Oct 1976, GK, JR (c); RA (a); A: Punisher. A: Nightcrawler	12.00
❑162, Nov 1976, JR, RA (c); RA (a); A: Punisher. A: Nightcrawler	11.00
❑163, Dec 1976, DC, JR (c); RA (a); V: Kingpin	10.00
❑164, Jan 1977, JR (c); RA (a); V: Kingpin	12.00
❑165, Feb 1977, JR (c); RA (a); V: Stegron. Newsstand edition (distributed by Curtis); issue number in box	9.00
❑165/Whitman, Feb 1977, JR (c); RA (a); V: Stegron. Special markets edition (usually sold in Whitman bagged prepacks); price appears in a diamond; UPC barcode appears	9.00
❑166, Mar 1977, JR (c); RA (a); V: Lizard. V: Stegron. Newsstand edition (distributed by Curtis); issue number in box	9.00
❑166/Whitman, Mar 1977, JR (c); RA (a); V: Lizard. V: Stegron. Special markets edition (usually sold in Whitman bagged prepacks); price appears in a diamond; UPC barcode appears	9.00

Other grades: Multiply price above by 5/6 for VF/NM • 2/3 for VERY FINE • 1/3 for FINE • 1/5 for VERY GOOD • 1/8 for GOOD

N-MINT | N-MINT | N-MINT

❑167, Apr 1977, JR (c); RA (a); 1: Will o' the Wisp. Newsstand edition (distributed by Curtis); issue number in box 6.50
❑167/Whitman, Apr 1977, JR (c); RA (a); 1: Will o' the Wisp. Special markets edition (usually sold in Whitman bagged prepacks); price appears in a diamond; UPC barcode appears 6.50
❑168, May 1977, JR (c); RA (a); V: Will o' the Wisp. Newsstand edition (distributed by Curtis); issue number in box 6.50
❑168/Whitman, May 1977, JR (c); RA (a); V: Will o' the Wisp. Special markets edition (usually sold in Whitman bagged prepacks); price appears in a diamond; UPC barcode appears 6.50
❑169, Jun 1977, AM (c); RA (a); Newsstand edition (distributed by Curtis); issue number in box; J. Jonah Jameson acquires photos showing Spider-Man disposing of clone's(?) body 10.00
❑169/Whitman, Jun 1977, AM (c); RA (a); Special markets edition (usually sold in Whitman bagged prepacks); price appears in a diamond; UPC barcode appears; J. Jonah Jameson acquires photos showing Spider-Man disposing of clone's(?) body... 10.00
❑169/35 cent, Jun 1977, AM (c); RA (a); 35 cent regional price variant; J. Jonah Jameson acquires photos showing Spider-Man disposing of clone's(?) body 15.00
❑170, Jul 1977, RA (c); RA (a); V: Doctor Faustus. Newsstand edition (distributed by Curtis); issue number in box 6.50
❑170/Whitman, Jul 1977, RA (c); RA (a); V: Doctor Faustus. Special markets edition (usually sold in Whitman bagged prepacks); price appears in a diamond; UPC barcode appears 6.50
❑170/35 cent, Jul 1977, RA (c); RA (a); V: Doctor Faustus. 35 cent regional price variant 15.00
❑171, Aug 1977, RA (c); RA (a); A: Nova. Newsstand edition (distributed by Curtis); issue number in box 6.50
❑171/Whitman, Aug 1977, RA (c); RA (a); A: Nova. Special markets edition (usually sold in Whitman bagged prepacks); price appears in a diamond; UPC barcode appears...... 6.50
❑171/35 cent, Aug 1977, RA (c); RA (a); 35 cent regional price variant........ 15.00
❑172, Sep 1977, RA (c); RA (a); 1: Rocket Racer. Newsstand edition (distributed by Curtis); issue number in box 8.00
❑172/Whitman, Sep 1977, RA (c); RA (a); 1: Rocket Racer. Special markets edition (usually sold in Whitman bagged prepacks); price appears in a diamond; UPC barcode appears... 8.00
❑172/35 cent, Sep 1977, RA (c); RA (a); 1: Rocket Racer. 35 cent regional price variant 15.00
❑173, Oct 1977, JR, RA (c); RA, JM (a); V: Molten Man. Newsstand edition (distributed by Curtis); issue number in box 18.00
❑173/Whitman, Oct 1977, JR, RA (c); RA, JM (a); V: Molten Man. Special markets edition (usually sold in Whitman bagged prepacks); price appears in a diamond; no UPC barcode 18.00
❑173/35 cent, Oct 1977, JR, RA (c); RA, JM (a); V: Molten Man. 35 cent regional price variant 25.00
❑174, Nov 1977, RA (c); RA, JM (a); A: Punisher. V: Hitman. Newsstand edition (distributed by Curtis); issue number in box 10.00
❑174/Whitman, Nov 1977, RA (c); RA, JM (a); A: Punisher. V: Hitman. Special markets edition (usually sold in Whitman bagged prepacks); price appears in a diamond; no UPC barcode 10.00
❑175, Dec 1977, RA (c); RA, JM (a); A: Punisher. V: Hitman. Newsstand edition (distributed by Curtis); issue number in box 10.00
❑175/Whitman, Dec 1977, RA (c); RA, JM (a); A: Punisher. V: Hitman. Special markets edition (usually sold in Whitman bagged prepacks); price appears in a diamond; no UPC barcode 10.00
❑176, Jan 1978, TD, RA (c); TD, RA (a); O: Green Goblin III (Doctor Barton Hamilton). 1: Green Goblin III (Doctor Barton Hamilton) 12.00
❑177, Feb 1978, RA, JSt (c); RA (a); A: Green Goblin III (Doctor Barton Hamilton). V: Silvermane 12.00
❑178, Mar 1978, RA, JSt (c); RA, JM (a); A: Green Goblin III (Doctor Barton Hamilton). V: Silvermane 11.00
❑179, Apr 1978, RA (c); RA (a); A: Green Goblin III (Doctor Barton Hamilton). V: Silvermane. Newsstand edition (distributed by Curtis); issue number in box 11.00
❑179/Whitman, Apr 1978, RA (c); RA (a); A: Green Goblin III (Doctor Barton Hamilton). V: Silvermane. Special markets edition (usually sold in Whitman bagged prepacks); price appears in a diamond; no UPC barcode 11.00
❑180, May 1978, RA (c); RA (a); A: Green Goblin III (Doctor Barton Hamilton). V: Silvermane. Newsstand edition (distributed by Curtis); issue number in box 11.00
❑180/Whitman, May 1978, RA (c); RA (a); A: Green Goblin III (Doctor Barton Hamilton). V: Silvermane. Special markets edition (usually sold in Whitman bagged prepacks); price appears in a diamond; no UPC barcode 11.00
❑181, Jun 1978, GK (c); SB (a); O: Spider-Man. Newsstand edition (distributed by Curtis); issue number in box 9.00
❑181/Whitman, Jun 1978, GK (c); SB (a); O: Spider-Man. Special markets edition (usually sold in Whitman bagged prepacks); price appears in a diamond; no UPC barcode 9.00
❑182, Jul 1978, RA (c); RA (a); V: Rocket Racer 8.00
❑183, Aug 1978, RA (c); RA, BMc (a); O: Big Wheel. 1: Big Wheel. D: Big Wheel. V: Tinkerer. V: Rocket Racer. Newsstand edition (distributed by Curtis); issue number in box 6.50
❑183/Whitman, Aug 1978, RA (c); RA, BMc (a); O: Big Wheel. 1: Big Wheel. D: Big Wheel. V: Tinkerer. V: Rocket Racer. Special markets edition (usually sold in Whitman bagged prepacks); price appears in a diamond; UPC barcode appears 6.50
❑184, Sep 1978, RA, BMc (c); RA (a); 1: White Dragon II. Newsstand edition (distributed by Curtis); issue number in box 6.00
❑184/Whitman, Sep 1978, RA, BMc (c); RA (a); 1: White Dragon II. Special markets edition (usually sold in Whitman bagged prepacks); price appears in a diamond; UPC barcode appears 6.00
❑185, Oct 1978, RA (c); RA (a); V: Dragon Gangs. V: White Dragon II. Newsstand edition (distributed by Curtis); issue number in box; Peter Parker graduates from college........ 6.50
❑185/Whitman, Oct 1978, RA (c); RA (a); V: Dragon Gangs. V: White Dragon II. Special markets edition (usually sold in Whitman bagged prepacks); price appears in a diamond; UPC barcode appears; Peter Parker graduates from college 6.50
❑186, Nov 1978, KP (c); KP (a); V: Chameleon. Newsstand edition (distributed by Curtis); issue number in box 8.00
❑186/Whitman, Nov 1978, KP (c); KP (a); V: Chameleon. Special markets edition (usually sold in Whitman bagged prepacks); price appears in a diamond; no UPC barcode........ 8.00
❑187, Dec 1978, KP (c); JSn (w); JSn, BMc (a); A: Shield. A: Captain America. V: Electro. Newsstand edition (distributed by Curtis); issue number in box 8.00
❑187/Whitman, Dec 1978, KP (c); JSn (w); JSn, BMc (a); A: Shield. A: Captain America. V: Electro. Special markets edition (usually sold in Whitman bagged prepacks); price appears in a diamond; no UPC barcode 8.00
❑188, Jan 1979, DC (c); KP (a); O: Jigsaw. 1: Jigsaw. V: Jigsaw. Newsstand edition (distributed by Curtis); issue number in box........ 6.50
❑188/Whitman, Jan 1979, DC (c); KP (a); O: Jigsaw. 1: Jigsaw. V: Jigsaw. Special markets edition (usually sold in Whitman bagged prepacks); price appears in a diamond; no UPC barcode 6.50
❑189, Feb 1979, JBy, BMc (c); JBy, JM (a); A: Man-Wolf. Newsstand edition (distributed by Curtis); issue number in box 6.00
❑189/Whitman, Feb 1979, JBy, BMc (c); JBy, JM (a); A: Man-Wolf. Special markets edition (usually sold in Whitman bagged prepacks); price appears in a diamond; no UPC barcode 6.00
❑190, Mar 1979, AM, KP (c); JBy, JM (a); A: Man-Wolf 6.50
❑191, Apr 1979, KP (a); V: Spider Slayer. V: Spencer Smythe........ 6.00
❑192, May 1979, KP, BMc (c); KP, JM (a); D: Spencer Smythe. V: The Fly. Newsstand edition (distributed by Curtis); issue number in box........ 6.00
❑192/Whitman, May 1979, KP, BMc (c); KP, JM (a); D: Spencer Smythe. V: The Fly. Special markets edition (usually sold in Whitman bagged prepacks); price appears in a diamond; no UPC barcode 6.00
❑193, Jun 1979, KP, JM (a); V: The Fly 6.00
❑194, Jul 1979, KP (a); 1: Black Cat... 21.00
❑195, Aug 1979, AM (c); AM, KP, JM (a); O: Black Cat. Peter Parker informed of Aunt May's death (faked death) 9.00
❑196, Sep 1979, KP (c); AM, JM (a); D: Aunt May (faked death). V: Kingpin. V: Mysterio 6.00
❑197, Oct 1979, KP, JM (a); V: Kingpin 6.00
❑198, Nov 1979, KP (c); SB, JM (a); V: Mysterio 6.00
❑199, Dec 1979, KP (c); SB, JM (a); V: Mysterio 6.00
❑200, Jan 1980, Giant sized; JR2 (c); KP, JM (a); O: Spider-Man. D: unnamed burglar that shot Uncle Ben. Aunt May revealed to be alive . 10.00
❑201, Feb 1980, JR2, BMc (c); KP, JM (a); A: Punisher 9.00
❑202, Mar 1980, KP (c); KP, JM (a); A: Punisher 7.00
❑203, Apr 1980, FM, JM (c); KP (a); 2: Dazzler. A: Dazzler 6.00
❑204, May 1980, AM, JR2 (c); KP (a); A: Black Cat 8.00
❑205, Jun 1980, AM (c); KP, JM (a); A: Black Cat 6.00
❑206, Jul 1980, AM (c); JBy, GD (a)... 6.00
❑207, Aug 1980, JM (a); V: Mesmero 5.00
❑208, Sep 1980, AM, JR2 (c); AM, JR2 (a); O: Fusion. 1: Lance Bannon. 1: Fusion 6.00
❑209, Oct 1980, KJ (a); O: Calypso. 1: Calypso. V: Kraven the Hunter 6.00
❑210, Nov 1980, AM, JR2 (c); JR2, JSt (a); O: Madame Web. 1: Madame Web 6.00
❑211, Dec 1980, AM, JR2 (c); JR2, JM (a); A: Sub-Mariner 6.00
❑212, Jan 1981, AM, JR2 (c); JR2, JM (a); O: Sandman (Marvel). O: Hydro-Man. 1: Hydro-Man 5.00
❑213, Feb 1981, AM, JR2 (c); JR2, JM (a); V: Wizard 5.00
❑214, Mar 1981, AM, JR2 (c); JR2, JM (a); A: Sub-Mariner. V: Frightful Four 5.00
❑215, Apr 1981, AM, JR2 (c); JR2, JM (a) 5.00
❑216, May 1981, AM, JR2 (c); JR2, JM (a) 5.00
❑217, Jun 1981, AM, JR2 (c); JR2, JM (a) 5.00
❑218, Jul 1981, AM, JR2, JM (a) 5.00
❑219, Aug 1981, FM (c); LMc, JM (a) 6.00
❑220, Sep 1981, BL (c); BMc (a); A: Moon Knight 6.00
❑221, Oct 1981, BWi (c); JM (a) 4.00
❑222, Nov 1981, BH, JM (a)........ 4.00
❑223, Dec 1981, JR2 (c); AM, JR2 (a) 4.00
❑224, Jan 1982, (c); JR2 (a) 4.00
❑225, Feb 1982, (c); JR2, BWi (a); A: Foolkiller II (Greg Salinger)........ 4.00
❑226, Mar 1982, (c); JR2, JM (a); A: Black Cat 7.00

Other grades: Multiply price above by 5/6 for VF/NM • 2/3 for VERY FINE • 1/3 for FINE • 1/5 for VERY GOOD • 1/8 for GOOD

Amazing Heroes Swimsuit Special

Cheesecake ish outlasted parent magazine

©Fantagraphics

Amazing High Adventure

Adventure stories by top-notch creative teams

©Marvel

Amazing Scarlet Spider

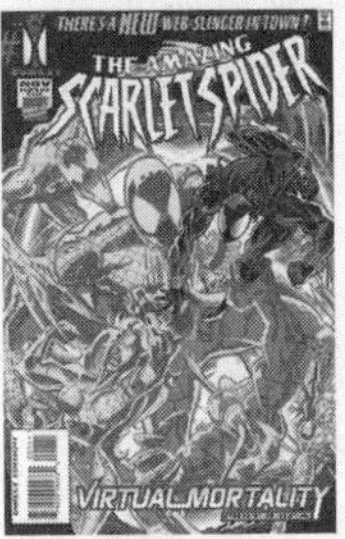

"Clone" series replaced Amazing Spider-Man

©Marvel

Amazing Screw-On Head

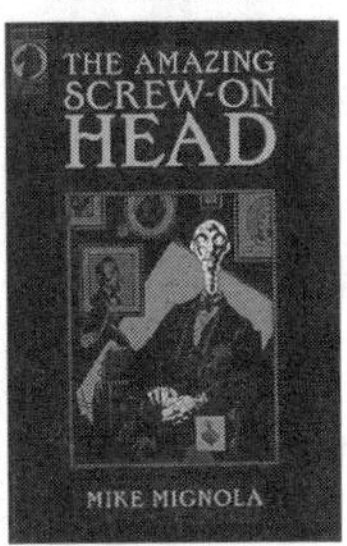

19th-century weirdness from Mike Mignola

©Dark Horse

Amazing Spider-Man

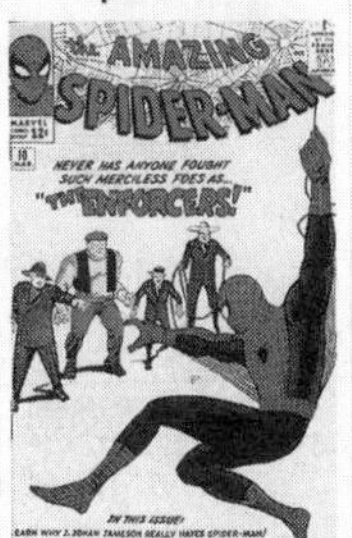

Marvel's flagship series swings high

©Marvel

	N-MINT
❑227, Apr 1982, (c); JR2, JM (a); A: Black Cat	6.00
❑228, May 1982, MN (c)	4.00
❑229, Jun 1982, AM, JR2 (c); JR2, JM (a)	11.00
❑230, Jul 1982, AM, JR2 (c); JR2, JM (a)	6.00
❑231, Aug 1982, AM, JR2 (c); JR2, JM (a)	6.00
❑232, Sep 1982, AM, JR2 (c); JR2, JM (a)	4.00
❑233, Oct 1982, AM, JR2 (c); JR2, JM (a)	4.00
❑234, Nov 1982, AM, JR2 (c); DGr, JR2 (a); Free 16 page insert-Marvel Guide to Collecting Comics	6.00
❑235, Dec 1982, AM, JR2 (c); JR2 (a); O: Will o' the Wisp	4.00
❑236, Jan 1983, JR2 (c); JR2 (a); D: Tarantula I (Anton Rodriguez)	5.00
❑237, Feb 1983, (c); BH (a)	5.00
❑238, Mar 1983, JR2 (c); JR2 (a); 1: Hobgoblin (Ned Leeds). Came with "Tattooz" temporary tattoo decal	22.00
❑239, Apr 1983, AM, JR2 (c); JR2 (a); 2: Hobgoblin	10.00
❑240, May 1983, BL, JR2 (c); BL, JR2 (a)	5.00
❑241, Jun 1983, JR2 (c); JR2 (a); O: Vulture	4.00
❑242, Jul 1983, JR2 (c); JR2 (a); V: Mad Thinker	5.00
❑243, Aug 1983, JR2 (c); JR2 (a)	6.00
❑244, Sep 1983, JR2, BWi (c); JR2, KJ (a); A: Hobgoblin (cameo). A: 3rd. V: Hobgoblin	5.00
❑245, Oct 1983, PS, JR2 (c); JR2 (a); A: 4th. Lefty Donovan becomes Hobgoblin	5.00
❑246, Nov 1983, DGr, JR2 (c); DGr, JR2 (a)	4.00
❑247, Dec 1983, JR2 (c); JR2 (a); V: Thunderball	3.00
❑248, Jan 1984, JR2 (c); JR2 (a); V: Thunderball	4.00
❑249, Feb 1984, (c); DGr, JR2 (a); V: Hobgoblin	5.00
❑250, Mar 1984, JR2, KJ (c); JR2, KJ (a); A: Hobgoblin	6.00
❑251, Apr 1984, KJ (c); KJ (a); V: Hobgoblin. Last old costume	6.00
❑252, May 1984, KJ (c); new costume	10.00
❑253, Jun 1984, 1: The Rose	5.00
❑254, Jul 1984, V: Jack O'Lantern	5.00
❑255, Aug 1984, V: Red Ghost	4.00
❑256, Sep 1984, O: Puma. 1: Puma. V: Puma	4.00
❑257, Oct 1984, 2: Puma. A: Hobgoblin. V: Puma	4.00
❑258, Nov 1984, A: Hobgoblin	4.00
❑259, Dec 1984, O: Mary Jane Watson. A: Hobgoblin. Spider-Man back to old costume	4.00
❑260, Jan 1985, A: Hobgoblin. V: Hobgoblin	5.00
❑261, Feb 1985, CV (c); A: Hobgoblin. V: Hobgoblin	5.00
❑262, Mar 1985, BL (w); BL (a); Spider-man unmasked	4.00
❑263, Apr 1985, 1: Spider-Kid	4.00

	N-MINT
❑264, May 1985	3.00
❑265, Jun 1985, 1: Silver Sable	4.00
❑265/2nd 1: Silver Sable	2.00
❑266, Jul 1985, PD (w); SB (a)	3.00
❑267, Aug 1985, (c); PD (w); BMc (a)	3.00
❑268, Sep 1985, JBy (c); A: Kingpin. A: Beyonder. Secret Wars II	4.00
❑269, Oct 1985, (c); V: Firelord	4.00
❑270, Nov 1985, BMc (a); 1: Kate Cushing (Peter Parker's supervisor at the Bugle). A: Avengers. V: Firelord	4.00
❑271, Dec 1985, (c); V: Manslaughter	5.00
❑272, Jan 1986, SB (a); V: Slyde	4.00
❑273, Feb 1986, A: Puma. Secret Wars II	4.00
❑274, Mar 1986, A: Zarathos (the spirit of vengeance). V: Beyonder. Secret Wars II	5.00
❑275, Apr 1986, double-sized; O: Spider-Man. Hobgoblin story	5.00
❑276, May 1986, A: Hobgoblin. D: Fly	5.00
❑277, Jun 1986, V: Kingpin	4.00
❑278, Jul 1986, D: Wraith	4.00
❑279, Aug 1986, Jack O' Lantern versus Silver Sable	4.00
❑280, Sep 1986	3.00
❑281, Oct 1986, V: Sinister Syndicate. Jack O' Lantern cover/story	5.00
❑282, Nov 1986	5.00
❑283, Dec 1986, V: Absorbing Man. V: Titania	4.00
❑284, Jan 1987, A: Punisher	5.00
❑285, Feb 1987, A: Punisher. A: Hobgoblin	6.00
❑286, Mar 1986	4.00
❑287, Apr 1987, EL (a); A: Hobgoblin. A: Daredevil	5.00
❑288, May 1987, A: Hobgoblin	6.00
❑289, Jun 1987, double-sized issue; PD (w); 1: Hobgoblin II (Jason Macendale). Hobgoblin unmasked; Hobgoblin's identity revealed; Jack O' Lantern becomes Hobgoblin	6.00
❑290, Jul 1987, JR2 (a); Peter Parker proposes to Mary Jane	5.00
❑291, Aug 1987, JR2 (a); V: Spider-Slayer	5.00
❑292, Sep 1987, V: Spider Slayer	5.00
❑293, Oct 1987, MZ (a); V: Kraven the Hunter	5.00
❑294, Nov 1987, MZ, BMc (a); D: Kraven. V: Kraven the Hunter	6.00
❑295, Dec 1987, BSz (a)	6.00
❑296, Jan 1988, V: Doctor Octopus	5.00
❑297, Feb 1988, V: Doctor Octopus	6.00
❑298, Mar 1988, TMc (a); 1: Venom (cameo). V: Chance I (Nicholas Powell). w/o costume	12.00
❑299, Apr 1988, TMc (a); 1: Venom (cameo). V: Chance I (Nicholas Powell)	9.00
❑300, May 1988, 25th anniversary; TMc (a); O: Venom. 1: Venom (Full). Last black costume for Spider-Man	35.00
❑301, Jun 1988, TMc (a)	6.00
❑302, Jul 1988, TMc (a)	4.00
❑303, Aug 1988, TMc (a); A: Silver Sable. A: Sandman	5.00
❑304, Sep 1988, TMc (a); V: The Fox.	4.00

	N-MINT
❑305, Sep 1988, TMc (a); V: The Prowler. V: The Fox	4.00
❑306, Oct 1988, TMc (a); V: Humbug.	4.00
❑307, Oct 1988, TMc (a); O: Chameleon. V: Chameleon	4.00
❑308, Nov 1988, TMc (a); V: Taskmaster	5.00
❑309, Nov 1988, TMc (a)	4.00
❑310, Dec 1988, TMc (a); V: Killer Shrike	5.00
❑311, Jan 1989, TMc (a); V: Mysterio. Inferno	5.00
❑312, Feb 1989, TMc (a); V: Hobgoblin. V: Green Goblin. Inferno; Hobgoblin vs. Green Goblin II (Harry Osborn) .	5.00
❑313, Mar 1989, TMc (a); V: Lizard. Inferno	5.00
❑314, Apr 1989, TMc (a)	4.00
❑315, May 1989, TMc (a); A: Venom. V: Venom	5.00
❑316, Jun 1989, TMc (a); A: Venom. V: Venom	5.00
❑317, Jul 1989, TMc (a); A: Venom. V: Venom	6.00
❑318, Aug 1989, TMc (a); A: Venom	6.00
❑319, Sep 1989, TMc (a)	5.00
❑320, Sep 1989, TMc (a); A: Silver Sable. V: Paladin	3.00
❑321, Oct 1989, TMc (a); A: Silver Sable	4.00
❑322, Oct 1989, TMc (a); A: Silver Sable. V: Ultimatum	5.00
❑323, Nov 1989, TMc (a); A: Silver Sable. V: Solo. V: Ultimatum	3.00
❑324, Nov 1989, TMc (c); TMc, EL (a); A: Sabretooth. V: Solo. V: Sabretooth	5.00
❑325, Nov 1989, TMc (a); A: Captain America. V: Red Skull	4.00
❑326, Dec 1989, V: Graviton. Acts of Vengeance	4.00
❑327, Dec 1989, EL (a); V: Magneto. cosmic Spider-Man; Acts of Vengeance	4.00
❑328, Jan 1990, TMc (a); Hulk; Acts of Vengeance; Last McFarlane Issue	5.00
❑329, Feb 1990, EL (a); V: Tri-Sentinel. Acts of Vengeance	3.00
❑330, Mar 1990, EL (a); A: Punisher. V: Punisher	3.00
❑331, Apr 1990, EL (a); A: Punisher. V: Punisher	3.00
❑332, May 1990, EL (a); A: Venom	3.00
❑333, Jun 1990, EL (a); A: Venom. V: Venom	3.00
❑334, Jul 1990, EL (a); V: Sinister Six (Doctor Octopus, Vulture, Electro, Sandman, Mysterio, Kraven the Hunter)	2.50
❑335, Jul 1990, EL (a)	2.50
❑336, Aug 1990, EL (a)	2.50
❑337, Aug 1990, EL (a)	2.50
❑338, Sep 1990, EL (a)	2.50
❑339, Sep 1990, EL (a)	2.50
❑340, Oct 1990, EL (a)	2.50
❑341, Nov 1990, EL (a); V: Tarantula. Powerless; Spider-Man loses powers	2.50
❑342, Dec 1990, EL (a); V: Scorpion. Powerless	2.50
❑343, Jan 1991, EL (a); V: Scorpion. V: Tarantula. Spider-Man gets his powers back	2.50

N-MINT

❑344, Feb 1991, EL (a); 1: Cardiac. 1: Cletus Kassidy (later becomes Carnage)-cameo. V: Rhino 4.00
❑345, Mar 1991, O: Cletus Kasady. A: Cletus Kassidy (later becomes Carnage)-full. V: Boomerang 3.00
❑346, Apr 1991, EL (a); A: Venom. V: Venom 3.00
❑347, May 1991, EL (a); A: Venom. V: Venom 3.00
❑348, Jun 1991, EL (a); A: Avengers .. 2.00
❑349, Jul 1991, EL (a) 2.00
❑350, Aug 1991, EL (a); V: Doctor Doom 2.00
❑351, Sep 1991, A: Nova. V: Tri-Sentinel 2.00
❑352, Oct 1991, A: Nova. V: Tri-Sentinel 2.00
❑353, Nov 1991, AM (w); A: Punisher. A: Moon Knight 2.00
❑354, Nov 1991, AM (w); A: Punisher. A: Moon Knight 3.00
❑355, Dec 1991, AM (w); A: Punisher. A: Moon Knight 2.00
❑356, Dec 1991, AM (w); A: Punisher. A: Moon Knight 2.00
❑357, Jan 1992, AM (w); A: Punisher. A: Moon Knight 2.00
❑358, Jan 1992, AM (w); A: Punisher. A: Moon Knight 6.00
❑359, Feb 1992 .... 2.00
❑360, Mar 1992, O: Cardiac. 1: Carnage (cameo) 3.00
❑361, Apr 1992, 1: Carnage (full appearance) 6.00
❑361/2nd, ca. 1992, silver cover 1.50
❑362, May 1992, A: Carnage. A: Venom 25.00
❑362/2nd, ca. 1992 .... 1.50
❑363, Jun 1992, A: Carnage. A: Venom 4.00
❑364, Jul 1992, V: Shocker. Peter Parker's parents (false parents) appear 3.00
❑365, Aug 1992, PD (w); 1: Spider-Man 2099. Hologram cover; Peter Parker meets his (false) parents; Gatefold poster with Venom and Carnage; Lizard back-up story 4.00
❑366, Sep 1992, A: Red Skull. V: Red Skull 2.00
❑367, Oct 1992 .... 2.00
❑368, Nov 1992, V: Spider-Slayers 2.00
❑369, Nov 1992, V: Spider-Slayers 2.00
❑370, Dec 1992, V: Spider-Slayers 3.00
❑371, Dec 1992, A: Black Cat. V: Spider-Slayers 2.00
❑372, Jan 1993, V: Spider-Slayers 2.00
❑373, Jan 1993, V: Spider-Slayers 2.00
❑374, Feb 1993, V: Venom 3.00
❑375, Mar 1993, 30th anniversary special; A: Venom. Metallic ink cover; Sets stage for Venom #1 .... 5.00
❑376, Apr 1993, O: Cardiac. V: Cardiac, Styx and Stone 4.00
❑377, May 1993, V: Cardiac 3.00
❑378, Jun 1993, A: Carnage. A: Venom 4.00
❑379, Jul 1993, A: Carnage. A: Venom 3.00
❑380, Aug 1993, A: Carnage. A: Venom. V: Carnage. V: Demogoblin 3.00
❑381, Sep 1993, A: Hulk. V: Hulk 3.00
❑382, Oct 1993, A: Hulk. V: Hulk 3.00
❑383, Nov 1993 .... 3.00
❑384, Dec 1993 .... 3.00
❑385, Jan 1994 .... 3.00
❑386, Feb 1994, V: Vulture 3.00
❑387, Mar 1994, V: Vulture 3.00
❑388, Apr 1994, Double-size D: Peter Parker's parents (false parents). V: Chameleon. V: Vulture 3.25
❑388/Variant, Apr 1994, Double-size; D: Peter Parker's parents (false parents). V: Vulture. foil cover 2.00
❑389, May 1994, V: Chameleon 3.00
❑390, Jun 1994 .... 3.00
❑390/CS, Jun 1994 .... 3.00
❑391, Jul 1994, V: Shriek. Aunt May suffers stroke 3.00
❑392, Aug 1994, V: Carrion. V: Shriek 3.00
❑393, Sep 1994, V: Carrion. V: Shriek. Carrion 3.00
❑394, Oct 1994, O: Ben Reilly. A: Ben Reilly 3.00
❑394/Variant, Oct 1994, Giant-size; O: Ben Reilly. A: Ben Reilly. enhanced cover 3.50
❑395, Nov 1994, V: Puma. continues in Spectacular Spider-Man #218 .... 3.00

N-MINT

❑396, Dec 1994, A: Daredevil. V: Owl. V: Vulture. continues in Spectacular Spider-Man #219 .... 3.00
❑397, Jan 1995, Double-size; V: Lizard. V: Doctor Octopus. flip book with illustrated story from The Ultimate Spider-Man back-up; continues in Spectacular Spider-Man #220 .... 3.00
❑398, Feb 1995, V: Doctor Octopus. continues in Spectacular Spider-Man #221 .... 3.00
❑399, Mar 1995, A: Scarlet Spider. A: Jackal. V: Jackal. continues in Spider-Man #56 .... 3.00
❑400, Apr 1995, SL (w); JR2 (a); D: Aunt May (fake death) 5.00
❑400/Gray, Apr 1995, white cover edition (no ads, back-up story); SL (w); JR2 (a); D: Aunt May (fake death). gray embossed cover 4.00
❑400/White, Apr 1995, SL (w); JR2 (a); D: Aunt May (fake death). Limited edition cover; 10,000 copies 30.00
❑401, May 1995, V: Kaine 1.50
❑402, Jun 1995, V: Traveller 1.50
❑403, Jul 1995, A: Carnage 1.50
❑404, Aug 1995 .... 1.50
❑405, Sep 1995 .... 1.50
❑406, Oct 1995, 1: Doctor Octopus II. OverPower cards inserted; (continues in Amazing Scarlet Spider) 1.50
❑407, Jan 1996, A: Silver Sable. A: Human Torch. A: Sandman 1.50
❑408, Feb 1996, V: Mysterio 1.50
❑409, Mar 1996, V: Rhino 1.50
❑410, Apr 1996, V: Cell 12 .... 1.50
❑411, May 1996 .... 1.50
❑412, Jun 1996 .... 1.50
❑413, Jul 1996 .... 1.50
❑414, Aug 1996, A: Delilah 1.50
❑415, Sep 1996, V: Sentinel. "Onslaught: Impact 2" 1.50
❑416, Oct 1996, post-Onslaught memories 1.50
❑417, Nov 1996 .... 1.50
❑418, Dec 1996, birth of Peter and Mary Jane's baby; Return of Norman Osborn (face shown) 2.00
❑419, Jan 1997, V: Black Tarantula 1.50
❑420, Feb 1997, A: X-Man. D: El Uno. 1.50
❑421, Mar 1997, O: The Dragonfly. 1: The Dragonfly 2.00
❑422, Apr 1997, O: Electro 2.00
❑423, May 1997, V: Electro 2.00
❑424, Jun 1997, A: Elektra. V: Elektra 2.00
❑425, Aug 1997 .... 2.00
❑426, Sep 1997, gatefold summary ... 2.00
❑427, Oct 1997, gatefold summary; return of Doctor Octopus 2.00
❑428, Nov 1997, gatefold summary V: Doctor Octopus 2.00
❑429, Dec 1997, gatefold summary V: Absorbing Man 2.00
❑430, Jan 1998, gatefold summary A: Silver Surfer. V: Carnage 2.00
❑431, Feb 1998, gatefold summary A: Silver Surfer. V: Carnage 2.00
❑432, Mar 1998, gatefold summary ... 2.00
❑432/Variant, Mar 1998; Variant "Wanted Dead or Alive" cover ....
❑433, Apr 1998, gatefold summary ... 2.00
❑434, May 1998, gatefold summary .. 2.00
❑435, Jun 1998, gatefold summary A: Ricochet 2.00
❑436, Jul 1998, gatefold summary 2.00
❑437, Aug 1998, gatefold summary A: Synch 2.00
❑438, Sep 1998, gatefold summary A: Daredevil 2.00
❑439, Sep 1998, gatefold summary A: Zack and Lana 2.00
❑440, Oct 1998, gatefold summary V: Molten Man 2.00
❑441, Nov 1998, gatefold summary A: Molten Man. D: Madame Web 2.00
❑500, Dec 2003, JR2 (a); numbering reverts to original series, adding in issues from Vol. 2 .... 5.00
❑501, Jan 2004, (c); JR2 (a) 4.00
❑502, Feb 2004, JR2 (a) 2.99
❑503, Mar 2004 .... 2.25
❑504, Apr 2004, JR2 (a) 2.25
❑505, May 2004, JR2 (a) 2.25

N-MINT

❑506, Jun 2004, JR2 (a) 2.25
❑507, Jul 2004, (c); JR2 (a) 2.25
❑508, Jul 2004 .... 2.25
❑509, Aug 2004 .... 2.25
❑509/DirCut, Aug 2004, Director's Cut 7.00
❑510, Sep 2004 .... 4.00
❑511, Oct 2004 .... 3.00
❑512, Nov 2004 .... 5.00
❑513, Dec 2004 .... 3.00
❑514, Jan 2005 .... 2.25
❑515, Feb 2005 .... 2.25
❑516, Mar 2005 .... 2.25
❑517, Apr 2005 .... 2.25
❑518, May 2005 .... 2.25
❑519, Jun 2005 .... 2.25
❑520, Jul 2005 .... 2.25
❑521, Aug 2005 .... 2.50
❑522, Sep 2005 .... 2.50
❑523, Oct 2005 .... 2.50
❑524, Nov 2005 .... 2.50
❑525, Dec 2005; Has 2005 Statement, filed 8/26/05 [earlier than allowed]; avg print run 150833; avg sales 102,377; avg subs 10,187; avg total paid 112,564 [statement had a one-copy math error]; samples 3,028; max existent 115,592; 23% of run returned 2.50
❑526, Jan 2006 .... 2.99
❑527, Feb 2006 .... 2.99
❑528, Mar 2006 .... 2.99
❑529, May 2006 .... 2.99
❑530, Jun 2006 .... 2.99
❑531, Jul 2006 .... 2.99
❑532, Aug 2006 .... 2.99
❑533, Sep 2006 .... 2.99
❑Aim Giveaway 1, ca. 1980; Giveaway from Aim Toothpaste; A: Doctor Octopus. Spider-Man vs. Doctor Octopus 4.00
❑Aim Giveaway 2; Aim toothpaste giveaway A: Green Goblin 2.00
❑Annual 1, ca. 1964 SD (c); SL (w); SD (a); 1: Sinister Six (Doctor Octopus, Vulture, Electro, Sandman, Mysterio, Kraven the Hunter) 700.00
❑Annual 2, ca. 1965; Cover reads "King-Size Special"; SD (c); SD, SL (w); SD (a); 1: Xandu. A: Doctor Strange. Cover reads King Size Special; reprints Amazing Spider-Man #1, 2, and 5, plus a new story. 550.00
❑Annual 3, Nov 1966; Cover reads "King-Size Special"; JR (c); SL (w); DH, JR (a); A: Daredevil. A: Avengers. V: Hulk. Cover reads King Size Special; New story; reprints Amazing Spider-Man #11 and 12 .... 115.00
❑Annual 4, Nov 1967; Cover reads "King-Size Special"; SL (w); A: Torch. V: Mysterio. V: Wizard. Cover reads King-Size Special 90.00
❑Annual 5, Nov 1968; Cover reads "King-Size Special"; JR (c); SL (w); 1: Peter Parker's parents. A: Red Skull. Cover reads King Size Special; fate of Peter Parker's parents revealed 75.00
❑Annual 5/2nd, ca. 1994; Cover reads "King-Size Special"; JR (c); SL (w); 1: Peter Parker's parents. A: Red Skull. Cover reads King-Size Special 2.50
❑Annual 6, Nov 1969; Cover reads "King-Size Special"; JR (c); SL (w); SD, JK (a); Cover reads King Size Special; reprints stories from Amazing Spider-Man #8, Annual #1 and Fantastic Four Annual #1 .... 35.00
❑Annual 7, Dec 1970; Cover reads "King-Size Special"; JR (c); SL (w); SD (a); Cover reads King Size Special; reprints stories from Amazing Spider-Man #1, 2, and 38. 35.00
❑Annual 8, Dec 1971; Cover reads "King-Size Special"; JR (c); SL (w); JR (a); A: Giant Man. Cover reads King Size Special; reprints stories from Amazing Spider-Man #46 and 50 and Tales to Astonish #57 .... 22.00
❑Annual 9, ca. 1973, reprints Spectacular Spider-Man (magazine) #2; JR, JM (c); JR, SL (w); JR, JM (a); A: Hobgoblin. Cover reads King Size Special; reprinted with changes from Spectacular Spider-Man #2 .... 22.00
❑Annual 10, Sep 1976, GK, JR (c); GK (a); O: Human Fly. 1: Human Fly 8.00

Other grades: Multiply price above by 5/6 for VF/NM • 2/3 for VERY FINE • 1/3 for FINE • 1/5 for VERY GOOD • 1/8 for GOOD

Amazing Spider-Man (Vol. 2)

Marvel restarted ASM ... then undid the restart

©Marvel

Amazing Spider-Man Giveaways

Comics giveaway covers child abuse problem

©Marvel

Amazing Spider-Man (Public Service Series)

Canadian public-service special issues

©Marvel

Amazing Spider-Man Soul of the Hunter

Kraven kauses khaos from beyond grave

©Marvel

Amazing Spider-Man Super Special

Venom and Carnage mix it up in special

©Marvel

N-MINT

❑Annual 11, Sep 1977, GK, JSt (c); AM, JR2, DP, JM (a) ... 8.00
❑Annual 12, Aug 1978, JBy (c); GK, JR (w); GK, JR (a); Reprints Hulk story from Amazing Spider-Man #119-120 ... 8.00
❑Annual 13, Nov 1979 KP, BMc (c); JBy, KP, TD, JM (a); V: Doctor Octopus.. 7.00
❑Annual 14, Dec 1980 FM, TP (a); A: Doctor Strange. V: Doctor Doom 6.00
❑Annual 15, ca. 1981 FM, KJ (c); FM, KJ (a); A: Punisher ... 7.00
❑Annual 16, ca. 1982 JR2 (c); JR2 (a); O: Captain Marvel II (Monica Rambeau). 1: Captain Marvel II (Monica Rambeau) 4.00
❑Annual 17, ca. 1983 KJ (c); JM (a)... 4.00
❑Annual 18, ca. 1984; BG (c); SL (w); BL, BG (a); Wedding of J. Jonah Jameson ... 4.00
❑Annual 19, ca. 1985 ... 4.00
❑Annual 20, ca. 1986 D: Blizzard ... 4.00
❑Annual 21, ca. 1987; newsstand edition; Wedding of Peter Parker and Mary Jane Watson ... 4.00
❑Annual 21/Direc, ca. 1987; Direct Market edition; Wedding of Peter Parker and Mary Jane Watson ... 5.00
❑Annual 22, ca. 1988 O: High Evolutionary. 1: Speedball. A: Daredevil ... 4.00
❑Annual 23, ca. 1989; O: Spider-Man. Atlantis Attacks ... 3.00
❑Annual 24, ca. 1990 SD, GK, MZ (a); A: Ant-Man ... 3.00
❑Annual 25, ca. 1991; O: Spider-Man. Vibranium Vendetta; 1st solo Venom story ... 3.00
❑Annual 26, ca. 1992 1: Dreadnought 2000 ... 4.00
❑Annual 27, ca. 1993; 1: Annex. trading card ... 3.00
❑Annual 28, ca. 1994; Carnage ... 3.00
❑Annual 1996, ca. 1996 ... 4.00
❑Annual 1997, ca. 1997; V: Sundown. wraparound cover ... 3.00
❑Ashcan 1, b&w; ashcan edition; O: Spider-Man. ashcan ... 0.75

AMAZING SPIDER-MAN (VOL. 2)

MARVEL

❑1 (442), Jan 1999; JBy (a); wraparound cover ... 7.00
❑1/DF Romita, Jan 1999; JR2 (c); JBy, JR2 (a); Sunburst variant cover; DFE alternate cover, signed John Romita Jr 12.00
❑1/DF Lee, Jan 1999; JBy (a); DFE alternate cover, signed Stan Lee 35.00
❑1/Dynamic, Jan 1999; JBy (a); Dynamic Forces Edition ... 5.00
❑1/Autographed, Jan 1999; JBy (a); Signed ... 10.00
❑1/Authentix, Jan 1999; Marvel Authentix edition JR2 (c); JBy, JR2 (a) ... 8.00
❑1/Sunburst, Jan 1999; JR2 (c); JBy (a); sunburst variant cover ... 18.00
❑2 (443), Feb 1999; gatefold summary; JBy (c); JBy (a); V: Shadrac. new Spider-Man's identity revealed; Skeleton grabbing Spider-Man on cover ... 2.50

N-MINT

❑2/Kubert, Feb 1999; gatefold summary; JBy (a); V: Shadrac. new Spider-Man's identity revealed ... 2.50
❑3 (444), Mar 1999 JBy (a); O: Shadrac 2.00
❑4 (445), Apr 1999 JBy (a); A: Fantastic Four. V: Trapster. V: Sandman ... 2.00
❑5 (446), May 1999 A: new Spider-Woman ... 2.00
❑6 (447), Jun 1999 V: Spider-Woman 2.00
❑7 (448), Jul 1999; Flash Thompson's fantasy ... 2.00
❑8 (449), Aug 1999 V: Mysterio ... 2.00
❑9 (450), Sep 1999 A: Doctor Octopus 2.00
❑10 (451), Oct 1999 A: Doctor Octopus. V: Captain Power ... 2.00
❑11 (452), Nov 1999 V: Blob ... 2.00
❑12 (453), Dec 1999; Giant-size ... 3.00
❑13 (454), Jan 2000 ... 2.00
❑14 (455), Feb 2000 JBy (w); JBy, DGr (a) ... 2.00
❑15 (456), Mar 2000 JBy (w); JBy (a) 2.00
❑16 (457), Apr 2000 ... 2.00
❑17 (458), May 2000 ... 2.00
❑18 (459), Jun 2000 ... 2.50
❑19 (460), Jul 2000 EL (a); A: Venom 2.50
❑20 (461), Aug 2000; EL (c); SL (w); SD, KP, JR, JM, EL (a); reprints Amazing Spider-Man (Vol. 1) #25, 58, and 192 ... 4.50
❑21 (462), Sep 2000 EL (c); EL (a); V: Spider-Slayers ... 2.25
❑22 (463), Oct 2000 ... 2.25
❑23 (464), Nov 2000 JR2 (a) ... 2.25
❑24 (465), Dec 2000 JR2 (a) ... 2.25
❑25 (466), Jan 2001; regular wraparound cover ... 3.00
❑25/Speckle, Jan 2001; Speckle foil cover ... 4.00
❑26 (467), Feb 2001 ... 2.25
❑27 (468), Mar 2001 JR2 (a); A: Mr. Q. A: Mr. P ... 2.25
❑28 (469), Apr 2001 ... 2.25
❑29 (470), May 2001; Return of Mary Jane ... 2.25
❑30 (471), Jun 2001 ... 5.00
❑31 (472), Jul 2001 ... 3.00
❑32 (473), Aug 2001 ... 4.00
❑33 (474), Sep 2001 ... 4.00
❑34 (475), Oct 2001 ... 5.00
❑35 (476), Nov 2001 ... 4.00
❑36 (477), Dec 2001 ... 9.00
❑36/Dynamic, Dec 2001, 9/11 tribute issue; Dynamic Forces special edition 20.00
❑37 (478), Jan 2002 ... 2.50
❑38 (479), Feb 2002 JR2 (a) ... 2.50
❑39 (480), ca. 2002 ... 2.50
❑40 (481), Jun 2002 ... 2.25
❑41 (482), Jul 2002 ... 4.00
❑42 (483), Aug 2002 ... 3.00
❑43 (484), Sep 2002 ... 3.00
❑44 (485), Oct 2002 ... 2.25
❑45 (486), Nov 2002 ... 2.25
❑46 (487), Dec 2002 ... 2.25
❑47 (488), Jan 2003 ... 2.25
❑48 (489), Feb 2003 ... 2.25
❑49 (490), Mar 2003 ... 2.25
❑50 (491), Apr 2003 ... 6.00

N-MINT

❑51 (492), May 2003 ... 2.25
❑52 (493), Jun 2003 JR2 (c); JR2 (a) 2.25
❑53 (494), Jul 2003; JR2 (c); JR2 (a); wraparound cover ... 2.25
❑54 (495), Aug 2003, JR2 (a) ... 2.49
❑55 (496), Sep 2003, JR2 (a) ... 2.49
❑56 (497), Oct 2003, JR2 (a) ... 2.00
❑57 (498), Oct 2003, (c); JR2 (a) ... 2.99
❑58 (499), Nov 2003, (c); JR2 (a); numbering restarts at 500 under Vol. 1 ... 2.99
❑Annual 1999, Jun 1999; V: Trapster. V: Wizard. 1999 Annual ... 3.50
❑Annual 2000, ca. 2000 ... 3.50
❑Annual 2001, ca. 2001; Cover B ... 2.99

AMAZING SPIDER-MAN 30TH ANNIVERSARY POSTER MAGAZINE

MARVEL

❑1 ... 3.95

AMAZING SPIDER-MAN GIVEAWAYS

MARVEL

❑1; (two different, both #1) ... 4.00
❑2; Managing Materials ... 4.00
❑3, Feb 1977; Planned Parenthood giveaway; miniature; ... vs. The Prodigy! ... 4.00
❑4, ca. 1979; No issue number; All Detergent giveaway ... 6.00
❑5, child abuse; with New Mutants ... 4.00

AMAZING SPIDER-MAN (PUBLIC SERVICE SERIES)

MARVEL

❑1, ca. 1990; TMc (c); TMc (a); Skating on Thin Ice! ... 2.50
❑1/2nd, Feb 1993; US Edition; TMc (c); TMc (a); Skating on Thin Ice ... 2.00
❑2, ca. 1993; TMc (a); Double Trouble! 2.50
❑2/2nd, Feb 1993; US Edition; TMc (a); Double Trouble ... 2.00
❑3, ca. 1991; TMc (a); Hit and Run! ... 2.50
❑3/2nd, Feb 1993; US Edition; TMc (a); A: Ghost Rider. Hit and Run ... 2.00
❑4, ca. 1992; TMc (a); 1: Turbine. Chaos in Calgary ... 2.50
❑4/2nd, Feb 1993; US Edition; Chaos in Calgary ... 2.00

AMAZING SPIDER-MAN, THE: SOUL OF THE HUNTER

MARVEL

❑1, Aug 1992 ... 5.95

AMAZING SPIDER-MAN SUPER SPECIAL

MARVEL

❑1, ca. 1995; Flip-book; two of the stories continue in Spider-Man Super Special #1; Amazing Scarlet Spider on other side ... 4.00

AMAZING STRIP

ANTARCTIC

❑1, Feb 1994 ... 2.95
❑2, Apr 1994; Indicia says April, cover says March ... 2.95
❑3, Apr 1994 ... 2.95
❑4, May 1994 ... 2.95
❑5, Jun 1994 ... 2.95

Other grades: Multiply price above by 5/6 for VF/NM • 2/3 for VERY FINE • 1/3 for FINE • 1/5 for VERY GOOD • 1/8 for GOOD

❑6, Jul 1994 .... 2.95
❑7, Aug 1994 .... 2.95
❑8, Sep 1994 .... 2.95
❑9, Nov 1994 .... 2.95
❑10, Dec 1994; #10 on cover, #4 in indicia (cover correct) 2.95
❑Book 1; Collects Amazing Strip #1-5 .... 10.95
❑Book 2; Collects Amazing Strip #6-10 .... 10.95

AMAZING WAHZOO
SOLSON

❑1 1986 .... 1.75

AMAZING WORLD OF SUPERMAN
DC

❑1 1973 .... 4.00

AMAZING X-MEN
MARVEL

❑1, Mar 1995; Age of Apocalypse 2.00
❑2, Apr 1995 .... 2.00
❑3, May 1995 .... 2.00
❑4, Jun 1995 .... 2.00

AMAZON
DC / AMALGAM

❑1, Apr 1996 .... 1.95

AMAZON ATTACK 3-D
3-D ZONE

❑1, ca. 1990, b&w 3.95

AMAZONS
FANTAGRAPHICS

❑1, b&w 2.95

AMAZON TALES
FANTACO

❑1 .... 2.95
❑2 .... 2.95
❑3 .... 2.95

AMAZON
COMICO

❑1, Mar 1989 .... 1.95
❑2, Apr 1989 .... 1.95
❑3, May 1989 .... 1.95

AMAZON WARRIORS
AC

❑1 1989; b&w Reprint 2.50

AMAZON WOMAN (1ST SERIES)
FANTACO

❑1, ca. 1994 .... 2.95
❑2, ca. 1994 .... 2.95

AMAZON WOMAN (2ND SERIES)
FANTACO

❑1, ca. 1994 .... 2.95
❑2, ca. 1994 .... 2.95
❑3, ca. 1994 .... 2.95
❑4, ca. 1994 .... 2.95

AMBER: NINE PRINCES IN AMBER (ROGER ZELAZNY'S...)
DC

❑1, ca. 1996, prestige format; adapts Zelazny story 6.95
❑2, ca. 1996, prestige format; adapts Zelazny story 6.95
❑3, ca. 1996, prestige format; adapts Zelazny story 6.95

AMBER: THE GUNS OF AVALON (ROGER ZELAZNY'S...)
DC

❑1, ca. 1996; prestige format 6.95
❑2, ca. 1996; prestige format 6.95
❑3, ca. 1996; prestige format 6.95

AMBUSH BUG
DC

❑1, Jun 1985 KG (w); KG (a) 1.00
❑2, Jul 1985 KG (w); KG (a) 1.00
❑3, Aug 1985 KG (w); KG (a) 1.00
❑4, Sep 1985 KG (w); KG (a) 1.00

AMBUSH BUG NOTHING SPECIAL
DC

❑1, Sep 1992 .... 2.50

AMBUSH BUG STOCKING STUFFER
DC

❑1, Mar 1986 .... 1.25

AMELIA RULES
RENAISSANCE

❑1, ca. 2001 .... 2.95
❑2, ca. 2001 .... 2.95
❑3, ca. 2001 .... 2.95
❑4, ca. 2001 .... 2.95
❑5, ca. 2002 .... 2.95
❑6, ca. 2002 .... 2.95
❑7, ca. 2002 .... 2.95
❑8, ca. 2002 .... 2.95
❑9, ca. 2003 .... 2.95
❑10, ca. 2003 .... 2.95

AMERICAN
DARK HORSE

❑1, Aug 1987, b&w 1.50
❑2, Oct 1987 .... 1.75
❑3, Dec 1987 .... 1.75
❑4, Apr 1988 .... 1.75
❑5, Jul 1988 .... 1.75
❑6, Sep 1988 .... 1.75
❑7, Oct 1988 .... 1.75
❑8, Feb 1989 .... 1.75
❑Special 1, b&w; Special edition 2.25

AMERICAN BOOK
DARK HORSE

❑1, Oct 1988, b&w 5.95

AMERICAN CENTURY
DC / VERTIGO

❑1, May 2001 .... 2.50
❑2, Jun 2001 .... 2.50
❑3, Jul 2001 .... 2.50
❑4, Aug 2001 .... 2.50
❑5, Aug 2001 .... 2.50
❑6, Sep 2001 .... 2.50
❑7, Oct 2001 .... 2.50
❑8, Nov 2001 .... 2.50
❑9, Dec 2001 .... 2.50
❑10, Jan 2002 .... 2.50
❑11, Feb 2002 .... 2.50
❑12, Mar 2002 .... 2.50
❑13, Apr 2002 .... 2.50
❑14, May 2002 .... 2.50
❑15, Jun 2002 .... 2.50
❑16, Aug 2002 .... 2.50
❑17, Sep 2002 .... 2.50
❑18, Oct 2002 .... 2.75
❑19, Nov 2002 .... 2.75
❑20, Jan 2003 .... 2.75
❑21, Feb 2003 .... 2.75
❑22, Mar 2003 .... 2.75
❑23, Jun 2003; Jun in indicia, Apr on cover 2.75
❑24, Jul 2003 .... 2.75
❑25, Aug 2003 .... 2.75
❑26, Sep 2003 .... 2.75
❑27, Oct 2003 .... 2.75

AMERICAN FLAGG
FIRST

❑1, Oct 1983 HC (a); 1: Reuben Flagg 2.50
❑2, Nov 1983 HC (a) 2.00
❑3, Dec 1983 HC (a) 2.00
❑4, Jan 1984 HC (a) 2.00
❑5, Feb 1984 HC (w); HC (a) 2.00
❑6, Mar 1984 HC (a) 1.50
❑7, Apr 1984 HC (a) 1.50
❑8, May 1984 HC (a) 1.50
❑9, Jun 1984 HC (a) 1.50
❑10, Jul 1984 HC (a) 1.50
❑11, Aug 1984 HC (a) 1.50
❑12, Sep 1984 HC (a) 1.50
❑13, Oct 1984 HC (a) 1.50
❑14, Nov 1984 PB (a) 1.25
❑15, Dec 1984 HC (a) 1.25
❑16, Jan 1985 HC (a) 1.25
❑17, Feb 1985 HC (a) 1.25
❑18, Mar 1985 HC (a) 1.25
❑19, Apr 1985 HC (a) 1.25
❑20, May 1985 HC (a) 1.25
❑21, Jun 1985 AMo (w) 1.25
❑22, Jul 1985 HC (c); AMo (w) 1.25
❑23, Aug 1985 HC (c); AMo (w) 1.25
❑24, Sep 1985 HC (c); AMo (w) 1.25
❑25, Oct 1985 HC (c); AMo (w) 1.25
❑26, Nov 1985 HC (c); AMo (w) 1.25
❑27, Dec 1985 HC (c); AMo (w); HC (a) 1.25
❑28, Apr 1986 HC, JSa (a) 1.25
❑29, May 1986 HC, JSa (a) 1.25
❑30, Jun 1986 HC, JSa (a) 1.25
❑31, Jul 1986 HC (a); O: Bob Violence 1.25
❑32, Aug 1986 HC (a) 1.25
❑33, Sep 1986 .... 1.25
❑34, Nov 1986 .... 1.25
❑35, Dec 1986 .... 1.25
❑36, Jan 1987 .... 1.25
❑37, Feb 1987 .... 1.25
❑38, Mar 1987 HC (a) 1.25
❑39, Apr 1987 HC (a) 1.25
❑40, May 1987 HC (a) 1.25
❑41, Jun 1987 HC (a) 1.25
❑42, Jul 1987 HC (a) 1.25
❑43, Aug 1987 HC (a) 1.25
❑44, Sep 1987 HC (a) 1.25
❑45, Oct 1987 .... 1.25
❑46, Nov 1987; HC (c); apology 1.75
❑47, Dec 1987 HC (a) 1.75
❑48, Jan 1988 HC (a) 1.75
❑49, Feb 1988 HC (a) 1.75
❑50, Mar 1988 HC (a) 1.75
❑Special 1, Nov 1986; HC (w); HC (a); Special #1 .... 1.75

AMERICAN FLAGG (HOWARD CHAYKIN'S...)
FIRST

❑1, May 1988 .... 2.00
❑2, Jun 1988 .... 1.75
❑3, Jul 1988 .... 1.75
❑4, Aug 1988 .... 1.75
❑5, Sep 1988 .... 1.75
❑6, Oct 1988 .... 1.95
❑7, Nov 1988 .... 1.95
❑8, Dec 1988 .... 1.95
❑9, Jan 1989 .... 1.95
❑10, Feb 1989 .... 1.95
❑11, Mar 1989 .... 1.95
❑12, Apr 1989 .... 1.95

AMERICAN FLYER
LAST GASP

❑1 .... 4.00
❑2 .... 4.00

AMERICAN FREAK: A TALE OF THE UN-MEN
DC / VERTIGO

❑1, Feb 1994 .... 2.00
❑2, Mar 1994 .... 2.00
❑3, Apr 1994 .... 2.00
❑4, May 1994 .... 2.00
❑5, Jun 1994 .... 2.00

AMERICAN HEROES
PERSONALITY

❑1, b&w 2.95

AMERICAN, THE: LOST IN AMERICA
DARK HORSE

❑1, Jul 1992 .... 2.50
❑2, Aug 1992 .... 2.50
❑3, Sep 1992 .... 2.50
❑4, Oct 1992 .... 2.50

AMERICAN PRIMITIVE
3-D ZONE

❑1, b&w; not 3-D 2.50

AMERICAN SPLENDOR
PEKAR

❑1, May 1976 .... 65.00
❑2, May 1977 .... 30.00
❑3, May 1978 .... 20.00
❑4, Oct 1979 .... 20.00
❑5, ca. 1980 .... 20.00
❑6, ca. 1981 .... 15.00
❑7, ca. 1982 .... 15.00
❑8, ca. 1983 .... 15.00
❑9, ca. 1984 .... 15.00
❑10, ca. 1985 .... 15.00
❑11, ca. 1986 .... 10.00
❑12, ca. 1987 .... 10.00
❑13, ca. 1988 .... 10.00
❑14, ca. 1989 .... 18.00
❑15, ca. 1990 .... 8.00
❑16, ca. 1991 .... 3.95
❑17, ca. 1993 .... 8.00

Amazing X-Men

"Age of Apocalypse" version of The X-Men

©Marvel

Ambush Bug

Corny character started out as a villain

©DC

American Century

Harry Block travels through America

©DC

American Flagg

It's 2076, and the world is falling apart...

©First

American Splendor

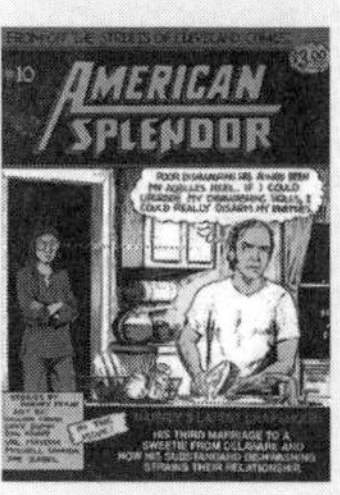

Slice-of-life from gruff Harvey Pekar

©Pekar

N-MINT

AMERICAN SPLENDOR: BEDTIME STORIES
DARK HORSE
❑1, Jun 2000 .... 3.95

AMERICAN SPLENDOR: COMIC-CON COMICS
DARK HORSE
❑1, Aug 1996, b&w 2.95

AMERICAN SPLENDOR: MUSIC COMICS
DARK HORSE
❑1, Nov 1997, b&w; collects Pekar's stories about music 2.95

AMERICAN SPLENDOR: ODDS & ENDS
DARK HORSE
❑1, Dec 1997, b&w; collects short pieces 2.95

AMERICAN SPLENDOR: ON THE JOB
DARK HORSE
❑1, May 1997, b&w 2.95

AMERICAN SPLENDOR: PORTRAIT OF THE AUTHOR IN HIS DECLINING YEARS
DARK HORSE
❑1, Apr 2001 .... 3.99

AMERICAN SPLENDOR: TERMINAL
DARK HORSE
❑1, Sep 1999 .... 2.95

AMERICAN SPLENDOR: TRANSATLANTIC COMICS
DARK HORSE
❑1, Jul 1998 .... 2.95

AMERICAN SPLENDOR: UNSUNG HERO
DARK HORSE
❑1, Aug 2002 .... 3.99
❑2, Sep 2002 .... 3.99
❑3, Oct 2002 .... 3.99

AMERICAN SPLENDOR: WINDFALL
DARK HORSE
❑1 1995, b&w 3.95
❑2, Oct 1995, b&w 3.95

AMERICAN SPLENDOR SPECIAL: A STEP OUT OF THE NEST
DARK HORSE
❑1, Aug 1994, b&w 2.95

AMERICAN TAIL, AN: FIEVEL GOES WEST
MARVEL
❑1 .... 1.25
❑2 .... 1.25
❑3, Feb 1992 .... 1.25

AMERICAN VIRGIN
DC / VERTIGO
❑1, May 2006 .... 2.99
❑2, Jun 2006 .... 2.99
❑3, Jul 2006 .... 2.99
❑4, Aug 2006 .... 2.99

N-MINT

AMERICAN WAY
DC / WILDSTORM
❑1, May 2006 .... 2.99
❑2, Jun 2006 .... 2.99
❑3, Jul 2006 .... 2.99
❑4, Aug 2006 .... 2.99
❑5, Sep 2006 .... 2.99

AMERICAN WOMAN
ANTARCTIC
❑1, Jun 1998 .... 2.95
❑2, Oct 1998 .... 2.95

AMERICA'S BEST COMICS
AMERICA'S BEST
❑Special 1 .... 6.95

AMERICA'S BEST COMICS PREVIEW
AMERICA'S BEST
❑1, AMo (w); KN (a); Included in Wizard #91 .... 1.50

AMERICA'S BEST COMICS SKETCHBOOK
DC / AMERICA'S BEST COMICS
❑1 .... 5.95

AMERICA'S BEST TV COMICS
ABC TV
❑1, ca. 1967; Giant-size; SL (w); JK, JR (a); promotional comic published by Marvel for ABC to promote Saturday morning cartoons 95.00

AMERICA VS. THE JUSTICE SOCIETY
DC
❑1, Jan 1985; Giant-size 1.50
❑2, Feb 1985 .... 1.00
❑3, Mar 1985; Wizard 1.00
❑4, Apr 1985; multiverse (Flash of Two Worlds) 1.00

AMERICOMICS
AC
❑1, Apr 1983 .... 2.00
❑2, Jun 1983 .... 2.00
❑3, Aug 1983 .... 2.00
❑4, Oct 1983 .... 2.00
❑5, Dec 1983 .... 2.00
❑6, Mar 1984 .... 2.00
❑Special 1, Jan 1983 .... 2.00

AMETHYST
DC
❑1, Jan 1985 RE (a); 1: Fire Jade 1.00
❑2, Feb 1985 .... 1.00
❑3, Mar 1985 .... 1.00
❑4, Apr 1985 .... 1.00
❑5, May 1985 .... 1.00
❑6, Jun 1985 .... 1.00
❑7, Jul 1985 .... 1.00
❑8, Aug 1985 .... 1.00
❑9, Sep 1985 .... 1.00
❑10, Oct 1985 .... 1.00
❑11, Nov 1985 .... 1.00
❑12, Dec 1985 .... 1.00
❑13, Feb 1986 A: Doctor Fate 1.00
❑14, Apr 1986 .... 1.00
❑15, Jun 1986 1: Child. 1: Flaw 1.00
❑16, Aug 1986 .... 1.00
❑Special 1, Oct 1986; Special 1.00

N-MINT

AMETHYST (MINI-SERIES)
DC
❑1, Nov 1987 .... 1.25
❑2, Dec 1987 .... 1.25
❑3, Jan 1988 .... 1.25
❑4, Feb 1988 .... 1.25

AMETHYST, PRINCESS OF GEMWORLD
DC
❑1, May 1983, O: Amethyst 1.00
❑1/75 cent, May 1983, O: Amethyst. 75 cent regional price variant 5.00
❑2, Jun 1983 .... 1.00
❑2/75 cent, Jun 1983, 75 cent regional price variant 5.00
❑3, Jul 1983 .... 1.00
❑4, Aug 1983 .... 1.00
❑5, Sep 1983 .... 1.00
❑6, Oct 1983 .... 1.00
❑7, Nov 1983 .... 1.00
❑8, Dec 1983 .... 1.00
❑9, Jan 1984 .... 1.00
❑10, Feb 1984 .... 1.00
❑11, Mar 1984 .... 1.00
❑12, Apr 1984 .... 1.00
❑Annual 1 .... 1.25

A MIDNIGHT OPERA
TOKYOPOP
❑1, Nov 2005 .... 9.95

AMMO ARMAGEDDON
ATOMEKA
❑1 .... 4.95

AMNESIA
NBM
❑1 .... 9.95

AMORA (GRAY MORROW'S...)
FANTAGRAPHICS / EROS
❑1, Apr 1991, b&w 2.95

AMUSING STORIES
RENEGADE
❑1, Mar 1987, b&w 2.00

AMY PAPUDA
NORTHSTAR
❑1 .... 2.50
❑2 .... 2.50

AMY RACECAR COLOR SPECIAL
EL CAPITAN
❑1, Jul 1997 .... 2.95
❑2, ca. 1999 .... 3.50

ANARCHY COMICS
LAST GASP
❑1 .... 2.50
❑2 .... 2.50
❑3 .... 2.50
❑4 .... 2.50

ANARKY (MINI-SERIES)
DC
❑1, May 1997 .... 2.50
❑2, Jun 1997 .... 2.50
❑3, Jul 1997 .... 2.50
❑4, Aug 1997 .... 2.50

Other grades: Multiply price above by 5/6 for VF/NM • 2/3 for VERY FINE • 1/3 for FINE • 1/5 for VERY GOOD • 1/8 for GOOD

ANARKY
DC

❑1, May 1999 .... 2.50
❑2, Jun 1999 .... 2.50
❑3, Jul 1999 .... 2.50
❑4, Aug 1999 .... 2.50
❑5, Sep 1999 .... 2.50
❑6, Oct 1999 .... 2.50
❑7, Nov 1999, Day of Judgment 2.50
❑8, Dec 1999 .... 2.50

ANCIENT JOE
DARK HORSE

❑1, ca. 2001 .... 3.50
❑2, ca. 2001 .... 3.50
❑3, ca. 2002 .... 3.50

ANDROMEDA (ANDROMEDA)
ANDROMEDA

❑1, Mar 1995 .... 2.50
❑2, Apr 1995 .... 2.50

ANDROMEDA (SILVER SNAIL)
SILVER SNAIL

❑1 .... 2.00
❑2 .... 2.00
❑3 .... 2.00
❑4 .... 2.00
❑5 .... 2.00
❑6 .... 2.00

ANDY PANDA (GOLD KEY)
GOLD KEY / WHITMAN

❑1, Aug 1973 .... 4.00
❑2, Nov 1973 .... 2.50
❑3, Feb 1974 .... 2.50
❑4, May 1974 .... 2.50
❑5, Aug 1974 .... 2.00
❑6, Nov 1974 .... 2.00
❑7, Feb 1975 .... 2.00
❑8, May 1975 .... 2.00
❑9, Aug 1975 .... 2.00
❑10, Nov 1975 .... 2.00
❑11, Feb 1976 .... 2.00
❑12, Apr 1976 .... 2.00
❑13, May 1976 .... 2.00
❑14, Jul 1976 .... 2.00
❑15, Sep 1976 .... 2.00
❑16, Nov 1976 .... 2.00
❑17, Jan 1977 .... 2.00
❑18, Mar 1977 .... 2.00
❑19, May 1977 .... 2.00
❑20, Jul 1977 .... 2.00
❑21, Sep 1977 .... 2.00
❑22, Nov 1977 .... 2.00
❑23, Jan 1978 .... 2.00

A-NEXT
MARVEL

❑1, Oct 1998; next generation of Avengers 1.99
❑2/A, Nov 1998; Figures busting out of comic page on cover 1.99
❑2/B, Nov 1998; Earth Sentry flying on cover 1.99
❑3, Dec 1998 .... 1.99
❑4, Jan 1999 .... 1.99
❑5, Feb 1999 .... 1.99
❑6, Mar 1999 .... 1.99
❑7, Apr 1999 .... 1.99
❑8, May 1999 .... 1.99
❑9, Jun 1999 .... 1.99
❑10, Jul 1999 .... 1.99
❑11, Aug 1999 .... 1.99

ANGEL (2ND SERIES)
DARK HORSE

❑1, Nov 1999 .... 3.00
❑1/A, Nov 1999; Dynamic Forces gold logo variant 3.00
❑1/Variant, Nov 1999 .... 3.00
❑2, Dec 1999 .... 3.00
❑2/Variant, Dec 1999 .... 3.00
❑3, Jan 2000 .... 3.00
❑3/A, Jan 2000; Valentine's Day Edition; Dynamic Forces purple foil variant (white cover) 3.00
❑3/Variant, Jan 2000 .... 3.00
❑4, Feb 2000 .... 3.00
❑4/Variant, Feb 2000 .... 3.00
❑5, Mar 2000 .... 3.00
❑5/Variant, Mar 2000 .... 3.00
❑6, Apr 2000 .... 3.00
❑6/Variant, Apr 2000 .... 3.00
❑7, May 2000 .... 3.00
❑7/A, May 2000; Dynamic Forces Lucky 7 foil variant (limited to 1500 copies) 3.00
❑7/Variant, May 2000 .... 3.00
❑8, Jun 2000 .... 3.00
❑8/Variant, Jun 2000 .... 3.00
❑9, Jul 2000 .... 3.00
❑9/Variant, Jul 2000 .... 3.00
❑10, Aug 2000 .... 3.00
❑10/Variant, Aug 2000 .... 3.00
❑11, Sep 2000 .... 2.95
❑11/Variant, Sep 2000 .... 2.95
❑12, Oct 2000 .... 2.99
❑12/Variant, Oct 2000 .... 2.99
❑13, Nov 2000 .... 2.99
❑13/Variant, Nov 2000 .... 2.99
❑14, Dec 2000 .... 2.99
❑14/Variant, Dec 2000 .... 2.99
❑15, Feb 2001 .... 2.99
❑15/Variant, Feb 2001 .... 2.99
❑16, Mar 2001 .... 2.99
❑16/Variant, Mar 2001 .... 2.99
❑17, Apr 2001 .... 2.99
❑17/Variant, Apr 2001 .... 2.99

ANGEL (3RD SERIES)
DARK HORSE

❑1, Sep 2001 .... 2.99
❑1/Variant, Sep 2001 .... 2.99
❑2, Oct 2001 .... 2.99
❑2/Variant, Oct 2001 .... 2.99
❑3, Nov 2001 .... 2.99
❑3/Variant, Nov 2001 .... 2.99
❑4, May 2002 .... 2.99
❑4/Variant, May 2002 .... 2.99

ANGELA
IMAGE

❑1, Dec 1994 NG (w); A: Spawn 3.50
❑1/A, Dec 1994; NG (w); A: Spawn. Pirate Spawn cover 3.50
❑2, Jan 1995 NG (w); A: Spawn 3.00
❑3, Feb 1995 NG (w) 3.00

ANGELA/GLORY: RAGE OF ANGELS
IMAGE

❑1/A, Mar 1996 .... 2.50
❑1/B, Mar 1996 .... 2.50

ANGEL AND THE APE
DC

❑1, Nov 1968 .... 40.00
❑2, Jan 1969 .... 20.00
❑3, Mar 1969 .... 15.00
❑4, May 1969 .... 15.00
❑5, Jul 1969 .... 15.00
❑6, Sep 1969 .... 15.00
❑7, Nov 1969 .... 15.00

ANGEL AND THE APE (MINI-SERIES)
DC

❑1, Mar 1991 PF (w); PF (a) 1.25
❑2, Apr 1991 PF (a) 1.25
❑3, May 1991 PF (a) 1.25
❑4, Jun 1991 PF (a) 1.25

ANGEL AND THE APE (VERTIGO)
DC / VERTIGO

❑1, Oct 2001 .... 2.95
❑2, Nov 2001 .... 2.95
❑3, Dec 2001 .... 2.95
❑4, Jan 2002 .... 2.95

ANGEL FIRE
CRUSADE

❑1/A, Jun 1997; wraparound photo cover 2.95
❑1/B, Jun 1997; black background cover 2.95
❑1/C, Jun 1997; white background cover 2.95
❑2, Aug 1997 .... 2.95
❑3, Oct 1997, b&w 2.95

ANGEL GIRL
ANGEL

❑0 .... 2.95
❑0/Nude; Nude cover 5.00

ANGEL GIRL: BEFORE THE WINGS
ANGEL

❑1, Aug 1997 .... 2.95

ANGEL GIRL VS. VAMPIRE GIRLS
ANGEL

❑1 .... 2.95
❑1/Nude; Nude edition 9.95

ANGELIC LAYER
TOKYOPOP

❑1, Jun 2002, b&w; printed in Japanese format 9.99

ANGEL LOVE
DC

❑1, Aug 1986 .... 1.00
❑2, Sep 1986 .... 1.00
❑3, Oct 1986 .... 1.00
❑4, Nov 1986 .... 1.00
❑5, Dec 1986 .... 1.00
❑6, Jan 1987 .... 1.00
❑7, Feb 1987 .... 1.00
❑8, Mar 1987 .... 1.00
❑Annual 1 .... 1.25
❑Special 1 .... 1.25

ANGEL OF DEATH
INNOVATION

❑1 .... 2.25
❑2 .... 2.25
❑3 .... 2.25
❑4 .... 2.25

ANGEL: OLD FRIENDS
IDEA & DESIGN WORKS

❑1, Jan 2006 .... 3.99
❑2, Jan 2006 .... 3.99
❑3, Feb 2006 .... 3.99
❑4, Mar 2006 .... 3.99
❑5, Apr 2006 .... 3.99

ANGELS 750
ANTARCTIC

❑1, Apr 2004 .... 2.99
❑2, May 2004 .... 2.99
❑3, Jul 2004 .... 2.99
❑4, Jul 2004 .... 2.99
❑5, Aug 2004 .... 2.99

ANGEL SANCTUARY
TOKYOPOP

❑1, Apr 2004 .... 9.95
❑2, Jun 2004 .... 9.95
❑3, Aug 2004 .... 9.95
❑4, Nov 2004 .... 9.95
❑5, Dec 2004 .... 9.95
❑6, 2003 2005 .... 9.95
❑7, Apr 2005 .... 9.95
❑8, Jun 2005 .... 9.95
❑9, Aug 2005 .... 9.95
❑10, Oct 2005 .... 9.95

ANGEL SCRIPTBOOK
IDEA & DESIGN WORKS

❑1, Jun 2006 .... 3.99
❑2, May 2006 .... 3.99
❑3, Jun 2006 .... 3.99
❑4, Jul 2006 .... 3.99

ANGELS OF DESTRUCTION
MALIBU

❑1, Oct 1996 .... 2.50

ANGEL SPOTLIGHT: GUNN
IDEA & DESIGN WORKS

❑1, Jun 2006 .... 3.99

ANGEL SPOTLIGHT: ILLYRIA
IDEA & DESIGN WORKS

❑1, May 2006 .... 3.99

ANGEL SPOTLIGHT: WESLEY
IDEA & DESIGN WORKS

❑1, Jun 2006 .... 3.99

ANGEL STOMP FUTURE (WARREN ELLIS'...)
AVATAR

❑1 2005 .... 3.50

ANGEL: THE CURSE
IDEA & DESIGN WORKS

❑1, Jul 2005 .... 3.99
❑1/Autographed, Jul 2005 .... 19.99
❑2/Byrne, Aug 2005 .... 5.00
❑2/ChrisCross, Aug 2005 .... 4.00

Other grades: Multiply price above by 5/6 for VF/NM • 2/3 for VERY FINE • 1/3 for FINE • 1/5 for VERY GOOD • 1/8 for GOOD

Angel (2nd series)

Based on TV Buffy spinoff series
©Dark Horse

Angel and the Ape

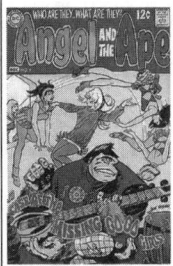

Silliness with Angel O'Day and Sam Simeon
©DC

Angel Love

DC's 1980s attempt at romance comic
©DC

Anima

Troubled teen gets super-hero treatment
©DC

Animal Man

Series that made a name for Grant Morrison
©DC

	N-MINT
❑2/Messina, Aug 2005	5.00
❑2/Shannon, Aug 2005	4.00
❑2/Photo, Aug 2005	15.00
❑3/Gardner, Sep 2005	3.99
❑3/Kordey, Sep 2005	3.99
❑3/Messina, Sep 2005	3.99
❑3/Wood, Sep 2005	3.99
❑4 2005	3.99
❑5 2005	3.99

ANGEL: THE CURSE COVER GALLERY
Idea & Design Works

❑1, Jul 2006	3.99

ANGELTOWN
DC

❑1, Jan 2005	2.95
❑2, Feb 2005	2.95
❑3, Mar 2005	2.95
❑4, Apr 2005	2.95
❑5, May 2005	2.95

ANGER GRRRL
Blatant

❑1, Jun 1999	2.95

ANGRYMAN
Caliber

❑1	2.50
❑2	2.50
❑3	2.50

ANGRYMAN (2ND SERIES)
Iconografix

❑1	2.50
❑2	2.50
❑3	2.50

ANGRY SHADOWS
Innovation

❑1, ca. 1989, b&w	4.95

ANIMA
DC

❑0, Oct 1994; Series continued in Anima #8	1.75
❑1, Mar 1994	1.75
❑2, Apr 1994	1.75
❑3, May 1994	1.75
❑4, Jun 1994	1.75
❑5, Jul 1994	1.75
❑6, Aug 1994	1.95
❑7, Sep 1994; Zero Hour	1.95
❑8, Nov 1994; Series continued from Anima #0	1.95
❑9, Dec 1994	1.95
❑10, Jan 1995	1.95
❑11, Feb 1995	1.95
❑12, Mar 1995	1.95
❑13, Apr 1995	1.95
❑14, Jun 1995	2.25
❑15, Jul 1995	2.25

ANIMAL CONFIDENTIAL
Dark Horse

❑1, May 1992, b&w	2.25

ANIMAL MAN
DC

	N-MINT
❑1, Sep 1988 BB (c)	4.00
❑2, Oct 1988 BB (c)	2.50
❑3, Nov 1988 BB (c)	2.00
❑4, Dec 1988 BB (c); A: B'wana Beast	2.00
❑5, Dec 1988; BB (c); Road Runner-Coyote	2.00
❑6, Jan 1989; BB (c); Invasion!	2.00
❑7, Jan 1989 BB (c)	2.00
❑8, Feb 1989 BB (c); V: Mirror Master	2.00
❑9, Mar 1989 BB (c); A: JLA	2.00
❑10, Apr 1989 BB (c); A: Vixen	2.00
❑11, May 1989 BB (c); A: Vixen	2.00
❑12, Jun 1989 BB (c); A: Vixen	2.00
❑13, Jul 1989 BB (c)	2.00
❑14, Aug 1989 BB (c)	2.00
❑15, Sep 1989 BB (c)	2.00
❑16, Oct 1989 BB (c)	2.00
❑17, Nov 1989 BB (c)	2.00
❑18, Dec 1989 BB (c)	2.00
❑19, Jan 1990 BB (c)	2.00
❑20, Feb 1990 BB (c)	2.00
❑21, Mar 1990 BB (c)	2.00
❑22, Apr 1990 BB (c)	2.00
❑23, May 1990; BB (c); A: Jason Blood. A: Phantom Stranger. Arkham Asylum story	2.00
❑24, Jun 1990 BB (c); A: Inferior Five	2.00
❑25, Jul 1990 BB (c)	2.00
❑26, Aug 1990; BB (c); Morrison puts himself in story	2.00
❑27, Sep 1990 BB (c)	2.00
❑28, Oct 1990 BB (c)	2.00
❑29, Nov 1990 BB (c); D: The Notional Man	2.00
❑30, Dec 1990 BB (c)	2.00
❑31, Jan 1991 BB (c)	2.00
❑32, Feb 1991 BB (c)	2.00
❑33, Mar 1991 BB (c)	2.00
❑34, Apr 1991 BB (c)	2.00
❑35, May 1991 BB (c)	2.00
❑36, Jun 1991 BB (c)	2.00
❑37, Jul 1991 BB (c)	2.00
❑38, Aug 1991; BB (c); Punisher parody	2.00
❑39, Sep 1991	2.00
❑40, Oct 1991	2.00
❑41, Nov 1991	2.00
❑42, Dec 1991	2.00
❑43, Jan 1992	2.00
❑44, Feb 1992	2.00
❑45, Mar 1992	2.00
❑46, Apr 1992	2.00
❑47, May 1992	2.00
❑48, Jun 1992	2.00
❑49, Jul 1992	2.00
❑50, Aug 1992; Giant-size	3.00
❑51, Sep 1992	2.00
❑52, Oct 1992	2.00
❑53, Nov 1992	2.00
❑54, Dec 1992	2.00
❑55, Jan 1993	2.00
❑56, Feb 1993; Giant-size	3.50
❑57, Mar 1993; Begin Vertigo line	2.00
❑58, Apr 1993	2.00
❑59, May 1993	2.00
❑60, Jun 1993 BB (c)	2.00
❑61, Jul 1993	2.00
❑62, Aug 1993	2.00
❑63, Sep 1993	2.00
❑64, Oct 1993	2.00
❑65, Nov 1993	2.00
❑66, Dec 1993	2.00
❑67, Jan 1994	2.00
❑68, Feb 1994	2.00
❑69, Mar 1994	2.00
❑70, Apr 1994	2.00
❑71, May 1994	1.95
❑72, Jun 1994	1.95
❑73, Jul 1994	1.95
❑74, Aug 1994	1.95
❑75, Sep 1994	1.95
❑76, Oct 1994	1.95
❑77, Nov 1994	1.95
❑78, Dec 1994	1.95
❑79, Jan 1995	1.95
❑80, Feb 1995	1.95
❑81, Mar 1995	1.95
❑82, Apr 1995	1.95
❑83, May 1995	2.25
❑84, Jun 1995	2.25
❑85, Jul 1995	2.25
❑86, Aug 1995	2.25
❑87, Sep 1995	2.25
❑88, Oct 1995	2.25
❑89, Nov 1995	2.25
❑Annual 1 BB (c)	4.00

ANIMAL MYSTIC
Cry for Dawn

❑1; published by Cry For Dawn Productions	10.00
❑1/Ltd.; limited edition with alternate cover and eight additional pages; limited edition with alternate cover and eight additional pages; published by Cry For Dawn Productions	10.00
❑1/2nd, May 1995, b&w; new cover; published by Sirius; new cover	5.00
❑2, Jun 1994, b&w 1: Klor	7.00
❑2/2nd, May 1995, b&w; New cover; art re-shot for superior reproduction	4.00
❑3, Oct 1994, b&w	5.00
❑3/2nd	3.00
❑4, Aug 1995, b&w	5.00
❑4/A, Aug 1995; Alternate centerfold	5.00
❑4/Ltd., Aug 1995; Limited edition with different covers and centerfold; Limited edition with different covers and centerfold; 1500 printed	5.00
❑4/2nd	4.00

ANIMAL MYSTIC WATER WARS
Sirius

❑1, Jun 1996	2.95
❑2, Sep 1996	2.95
❑3, Jan 1997	2.95
❑4, Aug 1997	2.95
❑5, May 1998	2.95
❑6, Oct 1998	2.95
❑Ashcan 1, Preview edition	2.50

ANIMAL RIGHTS COMICS
Stabur

❑1, Benefit comic for PETA	2.50

Other grades: Multiply price above by 5/6 for VF/NM • 2/3 for VERY FINE • 1/3 for FINE • 1/5 for VERY GOOD • 1/8 for GOOD

ANIMANIACS
DC

- ❑1, May 1995 A: Pinky & The Brain.... 2.50
- ❑2, Jun 1995 ... 2.00
- ❑3, Jul 1995 ... 2.00
- ❑4, Aug 1995 ... 2.00
- ❑5, Sep 1995 ... 2.00
- ❑6, Oct 1995 ... 2.00
- ❑7, Nov 1995 ... 2.00
- ❑8, Dec 1995 ... 2.00
- ❑9, Jan 1996; Pulp Fiction parody cover 2.00
- ❑10, Feb 1996; gratuitous pin-up cover 2.00
- ❑11, Mar 1996; Brain duplicates himself 1.75
- ❑12, Apr 1996 ... 1.75
- ❑13, May 1996 ... 1.75
- ❑14, Jun 1996 ... 1.75
- ❑15, Jul 1996 ... 1.75
- ❑16, Aug 1996; Wrestling issue ... 1.75
- ❑17, Sep 1996; Animaniacs judge a beauty contest... 1.75
- ❑18, Oct 1996; All France issue ... 1.75
- ❑19, Nov 1996 ... 1.75
- ❑20, Dec 1996; James Dean tribute.... 1.75
- ❑21, Jan 1997; Christmas issue ... 1.75
- ❑22, Feb 1997 ... 1.75
- ❑23, Mar 1997 ... 1.75
- ❑24, Apr 1997 ... 1.75
- ❑25, May 1997; Anniversary issue ... 1.75
- ❑26, Jun 1997; Tales from the Crypt cover parody... 1.75
- ❑27, Jul 1997; Slappy's plane is hijacked... 1.75
- ❑28, Aug 1997; Star Trek parody; Science issue ... 1.75
- ❑29, Sep 1997 ... 1.75
- ❑30, Oct 1997; "Electra Woman and Dyna Girl" parody... 1.75
- ❑31, Nov 1997; 101 Dalmations parody 1.75
- ❑32, Dec 1997; Dot hosts a slumber party ... 1.95
- ❑33, Jan 1998; 1: Sakko Warner. Lost World cover ... 1.95
- ❑34, Feb 1998 ... 1.95
- ❑35, Mar 1998 A: Freakazoid... 1.95
- ❑36, Apr 1998 ... 1.95
- ❑37, May 1998 ... 1.95
- ❑38, Jun 1998; manga-style cover ... 1.95
- ❑39, Jul 1998 A: Alfred Nobel ... 1.95
- ❑40, Sep 1998; Spice Girls parody ... 1.95
- ❑41, Oct 1998; Little Nemo and Little Mermaid parodies... 1.95
- ❑42, Nov 1998; Love Boat parody ... 1.99
- ❑43, Dec 1998; Pinky & the Brain... 1.99
- ❑44, Jan 1999; Pinky & the Brain... 1.99
- ❑45, Feb 1999; The Warner Twins; Featuring Pinky and the Brain ... 1.99
- ❑46, Mar 1999; Dot the Vampire Slayer; Featuring Pinky and the Brain ... 1.99
- ❑47, Apr 1999; Evita parody; Featuring Pinky and the Brain... 1.99
- ❑48, May 1999 ... 1.99
- ❑49, Jun 1999; literature issue; Featuring Pinky and the Brain; It's the Animaniacal Guide to the Classics!! 1.99
- ❑50, Jul 1999; Hello Nurse as super-hero; Featuring Pinky and the Brain 1.99
- ❑51, Aug 1999; Featuring Pinky and the Brain ... 1.99
- ❑52, Sep 1999; football; Featuring Pinky and the Brain... 1.99
- ❑53, Oct 1999; Featuring Pinky and the Brain ... 1.99
- ❑54, Nov 1999 ... 1.99
- ❑55, Dec 1999; Featuring Pinky and the Brain ... 1.99
- ❑56, Jan 2000; Featuring Pinky and the Brain ... 1.99
- ❑57, Feb 2000 ... 1.99
- ❑58, Mar 2000; Hello Nurse, Agent of H.U.B.B.A... 1.99
- ❑59, Apr 2000; Featuring Pinky and the Brain ... 1.99
- ❑Holiday 1, Dec 1994; double-sized ... 3.00

ANIMATION COMICS
VIZ

- ❑1 ... 3.95
- ❑2 ... 3.95
- ❑3 ... 3.95
- ❑4; PokÈmon the Movie 2000 ... 3.95

ANIMAX
MARVEL / STAR

- ❑1, Dec 1986... 1.00
- ❑2, Jan 1987 ... 1.00
- ❑3, Feb 1987 ... 1.00
- ❑4, Mar 1987 ... 1.00

ANIMERICA EXTRA
VIZ

- ❑1, ca. 1998... 4.95
- ❑2, ca. 1998... 4.95

ANIMERICA EXTRA (VOL. 2)
VIZ

- ❑1, Jan 1999... 4.95
- ❑2, Feb 1999... 4.95
- ❑3, Mar 1999 ... 4.95
- ❑4, Apr 1999... 4.95
- ❑5, May 1999... 4.95
- ❑6, Jun 1999... 4.95
- ❑7, Jul 1999... 4.95
- ❑8, Aug 1999 ... 4.95
- ❑9, Sep 1999... 4.95
- ❑10, Oct 1999 ... 4.95
- ❑11, Nov 1999 ... 4.95
- ❑12, Dec 1999... 4.95

ANIMERICA EXTRA (VOL. 3)
VIZ

- ❑1, Jan 2000... 4.95
- ❑2, Feb 2000... 4.95
- ❑3, Mar 2000 ... 4.95
- ❑4, Apr 2000... 4.95
- ❑5, May 2000 ... 4.95
- ❑6, Jun 2000; contains poster ... 4.95
- ❑7, Jul 2000... 4.95
- ❑8, Aug 2000 ... 4.95
- ❑9, Sep 2000... 4.95
- ❑10, Oct 2000 ... 4.95
- ❑11, Nov 2000 ... 4.95
- ❑12, Dec 2000... 4.95

ANIMERICA EXTRA (VOL. 4)
VIZ

- ❑1, Jan 2001 ... 4.95
- ❑2, Feb 2001 ... 4.95
- ❑3, Mar 2001 ... 4.95
- ❑4, Apr 2001 ... 4.95
- ❑5, May 2001 ... 4.95
- ❑6, Jun 2001 ... 4.95
- ❑7, Jul 2001 ... 4.95
- ❑8, Aug 2001 ... 4.95
- ❑9, Sep 2001... 4.95
- ❑10, Oct 2001 ... 4.95
- ❑11, Nov 2001 ... 4.95
- ❑12, Dec 2001... 4.95

ANIMERICA EXTRA (VOL. 5)
VIZ

- ❑1, Jan 2002... 4.95
- ❑2, Feb 2002... 4.95
- ❑3, Mar 2002 ... 4.95
- ❑4, Apr 2002 ... 4.95
- ❑5, May 2002 ... 4.95
- ❑6, Jun 2002... 4.95
- ❑7, Jul 2002... 4.95
- ❑8, Aug 2002 ... 4.95
- ❑9, Sep 2002... 4.95
- ❑10, Oct 2002 ... 4.95
- ❑11, Nov 2002 ... 4.95
- ❑12, Dec 2002... 4.95

ANIMERICA EXTRA (VOL. 6)
VIZ

- ❑1, Jan 2003... 4.95

ANIMISM
CENTURION

- ❑1, Jan 1987... 1.50

ANIVERSE
WEEBEE

- ❑1, Oct 1987 ... 1.95
- ❑2, Dec 1987... 1.95

ANNEX (MARVEL)
MARVEL

- ❑1, Aug 1994 ... 1.75
- ❑2, Sep 1994... 1.75
- ❑3, Oct 1994 ... 1.75
- ❑4, Nov 1994 ... 1.75

ANNIE
MARVEL

- ❑1, Oct 1982, Official movie adaptation 1.00
- ❑1/Special; Tabloid size ... 5.00
- ❑2, Nov 1982, Official movie adaptation 1.00

ANNIE OAKLEY AND TAGG (2ND SERIES)
GOLD KEY

- ❑1, Jul 1965; reuses photo cover from Dell #6 ... 40.00

ANNIE SPRINKLE IS MISS TIMED
RIP OFF

- ❑1, Sep 1991... 2.50
- ❑2, Oct 1991... 2.50
- ❑3, Nov 1991... 2.50
- ❑4, Dec 1991 ... 2.50

ANNIHILATION: NOVA
MARVEL

- ❑1, Jul 2006 ... 2.99
- ❑2, Aug 2006... 2.99

ANNIHILATION PROLOGUE
MARVEL

- ❑1, May 2006 ... 2.99

ANNIHILATION: RONAN THE ACCUSER
MARVEL

- ❑1, Jul 2006 ... 2.99
- ❑2, Aug 2006... 2.99
- ❑3, Sep 2006... 2.99

ANNIHILATION: SILVER SURFER
MARVEL

- ❑1, Jun 2006 ... 2.99
- ❑2, Jul 2006 ... 2.99
- ❑3, Aug 2006... 2.99

ANNIHILATION: SUPER-SKRULL
MARVEL

- ❑1, Jun 2006 ... 2.99
- ❑2, Jul 2006 ... 2.99
- ❑3, Aug 2006... 2.99

ANOMALIES
ABNORMAL FUN

- ❑1, Oct 2000... 2.95

ANOMALY
BUD PLANT

- ❑1 ... 8.00
- ❑2 ... 5.00
- ❑3 ... 5.00
- ❑4 ... 5.00

ANOMALY (BRASS RING)
BRASS RING

- ❑1 ... 3.95
- ❑2, Jun 2000 ... 3.95

ANOTHER CHANCE TO GET IT RIGHT
DARK HORSE

- ❑1 ... 9.95
- ❑1/2nd, Mar 1995... 9.95

ANOTHER DAY
RAISED BROW

- ❑1, Oct 1995, b&w ... 2.75
- ❑2, Aug 1997... 2.75

ANT
ARCANA

- ❑1, ca. 2004 ... 10.00
- ❑1/Red foil, ca. 2004, Red foil variant from Diamond 2004 Retailer Summit 35.00
- ❑2, ca. 2004 ... 5.00
- ❑3, ca. 2004 ... 5.00
- ❑3/Variant, ca. 2004 ... 6.00

ANT (VOL. 2)
IMAGE

- ❑1, Oct 2005... 2.99
- ❑1/Sketch, Oct 2005... 2.99
- ❑1/RRP, Oct 2005; Distributed at Baltimore 2005 retailer convention; red foil cover; 1 per store... 25.00
- ❑1/Conv, Oct 2005; Wizard World East 2005; 500 created... 15.00
- ❑2 ... 2.99
- ❑3, Dec 2005... 2.99
- ❑4, Mar 2006... 2.99
- ❑5, Apr 2006 ... 2.99
- ❑6, Jul 2006 ... 2.99

Other grades: Multiply price above by 5/6 for VF/NM • 2/3 for VERY FINE • 1/3 for FINE • 1/5 for VERY GOOD • 1/8 for GOOD

Animal Mystic

California girl awakens as a goddess
©Cry for Dawn

Animaniacs

Based on frenetic Warner Bros. cartoon
©DC

Animax

Star title inspired by a line of toys
©Marvel

Anthro

Life at the dawn of human history
©DC

Apathy Kat

Jazzy cartoon humor from Harold Buchholz
©Express

N-MINT

ANTABUSE
High Drive
- ❑1 ... 2.50
- ❑2 ... 2.50

ANTARCTIC PRESS JAM 1996
Antarctic
- ❑1, Dec 1996 ... 2.95

ANTARES CIRCLE
Antarctic
- ❑1 ... 1.95
- ❑2 ... 1.95

ANT BOY
Steeldragon
- ❑1 ... 1.75
- ❑2, Oct 1988 ... 1.75

ANT FARM
Gallant
- ❑1, Jun 1998 ... 2.50
- ❑2 ... 2.50

ANTHRO
DC
- ❑1, Aug 1968 ... 50.00
- ❑2, Oct 1968 ... 20.00
- ❑3, Dec 1968 ... 20.00
- ❑4, Feb 1969 ... 20.00
- ❑5, Apr 1969 ... 20.00
- ❑6, Aug 1969, WW (a) ... 20.00

ANTICIPATOR
Fantasy
- ❑1, ca. 1996 ... 2.25

ANTIETAM: THE FIERY TRAIL
Heritage Collection
- ❑1 1997 ... 3.50

ANTI-HITLER COMICS
New England
- ❑1 ... 2.75
- ❑2 ... 2.75

ANTI-SOCIAL
Helpless Anger
- ❑1, b&w ... 2.00
- ❑2 ... 2.50
- ❑3 ... 2.50
- ❑4 ... 2.75

ANTI SOCIAL FOR THE DISABLED
Helpless Anger
- ❑1, b&w ... 5.00

ANTI SOCIAL JR.
Helpless Anger
- ❑1, b&w ... 1.75

ANT-MAN'S BIG CHRISTMAS
Marvel
- ❑1, Feb 2000; prestige format ... 5.95

ANTON'S DREKBOOK
Fantagraphics / Eros
- ❑1, Mar 1991, b&w ... 2.50

ANUBIS
Super Crew
- ❑1 ... 2.50

N-MINT

ANUBIS (2ND SERIES)
Super Crew
- ❑1 ... 2.95

ANYTHING BUT MONDAY
Anything But Monday
- ❑1, Dec 1988 ... 2.00
- ❑2 ... 2.00

ANYTHING GOES!
Fantagraphics
- ❑1, Oct 1986 ... 2.00
- ❑2, Dec 1986 ... 2.00
- ❑3, Mar 1987 ... 2.00
- ❑4, May 1987 ... 2.00
- ❑5, Oct 1987; TMNT ... 2.00
- ❑6, Oct 1987, b&w ... 2.00

A-OK
Antarctic
- ❑1, Sep 1992 ... 2.50
- ❑2, Nov 1992 ... 2.50
- ❑3, Jan 1993 ... 2.50
- ❑4, Mar 1993 ... 2.50

APACHE DICK
Eternity
- ❑1, Feb 1990 ... 2.25
- ❑2, Mar 1990 ... 2.25
- ❑3, Apr 1990 ... 2.25
- ❑4, May 1990 ... 2.25
- ❑Book 1; Reprints ... 9.95

APACHE SKIES
Marvel
- ❑1, Sep 2002 ... 2.99
- ❑2, Oct 2002 ... 2.99
- ❑3, Nov 2002 ... 2.99
- ❑4, Dec 2002 ... 2.99

APACHE TRAIL
Steinway
- ❑1, Sep 1957 ... 58.00
- ❑2, Nov 1957 ... 36.00
- ❑3, Feb 1958 ... 36.00
- ❑4, Jun 1958 ... 36.00

APATHY KAT
Express / Entity
- ❑1, ca. 1995, b&w ... 2.50
- ❑2, ca. 1996 ... 2.75
- ❑3, ca. 1996 ... 2.75
- ❑4, ca. 1996 ... 2.75
- ❑Book 1; Kartoon Kollection; collects first three issues ... 7.95

APE CITY
Adventure
- ❑1; Planet of the Apes story ... 2.50
- ❑2; Planet of the Apes story ... 2.50
- ❑3; Planet of the Apes story ... 2.50
- ❑4; Planet of the Apes story ... 2.50

APE NATION
Adventure
- ❑1, Feb 1991, Alien Nation/Planet of Apes crossover ... 2.50
- ❑1/Ltd., limited edition; Alien Nation/Planet of the Apes crossover ... 4.00
- ❑2, Apr 1991; Alien Nation/Planet of the Apes crossover ... 2.00

N-MINT

- ❑3, May 1991; Alien Nation/Planet of the Apes crossover ... 2.00
- ❑4, Jun 1991; Alien Nation/Planet of the Apes crossover ... 2.00

APEX
Aztec
- ❑1, b&w ... 2.00

APEX PROJECT
Stellar
- ❑1 ... 1.00
- ❑2 ... 1.00

APHRODISIA
Fantagraphics / Eros
- ❑1 ... 2.95
- ❑2, Mar 1995 ... 2.95

APHRODITE IX
Image
- ❑0, Mar 2001; Posterior shot on cover 2.00
- ❑0/2nd, Oct 2001 ... 5.95
- ❑0/A, May 2001; Wizard Gold Foil Edition ... 9.00
- ❑0/B, May 2001; Wizard Blue Foil Edition ... 9.00
- ❑0/C, Mar 2001; Green foil behind logo 4.00
- ❑0/D, Mar 2001; Dynamic Forces Gold foil behind title ... 4.00
- ❑0/E, Mar 2001; Identical cover to #0; Limited to 250 ... 4.00
- ❑0/F, Mar 2001; Limited to 50 ... 4.00
- ❑1/A, Sep 2000; Aphrodite reclining against left edge of cover, gun up ... 4.00
- ❑1/B, Sep 2000; Aphrodite walking on metallic planks ... 2.50
- ❑1/C, Sep 2000; Red background, Aphrodite shooting on cover ... 2.50
- ❑1/D, Sep 2000; Green background, standing with guns up ... 2.50
- ❑1/E, Sep 2000; Tower records exclusive ... 5.00
- ❑1/F, Sep 2000; Tower records exclusive w/foil ... 5.00
- ❑1/G, Sep 2000; Wizard World exclusive ... 4.00
- ❑1/H, Sep 2000; Wizard World exclusive w/foil ... 4.00
- ❑1/I, Sep 2000; Chrome edition of 3,000; Dynamic Forces exclusive ... 5.00
- ❑2, Mar 2001 ... 2.00
- ❑2/A, Mar 2001; Graham Crackers comics exclusive ... 2.50
- ❑2/B, Mar 2001; Blue Foil behind title; connects to Dynamic Forces Exclusive; Graham Crackers Comics/Midwest Comics Co. Exclusive ... 2.50
- ❑2/C, Mar 2001; connects to Dynamic Forces Exclusive; Graham Crackers Comics/Midwest Comics Co. Exclusive; Green Foil behind title ... 2.50
- ❑2/D, Mar 2001; Several characters in profile on cover; connects to Graham Crackers Comics/Midwest Comics Co. Exclusive; Dynamic Forces Exclusive ... 2.50
- ❑2/E, Mar 2001; connects to Graham Crackers Comics/Midwest Comics Co. Exclusive; Dynamic Forces Exclusive ... 2.50

Other grades: Multiply price above by 5/6 for VF/NM • 2/3 for VERY FINE • 1/3 for FINE • 1/5 for VERY GOOD • 1/8 for GOOD

❑2/F, Mar 2001; connects to Graham Crackers Comics/Midwest Comics Co. Exclusive; Dynamic Forces Exclusive 2.50
❑2/G, Mar 2001; Blue Foil behind title; connects to Graham Crackers Comics/ Midwest Comics Co. Exclusive; Exclusive/Wizard World Authentic...... 2.50
❑2/H, Mar 2001; Blue Foil behind title; connects to Graham Crackers Comics/Midwest Comics Co. Exclusive; Dynamic Forces Exclusive/Wizard Authentic 2.50
❑2/I, Mar 2001; connects to Graham Crackers Comics/Midwest Comics Co. Exclusive; Dynamic Forces Exclusive; Green Foil behind title..... 2.50
❑2/J, Mar 2001; connects to Graham Crackers Comics/Midwest Comics Co. Exclusive; Dynamic Forces Exclusive; Green Foil behind title..... 2.50
❑2/K, Mar 2001; connects to Graham Crackers Comics/Midwest Comics Co. Exclusive; Dynamic Forces Exclusive 2.50
❑3, Dec 2001 .... 2.00
❑4, Mar 2002; Double-size 4.00
❑4/A, Mar 2002; sketch cover; Published/solicited by Jay Company Comics 4.95
❑Ashcan 1, Dec 2000; Convention Preview 6.00
❑Ashcan 1/Ltd., Dec 2000; Original color sketch and signature by Clarence Lansang; Solicited by Jay Company Comics 5.00

APOCALYPSE
APOCALYPSE

❑1 .... 3.95
❑2 .... 3.95
❑3 .... 3.95
❑4 .... 3.95
❑5 .... 3.95
❑6 .... 3.95
❑7; Makabre 3.95

APOCALYPSE NERD
DARK HORSE

❑1, 2005 .... 2.99
❑2 ....
❑3, Jul 2006 ....

APOLLO SMILE
MIXX

❑1, Jul 1998 .... 3.50
❑2, Sep 1998 .... 3.00

APPARITION
CALIBER

❑1 1996 .... 2.95
❑2 1996 .... 2.95
❑3 1996 .... 2.95
❑4 1996 .... 2.95
❑5 1996 .... 2.95

APPARITION, THE: ABANDONED
CALIBER

❑1 1995; prestige format 3.95

APPARITION, THE: VISITATIONS
CALIBER

❑1, Aug 1995 .... 3.95

APPLE, P.I.
PARROT COMMUNICATIONS

❑1, Sep 1996; pronounced "Apple Pie" 1.00

APPLESEED BOOK 1
ECLIPSE

❑1, Sep 1988 .... 7.00
❑2, Oct 1988 .... 5.00
❑3, Nov 1988, Squarebound 5.00
❑4, Jan 1989 .... 4.00
❑5, Feb 1989 .... 4.00
❑Book 1, Book One: The Promethean Challenge; Collects Appleseed Book 1 #1-5 .... 12.95
❑Book 1/2nd, Collects Appleseed Book 1 #1-5 .... 14.95

APPLESEED BOOK 2
ECLIPSE

❑1, Feb 1989 .... 5.00
❑2, Mar 1989 .... 4.00
❑3, Apr 1989 .... 3.50
❑4, May 1989 .... 3.50
❑5, Jun 1989 .... 3.50

APPLESEED BOOK 3
ECLIPSE

❑1, Aug 1989; Squarebound 4.00
❑2, Sep 1989 .... 3.50
❑3, Oct 1989 .... 3.50
❑4, Nov 1989 .... 3.50
❑5, Dec 1989 .... 3.50

APPLESEED BOOK 4
ECLIPSE

❑1, Jan 1991 .... 3.50
❑2, Mar 1991 .... 3.50
❑3, May 1991 .... 3.50
❑4, Aug 1991 .... 3.50

APPLESEED DATABOOK
DARK HORSE

❑1, Apr 1994 .... 3.50
❑2, May 1994; Flip-book; Squarebound 3.50

APRIL HORRORS
RIP OFF

❑1, Sep 1993, b&w 2.95

AQUABLUE
DARK HORSE

❑1, Nov 1989 .... 6.95

AQUABLUE: THE BLUE PLANET
DARK HORSE

❑1, Aug 1990 .... 8.95

AQUA KNIGHT
VIZ

❑1, ca. 2000 .... 2.95
❑2, ca. 2000 .... 3.50
❑3, ca. 2000 .... 3.50
❑4, ca. 2000 .... 3.50
❑5, ca. 2000 .... 3.50
❑6, ca. 2000 .... 3.50

AQUA KNIGHT PART 2
VIZ

❑1, Oct 2000 .... 3.50
❑2, Nov 2000 .... 3.50
❑3, Dec 2000 .... 3.50
❑4, Jan 2001 .... 3.50
❑5, Feb 2001 .... 3.50

AQUA KNIGHT PART 3
VIZ

❑1, ca. 2001 .... 3.50
❑2, ca. 2001 .... 3.50
❑3, ca. 2001 .... 3.50
❑4, ca. 2001 .... 3.50
❑5, ca. 2001 .... 3.50

AQUAMAN (1ST SERIES)
DC

❑1, Feb 1962, 1: Quisp 900.00
❑2, Apr 1962 .... 275.00
❑3, Jun 1962 .... 150.00
❑4, Aug 1962 .... 150.00
❑5, Oct 1962 .... 150.00
❑6, Dec 1962 .... 90.00
❑7, Feb 1963 .... 90.00
❑8, Apr 1963 .... 90.00
❑9, Jun 1963 .... 90.00
❑10, Aug 1963 .... 90.00
❑11, Oct 1963, 1: Mera 125.00
❑12, Dec 1963 .... 75.00
❑13, Feb 1964 .... 75.00
❑14, Apr 1964 .... 75.00
❑15, Jun 1964 .... 75.00
❑16, Aug 1964 .... 75.00
❑17, Oct 1964 .... 75.00
❑18, Dec 1964, A: Justice League of America. Aquaman marries Mera ... 90.00
❑19, Feb 1965 .... 60.00
❑20, Apr 1965 .... 60.00
❑21, Jun 1965, 1: Fisherman 60.00
❑22, Aug 1965 .... 60.00
❑23, Oct 1965, Birth of Aquababy 60.00
❑24, Dec 1965 .... 60.00
❑25, Feb 1966 .... 60.00
❑26, Apr 1966 .... 60.00
❑27, Jun 1966 .... 60.00
❑28, Aug 1966 .... 60.00
❑29, Oct 1966, 1: Ocean Master 75.00
❑30, Dec 1966 .... 50.00
❑31, Feb 1967 .... 45.00
❑32, Apr 1967 .... 50.00
❑33, Jun 1967, 1: Aqua-Girl 45.00
❑34, Aug 1967 .... 45.00
❑35, Oct 1967, 1: Black Manta 40.00
❑36, Dec 1967 .... 40.00
❑37, Feb 1968 .... 40.00
❑38, Apr 1968 .... 40.00
❑39, Jun 1968 .... 40.00
❑40, Aug 1968 .... 40.00
❑41, Oct 1968 .... 40.00
❑42, Dec 1968 .... 30.00
❑43, Feb 1969 .... 30.00
❑44, Apr 1969 .... 25.00
❑45, Jun 1969 .... 25.00
❑46, Aug 1969 .... 25.00
❑47, Oct 1969 .... 25.00
❑48, Dec 1969, JA (a); O: Aquaman ... 25.00
❑49, Feb 1970, JA (a) 25.00
❑50, Apr 1970, NA (a); A: Deadman ... 75.00
❑51, Jun 1970, NA (a); A: Deadman ... 50.00
❑52, Aug 1970, NA (a); A: Deadman .. 40.00
❑53, Oct 1970, JA (a) 20.00
❑54, Dec 1970, JA (a) 20.00
❑55, Feb 1971, JA (a) 20.00
❑56, Apr 1971, JA (a); O: Crusader. 1: Crusader 20.00
❑57, Aug 1977, JA (a) 20.00
❑58, Oct 1977, JA (a); O: Aquaman.... 20.00
❑59, Dec 1977 .... 10.00
❑60, Feb 1978 .... 10.00
❑61, Apr 1978 .... 10.00
❑62, Jun 1978 .... 10.00
❑63, Sep 1978 .... 10.00

AQUAMAN (2ND SERIES)
DC

❑1, Feb 1986; New costume 3.00
❑2, Mar 1986 .... 3.00
❑3, Apr 1986 .... 3.00
❑4, May 1986 .... 3.00
❑Special 1, Jun 1988 .... 2.00

AQUAMAN (3RD SERIES)
DC

❑1, Jun 1989 .... 1.00
❑2, Jul 1989 .... 1.00
❑3, Aug 1989 .... 1.00
❑4, Sep 1989 .... 1.00
❑5, Oct 1989 .... 1.00
❑Special 1, Apr 1989; Legend of Aquaman 2.00

AQUAMAN (4TH SERIES)
DC

❑1, Dec 1991 .... 1.50
❑2, Jan 1992 .... 1.00
❑3, Feb 1992 .... 1.00
❑4, Mar 1992 .... 1.00
❑5, Apr 1992 .... 1.00
❑6, May 1992 .... 1.25
❑7, Jun 1992 .... 1.25
❑8, Jul 1992 A: Batman. V: Nicodemus 1.25
❑9, Aug 1992 .... 1.25
❑10, Sep 1992 .... 1.25
❑11, Oct 1992 .... 1.25
❑12, Nov 1992 .... 1.25
❑13, Dec 1992 A: Scavanger. A: Scavenger 1.25

AQUAMAN (5TH SERIES)
DC

❑0, Oct 1994; PD (w); Aquaman gets harpoon for arm 3.00
❑1, Aug 1994 PD (w) 3.00
❑2, Sep 1994; PD (w); V: Charybdis. Aquaman loses hand 3.00
❑3, Nov 1994 PD (w); V: Superboy 2.00
❑4, Dec 1994 PD (w); A: Lobo. V: Lobo 2.00
❑5, Jan 1995 PD (w) 2.00
❑6, Feb 1995 PD (w) 1.50
❑7, Mar 1995 PD (w) 1.50
❑8, Apr 1995 PD (w) 1.50
❑9, Jun 1995 PD (w) 1.75
❑10, Jul 1995 PD (w) 1.75
❑11, Aug 1995 PD (w) 1.75
❑12, Sep 1995; PD (w); Mera returns. 1.75
❑13, Oct 1995 PD (w) 1.75
❑14, Nov 1995; PD (w); "Underworld Unleashed" 1.75
❑15, Dec 1995 PD (w) 1.75
❑16, Jan 1996 PD (w); V: Justice League 1.75
❑17, Feb 1996 PD (w) 1.75

Ape Nation

Alien Nation meets Planet of the Apes. Really!
©Adventure

Aphrodite IX

Green-haired killer questions her own existence
©Image

Aquaman (1st Series)

First attempt at a regular Aquaman series
©DC

Aquaman (5th Series)

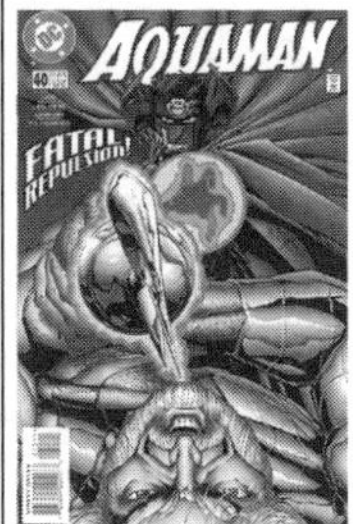

Fifth fishman try, this time from Peter David
©DC

Aquaman: Time and Tide

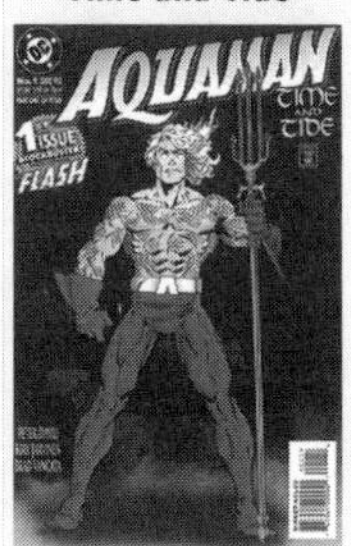

Peter David at his humorous best
©DC

N-MINT

❑18, Mar 1996 PD (w); O: Dolphin 1.75
❑19, Apr 1996; PD (w); Aqualad returns 1.75
❑20, May 1996 PD (w) 1.75
❑21, Jun 1996 PD (w) 1.75
❑22, Jul 1996 PD (w) 1.75
❑23, Aug 1996 PD (w); A: Sea Devils, Power Girl, Tsunami, Arion 1.75
❑24, Sep 1996 PD (w) 1.75
❑25, Oct 1996 PD (w) 1.75
❑26, Nov 1996; PD (w); "Final Night". 1.75
❑27, Dec 1996; PD (w); Aquaman declares war on Japan 1.75
❑28, Jan 1997 PD (w); A: Martian Manhunter 1.75
❑29, Feb 1997 PD (w); V: Black Manta 1.75
❑30, Mar 1997 PD (w) 1.75
❑31, Apr 1997 PD (w) 1.75
❑32, May 1997 PD (w); A: Swamp Thing 1.75
❑33, Jun 1997 PD (w) 1.75
❑34, Jul 1997 PD (w); V: Triton 1.75
❑35, Aug 1997; PD (w); A: Animal Man. V: Gamesman. Aquaman blind 1.75
❑36, Sep 1997 PD (w) 1.75
❑37, Oct 1997; PD (w); V: Parademons. "Genesis" 1.75
❑38, Nov 1997; PD (w); Poseidonis becomes a tourist attraction 1.75
❑39, Dec 1997; PD (w); A: Neptune Perkins. Face cover 2.00
❑40, Jan 1998 PD (w); V: Doctor Polaris 2.00
❑41, Feb 1998 PD (w); A: Maxima 2.00
❑42, Mar 1998 PD (w); V: Sea Wolf 2.00
❑43, Apr 1998; "Millennium Giants" ... 2.00
❑44, May 1998 A: Golden Age Flash. A: Sentinel 2.00
❑45, Jun 1998; Destruction of Poseidonis 2.00
❑46, Jul 1998 ..... 2.00
❑47, Aug 1998 ..... 2.00
❑48, Sep 1998 ..... 2.00
❑49, Oct 1998 ..... 2.00
❑50, Dec 1998 EL (c); EL (a) 2.00
❑51, Jan 1999 EL (c); EL (w); EL (a); A: King Noble 2.00
❑52, Feb 1999 EL (w); BSz, EL, JA (a); A: Fire Trolls. A: Mera. A: Lava Lord. A: Noble 2.00
❑53, Mar 1999 EL (w); EL (a); A: Superman. A: Shrapnel 2.00
❑54, Apr 1999 EL (w); EL (a); A: Sheeva the Mermaid. A: Shiva the Mermaid. A: Landlovers. A: Blubber. A: Lagoon Boy 2.00
❑55, May 1999 EL (w); EL (a) 2.00
❑56, Jun 1999 EL (w); EL (a) 2.00
❑57, Jul 1999 EL (w); EL (a) 2.00
❑58, Aug 1999 EL (w); EL (a) 2.00
❑59, Sep 1999 EL (w); EL (a) 2.00
❑60, Oct 1999; EL (w); EL (a); Wedding of Tempest and Dolphin 2.00
❑61, Nov 1999 ..... 2.00
❑62, Dec 1999 EL (w) 2.00
❑63, Jan 2000 ..... 2.00
❑64, Feb 2000 ..... 2.00
❑65, Mar 2000 ..... 2.00
❑66, Apr 2000 ..... 2.00
❑67, May 2000 ..... 2.00
❑68, Jun 2000 ..... 2.00
❑69, Jul 2000 ..... 2.00
❑70, Aug 2000; Cover incorrectly credits Raimondi and Rapmund 2.00
❑71, Sep 2000 A: Warlord 2.50
❑72, Oct 2000 ..... 2.50
❑73, Nov 2000 ..... 2.50
❑74, Dec 2000 ..... 2.50
❑75, Jan 2001 ..... 2.50
❑1000000, Nov 1998 ..... 2.00
❑Annual 1, ca. 1995 A: Superman,. A: Wonder Woman, Superman,. A: Wonder Woman 3.50
❑Annual 2, ca. 1996; Legends of the Dead Earth 2.95
❑Annual 3, Jul 1997; Pulp Heroes 3.95
❑Annual 4, Sep 1998; Ghosts 2.95
❑Annual 5, Sep 1999; JLApe 2.95

AQUAMAN (6TH SERIES)
DC

❑1, Feb 2003, Aquaman receives water hand 2.50
❑2, Mar 2003 ..... 2.50
❑3, Apr 2003 ..... 2.50
❑4, May 2003 ..... 2.50
❑5, Jun 2003 ..... 2.50
❑6, Jul 2003 ..... 2.50
❑7, Aug 2003 ..... 2.50
❑8, Sep 2003 ..... 2.50
❑9, Oct 2003 ..... 2.50
❑10, Nov 2003 ..... 2.50
❑11, Dec 2003 ..... 2.50
❑12, Jan 2004 ..... 2.50
❑13, Feb 2004 ..... 2.50
❑14, Mar 2004 ..... 2.50
❑15, Apr 2004 ..... 12.00
❑16, May 2004 ..... 6.00
❑17, Jun 2004 ..... 6.00
❑18, Jul 2004 ..... 2.50
❑19, Aug 2004 ..... 2.50
❑20, Jul 2004 ..... 2.50
❑21, Oct 2004 ..... 2.50
❑22, Nov 2004 ..... 2.50
❑23, Dec 2004 ..... 2.50
❑24, Jan 2005 ..... 2.50
❑25, Feb 2005 ..... 2.50
❑26, Mar 2005 ..... 2.50
❑27, Apr 2005 ..... 2.50
❑28, May 2005 ..... 2.50
❑29, May 2005 ..... 2.50
❑30, Jun 2005 ..... 2.50
❑31, Jul 2005 ..... 2.50
❑32, Aug 2005 ..... 2.50
❑33, Sep 2005 ..... 2.50
❑34, Oct 2005 ..... 2.99
❑35, Nov 2005 ..... 2.99
❑36, Jan 2006 ..... 2.99
❑37, Feb 2006 ..... 2.99
❑38, Mar 2006 ..... 2.99
❑39, Mar 2006 ..... 2.99
❑40, May 2006, Following the jump-year, this title's name switches to Aquaman: Sword of Atlantis with this issue 2.99
❑41, Jun 2006 ..... 2.99

AQUAMAN SECRET FILES
DC

❑1, Dec 1998 ..... 4.95
❑2, Mar 2003 ..... 4.95

AQUAMAN: TIME AND TIDE
DC

❑1, Dec 1993 PD (w); O: Aquaman 2.00
❑2, Jan 1994 PD (w) 2.00
❑3, Feb 1994 PD (w) 2.00
❑4, Mar 1994 PD (w); O: Ocean Master 2.00

AQUARIUM
CPM MANGA

❑1/A, Apr 2000, b&w; wraparound cover 2.95
❑1/B, Apr 2000, b&w; alternate wraparound cover 2.95
❑2, ca. 2000, b&w 2.95
❑3, ca. 2000, b&w 2.95
❑4, ca. 2000, b&w 2.95
❑5, ca. 2000, b&w 2.95
❑6, ca. 2000, b&w 2.95

ARABIAN NIGHTS ON THE WORLD OF MAGIC: THE GATHERING
ACCLAIM / ARMADA

❑1, Dec 1995 ..... 2.50
❑2 ..... 2.50

ARACHNOPHOBIA
DISNEY

❑1 ..... 2.95

ARAGONÉS 3-D
3-D ZONE

❑1; paperback 4.95

ARAKNIS
MUSHROOM

❑0, Apr 1996; Published by Mystic 2.50
❑1, May 1995 ..... 2.50
❑2, ca. 1996 ..... 2.50
❑3, ca. 1996 ..... 2.50
❑4, ca. 1996 ..... 2.50
❑5, ca. 1996 ..... 2.50
❑6, ca. 1996 ..... 2.50

ARAK SON OF THUNDER
DC

❑1, Sep 1981, O: Arak. 1: Angelica 1.00
❑2, Oct 1981, 1: Malagigi 1.00
❑3, Nov 1981, 1: Valda 1.00
❑4, Dec 1981 ..... 1.00
❑5, Jan 1982 ..... 1.00
❑6, Feb 1982 ..... 1.00
❑7, Mar 1982 ..... 1.00
❑8, Apr 1982 ..... 1.00
❑9, May 1982 ..... 1.00
❑10, Jun 1982 ..... 1.00
❑11, Jul 1982 ..... 1.00
❑12, Aug 1982 ..... 1.00
❑13, Sep 1982 ..... 1.00
❑14, Oct 1982 ..... 1.00
❑15, Nov 1982 ..... 1.00
❑16, Dec 1982 ..... 1.00
❑17, Jan 1983 ..... 1.00
❑18, Feb 1983 ..... 1.00
❑19, Mar 1983 ..... 1.00
❑20, Apr 1983, O: Angelica 1.00

N-MINT

- ❑21, May 1983 ... 1.00
- ❑22, Jun 1983 ... 1.00
- ❑23, Jul 1983 ... 1.00
- ❑24, Aug 1983 ... 1.00
- ❑25, Sep 1983 ... 1.00
- ❑26, Oct 1983 ... 1.00
- ❑27, Nov 1983 ... 1.00
- ❑28, Dec 1983 ... 1.00
- ❑29, Jan 1984 ... 1.00
- ❑30, Feb 1984 ... 1.00
- ❑31, Mar 1984 ... 1.00
- ❑32, Apr 1984 ... 1.00
- ❑33, May 1984 ... 1.00
- ❑34, Jun 1984 ... 1.00
- ❑35, Jul 1984 ... 1.00
- ❑36, Aug 1984 ... 1.00
- ❑37, Sep 1984 ... 1.00
- ❑38, Nov 1984 ... 1.00
- ❑39, Dec 1984 ... 1.00
- ❑40, Jan 1985 ... 1.00
- ❑41, Feb 1985 ... 1.00
- ❑42, Mar 1985 ... 1.00
- ❑43, Apr 1985 ... 1.00
- ❑44, May 1985 ... 1.00
- ❑45, Jun 1985 ... 1.00
- ❑46, Jul 1985 ... 1.00
- ❑47, Aug 1985 ... 1.00
- ❑48, Sep 1985 ... 1.00
- ❑49, Oct 1985 ... 1.00
- ❑50, Nov 1985; Giant-size ... 1.00
- ❑Annual 1 ... 2.00

ARAMIS
Comics Interview

- ❑1 ... 1.95
- ❑2 ... 1.95
- ❑3 ... 1.95

ARANA: HEART OF THE SPIDER
Marvel

- ❑1, Mar 2005 ... 4.00
- ❑1/Incentive, Mar 2005 ... 10.00
- ❑2, Apr 2005 ... 2.99
- ❑3, May 2005 ... 2.99
- ❑4, Jun 2005 ... 2.99
- ❑5, Jul 2005 ... 2.99
- ❑6, Aug 2005 ... 2.99
- ❑7, Sep 2005 ... 2.99
- ❑8, Oct 2005 ... 2.99
- ❑9 2005 ... 2.99
- ❑10, Dec 2005 ... 2.99
- ❑11, Jan 2006 ... 2.99
- ❑12, Feb 2006 ... 2.99

ARC (VOL. 2)
Arts Industria

- ❑1, Apr 1994 ... 2.95

ARCADE
Print Mint

- ❑1, Mar 1975 ... 10.00
- ❑2, Jun 1975 ... 8.00
- ❑3, Sep 1975 ... 8.00
- ❑4 1976 ... 7.00
- ❑5 1976 ... 7.00
- ❑6, Jun 1976 ... 7.00
- ❑7 1976 ... 5.00

ARCANA
DC / Vertigo

- ❑Annual 1, ca. 1994; "Children's Crusade" ... 4.00

ARCANA
Tokyopop

- ❑1, Jun 2005 ... 9.95
- ❑2, Sep 2005 ... 9.95
- ❑3, Dec 2005 ... 9.95

ARCANA (WELLS & CLARK)
Wells & Clark

- ❑1 1995 ... 3.00
- ❑2, Mar 1995 ... 3.00
- ❑3, May 1995 ... 3.00
- ❑4, Jul 1995 ... 2.25
- ❑5, Sep 1995 ... 2.25
- ❑6 1995 ... 2.25
- ❑7 1996 ... 2.25
- ❑8, Jul 1996 ... 2.25
- ❑9, Sep 1996 ... 2.25
- ❑10 1996 ... 2.25

N-MINT

ARCANE
Arcane

- ❑1 ... 2.00
- ❑2; Fly in My Eye ... 9.95

ARCANE (2ND SERIES)
Graphik

- ❑1, b&w ... 1.25

ARCANUM
Image

- ❑½, Dec 1997 ... 3.00
- ❑½/Gold, Dec 1997 ... 5.00
- ❑1, Apr 1997 ... 2.50
- ❑1/A, Apr 1997; variant cover ... 2.50
- ❑2, May 1997 ... 2.50
- ❑2/A, May 1997; variant cover ... 2.50
- ❑3, Jun 1997 ... 2.50
- ❑3/A, Jun 1997; variant cover ... 2.50
- ❑4, Jul 1997 ... 2.50
- ❑4/A, Jul 1997; variant cover ... 2.50
- ❑5, Sep 1997 ... 2.95
- ❑6, Nov 1997 ... 2.95
- ❑7, Jan 1998 ... 2.95
- ❑8, Feb 1998 ... 2.95

ARCHAIC
Fenickx Productions

- ❑1, ca. 2003, b&w ... 2.95
- ❑2, ca. 2003, b&w ... 2.95
- ❑3, ca. 2003, b&w ... 2.95
- ❑4, ca. 2003, b&w ... 2.95
- ❑5, ca. 2003, b&w ... 2.95

ARCHANGEL
Marvel

- ❑1, Feb 1996, b&w; wraparound cover 2.50

ARCHANGELS: THE SAGA
Eternal

- ❑1 1996 ... 2.50
- ❑1/2nd 1996 ... 2.50
- ❑2 1996 ... 2.50
- ❑3, Aug 1996 ... 2.50
- ❑4 1996 ... 2.50
- ❑5 1996 ... 2.50
- ❑6 1996 ... 2.50
- ❑7 1996 ... 2.50
- ❑8 1996 ... 2.50

ARCHARD'S AGENTS
CrossGen

- ❑1, Jan 2003 ... 2.95

ARCHENEMIES
Dark Horse

- ❑1, May 2006 ... 2.95
- ❑2, Jun 2006 ... 2.95
- ❑3, Jul 2006 ... 2.95

ARCHER & ARMSTRONG
Valiant

- ❑0, Jul 1992 BL (w); O: Archer & Armstrong ... 4.00
- ❑0/Gold, Jul 1992; Gold edition BL (w); O: Archer & Armstrong ... 25.00
- ❑1, Aug 1992; FM (c); FM (a); Unity .. 4.00
- ❑2, Sep 1992; Unity ... 3.00
- ❑3, Oct 1992 ... 2.00
- ❑4, Nov 1992 ... 2.00
- ❑5, Dec 1992 ... 2.00
- ❑6, Jan 1993 ... 2.00
- ❑7, Feb 1993 ... 2.00
- ❑8, Mar 1993; Double-sized: is also "Eternal Warrior #8"; 1: Timewalker (Ivar). Flip-book with Eternal Warrior #8 ... 3.00
- ❑9, Apr 1993 BL (w); 1: Mademoiselle Noir ... 2.00
- ❑10, May 1993 ... 1.00
- ❑11, Jun 1993 A: Solar ... 1.00
- ❑12, Jul 1993 ... 1.00
- ❑13, Aug 1993 ... 1.00
- ❑14, Sep 1993 ... 1.00
- ❑15, Oct 1993 ... 1.00
- ❑16, Nov 1993 ... 1.00
- ❑17, Dec 1993 ... 1.00
- ❑18, Jan 1994 ... 1.00
- ❑19, Feb 1994 ... 1.00
- ❑20, Mar 1994 ... 1.00
- ❑21, Apr 1994 A: Shadowman ... 1.00
- ❑22, May 1994; trading card ... 2.00
- ❑23, Jun 1994 ... 1.00

N-MINT

- ❑24, Aug 1994 ... 1.00
- ❑25, Sep 1994 A: Eternal Warrior ... 1.00
- ❑26, Oct 1994; Flip-book with Eternal Warrior #26; indicia says August ... 5.00

ARCHIE
Archie

- ❑83, Nov 1956 ... 44.00
- ❑84, Jan 1957 ... 44.00
- ❑85, Mar 1957 ... 44.00
- ❑86, May 1957 ... 44.00
- ❑87, Jul 1957 ... 44.00
- ❑88, Sep 1957 ... 44.00
- ❑89, Nov 1957 ... 44.00
- ❑90, Jan 1958 ... 44.00
- ❑91, Mar 1958 ... 34.00
- ❑92, May 1958 ... 34.00
- ❑93, Jul 1958 ... 34.00
- ❑94, Sep 1958 ... 34.00
- ❑95, Oct 1958 ... 34.00
- ❑96, Nov 1958 ... 34.00
- ❑97, Dec 1958 ... 34.00
- ❑98, Feb 1959 ... 34.00
- ❑99, Mar 1959 ... 34.00
- ❑100, Apr 1959 ... 55.00
- ❑101, Jun 1959 ... 22.00
- ❑102, Jul 1959 ... 22.00
- ❑103, Aug 1959 ... 22.00
- ❑104, Sep 1959 ... 22.00
- ❑105, Nov 1959 ... 22.00
- ❑106, Dec 1959 ... 22.00
- ❑107, Feb 1960 ... 22.00
- ❑108, Mar 1960 ... 22.00
- ❑109, Apr 1960 ... 22.00
- ❑110, Jun 1960 ... 22.00
- ❑111, Jul 1960 ... 22.00
- ❑112, Aug 1960 ... 22.00
- ❑113, Sep 1960 ... 22.00
- ❑114, Nov 1960 ... 22.00
- ❑115, Dec 1960 ... 22.00
- ❑116, Feb 1961 ... 22.00
- ❑117, Mar 1961 ... 22.00
- ❑118, Apr 1961 ... 22.00
- ❑119, Jun 1961 ... 22.00
- ❑120, Jul 1961 ... 22.00
- ❑121, Aug 1961 ... 16.00
- ❑122, Sep 1961 ... 16.00
- ❑123, Nov 1961 ... 16.00
- ❑124, Dec 1961 ... 16.00
- ❑125, Feb 1962 ... 16.00
- ❑126, Mar 1962 ... 16.00
- ❑127, Apr 1962 ... 16.00
- ❑128, Jun 1962 ... 16.00
- ❑129, Jul 1962 ... 16.00
- ❑130, Aug 1962 ... 16.00
- ❑131, Sep 1962 ... 16.00
- ❑132, Nov 1962 ... 16.00
- ❑133, Dec 1962 ... 16.00
- ❑134, Feb 1963 ... 16.00
- ❑135, Mar 1963 ... 16.00
- ❑136, Apr 1963 ... 16.00
- ❑137, Jun 1963 ... 16.00
- ❑138, Jul 1963 ... 16.00
- ❑139, Aug 1963 ... 16.00
- ❑140, Sep 1963 ... 16.00
- ❑141, Nov 1963 ... 13.00
- ❑142, Dec 1963 ... 13.00
- ❑143, Feb 1964 ... 13.00
- ❑144, Mar 1964 ... 13.00
- ❑145, Apr 1964 ... 13.00
- ❑146, Jun 1964 ... 13.00
- ❑147, Jul 1964 ... 13.00
- ❑148, Aug 1964 ... 13.00
- ❑149, Sep 1964 ... 13.00
- ❑150, Nov 1964 ... 13.00
- ❑151, Dec 1964 ... 8.50
- ❑152, Feb 1965 ... 8.50
- ❑153, Mar 1965 ... 8.50
- ❑154, Apr 1965 ... 8.50
- ❑155, Jun 1965 ... 8.50
- ❑156, Jul 1965 ... 8.50
- ❑157, Aug 1965 ... 8.50
- ❑158, Sep 1965 ... 8.50
- ❑159, Nov 1965 ... 8.50
- ❑160, Dec 1965 ... 8.50
- ❑161, Feb 1966 ... 8.50
- ❑162, Mar 1966 ... 8.50

Arabian Nights on the World of Magic: The Gathering

Game adaptation with ungainly title

©Acclaim

Arak Son of Thunder

Viking sword-and-sorcery tales from DC

©DC

Arcana

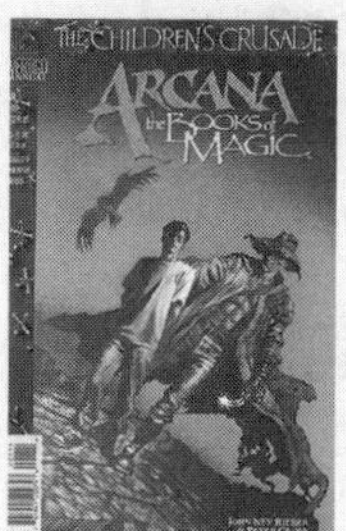

Part of the "Children's Crusade" story arc

©DC

Arcana (Wells & Clark)

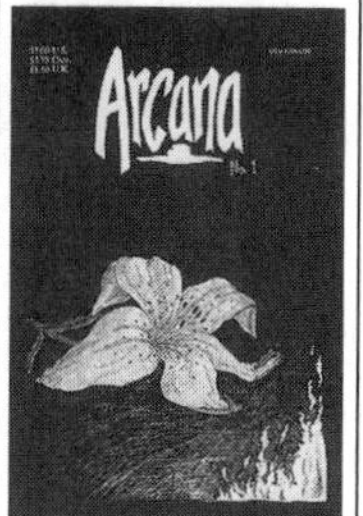

Independent series with magical medieval feel

©Wells & Clark

Arcanum

Short-lived series in the world of Witchblade

©Image

	N-MINT
❑163, Apr 1966	8.50
❑164, Jun 1966	8.50
❑165, Jul 1966	8.50
❑166, Aug 1966	8.50
❑167, Sep 1966	8.50
❑168, Nov 1966	8.50
❑169, Dec 1966	8.50
❑170, Feb 1967	8.50
❑171, Mar 1967	8.50
❑172, Apr 1967	8.50
❑173, Jun 1967	8.50
❑174, Jul 1967	8.50
❑175, Aug 1967	8.50
❑176, Sep 1967	8.50
❑177, Nov 1967	8.50
❑178, Dec 1967	8.50
❑179, Feb 1968	8.50
❑180, Mar 1968	8.50
❑181, Apr 1968	5.00
❑182, Jun 1968	5.00
❑183, Jul 1968	5.00
❑184, Aug 1968	5.00
❑185, Sep 1968	5.00
❑186, Nov 1968	5.00
❑187, Dec 1968	5.00
❑188, Feb 1969	5.00
❑189, Mar 1969	5.00
❑190, Apr 1969	5.00
❑191, Jun 1969	5.00
❑192, Jul 1969	5.00
❑193, Aug 1969	5.00
❑194, Sep 1969	5.00
❑195, Nov 1969	5.00
❑196, Dec 1969	5.00
❑197, Feb 1970	5.00
❑198, Mar 1970	5.00
❑199, Apr 1970	5.00
❑200, Jun 1970	5.00
❑201, Jul 1970	3.00
❑202, Aug 1970	3.00
❑203, Sep 1970	3.00
❑204, Nov 1970	3.00
❑205, Dec 1970	3.00
❑206, Feb 1971	3.00
❑207, Mar 1971	3.00
❑208, May 1971	3.00
❑209, Jun 1971	3.00
❑210, Jul 1971	3.00
❑211, Aug 1971	3.00
❑212, Sep 1971	3.00
❑213, Nov 1971	3.00
❑214, Dec 1971	3.00
❑215, Feb 1972	3.00
❑216, Mar 1972	3.00
❑217, Apr 1972	3.00
❑218, Jun 1972	3.00
❑219, Jul 1972	3.00
❑220, Aug 1972	3.00
❑221, Sep 1972	3.00
❑222, Nov 1972	3.00
❑223, Dec 1972	3.00
❑224, Feb 1973	3.00
❑225, Apr 1973	3.00
❑226, Jun 1973	3.00

	N-MINT
❑227, Jul 1973	3.00
❑228, Aug 1973	3.00
❑229, Sep 1973	3.00
❑230, Nov 1973	3.00
❑231, Dec 1973	3.00
❑232, Feb 1974	3.00
❑233, Mar 1974	3.00
❑234, Apr 1974	3.00
❑235, Jun 1974	3.00
❑236, Jul 1974	3.00
❑237, Aug 1974	3.00
❑238, Sep 1974	3.00
❑239, Nov 1974	3.00
❑240, Dec 1974	3.00
❑241, Feb 1975	3.00
❑242, Mar 1975	3.00
❑243, Apr 1975	3.00
❑244, Jun 1975	3.00
❑245, Jul 1975	3.00
❑246, Aug 1975	3.00
❑247, Sep 1975	3.00
❑248, Nov 1975	3.00
❑249, Dec 1975	3.00
❑250, Feb 1976	3.00
❑251, Mar 1976	2.00
❑252, Apr 1976	2.00
❑253, Jun 1976	2.00
❑254, Jul 1976	2.00
❑255, Aug 1976	2.00
❑256, Sep 1976	2.00
❑257, Nov 1976	2.00
❑258, Dec 1976	2.00
❑259, Feb 1977	2.00
❑260, Mar 1977	2.00
❑261, Apr 1977	2.00
❑262, Jun 1977	2.00
❑263, Jul 1977	2.00
❑264, Aug 1977	2.00
❑265, Sep 1977	2.00
❑266, Nov 1977	2.00
❑267, Dec 1977	2.00
❑268, Feb 1978	2.00
❑269, Mar 1978	2.00
❑270, Apr 1978	2.00
❑271, Jun 1978	2.00
❑272, Jul 1978	2.00
❑273, Aug 1978	2.00
❑274, Sep 1978	2.00
❑275, Nov 1978	2.00
❑276, Dec 1978	2.00
❑277, Feb 1979	2.00
❑278, Mar 1979	2.00
❑279, Apr 1979	2.00
❑280, May 1979	2.00
❑281, Jun 1979	2.00
❑282, Jul 1979	2.00
❑283, Aug 1979	2.00
❑284, Sep 1979	2.00
❑285, Oct 1979	2.00
❑286, Nov 1979	2.00
❑287, Dec 1979	2.00
❑288, Jan 1980	2.00
❑289, Feb 1980	2.00
❑290, Mar 1980	2.00

	N-MINT
❑291, Apr 1980	2.00
❑292, May 1980	2.00
❑293, Jun 1980	2.00
❑294, Jul 1980	2.00
❑295, Aug 1980	2.00
❑296, Sep 1980	2.00
❑297, Oct 1980	2.00
❑298, Nov 1980	2.00
❑299, Dec 1980	2.00
❑300, Jan 1981	2.00
❑301, Feb 1981	1.50
❑302, Mar 1981	1.50
❑303, Apr 1981	1.50
❑304, May 1981	1.50
❑305, Jun 1981	1.50
❑306, Jul 1981	1.50
❑307, Aug 1981	1.50
❑308, Sep 1981	1.50
❑309, Oct 1981	1.50
❑310, Nov 1981	1.50
❑311, Dec 1981	1.50
❑312, Jan 1982	1.50
❑313, Feb 1982	1.50
❑314, Mar 1982	1.50
❑315, Apr 1982	1.50
❑316, May 1982	1.50
❑317, Jun 1982	1.50
❑318, Jul 1982	1.50
❑319, Sep 1982	1.50
❑320, Nov 1982	1.50
❑321, Jan 1983	1.50
❑322, Mar 1983	1.50
❑323, May 1983	1.50
❑324, Jul 1983	1.50
❑325, Sep 1983	1.50
❑326, Nov 1983	1.50
❑327, Jan 1984	1.50
❑328, Mar 1984	1.50
❑329, May 1984	1.50
❑330, Jul 1984	1.50
❑331, Sep 1984	1.50
❑332, Nov 1984	1.50
❑333, Jan 1985	1.50
❑334, Mar 1985	1.50
❑335, May 1985	1.50
❑336, Jul 1985	1.50
❑337, Sep 1985	1.50
❑338, Nov 1985	1.50
❑339, Jan 1986	1.50
❑340, Mar 1986	1.50
❑341, May 1986	1.50
❑342, Jul 1986	1.50
❑343, Sep 1986	1.50
❑344, Nov 1986	1.50
❑345, Jan 1987	1.50
❑346, Mar 1987	1.50
❑347, May 1987	1.50
❑348, Jun 1987	1.50
❑349, Jul 1987	1.50
❑350, Aug 1987	1.50
❑351, Sep 1987	1.50
❑352, Oct 1987	1.50
❑353, Nov 1987	1.50
❑354, Jan 1988	1.50

Other grades: Multiply price above by 5/6 for VF/NM • 2/3 for VERY FINE • 1/3 for FINE • 1/5 for VERY GOOD • 1/8 for GOOD

	N-MINT
❑355, Mar 1988	1.50
❑356, May 1988	1.50
❑357, Jun 1988	1.50
❑358, Jul 1988	1.50
❑359, Aug 1988	1.50
❑360, Sep 1988	1.50
❑361, Oct 1988	1.50
❑362, Nov 1988	1.50
❑363, Jan 1989	1.50
❑364, Feb 1989	1.50
❑365, Mar 1989	1.50
❑366, Apr 1989	1.50
❑367, May 1989	1.50
❑368, Jul 1989	1.50
❑369, Aug 1993	1.50
❑370, Sep 1989	1.50
❑371, Oct 1989	1.50
❑372, Nov 1989	1.50
❑373, Jan 1990	1.50
❑374, Feb 1990	1.50
❑375, Mar 1990	1.50
❑376, Apr 1990	1.50
❑377, May 1990	1.50
❑378, Jul 1990	1.50
❑379, Aug 1990	1.50
❑380, Sep 1990	1.50
❑381, Oct 1990	1.50
❑382, Nov 1990	1.50
❑383, Dec 1990	1.50
❑384, Feb 1991	1.50
❑385, Mar 1991	1.50
❑386, Apr 1991	1.50
❑387, May 1991	1.50
❑388, Jun 1991	1.50
❑389, Jul 1991	1.50
❑390, Aug 1991	1.50
❑391, Sep 1991	1.50
❑392, Oct 1991	1.50
❑393, Nov 1991	1.50
❑394, Dec 1991	1.50
❑395, Jan 1992	1.50
❑396, Feb 1992	1.50
❑397, Mar 1992	1.50
❑398, Apr 1992	1.50
❑399, May 1992	1.50
❑400, Jun 1992	1.50
❑401, Jul 1992	1.50
❑402, Aug 1992	1.50
❑403, Sep 1992	1.50
❑404, Oct 1992	1.50
❑405, Nov 1992	1.50
❑406, Dec 1992	1.50
❑407, Jan 1993	1.50
❑408, Feb 1993	1.50
❑409, Mar 1993	1.50
❑410, Apr 1993	1.50
❑411, May 1993	1.50
❑412, Jun 1993	1.50
❑413, Jul 1993	1.50
❑414, Aug 1993, prom poster	1.50
❑415, Sep 1993	1.50
❑416, Oct 1993	1.50
❑417, Nov 1993	1.50
❑418, Dec 1993	1.50
❑419, Jan 1994	1.50
❑420, Feb 1994	1.50
❑421, Mar 1994	1.50
❑422, Apr 1994	1.50
❑423, May 1994	1.50
❑424, Jun 1994	1.50
❑425, Jul 1994	1.50
❑426, Aug 1994	1.50
❑427, Sep 1994	1.50
❑428, Oct 1994	1.50
❑429, Nov 1994	1.50
❑430, Dec 1994	1.50
❑431, Jan 1995	1.50
❑432, Feb 1995	1.50
❑433, Mar 1995	1.50
❑434, Apr 1995	1.50
❑435, May 1995	1.50
❑436, Jun 1995	1.50
❑437, Jul 1995	1.50
❑438, Aug 1995	1.50
❑439, Sep 1995	1.50
❑440, Oct 1995	1.50
❑441, Nov 1995	1.50
❑442, Dec 1995, continues in Betty & Veronica #95	1.50
❑443, Jan 1996	1.50
❑444, Feb 1996	1.50
❑445, Mar 1996	1.50
❑446, Apr 1996	1.50
❑447, May 1996	1.50
❑448, Jun 1996	1.50
❑449, Jul 1996	1.50
❑450, Aug 1996	1.50
❑451, Sep 1996	1.50
❑452, Oct 1996	1.50
❑453, Nov 1996	1.50
❑454, Dec 1996	1.50
❑455, Jan 1997	1.50
❑456, Feb 1997	1.50
❑457, Mar 1997	1.50
❑458, Apr 1997	1.50
❑459, May 1997	1.50
❑460, Jun 1997	1.50
❑461, Jul 1997	1.50
❑462, Aug 1997	1.50
❑463, Sep 1997	1.50
❑464, Oct 1997	1.50
❑465, Nov 1997	1.50
❑466, Dec 1997	1.50
❑467, Jan 1998	1.75
❑468, Feb 1998	1.75
❑469, Mar 1998	1.75
❑470, Apr 1998	1.75
❑471, May 1998	1.75
❑472, Jun 1998	1.75
❑473, Jul 1998	1.75
❑474, Aug 1998	1.75
❑475, Sep 1998	1.75
❑476, Oct 1998	1.75
❑477, Nov 1998	1.75
❑478, Dec 1998	1.75
❑479, Jan 1999	1.75
❑480, Feb 1999	1.75
❑481, Mar 1999	1.75
❑482, Apr 1999	1.79
❑483, May 1999	1.79
❑484, Jun 1999	1.79
❑485, Jul 1999	1.79
❑486, Aug 1999	1.79
❑487, Sep 1999	1.79
❑488, Oct 1999	1.75
❑489, Nov 1999	1.75
❑490, Dec 1999	1.75
❑491, Jan 2000	1.75
❑492, Feb 2000	1.75
❑493, Mar 2000	1.75
❑494, Apr 2000	1.99
❑495, May 2000	1.99
❑496, Jun 2000	1.99
❑497, Jul 2000	1.99
❑498, Aug 2000	1.99
❑499, Sep 2000	1.99
❑500, Oct 2000	1.99
❑501, Nov 2000	1.99
❑502, Dec 2000	1.99
❑503, Jan 2001	1.99
❑504, Feb 2001	1.99
❑505, Mar 2001	1.99
❑506, Apr 2001	1.99
❑507, May 2001	1.99
❑508, Jun 2001	1.99
❑509, Jul 2001	1.99
❑510, Aug 2001	1.99
❑511, Sep 2001	1.99
❑512, Oct 2001	1.99
❑513, Nov 2001	1.99
❑514, Nov 2001	2.19
❑515, Dec 2001	2.19
❑516, Jan 2002	2.19
❑517, Feb 2002	2.19
❑518, Mar 2002	2.19
❑519, Apr 2002	2.19
❑520, May 2002	2.19
❑521, Jun 2002	2.19
❑522, Jul 2002	2.19
❑523, ca. 2002	2.19
❑524, Aug 2002	2.19
❑525, Sep 2002	2.19
❑526, Oct 2002	2.19
❑527, Nov 2002	2.19
❑528, Dec 2002	2.19
❑529, Jan 2003	2.19
❑530, Feb 2003	2.19
❑531, Mar 2003	2.19
❑532, Apr 2003	2.19
❑533, May 2003	2.19
❑534, Jun 2003	2.19
❑535, Jul 2003	2.19
❑536, Jul 2003	2.19
❑537, Aug 2003	2.19
❑538, Sep 2003	2.19
❑539, Oct 2003	2.19
❑540, Nov 2003	2.19
❑541, Dec 2003	2.19
❑542, Jan 2004	2.19
❑543, Feb 2004	2.19
❑544, Mar 2004	2.19
❑545, Apr 2004, AM (a)	2.19
❑546, May 2004	2.19
❑547, Jun 2004	2.19
❑548, Jul 2004	2.19
❑549, Aug 2004	2.19
❑550, Sep 2004	2.19
❑551, Oct 2004	2.19
❑552, Dec 2004	2.19
❑553, Feb 2005	2.19
❑554, Mar 2005	2.19
❑555, Apr 2005	2.19
❑556, May 2005	2.19
❑557, Jun 2005	2.29
❑558, Jul 2005	2.29
❑559, Aug 2005	2.29
❑560, Sep 2005	2.29
❑561, Oct 2005	2.29
❑562, Nov 2005	2.29
❑563, Feb 2006	2.29
❑565, Jun 2006	2.29
❑566, Jun 2006	2.29
❑567, Aug 2006	2.29
❑Annual 7, ca. 1956	160.00
❑Annual 8, ca. 1957	135.00
❑Annual 9, ca. 1958	120.00
❑Annual 10, ca. 1959	110.00
❑Annual 11, ca. 1960	70.00
❑Annual 12, ca. 1961	60.00
❑Annual 13, ca. 1962	58.00
❑Annual 14, ca. 1963	50.00
❑Annual 15, ca. 1964	50.00
❑Annual 16, ca. 1965	26.00
❑Annual 17, ca. 1966	26.00
❑Annual 18, ca. 1967	22.00
❑Annual 19, ca. 1968	22.00
❑Annual 20, ca. 1969	14.00
❑Annual 21, ca. 1970	9.00
❑Annual 22, ca. 1971	9.00
❑Annual 23, ca. 1972	8.00
❑Annual 24, ca. 1973	8.00
❑Annual 25, ca. 1974	8.00
❑Annual 26, ca. 1975	8.00

ARCHIE ALL CANADIAN DIGEST

Archie

	N-MINT
❑1, Aug 1996, digest; reprints Archie stories set in Canada	2.00

ARCHIE AND FRIENDS

Archie

	N-MINT
❑1, Dec 1992, A: Great Rondo. A: Hiram Lodge	3.00
❑2, Feb 1992	2.00
❑3, Apr 1992	2.00
❑4, Jun 1992	2.00
❑5, Aug 1992	2.00
❑6, Oct 1992, A: Sabrina	2.00
❑7, Mar 1993	2.00
❑8 1993	2.00
❑9, Jun 1994	2.00
❑10, Aug 1994	2.00
❑11, Oct 1994	1.50
❑12, Dec 1994	1.50
❑13, Feb 1995	1.50
❑14, May 1995	1.50
❑15, Aug 1995	1.50
❑16, Nov 1995	1.50
❑17, Feb 1996	1.50
❑18, May 1996	1.50

Other grades: Multiply price above by 5/6 for VF/NM • 2/3 for VERY FINE • 1/3 for FINE • 1/5 for VERY GOOD • 1/8 for GOOD

Archangel

Unusual Marvel printed in glossy black and white

©Marvel

Archangels: The Saga

Independent comic with religious feel

©Eternal

Archard's Agents

Spinoff one-shot from CrossGen's Ruse

©CrossGen

Archer & Armstrong

Super-powered adventurers on the run

©Valiant

Archie

Flagship title for an American icon

©Archie

	N-MINT
❑19, Aug 1996, X-Men and E.R. parodies	1.50
❑20, Nov 1996	1.50
❑21, Feb 1997, The class puts on Romeo and Juliet	1.50
❑22, Apr 1997, Friends parody	1.50
❑23, Jun 1997	1.50
❑24, Aug 1997	1.50
❑25, Oct 1997	1.50
❑26, Dec 1997	1.50
❑27, Feb 1998	1.75
❑28, Apr 1998	1.75
❑29, Jun 1998, Pops opens a cyber-cafe	1.75
❑30, Aug 1998	1.75
❑31, Oct 1998	1.75
❑32, Dec 1998	1.75
❑33, Feb 1999	1.75
❑34, Apr 1999	1.75
❑35, Jun 1999	1.79
❑36, Aug 1999	1.79
❑37, Oct 1999	1.79
❑38, Dec 1999	1.79
❑39, Feb 2000	1.79
❑40, Apr 2000	1.79
❑41, Jun 2000	1.79
❑42, Aug 2000	1.99
❑43, Oct 2000	1.99
❑44, Dec 2000	1.99
❑45, Feb 2001	1.99
❑46, Apr 2001	1.99
❑47, Jun 2001	1.99
❑48, Sep 2001, A: Josie & the Pussycats	1.99
❑49, Oct 2001, A: Josie & the Pussycats	1.99
❑50, Nov 2001, A: Josie & the Pussycats	1.99
❑51, ca. 2001, A: Josie & the Pussycats	2.19
❑52, ca. 2001	2.19
❑53, Jan 2002, A: Josie & the Pussycats	2.19
❑54, ca. 2002	2.19
❑55, Apr 2002, A: Josie & the Pussycats	2.19
❑56, Jun 2002, A: Josie & the Pussycats	2.19
❑57, Jul 2002	2.19
❑58, Aug 2002, A: Josie & the Pussycats	2.19
❑59, Sep 2002	2.19
❑60, Oct 2002, A: Josie & the Pussycats	2.19
❑61, Oct 2002	2.19
❑62, Nov 2002	2.19
❑63, Dec 2002	2.19
❑64, Jan 2003	2.19
❑65, Feb 2003	2.19
❑66, Mar 2003	2.19
❑67, Apr 2003	2.19
❑68, May 2003	2.19
❑69, Jun 2003	2.19
❑70, Jul 2003	2.19
❑71, Aug 2003	2.19
❑72, Sep 2003, AM (a)	2.19
❑73, Oct 2003	2.19
❑74, Oct 2003	2.19
❑75, Nov 2003	2.19
❑76, Dec 2003	2.19
❑77, Jan 2004	2.19
❑78, Feb 2004	2.19
❑79, Mar 2004	2.19
❑80, Apr 2004	2.19
❑81, Jun 2004	2.19
❑82, Jul 2004, Mr. Weatherbee's past revealed	2.19
❑83, Aug 2004	2.19
❑84, Oct 2004	2.19
❑85, Nov 2004	2.19
❑86, Jan 2005	2.19
❑87, Feb 2005	2.19
❑88, Mar 2005	2.19
❑89, Apr 2005	2.19
❑90, May 2005	2.19
❑91, Jun 2005	2.19
❑92, Jul 2005	2.39
❑93, Aug 2005	2.39
❑94, Sep 2005	2.39
❑95, Oct 2005	2.39
❑96, Nov 2006	2.39
❑97, Dec 2005	2.39
❑98, Apr 2006	2.39
❑99, May 2006	2.39
❑100, Jul 2006	2.39
❑101, Aug 2006	2.39

ARCHIE AND ME
ARCHIE

	N-MINT
❑1, Oct 1964	125.00
❑2, Aug 1965	75.00
❑3, Sep 1965	45.00
❑4, Oct 1965	34.00
❑5, Dec 1965	34.00
❑6, Feb 1966	20.00
❑7, Apr 1966	20.00
❑8, Jun 1966	20.00
❑9, Aug 1966	20.00
❑10, Sep 1966	20.00
❑11, Oct 1966	12.00
❑12, Dec 1966	12.00
❑13, Feb 1967	12.00
❑14, Apr 1967	12.00
❑15, Jun 1967	12.00
❑16, Aug 1967	12.00
❑17, Oct 1967	12.00
❑18, Dec 1967	12.00
❑19, Feb 1968	12.00
❑20, Apr 1968	12.00
❑21, Jun 1968	8.00
❑22, Aug 1968	8.00
❑23, Sep 1968, Summer Camp issue	8.00
❑24, Oct 1968	8.00
❑25, Dec 1968, Election issue	8.00
❑26, Feb 1969, Christmas issue	8.00
❑27, Apr 1969	8.00
❑28, Jun 1969	8.00
❑29, Aug 1969	8.00
❑30, Sep 1969	8.00
❑31, Oct 1969	6.00
❑32, Dec 1969	6.00
❑33, Feb 1970	6.00
❑34, Apr 1970	6.00
❑35, Jun 1970	6.00
❑36, Aug 1970	6.00
❑37, Sep 1970, Japan's Expo 70	6.00
❑38, Oct 1970	6.00
❑39, Dec 1970	6.00
❑40, Feb 1971	6.00
❑41, Apr 1971	4.00
❑42, Jun 1971	4.00
❑43, Aug 1971	4.00
❑44, Sep 1971	4.00
❑45, Oct 1971	4.00
❑46, Dec 1971	4.00
❑47, Feb 1972	4.00
❑48, Apr 1972	4.00
❑49, Jun 1972	4.00
❑50, Aug 1972	4.00
❑51, Sep 1972	3.00
❑52, Oct 1972	3.00
❑53, Dec 1972	3.00
❑54, Feb 1973	3.00
❑55, Apr 1973	3.00
❑56, Jun 1973	3.00
❑57, Jul 1973	3.00
❑58, Aug 1973	3.00
❑59, Sep 1973	3.00
❑60, Oct 1973	3.00
❑61, Dec 1973	3.00
❑62, Jan 1974	3.00
❑63, Feb 1974	3.00
❑64, Apr 1974	3.00
❑65, Jun 1974	3.00
❑66, Jul 1974	3.00
❑67, Aug 1974	3.00
❑68, Sep 1974	3.00
❑69, Oct 1974	3.00
❑70, Dec 1974	3.00
❑71, Jan 1975	2.50
❑72, Feb 1975	2.50
❑73, Apr 1975	2.50
❑74, Jun 1975	2.50
❑75, Jul 1975	2.50
❑76, Aug 1975	2.50
❑77, Sep 1975	2.50
❑78, Oct 1975	2.50
❑79, Dec 1975	2.50
❑80, Jan 1976	2.50
❑81, Feb 1976	1.50
❑82, Apr 1976	1.50
❑83, Jun 1976	1.50
❑84, Jul 1976	1.50
❑85, Aug 1976	1.50
❑86, Sep 1976	1.50
❑87, Oct 1976	1.50
❑88, Dec 1976	1.50
❑89, Jan 1977	1.50
❑90, Feb 1977	1.50
❑91, Apr 1977	1.50
❑92, Jun 1977	1.50
❑93, Jul 1977	1.50
❑94, Aug 1977	1.50
❑95, Sep 1977	1.50
❑96, Oct 1977	1.50
❑97, Dec 1977	1.50
❑98, Jan 1978	1.50
❑99, Feb 1978	1.50
❑100, Apr 1978	1.50
❑101, Jun 1978	1.00
❑102, Jul 1978	1.00
❑103, Aug 1978	1.00
❑104, Sep 1978	1.00
❑105, Oct 1978	1.00

Other grades: Multiply price above by 5/6 for VF/NM • 2/3 for VERY FINE • 1/3 for FINE • 1/5 for VERY GOOD • 1/8 for GOOD

	N-MINT
❑106, Dec 1978	1.00
❑107, Jan 1979	1.00
❑108, Feb 1979	1.00
❑109, Apr 1979	1.00
❑110, Jun 1979	1.00
❑111, Jul 1979	1.00
❑112, Aug 1979	1.00
❑113, Sep 1979	1.00
❑114, Oct 1979	1.00
❑115, Dec 1979	1.00
❑116, Jan 1980	1.00
❑117, Feb 1980	1.00
❑118, Apr 1980	1.00
❑119, Jun 1980	1.00
❑120, Jul 1980	1.00
❑121, Aug 1980	1.00
❑122, Sep 1980	1.00
❑123, Oct 1980	1.00
❑124, Dec 1980	1.00
❑125, Feb 1981	1.00
❑126, Apr 1981	1.00
❑127, ca. 1981	1.00
❑128, ca. 1981	1.00
❑129, ca. 1981	1.00
❑130, ca. 1981	1.00
❑131, ca. 1981	1.00
❑132, Feb 1982	1.00
❑133, Apr 1982	1.00
❑134, Jun 1982	1.00
❑135, Aug 1982	1.00
❑136, Oct 1982	1.00
❑137, Dec 1982	1.00
❑138, Feb 1983	1.00
❑139, May 1983	1.00
❑140, ca. 1983	1.00
❑141, ca. 1983	1.00
❑142, ca. 1983	1.00
❑143, Feb 1984, DDC (c)	1.00
❑144, Apr 1984	1.00
❑145, Jun 1984	1.00
❑146, Aug 1984	1.00
❑147, Oct 1984	1.00
❑148, Dec 1984	1.00
❑149, Feb 1985	1.00
❑150, Apr 1985	1.00
❑151, Jun 1985	1.00
❑152, Aug 1985	1.00
❑153, Oct 1985	1.00
❑154, Dec 1985	1.00
❑155, Feb 1986	1.00
❑156, Apr 1986	1.00
❑157, Jun 1986	1.00
❑158, Aug 1986	1.00
❑159, Oct 1986	1.00
❑160, Dec 1986	1.00
❑161, Feb 1987	1.00

ARCHIE ANNUAL DIGEST MAGAZINE

ARCHIE

	N-MINT
❑66, Jun 1995	1.75
❑67, Oct 1995	1.75
❑68, Apr 1997	1.79

ARCHIE... ARCHIE ANDREWS, WHERE ARE YOU? DIGEST MAGAZINE

ARCHIE

	N-MINT
❑1, Feb 1977	5.00
❑2, May 1977	3.00
❑3, Aug 1977	3.00
❑4, Nov 1977	3.00
❑5, Feb 1978	3.00
❑6, May 1978	3.00
❑7, Aug 1978	3.00
❑8, Nov 1978, JK (a); reprints story from Adventures of the Fly #1	3.00
❑9, Feb 1979	3.00
❑10, May 1979	3.00
❑11, Aug 1979	2.00
❑12, Nov 1979	2.00
❑13, Feb 1980	2.00
❑14, May 1980	2.00
❑15, Aug 1980	2.00
❑16, Nov 1980	2.00
❑17, Feb 1981	2.00
❑18, May 1981	2.00
❑19, Aug 1981	2.00
❑20, Nov 1981	2.00
❑21, Feb 1982	1.50
❑22, May 1982	1.50
❑23, Aug 1982	1.50
❑24, Nov 1982	1.50
❑25, Feb 1983	1.50
❑26, May 1983	1.50
❑27, Aug 1983	1.50
❑28, Oct 1983	1.50
❑29, Dec 1983	1.50
❑30, Feb 1984	1.50
❑31, Apr 1984	1.50
❑32, Jun 1984	1.50
❑33, Aug 1984	1.50
❑34, Oct 1984	1.50
❑35, Dec 1984	1.50
❑36, Feb 1985	1.50
❑37, Apr 1985	1.50
❑38, Jun 1985	1.50
❑39, Aug 1985	1.50
❑40, Oct 1985	1.50
❑41, Dec 1985	1.50
❑42, Feb 1986	1.50
❑43, Apr 1986	1.50
❑44, Jun 1986	1.50
❑45, Aug 1986	1.50
❑46, Oct 1986	1.50
❑47, Dec 1986	1.50
❑48, Feb 1987	1.50
❑49, Apr 1987	1.50
❑50, Jun 1987	1.50
❑51, Aug 1987	1.50
❑52, Oct 1987	1.50
❑53, Dec 1987	1.50
❑54, Feb 1988	1.50
❑55, Apr 1988	1.50
❑56, Jun 1988	1.50
❑57, Aug 1988	1.50
❑58, Oct 1988	1.50
❑59, Dec 1988	1.50
❑60, Feb 1989	1.50
❑61, Apr 1989	1.50
❑62, Jun 1989	1.50
❑63, Aug 1989	1.50
❑64, Oct 1989	1.50
❑65, Dec 1989	1.50
❑66, Feb 1990	1.50
❑67, Apr 1990	1.50
❑68, Jun 1990	1.50
❑69, Aug 1990	1.50
❑70, Oct 1990	1.50
❑71, Dec 1990	1.50
❑72, Feb 1991	1.50
❑73, Apr 1991	1.50
❑74, Jun 1991	1.50
❑75, Aug 1991	1.50
❑76, Oct 1991	1.50
❑77, Dec 1991	1.50
❑78, Feb 1992	1.50
❑79, Apr 1992	1.50
❑80, Jun 1992	1.50
❑81, Aug 1992	1.50
❑82, Oct 1992	1.50
❑83, Dec 1992	1.50
❑84, Jan 1993	1.50
❑85, Feb 1993	1.50
❑86, Apr 1993	1.50
❑87, Jun 1993	1.50
❑88, Aug 1993	1.50
❑89, Oct 1993	1.50
❑90, Dec 1993	1.50
❑91, Feb 1994	1.75
❑92, Mar 1994	1.75
❑93, May 1994	1.75
❑94, Jul 1994	1.75
❑95, Sep 1994	1.75
❑96, Nov 1994	1.75
❑97, Jan 1995	1.75
❑98, Feb 1995	1.75
❑99, Apr 1995	1.75
❑100, Jun 1995	1.75
❑101, Aug 1995	1.75
❑102, Oct 1995	1.75
❑103, Dec 1995	1.75
❑104, Jan 1996	1.75
❑105, Mar 1996	1.75
❑106, May 1996	1.75
❑107, Aug 1996	1.75
❑108, Nov 1996	1.79
❑109, Feb 1997	1.79
❑110, May 1997	1.79
❑111, Sep 1997	1.79
❑112, Nov 1997	1.79
❑113, Feb 1998	1.95
❑114, May 1998	1.95
❑115, Sep 1998	1.95
❑116, Nov 1998	1.95
❑117, Feb 1999	1.95

ARCHIE AS PUREHEART THE POWERFUL

ARCHIE

	N-MINT
❑1, Sep 1966	55.00
❑2, Nov 1966	35.00
❑3, Jan 1967	25.00
❑4, May 1967	25.00
❑5, Aug 1967	25.00
❑6, Nov 1967	25.00

ARCHIE AT RIVERDALE HIGH

ARCHIE

	N-MINT
❑1, Aug 1972	42.00
❑2, Sep 1972	22.00
❑3, Oct 1972	16.00
❑4, Dec 1972	16.00
❑5, Feb 1973	16.00
❑6, Apr 1973	11.00
❑7, Jun 1973	11.00
❑8, Jul 1973	11.00
❑9, Aug 1973	11.00
❑10, Sep 1973	11.00
❑11, Oct 1973	8.00
❑12, Dec 1973	8.00
❑13, Feb 1974	8.00
❑14, Mar 1974	8.00
❑15, Apr 1974	8.00
❑16, Jun 1974	8.00
❑17, Jul 1974	8.00
❑18, Aug 1974	8.00
❑19, Sep 1974	8.00
❑20, ca. 1974	8.00
❑21	5.00
❑22, Feb 1975	5.00
❑23, Mar 1975	5.00
❑24, Apr 1975	5.00
❑25, Jun 1975	5.00
❑26, Jun 1975	5.00
❑27, Aug 1975	5.00
❑28, Sep 1975	5.00
❑29, Oct 1975	5.00
❑30, Nov 1975	5.00
❑31, Dec 1975	4.00
❑32, Jan 1976	4.00
❑33, Feb 1976	4.00
❑34, Mar 1976	4.00
❑35, May 1976	4.00
❑36, Jun 1976	4.00
❑37, Jul 1976	4.00
❑38, Aug 1976	4.00
❑39, Sep 1976	4.00
❑40, Oct 1976	4.00
❑41, Dec 1976	3.00
❑42, ca. 1977	3.00
❑43, Mar 1977	3.00
❑44, May 1977	3.00
❑45, Jun 1977	3.00
❑46, Jul 1977	3.00
❑47, Aug 1977	3.00
❑48, Sep 1977	3.00
❑49, Oct 1977	3.00
❑50, Dec 1977	3.00
❑51, Jan 1978	3.00
❑52, ca. 1978	3.00
❑53, May 1978	3.00
❑54, ca. 1978	3.00
❑55, ca. 1978	3.00
❑56, ca. 1978	3.00
❑57, ca. 1978	3.00
❑58, ca. 1978	3.00
❑59, Dec 1978	3.00
❑60, ca. 1979	3.00
❑61, ca. 1979	2.00
❑62, May 1979	2.00
❑63, ca. 1979	2.00
❑64, ca. 1979	2.00
❑65, ca. 1979	2.00

Other grades: Multiply price above by 5/6 for VF/NM • 2/3 for VERY FINE • 1/3 for FINE • 1/5 for VERY GOOD • 1/8 for GOOD

Archie and Friends

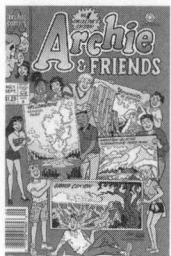

1990s version updates the supporting cast
©Archie

Archie and Me

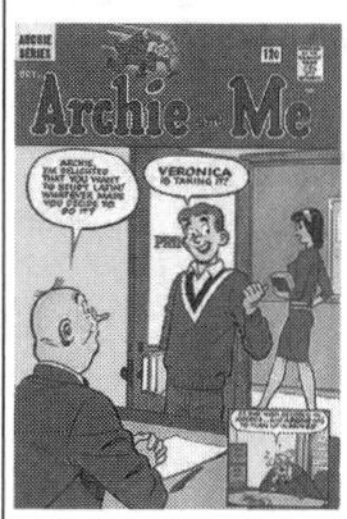

Long-lived Archie spinoff from the 1960s
©Archie

Archie As Pureheart the Powerful

Campy Batman series spawns Archie oddity
©Archie

Archie at Riverdale High

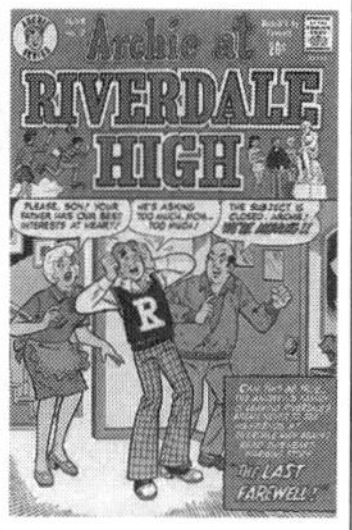

Series spotlights school supporting cast
©Archie

Archie Giant Series Magazine

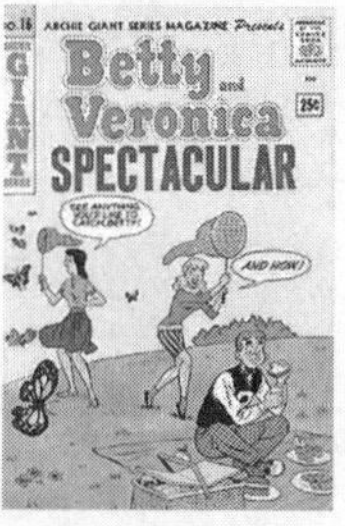

Ever-changing titles and weird numbering
©Archie

	N-MINT
❑66, ca. 1979	2.00
❑67, ca. 1979	2.00
❑68, Dec 1979	2.00
❑69, ca. 1980	2.00
❑70, ca. 1980	2.00
❑71, May 1980	2.00
❑72, ca. 1980	2.00
❑73, ca. 1980	2.00
❑74, ca. 1980	2.00
❑75, ca. 1980	2.00
❑76, ca. 1980	2.00
❑77, ca. 1980	2.00
❑78, Feb 1981	2.00
❑79, Apr 1981	2.00
❑80, Jun 1981	2.00
❑81, Aug 1981	2.00
❑82, Oct 1981	2.00
❑83, Dec 1981	2.00
❑84, Feb 1982	2.00
❑85, Apr 1982	2.00
❑86, ca. 1982	2.00
❑87	2.00
❑88	2.00
❑89	2.00
❑90	2.00
❑91, May 1983, DDC (c)	2.00
❑92, ca. 1983, DDC (c)	2.00
❑93, ca. 1983	2.00
❑94	2.00
❑95, Feb 1984	2.00
❑96, Apr 1984, Teen smoking issue	2.00
❑97, Jun 1984	2.00
❑98, Aug 1984	2.00
❑99, Oct 1984	2.00
❑100, Dec 1984, 100th anniversary issue	2.00
❑101, Feb 1985	1.00
❑102, Apr 1985	1.00
❑103, Jun 1985	1.00
❑104, Aug 1985	1.00
❑105, Oct 1985	1.00
❑106, Dec 1985	1.00
❑107, Feb 1986	1.00
❑108, Apr 1986	1.00
❑109, Jun 1986	1.00
❑110, Aug 1986, DDC (c)	1.00
❑111, Oct 1986	1.00
❑112, Dec 1986	1.00
❑113, Feb 1986, DDC (c)	1.00
❑114, ca. 1987	1.00

ARCHIE DIGEST MAGAZINE

ARCHIE

	N-MINT
❑1, Aug 1973	26.00
❑2, Oct 1973	10.00
❑3, Dec 1973	6.00
❑4, Feb 1974	6.00
❑5, Apr 1974	6.00
❑6, Jun 1974	4.00
❑7, Aug 1974	4.00
❑8, Oct 1974	4.00
❑9, Dec 1974	4.00
❑10, Feb 1975	4.00
❑11, Apr 1975	2.50
❑12, Jun 1975	2.50
❑13, Aug 1975	2.50
❑14, Oct 1975	2.50
❑15, Dec 1975	2.50
❑16, Feb 1976	2.50
❑17, Apr 1976	2.50
❑18, Jun 1976	2.50
❑19, Aug 1976	2.50
❑20, Oct 1976	2.50
❑21, Dec 1976	2.00
❑22, Feb 1977	2.00
❑23, Apr 1977	2.00
❑24, Jun 1977	2.00
❑25, Aug 1977	2.00
❑26, Oct 1977	2.00
❑27, Dec 1977	2.00
❑28, Feb 1978	2.00
❑29, Apr 1978	2.00
❑30, Jun 1978	2.00
❑31, Aug 1978	2.00
❑32, Oct 1978	2.00
❑33, Dec 1978	2.00
❑34, Feb 1979	2.00
❑35, Apr 1979	2.00
❑36, Jun 1979	2.00
❑37, Aug 1979	2.00
❑38, Oct 1979, Reprints Li'l Jinx story featuring comic-book collector paying $1,000 for old Red Circle comics	2.00
❑39, Dec 1979	2.00
❑40, Feb 1980	2.00
❑41, Apr 1980	2.00
❑42	2.00
❑43	2.00
❑44	2.00
❑45	2.00
❑46 1981	2.00
❑47 1981	2.00
❑48 1981	2.00
❑49 1981	2.00
❑50	2.00
❑51	1.50
❑52, Apr 1982	1.50
❑53	1.50
❑54	1.50
❑55	1.50
❑56	1.50
❑57	1.50
❑58 1983	1.50
❑59 1983	1.50
❑60 1983	1.50
❑61 1983	1.50
❑62	1.50
❑63	1.50
❑64	1.50
❑65	1.50
❑66, Jun 1984	1.50
❑67 1984	1.50
❑68	1.50
❑69	1.50
❑70	1.50
❑71	1.50
❑72 1985	1.50
❑73	1.50
❑74	1.50
❑75	1.50
❑76	1.50
❑77 1986	1.50
❑78	1.50
❑79	1.50
❑80	1.50
❑81	1.50
❑82 1987	1.50
❑83 1987	1.50
❑84 1987	1.50
❑85	1.50
❑86	1.50
❑87	1.50
❑88, Apr 1988	1.50
❑89 1988	1.50
❑90 1988	1.50
❑91 1988	1.50
❑92	1.50
❑93	1.50
❑94	1.50
❑95, Apr 1989	1.50
❑96	1.50
❑97	1.50
❑98	1.50
❑99	1.50
❑100	1.50
❑101	1.79
❑102	1.79
❑103 1990	1.79
❑104	1.79
❑105	1.79
❑106	1.79
❑107	1.79
❑108	1.79
❑109	1.79
❑110	1.79
❑111	1.79
❑112	1.79
❑113	1.79
❑114	1.79
❑115	1.79
❑116	1.79
❑117	1.79
❑118 1992	1.79
❑119	1.79
❑120	1.79
❑121	1.79
❑122	1.79
❑123	1.79
❑124 1993	1.79
❑125	1.79
❑126	1.79
❑127	1.79
❑128	1.79
❑129	1.79
❑130	1.79
❑131, Dec 1994, DDC (c)	1.79
❑132, Feb 1995	1.79
❑133, Apr 1995	1.79
❑134, May 1995	1.79
❑135, Jul 1995	1.79
❑136, Sep 1995	1.79
❑137, Nov 1995	1.79
❑138, Jan 1996	1.79
❑139, Mar 1996	1.79

Other grades: Multiply price above by 5/6 for VF/NM • 2/3 for VERY FINE • 1/3 for FINE • 1/5 for VERY GOOD • 1/8 for GOOD

	N-MINT
❑140, Apr 1996	1.79
❑141 1996	1.79
❑142 1996	1.79
❑143 1996	1.79
❑144, Dec 1996	1.79
❑145, Jan 1997	1.79
❑146, Mar 1997	1.79
❑147, Apr 1997	1.79
❑148, Jun 1997	1.79
❑149, Aug 1997	1.79
❑150, Sep 1997	1.79
❑151, Nov 1997	1.79
❑152, Jan 1998	1.95
❑153, Mar 1998	1.95
❑154, Apr 1998	1.95
❑155, Jun 1998	1.95
❑156, Jul 1998	1.95
❑157, Sep 1998	1.95
❑158, Oct 1998	1.95
❑159, Dec 1998	1.95
❑160, Jan 1999	1.95
❑161, Mar 1999	1.95
❑162, Apr 1999	1.99
❑163, Jun 1999	1.99
❑164, Jul 1999	1.99
❑165, Sep 1999	1.99
❑166, Oct 1999, DDC (c)	1.99
❑167, Nov 1999	1.99
❑168, Jan 2000	1.99
❑169, Feb 2000	1.99
❑170, Apr 2000	1.99
❑171, Jun 2000	1.99
❑172, Jul 2000	1.99
❑173, Aug 2000	2.19
❑174, Oct 2000	2.19
❑175, Nov 2000	2.19
❑176, Jan 2001	2.19
❑177, Feb 2001	2.19
❑178, Mar 2001	2.19
❑179, Apr 2001	2.19
❑180, Jun 2001	2.19
❑181, Jul 2001	2.19
❑182, Aug 2001	2.19
❑183, Sep 2001	2.19
❑184, Dec 2001	2.39
❑185, Jan 2002	2.39
❑186, Mar 2002	2.39
❑187, Apr 2002	2.39
❑188, May 2002	2.39
❑189, Jul 2002	2.39
❑190, Aug 2002	2.39
❑191, Oct 2002	2.39
❑192, Nov 2002	2.39
❑193, Dec 2002	2.39
❑194, Feb 2003	2.39
❑195, Mar 2003	2.39
❑196, Apr 2003	2.39
❑197, May 2003	2.39
❑198, Jul 2003	2.39
❑199, Aug 2003	2.39
❑200, Oct 2003	2.39
❑201, Nov 2003	2.39
❑202, Dec 2003	2.39
❑203, Jan 2004	2.39
❑204, Mar 2004	2.39
❑205, Apr 2004	2.39
❑206, Jun 2004	2.39
❑207, Jul 2004	2.39
❑208, Aug 2004	2.39
❑209, Sep 2004	2.39
❑210, Oct 2004	2.39
❑211, Nov 2004	2.39
❑212, Dec 2004	2.39
❑213, Jan 2005	2.39
❑214, Feb 2005	2.39
❑215, Mar 2005	2.39
❑216, Apr 2005	2.39
❑217, May 2005	2.39
❑218, Jun 2005	2.39
❑219, Jul 2005	2.39
❑220, Aug 2005	2.39
❑221, Nov 2005	2.39
❑222, Jan 2006	2.39
❑223, Apr 2006	2.39
❑224, May 2006	2.39
❑225, Jul 2006	2.39
❑226, Aug 2006	2.39

ARCHIE GIANT SERIES MAGAZINE

Archie

	N-MINT
❑1, Win 1954, Archie's Christmas Stocking (1954)	750.00
❑2, Win 1955, Archie's Christmas Stocking (1955)	475.00
❑3, Win 1956, Archie's Christmas Stocking (1956)	325.00
❑4, Win 1957, Archie's Christmas Stocking (1957)	325.00
❑5, Win 1958, Archie's Christmas Stocking (1958)	275.00
❑6, Win 1959, Archie's Christmas Stocking (1959)	275.00
❑7, Sep 1960, Katy Keene Holiday Fun	200.00
❑8, Oct 1960, Betty & Veronica Summer Fun	200.00
❑9, Dec 1960, The World of Jughead	185.00
❑10, Jan 1961, Archie's Christmas Stocking (1960)	185.00
❑11, Jun 1961	140.00
❑12, ca. 1961, Katy Keene Holiday Fun	125.00
❑13, ca. 1961	140.00
❑14, Dec 1961	110.00
❑15, Mar 1962, Archie's Christmas Stocking (1961)	110.00
❑16, Jun 1962	125.00
❑17, Sep 1962, Archie's Jokes	110.00
❑18, ca. 1962	125.00
❑19, ca. 1962	110.00
❑20, Jan 1963, Archie's Christmas Stocking (1962)	100.00
❑21, ca. 1963	85.00
❑22, ca. 1963	60.00
❑23, ca. 1963	80.00
❑24, ca. 1963, The World of Jughead	60.00
❑25, ca. 1964	60.00
❑26, ca. 1964	80.00
❑27, Jun 1964, Archie's Jokes	60.00
❑28, Sep 1964	80.00
❑29, ca. 1964	60.00
❑30, ca. 1964, The World of Jughead	60.00
❑31, ca. 1965	40.00
❑32, ca. 1965	40.00
❑33, ca. 1965	40.00
❑34, ca. 1965, Betty & Veronica Summer Fun	40.00
❑35, ca. 1965, Series continued in #136	40.00
❑136, ca. 1965	40.00
❑137, ca. 1966	40.00
❑138, ca. 1966	40.00
❑139, ca. 1966	40.00
❑140, ca. 1966	40.00
❑141, ca. 1966	40.00
❑142, ca. 1966, O: Captain Pureheart	45.00
❑143, ca. 1967, The World of Jughead	20.00
❑144, ca. 1967	20.00
❑145, ca. 1967	20.00
❑146, ca. 1967, Archie's Jokes	20.00
❑147, ca. 1967, Betty & Veronica Summer Fun	20.00
❑148, ca. 1967	20.00
❑149, ca. 1967, The World of Jughead	20.00
❑150, ca. 1967	20.00
❑151, ca. 1967	20.00
❑152, Feb 1968, The World of Jughead	20.00
❑153, ca. 1968	20.00
❑154, ca. 1968	20.00
❑155, ca. 1968	20.00
❑156, ca. 1968	20.00
❑157, ca. 1968	20.00
❑158, ca. 1969	20.00
❑159, ca. 1969	20.00
❑160, ca. 1969, The World of Archie	20.00
❑161, ca. 1969	12.00
❑162, ca. 1969	12.00
❑163, ca. 1969	12.00
❑164, ca. 1969	12.00
❑165, ca. 1969	12.00
❑166, ca. 1969	12.00
❑167, ca. 1970	12.00
❑168, ca. 1970	12.00
❑169, ca. 1970	12.00
❑170, ca. 1970, Jughead's Eat-Out	12.00
❑171, ca. 1970	12.00
❑172, ca. 1970, The World of Jughead	12.00
❑173, ca. 1970	12.00
❑174, ca. 1970	12.00
❑175, ca. 1970	12.00
❑176, ca. 1970	12.00
❑177, ca. 1970	12.00
❑178, ca. 1970	12.00
❑179, ca. 1971	12.00
❑180, ca. 1971	12.00
❑181, ca. 1971	10.00
❑182, ca. 1971, The World of Archie	10.00
❑183, ca. 1971, The World of Jughead	10.00
❑184, ca. 1971	10.00
❑185, ca. 1971	10.00
❑186, ca. 1971	10.00
❑187, ca. 1971	10.00
❑188, ca. 1971, The World of Archie	10.00
❑189, ca. 1971	10.00
❑190, ca. 1971	10.00
❑191, ca. 1972	10.00
❑192, ca. 1972	10.00
❑193, ca. 1972	10.00
❑194, ca. 1972	10.00
❑195, ca. 1972	10.00
❑196, ca. 1972	10.00
❑197, Jun 1972	10.00
❑198, ca. 1972, Archie's Jokes	10.00
❑199, ca. 1972	10.00
❑200, ca. 1972, The World of Archie	10.00
❑201, ca. 1972	8.00
❑202, ca. 1972	8.00
❑203, ca. 1972	8.00
❑204, ca. 1973	8.00
❑205, ca. 1973	8.00
❑206, ca. 1973	8.00
❑207, ca. 1973	8.00
❑208, ca. 1973	8.00
❑209, ca. 1973, The World of Jughead	8.00
❑210, Jun 1973	8.00
❑211, Jul 1973	8.00
❑212, Aug 1973	8.00
❑213, Oct 1973, Archie's Joke Book	8.00
❑214, Nov 1973	8.00
❑215, Nov 1973	8.00
❑216, Dec 1973, Archie's Christmas Stocking (1973)	8.00
❑217, Jan 1974	8.00
❑218, Feb 1974, Archie's Jokebook	8.00
❑219, Mar 1974	8.00
❑220, Apr 1974	8.00
❑221, May 1974	6.00
❑222, Jun 1974, Archie's Jokes	6.00
❑223, Jul 1974	6.00
❑224, Aug 1974	6.00
❑225, Sep 1974	6.00
❑226, Oct 1974	6.00
❑227, Nov 1974	6.00
❑228, Dec 1974, Archie's Christmas Stocking (1974)	6.00
❑229, Jan 1975, Betty & Veronica Christmas Spectacular	6.00
❑230, Feb 1975, Archie's Christmas Love-in	6.00
❑231, Mar 1975	6.00
❑232, Apr 1975	6.00
❑233, May 1975	6.00
❑234, Jun 1975	6.00
❑235, ca. 1975	6.00
❑236, ca. 1975, Betty & Veronica Summer Fun	6.00
❑237, ca. 1975	6.00
❑238, ca. 1975, Betty & Veronica Spectacular	6.00
❑239, ca. 1975	6.00
❑240, ca. 1975, Archie's Christmas Stocking (1975)	6.00
❑241, ca. 1975	6.00
❑242, ca. 1976	6.00
❑243, ca. 1976, Sabrina's Christmas Magic	6.00
❑244, ca. 1976	6.00
❑245, ca. 1976, The World of Jughead	6.00
❑246, ca. 1976	6.00
❑247, ca. 1976	6.00
❑248, ca. 1976	6.00
❑249, Sep 1976, The World of Archie	6.00
❑250, Oct 1976, Betty & Veronica Spectacular	6.00

Other grades: Multiply price above by 5/6 for VF/NM • 2/3 for VERY FINE • 1/3 for FINE • 1/5 for VERY GOOD • 1/8 for GOOD

Archie Meets the Punisher

The crossover nobody ever expected

©Marvel

Archie's Christmas Stocking (2nd Series)

A continuing seasonal classic

©Archie

Archie's Date Book

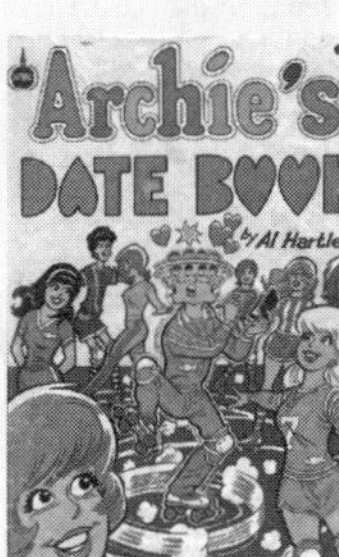

Religious comic preaches against premarital sex

©Spire

Archie's Family Album

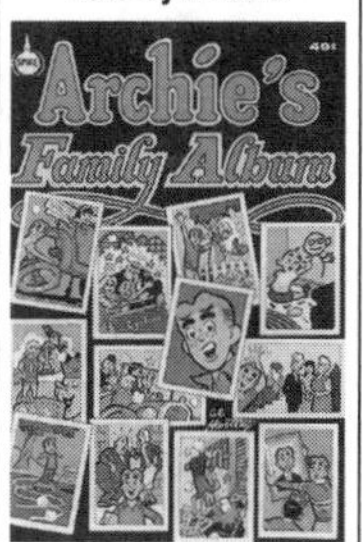

Another religious comic from Al Hartley

©Spire

Archie's Girls Betty & Veronica

First title by this name; see also "Betty..."

©Archie

	N-MINT
❑251, ca. 1976, Series continued in #452	4.00
❑452, ca. 1976	3.00
❑453, ca. 1976	3.00
❑454, ca. 1976	3.00
❑455, Jan 1977	3.00
❑456, ca. 1977	3.00
❑457, ca. 1977	3.00
❑458, Jun 1977, Betty & Veronica Spectacular	3.00
❑459, Aug 1977, Archie's Jokes	3.00
❑460, Aug 1977	3.00
❑461, Sep 1977, The World of Archie	3.00
❑462, Oct 1977, Betty & Veronica Spectacular	3.00
❑463, Oct 1977, The World of Jughead	3.00
❑464, ca. 1977	3.00
❑465, ca. 1978	3.00
❑466, Jan 1978, Archie's Christmas Love-in	3.00
❑467, ca. 1978	3.00
❑468, Mar 1978, The World of Archie	3.00
❑469, Apr 1978, The World of Jughead	3.00
❑470, Jun 1978	3.00
❑471, Jul 1978	3.00
❑472, Aug 1978	3.00
❑473, Sep 1978	3.00
❑474, Oct 1978	3.00
❑475, Nov 1978	3.00
❑476, Dec 1978	3.00
❑477, Dec 1979, Betty & Veronica Christmas Spectacular	3.00
❑478, Jan 1979, Archie's Christmas Love-in	3.00
❑479, Mar 1979	3.00
❑480, Apr 1979, The World of Archie	3.00
❑481, Apr 1979, The World of Jughead	3.00
❑482, Jun 1979, Betty & Veronica Spectacular	3.00
❑483, Aug 1979, Archie's Jokes	3.00
❑484, Sep 1979, Betty & Veronica Summer Fun	3.00
❑485, Sep 1979, The World of Archie	3.00
❑486, Oct 1979, Betty & Veronica Spectacular	3.00
❑487, Nov 1979, The World of Jughead	3.00
❑488, Dec 1979, Archie's Christmas Stocking (1979)	3.00
❑489, Dec 1980, Betty & Veronica Christmas Spectacular	3.00
❑490, Jan 1980, Archie's Christmas Love-in	3.00
❑491, Jan 1980, Sabrina's Christmas Magic	3.00
❑492, Mar 1980, The World of Archie	3.00
❑493, Apr 1980, World of Jughead	3.00
❑494, Jun 1980, DDC (c); Betty & Veronica Spectacular	3.00
❑495, Aug 1980, Archie's Jokes	3.00
❑496, Aug 1980, Betty & Veronica Summer Fun	3.00
❑497, Sep 1980, The World of Archie	3.00
❑498, Oct 1980, DDC (c); Betty & Veronica Spectacular	3.00
❑499, Oct 1980, The World of Jughead	3.00
❑500, Dec 1980, DDC (c); Archie's Christmas Stocking (1980)	2.50

	N-MINT
❑501, Dec 1981, Betty & Veronica Christmas Spectacular	2.50
❑502, Jan 1981, Archie's Christmas Love-in	2.50
❑503, Jan 1981, Sabrina's Christmas Magic	2.50
❑504, Mar 1981	2.50
❑505, Apr 1981, The World of Jughead	2.50
❑506, ca. 1981	2.50
❑507, ca. 1981	2.50
❑508, ca. 1981	2.50
❑509, ca. 1981	2.50
❑510, ca. 1981	2.50
❑511, Oct 1981, The World of Jughead	2.50
❑512, Dec 1981, Archie's Christmas Spectacular (1981)	2.50
❑513, Dec 1981, Betty & Veronica Christmas Spectacular	2.50
❑514, ca. 1982	2.50
❑515, ca. 1982	2.50
❑516, Mar 1982, The World of Archie	2.50
❑517, ca. 1982	2.50
❑518, ca. 1982	2.50
❑519, ca. 1982	2.50
❑520, ca. 1982	2.50
❑521, Sep 1982, The World of Archie	2.50
❑522, ca. 1982	2.50
❑523, ca. 1983	2.50
❑524, ca. 1983	2.50
❑525, ca. 1983	2.50
❑526, ca. 1983	2.50
❑527, ca. 1983	2.50
❑528, ca. 1983	2.50
❑529, ca. 1983	2.50
❑530, ca. 1983	2.50
❑531, ca. 1983	2.50
❑532, ca. 1983	2.50
❑533, ca. 1983	2.50
❑534, ca. 1984	2.50
❑535, ca. 1984	2.50
❑536, ca. 1984	2.50
❑537, ca. 1984	2.50
❑538, ca. 1984	2.50
❑539, ca. 1984	2.50
❑540, ca. 1984	2.50
❑541, Sep 1984, Betty & Veronica Spectacular	2.50
❑542, ca. 1984	2.50
❑543, ca. 1984	2.50
❑544, ca. 1984	2.50
❑545, Jan 1984, Little Archie	2.50
❑546, Jan 1984	2.50
❑547, Jan 1984, Betty & Veronica Christmas Spectacular	2.50
❑548, Jun 1984	2.50
❑549, ca. 1985, Betty & Veronica Spectacular	2.50
❑550, Aug 1985, Betty & Veronica Summer Fun	2.50
❑551, ca. 1985	2.00
❑552, ca. 1985	2.00
❑553, ca. 1985	2.00
❑554, ca. 1985	2.00
❑555, Aug 1985, Betty's Diary	2.00
❑556, ca. 1986	2.00

	N-MINT
❑557, Jan 1986, Archie's Christmas Stocking (1985)	2.00
❑558, Jan 1986, Betty & Veronica Christmas Spectacular	2.00
❑559, Jun 1986, Betty & Veronica Spectacular	2.00
❑560, Aug 1986, Little Archie	2.00
❑561, ca. 1986	2.00
❑562, ca. 1986	2.00
❑563, ca. 1986	2.00
❑564, ca. 1986	2.00
❑565, ca. 1986	2.00
❑566, ca. 1986	2.00
❑567, ca. 1986	2.00
❑568, ca. 1986	2.00
❑569, ca. 1987	2.00
❑570, Sep 1987, Little Archie	2.00
❑571, ca. 1987	2.00
❑572, ca. 1987	2.00
❑573, ca. 1987	2.00
❑574, ca. 1987	2.00
❑575, ca. 1987	2.00
❑576, ca. 1987	2.00
❑577, ca. 1987	2.00
❑578, ca. 1987	2.00
❑579, ca. 1987	2.00
❑580, Jan 1988, Betty & Veronica Christmas Spectacular	2.00
❑581, ca. 1988	2.00
❑582, ca. 1988	2.00
❑583, ca. 1988	2.00
❑584, ca. 1988	2.00
❑585, ca. 1988	2.00
❑586, ca. 1988	2.00
❑587, ca. 1988	2.00
❑588, ca. 1988	2.00
❑589, ca. 1988	2.00
❑590, Oct 1988, The World of Jughead	2.00
❑591, ca. 1988	2.00
❑592, ca. 1989	2.00
❑593, ca. 1989	2.00
❑594, ca. 1989	2.00
❑595, ca. 1989	2.00
❑596, ca. 1989	2.00
❑597, ca. 1989	2.00
❑598, ca. 1989	2.00
❑599, ca. 1989	2.00
❑600, ca. 1989	2.00
❑601, ca. 1989	1.50
❑602, ca. 1989	1.50
❑603, ca. 1990	1.50
❑604, ca. 1990	1.50
❑605, ca. 1990	1.50
❑606, ca. 1990	1.50
❑607, ca. 1990, Archie Giant Series Magazine Presents Little Archie A: Little Sabrina. A: Chester Punkett. A: South-Side Serpents. A: Mad Doctor Doom. A: Sue Stringly	1.50
❑608, ca. 1990	1.50
❑609, ca. 1990	1.50
❑610, ca. 1990	1.50
❑611, ca. 1990	1.50
❑612, ca. 1990	1.50
❑613, ca. 1990	1.50

Other grades: Multiply price above by 5/6 for VF/NM • 2/3 for VERY FINE • 1/3 for FINE • 1/5 for VERY GOOD • 1/8 for GOOD

❑614, Oct 1990, Pep Comics; Archie characters meet Archie Comics staff 1.50
❑615, ca. 1990 1.50
❑616, ca. 1990 1.50
❑617, ca. 1991 1.50
❑618, ca. 1991 1.50
❑619, ca. 1991 1.50
❑620, ca. 1991 1.50
❑621, ca. 1991 1.50
❑622, ca. 1991 1.50
❑623, ca. 1991 1.50
❑624, ca. 1991 1.50
❑625, ca. 1991 1.50
❑626, ca. 1992 1.50
❑627, ca. 1992 1.50
❑628, ca. 1992 1.50
❑629, ca. 1992 1.50
❑630, ca. 1992 1.50
❑631, Jun 1992 1.50
❑632, Jul 1992 1.50

ARCHIE MEETS THE PUNISHER
MARVEL

❑1, Aug 1994; Archie cover 3.25

ARCHIE'S CHRISTMAS STOCKING (2ND SERIES)
ARCHIE

❑1, Jan 1994, DDC (a); For 1993 holiday season 2.50
❑2, For 1994 holiday season 2.00
❑3, For 1995 holiday season 2.00
❑4, For 1996 holiday season 2.00
❑5, For 1997 holiday season 2.25
❑6, For 1998 holiday season 2.25
❑7, For 1999 holiday season 2.29

ARCHIE'S DATE BOOK
SPIRE

❑1, religious 4.00

ARCHIE'S DOUBLE DIGEST MAGAZINE
ARCHIE

❑1, Jan 1982 6.00
❑2, May 1982, DDC (c) 3.50
❑3, Jul 1982, DDC (c) 3.50
❑4, Oct 1982 3.50
❑5, Jan 1983 3.50
❑6, May 1983, DDC (c) 3.50
❑7, Jul 1983, DDC (c) 3.50
❑8, Oct 1983, DDC (c) 3.50
❑9, Jan 1984, DDC (c) 3.50
❑10, May 1984, DDC (c) 3.50
❑11, Jul 1984, DDC (c) 3.00
❑12, Sep 1984, DDC (c) 3.00
❑13, Nov 1984 3.00
❑14, Jan 1985 3.00
❑15, Mar 1985, DDC (c) 3.00
❑16, May 1985, DDC (c) 3.00
❑17, Jul 1985, DDC (c) 3.00
❑18, Sep 1985, DDC (c) 3.00
❑19, Nov 1985, DDC (c) 3.00
❑20, Jan 1986 3.00
❑21, Mar 1986, DDC (c) 3.00
❑22, May 1986, DDC (c) 3.00
❑23, Jul 1986, DDC (c) 3.00
❑24, Sep 1986, DDC (c) 3.00
❑25, Nov 1986, DDC (c) 3.00
❑26, Jan 1987, DDC (c) 3.00
❑27, Mar 1987, DDC (c) 3.00
❑28, May 1987, DDC (c) 3.00
❑29, Jul 1987, DDC (c) 3.00
❑30, Sep 1987, DDC (c) 3.00
❑31, Nov 1987, DDC (c) 3.00
❑32, Jan 1988, DDC (c) 3.00
❑33, Mar 1988, DDC (c) 3.00
❑34, May 1988, DDC (c) 3.00
❑35, Jul 1988, DDC (c) 3.00
❑36, Sep 1988, DDC (c) 3.00
❑37, Nov 1988, DDC (c) 3.00
❑38, Jan 1989, DDC (c) 3.00
❑39, Mar 1989, DDC (c) 3.00
❑40, May 1989, DDC (c) 3.00
❑41, Jul 1989 3.00
❑42, Sep 1989 3.00
❑43, Nov 1989 3.00
❑44, Jan 1990 3.00
❑45, Mar 1990 3.00
❑46, May 1990 3.00
❑47, Jul 1990 3.00
❑48, Sep 1990 3.00
❑49, Nov 1990 3.00
❑50, Jan 1991 3.00
❑51, Mar 1991 3.00
❑52, May 1991 3.00
❑53, Jul 1991 3.00
❑54, Sep 1991 3.00
❑55, Nov 1991 3.00
❑56, Dec 1991 3.00
❑57, Feb 1992 3.00
❑58, Apr 1992 3.00
❑59, Jun 1992 3.00
❑60, Aug 1992 3.00
❑61, Sep 1992 3.00
❑62, Nov 1992 3.00
❑63, Jan 1993 3.00
❑64, Mar 1993 3.00
❑65, May 1993 3.00
❑66, Jul 1993 3.00
❑67, Sep 1993 3.00
❑68, Oct 1993 3.00
❑69, Dec 1993 3.00
❑70, Feb 1994 3.00
❑71, Apr 1994 3.00
❑72, Jun 1994 3.00
❑73, Aug 1994 3.00
❑74, Oct 1994 3.00
❑75, Nov 1994 3.00
❑76, Jan 1995 3.00
❑77, Mar 1995 3.00
❑78, May 1995 3.00
❑79, Jul 1995 3.00
❑80, Aug 1995 2.75
❑81, Oct 1995 2.75
❑82, Dec 1995 2.75
❑83, Feb 1996 2.75
❑84, Apr 1996 2.75
❑85, May 1996 2.75
❑86, Jul 1996 2.75
❑87, Sep 1996 2.75
❑88, Oct 1996 2.75
❑89, Dec 1996 2.75
❑90, Feb 1997 2.75
❑91, Mar 1997 2.75
❑92, May 1997 2.75
❑93, Jul 1997 2.75
❑94, Aug 1997 2.75
❑95, Oct 1997 2.75
❑96, Dec 1997 2.75
❑97, Feb 1998 2.75
❑98, Mar 1998 2.75
❑99, May 1998 2.75
❑100, Jul 1998 2.75
❑101, Aug 1998 2.75
❑102, Sep 1998 2.75
❑103, Nov 1998, DDC (w) 2.95
❑104, Dec 1998 2.95
❑105, Feb 1999 2.95
❑106, Apr 1999 2.95
❑107, May 1999 2.99
❑108, Jun 1999 2.99
❑109, Aug 1999 2.99
❑110, Sep 1999 2.99
❑111, Nov 1999 2.95
❑112, Dec 1999 2.99
❑113, Feb 2000 2.95
❑114, Mar 2000 2.99
❑115, May 2000 2.95
❑116, Jul 2000 2.95
❑117, Aug 2000 3.19
❑118, Sep 2000 3.19
❑119, Nov 2000 3.19
❑120, Dec 2000 3.19
❑121, Jan 2001 3.19
❑122, Mar 2001 3.19
❑123, Apr 2001 3.29
❑124, May 2001 3.29
❑125, Jul 2001 3.29
❑126, Aug 2001 3.29
❑127, Sep 2001 3.29
❑128, Nov 2001 3.29
❑129, Dec 2001 3.29
❑130, Jan 2002 3.29
❑131, Mar 2002 3.29
❑132, Apr 2002 3.29
❑133, May 2002 3.29
❑134, Jul 2002 3.29
❑135, Aug 2002 3.29
❑136, Sep 2002 3.29
❑137, Nov 2002 3.29
❑138, Dec 2002 3.29
❑139, Jan 2003 3.59
❑140, Mar 2003 3.59
❑141, Apr 2003 3.59
❑142, May 2003 3.59
❑143, Jul 2003 3.59
❑144, Sep 2003 3.59
❑145, Oct 2003 3.59
❑146, Nov 2003 3.59
❑147, Jan 2004 3.59
❑148, Feb 2004, AM (a) 3.59
❑149, Mar 2004 3.59
❑150, May 2004, AM (a) 3.59
❑151, Jun 2004 3.59
❑152, Jul 2004 3.59
❑153, Aug 2004 3.59
❑154, Sep 2004 3.59
❑155, Oct 2004 3.59
❑156, Nov 2004 3.59
❑157, Dec 2004 3.59
❑158, Jan 2005 3.59
❑159 2005 3.59
❑160, May 2005 3.59
❑161, Jun 2005 3.59
❑162, Jul 2005 3.59
❑163, Aug 2005 3.59
❑164, Sep 2005 3.59
❑165, Oct 2005 3.59
❑166, Jan 2006 3.59
❑167, Feb 2006 3.59
❑168, May 2006 3.59
❑169, Jun 2006 3.59
❑170, Jun 2006 3.59
❑171, Aug 2006 3.59

ARCHIE'S FAMILY ALBUM
SPIRE

❑1 4.00

ARCHIE'S GIRLS BETTY & VERONICA
ARCHIE

❑1, ca. 1950 1400.00
❑2, Sum 1951 675.00
❑3, ca. 1951 485.00
❑4, ca. 1951 375.00
❑5, Sum 1952 375.00
❑6, Fal 1952 285.00
❑7, Win 1952 285.00
❑8, Spr 1953 285.00
❑9, Sum 1953 285.00
❑10, Fal 1953 285.00
❑11, Feb 1954 225.00
❑12, Apr 1954 225.00
❑13, Jun 1954 225.00
❑14, Aug 1954 225.00
❑15, Nov 1954 225.00
❑16, Jan 1955 225.00
❑17, Mar 1955 225.00
❑18, May 1955 225.00
❑19, Jul 1955 225.00
❑20, Sep 1955 165.00
❑21, Nov 1955 165.00
❑22, Jan 1956 165.00
❑23, Mar 1956 165.00
❑24, May 1956 165.00
❑25, Jul 1956 165.00
❑26, Sep 1956 165.00
❑27, Nov 1956 165.00
❑28, Jan 1957 165.00
❑29, Mar 1957 165.00
❑30, May 1957 115.00
❑31, Jul 1957 115.00
❑32, Sep 1957 115.00
❑33, Nov 1957 115.00
❑34, Jan 1958 115.00
❑35, Mar 1958 115.00
❑36, May 1958 115.00
❑37, Jul 1958 115.00
❑38, Sep 1958 115.00
❑39, Nov 1958 115.00
❑40, Jan 1959 85.00
❑41, Mar 1959 85.00
❑42, May 1959 85.00

Archie's Jokebook Magazine

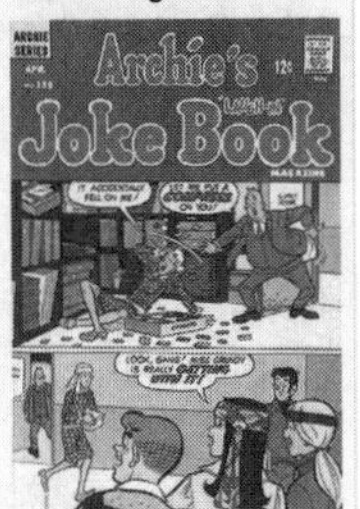

Lots and lots of simple gags with Archie
©Archie

Archie's Madhouse

The series that kept changing names
©Archie

Archie's Mysteries

More Scooby-Doo style Archie tales
©Archie

Archie's Pal Jughead Comics

Continuation of Jughead; not the 1950s series
©Archie

Archie's Pals 'n' Gals

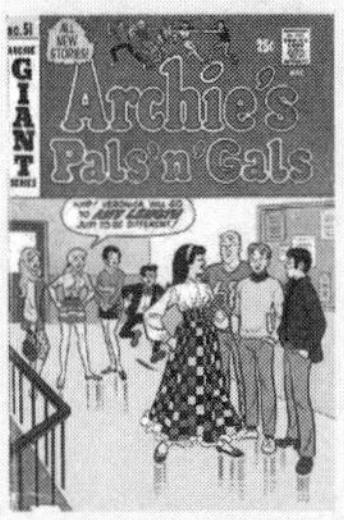

Title began as an annual special in the 1950s
©Archie

Issue	N-MINT
❑43, Jul 1959	85.00
❑44, Aug 1959	85.00
❑45, Sep 1959	85.00
❑46, Oct 1959	85.00
❑47, Nov 1959	85.00
❑48, Dec 1959	85.00
❑49, Jan 1960	85.00
❑50, Feb 1960	85.00
❑51, Mar 1960	55.00
❑52, Apr 1960	55.00
❑53, May 1960	55.00
❑54, Jun 1960	55.00
❑55, Jul 1960	55.00
❑56, Aug 1960	55.00
❑57, Sep 1960	55.00
❑58, Oct 1960	55.00
❑59, Nov 1960	55.00
❑60, Dec 1960	55.00
❑61, Jan 1961	45.00
❑62, Feb 1961	45.00
❑63, Mar 1961	45.00
❑64, Apr 1961	45.00
❑65, May 1961	45.00
❑66, Jun 1961	45.00
❑67, Jul 1961	45.00
❑68, Aug 1961	45.00
❑69, Sep 1961	45.00
❑70, Oct 1961	45.00
❑71, Nov 1961	32.00
❑72, Dec 1961	32.00
❑73, Jan 1962	32.00
❑74, Feb 1962	32.00
❑75, Mar 1962	32.00
❑76, Apr 1962	32.00
❑77, May 1962	32.00
❑78, Jun 1962	32.00
❑79, Jul 1962	32.00
❑80, Aug 1962	32.00
❑81, Sep 1962	32.00
❑82, Oct 1962	32.00
❑83, Nov 1962	32.00
❑84, Dec 1962	32.00
❑85, Jan 1963	32.00
❑86, Feb 1963	32.00
❑87, Mar 1963	32.00
❑88, Apr 1963	32.00
❑89, May 1963	32.00
❑90, Jun 1963	32.00
❑91, Jul 1963	24.00
❑92, Aug 1963	24.00
❑93, Sep 1963	24.00
❑94, Oct 1963	24.00
❑95, Nov 1963	24.00
❑96, Dec 1963	24.00
❑97, Jan 1964	24.00
❑98, Feb 1964	24.00
❑99, Mar 1964	24.00
❑100, Apr 1964	24.00
❑101, May 1964	24.00
❑102, Jun 1964	24.00
❑103, Jul 1964	24.00
❑104, Aug 1964	24.00
❑105, Sep 1964	24.00
❑106, Oct 1964	24.00
❑107, Nov 1964	24.00
❑108, Dec 1964	24.00
❑109, Jan 1965	24.00
❑110, Feb 1965	24.00
❑111, Mar 1965	16.00
❑112, Apr 1965	16.00
❑113, May 1965	16.00
❑114, Jun 1965	16.00
❑115, Jul 1965	16.00
❑116, Aug 1965	16.00
❑117, Sep 1965	16.00
❑118, Oct 1965	16.00
❑119, Nov 1965	16.00
❑120, Dec 1965	16.00
❑121, Jan 1966	16.00
❑122, Feb 1966	16.00
❑123, Mar 1966	16.00
❑124, Apr 1966	16.00
❑125, May 1966	16.00
❑126, Jun 1966	16.00
❑127, Jul 1966	16.00
❑128, Aug 1966	16.00
❑129, Sep 1966	16.00
❑130, Oct 1966	16.00
❑131, Nov 1966	16.00
❑132, Dec 1966	16.00
❑133, Jan 1967	16.00
❑134, Feb 1967	16.00
❑135, Mar 1967	16.00
❑136, Apr 1967	16.00
❑137, May 1967	16.00
❑138, Jun 1967	16.00
❑139, Jul 1967	16.00
❑140, Aug 1967	16.00
❑141, Sep 1967	13.00
❑142, Oct 1967	13.00
❑143, Nov 1967	13.00
❑144, Dec 1967	13.00
❑145, Jan 1968	13.00
❑146, Feb 1968	13.00
❑147, Mar 1968	13.00
❑148, Apr 1968	13.00
❑149, May 1968	13.00
❑150, Jun 1968	13.00
❑151, Jul 1968	13.00
❑152, Aug 1968	13.00
❑153, Sep 1968	13.00
❑154, Oct 1968	13.00
❑155, Nov 1968	13.00
❑156, Dec 1968	13.00
❑157, Jan 1969	13.00
❑158, Feb 1969	13.00
❑159, Mar 1969	13.00
❑160, Apr 1969	13.00
❑161, May 1969	10.00
❑162, Jun 1969	10.00
❑163, Jul 1969	10.00
❑164, Aug 1969	10.00
❑165, Sep 1969	10.00
❑166, Oct 1969	10.00
❑167, Nov 1969	10.00
❑168, Dec 1969	10.00
❑169, Jan 1970	10.00
❑170, Feb 1970	10.00
❑171, Mar 1970	10.00
❑172, Apr 1970	10.00
❑173, May 1970	10.00
❑174, Jun 1970	10.00
❑175, Jul 1970	10.00
❑176, Aug 1970	10.00
❑177, Sep 1970	10.00
❑178, Oct 1970	10.00
❑179, Nov 1970	10.00
❑180, Dec 1970	10.00
❑181, Jan 1971	7.00
❑182, Feb 1971	7.00
❑183, Mar 1971	7.00
❑184, Apr 1971	7.00
❑185, May 1971	7.00
❑186, Jun 1971	7.00
❑187, Jul 1971	7.00
❑188, Aug 1971	7.00
❑189, Sep 1971	7.00
❑190, Oct 1971	7.00
❑191, Nov 1971	7.00
❑192, Dec 1971	7.00
❑193, Jan 1972	7.00
❑194, Feb 1972	7.00
❑195, Mar 1972	7.00
❑196, Apr 1972	7.00
❑197, May 1972	7.00
❑198, Jun 1972	7.00
❑199, Jul 1972	7.00
❑200, Aug 1972	7.00
❑201, Sep 1972	5.00
❑202, Oct 1972	5.00
❑203, Nov 1972	5.00
❑204, Dec 1972	5.00
❑205, Jan 1973	5.00
❑206, Feb 1973	5.00
❑207, Mar 1973	5.00
❑208, Apr 1973	5.00
❑209, May 1973	5.00
❑210, Jun 1973	5.00
❑211, Jul 1973	5.00
❑212, Aug 1973	5.00
❑213, Sep 1973	5.00
❑214, Oct 1973	5.00
❑215, Nov 1973	5.00
❑216, Dec 1973	5.00
❑217, Jan 1974	5.00
❑218, Feb 1974	5.00
❑219, Mar 1974	5.00
❑220, Apr 1974	5.00
❑221, May 1974	5.00
❑222, Jun 1974	5.00
❑223, Jul 1974	5.00
❑224, Aug 1974	5.00
❑225, Sep 1974	5.00
❑226, Oct 1974	5.00
❑227, Nov 1974	5.00
❑228, Dec 1974	5.00
❑229, Jan 1975	5.00
❑230, Feb 1975	5.00
❑231, Mar 1975	5.00
❑232, Apr 1975	5.00
❑233, May 1975	5.00
❑234, Jun 1975	5.00

Other grades: Multiply price above by 5/6 for VF/NM • 2/3 for VERY FINE • 1/3 for FINE • 1/5 for VERY GOOD • 1/8 for GOOD

	N-MINT
❑235, Jul 1975	5.00
❑236, Aug 1975	5.00
❑237, Sep 1975	5.00
❑238, Oct 1975	5.00
❑239, Nov 1975	5.00
❑240, Dec 1975	5.00
❑241, Jan 1976	5.00
❑242, Feb 1976	5.00
❑243, Mar 1976	5.00
❑244, Apr 1976	5.00
❑245, May 1976	5.00
❑246, Jun 1976	5.00
❑247, Jul 1976	5.00
❑248, Aug 1976	5.00
❑249, Sep 1976	5.00
❑250, Oct 1976	5.00
❑251, Nov 1976	3.00
❑252, Dec 1976	3.00
❑253, Jan 1977	3.00
❑254, Feb 1977	3.00
❑255, Mar 1977	3.00
❑256, Apr 1977	3.00
❑257, May 1977	3.00
❑258, Jun 1977	3.00
❑259, Jul 1977	3.00
❑260, Aug 1977	3.00
❑261, Sep 1977	3.00
❑262, Oct 1977	3.00
❑263, Nov 1977	3.00
❑264, Dec 1977	3.00
❑265, Jan 1978	3.00
❑266, Feb 1978	3.00
❑267, Mar 1978	3.00
❑268, Apr 1978	3.00
❑269, May 1978	3.00
❑270, Jun 1978	3.00
❑271, Jul 1978	3.00
❑272, Aug 1978	3.00
❑273, Sep 1978	3.00
❑274, Oct 1978	3.00
❑275, Nov 1978	3.00
❑276, Dec 1978	3.00
❑277, Jan 1979	3.00
❑278, Feb 1979	3.00
❑279, Mar 1979	3.00
❑280, Apr 1979	3.00
❑281, May 1979	3.00
❑282, Jun 1979	3.00
❑283, Jul 1979	3.00
❑284, Aug 1979	3.00
❑285, Sep 1979	3.00
❑286, Oct 1979	3.00
❑287, Nov 1979	3.00
❑288, Dec 1979	3.00
❑289, Jan 1980	3.00
❑290, Feb 1980	3.00
❑291, Mar 1980	3.00
❑292, Apr 1980	3.00
❑293, May 1980	3.00
❑294, Jun 1980	3.00
❑295, Jul 1980	3.00
❑296, Aug 1980	3.00
❑297, Sep 1980	3.00
❑298, Oct 1980	3.00
❑299, Nov 1980	3.00
❑300, Dec 1980	3.00
❑301, Jan 1981	2.50
❑302, Feb 1981	2.50
❑303, Mar 1981	2.50
❑304, Apr 1981	2.50
❑305, May 1981	2.50
❑306, Jun 1981	2.50
❑307, Jul 1981	2.50
❑308, Aug 1981	2.50
❑309, Sep 1981	2.50
❑310, Oct 1981	2.50
❑311, Nov 1981	2.50
❑312, Dec 1981	2.50
❑313, Jan 1982	2.50
❑314, Feb 1982	2.50
❑315, Mar 1982	2.50
❑316, Apr 1982	2.50
❑317, May 1982	2.50
❑318, Jun 1982	2.50
❑319, Aug 1982	2.50
❑320, Oct 1982, 1: Cheryl Blossom	8.00
❑321, Dec 1982	4.00
❑322, Feb 1983	3.00
❑323, Apr 1983	3.00
❑324, Jun 1983	2.50
❑325, Aug 1983	2.50
❑326, Oct 1983	2.50
❑327, Dec 1983	2.50
❑328, Feb 1984	2.50
❑329, Apr 1984	2.50
❑330, Jun 1984	2.50
❑331, Aug 1984	2.50
❑332, Oct 1984	2.50
❑333, Dec 1984	2.50
❑334, Feb 1985	2.50
❑335, Apr 1985	2.50
❑336, Jun 1985	2.50
❑337, Aug 1985	2.50
❑338, Oct 1985	2.50
❑339, Dec 1985	2.50
❑340, Feb 1986	2.50
❑341, Apr 1986	2.50
❑342, Jun 1986	2.50
❑343, Aug 1986	2.50
❑344, Oct 1986	2.50
❑345, Dec 1986	2.50
❑346, Feb 1987	2.50
❑347, Apr 1987	2.50
❑Annual 1, ca. 1953	525.00
❑Annual 2, ca. 1954	325.00
❑Annual 3, ca. 1955	265.00
❑Annual 4, ca. 1956	265.00
❑Annual 5, ca. 1957	250.00
❑Annual 6, ca. 1958	175.00
❑Annual 7, ca. 1959	150.00
❑Annual 8, ca. 1960	100.00

ARCHIE'S HOLIDAY FUN DIGEST MAGAZINE

ARCHIE

	N-MINT
❑1, Feb 1997	1.95
❑2, Feb 1998	1.95
❑3, Feb 1999	1.95
❑4, Feb 2000	1.99
❑5, Jan 2001	2.19
❑6, Jan 2002	2.19
❑7, Jan 2003	2.19
❑8, Dec 2003	2.39
❑9 2004	2.39
❑10 2005	2.39

ARCHIE'S JOKEBOOK MAGAZINE

ARCHIE

	N-MINT
❑25, Nov 1956	100.00
❑26, Jan 1957	100.00
❑27, Mar 1957	100.00
❑28, May 1957	100.00
❑29, Jul 1957	100.00
❑30, Sep 1957	100.00
❑31, Nov 1957	75.00
❑32, Jan 1958	75.00
❑33, Mar 1958	75.00
❑34, May 1958	75.00
❑35, Jul 1958	75.00
❑36, Sep 1958	75.00
❑37, Nov 1958	75.00
❑38, Jan 1959	75.00
❑39, Mar 1959	75.00
❑40, May 1959	75.00
❑41, Jul 1959, NA (a); First pro work by Neal Adams	135.00
❑42, Sep 1959	65.00
❑43, Nov 1959	65.00
❑44, Jan 1960, NA (a)	70.00
❑45, Mar 1960, NA (a)	70.00
❑46, May 1960, NA (a)	70.00
❑47, Jul 1960, NA (a)	70.00
❑48, Sep 1960, NA (a)	70.00
❑49, Nov 1960	35.00
❑50, Dec 1960	35.00
❑51, Feb 1961	35.00
❑52, Apr 1961	35.00
❑53, May 1961	35.00
❑54, Jun 1961	35.00
❑55, Jul 1961	35.00
❑56, Aug 1961	35.00
❑57, Sep 1961	35.00
❑58, Oct 1961	35.00
❑59, Dec 1961	35.00
❑60, Feb 1962	35.00
❑61, Apr 1962	24.00
❑62, Jun 1962	24.00
❑63, Jul 1962	24.00
❑64, Aug 1962	24.00
❑65, Sep 1962	24.00
❑66, Oct 1962	24.00
❑67, Dec 1962	24.00
❑68, Feb 1963	24.00
❑69, Apr 1963	24.00
❑70, Jun 1963	24.00
❑71, Jul 1963	16.00
❑72, Aug 1963	16.00
❑73, Sep 1963	16.00
❑74, Oct 1963	16.00
❑75, Dec 1963	16.00
❑76, Feb 1964	16.00
❑77, Apr 1964	16.00
❑78, Jun 1964	16.00
❑79, Jul 1964	16.00
❑80, Aug 1964	16.00
❑81, Sep 1964	12.00
❑82, Oct 1964	12.00
❑83, Dec 1964	12.00
❑84, Jan 1965	12.00
❑85, Feb 1965	12.00
❑86, Mar 1965	12.00
❑87, Apr 1965	12.00
❑88, May 1965	12.00
❑89, Jun 1965	12.00
❑90, Jul 1965	12.00
❑91, Aug 1965	8.00
❑92, Sep 1965	8.00
❑93, Oct 1965	8.00
❑94, Nov 1965	8.00
❑95, Dec 1965	8.00
❑96, Jan 1966	8.00
❑97, Feb 1966	8.00
❑98, Mar 1966	8.00
❑99, Apr 1966	8.00
❑100, May 1966	8.00
❑101, Jun 1966	5.00
❑102, Jul 1966	5.00
❑103, Aug 1966	5.00
❑104, Sep 1966	5.00
❑105, Oct 1966	5.00
❑106, Nov 1966	5.00
❑107, Dec 1966	5.00
❑108, Jan 1967	5.00
❑109, Feb 1967	5.00
❑110, Mar 1967	5.00
❑111, Apr 1967	5.00
❑112, May 1967	5.00
❑113, Jun 1967	5.00
❑114, Jul 1967	5.00
❑115, Aug 1967	5.00
❑116, Aug 1967	5.00
❑117, Oct 1967	5.00
❑118, Nov 1967	5.00
❑119, Dec 1967	5.00
❑120, Jan 1968	5.00
❑121, Feb 1968	3.00
❑122, Mar 1968	3.00
❑123, Apr 1968	3.00
❑124, May 1968	3.00
❑125, Jun 1968	3.00
❑126, Jul 1968	3.00
❑127, Aug 1968	3.00
❑128, Sep 1968	3.00
❑129, Oct 1968	3.00
❑130, Nov 1968	3.00
❑131, Dec 1968	3.00
❑132, Jan 1969	3.00
❑133, Feb 1969	3.00
❑134, Mar 1969	3.00
❑135, Apr 1969	3.00
❑136, May 1969	3.00
❑137, Jun 1969	3.00
❑138, Jul 1969	3.00
❑139, Aug 1969	3.00
❑140, Sep 1969	3.00
❑141, Oct 1969	3.00
❑142, Nov 1969	3.00
❑143, Dec 1969	3.00
❑144, Jan 1970	3.00
❑145, Feb 1970	3.00

Other grades: Multiply price above by 5/6 for VF/NM • 2/3 for VERY FINE • 1/3 for FINE • 1/5 for VERY GOOD • 1/8 for GOOD

Archie's R/C Racers

Radio-control craze infects Riverdale

©Archie

Archie's Spring Break

Archie descends on the beach

©Archie

Archie's TV Laugh-Out

Title inspired by Rowan & Martin's Laugh-in

©Archie

Archie's Vacation Special

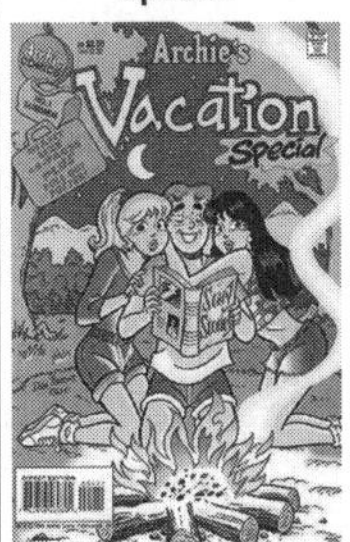

Deluxe format annuals featuring Archie

©Archie

Archie's Weird Mysteries

More horror-themed comedy from Archie

©Archie

	N-MINT
❑146, Mar 1970	3.00
❑147, Apr 1970	3.00
❑148, May 1970	3.00
❑149, Jun 1970	3.00
❑150, Jul 1970	3.00
❑151, Aug 1970	2.00
❑152, Sep 1970	2.00
❑153, Oct 1970	2.00
❑154, Nov 1970	2.00
❑155, Dec 1970	2.00
❑156, Jan 1971	2.00
❑157, Feb 1971	2.00
❑158, Mar 1971	2.00
❑159, Apr 1971	2.00
❑160, May 1971	2.00
❑161, Jun 1971	2.00
❑162, Jul 1971	2.00
❑163, Aug 1971	2.00
❑164, Sep 1971	2.00
❑165, Oct 1971	2.00
❑166, Nov 1971	2.00
❑167, Dec 1971	2.00
❑168, Jan 1972	2.00
❑169, Feb 1972	2.00
❑170, Mar 1972	2.00
❑171, Apr 1972	2.00
❑172, May 1972	2.00
❑173, Jun 1972	2.00
❑174, Jul 1972	2.00
❑175, Aug 1972	2.00
❑176, Sep 1972	2.00
❑177, Oct 1972	2.00
❑178, Nov 1972	2.00
❑179, Dec 1972	2.00
❑180, Jan 1973	2.00
❑181, Feb 1973	1.50
❑182, Mar 1973	1.50
❑183, Apr 1973	1.50
❑184, May 1973	1.50
❑185, Jun 1973	1.50
❑186, Jul 1973	1.50
❑187, Aug 1973	1.50
❑188, Sep 1973	1.50
❑189, Oct 1973	1.50
❑190, Nov 1973	1.50
❑191, Dec 1973	1.50
❑192, Jan 1974	1.50
❑193, Feb 1974	1.50
❑194, Mar 1974	1.50
❑195, Apr 1974	1.50
❑196, May 1974	1.50
❑197, Jun 1974	1.50
❑198, Jul 1974	1.50
❑199, Aug 1974	1.50
❑200, Sep 1974	1.50
❑201, Oct 1974	1.00
❑202, Nov 1974	1.00
❑203, Dec 1974	1.00
❑204, Jan 1975	1.00
❑205, Feb 1975	1.00
❑206, Mar 1975	1.00
❑207, Apr 1975	1.00
❑208, May 1975	1.00
❑209, Jun 1975	1.00
❑210, Jul 1975	1.00
❑211, Aug 1975	1.00
❑212, Sep 1975	1.00
❑213, Oct 1975	1.00
❑214, Nov 1975	1.00
❑215, Dec 1975	1.00
❑216, Jan 1976	1.00
❑217, Feb 1976	1.00
❑218, Mar 1976	1.00
❑219, Apr 1976	1.00
❑220, May 1976	1.00
❑221, Jun 1976	1.00
❑222, Jul 1976	1.00
❑223, Aug 1976	1.00
❑224, Sep 1976	1.00
❑225, Oct 1976	1.00
❑226, Nov 1976	1.00
❑227, Dec 1976	1.00
❑228, Jan 1977	1.00
❑229, Feb 1977	1.00
❑230, Mar 1977	1.00
❑231, Apr 1977	1.00
❑232, May 1977	1.00
❑233, Jun 1977	1.00
❑234, Jul 1977	1.00
❑235, Aug 1977	1.00
❑236, Sep 1977	1.00
❑237, Oct 1977	1.00
❑238, Nov 1977	1.00
❑239, Dec 1977	1.00
❑240, Jan 1978	1.00
❑241, Feb 1978	1.00
❑242, Mar 1978	1.00
❑243, Apr 1978	1.00
❑244, May 1978	1.00
❑245, Jun 1978	1.00
❑246, Jul 1978	1.00
❑247, Aug 1978	1.00
❑248, Sep 1978	1.00
❑249, Oct 1978	1.00
❑250, Nov 1978	1.00
❑251, Dec 1978	1.00
❑252, Jan 1979	1.00
❑253, Feb 1979	1.00
❑254, Mar 1979	1.00
❑255, Apr 1979	1.00
❑256, May 1979	1.00
❑257, Jun 1979	1.00
❑258, Jul 1979	1.00
❑259, Aug 1979	1.00
❑260, Sep 1979	1.00
❑261, Oct 1979	1.00
❑262, Nov 1979	1.00
❑263, Dec 1979	1.00
❑264, Jan 1980	1.00
❑265, Feb 1980	1.00
❑266, Mar 1980	1.00
❑267, Apr 1980	1.00
❑268, May 1980	1.00
❑269, Jun 1980	1.00
❑270, Jul 1980	1.00
❑271, Aug 1980	1.00
❑272, Sep 1980	1.00
❑273, Nov 1980	1.00
❑274, Jan 1981	1.00
❑275, Mar 1981	1.00
❑276, May 1981	1.00
❑277, Jun 1981	1.00
❑278, Jul 1981	1.00
❑279, Aug 1981	1.00
❑280, Sep 1981	1.00
❑281, Oct 1981	1.00
❑282, Nov 1981	1.00
❑283, Jan 1982	1.00
❑284, Mar 1982	1.00
❑285, May 1982	1.00
❑286, Jul 1982	1.00
❑287, Sep 1982	1.00
❑288, Nov 1982	1.00

ARCHIE'S MADHOUSE

ARCHIE

	N-MINT
❑1, Sep 1959	175.00
❑2, Nov 1959	95.00
❑3, Jan 1960	68.00
❑4, Mar 1960	50.00
❑5, Jun 1960	50.00
❑6, Aug 1960	38.00
❑7, Sep 1960	38.00
❑8, Oct 1960	38.00
❑9, Dec 1960	38.00
❑10, Feb 1961	38.00
❑11, Apr 1961	26.00
❑12, Jun 1961	26.00
❑13, Aug 1961	26.00
❑14, Sep 1961	26.00
❑15, Oct 1961	26.00
❑16, Dec 1961	23.00
❑17, Feb 1962	23.00
❑18, Apr 1962	23.00
❑19, Jun 1962	23.00
❑20, Aug 1962	23.00
❑21, Sep 1962	18.00
❑22, Oct 1962, 1: Sabrina the Teen-age Witch	100.00
❑23, Dec 1962	18.00
❑24, Feb 1963	18.00
❑25, Apr 1963	18.00
❑26, Jun 1963	14.00
❑27, Aug 1963	14.00
❑28, Sep 1963	14.00
❑29, Oct 1963	14.00
❑30, Dec 1963	14.00
❑31, Feb 1963	9.00
❑32, Apr 1964	9.00
❑33, Jun 1964	9.00
❑34, Aug 1964	9.00
❑35, Sep 1964	9.00
❑36, Oct 1964	9.00
❑37, Dec 1964	9.00
❑38, Feb 1965	9.00
❑39, Apr 1965	9.00
❑40, Jun 1965	9.00
❑41, Aug 1965	6.00
❑42, Sep 1965	6.00
❑43, Oct 1965	6.00
❑44, Dec 1965	6.00
❑45, Feb 1966	6.00
❑46, Apr 1966	6.00

Other grades: Multiply price above by 5/6 for VF/NM • 2/3 for VERY FINE • 1/3 for FINE • 1/5 for VERY GOOD • 1/8 for GOOD

	N-MINT
❑47, Jun 1966	6.00
❑48, Aug 1966	6.00
❑49, Sep 1966	6.00
❑50, Oct 1966	6.00
❑51, Dec 1966	3.50
❑52, Feb 1967	3.50
❑53, Apr 1967	3.50
❑54, Jun 1967	3.50
❑55, Aug 1967	3.50
❑56, Sep 1967	3.50
❑57, Oct 1967	3.50
❑58, Dec 1967	3.50
❑59, Feb 1968	3.50
❑60, Apr 1968	3.50
❑61, Jun 1968	3.50
❑62, Aug 1968	3.50
❑63, Sep 1968	3.50
❑64, Oct 1968	3.50
❑65, Dec 1968, Series continues as Madhouse Ma-ad Jokes	3.50
❑66, Jan 1969	3.50
❑Annual 1, ca. 1962	65.00
❑Annual 2, ca. 1964	25.00
❑Annual 3, ca. 1965	15.00
❑Annual 4, ca. 1966	10.00
❑Annual 5, ca. 1968	10.00
❑Annual 6, ca. 1969	10.00

ARCHIE'S MYSTERIES

ARCHIE

	N-MINT
❑25, Feb 2003, Continues numbering from Archie's Weird Mysteries	2.19
❑26, Apr 2003	2.19
❑27, Jun 2003	2.19
❑28, Aug 2003	2.19
❑29, Sep 2003	2.19
❑30, Oct 2003	2.19
❑31, Nov 2003	2.19
❑32, Jan 2004	2.19
❑33, Mar 2004	2.19
❑34, May 2004	2.19

ARCHIE'S PAL JUGHEAD

ARCHIE

	N-MINT
❑38, Oct 1956	38.00
❑39, Dec 1956	38.00
❑40, Feb 1957	38.00
❑41, Apr 1957	22.00
❑42, Jun 1957	22.00
❑43, Aug 1957	22.00
❑44, Oct 1957	22.00
❑45, Dec 1957	22.00
❑46, Feb 1958	22.00
❑47, Apr 1958	22.00
❑48, Jun 1958	22.00
❑49, Aug 1958	22.00
❑50, ca. 1958	22.00
❑51, ca. 1958	22.00
❑52, ca. 1959	22.00
❑53, ca. 1959	22.00
❑54, Jul 1959	22.00
❑55, ca. 1959	22.00
❑56, ca. 1959	22.00
❑57, ca. 1959	22.00
❑58, ca. 1960	22.00
❑59, ca. 1960	22.00
❑60, ca. 1960	22.00
❑61, ca. 1960	16.00
❑62, ca. 1960	16.00
❑63, Aug 1960	16.00
❑64, Sep 1960	16.00
❑65, Oct 1960	16.00
❑66, Nov 1960	16.00
❑67, Dec 1960	16.00
❑68, Jan 1961	16.00
❑69, Feb 1961	16.00
❑70, Mar 1961	16.00
❑71, Apr 1961	16.00
❑72, May 1961	16.00
❑73, Jun 1961	16.00
❑74, Jul 1961	16.00
❑75, Aug 1961	16.00
❑76, Sep 1961	16.00
❑77, Oct 1961	16.00
❑78, Nov 1961	16.00
❑79, Dec 1961	16.00
❑80, Jan 1962	16.00
❑81, Feb 1962	10.00
❑82, Mar 1962	10.00
❑83, Apr 1962	10.00
❑84, May 1962	10.00
❑85, Jun 1962	10.00
❑86, Jul 1962	10.00
❑87, Aug 1962	10.00
❑88, Sep 1962	10.00
❑89, Oct 1962	10.00
❑90, Nov 1962	10.00
❑91, Dec 1962	10.00
❑92, Jan 1963	10.00
❑93, Feb 1963	10.00
❑94, Mar 1963	10.00
❑95, Apr 1963	10.00
❑96, May 1963	10.00
❑97, Jun 1963	10.00
❑98, Jul 1963	10.00
❑99, Aug 1963	10.00
❑100, Sep 1963	10.00
❑101, Oct 1963	7.00
❑102, Nov 1963	7.00
❑103, Dec 1963	7.00
❑104, Jan 1964	7.00
❑105, Feb 1964	7.00
❑106, Mar 1964	7.00
❑107, Apr 1964	7.00
❑108, May 1964	7.00
❑109, Jun 1964	7.00
❑110, Jul 1964	7.00
❑111, Aug 1964	7.00
❑112, Sep 1964	7.00
❑113, Oct 1964	7.00
❑114, Nov 1964	7.00
❑115, Dec 1964	7.00
❑116, Jan 1965	7.00
❑117, Feb 1965	7.00
❑118, Mar 1965	7.00
❑119, Apr 1965	7.00
❑120, May 1965	7.00
❑121, Jun 1965	5.00
❑122, Jul 1965	5.00
❑123, Aug 1965	5.00
❑124, Sep 1965	5.00
❑125, Oct 1965	5.00
❑126, Nov 1965, Series continues as Jughead, Vol. 1	5.00
❑Annual 1, ca. 1953	650.00
❑Annual 2, ca. 1954	350.00
❑Annual 3, ca. 1955	145.00
❑Annual 4, ca. 1956	85.00
❑Annual 5, ca. 1957	65.00
❑Annual 6, ca. 1958	45.00
❑Annual 7, ca. 1959	45.00
❑Annual 8, ca. 1960	45.00

ARCHIE'S PAL JUGHEAD COMICS

ARCHIE

	N-MINT
❑46, Jun 1993, Series continued from Jughead #45	1.50
❑47, Jul 1993	1.50
❑48, Aug 1993	1.50
❑49, Sep 1993	1.50
❑50, Nov 1993	1.50
❑51, Dec 1993	1.50
❑52, Jan 1994	1.50
❑53, Feb 1994	1.50
❑54, Mar 1994	1.50
❑55, Apr 1994	1.50
❑56, May 1994	1.50
❑57, Jun 1994	1.50
❑58, Jul 1994	1.50
❑59, Aug 1994	1.50
❑60, Sep 1994	1.50
❑61, Oct 1994	1.50
❑62, Nov 1994	1.50
❑63, Dec 1994	1.50
❑64, Jan 1995	1.50
❑65, Feb 1995	1.50
❑66, Mar 1995	1.50
❑67, Apr 1995	1.50
❑68, May 1995	1.50
❑69, Jun 1995	1.50
❑70, Jul 1995	1.50
❑71, Aug 1995	1.50
❑72, Sep 1995, Jellybean's real name revealed	1.50
❑73, Oct 1995	1.50
❑74, Nov 1995	1.50
❑75, Dec 1995	1.50
❑76, Jan 1996	1.50
❑77, Feb 1996	1.50
❑78, Mar 1996	1.50
❑79, Apr 1996	1.50
❑80, May 1996	1.50
❑81, Jun 1996	1.50
❑82, Jul 1996	1.50
❑83, Aug 1996	1.50
❑84, Sep 1996	1.50
❑85, Oct 1996	1.50
❑86, Nov 1996	1.50
❑87, Dec 1996	1.50
❑88, Jan 1997	1.50
❑89, Feb 1997	1.50
❑90, Mar 1997, Jughead asks Trula out	1.50
❑91, Apr 1997, Trula Twyst's true plan revealed	1.50
❑92, May 1997	1.50
❑93, Jun 1997	1.50
❑94, Jul 1997	1.50
❑95, Aug 1997	1.50
❑96, Sep 1997	1.50
❑97, Oct 1997	1.50
❑98, Nov 1997	1.50
❑99, Dec 1997	1.50
❑100, Jan 1998, continues in Archie #467	1.50
❑101, Feb 1998	1.50
❑102, Mar 1998	1.50
❑103, Apr 1998	1.50
❑104, May 1998	1.50
❑105, Jun 1998	1.50
❑106, Jul 1998	1.50
❑107, Aug 1998	1.50
❑108, Sep 1998	1.75
❑109, Oct 1998	1.75
❑110, Nov 1998	1.75
❑111, Dec 1998	1.75
❑112, Jan 1999	1.75
❑113, Feb 1999	1.75
❑114, Mar 1999	1.75
❑115, Apr 1999	1.75
❑116, May 1999	1.75
❑117, Jun 1999	1.75
❑118, Jul 1999	1.75
❑119, Aug 1999, Ethel gets Jughead's baby pictures	1.75
❑120, Sep 1999	1.75
❑121, Oct 1999	1.75
❑122, Nov 1999	1.75
❑123, Dec 1999	1.75
❑124, Jan 2000	1.75
❑125, Feb 2000	1.75
❑126, Apr 2000	1.75
❑127, May 2000	1.75
❑128, Jul 2000	1.99
❑129, Aug 2000	1.99
❑130, Sep 2000	1.99
❑131, Oct 2000	1.99
❑132, Dec 2000	1.99
❑133, Jan 2001	1.99
❑134, Feb 2001	1.99
❑135, Apr 2001	1.99
❑136, May 2001	1.99
❑137, Jul 2001	1.99
❑138, Aug 2001	1.99
❑139, Sep 2001	1.99
❑140, Dec 2001	2.19
❑141, Feb 2002	2.19
❑142, Apr 2002	2.19
❑143, Jun 2002	2.19
❑144, Aug 2002	2.19
❑145, Sep 2002	2.19
❑146, Oct 2002	2.19
❑147, Dec 2002	2.19
❑148, Feb 2003	2.19
❑149, Apr 2003	2.19
❑150, Jun 2003	2.19
❑151, Jul 2003	2.19
❑152, Sep 2003	2.19
❑153, Oct 2003	2.19
❑154, Dec 2003	2.19
❑155, Feb 2004	2.19
❑156, Apr 2004	2.19
❑157, Jun 2004	2.19

Other grades: Multiply price above by 5/6 for VF/NM • 2/3 for VERY FINE • 1/3 for FINE • 1/5 for VERY GOOD • 1/8 for GOOD

Archie 3000	Area 52	Area 88	Areala: Angel of War	Argus

A look at Archie's life in the future ©Archie	Science-fiction military misfits in action ©Image	SF series was one of the earlier manga imports ©Eclipse	Warrior Nun Areala's Viking origins ©Antarctic	High-tech agent caught up in intrigue ©DC

	N-MINT
❑158, Aug 2004	2.19
❑159, Sep 2004	2.19
❑160, Oct 2004	2.19
❑161, Dec 2004	2.19
❑162, Jan 2004	2.19
❑163, Feb 2005	2.19
❑164 2005	2.39
❑165 2005	2.39
❑166, Aug 2005	2.39
❑167, Sep 2005	2.39
❑168, Oct 2005	2.39
❑169, Nov 2005	2.39
❑170, Jan 2006	2.39
❑172, May 2006	2.39
❑173, Jun 2006	2.39
❑174, Aug 2006	2.39

ARCHIE'S PALS 'N' GALS

ARCHIE

	N-MINT
❑1, ca. 1952	575.00
❑2, ca. 1954	290.00
❑3, ca. 1955	215.00
❑4, ca. 1956	185.00
❑5, ca. 1957	185.00
❑6, ca. 1957	135.00
❑7, ca. 1958	135.00
❑8, Spr 1959	80.00
❑9, Sum 1959	80.00
❑10, Fal 1959	80.00
❑11, Win 1959	45.00
❑12, Spr 1960	45.00
❑13, Sum 1960	45.00
❑14, Fal 1960	45.00
❑15, Win 1960	45.00
❑16, Spr 1961	45.00
❑17, Sum 1961	45.00
❑18, Fal 1961	45.00
❑19, Win 1961	45.00
❑20, Spr 1962	45.00
❑21, Sum 1962	22.00
❑22, Fal 1962	22.00
❑23, Win 1962	22.00
❑24, Spr 1963	22.00
❑25, Sum 1963	22.00
❑26, Fal 1963	22.00
❑27, Win 1963	22.00
❑28, Spr 1964	22.00
❑29, Sum 1964, A: The Beatles	45.00
❑30, Fal 1964	22.00
❑31, Win 1964	13.00
❑32, Spr 1965	13.00
❑33, Sum 1965	13.00
❑34, Fal 1965	13.00
❑35, Win 1965	13.00
❑36, Spr 1966	13.00
❑37, Sum 1966	13.00
❑38, Fal 1966	13.00
❑39, Win 1966	13.00
❑40, Spr 1967	13.00
❑41, Aug 1967	9.00
❑42, Oct 1967	9.00
❑43, Dec 1967	9.00
❑44, Feb 1968	9.00
❑45, Apr 1968	9.00
❑46, Jun 1968	9.00
❑47, Aug 1968	9.00
❑48, Oct 1968	9.00
❑49, Dec 1968	9.00
❑50, Feb 1969	9.00
❑51, Apr 1969	7.00
❑52, Jun 1969	7.00
❑53, Aug 1969	7.00
❑54, Oct 1969	7.00
❑55, Dec 1969	7.00
❑56, Feb 1970	7.00
❑57, Apr 1970	7.00
❑58, Jun 1970	7.00
❑59, Aug 1970	7.00
❑60, Oct 1970	7.00
❑61, Dec 1970	7.00
❑62, Feb 1971	7.00
❑63, Apr 1971	7.00
❑64, Jun 1971	7.00
❑65, Aug 1971	7.00
❑66, Oct 1971	7.00
❑67, Dec 1971	7.00
❑68, Feb 1972	7.00
❑69, Apr 1972	7.00
❑70, Jun 1972	7.00
❑71, Aug 1972	5.00
❑72, Sep 1972	5.00
❑73, Oct 1972	5.00
❑74, Dec 1972	5.00
❑75, Feb 1973	5.00
❑76, Apr 1973	5.00
❑77, Jun 1973	5.00
❑78, Jul 1973	5.00
❑79, Aug 1973	5.00
❑80, Sep 1973	5.00
❑81, Nov 1973	5.00
❑82, Dec 1973	4.00
❑83, Jan 1974	4.00
❑84, Apr 1974	4.00
❑85, Jun 1974	4.00
❑86, Jul 1974	4.00
❑87, Aug 1974	4.00
❑88, Sep 1974	4.00
❑89, Oct 1974	4.00
❑90, Nov 1974	4.00
❑91, Dec 1974	4.00
❑92, Mar 1975	4.00
❑93, Apr 1975	4.00
❑94, Jun 1975	4.00
❑95, Jul 1975	4.00
❑96, Aug 1975	4.00
❑97, Sep 1975	4.00
❑98, Oct 1975	4.00
❑99, Nov 1975	4.00
❑100, Dec 1975	4.00
❑101, Jan 1976	2.50
❑102, Feb 1976	2.50
❑103, Mar 1976	2.50
❑104, May 1976	2.50
❑105, Jun 1976	2.50
❑106, Jul 1976	2.50
❑107, Aug 1976	2.50
❑108, Sep 1976	2.50
❑109, Oct 1976	2.50
❑110, Dec 1976	2.50
❑111, Jan 1977	2.50
❑112, Mar 1977	2.50
❑113, May 1977	2.50
❑114, Jun 1977	2.50
❑115, Jul 1977	2.50
❑116, Aug 1977	2.50
❑117, Sep 1977	2.50
❑118, Oct 1977	2.50
❑119, Dec 1977	2.50
❑120, Jan 1978	2.50
❑121, Mar 1978	2.50
❑122, May 1978	2.50
❑123, Jun 1978	2.50
❑124, Jul 1978	2.50
❑125, Aug 1978	2.50
❑126, Sep 1978	2.50
❑127, Oct 1978	2.50
❑128, Dec 1978	2.50
❑129, Jan 1979	2.50
❑130, Mar 1979	2.50
❑131, May 1979	2.50
❑132, Jun 1979	2.50
❑133, Jul 1979	2.50
❑134, Aug 1979	2.50
❑135, Sep 1979	2.50
❑136, Oct 1979	2.50
❑137, Dec 1979	2.50
❑138, Jan 1980	2.50
❑139, Mar 1980	2.50
❑140, May 1980	2.50
❑141, Jun 1980	2.50
❑142, Jul 1980	2.50
❑143, Aug 1980	2.50
❑144, Sep 1980	2.50
❑145, Oct 1980	2.50
❑146, Dec 1980	2.50
❑147, Jan 1981	2.50
❑148, Mar 1981	2.50
❑149, May 1981	2.50
❑150, Jun 1981	2.50
❑151, Jul 1981	2.00
❑152, Aug 1981	2.00
❑153, Sep 1981	2.00
❑154, Oct 1981	2.00
❑155, Dec 1981	2.00
❑156, Jan 1982	2.00
❑157, Mar 1982	2.00
❑158, May 1982	2.00
❑159, Jul 1982	2.00
❑160, Sep 1982	2.00
❑161, Nov 1982	2.00
❑162, Jan 1983	2.00
❑163, May 1983	2.00
❑164, Jul 1983	2.00
❑165, Sep 1983	2.00
❑166, Nov 1983	2.00
❑167, Jan 1984	2.00
❑168, Mar 1984	2.00
❑169, May 1984	2.00
❑170, Jul 1984	2.00
❑171, Sep 1984	2.00
❑172, Nov 1984	2.00
❑173, Jan 1985	2.00
❑174, Mar 1985	2.00

Other grades: Multiply price above by 5/6 for VF/NM • 2/3 for VERY FINE • 1/3 for FINE • 1/5 for VERY GOOD • 1/8 for GOOD

	N-MINT
❑175, May 1985	2.00
❑176, Jul 1985	2.00
❑177, Sep 1985	2.00
❑178, Nov 1985	2.00
❑179, Jan 1986	2.00
❑180, Mar 1986	2.00
❑181, May 1986	2.00
❑182, Jul 1986	2.00
❑183, Sep 1986	2.00
❑184, Nov 1986	2.00
❑185, Jan 1987	2.00
❑186, Mar 1987	2.00
❑187, May 1987	2.00
❑188, Jun 1987	2.00
❑189, Jul 1987	2.00
❑190, Aug 1987	2.00
❑191, Sep 1987	2.00
❑192, Oct 1987	2.00
❑193, Nov 1987	2.00
❑194, Jan 1988	2.00
❑195, Mar 1988	2.00
❑196, May 1988	2.00
❑197, Jun 1988	2.00
❑198, Jul 1988	2.00
❑199, Aug 1988	2.00
❑200, Sep 1988	2.00
❑201, Oct 1988	1.50
❑202, Nov 1988	1.50
❑203, Jan 1989	1.50
❑204, Mar 1989	1.50
❑205, May 1989	1.50
❑206, Jun 1989	1.50
❑207, Jul 1989	1.50
❑208, Aug 1989	1.50
❑209, Sep 1989	1.50
❑210, Oct 1989	1.50
❑211, Nov 1989	1.50
❑212, Jan 1990	1.50
❑213, Mar 1990	1.50
❑214, May 1990	1.50
❑215, Jun 1990	1.50
❑216, Jul 1990	1.50
❑217, Aug 1990	1.50
❑218, Sep 1990	1.50
❑219, Nov 1990	1.50
❑220, Jan 1991	1.50
❑221, Mar 1991	1.50
❑222, May 1991	1.50
❑223, Jul 1991	1.50
❑224, Sep 1991	1.50

ARCHIE'S PALS 'N' GALS DOUBLE DIGEST

ARCHIE

	N-MINT
❑1	4.00
❑2	3.00
❑3	3.00
❑4	3.00
❑5	3.00
❑6	2.75
❑7	2.75
❑8	2.75
❑9, Jan 1995	2.75
❑10, Feb 1995	2.75
❑11, Apr 1995	2.75
❑12, Jun 1995	2.75
❑13, Aug 1995	2.75
❑14, Oct 1995	2.75
❑15, Dec 1995	2.75
❑16, Jan 1996	2.75
❑17, Mar 1996	2.75
❑18, May 1996	2.75
❑19, Jul 1996	2.75
❑20, Aug 1996	2.75
❑21, Oct 1996	2.75
❑22, Dec 1996	2.75
❑23, Jan 1997	2.75
❑24, Mar 1997	2.75
❑25, May 1997	2.75
❑26, Jul 1997	2.75
❑27, Aug 1997	2.75
❑28, Oct 1997	2.75
❑29, Dec 1997	2.75
❑30, Jan 1998	2.95
❑31, Mar 1998	2.95
❑32, May 1998	2.95
❑33, Jun 1998	2.95
❑34, Aug 1998	2.95
❑35, Sep 1998	2.95
❑36, Oct 1998	2.95
❑37, Dec 1998	2.95
❑38, Feb 1999	2.95
❑39, Apr 1999	2.95
❑40, May 1999	2.99
❑41, Jun 1999	2.99
❑42, Aug 1999	2.99
❑43, Sep 1999	2.99
❑44, Oct 1999	2.99
❑45, Dec 1999	2.99
❑46, Feb 2000	2.99
❑47, Mar 2000	2.99
❑48, May 2000	2.99
❑49, Jun 2000	3.19
❑50, Aug 2000	3.19
❑51, Sep 2000	3.19
❑52, Oct 2000	3.19
❑53, Dec 2000	3.19
❑54, Feb 2001	3.19
❑55, Mar 2001	3.19
❑56, May 2001	3.29
❑57, Jun 2001	3.29
❑58, Aug 2001	3.29
❑59, Sep 2001	3.29
❑60, Oct 2001	3.29
❑61, Dec 2001	3.29
❑62, Feb 2002	3.29
❑63, Mar 2002	3.29
❑64, May 2002	3.29
❑65, Jun 2002	3.29
❑66, Aug 2002	3.29
❑67, Sep 2002	3.29
❑68, Oct 2002	3.29
❑69, Dec 2002	3.29
❑70, Feb 2003	3.29
❑71, Mar 2003	3.59
❑72, May 2003	3.59
❑73, Jun 2003	3.59
❑74, Aug 2003	3.59
❑75, Sep 2003	3.59
❑76, Oct 2003	3.59
❑77, Sep 2003	3.59
❑78, Oct 2003	3.59
❑79, Dec 2003	3.59
❑80, Jan 2004	3.59
❑81, Feb 2004	3.59
❑82, Apr 2004	3.59
❑83, May 2004	3.59
❑84, Jun 2004	3.59
❑85, Jul 2004	3.59
❑86, Aug 2004	3.59
❑87, Sep 2004	3.59
❑88, Oct 2004	3.59
❑89, Jan 2005	3.59
❑90, Feb 2005	3.59
❑91, Mar 2005	3.59
❑92, Apr 2005	3.59
❑93, May 2005	3.59
❑94, Aug 2005	3.59
❑95, Sep 2005	3.59
❑96, Oct 2005	3.59
❑97, Nov 2005	3.59
❑98, Jan 2005	3.59
❑99, Feb 2005	3.59
❑100, Mar 2006	3.59
❑101, May 2006	3.59
❑102, Jun 2006	3.59
❑103, Aug 2006	3.59

ARCHIE'S R/C RACERS

ARCHIE

	N-MINT
❑1, Sep 1989; Reggie appearance	2.00
❑2, Nov 1989	1.50
❑3, Jan 1990	1.50
❑4, Mar 1990	1.50
❑5, May 1990; Tennessee tribute corner box	1.50
❑6, Jul 1990; Kentucky tribute corner box	1.50
❑7, Sep 1990; Ohio tribute corner box	1.50
❑8, Nov 1990; Missouri tribute corner box	1.50
❑9, Jan 1991; Texas tribute cover box	1.50
❑10, Mar 1991	1.50

ARCHIE'S SPRING BREAK

ARCHIE

	N-MINT
❑1 1996	2.50
❑2 1997	2.50
❑3 1998	2.50
❑4 1999	2.50
❑5 2000	2.50

ARCHIE'S STORY & GAME DIGEST MAGAZINE

ARCHIE

	N-MINT
❑32, Jul 1995	2.00
❑33, Sep 1995	2.00
❑34, Mar 1996	2.00
❑35, May 1996	2.00
❑36, ca. 1996	2.00
❑37, Jan 1997	2.00
❑38, Aug 1997	2.00
❑39, Jan 1998	2.00

ARCHIE'S SUPER-HERO SPECIAL

ARCHIE / RED CIRCLE

	N-MINT
❑1, Jan 1979, JK (a); reprints Adventures of the Fly #2; reprints Double Life of Private Strong #1	3.00
❑2, Aug 1979, JK (a); reprints Double Life of Private Strong #1; reprints Double Life of Private Strong #2	3.00

ARCHIE'S SUPER TEENS

ARCHIE

	N-MINT
❑1 1994, poster	2.50
❑2 1995	2.50
❑3 1995	2.50
❑4 1996	2.50

ARCHIE'S TV LAUGH-OUT

ARCHIE

	N-MINT
❑1, Dec 1969	42.00
❑2, Mar 1970	24.00
❑3, Jun 1970	16.00
❑4, Sep 1970	16.00
❑5 1971	16.00
❑6 1971	12.00
❑7 1971; Josie and the Pussycats features begin	22.00
❑8, Aug 1971	12.00
❑9 1971	12.00
❑10 1971	12.00
❑11, Feb 1972	9.00
❑12, May 1972	9.00
❑13, Aug 1972	9.00
❑14, Sep 1972	9.00
❑15, Oct 1972	9.00
❑16, Dec 1972	9.00
❑17 1973	9.00
❑18 1973	9.00
❑19 1973	9.00
❑20 1973	9.00
❑21 1973	7.00
❑22, Oct 1973	7.00
❑23, Dec 1973	7.00
❑24, May 1974	7.00
❑25, Jul 1974	7.00
❑26, Aug 1974	7.00
❑27, Sep 1974	7.00
❑28, Oct 1974	7.00
❑29, Dec 1974	7.00
❑30, Feb 1975	7.00
❑31, May 1975	6.00
❑32, Jul 1975	6.00
❑33, Aug 1975	6.00
❑34, Sep 1975	6.00
❑35, Oct 1975	6.00
❑36, Dec 1975	6.00
❑37, Feb 1976	6.00
❑38, Mar 1976	6.00
❑39, Apr 1976	6.00
❑40, Jun 1976	6.00
❑41, Jul 1976	4.00
❑42, Aug 1976	4.00
❑43, Sep 1976	4.00
❑44, Nov 1976	4.00
❑45, Dec 1976	4.00
❑46, Feb 1977	4.00
❑47, Mar 1977	4.00
❑48, Apr 1977	4.00
❑49, Jun 1977	4.00
❑50, Jul 1977	4.00
❑51, Aug 1977	4.00

Other grades: Multiply price above by 5/6 for VF/NM • 2/3 for VERY FINE • 1/3 for FINE • 1/5 for VERY GOOD • 1/8 for GOOD

Aria

Gods and faeries walk the streets

©Image

Aria: The Soul Market

Mischievous sprite arrives in modern times

©Image

Arion, Lord of Atlantis

Magical series spun off from Warlord #55

©DC

Aristocratic X-Traterrestrial Time-Traveling Thieves Micro-Series

Felon-for-hire title from the black-and-white glut

©Comics Interview

Aristokittens

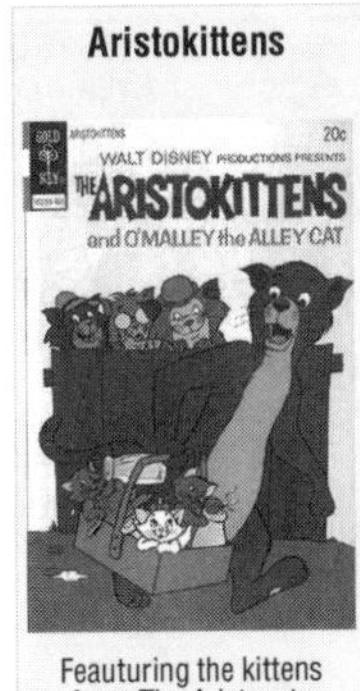

Feauturing the kittens from The Aristocats

©Gold Key

	N-MINT
❑52, Sep 1977	4.00
❑53, Nov 1977	4.00
❑54, Dec 1977	4.00
❑55, Feb 1978	4.00
❑56, Mar 1978	4.00
❑57, Apr 1978	4.00
❑58, Jun 1978	4.00
❑59, Jul 1978	4.00
❑60, Aug 1978	4.00
❑61, Sep 1978	3.00
❑62, Nov 1978	3.00
❑63, Dec 1978	3.00
❑64, Feb 1979	3.00
❑65, Mar 1979	3.00
❑66, Apr 1979	3.00
❑67, Jun 1979	3.00
❑68, Jul 1979	3.00
❑69, Aug 1979	3.00
❑70, Sep 1979	3.00
❑71, Nov 1979	3.00
❑72, Dec 1979	3.00
❑73, Feb 1980	3.00
❑74, Mar 1980	3.00
❑75, Apr 1980	3.00
❑76, Jun 1980	3.00
❑77, Jul 1980	3.00
❑78, Aug 1980	3.00
❑79, Oct 1980	3.00
❑80, Feb 1981	3.00
❑81, May 1981	2.50
❑82, Aug 1981	2.50
❑83, Oct 1981	2.50
❑84, Feb 1982	2.50
❑85, May 1982	2.50
❑86, Aug 1982	2.50
❑87, Feb 1983	2.50
❑88, Apr 1983	2.50
❑89, Jun 1983, DDC (c)	2.50
❑90, Aug 1983, DDC (c)	2.50
❑91, Oct 1983, DDC (c)	2.50
❑92, Dec 1983, DDC (c)	2.50
❑93, Feb 1984	2.50
❑94, Apr 1984	2.50
❑95, Jun 1984	2.50
❑96, Aug 1984	2.50
❑97, Oct 1984	2.50
❑98, Dec 1984	2.50
❑99, Feb 1985	2.50
❑100, Apr 1985, DDC (a); A: Jackie Maxon	2.50
❑101, Jun 1985	2.50
❑102, Aug 1985	2.50
❑103, Oct 1985	2.50
❑104, Dec 1985	2.50
❑105, Feb 1986	2.50
❑106, Apr 1986	2.50

ARCHIE'S VACATION SPECIAL
ARCHIE

❑1, Sum 1994 DDC (a)	2.50
❑2, Win 1995	2.50
❑3, Sum 1995	2.50
❑4, Sum 1996	2.50
❑5, Sum 1997	2.50
❑6, Sum 1998	2.50
❑7, Sum 1999	2.50
❑8, Sum 2000	2.50

ARCHIE'S WEIRD MYSTERIES
ARCHIE

❑1, Feb 2000	2.00
❑2, Mar 2000	2.00
❑3, Apr 2000	2.00
❑4, May 2000	2.00
❑5, Jun 2000	2.00
❑6, Jul 2000	2.00
❑7, Aug 2000	2.00
❑8, Sep 2000	2.00
❑9, Oct 2000	2.00
❑10, Dec 2000	2.00
❑11, Feb 2001	2.00
❑12, Apr 2001	2.00
❑13, ca. 2001	2.00
❑14, ca. 2001	2.00
❑15, ca. 2001	2.00
❑16, ca. 2001	2.00
❑17	2.19
❑18, Feb 2002	2.19
❑19, Apr 2002	2.19
❑20, Jun 2002	2.19
❑21, Aug 2002	2.19
❑22, Sep 2002	2.19
❑23, Oct 2002	2.19
❑24, Dec 2002; Series changes to Archie's Mysteries	2.19
❑Ashcan 1; Giveaway from Diamond	1.00

ARCHIE 3000
ARCHIE

❑1, May 1989	2.50
❑2, Jul 1989	2.00
❑3, Aug 1989	2.00
❑4, Oct 1989	2.00
❑5, Nov 1989	2.00
❑6, Jan 1990	1.00
❑7, Mar 1990	1.00
❑8, May 1990	1.00
❑9, Jul 1990	1.00
❑10, Aug 1990	1.00
❑11, Oct 1990	1.00
❑12, Nov 1990	1.00
❑13, Jan 1991	1.00
❑14, Mar 1991	1.00
❑15, May 1991	1.00

ARCOMICS PREMIERE
ARCOMICS

❑1, Jul 1993, b&w; lenticular animation cover	2.95

ARCTIC COMICS
NICK BURNS

❑1; souvenir	1.00

AREA 52
IMAGE

❑1, Jan 2001	2.95
❑1/A, Jan 2001; Gold Foil Title	2.95
❑1/B, Jan 2001; Red Foil Title	2.95
❑2, Mar 2001	2.95
❑3, Apr 2001	2.95
❑4, ca. 2001	2.95

AREA 88
ECLIPSE / VIZ

❑1, May 1987	3.50
❑1/2nd	2.00
❑2, Jun 1987	2.50
❑2/2nd	2.00
❑3, Jun 1987	2.00
❑4, Jul 1987	2.00
❑5, Jul 1987	2.00
❑6, Aug 1987	2.00
❑7, Aug 1987	2.00
❑8, Sep 1987	2.00
❑9, Sep 1987	2.00
❑10, Oct 1987	2.00
❑11, Oct 1987	2.00
❑12, Nov 1987	2.00
❑13, Nov 1987	2.00
❑14, Dec 1987	2.00
❑15, Dec 1987	2.00
❑16, Jan 1988	2.00
❑17, Jan 1988	2.00
❑18, Feb 1988	2.00
❑19, Feb 1988	2.00
❑20, Mar 1988	2.00
❑21, Mar 1988	2.00
❑22, Apr 1988	2.00
❑23, Apr 1988	2.00
❑24, May 1988	2.00
❑25, May 1988	2.00
❑26, Jun 1988	2.00
❑27, Jun 1988	2.00
❑28, Jul 1988	2.00
❑29, Jul 1988	2.00
❑30, Aug 1988	2.00
❑31, Aug 1988	2.00
❑32, Sep 1988	2.00
❑33, Sep 1988	2.00
❑34, Oct 1988	2.00
❑35, Oct 1988	2.00
❑36, Nov 1988	2.00
❑37, Nov 1988	2.00
❑38, Dec 1988	2.00
❑39, Dec 1988	2.00
❑40, Jan 1989	2.00
❑41, Jan 1989	2.00
❑42, Feb 1989	2.00
❑Book 1; b&w, reprint	12.95

AREALA: ANGEL OF WAR
ANTARCTIC

❑1, Sep 1998	2.95
❑2, Nov 1998	2.95
❑3, Feb 1999	2.95
❑4, Jun 1999	2.99

ARENA
ALCHEMY

❑1, b&w	1.50

ARES
MARVEL

❑1, Mar 2006	2.99
❑2, Apr 2006	2.99
❑3, Jun 2006	2.99
❑4, Jul 2006	2.99

Other grades: Multiply price above by 5/6 for VF/NM • 2/3 for VERY FINE • 1/3 for FINE • 1/5 for VERY GOOD • 1/8 for GOOD

N-MINT

ARGONAUTS (ETERNITY)
ETERNITY

❑1 ... 1.95
❑2 ... 1.95
❑3 ... 1.95
❑4 ... 1.95

ARGONAUTS, THE: SYSTEM CRASH
ALPHA PRODUCTIONS

❑1 ... 2.50
❑2 ... 2.50

ARGON ZARK!
ARCLIGHT

❑1 1997; based on on-line comics series ... 6.95

ARGUS
DC

❑1, Apr 1995 ... 1.50
❑2, Jun 1995 ... 1.50
❑3, Jul 1995 ... 1.50
❑4, Aug 1995 ... 1.50
❑5, Sep 1995 ... 1.50
❑6, Oct 1995 ... 1.50

ARIA
IMAGE

❑1, Jan 1999 ... 3.00
❑1/A, Jan 1999; white background cover ... 3.00
❑1/B, Jan 1999; Woman looking from balcony on cover ... 3.00
❑2, Apr 1999 ... 2.50
❑3, May 1999 ... 2.50
❑4/A, Nov 1999; Textured cover stock; Close-up shot of woman in green pointing at chest ... 2.50
❑4/B, Nov 1999; Variant cover with Angela ... 2.50
❑5, ca. 1999 ... 2.50
❑6, ca. 1999 ... 2.50
❑7, ca. 1999 ... 2.50
❑Ashcan 1, Nov 1998, b&w; preview issue ... 3.50

ARIA: A MIDWINTER'S DREAM
IMAGE

❑1, Jan 2002 ... 4.95

ARIA ANGELA
IMAGE

❑1/A, Feb 2000, Aria and Angela in profile on cover ... 2.95
❑1/B, Feb 2000, Aria sitting on stairs on cover ... 2.95
❑1/C, Feb 2000, Close-up on Aria (right half of 1/H cover in close-up) ... 2.95
❑1/D, Feb 2000, Woman walking through astral plane on cover ... 2.95
❑1/E, Feb 2000, Woman walking through astral plane on cover ... 2.95
❑1/F, Feb 2000, Two women, hawk on cover ... 2.95
❑1/G, Feb 2000, Tower records variant; Woman with sword (between legs) on cover ... 2.95
❑1/H, Feb 2000 ... 2.95
❑1/I, Feb 2000, chromium cover ... 2.95
❑2, Oct 2000 ... 2.95

ARIA ANGELA BLANC & NOIR
IMAGE

❑1, Apr 2000, Reprints Aria Angela #1 in black & white ... 2.95

ARIA BLANC & NOIR
IMAGE

❑1, Mar 1999; b&w reprint of Aria #1; wraparound cover ... 2.50
❑2, Sep 1999 ... 2.50

ARIA (MANGA)
ADV MANGA

❑1, ca. 2004 ... 9.99

ARIANE & BLUEBEARD
ECLIPSE

❑1, ca. 1989, Part of Eclipse's Night Music Series ... 3.95

ARIANNE
SLAVE LABOR

❑1, May 1991 ... 4.95
❑2, Oct 1991 ... 2.95

N-MINT

ARIANNE (MOONSTONE)
MOONSTONE

❑1, Dec 1995, b&w ... 4.95

ARIA SUMMER'S SPELL
IMAGE

❑1, Mar 2002 ... 2.95
❑2, Jun 2002 ... 2.95

ARIA: THE SOUL MARKET
IMAGE

❑1, Mar 2001 ... 2.95
❑2, Apr 2001 ... 2.95
❑3, May 2001 ... 2.95
❑4, Jun 2001 ... 2.95
❑5, Jul 2001 ... 2.95
❑6, Aug 2001 ... 2.95

ARIA: THE USES OF ENCHANTMENT
IMAGE

❑1, Feb 2003 ... 2.95
❑2, Apr 2003 ... 2.95
❑3, Jul 2003 ... 2.95
❑4, Sep 2003 ... 2.95

ARIK KHAN (A+)
A-PLUS

❑1; b&w, reprint ... 2.50
❑2 ... 2.50

ARIK KHAN (ANDROMEDA)
ANDROMEDA

❑1, Sep 1977 ... 1.95
❑2 ... 1.95
❑3 ... 1.95

ARION, LORD OF ATLANTIS
DC

❑1, Nov 1982, JDu (a); Story continued from Warlord #62 ... 1.00
❑2, Dec 1982, JDu (a); 1: Mara ... 1.00
❑3, Jan 1983, JDu (a) ... 1.00
❑4, Feb 1983, JDu (a) ... 1.00
❑5, Mar 1983, JDu (a) ... 1.00
❑6, Apr 1983, JDu (a) ... 1.00
❑7, May 1983, JDu (a) ... 1.00
❑8, Jun 1983 ... 1.00
❑9, Jul 1983 ... 1.00
❑10, Aug 1983 ... 1.00
❑11, Sep 1983 ... 1.00
❑12, Oct 1983, JDu (a) ... 1.00
❑13, Nov 1983 ... 1.00
❑14, Dec 1983 ... 1.00
❑15, Jan 1984 ... 1.00
❑16, Feb 1984 ... 1.00
❑17, Mar 1984 ... 1.00
❑18, Apr 1984 ... 1.00
❑19, May 1984 ... 1.00
❑20, Jun 1984 ... 1.00
❑21, Jul 1984 ... 1.00
❑22, Aug 1984 ... 1.00
❑23, Sep 1984 ... 1.00
❑24, Oct 1984 ... 1.00
❑25, Nov 1984 ... 1.00
❑26, Dec 1984 ... 1.00
❑27, Jan 1985 ... 1.00
❑28, Feb 1985 ... 1.00
❑29, Mar 1985 ... 1.00
❑30, Apr 1985 ... 1.00
❑31, May 1985 ... 1.00
❑32, Jun 1985 ... 1.00
❑33, Jul 1985 ... 1.00
❑34, Aug 1985 ... 1.00
❑35, Sep 1985 ... 1.00
❑Special 1, ca. 1985 ... 1.00

ARION THE IMMORTAL
DC

❑1, Jul 1992 ... 1.50
❑2, Aug 1992 ... 1.50
❑3, Sep 1992 ... 1.50
❑4, Oct 1992 ... 1.50
❑5, Nov 1992 ... 1.50
❑6, Dec 1992 ... 1.50

ARISTOCATS
GOLD KEY

❑1, Mar 1971, 30045-103; poster ... 3.50

N-MINT

ARISTOCRATIC X-TRATERRESTRIAL TIME-TRAVELING THIEVES
COMICS INTERVIEW

❑1, Feb 1987 ... 2.00
❑2, Apr 1987 ... 2.00
❑3, Jun 1987 ... 2.00
❑4, Aug 1987 ... 2.00
❑5, Oct 1987 ... 2.00
❑6, Dec 1987 ... 2.00
❑7, Feb 1988 ... 2.00
❑8, Apr 1988 ... 2.00
❑9, Jun 1988 ... 2.00
❑10, Aug 1988 ... 2.00
❑11, Oct 1988 ... 2.00
❑12, Dec 1988 ... 2.00

ARISTOCRATIC X-TRATERRESTRIAL TIME-TRAVELING THIEVES MICRO-SERIES
COMICS INTERVIEW

❑1, Aug 1986 ... 2.00
❑1/2nd ... 2.00

ARISTOKITTENS
GOLD KEY

❑1, Oct 1973 ... 16.00
❑2, Feb 1974 ... 10.00
❑3, Apr 1974 ... 8.00
❑4, Jul 1974 ... 8.00
❑5, Oct 1974 ... 8.00
❑6, Jan 1975 ... 6.00
❑7, Apr 1975 ... 6.00
❑8, Jul 1975 ... 6.00
❑9, Oct 1975 ... 6.00

ARIZONA: A SIMPLE HORROR
LONDON NIGHT

❑1, May 1998 ... 3.00
❑1/Nude, May 1998 ... 3.00

ARIZONA: WILD AT HEART
LONDON NIGHT

❑1, Feb 1998 ... 2.99

ARKAGA
IMAGE

❑1, Sep 1997 ... 2.95
❑2, Nov 1997 ... 2.95

ARK ANGELS
TOKYOPOP

❑1, Dec 2005 ... 9.99

ARKANIUM
DREAMWAVE

❑1, Sep 2002 ... 2.95
❑2, Nov 2002 ... 2.95
❑3, Jan 2003 ... 2.95
❑4, Feb 2003 ... 2.95
❑5, Mar 2003 ... 2.95

ARKEOLOGY
VALKYRIE

❑1, Apr 1989; companion one-shot for The Adventures of Luther Arkwright ... 2.00

ARKHAM ASYLUM LIVING HELL
DC

❑1, May 2003 ... 2.50
❑2, Jun 2003 ... 2.50
❑3, Jul 2003 ... 2.50
❑4, Aug 2003 ... 2.50
❑5, Sep 2003 ... 2.50
❑6, Oct 2003 ... 2.50

ARLINGTON HAMMER IN: GET ME TO THE CHURCH ON TIME
ONE SHOT

❑1 comic for sale at conventions only ... 2.50

A.R.M.
ADVENTURE

❑1, Introduction by Larry Niven ... 2.50
❑2 ... 2.50
❑3 ... 2.50

ARMADILLO COMICS
RIP OFF

❑1 ... 2.50
❑2 ... 2.50

ARMAGEDDON
LAST GASP

❑1 ... 2.50
❑2 ... 2.50

AGRONAUTS

Other grades: Multiply price above by 5/6 for VF/NM • 2/3 for VERY FINE • 1/3 for FINE • 1/5 for VERY GOOD • 1/8 for GOOD

Armorines

Valiant's special strike force of armored marines
©Valiant

Armorines (Vol. 2)

Acclaim reboots series under a new label
©Acclaim

Army of Darkness

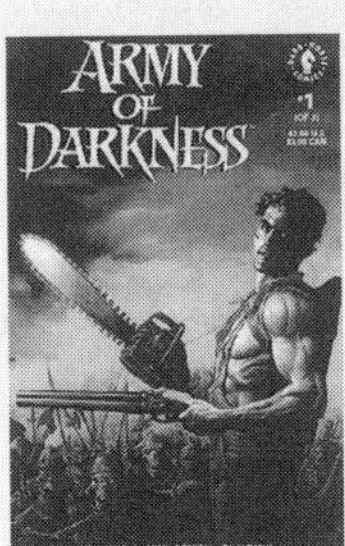

Big-budget sequel to Evil Dead movies
©Dark Horse

Army War Heroes

Charlton's tales of military courage
©Charlton

Artesia

Adult sword-and-sorcery with female lead
©Sirius

N-MINT

ARMAGEDDON (CHAOS)
CHAOS

- ❑1, Oct 1999 .... 2.95
- ❑2, Nov 1999 .... 2.95
- ❑3, Dec 1999 .... 2.95
- ❑4, Jan 2000 .... 2.95

ARMAGEDDON 2001
DC

- ❑1, May 1991 .... 2.00
- ❑1/2nd, May 1991 .... 2.00
- ❑1/3rd, May 1991; 3rd printing (silver ink on cover) 2.00
- ❑2, Oct 1991; Monarch's ID revealed.. 2.00

ARMAGEDDON: INFERNO
DC

- ❑1, Apr 1992 .... 1.00
- ❑2, May 1992 .... 1.00
- ❑3, Jun 1992 .... 1.00
- ❑4, Jul 1992; JSA returns from limbo 1.00

ARMAGEDDON: THE ALIEN AGENDA
DC

- ❑1, Nov 1991 .... 1.00
- ❑2, Dec 1991 .... 1.00
- ❑3, Jan 1992 .... 1.00
- ❑4, Feb 1992 .... 1.00

ARMAGEDDON FACTOR
AC

- ❑1, Jun 1987 .... 1.95
- ❑2, Aug 1987 .... 1.95
- ❑3 .... 1.95

ARMAGEDDON FACTOR, THE: THE CONCLUSION
AC

- ❑1 1990, b&w 3.95

ARMAGEDDONQUEST
STARHEAD

- ❑1 1994 .... 3.95
- ❑2 1994 .... 3.95

ARMAGEDDON RISING
MILLENNIUM

- ❑1 1997, b&w; special foil edition; features characters from Song of the Sirens 4.95

ARMAGEDDON SQUAD
HAZE

- ❑1, b&w 1.50

ARMATURE
OLYOPTICS

- ❑1, Nov 1996 .... 2.95
- ❑2, ca. 1997 .... 2.95

ARMED AND DANGEROUS (ACCLAIM)
ACCLAIM / ARMADA

- ❑1, Apr 1996, b&w 2.95
- ❑2, May 1996, b&w 2.95
- ❑3, Jun 1996, b&w 2.95
- ❑4, Jul 1996, b&w 2.95
- ❑Special 1, Aug 1996, b&w; one-shot special; later indicias show this is really issue #5 of series 2.95

N-MINT

ARMED & DANGEROUS: HELL'S SLAUGHTERHOUSE
ACCLAIM

- ❑1 .... 2.95
- ❑2 .... 2.95
- ❑3 .... 2.95
- ❑4 .... 2.95

ARMED & DANGEROUS (KITCHEN SINK)
KITCHEN SINK

- ❑1, Jul 1995; magazine-sized graphic novel 9.95

ARMEN DEEP & BUG BOY
DILEMMA

- ❑2 1995, b&w; cardstock cover 2.50

ARMITAGE
FLEETWAY-QUALITY

- ❑1; cardstock cover 2.95
- ❑2; cardstock cover 2.95

ARM OF KANNON
TOKYOPOP

- ❑1, May 2004 .... 9.99
- ❑2, Jul 2004 .... 9.99
- ❑3, Sep 2004 .... 9.99
- ❑4, Dec 2004 .... 9.99
- ❑5, Mar 2005 .... 9.99
- ❑6, Jun 2005 .... 9.99
- ❑7, Oct 2005 .... 9.99

ARMOR
CONTINUITY

- ❑4, Jul 1988; First three issues published as Revengers Featuring Armor and Silverstreak 2.00
- ❑5, Dec 1988 .... 2.00
- ❑6, Apr 1989 .... 2.00
- ❑7, Jan 1990 .... 2.00
- ❑8, Apr 1990 .... 2.00
- ❑9, Apr 1991 .... 2.00
- ❑10, Aug 1991 .... 2.00
- ❑11, Nov 1991 .... 2.00
- ❑12, Mar 1992 .... 2.00
- ❑13, Apr 1992 .... 2.00

ARMOR (2ND SERIES)
CONTINUITY

- ❑1, Apr 1993; wraparound foil cardstock cover; 2 trading cards; indicia calls title "Armor: Deathwatch 2000" 2.50
- ❑2, May 1993; trading card; diecut outer cover; indicia calls title "Armor: Deathwatch 2000" 2.50
- ❑3, Aug 1993; Indicia reverts to Armor as title 2.50
- ❑4, Oct 1993 .... 2.50
- ❑5, Nov 1993 .... 2.50
- ❑6, Nov 1993 .... 2.50

ARMORED TROOPER VOTOMS
CPM

- ❑1, Jul 1996 .... 2.95

N-MINT

ARMORINES
VALIANT

- ❑0/Gold, Feb 1993; Gold edition; gold edition 25.00
- ❑0, Feb 1993; "Fall Fling Preview Edition"; no cover price 1.00
- ❑0/StandAlone, Feb 1993 .... 30.00
- ❑1/VVSS, Jun 1994 .... 40.00
- ❑1, Jun 1994 .... 1.00
- ❑2, Aug 1994 .... 1.00
- ❑3, Sep 1994 .... 1.00
- ❑4, Oct 1994 .... 1.00
- ❑5, Nov 1994; Continues from Harbinger #34; Chaos Effect Delta 2 1.00
- ❑6, Dec 1994 A: X-O 1.00
- ❑7, Jan 1995; wraparound cover 1.00
- ❑8, Feb 1995 .... 1.00
- ❑9, Mar 1995 .... 2.00
- ❑10, Apr 1995 .... 2.00
- ❑11, May 1995 .... 2.00
- ❑12, Jun 1995 .... 4.00

ARMORINES (VOL. 2)
ACCLAIM

- ❑1, Oct 1999 .... 3.95
- ❑2, Nov 1999 .... 3.95
- ❑3, Dec 1999 .... 3.95
- ❑4, Jan 2000 A: X-O Manowar 3.95

ARMORQUEST
ALIAS

- ❑0 2005 .... 2.99
- ❑1, Sep 2005 .... 2.99
- ❑2, Dec 2005 ....

ARMOR X
IMAGE

- ❑1, Apr 2005 .... 2.95
- ❑2, May 2005 .... 2.95
- ❑3, Jun 2005 .... 2.95
- ❑4, Jul 2005 .... 2.95

ARM'S LENGTH
THIRD WIND

- ❑1, Jul 2000, b&w 3.95

ARMY ANTS (MICHAEL T. DESING'S...)
MICHAEL T. DESING

- ❑8, b&w 2.50

ARMY AT WAR
DC

- ❑1, Oct 1978 .... 10.00

ARMY OF DARKNESS
DARK HORSE

- ❑1, Nov 1992 .... 12.00
- ❑2, Nov 1992 .... 9.00
- ❑3, Oct 1993 .... 9.00

ARMY OF DARKNESS: ASHES 2 ASHES
DEVIL'S DUE

- ❑1, Jul 2004 .... 10.00
- ❑1/Incentive, Jul 2004 .... 5.00
- ❑1/Photo, Jul 2004 .... 4.00
- ❑1/Silvestri, Jul 2004 .... 3.00
- ❑1/Sketch, Jul 2004 .... 11.00
- ❑1/DirCut, Jul 2004 .... 7.00

Other grades: Multiply price above by 5/6 for VF/NM • 2/3 for VERY FINE • 1/3 for FINE • 1/5 for VERY GOOD • 1/8 for GOOD

❑1/Templesmith, Jul 2004 2.99
❑2, Aug 2004 4.00
❑2/B&W, Aug 2004 5.00
❑2/Photo, Aug 2004 3.00
❑2/Dynamic, Aug 2004 7.00
❑2/Land, Aug 2004 3.00
❑2/Isanove, Aug 2004 4.00
❑3, ca. 2004 3.00
❑4, ca. 2004 4.00
❑4/Garza, ca. 2004 3.00

ARMY OF DARKNESS: SHOP TIL YOU DROP (DEAD)
DEVIL'S DUE

❑1 2005; Bradshaw cover 2.99
❑1/Ebas 2005 4.00
❑1/Isanove 2005 3.00
❑1/Lee 2005 4.00
❑1/Rivera 2005 3.00
❑1/Glow 2005; 300 created 35.00
❑2 2005 2.99
❑2/Variant 2005 8.00
❑2/DF 2005 15.00
❑3 2005 2.99
❑4 2005 2.99

ARMY SURPLUS KOMIKZ FEATURING: CUTEY BUNNY
QUAGMIRE

❑1; Quagmire publishes 3.00
❑2 2.50
❑3 2.50
❑4 2.50
❑5 1985, b&w; X-Men parody; Eclipse publishes 2.50

ARMY WAR HEROES
CHARLTON

❑1, ca. 1963 20.00
❑2, ca. 1964 10.00
❑3, May 1964 8.00
❑4, Jul 1964 8.00
❑5, Oct 1964 8.00
❑6, Dec 1964 6.00
❑7, ca. 1965 6.00
❑8, May 1965 6.00
❑9, Aug 1965 6.00
❑10, Sep 1965 6.00
❑11, Nov 1965 6.00
❑12, Jan 1966 6.00
❑13, ca. 1966 6.00
❑14, Jun 1966 6.00
❑15, Aug 1966 6.00
❑16, Oct 1966 6.00
❑17, Dec 1966 6.00
❑18, Feb 1967 6.00
❑19, May 1967 6.00
❑20, Jul 1967 4.00
❑21, Sep 1967 4.00
❑22, Nov 1967, O: Iron Corporal. ❑1: Iron Corporal 6.00
❑23, Jan 1968 4.00
❑24, Mar 1968 4.00
❑25, Jun 1968 4.00
❑26, Aug 1968 4.00
❑27, Oct 1968 4.00
❑28, Nov 1968 4.00
❑29, Jan 1969 4.00
❑30, Feb 1969 4.00
❑31, Apr 1969 4.00
❑32, Jun 1969 4.00
❑33, Aug 1969 4.00
❑34, Oct 1969 4.00
❑35, Dec 1969 4.00
❑36, Feb 1970, A: Iron Corporal 4.00
❑37, Apr 1970 4.00
❑38, Jun 1970 4.00

AROMATIC BITTERS
TOKYOPOP

❑1, Mar 2004 9.99

AROUND THE WORLD UNDER THE SEA
DELL

❑1, Dec 1966 20.00

ARRGH!
MARVEL

❑1, Dec 1974, TS (a) 5.00
❑2, Feb 1975, TS (a) 4.00
❑3, May 1975, AA (a) 3.00
❑4, Jul 1975 3.00
❑5, Sep 1975, RA (a) 3.00

ARROW
MALIBU

❑1 1.95

ARROW ANTHOLOGY
ARROW

❑1, Nov 1997; The Fool, Jabberwocky, Great Scott, Night Streets, Battle Bot 3.95
❑2, Jan 1998; Simone & Ajax, Battle Bot, Night Streets, Miss Chevious, Dark Oz 3.95
❑3, Mar 1998; The Fool, Dragon Storm, Great Scott, Ninja Duck, Simone & Ajax, Samantha 3.95
❑4, Sep 1998; August, Land of Oz, Corhawk, Mr. Nightmare, Simone & Ajax; Flip book, with two front covers 3.95

ARROWMAN
PARODY

❑1, b&w 2.50

ARROWSMITH
DC / WILDSTORM

❑1, Jul 2003 2.95
❑2, Aug 2003 2.95
❑3, Sep 2003 2.95
❑4, Nov 2003 2.95
❑5, Jan 2004 2.95
❑6, May 2004 2.95
❑Book 1, ca. 2004 14.95

ARROWSMITH/ASTRO CITY
DC / WILDSTORM

❑1, Jun 2004 2.95

ARROW SPOTLIGHT
ARROW

❑1 1998, b&w; Simone & Ajax 2.95

ARSENAL
DC

❑1, Oct 1998 2.50
❑2, Nov 1998 2.50
❑3, Dec 1998 2.50
❑4, Jan 1999 2.50

ARSENAL SPECIAL
DC

❑1 1996 2.95

ARSENIC LULLABY
A. SILENT

❑1, Dec 1998 5.00
❑2, Mar 1999 2.50
❑3, May 1999 2.50
❑4, Jul 1999 2.50
❑5, Sep 1999 2.50
❑6 2000 2.50
❑7 2000 2.50
❑8 2000 2.50
❑9 2000 2.50
❑10, May 2001 2.50
❑11, Jun 2001 2.50
❑12, Jul 2001 2.50
❑13, Jan 2002, No number on cover; Jan/Feb issue 2.50

ARSINOE
FANTAGRAPHICS

❑1 2005 3.95
❑2 2005 3.95
❑3, Sep 2005 3.95
❑4, Nov 2005

ART & BEAUTY MAGAZINE
KITCHEN SINK

❑1, b&w; over-sized; cardstock cover 4.95
❑2 2003 4.95

ARTBABE (VOL. 2)
FANTAGRAPHICS

❑1, May 1997 2.95
❑2, Nov 1997 2.95
❑3, Aug 1998 2.95
❑4, Apr 1999 2.95

ART D'ECCO
FANTAGRAPHICS

❑1, Jan 1990, b&w 2.50
❑2, b&w 2.50
❑3 2.75

ARTEMIS: REQUIEM
DC

❑1, Jun 1996 1.75
❑2, Jul 1996 1.75
❑3, Aug 1996 1.75
❑4, Sep 1996 1.75
❑5, Oct 1996 1.75
❑6, Nov 1996 1.75

ARTESIA
SIRIUS

❑1, Jan 1999 2.95
❑2, Feb 1999 2.95
❑3, Mar 1999 2.95
❑4, Apr 1999 2.95
❑5, May 1999 2.95
❑6, Jun 1999 2.95

ARTESIA AFIELD
SIRIUS

❑1, Jul 2000; wraparound cover 2.95
❑2, Aug 2000; wraparound cover 2.95
❑3, Sep 2000; wraparound cover 2.95
❑4, Oct 2000; wraparound cover 2.95
❑5, Nov 2000 2.95
❑6, Dec 2000 2.95

ARTESIA AFIRE
ARCHAIA STUDIOS PRESS

❑1, Jun 2003 3.95
❑2, Jul 2003; cardstock wraparound cover 3.95
❑3, Aug 2003; cardstock wraparound cover 3.95
❑4, Oct 2003 3.95
❑5, Dec 2003 3.95
❑6, Mar 2004 3.95

ARTHUR KING OF BRITAIN
TOME

❑1, ca. 1993 2.95
❑2, ca. 1993 2.95
❑3 2.95
❑4 2.95
❑5 3.95

ARTHUR SEX
AIRCEL

❑1, b&w 2.50
❑2, b&w 2.50
❑3, Jul 1991, b&w 2.50
❑4, Aug 1991, b&w 2.50
❑5, Sep 1991, b&w 2.50
❑6, Oct 1991, b&w 2.50
❑7, Nov 1991, b&w 2.50
❑8, b&w 2.50

ARTILLERY ONE-SHOT
RED BULLET

❑1 1995, b&w 2.50

ARTISTIC COMICS (KITCHEN SINK)
KITCHEN SINK

❑1, Aug 1995, b&w; adults only; new printing; squarebound 3.00
❑1/2nd 2.50

ARTISTIC COMICS
GOLDEN GATE

❑0, Mar 1973 10.00

ARTISTIC LICENTIOUSNESS
STARHEAD

❑1, b&w 2.50
❑2, ca. 1994 2.95
❑3, ca. 1997, b&w 2.95

ART OF ABRAMS
LIGHTNING

❑1, Dec 1996; b&w pin-ups 3.50

ART OF AUBREY BEARDSLEY
TOME

❑1, b&w 2.95

ART OF HEATH ROBINSON
TOME

❑1, b&w 2.95

ART OF HOMAGE STUDIOS
IMAGE

❑1 1993 JLee (a); 1: Gen13 (pin-ups, sketches) 5.50

ART OF JAY ANACLETO
IMAGE

❑1, Apr 2002 5.95

Ascension

Springboard series took creator Batt to fame

©Image

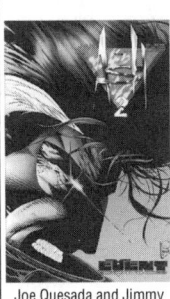

Ash

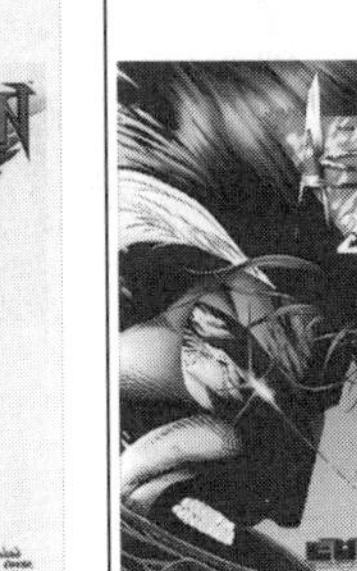

Joe Quesada and Jimmy Palmiotti's fireman hero

©Event

Astonishing Tales

Series gave rise to cyborg Deathlok

©Marvel

Astonishing X-Men (3rd Series)

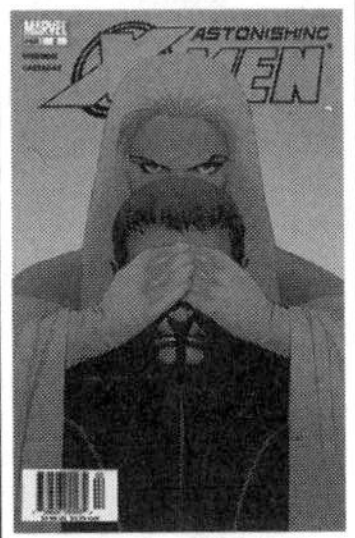

Buffy's Joss Whedon's spin on mutants

©Marvel

Astro City (Vol. 1) (Kurt Busiek's...)

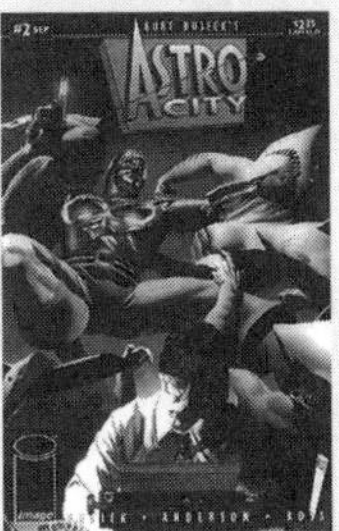

Critically acclaimed series about city of heroes

©Image

N-MINT

ART OF MUCHA
TOME

- ❑1, ca. 1992, b&w ... 2.95

ART OF PULP FICTION
A-LIST

- ❑1, Apr 1998 ... 2.95

ART OF USAGI YOJIMBO
RADIO

- ❑1, Apr 1997 ... 3.95
- ❑2, Jan 1998 ... 3.95

ASCENSION
IMAGE

- ❑0, Jun 1997; Included with Wizard Top Cow Special ... 3.00
- ❑0/Gold, Jun 1997; Gold edition ... 4.00
- ❑0/Ltd., Jun 1997; Gold cover; Wizard "Certified Authentic" ... 6.00
- ❑½, May 1998 ... 4.00
- ❑1, Oct 1997 ... 3.00
- ❑1/A, Oct 1997; Variant cover: Lucien holding head ... 3.00
- ❑1/B, Oct 1997; Fan club edition; Top Cow Fan Club exclusive ... 4.00
- ❑1/C, Oct 1997; American Entertainment exclusive ... 4.00
- ❑1/D, Oct 1997; Sendaway edition; angels on pile of bodies ... 4.00
- ❑2, Nov 1997 ... 2.50
- ❑2/A, Nov 1997; American Entertainment exclusive ... 4.00
- ❑2/Gold, Nov 1997; Gold edition ... 4.00
- ❑3, Dec 1997 ... 2.50
- ❑4, Feb 1998 ... 2.50
- ❑5, Mar 1998 ... 2.50
- ❑6, May 1998 ... 2.50
- ❑7, Jul 1998 ... 2.50
- ❑8, Aug 1998 ... 2.50
- ❑9, Oct 1998 ... 2.50
- ❑10, Nov 1998 ... 2.50
- ❑11, Feb 1999 ... 2.50
- ❑12, Apr 1999 ... 2.50
- ❑13, May 1999 ... 2.50
- ❑14, Jun 1999 ... 2.50
- ❑15, Jul 1999 ... 2.50
- ❑16, Jul 1999 ... 2.50
- ❑17, Aug 1999 ... 2.50
- ❑18, Sep 1999 ... 2.50
- ❑19, Oct 1999 ... 2.50
- ❑20, Nov 1999 ... 2.50
- ❑21, Dec 1999; cover says Nov, indicia says Dec ... 2.95
- ❑22, Mar 2000 ... 2.95
- ❑Ashcan 1, Jun 1997; Preview edition ... 4.00

ASH
EVENT

- ❑0, May 1996; "Present" edition; O: Ash. enhanced wraparound cover ... 3.50
- ❑0/A, May 1996; "Future" edition; O: Ash. alternate enhanced wraparound cover ... 3.50
- ❑0/B, May 1996; Red foil logo-Present edition ... 4.00
- ❑0/C, May 1996; Red foil logo-Future edition ... 4.00
- ❑½, Apr 1997 ... 2.50
- ❑½/Ltd., Apr 1997; Wizard authentic edition ... 4.00
- ❑½/Platinum, Apr 1997; Platinum edition ... 4.00
- ❑1, Nov 1994 1: Ash ... 3.00
- ❑1/A, Nov 1994; 1: Ash. Commemorative Omnichrome cover ... 4.00
- ❑1/B, Nov 1994; 1: Ash. Dynamic Forces exclusive (DF on cover) ... 3.00
- ❑2, Jan 1995 ... 3.00
- ❑3, May 1995 ... 3.00
- ❑4, Jul 1995 ... 3.00
- ❑4/A, Jul 1995; Red Edition ... 3.00
- ❑4/B, Jul 1995; White edition ... 3.00
- ❑4/Gold, Jul 1995; Gold edition ... 3.00
- ❑5, Sep 1995 ... 3.00
- ❑6, Dec 1995 ... 2.50
- ❑6/A, Dec 1995; alternate cover ... 2.50

ASH/22 BRIDES
EVENT

- ❑1, Dec 1996 ... 2.95
- ❑2, Apr 1997 ... 2.95

ASH: CINDER & SMOKE
EVENT

- ❑1, May 1997 ... 2.95
- ❑2, Jun 1997 ... 2.95
- ❑2/A, Jun 1997, variant cover ... 2.95
- ❑3, Jul 1997 ... 2.95
- ❑3/A, Jul 1997, variant cover ... 2.95
- ❑4, Aug 1997 ... 2.95
- ❑4/A, Aug 1997, variant cover ... 2.95
- ❑5, Sep 1997 ... 2.95
- ❑5/A, Sep 1997, variant cover ... 2.95
- ❑6, Oct 1997 ... 2.95
- ❑6/A, Oct 1997, variant cover ... 2.95

ASHEN VICTOR
VIZ

- ❑1, ca. 1997 ... 2.95
- ❑2, ca. 1997 ... 3.25
- ❑3, ca. 1997 ... 2.95
- ❑4, ca. 1997 ... 2.95

ASHES
CALIBER

- ❑1 ... 2.50
- ❑2 ... 2.50
- ❑3 ... 2.50
- ❑4 ... 2.50
- ❑5 ... 2.50

ASH FILES, THE
EVENT

- ❑1, Mar 1997; background on series ... 2.95

ASH: FIRE AND CROSSFIRE
EVENT

- ❑1, Jan 1999 JRo (w) ... 2.95
- ❑1/A, Jan 1999 JRo (w) ... 5.00
- ❑2 1999 JRo (w) ... 2.95

ASHLEY DUST
KNIGHT

- ❑1 ... 2.95
- ❑2, Dec 1994 ... 2.95
- ❑3, Mar 1995 ... 2.95

ASHPILE
SIDE SHOW

- ❑1 ... 8.95

ASH: THE FIRE WITHIN
EVENT

- ❑1, Sep 1996 ... 2.95
- ❑2 ... 2.95

ASKANI'SON
MARVEL

- ❑1, Jan 1996, cover says "Feb," indicia says "Jan" ... 2.95
- ❑2, Apr 1996, cover says "Mar", indicia says "Apr" ... 2.95
- ❑3, Apr 1996, cardstock wraparound cover ... 2.95
- ❑4, May 1996, cardstock wraparound cover ... 2.95

SORT OF HOMECOMING
ALTERNATIVE

- ❑1 ... 3.50
- ❑2, Feb 2004 ... 3.50
- ❑3, May 2004 ... 3.50

ASPEN EXTENDED EDITION
ASPEN

- ❑1, Jun 2004 ... 8.00
- ❑1/Conv, Jun 2004 ... 15.00

ASPEN (MICHAEL TURNER PRESENTS)
ASPEN

- ❑1, Jul 2003 ... 7.00
- ❑1/Variant, Jul 2003 ... 12.00
- ❑1/Conv, Jul 2003 ... 10.00
- ❑2, Jul 2003 ... 4.00
- ❑2/Variant, Jul 2003 ... 6.00
- ❑2/Convention, Jul 2003 ... 10.00
- ❑3, Aug 2003 ... 6.00
- ❑3/Variant, Aug 2003 ... 8.00
- ❑3/Convention, Aug 2003 ... 10.00

ASPEN SEASONS: SPRING 2005
ASPEN

- ❑0 2005 ... 2.99

ASPEN SKETCHBOOK
ASPEN

- ❑1, Feb 2004 ... 2.99

ASRIAL VS. CHEETAH
ANTARCTIC

- ❑1, Mar 1996 ... 2.95
- ❑2, Apr 1996 ... 2.95

ASSASSINATION OF MALCOLM X
ZONE

- ❑1 ... 2.95

ASSASSINETTE
POCKET CHANGE

- ❑1, ca. 1994; silver foil cover ... 2.50
- ❑2, ca. 1994 ... 2.50
- ❑3, ca. 1994 ... 2.50
- ❑4 ... 2.50
- ❑5, ca. 1995 ... 2.50
- ❑6, ca. 1995 ... 2.50
- ❑7 ... 2.50

Other grades: Multiply price above by 5/6 for VF/NM • 2/3 for VERY FINE • 1/3 for FINE • 1/5 for VERY GOOD • 1/8 for GOOD

ASSASSINETTE HARDCORE!
POCKET CHANGE
❑1, ca. 1995 .... 2.50
❑2, ca. 1995 .... 2.50

ASSASSINS
DC / AMALGAM
❑1, Apr 1996 .... 1.95

ASSASSIN SCHOOL
APCOMICS
❑0, ca. 2003 .... 2.99

ASSASSIN SCHOOL (VOL. 2)
APCOMICS
❑1, ca. 2003 .... 5.00
❑2 .... 4.00
❑3 .... 4.00
❑4 .... 4.00
❑5 .... 4.00
❑6 .... 4.00

ASSASSINS INC.
SILVERLINE
❑1 .... 1.95
❑2 .... 1.95

ASSEMBLY
ANTARCTIC
❑1, Nov 2003 .... 2.99
❑2, Dec 2003 .... 3.50
❑3, Jan 2004 .... 0.00

ASTER
EXPRESS / ENTITY
❑0, Oct 1994 .... 2.95
❑1, Oct 1994, b&w 2.95
❑1/Gold, Oct 1994, b&w; Gold edition 3.00
❑2, Nov 1994; enhanced cardstock cover 2.95
❑3, Jan 1995 .... 2.95
❑3/A, Jan 1995; alternate cover 2.95
❑3/B, Jan 1995; enhanced cover 2.95
❑Ashcan 1; no cover price; b&w preview 1.00

ASTER: THE LAST CELESTIAL KNIGHT
EXPRESS / ENTITY
❑1 1995, Chromium cover 3.75

ASTONISH!
WEHNER
❑1, b&w 2.00

ASTONISHING EXCITEMENT
ALL-JONH
❑501 .... 2.95
❑502 .... 2.95
❑503 .... 3.50

ASTONISHING TALES
MARVEL
❑1, Aug 1970, SL (w); JK, WW (a); A: Kraven the Hunter. Ka-Zar, Doctor Doom 40.00
❑2, Oct 1970, JK, WW (a); A: Kraven the Hunter. Ka-Zar, Doctor Doom 20.00
❑3, Dec 1970, WW (a); 1: Zaladane. Ka-Zar, Doctor Doom 20.00
❑4, Feb 1971, WW (a); Ka-Zar, Doctor Doom 20.00
❑5, Apr 1971, A: Red Skull. Ka-Zar, Doctor Doom 20.00
❑6, Jun 1971, 1: Mockingbird (as Bobbi Morse). Ka-Zar, Doctor Doom 12.00
❑7, Aug 1971, Ka-Zar, Doctor Doom .. 15.00
❑8, Oct 1971, Ka-Zar, Doctor Doom ... 15.00
❑9, Dec 1971, Ka-Zar 10.00
❑10, Feb 1972, SB (a); Ka-Zar 10.00
❑11, Apr 1972, O: Ka-Zar. Ka-Zar 10.00
❑12, Jun 1972, JB, NA, DA (a); A: Man-Thing. Ka-Zar 30.00
❑13, Aug 1972, RB, JB, DA (a); A: Man-Thing. Ka-Zar 10.00
❑14, Oct 1972, Ka-Zar; reprinted from Savage Tales #1 and Jungle Tales #2 10.00
❑15, Dec 1972, Ka-Zar 10.00
❑16, Feb 1973, Ka-Zar 10.00
❑17, Apr 1973, Ka-Zar 10.00
❑18, Jun 1973, Ka-Zar 10.00
❑19, Aug 1973, Ka-Zar 10.00
❑20, Oct 1973, Ka-Zar 10.00
❑21, Dec 1973, Reprinted from Amazing Adult Fantasy #9 .... 10.00
❑22, Feb 1974, Reprinted from Strange Tales #74 .... 10.00
❑23, Apr 1974, Reprinted from Strange Tales #89; Marvel Value Stamp #54: Shanna 10.00
❑24, Jun 1974, Marvel Value Stamp #18: Volstaag 10.00
❑25, Aug 1974, RB, GP (a); 1&O: Deathlok I (Luther Manning). 1st George Perez work; Marvel Value Stamp #68: Son of Satan 25.00
❑26, Oct 1974, A: Deathlok. Marvel Value Stamp #66: General Ross 10.00
❑27, Dec 1974, A: Deathlok. Marvel Value Stamp #22: Man-Thing 7.00
❑28, Feb 1975, A: Deathlok 7.00
❑29, Apr 1975, 1&O: Guardians of the Galaxy. Reprinted from Marvel Super-Heroes #18 .... 7.00
❑30, Jun 1975, RB, KP (a); A: Deathlok 5.00
❑31, Aug 1975, SL (w); RB, GC, KP (a); A: Deathlok. Reprinted from Silver Surfer #3 .... 5.00
❑32, Nov 1976, A: Deathlok 5.00
❑33, Jan 1976, A: Deathlok 10.00
❑34, Mar 1976, A: Deathlok 5.00
❑35, May 1976, A: Deathlok 7.00
❑35/30 cent, May 1976, A: Deathlok. 30 cent regional price variant 20.00
❑36, Jul 1976, A: Deathlok 10.00
❑36/30 cent, Jul 1976, A: Deathlok. 30 cent regional price variant 20.00

ASTONISHING X-MEN
MARVEL
❑1, Mar 1995; DGr (a); Age of Apocalypse 6.00
❑2, Apr 1995 DGr (a) 6.00
❑3, May 1995 JPH (w); AM (a) 6.00
❑4, Jun 1995 AM (a) 8.00

ASTONISHING X-MEN (2ND SERIES)
MARVEL
❑1, Sep 1999 .... 5.00
❑2, Oct 1999 .... 2.50
❑3, Nov 1999 .... 2.50

ASTONISHING X-MEN (3RD SERIES)
MARVEL
❑1, Jul 2004 .... 6.00
❑1/Cassaday, Jul 2004; John Cassaday cover 45.00
❑1/Del Otto, Jul 2004; Gabriel Del'Otto cover 12.00
❑1/DirCut, Aug 2004; Director's Cut ... 5.00
❑1/Dynamic 0.00
❑2, Aug 2004 .... 16.00
❑3, Sep 2004 .... 4.00
❑4, Oct 2004 .... 8.00
❑4/Variant, Oct 2004, Retailer variant, Colossus cover 25.00
❑5, Nov 2004 .... 8.00
❑6, Dec 2004 .... 5.00
❑7, Jan 2005 .... 4.00
❑8, Feb 2005 .... 2.99
❑9, Mar 2005 .... 2.99
❑10, Apr 2005 .... 2.99
❑10/Variant, Apr 2005 .... 5.00
❑11, Sep 2005 .... 2.99
❑12, Oct 2005 .... 2.99
❑13, May 2006 .... 2.99
❑14, Jul 2006 .... 2.99
❑15, Sep 2006 .... 2.99

ASTOUNDING SPACE THRILLS
DAY 1
❑1, May 1998, b&w 2.95
❑2, Jul 1998, b&w 2.95
❑3, Jan 1999, b&w 2.95

ASTOUNDING SPACE THRILLS: THE COMIC BOOK
IMAGE
❑1, Apr 2000 .... 2.95
❑2, Jul 2000 .... 2.95
❑3, Sep 2000 .... 2.95
❑4, Dec 2000 .... 2.95
❑Giant Size 1, Oct 2001 .... 4.95

ASTRIDER HUGO
RADIO
❑1, Jul 2000, b&w 3.95

ASTRO BOY (GOLD KEY)
GOLD KEY
❑1, Aug 1965 .... 265.00

ASTRO BOY (DARK HORSE)
DARK HORSE
❑1, ca. 2002 .... 9.95
❑2, ca. 2002 .... 9.95
❑3, ca. 2002 .... 9.95
❑4, ca. 2002 .... 9.95
❑5, ca. 2002 .... 9.95
❑6, ca. 2002 .... 9.95
❑7, ca. 2002 .... 9.95
❑8, ca. 2003 .... 9.95
❑9, ca. 2003 .... 9.95
❑10, ca. 2003 .... 9.95
❑11, ca. 2003 .... 9.95
❑12, ca. 2003 .... 9.95
❑13, ca. 2003 .... 9.95
❑14, ca. 2003 .... 9.95
❑15, ca. 2003 .... 9.95
❑16, ca. 2003 .... 9.95
❑17, ca. 2003 .... 9.95
❑18, ca. 2003 .... 9.95
❑19, ca. 2003 .... 9.95
❑20, ca. 2004 .... 9.95
❑21, ca. 2004 .... 9.95
❑22, ca. 2004 .... 9.95
❑23 2004 .... 9.95

ASTRO CITY: A VISITOR'S GUIDE
DC
❑1 2004 .... 5.95

ASTRO CITY LOCAL HEROES
DC
❑1, Apr 2003 .... 2.95
❑2, Jun 2003 .... 2.95
❑3, Aug 2003 .... 2.95
❑4, Dec 2003 .... 2.95
❑5, Feb 2004 .... 2.95

ASTRO CITY SPECIAL
DC / WILDSTORM
❑1, Oct 2004 .... 3.95

ASTRO CITY: THE DARK AGE
DC
❑1, Aug 2005 .... 2.99
❑2, Sep 2005 .... 2.99
❑3, Oct 2005 .... 2.99
❑4, Nov 2005 .... 2.99

ASTRO CITY (VOL. 1) (KURT BUSIEK'S...)
IMAGE
❑1, Aug 1995 ARo (c); KB (w); BA (a); 1: The Honor Guard. 1: The Menagerie Gang. 1: Doctor Saturday. 1: The Samaritan 5.00
❑2, Sep 1995 ARo (c); KB (w); BA (a); A: Silver Agent. A: Honor Guard 3.00
❑3, Oct 1995 ARo (c); KB (w); BA (a); A: Jack in the Box 3.00
❑4, Nov 1995 ARo (c); KB (w); BA (a); 1: The Hanged Man. A: First Family. A: Winged Victory 3.00
❑5, Dec 1995 ARo (c); KB (w); BA (a); A: Crackerjack. A: Astro City Irregulars .. 3.00
❑6, Jan 1996 ARo (c); KB (w); BA (a); O: The Samaritan 3.00

ASTRO CITY (VOL. 2) (KURT BUSIEK'S...)
IMAGE
❑½, Jan 2000, ARo (c); KB (w); BA (a); Wizard promotional item 3.00
❑½/Direct ed., Jan 1998, Direct Market edition; ARo (c); KB (w); BA (a); reprints "The Nearness of You" and "Clash of Titans" 3.00
❑1, Sep 1996, ARo (c); KB (w); BA (a) 4.00
❑1/3D, Dec 1997, ARo (c); KB (w); BA (a) 5.00
❑2, Oct 1996, ARo (c); KB (w); BA (a); A: First Family 3.00
❑3, Nov 1996, ARo (c); KB (w); BA (a); A: Astra, First Family 3.00
❑4, Dec 1996, ARo (c); KB (w); BA (a); 1: Brian Kinney (The Altar Boy) (out of costume) 3.00
❑5, Jan 1997, ARo (c); KB (w); BA (a); O: The Altar Boy. 1: The Altar Boy (Brian Kinney in costume) 3.00
❑6, Feb 1997, ARo (c); KB (w); BA (a); 1: The Gunslinger. The Confessor revealed as vampire 3.00
❑7, Mar 1997, ARo (c); KB (w); BA (a); O: The Confessor I 2.50

Atari Force

Ancient video game system inspires comics title

©DC

Atom

Ray Palmer gets small in Silver Age series

©DC

Atom and Hawkman

Continuation of The Atom series

©DC

Atomics

Madman spinoff from Mike Allred

©AAA Pop

Attack (4th Series)

Stand-alone reprints from Charlton's war titles

©Charlton

N-MINT

❑8, Apr 1997, ARo (c); KB (w); BA (a); D: The Confessor I 2.50
❑9, May 1997, ARo (c); KB (w); BA (a); 1: The Confessor II 2.50
❑10, Oct 1997, ARo (c); KB (w); BA (a); O: Junkman. O: The Junkman 2.50
❑11, Nov 1997, ARo (c); KB (w); BA (a); 1: The Box. 1: The Jackson. Jack-in-the-Box vs. alternate versions 2.50
❑12, Dec 1997, ARo (c); KB (w); BA (a); 1: Jack-in-the-Box II (Roscoe James) 2.50
❑13, Feb 1998, ARo (c); KB (w); BA (a); O: Loony Leo. 1: Loony Leo 2.50
❑14, Apr 1998, ARo (c); KB (w); BA (a); O: Steeljack. 1: Steeljack 2.50
❑15, Dec 1998, ARo (c); KB (w); BA (a); 1: new Goldenglove. 2: Steeljack. A: Steeljack 2.50
❑16, Mar 1999, ARo (c); KB (w); BA (a); O: El Hombre 2.50
❑17, May 1999, ARo (c); KB (w); BA (a); O: The Mock Turtle 2.50
❑18, Aug 1999, ARo (c); KB (w); BA (a) 2.50
❑19, Nov 1999, ARo (c); KB (w); BA (a) 2.50
❑20, Jan 2000, ARo (c); KB (w); BA (a) 2.50
❑21, Mar 2000, ARo (c); KB (w); BA (a) 2.50
❑22, Aug 2000, ARo (c); KB (w); BA (a); O: Crimson Cougar. 1: Crimson Cougar 2.50

ASTROCOMICS
HARVEY

❑1, Giveaway from American Airlines; Reprints Harvey Comics stories 2.50

ASTRONAUTS IN TROUBLE: SPACE 1959
AIT

❑1 .... 2.50

ASTROTHRILL
CHEEKY

❑1, May 1999; cardstock cover; new material and reprints from Nemesister; CD 12.95

ASYLUM (MAXIMUM)
MAXIMUM

❑1, Dec 1995, Flip-book; Beanworld/Avengelyne flip covers 2.95
❑1/A, Dec 1995, Warchild/Doubletake flip covers 2.95
❑2, Jan 1996, Flip-book 2.95
❑3, Apr 1996, Flip-book 2.95
❑4, May 1996, Flip-book; Flipbook 2.95
❑5, Jun 1996, Flipbook 2.95
❑6, Jul 1996, preview of planned Bionix series featuring The Six Million Dollar Man and Bionic Woman; flipbook 2.95
❑7, Sep 1996 .... 2.95
❑8, Sep 1996 .... 2.95
❑9, Nov 1996 .... 2.95
❑10, Dec 1996 .... 2.95
❑11, Jan 1997 .... 2.99
❑12, Feb 1997 .... 2.99
❑13, Mar 1997 .... 2.99

ASYLUM (MILLENNIUM)
MILLENNIUM

❑1 .... 2.50

N-MINT

❑2 .... 2.50
❑3 .... 4.95

ASYLUM (NCG)
NEW COMICS

❑1, b&w 1.95
❑2 .... 2.25

ATARI FORCE
DC

❑1, Jan 1984 JL (a); 1: Dark Destroyer. 1: Babe. 1: Atari Force (in standard comics). 1: Dart. 1: Blackjak 1.00
❑2, Feb 1984 1: Martin Champion 1.00
❑3, Mar 1984 .... 1.00
❑4, Apr 1984 .... 1.00
❑5, May 1984 .... 1.00
❑6, Jun 1984 .... 1.00
❑7, Jul 1984 .... 1.00
❑8, Aug 1984 .... 1.00
❑9, Sep 1984 .... 1.00
❑10, Oct 1984 .... 1.00
❑11, Nov 1984 .... 1.00
❑12, Dec 1984 .... 1.00
❑13, Jan 1985 .... 1.00
❑14, Feb 1985 .... 1.00
❑15, Mar 1985 .... 1.00
❑16, Apr 1985 .... 1.00
❑17, May 1985 .... 1.00
❑18, Jun 1985 .... 1.00
❑19, Jul 1985 .... 1.00
❑20, Aug 1985 .... 1.00
❑Special 1 1986; Giant-size MR (a).... 2.00

A-TEAM, THE
MARVEL

❑1, Mar 1984, based on TV series 2.00
❑2, Apr 1984, JM (a) 2.00
❑3, May 1984 .... 2.00

ATHEIST
IMAGE

❑1, May 2005 .... 3.50
❑2, Sep 2005 .... 3.50
❑3, Apr 206 ....

ATHENA
ANTARCTIC

❑0, Dec 1996, Antarctic publishes...... 2.95
❑1, Nov 1995, A.M. Press publishes .. 2.95
❑2, Dec 1995 .... 2.95
❑3, Feb 1996 .... 2.95
❑4, Apr 1996 .... 2.95
❑5, Jun 1996 .... 2.95
❑6, Aug 1996 .... 2.95
❑7, Mar 1997, b&w 2.95
❑8, Apr 1997, b&w 2.95
❑9, May 1997, b&w 2.95
❑10, Jun 1997, b&w 2.95
❑11, Aug 1997, b&w 2.95
❑12, Sep 1997, b&w 2.95
❑13, Nov 1997, b&w 2.95
❑14, Dec 1997, b&w 2.95

ATHENA INC. AGENTS ROSTER
IMAGE

❑1, Nov 2002 .... 5.95

N-MINT

ATHENA INC. THE BEGINNING
IMAGE

❑1, Jan 2001, b&w 5.95

ATHENA INC. THE MANHUNTER PROJECT
IMAGE

❑1 2002 .... 2.95
❑1/A 2002 .... 2.95
❑Ashcan 1 2002 .... 2.95
❑2/A, Apr 2002 .... 2.95
❑2/B, Apr 2002 .... 2.95
❑3/A, Aug 2002 .... 2.95
❑3/B, Aug 2002 .... 2.95
❑4/A, Oct 2002 .... 2.95
❑4/B, Oct 2002 .... 2.95
❑5/A, Jan 2003 .... 2.95
❑5/B, Jan 2003 .... 2.95
❑6/A, Apr 2003 .... 4.95
❑6/B, Apr 2003 .... 4.95

ATLANTIS CHRONICLES
DC

❑1, Mar 1990, PD (w) 3.00
❑2, Apr 1990, PD (w) 3.00
❑3, May 1990, PD (w) 3.00
❑4, Jun 1990, PD (w) 3.00
❑5, Jul 1990, PD (w) 3.00
❑6, Aug 1990, PD (w) 3.00
❑7, Sep 1990, PD (w); O: Aquaman.... 3.00

@LARGE
TOKYOPOP

❑1, Dec 2003 .... 9.95
❑2, Aug 2004 .... 9.95
❑3, Dec 2005 .... 9.95

ATLAS
DARK HORSE

❑1, Feb 1994 .... 2.50
❑2, Apr 1994 .... 2.50
❑3, Jun 1994 .... 2.50
❑4, Aug 1994 .... 2.50

ATLAS (AVATAR)
AVATAR

❑1/A, Aug 2002 .... 3.50
❑1/B, Aug 2002 .... 3.50
❑1/C, Aug 2002 .... 3.50
❑1/D, Aug 2002 .... 3.50
❑1/E, Aug 2002; M. Brooks cover....... 3.50
❑1/F, Aug 2002; Dealer incentive variant of #1/E; Platinum Foil title 3.50
❑1/G, Aug 2002; Judo Girl cover 3.50

ATOM
DC

❑1, Jul 1962, MA, GK (a); 1: Plant Master 750.00
❑2, Sep 1962, MA, GK (a) 300.00
❑3, Nov 1962, MA, GK (a); 1: Chronos 225.00
❑4, Jan 1963, MA, GK (a) 175.00
❑5, Mar 1963, MA, GK (a) 175.00
❑6, May 1963, MA, GK (a) 125.00
❑7, Jul 1963, MA, GK (a); A: Hawkman 250.00
❑8, Sep 1963, MA, GK (a); A: Justice League of America 125.00
❑9, Nov 1963, MA, GK (a) 90.00
❑10, Jan 1964, MA, GK (a) 85.00

❑11, Mar 1964, MA, GK (a) 85.00
❑12, May 1964, MA, GK (a) 85.00
❑13, Jul 1964 85.00
❑14, Sep 1964 95.00
❑15, Nov 1964 85.00
❑16, Jan 1965, MA, GK (a) 45.00
❑17, Mar 1965, MA, GK (a) 45.00
❑18, May 1965, MA, GK (a) 50.00
❑19, Jul 1965, MA, GK (a) 45.00
❑20, Sep 1965, MA, GK (a) 45.00
❑21, Nov 1965 35.00
❑22, Jan 1966 35.00
❑23, Mar 1966 35.00
❑24, May 1966 35.00
❑25, Jul 1966 35.00
❑26, Sep 1966, 1: Bug-Eyed Bandit 35.00
❑27, Nov 1966, V: Panther 35.00
❑28, Jan 1967 35.00
❑29, Mar 1967, A: Atom I (Al Pratt) 90.00
❑30, May 1967 35.00
❑31, Jul 1967, A: Hawkman 46.00
❑32, Sep 1967 35.00
❑33, Nov 1967 35.00
❑34, Jan 1968 35.00
❑35, Mar 1968, GK (a) 35.00
❑36, May 1968, A: Atom I (Al Pratt) 45.00
❑37, Jul 1968, A: Hawkman 45.00
❑38, Sep 1968, Series continued in Atom and Hawkman #39 30.00
❑Special 1, Jun 1993 2.50
❑Special 2, ca. 1995; LMc (a); 1995 2.50

ATOM AND HAWKMAN
DC

❑39, Oct 1968, JKu (a); Series continued from Atom #38 30.00
❑40, Dec 1968, DD (a) 30.00
❑41, Feb 1969 30.00
❑42, Apr 1969 30.00
❑43, Jun 1969, JKu (a) 30.00
❑44, Aug 1969 30.00
❑45, Oct 1969 30.00

ATOM ANT
GOLD KEY

❑1, Jan 1966 85.00

ATOMIC AGE
MARVEL / EPIC

❑1, Nov 1990 4.50
❑2, Dec 1990 4.50
❑3, Jan 1991 4.50
❑4, Feb 1991 4.50

ATOMIC AGE TRUCKSTOP WAITRESS
FANTAGRAPHICS / EROS

❑1, Jul 1991, b&w 2.25

ATOMIC CITY TALES
KITCHEN SINK

❑1 1996 2.95
❑2 1996 2.95
❑3, Sep 1996 2.95
❑Special 1 2.95

ATOMIC MAN
BLACKTHORNE

❑1 1986 1.75
❑2 1986 1.75
❑3 1986 1.75

ATOMIC MOUSE (VOL. 2)
CHARLTON

❑10, Sep 1985 5.00
❑11, Nov 1985 3.00
❑12, Jan 1986 3.00
❑13, Mar 1986 3.00

ATOMIC MOUSE (A+)
A+

❑1, ca. 1990 2.50
❑2 1990 2.50
❑3 1990 2.50

ATOMICOW
VISION

❑1, Aug 1990 2.50

ATOMIC RABBIT & FRIENDS
AVALON

❑1, b&w; reprints Charlton stories 2.50

ATOMICS
AAA POP

❑1, Jan 2000 2.95
❑2, Feb 2000 2.95
❑3, Mar 2000 2.95
❑4, Apr 2000 2.95
❑5, May 2000 2.95
❑6, Jun 2000 2.95
❑7, Jul 2000 2.95
❑8, Aug 2000 2.95
❑9, Sep 2000 2.95
❑10, Oct 2000 2.95
❑11, Nov 2000 2.95
❑12, Dec 2000 3.50
❑13, Jan 2001 3.50
❑14, Feb 2001 3.50
❑15, Mar 2001 3.50

ATOMIC TOYBOX
IMAGE

❑1, Nov 1999; cover says Dec, indicia says Nov 2.95
❑1/A, Nov 1999 2.95
❑1/B, Nov 1999 2.95

ATOMIKA
SPEAKEASY COMICS

❑1 2005 2.99
❑2 2005 2.99
❑3 2005 2.99
❑4/Turner, Sep 2005 2.99
❑4/Buzz, Sep 2005 2.99
❑4/Jay, Sep 2005 2.99
❑4/Rupps, Sep 2005 2.99

ATOMIK ANGELS (WILLIAM TUCCI'S...)
CRUSADE

❑1, May 1996 A: Freefall 2.95
❑1/Variant, May 1996; A: Freefall. variant cover 3.50
❑2, Jul 1996 2.95
❑3, Sep 1996 2.95
❑3/Variant, Sep 1996; alternate cover (orange background with Statue of Liberty) 3.50
❑4, Nov 1996; flipbook with Manga Shi 2000 preview 2.95
❑Special 1, Feb 1996, b&w; "The Intrep-edition"; promotional comic for U.S.S. Intrepid 3.00

ATOM THE ATOMIC CAT
AVALON

❑1 2.95

ATTACK (3RD SERIES)
CHARLTON

❑54, ca. 1958 0.00
❑55, ca. 1959 0.00
❑56, ca. 1959 0.00
❑57, ca. 1959 0.00
❑58, ca. 1959 0.00
❑59, ca. 1959 0.00
❑60, ca. 1959 0.00
❑1 1962, No number in indicia or cover 25.00
❑2 1963 15.00
❑3 1964 12.00
❑4 1964 12.00

ATTACK (4TH SERIES)
CHARLTON

❑1, Sep 1971 7.00
❑2, Nov 1971 4.00
❑3, Jan 1972 4.00
❑4, Mar 1972 3.00
❑5, May 1972 3.00
❑6, Jul 1972 2.50
❑7, Sep 1972 2.50
❑8, Nov 1972 2.50
❑9, Dec 1972 2.50
❑10, Feb 1973 2.50
❑11, May 1973 2.50
❑12, Jul 1973 2.50
❑13, Sep 1973 2.50
❑14, Nov 1973 2.50
❑15, Mar 1975 2.50
❑16, Aug 1979 2.50
❑17, Sep 1979 2.50
❑18, Nov 1979 2.50
❑19, Jan 1980 2.50
❑20, Mar 1980 2.50
❑21, May 1980 2.50
❑22 1980 2.50
❑23 1980 2.50
❑24, Oct 1980 2.50
❑25, Dec 1980 2.50
❑26, Feb 1981 2.50
❑27, Apr 1981 2.50
❑28, May 1981 2.50
❑29, Jul 1981 2.50
❑30, Sep 1981 2.50
❑31, Nov 1981 2.00
❑32, Jan 1982 2.00
❑33, Mar 1982 2.00
❑34, May 1982 2.00
❑35, Jul 1982 2.00
❑36, Sep 1982 2.00
❑37, Nov 1982 2.00
❑38, Jan 1983 2.00
❑39, Mar 1983 2.00
❑40, May 1983 2.00
❑41, Jul 1983 2.00
❑42, Sep 1983 2.00
❑43 1983 2.00
❑44 1984 2.00
❑45 1984 2.00
❑46 1984 2.00
❑47 1984 2.00
❑48, Oct 1984 2.00

ATTACK!
SPIRE

❑1, ca. 1975 5.00

ATTACK OF THE AMAZON GIRLS
FANTACO

❑1 4.95

ATTACK OF THE MUTANT MONSTERS
A-PLUS

❑1, b&w; Reprints 2.50

AT THE SEAMS
ALTERNATIVE

❑1, Jun 1997, b&w 2.95

ATTITUDE
NBM

❑1 13.95

ATTITUDE LAD
SLAVE LABOR

❑1 2.95

ATTU
4WINDS

❑1, b&w 9.95
❑2, b&w 9.95

AUGIE DOGGIE
GOLD KEY

❑1, Dec 1963 45.00

AUGUST
ARROW

❑1 2.95
❑2 2.95
❑3 2.95

AURORA COMIC SCENES
AURORA

❑181, ca. 1974; NA (a); really 181-140; small comic included in Aurora model kits (Tarzan) 30.00
❑182, ca. 1974; JR (a); really 182-140; small comic included in Aurora model kits (Amazing Spider-Man) 28.00
❑183, ca. 1974; GK (a); really 183-140; small comic included in Aurora model kits (Tonto) 27.00
❑184, ca. 1974; HT (a); really 184-140; small comic included in Aurora model kits (Incredible Hulk) 30.00
❑185, ca. 1974; CS (a); really 185-140; small comic included in Aurora model kits (Superman) 28.00
❑186, ca. 1974; DC (a); really 186-140; small comic included in Aurora model kits (Superboy) 27.00
❑187, ca. 1974; DG (a); really 187-140; small comic included in Aurora model kits (Batman) 26.00
❑188, ca. 1974; GK (a); really 188-140; small comic included in Aurora model kits (Lone Ranger) 25.00

Authority

Picks up where Stormwatch (Vol. 2) left off

©DC

Automaton

Martian energy creatures travel to Earth

©Image

Avalon

Anthology tryout series for new artists

©Harrier

Avengelyne (Mini-Series)

Angel who fell from grace battles demons

©Maximum

Avengers

Durable Marvel super-team gets its start

©Marvel

N-MINT

❑192, ca. 1974; really 192-140; small comic included in Aurora model kits (Captain America) 27.00
❑193, ca. 1974; really 193-140; small comic included in Aurora model kits (Robin) 30.00

AUTHORITY
DC / WILDSTORM

❑1, May 1999; wraparound cover 5.00
❑2, Jun 1999 .... 4.00
❑3, Jul 1999 .... 4.00
❑4, Aug 1999 .... 3.00
❑5, Oct 1999; cover says "Sep", indicia says "Oct" 3.00
❑6, Oct 1999 .... 3.00
❑7, Nov 1999 .... 3.00
❑8, Dec 1999 .... 3.00
❑9, Jan 2000 .... 3.00
❑10, Feb 2000 .... 3.00
❑11, Mar 2000 .... 2.50
❑12, Apr 2000 .... 2.50
❑13, May 2000 .... 2.50
❑14, Jun 2000 .... 2.50
❑15, Jul 2000 .... 2.50
❑16, Aug 2000 .... 2.50
❑17, Sep 2000 .... 2.50
❑18, Sep 2000 .... 2.50
❑19, Nov 2000 .... 2.50
❑20, Jan 2001 .... 2.50
❑21, Feb 2001 .... 2.50
❑22, Mar 2001 .... 2.50
❑23, Apr 2001 .... 2.50
❑24, May 2001 .... 2.50
❑25, Jun 2001 .... 2.50
❑26, Jul 2001 .... 2.50
❑27, Aug 2001 .... 2.50
❑28, Sep 2001 .... 2.50
❑29, Oct 2001 .... 2.50
❑Annual 2000, Dec 2000 .... 3.50

AUTHORITY (2ND SERIES)
DC / WILDSTORM

❑0, Aug 2003 .... 2.95
❑1, May 2003 .... 2.95
❑2, Jun 2003 .... 2.95
❑3, Jul 2003 .... 2.95
❑4, Aug 2003 .... 2.95
❑5, Sep 2003 .... 2.95
❑6, Oct 2003 .... 2.95
❑7, Nov 2003 .... 2.95
❑8, Dec 2003 .... 2.95
❑9, Jan 2004 .... 2.95
❑10, May 2004 .... 2.95
❑11, Jun 2004 .... 2.95
❑12, Jul 2004 .... 2.95
❑13, Aug 2004 .... 2.95
❑14, Oct 2004 .... 2.95

AUTHORITY: KEV
DC / WILDSTORM

❑nn, Oct 2002 .... 4.95

AUTHORITY/LOBO CHRISTMAS SPECIAL
DC / WILDSTORM

❑1, Dec 2003 .... 4.95

N-MINT

AUTHORITY/LOBO: SPRING BREAK MASSACRE
DC

❑0 2005 .... 4.99

AUTHORITY: THE MAGNIFICENT KEVIN
DC

❑1, Oct 2005 .... 2.99
❑2, Nov 2005 .... 2.99
❑3, Dec 2005 .... 2.99
❑4, Jan 2006 .... 2.99
❑5, Feb 2006 .... 2.99

AUTHORITY: MORE KEV
DC / WILDSTORM

❑1, Jul 2004 .... 2.95
❑2, Aug 2004 .... 2.95
❑3, Oct 2004 .... 2.95
❑4, Nov 2004 .... 2.95

AUTHORITY: REVOLUTION
DC / WILDSTORM

❑1, Dec 2004 .... 2.95
❑2, Jan 2005 .... 2.95
❑3, Feb 2005 .... 2.95
❑4, Apr 2005 .... 2.95
❑5, May 2005 .... 2.95
❑6, Jun 2005 .... 2.95
❑7, Jun 2005 .... 2.99
❑8, Jul 2005 .... 2.99
❑9, Aug 2005 .... 2.99
❑10, Sep 2005 .... 2.99
❑11, Oct 2005 .... 2.99
❑12, Dec 2005 .... 2.99

AUTHORITY: SCORCHED EARTH
DC / WILDSTORM

❑1, Feb 2003 .... 4.95

AUTOMATIC KAFKA
WILDSTORM

❑1, Sep 2002 .... 2.95
❑2, Oct 2002 .... 2.95
❑3, Nov 2002 .... 2.95
❑4, Dec 2002 .... 2.95
❑5, Jan 2003 .... 2.95
❑6, Feb 2003 .... 2.95
❑7, Mar 2003 .... 2.95
❑8, Apr 2003 .... 2.95
❑9, May 2003 .... 2.95

AUTOMATON
IMAGE

❑1, Sep 1998 .... 2.95
❑2, Oct 1998; no month of publication 2.95
❑3, Nov 1998; no month of publication 2.95

AUTUMN
CALIBER

❑1, ca. 1995 .... 2.95
❑2, ca. 1995 .... 2.95
❑3 .... 2.95

AUTUMN ADVENTURES (WALT DISNEY'S)
DISNEY

❑1 .... 2.95

N-MINT

AUTUMN...EARTH
ACID RAIN

❑1 .... 2.50

AVALON
HARRIER

❑1, Oct 1986 .... 1.95
❑2, ca. 1986 .... 1.95
❑3, ca. 1987 .... 1.95
❑4, ca. 1987 .... 1.95
❑5, ca. 1987 .... 1.95
❑6, ca. 1987 .... 1.95
❑7, ca. 1987 .... 1.95
❑8, ca. 1987 .... 1.95
❑9, ca. 1987 .... 1.95
❑10, ca. 1987 .... 1.95
❑11, ca. 1987 .... 1.95
❑12, ca. 1987 .... 1.95
❑13, ca. 1987 .... 1.95
❑14, ca. 1988 .... 1.95

AVANT GUARD: HEROES AT THE FUTURE'S EDGE
DAY ONE

❑1, Mar 1994, b&w 2.50
❑2, Jul 1994, b&w 2.50
❑3, Dec 1994, b&w 2.50

AVATAARS: COVENANT OF THE SHIELD
MARVEL

❑1, Sep 2000 .... 2.99
❑2, Oct 2000 .... 2.99
❑3, Nov 2000 .... 2.99

AVATAR
DC

❑1 .... 3.50
❑2 .... 3.50
❑3 .... 3.50

AVELON
DRAWBRIDGE

❑1 1997 .... 2.95
❑2 .... 2.95
❑3 .... 2.95
❑4 .... 2.95
❑5 .... 2.95
❑6 .... 2.95
❑7 .... 2.95
❑8 .... 2.95
❑9 .... 2.95

AVENGEBLADE
MAXIMUM

❑1, Jul 96 .... 2.95
❑2, Aug 96 .... 2.95

AVENGELYNE (MINI-SERIES)
MAXIMUM

❑1, May 1995 RL (w); RL (a); O: Avengelyne. 1: Avengelyne 3.00
❑1/A, May 1995 RL (w); O: Avengelyne. 1: Avengelyne 3.00
❑1/Gold, May 1995; Gold edition RL (w); O: Avengelyne. 1: Avengelyne 4.00
❑1/Variant, May 1995; RL (w); O: Avengelyne. 1: Avengelyne. chromium cover 3.50

Other grades: Multiply price above by 5/6 for VF/NM • 2/3 for VERY FINE • 1/3 for FINE • 1/5 for VERY GOOD • 1/8 for GOOD

❑2, Jun 1995; RL (w); polybagged with card 2.50
❑3/A, Jul 1995; RL (w); Avengelyne striking with sword on cover 2.50
❑3/B, Jul 1995; RL (w); Avengelyne standing with demons prominent on cover 2.50
❑Ashcan 1 RL (w) 3.50

AVENGELYNE (VOL. 2)
MAXIMUM

❑0, Oct 1996 3.00
❑½ 1996; Wizard promotional mail-in edition RL (w) 3.00
❑½/Platinum 1996; Platinum edition with certificate of authenticity (Wizard promo) RL (w) 3.50
❑1, Apr 1996 3.00
❑1/Variant, Apr 1996; alternate cover (photo wraparound) 3.00
❑2, May 1996 1: Darkchylde 4.00
❑2/A, May 1996 1: Darkchylde 4.00
❑2/B, May 1996; 1: Darkchylde. Nude cover 5.00
❑3, Jun 1996 2.50
❑4, Jul 1996 A: Cybrid 2.50
❑5, Aug 1996; RL (w); A: Cybrid. flipbook with Blindside preview 2.99
❑6, Sep 1996 RL (w) 2.99
❑7, Nov 1996 2.99
❑8, Dec 1996 RL (w) 2.99
❑9, Jan 1997 2.99
❑10, Feb 1997 RL (w) 2.99
❑11, Mar 1997 2.99
❑11/Variant, Mar 1997; alternate cover (multiple characters behind Avengelyne) 2.99
❑12 2.99
❑13 2.99
❑14 2.99
❑15 2.99

AVENGELYNE (VOL. 3)
AWESOME

❑1, Mar 1999 2.50

AVENGELYNE ARMAGEDDON
MAXIMUM

❑1, Dec 1996 2.99
❑2, Jan 1997 2.99
❑3, Feb 1997 2.99

AVENGELYNE BIBLE
MAXIMUM

❑1, Oct 1996 3.50

AVENGELYNE: DARK DEPTHS
AVATAR

❑½, Feb 2001 3.00
❑½/A, Feb 2001 3.00
❑½/B, Feb 2001 3.00
❑½/C, Feb 2001 3.00
❑1, Feb 2001 3.50
❑1/A, Feb 2001 3.50
❑1/B, Feb 2001 3.50
❑1/C, Feb 2001 3.50
❑1/D, Feb 2001 3.50
❑1/E, Feb 2001 3.50
❑2, Mar 2001 3.50
❑2/A, Mar 2001 3.50
❑2/B, Mar 2001 3.50
❑2/C, Mar 2001 3.50

AVENGELYNE: DEADLY SINS
MAXIMUM

❑1, Feb 1996 2.95
❑1/Variant, Feb 1996, alternate cover (photo) 3.50
❑2, Mar 1996 2.95

AVENGELYNE/GLORY
MAXIMUM

❑1, Sep 1995; wraparound chromium cover 3.95
❑1/Variant, Sep 1995; variant cover 3.95

AVENGELYNE/GLORY: THE GODYSSEY
MAXIMUM

❑1 2.99
❑1/Variant 2.99

AVENGELYNE: POWER
MAXIMUM

❑1/A, Nov 1995; Red background on cover 2.50
❑1/B, Nov 1995; Blue background on cover 2.50
❑2, Dec 1995 2.50
❑3, Jan 1996 2.50

AVENGELYNE-PROPHET
MAXIMUM

❑1/A, May 1996, Close-up of faces on cover 2.95
❑1, May 1996 2.95
❑2, Jun 1996 2.95

AVENGELYNE SWIMSUIT
MAXIMUM

❑1/D, Aug 1995; Black suit, wet hair on cover; pin-ups, both drawn and photographed 2.95
❑1/C, Aug 1995; pin-ups, both drawn and photographed; White suit on cover 2.95
❑1/B, Aug 1995; Black suit, dry hair, sitting on cliff on cover; pin-ups, both drawn and photographed 2.95
❑1/A, Aug 1995; Black swimsuit, dry hair, leaning against cliff on cover; pin-ups, both drawn and photographed 2.95
❑1, Aug 1995; Drawn cover; both drawn and photographed; n-ups 2.95

AVENGELYNE/WARRIOR NUN AREALA
MAXIMUM

❑1/A, Nov 1996; Avengelyne in front on cover 2.99
❑1/B, Nov 1996; Two women back-to-back on cover 2.99

AVENGERS
MARVEL

❑0, Wizard promotional edition 3.00
❑1, Sep 1963, JK, SL (w); JK (a); O: Avengers. 1st appearance/origin of the Avengers; Team consists of Thor, Ant-Man, Wasp, Hulk, and Iron Man 4200.00
❑1.5, Dec 1999, Issue #1-1/2 3.00
❑2, Nov 1963, JK, SL (w); JK (a); 1: Space Phantom. Hulk leaves Avengers; Ant-Man becomes Giant-Man 935.00
❑3, Jan 1964, JK, SL (w); JK (a); Avengers vs. Sub-Mariner and Hulk 750.00
❑4, Mar 1964, JK, SL (w); JK (a); 1: Baron Zemo. Captain America returns; Capt. America returns 1450.00
❑4/Golden Record, ca. 1966, Golden Records reprint 40.00
❑5, May 1964, JK, SL (w); JK (a); Hulk leaves team 350.00
❑6, Jul 1964, JK, SL (w); JK (a); 1: Masters of Evil 390.00
❑7, Aug 1964, JK, SL (w); JK (a) 460.00
❑8, Sep 1964, JK, SL (w); JK (a); O: Kang. 1: Kang 275.00
❑9, Oct 1964, SL (w); DH, JK (a); O: Wonder Man. 1: Wonder Man. D: Wonder Man 225.00
❑10, Nov 1964, SL (w); DH, JK (a); 1: Hercules. 1: Immortus 180.00
❑11, Dec 1964, SL (w); DH, JK (a); A: Spider-Man. Spider-Man 275.00
❑12, Jan 1965, JK (c); SL (w); DH, JK (a); 1: Monk Keefer (later becomes Ape-Man I). V: Mole Man 115.00
❑13, Feb 1965, SL (w); DH, JK (a); 1: Count Nefaria 135.00
❑14, Mar 1965, JK, SL (w); JK (a); 1: Ogor and Kallusians. The Watcher 150.00
❑15, Apr 1965, JK, SL (w); JK (a); D: Baron Zemo I (Heinrich Zemo). Death of Baron Zemo 100.00
❑16, May 1965, JK, SL (w); JK (a); Cap assembles new team of Hawkeye, Quicksilver, Scarlet Witch; New team begins: Captain America, Hawkeye, Quicksilver, and Scarlet Witch 125.00
❑17, Jun 1965, SL (w); JK (a) 115.00
❑18, Jul 1965, SL (w); DH, JK (a) 100.00
❑19, Aug 1965, SL (w); DH, JK (a); O: Hawkeye. 1: Swordsman. origin of Hawkeye 150.00
❑20, Sep 1965, SL (w); DH, WW (a); V: Swordsman 80.00
❑21, Oct 1965, SL (w); DH, JK (a); O: Power Man I (Erik Josten). 1: Power Man I (Erik Josten). Power Man 70.00
❑22, Nov 1965, SL (w); DH, JK (a) 70.00
❑23, Dec 1965, SL (w); DH, JK (a); 1: Ravonna 75.00
❑24, Jan 1966, SL (w); DH, JK (a); A: Kang. A: Doctor Doom. A: Princess Ravonna 70.00
❑25, Feb 1966, SL (w); DH, JK (a); A: Mr. Fantastic. A: Invisible Girl. A: Thing. A: Human Torch. A: Doctor Doom 70.00
❑26, Mar 1966, SL (w); DH, JK (a); A: Henry Pym. A: Puppet Master. A: Beetle. A: Tony Stark. A: Attuma. A: Sub-Mariner. A: The Wasp 65.00
❑27, Apr 1966, SL (w); DH, JK (a); A: Mr. Fantastic. A: Invisible Girl. A: Collector. A: Henry Pym. A: Beetle. A: Attuma 70.00
❑28, May 1966, SL (w); DH, JK (a); 1: The Collector. 1: Goliath. A: Beetle. Giant-Man becomes Goliath; Goliath rejoins Avengers; Wasp rejoins Avengers 50.00
❑29, Jun 1966, SL (w); DH, JK (a); 1: Hu Chen. 1: Doctor Yen. A: Black Widow. A: S.H.I.E.L.D.. A: Swordsman. Power Man I; Black Widow 50.00
❑30, Jul 1966, DH (c); SL (w); DH, JK (a); 1: Doctor Franz Anton. 1: Keeper of the Flame. 1: Prince Rey. A: Black Widow. A: Power Man I. A: Hu Chen. A: Swordsman. Quicksilver & Scarlet Witch leave Avengers 50.00
❑31, Aug 1966, SL (w); DH, JK (a) 43.00
❑32, Sep 1966, SL (w); DH (a); 1: Sons of the Serpent. 1: Supreme Serpent I. 1: Bill Foster (Giant-Man II). A: Black Widow. A: Scarlet Witch. A: Quicksilver. A: Nick Fury. A: Tony Stark. Black Widow 37.00
❑33, Oct 1966, SL (w); DH (a); A: Black Widow. Black Widow 50.00
❑34, Nov 1966, SL (w); DH (a);
❑0: Living Laser. 1: Living Laser. 1 : Lucy Barton 55.00
❑35, Dec 1966, SL (w); DH (a); 1: Ultrana (off page). 2: Living Laser. 2: Lucy Barton. A: Black Widow. A: Bill Foster 50.00
❑36, Jan 1967, DH (a); 1: Ultroids. 1: Ultrana (full). 1: Ixar. A: Black Widow. Quicksilver & Scarlet Witch rejoin Avengers 35.00
❑37, Feb 1967, DH (a); 2: Ultroids. 2: Ultrana. 2: Ixar. A: Black Widow. Black Widow; Ultroids consolidate into giant robot Ultroid 40.00
❑38, Mar 1967, DH (a); A: Hercules. A: Black Widow. Hercules; Captain America leaves Avengers 43.00
❑39, Apr 1967, DH (a); A: Hercules. A: Black Widow. A: S.H.I.E.L.D.. A: Jasper Sitwell. A: Dum Dum Dugan. A: Nick Fury. A: Mad Thinker. Hercules 40.00
❑40, May 1967, GT (c); DH (a); A: Hercules. A: Black Widow. A: Sub-Mariner. V: Sub-Mariner 40.00
❑41, Jun 1967, JB (a); 1: Colonel Ling. 2: Doctor Yen. A: Hercules. A: Black Widow. A: Dragon Man. A: Bill Foster. A: Diablo. Mr. Fantastic cameo; Human Torch cameo 40.00
❑42, Jul 1967, JB (a); V: Diablo, Dragon Man. Captain America rejoins the Avengers 50.00
❑43, Aug 1967, JB (a); 1: General Yuri Brushov. 1: Red Guardian I (Alexi Shostakov). A: Hercules. A: Black Widow. A: Edwin Jarvis. A: Colonel Ling 40.00
❑44, Sep 1967, JB (a); O: Red Guardian I (Alexi Shostakov). O: Black Widow (part). 2: Red Guardian I (Alexi Shostakov). A: Hercules. A: Black Widow. A: Colonel Ling. D: Red Guardian I (Alexi Shostakov) 40.00
❑45, Oct 1967, DH (w); DH (a); A: Super-Adaptoid. A: Iron Man I. A: Thor. V: Super-Adaptoid. Hercules joins team; Black Widow retires 50.00
❑46, Nov 1967, 1: Whirlwind. Goliath regains Ant-Man powers 30.00
❑47, Dec 1967, D: Black Knight II (Nathan Garrett). New Black Knight (Dr. Dane Whitman) origin part 1 37.00
❑48, Jan 1968, O: Aragorn. 1: Black Knight III (Dane Whitman). 1: Aragorn. New Black Knight (Dr. Dane Whitman) origin part 2 37.00

Avengers (Vol. 2)

Ill-fated Rob Liefeld "Heroes Reborn" relaunch

Avengers (Vol. 3)

Undid "Reborn" before being "Disassembled'

Avengers, The: Celestial Quest

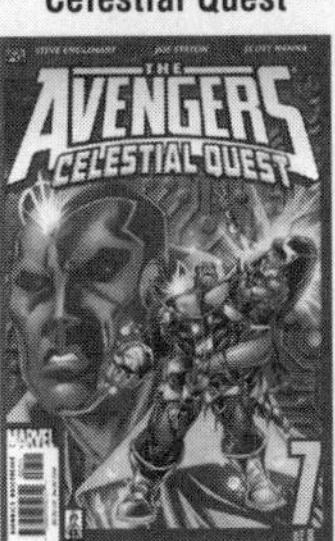

Arc from Steve Englehart and Jorge Santamaria

Avengers Forever

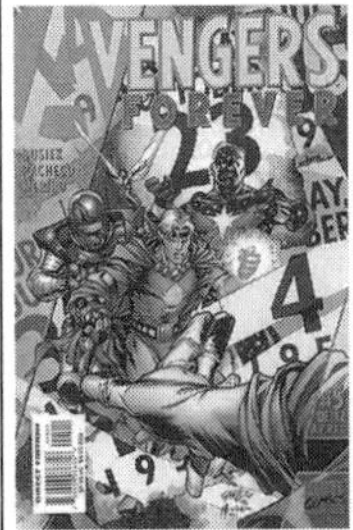

Sprawling story spans time and space

Avengers Infinity

Answering a distress call from Jack of Hearts

	N-MINT
❑49, Feb 1968, JB (a); A: Magneto. Quicksilver & Scarlet Witch leave Avengers; Goliath loses powers	32.00
❑50, Mar 1968, JB (a); Herculese leaves the Avengers	30.00
❑51, Apr 1968, JB (a); Thor, Iron Man; Goliath regains powers, new costume	40.00
❑52, May 1968, O: Grim Reaper. 1: Grim Reaper. Black Panther joins	41.00
❑53, Jun 1968, JB (a); A: X-Men	60.00
❑54, Jul 1968, JB (a); 1: Crimson Cowl	30.00
❑55, Aug 1968, JB (a); 1: Ultron-5	30.00
❑56, Sep 1968, JB (a)	50.00
❑57, Oct 1968, JB (a); 1: The Vision II (android). First Vision	110.00
❑58, Nov 1968, JB (a); O: The Vision II (android). Origin of the Vision; The Vision joins the Avengers; Thor, Captain America, Iron Man	65.00
❑59, Dec 1968, JB (a); 1: Yellowjacket. Goliath becomes Yellowjacket	40.00
❑60, Jan 1969, JB (a); Yellowjacket marries Wasp; Captain America	40.00
❑61, Feb 1969, JB (a); Doctor Strange	30.00
❑62, Mar 1969, JB (a); 1: W'Kabi. 1: The Man-Ape	30.00
❑63, Apr 1969, GC (a); O: Goliath-New (Hawkeye). 1: Goliath-New (Hawkeye)	30.00
❑64, May 1969, GC (a); Black Widow; Hawkeye's identity revealed	30.00
❑65, Jun 1969, GC (a); O: Hawkeye	30.00
❑66, Jul 1969	30.00
❑67, Aug 1969	45.00
❑68, Sep 1969, SB (a)	27.00
❑69, Oct 1969, SB (a); 1: Grandmaster. 1: Nighthawk II (Kyle Richmond)-Full. First Nighthawk; Captain America and Black Panther rejoin	22.00
❑70, Nov 1969, SB (a)	22.00
❑71, Dec 1969, SB (a); 1: Invaders (prototype). Human Torch, Golden Age Captain America and Sub-Mariner; Black Knight joins Avengers	50.00
❑72, Jan 1970, SB (a); 1: Zodiac I. 1: Taurus. 1: Pisces I	30.00
❑73, Feb 1970, HT (a); Quicksilver, Scarlet Witch return; Yellowjacket and Wasp leave	25.00
❑74, Mar 1970, JB (a)	25.00
❑75, Apr 1970, JB (a); 1: Arkon	25.00
❑76, May 1970, JB (a)	25.00
❑77, Jun 1970, JB (a); 1: the Split-Second Squad	20.00
❑78, Jul 1970, JB (a)	25.00
❑79, Aug 1970, JB (a)	23.00
❑80, Sep 1970, JB (a); O: Red Wolf. 1: Red Wolf	23.00
❑81, Oct 1970, JB (a)	23.00
❑82, Nov 1970, JB (a); Daredevil	25.00
❑83, Dec 1970, JB (a); 1: Valkyrie. First Valkyrie	36.00
❑84, Jan 1971, JB (a); Black Knight's sword destroyed	23.00
❑85, Feb 1971, JB (c); JB (a); 1: Whizzer II (Stanley Stewart). 1: Hawkeye II (Wyatt McDonald). 1: American Eagle II (James Dore Jr.). 1: Tom Thumb. 1: Doctor Spectrum I (Joe Ledger)	23.00
❑86, Mar 1971, JB, SB (a); 1: Brain-Child	23.00

	N-MINT
❑87, Apr 1971, O: Black Panther. Black Panther origin retold	40.00
❑88, May 1971, SB (a); 1: Psyklop	25.00
❑88/2nd, SB (a); 1: Psyklop	2.00
❑89, Jun 1971, SB (a); Kree/Skrull War part 1; Captain Marvel	20.00
❑90, Jul 1971, SB (a); Kree/Skrull War part 2; Captain Marvel origin retold	20.00
❑91, Aug 1971, SB (a); Kree/Skrull War part 3; Captain Marvel	20.00
❑92, Sep 1971, NA (c); SB, NA (a); Kree/Skrull War part 4; Captain Marvel	20.00
❑93, Nov 1971, Double-size; NA (a); Kree/Skrull War part 5; Captain Marvel	105.00
❑94, Dec 1971, JB, NA (a); 1: Mandroid armor. Kree/Skrull War part 6; Captain Marvel	35.00
❑95, Jan 1972, NA (a); O: Black Bolt. Kree/Skrull War part 7; Inhumans crosover with Amazing Adventures #5-8	35.00
❑96, Feb 1972, NA (a); Kree/Skrull War part 8; Captain Marvel	35.00
❑97, Mar 1972, NA (w); JB, BEv, SB, GK (a); Kree/Skrull War part 9; Captain Marvel	26.00
❑98, Apr 1972, 1: The Warhawks. Goliath becomes Hawkeye again	26.00
❑99, May 1972	30.00
❑100, Jun 1972, 100th anniversary issue; Black Knight regains magic sword	55.00
❑101, Jul 1972, RB (a); The Watcher	18.00
❑102, Aug 1972, RB (a)	16.00
❑103, Sep 1972, RB (a)	35.00
❑104, Oct 1972, RB (a)	20.00
❑105, Nov 1972, JB (a)	18.00
❑106, Dec 1972, RB, GT (a)	17.00
❑107, Jan 1973, JSn, GT, DC (a)	20.00
❑108, Feb 1973, DH (a)	12.00
❑109, Mar 1973, DH (a); 1: Imus Champion. Hawkeye leaves Avengers	18.00
❑110, Apr 1973, DH (a); A: X-Men. X-Men; crossover with Fantastic Four #132	25.00
❑111, May 1973, DH (a); A: X-Men. Daredevil	22.00
❑112, Jun 1973, DH (a); 1: Mantis. Black Widow leaves	25.00
❑113, Jul 1973, 1: The Living Bombs. D: The Living Bombs. Silver Surfer	11.00
❑114, Aug 1973, Silver Surfer	15.00
❑115, Sep 1973, D: The Living Bombs. Silver Surfer; Avengers and Defenders vs. Loki and Dormammu, part 1 - continues in Defenders #8	13.00
❑116, Oct 1973, Silver Surfer; Avengers and Defenders vs. Loki and Dormammu, part 3 - continues in Defenders #9	27.00
❑117, Nov 1973, Silver Surfer; Avengers and Defenders vs. Loki and Dormammu, part 5 - continues in Defenders #10	20.00
❑118, Dec 1973, Silver Surfer; Avengers and Defenders vs. Loki and Dormammu, part 7 - continues in Defenders #11	20.00

	N-MINT
❑119, Jan 1974, Silver Surfer	12.00
❑120, Feb 1974, JSn, DH, JSt (a)	12.00
❑121, Mar 1974, JB (a); Marvel Value Stamp #84: Dr. Doom	10.00
❑122, Apr 1974, Marvel Value Stamp #71: Vision	13.00
❑123, May 1974, O: Mantis. Origin of Mantis, part 1; Marvel Value Stamp #4: Thing	9.00
❑124, Jun 1974, Origin of Mantis, part 2; Marvel Value Stamp #81: rhino	12.00
❑125, Jul 1974, A: Thanos. Thanos; Crossover with Captain Marvel #32 and 33; Marvel Value Stamp #69: Marvel Girl	20.00
❑126, Aug 1974, Marvel Value Stamp #46: Mysterio	18.00
❑127, Sep 1974, SB, JSa (a); 1: Ultron-7. A: Fantastic Four. A: Inhumans. continues in Fantastic Four #150 (wedding of Crystal and Quicksilver); Marvel Value Stamp #13: Dr. Strange	12.00
❑128, Oct 1974, SB (a); Marvel Value Stamp #70: Super Skrull	12.00
❑129, Nov 1974, SB (a); Marvel Value Stamp #88: Leader	12.00
❑130, Dec 1974, SB (a); 1: The Slasher. V: Titanium Man, Radioactive Man, Crimson Dynamo, Slasher. Marvel Value Stamp #96: Dr. Octopus	12.00
❑131, Jan 1975, SB (a); Immortus; Marvel Value Stamp #70: Super Skrull	12.00
❑132, Feb 1975, SB (a); Iron Man dies (resurrected in Giant-Size Avengers #3); Marvel Value Stamp #78: Owl	10.00
❑133, Mar 1975, SB (a); origin of the Vision and Golden Age Human Torch, part 1	8.00
❑134, Apr 1975, SB (a); O: Vision II (android). origin of the Vision and Golden Age Human Torch, part 2	10.00
❑135, May 1975, GT (a); O: Moondragon. O: Vision II (android)-real origin. origin of the Vision and Golden Age Human Torch, part 3	10.00
❑136, Jun 1975, reprints with changes Amazing Adventures #12	8.00
❑137, Jul 1975, GT (a); membership becomes Beast, Iron Man, Moondragon, Thor, Wasp and Yellowjacket	8.00
❑138, Aug 1975, GT (a)	7.00
❑139, Sep 1975, GT (a)	7.00
❑140, Oct 1975, GT (a); Vision and Scarlet Witch return	7.00
❑141, Nov 1975, GP (a); 1: Golden Archer II (Wyatt McDonald). Squadron Sinister	10.00
❑142, Dec 1975, GP (a); Rawhide Kid, Two-Gun Kid, Kid Colt, Night Rider	9.00
❑143, Jan 1976, GP (a)	8.00
❑144, Feb 1976, GP (a); O: Hellcat. 1: Hellcat	8.00
❑145, Mar 1976, DH (a)	5.50
❑146, Apr 1976, KP, DH (a); Falcon	5.50
❑146/30 cent, Apr 1976, KP, DH (a); Falcon; 30 cent regional price variant	20.00
❑147, May 1976, Hellcat	5.50
❑147/30 cent, May 1976, Hellcat; 30 cent regional price variant	20.00
❑148, Jun 1976, 1: Cap'n Hawk	5.50

Other grades: Multiply price above by 5/6 for VF/NM • 2/3 for VERY FINE • 1/3 for FINE • 1/5 for VERY GOOD • 1/8 for GOOD

	N-MINT
❑148/30 cent, Jun 1976, 1: Cap'n Hawk. 30 cent regional price variant	17.00
❑149, Jun 1976	5.50
❑149/30 cent, Jun 1976, 30 cent regional price variant	15.00
❑150, Aug 1976, GP (a); New team: Captain America, Iron Man, Yellowjacket, Wasp, Beast, Vision II (android), and Scarlet Witch; Partial Reprint from Avengers #16, retitled from "The Old Order Changeth"	5.50
❑150/30 cent, Aug 1976, GP (a); New team: Captain America, Iron Man, Yellowjacket, Wasp, Beast, Vision II (android), and Scarlet Witch; Partial Reprint from Avengers #16, retitled from "The Old Order Changeth"	15.00
❑151, Sep 1976, GP (a); New Avengers lineup: Beast, Captain America, Iron Man, Scarlet Witch, Vision, Wasp, Yellowjacket; Wonder Man comes back from dead, new costume	5.50
❑152, Oct 1976, 1: Black Talon II	5.50
❑153, Nov 1976	5.50
❑154, Dec 1976	5.50
❑155, Jan 1977	5.50
❑156, Feb 1977, 1: Tyrack. Newsstand edition (distributed by Curtis); issue number in box	8.00
❑156/Whitman, Feb 1977, 1: Tyrack. Special markets edition (usually sold in Whitman bagged prepacks); price appears in a diamond; UPC barcode appears	8.00
❑157, Mar 1977, Newsstand edition (distributed by Curtis); issue number in box	5.50
❑157/Whitman, Mar 1977, Special markets edition (usually sold in Whitman bagged prepacks); price appears in a diamond; UPC barcode appears	5.50
❑158, Apr 1977, JK (c); SB (a); Newsstand edition (distributed by Curtis); issue number in box	5.50
❑158/Whitman, Apr 1977, JK (c); SB (a); Special markets edition (usually sold in Whitman bagged prepacks); price appears in a diamond; UPC barcode appears	5.50
❑159, May 1977, SB (a); Newsstand edition (distributed by Curtis); issue number in box	5.50
❑159/Whitman, May 1977, SB (a); Special markets edition (usually sold in Whitman bagged prepacks); price appears in a diamond; UPC barcode appears	5.50
❑160, Jun 1977, Newsstand edition (distributed by Curtis); issue number in box	5.50
❑160/Whitman, Jun 1977, Special markets edition (usually sold in Whitman bagged prepacks); price appears in a diamond; UPC barcode appears	5.50
❑160/35 cent, Jun 1977, 35 cent regional price variant; newsstand edition (distributed by Curtis); issue number in box	15.00
❑161, Jul 1977, GP, JBy (a); Newsstand edition (distributed by Curtis); issue number in box	5.50
❑161/Whitman, Jul 1977, GP, JBy (a); Special markets edition (usually sold in Whitman bagged prepacks); price appears in a diamond; UPC barcode appears	5.50
❑161/35 cent, Jul 1977, GP, JBy (a); 35 cent regional price variant; newsstand edition (distributed by Curtis); issue number in box	15.00
❑162, Aug 1977, GP, JBy (a); O: Jocasta. 1: Jocasta. Newsstand edition (distributed by Curtis); issue number in box	8.00
❑162/Whitman, Aug 1977, GP, JBy (a); O: Jocasta. 1: Jocasta. Special markets edition (usually sold in Whitman bagged prepacks); price appears in a diamond; UPC barcode appears	8.00
❑162/35 cent, Aug 1977, GP, JBy (a); 35 cent regional price variant; newsstand edition (distributed by Curtis); issue number in box	15.00
❑163, Sep 1977, GP, JBy (a); Newsstand edition (distributed by Curtis); issue number in box	5.50
❑163/Whitman, Sep 1977, GP, JBy (a); Special markets edition (usually sold in Whitman bagged prepacks); price appears in a diamond; UPC barcode appears	5.50
❑163/35 cent, Sep 1977, GP, JBy (a); 35 cent regional price variant; newsstand edition (distributed by Curtis); issue number in box	15.00
❑164, Oct 1977, GP, JBy (a); Newsstand edition (distributed by Curtis); issue number in box	5.50
❑164/Whitman, Oct 1977, GP, JBy (a); Special markets edition (usually sold in Whitman bagged prepacks); price appears in a diamond; no UPC barcode	5.50
❑164/35 cent, Oct 1977, GP, JBy (a); 35 cent regional price variant; newsstand edition (distributed by Curtis); issue number in box	15.00
❑165, Nov 1977, JBy (a); Newsstand edition (distributed by Curtis); issue number in box	5.50
❑165/Whitman, Nov 1977, JBy (a); Special markets edition (usually sold in Whitman bagged prepacks); price appears in a diamond; no UPC barcode	5.50
❑166, Dec 1977, JBy (a); Newsstand edition (distributed by Curtis); issue number in box	5.50
❑166/Whitman, Dec 1977, JBy (a); Special markets edition (usually sold in Whitman bagged prepacks); price appears in a diamond; no UPC barcode	5.50
❑167, Jan 1978, JBy (a)	5.00
❑168, Feb 1978, JBy (a)	7.00
❑169, Mar 1978, JBy (a)	4.00
❑170, Apr 1978, JBy (a)	4.00
❑171, May 1978, JBy (a); Newsstand edition (distributed by Curtis); issue number in box	4.00
❑171/Whitman, May 1978, JBy (a); Special markets edition (usually sold in Whitman bagged prepacks); price appears in a diamond; no UPC barcode	4.00
❑172, Jun 1978	4.00
❑173, Jul 1978	4.00
❑174, Aug 1978, Newsstand edition (distributed by Curtis); issue number in box	4.00
❑174/Whitman, Aug 1978, Special markets edition (usually sold in Whitman bagged prepacks); price appears in a diamond; UPC barcode appears	4.00
❑175, Sep 1978, Newsstand edition (distributed by Curtis); issue number in box	4.00
❑175/Whitman, Sep 1978, Special markets edition (usually sold in Whitman bagged prepacks); price appears in a diamond; no UPC barcode	4.00
❑176, Oct 1978, Newsstand edition (distributed by Curtis); issue number in box	4.00
❑176/Whitman, Oct 1978, Special markets edition (usually sold in Whitman bagged prepacks); price appears in a diamond; no UPC barcode	4.00
❑177, Nov 1978, Newsstand edition (distributed by Curtis); issue number in box	4.00
❑177/Whitman, Nov 1978, Special markets edition (usually sold in Whitman bagged prepacks); price appears in a diamond; UPC barcode appears	4.00
❑178, Dec 1978, CI, JBy (a)	5.00
❑179, Jan 1979, JM (a); 1: The Monolith. 1: The Stinger II. Newsstand edition (distributed by Curtis); issue number in box	4.00
❑179/Whitman, Jan 1979, JM (a); 1: The Monolith. 1: The Stinger II. Special markets edition (usually sold in Whitman bagged prepacks); price appears in a diamond; no UPC barcode	4.00
❑180, Feb 1979, JM (a); Newsstand edition (distributed by Curtis); issue number in box	4.00
❑180/Whitman, Feb 1979, JM (a); Special markets edition (usually sold in Whitman bagged prepacks); price appears in a diamond; no UPC barcode	4.00
❑181, Mar 1979, GP, JBy, TD (a); New team: Captain America, Falcon, Iron Man, Beast, Vision II (android), and Scarlet Witch	5.00
❑182, Apr 1979, JBy (a)	4.00
❑183, May 1979, JBy (a); Newsstand edition (distributed by Curtis); issue number in box	5.00
❑183/Whitman, May 1979, JBy (a); Special markets edition (usually sold in Whitman bagged prepacks); price appears in a diamond; no UPC barcode	5.00
❑184, Jun 1979, JBy (a)	6.00
❑185, Jul 1979, JBy (a); O: Scarlet Witch. O: Quicksilver. 1: Chthon (in human body)	7.00
❑186, Aug 1979, JBy (a)	5.00
❑187, Sep 1979, JBy (a); 1: Chthon (in real human form)	6.00
❑188, Oct 1979, JBy, DGr, FS (a)	6.00
❑189, Nov 1979, JBy (a)	6.00
❑190, Dec 1979, JBy (a); Daredevil	5.00
❑191, Jan 1980, GP, JBy (a)	5.00
❑192, Feb 1980	5.00
❑193, Mar 1980, FM, BMc (c); SB, DGr (a)	5.00
❑194, Apr 1980, GP (a)	5.00
❑195, May 1980, GP (a); 1: Taskmaster	5.00
❑196, Jun 1980, GP (a); O: Taskmaster	7.00
❑197, Jul 1980, GP, BMc (c); CI (a)	5.00
❑198, Aug 1980, GP (c); GP (a)	5.00
❑199, Sep 1980, GP (a)	5.00
❑200, Oct 1980, double-sized; GP (c); GP, DGr (a); Ms. Marvel leaves team	9.00
❑201, Nov 1980, GP (a)	2.50
❑202, Dec 1980, GP (a); V: Ultron	2.50
❑203, Jan 1981, CI (a)	2.50
❑204, Feb 1981, DN (a); A: Yellow Claw	2.50
❑205, Mar 1981, A: Yellow Claw	2.50
❑206, Apr 1981, GC (a)	2.50
❑207, May 1981, GC (a)	2.50
❑208, Jun 1981, GC (a)	2.50
❑209, Jul 1981	2.50
❑210, Aug 1981, GC, DG (a)	2.50
❑211, Sep 1981, GC, DG (a); Moon Knight, Dazzler; New team begins	2.50
❑212, Oct 1981, BH (c)	2.50
❑213, Nov 1981, BH (c); BH (a); Yellowjacket's court martial; Yellowjacket leaves	2.50
❑214, Dec 1981, BH (c); BH (a); A: Ghost Rider	3.00
❑215, Jan 1982, A: Silver Surfer	2.50
❑216, Feb 1982, A: Silver Surfer	2.50
❑217, Mar 1982, BH (c); BH (a); Yellowjacket jailed; Yellowjacket & Wasp return	3.00
❑218, Apr 1982, DP (a)	3.00
❑219, May 1982, BH (c); BH (a); A: Drax	2.00
❑220, Jun 1982, BH (c); BH (a); A: Drax. D: Drax the Destroyer	2.00
❑221, Jul 1982, BH (c); BH (a); Hawkeye rejoins; She-Hulk joins; Wolverine on cover, not in issue	2.00
❑222, Aug 1982, V: Masters of Evil	2.00
❑223, Sep 1982, A: Ant-Man	2.00
❑224, Oct 1982, Tony Stark/Wasp romance	2.00
❑225, Nov 1982, 1: Balor. A: Black Knight	3.00
❑226, Dec 1982, 1: Valinor. A: Black Knight	2.00
❑227, Jan 1983, SB (a); O: Yellowjacket. O: Ant-Man. O: Goliath. O: Wasp. O: Giant-Man. O: Avengers. Captain Marvel II joins team; Captain Marvel II (female) joins team	2.00
❑228, Feb 1983, AM (a)	2.00
❑229, Mar 1983, AM (c); AM (a); V: Egghead	2.00
❑230, Apr 1983, AM (a); D: Egghead. Yellowjacket leaves	2.00
❑231, May 1983, AM (a); Iron Man leaves	2.00
❑232, Jun 1983, AM (a); A: Starfox. Starfox (Eros) joins	2.00
❑233, Jul 1983, JBy (w); JBy, JSt (a)	2.00
❑234, Aug 1983, AM (a); O: Scarlet Witch. O: Quicksilver	2.00
❑235, Sep 1983, AM, JSt (c); V: Wizard	2.00
❑236, Oct 1983, AM, JSt (c); AM (a); Spider-Man; New logo	2.00

Other grades: Multiply price above by 5/6 for VF/NM • 2/3 for VERY FINE • 1/3 for FINE • 1/5 for VERY GOOD • 1/8 for GOOD

Avengers Spotlight

Renamed title had been called Solo Avengers

©Marvel

Avengers/ Thunderbolts

Crossover title from Kurt Busiek

©Marvel

Avengers: United They Stand

Adaptation of the Avengers cartoon series

©Marvel

Avengers Unplugged

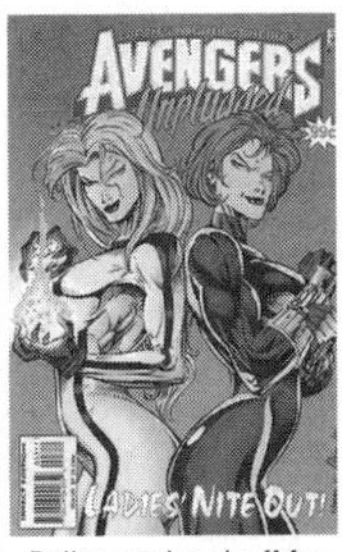

Dollar-comic spinoff for bargain hunters

©Marvel

Avengers West Coast

Renamed version of West Coast Avengers

©Marvel

	N-MINT
❑237, Nov 1983, AM, JSt (c); AM, JSt (a); Spider-Man	2.00
❑238, Dec 1983, AM, JSt (c); AM, JSt (a); O: Blackout I (Marcus Daniels)	2.00
❑239, Jan 1984, AM (a); A: David Letterman. D: Blackout I (Marcus Daniels)	2.00
❑240, Feb 1984, AM, JSt (a); A: Spider-Woman. Spider-Woman revived	2.00
❑241, Mar 1984, AM (c); AM, JSt (a); A: Spider-Woman	2.00
❑242, Apr 1984, AM, JSt (c); AM (a)	2.00
❑243, May 1984, AM, JSt (c); AM, JSt (a)	2.00
❑244, Jun 1984, AM, JSt (c); AM, Cl, JSt (a); V: Dire Wraiths	2.00
❑245, Jul 1984, AM, JSt (c); AM, JSt (a); V: Dire Wraiths	2.00
❑246, Aug 1984, AM, JSt (c); AM, JSt (a); A: Sersi	2.00
❑247, Sep 1984, AM, JSt (c); AM, JSt (a); A: Uni-Mind	2.00
❑248, Oct 1984, AM, JSt (c); AM, JSt (a); A: Eternals	2.00
❑249, Nov 1984, AM, JSt (c); AM, JSt (a); A: Fantastic Four	2.00
❑250, Dec 1984, AM, JSt (c); AM, JSt (a); Maelstrom	2.50
❑251, Jan 1985, BH, JSt (c); BH, JSt (a)	1.75
❑252, Feb 1985, BH (c); BH, JSt (a)	1.75
❑253, Mar 1985, KP (c); BH (a)	1.75
❑254, Apr 1985, BH (c); BH (a)	1.75
❑255, May 1985, TP (c); JB, TP (a)	1.75
❑256, Jun 1985, JB, TP (c); JB, TP (a); Savage Land	1.75
❑257, Jul 1985, JB (a); 1: Nebula	1.75
❑258, Aug 1985, Spider-Man vs. Firelord	1.75
❑259, Sep 1985, V: Skrulls	1.75
❑260, Oct 1985, JBy (c); JB, TP (a); A: Nebula. Secret Wars II	1.75
❑261, Nov 1985, JB (a); Secret Wars II	1.75
❑262, Dec 1985, JB, TP (c); JB, TP (a); A: Sub-Mariner	1.75
❑263, Jan 1986, 1: X-Factor. D: Melter	3.00
❑264, Feb 1986	1.75
❑265, Mar 1986, JB (a); Secret Wars II	1.75
❑266, Apr 1986, JB, TP (c); JB, TP (a); Secret Wars II Epilogue	1.50
❑267, May 1986, JB, TP (c); JB, TP (a); V: Kang	1.50
❑268, Jun 1986, JB (a); V: Kang	1.50
❑269, Jul 1986, JB, TP (c); JB, TP (a); O: Rama-Tut. V: Kang	1.50
❑270, Aug 1986, JB, TP (c); JB, TP (a); A: Namor	1.50
❑271, Sep 1986, JB (a)	1.50
❑272, Oct 1986, JB (a); A: Alpha Flight	1.50
❑273, Nov 1986, JB (a)	1.50
❑274, Dec 1986, JB (a)	1.50
❑275, Jan 1987, JB (a)	1.50
❑276, Feb 1987, JB (a)	1.50
❑277, Mar 1987, JB (a); D: Blackout	1.50
❑278, Apr 1987, JB (a)	1.50
❑279, May 1987	1.50
❑280, Jun 1987, BH (a)	1.50
❑281, Jul 1987	1.50

	N-MINT
❑282, Aug 1987, JB, TP (c); JB, TP (a); V: Neptune	1.50
❑283, Sep 1987, JB, TP (c); JB, TP (a)	1.50
❑284, Oct 1987, JB, TP (c); JB, TP (a); on Olympus	1.50
❑285, Nov 1987, JB, TP (c); JB, TP (a); V: Zeus	1.50
❑286, Dec 1987, JB, TP (c); JB, TP (a); V: Super Adaptoid	1.50
❑287, Jan 1988, JB, TP (c); JB, TP (a); V: Fixer	1.50
❑288, Feb 1988, JB, TP (c); JB, TP (a); V: Sentry Sinister	1.50
❑289, Mar 1988, JB, TP (c); JB, TP (a); V: Super Adaptoid, Sentry Sinister, Machine Man, Tess-One, Fixer	1.50
❑290, Apr 1988, JB (a)	1.50
❑291, May 1988, JB (a)	1.50
❑292, Jun 1988, JB (a); 1: Leviathan III (Marina). D: Leviathan III (Marina)	1.50
❑293, Jul 1988, JB (a); 1: Nebula. D: Marina. D: Marrina	1.50
❑294, Aug 1988, JB (a); Captain Marvel leaves team; Capt. Marvel leaves team	1.50
❑295, Sep 1988, JB (a)	1.50
❑296, Oct 1988, JB (a)	1.50
❑297, Nov 1988, JB (a); D: Doctor Druid. Thor, Black Knight, She-Hulk leaves team; She-Hulk, Thor, and Black Knight leave	1.50
❑298, Dec 1988, JB (a); Inferno	1.50
❑299, Jan 1989, JB (a); Inferno	1.50
❑300, Feb 1989, 300th anniversary issue; JB (a); Inferno; new team; Thor Joins	2.00
❑301, Mar 1989, BH (c); BH (a)	1.50
❑302, Apr 1989, JB, TP (c); RB, TP (a)	1.50
❑303, May 1989, JB, TP (c); RB, TP (a)	1.50
❑304, Jun 1989, RB, TP (a); 1: Portal. A: Puma. V: U-Foes	1.50
❑305, Jul 1989, JBy (w); JBy (a)	1.50
❑306, Aug 1989, JBy (w)	1.50
❑307, Sep 1989, JBy (w)	1.50
❑308, Oct 1989, JBy (w)	1.50
❑309, Nov 1989, JBy (w); TP (a)	1.50
❑310, Nov 1989, JBy (w)	1.50
❑311, Dec 1989, TP (c); JBy (w); TP (a); "Acts of Vengeance"	1.50
❑312, Dec 1989, TP (c); JBy (w); TP (a); "Acts of Vengeance"	1.50
❑313, Jan 1990, TP (c); JBy (w); "Acts of Vengeance"	1.50
❑314, Feb 1990, JBy (w); Spider-Man	1.50
❑315, Mar 1990, JBy (w); TP (a); Spider-Man; Spider-Man x-over	1.50
❑316, Apr 1990, JBy (w); Spider-Man	1.50
❑317, May 1990, JBy (w); Spider-Man	1.50
❑318, Jun 1990, Spider-Man	1.50
❑319, Jul 1990	1.50
❑320, Aug 1990, A: Alpha Flight	1.50
❑321, Aug 1990	1.50
❑322, Sep 1990, A: Alpha Flight	1.50
❑323, Sep 1990, A: Alpha Flight	1.50
❑324, Oct 1990	1.50
❑325, Oct 1990	1.50
❑326, Nov 1990, 1: Rage	1.50
❑327, Dec 1990	1.50
❑328, Jan 1991, O: Rage. O: Turbo	1.50

	N-MINT
❑329, Feb 1991	1.50
❑330, Mar 1991	1.50
❑331, Apr 1991	1.50
❑332, May 1991	1.50
❑333, Jun 1991, HT (a)	1.50
❑334, Jul 1991	1.50
❑335, Aug 1991	1.50
❑336, Aug 1991	1.50
❑337, Sep 1991	1.50
❑338, Sep 1991, TP (c); TP (a); numbering of story arc wrong on cover, really Part 5 of story	1.50
❑339, Oct 1991	1.50
❑340, Oct 1991	1.50
❑341, Nov 1991	1.50
❑342, Dec 1991, TP (c); TP (a); A: New Warriors	1.50
❑343, Jan 1992	1.50
❑344, Feb 1992	1.50
❑345, Mar 1992, TP (c); TP (a)	1.50
❑346, Apr 1992, TP (c); TP (a)	1.50
❑347, May 1992, TP (c); TP (a); D: Supreme Intelligence (apparent death). Conclusion to Operation: Galactic Storm	2.00
❑348, Jun 1992, TP (c); TP (a)	1.50
❑349, Jul 1992, TP (c); TP (a)	1.50
❑350, Aug 1992, Dbl. Size; Gatefold covers	2.50
❑351, Aug 1992, TP (c)	1.25
❑352, Sep 1992, TP (c); TP (a); V: Grim Reaper	1.25
❑353, Sep 1992, TP (c); V: Grim Reaper	1.25
❑354, Oct 1992, TP (c); V: Grim Reaper	1.25
❑355, Oct 1992	1.25
❑356, Nov 1992	1.25
❑357, Dec 1992	1.25
❑358, Jan 1993	1.25
❑359, Feb 1993, TP (c); TP (a)	1.25
❑360, Mar 1993, TP (a); foil cover	2.95
❑361, Apr 1993	1.25
❑362, May 1993	1.25
❑363, Jun 1993, Silver embossed cover	2.95
❑364, Jul 1993	1.25
❑365, Aug 1993, TP (c); TP (a)	1.25
❑366, Sep 1993, sculpted foil cover	3.95
❑367, Oct 1993, TP (c); A: Sersi. A: Black Knight	1.25
❑368, Nov 1993, TP (c); TP (a)	1.25
❑369, Dec 1993, sculpted foil cover	2.95
❑370, Jan 1994	1.25
❑371, Feb 1994, MGu, TP (a)	1.25
❑372, Mar 1994, TP (c); TP (a)	1.25
❑373, Apr 1994	1.25
❑374, May 1994, cards	1.25
❑375, Jun 1994, Giant-size; D: Proctor. poster; Dane Whitman and Sersi leave the Avengers	2.00
❑375/Collector's, Jun 1994, Giant-size; D: Proctor. Dane Whitman and Sersi leave the Avengers	2.50
❑376, Jul 1994, (c)	1.50
❑377, Aug 1994	1.50
❑378, Sep 1994	1.50
❑379, Oct 1994, (c)	1.50

Other grades: Multiply price above by 5/6 for VF/NM • 2/3 for VERY FINE • 1/3 for FINE • 1/5 for VERY GOOD • 1/8 for GOOD

	N-MINT
❑379/Double, Oct 1994, Double-feature with Giant-Man	2.50
❑380, Nov 1994, TP (c); TP (a); V: High Evolutionary	1.50
❑380/Double, Nov 1994, TP (c); TP (a); second indicia gives name as "Marvel Double Feature ... The Avengers/Giant Man"	2.50
❑381, Dec 1994, TP (c); TP (a)	1.50
❑381/Double, Dec 1994, TP (c); GP (w); TP (a); second indicia gives name as "Marvel Double Feature ... The Avengers/Giant Man"	2.50
❑382, Jan 1995, TP (a)	1.50
❑382/Double, Jan 1995, TP (a); second indicia gives name as "Marvel Double Feature ... The Avengers/Giant Man"	2.50
❑383, Feb 1995, MGu (a)	1.50
❑384, Mar 1995, TP (c); TP (a)	1.50
❑385, Apr 1995, TP (c); JB, TP (a)	1.50
❑386, May 1995, (c); continues in Captain America #440	1.50
❑387, Jun 1995, TP (a); continues in Captain America #441	1.50
❑388, Jul 1995, TP (c); TP (a)	1.50
❑389, Aug 1995	1.50
❑390, Sep 1995	1.50
❑391, Oct 1995	1.50
❑392, Nov 1995, Mantis returns	1.50
❑393, Dec 1995, A: Tony Stark. "The Crossing"; Wasp critically injured	1.50
❑394, Jan 1996, 1: New Wasp. "The Crossing"	1.50
❑395, Feb 1996, D: Tony Stark	1.50
❑396, Mar 1996	1.50
❑397, Apr 1996	1.50
❑398, May 1996	1.50
❑399, Jun 1996	1.50
❑400, Jul 1996, MWa (w); wraparound cover	4.00
❑401, Aug 1996, MWa (w); A: Magneto, Rogue	2.50
❑402, Sep 1996, MWa (w); "Onslaught: Impact 2"; story continues in X-Men #56 and Onslaught: Marvel	2.50
❑Annual 1, Sep 1967, Cover reads "King-Size Special"; DH (a); A: Hercules. A: Iron Man I. A: Mandarin. A: Black Widow. A: Edwin Jarvis. A: Power Man I. A: Living Laser. A: Thor. Cover reads King-Size Special	125.00
❑Annual 2, Sep 1968, Cover reads "King-Size Special"; Cover reads King-Size Special	115.00
❑Annual 3, Sep 1969, Cover reads "King-Size Special"; Cover reads King Size Special; Reprinted from Avengers #4 and Tales of Suspense #66, #67, and #68 respectively	26.00
❑Annual 4, Jan 1971, Cover reads "King-Size Special"; SB (c); SL (w); JK (a); O: Moondragon. Cover reads King Size Special; Reprinted from Avengers #5 & #6 respectively	23.00
❑Annual 5, Jan 1972, Cover reads "King-Size Special"; DH, JK (a); Cover reads King Size Special; Reprinted from Avengers #8 and 11	25.00
❑Annual 6, ca. 1976, JK (c); GP, HT (a); V: Nuklo	7.00
❑Annual 7, ca. 1977, JSn, JSt (a); D: Gamora. D: Warlock. Warlock	12.00
❑Annual 8, ca. 1978, GP (a); A: Ms. Marvel	8.00
❑Annual 9, ca. 1979, DN (a)	4.00
❑Annual 10, ca. 1981, AM (c); MG (a); 1: Rogue. 1: Destiny. X-Men	9.00
❑Annual 11, ca. 1982, AM (c); AM, JAb (a)	3.50
❑Annual 12, ca. 1983, AM, JSt (c); BG (a); A: Inhumans	3.50
❑Annual 13, ca. 1984, SD, JBy (a); D: Nebulon	3.50
❑Annual 14, ca. 1985, JBy (a)	3.50
❑Annual 15, ca. 1986, SD (a)	3.50
❑Annual 16, ca. 1987, BL (c); AW, BSz, KP, BL, BG, JR2, TP, BH, KN, MR, BWi (a)	3.50
❑Annual 17, ca. 1988, SB (c); MGu, TD (a)	3.00
❑Annual 18, ca. 1989, JBy (c); MGu (a); Atlantis Attacks	2.50
❑Annual 19, ca. 1990, KB (w); RHo, HT (a); Terminus	2.50
❑Annual 20, ca. 1991, Subterranean Wars	2.50
❑Annual 21, ca. 1992, HT (a); O: Terminatrix. 1: Terminatrix. Citizen Kang	2.50
❑Annual 22, ca. 1993, AM, MGu (a); 1: Bloodwraith. Polybagged with trading card	2.95
❑Annual 23, ca. 1994, JB (c); AM (w); AM, JB (a)	2.95

AVENGERS (VOL. 2)

Marvel

	N-MINT
❑1 (403), Nov 1996; RL (c); RL (w); RL (a); Thor revived	3.00
❑1/A, Nov 1996; RL (w); RL (a); alternate cover; Thor revived	3.00
❑2 (404), Dec 1996 JPH, RL (w); A: Mantis. V: Kang	2.00
❑3 (405), Jan 1997 JPH, RL (w); A: Mantis, Nick Fury	2.00
❑4 (406), Feb 1997 RL (c); JPH, RL (w); V: Hulk	2.00
❑5 (407), Mar 1997; RL (c); JPH, RL (w); RL (a); Thor vs. Hulk	2.00
❑5/A, Mar 1997; JPH, RL (w); RL (a); White cover; Thor vs. Hulk	2.00
❑6 (408), Apr 1997; (c); JPH, RL (w); continues in Iron Man #6	1.95
❑7 (409), May 1997 JPH, RL (w); V: Lethal Legion (Enchantress, Wonder Man, Ultron 5, Executioner, Scarlet Witch)	1.95
❑8 (410), Jun 1997 JLee (c)	1.95
❑9 (411), Jul 1997 V: Masters of Evil.	1.95
❑10 (412), Aug 1997; gatefold summary V: dopplegangers	1.95
❑11 (413), Sep 1997; gatefold summary D: Thor. V: Loki	1.95
❑12 (414), Oct 1997; cover forms quadtych with Fantastic Four #12, Iron Man #12, and Captain America #12	2.99
❑13 (415), Nov 1997; JRo (w); cover forms quadtych with Fantastic Four #13, Iron Man #13, and Captain America #13	1.95

AVENGERS (VOL. 3)

Marvel

	N-MINT
❑0; Promotional edition included with Wizard KB (w)	2.00
❑1 (416), Feb 1998; gatefold summary GP (c); KB (w); GP (a)	4.00
❑1/Chromium, Feb 1998; GP (c); KB (w); GP (a); chromium cover	6.00
❑1/RoughCut, Jul 1998; GP (c); KB (w); GP (a); Avengers Rough Cut; cardstock cover	4.00
❑1/Variant, Feb 1998; gatefold summary; GP (c); KB (w); GP (a); alternate cover	4.00
❑2 (417), Mar 1998; gatefold summary GP (c); KB (w); GP (a)	3.00
❑2/Variant, Mar 1998; gatefold summary; KB (w); GP (a); alternate cover	3.00
❑3 (418), Apr 1998 GP (c); KB (w); GP (a); A: Wonder Man gatefold summary	2.50
❑4 (419), May 1998; GP (c); KB (w); GP (a); New team announced gatefold summary; New team begins	2.50
❑5 (420), Jun 1998; gatefold summary GP (c); KB (w); GP (a); V: Squadron Supreme	2.50
❑6 (421), Jul 1998; gatefold summary GP (c); KB (w); GP (a); V: Squadron Supreme	2.00
❑7 (422), Aug 1998; gatefold summary; GP (c); KB (w); GP (a); A: Supreme Intelligence. Warbird leaves	2.00
❑8 (423), Sep 1998; gatefold summary GP (c); KB (w); GP (a); 1: Silverclaw. 1: Triathlon	2.00
❑9 (424), Oct 1998; gatefold summary GP (c); KB (w); GP (a); V: Moses Magnum	2.00
❑10 (425), Nov 1998; Anniversary issue GP (c); KB (w); GP (a); V: Grim Reaper	2.00
❑11 (426), Dec 1998; gatefold summary GP (c); KB (w); GP (a); A: Captain Marvel appearance, Thunderstrike. A: Wonder Man. A: Mockingbird. A: Doctor Druid. A: Captain Marvel. A: Hellcat. A: Swordsman. V: Grim Reaper	2.00
❑12 (427), Jan 1999; double-sized; GP (c); KB (w); GP (a); V: Thunderbolts. Continued from Thunderbolts #22; wraparound cover	3.00
❑12/Dynamic, Jan 1999; GP (c); KB (w); GP (a); Continued from Thunderbolts #22; DFE alternate cover	12.00
❑12/White, Jan 1999; GP (c); KB (w); GP (a); Headshot cover (white background); Continued from Thunderbolts #22	5.00
❑13 (428), Feb 1999 GP (c); KB (w); GP (a); A: New Warriors	2.00
❑14 (429), Mar 1999; GP (c); KB (w); GP (a); A: Lord Templar. A: George P…rez. A: Beast. A: Kurt Busiek. Return of Beast to team	2.00
❑15 (430), Apr 1999 GP (c); KB (w); GP (a); A: Lord Templar. A: Triathalon	2.00
❑16 (431), May 1999 JOy (c); JOy (w); JOy (a); V: Wrecking Crew	2.00
❑16/A, May 1999; JOy (c); JOy (w); JOy (a); 1 in 4 variant cover (purple background with team charging)	2.00
❑17 (432), Jun 1999 JOy (c); JOy (w); JOy (a); V: Doomsday Man	2.00
❑18 (433), Jul 1999 JOy (c); JOy (w); JOy (a); V: Wrecking Crew	2.00
❑19 (434), Aug 1999 GP (c); KB (w); GP (a); A: Black Panther. V: Ultron	2.00
❑20 (435), Sep 1999 GP (c); KB (w); GP (a); V: Ultron	2.00
❑21 (436), Oct 1999 GP (c); KB (w); GP (a); V: Ultron	2.00
❑22 (437), Oct 1999 GP (c); KB (w); GP (a); V: Ultron	2.00
❑23 (438), Dec 1999; GP (c); KB (w); GP (a); Wonder Man versus Vision.	2.00
❑24 (439), Jan 2000 GP (c); KB (w); GP (a)	2.00
❑25 (440), Feb 2000; Giant-size GP (c); KB (w); GP (a); A: Juggernaut	3.00
❑26 (441), Mar 2000; GP (c); KB (w); new team (Warbird, Captain Marvel, Ant-Man, Silverclaw, and Captain America)	2.00
❑27 (442), Apr 2000; GP (c); KB, SL (w); RB, RHo, GP, JK, DA (a); 100 pages; reprints material from Avengers Vol. 1 #16, #101, #150-151, and Annual #19	3.00
❑28 (443), May 2000 GP (c); KB (w); GP (a)	2.00
❑29 (444), Jun 2000 GP (c); KB (w); GP (a)	2.25
❑30 (445), Jul 2000 GP (c); KB (w); GP (a)	2.25
❑31 (446), Aug 2000 GP (c); KB (w); GP (a); A: Madame Masque. A: Grim Reaper	2.25
❑32 (447), Sep 2000 GP (c); KB (w); GP (a); A: Madame Masque	2.25
❑33 (448), Oct 2000 GP (c); KB (w); GP (a); A: Madame Masque. A: Thunderbolts. V: Count Nefaria	2.25
❑34 (449), Nov 2000; double-sized issue GP (c); KB (w); GP (a); A: Madame Masque. A: Thunderbolts. V: Count Nefaria	2.99
❑35 (450), Dec 2000 JR2 (c); KB (w); JR2 (a)	2.25
❑36 (451), Jan 2001 KB (w); A: Ten-Thirtifor	2.25
❑37 (452), Feb 2001 KB (w); A: Bloodwraith	2.25
❑38 (453), Mar 2001; KB (w); Slashback issue; price reduced	1.99
❑39 (454), Apr 2001 KB (w)	2.25
❑40 (455), May 2001 KB (w)	2.25
❑41 (456), Jun 2001 KB (w)	2.25
❑42 (457), Jul 2001 KB (w)	2.25
❑43 (458), Aug 2001 KB (w)	2.25
❑44 (459), Sep 2001 KB (w); BL (a)	2.25
❑45 (460), Oct 2001 KB (w); BL (a)	2.25
❑46 (461), Nov 2001; KB (w); BL (a); index numbering out of sequence, should be #461, not #463	2.25
❑47 (462), Dec 2001 KB (w); BL (a)	2.25
❑48 (463), Jan 2002; KB (w); TS, SB, JSt, BS (a); 100 pages; reprints Avengers Vol. 1 #98-100	3.50
❑49 (464), Feb 2002; KB (w); silent issue	2.25
❑50 (465), Mar 2002 KB (w)	2.99
❑51 (466), Apr 2002 KB (w); BA, TP (a)	2.25
❑52 (467), May 2002 KB (w)	2.25

Other grades: Multiply price above by 5/6 for VF/NM • 2/3 for VERY FINE • 1/3 for FINE • 1/5 for VERY GOOD • 1/8 for GOOD

Awesome Preview

San Diego giveaway from Rob Liefeld company

©Awesome

Axel Pressbutton

Early Eclipse title reprints from U.K.'s Warrior

©Eclipse

Azrael

Batman's replacement gets his own series

©DC

Aztec Ace

Future warrior who's a defender of time itself

©Eclipse

Aztek: The Ultimate Man

Short-lived Grant Morrison title

©DC

	N-MINT
❑53 (468), Jun 2002 KB (w)	2.25
❑54 (469), Jul 2002 KB (w)	2.25
❑55 (470), Aug 2002 KB (w)	2.25
❑56 (471), Sep 2002 KB (w)	2.25
❑57 (472), Oct 2002	2.25
❑58 (473), Nov 2002	2.25
❑59 (474), Dec 2002	2.25
❑60 (475), Jan 2003	2.25
❑61 (476), Feb 2003	2.25
❑62 (477), Feb 2003	2.25
❑63 (478), Mar 2003	2.25
❑64 (479), Apr 2003	2.25
❑65 (480), May 2003	2.25
❑66 (481), Jun 2003	2.25
❑67 (482), Jul 2003	2.25
❑68 (483), Aug 2003	2.25
❑69 (484), Sep 2003	2.25
❑70 (485), Oct 2003	2.25
❑71 (486), Nov 2003	2.25
❑72 (487), Nov 2003	2.25
❑73 (488), Dec 2003	2.25
❑74 (489), Jan 2004	2.25
❑75 (490), Feb 2004	2.25
❑76 (491), Feb 2004	2.25
❑77 (492), Mar 2004	2.25
❑78 (493), Apr 2004	2.25
❑79 (494), Apr 2004	2.25
❑80 (495), May 2004	2.25
❑81 (496), Jun 2004	2.99
❑82 (497), Jul 2004	2.99
❑83 (498), Jul 2004	2.25
❑84 (499), Aug 2004, concludes in Invaders #0	2.25
❑500, Sep 2004, BMB (w); numbering reverts back to Vol. 1, however, indicia does not	12.00
❑500/DirCut, Oct 2004, BMB (w); Director's Cut	18.00
❑501, Oct 2004, BMB (w)	5.00
❑502, Nov 2004, BMB (w)	7.00
❑503, Dec 2004, BMB (w); events continue in Avengers Finale	3.50
❑Annual 1998, ca. 1998, gatefold summary; GP (c); KB (w); BWi (a); wraparound cover	2.99
❑Annual 1999, Jul 1999, Jarvis' story	3.50
❑Annual 2000, ca. 2000, KB (w); RHo (a); wraparound cover	3.50
❑Annual 2001, ca. 2001, KB (w)	2.99

AVENGERS AND POWER PACK ASSEMBLE!
Marvel

	N-MINT
❑1, Jul 2006	2.99
❑2, Aug 2006	2.99
❑3, Sep 2006	2.99

AVENGERS CASEBOOK
Marvel

	N-MINT
❑1999, ca. 1999	2.99

AVENGERS, THE: CELESTIAL QUEST
Marvel

	N-MINT
❑1, Sep 2001	2.50
❑2, Oct 2001	2.50
❑3, Nov 2001	2.50
❑4, Dec 2001	2.50
❑5, Jan 2002	2.50
❑6, Feb 2002	2.50
❑7, Mar 2002	2.50
❑8, Apr 2002	3.50

AVENGERS: DEATH TRAP, THE VAULT
Marvel

	N-MINT
❑1, Sep 1991; also published as Venom: Deathtrap - The Vault	9.95

AVENGERS: EARTH'S MIGHTIEST HEROES
Marvel

	N-MINT
❑1, Nov 2004	3.50
❑2, Jan 2005	3.50
❑3, Feb 2005	3.50
❑4, Feb 2005	3.50
❑5, Mar 2005	3.50
❑6, Apr 2005	3.50
❑7, May 2005	3.50
❑8, Jun 2005	3.50

AVENGERS FINALE
Marvel

	N-MINT
❑1, Jan 2005	3.50

AVENGERS FOREVER
Marvel

	N-MINT
❑1, Dec 1998	2.99
❑1/WF, Dec 1998; Westfield alternate cover	4.95
❑2, Jan 1999	2.99
❑3, Feb 1999	2.99
❑4/A, Mar 1999; Avengers of Tomorrow cover	2.99
❑4/B, Mar 1999; Kang in the Old West cover	2.99
❑4/C, Mar 1999; Avengers throughout time cover	2.99
❑4/D, Mar 1999; Avengers of the '50s cover	2.99
❑5, Apr 1999	2.99
❑6, May 1999	2.99
❑7, Jun 1999	2.99
❑8, Jul 1999	2.99
❑9, Aug 1999	2.99
❑10, Oct 1999	2.99
❑11, Jan 2000	2.99
❑12, Feb 2000	2.99

AVENGERS (TV)
Gold Key

	N-MINT
❑1, Nov 1968, based on TV series	125.00
❑1/Variant, Nov 1968	200.00

AVENGERS ICONS: THE VISION
Marvel

	N-MINT
❑1	2.99
❑2	2.99
❑3	2.99
❑4	2.99

AVENGERS INFINITY
Marvel

	N-MINT
❑1/Dynamic, Sep 2000; Dynamic Forces variant (Thor brandishing hammer)	10.00
❑1, Sep 2000	2.99
❑2, Oct 2000	2.99
❑3, Nov 2000	2.99
❑4, Dec 2000	2.99

AVENGERS/JLA
DC

	N-MINT
❑2, Oct 2003	7.00
❑4, Jun 2004	5.95

AVENGERS LEGENDS
Marvel

	N-MINT
❑1	0.00
❑2, ca. 2003	19.95
❑3, ca. 2004	16.99

AVENGERS LOG
Marvel

	N-MINT
❑1, Feb 1994	1.95

AVENGERS SPOTLIGHT
Marvel

	N-MINT
❑21, Aug 1989; Starfox; Series continued from Solo Avengers #20.	1.00
❑22, Sep 1989; Swordsman	1.00
❑23, Oct 1989; Vision	1.00
❑24, Nov 1989 A: Trickshot	1.00
❑25, Nov 1989 A: Crossfire. A: Mockingbird. A: Trickshot	1.00
❑26, Dec 1989; "Acts of Vengeance"	1.00
❑27, Dec 1989; AM (a); "Acts of Vengeance"	1.00
❑28, Jan 1990; "Acts of Vengeance"	1.00
❑29, Feb 1990; "Acts of Vengeance"	1.00
❑30, Mar 1990; new Hawkeye costume	1.00
❑31, Apr 1990	1.00
❑32, May 1990	1.00
❑33, Jun 1990	1.00
❑34, Jul 1990	1.00
❑35, Aug 1990 A: Gilgamesh	1.00
❑36, Sep 1990	1.00
❑37, Oct 1990 BH (a)	1.00
❑38, Nov 1990	1.00
❑39, Dec 1990	1.00
❑40, Jan 1991	1.00

AVENGERS STRIKE FILE
Marvel

	N-MINT
❑1, Jan 1994	1.75

AVENGERS: THE CROSSING
Marvel

	N-MINT
❑1, Sep 1995, Chromium cover	4.95

AVENGERS: THE TERMINATRIX OBJECTIVE
Marvel

	N-MINT
❑1, Sep 1993; Holo-grafix cover; U.S. Agent, Thunderstrike, War Machine	2.50
❑2, Oct 1993; New Avengers vs. Old Avengers	1.25
❑3, Nov 1993	1.25
❑4, Dec 1993	1.25

AVENGERS: THE ULTRON IMPERATIVE
Marvel

	N-MINT
❑1, Oct 2001	5.99

AVENGERS/THUNDERBOLTS
Marvel

	N-MINT
❑1, May 2004	2.99
❑2, Jun 2004	2.99
❑3, Jun 2004	2.99
❑4, Aug 2004	2.99
❑5, Aug 2004	2.99
❑6, Oct 2004	2.99

N-MINT

AVENGERS: TIMESLIDE
MARVEL

❑1, Feb 1996; enhanced wraparound cardstock cover 4.95

AVENGERS TWO: WONDER MAN & BEAST
MARVEL

❑1, May 2000 ..... 2.99
❑2, Jun 2000 ..... 2.99
❑3, Jul 2000 ..... 2.99

AVENGERS/ULTRAFORCE
MARVEL

❑1, Oct 1995, continues in UltraForce/ Avengers #1; Foil logo 3.95

AVENGERS: ULTRON UNLEASHED
MARVEL

❑1, Aug 1999; collects Avengers (1st series) #57-58 and #170-171 ..... 3.50

AVENGERS: UNITED THEY STAND
MARVEL

❑1, Nov 1999 ..... 2.99
❑2, Dec 1999 ..... 1.99
❑3, Jan 2000 ..... 1.99
❑4, Feb 2000 ..... 1.99
❑5, Mar 2000 ..... 1.99
❑6, Apr 2000 ..... 1.99
❑7, May 2000 ..... 1.99

AVENGERS UNIVERSE
MARVEL

❑1, Aug 2000 ..... 2.99
❑2, Sep 2000 ..... 2.99
❑3, Oct 2000 ..... 2.99
❑4, Nov 2000; reprints Iron Fist: Wolverine #1; indicia is for Iron Fist: Wolverine #1 ..... 2.99
❑5, Dec 2000; reprints Iron Fist: Wolverine #2; indicia is for Iron Fist: Wolverine #2 ..... 2.99
❑6, Jan 2001; reprints Iron Fist: Wolverine #3; indicia is for Iron Fist: Wolverine #3 ..... 2.99

AVENGERS UNPLUGGED
MARVEL

❑1, Oct 1995 ..... 1.25
❑2, Dec 1995; A: Gravitron. Untold Tales of Spider-Man #4 ..... 1.00
❑3, Dec 1996; Luna; Black Widow 1.00
❑4, Feb 1996; Wedding of Thunderball and Titania; Peter David appears as reverend in story; Untold Tales of Spider-Man #8 ..... 1.00
❑5, Jun 1996 A: Captain Marvel 1.00
❑6, Aug 1996 ..... 1.00

AVENGERS WEST COAST
MARVEL

❑47, Aug 1989 ..... 1.00
❑48, Sep 1989 ..... 1.00
❑49, Oct 1989 ..... 1.00
❑50, Nov 1989; Golden Age Human Torch returns 1.00
❑51, Nov 1989 ..... 1.00
❑52, Dec 1989 ..... 1.00
❑53, Dec 1989; "Acts of Vengeance" 1.00
❑54, Jan 1990; Fantastic Four #1 cover homage; "Acts of Vengeance" 1.00
❑55, Feb 1990; "Acts of Vengeance" 1.00
❑56, Mar 1990 ..... 1.00
❑57, Apr 1990 ..... 1.00
❑58, May 1990 ..... 1.00
❑59, Jun 1990 ..... 1.00
❑60, Jul 1990 ..... 1.00
❑61, Aug 1990 ..... 1.00
❑62, Sep 1990 ..... 1.00
❑63, Oct 1990 ..... 1.00
❑64, Nov 1990 ..... 1.00
❑65, Dec 1990 ..... 1.00
❑66, Jan 1991 ..... 1.00
❑67, Feb 1991 ..... 1.00
❑68, Mar 1991 ..... 1.00
❑69, Apr 1991 ..... 1.00
❑70, May 1991 ..... 1.00
❑71, Jun 1991 ..... 1.00
❑72, Jul 1991 ..... 1.00
❑73, Aug 1991 ..... 1.00
❑74, Sep 1991 ..... 1.00
❑75, Oct 1991; Double-size issue 1.50
❑76, Nov 1991 ..... 1.00

N-MINT

❑77, Dec 1991 ..... 1.00
❑78, Jan 1992 ..... 1.00
❑79, Feb 1992 ..... 1.25
❑80, Mar 1992; Galactic Storm 1.25
❑81, Apr 1992; Galactic Storm 1.25
❑82, May 1992; Galactic Storm 1.25
❑83, Jun 1992 ..... 1.25
❑84, Jul 1992 ..... 1.25
❑85, Aug 1992 ..... 1.25
❑86, Sep 1992 ..... 1.25
❑87, Oct 1992 ..... 1.25
❑88, Nov 1992 ..... 1.25
❑89, Dec 1992 ..... 1.25
❑90, Jan 1993 ..... 1.25
❑91, Feb 1993 ..... 1.25
❑92, Mar 1993 ..... 1.25
❑93, Apr 1993 ..... 1.25
❑94, May 1993 ..... 1.25
❑95, Jun 1993 ..... 1.25
❑96, Jul 1993 ..... 1.25
❑97, Aug 1993 ..... 1.25
❑98, Sep 1993 ..... 1.25
❑99, Oct 1993 ..... 1.25
❑100, Nov 1993; sculpted foil cover 1.25
❑101, Dec 1993 ..... 1.25
❑102, Jan 1994 ..... 1.25
❑Annual 4, ca. 1989; see West Coast Avengers for previous Annuals; "Atlantis Attacks" 2.00
❑Annual 5, ca. 1990; "Terminus Factor" 2.00
❑Annual 6 ..... 2.00
❑Annual 7, ca. 1992 ..... 2.25
❑Annual 8; Polybagged with trading card 2.95

AVENGERS/X-MEN: BLOODTIES
MARVEL

❑1, Jan 1995; Trade Paperback; collects Avengers #368 and 369, Avengers West Coast #101, Uncanny X-Men #307, and X-Men #26 ..... 15.95

AVENUE D
FANTAGRAPHICS

❑1, b&w 3.50

AVENUE X
PURPLE SPIRAL

❑1, ca. 1992 ..... 2.50
❑2, ca. 1992 ..... 2.50
❑3, ca. 1992 ..... 3.00

AVIGON
IMAGE

❑1, Oct 2000 ..... 5.95

A-V IN 3-D
AARDVARK-VANAHEIM

❑1, Dec 1984, glasses 3.00

AWAKENING
IMAGE

❑1, Oct 1997 ..... 2.95
❑2, Dec 1997 ..... 2.95
❑3, Feb 1998 ..... 2.95
❑4, Apr 1998 ..... 2.95

AWAKENING COMICS
AWAKENING COMICS

❑1 1997 ..... 3.50
❑2, Nov 1997 A: Cerebus the Aardvark. A: Cerebus 3.50
❑3, Aug 1998; wraparound cover; "The Everwinds Awakening War" 2.95
❑4, Nov 1998 1: Melvin G. Moose, Private Eye 2.95

AWAKENING COMICS 1999
AWAKENING COMICS

❑1 1999, b&w 3.50

AWESOME ADVENTURES
AWESOME

❑1/A, Aug 1999, Woman standing (full length) on cover 2.50
❑1/B, Aug 1999, Woman standing (3/4 length) on cover 2.50

AWESOME HOLIDAY SPECIAL
AWESOME

❑1, Dec 1997; Flip cover; Youngblood side has gold foil logo 2.50

N-MINT

AWESOME MAN
ASTONISH

❑1, ca. 2002 ..... 2.95
❑2, Aug 2003 ..... 3.50

AWESOME PREVIEW
AWESOME

❑1 1997; ARo (c); ARo (a); b&w and color previews of upcoming Awesome series given out at Comic-Con International: San Diego '97 ..... 1.00

AWKWARD
SLAVE LABOR

❑1 ..... 4.95

AWKWARD UNIVERSE
SLAVE LABOR

❑1, Dec 1995 ..... 9.95

AXA (ECLIPSE)
ECLIPSE

❑1, ca. 1987 ..... 2.00
❑2 1987, b&w 2.00

AXA (KEN PIERCE)
KEN PIERCE

❑1, ca. 1981 ..... 5.95
❑2, ca. 1982 ..... 5.95
❑3, ca. 1983 ..... 5.95
❑4, ca. 1983 ..... 5.95
❑5, ca. 1984 ..... 5.95
❑6, ca. 1984 ..... 5.95
❑7, ca. 1985 ..... 5.95
❑8, ca. 1986 ..... 5.95
❑GN 1 ..... 5.95

AXED FILES
EXPRESS / PARODY

❑1 1995, b&w 2.50

AXEL PRESSBUTTON
ECLIPSE

❑1, Nov 1984 ..... 2.00
❑2, Jan 1985 ..... 2.00
❑3, Mar 1985 ..... 2.00
❑4, May 1985 ..... 2.00
❑5, Jul 1985; Continues as Pressbutton 2.00
❑6, Jul 1985 ..... 2.00

AXIOM
ICON CREATIONS

❑1, Aug 94 ..... 1.25

AXIS ALPHA
AXIS

❑1, Feb 1994; Previews of five upcoming titles; only B.E.A.S.T.I.E.S. and Tribe ever published 2.50

AXIS MUNDI
AMAZE INK

❑2, Dec 1996, b&w; no indicia; wraparound cover 2.95

AZ
COMICO

❑1, ca. 1983, b&w 1.50
❑2, ca. 1983, b&w 1.50

AZRACH
DARK HORSE / BIG BANG

❑nn, ca. 1996 ..... 6.95

AZRAEL
DC

❑1, Feb 1995 ..... 3.00
❑2, Mar 1995 ..... 2.00
❑3, Apr 1995 ..... 2.00
❑4, May 1995 ..... 2.00
❑5, Jun 1995 ..... 2.00
❑6, Jul 1995 ..... 2.00
❑7, Aug 1995 ..... 2.00
❑8, Sep 1995 ..... 2.00
❑9, Oct 1995 ..... 2.00
❑10, Nov 1995; "Underworld Unleashed" 2.00
❑11, Dec 1995 ..... 1.95
❑12, Jan 1996 ..... 1.95
❑13, Feb 1996 ..... 1.95
❑14, Mar 1996 ..... 1.95
❑15, Mar 1996; Marked as Contagion, Part 4 on cover 1.95
❑16, Apr 1996 ..... 1.95
❑17, May 1996 ..... 1.95
❑18, Jun 1996 ..... 1.95
❑19, Jul 1996 ..... 1.95
❑20, Aug 1996 ..... 1.95

Other grades: Multiply price above by 5/6 for VF/NM • 2/3 for VERY FINE • 1/3 for FINE • 1/5 for VERY GOOD • 1/8 for GOOD

Baby Huey The Baby Giant

Cartoon antics with brain-damaged duck

©Harvey

Babylon 5

Series creator had a hand in comics spinoff

©DC

Babylon 5: In Valen's Name

Babylon 4 station reappears in limited series

©DC

Baby's First Deadpool Book

Silly spoof on children's books

©Marvel

Bacchus (Eddie Campbell's...)

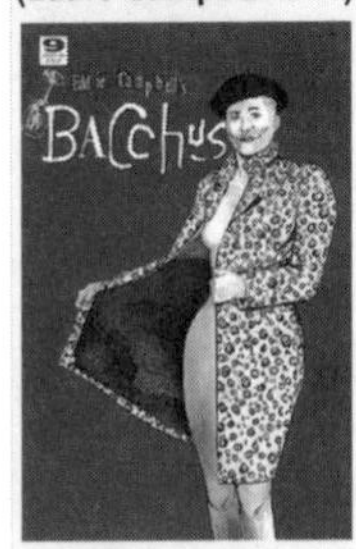

Greek god of wine and poetry hits comics

©Eddie Campbell

	N-MINT
❑21, Sep 1996	1.95
❑22, Oct 1996	1.95
❑23, Oct 1996	1.95
❑24, Dec 1996	1.95
❑25, Jan 1997	1.95
❑26, Feb 1997	1.95
❑27, Mar 1997	1.95
❑28, Apr 1997	1.95
❑29, May 1997	1.95
❑30, Jun 1997	1.95
❑31, Jul 1997	1.95
❑32, Aug 1997	1.95
❑33, Sep 1997	1.95
❑34, Oct 1997; "Genesis"	1.95
❑35, Nov 1997	1.95
❑36, Dec 1997; Face cover	1.95
❑37, Jan 1998	1.95
❑38, Feb 1998	1.95
❑39, Mar 1998	1.95
❑40, Apr 1998; continues in Detective Comics #720	1.95
❑41, May 1998	1.95
❑42, Jun 1998	1.95
❑43, Jul 1998	1.95
❑44, Aug 1998	1.95
❑45, Sep 1998	2.25
❑46, Oct 1998	1.99
❑47, Dec 1998; Signed extra-sized flip-book; Title changes to "Azrael: Agent of the Bat"; "Road to No Man's Land"; flipbook with Batman: Shadow of the Bat #80 (true title)	3.95
❑47/Ltd., Dec 1998	6.00
❑48, Jan 1999; "Road to No Man's Land"; Batman cameo	2.25
❑49, Feb 1999; "Road to No Man's Land"	2.25
❑50, Mar 1999; "No Man's Land"	2.25
❑51, Apr 1999; "No Man's Land"; new costume	2.25
❑52, May 1999; "No Man's Land"	2.25
❑53, Jun 1999; "No Man's Land"	2.25
❑54, Jul 1999; "No Man's Land"	2.25
❑55, Aug 1999; "No Man's Land"	2.25
❑56, Sep 1999; "No Man's Land"	2.25
❑57, Oct 1999; "No Man's Land"	2.25
❑58, Nov 1999; "No Man's Land"; Day of Judgment	2.25
❑59, Dec 1999; No Man's Land	2.25
❑60, Jan 2000; No Man's Land	2.25
❑61, Feb 2000	2.25
❑62, Mar 2000	2.25
❑63, Apr 2000	2.25
❑64, May 2000	2.25
❑65, Jun 2000	2.25
❑66, Jul 2000	2.25
❑67, Aug 2000	2.25
❑68, Sep 2000	2.25
❑69, Oct 2000	2.50
❑70, Nov 2000	2.50
❑71, Dec 2000	2.50
❑72, Jan 2001	2.50
❑73, Feb 2001	2.50
❑74, Mar 2001	2.50
❑75, Apr 2001; Giant-size	3.95
❑76, May 2001	2.50
❑77, Jun 2001	2.50
❑78, Jul 2001	2.50
❑79, Aug 2001	2.50
❑80, Sep 2001	2.50
❑81, Oct 2001	2.50
❑82, Nov 2001	2.50
❑83, Dec 2001; Joker: Last Laugh crossover	2.50
❑84, Jan 2002	2.50
❑85, Feb 2002	2.50
❑86, Mar 2002	2.50
❑87, Apr 2002	2.50
❑88, May 2002	2.50
❑89, Jun 2002	2.50
❑91, Aug 2002	2.50
❑90, Jul 2002	2.50
❑92, Sep 2002	2.50
❑93, Oct 2002	2.95
❑94, Nov 2002	2.95
❑95, Dec 2002	2.95
❑96, Jan 2003	2.95
❑97, Feb 2003	2.95
❑98, Mar 2003	2.95
❑99, Apr 2003	2.95
❑100, May 2003	2.95
❑1000000, Nov 1998; becomes Azrael: Agent of the Bat	3.00
❑Annual 1, ca. 1995; Year One; 1995 Annual	3.95
❑Annual 2, ca. 1996; Legends of the Dead Earth	2.95
❑Annual 3, ca. 1997; Pulp Heroes	3.95

AZRAEL/ASH
DC

	N-MINT
❑1, ca. 1997	4.95

AZRAEL PLUS
DC

	N-MINT
❑1, Dec 1996	2.95

AZTEC ACE
ECLIPSE

	N-MINT
❑1, Mar 1984; Giant-size 1: Aztec Ace	2.50
❑2 1984	2.00
❑3 1984	2.00
❑4 1984	2.00
❑5 1984	2.00
❑6 1984	2.00
❑7 1984	2.00
❑8 1984	2.00
❑9, Jan 1985	2.00
❑10 1985	2.00
❑11 1985	2.00
❑12 1985	2.00
❑13 1985	2.00
❑14 1985	2.00
❑15, Sep 1985	2.00

AZTEC ANTHROPOMORPHIC AMAZONS
ANTARCTIC

	N-MINT
❑1, Mar 1994, b&w	2.75

AZTEC OF THE CITY
EL SALTO

	N-MINT
❑1, May 1993	2.25

AZTEC OF THE CITY (VOL. 2)
EL SALTO

	N-MINT
❑1 1996	2.50
❑2, May 1996	2.50

AZTEK: THE ULTIMATE MAN
DC

	N-MINT
❑1, Aug 1996	1.75
❑2, Sep 1996	1.75
❑3, Oct 1996	1.75
❑4, Nov 1996	1.75
❑5, Dec 1996	1.75
❑6, Jan 1997	1.75
❑7, Feb 1997	1.75
❑8, Mar 1997	1.75
❑9, Apr 1997	1.75
❑10, May 1997	1.75

AZUMANGA DAIOH
ADV MANGA

	N-MINT
❑1, ca. 2003	9.99
❑2, ca. 2003	9.99
❑3, ca. 2004	9.99
❑4, ca. 2004	9.99

BABE
DARK HORSE / LEGEND

	N-MINT
❑1, Jul 1994	2.50
❑2, Aug 1994	2.50
❑3, Sep 1994	2.50
❑4, Oct 1994	2.50

BABE 2
DARK HORSE / LEGEND

	N-MINT
❑1, Mar 1995	2.50
❑2, Apr 1995	2.50

BABES OF BROADWAY
BROADWAY

	N-MINT
❑1, May 1996, pin-ups and previews of upcoming Broadway series	2.95

BABEWATCH
EXPRESS / PARODY

	N-MINT
❑1 1995, b&w	2.50
❑1/A 1995	2.95

BABY ANGEL X
BRAINSTORM

	N-MINT
❑1, b&w	2.95

BABY HUEY DIGEST
HARVEY

	N-MINT
❑1	1.75

BABY HUEY IN 3-D
BLACKTHORNE

	N-MINT
❑1	2.50

BABY HUEY THE BABY GIANT
HARVEY

	N-MINT
❑1, Sep 1956	175.00
❑2, Nov 1956	90.00
❑3, Jan 1957	50.00
❑4, Mar 1957	36.00
❑5, May 1957	36.00
❑6, Jul 1957	20.00
❑7, Sep 1957	20.00
❑8, Nov 1957	20.00
❑9, Jan 1958	20.00
❑10, Mar 1958	20.00
❑11, ca. 1958	15.00

Other grades: Multiply price above by 5/6 for VF/NM • 2/3 for VERY FINE • 1/3 for FINE • 1/5 for VERY GOOD • 1/8 for GOOD

N-MINT

❑12, ca. 1958 15.00
❑13, ca. 1958 15.00
❑14, ca. 1958 15.00
❑15, ca. 1958 15.00
❑16, Feb 1959 15.00
❑17, Apr 1959 15.00
❑18, Jun 1959 15.00
❑19, Aug 1959 15.00
❑20, Oct 1959 15.00
❑21, Dec 1959 12.00
❑22, Feb 1960 12.00
❑23, Apr 1960 12.00
❑24, Jun 1960 12.00
❑25, Aug 1960 12.00
❑26, Sep 1960 12.00
❑27, Oct 1960 12.00
❑28, Nov 1960 12.00
❑29, Dec 1960 12.00
❑30, Jan 1961 12.00
❑31, Feb 1961 9.00
❑32, Mar 1961 9.00
❑33, Apr 1961 9.00
❑34, May 1961 9.00
❑35, Jun 1961 9.00
❑36, Jul 1961 9.00
❑37, Aug 1961 9.00
❑38, Sep 1961 9.00
❑39, Oct 1961 9.00
❑40, Nov 1961 9.00
❑41, Dec 1961 6.00
❑42, Jan 1962 6.00
❑43, Feb 1962 6.00
❑44, Mar 1962 6.00
❑45, Apr 1962 6.00
❑46, Jun 1962 6.00
❑47, Aug 1962 6.00
❑48, Oct 1962 6.00
❑49, Dec 1962 6.00
❑50, Feb 1963 6.00
❑51, Apr 1963 4.00
❑52, Jun 1963 4.00
❑53, Aug 1963 4.00
❑54, Oct 1963 4.00
❑55, Dec 1963 4.00
❑56, Feb 1964 4.00
❑57, Apr 1964 4.00
❑58, Jun 1964 4.00
❑59, Aug 1964 4.00
❑60, Oct 1964 4.00
❑61, Dec 1964 4.00
❑62, Feb 1965 4.00
❑63, Apr 1965 4.00
❑64, Jun 1965 4.00
❑65, Aug 1965 4.00
❑66, Oct 1965 4.00
❑67, Dec 1965 4.00
❑68, Feb 1966 4.00
❑69, Apr 1966 4.00
❑70, Jun 1966 4.00
❑71, Aug 1966 2.50
❑72, Oct 1966 2.50
❑73, Dec 1966 2.50
❑74, Feb 1967 2.50
❑75, Apr 1967 2.50
❑76, Jun 1967 2.50
❑77, Aug 1967 2.50
❑78, Oct 1967 2.50
❑79, Dec 1967 2.50
❑80, Dec 1968, Giant-size 2.50
❑81, Feb 1969, Giant-size 2.50
❑82, Apr 1969, Giant-size 2.50
❑83, Jun 1969, Giant-size 2.50
❑84, Aug 1969, Giant-size 2.50
❑85, Oct 1969, Giant-size 2.50
❑86, Dec 1969, Giant-size 2.50
❑87, Feb 1970, Giant-size 2.50
❑88, Apr 1970, Giant-size 2.50
❑89, Jun 1970, Giant-size 2.50
❑90, Aug 1970, Giant-size 2.50
❑91, Oct 1970, Giant-size 2.50
❑92, Dec 1970, Giant-size 2.50
❑93, Feb 1971, Giant-size 2.50
❑94, Apr 1971, Giant-size 2.50
❑95, Jun 1971, Giant-size 2.50
❑96, Aug 1971, Giant-size 2.50
❑97, Oct 1971, Giant-size 2.50
❑98, Oct 1972 2.50
❑99 2.50
❑100, Oct 1990, Series begins again after hiatus 1.00
❑101 1.00
❑102 1.00

BABY HUEY (VOL. 2)
HARVEY

❑1 1991 1.25
❑2, Jan 1992 1.25
❑3, Apr 1992 1.25
❑4, Aug 1992 1.25
❑5, Nov 1992 1.25
❑6, Mar 1993 1.25
❑7, Jun 1993 1.25
❑8 1.25
❑9 1.25

BABYLON 5
DC

❑1, Jan 1995 5.00
❑2, Feb 1995 4.00
❑3, Mar 1995 3.50
❑4, Apr 1995 3.50
❑5, Jun 1995 3.00
❑6, Jul 1995 3.00
❑7, Aug 1995 3.00
❑8, Sep 1995 2.50
❑9, Oct 1995 2.50
❑10, Nov 1995 2.50
❑11, Dec 1995 2.50
❑Book 1/Ltd 24.95

BABYLON 5: IN VALEN'S NAME
DC

❑1, Mar 1998 3.50
❑2, Apr 1998 3.00
❑3, May 1998 3.00

BABYLON CRUSH
BONEYARD

❑1, May 1995; cardstock cover, b&w. 2.95
❑2, Jul 1995; cardstock cover, b&w... 2.95
❑3, Oct 1995, b&w 2.95
❑4 2.95
❑Xmas 1, Jan 1998 2.95

BABY'S FIRST DEADPOOL BOOK
MARVEL

❑1, Dec 1998; children's-book style stories 2.99

BABY SNOOTS
GOLD KEY

❑1, Aug 1970 12.00
❑2, Nov 1970 10.00
❑3, Feb 1971 8.00
❑4, May 1971 6.00
❑5, Aug 1971 6.00
❑6, Nov 1971 6.00
❑7, Feb 1972 6.00
❑8, May 1972 6.00
❑9, Aug 1972 6.00
❑10, Nov 1972 6.00
❑11, Feb 1973 6.00
❑12, May 1973 6.00
❑13, Aug 1973 5.00
❑14, Nov 1973 5.00
❑15, Feb 1974 5.00
❑16, May 1974 5.00
❑17, Aug 1974 5.00
❑18, Nov 1974 5.00
❑19, Feb 1975 5.00
❑20, May 1975 5.00
❑21, Aug 1975 5.00
❑22, Nov 1975 5.00

BABY, YOU'RE REALLY SOMETHING!
FANTAGRAPHICS / EROS

❑1, b&w; Reprints 2.50

BACCHUS (HARRIER)
HARRIER

❑1, ca. 1988 5.00
❑2, ca. 1988 4.00

BACCHUS COLOR SPECIAL
DARK HORSE

❑1, Apr 1995 3.25

BACCHUS (EDDIE CAMPBELL'S...)
EDDIE CAMPBELL

❑1, May 1995 6.00
❑1/2nd, May 1999 3.00
❑2, Jun 1995 4.00
❑3, Jul 1995 4.00
❑4, Aug 1995 3.50
❑5, Sep 1995 3.50
❑6, Oct 1995 3.00
❑7, Nov 1995 3.00
❑8, Dec 1995 3.00
❑9, Jan 1996 3.00
❑10, Feb 1996 3.00
❑11, Mar 1996 3.00
❑12, Apr 1996 3.00
❑13, May 1996 3.00
❑14, Jun 1996 3.00
❑15, Jul 1996 3.00
❑16, Aug 1996 3.00
❑17, Sep 1996 3.00
❑18, Oct 1996, b&w 3.00
❑19, Nov 1996 3.00
❑20, Dec 1996 3.00
❑21, Jan 1997 2.95
❑22, Feb 1997 2.95
❑23, Mar 1997 2.95
❑24, ca. 1997 2.95
❑25, ca. 1997 2.95
❑26, ca. 1997 2.95
❑27, Aug 1997 2.95
❑28, Sep 1997 2.95
❑29, Oct 1997 2.95
❑30, Nov 1997 2.95
❑31, Dec 1997 2.95
❑32, ca. 1998 2.95
❑33, ca. 1998 2.95
❑34, Apr 1998 2.95
❑35, ca. 1998 2.95
❑36, ca. 1998 2.95
❑37, ca. 1998 2.95
❑38, Sep 1998 2.95
❑39, Oct 1998 2.95
❑40, Dec 1998 2.95
❑41, Jan 1999 2.95
❑42, Feb 1999 2.95

BACHELOR FATHER
DELL

❑2, Nov 1962 50.00

BACK DOWN THE LINE
ECLIPSE

❑1 8.95

BACKLASH
IMAGE

❑1, Nov 1994; Double cover 2.50
❑2, Dec 1994 2.50
❑3, Jan 1995 2.50
❑4, Feb 1995 2.50
❑5, Feb 1995 2.50
❑6, Mar 1995 2.50
❑7, Apr 1995 2.50
❑8, May 1995; bound-in trading cards 2.50
❑9, Jun 1995 2.50
❑10, Jul 1995; indicia says Jul, cover says Aug 2.50
❑11, Aug 1995 2.50
❑12, Sep 1995; indicia says Sep, cover says Oct 2.50
❑13, Nov 1995 2.50
❑14, Nov 1995; indicia says Nov, cover says Dec 2.50
❑15, Dec 1995; indicia says Dec, cover says Jan 2.50
❑16, Jan 1996; indicia says Jan, cover says Feb 2.50
❑17, Feb 1996 2.50
❑18, Mar 1996 2.50
❑19, Apr 1996 2.50
❑20, May 1996 2.50
❑21, Jun 1996 2.50
❑22, Jul 1996 2.50
❑23, Aug 1996 2.50
❑24, Sep 1996 2.50
❑25, Nov 1996; Giant-size 2.50
❑26, Nov 1996 2.50
❑27, Dec 1996 2.50
❑28, Jan 1997 2.50
❑29, Feb 1997 2.50

Other grades: Multiply price above by 5/6 for VF/NM • 2/3 for VERY FINE • 1/3 for FINE • 1/5 for VERY GOOD • 1/8 for GOOD

Backlash

Solo series spinoff from Stormwatch
©Image

Badger

Series gives Madison, Wis., its own hero
©Capital

Badrock/Wolverine

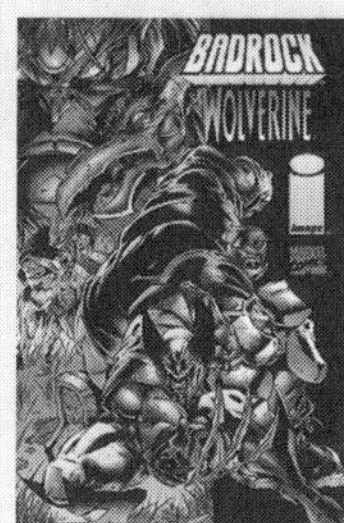

Crossover between Image and Marvel
©Image

Balder the Brave

Thor's friend is Balder, yet has plenty of hair
©Marvel

Ballad Of Utopia

Dark, forbidding Western comics series
©Black Daze

	N-MINT
❑30, Mar 1997	2.50
❑31, Apr 1997	2.50
❑32, May 1997	2.50

BACKLASH & TABOO'S AFRICAN HOLIDAY
DC / WILDSTORM

	N-MINT
❑1, Sep 1999	5.95

BACKLASH/SPIDER-MAN
IMAGE

	N-MINT
❑1, Aug 1996	2.50
❑1/A, Aug 1996; crossover with Marvel, cover says Jul, indicia says Aug	2.50
❑1/B, Aug 1996; alternate cover, crossover with Marvel, cover says Jul, indicia says Aug	2.50
❑2, Oct 1996; crossover with Marvel..	2.50

BACKPACK MARVELS: AVENGERS
MARVEL

	N-MINT
❑1, Jan 2001	6.95

BACKPACK MARVELS: X-MEN
MARVEL

	N-MINT
❑1, Nov 2000	6.95
❑2, Nov 2000; Reprints Uncanny X-Men #167-173	6.95

BACK TO THE FUTURE
HARVEY

	N-MINT
❑1, Nov 1991, GK (c); GK (a)	1.50
❑2, Nov 1991	1.50
❑3, Jan 1992	1.50
❑4, Jun 1992	1.50
❑Special 1, Universal Studios-Florida giveaway	1.00

BACK TO THE FUTURE: FORWARD TO THE FUTURE
HARVEY

	N-MINT
❑1, Oct 1992	1.50
❑2, Nov 1992	1.50
❑3, Jan 1993	1.50

BAD APPLES
HIGH IMPACT

	N-MINT
❑1, Jan 1997	2.95
❑2, ca. 1997	2.95

BAD ART COLLECTION
SLAVE LABOR

	N-MINT
❑1, Apr 1996; Oversized	1.95

BADAXE
ADVENTURE

	N-MINT
❑1	1.00
❑2	1.00
❑3	1.00

BAD BOY
ONI

	N-MINT
❑1, Dec 1997; oversized one-shot	4.95

BAD COMICS
CAT-HEAD

	N-MINT
❑1, b&w	2.75

BAD COMPANY
FLEETWAY-QUALITY

	N-MINT
❑1	1.50
❑2	1.50
❑3	1.50
❑4	1.50
❑5	1.50
❑6	1.50
❑7	1.50
❑8	1.50
❑9	1.50
❑10	1.50
❑11	1.50
❑12	1.50
❑13	1.50
❑14	1.50
❑15	1.50
❑16	1.75
❑17	1.75
❑18	1.75
❑19	1.75

BADE BIKER & ORSON
MIRAGE

	N-MINT
❑1, Nov 1986	1.50
❑2, Jan 1987	1.50
❑3, Mar 1987	1.50
❑4, Jun 1987	1.50

BAD EGGS
ACCLAIM / ARMADA

	N-MINT
❑1, Jun 1996	2.95
❑2, Jul 1996	2.95
❑3, Aug 1996	2.95
❑4, Sep 1996	2.95
❑5, Sep 1996; cover says Oct, indicia says Sep	2.95
❑6, Nov 1996; shoplifting instructions on cover	2.95
❑7, Dec 1996	2.95
❑8, Jan 1997	2.95

BADGE
VANGUARD

	N-MINT
❑1 1981	2.95

BADGER
CAPITAL

	N-MINT
❑1, Oct 1983 SR (a); 1: Badger. 1: Ham	4.00
❑2, Feb 1984	2.50
❑3, Mar 1984	2.50
❑4, Apr 1984	2.50
❑5, May 1985; First Comics begins publishing	2.50
❑6, Jul 1985	2.00
❑7, Sep 1985	2.00
❑8, Nov 1985	2.00
❑9, Jan 1986	2.00
❑10, Mar 1986	2.00
❑11, May 1986	2.00
❑12, Jun 1986	2.00
❑13, Jul 1986	2.00
❑14, Aug 1986	2.00
❑15, Sep 1986	2.00
❑16, Oct 1986	2.00
❑17, Nov 1986	2.00
❑18, Dec 1986	2.00
❑19, Jan 1987	2.00
❑20, Feb 1987	2.00
❑21, Mar 1987	2.00
❑22, Apr 1987	2.00
❑23, May 1987	2.00
❑24, Jun 1987	2.00
❑25, Jul 1987	2.00
❑26, Aug 1987; Roach Wrangler	2.00
❑27, Sep 1987; Roach Wrangler	2.00
❑28, Oct 1987	2.00
❑29, Nov 1987	2.00
❑30, Dec 1987	2.00
❑31, Jan 1988	2.00
❑32, Feb 1988	2.00
❑33, Mar 1988	2.00
❑34, Apr 1988	2.00
❑35, May 1988	2.00
❑36, Jun 1988	2.00
❑37, Jul 1988	2.00
❑38, Aug 1988	2.00
❑39, Sep 1988	2.00
❑40, Oct 1988	2.00
❑41, Nov 1988	2.00
❑42, Dec 1988	2.00
❑43, Jan 1989	2.00
❑44, Feb 1989 1: Steve Marmel (The Hilariator-in comics)	2.00
❑45, Mar 1989	2.00
❑46, Apr 1989	2.00
❑47, May 1989	2.00
❑48, Jun 1989	2.00
❑49, Jul 1989	2.00
❑50, Aug 1989; Double-size	3.95
❑51, Sep 1989	2.00
❑52, Oct 1989	3.00
❑53, Nov 1989	3.00
❑54, Dec 1989	3.00
❑55, Jan 1990	2.00
❑56, Feb 1990	2.00
❑57, Mar 1990	2.00
❑58, Apr 1990	2.00
❑59, May 1990	2.00
❑60, Jun 1990	2.00
❑61, Jul 1990	2.00
❑62, Aug 1990	2.00
❑63, Sep 1990	2.00
❑64, Oct 1990	2.25
❑65, Nov 1990	2.25
❑66, Dec 1990	2.25
❑67, Jan 1991	2.25
❑68, Feb 1991	2.25
❑69, Mar 1991	2.25
❑70, Apr 1991	2.25

BADGER (VOL. 2)
FIRST

	N-MINT
❑1, May 1991; Badger Bedlam	4.95

BADGER (VOL. 3)
IMAGE

	N-MINT
❑1, May 1997, b&w; indicia says #78 in series	2.95
❑2, Jun 1997, b&w; indicia says #79 in series	2.95
❑3, Jul 1997, b&w; indicia says #80 in series	2.95
❑4, Aug 1997, b&w; indicia says #81 in series	2.95
❑5, Sep 1997, b&w; indicia says #82 in series	2.95
❑6, Oct 1997, b&w; indicia says #83 in series	2.95

❑7, Nov 1997, b&w; indicia says #84 in series 2.95
❑8, Dec 1997, b&w; indicia says #85 in series 2.95
❑9, Jan 1998, b&w; indicia says #86 in series 2.95
❑10, Feb 1998, b&w; indicia says #87 in series 2.95
❑11, Apr 1998, b&w; indicia says #88 in series 2.95

BADGER GOES BERSERK
FIRST

❑1, Sep 1989 .... 2.00
❑2, Oct 1989 .... 2.00
❑3, Nov 1989 .... 2.00
❑4, Dec 1989 .... 2.00

BADGER: SHATTERED MIRROR
DARK HORSE

❑1, Jul 1994 .... 2.50
❑2, Aug 1994 .... 2.50
❑3, Sep 1994 .... 2.50
❑4, Oct 1994 .... 2.50

BADGER: ZEN POP FUNNY-ANIMAL VERSION
DARK HORSE

❑1, Jul 1994 .... 2.50
❑2, Aug 1994 .... 2.50

BAD GIRLS
DC

❑1, Aug 2003 .... 2.50
❑2, Sep 2003 .... 2.50
❑3, Oct 2003 .... 2.50
❑4, Nov 2003 .... 2.50
❑5, Dec 2003 .... 2.50

BAD GIRLS (BILL WARD'S...)
FORBIDDEN FRUIT

❑1 .... 1.50

BAD GIRLS OF BLACKOUT
BLACKOUT

❑0 1995 .... 3.50
❑1 1995 .... 3.50
❑Annual 1, ca. 1995 .... 3.50

BAD HAIR DAY
SLAB-O-CONCRETE

❑1; Postcard Comic 1.00

BAD IDEAS
IMAGE

❑1, Apr 2004 .... 5.95
❑2, Sep 2004 .... 6.00

BAD KITTY
CHAOS

❑1, Feb 2001 .... 2.99
❑1/A, Mar 2001; Alternate cover (nude w/cat) 2.99
❑Ashcan 1; 1,000 copies printed ....
❑2, Mar 2001 .... 2.99
❑3, Apr 2001 .... 2.99

BAD KITTY: MISCHIEF NIGHT
CHAOS

❑1, Nov 2001; Events take place after Lady Death/Bad Kitty #1 .... 3.00
❑1/A, Nov 2001; Events take place after Lady Death/Bad Kitty #1 .... 2.99
❑1/B, Nov 2001; Events take place after Lady Death/Bad Kitty #1; Posing next to car on white background 2.99
❑1/C, Nov 2001; Events take place after Lady Death/Bad Kitty #1; Posing next to car on white background 2.99
❑1/D, Nov 2001; Otherwise same as #1 .... 2.99

BADLANDS
DARK HORSE

❑1, Jul 1991 .... 2.50
❑2 .... 2.50
❑3 .... 2.50
❑4 .... 2.50
❑5 .... 2.50
❑6 .... 2.50

BAD LUCK AND RICK DEES SENTINEL OF JUSTICE
KING COMICS

❑1, Feb 1994 .... 2.95

BAD MEAT
FANTAGRAPHICS / EROS

❑1, Jul 1991, b&w 2.25
❑2 .... 2.25

BAD NEWS
FANTAGRAPHICS

❑3, b&w 3.50

BAD PLANET
IMAGE

❑1, Dec 2005 .... 2.99

BADROCK
IMAGE

❑1/A, Mar 1995 .... 1.75
❑1/B, Mar 1995 .... 1.75
❑1/C, Mar 1995 .... 1.75
❑2 .... 1.75
❑3 .... 1.75
❑Annual 1, Jul 1995 .... 2.95

BADROCK & COMPANY
IMAGE

❑1, Sep 1994 .... 2.50
❑2, Oct 1994 .... 2.50
❑3, Nov 1994 .... 2.50
❑4, Dec 1994 .... 2.50
❑5, Jan 1995 .... 2.50
❑6, Oct 1995; cover says Feb 95, indicia says Oct 94 .... 2.50
❑Special 1, Sep 1994; San Diego Comic-Con edition 2.50

BADROCK/WOLVERINE
IMAGE

❑1/A, Jun 1996 .... 4.95
❑1/B, Jun 1996 .... 4.95
❑1/C, Jun 1996 .... 4.95
❑1/D, Jun 1996 .... 4.95

BAKERS
KYLE BAKER PUBLISHING

❑1, Oct 2005 .... 4.95

BAKER STREET
CALIBER

❑1, Mar 1989 .... 2.50
❑2 .... 2.50
❑3 .... 2.50
❑4 .... 2.50
❑5 .... 2.50
❑6 .... 2.50
❑7 .... 2.50
❑8 .... 2.50
❑9 .... 2.50
❑10 .... 2.50

BAKER STREET GRAFFITI
CALIBER

❑1, b&w 2.50

BAKER STREET SKETCHBOOK
CALIBER

❑1 .... 3.95

BALANCE OF POWER
MU

❑1, b&w 2.50
❑2 .... 2.50
❑3, Mar 1991 .... 2.50
❑4, Jul 1991 .... 2.50

BALDER THE BRAVE
MARVEL

❑1, Nov 1985 SB (a) 1.00
❑2, Jan 1986 .... 1.00
❑3, Mar 1986 .... 1.00
❑4, May 1986 .... 1.00

BALLAD OF HALO JONES
FLEETWAY-QUALITY

❑1, Sep 1987; AMo (w); 1: Halo Jones. Reprints The Ballad of Halo Jones from 2000 A.D 1.50
❑2, Oct 1987 AMo (w) 1.50
❑3 AMo (w) 1.50
❑4 AMo (w) 1.50
❑5 AMo (w) 1.50
❑6 AMo (w) 1.50
❑7 AMo (w) 1.50
❑8 AMo (w) 1.50
❑9 AMo (w) 1.50
❑10 AMo (w) 1.50
❑11 AMo (w) 1.50
❑12 AMo (w) 1.50

BALLAD OF UTOPIA
BLACK DAZE

❑1, Mar 2000, b&w 2.95
❑2, Apr 2000, b&w 2.95
❑3, May 2000, b&w 2.95
❑4, Feb 2002, b&w; Amryl Entertainment begins publishing 2.95
❑5, Jun 2002, b&w 2.95
❑6, Feb 2003, b&w 2.95
❑7, ca. 2003, b&w 2.95
❑8, Nov 2003, b&w; Antimatter/Hoffman International publishes 2.95

BALL AND CHAIN
DC / HOMAGE

❑1, Nov 1999 .... 2.50
❑2, Dec 1999 .... 2.50
❑3, Jan 2000 .... 2.50
❑4, Feb 2000 .... 2.50

BALLAST
ACTIVE IMAGES

❑0, Sep 2005 .... 4.00

BALLISTIC
IMAGE

❑1, Sep 1995 .... 2.50
❑2, Oct 1995 .... 2.50
❑3, Nov 1995 .... 2.50

BALLISTIC ACTION
IMAGE

❑1, May 1996; pin-ups 2.95

BALLISTIC IMAGERY
IMAGE

❑1, Jan 1996 .... 2.50
❑2 .... 2.50

BALLISTIC STUDIOS SWIMSUIT SPECIAL
IMAGE

❑1, May 1995; pin-ups 2.95

BALLISTIC/WOLVERINE
TOP COW

❑1, Feb 1997; crossover with Marvel, continues in Wolverine/Witchblade. 3.50

BALLOONATIKS
BEST

❑1, Oct 1991 .... 2.50

BALOO & LITTLE BRITCHES
GOLD KEY

❑1, Apr 1968 .... 25.00

BAMBEANO BOY
MOORDAM

❑1, May 1998 .... 2.50

BAMBI
DELL

❑3, Apr 1956, Reprints Four-Color #186 .... 30.00
❑3/A, Apr 1956, 15 cent regional price variant; reprints Four-Color #186 .... 50.00

BAMBI (WALT DISNEY...)
WHITMAN

❑1, Reprint of 1942 story 2.50

BAMBI AND HER FRIENDS
FRIENDLY

❑1, Jan 1991 .... 2.50
❑2, Feb 1991 .... 2.50
❑3, Mar 1991 .... 2.95
❑4, Apr 1991 .... 2.95
❑5, May 1991 .... 2.95
❑6, Jun 1991 .... 2.95
❑7, Jul 1991 .... 2.95
❑8, Aug 1991 .... 2.95
❑9, Sep 1991 .... 2.95

BAMBI IN HEAT
FRIENDLY

❑1 .... 2.95
❑2 .... 2.95
❑3 .... 2.95

BAMBI THE HUNTER
FRIENDLY

❑1 .... 2.95
❑2 .... 2.95
❑3, Mar 1992 .... 2.95
❑4 .... 2.95
❑5 .... 2.95

BAMM-BAMM AND PEBBLES FLINTSTONE
GOLD KEY

❑1, ca. 1964 .... 75.00

Other grades: Multiply price above by 5/6 for VF/NM • 2/3 for VERY FINE • 1/3 for FINE • 1/5 for VERY GOOD • 1/8 for GOOD

Banana Splits (Hanna Barbera...)

Awful live-action TV show spins off a comic book

©Gold Key

Barbie

Marvel/Mattel project had many subscribers

©Marvel

Barb Wire

The comic book was better than the movie

©Dark Horse

Barney and Betty Rubble

Flintstone neighbors get their own series

©Charlton

Bartman

Adventures of Bart Simpson's alter ego

©Bongo

N-MINT

BANANA FISH
TOKYOPOP

- ❑1, May 2004 .... 9.95
- ❑2, Jul 2004 .... 9.95
- ❑3, Aug 2004 .... 9.95
- ❑4, Oct 2004 .... 9.95
- ❑5, Dec 2004 .... 9.95
- ❑6, Feb 2005 .... 9.95
- ❑7, Apr 2005 .... 9.95
- ❑8, Jun 2005 .... 9.95
- ❑9, Aug 2005 .... 9.95
- ❑10, Oct 2005 .... 9.95

BANANA SPLITS (HANNA BARBERA...)
GOLD KEY

- ❑1, Jun 1969, 1: Snorky (in comics). 1: Fleegle (in comics). 1: Drooper (in comics). 1: Bingo (in comics).... 30.00
- ❑2, Apr 1970 .... 18.00
- ❑3, Jul 1970 .... 14.00
- ❑4, Oct 1970 .... 14.00
- ❑5, Jan 1971 .... 14.00
- ❑6, Apr 1971 .... 12.00
- ❑7, Jul 1971 .... 12.00
- ❑8, Oct 1971 .... 12.00

BANANA SUNDAYS
ONI

- ❑1, Aug 2005 .... 2.99
- ❑2, Sep 2005 .... 2.99
- ❑3, Oct 2005 .... 2.99
- ❑4, Nov 2005 .... 2.99

BANDY MAN
CALIBER

- ❑1, ca. 1996, b&w 2.95
- ❑2, ca. 1996, b&w 2.95
- ❑3, ca. 1997, b&w 2.95

BANG GANG
FANTAGRAPHICS / EROS

- ❑1, b&w 2.50

BANGS AND THE GANG
SHHWINNG

- ❑1, Feb 1994, b&w 2.95

BANISHED KNIGHTS
IMAGE

- ❑1, Dec 2001; no cover price 6.50
- ❑1/A, Dec 2001 .... 3.00
- ❑1/B, Dec 2001 .... 3.00
- ❑2/A, Feb 2002 .... 3.00
- ❑2/B, Feb 2002 .... 3.00

BANZAI GIRL
SIRIUS

- ❑1 2002 .... 2.95
- ❑2 2002 .... 2.95
- ❑3, Feb 2003 .... 2.95
- ❑4, May 2003 .... 2.95
- ❑Annual 1, Jan 2004 .... 3.50

BAOBAB
FANTAGRAPHICS

- ❑1 2005 .... 4.95

N-MINT

BAOH
VIZ

- ❑1 .... 3.50
- ❑2 .... 3.00
- ❑3 .... 3.00
- ❑4 .... 3.00
- ❑5 .... 3.00
- ❑6 .... 3.00
- ❑7 .... 3.00
- ❑8 .... 3.00
- ❑Book 1, May 1995 .... 14.95
- ❑Book 2 .... 14.95

BARABBAS
SLAVE LABOR

- ❑1, Aug 1986 .... 1.50
- ❑2, Nov 1985 .... 1.50

BARBARIAN COMICS
CALIFORNIA

- ❑1, ca. 1972 .... 3.00
- ❑2, ca. 1973 .... 2.50

BARBARIANS
ATLAS-SEABOARD

- ❑1, Jun 1975 O: Andrax. 1: Ironjaw ... 8.00

BARBARIANS (AVALON)
AVALON

- ❑1 .... 2.95
- ❑2 .... 2.95

BARBARIANS AND BEAUTIES
AC

- ❑1 1990 .... 2.75

BARBARIC TALES
PYRAMID

- ❑1 .... 1.70
- ❑2 .... 1.70

BARBARIENNE (FANTAGRAPHICS)
FANTAGRAPHICS / EROS

- ❑2, b&w 2.50
- ❑3, b&w 2.50
- ❑4 .... 3.50
- ❑5 .... 3.50
- ❑6 .... 3.50
- ❑7 .... 3.50
- ❑8 .... 3.95
- ❑9 .... 3.95
- ❑10 .... 3.95

BARBARIENNE (HARRIER)
HARRIER

- ❑1, Mar 1987 .... 2.00
- ❑2 .... 2.00
- ❑3 .... 2.00
- ❑4 .... 2.00
- ❑5 .... 2.00
- ❑6 V: Cuirass 2.00
- ❑7 V: Cuirass 2.00
- ❑8 V: Cuirass 2.00

BARBIE
MARVEL

- ❑1, Jan 1991 .... 3.00
- ❑1/A, Jan 1991 .... 3.00
- ❑2, Feb 1991 .... 2.00
- ❑3, Mar 1991 .... 2.00

N-MINT

- ❑4, Apr 1991 .... 2.00
- ❑5, May 1991 .... 2.00
- ❑6, Jun 1991 .... 1.50
- ❑7, Jul 1991 .... 1.50
- ❑8, Aug 1991 .... 1.50
- ❑9, Sep 1991 .... 1.50
- ❑10, Oct 1991 .... 1.50
- ❑11, Nov 1991 .... 1.50
- ❑12, Dec 1991 .... 1.50
- ❑13, Jan 1992 .... 1.50
- ❑14, Feb 1992 .... 1.50
- ❑15, Mar 1992 .... 1.50
- ❑16, Apr 1992 .... 1.50
- ❑17, May 1992 .... 1.50
- ❑18, Jun 1992 .... 1.50
- ❑19, Jul 1992 .... 1.50
- ❑20, Aug 1992 .... 1.50
- ❑21, Sep 1992 .... 1.50
- ❑22, Oct 1992 .... 1.50
- ❑23, Nov 1992 .... 1.50
- ❑24, Dec 1992 .... 1.50
- ❑25, Jan 1993 .... 1.50
- ❑26, Feb 1993 .... 1.50
- ❑27, Mar 1993 .... 1.50
- ❑28, Apr 1993 .... 1.50
- ❑29, May 1993 .... 1.50
- ❑30, Jun 1993 .... 1.50
- ❑31, Jul 1993 .... 1.50
- ❑32, Aug 1993 GM (a) 1.50
- ❑33, Sep 1993 .... 1.50
- ❑34, Oct 1993 A: Teresa 1.50
- ❑35, Nov 1993 .... 1.50
- ❑36, Dec 1993 .... 1.50
- ❑37, Jan 1994 .... 1.50
- ❑38, Feb 1994 .... 1.50
- ❑39, Mar 1994 .... 1.50
- ❑40, Apr 1994 .... 1.50
- ❑41, May 1994 .... 1.50
- ❑42, Jun 1994 .... 1.50
- ❑43, Jul 1994 .... 1.50
- ❑44, Aug 1994 .... 1.50
- ❑45, Sep 1994 .... 1.50
- ❑46, Oct 1994 .... 1.50
- ❑47, Nov 1994 .... 1.50
- ❑48, Dec 1994 .... 1.50
- ❑49, Jan 1995 .... 1.50
- ❑50, Feb 1995; Giant-size 2.25
- ❑51, Mar 1995 .... 1.50
- ❑52, Apr 1995 .... 1.50
- ❑53, May 1995 .... 1.50
- ❑54, Jun 1995 .... 1.50
- ❑55, Jul 1995 .... 1.50
- ❑56, Aug 1995 .... 1.50
- ❑57, Sep 1995 .... 1.50
- ❑58, Oct 1995 .... 1.50
- ❑59, Nov 1995 .... 1.50
- ❑60, Dec 1995 .... 1.50
- ❑61, Jan 1996 .... 1.50
- ❑62, Feb 1996; Nutcracker Suite references 1.50
- ❑63, Mar 1996 .... 1.50

Other grades: Multiply price above by 5/6 for VF/NM • 2/3 for VERY FINE • 1/3 for FINE • 1/5 for VERY GOOD • 1/8 for GOOD

BARBIE AND KEN
DELL

- ❑1, May 1962 ... 200.00
- ❑2, Aug 1962 ... 150.00
- ❑3, May 1963 ... 150.00
- ❑4, Aug 1963 ... 150.00
- ❑5, Nov 1963 ... 165.00

BARBIE FASHION
MARVEL

- ❑1, Jan 1991 ... 3.00
- ❑1/A, Jan 1991 ... 3.00
- ❑2, Feb 1991 ... 2.00
- ❑3, Mar 1991 ... 2.00
- ❑4, Apr 1991 ... 1.50
- ❑5, May 1991 ... 1.50
- ❑6, Jun 1991 ... 1.50
- ❑7, Jul 1991 ... 1.50
- ❑8, Aug 1991 ... 1.50
- ❑9, Sep 1991 ... 1.50
- ❑10, Oct 1991 ... 1.50
- ❑11, Nov 1991 ... 1.50
- ❑12, Dec 1991 ... 1.50
- ❑13, Jan 1992 ... 1.50
- ❑14, Feb 1992 ... 1.50
- ❑15, Mar 1992 ... 1.50
- ❑16, Apr 1992 ... 1.50
- ❑17, May 1992 ... 1.50
- ❑18, Jun 1992 ... 1.50
- ❑19, Jul 1992 ... 1.50
- ❑20, Aug 1992 ... 1.50
- ❑21, Sep 1992 ... 1.50
- ❑22, Oct 1992 ... 1.50
- ❑23, Nov 1992 ... 1.50
- ❑24, Dec 1992 ... 1.50
- ❑25, Jan 1993 ... 1.50
- ❑26, Feb 1993 ... 1.50
- ❑27, Mar 1993 ... 1.50
- ❑28, Apr 1993 ... 1.50
- ❑29, May 1993 ... 1.50
- ❑30, Jun 1993 ... 1.50
- ❑31, Jul 1993, GM (a) ... 1.50
- ❑32, Aug 1993 ... 1.50
- ❑33, Sep 1993 ... 1.50
- ❑34, Oct 1993 ... 1.50
- ❑35, Nov 1993 ... 1.50
- ❑36, Dec 1993 ... 1.50
- ❑37, Jan 1994 ... 1.50
- ❑38, Feb 1994 ... 1.50
- ❑39, Mar 1994 ... 1.50
- ❑40, Apr 1994 ... 1.50
- ❑41, May 1994 ... 1.50
- ❑42, Jun 1994 ... 1.50
- ❑43, Jul 1994 ... 1.50
- ❑44, Aug 1994 ... 1.50
- ❑45, Sep 1994 ... 1.50
- ❑46, Oct 1994 ... 1.50
- ❑47, Nov 1994 ... 1.50
- ❑48, Dec 1994 ... 1.50
- ❑49, Jan 1995 ... 1.50
- ❑50, Feb 1995, Giant-size ... 2.25
- ❑51, Mar 1995 ... 1.50
- ❑52, Apr 1995 ... 1.50
- ❑53, May 1995 ... 1.50
- ❑54 ... 1.50
- ❑55 ... 1.50

BARBI TWINS ADVENTURES
TOPPS

- ❑1, Jul 1995; Flip-book ... 2.50

BARB WIRE
DARK HORSE

- ❑1, Apr 1994 ... 2.50
- ❑2, May 1994 ... 2.50
- ❑3, Jun 1994 ... 2.50
- ❑4, Aug 1994 ... 2.50
- ❑5, Sep 1994 ... 2.50
- ❑6, Oct 1994 ... 2.50
- ❑7, Nov 1994 ... 2.50
- ❑8, Jan 1995 ... 2.50
- ❑9, Feb 1995 ... 2.50

BARB WIRE: ACE OF SPADES
DARK HORSE

- ❑1, May 1996 ... 2.95
- ❑2, Jun 1996 ... 2.95
- ❑3, Jul 1996 ... 2.95
- ❑4, Sep 1996 ... 2.95

BARB WIRE COMICS MAGAZINE SPECIAL
DARK HORSE

- ❑1, May 1996; magazine-sized adaptation of movie, b&w, poster... 3.50

BARB WIRE MOVIE SPECIAL
DARK HORSE

- ❑1, May 1996; adapts movie ... 3.95

BAR CRAWL OF THE DAMNED
MORTCO

- ❑1 1997, b&w ... 2.50

BAREFOOTZ FUNNIES
KITCHEN SINK

- ❑1, Jul 1975, b&w ... 3.00
- ❑2, Apr 1976, b&w ... 2.00
- ❑3, Dec 1979, b&w ... 2.00

BAREFOOTZ THE COMIX BOOK STORIES (HOWARD CRUSE'S...)
RENEGADE

- ❑1 A: Dolly. A: Barefootz. A: Headrack ... 2.50

BARF
REVOLUTIONARY

- ❑1, Apr 1990, b&w ... 1.95
- ❑2, Jun 1990, b&w ... 2.50
- ❑3, Sep 1990, b&w ... 2.50

BARNEY AND BETTY RUBBLE
CHARLTON

- ❑1, Jan 1973 ... 15.00
- ❑2, Jan 1973 ... 10.00
- ❑3, Mar 1973 ... 6.00
- ❑4, May 1973 ... 6.00
- ❑5, Jul 1973 ... 6.00
- ❑6, Sep 1973 ... 6.00
- ❑7, May 1974 ... 6.00
- ❑8, Jul 1974 ... 6.00
- ❑9, Sep 1974 ... 6.00
- ❑10, Nov 1974 ... 6.00
- ❑11, Feb 1975 ... 6.00
- ❑12, Mar 1975 ... 5.00
- ❑13, May 1975 ... 5.00
- ❑14, Jun 1975 ... 5.00
- ❑15, Aug 1975 ... 5.00
- ❑16, Oct 1975 ... 5.00
- ❑17, Dec 1975 ... 5.00
- ❑18, Feb 1976 ... 5.00
- ❑19, Apr 1976 ... 5.00
- ❑20, Jun 1976 ... 5.00
- ❑21, Aug 1976 ... 5.00
- ❑22, Oct 1976 ... 5.00
- ❑23, Dec 1976 ... 5.00

BARNEY THE INVISIBLE TURTLE
AMAZING

- ❑1 ... 1.95

BARR GIRLS
ANTARCTIC / VENUS

- ❑1, b&w ... 2.95

BARRON STOREY'S WATCH ANNUAL (VOL. 2)
VANGUARD

- ❑1; b&w anthology, squarebound ... 5.95

BARRY WINDSOR-SMITH: STORYTELLER
DARK HORSE

- ❑1, Oct 1996 ... 4.95
- ❑1/Variant, Oct 1996, alternate cover (logoless), cover with logos appears as back cover ... 4.95
- ❑2, Nov 1996 ... 4.95
- ❑3, Dec 1996 ... 4.95
- ❑4, Jan 1997 ... 4.95
- ❑5, Feb 1997 ... 4.95
- ❑6, Mar 1997 ... 4.95
- ❑7, May 1997 ... 4.95
- ❑8, Jun 1997 ... 4.95
- ❑9, Jul 1997 ... 4.95

BAR SINISTER
WINDJAMMER / ACCLAIM

- ❑1, Jun 1995 ... 2.50
- ❑2, Jul 1995 ... 2.50
- ❑3, Aug 1995 ... 2.50
- ❑4, Sep 1995 ... 2.50

BARTMAN
BONGO

- ❑1, ca. 1993; Silver ink cover ... 4.00
- ❑2, ca. 1994 ... 3.00
- ❑3, ca. 1994; trading card ... 3.00
- ❑4, ca. 1995 ... 2.50
- ❑5, ca. 1995 1: Lisa the Conjuror. 1: The Great Maggeena ... 2.50
- ❑6, ca. 1995 O: Bart Dog. 1: Bart Dog ... 2.50

BASARA
VIZ

- ❑1, Aug 2003 ... 9.95
- ❑2, Oct 2003 ... 9.95
- ❑3, Dec 2003 ... 9.95
- ❑4, Feb 2004 ... 9.95
- ❑5, Apr 2004 ... 9.95
- ❑6, Jun 2004 ... 9.95
- ❑7, Aug 2004 ... 9.95
- ❑8, Oct 2004 ... 9.95
- ❑9, Dec 2004 ... 9.95
- ❑10, Feb 2005 ... 9.95
- ❑11, Apr 2005 ... 9.95
- ❑12, Jun 2005 ... 9.95
- ❑13, Aug 2005 ... 9.95
- ❑14, Oct 2005 ... 9.95

BASEBALL CLASSICS
PERSONALITY

- ❑1 ... 2.95
- ❑2 ... 2.95

BASEBALL COMICS
KITCHEN SINK

- ❑1, May 1991; trading cards ... 3.95
- ❑2, ca. 1992; cards on back cover ... 2.95

BASEBALL COMICS (PERSONALITY)
PERSONALITY

- ❑1 ... 2.95
- ❑2 ... 2.95

BASEBALL GREATS
DARK HORSE

- ❑1, Oct 1992; Jimmy Piersall, with cards ... 2.95
- ❑2; Bob Gibson ... 2.95
- ❑3; 2 trading cards ... 2.95

BASEBALL HALL OF SHAME IN 3-D
BLACKTHORNE

- ❑1 ... 2.50

BASEBALL LEGENDS
REVOLUTIONARY

- ❑1, Mar 1992, b&w; Babe Ruth ... 2.50
- ❑2, Apr 1992, b&w; Ty Cobb ... 2.50
- ❑3, May 1992, b&w; Ted Williams ... 2.50
- ❑4, Jun 1992, b&w; Mickey Mantle ... 2.50
- ❑5, Jul 1992, b&w; Joe Dimaggio ... 2.50
- ❑6, Aug 1992, b&w; Jackie Robinson ... 2.50
- ❑7, Sep 1992, b&w; Sandy Koufax ... 2.50
- ❑8, Oct 1992, b&w; Willie Mays ... 2.50
- ❑9, Nov 1992, b&w; Honus Wagner ... 2.50
- ❑10, Dec 1992, Roberto Clemente ... 2.75
- ❑11, Jan 1993, Yogi Berra ... 2.75
- ❑12, Feb 1993, Billy Martin ... 2.75
- ❑13, Mar 1993, Hank Aaron ... 2.95
- ❑14, Apr 1993, b&w; Carl Yastrzemski ... 2.95
- ❑15, May 1993, b&w; Satchel Paige ... 2.95
- ❑16, Jun 1993, b&w; Johnny Bench ... 2.95
- ❑17, Jul 1993, b&w; Shoeless Joe Jackson ... 2.95
- ❑18, Aug 1993, b&w; Lou Gehrig ... 2.95
- ❑19, Sep 1993, b&w; Casey Stengel ... 2.95

BASEBALL'S GREATEST HEROES
MAGNUM

- ❑1, Dec 1991; Mickey Mantle ... 2.50
- ❑2 ... 2.50

BASEBALL SLUGGERS
PERSONALITY

- ❑1 ... 2.95
- ❑2 ... 2.95
- ❑3 ... 2.95
- ❑4 ... 2.95

BASEBALL SUPERSTARS COMICS
REVOLUTIONARY

- ❑1, Nov 1991; Nolan Ryan ... 2.50
- ❑2, Feb 1992; Bo Jackson ... 2.50
- ❑3, Mar 1992; Ken Griffey Jr ... 2.50
- ❑4, Apr 1992; Pete Rose ... 2.50

Baseball Superstars Comics

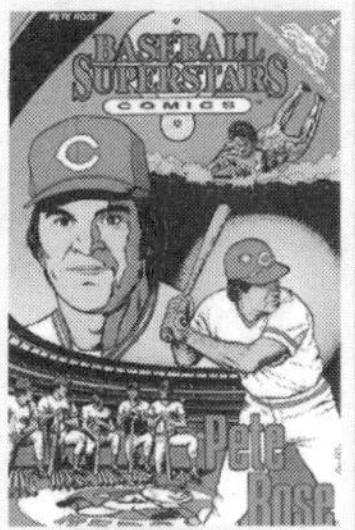

Unauthorized bio comics from Revolutionary

©Revolutionary

Bastard Samurai

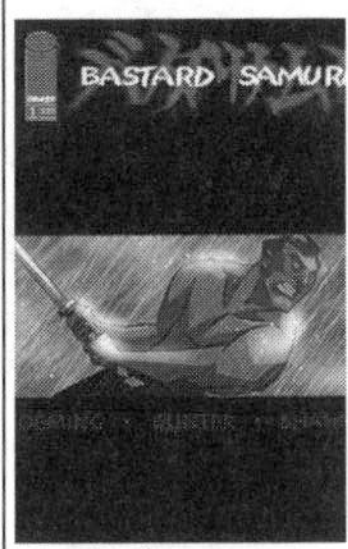

Character raves and rants about everything

©Image

Batgirl

Batgirl's first solo series was hot seller for a while

©DC

Bat Lash

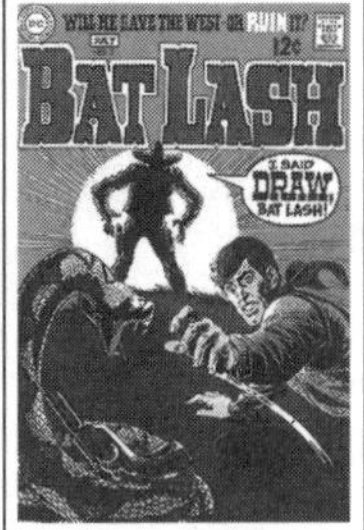

Humorous Western adventure series from DC

©DC

Batman

Caped Crusader's title spun off from Detective

©DC

	N-MINT
❑5, May 1992; Rickey Henderson	2.50
❑6, Jun 1992; Jose Canseco	2.50
❑7, Jul 1992; Cal Ripkin Jr	2.50
❑8, Aug 1992; Carlton Fisk	2.50
❑9, Sep 1992; George Brett	2.50
❑10, Oct 1992; Darryl Strawberry	2.50
❑11, Nov 1992; Frank Thomas	2.50
❑12, Dec 1992, Ryne Sandberg	2.75
❑13, Jan 1993, Kirby Puckett	2.75
❑14, Feb 1993, Roberto and Sandi Alomar	2.75
❑15, Mar 1993, Roger Clemens	2.95
❑16, Apr 1993, b&w; Mark McGuire	2.95
❑17, May 1993, b&w; Avery/Glavine	2.95
❑18, Jun 1993, b&w; Dennis Eckersley	2.95
❑19, Jul 1993, b&w; Dave Winfield	2.95
❑20, Aug 1993, b&w; Jim Abbott	2.95

BASEBALL THRILLS 3-D
3-D ZONE

❑1	2.95

BASICALLY STRANGE
JOHN C.

❑1, Nov 1982 WW (w); ATh, FT, WW (a)	4.00

BASTARD
VIZ

❑1, Dec 2001	3.95
❑2, Jan 2002	3.95
❑3, Feb 2002	3.95
❑4, Mar 2002	3.95
❑5, Apr 2002	3.95
❑6, May 2002	3.95
❑7, Jun 2002	3.95
❑8, Jul 2002	3.95
❑9, Aug 2002	3.95
❑10, Sep 2002	3.95
❑11, Oct 2002	3.95
❑12, Nov 2002	3.95
❑13, Dec 2002	3.95
❑14, Jan 2003	3.95
❑15, Feb 2003	3.95
❑Book 1 2002	14.95

BASTARD SAMURAI
IMAGE

❑1, Apr 2002	2.95
❑2, Jun 2002	2.95
❑3, Aug 2002	2.95
❑Book 1, ca. 2003	12.95

BASTARD TALES
BABOON BOOKS

❑1 1998, b&w	2.95

BAT (APPLE)
APPLE

❑1, Mar 1994, b&w	2.50

BATBABE
SPOOF

❑2	2.50

BATCH
CALIBER

❑1, b&w	2.95

BATGIRL
DC

	N-MINT
❑1, Apr 2000	4.00
❑1/2nd, Apr 2000	3.00
❑2, May 2000	3.50
❑3, Jun 2000	3.50
❑4, Jul 2000	3.50
❑5, Aug 2000	3.50
❑6, Sep 2000	3.00
❑7, Oct 2000	3.00
❑8, Nov 2000	3.00
❑9, Dec 2000	3.00
❑10, Jan 2001	3.00
❑11, Feb 2001	2.50
❑12, Mar 2001; Officer Down	2.50
❑13, Apr 2001	2.50
❑14, May 2001	2.50
❑15, Jun 2001	2.50
❑16, Jul 2001	2.50
❑17, Aug 2001	2.50
❑18, Sep 2001	2.50
❑19, Oct 2001	2.50
❑20, Nov 2001	2.50
❑21, Dec 2001	2.50
❑22, Jan 2002	2.50
❑23, Feb 2002	2.50
❑24, Mar 2002	2.50
❑25, Apr 2002; Giant-size	3.25
❑26, May 2002	2.50
❑27, Jun 2002	2.50
❑28, Jul 2002	2.50
❑29, Aug 2002	2.50
❑30, Sep 2002	2.50
❑31, Oct 2002	2.50
❑32, Nov 2002	2.50
❑33, Dec 2002	2.50
❑34, Jan 2003	2.50
❑35, Feb 2003	2.50
❑36, Mar 2003	2.50
❑37, Apr 2003	2.50
❑38, May 2003	2.50
❑39, Jun 2003	2.50
❑40, Jul 2003	2.50
❑41, Aug 2003	2.50
❑42, Sep 2003	2.50
❑43, Oct 2003	2.50
❑44, Nov 2003	2.50
❑45, Dec 2003	2.50
❑46, Jan 2004	2.50
❑47, Feb 2004	2.50
❑48, Mar 2004	2.50
❑49, Apr 2004	2.50
❑50, May 2004	2.50
❑51, Jun 2004	2.50
❑52, Jul 2004	2.50
❑53, Aug 2004	2.50
❑54, Jul 2004	2.50
❑55, Oct 2004	2.50
❑56, Nov 2004	2.50
❑57, Jan 2005	2.50
❑58, Feb 2005	2.50
❑59, Mar 2005	2.50
❑60, Apr 2005	2.50
❑61, May 2005	2.50
❑62, Jun 2005	2.50
❑63, Jun 2005	2.50
❑64, Jul 2005	2.50
❑65, Aug 2005	2.50
❑66, Sep 2005	2.50
❑67, Oct 2005	2.50
❑68, Nov 2005	2.99
❑69, Dec 2005	2.99
❑70, Jan 2006	2.99
❑71, Feb 2006	2.99
❑72, Mar 2006	2.99
❑73, Apr 2006	2.99
❑Annual 1, ca. 2002; 1: Aruna. Planet DC	4.00

BATGIRL ADVENTURES
DC

❑1, Feb 1998 V: Harley Quinn, Poison Ivy	3.50

BATGIRL SECRET FILES AND ORIGINS
DC

❑1, Aug 2002	4.95

BATGIRL SPECIAL
DC

❑1, Jul 1988	3.00

BATGIRL: YEAR ONE
DC

❑1, Feb 2003	2.95
❑2, Mar 2003	2.95
❑3, Apr 2003	2.95
❑4, May 2003	2.95
❑5, Jun 2003	2.95
❑6, Jul 2003	2.95
❑7, Aug 2003	2.95
❑8, Sep 2003	2.95
❑9, Oct 2003	2.95

BATHING MACHINE
C&T

❑1, ca. 1987, b&w	2.50
❑2, ca. 1987	1.50
❑3, ca. 1987	1.50

BATHROOM GIRLS
MODERN

❑1 1997, b&w	2.95
❑2 1998, b&w	2.95

BAT LASH
DC

❑1, Nov 1968	25.00
❑2, Jan 1969	15.00
❑3, Mar 1969	15.00
❑4, May 1969	15.00
❑5, Jul 1969	15.00
❑6, Sep 1969	15.00
❑7, Nov 1969, SA (w); NC (a)	15.00

BATMAN
DC

❑103, Oct 1956	400.00
❑104, Dec 1956	400.00
❑105, Feb 1957 2: Batwoman. A: Batwoman	490.00
❑106, Mar 1957	400.00
❑107, Apr 1957	400.00
❑108, Jun 1957	400.00
❑109, Jul 1957	400.00
❑110, Sep 1957, A: Joker. V: Joker	425.00
❑111, Oct 1957	290.00
❑112, Dec 1957, 1: The Signalman	290.00

Other grades: Multiply price above by 5/6 for VF/NM • 2/3 for VERY FINE • 1/3 for FINE • 1/5 for VERY GOOD • 1/8 for GOOD

	N-MINT
❑113, Feb 1958 1: Fatman	290.00
❑114, Mar 1958	290.00
❑115, Apr 1958	290.00
❑116, Jun 1958	290.00
❑117, Jul 1958	290.00
❑118, Sep 1958	290.00
❑119, Oct 1958	290.00
❑120, Dec 1958	290.00
❑121, Feb 1959, O: Mr. Zero (later Mr. Freeze). 1: Mr. Zero (later Mr. Freeze)	375.00
❑122, Mar 1959	225.00
❑123, Apr 1959, A: Joker	220.00
❑124, Jun 1959	195.00
❑125, Aug 1959	195.00
❑126, Sep 1959	195.00
❑127, Oct 1959, A: Joker. A: Superman	240.00
❑128, Dec 1959	195.00
❑129, Feb 1960, O: Robin I (Dick Grayson)	250.00
❑130, Mar 1960, A: Lex Luthor. A: Bat-Hound ("Ace")	195.00
❑131, Apr 1960, 1: 2nd Batman	145.00
❑132, Jun 1960	130.00
❑133, Aug 1960	130.00
❑134, Sep 1960	130.00
❑135, Oct 1960	130.00
❑136, Dec 1960, A: Joker. V: Joker	215.00
❑137, Feb 1961, A: Mr. Marvel	140.00
❑138, Mar 1961	140.00
❑139, Apr 1961, 1: Batgirl (Golden Age)	140.00
❑140, Jun 1961, A: Joker	140.00
❑141, Aug 1961	140.00
❑142, Sep 1961	140.00
❑143, Oct 1961	140.00
❑144, Dec 1961, A: Joker	140.00
❑145, Feb 1962, A: Joker	140.00
❑146, Mar 1962	110.00
❑147, May 1962	110.00
❑148, Jul 1962, A: Joker	140.00
❑149, Aug 1962	110.00
❑150, Oct 1962	110.00
❑151, Nov 1962	90.00
❑152, Dec 1962, A: Joker	100.00
❑153, Feb 1963	85.00
❑154, Mar 1963	85.00
❑155, Apr 1963, 1: Penguin (in Silver Age)	300.00
❑156, Jun 1963	85.00
❑157, Aug 1963	85.00
❑158, Sep 1963	85.00
❑159, Nov 1963, A: Joker	85.00
❑160, Dec 1963	85.00
❑161, Feb 1964	85.00
❑162, Mar 1964	85.00
❑163, May 1964, A: Joker	85.00
❑164, Jun 1964	85.00
❑165, Aug 1964	85.00
❑166, Sep 1964	85.00
❑167, Nov 1964	85.00
❑168, Dec 1964	85.00
❑169, Feb 1965, A: Penguin	90.00
❑170, Mar 1965	85.00
❑171, May 1965, CI (a); A: Riddler	450.00
❑172, Jun 1965	75.00
❑173, Aug 1965	75.00
❑174, Sep 1965	75.00
❑175, Nov 1965	75.00
❑176, Dec 1965; 80-Page Giant; A: Joker. aka 80 Page Giant #G-17	85.00
❑177, Dec 1965	75.00
❑178, Feb 1966	75.00
❑179, Mar 1966, A: Riddler	120.00
❑180, May 1966	60.00
❑181, Jun 1966, 1: Poison Ivy	175.00
❑182, Aug 1966; A: Joker. aka 80 Page Giant #G-24; Reprints	60.00
❑183, Aug 1966, TV show reference	60.00
❑184, Sep 1966	60.00
❑185, Nov 1966; 80-Page Giant; aka 80 Page Giant #G-27	60.00
❑186, Nov 1966, A: Joker	60.00
❑187, Dec 1966; 80-Page Giant; A: Joker. aka 80 Page Giant #G-30	65.00
❑188, Jan 1967	40.00
❑189, Feb 1967, 1: The Scarecrow (in Silver Age)	200.00
❑190, Mar 1967, A: Penguin	45.00
❑191, May 1967	40.00

	N-MINT
❑192, Jun 1967	40.00
❑193, Aug 1967; 80-Page Giant; aka 80 Page Giant #G-37	70.00
❑194, Aug 1967	40.00
❑195, Sep 1967	40.00
❑196, Nov 1967	40.00
❑197, Dec 1967, A: Catwoman	100.00
❑198, Jan 1968; 80-Page Giant; O: Batman. A: Joker. aka 80 Page Giant #G-43	85.00
❑199, Feb 1968	40.00
❑200, Mar 1968, NA (a); O: Robin I (Dick Grayson). O: Batman. A: Joker	100.00
❑201, May 1968, A: Joker	35.00
❑202, Jun 1968	30.00
❑203, Aug 1968; 80-Page Giant; aka 80 Page Giant #G-49	30.00
❑204, Aug 1968	30.00
❑205, Sep 1968	30.00
❑206, Nov 1968	30.00
❑207, Dec 1968	30.00
❑208, Jan 1969; 80-Page Giant; O: Batman (new origin). aka 80 Page Giant #G-55	30.00
❑209, Jan 1969	30.00
❑210, Mar 1969	30.00
❑211, May 1969	30.00
❑212, Jun 1969	30.00
❑213, Aug 1969; Giant-size; O: Robin I (Dick Grayson-new origin). A: Joker. aka Giant #G-61; Joker reprint	45.00
❑214, Aug 1969	30.00
❑215, Sep 1969	30.00
❑216, Nov 1969	30.00
❑217, Dec 1969	30.00
❑218, Feb 1970; Giant-size; aka Giant #G-67	70.00
❑219, Feb 1970, NA (a)	50.00
❑220, Mar 1970, NA (a)	30.00
❑221, May 1970, NA (a)	30.00
❑222, Jun 1970, NA (a); A: The Beatles	50.00
❑223, Aug 1970; Giant-size; CS (c); MA (a); aka Giant #G-73; Reprints stories from Batman #79 & #93, Detective #196 & #248, and Sunday strips from August 8 through September 17, 1944	40.00
❑224, Aug 1970, NA (a)	30.00
❑225, Sep 1970, NA (a)	30.00
❑226, Nov 1970, NA (a)	30.00
❑227, Dec 1970, NA (a); Robin back-up	30.00
❑228, Feb 1971; Giant-size; MA (a); aka Giant #G-79	40.00
❑229, Feb 1971	30.00
❑230, Mar 1971	30.00
❑231, May 1971	30.00
❑232, Jun 1971, DG, NA (a); O: Batman. 1: Ra's Al Ghul	350.00
❑233, Aug 1971; Giant-size; aka Giant #G-85	30.00
❑234, Aug 1971 CI, NA (a); 1: Two-Face (in Silver Age)	115.00
❑235, Sep 1971 CI (a)	17.00
❑236, Nov 1971 NA (a)	17.00
❑237, Dec 1971 NA (a); 1: The Reaper	75.00
❑238, Jan 1972, Giant-size; JKu, NA (a); a.k.a. DC 100-Page Super Spectacular #DC-8, wraparound cover	65.00
❑239, Feb 1972 RB, NA (a)	17.00
❑240, Mar 1972 RB, NA (a)	17.00
❑241, May 1972 RB, NA (a)	17.00
❑242, Jun 1972 RB (a)	17.00
❑243, Aug 1972, DG, NA (a); Ra's al Ghul	70.00
❑244, Sep 1972, DG, NA (a); Ra's al Ghul	60.00
❑245, Oct 1972, FM (c); DG, NA, IN (a)	50.00
❑246, Dec 1972	15.00
❑247, Feb 1973	15.00
❑248, Apr 1973	15.00
❑249, Jun 1973	15.00
❑250, Jul 1973	15.00
❑251, Sep 1973, NA (a); A: Joker	60.00
❑252, Sep 1973	14.00
❑253, Nov 1973	14.00
❑254, Feb 1974, 100 Page giant NA, GK (a)	32.00
❑255, Apr 1974, 100 Page giant CI, DG, NA, GK (a)	32.00
❑256, Jun 1974, 100 Page giant	32.00
❑257, Aug 1974, 100 Page giant	32.00

	N-MINT
❑258, Oct 1974, 100 Page giant	32.00
❑259, Dec 1974, 100 Page giant	32.00
❑260, Feb 1975, 100 Page giant A: Joker	32.00
❑261, Mar 1975, 100 Page giant	32.00
❑262, Apr 1975, Giant-size	13.00
❑263, May 1975	9.00
❑264, Jun 1975 DG (a); V: Devil Dayre	9.00
❑265, Jul 1975	9.00
❑266, Aug 1975; A: Catwoman. Catwoman goes back to old costume	9.00
❑267, Sep 1975	8.00
❑268, Oct 1975	8.00
❑269, Nov 1975	8.00
❑270, Dec 1975	8.00
❑271, Jan 1976	8.00
❑272, Feb 1976	8.00
❑273, Mar 1976	8.00
❑274, Apr 1976	8.00
❑275, May 1976	8.00
❑276, Jun 1976	8.00
❑277, Jul 1976, Bicentennial #11	8.00
❑278, Aug 1976	8.00
❑279, Sep 1976	8.00
❑280, Oct 1976	8.00
❑281, Nov 1976	8.00
❑282, Dec 1976	8.00
❑283, Jan 1977, V: Omega	8.00
❑284, Feb 1977	8.00
❑285, Mar 1977	8.00
❑286, Apr 1977, A: Joker	12.00
❑287, May 1977	9.00
❑288, Jun 1977	9.00
❑289, Jul 1977	9.00
❑290, Aug 1977	9.00
❑291, Sep 1977, A: Joker	9.00
❑292, Oct 1977	9.00
❑293, Nov 1977, A: Lex Luthor. A: Superman	9.00
❑294, Dec 1977, A: Joker	9.00
❑295, Jan 1978	8.00
❑296, Feb 1978, V: Scarecrow	8.00
❑297, Mar 1978	8.00
❑298, Apr 1978	8.00
❑299, May 1978	8.00
❑300, Jun 1978, Double-size	15.00
❑301, Jul 1978	7.00
❑302, Aug 1978	7.00
❑303, Sep 1978	7.00
❑304, Oct 1978	7.00
❑305, Nov 1978	7.00
❑306, Dec 1978	7.00
❑306/Whitman, Dec 1978, Whitman variant	14.00
❑307, Jan 1979	7.00
❑307/Whitman, Jan 1979, Whitman variant	14.00
❑308, Feb 1979	7.00
❑308/Whitman, Feb 1979, Whitman variant	14.00
❑309, Mar 1979	7.00
❑310, Apr 1979	7.00
❑311, May 1979	7.00
❑311/Whitman, May 1979, Whitman variant	20.00
❑312, Jun 1979	7.00
❑312/Whitman, Jun 1979, Whitman variant	14.00
❑313, Jul 1979	7.00
❑313/Whitman, Jul 1979, Whitman variant	14.00
❑314, Aug 1979	7.00
❑314/Whitman, Aug 1979, Whitman variant	14.00
❑315, Sep 1979	7.00
❑315/Whitman, Sep 1979, Whitman variant	14.00
❑316, Oct 1979	7.00
❑316/Whitman, Oct 1979, Whitman variant	14.00
❑317, Nov 1979	7.00
❑317/Whitman, Nov 1979, Whitman variant	17.00
❑318, Dec 1979, 1: Firebug	7.00
❑318/Whitman, Dec 1979, 1: Firebug. Whitman variant	17.00
❑319, Jan 1980	7.00
❑319/Whitman, Jan 1980, Whitman variant	17.00
❑320, Feb 1980	7.00

Other grades: Multiply price above by 5/6 for VF/NM • 2/3 for VERY FINE • 1/3 for FINE • 1/5 for VERY GOOD • 1/8 for GOOD

Batman Adventures

Art has the look of the Fox cartoon series

©DC

Batman Adventures: Mad Love

Critically acclaimed Harley Quinn story

©DC

Batman/Aliens II

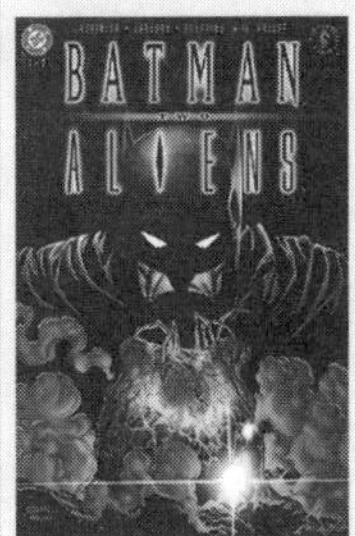

Second crossover for these franchises

©DC-Dark Horse

Batman and Robin Adventures

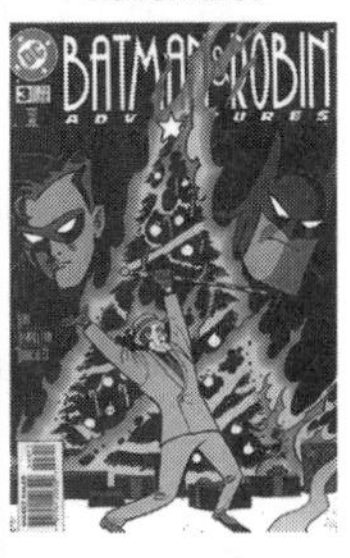

Younger-reader Batman series adds sidekick

©DC

Batman and Superman: World's Finest

Prestige format series reteaming heroes

©DC

	N-MINT
❑320/Whitman, Feb 1980, Whitman variant	14.00
❑321, Mar 1980, A: Catwoman. A: Joker	7.00
❑322, Apr 1980	7.00
❑323, May 1980	7.00
❑323/Whitman, May 1980, Whitman variant	7.00
❑324, Jun 1980	7.00
❑324/Whitman, Jun 1980, Whitman variant	7.00
❑325, Jul 1980	7.00
❑326, Aug 1980, 1: Arkham Asylum	7.00
❑326/Whitman, Aug 1980, 1: Arkham Asylum. Whitman variant	7.00
❑327, Sep 1980	7.00
❑328, Oct 1980	7.00
❑329, Nov 1980	7.00
❑330, Dec 1980	7.00
❑331, Jan 1981, 1: Electrocutioner	7.00
❑332, Feb 1981, 1st solo Catwoman story	8.00
❑333, Mar 1981	7.00
❑334, Apr 1981	7.00
❑335, May 1981	7.00
❑336, Jun 1981	7.00
❑337, Jul 1981	7.00
❑338, Aug 1981	7.00
❑339, Sep 1981	7.00
❑340, Oct 1981	7.00
❑341, Nov 1981	7.00
❑342, Dec 1981	7.00
❑343, Jan 1982	7.00
❑344, Feb 1982	7.00
❑345, Mar 1982	7.00
❑346, Apr 1982, V: Two-Face	7.00
❑347, May 1982	7.00
❑348, Jun 1982	7.00
❑349, Jul 1982	7.00
❑350, Aug 1982	7.00
❑351, Sep 1982	7.00
❑352, Oct 1982	7.00
❑353, Nov 1982, A: Joker	5.00
❑354, Dec 1982	7.00
❑355, Jan 1983	7.00
❑356, Feb 1983	7.00
❑357, Mar 1983, 1: Killer Croc. 1: Jason Todd	9.00
❑358, Apr 1983	7.00
❑359, May 1983, A: Joker	7.00
❑360, Jun 1983	7.00
❑361, Jul 1983, 1: Harvey Bullock	7.00
❑362, Aug 1983	7.00
❑363, Sep 1983	7.00
❑364, Oct 1983	7.00
❑365, Nov 1983	7.00
❑366, Dec 1983 1: Jason Todd in Robin costume. A: Joker	6.00
❑367, Jan 1984	7.00
❑368, Feb 1984 DN, AA (a); 1: Robin II (Jason Todd)	8.00
❑369, Mar 1984 V: Deadshot	6.00
❑370, Apr 1984	6.00
❑371, May 1984 V: Catman	5.00
❑372, Jun 1984	5.00
❑373, Jul 1984 V: Scarecrow	5.00

	N-MINT
❑374, Aug 1984 V: Penguin	5.00
❑375, Sep 1984 V: Mr. Freeze	5.00
❑376, Oct 1984	5.00
❑377, Nov 1984	5.00
❑378, Dec 1984 V: Mad Hatter	5.00
❑379, Jan 1985 V: Mad Hatter	5.00
❑380, Feb 1985	5.00
❑381, Mar 1985	5.00
❑382, Apr 1985 GK (c); A: Catwoman	5.00
❑383, May 1985	5.00
❑384, Jun 1985 V: Calendar Man	5.00
❑385, Jul 1985	5.00
❑386, Aug 1985 1: Black Mask	5.00
❑387, Sep 1985 V: Black Mask	5.00
❑388, Oct 1985 V: Mirror Master. V: Capt. Boomerang. V: Captain Boomerang	5.00
❑389, Nov 1985 A: Catwoman	5.00
❑390, Dec 1985 A: Catwoman	5.00
❑391, Jan 1986 A: Catwoman	5.00
❑392, Feb 1986	5.00
❑393, Mar 1986 PG (c); PG (a)	5.00
❑394, Apr 1986 PG (c); PG (a)	5.00
❑395, May 1986	5.00
❑396, Jun 1986	5.00
❑397, Jul 1986 V: Two-Face	5.00
❑398, Aug 1986 A: Catwoman. A: Two-Face. V: Two-Face	5.00
❑399, Sep 1986	5.00
❑400, Oct 1986; Anniversary edition	10.00
❑401, Nov 1986; V: Magpie. Legends	4.00
❑402, Dec 1986	4.00
❑403, Jan 1987	4.00
❑404, Feb 1987 FM (w); O: Batman. 1: Catwoman (new)	5.00
❑405, Mar 1987; FM (w); Year One	6.00
❑406, Apr 1987; FM (w); Year One	5.00
❑407, May 1987; FM (w); Year One	5.00
❑408, Jun 1987 O: Jason Todd (new origin)	5.00
❑409, Jul 1987	3.00
❑410, Aug 1987 V: Two-Face	3.00
❑411, Sep 1987	3.00
❑412, Oct 1987 O: Mime. 1: Mime	3.00
❑413, Nov 1987	3.00
❑414, Dec 1987; JSn (w); JA (a); Millennium	3.00
❑415, Jan 1988; Millennium	3.00
❑416, Feb 1988 JA (a); A: Nightwing	3.00
❑417, Mar 1988 MZ (c); 1: KGBeast. V: KGBeast	5.00
❑418, Apr 1988 MZ (c); V: KGBeast	4.00
❑419, May 1988 MZ (c); V: KGBeast	4.00
❑420, Jun 1988 MZ (c); V: KGBeast	4.00
❑421, Jul 1988	3.00
❑422, Aug 1988	3.00
❑423, Sep 1988 TMc (c); DC (a)	3.00
❑424, Oct 1988	3.00
❑425, Nov 1988	3.00
❑426, Dec 1988	6.00
❑427, Dec 1988 D: Robin, newsstand	6.00
❑427/Direct ed., Dec 1988 D: Robin, direct sale	4.00
❑428, Jan 1989; D: Robin II (Jason Todd). Robin declared dead	6.00
❑429, Jan 1989 JSn (w); JA (a)	4.00

	N-MINT
❑430, Feb 1989	3.00
❑431, Mar 1989	2.00
❑432, Apr 1989	2.00
❑433, May 1989 JBy (w); JBy, JA (a)	2.00
❑434, Jun 1989 JBy (w); JBy, JA (a)	2.00
❑435, Jul 1989 JBy (w); JBy, JA (a)	2.00
❑436, Aug 1989	2.50
❑436/2nd	1.25
❑437, Aug 1989 PB (a)	2.00
❑438, Sep 1989	2.00
❑439, Sep 1989	2.00
❑440, Oct 1989 JA (a); 1: Timothy Drake	2.00
❑441, Nov 1989	2.00
❑442, Dec 1989 1: Robin III (Timothy Drake)	2.50
❑443, Jan 1990	1.50
❑444, Feb 1990 JA (a); V: Crimesmith	1.50
❑445, Mar 1990 JA (a); 1: NKVDemon. V: NKVDemon	1.50
❑446, Apr 1990 V: NKVDemon	1.50
❑447, May 1990 V: NKVDemon	1.50
❑448, Jun 1990 V: Penguin	1.50
❑449, Jun 1990 V: Penguin	1.50
❑450, Jul 1990 V: Joker	1.50
❑451, Jul 1990 V: Joker	1.50
❑452, Aug 1990 V: Riddler	1.50
❑453, Aug 1990 V: Riddler	1.50
❑454, Sep 1990 V: Riddler	1.50
❑455, Oct 1990	1.50
❑456, Nov 1990	1.50
❑457, Dec 1990; 1: new Robin costume. Timothy Drake as Robin	2.50
❑457/Direct ed., Dec 1990; with #000 on indicia	4.00
❑457/2nd, Dec 1990; Timothy Drake as Robin	2.00
❑458, Jan 1991 1: Harold	1.50
❑459, Feb 1991	1.50
❑460, Mar 1991 A: Catwoman	1.50
❑461, Apr 1991 A: Catwoman	1.50
❑462, May 1991	1.50
❑463, Jun 1991	1.50
❑464, Jul 1991	1.50
❑465, Jul 1991; Robin	1.50
❑466, Aug 1991; Robin	1.50
❑467, Aug 1991; A: Robin. covers form triptych	1.50
❑468, Sep 1991; A: Robin. covers form triptych	1.50
❑469, Sep 1991; A: Robin. covers form triptych	1.50
❑470, Oct 1991; War of the Gods	1.50
❑471, Nov 1991	1.50
❑472, Dec 1991	1.50
❑473, Jan 1992	1.50
❑474, Feb 1992; Anton Furst's Gotham City	1.50
❑475, Mar 1992 V: Two-Face. V: Scarface. V: Ventriloquist	1.50
❑476, Apr 1992	1.50
❑477, May 1992	1.50
❑478, May 1992	1.50
❑479, Jun 1992	1.50
❑480, Jun 1992 JA (a)	1.50
❑481, Jul 1992 JA (a)	1.50
❑482, Jul 1992 JA (a)	1.50

Other grades: Multiply price above by 5/6 for VF/NM • 2/3 for VERY FINE • 1/3 for FINE • 1/5 for VERY GOOD • 1/8 for GOOD

	N-MINT
❑483, Aug 1992 JA (a)	1.50
❑484, Sep 1992	1.50
❑485, Oct 1992	1.50
❑486, Nov 1992 V: Metalhead	1.50
❑487, Dec 1992	1.25
❑488, Jan 1993; JA (a); Robin trains Azrael	2.50
❑489, Feb 1993 JA (a); 1: Azrael (as Batman). A: Bane	2.50
❑490, Mar 1993; JA (a); Riddler on Venom	2.50
❑491, Apr 1993; JA (a); Knightfall prequel	2.50
❑492, May 1993	2.50
❑492/Silver, May 1993; Silver edition printing	4.50
❑492/2nd, May 1993	2.00
❑493, May 1993 V: Mr. Zsasz	3.00
❑494, Jun 1993 JA (a); V: Scarecrow	2.00
❑495, Jun 1993 JA (a); V: Poison Ivy	2.00
❑496, Jul 1993 JA (a); V: Joker	2.00
❑497, Jul 1993; JA (a); partial overlay outer cover; Bane cripples Batman	3.00
❑497/2nd, Jul 1993; JA (a); 2nd Printing, also has partial overlay; Bane cripples Batman	2.00
❑498, Aug 1993; JA (a); Azrael takes on role of Batman	2.00
❑499, Sep 1993 JA (a)	2.00
❑500, Oct 1993; Giant-size; JA (a); Azrael vs. Bane, with poster	2.00
❑500/CS, Oct 1993; Giant-size; JA (a); diecut; two-level cover; Azrael vs. Bane; Collector's set	4.00
❑501, Nov 1993	2.00
❑502, Dec 1993	2.00
❑503, Jan 1994 A: Catwoman	2.00
❑504, Feb 1994 A: Catwoman	2.00
❑505, Mar 1994	2.00
❑506, Apr 1994	2.00
❑507, May 1994	2.00
❑508, Jun 1994 D: Abattoir	2.00
❑509, Jul 1994	2.00
❑510, Aug 1994	2.00
❑511, Sep 1994; A: Batgirl. Zero Hour, A: Batgirl	2.00
❑512, Nov 1994 MGu, RT (a)	2.00
❑513, Dec 1994 MGu, RT (a)	2.00
❑514, Jan 1995	2.00
❑515, Feb 1995; Return of Bruce Wayne as Batman	2.00
❑515/Variant, Feb 1995; Embossed cover; Return of Bruce Wayne as Batman	4.00
❑516, Mar 1995	2.00
❑517, Apr 1995	2.00
❑518, May 1995 V: Black Mask	2.00
❑519, Jun 1995	2.00
❑520, Jul 1995	2.00
❑521, Aug 1995 V: Killer Croc	2.00
❑522, Sep 1995 V: Killer Croc, Swamp Thing	2.00
❑523, Oct 1995 V: Scarecrow	2.00
❑524, Nov 1995 V: Scarecrow	2.00
❑525, Dec 1995; V: Mr. Freeze. Underworld Unleashed, V: Mr. Freeze	2.00
❑526, Jan 1996	2.00
❑527, Feb 1996 V: Two-Face	2.00
❑528, Mar 1996	2.00
❑529, Apr 1996	2.00
❑530, May 1996; Glow-in-the-dark cover	1.95
❑530/Variant, May 1996; Glow-in-the-dark cover	2.50
❑531, Jun 1996; Glow-in-the-dark cover	1.95
❑531/Variant, Jun 1996; Glow-in-the-dark cover	2.50
❑532, Jul 1996; Glow-in-the-dark cover	1.95
❑532/Variant, Jul 1996; glow-in-the-dark cardstock cover	2.50
❑533, Aug 1996 JA (a)	2.00
❑534, Sep 1996	2.00
❑535, Oct 1996; self-contained story, V: The Ogre and The Ape	2.00
❑535/Variant, Oct 1996; V: The Ogre and The Ape. Die-cut cover; self-contained story	4.00
❑536, Nov 1996; Final Night	2.00
❑537, Dec 1996 A: Man-Bat. V: Man-Bat	2.00
❑538, Jan 1997 A: Man-Bat	2.00
❑539, Feb 1997	2.00

	N-MINT
❑540, Mar 1997 A: Spectre	2.00
❑541, Apr 1997 A: Spectre	2.00
❑542, May 1997	2.00
❑543, Jun 1997	2.00
❑544, Jul 1997 A: Demon	2.00
❑545, Aug 1997 A: Demon	2.00
❑546, Sep 1997 A: Demon	2.00
❑547, Oct 1997; Genesis	2.00
❑548, Nov 1997 V: Penguin	2.00
❑549, Dec 1997; V: Penguin. Face cover	2.00
❑550, Jan 1998 2: Chase	3.00
❑550/Variant, Jan 1998 2: Chase	3.50
❑551, Feb 1998 A: Ragman	2.00
❑552, Mar 1998 A: Ragman	2.00
❑553, Apr 1998; KJ (a); continues in Azrael #40	2.00
❑554, May 1998 KJ (a); V: Quakemaster	2.00
❑555, Jun 1998; V: Ratcatcher. Aftershock	2.00
❑556, Jul 1998; Aftershock	2.00
❑557, Aug 1998; SB (a); A: Ballistic. Aftershock	2.00
❑558, Sep 1998; Aftershock	2.00
❑559, Oct 1998; Aftershock	2.00
❑560, Dec 1998; Road to No Man's Land, Bruce Wayne testifies	2.00
❑561, Jan 1999; JA (a); Road to No Man's Land, Bruce Wayne testifies	2.00
❑562, Feb 1999; JA (a); A: Mayor Grange. Road to No Man's Land, Gotham City is cut off	2.00
❑563, Mar 1999; A: Oracle. V: Joker. No Man's Land	3.00
❑564, Apr 1999; A: Scarecrow. A: Huntress. No Man's Land	2.50
❑565, May 1999; No Man's Land	2.00
❑566, Jun 1999; A: Superman. No Man's Land	2.00
❑567, Jul 1999; No Man's Land	2.00
❑568, Aug 1999; BSz (a); A: Poison Ivy. No Man's Land	2.00
❑569, Sep 1999; No Man's Land	2.00
❑570, Oct 1999; V: Joker. No Man's Land	2.00
❑571, Nov 1999; V: Bane. No Man's Land	2.00
❑572, Dec 1999; No Man's Land	2.00
❑573, Jan 2000; No Man's Land	2.00
❑574, Feb 2000; No Man's Land	2.00
❑575, Mar 2000	2.00
❑576, Apr 2000	2.00
❑577, May 2000	2.00
❑578, Jun 2000	2.00
❑579, Jul 2000	2.00
❑580, Aug 2000 V: Orca	2.25
❑581, Sep 2000 V: Orca	2.25
❑582, Oct 2000	2.25
❑583, Nov 2000	2.25
❑584, Dec 2000	2.25
❑585, Jan 2001	2.25
❑586, Feb 2001	2.25
❑587, Mar 2001	2.25
❑588, Apr 2001	2.25
❑589, May 2001	2.25
❑590, Jun 2001	2.25
❑591, Jul 2001	2.25
❑592, Aug 2001	2.25
❑593, Sep 2001	2.25
❑594, Oct 2001	2.25
❑595, Nov 2001	2.25
❑596, Dec 2001; Joker: Last Laugh crossover	2.25
❑597, Jan 2002	2.25
❑598, Feb 2002	2.25
❑599, Mar 2002	2.25
❑600, Apr 2002; Giant-size anniversary issue	3.95
❑601, May 2002	2.25
❑602, Jun 2002	2.25
❑603, Jul 2002	2.25
❑604, Aug 2002	2.25
❑605, Sep 2002	2.25
❑606, Oct 2002	2.25
❑607, Nov 2002	2.25
❑608, Dec 2002 JPH (w); JLee (a)	5.00
❑608/2nd, Dec 2002	2.25
❑608/Dynamic, Dec 2002; Dynamic Forces signed edition	25.00
❑608/Retailer ed, Dec 2002; Retailer incentive promo (aka RRP edition); alternate cover with no cover price.	500.00

	N-MINT
❑608/NYPost 2005, Distributed in July 13, 2005, N.Y. Post newspapers in conjunction with the release of Batman Begins movie. New Jim Lee cover. Included in Sports Extra and Late City Final editions of The Post in the tri-state area	5.00
❑609, Jan 2003 JPH (w); JLee (a)	4.00
❑610, Feb 2003 JPH (w); JLee (a)	2.25
❑611, Mar 2003 JPH (w); JLee (a)	2.25
❑612, Apr 2003; JPH (w); JLee (a); A: Superman. alternate cover with no cover price	2.25
❑612/2nd, Apr 2003; alternate cover with no cover price	2.25
❑613, May 2003; JPH (w); JLee (a); alternate cover with no cover price	2.25
❑614, Jun 2003	2.25
❑615, Jul 2003	2.25
❑616, Aug 2003	2.25
❑617, Sep 2003	4.00
❑618, Oct 2003	4.00
❑619, Nov 2003, O: Batman	3.00
❑619/2nd, Nov 2003	2.25
❑620, Dec 2003	2.25
❑621, Jan 2004	2.25
❑622, Feb 2004	2.25
❑623, Mar 2004	2.25
❑624, Apr 2004	2.25
❑625, May 2004	2.25
❑626, Jun 2004	2.25
❑627, Jul 2004	2.25
❑628, Jul 2004	2.25
❑629, Aug 2004	2.25
❑630, Sep 2004	2.50
❑631, Oct 2004	2.25
❑632, Nov 2004	2.25
❑633, Dec 2004	2.95
❑634, Jan 2005	6.00
❑635, Feb 2005	15.00
❑636, Mar 2005	12.00
❑637, Apr 2005	12.00
❑638, May 2005	11.00
❑638/2nd, May 2005	6.00
❑639, Jun 2005	16.00
❑640, Jul 2005	6.00
❑641, Aug 2005	6.00
❑642, Sep 2005	3.00
❑643, Sep 2005	3.00
❑644, Oct 2005	2.99
❑645, Nov 2005	2.99
❑646, Dec 2005	2.99
❑647, Jan 2006	2.99
❑648, Feb 2006	2.99
❑649, Mar 2006	2.99
❑650, May 2006	2.99
❑651, Jun 2006	2.99
❑652, Jul 2006	2.99
❑653, Aug 2006	2.99
❑654, Sep 2006	2.99
❑1000000, Nov 1998 SB (a)	4.00
❑Annual 1, ca. 1961 CS (a); O: The Batcave	540.00
❑Annual 1/2nd, ca. 1999; O: The Batcave. cardstock cover; Reprint	5.50
❑Annual 2, ca. 1961	275.00
❑Annual 3, Sum 1962; 80-Page Giant	215.00
❑Annual 4, Win 1963; 80-Page Giant	110.00
❑Annual 5, Sum 1963; 80-Page Giant	110.00
❑Annual 6, Win 1964	85.00
❑Annual 7, Sum 1964	85.00
❑Annual 8 1982 A: Ra's Al Ghul	7.00
❑Annual 9 1985 JOy, PS, AN (a)	6.00
❑Annual 10 1986	6.00
❑Annual 11 1987 AMo (w)	6.00
❑Annual 12 1988	5.00
❑Annual 13 1989; Who's Who entries	5.00
❑Annual 14 1990 O: Two-Face	3.00
❑Annual 15 1991 A: Joker	3.00
❑Annual 15/2nd 1991	2.00
❑Ann 15/Silver/3 1991	4.00
❑Annual 16 1992; A: Joker. Eclipso	3.00
❑Annual 17 1993; 1: Ballistic. Bloodlines: Earthplague	3.00
❑Annual 18 1994; Elseworlds	3.00
❑Annual 19 1995; O: Scarecrow. Year One	4.00
❑Annual 20 1996; Legends of the Dead Earth	3.00

Other grades: Multiply price above by 5/6 for VF/NM • 2/3 for VERY FINE • 1/3 for FINE • 1/5 for VERY GOOD • 1/8 for GOOD

Batman and the Outsiders

Batman team-up series with hard-luck bunch

©DC

Batman: Bane of the Demon

Bane goes on a journey to learn his origins

©DC

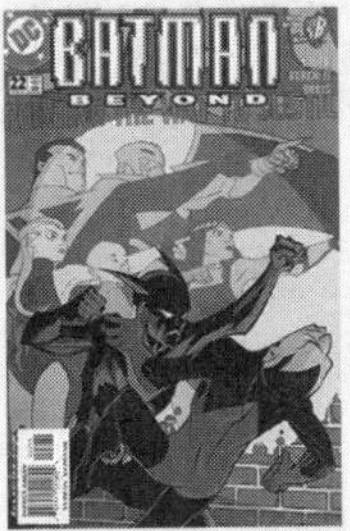
Batman Beyond

Another series kicked off by a cartoon

©DC

Batman Black and White

Anthology series published in black and white

©DC

Batman Chronicles

Quarterly filled "13th week" gap in Bat-titles

©DC

N-MINT

❑Annual 21 1997; Pulp Heroes 3.95
❑Annual 22 1998; Ghosts 2.95
❑Annual 23 1999; JLApe 2.95
❑Annual 24 2000 JA (a); 1: The Boggart 3.50
❑Annual 25 2006 ....
❑Giant Size 1, Aug 1998 KJ, DGry (w); KJ (a) 4.95
❑Giant Size 2, Oct 1999 SB (a) 4.95
❑Giant Size 3, Jul 2000 BSz, JSa (a) .. 5.95

BATMAN ADVENTURES
DC

❑1, Oct 1992; A: Penguin. based on animated series, V: Penguin........... 3.00
❑1/Silver, Oct 1992; silver edition 4.00
❑2, Nov 1992 A: Catwoman. V: Catwoman 2.00
❑3, Dec 1992 A: Joker. V: Joker.......... 2.00
❑4, Jan 1993; Robin 2.00
❑5, Feb 1993 A: Scarecrow. V: Scarecrow 2.00
❑6, Mar 1993 .... 2.00
❑7, Apr 1993 V: Killer Croc 2.00
❑7/CS, Apr 1993; trading card, V: Killer Croc 3.00
❑8, May 1993 .... 2.00
❑9, Jun 1993 .... 2.00
❑10, Jul 1993 V: Riddler 2.00
❑11, Aug 1993 V: Man-Bat 1.50
❑12, Sep 1993; Batgirl 1.50
❑13, Oct 1993 .... 1.50
❑14, Nov 1993; Robin 1.50
❑15, Dec 1993 .... 1.50
❑16, Jan 1994 A: Joker. V: Joker 1.50
❑17, Feb 1994 .... 1.50
❑18, Mar 1994; Batgirl-Robin 1.50
❑19, Apr 1994 V: Scarecrow 1.50
❑20, May 1994 .... 1.50
❑21, Jun 1994; Holiday special A: Catwoman. V: Man-Bat. V: Mr. Freeze 1.50
❑22, Jul 1994 V: Two-Face 1.50
❑23, Aug 1994 V: Poison Ivy 1.50
❑24, Sep 1994 .... 1.50
❑25, Nov 1994; Giant-size A: Lex Luthor. A: Superman 2.50
❑26, Nov 1994 A: Batgirl 1.50
❑27, Dec 1994 .... 1.50
❑28, Jan 1995 A: Harley Quinn 1.50
❑29, Feb 1995 V: Ra's Al Ghul 1.50
❑30, Mar 1995 O: The Perfesser. O: Mister Nice. O: Mastermind (DC) 1.50
❑31, Apr 1995 .... 1.50
❑32, Jun 1995 .... 1.50
❑33, Jul 1995 .... 1.75
❑34, Aug 1995 : . A: Catwoman. V: Hugo Strange 1.75
❑35, Sep 1995 : . A: Catwoman. V: Hugo Strange 1.75
❑36, Oct 1995 : . A: Catwoman. V: Hugo Strange 1.75
❑Annual 1 1994 DDC, KJ (a) 2.95
❑Annual 2 1995 A: The Demon 3.50

BATMAN ADVENTURES (VOL. 2)
DC

❑1, Apr 2003 .... 2.25
❑2, May 2003 .... 2.25
❑3, Jun 2003 .... 2.25

N-MINT

❑4, Jul 2003 .... 2.25
❑5, Aug 2003 .... 2.25
❑6, Sep 2003 .... 2.25
❑7, Oct 2003 .... 2.25
❑8, Nov 2003 .... 2.25
❑9, Dec 2003 .... 2.25
❑10, Jan 2004 .... 2.25
❑11, Apr 2004 .... 2.25
❑12, May 2004 .... 2.25
❑13, Jun 2004 .... 2.25
❑14, Jul 2004 .... 2.25
❑15, Aug 2004 .... 2.25
❑16, Sep 2004 .... 2.25
❑17, Oct 2004 .... 2.25

BATMAN ADVENTURES, THE: MAD LOVE
DC

❑1, Feb 1994 O: Harley Quinn. A: Joker 7.50
❑1/2nd 1994; prestige format O: Harley Quinn. A: Joker 5.50

BATMAN ADVENTURES, THE: THE LOST YEARS
DC

❑1, Jan 1998, fills in time between first and second Batman animated series 2.00
❑2, Feb 1998, A: Robin II 2.00
❑3, Mar 1998, V: Two-Face 2.00
❑4, Apr 1998 .... 2.00
❑5, May 1998, A: Nightwing 2.00

BATMAN/ALIENS
DARK HORSE

❑1, Mar 1997; prestige format; BWr (a); crossover with DC 5.00
❑2, Apr 1997; prestige format; BWr (a); crossover with DC 5.00

BATMAN/ALIENS II
DC-DARK HORSE

❑1 2003 .... 5.95
❑2 2003 .... 5.95
❑3 2003 .... 5.95

BATMAN ALLIES SECRET FILES 2005
DC

❑0, Jul 2005 .... 4.99

BATMAN: A LONELY PLACE OF DYING
DC

❑Book 1, Sep 1990 .... 5.00

BATMAN AND OTHER DC CLASSICS
DC

❑1, ca. 1989, FM (c); KG (w); GP, BB, FM (a); O: Batman. Includes guide to collecting comics by Don & Maggie Thompson 2.00

BATMAN AND ROBIN ADVENTURES
DC

❑1, Nov 1995 .... 3.00
❑2, Dec 1995 V: Two-Face 2.00
❑3, Jan 1996 V: Riddler 2.00
❑4, Feb 1996 V: Penguin 2.00
❑5, Mar 1996 V: Joker 2.00
❑6, May 1996 .... 1.75
❑7, Jun 1996 V: Scarface 1.75
❑8, Jul 1996; Robin is enslaved by Poison Ivy 1.75

N-MINT

❑9, Aug 1996; Batgirl versus Talia 1.75
❑10, Sep 1996 V: Ra's Al Ghul 1.75
❑11, Oct 1996 .... 1.75
❑12, Nov 1996 V: Bane 1.75
❑13, Dec 1996 V: Scarecrow 1.75
❑14, Jan 1997 .... 1.75
❑15, Feb 1997 A: Deadman 1.75
❑16, Mar 1997 A: Catwoman 1.75
❑17, Apr 1997 .... 1.75
❑18, May 1997 V: Joker 1.75
❑19, Jun 1997 .... 1.75
❑20, Jul 1997 .... 1.75
❑21, Aug 1997; JSa (a); Batgirl vs. Riddler 1.75
❑22, Sep 1997 V: Two-Face 1.75
❑23, Oct 1997 V: Killer Croc 1.75
❑24, Nov 1997 V: Poison Ivy 1.75
❑25, Dec 1997; Giant-size; V: Ra's Al Ghul. Face cover 2.95
❑Annual 1, Nov 1996; sequel to Batman: Mask of the Phantasm 4.00
❑Annual 2, Nov 1997; JSa (a); A: Zatara. A: Zatanna. ties in with Adventures in the DC Universe Annual #1 and Superman Adventures Annual #1 ... 3.95

BATMAN AND ROBIN ADVENTURES, THE: SUB-ZERO
DC

❑1 1998, cover says 98; adapts direct-to-video movie; indicia says 97 .... 3.95

BATMAN AND ROBIN: THE OFFICIAL ADAPTATION OF THE WARNER BROS. MOTION PICTURE
DC

❑1, ca. 1997; prestige format 5.95

BATMAN & SUPERMAN ADVENTURES: WORLD'S FINEST
DC

❑1 1997; prestige format; adapts 90-minute special 6.95

BATMAN AND SUPERMAN: WORLD'S FINEST
DC

❑1, Apr 1999; prestige format 2.50
❑1/Autographed 18.95
❑2, May 1999 .... 2.00
❑3, Jun 1999 V: Joker 2.00
❑4, Jul 1999 .... 2.00
❑5, Aug 1999 A: Batgirl 2.00
❑6, Sep 1999 A: Bat-Mite. A: Mr. Mxyzptlk 2.00
❑7, Oct 1999 .... 2.00
❑8, Nov 1999 .... 2.00
❑9, Dec 1999 .... 2.00
❑10, Jan 2000 .... 2.00

BATMAN AND THE MONSTER MEN
DC

❑1, Jan 2006 .... 3.99
❑2, Jan 2006 .... 3.99
❑3, Feb 2006 .... 3.99
❑4, Mar 2006 .... 3.99
❑5, May 2006 .... 3.99
❑6, Jun 2006 .... 3.99

BATMAN AND THE OUTSIDERS
DC

❑1, Aug 1983, O: Geo-Force. 1: Baron Bedlam 3.00
❑2, Sep 1983, JA (a); V: Baron Bedlam 2.00
❑3, Oct 1983, JA (a); V: Agent Orange 2.00
❑4, Nov 1983, JA (a) 2.00
❑5, Dec 1983 JA (a); A: New Teen Titans 2.00
❑6, Jan 1984 1.50
❑7, Feb 1984 1.50
❑8, Mar 1984 1.50
❑9, Apr 1984 1: Masters of Disaster 1.50
❑10, May 1984 V: Masters of Disaster 1.50
❑11, Jun 1984 O: Katana 1.50
❑12, Jul 1984 O: Katana 1.50
❑13, Aug 1984 1.50
❑14, Oct 1984 V: Maxie Zeus 1.50
❑15, Nov 1984 V: Maxie Zeus 1.50
❑16, Dec 1984 1.50
❑17, Jan 1985 1.50
❑18, Feb 1985 1.50
❑19, Mar 1985 1.50
❑20, Apr 1985 1: Syonide II 1.50
❑21, May 1985 1.50
❑22, Jun 1985 1.50
❑23, Jul 1985 1.50
❑24, Aug 1985 1.50
❑25, Sep 1985 1.50
❑26, Oct 1985 V: Kobra 1.50
❑27, Nov 1985 1.50
❑28, Dec 1985 1.50
❑29, Jan 1986 1.50
❑30, Feb 1986 1.50
❑31, Mar 1986 1.50
❑32, Apr 1986; Series continues as Adventures of the Outsiders; Batman leaves 1.50
❑Annual 1, ca. 1984 FM (c); FM (a); 1: Force of July. 1: Major Victory 3.00
❑Annual 2, ca. 1985; JA (a); Wedding of Metamorpho and Sapphire Stag 2.00

BATMAN: ARKHAM ASYLUM - TALES OF MADNESS
DC

❑1, May 1998 2.95

BATMAN: ARROW, RING AND BAT
DC

❑1, ca. 2003 19.95

BATMAN: A WORD TO THE WISE
DC

❑1; (DC giveaway) 1.25

BATMAN: BANE
DC

❑1, Jul 1997; prestige format one-shot, cover is part of quadtych 4.95

BATMAN: BANE OF THE DEMON
DC

❑1, Mar 1998 1.95
❑2, Apr 1998 1.95
❑3, May 1998 1.95
❑4, Jun 1998 1.95

BATMAN: BATGIRL
DC

❑1, Jul 1997; prestige format one-shot; cover is part of quadtych 4.95

BATMAN: BATGIRL (GIRLFRENZY)
DC

❑1, Jun 1998; Girlfrenzy; one-shot, V: Mr. Zsasz 1.95

BATMAN BEGINS MOVIE ADAPTATION
DC

❑0 2005 6.99

BATMAN BEYOND (MINI-SERIES)
DC

❑1, Mar 1999; O: Batman II (Terry McGuiness). adapts first episode 2.50
❑2, Apr 1999; O: Batman II (Terry McGuiness). A: Derek Powers. adapts first episode 2.00
❑3, May 1999 V: Blight 2.00
❑4, Jun 1999 JSa (a); A: Demon 2.00
❑5, Jul 1999 2.00
❑6, Aug 1999 JSa (a) 2.00

BATMAN BEYOND
DC

❑1, Nov 1999; adapts first episode 2.50
❑2, Dec 1999; adapts first episode 2.00
❑3, Jan 2000 V: Blight 2.00
❑4, Feb 2000 A: Demon 1.99
❑5, Mar 2000 1.99
❑6, Apr 2000 1.99
❑7, May 2000 1.99
❑8, Jun 2000 1.99
❑9, Jul 2000 1.99
❑10, Aug 2000 V: Golem 1.99
❑11, Sep 2000 1.99
❑12, Oct 2000 V: Terminal 1.99
❑13, Nov 2000 A: Scarecrow. A: Batgirl 1.99
❑14, Dec 2000 A: Demon 1.99
❑15, Jan 2001 1.99
❑16, Feb 2001 1.99
❑17, Mar 2001 1.99
❑18, Apr 2001 1.99
❑19, May 2001 1.99
❑20, Jun 2001 1.99
❑21, Jul 2001 1.99
❑22, Aug 2001 1.99
❑23, Sep 2001 1.99
❑24, Oct 2001 1.99

BATMAN BEYOND: RETURN OF THE JOKER
DC

❑1, Feb 2001 2.95

BATMAN BEYOND SPECIAL ORIGIN ISSUE
DC

❑1, Jun 1999, Free 1.00

BATMAN BLACK AND WHITE
DC

❑1, Jun 1996, b&w JLee (c); HC, JKu (a) 3.50
❑2, Jul 1996, b&w FM (c) 3.00
❑3, Aug 1996, b&w MW, BSz, KJ (a) 3.00
❑4, Sep 1996, b&w ATh (c) 3.00

BATMAN: BLACKGATE
DC

❑1, Jan 1997 3.95

BATMAN: BLACKGATE, ISLE OF MEN
DC

❑1, Apr 1998; one-shot, continues in Batman: Shadow of the Bat #74 2.95

BATMAN: BLIND JUSTICE
DC

❑Book 1; Reprints 7.50

BATMAN: BOOK OF THE DEAD
DC

❑1, Jun 1999 4.95
❑2, Jul 1999 4.95

BATMAN: BULLOCK'S LAW
DC

❑1, Aug 1999 4.95

BATMAN/CAPTAIN AMERICA
DC

❑1 1996; prestige format crossover with Marvel, Elseworlds; prestige format crossover with Marvel; Elseworlds 5.95

BATMAN: CASTLE OF THE BAT
DC

❑1 1994; prestige format; Elseworlds 5.95

BATMAN: CATWOMAN DEFIANT
DC

❑1, ca. 1992; prestige format; cover forms diptych with Batman: Penguin Triumphant 5.00

BATMAN/CATWOMAN: TRAIL OF THE GUN
DC

❑1, Oct 2004 5.95
❑2, Nov 2004 5.95

BATMAN CHRONICLES
DC

❑1, Jun 1995; Giant-size BSz (a) 4.00
❑2, Sep 1995 3.50
❑3, Dec 1995 BB (c); BSz (a); O: Mr. Zsasz. A: Riddler. A: Killer Croc 3.50
❑4, Mar 1996 A: Hitman 4.00
❑5, Jun 1996 HC (c); O: Oracle 3.50
❑6, Sep 1996 CS (a) 3.50
❑7, Dec 1996 JO (c); JA (a); A: Superman 3.50
❑8, Mar 1997 SB (a); V: Ra's Al Ghul 3.50
❑9, Jun 1997; Movie poster cover 3.50
❑10, Sep 1997 BSz (a) 3.50
❑11, Dec 1997 3.50
❑12, Mar 1998 BSz, KJ (a) 3.50
❑13, Jun 1998 SB, DG (a) 3.00
❑14, Sep 1998; Aftershock 3.00
❑15, Dec 1998; A: Man-Bat. A: Green Lantern. A: Question. A: Oracle. team-up issue 3.00
❑16, Mar 1999; A: Renee Montoya. A: Batgirl. A: Two Face. No Man's Land 3.00
❑17, Jun 1999; BSz (a); No Man's Land; Man-Bat's child 3.00
❑18, Sep 1999; DGry (w); No Man's Land 3.00
❑19, Dec 1999 3.00
❑20, Mar 2000 DGry (w) 3.00
❑21, Jun 2000 2.95
❑22, Sep 2000 2.95
❑23, Dec 2000 KN (w); KN (a) 2.95

BATMAN CHRONICLES GALLERY
DC

❑1, May 1997; pin-ups 3.50

BATMAN CHRONICLES: THE GAUNTLET
DC

❑1 1997, prestige format; 1st Robin solo adventure 4.95

BATMAN: CITY OF LIGHT
DC

❑1, Dec 2003 2.95
❑2, Jan 2004 2.95
❑3, Feb 2004 2.95
❑4, Mar 2004 2.95
❑5, Apr 2004 2.95
❑6, May 2004 2.95
❑7, Jun 2004 2.95
❑8, Jul 2004 2.95

BATMAN/DANGER GIRL
DC

❑1 2005 4.95

BATMAN/DAREDEVIL
DC

❑1 2000 5.95

BATMAN: DARK ALLEGIANCES
DC

❑1 1996 5.95

BATMAN: DARK DETECTIVE
DC

❑1, Jun 2005 2.99
❑2 2005 2.99
❑3 2005 2.99
❑4 2005 2.99
❑5 2005 2.99
❑6, Sep 2005 2.99

BATMAN: DARK JOKER: THE WILD
DC

❑Book 1; Elseworlds story 9.95
❑Book 1/HC; hardcover 24.95

BATMAN: THE DARK KNIGHT ADVENTURES
DC

❑1 7.95

BATMAN: DARK KNIGHT GALLERY
DC

❑1, Jan 1996, pin-ups 3.50

BATMAN: DARK KNIGHT OF THE ROUND TABLE
DC

❑1, ca. 1999; prestige format; Elseworlds story 4.95
❑2, ca. 1999; prestige format; Elseworlds story 4.95

BATMAN: DARK VICTORY
DC

❑0, ca. 1999; Wizard giveaway 1.00
❑1, Dec 1999; prestige format 5.00
❑2, Jan 2000; cardstock cover 3.00
❑3, Feb 2000; cardstock cover 3.00
❑4, Mar 2000; cardstock cover 3.00
❑5, Apr 2000; cardstock cover 3.00
❑6, May 2000; cardstock cover 3.00
❑7, Jun 2000; cardstock cover 3.00
❑8, Jul 2000; cardstock cover 3.00

Batman: Dark Victory

Sequel to Batman: The Long Halloween

©DC

Batman Family

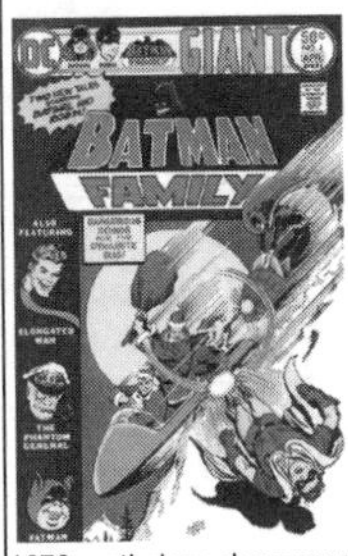

1970s anthology showcased Batgirl and Robin

©DC

Batman: Gotham Adventures

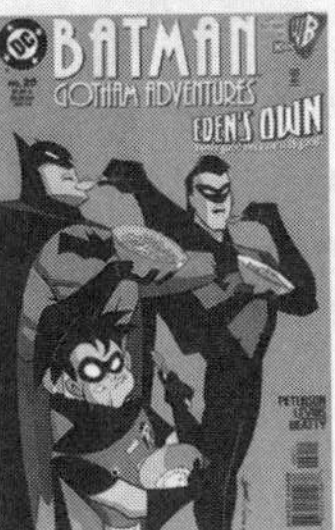

Another series in the "animated" DC universe

©DC

Batman: Gotham By Gaslight

Notable as the first DC "Elseworlds" story

©DC

Batman: Gotham Knights

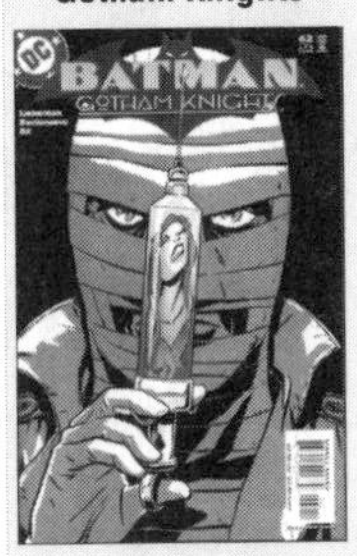

Spotlights members of the Batman family

©DC

N-MINT

❑9, Aug 2000; cardstock cover........... 3.00
❑10, Sep 2000; cardstock cover......... 3.00
❑11, Oct 2000; cardstock cover.......... 3.00
❑12, Nov 2000; cardstock cover......... 3.00
❑13, Dec 2000; prestige format.......... 3.00

BATMAN: DAY OF JUDGMENT
DC

❑1, Nov 1999...................................... 3.95

BATMAN: DEATH AND THE MAIDENS
DC

❑1, Oct 2003...................................... 2.95
❑2, Nov 2003...................................... 2.95
❑3, Dec 2003...................................... 2.95
❑4, Jan 2004...................................... 2.95
❑5, Feb 2004...................................... 2.95
❑6, Mar 2004...................................... 2.95
❑7, Apr 2004...................................... 2.95
❑8, Jun 2004...................................... 2.95
❑9, Jun 2004...................................... 2.95

BATMAN/DEATHBLOW: AFTER THE FIRE
DC

❑1, May 2002...................................... 5.95
❑2, Jun 2002...................................... 5.95
❑3, Oct 2002...................................... 5.95

BATMAN: DEATH OF INNOCENTS
DC

❑1, Dec 1996, one-shot about the dangers of landmines and unexploded ordnance...................... 3.95

BATMAN/DEMON
DC

❑1 1996; prestige format one-shot..... 4.95

BATMAN/DEMON: A TRAGEDY
DC

❑1 2000.. 5.95

BATMAN: DOA
DC

❑1, Jan 2000...................................... 6.95

BATMAN: DREAMLAND
DC

❑1, Jul 2000....................................... 5.95

BATMAN: EGO
DC

❑1, Oct 2000....................................... 6.95

BATMAN FAMILY
DC

❑1, Oct 1975...................................... 14.00
❑2, Dec 1975...................................... 10.00
❑3, Feb 1976...................................... 8.00
❑4, Apr 1976, CI (a); A: Fatman.......... 8.00
❑5, Jun 1976...................................... 8.00
❑6, Aug 1976...................................... 8.00
❑7, Sep 1976...................................... 6.00
❑8, Nov 1976...................................... 6.00
❑9, Jan 1977, A: Duela Dent............... 7.00
❑10, Mar 1977.................................... 7.00
❑11, May 1977.................................... 7.00
❑12, Jul 1977...................................... 7.00
❑13, Sep 1977, A: Man-Bat. V: Outsider. 5.00
❑14, Oct 1977..................................... 5.00
❑15, Dec 1977..................................... 5.00
❑16, Feb 1978..................................... 5.00
❑17, Apr 1978..................................... 7.00
❑18, Jun 1978..................................... 7.00
❑19, Aug 1978..................................... 7.00
❑20, Oct 1978..................................... 7.00

BATMAN: FAMILY
DC

❑1, Dec 2002...................................... 2.95
❑2, Jan 2003...................................... 2.95
❑3, Jan 2003...................................... 2.95
❑4, Jan 2003...................................... 2.95
❑5, Jan 2003...................................... 2.95
❑6, Feb 2003...................................... 2.95
❑7, Feb 2003...................................... 2.95
❑8, Feb 2003...................................... 2.95

BATMAN FOREVER: THE OFFICIAL COMIC ADAPTATION OF THE WARNER BROS. MOTION PICTURE
DC

❑1 1995.. 3.95
❑1/Prestige; movie adaptation, prestige format............................ 5.95

BATMAN: FULL CIRCLE
DC

❑1, ca. 1991, b&w; prestige format.... 6.00

BATMAN GALLERY
DC

❑1.. 2.95

BATMAN: GCPD
DC

❑1, Aug 1996...................................... 2.25
❑2, Sep 1996...................................... 2.25
❑3, Oct 1996...................................... 2.25
❑4, Nov 1996...................................... 2.25

BATMAN: GHOSTS
DC

❑1 1995; prestige format one-shot 4.95

BATMAN: GORDON OF GOTHAM
DC

❑1, Jun 1998...................................... 1.95
❑2, Jul 1998....................................... 1.95
❑3, Aug 1998...................................... 1.95
❑4, Sep 1998...................................... 1.95

BATMAN: GORDON'S LAW
DC

❑1, Dec 1996...................................... 1.95
❑2, Jan 1997...................................... 1.95
❑3, Feb 1997...................................... 1.95
❑4, Mar 1997...................................... 1.95

BATMAN: GOTHAM ADVENTURES
DC

❑1, Jun 1998; based on animated series, Joker has a price on his head 3.00
❑2, Jul 1998 V: Two-Face.................. 2.50
❑3, Aug 1998; cover is toy package mock-up.. 2.50
❑4, Sep 1998 V: Catwoman................ 2.50
❑5, Oct 1998...................................... 2.50
❑6, Nov 1998 A: Deadman.................. 2.50
❑7, Dec 1998...................................... 2.50
❑8, Jan 1999 1: Hunchback. A: Batgirl. 2.50
❑9, Feb 1999 A: League of Assassins. A: Batgirl. V: Sensei........................ 2.50
❑10, Mar 1999 A: Joker. A: Nightwing. A: Harley Quinn. A: Robin III (Timothy Drake)............................ 2.50
❑11, Apr 1999 A: Riddler. V: Riddler... 2.00
❑12, May 1999 V: Two-Face.............. 2.00
❑13, Jun 1999.................................... 2.00
❑14, Jul 1999 V: Harley Quinn............ 2.00
❑15, Aug 1999 A: Bane. V: Venom..... 2.00
❑16, Sep 1999; Alfred is kidnapped.... 2.00
❑17, Oct 1999.................................... 2.00
❑18, Nov 1999 A: Man-Bat................ 2.00
❑19, Dec 1999.................................... 2.00
❑20, Jan 2000.................................... 2.00
❑21, Feb 2000.................................... 2.00
❑22, Mar 2000.................................... 2.00
❑23, Apr 2000.................................... 2.00
❑24, May 2000.................................... 2.00
❑25, Jun 2000.................................... 2.00
❑26, Jul 2000..................................... 2.00
❑27, Aug 2000.................................... 2.00
❑28, Sep 2000.................................... 2.00
❑29, Oct 2000 JSa (a)........................ 2.00
❑30, Nov 2000.................................... 2.00
❑31, Dec 2000 A: Joker...................... 2.00
❑32, Jan 2001.................................... 2.00
❑33, Feb 2001.................................... 2.00
❑34, Mar 2001.................................... 2.00
❑35, Apr 2001.................................... 2.00
❑36, May 2001.................................... 2.00
❑37, Jun 2001 A: Joker....................... 2.00
❑38, Jul 2001..................................... 2.00
❑39, Aug 2001.................................... 2.00
❑40, Sep 2001.................................... 2.00
❑41, Oct 2001.................................... 2.00
❑42, Nov 2001.................................... 2.00
❑43, Dec 2001.................................... 2.00
❑44, Jan 2002 A: Two-Face................ 2.00
❑45, Feb 2002.................................... 2.00
❑46, Mar 2002.................................... 2.00
❑47, Apr 2002.................................... 2.00
❑48, May 2002.................................... 2.00
❑49, Jun 2002.................................... 2.00
❑50, Jul 2002..................................... 2.00
❑51, Aug 2002.................................... 2.00
❑52, Sep 2002.................................... 2.00
❑53, Oct 2002.................................... 2.25
❑54, Nov 2002.................................... 2.25
❑55, Dec 2002.................................... 2.25
❑56, Jan 2003.................................... 2.25
❑57, Feb 2003.................................... 2.25
❑58, Mar 2003.................................... 2.25
❑59, Apr 2003.................................... 2.25
❑60, May 2003.................................... 2.25

BATMAN: GOTHAM BY GASLIGHT
DC

❑1, ca. 1989; prestige format; CR (a); first Elseworlds story; Victorian-era Batman; Prelude by Robert Bloch... 4.00

BATMAN GOTHAM CITY SECRET FILES
DC

❑1, Apr 2000...................................... 4.95

Other grades: Multiply price above by 5/6 for VF/NM • 2/3 for VERY FINE • 1/3 for FINE • 1/5 for VERY GOOD • 1/8 for GOOD

N-MINT

BATMAN: GOTHAM COUNTY LINE
DC

❑1 2005 ... 3.95
❑2, Jan 2006 ... 3.95
❑3, Feb 2006 ... 3.95

BATMAN: GOTHAM KNIGHTS
DC

❑1, Mar 2000 ... 4.00
❑2, Apr 2000 DGry (w) ... 2.50
❑3, May 2000 DGry (w) ... 2.50
❑4, Jun 2000 ... 2.50
❑5, Jul 2000 ... 2.50
❑6, Aug 2000 ... 2.50
❑7, Sep 2000 DGry (w) ... 2.50
❑8, Oct 2000 DGry (w) ... 2.50
❑9, Nov 2000 DGry (w) ... 2.50
❑10, Dec 2000 DGry (w) ... 2.50
❑11, Jan 2001 DGry (w) ... 2.50
❑12, Feb 2001 ... 2.50
❑13, Mar 2001 ... 2.50
❑14, Apr 2001 DGry (w) ... 2.50
❑15, May 2001 DGry (w) ... 2.50
❑16, Jun 2001 ... 2.50
❑17, Jul 2001 ... 2.50
❑18, Aug 2001 ... 2.50
❑19, Sep 2001 ... 2.50
❑20, Oct 2001 ... 2.50
❑21, Nov 2001 ... 2.50
❑22, Dec 2001; Joker: Last Laugh crossover ... 2.50
❑23, Jan 2002 A: Scarecrow. ... 2.50
❑24, Feb 2002 ... 2.50
❑25, Mar 2002 ... 2.50
❑26, Apr 2002 ... 2.50
❑27, May 2002 ... 2.50
❑28, Jun 2002 ... 2.50
❑29, Jul 2002 ... 2.50
❑30, Aug 2002 ... 2.50
❑31, Sep 2002 ... 2.50
❑32, Oct 2002 ... 2.75
❑33, Nov 2002 ... 2.75
❑34, Dec 2002 ... 2.75
❑35, Jan 2003 ... 2.75
❑36, Feb 2003 ... 2.75
❑37, Mar 2003 ... 2.75
❑38, Apr 2003 ... 2.75
❑39, May 2003 ... 2.75
❑40, Jun 2003 ... 2.75
❑41, Jul 2003 ... 2.75
❑42, Aug 2003 ... 2.75
❑43, Sep 2003 ... 2.75
❑44, Oct 2003 ... 2.75
❑45, Nov 2003 ... 2.75
❑46, Dec 2003 ... 2.75
❑47, Jan 2004 ... 2.75
❑48, Feb 2004 ... 2.75
❑49, Mar 2004 ... 2.75
❑50, Apr 2004 ... 2.75
❑51, May 2004 ... 2.75
❑52, Jun 2004 ... 2.75
❑52/2nd, Jul 2004, 2nd printing ... 2.95
❑53, Jul 2004 ... 2.95
❑54, Aug 2004 ... 2.95
❑55, Sep 2004 ... 3.75
❑56, Oct 2004 ... 2.50
❑57, Nov 2004 ... 2.95
❑58, Jan 2005 ... 2.50
❑59, Feb 2005 ... 2.50
❑60, Mar 2005 ... 2.50
❑61, Apr 2005 ... 2.50
❑62, May 2005 ... 2.50
❑63, Jun 2005 ... 2.50
❑64, Jul 2005 ... 2.50
❑65 2005 ... 2.50
❑66, Aug 2005 ... 2.50
❑67, Sep 2005 ... 2.50
❑68, Oct 2005 ... 2.50
❑69, Nov 2005 ... 2.50
❑70, Dec 2005 ... 2.50
❑71, Jan 2006 ... 2.50
❑72, Feb 2006 ... 2.50
❑73, Mar 2006 ... 2.50
❑74, Apr 2006 ... 2.50

BATMAN: GOTHAM NOIR
DC

❑1, May 2001; Elseworlds ... 6.95

N-MINT

BATMAN/GREEN ARROW: THE POISON TOMORROW
DC

❑1 1992; prestige format ... 6.00

BATMAN/GRENDEL (1ST SERIES)
DC / COMICO

❑1, ca. 1993; prestige format MW (a) ... 6.00
❑2, ca. 1993; MW (a); Index title: Grendel/Batman: Devil's Masque; prestige format, cover indicates Grendel/Batman ... 6.00

BATMAN/GRENDEL (2ND SERIES)
DC / DARK HORSE

❑1, Jun 1996; Batman/Grendel: Devil's Bones; prestige format crossover with Dark Horse; concludes in Grendel/Batman: Devil's Dance ... 5.00
❑2, Jul 1996; prestige format; MW (w); MW (a); Grendel/Batman: Devil's Dance; continued from Batman/Grendel: Devil's Bones ... 5.00

BATMAN: HARLEY & IVY
DC / WILDSTORM

❑1, Jun 2004 ... 2.50
❑2, Jul 2004 ... 2.50
❑3, Aug 2004 ... 2.50

BATMAN: HARLEY QUINN
DC

❑1, ca. 1999; prestige format ARo (c); ARo (a) ... 12.00
❑1/2nd, ca. 1999 ARo (c); ARo (a) ... 6.00

BATMAN: HAUNTED GOTHAM
DC

❑1 2000; prestige format; Elseworlds 4.95
❑2 2000; prestige format; Elseworlds 4.95
❑3 2000; prestige format; Elseworlds 4.95
❑4 2000; prestige format; Elseworlds 4.95

BATMAN/HELLBOY/STARMAN
DC / DARK HORSE

❑1, Jan 1999 ... 3.00
❑1/Autographed, Jan 1999 ... 10.00
❑2, Feb 1999 ... 3.00

BATMAN: HOLLYWOOD KNIGHT
DC

❑1, Apr 2001; Elseworlds ... 2.50
❑2, May 2001; Elseworlds ... 2.50
❑3, Jun 2001; Elseworlds ... 2.50

BATMAN: HOLY TERROR
DC

❑1, Oct 1991; prestige format; Elseworlds ... 5.00

BATMAN/HOUDINI: THE DEVIL'S WORKSHOP
DC

❑1; prestige format; Elseworlds ... 4.50

BATMAN/HUNTRESS: CRY FOR BLOOD
DC

❑1, Jun 2000 ... 2.50
❑2, Jul 2000 ... 2.50
❑3, Aug 2000 ... 2.50
❑4, Sep 2000 ... 2.50
❑5, Oct 2000 ... 2.50
❑6, Nov 2000 ... 2.50

BATMAN: HUSH DOUBLE FEATURE
DC

❑1 2003; Reprints Batman #608-609. 4.95

BATMAN: I, JOKER
DC

❑1, Oct 1998; prestige format; Elseworlds ... 4.95

BATMAN: IN DARKEST KNIGHT
DC

❑1, ca. 1994, prestige format; Elseworlds; Bruce Wayne as Green Lantern ... 4.95

BATMAN: JEKYLL AND HYDE
DC

❑1, Jun 2005 ... 2.99
❑2, Jul 2005 ... 2.99
❑3, Aug 2005 ... 2.99
❑4, Sep 2005 ... 2.99
❑5, Oct 2005 ...

BATMAN: JOKER'S APPRENTICE
DC

❑1, May 1999 ... 3.95

N-MINT

BATMAN: JOKER TIME
DC

❑1, ca. 2000; prestige format ... 4.95
❑2, ca. 2000; prestige format ... 4.95
❑3, ca. 2000; prestige format ... 4.95

BATMAN: JOURNEY INTO KNIGHT
DC

❑1, Oct 2005 ... 2.50
❑2 2005 ... 2.50
❑3, Dec 2005 ... 2.50
❑4, Jan 2006 ... 2.50
❑5, Feb 2006 ... 2.50
❑6, Mar 2006 ... 2.50
❑7, May 2006 ... 2.50
❑8, Jun 2006 ... 2.50
❑9, Jul 2006 ... 2.50
❑10, Aug 2006 ... 2.50

BATMAN/JUDGE DREDD: DIE LAUGHING
DC

❑1; prestige format; Joker in Mega-City One ... 4.95
❑2; prestige format; Joker in Mega-City One ... 4.95

BATMAN/JUDGE DREDD: JUDGMENT ON GOTHAM
DC

❑1 ... 5.95

BATMAN/JUDGE DREDD: THE ULTIMATE RIDDLE
DC

❑1; prestige format ... 5.00

BATMAN/JUDGE DREDD: VENDETTA IN GOTHAM
DC

❑1 1993 ... 6.00

BATMAN: LEAGUE OF BATMEN
DC

❑1, Jun 2001 ... 5.95
❑2, Jul 2001 ... 5.95

BATMAN: LEGENDS OF THE DARK KNIGHT
DC

❑1, Nov 1989; Outer cover comes in four different colors (yellow, blue, orange, pink); poster ... 3.00
❑2, Dec 1989 ... 2.75
❑3, Jan 1990 ... 2.75
❑4, Feb 1990 ... 2.75
❑5, Mar 1990 ... 2.75
❑6, Apr 1990 KJ (a) ... 2.50
❑7, May 1990 KJ (a) ... 2.50
❑8, Jun 1990 KJ (a) ... 2.50
❑9, Jul 1990 KJ (a) ... 2.50
❑10, Aug 1990 KJ (a) ... 2.50
❑11, Sep 1990 PG (c); PG, TD (a) ... 2.50
❑12, Oct 1990 PG (c); PG, TD (a) ... 2.50
❑13, Nov 1990 PG (c); PG, TD (a) ... 2.50
❑14, Dec 1990 PG (c); PG, TD (a) ... 2.50
❑15, Feb 1991 PG (c); PG, TD (a) ... 2.50
❑16, Mar 1991; TVE (a); Tie-in to Bane/KnightsEnd ... 3.50
❑17, Apr 1991; TVE (a); Tie-in to Bane/KnightsEnd ... 2.50
❑18, May 1991; TVE (a); Tie-in to Bane/KnightsEnd ... 2.50
❑19, Jun 1991; TVE (a); Tie-in to Bane/KnightsEnd ... 2.50
❑20, Jul 1991; TVE (a); Tie-in to Bane/KnightsEnd ... 2.50
❑21, Aug 1991 (a) ... 2.00
❑22, Sep 1991 (a) ... 2.00
❑23, Oct 1991 (a) ... 2.00
❑24, Nov 1991 HC (w); GK (a) ... 2.00
❑25, Dec 1991 HC (w); GK (a) ... 2.00
❑26, Jan 1992 HC (w); GK (a) ... 2.00
❑27, Feb 1992; Gotham City Visions by Anton Furst feature ... 2.50
❑28, Mar 1992; MW (a); Two-Face ... 2.00
❑29, Apr 1992; MW (a); Two-Face ... 2.00
❑30, May 1992; MW (a); Two-Face ... 2.00
❑31, Jun 1992 BA (a) ... 2.00
❑32, Jun 1992 JRo (w) ... 2.00
❑33, Jul 1992 JRo (w) ... 2.00
❑34, Jul 1992 JRo (w) ... 2.00
❑35, Aug 1992 ... 2.00

Batman: Joker Time

Reality TV goes too far with Joker show
©DC

Batman: Legends of the Dark Knight

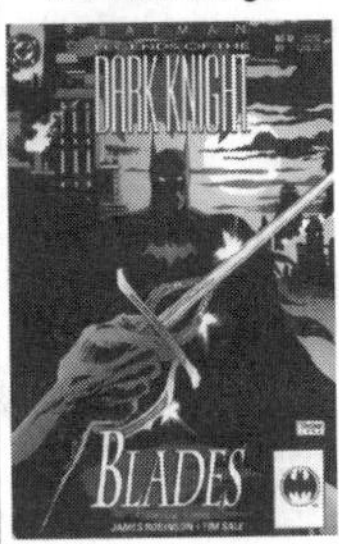

First issue launched the variant cover craze
©DC

Batman: Manbat

Elseworlds story pits bat versus bat
©DC

Batman: Mr. Freeze

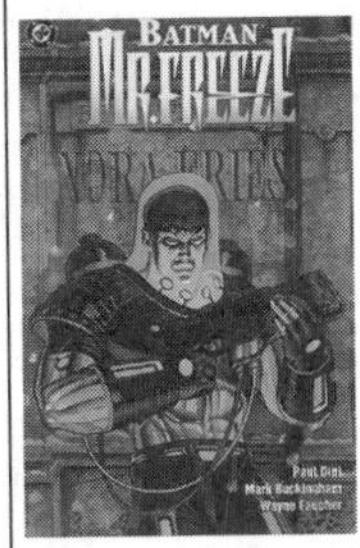

Cover forms quadritych with other movie spinoffs
©DC

Batman: No Man's Land

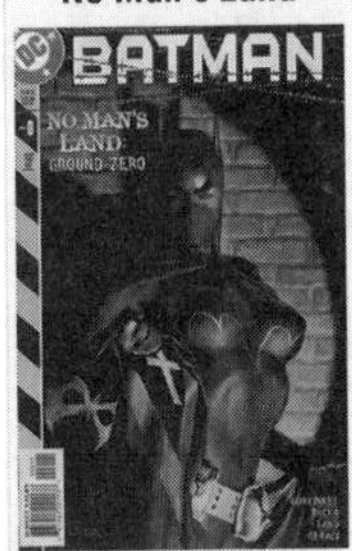

Events after an earthquake levels Gotham
©DC

	N-MINT
❑36, Aug 1992	2.00
❑37, Aug 1992; Series continues as Batman: Legends of the Dark Knight	2.00
❑38, Oct 1992 A: Bat-Mite.	2.00
❑39, Nov 1992 BT (a)	2.00
❑40, Dec 1992 BT (w); BT (a)	2.00
❑41, Jan 1993	2.00
❑42, Feb 1993 CR (a)	2.00
❑43, Mar 1993 CR (a)	2.00
❑44, Apr 1993	2.00
❑45, May 1993	2.00
❑46, Jun 1993 RH (a); A: Catwoman. V: Catwoman. V: Catman	2.00
❑47, Jul 1993 RH (a); A: Catwoman. V: Catwoman. V: Catman	2.00
❑48, Aug 1993 RH (a); A: Catwoman. V: Catwoman. V: Catman	2.00
❑49, Aug 1993 RH (a); A: Catwoman. V: Catwoman. V: Catman	2.00
❑50, Sep 1993; Giant-size; A: Joker. foil cover	4.00
❑51, Sep 1993 JKu (c)	2.00
❑52, Oct 1993	2.00
❑53, Oct 1993	2.00
❑54, Nov 1993	2.00
❑55, Dec 1993	2.00
❑56, Jan 1994	2.00
❑57, Feb 1994	2.00
❑58, Mar 1994	2.00
❑59, Apr 1994	2.00
❑60, May 1994	2.00
❑61, Jun 1994	2.00
❑62, Jul 1994	2.00
❑63, Aug 1994	2.00
❑64, Sep 1994	2.00
❑0, Oct 1994	2.50
❑65, Nov 1994 JSa (a); A: Joker. V: Joker.	2.00
❑66, Dec 1994 JSa (a); A: Joker. V: Joker.	2.00
❑67, Jan 1995 JSa (a); A: Joker. V: Joker.	2.00
❑68, Feb 1995 JSa (a); V: Joker.	2.00
❑69, Mar 1995 MZ (a)	2.00
❑70, Apr 1995 MZ (a)	2.00
❑71, May 1995	2.00
❑72, Jun 1995	2.00
❑73, Jul 1995	2.00
❑74, Aug 1995	2.00
❑75, Sep 1995	2.00
❑76, Oct 1995	2.00
❑77, Nov 1995	2.00
❑78, Dec 1995	2.00
❑79, Jan 1996	2.00
❑80, Feb 1996	2.00
❑81, Mar 1996	2.00
❑82, May 1996	2.00
❑83, Jun 1996	2.00
❑84, Jul 1996	2.00
❑85, Aug 1996	2.00
❑86, Sep 1996	2.00
❑87, Oct 1996	2.00
❑88, Nov 1996	2.00
❑89, Dec 1996 O: Clayface (Matt Hagen).	2.00
❑90, Jan 1997	2.00

	N-MINT
❑91, Feb 1997	2.00
❑92, Mar 1997	2.00
❑93, Apr 1997	2.00
❑94, May 1997; three eras of Batman	2.00
❑95, Jun 1997	2.00
❑96, Jul 1997	2.00
❑97, Aug 1997	2.00
❑98, Sep 1997	2.00
❑99, Oct 1997	2.00
❑100, Nov 1997; Double-size; ARo (c); JRo (w); ARo, FM, CS, KJ (a); O: Robin I and Robin II, pin-up gallery. O: Robin I and Robin II. A: Joker. pin-up gallery	4.50
❑101, Dec 1997; Face cover; 100 years in the future	2.00
❑102, Jan 1998 JRo (w)	2.00
❑103, Feb 1998 JRo (w)	2.00
❑104, Mar 1998 JRo (w)	2.00
❑105, Apr 1998	2.00
❑106, May 1998; Gordon vs. Joker	2.00
❑107, Jun 1998	2.00
❑108, Jul 1998	2.00
❑109, Aug 1998 V: Riddler.	2.00
❑110, Sep 1998 V: Riddler.	2.00
❑111, Oct 1998 V: Riddler.	2.00
❑112, Nov 1998	2.00
❑113, Dec 1998	2.00
❑114, Jan 1999	2.00
❑115, Feb 1999 LMc (a)	2.00
❑116, Apr 1999; A: Scarecrow. A: Huntress. No Man's Land	2.00
❑117, May 1999; V: Penguin. No Man's Land	2.00
❑118, Jun 1999; No Man's Land	2.00
❑119, Jul 1999; A: Two-Face. No Man's Land	2.00
❑120, Aug 1999; 1: Batgirl III (in costume). A: Huntress. A: Nightwing. A: Robin. No Man's Land	3.50
❑121, Sep 1999; V: Mr. Freeze. No Man's Land	2.00
❑122, Oct 1999; PG (a); A: Lynx. No Man's Land	2.00
❑123, Nov 1999; No Man's Land	2.00
❑124, Dec 1999; No Man's Land	2.00
❑125, Jan 2000; No Man's Land; Batman attempts to reveal identity to Commissioner Gordon	2.00
❑126, Feb 2000; DGry (w); No Man's Land	2.00
❑127, Mar 2000	2.00
❑128, Apr 2000	2.00
❑129, May 2000	2.00
❑130, Jun 2000	2.00
❑131, Jul 2000	2.00
❑132, Aug 2000 JRo (a); A: Silver St. Cloud	2.00
❑133, Sep 2000 JRo (a); A: Silver St. Cloud	2.25
❑134, Oct 2000 JRo (a); A: Silver St. Cloud	2.25
❑135, Nov 2000 JRo (a)	2.25
❑136, Dec 2000 JRo (a)	2.25
❑137, Jan 2001 PG (c); PG (a)	2.25
❑138, Feb 2001 PG (c); PG (a)	2.25
❑139, Mar 2001 PG (c); PG (a)	2.25

	N-MINT
❑140, Apr 2001 PG (c); PG (a)	2.25
❑141, May 2001 PG (c); PG (a)	2.25
❑142, Jun 2001 JA (a)	2.25
❑143, Jul 2001 JA (a)	2.25
❑144, Aug 2001 JA (a)	2.25
❑145, Sep 2001 JA (a)	2.25
❑146, Oct 2001	2.25
❑147, Nov 2001	2.25
❑148, Dec 2001	2.25
❑149, Jan 2002 TVE (a)	2.25
❑150, Feb 2002 TVE (a)	2.25
❑151, Mar 2002 TVE (a)	2.25
❑152, Apr 2002 TVE (a)	2.25
❑153, May 2002 TVE (a)	2.25
❑154, Jun 2002	2.25
❑155, Jul 2002	2.25
❑156, Aug 2002	2.25
❑157, Sep 2002	2.25
❑158, Oct 2002	2.50
❑159, Nov 2002	2.50
❑160, Dec 2002	2.50
❑161, Jan 2003	2.50
❑162, Feb 2003	2.50
❑163, Mar 2003	2.50
❑164, Apr 2003	2.50
❑165, May 2003	2.50
❑166, Jun 2003	2.50
❑167, Jul 2003	2.50
❑168, Aug 2003	2.50
❑169, Sep 2003	2.50
❑170, Oct 2003	2.50
❑171, Nov 2003	2.50
❑172, Dec 2003	2.50
❑173, Jan 2004	2.50
❑174, Feb 2004	2.50
❑175, Mar 2004	2.50
❑176, Apr 2004	2.50
❑177, May 2004, (c); DGry (w)	2.50
❑178, Jun 2004	2.50
❑179, Jul 2004	2.50
❑180, Aug 2004	2.50
❑181, Sep 2004	2.50
❑182, Oct 2004; War Games	2.50
❑183, Nov 2004, War Games	2.50
❑184, Dec 2004, War Games	2.50
❑185, Jan 2005	2.50
❑186, Feb 2005	2.50
❑187, Mar 2005	2.50
❑188, Apr 2005	2.50
❑189, May 2005	2.50
❑190, Jun 2005	2.50
❑191, Jul 2005	2.50
❑192, Aug 2005	2.50
❑193, Sep 2005	2.50
❑194, Oct 2005	2.50
❑195, Nov 2005	2.50
❑196	2.50
❑197, Jan 2006	2.50
❑198, Feb 2006	2.50
❑200, Apr 2006	2.50
❑201, May 2006	2.50
❑202, Jun 2006	2.50
❑203, Jun 2006	2.50
❑204, Jul 2006	2.50

Other grades: Multiply price above by 5/6 for VF/NM • 2/3 for VERY FINE • 1/3 for FINE • 1/5 for VERY GOOD • 1/8 for GOOD

N-MINT

❑206, Aug 2006 .... 2.50
❑207, Aug 2006 .... 2.50
❑Annual 1, Dec 1991 MG, KG, DS, JA (a) 4.50
❑Annual 2, ca. 1992; Wedding of James Gordon 3.50
❑Annual 3, ca. 1993 GM, LMc (a); 1: Cardinal Sin. 3.50
❑Annual 4, ca. 1994 MWa (w); JSa (a) 3.50
❑Annual 5, ca. 1995; O: Man-Bat. Year One 3.95
❑Annual 6, ca. 1996; Legends of the Dead Earth 2.95
❑Annual 7, ca. 1997; A: Balloon Buster. Pulp Heroes 3.95
❑Special 1, ca. 1993; prestige format. 6.95

BATMAN: LEGENDS OF THE DARK KNIGHT: JAZZ
DC

❑1, Apr 1995 .... 2.50
❑2, May 1995 .... 2.50
❑3, Jun 1995 .... 2.50

BATMAN: MADNESS A LEGENDS OF THE DARK KNIGHT HALLOWEEN SPECIAL
DC

❑1, ca. 1994, prestige format 4.95

BATMAN: MANBAT
DC

❑1, prestige format; Elseworlds 5.00
❑2, prestige format; Elseworlds 5.00
❑3, prestige format; Elseworlds 5.00

BATMAN: MASK OF THE PHANTASM-THE ANIMATED MOVIE
DC

❑1, ca. 1993, newstand 2.95
❑1/Prestige, ca. 1993, slick paper 4.95
❑1/Video, ca. 1993, Included with video release; smaller than regular comic book 5.00

BATMAN: MASQUE
DC

❑1, Jan 1997; prestige format; Elseworlds; Phantom of the Opera theme 6.95

BATMAN: MASTER OF THE FUTURE
DC

❑1, ca. 1991 .... 5.95

BATMAN: MR. FREEZE
DC

❑1, May 1997; prestige format; cover is part of quadtych 4.95

BATMAN: MITEFALL
DC

❑1; prestige format; prestige format one-shot 4.95

BATMAN: NEVERMORE
DC

❑1, Jun 2003 .... 2.50
❑2, Jul 2003 .... 2.50
❑3, Aug 2003 .... 2.50
❑4, Sep 2003 .... 2.50
❑5, Oct 2003 .... 2.50

BATMAN/NIGHTWING: BLOODBORNE
DC

❑1, Mar 2002, prestige format 5.95

BATMAN: NO MAN'S LAND
DC

❑0, Dec 1999 .... 4.95
❑1, Mar 1999 ARo (c); ARo (a) 2.95
❑1/Autographed, Mar 1999 ARo (c); ARo (a) 17.95
❑1/Variant, Mar 1999; ARo (c); ARo (a); lenticular animation cover 3.95
❑2, ca. 1999 .... 2.95
❑3, ca. 1999 .... 2.95
❑4, ca. 1999 .... 2.95

BATMAN: NO MAN'S LAND GALLERY
DC

❑1, Jul 1999; pin-ups 3.95

BATMAN: NO MAN'S LAND SECRET FILES
DC

❑1, Dec 1999 .... 4.95

N-MINT

BATMAN: NOSFERATU
DC

❑1, May 1999; prestige format; Elseworlds 5.95

BATMAN OF ARKHAM
DC

❑1 .... 5.95

BATMAN: ORDER OF THE BEASTS
DC

❑1, Jul 2004 .... 5.95

BATMAN: ORPHEUS RISING
DC

❑1, Oct 2001 .... 2.50
❑2, Nov 2001 .... 2.50
❑3, Dec 2001 .... 2.50
❑4, Jan 2002 .... 2.50
❑5, Feb 2002 .... 2.50

BATMAN: OUR WORLDS AT WAR
DC

❑1, Aug 2001 .... 2.95

BATMAN: OUTLAWS
DC

❑1, Sep 2000 .... 4.95
❑2, Oct 2000 .... 4.95
❑3, Nov 2000 .... 4.95

BATMAN: PENGUIN TRIUMPHANT
DC

❑1, ca. 1992; prestige format; JSa (a); cover forms diptych with Batman: Catwoman Defiant 5.00

BATMAN/PHANTOM STRANGER
DC

❑1, Dec 1997, prestige format 5.00

BATMAN PLUS
DC

❑1, Feb 1997 .... 2.95

BATMAN: POISON IVY
DC

❑1, Jul 1997, prestige format; O: Poison Ivy. A: Croc. A: Batman. A: Poison Ivy. cover is part of quadtych 5.00

BATMAN/POISON IVY: CAST SHADOWS
DC

❑1, ca. 2004 .... 6.95

BATMAN/PREDATOR III
DC

❑1, Nov 1997 .... 1.95
❑2, Dec 1997 .... 1.95
❑3, Jan 1998 .... 1.95
❑4, Feb 1998 .... 1.95

BATMAN/PUNISHER: LAKE OF FIRE
DC / MARVEL

❑1 1994 .... 5.00

BATMAN: REIGN OF TERROR
DC

❑1, Feb 1999; prestige format; Elseworlds 4.95

BATMAN RETURNS: THE OFFICIAL COMIC ADAPTATION OF THE WARNER BROS. MOTION PICTURE
DC

❑1, ca. 1992; Comic adaptation of Warner Bros. Movie 4.00
❑1/Prestige, ca. 1992; prestige format; Comic adaptation of Warner Bros. Movie 6.00

BATMAN: RIDDLER: THE RIDDLE FACTORY
DC

❑1; prestige format; cover forms diptych with Batman: Two-Face - Crime and Punishment 4.95

BATMAN: ROOMFUL OF STRANGERS
DC

❑1, Apr 2004 .... 5.95

BATMAN: RUN, RIDDLER, RUN
DC

❑1 1992, prestige format 5.00
❑2 1992, prestige format 5.00
❑3 1992, prestige format 5.00

N-MINT

BATMAN/SCARECROW 3-D
DC

❑1, Dec 1998; with glasses 3.95
❑1/Variant, Dec 1998 .... 7.50

BATMAN/SCARFACE: A PSYCHODRAMA
DC

❑1, Mar 2001 .... 5.95

BATMAN: SCAR OF THE BAT
DC

❑1; prestige format; Elseworlds 4.95

BATMAN: SCOTTISH CONNECTION
DC

❑1, ca. 1998, prestige format 5.95

BATMAN SECRET FILES
DC

❑1, Oct 1997, background information 4.95

BATMAN: SECRETS
DC

❑1, May 2006 .... 3.99
❑2, Jun 2006 .... 3.99
❑3, Jul 2006 .... 3.99
❑4, Aug 2006 .... 3.96

BATMAN: SEDUCTION OF THE GUN
DC

❑1, Feb 1993, Special edition on gun control; dedicated to John Reisenbach (Son of DC editor slain in gun killing) 3.50

BATMAN: SHADOW OF THE BAT
DC

❑0, Oct 1994; O: Batman. falls between issues #31 and 32 .... 2.50
❑1, Jun 1992; Last Arkham 2.50
❑1/CS, Jun 1992; collector's set 3.50
❑2, Jul 1992; Last Arkham 2.75
❑3, Aug 1992; Last Arkham 2.75
❑4, Sep 1992; Last Arkham 2.75
❑5, Oct 1992 .... 2.75
❑6, Nov 1992 .... 2.50
❑7, Dec 1992 .... 2.50
❑8, Jan 1993; Misfits 2.50
❑9, Feb 1993 .... 2.50
❑10, Mar 1993 .... 2.50
❑11, Apr 1993 .... 2.50
❑12, May 1993 .... 2.50
❑13, Jun 1993 .... 2.50
❑14, Jul 1993 JSa (a) 2.50
❑15, Aug 1993 JSa (a) 2.50
❑16, Sep 1993 V: Scarecrow. 2.50
❑17, Sep 1993 V: Scarecrow. 2.50
❑18, Oct 1993 V: Scarecrow. 2.50
❑19, Oct 1993 V: Tally Man. 2.50
❑20, Nov 1993 V: Tally Man. 2.50
❑21, Nov 1993 .... 2.50
❑22, Dec 1993 .... 2.50
❑23, Jan 1994 .... 2.50
❑24, Feb 1994 .... 2.50
❑25, Mar 1994 A: Joe Public. 2.50
❑26, Apr 1994 V: Clayface. 2.50
❑27, May 1994 .... 2.50
❑28, Jun 1994 .... 2.50
❑29, Jul 1994; Giant-size 2.50
❑30, Aug 1994 .... 2.50
❑31, Sep 1994; Zero Hour, R: Alfred as detective 2.50
❑32, Nov 1994 .... 2.50
❑33, Dec 1994 .... 2.50
❑34, Jan 1995 .... 2.50
❑35, Feb 1995 .... 4.00
❑35/Variant, Feb 1995; enhanced cover 2.95
❑36, Mar 1995 A: Black Canary. 2.00
❑37, Apr 1995 .... 2.00
❑38, May 1995 .... 2.00
❑39, Jun 1995 V: Anarky. 2.00
❑40, Jul 1995 V: Anarky. 2.00
❑41, Aug 1995 .... 2.00
❑42, Sep 1995 .... 2.00
❑43, Oct 1995 .... 2.00
❑44, Nov 1995 .... 2.00
❑45, Dec 1995; Wayne Manor history 2.00
❑46, Jan 1996 .... 2.00
❑47, Feb 1996 .... 2.00
❑48, Mar 1996; trading card bound in 2.00
❑49, Apr 1996 .... 2.00

Other grades: Multiply price above by 5/6 for VF/NM • 2/3 for VERY FINE • 1/3 for FINE • 1/5 for VERY GOOD • 1/8 for GOOD

Batman/Predator III

Earlier series called "Batman Vs. Predator"
©DC

Batman: Shadow of the Bat

Batman Returns film prompted third Bat-title
©DC

Batman: The Dark Knight

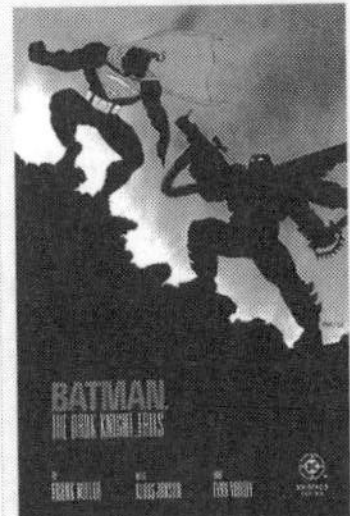
Real name of spectacular "Dark Knight Returns"
©DC

Batman: The Killing Joke

Infamous Alan Moore one-shot crippled Batgirl
©DC

Batman: The Long Halloween

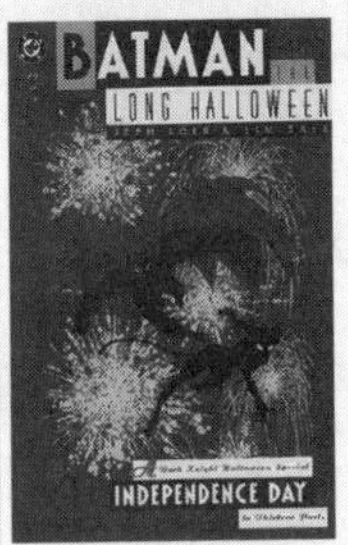
Popular Jeph Loeb/ Tim Sale production
©DC

N-MINT

- ❑50, May 1996 ... 2.00
- ❑51, Jun 1996 ... 2.00
- ❑52, Jul 1996 ... 2.00
- ❑53, Aug 1996 A: Huntress. ... 2.00
- ❑54, Sep 1996 ... 2.00
- ❑55, Oct 1996 KJ (a) ... 2.00
- ❑56, Nov 1996 V: Poison Ivy. ... 2.00
- ❑57, Dec 1996 V: Poison Ivy. ... 2.00
- ❑58, Jan 1997 V: Floronic Man. ... 2.00
- ❑59, Feb 1997 V: Scarface. ... 2.00
- ❑60, Mar 1997 V: Scarface. ... 2.00
- ❑61, Apr 1997 JA (a) ... 2.00
- ❑62, May 1997 V: Two-Face. ... 2.00
- ❑63, Jun 1997 V: Two-Face. ... 2.00
- ❑64, Jul 1997 ... 2.00
- ❑65, Aug 1997 ... 2.00
- ❑66, Sep 1997 ... 2.00
- ❑67, Oct 1997 ... 2.00
- ❑68, Nov 1997 ... 2.00
- ❑69, Dec 1997 A: Fate. ... 2.00
- ❑70, Jan 1998 A: Fate. ... 2.00
- ❑71, Feb 1998 ... 2.00
- ❑72, Mar 1998 1: Drakken. ... 2.00
- ❑73, Apr 1998; continues in Nightwing #19 ... 2.00
- ❑74, May 1998; continues in Batman Chronicles #12 ... 2.00
- ❑75, Jun 1998; V: Clayface. V: Mr. Freeze. Aftershock ... 2.00
- ❑76, Jul 1998; Aftershock ... 2.00
- ❑77, Aug 1998; Aftershock ... 2.00
- ❑78, Sep 1998; Aftershock ... 2.00
- ❑79, Oct 1998; Aftershock ... 2.00
- ❑80, Dec 1998; Road to No Man's Land; flipbook with Azrael: Agent of the Bat #47 ... 3.95
- ❑80/Ltd., Dec 1998; Extra-sized flip-book 5.00
- ❑81, Jan 1999; A: Jeremiah Arkham. Road to No Man's Land ... 2.00
- ❑82, Feb 1999; Road to No Man's Land 2.00
- ❑83, Mar 1999; 1: new Batgirl. No Man's Land ... 9.00
- ❑84, Apr 1999; A: Scarecrow. A: Huntress. A: Batgirl. No Man's Land 2.00
- ❑85, May 1999; A: Batgirl. V: Penguin. No Man's Land ... 2.00
- ❑86, Jun 1999; No Man's Land ... 2.00
- ❑87, Jul 1999; A: Two-Face. No Man's Land ... 2.00
- ❑88, Aug 1999; BSz (a); A: Poison Ivy. V: Clayface. No Man's Land; continues in Batman #568 ... 2.00
- ❑89, Sep 1999; V: Killer Croc. No Man's Land ... 2.00
- ❑90, Oct 1999; PG (a); A: Lynx. No Man's Land ... 2.00
- ❑91, Nov 1999 ... 2.00
- ❑92, Dec 1999; DGry (w); No Man's Land ... 2.00
- ❑93, Jan 2000; BSz (a); No Man's Land 2.00
- ❑94, Feb 2000 ... 2.00
- ❑1000000, Nov 1998; Aftershock ... 3.00
- ❑Annual 1, ca. 1993 TVE (a); 1: Joe Public ... 4.00
- ❑Annual 2, ca. 1994; JSa (a); Elseworlds 3.95
- ❑Annual 3, ca. 1995; O: Poison Ivy. Year One ... 3.95
- ❑Annual 4, Nov 1996; Legends of the Dead Earth; 1996 Annual ... 2.95
- ❑Annual 5, Oct 1997; V: Poison Ivy. 1997 Annual; Pulp Heroes ... 3.95

BATMAN-SPAWN: WAR DEVIL
DC

- ❑1, ca. 1994; prestige format; crossover with Image ... 4.95

BATMAN SPECIAL
DC

- ❑1, ca. 1984, MG (a) ... 2.50

BATMAN/SPIDER-MAN
DC

- ❑1, Oct 1997, prestige format; crossover with Marvel ... 4.95

BATMAN: SPOILER/HUNTRESS: BLUNT TRAUMA
DC

- ❑1, May 1998 ... 2.95
- ❑2, ca. 1998 ... 2.95
- ❑3, ca. 1998 ... 2.95
- ❑4, ca. 1998 ... 2.95

BATMAN STRIKES
DC

- ❑1, Nov 2004 ... 2.25
- ❑2, Dec 2004 ... 2.25
- ❑3, Jan 2005 ... 2.25
- ❑4, Feb 2005 ... 2.25
- ❑5, Mar 2005 ... 2.25
- ❑6, Apr 2005 ... 2.25
- ❑7, May 2005 ... 2.25
- ❑8, Jun 2005 ... 2.25
- ❑9, Jun 2005 ... 2.25
- ❑10, Jul 2005 ... 2.25
- ❑11, Aug 2005 ... 2.25
- ❑12, Sep 2005 ... 2.25
- ❑13, Oct 2005 ... 2.25
- ❑14 ... 2.25
- ❑15, Jan 2006 ... 2.25
- ❑16, Feb 2006 ... 2.25
- ❑17, Mar 2006 ... 2.25
- ❑18, Apr 2006 ... 2.25
- ❑19, May 2006 ... 2.25
- ❑20, Jun 2006 ... 2.25
- ❑21, Jul 2006 ... 2.25
- ❑22, Aug 2006 ... 2.25

BATMAN/SUPERMAN/WONDER WOMAN TRINITY
DC

- ❑1, Aug 2003 ... 9.00
- ❑2, Oct 2003 ... 8.00
- ❑3, Dec 2003 ... 6.95

BATMAN: SWORD OF AZRAEL
DC

- ❑1, Oct 1992, 1: Azrael. Wraparound, gatefold cover ... 4.00
- ❑1/Silver, Oct 1992, silver edition ... 2.00
- ❑2, Nov 1992 ... 3.00
- ❑2/Silver, Nov 1992, silver edition ... 2.00
- ❑3, Dec 1992 ... 3.00
- ❑3/Silver, Dec 1992, silver edition ... 2.00
- ❑4, Jan 1993 ... 2.50
- ❑4/Silver, Jan 1993, silver edition ... 2.00

BATMAN/TARZAN: CLAWS OF THE CAT-WOMAN
DARK HORSE

- ❑1, Sep 1999 ... 2.95
- ❑2, Oct 1999 ... 2.95
- ❑3, Nov 1999 ... 2.95
- ❑4, Dec 1999 ... 2.95

BATMAN: TENSES
DC

- ❑1, Oct 2003 ... 6.95
- ❑2 2003 ... 6.95

BATMAN: THE ABDUCTION
DC

- ❑1, Jun 1998; prestige format; Batman kidnapped by aliens ... 5.95

BATMAN: THE ANKH
DC

- ❑1, Jan 2002 ... 5.95
- ❑2, Feb 2002 ... 5.95

BATMAN: THE BLUE, THE GREY, AND THE BAT
DC

- ❑1 1992; prestige format; Elseworlds. 5.95

BATMAN: THE BOOK OF SHADOWS
DC

- ❑1; prestige format ... 5.95

BATMAN: THE CULT
DC

- ❑1, Aug 1988 JSn (w); JSn, BWr (a) .. 5.00
- ❑2, Sep 1988 JSn (w); JSn, BWr (a) .. 4.00
- ❑3, Oct 1988 JSn (w); JSn, BWr (a) ... 4.00
- ❑4, Nov 1988 JSn (w); JSn, BWr (a) .. 4.00

BATMAN: THE DARK KNIGHT
DC

- ❑1, Mar 1986; FM (w); FM (a); Squarebound ... 25.00
- ❑1/2nd, Mar 1986 FM (w); FM (a) ... 7.00
- ❑1/3rd, ca. 1986 FM (w); FM (a) ... 5.00
- ❑2, Mar 1986 FM (w); FM (a) ... 9.00
- ❑2/2nd, ca. 1986 FM (w); FM (a) ... 3.00
- ❑2/3rd, ca. 1986 FM (w); FM (a) ... 3.00
- ❑3, ca. 1986 FM (w); FM (a); D: Joker (future). ... 6.00
- ❑3/2nd, ca. 1986 FM (w); FM (a); D: Joker (future). ... 3.00
- ❑4, ca. 1986 FM (w); FM (a); D: Alfred (future). ... 5.00

BATMAN: THE DOOM THAT CAME TO GOTHAM
DC

- ❑1, Nov 2000 ... 4.95
- ❑2, Dec 2000 ... 4.95
- ❑3, Jan 2001 ... 4.95

BATMAN: THE HILL
DC

- ❑1, May 2000 ... 2.95

BATMAN: THE KILLING JOKE
DC

- ❑1, Jul 1988; prestige format; BB (c); AMo (w); BB (a); O: Joker. V: Joker. first printing; green logo ... 7.00

Other grades: Multiply price above by 5/6 for VF/NM • 2/3 for VERY FINE • 1/3 for FINE • 1/5 for VERY GOOD • 1/8 for GOOD

❑1/2nd, ca. 1988; prestige format; BB (c); AMo (w); BB (a); O: Joker. V: Joker. second printing; pink logo.... 5.50
❑1/3rd, ca. 1988; prestige format; BB (c); AMo (w); BB (a); O: Joker. V: Joker. third printing; yellow logo..... 5.00
❑1/4th, ca. 1988; prestige format; BB (c); AMo (w); BB (a); O: Joker. V: Joker. fourth printing; orange logo.. 5.00
❑1/5th, ca. 1988; prestige format BB (c); AMo (w); BB (a); O: Joker. V: Joker. 5.00
❑1/6th, ca. 1988; prestige format BB (c); AMo (w); BB (a); O: Joker. V: Joker. 5.00
❑1/7th, ca. 1988; prestige format BB (c); AMo (w); BB (a); O: Joker. V: Joker. 5.00
❑1/8th, ca. 1988; prestige format BB (c); AMo (w); BB (a); O: Joker. V: Joker. 5.00

BATMAN: THE LONG HALLOWEEN
DC

❑1, Dec 1996; prestige format JPH (w) 8.50
❑2, Jan 1997; JPH (w); V: Solomon Grundy. cardstock cover 6.50
❑3, Feb 1997; JPH (w); V: Joker. cardstock cover 5.50
❑4, Mar 1997; JPH (w); V: Joker. cardstock cover 5.00
❑5, Apr 1997; JPH (w); A: Catwoman. A: Poison Ivy. cardstock cover 4.50
❑6, May 1997; JPH (w); V: Poison Ivy. cardstock cover 4.50
❑7, Jun 1997; JPH (w); V: Riddler. cardstock cover 3.50
❑8, Jul 1997; JPH (w); V: Scarecrow. cardstock cover 3.50
❑9, Aug 1997; JPH (w); cardstock cover 3.50
❑10, Sep 1997; JPH (w); A: Catwoman. V: Scarecrow. V: Mad Hatter. cardstock cover 3.50
❑11, Oct 1997; JPH (w); O: Two-Face. cardstock cover 3.50
❑12, Nov 1997; JPH (w); D: Maroni. cardstock cover; identity of Holiday revealed 3.50
❑13, Dec 1997; prestige format JPH (w); 1: Holiday. V: Arkham inmates. 5.50

BATMAN: THE MAN WHO LAUGHS
DC

❑1 2005 6.95

BATMAN: THE OFFICIAL COMIC ADAPTATION OF THE WARNER BROS. MOTION PICTURE
DC

❑1, ca. 1989; regular edition; JOy (a); newsstand format; Comic adaptation of Warner Bros. Movie 3.00
❑1/Prestige, ca. 1989; prestige format; Comic adaptation of Warner Bros. Movie 5.00

BATMAN: THE 10-CENT ADVENTURE
DC

❑1, Mar 2002 1.00

BATMAN: THE ULTIMATE EVIL
DC

❑1; prestige format; adapts Andrew Vachss novel 6.00
❑2; prestige format; adapts Andrew Vachss novel 6.00

BATMAN 3-D
DC

❑1, ca. 1990 9.95

BATMAN: TOYMAN
DC

❑1, Nov 1998 2.25
❑2, Dec 1998 2.25
❑3, Jan 1999; Wordless issue 2.25
❑4, Feb 1999 2.25

BATMAN: TURNING POINTS
DC

❑1, Jan 2001 2.50
❑2, Jan 2001 2.50
❑3, Jan 2001 2.50
❑4, Jan 2001 2.50
❑5, Jan 2001 2.50

BATMAN: TWO-FACE: CRIME AND PUNISHMENT
DC

❑1; prestige format; cover forms diptych with Batman: Riddler - The Riddle Factory 4.95

BATMAN: TWO FACES
DC

❑1, Nov 1998; Elseworlds 4.95
❑1/Ltd., Nov 1998; Signed edition 10.00

BATMAN: TWO-FACE STRIKES TWICE
DC

❑1 JSa (a) 5.00
❑2 5.00

BATMAN: VENGEANCE OF BANE II
DC

❑1 4.00

BATMAN: VENGEANCE OF BANE SPECIAL
DC

❑1, Jan 1993 O: Bane. 1: Bane. 4.00

BATMAN VERSUS PREDATOR
DC / DARK HORSE

❑1, ca. 1991; DaG (w); newsstand 2.50
❑1/Prestige Batm, ca. 1991; prestige format; trading cards; Batman on front cover 5.00
❑1/Prestige Pred, ca. 1991; prestige format; trading cards; Predator on front; Batman on back cover 5.00
❑2, ca. 1992; DaG (w); newsstand 2.50
❑2/Prestige, ca. 1992; prestige format; DaG (w); pin-ups 5.00
❑3, ca. 1992; DaG (w); newsstand 2.50
❑3/Prestige, ca. 1992; prestige format DaG (w) 5.00

BATMAN VERSUS PREDATOR II: BLOODMATCH
DC / DARK HORSE

❑1, ca. 1994; Crossover, no year in indicia 2.50
❑2, ca. 1994; Crossover 2.50
❑3, ca. 1995; Crossover 2.50
❑4, ca. 1995; Crossover 2.50

BATMAN VS. THE INCREDIBLE HULK
DC

❑1, Fal 1981; oversized, (DC Special Series #27) 2.50
❑1/2nd; 2nd Printing, comics-sized 3.95

BATMAN VILLAINS SECRET FILES
DC

❑1, Oct 1998 4.95

BATMAN VILLAINS SECRET FILES 2005
DC

❑0, Jul 2005 4.99

BATMAN/WILDCAT
DC

❑1, Apr 1997 2.25
❑2, May 1997 2.25
❑3, Jun 1997 2.25

BATMAN: YEAR 100
DC

❑1, Apr 2006 5.95
❑2, May 2006 5.95
❑3, Jun 2006 5.95

BAT (MARY ROBERTS RINEHART'S)
ADVENTURE

❑1, Aug 1992, b&w 2.50

BAT MEN
AVALON

❑1 2.95

BATS, CATS & CADILLACS
NOW

❑1, Oct 1990 2.00
❑2, Nov 1990 2.00

BAT-THING
DC / AMALGAM

❑1, Jun 1997 1.95

BATTLE ANGEL ALITA PART 1
VIZ

❑1, Jul 1992 1: Alita. 4.00
❑2, Aug 1992 3.50
❑3, Sep 1992 3.50
❑4, Oct 1992 3.00
❑5, Nov 1992 3.00
❑6, Dec 1992 3.00
❑7, Jan 1993 3.00
❑8, Feb 1993 3.00
❑9, Mar 1993 3.00

BATTLE ANGEL ALITA PART 2
VIZ

❑1, Apr 1993 3.00
❑2, May 1993 2.75
❑3, Jun 1993 2.75
❑4, Jul 1993 2.75
❑5, Aug 1993 2.75
❑6, Sep 1993 2.75
❑7, Oct 1993 2.75

BATTLE ANGEL ALITA PART 3
VIZ

❑1, Nov 1993 2.75
❑2, Dec 1993 2.75
❑3, Jan 1994 2.75
❑4, Feb 1994 2.75
❑5, Mar 1994 2.75
❑6, Apr 1994 2.75
❑7, May 1994 2.75
❑8, Jun 1994 2.75
❑9, Jul 1994 2.75
❑10, Aug 1994 2.75
❑11, Sep 1994 2.75
❑12, Oct 1994 2.75
❑13, Nov 1994 2.75

BATTLE ANGEL ALITA PART 4
VIZ

❑1, Dec 1994 2.75
❑2, Jan 1995 2.75
❑3, Feb 1995 2.75
❑4, Mar 1995 2.75
❑5, Apr 1995 2.75
❑6, May 1995 2.75
❑7, Jun 1995 2.75

BATTLE ANGEL ALITA PART 5
VIZ

❑1, Jul 1995 2.75
❑2, Aug 1995 2.75
❑3, Sep 1995 2.75
❑4, Oct 1995 2.75
❑5, Nov 1995 2.75
❑6, Dec 1995 2.75
❑7, Jan 1996 2.95

BATTLE ANGEL ALITA PART 6
VIZ

❑1, Feb 1996 2.95
❑2, Mar 1996 2.95
❑3, Apr 1996 2.95
❑4, May 1996 2.95
❑5, Jun 1996 2.95
❑6, Jul 1996 2.95
❑7, Aug 1996 2.95
❑8, Sep 1996 2.95

BATTLE ANGEL ALITA PART 7
VIZ

❑1, Oct 1996 2.95
❑2, Nov 1996 2.95
❑3, Dec 1996 2.95
❑4, Jan 1997 2.95
❑5, Feb 1997 2.95
❑6, Mar 1997 2.95
❑7, Apr 1997 2.95
❑8, May 1997 2.95

BATTLE ANGEL ALITA PART 8
VIZ

❑1, Jun 1997 2.95
❑2, Jul 1997 2.95
❑3, Aug 1997 2.95
❑4, Sep 1997 2.95
❑5, Oct 1997 2.95
❑6, Nov 1997 2.95
❑7, Dec 1997 2.95
❑8, Jan 1998 2.95
❑9, Feb 1998 2.95

BATTLE ANGEL ALITA: LAST ORDER PART 1
VIZ

❑1, Sep 2002 2.95
❑2, Oct 2002 2.95

Batman Versus Predator

First of a trio of Bats/ Predator crossovers
©DC

Battle Angel Alita Part 1

Scavenger rebuilds robot martial artist
©Viz

Battle Chasers

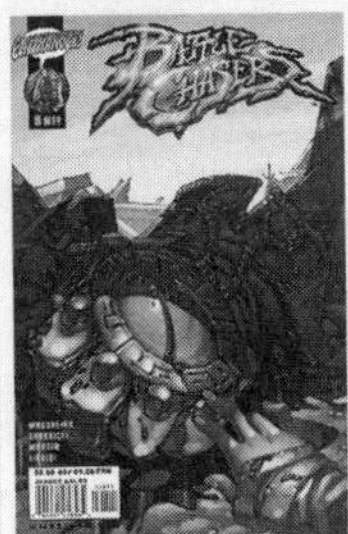

Infamously late-shipping Cliffhanger title
©Image

Battlefield Action

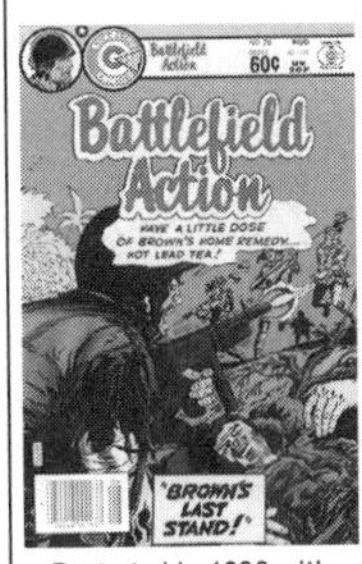

Restarted in 1980 with nothing but reprints
©Charlton

Battle of the Planets

Early anime adaptation from Gold Key
©Gold Key

	N-MINT
❑3, Nov 2002	2.95
❑4, Dec 2002	2.95
❑5, Jan 2003	2.95
❑6, Feb 2003	2.95

BATTLE ARMOR
ETERNITY

	N-MINT
❑1, Oct 1988	1.95
❑2	1.95
❑3	1.95

BATTLE AXE
COMICS INTERVIEW

	N-MINT
❑1, b&w	2.50

BATTLEAXES
DC / VERTIGO

	N-MINT
❑1, May 2000	2.50
❑2, Jun 2000	2.50
❑3, Jul 2000	2.50
❑4, Aug 2000	2.50

BATTLE AXIS
INTREPID

	N-MINT
❑1, Feb 1993	2.95

BATTLE BEASTS
BLACKTHORNE

	N-MINT
❑1, Feb 1988	1.75
❑2, ca. 1988	1.50
❑3, ca. 1988	1.50
❑4, ca. 1988	1.75

BATTLE BINDER PLUS
ANTARCTIC / VENUS

	N-MINT
❑1, Nov 1994	2.95
❑2, Dec 1994	2.95
❑3, Jan 1995	2.95
❑4, Feb 1995	2.95
❑5, Mar 1995	2.95
❑6, Apr 1995	2.95

BATTLE CHASERS
IMAGE / CLIFFHANGER

	N-MINT
❑1, Apr 1998	5.00
❑1/Wraparound, Apr 1998; alternate cover, logo on back side of wraparound cover	8.00
❑1/Holochrome, Apr 1998; Limited holochrome cover (limited to 5,000 copies); Wrap-around	16.50
❑1/Gold, Apr 1998; Gold "Come on, take a peek" cover (Monika)	14.00
❑1/2nd, Apr 1998	3.00
❑2, May 1998	4.00
❑2/Dynamic, May 1998; Special "omnichrome" cover from Dynamic Forces	5.00
❑2/B, May 1998; Battlechrome edition	6.00
❑3, Jul 1998	3.00
❑4/A, Oct 1998; four alternate back covers form quadtych	2.50
❑4/B, Oct 1998; Old man on cover	2.50
❑4/C, Oct 1998; four alternate back covers form quadtych	2.50
❑4/D, Oct 1998; four alternate back covers form quadtych	2.50
❑5, May 1999	2.50
❑6, Aug 1999	2.50
❑7, Jan 2001	2.50
❑8, May 2001	2.50
❑9, Jun 2001; Flip book with bonus story	3.50
❑Ashcan 1, Aug 1998; Preview edition 1: Battle Chasers.	5.00
❑Ashcan 1/Gold, Aug 1998; Preview edition; 1: Battle Chasers. Gold logo	7.00

BATTLE CLASSICS
DC

	N-MINT
❑1, Oct 1978, Reprints	4.00

BATTLEFIELD ACTION
CHARLTON

	N-MINT
❑16 1957, Continued from Foreign Intrigues #15	28.00
❑17 1957	13.00
❑18, Mar 1958	10.00
❑19, May 1958	10.00
❑20, Jul 1958	10.00
❑21, Sep 1958	9.00
❑22, Dec 1958	9.00
❑23 1959	9.00
❑24 1959	9.00
❑25, Jul 1959	9.00
❑26, Sep 1959, Swimming pool contest	9.00
❑27 1959	9.00
❑28, Jan 1960	9.00
❑29 1960	9.00
❑30, Jun 1960	9.00
❑31, Aug 1960	7.00
❑32, Oct 1960	7.00
❑33 1961	7.00
❑34 1961	7.00
❑35 1961	7.00
❑36 1961	7.00
❑37 1961	7.00
❑38, Nov 1961	7.00
❑39, Dec 1961	7.00
❑40, Feb 1962	7.00
❑41, May 1962	6.00
❑42, ca. 1962	6.00
❑43, ca. 1962	6.00
❑44, ca. 1962	6.00
❑45, Jan 1963	6.00
❑46, Mar 1963	6.00
❑47, May 1963	6.00
❑48, Jul 1963	6.00
❑49, Sep 1963	6.00
❑50, Nov 1963	6.00
❑51, Jan 1964	5.00
❑52, ca. 1964	5.00
❑53, Jun 1964	5.00
❑54, ca. 1964	5.00
❑55, Nov 1964	5.00
❑56, Jan 1965	5.00
❑57, ca. 1965	5.00
❑58, Jul 1965	5.00
❑59, ca. 1965	5.00
❑60, Oct 1965	5.00
❑61, Mar 1963	5.00
❑62, Feb 1966, Last issue of 1960s run	5.00
❑63, Jul 1980, Series begins again	2.50
❑64, Sep 1980	2.50
❑65, Nov 1980	2.50
❑66, Jan 1981	2.50
❑67, Mar 1981	2.50
❑68, Apr 1981	2.50
❑69, Jun 1981	2.50
❑70, Aug 1981	2.50
❑71, Oct 1981	2.50
❑72, Dec 1981	2.50
❑73, Feb 1982	2.50
❑74, Apr 1982	2.50
❑75, Jun 1982	2.50
❑76, Aug 1982	2.50
❑77, Oct 1982	2.50
❑78, Dec 1982	2.50
❑79, Feb 1983	2.50
❑80, Apr 1983	2.50
❑81, Jun 1983	2.50
❑82, Aug 1983	2.50
❑83, Oct 1983	2.50
❑84, Dec 1983, Reprints from Foxhole #6 ("Boidie" & "Steven"), and #5 ("Stiff")	2.50
❑85 1984	2.50
❑86 1984	2.50
❑87 1984	2.50
❑88, Sep 1984	2.50
❑89, Nov 1984	2.50

BATTLE FOR A THREE DIMENSIONAL WORLD
3-D COSMIC

	N-MINT
❑1, ca. 1982, b&w; JK (a); no cover price	2.50

BATTLEFORCE
BLACKTHORNE

	N-MINT
❑1	1.75
❑2, b&w	1.75

BATTLE GIRLZ
ANTARCTIC

	N-MINT
❑1, ca. 2002, b&w	2.99

BATTLE GODS: WARRIORS OF THE CHAAK
DARK HORSE

	N-MINT
❑1, Apr 2000	2.95
❑2, May 2000	2.95
❑3, Jun 2000	2.95

BATTLEGROUND EARTH
BEST

	N-MINT
❑1, b&w	2.50
❑2, b&w	2.50

BATTLE GROUP PEIPER
TOME

	N-MINT
❑1, b&w	2.95

BATTLE HYMN
IMAGE

	N-MINT
❑1, ca. 2005	2.95
❑2, ca. 2005	2.95
❑3 2005	2.95
❑4 2005	2.95
❑5, Jan 2006	2.95

BATTLE OF THE PLANETS
GOLD KEY / WHITMAN

	N-MINT
❑1, Jun 1979	20.00
❑2, Aug 1979	15.00
❑3, Oct 1979	12.00

Other grades: Multiply price above by 5/6 for VF/NM • 2/3 for VERY FINE • 1/3 for FINE • 1/5 for VERY GOOD • 1/8 for GOOD

❑4, Dec 1979 .... 12.00
❑5, Feb 1980 .... 12.00
❑6, Apr 1980 .... 12.00
❑7, Oct 1980 .... 30.00
❑8, Nov 1980 .... 20.00
❑9, Dec 1980 .... 20.00
❑10, Feb 1981 .... 20.00

BATTLE OF THE PLANETS ARTBOOK
IMAGE

❑1, ca. 2003 .... 4.99

BATTLE OF THE PLANETS (IMAGE)
IMAGE

❑½, Jul 2002; Black & white cover 3.00
❑½/Gold, Jul 2002; Black & white cover 5.00
❑1/A, Aug 2002 ARo (c) 3.00
❑1/B, Aug 2002 .... 3.00
❑1/C, Aug 2002 .... 3.00
❑1/D, Aug 2002 .... 3.00
❑1/E, Aug 2002; ARo (c); Holofoil cover 3.00
❑1/F, Aug 2002; Wizard World 2002 Convention Edition, limited to 5,000 copies 3.00
❑1/G, Aug 2002; ARo (c); Limited to 7,000 copies; DFE red foil cover 3.00
❑1/H, Aug 2002; ARo (c); Limited to 2,000 copies; DFE blue foil cover 3.00
❑1/I, Aug 2002; ARo (c); Limited to 1,978 copies; DFE gold foil cover 3.00
❑1/J, Aug 2002; "Virgin" cover without price or logo 3.00
❑1/K, Aug 2002; Black & white cover 3.00
❑2, Sep 2002 .... 2.99
❑2/Variant, Sep 2002; Animation cover; Limited to 5,000 copies 3.00
❑2/A, Sep 2002; 2002 San Diego Convention exclusive; Limited to 1,000 copies 3.00
❑2/B, Sep 2002; "Virgin" cover without price or logo 3.00
❑3, Oct 2002 ARo (c) 2.99
❑4, Nov 2002 .... 2.99
❑5, Dec 2002 .... 2.99
❑6, Feb 2003 .... 2.99
❑7, Mar 2003 .... 2.99
❑7/A, Mar 2003; Retailer incentive; variant cover 5.00
❑8, Apr 2003 .... 2.99
❑9, May 2003 .... 2.99
❑10, Jun 2003 .... 2.99
❑11, Jul 2003 .... 2.99
❑12, Aug 2003 .... 4.99

BATTLE OF THE PLANETS: JASON
IMAGE

❑1, Jun 2003 .... 4.99

BATTLE OF THE PLANETS: MANGA
IMAGE

❑1, Oct 2003 .... 2.99
❑2, Nov 2003 .... 2.99
❑3, Dec 2003 .... 2.99

BATTLE OF THE PLANETS: MARK
IMAGE

❑1, May 2003 .... 4.99

BATTLE OF THE PLANETS: PRINCESS
IMAGE

❑1, Nov 2004 .... 2.99
❑2, Dec 2004 .... 2.99
❑3, Jan 2005 .... 2.99
❑4, Feb 2005 .... 2.99
❑5, Mar 2005 .... 2.99
❑6, Apr 2005 .... 2.99

BATTLE OF THE PLANETS/ THUNDERCATS
IMAGE

❑1, May 2003 .... 4.99

BATTLE OF THE PLANETS/ WITCHBLADE
IMAGE

❑1, Feb 2003 .... 5.95

BATTLE OF THE ULTRA-BROTHERS
VIZ

❑1 .... 4.95
❑2 .... 4.95
❑3 .... 4.95
❑4 .... 4.95
❑5 .... 4.95

BATTLE POPE
FUNK-O-TRON

❑1 .... 5.00
❑2 .... 4.00
❑3 .... 4.00

BATTLEPOPE
FUNK-O-TRON

❑1, Jun 2000, b&w 2.95
❑2, Jul 2000, b&w 2.95
❑3, Aug 2000, b&w 2.95
❑4, Sep 2000, b&w 2.95
❑5, Mar 2001, b&w; A.K.A. Battle Pope Shorts #1 .... 2.95
❑6, Jun 2001, b&w; A.K.A. Battle Pope: Mayhem #1 .... 2.95
❑7, Jul 2001, b&w; A.K.A. Battle Pope: Mayhem #2 .... 2.95

BATTLE POPE COLOR
IMAGE

❑1, Sep 2005 .... 2.95
❑2, Oct 2005 .... 2.95
❑3, Nov 2005 .... 2.95
❑6, Apr 2006 .... 2.95
❑7, May 2006 .... 2.95
❑8, Jul 2006 .... 2.95

BATTLE ROYALE
TOKYOPOP

❑1, May 2003 .... 9.99
❑2, Jul 2003 .... 9.99
❑3, Nov 2003 .... 9.99
❑4, Dec 2003 .... 9.99
❑5, Jan 2004 .... 9.99
❑6, Mar 2004 .... 9.99
❑7, Jun 2004 .... 9.99
❑8, Aug 2004 .... 9.99
❑9, Oct 2004 .... 9.99
❑10, Dec 2004 .... 9.99
❑11, Feb 2005 .... 9.99
❑12, Apr 2005 .... 9.99
❑13, Jul 2005 .... 9.99
❑14, Nov 2005 .... 9.99

BATTLESTAR GALACTICA 1999 TOUR BOOK
REALM

❑1/A, May 1999 .... 2.99
❑1/B, May 1999; Dynamic Forces Edition, no cover price; Dynamic Forces Edition, no cover price 3.00
❑1/C, May 1999; cardstock cover version 6.99

BATTLESTAR GALACTICA: APOLLO'S JOURNEY
MAXIMUM

❑1, Apr 1996, Wrong year listed in indicia; came out in 1996, not 1995 .... 2.95
❑2, Jun 1996 .... 2.50
❑3, Jun 1996 .... 2.95

BATTLESTAR GALACTICA: EVE OF DESTRUCTION PRELUDE
REALM

❑nn, Dec 1999 .... 3.99

BATTLESTAR GALACTICA: JOURNEY'S END
MAXIMUM

❑1, Aug 1996 .... 2.99
❑2, Sep 1996 .... 2.99
❑3, Oct 1996 .... 2.99
❑4, Nov 1996 .... 2.99

BATTLESTAR GALACTICA (MARVEL)
MARVEL

❑1, Mar 1979, Pilot movie adaptation; reformatted from Marvel Super Special #8; newsstand edition (issue number appears in box) 4.00
❑1/Whitman, Mar 1979, Special markets edition (usually sold in Whitman bagged prepacks); price appears in a diamond; no UPC barcode 4.00
❑1/2nd, 20 Yahren reunion edition; reprint 5.00
❑2, Apr 1979, Pilot movie adaptation; reformatted from Marvel Super Special #8; newsstand edition (issue number appears in box) 3.00
❑2/Whitman, Apr 1979, Special markets edition (usually sold in Whitman bagged prepacks); price appears in a diamond; no UPC barcode 3.00
❑3, May 1979, Pilot movie adaptation; reformatted from Marvel Super Special #8; newsstand edition (issue number appears in box) 3.00
❑3/Whitman, May 1979, Special markets edition (usually sold in Whitman bagged prepacks); price appears in a diamond; no UPC barcode 3.00
❑4, Jun 1979, Adapts first hour-long episode of TV series 3.00
❑5, Jul 1979, Adapts second hour-long episode of TV series 3.00
❑6, Aug 1979, First original comics story 3.00
❑7, Sep 1979, Adama trapped in Memory Machine 3.00
❑8, Oct 1979, Young Adama on Scorpia; fill-in issue 3.00
❑9, Nov 1979 .... 3.00
❑10, Dec 1979, PB (a); Flashback story 3.00
❑11, Jan 1980, KJ (a) 2.00
❑12, Feb 1980, Adama leaves Memory Machine 2.00
❑13, Mar 1980 .... 2.00
❑14, Apr 1980, Muffit Two is melted 2.00
❑15, May 1980, KJ (a); Boomer discovers Adama's wife alive 2.00
❑16, Jun 1980 .... 2.00
❑17, Jul 1980, Red "Hulks" 2.00
❑18, Aug 1980, Red "Hulks" 2.00
❑19, Sep 1980, Starbuck returns 2.00
❑20, Oct 1980 .... 2.00
❑21, Nov 1980, BA (a) 2.00
❑22, Dec 1980 .... 2.00
❑23, Jan 1981, Last issue 2.00

BATTLESTAR GALACTICA (MAXIMUM)
MAXIMUM

❑1, Jul 1995 .... 2.50
❑2, Aug 1995 .... 2.50
❑3, Sep 1995 .... 2.50
❑4, Nov 1995 .... 2.50
❑Special 1, Jan 1997 .... 2.99

BATTLESTAR GALACTICA (REALM)
REALM

❑1/A, Dec 1997; Spaceships cover 2.99
❑1/B, Dec 1997; Cylons cover 2.99
❑2, Jan 1998 .... 2.99
❑3, Mar 1998 .... 2.99
❑3/Variant, Mar 1998; alternate cover (eyes in background) 2.99
❑4, Jun 1998 .... 2.99
❑5, Jul 1998 .... 2.99

BATTLESTAR GALACTICA: SEARCH FOR SANCTUARY
REALM

❑1, Sep 1998 .... 2.99
❑Special 1, Sep 1998 .... 3.99

BATTLESTAR GALACTICA: SEASON III
REALM

❑1, Jun 1999 .... 2.99
❑1/A, Jun 1999; Special Convention Edition 5.00
❑1/B, Jun 1999 .... 4.99
❑2, Jul 1999 .... 4.99
❑2/Convention, Jul 1999; Convention edition 5.00
❑3/A, Sep 1999 .... 2.99
❑3/B, Sep 1999; Alternate cover 2.99
❑3/Convention, Sep 1999; Convention edition 5.00

BATTLESTAR GALACTICA: STARBUCK
MAXIMUM

❑1 .... 2.50
❑2 .... 2.50
❑3, Mar 1996 .... 2.50

BATTLESTAR GALACTICA: THE COMPENDIUM
MAXIMUM

❑1, Feb 1997, b&w 2.95

BATTLESTAR GALACTICA: THE ENEMY WITHIN
MAXIMUM

❑1, Nov 1995 .... 2.50
❑2, Jan 1996 .... 2.50
❑3, Feb 1996 .... 2.95
❑3/Variant, Feb 1996; alternate cover 2.95

Battlestar Galactica (Marvel)

TV series launched comics adventures

©Marvel

Beagle Boys

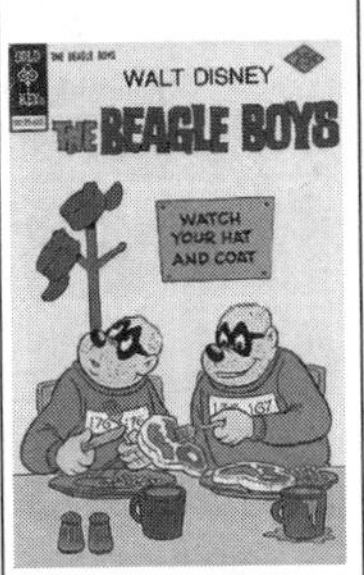

Uncle Scrooge's arch-enemies go wild

©Gold Key

Beast Boy

Changeling uses his older, sillier name

©DC

Beatles Experience

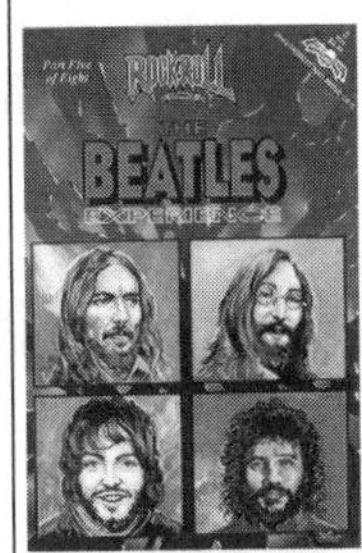

Unauthorized tales of the Fab Four

©Revolutionary

Beautiful Stories for Ugly Children

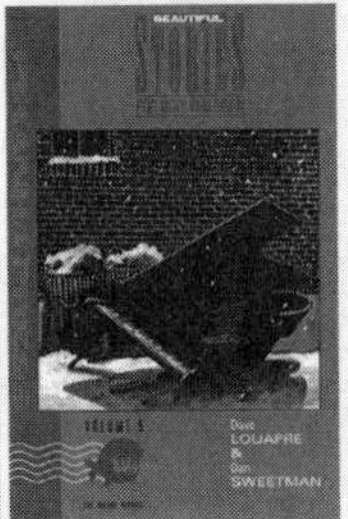

Piranha series ventures into the grotesque

©DC

N-MINT

BATTLESTONE
IMAGE

❑1 ... 2.50
❑1/A, Nov 1994 ... 2.50
❑1/B, Nov 1994, alternate cover ... 2.50
❑2, Dec 1994 ... 2.50

BATTLETECH
MALIBU

❑0 ... 2.95

BATTLETECH (BLACKTHORNE)
BLACKTHORNE

❑1, Oct 1997 ... 2.00
❑2, b&w ... 2.00
❑3, b&w ... 2.00
❑4, b&w ... 2.00
❑5, b&w ... 2.00
❑6, b&w ... 2.00

BATTLETECH: FALLOUT
MALIBU

❑1 ... 2.50
❑2 ... 2.50
❑3 ... 2.50
❑4 ... 2.50

BATTLETECH IN 3-D
BLACKTHORNE

❑1 ... 2.50

BATTLETIDE
MARVEL

❑1, Dec 1992 ... 1.75
❑2, Jan 1993 ... 1.75
❑3, Feb 1993 ... 1.75
❑4, Mar 1993 ... 1.75

BATTLETIDE II
MARVEL

❑1, Aug 1993; Embossed cover ... 2.50
❑2, Sep 1993 ... 1.75
❑3, Oct 1993 ... 1.75
❑4, Nov 1993 ... 1.75

BATTLE TO THE DEATH
IMPERIAL

❑1, b&w ... 1.50
❑2 ... 1.50
❑3 ... 1.50

BATTLE VIXENS
TOKYOPOP

❑1, Apr 2004 ... 9.99

BATTLEZONES: DREAM TEAM 2
MALIBU

❑1, Mar 1996; pin-ups of battles between Malibu and Marvel characters ... 3.95

BATTRON
NEC

❑1, b&w ... 2.75
❑2, b&w ... 2.75

BATTRON'S 4 QUEENS: GUNS, BABES & INTRIGUE
COMMODE

❑1 ... 3.50

N-MINT

BAY CITY JIVE
DC / WILDSTORM

❑1, Jul 2001 ... 2.95
❑1/A, Jul 2001, alternate cover ... 2.95
❑2, Aug 2001 ... 2.95
❑3, Sep 2001 ... 2.95

BAYWATCH COMIC STORIES
ACCLAIM / ARMADA

❑1 ... 4.95
❑2 ... 4.95
❑3 ... 4.95
❑4 ... 4.95

BAZOOKA JULES
COM.X

❑1, ca. 2001 ... 2.99
❑2, ca. 2001 ... 2.95

BEACH HIGH
BIG

❑1, Feb 1997, illustrated text story, one-shot ... 3.25

BEACH PARTY
ETERNITY

❑1; b&w pin-ups ... 2.50

BEAGLE BOYS
GOLD KEY

❑1, Nov 1964 ... 22.00
❑2, Nov 1965 ... 16.00
❑3, Aug 1966 ... 16.00
❑4, Nov 1966 ... 16.00
❑5, Feb 1967 ... 16.00
❑6, May 1967 ... 12.00
❑7, ca. 1968 ... 12.00
❑8, Oct 1968 ... 12.00
❑9, Apr 1970 ... 12.00
❑10, ca. 1970 ... 12.00
❑11, ca. 1971 ... 8.00
❑12, Sep 1971 ... 8.00
❑13, Jul 1972 ... 8.00
❑14, Sep 1972 ... 8.00
❑15, ca. 1973 ... 8.00
❑16, Apr 1973, A: Uncle Scrooge ... 8.00
❑17, Jul 1973 ... 8.00
❑18, Oct 1973 ... 8.00
❑19, Jan 1974 ... 8.00
❑20, Apr 1974 ... 8.00
❑21, Jul 1974 ... 6.00
❑22, Oct 1974 ... 6.00
❑23, Jan 1975 ... 6.00
❑24, Apr 1975 ... 6.00
❑25, Jul 1975 ... 6.00
❑26, Oct 1975 ... 6.00
❑27, Jan 1976 ... 6.00
❑28, Mar 1976 ... 6.00
❑29, May 1976 ... 6.00
❑30, Jul 1976 ... 6.00
❑31, Sep 1976 ... 4.00
❑32, Nov 1976 ... 4.00
❑33, Jan 1977 ... 4.00
❑34, Apr 1977 ... 4.00
❑35, Jun 1977 ... 4.00
❑36, Aug 1977 ... 4.00
❑37, Sep 1977 ... 4.00
❑38, Oct 1977 ... 4.00

N-MINT

❑39, Dec 1977 ... 4.00
❑40, Jan 1978 ... 4.00
❑41, Apr 1978 ... 3.00
❑42, Jun 1978 ... 3.00
❑43, Aug 1978 ... 3.00
❑44, Sep 1978 ... 3.00
❑45, Oct 1978 ... 3.00
❑46, Dec 1978 ... 3.00
❑47 1979 ... 3.00

BEAGLE BOYS VERSUS UNCLE SCROOGE
WHITMAN

❑1, Mar 1979 ... 6.00
❑2, Apr 1979 ... 5.00
❑3, May 1979 ... 4.00
❑4, Jun 1979 ... 4.00
❑5, Jul 1979 ... 4.00
❑6, Aug 1979 ... 4.00
❑7, Sep 1979 ... 4.00
❑8, Oct 1979 ... 3.00
❑9, Nov 1979 ... 3.00
❑10, Dec 1979 ... 3.00
❑11, Jan 1980 ... 3.00
❑12, Feb 1980 ... 3.00

BEANY AND CECIL
DELL

❑1, Jul 1962 ... 75.00
❑2, Oct 1962 ... 60.00
❑3, Jan 1963 ... 60.00
❑4, Apr 1963 ... 60.00
❑5, Jul 1963 ... 60.00

BEAR
SLAVE LABOR

❑1, ca. 2003 ... 2.95
❑2, ca. 2003 ... 2.95
❑3, ca. 2003 ... 2.95
❑4, ca. 2004 ... 2.95
❑5, ca. 2004 ... 2.95
❑6, ca. 2004 ... 2.95
❑7 ... 2.95
❑8 ... 2.95
❑9, Sep 2005 ... 2.95
❑10, Jan 2006 ... 2.95

BEARFAX FUNNIES
TREASURE

❑1 ... 2.75

BEARSKIN: A GRIMM TALE
THECOMIC.COM

❑1, b&w; no cover price ... 1.50

BEAST
MARVEL

❑1, May 1997 ... 2.50
❑2, Jun 1997 ... 2.50
❑3, Jul 1997 ... 2.50

BEAST BOY
DC

❑1, Jan 2000 ... 2.95
❑2, Feb 2000 ... 2.95
❑3, Mar 2000 ... 2.95
❑4, Apr 2000 ... 2.95

Other grades: Multiply price above by 5/6 for VF/NM • 2/3 for VERY FINE • 1/3 for FINE • 1/5 for VERY GOOD • 1/8 for GOOD

N-MINT

B.E.A.S.T.I.E.S.
Axis
- ❑1, Apr 1994 ... 1.95

BEAST WARRIORS OF SHAOLIN
Pied Piper
- ❑1, Jul 1987 ... 1.95
- ❑2 ... 1.95
- ❑3 ... 1.95

BEATLES (DELL)
Dell
- ❑1, Sep 1964 ... 440.00

BEATLES EXPERIENCE
Revolutionary
- ❑1, Mar 1991 ... 2.50
- ❑2, May 1991 ... 2.50
- ❑3, Jul 1991 ... 2.50
- ❑4, Sep 1991 ... 2.50
- ❑5, Nov 1991 ... 2.50
- ❑6, Jan 1992 ... 2.50
- ❑7, Mar 1992 ... 2.50
- ❑8, May 1992 ... 2.50

BEATLES (PERSONALITY)
Personality
- ❑1, b&w ... 5.00
- ❑1/Ltd.; limited edition, b&w ... 8.00
- ❑2, b&w ... 4.00

BEATLES VS. THE ROLLING STONES
Celebrity
- ❑1, May 1992 ... 2.95

BEATRIX
Vision
- ❑1 ... 2.95
- ❑2, Mar 1997 ... 2.95

BEAUTIES & BARBARIANS
AC
- ❑1 WW (a) ... 1.50

BEAUTIFUL PEOPLE
Slave Labor
- ❑1, Apr 1994; Oversized ... 4.50

BEAUTIFUL STORIES FOR UGLY CHILDREN
DC / Piranha
- ❑1, ca. 1989 ... 2.50
- ❑2, ca. 1989 ... 2.50
- ❑3, ca. 1989 ... 2.50
- ❑4, ca. 1989 ... 2.50
- ❑5, ca. 1989 ... 2.50
- ❑6, ca. 1989 ... 2.50
- ❑7, ca. 1989 ... 2.50
- ❑8, ca. 1990 ... 2.50
- ❑9, ca. 1990 ... 2.50
- ❑10, ca. 1990 ... 2.50
- ❑11, ca. 1990 ... 2.50
- ❑12, ca. 1990 ... 2.50
- ❑13, ca. 1990 ... 2.50
- ❑14, ca. 1990 ... 2.50
- ❑15, ca. 1990 ... 2.50
- ❑16, ca. 1990 ... 2.50
- ❑17, ca. 1990 ... 2.50
- ❑18, ca. 1990 ... 2.50
- ❑19, ca. 1991 ... 2.50
- ❑20, ca. 1991 ... 2.50
- ❑21, ca. 1991 ... 2.50
- ❑22, ca. 1991 ... 2.50
- ❑23, ca. 1991 ... 2.50
- ❑24, ca. 1992 ... 2.50
- ❑25, ca. 1992 ... 2.50
- ❑26, ca. 1992 ... 2.50
- ❑27, ca. 1992 ... 2.50
- ❑28, ca. 1992 ... 2.50
- ❑29, ca. 1992 ... 2.50
- ❑30, ca. 1992 ... 2.50

BEAUTY AND THE BEAST
Disney
- ❑1 ... 2.50
- ❑1/Direct ed.; squarebound ... 4.95

BEAUTY AND THE BEAST (DISNEY'S...)
Disney
- ❑1, Sep 1994 ... 1.50
- ❑2, Oct 1994 ... 1.50
- ❑3, Nov 1994 ... 1.50
- ❑4, Dec 1994 ... 1.50
- ❑5, Jan 1995 ... 1.50
- ❑6, Feb 1995 ... 1.50
- ❑7, Mar 1995 ... 1.50
- ❑8, Apr 1995 ... 1.50
- ❑9, May 1995 ... 1.50
- ❑10, Jun 1995 ... 1.50
- ❑11, Jul 1995 ... 1.50
- ❑12, Aug 1995 ... 1.50
- ❑13, Sep 1995 ... 1.50
- ❑Holiday 1; digest; based on direct-to-video feature ... 4.50

BEAUTY AND THE BEAST (INNOVATION)
Innovation
- ❑1, May 1993 ... 2.50
- ❑1/CS ... 3.95
- ❑2, Jun 1993 ... 2.50
- ❑3, Jul 1993 ... 2.50
- ❑4, Aug 1993 ... 2.50
- ❑5, Sep 1993 ... 2.50
- ❑6, Oct 1993, indicia says Jul, should be Oct ... 2.50

BEAUTY AND THE BEAST (MARVEL)
Marvel
- ❑1, Dec 1984 DP (a) ... 2.00
- ❑2, Feb 1985 DP (a) ... 2.00
- ❑3, Apr 1985 DP (a) ... 2.00
- ❑4, Jun 1985 DP (a) ... 2.00

BEAUTY AND THE BEAST: NIGHT OF BEAUTY
First
- ❑1, Mar 1990 ... 5.95

BEAUTY AND THE BEAST: PORTRAIT OF LOVE
First
- ❑1, May 1989 ... 5.95

BEAUTY AND THE BEAST (STAN SHAW'S...)
Dark Horse
- ❑1 ... 4.95

BEAUTY IS THE BEAST
Viz
- ❑1, Dec 2005 ... 9.95

BEAUTY OF THE BEASTS
Mu
- ❑1, Nov 1991, b&w ... 2.50
- ❑2, May 1992, b&w ... 2.50
- ❑3, Jul 1993 ... 2.50

BEAVIS & BUTT-HEAD
Marvel
- ❑1, Mar 1994 1: Beavis & Butt-Head (in comics). A: Punisher. ... 2.50
- ❑1/2nd, Mar 1994 ... 1.95
- ❑2, Apr 1994 ... 2.50
- ❑3, May 1994 JR (a) ... 2.50
- ❑4, Jun 1994 ... 2.50
- ❑5, Jul 1994 ... 2.50
- ❑6, Aug 1994 ... 2.00
- ❑7, Sep 1994 ... 2.00
- ❑8, Oct 1994 ... 2.00
- ❑9, Nov 1994 ... 2.00
- ❑10, Dec 1994 ... 2.00
- ❑11, Jan 1995 ... 2.00
- ❑12, Feb 1995 ... 2.00
- ❑13, Mar 1995 ... 2.00
- ❑14, Apr 1995 ... 2.00
- ❑15, May 1995 ... 2.00
- ❑16, Jun 1995 ... 2.00
- ❑17, Jul 1995 ... 2.00
- ❑18, Aug 1995 ... 2.00
- ❑19, Sep 1995 ... 2.00
- ❑20, Oct 1995 ... 2.00
- ❑21, Nov 1995 ... 2.00
- ❑22, Dec 1995 ... 2.00
- ❑23, Jan 1996 ... 2.00
- ❑24, Feb 1996 ... 2.00
- ❑25, Mar 1996 ... 2.00
- ❑26, Apr 1996 ... 2.00
- ❑27, May 1996 ... 2.00
- ❑28, Jun 1996 ... 2.00

BECK & CAUL INVESTIGATIONS
Caliber
- ❑1, Jan 1994 ... 2.95
- ❑2, Mar 1994 ... 2.95
- ❑3, May 1994 ... 2.95
- ❑4, Aug 1994 ... 2.95
- ❑5 ... 2.95
- ❑Annual 1, May 1995 ... 3.50

BECK: MONGOLIAN CHOP SQUAD
Tokyopop
- ❑1, Jul 2005 ... 9.95
- ❑2, Nov 2005 ... 9.95

BEDLAM!
Eclipse
- ❑1, Aug 1985 ... 1.75
- ❑2, Sep 1985 ... 1.75

BEDLAM (CHAOS)
Chaos
- ❑1, Sep 2000 ... 2.95
- ❑1/Variant, Sep 2000 ... 2.95

BEELZELVIS
Slave Labor
- ❑1, Feb 1994 ... 2.95

BEEP BEEP
Dell
- ❑4, Feb 1960 ... 24.00
- ❑5, May 1960 ... 24.00
- ❑6, Aug 1960 ... 24.00
- ❑7, Nov 1960 ... 24.00
- ❑8, Feb 1961 ... 24.00
- ❑9, May 1961 ... 24.00
- ❑10, Aug 1961 ... 16.00
- ❑11, Nov 1961 ... 16.00
- ❑12, Feb 1962 ... 16.00
- ❑13, May 1962 ... 16.00
- ❑14, Aug 1962 ... 16.00

BEEP BEEP, THE ROAD RUNNER (GOLD KEY)
Gold Key
- ❑1, Oct 1966 ... 50.00
- ❑2, Jan 1967 ... 30.00
- ❑3, Apr 1967 ... 30.00
- ❑4, Jul 1967 ... 30.00
- ❑5, Oct 1967 ... 30.00
- ❑6, Jan 1968 ... 15.00
- ❑7, Apr 1968 ... 15.00
- ❑8, Jul 1968 ... 15.00
- ❑9, Oct 1968 ... 15.00
- ❑10, Feb 1969 ... 15.00
- ❑11, Apr 1969 ... 15.00
- ❑12, Jun 1969 ... 15.00
- ❑13, Aug 1969 ... 15.00
- ❑14, Oct 1969 ... 15.00
- ❑15, Dec 1969 ... 15.00
- ❑16, Feb 1970 ... 10.00
- ❑17, Apr 1970 ... 10.00
- ❑18, Jun 1970, Cover code 10189-006 ... 10.00
- ❑19, Aug 1970 ... 10.00
- ❑20, Oct 1970 ... 10.00
- ❑21, Dec 1970 ... 10.00
- ❑22, Feb 1971 ... 10.00
- ❑23, Apr 1971, Cover code 10189-104 ... 10.00
- ❑24, Jun 1971 ... 10.00
- ❑25, Aug 1971 ... 10.00
- ❑26, Oct 1971 ... 10.00
- ❑27, Dec 1971 ... 10.00
- ❑28, Feb 1972 ... 10.00
- ❑29, Apr 1972 ... 10.00
- ❑30, Jun 1972 ... 10.00
- ❑31, Aug 1972 ... 10.00
- ❑32, Oct 1972 ... 10.00
- ❑33, Dec 1972 ... 10.00
- ❑34, Feb 1973 ... 10.00
- ❑35, Apr 1973, Cover code 90189-304; Wile's triplet nephews appear ... 10.00
- ❑36, Jun 1973 ... 10.00
- ❑37, Aug 1973 ... 10.00
- ❑38, Sep 1973 ... 10.00
- ❑39, Oct 1973 ... 10.00
- ❑40, Dec 1973 ... 10.00
- ❑41, Feb 1974 ... 8.00
- ❑42, Apr 1974 ... 8.00
- ❑43, Jun 1974 ... 8.00
- ❑44, Aug 1974 ... 8.00
- ❑45, Sep 1974 ... 8.00
- ❑46, Oct 1974 ... 8.00
- ❑47, Dec 1974 ... 8.00
- ❑48, Feb 1975 ... 8.00
- ❑49, Apr 1975 ... 8.00

Other grades: Multiply price above by 5/6 for VF/NM • 2/3 for VERY FINE • 1/3 for FINE • 1/5 for VERY GOOD • 1/8 for GOOD

Beauty and the Beast (Marvel)

Odd romantic pairing of Beast and Dazzler

©Marvel

Beavis & Butt-Head

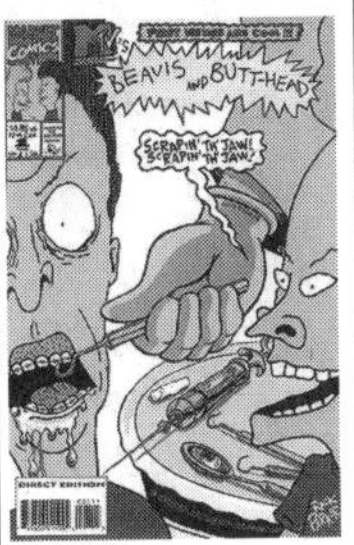

Dim duo goes from MTV to Marvel

©Marvel

Beep Beep

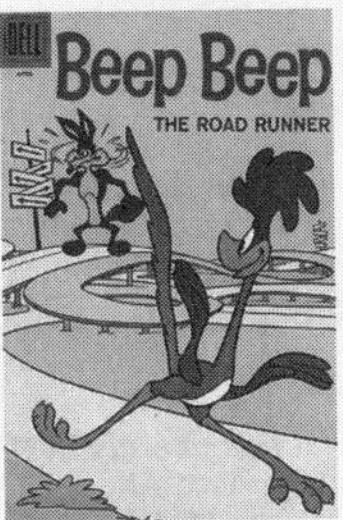

First series starring pesky running fowl

©Dell

Beetle Bailey (Vol. 1)

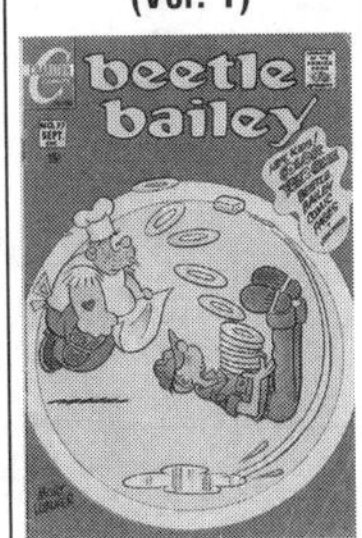

Misadventures with comic strip soldier

©Dell

Beowulf

Medieval tale updated for 1970s DC series

©DC

N-MINT

❑50, Jun 1975 ... 8.00
❑51, Jul 1975 ... 8.00
❑52, Aug 1975 ... 8.00
❑53, Oct 1975 ... 8.00
❑54, Dec 1975 ... 8.00
❑55, Jan 1976 ... 8.00
❑56, Mar 1976 ... 8.00
❑57, May 1976 ... 8.00
❑58, Jul 1976 ... 8.00
❑59, Sep 1976 ... 8.00
❑60, Oct 1976 ... 6.00
❑61, Nov 1976 ... 6.00
❑62, Jan 1977 ... 6.00
❑63, Mar 1977 ... 6.00
❑64, May 1977 ... 6.00
❑65, Jul 1977 ... 6.00
❑66, Sep 1977 ... 6.00
❑67, Oct 1977 ... 6.00
❑68, Nov 1977 ... 6.00
❑69, Jan 1978 ... 6.00
❑70, Mar 1978 ... 6.00
❑71, May 1978 ... 6.00
❑72, Jul 1978 ... 6.00
❑73, Sep 1978 ... 6.00
❑74, Oct 1978 ... 6.00
❑75, Nov 1978 ... 6.00
❑76, Jan 1979 ... 6.00
❑77, Mar 1979 ... 6.00
❑78, Apr 1979 ... 6.00
❑79, May 1979 ... 6.00
❑80, Jun 1979 ... 3.00
❑81, Jul 1979 ... 3.00
❑82, Aug 1979 ... 3.00
❑83, Sep 1979 ... 3.00
❑84, Oct 1979 ... 3.00
❑85, Nov 1979 ... 3.00
❑86, Dec 1979 ... 3.00
❑87, Jan 1980 ... 3.00
❑88, Feb 1980 ... 3.00
❑89, Apr 1980, (c); (w); (a) ... 3.00
❑90, Jul 1980, (c); (w); (a) ... 3.00
❑91, Aug 1980, (c); (w); (a) ... 12.00
❑92, Sep 1980, (c); (w); (a) ... 12.00
❑93, Oct 1980, (c); (w); (a) ... 17.00
❑94, Feb 1981, (c); (w); (a) ... 3.00
❑95 1981, (c); (w); (a) ... 3.00
❑96 1981, (c); (w); (a) ... 3.00
❑97, Sep 1981, (c); (w); (a) ... 3.00
❑98 1981, (c); (w); (a) ... 3.00
❑99 1981, (c); (w); (a) ... 3.00
❑100 1982, (c); (w); (a) ... 3.00
❑101, Apr 1982, (c); (w); (a) ... 3.00
❑102, Jun 1983, (c); (w); (a) ... 12.00
❑103, Jul 1983, (c); (w); (a) ... 12.00
❑104, ca. 1983, (c); (w); (a) ... 12.00
❑105, Jun 1984, (c); (w); (a) ... 12.00

BEER & ROAMING IN LAS VEGAS
SLAVE LABOR

❑1, ca. 1998, b&w ... 2.95
❑Ashcan 1 ... 1.00

N-MINT

BEER NUTZ
TUNDRA

❑1 ... 2.95
❑2 ... 2.00
❑3, b&w ... 2.25

BEETHOVEN
HARVEY

❑1, Mar 1994 ... 1.50
❑2, May 1994 ... 1.50
❑3, Jul 1994 ... 1.50

BEETLE BAILEY (VOL. 1)
DELL

❑5, Apr 1956, Earlier issues appeared as Four Color #469, #521, #552, and #622 ... 24.00
❑6, Jun 1956 ... 24.00
❑7, Aug 1956 ... 24.00
❑8, Nov 1956 ... 24.00
❑9, Feb 1957 ... 24.00
❑10, May 1957 ... 24.00
❑11, Aug 1957 ... 18.00
❑12, Nov 1957 ... 18.00
❑13, Feb 1958 ... 18.00
❑14, Apr 1958 ... 18.00
❑15, Jun 1958 ... 18.00
❑16, Aug 1958 ... 18.00
❑17, Oct 1958 ... 18.00
❑18, Dec 1958 ... 18.00
❑19, Feb 1959 ... 18.00
❑20, Apr 1959 ... 18.00
❑21, Jun 1959 ... 14.00
❑22, Aug 1959 ... 14.00
❑23, Oct 1959 ... 14.00
❑24, Dec 1959 ... 14.00
❑25, Feb 1960 ... 14.00
❑26, Apr 1960 ... 14.00
❑27, Jun 1960 ... 14.00
❑28 1960 ... 14.00
❑29 1960 ... 14.00
❑30 1960 ... 14.00
❑31, Mar 1961 ... 10.00
❑32, May 1961 ... 10.00
❑33, Jul 1961 ... 10.00
❑34, Sep 1961 ... 10.00
❑35, Nov 1961 ... 10.00
❑36, Jan 1962 ... 10.00
❑37, Mar 1962 ... 10.00
❑38, May 1962 ... 10.00
❑39, Nov 1962 ... 10.00
❑40, Feb 1963 ... 10.00
❑41, May 1963 ... 8.00
❑42, Aug 1963 ... 8.00
❑43, Nov 1963 ... 8.00
❑44, Feb 1964 ... 8.00
❑45, May 1964 ... 8.00
❑46, Aug 1964 ... 8.00
❑47, Nov 1964 ... 8.00
❑48, Feb 1965 ... 8.00
❑49, May 1965 ... 8.00
❑50, Aug 1965 ... 8.00
❑51, Nov 1965 ... 7.00
❑52, Feb 1966 ... 7.00
❑53, May 1966, Last Dell/Gold Key issue ... 7.00

N-MINT

❑54, Aug 1966, First King issue ... 7.00
❑55, Oct 1966 ... 7.00
❑56, Dec 1966 ... 7.00
❑57, Feb 1967 ... 7.00
❑58, Apr 1967 ... 7.00
❑59, Jun 1967 ... 7.00
❑60, Jul 1967 ... 7.00
❑61, Aug 1967 ... 6.00
❑62, Sep 1967 ... 6.00
❑63 1968 ... 6.00
❑64 1968 ... 6.00
❑65 1968 ... 6.00
❑66 1968, Last King issue ... 6.00
❑67, Feb 1969, First Charlton issue ... 6.00
❑68, Apr 1969 ... 6.00
❑69, Jun 1969 ... 6.00
❑70, ca. 1969 ... 6.00
❑71, Oct 1969 ... 4.00
❑72, Nov 1969 ... 4.00
❑73, Jan 1970 ... 4.00
❑74, Mar 1970 ... 4.00
❑75, May 1970 ... 4.00
❑76, Jul 1970 ... 4.00
❑77, Sep 1970 ... 4.00
❑78, Nov 1970 ... 4.00
❑79, Jan 1971 ... 4.00
❑80, Mar 1971 ... 4.00
❑81, May 1971 ... 4.00
❑82, Jul 1971 ... 4.00
❑83, Sep 1971 ... 4.00
❑84, Oct 1971 ... 4.00
❑85, Nov 1971 ... 4.00
❑86, Dec 1971 ... 4.00
❑87, Jan 1972 ... 4.00
❑88, Mar 1972 ... 4.00
❑89, Apr 1972 ... 4.00
❑90, Jun 1972 ... 4.00
❑91, Jul 1972 ... 4.00
❑92, Aug 1972 ... 4.00
❑93, Oct 1972 ... 4.00
❑94, Nov 1972 ... 4.00
❑95, Dec 1972 ... 4.00
❑96, Jan 1973 ... 4.00
❑97, Mar 1973 ... 4.00
❑98, Apr 1973 ... 4.00
❑99, Jun 1973 ... 4.00
❑100, Jul 1973 ... 4.00
❑101, Aug 1973 ... 3.00
❑102, Oct 1973 ... 3.00
❑103, Nov 1973 ... 3.00
❑104 1974 ... 3.00
❑105, May 1974 ... 3.00
❑106, Jul 1974 ... 3.00
❑107, Oct 1974 ... 3.00
❑108 1974 ... 3.00
❑109 1975 ... 3.00
❑110, Apr 1975 ... 3.00
❑111, Jun 1975 ... 3.00
❑112, Sep 1975 ... 3.00
❑113 1975 ... 3.00
❑114 1976 ... 3.00
❑115, Mar 1976 ... 3.00
❑116, May 1976 ... 3.00
❑117, Jul 1976 ... 3.00

Other grades: Multiply price above by 5/6 for VF/NM • 2/3 for VERY FINE • 1/3 for FINE • 1/5 for VERY GOOD • 1/8 for GOOD

N-MINT | N-MINT | N-MINT

❑118, Sep 1976 .... 3.00
❑119; Last Charlton issue 3.00
❑120, Apr 1978, Returns to Gold Key. 3.00
❑121, Jun 1978 .... 3.00
❑122, Aug 1978 .... 3.00
❑123, Oct 1978 .... 3.00
❑124, Dec 1978 .... 3.00
❑125, Feb 1979 .... 3.00
❑126, Apr 1979 .... 3.00
❑127, Jun 1979 .... 3.00
❑128, Aug 1979 .... 3.00
❑129, Oct 1979 .... 3.00
❑130, Dec 1979 .... 3.00
❑131, Feb 1980 .... 3.00
❑132, Apr 1980 .... 3.00

BEETLE BAILEY (VOL. 2)
HARVEY

❑1, Sep 1992 .... 2.00
❑2, Jan 1993 .... 2.00
❑3, Apr 1993 .... 2.00
❑4, Jul 1993 .... 2.00
❑5, Oct 1993 .... 2.00
❑6, Jan 1994 .... 2.00
❑7, Apr 1994 .... 2.00
❑8, Jun 1994 .... 2.00
❑9, Aug 1994 .... 2.00
❑Giant Size 1, Giant-size 2.25
❑Giant Size 2, Giant-size 2.25

BEETLE BAILEY BIG BOOK
HARVEY

❑2 .... 2.00

BEETLEJUICE
HARVEY

❑1 .... 1.50
❑2 .... 1.50

BEETLEJUICE: ELLIOT MESS AND THE UNWASHABLES
HARVEY

❑1 .... 1.50
❑2, Oct 1992 .... 1.50
❑3, Nov 1992 .... 1.50

BEETLEJUICE HOLIDAY SPECIAL
HARVEY

❑1, Feb 1992 .... 1.50

BEETLEJUICE IN THE NEITHERWORLD
HARVEY

❑1 .... 1.50
❑2 .... 1.50

BEET THE VANDEL BUSTER
VIZ

❑1, Oct 2004 .... 9.99
❑2, Dec 2004 .... 9.99
❑3, Feb 2005 .... 9.99
❑4, Apr 2005 .... 9.99
❑5, May 2005 .... 9.99
❑6, Aug 2005 .... 9.99
❑7, Oct 2005 .... 9.99

BEFORE THE FANTASTIC FOUR: BEN GRIMM AND LOGAN
MARVEL

❑1, Jul 2000 .... 2.99
❑2, Aug 2000 .... 2.99
❑3, Sep 2000 .... 2.99

BEFORE THE FF: REED RICHARDS
MARVEL

❑1, Sep 2000 .... 2.99
❑2, Oct 2000 .... 2.99
❑3, Dec 2000 .... 2.99

BEFORE THE FF: THE STORMS
MARVEL

❑1, Dec 2000 .... 2.99
❑2, Jan 2001 .... 2.99
❑3, Feb 2001 .... 2.99

BEHOLD 3-D
EDGE GROUP

❑1 .... 3.95

BELIEVE IN YOURSELF PRODUCTIONS
BELIEVE IN YOURSELF PRODUCTIONS

❑1/Ashcan; Ashcan Edition. Cardstock cover. Includes 6 page story only available in Ashcan format with 14 pin-u; Cardstock cover. Includes six-page story only available in Ashcan format with 14 pin-up pages 1.00

❑1/B; Sapphire Edition. Only 25 made 1.00
❑1/Ltd 1.00

BELLA DONNA
PINNACLE

❑1, b&w 1.75

BELLY BUTTON
FANTAGRAPHICS

❑1, Oct 2004 .... 4.95
❑2, Dec 2004 .... 4.95

BEN CASEY FILM STORIES
GOLD KEY

❑1, ca. 1962 .... 55.00

BENEATH THE PLANET OF THE APES
GOLD KEY

❑1, Dec 1970 .... 35.00

BENZANGO OBSCURO
STARHEAD

❑1 .... 2.75

BENZINE
ANTARCTIC

❑1, Oct 2000 .... 4.95
❑2, Nov 2000 .... 4.95
❑3, Dec 2000 .... 4.95
❑4, Jan 2001 .... 4.95
❑5, Feb 2001 .... 4.95
❑6, Mar 2001 .... 4.95
❑7, May 2001 .... 4.95

BEOWULF
DC

❑1, May 1975 1: Grendel (monster). 1: Beowulf. 5.00
❑2, Jul 1975 .... 3.00
❑3, Sep 1975 .... 1.50
❑4, Nov 1975 .... 1.50
❑5, Jan 1976 .... 1.50
❑6, Mar 1976 .... 1.50

BEOWULF (THECOMIC.COM)
COMIC.COM

❑1, ca. 1999 .... 4.95
❑2 1999 .... 4.95
❑3 1999 .... 4.95

BEOWULF (SPEAKEASY)
SPEAKEASY COMICS

❑1 2005 .... 2.99
❑2 2005 .... 2.99
❑3, Sep 2005 .... 2.99
❑4, Oct 2005 ....

BERLIN
DRAWN & QUARTERLY

❑1, Apr 1996 .... 2.50
❑2, Jul 1996 .... 2.50
❑3, Feb 1997 .... 2.50
❑4, Feb 1998 .... 2.50
❑5, ca. 1998 .... 2.95
❑6, ca. 1999 .... 2.95
❑7, Apr 2000, b&w; smaller than normal comic book 2.95
❑8, b&w 2.95
❑9 .... 0.00
❑10 2003 .... 3.50
❑11 2005 .... 3.95
❑12, Dec 2005 .... 3.95

BERNIE WRIGHTSON, MASTER OF THE MACABRE
PACIFIC

❑1, Jun 1983; BWr (w); BWr (a); Edgar Allen Poe adaptation ("The Black Cat") 2.50
❑2, Aug 1983 BWr (w); BWr (a) 2.50
❑3, Aug 1983 BWr (w); BWr (a) 2.50
❑4, Aug 1984 BWr (w); BWr (a) 2.50
❑5, Nov 1984 BWr (w); BWr (a) 2.50

BERSERK
DARK HORSE

❑1, ca. 2003 .... 13.95
❑2, ca. 2004 .... 13.95
❑3, ca. 2004 .... 13.95

BERZERKER
GAUNTLET

❑1, Feb 1993; Medina 2.95
❑2 .... 2.95
❑3 .... 2.95
❑4 .... 2.95
❑5 .... 2.95

BERZERKERS
IMAGE

❑1, Aug 1995 .... 2.50
❑1/Variant, Aug 1995; alternate cover 2.50
❑2, Sep 1995 .... 2.50
❑3, Oct 1995 .... 2.50

BEST CELLARS
OUT OF THE CELLAR

❑1 .... 2.50

BEST OF BARRON STOREY'S W.A.T.C.H. MAGAZINE
VANGUARD

❑1, Dec 1993 .... 2.95

BEST OF DARK HORSE PRESENTS
DARK HORSE

❑1, b&w; Reprints 5.95
❑2, b&w; Reprints 8.95

BEST OF DC
DC

❑1, Sep 1979 JO, DG, RA (c); MA, CS, KS (a) 5.00
❑2, Nov 1979 NA (a) 4.00
❑3, Jan 1980 JO, JL (c) 4.00
❑4, Mar 1980 .... 4.00
❑5, May 1980, DG, RA (c); DN, JSa, CS, JL, KS, DA, JAb (a) 4.00
❑6, Jul 1980, DG, RA (c); CS, KS (a) .. 4.00
❑7, Sep 1980, DG, RA (c); FR (w); MA, CS (a); Superboy 4.00
❑8, Nov 1980; DG, RA (c); MA, CS (a); Superman, Other Identities 4.00
❑9, Jan 1981 JA (c); FR (w); DG, JA, IN (a) 4.00
❑10, Mar 1981 DG, RA (c); MA, CI, JKu, GK, NC, RT (a) 4.00
❑11, Apr 1981 DG, RA (c); DG, CS, TVE, DS, JL (a) 4.00
❑12, May 1981 DG, RA (c); MA, CS (a) 4.00
❑13, Jun 1981 DG, RA (c); DD, CS (a) 4.00
❑14, Jul 1981, DG, RA (c); DG, NA, MR, IN (a) 4.00
❑15, Aug 1981; DG, RA (c); MA, WW (a); Superboy 4.00
❑16, Sep 1981, RB, DG (c); Superman Anniversaries 4.00
❑17, Oct 1981 DG (c); BO, JM (a) 4.00
❑18, Nov 1981, RT (c); NA (w); CI, NA, GK, NC, RT (a) 4.00
❑19, Dec 1981; DG, RA (c); BO, CS, KS, JAb (a); Superman, Imaginary Stories 4.00
❑20, Jan 1982 DG, RA (c); DD (a) 4.00
❑21, Feb 1982; MA, BL, JSa (a); Justice Society 4.00
❑22, Mar 1982, RB, DG (c); DG, JK, DD, NC, IN (a); Sandman 4.00
❑23, Apr 1982, DG (c); DN, FMc, DG, JSa, CS, DS, DA, RT (a) 4.00
❑24, May 1982; EC (c); CI, GT, CS, JAb (a); Legion 4.00
❑25, Jun 1982, RA (c); BO, MA, NA, CS (a) 4.00
❑26, Jul 1982; JA (c); JKu, NA, TVE, RA, RH, JA, IN (a); Brave and the Bold 4.00
❑27, Aug 1982; DG, RA (c); BO, MA, CS, KS, JAb (a); Superman vs. Luthor.... 4.00
❑28, Sep 1982 BO (c) 4.00
❑29, Oct 1982 .... 4.00
❑30, Nov 1982, JA (c); FR (w); CI, FR, DG, GK, IN (a); Batman 4.00
❑31, Dec 1982, GK (c); Justice League 4.00
❑32, Jan 1983, RB (c); Superman 4.00
❑33, Feb 1983, KG (c) 4.00
❑34, Mar 1983, Metal Men 4.00
❑35, Apr 1983, Year's Best 82 .... 4.00
❑36, May 1983; Superman vs. Kryptonite 4.00
❑37, Jun 1983 .... 4.00
❑38, Jul 1983 .... 4.00
❑39, Aug 1983 .... 4.00
❑40, Sep 1983; Superman, Krypton ... 4.00
❑41, Oct 1983 .... 4.00
❑42, Nov 1983 .... 4.00
❑43, Dec 1983 .... 4.00
❑44, Jan 1984, KS (c); KG, KS (a); Legion 4.00
❑45, Feb 1984; Binky 4.00
❑46, Mar 1984; Jimmy Olsen 4.00
❑47, Apr 1984 .... 4.00
❑48, May 1984 .... 4.00
❑49, Jun 1984 .... 4.00

Other grades: Multiply price above by 5/6 for VF/NM • 2/3 for VERY FINE • 1/3 for FINE • 1/5 for VERY GOOD • 1/8 for GOOD

Berzerkers

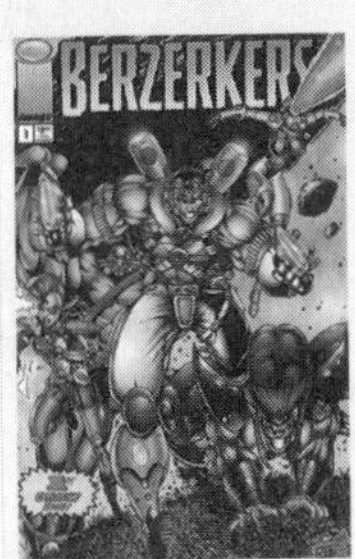

Prison escapees live a life of violence

©Image

Best of Furrlough

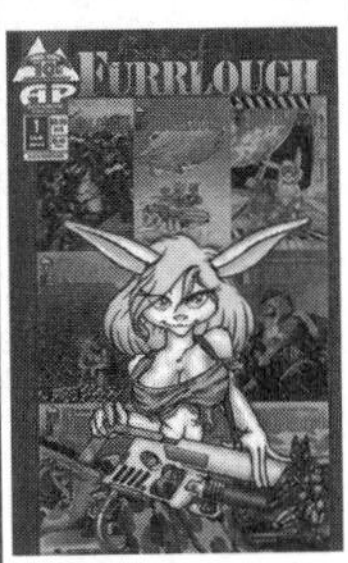

Reprinting adventures from anthropomorphic title

©Antarctic

Bettie Page: Queen of the Nile

Jim Silke's risqué Bettie Page adventures

©Dark Horse

Betty

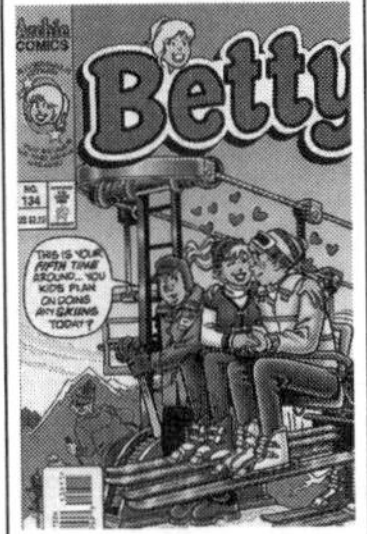

Nice-girl Archie character gets own series

©Archie

Betty & Me

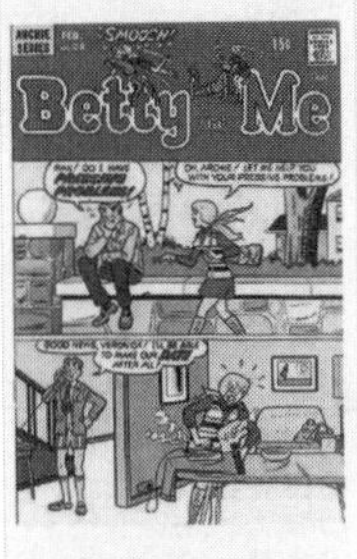

But there was no "Veronica & Me." Hmmm...

©Archie

N-MINT

❑50, Jul 1984; Superman ... 4.00
❑51, Aug 1984 ... 4.00
❑52, Sep 1984; Year's Best 83 ... 4.00
❑53, Oct 1984 ... 4.00
❑54, Nov 1984 ... 4.00
❑55, Dec 1984 ... 4.00
❑56, Jan 1985; Superman ... 4.00
❑57, Feb 1985; Legion ... 4.00
❑58, Mar 1985; Superman Jrs ... 4.00
❑59, Apr 1985; Superman ... 4.00
❑60, May 1985 ... 4.00
❑61, Jun 1985 ... 4.00
❑62, Jul 1985; Batman ... 4.00
❑63, Aug 1985, WW (c); SA (w); SA, SD, BWr, BW, AA, WW, NC (a) ... 4.00
❑64, Sep 1985; Legion ... 4.00
❑65, Oct 1985; Sugar & Spike ... 4.00
❑66, Nov 1985; Superman ... 4.00
❑67, Dec 1985 ... 4.00
❑68, Jan 1986; Sugar & Spike ... 4.00
❑69, Feb 1986; Year's Best 85 ... 4.00
❑70, Mar 1986; Binky's Buddies ... 4.00

BEST OF DONALD DUCK AND UNCLE SCROOGE
GOLD KEY

❑1, Nov 1964, Reprints stories from Four Color Comics #189 and 408 (Donald Duck) ... 50.00
❑2, Sep 1967, CB (a); Reprints stories from Four Color Comics #256 (Donald Duck) and Uncle Scrooge #7 and 8 ... 50.00

BEST OF DORK TOWER
DORK STORM

❑1, ca. 2001, b&w ... 2.00

BEST OF FURRLOUGH
ANTARCTIC

❑1, Jan 1995, b&w ... 3.95
❑2 ... 3.95

BEST OF GOLD DIGGER
ANTARCTIC

❑Annual 1, May 1999, b&w ... 2.99

BEST OF NORTHSTAR
NORTHSTAR

❑1, b&w ... 1.95

BEST OF THE BRAVE AND THE BOLD
DC

❑1, Oct 1988, Batman, Green Arrow ... 2.50
❑2, Nov 1988, Batman, Flash ... 2.50
❑3, Dec 1988, Batman, Aquaman ... 2.50
❑4, Dec 1988, Batman, Creeper ... 2.50
❑5, Jan 1989, Batman, House of Mystery ... 2.50
❑6, Jan 1989, Batman, Teen Titans ... 2.50

BEST OF THE BRITISH INVASION
REVOLUTIONARY

❑1, Sep 1993, b&w ... 2.50
❑2, Jan 1994, b&w ... 2.50

BEST OF TRIBUNE CO.
DRAGON LADY

❑1 ... 2.95
❑2 ... 2.95
❑3 ... 2.95
❑4; (becomes Thrilling Adventure Strips) ... 2.95

N-MINT

BEST OF UNCLE SCROOGE & DONALD DUCK
GOLD KEY

❑1, Nov 1968; reprints parts of Four Color #159 and #456 and Uncle Scrooge #6 and #7 ... 45.00

BEST OF WALT DISNEY COMICS
WESTERN

❑1, ca. 1974; 96170; Reprints stories from Four Color Comics #62 (Donald Duck) ... 15.00
❑2, ca. 1974; 96171 ... 12.00
❑3, ca. 1974; 96172; Reprints stories from Four Color Comics #386 and 495 (Uncle Scrooge) and Uncle Scrooge #7 ... 12.00
❑4, ca. 1974; 96173; Reprints stories from Four Color Comics #159 and 178 (Donald Duck) ... 12.00

BETA SEXUS
FANTAGRAPHICS / EROS

❑1, b&w ... 2.75
❑2, Jul 1994, b&w ... 2.75

BETTA: TIME WARRIOR
IMMORTAL / EROS

❑1 ... 2.95
❑2 ... 2.95
❑3 ... 2.95

BETTI COZMO
ANTARCTIC

❑1, Apr 1999 ... 2.99
❑2, Jun 1999 ... 2.99

BETTIE PAGE COMICS
DARK HORSE

❑1, Mar 1996; one-shot, cardstock cover ... 3.95

BETTIE PAGE COMICS: SPICY ADVENTURE
DARK HORSE

❑1, Jan 1997 ... 2.95

BETTIE PAGE: QUEEN OF THE NILE
DARK HORSE

❑1, Dec 1999 ... 2.95
❑2, Feb 2000 ... 2.95
❑3, Apr 2000 ... 2.95

BETTY
ARCHIE

❑1, Sep 1992 ... 4.00
❑2, Oct 1992 ... 2.00
❑3, Dec 1992 ... 2.00
❑4, Feb 1993 ... 2.00
❑5, Apr 1993 ... 2.00
❑6, Jun 1993 ... 1.50
❑7, Aug 1993 ... 1.50
❑8, Sep 1993 ... 1.50
❑9, Oct 1993 ... 1.50
❑10, Nov 1993 ... 1.50
❑11, Dec 1993 ... 1.50
❑12, Feb 1994 ... 1.50
❑13, Apr 1994 ... 1.50
❑14, Jun 1994 ... 1.50
❑15, Jul 1994 ... 1.50
❑16, Aug 1994 ... 1.50
❑17, Sep 1994 ... 1.50

N-MINT

❑18, Oct 1994 ... 1.50
❑19, Nov 1994 ... 1.50
❑20, Dec 1994 ... 1.50
❑21, Jan 1995 ... 1.50
❑22, Feb 1995 ... 1.50
❑23, Mar 1995 ... 1.50
❑24, Apr 1995 ... 1.50
❑25, May 1995 ... 1.50
❑26, Jun 1995 ... 1.50
❑27, Jul 1995 ... 1.50
❑28, Aug 1995 ... 1.50
❑29, Sep 1995 ... 1.50
❑30, Oct 1995 ... 1.50
❑31, Nov 1995 ... 1.50
❑32, Dec 1995 ... 1.50
❑33, Jan 1996 ... 1.50
❑34, Feb 1996 ... 1.50
❑35, Mar 1996 ... 1.50
❑36, Apr 1996 ... 1.50
❑37, May 1996 ... 1.50
❑38, Jun 1996 ... 1.50
❑39, Jul 1996 ... 1.50
❑40, Aug 1996 ... 1.50
❑41, Sep 1996 ... 1.50
❑42, Oct 1996, cover has reader sketches of Betty ... 1.50
❑43, Nov 1996 ... 1.50
❑44, Dec 1996 ... 1.50
❑45, Jan 1997 ... 1.50
❑46, Feb 1997 ... 1.50
❑47, Mar 1997 ... 1.50
❑48, Apr 1997 ... 1.50
❑49, May 1997 ... 1.50
❑50, Jun 1997 ... 1.50
❑51, Jul 1997 ... 1.50
❑52, Aug 1997 ... 1.50
❑53, Sep 1997 ... 1.50
❑54, Oct 1997 ... 1.50
❑55, Nov 1997 ... 1.50
❑56, Dec 1997, return of Polly Cooper 1.50
❑57, Jan 1998 ... 1.75
❑58, Feb 1998, Virtual Pets ... 1.75
❑59, Mar 1998 ... 1.75
❑60, Apr 1998 ... 1.75
❑61, May 1998 ... 1.75
❑62, Jun 1998 ... 1.75
❑63, Jul 1998 ... 1.75
❑64, Aug 1998 ... 1.75
❑65, Sep 1998 ... 1.75
❑66, Oct 1998 ... 1.75
❑67, Nov 1998 ... 1.75
❑68, Dec 1998 ... 1.75
❑69, Jan 1999 ... 1.75
❑70, Feb 1999 ... 1.75
❑71, Mar 1999 ... 1.75
❑72, Apr 1999 ... 1.79
❑73, May 1999 ... 1.79
❑74, Jun 1999 ... 1.79
❑75, Jul 1999 ... 1.79
❑76, Aug 1999 ... 1.79
❑77, Sep 1999 ... 1.79
❑78, Oct 1999 ... 1.79
❑79, Nov 1999 ... 1.79
❑80, Dec 1999 ... 1.79

	N-MINT
❑81, Jan 2000	1.79
❑82, Feb 2000	1.79
❑83, Mar 2000	1.79
❑84, Apr 2000	1.79
❑85, May 2000	1.79
❑86, Jun 2000	1.79
❑87, Jul 2000	1.99
❑88, Aug 2000	1.99
❑89, Sep 2000	1.99
❑90, Oct 2000	1.99
❑91, Nov 2000	1.99
❑92, Dec 2000	1.99
❑93, Jan 2001	1.99
❑94, Feb 2001	1.99
❑95, Mar 2001	1.99
❑96, Apr 2001	1.99
❑97, May 2001	1.99
❑98, Jun 2001	1.99
❑99, Jul 2001	1.99
❑100, Aug 2001	1.99
❑101, Sep 2001	1.99
❑102, Oct 2001	1.99
❑103, Oct 2001	2.19
❑104, Nov 2001	2.19
❑105, Dec 2001	2.19
❑106, Jan 2002	2.19
❑107, Feb 2002	2.19
❑108, Mar 2002	2.19
❑109, Apr 2002	2.19
❑110, May 2002	2.19
❑111, Jun 2002	2.19
❑112, Jul 2002	2.19
❑113, Aug 2002	2.19
❑114, Sep 2002	2.19
❑115, Oct 2002	2.19
❑116, Oct 2002	2.19
❑117, Nov 2002	2.19
❑118, Dec 2002	2.19
❑119, Jan 2003	2.19
❑120, Feb 2003	2.19
❑121, Mar 2003	2.19
❑122, Apr 2003	2.19
❑123, May 2003	2.19
❑124, Jun 2003	2.19
❑125, Jul 2003	2.19
❑126, Aug 2003	2.19
❑127, Sep 2003	2.19
❑128, Oct 2003	2.19
❑129, Oct 2003	2.19
❑130, Nov 2003	2.19
❑131, Dec 2003	2.19
❑132, Jan 2004	2.19
❑133, Feb 2004	2.19
❑134, Mar 2004	2.19
❑135, Apr 2004	2.19
❑136, May 2004	2.19
❑137, Jul 2004	2.19
❑138, Aug 2004	2.19
❑139, Sep 2004	2.19
❑140, Oct 2004	2.19
❑141, Nov 2004	2.19
❑142, Jan 2005	2.19
❑143, Feb 2005 AM (a)	2.19
❑144, Mar 2005	2.19
❑145, Apr 2005	2.19
❑146, May 2005	2.19
❑147, Jun 2005	2.19
❑148, Aug 2005	2.19
❑149, Aug 2005	2.19
❑150, Oct 2005	2.19
❑151, Nov 2005	2.19
❑152, Dec 2005	2.19
❑153, Mar 2006	2.19
❑154, May 2006	2.19
❑156, Aug 2006	2.19
❑157, Aug 2006	2.19

BETTY & ME
ARCHIE

	N-MINT
❑1, Aug 1965	65.00
❑2, Nov 1965	40.00
❑3, Aug 1966	24.00
❑4, Oct 1966	24.00
❑5, Dec 1966	24.00
❑6, Feb 1967	15.00
❑7, Apr 1967	15.00
❑8, Jun 1967	15.00
❑9, Aug 1967	15.00
❑10, Oct 1967	15.00
❑11, Dec 1967	10.00
❑12, Feb 1968	10.00
❑13, Apr 1968	10.00
❑14, Jun 1968	10.00
❑15, Aug 1968	10.00
❑16, Sep 1968	10.00
❑17, Oct 1968	10.00
❑18, Dec 1968	10.00
❑19, Feb 1969	10.00
❑20, Apr 1969	10.00
❑21, Jun 1969	7.00
❑22, Aug 1969	7.00
❑23, Sep 1969	7.00
❑24, Oct 1969	7.00
❑25, Dec 1969	7.00
❑26, Feb 1970	7.00
❑27, Apr 1970	7.00
❑28, Jun 1970	7.00
❑29, Aug 1970	7.00
❑30, Sep 1970	7.00
❑31, Oct 1970	6.00
❑32, Dec 1970	6.00
❑33, Feb 1971	6.00
❑34, Apr 1971	6.00
❑35, Jun 1971	6.00
❑36, Aug 1971	6.00
❑37, Sep 1971	6.00
❑38, Oct 1971	6.00
❑39, Dec 1971	6.00
❑40, Feb 1972	6.00
❑41, Apr 1972	5.00
❑42, Jun 1972	5.00
❑43, Aug 1972	5.00
❑44, Sep 1972	5.00
❑45, Oct 1972	5.00
❑46, Dec 1972	5.00
❑47, Feb 1973	5.00
❑48, Apr 1973	5.00
❑49, Jun 1973	5.00
❑50, Jul 1973	5.00
❑51, Aug 1973	4.00
❑52, Sep 1973	4.00
❑53, Oct 1973	4.00
❑54, Dec 1973	4.00
❑55, Feb 1974	4.00
❑56, Apr 1974	4.00
❑57, Jun 1974	4.00
❑58, Jul 1974	4.00
❑59, Aug 1974	4.00
❑60, Sep 1974	4.00
❑61, Oct 1974	3.00
❑62, Dec 1974	3.00
❑63, Feb 1975	3.00
❑64, Mar 1975	3.00
❑65, Apr 1975	3.00
❑66, May 1975	3.00
❑67, Jul 1975	3.00
❑68, Aug 1975	3.00
❑69, Sep 1975	3.00
❑70, Oct 1975	3.00
❑71, Dec 1975	2.00
❑72, Feb 1976	2.00
❑73, Mar 1976	2.00
❑74, Apr 1976	2.00
❑75, May 1976	2.00
❑76, Jul 1976	2.00
❑77, Aug 1976	2.00
❑78, Sep 1976	2.00
❑79, Oct 1976	2.00
❑80, Dec 1976	2.00
❑81, Feb 1977	2.00
❑82, Mar 1977	2.00
❑83, Apr 1977	2.00
❑84, May 1977	2.00
❑85, Jul 1977	2.00
❑86, Aug 1977	2.00
❑87, Sep 1977	2.00
❑88, Oct 1977	2.00
❑89, Dec 1977	2.00
❑90, Feb 1978	2.00
❑91, Mar 1978	2.00
❑92, Apr 1978	2.00
❑93, May 1978	2.00
❑94, Jul 1978	2.00
❑95, Aug 1978	2.00
❑96, Sep 1978	2.00
❑97, Oct 1978	2.00
❑98, Dec 1978	2.00
❑99, Feb 1979	2.00
❑100, Mar 1979	2.00
❑101, Apr 1979	2.00
❑102, May 1979	2.00
❑103, Jul 1979	2.00
❑104, Aug 1979	2.00
❑105, Sep 1979	2.00
❑106, Oct 1979	2.00
❑107, Dec 1979	2.00
❑108, Feb 1980	2.00
❑109, Mar 1980	2.00
❑110 1980	2.00
❑111 1980	2.00
❑112 1980	2.00
❑113 1980	2.00
❑114	2.00
❑115	2.00
❑116	2.00
❑117	2.00
❑118	2.00
❑119	2.00
❑120	2.00
❑121	2.00
❑122	2.00
❑123	2.00
❑124	2.00
❑125	2.00
❑126 1982	2.00
❑127 1982	2.00
❑128 1982	2.00
❑129 1982	2.00
❑130 1982	2.00
❑131 1982	2.00
❑132, Jan 1983	2.00
❑133 1983	2.00
❑134, Jul 1983	2.00
❑135, Sep 1983	2.00
❑136, Nov 1983	2.00
❑137, Jan 1984	2.00
❑138, Mar 1984	2.00
❑139, May 1984	2.00
❑140, Jul 1984	2.00
❑141, Sep 1984	2.00
❑142, Nov 1984	2.00
❑143, Jan 1985	2.00
❑144, Mar 1985	2.00
❑145, May 1985	2.00
❑146, Jul 1985	2.00
❑147, Sep 1985	2.00
❑148, Nov 1985	2.00
❑149, Jan 1986	2.00
❑150, Mar 1986	2.00
❑151, May 1986	1.50
❑152, Jul 1986	1.50
❑153, Sep 1986	1.50
❑154, Nov 1986	1.50
❑155, Jan 1987	1.50
❑156, Mar 1987	1.50
❑157, May 1987	1.50
❑158, Jun 1987	1.50
❑159, Jul 1987	1.50
❑160, Aug 1987	1.50
❑161, Sep 1987	1.50
❑162, Oct 1987	1.50
❑163, Dec 1987	1.50
❑164, Jan 1988	1.50
❑165, Mar 1988	1.50
❑166, May 1988	1.50
❑167, Jun 1988	1.50
❑168, Jul 1988	1.50
❑169, Aug 1988	1.50
❑170, Sep 1988	1.50
❑171, Oct 1988	1.50
❑172, Jan 1989	1.50
❑173, Mar 1989	1.50
❑174, May 1989	1.50
❑175, Jun 1989	1.50
❑176, Jul 1989	1.50
❑177, Aug 1989	1.50
❑178, Sep 1989 A: Veronica Lodge.	1.50
❑179, Oct 1989	1.50
❑180, Jan 1990	1.50

Other grades: Multiply price above by 5/6 for VF/NM • 2/3 for VERY FINE • 1/3 for FINE • 1/5 for VERY GOOD • 1/8 for GOOD

Betty and Veronica

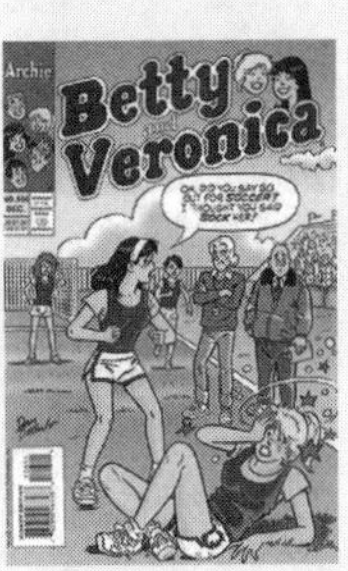

Mid-1980s restart for Archie's girls

©Archie

Betty and Veronica Spectacular

More comics focusing on the competitive girls

©Archie

Betty & Veronica Summer Fun

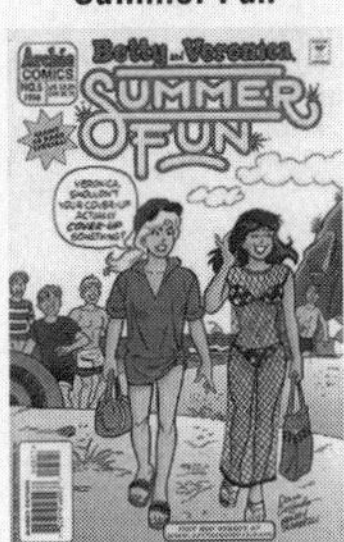

Giant annual specials take girls to the beach

©Archie

Betty Boop 3-D

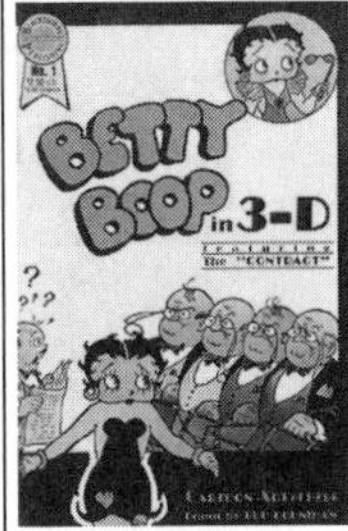

One of many 3-D specials from Blackthorne

©Blackthorne

Betty Boop's Big Break

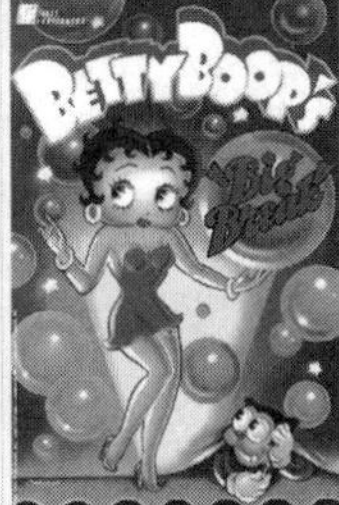

Success finds the wide-eyed animation star

©First

	N-MINT
❑181, Mar 1990	1.50
❑182, May 1990	1.50
❑183, Jun 1990	1.50
❑184, Jul 1990	1.50
❑185, Aug 1990	1.50
❑186, Sep 1990	1.50
❑187, Oct 1990	1.50
❑188, Jan 1991	1.50
❑189, Mar 1991	1.50
❑190, May 1991	1.50
❑191, Jul 1991	1.50
❑192, Aug 1991	1.50
❑193, Sep 1991	1.50
❑194, Oct 1991	1.50
❑195, Nov 1991	1.50
❑196, Jan 1992	1.50
❑197, Mar 1992	1.50
❑198, May 1992	1.50
❑199, Jul 1992	1.50
❑200, Aug 1992	1.50

BETTY AND VERONICA

ARCHIE

	N-MINT
❑1, Jun 1987	6.00
❑2 1987	4.00
❑3 1987	4.00
❑4	3.00
❑5	3.00
❑6	3.00
❑7	3.00
❑8 1988	3.00
❑9 1988	3.00
❑10 1988	3.00
❑11 1988	2.50
❑12 1988	2.50
❑13 1988	2.50
❑14	2.50
❑15	2.50
❑16	2.50
❑17	2.50
❑18	2.50
❑19	2.50
❑20 1989	2.50
❑21 1989	2.00
❑22 1989	2.00
❑23 1989	2.00
❑24 1989	2.00
❑25 1989	2.00
❑26	2.00
❑27	2.00
❑28 1990	2.00
❑29 1990	2.00
❑30, May 1990	2.00
❑31 1990	2.00
❑32 1990	2.00
❑33 1990	2.00
❑34 1990	2.00
❑35 1990	2.00
❑36	2.00
❑37 1991	2.00
❑38 1991	2.00
❑39 1991	2.00
❑40 1991	2.00
❑41 1991	2.00
❑42 1991	2.00
❑43 1991	2.00
❑44 1991	2.00
❑45 1991	2.00
❑46 1991	2.00
❑47, Jan 1992	2.00
❑48, Feb 1992	2.00
❑49, Mar 1992	2.00
❑50, Apr 1992	2.00
❑51, May 1992	1.50
❑52, Jun 1992	1.50
❑53, Jul 1992	1.50
❑54, Aug 1992	1.50
❑55, Sep 1992	1.50
❑56, Oct 1992	1.50
❑57, Nov 1992	1.50
❑58, Dec 1992	1.50
❑59, Jan 1993	1.50
❑60, Feb 1993	1.50
❑61, Mar 1993	1.50
❑62, Apr 1993	1.50
❑63, May 1993	1.50
❑64, Jun 1993	1.50
❑65, Jul 1993	1.50
❑66, Aug 1993, DDC (a)	1.50
❑67, Sep 1993	1.50
❑68, Oct 1993	1.50
❑69, Nov 1993	1.50
❑70, Dec 1993	1.50
❑71, Jan 1994	1.50
❑72, Feb 1994	1.50
❑73, Mar 1994	1.50
❑74, Apr 1994	1.50
❑75, May 1994	1.50
❑76, Jun 1994	1.50
❑77, Jul 1994	1.50
❑78, Aug 1994	1.50
❑79, Sep 1994	1.50
❑80, Oct 1994	1.50
❑81, Nov 1994	1.50
❑82, Dec 1994	1.50
❑83, Jan 1995	1.50
❑84, Feb 1995	1.50
❑85, Mar 1995	1.50
❑86, Apr 1995	1.50
❑87, May 1995	1.50
❑88, Jun 1995	1.50
❑89, Jul 1995	1.50
❑90, Aug 1995	1.50
❑91, Sep 1995	1.50
❑92, Oct 1995	1.50
❑93, Nov 1995	1.50
❑94, Dec 1995	1.50
❑95, Jan 1996, concludes in Archie's Pal Jughead #76	1.50
❑96, Feb 1996	1.50
❑97, Mar 1996	1.50
❑98, Apr 1996	1.50
❑99, May 1996	1.50
❑100, Jun 1996	1.50
❑101, Jul 1996	1.50
❑102, Aug 1996	1.50
❑103, Sep 1996	1.50
❑104, Oct 1996	1.50
❑105, Nov 1996	1.50
❑106, Dec 1996	1.50
❑107, Jan 1997	1.50
❑108, Feb 1997	1.50
❑109, Mar 1997	1.50
❑110, Apr 1997	1.50
❑111, May 1997	1.50
❑112, Jun 1997	1.50
❑113, Jul 1997	1.50
❑114, Aug 1997	1.50
❑115, Sep 1997	1.50
❑116, Oct 1997	1.50
❑117, Nov 1997	1.50
❑118, Dec 1997	1.50
❑119, Jan 1998	1.75
❑120, Feb 1998	1.75
❑121, Mar 1998	1.75
❑122, Apr 1998	1.75
❑123, May 1998	1.75
❑124, Jun 1998	1.75
❑125, Jul 1998	1.75
❑126, Aug 1998	1.75
❑127, Sep 1998, DDC (a)	1.75
❑128, Oct 1998	1.75
❑129, Nov 1998, DDC (a)	1.75
❑130, Dec 1998	1.75
❑131, Jan 1999	1.75
❑132, Feb 1999	1.75
❑133, Mar 1999, DDC (a)	1.75
❑134, Apr 1999	1.79
❑135, May 1999, DDC (a)	1.79
❑136, Jun 1999	1.79
❑137, Jul 1999	1.79
❑138, Aug 1999	1.79
❑139, Sep 1999	1.79
❑140, Oct 1999	1.79
❑141, Nov 1999	1.79
❑142, Dec 1999	1.79
❑143, Jan 2000	1.79
❑144, Feb 2000	1.79
❑145, Mar 2000	1.79
❑146, Apr 2000	1.79
❑147, May 2000	1.79
❑148, Jun 2000	1.79
❑149, Jul 2000	1.99
❑150, Aug 2000	1.99
❑151, Sep 2000	1.99
❑152, Oct 2000	1.99
❑153, Nov 2000	1.99
❑154, Dec 2000	1.99
❑155, Jan 2001	1.99
❑156, Feb 2001	1.99
❑157, Mar 2001	1.99
❑158, Apr 2001	1.99
❑159, May 2001	1.99
❑160, May 2001	1.99
❑161, Jun 2001	1.99
❑162, Jul 2001	1.99
❑163, Aug 2001	1.99
❑164, Sep 2001	1.99
❑165, Oct 2001	1.99
❑166, Nov 2001	2.19
❑167, Dec 2001	2.19
❑168, Jan 2002	2.19
❑169, Feb 2002	2.19

	N-MINT
❑170, Mar 2002	2.19
❑171, Apr 2002	2.19
❑172, Apr 2002	2.19
❑173, May 2002	2.19
❑174, Jun 2002	2.19
❑175, Jul 2002	2.19
❑176, Aug 2002	2.19
❑177, Sep 2002	2.19
❑178, Oct 2002	2.19
❑179, Nov 2002	2.19
❑180, Dec 2002	2.19
❑181, Jan 2003	2.19
❑182, Feb 2003	2.19
❑183, Mar 2003	2.19
❑184, Apr 2003	2.19
❑185, Apr 2003	2.19
❑186, May 2003	2.19
❑187, Jun 2003	2.19
❑188, Jul 2003	2.19
❑189, Aug 2003	2.19
❑190, Sep 2003	2.19
❑191, Oct 2003	2.19
❑192, Nov 2003	2.19
❑193, Dec 2003	2.19
❑194, Jan 2004	2.19
❑195, Feb 2004	2.19
❑196, Mar 2004	2.19
❑197, Mar 2004	2.19
❑198, May 2004	2.19
❑199, Jun 2004	2.19
❑200, Jul 2004	2.19
❑201, Aug 2004	2.19
❑202, Sep 2004	2.19
❑203, Oct 2004	2.19
❑204, Nov 2004	2.19
❑205, Dec 2004	2.19
❑206, Apr 2005	2.19
❑207, May 2005	2.19
❑208, Jun 2005	2.19
❑209, Aug 2005	2.19
❑210, Sep 2005	2.19
❑211, Oct 2005	2.19
❑212, Dec 2005	2.19
❑213, Jan 2006	2.19
❑214, Jan 2006	2.19
❑215, Apr 2006	2.19
❑216, May 2006	2.19
❑217, Jun 2006	2.19
❑218, Aug 2006	2.19

BETTY & VERONICA ANNUAL DIGEST MAGAZINE

ARCHIE

	N-MINT
❑12, Jan 1995	1.75
❑13, Sep 1995	1.75
❑14, Feb 1996	1.75
❑15, Jul 1996	1.75
❑16, Aug 1997	1.79

BETTY AND VERONICA COMICS DIGEST

ARCHIE

	N-MINT
❑1, Aug 1982	9.00
❑2, Nov 1982	5.00
❑3, Feb 1983	5.00
❑4, May 1983	4.00
❑5, Aug 1983	4.00
❑6, Nov 1983	4.00
❑7, Feb 1984	4.00
❑8, May 1984	4.00
❑9, Aug 1984	4.00
❑10, Nov 1984	4.00
❑11, Feb 1985	3.00
❑12, Apr 1985	3.00
❑13, Jun 1985	3.00
❑14, Aug 1985	3.00
❑15, Oct 1985	3.00
❑16, Dec 1985	3.00
❑17, Feb 1986	3.00
❑18, Apr 1986	3.00
❑19, Jun 1986	3.00
❑20, Aug 1986	3.00
❑21, Oct 1986	3.00
❑22, Dec 1986	3.00
❑23, Feb 1987	3.00
❑24, Apr 1987	3.00
❑25, Jun 1987	3.00
❑26, Aug 1987	3.00
❑27, Nov 1987	3.00
❑28, Jan 1988	3.00
❑29, Mar 1988	3.00
❑30, May 1988	3.00
❑31, Jul 1988	2.50
❑32, Sep 1988	2.50
❑33, Nov 1988	2.50
❑34, Jan 1989	2.50
❑35, Mar 1989	2.50
❑36, May 1989	2.50
❑37, Jul 1989	2.50
❑38, Sep 1989	2.50
❑39, Nov 1989	2.50
❑40, Jan 1990	2.50
❑41, Mar 1990	2.50
❑42, May 1990	2.50
❑43, Jul 1990, becomes Betty and Veronica Digest Magazine	2.50

BETTY AND VERONICA DIGEST MAGAZINE

ARCHIE

	N-MINT
❑44, Sep 1990	2.50
❑45, Nov 1990	2.50
❑46, Jan 1991	2.50
❑47, Mar 1991	2.50
❑48, May 1991	2.50
❑49, Jul 1991	2.50
❑50, Sep 1991	2.50
❑51, Nov 1991	2.00
❑52, ca. 1992	2.00
❑53, ca. 1992	2.00
❑54, ca. 1992	2.00
❑55, ca. 1992	2.00
❑56, ca. 1992	2.00
❑57, ca. 1992	2.00
❑58, ca. 1992	2.00
❑59, ca. 1992	2.00
❑60, Feb 1993	2.00
❑61, Apr 1993	2.00
❑62, Jun 1993	2.00
❑63, Aug 1993	2.00
❑64, Oct 1993	2.00
❑65, Dec 1993	2.00
❑66, Feb 1994	2.00
❑67, Apr 1994	2.00
❑68, ca. 1994	2.00
❑69, Jul 1994	2.00
❑70, ca. 1994	2.00
❑71, ca. 1994	2.00
❑72, Jan 1995	2.00
❑73, Mar 1995	2.00
❑74, Apr 1995	2.00
❑75, Jun 1995	2.00
❑76, Aug 1995	2.00
❑77, Oct 1995	2.00
❑78, Dec 1995	2.00
❑79, Feb 1996	2.00
❑80, Apr 1996	2.00
❑81, Jun 1996	2.00
❑82, Jul 1996	2.00
❑83, Sep 1996	2.00
❑84, Nov 1996	2.00
❑85, Jan 1997	2.00
❑86, Feb 1997	2.00
❑87, Apr 1997	2.00
❑88, Jun 1997	2.00
❑89, Jul 1997	2.00
❑90, Sep 1997	2.00
❑91, Oct 1997	2.00
❑92, Dec 1997	2.00
❑93, Feb 1998	2.00
❑94, Apr 1998	2.00
❑95, May 1998	2.00
❑96, Jul 1998	2.00
❑97, Aug 1998	2.00
❑98, Sep 1998	2.00
❑99, Nov 1998, DDC (a)	2.00
❑100, Dec 1998	2.00
❑101, Feb 1999	2.00
❑102, Apr 1999	2.00
❑103, May 1999	2.00
❑104, Jul 1999	2.00
❑105, Aug 1999	2.00
❑106, Sep 1999	2.00
❑107, Nov 1999	2.00
❑108, Sep 1999	2.00
❑109, Feb 2000	2.00
❑110, Apr 2000	2.00
❑111, May 2000	2.00
❑112, Jul 2000	2.19
❑113, Aug 2000	2.19
❑114, Oct 2000	2.19
❑115, Nov 2000	2.19
❑116, Dec 2000	2.19
❑117, Feb 2001	2.19
❑118, Apr 2001	2.19
❑119, May 2001	2.19
❑120, Jun 2001	2.19
❑121, Aug 2001	2.19
❑122, Sep 2001	2.19
❑123, Oct 2001	2.19
❑124, Dec 2001	2.19
❑125, Jan 2002	2.19
❑126, Mar 2002	2.19
❑127, Apr 2002	2.19
❑128, May 2002	2.19
❑129, Jul 2002	2.19
❑130, Aug 2002	2.19
❑131, Oct 2002	2.19
❑132, Nov 2002	2.19
❑133, Dec 2002	2.19
❑134, Feb 2003	2.19
❑135, Mar 2003	2.39
❑136, Apr 2003	2.39
❑137, May 2003	2.39
❑138, Jul 2003	2.39
❑139, Aug 2003	2.39
❑140, Sep 2003	2.39
❑141, Oct 2003	2.39
❑142, Dec 2003	2.39
❑143, Jan 2004	2.39
❑144, Mar 2004	2.39
❑145, Apr 2004	2.39
❑146, May 2004	2.39
❑147, Jul 2004	2.39
❑148, Aug 2004	2.39
❑149, Sep 2004	2.39
❑150, Oct 2004	2.39
❑151, Nov 2004	2.39
❑152, Dec 2004	2.39
❑153, Jan 2004	2.39
❑154, Apr 2005	2.39
❑155, May 2005	2.39
❑156, Jun 2005	2.39
❑157, Aug 2005	2.39
❑158, Sep 2005	2.39
❑159, Oct 2005	2.39
❑160, Nov 2005	2.39
❑161, Dec 2005	2.39
❑162, Jan 2006	2.39
❑163, Feb 2006	2.39
❑164, May 2006	2.39
❑165, Jun 2006	2.39
❑166, Aug 2006	2.39

BETTY AND VERONICA DOUBLE DIGEST

ARCHIE

	N-MINT
❑1, Jun 1987	8.00
❑2, Aug 1987	5.00
❑3, Oct 1987	5.00
❑4, Dec 1987	4.00
❑5, Feb 1988	4.00
❑6, Apr 1988	4.00
❑7, Jun 1988	4.00
❑8, Aug 1988	4.00
❑9, Oct 1988	4.00
❑10, Dec 1988	4.00
❑11, Feb 1989	3.00
❑12, Apr 1989	3.00
❑13, Jun 1989	3.00
❑14, Aug 1989	3.00
❑15, Oct 1989	3.00
❑16, Dec 1989	3.00
❑17, Feb 1990	3.00
❑18, Apr 1990	3.00
❑19, Jun 1990	3.00
❑20, Aug 1990	3.00
❑21, Oct 1990	3.00
❑22, Dec 1990	3.00
❑23, Feb 1991	3.00
❑24, Apr 1991	3.00
❑25, Jun 1991	3.00
❑26, Aug 1991	3.00

Other grades: Multiply price above by 5/6 for VF/NM • 2/3 for VERY FINE • 1/3 for FINE • 1/5 for VERY GOOD • 1/8 for GOOD

Betty's Diary

Another title for the smiling tomboy

©Archie

Beverly Hillbillies

Load up the truck and head for comics-land

©Dell

Beware (Marvel)

Part of Marvel's return to horror comics

©Marvel

Beware the Creeper

More with the character from Showcase #73

©DC

Bewitched

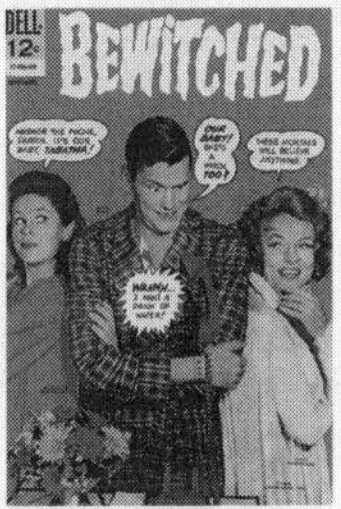

Does the comics version count as a third Darren?

©Dell

	N-MINT
❑27, Oct 1991	3.00
❑28, Nov 1991	3.00
❑29, Jan 1992	3.00
❑30, Mar 1992	3.00
❑31, May 1992	3.00
❑32, Jul 1992	3.00
❑33, Sep 1992	3.00
❑34, Oct 1992	3.00
❑35, Dec 1992	3.00
❑36, Feb 1993	3.00
❑37, Apr 1993	3.00
❑38, Jun 1993	3.00
❑39, Aug 1993	3.00
❑40, Sep 1993	3.00
❑41, Nov 1993	3.00
❑42, Jan 1994	3.00
❑43, Apr 1994	3.00
❑44, May 1994	3.00
❑45, Jul 1994	3.00
❑46, Aug 1994	3.00
❑47, Oct 1994	3.00
❑48, Dec 1994, DDC (c)	3.00
❑49, Feb 1995	3.00
❑50, Apr 1995	3.00
❑51, Jun 1995	3.00
❑52, Aug 1995	3.00
❑53, Sep 1995	3.00
❑54, Nov 1995	3.00
❑55, Jan 1996	3.00
❑56, Mar 1996	3.00
❑57, Apr 1996	3.00
❑58, Jun 1996	3.00
❑59, Aug 1996	3.00
❑60, Oct 1996	3.00
❑61, Nov 1996	3.00
❑62, Jan 1997	3.00
❑63, Mar 1997	3.00
❑64, Apr 1997	3.00
❑65, Jun 1997	3.00
❑66, Aug 1997	3.00
❑67, Sep 1997	3.00
❑68, Nov 1997	3.00
❑69, Jan 1998	3.00
❑70, Mar 1998	3.00
❑71, Apr 1998	3.00
❑72, Jun 1998	3.00
❑73, Jul 1998	3.00
❑74, Sep 1998	3.00
❑75, Oct 1998	3.00
❑76, Dec 1998	3.00
❑77, Jan 1999	3.00
❑78, Mar 1999	3.00
❑79, Apr 1999	3.00
❑80, Jun 1999	3.00
❑81, Jul 1999	3.00
❑82, Sep 1999	3.00
❑83, Oct 1999	3.00
❑84, Dec 1999	3.00
❑85, Jan 2000	3.00
❑86, Mar 2000	3.00
❑87, Apr 2000	3.00
❑88, Jun 2000	3.00
❑89, Jul 2000	3.00
❑90, Sep 2000	3.19

	N-MINT
❑91, Oct 2000	3.19
❑92, Nov 2000	3.19
❑93, Jan 2001	3.19
❑94, Feb 2001	3.19
❑95, Apr 2001	3.29
❑96, Jun 2001	3.29
❑97, Jul 2001	3.29
❑98, Sep 2001	3.29
❑99, Oct 2001	3.29
❑100, Nov 2001	3.29
❑101, Dec 2001	3.29
❑102, Feb 2002	3.29
❑103, Mar 2002	3.29
❑104, Apr 2002	3.29
❑105, Jun 2002	3.29
❑106, Jul 2002	3.29
❑107, Sep 2002	3.29
❑108, Oct 2002	3.29
❑109, Nov 2002	3.59
❑110, Dec 2002	3.59
❑111, Feb 2003	3.59
❑112, Mar 2003	3.59
❑113, Apr 2003	3.59
❑114, Jun 2003	3.59
❑115, Jul 2003	3.59
❑116, Sep 2003	3.59
❑117, Oct 2003	3.59
❑118, Nov 2003	3.59
❑119, Dec 2003	3.59
❑120, Feb 2004	3.59
❑121, Mar 2004	3.59
❑122, Apr 2004	3.59
❑123, May 2004	3.59
❑124, Jun 2004	3.59
❑125, Jul 2004	3.59
❑126, Aug 2004	3.59
❑127, Sep 2004	3.59
❑128, Oct 2004	3.59
❑129, Nov 2004	3.59
❑130, Dec 2004	3.59
❑131, Jan 2005	3.59
❑132, Feb 2005	3.59
❑133 2005	3.59
❑134 2005	3.59
❑135 2005	3.59
❑136 2005	3.59
❑137 2005	3.59
❑138, Dec 2005	3.59
❑139, Jan 2006	3.59
❑140, Apr 2006	3.59
❑141, May 2006	3.59
❑142, Jul 2006	3.59
❑143, Aug 2006	3.59

BETTY AND VERONICA SPECTACULAR
ARCHIE

	N-MINT
❑1, Oct 1992	4.00
❑2	3.00
❑3, May 1993	3.00
❑4 1993	2.50
❑5, Oct 1993	2.50
❑6, Feb 1994	2.00
❑7, Apr 1994	2.00
❑8, May 1994	2.00
❑9, Jul 1994	2.00
❑10, Sep 1994	2.00
❑11, Nov 1994	2.00
❑12, Jan 1995	2.00
❑13, Feb 1995	2.00
❑14, Apr 1995	2.00
❑15, Jul 1995	2.00
❑16, Oct 1995	2.00
❑17, Jan 1996	2.00
❑18, Apr 1996	2.00
❑19, Jul 1996	2.00
❑20, Oct 1996	2.00
❑21, Jan 1997, Betty becomes a fashion model	2.00
❑22, Mar 1997	2.00
❑23, May 1997	2.00
❑24, Jul 1997, Betty and Veronica set up web pages	2.00
❑25, Sep 1997	2.00
❑26, Nov 1997	2.00
❑27, Feb 1998	2.00
❑28, Mar 1998	2.00
❑29, May 1998	2.00
❑30, Jul 1998	2.00
❑31, Sep 1998	2.00
❑32, Nov 1998, Betty and Veronica are maids for each other	2.00
❑33, Jan 1999, talent competition	2.00
❑34, Mar 1999	2.00
❑35, May 1999, Swing issue	2.00
❑36, Jul 1999	2.00
❑37, Sep 1999	2.00
❑38, Nov 1999	2.00
❑39, Jan 2000	2.00
❑40, Mar 2000	2.00
❑41, May 2000	2.00
❑42, Jul 2000	2.00
❑43, Sep 2000	2.00
❑44, Nov 2000	2.00
❑45, Jan 2001	2.00
❑46, Mar 2001	2.00
❑47, May 2001	2.00
❑48, Jul 2001	2.00
❑49, Sep 2001	2.00
❑50, Nov 2001	2.00
❑51, Jan 2002	2.00
❑52, Mar 2002	2.00
❑53, May 2002	2.00
❑54, Jul 2002	2.00
❑55, Sep 2002	2.00
❑56, Nov 2002	2.00
❑57, Jan 2003	2.00
❑58, Mar 2003	2.20
❑59, May 2003	2.20
❑60, Jul 2003	2.20
❑61, Sep 2003	2.19
❑62, Nov 2003	2.19
❑63, Dec 2003	2.19
❑64, Feb 2004	2.19
❑65, May 2004	2.19
❑66, Jul 2004	2.19
❑67, Aug 2004	2.19
❑68, Jan 2005	2.19
❑69 2005	2.19

Other grades: Multiply price above by 5/6 for VF/NM • 2/3 for VERY FINE • 1/3 for FINE • 1/5 for VERY GOOD • 1/8 for GOOD

N-MINT

❑72, Dec 2005 .... 2.19
❑73, Feb 2006 .... 2.19

BETTY & VERONICA SUMMER FUN
ARCHIE

❑1, Sum 1994 .... 3.00
❑2, Sum 1995 .... 2.50
❑3, Sum 1996 .... 2.50
❑4, Sum 1997 .... 2.50
❑5, Sum 1998 .... 2.25
❑6, Sum 1999 .... 2.29

BETTY BOOP 3-D
BLACKTHORNE

❑1, Nov 1986 .... 2.50

BETTY BOOP'S BIG BREAK
FIRST

❑1, Oct 1990 .... 5.95

BETTY IN BONDAGE: BETTY MAE
SHUNGA

❑1 .... 6.95

BETTY IN BONDAGE (TEO JONELLI'S...)
SHUNGA

❑1, b&w 3.00
❑2, b&w 3.00
❑3, b&w 3.00
❑4, b&w 3.00
❑5 .... 3.00
❑6 .... 3.00
❑7 .... 3.00
❑8 .... 3.00
❑Annual 1; 1993 Annual 5.95
❑Annual 2; 1994 Annual 5.95
❑Annual 3; 1995 Annual 5.95

BETTY PAGE 3-D COMICS
3-D ZONE

❑1 .... 3.95

BETTY PAGE 3-D PICTURE BOOK
3-D ZONE

❑1; photos, adult 3.95

BETTY PAGE CAPTURED JUNGLE GIRL 3-D
3-D ZONE

❑1; photos 3.95

BETTY PAGES
PURE IMAGINATION

❑1; DSt (a); Ward, photos 6.00
❑1/2nd 5.00
❑2 .... 5.00
❑2/2nd 5.00
❑3 .... 5.00
❑4 .... 5.00
❑5, Win 1989 .... 4.50
❑6 .... 4.50
❑7 .... 4.50
❑8 .... 4.50
❑9 .... 5.00

BETTY PAGE: THE 50'S RAGE
ILLUSTRATION

❑1/A, Jan 1993; tame cover 3.25
❑1/B, Jan 1993; Adult cover 3.25
❑2/A; tame cover 3.25
❑2/B; Adult cover 3.25

BETTY'S DIARY
ARCHIE

❑1, Apr 1986 .... 4.00
❑2 1986 .... 2.50
❑3 1986 .... 2.50
❑4 1986 .... 2.50
❑5 1986 .... 2.50
❑6 1986 .... 2.00
❑7 1987 .... 2.00
❑8 1987 .... 2.00
❑9 1987 .... 2.00
❑10, Aug 1987 .... 2.00
❑11, Sep 1987 .... 1.50
❑12, Oct 1987 .... 1.50
❑13 1987 .... 1.50
❑14 1987 .... 1.50
❑15 1988 .... 1.50
❑16 1988 .... 1.50
❑17 1988 .... 1.50
❑18 1988 .... 1.50
❑19 1988 .... 1.50
❑20 1988 .... 1.50
❑21 1988 .... 1.50
❑22 1988 .... 1.50
❑23 1989 .... 1.50
❑24 1989 .... 1.50
❑25 1989 .... 1.50
❑26 1989 .... 1.50
❑27 1989 .... 1.50
❑28 1989 .... 1.50
❑29 1989 .... 1.50
❑30 1989 .... 1.50
❑31 1990 .... 1.50
❑32 1990 .... 1.50
❑33 1990 .... 1.50
❑34 1990 .... 1.50
❑35 1990 .... 1.50
❑36 1990 .... 1.50
❑37 1990 .... 1.50
❑38 1990 .... 1.50
❑39 1991 .... 1.50
❑40 1991 .... 1.50

BETTY'S DIGEST MAGAZINE
ARCHIE

❑1, Nov 1996 .... 2.00
❑2, Nov 1997 .... 2.00

BETWEEN THE SHEETS
TOKYOPOP

❑1, May 2003, b&w; printed in Japanese format 9.99

BEVERLY HILLBILLIES
DELL

❑1, Apr 1963 .... 60.00
❑2, Jul 1963 .... 38.00
❑3, Oct 1963 .... 28.00
❑4, Jan 1964 .... 24.00
❑5, Apr 1964 .... 24.00
❑6, Jul 1964 .... 18.00
❑7, Oct 1964 .... 18.00
❑8, Jan 1965 .... 18.00
❑9, Apr 1965 .... 18.00
❑10, ca. 1965, Not a photo cover; cartoon Clampetts appear on cover, but actors' names still listed with them 18.00
❑11, Dec 1965 .... 15.00
❑12, Mar 1966 .... 15.00
❑13, Jun 1966 .... 15.00
❑14, Sep 1966 .... 15.00
❑15, Dec 1966 .... 15.00
❑16, Mar 1967 .... 15.00
❑17, May 1967 .... 15.00
❑18, Aug 1967 .... 12.00
❑19, Oct 1969, Same cover as #1 .... 12.00
❑20, Oct 1970 .... 12.00
❑21, Oct 1971 .... 12.00

BEWARE (MARVEL)
MARVEL

❑1, Mar 1973, "Witch" reprinted from Tales of Suspense #27 .... 8.00
❑2, May 1973 .... 5.00
❑3, Jul 1973 .... 5.00
❑4, Sep 1973 .... 5.00
❑5, Nov 1973 .... 5.00
❑6, Jan 1974 .... 5.00
❑7, Mar 1974 .... 5.00
❑8, May 1974; Series continued in Tomb of Darkness #9 .... 5.00

BEWARE THE CREEPER
DC

❑1, Jun 1968, SD (a) 45.00
❑2, Aug 1968, SD (a) 32.00
❑3, Oct 1968, SD (a) 32.00
❑4, Dec 1968, SD (a) 32.00
❑5, Feb 1969, SD (a) 32.00
❑6, Apr 1969, SD (a) 40.00

BEWARE THE CREEPER (2ND SERIES)
DC

❑1, Jun 2003 .... 2.95
❑2, Jul 2003 .... 2.95
❑3, Aug 2003 .... 2.95
❑4, Sep 2003 .... 2.95
❑5, Oct 2003 .... 2.95

BEWITCHED
DELL

❑1, Apr 1965 .... 85.00
❑2, Jul 1965 .... 50.00
❑3, Oct 1965 .... 40.00
❑4, Mar 1966 .... 40.00
❑5, Jun 1966 .... 40.00
❑6, Sep 1966 .... 40.00
❑7, Dec 1966 .... 40.00
❑8, Mar 1967 .... 40.00
❑9, Apr 1967 .... 40.00
❑10, Jul 1967 .... 40.00
❑11, Oct 1967 .... 30.00
❑12, Oct 1968 .... 30.00
❑13, Jan 1969 .... 30.00
❑14, Oct 1969 .... 30.00

BEYBLADE
VIZ

❑1, Oct 2004 .... 9.95
❑2, Dec 2004 .... 9.95
❑3, Feb 2005 .... 9.95
❑4, Apr 2005 .... 9.95
❑5, May 2005 .... 9.95
❑6, Aug 2005 .... 9.95
❑7, Oct 2005 .... 9.95

BEYOND (BLUE)
BLUE

❑1, Jun 1996 .... 2.95

BEYOND AVALON
IMAGE

❑1, Feb 2005 .... 2.95
❑2, May 2005 .... 3.50
❑3, Apr 2006 ....

BEYOND COMMUNION
CALIBER

❑1 .... 2.95

BEYOND MARS
BLACKTHORNE

❑1, Jan 1989, b&w 2.00
❑2, Feb 1989, b&w 2.00
❑3, Mar 1989 .... 2.00
❑4, ca. 1989 .... 2.00
❑5, ca. 1989 .... 2.00
❑Book 2 .... 6.95

BEYOND THE GRAVE
CHARLTON

❑1, Jul 1975 .... 6.50
❑2, Oct 1975 .... 4.00
❑3, Dec 1975 .... 4.00
❑4, Feb 1976 .... 3.00
❑5 .... 3.00
❑6, Jun 1976 .... 2.50
❑7 .... 2.50
❑8 .... 2.50
❑9 .... 2.50
❑10, Aug 1983 .... 2.50
❑11 1983 .... 2.50
❑12 1983 .... 2.50
❑13, Feb 1984 .... 2.50
❑14, Apr 1984 .... 2.50
❑15, Jun 1984 .... 2.50
❑16, Aug 1984 .... 2.50
❑17 .... 2.50

BICENTENNIAL GROSS-OUTS
YENTZER AND GONIF

❑1, Jul 1976 .... 25.00

BIFF BANG POW!
PAISANO

❑1 .... 2.95
❑2, Feb 1992 .... 2.95

BIG
DARK HORSE

❑1, Mar 1989; adaptation 2.50

BIG ASS COMICS
RIP OFF

❑1, Jun 1969 .... 50.00
❑1/2nd 24.00
❑1/3rd 10.00
❑1/4th 10.00
❑1/5th 6.00
❑1/6th 6.00
❑2, Aug 1971 .... 25.00
❑2/2nd 15.00

Other grades: Multiply price above by 5/6 for VF/NM • 2/3 for VERY FINE • 1/3 for FINE • 1/5 for VERY GOOD • 1/8 for GOOD

Beyond the Grave

Ghosts, witches, and demons from Charlton

©Charlton

Big Bang Comics (Vol. 1)

Silver Age tributes abound in this series

©Caliber

Big Bang Comics (Vol. 2)

Image takes on the Silver Age here

©Image

Bill & Ted's Excellent Comic Book

Marvel's take on the future Wild Stallyns

©Marvel

Bill, the Galactic Hero

Based on the Harry Harrison novel series

©Topps

N-MINT

BIG BAD BLOOD OF DRACULA
APPLE

❑1; reprints, b&w 2.75
❑2 2.95

BIG BANG COMICS: ROUND TABLE OF AMERICA
IMAGE

❑1, Mar 2004 3.95

BIG BANG COMICS (VOL. 1)
CALIBER / BIG BANG

❑0, May 1995, ARo (c); ARo (a) 3.50
❑1, Spr 1994, b&w 2.50
❑2, Sum 1994, b&w 2.50
❑3, Oct 1994, b&w 2.50
❑4, Feb 1995, b&w 2.50

BIG BANG COMICS (VOL. 2)
IMAGE

❑1, May 1996; Mighty Man, Knight Watchman, Doctor Weird 3.00
❑2, Jun 1996; Silver Age Shadowhawk, Knight Watchman, The Badge 2.75
❑3, Jul 1996; Knight Watchman, Ultiman, Thunder Girl 2.75
❑4, Sep 1996 2.75
❑5, Oct 1996; origins issue 2.95
❑6, Nov 1996 CS (c); CS (a) 2.95
❑7, Dec 1996; Mighty Man vs. Mighty Man 2.95
❑8, Jan 1997 1: Mister U.S. 2.95
❑9, Mar 1997; A: Sphinx. A: Blitz. Showplace 2.95
❑10, May 1997 2.95
❑11, Jul 1997; Knight Watchman vs. Faulty Towers 2.95
❑12, Sep 1997 A: Savage Dragon. 2.95
❑13, Aug 1997; cover says Jul, indicia says Aug 2.95
❑14, Oct 1997 A: Savage Dragon 2.95
❑15, Oct 1997; Doctor Weird vs. Bog Swamp Demon, cover says Dec, indicia says Oct/Nov 2.95
❑16, Jan 1998; Thunder Girl 2.95
❑17, Feb 1998; Shadow Lady 2.95
❑18, Apr 1998 DC (c); DC (a); A: Savage Dragon, Pantheon of Heroes 2.95
❑19, Jun 1998; O: The Beacon II (Doctor Julia Gardner). O: The Hummingbird. O: The Beacon I (Scott Martin). cover says Apr, indicia says Jun 2.95
❑20, Jul 1998; A: Dimensioneer. A: Knight Watchman. A: The Blitz. A: The Sphinx. photo back cover 2.95
❑21, Aug 1998; Shadow Lady 2.95
❑22, Sep 1998; Knight Watchman 2.95
❑23, Nov 1998; Tales of the Sphinx, Book 2 3.95
❑24, Apr 1999; The Big Bang History of Comics 2.95
❑25, Jun 1999 2.95
❑26, Jul 1999 2.95
❑27, Oct 1999; The Big Bang History of Comics, Part 2 3.95
❑28, Dec 1999; Knight Watchman 3.95
❑29, Feb 2000 3.95
❑30, Mar 2000 3.95
❑31, Apr 2000 3.95
❑32, Jun 2000 3.95
❑33, Jul 2000 3.95
❑34, Aug 2000 3.95
❑35, Jan 2001 3.95

BIG BANG PRESENTS: ULTIMAN FAMILY
IMAGE

❑1, Mar 2005 3.50

BIG BANG (RED CALLOWAY'S...)
ZOO ARSONIST

❑1 2.95

BIG BANG SUMMER SPECIAL
IMAGE

❑1, Aug 2003 4.95

BIG BLACK KISS
VORTEX

❑1, Sep 1989 HC (w); HC (a) 3.95
❑2, Oct 1989 HC (w); HC (a) 3.95
❑3, Nov 1989 HC (w); HC (a) 3.95

BIG BLACK THING (COLIN UPTON'S...)
UPTON

❑1, b&w 3.25

BIG BLOWN BABY
DARK HORSE

❑1, Aug 1996 2.95
❑2, Sep 1996 2.95
❑3, Oct 1996, 2.95
❑4, Nov 1996 2.95

BIG BLUE COUCH COMIX
COUCH

❑1, b&w 2.00

BIG BOOB BONDAGE
ANTARCTIC / VENUS

❑1, Jan 1997; b&w pin-ups, adult 2.95

BIG BRUISERS
IMAGE

❑1, Jul 1996 3.50

BIG DADDY DANGER
DC

❑1, Oct 2002 2.95
❑2, Nov 2002 2.95
❑3, Dec 2002 2.95
❑4, Jan 2003 2.95
❑5, Feb 2003 2.95
❑6, Mar 2003 2.95
❑7, Apr 2003 2.95
❑8, May 2003 2.95
❑9, Jun 2003 2.95

BIG DOG FUNNIES
RIP OFF

❑1, Jun 1992 2.50

BIG FUNNIES
RADIO

❑1, ca. 2001 3.95
❑2, ca. 2001 3.99
❑3, ca. 2001 3.99

BIGGER
FREE LUNCH

❑1, ca. 1998, b&w 3.00

BIGGER: WILL RISON & THE DEVIL'S CONCUBINE
FREE LUNCH

❑1, Dec 1998 2.95
❑2, Feb 1999 2.95
❑3, Apr 1999 2.95
❑4, Jun 1999; Indicia says #3, really #4

BIG GUY AND RUSTY THE BOY ROBOT
DARK HORSE / LEGEND

❑1, Jul 1995 FM (w) 10.00
❑2, Aug 1995 FM (w) 10.00

BIG HAIR PRODUCTIONS
IMAGE

❑1, Mar 2000 3.50
❑2, Apr 2000 3.50

BIG LOU
SIDE SHOW

❑1 2.95

BIG MONSTER FIGHT
KIDGANG COMICS

❑0 2.50
❑1 2.50

BIG MOUTH
STARHEAD

❑1, b&w 2.95
❑2, b&w 2.95
❑3 2.95
❑4 2.95
❑5; no indicia, b&w 2.95
❑6, Dec 1996 2.95
❑7, Jan 1998 2.95

BIG NUMBERS
MAD LOVE

❑1 5.50
❑2; Final published issue 5.50

BIG O PART 1
VIZ

❑1, Feb 2002 3.50
❑2, Mar 2002 3.50
❑3, Apr 2002 3.50
❑4, May 2002 3.50
❑5, Jun 2002 3.50

BIG O PART 2
VIZ

❑1, Jul 2002 3.50
❑2, Aug 2002 3.50
❑3, Sep 2002 3.50
❑4, Oct 2002 3.50

BIG O PART 3
VIZ

❑1, Nov 2002 3.50
❑2, Dec 2002 3.50
❑3, Jan 2003 3.50
❑4, Feb 2003 3.50

Other grades: Multiply price above by 5/6 for VF/NM • 2/3 for VERY FINE • 1/3 for FINE • 1/5 for VERY GOOD • 1/8 for GOOD

BIG O PART 4
VIZ

❑1, Mar 2003 ... 3.50
❑2, Apr 2003 ... 3.50
❑3, May 2003 ... 3.50
❑4, Jun 2003 ... 3.50

BIG PRIZE
ETERNITY

❑1, May 1988, b&w ... 1.95
❑2, Aug 1985, b&w ... 1.95

BIG TIME
DELTA

❑1, Mar 1996 ... 1.95

BIG TOP BONDAGE
FANTAGRAPHICS / EROS

❑1, b&w ... 2.50

BIG TOWN (MARVEL)
MARVEL

❑1, Jan 2001; A: X-Men. A: Avengers. says Fantastic Four Big Town on cover; alternate Marvel history ... 3.50
❑2, Feb 2001 A: Hulk. A: Avengers. A: Sub-Mariner ... 3.50
❑3, Mar 2001 A: Hulk. A: Avengers. A: Sub-Mariner ... 3.50
❑4, Apr 2001 A: Hulk. A: Avengers. A: Sub-Mariner ... 3.50

BIG VALLEY
DELL

❑1, ca. 1966 ... 40.00
❑2, ca. 1966 ... 25.00
❑3, ca. 1967 ... 25.00
❑4, ca. 1967 ... 25.00
❑5, ca. 1967 ... 25.00
❑6, ca. 1967 ... 25.00

BIJOU FUNNIES
KITCHEN SINK

❑1, ca. 1968 ... 85.00
❑1/2nd, May 1968 ... 30.00
❑2, ca. 1969 ... 30.00
❑3, Oct 1969 ... 25.00
❑3/2nd, ca. 1970 ... 15.00
❑3/3rd, ca. 1972 ... 10.00
❑4, ca. 1970 ... 25.00
❑5, ca. 1970 ... 20.00
❑6, Sep 1971 ... 18.00
❑7, Apr 1972 ... 18.00
❑8, ca. 1973 ... 18.00
❑8/2nd, ca. 1974 ... 4.00

BIKER MICE FROM MARS
MARVEL

❑1, Nov 1993, O: The Biker Mice From Mars. ... 2.00
❑2, Dec 1993, O: The Biker Mice From Mars. ... 2.00
❑3, Jan 1994 ... 2.00

BIKINI ASSASSIN TEAM
CATFISH

❑1 ... 2.50

BIKINI BATTLE 3-D
3-D ZONE

❑1 ... 3.95

BILL & TED'S BOGUS JOURNEY
MARVEL

❑1, Sep 1991; adapts movie ... 2.95

BILL & TED'S EXCELLENT ADVENTURE MOVIE ADAPTATION
DC

❑1; adapts movie, wraparound cover, no cover price ... 1.50

BILL & TED'S EXCELLENT COMIC BOOK
MARVEL

❑1, Dec 1991 ... 1.50
❑2, Jan 1992 ... 1.50
❑3, Feb 1992 ... 1.50
❑4, Mar 1992 ... 1.50
❑5, Apr 1992 ... 1.50
❑6, May 1992 ... 1.50
❑7, Jun 1992 ... 1.50
❑8, Jul 1992 ... 1.50
❑9, Aug 1992 ... 1.50
❑10, Sep 1992 ... 1.50
❑11, Oct 1992 ... 1.50
❑12, Nov 1992 ... 1.50

BILL, THE GALACTIC HERO
TOPPS

❑1, Jul 1994; prestige format, based on Harry Harrison novel series ... 4.95
❑2, Sep 1994 ... 4.95
❑3, Nov 1994 ... 4.95

BILLI 99
DARK HORSE

❑1 ... 3.50
❑2 ... 3.50
❑3 ... 3.50
❑4 ... 3.50

BILL THE BULL: BURNT CAIN
BONEYARD

❑1, Jul 1992 ... 4.95
❑2 ... 4.95
❑3 ... 4.95

BILL THE BULL: ONE SHOT, ONE BOURBON, ONE BEER
BONEYARD

❑1, Dec 1994 ... 2.95
❑2, indicia says Mar 94, a misprint ... 2.95

BILL THE CLOWN
SLAVE LABOR

❑1, Feb 1992, b&w; 2nd Printing, b&w ... 2.50
❑1/2nd, 2nd Printing, b&w ... 2.95

BILL THE CLOWN: COMEDY ISN'T PRETTY
SLAVE LABOR

❑1, Nov 1992, b&w ... 2.50

BILL THE CLOWN: DEATH & CLOWN WHITE
SLAVE LABOR

❑1, Sep 1993, b&w ... 2.95

BILLY BOY THE SICK LITTLE FAT KID
ASYLUM

❑1, ca. 2001 ... 2.95

BILLY COLE
CULT

❑1, Jun 1994, b&w ... 2.75
❑2 ... 2.75
❑3 ... 2.75
❑4 ... 2.75

BILLY DOGMA
MODERN

❑1, Apr 1997 ... 2.95
❑2, Aug 1997 ... 2.95
❑3, Dec 1997 ... 2.95

BILLY JOE VAN HELSING: REDNECK VAMPIRE HUNTER
ALPHA

❑1 ... 2.50

BILLY NGUYEN, PRIVATE EYE
ATTITUDE

❑1, Mar 1988 ... 2.00
❑2 ... 2.00
❑3 ... 2.00

BILLY NGUYEN, PRIVATE EYE (VOL. 2)
CALIBER

❑1, b&w ... 2.50

BILLY RAY CYRUS
MARVEL MUSIC

❑1; prestige format ... 5.95

BILLY THE KID
CHARLTON

❑9, Nov 1957, Series continued from Masked Raider #8 ... 58.00
❑10, Dec 1957 ... 35.00
❑11 1958, Double-size ... 40.00
❑12 1958 ... 30.00
❑13 1958, AW (a) ... 40.00
❑14 1958 ... 30.00
❑15 1958, O: Billy the Kid. ... 40.00
❑16 1959 ... 40.00
❑17, Jun 1959 ... 30.00
❑18, Aug 1959 ... 30.00
❑19, Oct 1959 ... 30.00
❑20, Dec 1959 ... 35.00
❑21, Mar 1960, JSe (a) ... 35.00
❑22, May 1960 ... 35.00
❑23, Jul 1960 ... 20.00
❑24 1960 ... 35.00
❑25 1960 ... 35.00
❑26 1960 ... 35.00
❑27, Mar 1961 ... 20.00
❑28, May 1961 ... 20.00
❑29, Jul 1961 ... 20.00
❑30, Sep 1961 ... 20.00
❑31, Nov 1961 ... 14.00
❑32, Jan 1962 ... 14.00
❑33, Apr 1962 ... 14.00
❑34 1962 ... 14.00
❑35 1962 ... 14.00
❑36 ... 14.00
❑37 1963 ... 14.00
❑38 1963 ... 14.00
❑39 1963 ... 14.00
❑40, Jun 1963 ... 14.00
❑41 ... 8.00
❑42 ... 8.00
❑43 1964 ... 8.00
❑44 1964 ... 8.00
❑45, May 1964 ... 8.00
❑46 1964 ... 8.00
❑47 ... 8.00
❑48 ... 8.00
❑49 1965 ... 8.00
❑50, Jun 1965 ... 8.00
❑51 1965 ... 7.00
❑52, Oct 1965 ... 7.00
❑53, Dec 1965 ... 7.00
❑54, Mar 1966 ... 7.00
❑55, May 1966 ... 7.00
❑56, Jul 1966 ... 7.00
❑57, Sep 1966 ... 7.00
❑58, Nov 1966 ... 7.00
❑59, Jan 1967 ... 7.00
❑60, Mar 1967 ... 7.00
❑61 1967 ... 5.00
❑62, Aug 1967 ... 5.00
❑63, Oct 1967 ... 5.00
❑64, Dec 1967 ... 5.00
❑65, Feb 1968 ... 5.00
❑66, May 1968 ... 5.00
❑67, ca. 1968 ... 5.00
❑68, Sep 1968 ... 5.00
❑69, Nov 1968 ... 5.00
❑70, Jan 1969 ... 5.00
❑71, Mar 1969 ... 4.00
❑72, May 1969 ... 4.00
❑73, Jul 1969 ... 4.00
❑74, Sep 1969 ... 4.00
❑75, Nov 1969 ... 4.00
❑76, Jan 1970 ... 4.00
❑77, Mar 1970 ... 4.00
❑78, May 1970 ... 4.00
❑79, Jul 1970 ... 4.00
❑80, Sep 1970 ... 4.00
❑81, Nov 1970 ... 3.50
❑82, Jan 1971 ... 3.50
❑83, Mar 1971 ... 3.50
❑84, May 1971 ... 3.50
❑85, Jul 1971 ... 3.50
❑86, Sep 1971 ... 3.50
❑87, Nov 1971 ... 3.50
❑88, Dec 1971 ... 3.50
❑89, Feb 1972 ... 3.50
❑90, Mar 1972 ... 3.50
❑91, Apr 1972 ... 3.50
❑92, May 1972 ... 3.50
❑93, Jul 1972 ... 3.50
❑94, Aug 1972 ... 3.50
❑95, Oct 1972 ... 3.50
❑96, Nov 1972 ... 3.50
❑97, Dec 1972 ... 3.50
❑98, Jan 1973 ... 3.50
❑99, Feb 1973 ... 3.50
❑100, Mar 1973 ... 3.50
❑101 1973 ... 3.00
❑102 1973 ... 3.00
❑103, Aug 1973, Spanish lesson text piece; no credits listed ... 3.00
❑104, Sep 1973 ... 3.00
❑105, Nov 1973 ... 3.00
❑106, Dec 1973 ... 3.00
❑107, May 1974 ... 3.00
❑108, Jul 1974 ... 3.00
❑109, Oct 1974 ... 3.00

Billy the Kid

William Bonney gets the hero treatment

©Charlton

Binky

Continuation of "Leave It to Binky" series

©DC

Birds of Prey

Oracle and Black Canary fight crime

©DC

Bishop

Mutant from the future returns to star in comic

©Marvel

Bishop: XSE

It stands for "Xavier Security Enforcers"

©Marvel

	N-MINT
❑110, Dec 1974	3.00
❑111, Feb 1975	3.00
❑112, Apr 1975	3.00
❑113, Jun 1975	3.00
❑114, Oct 1975	3.00
❑115, Dec 1975	3.00
❑116, Feb 1976	3.00
❑117, Apr 1976	3.00
❑118, Jun 1976	3.00
❑119, Aug 1976	3.00
❑120, Oct 1976	3.00
❑121	3.00
❑122, Sep 1977	3.00
❑123, Nov 1977	3.00
❑124, Feb 1978	3.00
❑125, Oct 1978	3.00
❑126, Jan 1979	3.00
❑127, Feb 1979	3.00
❑128, Apr 1979	3.00
❑129, Jun 1979	3.00
❑130, Aug 1979	3.00
❑131, Sep 1979	3.00
❑132, Oct 1979	3.00
❑133, Dec 1979	3.00
❑134, Feb 1980	3.00
❑135, Apr 1980	3.00
❑136, Jun 1980	3.00
❑137, Aug 1980	3.00
❑138, Oct 1980	3.00
❑139, Dec 1980	3.00
❑140, Feb 1981	3.00
❑141, Apr 1981	3.00
❑142, Jun 1981	3.00
❑143, Aug 1981	3.00
❑144, Oct 1981	3.00
❑145, Nov 1981	3.00
❑146, Jan 1982	3.00
❑147, Mar 1982	3.00
❑148 1982	3.00
❑149, Aug 1982	3.00
❑150, Oct 1982	3.00
❑151, Dec 1982	3.00
❑152	3.00
❑153, Mar 1983	3.00

BILLY THE KID'S OLD-TIMEY ODDITIES
DARK HORSE

❑1, May 2005	2.99
❑2, Jun 2005	2.99
❑3, Jul 2005	2.99
❑4, Aug 2005	2.99

B1N4RY
APCOMICS

❑0, ca. 2004	3.50
❑1 2004	3.50
❑2 2004	3.50
❑3 2004	5.00
❑3/Sketch 2004	6.00
❑4 2004	3.50

BINKY
DC

	N-MINT
❑72, May 1970; Series continued from "Leave it to Binky #71"	7.00
❑73, Jul 1970	7.00
❑74, Sep 1970	7.00
❑75, Nov 1970	7.00
❑76, Jan 1971	6.00
❑77, Mar 1971	6.00
❑78, May 1971	6.00
❑79, Jul 1971	6.00
❑80, Sep 1971	6.00
❑81, Nov 1971; Final issue of original series	6.00
❑82, Sum 1977; 1977 one-shot revival	3.00

BINKY'S BUDDIES
DC

❑1, Jan 1969	26.00
❑2, Mar 1969	16.00
❑3, May 1969	12.00
❑4, Jul 1969	10.00
❑5, Sep 1969	10.00
❑6, Nov 1969	10.00
❑7, Jan 1970	10.00
❑8, Mar 1970	10.00
❑9, May 1970	10.00
❑10, Jul 1970	10.00
❑11, Sep 1970	10.00
❑12, Nov 1970	10.00

BIO 90
BULLET

❑1, Aug 1992, b&w	2.50

BIO-BOOSTER ARMOR GUYVER
VIZ

❑1	4.00
❑2	3.50
❑3	3.50
❑4	3.50
❑5	3.50
❑6	3.00
❑7	3.00
❑8	3.00
❑9	3.00
❑10	3.00
❑11	3.00
❑12	3.00

BIO-BOOSTER ARMOR GUYVER PART 2
VIZ

❑1, Oct 1994	3.00
❑2, Nov 1994	3.00
❑3, Dec 1994	3.00
❑4, Jan 1995	3.00
❑5, Feb 1995	3.00
❑6, Mar 1995	3.00

BIO-BOOSTER ARMOR GUYVER PART 3
VIZ

❑1, Apr 1995	2.75
❑2, May 1995	2.75
❑3, Jun 1995	2.75
❑4, Jul 1995	2.75
❑5, Aug 1995	2.75
❑6, Sep 1995	2.75
❑7, Oct 1995	2.75

BIO-BOOSTER ARMOR GUYVER PART 4
VIZ

	N-MINT
❑1, Nov 1995	2.75
❑2, Dec 1995	2.75
❑3, Jan 1996	2.95
❑4, Feb 1996	2.95
❑5, Mar 1996	2.95
❑6, Apr 1996	2.95

BIO-BOOSTER ARMOR GUYVER PART 5
VIZ

❑1, May 1996	2.95
❑2, Jun 1996	2.95
❑3, Jul 1996	2.95
❑4, Aug 1996	2.95
❑5, Sep 1996	2.95
❑6, Oct 1996	2.95
❑7, Nov 1996	2.95

BIO-BOOSTER ARMOR GUYVER PART 6
VIZ

❑1, Dec 1996	2.95
❑2, Jan 1997	2.95
❑3, Feb 1997	2.95
❑4, Mar 1997	2.95
❑5, Apr 1997	2.95
❑6, May 1997	2.95

BIOLOGIC SHOW
FANTAGRAPHICS

❑0, Oct 1994, b&w; magazine; cardstock cover	2.95
❑1, Jan 1995, b&w	2.75

BIONEERS
MIRAGE

❑1, Aug 1994	2.75
❑2	2.75
❑3	2.75

BIONIC DOG
HUGO REX

❑1	3.25

BIONICLE
DC

❑1, ca. 2001	2.25
❑2 2001	2.25
❑3, Oct 2001	2.25
❑4 2002	2.25
❑5, Apr 2002	2.25
❑6, May 2002	2.25
❑7 2002	2.25
❑8 2002	2.25
❑9, Dec 2002	2.25

BIONIC WOMAN
CHARLTON

❑1, Oct 1977	14.00
❑2, Feb 1978	6.00
❑3, Mar 1978	6.00
❑4, May 1978	6.00
❑5, Jun 1978	6.00

BIONIX
MAXIMUM

❑1, ca. 1996	2.99

BIRDLAND
FANTAGRAPHICS / EROS

❑1, b&w	1.95
❑2	2.25
❑3	2.25

BIRDLAND (VOL. 2)
FANTAGRAPHICS / EROS

❑1, Jun 1994, b&w	2.95

BIRDS OF PREY
DC

❑1, Jan 1999 A: Hellhound. A: Oracle. 4.00
❑2, Feb 1999 A: Hellhound. A: Black Canary. A: Jackie Pajamas. 3.00
❑3, Mar 1999 A: Hellhound. A: Black Canary. 3.00
❑4, Apr 1999 A: Ravens. A: Kobra. 3.00
❑5, May 1999 A: Ravens. 3.00
❑6, Jun 1999 3.00
❑7, Jul 1999 3.00
❑8, Aug 1999 A: Nightwing. 12.00
❑9, Sep 1999 3.00
❑10, Oct 1999 3.00
❑11, Nov 1999 DG (a) 3.00
❑12, Dec 1999 3.00
❑13, Jan 2000 3.00
❑14, Feb 2000 3.00
❑15, Mar 2000 3.00
❑16, Apr 2000 BG (a); A: Joker. 3.00
❑17, May 2000 BG (a) 3.00
❑18, Jun 2000 BG (a) 3.00
❑19, Jul 2000 BG (a) 3.00
❑20, Aug 2000 BG (a) 3.00
❑21, Sep 2000 BG (a) 3.00
❑22, Oct 2000 BSz, BG (a) 3.00
❑23, Nov 2000 BG (a) 3.00
❑24, Dec 2000 BG (a) 3.00
❑25, Jan 2001 BG (a) 3.00
❑26, Feb 2001 BG (a) 3.00
❑27, Mar 2001 3.00
❑28, Apr 2001 BG (a) 3.00
❑29, May 2001 BG (a) 3.00
❑30, Jun 2001 BG (a) 3.00
❑31, Jul 2001 2.50
❑32, Aug 2001 2.50
❑33, Sep 2001 BG (a) 2.50
❑34, Oct 2001 BG (a) 2.50
❑35, Nov 2001 2.50
❑36, Dec 2001 2.50
❑37, Jan 2002 2.50
❑38, Feb 2002 2.50
❑39, Mar 2002 2.50
❑40, Apr 2002 2.50
❑41, May 2002 2.50
❑42, Jun 2002 2.50
❑43, Jul 2002 2.50
❑44, Aug 2002 2.50
❑45, Sep 2002 2.50
❑46, Oct 2002 2.50
❑47, Nov 2002 2.50
❑48, Dec 2002 2.50
❑49, Jan 2003 2.50
❑50, Feb 2003 2.50
❑51, Mar 2003 2.50
❑52, Apr 2003 2.50
❑53, May 2003 2.50
❑54, Jun 2003 2.50
❑55, Jul 2003 2.50
❑56, Aug 2003 2.50
❑57, Sep 2003 2.50
❑58, Oct 2003 2.50
❑59, Nov 2003 2.50
❑60, Dec 2003 2.50
❑61, Jan 2004 2.50
❑62, Feb 2004 2.50
❑63, Mar 2004 2.50
❑64, Apr 2004 2.50
❑65, May 2004 2.50
❑66, Jun 2004 2.50
❑67, Jul 2004 2.50
❑68, Aug 2004 2.50
❑69, Sep 2004 2.50
❑70, Sep 2004 2.50
❑71, Oct 2004 2.50
❑72, Oct 2004 2.50
❑73, Nov 2004 2.50
❑74, Dec 2004 2.50
❑75, Jan 2005 2.95
❑76, Feb 2005 2.50
❑77, Mar 2005 2.50
❑78, Apr 2005 2.50
❑79, May 2005 2.50
❑80, Jun 2005 2.50
❑81, Jun 2005 2.50
❑82, Jul 2005 2.50
❑83, Aug 2005 2.50
❑84, Sep 2005 2.50
❑85, Oct 2005 2.50
❑86 2005 2.50
❑87, Dec 2005 2.50
❑88, Jan 2006 2.50
❑89, Feb 2006 2.50
❑90, Mar 2006 2.50
❑91, Apr 2006 2.50
❑92, May 2006 2.50
❑93, Jun 2006 2.50
❑94, Aug 2006 2.50
❑95, Sep 2006 2.50

BIRDS OF PREY: BATGIRL
DC

❑1, Feb 1998 3.00

BIRDS OF PREY: CATWOMAN
DC

❑1, Feb 2003 5.95
❑2, Mar 2003 5.95

BIRDS OF PREY: MANHUNT
DC

❑1, Sep 1996 2.25
❑2, Oct 1996 2.00
❑3, Nov 1996 2.00
❑4, Dec 1996 SB (a) 2.00

BIRDS OF PREY: REVOLUTION
DC

❑1, Apr 1997 2.95

BIRDS OF PREY: SECRET FILES 2003
DC

❑1, Jun 2003 4.95

BIRDS OF PREY: THE RAVENS
DC

❑1, Jun 1998; Girlfrenzy 1.95

BIRDS OF PREY: WOLVES
DC

❑1, Oct 1997 2.95

BIRTH CAUL
EDDIE CAMPBELL

❑1, Jun 1999 5.95

BIRTHRIGHT
FANTAGRAPHICS

❑1 2.50
❑2 2.50
❑3 2.50

BIRTHRIGHT (TSR)
TSR

❑1 1.50

BIRTH RITE
CONGRESS

❑1 2.50
❑2 2.50
❑3 2.50
❑4 2.50

BISHOP
MARVEL

❑1, Dec 1994; 1: Mountjoy. foil cover 4.00
❑2, Jan 1995 2.95
❑3, Feb 1995 2.95
❑4, Mar 1995 2.95

BISHOP THE LAST X-MAN
MARVEL

❑1, Oct 1999 2.99
❑2, Nov 1999 2.99
❑3, Dec 1999 2.99
❑4, Jan 2000 2.99
❑5, Feb 2000 2.99
❑6, Mar 2000 2.99
❑7, Apr 2000 2.99
❑8, May 2000 2.99
❑9, Jun 2000 2.99
❑10, Jul 2000 2.99
❑11, Aug 2000 2.99
❑12, Sep 2000; double-sized 2.99
❑13, Oct 2000 2.25
❑14, Nov 2000 2.25
❑15, Dec 2000 2.25
❑16, Jan 2001 2.25

BISHOP: XSE
MARVEL

❑1, Jan 1998; gatefold summary 2.50
❑2, Feb 1998; gatefold summary 2.50
❑3, Mar 1998 2.50

BISLEY'S SCRAPBOOK
ATOMEKA

❑1 2.50

BITCH IN HEAT
FANTAGRAPHICS / EROS

❑1, Mar 1997 2.95
❑2 2.95
❑3 2.95
❑4 2.95
❑5, Jul 1998 2.95
❑6, Sep 1998 2.95
❑7, Jan 1999 2.95
❑8, Apr 1999 2.95
❑9, ca. 1999 2.95
❑10, ca. 2000 2.95

BITE CLUB
DC / VERTIGO

❑1, May 2004 2.95
❑2, Jun 2004 4.00
❑3, Aug 2004 2.95
❑4, Sep 2004 2.95
❑5, Oct 2004 2.95
❑6, Nov 2004 2.95

BITE CLUB: VAMPIRE CRIME UNIT
DC / VERTIGO

❑1, Jun 2006 2.99
❑3, Sep 2006 2.99

BITS AND PIECES
MORTIFIED

❑1, Nov 1994 3.00

BITTER CAKE
TIN CUP

❑1, b&w 2.00

BIZARRE 3-D ZONE
BLACKTHORNE

❑1, Jul 1986 2.25
❑2 2.25
❑3 2.25
❑4 2.25
❑5, Jul 1986; #1 on cover 2.25

BIZARRE ADVENTURES
MARVEL

❑25, Mar 1981, A: Black Widow. Lethal Ladies; Was Marvel Preview 2.50
❑26, May 1981, King Kull 2.50
❑27, Jul 1981, X-Men 4.00
❑28, Oct 1981, FM (w); FM (a); A: Elektra. Unlikely Heroes 3.00
❑29, Dec 1981, Stephen King; Horror 2.50
❑30, Feb 1982, Paradox; Tomorrow 2.50
❑31, Apr 1982, FM (a); After the Violence Stops 2.50
❑32, Aug 1982, Thor and other Gods. 2.50
❑33, ca. 1982, 1: Varnae. Dracula; Zombie; Horror 2.50
❑34, Feb 1983, gatefold summary; AM (w); AM, PS (a); A: Howard the Duck. Format changes to comic book 2.50

BIZARRE FANTASY
FLASHBACK

❑0 2.50
❑0/Autographed; 1500 copies printed 9.95
❑1 2.50
❑2 2.50

BIZARRE HEROES
KITCHEN SINK

❑1, May 1990; parody, b&w 2.50

BIZARRE HEROES (DON SIMPSON'S...)
FIASCO

❑0, Dec 1994 2.95
❑1, May 1994 3.25
❑2, Jun 1994 2.95
❑3, Jul 1994 2.95
❑4, Aug 1994 2.95
❑5, Sep 1994 2.95
❑6, Oct 1994 2.95
❑7, Nov 1994 2.95
❑8, Dec 1994 2.95
❑9 2.95
❑10 2.95
❑11 2.95
❑12 2.95
❑13 2.95

Black Axe

50,000-year-old asssassin in Marvel UK import
©Marvel

Black Canary (Mini-Series)

Sonic-screaming heroine gets own title
©DC

Black Condor

Reuses name from an old Quality character
©DC

Black Goliath

Short-lived 1970s African-American superhero title
©Marvel

Blackhawk (1st Series)

Allied ace fighters star in aerial series
©DC

N-MINT

❑14, Oct 1995, Title changes to Bizarre Heroes 2.95
❑15, Jan 1996, O: The Slick. 2.95

BIZARRE SEX
KITCHEN SINK

❑1, May 1972 15.00
❑2, Nov 1972 9.00
❑3, Jun 1973; White "remove this outer cover at your own risk" cover 7.00
❑4, Oct 1975; White "remove this outer cover at your own risk" cover 5.00
❑4/2nd, Sep 1976; White "remove this outer cover at your own risk" cover 4.00
❑4/3rd, Jul 1977 4.00
❑5, Oct 1976 5.00
❑6, Oct 1977 5.00
❑7, Jan 1979 5.00
❑8, Mar 1980 5.00
❑9, Aug 1981, b&w 1: Omaha. 18.00

BIZZARIAN
IRONCAT

❑1, ca. 2000 2.95
❑2, ca. 2000 2.95
❑3, ca. 2000 2.95
❑4, ca. 2000 2.95
❑5, ca. 2001 2.95
❑6, ca. 2001 2.95
❑7, ca. 2001 2.95
❑8, ca. 2001 2.95

B. KRIGSTEIN SAMPLER, A
INDEPENDENT

❑1 BK (c); BK (w); BK (a) 2.50

BLAB!
KITCHEN SINK

❑8, Sum 1995; odd-sized anthology 16.95
❑9, Fal 1997; odd-sized anthology 18.95
❑10, Fal 1998; odd-sized anthology 19.95

BLACK & WHITE (MINI-SERIES)
IMAGE

❑1, Oct 1994 1.95
❑2, Nov 1994 1.95
❑3, Jan 1995 1.95

BLACK & WHITE
IMAGE

❑1, Feb 1996 2.50
❑Ashcan 1; No cover price; ashcan preview of series 1.00

BLACK & WHITE (VIZ)
VIZ

❑1, Aug 1999 3.25
❑2 1999 3.25
❑3 1999 3.25

BLACK AND WHITE BONDAGE
VEROTIK

❑1 4.95

BLACK AND WHITE COMICS
APEX NOVELTIES

❑1 4.00

BLACK AND WHITE THEATER
DOUBLE M

❑1, Jun 1996, b&w 2.95
❑2, b&w 2.95

N-MINT

BLACK AXE
MARVEL

❑1, Apr 1993 1.75
❑2, May 1993 1.75
❑3, Jun 1993 1.75
❑4, Jul 1993 1.75
❑5, Aug 1993 1.75
❑6, Sep 1993 1.75
❑7, Oct 1993 1.75

BLACKBALL COMICS
BLACKBALL

❑1, Mar 1994 3.00

BLACK BOOK (BRIAN BOLLAND'S...)
ECLIPSE

❑1 BB (a) 2.00

BLACK BOW
ARTLINE

❑1 2.50

BLACKBURNE COVENANT
DARK HORSE

❑1, Jun 2003 2.99
❑2, Jul 2003 2.99
❑3, Aug 2003 2.99
❑4, Sep 2003 2.99

BLACK CANARY (MINI-SERIES)
DC

❑1, Nov 1991 TVE (a) 2.50
❑2, Dec 1991 TVE (a) 2.50
❑3, Jan 1992 TVE (a) 2.50
❑4, Feb 1992 TVE (a) 2.50

BLACK CANARY
DC

❑1, Jan 1993, TVE (a) 2.00
❑2, Feb 1993, TVE (a) 2.00
❑3, Mar 1993, TVE (a) 2.00
❑4, Apr 1993, TVE (a) 2.00
❑5, May 1993, TVE (a) 2.00
❑6, Jun 1993, TVE (a) 2.00
❑7, Jul 1993, TVE (a) 2.00
❑8, Aug 1993, A: The Ray. 2.00
❑9, Sep 1993, TVE (a) 2.00
❑10, Oct 1993, TVE (a) 2.00
❑11, Nov 1993, TVE (a) 2.00
❑12, Dec 1993 2.00

BLACK CANARY/ORACLE: BIRDS OF PREY
DC

❑1, Jun 1996 3.95

BLACK CAT (THE ORIGINS)
LORNE-HARVEY

❑1 and b&w; reprints Black Cat and Sad Sack strips; text feature on Alfred Harvey 3.50

BLACK CAT THE WAR YEARS
RECOLLECTIONS

❑1; Golden Age reprints, b&w 1.00

BLACK CONDOR
DC

❑1, Jun 1992 O: Black Condor II. 1: Black Condor II. 1.50
❑2, Jul 1992 1.25
❑3, Aug 1992 1.25

N-MINT

❑4, Sep 1992 1.25
❑5, Oct 1992 1.25
❑6, Nov 1992 1.25
❑7, Dec 1992 1.25
❑8, Jan 1993 MGu (a) 1.25
❑9, Feb 1993 1.25
❑10, Mar 1993 A: The Ray. 1.25
❑11, Apr 1993 1.25
❑12, May 1993 A: Batman. 1.25

BLACK CROSS: DIRTY WORK
DARK HORSE

❑1, Apr 1997 2.95

BLACK CROSS SPECIAL
DARK HORSE

❑1, Jan 1988, b&w 2.50
❑1/2nd 1.75

BLACK DIAMOND
AC

❑1, May 1983 2.00
❑2, Jul 1983 2.00
❑3, Dec 1983 2.00
❑4, Feb 1984 2.00
❑5, May 1984 2.00

BLACK DIAMOND EFFECT
BLACK DIAMOND EFFECT

❑1 3.00
❑2, Oct 1991 3.10
❑3 3.10
❑4 3.10
❑5 3.10
❑6, Dec 1992 3.00
❑7 3.10

BLACK DRAGON
MARVEL / EPIC

❑1, May 1985 3.00
❑2, Jun 1985 2.50
❑3, Jul 1985 2.50
❑4, Aug 1985 2.50
❑5, Sep 1985 2.00
❑6, Oct 1985 2.00

BLACK FLAG (IMAGE)
IMAGE

❑1, Jun 1994, b&w; Fold-out cover 1.95
❑Ashcan 1; Preview edition 1.95

BLACK FLAG (MAXIMUM)
MAXIMUM

❑0, Jul 1995 2.50
❑1, Jan 1995 2.50
❑2/A, Feb 1995; Woman on cover 2.50
❑2/B; Variant cover with man 2.50
❑3, Mar 1995 2.50
❑4/A, cover has black background 2.50
❑4/B, cover has white background 2.50

BLACK FOREST
IMAGE

❑1, ca. 2003 9.95

BLACK GOLIATH
MARVEL

❑1, Feb 1976, RB (c); GT (a); O: Black Goliath. 11.00
❑2, Apr 1976, RB (c); GT (a) 5.00

Other grades: Multiply price above by 5/6 for VF/NM • 2/3 for VERY FINE • 1/3 for FINE • 1/5 for VERY GOOD • 1/8 for GOOD

❑2/30 cent, Apr 1976, RB (c); GT (a); 30-cent regional price variant 20.00
❑3, Jun 1976, GT (a) 4.00
❑3/30 cent, Jun 1976, GT (a); 30-cent regional price variant 20.00
❑4, Aug 1976, JK (c); RB, DH (a) 4.00
❑4/30 cent, Aug 1976, JK (c); RB, DH (a); 30-cent regional price variant 20.00
❑5, Nov 1976, AM, GK (c); KP (a) 4.00

BLACK HARVEST
DEVIL'S DUE

❑1, Nov 2005 .... 3.95
❑2, Jan 2006 .... 3.95
❑3, Feb 2006 .... 3.95
❑4, Mar 2006 .... 3.95
❑5, Apr 2006 .... 3.95

BLACKHAWK (1ST SERIES)
DC

❑105, Oct 1956 .... 105.00
❑106, Nov 1956 .... 105.00
❑107, Dec 1956 .... 105.00
❑108, Jan 1957, DC begins publishing (formerly Quality) 325.00
❑109, Feb 1957 .... 130.00
❑110, Mar 1957 .... 110.00
❑111, Apr 1957 .... 110.00
❑112, May 1957 .... 110.00
❑113, Jun 1957 .... 110.00
❑114, Jul 1957 .... 110.00
❑115, Aug 1957 .... 110.00
❑116, Sep 1957 .... 110.00
❑117, Oct 1957 .... 110.00
❑118, Nov 1957, FF (a) 135.00
❑119, Dec 1957 .... 85.00
❑120, Jan 1958 .... 85.00
❑121, Feb 1958 .... 85.00
❑122, Mar 1958 .... 85.00
❑123, Apr 1958 .... 85.00
❑124, May 1958 .... 85.00
❑125, Jun 1958 .... 85.00
❑126, Jul 1958 .... 85.00
❑127, Aug 1958 .... 85.00
❑128, Sep 1958 .... 85.00
❑129, Oct 1958 .... 85.00
❑130, Nov 1958 .... 85.00
❑131, Dec 1958 .... 65.00
❑132, Jan 1959 .... 65.00
❑133, Feb 1959, 1: Lady Blackhawk 65.00
❑134, Mar 1959 .... 65.00
❑135, Apr 1959 .... 65.00
❑136, May 1959 .... 65.00
❑137, Jun 1959 .... 65.00
❑138, Jul 1959 .... 65.00
❑139, Aug 1959 .... 65.00
❑140, Sep 1959 .... 65.00
❑141, Oct 1959 .... 50.00
❑142, Nov 1959 .... 50.00
❑143, Dec 1959 .... 50.00
❑144, Jan 1960 .... 50.00
❑145, Feb 1960 .... 50.00
❑146, Mar 1960 .... 50.00
❑147, Apr 1960 .... 50.00
❑148, May 1960 .... 50.00
❑149, Jun 1960 .... 50.00
❑150, Jul 1960 .... 48.00
❑151, Aug 1960 .... 48.00
❑152, Sep 1960 .... 48.00
❑153, Oct 1960 .... 48.00
❑154, Nov 1960 .... 48.00
❑155, Dec 1960 .... 48.00
❑156, Jan 1961 .... 48.00
❑157, Feb 1961 .... 48.00
❑158, Mar 1961 .... 48.00
❑159, Apr 1961 .... 48.00
❑160, May 1961 .... 48.00
❑161, Jun 1961 .... 48.00
❑162, Jul 1961 .... 48.00
❑163, Aug 1961 .... 48.00
❑164, Sep 1961, O: Blackhawks. O: Blackhawk 60.00
❑165, Oct 1961 .... 48.00
❑166, Nov 1961 .... 48.00
❑167, Dec 1961 .... 22.00
❑168, Jan 1962 .... 22.00
❑169, Feb 1962 .... 22.00
❑170, Mar 1962 .... 22.00
❑171, Apr 1962 .... 22.00
❑172, May 1962 .... 22.00
❑173, Jun 1962 .... 22.00
❑174, Jul 1962 .... 22.00
❑175, Aug 1962 .... 22.00
❑176, Sep 1962 .... 22.00
❑177, Oct 1962 .... 22.00
❑178, Nov 1962 .... 22.00
❑179, Dec 1962 .... 22.00
❑180, Jan 1963 .... 22.00
❑181, Feb 1963 .... 16.00
❑182, Mar 1963 .... 16.00
❑183, Apr 1963 .... 16.00
❑184, May 1963 .... 16.00
❑185, Jun 1963 .... 16.00
❑186, Jul 1963 .... 16.00
❑187, Aug 1963 .... 16.00
❑188, Sep 1963 .... 16.00
❑189, Oct 1963, O: Blackhawks 16.00
❑190, Nov 1963 .... 16.00
❑191, Dec 1963 .... 16.00
❑192, Jan 1964 .... 16.00
❑193, Feb 1964 .... 16.00
❑194, Mar 1964 .... 16.00
❑195, Apr 1964 .... 16.00
❑196, May 1964, Biographies of Dick Dillon and Chuck Cuidera (Blackhawk artists) 16.00
❑197, Jun 1964, new look 16.00
❑198, Jul 1964, O: Blackhawks. O: Blackhawk 16.00
❑199, Aug 1964 .... 16.00
❑200, Sep 1964 .... 16.00
❑201, Oct 1964 .... 15.00
❑202, Nov 1964 .... 15.00
❑203, Dec 1964, O: Chop-Chop 15.00
❑204, Jan 1965 .... 15.00
❑205, Feb 1965 .... 15.00
❑206, Mar 1965 .... 15.00
❑207, Apr 1965 .... 15.00
❑208, May 1965 .... 15.00
❑209, Jun 1965 .... 15.00
❑210, Jul 1965 .... 15.00
❑211, Aug 1965 .... 15.00
❑212, Sep 1965 .... 15.00
❑213, Oct 1965 .... 15.00
❑214, Nov 1965 .... 15.00
❑215, Dec 1965 .... 15.00
❑216, Jan 1966 .... 15.00
❑217, Feb 1966 .... 15.00
❑218, Mar 1966 .... 15.00
❑219, Apr 1966 .... 15.00
❑220, May 1966 .... 15.00
❑221, Jun 1966 .... 15.00
❑222, Jul 1966 .... 15.00
❑223, Aug 1966 .... 15.00
❑224, Sep 1966 .... 15.00
❑225, Oct 1966 .... 15.00
❑226, Nov 1966 .... 15.00
❑227, Dec 1966 .... 15.00
❑228, Jan 1967 .... 30.00
❑229, Feb 1967 .... 15.00
❑230, Mar 1967, Blackhawks become super-heroes; New costumes 15.00
❑231, Apr 1967, Blackhawks as super-heroes 15.00
❑232, May 1967, Blackhawks as super-heroes 15.00
❑233, Jun 1967, Blackhawks as super-heroes 15.00
❑234, Jul 1967, Blackhawks as super-heroes 15.00
❑235, Aug 1967, Blackhawks as super-heroes 15.00
❑236, Sep 1967, Blackhawks as super-heroes 15.00
❑237, Nov 1967, Blackhawks as super-heroes 15.00
❑238, Jan 1968, Blackhawks as super-heroes 15.00
❑239, Mar 1968, Blackhawks as super-heroes 15.00
❑240, May 1968, Blackhawks as super-heroes 15.00
❑241, Jul 1968, Blackhawks as super-heroes 15.00
❑242, Sep 1968, Blackhawks back to old costumes 15.00
❑243, Nov 1968, Last issue of 1960s run 15.00
❑244, Feb 1976; GE (a); New issues begin with old # sequence 4.00
❑245, Apr 1976 .... 4.00
❑246, Jun 1976 .... 4.00
❑247, Aug 1976, Bicentennial #25 .... 4.00
❑248, Sep 1976 .... 4.00
❑249, Nov 1976 .... 4.00
❑250, Jan 1977, D: Chuck 4.00
❑251, Oct 1982 .... 4.00
❑252, Nov 1982, DS (a); V: War Wheel 4.00
❑253, Dec 1982 .... 4.00
❑254, Jan 1983 .... 4.00
❑255, Feb 1983 .... 4.00
❑256, Mar 1983 .... 4.00
❑257, Apr 1983, HC (c) 4.00
❑258, May 1983, HC (c) 4.00
❑259, Jun 1983, HC (c) 4.00
❑260, Jul 1983, HC (c); ME (w); HC (a) 4.00
❑261, Aug 1983 .... 3.00
❑262, Sep 1983, HC (c); ME (w); DS (a) 3.00
❑263, Oct 1983, GK (c); V: War Wheel 3.00
❑264, Nov 1983 .... 3.00
❑265, Dec 1983 .... 3.00
❑266, Jan 1984 .... 3.00
❑267, Feb 1984 .... 3.00
❑268, Mar 1984 .... 3.00
❑269, Apr 1984 1: Killer Shark I (General Haifisch) 3.00
❑270, May 1984 .... 3.00
❑271, Jul 1984 .... 3.00
❑272, Sep 1984 .... 3.00
❑273, Nov 1984 HC (c) 3.00

BLACKHAWK (2ND SERIES)
DC

❑1, Mar 1988; HC (w); HC (a); no mature readers advisory 3.50
❑2, Apr 1988 HC (w); HC (a) 3.50
❑3, May 1988 HC (w); HC (a) 3.50

BLACKHAWK (3RD SERIES)
DC

❑1, Mar 1989 .... 2.00
❑2, Apr 1989 .... 1.75
❑3, May 1989 .... 1.75
❑4, Jun 1989 .... 1.75
❑5, Aug 1989 .... 1.75
❑6, Sep 1989 .... 1.50
❑7, Oct 1989; Double-size; WE (w); Reprints 2.50
❑8, Nov 1989 .... 1.50
❑9, Dec 1989 .... 1.50
❑10, Jan 1990 .... 1.50
❑11, Feb 1990 .... 1.50
❑12, Mar 1990 .... 1.50
❑13, Apr 1990 .... 1.50
❑14, May 1990 .... 1.50
❑15, Jul 1990 .... 1.50
❑16, Aug 1990 .... 1.50
❑Annual 1, ca. 1989 .... 2.95
❑Special 1, ca. 1992; Special edition (1992) 3.50

BLACK HEART: ASSASSIN
IGUANA

❑1 .... 2.95

BLACK HEART BILLY
SLAVE LABOR

❑1, Mar 2000, b&w 2.95

BLACK HOLE
KITCHEN SINK

❑1 .... 3.50
❑2, Nov 1995 .... 3.50
❑3, Jul 1996 .... 3.50
❑4, Jun 1997 .... 3.50
❑5, Mar 1998 .... 3.95
❑6, Dec 1998 .... 4.50
❑7, ca. 1999 .... 4.50
❑8, ca. 2000 .... 4.50
❑9, ca. 2001 .... 4.50

BLACK HOLE (WALT DISNEY...)
WHITMAN

❑1, Mar 1980 .... 2.00
❑2, May 1980 .... 2.00
❑3, Jul 1980 .... 2.00
❑4, Sep 1980 .... 2.00

Blackhawk (2nd Series)
Racy Chaykin version angered retailers
©DC

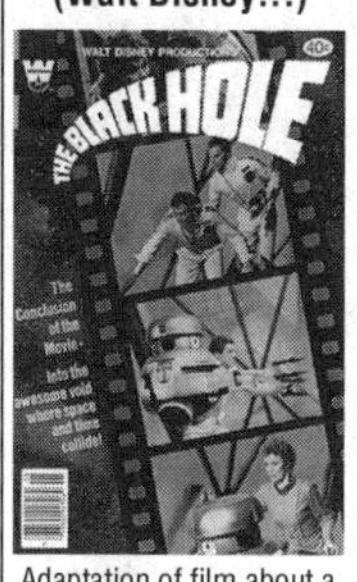
Black Hole (Walt Disney...)
Adaptation of film about a bathtub drain in space
©Whitman

Black Lightning (1st Series)
Teacher turns vigilante in Isabella series
©DC

Black Panther
Jack Kirby handled the 1977 return of T'Challa
©Marvel

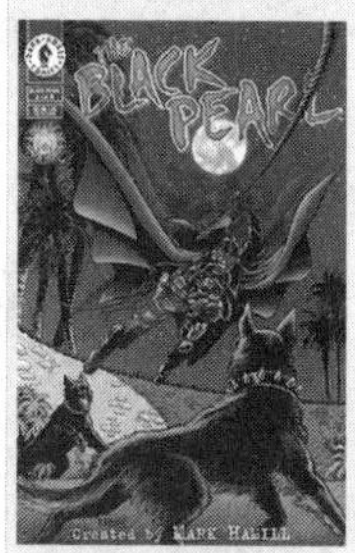
Black Pearl
Series from actor and comics fan Mark Hamill
©Dark Horse

N-MINT

BLACK HOOD
DC / IMPACT
❑1, Dec 1991 1.00
❑2, Jan 1992 1.00
❑3, Feb 1992 1.00
❑4, Mar 1992 1.00
❑5, Apr 1992 1.00
❑6, May 1992 1.00
❑7, Jun 1992 1.00
❑8, Aug 1992 1.00
❑9, Sep 1992 1.00
❑10, Oct 1992 1.00
❑11, Nov 1992 1.00
❑12, Dec 1992 1.00
❑Annual 1, trading card 1.50

BLACK HOOD (RED CIRCLE)
ARCHIE / RED CIRCLE
❑1, Jun 1983, ATh, GM (a) 3.00
❑2, Aug 1983, ATh, GM (a) 2.00
❑3, Oct 1983, ATh, GM (a) 2.00

BLACKJACK (VOL. 1)
DARK ANGEL
❑1, Sep 1996 2.95
❑2, Oct 1996 2.95
❑3, Jan 1997 2.95
❑4 1997 2.95
❑Special 1, Sep 1998 3.50

BLACKJACK (VOL. 2)
DARK ANGEL
❑1, Apr 1997 2.95
❑2, Feb 1998 2.95

BLACK KISS
VORTEX
❑1, Jun 1988 HC (w); HC (a) 2.50
❑1/2nd, Jun 1988 HC (w); HC (a) 2.00
❑1/3rd HC (w); HC (a) 2.00
❑2, Jul 1988 HC (w); HC (a) 2.50
❑2/2nd HC (w); HC (a) 2.00
❑3, Aug 1988 HC (w); HC (a) 2.00
❑4, Sep 1988; HC (w); HC (a); polybagged with black insert card covering actual cover 2.00
❑5, Oct 1988 HC (w); HC (a) 2.00
❑6, Nov 1988 HC (w); HC (a) 2.00
❑7, Dec 1988 HC (w); HC (a) 2.00
❑8, Jan 1989; HC (w); HC (a); indicia says 88 (misprint) 2.00
❑9, Feb 1989; HC (w); HC (a); indicia says 88 (misprint) 2.00
❑10, Mar 1989; HC (w); HC (a); indicia says 88 (misprint) 2.00
❑11, May 1989 HC (w); HC (a) 2.00
❑12, Jul 1989 HC (w); HC (a) 2.00

BLACK KNIGHT (LTD. SERIES)
MARVEL
❑1, Jun 1990 TD (a); O: Black Knight III (Dane Whitman). O: Black Knight I (Sir Percy). O: Black Knight II (Nathan Garrett) 2.00
❑2, Jul 1990 A: Captain Britain. 1.50
❑3, Aug 1990 RB (a); 1: new Valkyrie. A: Doctor Strange. 1.50
❑4, Sep 1990 A: Doctor Strange. A: Valkyrie. 1.50

N-MINT

BLACK KNIGHT: EXODUS
MARVEL
❑1, Dec 1996 2.50

BLACK LAMB
DC / HELIX
❑1, Nov 1996 2.50
❑2, Dec 1996 2.50
❑3, Jan 1997 2.50
❑4, Feb 1997 2.50
❑5, Mar 1997 2.50
❑6, Apr 1997 2.50

BLACKLIGHT
IMAGE
❑1, Jul 2005 2.99
❑2, Dec 2005 2.99

BLACK LIGHTNING (1ST SERIES)
DC
❑1, Apr 1977, TVE, FS (a); O: Black Lightning. 1: Black Lightning 10.00
❑2, May 1977 5.00
❑3, Jul 1977 5.00
❑4, Sep 1977 5.00
❑5, Nov 1977 5.00
❑6, Jan 1978, 1: Syonide I. 5.00
❑7, Mar 1978 5.00
❑8, Apr 1978 5.00
❑9, May 1978 5.00
❑10, Jul 1978 5.00
❑11, Sep 1978, A: The Ray. 5.00

BLACK LIGHTNING (2ND SERIES)
DC
❑1, Feb 1995 2.50
❑2, Mar 1995 2.00
❑3, Apr 1995 2.00
❑4, May 1995 2.00
❑5, Jun 1995 2.00
❑6, Jul 1995 A: Gangbuster. 2.75
❑7, Aug 1995 A: Gangbuster. 2.25
❑8, Sep 1995 2.25
❑9, Oct 1995 2.25
❑10, Nov 1995 2.25
❑11, Dec 1995 2.25
❑12, Jan 1996 2.25
❑13, Feb 1996 2.25

BLACK LION THE BANTU WARRIOR
HEROES FROM THE HOOD
❑1, ca. 1997, b&w 2.50

BLACK MAGIC (DC)
DC
❑1, Nov 1973 15.00
❑2, Dec 1973 7.00
❑3, Apr 1974 7.00
❑4, Jun 1974, JK (a) 7.00
❑5, Aug 1974 7.00
❑6, Oct 1974 7.00
❑7, Dec 1974 7.00
❑8, Feb 1975 7.00
❑9, Apr 1975 7.00

BLACK MAGIC (ECLIPSE)
ECLIPSE
❑1, Apr 1990; Japanese, b&w 3.50
❑2, Jun 1990 2.75

N-MINT

❑3, Aug 1990 2.75
❑4, Oct 1990 2.75

BLACKMASK
DC
❑1, ca. 2000 4.95
❑2, ca. 2000 4.95
❑3, ca. 2000 4.95

BLACKMASK (EASTERN)
EASTERN
❑1, ca. 1988, Translated by Franz Hankel 1.75
❑2, ca. 1988 1.75
❑3, ca. 1988 1.75

BLACK MIST
CALIBER
❑1, ca. 1994 2.95
❑2, ca. 1994 2.95
❑3, ca. 1994 2.95
❑4, ca. 1994 2.95

BLACK MIST: BLOOD OF KALI
CALIBER
❑1, Jan 1998 2.95
❑2, ca. 1998 2.95
❑3, ca. 1998 2.95

BLACKMOON
U.S.COMICS
❑1 1985 O: Blackmoon. 2.00
❑2 2.00
❑3 2.00

BLACK OPS
IMAGE
❑1, Jan 1996 2.50
❑2, Feb 1996 2.50
❑3, Mar 1996 2.50
❑4, Apr 1996 2.50
❑5/A, Jun 1996 2.50
❑5/B, Jun 1996; alternate cover 2.50

BLACK ORCHID
DC / VERTIGO
❑1, Sep 1993 2.50
❑1/Platinum, Sep 1993, Platinum edition 5.00
❑2, Oct 1993 2.25
❑3, Nov 1993 2.25
❑4, Dec 1993 2.25
❑5, Jan 1994 2.25
❑6, Feb 1994 2.00
❑7, Mar 1994 2.00
❑8, Apr 1994 2.00
❑9, May 1994 2.00
❑10, Jun 1994 2.00
❑11, Jul 1994 2.00
❑12, Aug 1994 2.00
❑13, Sep 1994 2.00
❑14, Oct 1994 2.00
❑15, Nov 1994 2.00
❑16, Dec 1994 2.00
❑17, Jan 1995 1.95
❑18, Feb 1995 1.95
❑19, Mar 1995 1.95
❑20, Apr 1995 1.95
❑21, May 1995 2.25

❑22, Jun 1995 .... 2.25
❑Annual 1, Children's Crusade 4.00

BLACK ORCHID (MINI-SERIES)
DC

❑1 1988, NG (w); 1st Neil Gaiman U.S. comics work 6.00
❑2 1989, NG (w); A: Batman 5.00
❑3 1989, NG (w) 5.00

BLACK PANTHER
MARVEL

❑1, Jan 1977, JK (c); JK (w); JK (a) 12.00
❑2, Mar 1977, JK (c); JK (w); JK (a) 7.00
❑3, May 1977, JK (c); JK (w); JK (a) 5.00
❑4, Jul 1977, JK (c); JK (w); JK (a) 5.00
❑4/35 cent, Jul 1977, JK (c); JK (w); JK (a); 35 cent regional price variant 15.00
❑5, Sep 1977, JK (c); JK (w); JK (a) 5.00
❑5/35 cent, Sep 1977, JK (c); JK (w); JK (a); 35 cent regional price variant 15.00
❑6, Nov 1977, JK (c); JK (w); JK (a) 5.00
❑7, Jan 1978, JK (c); JK (w); JK (a) 5.00
❑8, Mar 1978, JK (c); JK (w); JK (a) 5.00
❑9, May 1978, JK (c); JK (w); JK (a) 5.00
❑10, Jul 1978, JK, JSt (c); JK (w); JK (a) 5.00
❑11, Sep 1978, JK, JSt (c); JK (w); JK (a) 4.00
❑12, Nov 1978, JK, TP (c); JK (w); JK (a) 4.00
❑13, Jan 1979, BL (c); GD (a) 4.00
❑14, Mar 1979, TP (c); GD (a) 4.00
❑15, May 1979, AM, JB (c); GD (a); A: Klaw 4.00

BLACK PANTHER (VOL. 2)
MARVEL

❑1, Nov 1998; gatefold summary 5.00
❑1/Variant, Nov 1998; DFE alternate cover 7.00
❑2/A, Dec 1998; gatefold summary 4.00
❑2/B, Dec 1998; gatefold summary 4.00
❑3, Jan 1999; gatefold summary; A: Fantastic Four. gatefold summary, A: Fantastic Four 3.00
❑4, Feb 1999 A: Mephisto 3.00
❑5, Mar 1999 A: Mephisto. 3.00
❑6, Apr 1999 V: Kraven the Hunter. 3.00
❑7, May 1999 .... 3.00
❑8, Jun 1999 .... 3.00
❑9, Jul 1999 .... 3.00
❑10, Aug 1999 .... 3.00
❑11, Sep 1999 .... 3.00
❑12, Oct 1999 .... 3.00
❑13, Dec 1999 .... 3.00
❑14, Jan 2000 .... 3.00
❑15, Feb 2000 .... 3.00
❑16, Mar 2000 .... 3.00
❑17, Apr 2000 .... 3.00
❑18, May 2000 .... 3.00
❑19, Jun 2000 .... 3.00
❑20, Jul 2000 .... 3.00
❑21, Aug 2000 .... 2.50
❑22, Sep 2000 .... 2.50
❑23, Oct 2000 .... 2.50
❑24, Nov 2000 .... 2.50
❑25, Dec 2000 .... 2.50
❑26, Jan 2001 A: Storm. 2.50
❑27, Feb 2001 .... 2.50
❑28, Mar 2001 .... 2.50
❑29, Apr 2001 .... 2.50
❑30, May 2001; A: Captain America. World War II story 2.50
❑31, Jun 2001 .... 2.50
❑32, Jul 2001 .... 2.50
❑33, Aug 2001 .... 2.50
❑34, Sep 2001 .... 2.50
❑35, Oct 2001 .... 2.50
❑36, Nov 2001 .... 2.50
❑37, Dec 2001 .... 2.50
❑38, Jan 2002 .... 2.50
❑39, Feb 2002 .... 2.50
❑40, Mar 2002 .... 2.50
❑41, Apr 2002 .... 2.50
❑42, May 2002 .... 2.50
❑43, Jun 2002 .... 2.50
❑44, Jul 2002; wraparound cover 2.50
❑45, Aug 2002; wraparound cover 2.50
❑46, Aug 2002; wraparound cover 2.50
❑47, Sep 2002; wraparound cover 2.50
❑48, Oct 2002; wraparound cover 2.50
❑49, Nov 2002; wraparound cover 2.50
❑50, Dec 2002; wraparound cover 2.50
❑51, Jan 2003; wraparound cover 2.50
❑52, Feb 2003; wraparound cover 2.50
❑53, Mar 2003; wraparound cover 2.50
❑54, Apr 2003 .... 2.99
❑55, May 2003 .... 2.99
❑56, May 2003 .... 2.99
❑57, Jun 2003 .... 2.99
❑58, Jun 2003 .... 2.99
❑59, Jul 2003 .... 2.99
❑60, Jul 2003 .... 2.99
❑61, Sep 2003 .... 2.99
❑62, Sep 2003 .... 2.99

BLACK PANTHER (LTD. SERIES)
MARVEL

❑1, Jul 1988 .... 2.00
❑2, Aug 1988 .... 2.00
❑3, Sep 1988 .... 2.00
❑4, Oct 1988 .... 2.00

BLACK PANTHER: PANTHER'S PREY
MARVEL

❑1, May 1991 .... 4.95
❑2, Jun 1991 .... 4.95
❑3, Aug 1991 .... 4.95
❑4, Oct 1991 .... 4.95

BLACK PANTHER (VOL. 3)
MARVEL

❑1, Mar 2005 .... 6.00
❑1/2nd, Mar 2005 .... 4.00
❑1/Ribic, Mar 2005 .... 20.00
❑2, Apr 2005 .... 2.99
❑3, May 2005 .... 2.99
❑4, Jun 2005 .... 2.99
❑5, Jul 2005 .... 2.99
❑6, Aug 2005 .... 2.99
❑7, Sep 2005 .... 2.99
❑8 2005 .... 2.99
❑9, Dec 2005 .... 2.99
❑10, Jan 2006 .... 2.99
❑11, Feb 2006 .... 2.99
❑12, Mar 2006 .... 2.99
❑13, May 2006 .... 2.99
❑14, Jun 2006 .... 2.99
❑15, Jul 2006 .... 2.99
❑16, Aug 2006 .... 2.99
❑17, Sep 2006 .... 2.99

BLACK PEARL
DARK HORSE

❑1, Sep 1996 .... 3.50
❑2, Oct 1996 .... 3.00
❑3, Nov 1996 .... 3.00
❑4, Dec 1996 .... 3.00
❑5, Jan 1997 .... 3.00

BLACK PHANTOM
AC

❑1, b&w 2.50
❑2 .... 2.50
❑3, b&w 2.75

BLACK RAVEN
ARTEFFECT ENTERTAINMENT

❑1, ca. 1998 .... 2.50

BLACK SABBATH
ROCK-IT / MALIBU

❑1, Feb 1994 .... 3.95

BLACK SCORPION
SPECIAL STUDIO

❑1, b&w 2.75
❑2, b&w 2.75
❑3, b&w 2.75

BLACK SEPTEMBER
MALIBU / ULTRAVERSE

❑Infinity, Sep 1993; events affect the Infinity issues of the other Ultraverse titles 1.00

BLACKSTAR
IMPERIAL

❑1 .... 2.00
❑2 .... 2.00

BLACK SUN
WILDSTORM

❑1, Nov 2002 .... 2.95
❑2, Dec 2002 .... 2.95
❑3, Jan 2003 .... 2.95
❑4, Feb 2003 .... 2.95
❑5, Mar 2003 .... 2.95
❑6, Apr 2003 .... 2.95

BLACK SUN: X-MEN
MARVEL

❑1, Nov 2000 .... 2.99
❑1/A, Nov 2000; Dynamic Forces cover 6.00
❑2, Nov 2000 .... 2.99
❑3, Nov 2000 .... 2.99
❑4, Nov 2000 .... 2.99
❑5, Nov 2000 .... 2.99

BLACK TERROR (ECLIPSE)
ECLIPSE

❑1, Oct 1989 .... 4.95
❑1/Autographed, Oct 1989 .... 3.50
❑2, Mar 1990 .... 4.95
❑2/Autographed, Mar 1990 .... 3.50
❑3, Jun 1990 .... 4.95
❑3/Autographed, Jun 1990 .... 3.50

BLACKTHORNE'S 3 IN 1
BLACKTHORNE

❑1, Nov 1986 .... 1.75
❑2, Feb 1987 .... 1.75

BLACKTHORNE'S HARVEY FLIP BOOK
BLACKTHORNE

❑1, b&w 2.00

BLACK TIDE
IMAGE

❑1/A, Nov 2001; Grey background; 3 figures standing on cover 2.95
❑1/B, Nov 2001; 2 figures charging on cover 2.95
❑1/C, Nov 2001; Sun in background; 3 figures posing on cover 2.95
❑2, Jan 2002 .... 2.95
❑3, Mar 2002 .... 2.95
❑4, May 2002 .... 2.95

BLACK TIDE (VOL. 2)
AVATAR

❑1 .... 2.95
❑1/A 2.95
❑1/C, Wrap-Around cover 2.95
❑2 .... 2.95
❑2/A 2.95
❑3 .... 2.95
❑3/A 2.95
❑4 .... 2.95
❑4/A 2.95
❑5, May 2003 .... 2.95
❑5/A, May 2003 .... 2.95
❑6, Jun 2003 .... 2.95
❑6/A, Jun 2003 .... 2.95
❑7, Sep 2003 .... 2.95
❑7/A, Sep 2003 .... 2.95
❑8, Nov 2003 .... 2.95
❑8/A, Nov 2003 .... 2.95
❑9, Feb 2004 .... 2.95
❑9/A, Feb 2004 .... 2.95
❑10 2004 .... 2.95

BLACK WEB
INKS

❑1 .... 2.95

BLACK WIDOW (VOL. 1)
MARVEL

❑1, Jun 1999 .... 3.50
❑2, Jul 1999 .... 3.00
❑3, Aug 1999 .... 3.00

BLACK WIDOW (VOL. 2)
MARVEL

❑1, Jan 2001 .... 2.99
❑2, Feb 2001 .... 2.99
❑3, May 2001 .... 2.99

BLACK WIDOW (3RD SERIES)
MARVEL

❑1, Nov 2004 .... 2.99
❑2, Dec 2004 .... 2.99
❑3, Jan 2005 .... 2.99
❑4, Feb 2005 .... 2.99
❑5, Mar 2005 .... 2.99
❑6, Apr 2005 .... 2.99

Blackwulf

One of 3 Marvel 1994 titles starting with "Bla"

©Marvel

Blade of the Immortal

Hiroaki Samura's manga, faithfully reprinted

©Dark Horse

Blade: The Vampire-Hunter

Tomb of Dracula character returns

©Marvel

Blair Witch Project

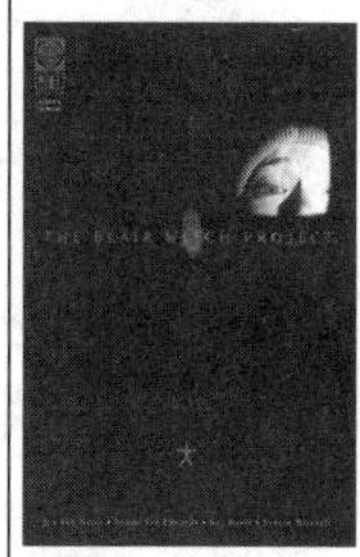

Oni struck oil with cult movie comic

©Oni

Blaze

Relic from the short-lived Ghost Rider craze

©Marvel

N-MINT

BLACK WIDOW: PALE LITTLE SPIDER
MARVEL

❑1, Jun 2002 .... 2.99
❑2, Jul 2002 .... 2.99
❑3, Aug 2002 .... 2.99

BLACK WIDOW: THINGS THEY SAY ABOUT HER
MARVEL

❑1, Nov 2005 .... 2.99
❑2, Dec 2005 .... 2.99

BLACK WIDOW 2
MARVEL

❑1 2005 .... 2.99
❑3, Jan 2006 .... 2.99
❑4, Feb 2006 .... 2.99
❑5, Apr 2006 .... 2.99
❑6, May 2006 .... 2.99

BLACK WIDOW: WEB OF INTRIGUE
MARVEL

❑1, Jun 1999; collects Marvel Fanfare #10-13 .... 3.50

BLACKWULF
MARVEL

❑1, Jun 1994; Embossed cover 2.50
❑2, Jul 1994 .... 1.50
❑3, Aug 1994 .... 1.50
❑4, Sep 1994 .... 1.50
❑5, Oct 1994 .... 1.50
❑6, Nov 1994 .... 1.50
❑7, Dec 1994 .... 1.50
❑8, Jan 1995 .... 1.50
❑9, Feb 1995 .... 1.50
❑10, Mar 1995 .... 1.50

BLACK ZEPPELIN (GENE DAY'S...)
RENEGADE

❑1, Apr 1985, GD (w); GD (a) 2.00
❑2 .... 2.00
❑3 .... 2.00
❑4 .... 2.00
❑5 .... 2.00

BLADE (BUCCANEER)
BUCCANEER

❑1, Dec 1989 .... 2.00
❑2 .... 2.00

BLADE (1ST SERIES)
MARVEL

❑1, May 1997; giveaway; GC, TP (a); O: Blade. Reprints 1.50

BLADE (2ND SERIES)
MARVEL

❑1, Mar 1998 .... 3.50

BLADE (3RD SERIES)
MARVEL

❑1, Oct 1998; gatefold summary 2.99

BLADE (4TH SERIES)
MARVEL

❑1, Nov 1998; gatefold summary 3.50
❑2/A, Dec 1998; gatefold summary; cover says Nov, indicia says Dec 2.99
❑2/B, Dec 1998 .... 2.99
❑3, Jan 1999; gatefold summary; cover says Dec, indicia says Jan 2.99

N-MINT

BLADE OF HEAVEN
TOKYOPOP

❑1, Mar 2005 .... 9.95
❑2, May 2005 .... 9.95
❑3, Jul 2005 .... 9.95
❑4, Sep 2005 .... 9.95
❑5, Nov 2005 .... 9.95
❑6, Jan 2006 .... 9.95

BLADE OF KUMORI
DEVIL'S DUE

❑1, Jan 2005 .... 2.95
❑2, Feb 2005 .... 2.95
❑3, Mar 2005 .... 2.95
❑4, Apr 2005 .... 2.95
❑5, May 2005 .... 2.95

BLADE OF SHURIKEN
ETERNITY

❑1, May 1987 .... 1.95
❑2, Jul 1987 .... 1.95
❑3, Sep 1987 .... 1.95
❑4, Nov 1987 .... 1.95
❑5, Jan 1988 .... 1.95

BLADE OF THE IMMORTAL
DARK HORSE

❑1, Jun 1996 .... 3.50
❑2, Jul 1996 .... 3.00
❑3, Aug 1996 .... 3.00
❑4, Sep 1996 .... 3.00
❑5, Oct 1996 .... 3.00
❑6, Nov 1996 .... 2.95
❑7, Dec 1996 .... 2.95
❑8, Jan 1997 .... 2.95
❑9, Apr 1997, Giant-size SA (a) 3.95
❑10, May 1997, Giant-size DG (a) 3.95
❑11, Jun 1997, Giant-size GK (a) 3.95
❑12, Jul 1997 .... 2.95
❑13, Aug 1997 .... 2.95
❑14, Sep 1997 .... 2.95
❑15, Oct 1997 .... 2.95
❑16, Nov 1997 .... 2.95
❑17, Dec 1997 .... 2.95
❑18, Jan 1998 .... 2.95
❑19, Mar 1998 .... 2.95
❑20, Apr 1998 .... 2.95
❑21, May 1998 .... 2.95
❑22, Jun 1998 .... 2.95
❑23, Jul 1998 .... 2.95
❑24, Aug 1998 .... 2.95
❑25, Sep 1998 .... 2.95
❑26, Oct 1998 .... 2.95
❑27, Nov 1998 .... 2.95
❑28, Dec 1998 .... 2.95
❑29, Jan 1999 .... 2.95
❑30, Feb 1999 .... 2.95
❑31, Mar 1999 .... 2.95
❑32, Apr 1999 .... 2.95
❑33, May 1999 .... 2.95
❑34, Jun 1999 .... 3.95
❑35, Jul 1999 .... 2.95
❑36, Aug 1999 .... 3.95
❑37, Sep 1999 .... 3.95
❑38, Oct 1999 .... 3.95
❑39, Nov 1999 .... 2.99

N-MINT

❑40, Dec 1999 .... 2.99
❑41, Jan 2000 .... 2.99
❑42, Feb 2000 .... 2.99
❑43, Mar 2000 .... 2.99
❑44, Apr 2000 .... 2.99
❑45, May 2000 .... 2.99
❑46, Jun 2000 .... 2.99
❑47, Jul 2000 .... 2.99
❑48, Aug 2000 .... 2.99
❑49, Sep 2000 .... 2.99
❑50, Oct 2000 .... 2.99
❑51, Nov 2000 .... 2.99
❑52, Dec 2000 .... 2.99
❑53, Jan 2001 .... 2.99
❑54, Feb 2001 .... 2.99
❑55, Mar 2001 .... 2.99
❑56, Apr 2001 .... 2.99
❑57, May 2001 .... 2.99
❑58, Jun 2001 .... 2.99
❑59, Jul 2001 .... 2.99
❑60, Aug 2001 .... 2.99
❑61, Sep 2001 .... 2.99
❑62, Oct 2001 .... 2.99
❑63, Nov 2001 .... 2.99
❑64, Dec 2001 .... 2.99
❑65, Feb 2002 .... 2.99
❑66, Mar 2002 .... 2.99
❑67, Apr 2002 .... 2.99
❑68, May 2002 .... 2.99
❑69, Jun 2002 .... 2.99
❑70, Jul 2002 .... 2.99
❑71, Aug 2002 .... 2.99
❑72, Sep 2002 .... 2.99
❑73, Nov 2002 .... 2.99
❑74, Dec 2002 .... 2.99
❑75, Jan 2003 .... 2.99
❑76, Feb 2003 .... 2.99
❑77, Mar 2003 .... 2.99
❑78, Apr 2003 .... 2.99
❑79, Jun 2003 .... 2.99
❑80, Jul 2003 .... 2.99
❑81, Aug 2003 .... 2.99
❑82, Sep 2003 .... 2.99
❑83, Oct 2003 .... 2.99
❑84, Nov 2003 .... 2.99
❑85, Dec 2003 .... 2.99
❑86, Jan 2004 .... 2.99
❑87, Feb 2004 .... 2.99
❑88, Apr 2004 .... 2.99
❑89, Jul 2004 .... 2.99
❑90, Aug 2004 .... 2.99
❑91, Sep 2004 .... 2.99
❑92, Oct 2004 .... 2.99
❑93, Nov 2004 .... 2.99
❑94, Dec 2004 .... 2.99
❑95, Jan 2005, b&w 2.99
❑96, Feb 2005, b&w 2.99
❑97, Mar 2005 .... 2.99
❑98, Apr 2005 .... 2.99
❑99, May 2005 .... 2.99
❑100, Jun 2005 .... 5.99
❑101, Jul 2005, b&w 2.99
❑102, Aug 2005 .... 2.99
❑103, Sep 2005 .... 2.99

Other grades: Multiply price above by 5/6 for VF/NM • 2/3 for VERY FINE • 1/3 for FINE • 1/5 for VERY GOOD • 1/8 for GOOD

❑104, Oct 2005 2.99
❑105, Nov 2005 2.99
❑106, Dec 2005 2.99
❑107, Nov 2005 2.99
❑108, Dec 2005, b&w 2.99
❑109, Feb 2006, b&w 2.99
❑110, Mar 2006, b&w 2.99
❑111, Apr 2006 2.99
❑112, May 2006 2.99
❑113, Jun 2006 2.99
❑114, Jul 2006 2.99

BLADE RUNNER
MARVEL
❑1, Oct 1982, AW (a) 1.50
❑2, Nov 1982, BA (c); AW, BA (a) 1.00

BLADE: SINS OF THE FATHER
MARVEL
❑1, Oct 1998 5.99

BLADESMEN
BLUE COMET
❑0, b&w 2.00
❑1, b&w 2.00
❑2 2.00

BLADE: THE VAMPIRE-HUNTER
MARVEL
❑1, Jul 1994; foil cover 2.95
❑2, Aug 1994 1.95
❑3, Sep 1994 1.95
❑4, Oct 1994 1.95
❑5, Nov 1994 1.95
❑6, Dec 1994 1.95
❑7, Jan 1995 1.95
❑8, Feb 1995 1.95
❑9, Mar 1995 1.95
❑10, Apr 1995 1.95

BLADE: VAMPIRE HUNTER
MARVEL
❑1, Dec 1999 3.50
❑2, Jan 2000; Art cover 2.50
❑2/Photo, Jan 2000; Photo variant 2.50
❑3, Feb 2000 2.50
❑4, Mar 2000 2.50
❑5, Apr 2000 2.50
❑6, May 2000 2.50

BLADE 2: MOVIE ADAPTATION
MARVEL
❑1, May 2002, b&w 5.95

BLAIR WHICH? (SERGIO ARAGONÉS')
DARK HORSE
❑1, Dec 1999 2.95

BLAIR WITCH CHRONICLES
ONI
❑1, Mar 2000, b&w 2.95
❑2, Apr 2000 2.95
❑3, Jun 2000 2.95
❑4, Jul 2000 2.95

BLAIR WITCH: DARK TESTAMENTS
IMAGE
❑1, Oct 2000 2.95

BLAIR WITCH PROJECT
ONI
❑1, Aug 1999; prequel to movie 10.00
❑1/2nd 3.00

BLAME!
TOKYOPOP
❑1, Aug 2005 9.95
❑2, Nov 2005 9.95

BLANCHE GOES TO HOLLYWOOD
DARK HORSE
❑1, b&w 2.95

BLANCHE GOES TO NEW YORK
DARK HORSE
❑1, Nov 1992, b&w 2.95

BLARNEY
DISCOVERY
❑1; cardstock cover, b&w 2.95

BLAST CORPS
DARK HORSE
❑1, Oct 1998; based on Nintendo 64 games 2.50

BLASTERS SPECIAL
DC
❑1, May 1989 2.00

BLAST-OFF
HARVEY
❑1, Oct 1965, AW, JK (w); AW, JK (a); A: The Three Rocketeers 28.00

BLAZE
MARVEL
❑1, Aug 1994; silver enhanced cover 2.95
❑2, Sep 1994 1.95
❑3, Oct 1994 1.95
❑4, Nov 1994 1.95
❑5, Dec 1994 1.95
❑6, Jan 1995 1.95
❑7, Feb 1995 1.95
❑8, Mar 1995 1.95
❑9, Apr 1995 1.95
❑10, May 1995 1.95
❑11, Jun 1995 1.95
❑12, Jul 1995 1.95

BLAZE: LEGACY OF BLOOD
MARVEL
❑1, Dec 1993 1.75
❑2, Jan 1994 1.75
❑3, Feb 1994 1.75
❑4, Mar 1994 1.75

BLAZE OF GLORY
MARVEL
❑1, Feb 2000, biweekly mini-series 2.95
❑2, Feb 2000 2.95
❑3, Mar 2000 2.95
❑4, Mar 2000 2.99

BLAZIN' BARRELS
TOKYOPOP
❑1, Jun 2005 9.95
❑2, Sep 2005 9.95
❑3, Dec 2005 9.95

BLAZING BATTLE TALES
SEABOARD / ATLAS
❑1, Jul 1975 2.50

BLAZING COMBAT
WARREN
❑1, Oct 1965, FF (c); FF (a); scarcer 90.00
❑2 1965, FF (c); FF (a) 30.00
❑3 1966, FF (c); FF (a) 30.00
❑4 1966, FF (c); FF (a) 30.00
❑Annual 1 45.00

BLAZING COMBAT (APPLE)
APPLE
❑1 4.50
❑2, b&w; Reprints 4.50

BLAZING COMBAT: WORLD WAR I AND WORLD WAR II
APPLE
❑1; Reprints 3.75
❑2, Jun 1994; Reprints 3.75

BLAZING FOXHOLES
FANTAGRAPHICS / EROS
❑1, Sep 1994 2.95
❑2 2.95
❑3, Jan 1995 2.95

BLAZING WESTERN (AC)
AC
❑1, b&w 2.50

BLAZING WESTERN (AVALON)
AVALON
❑1, ca. 1997, b&w 2.75

BLEACH
VIZ
❑1, Jun 2004 9.95
❑2, Aug 2004 9.95
❑3, Oct 2004 9.95
❑4, Dec 2004 9.95
❑5, Feb 2005 9.95
❑6, Apr 2005 9.95
❑7, May 2005 9.95
❑8, Aug 2005 9.95
❑9, Oct 2005 9.95

BLEAT
SLAVE LABOR
❑1, Aug 1995 2.95

BLEEDING HEART
FANTAGRAPHICS
❑1 2.50
❑2, Spr 1992 2.50
❑3 2.50
❑4 2.50
❑5, Aug 1993 2.50

BLINDSIDE
IMAGE
❑1, Feb 1998; video game magazine in comic-book format 1.00
❑1/A, Aug 1996 2.50
❑1/B, Aug 1996; white background cover 2.50
❑2, Sep 1996 1.00
❑3, Dec 1996 1.00
❑4 1997 1.00
❑5 1997 1.00
❑6 1997 1.00
❑7 1997 1.00

BLINK
MARVEL
❑1, Mar 2001 2.99
❑2, Apr 2001 2.99
❑3, May 2001 2.99
❑4 2.99

BLIP
MARVEL
❑1, Feb 1983; video game magazine in comic-book format 1.00
❑2, Mar 1983 1.00
❑3, Apr 1983 1.00
❑4, May 1983 1.00
❑5, Jun 1983 1.00
❑6, Jul 1983 1.00
❑7, Aug 1983 1.00

BLIP (BARDIC)
BARDIC
❑1, Feb 1998 1.25

BLIP AND THE C.C.A.D.S.
AMAZING
❑1 2.00
❑2 2.00

BLISS ALLEY
IMAGE
❑1, Jul 1997 2.95
❑2, Sep 1997 2.95

BLITE
FANTAGRAPHICS
❑1, b&w 2.25

BLITZ
NIGHTWYND
❑1 2.50
❑2 2.50
❑3 2.50
❑4 2.50

BLITZKRIEG
DC
❑1, Jan 1976 RE (a) 16.00
❑2, Mar 1976 8.00
❑3, May 1976, RE (a) 6.00
❑4, Jul 1976, Bicentennial #20 6.00
❑5, Sep 1976 6.00

BLOKHEDZ
IMAGE
❑1, Dec 2003 2.95
❑2 2004 2.95

BLONDE
FANTAGRAPHICS / EROS
❑1 2.50
❑2 2.50
❑3 2.50

BLONDE ADDICTION
BLITZWEASEL
❑1 2.95
❑2 2.95
❑3 2.95
❑4; flip-book with Blonde Avenger's Subplots 2.95

BLONDE AVENGER
BLITZ WEASEL
❑27/A 3.95
❑27/B 3.95

Other grades: Multiply price above by 5/6 for VF/NM • 2/3 for VERY FINE • 1/3 for FINE • 1/5 for VERY GOOD • 1/8 for GOOD

Blip

Marvel's comic-book-sized video game entry

©Marvel

Blitzkrieg

A unusual twist on the war comics genre

©DC

Blondie Comics

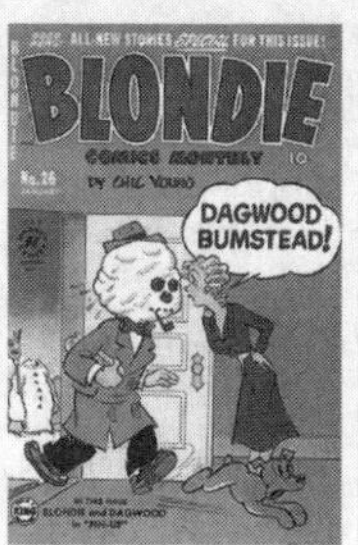

King and Charlton later published this title

©David McKay

Bloodfire

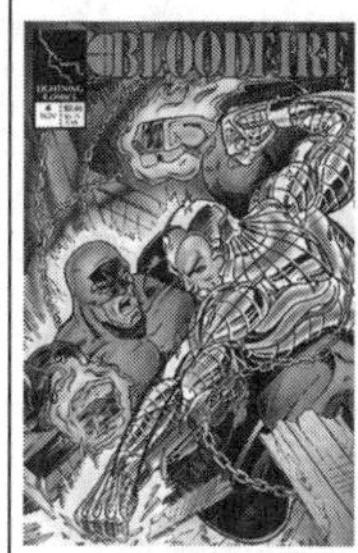

Yet another "super-soldier serum" story

©Lightning

Blood of Dracula

Serial anthology had three stories per issue

©Apple

N-MINT

BLONDE AVENGER: CROSSOVER CRAZZEEE
BLITZWEASEL

- ❑1 .... 3.95

BLONDE AVENGER (MINI-SERIES)
FANTAGRAPHICS / EROS

- ❑1, Mar 1993 .... 2.75
- ❑2, ca. 1993 .... 2.75
- ❑3 .... 2.75
- ❑4, Apr 1994 .... 2.75

BLONDE AVENGER MONTHLY
BLITZWEASEL

- ❑1, Mar 1996, b&w 4.00
- ❑2, Apr 1996 .... 3.00
- ❑3, May 1996 .... 2.95
- ❑4, Jun 1996 .... 2.95
- ❑5 .... 2.95
- ❑6 .... 2.95

BLONDE AVENGER ONE-SHOT SPECIAL: THE SPYING GAME
BLITZWEASEL

- ❑1, Mar 1996, b&w 2.95

BLONDE, THE: BONDAGE PALACE
FANTAGRAPHICS / EROS

- ❑1 .... 2.95
- ❑2 .... 2.95
- ❑3 .... 2.95
- ❑5, May 1994 .... 2.95

BLONDIE COMICS
DAVID MCKAY

- ❑95, Oct 1956 .... 9.00
- ❑96, Nov 1956 .... 9.00
- ❑97, Dec 1956 .... 9.00
- ❑98, Jan 1957 .... 9.00
- ❑99, Feb 1957 .... 9.00
- ❑100, Mar 1957, 100th anniversary issue 10.00
- ❑101, Apr 1957 .... 8.00
- ❑102, May 1957 .... 8.00
- ❑103, Jun 1957 .... 8.00
- ❑104, Jul 1957 .... 8.00
- ❑105, Aug 1957 .... 8.00
- ❑106, Sep 1957 .... 8.00
- ❑107, Oct 1957 .... 8.00
- ❑108, Nov 1957 .... 8.00
- ❑109, Dec 1957 .... 8.00
- ❑110 1958 .... 8.00
- ❑111 1958 .... 8.00
- ❑112 1958 .... 8.00
- ❑113 1958 .... 8.00
- ❑114 1958 .... 8.00
- ❑115 1958 .... 8.00
- ❑116 1958 .... 8.00
- ❑117 1958 .... 8.00
- ❑118 1958 .... 8.00
- ❑119 1958 .... 8.00
- ❑120 1958 .... 8.00
- ❑121, Jan 1959 .... 8.00
- ❑122, Feb 1959 .... 8.00
- ❑123, Mar 1959 .... 8.00
- ❑124, Apr 1959 .... 8.00
- ❑125, May 1959, Double-size 9.00
- ❑126, Jun 1959 .... 8.00

N-MINT

- ❑127, Jul 1959 .... 8.00
- ❑128, Aug 1959 .... 8.00
- ❑129, Sep 1959 .... 8.00
- ❑130 1959 .... 8.00
- ❑131 1959 .... 7.00
- ❑132 1960 .... 7.00
- ❑133 1960 .... 7.00
- ❑134 1960 .... 7.00
- ❑135 1960 .... 7.00
- ❑136, Aug 1960 .... 7.00
- ❑137, Sep 1960 .... 7.00
- ❑138, Oct 1960 .... 7.00
- ❑139, Nov 1960 .... 7.00
- ❑140, Dec 1960 .... 7.00
- ❑141, Jan 1960 .... 8.00
- ❑142, Feb 1961 .... 8.00
- ❑143, Mar 1961 .... 8.00
- ❑144, Apr 1961 .... 8.00
- ❑145, Jun 1961 .... 8.00
- ❑146, Aug 1961 .... 8.00
- ❑147, Oct 1961 .... 8.00
- ❑148 1961 .... 8.00
- ❑149 1961 .... 8.00
- ❑150 1962 .... 8.00
- ❑151 1962 .... 8.00
- ❑152 1962 .... 8.00
- ❑153 1962 .... 8.00
- ❑154, Oct 1962 .... 8.00
- ❑155 1963 .... 8.00
- ❑156 1963 .... 8.00
- ❑157 1963 .... 8.00
- ❑158 1963 .... 8.00
- ❑159, Nov 1963 .... 8.00
- ❑160, Mar 1965 .... 8.00
- ❑161 1965 .... 8.00
- ❑162, Sep 1965 .... 8.00
- ❑163, Nov 1965 .... 8.00
- ❑164, Aug 1966, King Features Syndicate begins publishing 8.00
- ❑165, Oct 1966 .... 8.00
- ❑166, Dec 1966 .... 8.00
- ❑167, Feb 1967 .... 8.00
- ❑168, Apr 1967 .... 5.00
- ❑169, Jun 1967 .... 5.00
- ❑170, Jul 1967 .... 5.00
- ❑171, Aug 1967 .... 5.00
- ❑172, Sep 1967 .... 5.00
- ❑173, Oct 1967 .... 5.00
- ❑174, Nov 1967 .... 5.00
- ❑175, Dec 1967 .... 5.00
- ❑177, Feb 1969, #176 appears not to have been published 5.00
- ❑178, Apr 1969 .... 5.00
- ❑179, Jun 1969 .... 5.00
- ❑180, Aug 1969 .... 5.00
- ❑181, Oct 1969 .... 4.00
- ❑182, Nov 1969 .... 4.00
- ❑183, Jan 1970 .... 4.00
- ❑184, Mar 1970 .... 4.00
- ❑185, May 1970 .... 4.00
- ❑186, Jul 1970 .... 4.00
- ❑187, Sep 1970 .... 4.00
- ❑188, Nov 1970 .... 4.00
- ❑189, Jan 1971 .... 4.00

N-MINT

- ❑190, Mar 1971 .... 4.00
- ❑191, May 1971 .... 4.00
- ❑192, Jul 1971 .... 4.00
- ❑193, Sep 1971 .... 4.00
- ❑194, Nov 1971 .... 4.00
- ❑195, Jan 1971 .... 4.00
- ❑196, Mar 1972 .... 4.00
- ❑197, Apr 1972 .... 4.00
- ❑198, May 1972 .... 4.00
- ❑199, Jul 1972 .... 4.00
- ❑200, Oct 1972, Anniversary issue 4.00
- ❑201, Dec 1972 .... 3.00
- ❑202, Jan 1973 .... 3.00
- ❑203, Mar 1973 .... 3.00
- ❑204, May 1973 .... 3.00
- ❑205, Jul 1973 .... 3.00
- ❑206, Sep 1973 .... 3.00
- ❑207, Nov 1973 .... 3.00
- ❑208, May 1974 .... 3.00
- ❑209 1974 .... 3.00
- ❑210, Oct 1974 .... 3.00
- ❑211, Dec 1974 .... 3.00
- ❑212, Feb 1975 .... 3.00
- ❑213, Apr 1975 .... 3.00
- ❑214, Jun 1975 .... 3.00
- ❑215, Sep 1975 .... 3.00
- ❑216, Nov 1975 .... 3.00
- ❑217, Jan 1976 .... 3.00
- ❑218, Mar 1976 .... 3.00
- ❑219, May 1976 .... 3.00
- ❑220, Jul 1976 .... 3.00
- ❑221 1976 .... 3.00
- ❑222, Nov 1976 .... 3.00

BLOOD
FANTACO

- ❑1, b&w 3.95

BLOOD AND GLORY
MARVEL

- ❑1; Embossed cover 5.95
- ❑2 .... 5.95
- ❑3 .... 5.95

BLOOD & KISSES
FANTACO

- ❑1 .... 2.95
- ❑2 .... 3.95

BLOOD & ROSES ADVENTURES
KNIGHT

- ❑1, May 1995, b&w 2.95

BLOOD & ROSES: FUTURE PAST TENSE
SKY

- ❑1, Dec 1993; Silver logo regular edition 2.25
- ❑1/Ashcan; ashcan edition 3.00
- ❑1/Gold; Gold logo promotional edition 3.00
- ❑2 .... 2.25

BLOOD & ROSES: SEARCH FOR THE TIME-STONE
SKY

- ❑1, Apr 1994 .... 2.50
- ❑1/Ashcan, Apr 1994; ashcan edition 3.00
- ❑2, Jan 1995; Indicia has incorrect initial date, really Jan 1995 .... 2.50

Other grades: Multiply price above by 5/6 for VF/NM • 2/3 for VERY FINE • 1/3 for FINE • 1/5 for VERY GOOD • 1/8 for GOOD

BLOOD & ROSES SPECIAL
KNIGHT

❑1, Mar 1996, b&w 2.50

BLOOD AND SHADOWS
DC / VERTIGO

❑1 .... 5.95
❑2 .... 5.95
❑3 .... 5.95
❑4 .... 5.95

BLOOD AND THUNDER
CONQUEST

❑1, b&w 2.95

BLOOD & WATER
SLAVE LABOR

❑1, Oct 1991, b&w 2.95

BLOOD AND WATER (DC)
DC / VERTIGO

❑1, May 2003 .... 2.95
❑2, Jun 2003 .... 2.95
❑3, Jul 2003 .... 2.95
❑4, Aug 2003 .... 2.95
❑5, Sep 2003 .... 2.95

BLOOD: A TALE
MARVEL / EPIC

❑1 1987 .... 3.25
❑2 1987 .... 3.25
❑3 1987 .... 3.25
❑4 1987 .... 3.25

BLOOD: A TALE (VERTIGO)
DC / VERTIGO

❑1, Nov 1996 .... 2.95
❑2, Dec 1996 .... 2.95
❑3, Jan 1997 .... 2.95
❑4, Feb 1997 .... 2.95

BLOODBATH
DC

❑1, Dec 1993 .... 3.50
❑2, Dec 1993 .... 3.50

BLOOD BOUNTY
HIGHLAND

❑1 .... 2.00

BLOODBROTHERS
ETERNITY

❑1 .... 1.95
❑2 .... 1.95
❑3 .... 1.95
❑4 .... 1.95

BLOODCHILDE
MILLENNIUM

❑1, Dec 1994 .... 2.50
❑2, Feb 1995 .... 2.50
❑3, May 1995 .... 2.50
❑4, Jul 1995 .... 2.95

BLOOD CLUB
KITCHEN SINK

❑2; Cover says "Blood Club Featuring Big Baby" 5.95

BLOODFANG
EPITAPH

❑0, Mar 1996 .... 2.50
❑1 .... 2.50

BLOOD FEAST
ETERNITY

❑1, b&w; tame cover 2.50
❑1/Variant, b&w; Explicit cover 2.50
❑2, b&w 2.50
❑2/Variant, b&w; Explicit cover 2.50

BLOOD FEAST: THE SCREENPLAY
ETERNITY

❑1, b&w; not comics 4.95

BLOODFIRE
LIGHTNING

❑0, Jun 1994; Giant-size 3.50
❑0/A, Jun 1994; Giant-size; Yellow logo on cover 3.50
❑1, Mar 1993, b&w; promotional copy 3.50
❑1/Platinum, Jun 1993; platinum 3.50
❑1/Variant, Jun 1993; red foil 3.50
❑2, Jul 1993 .... 2.95
❑8, Jan 1994 .... 2.95
❑3, Aug 1993 .... 2.95
❑4, Sep 1993 .... 2.95
❑5, Oct 1993; trading card 2.95
❑6, Nov 1993 .... 2.95
❑7, Dec 1993 .... 2.95
❑9, Feb 1994 .... 2.95
❑10, Mar 1994 .... 2.95
❑11, Apr 1994 .... 2.95
❑12, May 1994 .... 2.95

BLOODFIRE/HELLINA
LIGHTNING

❑1, Aug 1995 .... 3.00
❑1/Nude, Aug 1995; Nude edition 4.00
❑1/Platinum; Platinum edition 3.00

BLOOD GOTHIC
FANTACO

❑1 .... 4.95
❑2 .... 4.95

BLOODHOUND
DC

❑1, Sep 2004 .... 2.95
❑2, Oct 2004 .... 2.95
❑3, Nov 2004 .... 2.95
❑4, Dec 2004 .... 2.95
❑5, Jan 2005 .... 2.95
❑6, Feb 2005 .... 2.95
❑7, Mar 2005 .... 2.95
❑8, Apr 2005 .... 2.95
❑9, May 2005 .... 2.95
❑10, Jun 2005 .... 2.95

BLOODHUNTER
BRAINSTORM

❑1, Oct 1996, b&w; cardstock cover 2.95

BLOOD IS THE HARVEST (ECLIPSE)
ECLIPSE

❑1, Jul 1992 .... 2.50
❑2 .... 2.50
❑3 .... 2.50
❑4 .... 2.50

BLOOD JUNKIES
ETERNITY

❑1 .... 2.50
❑2 .... 2.50

BLOOD LEGACY: THE STORY OF RYAN
IMAGE

❑1, Jul 2000 .... 2.50
❑2, Aug 2000 .... 2.50
❑3, Sep 2000 .... 2.50
❑4, Nov 2000 .... 2.50
❑Book 1 .... 6.95

BLOOD LEGACY/ YOUNG ONES ONE SHOT
IMAGE

❑1, Apr 2003 .... 4.99

BLOODLETTING (1ST SERIES)
FANTACO

❑1 .... 2.95

BLOODLETTING (2ND SERIES)
FANTACO

❑1 .... 3.95
❑2 .... 3.95

BLOODLINES
AIRCEL

❑1; Aircel publishes 2.50
❑2 .... 2.50
❑3; Blackburn begins as publisher 2.50
❑4 .... 2.50
❑5 .... 2.50
❑6 .... 2.50

BLOODLINES: A TALE FROM THE HEART OF AFRICA
MARVEL / EPIC

❑1, ca. 1992 .... 5.95

BLOODLUST
SLAVE LABOR

❑1, Dec 1990 .... 2.25

BLOOD 'N' GUTS
AIRCEL

❑1, Nov 1990, b&w 2.50
❑2 .... 2.50
❑3 .... 2.50
❑4 .... 2.50

BLOOD OF DRACULA
APPLE

❑1, Nov 1987 .... 2.00
❑2, Dec 1987 .... 2.00
❑3, Jun 1988 .... 2.00
❑4, Jul 1988 .... 2.00
❑5, Aug 1988 .... 2.00
❑6, Sep 1988 .... 2.00
❑7, Oct 1988 .... 2.00
❑8, Nov 1988 .... 2.00
❑9, Jan 1989 .... 2.00
❑10, Mar 1989 .... 2.00
❑11, May 1989 .... 2.00
❑12, Jun 1989 .... 2.00
❑13, Jul 1989 BWr (a) 2.00
❑14, Sep 1989 BWr (a) 2.25
❑15, Nov 1989; flexidisc 3.75
❑16, May 1990 BWr (a) 2.25
❑17, Jul 1990 BWr (a) 2.25
❑18, Sep 1990 BWr (a) 2.25
❑19, Mar 1991 BWr (a) 2.25

BLOOD OF THE DEMON
DC

❑1, Apr 2005 .... 4.00
❑2, May 2005 .... 2.50
❑3, Jun 2005 .... 2.50
❑4, Jul 2005 .... 2.50
❑5, Aug 2005 .... 2.50
❑6, Sep 2005 .... 2.50
❑7, Oct 2005 .... 2.50
❑8, Nov 2005 .... 2.50
❑9, Dec 2005 .... 2.50
❑10, Jan 2006 .... 2.50
❑11, Mar 2006 .... 2.50
❑12, Mar 2006 .... 2.50
❑13, May 2006 .... 2.50
❑14, Jun 2006 .... 2.50
❑15, Jul 2006 .... 2.50
❑16, Aug 2006 .... 2.50

BLOOD OF THE INNOCENT
WARP

❑1 .... 2.00
❑2 .... 2.00
❑3 .... 2.00
❑4 .... 2.00

BLOOD PACK
DC

❑1, Mar 1995 .... 1.50
❑2, Apr 1995 .... 1.50
❑3, May 1995 .... 1.50
❑4, Jun 1995 .... 1.50

BLOODPOOL
IMAGE

❑1, Aug 1995 .... 2.50
❑1/Variant, Aug 1995, alternate cover 2.50
❑2, Sep 1995 .... 2.50
❑3, Oct 1995 .... 2.50
❑4, Nov 1995 .... 2.50
❑Special 1, Mar 1996, Special 4.00

BLOOD REIGN
FATHOM

❑1 .... 2.95
❑2, Sep 1991 .... 2.95
❑3, Oct 1991 .... 2.95

BLOODSCENT
COMICO

❑1, Oct 1988 .... 2.00

BLOODSEED
MARVEL

❑1, Oct 1993 .... 1.95
❑2, Nov 1993; Gold cover; nudity; Final issue (series was rescheduled as 2-issue series) 1.95

BLOODSHED
DAMAGE!

❑1 .... 2.95
❑1/Ltd.; no cover price, b&w 2.95
❑2 .... 2.95
❑3, ca. 1994; no cover price; cardstock cover 2.95
❑Ashcan 1, ca. 1997; no cover price; "Promo Edition" on cover; retailer promotional item 2.00

Other grades: Multiply price above by 5/6 for VF/NM • 2/3 for VERY FINE • 1/3 for FINE • 1/5 for VERY GOOD • 1/8 for GOOD

Bloodshot

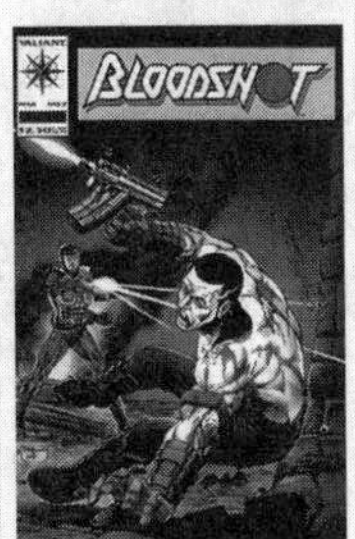

Valiant title about an enhanced warrior
©Valiant

Bloodstrike

Rob Liefeld's elite strike force
©Image

Blood Sword

One of many Jademan imports from Hong Kong
©Jademan

Blue Beetle (DC)

Good-natured import into the DC universe
©DC

Blue Devil

Stuntman becomes supernatural super-hero
©DC

BLOODSHOT
VALIANT

	N-MINT
❑0/VVSS	25.00
❑0/PlatError, Mar 1994	750.00
❑0, Mar 1994; O: Bloodshot. A: Eternal Warrior. chromium cover	3.00
❑0/Gold, Mar 1994; Gold edition; O: Bloodshot. A: Eternal Warrior. no cover price	25.00
❑1, Feb 1993; DP, BWi (a); Metallic embossed foil cover	2.00
❑2, Mar 1993 DP, BWi (a); V: X-O Manowar.	1.00
❑3, Apr 1993 DP, BWi (a)	1.00
❑4, May 1993 DP, BWi (a); A: Eternal Warrior.	1.00
❑5, Jun 1993 DP, BWi (a); A: Rai. A: Eternal Warrior.	1.00
❑6, Jul 1993 DP, BWi (a); 1: Ninjak.	1.00
❑6/VVSS, Jul 1993, DP, BWi (a)	50.00
❑7, Aug 1993 A: Ninjak.	1.00
❑8, Sep 1993	1.00
❑9, Oct 1993	1.00
❑10, Nov 1993	1.00
❑11, Dec 1993	1.00
❑12, Jan 1994 DP (a)	1.00
❑13, Feb 1994	1.00
❑14, Mar 1994	1.00
❑15, Apr 1994	1.00
❑16, May 1994; trading card	2.00
❑17, Jun 1994 A: H.A.R.D.Corps.	1.00
❑18, Aug 1994	1.00
❑19, Sep 1994	1.00
❑20, Oct 1994; Chaos Effect Gamma 1	1.00
❑21, Nov 1994 V: Ax.	1.00
❑22, Dec 1994	1.00
❑23, Jan 1995	1.00
❑24, Feb 1995	1.00
❑25, Mar 1995	2.00
❑26, Apr 1995	2.00
❑27, May 1995	2.00
❑28, May 1995 V: Ninjak.	2.00
❑29, Jun 1995; Valiant becomes Acclaim imprint	2.00
❑30, Jul 1995; Birthquake	2.00
❑31, Jul 1995; Birthquake	2.00
❑32, Aug 1995; Birthquake	2.00
❑33, Aug 1995; Birthquake	2.00
❑34, Sep 1995	2.00
❑35, Sep 1995 V: Rampage.	2.00
❑36, Oct 1995 MGr, BA (a)	2.00
❑37, Oct 1995 BA (a)	2.00
❑38, Nov 1995	3.00
❑39, Nov 1995	3.00
❑40, Dec 1995	3.00
❑41, Dec 1995 PG (a)	3.00
❑42, Jan 1996	3.00
❑43, Jan 1996	3.00
❑44, Feb 1996	4.00
❑45, Mar 1996	4.00
❑46, Apr 1996	4.00
❑47, May 1996	4.00
❑48, May 1996	5.00
❑49, Jun 1996	5.00
❑50, Jul 1996	6.00
❑51, Aug 1996	10.00
❑Yearbook 1, ca. 1994; Yearbook (annual) #1	5.00

BLOODSHOT: LAST STAND
VALIANT

	N-MINT
❑0, Mar 1996	10.00

BLOODSHOT (VOL. 2)
ACCLAIM

	N-MINT
❑1, Jul 1997	2.50
❑1/Variant, Jul 1997; alternate painted cover	2.50
❑2, Aug 1997	2.50
❑3, Sep 1997	2.50
❑4, Oct 1997	2.50
❑5, Nov 1997; Steranko tribute cover	2.50
❑6, Dec 1997	2.50
❑7, Jan 1998 V: X-O Manowar.	2.50
❑8, Feb 1998 V: X-O Manowar.	2.50
❑9, Mar 1998	2.50
❑10, Apr 1998; in Area 51	2.50
❑11, May 1998	2.50
❑12, Jun 1998; No cover date; indicia says Feb	2.50
❑13, Jul 1998; No cover date; indicia says Mar	2.50
❑14, Aug 1998; No cover date; indicia says Apr	2.50
❑15, Sep 1998; No cover date; indicia says May	2.50
❑16, Oct 1998; No cover date; indicia says Jun	2.50
❑Ashcan 1, Mar 1997; No cover price; b&w preview of upcoming series	1.00

BLOODSTONE
MARVEL

	N-MINT
❑1, Dec 2001	2.99
❑2, Jan 2002	2.99
❑3, Feb 2002	2.99
❑4, Mar 2002	2.99

BLOODSTREAM
IMAGE

	N-MINT
❑1, Jan 2004	2.95
❑2, Mar 2004	2.95
❑3, Jul 2004	2.95
❑4, Nov 2004	2.95

BLOODSTRIKE
IMAGE

	N-MINT
❑1, Apr 1993; RL (a); 1: Tag. 1: Deadlock. 1: Shogun. 1: Col. Cabbot. 1: Fourplay. fading blood cover	3.00
❑2, Jun 1993 1: Lethal.	2.00
❑3, Jul 1993	2.00
❑4, Oct 1993 KG (w)	2.00
❑5, Nov 1993 1: Noble. A: Supreme.	2.00
❑6, Dec 1993; Chapel becomes team leader	2.00
❑7, Jan 1994 A: Chapel.	2.00
❑8, Feb 1994	2.00
❑9, Mar 1994	2.00
❑10, Apr 1994	2.00
❑11, Jul 1994	2.00
❑12, Aug 1994	2.00
❑13, Aug 1994	2.50
❑14, Sep 1994	2.50
❑15, Oct 1994	2.50
❑16, Nov 1994	2.50
❑17, Dec 1994	2.50
❑18, Jan 1995; polybagged with trading card	2.50
❑19, Feb 1995; polybagged	2.50
❑20, Mar 1995	2.50
❑21, Apr 1995	2.50
❑22, May 1995	2.50
❑23	2.50
❑24	2.50
❑25, May 1994; Images of Tomorrow; Published out of sequence as a preview of the future	1.95

BLOODSTRIKE ASSASSIN
IMAGE

	N-MINT
❑0, Oct 1995	2.50
❑1/A, Jun 1995	2.50
❑1/B, Jun 1995, alternate cover	2.50
❑2, Jul 1995	2.50
❑3, Aug 1995	2.50
❑4	2.50

BLOODSUCKER
FANTAGRAPHICS / EROS

	N-MINT
❑1, b&w	2.50

BLOOD SWORD
JADEMAN

	N-MINT
❑1, Aug 1988	1.95
❑2, Sep 1988	1.95
❑3, Oct 1988	1.95
❑4, Nov 1988	1.95
❑5, Dec 1988	1.95
❑6, Jan 1989	1.95
❑7, Feb 1989	1.95
❑8, Mar 1989	1.95
❑9, Apr 1989	1.95
❑10, May 1989	1.95
❑11, Jun 1989	1.95
❑12, Jul 1989	1.95
❑13, Aug 1989	1.95
❑14, Sep 1989	1.95
❑15, Oct 1989	1.95
❑16, Nov 1989	1.95
❑17, Dec 1989	1.95
❑18, Jan 1990	1.95
❑19, Feb 1990	1.95
❑20, Mar 1990	1.95
❑21, Apr 1990	1.95
❑22, May 1990	1.95
❑23, Jun 1990	1.95
❑24, Jul 1990	1.95
❑25, Aug 1990	1.95
❑26, Sep 1990	1.95
❑27, Oct 1990	1.95
❑28, Nov 1990	1.95
❑29, Dec 1990	1.95
❑30, Jan 1991	1.95
❑31, Feb 1991	1.95
❑32, Mar 1991	1.95
❑33, Apr 1991	1.95
❑34, May 1991	1.95
❑35, Jun 1991	1.95
❑36, Jul 1991	1.95
❑37, Aug 1991	1.95

Other grades: Multiply price above by 5/6 for VF/NM • 2/3 for VERY FINE • 1/3 for FINE • 1/5 for VERY GOOD • 1/8 for GOOD

❑38, Sep 1991 1.95
❑39, Oct 1991 1.95
❑40, Nov 1991 1.95
❑41, Dec 1991 1.95
❑42, Jan 1992 1.95

BLOOD SWORD DYNASTY
JADEMAN

❑1, Sep 1989 1.25
❑2, Oct 1989 1.25
❑3, Nov 1989 1.25
❑4, Dec 1989 1.25
❑5, Jan 1990 1.25
❑6, Feb 1990 1.25
❑7, Mar 1990 1.25
❑8, Apr 1990 1.25
❑9, May 1990 1.25
❑10, Jun 1990 1.25
❑11, Jul 1990 1.25
❑12, Aug 1990 1.25
❑13, Sep 1990 1.25
❑14, Oct 1990 1.25
❑15, Nov 1990 1.25
❑16, Dec 1990 1.25
❑17, Jan 1991 1.25
❑18, Feb 1991 1.25
❑19, Mar 1991 1.25
❑20, Apr 1991 1.25
❑21, May 1991 1.25
❑22, Jun 1991 1.25
❑23, Jul 1991 1.25
❑24, Aug 1991 1.25
❑25, Sep 1991 1.25
❑26, Oct 1991 1.25
❑27, Nov 1991 1.25
❑28, Dec 1991 1.25
❑29, Jan 1992 1.25

BLOOD SYNDICATE
DC / MILESTONE

❑1, Apr 1993, TVE (a); 1: Blood Syndicate. 1: Rob Chaplik 1.50
❑1/CS, Apr 1993, TVE (a); 1: Blood Syndicate. 1: Rob Chaplik. poster, trading card 2.95
❑2, May 1993, 1: Boogieman. V: Holocaust 1.50
❑3, Jun 1993, 1: MOM. A: Boogieman. 1.50
❑4, Jul 1993, D: Tech-9. 1.50
❑5, Aug 1993, 1: Demon Fox. 1: John Wing. 1: Kwai. 1.50
❑6, Sep 1993 1.50
❑7, Oct 1993, 1: Edmund. 1: Cornelia. 1.50
❑8, Nov 1993, 1: Kwai. 1.50
❑9, Dec 1993, O: Blood Syndicate. 1: Templo. 1.50
❑10, Jan 1994, Giant-size; 1: Bubbasaur. Metallic ink cover 2.50
❑11, Feb 1994, Aquamaria joins Blood Syndicate 1.50
❑12, Mar 1994, 1: The Rat Congress. 1.50
❑13, Apr 1994, 1: The White Roaches. 1.50
❑14, May 1994 1.50
❑15, Jun 1994 1.50
❑16, Jul 1994, A: Superman. 1.50
❑17, Aug 1994 1.75
❑18, Sep 1994 1.75
❑19, Oct 1994 1.75
❑20, Nov 1994, A: Shadow Cabinet. 1.75
❑21, Dec 1994 1.75
❑22, Jan 1995 1.75
❑23, Feb 1995 1.75
❑24, Mar 1995 1.75
❑25, Apr 1995, Giant-size; Tech-9 returns 2.95
❑26, May 1995 1.75
❑27, Jun 1995 1.75
❑28, Jul 1995 2.50
❑29, Aug 1995 1.00
❑30, Sep 1995 2.50
❑31, Oct 1995 2.50
❑32, Nov 1995 2.50
❑33, Dec 1995 0.99
❑34, Jan 1996 2.50
❑35, Feb 1996 3.50

BLOODTHIRST: TERMINUS OPTION
ALPHA PRODUCTIONS

❑1, b&w 2.50
❑2 2.50

BLOODTHIRST: THE NIGHTFALL CONSPIRACY
ALPHA

❑1 2.50
❑2 2.50

BLOODTHIRSTY PIRATE TALES
BLACK SWAN

❑1 2.50
❑2 2.50
❑3, Win 1995 2.50
❑4, Fal 1996 2.50
❑5, Spr 1997 2.50
❑6, Win 1997 2.50
❑7 2.50
❑8 2.50

BLOOD TIES
FULL MOON

❑1, ca. 1991 2.25

BLOODWING
ETERNITY

❑1, Jan 1988 1.95
❑2, Feb 1988 1.95
❑3, Mar 1988 1.95
❑4, Apr 1988 1.95
❑5, May 1988 1.95
❑6 1.95

BLOODWULF
IMAGE

❑1, Feb 1995; five different covers 2.50
❑2, Mar 1995 2.50
❑3, Apr 1995 2.50
❑4, May 1995 2.50
❑Summer 1, Aug 1995; Summer Special 2.50

BLOODY BONES & BLACKEYED PEAS
GALAXY

❑1 1.00

BLOODYHOT
PARODY

❑1 2.95

BLOODY MARY
DC / HELIX

❑1, Oct 1996 2.25
❑2, Nov 1996 2.25
❑3, Dec 1996 2.25
❑4, Jan 1997 2.25

BLOODY MARY: LADY LIBERTY
DC / HELIX

❑1, Sep 1997 2.50
❑2, Oct 1997 2.50
❑3, Nov 1997 2.50
❑4, Dec 1997 2.50

BLOODY SCHOOL
CURTIS COMIC

❑1 2.95

BLUE
IMAGE

❑1, Aug 1999 2.50
❑2, Apr 2000 2.50

BLUEBEARD
SLAVE LABOR

❑1, b&w 2.95
❑2, b&w 2.95
❑3, b&w 2.95
❑Book 1, b&w; collects mini-series 9.95

BLUE BEETLE (VOL. 2)
CHARLTON

❑1, Jun 1964, SD (a) 45.00
❑2, Sep 1964, SD (a) 30.00
❑3, Nov 1964, SD (a) 20.00
❑4, Jan 1965, SD (a) 20.00
❑5, Apr 1965, SD (a) 20.00

BLUE BEETLE (VOL. 3)
CHARLTON

❑50, Jul 1965 27.00
❑51, Aug 1965 27.00
❑52, Oct 1965, SD (a) 27.00
❑53, Dec 1965, SD (a) 27.00
❑54, Feb 1966 27.00
❑1, Jun 1967, SD (c); SD (a) 60.00
❑2, Aug 1967, SD (c); SD (w); SD (a); O: Blue Beetle. 40.00
❑3, Oct 1967, SD (c); SD (w); SD (a). 27.00
❑4, Dec 1967, SD (c); SD (w); SD (a). 27.00
❑5, Nov 1968, SD (c); SD (w); SD (a) 27.00

BLUE BEETLE (DC)
DC

❑1, Jun 1986 O: Blue Beetle. V: Firefist. 1.00
❑2, Jul 1986 O: Firefist. V: Firefist. 1.00
❑3, Aug 1986 V: Madmen. 1.00
❑4, Sep 1986 V: Doctor Alchemy. 1.00
❑5, Oct 1986 A: The Question 1.00
❑6, Nov 1986 A: The Question 1.00
❑7, Dec 1986 A: The Question. D: Muse. 1.00
❑8, Jan 1987 V: Calculator 1.00
❑9, Feb 1987; A: Chronos. Legends tie-in 1.00
❑10, Mar 1987; V: Chronos. Legends tie-in 1.00
❑11, Apr 1987 A: Teen Titans. 1.00
❑12, May 1987 A: Teen Titans. 1.00
❑13, Jun 1987 A: Teen Titans. 1.00
❑14, Jul 1987 1: Carapax 1.00
❑15, Aug 1987 RA (c); RA (a); A: Carapax. 1.00
❑16, Sep 1987 RA (c); RA (a) 1.00
❑17, Oct 1987 A: Blue Beetle (Dan Garrett) 1.00
❑18, Nov 1987 V: Blue Beetle (Dan Garrett) 1.00
❑19, Dec 1987 DG (c); RA (a) 1.00
❑20, Jan 1988; DG (c); RA (a); Millennium tie-in 1.00
❑21, Feb 1988; RA (a); A: Mister Miracle. Millennium tie-in 1.00
❑22, Mar 1988 RA (a); A: Chronos. 1.00
❑23, Apr 1988 DH (a); V: Madmen. 1.00
❑24, May 1988 DH (a); V: Carapax. 1.00

BLUE BEETLE (MODERN)
MODERN

❑1, ca. 1977; reprints Charlton's Blue Beetle (Vol. 3) #1; no #2 2.00
❑3, ca. 1977; reprints Charlton's Blue Beetle (Vol. 3) #3 2.00

BLUE BEETLE (2ND SERIES)
DC

❑1, Jun 2006 2.99
❑1/2nd, Jun 2006 2.99
❑2, Jul 2006 2.99
❑3, Aug 2006 2.99
❑4, Sep 2006 2.99

BLUE BLOCK
KITCHEN SINK

❑1 2.95

BLUE BULLETEER
AC

❑1, b&w O: Blue Bulleteer. 2.50

BLUE DEVIL
DC

❑1, Jun 1984 O: Blue Devil. 1.00
❑2, Jul 1984 V: Shockwave. 1.00
❑3, Aug 1984 V: Metallo. 1.00
❑4, Sep 1984 A: Zatanna. 1.00
❑5, Oct 1984 A: Zatanna. 1.00
❑6, Nov 1984 1: Bolt. 1.00
❑7, Dec 1984 V: Bolt. V: Trickster. 1.00
❑8, Jan 1985 V: Bolt. V: Trickster. 1.00
❑9, Feb 1985 V: Bolt. V: Trickster. 1.00
❑10, Mar 1985 1.00
❑11, Apr 1985 1.00
❑12, May 1985 A: Demon 1.00
❑13, Jun 1985 A: Green Lantern. A: Zatanna. 1.00
❑14, Jul 1985 1: Kid Devil. 1.00
❑15, Aug 1985 1.00
❑16, Sep 1985 1.00
❑17, Oct 1985; Crisis 1.00
❑18, Nov 1985; Crisis 1.00
❑19, Dec 1985 1.00
❑20, Jan 1986 1.00
❑21, Feb 1986 1.00
❑22, Mar 1986 1.00
❑23, Apr 1986 A: Firestorm. 1.00
❑24, May 1986 1.00
❑25, Jun 1986 1.00
❑26, Jul 1986 V: Green Gargoyle. 1.00
❑27, Aug 1986 1.00
❑28, Sep 1986 1.00
❑29, Oct 1986 1.00

Blue Ribbon Comics (Vol. 2)

Archie dusts off its old super-heroes again

©Archie

Boffo Laffs

Humor title had the first holographic cover

©Paragraphics

Bomba

Based on children's adventure novels

©DC

Bonanza

Saddle up for the Ponderosa

©Gold Key

Bone

Jeff Smith's 1990s classic series

©Cartoon Books

N-MINT

❑30, Nov 1986; Double-size V: Flash's Rogues' Gallery.......... 1.25
❑31, Dec 1986; Giant-size.......... 1.25
❑Annual 1, Nov 1985.......... 2.00

BLUE HOLE
CHRISTINE SHIELDS

❑1.......... 2.95

BLUE ICE
MARTYR

❑1, ca. 1992.......... 2.50
❑2, ca. 1992..........

BLUE LILY
DARK HORSE

❑1, Mar 1993.......... 3.95
❑2.......... 3.95
❑3.......... 3.95
❑4.......... 3.95

BLUE LOCO
KITCHEN SINK

❑1, Feb 1997; cardstock cover.......... 5.95

BLUE MONDAY: ABSOLUTE BEGINNERS
ONI

❑1, ca. 2001.......... 2.95
❑2, ca. 2001.......... 2.95
❑3, ca. 2001.......... 2.95
❑4, ca. 2001.......... 2.95

BLUE MONDAY: LOVECATS
ONI

❑1, ca. 2002.......... 2.95

BLUE MONDAY: PAINTED MOON
ONI

❑1 2004.......... 2.99
❑2 2004.......... 2.99
❑3 2004.......... 2.99
❑4 2004.......... 2.99

BLUE MONDAY: THE KIDS ARE ALRIGHT
ONI

❑1, ca. 2000.......... 2.95
❑2, ca. 2000.......... 2.95
❑3, ca. 2000.......... 2.95

BLUE MOON
MU

❑1, Sep 1992.......... 2.50
❑2, Nov 1992.......... 2.50
❑3, Feb 1993.......... 2.50
❑4, May 1993.......... 2.50
❑5, Dec 1993.......... 2.50

BLUE MOON (VOL. 2)
AEON

❑1, Aug 1994, b&w.......... 2.95

BLUE RIBBON COMICS (VOL. 2)
ARCHIE / RED CIRCLE

❑1, Nov 1983, SD (c); AW, JK (a); Red Circle publishes.......... 2.50
❑2, Nov 1983, RB (c); AN (a).......... 1.50
❑3, Dec 1983.......... 1.50
❑4, Jan 1984.......... 1.50
❑5, Feb 1984, A: Steel Sterling. All reprinted from "The Double Life of Private Strong" #1.......... 1.50

N-MINT

❑6, Mar 1984.......... 1.50
❑7, Apr 1984, RB (w); TD (a).......... 1.50
❑8, May 1984.......... 1.50
❑9, Jun 1984.......... 1.50
❑10, Jul 1984.......... 1.50
❑11, Aug 1984.......... 1.50
❑12, Sep 1984.......... 1.50
❑13, Oct 1984.......... 1.50
❑14, Dec 1984.......... 1.50

B-MOVIE PRESENTS
B-MOVIE

❑1.......... 1.70
❑2.......... 1.70
❑3.......... 1.70
❑4.......... 1.70

BMW FILMS: THE HIRE
DARK HORSE

❑1 2004.......... 2.99
❑2 2005.......... 2.99
❑3, Oct 2005.......... 2.99
❑4, Jan 2006.......... 2.99

BOARD OF SUPERHEROS
NOT AVAILABLE

❑1.......... 1.00

BOBBY BENSON'S B-BAR-B RIDERS
AC

❑1, ca. 1990, b&w.......... 2.75

BOBBY RUCKERS
ART

❑1.......... 2.95

BOBBY SHERMAN
CHARLTON

❑1, Feb 1972.......... 15.00
❑2, Mar 1972.......... 10.00
❑3, May 1972.......... 10.00
❑4, Jun 1972.......... 10.00
❑5, Jul 1972.......... 10.00
❑6, Sep 1972.......... 10.00
❑7, Oct 1972.......... 10.00

BOB, THE GALACTIC BUM
DC

❑1, Feb 1995.......... 2.00
❑2, Mar 1995.......... 2.00
❑3, Apr 1995.......... 2.00
❑4, Jun 1995.......... 2.00

BOB MARLEY, TALE OF THE TUFF GONG
MARVEL

❑1.......... 5.95
❑2.......... 5.95
❑3.......... 5.95

BOBOBO-BO BO-BOBO
VIZ

❑1, Dec 2005.......... 9.95

"BOB'S" FAVORITE COMICS
RIP OFF

❑1, b&w.......... 2.50
❑1/2nd, b&w.......... 2.50
❑1/3rd, b&w.......... 2.50

N-MINT

BOB STEELE WESTERN (AC)
AC

❑1 1990, b&w; Reprints.......... 2.75

BODY BAGS
DARK HORSE / BLANC NOIR

❑1, Sep 1996.......... 3.50
❑2, Oct 1996.......... 3.00
❑3, Nov 1996.......... 3.00
❑4, Jan 1997.......... 3.00
❑Ashcan 1.......... 3.00

BODY BAGS: FATHER'S DAY
IMAGE

❑1, Aug 2005.......... 5.99
❑2, Oct 2005.......... 5.99

BODY COUNT (AIRCEL)
AIRCEL

❑1; TMNT storyline.......... 2.25
❑2; TMNT storyline.......... 2.25
❑3; TMNT storyline.......... 2.25
❑4; TMNT storyline.......... 2.25

BODYCOUNT (IMAGE)
IMAGE

❑1, Mar 1996.......... 2.50
❑2, Apr 1996.......... 2.50
❑3, May 1996.......... 2.50
❑4.......... 2.50

BODY DOUBLES
DC

❑1, Oct 1999.......... 2.50
❑2, Nov 1999.......... 2.50
❑3, Dec 1999.......... 2.50
❑4, Jan 2000.......... 2.50

BODY DOUBLES (VILLAINS)
DC

❑1, Feb 1998; New Year's Evil.......... 2.00

BODYGUARD
AIRCEL

❑1, Sep 1990, b&w; intro by Todd McFarlane.......... 2.50
❑2, Oct 1990, b&w.......... 2.50
❑3, Nov 1990, b&w.......... 2.50

BODY PAINT
FANTAGRAPHICS / EROS

❑1.......... 2.95
❑2, Jun 1995.......... 2.95

BODY SWAP
ROGER MASON

❑1.......... 2.95

BOFFO IN HELL
NEATLY CHISELED FEATURES

❑1.......... 2.50

BOFFO LAFFS
PARAGRAPHICS

❑1; first hologram cover.......... 2.50
❑2.......... 1.95
❑3.......... 1.95
❑4.......... 1.95
❑5.......... 1.95

Other grades: Multiply price above by 5/6 for VF/NM • 2/3 for VERY FINE • 1/3 for FINE • 1/5 for VERY GOOD • 1/8 for GOOD

BOFFY THE VAMPIRE SLAYER
FANTAGRAPHICS / EROS

❑1, ca. 2000 ... 2.95
❑2, ca. 2000 ... 2.95
❑3, ca. 2001 ... 2.95

BOGIE MAN
FAT MAN

❑1 ... 2.50
❑2 ... 2.50
❑3 ... 2.50
❑4 ... 2.50

BOGIE MAN, THE: CHINATOON
ATOMEKA

❑1 ... 2.95
❑2 ... 2.95
❑3 ... 2.95
❑4 ... 2.95

BOGIE MAN, THE: THE MANHATTAN PROJECT
TUNDRA

❑1, Jul 1992 ... 4.95

BOG SWAMP DEMON
HALL OF HEROES

❑1, Aug 1996 ... 2.50
❑1/Variant, Aug 1996; alternate cover
❑1/Commem, Aug 1996; Commemorative Edition; limited to 500 copies ...
❑2, Oct 1996; no indicia ... 2.50
❑2/Variant, Oct 1996; alternate cover .
❑3, Dec 1996 ... 2.50
❑4, Mar 1997 ... 2.50

BOHOS
IMAGE

❑1, May 1998; cover says Jun, indicia says May ... 2.95
❑2, Jun 1998 ... 2.95
❑3, Jul 1998; no month of publication 2.95
❑Book 1 ... 12.95

BO JACKSON VS. MICHAEL JORDAN
CELEBRITY

❑1 ... 2.95
❑2 ... 2.95

BOLD ADVENTURE
PACIFIC

❑1 ... 2.00
❑2 ... 2.00
❑3 ... 2.00

BOLT AND STARFORCE SIX
AC

❑1, Jul 1984 ... 1.75

BOLT SPECIAL
AC

❑1 ... 2.00

BOMARC
NIGHTWYND

❑1 ... 2.50
❑2 ... 2.50
❑3 ... 2.50

BOMBA
DC

❑1, Sep 1967, 1: Bomba. ... 16.00
❑2, Nov 1967 ... 8.00
❑3, Jan 1968 ... 8.00
❑4, Mar 1968 ... 8.00
❑5, May 1968 ... 8.00
❑6, Jul 1968 ... 8.00
❑7, Sep 1968 ... 8.00

BOMBAST
TOPPS

❑1, Apr 1993; Savage Dragon, #1 - Factory bagged ... 2.95

BOMBASTIC
SCREAMING DODO

❑1, Nov 1996 ... 2.50
❑2, Feb 1997 ... 2.50
❑3, May 1997 ... 2.50
❑4, Aug 1997 ... 2.50
❑5, Dec 1997; cardstock cover ... 2.50

BOMB QUEEN
IMAGE

❑1, Mar 2006 ... 2.95
❑2, Apr 2006 ... 2.95
❑3, May 2006 ... 2.95

BONAFIDE
BONAFIDE

❑0/2nd, Mar 1994 ... 3.95
❑0 ... 3.95

BONANZA
GOLD KEY

❑1, Dec 1962 ... 110.00
❑2, Mar 1963 ... 75.00
❑3, Jun 1963 ... 50.00
❑4, Sep 1963 ... 50.00
❑5, Dec 1963 ... 50.00
❑6, Feb 1964 ... 32.00
❑7, Apr 1964 ... 32.00
❑8, Jun 1964 ... 32.00
❑9, Aug 1964 ... 32.00
❑10, Oct 1964 ... 32.00
❑11, Dec 1964 ... 22.00
❑12, Feb 1965 ... 22.00
❑13, Apr 1965 ... 22.00
❑14, Jun 1965 ... 22.00
❑15, Aug 1965 ... 22.00
❑16, Oct 1965 ... 22.00
❑17, Dec 1965 ... 22.00
❑18, Feb 1966 ... 22.00
❑19, Apr 1966 ... 22.00
❑20, Jun 1966 ... 22.00
❑21, Aug 1966 ... 15.00
❑22, Oct 1966 ... 15.00
❑23, Feb 1967 ... 15.00
❑24, May 1967 ... 15.00
❑25, Aug 1967 ... 15.00
❑26, Nov 1967 ... 15.00
❑27, Feb 1968 ... 15.00
❑28, May 1968 ... 15.00
❑29, Aug 1968 ... 15.00
❑30, Nov 1968 ... 15.00
❑31, Feb 1969 ... 12.00
❑32, May 1969 ... 12.00
❑33, Aug 1969 ... 12.00
❑34, Nov 1969 ... 12.00
❑35, Feb 1970 ... 12.00
❑36, May 1970 ... 12.00
❑37, Aug 1970 ... 12.00

BONDAGE CONFESSIONS
FANTAGRAPHICS / EROS

❑1 ... 2.95
❑2 ... 2.95
❑3 ... 2.95
❑4, Nov 1998 ... 2.95

BONDAGE FAIRIES
ANTARCTIC / VENUS

❑1, Mar 1994 ... 4.00
❑1/2nd, May 1994 ... 2.95
❑1/3rd, Aug 1994 ... 2.95
❑1/4th, Jan 1995 ... 2.95
❑2, Apr 1994 ... 4.00
❑2/2nd, Jun 1994 ... 2.95
❑2/3rd, Oct 1994 ... 2.95
❑2/4th, Apr 1995 ... 2.95
❑3, May 1994 ... 3.25
❑3/2nd, Sep 1994 ... 2.95
❑3/3rd, Dec 1994 ... 2.95
❑4, Jun 1994 ... 3.25
❑4/2nd, Nov 1994 ... 2.95
❑4/3rd, Jan 1995 ... 2.95
❑5, Jul 1994 ... 3.25
❑5/2nd, Nov 1994 ... 2.95
❑5/3rd, Feb 1995 ... 2.95
❑6, Aug 1994 ... 2.95
❑6/2nd, Feb 1995 ... 2.95

BONDAGE FAIRIES EXTREME
FANTAGRAPHICS / EROS

❑1, Oct 1999 ... 3.50
❑2, Nov 1999 ... 3.50
❑3, Dec 1999 ... 3.50
❑4, Jan 2000 ... 3.50
❑5, Feb 2000 ... 3.50
❑6, Mar 2000 ... 3.50
❑7, Apr 2000 ... 3.50
❑8, May 2000 ... 3.95
❑9, Jun 2000 ... 3.50
❑10, Jul 2000 ... 3.50
❑11, Sep 2000 ... 3.50
❑12, Oct 2000 ... 3.50
❑13, Nov 2000 ... 3.95
❑14, ca. 2000 ... 3.50

BONDAGE GIRLS AT WAR
FANTAGRAPHICS / EROS

❑1 1996 ... 2.95
❑2 1996 ... 2.95
❑3 1996 ... 2.95
❑4 1996 ... 2.95
❑5, Feb 1997 ... 2.95
❑6, ca. 1997 ... 2.95

BONE
CARTOON BOOKS

❑1, Jul 1991, b&w; 1: Phoney Bone. 1: Smiley Bone. 1: Fone Bone. 3000 printed ... 80.00
❑1/2nd 1: Phoney Bone. 1: Fone Bone. 8.00
❑1/3rd 1: Phoney Bone. 1: Fone Bone. 3.00
❑1/4th, Jan 1993 1: Phoney Bone. 1: Fone Bone. ... 3.00
❑1/5th; 1: Phoney Bone. 1: Fone Bone. fifth printing ... 3.00
❑1/6th; 1: Phoney Bone. 1: Fone Bone. sixth printing ... 3.00
❑1/7th; 1: Phoney Bone. 1: Fone Bone. seventh printing ... 3.00
❑1/8th; 1: Phoney Bone. 1: Fone Bone. eighth printing ... 3.00
❑1/9th, 1: Phoney Bone. 1: Fone Bone. Image reprint ... 3.00
❑2, Sep 1991, b&w 1: Thorn. ... 45.00
❑2/2nd 1: Thorn. ... 6.00
❑2/3rd, Jan 1993 1: Thorn. ... 3.00
❑2/4th 1: Thorn. ... 3.00
❑2/5th; 1: Thorn. fifth printing ... 3.00
❑2/6th; 1: Thorn. sixth printing ... 3.00
❑2/7th; 1: Thorn. seventh printing ... 3.00
❑2/8th, Image reprint ... 3.00
❑3, Dec 1991, b&w ... 25.00
❑3/2nd ... 3.00
❑3/3rd, Jan 1993 ... 3.00
❑3/4th ... 3.00
❑3/5th; fifth printing ... 3.00
❑3/6th; sixth printing ... 3.00
❑3/7th; seventh printing ... 3.00
❑3/8th, Image reprint ... 3.00
❑4, Mar 1992, b&w ... 16.00
❑4/2nd, Sep 1992 ... 3.00
❑4/3rd, Image reprint ... 3.00
❑4/4th ... 3.00
❑4/5th ... 3.00
❑4/6th ... 3.00
❑5, Jun 1992, b&w ... 12.00
❑5/2nd, Sep 1992; Image reprint ... 3.00
❑5/3rd, Image reprint ... 3.00
❑5/4th ... 3.00
❑5/5th ... 3.00
❑5/6th ... 3.00
❑5/7th ... 3.00
❑6, Nov 1992, b&w ... 7.00
❑6/2nd ... 3.00
❑6/3rd, Image reprint ... 3.00
❑6/4th ... 3.00
❑6/5th ... 3.00
❑6/6th ... 3.00
❑7, Dec 1992, b&w ... 7.00
❑7/2nd ... 3.00
❑7/3rd, Image reprint ... 3.00
❑7/4th ... 3.00
❑7/5th ... 3.00
❑8, Feb 1993, b&w; Eisner award-winning story (1994) ... 7.00
❑8/2nd; second printing; Eisner award-winning story (1994) ... 3.00
❑8/3rd; third printing; Eisner award-winning story (1994) ... 3.00
❑8/4th; fourth printing; Eisner award-winning story (1994) ... 3.00
❑8/5th; fifth printing; Eisner award-winning story (1994) ... 3.00
❑8/6th; sixth printing; Eisner award-winning story (1994) ... 3.00
❑8/7th, Image reprint ... 3.00
❑9, Jul 1993, b&w; Eisner award-winning story (1994) ... 4.00
❑9/2nd; second printing; Eisner award-winning story (1994) ... 3.00
❑9/3rd, Image reprint; Eisner award-winning story (1994) ... 3.00

Other grades: Multiply price above by 5/6 for VF/NM • 2/3 for VERY FINE • 1/3 for FINE • 1/5 for VERY GOOD • 1/8 for GOOD

Bone (2nd Series)

Image reprints of Cartoon Books issues
©Image

Boof (Image)

Short, fat warrior from planet Smashmouth
©Image

Book of Fate

Keith Giffen's relaunch of Doctor Fate
©DC

Books of Faerie

Mini-series explores the origins of Titania
©DC

Books of Magic

All-powerful boy magician learns tricks
©DC

	N-MINT
❑9/4th; fourth printing; Eisner award-winning story (1994)	3.00
❑10, Sep 1993, b&w; Eisner award-winning story (1994)	3.50
❑10/2nd; second printing; Eisner award-winning story (1994)	2.95
❑10/3rd, Image reprint; Eisner award-winning story (1994)	2.95
❑11, Dec 1993, b&w	3.50
❑11/2nd, Image reprint	2.95
❑12, Feb 1994, b&w	3.50
❑12/2nd, Image reprint	2.95
❑12/3rd	2.95
❑13, Mar 1994, b&w	3.50
❑13/2nd, Image reprint	2.95
❑13.5; Wizard promotional edition	3.50
❑13.5/Gold; Gold edition	3.50
❑14, May 1994, b&w	2.95
❑14/2nd, Image reprint	2.95
❑15, Aug 1994, b&w	2.95
❑15/2nd, Image reprint	2.95
❑16, Oct 1994, b&w	2.95
❑16/2nd, Image reprint	2.95
❑17, Jan 1995, b&w	2.95
❑17/2nd, Image reprint	2.95
❑18, Apr 1995, b&w	2.95
❑18/2nd, Image reprint	2.95
❑19, Jun 1995, b&w	2.95
❑19/2nd, Image reprint	2.95
❑20, Oct 1995, b&w; moves to Image	2.95
❑20/2nd, Image reprint	2.95
❑21, Dec 1995, b&w; Image begins as publisher	2.95
❑22, Feb 1996, b&w	2.95
❑23, May 1996, b&w 1: Baby Rat Creature.	2.95
❑24, Jun 1996, b&w	2.95
❑25, Aug 1996, b&w	2.95
❑26, Dec 1996, b&w	2.95
❑27, Apr 1997, b&w; Phoney captures Red Dragon; series returns to Cartoon Books	2.95
❑28, Aug 1997, b&w; Cartoon Books begins as publisher	2.95
❑29, Nov 1997, b&w	2.95
❑30, Jan 1998, b&w	2.95
❑31, Apr 1998, b&w	2.95
❑32, Jun 1998, b&w	2.95
❑33, Aug 1998, b&w	2.95
❑34, Dec 1998, b&w	2.95
❑35, Mar 1999, b&w	2.95
❑36, May 1999, b&w	2.95
❑37, Aug 1999, b&w; cover says Sep, indicia says Aug	2.95
❑38/A, Aug 2000, b&w	2.95
❑38/B, Aug 2000, b&w; FM (c); FM (a); alternate cover	2.95
❑38/C, Aug 2000, b&w; ARo (c); ARo (a); alternate cover	2.95
❑39, Oct 2000, b&w	2.95
❑40, Jan 2001, b&w	2.95
❑41, Mar 2001, b&w	2.95
❑42, May 2001, b&w	2.95
❑43, Jul 2001, b&w	2.95
❑44, Sep 2001, b&w	2.95
❑45 2001	2.95

	N-MINT
❑46 2001	2.95
❑47 2002	2.95
❑48 2002	2.95
❑49 2002	2.95
❑50 2002	2.95
❑51 2002	2.95
❑52 2003	3.00
❑53 2003	3.00
❑54 2003	3.00
❑55, Jun 2004	3.00
❑Special 1, ca. 1993; Special edition; Holiday Special polybagged with Hero Illustrated	2.00

BONE (2ND SERIES)
IMAGE

	N-MINT
❑1; Reprints Bone (1st Series) #1 with new cover	3.00
❑2; Reprints Bone (1st Series) #2 with new cover	3.00
❑3; Reprints Bone (1st Series) #3 with new cover	3.00
❑4; Reprints Bone (1st Series) #4 with new cover	3.00
❑5; Reprints Bone (1st Series) #5 with new cover	3.00
❑6; Reprints Bone (1st Series) #6 with new cover	3.00
❑7; Reprints Bone (1st Series) #7 with new cover	3.00
❑8; Reprints Bone (1st Series) #8 with new cover	3.00
❑9; Reprints Bone (1st Series) #9 with new cover	3.00
❑10; Reprints Bone (1st Series) #10 with new cover	3.00
❑11, Sep 1996; Reprints Bone (1st Series)#11 with new cover	3.00
❑12, Oct 1996; Reprints Bone (1st Series)#12 with new cover	3.00
❑13, Nov 1996; Reprints Bone (1st Series)#13 with new cover	3.00
❑14, Dec 1996; Reprints Bone (1st Series)#14 with new cover	3.00
❑15, Jan 1997; Reprints Bone (1st Series)#15 with new cover	3.00
❑16, Feb 1997; Reprints Bone (1st Series)#16 with new cover	3.00
❑17, Mar 1997; Reprints Bone (1st Series)#17 with new cover	3.00
❑18, Apr 1997; Reprints Bone (1st Series)#18 with new cover	3.00
❑19, May 1997; Reprints Bone (1st Series)#19 with new cover	3.00
❑20, Jun 1997	3.00

BONE SOURCEBOOK
IMAGE

	N-MINT
❑1/A, Nov 1995, b&w; No cover price; promotional handout	2.00
❑1/B, Nov 1995; San Diego Comic-Con edition	2.00

BONEREST
IMAGE

	N-MINT
❑1, Aug 2005	2.95
❑1, Jul 2005	2.95
❑1/Variant, Jul 2005	2.95
❑2, Sep 2005	2.95
❑3, Oct 2005	2.95
❑4, Nov 2005	2.95
❑5, Dec 2005	2.95
❑6, Jan 2006	2.95
❑7, Jan 2006	2.95
❑8, Mar 2006	2.95

BONES
MALIBU

	N-MINT
❑1	1.95
❑2	1.95
❑3, Oct 1987	1.95
❑4, Nov 1987	1.95

BONESHAKER
CALIBER

	N-MINT
❑1, ca. 1994, b&w; Collects serial from Negative Burn	3.50

BONEYARD
NBM

	N-MINT
❑1, ca. 2001	2.95
❑2, ca. 2001	2.95
❑3, ca. 2001	2.95
❑4, ca. 2002	2.95
❑5, ca. 2002	2.95
❑6	2.95
❑7	2.95
❑8	2.95
❑9 2003	2.95
❑10, ca. 2003	2.95
❑11 2003	2.95
❑12 2003	2.95
❑13 2004	2.95
❑14 2004	2.95
❑15 2004	2.95
❑16 2004	2.95
❑17 2005	2.95
❑18 2005	2.95
❑19 2005	2.95
❑20, Jan 2006	2.95

BONEYARD PRESS 1993 TOURBOOK
BONEYARD

	N-MINT
❑1; Distributor giveaway previewing Boneyard Press books	1.50

BOOF (ICONOGRAFIX)
ICONOGRAFIX

	N-MINT
❑1, b&w	2.50

BOOF (IMAGE)
IMAGE

	N-MINT
❑1, Jul 1994	1.95
❑1/A, Jul 1994; alternate cover	1.95
❑2, Aug 1994	1.95
❑2/A, Aug 1994; alternate cover	1.95
❑3, Sep 1994	1.95
❑3/A, Sep 1994; alternate cover	1.95
❑4, Oct 1994	1.95
❑5, Nov 1994	1.95
❑6, Dec 1994	1.95

BOOF AND THE BRUISE CREW
IMAGE

	N-MINT
❑1, Jul 1994	1.95
❑1/A, Jul 1994, alternate cover	1.95
❑2, Aug 1994	1.95
❑2/A, Aug 1994, alternate cover	1.95
❑3, Sep 1994	1.95

Other grades: Multiply price above by 5/6 for VF/NM • 2/3 for VERY FINE • 1/3 for FINE • 1/5 for VERY GOOD • 1/8 for GOOD

N-MINT | N-MINT | N-MINT

❑3/A, Sep 1994, alternate cover 1.95
❑4, Oct 1994 .... 1.95
❑5, Nov 1994 .... 1.95
❑6, Dec 1994 .... 1.95

BOOGEYMAN (SERGIO ARAGONÉS')
DARK HORSE

❑1, Jun 1998 .... 2.95
❑2, Jul 1998 .... 2.95
❑3, Aug 1998 .... 2.95
❑4, Sep 1998 .... 2.95

BOOGIEMAN
RION

❑1, b&w 1.50

BOOK
DREAMSMITH

❑1, May 1998, b&w 3.50
❑2, Aug 1998 .... 3.50

BOOK OF ANGELS
CALIBER

❑1, ca. 1997, b&w; cardstock cover ... 3.95

BOOK OF BALLADS AND SAGAS
GREEN MAN

❑1 1996, b&w 2.95
❑2 1996, b&w 2.95
❑3, Jun 1996, b&w 3.50
❑4, Dec 1996, b&w 3.50

BOOK OF FATE
DC

❑1, Feb 1997 .... 2.25
❑2, Mar 1997 .... 2.25
❑3, Apr 1997 .... 2.25
❑4, May 1997 .... 2.25
❑5, Jun 1997 .... 2.25
❑6, Jul 1997; continues in Night Force #8 .... 2.25
❑7, Aug 1997 .... 2.25
❑8, Sep 1997 .... 2.25
❑9, Oct 1997 .... 2.25
❑10, Nov 1997 .... 2.25
❑11, Dec 1997; Face cover 2.25
❑12, Jan 1998 .... 2.50

BOOK OF LOST SOULS
MARVEL

❑1, Dec 2005 .... 2.99
❑2, Jan 2006 .... 2.99
❑3, Feb 2006 .... 2.99
❑4, Mar 2006 .... 2.99
❑5, May 2006 .... 2.99
❑6, Jun 2006 .... 2.99

BOOK OF NIGHT
DARK HORSE

❑1, Jul 1987 CV (w); CV (a) 2.50
❑2, Aug 1987 CV (w); CV (a) 2.00
❑3, Sep 1987 CV (w); CV (a) 2.00

BOOK OF SHADOWS
IMAGE

❑1, May 2006 .... 2.99
❑2, Jun 2006 .... 2.99

BOOK OF SPELLS
DOUBLE EDGE

❑1 .... 2.00
❑2, Sep 1994 .... 2.00
❑3 .... 2.00
❑4 .... 2.00

BOOK OF THE DAMNED: A HELLRAISER COMPANION (CLIVE BARKER'S...)
MARVEL / EPIC

❑1, Oct 1991 .... 4.95
❑2, Apr 1992 .... 4.95
❑3 .... 4.95
❑4 .... 4.95

BOOK OF THE DEAD
MARVEL

❑1, Dec 1993, MP (a) 2.00
❑2, Jan 1994, GM, HC, MP (a) 2.00
❑3, Feb 1994, MP (a) 2.00
❑4, Mar 1994, MP (a) 2.00

BOOK OF THE TAROT
CALIBER / TOME

❑1, b&w 3.95

BOOK OF THOTH
CIRCLE

❑1, Jun 1995 .... 2.50

BOOKS OF DOOM
MARVEL

❑1, Jan 2006 .... 2.99
❑2, Feb 2006 .... 2.99
❑3, Mar 2006 .... 2.99
❑4, May 2006 .... 2.99
❑5, Jun 2006 .... 2.99
❑6, Aug 2006 .... 2.99

BOOKS OF FAERIE
DC / VERTIGO

❑1, Mar 1997 .... 2.50
❑2, Apr 1997 .... 2.50
❑3, May 1997 .... 2.50

BOOKS OF FAERIE, THE: AUBERON'S TALE
DC / VERTIGO

❑1, Aug 1998 .... 2.50
❑2, Sep 1998 .... 2.50
❑3, Oct 1998 .... 2.50

BOOKS OF FAERIE, THE: MOLLY'S STORY
DC / VERTIGO

❑1, Sep 1999 .... 2.50
❑2, Oct 1999 .... 2.50
❑3, Nov 1999 .... 2.50
❑4, Dec 1999 .... 2.50

BOOKS OF LORE: SPECIAL EDITION
PEREGRINE ENTERTAINMENT

❑1, Sep 1997, b&w; cardstock cover, b&w 2.95
❑1/Ltd., Collector's Edition, bagged with poster and limited and regular editions of #1 .... 5.00
❑2, Nov 1997 .... 2.95

BOOKS OF LORE: STORYTELLER
PEREGRINE ENTERTAINMENT

❑1 .... 2.95

BOOKS OF LORE: THE KAYNIN GAMBIT
PEREGRINE ENTERTAINMENT

❑0, Dec 1998 .... 2.95
❑1, Nov 1998 .... 2.95
❑1/Variant, Nov 1998; alternate cover 2.95
❑2, Jan 1999 .... 2.95
❑3, Mar 1999 .... 2.95
❑Ashcan 1, Jul 1998; b&w preview of Books Of Lore: The Kaynin Gambit. 3.00

BOOKS OF MAGIC (MINI-SERIES)
DC

❑1, Dec 1990 NG (w); 1: Timothy Hunter 4.00
❑2, Jan 1991 NG (w) 4.00
❑3, Feb 1991 NG (w); CV (a) 4.00
❑4, Mar 1991; NG (w); Paul Johnson. 4.00

BOOKS OF MAGIC
DC / VERTIGO

❑1, May 1994 .... 3.00
❑1/Silver, May 1994; Silver (limited promotional) edition; no cover price 4.00
❑2, Jun 1994 .... 2.50
❑3, Jul 1994 .... 2.50
❑4, Aug 1994 .... 2.50
❑5, Sep 1994 .... 2.50
❑6, Oct 1994 .... 2.50
❑7, Nov 1994 .... 2.50
❑8, Dec 1994 .... 2.50
❑9, Jan 1995 .... 2.50
❑10, Feb 1995 .... 2.50
❑11, Mar 1995 .... 2.50
❑12, Apr 1995 .... 2.50
❑13, May 1995 .... 2.50
❑14, Jul 1995 .... 2.50
❑15, Aug 1995 .... 2.50
❑16, Sep 1995 .... 2.50
❑17, Oct 1995 .... 2.50
❑18, Nov 1995 .... 2.50
❑19, Dec 1995 .... 2.50
❑20, Jan 1996 .... 2.50
❑21, Feb 1996 .... 2.50
❑22, Mar 1996 .... 2.50
❑23, Apr 1996 .... 2.50
❑24, May 1996 .... 2.50
❑25, Jun 1996 A: Death (Sandman). .. 2.50
❑26, Jul 1996 .... 2.50
❑27, Aug 1996 .... 2.50
❑28, Sep 1996 .... 2.50
❑29, Oct 1996 .... 2.50
❑30, Nov 1996 .... 2.50
❑31, Dec 1996 .... 2.50
❑32, Jan 1997 .... 2.50
❑33, Feb 1997 .... 2.50
❑34, Mar 1997 .... 2.50
❑35, Apr 1997 .... 2.50
❑36, May 1997 .... 2.50
❑37, Jun 1997 .... 2.50
❑38, Jul 1997 .... 2.50
❑39, Aug 1997 .... 2.50
❑40, Sep 1997 .... 2.50
❑41, Oct 1997 .... 2.50
❑42, Nov 1997 .... 2.50
❑43, Dec 1997 .... 2.50
❑44, Jan 1998 .... 2.50
❑45, Feb 1998 .... 2.50
❑46, Mar 1998 .... 2.50
❑47, Apr 1998 .... 2.50
❑48, May 1998 .... 2.50
❑49, Jun 1998 .... 2.50
❑50, Jul 1998; preview of issue #51 ... 2.50
❑51, Aug 1998 .... 2.50
❑52, Sep 1998 .... 2.50
❑53, Oct 1998 .... 2.50
❑54, Nov 1998 .... 2.50
❑55, Dec 1998 .... 2.50
❑56, Jan 1999 A: Cain. 2.50
❑57, Feb 1999; Books of Faerie back-up 2.50
❑58, Mar 1999; Books of Faerie back-up 2.50
❑59, Apr 1999; Books of Faerie back-up 2.50
❑60, May 1999 .... 2.50
❑61, Jun 1999 .... 2.50
❑62, Jul 1999; Books of Faerie back-up 2.50
❑63, Aug 1999 .... 2.50
❑64, Sep 1999 .... 2.50
❑65, Oct 1999 .... 2.50
❑66, Nov 1999 .... 2.50
❑67, Dec 1999 .... 2.50
❑68, Jan 2000 .... 2.50
❑69, Feb 2000 .... 2.50
❑70, Mar 2000 .... 2.50
❑71, Apr 2000 .... 2.50
❑72, May 2000 .... 2.50
❑74, Jul 2000 .... 2.50
❑73, Jun 2000 .... 2.50
❑75, Aug 2000 .... 2.50
❑Annual 1, Feb 1997; 1997 Annual..... 3.95
❑Annual 2, Feb 1998; 1998 Annual..... 3.95
❑Annual 3, Jun 1999; 1999 Annual 3.95

BOOKS OF MAGICK: LIFE DURING WARTIME
DC / VERTIGO

❑1, Sep 2004 .... 2.50
❑2, Oct 2004 .... 2.50
❑3, Nov 2004 .... 2.50
❑4, Dec 2004 .... 2.50
❑5, Jan 2005 .... 2.50
❑6, Feb 2005 .... 2.50
❑7, Mar 2005 .... 2.50
❑8, Apr 2005 .... 2.50
❑9, May 2005 .... 2.50
❑10, Jun 2005 .... 2.50
❑11, Jul 2005 .... 2.50
❑12, Aug 2005 .... 2.50
❑13, Sep 2005 .... 2.75
❑14 2005 .... 2.75
❑15, Dec 2005 .... 2.75

BOOM BOOM
AEON

❑1, b&w 2.50
❑2, Sep 1994, b&w 2.50
❑3 .... 2.50
❑4, ca. 1995 .... 2.50

BOONDOGGLE
KNIGHT

❑1, Mar 1995 .... 2.95
❑2, Jul 1995, b&w 2.95
❑3, Nov 1995 .... 2.95
❑4, Jan 1996, b&w 2.95
❑Special 1, Nov 1996, b&w 2.95

Other grades: Multiply price above by 5/6 for VF/NM • 2/3 for VERY FINE • 1/3 for FINE • 1/5 for VERY GOOD • 1/8 for GOOD

Booster Gold

Super-hero is only in it for the money

©DC

Boris Karloff Tales of Mystery

Horror star "introduces" horror tales

©Gold Key

Boris the Bear

Violent ursine parodies many in series

©Dark Horse

Box Office Poison

Relationship humor from Alex Robinson

©Antarctic

Bradleys

Peter Bagge's take on a dysfunctional family

©Fantagraphics

N-MINT

BOONDOGGLE (VOL. 2)
CALIBER / TAPESTRY

❑1, Jan 1997 .... 2.95
❑2, Apr 1997 .... 2.95

BOOSTER GOLD
DC

❑1, Feb 1986 1: Booster Gold. V: Blackguard 1.00
❑2, Mar 1986 1: Mindancer. 1.00
❑3, Apr 1986 .... 1.00
❑4, May 1986 .... 1.00
❑5, Jun 1986 .... 1.00
❑6, Jul 1986 A: Superman. 1.00
❑7, Aug 1986 A: Superman. 1.00
❑8, Sep 1986 A: Legion. 1.00
❑9, Oct 1986 A: Legion. 1.00
❑10, Nov 1986 .... 1.00
❑11, Dec 1986 .... 1.00
❑12, Jan 1987 .... 1.00
❑13, Feb 1987 .... 1.00
❑14, Mar 1987; back to future 1.00
❑15, Apr 1987 .... 1.00
❑16, May 1987 1: Booster Gold International 1.00
❑17, Jun 1987 A: CheshireHawk. 1.00
❑18, Jul 1987 .... 1.00
❑19, Aug 1987 V: Rainbow Raider. 1.00
❑20, Sep 1987; blind 1.00
❑21, Oct 1987 .... 1.00
❑22, Nov 1987 A: Justice League International 1.00
❑23, Dec 1987 A: Superman 1.00
❑24, Jan 1988; Millennium 1.00
❑25, Feb 1988; Millennium; final issue 1.00

BOOTS OF THE OPPRESSOR
NORTHSTAR

❑1, Apr 1993 .... 2.95

BORDERGUARD
ETERNITY

❑1, Nov 1987 .... 1.95
❑2, Dec 1987 .... 1.95

BORDERLINE
KARDIA

❑1, Jun 1992 .... 2.25

BORDER WORLDS (VOL. 1)
KITCHEN SINK

❑1, Jul 1986; Reprinted from Megaton Man 1.95
❑2, Sep 1986 .... 1.95
❑3, Nov 1986 .... 1.95
❑4, Jan 1987 .... 1.95
❑5, Apr 1987 .... 1.95
❑6, Jun 1987 .... 1.95
❑7, Aug 1987; pages 4-5 transposed .. 2.00
❑7/A; Corrected edition; corrected 2.00

BORDER WORLDS (VOL. 2)
KITCHEN SINK

❑1, b&w 2.00

BORIS' ADVENTURE MAGAZINE
NICOTAT

❑1, Aug 1988, b&w; Rocketeer Adventure Magazine parody 2.00
❑2, Punishbear 2.95

N-MINT

❑3, Sep 1996 .... 2.95
❑4, BlackBear 2.95

BORIS KARLOFF TALES OF MYSTERY
GOLD KEY

❑3, Apr 1963 .... 27.00
❑4, Jul 1963 .... 25.00
❑5, Oct 1963 .... 25.00
❑6, Jan 1964 .... 20.00
❑7, Sep 1964 .... 20.00
❑8, Dec 1965 .... 20.00
❑9, Mar 1965, WW (a) 25.00
❑10, Jun 1965 .... 15.00
❑11, Sep 1965 .... 22.00
❑12, Dec 1965, back cover pin-up 15.00
❑13, Mar 1966 .... 12.00
❑14, Jun 1966 .... 12.00
❑15, Sep 1966 .... 15.00
❑16, Dec 1966 .... 12.00
❑17, Mar 1967 .... 12.00
❑18, Jun 1967 .... 12.00
❑19, Sep 1967 .... 12.00
❑20, Dec 1967 .... 12.00
❑21, Mar 1968, JJ (a) 18.00
❑22, Jun 1968 .... 10.00
❑23, Sep 1968, 10053-809 .... 10.00
❑24, Dec 1968 .... 10.00
❑25, Mar 1969 .... 10.00
❑26, Jun 1969 .... 10.00
❑27, Sep 1969 .... 10.00
❑28, Dec 1969 .... 10.00
❑29, Feb 1970 .... 10.00
❑30, May 1970 .... 10.00
❑31, Aug 1970 .... 8.50
❑32, Nov 1970 .... 8.50
❑33, Feb 1971 .... 8.50
❑34, Apr 1971 .... 8.50
❑35, Jun 1971 .... 8.50
❑36, Aug 1971 .... 8.50
❑37, Oct 1971 .... 8.50
❑38, Dec 1971 .... 8.50
❑39, Feb 1972 .... 8.50
❑40, Apr 1972 .... 8.50
❑41, Jun 1972 .... 7.50
❑42, Oct 1972 .... 7.50
❑43, Dec 1972 .... 7.50
❑44, Feb 1973 .... 7.50
❑45, Apr 1973 .... 7.50
❑46, May 1973 .... 7.50
❑47, Jun 1973 .... 7.50
❑48, Jul 1973 .... 7.50
❑49, Aug 1973, 90053-308 .... 7.50
❑50, Oct 1973 .... 7.50
❑51, Dec 1973 .... 6.00
❑52, Feb 1974 .... 6.00
❑53, Apr 1974 .... 6.00
❑54, Jun 1974 .... 6.00
❑55, Jul 1974 .... 6.00
❑56, Aug 1974 .... 6.00
❑57, Oct 1974 .... 6.00
❑58, Dec 1974 .... 6.00
❑59, Feb 1975 .... 6.00
❑60, Apr 1975 .... 5.00
❑61, ca. 1975 .... 5.00
❑62, ca. 1975 .... 5.00

N-MINT

❑63, Aug 1975 .... 5.00
❑64, Oct 1975 .... 5.00
❑65, Dec 1975 .... 5.00
❑66, Feb 1976 .... 5.00
❑67, Apr 1976 .... 5.00
❑68, Jun 1976 .... 5.00
❑69, ca. 1976 .... 5.00
❑70, Sep 1976 .... 5.00
❑71, ca. 1976 .... 5.00
❑72, Dec 1976 .... 5.00
❑73, ca. 1977 .... 5.00
❑74, Apr 1977 .... 5.00
❑75, ca. 1977 .... 3.00
❑76, ca. 1977 .... 3.00
❑77, ca. 1977 .... 3.00
❑78, Oct 1977 .... 3.00
❑79, ca. 1977 .... 3.00
❑80, Feb 1978 .... 7.00
❑81, Apr 1978 .... 6.00
❑82, ca. 1978 .... 5.00
❑83, Aug 1978 .... 6.00
❑84, Sep 1978 .... 5.00
❑85, Oct 1978 .... 6.00
❑86, Nov 1978 .... 3.00
❑87, Dec 1978 .... 3.00
❑88, Jan 1979 .... 3.00
❑89, Feb 1979 .... 3.00
❑90, ca. 1979 .... 3.00
❑91, May 1979 .... 3.00
❑92, Jul 1979 .... 3.00
❑93, Aug 1979 .... 3.00
❑94, Sep 1979 .... 3.00
❑95, Oct 1979 .... 3.00
❑96, Nov 1979 .... 3.00
❑97, Feb 1980 .... 3.00

BORIS KARLOFF THRILLER
GOLD KEY

❑1, Oct 1962 .... 75.00
❑2, Jan 1963 .... 55.00

BORIS THE BEAR
DARK HORSE

❑1, ca. 1986, b&w 3.00
❑1/2nd, ca. 1986, b&w 1.75
❑2, ca. 1986, b&w V: Transformers.... 2.25
❑3, ca. 1986, b&w; Boris takes on Marvel Comics for Jack Kirby 2.50
❑4, ca. 1986, b&w; O: Boris the Bear. two different covers; Man of Steel parody cover (far shot) 2.50
❑4/A, ca. 1986; Man of Steel parody cover (close-up) 2.50
❑5, ca. 1986, b&w; Swamp Thing parody 2.50
❑6, ca. 1987, b&w; Batman parody 2.50
❑7, ca. 1987, b&w; Elfquest parody ... 2.25
❑8, ca. 1987, b&w 2.25
❑9, ca. 1987, b&w; G.I. Joe parody; Wacky Squirrel backup 2.25
❑10, May 1987, b&w; G.I. Joe parody continues; Wacky Squirrel backup .. 2.25
❑11, Jun 1987, b&w; DA (a); T.H.U.N.D.E.R. Agents 2.25
❑12, Jul 1987, b&w; PG (a); Boris' Birthday; Last Dark Horse issue 2.25

❏13, Nov 1987, b&w; 1: Punishbear. Drug abuse issue; First Nicotat issue, remaining issues scarce.......... 2.25
❏14, Dec 1987, b&w V: Number Two.. 2.25
❏15, ca. 1988, b&w.......... 2.25
❏16, Mar 1988, b&w; Indiana Jones parody.......... 2.25
❏17, ca. 1988, b&w; BlackHawk parody; Sininju Coneys back-up...... 2.25
❏18, ca. 1988, b&w; Spider-Slayer (Spider-Man) parody.......... 2.25
❏19, Sep 1988, b&w; PG (c); The Old Swap Shop back-up.......... 2.25
❏20, Nov 1988, b&w; The Old Swap Shop back-up.......... 2.25
❏21, Feb 1989, b&w; The Old Swap Shop back-up.......... 2.00
❏22, Apr 1989, b&w; Kraven the Hunter/Sonny and Cher parody....... 2.00
❏23, May 1989, b&w.......... 2.00
❏24, Jul 1989, b&w; Bingo Glumm back-up.......... 2.00
❏25, ca. 1989, b&w A: Southern Squadron.......... 2.00
❏26, Jul 1990, b&w; A: Beardevil. Tom & Jerry parody.......... 2.00
❏27, Oct 1990, b&w.......... 2.00
❏28, Dec 1990, b&w.......... 2.00
❏29, Jan 1991, b&w.......... 2.00
❏30, Apr 1991, b&w; Gulf War issue/ parody.......... 2.50
❏31, Jun 1991, b&w.......... 2.50
❏32, Jul 1991, b&w; Dinosaurs; very scarce.......... 2.50
❏33, Sep 1991, b&w; very scarce....... 2.50
❏34, Nov 1991, b&w; A: BlackBear. #1 of 4, but series cancelled; very scarce 2.50

BORIS THE BEAR INSTANT COLOR CLASSICS
DARK HORSE

❏1, Jul 1987; 1: Boris the Bear. Reprints Boris the Bear #1 in color.......... 2.00
❏2, Aug 1987.......... 2.00
❏3, Dec 1987.......... 2.00

BORN
MARVEL / MAX

❏1, Aug 2003, TP (a); O: Frank Castle (Punisher). cardstock cover; Vietnam 5.00
❏2, Sep 2003, TP (a); cardstock cover; Vietnam.......... 3.50
❏3, Oct 2003, TP (a); cardstock cover; Vietnam.......... 3.50
❏4, Nov 2003, TP (a); cardstock cover; Vietnam.......... 3.50
❏Book 1/HC, ca. 2004.......... 17.99

BORN AGAIN
SPIRE

❏1; Chuck Colson.......... 3.50

BORN TO KILL
AIRCEL

❏1, May 1991, b&w.......... 2.50
❏2.......... 2.50
❏3.......... 2.50

BOSTON BOMBERS
CALIBER

❏1, ca. 1990.......... 2.50
❏2, ca. 1990.......... 2.50
❏3, ca. 1990.......... 2.50
❏4.......... 2.50
❏5.......... 2.50
❏6.......... 2.50
❏Special 1, ca. 1997.......... 3.95

BOULEVARD OF BROKEN DREAMS
FANTAGRAPHICS

❏1.......... 3.95

BOUND AND GAGGED
ICONOGRAFIX

❏1.......... 2.50

BOUND IN DARKNESS: INFINITY ISSUE
CFD

❏1, b&w.......... 2.50

BOUNTY
CALIBER

❏1, ca. 1991.......... 2.50
❏2, ca. 1991.......... 2.50
❏3, ca. 1991.......... 2.50

BOUNTY OF ZONE-Z
SUNSET STRIPS

❏1.......... 2.50

BOWIE BUTANE
MIKE MURDOCK

❏1, ca. 1995, b&w.......... 1.95

BOX
FANTAGRAPHICS / EROS

❏1.......... 2.25
❏2.......... 2.25
❏3.......... 2.25
❏4.......... 2.25
❏5.......... 2.25
❏6.......... 2.25

BOXBOY
SLAVE LABOR

❏1, Aug 1993.......... 1.00
❏1/2nd, May 1995.......... 1.25
❏2, Jul 1995.......... 1.25

BOX OFFICE POISON
ANTARCTIC

❏0; Collects stories from mini-comics 4.00
❏1, Oct 1996.......... 8.00
❏2, Dec 1996.......... 5.00
❏3, Feb 1997.......... 4.00
❏4, Mar 1997.......... 4.00
❏5, ca. 1997.......... 3.00
❏6, ca. 1997.......... 3.00
❏7, Nov 1997.......... 3.00
❏8, Feb 1998; cover says Feb 97, indicia says Feb 98.......... 2.95
❏9, Apr 1998; cover says May, indicia says Apr.......... 2.95
❏10, Jul 1998.......... 2.95
❏11, Oct 1998.......... 2.95
❏12, Dec 1998; wraparound cover..... 2.95
❏13, Feb 1999.......... 2.99
❏14, Jun 1999.......... 2.99
❏15, Aug 1999.......... 2.99
❏16 1999.......... 2.99
❏17 2000.......... 2.99
❏18, ca. 2000.......... 2.99
❏20, Aug 2000, b&w.......... 2.99
❏SS 1, May 1997; Super Special........ 4.95

BOX OFFICE POISON: KOLOR KARNIVAL
ANTARCTIC

❏1, May 1999; cover says Apr, indicia says May; Kolor Karnival.......... 3.50

BOY AND HIS 'BOT
NOW

❏1, Jan 1987; digest-sized.......... 1.95

BOY COMMANDOS (2ND SERIES)
DC

❏1, Oct 1973, JK (a); Reprinted from Detective Comics #66 ("Sphinx") and Boy Commandos #1 ("Heroes") 8.00
❏2, Dec 1973, JK (a); Reprinted from Boy Commandos #2 & #6 respectively.......... 5.00

BOYS BE ...
TOKYOPOP

❏1, Nov 2004.......... 9.95
❏2, Jan 2005.......... 9.95
❏3, Mar 2005.......... 9.95
❏4, May 2005.......... 9.95
❏5, Jul 2005.......... 9.95
❏6, Sep 2005.......... 9.95
❏7, Nov 2005.......... 9.95

BOYS OVER FLOWERS
VIZ

❏1, Aug 2003.......... 9.95
❏2, Oct 2003.......... 9.95
❏3, Dec 2003.......... 9.95
❏4, Feb 2004.......... 9.95
❏5, Apr 2004.......... 9.95
❏6, Jun 2004.......... 9.95
❏7, Aug 2004.......... 9.95
❏8, Oct 2004.......... 9.95
❏9, Dec 2004.......... 9.95
❏10, Feb 2005.......... 9.95
❏11, Apr 2005.......... 9.95
❏12, Jun 2005.......... 9.95
❏13, Aug 2005.......... 9.95
❏14, Oct 2005.......... 9.95

BOZO (2ND SERIES)
DELL

❏1, May 1962, 01-073-207.......... 60.00
❏2, Apr 1963.......... 35.00
❏3, Jul 1963.......... 35.00
❏4, Oct 1963.......... 28.00

BOZO: THE WORLD'S MOST FAMOUS CLOWN (LARRY HARMON'S...)
INNOVATION

❏1; some reprint; Reprints Four Color Comics #285.......... 6.00

BOZZ CHRONICLES
MARVEL / EPIC

❏1, Dec 1985, O: Bozz. 1: Bozz.......... 2.00
❏2, Feb 1986.......... 2.00
❏3, Apr 1986.......... 2.00
❏4, Jun 1986.......... 2.00
❏5, Aug 1986.......... 2.00
❏6, Oct 1986.......... 2.00

BPRD: A PLAGUE OF FROGS
DARK HORSE

❏1, Mar 2004.......... 2.99
❏2, Apr 2004.......... 2.99
❏3, May 2004.......... 2.99
❏4, Aug 2004.......... 2.99
❏5, Sep 2004.......... 3.00

BPRD: DARK WATERS
DARK HORSE

❏1, Jul 2003.......... 2.99

BPRD: HOLLOW EARTH
DARK HORSE

❏1, Jan 2002.......... 2.99
❏2, Apr 2002.......... 2.99
❏3, Jun 2002.......... 2.99

BPRD: NIGHT TRAIN
DARK HORSE

❏1, Sep 2003.......... 2.99

BPRD: SOUL OF VENICE
DARK HORSE

❏1, May 2003.......... 2.99

BPRD: THE BLACK FLAME
DARK HORSE

❏1, Aug 2005.......... 2.99
❏2, Sep 2005.......... 2.99
❏3, Oct 2005.......... 2.99
❏4, Nov 2005.......... 2.99
❏5, Dec 2005.......... 2.99
❏6, Jan 2006.......... 2.99

BPRD: THE DEAD
DARK HORSE

❏1, Nov 2004.......... 2.99
❏2, Dec 2004.......... 2.99
❏3, Jan 2005.......... 2.99
❏4, Feb 2005.......... 2.99
❏5, Mar 2005.......... 2.99

BPRD: THERE'S SOMETHING UNDER MY BED
DARK HORSE

❏1, Nov 2003.......... 2.99

BPRD: THE UNIVERSAL MACHINE
DARK HORSE

❏1, May 2006.......... 2.99
❏2, Jun 2006.......... 2.99
❏3, Jul 2006.......... 2.99

BRADLEYS
FANTAGRAPHICS

❏1, Apr 1999.......... 2.95
❏2, May 1999.......... 2.95
❏3, Jul 1999.......... 2.95

BRADY BUNCH
DELL

❏1, ca. 1970.......... 45.00
❏2, ca. 1970.......... 30.00

BRAGADE
PARODY

❏1, Mar 1993.......... 2.50

BRAINBANX
DC / HELIX

❏1, Mar 1997.......... 2.50
❏2, Apr 1997.......... 2.50
❏3, May 1997.......... 2.50
❏4, Jun 1997.......... 2.50

Brain Boy

Matt Price's mental magic adventures

©Dell

Brass (WildStorm)

Soldiers prepare for alien invasion

©DC

Brave and the Bold

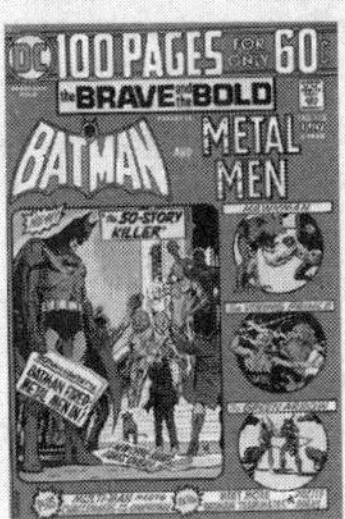

Batman team-ups in the Haney-verse

©DC

Brave and the Bold (Mini-Series)

Green Arrow, Question team up

©DC

Brave Old World

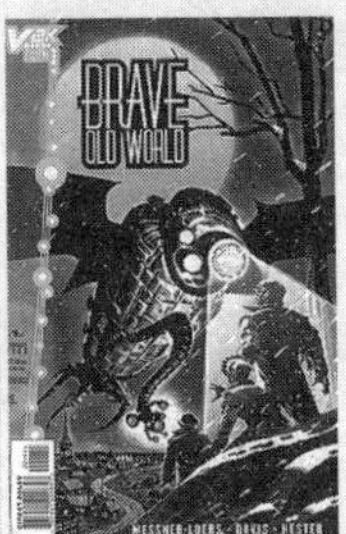

It's "1900 House" for the entire planet

©DC

N-MINT

❑5, Jul 1997 ... 2.50
❑6, Aug 1997 ... 2.50

BRAIN BAT 3-D
3-D ZONE

❑1, ca. 1992, b&w; No cover price; Oversized ... 3.95

BRAIN BOY
DELL

❑2, Jul 1962 ... 65.00
❑3, Dec 1962 ... 50.00
❑4, Mar 1963 ... 45.00
❑5, Jun 1963 ... 45.00
❑6, Sep 1963 ... 45.00

BRAIN CAPERS
FANTAGRAPHICS

❑1 ... 3.95

BRAIN FANTASY
LAST GASP

❑1 ... 3.00

BRAIN (I.W.)
I.W.

❑1, Sep 1958 ... 12.00
❑2 ... 9.00
❑3 ... 9.00
❑4 ... 9.00
❑5, Exists? ... 9.00
❑6; Exists? ... 9.00
❑7, Exists? ... 9.00
❑8 ... 9.00
❑9 ... 9.00
❑10, ca. 1963 ... 9.00
❑11; Exists? ... 8.00
❑12; Exists? ... 8.00
❑13; Exists? ... 8.00
❑14, Exists? ... 8.00
❑15; Exists? ... 8.00
❑16; Exists? ... 8.00
❑17 ... 8.00
❑18 ... 8.00

BRAINTRUST KOMICKS
SPOON

❑1, Mar 1993 ... 2.75

BRAND NEW YORK
MEAN

❑1, Jul 1997, cardstock cover ... 3.95
❑2 ... 3.95

BRASS
IMAGE

❑1, Aug 1996 ... 2.50
❑1/Deluxe, Aug 1996, Folio edition ... 4.50
❑2, Sep 1996 ... 2.50
❑3, May 1997 ... 2.50

BRASS (WILDSTORM)
DC / WILDSTORM

❑1, Aug 2000 ... 2.50
❑2, Sep 2000 ... 2.50
❑3, Oct 2000 ... 2.50
❑4, Nov 2000 ... 2.50
❑5, Dec 2000 ... 2.50
❑6, Jan 2001 ... 2.50

N-MINT

BRATH
CROSSGEN

❑1, Mar 2003 ... 2.95
❑2, Apr 2003 ... 2.95
❑3, May 2003 ... 2.95
❑4, Jun 2003 ... 2.95
❑5, Jul 2003 ... 2.95
❑6, Aug 2003 ... 2.95
❑7, Sep 2003 ... 2.95
❑8, Oct 2003 ... 2.95
❑9, Nov 2003 ... 2.95
❑10, Dec 2003 ... 2.95
❑11, Jan 2004 ... 2.95
❑12, Feb 2004 ... 2.95
❑13, Apr 2004 ... 2.95
❑14, May 2004 ... 2.95

BRATPACK
KING HELL

❑1, Aug 1990, b&w 1: Doctor Blasphemy. 1: Luna. 1: Kid Vicious. 1: Wild Boy. ... 3.00
❑1/2nd, 1: Doctor Blasphemy. 1: Luna. 1: Kid Vicious. 1: Wild Boy. ... 3.00
❑1/3rd, 1: Doctor Blasphemy. 1: Luna. 1: Kid Vicious. 1: Wild Boy. ... 3.00
❑2, Nov 1990 ... 2.95
❑3, Jan 1991 ... 2.95
❑4, Mar 1991 ... 2.95
❑5, May 1991 ... 2.95

BRAT PACK/MAXIMORTAL SUPER SPECIAL
KING HELL

❑1, Sep 1996 ... 2.95

BRATS BIZARRE
MARVEL / EPIC

❑1, May 1994 ... 2.50
❑2, Jun 1994 ... 2.50
❑3, Jul 1994; trading card ... 2.50
❑4, Aug 1994 ... 2.50

BRAVE AND THE BOLD
DC

❑1, Aug 1955; JKu (a); Viking Prince, Golden Gladiator, Silent Knight ... 3000.00
❑2, Oct 1955; Viking Prince, Golden Gladiator, Silent Knight ... 1500.00
❑3, Dec 1955, Viking Prince, Golden Gladiator, Silent Knight ... 700.00
❑4, Feb 1956; Viking Prince, Golden Gladiator, Silent Knight ... 650.00
❑5, Apr 1956; Robin Hood, Silent Knight, Viking Prince ... 650.00
❑6, Jun 1956; JKu (a); Robin Hood, Silent Knight, Golden Gladiator ... 500.00
❑7, Aug 1956; JKu (a); Robin Hood, Silent Knight, Viking Prince ... 500.00
❑8, Oct 1956; JKu (a); Robin Hood, Silent Knight, Golden Gladiator ... 500.00
❑9, Dec 1956; JKu (a); Robin Hood, Silent Knight, Viking Prince ... 500.00
❑10, Feb 1957, JKu (a); Robin Hood, Silent Knight, Viking Prince ... 500.00
❑11, Apr 1957; JKu (a); Robin Hood, Silent Knight, Viking Prince ... 400.00
❑12, Jun 1957; JKu (a); Robin Hood, Silent Knight, Viking Prince ... 400.00

N-MINT

❑13, Sep 1957; JKu (a); Robin Hood, Silent Knight, Viking Prince ... 400.00
❑14, Nov 1957; JKu (a); Robin Hood, Silent Knight, Viking Prince ... 400.00
❑15, Jan 1958; JKu (a); Robin Hood, Silent Knight, Viking Prince ... 400.00
❑16, Mar 1958; JKu (a); Silent Knight, Viking Prince ... 400.00
❑17, May 1958; JKu (a); Silent Knight, Viking Prince ... 400.00
❑18, Jul 1958; JKu (a); Silent Knight, Viking Prince ... 400.00
❑19, Sep 1958; JKu (a); Silent Knight, Viking Prince ... 400.00
❑20, Nov 1958; JKu (a); Silent Knight, Viking Prince ... 400.00
❑21, Jan 1959; JKu (a); Silent Knight, Viking Prince ... 400.00
❑22, Mar 1959; JKu (a); Silent Knight, Viking Prince ... 400.00
❑23, May 1959; JKu (a); O: Viking Prince. Viking Prince ... 500.00
❑24, Jul 1959; JKu (a); Viking Prince. 350.00
❑25, Sep 1959 1: The Suicide Squad (Golden Age) ... 500.00
❑26, Nov 1959 2: Suicide Squad. ... 325.00
❑27, Jan 1960 A: Suicide Squad ... 330.00
❑28, Mar 1960 1: Justice League of America. 1: Starro the Conqueror. 1: Snapper Carr. ... 5000.00
❑29, May 1960, 2: Justice League of America. ... 2000.00
❑30, Jul 1960 1: Amazo. 1: Professor Ivo. A: Justice League of America... 1750.00
❑31, Sep 1960, 1: Cave Carson. ... 350.00
❑32, Nov 1960; Cave Carson ... 200.00
❑33, Jan 1961; Cave Carson ... 200.00
❑34, Mar 1961 JK, JKu (a); 1: Thanagar. 1: Byth. 1: Hawkwoman II (Shayera Thal). 1: Hawkman II (Katar Hol). ... 1750.00
❑35, May 1961; JK, JKu (a); 1: Matter Master. Hawkman ... 400.00
❑36, Jul 1961; JK, JKu (a); 1: Shadow-Thief. Hawkman ... 400.00
❑37, Sep 1961; Suicide Squad ... 250.00
❑38, Nov 1961, Suicide Squad ... 225.00
❑39, Jan 1962; Suicide Squad ... 225.00
❑40, Mar 1962, Cave Carson ... 140.00
❑41, May 1962, Cave Carson ... 140.00
❑42, Jul 1962, JK, JKu (a); A: Hawkman. 300.00
❑43, Sep 1962, JK, JKu (a); O: Hawkman (Silver Age). 1: Manhawks. ... 350.00
❑44, Nov 1962, JK, JKu (a); A: Hawkman. 260.00
❑45, Jan 1963, CI (a); Strange Sports Stories ... 60.00
❑46, Mar 1963, CI (a); Strange Sports Stories ... 60.00
❑47, May 1963, CI (a); Strange Sports Stories ... 60.00
❑48, Jul 1963, CI (a); Strange Sports Stories ... 60.00
❑49, Sep 1963, CI (a); Strange Sports Stories ... 60.00
❑50, Nov 1963, Green Arrow; Team-ups begin ... 175.00
❑51, Jan 1964, Aquaman, Hawkman; Early Hawkman/Aquaman team-up. 225.00
❑52, Mar 1964, JK (a); Sgt. Rock ... 125.00
❑53, May 1964, ATh (a); Atom & Flash 75.00

Other grades: Multiply price above by 5/6 for VF/NM • 2/3 for VERY FINE • 1/3 for FINE • 1/5 for VERY GOOD • 1/8 for GOOD

	N-MINT
❑54, Jul 1964, O: Teen Titans. 1: Teen Titans	350.00
❑55, Sep 1964, Metal Men, Atom	45.00
❑56, Nov 1964, 1: Wynde. Flash	45.00
❑57, Jan 1965, O: Metamorpho. 1: Metamorpho	150.00
❑58, Mar 1965, 2: Metamorpho	65.00
❑59, May 1965, Batman; Batman/ Green Lantern team-up	80.00
❑60, Jul 1965, NC (c); 1: Wonder Girl (Donna Troy). Teen Titans	100.00
❑61, Sep 1965, MA (a); O: Starman I (Ted Knight). O: Black Canary. Starman, Black Canary	125.00
❑62, Nov 1965, MA (a); Starman, Black Canary	100.00
❑63, Jan 1966, Supergirl	40.00
❑64, Mar 1966, A: Eclipso. Batman	60.00
❑65, May 1966, Doom Patrol	22.00
❑66, Jul 1966, Metamorpho, Metal Men	22.00
❑67, Sep 1966, CI (a); Batman, Flash; Batman in all remaining issues	65.00
❑68, Nov 1966, A: Joker. Metamorpho	80.00
❑69, Jan 1967, Green Lantern	50.00
❑70, Mar 1967, Hawkman	50.00
❑71, May 1967, Green Arrow	50.00
❑72, Jul 1967, CI (a); Spectre	50.00
❑73, Sep 1967, Aquaman, Atom	40.00
❑74, Nov 1967, Metal Men	40.00
❑75, Jan 1968, Spectre	40.00
❑76, Mar 1968, Plastic Man	40.00
❑77, May 1968	40.00
❑78, Jul 1968, 1: Copperhead. Wonder Woman	40.00
❑79, Sep 1968, NA (a); A: Deadman. Deadman	75.00
❑80, Nov 1968, NA (a); A: Creeper. Creeper	50.00
❑81, Jan 1969, NA (a); A: Deadman. Flash	50.00
❑82, Mar 1969, NA (a); O: Ocean Master. A: Deadman	50.00
❑83, May 1969, NA (a); Titans	60.00
❑84, Jul 1969, NA (a); Sgt. Rock	50.00
❑85, Sep 1969, NA (a); Green Arrow gets new costume	50.00
❑86, Nov 1969, NA (a); Deadman	50.00
❑87, Jan 1970, Wonder Woman	20.00
❑88, Mar 1970, Wildcat	20.00
❑89, May 1970, Phantom Stranger	20.00
❑90, Jul 1970, Adam Strange	20.00
❑91, Sep 1970, Black Canary	18.00
❑92, Nov 1970, Bat Squad	18.00
❑93, Jan 1971, NA (a); House of Mystery	30.00
❑94, Mar 1971, Titans	18.00
❑95, May 1971, Plastic Man	15.00
❑96, Jul 1971, Sgt. Rock	15.00
❑97, Sep 1971; Wildcat	15.00
❑98, Nov 1971; Phantom Stranger	15.00
❑99, Jan 1972; NC (a); Flash	15.00
❑100, Mar 1972; Double-size; NA (a); Green Arrow	30.00
❑101, May 1972; Metamorpho	12.00
❑102, Jul 1972; NA (a); Titans	15.00
❑103, Oct 1972, Metal Men	12.00
❑104, Dec 1972, JA (a); Deadman	12.00
❑105, Feb 1973, JA (a); Wonder Woman	12.00
❑106, Apr 1973, JA (a); Green Arrow	12.00
❑107, Jul 1973, Black Canary	12.00
❑108, Sep 1973, JA (a); Sgt. Rock	12.00
❑109, Nov 1973, JA (a); Demon	12.00
❑110, Jan 1974, JA (a); Wildcat	12.00
❑111, Mar 1974, JA (a); Joker	18.00
❑112, May 1974, 100 Page giant; Mr. Miracle	18.00
❑113, Jul 1974, 100 Page giant; JA (a); Metal Men	18.00
❑114, Sep 1974, 100 Page giant; JA (a); Aquaman	18.00
❑115, Nov 1974, 100 Page giant JA (a); O: Viking Prince	18.00
❑116, Jan 1975, 100 Page giant; JA (a); Spectre	18.00
❑117, Mar 1975, 100 Page giant; JA (a); Sgt. Rock; reprints Secret Six #1	18.00
❑118, Apr 1975; JA (a); Wildcat, Joker	18.00
❑119, Jun 1975; JA (a); Man-Bat	6.00
❑120, Jul 1975, JA (a); Kamandi, 68 pgs., reprints Secret Six #2	6.00
❑121, Sep 1975; JA (a); Metal Men	6.00
❑122, Oct 1975; Swamp Thing	6.00
❑123, Dec 1975; JA (a); Plastic Man, Metamorpho	6.00
❑124, Jan 1976; JA (a); Sgt. Rock	6.00
❑125, Mar 1976; JA (a); Flash	6.00
❑126, Apr 1976, JA (a); Aquaman	6.00
❑127, Jun 1976, JA (a); Wildcat	6.00
❑128, Jul 1976, JA (a); Mr. Miracle; Bicentennial #19	6.00
❑129, Sep 1976, Green Arrow/Joker	11.00
❑130, Oct 1976, Green Arrow/Joker	11.00
❑131, Dec 1976, JA (a); A: Catwoman. Wonder Woman	6.00
❑132, Feb 1977, JA (a); Kung Fu Fighter	4.00
❑133, Apr 1977, JA (a); Deadman	4.00
❑134, May 1977, JA (a); Green Lantern	4.00
❑135, Jul 1977, JA (a); Metal Men	4.00
❑136, Sep 1977, Green Arrow, Metal Men	4.00
❑137, Oct 1977, Demon	4.00
❑138, Nov 1977, JA (a); Mr. Miracle	4.00
❑139, Jan 1978, JA (a); Hawkman	4.00
❑140, Mar 1978, JA (a); Wonder Woman	4.00
❑141, May 1978, Black Canary, Joker	10.00
❑142, Jul 1978, JA (a); Aquaman	4.00
❑143, Sep 1978, JA (a); O: Human Target	4.00
❑144, Nov 1978, JA (a); Green Arrow	4.00
❑145, Dec 1978, JA (a); Phantom Stranger	4.00
❑145/Whitman, Dec 1978, JA (a); Phantom Stranger; Whitman variant	8.00
❑146, Jan 1979, JA (a); E-2 Batman/ Unknown Soldier	4.00
❑146/Whitman, Jan 1979, JA (a); E-2 Batman/Unknown Soldier; Whitman variant	8.00
❑147, Feb 1979, JA (a); A: Doctor Light	4.00
❑147/Whitman, Feb 1979, JA (a); A: Doctor Light. Whitman variant	8.00
❑148, Mar 1979, Plastic Man	4.00
❑149, Apr 1979, JA (a); Teen Titans	4.00
❑149/Whitman, Apr 1979, JA (a); Teen Titans; Whitman variant	8.00
❑150, May 1979, JA (a); Superman	4.00
❑150/Whitman, May 1979, JA (a); Superman; Whitman variant	12.00
❑151, Jun 1979, JA (a); Flash	4.00
❑151/Whitman, Jun 1979, JA (a); Flash; Whitman variant	8.00
❑152, Jul 1979, JA (a); Atom	4.00
❑152/Whitman, Jul 1979, JA (a); Atom; Whitman variant	8.00
❑153, Aug 1979, DN (a); Red Tornado	4.00
❑153/Whitman, Aug 1979, DN (a); Red Tornado; Whitman variant	20.00
❑154, Sep 1979, JA (a); Metamorpho	4.00
❑154/Whitman, Sep 1979, JA (a); Metamorpho; Whitman variant	8.00
❑155, Oct 1979, JA (a); Green Lantern	4.00
❑155/Whitman, Oct 1979, JA (a); Green Lantern; Whitman variant	8.00
❑156, Nov 1979, DN (a); Doctor Fate	4.00
❑156/Whitman, Nov 1979, DN (a); Doctor Fate; Whitman variant	8.00
❑157, Dec 1979, JA (a); Kamandi, continues story from Kamandi #59	4.00
❑157/Whitman, Dec 1979, JA (a); Kamandi, continues story from Kamandi #59; Whitman variant	8.00
❑158, Jan 1980, JA (a); Wonder Woman	4.00
❑158/Whitman, Jan 1980, JA (a); Wonder Woman; Whitman variant	8.00
❑159, Feb 1980, JA (a); Ra's al Ghul	4.00
❑159/Whitman, Feb 1980, JA (a); Ra's al Ghul; Whitman variant	8.00
❑160, Mar 1980, JA (a); Supergirl	4.00
❑160/Whitman, Mar 1980, JA (a); Supergirl; Whitman variant	8.00
❑161, Apr 1980, JA (a); Adam Strange	4.00
❑161/Whitman, Apr 1980, JA (a); Adam Strange; Whitman variant	8.00
❑162, May 1980, JA (a); Sgt. Rock	4.00
❑162/Whitman, May 1980, JA (a); Sgt. Rock; Whitman variant	8.00
❑163, Jun 1980, DG (a); Black Lightning	4.00
❑163/Whitman, Jun 1980, DG (a); Black Lightning; Whitman variant	8.00
❑164, Jul 1980, JL (a); A: Hawkgirl. A: Hawkman. Hawkman	4.00
❑164/Whitman, Jul 1980, JL (a); A: Hawkgirl. A: Hawkman. Hawkman; Whitman variant	8.00
❑165, Aug 1980, DN (a); Man-Bat	4.00
❑165/Whitman, Aug 1980, DN (a); Man-Bat; Whitman variant	8.00
❑166, Sep 1980, DS, TD (a); 1: Nemesis. Black Canary	4.00
❑167, Oct 1980, DC, DA (a); Blackhawk	4.00
❑168, Nov 1980, JA (a); Green Arrow	4.00
❑169, Dec 1980, JA (a); Zatanna	4.00
❑170, Jan 1981, JA (a); Nemesis	4.00
❑171, Feb 1981, GC, JL (a); Scalphunter	4.00
❑172, Mar 1981, CI (a); Firestorm	4.00
❑173, Apr 1981, JA (a); Guardians	4.00
❑174, May 1981, JA (a); Green Lantern	4.00
❑175, Jun 1981, JA (a); Lois Lane	4.00
❑176, Jul 1981, JA (a); Swamp Thing	4.00
❑177, Aug 1981, JA (a); Elongated Man	4.00
❑178, Sep 1981, JA (a); Creeper	4.00
❑179, Oct 1981, Legion	4.00
❑180, Nov 1981, JA (a); Spectre, Nemesis	3.00
❑181, Dec 1981, JA (a); Hawk & Dove, Nemesis	3.00
❑182, Jan 1982, JA (a); E-2 Robin	3.00
❑183, Feb 1982, CI (a); Riddler, Nemesis	3.00
❑184, Mar 1982, JA (a); Huntress	3.00
❑185, Apr 1982, Green Lantern	3.00
❑186, May 1982, JA (a); Hawkman, Nemesis	3.00
❑187, Jun 1982, JA (a); Metal Men, Nemesis	3.00
❑188, Jul 1982, JA (a); Rose & Thorn	3.00
❑189, Aug 1982, JA (a); Thorn, Nemesis	3.00
❑190, Sep 1982, JA (a); Adam Strange, Nemesis	3.00
❑191, Oct 1982, JA (a); A: Penguin. A: Nemesis. Joker	8.00
❑192, Nov 1982, JA (a); V: Mr. IQ. Superboy	3.00
❑193, Dec 1982, JA (a); D: Nemesis.	3.00
❑194, Jan 1983, CI (a); V: Double-X. V: Rainbow Raider. Flash; V: Rainbow Raider, Double-X	3.00
❑195, Feb 1983, JA (a); I...Vampire	3.00
❑196, Mar 1983, JA (a); Ragman	3.00
❑197, Apr 1983, Catwoman; Wedding of Earth-2 Batman & Earth-2 Catwoman	4.00
❑198, May 1983, Karate Kid	3.00
❑199, Jun 1983, RA (a); Spectre	3.00
❑200, Jul 1983; Giant-size; JA (a); 1: Halo. 1: Katana. 1: Geo-Force. 1: Outsiders. E-1 and E-2 Batman	7.00
❑Annual 1, ca. 2001; SD, CI (a); Revival issue (2001)	5.95

BRAVE AND THE BOLD (MINI-SERIES)
DC

❑1, Dec 1991 MGr (w)	2.50
❑2, Jan 1992 MGr (w)	2.00
❑3, Feb 1992 MGr (w)	2.00
❑4, Mar 1992 MGr (w)	2.00
❑5, May 1992 MGr (w)	2.00
❑6, Jun 1992 MGr (w)	2.00

BRAVE OLD WORLD
DC / VERTIGO

❑1, Feb 2000	2.50
❑2, Mar 2000	2.50
❑3, Apr 2000	2.50
❑4, May 2000	2.50

BRAVESTARR IN 3-D
BLACKTHORNE

❑1	2.50
❑2	2.50

BRAVO FOR ADVENTURE
DRAGON LADY

❑1	5.95

BRAVURA PREVIEW BOOK
MALIBU / BRAVURA

❑0, Jan 1995, JSn, HC (w); JSn, HC, GK (a); Coupon redemption promotion	3.00
❑1, Nov 1993, No cover price; 1994 Preview book	1.50
❑2, Aug 1994, 1995 Preview book (#1 on cover)	1.50

Brigade (Mini-Series)

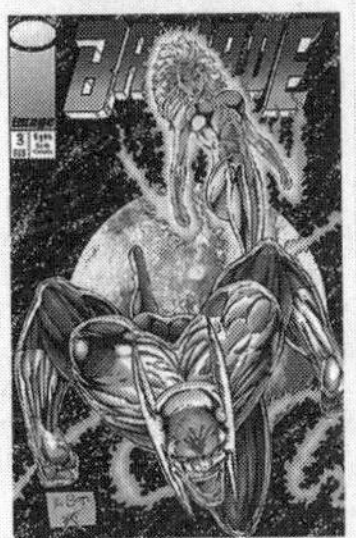

Rob Liefeld published this super-hero team

©Image

Brilliant Boy

The new kid has some strange habits

©Circus

Brother Power, the Geek

Joe Simon's take on hippie culture

©DC

Brothers of the Spear

Originally appeared as back-ups in Tarzan

©Gold Key

Bru-Hed

Lovable loser has no tact at all

©Schism

N-MINT

BREACH
DC

❑1 2005 .... 2.95
❑2, Mar 2005 .... 2.50
❑3, Apr 2005 .... 5.00
❑4, May 2005 .... 2.50
❑5, Jun 2005 .... 2.50
❑6, Jul 2005 .... 2.50
❑7, Aug 2005 .... 2.50
❑8, Sep 2005 .... 2.50
❑9, Oct 2005 .... 2.50
❑10 .... 2.50
❑11, Jan 2006 .... 2.50

BREAKDOWN
DEVIL'S DUE

❑1, Oct 2004 .... 4.00
❑1/Variant, Oct 2004 .... 5.00
❑2, Nov 2004 .... 4.00
❑2/Variant, Nov 2004 .... 5.00
❑3, Dec 2004 .... 3.00
❑4, Feb 2005 .... 3.00
❑5, Mar 2005 .... 2.95
❑6, Apr 2005 .... 2.95

BREAKDOWNS
INFINITY

❑1, Oct 1986, b&w 1.70

BREAKFAST AFTER NOON
ONI

❑1, May 2000, b&w 2.95
❑2, Aug 2000, b&w 2.95
❑3, Sep 2000, b&w 2.95
❑4, Nov 2000, b&w 2.95
❑5, Dec 2000, b&w 2.95
❑6, Jan 2001, b&w 2.95

BREAKNECK BLVD. (MOTION)
MOTION

❑0, Feb 1994, b&w 2.50
❑1, Jul 1994, b&w 2.50
❑2, Sep 1994, b&w 2.50

BREAKNECK BLVD. (SLAVE LABOR)
SLAVE LABOR

❑1, Jul 1995 .... 2.95
❑2, Oct 1995 .... 2.95
❑3, Jan 1996 .... 2.95
❑4, May 1996 .... 2.95
❑5, Aug 1996 .... 2.95
❑6, Dec 1996 .... 2.95

BREAK THE CHAIN
MARVEL MUSIC

❑1; polybagged with KRS-1 cassette tape 6.95

BREAK-THRU
MALIBU

❑1, Dec 1993 GP (a) 2.50
❑1/Ltd., Dec 1993; Ultra Limited; foil logo 4.00
❑2, Jan 1994 GP (a) 2.50

BREATHTAKER
DC

❑1, Jul 1990 1: The Man. 1: Breathtaker. 5.00
❑2, Aug 1990 .... 5.00
❑3, Sep 1990 O: Breathtaker. 5.00
❑4, Oct 1990 .... 5.00

N-MINT

'BREED
MALIBU / BRAVURA

❑1, Jan 1994, JSn (w); JSn (a) 2.50
❑1/Gold, Jan 1994; sendaway with gold ink on the cover ....
❑2, Feb 1994, JSn (w); JSn (a) 2.50
❑3, Mar 1994, JSn (w); JSn (a) 2.50
❑4, Apr 1994, JSn (w); JSn (a) 2.50
❑5, May 1994, JSn (w); JSn (a) 2.50
❑6, Jun 1994, JSn (w); JSn (a) 2.50

'BREED II
MALIBU / BRAVURA

❑1, Nov 1994 .... 2.95
❑2, Dec 1994 .... 2.95
❑3, Jan 1995 .... 2.95
❑4, Feb 1995 .... 2.95
❑5, Mar 1995 .... 2.95
❑6, Apr 1995 .... 2.95

BRENDA LEE'S LIFE STORY
DELL

❑1, Sep 1962 .... 50.00

BRENDA STARR (AVALON)
AVALON

❑1 .... 2.95
❑2 .... 2.95

BRENDA STARR CUT-OUTS AND COLORING BOOK
BLACKTHORNE

❑1 .... 6.95

BRICKMAN
HARRIER

❑1 .... 1.95

BRIDES IN LOVE
CHARLTON

❑1 1956 .... 60.00
❑2 1957 .... 35.00
❑3 1957 .... 24.00
❑4 1957 .... 24.00
❑5 1957 .... 24.00
❑6 1957 .... 24.00
❑7 1957 .... 24.00
❑8 1958 .... 24.00
❑9 1958 .... 24.00
❑10 1958 .... 24.00
❑11 1959 .... 18.00
❑12 1959 .... 18.00
❑13 1959 .... 18.00
❑14 1959 .... 18.00
❑15 1959 .... 18.00
❑16 1960 .... 18.00
❑17 1960 .... 18.00
❑18 1960 .... 18.00
❑19, Jul 1960 .... 18.00
❑20, Sep 1960 .... 18.00
❑21, Nov 1960, DG (a) 18.00
❑22, Jan 1961 .... 18.00
❑23, Mar 1961 .... 18.00
❑24, May 1961 .... 18.00
❑25, Jul 1961 .... 18.00
❑26, Sep 1961 .... 18.00
❑27, Nov 1961 .... 18.00
❑28, Jan 1962 .... 18.00
❑29, Mar 1962 .... 18.00

N-MINT

❑30, May 1962 .... 18.00
❑31, Jul 1962 .... 12.00
❑32, Sep 1962 .... 12.00
❑33, Nov 1962, DG (c) 12.00
❑34, Jan 1963 .... 12.00
❑35, Mar 1963 .... 12.00
❑36, May 1963 .... 12.00
❑37, Jul 1963 .... 12.00
❑38, Sep 1963 .... 12.00
❑39, Nov 1963 .... 12.00
❑40, ca. 1964 .... 12.00
❑41, ca. 1964 .... 12.00
❑42, Jul 1964 .... 12.00
❑43, Sep 1964, Swimsuit cover 12.00
❑44, Nov 1964 .... 12.00
❑45, Feb 1965 .... 12.00

BRIDGMAN'S CONSTRUCTIVE ANATOMY
A-LIST

❑1, Apr 1998, b&w 2.95

BRIGADE (MINI-SERIES)
IMAGE

❑1, Aug 1992 .... 2.00
❑1/Gold, Aug 1992; Gold edition 2.00
❑2, Oct 1992 .... 3.50
❑2/Gold, Oct 1992; Gold edition 3.50
❑3, Feb 1993 .... 2.00
❑4, Jul 1993; flip side of Youngblood #5 .... 2.00

BRIGADE
IMAGE

❑0, Sep 1993; RL (w); 1: Warcry. gatefold cover 2.00
❑1, May 1993 RL (w); 1: Boone. 1: Hacker. 2.00
❑2, Jun 1993 RL (w) 2.00
❑2/A, Jun 1993; foil alternate cover 2.95
❑3, Sep 1993; RL (w); 1: Roman. Indicia says Volume 1 instead of Volume 2 .... 2.00
❑4, Oct 1993 .... 2.00
❑5, Nov 1993 .... 2.00
❑6, Dec 1993 1: Worlok. 1: Coral. 1.95
❑7, Feb 1994 .... 1.95
❑8, Mar 1994 .... 1.95
❑9, Apr 1994 .... 1.95
❑10, Jun 1994 .... 1.95
❑11, Aug 1994 A: WildC.A.T.s. 1.95
❑12, Sep 1994 A: WildC.A.T.s. 2.50
❑13, Oct 1994 .... 2.50
❑14, Nov 1994 .... 2.50
❑15, Dec 1994 .... 2.50
❑16, Jan 1995 .... 2.50
❑17, Feb 1995 .... 2.50
❑18, Mar 1995 .... 2.50
❑18/Variant, Mar 1995; alternate cover 2.50
❑19, Apr 1995 A: Glory. 2.50
❑20/A, May 1995 A: Glory. 2.50
❑20/B, May 1995; A: Glory. alternate cover 2.50
❑21, Jun 1995; Funeral of Shadowhawk 2.50
❑22, Jul 1995 .... 2.50
❑25, May 1994; Images of Tomorrow; Published out of sequence as a preview of the future 1.95

Other grades: Multiply price above by 5/6 for VF/NM • 2/3 for VERY FINE • 1/3 for FINE • 1/5 for VERY GOOD • 1/8 for GOOD

❑26, Jun 1994; Published out of sequence as a preview of the future ... 1.95
❑27, Jul 1994 ... 2.50

BRIGADE (AWESOME)
Awesome

❑1, Jul 2000 ... 2.99

BRIGADE SOURCEBOOK
Image

❑1, Aug 1994 ... 2.95

BRIK HAUSS
Blackthorne

❑1, Jul 1987 ... 1.75

BRILLIANT BOY
Circus

❑1, Jan 1997 ... 2.95
❑2, Mar 1997 ... 2.50
❑3, May 1997 ... 2.50
❑4 ... 2.50
❑5 ... 2.50

BRINKE OF DESTRUCTION
High-Top

❑1, Dec 1995 ... 2.95
❑1/CS, Dec 1995; packaged with audio tape ... 6.99
❑2 ... 2.95
❑3, Jan 1997 ... 2.95
❑Special 1 ... 6.95

BRINKE OF DISASTER
High-Top

❑1, Sep 1996 ... 2.25

BRINKE OF ETERNITY
Chaos

❑1, Apr 1994 ... 2.75

BRIT
Image

❑1, Jul 2003 ... 4.95

BRIT-CIT BABES
Fleetway-Quality

❑1 ... 5.95

BRIT/COLD DEATH ONE SHOT
Image

❑1, Jan 2004 ... 4.95

BRIT: RED, WHITE, BLACK & BLUE ONE-SHOT
Image

❑1 2004 ... 5.00

BROADWAY BABES
Avalon

❑1, reprints Moronica stories, b&w ... 2.95

BROADWAY VIDEO SPECIAL COLLECTORS EDITION
Broadway

❑1, Promotional giveaway; 1150 copies printed; cardstock cover ... 1.00

BROID
Eternity

❑1, May 1990, b&w ... 2.75
❑2 ... 2.25
❑3 ... 2.25
❑4 ... 2.25

BROKEN AXIS
Antarctic

❑1, b&w ... 2.95

BROKEN FENDER
Top Shelf Productions

❑1, ca. 1997, b&w ... 2.95
❑2, b&w ... 2.95

BROKEN HALO: IS THERE NOTHING SACRED?
Broken Halos

❑2, Oct 1998, b&w ... 2.95
❑2/Nude, Oct 1998, b&w; nude cover edition; Nude cover edition ... 4.95

BROKEN HEROES
Sirius

❑1, Mar 1998 ... 2.50
❑2, Apr 1998 ... 2.50
❑3, May 1998 ... 2.50
❑4, Jun 1998 ... 2.50
❑5, Jul 1998 ... 2.50
❑6, Aug 1998 ... 2.50
❑7, Sep 1998 ... 2.50
❑8, Oct 1998 ... 2.50
❑9, Nov 1998 ... 2.50
❑10, Dec 1998 ... 2.50
❑11, Jan 1999 ... 2.50
❑12, Feb 1999 ... 2.50

BRONTE'S INFERNAL ANGRIA
Headless Shakespeare Press

❑1, Aug 2005 ... 4.00

BRONX
Eternity

❑1 ... 2.50
❑2 ... 2.50
❑3 ... 2.50

ROOKLYN DREAMS
DC / Paradox

❑1 1994, b&w ... 4.95
❑2 1994, b&w ... 4.95
❑3 1994, b&w ... 4.95
❑4 1994, b&w ... 4.95

BROTHER BILLY THE PAIN FROM PLAINS
Marvel

❑1, Jun 1979; Billy Carter parody ... 20.00

BROTHER DESTINY
Mecca

❑1 2004 ... 2.99
❑2, Nov 2004; Cover says July, indicia says November ... 2.99
❑3 2004 ... 2.99

BROTHERHOOD
Marvel

❑1, Jul 2001 ... 2.25
❑2, Aug 2001 ... 2.25
❑3, Sep 2001 ... 2.25
❑4, Oct 2001 ... 2.25
❑5, Nov 2001 ... 2.25
❑6, Dec 2001 ... 2.25
❑7, Jan 2002 ... 2.25
❑8, Feb 2002 ... 2.25
❑9, Mar 2002 ... 2.25

BROTHERMAN
Big City

❑1 ... 2.00
❑2 ... 2.00
❑3 ... 2.00
❑4 ... 2.00
❑5 ... 2.00
❑6 ... 2.00
❑7 ... 2.00
❑8 ... 2.00

BROTHER MAN: DICTATOR OF DISCIPLINE
Big City

❑11, Jul 1996; magazine-sized ... 2.95

BROTHER POWER, THE GEEK
DC

❑1, Sep 1968, 1: Brother Power, the Geek. ... 45.00
❑2, Nov 1968 ... 20.00

BROTHERS OF THE SPEAR
Gold Key

❑1, Jun 1972 ... 20.00
❑2, Sep 1972 ... 10.00
❑3, Dec 1972 ... 6.00
❑4, Mar 1973 ... 6.00
❑5, Jun 1973 ... 6.00
❑6, Sep 1973 ... 4.00
❑7, Dec 1973 ... 4.00
❑8, Mar 1974 ... 4.00
❑9, Jun 1974 ... 4.00
❑10, Sep 1974 ... 4.00
❑11, Dec 1974 ... 4.00
❑12, Mar 1975 ... 4.00
❑13, May 1975 ... 4.00
❑14, Jul 1975 ... 4.00
❑15, Aug 1975 ... 4.00
❑16, Nov 1975 ... 4.00
❑17, Feb 1976, Original series ends (1976) ... 4.00
❑18, ca. 1982, One-shot continuation of series (1982) ... 2.50

BRUCE LEE
Malibu

❑1, Jul 1994 ... 2.95
❑2, Aug 1994 ... 2.95
❑3, Sep 1994 ... 2.95
❑4, Oct 1994 ... 2.95
❑5, Nov 1994 ... 2.95
❑6, Dec 1994 ... 2.95

BRUCE WAYNE: AGENT OF S.H.I.E.L.D.
Marvel / Amalgam

❑1, Apr 1996 ... 1.95

BRU-HED
Schism

❑1, Mar 1994 1: Bru-Hed. 1: Grrim & Grritty ... 3.00
❑1/Ashcan, ca. 1993; Test-Market Ashcan edition 1: Bru-Hed. 1: Grrim & Grritty. ... 3.00
❑1/Variant, Mar 1994; metallic foil logo on cover ... 2.50
❑2, Jul 1994, b&w ... 2.50
❑3, ca. 1995, b&w; D: Grrim & Grritty. Pete Bickford thanked on letters page ... 2.50
❑4, ca. 1996 ... 2.50

BRU-HED'S BREATHTAKING BEAUTIES
Schism

❑1, Jun 1995, b&w pin-ups, cardstock cover ... 2.50

BRU-HED'S BUNNIES, BADDIES & BUDDIES
Schism

❑1 ... 2.50

BRU-HED'S GUIDE TO GETTIN' GIRLS NOW!
Schism

❑1 ... 2.95
❑2 ... 2.50

BRUISER
Anthem

❑1, Feb 1994 ... 2.45

BRUISER
Mythic

❑1, No cover price ... 2.50

BRUNNER'S BEAUTIES
Fantagraphics / Eros

❑1; pin-ups, adult, b&w ... 4.95

BRUTE
Atlas-Seaboard

❑1, Feb 1975 O: Brute. 1: Brute. ... 7.00
❑2, Apr 1975 ... 5.00
❑3, Jul 1975 ... 5.00

BRUTE FORCE
Marvel

❑1, Aug 1990 ... 1.00
❑2, Sep 1990 ... 1.00
❑3, Oct 1990 ... 1.00
❑4, Nov 1990 ... 1.00

B-SIDES
Marvel

❑1, Nov 2002, b&w ... 3.50
❑2, Dec 2002; No indicia inside ... 2.99
❑3, Jan 2003 ... 2.99

B'TX
Tokyopop

❑1, Jan 2006 ... 9.95

BUBBLEGUM CRISIS: GRAND MAL
Dark Horse

❑1, Mar 1994 ... 2.50
❑2, Apr 1994 ... 2.50
❑3, May 1994 ... 2.50
❑4, Jun 1994 ... 2.50

BUCKAROO BANZAI
Marvel

❑1, Dec 1984 ... 1.00
❑2, Feb 1985 ... 1.00

BUCK GODOT, ZAP GUN FOR HIRE
Palliard

❑1, Jul 1993, PF (w); PF (a) ... 3.50
❑2, Nov 1993, PF (w); PF (a) ... 3.00
❑3, Apr 1994, PF (w); PF (a) ... 2.95
❑4, Aug 1994, PF (w); PF (a) ... 2.95
❑5, Sep 1995, PF (w); PF (a) ... 2.95
❑6, Oct 1995, PF (w); PF (a) ... 2.95
❑7, Aug 1997, PF (w); PF (a) ... 2.95
❑8, Mar 1998, PF (w); PF (a) ... 2.95

Other grades: Multiply price above by 5/6 for VF/NM • 2/3 for VERY FINE • 1/3 for FINE • 1/5 for VERY GOOD • 1/8 for GOOD

Buckaroo Banzai

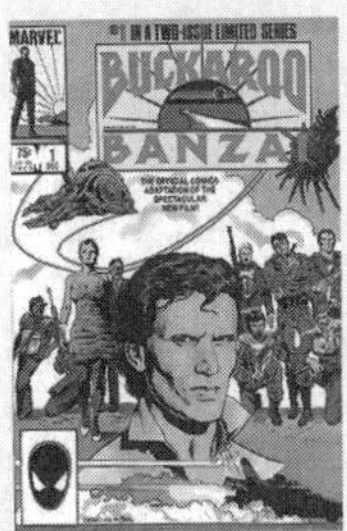

Cult-movie adventures adapted for comics

©Marvel

Buck Rogers (Gold Key/Whitman)

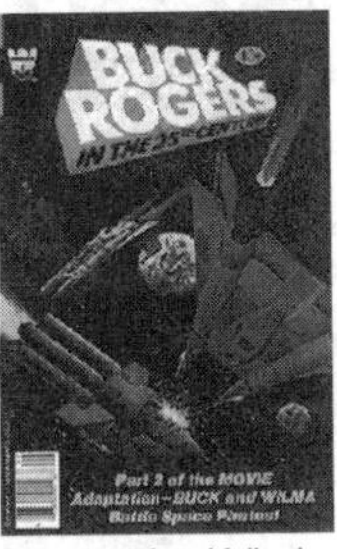

Series resurfaced following TV show launch

©Gold Key

Bucky O'Hare

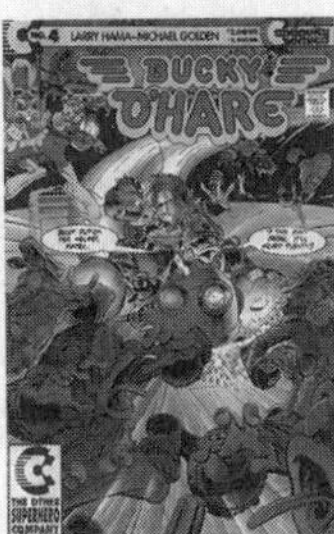

Kid is trapped in dimension of funny animals

©Continuity

Buffy the Vampire Slayer

Lots and lots of Sarah Michelle Gellar photos

©Dark Horse

Bugs Bunny (Gold Key)

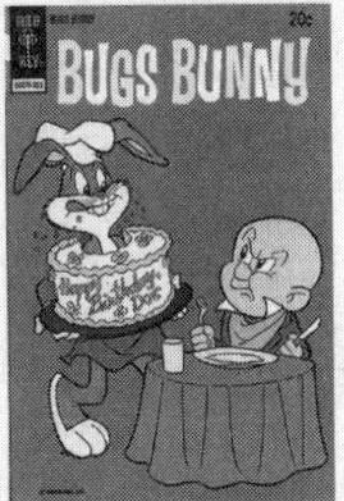

Wascally wabbit wreaks woe, wegulawly

©Gold Key

	N-MINT

BUCK ROGERS (GOLD KEY/WHITMAN)
Gold Key / Whitman

- ❑1, Oct 1964, Gold Key publishes 36.00
- ❑2, Aug 1979 ...... 5.00
- ❑3, Sep 1979 ...... 4.00
- ❑4, Oct 1979 ...... 4.00
- ❑5, Dec 1979 ...... 3.00
- ❑6, Feb 1980 ...... 3.00
- ❑7, Apr 1980, Series begins under Whitman imprint 3.00
- ❑8, ca. 1980 ...... 3.00
- ❑9, ca. 1980 ...... 3.00
- ❑11, Feb 1981, #10 never printed 3.00
- ❑12, Jul 1981 ...... 3.00
- ❑13, Oct 1981 ...... 3.00
- ❑14, Feb 1982 ...... 3.00
- ❑15, ca. 1982 ...... 3.00
- ❑16, May 1982 ...... 3.00

BUCK ROGERS COMICS MODULE
TSR

- ❑1; Listed as 1 of 3 ...... 2.95
- ❑2 ...... 2.95
- ❑3 ...... 2.95
- ❑4 ...... 2.95
- ❑5 ...... 2.95
- ❑6 ...... 2.95
- ❑7 ...... 2.95
- ❑8 ...... 2.95
- ❑9 ...... 2.95

BUCKY O'HARE
Continuity

- ❑1, Jan 1991 ...... 2.50
- ❑2, May 1991 ...... 2.00
- ❑3, Jul 1991 ...... 2.00
- ❑4, Dec 1991 ...... 2.00
- ❑5, Mar 1992 ...... 2.00

BUDDHA ON THE ROAD
Aeon

- ❑1, Aug 1996 ...... 2.95
- ❑2, Nov 1996 ...... 2.95
- ❑3, Feb 1997 ...... 2.95
- ❑4, May 1997 ...... 2.95
- ❑5, Sep 1997 ...... 2.95
- ❑6, Mar 1997, Indicia says 1997, should be 1998 ...... 2.95

BUFFALO BILL JR.
Dell

- ❑7, Feb 1958, First six issues appeared as Dell Four Color 30.00
- ❑8, May 1958 ...... 30.00
- ❑9, Aug 1958 ...... 30.00
- ❑10, Nov 1958 ...... 30.00
- ❑11, Feb 1959 ...... 30.00
- ❑12, May 1959 ...... 30.00
- ❑13, Aug 1959 ...... 30.00

BUFFALO BILL JR. (2ND SERIES)
Gold Key

- ❑1, Jun 1965, reprints Four-Color #798 30.00

BUFFALO WINGS
Antarctic

- ❑1, Sep 1993, b&w 2.50
- ❑2, Nov 1993, b&w 2.75

	N-MINT

BUFFY THE VAMPIRE SLAYER
Dark Horse

- ❑½, Wizard promotional edition 4.00
- ❑½/Gold, Wizard promotional edition; Gold logo 8.00
- ❑½/Platinum, Wizard promotional edition; Platinum logo 10.00
- ❑1, Sep 1998, no month of publication 5.00
- ❑1/A, Sep 1998, Another Universe foil logo variant 10.00
- ❑1/B, Sep 1998, Another Universe edition; depicts Buffy holding gate without foil logo 5.00
- ❑1/Gold, Sep 1998, Gold art cover with gold foil logooil logo 10.00
- ❑1/Variant, Sep 1998 ...... 10.00
- ❑1/2nd, Feb 1999 ...... 4.00
- ❑2, Oct 1998 ...... 4.00
- ❑2/Variant, Oct 1998 ...... 5.00
- ❑3, Nov 1998, no month of publication 5.00
- ❑3/Variant, Nov 1998 ...... 5.00
- ❑4, Dec 1998 ...... 4.00
- ❑4/Variant, Dec 1998 ...... 4.00
- ❑5, Jan 1999 ...... 4.00
- ❑5/Variant, Jan 1999 ...... 4.00
- ❑6, Feb 1999 ...... 3.50
- ❑6/Variant, Feb 1999 ...... 3.50
- ❑7, Mar 1999 ...... 3.50
- ❑7/Variant, Mar 1999 ...... 3.50
- ❑8, Apr 1999 ...... 3.50
- ❑8/Variant, Apr 1999 ...... 3.50
- ❑9, May 1999 ...... 3.50
- ❑9/Variant, May 1999 ...... 3.50
- ❑10, Jun 1999, teen magazine-style cover; teen magazine-style cover ... 3.50
- ❑10/Variant, Jun 1999 ...... 3.50
- ❑11, Jul 1999 ...... 3.50
- ❑11/Variant, Jul 1999 ...... 3.50
- ❑12, Aug 1999 ...... 3.50
- ❑12/Variant, Aug 1999 ...... 3.50
- ❑13, Sep 1999 ...... 3.50
- ❑13/Variant, Sep 1999 ...... 3.50
- ❑14, Oct 1999 ...... 3.50
- ❑14/Variant, Oct 1999 ...... 3.50
- ❑15, Nov 1999 ...... 3.50
- ❑15/Variant, Nov 1999 ...... 3.50
- ❑16, Dec 1999 ...... 3.50
- ❑16/Variant, Dec 1999 ...... 3.50
- ❑17, Jan 2000 ...... 3.50
- ❑17/Variant, Jan 2000 ...... 3.50
- ❑18, Feb 2000 ...... 3.50
- ❑18/Variant, Feb 2000 ...... 3.50
- ❑19, Mar 2000 ...... 3.50
- ❑19/Variant, Mar 2000 ...... 3.50
- ❑20, Apr 2000 ...... 3.50
- ❑20/Variant, Apr 2000 ...... 3.00
- ❑21, May 2000 ...... 3.00
- ❑21/Variant, May 2000 ...... 3.00
- ❑22, Jun 2000 ...... 3.00
- ❑22/Variant, Jun 2000 ...... 3.00
- ❑23, Jul 2000 ...... 3.00
- ❑23/Variant, Jul 2000 ...... 3.00
- ❑24, Aug 2000 ...... 3.00
- ❑24/Variant, Aug 2000 ...... 3.00
- ❑25, Sep 2000 ...... 3.00

	N-MINT

- ❑25/Variant, Sep 2000 ...... 3.00
- ❑26, Oct 2000 ...... 3.00
- ❑26/Variant, Oct 2000 ...... 3.00
- ❑27, Nov 2000 ...... 3.00
- ❑27/Variant, Nov 2000 ...... 3.00
- ❑28, Dec 2000 ...... 3.00
- ❑28/Variant, Dec 2000 ...... 3.00
- ❑29, Jan 2001 ...... 3.00
- ❑29/Variant, Jan 2001 ...... 3.00
- ❑30, Feb 2001 ...... 3.00
- ❑30/Variant, Feb 2001 ...... 3.00
- ❑31, Mar 2001 ...... 3.00
- ❑31/Variant, Mar 2001 ...... 3.00
- ❑32, Apr 2001 ...... 3.00
- ❑32/Variant, Apr 2001 ...... 3.00
- ❑33, May 2001 ...... 3.00
- ❑33/Variant, May 2001 ...... 3.00
- ❑34, Jun 2001 ...... 3.00
- ❑34/Variant, Jun 2001 ...... 3.00
- ❑35, Jul 2001 ...... 3.00
- ❑35/Variant, Jul 2001 ...... 3.00
- ❑36, Aug 2001 ...... 3.00
- ❑36/Variant, Aug 2001 ...... 3.00
- ❑37, Sep 2001 ...... 3.00
- ❑37/Variant, Sep 2001 ...... 3.00
- ❑38, Oct 2001 ...... 3.00
- ❑38/Variant, Oct 2001 ...... 3.00
- ❑39, Nov 2001 ...... 3.00
- ❑39/Variant, Nov 2001 ...... 3.00
- ❑40, Dec 2001 ...... 3.00
- ❑40/Variant, Dec 2001 ...... 3.00
- ❑41, Jan 2002 ...... 3.00
- ❑41/Variant, Jan 2002 ...... 3.00
- ❑42, Feb 2002 ...... 3.00
- ❑42/Variant, Feb 2002 ...... 3.00
- ❑43, Mar 2002 ...... 3.00
- ❑43/Variant, Mar 2002 ...... 3.00
- ❑44, Apr 2002 ...... 3.00
- ❑44/Variant, Apr 2002 ...... 3.00
- ❑45, May 2002 ...... 3.00
- ❑45/Variant, May 2002 ...... 3.00
- ❑46, Jun 2002 ...... 3.00
- ❑46/Variant, Jun 2002 ...... 3.00
- ❑47, Jul 2002 ...... 3.00
- ❑47/Variant, Jul 2002 ...... 3.00
- ❑48, Aug 2002 ...... 3.00
- ❑48/Variant, Aug 2002 ...... 3.00
- ❑49, Sep 2002 ...... 3.00
- ❑49/Variant, Sep 2002 ...... 3.00
- ❑50, Oct 2002 ...... 3.50
- ❑50/Variant, Oct 2002 ...... 3.50
- ❑51, Nov 2002 ...... 3.00
- ❑51/Variant, Nov 2002 ...... 3.00
- ❑52, Dec 2002 ...... 3.00
- ❑52/Variant, Dec 2002 ...... 3.00
- ❑53, Jan 2003 ...... 3.00
- ❑53/Variant, Jan 2003 ...... 3.00
- ❑54, Feb 2003 ...... 3.00
- ❑55, Mar 2003 ...... 3.00
- ❑56, Apr 2003 ...... 3.00
- ❑57, May 2003 ...... 3.00
- ❑58, Jun 2003 ...... 2.99
- ❑59, Jul 2003 ...... 2.99
- ❑60, Aug 2003 ...... 2.99

Other grades: Multiply price above by 5/6 for VF/NM • 2/3 for VERY FINE • 1/3 for FINE • 1/5 for VERY GOOD • 1/8 for GOOD

- ❑61, Sep 2003 ... 2.99
- ❑62, Oct 2003 ... 2.99
- ❑63, Nov 2003 ... 2.99
- ❑Annual 1999, Aug 1999, squarebound; 1999 Annual ... 5.50

BUFFY THE VAMPIRE SLAYER: ANGEL
DARK HORSE

- ❑1, May 1999 ... 4.00
- ❑1/Variant, May 1999 ... 4.00
- ❑2, Jun 1999 ... 3.00
- ❑2/Variant, Jun 1999 ... 3.00
- ❑3, Jul 1999 ... 3.00
- ❑3/Variant, Jul 1999 ... 3.00
- ❑Book 1 ... 3.50

BUFFY THE VAMPIRE SLAYER: CHAOS BLEEDS
DARK HORSE

- ❑1, Jun 2003 ... 2.99

BUFFY THE VAMPIRE SLAYER: GILES
DARK HORSE

- ❑1, Oct 2000 ... 3.00
- ❑1/Variant, Oct 2000 ... 3.00

BUFFY THE VAMPIRE SLAYER: HAUNTED
DARK HORSE

- ❑1, Dec 2001 ... 3.00
- ❑2, Jan 2002 ... 3.00
- ❑3, Feb 2002 ... 3.00
- ❑4, Mar 2002 ... 3.00

BUFFY THE VAMPIRE SLAYER: JONATHAN
DARK HORSE

- ❑1, Jan 2001 ... 3.00
- ❑1/Variant, Jan 2001 ... 3.00
- ❑1/Gold, Jan 2001 ... 10.00
- ❑1/Platinum, Jan 2001 ... 20.00

BUFFY THE VAMPIRE SLAYER: LOST AND FOUND
DARK HORSE

- ❑1, Mar 2002, b&w ... 3.00

BUFFY THE VAMPIRE SLAYER: LOVER'S WALK
DARK HORSE

- ❑1, Feb 2001 ... 3.00
- ❑1/Variant, Feb 2001 ... 3.00
- ❑1/Dynamic, Feb 2001 ... 10.00

BUFFY THE VAMPIRE SLAYER: OZ
DARK HORSE

- ❑1, Jul 2001 ... 3.00
- ❑1/Variant, Jul 2001 ... 3.00
- ❑2, Aug 2001 ... 3.00
- ❑2/Variant, Aug 2001 ... 3.00
- ❑3, Sep 2001 ... 3.00
- ❑3/Variant, Sep 2001 ... 3.00

BUFFY THE VAMPIRE SLAYER: REUNION
DARK HORSE

- ❑1, Jun 2002, b&w ... 3.50

BUFFY THE VAMPIRE SLAYER: SPIKE AND DRU
DARK HORSE

- ❑1, Apr 1999 ... 2.95
- ❑2, May 1999 ... 2.95
- ❑3, Jun 1999 ... 2.95
- ❑3/Variant, Dec 2000 ... 2.95

BUFFY THE VAMPIRE SLAYER, TALES OF THE SLAYERS
DARK HORSE

- ❑1/Variant, Oct 2002 ... 3.50
- ❑1, Oct 2002 ... 3.50

BUFFY THE VAMPIRE SLAYER: THE DUST WALTZ
DARK HORSE

- ❑1, Oct 1998 ... 9.95

BUFFY THE VAMPIRE SLAYER: THE ORIGIN
DARK HORSE

- ❑1, Jan 1999 ... 3.50
- ❑1/Ltd., Jan 1999; Limited edition foil cover; Limited edition foil cover ... 15.00
- ❑1/Variant, Jan 1999 ... 4.00
- ❑2, Feb 1999 ... 2.95
- ❑2/Variant, Feb 1999 ... 2.95

- ❑3, Mar 1999 ... 2.95
- ❑3/Variant, Mar 1999 ... 2.95

BUFFY THE VAMPIRE SLAYER: WILLOW & TARA
DARK HORSE

- ❑1, Apr 2001 ... 5.00
- ❑1/Variant, Apr 2001 ... 5.00

BUFFY THE VAMPIRE SLAYER: WILLOW & TARA: WILDERNESS
DARK HORSE

- ❑1, Aug 2002 ... 2.99
- ❑2, Sep 2002 ... 2.99

BUG (MARVEL)
MARVEL

- ❑1, Mar 1997 ... 2.99

BUG (PLANET-X)
PLANET-X

- ❑1 ... 1.50

BUG & STUMP
AAARGH!

- ❑1, Aut 1993, b&w; Australian, distributed in U.S. ... 2.95
- ❑2, Spr 1994, b&w; Australian, distributed in U.S. ... 2.95

BUGBOY
IMAGE

- ❑1, Jun 1998, b&w ... 3.95

B.U.G.G.'S
ACETYLENE COMICS

- ❑Ashcan 1, ca. 2001 ... 2.25
- ❑1, ca. 2001 ... 2.25
- ❑2, ca. 2001 ... 2.25

B.U.G.G.'S (VOL. 2)
ACETYLENE COMICS

- ❑1/A, ca. 2001 ... 2.50
- ❑1, ca. 2001 ... 2.25
- ❑2, ca. 2001 ... 2.25
- ❑3/A, ca. 2001; Fighting on cover, orange stripe down center ... 2.50
- ❑3, ca. 2001; Woman posing on cover ... 2.50
- ❑4, ca. 2001 ... 2.50

BUGHOUSE (CAT-HEAD)
CAT-HEAD

- ❑1, ca. 1994, b&w ... 2.95
- ❑2, Nov 1994, b&w ... 2.95
- ❑3, Jun 1995, b&w ... 2.95
- ❑4, ca. 1996, b&w; cardstock cover ... 2.95
- ❑5, Spr 1997, b&w ... 2.95

BUG-HUNTERS
TRIDENT

- ❑1, b&w ... 5.95

BUGNUT
COMICOSLEY

- ❑1, Jul 1999 ... 2.95

BUGS BUNNY (DELL)
DELL

- ❑51, Oct 1956 ... 25.00
- ❑52, Dec 1956 ... 25.00
- ❑53, Feb 1957 ... 25.00
- ❑54, Apr 1957 ... 25.00
- ❑55, Jun 1957 ... 25.00
- ❑56, Aug 1957 ... 25.00
- ❑57, Oct 1957 ... 25.00
- ❑58, Dec 1957 ... 25.00
- ❑59, Feb 1958 ... 25.00
- ❑60, Apr 1958 ... 25.00
- ❑61, Jun 1958 ... 20.00
- ❑62, Aug 1958 ... 20.00
- ❑63, Oct 1958 ... 20.00
- ❑64, Dec 1958 ... 20.00
- ❑65, Feb 1959 ... 20.00
- ❑66, Apr 1959 ... 20.00
- ❑67, Jun 1959 ... 20.00
- ❑68, Aug 1959 ... 20.00
- ❑69, Oct 1959 ... 20.00
- ❑70, Dec 1959 ... 20.00
- ❑71, Feb 1960 ... 20.00
- ❑72, Apr 1960 ... 20.00
- ❑73, Jun 1960 ... 20.00
- ❑74, Aug 1960 ... 20.00
- ❑75, Oct 1960 ... 20.00
- ❑76, Dec 1960 ... 20.00
- ❑77, Mar 1961 ... 20.00
- ❑78, May 1961 ... 20.00

- ❑79, Jul 1961 ... 20.00
- ❑80, Sep 1961 ... 20.00
- ❑81, Nov 1961 ... 15.00
- ❑82, Jan 1962 ... 15.00
- ❑83, Mar 1962 ... 15.00
- ❑84, May 1962 ... 15.00
- ❑85, Jul 1962 ... 15.00

BUGS BUNNY (GOLD KEY)
GOLD KEY

- ❑86, Oct 1962 ... 7.00
- ❑87, Dec 1962 ... 7.00
- ❑88, Mar 1963 ... 7.00
- ❑89, Jun 1963 ... 7.00
- ❑90, Sep 1963 ... 7.00
- ❑91, Dec 1963 ... 7.00
- ❑92, Mar 1964 ... 7.00
- ❑93, May 1964 ... 7.00
- ❑94, Jul 1964 ... 7.00
- ❑95, Sep 1964 ... 7.00
- ❑96, Nov 1964 ... 7.00
- ❑97, Jan 1965 ... 7.00
- ❑98, Mar 1965 ... 7.00
- ❑99, May 1965 ... 7.00
- ❑100, Jul 1965 ... 7.00
- ❑101, Sep 1965 ... 7.00
- ❑102, Nov 1965 ... 6.00
- ❑103, Jan 1966 ... 6.00
- ❑104, Mar 1966 ... 6.00
- ❑105, May 1966 ... 6.00
- ❑106, Jul 1966 ... 6.00
- ❑107, Sep 1966 ... 6.00
- ❑108, Nov 1966 ... 6.00
- ❑109, Jan 1967 ... 6.00
- ❑110, Mar 1967 ... 6.00
- ❑111, May 1967 ... 6.00
- ❑112, Jul 1967 ... 6.00
- ❑113, Sep 1967 ... 6.00
- ❑114, Nov 1967 ... 6.00
- ❑115, Jan 1968 ... 6.00
- ❑116, Mar 1968 ... 6.00
- ❑117, May 1968 ... 6.00
- ❑118, Jul 1968 ... 6.00
- ❑119, Sep 1968 ... 6.00
- ❑120, Nov 1968 ... 6.00
- ❑121, Jan 1969 ... 6.00
- ❑122, Mar 1969 ... 6.00
- ❑123, May 1969 ... 6.00
- ❑124, Jul 1969 ... 6.00
- ❑125, Sep 1969 ... 6.00
- ❑126, Nov 1969 ... 6.00
- ❑127, Jan 1970 ... 6.00
- ❑128, Mar 1970 ... 6.00
- ❑129, May 1970 ... 6.00
- ❑130, Jul 1970 ... 6.00
- ❑131, Sep 1970 ... 6.00
- ❑132, Nov 1970 ... 6.00
- ❑133, Jan 1971 ... 6.00
- ❑134, Mar 1971 ... 6.00
- ❑135, May 1971 ... 6.00
- ❑136, Jul 1971 ... 6.00
- ❑137, Sep 1971 ... 6.00
- ❑138, Oct 1971 ... 6.00
- ❑139, Dec 1971 ... 6.00
- ❑140, Jan 1971 ... 6.00
- ❑141, Mar 1972 ... 6.00
- ❑142, May 1972 ... 6.00
- ❑143, Jul 1972 ... 6.00
- ❑144, Sep 1972 ... 6.00
- ❑145, Oct 1972 ... 6.00
- ❑146, Dec 1972 ... 6.00
- ❑147, Jan 1973 ... 6.00
- ❑148, Mar 1973 ... 6.00
- ❑149, May 1973 ... 6.00
- ❑150, Jul 1973 ... 6.00
- ❑151, Aug 1973 ... 5.00
- ❑152, Sep 1973 ... 5.00
- ❑153, Nov 1973 ... 5.00
- ❑154, Jan 1974 ... 5.00
- ❑155, Mar 1974 ... 5.00
- ❑156, May 1974 ... 5.00
- ❑157, Jul 1974 ... 5.00
- ❑158, Aug 1974, Bugs becomes a telekinetic ... 5.00
- ❑159, Sep 1974 ... 5.00
- ❑160, Nov 1974 ... 5.00
- ❑161, Jan 1975 ... 5.00

Other grades: Multiply price above by 5/6 for VF/NM • 2/3 for VERY FINE • 1/3 for FINE • 1/5 for VERY GOOD • 1/8 for GOOD

Bulletproof Monk

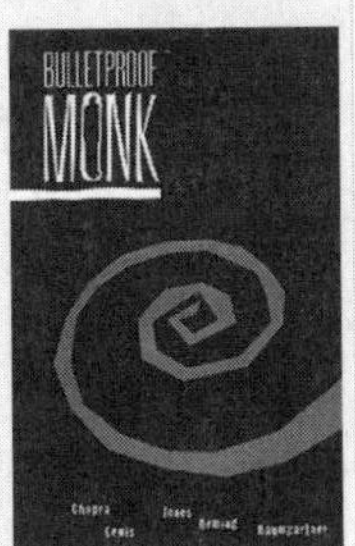

Ancient legends meet modern gang wars

©Image

Bullwinkle and Rocky (Gold Key)

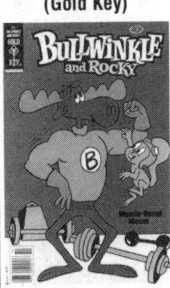

"Now here's something you'll really like!"

©Gold Key

Burke's Law

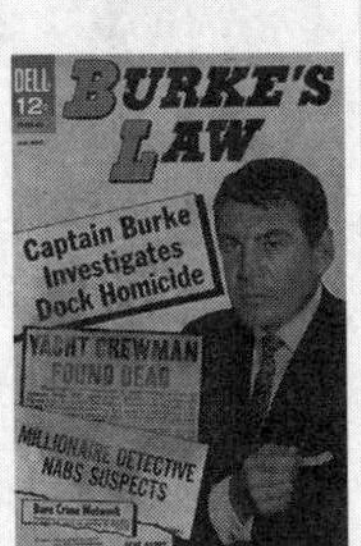

TV police drama spawns comics spinoff

©Dell

Burrito

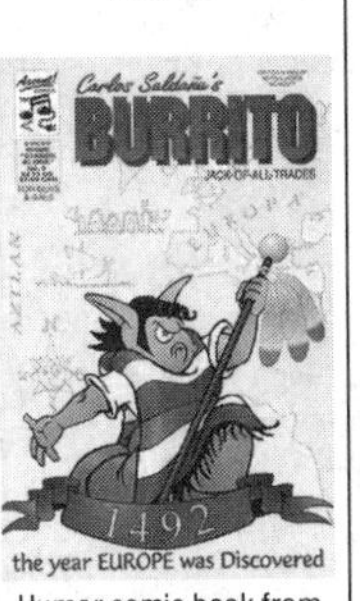

Humor comic book from Carlos Saldaña

©Accent!

Butcher

Native American adventure from Mike Baron

©DC

N-MINT

❑162, Mar 1975 5.00
❑163, May 1975 5.00
❑164, Jul 1975 5.00
❑165, Aug 1975 5.00
❑166, Sep 1975 5.00
❑167, Oct 1975 5.00
❑168, Nov 1975 5.00
❑169, Jan 1976 5.00
❑170, Mar 1976 5.00
❑171, Apr 1976 5.00
❑172, May 1976 5.00
❑173, Jun 1976 5.00
❑174, Jul 1976 5.00
❑175, Aug 1976 5.00
❑176, Sep 1976 5.00
❑177, Oct 1976 5.00
❑178, Nov 1976 5.00
❑179, Dec 1976 5.00
❑180, Jan 1977 5.00
❑181, Feb 1977 5.00
❑182, Mar 1977 5.00
❑183, Apr 1977 5.00
❑184, May 1977 5.00
❑185, Jun 1977 5.00
❑186, Jul 1977 5.00
❑187, Aug 1977 5.00
❑188, Sep 1977 5.00
❑189, Oct 1977 5.00
❑190, Nov 1977 5.00
❑191, Dec 1977 5.00
❑192, Jan 1978 5.00
❑193, Feb 1978 5.00
❑194, Mar 1978 5.00
❑195, Apr 1978 5.00
❑196, May 1978 5.00
❑197, Jun 1978 5.00
❑198, Jul 1978 5.00
❑199, Aug 1978 5.00
❑200, Sep 1978 5.00
❑201, Oct 1978 3.00
❑202, Nov 1978 3.00
❑203, Dec 1978 3.00
❑204, Jan 1979 3.00
❑205, Feb 1979 3.00
❑206, Mar 1979 3.00
❑207, Apr 1979 3.00
❑208, May 1979 3.00
❑209, Jun 1979 3.00
❑210, Jul 1979 3.00
❑211, Aug 1979 3.00
❑212, Sep 1979 3.00
❑213, Oct 1979 2.00
❑214, Nov 1979 2.00
❑215, Dec 1979 2.00
❑216, Jan 1980 2.00
❑217, Feb 1980 2.00
❑218, Mar 1980 2.00
❑219, ca. 1980 2.00
❑220, ca. 1980 2.00
❑221, Sep 1980 2.00
❑222, Nov 1980 2.00
❑223, Jan 1981 2.00
❑224, Mar 1981 2.00
❑225, Jun 1981 2.00

N-MINT

❑226, Jul 1981 2.00
❑227, Aug 1981 2.00
❑228, Sep 1981 2.00
❑229, Oct 1981 2.00
❑230, Nov 1981 2.00
❑231, Dec 1981 2.00
❑232, ca. 1982 2.00
❑233, ca. 1982 2.00
❑234, ca. 1982, (w) 2.00
❑235, ca. 1982 2.00
❑236, ca. 1982 2.00
❑237, ca. 1982 2.00
❑238, ca. 1982 2.00
❑239, ca. 1982 2.00
❑240, ca. 1982 2.00
❑241, ca. 1982 2.00
❑242, ca. 1983 2.00
❑243, Aug 1983 2.00
❑244, ca. 1983 2.00
❑245 2.00

BUGS BUNNY
DC

❑1, Jun 1990 2.00
❑2, Jul 1990 1.50
❑3, Aug 1990 1.50

BUGS BUNNY AND PORKY PIG
DELL

❑1, ca. 1965 26.00

BUGS BUNNY MONTHLY
DC

❑1 1.95
❑2 1.95
❑3 1.95

BUGS BUNNY WINTER FUN
GOLD KEY

❑1, Dec 1967 30.00

BUG'S GIFT
DISCOVERY

❑1 1.95

BUG WARS
AVALON COMMUNICATIONS / ACG

❑1, ca. 1998 2.95

BULLDOG
FIVE STAR

❑1 2.95

BULLET CROW, FOWL OF FORTUNE
ECLIPSE

❑1 2.00
❑2 2.00

BULLETPROOF
KNOWN ASSOCIATES

❑1, b&w 3.95

BULLETPROOF COMICS
WET PAINT GRAPHICS

❑1 2.25
❑2, May 1999 2.25
❑3, Sep 1999 2.25

BULLETPROOF MONK
IMAGE

❑1, Nov 1998 3.00

N-MINT

❑2, Dec 1998 3.00
❑3, Jan 1999 3.00

BULLETPROOF MONK: TALES OF THE BULLETPROOF MONK
IMAGE

❑1, Mar 2003 2.95

BULLETS AND BRACELETS
MARVEL / AMALGAM

❑1, Apr 1996 1.95

BULLSEYE GREATEST HITS
MARVEL

❑1, Nov 2004 2.99
❑2, Dec 2004 2.99
❑3, Jan 2005 2.99
❑4, Feb 2005 2.99
❑5, Mar 2005 2.99

BULLWINKLE
DELL

❑1, Jul 1962 100.00

BULLWINKLE AND ROCKY (GOLD KEY)
GOLD KEY

❑1, Nov 1962 90.00
❑2, Feb 1963 68.00
❑3, Apr 1972 45.00
❑4, Jul 1972 40.00
❑5, Sep 1972 40.00
❑6, Jan 1973, Reprints 28.00
❑7, Apr 1973, Reprints 28.00
❑8, Jul 1973 28.00
❑9, Oct 1973 28.00
❑10, Jan 1974 28.00
❑11, Apr 1974, Last issue of original run 28.00
❑12, Jun 1976, Series picks up after hiatus 14.00
❑13, Sep 1976 20.00
❑14, Dec 1976 16.00
❑15, Mar 1977 10.00
❑16, Jun 1977 10.00
❑17, Sep 1977 10.00
❑18, Dec 1977 10.00
❑19 10.00
❑20 10.00
❑21 8.00
❑22 8.00
❑23, Oct 1979 8.00
❑24, Dec 1979 8.00
❑25 8.00

BULLWINKLE AND ROCKY (CHARLTON)
CHARLTON

❑1, Jul 1970, poster 30.00
❑2, Sep 1970 18.00
❑3, Nov 1970 15.00
❑4, Jan 1971 12.00
❑5, Mar 1971 12.00
❑6, May 1971 12.00
❑7, Jul 1971 12.00

N-MINT

BULLWINKLE AND ROCKY (STAR)
MARVEL / STAR

- ❑1, Nov 1987 ... 2.00
- ❑2, Jan 1988 ... 1.50
- ❑3, Mar 1988 ... 1.50
- ❑4, May 1988 ... 1.50
- ❑5, Jul 1988 ... 1.50
- ❑6, Sep 1988 ... 1.50
- ❑7, Nov 1988 ... 1.50
- ❑8, Jan 1989; Marvel publishes ... 1.50
- ❑9, Mar 1989 ... 1.50
- ❑Book 1, Jan 1992 ... 4.95

BULLWINKLE & ROCKY (BLACKTHORNE)
BLACKTHORNE

- ❑1 ... 2.50
- ❑2 ... 2.50
- ❑3 ... 2.50
- ❑3D 1, Mar 1987 ... 2.50

BULLWINKLE FOR PRESIDENT IN 3-D
BLACKTHORNE

- ❑1, Mar 1987, b&w; no cover price ... 2.50

BULLWINKLE MOTHER MOOSE NURSERY POMES
DELL

- ❑1, May 1962 ... 85.00

BUMBERCOMIX
STARHEAD

- ❑1; Giveaway from arts festival ... 1.00

BUNKER
IMAGE

- ❑Book 1, ca. 2003 ... 9.95

BUNNY TOWN
RADIO

- ❑1, Jan 2002, b&w ... 2.95

BURGER BOMB
FUNNY BOOK INSTITUTE

- ❑1, Nov 1999 ... 2.95
- ❑½, Mar 2000, b&w ... 2.95

BURGLAR BILL
IMAGE

- ❑1 ... 3.00
- ❑2 2005 ... 3.00
- ❑3, Jul 2005 ... 2.95
- ❑4 2005 ...

BURIAL OF THE RATS (BRAM STOKER'S...)
ROGER CORMAN'S COSMIC COMICS

- ❑1 ... 2.50
- ❑2, May 1995 ... 2.50

BURIED TERROR
NEC

- ❑1, Mar 1995 ... 2.75

BURIED TREASURE
PURE IMAGINATION

- ❑1 ... 5.95
- ❑2 ... 5.95
- ❑3; moves to Caliber ... 5.95

BURIED TREASURE (2ND SERIES)
CALIBER

- ❑1; reprints, b&w ... 2.50
- ❑2; Reprints ... 2.50
- ❑3; reprints Frankenstein ... 2.50
- ❑4 ... 2.50

BURKE'S LAW
DELL

- ❑1, Jan 1964 ... 24.00
- ❑2, ca. 1964 ... 20.00
- ❑3, Mar 1965 ... 20.00

BURRITO
ACCENT!

- ❑1, Jan 1995 ... 2.75
- ❑2, Apr 1995 ... 2.75
- ❑3, Jul 1995 ... 2.75
- ❑4, Nov 1995 ... 2.75
- ❑5, Jul 1996 ... 2.75

BUSHIDO
ETERNITY

- ❑1, Jul 1988 ... 1.95
- ❑2 ... 1.95
- ❑3 ... 1.95
- ❑4 ... 1.95

N-MINT

BUSHIDO BLADE OF ZATOICHI WALRUS
SOLSON

- ❑1 ... 2.00
- ❑2, ca. 1987, b&w ... 2.00

BUSHWHACKED
FANTAGRAPHICS / EROS

- ❑1 ... 2.95

BUSTER
CRISIS

- ❑1 ... 2.50
- ❑2 ... 2.50

BUSTER THE AMAZING BEAR
URSUS

- ❑1, Aug 1992; says Aug 93 on cover, Aug 92 in indicia; Surprise Poster Insert ... 2.50
- ❑2, Oct 1993 ... 2.50
- ❑2/2nd, Oct 1994 ... 2.50
- ❑3, Jan 1994 ... 2.50
- ❑4, May 1994 ... 2.50
- ❑5, Nov 1994 ... 2.50

BUSTLINE COMBAT
FANTAGRAPHICS / EROS

- ❑1, May 1999 ... 2.95

BUTCHER
DC

- ❑1, May 1990 1: John Butcher. ... 2.50
- ❑2, Jun 1990 ... 2.00
- ❑3, Jul 1990 ... 2.00
- ❑4, Aug 1990 ... 2.00
- ❑5, Sep 1990 ... 2.00

BUTCHER KNIGHT
IMAGE

- ❑1/A, Dec 2000; Demon's teeth cover ... 2.50
- ❑1/B, Dec 2000; Woman standing next to demon on cover ... 2.50
- ❑1/C, Dec 2000; Woman posing on demon on cover ... 2.50
- ❑1/D, Dec 2000; White cover ... 2.50
- ❑2, Jan 2001 ... 2.50
- ❑3, Apr 2001 ... 2.95
- ❑4, May 2001 ... 2.95

BUTT BISCUIT
FANTAGRAPHICS

- ❑1 ... 2.25
- ❑2 ... 2.25
- ❑3, Sep 1992 ... 2.25

BUTTERSCOTCH
FANTAGRAPHICS / EROS

- ❑1 ... 2.50
- ❑2 ... 2.50
- ❑3 ... 2.50

BUTTON MAN: THE KILLING GAME
KITCHEN SINK

- ❑1, Aug 1995; oversized graphic novel ... 15.95

BUZ SAWYER QUARTERLY
DRAGON LADY

- ❑1, Nov 1986 ... 5.95
- ❑2, Apr 1987 ... 5.95
- ❑3, Apr 1987 ... 5.95

BUZZ
KITCHEN SINK

- ❑1 ... 2.95
- ❑2 ... 2.95
- ❑3 ... 2.95

BUZZ
MARVEL

- ❑1, Jul 2000 ... 2.99
- ❑2, Aug 2000 ... 2.99
- ❑3, Sep 2000 ... 2.99

BUZZ AND COLONEL TOAD
BELMONT

- ❑1 ... 2.50
- ❑2 ... 2.50
- ❑3, Jan 1998 ... 2.50

BUZZARD
CAT-HEAD

- ❑1 ... 3.00
- ❑2, Oct 1990 ... 3.00
- ❑3 ... 3.00
- ❑4 ... 3.00
- ❑5 ... 3.00

N-MINT

- ❑6, Aug 1992 ... 3.00
- ❑7, Feb 1993 ... 3.00
- ❑8 ... 3.00
- ❑9 ... 3.00
- ❑10 ... 3.00
- ❑11 ... 3.25
- ❑12 ... 3.50
- ❑13 ... 3.50
- ❑14 ... 3.50
- ❑15 ... 3.50
- ❑16 ... 3.50
- ❑17 ... 3.50
- ❑18 ... 3.75
- ❑19 ... 3.75
- ❑20 ... 3.75

BUZZBOY
SKYDOG

- ❑1, May 1998 ... 2.95
- ❑2, Aug 1998 ... 2.95
- ❑3, Oct 1998 ... 2.95
- ❑4, Win 1998 ... 2.95

BY BIZARRE HANDS
DARK HORSE

- ❑1, Apr 1994 ... 2.50
- ❑2, May 1994 ... 2.50
- ❑3, Jun 1994 ... 2.50

BY BIZARRE HANDS (JOE LANSDALE'S)
AVATAR

- ❑1, Apr 2004 ... 3.50
- ❑1/Red foil ... 10.00
- ❑1/Wraparound ... 5.00
- ❑2, May 2004 ... 3.50
- ❑2/Red foil ... 8.00
- ❑2/Wraparound ... 5.00
- ❑3 ... 3.50
- ❑3/Red foil ... 8.00
- ❑3/Wraparound ... 5.00
- ❑4 ... 3.50
- ❑4/Red foil ... 8.00
- ❑4/Wraparound ... 5.00
- ❑5 ... 3.50
- ❑5/Red foil ... 8.00
- ❑5/Wraparound ... 5.00
- ❑6 ... 3.50
- ❑6/Red foil ... 8.00
- ❑6/Wraparound ... 5.00

BY THE TIME I GET TO WAGGA WAGGA
HARRIER

- ❑1 ... 1.50

C•23
IMAGE

- ❑1, Apr 1998 1: Fluxus. 1: Zum. 1: A-Mortal. 1: The Hyperclan. 1: Armek. 1: Tronix. 1: Primaid. 1: Zenturion. 1: Protex. ... 5.00
- ❑1/Ashcan, Apr 1998 ... 4.00
- ❑2, May 1998 ... 2.50
- ❑2/Variant, May 1998 ... 2.00
- ❑3, Jun 1998; bound-in card ... 2.50
- ❑4, Jul 1998 ... 2.50
- ❑5, Aug 1998 ... 2.50
- ❑6, Sep 1998 ... 2.50
- ❑7, Oct 1998 ... 2.50
- ❑8, Nov 1998 ... 2.50
- ❑8/Variant, Nov 1998; alternate cover (group) ... 4.00

CABBOT: BLOODHUNTER
MAXIMUM

- ❑1, Jan 1997 ... 2.50

CABINET OF DR. CALIGARI
MONSTER

- ❑1, Apr 1992 ... 2.25
- ❑2, Jun 1992 ... 2.25
- ❑3, Sep 1992 ... 2.25

CABLE
MARVEL

- ❑-1, Jul 1997; JRo (w); Flashback; Alpha Flight, Vol. 2 preview ... 2.25
- ❑1, May 1993; Embossed cover ... 4.00
- ❑2, Jun 1993 ... 2.50
- ❑3, Jul 1993 AM, PS, TP, KGa, KJ, BWi (a) ... 2.50
- ❑4, Aug 1993 RL (a) ... 2.50

Other grades: Multiply price above by 5/6 for VF/NM • 2/3 for VERY FINE • 1/3 for FINE • 1/5 for VERY GOOD • 1/8 for GOOD

Cadillacs & Dinosaurs

Renamed version of Xenozoic Tales

©Marvel

Cage

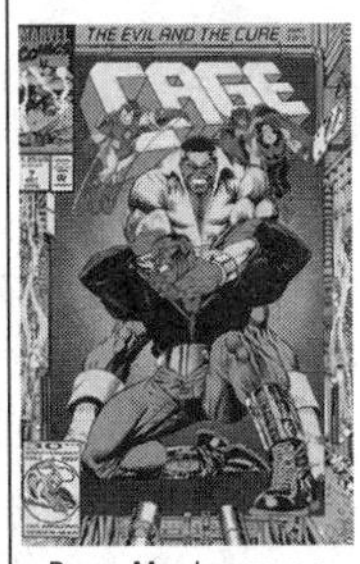

Power Man becomes a not-very-nice guy

©Marvel

Cage (2nd series)

A not-very-nice guy gets worse in "mature" title

©Marvel

Caliber Presents

Series had early appearance of The Crow

©Caliber

California Raisins in 3-D

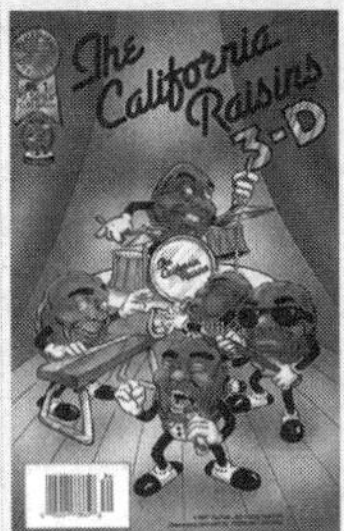

This fad was left out in the sun too long

©Blackthorne

	N-MINT
❑5, Nov 1993	2.50
❑6, Dec 1993 A: Other. A: Sinsear.	2.50
❑7, Jan 1994	2.50
❑8, Feb 1994	2.50
❑9, Mar 1994 A: Omega Red.	2.50
❑10, Apr 1994	2.50
❑11, May 1994 A: Colossus.	2.25
❑12, Jun 1994	2.25
❑13, Jul 1994	2.25
❑14, Aug 1994	2.25
❑15, Sep 1994	2.25
❑16, Oct 1994	2.25
❑16/Variant, Oct 1994; Prismatic foil cover	4.00
❑17, Nov 1994	1.50
❑17/Deluxe, Nov 1994; Deluxe edition	2.00
❑18, Dec 1994	1.50
❑18/Deluxe, Dec 1994; Deluxe edition	2.00
❑19, Jan 1995	1.50
❑19/Deluxe, Jan 1995; Deluxe edition	2.00
❑20, Feb 1995; A: X-Men. Legion Quest Addendum	1.50
❑20/Deluxe, Feb 1995; Deluxe edition; JPH (w); A: X-Men. Legion Quest Addendum	2.00
❑21, Jul 1995	2.00
❑22, Aug 1995	2.00
❑23, Sep 1995	2.00
❑24, Oct 1995; no issue number on cover	2.00
❑25, Nov 1995; Giant-size; JPH (w); enhanced wraparound fold-out cardstock cover; 25th Issue Extravaganza	4.00
❑26, Dec 1995 A: Weapon X.	2.00
❑27, Jan 1996 V: Sugar Man.	2.00
❑28, Feb 1996 V: Sugar Man.	2.00
❑29, Mar 1996 JPH (w)	2.00
❑30, Apr 1996; JPH (w); A: X-Man. Cable meets X-Man	2.00
❑31, May 1996 V: X-Man.	2.00
❑32, Jun 1996	2.00
❑33, Jul 1996	2.00
❑34, Aug 1996 V: Hulk.	2.00
❑35, Sep 1996 V: Apocalypse.	2.00
❑36, Oct 1996	2.00
❑37, Nov 1996 A: Weapon X.	2.00
❑38, Dec 1996 JPH (w); A: Micronauts.	2.00
❑39, Jan 1997 JPH (w); A: Micronauts.	2.00
❑40, Feb 1997	2.00
❑41, Mar 1997 A: Bishop.	2.00
❑42, Apr 1997	2.00
❑43, May 1997	2.00
❑44, Jun 1997 JRo (w)	2.00
❑45, Aug 1997; gatefold summary; Operation Zero Tolerance	2.00
❑46, Sep 1997; gatefold summary; JRo (w); Operation Zero Tolerance	2.00
❑47, Oct 1997; gatefold summary; Operation Zero Tolerance	2.00
❑48, Nov 1997; gatefold summary	2.00
❑49, Dec 1997; gatefold summary	2.00
❑50, Jan 1998; Giant-size	2.95
❑51, Feb 1998; gatefold summary	1.99
❑52, Mar 1998; gatefold summary	1.99
❑53, Apr 1998; gatefold summary	1.99
❑54, May 1998; gatefold summary A: Black Panther. V: Klaw.	1.99
❑55, Jun 1998; gatefold summary A: Domino.	1.99
❑56, Jul 1998; gatefold summary	1.99
❑57, Aug 1998; gatefold summary	1.99
❑58, Sep 1998; gatefold summary	1.99
❑59, Oct 1998; gatefold summary V: Zzzax.	1.99
❑60, Nov 1998; gatefold summary 1: Agent 18.	1.99
❑61, Nov 1998; gatefold summary; captured by S.H.I.E.L.D	1.99
❑62, Dec 1998; gatefold summary A: Nick Fury.	1.99
❑63, Jan 1999; gatefold summary A: Stryfe. V: Stryfe.	1.99
❑64, Feb 1999; gatefold summary O: Cable. A: Ozymandias.	1.99
❑65, Mar 1999 1: Acidroid. A: Rachel Summers.	1.99
❑66, Apr 1999	1.99
❑67, May 1999 A: Avengers.	1.99
❑68, Jun 1999 A: Avengers.	1.99
❑69, Jul 1999	1.99
❑70, Aug 1999	1.99
❑71, Sep 1999 V: Hound Master.	1.99
❑72, Oct 1999	1.99
❑73, Nov 1999	1.99
❑74, Dec 1999	1.99
❑75, Jan 2000	2.25
❑76, Feb 2000	2.25
❑77, Mar 2000	2.25
❑78, Apr 2000	2.25
❑79, May 2000	2.25
❑80, Jun 2000	2.25
❑81, Jul 2000	2.25
❑82, Aug 2000	2.25
❑83, Sep 2000	2.25
❑84, Oct 2000	2.25
❑85, Nov 2000	2.25
❑86, Dec 2000	2.25
❑87, Jan 2001	2.25
❑88, Feb 2001 A: Nightcrawler.	2.25
❑89, Mar 2001	2.25
❑90, Apr 2001	2.25
❑91, May 2001	2.25
❑92, Jun 2001	2.25
❑93, Jul 2001	2.25
❑94, Aug 2001	2.25
❑95, Sep 2001	2.25
❑96, Oct 2001	2.25
❑97, Nov 2001	2.25
❑98, Dec 2001	2.25
❑99, Jan 2002	2.25
❑100, Feb 2002; Giant-size	3.99
❑101, Mar 2002	2.25
❑102, Apr 2002	2.25
❑103, May 2002	2.25
❑104, Jun 2002	2.25
❑105, Jul 2002	2.25
❑106, Aug 2002	2.25
❑107, Sep 2002	2.25
❑Annual 1998, Cable/Machine Man '98; continues in Machine Man/Bastion '98; wraparound cover	2.99
❑Annual 1999, V: Sinister.	3.50

CABLE: BLOOD AND METAL

MARVEL

	N-MINT
❑1, Oct 1992 JR2 (a)	3.50
❑2, Nov 1992 JR2 (a)	3.00

CABLE/DEADPOOL

MARVEL

	N-MINT
❑1, May 2004	4.00
❑2, Jun 2004	2.99
❑3, Jul 2004	2.99
❑4, Aug 2004	2.99
❑5, Sep 2004	2.99
❑6, Oct 2004	2.99
❑7, Nov 2004	2.99
❑8, Dec 2004	2.99
❑9, Jan 2005	2.99
❑10, Feb 2005	2.99
❑11, Mar 2005	2.99
❑12, Apr 2005	2.99
❑13, May 2005	2.99
❑14, Jun 2005	2.99
❑15, Jul 2005	2.99
❑16, Aug 2005	2.99
❑17, Sep 2005	2.99
❑18, Oct 2005	2.99
❑19 2005	2.99
❑20 2005	2.99
❑21 2005	2.99
❑22, Jan 2006	2.99
❑23, Feb 2006	2.99
❑24, Mar 2006	2.99
❑25, Apr 2006	2.99
❑26, May 2006	2.99
❑27, Jun 2006	2.99
❑28, Jul 2006	2.99
❑29, Aug 2006	2.99

CABLE: SECOND GENESIS

MARVEL

	N-MINT
❑1, Sep 1999; collects New Mutants #1-2 and X-Force #1	3.99

CABLE TV

PARODY

	N-MINT
❑1, b&w	2.50

CADAVERA

MONSTER

	N-MINT
❑1, b&w	1.95
❑2, b&w	1.95

CADILLACS & DINOSAURS

MARVEL / EPIC

	N-MINT
❑1, Nov 1990; Reprints Xenozoic Tales #1 in color	2.50
❑2, Dec 1990; Reprints Xenozoic Tales #2 in color	2.50
❑3, Jan 1991; Reprints Xenozoic Tales #3 in color	2.50
❑4, Feb 1991; Reprints Xenozoic Tales #4 in color	2.50
❑5, Mar 1991; Reprints Xenozoic Tales #5 in color	2.50
❑6, Apr 1991; Reprints Xenozoic Tales #6 in color	2.50
❑3D 1, Jul 1992; 100 Page giant	3.95

CADILLACS & DINOSAURS (KITCHEN SINK)
KITCHEN SINK

❑1, Dec 1993 .... 4.00

CADILLACS & DINOSAURS (VOL. 2)
TOPPS

❑1, Feb 1994 .... 2.50
❑1/Variant, Feb 1994; foil cover 2.95
❑2, Mar 1994 .... 2.50
❑2/Deluxe, Mar 1994; poster by Moebius 2.50
❑3, Apr 1994 .... 2.50
❑3/Deluxe, Apr 1994; poster 2.50
❑4, Jun 1994 .... 2.50
❑4/Variant, Jun 1994 .... 2.50
❑5, Aug 1994 .... 2.50
❑6, Oct 1994 .... 2.50
❑7, Dec 1994 .... 2.50
❑8, Feb 1995 .... 2.50
❑9, Apr 1995 .... 2.50
❑10, Jun 1995 .... 2.50

CAFFEINE
SLAVE LABOR

❑1, Jan 1996 .... 2.95
❑2, Apr 1996 .... 2.95
❑3, Jul 1996 .... 2.95
❑4, Nov 1996 .... 2.95
❑5, Jan 1997 .... 2.95
❑6, Apr 1997 .... 2.95
❑7, Jul 1997; flip book 2.95
❑8, Nov 1997 .... 2.95
❑9, Jan 1998 .... 2.95
❑10, Apr 1998 .... 2.95

CAGE
MARVEL

❑1, Apr 1992 .... 3.00
❑2, May 1992 .... 1.00
❑3, Jun 1992 .... 1.00
❑4, Jul 1992 .... 1.00
❑5, Aug 1992 .... 1.00
❑6, Sep 1992 .... 1.00
❑7, Oct 1992 .... 1.00
❑8, Nov 1992 .... 1.00
❑9, Dec 1992 .... 1.00
❑10, Jan 1993 .... 1.00
❑11, Feb 1993 .... 1.00
❑12, Mar 1993; Giant-size; Iron Fist 1.00
❑13, Apr 1993 .... 1.00
❑14, May 1993 .... 1.00
❑15, Jun 1993 .... 1.00
❑16, Jul 1993 .... 1.00
❑17, Aug 1993 .... 1.00
❑18, Sep 1993 .... 1.00
❑19, Oct 1993 .... 1.00
❑20, Nov 1993 .... 1.00

CAGE (2ND SERIES)
MARVEL / MAX

❑1, Mar 2002 .... 4.00
❑2, May 2002 .... 2.99
❑3, Jul 2002 .... 2.99
❑4, Aug 2002 .... 2.99
❑5, Sep 2002 .... 2.99

CAGED HEAT 3000
ROGER CORMAN'S COSMIC COMICS

❑1 .... 2.50
❑2 .... 2.50

CAGES
TUNDRA

❑1, b&w 5.00
❑2, b&w 4.00
❑3, b&w 4.00
❑4 .... 4.00
❑5 .... 4.00
❑6 .... 4.00
❑7 .... 4.00
❑8 .... 4.00
❑9 .... 4.00
❑10 .... 5.00

CAIN
HARRIS

❑1; trading card 2.95
❑2, Oct 1993; two alternate covers 2.95

CALCULATED RISK
GENESIS

❑1, Mar 1990, b&w 2.00

CALIBER CHRISTMAS (1ST SERIES)
CALIBER

❑1 .... 5.95

CALIBER CHRISTMAS (2ND SERIES)
CALIBER

❑1, Dec 1998; Crow; sampler 3.95

CALIBER CORE
CALIBER

❑0, b&w; intro to imprint 2.95
❑Ashcan 1, b&w; No cover price; intro to imprint 1.00

CALIBER PRESENTS
CALIBER

❑1, Jan 1989, b&w; Crow 15.00
❑2 1989, b&w 2.50
❑3 1989, b&w 2.50
❑4 1989, b&w 2.50
❑5 1989, b&w 2.50
❑6, Aug 1989 .... 2.50
❑7, Nov 1989, b&w 2.50
❑8 .... 2.00
❑9 .... 2.50
❑10 .... 2.95
❑11 .... 2.95
❑12 .... 2.50
❑13 .... 2.95
❑14 .... 2.50
❑15, Sep 1990 .... 3.00
❑16 .... 3.00
❑17 .... 3.00
❑18 .... 3.00
❑19 .... 3.00
❑20 .... 3.00
❑21 .... 3.00
❑22 .... 3.00
❑23 .... 3.00
❑24 .... 3.00

CALIBER PRESENTS: CINDERELLA ON FIRE
CALIBER

❑1, ca. 1994, b&w 2.95

CALIBER PRESENTS: GENERATOR COMICS
CALIBER

❑1, b&w 2.95

CALIBER PRESENTS: HYBRID STORIES
CALIBER

❑1, b&w 2.95

CALIBER PRESENTS: PETIT MAL
CALIBER

❑1, b&w 2.95

CALIBER PRESENTS: ROMANTIC TALES
CALIBER

❑1, ca. 1995, b&w 2.95

CALIBER PRESENTS: SEPULCHER OPUS
CALIBER

❑1, ca. 1993, b&w 2.95

CALIBER PRESENTS: SOMETHING INSIDE
CALIBER

❑1, b&w 3.50

CALIBER PRESENTS: SUB-ATOMIC SHOCK
CALIBER

❑1, b&w 2.95

CALIBER SPOTLIGHT
CALIBER

❑1, May 1995; b&w anthology with A.K.A. Goldfish, Kabuki, Kilroy is Here, Oz, and previews 2.95

CALIBRATIONS (1ST SERIES)
CALIBER

❑1, b&w 1.00
❑2 .... 1.00
❑3 .... 1.00
❑4 .... 1.00
❑5 .... 1.00

CALIBRATIONS (3RD SERIES)
CALIBER

❑1, Jun 1996; preview of The Lost and Atmospherics 1.00
❑2, Jul 1996 .... 1.00
❑3, Aug 1996 .... 1.00
❑4, Sep 1996 .... 1.00
❑5, Oct 1996 .... 1.00

CALIFORNIA COMICS
CALIFORNIA

❑1 .... 5.00
❑2 .... 4.00

CALIFORNIA GIRLS
ECLIPSE

❑1, Jun 1987 .... 2.00
❑2, Jul 1987 .... 2.00
❑3, Aug 1987 .... 2.00
❑4, Sep 1987 .... 2.00
❑5, Oct 1987 .... 2.00
❑6, Nov 1987 .... 2.00
❑7, Dec 1987 .... 2.00
❑8, Jan 1988 .... 2.00

CALIFORNIA RAISINS IN 3-D
BLACKTHORNE

❑1, Dec 1987; a.k.a. Blackthorne in 3-D #31 .... 2.50
❑1/2nd 2.50
❑1/3rd 2.50
❑2 .... 2.50
❑3 .... 2.50
❑4 .... 2.50
❑5 .... 2.50

CALIGARI 2050
MONSTER

❑1, Apr 1992 .... 2.25
❑2 .... 2.25
❑3 .... 2.25

CALIGARI 2050: ANOTHER SLEEPLESS NIGHT
CALIBER

❑1, ca. 1993 .... 2.25

CALL
MARVEL

❑1, Jun 2003 .... 2.25
❑2, Jul 2003 .... 2.25
❑3, Aug 2003 .... 2.25
❑4, Sep 2003, cardstock cover 2.25

CALLED FROM DARKNESS
ANARCHY

❑1/2nd 2.95
❑1 .... 2.95

CALL ME PRINCESS
CPM

❑1, May 1999, b&w 2.95
❑1/A, May 1999, b&w 2.95
❑2 1999, b&w 2.95
❑3 1999, b&w 2.95
❑4 1999, b&w 2.95
❑5 1999, b&w 2.95
❑6 1999, b&w 2.95

CALL OF DUTY: THE BROTHERHOOD
MARVEL

❑1, Aug 2002 .... 2.25
❑2, Sep 2002 .... 2.25
❑3, Oct 2002 .... 2.25
❑4, Nov 2002 .... 2.25
❑5, Dec 2002 .... 2.25
❑6, Jan 2003 .... 2.25

CALL OF DUTY: THE PRECINCT
MARVEL

❑1, Sep 2002 .... 2.25
❑2, Oct 2002 .... 2.25
❑3, Nov 2002 .... 2.25
❑4, Dec 2002 .... 2.25
❑5, Jan 2003 .... 2.25

CALL OF DUTY: THE WAGON
MARVEL

❑1, Oct 2002 .... 2.25
❑2, Nov 2002 .... 2.25
❑3, Dec 2002 .... 2.25
❑4, Jan 2003 .... 2.25

Camelot 3000

Even Merlin couldn't keep it from shipping late
©DC

Camp Candy

Humor title based on John Candy cartoon
©Marvel

Cap'n Quick & a Foozle

Lighthearted fare from Marshall Rogers
©Eclipse

Captain Action (DC)

Early toy tie-in from 1960s
©DC

Captain America (1st Series)

Title picked up from Tales of Suspense
©Marvel

N-MINT

CAMBION
SLAVE LABOR

❑1, Dec 1995 ..... 2.95
❑2, Feb 1996 ..... 2.95
❑3, Feb 1997, b&w; Published by Moonstone 2.95

CAMELOT ETERNAL
CALIBER

❑1 ..... 2.50
❑2 ..... 2.50
❑3 ..... 2.50
❑4 ..... 2.50
❑5 ..... 2.50
❑6 ..... 2.50
❑7 ..... 2.50
❑8 ..... 2.50

CAMELOT 3000
DC

❑1, Dec 1982 BB (a); O: Merlin. O: Arthur. 2.50
❑2, Jan 1983 BB (a) 2.00
❑3, Feb 1983 BB (a) 2.00
❑4, Mar 1983 BB (a) 2.00
❑5, Apr 1983 BB (a) 2.00
❑6, Jul 1983 BB (a) 2.00
❑7, Aug 1983 BB (a) 2.00
❑8, Sep 1983 BB (a) 2.00
❑9, Dec 1983 BB (a) 2.00
❑10, Mar 1984 BB (a) 2.00
❑11, Jul 1984 BB (a) 2.00
❑12, Apr 1985 BB (a) 2.00

CAMP CANDY
MARVEL

❑1, May 1990 ..... 1.00
❑2, Jun 1990 ..... 1.00
❑3, Jul 1990 ..... 1.00
❑4, Aug 1990 ..... 1.00
❑5, Sep 1990 ..... 1.00
❑6, Oct 1990 ..... 1.00
❑7, Nov 1990 ..... 1.00

CAMPFIRE STORIES
GLOBAL

❑1, ca. 1992 ..... 2.25

CAMPING WITH BIGFOOT
SLAVE LABOR

❑1, Sep 1995 ..... 2.95

CAMP RUNAMUCK
DELL

❑1, Apr 1966, Based on 1965-66 NBC TV show 40.00

CANADIAN ROCK SPECIAL
REVOLUTIONARY

❑1, Apr 1994, b&w; Rush 2.50

CANCER: THE CRAB BOY
SABRE'S EDGE

❑1 ..... 2.95
❑2 ..... 2.95
❑3 ..... 2.95
❑4 ..... 2.95
❑5 ..... 2.95

CANDIDATE GODDESS
TOKYOPOP

❑1, Apr 2004 ..... 9.99

N-MINT

CANDIDE REVEALED
FANTAGRAPHICS / EROS

❑1, b&w 2.25

CANDYAPPLEBLACK
GOOD INTENTIONS PAVING

❑1 2004 ..... 3.50
❑2 2004 ..... 3.50
❑3 2004 ..... 3.50
❑4 2004 ..... 3.50
❑5 2004 ..... 3.50

CANNIBALIS
RAGING RHINO

❑1, b&w 2.95

CANNON
FANTAGRAPHICS / EROS

❑1, Feb 1991, b&w WW (w); WW (a). 2.75
❑1/2nd, WW (a) 2.95
❑2, Mar 1991, b&w WW (w); WW (a) 2.95
❑2/2nd, WW (a) 2.95
❑3, Apr 1991, WW (w); WW (a); O: Madame Toy. O: Sue Stevens. 2.95
❑3/2nd, WW (a); O: Madame Toy. O: Sue Stevens. 2.95
❑4, May 1991, WW (w); WW (a) 2.95
❑5, Jun 1991, WW (w); WW (a) 2.95
❑6, Jul 1991, WW (w); WW (a) 2.95
❑7, Aug 1991, WW (w); WW (a) 2.95
❑8, Sep 1991, WW (w); WW (a) 2.95

CANNON BUSTERS
DEVIL'S DUE

❑0 2004; Available at 2004 San Diego Comic Con 15.00
❑1 2004 ..... 2.95
❑1/Variant 2004 ..... 4.00
❑2 2004 ..... 2.95
❑2/Variant 2004 ..... 4.00

CANNON GOD EXAXXION
DARK HORSE

❑1, Nov 2001; Stage 1.1 ..... 2.99
❑2, Dec 2001; Stage 1.2 ..... 2.99
❑3, Jan 2002; Stage 1.3 ..... 2.99
❑4, Feb 2002; Stage 1.4 ..... 2.99
❑5, Mar 2002; Stage 1.5 ..... 2.99
❑6, Apr 2002; Stage 1.6 ..... 2.99
❑7, May 2002; Stage 1.7 ..... 2.99
❑8, Jun 2002; Stage 1.8 ..... 2.99
❑9, Sep 2002; 48 pages; Stage 2.1 ..... 3.99
❑10, Oct 2002; Stage 2.2 ..... 3.50
❑11, Nov 2002 ..... 3.50
❑12, Dec 2002 ..... 3.50
❑13, Jan 2003 ..... 3.50
❑14, Jun 2003 ..... 3.50
❑15, Jul 2003 ..... 2.99
❑16, Aug 2003 ..... 2.99
❑17, Sep 2003 ..... 2.99
❑18, Oct 2003 ..... 2.99
❑19, Nov 2003 ..... 2.99
❑20, Dec 2003 ..... 2.99

CANNON HAWKE: DAWN OF WAR (MICHAEL TURNER'S)
ASPEN

❑1, Jun 2004 ..... 6.00

N-MINT

CANYON COMICS PRESENTS
GRAND CANYON ASSOCIATION

❑1, Fal 1995, Sold at Grand Canyon Information Center 3.00
❑2, Sum 1996; Sold at Grand Canyon Information Center 3.00

CAPE CITY
DIMENSION X

❑1, b&w 2.75
❑2, b&w 2.75

CAPER
DC

❑1, Dec 2003 ..... 2.95
❑2, Jan 2004 ..... 2.95
❑3, Feb 2004 ..... 2.95
❑4, Mar 2004 ..... 2.95
❑5, Apr 2004 ..... 2.95
❑6, May 2004 ..... 2.95
❑7, Jun 2004 ..... 2.95
❑8, Jul 2004 ..... 2.95
❑9, Aug 2004 ..... 2.95
❑10, Sep 2004 ..... 2.95
❑11, Oct 2004 ..... 2.95
❑12, Nov 2004 ..... 2.95

CAPES
IMAGE

❑1, Oct 2003 ..... 3.50
❑2, Nov 2003 ..... 3.50
❑3, Dec 2003 ..... 3.50

CAPITAL CAPERS PRESENTS
BLT

❑1, Oct 1994, b&w 2.95

CAP'N OATMEAL
ALL AMERICAN

❑1, b&w 2.25

CAP'N QUICK & A FOOZLE
ECLIPSE

❑1, Jul 1984 ..... 1.50
❑2, Mar 1985 ..... 1.50
❑3; Title changes to The Foozle 1.50

CAPTAIN ACTION
KARL ART

❑0; preview of ongoing series; Insert in Space Bananas #1 ..... 1.95

CAPTAIN ACTION (DC)
DC

❑1, Nov 1968, WW (a); O: Captain Action. 45.00
❑2, Jan 1969, GK, WW (a) 35.00
❑3, Mar 1969, GK, WW (a) 35.00
❑4, May 1969, GK (a) 35.00
❑5, Jul 1969, GK, WW (a) 20.00

CAPTAIN AFRICA
AFRICAN PRINCE PRODUCTIONS

❑1, Jun 1992, b&w 1.00

CAPTAIN AMERICA (1ST SERIES)
MARVEL

❑100, Apr 1968, JK (a); A: Avengers. Series continued from Tales of Suspense #99 ..... 210.00
❑101, May 1968, JK (a); 1: 4th Sleeper. 55.00
❑102, Jun 1968, JK (a) 35.00

Other grades: Multiply price above by 5/6 for VF/NM • 2/3 for VERY FINE • 1/3 for FINE • 1/5 for VERY GOOD • 1/8 for GOOD

Issue	N-MINT
❑103, Jul 1968, JK (a); A: Red Skull. Agent 13's identity revealed as Sharon Carter	35.00
❑104, Aug 1968, JK (a); V: Red Skull.	35.00
❑105, Sep 1968, JK (a); V: Batroc.	35.00
❑106, Oct 1968, SL (w); JK (a)	35.00
❑107, Nov 1968, SL (w); JK (a); 1: Doctor Faustus. A: Red Skull.	35.00
❑108, Dec 1968, JK (a)	35.00
❑109, Jan 1969, SL (w); JK (a); O: Captain America.	45.00
❑109/2nd, ca. 1994, JK (a); O: Captain America. Reprint	2.50
❑110, Feb 1969, JSo (a); 1: Viper II (as Madame Hydra). 1: Viper. A: Hulk. A: Rick Jones. Rick Jones dons Bucky costume	75.00
❑111, Mar 1969, JSo (a)	65.00
❑112, Apr 1969, GT, JK (a); O: Viper II (as Madame Hydra). O: Captain America. album	50.00
❑113, May 1969, JSo (a); Avengers	60.00
❑114, Jun 1969, JR (a)	30.00
❑115, Jul 1969	30.00
❑116, Aug 1969	30.00
❑117, Sep 1969, GC, JSt (a); 1: Falcon.	95.00
❑118, Oct 1969, SL (w); GC, JSt (a); A: Falcon.	25.00
❑119, Nov 1969, SL (w); GC, JSt (a); A: Falcon.	25.00
❑120, Dec 1969, SL (w); GC, JSt (a); A: Falcon.	25.00
❑121, Jan 1970, SL (w); GC (a); O: Captain America.	25.00
❑122, Feb 1970, SL (w); GC (a)	25.00
❑123, Mar 1970, SL (w); GC (a); 1: Suprema (later becomes Mother Night).	25.00
❑124, Apr 1970, SL (w); GC (a)	25.00
❑125, May 1970, SL (w); GC (a)	20.00
❑126, Jun 1970, SL (w); GC (a); 1: Diamond Head. A: Falcon.	20.00
❑127, Jul 1970, SL (w); GC (a)	20.00
❑128, Aug 1970, SL (w); GC (a)	15.00
❑129, Sep 1970, SL (w); GC (a)	15.00
❑130, Oct 1970, SL (w); GC (a)	15.00
❑131, Nov 1970, SL (w); GC (a)	18.00
❑132, Dec 1970, SL (w); GC (a)	18.00
❑133, Jan 1971, SL (w); GC (a); O: Modok. Falcon becomes Captain America's partner	15.00
❑134, Feb 1971, SL (w); GC (a)	18.00
❑135, Mar 1971, JR (c); SL (w); GC (a)	18.00
❑136, Apr 1971, SL (w); GC (a)	18.00
❑137, May 1971, GC, BEv (a); A: Spider-Man.	35.00
❑138, Jun 1971, JR (a); A: Spider-Man.	30.00
❑139, Jul 1971, SL (w); GC, JR (a)	25.00
❑140, Aug 1971, JR (a); O: Grey Gargoyle.	25.00
❑141, Sep 1971, SL (w); JR (a)	25.00
❑142, Oct 1971, JR (a); V: Grey Gargoyle.	25.00
❑143, Nov 1971, Giant-size JR (a)	25.00
❑144, Dec 1971, JR (a)	25.00
❑145, Jan 1972, GK (a)	25.00
❑146, Feb 1972, SB (a)	25.00
❑147, Mar 1972	15.00
❑148, Apr 1972	15.00
❑149, May 1972, SB (a)	15.00
❑150, Jun 1972	25.00
❑151, Jul 1972	15.00
❑152, Aug 1972, SB (a)	15.00
❑153, Sep 1972, 1: Bucky III (Jack Monroe). 1: Captain America IV. V: Red Skull.	15.00
❑154, Oct 1972	15.00
❑155, Nov 1972, SB (a); O: Captain America II (Jack Monroe). O: Captain America.	25.00
❑156, Dec 1972	15.00
❑157, Jan 1973	10.00
❑158, Feb 1973	10.00
❑159, Mar 1973	10.00
❑160, Apr 1973, 1: Solarr.	10.00
❑161, May 1973, SB (a)	10.00
❑162, Jun 1973, SB (a); O: Sharon Carter.	10.00
❑163, Jul 1973, SB (a); 1: Dave Cox.	10.00
❑164, Aug 1973, 1: Nightshade.	10.00
❑165, Sep 1973, SB (a)	10.00
❑166, Oct 1973, SB (a)	10.00
❑167, Nov 1973, SB (a)	10.00
❑168, Dec 1973, SB (a); 1: Phoenix I (Helmut Zemo). A: Baron Zemo (Helmut). D: Phoenix I (Helmut Zemo).	12.00
❑169, Jan 1974, 1: Moonstone I (Lloyd Bloch)-cameo.	10.00
❑170, Feb 1974, SB (a); 1: Moonstone I (Lloyd Bloch)-full.	10.00
❑171, Mar 1974, Marvel Value Stamp #50: Black Panther	10.00
❑172, Apr 1974, SB (a); A: X-Men. A: Banshee. Marvel Value Stamp #43: Enchantress	10.00
❑173, May 1974, SB (a); A: X-Men. Marvel Value Stamp #61: Red Ghost	10.00
❑174, Jun 1974, SB (a); A: X-Men. Marvel Value Stamp #48: Kraven	10.00
❑175, Jul 1974, SB (a); A: X-Men. Marvel Value Stamp #77: Swordsman	10.00
❑176, Aug 1974, SB (a); Marvel Value Stamp #15: Iron Man	7.00
❑177, Sep 1974, SB (a); recalls origin and quits; Marvel Value Stamp #26: Mephisto	7.00
❑178, Oct 1974, SB (a); Marvel Value Stamp #89: Hammerhead	7.00
❑179, Nov 1974, SB (a); Marvel Value Stamp #52: Quicksilver	7.00
❑180, Dec 1974, SB (a); O: Nomad. 1: Nomad (Steve Rogers). 1: Viper II. Marvel Value Stamp #61: Red Ghost	7.00
❑181, Jan 1975, SB (a); O: Captain America (new). 1: Captain America (new). Marvel Value Stamp #46 Mysterio	7.00
❑182, Feb 1975, Marvel Value Stamp #36: Ancient One	7.00
❑183, Mar 1975, D: Captain America (new). Steve Rogers becomes Captain America again	7.00
❑184, Apr 1975, Marvel Value Stamp #94: Electro	5.00
❑185, May 1975	5.00
❑186, Jun 1975, O: Falcon (real origin).	5.00
❑187, Jul 1975	5.00
❑188, Aug 1975, SB (a)	5.00
❑189, Sep 1975, FR (a)	5.00
❑190, Oct 1975, FR (a)	5.00
❑191, Nov 1975, FR (a)	5.00
❑192, Dec 1975, FR (a); 1: Karla Sofen (becomes Moonstone). Marvel Value Stamp #56: Rawhide Kid	5.00
❑193, Jan 1976, JK (w); JK (a)	5.00
❑194, Feb 1976, JK (w); JK (a)	5.00
❑195, Mar 1976, JK (w); JK (a)	5.00
❑196, Apr 1976, JK (w); JK (a)	5.00
❑196/30 cent, Apr 1976, JK (w); JK (a); 30 cent regional price variant	20.00
❑197, May 1976, JK (w); JK (a)	5.00
❑197/30 cent, May 1976, JK (w); JK (a); 30 cent regional price variant	20.00
❑198, Jun 1976, JK (w); JK (a)	5.00
❑198/30 cent, Jun 1976, JK (w); JK (a); 30 cent regional price variant	20.00
❑199, Jul 1976, JK (w); JK (a)	5.00
❑199/30 cent, Jul 1976, JK (w); JK (a); 30 cent regional price variant	20.00
❑200, Aug 1976, 200th anniversary issue JK (w); JK (a)	6.00
❑200/30 cent, Aug 1976, JK (w); JK (a); 30 cent regional price variant	20.00
❑201, Sep 1976, JK (w); JK (a)	4.00
❑202, Oct 1976, JK (a)	4.00
❑203, Nov 1976, JK (w); JK (a)	4.00
❑204, Dec 1976, JK (w); JK (a)	4.00
❑205, Jan 1977, JK (w); JK (a)	4.00
❑206, Feb 1977, JK (w); JK (a); 1: Donna Maria Puentes. Newsstand edition (distributed by Curtis); issue number in box	4.00
❑206/Whitman, Feb 1977, JK (w); JK (a); 1: Donna Maria Puentes. Special markets edition (usually sold in Whitman bagged prepacks); price appears in a diamond; UPC barcode appears	4.00
❑207, Mar 1977, JK (w); JK (a); Newsstand edition (distributed by Curtis); issue number in box	4.00
❑207/Whitman, Mar 1977, JK (w); JK (a); Special markets edition (usually sold in Whitman bagged prepacks); price appears in a diamond; UPC barcode appears	4.00
❑208, Apr 1977, JK (w); JK (a); 1: Arnim Zola. Newsstand edition (distributed by Curtis); issue number in box	4.00
❑208/Whitman, Apr 1977, JK (w); JK (a); 1: Arnim Zola. Special markets edition (usually sold in Whitman bagged prepacks); price appears in a diamond; UPC barcode appears	4.00
❑209, May 1977, JK (w); JK (a); 1: Arnim Zola. 1: Doughboy. Newsstand edition (distributed by Curtis); issue number in box	4.00
❑209/Whitman, May 1977, JK (w); JK (a); 1: Arnim Zola. 1: Doughboy. Special markets edition (usually sold in Whitman bagged prepacks); price appears in a diamond; UPC barcode appears	4.00
❑210, Jun 1977, JK (w); JK (a); Newsstand edition (distributed by Curtis); issue number in box	4.00
❑210/Whitman, Jun 1977, JK (w); JK (a); Special markets edition (usually sold in Whitman bagged prepacks); price appears in a diamond; UPC barcode appears	4.00
❑210/35 cent, Jun 1977, JK (w); JK (a); 35 cent regional price variant; newsstand edition (distributed by Curtis); issue number in box	15.00
❑211, Jul 1977, JK (w); JK (a); Newsstand edition (distributed by Curtis); issue number in box	4.00
❑211/Whitman, Jul 1977, JK (w); JK (a); Special markets edition (usually sold in Whitman bagged prepacks); price appears in a diamond; UPC barcode appears	4.00
❑211/35 cent, Jul 1977, JK (w); JK (a); 35 cent regional price variant; newsstand edition (distributed by Curtis); issue number in box	15.00
❑212, Aug 1977, JK (w); JK (a); Newsstand edition (distributed by Curtis); issue number in box	4.00
❑212/Whitman, Aug 1977, JK (w); JK (a); Special markets edition (usually sold in Whitman bagged prepacks); price appears in a diamond; UPC barcode appears	4.00
❑212/35 cent, Aug 1977, JK (w); JK (a); 35 cent regional price variant; newsstand edition (distributed by Curtis); issue number in box	15.00
❑213, Sep 1977, JK (w); JK (a); Newsstand edition (distributed by Curtis); issue number in box	4.00
❑213/Whitman, Sep 1977, JK (w); JK (a); Special markets edition (usually sold in Whitman bagged prepacks); price appears in a diamond; UPC barcode appears	4.00
❑213/35 cent, Sep 1977, JK (w); JK (a); 35 cent regional price variant; newsstand edition (distributed by Curtis); issue number in box	15.00
❑214, Oct 1977, JK (w); JK (a); Newsstand edition (distributed by Curtis); issue number in box	4.00
❑214/Whitman, Oct 1977, JK (w); JK (a); Special markets edition (usually sold in Whitman bagged prepacks); price appears in a diamond; no UPC barcode	4.00
❑214/35 cent, Oct 1977, JK (w); JK (a); 35 cent regional price variant; newsstand edition (distributed by Curtis); issue number in box	15.00
❑215, Nov 1977, GK (a); Newsstand edition (distributed by Curtis); issue number in box	4.00
❑215/Whitman, Nov 1977, GK (a); Special markets edition (usually sold in Whitman bagged prepacks); price appears in a diamond; no UPC barcode	4.00
❑216, Dec 1977, GK (a); Reprinted from Strange Tales #114; newsstand edition (distributed by Curtis); issue number in box	4.00
❑216/Whitman, Dec 1977, GK (a); Reprinted from Strange Tales #114; special markets edition (usually sold in Whitman bagged prepacks); price appears in a diamond; no UPC barcode	4.00
❑217, Jan 1978, JB (a); 1: Quasar (Marvel Man). 1: Blue Streak.	4.00
❑218, Feb 1978, SB (a)	4.00

Other grades: Multiply price above by 5/6 for VF/NM • 2/3 for VERY FINE • 1/3 for FINE • 1/5 for VERY GOOD • 1/8 for GOOD

Captain America (2nd Series)

Liefeld rewrote Cap's Origin for restart
©Marvel

Captain America (3rd Series)

Second restart after "Heroes Reborn"
©Marvel

Captain America (4th Series)

Third restart didn't outlast the second one
©Marvel

Captain America (5th Series)

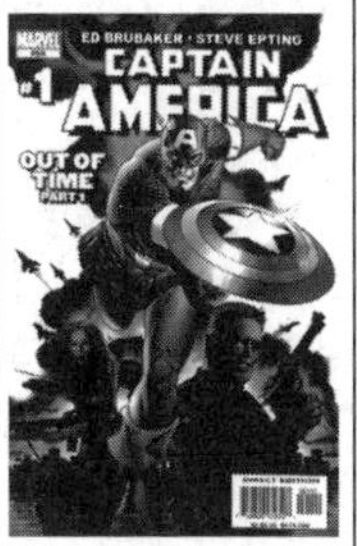

Fourth restart features "return" of Bucky
©Marvel

Captain America & The Falcon

Team-up title revives old partnership
©Marvel

	N-MINT
❑219, Mar 1978, SB (a)	4.00
❑220, Apr 1978, SB, GK (a); Newsstand edition (distributed by Curtis); issue number in box	4.00
❑220/Whitman, Apr 1978, SB, GK (a); Special markets edition (usually sold in Whitman bagged prepacks); price appears in a diamond; no UPC barcode	4.00
❑221, May 1978, SB, GK (a); Newsstand edition (distributed by Curtis); issue number in box	4.00
❑221/Whitman, May 1978, SB, GK (a); Special markets edition (usually sold in Whitman bagged prepacks); price appears in a diamond; no UPC barcode	4.00
❑222, Jun 1978, SB (a); Newsstand edition (distributed by Curtis); issue number in box	4.00
❑222/Whitman, Jun 1978, SB (a); Special markets edition (usually sold in Whitman bagged prepacks); price appears in a diamond; no UPC barcode	4.00
❑223, Jul 1978, SB, JBy (a)	4.00
❑224, Aug 1978, MZ (a); 1: Señor Muerte II (Philip Garcia). Newsstand edition (distributed by Curtis); issue number in box	4.00
❑224/Whitman, Aug 1978, MZ (a); 1: Señor Muerte II (Philip Garcia). Special markets edition (usually sold in Whitman bagged prepacks); price appears in a diamond; no UPC barcode	4.00
❑225, Sep 1978, SB (a); Newsstand edition (distributed by Curtis); issue number in box	4.00
❑225/Whitman, Sep 1978, SB (a); Special markets edition (usually sold in Whitman bagged prepacks); price appears in a diamond; UPC barcode appears	4.00
❑226, Oct 1978, SB (a); Newsstand edition (distributed by Curtis); issue number in box	4.00
❑226/Whitman, Oct 1978, SB (a); Special markets edition (usually sold in Whitman bagged prepacks); price appears in a diamond; no UPC barcode	4.00
❑227, Nov 1978, SB (a); Newsstand edition (distributed by Curtis); issue number in box	4.00
❑227/Whitman, Nov 1978, SB (a); Special markets edition (usually sold in Whitman bagged prepacks); price appears in a diamond; no UPC barcode	4.00
❑228, Dec 1978, SB (a); Newsstand edition (distributed by Curtis); issue number in box	4.00
❑228/Whitman, Dec 1978, SB (a); Special markets edition (usually sold in Whitman bagged prepacks); price appears in a diamond; no UPC barcode	4.00
❑229, Jan 1979, SB (a); A: Marvel Man (Quasar). Newsstand edition (distributed by Curtis); issue number in box	4.00
❑229/Whitman, Jan 1979, SB (a); A: Marvel Man (Quasar). Special markets edition (usually sold in Whitman bagged prepacks); price appears in a diamond; no UPC barcode	4.00

	N-MINT
❑230, Feb 1979, SB, DP (a); A: Hulk. V: Hulk. Newsstand edition (distributed by Curtis); issue number in box	4.00
❑230/Whitman, Feb 1979, SB, DP (a); A: Hulk. V: Hulk. Special markets edition (usually sold in Whitman bagged prepacks); price appears in a diamond; no UPC barcode	4.00
❑231, Mar 1979, SB, DP (a); V: Grand Director	4.00
❑232, Apr 1979, SB, DP (a)	4.00
❑233, May 1979, SB, DP (a); D: Sharon Carter. Newsstand edition (distributed by Curtis); issue number in box	4.00
❑233/Whitman, May 1979, SB, DP (a); D: Sharon Carter. Special markets edition (usually sold in Whitman bagged prepacks); price appears in a diamond; no UPC barcode	4.00
❑234, Jun 1979, A: Daredevil.	4.00
❑235, Jul 1979, SB, FM, JAb (a); A: Daredevil.	4.00
❑236, Aug 1979, SB, DP (a); D: Captain America IV.	4.00
❑237, Sep 1979, SB, DP (a); 1: Anna Kappelbaum. 1: Joshua Cooper. 1: Copperhead. 1: Mike Farrel. Steve moves to Brooklyn	4.00
❑238, Oct 1979, JBy (a)	4.00
❑239, Nov 1979, JBy (a)	4.00
❑240, Dec 1979	4.00
❑241, Jan 1980, FM (c); FM (a); A: Punisher. Human Torch in Hostess ad ("The Icemaster Cometh")	4.00
❑242, Feb 1980, DP, JSt (a); Mr. Fantastic in Hostess ad ("A Passion for Gold").	4.00
❑243, Mar 1980, RB, GP, DP (a); Iron Man in Hostess ad ("The Hungry Battleaxe")	4.00
❑244, Apr 1980, FM (c); FM, DP (a); Human Torch in Hostess ad ("A Hot Time in the Old Town")	4.00
❑245, May 1980, FM (a); Thor in Hostess ad ("Meets the Ricochet Monster!")	4.00
❑246, Jun 1980, GP (a); Spider-Man in Hostess ad ("The Trap")	4.00
❑247, Jul 1980, JBy (a); 1: Machinesmith. Thing in Hostess ad ("Sunday Punch!")	4.00
❑248, Aug 1980, JBy (a); 1: Bernie Rosenthal. Hulk in Hostess ad ("vs. the Roller Disco Devils!")	4.00
❑249, Sep 1980, JBy (a); O: Machinesmith. Captain Marvel in Hostess ad ("Defends the Earth!") .	4.00
❑250, Oct 1980, JBy (a); Human Torch in Hostess ad ("Saves the Valley!")	4.00
❑251, Nov 1980, JBy (a); Mr. Fantastic in Hostess ad ("The Power of Gold")	4.00
❑252, Dec 1980, JBy (a); Iron Man in Hostess ad ("vs. The Bank Robbers")	4.00
❑253, Jan 1981, JBy (a); 1: Joe Chapman (becomes Union Jack III). D: Union Jack II (Brian Falsworth). Iron Man in Hostess ad ("vs. The Bank Robbers")	4.00
❑254, Feb 1981, JBy (a); O: Union Jack III (Joe Chapman). 1: Union Jack III (Joe Chapman). D: Baron Blood. D: Union Jack I (Lord Falsworth). Daredevil in Hostess ad ("vs. Johnny Punk!")	4.00

	N-MINT
❑255, Mar 1981, 40th anniversary; FM (c); JBy, FM (a); O: Captain America. 1: Sarah Rogers (Steve's mother). Human Torch in Hostess ad ("Blown About")	4.00
❑256, Apr 1981, GC (a); Spider-Man in Hostess ad ("The Rescue")	2.00
❑257, May 1981, A: Hulk. Has Not Brand Ecch reprints; Thing in Hostess ad ("Earthly Delights")	2.00
❑258, Jun 1981, MZ (a)	2.00
❑259, Jul 1981, MZ (c); MZ (a); V: Doctor Octopus. Spider-Man in Hostess ad ("Versus The Human Computer")	2.00
❑260, Aug 1981, AM (w); AM (a)	2.00
❑261, Sep 1981, MZ (c); MZ (a); A: Avengers. Human Torch in Hostess ad ("Hot-Tempered Heroes!")	2.00
❑262, Oct 1981, MZ (c); MZ (a); Hulk in Hostess ad ("vs. The Phoomie Goonies")	2.00
❑263, Nov 1981, MZ (a); Thing in Hostess ad ("A Lesson to Be Learned"); D&D ad comic #2	2.00
❑264, Dec 1981, MZ (a); A: X-Men. X-Men cameo; Spider-Man in Hostess ad ("Dream Girl")	2.00
❑265, Jan 1982, MZ (a); A: Nick Fury & Spider-Man. Captain Marvel in Hostess ad ("Flea Bargaining")	2.00
❑266, Feb 1982, MZ (a); Daredevil in Hostess ad ("Daredevil's Longest Fight"); D&D ad comic #3	2.00
❑267, Mar 1982, MZ (a); 1: Everyman. Daredevil in Hostess ad ("Daredevil's Longest Fight"); D&D ad comic #4 .	2.00
❑268, Apr 1982, MZ (a); Daredevil in Hostess ad ("Daredevil's Longest Fight")	2.00
❑269, May 1982, MZ (a); 1: Team America. D&D ad comic #5	2.00
❑270, Jun 1982, MZ (a)	2.00
❑271, Jul 1982, D&D ad comic #6	2.00
❑272, Aug 1982, MZ (a); 1: Vermin. D&D ad comic #7	3.00
❑273, Sep 1982, MZ (a); D&D ad comic #8	2.00
❑274, Oct 1982, MZ (a); D: General Samuel "Happy Sam" Sawyer.	2.00
❑275, Nov 1982, MZ (a); Bernie Rosenthal learns Cap's identity	2.00
❑276, Dec 1982, MZ (a); 1: Baron Zemo II (Helmut Zemo). Later becomes Citizen V	4.00
❑277, Jan 1983, MZ (a)	2.00
❑278, Feb 1983, MZ (a)	2.00
❑279, Mar 1983, MZ (a)	2.00
❑280, Apr 1983, MZ (a)	2.00
❑281, May 1983, MZ (a); A: Jack Monroe.	2.00
❑282, Jun 1983, MZ (a); 1: Joseph Rogers (Steve's father). 1: Nomad II (Jack Monroe).	3.00
❑282/2nd, Jun 1983, MZ (a); 1: Nomad II (Jack Monroe). silver ink	2.00
❑283, Jul 1983, MZ (a); 2: Nomad (Jack Monroe).	2.00
❑284, Aug 1983, MZ (a); A: Patriot (Jeffrey Mace)	3.00
❑285, Sep 1983, SB, MZ (a); D: Patriot (Jeffrey Mace). V: Porcupine	2.00

Other grades: Multiply price above by 5/6 for VF/NM • 2/3 for VERY FINE • 1/3 for FINE • 1/5 for VERY GOOD • 1/8 for GOOD

N-MINT

❑286, Oct 1983, MZ (a); A: Deathlok. . 3.00
❑287, Nov 1983, MZ (a); A: Deathlok. 3.00
❑288, Dec 1983, MZ (a); A: Deathlok. 3.00
❑289, Jan 1984, MZ (a); A: Bernie America. Assistant Editors' Month.. 2.00
❑290, Feb 1984, JBy (a); 1: Black Crow (in crow form). A: Mother Night. Zemo 2.00
❑291, Mar 1984, JBy (c); HT (a)........ 2.00
❑292, Apr 1984, O: Black Crow. 1: Black Crow (in human form)................... 2.00
❑293, May 1984 .... 2.00
❑294, Jun 1984 .... 2.00
❑295, Jul 1984 .... 2.00
❑296, Aug 1984 .... 2.00
❑297, Sep 1984 .... 2.00
❑298, Oct 1984, O: Red Skull. 3.00
❑299, Nov 1984, O: Red Skull. 2.00
❑300, Dec 1984, MZ (a); V: Red Skull. 2.00
❑301, Jan 1985 .... 2.00
❑302, Feb 1985, 1: Machete. 2.00
❑303, Mar 1985, V: Batroc. 2.00
❑304, Apr 1985 .... 2.00
❑305, May 1985, A: Captain Britain. ... 2.00
❑306, Jun 1985, A: Captain Britain. 2.00
❑307, Jul 1985, 1: Madcap. 2.00
❑308, Aug 1985, JBy (a); Secret Wars II 2.00
❑309, Sep 1985, O: Madcap. V: Madcap. Nomad leaves team 2.00
❑310, Oct 1985, 1: Diamondback. 1: Rattler. 1: Cottonmouth II. 1: Serpent Society. 1: Bushmaster. 1: Asp II (Cleo)............................. 2.00
❑311, Nov 1985, V: Super-Adaptoid. .. 2.00
❑312, Dec 1985, O: Flag-Smasher. 1: Flag-Smasher............................. 2.00
❑313, Jan 1986, JBy (a) 2.00
❑314, Feb 1986 .... 2.00
❑315, Mar 1986, D: Porcupine. V: Serpent Society.......................... 2.00
❑316, Apr 1986 .... 2.00
❑317, May 1986 .... 2.00
❑318, Jun 1986, D: The Blue Streak. D: Death-Adder............................ 2.00
❑319, Jul 1986, D: Bird-Man II. 2.00
❑320, Aug 1986, V: Scourge............. 2.00
❑321, Sep 1986, MZ (a); 1: Ultimatum. 2.00
❑322, Oct 1986, 1: Super-Patriot........ 2.00
❑323, Nov 1986, MZ (a); 1: Super-Patriot II (later becomes USAgent). 2.00
❑324, Dec 1986 .... 2.00
❑325, Jan 1987, MZ (a); 1: Slug......... 2.00
❑326, Feb 1987, MZ (a)..................... 2.00
❑327, Mar 1987, MZ (a) 2.00
❑328, Apr 1987, MZ (a); O: Demolition-Man. 1: Demolition-Man. 2.00
❑329, May 1987, MZ (a).................... 2.00
❑330, Jun 1987, MZ (a); A: Demolition-Man... 2.00
❑331, Jul 1987, MZ (a) 2.00
❑332, Aug 1987, MZ (a); Steve Rogers quits as Captain America................ 3.00
❑333, Sep 1987, MZ (a); 1: Captain America VI (John Walker). John Walker (Super-Patriot II) becomes Captain America............................ 2.00
❑334, Oct 1987, MZ (a); 1: Bucky IV (Lemar Hoskins)............................ 2.00
❑335, Nov 1987, 1: Watchdogs. 2.00
❑336, Dec 1987, MZ (a) 2.00
❑337, Jan 1988, MZ (a); 1: Fer-de-Lance. 1: The Captain. 1: Puff Adder. 2.00
❑338, Feb 1988, D: Professor Power. . 2.00
❑339, Mar 1988, Fall of Mutants 2.00
❑340, Apr 1988 .... 2.00
❑341, May 1988, 1: Left-Winger. 1: Rock Python (cameo). 1: Battle Star. A: Iron Man........................... 2.00
❑342, Jun 1988, 1: Rock Python (full appearance)........................... 2.00
❑343, Jul 1988, 1: Quill. 2.00
❑344, Aug 1988, Giant-size 2.00
❑345, Sep 1988 .... 2.00
❑346, Oct 1988............................. 2.00
❑347, Nov 1988, D: Left-Winger......... 2.00
❑348, Dec 1988, V: Flag Smasher....... 2.00
❑349, Jan 1989 .... 2.00
❑350, Feb 1989, Giant-size; The Captain and Super-Patriot fight for title of Captain America.................. 3.00
❑351, Mar 1989, A: Nick Fury. D: Watchdog............................... 2.00

N-MINT

❑352, Apr 1989, 1: Machete. A: Soviet Super Soldiers.............................. 2.00
❑353, May 1989, A: Soviet Super Soldiers.. 2.00
❑354, Jun 1989, 1: U.S. Agent. A: Fabian Stankowitz. Super-Patriot becomes USAgent......................... 2.00
❑355, Jul 1989, RB (a) 2.00
❑356, Aug 1989, AM (a); 1: Mother Night. 2.00
❑357, Sep 1989, CBG Fan Awards parody ballot 2.00
❑358, Sep 1989, A: John Jameson. ... 2.00
❑359, Oct 1989, 1: Crossbones (cameo). 2.00
❑360, Oct 1989, 1: Crossbones (full appearance). 2.00
❑361, Nov 1989 .... 2.00
❑362, Nov 1989 .... 2.00
❑363, Nov 1989 .... 2.00
❑364, Dec 1989............................. 2.00
❑365, Dec 1989, Acts of Vengeance... 2.00
❑366, Jan 1990, Acts of Vengeance ... 2.00
❑367, Feb 1990, Acts of Vengeance; Red Skull vs. Magneto................... 2.00
❑368, Mar 1990, O: Machinesmith..... 2.00
❑369, Apr 1990, 1: Skeleton Crew...... 2.00
❑370, May 1990............................. 2.00
❑371, Jun 1990............................. 2.00
❑372, Jul 1990 .... 2.00
❑373, Jul 1990 .... 2.00
❑374, Aug 1990 .... 2.00
❑375, Aug 1990 .... 2.00
❑376, Sep 1990............................. 2.00
❑377, Sep 1990............................. 2.00
❑378, Oct 1990 .... 2.00
❑379, Nov 1990, O: Nefarius. 1: Nefarius. A: Quasar. V: Nefarius.. 2.00
❑380, Dec 1990............................. 2.00
❑381, Jan 1991 .... 2.00
❑382, Feb 1991 .... 2.00
❑383, Mar 1991, 50th anniversary issue JLee (c); JLee (a) 3.00
❑384, Apr 1991, A: Jack Frost........... 2.00
❑385, May 1991............................. 2.00
❑386, Jun 1991, A: U.S. Agent.......... 2.00
❑387, Jul 1991, Red Skull back-up stories 2.00
❑388, Jul 1991, 1: Impala. Red Skull back-up stories............................ 2.00
❑389, Aug 1991, Red Skull back-up stories 2.00
❑390, Aug 1991 .... 2.00
❑391, Sep 1991............................. 2.00
❑392, Sep 1991............................. 2.00
❑393, Oct 1991 .... 2.00
❑394, Nov 1991 .... 2.00
❑395, Dec 1991............................. 2.00
❑396, Jan 1992, 1: Jack O'Lantern II. 2.00
❑397, Feb 1992 .... 2.00
❑398, Mar 1992, Galactic Storm 2.00
❑399, Apr 1992, Galactic Storm......... 2.00
❑400, May 1992, O: Cutthroat. O: Diamondback. Double-gatefold cover; Galactic Storm; reprints Avengers #4 .... 3.00
❑401, Jun 1992............................. 2.00
❑402, Jul 1992, 1: Dredmund Druid. A: Wolverine.................................. 2.00
❑403, Jul 1992, 2: Dredmund Druid. A: Wolverine.................................. 2.00
❑404, Aug 1992, A: Wolverine. 2.00
❑405, Aug 1992, A: Wolverine. 2.00
❑406, Sep 1992, A: Wolverine........... 2.00
❑407, Sep 1992, A: Wolverine. A: Cable. 2.00
❑408, Oct 1992, D: Cutthroat. 2.00
❑409, Nov 1992 .... 2.00
❑410, Dec 1992............................. 2.00
❑411, Jan 1993............................. 2.00
❑412, Feb 1993............................. 2.00
❑413, Mar 1993, V: Modam. 2.00
❑414, Apr 1993, Savage Land 2.00
❑415, May 1993............................. 2.00
❑416, Jun 1993............................. 2.00
❑417, Jul 1993 .... 2.00
❑418, Aug 1993 .... 2.00
❑419, Sep 1993, A: Silver Sable......... 2.00
❑420, Oct 1993, A: Nomad. A: Blazing Skull. A: Viper.............................. 2.00
❑420/CS, Oct 1993, Includes copy of Dirt Magazine A: Nomad. A: Blazing Skull. A: Viper. 3.00

N-MINT

❑421, Nov 1993, A: Nomad............... 2.00
❑422, Dec 1993............................. 2.00
❑423, Jan 1994, V: Namor................. 2.00
❑424, Feb 1994 .... 2.00
❑425, Mar 1994, Giant-size 3.00
❑425/Variant, Mar 1994, Giant-size; Foil-embossed cover...................... 4.00
❑426, Apr 1994 .... 2.00
❑427, May 1994 .... 2.00
❑428, Jun 1994 .... 2.00
❑429, Jul 1994, 1: Kono the Sumo..... 2.00
❑430, Aug 1994............................. 2.00
❑431, Sep 1994, 1: Free Spirit............ 2.00
❑432, Oct 1994............................. 2.00
❑433, Nov 1994............................. 2.00
❑434, Dec 1994, 1: Jack Flag. 2.00
❑435, Jan 1995, V: new Cobra. 2.00
❑436, Feb 1995 .... 2.00
❑437, Mar 1995............................. 2.00
❑438, Apr 1995, 1: Cap-Armor. 2.00
❑439, May 1995, V: Death-Stalker...... 2.00
❑440, Jun 1995............................. 2.00
❑441, Jul 1995 .... 2.00
❑442, Aug 1995............................. 2.00
❑443, Sep 1995, D: Captain America.. 2.00
❑444, Oct 1995, MWa (w); Title changes to Steve Rogers, Captain America; Red Skull brings Cap back to life; Return of Sharon Carter 3.00
❑445, Nov 1995, MWa (w); Return of Sharon Carter; Cap revived 2.00
❑446, Dec 1995, MWa (w); A: Red Skull. 2.00
❑447, Jan 1996, MWa (w)................. 2.00
❑448, Feb 1996, Giant-size MWa (w) . 3.00
❑449, Mar 1996, MWa (w) 2.00
❑450, Apr 1996, MWa (w); Title returns to Captain America; Cap's American citizenship is revoked..................... 2.00
❑450/A, Apr 1996, MWa (w); alternate cover.. 2.00
❑451, May 1996, MWa (w)................ 2.00
❑452, Jun 1996, MWa (w)................. 2.00
❑453, Jul 1996, MWa (w); Cap's citizenship restored........................ 2.00
❑454, Aug 1996, MWa (w) 2.00
❑Annual 1, ca. 1971, Cover reads "King-Size Special"; Cover reads King Size Special; Reprints from Tales of Suspense #63, 69-71, 75... 30.00
❑Annual 2, Jan 1972, Cover reads "King-Size Special"; GC, GT, JK (a); Cover reads King Size Special; Reprints from Tales of Suspense #72-74; Not Brand Ecch #3............ 10.00
❑Annual 3, ca. 1976, JK (a)................ 7.00
❑Annual 4, ca. 1977, JK (a); 1: Slither. 1: Crucible (Marvel)...................... 7.00
❑Annual 5, ca. 1981, FM (c); FM (a).... 3.00
❑Annual 6, ca. 1982, Four Caps.......... 3.00
❑Annual 7, ca. 1983, O: Kubik (Cosmic Cube)............................ 3.00
❑Annual 8, ca. 1986, A: Wolverine...... 12.00
❑Annual 9, ca. 1990, A: Iron Man....... 3.00
❑Annual 10, ca. 1991, DH (a); O: Captain America. O: Bushmaster. 3.00
❑Annual 11, ca. 1992 .... 3.00
❑Annual 12, ca. 1993, 1: Battling Bantam. Polybagged with trading card 3.00
❑Annual 13, ca. 1994, V: Red Skull. ... 3.00
❑Ashcan 1, ashcan edition; no indicia; Mini "Ashcan" preview.................... 1.00
❑Special 1, Feb 1984, Special Edition #1; JSo (c); JSo (a); reprint of Steranko issues 4.00
❑Special 2, Mar 1984, Special Edition #2; JSo (c); JSo (a); reprint of Steranko issues; Double-gatefold cover.. 4.00

CAPTAIN AMERICA (2ND SERIES)

MARVEL

❑1, Nov 1996; Steve Rogers regains memories of WW II action; Captain America jumping forward on cover. 3.00
❑1/Flag, Nov 1996; Variant cover (flag background) 4.00
❑1/Convention, Nov 1996; variant cover.. 5.00
❑2, Dec 1996 .... 2.00
❑3, Jan 1997 .... 2.00
❑4, Feb 1997 .... 2.00
❑5, Mar 1997............................... 2.00

Other grades: Multiply price above by 5/6 for VF/NM • 2/3 for VERY FINE • 1/3 for FINE • 1/5 for VERY GOOD • 1/8 for GOOD

Captain America: Dead Man Running

Series interlude between 3rd and 4th series

©Marvel

Captain America: The Movie Special

And it's the only thing special about the movie

©Marvel

Captain Atom (Charlton)

Title picked up from Strange Suspense Stories

©Charlton

Captain Atom (DC)

Learn how to cope with disintegration

©DC

Captain Carrot and His Amazing Zoo Crew

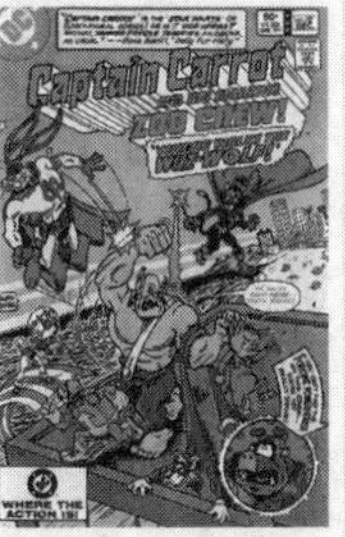

Very funny funny-animal super-hero title

©DC

	N-MINT
❑6, Apr 1997	2.00
❑7, May 1997	2.00
❑8, Jun 1997	2.00
❑9, Jul 1997	2.00
❑10, Aug 1997; gatefold summary	2.00
❑11, Sep 1997; gatefold summary	2.00
❑12, Oct 1997; gatefold summary; cover forms quadtych with Avengers #12, Iron Man #12; and Fantastic Four #12	2.00
❑13, Nov 1997; gatefold summary	2.00
❑Ashcan 1, Mar 1995; Collector's Preview	1.00
❑Ashcan 1/A; Special Comicon Edition; No cover price; preview of Vol. 2	1.00

CAPTAIN AMERICA (3RD SERIES)
MARVEL

	N-MINT
❑1, Jan 1998; gatefold summary; follows events in Heroes Return; Cap in Japan; wraparound cover	3.50
❑1/Sunburst, Jan 1998; gatefold summary; alternate cover; follows events in Heroes Return; Cap in Japan	5.00
❑2, Feb 1998; gatefold summary; Cap loses his shield	2.50
❑2/Variant, Feb 1998; variant cover	4.00
❑3, Mar 1998; gatefold summary	2.00
❑4, Apr 1998; gatefold summary; true identity of Sensational Hydra revealed	2.00
❑5, May 1998; gatefold summary; Cap replaced by Skrull	2.00
❑6, Jun 1998; gatefold summary; Skrulls revealed	2.00
❑7, Jul 1998; gatefold summary	2.00
❑8, Aug 1998; gatefold summary; Cap's shield destroyed; continues in Quicksilver #10	2.00
❑9, Sep 1998; gatefold summary; Cap gets new virtual shield	2.00
❑10, Oct 1998; gatefold summary; Nightmare	2.00
❑11, Nov 1998; gatefold summary	2.00
❑12, Dec 1998; double-sized; wraparound cover	2.00
❑12/Ltd., Dec 1998	6.00
❑13, Jan 1999; gatefold summary	2.00
❑14, Feb 1999; gatefold summary	2.00
❑15, Mar 1999	2.00
❑16, Apr 1999	2.00
❑17, May 1999	2.00
❑18, Jun 1999	2.00
❑19, Jul 1999	2.00
❑20, Aug 1999; Sgt. Fury back-up (b&w)	2.00
❑21, Sep 1999; Sgt. Fury back-up (b&w)	2.00
❑22, Oct 1999; Cap's shield restored	2.00
❑23, Nov 1999	2.00
❑24, Dec 2000	2.00
❑25, Jan 2000; Giant-size	3.00
❑26, Feb 2000	2.25
❑27, Mar 2000	2.25
❑28, Apr 2000	2.25
❑29, May 2000	2.25
❑30, Jun 2000	2.25
❑31, Jul 2000	2.25
❑32, Aug 2000; World War II story	2.25
❑33, Sep 2000	2.25
❑34, Oct 2000	2.25
❑35, Nov 2000	2.25
❑36, Dec 2000	2.25
❑37, Jan 2001	2.25
❑38, Feb 2001	2.25
❑39, Mar 2001	2.25
❑40, Apr 2001	2.25
❑41, May 2001	2.25
❑42, Jun 2001	2.25
❑43, Jul 2001	2.25
❑44, Aug 2001	2.25
❑45, Sep 2001	2.25
❑46, Oct 2001	2.25
❑47, Nov 2001	2.25
❑48, Dec 2001	2.25
❑49, Jan 2002	2.25
❑50, Feb 2002	5.95
❑Annual 1998, ca. 1998; wraparound cover	3.50
❑Annual 1999, ca. 1999	3.50
❑Annual 2000, ca. 2000; continued from Captain America #35	3.50
❑Annual 2001, ca. 2001	2.99

CAPTAIN AMERICA (4TH SERIES)
MARVEL

	N-MINT
❑1, Jun 2002	4.00
❑2, Jul 2002	3.00
❑3, Aug 2002	3.00
❑4, Sep 2002	3.00
❑5, Oct 2002	3.00
❑6, Dec 2002	3.00
❑7, Feb 2003	3.00
❑8, Mar 2003	3.00
❑9, Apr 2003	3.00
❑10, May 2003	3.00
❑11, Jun 2003	3.00
❑12, Jun 2003	3.00
❑13, Jul 2003	3.00
❑14, Aug 2003	3.00
❑15, Sep 2003	3.00
❑16, Oct 2003	3.00
❑17, Nov 2003, DaG (w); JK, JR, TP (a)	3.00
❑18, Nov 2003, DaG (w); TP (a)	3.00
❑19, Dec 2003, DaG (w); TP (a)	3.00
❑20, Jan 2004, DaG (w); TP (a)	3.00
❑21, Feb 2004	3.00
❑22, Mar 2004	3.00
❑23, Apr 2004	3.00
❑24, May 2004	3.00
❑25, Jun 2004	3.00
❑26, Jul 2004	2.99
❑27, Aug 2004	2.99
❑28, Aug 2004	2.99
❑29, Sep 2004	2.99
❑30, Oct 2004	2.99
❑31, Nov 2004	2.99
❑32, Dec 2004	2.99

CAPTAIN AMERICA (5TH SERIES)
MARVEL

	N-MINT
❑1, Jan 2005	8.00
❑2, Feb 2005	5.00
❑3, Mar 2005	5.00
❑4, Apr 2005	2.99
❑5, May 2005	2.99
❑6, Jun 2005	7.00
❑6/Variant, Jun 2005	5.00
❑7, Jul 2005	2.99
❑8, Aug 2005	2.99
❑9, Sep 2005	2.99
❑10, Oct 2005	2.99
❑11, Nov 2005	2.99
❑12, Jan 2006	2.99
❑13, Feb 2006	2.99
❑14, Mar 2006	2.99
❑15, May 2006	2.99
❑16, Jun 2006	2.99
❑17, Jul 2006	2.99
❑19, Sep 2006	2.99

CAPTAIN AMERICA AND HE CAMPBELL KIDS
MARVEL

	N-MINT
❑1, ca. 1980; giveaway	3.00

CAPTAIN AMERICA & THE FALCON
MARVEL

	N-MINT
❑1, May 2004	2.99
❑2, Jun 2004, (c)	2.99
❑3, Jul 2004	2.99
❑4, Aug 2004	2.99
❑5, Sep 2004	2.99
❑6, Oct 2004	4.00
❑7, Nov 2004	2.99
❑8, Dec 2004	2.99
❑9, Jan 2005	2.99
❑10, Feb 2005	2.99
❑11, Mar 2005	2.99
❑12, Apr 2005	2.99
❑13, May 2005	2.99
❑14, Jun 2005	2.99

CAPTAIN AMERICA: DEAD MAN RUNNING
MARVEL

	N-MINT
❑1, Mar 2002	2.99
❑2, Apr 2002	2.99
❑3, May 2002	2.99

CAPTAIN AMERICA: DRUG WAR
MARVEL

	N-MINT
❑1, Apr 1993	2.00

CAPTAIN AMERICA GOES TO WAR AGAINST DRUGS
MARVEL

	N-MINT
❑1, ca. 1990; Anti-drug giveaway PD (w)	1.00

CAPTAIN AMERICA: MEDUSA EFFECT
MARVEL

	N-MINT
❑1, Mar 1994	2.95

CAPTAIN AMERICA/NICK FURY: BLOOD TRUCE
MARVEL

	N-MINT
❑1, Feb 1995; prestige format one-shot	5.95

CAPTAIN AMERICA/NICK FURY: THE OTHERWORLD WAR
MARVEL

	N-MINT
❑1, Oct 2001	6.95

Other grades: Multiply price above by 5/6 for VF/NM • 2/3 for VERY FINE • 1/3 for FINE • 1/5 for VERY GOOD • 1/8 for GOOD

CAPTAIN AMERICA: SENTINEL OF LIBERTY
MARVEL

- ❑1, Sep 1998; gatefold summary; wraparound cover 1.99
- ❑1/Variant, Sep 1988; Roughcut edition 2.99
- ❑2, Oct 1998; gatefold summary; Invaders 1.99
- ❑2/Variant, Oct 1998 1.99
- ❑3, Nov 1998; gatefold summary; Invaders 1.99
- ❑4, Dec 1998; gatefold summary; Invaders 1.99
- ❑5, Jan 1999; gatefold summary; Tales of Suspense tribute 1.99
- ❑6, Feb 1999; double-sized; Tales of Suspense tribute 2.99
- ❑7, Mar 1999; Bicentennial story 1.99
- ❑8, Apr 1999 1.99
- ❑9, May 1999 1.99
- ❑10, Jun 1999 1.99
- ❑11, Jul 1999 1.99
- ❑12, Aug 1999 2.99

CAPTAIN AMERICA 65TH ANNIVERSARY SPECIAL
MARVEL

- ❑1, Jun 2006 4.99

CAPTAIN AMERICA: THE LEGEND
MARVEL

- ❑1, Sep 1996; background on Cap and his supporting cast; wraparound cover 4.00

CAPTAIN AMERICA: THE MOVIE SPECIAL
MARVEL

- ❑1, May 1992 3.50

CAPTAIN AMERICA: WHAT PRICE GLORY
MARVEL

- ❑1, May 2003 2.99
- ❑2, May 2003 2.99
- ❑3, May 2003 2.99
- ❑4, May 2003 2.99

CAPTAIN ARMADILLO: THE ADVENTURE BEGINS
STATON GRAPHICS

- ❑1, ca. 1989, b&w 2.00

CAPTAIN ATOM (CHARLTON)
CHARLTON

- ❑78, Dec 1965, SD (c); SD (w); SD (a); O: Captain Atom. Series continued from Strange Suspense Stories #77 40.00
- ❑79, Mar 1966, SD (c); SD (w); SD (a) 25.00
- ❑80, May 1966, SD (c); SD (w); SD (a) 25.00
- ❑81, Jul 1966, SD (c); SD (w); SD (a) 25.00
- ❑82, Sep 1966, SD (c); SD (a) 25.00
- ❑83, Nov 1966, SD (c); SD (w); SD (a); 1: Ted Kord (Blue Beetle). 25.00
- ❑84, Jan 1967, SD (c); SD (a); 1: Captain Atom (new). 25.00
- ❑85, Mar 1967, SD (c); SD (a) 25.00
- ❑86, Jun 1967, SD (c); SD (a) 20.00
- ❑87, Aug 1967, SD (c); SD, JA (a); Nightshade back-up story 20.00
- ❑88, Oct 1967, FMc, SD (c); FMc, SD (a) 20.00
- ❑89, Dec 1967, FMc, SD (c); FMc, SD (a) 20.00

CAPTAIN ATOM (DC)
DC

- ❑1, Mar 1987; PB (a); O: Captain Atom. New costume 1.00
- ❑2, Apr 1987 1.00
- ❑3, May 1987 O: Captain Atom (fake origin). 1.00
- ❑4, Jun 1987 1.00
- ❑5, Jul 1987 A: Firestorm. 1.00
- ❑6, Aug 1987 V: Doctor Spectro. 1.00
- ❑7, Sep 1987 1.00
- ❑8, Oct 1987 A: Plastique. 1.00
- ❑9, Nov 1987 1.00
- ❑10, Dec 1987 1.00
- ❑11, Jan 1988; A: Firestorm. Millennium 1.00
- ❑12, Feb 1988 1: Major Force. 1.00
- ❑13, Mar 1988 1.00
- ❑14, Apr 1988 1.00
- ❑15, May 1988 V: Major Force. 1.00
- ❑16, Jun 1988 A: JLI. 1.00
- ❑17, Jul 1988 A: Swamp Thing. 1.00
- ❑18, Aug 1988 1.00
- ❑19, Sep 1988 1.00
- ❑20, Oct 1988 A: Blue Beetle. 1.00
- ❑21, Nov 1988 1.00
- ❑22, Dec 1988; Plastique vs. Nightshade 1.00
- ❑23, ca. 1988; V: Ghost. no month of publication 1.00
- ❑24, ca. 1989; Invasion!; no month of publication 1.00
- ❑25, Jan 1989; Invasion!; no month of publication 1.00
- ❑26, Feb 1989 O: Captain Atom. A: JLA. 1.00
- ❑27, Mar 1989 PB (a); O: Captain Atom. 1.00
- ❑28, Apr 1989 O: Captain Atom. V: Ghost. 1.00
- ❑29, May 1989 1.00
- ❑30, Jun 1989 1.00
- ❑31, Jul 1989 V: Rocket Red. 1.00
- ❑32, Aug 1989 1.00
- ❑33, Sep 1989; Batman; new costume 1.00
- ❑34, Oct 1989 V: Doctor Spectro. 1.00
- ❑35, Nov 1989; A: Major Force. back to old costume 1.00
- ❑36, Dec 1989 1.00
- ❑37, Jan 1990 1.00
- ❑38, Feb 1990 V: Black Racer. 1.00
- ❑39, Mar 1990 1.00
- ❑40, Apr 1990 1.00
- ❑41, May 1990 1.00
- ❑42, Jun 1990 1.00
- ❑43, Jul 1990 1.00
- ❑44, Aug 1990 A: Plastique. 1.00
- ❑45, Sep 1990 1.00
- ❑46, Oct 1990; Superman 1.00
- ❑47, Nov 1990 1.00
- ❑48, Dec 1990 1.00
- ❑49, Jan 1991; Trial of Plastique 1.00
- ❑50, Feb 1991; Giant-size D: Megala. 2.00
- ❑51, Mar 1991 1.00
- ❑52, Apr 1991 1.00
- ❑53, May 1991 1.00
- ❑54, Jun 1991 1.00
- ❑55, Jul 1991 1.00
- ❑56, Aug 1991 1.00
- ❑57, Sep 1991 1.00
- ❑Annual 1, ca. 1988; 1: Major Force. V: Major Force. says 88 on cover, 87 in indicia 2.00
- ❑Annual 2, ca. 1989 V: Queen Bee. 1.50

CAPTAIN ATOM: ARMAGEDDON
DC

- ❑1, Dec 2005 2.99
- ❑2, Jan 2006 2.99
- ❑3, Feb 2006 2.99
- ❑4, Mar 2006 2.99
- ❑5, Apr 2006 2.99
- ❑6, May 2006 2.99
- ❑7, Jun 2006 2.99
- ❑8, Jul 2006 2.99
- ❑9, Aug 2006 2.99

CAPTAIN ATOM (MODERN)
MODERN

- ❑83, ca. 1977; reprints Charlton series #83 5.00
- ❑84, ca. 1977; reprints Charlton series #84 5.00
- ❑85, ca. 1977; reprints Charlton series #85 5.00

CAPTAIN BRITAIN
MARVEL UK

- ❑1, Jan 1985, O: The Free-Fall Warriors. 2.50
- ❑2, Feb 1985, b&w; No logo, Gold cover 2.00
- ❑3, Mar 1985, b&w; No logo, Gold cover 2.00
- ❑4, Apr 1985, b&w; No logo, Gold cover 2.00
- ❑5, May 1985, b&w; No logo, Gold cover 2.00
- ❑6, Jun 1985, b&w; No logo, Gold cover 2.00
- ❑7, Jul 1985, b&w; No logo, Gold cover 2.00
- ❑8, Aug 1985, b&w; No logo, Gold cover 2.00
- ❑9, Sep 1985, b&w; No logo, Gold cover 2.00
- ❑10, Oct 1985, b&w; No logo, Gold cover 2.00
- ❑11, Nov 1985, b&w; No logo, Gold cover 2.00
- ❑12, Dec 1985, b&w; No logo, Gold cover 2.00
- ❑13, Jan 1986, b&w; No logo, Gold cover 2.00
- ❑14, Feb 1986 2.00

CAPTAIN CANUCK
COMELY

- ❑1, Jul 1975 3.00
- ❑2, ca. 1975, no month of publication 2.00
- ❑3, ca. 1976, no month of publication 2.00
- ❑4, Aug 1979, New publisher 1.50
- ❑5, Sep 1979 1.50
- ❑6, Nov 1979 1.50
- ❑7, Jan 1980 1.50
- ❑8, Mar 1980 1.50
- ❑9, May 1980, says Jun on cover; May in indicia 1.50
- ❑10, Aug 1980 1.50
- ❑11, Oct 1980 1.50
- ❑12, Dec 1980 1.50
- ❑13, Feb 1981 1.50
- ❑14, Apr 1981 1.50

CAPTAIN CANUCK FIRST SUMMER SPECIAL
COMELY

- ❑1, Sep 1980 1.50

CAPTAIN CANUCK REBORN
SEMPLE

- ❑0, Sep 1993 1.50
- ❑1, Jan 1994 2.50
- ❑1/Gold; Gold polybagged edition with trading cards 2.95
- ❑2, Jul 1994 2.50
- ❑3, b&w; strip reprints; cardstock cover 2.50

CAPTAIN CARROT AND HIS AMAZING ZOO CREW
DC

- ❑1, Mar 1982, RA (c); A: Superman. A: Starro. 1.50
- ❑2, Apr 1982, AA (a); A: Superman. 1.00
- ❑3, May 1982 1.00
- ❑4, Jun 1982 1.00
- ❑5, Jul 1982, A: Oklahoma Bones. 1.00
- ❑6, Aug 1982, V: Bunny from Beyond. Back-up stories begin 1.00
- ❑7, Sep 1982, A: Bow-zar the Barbarian. 1.00
- ❑8, Oct 1982, 1: Z-Building (Zoo Crew's Headquarters). 1.00
- ❑9, Nov 1982, A: Terrific Whatzie. A: Three Mouseketeers. Masters of the Universe preview 1.00
- ❑10, Dec 1982 1.00
- ❑11, Jan 1983 1.00
- ❑12, Feb 1983, 1: Little Cheese. 1st Art Adams art (pin-up of Fara Foxette). 1.00
- ❑13, Mar 1983 1.00
- ❑14, Apr 1983, Justa Lotta Animals 1.00
- ❑15, May 1983, Justa Lotta Animals 1.00
- ❑16, Jun 1983 1.00
- ❑17, Jul 1983 1.00
- ❑18, Aug 1983 1.00
- ❑19, Sep 1983, V: Frogzilla. Superman III movie contest 1.00
- ❑20, Nov 1983, A: Changeling. V: Gorilla Grodd. 1.00

CAPTAIN CONFEDERACY (STEELDRAGON)
STEELDRAGON

- ❑1 1.50
- ❑2 1.50
- ❑3 1.50
- ❑4 1.50
- ❑5 1.50
- ❑6, Sum 1987 1.50
- ❑7, Aut 1987 1.75
- ❑8, Win 1987 1.75
- ❑9, Spr 1988 1.75
- ❑10, Jun 1988 1.75
- ❑11, Jun 1988 1.75
- ❑12, Oct 1988 1.75
- ❑Special 1, Sum 1987 1.75
- ❑Special 2, Sum 1987 1.75

CAPTAIN CONFEDERACY (EPIC)
MARVEL / EPIC

- ❑1, Nov 1991 2.00
- ❑2, Dec 1991 2.00
- ❑3, Jan 1992 2.00
- ❑4, Feb 1992 2.00

Other grades: Multiply price above by 5/6 for VF/NM • 2/3 for VERY FINE • 1/3 for FINE • 1/5 for VERY GOOD • 1/8 for GOOD

Captain Marvel (1st Series)

Adventures of Mar-Vell of the Kree

©Marvel

Captain Planet and the Planeteers

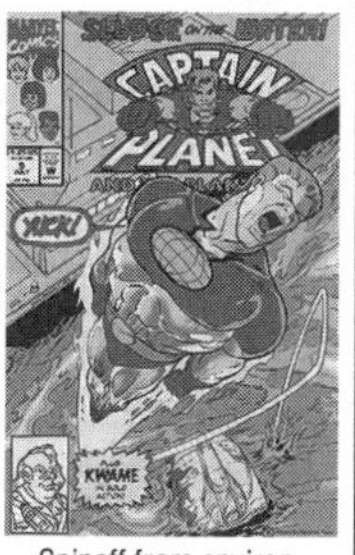

Spinoff from environmentalist TV cartoon

©Marvel

Capt. Savage and His Leatherneck Raiders

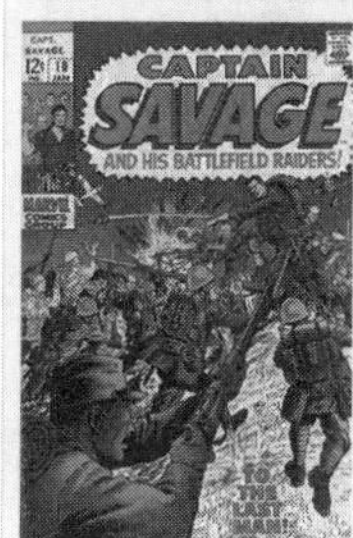

One of the more action-packed war comics

©Marvel

Captain Sternn: Running Out of Time

Bernie Wrightson's SF satire goes glossy

©Kitchen Sink

Capt. Storm

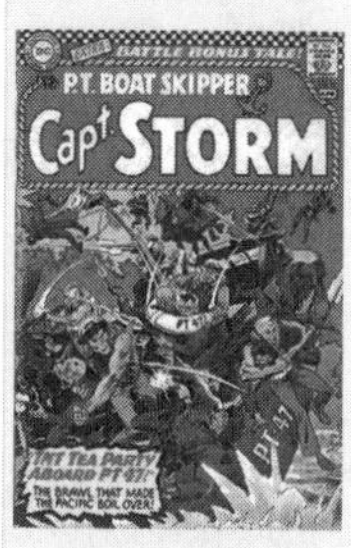

One-legged captain commands PT boat

©DC

N-MINT

CAPTAIN COSMOS, THE LAST STARVEYOR
YBOR CITY

❑1 .... 2.95

CAPTAIN CRAFTY
CONCEPTION

❑1, Jun 1994, b&w; wraparound cover 2.50
❑2, Win 1994, b&w; wraparound cover 2.50
❑2.5, Apr 1998 .... 1.00

CAPTAIN CRAFTY COLOR SPECTACULAR
CONCEPTION

❑1, Aug 1996; wraparound cover 2.50
❑2, Dec 1996; wraparound cover 2.50

CAPTAIN CRUSADER
TPI

❑1, Aug 1990 .... 1.25

CAPTAIN CULT
HAMMAC

❑1, b&w; 1st appearance of Captain Cult 2.00

CAPTAIN DINGLEBERRY
SLAVE LABOR

❑1, Aug 1998 .... 2.95
❑2, Sep 1998 .... 2.95
❑3, Oct 1998 .... 2.95
❑4 1998 .... 2.95
❑5, Jan 1999 .... 2.95
❑6, Feb 1999 .... 2.95

CAPTAIN D'S ADVENTURE MAGAZINE
PARAGON

❑1, ca. 1983, Promotional comic book for Shoney's Captain D's seafood restaurants in the Southeast 1.00
❑2, ca. 1983 .... 1.00
❑3, ca. 1984 .... 1.00
❑4, ca. 1984 .... 1.00
❑5, ca. 1984 .... 1.00
❑6, ca. 1984 .... 1.00

CAPTAIN EO 3-D
ECLIPSE

❑1, Aug 1987; oversized (11x17) 5.00

CAPTAIN FORTUNE
RIP OFF

❑1 .... 2.95
❑2 .... 3.25
❑3 .... 3.25
❑4 .... 3.25

CAPTAIN GLORY
TOPPS

❑0, Apr 1993; trading card 2.95
❑1, Apr 1993 .... 2.95

CAPTAIN GRAVITY
PENNY-FARTHING

❑1, Dec 1998 .... 2.75
❑1/Autographed, Dec 1998; Autographed edition 3.50
❑2, Jan 1999 .... 2.75
❑3, Feb 1999 .... 2.75
❑4, Mar 1999 .... 2.75

N-MINT

CAPTAIN GRAVITY: ONE TRUE HERO
PENNY-FARTHING

❑1, Aug 1999 .... 2.95

CAPTAIN HARLOCK
ETERNITY

❑1, b&w; Character created by Leiji Matsumoto 2.50
❑2 .... 2.50
❑3 .... 2.50
❑4 .... 2.50
❑5 .... 2.50
❑6 .... 2.50
❑7 .... 2.50
❑8 .... 2.50
❑9 .... 2.50
❑10 .... 2.50
❑11 .... 2.50
❑12 .... 2.50
❑13 .... 2.50
❑Book 1; Captain Harlock Returns 9.95
❑Holiday 1, b&w; prestige format 2.50

CAPTAIN HARLOCK: DEATHSHADOW RISING
ETERNITY

❑1 .... 2.25
❑2 .... 2.25
❑3 .... 2.25
❑4 .... 2.25
❑5 .... 2.25
❑6 .... 2.25

CAPTAIN HARLOCK: THE FALL OF THE EMPIRE
ETERNITY

❑1 .... 2.50
❑2, Aug 1992 .... 2.50
❑3 .... 2.50
❑4 .... 2.50

CAPTAIN HARLOCK: THE MACHINE PEOPLE
ETERNITY

❑1 .... 2.50
❑2 .... 2.50
❑3 .... 2.50
❑4 .... 2.50

CAPTAIN JOHNER & THE ALIENS
VALIANT

❑1, May 1995, PS (c); RM (w); PS, RM (a); reprints back-ups from Magnus, Robot Fighter (Gold Key) #1-7; cardstock cover 6.00
❑2, May 1995, RM (w); RM (a); reprints back-ups from Magnus, Robot Fighter (Gold Key); cardstock cover 6.00

CAPTAIN JUSTICE
MARVEL

❑1, ca. 1988; TV show 1.25
❑2, Apr 1988; TV show 1.25

CAPTAIN MARVEL
M.F.

❑1, Apr 1966 .... 40.00
❑2, Jun 1966 .... 25.00
❑3, Sep 1966 .... 25.00
❑4, Nov 1966 .... 25.00

N-MINT

CAPTAIN MARVEL (1ST SERIES)
MARVEL

❑1, May 1968, GC (a); Indicia: Marvel's Space-Born Superhero: Captain Marvel 60.00
❑2, Jun 1968, GC (a); A: Sub-Mariner. V: Skrull. 18.00
❑3, Jul 1968, GC (a); V: Skrull. 18.00
❑4, Aug 1968, GC (a); A: Sub-Mariner. V: Sub-Mariner. 22.00
❑5, Sep 1968, DH (a) 15.00
❑6, Oct 1968, DH (a) 20.00
❑7, Nov 1968, DH (a); V: Quasimodo. 15.00
❑8, Dec 1968, DH (a); 1: Aakon (alien race) 15.00
❑9, Jan 1969, DH (a) 15.00
❑10, Feb 1969, DH (a) 13.00
❑11, Mar 1969, D: Una. 13.00
❑12, Apr 1969 .... 13.00
❑13, May 1969 .... 13.00
❑14, Jun 1969, A: Iron Man. 13.00
❑15, Aug 1969 .... 13.00
❑16, Sep 1969 .... 13.00
❑17, Oct 1969, GK, DA (c); GK, DA (a); O: Rick Jones retold. new costume; crossover with Captain America #114-116 .... 13.00
❑18, Nov 1969 .... 13.00
❑19, Dec 1969, GK, DA (a); series goes on hiatus 13.00
❑20, Jun 1970, GK, DA (c); GK, DA (a) 13.00
❑21, Aug 1970, A: Hulk. series goes on hiatus 13.00
❑22, Sep 1972, V: Megaton. Title changes to Captain Marvel after hiatus 13.00
❑23, Nov 1972, V: Megaton. 13.00
❑24, Jan 1973 .... 13.00
❑25, Mar 1973, JSn (a); Thanos War begins 25.00
❑26, May 1973, JSn (a); A: Thanos. Thing; Masterlord revealed as Thanos 25.00
❑27, Jul 1973, JSn (a); 1: Death (Marvel). A: Thanos. death of Super Skrull 25.00
❑28, Sep 1973, AM, JSn (a); A: Thanos. Avengers 30.00
❑29, Nov 1973, AM, JSn (a); O: Kronos. A: Thanos. Captain Marvel gets new powers 15.00
❑30, Jan 1974, AM, JSn (a); A: Thanos. V: Controller. 12.00
❑31, Mar 1974, JSn (a); 1: ISAAC. A: Thanos. Avengers 15.00
❑32, May 1974, JSn (a); O: Moondragon. O: Drax. A: Thanos. Rick Jones vs. Thanos; continued in Avengers #125; Marvel Value Stamp #19: Balder, Hogun, Fandral 12.00
❑33, Jul 1974, JSn (a); O: Thanos. Thanos War ends; continued from Avengers #125; Marvel Value Stamp #6: Thor 12.00
❑34, Sep 1974, JSn, JAb (a); 1: Nitro. Captain Marvel contracts cancer (will eventually die from it); Marvel Value Stamp #25: Torch 6.00
❑35, Nov 1974, AA (a); V: Living Laser. Ant-Man, Wasp; Marvel Value Stamp #1: Spider-Man 3.00

Other grades: Multiply price above by 5/6 for VF/NM • 2/3 for VERY FINE • 1/3 for FINE • 1/5 for VERY GOOD • 1/8 for GOOD

❑36, Jan 1975, JSn (a); A: Thanos. Watcher; Marvel Value Stamp #25: Torch 3.00
❑37, Mar 1975, AM (w); Watcher 3.00
❑38, May 1975, AM (w); Trial of the Watcher 3.00
❑39, Jul 1975, AM (w); 1: Aron the Rogue Watcher. Watcher (Uatu) 3.00
❑40, Sep 1975, AM (w); Watcher 3.00
❑41, Nov 1975, AM (w); A: Supreme Intelligence. V: Ronan. Marvel Value Stamp #2: Hulk 3.00
❑42, Jan 1976, AM (w); V: Stranger. 3.00
❑43, Mar 1976, AM (a); V: Drax 3.00
❑44, May 1976, AM (w); V: Drax. 3.00
❑44/30 cent, May 1976, AM (w); V: Drax. 30 cent regional price variant 20.00
❑45, Jul 1976, AM (w) 3.00
❑45/30 cent, Jul 1976, AM (w); 30 cent regional price variant 20.00
❑46, Sep 1976, 1: Supremor 3.00
❑47, Nov 1976, A: Human Torch. V: Sentry Sinister. 3.00
❑48, Jan 1977, 1: Cheetah (Esteban Carracus). V: Cheetah. V: Sentry Sinister. 3.00
❑49, Mar 1977, V: Ronan. 3.00
❑50, May 1977, AM (a); 1: Doctor Minerva. A: Avengers. A: Adaptoid. 3.00
❑51, Jul 1977, V: Mercurio. 4.00
❑52, Sep 1977 3.00
❑52/35 cent, Sep 1977, 35 cent regional price variant 15.00
❑53, Nov 1977 3.00
❑54, Jan 1978 3.00
❑55, Mar 1978, V: Death-Grip 3.00
❑56, May 1978, PB (a); V: Death-Grip. 3.00
❑57, Jul 1978, PB, BWi (a); A: Thanos. V: Thor. Flashback 6.00
❑58, Sep 1978, V: Drax 3.00
❑59, Nov 1978, 1: Elysius. V: Drax. 3.00
❑60, Jan 1979 3.00
❑61, Mar 1979, PB (a) 3.00
❑62, May 1979 3.00

CAPTAIN MARVEL (2ND SERIES)
MARVEL

❑1, Nov 1989; New Captain Marvel (Monica Rambeau) gets her powers back 2.00

CAPTAIN MARVEL (3RD SERIES)
MARVEL

❑1, Feb 1994 2.00

CAPTAIN MARVEL (4TH SERIES)
MARVEL

❑1, Dec 1995; enhanced cardstock cover 2.95
❑2, Jan 1996 1.95
❑3, Feb 1996 1.95
❑4, Mar 1996 1.95
❑5, Apr 1996 1.95
❑6, May 1996 1.95

CAPTAIN MARVEL (5TH SERIES)
MARVEL

❑0; Wizard promotional edition 3.00
❑1, Jan 2000; PD (w); Regular cover (space background w/rocks) 3.00
❑1/A, Jan 2000; PD (w); 1: 10 ratio. Variant cover (Marvel against white background) 4.00
❑2, Feb 2000 PD (w); A: Wendigo. A: Moondragon. A: Hulk 2.50
❑3, Mar 2000 PD (w); A: Wendigo. A: Moondragon. A: Hulk. A: Drax. D: Lorraine. 2.50
❑4, Apr 2000 PD (w); A: Moondragon. A: Drax. 2.50
❑5, May 2000; PD (w); A: Moondragon. A: Drax. in microverse 2.50
❑6, Jun 2000 PD (w) 2.50
❑7, Jul 2000 2.50
❑8, Aug 2000 2.50
❑9, Sep 2000 PD (w); A: Super Skrull. A: Silver Surfer. 2.50
❑10, Oct 2000 2.50
❑11, Nov 2000 PD (w); JSn (a); A: Moondragon. A: Silver Surfer. A: Mar-Vell. 2.50
❑12, Dec 2000 PD (w) 2.50
❑13, Jan 2001 PD (w) 2.50
❑14, Feb 2001 2.50
❑15, Mar 2001 PD (w) 2.50
❑16, Apr 2001 PD (w) 2.50
❑17, May 2001 PD (w); JSn (a); A: Thor. 2.50
❑18, Jun 2001 2.50
❑19, Jul 2001 2.50
❑20, Aug 2001 2.50
❑21, Sep 2001 2.50
❑22, Oct 2001 2.50
❑23, Nov 2001 2.50
❑24, Dec 2001 2.50
❑25, Jan 2002 2.50
❑26, Feb 2002 2.50
❑27, Mar 2002 2.50
❑29, Apr 2002 2.50
❑28, Mar 2002 2.50
❑30, May 2002 2.50
❑31, Jun 2002 2.50
❑32, Jul 2002 2.50
❑33, Aug 2002 2.50
❑34, Sep 2002 2.50
❑35, Oct 2002 2.50

CAPTAIN MARVEL (6TH SERIES)
MARVEL

❑1, Nov 2002 2.25
❑2, Dec 2002 2.25
❑3, Jan 2003 2.25
❑4, Feb 2003 2.25
❑5, Mar 2003 2.99
❑6, Apr 2003 2.99
❑7, May 2003 2.99
❑8, Jun 2003 2.99
❑9, Jul 2003 2.99
❑10, Jul 2003 2.99
❑11, Aug 2003 2.99
❑12, Sep 2003 2.99
❑13, Oct 2003 2.99
❑14, Oct 2003 2.99
❑15, Nov 2003 2.99
❑16, Jan 2004 2.99
❑17, Feb 2004 2.99
❑18, Mar 2004 2.99
❑19, Apr 2004 2.99
❑20, May 2004 2.99
❑21, May 2004 2.99
❑22, Jun 2004 2.99
❑23, Jul 2004 2.99
❑24, Aug 2004 2.99
❑25, Sep 2004 2.99

CAPTAIN NAUTICUS & THE OCEAN FORCE
EXPRESS / ENTITY

❑1, May 1994 2.95
❑1/Ltd., Oct 1994; limited promotional edition 2.95
❑2, Dec 1994; for The National Maritime Center Authority 2.95

CAPTAIN NICE
GOLD KEY

❑1, Nov 1967 35.00

CAPTAIN N: THE GAME MASTER
VALIANT

❑1, ca. 1990 1.95
❑2, ca. 1990 1.95
❑3, ca. 1990 1.95
❑4, ca. 1990 1.95
❑5, ca. 1990 1.95
❑6, ca. 1990 1.95

CAPTAIN OBLIVION
HARRIER

❑1, Aug 1987 1.95

CAPTAIN PARAGON
AC

❑1, Dec 1983 1.50
❑2 1.50
❑3 1.50
❑4 1.50

CAPTAIN PARAGON AND THE SENTINELS OF JUSTICE
AC

❑1 1.75
❑2 1.75
❑3 1.75
❑4 1.75
❑5; O: Captain Paragon. Title changes to Sentinels of Justice 1.75
❑6 1.75

CAPTAIN PHIL
STEELDRAGON

❑1 1.50

CAPTAIN PLANET AND THE PLANETEERS
MARVEL

❑1, Oct 1991; TV 1.00
❑2, Nov 1991 1.00
❑3, Dec 1991 1.00
❑4, Jan 1992 1.00
❑5, Feb 1992 1.00
❑6, Mar 1992 1.00
❑7, Apr 1992 1.00
❑8, Jun 1992 1.00
❑9, Jul 1992 1.00
❑10, Aug 1992 1.00
❑11, Sep 1992 1.00
❑12, Oct 1992 1.00

CAPTAIN POWER AND THE SOLDIERS OF THE FUTURE
CONTINUITY

❑1, Aug 1988; newsstand cover: Captain Power standing 2.00
❑1/Direct ed. 1988; direct-sale cover: Captain Power kneeling 2.00
❑2, Jan 1989 2.00

CAPTAIN SALVATION
STREETLIGHT

❑1 1.95

CAPTAIN SATAN
MILLENNIUM

❑1; Flip-book format 2.95
❑2; Flip-book format 2.95

CAPT. SAVAGE AND HIS LEATHERNECK RAIDERS
MARVEL

❑1, Jan 1968, O: Captain Savage and his Leatherneck Raiders. A: Sgt. Fury. 35.00
❑2, Mar 1968, O: Hydra. V: Baron Strucker. 25.00
❑3, May 1968, V: Baron Strucker, Hydra. 15.00
❑4, Jul 1968, V: Baron Strucker 15.00
❑5, Aug 1968 15.00
❑6, Sep 1968, A: Izzy Cohen 15.00
❑7, Oct 1968, A: Ben Grimm. 15.00
❑8, Nov 1968, (becomes Captain Savage) 15.00
❑9, Dec 1968, Title changes to Captain Savage (and his Battlefield Raiders) 15.00
❑10, Jan 1969, JSe (c); JSe (a) 15.00
❑11, Feb 1969, A: Sgt. Fury. D: Baker. Story continued in Sgt. Fury #64 15.00
❑12, Mar 1969, DH (c) 10.00
❑13, Apr 1969, DH (c); DH (a) 10.00
❑14, May 1969, DH (c); DH (a) 10.00
❑15, Jul 1969, JSe (c); DH (a); Title changes to Capt. Savage 10.00
❑16, Sep 1969, JSe (c); DH, JSe (a) 10.00
❑17, Nov 1969, JSe (c); JSe (a) 10.00
❑18, Jan 1970, JSe (c); JSe (a) 10.00
❑19, Mar 1970, JSe (c); JSe (a) 10.00

CAPTAIN'S JOLTING TALES
ONE SHOT

❑1, Aug 1991 2.95
❑2, Oct 1991 3.50
❑3; trading card 3.50
❑3/Deluxe, Dec 1992 3.50
❑4 3.50

CAPTAIN STERNN: RUNNING OUT OF TIME
KITCHEN SINK

❑1, Sep 1993, b&w BWr (w); BWr (a) 5.50
❑2, Dec 1993, b&w BWr (w); BWr (a) 5.00
❑3, Mar 1994 BWr (w); BWr (a) 5.00
❑4, May 1994 BWr (w); BWr (a) 5.00
❑5, Sep 1994 BWr (w); BWr (a) 5.00

CAPT. STORM
DC

❑1, Jun 1964, O: Captain Storm. 28.00
❑2, Aug 1964 18.00
❑3, Oct 1964 18.00
❑4, Dec 1964 18.00
❑5, Feb 1965 18.00
❑6, Apr 1965 14.00
❑7, Jun 1965 12.00
❑8, Aug 1965 12.00

Other grades: Multiply price above by 5/6 for VF/NM • 2/3 for VERY FINE • 1/3 for FINE • 1/5 for VERY GOOD • 1/8 for GOOD

Captain Victory and the Galactic Rangers

Independent space-spanning Kirby work

©Pacific

Care Bears

Cavity-causing cartoon spreads to comics

©Marvel

Cartoon Cartoons

DC's catchall for other Cartoon Network titles

©DC

Cartoon Network Presents

DC's first Cartoon Network anthology

©DC

Cartoon Network Starring

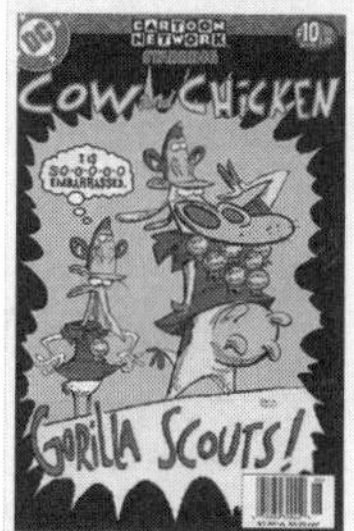

Anthology evolved into Cartoon Cartoons

©DC

	N-MINT
❑9, Oct 1965	12.00
❑10, Dec 1965	12.00
❑11, Feb 1966	12.00
❑12, Apr 1966	12.00
❑13, Jun 1966	12.00
❑14, Aug 1966	12.00
❑15, Oct 1966	12.00
❑16, Dec 1966	9.00
❑17, Feb 1967	9.00
❑18, Apr 1967	9.00

CAPTAIN TAX TIME
PAUL HAYNES COMICS

❑1	4.00

CAPTAIN THUNDER AND BLUE BOLT
HERO

❑1 1987	1.95
❑2, Oct 1987	1.95
❑3 1988	1.95
❑4 1988	1.95
❑5 1988	1.95
❑6	1.95
❑7 1989	1.95
❑8	1.95
❑9	1.95
❑10	1.95

CAPTAIN THUNDER AND BLUE BOLT (VOL. 2)
HERO

❑1, Aug 1992	3.50
❑2	3.50

CAPTAIN UNIVERSE/DAREDEVIL
MARVEL

❑1, Jan 2006, b&w	2.99

CAPTAIN UNIVERSE/ INVISIBLE WOMAN
MARVEL

❑1, Jan 2006	2.99

CAPTAIN UNIVERSE/THE INCREDIBLE HULK
MARVEL

❑1, Jan 2006	2.99

CAPTAIN UNIVERSE/SILVER SURFER
MARVEL

❑1, Jan 2006	2.99

CAPTAIN UNIVERSE/X-23
MARVEL

❑1, Jan 2006	2.99

CAPTAIN VENTURE AND THE LAND BENEATH THE SEA
GOLD KEY

❑1, Oct 1968	26.00
❑2, Oct 1969, DS (a)	18.00

CAPTAIN VICTORY AND THE GALACTIC RANGERS
PACIFIC

	N-MINT
❑1, Nov 1981	1.00
❑2, Jan 1982	1.00
❑3, Mar 1982	1.00
❑4, May 1982; Goozlebobber	1.00
❑5, Jul 1982; Goozlebobber	1.00
❑6, Sep 1982; Goozlebobber	1.00
❑7, Oct 1982; Martius Klavus	1.00
❑8, Dec 1982; Martius Klavus	1.00
❑9, Feb 1983; Martius Klavus	1.00
❑10, Apr 1983	1.00
❑11, Jun 1983	1.00
❑12, Oct 1983	1.00
❑13, Jan 1984; indicia lists title as Captain Victory	1.50
❑Special 1, Oct 1983	1.50

CAPTAIN VICTORY AND THE GALACTIC RANGERS (MINI-SERIES)
JACK KIRBY

❑1, Jul 2000, b&w; no cover price	2.95
❑2, Sep 2000	2.95
❑3, Nov 2000	2.95

CAPTAIN WINGS COMPACT COMICS
AC

❑1; Reprints	3.95
❑2; Reprints	3.95

CARAVAN KIDD
DARK HORSE

❑1, Jul 1992	2.50
❑2, Aug 1992	2.50
❑3, Sep 1992	2.50
❑4, Oct 1992	2.50
❑5, Nov 1992	2.50
❑6, Dec 1992	2.50
❑7, Jan 1993	2.50
❑8, Feb 1993	2.50
❑9, Mar 1993	2.50
❑10, Apr 1993	2.50

CARAVAN KIDD PART 2
DARK HORSE

❑1, May 1993	2.50
❑2, Jun 1993	2.50
❑3, Jul 1993	2.95
❑4, Aug 1993	2.50
❑5, Sep 1993	2.50
❑6, Oct 1993	2.50
❑7	2.50
❑8	2.50
❑9, Mar 1994	2.50
❑10, Apr 1994	2.50

CARAVAN KIDD PART 3
DARK HORSE

❑1, May 1994	2.50
❑2, Jun 1994	2.50
❑3, Jul 1994	2.50
❑4, Aug 1994	2.50
❑5, Sep 1994	2.50
❑6, Oct 1994	2.50
❑7, Nov 1994	2.95
❑8, Dec 1994	2.50

CARBON KNIGHT
LUNAR

❑1, b&w	2.95
❑2, b&w	2.95
❑3, ca. 1997, b&w	2.95
❑4, ca. 1998, b&w	2.95

CARDCAPTOR SAKURA COMIC
MIXX

	N-MINT
❑1, ca. 2000	2.95
❑2, ca. 2000	2.95
❑3 2000	2.95
❑4 2000	2.95
❑5 2000	2.95
❑6 2000	2.95
❑7 2000	2.95
❑8 2000	2.95
❑9 2000	2.95
❑10 2000	2.95
❑11 2000	2.95
❑12 2000	2.95
❑13, ca. 2001	2.95
❑14 2001	2.95
❑15 2001	2.95
❑16 2001	2.95
❑17 2001	2.95
❑18 2001	2.95
❑19 2001	2.95
❑20 2001	2.95
❑21 2001	2.95
❑22 2001	2.95
❑23 2001	2.95
❑24, Jan 2002	2.95
❑25, Feb 2002	2.95
❑26, Mar 2002	2.95
❑27, Apr 2002	2.95
❑28, May 2002	2.99
❑29, Jun 2002	2.99
❑30, Jul 2002	2.99
❑31, Aug 2002	2.99
❑32, Sep 2002	2.99
❑33, Oct 2002	2.99
❑34, Nov 2002	2.99

CARDCAPTOR SAKURA: MASTER OF THE CLOW
TOKYOPOP

❑1, Aug 2002, b&w; printed in Japanese format	9.99

CARE BEARS
MARVEL / STAR

❑1, Nov 1985	1.00
❑2, Jan 1986	1.00
❑3, Mar 1986	1.00
❑4, May 1986	1.00
❑5, Jul 1986	1.00
❑6, Sep 1986	1.00
❑7, Nov 1986	1.00
❑8, Jan 1987	1.00
❑9, Mar 1987	1.00
❑10, May 1987	1.00
❑11, Jul 1987	1.00
❑12, Sep 1987	1.00
❑13, Nov 1987 A: Madballs.	1.00
❑14, Jan 1988	1.00
❑15, Mar 1988	1.00
❑16, May 1988	1.00
❑17, Jul 1988	1.00
❑18, Sep 1988	1.00
❑19, Nov 1988	1.00
❑20, Jan 1989	1.00

Other grades: Multiply price above by 5/6 for VF/NM • 2/3 for VERY FINE • 1/3 for FINE • 1/5 for VERY GOOD • 1/8 for GOOD

CAR 54 WHERE ARE YOU?
DELL

❑2, Aug 1962 .... 75.00
❑3, Oct 1962 .... 45.00
❑4, Dec 1962 .... 40.00
❑5, Mar 1963 .... 40.00
❑6, Jun 1963 .... 35.00
❑7, Sep 1963 .... 35.00

CARL AND LARRY CHRISTMAS SPECIAL
COMICS INTERVIEW

❑1, b&w 2.25

CARMILLA
AIRCEL

❑1, Feb 1991, b&w; outer paper wrapper to cover nude cover 2.50
❑2, Mar 1991, b&w 2.50
❑3, Apr 1991, b&w 2.50
❑4, b&w 2.50
❑5, b&w 2.50
❑6, b&w 2.50

CARNAGE
ETERNITY

❑1 .... 1.95

CARNAGE: IT'S A WONDERFUL LIFE
MARVEL

❑1, Oct 1996 .... 1.95

CARNAGE: MINDBOMB
MARVEL

❑1, Feb 1996; foil cover 2.95

CARNAL COMICS PRESENTS DEMI'S WILD KINGDOM ADVENTURE
REVISIONARY

❑1, Sep 1999, b&w; no cover price 3.50

CARNAL COMICS PRESENTS GINGER LYNN IS TORN
REVISIONARY

❑1, Sep 1999, b&w; Drawn cover 3.50
❑1/A, Sep 1999, b&w; adult 3.50

CARNEYS
ARCHIE

❑1, Sum 1994 .... 2.00

CARNOSAUR CARNAGE
ATOMEKA

❑1 .... 4.95

CARTOON CARTOONS
DC

❑1, Mar 2001 .... 2.25
❑2, Apr 2001 .... 2.00
❑3, May 2001 .... 2.00
❑4, Jun 2001 .... 2.00
❑5, Jul 2001 .... 2.00
❑6, Aug 2001 .... 2.00
❑7, Sep 2001 .... 2.00
❑8, Jan 2002 .... 2.00
❑9, Mar 2002 .... 2.00
❑10, May 2002 .... 2.00
❑11, Jun 2002 .... 2.00
❑12, Sep 2002 .... 2.00
❑13, Nov 2002 .... 2.25
❑14, Jan 2003 .... 2.25
❑15, Mar 2003 .... 2.25
❑16, May 2003 .... 2.25
❑17, Jun 2003 .... 2.25
❑18, Jul 2003 .... 2.25
❑19, Jul 2003 .... 2.25
❑20, Aug 2003 .... 2.25
❑21, Sep 2003 .... 2.25
❑22, Oct 2003 .... 2.25
❑23, Nov 2003 .... 2.25
❑24, Dec 2003 .... 2.25
❑25, Jan 2004 .... 2.25
❑26, Feb 2004 .... 2.25
❑27, Apr 2004 .... 2.25
❑28, May 2004 .... 2.25
❑29, Jun 2005 .... 2.25
❑30, Jul 2004 .... 2.25
❑31, Aug 2004 .... 2.25
❑32, Sep 2004 .... 2.25
❑33, Oct 2004 .... 2.25

CARTOON HISTORY OF THE UNIVERSE
RIP OFF

❑1, b&w; cardstock cover 4.50
❑2, b&w; cardstock cover 3.50
❑3, b&w; cardstock cover 3.50
❑4, b&w; cardstock cover 3.50
❑5, b&w; cardstock cover 3.50
❑6, b&w; cardstock cover 2.50
❑7, b&w; cardstock cover 2.50
❑8, b&w 2.95
❑9, b&w 2.95

CARTOONIST
SIRIUS / DOG STAR

❑1, b&w; collects strips 2.95

CARTOON NETWORK
DC

❑1, Giveaway from DC Comics to promote comics; Reprints stories from Cartoon Networks Presents #6 .... 1.00

CARTOON NETWORK ACTION PACK
DC

❑1, Jul 2006 ....
❑2, Aug 2006 ....

CARTOON NETWORK BLOCK PARTY
DC

❑1, Dec 2004 .... 2.25
❑2, Jan 2005 .... 2.25
❑3, Feb 2005 .... 2.95
❑4, Mar 2005 .... 2.25
❑5, Apr 2005 .... 2.25
❑6, May 2005 .... 2.25
❑7, Jun 2005 .... 2.25
❑8, Jun 2005 .... 2.25
❑9, Jul 2005 .... 2.25
❑10, Aug 2005 .... 2.25
❑11, Sep 2005 .... 2.25
❑13 2005 .... 2.25
❑14 .... 2.25
❑15, Jan 2006 .... 2.25
❑16, Feb 2006 .... 2.25
❑17, Mar 2006 .... 2.25
❑18, May 2006 .... 2.25
❑19, Jun 2006 .... 2.25
❑20, Jul 2006 .... 2.25
❑21, Aug 2006 .... 2.25
❑22, Sep 2006 .... 2.25

CARTOON NETWORK CHRISTMAS SPECTACULAR
ARCHIE

❑1 .... 2.00

CARTOON NETWORK PRESENTS
DC

❑1, Aug 1997; Dexter's Laboratory, Top Cat 2.00
❑2, Sep 1997; Space Ghost, Yogi Bear 2.00
❑3, Oct 1997; Hanna-Barbera crossover with Mr. Peebles, Ranger Smith, Officer Dibble, Mr. Twiddle, and Colonel Fusby; Wally Gator back-up; Cartoon All-Stars 2.00
❑4, Nov 1997; Dial M for Monkey 2.00
❑5, Dec 1997; A: Birdman, Herculoids. Toonami 2.00
❑6, Jan 1998; Cow and Chicken 2.00
❑7, Feb 1998; Wacky Races 2.00
❑8, Mar 1998; Fighting Monkies; Johnny Bravo 2.00
❑9, Apr 1998; A: Herculoids, Birdman. Toonami 2.00
❑10, May 1998; Cow & Chicken 2.00
❑11, Jun 1998; Wacky Races 2.00
❑12, Aug 1998; Cartoon All-Stars; Peter Potamus 2.00
❑13, Sep 1998; Toonami, Birdman, Herculoids 2.00
❑14, Oct 1998; Cow and Chicken 2.00
❑15, Nov 1998; Wacky Races 1.99
❑16, Dec 1998; Cartoon All-Stars; Top Cat 1.99
❑17, Jan 1999; Toonami, Herculoids, Galaxy Trio; Toonami 1.99
❑18, Feb 1999; Cartoon All-Stars; Funtastic Treasure Hunt 1.99
❑19, Mar 1999; Cow and Chicken 1.99
❑20, Apr 1999; Cartoon All-Stars; Hong Kong Phooey, Atom Ant, Secret Squirrel 1.99
❑21, May 1999; Toonami, Blue Falcon and Dyno-Mutt, Galtar and the Golden Lance; Toonami 1.99
❑22, Jun 1999; A: Yogi Bear. A: Quick Draw McGraw. A: Magilla Gorilla. A: Boo Boo Bear. A: El Kabonng. A: Ranger Jones. A: Ranger Smith. Cartoon All-Stars; Baba Looey 1.99
❑23, Jul 1999; Jabberjaw, Speed Buggy, Captain Caveman; Jabberjaw; Speed Buggy; Captain Caveman 1.99
❑24, Aug 1999; Scrappy-Doo 1.99

CARTOON NETWORK PRESENTS SPACE GHOST
ARCHIE

❑1, Mar 1997 .... 2.00

CARTOON NETWORK STARRING
DC

❑1, Sep 1999; The Powerpuff Girls..... 3.00
❑2, Oct 1999 1: Johnny Bravo (in comics). 3.00
❑3, Nov 1999 .... 2.00
❑4, Dec 1999; Space Ghost 2.00
❑5, Jan 2000 .... 2.00
❑6, Feb 2000 .... 2.00
❑7, Mar 2000 .... 2.00
❑8, Apr 2000 .... 2.00
❑9, May 2000; Space Ghost 2.00
❑10, Jun 2000 .... 2.00
❑11, Jul 2000 .... 2.00
❑12, Aug 2000 .... 2.00
❑13, Sep 2000 .... 2.00
❑14, Oct 2000; Johnny Bravo 2.00
❑15, Nov 2000; Space Ghost 2.00
❑16, Dec 2000; Cow and Chicken 2.00
❑17, Jan 2001; Johnny Bravo 2.00
❑18, Feb 2001; Space Ghost 2.00

CARTOON QUARTERLY
GLADSTONE

❑1; Mickey Mouse 5.00

CARTOON TALES (DISNEY'S...)
DISNEY

❑1, ca. 1992 .... 2.95
❑2, ca. 1992; 21809; Darkwing Duck . 2.95
❑3, ca. 1992; 21810; Tale Spin: Surprise in the Skies; Reprints stories from Disney's Tale Spin #4, 6 .... 2.95
❑4; Beauty and the Beast 2.95

CARTUNE LAND
MAGIC CARPET

❑1, b&w 1.50
❑2, Jul 1987, b&w 1.50

CARVERS
IMAGE

❑1, Oct 1998 .... 2.95
❑2, Nov 1998 .... 2.95
❑3, Dec 1998 .... 2.95

CAR WARRIORS
MARVEL / EPIC

❑1, Jun 1991 .... 2.25
❑2, Jul 1991 .... 2.25
❑3, Aug 1991 .... 2.25
❑4, Sep 1991 .... 2.25

CASANOVA
IMAGE

❑1, Jul 2006 .... 2.99

CASANOVA
AIRCEL

❑1, b&w 2.50
❑2, b&w 2.50
❑3, b&w 2.50
❑4, b&w 2.50
❑5, b&w 2.50
❑6, b&w 2.50
❑7, b&w 2.50
❑8, b&w 2.50
❑9, Nov 1991, b&w 2.95
❑10, b&w 2.95

CASEFILES: SAM & TWITCH
IMAGE

❑1, Jun 2003 .... 2.50
❑2, Aug 2003 .... 2.50
❑3, Sep 2003 .... 2.50
❑4, Oct 2003 .... 2.50
❑5, Nov 2003 .... 2.50
❑6, Dec 2003 .... 2.50
❑7, Mar 2004 .... 2.50
❑8, Apr 2004 .... 2.50

Cases of Sherlock Holmes

Reprinted actual stories with illustrations

©Renegade

Casper the Friendly Ghost (3rd Series)

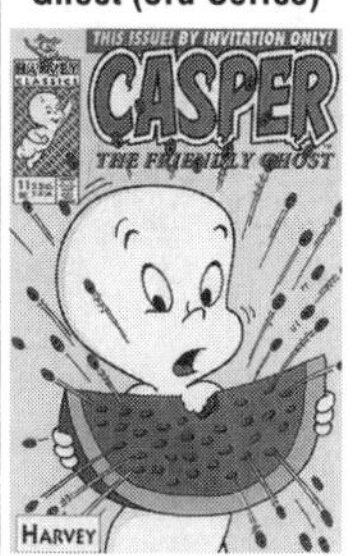

Earlier title was called "Friendly Ghost, Casper"

©Harvey

Castle Waiting (Cartoon Books)

Linda Medley's medieval fantasyland

©Cartoon Books

Cat

She got cattier when she became Tigra

©Marvel

Catwoman (2nd Series)

Long-running Catwoman series from 1990s

©DC

	N-MINT
❑9, ca. 2004	2.50
❑10, ca. 2004	2.50
❑11, Dec 2004	2.50
❑12, Jan 2005	2.50
❑13, Feb 2005	2.95
❑14, ca. 2005	2.50
❑15, May 2005	2.50
❑16, Jun 2005	2.50
❑17, Jul 2005	2.50
❑18, Aug 2005	2.50
❑19 2005	2.50
❑20, Dec 2005	2.50
❑21, Jan 2006	2.50
❑22, Mar 2006	2.50

CASE MORGAN, GUMSHOE PRIVATE EYE
FORBIDDEN FRUIT

❑1, b&w	2.95
❑2, b&w	2.95
❑3, b&w	2.95
❑4, b&w	2.95
❑5, b&w	2.95
❑6, b&w	2.95
❑7, b&w	2.95
❑8, b&w	2.95
❑9, b&w	2.95
❑10, b&w	2.95
❑11, b&w	3.50

CASE OF BLIND FEAR
ETERNITY

❑1, Jan 1989, b&w; Sherlock Holmes, Invisible Man	1.95
❑2, Apr 1989, b&w; Sherlock Holmes, Invisible Man	1.95
❑3, b&w; Sherlock Holmes, Invisible Man	1.95
❑4, b&w; Sherlock Holmes, Invisible Man	1.95

CASES OF SHERLOCK HOLMES
RENEGADE

❑1, May 1986, b&w; Renegade publishes	2.00
❑2, Jul 1986, b&w	2.00
❑3, Sep 1986	2.00
❑4, Nov 1986	2.00
❑5, Jan 1987	2.00
❑6, Mar 1987	2.00
❑7, May 1987	2.00
❑8, Jul 1987	2.00
❑9, Sep 1987	2.00
❑10, Nov 1987	2.00
❑11, Jan 1988	2.00
❑12, Mar 1988	2.00
❑13, May 1988	2.00
❑14, Jul 1988	2.00
❑15, Sep 1988	2.00
❑16, Nov 1988, b&w; Northstar begins as publisher	2.25
❑17, Jan 1989, b&w	2.25
❑18, Mar 1989, b&w	2.25
❑19, May 1989	2.25
❑20, Jul 1989	2.25
❑21, Sep 1989	2.25
❑22, Nov 1989	2.25

	N-MINT
❑23, Jan 1990	2.25
❑24, Mar 1990	2.25

CASEY JONES & RAPHAEL
MIRAGE

❑1, Oct 1994	2.75

CASEY JONES: NORTH BY DOWNEAST
MIRAGE

❑1, May 1994	2.75
❑2, Jul 1994	2.75

CASPER ADVENTURE DIGEST
HARVEY

❑1, Oct 1992	2.00
❑2, Dec 1992	1.75
❑3, Jan 1993	1.75
❑4, Apr 1993	1.75
❑5, Jul 1993	1.75
❑6, Oct 1993	1.75
❑7	1.75
❑8	1.75

CASPER AND FRIENDS
HARVEY

❑1, ca. 1991	1.50
❑2, ca. 1991	1.50
❑3, ca. 1992	1.50
❑4, ca. 1992	1.50
❑5, ca. 1992	1.50

CASPER AND FRIENDS MAGAZINE
MARVEL

❑1, Mar 1997, magazine	3.99
❑2, May 1997, magazine	3.99
❑3, Jul 1997, magazine	3.99

CASPER AND NIGHTMARE
HARVEY

❑6, Nov 1964; was Nightmare & Casper	35.00
❑7, Feb 1965	24.00
❑8, May 1965	24.00
❑9, Aug 1965	24.00
❑10, Nov 1965	24.00
❑11, Feb 1966	16.00
❑12, May 1966	16.00
❑13, Aug 1966	16.00
❑14, Oct 1966	16.00
❑15, Dec 1966	16.00
❑16, Feb 1967	16.00
❑17, May 1967	16.00
❑18, Aug 1967	16.00
❑19, ca. 1968	16.00
❑20, ca. 1968	16.00
❑21, ca. 1968	14.00
❑22, ca. 1968	14.00
❑23, Apr 1969	14.00
❑24, ca. 1969	14.00
❑25, ca. 1969	14.00
❑26, ca. 1969	14.00
❑27, ca. 1970	14.00
❑28, ca. 1970	14.00
❑29, Sep 1970	14.00
❑30, ca. 1970	14.00
❑31, ca. 1971	14.00
❑32, ca. 1971	14.00
❑33, ca. 1971	14.00

	N-MINT
❑34, Nov 1971	14.00
❑35, Feb 1972	14.00
❑36, May 1972	10.00
❑37, Aug 1972	10.00
❑38, Nov 1972	10.00
❑39, ca. 1973	10.00
❑40, ca. 1973	10.00
❑41, ca. 1973	10.00
❑42, Jun 1973	10.00
❑43, Aug 1973	10.00
❑44, Oct 1973	10.00
❑45, Jun 1974	10.00
❑46, Aug 1974	10.00

CASPER AND THE GHOSTLY TRIO
HARVEY

❑1, Nov 1972	20.00
❑2, Jan 1973	15.00
❑3, Mar 1973	15.00
❑4, May 1973	15.00
❑5, Jul 1973	12.00
❑6, Sep 1973	12.00
❑7, Nov 1973	12.00
❑8, Aug 1990	1.50
❑9, Oct 1990	1.50
❑10, Dec 1990	1.50

CASPER & WENDY
HARVEY

❑1, Sep 1972, (c); (w); (a); Alice in Wonderland	9.00
❑2, Nov 1972, (c); (w); (a)	5.00
❑3, Jan 1973, (c); (w); (a)	4.00
❑4, Mar 1973, (c); (w); (a)	4.00
❑5, May 1973, (c); (w); (a)	4.00
❑6, Jul 1973, (c); (w); (a)	3.00
❑7, Sep 1973, (c); (w); (a)	3.00
❑8, Nov 1973, (c); (w); (a)	3.00

CASPER DIGEST MAGAZINE
HARVEY

❑1	2.50
❑2	2.00
❑3	2.00
❑4	2.00
❑9, Sep 1989	2.00
❑10, Feb 1990	2.00
❑11, May 1990	2.00
❑12, Jul 1990	2.00
❑13, Aug 1990	2.00

CASPER DIGEST MAGAZINE (VOL. 2)
HARVEY

❑1, Sep 1991	2.00
❑2, Jan 1992	1.75
❑3, Apr 1992	1.75
❑4, Jul 1992, indicia says Casper Digest	1.75
❑5, Nov 1992	1.75
❑6, Feb 1993	1.75
❑7, May 1993	1.75
❑8, Aug 1993	1.75
❑9, Nov 1993	1.75
❑10, Feb 1994	1.75
❑11, May 1994	1.75
❑12, Jul 1994	1.75

	N-MINT
❑13, Aug 1994	1.75
❑14, Nov 1994	1.75

CASPER ENCHANTED TALES DIGEST
HARVEY

	N-MINT
❑1, May 1992	2.00
❑2, Sep 1992	1.75
❑3 1993	1.75
❑4, Jun 1993	1.75
❑5, Sep 1993	1.75
❑6, Dec 1993	1.75
❑7 1994	1.75
❑8, Jun 1994	1.75
❑9, Aug 1994	1.75
❑10, Oct 1994	1.75

CASPER GHOSTLAND
HARVEY

	N-MINT
❑1, ca. 1992	1.50

CASPER GIANT SIZE
HARVEY

	N-MINT
❑1	2.25
❑2	2.25
❑3	2.25
❑4	2.25

CASPER IN 3-D
BLACKTHORNE

	N-MINT
❑1, Win 1988	2.50

CASPER'S GHOSTLAND
HARVEY

	N-MINT
❑1, Win 1958	175.00
❑2, Spr 1959	75.00
❑3, Sum 1959	50.00
❑4, Fal 1959	50.00
❑5, Apr 1960	50.00
❑6 1960	40.00
❑7 1960	40.00
❑8 1961	40.00
❑9 1961	40.00
❑10, Jul 1961	40.00
❑11, Oct 1961	25.00
❑12, Jan 1962	25.00
❑13, Apr 1962	25.00
❑14, Jul 1962	25.00
❑15, Oct 1962	25.00
❑16, Jan 1963	25.00
❑17, Apr 1963	25.00
❑18, Jul 1963	25.00
❑19, Oct 1963	25.00
❑20, Jan 1964	25.00
❑21, Apr 1964	20.00
❑22, Jul 1964	20.00
❑23, Oct 1964	20.00
❑24, Jan 1965	20.00
❑25, Apr 1965	20.00
❑26, Jul 1965	20.00
❑27, Oct 1965	20.00
❑28, Jan 1966	20.00
❑29, Apr 1966	20.00
❑30, Jun 1966	20.00
❑31, Aug 1966	15.00
❑32, Oct 1966	15.00
❑33, Dec 1966	15.00
❑34, Feb 1967	15.00
❑35, Apr 1967	15.00
❑36, Jun 1967	15.00
❑37, Aug 1967	15.00
❑38, Oct 1967	15.00
❑39, Dec 1967	15.00
❑40, Feb 1968	15.00
❑41, Apr 1968	10.00
❑42, Jun 1968	10.00
❑43, Aug 1968	10.00
❑44, Oct 1968	10.00
❑45, Dec 1968	10.00
❑46, Jan 1969	10.00
❑47, Mar 1969	10.00
❑48, May 1969	10.00
❑49, Jul 1969	10.00
❑50, Sep 1969	10.00
❑51, Nov 1969	10.00
❑52, Jan 1970	10.00
❑53, Mar 1970	10.00
❑54, May 1970	10.00
❑55, Jul 1970	10.00
❑56, Sep 1970	10.00
❑57, Nov 1970	10.00
❑58, Jan 1971	10.00
❑59, Mar 1971	10.00
❑60, May 1971	10.00
❑61, Jul 1971	5.00
❑62, Sep 1971	5.00
❑63, Nov 1971	5.00
❑64, Jan 1972	5.00
❑65, Mar 1972	5.00
❑66, May 1972	5.00
❑67, Jul 1972	5.00
❑68, Sep 1972	5.00
❑69, Nov 1972	5.00
❑70, Jan 1973	5.00
❑71, Mar 1973	5.00
❑72, May 1973	5.00
❑73, Jul 1973	5.00
❑74, Sep 1973	5.00
❑75, Nov 1973	5.00
❑76, Jan 1974	5.00
❑77, Mar 1974	5.00
❑78, May 1974	5.00
❑79, Jul 1974	5.00
❑80, Sep 1974	5.00
❑81, Nov 1974	5.00
❑82, Jan 1975	4.00
❑83, Mar 1975	4.00
❑84, May 1975	4.00
❑85, Jul 1975	4.00
❑86, Sep 1975	4.00
❑87, Nov 1975	4.00
❑88, Feb 1976	4.00
❑89, Apr 1976	4.00
❑90, Jun 1976	4.00
❑91, Aug 1976	4.00
❑92, Oct 1976	4.00
❑93, Dec 1976	4.00
❑94, Feb 1977, Richie Rich in Hostess Ad ("Aunt Chatter Bucks")	4.00
❑95 1977	4.00
❑96 1977	4.00
❑97, Dec 1977	4.00
❑98	4.00

CASPER SPACE SHIP
HARVEY

	N-MINT
❑1, Aug 1972	16.00
❑2, Oct 1972	13.00
❑3, Dec 1972	13.00
❑4, Feb 1973	10.00
❑5, Apr 1973	10.00

CASPER THE FRIENDLY GHOST (2ND SERIES)
HARVEY

	N-MINT
❑254, Jul 1990; was Friendly Ghost, Casper, The	1.25
❑255, Aug 1990	1.25
❑256, Sep 1990	1.25
❑257, Oct 1990	1.25
❑258, Nov 1990	1.25
❑259, Dec 1990	1.25
❑260, Jan 1991	1.25

CASPER THE FRIENDLY GHOST (3RD SERIES)
HARVEY

	N-MINT
❑1, Mar 1991	2.00
❑2, May 1991	1.50
❑3, Jul 1991	1.50
❑4, Sep 1991	1.50
❑5, Nov 1991	1.50
❑6, Jan 1992	1.50
❑7, Mar 1992	1.50
❑8 1992	1.50
❑9 1992	1.50
❑10 1992	1.50
❑11, Dec 1992	1.50
❑12 1993	1.50
❑13 1993	1.50
❑14 1993	1.50
❑15, Oct 1993	1.50
❑16, Nov 1993	1.50
❑17, Dec 1993	1.50
❑18, Jan 1994	1.50
❑19, Feb 1994	1.50
❑20, Mar 1994	1.50
❑21, Apr 1994	1.50
❑22, May 1994	1.50
❑23, Jun 1994	1.50
❑24, Jul 1994	1.50
❑25, Aug 1994	1.50
❑26, Sep 1994	1.50
❑27, Oct 1994	1.50
❑28, Nov 1994, (c)	1.50
❑Giant Size 1	2.25
❑Giant Size 2	2.25
❑Giant Size 3	2.25
❑Giant Size 4	2.25

CASPER THE FRIENDLY GHOST BIG BOOK
HARVEY

	N-MINT
❑1	2.00
❑2	2.00
❑3	2.00

CAST
NAUTILUS COMICS

	N-MINT
❑1 2005	2.99
❑2, Sep 2005	2.99

CASTLEVANIA: THE BELMONT LEGACY
IDEA & DESIGN WORKS

	N-MINT
❑1, ca. 2005	3.99
❑2, ca. 2005	3.99
❑3 2005	3.99
❑4 2005	3.99
❑5, Sep 2005	3.99

CASTLE WAITING
OLIO

	N-MINT
❑1, b&w	4.50
❑1/2nd	3.50
❑1/3rd	3.50
❑2, b&w	3.00
❑2/2nd	3.00
❑3, ca. 1997, b&w; Akiko pin-up	3.00
❑3/2nd	3.00
❑4, b&w; Scott Roberts pin-up	3.00
❑4/2nd	3.00
❑5, Mar 1998, b&w	3.00
❑5/2nd	3.00
❑6, May 1998, b&w; profiles of 12 Witches begins	3.00
❑7, Oct 1998, b&w; Series moves to Cartoon Books, where there are four issues; returns to Olio for #12	3.00
❑12, ca. 2001, b&w; Also known as Vol. 2 #5 after the Cartoon Books numbering	3.00
❑13, ca. 2001; Also known as Vol. 2 #6 after the Cartoon Books numbering	3.00
❑14, ca. 2002; Also known as Vol. 2 #7 after the Cartoon Books numbering	3.00
❑15, ca. 2002	3.00
❑16, ca. 2003	3.00
❑Ashcan 1, Jan 1999; Limited ashcan edition given away (20 printed); Hiatus issue	10.00

CASTLE WAITING (CARTOON BOOKS)
CARTOON BOOKS

	N-MINT
❑1, Jul 2000, b&w; follows events of Olio series; also considered #8 in the Olio numbering	3.00
❑2, Oct 2000; follows events of Olio series; also considered #9 in the Olio numberingfollows events of Olio series; also considered #8 in the Olio numbering	3.00
❑3, Dec 2000; follows events of Olio series; also considered #10 in the Olio numbering	3.00
❑4, Mar 2001; follows events of Olio series; also considered #11 in the Olio numbering	3.00

CASUAL HEROES
IMAGE

	N-MINT
❑1, Apr 1996	2.25

CAT
MARVEL

	N-MINT
❑1, Nov 1972, WW (a); O: Cat. 1: Cat. Cat later becomes Tigra	35.00
❑2, Jan 1973	15.00
❑3, Apr 1973, A: Contains letter by Frank Miller (1st Miller).	12.00
❑4, Jun 1973	10.00

CAT (AIRCEL)
AIRCEL

	N-MINT
❑1, b&w	2.50
❑2, b&w	2.50

Catwoman (3rd Series)

Restarted series somehow survived movie

©DC

Cave Kids

Pebbles and Bamm Bamm dropped in

©Gold Key

Cavewoman Color Special

Jungle titillation with overendowed heroine

©Avatar

Centurions

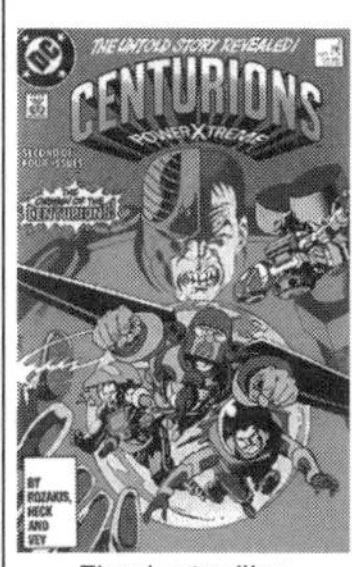

They kept yelling "Power Xtreme!"

©DC

Cerebus Bi-Weekly

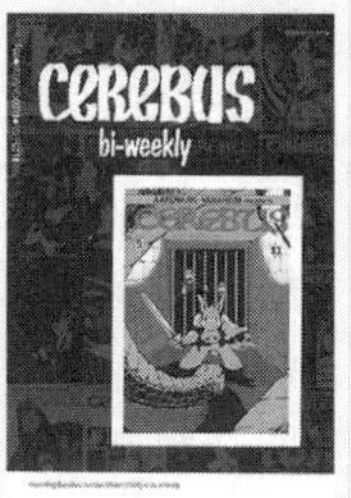

Faithful reprinting of Cerebus the Aardvark

©Aardvark-Vanaheim

N-MINT

CATALYST: AGENTS OF CHANGE
DARK HORSE

- ❑1, Feb 1994; cardstock cover with foil logo 2.00
- ❑2, Mar 1994 .... 2.00
- ❑3, Apr 1994 .... 2.00
- ❑4, May 1994 .... 2.00
- ❑5 .... 2.00
- ❑6, Aug 1994 .... 2.00
- ❑7, Sep 1994 .... 2.00

CAT & MOUSE
EF GRAPHICS

- ❑1, Jan 1989, part color 2.00
- ❑1/2nd 1.75

CAT & MOUSE (AIRCEL)
AIRCEL

- ❑1, Mar 1990, b&w 2.25
- ❑2, Apr 1990, b&w 2.25
- ❑3, May 1990, b&w 2.25
- ❑4, Jun 1990, b&w 2.25
- ❑5, Jul 1990, b&w 2.25
- ❑6, Aug 1990, b&w 2.25
- ❑7, Sep 1990, b&w 2.25
- ❑8, Oct 1990, b&w 2.25
- ❑9, Nov 1990, b&w 2.25
- ❑10, Dec 1990, b&w 2.25
- ❑11, Jan 1991, b&w 2.25
- ❑12, Feb 1991, b&w 2.25
- ❑13, Mar 1991, b&w 2.25
- ❑14, Apr 1991, b&w 2.25
- ❑15, May 1991, b&w 2.25
- ❑16, Jun 1991, b&w 2.25
- ❑17, Aug 1991, b&w 2.25
- ❑18, Sep 1991, b&w 2.25
- ❑Book 1, Oct 1990; Reprints 9.95
- ❑Book 2; Wearin' 'n' Tearin' 9.95

CAT CLAW
ETERNITY

- ❑1, Sep 1990, b&w 2.50
- ❑1/2nd 2.50
- ❑2, Nov 1990 .... 2.50
- ❑3, Jan 1991 .... 2.50
- ❑4, Feb 1991 .... 2.50
- ❑5, Apr 1991 .... 2.50
- ❑6, Jun 1991 .... 2.50
- ❑7 .... 2.50
- ❑8 .... 2.50
- ❑9 .... 2.50
- ❑Book 1, b&w; Cat Scratch Fever 9.95

CATFIGHT
INSOMNIA

- ❑1, Mar 1995, b&w 2.75
- ❑1/Gold; Gold edition 3.00

CATFIGHT: DREAM INTO ACTION
LIGHTNING

- ❑1, Mar 1996, b&w; Creed Guest Star 2.75

CATFIGHT: DREAM WARRIOR
LIGHTNING

- ❑1 .... 2.75

CATFIGHT: ESCAPE FROM LIMBO
LIGHTNING

- ❑1, Nov 1996 .... 2.75

N-MINT

CATFIGHT: SWEET REVENGE
LIGHTNING

- ❑1, Apr 1997, b&w; alternate cover B 2.95

CATHARSIS
BEING

- ❑1, Oct 1994 .... 2.50

CATNIP
SIDE SHOW

- ❑1 .... 2.95

CATSEYE
MANIC

- ❑1, Dec 1998 .... 2.50
- ❑2 1999 .... 2.50
- ❑3 1999 .... 2.50
- ❑4 1999 .... 2.50
- ❑5 1999 .... 2.50
- ❑6 1999 .... 2.50
- ❑7 1999 .... 2.50
- ❑8 1999 .... 2.50

CATSEYE AGENCY
RIP OFF

- ❑1, Sep 1992, b&w 2.50
- ❑2, Oct 1992, b&w 2.50

CAT, T.H.E. (DELL)
DELL

- ❑1, ca. 1967 .... 18.00
- ❑2, ca. 1967 .... 12.00
- ❑3, ca. 1967 .... 12.00
- ❑4, Oct 1967 .... 12.00

CATTLE BRAIN
ITCHY EYEBALL

- ❑1, b&w 2.75
- ❑2, b&w 2.75
- ❑3, b&w 2.75

CATWOMAN (1ST SERIES)
DC

- ❑1, Feb 1989 O: Catwoman (new origin). 3.00
- ❑2, Mar 1989 .... 2.50
- ❑3, Apr 1989 .... 2.00
- ❑4, May 1989 .... 2.00

CATWOMAN (2ND SERIES)
DC

- ❑0, Oct 1994 O: Catwoman. 2.00
- ❑1, Aug 1993 O: Catwoman. 3.00
- ❑2, Sep 1993 .... 3.00
- ❑3, Oct 1993 .... 2.50
- ❑4, Nov 1993 .... 2.50
- ❑5, Dec 1993 .... 2.50
- ❑6, Jan 1994 .... 2.50
- ❑7, Feb 1994 .... 2.50
- ❑8, Mar 1994 .... 2.50
- ❑9, Apr 1994 .... 2.50
- ❑10, May 1994 .... 2.50
- ❑11, Jun 1994 .... 2.00
- ❑12, Jul 1994 .... 2.00
- ❑13, Aug 1994 .... 2.00
- ❑14, Sep 1994; Zero Hour 2.00
- ❑15, Nov 1994 .... 2.00
- ❑16, Dec 1994 .... 2.00
- ❑17, Jan 1995 .... 2.00
- ❑18, Feb 1995 .... 2.00
- ❑19, Mar 1995 .... 2.00

N-MINT

- ❑20, Apr 1995 .... 2.00
- ❑21, May 1995 .... 2.00
- ❑22, Jul 1995 .... 2.00
- ❑23, Aug 1995 .... 2.00
- ❑24, Sep 1995 .... 2.00
- ❑25, Oct 1995; Giant-size A: Psyba-Rats. A: Robin. 2.00
- ❑26, Nov 1995 .... 2.00
- ❑27, Dec 1995 .... 2.00
- ❑28, Jan 1996 .... 2.00
- ❑29, Feb 1996 .... 2.00
- ❑30, Mar 1996 .... 2.00
- ❑31, Mar 1996 .... 2.00
- ❑32, Apr 1996 .... 2.00
- ❑33, May 1996 .... 2.00
- ❑34, Jun 1996 .... 2.00
- ❑35, Jul 1996 .... 2.00
- ❑36, Aug 1996 .... 2.00
- ❑37, Sep 1996 .... 2.00
- ❑38, Oct 1996 .... 2.00
- ❑39, Nov 1996 .... 2.00
- ❑40, Dec 1996 V: Two-Face, Penguin. 2.00
- ❑41, Jan 1997 .... 2.00
- ❑42, Feb 1997 1: Cybercat. 2.00
- ❑43, Mar 1997 A: She-Cat. 2.00
- ❑44, Apr 1997 .... 2.00
- ❑45, May 1997 .... 2.00
- ❑46, Jun 1997 V: Two-Face. 2.00
- ❑47, Jul 1997 V: Two-Face. 2.00
- ❑48, Aug 1997 .... 2.00
- ❑49, Sep 1997 .... 2.00
- ❑50, Oct 1997 .... 2.00
- ❑50/A, Oct 1997; yellow logo 2.95
- ❑50/B, Oct 1997; purple logo 2.95
- ❑51, Nov 1997 V: Huntress. 2.00
- ❑52, Dec 1997; Face cover 2.00
- ❑53, Jan 1998 .... 2.00
- ❑54, Feb 1998; DGry (w); self-contained story; 1st Devin Grayson script 2.00
- ❑55, Mar 1998; DGry (w); self-contained story 2.00
- ❑56, Apr 1998; continues in Robin #52 2.00
- ❑57, May 1998; V: Poison Ivy. continues in Batman: Arkham Asylum - Tales of Madness #1 .... 2.00
- ❑58, Jun 1998 V: Scarecrow. 2.00
- ❑59, Jul 1998 V: Scarecrow. 2.00
- ❑60, Aug 1998 V: Scarecrow. 2.00
- ❑61, Sep 1998 .... 2.00
- ❑62, Oct 1998 A: Nemesis. 2.00
- ❑63, Dec 1998 V: Joker. 2.00
- ❑64, Jan 1999 DGry (w); A: Joker. A: Batman. V: Joker. 2.00
- ❑65, Feb 1999 DGry (w); A: Scarecrow. A: Joker. A: Batman. V: Joker. 2.00
- ❑66, Mar 1999 DGry (w) 2.00
- ❑67, Apr 1999 DGry (w) 2.00
- ❑68, May 1999; DGry (w); V: Body Doubles. Lady Vic 2.00
- ❑69, Jun 1999 DGry (w); A: Trickster. 2.00
- ❑70, Jul 1999 DGry (w) 2.00
- ❑71, Aug 1999 DGry (w) 2.00
- ❑72, Sep 1999; DGry (w); No Man's Land 2.00
- ❑73, Oct 1999; No Man's Land 2.00

❑74, Nov 1999; No Man's Land 2.00
❑75, Dec 1999; No Man's Land 2.00
❑76, Jan 2000; No Man's Land 2.00
❑77, Feb 2000 .... 2.00
❑78, Mar 2000 .... 2.00
❑79, Apr 2000 .... 2.00
❑80, May 2000 .... 2.00
❑81, Jun 2000 .... 2.00
❑82, Jul 2000 .... 2.00
❑83, Aug 2000 .... 2.25
❑84, Sep 2000 .... 2.25
❑85, Oct 2000 .... 2.25
❑86, Nov 2000 .... 2.25
❑87, Dec 2000 .... 2.25
❑88, Jan 2001 .... 2.25
❑89, Feb 2001 .... 2.25
❑90, Mar 2001 .... 2.25
❑91, Apr 2001 .... 2.25
❑92, May 2001 .... 2.25
❑93, Jun 2001 .... 2.25
❑94, Jul 2001 .... 2.25
❑1000000, Nov 1998 .... 3.00
❑Annual 1, ca. 1994; Elseworlds 3.50
❑Annual 2, ca. 1995; Year One 3.95
❑Annual 3, ca. 1996; Legends of the Dead Earth 2.95
❑Annual 4, ca. 1997; Pulp Heroes 3.95

CATWOMAN (3RD SERIES)
DC

❑1, Jan 2002 .... 4.00
❑2, Feb 2002 .... 2.50
❑3, Mar 2002 .... 2.50
❑4, Apr 2002 .... 2.50
❑5, May 2002 .... 2.50
❑6, Jun 2002 .... 2.50
❑7, Jul 2002 .... 2.50
❑8, Aug 2002 .... 2.50
❑9, Sep 2002 .... 2.50
❑10, Oct 2002 .... 2.50
❑11, Nov 2002 .... 2.50
❑12, Dec 2002 .... 2.50
❑13, Jan 2003 .... 2.50
❑14, Feb 2003 .... 2.50
❑15, Mar 2003 .... 2.50
❑16, Apr 2003 .... 2.50
❑17, May 2003 .... 2.50
❑18, Jun 2003 .... 2.50
❑19, Jul 2003 .... 2.50
❑20, Aug 2003 .... 2.50
❑21, Sep 2003 .... 2.50
❑22, Oct 2003 .... 2.50
❑23, Nov 2003 .... 2.50
❑24, Dec 2003 .... 2.50
❑25, Jan 2004 .... 2.50
❑26, Feb 2004 PG (c); PG (a) 2.50
❑27, Mar 2004 PG (c); PG (a) 2.50
❑28, Apr 2004, PG (c); PG (a) 2.50
❑29, May 2004 PG (c); PG (a) 2.50
❑30, Jun 2004 PG (c); PG (a) 2.50
❑31, Jul 2004 .... 2.50
❑32, Aug 2004 .... 2.50
❑33, Jul 2004 .... 2.50
❑34, Oct 2004 .... 2.50
❑35, Nov 2004 .... 2.50
❑36, Dec 2004 .... 2.50
❑37, Jan 2005 .... 2.50
❑38, Feb 2005 .... 2.50
❑39, Mar 2005 .... 2.50
❑40, Apr 2005 .... 2.50
❑41, May 2005 .... 2.50
❑42, Jun 2005 .... 2.50
❑43, Jul 2005 .... 2.50
❑44, Aug 2005 .... 2.50
❑45, Sep 2005 .... 2.50
❑46, Oct 2005 .... 2.50
❑47, Nov 2005 .... 2.50
❑48, Dec 2005 .... 2.50
❑49, Jan 2006 .... 2.50
❑50, Feb 2006 .... 2.50
❑51, Mar 2006 .... 2.50
❑52, May 2006 .... 2.50
❑53, Jun 2006 .... 2.50
❑54, Jul 2006 .... 2.50
❑55, Aug 2006 .... 2.50
❑56, Sep 2006 .... 2.50

CATWOMAN: GUARDIAN OF GOTHAM
DC

❑1, ca. 1999 .... 5.95
❑2, ca. 1999 .... 5.95

CATWOMAN: NINE LIVES OF A FELINE FATALE
DC

❑1, ca. 2004 .... 14.95

CATWOMAN PLUS
DC

❑1, Nov 1997; continues in Robin Plus #2 .... 2.95

CATWOMAN SECRET FILES AND ORIGINS
DC

❑1, Nov 2002 .... 4.95

CATWOMAN THE MOVIE
DC / VERTIGO

❑1, Sep 2004 .... 4.95

CATWOMAN/VAMPIRELLA: THE FURIES
DC

❑1, Feb 1997, prestige format; crossover with Harris 4.95

CATWOMAN: WHEN IN ROME
DC

❑1, Nov 2004 .... 3.50
❑2, Dec 2004 .... 3.50
❑3, Jan 2005 .... 3.50
❑4, Feb 2005 .... 3.50
❑5, Jun 2005 .... 3.50

CATWOMAN/WILDCAT
DC

❑1, Aug 1998 .... 2.50
❑2, Sep 1998 .... 2.50
❑3, Oct 1998 .... 2.50
❑4, Nov 1998 .... 2.50

CAVE BANG
FANTAGRAPHICS / EROS

❑1, Oct 1996 .... 2.95
❑2, Jul 2000 .... 2.95

CAVE GIRL
AC

❑1 .... 2.95

CAVE KIDS
GOLD KEY

❑1, Feb 1963 .... 35.00
❑2, ca. 1963 .... 18.00
❑3, Nov 1963 .... 15.00
❑4, Mar 1964 .... 15.00
❑5, Jun 1964 .... 15.00
❑6, Sep 1964 .... 12.00
❑7, Dec 1964 .... 12.00
❑8, Mar 1965 .... 12.00
❑9, Jun 1965 .... 12.00
❑10, Sep 1965 .... 12.00
❑11, Dec 1965 .... 12.00
❑12, Mar 1966 .... 12.00
❑13, Jun 1966 .... 9.00
❑14, Sep 1966 .... 9.00
❑15, Dec 1966 .... 9.00
❑16, Mar 1967 .... 9.00

CAVEMAN
CAVEMAN

❑1, Apr 1998 .... 3.50
❑2, Jun 1998 .... 3.50
❑3, Aug 1998 .... 3.50
❑4, Oct 1998 .... 3.50
❑GN 1, b&w; graphic novel 9.95

CAVEWOMAN
BASEMENT

❑1, Jan 1994, b&w 26.00
❑2, ca. 1994, b&w 20.00
❑3, Jul 1994, b&w 15.00
❑4, Nov 1994, b&w 12.00
❑5, b&w 10.00
❑6, b&w 10.00

CAVEWOMAN COLOR SPECIAL
AVATAR

❑1 .... 3.50

CAVEWOMAN: MISSING LINK
BASEMENT

❑1, Sep 1997, b&w 2.95
❑2, Nov 1997, b&w 2.95

CAVEWOMAN: ODYSSEY
CALIBER

❑1 .... 2.95

CAVEWOMAN ONE-SHOT
BASEMENT

❑1, Apr 2001, Klyde & Meriem 4.00

CAVEWOMAN: PANGAEAN SEA
AVATAR

❑Ashcan 1, Oct 1999 .... 4.95

CAVEWOMAN: RAIN
BASEMENT

❑1, ca. 1996 .... 3.00
❑1/2nd 2.95
❑1/3rd 2.95
❑2 .... 3.50
❑2/2nd 2.95
❑2/3rd 2.95
❑3, ca. 1997 .... 3.50
❑3/2nd 2.95
❑4 .... 3.00
❑4/2nd 2.95
❑5, Nov 1996 .... 3.00
❑5/2nd 2.95
❑6, Feb 1997 .... 3.00
❑7, May 1997 .... 3.00
❑8, Sep 1997 .... 3.00

CAVEWOMAN: RAPTOR
BASEMENT

❑1, Jul 2002 .... 3.25

CECIL KUNKLE (2ND SERIES)
DARKLINE

❑1 .... 3.50
❑2 .... 3.50
❑3, b&w; Santa cover 2.00

CECIL KUNKLE (CHARLES A. WAGNER'S...)
RENEGADE

❑1, May 1986, b&w 2.00

CELESTIAL MECHANICS: THE ADVENTURES OF WIDGET WILHELMINA JONES
INNOVATION

❑1, Dec 1990, b&w 2.25
❑2, Feb 1991, b&w 2.25
❑3, b&w 2.25

CELESTINE
IMAGE

❑1, May 1996 .... 2.50
❑1/Variant, May 1996; alternate cover 2.50
❑2, Jun 1996 .... 2.50

CELL
ANTARCTIC

❑1, Sep 1996, b&w 2.95
❑2, Nov 1996, b&w 2.95
❑3, Jan 1997, b&w 2.95

CEMENT SHOOZ
HORSE FEATHERS

❑1, Sep 1991 .... 2.50

CENOTAPH
NORTHSTAR

❑1 .... 3.95

CENTRIFUGAL BUMBLE-PUPPY
FANTAGRAPHICS

❑1, b&w 2.25
❑2, b&w 2.25
❑3, b&w 2.25
❑4, b&w 2.25
❑5, b&w 2.25
❑6, b&w 2.25
❑7 .... 2.25
❑8 .... 2.50

CENTURIONS
DC

❑1, Jun 1987 O: Centurions 1.00
❑2, Jul 1987 DH (a); O: Centurions. 1.00
❑3, Aug 1987 .... 1.00
❑4, Sep 1987 .... 1.00

Other grades: Multiply price above by 5/6 for VF/NM • 2/3 for VERY FINE • 1/3 for FINE • 1/5 for VERY GOOD • 1/8 for GOOD

Cerebus Guide to Self Publishing

Excellent primer from Dave Sim

©Aardvark-Vanaheim

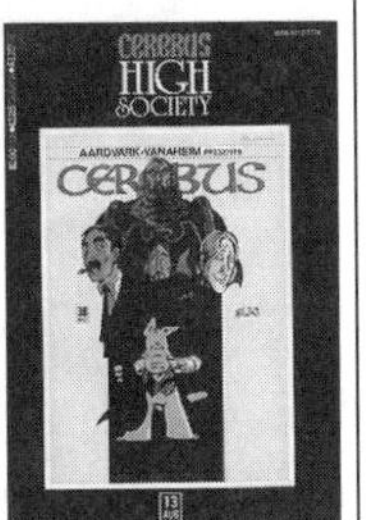
Cerebus High Society

Reprinting the second Cerebus story arc

©Aardvark-Vanaheim

Cerebus Jam

Will Eisner and more contributed

©Aardvark-Vanaheim

Cerebus the Aardvark

Amazing "6,000-page graphic novel"

©Aardvark-Vanaheim

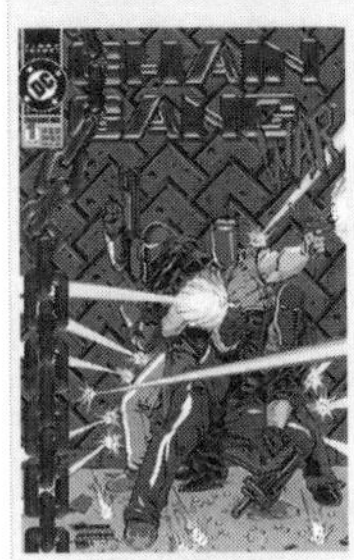
Chain Gang War

Vigilantes seek to make villains serve time

©DC

N-MINT

CENTURY: DISTANT SONS
MARVEL
❑1, Feb 1996 .... 2.95

CEREAL KILLINGS
FANTAGRAPHICS
❑1, Mar 1992, b&w 2.50
❑2, ca. 1992, b&w 2.50
❑3, ca. 1992, b&w 2.50
❑4, Mar 1993, b&w 2.50
❑5, ca. 1993, b&w 2.50

CEREBUS BI-WEEKLY
AARDVARK-VANAHEIM
❑1, Dec 1988, b&w; A: Reprints Cerebus the Aardvark #1, 1st. Reprints Cerebus the Aardvark #1 .. 1.50
❑2, Dec 1988, b&w; Reprints Cerebus the Aardvark #2........ 1.50
❑3, Dec 1988, b&w; Reprints Cerebus the Aardvark #3........ 1.50
❑4, Jan 1989, b&w; Reprints Cerebus the Aardvark #4........ 1.50
❑5, Jan 1989, b&w; Reprints Cerebus the Aardvark #5........ 1.50
❑6, Feb 1989, b&w; Reprints Cerebus the Aardvark #6........ 1.50
❑7, Feb 1989, b&w; Reprints Cerebus the Aardvark #7........ 1.50
❑8, Mar 1989, b&w; Reprints Cerebus the Aardvark #8........ 1.50
❑9, Mar 1989, b&w; Reprints Cerebus the Aardvark #9........ 1.50
❑10, Apr 1989, b&w; Reprints Cerebus the Aardvark #10........ 1.50
❑11, Apr 1989, b&w; Reprints Cerebus the Aardvark #11........ 1.50
❑12, May 1989, b&w; Reprints Cerebus the Aardvark #12........ 1.50
❑13, May 1989, b&w; Reprints Cerebus the Aardvark #13........ 1.50
❑14, May 1989, b&w; Reprints Cerebus the Aardvark #14........ 1.50
❑15, Jun 1989, b&w; Reprints Cerebus the Aardvark #15........ 1.50
❑16, Jun 1989, b&w; Reprints Cerebus the Aardvark #16........ 1.50
❑17, Jul 1989, b&w; 1: Hepcats. Reprints Cerebus the Aardvark #17 with new material........ 4.00
❑18, Jul 1989, b&w; Reprints Cerebus the Aardvark #18........ 1.50
❑19, Aug 1989, b&w; Reprints Cerebus the Aardvark #19........ 1.50
❑20, Aug 1989, b&w; 1: Milk & Cheese. Reprints Cerebus the Aardvark #20 with new material........ 6.00
❑21, Sep 1989, b&w; Reprints Cerebus the Aardvark #21........ 1.50
❑22, Sep 1989, b&w; Reprints Cerebus the Aardvark #22........ 1.50
❑23, Oct 1989, b&w; Reprints Cerebus the Aardvark #23........ 1.50
❑24, Oct 1989, b&w; Reprints Cerebus the Aardvark #24........ 1.50
❑25, Nov 1989, b&w; Reprints Cerebus the Aardvark #25........ 1.50

N-MINT

❑26, Nov 1989, b&w; Reprints Cerebus the Aardvark "Prince Silverspoon" strips from The Buyer's Guide for Comic Fandom no indicia or cover number........ 1.50

CEREBUS: CHURCH & STATE
AARDVARK-VANAHEIM
❑1, Feb 1991, b&w; Reprints Cerebus the Aardvark #51........ 2.00
❑2, Feb 1991, b&w; Reprints Cerebus the Aardvark #52........ 2.00
❑3, Mar 1991, b&w; Reprints Cerebus the Aardvark #53........ 2.00
❑4, Mar 1991, b&w; Reprints Cerebus the Aardvark #54........ 2.00
❑5, Apr 1991, b&w; Reprints Cerebus the Aardvark #55........ 2.00
❑6, Apr 1991, b&w; Reprints Cerebus the Aardvark #56........ 2.00
❑7, May 1991, b&w; Reprints Cerebus the Aardvark #57........ 2.00
❑8, May 1991, b&w; Reprints Cerebus the Aardvark #58........ 2.00
❑9, Jun 1991, b&w; Reprints Cerebus the Aardvark #59........ 2.00
❑10, Jun 1991, b&w; Reprints Cerebus the Aardvark #60........ 2.00
❑11, Jul 1991, b&w; Reprints Cerebus the Aardvark #61........ 2.00
❑12, Jul 1991, b&w; Reprints Cerebus the Aardvark #62........ 2.00
❑13, Aug 1991, b&w; Reprints Cerebus the Aardvark #63........ 2.00
❑14, Aug 1991, b&w; Reprints Cerebus the Aardvark #64........ 2.00
❑15, Sep 1991, b&w; Reprints Cerebus the Aardvark #65........ 2.00
❑16, Sep 1991, b&w; Reprints Cerebus the Aardvark #66........ 2.00
❑17, Oct 1991, b&w; Reprints Cerebus the Aardvark #67........ 2.00
❑18, Oct 1991, b&w; Reprints Cerebus the Aardvark #68........ 2.00
❑19, Nov 1991, b&w; Reprints Cerebus the Aardvark #69........ 2.00
❑20, Nov 1991, b&w; Reprints Cerebus the Aardvark #70........ 2.00
❑21, Dec 1991, b&w; Reprints Cerebus the Aardvark #71........ 2.00
❑22, Dec 1991, b&w; Reprints Cerebus the Aardvark #72........ 2.00
❑23, Jan 1992, b&w; Reprints Cerebus the Aardvark #73........ 2.00
❑24, Jan 1992, b&w; Reprints Cerebus the Aardvark #74........ 2.00
❑25, Feb 1992, b&w; Reprints Cerebus the Aardvark #75........ 2.00
❑26, Feb 1992, b&w; Reprints Cerebus the Aardvark #76........ 2.00
❑27, Mar 1992, b&w; Reprints Cerebus the Aardvark #77........ 2.00
❑28, Mar 1992, b&w; Reprints Cerebus the Aardvark #78........ 2.00
❑29, Apr 1992, b&w; Reprints Cerebus the Aardvark #79........ 2.00
❑30, Apr 1992, b&w; Reprints Cerebus the Aardvark #80........ 2.00

N-MINT

CEREBUS COMPANION
WIN-MILL
❑1, Dec 1993, b&w........ 3.95
❑2, Dec 1994, b&w........ 3.95

CEREBUS GUIDE TO SELF PUBLISHING
AARDVARK-VANAHEIM
❑1, Nov 1997, b&w; collects Sim text pieces on the subject from Cerebus 3.95

CEREBUS: GUYS PARTY PACK
AARDVARK-VANAHEIM
❑1, b&w; Reprints Cerebus the Aardvark #201-204........ 3.95

CEREBUS HIGH SOCIETY
AARDVARK-VANAHEIM
❑1, Feb 1990, b&w........ 2.00
❑2, Feb 1990, b&w........ 2.00
❑3, Mar 1990, b&w........ 2.00
❑4, Mar 1990, b&w........ 2.00
❑5, Apr 1990, b&w........ 2.00
❑6, Apr 1990, b&w........ 2.00
❑7, May 1990, b&w........ 2.00
❑8, May 1990, b&w........ 2.00
❑9, Jun 1990, b&w........ 2.00
❑10, Jun 1990, b&w........ 2.00
❑11, Jul 1990, b&w........ 2.00
❑12, Jul 1990, b&w........ 2.00
❑13, Aug 1990, b&w........ 2.00
❑14, Aug 1990, b&w........ 2.00
❑15, Sep 1990, b&w........ 2.00
❑16, Sep 1990, b&w........ 2.00
❑17, Oct 1990, b&w........ 2.00
❑18, Oct 1990, b&w........ 2.00
❑19, Nov 1990, b&w........ 2.00
❑20, Nov 1990, b&w........ 2.00
❑21, Dec 1990, b&w........ 2.00
❑22, Dec 1990, b&w........ 2.00
❑23, Jan 1991, b&w........ 2.00
❑24, Jan 1991, b&w........ 2.00
❑25, Feb 1991, b&w........ 2.00

CEREBUS JAM
AARDVARK-VANAHEIM
❑1, Apr 1985, b&w........ 3.00

CEREBUS THE AARDVARK
AARDVARK-VANAHEIM
❑0, Jun 1993, b&w; Reprints Cerebus the Aardvark #51, 112/113, 137/138 4.00
❑0/Gold, b&w; Reprints Cerebus the Aardvark #51, 112/113, 137/138; Gold logo on cover........ 6.00
❑1, Dec 1977, b&w; 1: Cerebus. genuine; Low circulation........ 700.00
❑1/Counterfeit, b&w; Counterfeit edition (glossy cover stock on inside cover); 1: Cerebus. Counterfeit edition (glossy cover stock on inside cover); Low circulation........ 60.00
❑2 1978, b&w........ 150.00
❑3 1978, b&w 1: Red Sophia........ 90.00
❑4 1978, b&w 1: Elrod the Albino........ 75.00
❑5, Aug 1978, b&w........ 50.00
❑6, Oct 1978, b&w 1: Jaka........ 35.00
❑7, Dec 1978, b&w........ 20.00
❑8, Feb 1979, b&w........ 15.00
❑9, Apr 1979, b&w........ 15.00

Other grades: Multiply price above by 5/6 for VF/NM • 2/3 for VERY FINE • 1/3 for FINE • 1/5 for VERY GOOD • 1/8 for GOOD

	N-MINT
❑10, Jun 1979, b&w	15.00
❑11, Aug 1979, b&w 1: Captain Cockroach.	12.00
❑12, Oct 1979, b&w	10.00
❑13, Dec 1979, b&w	10.00
❑14, Mar 1980, b&w 1: Lord Julius.	10.00
❑15, Apr 1980, b&w	10.00
❑16, May 1980, b&w	10.00
❑17, Jun 1980, b&w	10.00
❑18, Jul 1980, b&w	10.00
❑19, Aug 1980, b&w	10.00
❑20, Sep 1980, b&w	10.00
❑21, Oct 1980, b&w; 1: Weisshaupt. Low circulation	10.00
❑22, Nov 1980, b&w; no cover price	10.00
❑23, Dec 1980, b&w	6.00
❑24, Jan 1981, b&w	6.00
❑25, Mar 1981, b&w	6.00
❑26, May 1981, b&w	6.00
❑27, Jun 1981, b&w	6.00
❑28, Jul 1981, b&w	6.00
❑29, Aug 1981, b&w 1: Elf.	6.00
❑30, Sep 1981, b&w	6.00
❑31, Oct 1981, b&w 1: Astoria.	6.00
❑32, Nov 1981, b&w; First "Unique Story" backup	5.00
❑33, Dec 1981, b&w	5.00
❑34, Jan 1982, b&w	5.00
❑35, Feb 1982, b&w	5.00
❑36, Mar 1982, b&w	5.00
❑37, Apr 1982, b&w	5.00
❑38, May 1982, b&w	5.00
❑39, Jun 1982, b&w	5.00
❑40, Jul 1982, b&w	5.00
❑41, Aug 1982, b&w	4.00
❑42, Sep 1982, b&w	4.00
❑43, Oct 1982, b&w	4.00
❑44, Nov 1982, b&w; sideways	4.00
❑45, Dec 1982, b&w; sideways	4.00
❑46, Jan 1983, b&w; sideways	4.00
❑47, Feb 1983, b&w; sideways	4.00
❑48, Mar 1983, b&w; sideways	4.00
❑49, Apr 1983, b&w; rotating issue	4.00
❑50, May 1983, b&w	4.00
❑51, Jun 1983, b&w; Low circulation	6.00
❑52, Jul 1983, b&w	4.00
❑53, Aug 1983, b&w 1: Wolveroach (cameo).	4.00
❑54, Sep 1983, b&w 1: Wolveroach (full story). A: Wolveroach.	4.00
❑55, Oct 1983, b&w A: Wolveroach.	4.00
❑56, Nov 1983, b&w 1: Normalman. A: Wolveroach.	4.00
❑57, Dec 1983, b&w 2: Normalman.	4.00
❑58, Jan 1984, b&w	3.00
❑59, Feb 1984, b&w	3.00
❑60, Mar 1984, b&w	3.00
❑61, Apr 1984, b&w; A: Flaming Carrot. Flaming Carrot	4.00
❑62, May 1984, b&w; A: Flaming Carrot. Flaming Carrot.	4.00
❑63, Jun 1984, b&w	2.50
❑64, Jul 1984, b&w	2.50
❑65, Aug 1984, b&w; Gerhard begins as background artist	2.50
❑66, Sep 1984, b&w	2.50
❑67, Oct 1984, b&w	2.50
❑68, Nov 1984, b&w	2.50
❑69, Dec 1984, b&w	2.50
❑70, Jan 1985, b&w	2.50
❑71, Feb 1985, b&w; Last "Unique Story" backup	2.50
❑72, Mar 1985, b&w	2.50
❑73, Apr 1985, b&w	2.50
❑74, May 1985, b&w	2.50
❑75, Jun 1985, b&w	2.50
❑76, Jul 1985, b&w	2.50
❑77, Aug 1985, b&w	2.50
❑78, Sep 1985, b&w	2.50
❑79, Oct 1985, b&w	2.50
❑80, Nov 1985, b&w	2.50
❑81, Dec 1985, b&w	2.50
❑82, Jan 1986, b&w	2.50
❑83, Feb 1986, b&w	2.50
❑84, Mar 1986, b&w	2.50
❑85, Apr 1986, b&w	2.50
❑86, May 1986, b&w	2.50
❑87, Jun 1986, b&w	2.50

	N-MINT
❑88, Jul 1986, b&w	2.50
❑89, Aug 1986, b&w	2.50
❑90, Sep 1986, b&w	2.50
❑91, Oct 1986, b&w	2.50
❑92, Nov 1986, b&w	2.50
❑93, Dec 1986, b&w	2.50
❑94, Jan 1987, b&w	2.50
❑95, Feb 1987, b&w	2.50
❑96, Mar 1987, b&w	2.50
❑97, Apr 1987, b&w	2.50
❑98, May 1987, b&w	2.50
❑99, Jun 1987, b&w 1: Cirin.	2.50
❑100, Jul 1987, b&w	2.50
❑101, Aug 1987, b&w	2.00
❑102, Sep 1987, b&w	2.00
❑103, Oct 1987, b&w	2.00
❑104, Nov 1987, b&w A: Flaming Carrot.	2.00
❑105, Dec 1987, b&w	2.00
❑106, Jan 1988, b&w	2.00
❑107, Feb 1988, b&w	2.00
❑108, Mar 1988, b&w	2.00
❑109, Apr 1988, b&w	2.00
❑110, May 1988, b&w	2.00
❑111, Jun 1988, b&w	2.00
❑112, Jul 1988, b&w; Double-issue #112 and #113	2.00
❑114, Sep 1988, b&w	2.00
❑115, Oct 1988, b&w	2.00
❑116, Nov 1988, b&w	2.00
❑117, Dec 1988, b&w	2.00
❑118, Jan 1989, b&w	2.00
❑119, Feb 1989, b&w	2.00
❑120, Mar 1989, b&w	2.00
❑121, Apr 1989, b&w	2.00
❑122, May 1989, b&w	2.00
❑123, Jun 1989, b&w	2.00
❑124, Jul 1989, b&w	2.00
❑125, Aug 1989, b&w	2.00
❑126, Sep 1989, b&w	2.00
❑127, Oct 1989, b&w	2.00
❑128, Nov 1989, b&w	2.00
❑129, Dec 1989, b&w	2.00
❑130, Jan 1990, b&w	2.00
❑131, Feb 1990, b&w	2.00
❑132, Mar 1990, b&w	2.00
❑133, Apr 1990, b&w	2.00
❑134, May 1990, b&w	2.00
❑135, Jun 1990, b&w	2.00
❑136, Jul 1990, b&w	2.00
❑137, Aug 1990, b&w	2.25
❑138, Sep 1990, b&w	2.25
❑139, Oct 1990, b&w	2.25
❑140, Nov 1990, b&w	2.25
❑141, Dec 1990, b&w	2.25
❑142, Jan 1991, b&w	2.25
❑143, Feb 1991, b&w	2.25
❑144, Mar 1991, b&w	2.25
❑145, Apr 1991, b&w	2.25
❑146, May 1991, b&w	2.25
❑147, Jun 1991, b&w	2.25
❑148, Jul 1991, b&w	2.25
❑149, Aug 1991, b&w	2.25
❑150, Sep 1991, b&w	2.25
❑151, Oct 1991, b&w	2.25
❑152, Nov 1991, b&w	2.25
❑153, Dec 1991, b&w	2.25
❑154, Jan 1992, b&w	2.25
❑155, Feb 1992, b&w	2.25
❑156, Mar 1992, b&w	2.25
❑157, Apr 1992, b&w	2.25
❑158, May 1992, b&w	2.25
❑159, Jun 1992, b&w	2.25
❑160, Jul 1992, b&w	2.25
❑161, Aug 1992, b&w; Bone back-up	2.25
❑162, Sep 1992, b&w	2.25
❑163, Oct 1992, b&w	2.25
❑164, Nov 1992, b&w	2.25
❑165, Dec 1992, b&w	2.25
❑165/2nd, Dec 1992, b&w	2.25
❑166, Jan 1993, b&w	2.25
❑167, Feb 1993, b&w	2.25
❑168, Mar 1993, b&w	2.25
❑169, Apr 1993, b&w	2.25
❑170, May 1993, b&w	2.25
❑171, Jun 1993, b&w	2.25
❑172, Jul 1993, b&w	2.25

	N-MINT
❑173, Aug 1993, b&w	2.25
❑174, Sep 1993, b&w	2.25
❑175, Oct 1993, b&w	2.25
❑176, Nov 1993, b&w	2.25
❑177, Dec 1993, b&w	2.25
❑178, Jan 1994, b&w	2.25
❑179, Feb 1994, b&w	2.25
❑180, Mar 1994, b&w	2.25
❑181, Apr 1994, b&w	2.25
❑182, May 1994, b&w	2.25
❑183, Jun 1994, b&w	2.25
❑184, Jul 1994, b&w	2.25
❑185, Aug 1994, b&w	2.25
❑186, Sep 1994, b&w	2.25
❑187, Oct 1994, b&w	2.25
❑188, Nov 1994, b&w	2.25
❑189, Dec 1994, b&w	2.25
❑190, Jan 1994, b&w	2.25
❑191, Feb 1994, b&w	2.25
❑192, Mar 1994, b&w	2.25
❑193, Apr 1994, b&w	2.25
❑194, May 1995, b&w	2.25
❑195, Jun 1995, b&w	2.25
❑196, Jul 1995, b&w	2.25
❑197, Aug 1995, b&w	2.25
❑198, Sep 1995, b&w	2.25
❑199, Oct 1995, b&w	2.25
❑200, Nov 1995, b&w; Patty Cake back-up	2.25
❑201, Dec 1995, b&w	2.25
❑202, Jan 1996, b&w	2.25
❑203, Feb 1996, b&w	2.25
❑204, Mar 1996, b&w	2.25
❑205, Apr 1996, b&w	2.25
❑206, May 1996, b&w	2.25
❑207, Jun 1996, b&w	2.25
❑208, Jul 1996, b&w	2.25
❑209, Aug 1996, b&w	2.25
❑210, Sep 1996, b&w	2.25
❑211, Oct 1996, b&w	2.25
❑212, Nov 1996, b&w	2.25
❑213, Dec 1996, b&w	2.25
❑214, Jan 1997, b&w	2.25
❑215, Feb 1997, b&w	2.25
❑216, Mar 1997, b&w	2.25
❑217, Apr 1997, b&w	2.25
❑218, May 1997, b&w	2.25
❑219, Jun 1997, b&w	2.25
❑220, Jul 1997, b&w	2.25
❑221, Aug 1997, b&w	2.25
❑222, Sep 1997, b&w	2.25
❑223, Oct 1997, b&w	2.25
❑224, Nov 1997, b&w	2.25
❑225, Dec 1997, b&w	2.25
❑226, Jan 1998, b&w	2.25
❑227, Feb 1998, b&w	2.25
❑228, Mar 1998, b&w	2.25
❑229, Apr 1998, b&w	2.25
❑230, May 1998, b&w A: Jaka.	2.25
❑231, Jun 1998, b&w	2.25
❑232, Jul 1998, b&w	2.25
❑233, Aug 1998, b&w	2.25
❑234, Sep 1998, b&w	2.25
❑235, Oct 1998, b&w	2.25
❑236, Nov 1998, b&w	2.25
❑237, Dec 1998, b&w	2.25
❑238, Jan 1999, b&w	2.25
❑239, Feb 1999, b&w	2.25
❑240, Mar 1999, b&w	2.25
❑241, Apr 1999, b&w	2.25
❑242, May 1999, b&w	2.25
❑243, Jun 1999, b&w	2.25
❑244, Jul 1999, b&w	2.25
❑245, Aug 1999, b&w	2.25
❑246, Sep 1999, b&w	2.25
❑247, Oct 1999, b&w	2.25
❑248, Nov 1999, b&w	2.25
❑249, Dec 1999, b&w	2.25
❑250, Jan 2000, b&w	2.25
❑251, Feb 2000, b&w	2.25
❑252, Mar 2000, b&w	2.25
❑253, Apr 2000, b&w	2.25
❑254, May 2000, b&w	2.25
❑255, Jun 2000, b&w	2.25
❑256, Jul 2000, b&w	2.25
❑257, Aug 2000, b&w	2.25

Challengers of the Unknown

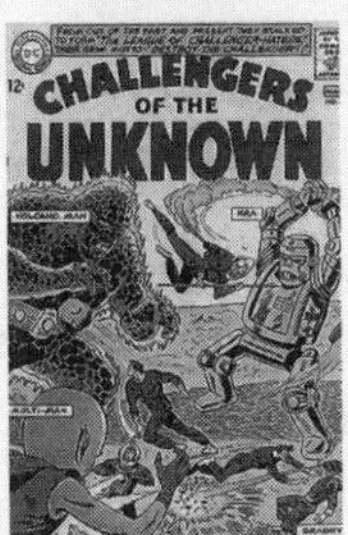

Team of adventurers g oes exploring

©DC

Chamber of Chills

Dungeons, werewolves, and dragons abound

©Marvel

Chamber of Darkness

Marvel's horror and suspense anthology

©Marvel

Champions (Marvel)

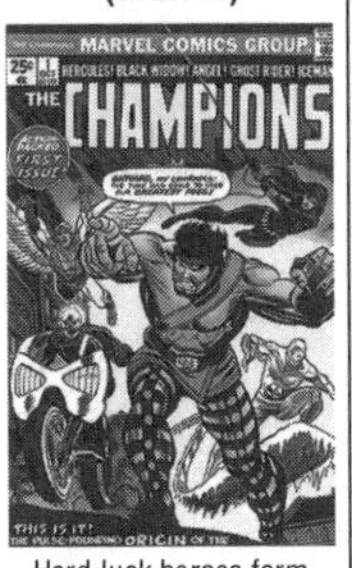

Hard-luck heroes form forgettable super-team

©Marvel

Champion Sports

Some inspirational stories, some unbelievable

©DC

N-MINT

❑258, Sep 2000, b&w 2.25
❑259, Oct 2000, b&w 2.25
❑260, Nov 2000, b&w 2.25
❑261, Dec 2000, b&w 2.25
❑262, Jan 2001, b&w 2.25
❑263, Feb 2001, b&w 2.25
❑264, Mar 2001, b&w 2.25
❑265, Apr 2001, b&w 2.25
❑266, May 2001, b&w 2.25
❑267, Jun 2001, b&w 2.25
❑268, Jul 2001, b&w 1: The Three Wise Fellows 2.25
❑269, Aug 2001, b&w 2.25
❑270, Sep 2001, b&w 2.25
❑271, Oct 2001, b&w 2.25
❑272, Nov 2001, b&w 1: Rabbi. 2.25
❑273, Dec 2001, b&w 2.25
❑274, Jan 2002, b&w 2.25
❑275, Feb 2002, b&w 2.25
❑276, Mar 2002, b&w 2.25
❑277, Apr 2002, b&w 2.25
❑278, May 2002, b&w 2.25
❑279, Jun 2002, b&w 2.25
❑280, Jul 2002, b&w 2.25
❑281, Aug 2002, b&w 2.25
❑282, Sep 2002, b&w 2.25
❑283, Oct 2002, b&w 2.25
❑284, Nov 2002, b&w 2.25
❑285, Dec 2002, b&w 2.25
❑286, Jan 2003, b&w 2.25
❑287, Feb 2003, b&w 2.25
❑288, Mar 2003, b&w 2.25
❑289, Apr 2003, b&w 2.25
❑290, May 2003, b&w 2.25
❑291, Jun 2003, b&w 2.25
❑292, Jul 2003, b&w 2.25
❑293, Aug 2003, b&w 2.25
❑294, Sep 2003, b&w 2.25
❑295, Oct 2003, b&w 2.25
❑296, Nov 2003, b&w 2.25
❑297, Dec 2003, b&w 2.25
❑298, Jan 2004, b&w 2.25
❑299, Feb 2004, b&w 2.25
❑300, Mar 2004, b&w D: Cerebus. 4.00

CEREBUS WORLD TOUR BOOK
AARDVARK-VANAHEIM

❑1, b&w 3.00

CERES CELESTIAL LEGEND PART 1
VIZ

❑1, Jun 2001 .... 3.25
❑2, Jul 2001 .... 2.95
❑3, Aug 2001 .... 2.95
❑4, Sep 2001 .... 2.95
❑5, Oct 2001 .... 2.95
❑6, Nov 2001 .... 2.95

CERES CELESTIAL LEGEND PART 2
VIZ

❑1, Dec 2001 .... 2.95
❑2, Jan 2002 .... 2.95
❑3, Feb 2002 .... 2.95
❑4, Mar 2002 .... 2.95
❑5, Apr 2002 .... 2.95
❑6, May 2002 .... 2.95

N-MINT

CERES CELESTIAL LEGEND PART 3
VIZ

❑1, Jun 2002 .... 2.95
❑2, Jul 2002 .... 3.50
❑3, Aug 2002 .... 3.50
❑4, Sep 2002 .... 3.50

CERES CELESTIAL LEGEND PART 4
VIZ

❑1, Oct 2002 .... 3.50
❑2, Nov 2002 .... 3.50
❑3, Dec 2002 .... 3.50
❑4, Jan 2003 .... 3.50

CERES CELESTIAL LEGEND PART 5
VIZ

❑1, Feb 2003 .... 3.50

CHADZ FRENDZ
SMILING FACE

❑1, Jan 1998 .... 1.50

CHAINGANG
NORTHSTAR

❑1, b&w 2.50
❑2 .... 2.50

CHAIN GANG WAR
DC

❑1, Jul 1993; Foil embossed cover 2.50
❑1/Silver, Jul 1993; Silver promotional edition 2.50
❑2, Aug 1993 .... 1.75
❑3, Sep 1993 .... 1.75
❑4, Oct 1993 .... 1.75
❑5, Nov 1993; Embossed cover 2.50
❑6, Dec 1993 .... 1.75
❑7, Jan 1994 .... 1.75
❑8, Feb 1994 .... 1.75
❑9, Mar 1994 .... 1.75
❑10, Apr 1994 .... 1.75
❑11, May 1994 .... 1.75
❑12, Jun 1994; End of Chain Gang 1.75

CHAINSAW VIGILANTE
NEC

❑1 .... 3.50
❑1/A; Orange cover 5.00
❑1/B; Gold foil cover 6.00
❑1/C; Pseudo-3D "platinum" foil cover 6.00
❑2 .... 2.75
❑3 .... 2.75

CHAINS OF CHAOS
HARRIS

❑1, Nov 1994 .... 2.95
❑2, Dec 1994 .... 2.95
❑3, Jan 1995 .... 2.95

CHAKAN
RAK

❑1, b&w 4.00

CHALLENGERS OF THE FANTASTIC
MARVEL / AMALGAM

❑1, Jun 1997 .... 2.00

CHALLENGERS OF THE UNKNOWN
DC

❑1, May 1958 JK (a) 1450.00
❑2, Jul 1958 JK (a) 375.00
❑3, Sep 1958 JK (a) 220.00

N-MINT

❑4, Nov 1958 JK, WW (a) 220.00
❑5, Jan 1959 JK, WW (a) 220.00
❑6, Mar 1959 JK, WW (a) 220.00
❑7, May 1959 JK, WW (a) 220.00
❑8, Jul 1959, JK, WW (a) 220.00
❑9, Sep 1959 .... 140.00
❑10, Nov 1959 .... 140.00
❑11, Jan 1960 .... 90.00
❑12, Mar 1960 .... 90.00
❑13, May 1960 .... 90.00
❑14, Jul 1960 O: Multi-Man. 1: Multi-Man. 90.00
❑15, Sep 1960 .... 90.00
❑16, Nov 1960 .... 52.00
❑17, Jan 1961 .... 52.00
❑18, Mar 1961 1: Cosmo (Challengers of the Unknown's Pet). 52.00
❑19, May 1961 .... 52.00
❑20, Jul 1961 .... 52.00
❑21, Sep 1961 .... 52.00
❑22, Nov 1961 .... 52.00
❑23, Jan 1962 .... 52.00
❑24, Mar 1962 .... 25.00
❑25, May 1962 .... 25.00
❑26, Jul 1962 .... 25.00
❑27, Sep 1962 .... 25.00
❑28, Nov 1962 .... 25.00
❑29, Jan 1963 .... 25.00
❑30, Mar 1963 .... 25.00
❑31, May 1963, O: Challengers of the Unknown. 25.00
❑32, Jul 1963 .... 20.00
❑33, Sep 1963 .... 20.00
❑34, Nov 1963, O: Multi-Woman. 1: Multi-Woman. 20.00
❑35, Jan 1964 .... 20.00
❑36, Mar 1964 .... 20.00
❑37, May 1964 .... 20.00
❑38, Jul 1964 .... 20.00
❑39, Sep 1964 .... 20.00
❑40, Nov 1964 .... 20.00
❑41, Jan 1965 .... 20.00
❑42, Mar 1965 .... 20.00
❑43, May 1965, Challengers of the Unknown get new uniforms 20.00
❑44, Jul 1965 .... 20.00
❑45, Sep 1965 .... 20.00
❑46, Nov 1965 .... 20.00
❑47, Jan 1966 .... 20.00
❑48, Mar 1966, A: The Doom Patrol. 20.00
❑49, May 1966 .... 20.00
❑50, Jul 1966, 1: Villo. 15.00
❑51, Sep 1966, A: Sea Devils. V: Sponge Man. 15.00
❑52, Nov 1966 .... 15.00
❑53, Jan 1967 .... 15.00
❑54, Mar 1967 .... 15.00
❑55, May 1967, 1: Tino Manarry. D: Red Ryan. 15.00
❑56, Jul 1967 .... 15.00
❑57, Sep 1967 .... 11.00
❑58, Nov 1967, V: Neutro. 11.00
❑59, Jan 1968 .... 11.00
❑60, Mar 1968, Red Ryan returns 11.00
❑61, May 1968 .... 11.00

Other grades: Multiply price above by 5/6 for VF/NM • 2/3 for VERY FINE • 1/3 for FINE • 1/5 for VERY GOOD • 1/8 for GOOD

❑62, Jul 1968 .... 11.00
❑63, Sep 1968 .... 11.00
❑64, Nov 1968, JK (a); O: Challengers of the Unknown. reprints Showcase #6 . 11.00
❑65, Jan 1969, JK (a); O: Challengers of the Unknown. reprints Showcase #6 11.00
❑66, Mar 1969 .... 11.00
❑67, May 1969 .... 11.00
❑68, Jul 1969 .... 11.00
❑69, Sep 1969, 1: Corinna. 11.00
❑70, Nov 1969 .... 7.00
❑71, Jan 1970 .... 7.00
❑72, Mar 1970 .... 7.00
❑73, May 1970 .... 7.00
❑74, Jul 1970, NA (a); A: Deadman. ... 14.00
❑75, Sep 1970, JK (a); V: Ultivac. reprints Showcase #7 .... 7.00
❑76, Nov 1970, Reprints stories from Challengers of the Unknown #2 & #3 7.00
❑77, Jan 1971, reprints Showcase #12 7.00
❑78, Feb 1973, Reprints stories from Challengers of the Unknown #6 & #7 7.00
❑79, Apr 1973, JKu (c); reprints stories from Challengers of the Unknown #1 and 2 .... 7.00
❑80, Jul 1973, reprints Showcase #11; series goes on hiatus for four years 7.00
❑81, Jul 1977 .... 6.00
❑82, Aug 1977, A: Swamp Thing. 5.00
❑83, Oct 1977 .... 5.00
❑84, Dec 1977 .... 5.00
❑85, Feb 1978, A: Deadman, Swamp Thing 5.00
❑86, Apr 1978, A: Deadman, Swamp Thing 5.00
❑87, Jul 1978, KG (a); A: Deadman, Swamp Thing, Rip Hunter. 5.00

CHALLENGERS OF THE UNKNOWN (2ND SERIES)
DC

❑1, Feb 1997; new team 2.25
❑2, Mar 1997 .... 2.25
❑3, Apr 1997 .... 2.25
❑4, May 1997 .... 2.25
❑5, Jun 1997 .... 2.25
❑6, Jul 1997; concludes in Scare Tactics #8 .... 2.25
❑7, Aug 1997; return of original Challengers 2.25
❑8, Sep 1997 .... 2.25
❑9, Oct 1997 .... 2.25
❑10, Nov 1997 .... 2.25
❑11, Dec 1997; Face cover 2.25
❑12, Jan 1998 .... 2.25
❑13, Feb 1998 .... 2.25
❑14, Mar 1998 .... 2.25
❑15, Apr 1998; Millennium Giants; continues in Superman #134 .... 2.25
❑16, May 1998; tales of the original Challengers 2.25
❑17, Jun 1998 .... 2.25
❑18, Jul 1998 .... 2.50

CHALLENGERS OF THE UNKNOWN (MINI-SERIES)
DC

❑1, Mar 1991 .... 1.75
❑2, Apr 1991 .... 1.75
❑3, May 1991 .... 1.75
❑4, Jun 1991 .... 1.75
❑5, Jul 1991 .... 1.75
❑6, Aug 1991 .... 1.75
❑7, Sep 1991 .... 1.75
❑8, Oct 1991 .... 1.75

CHALLENGERS OF THE UNKNOWN (2ND MINI-SERIES)
DC

❑1, Aug 2004 .... 2.95
❑2, Sep 2004 .... 2.95
❑3, Oct 2004 .... 2.95
❑4, Nov 2004 .... 2.95
❑5, Dec 2004 .... 2.95
❑6, Jan 2005 .... 2.95

CHAMBER
MARVEL

❑1, Oct 2002 .... 3.00
❑2, Nov 2002 .... 3.00
❑3, Dec 2002 .... 3.00
❑4, Jan 2003 .... 3.00

CHAMBER OF CHILLS
MARVEL

❑1, Nov 1972 .... 25.00
❑2, Jan 1973 .... 15.00
❑3, Mar 1973 .... 15.00
❑4, May 1973 .... 15.00
❑5, Jul 1973 .... 15.00
❑6, Sep 1973 .... 15.00
❑7, Nov 1973 .... 15.00
❑8, Jan 1974 .... 15.00
❑9, Mar 1974 .... 15.00
❑10, May 1974 .... 15.00
❑11, Jul 1974, Reprints story from Tales of Suspense #28 .... 12.00
❑12, Sep 1974 .... 12.00
❑13, Nov 1974 .... 12.00
❑14, Jan 1975 .... 12.00
❑15, Mar 1975 .... 12.00
❑16, May 1975 .... 12.00
❑17, Jul 1975 .... 12.00
❑18, Sep 1975, Reprints story from Tales to Astonish #11 .... 12.00
❑19, Nov 1975, Reprints story from Tales to Astonish #26 .... 12.00
❑20, Jan 1976 .... 12.00
❑21, Mar 1976 .... 12.00
❑22, May 1976, Reprints story from Tales to Astonish #26 .... 12.00
❑22/30 cent, May 1976, Reprints story from Tales to Astonish #26; 30 cent regional price variant 20.00
❑23, Jul 1976 .... 12.00
❑23/30 cent, Jul 1976 .... 20.00
❑24, Sep 1976 .... 12.00
❑25, Nov 1976 .... 12.00

CHAMBER OF DARKNESS
MARVEL

❑1, Oct 1968, SL (w); JB, DH (a) 60.00
❑2, Dec 1968 .... 35.00
❑3, Feb 1969 .... 30.00
❑4, Apr 1969, Conan try-out 60.00
❑5, Jun 1969 .... 30.00
❑6, Aug 1969 .... 30.00
❑7, Oct 1969, BWr (a); 1st Bernie Wrightson work; reprints story from Tales to Astonish #13 .... 30.00
❑8, Dec 1969 .... 20.00
❑1/Special 1972; Special Edition 20.00

CHAMBER OF EVIL
COMAX

❑1 .... 2.95

CHAMPION
SPECIAL STUDIO

❑1, b&w 2.50

CHAMPION OF KATARA
MU

❑1, Jan 1992, b&w 2.50
❑2, Apr 1992 .... 2.50

CHAMPION OF KATARA: DUM-DUMS & DRAGONS
MU

❑1, Jun 1995, b&w 2.95
❑2, Jul 1995, b&w 2.95
❑3, Aug 1995, b&w 2.95

CHAMPIONS CLASSICS
HERO

❑1; Reprints 1.00
❑13, Oct 1993; b&w reprint 3.95
❑14, Jan 1994; b&w reprint 3.95

CHAMPIONS CLASSICS/FLARE ADVENTURES
HERO

❑2; flip-format 2.95
❑3; flip-format 2.95
❑4; flip-format 3.50
❑5; flip-format 3.50
❑6; flip-format 3.50
❑7; flip-format 3.50

CHAMPIONS (ECLIPSE)
ECLIPSE

❑1, Jun 1986 .... 1.25
❑2, Sep 1986 .... 1.25
❑3, Oct 1986 .... 1.25
❑4, Nov 1986 .... 1.25
❑5, Feb 1987 .... 1.25
❑6, Feb 1987 .... 1.25

CHAMPIONS (HERO)
HERO

❑1, Sep 1987 1: 1: The Galloping Galooper. 1: Madame Synn. 1.95
❑2, Oct 1987 1: 1: Black Enchantress. 1: The Fat Man. 1.95
❑3, Nov 1987 O: Flare. 1: Icicle. 1: Sparkplug. 1.95
❑4, Dec 1987 1: 1: Pulsar. 1: Exo-Skeleton Man. 1.95
❑5, Jan 1988 .... 1.95
❑6, Feb 1988 1: Mechanon. 1.95
❑7, Mar 1988 .... 1.95
❑8, May 1988 O: Foxbat. 1.95
❑9, Jun 1988; (also was Flare #0) 1.95
❑10, Jul 1988 .... 1.95
❑11, Sep 1988 .... 1.95
❑12, Oct 1988 .... 1.95
❑13 .... 1.95
❑14 .... 1.95
❑15, b&w 3.95
❑Annual 1, Dec 1988 O: Giant. O: Dark Malice. 2.75
❑Annual 2 .... 3.95

CHAMPIONS (MARVEL)
MARVEL

❑1, Oct 1975, DH (a); O: The Champions. 1: The Champions. A: Venus. 15.00
❑2, Jan 1976 .... 6.00
❑3, Feb 1976 .... 6.00
❑4, Mar 1976 .... 5.00
❑5, Apr 1976, DH (a); O: Rampage (Marvel). 1: Rampage (Marvel). A: Ghost Rider. 5.00
❑5/30 cent, Apr 1976, DH (a); 30 cent regional price variant 20.00
❑6, Jun 1976 .... 4.00
❑6/30 cent, Jun 1976, 30 cent regional price variant 20.00
❑7, Aug 1976 .... 4.00
❑7/30 cent, Aug 1976, 30 cent regional price variant 20.00
❑8, Oct 1976, GK, BH (a) 4.00
❑9, Dec 1976, GK, BH (a); V: Darkstar, Titanium Man, Crimson Dynamo. ... 4.00
❑10, Jan 1977, DC, BH (a) 4.00
❑11, Feb 1977, JBy (a) 4.00
❑12, Mar 1977, JBy (a) 4.00
❑13, May 1977, JBy (a) 4.00
❑14, Jul 1977, JBy (a); 1: Swarm. 4.00
❑14/35 cent, Jul 1977, JBy (a); 1: Swarm. 35 cent regional price variant 15.00
❑15, Sep 1977, JBy (a) 4.00
❑15/35 cent, Sep 1977, JBy (a); 35 cent regional price variant 15.00
❑16, Nov 1977, JBy, BH (a); A: Doctor Doom. 4.00
❑17, Jan 1978, JBy, GT (a); V: Sentinels. 4.00

CHAMPION SPORTS
DC

❑1, Nov 1973 .... 5.00
❑2, Jan 1974 .... 3.50
❑3, Mar 1974 .... 3.50

CHANGE COMMANDER GOKU (1ST SERIES)
ANTARCTIC

❑1, Oct 1993 .... 2.95
❑2, Nov 1993 .... 2.95
❑3, Dec 1993 .... 2.95
❑4, Jan 1994 .... 2.95
❑5, Feb 1994 .... 2.95

CHANGE COMMANDER GOKU 2
ANTARCTIC

❑1, Sep 1996 .... 2.95
❑2, Nov 1996 .... 2.95
❑3, Jan 1997 .... 2.95
❑4, Mar 1997 .... 2.95

CHANGES
TUNDRA

❑1 .... 7.95

CHANNEL ZERO
IMAGE

❑1, Feb 1998 .... 2.95
❑2, Apr 1998 .... 2.95
❑3, Jun 1998 .... 2.95
❑4, Aug 1998 .... 2.95
❑5, Nov 1998 .... 2.95
❑6, Feb 1999 .... 2.95

Charlton Bullseye

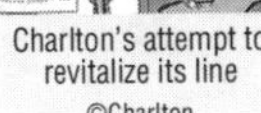

Charlton's attempt to revitalize its line

©Charlton

Checkmate (Gold Key)

TV private detective series from 1960-62

©Gold Key

Checkmate

Secret organization for dealing with criminals

©DC

Cheryl Blossom (2nd Series)

Redhead competitor to Betty and Veronica

©Archie

Cheyenne

Western ran on TV from 1955-63

©Dell

N-MINT

CHANNEL ZERO: DUPE
IMAGE

❑1, Jan 1999, b&w 2.95

CHAOS! BIBLE
CHAOS

❑1, Nov 1995 ..... 3.50

CHAOS! CHRONICLES
CHAOS

❑1, Feb 2000 ..... 3.50

CHAOS EFFECT, THE: ALPHA
VALIANT

❑1, ca. 1994; giveaway; BL (w); A: Timewalker. no cover price 3.00
❑1/Red foil, ca. 1994; Approx. 2,500 printed; retailers needed to order 100 Chaos Effect comics to receive one copy of the Red variant. Copies also given away for completing a Valiant survey in 1995 ..... 90.00

CHAOS EFFECT, THE: EPILOGUE
VALIANT

❑1, Dec 1994; Magnus in 20th century; cardstock cover 2.00
❑2, Jan 1995; Magnus in 20th century; cardstock cover 2.00

CHAOS EFFECT, THE: OMEGA
VALIANT

❑1, Nov 1994; Magnus in 20th century; cardstock cover 2.00
❑1/Gold, Nov 1994; Gold edition; Magnus in 20th century; cardstock cover 20.00

CHAOS EFFECT, THE: BETA
VALIANT

❑1 ..... 2.25

CHAOS! GALLERY
CHAOS!

❑1, Aug 1997; pin-ups 2.95

CHAOS! PRESENTS JADE
CHAOS

❑1, May 2001 ..... 2.99
❑2, Jun 2001 ..... 2.99
❑3, Jul 2001 ..... 2.99
❑4, Aug 2001 ..... 2.99

CHAOS! QUARTERLY
CHAOS

❑1 ..... 4.95
❑2 ..... 4.95
❑3 ..... 3.95

CHAPEL
IMAGE

❑1, Feb 1995 ..... 2.50
❑2, Mar 1995 ..... 2.50
❑2/Variant, Mar 1995, Alternate cover; Chapel firing right, white lettering in logo 4.00

CHAPEL (MINI-SERIES)
IMAGE

❑1 ..... 2.50
❑2, Mar 1995 ..... 2.50

CHAPEL (VOL. 2)
IMAGE

❑1, Aug 1995 ..... 2.50
❑1/Variant, Aug 1995, alternate cover 2.50
❑2, Sep 1995 ..... 2.50
❑3, Oct 1995 ..... 2.50
❑4, Nov 1995, Babewatch 2.50
❑5, Dec 1995 ..... 2.50
❑6, Feb 1996 ..... 2.50
❑7, Apr 1996 ..... 2.50

CHAPEL (3RD SERIES)
AWESOME

❑1, Sep 1997; Says "Vol. 1" in indicia

CHARLEMAGNE
DEFIANT

❑0, Feb 1994, giveaway 1.00
❑1, Mar 1994 ..... 3.25
❑2, Apr 1994 ..... 2.50
❑3, May 1994 ..... 2.50
❑4, Jun 1994 ..... 2.50
❑5, Jul 1994 ..... 2.50
❑6 ..... 2.50
❑7 ..... 2.50
❑8 ..... 2.50

CHARLES BURNS' MODERN HORROR SKETCHBOOK
KITCHEN SINK

❑1 ..... 6.95

CHARLIE CHAN (ETERNITY)
ETERNITY

❑1, Mar 1989; b&w strip reprint 1.95
❑2, Mar 1989; b&w strip reprint 1.95
❑3, Apr 1989; b&w strip reprint 1.95
❑4, May 1989; b&w strip reprint 1.95
❑5, Jul 1989 ..... 2.25
❑6, Aug 1989 ..... 2.25

CHARLIE THE CAVEMAN
FANTASY GENERAL

❑1, b&w 2.00

CHARLTON ACTION FEATURING STATIC
CHARLTON

❑11, Oct 1985 ..... 1.50
❑12, Dec 1985 ..... 1.50

CHARLTON BULLSEYE
CHARLTON

❑1, Jun 1981 ..... 7.00
❑2, Jul 1981 ..... 2.00
❑3, Sep 1981 ..... 2.00
❑4, Nov 1981 ..... 2.00
❑5, Jan 1982 ..... 2.00
❑6, Mar 1982 ..... 2.00
❑7, May 1982, A: Captain Atom. 2.00
❑8, Jul 1982 ..... 2.00
❑9, Sep 1982, GD (w); GD (a) 2.00
❑10, Dec 1982 ..... 2.00

CHARLTON CLASSICS
CHARLTON

❑1, Apr 1980 ..... 3.00
❑2, Jun 1980 ..... 2.00
❑3, Aug 1980 ..... 2.00
❑4, Oct 1980 ..... 2.00
❑5, Dec 1980 ..... 2.00
❑6, Feb 1981 ..... 2.00
❑7, Apr 1981 ..... 2.00
❑8, Jun 1981, Hercules; Joe Gill story, Sam Glanzman art credits; Tom Sutton script and art 2.00
❑9, Aug 1981 ..... 2.00

CHARLTON PREMIERE (VOL. 1)
CHARLTON

❑19, Jul 1967 ..... 20.00

CHARLTON PREMIERE (VOL. 2)
CHARLTON

❑1, Sep 1967, Restarted; Vol. 1, #19 was the end of Marine War Heroes. 6.00
❑2, Nov 1967 ..... 4.00
❑3, Jan 1968 ..... 4.00
❑4, May 1968 ..... 4.00

CHARLTON SPORT LIBRARY: PROFESSIONAL FOOTBALL
CHARLTON

❑1, Win 1969 ..... 35.00

CHARM SCHOOL
SLAVE LABOR

❑1, Apr 2000, b&w 2.95
❑2, Jul 2000, b&w 2.95
❑3, Dec 2000, b&w 2.95

CHASE
DC

❑1, Feb 1998; bound-in trading cards 2.50
❑2, Mar 1998 ..... 2.50
❑3, Apr 1998 ..... 2.50
❑4, May 1998 ..... 2.50
❑5, Jun 1998 ..... 2.50
❑6, Jul 1998 ..... 2.50
❑7, Aug 1998 ..... 2.50
❑8, Sep 1998 ..... 2.50
❑9, Oct 1998 ..... 2.50
❑1000000, Nov 1998 ..... 2.00

CHASE
APCOMICS

❑1 2004 ..... 3.50
❑1/Sketch 2004 ..... 5.00
❑2 2004 ..... 3.50

CHASER PLATOON
AIRCEL

❑1, Feb 1991, b&w 2.25
❑2, Mar 1991, b&w 2.25
❑3, Apr 1991, b&w 2.25
❑4, May 1991, b&w 2.25
❑5, b&w 2.25
❑6, b&w 2.25

CHASSIS (VOL. 1)
MILLENNIUM / EXPAND

❑1; foil logo 2.95
❑1/2nd, May 1997 ..... 2.95
❑2 ..... 2.95
❑3, Apr 1998 ..... 2.95

CHASSIS (VOL. 2)
HURRICANE

❑0, Apr 1999, biographical information on Chassis characters 2.95
❑1, Jun 1998 ..... 2.95
❑2, Sep 1998 ..... 2.95
❑3, Jan 1999 ..... 2.95

Other grades: Multiply price above by 5/6 for VF/NM • 2/3 for VERY FINE • 1/3 for FINE • 1/5 for VERY GOOD • 1/8 for GOOD

CHASSIS (VOL. 3)
IMAGE

❑0, Apr 1999; background information 2.95
❑1, Nov 1999 2.95
❑1/A, Nov 1999; Alternate cover with Chassis standing against blueprint background 2.95
❑2, Dec 1999 2.95
❑3, Mar 2000 2.95
❑4, Mar 2000 2.95

CHASTITY
CHAOS!

❑½, Jan 2001 2.95

CHASTITY: LUST FOR LIFE
CHAOS!

❑1/Dynamic, May 1999; Dynamic Forces cover (falling with two outstretched swords) 5.00
❑1/Ltd., May 1999 5.00
❑1, May 1999 3.50
❑2, Jun 1999 2.95

CHASTITY: REIGN OF TERROR
CHAOS!

❑1, Oct 2000 2.95

CHASTITY: ROCKED
CHAOS!

❑1, Nov 1998 2.95
❑2, Dec 1998 2.95
❑3, Jan 1999 2.95
❑4, Feb 1999 2.95

CHASTITY: THEATRE OF PAIN
CHAOS!

❑1, Feb 1997 2.95
❑1/Variant, Feb 1997; Onyx Premium Edition; cardstock cover 4.00
❑2, Apr 1997 2.95
❑3, Jun 1997; back cover pin-up 2.95
❑3/Variant, Jun 1997; Final Curtain Edition; No cover price; Limited Engagement 4.00

CHEAPSKIN
FANTAGRAPHICS / EROS

❑1, b&w 2.95

CHECKMATE (GOLD KEY)
GOLD KEY

❑1, Oct 1962 30.00
❑2, Dec 1962 20.00

CHECKMATE
DC

❑1, Apr 1988 1.25
❑2, May 1988 1.25
❑3, Jun 1988 1.25
❑4, Jul 1988 1.25
❑5, Aug 1988 1.25
❑6, Sep 1988 1.25
❑7, Oct 1988 1.25
❑8, Nov 1988 1.25
❑9, Dec 1988 1.25
❑10, Win 1988 1.25
❑11, Hol 1988; Invasion! First Strike 1.25
❑12, Feb 1989; Invasion! Aftermath 1.25
❑13, Mar 1989 1.50
❑14, Apr 1989 1.50
❑15, May 1989; continues in Suicide Squad #27 1.50
❑16, May 1989; continues in Suicide Squad #28 1.50
❑17, Jun 1989; continues in Manhunter #14 1.50
❑18, Jun 1989; continues in Suicide Squad #30 1.50
❑19, Jul 1989 1.50
❑20, Aug 1989 1.50
❑21, Oct 1989 1.50
❑22, Nov 1989 1.50
❑23, Dec 1989 1.50
❑24, Jan 1990 1.50
❑25, Feb 1990 1.50
❑26 1.50
❑27 1.50
❑28, Jun 1990 1.50
❑29, Jul 1990 1.50
❑30, Aug 1990 1.50
❑31, Oct 1990 1.50
❑32, Dec 1990 1.50
❑33 1991 1.50

CHECKMATE (2ND SERIES)
DC

❑1, Jul 2006 2.99
❑2, Aug 2006 2.99
❑3, Aug 2006 2.99

CHECK-UP
FANTAGRAPHICS

❑1, b&w 2.75

CHEECH WIZARD
LAST GASP

❑1 3.00

CHEEKY ANGEL
VIZ

❑1, Jul 2004 9.95
❑2, Sep 2004 9.95
❑3, Nov 2004 9.95
❑4, Jan 2005 9.95
❑5, Mar 2005 9.95
❑6, May 2005 9.95
❑7, Jul 2005 9.95
❑8, Sep 2005 9.95

CHEERLEADERS FROM HELL
CALIBER

❑1, b&w 2.50

CHEESE HEADS
TRAGEDY STRIKES

❑1, b&w; second edition 2.50
❑1/2nd, b&w; second edition 2.95
❑2, b&w 2.50
❑3 2.95
❑4 2.95
❑5 2.95

CHEESE WEASEL
SIDE SHOW

❑1; Color cover 2.95
❑2; Black & white covers begin 2.95
❑3 2.95
❑4 2.95
❑5 2.95
❑6 2.95
❑7 2.95

CHEESE WEASEL: INNOCENT UNTIL PROVEN GUILTY
SIDE SHOW

❑1 9.95

CHEETA POP SCREAM QUEEN
ANTARCTIC / VENUS

❑1, May 1994 2.95
❑2, Nov 1994 2.95
❑3, Jan 1995 2.95
❑4, Mar 1995 2.95
❑5, May 1995 2.95

CHEETA POP (VOL. 2)
FANTAGRAPHICS / EROS

❑1 2.95
❑2 2.95
❑3, Jan 1996 2.95

CHEMICAL WARFARE
CHECKER COMICS

❑1, b&w 2.95
❑2, Sum 1998, b&w 2.95
❑3 2.95

CHEQUE, MATE
FANTAGRAPHICS

❑1, b&w 3.50

CHERRY
LAST GASP

❑1, ca. 1982; 1: Cherry Poptart. 1977 8.00
❑1/2nd; 1: Cherry Poptart. 1982 4.00
❑2 4.00
❑3; Title changes to Cherry; indicia says Cherry (nee Poptart) 4.00
❑4 3.50
❑5 3.50
❑6 3.50
❑7 3.50
❑8; Oz parody Land of Woz 3.50
❑9 3.50
❑10 3.50
❑11; 3-D issue; 3-D issue 4.00
❑11/2nd; Kitchen Sink reprint 4.00
❑12, Sum 1991; Cherry goes to Iraq 3.00
❑13; Last Cherry issue from Last Gasp 3.00
❑14, Feb 1993; O: Cherry. moves to Kitchen Sink; 1st issue at Kitchen Sink 3.00
❑15, Nov 1993 3.00
❑16, Nov 1994 3.00
❑17, Apr 1995; TMNT parody 3.00
❑18, Oct 1995 3.00
❑19, Sep 1996; moves to Cherry Comics 3.00
❑20, Mar 1999; was Kitchen Sink 3.00

CHERRY DELUXE
CHERRY

❑1, Aug 1998, b&w 4.00

CHERRY'S JUBILEE
TUNDRA

❑1 2.95
❑2 2.95
❑3 2.95
❑4 2.95

CHERYL BLOSSOM (1ST SERIES)
ARCHIE

❑1, Sep 1995 2.50
❑2, Oct 1995 2.00
❑3, Nov 1995 2.00

CHERYL BLOSSOM (2ND SERIES)
ARCHIE

❑1, Jul 1996, DDC (a) 2.00
❑2, Aug 1996 1.50
❑3, Sep 1996 1.50

CHERYL BLOSSOM (3RD SERIES)
ARCHIE

❑1, Apr 1997 2.00
❑2, May 1997 1.50
❑3, Jun 1997 1.50
❑4, Aug 1997 1.50
❑5, Sep 1997 1.50
❑6, Oct 1997 1.50
❑7, Nov 1997 1.50
❑8, Jan 1998 1.75
❑9, Feb 1998 1.75
❑10, Mar 1998 1.75
❑11, Apr 1998 1.75
❑12, May 1998 1.75
❑13, Jun 1998 1.75
❑14, Aug 1998 1.75
❑15, Sep 1998, cover forms triptych with issue #16 and #17 1.75
❑16, Oct 1998 1.75
❑17, Nov 1998 1.75
❑18, Jan 1999, Cheryl as super-model with readers' fashions 1.75
❑19, Feb 1999 1.75
❑20, Mar 1999 1.75
❑21, Apr 1999 1.79
❑22, May 1999 1.79
❑23, Jun 1999 1.79
❑24, Aug 1999 1.79
❑25, Sep 1999 1.79
❑26, Oct 1999 1.79
❑27, Nov 1999 1.79
❑28, Jan 2000 1.79
❑29, Feb 2000 1.79
❑30, Mar 2000 1.79
❑31, May 2000 1.79
❑32, Jul 2000, Indicia says May, cover says Jul 1.79
❑33, Aug 2000 1.79
❑34, Sep 2000 1.79
❑35, Oct 2000 1.79
❑36, Jan 2001 1.79
❑37, Mar 2001 1.79

CHERYL BLOSSOM GOES HOLLYWOOD
ARCHIE

❑1, Dec 1996 1.50
❑2, Jan 1997 1.50
❑3, Feb 1997 1.50

CHERYL BLOSSOM SPECIAL
ARCHIE

❑1 2.00
❑2 2.00
❑3 2.00
❑4 2.00

CHESTY SANCHEZ
ANTARCTIC

❑1, Nov 1995, b&w 2.95
❑2, Mar 1996, b&w 2.95
❑3 2.95

Other grades: Multiply price above by 5/6 for VF/NM • 2/3 for VERY FINE • 1/3 for FINE • 1/5 for VERY GOOD • 1/8 for GOOD

Chiaroscuro	Chip 'n' Dale (2nd Series)	Choo-Choo Charlie	Chroma-Tick	Chromium Man
	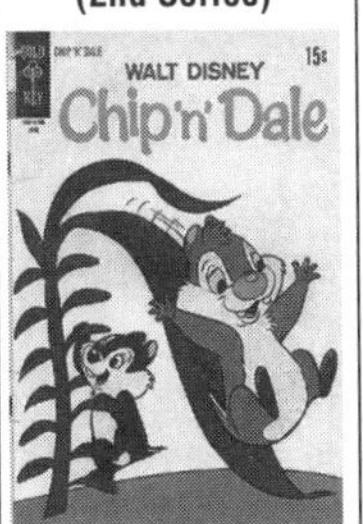	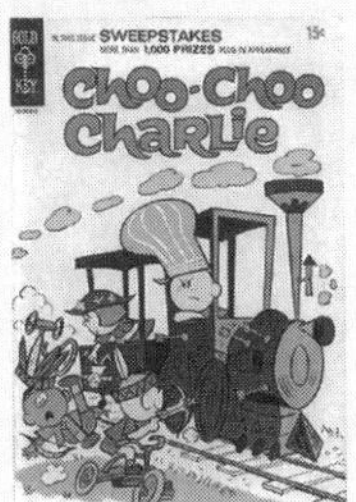		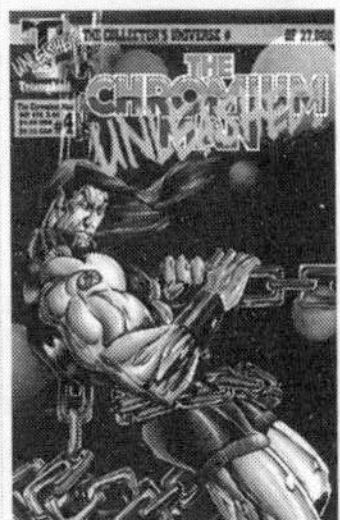
The life of Leonardo da Vinci ©DC	Less annoying when you can't hear their voices ©Gold Key	Good & Plenty candy mascot hits comics ©Gold Key	Color! Color! Color! Color! Color! Color! Color! ©New England	Publisher serially numbered all copies ©Triumphant

N-MINT

CHEVAL NOIR
DARK HORSE

❑1, Aug 1989, b&w DSt (c) 3.50
❑2, Oct 1989, b&w DSt (c) 3.50
❑3 .... 3.50
❑4 1990 .... 3.50
❑5, Mar 1990, BB (a) 3.50
❑6 1990, BB (w); BB (a) 3.50
❑7 1990, DSt (c) 3.50
❑8 1990 .... 3.50
❑9 1990 .... 3.50
❑10 1990 .... 3.50
❑11 1990 .... 3.50
❑12 1990 .... 3.50
❑13 1990 .... 3.50
❑14 .... 3.50
❑15 1991 .... 3.50
❑16 1991, trading cards 3.75
❑17 1991, trading cards 3.50
❑18 1991, trading cards 3.50
❑19 1991, trading cards 3.50
❑20 1991 .... 3.50
❑21 1991 .... 3.50
❑22 1991 .... 3.50
❑23 1991 .... 3.50
❑24 1991 .... 3.50
❑25 1991 .... 3.50
❑26, Jan 1992 .... 3.50
❑27, Feb 1992 .... 2.95
❑28, Mar 1992 .... 2.95
❑29, Apr 1992 .... 2.95
❑30, May 1992 .... 2.95
❑31, Jun 1992 .... 2.95
❑32, Jul 1992 .... 2.95
❑33, Aug 1992 .... 2.95
❑34, Sep 1992 .... 2.95
❑35, Oct 1992 .... 2.95
❑36, Nov 1992 .... 2.95
❑37, Dec 1992 .... 2.95
❑38, Jan 1993 .... 2.95
❑39, Feb 1993 .... 2.95
❑40, Mar 1993 .... 2.95
❑41, Apr 1993 .... 2.95
❑42, May 1993 .... 2.95
❑43, Jun 1993 .... 2.95
❑44, Jul 1993 .... 2.95
❑45, Aug 1993 .... 2.95
❑46, Sep 1993 .... 2.95
❑47, Oct 1993 .... 2.95
❑48, Nov 1993 .... 2.95
❑49, Dec 1993 .... 2.95
❑50, Jan 1994 .... 2.95

CHEYENNE
DELL

❑4, Aug 1957; Series continued from appearances in Four Color Comics.. 35.00
❑5, Nov 1957 .... 35.00
❑6, Feb 1958 .... 25.00
❑7, May 1958 .... 25.00
❑8, Aug 1958 .... 25.00
❑9, Nov 1958 .... 25.00
❑10, Feb 1959 .... 25.00
❑11, May 1959 .... 20.00
❑12, Aug 1959 .... 20.00
❑13, Nov 1959 .... 20.00
❑14, Feb 1960 .... 20.00
❑15, Apr 1960 .... 20.00
❑16, Jun 1960 .... 20.00
❑17, Aug 1960 .... 20.00
❑18, Oct 1960 .... 20.00
❑19, Dec 1960 .... 20.00
❑20, Feb 1961 .... 20.00
❑21, Apr 1961 .... 20.00
❑22, Jun 1961 .... 20.00
❑23, Aug 1961 .... 20.00
❑24, Oct 1961 .... 20.00
❑25, Dec 1961 .... 20.00

CHIAROSCURO
DC / VERTIGO

❑1, Jul 1995 .... 2.50
❑2, Aug 1995 .... 2.50
❑3, Sep 1995 .... 2.50
❑4, Oct 1995 .... 2.50
❑5, Nov 1995 .... 2.50
❑6, Dec 1995 .... 2.50
❑7, Jan 1996 .... 2.50
❑8, Feb 1996 .... 2.50
❑9, Mar 1996 .... 2.95
❑10, Apr 1996 .... 2.95

CHICANOS
IDEA & DESIGN WORKS

❑1, Dec 2005 .... 3.95
❑2, Jan 2006 .... 3.95
❑3, Jan 2006 .... 3.95
❑4, Feb 2006 .... 3.95
❑5, Apr 2006 .... 3.95
❑6, Apr 2006 .... 3.95
❑7, May 2006 .... 3.95
❑8, Jun 2006 .... 3.95

CHI CHIAN
SIRIUS

❑1, Oct 1997 .... 2.95
❑2, Dec 1997, b&w; Rough & Pulpy cover 2.95
❑2/2nd 2.95
❑2/3rd, b&w; Rough & Pulpy cover ... 2.95
❑3, Feb 1998 .... 2.95
❑4, Apr 1998 .... 2.95
❑5, Jun 1998 .... 2.95
❑6, Aug 1998 .... 2.95

CHICK MAGNET
VOLUPTUOUS

❑1 .... 2.95

CHILDHOOD'S END
IMAGE

❑1, Oct 1997, b&w 2.95

CHILDREN OF FIRE
FANTAGOR

❑1 .... 2.00
❑2 .... 2.00
❑3 .... 2.00

CHILDREN OF THE FALLEN ANGEL
ACE

❑1, Feb 1997 .... 2.95

CHILDREN OF THE NIGHT
NIGHTWYND

❑1, b&w 2.50
❑2, b&w 2.50
❑3, b&w 2.50
❑4, b&w 2.50

CHILDREN OF THE VOYAGER
MARVEL

❑1, Sep 1993; Embossed cover 2.95
❑2, Oct 1993 .... 1.95
❑3, Nov 1993 .... 1.95
❑4, Dec 1993 .... 1.95

CHILDREN'S CRUSADE
DC / VERTIGO

❑1, Dec 1993 NG (w) 4.50
❑2, Jan 1994 NG (w) 4.00

CHILD'S PLAY 2: THE OFFICIAL MOVIE ADAPTATION
INNOVATION

❑1; Adapted from the screenplay by Don Mancini 2.50
❑2 .... 2.50
❑3 .... 2.50
❑Book 1; collection 6.95

CHILD'S PLAY 3
INNOVATION

❑1 .... 2.50
❑2 .... 2.50
❑3 .... 2.50
❑4 .... 2.50

CHILD'S PLAY: THE SERIES
INNOVATION

❑1 .... 2.50
❑2 .... 2.50
❑3 .... 2.50
❑4 .... 2.50
❑5 .... 2.50

CHILLER
MARVEL / EPIC

❑1 .... 3.00
❑2 .... 3.00

CHILLING TALES OF HORROR (1ST SERIES)
STANLEY

❑1 .... 12.00
❑2, Aug 1969 .... 10.00
❑3 .... 10.00
❑4 .... 10.00
❑5 .... 10.00
❑6 .... 10.00
❑7 .... 10.00

CHILLING TALES OF HORROR (2ND SERIES)
STANLEY

❑1 .... 9.00
❑2/A, Feb 1971 .... 8.00
❑2/B 8.00
❑3 .... 6.00
❑4 .... 6.00
❑5 .... 6.00

Other grades: Multiply price above by 5/6 for VF/NM • 2/3 for VERY FINE • 1/3 for FINE • 1/5 for VERY GOOD • 1/8 for GOOD

CHIMERA
CROSSGEN

Issue	N-MINT
❑1, Mar 2003	2.95
❑2, Apr 2003	2.95
❑3, May 2003	2.95
❑4, Jul 2003	2.95

CHINAGO AND OTHER STORIES
TOME

Issue	N-MINT
❑1, b&w	2.50

CHINA SEA
NIGHTWYND

Issue	N-MINT
❑1, b&w	2.50
❑2, b&w	2.50
❑3, b&w	2.50
❑4, b&w	2.50
❑Book 1; album b&w	6.95

CHIPMUNKS & SQUIRRELS
ORIGINAL SYNDICATE

Issue	N-MINT
❑1, Dec 1994	5.95

CHIP 'N' DALE (1ST SERIES)
DELL

Issue	N-MINT
❑4, Dec 1955, Previous issues published as Dell Four Color	35.00
❑5, Feb 1956	35.00
❑6, Jun 1956	30.00
❑7, Sep 1956	30.00
❑8, Dec 1956	30.00
❑9, Mar 1957	30.00
❑10, Jun 1957	30.00
❑11, Sep 1957	24.00
❑12, Dec 1957	24.00
❑13, Mar 1958	24.00
❑14/A, Jun 1958, 15¢ listed as price on front cover	30.00
❑14, Jun 1958	24.00
❑15, Sep 1958	24.00
❑16, Dec 1958	24.00
❑17, Mar 1959	24.00
❑18, Jun 1959	24.00
❑19, Sep 1959	24.00
❑20, Dec 1959	24.00
❑21, Mar 1960	20.00
❑22, Jun 1960	20.00
❑23, Sep 1960	20.00
❑24, Dec 1960	20.00
❑25, Mar 1961	20.00
❑26, Jun 1961	20.00
❑27, Sep 1961	20.00
❑28, Dec 1961	20.00
❑29, Mar 1962	20.00
❑30, Jun 1962	20.00

CHIP 'N' DALE (2ND SERIES)
GOLD KEY

Issue	N-MINT
❑1, May 1967	20.00
❑2, Aug 1968	12.00
❑3, Apr 1969	8.00
❑4, Aug 1969	8.00
❑5, Dec 1969	8.00
❑6, Mar 1970	5.00
❑7, Jun 1970	5.00
❑8, Sep 1970	5.00
❑9, Dec 1970	5.00
❑10, Mar 1971	5.00
❑11, Jun 1971	5.00
❑12, Sep 1971	5.00
❑13, Dec 1971	5.00
❑14, Mar 1972	5.00
❑15, May 1972	5.00
❑16, Jul 1972	5.00
❑17, Sep 1972	5.00
❑18, Nov 1972	5.00
❑19, Jan 1973	5.00
❑20, Mar 1973	5.00
❑21, May 1973	3.00
❑22, Jul 1973	3.00
❑23, Sep 1973	3.00
❑24, Nov 1973	3.00
❑25, Jan 1974	3.00
❑26, Mar 1974	3.00
❑27, May 1974	3.00
❑28, Jul 1974	3.00
❑29, Sep 1974	3.00
❑30, Nov 1974	3.00
❑31, Jan 1975	3.00
❑32, Mar 1975	3.00
❑33, May 1975	3.00
❑34, Jul 1975	3.00
❑35, Sep 1975	3.00
❑36, Nov 1975	3.00
❑37, Jan 1976	3.00
❑38, Mar 1976	3.00
❑39, May 1976	3.00
❑40, Jul 1976	3.00
❑41, Aug 1976	2.50
❑42, Sep 1976	2.50
❑43, Nov 1976	2.50
❑44, Jan 1977	2.50
❑45, Mar 1977	2.50
❑46, May 1977	2.50
❑47, Jul 1977	2.50
❑48, Aug 1977	2.50
❑49, Nov 1977	2.50
❑50, Jan 1978	2.50
❑51, Mar 1978	2.50
❑52, May 1978	2.50
❑53, Jul 1978	2.50
❑54, Sep 1978	2.50
❑55, Nov 1978	2.50
❑56, Jan 1979	2.50
❑57, Mar 1979	2.50
❑58, May 1979	2.50
❑59, Jul 1979	2.50
❑60, Aug 1979	2.50
❑61, Sep 1979	2.50
❑62, Oct 1979	2.50
❑63, Nov 1979	2.50
❑64, Feb 1980	2.50
❑65, Apr 1980	5.00
❑66, Jun 1980	5.00
❑67, Aug 1980	20.00
❑68, Oct 1980	17.00
❑69, ca. 1980	17.00
❑70 1981	2.50
❑71, Jun 1981	2.50
❑72, Aug 1982	2.50
❑73, Oct 1982	2.50
❑74, Dec 1982	2.50
❑75, Feb 1982	2.50
❑76 1982	2.50
❑77, Mar 1982	2.50
❑78 1982	10.00
❑79 1982	10.00
❑80, Jul 1983	10.00
❑81 1983	10.00
❑82 1983	10.00
❑83, Jul 1984	10.00

CHIP 'N' DALE (ONE-SHOT)
DISNEY

Issue	N-MINT
❑1	3.50

CHIP 'N' DALE RESCUE RANGERS (DISNEY'S...)
DISNEY

Issue	N-MINT
❑1, Jun 1990	1.50
❑2, Jul 1990	1.50
❑3, Aug 1990	1.50
❑4, Sep 1990	1.50
❑5, Oct 1990	1.50
❑6, Nov 1990	1.50
❑7, Dec 1990	1.50
❑8, Jan 1991	1.50
❑9, Feb 1991	1.50
❑10, Mar 1991	1.50
❑11, Apr 1991	1.50
❑12, May 1991	1.50
❑13, Jun 1991	1.50
❑14, Jul 1991	1.50
❑15, Aug 1991	1.50
❑16, Sep 1991	1.50
❑17, Oct 1991	1.50
❑18, Nov 1991	1.50
❑19, Dec 1991	1.50

CHIPS AND VANILLA
KITCHEN SINK

Issue	N-MINT
❑1, Jun 1988, b&w	1.75

CHIRALITY
CPM

Issue	N-MINT
❑1, Mar 1997	2.95
❑2, Apr 1997; Carol reveals morph power	2.95
❑3, May 1997	2.95
❑4, Jun 1997	2.95
❑5, Jul 1997	2.95
❑6, Aug 1997	2.95
❑7, Sep 1997	2.95
❑8, Oct 1997	2.95
❑9, Nov 1997	2.95
❑10, Dec 1997	2.95
❑11, Jan 1998	2.95
❑12, Feb 1998	2.95
❑13, Mar 1998	2.95
❑14, Apr 1998	2.95
❑15, May 1998	2.95
❑16, Jun 1998	2.95
❑17, Jul 1998	2.95
❑18, Aug 1998	2.95

CHIRÖN
HAMMAC

Issue	N-MINT
❑1, b&w; Hammac Publications	2.00
❑2, b&w; Hammac Publications	2.00
❑3, b&w; Alpha Productions takes over	2.00

CHITTY CHITTY BANG BANG
GOLD KEY

Issue	N-MINT
❑1, Feb 1969	35.00

C.H.I.X.
IMAGE

Issue	N-MINT
❑1, Jan 1998; Bad Girl parody comic book	2.50
❑1/Variant, Jan 1998; X-Ray edition; Bad Girl parody comic book; Comic Cavalcade alternate	2.50

C.H.I.X. THAT TIME FORGOT
IMAGE

Issue	N-MINT
❑1, Aug 1998	2.95

CHOBITS
TOKYOPOP

Issue	N-MINT
❑1, Apr 2003, b&w; printed in Japanese format	9.99
❑2, Jul 2002, b&w; printed in Japanese format	9.99
❑3, Oct 2002, b&w; printed in Japanese format	9.99

CHOICES
ANGRY ISIS

Issue	N-MINT
❑1	4.00

CHOKE
ANUBIS

Issue	N-MINT
❑1	2.95
❑2	2.95
❑2/Ltd., Centaur cover	2.95
❑Annual 1, Jul 1994	2.75

CHOLLY & FLYTRAP
IMAGE

Issue	N-MINT
❑1, ca. 2004	4.95
❑2, May 2005	4.95
❑3, ca. 2005	4.95
❑4, Aug 2005	4.95

CHOO-CHOO CHARLIE
GOLD KEY

Issue	N-MINT
❑1, Dec 1969	60.00

CHOPPER: EARTH, WIND & FIRE
FLEETWAY-QUALITY

Issue	N-MINT
❑1; cardstock cover	2.95
❑2	2.95

CHOPPER: SONG OF THE SURFER
FLEETWAY-QUALITY

Issue	N-MINT
❑1	9.95

CHOSEN
MARTINEZ

Issue	N-MINT
❑1, Jul 1995; cover indicates Premiere Issue	2.50

CHOSEN (DARK HORSE)
DARK HORSE

Issue	N-MINT
❑1, Feb 2004	2.99
❑1/2nd, Feb 2004; Reprints	2.99
❑2, Apr 2004	2.99
❑3 2004	3.00

CHRISTIAN COMICS & GAMES MAGAZINE
AIDA-ZEE

Issue	N-MINT
❑0, b&w	3.50
❑1, b&w	3.50

CHRISTINA WINTERS: AGENT OF DEATH
FANTAGRAPHICS / EROS

Issue	N-MINT
❑1	2.95
❑2, Mar 1995	2.95

Chronos

DC's time-spanning super-hero
©DC

Chuck Norris

Fighter beats people up for Marvel's kids' line
©Marvel

Clan Apis

Educational independent comic about bees
©Active Synapse

Classics Illustrated (First)

Outstanding adaptations of classic fiction
©First

Classic X-Men

Retold new X-Men tales plus new material
©Marvel

N-MINT

CHRISTMAS CLASSICS (WALT KELLY'S...)
ECLIPSE

❑1, Dec 1987; Peter Wheat 1.75

CHRISTMAS WITH SUPERSWINE
FANTAGRAPHICS

❑1, b&w 2.00

CHRISTMAS WITH THE SUPER-HEROES
DC

❑1, Dec 1988; MA, DG, FM, NA, DD, CS, NC, JL (a); Reprints stories from DC Special Series #21, Justice League of America #110; Teen Titans #13; DC Comics Presents #67, and Batman #219; Mark Waid editorial.. 3.00

❑2, Dec 1989; DaG, JBy, ES (w); GM, JBy, DG, ES (a); New stories; Mark Waid editorial; Cover says 1989, indicia says 1988 .... 3.00

CHROMA-TICK
NEW ENGLAND

❑1, Feb 1992, trading cards; Reprints The Tick #1 in color 3.95

❑2, Jun 1992, "Special Edition #2"; trading cards 3.95

❑3, Aug 1992, Reprints 3.50

❑4, Oct 1992, Bush cover 3.50

❑4/A, Oct 1992; Perot cover 3.50

❑4/B, Oct 1992; Clinton cover 3.50

❑5 .... 3.50

❑6, Jun 1993 .... 3.50

❑7 .... 3.50

❑8 .... 3.50

❑9 .... 3.50

CHROME
HOT COMICS

❑1, Oct 1986 .... 1.50

❑2, Oct 1986; Reprints indicia from issue #1 .... 1.50

❑3, Mar 1987 .... 1.50

CHROMIUM MAN
TRIUMPHANT

❑0, Apr 1994 .... 2.50

❑1, Jan 1994 .... 2.50

❑1/Ashcan 1994; ashcan edition 2.50

❑2 1994; indicia not updated through issue #7; says Jan 94; Violent Past. 2.50

❑3 1994 .... 2.50

❑4 1994; Unleashed! 2.50

❑5 1994; Unleashed! 2.50

❑6 1994 .... 2.50

❑7 1994 .... 2.50

❑8, Mar 1994 .... 2.50

❑9, Mar 1994 .... 2.50

❑10, May 1994 .... 2.50

❑11 .... 2.50

❑12 .... 2.50

❑13 .... 2.50

❑14 .... 2.50

❑15 .... 2.50

N-MINT

CHROMIUM MAN, THE: VIOLENT PAST
TRIUMPHANT

❑1 .... 2.50

❑2 .... 2.50

CHRONIC APATHY
ILLITERATURE

❑1, Aug 1995, b&w 2.95

❑2, Sep 1995, b&w 2.95

❑3, Oct 1995, b&w 2.95

❑4, Dec 1995, b&w 2.95

CHRONIC IDIOCY
CALIBER

❑1, b&w 2.50

❑2, b&w 2.50

❑3, b&w 2.50

CHRONICLES OF CORUM
FIRST

❑1, Jan 1987 .... 2.00

❑2, Mar 1987 .... 2.00

❑3, May 1987 .... 2.00

❑4, Jul 1987 .... 2.00

❑5, Sep 1987 .... 2.00

❑6, Nov 1987 .... 2.00

❑7, Jan 1988 .... 2.00

❑8, Mar 1988 .... 2.00

❑9, May 1988 .... 2.00

❑10, Jul 1988 .... 2.00

❑11, Sep 1988 .... 2.00

❑12, Nov 1988 .... 2.00

CHRONICLES OF CRIME AND MYSTERY: SHERLOCK HOLMES
NORTHSTAR

❑1, b&w 2.25

CHRONICLES OF PANDA KHAN
ABACUS

❑1 .... 1.50

❑2 .... 1.50

❑3 .... 1.50

❑4 .... 1.50

CHRONICLES OF THE CURSED SWORD
TOKYOPOP

❑1, Jul 2003 .... 9.95

❑2, Sep 2003 .... 9.95

❑3, Nov 2003 .... 9.95

❑4, Jan 2004 .... 9.95

❑5, Mar 2004 .... 9.95

❑6, May 2004 .... 9.95

❑7, Jul 2004 .... 9.95

❑8, Sep 2004 .... 9.95

❑9, Nov 2004 .... 9.95

❑10, Jan 2005 .... 9.95

❑11, Mar 2005 .... 9.95

❑12, Jun 2005 .... 9.95

❑13, Oct 2005 .... 9.95

❑14, Jan 2006 .... 9.95

CHRONO CODE
TOKYOPOP

❑1, Jul 2005 .... 9.95

❑2, Oct 2005 .... 9.95

N-MINT

CHRONO CRUSADE
ADV MANGA

❑1, ca. 2004 .... 9.99

CHRONOS
DC

❑1, Mar 1998 .... 2.50

❑2, Apr 1998 .... 2.50

❑3, May 1998 .... 2.50

❑4, Jun 1998 D: original Chronos 2.50

❑5, Jul 1998 .... 2.50

❑6, Aug 1998; A: Tattooed Man. funeral of original Chronos 2.50

❑7, Sep 1998 .... 2.50

❑8, Oct 1998 .... 2.50

❑9, Dec 1998 A: Destiny. 2.50

❑10, Jan 1999 A: Azrael 2.50

❑11, Feb 1999 .... 2.50

❑1000000, Nov 1998 A: Hourman. 3.50

CHRONOWAR
DARK HORSE / MANGA

❑1, Aug 1996, b&w 2.95

❑2, Sep 1996, b&w 2.95

❑3, Oct 1996, b&w 2.95

❑4, Nov 1996, b&w 2.95

❑5, Dec 1996, b&w 2.95

❑6, Jan 1997, b&w 2.95

❑7, Feb 1997, b&w 2.95

❑8, Mar 1997, b&w 2.95

❑9, Apr 1997, b&w 2.95

CHUCK NORRIS
MARVEL / STAR

❑1, Jan 1987 SD (a) 1.50

❑2, Mar 1987 SD (a) 1.25

❑3, May 1987 SD (a) 1.25

❑4, Jul 1987 .... 1.25

❑5, Sep 1987 .... 1.25

CHUK THE BARBARIC
AVATAR

❑3; no color cover 1.25

CHYNA
CHAOS!

❑1, Sep 2000 .... 2.95

❑1/Variant, Sep 2000; Special cover... 2.95

CINDERALLA
VIZ

❑1, Jun 2002 .... 15.95

CINDER AND ASHE
DC

❑1, May 1988 .... 1.75

❑2, Jun 1988 .... 1.75

❑3, Jul 1988 .... 1.75

❑4, Aug 1988 .... 1.75

CINDERELLA
GOLD KEY

❑1, Aug 1965, reprints Four-Color #786 24.00

CINNAMON EL CICLO
DC

❑1, Oct 2003 .... 2.50

❑2, Nov 2003 .... 2.50

❑3, Dec 2003 .... 2.50

❑4, Jan 2004 .... 2.50

❑5, Feb 2004 .... 2.50

Other grades: Multiply price above by 5/6 for VF/NM • 2/3 for VERY FINE • 1/3 for FINE • 1/5 for VERY GOOD • 1/8 for GOOD

CIRCLE UNLEASHED
EPOCH

❑1, May 1995 ... 3.00

CIRCLE WEAVE, THE: APPRENTICE TO A GOD
ABALONE

❑1, b&w ... 2.00
❑2, b&w ... 2.00

CIRCUS WORLD
HAMMAC

❑1, b&w ... 2.50
❑2 ... 2.50
❑3 ... 2.50

CITIZEN V AND THE V-BATTALION
MARVEL

❑1, Jun 2001 ... 2.99
❑2, Jul 2001 ... 2.99
❑3, Aug 2001 ... 2.99

CITIZEN V AND THE V BATTALION: THE EVERLASTING
MARVEL

❑1, Apr 2002 ... 2.99
❑2, May 2002 ... 2.99
❑3, Jun 2002 ... 2.99
❑4, Jul 2002 ... 2.99

CITY OF HEROES (1ST SERIES)
BLUE KING STUDIOS

❑1, Jun 2004, based on online videogame; player's guide in back ... 2.95
❑2, Jul 2004 ... 2.95
❑3, Aug 2004 ... 2.95
❑4, Sep 2004 ... 2.95
❑5, Oct 2004 ... 2.95
❑6, Nov 2004 ... 2.95
❑7, Dec 2004 ... 2.95
❑8, Jan 2005 ... 2.95
❑9, Feb 2005 ... 2.95
❑10, Mar 2005 ... 2.95
❑11, Apr 2005 ... 2.95
❑12, May 2005 ... 2.95

CITY OF HEROES (2ND SERIES)
IMAGE

❑1, Jun 2005 MWa (w) ... 2.99
❑1/Keown, Jun 2005 MWa (w) ... 5.00
❑1/Perez, Jun 2005 GP (c); MWa (w) . 4.00
❑2, Jul 2005 MWa (w) ... 2.99
❑3, Aug 2005 MWa (w) ... 2.99
❑4, Sep 2005 ... 2.99
❑5, Oct 2005 ... 2.99
❑6, Nov 2005 ... 2.99
❑7, Dec 2005 ... 2.99
❑8, Jan 2006 ... 2.99
❑9, Jan 2006 ... 2.99
❑10, Feb 2006 ... 2.99
❑11, Mar 2006 ... 2.99
❑12, May 2006 ... 2.99
❑13, Jun 2006 ... 2.99
❑14, Jul 2006 ... 2.99

CITY OF SILENCE
IMAGE

❑1, May 2000 ... 2.50
❑2, Jun 2000 ... 2.50
❑3, Jul 2000 ... 2.50

CITY OF TOMORROW
DC

❑1, Jun 2005 ... 2.99
❑2, Jul 2005 ... 2.99
❑3, Aug 2005 ... 2.99
❑4, Sep 2005 ... 2.99
❑5, Oct 2005 ... 2.99
❑6, Nov 2005 ... 2.99

CITY SURGEON
GOLD KEY

❑1, Aug 1963 ... 18.00

CIVIL WAR
MARVEL

❑1, Jul 2006 ... 10.00
❑2, Aug 2006 ... 7.00
❑2/Variant, Aug 2006 ... 7.00

CIVIL WAR: FRONT LINE
MARVEL

❑1, Aug 2006 ... 5.00
❑2, Sep 2006 ... 4.00

CLAIR VOYANT
LIGHTNING

❑1, Jun 1996, b&w ... 3.50

CLAN APIS
ACTIVE SYNAPSE

❑1, b&w; educational comic about bees 2.95
❑2, Dec 1998 ... 2.95
❑3, Feb 1999 ... 2.95
❑4, Apr 1999 ... 2.95
❑5, Apr 1999, b&w ... 3.95

CLANDESTINE
MARVEL

❑1, Oct 1994; foil cover ... 2.95
❑2, Nov 1994 ... 2.50
❑3, Dec 1994 ... 2.50
❑4, Jan 1995 ... 2.50
❑5, Feb 1995 ... 2.50
❑6, Mar 1995 ... 2.50
❑7, Apr 1995 ... 2.50
❑8, May 1995 ... 2.50
❑9, Jun 1995 ... 2.50
❑10, Jul 1995 ... 2.50
❑11, Aug 1995 ... 2.50
❑12, Sep 1995 ... 2.50
❑Ashcan 1, Oct 1994; Preview ... 1.50

CLASH
DC

❑1, ca. 1991 ... 4.95
❑2, ca. 1991 ... 4.95
❑3, ca. 1991 ... 4.95

CLASSIC ADVENTURE STRIPS
DRAGON LADY

❑1, May 1985; King of the Royal Mounted ... 4.00
❑2, Jul 1985; Red Ryder ... 4.00
❑3, Sep 1985; Dickie Dare, Flash Gordon 4.00
❑4, Nov 1985; FR (w); FR (a); Buz Sawyer; Johnny Hazard; Steve Canyon 4.00
❑5, Jan 1986; Wash Tubbs ... 4.00
❑6, Mar 1986; Mandrake the Magician, Johnny Hazard, Rip Kirby ... 4.00
❑7, Jul 1986; Buz Sawyer ... 4.00
❑8, Oct 1986 ... 4.00
❑9, Jan 1987 ... 4.00
❑10, Apr 1987 MA (w); MA (a) ... 4.00

CLASSIC ALEX TOTH ZORRO
IMAGE

❑1, Jul 1998; Trade Paperback; reprints Eclipse collection ... 15.95
❑2, Aug 1998; Trade Paperback; reprints Eclipse collection ... 15.95

CLASSIC GIRLS
ETERNITY

❑1, b&w; Reprints ... 2.50
❑2, b&w; Reprints ... 2.50
❑3, b&w; Reprints ... 2.50
❑4, b&w; Reprints ... 2.50

CLASSIC JONNY QUEST: SKULL & DOUBLE CROSSBONES
ILLUSTRATED PRODUCTIONS

❑1, Mar 1996; smaller than normal size comic book; No cover price; inserted with Jonny Quest videos ... 1.00

CLASSIC JONNY QUEST: THE QUETONG MISSILE MYSTERY
ILLUSTRATED PRODUCTIONS

❑1, Mar 1996; smaller than normal size comic book; No cover price; inserted with Jonny Quest videos ... 1.00

CLASSIC PUNISHER
MARVEL

❑1, Dec 1989, b&w; prestige format; Reprints Punisher stories from Marvel Preview #2, Marvel Super Action #1 ... 4.95

CLASSICS ILLUSTRATED (FIRST)
FIRST

❑1, Feb 1990 ... 4.00
❑2, Feb 1990 ... 4.00
❑3, Feb 1990 ... 4.00
❑4, Feb 1990 BSz (c); BSz (a) ... 4.00
❑5, Mar 1990 ... 4.00
❑6, Mar 1990 CR (a) ... 4.00
❑7, Apr 1990 DS (a) ... 4.00
❑8, Apr 1990 JK (a) ... 4.00
❑9, May 1990 MP (a) ... 4.00
❑10, Jun 1990 ... 4.00
❑11, Jul 1990 ... 4.00
❑12, Aug 1990 ... 4.00
❑13, Oct 1990 ... 4.00
❑14, Sep 1990 CR (a) ... 4.00
❑15, Nov 1990 ... 4.00
❑16, Dec 1990 JSa (w); JSa (a) ... 4.00
❑17 1991 ... 4.00
❑18 1991 ... 4.00
❑19, Feb 1991 ... 4.00
❑20, Mar 1991 ... 4.00
❑21 1991 ... 4.00
❑22 1991 ... 4.00
❑23, Apr 1991 ... 4.00
❑24, May 1991 ... 4.00
❑25, May 1991 ... 4.00
❑26, Jun 1991 ... 4.00
❑27 ... 4.00

CLASSICS ILLUSTRATED STUDY GUIDE
ACCLAIM

❑1 1997; All Quiet on the Western Front 4.99
❑2 1997; Around the World in 80 Days 4.99
❑3, Sep 1997; The Call of the Wild ... 4.99
❑4 1997; Captains Courageous ... 4.99
❑5 1997; A Christmas Carol ... 4.99
❑6 1997; The Count of Monte Cristo .. 4.99
❑7, Aug 1997; David Copperfield ... 4.99
❑8 1997; Doctor Jekyll and Mr. Hyde . 4.99
❑9 1997; Don Quixote ... 5.25
❑10 1997; Faust ... 4.99
❑11 1997; Frankenstein ... 4.99
❑12 1997; Great Expectations ... 4.99
❑13, Sep 1997; The Hunchback of Notre Dame ... 4.99
❑14 1997; The Iliad ... 4.99
❑15 1997; The Invisible Man ... 4.99
❑16, Aug 1997; Julius Caesar ... 4.99
❑17, Aug 1997; The Jungle Book ... 4.99
❑18 1997; Kidnapped ... 4.99
❑19 1997; Kim ... 4.99
❑20 1997; The Last of the Mohicans .. 4.99
❑21, Sep 1997; Lord Jim ... 4.99
❑22, Aug 1997; The Man in the Iron Mask ... 4.99
❑23 1997; The Master of Ballantrae ... 4.99
❑24, Apr 1997; A Midsummer Night's Dream ... 4.99
❑25, Apr 1997; Moby Dick ... 4.99
❑26 1997; new adaptation of Narrative of the Life of Frederick Douglass ... 4.99
❑27 1997; The Prince and the Pauper 4.99
❑28, Aug 1997; Pudd'nhead Wilson ... 4.99
❑29, Sep 1997; Robinson Crusoe ... 4.99
❑30 1997; new adaptation of The Scarlet Pimpernel ... 4.99
❑31 1997; Silas Marner ... 4.99
❑32 1997; War of the Worlds ... 4.99
❑33 1997; Wuthering Heights ... 4.99
❑34, Feb 1997 ... 4.99
❑35 1997 ... 4.99
❑36, Feb 1997 ... 4.99
❑37, Jul 1997 ... 4.99
❑38, Feb 1997 ... 4.99

CLASSIC STAR WARS
DARK HORSE

❑1, Aug 1992, AW (c); AW (a) ... 4.00
❑2, Sep 1992, AW (c); AW (a) ... 3.50
❑3, Oct 1992, AW (c); AW (a) ... 3.50
❑4, Nov 1992, AW (c); AW (a) ... 3.25
❑5, Dec 1992, AW (c); AW (a) ... 3.25
❑6, Jan 1993, AW (c); AW (a) ... 3.00
❑7, Feb 1993, AW (c); AW (a) ... 3.00
❑8, Apr 1993, AW (c); AW (a); trading card ... 3.00
❑9, May 1993, AW (c); AW (a) ... 3.00
❑10, Jun 1993, AW (c); AW (a) ... 3.00
❑11, Aug 1993, AW (a) ... 3.00
❑12, Sep 1993, AW (a) ... 3.00
❑13, Oct 1993, TY (c); AW (a) ... 3.00
❑14, Nov 1993, AW (c); AW (a) ... 3.00
❑15, Jan 1994, AW (c); AW (a) ... 3.00
❑16, Feb 1994, AW (a) ... 3.00
❑17, Mar 1994, AW (a) ... 3.00
❑18, Apr 1994, AW (a) ... 3.00
❑19, May 1994, GE (c); AW (a) ... 3.00
❑20, Jun 1994, Giant-size AW (c); AW (a) ... 3.50

Other grades: Multiply price above by 5/6 for VF/NM • 2/3 for VERY FINE • 1/3 for FINE • 1/5 for VERY GOOD • 1/8 for GOOD

Clerks: The Comic Book

Kevin Smith book was hot at inception

©Oni

Cloak & Dagger

Limited series about drug-induced mutants

©Marvel

Cold-Blooded Chameleon Commandos

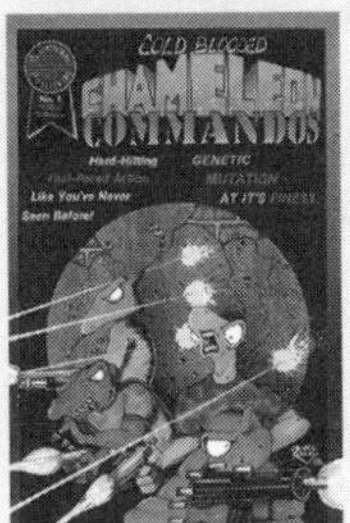

Lesser-known series from the Turtles age

©Blackthorne

Colonia

Jeff Nicholson's fantasy about a strange island

©Colonia

Combat Kelly (2nd Series)

Most of cast run over by a tank in last issue

©Marvel

N-MINT

CLASSIC STAR WARS: A LONG TIME AGO
DARK HORSE

- ❑1, Mar 1999 ... 12.95
- ❑2, Apr 1999 ... 12.95
- ❑3, May 1999; no cover price ... 12.95
- ❑4, Jun 1999; no cover price ... 12.95
- ❑5, Jul 1999; no cover price ... 12.95
- ❑6, Aug 1999 ... 12.95

CLASSIC STAR WARS: A NEW HOPE
DARK HORSE

- ❑1, Jun 1994; prestige format; Collects Star Wars (Marvel) #1-3 ... 3.95
- ❑2, Jul 1994; prestige format; Collects Star Wars (Marvel) #4-6 ... 3.95

CLASSIC STAR WARS: DEVILWORLDS
DARK HORSE

- ❑1, Aug 1996 ... 2.50
- ❑2, Sep 1996 ... 2.50

CLASSIC STAR WARS: HAN SOLO AT STARS' END
DARK HORSE

- ❑1, Mar 1997; adapts Brian Daley novel; cardstock cover ... 2.95
- ❑2, Apr 1997; adapts Brian Daley novel; cardstock cover ... 2.95
- ❑3, May 1997; adapts Brian Daley novel; cardstock cover ... 2.95

CLASSIC STAR WARS: RETURN OF THE JEDI
DARK HORSE

- ❑1, Oct 1994, AW (a); polybagged with trading card ... 3.50
- ❑2, Nov 1994, AW (a) ... 3.95

CLASSIC STAR WARS: THE EARLY ADVENTURES
DARK HORSE

- ❑1, Aug 1994 ... 2.50
- ❑2, Sep 1994 ... 2.50
- ❑3, Oct 1994 ... 2.50
- ❑4, Nov 1994 ... 2.50
- ❑5, Dec 1994 ... 2.50
- ❑6, Jan 1995 ... 2.50
- ❑7, Feb 1995 ... 2.50
- ❑8, Mar 1995 ... 2.50
- ❑9, Apr 1995 ... 2.50

CLASSIC STAR WARS: THE EMPIRE STRIKES BACK
DARK HORSE

- ❑1, Aug 1994; prestige format ... 3.95
- ❑2, Sep 1994; prestige format ... 3.95

CLASSIC STAR WARS: THE VANDELHELM MISSION
DARK HORSE

- ❑1, Mar 1995 ... 2.50

CLASSIC X-MEN
MARVEL

- ❑1, Sep 1986 ... 6.00
- ❑2, Oct 1986; DC (a); Reprints X-Men (1st Series) #94 ... 4.00
- ❑3, Nov 1986 ... 3.00
- ❑4, Dec 1986 ... 3.00
- ❑5, Jan 1987 ... 3.00
- ❑6, Feb 1987 ... 2.50
- ❑7, Mar 1987 ... 2.50
- ❑8, Apr 1987 ... 2.50
- ❑9, May 1987 ... 2.50
- ❑10, Jun 1987 ... 2.50
- ❑11, Jul 1987 ... 2.50
- ❑12, Aug 1987 ... 2.50
- ❑13, Sep 1987 ... 2.50
- ❑14, Oct 1987 ... 2.50
- ❑15, Nov 1987 ... 2.50
- ❑16, Dec 1987 ... 2.50
- ❑17, Jan 1988 ... 2.50
- ❑18, Feb 1988 ... 2.50
- ❑19, Mar 1988 ... 2.50
- ❑20, Apr 1988 ... 2.50
- ❑21, May 1988 ... 2.50
- ❑22, Jun 1988 FM (a) ... 2.50
- ❑23, Jul 1988 ... 2.50
- ❑24, Aug 1988 ... 2.50
- ❑25, Sep 1988 ... 2.50
- ❑26, Oct 1988 ... 2.50
- ❑27, Nov 1988 ... 2.50
- ❑28, Dec 1988 ... 2.50
- ❑29, Jan 1989 ... 2.50
- ❑30, Feb 1989 ... 2.00
- ❑31, Mar 1989; JBy (a); Reprints X-Men (1st Series) #125 ... 2.00
- ❑32, Apr 1989 ... 2.00
- ❑33, May 1989 ... 2.00
- ❑34, Jun 1989 ... 2.00
- ❑35, Jul 1989 ... 2.00
- ❑36, Aug 1989 ... 2.00
- ❑37, Sep 1989 ... 2.00
- ❑38, Oct 1989 ... 2.00
- ❑39, Nov 1989 ... 2.00
- ❑40, Nov 1989 ... 2.00
- ❑41, Dec 1989 ... 2.00
- ❑42, Dec 1989 ... 2.00
- ❑43, Jan 1990 ... 2.00
- ❑44, Feb 1990 ... 2.00
- ❑45, Mar 1990; Series continued in X-Men Classic #46 ... 2.00

CLAUS
DRACO

- ❑1, Dec 1997 ... 2.95
- ❑2, Feb 1998 ... 2.95

CLAWS
CONQUEST

- ❑1, b&w ... 2.95

CLAW THE UNCONQUERED
DC

- ❑1, Jun 1975, 1: Claw the Unconquered. ... 7.00
- ❑2, Aug 1975 ... 4.00
- ❑3, Oct 1975 ... 3.00
- ❑4, Dec 1975 ... 2.00
- ❑5, Feb 1976 ... 2.00
- ❑6, Apr 1976 ... 2.00
- ❑7, Jun 1976 ... 2.00
- ❑8, Aug 1976, Bicentennial #18 ... 2.00
- ❑9, Oct 1976, O: Claw the Unconquered. ... 2.00
- ❑10, May 1978 ... 2.00
- ❑11, Jul 1978 ... 2.00
- ❑12, Sep 1978 ... 2.00

CLAW THE UNCONQUERED (2ND SERIES)
DC

- ❑1, Sep 2006 ... 2.99

CLEM: MALL SECURITY
SPIT TAKE

- ❑0, ca. 1997, b&w ... 2.00

CLEOPATRA
RIP OFF

- ❑1, Feb 1992, b&w ... 2.50

CLERKS: THE COMIC BOOK
ONI

- ❑1, Feb 1998 KSm (w) ... 5.00
- ❑1/2nd KSm (w) ... 3.00
- ❑1/3rd KSm (w) ... 3.00
- ❑1/4th, May 1998 ... 3.00
- ❑2 ... 3.00
- ❑Holiday 1, Dec 1998, b&w; Double-size KSm (w) ... 4.00

CLETUS AND FLOYD SHOW
ASYLUM

- ❑1, Mar 2002 ... 2.95

CLF: CYBERNETIC LIBERATION FRONT
ANUBIS

- ❑1 ... 2.75

CLIFFHANGER!
IMAGE

- ❑1, ca. 1997 ... 3.00

CLIFFHANGER COMICS
AC

- ❑1, ca. 1989, b&w; Tom Mix Western; Don Winslow serial (photo-text)
- ❑ ... 2.50
- ❑2, ca. 1989, b&w; Tom Mix Western 2.50

CLIFFHANGER COMICS (2ND SERIES)
AC

- ❑1/A 1990, b&w; new and reprint ... 2.75
- ❑2/A, Aug 1990, b&w; new and reprint 2.75

CLIMAXXX
AIRCEL

- ❑1, Apr 1991 ... 3.50
- ❑2, May 1991 ... 3.50
- ❑3, Jun 1991 ... 3.50
- ❑4, Jul 1991 ... 3.50

CLINT
TRIGON

- ❑1, Sep 1986 ... 1.50
- ❑2, Jan 1987 ... 1.50

CLINT: THE HAMSTER TRIUMPHANT
ECLIPSE

- ❑1, b&w ... 1.50
- ❑2, b&w ... 1.50

CLIVE BARKER'S THE GREAT AND SECRET SHOW
IDEA & DESIGN WORKS

- ❑1, Apr 2006 ... 4.95
- ❑2, May 2006 ... 4.95
- ❑3, Jun 2006 ... 4.95

N-MINT

CLOAK & DAGGER
Marvel

- ❑1, Oct 1983, TD (a); 1: Brigid O'Reilly. 2.95
- ❑2, Nov 1983, TD (a) 2.95
- ❑3, Dec 1983, TD (a) 2.00
- ❑4, Jan 1984, TD (a); O: Cloak & Dagger. 2.00

CLOAK & DAGGER
Marvel

- ❑1, Jul 1985 2.00
- ❑2, Sep 1985, TD (a) 1.50
- ❑3, Nov 1985, TD (a); A: Spider-Man. 1.50
- ❑4, Jan 1986, Secret Wars II 1.50
- ❑5, Mar 1985 TD (a); O: Mayhem. 1: Mayhem. 1.25
- ❑6, May 1985 TD (a) 1.25
- ❑7, Jul 1985 TD (a) 1.25
- ❑8, Sep 1985 TD (a) 1.25
- ❑9, Nov 1985 TD (a) 1.25
- ❑10, Jan 1986 TD (a) 1.25
- ❑11, Mar 1986; Giant-size TD (a) 1.50

CLOAK AND DAGGER IN PREDATOR AND PREY
Marvel

- ❑1; prestige format 5.95

CLOCK!
Top Shelf

- ❑3, b&w 2.95

CLOCKMAKER
Image

- ❑1, Feb 2003 2.50
- ❑2, Mar 2003 2.50
- ❑3, May 2003 2.50
- ❑4, Jun 2003 2.50

CLOCKMAKER ACT 2
Image

- ❑1 2003 4.95
- ❑2, Aug 2004 4.95

CLONEZONE SPECIAL
Dark Horse

- ❑1, b&w 2.00

CLOSE SHAVES OF PAULINE PERIL
Gold Key

- ❑1, Jun 1970 20.00
- ❑2, Sep 1970 14.00
- ❑3, Dec 1970 14.00
- ❑4, Mar 1971 14.00

CLOUDFALL
Image

- ❑1, Dec 2003 4.95

CLOWN FIGURE
Image

- ❑1, ca. 1994; packaged with Todd Toys' Clown action figure 1.00

CLOWN: NOBODY'S LAUGHING NOW
Fleetway-Quality

- ❑1 4.95

CLOWNS
Yahoo Pro

- ❑1 3.00

CLOWNS
Dark Horse

- ❑1, Apr 1998, b&w; adapts Leoncavallo opera 2.95

CLYDE CRASHCUP
Dell

- ❑1, Aug 1963 90.00
- ❑2 1963 65.00
- ❑3, May 1964 48.00
- ❑4, Jun 1964 48.00
- ❑5, Sep 1964 48.00

COBALT 60
Tundra

- ❑1 4.95
- ❑2 4.95

COBALT BLUE
Power

- ❑1, Jan 1978, MGu (a) 2.00

COBALT BLUE (INNOVATION)
Innovation

- ❑1, Sep 1989 MGu (a) 2.00
- ❑2, Oct 1989 MGu (a) 2.00
- ❑GN 1; KP (a); Graphic novel 5.95

COBB: OFF THE LEASH
Idea & Design Works

- ❑1, Jun 2006 3.99

COBRA
Viz

- ❑1 2.95
- ❑2 2.95
- ❑3 2.95
- ❑4 2.95
- ❑5 2.95
- ❑6 2.95
- ❑7 3.25
- ❑8 3.25
- ❑9 3.25
- ❑10 3.25
- ❑11 3.25
- ❑12 3.25

COCOPIAZO
Slave Labor

- ❑1 2004 2.95
- ❑2 2005 2.95
- ❑3 2005 2.95
- ❑4, Sep 2005 2.95

CODA
Coda

- ❑1 2.00
- ❑2 2.00
- ❑3 2.00
- ❑4 2.00

CODE BLUE
Image

- ❑1, Apr 1998 2.95

CODENAME: DANGER
Lodestone

- ❑1, Aug 1985 RB (a) 2.00
- ❑2, Oct 1985 1.75
- ❑3, Jan 1986 PS (a) 1.75
- ❑4, May 1986 1.75

CODENAME: FIREARM
Malibu

- ❑0, Jun 1995, b&w 2.95
- ❑1, Jun 1995, b&w 2.95
- ❑2, Jul 1995, b&w 2.95
- ❑3, Jul 1995, b&w 2.95
- ❑4, Aug 1995, b&w 2.95
- ❑5, Aug 1995, b&w 2.95

CODENAME: GENETIX
Marvel

- ❑1, Feb 1993 1.75
- ❑2, Mar 1993 1.75
- ❑3, Apr 1993 1.75
- ❑4, May 1993 1.75

CODENAME: KNOCKOUT
DC / Vertigo

- ❑0, Jun 2001 2.50
- ❑1, Jul 2001 2.50
- ❑2, Aug 2001 2.50
- ❑3, Sep 2001 2.50
- ❑4, Oct 2001 2.50
- ❑5, Nov 2001 2.50
- ❑6, Dec 2001 2.50
- ❑7, Jan 2002 2.50
- ❑8, Feb 2002 2.50
- ❑9, Mar 2002 2.50
- ❑10, Apr 2002 2.50
- ❑11, May 2002 2.50
- ❑12, Jun 2002 2.50
- ❑13, Jul 2002 2.50
- ❑14, Aug 2002 2.50
- ❑15, Sep 2002 2.50
- ❑16, Oct 2002 2.75
- ❑17, Nov 2002 2.75
- ❑18, Dec 2002 2.75
- ❑19, Feb 2003 2.75
- ❑20, Mar 2003 2.75
- ❑21, Apr 2003 2.75
- ❑22, May 2003 2.75
- ❑23, Jun 2003 2.75

CODE NAME NINJA
Solson

- ❑1, b&w 2.00

CODENAME: SCORPIO
Antarctic

- ❑1, Oct 1996, b&w 2.95
- ❑2, Apr 1997, b&w 2.95
- ❑3, Jul 1997, b&w 2.95
- ❑4, Sep 1997, b&w 2.95

CODENAME: SPITFIRE
Marvel

- ❑10, Jul 1987; Series continued from Spitfire and the Troubleshooters #9 1.00
- ❑11, Aug 1987 1.00
- ❑12, Sep 1987 1.00
- ❑13, Oct 1987 1.00

CODENAME: STRIKEFORCE
Spectrum

- ❑1, Jun 1984 1.50

CODENAME: STRYKE FORCE
Image

- ❑0, Jun 1995, indicia says Jun, cover says Jul 2.50
- ❑1, Jan 1994 2.50
- ❑1/Gold, Jan 1994, Gold promotional edition 3.00
- ❑1/Variant, Jan 1994, blue embossed edition 2.50
- ❑2, Mar 1994 1.95
- ❑3, Apr 1994 1.95
- ❑4, Jun 1994 1.95
- ❑5, Jul 1994 1.95
- ❑6, Aug 1994 1.95
- ❑7, Oct 1994 1.95
- ❑8/A, Nov 1994, same cover, different poster 1.95
- ❑8/B, Nov 1994, same cover, different poster 1.95
- ❑8/C, Nov 1994, same cover, different poster 1.95
- ❑9, Dec 1994 1.95
- ❑10, Jan 1995 1.95
- ❑11, Mar 1995 1.95
- ❑12, Apr 1995 1.95
- ❑13, May 1995 2.25
- ❑14, Aug 1995 2.25

CODE OF HONOR
Marvel

- ❑1, Jan 1997 5.95
- ❑2, Mar 1997 5.95
- ❑3, Apr 1997 5.95
- ❑4, May 1997 5.95

CODY STARBUCK
Star*Reach

- ❑1 2.00

CO-ED SEXXTASY
Fantagraphics / Eros

- ❑1, Dec 1999 3.50
- ❑2, Jan 2000 3.50
- ❑3, Feb 2000 3.50
- ❑4, Mar 2000 3.50
- ❑5, Apr 2000 3.50
- ❑6, May 2000 3.50
- ❑7, Jun 2000 3.50
- ❑8, Jul 2000 3.50
- ❑9, Aug 2000 3.50
- ❑10, Sep 2000 3.50
- ❑11, Oct 2000 3.50

COFFIN
Oni

- ❑1, Sep 2000, b&w 40.00
- ❑2 25.00

COFFIN BLOOD
Monster

- ❑1, b&w 3.95

COLD BLOODED
Northstar

- ❑1, b&w 2.95
- ❑2, Sep 1993, b&w 2.95
- ❑3, Dec 1993, b&w 4.95

COLD-BLOODED CHAMELEON COMMANDOS
Blackthorne

- ❑1 1.50
- ❑2 1.50
- ❑3 1.50
- ❑4 1.50
- ❑5 1.50

Other grades: Multiply price above by 5/6 for VF/NM • 2/3 for VERY FINE • 1/3 for FINE • 1/5 for VERY GOOD • 1/8 for GOOD

Comet Man

Obscure Marvel mini-series from 1987

©Marvel

Command Review

Features reprints from Albedo

©Thoughts & Images

Conan

Marvel's "adjective-less" series relaunch

©Marvel

Conan (Dark Horse)

Dark Horse version was red hot in 2004

©Dark Horse

Conan Saga

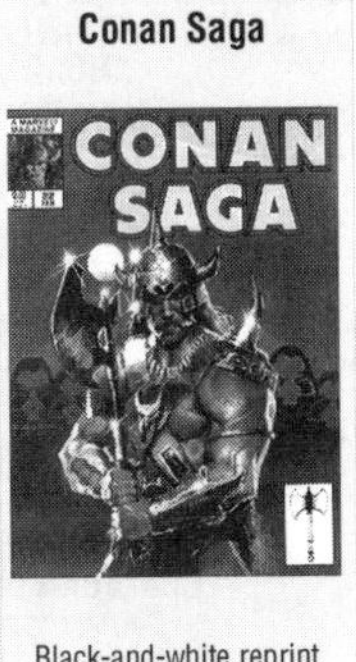

Black-and-white reprint magazine

©Marvel

N-MINT

COLD BLOODED: THE BURNING KISS
NORTHSTAR
- ❑1, Nov 1993, b&w; cardstock cover . 4.95

COLD EDEN
LEGACY
- ❑4, Nov 1995, b&w; cover says Feb 96, indicia says Nov 95 .... 2.35

COLLECTION
ETERNITY
- ❑1 .... 2.95

COLLECTOR'S DRACULA
MILLENNIUM
- ❑1 .... 3.95
- ❑2 .... 3.95

COLLECTORS GUIDE TO THE ULTRAVERSE
MALIBU / ULTRAVERSE
- ❑1, Aug 1994 .... 1.00

COLLIER'S
FANTAGRAPHICS
- ❑1, b&w 2.75
- ❑2, b&w 3.25

COLONIA
COLONIA
- ❑1, Oct 1998, b&w 2.95
- ❑1/2nd, ca. 1998, b&w 2.95
- ❑2, ca. 1999, b&w 2.95
- ❑3, ca. 1999, b&w 2.95
- ❑4, ca. 2000, b&w 2.95
- ❑5, ca. 2001, b&w 2.95
- ❑6, ca. 2002, b&w 2.95
- ❑7, ca. 2002, b&w 2.95
- ❑8, ca. 2003, b&w 2.95
- ❑9, ca. 2004, b&w 2.95
- ❑10, ca. 2004, b&w 2.95
- ❑11, Nov 2004 .... 3.50

COLORS IN BLACK
DARK HORSE
- ❑1, Mar 1995 .... 2.95
- ❑2 1995 .... 2.95
- ❑3 1995 .... 2.95
- ❑4 1995 .... 2.95

COLOSSAL SHOW
GOLD KEY
- ❑1, Oct 1969 .... 25.00

COLOSSUS
MARVEL
- ❑1, Oct 1997; gatefold summary; gatefold cover 2.99

COLOSSUS: GOD'S COUNTRY
MARVEL
- ❑1; prestige format 6.95

COLOUR OF MAGIC (TERRY PRATCHETT'S...)
INNOVATION
- ❑1 .... 2.50
- ❑2 .... 2.50
- ❑3 .... 2.50
- ❑4 .... 2.50

N-MINT

COLT SPECIAL
AC
- ❑1, Aug 1985 .... 1.50

COLUMBUS
DARK HORSE
- ❑1, b&w 2.50

COLVILLE
KING INK
- ❑1, Sep 1997, b&w 3.00

COMBAT (IMAGE)
IMAGE
- ❑1, Jan 1996 .... 2.50
- ❑2, Jan 1996 .... 2.50

COMBAT KELLY (2ND SERIES)
MARVEL
- ❑1, Jun 1972, JSe (c); JM (a); O: Combat Kelly. Combat Kelly becomes leader of Dum-Dum Dugan's Deadly Dozen (from Sgt. Fury #98) 10.00
- ❑2, Aug 1972, JSe (c) 6.00
- ❑3, Oct 1972, (c); O: Combat Kelly. 6.00
- ❑4, Dec 1972, (c); A: Sgt. Fury and his Howling Commandos. 4.00
- ❑5, Feb 1973, (c) 4.00
- ❑6, Apr 1973, (c) 4.00
- ❑7, Jun 1973, (c) 4.00
- ❑8, Aug 1973, (c) 4.00
- ❑9, Oct 1973, D: Deadly Dozen. Combat Kelly leaves team 4.00

COMBAT ZONE
AVALON
- ❑1, b&w; Reprints 2.95

COME AGAIN
FANTAGRAPHICS / EROS
- ❑1, Feb 1997 .... 2.95
- ❑2, May 1997 .... 2.95

COMET (RED CIRCLE)
ARCHIE / RED CIRCLE
- ❑1, Oct 1983 .... 1.00
- ❑2, Dec 1983 .... 1.00

COMET (IMPACT)
DC / IMPACT
- ❑1, Jul 1991 .... 1.00
- ❑2, Aug 1991 .... 1.00
- ❑3, Sep 1991 .... 1.00
- ❑4, Oct 1991 .... 1.00
- ❑5, Nov 1991 .... 1.00
- ❑6, Dec 1991 .... 1.00
- ❑7, Jan 1992 .... 1.00
- ❑8, Feb 1992 .... 1.00
- ❑9, Mar 1992 .... 1.00
- ❑10, Apr 1992; trading card 1.00
- ❑11, May 1992 .... 1.00
- ❑12, Jun 1992 .... 1.00
- ❑13, Jul 1992 .... 1.00
- ❑14, Aug 1992 .... 1.00
- ❑15, Sep 1992 .... 1.00
- ❑16, Oct 1992 .... 1.00
- ❑17, Nov 1992 .... 1.00
- ❑18, Dec 1992 .... 1.00
- ❑Annual 1; trading card 2.00

N-MINT

COMET MAN
MARVEL
- ❑1, Feb 1987 .... 1.00
- ❑2, Mar 1987 .... 1.00
- ❑3, Apr 1987 .... 1.00
- ❑4, May 1987 .... 1.00
- ❑5, Jun 1987 .... 1.00
- ❑6, Jul 1987 .... 1.00

COMET TALES
ROCKET
- ❑1 .... 1.00
- ❑2 .... 1.00
- ❑3 .... 1.00

COMIC BOOK
MARVEL / SPUMCO
- ❑1, ca. 1996; oversized anthology...... 6.95
- ❑2, ca. 1997; oversized anthology...... 6.95

COMIC BOOK CONFIDENTIAL
SPHINX
- ❑1, ca. 1988, b&w; giveaway promo for documentary film of same name; No cover price; Film promo 2.00

COMIC BOOK HEAVEN
SLAVE LABOR
- ❑1 .... 2.00
- ❑2 .... 2.00

COMIC BOOK TALENT SEARCH
SILVERWOLF
- ❑1, Feb 1987 .... 1.50

COMICO BLACK BOOK
COMICO
- ❑1, ca. 1987 .... 2.00

COMICO CHRISTMAS SPECIAL
COMICO
- ❑1, Dec 1988 .... 2.50

COMIC PARTY
TOKYOPOP
- ❑1, Jun 2004 .... 9.95
- ❑2, Aug 2004 .... 9.95
- ❑3, Oct 2004 .... 9.95
- ❑4, Dec 2004 .... 9.95
- ❑5, Jan 2006 .... 9.95

COMICS AND STORIES
DARK HORSE
- ❑1, Apr 1996; Wolf & Red 2.95
- ❑2, May 1996 .... 2.95
- ❑3, Jun 1996; Bad Luck Blackie 2.95
- ❑4, Jan 1997; Screwball Squirrel........ 2.95

COMICS ARE DEAD
SLAP HAPPY
- ❑1, Mar 1999, b&w 4.95

COMICS ARTIST SHOWCASE
SHOWCASE
- ❑1 .... 1.00

COMICS FOR STONERS
JASON NEUMAN
- ❑1 .... 1.00

COMICS' GREATEST WORLD
DARK HORSE
- ❑1, Jun 1993; preview copy of Comics' Greatest World: X; 1500 printed 1.00

COMICS' GREATEST WORLD: ARCADIA
DARK HORSE

❑1, Jun 1993; FM (c); FM (a); 1: X. X; Arcadia, Week 1 .... 2.00
❑1/Ltd., Jun 1993; limited edition for Heroes World Distribution; FM (c); FM (a); enhanced cardstock cover; X 2.50
❑2, Jun 1993; Pit Bulls; Arcadia, Week 2 .... 1.00
❑3, Jun 1993; 1: Ghost. Ghost; Arcadia, Week 3 .... 3.00
❑4; Monster; continues in Comics' Greatest World - Golden City; Arcadia, Week 4 .... 1.00

COMICS' GREATEST WORLD: CINNABAR FLATS
DARK HORSE

❑1, Jun 1993; Division 13; Vortex, Week 1 .... 1.00
❑1/A, Aug 1993; limited edition for American Distribution; Division 13; Vortex, Week 1; cardstock cover 2.50
❑1/Ltd., Aug 1993; limited edition; Division 13; cardstock cover 2.50
❑2, Jun 1993; Hero Zero; Vortex, Week 2 .... 1.00
❑3, Jun 1993; King Tiger; Vortex, Week 3 .... 1.00
❑4, Jun 1993; Out of the Vortex; continues in Out of the Vortex (Comics' Greatest World...), Week 4 .... 1.00

COMICS' GREATEST WORLD: GOLDEN CITY
DARK HORSE

❑1, Jul 1993; JO (c); Rebel; Golden City, Week 1 .... 1.00
❑1/Ltd.; limited edition for Heroes World Distribution; JO (c); enhanced cardstock cover; Rebel; Golden City, Week 1 .... 2.50
❑2, Jul 1993; Mecha; Golden City, Week 2 .... 1.00
❑3, Jul 1993; Titan; Golden City, Week 3 .... 1.00
❑4, Aug 1993; JDu (a); continues in Comics' Greatest World - Steel Harbor; Catalyst: Agents of Change; Golden City, Week 4 .... 1.00

COMICS' GREATEST WORLD: OUT OF THE VORTEX
DARK HORSE

❑1, Oct 1993, Foil embossed cover 2.50
❑2, Nov 1993 .... 2.50
❑3, Dec 1993 .... 2.50
❑4, Jan 1994, becomes Out of the Vortex 2.50

COMICS' GREATEST WORLD SOURCEBOOK
DARK HORSE

❑1, Mar 1993 .... 1.00

COMICS' GREATEST WORLD: STEEL HARBOR
DARK HORSE

❑1, Aug 1993; PG (a); 1: Barb Wire. Barb Wire; Steel Harbor, Week 1 .... 2.50
❑2; The Machine; Steel Harbor, Week 2 .... 1.00
❑3, Aug 1993; Wolf Gang; Steel Harbor, Week 3 .... 1.00
❑4, Aug 1993; Motorhead; continues in Comics' Greatest World - Cinnabar Flats; Steel Harbor, Week 4 .... 1.00

COMICS 101 PRESENTS
CHEAP THRILLS

❑1, Aug 1994, b&w; two covers, one inside the other 1.50

COMING OF APHRODITE
HERO

❑1, b&w 3.95

COMIX BOOK
MARVEL

❑1, ca. 1974 .... 10.00
❑2, ca. 1974 .... 8.00
❑3, ca. 1975 .... 8.00
❑4, ca. 1975 .... 5.00
❑5, ca. 1975 .... 5.00

COMIX INTERNATIONAL
WARREN

❑1, Jul 1974 .... 125.00
❑2 .... 90.00
❑3 .... 75.00
❑4 .... 75.00
❑5, Spr 1977 .... 75.00

COMMAND REVIEW
THOUGHTS & IMAGES

❑1, Jul 1986, b&w; collects stories from Albedo #1-4 .... 4.00
❑2, Aug 1987, b&w; collects stories from Albedo #5-8 .... 4.00
❑3, b&w 5.00
❑4, Jan 1994 .... 4.95

COMMIES FROM MARS
LAST GASP

❑1 .... 2.00
❑2 .... 2.00
❑3 .... 2.00
❑4 .... 2.00
❑5 .... 2.00
❑6 .... 2.50

COMMON FOE
IMAGE

❑1, Aug 2005 .... 3.50
❑2, Sep 2005 .... 3.50
❑3, Nov 2005 ....

COMMON GROUNDS
IMAGE

❑1, Jan 2004 .... 2.99
❑2, Feb 2004 .... 2.99
❑3, Mar 2004 .... 2.99
❑4, Apr 2004 .... 2.99
❑5, Jun 2004 .... 2.99
❑6, Aug 2004 .... 2.99

COMMUNION
FANTAGRAPHICS / EROS

❑1, b&w 2.75

COMPLETE CHEECH WIZARD
RIP OFF

❑1, Oct 1986, b&w 2.25
❑2, Jan 1987, b&w 2.25
❑3, May 1987 .... 2.50
❑4, Nov 1987 .... 2.50

COMPLETELY BAD BOYS
FANTAGRAPHICS

❑1, b&w 2.50

COMPLEX CITY
BETTER

❑1, Oct 2000 .... 2.50
❑2, Dec 2000 .... 2.50
❑3, Mar 2001 .... 2.50
❑4, May 2001 .... 2.50

COMPU-M.E.C.H.
MONOLITH

❑1, Oct 1999 .... 2.75
❑2, Jul 2000 .... 2.75
❑3, ca. 2004; squarebound 7.95
❑4, ca. 2004; squarebound 7.95
❑5, ca. 2004; squarebound 7.95
❑6, ca. 2004; squarebound 7.95
❑7, ca. 2004; squarebound 7.95
❑8, ca. 2004; squarebound 7.95
❑9, ca. 2004; squarebound 7.95
❑10, ca. 2004; squarebound 7.95

CONAN
MARVEL

❑1, Aug 1995, cardstock cover 2.95
❑2, Sep 1995, cardstock cover 2.95
❑3, Oct 1995, cardstock cover 2.95
❑4, Nov 1995, A: Rune. cardstock cover 2.95
❑5, Dec 1995, A: yeti. cardstock cover 2.95
❑6, Jan 1996, cardstock cover 2.95
❑7, Feb 1996, V: Man of Iron. 2.95
❑8, Mar 1996, cardstock cover 2.95
❑9, Apr 1996, cardstock cover 2.95
❑10, May 1996, cardstock cover 2.95
❑11, Jun 1996, cardstock cover 2.95
❑12, Jul 1996 .... 2.95

CONAN (DARK HORSE)
DARK HORSE

❑0 2004 .... 4.00
❑1, Feb 2004 .... 10.00
❑1/2nd, Aug 2004, re-print 3.00
❑2, Mar 2004 .... 5.00
❑2/2nd, Aug 2004, re-print 2.99
❑3, Apr 2004 .... 2.99
❑4, Jun 2004 .... 2.99
❑5, Aug 2004 .... 2.99
❑6, Sep 2004 .... 2.99
❑7, Oct 2004 .... 2.99
❑8, Nov 2004 .... 2.99
❑9, Dec 2004 .... 2.99
❑10, Jan 2005 .... 2.99
❑11, Feb 2005 .... 2.99
❑12, Mar 2005 .... 2.99
❑13, Apr 2005 .... 2.99
❑14, May 2005 .... 2.99
❑15, May 2005 .... 2.99
❑16, Jun 2005 .... 2.99
❑17, Jul 2005 .... 2.99
❑18, Aug 2005 .... 2.99
❑19, Sept 2005 .... 2.99
❑20, Oct 2005 .... 2.99
❑21, Nov 2005 .... 2.99
❑22, Dec 2005 .... 2.99
❑23, Jan 2006 .... 2.99
❑24, Feb 2006 .... 2.99
❑25, Mar 2006 .... 2.99
❑26, Apr 2006 .... 2.99
❑27, Apr 2006 .... 2.99
❑28, May 2006 .... 2.99
❑29, Jun 2006 .... 2.99

CONAN CLASSIC
MARVEL

❑1, Jun 1994; Reprints Conan the Barbarian #1 .... 1.50
❑2, Jul 1994 .... 1.50
❑3, Aug 1994 .... 1.50
❑4, Sep 1994 .... 1.50
❑5, Oct 1994 .... 1.50
❑6, Nov 1994 .... 1.50
❑7, Dec 1994 .... 1.50
❑8, Jan 1995 .... 1.50
❑9, Feb 1995 .... 1.50
❑10, Mar 1995 .... 1.50
❑11, Apr 1995 .... 1.50

CONAN AND THE DAUGHTERS OF MIDORA
DARK HORSE

❑1, Nov 2004 .... 5.00

CONAN AND THE DEMONS OF KHITAI
DARK HORSE

❑1, ... 2.99
❑2, Oct 2005 .... 2.99
❑3, Nov 2005 .... 2.99
❑4, Dec 2005 .... 2.99

CONAN: BOOK OF THOTH
DARK HORSE

❑1, Apr 2006 .... 2.99
❑2, Apr 2006 .... 2.99
❑3, May 2006 .... 2.99
❑4, Jun 2006 .... 2.99

CONAN AND THE JEWELS OF GWAHLUR
DARK HORSE

❑1 2005 .... 2.99
❑2, Jun 2005 .... 2.99
❑3, Jul 2005 .... 2.99

CONAN: DEATH COVERED IN GOLD
MARVEL

❑1, Sep 1999 .... 2.99
❑3, Nov 1999 .... 2.99

CONAN: FLAME AND THE FIEND
MARVEL

❑1, Aug 2000 .... 2.99
❑2, Sep 2000 .... 2.99
❑3, Oct 2000 .... 2.99

CONAN: RETURN OF STYRM
MARVEL

❑1, Sep 1998; gatefold summary 2.99
❑2, Oct 1998; gatefold summary 2.99
❑3, Nov 1998; gatefold summary 2.99

CONAN: RIVER OF BLOOD
MARVEL

❑1, Jun 1998 .... 2.50
❑2, Jul 1998 .... 2.50
❑3, Aug 1998 .... 2.50

CONAN SAGA
MARVEL

❑1, May 1987, b&w; Reprints 3.00
❑2, Jun 1987 .... 2.50

Other grades: Multiply price above by 5/6 for VF/NM • 2/3 for VERY FINE • 1/3 for FINE • 1/5 for VERY GOOD • 1/8 for GOOD

Conan the Adventurer

Relaunch followed 275-issue series

©Marvel

Conan the Barbarian

Most important title of the early 1970s

©Marvel

Conan the Barbarian (Vol. 2)

Volume 1: 275 issues. Volume 2: Three.

©Marvel

Conan the Destroyer

Adaptation of second Conan film

©Marvel

Conan the King

Series continued from King Conan

©Marvel

N-MINT

❑3, Jul 1987 .... 2.50
❑4, Aug 1987 .... 2.50
❑5, Sep 1987 .... 2.50
❑6, Oct 1987 .... 2.50
❑7, Nov 1987 .... 2.50
❑8, Dec 1987 .... 2.50
❑9, Jan 1988 .... 2.50
❑10, Feb 1988 .... 2.50
❑11, Mar 1988 .... 2.50
❑12, Apr 1988 .... 2.50
❑13, May 1988 .... 2.50
❑14, Jun 1988 .... 2.50
❑15, Jul 1988 .... 2.50
❑16, Aug 1988 .... 2.50
❑17, Sep 1988 .... 2.50
❑18, Oct 1988 .... 2.50
❑19, Nov 1988 .... 2.50
❑20, Dec 1988 .... 2.50
❑21, Jan 1989 .... 2.50
❑22, Feb 1989 .... 2.50
❑23, Mar 1989 .... 2.50
❑24, Apr 1989 .... 2.50
❑25, May 1989 .... 2.50
❑26, Jun 1989 .... 2.50
❑27, Jul 1989 .... 2.50
❑28, Aug 1989, b&w; Reprints 2.50
❑29, Sep 1989, b&w; Reprints 2.50
❑30, Oct 1989, b&w; Reprints 2.50
❑31, Nov 1989, b&w; Reprints 2.50
❑32, Dec 1989, b&w; Reprints 2.50
❑33, Dec 1989, b&w; Reprints 2.50
❑34, Jan 1990, b&w; Reprints 2.50
❑35, Feb 1990, b&w; Reprints 2.50
❑36, Mar 1990, b&w; Reprints 2.50
❑37, Apr 1990, b&w; Reprints 2.50
❑38, May 1990, b&w; Reprints 2.50
❑39, Jun 1990, b&w; Reprints 2.50
❑40, Jul 1990, b&w; Reprints 2.50
❑41, Aug 1990, b&w; Reprints 2.50
❑42, Sep 1990, b&w; Reprints 2.50
❑43, Oct 1990, b&w; Reprints 2.50
❑44, Nov 1990, b&w; Reprints 2.50
❑45, Dec 1990, b&w; Reprints 2.50
❑46, Jan 1991, b&w; Reprints 2.50
❑47, Feb 1991, b&w; Reprints 2.50
❑48, Mar 1991, b&w; Reprints 2.50
❑49, Apr 1991, b&w; Reprints 2.50
❑50, May 1991, b&w; Reprints 2.50
❑51, Jun 1991, b&w; Reprints 2.50
❑52, Jul 1991, b&w; Reprints 2.50
❑53, Aug 1991, b&w; Reprints 2.50
❑54, Sep 1991, b&w; JB (a); Reprints 2.50
❑55, Oct 1991, b&w; JB (a); Reprints. 2.50
❑56, Nov 1991, b&w; JB (a); Reprints 2.50
❑57, Dec 1991, b&w; FB (a); Reprints 2.50
❑58, Jan 1992, b&w; Reprints 2.50
❑59, Feb 1992, b&w; Reprints 2.50
❑60, Mar 1992, b&w; JB (a); Reprints 2.50
❑61, Apr 1992, b&w; JB (a); Reprints 2.50
❑62, May 1992, b&w; JB (a); Reprints 2.50
❑63, Jun 1992, b&w; JB (a); Reprints 2.50
❑64, Jul 1992, b&w; Reprints 2.50
❑65, Aug 1992, b&w; JB (a); Reprints 2.50
❑66, Sep 1992, b&w; Reprints 2.50

N-MINT

❑67, Oct 1992, b&w; JB (a); Reprints 2.50
❑68, Nov 1992, b&w; JB (a); Reprints 2.50
❑69, Dec 1992, b&w; Reprints 2.50
❑70, Jan 1993, b&w; Reprints 2.50
❑71, Feb 1993, b&w; JB (a); Reprints 2.50
❑72, Mar 1993, b&w; JB, MP (a); Reprints 2.50
❑73, Apr 1993, b&w; JB (a); Reprints 2.50
❑74, May 1993, b&w; JB (a); Reprints 2.50
❑75, Jun 1993; poster, handbook 4.00
❑76, Jul 1993, b&w; Reprints 2.25
❑77, Aug 1993, b&w; Reprints 2.25
❑78, Sep 1993, b&w; Reprints 2.25
❑79, Oct 1993, b&w; JB, FT, NA (a); A: Red Sonja. Reprints Conan the Barbarian #43-45 .... 2.25
❑80, Nov 1993, b&w; JB (a); Reprints 2.25
❑81, Dec 1993, b&w; JB (a); Reprints 2.25
❑82, Jan 1994, b&w; JB (a); Reprints 2.25
❑83, Feb 1994, b&w; Reprints 2.25
❑84, Mar 1994, b&w; Reprints 2.25
❑85, Apr 1994, b&w; Reprints 2.25
❑86, May 1994, b&w; JB (a); Reprints 2.25
❑87, Jun 1994, b&w; JB (a); Reprints 2.25
❑88, Jul 1994, b&w; JB (a); Reprints. 2.25
❑89, Aug 1994, b&w; JB (a); Reprints 2.25
❑90, Sep 1994, b&w; Reprints 2.25
❑91, Oct 1994, b&w; HC (a); Reprints 2.25
❑92, Nov 1994, b&w; JB (a); Reprints 2.25
❑93, Dec 1994, b&w; JB (a); Reprints 2.25
❑94, Jan 1995, b&w; JB (a); Reprints 2.25
❑95, Feb 1995, b&w; JB (a); Reprints 2.25
❑96, Mar 1995, b&w; JB (a); Reprints Conan the Barbarian #101-103 in black and white 2.25
❑97, Apr 1995, b&w; JB (a); Reprints 2.25

CONAN: SCARLET SWORD

MARVEL

❑1, Dec 1998, gatefold summary 2.99
❑2, Jan 1999, gatefold summary 2.99
❑3, Feb 1999 .... 2.99

CONAN THE ADVENTURER

MARVEL

❑1, Jun 1994; Embossed foil cover 2.00
❑2, Jul 1994 .... 1.50
❑3, Aug 1994 .... 1.50
❑4, Sep 1994 .... 1.50
❑5, Oct 1994 .... 1.50
❑6, Nov 1994 .... 1.50
❑7, Dec 1994 .... 1.50
❑8, Jan 1995 .... 1.50
❑9, Feb 1995 .... 1.50
❑10, Mar 1995 .... 1.50
❑11, Apr 1995 .... 1.50
❑12, May 1995 .... 1.50
❑13, Jun 1995 .... 1.50
❑14, Jul 1995 .... 1.50

CONAN THE BARBARIAN

MARVEL

❑1, Oct 1970, DA (a); O: Conan. 1: Conan. A: Kull. Hyborian Age map 160.00
❑2, Dec 1970 .... 55.00
❑3, Feb 1971, TS (a); low dist 72.00
❑4, Apr 1971, TS, SB (a) 26.00

N-MINT

❑5, May 1971, TS (a) 30.00
❑6, Jun 1971 .... 26.00
❑7, Jul 1971, 1: Thoth Amon. Howard story 26.00
❑8, Aug 1971 .... 30.00
❑9, Aug 1971 .... 20.00
❑10, Oct 1971, Giant-size A: King Kull. 35.00
❑11, Nov 1971, Giant-size 35.00
❑12, Dec 1971 .... 15.00
❑13, Jan 1972 .... 20.00
❑14, Mar 1972, 1: Elric. Michael Moorcock characters 20.00
❑15, May 1972, A: Elric. Michael Moorcock characters 17.00
❑16, Jul 1972, TS (a); reprinted from Savage Tales #1 and Chamber of Darkness #4 .... 20.00
❑17, Aug 1972, GK (a) 17.00
❑18, Aug 1972, GK (a) 20.00
❑19, Oct 1972 .... 17.00
❑20, Nov 1972 .... 27.00
❑21, Dec 1972 .... 20.00
❑22, Jan 1973, reprinted from Conan the Barbarian #1 .... 20.00
❑23, Feb 1973, TS, GK (a); 1: Red Sonja. 20.00
❑24, Mar 1973, A: Red Sonja. 1st full Red Sonja story 20.00
❑25, Apr 1973, TS, JB, GK (a) 10.00
❑26, May 1973, JB (a) 8.00
❑27, Jun 1973, JB (a) 8.00
❑28, Jul 1973, TS, JB, GK (a) 8.00
❑29, Aug 1973, TS, JB, GK (a) 8.00
❑30, Sep 1973, TS, JB, GK (a) 8.00
❑31, Oct 1973, JB (a) 7.00
❑32, Nov 1973, JB (a) 7.00
❑33, Dec 1973, JB (a) 7.00
❑34, Jan 1974, JB (a) 7.00
❑35, Feb 1974, JB (a) 7.00
❑36, Mar 1974, JB (a); Marvel Value Stamp #10: Power Man 9.00
❑37, Apr 1974, TS, NA (a); Marvel Value Stamp #8: Captain America 9.00
❑38, May 1974, Marvel Value Stamp #30: Grey Gargoyle 9.00
❑39, Jun 1974, JB (a); Marvel Value Stamp #72: Lizard 7.00
❑40, Jul 1974, RB (a); Marvel Value Stamp #31: Modok 7.00
❑41, Aug 1974, JB, GK (a); Marvel Value Stamp #91: Hela 7.00
❑42, Sep 1974, JB, GK (a); Marvel Value Stamp #24: Falcon 7.00
❑43, Oct 1974, JB, GK (a); Red Sonja; Marvel Value Stamp #55: Medusa .. 7.00
❑44, Nov 1974, JB (a); Red Sonja; Marvel Value Stamp #71: Vision 7.00
❑45, Dec 1974, NA (a) 7.00
❑46, Jan 1975, JB (a) 7.00
❑47, Feb 1975, JB (a) 7.00
❑48, Mar 1975, JB (a); O: Conan. 6.00
❑49, Apr 1975, JB (a); Marvel Value Stamp #80: Ghost Rider 6.00
❑50, May 1975, JB (a) 6.00
❑51, Jun 1975, JB (a); V: Unos. 5.00
❑52, Jul 1975, JB (a) 5.00
❑53, Aug 1975, JB (a) 5.00

Other grades: Multiply price above by 5/6 for VF/NM • 2/3 for VERY FINE • 1/3 for FINE • 1/5 for VERY GOOD • 1/8 for GOOD

	N-MINT
❑54, Sep 1975, JB (a)	5.00
❑55, Oct 1975, JB (a)	5.00
❑56, Nov 1975, JB (a)	5.00
❑57, Dec 1975, MP (a)	5.00
❑58, Jan 1976, JB (a); 2: of Bélit.	5.00
❑59, Feb 1976, JB (a); O: Bélit.	5.00
❑60, Mar 1976, JB (a)	5.00
❑61, Apr 1976, JB (a)	5.00
❑61/30 cent, Apr 1976, 30 cent regional price variant	20.00
❑62, May 1976, JB (a)	5.00
❑62/30 cent, May 1976, 30 cent regional price variant	20.00
❑63, Jun 1976, JB (a)	5.00
❑63/30 cent, Jun 1976, 30 cent regional price variant	20.00
❑64, Jul 1976, AM, JSn (a)	5.00
❑64/30 cent, Jul 1976, 30 cent regional price variant	20.00
❑65, Aug 1976, JB, GK (a)	5.00
❑65/30 cent, Aug 1976, 30 cent regional price variant	20.00
❑66, Sep 1976, JB, GK (a); V: Dagon.	5.00
❑67, Oct 1976, JB, GK (a); A: Red Sonja. Red Sonja	5.00
❑68, Nov 1976, JB, GK (a); A: Red Sonja. (continued from Marvel Feature #7)	5.00
❑69, Dec 1976	5.00
❑70, Jan 1977, JB (a)	5.00
❑71, Feb 1977, JB (a); Newsstand edition (distributed by Curtis); issue number in box	5.00
❑71/Whitman, Feb 1977, JB (a); Special markets edition (usually sold in Whitman bagged prepacks); price appears in a diamond; UPC barcode appears	5.00
❑72, Mar 1977, JB (a); Newsstand edition (distributed by Curtis); issue number in box	5.00
❑72/Whitman, Mar 1977, JB (a); Special markets edition (usually sold in Whitman bagged prepacks); price appears in a diamond; UPC barcode appears	5.00
❑73, Apr 1977, JB (a)	5.00
❑74, May 1977, JB (a); Newsstand edition (distributed by Curtis); issue number in box	5.00
❑74/Whitman, May 1977, JB (a); Special markets edition (usually sold in Whitman bagged prepacks); price appears in a diamond; UPC barcode appears	5.00
❑75, Jun 1977, JB (a); Newsstand edition (distributed by Curtis); issue number in box	5.00
❑75/Whitman, Jun 1977, JB (a); Special markets edition (usually sold in Whitman bagged prepacks); price appears in a diamond; UPC barcode appears	5.00
❑75/35 cent, Jun 1977, 35 cent regional price variant; newsstand edition (distributed by Curtis); issue number in box	15.00
❑76, Jul 1977, JB (a); Newsstand edition (distributed by Curtis); issue number in box	5.00
❑76/Whitman, Jul 1977, JB (a); Special markets edition (usually sold in Whitman bagged prepacks); price appears in a diamond; UPC barcode appears	5.00
❑76/35 cent, Jul 1977, JB (a); 35 cent regional price variant; newsstand edition (distributed by Curtis); issue number in box	15.00
❑77, Aug 1977, JB (a); Newsstand edition (distributed by Curtis); issue number in box	5.00
❑77/Whitman, Aug 1977, JB (a); Special markets edition (usually sold in Whitman bagged prepacks); price appears in a diamond; UPC barcode appears	5.00
❑77/35 cent, Aug 1977, 35 cent regional price variant; newsstand edition (distributed by Curtis); issue number in box	15.00
❑78, Sep 1977, JB (a); Newsstand edition (distributed by Curtis); issue number in box	5.00

	N-MINT
❑78/Whitman, Sep 1977, JB (a); Special markets edition (usually sold in Whitman bagged prepacks); price appears in a diamond; UPC barcode appears	5.00
❑78/35 cent, Sep 1977, JB (a); 35 cent regional price variant; newsstand edition (distributed by Curtis); issue number in box	15.00
❑79, Oct 1977, HC (a); Newsstand edition (distributed by Curtis); issue number in box	5.00
❑79/Whitman, Oct 1977, HC (a); Special markets edition (usually sold in Whitman bagged prepacks); price appears in a diamond; no UPC barcode	5.00
❑79/35 cent, Oct 1977, HC (a); 35 cent regional price variant; newsstand edition (distributed by Curtis); issue number in box	15.00
❑80, Nov 1977, HC (a); Newsstand edition (distributed by Curtis); issue number in box	5.00
❑80/Whitman, Nov 1977, HC (a); Special markets edition (usually sold in Whitman bagged prepacks); price appears in a diamond; no UPC barcode	5.00
❑81, Dec 1977, HC (a); Newsstand edition (distributed by Curtis); issue number in box	5.00
❑81/Whitman, Dec 1977, HC (a); Special markets edition (usually sold in Whitman bagged prepacks); price appears in a diamond; no UPC barcode	5.00
❑82, Jan 1978, HC (a)	5.00
❑83, Feb 1978, HC (a)	5.00
❑84, Mar 1978, JB (a); 1: Zula.	5.00
❑85, Apr 1978, JB (a); O: Zula.	5.00
❑86, May 1978, JB (a); Newsstand edition (distributed by Curtis); issue number in box	5.00
❑86/Whitman, May 1978, JB (a); Special markets edition (usually sold in Whitman bagged prepacks); price appears in a diamond; no UPC barcode	5.00
❑87, Jun 1978, JB (a); Reprints Savage Sword of Conan #3 in color	5.00
❑88, Jul 1978, JB (a); Return of Belit.	5.00
❑89, Aug 1978, JB (a); V: Thoth-Amon. Newsstand edition (distributed by Curtis); issue number in box	5.00
❑89/Whitman, Aug 1978, JB (a); V: Thoth-Amon. Special markets edition (usually sold in Whitman bagged prepacks); price appears in a diamond; no UPC barcode	5.00
❑90, Sep 1978, JB (a); Newsstand edition (distributed by Curtis); issue number in box	5.00
❑90/Whitman, Sep 1978, JB (a); Special markets edition (usually sold in Whitman bagged prepacks); price appears in a diamond; no UPC barcode	5.00
❑91, Oct 1978, JB (a); Newsstand edition (distributed by Curtis); issue number in box	5.00
❑91/Whitman, Oct 1978, JB (a); Special markets edition (usually sold in Whitman bagged prepacks); price appears in a diamond; no UPC barcode	5.00
❑92, Nov 1978, JB (a); Newsstand edition (distributed by Curtis); issue number in box	5.00
❑92/Whitman, Nov 1978, JB (a); Special markets edition (usually sold in Whitman bagged prepacks); price appears in a diamond; UPC barcode appears	5.00
❑93, Dec 1978, JB (a); Belit regains throne; newsstand edition (distributed by Curtis); issue number in box	5.00
❑93/Whitman, Dec 1978, JB (a); Belit regains throne; special markets edition (usually sold in Whitman bagged prepacks); price appears in a diamond; no UPC barcode	5.00
❑94, Jan 1979, JB (a); Newsstand edition (distributed by Curtis); issue number in box	4.00
❑94/Whitman, Jan 1979, JB (a); Special markets edition (usually sold in Whitman bagged prepacks); price appears in a diamond; no UPC barcode	4.00

	N-MINT
❑95, Feb 1979, JB (a); Newsstand edition (distributed by Curtis); issue number in box	4.00
❑95/Whitman, Feb 1979, JB (a); Special markets edition (usually sold in Whitman bagged prepacks); price appears in a diamond; no UPC barcode	4.00
❑96, Mar 1979, JB (a)	4.00
❑97, Apr 1979, JB (a)	4.00
❑98, May 1979, JB (a); Newsstand edition (distributed by Curtis); issue number in box	4.00
❑98/Whitman, May 1979, JB (a); Special markets edition (usually sold in Whitman bagged prepacks); price appears in a diamond; no UPC barcode	4.00
❑99, Jun 1979, JB (a)	4.00
❑100, Jul 1979, Double-size issue TS, JB (a); D: Bélit	6.00
❑101, Aug 1979, JB (a)	2.00
❑102, Sep 1979, JB (a)	2.00
❑103, Oct 1979, JB (a)	2.00
❑104, Nov 1979, JB (a)	2.00
❑105, Dec 1979, JB (a)	2.00
❑106, Jan 1980, JB (a)	2.00
❑107, Feb 1980, JB (a)	2.00
❑108, Mar 1980, JB (a)	2.00
❑109, Apr 1980, JB (a)	2.00
❑110, May 1980, JB (a)	2.00
❑111, Jun 1980, JB (a)	2.00
❑112, Jul 1980, JB (a)	2.00
❑113, Aug 1980, JB (a)	2.00
❑114, Sep 1980, JB (a)	2.00
❑115, Oct 1980, double-sized JB (a)	2.00
❑116, Nov 1980, JB, NA (a); Reprints	2.00
❑117, Dec 1980, JB (a)	2.00
❑118, Jan 1981, JB (a)	2.00
❑119, Feb 1981, JB (a)	2.00
❑120, Mar 1981, JB (a)	2.00
❑121, Apr 1981, JB (a)	2.00
❑122, May 1981, JB (a)	2.00
❑123, Jun 1981, JB (a)	2.00
❑124, Jul 1981, JB (a)	2.00
❑125, Aug 1981, JB (a)	2.00
❑126, Sep 1981, JB (a)	2.00
❑127, Oct 1981, JB (a)	2.00
❑128, Nov 1981, GK (c); GK (a)	2.00
❑129, Dec 1981	2.00
❑130, Jan 1982, GK (a)	2.00
❑131, Feb 1982, GK (a)	2.00
❑132, Mar 1982, GK (a)	2.00
❑133, Apr 1982, GK (a)	2.00
❑134, May 1982, GK (a)	2.00
❑135, Jun 1982	2.00
❑136, Jul 1982, JB (a)	2.00
❑137, Aug 1982, AA (a)	2.00
❑138, Sep 1982, VM (a)	2.00
❑139, Oct 1982, VM (a)	2.00
❑140, Nov 1982, JB (a)	2.00
❑141, Dec 1982, JB (a)	2.00
❑142, Jan 1983, JB (a)	2.00
❑143, Feb 1983, JB (a)	2.00
❑144, Mar 1983, JB (a)	2.00
❑145, Apr 1983, JB (a)	2.00
❑146, May 1983, JB (a)	2.00
❑147, Jun 1983, JB (a)	2.00
❑148, Jul 1983, JB (a)	2.00
❑149, Aug 1983, JB (a)	2.00
❑150, Sep 1983, JB (a)	2.00
❑151, Oct 1983, JB (a)	2.00
❑152, Nov 1983, JB (a)	2.00
❑153, Dec 1983, JB (a)	2.00
❑154, Jan 1984, Assistant Editors' Month	2.00
❑155, Feb 1984, JB (a)	2.00
❑156, Mar 1984, JB (a)	2.00
❑157, Apr 1984, JB (a)	2.00
❑158, May 1984, JB (a)	2.00
❑159, Jun 1984, JB (a)	2.00
❑160, Jul 1984	2.00
❑161, Aug 1984, JB (a)	2.00
❑162, Sep 1984, JB (a)	2.00
❑163, Oct 1984, JB (a)	2.00
❑164, Nov 1984	2.00
❑165, Dec 1984, JB (a)	2.00
❑166, Jan 1985, JB (a)	2.00
❑167, Feb 1985, JB (a)	2.00
❑168, Mar 1985, JB (a)	2.00
❑169, Apr 1985, JB (a)	2.00

Other grades: Multiply price above by 5/6 for VF/NM • 2/3 for VERY FINE • 1/3 for FINE • 1/5 for VERY GOOD • 1/8 for GOOD

Concrete

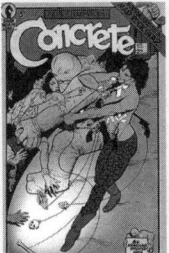

Interesting series with environmentalist themes

©Dark Horse

Condorman (Walt Disney)

Adaptation of Disney film almost nobody saw

©Whitman

Contest of Champions II

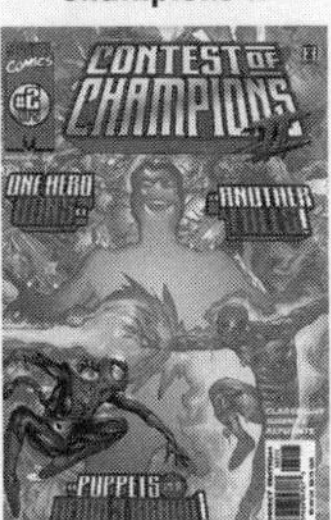

Sequel had little of the original's charm

©Marvel

Cop Called Tracy

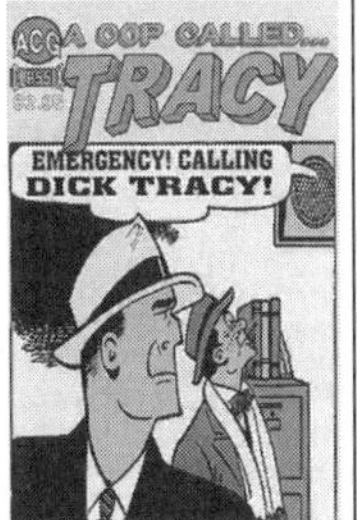

Avalon reprinting of early comic strips

©Avalon

COPS

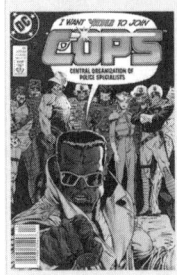

"Central Organization of Police Specialists"

©DC

N-MINT

- ❑170, May 1985, JB (a) ... 2.00
- ❑171, Jun 1985, JB (a) ... 2.00
- ❑172, Jul 1985, JB (a) ... 2.00
- ❑173, Aug 1985, JB (a) ... 2.00
- ❑174, Sep 1985, JB (a) ... 2.00
- ❑175, Oct 1985, JB (a) ... 2.00
- ❑176, Nov 1985, JB (a) ... 2.00
- ❑177, Dec 1985, JB (a) ... 2.00
- ❑178, Jan 1986, JB (a) ... 2.00
- ❑179, Feb 1986, JB (a) ... 2.00
- ❑180, Mar 1986, JB (a) ... 2.00
- ❑181, Apr 1986, JB (a) ... 2.00
- ❑182, May 1986, JB (a) ... 2.00
- ❑183, Jun 1986, JB (a) ... 2.00
- ❑184, Jul 1986 ... 2.00
- ❑185, Aug 1986 ... 2.00
- ❑186, Sep 1986 ... 2.00
- ❑187, Oct 1986, JB (a) ... 2.00
- ❑188, Nov 1986 ... 2.00
- ❑189, Dec 1986 ... 2.00
- ❑190, Jan 1987 ... 2.00
- ❑191, Feb 1987 ... 2.00
- ❑192, Mar 1987 ... 2.00
- ❑193, Apr 1987 ... 2.00
- ❑194, May 1987 ... 2.00
- ❑195, Jun 1987 ... 2.00
- ❑196, Jul 1987 ... 2.00
- ❑197, Aug 1987 ... 2.00
- ❑198, Sep 1987 ... 2.00
- ❑199, Oct 1987 ... 2.00
- ❑200, Nov 1987, 200th issue anniversary ... 2.00
- ❑201, Dec 1987 ... 2.00
- ❑202, Jan 1988 ... 2.00
- ❑203, Feb 1988 ... 2.00
- ❑204, Mar 1988 ... 2.00
- ❑205, Apr 1988 ... 2.00
- ❑206, May 1988 ... 2.00
- ❑207, Jun 1988 ... 2.00
- ❑208, Jul 1988 ... 2.00
- ❑209, Aug 1988 ... 2.00
- ❑210, Sep 1988 ... 2.00
- ❑211, Oct 1988 ... 2.00
- ❑212, Nov 1988 ... 2.00
- ❑213, Dec 1988 ... 2.00
- ❑214, Jan 1989 ... 2.00
- ❑215, Feb 1989 ... 2.00
- ❑216, Mar 1989 ... 2.00
- ❑217, Apr 1989 ... 2.00
- ❑218, May 1989 ... 2.00
- ❑219, Jun 1989 ... 2.00
- ❑220, Jul 1989 ... 2.00
- ❑221, Aug 1989 ... 2.00
- ❑222, Sep 1989 ... 2.00
- ❑223, Oct 1989 ... 2.00
- ❑224, Nov 1989 ... 2.00
- ❑225, Nov 1989 ... 2.00
- ❑226, Dec 1989 ... 2.00
- ❑227, Dec 1989 ... 2.00
- ❑228, Jan 1990 ... 2.00
- ❑229, Feb 1990 ... 2.00
- ❑230, Mar 1990 ... 2.00
- ❑231, Apr 1990 ... 2.00
- ❑232, May 1990, starts over ... 2.00

N-MINT

- ❑233, Jun 1990 ... 2.00
- ❑234, Jul 1990 ... 2.00
- ❑235, Aug 1990 ... 2.00
- ❑236, Sep 1990 ... 2.00
- ❑237, Oct 1990 ... 2.00
- ❑238, Nov 1990 ... 2.00
- ❑239, Dec 1990 ... 2.00
- ❑240, Jan 1991 ... 2.00
- ❑241, Feb 1991, TMc (c); TMc (a) ... 2.00
- ❑242, Mar 1991, JLee (c); JLee (a) ... 2.00
- ❑243, Apr 1991, Red Sonja ... 2.00
- ❑244, May 1991, Red Sonja ... 2.00
- ❑245, Jun 1991, Red Sonja ... 2.00
- ❑246, Jul 1991, Red Sonja ... 2.00
- ❑247, Aug 1991, Red Sonja ... 2.00
- ❑248, Sep 1991, Red Sonja ... 2.00
- ❑249, Oct 1991, Red Sonja ... 2.00
- ❑250, Nov 1991, 250th issue anniversary ... 2.00
- ❑251, Dec 1991 ... 2.00
- ❑252, Jan 1992 ... 2.00
- ❑253, Feb 1992 ... 2.00
- ❑254, Mar 1992 ... 2.00
- ❑255, Apr 1992 ... 2.00
- ❑256, May 1992 ... 2.00
- ❑257, Jun 1992, V: Thoth-Amon. ... 2.00
- ❑258, Jul 1992, returns to Cimmeria . 2.00
- ❑259, Aug 1992 ... 2.00
- ❑260, Sep 1992 ... 2.00
- ❑261, Oct 1992 ... 2.00
- ❑262, Nov 1992 ... 2.00
- ❑263, Dec 1992 ... 2.00
- ❑264, Jan 1993 ... 2.00
- ❑265, Feb 1993 ... 2.00
- ❑266, Mar 1993 ... 2.00
- ❑267, Apr 1993 ... 2.00
- ❑268, May 1993 ... 2.00
- ❑269, Jun 1993 ... 2.00
- ❑270, Jul 1993 ... 2.00
- ❑271, Aug 1993 ... 2.00
- ❑272, Sep 1993 ... 2.00
- ❑273, Oct 1993, A: Lord of the Purple Lotus. ... 2.00
- ❑274, Nov 1993 ... 2.00
- ❑275, Dec 1993 ... 2.50
- ❑Annual 1, ca. 1973, Cover reads "King-Size Special"; Cover reads King Size Special; Reprints Conan the Barbarian #2 and 4 ... 10.00
- ❑Annual 2, Jan 1976, JB (a) ... 6.00
- ❑Annual 3, ca. 1977, JB, HC, NA (a); A: King Kull. Reprints Savage Sword of Conan #2 ... 6.00
- ❑Annual 4, ca. 1978, JB (a); King Conan story ... 2.00
- ❑Annual 5, ca. 1979, JB (a) ... 2.00
- ❑Annual 6, ca. 1981, JB (a) ... 2.00
- ❑Annual 7, ca. 1982, JB (a) ... 1.50
- ❑Annual 8, ca. 1983, VM (a) ... 1.50
- ❑Annual 9, ca. 1984 ... 1.50
- ❑Annual 10, ca. 1985 ... 1.50
- ❑Annual 11, ca. 1986 ... 1.50
- ❑Annual 12, ca. 1987 ... 1.50
- ❑Special 1; Reprints ... 2.50

N-MINT

CONAN THE BARBARIAN (VOL. 2)

Marvel

- ❑1, Jul 1997 ... 2.50
- ❑2, Aug 1997 ... 2.50
- ❑3, Oct 1997 ... 2.50

CONAN THE BARBARIAN MOVIE SPECIAL

Marvel

- ❑1, Oct 1982, JB (w); JB (a) ... 1.00
- ❑2, Nov 1982, JB (w); JB (a) ... 1.00

CONAN THE BARBARIAN: THE USURPER

Marvel

- ❑1, Dec 1997; gatefold summary; gatefold cover ... 2.50
- ❑2, Jan 1998; gatefold summary ... 2.50
- ❑3, Feb 1998 ... 2.50
- ❑4, Mar 1998 ... 2.50

CONAN THE DESTROYER

Marvel

- ❑1, Jan 1985 ... 1.00
- ❑2, Mar 1985 ... 1.00

CONAN THE KING

Marvel

- ❑20, Jan 1984; Continued from King Conan #19 ... 1.50
- ❑21, Mar 1984 ... 1.50
- ❑22, May 1984 ... 1.50
- ❑23, Jul 1984 ... 1.50
- ❑24, Sep 1984 ... 1.50
- ❑25, Nov 1984 ... 1.50
- ❑26, Jan 1985 ... 1.50
- ❑27, Mar 1985 ... 1.50
- ❑28, May 1985 ... 1.50
- ❑29, Jul 1985 ... 1.50
- ❑30, Sep 1985 ... 1.50
- ❑31, Nov 1985 ... 1.50
- ❑32, Jan 1986 ... 1.50
- ❑33, Mar 1986 ... 1.50
- ❑34, May 1986 ... 1.50
- ❑35, Jul 1986 ... 1.50
- ❑36, Sep 1986 ... 1.50
- ❑37, Nov 1986 ... 1.50
- ❑38, Jan 1987 ... 1.50
- ❑39, Mar 1987 ... 1.50
- ❑40, May 1987 ... 1.50
- ❑41, Jul 1987 ... 1.50
- ❑42, Sep 1987 ... 1.50
- ❑43, Nov 1987 ... 1.50
- ❑44, Jan 1988 ... 1.50
- ❑45, Mar 1988 ... 1.50
- ❑46, May 1988 ... 1.50
- ❑47, Jul 1988 ... 1.50
- ❑48, Sep 1988 ... 1.50
- ❑49, Nov 1988 ... 1.50
- ❑50, Jan 1989 ... 1.50
- ❑51, Mar 1989 ... 1.50
- ❑52, May 1989 ... 1.50
- ❑53, Jul 1989 ... 1.50
- ❑54, Sep 1989 ... 1.50
- ❑55, Nov 1989 ... 1.50

Other grades: Multiply price above by 5/6 for VF/NM • 2/3 for VERY FINE • 1/3 for FINE • 1/5 for VERY GOOD • 1/8 for GOOD

CONAN: THE LORD OF THE SPIDERS
MARVEL
- ❑1, Mar 1998; gatefold summary; gatefold cover 2.50
- ❑2, Apr 1998; gatefold summary 2.50
- ❑3, May 1998; gatefold summary 2.50

CONAN THE SAVAGE
MARVEL
- ❑1, Aug 1995; b&w magazine 2.95
- ❑2, Sep 1995; b&w magazine 2.95
- ❑3, Oct 1995; b&w magazine 2.95
- ❑4, Nov 1995; b&w magazine; indicia gives title as Conan 2.95
- ❑5, Dec 1995; b&w magazine 2.95
- ❑6, Jan 1996; b&w magazine 2.95
- ❑7, Feb 1996; b&w magazine 2.95
- ❑8, Mar 1996; b&w magazine 2.95
- ❑9, Apr 1996; b&w magazine 2.95
- ❑10, May 1996; b&w magazine 2.95
- ❑11, Jun 1996 2.95
- ❑12, Jul 1996 2.95

CONAN VS. RUNE
MARVEL
- ❑1, Nov 1995 2.95

CONCRETE
DARK HORSE
- ❑1, Mar 1987 2.50
- ❑1/2nd 1.50
- ❑2, Jun 1987 2.00
- ❑3, Aug 1987 O: Concrete. 2.00
- ❑4, Oct 1987 O: Concrete. 2.00
- ❑5, Dec 1987 2.00
- ❑6, Feb 1988 2.00
- ❑7, Apr 1988 2.00
- ❑8, Jun 1988 2.00
- ❑9, Sep 1988 2.00
- ❑10 2.00
- ❑Hero ed. 1; Hero Special edition; Included with Hero Illustrated #23 1.00

CONCRETE: A NEW LIFE
DARK HORSE
- ❑1, Oct 1989; b&w reprint 2.95

CONCRETE CELEBRATES EARTH DAY
DARK HORSE
- ❑1, Apr 1990; Moebius 3.50

CONCRETE COLOR SPECIAL
DARK HORSE
- ❑1, Feb 1989; reprint in color 2.95

CONCRETE: ECLECTICA
DARK HORSE
- ❑1, Apr 1993; wraparound cover from 1992 WonderCon program book 2.95
- ❑2, May 1993; wraparound cover 2.95

CONCRETE: FRAGILE CREATURE
DARK HORSE
- ❑1, Jun 1991, wraparound cover 2.50
- ❑2, Jul 1991, wraparound cover 2.50
- ❑3, Aug 1991, wraparound cover 2.50
- ❑4, Feb 1992, wraparound cover 2.50

CONCRETE JUNGLE: THE LEGEND OF THE BLACK LION
ACCLAIM
- ❑1, Apr 1998 2.50

CONCRETE: KILLER SMILE
DARK HORSE / LEGEND
- ❑1, Jul 1994 2.95
- ❑2, Aug 1994 2.95
- ❑3, Sep 1994 2.95
- ❑4, Oct 1994 2.95

CONCRETE: LAND & SEA
DARK HORSE
- ❑1, Feb 1989, b&w; reprints first two Concrete stories with additional material; wraparound cardstock cover 2.95

CONCRETE: ODD JOBS
DARK HORSE
- ❑1, Jul 1990; b&w reprint; Collects Concrete #5-6 3.50

CONCRETE: STRANGE ARMOR
DARK HORSE
- ❑1, Dec 1997 2.95
- ❑2, Jan 1998 2.95
- ❑3, Mar 1998 2.95
- ❑4, Apr 1998 2.95
- ❑5, May 1998 2.95

CONCRETE: THE HUMAN DILEMMA
DARK HORSE
- ❑1 2005 3.50
- ❑2 2005 3.50
- ❑3 2005 3.50
- ❑4 2005 3.50
- ❑5, May 2005 3.50
- ❑6 2005 3.50

CONCRETE: THINK LIKE A MOUNTAIN
DARK HORSE / LEGEND
- ❑1, Mar 1996, b&w; promotional giveaway for mini-series 2.95
- ❑2, Apr 1996 2.95
- ❑3, May 1996 2.95
- ❑4, Jun 1996 2.95
- ❑5, Jul 1996 2.95
- ❑6, Aug 1996 2.95
- ❑Ashcan 1, b&w; promotional giveaway for mini-series; promotional giveaway for mini-series 1.00

CONDOM-MAN
AAAAHH!!
- ❑1; Gold ink limited edition 3.95

CONDORMAN (WALT DISNEY)
WHITMAN
- ❑1, Nov 1981, Adapts Disney film; sold only in bagged three-packs 2.00
- ❑2, Dec 1981, Adapts Disney film; sold only in bagged three-packs 2.00
- ❑3, Jan 1982, Original material; sold only in bagged three-packs 2.00

CONEHEADS
MARVEL
- ❑1, Jun 1994 1.75
- ❑2, Jul 1994 1.75
- ❑3, Aug 1994 1.75
- ❑4, Sep 1994 1.75

CONFESSIONS OF A CEREAL EATER
NBM
- ❑1, ca. 2000, b&w 2.95
- ❑2, ca. 2000, b&w 2.95
- ❑3, ca. 2000, b&w 2.95
- ❑4, ca. 2001 2.95

CONFESSIONS OF A TEENAGE VAMPIRE: THE TURNING
SCHOLASTIC
- ❑1, Jul 1997; digest 4.99

CONFESSIONS OF A TEENAGE VAMPIRE: ZOMBIE SATURDAY NIGHT
SCHOLASTIC
- ❑1, Jul 1997; digest 4.99

CONFESSOR (DEMONICUS EX DEO)
DARK MATTER
- ❑1, b&w 2.95

CONFIDENTIAL CONFESSIONS
TOKYOPOP
- ❑1, Jul 2003, b&w; printed in Japanese format 9.99

CONFRONTATION
SACRED ORIGIN
- ❑1, Jul 1997 2.95
- ❑2, Oct 1997 2.95
- ❑3 1997 2.95
- ❑4 1998 2.95
- ❑Special 1; Convention exclusive edition 5.00

CONGO BILL (VERTIGO)
DC / VERTIGO
- ❑1, Oct 1999 2.95
- ❑2, Nov 1999 2.95
- ❑3, Dec 1999 2.95
- ❑4, Jan 2000 2.95

CONGORILLA
DC
- ❑1, Nov 1992 2.00
- ❑2, Dec 1992 1.75
- ❑3, Jan 1993 1.75
- ❑4, Feb 1993 1.75

CONJURORS
DC
- ❑1, Apr 1999; Elseworlds story 2.95
- ❑2, May 1999; Elseworlds story 2.95
- ❑3, Jun 1999; Elseworlds story 2.95

CONQUEROR
HARRIER
- ❑1, Aug 1984 1.75
- ❑2, Oct 1984 1.75
- ❑3, Dec 1984 1.75
- ❑4, Feb 1985 1.75
- ❑5, Apr 1985 1.75
- ❑6, Jun 1985 1.75
- ❑7, Aug 1985 1.75
- ❑8, Oct 1985 1.75
- ❑9, Dec 1985 1.75
- ❑Special 1; Special edition (1987) 1.95

CONQUEROR OF THE BARREN EARTH
DC
- ❑1, Feb 1983 1.00
- ❑2, Mar 1983 1.00
- ❑3, Apr 1983 1.00
- ❑4, May 1983 1.00

CONQUEROR UNIVERSE
HARRIER
- ❑1 2.75

CONSERVATION CORPS
ARCHIE
- ❑1, Aug 1993 1.25
- ❑2, Sep 1993 1.25
- ❑3, Nov 1993 1.25

CONSPIRACY
MARVEL
- ❑1, Feb 1998 2.99
- ❑2, Mar 1998 2.99

CONSPIRACY COMICS
REVOLUTIONARY
- ❑1, Oct 1991; Marilyn Monroe 2.50
- ❑2, Feb 1992, b&w; John F. Kennedy 2.50
- ❑3, Jul 1992, b&w; Robert F. Kennedy 2.50

CONSTELLATION GRAPHICS
STAGES
- ❑1 1.50
- ❑2 1.50

CONSTRUCT
CALIBER
- ❑1 2.95
- ❑2 2.95
- ❑3 2.95
- ❑4 2.95
- ❑5 2.95
- ❑6 2.95

CONTAINMENT (ERIC RED'S)
IDEA & DESIGN WORKS
- ❑1, ca. 2004 3.99
- ❑2, ca. 2005 3.99
- ❑3, ca. 2005 3.99
- ❑4, ca. 2005 3.99

CONTAMINATED ZONE
BRAVE NEW WORDS
- ❑1, Apr 1991, b&w 2.50
- ❑2 1991, b&w 2.50
- ❑3 1991, b&w 2.50

CONTEMPORARY BIO-GRAPHICS
REVOLUTIONARY
- ❑1, Dec 1991, b&w; Stan Lee 2.50
- ❑2, Apr 1992, b&w; Boris Yeltsin 2.50
- ❑3, May 1992, b&w; Gene Roddenberry 2.50
- ❑4, Jun 1992; Pee Wee Herman 2.50
- ❑5, Sep 1992, b&w; David Lynch 2.50
- ❑6, Oct 1992; Ross Perot 2.50
- ❑7, Dec 1992, b&w; Spike Lee 2.50
- ❑8, Jun 1993, b&w; Image story 2.50

CONTENDER COMICS SPECIAL
CONTENDER
- ❑1, b&w 1.00

CONTEST OF CHAMPIONS II
MARVEL
- ❑1, Sep 1999; Iron Man vs. Psylocke; Iron Man vs. X-Force 2.50
- ❑2, Sep 1999; Human Torch vs. Spider-Girl, Storm, She-Hulk; Mr. Fantastic vs. Hulk 2.50
- ❑3, Oct 1999; Thor vs. Storm; Cable vs. Scarlet Witch; New Warriors vs. Slingers 2.50
- ❑4, Nov 1999; Black Panther vs Captain America 2.50
- ❑5, Nov 1999; Rogue vs Warbird 2.50

Cosmic Boy

Legionnaires spin-off limited series

©DC

Cosmic Powers

Marvel's stellar characters are showcased

©Marvel

Courtship of Eddie's Father

"People, let me tell you 'bout my best friend..."

©Dell

Cow-Boy

Comics Buyer's Guide strip gets a comic book

©Ogre

Coyote

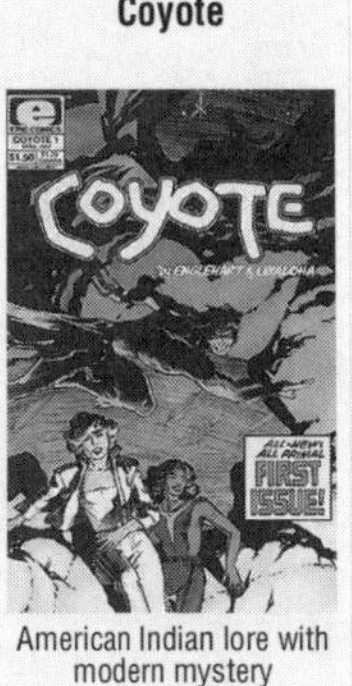

American Indian lore with modern mystery

©Marvel

CONTINÜM PRESENTS
CONTINÜM

	N-MINT
❑1, Oct 1988	1.75
❑2, Fal 1989	1.75

CONTRACTORS
ECLIPSE

	N-MINT
❑1, Jun 1987, b&w	2.00

CONVOCATIONS: A MAGIC: THE GATHERING GALLERY
ACCLAIM / ARMADA

	N-MINT
❑1, Jan 1995; pin-ups; reproduces covers from several Magic mini-series	2.50

COOL WORLD
DC

	N-MINT
❑1, Apr 1992	1.75
❑2, May 1992	1.75
❑3, Jun 1992	1.75
❑4, Sep 1992	1.75

COOL WORLD MOVIE ADAPTATION
DC

	N-MINT
❑1	3.50

COP CALLED TRACY
AVALON

	N-MINT
❑1	2.95
❑2	2.95
❑3	2.95
❑4	2.95
❑5	2.95
❑6	2.95
❑7	2.95
❑8	2.95
❑9	2.95
❑10	2.95
❑11	2.95
❑12	2.95
❑13	2.95
❑14	2.95
❑15	2.95
❑16	2.95
❑17	2.95
❑18	2.95
❑19	2.95
❑20	2.95
❑21	2.95
❑22	2.95

COPS
DC

	N-MINT
❑1, Aug 1988; Giant-size	1.00
❑2, Sep 1988	1.00
❑3, Oct 1988	1.00
❑4, Nov 1988	1.00
❑5, Dec 1988	1.00
❑6, Win 1988; Winter, 1988	1.00
❑7, Hol 1988; Holdays, 1988	1.00
❑8, Jan 1989	1.00
❑9, Feb 1989	1.00
❑10, Mar 1989	1.00
❑11, Apr 1989	1.00
❑12, May 1989	1.00
❑13, Jun 1989	1.00
❑14, Jul 1989	1.00
❑15, Aug 1989	1.00

COPS: THE JOB
MARVEL

	N-MINT
❑1, Jun 1992	1.25
❑2, Jul 1992	1.25
❑3, Aug 1992	1.25
❑4, Sep 1992	1.25

COPYBOOK TALES
SLAVE LABOR

	N-MINT
❑1, Jul 1996, b&w	2.95
❑2, Oct 1996, b&w	2.95
❑3, Jan 1997, b&w	2.95
❑4, Apr 1997, b&w	2.95
❑5, Jul 1997, b&w	2.95
❑6, Aug 1997; Cover swipe of X-Men (1st Series) #141	2.95

CORBEN SPECIAL
PACIFIC

	N-MINT
❑1, May 1984, Adapted From Edgar Allan Poe	1.50

CORBO
SWORD IN STONE

	N-MINT
❑1	1.75

CORMAC MAC ART
DARK HORSE

	N-MINT
❑1, Jul 1989, b&w	1.95
❑2, Aug 1989, b&w	1.95
❑3, Mar 1990, b&w	1.95
❑4, Apr 1990, b&w	1.95

CORNY'S FETISH
DARK HORSE

	N-MINT
❑1, Apr 1998, b&w	4.95

CORPORATE CRIME COMICS
KITCHEN SINK

	N-MINT
❑1	2.50
❑2	2.50

CORPORATE NINJA
SLAVE LABOR

	N-MINT
❑1, Nov 2005	2.99

CORTEZ AND THE FALL OF THE AZTECS
TOME

	N-MINT
❑1, b&w	2.95
❑2, b&w	2.95

CORTO MALTESE: BALLAD OF THE SALT SEA
NBM

	N-MINT
❑1	2.95
❑2	2.95
❑3	2.95
❑4	2.95

CORUM: THE BULL AND THE SPEAR
FIRST

	N-MINT
❑1	1.50
❑2	1.50
❑3	1.50
❑4	1.50

CORVUS REX: A LEGACY OF SHADOWS
CROW

	N-MINT
❑1, Feb 1996, b&w; Prologue	1.95

COSMIC BOOK
ACE

	N-MINT
❑1	1.95

COSMIC BOY
DC

	N-MINT
❑1, Dec 1986; KG (a); Legends Spin-Off, Part 4	1.00
❑2, Jan 1987; Legends Spin-Off, Part 8	1.00
❑3, Feb 1987; Legends Spin-Off, Part 13	1.00
❑4, Mar 1987; V: Time Trapper. Legends Spin-Off, Part 20	1.00

COSMIC GUARD
DEVIL'S DUE

	N-MINT
❑1, Nov 2004	5.00
❑2, Dec 2004	4.00
❑3, Jan 2005	2.99
❑4, Feb 2005	2.99
❑5, Mar 2005	2.99
❑6, Apr 2005	2.99

COSMIC HEROES
ETERNITY

	N-MINT
❑1, b&w; Buck Rogers	1.95
❑2, b&w; Buck Rogers	1.95
❑3, b&w; Buck Rogers	1.95
❑4, b&w; Buck Rogers	1.95
❑5, b&w; Buck Rogers	1.95
❑6, b&w; Buck Rogers	1.95
❑7	2.25
❑8	2.25
❑9	2.95
❑10	3.50
❑11	3.95

COSMIC KLITI
FANTAGRAPHICS / EROS

	N-MINT
❑1, b&w	2.25

COSMIC ODYSSEY
DC

	N-MINT
❑1, Nov 1988	3.50
❑2, Dec 1988	3.50
❑3, Dec 1988	3.50
❑4, Jan 1989	3.50

COSMIC POWERS
MARVEL

	N-MINT
❑1, Mar 1994; Thanos	2.50
❑2, Apr 1994; Terrax	2.50
❑3, May 1994; Jack of Hearts & Ganymede	2.50
❑4, Jun 1994	2.50
❑5, Jul 1994; Morg	2.50
❑6, Aug 1994; Tyrant	2.50

COSMIC POWERS UNLIMITED
MARVEL

	N-MINT
❑1, May 1995	3.95
❑2, Aug 1995; indicia says Aug; cover says Sep	3.95
❑3, Dec 1995	3.95
❑4, Feb 1996	3.95
❑5, May 1996	3.95

COSMIC RAY
IMAGE

	N-MINT
❑1/A, Jun 1999; green sunglasses cover	2.95

Other grades: Multiply price above by 5/6 for VF/NM • 2/3 for VERY FINE • 1/3 for FINE • 1/5 for VERY GOOD • 1/8 for GOOD

❑1/B, Jun 1999; Murderer or Hero cover 2.95
❑2, Aug 1999 2.95
❑3, Oct 1999 2.95

COSMIC STELLER REBELLERS
HAMMAC

❑1 1.50
❑2 1.50

COSMIC WAVES
AMF

❑1, Aug 1994, Science-fiction anthology

COUGAR
ATLAS-SEABOARD

❑1, Apr 1975 FS, DA (a) 5.00
❑2, Jul 1975 O: Cougar. 3.00

COUNTDOWN
DC / WILDSTORM

❑1, Jun 2000 2.95
❑2, Jul 2000 2.95
❑3, Aug 2000 2.95
❑4, Sep 2000 2.95
❑5, Oct 2000 2.95
❑6, Nov 2000 2.95
❑7, Dec 2000 2.95
❑8, Jan 2001 2.95

COUNT DUCKULA
MARVEL

❑1, Jan 1989 1.00
❑2, Feb 1989 1.00
❑3, Mar 1989 1.00
❑4, Apr 1989, Danger Mouse 1.00
❑5, May 1989, Danger Mouse 1.00
❑6, Jun 1989, Danger Mouse 1.00
❑7, Jul 1989, Danger Mouse 1.00
❑8, Aug 1989, Geraldo Rivera 1.00
❑9, Sep 1989 1.00
❑10, Oct 1989 1.00
❑11, Nov 1989 1.00
❑12, Dec 1989 1.00
❑13, Jan 1990 1.00
❑14, Feb 1990 1.00
❑15, Mar 1990 1.00

COUNTER OPS
ANTARCTIC

❑1, Mar 2003 3.95
❑2, Apr 2003 3.95
❑3, May 2003 3.95
❑4, Jun 2003 3.95

COUNTERPARTS
TUNDRA

❑1, Jan 1993, b&w 2.95
❑2, Mar 1993, b&w 2.95
❑3 2.95

COUP D'ETAT: AFTERWORD
DC / WILDSTORM

❑1, May 2004; follows other Coup D'Etat issues; Wetworks Vol. 2 and Sleeper Season Two preludes 2.95

COUP D'ETAT: THE AUTHORITY
DC / WILDSTORM

❑1, Apr 2004; Says "Four of Four" on cover 4.00

COUP D'ETAT: SLEEPER
DC / WILDSTORM

❑1, Apr 2004; Says "One of Four" on cover; story continues in Coup D'Etat: Stormwatch 6.00
❑1/Variant, Apr 2004; Says "One of Four" on cover; story continues in Coup D'Etat: Stormwatch 10.00

COUP D'ETAT: STORMWATCH
DC / WILDSTORM

❑1, Apr 2004; Says "Two of Four" on cover; story continues in Coup D'Etat: Wildcats Version 3.0 5.00
❑1/Variant, Apr 2004; Says "Two of Four" on cover; story continues in Coup D'Etat: Wildcats Version 3.0 7.00

COUP D'ETAT: WILDCATS VERSION 3.0
DC / WILDSTORM

❑1, Apr 2004; Says "Three of Four" on cover; story concludes in Coup D'Etat: Authority 5.00
❑1/Variant, Apr 2004; Says "Three of Four" on cover; story concludes in Coup D'Etat: Authority 6.00

COUPLE OF WINOS
FANTAGRAPHICS

❑1, ca. 1991, b&w 2.25

COURAGEOUS MAN ADVENTURES
MOORDAM

❑1, b&w; Mr. Beat back-up 2.95
❑2, b&w 2.95
❑3, Oct 1998 2.95

COURAGEOUS PRINCESS
ANTARCTIC

❑1, Apr 2000 11.95

COURTNEY CRUMRIN & THE NIGHT THINGS
ONI

❑1, Mar 2002 2.95
❑2, Apr 2002 2.95
❑3, May 2002 2.95
❑4, Jun 2002 2.95

COURTNEY CRUMRIN TALES
ONI

❑1, Sep 2005 5.95

COURTSHIP OF EDDIE'S FATHER
DELL

❑1, Jan 1970 30.00
❑2, May 1970 24.00

COURTYARD (ALAN MOORE'S)
AVATAR

❑1, Feb 2003, b&w 3.50
❑1/A, Feb 2003, b&w; Wraparound art cover 3.95
❑2, Mar 2003, b&w 3.50
❑2/A, Mar 2003, b&w; Wraparound art cover 3.95

COUTOO
DARK HORSE

❑1, b&w 3.50

COVEN
AWESOME

❑1/A, Aug 1997; RL (c); JPH (w); RL (a); "Butt" cover 5.00
❑1/B, Aug 1997; JPH (w); Man with flaming hands on cover; Red border 2.50
❑1/C, Aug 1997; JPH (w); "Wizard Authentic" cover 4.00
❑1/D, Aug 1997; JPH (w); Team on cover; White border 2.50
❑1/E, Aug 1997; Dynamic Forces edition; RL (c); JPH (w); RL (a); Chromium cover otherwise same as 1/A 2.50
❑1/F, Aug 1997; 1st Edition; JPH (w); Flip book with Kaboom 1+ 2.50
❑1/G, Aug 1997; JPH (w); "Flame Hands" cover 2.50
❑1/2nd 1997; "Fan Appreciation Edition"; JPH (w); Is really 2nd Printing 2.50
❑2, Sep 1997 JPH (w) 2.50
❑2/Gold, Sep 1997; Gold edition limited to 5000 copies JPH (w) 2.50
❑3, Oct 1997 JPH (w) 2.50
❑3/A, Oct 1997; JPH (w); Red foil logo on cover 2.50
❑4, Nov 1998 JPH (w) 2.50
❑5, Jan 1998 JPH (w) 2.50
❑5/A, Jan 1998; JPH (w); Variant cover, woman, ghouls standing in water 2.50
❑6, Feb 1998 JPH (w) 2.50

COVEN (VOL. 2)
AWESOME

❑1, Jan 1999; regular cover: Woman with glowing gloves facing forward 2.50
❑1/A, Jan 1999; Chrome ("Covenchrome") edition with certificate of authenticity; Two team-members flying on cover with white Coven logo 2.50
❑1/B, Jan 1999; Variant "scratch" cover by Ian Churchill 2.50
❑1/C, Jan 1999; Gold edition 2.50
❑1/D, Jan 1999; "Spellcaster" cover by Rob Liefeld 2.50
❑1/E, Jan 1999; "Black Mass" cover 2.50
❑1/F, Jan 1999; Dynamic Forces exclusive cover with two women surfing 2.50
❑2, Feb 1999 2.50
❑3, Mar 1999 2.50
❑4, Apr 1999 2.50

COVEN BLACK AND WHITE
AWESOME

❑1, Sep 1998 2.95

COVEN: DARK ORIGINS
AWESOME

❑1, Jun 1999 2.50

COVEN, THE: FANTOM
AWESOME

❑1, Feb 1998 JPH (w) 3.00
❑1/Gold, Feb 1998; JPH (w); Gold logo 3.00

COVEN OF ANGELS
JITTERBUG

❑1, Nov 1995 4.00
❑2 4.00
❑Ashcan 1; Ashcan edition with Linsner cover 8.00

COVEN 13
NO MERCY

❑1, Aug 1997 2.50

COVEN, THE: TOOTH AND NAIL
AVATAR

❑1 2.95
❑1/Ltd.; White foil-embossed leatherette cover; No indicia 29.95

COVENTRY
FANTAGRAPHICS

❑1, Nov 1996, b&w; cardstock cover 3.95
❑2, Mar 1997, b&w; cardstock cover 3.95
❑3, Jul 1997, b&w; cardstock cover 3.95

COVERT VAMPIRIC OPERATIONS
IDEA & DESIGN WORKS

❑1, ca. 2003 5.99

COVERT VAMPIRIC OPERATIONS: ARTIFACT
IDEA & DESIGN WORKS

❑1, Oct 2003 3.99
❑2, Nov 2003 3.99
❑3, Jan 2004 3.99

COW
MONSTERPANTS

❑1 1.99
❑2 1.99
❑3 1.99

COW-BOY
OGRE

❑1, ca. 1997, b&w 4.00

COWBOY IN AFRICA
GOLD KEY

❑1, Mar 1968 40.00

COWBOY LOVE (AVALON)
AVALON

❑1, b&w; Reprints 2.95

COW SPECIAL, THE (VOL. 2)
IMAGE

❑1, Jun 2001, b&w; Spring/Summer issue 2.95

COYOTE
MARVEL / EPIC

❑1, Apr 1983 O: Coyote. 2.50
❑2, Jun 1983 2.00
❑3, Sep 1983 2.00
❑4, Jan 1984 1.50
❑5, Apr 1984 1.50
❑6, Jun 1984 1.50
❑7, Jul 1984 SD (a) 1.50
❑8, Oct 1984 SD (a) 1.50
❑9, Dec 1984 SD (a) 1.50
❑10, Jan 1985 1.50
❑11, Mar 1985; TMc (a); 1st Todd McFarlane art 2.50
❑12, May 1985 TMc (a) 2.00
❑13, Jul 1985 TMc (a) 2.00
❑14, Sep 1985 TMc (a); A: Badger 1.50
❑15, Nov 1985 1.50
❑16, Jan 1986 1.50

Cracked

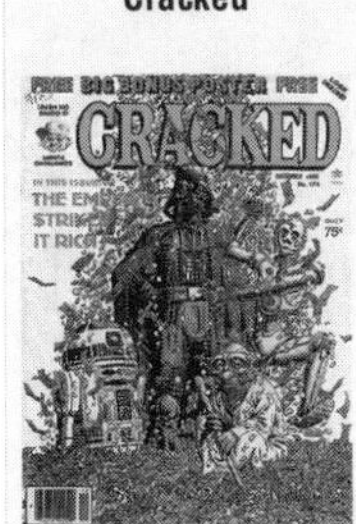

Mad copycat had great John Severin art

©Globe

Cracked Collectors' Edition

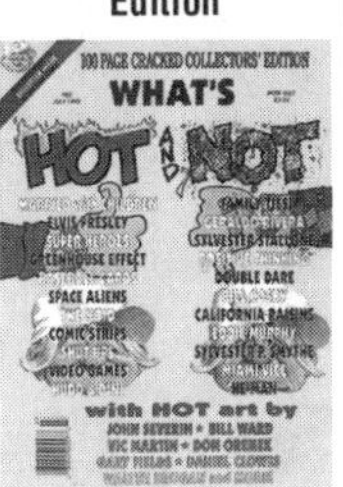

Issues #24-63 have no numbers

©Globe

Crash Dummies

Comic based on cartoon based on commercial

©Harvey

Crash Ryan

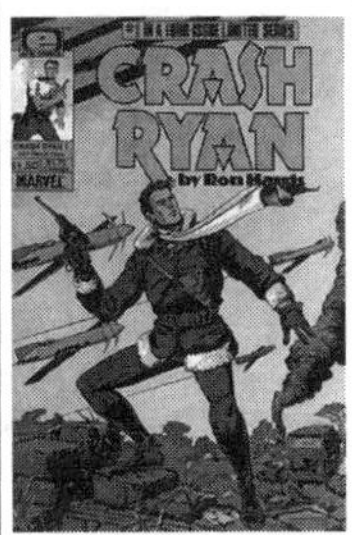

Pilot becomes involved in adventure

©Marvel

Crazy (Marvel)

Reprints from Marvel's Not Brand Ecch

©Marvel

CRABBS
Cat-Head

	N-MINT
❑1, b&w	3.75

CRACK BUSTERS
Showcase

	N-MINT
❑1, Nov 1986	1.95
❑2	1.95

CRACKED
Globe

	N-MINT
❑1, Mar 1958, b&w JSe (a)	125.00
❑2, Apr 1958, b&w JSe (a)	60.00
❑3, Jun 1958, b&w JSe (a)	35.00
❑4, Sep 1958, b&w JSe (a)	35.00
❑5, Oct 1958, b&w JSe (a)	35.00
❑6, Dec 1958, b&w JSe (a)	20.00
❑7, Feb 1959, b&w; JSe (a); First anniversary issue (past covers on cover)	20.00
❑8, ca. 1959, b&w JSe (a)	20.00
❑9, ca. 1959, b&w JSe (a)	20.00
❑10, ca. 1959, b&w JSe (a)	20.00
❑11, Oct 1959, b&w JSe (c); JSe (a)	12.00
❑12, b&w JSe (a)	12.00
❑13, b&w JSe (a)	12.00
❑14, Jun 1960, b&w; JSe (a); Descent of Man cover	12.00
❑15, Aug 1960, b&w JSe (a)	12.00
❑16, Apr 1961, b&w JSe (a)	12.00
❑17, b&w JSe (a)	12.00
❑18, ca. 1961, b&w JSe (a)	12.00
❑19, ca. 1961, b&w JSe (a)	12.00
❑20, ca. 1961, b&w JSe (a)	12.00
❑21, b&w JSe (a)	10.00
❑22, ca. 1962, b&w JSe (a)	10.00
❑23, ca. 1962, b&w JSe (a)	10.00
❑24, ca. 1962, b&w JSe (a)	10.00
❑25, Jul 1962, b&w JSe (a)	10.00
❑26, b&w JSe (a)	10.00
❑27, Feb 1962, b&w JSe (a)	10.00
❑28, ca. 1963, b&w JSe (a)	10.00
❑29, ca. 1963, b&w JSe (a)	10.00
❑30, ca. 1963, b&w JSe (a)	10.00
❑31, Sep 1963, b&w JSe (a)	8.00
❑32 1963, b&w JSe (a)	8.00
❑33, Dec 1963, b&w JSe (c); JSe (a)	8.00
❑34, b&w JSe (a)	8.00
❑35, ca. 1964, b&w JSe (a)	8.00
❑36, ca. 1964, b&w JSe (a)	8.00
❑37, ca. 1964, b&w JSe (a)	8.00
❑38, ca. 1964, b&w JSe (a)	8.00
❑39, b&w JSe (a)	8.00
❑40, b&w JSe (a)	8.00
❑41, b&w JSe (a)	8.00
❑42, b&w JSe (a)	8.00
❑43, May 1965, b&w JSe (a)	8.00
❑44, ca. 1965, b&w JSe (a)	8.00
❑45, ca. 1965, b&w JSe (a)	8.00
❑46 1965, b&w JSe (a)	8.00
❑47, b&w JSe (a)	8.00
❑48, b&w JSe (a)	8.00
❑49, b&w JSe (a)	8.00
❑50, b&w JSe (a)	8.00
❑51, ca. 1966, b&w JSe (a)	5.00
❑52, ca. 1966, b&w JSe (a)	5.00
❑53, ca. 1966, b&w JSe (a)	5.00
❑54 1966, b&w JSe (a)	5.00
❑55, Sep 1966, b&w JSe (a)	5.00
❑56, b&w JSe (a)	5.00
❑57, b&w JSe (a)	5.00
❑58, b&w JSe (a)	5.00
❑59 1967, b&w JSe (a)	5.00
❑60 1967, b&w JSe (a)	5.00
❑61, Jul 1967, b&w JSe (a)	5.00
❑62, Aug 1967, b&w JSe (a)	5.00
❑63, Sep 1967, b&w JSe (a)	5.00
❑64, Oct 1967, b&w JSe (a)	5.00
❑65, Nov 1967, b&w JSe (a)	5.00
❑66, b&w JSe (a)	5.00
❑67 1968, b&w JSe (a)	5.00
❑68 1968, b&w JSe (c); JSe (a)	5.00
❑69 1968, b&w JSe (a)	5.00
❑70 1968, b&w JSe (a)	5.00
❑71 1968, b&w JSe (c); JSe (a)	5.00
❑72 1968, b&w JSe (a)	5.00
❑73 1968, b&w JSe (a)	5.00
❑74, Jan 1969, b&w JSe (a)	5.00
❑75 1969, b&w JSe (a)	5.00
❑76, May 1969, b&w JSe (a)	5.00
❑77 1969, b&w JSe (a)	5.00
❑78 1969, b&w JSe (a)	5.00
❑79 1969, b&w JSe (a)	5.00
❑80 1969, b&w JSe (a)	5.00
❑81 1969, b&w JSe (a)	5.00
❑82, Jan 1970, b&w JSe (a)	5.00
❑83 1970, b&w JSe (a)	5.00
❑84 1970, b&w JSe (a)	5.00
❑85 1970, b&w JSe (a)	5.00
❑86 1970, b&w JSe (a)	5.00
❑87, Sep 1970, b&w JSe (a)	5.00
❑88, Oct 1970, b&w JSe (a)	5.00
❑89, Nov 1970, b&w JSe (a)	5.00
❑90, Jan 1971, b&w JSe (a)	5.00
❑91, Mar 1971, b&w JSe (a)	5.00
❑92, May 1971, b&w JSe (a)	5.00
❑93, Jul 1971, b&w JSe (a)	5.00
❑94, Aug 1971, b&w JSe (a)	5.00
❑95, Sep 1971, b&w JSe (a)	5.00
❑96, Oct 1971, b&w JSe (a)	5.00
❑97, Nov 1971, b&w JSe (a)	5.00
❑98, Jan 1972, b&w JSe (a)	5.00
❑99, Mar 1972, b&w JSe (a)	5.00
❑100, May 1972, b&w JSe (a)	5.00
❑101, Jul 1972, b&w JSe (a)	4.00
❑102, Aug 1972, b&w JSe (a)	4.00
❑103, Sep 1972, b&w JSe (a)	4.00
❑104, Oct 1972, b&w JSe (a)	4.00
❑105, Nov 1972, b&w JSe (a)	4.00
❑106, Jan 1973, b&w JSe (a)	4.00
❑107, Mar 1973, b&w JSe (a)	4.00
❑108, May 1973, b&w JSe (a)	4.00
❑109, Jul 1973, b&w JSe (a)	4.00
❑110, Aug 1973, b&w JSe (a)	4.00
❑111, Sep 1973, b&w; JSe (a); Poseidon Adventure, McCloud parodies	4.00
❑112, Oct 1973, b&w; JSe (c); JSe (a); Kung Fu parody	4.00
❑113, Nov 1973, b&w JSe (a)	4.00
❑114, Jan 1974, b&w JSe (a)	4.00
❑115, Mar 1974, b&w JSe (a)	4.00
❑116, May 1974, b&w JSe (a)	4.00
❑117, Jul 1974, b&w JSe (a)	4.00
❑118, Aug 1974, b&w; JSe (c); JSe (a); Sting parody	4.00
❑119, Sep 1974, b&w JSe (a)	4.00
❑120, Oct 1974, b&w JSe (a)	4.00
❑121, Nov 1974, b&w JSe (a)	4.00
❑122, Jan 1975, b&w JSe (a)	4.00
❑123, Mar 1975, b&w JSe (a)	4.00
❑124, May 1975, b&w JSe (a)	4.00
❑125, Jul 1975, b&w; JSe (a); Earthquake parody	4.00
❑126, Aug 1975, b&w JSe (a)	4.00
❑127, Sep 1975, b&w JSe (a)	4.00
❑128, Oct 1975, b&w; JSe (c); JSe (a); Capone parody	4.00
❑129, Nov 1975, b&w; JSe (a); Jaws parody	4.00
❑130, Jan 1976, b&w BWa, JSe (a)	4.00
❑131, Mar 1976, b&w; JSe (c); BWa, JSe (a); Godfather, Jaws parodies	4.00
❑132, May 1976, b&w; JSe (c); JSe (a); Baretta parody	4.00
❑133, Jul 1976, b&w BWa, JSe (a)	4.00
❑134, Aug 1976, b&w JSe (a)	4.00
❑135, Sep 1976, b&w BWa, JSe (a)	4.00
❑136, Oct 1976, b&w BWa, JSe (a)	4.00
❑137, Nov 1976, b&w; JSe (a); Welcome Back Kotter parody	4.00
❑138, Dec 1976, b&w JSe (a)	4.00
❑139, Jan 1977, b&w JSe (a)	4.00
❑140, Mar 1977, b&w BWa, JSe (a)	4.00
❑141, May 1977, b&w JSe (a)	4.00
❑142, Jul 1977, b&w JSe (a)	4.00
❑143, Aug 1977, b&w; JSe (a); Rocky parody	4.00
❑144, Sep 1977, b&w JSe (a)	4.00
❑145, Oct 1977, b&w JSe (a)	4.00
❑146, Nov 1977, b&w; JSe (c); JSe (a); Star Wars parody; Cracked cover stickers	8.00
❑147, Dec 1977, b&w; JSe (a); Star Wars II, What's Happening parodies; postcards	5.00
❑148, Jan 1978, b&w; JSe (a); Star Wars Cantina parody	5.00
❑149, Mar 1978, b&w; JSe (c); JSe (a); Star Wars, Bionic Man parodies; poster inside	5.00
❑150, May 1978, b&w; JSe (a); Close Encounters parody	4.00
❑151, Jul 1978, b&w JSe (a)	3.00
❑152, Aug 1978, b&w JSe (a)	3.00
❑153, Sep 1978, b&w JSe (a)	3.00
❑154, Oct 1978, b&w; JSe (c); JSe (a); Jaws 2 parody; T-shirt iron-on inside	3.00
❑155, Nov 1978, b&w JSe (a)	3.00
❑156, Dec 1978, b&w; JSe (c); JSe (a); Grease parody; poster inside	3.00
❑157, Jan 1979, b&w; JSe (a); Battlestar Galactica parody	6.00
❑158, Mar 1979, b&w JSe (c); JSe (a)	3.00
❑159, May 1979, b&w JSe (a)	3.00
❑160, Jul 1979, b&w; JSe (c); JSe (a); Superman parody; poster inside	3.00

	N-MINT
❑161, Aug 1979, b&w JSe (a)	3.00
❑162, Sep 1979, b&w BWa, JSe (a)	3.00
❑163, Oct 1979, b&w; JSe (c); JSe (a); Mork and Mindy parody; postcards inside	3.00
❑164, Nov 1979, b&w; JSe (c); JSe (a); Alien parody	4.00
❑165, Dec 1979, b&w JSe (a)	3.00
❑166, Jan 1980, b&w JSe (a)	3.00
❑167, Mar 1980, b&w; JSe (c); JSe (a); Mork and Mindy parody; infinity cover; poster inside	3.00
❑168, May 1980, b&w; JSe (c); JSe (a); M*A*S*H parody	3.00
❑169, Jul 1980, b&w; JSe (c); JSe (a); Star Trek: The Motion Picture parody; poster inside	4.00
❑170, Aug 1980, b&w JSe (a)	3.00
❑171, Sep 1980, b&w JSe (a)	3.00
❑172, Oct 1980, b&w; JSe (c); JSe (a); ChiPs/Dukes of Hazzard cross-over; iron-ons	3.00
❑173, Nov 1980, b&w JSe (a)	3.00
❑174, Dec 1980, b&w JSe (a)	3.00
❑175, Jan 1981, b&w JSe (a)	3.00
❑176, Mar 1981, b&w JSe (a)	3.00
❑177, May 1981, b&w JSe (a)	3.00
❑178, Jul 1981, b&w JSe (a)	3.00
❑179, Aug 1981, b&w JSe (a)	3.00
❑180, Sep 1981, b&w JSe (a)	3.00
❑181, Oct 1981, b&w JSe (a)	3.00
❑182, Nov 1981, b&w; JSe (c); JSe (a); Hulk parody; Alfred E. Neuman on cover	4.00
❑183, Dec 1981, b&w JSe (a)	3.00
❑184, Jan 1982, b&w JSe (a)	3.00
❑185, Mar 1982, b&w JSe (a)	3.00
❑186, May 1982, b&w; JSe (a); Barney Miller, Three's Company parodies	3.00
❑187, Jul 1982, b&w JSe (a)	3.00
❑188, Aug 1982, b&w JSe (a)	3.00
❑189, Sep 1982, b&w JSe (a)	3.00
❑190, Oct 1982, b&w JSe (a)	3.00
❑191, Nov 1982, b&w BWa, JSe (a)	3.00
❑192, Jan 1983, b&w JSe (a)	3.00
❑193, Mar 1983, b&w JSe (a)	3.00
❑194, May 1983, b&w; JSe (a); M.A.S.H. parody	3.00
❑195, Jul 1983, b&w JSe (a)	3.00
❑196, Aug 1983, b&w JSe (a)	3.00
❑197, Sep 1983, b&w JSe (a)	3.00
❑198, Oct 1983, b&w; JSe (c); JSe (a); Jaws 3-D, Fall Guy parodies; poster inside	3.00
❑199, Nov 1983, b&w JSe (a)	3.00
❑200, Dec 1983, b&w JSe (a)	3.00
❑201, Jan 1984, b&w JSe (a)	2.50
❑202, Mar 1984, b&w; JSe (a); Alfred E. Neuman/Smythe cover	3.00
❑203, May 1984, b&w JSe (a)	2.50
❑204, Jul 1984, b&w JSe (a)	2.50
❑205, Aug 1984, b&w JSe (a)	2.50
❑206, Sep 1984, b&w JSe (a)	2.50
❑207, Oct 1984, b&w JSe (a)	2.50
❑208, Nov 1984, b&w JSe (a)	2.50
❑209, Jan 1985, b&w JSe (a)	2.50
❑210, Mar 1985, b&w JSe (a)	2.50
❑211, May 1985, b&w JSe (a)	2.50
❑212, Jul 1985, b&w JSe (a)	2.50
❑213, Aug 1985, b&w; JSe (a); Boy George, Transformer parodies	2.50
❑214, Sep 1985, b&w JSe (a)	2.50
❑215, Oct 1985, b&w JSe (a)	2.50
❑216, Nov 1985, b&w JSe (a)	2.50
❑217, Dec 1985, b&w JSe (a)	2.50
❑218, Jan 1986, b&w; JSe (a); G.I. Joe, Back to the Future parodies	2.50
❑219, Mar 1986, b&w; JSe (a); Sylvester P. Smythe as Rambo	2.50
❑220, May 1986, b&w JSe (a)	2.50
❑221, Jul 1986, b&w JSe (a)	2.50
❑222, Aug 1986, b&w JSe (a)	2.50
❑223, Sep 1986, b&w JSe (a)	2.50
❑224, Nov 1986, b&w; JSe (a); Music-themed issue	2.50
❑225, Jan 1987, b&w JSe (a)	2.50
❑226, Mar 1987, b&w JSe (a)	2.50
❑227, Apr 1987, b&w; JSe (c); SD, JSe (a); Soviet-themed issue	2.50
❑228, Jul 1987, b&w JSe (a)	2.50

	N-MINT
❑229, Aug 1987, b&w JSe (a)	2.50
❑230, Sep 1987, b&w; JSe (a); Monkees, Growing Pains, Murder She Wrote, Gumby parodies	2.50
❑231, Oct 1987, b&w JSe (a)	2.50
❑232, Nov 1987, b&w; JSe (c); JSe (a); Cheers, Max Headroom, others parodied	2.50
❑233, Jan 1988, b&w JSe (a)	2.50
❑234, Mar 1988, b&w JSe (a)	2.50
❑235, May 1988, b&w JSe (a)	2.50
❑236, Jul 1988, b&w JSe (a)	2.50
❑237, Aug 1988, b&w JSe (a)	2.50
❑238, Sep 1988, b&w JSe (a)	2.50
❑239, Oct 1988, b&w JSe (a)	2.50
❑240, Nov 1988, b&w JSe (a)	2.50
❑241, Dec 1988, b&w JSe (a)	2.50
❑242, Jan 1989, b&w JSe (a)	2.50
❑243, Mar 1989, b&w JSe (a)	2.50
❑244, May 1989, b&w JSe (a)	2.50
❑245, Jul 1989, b&w JSe (a)	2.50
❑246, Aug 1989, b&w JSe (a)	2.50
❑247, Sep 1989, b&w JSe (a)	2.50
❑248, Oct 1989, b&w JSe (a)	2.50
❑249, Nov 1989, b&w JSe (a)	2.50
❑250, Dec 1989, b&w JSe (a)	2.50
❑251, Jan 1990, b&w JSe (a)	2.00
❑252, Mar 1990, b&w JSe (a)	2.00
❑253, May 1990, b&w JSe (a)	2.00
❑254, Jul 1990, b&w JSe (a)	2.00
❑255, Aug 1990, b&w JSe (a)	2.00
❑256, Sep 1990, b&w JSe (a)	2.00
❑257, Oct 1990, b&w JSe (a)	2.00
❑258, Nov 1990, b&w JSe (a)	2.00
❑259, Dec 1990, b&w JSe (a)	2.00
❑260, Jan 1991, b&w	2.00
❑261, Mar 1991, b&w JSe (a)	2.00
❑262, May 1991, b&w JSe (a)	2.00
❑263, Jul 1991, b&w JSe (a)	2.00
❑264, Aug 1991, b&w JSe (a)	2.00
❑265, Sep 1991, b&w JSe (a)	2.00
❑266, Oct 1991, b&w JSe (a)	2.00
❑267, Nov 1991, b&w JSe (a)	2.00
❑268, Dec 1991, b&w JSe (a)	2.00
❑269, Jan 1992, b&w JSe (a)	2.00
❑270, Mar 1992, b&w JSe (a)	2.00
❑271, May 1992, b&w JSe (a)	2.00
❑272, Jul 1992, b&w JSe (a)	2.00
❑273, Aug 1992, b&w JSe (a)	2.00
❑274, Sep 1992, b&w JSe (a)	2.00
❑275, Oct 1992, b&w JSe (a)	2.00
❑276, Nov 1992, b&w JSe (a)	2.00
❑277, Dec 1992, b&w JSe (a)	2.00
❑278, Jan 1993, b&w JSe (a)	2.00
❑279, Mar 1993, b&w JSe (a)	2.00
❑280, May 1993, b&w JSe (a)	2.00
❑281, Jul 1993, b&w JSe (a)	2.00
❑282, Aug 1993, b&w JSe (a)	2.00
❑283, Sep 1993, b&w JSe (a)	2.00
❑284, Oct 1993, b&w JSe (a)	2.00
❑285, Nov 1993, b&w JSe (a)	2.00
❑286, Dec 1993, b&w JSe (a)	2.00
❑287, Jan 1994, b&w JSe (a)	2.00
❑288, Mar 1994, b&w JSe (a)	2.00
❑289, May 1994, b&w JSe (a)	2.00
❑290, Jul 1994, b&w JSe (a)	2.00
❑291, Aug 1994, b&w; b&w magazine JSe (c); JSe (a)	2.00
❑292, Sep 1994, b&w; b&w magazine JSe (a)	2.00
❑293, Oct 1994, b&w JSe (a)	2.00
❑294, Nov 1994, b&w; b&w magazine JSe (a)	2.00
❑295, Dec 1994, b&w; b&w magazine JSe (a)	2.00
❑296, Jan 1995, b&w; b&w magazine JSe (a)	2.00
❑297, Mar 1995, b&w; b&w magazine JSe (a)	2.00
❑298, May 1995, b&w JSe (a)	2.00
❑299, Jul 1995, b&w JSe (a)	2.00
❑300, Aug 1995, b&w JSe (a)	2.00
❑301, Sep 1995, b&w JSe (a)	2.00
❑302, Oct 1995, b&w; b&w magazine JSe (a)	2.00
❑303, Nov 1995, b&w JSe (a)	2.00
❑304, Dec 1995, b&w JSe (a)	2.00
❑305, Jan 1996, b&w JSe (a)	2.00

	N-MINT
❑306, Mar 1996, b&w; b&w magazine JSe (a)	2.00
❑307, ca. 1996, b&w JSe (a)	2.00
❑308, ca. 1996, b&w JSe (a)	2.00
❑309, Aug 1996, b&w JSe (a)	2.00
❑310, Sep 1996, b&w JSe (a)	2.00
❑311, Oct 1996, b&w JSe (a)	2.00
❑312, Nov 1996, b&w JSe (a)	2.00
❑313 1997, b&w JSe (a)	2.00
❑314 1997, b&w JSe (a)	2.00
❑315, Mar 1997, b&w JSe (a)	2.00
❑316 1997, b&w JSe (a)	2.00
❑317 1997, b&w JSe (a)	2.00
❑318, Aug 1997, b&w JSe (a)	2.00
❑319 1997, b&w JSe (a)	2.00
❑320, b&w JSe (a)	2.00
❑321, b&w JSe (a)	2.00
❑322, b&w JSe (a)	2.00
❑323, b&w JSe (a)	2.00
❑324, b&w JSe (a)	2.00
❑325, May 1998, b&w; JSe (a); 40th anniversary issue; Titanic parody	2.00
❑326, Jul 1998, b&w; JSe (a); King of the Hill, Flubber parodies	2.00
❑327, b&w JSe (a)	2.00
❑328, b&w; JSe (a); Simpsons, South Park, King of the Hill parody	2.00
❑329, b&w JSe (a)	2.00
❑330, b&w JSe (a)	2.00
❑331, b&w JSe (a)	2.00
❑332, Jan 1999, b&w; JSe (a); Armageddon, Saving Private Ryan parodies	2.00
❑333, b&w JSe (a)	2.00
❑334, b&w JSe (a)	2.00
❑335, b&w JSe (a)	2.00
❑336, b&w JSe (a)	2.00
❑337, b&w JSe (a)	2.00
❑338, Oct 1999, b&w; JSe (a); Star Wars, Mystery Men, Inspector Gadget parodies	2.00
❑339, Nov 1999, b&w; JSe (a); Tarzan, Animorphs, American Pie parodies	2.00
❑340 2000, b&w JSe (a)	2.00
❑341 2000, b&w JSe (a)	2.00
❑342 2000, b&w JSe (a)	2.00
❑343 2000, b&w JSe (a)	2.00
❑344 2000 JSe (a)	2.00
❑345 2000 JSe (a)	2.00
❑346 2000 JSe (a)	2.00
❑347 2000 JSe (a)	2.00
❑348 2000 JSe (a)	2.00
❑349 2000 JSe (a)	2.00
❑350, Dec 2000 JSe (a)	2.00
❑351, Jan 2001, First issue without John Severin	2.95
❑352, Feb 2001	2.95
❑353, Mar 2001; Pokemon, X-Men movie parodies	2.95
❑354 2001; Eminem parody; super-hero issue	2.95
❑Annual 1, b&w JSe (a)	7.00
❑Annual 2, b&w JSe (a)	5.00
❑Annual 3, b&w JSe (a)	5.00
❑Annual 4, b&w JSe (a)	4.00
❑Annual 5, b&w JSe (a)	4.00
❑Annual 6, b&w JSe (a)	4.00
❑Annual 7, b&w JSe (a)	4.00
❑Annual 8, b&w JSe (a)	4.00
❑Annual 9 1975, b&w JSe (a)	4.00
❑Annual 10 1976 JSe (a)	4.00
❑Annual 11 1977 JSe (a)	4.00
❑Annual 12 1978 JSe (a)	4.00
❑Annual 13 1979 JSe (a)	4.00
❑Annual 14 1980 JSe (a)	4.00
❑Annual 15 1981 JSe (a)	4.00
❑Annual 16 1982 JSe (a)	4.00
❑Annual 17 1983 JSe (a)	4.00
❑Annual 18 1984 JSe (a)	4.00
❑Annual 19, Sum 1985; JSe (a); Knight Rider, Raiders of the Lost Ark, Too Close for Comfort parodies	4.00

CRACKED COLLECTORS' EDITION

GLOBE

❑4, ca. 1973, JSe (a); No #1-3	10.00
❑5 1973, JSe (a)	8.00
❑6 1974, JSe (a); Gangster issue	6.00
❑7 1974, JSe (c); JSe (a); TV issue	6.00

Other grades: Multiply price above by 5/6 for VF/NM • 2/3 for VERY FINE • 1/3 for FINE • 1/5 for VERY GOOD • 1/8 for GOOD

Crazy (Magazine)

Marvel joins satire magazine crowd
©Marvel

Creature Commandos

Monsters team up in short-lived DC book
©DC

Creatures on the Loose

Later incarnation of Tower of Shadows
©Marvel

Creeper

Journalist is haunted by other self
©DC

Crime Patrol (Gemstone)

Gemstone reprinting of E.C. series
©Gemstone

	N-MINT
❑8 1975, JSe (a)	6.00
❑9 1975, JSe (a)	6.00
❑10 1975, JSe (a)	6.00
❑11 1975, JSe (c); JSe (a); World of Advertising	5.00
❑12 1975, JSe (a)	5.00
❑13 1976, JSe (a)	5.00
❑14 1976, JSe (a)	5.00
❑15 1976, JSe (a)	5.00
❑16 1976, JSe (c); JSe (a); Fonz for President cover	5.00
❑17 1976 JSe (a)	5.00
❑18 1976 JSe (a)	5.00
❑19 1977; JSe (a); TV issue	5.00
❑20 1977 JSe (a)	5.00
❑21 1977 JSe (a)	5.00
❑22 1978 JSe (a)	5.00
❑23, May 1978; JSe (a); Cracked Visits Outer Space	5.00
❑nn (24), Jul 1978; JSe (a); No number	5.00
❑nn (25), Sep 1978; JSe (a); No number	5.00
❑nn (26), Nov 1978; JSe (c); JSe (a); Sharks special; no number	5.00
❑nn (27), Dec 1978; JSe (a); No number	5.00
❑nn (28), Feb 1979; JSe (a); No number	
❑nn (29), May 1979; JSe (c); JSe (a); Mork issue; No number	10.00
❑nn (30), Jul 1979; JSe (a); No number	5.00
❑nn (31), Sep 1979; JSe (a); No number	4.00
❑nn (32), Nov 1979; JSe (c); JSe (a); Summer Fun; No number	4.00
❑nn (33), Dec 1979; JSe (a); No number	4.00
❑nn (34), Feb 1980; JSe (a); No number	4.00
❑nn (35), May 1980; JSe (a); No number	4.00
❑nn (36), Jul 1980; JSe (a); No number	4.00
❑nn (37), Sep 1980; JSe (a); No number	4.00
❑nn (38), Nov 1980; JSe (a); No number	4.00
❑nn (39), Dec 1980; JSe (a); No number	4.00
❑nn (40), Feb 1981; JSe (c); JSe (a); TV special; No number	4.00
❑41, May 1981 JSe (a)	4.00
❑nn (42), Jul 1981; JSe (a); No number	4.00
❑nn (43), Sep 1981; JSe (a); No number	4.00
❑nn (44), Nov 1981; JSe (a); No number	4.00
❑nn (45), Dec 1981; JSe (a); No number	4.00
❑nn (46), Feb 1982; JSe (a); No number	4.00
❑nn (47), May 1982; JSe (a); No number	4.00
❑nn (48), Jul 1982; JSe (a); No number	4.00
❑nn (49), Sep 1982; JSe (a); No number	4.00
❑nn (50), Nov 1982; JSe (a); No number	4.00
❑nn (51), Dec 1982; JSe (a); No number	3.00
❑nn (52), Feb 1983; JSe (a); No number	3.00
❑nn (53), May 1983; JSe (a); No number	3.00
❑nn (54), Sep 1983; JSe (a); No number	3.00
❑nn (55), Nov 1983; JSe (a); No number	3.00
❑nn (56), Dec 1983; JSe (a); ❑No number	3.00
❑nn (57), Feb 1984; JSe (a); No number	3.00
❑nn (58), May 1984; JSe (a); No number	3.00
❑nn (59), Jul 1984; JSe (a); No number	3.00
❑nn (60), Nov 1984; JSe (a); No number	3.00
❑nn (61), Feb 1985; JSe (a); No number	3.00
❑nn (62), Sep 1985; JSe (a); No number	3.00
❑nn (63), Nov 1985; JSe (a); No number	3.00
❑64, Dec 1985 JSe (a)	3.00
❑65 1986 JSe (a)	3.00
❑66 1986 JSe (a)	3.00
❑67 1986 JSe (a)	3.00
❑68 1986 JSe (a)	3.00
❑69 1987 JSe (a)	3.00
❑70 1987 JSe (a)	3.00
❑71 1987 JSe (a)	3.00
❑72, Sep 1987 JSe (a)	3.00
❑73, Jan 1988 JSe (a)	3.00
❑74 1988 JSe (a)	3.00
❑75 1988 JSe (a)	3.00
❑76 1988 JSe (a)	3.00
❑77 1989 JSe (a)	3.00
❑78 1989 JSe (a)	3.00
❑79 1989 JSe (a)	3.00
❑80 1989 JSe (a)	3.00
❑81 1990 JSe (a)	3.00
❑82 1990 JSe (a)	3.00
❑83 1990 JSe (a)	3.00
❑84 1990 JSe (a)	3.00
❑85 1991 JSe (a)	3.00
❑86 1991 JSe (a)	3.00
❑87 1991 JSe (a)	3.00
❑88 1991 JSe (a)	3.00
❑89 1992 JSe (a)	3.00
❑90 1992 JSe (a)	3.00
❑91 1992 JSe (a)	3.00
❑92, Sep 1992; JSe (a); Family Matters, Robin Hood, Funniest Home Videos parodies	3.00
❑93 1993 JSe (a)	3.00
❑94 1993 JSe (a)	3.00
❑95 1993 JSe (a)	3.00
❑96 1993 JSe (a)	3.00
❑97, Jan 1994; JSe (a); 35th Anniversary issue; polybagged with reprint of #1	3.00
❑98, Apr 1994 JSe (a)	3.00
❑99, Jul 1994 JSe (a)	3.00
❑100, Oct 1994 JSe (a)	3.00
❑101, Jan 1995; b&w magazine JSe (a)	3.00
❑102, Apr 1995 JSe (a)	3.00
❑103, Jul 1995 JSe (a)	3.00
❑104, Oct 1995 JSe (a)	3.00
❑105, Jan 1996 JSe (a)	3.00
❑106, Apr 1996 JSe (a)	3.00
❑107, Jul 1996 JSe (a)	3.00
❑108, Oct 1996; JSe (a); Year's Best	3.00
❑109, Jan 1997 JSe (a)	3.00
❑110, Apr 1997 JSe (a)	3.00
❑111 1997 JSe (a)	3.00
❑112 1997 JSe (a)	3.00
❑113 1998 JSe (a)	3.00
❑114 1998 JSe (a)	3.00
❑115 1998 JSe (a)	3.00
❑116 1998 JSe (a)	3.00
❑117 1998 JSe (a)	3.00
❑118 1999 JSe (a)	3.00
❑119 1999 JSe (a)	3.00
❑120 1999 JSe (a)	3.00
❑121 1999 JSe (a)	3.00
❑122 1999 JSe (a)	3.00
❑123 2000 JSe (a)	3.00
❑124 2000 JSe (a)	3.00
❑125, Fal 2000 JSe (a)	3.00

CRAP
Fantagraphics

	N-MINT
❑1, Aug 1993	2.50
❑2, Oct 1993	2.50
❑3, Feb 1994	2.50
❑4, May 1994	2.50
❑5, Aug 1994	2.50

CRASH DUMMIES
Harvey

	N-MINT
❑1 1994	1.50
❑2 1994	1.50
❑3, Jun 1994	1.50

CRASH METRO & THE STAR SQUAD
Oni

	N-MINT
❑1, May 1999, b&w	2.95

CRASH RYAN
Marvel / Epic

	N-MINT
❑1, Oct 1984	1.50
❑2, Nov 1984	1.50
❑3, Dec 1984	1.50
❑4, Jan 1985	1.50

CRAY BABY ADVENTURES SPECIAL
Electric Milk

	N-MINT
❑1	2.95

CRAY-BABY ADVENTURES, THE: WRATH OF THE PEDIDDLERS
Destination Entertainment

	N-MINT
❑1, b&w	2.95
❑2, ca. 1998	2.95
❑3, ca. 1998	2.95

CRAZY (MARVEL)
Marvel

	N-MINT
❑1, Feb 1973, reprints Not Brand Ecch	16.00
❑2, Apr 1973, reprints Not Brand Ecch #6	10.00
❑3, Jun 1973, reprints Not Brand Ecch #7	10.00

CRAZY (MAGAZINE)
Marvel

	N-MINT
❑1, Oct 1973, b&w	16.00
❑2 1973, b&w	10.00
❑3, Mar 1974, b&w	10.00
❑4, May 1974, b&w	5.00
❑5, Jul 1974, b&w	5.00

Other grades: Multiply price above by 5/6 for VF/NM • 2/3 for VERY FINE • 1/3 for FINE • 1/5 for VERY GOOD • 1/8 for GOOD

	N-MINT
❑6, Aug 1974, b&w	3.00
❑7, Oct 1974, b&w	3.00
❑8, Dec 1974, b&w	3.00
❑9, Feb 1975, b&w	3.00
❑10, Apr 1975, b&w	3.00
❑11, Jun 1975, b&w	3.00
❑12, Aug 1975, b&w	3.00
❑13, Oct 1975, b&w	3.00
❑14, Nov 1975, b&w	3.00
❑15, Jan 1976, b&w	3.00
❑16, Mar 1976, b&w	2.00
❑17, May 1976, b&w	2.00
❑18, Jul 1976, b&w	2.00
❑19, Aug 1976, b&w	2.00
❑20, Oct 1976, b&w	2.00
❑21, Nov 1976, b&w	2.00
❑22, Jan 1977, b&w	2.00
❑23 1977, b&w	2.00
❑24 1977, b&w	2.00
❑25 1977, b&w	2.00
❑26, Jun 1977, b&w	2.00
❑27, Jul 1977, b&w	2.00
❑28, Aug 1977, b&w	2.00
❑29, Sep 1977, b&w	2.00
❑30, Oct 1977, b&w	2.00
❑31, Nov 1977, b&w	2.00
❑32, Dec 1977, b&w	2.00
❑33, Jan 1978, b&w	2.00
❑34, Feb 1978, b&w	2.00
❑35, Mar 1978, b&w	2.00
❑36, Apr 1978, b&w	2.00
❑37, May 1978, b&w	2.00
❑38, Jun 1978, b&w	2.00
❑39, Jul 1978, b&w	2.00
❑40, Aug 1978, b&w	2.00
❑41, Sep 1978, b&w	2.00
❑42, Sep 1978, b&w	2.00
❑43, Oct 1978, b&w	2.00
❑44, Nov 1978, b&w	2.00
❑45, Dec 1978, b&w	2.00
❑46, Jan 1979, b&w	2.00
❑47, Feb 1979, b&w	2.00
❑48, Mar 1979, b&w	2.00
❑49, Apr 1979, b&w	2.00
❑50, May 1979, b&w	2.00
❑51, Jun 1979, b&w	2.00
❑52, Jul 1979, b&w	2.00
❑53, Aug 1979, b&w	2.00
❑54, Sep 1979, b&w	2.00
❑55, Oct 1979, b&w	2.00
❑56, Nov 1979, b&w	2.00
❑57, Dec 1979, b&w	2.00
❑58, Jan 1980, b&w	2.00
❑59, Feb 1980, b&w	2.00
❑60, Mar 1980, b&w	2.00
❑61, Apr 1980, b&w	2.00
❑62, May 1980, b&w	2.00
❑63, Jun 1980, b&w	2.00
❑64, Jul 1980, b&w	2.00
❑65, Aug 1980, b&w	2.00
❑66, Sep 1980, b&w; "Creatures" parodies Journey into Mystery #51.	2.00
❑67, Oct 1980, b&w	2.00
❑68, Nov 1980, b&w	2.00
❑69, Dec 1980, b&w	2.00
❑70, Jan 1981, b&w	2.00
❑71, Feb 1981, b&w	2.00
❑72, Mar 1981, b&w	2.00
❑73, Apr 1981, b&w	2.00
❑74, May 1981, b&w	2.00
❑75, Jun 1981, b&w	2.00
❑76, Jul 1981, b&w	2.00
❑77, Aug 1981, b&w	2.00
❑78, Sep 1981, b&w	2.00
❑79, Oct 1981, b&w	2.00
❑80, Nov 1981, b&w	2.00
❑81, Dec 1981, b&w	2.00
❑82, Jan 1982, b&w; parodies Amazing Spider-Man #8	2.00
❑83, Feb 1982, b&w; Raiders of the Lost Ark parody	2.00
❑84, Mar 1982, b&w	2.00
❑85, Apr 1982, b&w	2.00
❑86, May 1982, b&w	2.00
❑87, Jun 1982, b&w	2.00
❑88, Jul 1982, b&w	2.00
❑89, Aug 1982, b&w	2.00
❑90, Sep 1982, b&w	2.00
❑91, Oct 1982, b&w; Blade Runner parody	2.00
❑92, Dec 1982, b&w; Star Trek II parody	2.00
❑93, Feb 1983, b&w	2.00
❑94, Apr 1983, b&w	2.00

CRAZY BOB
BLACKBIRD

	N-MINT
❑1, b&w	2.75
❑2, b&w	2.00

CRAZYFISH PREVIEW
CRAZYFISH

	N-MINT
❑1	0.50
❑2	0.50

CRAZY LOVE STORY
TOKYOPOP

	N-MINT
❑1, Oct 2004	9.95
❑2, Jan 2005	9.95
❑3, Apr 2005	9.95
❑4, Sep 2005	9.95
❑5, Jan 2006	9.95

CRAZYMAN
CONTINUITY

	N-MINT
❑1, Apr 1992; enhanced cover	3.95
❑2, May 1992	2.50
❑3, Jul 1992	2.50

CRAZYMAN (2ND SERIES)
CONTINUITY

	N-MINT
❑1, May 1993; Die-cut comic book	3.95
❑2, Dec 1993	2.50
❑3, Dec 1993	2.50
❑4, Jan 1994; indicia says #3	2.50

CREATURE
ANTARCTIC

	N-MINT
❑1, Oct 1997, b&w	2.95
❑2, Dec 1997, b&w	2.95

CREATURE COMMANDOS
DC

	N-MINT
❑1, May 2000	2.50
❑2, Jun 2000	2.50
❑3, Jul 2000	2.50
❑4, Aug 2000	2.50
❑5, Sep 2000	2.50
❑6, Oct 2000	2.50
❑7, Nov 2000	2.50
❑8, Dec 2000	2.50

CREATURE FEATURES
MOJO

	N-MINT
❑1, b&w; prestige format one-shot	4.95

CREATURES OF THE ID
CALIBER

	N-MINT
❑1, Jan 1990, b&w 1: Madman (Frank Einstein).	11.00

CREATURES ON THE LOOSE
MARVEL

	N-MINT
❑10, Mar 1971, SL (w); BWr, JK (a); Title changes to Creatures on the Loose; first King Kull story; Series continued from Tower of Shadows #9; "Trull" reprints story from Tales to Astonish #21	50.00
❑11, May 1971, reprints story from Tales to Astonish #23	15.00
❑12, Jul 1971, reprints story from Journey into Mystery #69	15.00
❑13, Sep 1971, reprints stories from Tales to Astonish #25 & #28	15.00
❑14, Nov 1971, reprints story from Tales to Astonish #33	15.00
❑15, Jan 1972, Reprints	15.00
❑16, Mar 1972, GK (a); O: Gulliver Jones, Warrior of Mars	10.00
❑17, May 1972, GK (a); A: Gulliver Jones, Warrior of Mars	7.00
❑18, Jul 1972, RA (a); A: Gulliver Jones, Warrior of Mars	7.00
❑19, Sep 1972, JM (a); A: Gulliver Jones, Warrior of Mars	7.00
❑20, Nov 1972, GM (a); A: Gulliver Jones, Warrior of Mars	7.00
❑21, Jan 1973, JSo (c); GM, JSo (a); A: Gulliver Jones, Warrior of Mars.	6.00
❑22, Mar 1973, VM (a); A: Thongor.	10.00
❑23, May 1973, VM (a); A: Thongor.	5.00
❑24, Jul 1973, VM (a); A: Thongor.	4.00
❑25, Sep 1973, VM (a); A: Thongor.	4.00
❑26, Nov 1973, VM (a); A: Thongor.	4.00
❑27, Jan 1974, VM (a); A: Thongor.	3.00
❑28, Mar 1974, A: Thongor. Marvel Value Stamp #15: Iron Man	3.00
❑29, May 1974; A: Thongor. Marvel Value Stamp #37: Watcher	3.00
❑30, Jul 1974; A: Man-Wolf. Marvel Value Stamp #65: Iceman	25.00
❑31, Sep 1974; GT (a); A: Man-Wolf. Marvel Value Stamp #30: Grey Gargoyle	20.00
❑32, Nov 1974; A: Man-Wolf. Marvel Value Stamp #34: Mr. Fantastic	10.00
❑33, Jan 1975; A: Man-Wolf. Marvel Value Stamp #24: Falcon	10.00
❑34, Mar 1975 A: Man-Wolf.	10.00
❑35, May 1975 A: Man-Wolf	10.00
❑36, Jul 1975; A: Man-Wolf. Marvel Value Stamp #73: Kingpin	10.00
❑37, Sep 1975 A: Man-Wolf.	12.00
❑King Size 1; King-size special	10.00

CREECH
IMAGE

	N-MINT
❑1, Oct 1997	1.95
❑1/A, Oct 1997; alternate cover	1.95
❑2, Nov 1997	2.50
❑3, Dec 1997	2.50
❑Book 1	9.95

CREECH, THE: OUT FOR BLOOD
IMAGE

	N-MINT
❑1, Jul 2001	4.95
❑2, Sep 2001	4.95

CREED (1ST SERIES)
HALL OF HEROES

	N-MINT
❑1	4.00
❑2, Dec 1994	3.00

CREED (2ND SERIES)
LIGHTNING

	N-MINT
❑1, Sep 1995, b&w; reprints Hall of Heroes #1 and #2 with corrections; Black and white	3.00
❑1/A, Sep 1995	3.00
❑1/B, Sep 1995; Purple edition	3.00
❑1/Platinum, Sep 1995; Collector's edition; enhanced cover	3.00
❑2, Jan 1996	3.00
❑2/Platinum, Jan 1996; Platinum edition; alternate cover	4.00
❑3, Jul 1996; bagged with trading card	3.00
❑3/Platinum; Platinum edition	3.00

CREED: APPLE TREE
GEARBOX

	N-MINT
❑1, Dec 2000, b&w	2.95

CREED: CRANIAL DISORDER
LIGHTNING

	N-MINT
❑1, Nov 1996	3.00
❑2, Nov 1996; alternate cover, cover says Dec, indicia says Nov	3.00
❑3, Apr 1997; alternate cover	3.00

CREED: MECHANICAL EVOLUTION
GEARBOX

	N-MINT
❑1, Sep 2000	2.95
❑1/Variant, Sep 2000	2.95
❑2, Oct 2000	2.95

CREED/TEENAGE MUTANT NINJA TURTLES
LIGHTNING

	N-MINT
❑1, May 1996	3.00

CREED: THE GOOD SHIP AND THE NEW JOURNEY HOME
LIGHTNING

	N-MINT
❑1, Jul 1997, b&w	2.95

CREED USE YOUR DELUSION
AVATAR

	N-MINT
❑1, Jan 1998	3.00
❑2, Feb 1998	3.00

CREED: UTOPIATE
IMAGE

	N-MINT
❑1, Jan 2002	2.95
❑2/A, Mar 2002; Indicia is from #1	2.95
❑2/B, Mar 2002; Indicia is from #1	2.95
❑3, Aug 2002	2.95
❑4 2002	2.95

Crime SuspenStories (RCP)

Russ Cochran reprinting of the E.C. classic

©Gemstone

Crimson

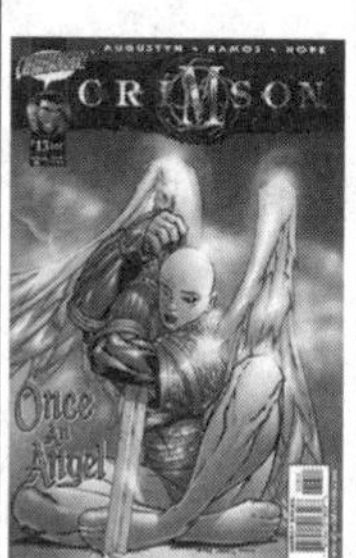

Contemporary spin on vampire legends

©Image

Crimson Dynamo

Only completed series in Epic's second run

©Marvel

Crisis on Infinite Earths

Maxi-series pared DC universe mightily

©DC

Crow (Caliber)

Series that spawned a successful movie

©Caliber

N-MINT

CREEPER
DC

❑1, Dec 1997 .... 2.50
❑2, Jan 1998 .... 2.50
❑3, Feb 1998 .... 2.50
❑4, Mar 1998 .... 2.50
❑5, Apr 1998 .... 2.50
❑6, May 1998 .... 2.50
❑7, Jun 1998 V: Joker. 2.50
❑8, Jul 1998 A: Batman. 2.50
❑9, Aug 1998 .... 2.50
❑10, Sep 1998 .... 2.50
❑11, Oct 1998 .... 2.50
❑1000000, Nov 1998 .... 3.00

CREEPS
IMAGE

❑1, Oct 2001 .... 2.95
❑2 .... 2.95
❑3, Feb 2002 .... 2.95
❑4, May 2002 .... 2.95

CREEPSVILLE
GO-GO

❑1, b&w; trading cards 2.95
❑2, b&w; trading cards 2.95
❑3 .... 2.95
❑4 .... 2.95
❑5 .... 2.95

CREEPY TALES
PINNACLE

❑1 1975 .... 1.75

CREEPY: THE LIMITED SERIES
DARK HORSE

❑1, ca. 1992, b&w; prestige format 4.00
❑2, ca. 1992, b&w; prestige format KB (w) 4.00
❑3, ca. 1992, b&w; prestige format RHo, PD (w); BG, JM (a) 4.00
❑4, ca. 1992, b&w; prestige format 4.00
❑FB 1993, ca. 1993; KB (w); A: Vampirella. 1993 "Fearbook"; Relaunch of Vampirella for '90s 12.00

CREMATOR
CHAOS

❑1, Dec 1998 .... 2.95
❑2, Dec 1999 .... 2.95
❑3, Jan 1999 .... 2.95
❑4, Feb 1999 .... 2.95
❑5, Apr 1999 .... 2.95

CRESCENT
B-LINE

❑0, May 1996 .... 1.00

CRESCENT MOON
TOKYOPOP

❑1, May 2004 .... 9.99

CREW
MARVEL

❑1, Jul 2003 .... 2.50
❑2, Aug 2003 .... 2.50
❑3, Sep 2003 .... 2.50
❑4, Oct 2003 .... 2.99
❑5, Nov 2003 .... 2.99
❑6, Dec 2003 .... 2.99
❑7, Jan 2004 .... 2.99

N-MINT

CRIME & JUSTICE
AVALON

❑1, Mar 1998, b&w 2.95

CRIME AND PUNISHMENT MARSHAL LAW TAKES MANHATTAN
MARVEL / EPIC

❑1, ca. 1989, prestige format 4.95

CRIMEBUSTER
AC

❑0 .... 2.95

CRIMEBUSTER CLASSICS
AC

❑1 .... 3.50

CRIME CLASSICS
ETERNITY

❑1, Jul 1988, The Shadow 1.95
❑2, Jul 1988, The Shadow 1.95
❑3, Aug 1988, The Shadow 1.95
❑4, Sep 1989, The Shadow 1.95
❑5, Jan 1989, The Shadow 1.95
❑6, Feb 1989, The Shadow 1.95
❑7, Mar 1989, The Shadow 1.95
❑8, Apr 1989, The Shadow 1.95
❑9, May 1989, The Shadow 1.95
❑10, Jun 1989, The Shadow 1.95
❑11, Aug 1989, The Shadow 1.95
❑12, Sep 1989, The Shadow 1.95
❑13, Oct 1989, The Shadow 1.95

CRIME CLINIC
SLAVE LABOR

❑1, Nov 1995 .... 2.95
❑2, May 1995 .... 2.95

CRIME PATROL (GEMSTONE)
GEMSTONE

❑1, Apr 2000; Reprints Crime Patrol #1 (#7) 2.50
❑2, May 2000; Reprints Crime Patrol #2 (#8) 2.50
❑3, Jun 2000; Reprints Crime Patrol #3 (#9) 2.50
❑4, Jul 2000; Reprints Crime Patrol #4 .... 2.50
❑5, Aug 2000; Reprints Crime Patrol #5 .... 2.50
❑Annual 1, ca. 2000; Collects issues #1-5 .... 13.50

CRIME PAYS
BONEYARD

❑1, Oct 1996, b&w 2.95
❑2, Sep 1997 .... 2.95

CRIME-SMASHER (BLUE COMET)
BLUE COMET

❑Special 1, Jul 1987 .... 2.00

CRIME SUSPENSTORIES (RCP)
GEMSTONE

❑1, Nov 1992; HK, JCr, WW, GI (w); HK, JCr, WW, GI (a); Reprints Crime SuspenStories (EC) #1 .... 2.00
❑2, Nov 1992; Reprints Crime SuspenStories (EC) #2 .... 2.00
❑3, Feb 1993; Reprints Crime SuspenStories (EC) #3 .... 2.00
❑4, May 1993; JCr, JKa, GI (w); JCr, JKa, GI (a); Reprints Crime SuspenStories (EC) #4 .... 2.00

N-MINT

❑5, Aug 1993; Reprints Crime SuspenStories (EC) #5 .... 2.00
❑6, Nov 1993; Reprints Crime SuspenStories (EC) #6 .... 2.00
❑7, Feb 1994; Reprints Crime SuspenStories (EC) #7 .... 2.00
❑8, May 1994; Reprints Crime SuspenStories (EC) #8 .... 2.00
❑9, Aug 1994; Reprints Crime SuspenStories (EC) #9 .... 2.00
❑10, Nov 1994; Reprints Crime SuspenStories (EC) #10 .... 2.00
❑11, Feb 1995; Reprints Crime SuspenStories (EC) #11 .... 2.00
❑12, May 1995; Reprints Crime SuspenStories (EC) #12 .... 2.00
❑13, Aug 1995; Reprints Crime SuspenStories (EC) #13 .... 2.00
❑14, Nov 1995; Reprints Crime SuspenStories (EC) #14 .... 2.00
❑15, Feb 1996; Ray Bradbury story; Reprints Crime SuspenStories (EC) #15 .... 2.00
❑16, May 1996; AW, JO, JCr, JKa (w); AW, JO, JCr, JKa (a); Reprints Crime SuspenStories (EC) #16 .... 2.50
❑17, Aug 1996; AW, JCr, FF, BE, JKa (w); AW, JCr, FF, BE, JKa (a); Ray Bradbury story; Reprints Crime SuspenStories (EC) #17 .... 2.50
❑18, Nov 1996; JCr, BE, JKa (w); JCr, BE, JKa (a); Reprints Crime SuspenStories (EC) #18 .... 2.50
❑19, Feb 1997; GE, JCr (w); GE, JCr (a); Reprints Crime SuspenStories (EC) #19 .... 2.50
❑20, May 1997; Reprints Crime SuspenStories (EC) #20 .... 2.50
❑21, Aug 1997; Reprints Crime SuspenStories (EC) #21 .... 2.50
❑22, Nov 1997; Reprints Crime SuspenStories (EC) #22 .... 2.50
❑23, Feb 1998; Reprints Crime SuspenStories (EC) #23 .... 2.50
❑24, May 1998; JO, BK, JKa (a); Reprints Crime SuspenStories (EC) #24 .... 2.50
❑25, Aug 1998; GE, BK, JKa (a); Reprints Crime SuspenStories (EC) #25 .... 2.50
❑26, Nov 1998; JO, JKa (a); Reprints Crime SuspenStories (EC) #26 .... 2.50
❑27, Feb 1999; GE, BK, JKa, GI (a); Reprints Crime SuspenStories (EC) #27 .... 2.50
❑Annual 1; Reprints Crime SuspenStories (EC) #1-5 .... 8.95
❑Annual 2; Reprints Crime SuspenStories (EC) #6-10 .... 9.95
❑Annual 3; Reprints Crime SuspenStories (EC) #11-15 .... 9.95
❑Annual 4; Reprints Crime SuspenStories (EC) #15-19 .... 10.50
❑Annual 5; Reprints Crime SuspenStories (EC) #20-23 .... 10.95
❑Annual 6; Reprints Crime SuspenStories (EC) #24-27 .... 10.95

CRIMINAL MACABRE
DARK HORSE
- ❑1, May 2003 .... 2.99
- ❑2, Jun 2003 .... 2.99
- ❑3, Jul 2003 .... 2.99
- ❑4, Aug 2003 .... 2.99
- ❑5, Sep 2003 .... 2.99

CRIMINAL MACABRE: FEAT OF CLAY
DARK HORSE
- ❑1, Jun 2006 .... 2.95

CRIMSON
IMAGE / CLIFFHANGER
- ❑1, May 1998, Several figures on cover, one in cowboy hat smoking 3.50
- ❑1/A, May 1998, Boy covered in blood/ rain 3.50
- ❑1/B, May 1998, chromium cover; Three figures on ledge 6.00
- ❑1/C, May 1998, Dynamic Forces chromium edition with certificate of authenticity; Boy in graveyard; chromium cover 6.00
- ❑2, May 1998 .... 3.00
- ❑2/A, Jun 1998, alternate cover (vampire) 6.00
- ❑2/B, Jun 1998, Crimson chrome edition 6.00
- ❑3, Jun 1998 .... 3.00
- ❑3/A, Jul 1998, alternate cover ❑(red background) 3.50
- ❑4, Jul 1998 .... 2.50
- ❑5, Aug 1998 .... 2.50
- ❑6, Sep 1998 .... 2.50
- ❑7, Dec 1998, Last published by Image 2.50
- ❑7/A, Nov 1998, DFE Hard-to-Get Foil covers pack 15.00
- ❑7/B, Dec 1998, alternate cover (angels) 3.00
- ❑7/C, Dec 1998, alternate cover (archway) 3.00
- ❑8, Dec 1999, First published by DC .. 2.50
- ❑9, Mar 1999 .... 2.50
- ❑10, May 1999 .... 2.50
- ❑11, Jun 1999 .... 2.50
- ❑12, Aug 1999 .... 2.50
- ❑13, Dec 1999 .... 2.50
- ❑14, Jan 2000 .... 2.50
- ❑15, Feb 2000 .... 2.50
- ❑16, Mar 2000 .... 2.50
- ❑17, Apr 2000 .... 2.50
- ❑18, Jul 2000 .... 2.50
- ❑19, Sep 2000 .... 2.50
- ❑20, Oct 2000 .... 2.50
- ❑21, Nov 2000 .... 2.50
- ❑22, Dec 2000 .... 2.50
- ❑23, Jan 2001 .... 2.50
- ❑24, Apr 2001 .... 2.50
- ❑Special 1 .... 6.95
- ❑Special 1/A, European cover 8.00
- ❑Special 1/Autog, DFE alternate cover 7.00
- ❑Special 1/Varia, DFE alternate cover . 7.00

CRIMSON AVENGER
DC
- ❑1, Jun 1988 .... 1.50
- ❑2, Jul 1988 .... 1.50
- ❑3, Aug 1988 MGu (a) 1.50
- ❑4, Sep 1988 MGu (a) 1.50

CRIMSON DREAMS
CRIMSON
- ❑1 .... 2.00
- ❑2 .... 2.00
- ❑3 .... 2.00
- ❑4 .... 2.00
- ❑5 .... 2.00
- ❑6 .... 2.00
- ❑7, ca. 1985 .... 2.00
- ❑8, ca. 1986 .... 2.00
- ❑9, Sum 1986 .... 2.00
- ❑10, ca. 1986 .... 2.00
- ❑11, ca. 1986 .... 2.00

CRIMSON DYNAMO
MARVEL / EPIC
- ❑1, Oct 2003 .... 2.50
- ❑2, Nov 2003 .... 2.50
- ❑3, Dec 2003 .... 2.50
- ❑4, Jan 2004, Going Up! 2.50
- ❑5, Jan 2004, Retells origin of Crimson Dynamo; price erroneously printed as $2.99, retailers charged $2.50 .... 2.95
- ❑6, May 2004 .... 2.50

CRIMSON LETTERS
ADVENTURE
- ❑1 Adventurers b&w 2.25

CRIMSON NUN
ANTARCTIC
- ❑1, May 1997 .... 2.95
- ❑2, Jul 1997 .... 2.95
- ❑3, Sep 1997 .... 2.95
- ❑4, Nov 1997 .... 2.95

CRIMSON PLAGUE
EVENT
- ❑1, Jun 1997 .... 2.95
- ❑1/Ltd., Jun 1997; alternate limited edition only sold at 1997 Heroes Con 5.00

CRIMSON PLAGUE (GEORGE PÉREZ'S...)
IMAGE
- ❑1, Jun 2000 .... 2.95
- ❑2, Aug 2000 .... 2.50

CRIMSON: SCARLET X BLOOD ON THE MOON
DC / CLIFFHANGER
- ❑1, Oct 1999 .... 3.95

CRIMSON SOURCEBOOK
WILDSTORM
- ❑1, Nov 1999 .... 2.95

CRISIS AFTERMATH: THE BATTLE FOR BLUDHAVEN
- ❑1, Jun 2006 .... 2.99
- ❑2, Jul 2006 .... 2.99
- ❑3, Jul 2006 .... 2.99
- ❑4, Aug 2006 .... 2.99
- ❑5, Aug 2006 .... 2.99

CRISIS AFTERMATH: THE SPECTRE
DC
- ❑1, Aug 2006 .... 2.99
- ❑2, Sep 2006 .... 2.99

CRISIS ON INFINITE EARTHS
DC
- ❑1, Apr 1985; wraparound cover 5.00
- ❑2, May 1985 .... 4.00
- ❑3, Jun 1985 .... 4.00
- ❑4, Jul 1985 .... 3.00
- ❑5, Aug 1985 .... 5.00
- ❑6, Sep 1985 .... 3.00
- ❑7, Oct 1985; Double-size 5.00
- ❑8, Nov 1985 .... 5.00
- ❑9, Dec 1985 .... 3.00
- ❑10, Jan 1986 .... 3.00
- ❑11, Feb 1986 .... 3.00
- ❑12, Mar 1986 .... 3.00

CRISP
CRISP BISCUIT
- ❑1, Apr 1997 .... 3.00
- ❑2, Apr 1998 .... 3.00

CRISP BISCUIT
CRISP BISCUIT
- ❑1, Jul 1991 .... 2.00

CRISTIAN DARK
DARQUE
- ❑1 1993 .... 2.50
- ❑2 1993 .... 2.50
- ❑3, Dec 1993 .... 2.50

CRITICAL ERROR
DARK HORSE
- ❑1, Jul 1992; color reprint of silent story from The Art of John Byrne ... 2.50

CRITICAL MASS
MARVEL / EPIC
- ❑1, Jan 1989 .... 4.95
- ❑2, Feb 1989 .... 4.95
- ❑3, Mar 1989 .... 4.95
- ❑4, Apr 1989 .... 4.95
- ❑5, May 1989 .... 4.95
- ❑6, Jun 1989 .... 4.95
- ❑7, Jul 1989 .... 4.95

CRITTERS
FANTAGRAPHICS
- ❑1, Jun 1986, b&w A: Usagi Yojimbo. 10.00
- ❑2, Jul 1986; Captain Jack debut 3.00
- ❑3, Aug 1986 A: Usagi Yojimbo 8.00
- ❑4, Sep 1986 .... 3.00
- ❑5, Oct 1986 .... 3.00
- ❑6, Nov 1986 A: Usagi Yojimbo 5.00
- ❑7, Dec 1986 A: Usagi Yojimbo 5.00
- ❑8, Jan 1987 .... 3.00
- ❑9, Feb 1987 .... 3.00
- ❑10, Mar 1987 A: Usagi Yojimbo 4.00
- ❑11, Apr 1987 .... 3.00
- ❑12, May 1987 .... 3.00
- ❑13, Jun 1987; Gnuff story; Birthright II story 3.00
- ❑14, Jul 1987 A: Usagi Yojimbo 3.00
- ❑15, Aug 1987 .... 3.00
- ❑16, Sep 1987 .... 3.00
- ❑17, Oct 1987 .... 3.00
- ❑18, Nov 1987; indicia says Sep 87 ... 3.00
- ❑19, Dec 1987 .... 3.00
- ❑20, Jan 1988 .... 3.00
- ❑21, Feb 1988 .... 2.50
- ❑22, Mar 1988; Watchmen parody cover; indicia repeated from issue #21 .... 2.50
- ❑23, Apr 1988 AMo (w) 3.95
- ❑24, May 1988 .... 2.50
- ❑25, Jun 1988 .... 2.50
- ❑26, Jul 1988 .... 2.50
- ❑27, Aug 1988 .... 2.50
- ❑28, Sep 1988 .... 2.50
- ❑29, Oct 1988 .... 2.50
- ❑30, Nov 1988 .... 2.50
- ❑31, Dec 1988 .... 2.50
- ❑32, Jan 1989 .... 2.50
- ❑33, Feb 1989 .... 2.50
- ❑34, Mar 1989 .... 2.50
- ❑35, Apr 1989 .... 2.50
- ❑36, May 1989 .... 2.50
- ❑37, Jun 1989 .... 2.50
- ❑38, Jul 1989; 1: Stinz. Usagi Yojimbo 2.50
- ❑39, Aug 1989; Fission Chicken 2.50
- ❑40, Aug 1989 .... 2.50
- ❑41, Sep 1989; Platypus 2.00
- ❑42, Sep 1989; Captain Jack 2.00
- ❑43 1989 .... 2.00
- ❑44 1989 .... 2.00
- ❑45 1989 .... 2.00
- ❑46 1989 .... 2.00
- ❑47 1990 .... 2.00
- ❑48 1990 .... 2.00
- ❑49 1990 .... 2.00
- ❑50 1990 .... 4.95
- ❑Special 1, Jan 1988; A: Usagi Yojimbo. Special #1 .... 2.00

CRITTURS
MU
- ❑0, Nov 1992 .... 2.50

CROMWELL STONE
DARK HORSE
- ❑1, b&w 3.50

CROSS
DARK HORSE
- ❑0, Oct 1995 .... 2.95
- ❑1, Nov 1995 .... 2.95
- ❑2, Dec 1995 .... 2.95
- ❑3, Jan 1996 .... 2.95
- ❑4, Feb 1996 .... 2.95
- ❑5, Mar 1996 .... 2.95
- ❑6, Apr 1996 .... 2.95

CROSS
TOKYOPOP
- ❑1, Nov 2004 .... 9.95
- ❑2, Feb 2005 .... 9.95
- ❑3, May 2005 .... 9.95
- ❑4, Aug 2005 .... 9.95
- ❑5, Jan 2006 .... 9.95

CROSS AND THE SWITCHBLADE
SPIRE
- ❑1, Based on the book, The Cross and the Switchblade 3.00
- ❑1/2nd, ca. 1972 .... 2.00
- ❑1/Barbour, ca. 1993, Barbour Christian Comics reprint with newsprint covers 2.00

Other grades: Multiply price above by 5/6 for VF/NM • 2/3 for VERY FINE • 1/3 for FINE • 1/5 for VERY GOOD • 1/8 for GOOD

Crusaders

Super-team combining Archie super-heroes

©DC

Crux

Six Atlantean survivors rudely awaken

©CrossGen

Cry for Dawn

Linsner's shapely horror-comics character

©Cry for Dawn

Crying Freeman Part 1

Chinese mafia changes painter's life

©Viz

CSI: Crime Scene Investigation

First TV cop series-turned-comic in years

©Idea & Design Works

N-MINT

CROSSED SWORDS
K-Z

❑1, Dec 1986 .... 1.00

CROSSFIRE
ECLIPSE

❑1, May 1984, DS, ME (w); DS (a) 2.50
❑2, Jun 1984, DS (a) 1.75
❑3, Jul 1984, DS (a) 1.75
❑4, Aug 1984, DS (a) 1.75
❑5, Sep 1984, DS (a) 1.75
❑6, Nov 1984, DS (a) 1.75
❑7, Dec 1984, DS (a) 1.75
❑8, Jan 1985, DS (a) 1.75
❑9, Mar 1985, DS (a) 1.75
❑10, Apr 1985, DS (a) 1.75
❑11, May 1985, DS (a) 1.75
❑12, Jun 1985, DSt (c); DS (a); Marilyn Monroe story, cover 1.75
❑13, Jul 1985, DS (a) 1.75
❑14, Aug 1985, DS (a) 1.75
❑15, Oct 1985, DS (a) 1.75
❑16, Jan 1986, BA (c); BA, DS (a) 1.75
❑17, Mar 1986, DS (a) 1.75
❑18, Jan 1987, Black & white issues begin 1.75
❑19, Feb 1987 .... 1.75
❑20, Mar 1987 .... 1.75
❑21, Apr 1987 .... 1.75
❑22, Jun 1987 .... 1.75
❑23, Jul 1987 .... 1.75
❑24, Aug 1987 .... 1.75
❑25, Oct 1987 .... 1.75
❑26, Feb 1988 .... 1.75

CROSSFIRE AND RAINBOW
ECLIPSE

❑1, Jun 1986 .... 1.25
❑2, Jul 1986 .... 1.25
❑3, Aug 1986 .... 1.25
❑4, Sep 1986 .... 1.25

CROSSGEN CHRONICLES
CROSSGEN

❑1, Jun 2000; lead-in to ongoing CrossGen series; background info on creators and series 3.95
❑2, Mar 2001 .... 3.95
❑3, Jun 2001 .... 3.95
❑4, Sep 2001 .... 3.95
❑5, Dec 2001 .... 3.95
❑6, Mar 2002; The First 3.95
❑7, May 2002; Negation 3.95

CROSSGENESIS
CROSSGEN

❑1, Jan 2000; No cover price; serves as basis for first four CrossGen titles: Mystic, Sigil, Scion, and Meridian 1.00

CROSSGEN SAMPLER
CROSSGEN

❑1, Feb 2000; No cover price; previews of upcoming series 1.00

CROSSOVERS
CROSSGEN

❑1, Feb 2003 .... 2.95
❑2, Mar 2003 .... 2.95
❑3, Apr 2003 .... 2.95
❑4, May 2003 .... 2.95
❑5, Jun 2003 .... 2.95
❑6, Jul 2003 .... 2.95
❑7, Oct 2003 .... 2.95
❑8, Nov 2003 .... 2.95
❑9, Dec 2003 .... 2.95

CROSSROADS
FIRST

❑1, Jul 1988; Sable, Whisper 3.50
❑2, Aug 1988; Sable, Badger 3.50
❑3, Sep 1988; Badger, Luther Ironheart 3.50
❑4, Oct 1988; Grimjack, Judah 3.50
❑5, Nov 1988; Grimjack, Nexus, Dreadstar 3.50

CROW (CALIBER)
CALIBER

❑1, Feb 1989; O: The Crow. b&w (10, 000 print run) 22.00
❑1/2nd; O: The Crow. 2nd Printing (5, 000 print run) 3.50
❑1/3rd; O: The Crow. 3rd printing (5, 000 print run) 3.00
❑2, Mar 1989; (7000 print run) 12.00
❑2/2nd, Dec 1989; 2nd Printing (5, 000 print run) 3.50
❑2/3rd, Jun 1990; 3rd printing (5, 000 print run) 3.00
❑3, Aug 1989; (5000 print run) 10.00
❑3/2nd; 2nd Printing (5, 000 print run) 3.50
❑4, ca. 1989; only printing (12, 000 print run) 10.00

CROW (TUNDRA)
TUNDRA

❑1, Jan 1992, b&w; prestige format 4.95
❑2, Mar 1992, b&w; prestige format 4.95
❑3, May 1992, b&w; prestige format 4.95
❑4 .... 4.95

CROW (IMAGE)
IMAGE

❑1, Feb 1999 .... 3.00
❑1/A, Feb 1999; gravestones 3.00
❑2, Mar 1999 .... 2.50
❑3, Apr 1999 .... 2.50
❑4, May 1999 .... 2.50
❑5, Jun 1999 .... 2.50
❑6, Jul 1999 .... 2.50
❑7, Aug 1999 .... 2.50
❑8, Sep 1999 .... 2.50
❑9, Oct 1999 .... 2.50
❑10, Nov 1999 .... 2.50

CROW, THE: CITY OF ANGELS
KITCHEN SINK

❑1, Jul 1996; adapts movie 2.95
❑1/Variant, Jul 1996; adapts movie 2.95
❑2, Aug 1996; adapts movie 2.95
❑2/Variant, Aug 1996; adapts movie 2.95
❑3, Sep 1996 .... 2.95
❑3/Variant, Sep 1996 .... 2.95

CROW, THE: DEAD TIME
KITCHEN SINK

❑1, Jan 1996, b&w 2.95
❑2, Feb 1996 .... 2.95
❑3, Mar 1996 .... 2.95

CROW, THE: FLESH & BLOOD
KITCHEN SINK

❑1, May 1996, b&w 2.95
❑2, Jun 1996, b&w 2.95
❑3, Jul 1996, b&w 2.95

CROW OF THE BEARCLAN
BLACKTHORNE

❑1, Oct 1986 .... 1.50
❑2 1987 .... 1.50
❑3 1987 .... 1.50
❑4 1987 .... 1.50
❑5 1987 .... 1.50
❑6, Mar 1988 .... 1.50

CROW, THE: WAKING NIGHTMARES
KITCHEN SINK

❑1, Jan 1997, b&w 2.95
❑2, Jan 1998, b&w 2.95
❑3, Feb 1998, b&w 2.95
❑4, May 1998, b&w 2.95

CROW, THE: WILD JUSTICE
KITCHEN SINK

❑1, Oct 1996, b&w 2.95
❑2, Nov 1996, b&w 2.95
❑3, Dec 1996, b&w 2.95

CROZONIA
IMAGE

❑1 .... 2.95

CRUCIAL FICTION
FANTAGRAPHICS

❑1, Mar 1992, b&w 2.50
❑2, b&w 2.25
❑3, b&w 2.25

CRUCIBLE
DC / IMPACT

❑1, Feb 1993 MWa (w) 1.50
❑2, Mar 1993 .... 1.25
❑3, Apr 1993 .... 1.25
❑4, May 1993 .... 1.25
❑5, Jun 1993 .... 1.25
❑6, Jul 1993 .... 1.25

CRUEL AND UNUSUAL
DC / VERTIGO

❑1, Jun 1999 .... 2.95
❑2, Jul 1999 .... 2.95
❑3, Aug 1999 .... 2.95
❑4, Sep 1999 .... 2.95

CRUEL & UNUSUAL PUNISHMENT
STARHEAD

❑1, Nov 1993, b&w 2.50
❑2, Oct 1994, b&w 2.95

CRUEL WORLD
FANTAGRAPHICS

❑1, b&w 3.50

CRUSADERS
GUILD

❑1; Title continued in Southern Nights #2 .... 1.00

CRUSADERS
DC / IMPACT

❑1, May 1992 .... 1.00
❑2, Jun 1992 .... 1.00

Other grades: Multiply price above by 5/6 for VF/NM • 2/3 for VERY FINE • 1/3 for FINE • 1/5 for VERY GOOD • 1/8 for GOOD

N-MINT

❑3, Jul 1992 .... 1.00
❑4, Aug 1992 .... 1.00
❑5, Sep 1992 .... 1.00
❑6, Oct 1992 .... 1.00
❑7, Nov 1992 .... 1.00
❑8, Dec 1992 .... 1.00

CRUSADES
DC / Vertigo

❑1, May 2001 .... 2.50
❑2, Jun 2001 .... 2.50
❑3, Jul 2001 .... 2.50
❑4, Aug 2001 .... 2.50
❑5, Sep 2001 .... 2.50
❑6, Oct 2001 .... 2.50
❑7, Nov 2001 .... 2.50
❑8, Dec 2001 .... 2.50
❑9, Jan 2002 .... 2.50
❑10, Feb 2002 .... 2.50
❑11, Mar 2002 .... 2.50
❑12, Apr 2002 .... 2.50
❑13, May 2002 .... 2.50
❑14, Jun 2002 .... 2.50
❑15, Jul 2002 .... 2.50
❑16, Aug 2002 .... 2.50
❑17, Sep 2002 .... 2.50
❑18, Oct 2002 .... 2.95
❑19, Nov 2002 .... 2.95
❑20, Dec 2002 .... 2.95

CRUSADES, THE: URBAN DECREE
DC / Vertigo

❑1, Apr 2001 .... 3.95

CRUSH
Aeon

❑1, Nov 1995, b&w; cardstock cover . 2.95
❑2, Dec 1995, b&w; cardstock cover.. 2.95
❑3, Jan 1996, b&w; cardstock cover .. 2.95
❑4, Feb 1996, b&w; cardstock cover .. 2.95

CRUSH (DARK HORSE)
Dark Horse

❑1, Oct 2003 .... 2.99
❑2, Dec 2003 .... 2.99
❑3, Feb 2004 .... 2.99
❑4, Mar 2004 .... 2.99

CRUSH
Image

❑1, Jan 1996; cover says Mar, indicia says Jan 2.25
❑2, Apr 1996 .... 2.25
❑3, May 1996 .... 2.25
❑4, Jun 1996 .... 2.25
❑5, Jul 1996 .... 2.25

CRUSHER JOE
Ironcat

❑1 1999 .... 2.25
❑2 1999 .... 2.25
❑3, Mar 1999 .... 2.25

CRUST
Top Shelf

❑1, b&w; no cover date 3.00

CRUX
CrossGen

❑1, May 2001 .... 2.95
❑2, Jun 2001 .... 2.95
❑3, Jul 2001 .... 2.95
❑4, Aug 2001 .... 2.95
❑5, Sep 2001 .... 2.95
❑6, Oct 2001 .... 2.95
❑7, Nov 2001 .... 2.95
❑8, Dec 2001 .... 2.95
❑9, Jan 2002 .... 2.95
❑10, Feb 2002 .... 2.95
❑11, Mar 2002 .... 2.95
❑12, Apr 2002 .... 2.95
❑13, May 2002 .... 2.95
❑14, Jun 2002 .... 2.95
❑15, Jul 2002 .... 2.95
❑16, Aug 2002 .... 2.95
❑17, Sep 2002 .... 2.95
❑18, Oct 2002 .... 2.95
❑19, Nov 2002 .... 2.95
❑20, Dec 2002 .... 2.95
❑21, Jan 2003 .... 2.95
❑22, Feb 2003 .... 2.95
❑23, Mar 2003 .... 2.95

N-MINT

❑24, Apr 2003 .... 2.95
❑25, May 2003 .... 2.95
❑26, Jun 2003 .... 2.95
❑27, Jul 2003 .... 2.95
❑28, Aug 2003 .... 2.95
❑29, Nov 2003 .... 2.95
❑30, Nov 2003 .... 2.95
❑31, Dec 2003 .... 2.95
❑32, Dec 2003 .... 2.95
❑33, Feb 2004 .... 2.95

CRY FOR DAWN
Cry for Dawn

❑1, Apr 1989, b&w 1: Dawn 45.00
❑1/A; Black light edition 15.00
❑1/Counterfeit; Counterfeit version of #1; Has blotchy tones on cover 2.25
❑1/2nd 1: Dawn 20.00
❑1/3rd 1: Dawn 18.00
❑2, ca. 1990 .... 30.00
❑2/2nd 15.00
❑3 .... 25.00
❑4, Win 1991 .... 15.00
❑4/Autographed, Win 1991 .... 30.00
❑5, b&w 15.00
❑5/Autographed 25.00
❑5/2nd 8.00
❑6, Fal 1991, b&w 15.00
❑6/Autographed, Fal 1991 .... 25.00
❑7, b&w 15.00
❑7/Autographed 15.00
❑8, Win 1992, b&w 10.00
❑8/Autographed, Win 1992 .... 15.00
❑9, Spr 1992, b&w 10.00
❑9/Autographed, Spr 1992 .... 15.00

CRYING FREEMAN PART 1
Viz

❑1 1989; O: The 108 Dragons. O: Emu Hino. 1: Koh Tokugen. 1: Yo Hinomura a.k.a. Crying Freeman. 1: Emu Hino. 1st appearance of Crying Freeman ... 4.00
❑2 1: Ryuji The Blade. 1: Detective Nitta. 4.00
❑3 .... 4.00
❑4 1990 O: Crying Freeman. 1: Rushichiryu a.k.a. The Seven Crying Dragons a.k.a. Father Dragon. 4.00
❑5 1990; 1: Fuh Fung Ling a.k.a. The Tigress a.k.a. Mother Tiger. Crying Freeman gets tattooed 4.00
❑6 1990 .... 4.00
❑7 1990 .... 4.00
❑8 1990 .... 4.00

CRYING FREEMAN PART 2
Viz

❑1 1990 .... 4.00
❑2 .... 4.00
❑3 1: Kitche. 4.00
❑4 D: Koh Tokugen. D: Kitche. 4.00
❑5 1: Shikebaro. 4.00
❑6 D: Old Man Venus. D: Old Man Earth. D: Old Man Jupiter. D: Old Man Saturn. D: Old Man Mars. 4.00
❑7 D: Shikeb. 4.00
❑8 .... 4.00
❑9 1991 O: Muramasa. 1: Goken Ishida. 4.00

CRYING FREEMAN PART 3
Viz

❑1 1991, 1: Tohgoku Oshu. 1st issue in color 5.50
❑2 .... 5.00
❑3 .... 5.00
❑4 .... 5.00
❑5 .... 5.00
❑6 .... 5.00
❑7 .... 5.00
❑8 .... 5.00
❑9, D: Detective Nitta. color 5.00
❑10 1992, D: Master Naiji. D: Tohgoku Oshu. color 5.00

CRYING FREEMAN PART 4
Viz

❑1 1: Wong Da Ren. 1: Wong Shaku.. 5.00
❑2 1: Lucky Boyd. 5.00
❑3 1: Wong Woh-Pei. 5.00
❑4 1: Larry Buck. 3.00
❑5 O: Kidnappers Organization. 1: Nina Heaven. 3.00
❑6 O: Nina Heaven. 3.00

N-MINT

❑7 .... 3.00
❑8 D: Nina Heaven. D: Larry Buck. 3.00

CRYING FREEMAN PART 5
Viz

❑1, b&w 2.75
❑2, b&w 2.75
❑3, b&w 2.75
❑4, b&w 2.75
❑5, b&w 2.75
❑6, b&w 2.75
❑7, b&w 2.75
❑8, b&w 2.75
❑9, b&w 2.75
❑10, b&w 2.75
❑11, b&w 2.75

CRYPT
Image

❑1, Aug 1995 .... 2.50
❑2, Oct 1995 .... 2.50

CRYPTIC TALES
Showcase

❑1 .... 1.95

CRYPTIC WRITINGS OF MEGADETH
Chaos!

❑1, Sep 1997; Necro Limited Premium Edition; comics adaptation of Megadeath songs; alternate cardstock cover 2.95
❑2, Dec 1997; comics adaptation of Megadeath songs 2.95

CRYPT OF C*M
Fantagraphics / Eros

❑1, Feb 1999 .... 2.95

CRYPT OF DAWN
Sirius

❑1, Oct 1996 .... 3.50
❑1/Ltd., Oct 1996 .... 6.00
❑2, Apr 1997 .... 3.00
❑3, Feb 1998 .... 3.00
❑4, Jun 1998 story 2.95
❑5, Nov 1998 .... 2.95
❑6, Mar 1999 .... 2.95

CRYPT OF SHADOWS
Marvel

❑1, Jan 1973, BW (a); Reprints Adventures into Terror #7 .... 35.00
❑2, Mar 1973 .... 16.00
❑3, May 1973 .... 15.00
❑4, Jul 1973 .... 12.00
❑5, Sep 1973 .... 12.00
❑6, Oct 1973 .... 10.00
❑7, Nov 1973 .... 10.00
❑8, Jan 1974 .... 10.00
❑9, Mar 1974 .... 10.00
❑10, May 1974 .... 10.00
❑11, Jul 1974 .... 10.00
❑12, Sep 1974 .... 10.00
❑13, Oct 1974 .... 10.00
❑14, Nov 1974 .... 10.00
❑15, Jan 1975 .... 8.00
❑16, Mar 1975 .... 8.00
❑17, May 1975 .... 8.00
❑18, Jul 1975, Reprints Tales to Astonish #11 .... 8.00
❑19, Sep 1975 .... 8.00
❑20, Oct 1975, Reprints Tales of Suspense #29 .... 8.00
❑21, Nov 1975 .... 8.00

CRYSTAL BALLS
Fantagraphics / Eros

❑1 .... 2.95
❑2, Sep 1995 .... 2.95

CRYSTAL BREEZE UNLEASHED
High Impact

❑1, Oct 1996, b&w; no cover price 3.00

CRYSTAL WAR
Atlantis

❑1 .... 3.50

CSI: BAD RAP
Idea & Design Works

❑1, ca. 2003 .... 6.00
❑2, ca. 2003 .... 4.00
❑3, ca. 2003 .... 4.00
❑4, ca. 2004 .... 4.00
❑5, ca. 2004 .... 4.00

Other grades: Multiply price above by 5/6 for VF/NM • 2/3 for VERY FINE • 1/3 for FINE • 1/5 for VERY GOOD • 1/8 for GOOD

Curse of the Spawn

Spinoff from Todd McFarlane's series
©Image

Cyberella

Howard Chaykin's addition to DC's SF line
©DC

Cyberforce (Vol. 1)

One of the first titles from the Image line
©Image

CyberFrog (Harris)

Big armored amphibian causes trouble
©Harris

Cyberspace 3000

Galactus pays a call to a space station
©Marvel

N-MINT

CSI: CRIME SCENE INVESTIGATION
IDEA & DESIGN WORKS
❑1 2003 ... 3.00
❑1/A 2003 ... 3.00
❑2 2003 ... 3.00
❑2/A 2003 ... 3.00
❑3 2003 ... 3.00
❑3/A 2003 ... 3.00
❑4 2003 ... 3.00
❑4/A 2003 ... 3.00
❑5 2003 ... 3.00
❑5/A 2003 ... 3.00

CSI: DEMON HOUSE
IDEA & DESIGN WORKS
❑1, ca. 2004 ... 5.00
❑2, ca. 2004 ... 4.00
❑3, ca. 2004 ... 4.00
❑4, Jun 2004 ... 3.99
❑5, Jul 2004 ... 3.99

CSI MIAMI: SMOKING GUN
IDEA & DESIGN WORKS
❑1, ca. 2003 ... 6.99

CSI MIAMI: THOU SHALT NOT
IDEA & DESIGN WORKS
❑1, ca. 2004 ... 6.99

CSI: NEW YORK BLOODY MURDER
IDEA & DESIGN WORKS
❑1, Sep 2005 ... 3.99
❑2, Oct 2005 ... 3.99
❑3, Nov 2005 ... 3.99
❑4, Dec 2005 ... 3.99
❑5, Jan 2006 ... 3.99

CSI: SECRET IDENTITY
IDEA & DESIGN WORKS
❑1, ca. 2005 ... 3.99
❑2, ca. 2005 ... 3.99
❑3, ca. 2005 ... 3.99
❑4 2005 ... 3.99
❑5 2005 ... 3.99

CSI: SERIAL
IDEA & DESIGN WORKS
❑1, ca. 2003 ... 19.99

CSI: THICKER THAN BLOOD
IDEA & DESIGN WORKS
❑1, ca. 2003 ... 6.99

CTHULHU (H.P. LOVECRAFT'S...)
MILLENNIUM
❑1 ... 2.50
❑1/CS; trading cards ... 3.50
❑2; trading cards ... 2.50
❑3 ... 2.50

CUCKOO
GREEN DOOR
❑1, b&w; cardstock cover ... 2.75
❑2, Win 1996, b&w; cardstock cover ... 2.75
❑3, Spr 1997, b&w; cardstock cover ... 2.75
❑4, Sum 1997, b&w; cardstock cover ... 2.75
❑5, Fal 1997, b&w; cardstock cover ... 2.75

CUD
FANTAGRAPHICS
❑1, b&w ... 3.00
❑2, b&w ... 2.50
❑3, b&w ... 2.50
❑4, b&w ... 2.50
❑5, b&w ... 2.50
❑6, b&w ... 2.50
❑7, Aug 1994, b&w ... 2.50

CUDA
AVATAR
❑1/C, Oct 1998; Woman bathing on cover ... 3.50
❑1/B, Oct 1998; Nude cover ... 3.50
❑1/A, Oct 1998; Woman battling man on cover ... 3.50
❑1, Oct 1998; wraparound cover ... 3.50

CUDA B.C.
REBEL
❑1 ... 2.00

CUD COMICS
DARK HORSE
❑1, Nov 1995, b&w ... 2.95
❑2, Jan 1996, b&w ... 2.95
❑3, Mar 1996, b&w ... 2.95
❑4, Jun 1996 ... 2.95
❑5, Sep 1996, b&w ... 2.95
❑6, Dec 1996, b&w ... 2.95
❑7, Apr 1997, b&w ... 2.95
❑8, Sep 1997, b&w ... 2.95
❑Ashcan 1, Ashcan promotional giveaway from comic con appearances; Promotional giveaway from comic con ... 1.00

CUIRASS
HARRIER
❑1, b&w ... 1.95

CULT TELEVISION
ZONE
❑1, Nov 1992 ... 2.95

CULTURAL JET LAG
FANTAGRAPHICS
❑1, Jul 1991, b&w ... 2.50

CULTURE VULTURES
ICONOGRAFIX
❑1 ... 2.95

CUPID'S REVENGE
FANTAGRAPHICS / EROS
❑1 ... 2.95
❑2 ... 2.95

CURIO SHOPPE
PHOENIX
❑1, Mar 1995, b&w ... 2.50

CURSED
IMAGE
❑1, Oct 2003 ... 2.99
❑2, Nov 2003 ... 2.99
❑3, Dec 2003 ... 2.99
❑4, Jan 2004 ... 2.99

CURSED WORLDS SOURCE BOOK
BLUE COMET
❑1 ... 2.95

CURSE OF DRACULA
DARK HORSE
❑1, Jul 1998 ... 2.95
❑2, Aug 1998 ... 2.95
❑3, Sep 1998 ... 2.95

CURSE OF DREADWOLF
LIGHTNING
❑1, Sep 1994, b&w ... 2.75

CURSE OF RUNE
MALIBU
❑1, May 1995 ... 2.50
❑2, Jun 1995, b&w; no indicia ... 2.50
❑3, Jul 1995, b&w ... 2.50
❑4, Aug 1995, b&w ... 2.50

CURSE OF THE MOLEMEN
KITCHEN SINK
❑1 ... 4.95

CURSE OF THE SHE-CAT
AC
❑1, Feb 1989, b&w ... 2.50

CURSE OF THE SPAWN
IMAGE
❑1, Sep 1996; b&w promo ... 3.00
❑1/A, Sep 1996, b&w; softcover; promo ... 4.00
❑2, Oct 1996 ... 3.00
❑3, Nov 1996 ... 3.00
❑4, Dec 1996 ... 2.50
❑5, Dec 1996 ... 2.50
❑6, Feb 1997 ... 2.50
❑7, Mar 1997 ... 2.50
❑8, Apr 1997 ... 2.50
❑9, May 1997 A: Angela. ... 2.50
❑10, Jun 1997 A: Angela. ... 2.50
❑11, Aug 1997 A: Angela. ... 2.50
❑12, Sep 1997 ... 2.50
❑13, Oct 1997 ... 2.50
❑14, Nov 1997 ... 2.50
❑15, Dec 1997 ... 2.50
❑16, Jan 1998 ... 2.00
❑17, Feb 1998 ... 2.00
❑18, Mar 1998 ... 2.00
❑19, Apr 1998 ... 2.00
❑20, May 1998 ... 2.00
❑21, Jun 1998 ... 2.00
❑22, Jul 1998 ... 2.00
❑23, Aug 1998 ... 2.00
❑24, Sep 1998 ... 1.95
❑25, Oct 1998 ... 1.95
❑26, Nov 1998 ... 1.95
❑27, Dec 1998 ... 1.95
❑28, Feb 1999 TMc (a) ... 1.95
❑29, Mar 1999 TMc (a) ... 1.95

CURSE OF THE WEIRD
MARVEL
❑1, Dec 1993; RH (a); Reprints stories from Adventures in Terror #4, Astonishing Tales #10, others ... 1.50
❑2, Jan 1994; Reprints ... 1.50
❑3, Feb 1994; BW, RH (a); Reprints ... 1.50
❑4, Mar 1994; Reprints ... 1.50

CURSE OF THE ZOMBIE
MARVEL
❑4; Reprints ... 1.25

CUTEGIRL
NOT AVAILABLE
❑1 ... 0.50
❑2 ... 0.50

CUTTING CLASS
B Comics

❑1, Sep 1995 .... 2.00

CUTTING EDGE
Marvel

❑1, Dec 1995; continued from The Incredible Hulk #436; continues in The Incredible Hulk #437 .... 2.95

CVO: COVERT VAMPIRIC OPERATIONS ROGUE STATE
Idea & Design Works

❑1 2004 .... 3.99
❑2 2004 .... 3.99
❑3 2004 .... 3.99
❑4 2005 .... 3.99
❑5 2005 .... 3.99

CYBER 7
Eclipse

❑1, Mar 1989, b&w; Japanese 2.00
❑2, Apr 1989, b&w; Japanese 2.00
❑3, May 1989, b&w; Japanese 2.00
❑4, Jun 1989, b&w; Japanese 2.00
❑5, Jul 1989, b&w; Japanese 2.00
❑6, Aug 1989, b&w; Japanese 2.00
❑7, Sep 1989, b&w; Japanese 2.00

CYBER 7 BOOK TWO
Eclipse

❑1, Oct 1989, b&w; Japanese 2.00
❑2, Nov 1989, b&w; Japanese 2.00
❑3, Dec 1989, b&w; Japanese 2.00
❑4, Jan 1990, b&w; Japanese 2.00
❑5, Mar 1990, b&w; Japanese 2.00
❑6, Apr 1990, b&w; Japanese 2.00
❑7, May 1990, b&w; Japanese 2.00
❑8, Jun 1990, b&w; Japanese 2.00
❑9, Sep 1990, b&w; Japanese 2.00
❑10, Nov 1990, b&w; Japanese 2.00

CYBER CITY: PART 1
CPM

❑1, Sep 1995, adapts anime 2.95
❑2, Sep 1995, adapts anime 2.95

CYBER CITY: PART 2
CPM

❑1, Oct 1995; adapts anime 2.95
❑2, Nov 1995; adapts anime 2.95

CYBER CITY: PART 3
CPM

❑1, Dec 1995; adapts anime 2.95
❑2, Jan 1996; adapts anime 2.95

CYBERCOM, HEART OF THE BLUE MESA
Matrix

❑1, Dec 1987, b&w 2.00

CYBER CRUSH: ROBOTS IN REVOLT
Fleetway-Quality

❑1, Sep 1991 .... 1.95
❑2, Oct 1991 .... 1.95
❑3, Nov 1991 .... 1.95
❑4, Dec 1991 .... 1.95
❑5, Feb 1992 .... 1.95
❑6, Mar 1992 .... 1.95
❑7, Apr 1992 .... 1.95
❑8, May 1992 .... 1.95
❑9, Jun 1992 .... 1.95
❑10, Jul 1992 .... 1.95
❑11, Aug 1992 .... 1.95
❑12, Sep 1992 .... 1.95
❑13, Oct 1992 .... 1.95
❑14, Nov 1992 .... 1.95

CYBERELLA
DC / Helix

❑1, Sep 1996 .... 2.25
❑2, Oct 1996 .... 2.25
❑3, Nov 1996 .... 2.25
❑4, Dec 1996 .... 2.25
❑5, Jan 1997 .... 2.25
❑6, Feb 1997 .... 2.25
❑7, Mar 1997 .... 2.50
❑8, Apr 1997 .... 2.50
❑9, May 1997 .... 2.50
❑10, Jun 1997 .... 2.50
❑11, Jul 1997 .... 2.50
❑12, Aug 1997 .... 2.50

CYBERFARCE
Parody

❑1, b&w 2.50

CYBER FEMMES
Spoof

❑1 .... 2.95

CYBERFORCE (VOL. 1)
Image

❑1, Oct 1992 1: Cyberforce. 3.00
❑2, Mar 1993 .... 2.50
❑3, May 1993 A: Pitt. 2.00
❑4, Jul 1993; foil cover 2.00

CYBERFORCE (VOL. 2)
Image

❑0, Sep 1993 O: Cyberforce. 2.50
❑1, Nov 1993 .... 2.50
❑1/Gold, Gold edition 3.00
❑1/2nd, Nov 1993 .... 1.25
❑2, Feb 1994 .... 2.50
❑2/Platinum, Feb 1994; Platinum edition; foil-embossed outer wrap.. 3.00
❑3, Mar 1994 .... 2.50
❑3/Gold, Mar 1994; Gold edition 2.50
❑4, Apr 1994 .... 2.50
❑5, Jun 1994 .... 2.50
❑6, Jul 1994 .... 2.00
❑7, Sep 1994 .... 2.00
❑8, Oct 1994; TMc (a); Image X-Month 2.50
❑9, Dec 1994 .... 2.50
❑10, Feb 1995 .... 2.50
❑10/Gold, Feb 1995; Gold edition 2.50
❑10/Platinum, Feb 1995; Platinum edition 2.50
❑10/Variant, Feb 1995; alternate cover 2.50
❑11, Mar 1995 .... 2.00
❑12, Apr 1995 .... 2.00
❑13, Jun 1995 .... 2.50
❑14, Jul 1995 .... 2.50
❑15, Aug 1995 .... 2.50
❑16, Nov 1995 .... 2.50
❑17, Dec 1995 .... 2.25
❑18, Jan 1996 .... 2.50
❑18/A, Jan 1996; alternate cover 2.50
❑19, Feb 1996 .... 2.50
❑20, Mar 1996 .... 2.50
❑21, May 1996 .... 2.50
❑22, May 1996 .... 2.50
❑23, Jun 1996 .... 2.50
❑24, Jun 1996 .... 2.50
❑25, Aug 1996; enhanced wraparound cardstock cover 3.95
❑26, Sep 1996 .... 2.50
❑27, Oct 1996 .... 2.50
❑27/Variant, Oct 1996; A: Ash. alternate cover 2.50
❑28, Nov 1996 A: Gabriel (from Ash). 2.50
❑29, Dec 1996 .... 2.50
❑30, Feb 1997 .... 2.50
❑31, Mar 1997 .... 2.50
❑32, Apr 1997 .... 2.50
❑33, May 1997 .... 2.50
❑34, Jul 1997 .... 2.50
❑35, Sep 1997 .... 2.50
❑Annual 1, Mar 1995 .... 4.00
❑Annual 2, Aug 1996 .... 2.95

CYBERFORCE ORIGINS
Image

❑1, Jan 1995 O: Cyblade. 2.50
❑1/Gold, Jan 1995; Gold edition O: Cyblade. 3.00
❑1/2nd, Mar 1996 O: Cyblade. 1.25
❑2, Feb 1995 O: Stryker. 2.50
❑3, Nov 1995 O: Impact. 2.50

CYBERFORCE, STRYKE FORCE: OPPOSING FORCES
Image

❑1, Sep 1995 .... 2.50
❑2, Oct 1995 .... 2.50

CYBERFORCE UNIVERSE SOURCEBOOK
Image

❑1, Aug 1994 .... 2.50
❑2, Feb 1995 .... 2.50

CYBERFORCE (VOL. 3)
Image

❑0, ca. 2006 .... 2.99
❑1, Apr 2006 .... 2.99
❑1/Variant, Apr 2006 .... 2.99
❑2, May 2006 .... 2.99

CYBERFROG (HARRIS)
Harris

❑1/A, Feb 1996; Alternate cover (titles along left side) 2.95
❑0, Mar 1997 .... 3.00
❑0/A, Mar 1997 .... 3.00
❑2/A; Alternate cover ("Wax the Kutyack!") 2.95
❑1, Feb 1996 .... 3.00
❑3/A; Alternate cover (rendered) 2.95
❑4/A; Alternate cover (holding man's face against wall).... 2.95
❑2 1996 .... 3.00
❑3 1996 .... 3.00
❑4 1996 .... 3.00

CYBERFROG: RESERVOIR FROG
Harris

❑1, Sep 1996 .... 2.95
❑1/A 2.95
❑2, Oct 1996 .... 2.95
❑2/A 2.95

CYBERFROG: 3RD ANNIVERSARY SPECIAL
Harris

❑1, Jan 1997, b&w; Reprints from Hall of Heroes 2.50
❑2, Feb 1997, b&w; Reprints from Hall of Heroes 2.50

CYBERFROG VS CREED
Harris

❑1, Jul 1997 .... 2.95

CYBERGEN
CFD

❑1, Jan 1996 .... 2.50

CYBERHAWKS
Pyramid

❑1, Jul 1987, b&w 1.80
❑2, b&w 1.80

CYBERLUST
Aircel

❑1, b&w 2.95
❑2, b&w 2.95
❑3, b&w 2.95

CYBERNARY
Image

❑1, Nov 1995 .... 2.50
❑2, Dec 1995 .... 2.50
❑3, Jan 1996 .... 2.50
❑4, Feb 1996 .... 2.50
❑5, Mar 1996 .... 2.50

CYBERNARY 2.0
DC / Wildstorm

❑1, Sep 2001 .... 2.95
❑2, Oct 2001 .... 2.95
❑3, Nov 2001 .... 2.95
❑4, Dec 2001 .... 2.95
❑5, Jan 2002 .... 2.95
❑6, Apr 2002 .... 2.95

CYBERPUNK (BOOK 1)
Innovation

❑1 .... 1.95
❑2 .... 1.95

CYBERPUNK (BOOK 2)
Innovation

❑1 .... 2.25
❑2 .... 2.25

CYBERPUNK GRAPHIC NOVEL
Innovation

❑1 .... 6.95

CYBERPUNK: THE SERAPHIM FILES
Innovation

❑1 .... 2.50
❑2 .... 2.50

CYBERPUNX
Image

❑1/A, Mar 1996; Woman with purple/white costume at bottom of cover .. 2.50
❑1/B, Mar 1996; Man with green hair at bottom of cover 2.50

Other grades: Multiply price above by 5/6 for VF/NM • 2/3 for VERY FINE • 1/3 for FINE • 1/5 for VERY GOOD • 1/8 for GOOD

Daffy Duck

Waterfowl is less hyperactive in comics
©Dell

Daffy Qaddafi

Dated artifact spoofing Libyan dictator
©Comics Unlimited

Dagar the Invincible (Tales of Sword and Sorcery...)

Sword-wielding barbarian swears revenge
©Gold Key

Dagwood Comics (Chic Young's...)

Sandwich-chomper loses series in 1965
©Harvey

Daisy and Donald

Fairly clever tales of social-climber Daisy
©Gold Key

	N-MINT
❑1/C, Mar 1996; variant cover	2.50
❑1/D, Mar 1996; variant cover	2.50

CYBERRAD (1ST SERIES)
CONTINUITY

❑1, Jan 1991	2.00
❑2, Apr 1991	2.00
❑3, May 1991	2.00
❑4, Jun 1991	2.00
❑5, glow cover	2.00
❑6, Nov 1991, foldout poster	2.00
❑7, Mar 1992	2.00

CYBERRAD (2ND SERIES)
CONTINUITY

❑1, Nov 1992; Hologram cover	2.95
❑1/A, Nov 1992; With regular cover	2.00

CYBERRAD DEATHWATCH 2000
CONTINUITY

❑1, Apr 1993; trading card	2.50
❑2, Jul 1993; trading card; indicia drops Deathwatch 2000	2.50

CYBER REALITY COMIX
WONDER COMIX

❑1, Fal 1994	3.95
❑2, Win 1995	3.95

CYBERSEXATION
ANTARCTIC / VENUS

❑1, Mar 1997, b&w	2.95

CYBERSPACE 3000
MARVEL

❑1, Jul 1993; Glow-in-the-dark cover	2.95
❑2, Aug 1993	1.75
❑3, Sep 1993	1.75
❑4, Oct 1993	1.75
❑5, Nov 1993	1.75
❑6, Dec 1993	1.75
❑7, Jan 1994	1.75
❑8, Feb 1994	1.75

CYBERSUIT ARKADYNE
IANUS

❑1, b&w	2.50
❑2, b&w	2.50
❑3, Jun 1992, b&w	2.50
❑4	2.50
❑5	2.50
❑6	2.50

CYBERTRASH AND THE DOG
SILVERLINE

❑1, May 1998	2.95

CYBERZONE
JET-BLACK GRAFIKS

❑1, Jul 1994	2.50
❑2, Sep 1994	2.50
❑3, Dec 1994	2.50
❑4, Mar 1995	2.50
❑5, May 1995	2.50
❑6, Sep 1995	2.50
❑7, Feb 1996	2.50
❑8	2.50

CYBLADE/GHOST RIDER
MARVEL

❑1, Jan 1997; crossover with Top Cow; continues in Ghost Rider/Ballistic	2.95

CYBLADE/SHI: THE BATTLE FOR INDEPENDENTS
IMAGE

	N-MINT
❑1 1: Witchblade.	6.00
❑1/A; 1: Witchblade. alternate cover; crossover; concludes in Shi/Cyblade: The Battle for Independents #2	6.00
❑1/B; crossover; concludes in Shi/Cyblade: The Battle for Independents #2; San Diego Preview	6.00
❑1/CS; boxed set; crossover with Crusade; also contains Shi/Cyblade: The Battle for Independents #2	10.00
❑Ashcan 1, ca. 1995; preview of crossover with Crusade	3.00

CYBOARS
VINTAGE

❑1, Aug 1996	1.95
❑1/A, Aug 1996, alternate cover	1.95

CYBORG, THE COMIC BOOK
CANNON

❑1, Jun 1989	1.00

CYBRID
MAXIMUM

❑1, Jul 1995	2.95

CYCLOPS
MARVEL

❑1, Oct 2000	2.50
❑2, Nov 2000	2.50
❑3, Dec 2000	2.50
❑4, Jan 2001	2.50

CYCOPS
COMICS INTERVIEW

❑1, Jun 1988, b&w	1.95
❑2, Sum 1988, b&w	1.95
❑3, b&w	1.95

CYGNUS X-1
TWISTED PEARL PRESS

❑1, ca. 1994	2.00
❑2, ca. 1995	2.00

CY-GOR
IMAGE

❑1, Jul 1999	2.50
❑2, Aug 1999	2.50
❑3, Sep 1999	2.50
❑4, Oct 1999	2.50
❑5, Nov 1999	2.50

CYLINDERHEAD
SLAVE LABOR

❑1, Feb 1989, b&w	1.95

CYNDER
IMMORTELLE

❑1	2.50
❑2	2.50
❑3	2.50
❑Annual 1, Nov 1996	2.95

CYNDER/HELLINA SPECIAL
IMMORTELLE

❑1, Nov 1996	2.95

CYNOSURE
CYNOSURE

❑1, Nov 1994	1.95

CYNTHERITA
SIDE SHOW

	N-MINT
❑1	2.95

CZAR CHASM
C&T

❑1, b&w	2.00
❑2, b&w	2.00

DADAVILLE
CALIBER

❑1, b&w	2.95

DAEMONIFUGE: THE SCREAMING CAGE
BLACK LIBRARY

❑1, Mar 2002	2.50
❑2	2.50
❑3	2.50

DAEMON MASK
AMAZING

❑1	1.95

DAEMONSTORM
CALIBER

❑1 1997, b&w; TMc (c); Partial color	3.95
❑Ashcan 1, b&w; preview of upcoming series	1.00

DAFFY DUCK
DELL / GOLD KEY/WHITMAN

❑4, Jan 1956, Earlier issues appeared as Dell Four Color #457, #536, and #615	18.00
❑5, Apr 1956	18.00
❑6, Jul 1956	18.00
❑7, Oct 1956	18.00
❑8, Jan 1957	18.00
❑9, Apr 1957	18.00
❑10, Jul 1957	18.00
❑11, Oct 1957	10.00
❑12, Jan 1958	10.00
❑13, Apr 1958	10.00
❑14, Jul 1958	10.00
❑15, Oct 1958	10.00
❑16, Jan 1959	10.00
❑17, Apr 1959	10.00
❑18, Jul 1959	10.00
❑19, Oct 1959	10.00
❑20, Jan 1960	10.00
❑21, Apr 1960	7.00
❑22, Jul 1960	7.00
❑23, Oct 1960	7.00
❑24, Mar 1961	7.00
❑25, Jun 1961	7.00
❑26, Sep 1961	7.00
❑27, Dec 1961	7.00
❑28 1962	7.00
❑29 1962	7.00
❑30, Jul 1962	7.00
❑31 1962	7.00
❑32 1963	7.00
❑33, Jun 1963	7.00
❑34, Sep 1963	7.00
❑35, Nov 1963	7.00
❑36, Mar 1964	7.00
❑37, Jun 1964	7.00
❑38, Sep 1964	7.00

Other grades: Multiply price above by 5/6 for VF/NM • 2/3 for VERY FINE • 1/3 for FINE • 1/5 for VERY GOOD • 1/8 for GOOD

❑39, Dec 1964 ..... 7.00
❑40, Mar 1965 ..... 7.00
❑41, Jun 1965 ..... 5.00
❑42, Sep 1965 ..... 5.00
❑43, Dec 1965 ..... 5.00
❑44, Mar 1966 ..... 5.00
❑45, Jun 1966 ..... 5.00
❑46, Sep 1966 ..... 5.00
❑47, Dec 1966 ..... 5.00
❑48, Mar 1967 ..... 5.00
❑49, Jun 1967 ..... 5.00
❑50, Sep 1967 ..... 5.00
❑51, Dec 1967 ..... 5.00
❑52, Mar 1968 ..... 5.00
❑53, Jun 1968 ..... 5.00
❑54, Sep 1968 ..... 5.00
❑55, Dec 1968 ..... 5.00
❑56, Mar 1969 ..... 5.00
❑57, May 1969 ..... 5.00
❑58, Jul 1969 ..... 5.00
❑59, Sep 1969 ..... 5.00
❑60, Nov 1969 ..... 5.00
❑61, Jan 1970 ..... 4.00
❑62, Mar 1970 ..... 4.00
❑63, May 1970 ..... 4.00
❑64, Jul 1970 ..... 4.00
❑65, Sep 1970 ..... 4.00
❑66, Nov 1970 ..... 4.00
❑67, Jan 1971 ..... 4.00
❑68, Mar 1971 ..... 4.00
❑69, May 1971 ..... 4.00
❑70, Jul 1971 ..... 4.00
❑71, Sep 1971, Cover code 10029-109 4.00
❑72, Nov 1971 ..... 4.00
❑73, Jan 1972 ..... 4.00
❑74, Mar 1972 ..... 4.00
❑75, May 1972 ..... 4.00
❑76, Jul 1972, Cover code 90029-207; cover reads ...and the Road Runner 4.00
❑77, Aug 1972 ..... 4.00
❑78, Oct 1972 ..... 4.00
❑79, Dec 1972 ..... 4.00
❑80, Feb 1973 ..... 4.00
❑81, Apr 1973 ..... 2.50
❑82, Jun 1973 ..... 2.50
❑83, Aug 1973 ..... 2.50
❑84, Oct 1973 ..... 2.50
❑85, Dec 1973, Cover code 90029-312; contains 16-page run-of-press Kenner catalog, reprinting many Kenner ads 2.50
❑86, Feb 1974 ..... 2.50
❑87, Apr 1974 ..... 2.50
❑88, Jun 1974 ..... 2.50
❑89, Aug 1974 ..... 2.50
❑90, Oct 1974 ..... 2.50
❑91, Dec 1974 ..... 2.50
❑92, Feb 1975 ..... 2.50
❑93, Apr 1975 ..... 2.50
❑94, Jun 1975 ..... 2.50
❑95, Aug 1975 ..... 2.50
❑96, Sep 1975 ..... 2.50
❑97, Oct 1975 ..... 2.50
❑98, Dec 1975 ..... 2.50
❑99, Feb 1976 ..... 2.50
❑100, Apr 1976 ..... 2.50
❑101, Jun 1976 ..... 2.00
❑102, Jul 1976 ..... 2.00
❑103, Aug 1976 ..... 2.00
❑104, Oct 1976 ..... 2.00
❑105, Dec 1976 ..... 2.00
❑106, Feb 1977 ..... 2.00
❑107, Apr 1977 ..... 2.00
❑108, Jun 1977 ..... 2.00
❑109, Jul 1977 ..... 2.00
❑110, Aug 1977 ..... 2.00
❑111, Oct 1977 ..... 2.00
❑112, Dec 1977 ..... 2.00
❑113, Feb 1978 ..... 2.00
❑114, Apr 1978 ..... 2.00
❑115, Jun 1978 ..... 2.00
❑116, Jul 1978 ..... 2.00
❑117, Aug 1978 ..... 2.00
❑118, Oct 1978 ..... 2.00
❑119, Dec 1978 ..... 2.00
❑120, Feb 1979 ..... 2.00
❑121, Apr 1979 ..... 2.00
❑122, Jun 1979 ..... 2.00
❑123, Aug 1979 ..... 2.00
❑124, Oct 1979, (c); (w); (a) 2.00
❑125, Dec 1979, (c); (w); (a) 2.00
❑126, Feb 1980, (c); (w); (a) 2.00
❑127, Apr 1980, (c); (w); (a) 2.00
❑128, Jun 1980, (c); (w); (a) 2.00
❑129, Aug 1980, (c); (w); (a) 18.00
❑130, Oct 1980, (c); (w); (a) 25.00
❑131, Dec 1980, (c); (w); (a) 15.00
❑134, Mar 1981, (c); (w); (a); #132 and #133 never printed 15.00
❑135, Jul 1981, (c); (w); (a) 5.00
❑136, Nov 1981, (c); (w); (a) 5.00
❑137, Dec 1981, (c); (w); (a) 5.00
❑138, Jan 1982, (c); (w); (a) 2.00
❑139, Feb 1982, (c); (w); (a) 5.00
❑140, Mar 1982, (c); (w); (a) 5.00
❑141, Apr 1982, (c); (w); (a) 5.00
❑142 1982, (c); (w); (a) 15.00
❑143 1982, (c); (w); (a) 15.00
❑144 1983, (c); (w); (a) 15.00
❑145 1983, (c); (w); (a) 7.00

DAFFY QADDAFI
Comics Unlimited

❑1 1986, b&w; A: Oliver North. A: Moammar Qaddafi. A: Daffy Duck. A: Ronald Reagan. Nancy Reagan cameo 2.00

DAGAR, DESERT HAWK
Fox

❑14, Feb 1948 ..... 475.00
❑15, Apr 1948 ..... 400.00
❑16, Jun 1948 ..... 300.00
❑17 1948 ..... 300.00
❑18 1948 ..... 300.00
❑19, Aug 1948 ..... 300.00
❑20, Oct 1948 ..... 300.00
❑21, Dec 1948 ..... 300.00
❑22, Feb 1949 ..... 300.00
❑23, Apr 1949 ..... 300.00

DAGAR THE INVINCIBLE (TALES OF SWORD AND SORCERY...)
Gold Key

❑1, Oct 1972, O: Dagar. 1: Scorpio. 1: Ostellon 16.00
❑2, Jan 1973 ..... 11.00
❑3, Apr 1973, 1: Graylin 7.00
❑4, Jul 1973 ..... 7.00
❑5, Oct 1973 ..... 7.00
❑6, Jan 1974, Dark Gods story 7.00
❑7, Apr 1974 ..... 7.00
❑8, Jul 1974 ..... 7.00
❑9, Oct 1974 ..... 7.00
❑10, Jan 1975 ..... 7.00
❑11, Apr 1975 ..... 7.00
❑12, Jul 1975 ..... 5.00
❑13, Oct 1975 ..... 5.00
❑14, Jan 1976 ..... 5.00
❑15, Apr 1976 ..... 3.00
❑16, Jul 1976 ..... 3.00
❑17, Oct 1976 ..... 3.00
❑18, Dec 1976, Final issue of original run (1976) 3.00
❑19, Apr 1982, O: Dagar. One-shot revival: 1982; Reprints Dagar #1 ..... 2.00

DAGWOOD COMICS (CHIC YOUNG'S...)
Harvey

❑70, Oct 1956 ..... 13.00
❑71, Nov 1956 ..... 10.00
❑72, Dec 1956 ..... 10.00
❑73, Jan 1957 ..... 10.00
❑74, Feb 1957 ..... 10.00
❑75, Mar 1957 ..... 10.00
❑76, Apr 1957 ..... 10.00
❑77, May 1957 ..... 10.00
❑78, Jun 1957 ..... 10.00
❑79, Jul 1957 ..... 10.00
❑80, Aug 1957 ..... 10.00
❑81, Sep 1957 ..... 8.00
❑82, Oct 1957 ..... 8.00
❑83, Nov 1957 ..... 8.00
❑84, Dec 1957 ..... 8.00
❑85, Jan 1958 ..... 8.00
❑86, Feb 1958 ..... 8.00
❑87, Mar 1958 ..... 8.00
❑88, Apr 1958 ..... 8.00
❑89, May 1958 ..... 8.00
❑90, Jun 1958 ..... 8.00
❑91, Jul 1958 ..... 8.00
❑92, Aug 1958 ..... 8.00
❑93, Sep 1958 ..... 8.00
❑94, Oct 1958 ..... 8.00
❑95, Dec 1958 ..... 8.00
❑96, Jan 1959 ..... 8.00
❑97, Feb 1959 ..... 8.00
❑98, Mar 1959 ..... 8.00
❑99, Apr 1959 ..... 8.00
❑100, May 1959 ..... 8.00
❑101, Jun 1959 ..... 7.00
❑102, Jul 1959 ..... 7.00
❑103, Aug 1959 ..... 7.00
❑104, Sep 1959 ..... 7.00
❑105, Oct 1959 ..... 7.00
❑106 1959 ..... 7.00
❑107 ..... 7.00
❑108 1960 ..... 7.00
❑109 1960 ..... 7.00
❑110 1960 ..... 7.00
❑111 1960 ..... 7.00
❑112 1960 ..... 7.00
❑113 1960 ..... 7.00
❑114 1960 ..... 7.00
❑115, Sep 1960 ..... 7.00
❑116 ..... 7.00
❑117, ca. 1961 ..... 7.00
❑118, ca. 1961 ..... 7.00
❑119, May 1961 ..... 7.00
❑120, Jul 1961 ..... 7.00
❑121, Sep 1961 ..... 6.00
❑122, Oct 1961 ..... 6.00
❑123, Nov 1961 ..... 6.00
❑124, Jan 1962 ..... 6.00
❑125, Mar 1962 ..... 6.00
❑126, May 1962 ..... 6.00
❑127, Jul 1962 ..... 6.00
❑128, Sep 1962 ..... 6.00
❑129, Oct 1962 ..... 6.00
❑130, Nov 1962 ..... 6.00
❑131 ..... 6.00
❑132, Apr 1963 ..... 6.00
❑133 1963 ..... 6.00
❑134 1963 ..... 6.00
❑135 ..... 6.00
❑136 ..... 6.00
❑137, Sep 1964 ..... 6.00
❑138 1965 ..... 6.00
❑139, Sep 1965 ..... 6.00
❑140, Nov 1965 ..... 6.00

DAHMER'S ZOMBIE SQUAD
Boneyard

❑1, Feb 1993 ..... 3.95

DAI KAMIKAZE!
Now

❑1, Jun 1987; Preview of Speed Racer 1.50
❑1/2nd, Sep 1987 ..... 1.75
❑2, Jul 1987 ..... 1.50
❑3, Aug 1987 ..... 1.50
❑4, Oct 1987 ..... 1.50
❑5, Nov 1987 ..... 1.75
❑6, Dec 1987 ..... 1.75
❑7, Jan 1988 ..... 1.75
❑8, Feb 1988 ..... 1.75
❑9, Mar 1988 ..... 1.75
❑10, Apr 1988 ..... 1.75
❑11, Jun 1988 ..... 1.75
❑12, Jul 1988 ..... 1.75

DAIKAZU
Ground Zero

❑1, b&w 1.50
❑1/2nd, b&w 1.50
❑2, b&w 1.50
❑2/2nd, b&w 1.50
❑3, Jul 1988, b&w 1.50
❑4, b&w 1.50
❑5, b&w 1.50
❑6, b&w 1.50
❑7, b&w 1.50
❑8, b&w 1.75

Other grades: Multiply price above by 5/6 for VF/NM • 2/3 for VERY FINE • 1/3 for FINE • 1/5 for VERY GOOD • 1/8 for GOOD

Damage Control (Vol. 1)

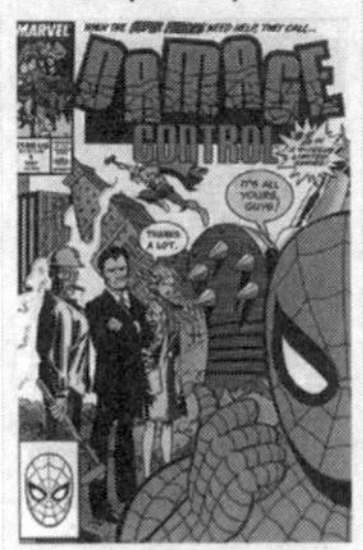

Team cleans up after super-hero fights

©Marvel

Danger Girl

First Cliffhanger title was popular for a while

©Image

Daniel Boone

Fess Parker follows trail from TV to comics

©Gold Key

Darby O'Gill and the Little People

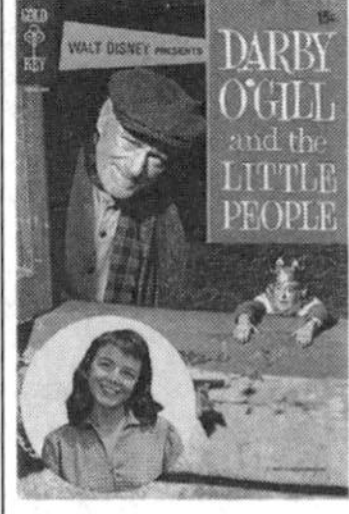

Sean Connery sings, but you can't hear him here

©Gold Key

Daredevil

Blind super-hero gets popular under Frank Miller

©Marvel

N-MINT

DAILY BUGLE
Marvel

- ❑1, Dec 1996, b&w 2.50
- ❑2, Jan 1997, b&w 2.50
- ❑3, Feb 1997, b&w 2.50

DAILY PLANET INVASION! EXTRA
DC

- ❑1; newspaper 2.00

DAIMONS
Cry for Dawn

- ❑1 2.50

DAISY AND DONALD
Gold Key

- ❑1, May 1973, CB (w); CB (a); A: June. A: May. A: April. Reprints story from Walt Disney's Comics #308 25.00
- ❑2, Aug 1973 15.00
- ❑3, Nov 1973 15.00
- ❑4, Jan 1974, CB (w); CB (a); Reprints story from Walt Disney's Comics #224 15.00
- ❑5, May 1974 10.00
- ❑6, Aug 1974 10.00
- ❑7, Nov 1974 10.00
- ❑8, Jan 1975 4.00
- ❑9, Mar 1975 4.00
- ❑10, May 1975 4.00
- ❑11, Jul 1975 3.00
- ❑12, Sep 1975 3.00
- ❑13, Nov 1975 3.00
- ❑14, Jan 1976 3.00
- ❑15, Mar 1976 3.00
- ❑16, May 1976, Road Runner in Hostess ad ("Phony Express") 3.00
- ❑17, Jul 1976 3.00
- ❑18, Aug 1976 3.00
- ❑19, Sep 1976 3.00
- ❑20, Nov 1976 3.00
- ❑21, Jan 1977 3.00
- ❑22, Mar 1977, Casper in Hostess ad ("The Boogy-Woogy Man") 3.00
- ❑23, May 1977 3.00
- ❑24, Jul 1977 3.00
- ❑25, Aug 1977 3.00
- ❑26, Sep 1977 3.00
- ❑27, Nov 1977 3.00
- ❑28, Jan 1978 3.00
- ❑29, Mar 1978 3.00
- ❑30, May 1978 3.00
- ❑31, Jul 1978 2.50
- ❑32, Aug 1978, CB (w); CB (a); Reprints stories from Walt Disney Comics & Stories #280 and #308 2.50
- ❑33, Sep 1978, Captain America in Hostess ad ("Vs. The Aliens") 2.50
- ❑34, Nov 1978 2.50
- ❑35, Jan 1979, Thor in Hostess ad ("The Storm Meets Its Master") 2.50
- ❑36, Mar 1979 2.50
- ❑37, May 1979 2.50
- ❑38, Jul 1979 2.50
- ❑39, Aug 1979 2.50
- ❑40, Sep 1979 2.50
- ❑41, Nov 1979 2.50
- ❑42, Mar 1980, Spider-Man in Hostess ad ("Puts Himself in the Picture") 2.50
- ❑43, Apr 1980 2.50
- ❑44, May 1980 2.50
- ❑45, Jun 1980 25.00
- ❑46, Oct 1980 25.00
- ❑47, Dec 1980 60.00
- ❑49 1981, #48 never printed 10.00
- ❑50, Aug 1981 10.00
- ❑51, Oct 1981 10.00
- ❑52, Dec 1981 10.00
- ❑53, Feb 1982 10.00
- ❑54 1982 10.00
- ❑55 1982 15.00
- ❑56 1982 15.00
- ❑57 1983 15.00
- ❑58, Aug 1983 15.00
- ❑59, Jul 1984 15.00

DAISY KUTTER: THE LAST TRAIN
Viper

- ❑1 2004 5.00
- ❑1/Convention 2004, 2004 San Diego Con premium 6.00
- ❑2 2004 4.00
- ❑3 2004 4.00
- ❑4 3.99

DAKOTA NORTH
Marvel

- ❑1, Jun 1986 1.50
- ❑2, Aug 1986 1.50
- ❑3, Oct 1986 1.50
- ❑4, Dec 1986 1.50
- ❑5, Feb 1987 1.50

DAKTARI
Dell

- ❑1, Jul 1967 35.00
- ❑2, Nov 1967, Yale Summers' name misspelled on cover 30.00
- ❑3, Oct 1968, Yale Summers' name misspelled again on cover, a different way; same for Hedley Mattingly; no interior ads 30.00
- ❑4, Oct 1969, Cover from #1 reused 30.00

DALGODA
Fantagraphics

- ❑1, Aug 1984, b&w 2.25
- ❑2, Dec 1984, b&w 1.50
- ❑3, Feb 1985, b&w 1.50
- ❑4, Apr 1985, b&w 1.50
- ❑5, Jun 1985, b&w 2.00
- ❑6, Oct 1985, b&w 2.00
- ❑7, Jan 1986, b&w 2.00
- ❑8, Apr 1986, b&w 2.00

DALKIEL: THE PROPHECY
Verotik

- ❑1, Aug 1998; cardstock cover 3.95

DAM
Dam

- ❑1 2.95

DAMAGE
DC

- ❑0, Oct 1994, Follows Damage #6 1.95
- ❑1, Apr 1994 1.75
- ❑2, May 1994 1.75
- ❑3, Jun 1994 1.75
- ❑4, Jul 1994 1.75
- ❑5, Aug 1994, Iron Munro 1.95
- ❑6, Sep 1994, A: New Titans. Zero Hour 1.95
- ❑7, Nov 1994 1.95
- ❑8, Dec 1994 1.95
- ❑9, Jan 1995, A: Iron Munro. 1.95
- ❑10, Feb 1995, A: Iron Munro. 1.95
- ❑11, Mar 1995 1.95
- ❑12, Apr 1995 1.95
- ❑13, Jun 1995 2.25
- ❑14, Jul 1995, A: Ray. 2.25
- ❑15, Aug 1995 2.25
- ❑16, Sep 1995 2.25
- ❑17, Oct 1995 2.25
- ❑18, Nov 1995, Underworld Unleashed 2.25
- ❑19, Dec 1995 2.25
- ❑20, Jan 1996 2.25

DAMAGE CONTROL (VOL. 1)
Marvel

- ❑1, May 1989, A: Spider-Man. A: Thor. 1.50
- ❑2, Jun 1989, A: Doctor Doom 1.00
- ❑3, Jul 1989, A: Iron Man 1.00
- ❑4, Aug 1989, A: Wolverine. Inferno 1.00

DAMAGE CONTROL (VOL. 2)
Marvel

- ❑1, Dec 1989, A: Captain America. A: Thor. Acts of Vengeance 1.50
- ❑2, Dec 1989, A: Punisher. Acts of Vengeance 1.00
- ❑3, Jan 1990, A: She-Hulk. Acts of Vengeance 1.00
- ❑4, Feb 1990, A: Punisher. A: Shield. A: Captain America. A: Thor. Acts of Vengeance 1.00

DAMAGE CONTROL (VOL. 3)
Marvel

- ❑1, Jun 1991 1.50
- ❑2, Jul 1991 1.00
- ❑3, Aug 1991 1.00
- ❑4, Sep 1991 1.00

DAME PATROL
Spoof

- ❑1, b&w 2.95

DAMLOG
Pyramid

- ❑1, b&w 2.00

DAMNATION
Fantagraphics

- ❑1, Sum 1994, b&w; magazine 2.95

DAMNED
Image

- ❑1, Jun 1997 2.50
- ❑2, Jul 1997 2.50
- ❑3, Aug 1997 2.50
- ❑4, Sep 1997 2.50

DAMN NATION
Dark Horse

- ❑1 2005 2.99
- ❑2 2005 2.99
- ❑3, Jun 2005 3.00

Other grades: Multiply price above by 5/6 for VF/NM • 2/3 for VERY FINE • 1/3 for FINE • 1/5 for VERY GOOD • 1/8 for GOOD

DAMPYR
IDEA & DESIGN WORKS
- ❑1, ca. 2005 ... 7.99
- ❑2 2005 ... 7.99
- ❑3 2005 ... 7.99
- ❑4, Aug 2005, Nocturne in Red ... 7.99
- ❑5, Sep 2005, Under the Stone Bridge
- ❑6 2005 ... 7.99
- ❑7, Dec 2005 ... 7.99
- ❑8, Jan 2006 ... 7.99

DANCE OF LIFEY DEATH
DARK HORSE
- ❑1, Jan 1994 ... 3.95

DANCE PARTY DOA
SLAVE LABOR
- ❑1, Nov 1993 ... 3.95

DANCES WITH DEMONS
MARVEL
- ❑1, Sep 1993; Embossed foil cover ... 2.95
- ❑2, Oct 1993 ... 1.95
- ❑3, Nov 1993 ... 1.95
- ❑4, Dec 1993 ... 1.95

DANGER GIRL
IMAGE / CLIFFHANGER
- ❑1, Mar 1998 ... 5.00
- ❑1/Chromium, Mar 1998; chromium cover ... 8.00
- ❑1/Mag sized, Mar 1998; magazine-sized ... 20.00
- ❑1/Tour ed, Mar 1998; Tour Edition; Woman holding rifle, white background Tour Edition ... 8.00
- ❑1/Go-go cover, Mar 1988; Chromium a-go-go cover ... 31.00
- ❑2, May 1998 ... 3.00
- ❑2/Chrome, May 1998; Special holochrome cover ... 8.00
- ❑2/Dynamic, May 1988; Dynamic Forces cover, later recalled ... 45.00
- ❑2/Gold, May 1998; Gold logo ... 6.00
- ❑3, Aug 1998; White background, 3 girls on cover ... 3.00
- ❑3/A, Aug 1998; Girls surrounding guy, knife cover ... 5.00
- ❑3/B, Aug 1998; "Filled to the Brim with Danger" cover ... 3.00
- ❑4, Dec 1998 ... 3.00
- ❑4/A, Dec 1998; alternate cover (purple background) ... 7.00
- ❑5, Jul 1999 ... 2.50
- ❑5/Dynamic red, Jul 1999; Dynamic Forces variant; Woman in red bikini ... 6.00
- ❑5/Dynamic blue, Jul 1999; Dynamic Forces variant; Woman in blue bikini ... 6.00
- ❑6, Dec 1999 ... 2.50
- ❑6/Dynamic, Dec 1999; DFE gold foil edition ... 15.00
- ❑6/Gold, Dec 1999; DFE gold foil edition ... 5.00
- ❑7, Feb 2001 ... 5.95
- ❑Ashcan 1; Preview edition ... 5.00
- ❑Ashcan 1/Gold; Preview edition; Gold logo ... 6.00
- ❑SP 1, Feb 2000 ... 3.50

DANGER GIRL 3-D
DC
- ❑1, Apr 2003 ... 4.95

DANGER GIRL: BACK IN BLACK
DC
- ❑1, Jan 2006 ... 2.99
- ❑2, Jan 2006 ... 2.99
- ❑3, Mar 2006 ... 2.99
- ❑4, Apr 2006 ... 2.99

DANGER GIRL: HAWAIIAN PUNCH
DC
- ❑1, May 2003 ... 4.95

DANGER GIRL KAMIKAZE
DC / WILDSTORM
- ❑1, Nov 2001 ... 2.95
- ❑2, Dec 2001 ... 2.95

DANGER GIRL SKETCHBOOK
DC / WILDSTORM
- ❑1 ... 6.95

DANGER GIRL: VIVA LAS DANGER
DC
- ❑1, Jan 2004 ... 4.95

DANGEROUS TIMES
EVOLUTION
- ❑1 ... 1.75
- ❑1/2nd ... 1.75
- ❑2 ... 1.75
- ❑2/2nd ... 1.75
- ❑3 ... 1.95
- ❑3/2nd ... 1.95
- ❑4 ... 1.95
- ❑4/2nd ... 1.95
- ❑5 ... 1.95
- ❑5/2nd ... 1.95
- ❑6 ... 1.95
- ❑6/2nd ... 2.25

DANGER RANGER
CHECKER
- ❑1, Sum 1998 ... 1.95
- ❑2, Fal 1998 ... 1.95

DANGER TRAIL (MINI-SERIES)
DC
- ❑1, Apr 1993 ... 1.50
- ❑2, May 1993 ... 1.50
- ❑3, Jun 1993 ... 1.50
- ❑4, Jul 1993 ... 1.50

DANGER UNLIMITED
DARK HORSE / LEGEND
- ❑1, Feb 1994 ... 2.00
- ❑2, Mar 1994 ... 2.00
- ❑3, Apr 1994 ... 2.00
- ❑4, May 1994 ... 2.00

DANIEL BOONE
GOLD KEY
- ❑1, Jan 1965 ... 45.00
- ❑2, May 1965 ... 28.00
- ❑3, Nov 1965 ... 24.00
- ❑4, Feb 1966 ... 24.00
- ❑5, May 1966 ... 24.00
- ❑6, Aug 1966 ... 18.00
- ❑7, Nov 1966 ... 18.00
- ❑8, Feb 1967 ... 18.00
- ❑9, May 1967 ... 18.00
- ❑10, Aug 1967 ... 18.00
- ❑11, Nov 1967 ... 18.00
- ❑12, Feb 1968 ... 18.00
- ❑13, Oct 1968 ... 18.00
- ❑14, Jan 1969 ... 18.00
- ❑15, Apr 1969 ... 18.00

DAN TURNER: ACE IN THE HOLE
ETERNITY
- ❑1, b&w ... 2.50

DAN TURNER: DARK STAR OF DEATH
ETERNITY
- ❑1, b&w ... 2.50

DAN TURNER: HOMICIDE HUNCH
ETERNITY
- ❑1, Jul 1991, b&w ... 2.50

DAN TURNER: STAR CHAMBER
ETERNITY
- ❑1, Sep 1991, b&w ... 2.50

DARBY O'GILL AND THE LITTLE PEOPLE
GOLD KEY
- ❑1, Jan 1970, Reprints Four Color Comics (2nd Series) #1024 ... 20.00

D'ARC TANGENT
FFANTASY FFACTORY
- ❑1, Aug 1982 ... 2.00

DAREDEVIL
MARVEL
- ❑-1, Jul 1997, GC (c); GC (a); Flashback ... 2.25
- ❑1, Apr 1964, BEv, JK (c); SL (w); SD, BEv (a); O: Daredevil. 1: Karen Page. 1: Battling Jack Murdock. 1: Daredevil. 1: Foggy Nelson. D: Battling Jack Murdock ... 3250.00
- ❑2, Jun 1964, JK (c); SL (w); JO (a); A: Fantastic Four. V: Electro. ... 850.00
- ❑3, Aug 1964, JK (c); SL (w); JO (a); O: Owl. 1: Owl. ... 550.00
- ❑4, Oct 1964, JK (c); SL (w); JO (a); O: The Purple Man. 1: The Purple Man. V: Killgrave. ... 400.00
- ❑5, Dec 1964, WW (c); SL (w); WW (a); V: Masked Matador. ... 300.00
- ❑6, Feb 1965, WW (c); SL (w); WW (a); 1: Mister Fear I (Zoltan Drago). V: Fellowship of Fear. ... 225.00
- ❑7, Apr 1965, WW (c); SL (w); WW (a); 1: red costume. A: Sub-Mariner. ... 675.00
- ❑8, Jun 1965, WW (c); SL (w); WW (a); O: Stilt Man. 1: Stilt Man. ... 135.00
- ❑9, Aug 1965, WW (c); SL (w); WW (a) ... 135.00
- ❑10, Oct 1965, WW (c); WW (w); WW (a); 1: Ape-Man I (Gordon Monk Keefer). 1: Frog-Man I (Francois LeBlanc). 1: Ani-Men. 1: Cat-Man I (Townshend Horgan). 1: Bird-Man I (Henry Hawk). ... 135.00
- ❑11, Dec 1965, WW (c); SL (w); WW (a) ... 85.00
- ❑12, Jan 1966, SL (w); JK (a); 2: Ka-Zar. ... 85.00
- ❑13, Feb 1966, SL (w); JK (a); O: Ka-Zar. ... 85.00
- ❑14, Mar 1966, SL (w); A: Ka-Zar. ... 85.00
- ❑15, Apr 1966, SL (w) ... 85.00
- ❑16, May 1966, SL (w); 1: Masked Marauder. A: Spider-Man. ... 120.00
- ❑17, Jun 1966, SL (w); A: Spider-Man. ... 120.00
- ❑18, Jul 1966, SL (w); O: Gladiator I (Melvin Potter). 1: Gladiator I (Melvin Potter). ... 70.00
- ❑19, Aug 1966, SL (w); A: Gladiator I (Melvin Potter). ... 60.00
- ❑20, Sep 1966, SL (w); GC (a); V: Owl. ... 55.00
- ❑21, Oct 1966, GC (c); SL (w); GC, BEv (a); V: Owl. ... 50.00
- ❑22, Nov 1966, GC (c); SL (w); GC (a) ... 50.00
- ❑23, Dec 1966, GC (c); SL (w); GC (a) ... 50.00
- ❑24, Jan 1967, GC (c); SL (w); GC (a); A: Ka-Zar. ... 50.00
- ❑25, Feb 1967, GC (c); SL (w); GC (a) ... 50.00
- ❑26, Mar 1967, GC (c); GC (a) ... 50.00
- ❑27, Apr 1967, GC (c); GC (a); A: Spider-Man. ... 50.00
- ❑28, May 1967, GC (c); SL (w); GC (a) ... 45.00
- ❑29, Jun 1967, GC (c); SL (w); GC (a) ... 45.00
- ❑30, Jul 1967, GC (c); GC (a); A: Thor. ... 45.00
- ❑31, Aug 1967, GC (c); GC (a); Cobra ... 40.00
- ❑32, Sep 1967, GC (c); GC (a) ... 40.00
- ❑33, Oct 1967, GC (c); SL (w); GC (a) ... 40.00
- ❑34, Nov 1967, GC (c); GC (a) ... 40.00
- ❑35, Dec 1967, GC (c); SL (w); GC (a); A: Invisible Girl. V: Trapster. ... 40.00
- ❑36, Jan 1968, GC (c); GC (a); A: Fantastic Four. A: Doctor Doom. ... 40.00
- ❑37, Feb 1968, GC (c); GC (a); A: Doctor Doom. V: Doctor Doom. ... 40.00
- ❑38, Mar 1968, GC (c); SL (w); GC (a); A: Fantastic Four. A: Doctor Doom. ... 40.00
- ❑39, Apr 1968, GC (c); GC (a); 1: Exterminator (later Death-Stalker). ... 40.00
- ❑40, May 1968, GC (c); SL (w); GC (a) ... 40.00
- ❑41, Jun 1968, GC (c); SL (w); GC (a); D: Mike Murdock (Daredevil's "twin brother"). ... 40.00
- ❑42, Jul 1968, GC (c); GC (a); 1: Jester. ... 40.00
- ❑43, Aug 1968, JK, JSt (c); SL (w); GC (a); O: Daredevil. V: Captain America. ... 45.00
- ❑44, Sep 1968, GC (a) ... 30.00
- ❑45, Oct 1968, GC (a); Characters drawn on Statue of Liberty photo ... 30.00
- ❑46, Nov 1968, GC (a) ... 30.00
- ❑47, Dec 1968, GC (a) ... 30.00
- ❑48, Jan 1969, GC (a) ... 30.00
- ❑49, Feb 1969, SL (w); GC (a); 1: Samuel Starr Saxon. ... 30.00
- ❑50, Mar 1969 ... 33.00
- ❑51, Apr 1969, A: Captain America. ... 33.00
- ❑52, May 1969, A: Black Panther. ... 33.00
- ❑53, Jun 1969, GC (a); O: Daredevil. ... 20.00
- ❑54, Jul 1969, GC (a); 1: Mister Fear II (Samuel Starr Saxon). A: Spider-Man. ... 20.00
- ❑55, Aug 1969, GC (a) ... 20.00
- ❑56, Sep 1969, GC (a) ... 20.00
- ❑57, Oct 1969, GC (a); Daredevil reveals identity to Karen Page ... 20.00
- ❑58, Nov 1969, GC (a) ... 20.00
- ❑59, Dec 1969, GC (a) ... 20.00
- ❑60, Jan 1970, GC (a) ... 20.00
- ❑61, Feb 1970, GC (a) ... 20.00
- ❑62, Mar 1970, GC (a); O: Nighthawk II (Kyle Richmond). ... 20.00
- ❑63, Apr 1970, GC (a) ... 20.00
- ❑64, May 1970, GC (a) ... 20.00
- ❑65, Jun 1970, GC (a) ... 20.00
- ❑66, Jul 1970, GC (a) ... 20.00

Daredevil (Vol. 2)

Kevin Smith relaunch got hot quickly

Daredevil/Black Widow: Abattoir

Terrifying 1993 graphic novel reunion

Daredevil: Father

Joe Quesada's take on Daredevil

Daredevil: Ninja

Ninja steals from under Daredevil's nose

Daredevil: Yellow

Jeph Loeb and Tim Sale "color" mini-series

	N-MINT
❑67, Aug 1970, GC (a)	20.00
❑68, Sep 1970, GC (a)	20.00
❑69, Oct 1970, GC (a); 1: William Carver (Thunderbolt).	20.00
❑70, Nov 1970, GC (a)	20.00
❑71, Dec 1970, GC (a)	20.00
❑72, Jan 1971, GC (a); 1: Tagak the Leopard Lord.	17.00
❑73, Feb 1971, GC (a)	17.00
❑74, Mar 1971, GC (a)	17.00
❑75, Apr 1971, GC (a)	17.00
❑76, May 1971, GC (a)	17.00
❑77, Jun 1971, GC (a)	17.00
❑78, Jul 1971, GC (a)	17.00
❑79, Aug 1971, GC (a)	17.00
❑80, Sep 1971, GC (a)	17.00
❑81, Nov 1971, GC (a); A: Human Torch. giant; reprints story from Strange Tales #132	25.00
❑82, Dec 1971, GC (a)	17.00
❑83, Jan 1972, V: Mr. Hyde.	17.00
❑84, Feb 1972, GC (a)	14.00
❑85, Mar 1972	14.00
❑86, Apr 1972	14.00
❑87, May 1972	14.00
❑88, Jun 1972, GC (a); O: Black Widow.	14.00
❑89, Jul 1972	14.00
❑90, Aug 1972	14.00
❑91, Sep 1972, 1: Mister Fear III (Larry Cranston).	14.00
❑92, Oct 1972, GC (a)	14.00
❑93, Nov 1972	14.00
❑94, Dec 1972	14.00
❑95, Jan 1973	14.00
❑96, Feb 1973	14.00
❑97, Mar 1973, GC (a); 1: Dark Messiah. 1: Disciples of Doom	14.00
❑98, Apr 1973	14.00
❑99, May 1973, story continues in Avengers #110	14.00
❑100, Jun 1973, 100th anniversary issue RB (c); GC (a); 1: Angar the Screamer.	30.00
❑101, Jul 1973	8.00
❑102, Aug 1973	8.00
❑103, Sep 1973, DH (a); O: Ramrod I. 1: Ramrod I.	8.00
❑104, Oct 1973	8.00
❑105, Nov 1973, O: Moondragon. 1: Moondragon. A: Thanos.	8.00
❑106, Dec 1973, DH (a); 1: Black Spectre (female group). A: Black Widow.	8.00
❑107, Jan 1974, SB (a); A: Captain Marvel.	8.00
❑108, Mar 1974, Marvel Value Stamp #22: Man-Thing	8.00
❑109, May 1974, Story continues in Marvel Two-In-One #3; Marvel Value Stamp #52: Quicksilver	8.00
❑110, Jun 1974, GC (a); Marvel Value Stamp #51: Bucky Barnes	8.00
❑111, Jul 1974, 1: Silver Samurai. Marvel Value Stamp #70: Super Skrull	8.00
❑112, Aug 1974, Marvel Value Stamp #63: Sub-Mariner	8.00

	N-MINT
❑113, Sep 1974, Marvel Value Stamp #85: Lilith	8.00
❑114, Oct 1974, 1: Death-Stalker. Marvel Value Stamp #7: Werewolf.	8.00
❑115, Nov 1974, Marvel Value Stamp #35: Killraven	8.00
❑116, Dec 1974, Marvel Value Stamp #95: Mole-Man	8.00
❑117, Jan 1975, Marvel Value Stamp #88: Leader	8.00
❑118, Feb 1975, DH (a); 1: Blackwing. Marvel Value Stamp #28: Hawkeye	8.00
❑119, Mar 1975	8.00
❑120, Apr 1975, Marvel Value Stamp #99: Sandman	8.00
❑121, May 1975	8.00
❑122, Jun 1975	8.00
❑123, Jul 1975	8.00
❑124, Aug 1975, GC, KJ (a); 1: Blake Tower. 1: Copperhead.	8.00
❑125, Sep 1975, KJ (a)	8.00
❑126, Oct 1975, KJ (a); 1: Torpedo.	8.00
❑127, Nov 1975, KJ (a); Marvel Value Stamp #80: Ghost Rider	8.00
❑128, Dec 1975, KJ (a)	8.00
❑129, Jan 1976, KJ (a)	8.00
❑130, Feb 1976, KJ (a)	8.00
❑131, Mar 1976, KJ (a); O: Bullseye. First Bullseye	75.00
❑132, Apr 1976	15.00
❑132/30 cent, Apr 1976, 30 cent regional variant	20.00
❑133, May 1976, 1: Mind-Wave.	6.00
❑133/30 cent, May 1976, 30 cent regional variant	20.00
❑134, Jun 1976	6.00
❑134/30 cent, Jun 1976, 30 cent regional variant	20.00
❑135, Jul 1976	6.00
❑135/30 cent, Jul 1976, 30 cent regional variant	20.00
❑136, Aug 1976, JB (a)	6.00
❑136/30 cent, Aug 1976, JB (a); 30 cent regional variant	20.00
❑137, Sep 1976, JB (a)	6.00
❑138, Oct 1976, JBy (a); A: Ghost Rider. A: Death's Head (monster).	6.00
❑139, Nov 1976, SB (a)	6.00
❑140, Dec 1976, SB (a)	6.00
❑141, Jan 1977, GK (a)	6.00
❑142, Feb 1977, JM (a); V: Cobra, Mr. Hyde.	6.00
❑143, Mar 1977	6.00
❑144, Apr 1977	6.00
❑145, May 1977, GT, JM (a)	6.00
❑146, Jun 1977, GK (a); A: Bullseye. V: Bullseye. Newsstand edition (distributed by Curtis); issue number in box	6.00
❑146/Whitman, Jun 1977, GK (a); A: Bullseye. V: Bullseye. Special markets edition (usually sold in Whitman bagged prepacks); price appears in a diamond; UPC barcode appears	6.00
❑146/35 cent, Jun 1977, GK (a); A: Bullseye. V: Bullseye. 35 cent regional price variant; newsstand edition (distributed by Curtis); issue number in box	15.00

	N-MINT
❑147, Jul 1977, GK, KJ (a)	6.00
❑147/35 cent, Jul 1977, GK, KJ (a); 35 cent regional price variant	15.00
❑148, Sep 1977, GK, KJ (a)	6.00
❑148/35 cent, Sep 1977, GK, KJ (a); 35 cent regional variant	15.00
❑149, Nov 1977, CI, KJ (a)	6.00
❑150, Jan 1978, CI, KJ (a); 1: Paladin.	6.00
❑151, Mar 1978, GK, KJ (a); Daredevil reveals identity to Heather Glenn	6.00
❑152, May 1978, CI, KJ (a); A: Paladin.	6.00
❑153, Jul 1978, 1: Ben Urich.	6.00
❑154, Sep 1978, GC (a)	6.00
❑155, Nov 1978, FR (a); Black Widow returns	6.00
❑156, Jan 1979, GC (a); A: 1960's Daredevil. Newsstand edition (distributed by Curtis); issue number in box	6.00
❑156/Whitman, Jan 1979, GC (a); A: 1960's Daredevil. Special markets edition (usually sold in Whitman bagged prepacks); price appears in a diamond; no UPC barcode	6.00
❑157, Mar 1979, GC, KJ (a); 1: Bird-Man II (Achille DiBacco). 1: Cat-Man II (Sebastian Patane). 1: Ape-Man II (Roy McVey).	6.00
❑158, May 1979, FM (w); FM (a); O: Death-Stalker. D: Cat-Man II (Sebastian Patane). D: Ape-Man II (Roy McVey). D: Death-Stalker. V: Deathstalker. First Miller Daredevil	50.00
❑159, Jul 1979, FM, KJ (c); FM, KJ (a); A: Bullseye. V: Bullseye.	22.00
❑160, Sep 1979, FM, KJ (c); FM, KJ (a); V: Bullseye.	17.00
❑161, Nov 1979, FM, KJ (a); V: Bullseye.	17.00
❑162, Jan 1980, SD (a)	9.00
❑163, Mar 1980, FM, KJ (a)	18.00
❑164, May 1980, FM, KJ (a)	11.00
❑165, Jul 1980, FM (a)	11.00
❑166, Sep 1980, FM (a)	11.00
❑167, Nov 1980, FM (a)	11.00
❑168, Jan 1981, FM (w); FM (a); O: Elektra. 1: Elektra.	75.00
❑169, Mar 1981, FM (w); FM (a); A: Elektra. V: Bullseye.	16.00
❑170, May 1981, FM (w); FM (a); V: Bullseye.	10.00
❑171, Jun 1981, FM (w); FM (a)	12.00
❑172, Jul 1981, FM (w); FM (a)	7.00
❑173, Aug 1981, FM (w); FM (a)	7.00
❑174, Sep 1981, FM (w); FM (a)	7.00
❑175, Oct 1981, FM (w); FM (a)	7.00
❑176, Nov 1981, FM (w); FM (a); 1: Stick. A: Elektra.	7.00
❑177, Dec 1981, FM (w); FM (a); A: Elektra.	7.00
❑178, Jan 1982, FM (w); FM (a); A: Elektra.	6.00
❑179, Feb 1982, FM (w); FM (a); A: Elektra.	6.00
❑180, Mar 1982, FM (w); FM (a); A: Elektra.	6.00
❑181, Apr 1982, double-sized; FM (w); FM (a); D: Elektra. V: Bullseye. Punisher cameo out of costume	15.00

Other grades: Multiply price above by 5/6 for VF/NM • 2/3 for VERY FINE • 1/3 for FINE • 1/5 for VERY GOOD • 1/8 for GOOD

	N-MINT
❑182, May 1982, FM (w); FM (a); A: Punisher. V: Punisher.	7.00
❑183, Jun 1982, FM (w); FM (a); A: Punisher. V: Punisher.	7.00
❑184, Jul 1982, FM (c); FM (w); FM, KJ (a); A: Punisher. V: Punisher.	6.00
❑185, Aug 1982, FM (w); FM, KJ (a)	5.00
❑186, Sep 1982, FM (w); FM, KJ (a)	6.00
❑187, Oct 1982, FM (c); FM (w); FM, KJ (a); A: Black Widow.	5.00
❑188, Nov 1982, FM (c); FM (w); FM, KJ (a)	5.00
❑189, Dec 1982, FM (w); FM, KJ (a); D: Stick.	5.00
❑190, Jan 1983, Double-size FM (w); FM, KJ (a); O: Elektra. A: Elektra.	5.00
❑191, Feb 1983, FM (w); FM (a)	6.00
❑192, Mar 1983, KJ (a)	3.00
❑193, Apr 1983, KJ (a)	3.00
❑194, May 1983, KJ (a)	3.00
❑195, Jun 1983, KJ (a)	3.00
❑196, Jun 1983, KJ (a); A: Wolverine.	6.00
❑197, Aug 1983, KJ (a); V: Bullseye.	3.00
❑198, Sep 1983	3.00
❑199, Oct 1983	3.00
❑200, Nov 1983, JBy (c); V: Bullseye.	3.00
❑201, Dec 1983, JBy (c); A: Black Widow.	3.00
❑202, Jan 1984	3.00
❑203, Feb 1984, 1: Trump.	3.00
❑204, Mar 1984, LMc (a)	3.00
❑205, Apr 1984	4.00
❑206, May 1984	3.00
❑207, Jun 1984	3.00
❑208, Jul 1984	3.00
❑209, Aug 1984	3.00
❑210, Sep 1984, MZ, BWi (c)	3.00
❑211, Oct 1984	3.00
❑212, Nov 1984	3.00
❑213, Dec 1984	3.00
❑214, Jan 1985	3.00
❑215, Feb 1985, A: Two-Gun Kid.	3.00
❑216, Mar 1985	3.00
❑217, Apr 1985, FM (c)	3.00
❑218, May 1985, KP (c); SB (a)	3.00
❑219, Jun 1985, FM (c); FM (w); JB, FM (a)	3.00
❑220, Jul 1985	3.00
❑221, Aug 1985	3.00
❑222, Sep 1985, KP (c); A: Black Widow.	3.00
❑223, Oct 1985, Secret Wars II	3.00
❑224, Nov 1985, BL (c); V: Sunturion.	3.00
❑225, Dec 1985, (c); V: Vulture.	3.00
❑226, Jan 1986, FM (w)	3.00
❑227, Feb 1986, FM (w); A: Kingpin.	4.00
❑228, Mar 1986, FM (w)	3.00
❑229, Apr 1986, FM (w); FM (a); 1: Sister Maggie.	3.00
❑230, May 1986, FM (w)	3.00
❑231, Jun 1986, FM (w)	3.00
❑232, Jul 1986, FM (w)	3.00
❑233, Aug 1986, FM (w)	3.00
❑234, Sep 1986, SD (a)	3.00
❑235, Oct 1986, SD (a)	3.00
❑236, Nov 1986	3.00
❑237, Dec 1986	3.00
❑238, Jan 1987, SB (a); A: Sabretooth.	3.00
❑239, Feb 1987	3.00
❑240, Mar 1987	3.00
❑241, Apr 1987, TMc (a)	3.00
❑242, May 1987, KP (c); KP (a)	3.00
❑243, Jun 1987	3.00
❑244, Jul 1987	3.00
❑245, Aug 1987, A: Black Panther.	3.00
❑246, Sep 1987	3.00
❑247, Oct 1987, KP (a)	3.00
❑248, Nov 1987, A: Wolverine.	4.00
❑249, Dec 1987, A: Wolverine.	4.00
❑250, Jan 1988, JR2 (a); 1: Bullet.	3.00
❑251, Feb 1988, JR2 (a)	5.00
❑252, Mar 1988, double-sized; JR2 (a); Fall of Mutants	4.00
❑253, Apr 1988, JR2 (a)	3.00
❑254, May 1988, JR2 (a); O: Typhoid Mary. 1: Typhoid Mary.	6.00
❑255, Jun 1988, JR2 (a); 2: Typhoid Mary.	2.50
❑256, Jul 1988, JR2 (a); A: Typhoid Mary.	2.50
❑257, Aug 1988, JR2 (a); A: Punisher.	2.50
❑258, Sep 1988, O: Bengal. 1: Bengal.	4.00
❑259, Oct 1988, JR2 (a); A: Typhoid Mary.	3.00
❑260, Nov 1988, double-sized JR2 (a)	3.00
❑261, Dec 1988, JR2 (a); A: Human Torch.	3.00
❑262, Jan 1989, JR2 (a); Inferno	3.00
❑263, Feb 1989, JR2 (a); Inferno	3.00
❑264, Mar 1989, SD (a)	3.00
❑265, Apr 1989, JR2 (a); Inferno	3.00
❑266, May 1989, JR2 (a)	3.00
❑267, Jun 1989, JR2 (a)	3.00
❑268, Jul 1989, JR2 (a)	3.00
❑269, Aug 1989, JR2 (a)	3.00
❑270, Sep 1989, JR2 (a); O: Blackheart. 1: Blackheart. A: Spider-Man.	3.00
❑271, Oct 1989, JR2 (a)	3.00
❑272, Nov 1989, JR2 (a); 1: Shotgun II.	3.00
❑273, Nov 1989, JR2 (a)	3.00
❑274, Dec 1989, JR2 (a)	3.00
❑275, Dec 1989, JR2 (a); Acts of Vengeance	3.00
❑276, Jan 1990, JR2 (a); Acts of Vengeance	3.00
❑277, Feb 1990	3.00
❑278, Mar 1990, JR2 (a)	3.00
❑279, Apr 1990, JR2 (a)	3.00
❑280, May 1990, JR2 (a)	3.00
❑281, Jun 1990, JR2 (a); Silver Surfer cameo	3.00
❑282, Jul 1990, A: Silver Surfer.	3.00
❑283, Aug 1990, A: Captain America.	3.00
❑284, Sep 1990	3.00
❑285, Oct 1990	3.00
❑286, Nov 1990, AW (c)	3.00
❑287, Dec 1990	3.00
❑288, Jan 1991	3.00
❑289, Feb 1991	3.00
❑290, Mar 1991	3.00
❑291, Apr 1991	3.00
❑292, May 1991, A: Punisher.	3.00
❑293, Jun 1991, A: Punisher.	3.00
❑294, Jul 1991	3.00
❑295, Aug 1991, A: Ghost Rider.	3.00
❑296, Sep 1991	1.50
❑297, Oct 1991, AW (a); A: Typhoid Mary. V: Typhoid Mary.	1.50
❑298, Nov 1991, AW (a)	1.50
❑299, Dec 1991, AW (a)	1.50
❑300, Jan 1992, double-sized; AW (a); Kingpin deposed	3.00
❑301, Feb 1992, V: Owl.	1.50
❑302, Mar 1992, V: Owl.	1.50
❑303, Apr 1992, V: Owl.	1.50
❑304, May 1992	3.00
❑305, Jun 1992, 1: Surgeon General.	1.50
❑306, Jul 1992	1.50
❑307, Aug 1992	1.50
❑308, Sep 1992, (c)	1.50
❑309, Oct 1992	1.50
❑310, Nov 1992	1.50
❑311, Dec 1992	1.50
❑312, Jan 1993	3.00
❑313, Feb 1993	1.50
❑314, Mar 1993	1.50
❑315, Apr 1993, V: Mr. Fear.	1.50
❑316, May 1993	1.50
❑317, Jun 1993, (c); V: Stiltman.	1.50
❑318, Jul 1993, V: Stiltman. V: Devil-Man.	1.50
❑319, Aug 1993, first printing (white); Elektra returns	5.00
❑319/2nd, Aug 1993, 2nd Printing (black); Elektra returns	2.00
❑320, Sep 1993, A: Silver Sable. red costume destroyed; New costume.	2.00
❑321, Oct 1993	2.00
❑321/Variant, Oct 1993, Special glow-in-the-dark cover	3.00
❑322, Nov 1993	2.00
❑323, Dec 1993, V: Venom.	2.00
❑324, Jan 1994	2.00
❑325, Feb 1994, Double-size; D: Hellspawn. poster	3.00
❑326, Mar 1994	1.50
❑327, Apr 1994	1.50
❑328, May 1994	1.50
❑329, Jun 1994	1.50
❑330, Jul 1994, Gambit	1.50
❑331, Aug 1994	1.50
❑332, Sep 1994	1.50
❑333, Oct 1994	1.50
❑334, Nov 1994	1.50
❑335, Dec 1994, (c)	1.50
❑336, Jan 1995	1.50
❑337, Feb 1995	1.50
❑338, Mar 1995	1.50
❑339, Apr 1995, (c)	1.50
❑340, May 1995	1.50
❑341, Jun 1995, (c); KP (a)	1.50
❑342, Jul 1995	1.50
❑343, Aug 1995	1.50
❑344, Sep 1995, Yellow and red-costumed Daredevil returns	2.00
❑345, Oct 1995, Red-costumed Daredevil returns; OverPower card inserted	2.00
❑346, Nov 1995	2.00
❑347, Dec 1995, Identity of both Daredevils revealed	2.00
❑348, Jan 1996, A: Sister Maggie. A: Stick. cover says Dec, indicia says Jan	2.00
❑349, Feb 1996, AW (c); AW (a); A: Sister Maggie. A: Stick.	2.00
❑350, Mar 1996, Giant-size; Daredevil switches back to red costume	2.95
❑350/Variant, Mar 1996, Giant-size; gold ink on cover; Daredevil switches back to red costume	3.50
❑351, Apr 1996, 1: The Vice Cop.	2.00
❑352, May 1996, A: Bullseye. V: Bullseye.	2.00
❑353, Jun 1996, V: Mr. Hyde.	2.00
❑354, Jul 1996, A: Spider-Man.	1.50
❑355, Aug 1996, V: Pyro.	1.50
❑356, Sep 1996, V: Enforcers.	1.50
❑357, Oct 1996, V: Enforcers.	1.50
❑358, Nov 1996, V: Mysterio.	1.50
❑359, Dec 1996	1.50
❑360, Jan 1997, V: Absorbing Man.	1.50
❑361, Feb 1997, A: Black Widow.	1.50
❑362, Mar 1997	1.99
❑363, Apr 1997, GC (c); GC (a); 1: Insomnia. V: Insomnia.	1.95
❑364, May 1997, (c)	1.95
❑365, Jun 1997, V: Molten Man.	1.99
❑366, Aug 1997, gatefold summary (c); AW, GC (a)	1.99
❑367, Sep 1997, gatefold summary GC (c); GC (a)	1.99
❑368, Oct 1997, gatefold summary GC (a); V: Omega Red.	1.99
❑369, Nov 1997, gatefold summary (c)	1.99
❑370, Dec 1997, gatefold summary (c); GC (a); A: Black Widow.	1.99
❑371, Jan 1998, gatefold summary; Ghost Rider	1.99
❑372, Feb 1998, gatefold summary A: Ghost Rider.	1.99
❑373, Mar 1998, gatefold summary (c)	1.99
❑374, Apr 1998, gatefold summary	1.99
❑375, May 1998, Giant-size (c); V: Mr. Fear.	2.95
❑376, Jun 1998, gatefold summary; Matt sent deep undercover, regains eyesight	1.99
❑377, Jul 1998, gatefold summary; Matt as Laurent Levasseur with new costume	1.99
❑378, Aug 1998, gatefold summary	1.99
❑379, Sep 1998, gatefold summary; Matt regains his identity and loses sight	1.99
❑380, Oct 1998, Giant-size A: Kingpin.	2.99
❑Annual 1, Sep 1967, Cover reads "King-Size Special"; GC (a); Cover reads King-Size Special	40.00
❑Annual 2, Feb 1971, Cover reads "King-Size Special"; Cover reads King-Size Special	9.00
❑Annual 3, Jan 1972, Cover reads "King-Size Special"; JR (a); Cover reads King-Size Special; Reprints Daredevil #16-17	9.00
❑Annual 4, ca. 1976, JSt (c); AM, JR2, JLee, KJ (a); Reprints	6.00

Other grades: Multiply price above by 5/6 for VF/NM • 2/3 for VERY FINE • 1/3 for FINE • 1/5 for VERY GOOD • 1/8 for GOOD

Daring New Adventures of Supergirl

Series continues as simply "Supergirl"

©DC

Darkchylde (Image)

Troubled girl's nightmares become reality

©Image

Dark Crystal

Henson movie spawns two-issue adaptation

©Marvel

Darker Image

The shadowy reaches of the Image universe

©Image

Darkhawk

Ebony amulet changes teen's life

©Marvel

N-MINT

❑Annual 5, JR2 (a); Cover issue number reads #4, seems to be a mistake; Atlantis Attacks; 1989 annual 4.00
❑Annual 6, TS (a); Lifeform 3.00
❑Annual 7, ca. 1991, BG (a); O: Crippler. 1: Crippler. Von Strucker Gambit..... 2.50
❑Annual 8, ca. 1992, AW (c).............. 2.50
❑Annual 9, ca. 1993, O: Devourer. 1: Devourer. trading card 2.95
❑Annual 10 .... 2.95
❑Annual 1997, Sep 1997, gatefold summary; Daredevil/Deadpool '97; combined annuals for Daredevil and Deadpool... 4.00

DAREDEVIL (VOL. 2)

Marvel

❑½, Nov 1998; gatefold summary KSm (w); JR, KN (a)............................... 5.00
❑1, Nov 1998; gatefold summary KSm (w).. 9.00
❑1/Ltd., Nov 1998; KSm (w); DFE alternate cover signed............. 50.00
❑1/Variant, Nov 1998; KSm (w); DFE alternate cover 11.00
❑2/A, Dec 1998; gatefold summary KSm (w).. 5.00
❑2/B, Dec 1998 KSm (w).................... 5.00
❑3, Jan 1999; gatefold summary; KSm (w); A: Karen Page. A: Foggy Nelson. Matt quits law firm......................... 4.00
❑4, Feb 1999 KSm (w)........................ 4.00
❑5, Mar 1999; KSm (w); A: Mephisto. A: Doctor Strange. D: Karen Page. V: Bullseye. Bullseye cover 4.00
❑5/A, Mar 1999; KSm (w); Black/white/ red cover... 5.00
❑6, Apr 1999 KSm (w); V: Mysterio.... 3.00
❑7, May 1999 KSm (w); D: Karen Page. D: Mysterio. 4.00
❑8, Jun 1999; KSm (w); A: Spider-Man. Karen's funeral 3.00
❑9, Dec 1999 A: Echo. 3.00
❑10, Mar 2000 A: Echo. 3.00
❑11, May 2000 A: Echo. 3.00
❑12, Jun 2000 A: Echo. 3.00
❑13, Oct 2000; A: Echo. Trial of Kingpin 3.00
❑14, Mar 2001 A: Echo....................... 3.00
❑15, Apr 2001 A: Echo. 3.00
❑16, May 2001 BMB (w) 5.00
❑16/Unlimited, May 2001 .... 6.00
❑17, Jun 2001 BMB (w) 3.00
❑17/Unlimited, Jun 2001; Marvel Unlimited newsstand variant........... 5.00
❑18, Jul 2001 BMB (w) 3.00
❑19, Aug 2001 BMB (w) 3.00
❑20, Sep 2001 .... 3.00
❑20/Unlimited, Sep 2001 .... 5.00
❑21, Oct 2001 .... 2.99
❑21/Unlimited, Oct 2001 .... 5.00
❑22, Oct 2001 .... 2.99
❑22/Unlimited, Oct 2001 .... 5.00
❑23, Nov 2001 .... 2.99
❑23/Unlimited, Nov 2001 .... 5.00
❑24, Nov 2001 .... 2.99
❑25, Dec 2001 .... 2.99
❑26, Jan 2002 BMB (w)........................ 2.99
❑27, Feb 2002 BMB (w)........................ 2.99

N-MINT

❑28, Mar 2002; BMB (w); Silent issue 2.99
❑29, Apr 2002 BMB (w) 2.99
❑30, May 2002 BMB (w) 2.99
❑31, Jun 2002 BMB (w) 2.99
❑32, Jul 2002 BMB (w) 2.99
❑33, Aug 2002; BMB (w); Has part 3 of Spider-Man/Jay Leno team-up 2.99
❑34, Sep 2002 BMB (w)....................... 2.99
❑35, Oct 2002 BMB (w); A: Spider-Man. 2.99
❑36, Nov 2002 BMB (w) 2.99
❑36/No #, Nov 2002 .... 5.00
❑37, Dec 2002 BMB (w); A: Elektra.... 2.99
❑37/Unlimited, Dec 2002 .... 5.00
❑37/No #, Dec 2002 .... 4.00
❑38, Dec 2002 BMB (w)........................ 2.99
❑39, Jan 2003 BMB (w) 2.99
❑40, Feb 2003 BMB (w) 2.99
❑41, Mar 2003 BMB (w) 2.99
❑42, Apr 2003 BMB (w) 2.99
❑43, Apr 2003 BMB (w) 2.99
❑44, Apr 2003 BMB (w) 2.99
❑45, May 2003 BMB (w) 2.99
❑46, Jun 2003 BMB (w) 2.99
❑47, Jul 2003 BMB (w) 2.99
❑48, Aug 2003, BMB (w) 2.99
❑49, Sep 2003, BMB (w)....................... 2.99
❑50, Oct 2003, BMB (w) 2.99
❑51, Nov 2003 .... 2.99
❑52, Nov 2003 .... 2.99
❑53, Dec 2003..................................... 2.99
❑54, Jan 2004 .... 2.99
❑55, Feb 2004 .... 2.99
❑56, Mar 2004, BMB (w) 2.99
❑57, Apr 2004, BMB (w) 4.00
❑58, May 2004, BMB (w) 2.99
❑59, Jun 2004, BMB (w) 2.99
❑60, Jul 2004, BMB (w) 2.99
❑61, Aug 2004, BMB (w) 2.99
❑62, Sep 2004, BMB (w)....................... 2.99
❑63, Oct 2004, BMB (w) 2.99
❑64, Nov 2004 .... 2.99
❑65, Dec 2004..................................... 3.99
❑66, Jan 2005 .... 2.99
❑67, Feb 2005 .... 2.99
❑68, Feb 2005 .... 2.99
❑69, Mar 2005 .... 2.99
❑70, Apr 2005 .... 2.99
❑71, May 2005 .... 2.99
❑72, Jun 2005 .... 2.99
❑73, Jul 2005 .... 2.99
❑74, Aug 2005 .... 2.99
❑75, Sep 2005 .... 2.99
❑76, Oct 2005 .... 2.99
❑77, Nov 2005 .... 2.99
❑78, Dec 2005...................................... 2.99
❑79, Jan 2006 .... 2.99
❑80, Feb 2006 .... 2.99
❑81, Mar 2006 .... 2.99
❑82, Apr 2006 .... 2.99
❑83, Jun 2006 .... 2.99
❑84, Jul 2006 .... 2.99
❑85, Aug 2006 .... 2.99
❑86, Sep 2006....................................... 2.99

N-MINT

DAREDEVIL/BATMAN

Marvel

❑1, ca. 1997; prestige format; crossover with DC 5.99

DAREDEVIL: FATHER

Marvel

❑1, Jun 2004 .... 3.50
❑1/DirCut, Sep 2005........................... 2.99
❑2, Oct 2005.. 2.99
❑3 2005 .... 2.99
❑4, Jan 2006 .... 2.99
❑5, Feb 2006 .... 2.99

DAREDEVIL: NINJA

Marvel

❑1, Dec 2000....................................... 2.99
❑1/A, Dec 2000.................................... 2.99
❑2, Jan 2001 .... 2.99
❑3, May 2001 .... 2.99

DAREDEVIL/PUNISHER: CHILD'S PLAY

Marvel

❑nn; Reprints Daredevil #182-184...... 4.95

DAREDEVIL: REDEMPTION

Marvel

❑1, Mar 2005....................................... 2.99
❑2, Apr 2005 .... 2.99
❑3, May 2005 .... 2.99
❑4, Jun 2005.. 2.99
❑5, Jul 2005 .... 2.99
❑6, Aug 2005....................................... 2.99

DAREDEVIL/SHI

Marvel

❑1, Feb 1997, AW (a); crossover with Crusade 3.00

DAREDEVIL/SPIDER-MAN

Marvel

❑1, Jan 2001 .... 2.99
❑1/A, Jan 2000.................................... 2.99
❑2, Feb 2001 .... 2.99
❑3, Mar 2001....................................... 2.99
❑4, Apr 2001 .... 2.99

DAREDEVIL THE MAN WITHOUT FEAR

Marvel

❑1, Oct 1993; FM (w); AW, JR2 (a); O: Daredevil. Partial foil cover......... 3.50
❑2, Nov 1993; FM (w); AW, JR2 (a); Partial foil cover............................. 3.50
❑3, Dec 1993; FM (w); AW, JR2 (a); cardstock cover 3.50
❑4, Jan 1994; FM (w); AW, JR2 (a); Partial foil cover............................. 3.00
❑5, Feb 1994; FM (w); AW, JR2 (a); cardstock cover 3.00

DAREDEVIL: THE TARGET

Marvel

❑1, Jan 2003 .... 3.50

DAREDEVIL VS. VAPORA

Marvel

❑nn, ca. 1996, Fire-prevention comic; giveaway 1.25

N-MINT

DAREDEVIL VS. PUNISHER
MARVEL

❑1, Aug 2005 ... 2.99
❑2, Sep 2005 ... 2.99
❑3, Oct 2005 ... 2.99
❑4, Nov 2005 ... 2.99
❑5, Dec 2005 ... 2.99
❑6, Jan 2006 ... 2.99

DAREDEVIL: YELLOW
MARVEL

❑1, Aug 2001 ... 3.50
❑2, Sep 2001 ... 3.50
❑3, Oct 2001 ... 3.50
❑4, Nov 2001 ... 3.50
❑5, Dec 2001 ... 3.50
❑6, Jan 2002 ... 3.50

DARERAT/TADPOLE
MIGHTY PUMPKIN

❑1, Feb 1987, b&w; parody of Frank Miller's Daredevil work; flip book with Tadpole: Prankster back-up; color poster ... 1.95

DARIA JONTAK
JMJ

❑1, Jan 2001 ... 4.99

DARING ADVENTURES (2ND SERIES)
I.W.

❑9, ca. 1963 ... 20.00
❑10, ca. 1963 ... 20.00
❑11, ca. 1964 ... 20.00
❑12, ca. 1964 ... 40.00
❑13, ca. 1964 ... 20.00
❑14, ca. 1964 ... 20.00
❑15, ca. 1964 ... 20.00
❑16, ca. 1964 ... 20.00
❑17, ca. 1964 ... 20.00
❑18, ca. 1964 ... 20.00

DARING ADVENTURES (3RD SERIES)
B COMICS

❑1 1993 ... 2.00
❑2, Jul 1993 ... 2.00
❑3 1993 ... 2.00

DARING COMICS
MARVEL

❑9, Fal 1944 ... 1100.00
❑10, Win 1944 ... 950.00
❑11, Sum 1945 ... 875.00
❑12, Fal 1945 ... 875.00

DARING ESCAPES
IMAGE

❑1, Sep 1998 ... 2.50
❑1/Variant, Sep 1998; alternate cover ... 2.50
❑2, Oct 1998 ... 2.50
❑3, Nov 1998 ... 2.50
❑4, Dec 1998 ... 2.50

DARING NEW ADVENTURES OF SUPERGIRL
DC

❑1, Nov 1982, Cl (a); O: Supergirl. 1: Psi ... 2.50
❑2, Dec 1982 ... 2.00
❑3, Jan 1983, 1: The Council. ... 2.00
❑4, Feb 1983, 1: The Gang. ... 1.50
❑5, Mar 1983 ... 1.50
❑6, Apr 1983, 1: Matrix-Prime. ... 1.50
❑7, May 1983 ... 1.50
❑8, Jun 1983, 1: Reactron. A: The Doom Patrol ... 1.50
❑9, Jul 1983, A: The Doom Patrol. ... 1.50
❑10, Aug 1983 ... 1.50
❑11, Sep 1983 ... 1.50
❑12, Oct 1983 ... 1.50
❑13, Nov 1983, 1: Blackstarr. New costume; Series continues as Supergirl ... 1.50

DARK (VOL. 1)
CONTINUÜM

❑1, Jun 1993, blue foil cover ... 2.00
❑1/Variant, Jun 1993; red foil cover ... 2.00
❑1/2nd, Jun 1993; blue foil cover ... 2.00
❑1/3rd, Oct 1993, blue foil cover ... 2.00
❑2, Jul 1993 ... 2.00
❑3, Aug 1993; GP (c); GP (a); foil cover ... 2.00
❑3/Autographed, Aug 1993; GP (a); foil cover ... 2.00
❑4, Sep 1993 ... 2.00
❑5, Feb 1994 ... 2.00
❑6, Mar 1994 ... 2.00
❑7, Jul 1994 ... 2.00
❑7/2nd, Jul 1994; blue foil cover ... 2.00

DARK (VOL. 2)
CONTINUÜM

❑1, Jan 1995 ... 2.00
❑1/A, Jan 1995; enhanced cover ... 2.50
❑2, Feb 1995 ... 2.25
❑3, Mar 1995 ... 2.50
❑4, Apr 1995 ... 2.50

DARK (AUGUST HOUSE)
AUGUST HOUSE

❑1, May 1995; enhanced cover ... 2.50
❑2, Jun 1995 ... 2.50

DARK ADVENTURES
DARKLINE

❑1 ... 1.25
❑2 ... 1.75
❑3 ... 1.50
❑4 ... 1.25

DARK ANGEL (1ST SERIES)
BONEYARD

❑1, May 1997, b&w ... 2.25
❑2, Sep 1991 ... 2.25
❑3, Oct 1991 ... 2.25

DARK ANGEL (2ND SERIES)
MARVEL

❑6, Dec 1992, Title changes to Dark Angel; Series continued from Hell's Angel #5 ... 1.75
❑7, Jan 1993 ... 1.75
❑8, Feb 1993 ... 1.75
❑9, Apr 1993 ... 1.75
❑10, May 1993 ... 1.75
❑11, Jun 1993 ... 1.75
❑12, Jul 1993 ... 1.75
❑13, Aug 1993 ... 1.75
❑14, Sep 1993 ... 1.75
❑15, Oct 1993 ... 1.75
❑16, Nov 1993 ... 1.75
❑17, Dec 1993 ... 1.75

DARK ANGEL (3RD SERIES)
BONEYARD

❑1 1997 ... 4.95
❑2, Aug 1997 ... 1.95
❑3, Sep 1997 ... 1.95

DARK ANGEL (4TH SERIES)
CPM MANGA

❑1, ... 2.95
❑2, Jun 1999 ... 2.95
❑3, Jul 1999 ... 2.95
❑4, Aug 1999 ... 2.95
❑5, Sep 1999 ... 2.95
❑6, Oct 1999 ... 2.95
❑7, Nov 1999 ... 2.95
❑8, Dec 1999 ... 2.95
❑9, Jan 2000 ... 2.95
❑10, Feb 2000 ... 2.95
❑11, Mar 2000 ... 2.95
❑12, Apr 2000 ... 2.95
❑13, May 2000 ... 2.95
❑14, Jun 2000 ... 2.95
❑15, Jul 2000 ... 2.95
❑16, Aug 2000 ... 2.95
❑17, Sep 2000 ... 2.95
❑18, Oct 2000 ... 2.95
❑19, Nov 2000 ... 2.95
❑20, Dec 2000 ... 2.95
❑21, Jan 2001 ... 2.95
❑22, Feb 2001 ... 2.95
❑23, Mar 2001 ... 2.95
❑24, Apr 2001 ... 2.95
❑25, May 2001 ... 2.95
❑26, Jun 2001 ... 2.95
❑27, Jul 2001 ... 2.95
❑28, Aug 2001 ... 2.95
❑29, Sep 2001 ... 2.95

DARK ANGEL: PHOENIX RESURRECTION
IMAGE

❑1, May 2000 ... 2.95
❑2, Aug 2000 ... 2.95
❑3, Mar 2001 ... 2.95
❑4, Oct 2001 ... 2.95

DARK ASSASSIN
SILVERWOLF

❑1, Feb 1987, b&w; cardstock cover ... 1.50

DARK ASSASSIN (VOL. 2)
GREATER MERCURY

❑1, Jul 1989 ... 1.50
❑2, Aug 1989 ... 1.50
❑3, Sep 1989; Cover says Sep, indicia says Aug ... 1.50
❑4, Jul 1990 ... 1.50
❑5, Sep 1990 ... 1.50
❑6, ca. 1990 ... 1.50
❑7, Dec 1990; Title changes to Dark Assassin and Chance ... 1.50
❑8, Mar 1991 ... 1.50
❑9, May 1991 ... 1.50

DARKCHYLDE (MAXIMUM)
MAXIMUM

❑1, Jun 1996 ... 3.00
❑2, Jul 1996 ... 2.50
❑3, Sep 1996 ... 2.50

DARKCHYLDE (IMAGE)
IMAGE

❑0/A, Mar 1998 ... 2.50
❑0/B, Mar 1998, b&w; Variant Cover Another Universe ... 2.50
❑0/C, Mar 1998 ... 2.50
❑½, Aug 1997; Wizard 1/2 edition; purple background, girl sitting on skull ... 3.00
❑½/Variant, Aug 1997; Wizard 1/2 edition; Black background, demoness ... 3.00
❑1 ... 5.00
❑1/American Ent; American Entertainment variant ... 5.00
❑1/B; Magazine-style variant ... 7.00
❑1/Convention; San Diego Comic-Con variant (Darkchylde with wings standing on front); Flip-book with Glory/Angela #1 ... 5.00
❑2 ... 5.00
❑2/A; Spider-Web/Moon variant cover ... 5.00
❑3 ... 5.00
❑3/A; All-white variant ... 2.50
❑4/A, Mar 1997; was Maximum Press title; Image begins as publisher ... 2.50
❑4/B, Mar 1997; "Fear" Edition; alternate cover; Image begins as publisher ... 2.50
❑5/A, Sep 1997; variant cover ... 2.50
❑5/B, Sep 1997; alternate cover ... 2.50
❑5/C, Sep 1997; alternate cover ... 2.50
❑Ashcan 1; Preview edition ... 2.00
❑Ashcan 1/Gold; Preview edition; Gold logo ... 3.00
❑Ashcan 1/Ltd. ... 5.00

DARKCHYLDE REMASTERED
IMAGE

❑0, Mar 1998 ... 2.50
❑1/A, May 1997; reprints Darkchylde #1 with corrections ... 2.50
❑1/B, May 1997; alternate cover; reprints Darkchylde #1 with corrections ... 2.50
❑2, Sep 1998; reprints Darkchylde #2 with corrections ... 2.50
❑3, Nov 1998; reprints Darkchylde #3 with corrections ... 2.50

DARKCHYLDE SKETCHBOOK
IMAGE

❑1, ca. 1998 ... 3.00

DARKCHYLDE SUMMER SWIMSUIT SPECTACULAR
DC / WILDSTORM

❑1, Aug 1999; pin-ups ... 3.95

DARKCHYLDE SWIMSUIT ILLUSTRATED
IMAGE

❑1, ca. 1998; JLee (a); pin-ups ... 3.50
❑1/Gold; JLee (a); Gold logo ... 4.50

DARKCHYLDE THE DIARY
IMAGE

❑1/A, Jun 1997; pin-ups with diary entries ... 2.50
❑1/B, Jun 1997; alternate cover; pin-ups with diary entries ... 2.50

Darkhold

Pages of ancient book cause chaos
©Marvel

Dark Horse Comics

Companion series to Dark Horse Presents
©Dark Horse

Dark Horse Presents

Long-running anthology spawned many titles
©Dark Horse

Dark Horse Presents: Aliens

Color reprints of Dark Horse Presents stories
©Dark Horse

Dark Knight Strikes Again

Less-beloved sequel to Miller's blockbuster
©DC

N-MINT

❑1/C, Jun 1997; alternate cover; pin-ups with diary entries 2.50
❑1/D, Jun 1997; alternate cover; pin-ups with diary entries 2.50

DARKCHYLDE: THE LEGACY
IMAGE

❑1, Aug 1998; cardstock cover 2.50
❑1/A, Aug 1998; DFE alternate chrome cover 4.00
❑1/Variant, Aug 1998; DFE alternate chrome cover 4.00
❑2, Dec 1998 ..... 2.50
❑2/Variant, Dec 1998; alternate cover. 2.50
❑3, Jun 1999 ..... 2.50

DARK CLAW ADVENTURES
DC / AMALGAM

❑1, Jun 1997 ..... 1.95

DARK CONVENTION BOOK
CONTINUÜM

❑1 ..... 1.95

DARK CROSSINGS: DARK CLOUD RISING
IMAGE

❑1, Sep 2003 ..... 5.95

DARK CROSSINGS
IMAGE

❑1, Jun 2000 ..... 5.95
❑2, Oct 2000 ..... 5.95

DARK CROSSINGS: DARK CLOUDS OVERHEAD
IMAGE

❑1, Jun 2000; prestige format; cover says Dark Crossings: Dark Clouds Rising 5.95

DARK CRYSTAL
MARVEL

❑1, Apr 1983 ..... 1.25
❑2, May 1983 ..... 1.25

DARK DAYS: A 30 DAYS OF NIGHT SEQUEL
IDEA & DESIGN WORKS

❑1, ca. 2003 ..... 8.00
❑2, ca. 2003 ..... 5.00
❑3, ca. 2003 ..... 4.00
❑4, ca. 2003 ..... 4.00
❑5, ca. 2003 ..... 4.00
❑6, ca. 2004 ..... 4.00
❑Book 1, ca. 2004 ..... 19.99

DARK DESTINY
ALPHA

❑1, Oct 1994, b&w; cardstock cover .. 3.50

DARKDEVIL
MARVEL

❑1, Nov 2000 ..... 2.99
❑2, Dec 2000 ..... 2.99
❑3, Jan 2001 ..... 2.99

DARK DOMINION
DEFIANT

❑1, Oct 1993 ..... 2.50
❑2, Nov 1993 ..... 2.50
❑3, Dec 1993 ..... 2.50
❑4, Jan 1994 ..... 2.50
❑5, Feb 1994 ..... 2.50
❑6, Mar 1994 ..... 2.50
❑7, Apr 1994 ..... 2.50
❑8, May 1994 ..... 2.50
❑9, Jun 1994 ..... 2.50
❑10, Jul 1994 ..... 2.50
❑11, Aug 1994 ..... 2.50
❑12, Sep 1994 ..... 2.50
❑13, Oct 1994 ..... 2.50

DARKER IMAGE
IMAGE

❑1, Mar 1993 RL, JLee (a); 1: Maxx. 1: Deathblow. 2.50
❑1/Gold, Mar 1993; RL, JLee (a); 1: Maxx. 1: Deathblow. Gold logo... 4.00
❑1/Ltd., Mar 1993; White limited edition cover; RL, JLee (a); 1: Maxx. 1: Deathblow. White cover. 4.00

DARK FANTASY
APPLE

❑1, Sep 1992, b&w 2.75

DARK FRINGE
BRAINSTORM

❑2, Dec 1996, b&w 2.95

DARK GUARD
MARVEL

❑1, Oct 1993; 1: The Time Guardian. Prism cover 2.95
❑2, Nov 1993 ..... 1.75
❑3, Dec 1993 ..... 1.75
❑4, Jan 1994 ..... 1.75
❑5 ..... 1.75

DARKHAWK
MARVEL

❑1, Mar 1991 O: Darkhawk. 1: Darkhawk. A: Hobgoblin. 2.00
❑2, Apr 1991 A: Hobgoblin. A: Spider-Man. 1.50
❑3, May 1991 A: Hobgoblin. A: Spider-Man. 1.50
❑4, Jun 1991 ..... 1.50
❑5, Jul 1991 ..... 1.50
❑6, Aug 1991 A: Daredevil. A: Captain America. 1.50
❑7, Sep 1991 ..... 1.50
❑8, Oct 1991 ..... 1.50
❑9, Nov 1991 A: Punisher. 1.50
❑10, Dec 1991 ..... 1.50
❑11, Jan 1992 ..... 1.50
❑12, Feb 1992 V: Tombstone. 1.50
❑13, Mar 1992 A: Venom. 1.50
❑14, Apr 1992 A: Venom. 1.50
❑15, May 1992 ..... 1.25
❑16, Jun 1992 V: Peristrike Force. 1.25
❑17, Jul 1992 V: Peristrike Force. 1.25
❑18, Aug 1992 ..... 1.25
❑19, Sep 1992 A: Spider-Man. 1.25
❑20, Oct 1992 A: Sleepwalker. A: Spider-Man. 1.25
❑21, Nov 1992 O: Darkhawk. 1.25
❑22, Dec 1992 A: Ghost Rider. 1.25
❑23, Jan 1993 ..... 1.25
❑24, Feb 1993 ..... 1.25
❑25, Mar 1993; Double-size; O: Darkhawk armor. foil cover 2.95
❑26, Apr 1993 A: New Warriors. 1.25
❑27, May 1993 ..... 1.25
❑28, Jun 1993 ..... 1.25
❑29, Jul 1993 ..... 1.25
❑30, Aug 1993; Infinity Crusade crossover 1.25
❑31, Sep 1993; Infinity Crusade crossover 1.25
❑32, Oct 1993 ..... 1.25
❑33, Nov 1993 ..... 1.25
❑34, Dec 1993 ..... 1.25
❑35, Jan 1994 A: Venom. 1.25
❑36, Feb 1994 A: Venom. 1.25
❑37, Mar 1994 A: Venom. 1.25
❑38, Apr 1994 ..... 1.25
❑39, May 1994 ..... 1.50
❑40, Jun 1994 ..... 1.50
❑41, Jul 1994 ..... 1.50
❑42, Aug 1994 ..... 1.50
❑43, Sep 1994 ..... 1.50
❑44, Oct 1994 ..... 1.50
❑45, Nov 1994 ..... 1.50
❑46, Dec 1994 ..... 1.50
❑47, Jan 1995 ..... 1.50
❑48, Feb 1995 ..... 1.50
❑49, Mar 1995 ..... 1.50
❑50, Apr 1995; Giant-size 2.50
❑Annual 1 ..... 2.50
❑Annual 2 1: Dreamkiller. 2.95
❑Annual 3 ..... 2.95

DARKHOLD
MARVEL

❑1/CS, Oct 1992; Midnight Sons 2.75
❑2, Nov 1992 ..... 1.75
❑3, Dec 1992 ..... 1.75
❑4, Jan 1993 ..... 1.75
❑5, Feb 1993 ..... 1.75
❑6, Mar 1993 ..... 1.75
❑7, Mar 1993 ..... 1.75
❑8, Apr 1993 ..... 1.75
❑9, May 1993 ..... 1.75
❑10, Jun 1993 ..... 1.75
❑11, Jul 1993; Double-cover 1.75
❑12, Aug 1993 ..... 1.75
❑13, Sep 1993; Missing CCA approval stamp 1.75
❑14, Oct 1993 ..... 1.75
❑15, Nov 1993 ..... 1.75
❑16, Dec 1993 ..... 1.75

DARK HORSE CLASSICS: ALIENS VERSUS PREDATOR
DARK HORSE

❑1, Feb 1997; Reprints Aliens Vs. Predator #1 with new cover 2.95
❑2, Mar 1997; Reprints Aliens Vs. Predator #2 with new cover 2.95
❑3, Apr 1997; Reprints Aliens Vs. Predator #3 with new cover 2.95
❑4, May 1997; Reprints Aliens Vs. Predator #4 with new cover 2.95
❑5, Jun 1997; Reprints Aliens Vs. Predator #5 with new cover 2.95

Other grades: Multiply price above by 5/6 for VF/NM • 2/3 for VERY FINE • 1/3 for FINE • 1/5 for VERY GOOD • 1/8 for GOOD

- ❑6, Jul 1997; Reprints Aliens Vs. Predator #6 with new cover ... 2.95

DARK HORSE CLASSICS: GODZILLA
DARK HORSE

- ❑1, Apr 1998 ... 2.95

DARK HORSE CLASSICS: GODZILLA: KING OF THE MONSTERS
DARK HORSE

- ❑1, Jul 1998 ... 2.95
- ❑2, Aug 1998; Can G-Force Survive? In the Grip of Godzilla! ... 2.95
- ❑3, Sep 1998; No Blast from the Past-Godzilla Rules! ... 2.95
- ❑4, Oct 1998 ... 2.95
- ❑5, Nov 1998 ... 2.95
- ❑6, Dec 1998 ... 2.95

DARK HORSE CLASSICS: STAR WARS: DARK EMPIRE
DARK HORSE

- ❑1, Mar 1997 ... 2.95
- ❑2, Apr 1997 ... 2.95
- ❑3, May 1997 ... 2.95
- ❑4, Jun 1997 ... 2.95
- ❑5, Jul 1997 ... 2.95
- ❑6, Aug 1997 ... 2.95

DARK HORSE CLASSICS: TERROR OF GODZILLA
DARK HORSE

- ❑1, Aug 1998; Translation by Mike Richardson and Randy Stradley of Viz Communications ... 2.95
- ❑2, Sep 1998; Translation by Mike Richardson and Randy Stradley of Viz Communications ... 2.95
- ❑3, Oct 1998; Translation by Mike Richardson and Randy Stradley of Viz Communications ... 2.95
- ❑4, Nov 1998 ... 2.95
- ❑5, Dec 1998 ... 2.95
- ❑6, Jan 1999 ... 2.95

DARK HORSE COMICS
DARK HORSE

- ❑1, Aug 1992; 1: Time Cop. wraparound gatefold cover; Predator, RoboCop, Time Cop, Renegade ... 3.50
- ❑2, Sep 1992; RoboCop, Renegade, Time Cop, Predator ... 2.50
- ❑3, Oct 1992 ... 2.50
- ❑4, Nov 1992; Aliens, Predator, Indiana Jones, Mad Dogs ... 2.50
- ❑5, Dec 1992; Aliens, Predator, Indiana Jones, Mad Dogs ... 2.50
- ❑6, Jan 1993; RoboCop, Predator, Indiana Jones, Mad Dogs ... 2.50
- ❑7, Feb 1993; RoboCop, Star Wars, Mad Dogs, Predator ... 5.00
- ❑8, Mar 1993; 1: X. RoboCop, James Bond, Star Wars ... 5.00
- ❑9, Apr 1993; 2: X. 2: X. James Bond, Star Wars, RoboCop ... 4.00
- ❑10, May 1993; X, Predator, Godzilla, James Bond ... 3.00
- ❑11, Jul 1993; Predator, Godzilla, James Bond, Aliens ... 2.50
- ❑12, Aug 1993; Aliens, Predator ... 2.50
- ❑13, Sep 1993; Aliens, Predator, Thing from Another World ... 2.50
- ❑14, Oct 1993; Predator, The Mark, Thing from Another World ... 2.50
- ❑15, Nov 1993 ... 2.50
- ❑16, Dec 1993 ... 2.50
- ❑17, Jan 1994 ... 2.50
- ❑18, Feb 1994; Aliens, Star Wars: Droids, Predator ... 2.50
- ❑19, Mar 1994; X, Aliens, Star Wars: Droids ... 2.50
- ❑20, Apr 1994 ... 2.50
- ❑21, May 1994 ... 2.50
- ❑22, Jun 1994 ... 2.50
- ❑23, Jul 1994; Aliens, The Machine ... 2.50
- ❑24, Aug 1994 ... 2.50
- ❑25, Sep 1994; Flip-book ... 2.50

DARK HORSE DOWN UNDER
DARK HORSE

- ❑1, Jun 1994, b&w ... 2.50
- ❑2, Aug 1994, b&w ... 2.50
- ❑3, Oct 1994, b&w ... 2.50

DARK HORSE MAVERICK 2000
DARK HORSE

- ❑0, Jul 2000 ... 3.95

DARK HORSE MAVERICK 2001
DARK HORSE / MAVERICK

- ❑1, Jul 2001 ... 4.99

DARK HORSE MONSTERS
DARK HORSE

- ❑1, Feb 1997; Reprinted from Dark Horse Presents #33 & #47 ... 2.95

DARK HORSE PRESENTS
DARK HORSE

- ❑1, Jul 1986 1: Concrete. A: Black Cross. ... 4.00
- ❑1/2nd Green, ca. 1992; Commemorative edition; 1: Concrete. A: Black Cross. Green border ... 2.25
- ❑1/2nd Silver, ca. 1992; Silver border ... 2.25
- ❑2, ca. 1986, b&w 2: Concrete. ... 2.50
- ❑3, Nov 1986 A: Concrete. ... 2.50
- ❑4, Jan 1987 A: Concrete. ... 2.50
- ❑5, Feb 1987 PG (c); A: Concrete. ... 2.00
- ❑6, Apr 1987 A: Concrete. ... 2.00
- ❑7, May 1987 ... 2.00
- ❑8, Jun 1987 A: Concrete. ... 2.00
- ❑9, Jul 1987 PG (c); ... 2.00
- ❑10, Sep 1987 1: The Mask. A: Concrete. ... 3.00
- ❑11, Oct 1987 2: The Mask. ... 2.50
- ❑12, Nov 1987 A: Concrete. A: The Mask. ... 2.50
- ❑13, Dec 1987 A: The Mask. ... 2.50
- ❑14, Jan 1987 A: Concrete. A: The Mask. ... 2.50
- ❑15, Feb 1988 A: The Mask. ... 2.50
- ❑16, Mar 1988 A: Concrete. A: The Mask. ... 2.50
- ❑17, Apr 1988 ... 2.00
- ❑18, Jun 1988 A: Concrete. A: The Mask. ... 2.50
- ❑19, Jul 1988 A: The Mask. ... 2.00
- ❑20, Aug 1988; Double Size; A: Flaming Carrot. A: Concrete. A: The Mask. 64 page Annual ... 2.00
- ❑21, Aug 1988 A: The Mask. ... 2.00
- ❑22, Sep 1988 1: Duckman. ... 2.00
- ❑23, Oct 1988 ... 2.00
- ❑24, Nov 1988 O: Aliens. 1: Aliens. ... 6.00
- ❑25, Dec 1988 ... 2.00
- ❑26, Jan 1989 ... 2.00
- ❑27, Feb 1989 ... 2.00
- ❑28, Mar 1989; Double Size ... 3.00
- ❑29, Apr 1989 ... 2.00
- ❑30, May 1989 ... 2.00
- ❑31, Jul 1989 ... 2.00
- ❑32, Aug 1989; Giant-size A: Concrete. ... 3.50
- ❑33, Sep 1989; Giant-size ... 2.50
- ❑34, Nov 1989 ... 3.00
- ❑35, Dec 1989 ... 3.00
- ❑36, Feb 1990; regular cover; Predator pin-up on back cover ... 4.00
- ❑36/A, Feb 1990; painted cover; Predator pin-up on back cover ... 3.00
- ❑37, Mar 1990; Delia & Celia pin-up on back cover ... 2.00
- ❑38, Apr 1990 A: Concrete. ... 2.00
- ❑39, May 1990 ... 2.00
- ❑40, May 1990; Giant-size; MW (a); Wacky Squirrel fold-in on back cover ... 3.00
- ❑41, Jun 1990 ... 2.00
- ❑42, Jul 1990 ... 2.00
- ❑43, Aug 1990 ... 2.00
- ❑44, Sep 1990 ... 2.00
- ❑45, Nov 1990 MW (a); ... 2.00
- ❑46, Nov 1990 ... 2.00
- ❑47, Jan 1991 ... 2.00
- ❑48, Feb 1991; contains Aliens: Earth Wars and Starstruck trading cards ... 2.00
- ❑49, Mar 1991; contains The Mask and checklist trading cards ... 2.00
- ❑50, Apr 1991; contains Bob the Alien and Black Cross trading cards ... 3.00
- ❑51, Jun 1991; FM (w); FM (a); Sin City story continued from Dark Horse Presents Fifth Anniversary Special ... 4.00
- ❑52, Jul 1991 FM (w); FM (a); ... 3.00
- ❑53, Aug 1991 FM (w); FM (a); ... 3.00
- ❑54, Sep 1991 JBy (w); GM, JBy, FM (a); 1: Next Men ... 4.00
- ❑55, Oct 1991 JBy, FM (w); JBy, FM (a); 2: Next Men. ... 2.25
- ❑56, Nov 1991; Double-size; FM (w); JBy, FM (a); "Silverware Anniversary Issue"; cover homage to DC silver anniversary issues ... 3.95
- ❑57, Dec 1991; Giant-size; FM (w); JBy, FM (a); 48-page "Post-Annual"; cover homage to Daredevil #1 ... 3.50
- ❑58, Jan 1992 FM (w); FM (a); ... 2.00
- ❑59, Feb 1992 FM (w); FM (a); ... 2.50
- ❑60, Mar 1992 FM (w); FM (a); ... 2.50
- ❑61, Apr 1992 FM (w); FM (a); ... 2.50
- ❑62, May 1992; FM (w); FM (a); all Sin City issue ... 2.50
- ❑63, Jun 1992 FM (w) ... 2.50
- ❑64, Jul 1992 ... 2.50
- ❑65, Aug 1992; Interact-o-Rama is a scriptwriting contest ... 2.50
- ❑66, Sep 1992 ES (a); ... 2.50
- ❑67, Nov 1992; Double-size issue; CR, ES (a); A: Zoo-Lou. Flash #123 homage cover ... 3.95
- ❑68, Dec 1992 ... 2.50
- ❑69, Feb 1993 ... 2.50
- ❑70, Feb 1993 ... 2.50
- ❑71, Mar 1993 ... 2.50
- ❑72, Apr 1993 ... 2.50
- ❑73, Jun 1993 ... 2.50
- ❑74, Jun 1993 ... 2.50
- ❑75, Jul 1993 CV (a) ... 2.50
- ❑76, Aug 1993 ... 2.50
- ❑77, Sep 1993 ... 2.50
- ❑78, Oct 1993 ... 2.50
- ❑79, Nov 1993 ... 2.50
- ❑80, Dec 1993 ... 3.00
- ❑81, Jan 1994 ... 2.50
- ❑82, Feb 1994 ... 2.50
- ❑83, Mar 1994 ... 2.50
- ❑84, Apr 1994 ... 2.50
- ❑85, May 1994 ... 2.50
- ❑86, Jun 1994 ... 2.50
- ❑87, Jul 1994 ... 2.50
- ❑88, Aug 1994; Hellboy ... 2.50
- ❑89, Sep 1994; Hellboy ... 2.50
- ❑90, Oct 1994 ... 2.50
- ❑91, Nov 1994 ... 2.50
- ❑92, Dec 1994 A: Too Much Coffee Man. ... 2.50
- ❑93, Jan 1995 A: Too Much Coffee Man. ... 2.50
- ❑94, Feb 1995 ... 2.50
- ❑95, Mar 1995 A: Too Much Coffee Man. ... 2.50
- ❑96, Apr 1995 ... 2.50
- ❑97, May 1995 ... 2.50
- ❑98, Jun 1995 ... 2.50
- ❑99, Jul 1995 ... 2.50
- ❑100.1, Aug 1995; FM, DSt (c); FM, DSt (w); FM, DSt (a); Issue 100 #1 ... 2.50
- ❑100.2, Aug 1995; Issue 100 #2: Hellboy cover and story ... 2.50
- ❑100.3, Aug 1995; Issue 100 #3; Concrete cover and story ... 2.50
- ❑100.4, Aug 1995; DaG (c); FM (w); Martha Washington story; Issue 100 #4 ... 2.50
- ❑100½, Aug 1995; Issue 100 #5 ... 2.50
- ❑101, Sep 1995 BWr (a); A: Aliens ... 2.50
- ❑102, Oct 1995 ... 2.50
- ❑103, Nov 1995; JK (a); Kirby centerfold; Mr. Painter, One-Trick Rip-Off, The Pink Tornado, Hairball ... 2.95
- ❑104, Dec 1995 ... 2.95
- ❑105, Jan 1996 ... 2.95
- ❑106, Feb 1996 ... 2.95
- ❑107, Mar 1996 ... 2.95
- ❑108, Apr 1996 ... 2.95
- ❑109, May 1996 ... 2.95
- ❑110, Jun 1996 ... 2.95
- ❑111, Jul 1996 ... 2.95
- ❑112, Aug 1996 ... 2.95
- ❑113, Sep 1996 ... 2.95
- ❑114, Oct 1996; FM (w); FM (a); Star Slammers, Lance Blastoff, Lowlife, Trypto the Acid Dog ... 2.95
- ❑115, Nov 1996; FM (c); Doctor Spin, The Creep, Lowlife, Trypto the Acid Dog ... 2.95
- ❑116, Dec 1996; Fat Dog Mendoza, Trypto the Acid Dog, Doctor Spin ... 2.95
- ❑117, Jan 1997; GC (a); Aliens, Trypto the Acid Dog, Doctor Spin ... 2.95
- ❑118, Feb 1997; Monkeyman & O'Brien, Hectic Planet, Trypto the Acid Dog, Doctor Spin ... 2.95
- ❑119, Mar 1997; Monkeyman & O'Brien, Hectic Planet, Trout, Predator ... 2.95

Other grades: Multiply price above by 5/6 for VF/NM • 2/3 for VERY FINE • 1/3 for FINE • 1/5 for VERY GOOD • 1/8 for GOOD

Darkman (Vol. 1)

Rare case of movie super-hero coming to comics

©Marvel

Dark Mansion of Forbidden Love

Horror meets romance in hotly collected series

©DC

Darkness

Mob hit man makes deal with devil

©Top Cow

Dark Shadows (Gold Key)

Creepy Gothic soap opera comes to comics

©Gold Key

Darkstars

Intergalactic security-for-hire force

©DC

N-MINT

❑120, Apr 1997; One Last Job, The Lords of Misrule, Trout, Hectic Planet ... 2.95
❑121, May 1997; Jack Zero, Aliens, The Lords of Misrule, Trout ... 2.95
❑122, Jun 1997; Jack Zero, Imago, Trout, The Lords of Misrule ... 2.95
❑123, Jul 1997; Imago, Jack Zero, Trout ... 2.95
❑124, Aug 1997; Predator, Jack Zero, Outside, Inside ... 2.95
❑125, Sep 1997 ... 2.95
❑126, Oct 1997 ... 2.95
❑127, Nov 1997; Nocturnals, Metalfer, Stiltskin, Blue Monday ... 2.95
❑128, Jan 1998; Dan & Larry, Metalfer, Stiltskin ... 2.95
❑129, Feb 1998 ... 2.95
❑130, Mar 1998; Dan & Larry, Wanted Man, Mary Walker: The Woman ... 2.95
❑131, Apr 1998; Girl Crazy, The Fall, Dan & Larry, Boogie Picker ... 2.95
❑132, Apr 1998; The Fall, Dan & Larry, Dirty Pair ... 2.95
❑133, May 1998; Carson of Venus, The Fall, Dirty Pair, Blue Monday ... 2.95
❑134, Jul 1998 ... 2.95
❑135, Sep 1998; Carson of Venus, The Mark, The Fall, The Ark ... 3.50
❑136, Oct 1998; The Ark, Spirit of the Badlander ... 2.95
❑137, Nov 1998; Predator, The Ark, My Vagabond Days ... 2.95
❑138, Dec 1998; Terminator, The Moth, My Vagabond Days ... 2.95
❑139, Jan 1999; Roachmill, Saint Slayer ... 2.95
❑140, Feb 1999; Aliens, Usagi Yojimbo, Saint Slayer ... 2.95
❑141, Mar 1999; Buffy the Vampire Slayer ... 2.95
❑142, Apr 1999; 1: Doctor Gosburo Coffin. Codex Arcana ... 2.95
❑143, May 1999; TY (w); TY (a); Tarzan: Tales of Pellucidar ... 2.95
❑144, Jun 1999; The Vortex, Burglar Girls, Galactic Jack ... 2.95
❑145, Jul 1999; Burglar Girls ... 2.95
❑146, Sep 1999; Aliens vs Predator ... 2.95
❑147, Oct 1999; Ragnok ... 2.95
❑148, Oct 1999 ... 2.95
❑149, Dec 1999 ... 2.95
❑150, Jan 2000; Giant-size ... 4.50
❑151, Feb 2000, b&w ... 2.95
❑152, Mar 2000, b&w ... 2.95
❑153, Apr 2000, b&w; Flipbook ... 2.95
❑154, May 2000, b&w ... 2.95
❑155, Jul 2000, b&w ... 2.95
❑156, Aug 2000, b&w ... 2.95
❑157, Sep 2000, b&w; Last issue of the series ... 2.95
❑Annual 1997, Feb 1998, b&w; GM (a); cover says 1997, indicia says 1998 ... 4.95
❑Annual 1998, Sep 1998, b&w; Hellboy, Buffy, Skeleton Key, The Ark, My Vagabond Days, Infirmary ... 4.95
❑Annual 1999, Aug 1999; SA, ME (w); SA (a); Dark Horse Jr. ... 4.95
❑Annual 2000, Jun 2000; Flip-book PD (w) ... 4.95

N-MINT

DARK HORSE PRESENTS: ALIENS
DARK HORSE

❑1, ca. 1992; color reprints; Reprints Aliens stories from Dark Horse Presents ... 4.95
❑1/A, ca. 1992; Promotion only ... 4.95

DARK ISLAND
DAVDEZ

❑1, May 1998, b&w ... 2.95
❑2, Jun 1998, b&w ... 2.95
❑3, Jul 1998, b&w ... 2.50

DARK KNIGHT STRIKES AGAIN
DC

❑1, ca. 2001; Only DK2 on cover ... 3.00
❑1/A, ca. 2001; Full title on cover; Variant cover edition ... 5.00
❑2, ca. 2002; Only DK2 on cover ... 3.00
❑2/A, ca. 2002; Full title on cover; Variant cover edition ... 4.00
❑3, ca. 2002; Only DK2 on cover ... 3.00
❑3/A, ca. 2002; Full title on cover; Variant cover edition ... 4.00

DARKLIGHT: PRELUDE
SIRIUS

❑1, Jan 1994, b&w ... 2.95
❑2, b&w ... 2.95
❑3, b&w ... 2.95

DARKLON THE MYSTIC
PACIFIC

❑1, Nov 1983 ... 2.00

DARKMAN (VOL. 1)
MARVEL

❑1, Oct 1990 BH (c); BH (a) ... 2.00
❑2, Nov 1990 BH (c); BH (a) ... 1.50
❑3, Dec 1990 BH (c); BH (a) ... 1.50

DARKMAN (VOL. 2)
MARVEL

❑1, Apr 1993 ... 3.95
❑2, May 1993 ... 2.95
❑3, Jun 1993 ... 2.95
❑4, Jul 1993 ... 2.95
❑5, Aug 1993 ... 2.95
❑6, Sep 1993 ... 2.95

DARKMAN (MAGAZINE)
MARVEL

❑1, Sep 1990, b&w; Magazine size ... 2.25

DARK MANSION OF FORBIDDEN LOVE
DC

❑1, Sep 1971 TD (a) ... 125.00
❑2, Nov 1971 ... 50.00
❑3, Jan 1972 DH (a) ... 50.00
❑4, Mar 1972; Series continued in Forbidden Tales of Dark Mansion #5 ... 50.00

DARKMINDS
IMAGE

❑½, May 1999 ... 2.50
❑1, Jul 1998 ... 3.50
❑1/Gold, Aug 1998; DFE gold foil edition ... 4.00
❑1/Variant, Jul 1998; alternate cover (solo figure) ... 3.50
❑1/2nd ... 2.50
❑2, Aug 1998 ... 3.00
❑2/Variant, Aug 1998; alternate cover ... 3.00

N-MINT

❑3, Sep 1998 ... 3.00
❑3/Variant, Sep 1998; alternate cover. 3.00
❑4, Oct 1998; cover says Dec, indicia says Oct ... 3.00
❑5, Nov 1998 ... 2.50
❑6, Dec 1998 ... 2.50
❑7, Feb 1999 ... 2.50
❑8, Apr 1999 ... 2.50

DARKMINDS (VOL. 2)
IMAGE

❑0, Jul 2000 ... 2.50
❑1, Feb 2000 ... 2.50
❑2, Mar 2000 ... 2.50
❑3, Apr 2000 ... 2.50
❑4, May 2000 ... 2.50
❑5, Jun 2000 ... 2.50
❑6, Sep 2000 ... 2.50
❑7, Oct 2000 ... 2.50
❑8, Nov 2000 ... 2.50
❑9, Feb 2001 ... 2.50
❑10, Apr 2001 ... 2.50

DARKMINDS: MACROPOLIS
IMAGE

❑1/A ... 2.95
❑1/B ... 2.95
❑2/A, Mar 2002 ... 2.95
❑2/B, Mar 2002 ... 2.95

DARKMINDS: MACROPOLIS (VOL. 2)
DREAMWAVE

❑1, Sep 2003, ... 2.95
❑2, Oct 2003, ... 2.95
❑3, Dec 2003, ... 2.95
❑4, Sep 2004, ... 2.95

DARKMINDS/WITCHBLADE
IMAGE

❑1, Aug 2000 ... 5.95

DARK MISTS
APCOMICS

❑1, Jul 2005 ... 3.50
❑2, Sep 2005 ... 3.50

DARK MOON PROPHESY
DARK MOON PRODUCTIONS

❑1, May 1995; free color and b&w preview of Dark Moon line ... 1.00

DARK NEMESIS (VILLAINS)
DC

❑1, Feb 1998; New Year's Evil ... 1.95

DARKNESS
TOP COW

❑0 ... 3.00
❑½, ca. 1996; Wizard mail-away promotion ... 3.00
❑½/Variant, ca. 1996; Christmas cover; Wizard mail-away promotion ... 3.00
❑½/2nd, Mar 2001 ... 2.95
❑1, Dec 1996 ... 3.00
❑1/A, Dec 1996; Dark cover variant ... 3.00
❑1/B, Dec 1996; Wizard Ace edition; Variant ... 3.00
❑1/C, Dec 1996; Fan club edition ... 3.00
❑1/Gold, Dec 1996; Gold edition ... 3.00
❑1/Platinum, Dec 1996; Platinum edition; Platinum cover ... 8.00

Other grades: Multiply price above by 5/6 for VF/NM • 2/3 for VERY FINE • 1/3 for FINE • 1/5 for VERY GOOD • 1/8 for GOOD

❑2, Jan 1997 ... 3.00
❑3, Mar 1997 ... 3.00
❑4, May 1997 ... 3.00
❑5, Jun 1997 ... 3.00
❑6, Jul 1997 ... 3.00
❑7, Aug 1997 ... 2.50
❑7/A, Aug 1997; Variant cover with Michael Turner and babes ... 2.50
❑8, Oct 1997 ... 2.50
❑8/A, Oct 1997; alternate cover ... 2.50
❑8/B, Oct 1997; alternate cover ... 2.50
❑8/C, Oct 1997; alternate cover ... 2.50
❑9, Nov 1997 ... 2.50
❑9/A, Nov 1997; alternate cover ... 2.50
❑10, Dec 1997 ... 2.50
❑10/A, Dec 1997; alternate cover (gold) 2.50
❑10/B, Dec 1997; alternate cover (gold) 2.50
❑11/A, Jan 1998; chromium cover ... 8.00
❑11/B, Jan 1998 ... 2.50
❑11/C, Jan 1998 ... 2.50
❑11/D, Jan 1998 ... 2.50
❑11/E, Jan 1998 ... 2.50
❑11/F, Jan 1998 ... 2.50
❑11/G, Jan 1998 ... 2.50
❑11/H, Jan 1998 ... 2.50
❑11/I, Jan 1998 ... 2.50
❑11/J, Jan 1998; Museum Edition ... 2.50
❑12, Feb 1998 ... 2.50
❑13, Mar 1998 ... 2.50
❑14, Apr 1998 ... 2.50
❑15, Jun 1998 ... 2.50
❑16, Jul 1998 ... 2.50
❑17, Sep 1998 O: Magdalena. ... 2.50
❑18, Nov 1998 ... 2.50
❑19, Jan 1999 ... 2.50
❑20/A, Apr 1999; Regular Cover (with Darklings) ... 2.50
❑20/B, Apr 1999; Museum Edition ... 2.50
❑20/C, Apr 1999; Alternate Cover (With Darklings) ... 2.50
❑21, May 1999 ... 2.50
❑22, Jun 1999 ... 2.50
❑23, Jul 1999 ... 2.50
❑24, Aug 1999 ... 2.50
❑25, Sep 1999 ... 3.99
❑25/A, Sep 1999; Chrome Holofoil variant ... 20.00
❑26, Oct 1999 ... 2.50
❑27, Oct 1999 ... 2.50
❑28, Jan 2000 ... 2.50
❑28/Graham, Jan 2000, Exclusive for Graham Crackers Comics (Naperville, Ill.). Features Keu Cha cover ... 5.00
❑29 2000 ... 2.50
❑30, Apr 2000 ... 2.50
❑31, May 2000 ... 2.50
❑32, Jul 2000 ... 2.50
❑33, Aug 2000 ... 2.50
❑34, Oct 2000 ... 2.50
❑35, Nov 2000 ... 2.50
❑36, Dec 2000 ... 2.50
❑37, Feb 2001 ... 2.50
❑38, Apr 2001 ... 2.50
❑39, May 2001 ... 2.50
❑40, Aug 2001 ... 2.50
❑Ashcan 1, Jul 1996; No cover price; preview of upcoming series ... 3.00
❑Ashcan 1/A; Prelude; "Wizard Authentic" variant ... 3.00

DARKNESS (VOL. 2)
IMAGE

❑1, Dec 2002 ... 4.00
❑1/A, Dec 2002; Black and White ... 2.99
❑1/B, Dec 2002; DF Cover ... 2.99
❑1/C, Dec 2002; Holofoil Cover ... 2.99
❑1/D, Dec 2002; Sketch Cover ... 2.99
❑2, Feb 2003 ... 2.99
❑3, Apr 2003 ... 2.99
❑4, Jun 2003 ... 2.99
❑5, Sep 2003 ... 2.99
❑6, Nov 2003 ... 2.99
❑7, Apr 2004 ... 2.99
❑8, Apr 2004 ... 2.99
❑9, May 2004 ... 2.99
❑10, May 2004 ... 2.99
❑11, Jun 2004 ... 2.99
❑12, Aug 2004 ... 2.99
❑13, Sep 2004 ... 2.99
❑14, Oct 2004 ... 2.99
❑15, Nov 2004 ... 2.99
❑16, Dec 2004 ... 2.99
❑17, Jan 2005 ... 2.99
❑18, Feb 2005 ... 2.99
❑19, Mar 2005 ... 2.99
❑20, Apr 2005 ... 2.99
❑21 2005 ... 2.99
❑22, Sep 2005 ... 2.99
❑23, Oct 2005 ... 2.99
❑24, Nov 2005 ... 2.99

DARKNESS & TOMB RAIDER
TOP COW

❑1 2005 ... 2.99

DARKNESS/BATMAN
IMAGE

❑1, Aug 1999 ... 5.95

DARKNESS COLLECTED EDITION
IMAGE

❑1, Oct 2003 ... 4.95

DARKNESS FALLS: THE TRAGIC LIFE OF MATILDA DIXON
DARK HORSE

❑1, Dec 2002; Movie-based one-shot 2.99

DARKNESS/HULK
IMAGE

❑1, Jul 2004 ... 5.00

DARKNESS INFINITY
IMAGE

❑1, Aug 1999 ... 3.50

DARKNESS: MEGACON ISSUE
IMAGE

❑1, Aug 2003 ... 0.00

DARKNESS/PAINKILLER JANE
IMAGE

❑Ashcan 1 ... 3.00
❑Ashcan 1/A; variant cover ... 3.00

DARKNESS PRELUDE
IMAGE

❑0, Jan 2003, Dynamic Foces Exclusive 4.00
❑0/Dynamic ... 0.00
❑0/A, Jan 2003 ... 4.00

DARKNESS/SUPERMAN
IMAGE

❑1, Feb 2005 ... 2.99
❑2, Mar 2005 ... 2.99

DARKNESS: WANTED DEAD ONE SHOT
IMAGE

❑1, Aug 2003 ... 2.99

DARKNESS/WITCHBLADE SPECIAL
IMAGE

❑1, Dec 1999 ... 3.95

DARK OZ
ARROW

❑1 1997 ... 2.75
❑2 1997 ... 2.75
❑3 1998 ... 2.75
❑4 1998 ... 2.75
❑5 1998; indicia says 97, a misprint .. 2.75

DARK RAT
MAVERICK PULP COMIX

❑1, Sep 1997, b&w ... 2.50

DARK REALM
IMAGE

❑1, Oct 2000 ... 2.95
❑2, Dec 2000 ... 2.95
❑3, Feb 2001 ... 2.95
❑4, Jun 2001 ... 2.95

DARK REGIONS
WHITE WOLF

❑1, Feb 1987 ... 1.75
❑2 ... 1.75
❑3, May 1987 ... 1.75

DARKSEID (VILLAINS)
DC

❑1, Feb 1998; New Year's Evil ... 1.95

DARK SHADOWS (GOLD KEY)
GOLD KEY

❑1, Mar 1969, based on TV series ... 175.00
❑1/A, based on TV series; without poster ... 25.00
❑2, Aug 1969 ... 44.00
❑3, Nov 1969 ... 44.00
❑4, Feb 1970 ... 35.00
❑5, May 1970 ... 35.00
❑6, Aug 1970 ... 25.00
❑7, Nov 1970 ... 25.00
❑8, Feb 1971 ... 25.00
❑9, May 1971 ... 25.00
❑10, Aug 1971 ... 25.00
❑11, Nov 1971 ... 25.00
❑12, Feb 1972 ... 25.00
❑13, Apr 1972 ... 25.00
❑14, Jun 1972, Painted cover ... 25.00
❑15, Aug 1972 ... 25.00
❑16, Oct 1972 ... 16.00
❑17, Dec 1972 ... 16.00
❑18, Feb 1973 ... 16.00
❑19, Apr 1973 ... 16.00
❑20, Jun 1973 ... 16.00
❑21, Aug 1973 ... 14.00
❑22, Oct 1973 ... 14.00
❑23, Dec 1973 ... 14.00
❑24, Feb 1974 ... 14.00
❑25, Apr 1974 ... 14.00
❑26, Jun 1974 ... 14.00
❑27, Aug 1974 ... 14.00
❑28, Oct 1974 ... 14.00
❑29, Nov 1974 ... 14.00
❑30, Dec 1974 ... 14.00
❑31, Apr 1975 ... 14.00
❑32, Jun 1975 ... 14.00
❑33, Aug 1975 ... 14.00
❑34, Nov 1975 ... 14.00
❑35, Feb 1976 ... 14.00
❑Book 1, Synopsis of TV Episodes ... 35.00

DARK SHADOWS (INNOVATION)
INNOVATION

❑1, Jun 1992, TV series ... 3.00
❑2, Aug 1992, TV series ... 2.50
❑3, Nov 1992, TV series ... 2.50
❑4, Spr 1993, TV series ... 2.50
❑5, Jun 1993, Book 2, #1 ... 2.50
❑5/Autographed, Jun 1993, Book 2, #1 2.50
❑6, Jun 1993, Book 2, #2 ... 2.50
❑7, Jun 1993, Book 2, #3 ... 2.50
❑8, Book 2, #4 ... 2.50
❑9, Book 3 #1 ... 2.50

DARK SHRINE
ANTARCTIC

❑1, May 1999 ... 2.99
❑2, Jun 1999 ... 2.50

DARK SHRINE GALLERY
BASEMENT

❑1 ... 3.25

DARKSIDE BLUES
ADV MANGA

❑1, Mar 2004 ... 14.98

DARKSTALKERS
DEVIL'S DUE

❑1 2004 ... 3.00
❑1/Variant 2004 ... 4.00
❑2 2004 ... 3.00
❑2/Variant 2004 ... 4.00
❑3 2005 ... 3.00
❑3/Variant 2005 ... 4.00
❑4 2005 ... 3.00
❑4/Variant 2005 ... 4.00
❑4/Foil 2005 ... 3.00
❑5 2005 ... 4.00
❑5/Variant 2005 ... 3.00
❑5/Foil 2005 ... 4.00

DARKSTARS
DC

❑0, Oct 1994; Series continued in Darkstars #24 ... 2.00
❑1, Oct 1992 ... 1.75
❑2, Nov 1992 ... 1.75
❑3, Dec 1992 ... 1.75
❑4, Jan 1993 ... 1.75
❑5, Feb 1993 ... 1.75
❑6, Mar 1993 ... 1.75
❑7, Apr 1993 ... 1.75
❑8, May 1993 ... 1.75
❑9, Jun 1993 ... 1.75
❑10, Jun 1993 ... 1.75
❑11, Aug 1993 ... 1.75

Other grades: Multiply price above by 5/6 for VF/NM • 2/3 for VERY FINE • 1/3 for FINE • 1/5 for VERY GOOD • 1/8 for GOOD

Date with Debbi

Late 1960s DC teen romance title

©DC

David Cassidy

Partridge Family heartthrob in action

©Charlton

Dazzler

Disco darling turns sound into light

©Marvel

DC Challenge

Different writer/artist team each issue

©DC

DC Comics Presents

It's a Superman team-up series

©DC

N-MINT

❑12, Sep 1993 .... 1.75
❑13, Oct 1993 .... 1.75
❑14, Nov 1993 .... 1.75
❑15, Dec 1993 .... 1.75
❑16, Jan 1994 .... 1.75
❑17, Feb 1994 .... 1.75
❑18, Mar 1994 .... 1.75
❑19, Apr 1994; Flash 1.75
❑20, May 1994; Flash 1.75
❑21, Jun 1994 .... 1.75
❑22, Jul 1994 .... 1.75
❑23, Aug 1994; Series continued in Darkstars #0, Donna Troy joins Darkstars 1.95
❑24, Sep 1994; Zero Hour 1.95
❑25, Nov 1994 .... 1.95
❑26, Dec 1994 .... 1.95
❑27, Jan 1995 .... 1.95
❑28, Feb 1995 .... 1.95
❑29, Mar 1995 .... 1.95
❑30, Apr 1995 .... 1.95
❑31, Jun 1995 .... 2.25
❑32, Jul 1995 .... 2.25
❑33, Aug 1995 .... 2.25
❑34, Sep 1995 .... 2.25
❑35, Oct 1995 .... 2.25
❑36, Nov 1995 .... 2.25
❑37, Dec 1995 .... 2.25
❑38, Jan 1996 .... 2.25

DARK TALES OF DAILY HORROR
ANTARCTIC

❑1, Feb 1994, b&w 2.95

DARK VISIONS
PYRAMID

❑1, Nov 1986 .... 2.00
❑2 .... 2.00

DARKWING DUCK
DISNEY

❑1 .... 1.50
❑2 .... 1.50
❑3 .... 1.50
❑4 .... 1.50

DARKWING DUCK LIMITED SERIES (DISNEY'S...)
DISNEY

❑1, Nov 1991 .... 1.50
❑2, Dec 1991 .... 1.50
❑3, Jan 1992 .... 1.50
❑4, Feb 1992 .... 1.50

DARK WOLF
ETERNITY

❑1 1988, b&w 1.95
❑2 1988, b&w 1.95
❑3 1988, b&w 1.95
❑4 1988, b&w 1.95
❑5, Jun 1988, b&w 1.95
❑6 1988, b&w 1.95
❑7 1988, b&w 1.95
❑8 1988, b&w 1.95
❑9, b&w 1.95
❑10, b&w 1.95
❑11, b&w 1.95
❑12, b&w 1.95

N-MINT

❑13, b&w 1.95
❑14, b&w 1.95
❑Annual 1, b&w 2.25

DARK WOLF (VOL. 2)
MALIBU

❑1 .... 1.95
❑2 .... 1.95
❑3 .... 1.95
❑4 .... 1.95

DARQUE PASSAGES
VALIANT

❑1, Jan 1994 .... 2.00

DARQUE PASSAGES (VOL. 2)
ACCLAIM

❑1, Apr 1998 .... 2.50
❑2, Jan 1998; No cover date; indicia says Jan 2.50
❑3, Feb 1998; No cover date; indicia says Feb 2.50
❑4, Mar 1998; No cover date; indicia says Mar ....

DARQUE RAZOR
LONDON NIGHT

❑1, Oct 1997 .... 3.00

DART
IMAGE

❑1, Feb 1996 .... 2.50
❑1/A, Feb 1996; alternate cover 2.50
❑2, Apr 1996 .... 2.50
❑3, May 1996 .... 2.50

DATE WITH DEBBI
DC

❑1, Feb 1969 .... 16.00
❑2, Apr 1969 .... 12.00
❑3, Jun 1969 .... 10.00
❑4, Aug 1969 .... 10.00
❑5, Oct 1969 .... 10.00
❑6, Dec 1969 .... 10.00
❑7, Feb 1970, Includes note from Dawn Giordano in "Debbi Makes the Teen Scene" 10.00
❑8, Apr 1970 .... 10.00
❑9, Jun 1970, ... 10.00
❑10, Aug 1970 .... 10.00
❑11, Oct 1970 .... 10.00
❑12, Dec 1970 .... 10.00
❑13, Feb 1971 .... 12.00
❑14, Apr 1971 .... 12.00
❑15, Jun 1971 .... 12.00
❑16, Aug 1971 .... 12.00
❑17, Oct 1971 .... 12.00
❑18, ca. 1972 .... 10.00

DAUGHTERS OF THE DRAGON
MARVEL

❑1, Mar 2006 .... 3.99
❑2, May 2006 .... 3.99
❑3, Jun 2006 .... 3.99
❑4, Jul 2006 .... 3.99
❑5, Aug 2006 .... 3.99

DAUGHTERS OF THE DRAGON: DEADLY HANDS
MARVEL

❑1, Feb 2006 .... 3.99

N-MINT

DAUGHTERS OF TIME 3-D
3-D ZONE

❑1 .... 3.95

DAVID & GOLIATH
IMAGE

❑1, Sep 2003 .... 2.95
❑2, Dec 2003 .... 2.95
❑3, Jun 2004 .... 2.95

DAVID CASSIDY
CHARLTON

❑1, Feb 1972 .... 25.00
❑2, Mar 1972 .... 16.00
❑3, May 1972 .... 16.00
❑4 1972 .... 16.00
❑5, Aug 1972 .... 16.00
❑6, Sep 1972 .... 14.00
❑7, Oct 1972 .... 14.00
❑8, Nov 1972 .... 14.00
❑9, Dec 1972 .... 14.00
❑10, Feb 1973 .... 12.00
❑11, Mar 1973 .... 12.00
❑12, May 1973 .... 12.00
❑13, Jul 1973 .... 12.00
❑14, Sep 1973 .... 12.00

DAVID CHELSEA IN LOVE
ECLIPSE

❑1, b&w 3.50
❑2, b&w 3.50
❑3, b&w 3.50
❑4, b&w 3.50

DAVID SHEPHERD'S SONG
ALIAS

❑1, Nov 2005 .... 3.95

DAVY CROCKETT
GOLD KEY

❑1, Dec 1963 .... 115.00
❑2, Nov 1969 .... 30.00

DAWN
SIRIUS ENTERTAINMENT

❑½, ca. 1996, Wizard mail-away 3.00
❑½/Variant, ca. 1996, Wizard mail-away; "Hey Kids" Variant cover 5.00
❑1, Jul 1995 .... 3.00
❑1/Black, Jul 1995, blacklight edition; "Black light" cover 8.00
❑1/Sharp, Jul 1995; "White Trash" edition; Look Sharp Edition 6.00
❑1/Kids, Jul 1995; "Look Sharp" edition; Kids 5.00
❑2, Sep 1995 .... 3.00
❑2/Mystery, Sep 1995, Signed, limited edition; Mystery Book 6.00
❑3, ca. 1996 .... 3.00
❑4, ca. 1996 .... 3.00
❑5, Sep 1996 .... 3.00
❑6, Oct 1996 .... 3.00
❑Book 1 .... 19.95

DAWN 15TH ANNIVERSARY POSTER BOOK
IMAGE

❑1, Dec 2004 .... 4.95

Other grades: Multiply price above by 5/6 for VF/NM • 2/3 for VERY FINE • 1/3 for FINE • 1/5 for VERY GOOD • 1/8 for GOOD

DAWN 2004 CON SKETCHBOOK ONE-SHOT
IMAGE

❑1, May 2004 .... 2.95

DAWN CONVENTION SKETCH BOOK
IMAGE

❑1, Apr 2003 .... 2.95

DAWN: CONVENTION SKETCHBOOK
IMAGE

❑1, Mar 2002 .... 2.95

DAWN OF THE DEAD (GEORGE ROMERO'S)
IDEA & DESIGN WORKS

❑1, Apr 2004 .... 3.99
❑2, May 2004 .... 3.99
❑3, Jun 2004 .... 3.99

DAWN TENTH ANNIVERSARY SPECIAL
SIRIUS ENTERTAINMENT

❑1, Sep 1999 .... 2.95

DAWN: THE RETURN OF THE GODDESS
SIRIUS ENTERTAINMENT

❑1, Apr 1999 .... 2.95
❑1/Ltd., Apr 1999 .... 8.00
❑2, May 1999 .... 2.95
❑3, Nov 1999 .... 2.95
❑4, Jul 2000 .... 2.95

DAWN: THREE TIERS
IMAGE

❑1, Jul 2003 .... 2.95
❑2, Sep 2003 .... 2.95
❑3, Feb 2004 .... 2.95
❑4 2004 .... 2.95
❑5 2005 .... 2.95
❑6, Oct 2005 .... 2.95

DAYDREAMERS
MARVEL

❑1, Aug 1997; gatefold summary; teams Howard the Duck, Man-Thing, Franklin Richards, Leech, Artie, and Tana 2.50
❑2, Sep 1997; gatefold summary 2.50
❑3, Oct 1997; gatefold summary 2.50

DAY OF JUDGMENT
DC

❑1, Nov 1999 .... 2.50
❑2, Nov 1999 .... 2.50
❑3, Nov 1999 .... 2.50
❑4, Nov 1999 .... 2.50
❑5, Nov 1999, Hal Jordan becomes Spectre 2.50

DAY OF JUDGMENT SECRET FILES
DC

❑1, Nov 1999; background on participants in event 4.95

DAY OF THE DEFENDERS
MARVEL

❑1, Mar 2001; Reprints 3.50

DAY OF VENGEANCE
DC

❑1, Jun 2005 .... 10.00
❑1/Variant, Jun 2005 .... 5.00
❑1/3rd variant, Jul 2005 .... 6.00
❑2, Jul 2005 .... 5.00
❑2/2nd variant, Jul 2005 .... 4.00
❑3, Aug 2005 .... 2.50
❑4, Sep 2005 .... 2.50
❑5, Oct 2005 .... 2.50
❑6 2005 .... 2.50

DAY OF VENGEANCE: INFINITE CRISIS SPECIAL
DC

❑1, Feb 206 .... 4.95

DAYS OF WRATH
APPLE

❑1, b&w 2.75
❑2, b&w 2.75
❑3, b&w 2.75
❑4, Jun 1994, b&w 2.75

DAZZLE
TOKYOPOP

❑1, Jan 2006 .... 9.95

DAZZLER
MARVEL

❑1, Mar 1981, JR2 (a); O: Dazzler. A: X-Men. First Marvel direct market-only comic 5.00
❑2, Apr 1981, JR2, AA (a); A: X-Men. 1.50
❑3, May 1981, BA (c); JR2, BA (a); A: Doctor Doom. V: Doctor Doom. . 1.00
❑4, Jun 1981, FS (a); V: Doctor Doom. 1.00
❑5, Jul 1981, 1: Blue Shield. 1.00
❑6, Aug 1981 .... 1.00
❑7, Sep 1981 .... 1.00
❑8, Oct 1981 .... 1.00
❑9, Nov 1981 .... 1.00
❑10, Dec 1981, A: Galactus. 1.00
❑11, Jan 1982, A: Galactus. 1.00
❑12, Feb 1982 .... 1.00
❑13, Mar 1982 .... 1.00
❑14, Apr 1982 .... 1.00
❑15, May 1982, FS (a) 1.00
❑16, Jun 1982, FS (a) 1.00
❑17, Jul 1982, FS (a); Angel 1.00
❑18, Aug 1982, FS (a); 1.00
❑19, Sep 1982 .... 1.00
❑20, Oct 1982 .... 1.00
❑21, Nov 1982; Double-size 1.00
❑22, Dec 1982, A: Rogue. V: Rogue... 1.00
❑23, Jan 1983 .... 1.00
❑24, Feb 1983 .... 1.00
❑25, Mar 1983 .... 1.00
❑26, May 1983 .... 1.00
❑27, Jul 1983, BSz (c); 1.00
❑28, Sep 1983, BSz (c); A: Rogue...... 1.00
❑29, Nov 1983 .... 1.00
❑30, Jan 1984, BSz (c) 1.00
❑31, Mar 1984, BSz (c) 1.00
❑32, Jun 1984, BSz (c); A: Inhumans. 1.00
❑33, Aug 1984, BSz (c) 1.00
❑34, Oct 1984, BSz (c) 1.00
❑35, Jan 1985, BSz (c) 1.00
❑36, Mar 1985, JBy (c) 1.00
❑37, May 1985 .... 1.00
❑38, Jul 1985, A: X-Men. 1.00
❑39, Sep 1985 .... 1.00
❑40, Nov 1985, Secret Wars II 1.00
❑41, Jan 1986 .... 1.00
❑42, Mar 1986 .... 1.00

DC 100-PAGE SUPER SPECTACULAR: WORLD'S GREATEST SUPER-HEROES
DC

❑1, Jul 2004 .... 6.95

DC CHALLENGE
DC

❑1, Nov 1985 ME (w); GC (a) 1.50
❑2, Dec 1985 .... 1.50
❑3, Jan 1986 CI (a) 1.50
❑4, Feb 1986 GK, KJ (a) 1.50
❑5, Mar 1986 DaG (a) 1.50
❑6, Apr 1986 .... 1.50
❑7, May 1986 JSa (a) 1.50
❑8, Jun 1986 DG (a) 1.50
❑9, Jul 1986 DH (a) 1.50
❑10, Aug 1986 CS (a) 1.50
❑11, Sep 1986 KG, RT (a) 1.50
❑12, Oct 1986 GP (a) 2.00

DC COMICS PRESENTS
DC

❑1, Jul 1978, JL, DA (a); Flash 11.00
❑1/Whitman, Jul 1978, JL, DA (a); Flash; Whitman variant 14.00
❑2, Sep 1978, JL, DA (a); Flash 7.00
❑2/Whitman, Sep 1978, JL, DA (a); Flash; Whitman variant 12.00
❑3, Oct 1978, JL (a); Adam Strange... 4.00
❑3/Whitman, Oct 1978, JL (a); Adam Strange; Whitman variant 8.00
❑4, Dec 1978, JL (a); Metal Men 2.00
❑4/Whitman, Dec 1978, JL (a); Metal Men; Whitman variant 4.00
❑5, Jan 1979, MA (a); Aquaman 2.00
❑6, Feb 1979, CS (a); Green Lantern .. 6.00
❑7, Mar 1979, DD (a); Red Tornado ... 2.00
❑8, Apr 1979, MA (a); Swamp Thing.. 2.00
❑9, May 1979, JSa (a); Wonder Woman 2.00
❑9/Whitman, May 1979 .... 6.00
❑10, Jun 1979, JSa (a); Sgt. Rock 2.00
❑10/Whitman, Jun 1979, JSa (a); Sgt. Rock; Whitman variant 4.00
❑11, Jul 1979, JSa (a); Hawkman 2.00
❑11/Whitman, Jul 1979, JSa (a); Hawkman; Whitman variant 4.00
❑12, Aug 1979, RB, DG (a); Mr. Miracle 2.00
❑12/Whitman, Aug 1979, RB, DG (a); Mr. Miracle; Whitman variant 4.00
❑13, Sep 1979, DG, DD (a); Legion of Super-Heroes 2.00
❑14, Oct 1979, DG, DD (a); Superboy 1.50
❑14/Whitman, Oct 1979, DG, DD (a); Superboy; Whitman variant 3.00
❑15, Nov 1979, JSa (a); Atom 1.50
❑15/Whitman, Nov 1979, JSa (a); Atom; Whitman variant 3.00
❑16, Dec 1979, Black Lightning 1.50
❑16/Whitman, Dec 1979, Black Lightning; Whitman variant 3.00
❑17, Jan 1980, JL (a); Firestorm 1.50
❑18, Feb 1980, DD (a); Zatanna 1.50
❑19, Mar 1980, JSa (a); Batgirl 1.50
❑19/Whitman, Mar 1980, JSa (a); Batgirl; Whitman variant 3.00
❑20, Apr 1980, JL (a); Green Arrow ... 1.50
❑20/Whitman, Apr 1980, JL (a); Green Arrow; Whitman variant 3.00
❑21, May 1980, JSa (a); Elongated Man 1.50
❑21/Whitman, May 1980, JSa (a); Elongated Man; Whitman variant 3.00
❑22, Jun 1980, Captain Comet 1.50
❑22/Whitman, Jun 1980, Whitman variant 3.00
❑23, Jul 1980, JSa (a); Doctor Fate 1.50
❑24, Aug 1980, JL (a); Deadman 1.50
❑25, Sep 1980, Phantom Stranger 1.50
❑26, Oct 1980, JSn (w); JSn, GP (a); 1: New Teen Titans. 1: Raven. 1: Starfire II (Koriand'r). 1: Cyborg. Green Lantern 22.00
❑27, Nov 1980, JSn (a); 1: Mongul. Martian Manhunter; Congorilla back-up 2.50
❑28, Dec 1980, JSn (a); V: Mongul. Supergirl; Johnny Thunder Lawman back-up 1.50
❑29, Jan 1981, JSn, RT (a); Spectre... 1.50
❑30, Feb 1981, CS (a); Black Canary .. 1.50
❑31, Mar 1981, DG, JL (a); Robin; Robotman back-up 1.50
❑32, Apr 1981, Wonder Woman 1.50
❑33, May 1981, Captain Marvel 1.50
❑34, Jun 1981, Marvel Family 1.50
❑35, Jul 1981, CS (a); Man-Bat 1.50
❑36, Aug 1981, JSn (a); Starman 1.50
❑37, Sep 1981, JSn, RT (a); Hawkgirl; Rip Hunter back-up 1.50
❑38, Oct 1981, D: Crimson Avenger. Flash 1.50
❑39, Nov 1981, JSn (a); A: Toyman 1.50
❑40, Dec 1981, Metamorpho 1.50
❑41, Jan 1982, 1: new Wonder Woman. A: Joker. 2.25
❑42, Feb 1982, Unknown Soldier; Golden Age Sandman back-up 1.25
❑43, Mar 1982, CS (a); Legion 1.25
❑44, Apr 1982, A: Joker. Dial 'H' for Hero 2.25
❑45, May 1982, RB (a); Firestorm 1.25
❑46, Jun 1982, 1: Global Guardians... 1.25
❑47, Jul 1982, 1: Masters of Universe. 17.00
❑48, Aug 1982, Aquaman; Black Pirate back-up 1.25
❑49, Sep 1982, RB (a); Captain Marvel 1.25
❑50, Oct 1982, CS (a); Clark Kent 1.25
❑51, Nov 1982, FMc (a); Atom 6.00
❑52, Dec 1982, KG (a); 1: Ambush Bug. Doom Patrol 2.50
❑53, Jan 1983, 1: Atari Force. House of Mystery 1.00
❑54, Feb 1983, DN (a); Green Arrow, Black Canary 1.00
❑55, Mar 1983, A: Superboy. V: Parasite. Air Wave 1.00
❑56, Apr 1983, CS (a); 1: Maaldor the Darklord. Power Girl 1.00
❑57, May 1983, Atomic Knights 1.00
❑58, Jun 1983, GK (c); CS (a); 1: The Untouchables (DC). Robin, Elongated Man 1.00
❑59, Jul 1983, KG (a); Legion of Super-Heroes, Ambush Bug 1.00

Other grades: Multiply price above by 5/6 for VF/NM • 2/3 for VERY FINE • 1/3 for FINE • 1/5 for VERY GOOD • 1/8 for GOOD

DC One Million

Comics from the 853rd Century
©DC

DC Special

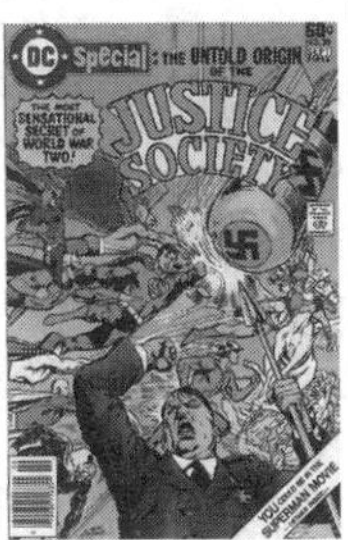

Double-sized issues spotlighting the DC world
©DC

DC Super-Stars

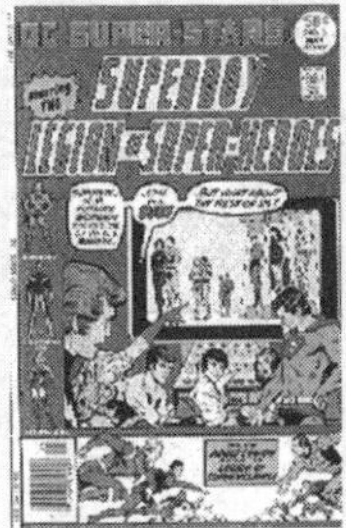

Giant-sized issues reprinting classic DC stories
©DC

Dead (2nd Series)

Blood and gore from Arrow Comics
©Arrow

Deadbeats

Black-and-white vampire soap opera
©Claypool

N-MINT

❑60, Aug 1983, Guardians of the Universe ... 1.00
❑61, Sep 1983, OMAC ... 1.00
❑62, Oct 1983, Freedom Fighters ... 1.00
❑63, Nov 1983, Amethyst ... 1.00
❑64, Dec 1983; Kamandi ... 1.00
❑65, Jan 1984; Madame Xanadu ... 1.00
❑66, Feb 1984; JK (a); 1: Blackbriar Thorn. Demon ... 1.00
❑67, Mar 1984; V: Toyman. Santa Claus ... 1.00
❑68, Apr 1984; MA, CS (a); Vixen ... 1.00
❑69, May 1984; IN (a); Blackhawk ... 1.00
❑70, Jun 1984; Metal Men ... 1.00
❑71, Jul 1984; CS (a); Bizarro ... 1.00
❑72, Aug 1984; Phantom Stranger, Joker ... 1.50
❑73, Sep 1984; CI (a); Flash ... 1.00
❑74, Oct 1984; Hawkman ... 1.00
❑75, Nov 1984; Arion ... 1.00
❑76, Dec 1984; A: Monitor. Wonder Woman ... 1.00
❑77, Jan 1985; 1: The Forgotten Villains. Animal Man, Dolphin, Congorilla, Cave Carson, Immortal Man, Rip Hunter, Rick Flagg ... 3.00
❑78, Feb 1985; Animal Man, Dolphin, Congorilla, Cave Carson, Immortal Man, Rip Hunter, Rick Flagg ... 3.00
❑79, Mar 1985; Clark Kent ... 1.00
❑80, Apr 1985; Legion ... 1.00
❑81, May 1985; V: Kobra. Ambush Bug ... 1.00
❑82, Jun 1985; Adam Strange ... 1.00
❑83, Jul 1985; Outsiders ... 1.00
❑84, Aug 1985; Challengers of the Unknown ... 1.00
❑85, Sep 1985; AMo (w); Swamp Thing ... 6.00
❑86, Oct 1985; V: Blackstarr. Crisis; Supergirl ... 1.00
❑87, Nov 1985; 1: Superboy of Earth-Prime. Crisis ... 1.00
❑88, Dec 1985; Crisis ... 1.00
❑89, Jan 1986; Omega Men ... 1.00
❑90, Feb 1986; O: Captain Atom. Firestorm ... 1.00
❑91, Mar 1986; Captain Comet ... 1.00
❑92, Apr 1986; Vigilante ... 1.00
❑93, May 1986; Plastic Man, Elongated Man, Elastic Lad ... 2.00
❑94, Jun 1986; Harbinger, Lady Quark, Pariah ... 1.00
❑95, Jul 1986; Hawkman ... 1.00
❑96, Aug 1986; Blue Devil ... 1.00
❑97, Sep 1986; Double-size A: Bizarro. A: Mxyzptlk. V: Phantom Zone Criminals ... 1.25
❑Annual 1, ca. 1982; RB (a); Superman & E-2 Superman ... 3.00
❑Annual 2, ca. 1983 O: Superwoman. 1: Superwoman ... 3.00
❑Annual 3, ca. 1984; Doctor Sivana gains the Shazam! powers ... 3.00
❑Annual 4, ca. 1985 A: Superwoman. ... 3.00

DC COMICS PRESENTS: BATMAN
DC

❑1, Sep 2004 ... 2.50

N-MINT

DC COMICS PRESENTS: GREEN LANTERN
DC

❑1, Sep 2004 ... 2.50

DC COMICS PRESENTS: HAWKMAN
DC

❑1, Sep 2004 ... 2.50

DC COMICS PRESENTS: JLA
DC

❑1, Oct 2004 ... 2.50

DC COMICS PRESENTS: MYSTERY IN SPACE
DC

❑1, Sep 2004 ... 2.50

DC COMICS PRESENTS: SUPERMAN
DC

❑1, Oct 2004 ... 2.50

DC COMICS PRESENTS: THE ATOM
DC

❑1, Oct 2004 ... 2.50

DC COMICS PRESENTS: THE FLASH
DC

❑1, Oct 2004 ... 2.50

DC COUNTDOWN
DC

❑1, May 2005 D: Blue Beetle. ... 6.00
❑1/2nd, May 2005; Second print ... 3.00
❑1/DF Ross, May 2005 ... 25.00
❑1/DF Lee & Ross, May 2005 ... 50.00

DC FIRST: BATGIRL/JOKER
DC

❑1, Jul 2002 ... 3.50

DC FIRST: FLASH/SUPERMAN
DC

❑1, Jul 2002 ... 3.50

DC FIRST: GREEN LANTERN/ GREEN LANTERN
DC

❑1, Jul 2002 ... 3.50

DC FIRST: SUPERMAN/LOBO
DC

❑1, Jul 2002 ... 3.50

DC GRAPHIC NOVEL
DC

❑1, Star Raiders ... 5.95
❑2, Warlords ... 5.95
❑3, Medusa Chain ... 5.95
❑4, Hunger Dogs ... 5.95
❑5, Me and Joe Priest ... 5.95
❑6, Metalzoic ... 6.95
❑7, Space Clusters ... 5.95

DC/MARVEL: ALL ACCESS
DC

❑1, Dec 1996; BG (a); A: Superman, Spider-Man, Venom. crossover with Marvel ... 2.95
❑2, Jan 1997; BG (a); A: Jubilee, Robin, Two-Face, Scorpion. crossover with Marvel ... 2.95
❑3, Jan 1997; BG (a); A: Jubilee, Robin, Batman, Doctor Strange, Scorpion, JLA, X-Men. crossover with Marvel ... 2.95

N-MINT

❑4, Feb 1997; BG (a); A: JLA, X-Men, Doctor Strangefate, Amalgam universe. crossover with Marvel ... 2.95

DC 100 PAGE SUPER SPECTACULAR
DC

❑4, ca. 1971, BWr (c); SA, BWr (a); Weird Mystery Tales; reprints; back cover pin-up ... 175.00
❑5, ca. 1971, BO, MD, RE (a); Love Stories; back cover pin-up ... 350.00
❑5/2nd; Replica edition; BO, MD, RE (a); Love Stories ... 7.00
❑6, ca. 1971, World's Greatest Super-Heroes; reprints JLA #21-22; wraparound cover ... 165.00
❑7, Dec 1971, really DC-7; a.k.a. Superman #245; back cover pin-up ... 60.00
❑8, Jan 1972, really DC-8; a.k.a. Batman #238; wraparound cover ... 75.00
❑9, Feb 1972, really DC-9; a.k.a. Our Army at War #242; Sgt. Rock, wraparound cover ... 75.00
❑10, Mar 1972, really DC-10; a.k.a. Adventure Comics #416; Supergirl; wraparound cover ... 60.00
❑11, Apr 1972, really DC-11; a.k.a. Flash #214; wraparound cover ... 60.00
❑12, May 1972, really DC-12; a.k.a. Superboy #185; wraparound cover. ... 60.00
❑13, Jun 1972, really DC-13; a.k.a. Superman #252; wraparound cover ... 60.00
❑14, Feb 1973, really DC-14; Batman; wraparound cover ... 50.00
❑15, Mar 1973, really DC-15; Superboy; back cover pin-up ... 50.00
❑16, Apr 1973, really DC-16; Sgt. Rock; back cover cover gallery ... 50.00
❑17, Jun 1973, really DC-17; JLA; back cover cover gallery ... 50.00
❑18, Jul 1973, Superman's 35th anniversary; NC (c); MA, GK, CS (a); really DC-18; back cover cover gallery; Superman cast, Golden Age Atom, TNT, Hourman, Captain Triumph; Reprints from Superman #25, #97, & #162, Flash Comics #90, Atom #8, World's Finest Comics #5, Adventure #57, and Crack Comics #42 ... 30.00
❑19, Aug 1973, JKu (c); (w); RM (a); really DC-19; Tarzan; back cover pin-up ... 22.00
❑20, Sep 1973, O: Two-Face. really DC-20; Batman; back cover cover gallery ... 22.00
❑21, Oct 1973, really DC-21; Superboy; back cover cover gallery ... 22.00
❑22, Nov 1973, really DC-22; Flash; Super Specs become part of individual series beginning with Shazam! #8 ... 22.00

DC ONE MILLION
DC

❑1, Nov 1998 ... 2.00
❑1/Variant, Nov 1998; Signed edition. ... 14.99
❑2, Nov 1998 ... 2.00
❑3, Nov 1998 ... 2.00
❑4, Nov 1998 ... 2.00
❑Giant Size 1, Aug 1999; 80-Page Giant ... 4.95

DC SAMPLER
DC

❑1, Sep 1983; Promotional giveaway; CI (a); no cover price 1.50
❑2, Sep 1984; Promotional giveaway; FH, JL (a); No cover price; Atari Force, etc. 1.00
❑3; Promotional giveaway; FH (c); AMo (w); FH (a); No cover price; The Saga of the Swamp Thing, etc. 1.00

DC SCIENCE FICTION GRAPHIC NOVEL
DC

❑1, Hell on Earth 5.95
❑2, Nightwings 5.95
❑3 ..... 5.95
❑4, Merchants Venus 5.95
❑5 ..... 5.95
❑6, Magic Goes Away 5.95
❑7, Sand Kings 5.95

DC SILVER AGE CLASSICS ACTION COMICS
DC

❑252, reprints Action Comics #252 ..... 1.00

DC SILVER AGE CLASSICS ADVENTURE COMICS
DC

❑247, reprints Adventure Comics #247 ..... 1.00

DC SILVER AGE CLASSICS DETECTIVE COMICS
DC

❑225, reprints Detective Comics #225 ..... 1.00
❑327, reprints Detective Comics #327 ..... 1.00

DC SILVER AGE CLASSICS GREEN LANTERN
DC

❑76, reprints Green Lantern #76 ..... 1.00

DC SILVER AGE CLASSICS HOUSE OF SECRETS
DC

❑92, reprints House of Secrets #92 ..... 1.00

DC SILVER AGE CLASSICS SHOWCASE
DC

❑4, reprints Showcase #4 ..... 1.00
❑22, reprints Showcase #22 ..... 1.00

DC SILVER AGE CLASSICS SUGAR & SPIKE
DC

❑99, not a reprint; first publication of Sugar and Spike #99 ..... 2.00

DC SILVER AGE CLASSICS THE BRAVE AND THE BOLD
DC

❑28, 1: JLA. 1: The Justice League of America. reprints The Braveand the Bold #28 ..... 1.25

DC SPECIAL
DC

❑1, Dec 1968; CI (a); Flash, Batman, Adam Strange 60.00
❑2, Mar 1969; teen 50.00
❑3, Jun 1969; ATh, GK, JM (a); All female issue; Wonder Woman, Green Lantern/Star Sapphire, Green Arrow/ Black Canary, Supergirl/Black Flame; Reprints stories from Green Lantern (2nd series) #16 and Action #304 ..... 35.00
❑4, Sep 1969; JK (a); Partial reprint from Tales of the Unexpected #16 ..... 25.00
❑5, Dec 1969 ..... 25.00
❑6, Mar 1970 ..... 20.00
❑7, Jun 1970; Strange Sports 20.00
❑8, Sep 1970; Wanted 20.00
❑9, Dec 1970 ..... 20.00
❑10, Feb 1971 ..... 20.00
❑11, Apr 1971; Monsters 20.00
❑12, Jun 1971; JKu, RH, IN (a); Viking Prince 20.00
❑13, Aug 1971; Strange Sports 20.00
❑14, Oct 1971; Giant-size; Wanted: The World's Most Dangerous Villains 20.00
❑15, Dec 1971; Giant-size; O: Woozy Winks. O: Plastic Man (Golden Age). Plastic Man reprints 25.00
❑16, Spr 1975, CI, RA (a); Gorillas 10.00
❑17, Sum 1975 ..... 10.00
❑18, Nov 1975, Earth-Shaking Stories 10.00
❑19, Jan 1976 ..... 10.00
❑20, Mar 1976, Green Lantern 10.00
❑21, May 1976, Monsters, War That Time Forgot 10.00
❑22, Jul 1976, Three Musketeers, Robin Hood 10.00
❑23, Sep 1976, Three Musketeers, Robin Hood 10.00
❑24, Oct 1976, Robin Hood, Viking Prince 10.00
❑25, Dec 1976, Robin Hood, Viking Prince 10.00
❑26, Feb 1977, Enemy Ace 10.00
❑27, Apr 1977, Captain Comet 10.00
❑28, Jun 1977, Batman; new Legion of Super-Heroes story 10.00
❑29, Sep 1977, BL, JSa (a); O: Justice Society of America (Secret Origin). 10.00

DC SPECIAL BLUE RIBBON DIGEST
DC

❑1, Apr 1980; Legion of Super Heroes 5.00
❑2, Jun 1980; Flash 4.00
❑3, Aug 1980; Justice Society 4.00
❑4, Oct 1980; Green Lantern 4.00
❑5, Dec 1980; Secret Origins 4.00
❑6, Jan 1981; AA, TD, JA (a); House of Mystery 3.00
❑7, Mar 1981; Flying Tigers, Haunted Tank, War That Time Forgot, Enemy Ace 3.00
❑8, Apr 1981; Legion 3.00
❑9, May 1981; The Atom 3.00
❑10, Jun 1981; Warlord 3.00
❑11, Jul 1981; Justice League, Justice Society, Seven Soldiers 3.00
❑12, Aug 1981; Haunted Tank 3.00
❑13, Sep 1981; Strange Sports 3.00
❑14, Oct 1981; Science Fiction 3.00
❑15, Nov 1981; Superboy, Green Lantern, Batman 3.00
❑16, Dec 1981; Green Lantern/Green Arrow 3.00
❑17, Jan 1982; Mystery 3.00
❑18, Feb 1982; Sgt. Rock 4.00
❑19, Mar 1982; Reprints My Greatest Adventure #80 and Doom Patrol #86, 90 and 91 ..... 3.00
❑20, Apr 1982; Mystery 7.00
❑21, May 1982; JK (a); War 3.00
❑22, Jun 1982; Secret Origins 3.00
❑23, Jul 1982; Green Arrow 3.00

DC SPECIAL SERIES
DC

❑1, Sep 1977; FMc, MN, DD, JR, IN (a); 5-Star Super-Hero Spectacular 10.00
❑2, Sep 1977, BWr (a); Swamp Thing reprint; Swamp Thing 7.00
❑3, Oct 1977, JK (a); Sgt. Rock 7.00
❑4, Oct 1977; Unexpected Annual 7.00
❑5, Nov 1977; A: Superman. A: Luthor. A: Brainiac. a.k.a. Superman Spectacular; first DC Dollar Comic; Superman, Luthor 7.00
❑6, Nov 1977, JLA 6.00
❑7, Dec 1977, Ghosts 6.00
❑8, Feb 1978, DG (a); Brave & Bold 6.00
❑9, Mar 1978; SD, RH (a); Wonder Woman vs. Hitler 16.00
❑10, Apr 1978, MN (a); Super-Heroes 6.00
❑11, May 1978; MA, WW, KS, IN (a); A: Johnny Quick. Flash; a.k.a. Flash Spectacular 6.00
❑12, Jun 1978; Secrets of Haunted House 6.00
❑13, Jul 1978; Sgt. Rock 6.00
❑14, Jul 1978, Swamp Thing reprint 6.00
❑15, Aug 1978; Batman, Ra's al Ghul. 8.00
❑16, Sep 1978 RH (a); D: Jonah Hex. 20.00
❑17, Sep 1979; Swamp Thing reprint 5.00
❑18, Oct 1979; digest Sgt. Rock 5.00
❑19, Oct 1979; digest; O: Wonder Woman. Secret Origins 6.00
❑20, Jan 1980; BWr (a); Swamp Thing reprint; a.k.a. Original Swamp Thing Saga 6.00
❑21, Mar 1980; FM (a); Batman; Legion; 1st Frank Miller Batman 21.00
❑22, Sep 1980; G.I. Combat 6.00
❑23, Feb 1981; digest; Flash 6.00
❑24, Feb 1981; Flash 6.00
❑25, Sum 1981; treasury-sized; Superman II movie adaptation 6.00
❑26, Sum 1981; treasury-sized; RA, RT (a); Superman's Fortress 6.00
❑27, Dec 1981; treasury-sized; Batman vs. The Incredible Hulk 18.00

DC SPECIAL: THE RETURN OF DONNA TROY
DC

❑1, Aug 2005 ..... 8.00
❑2, Sep 2005 ..... 5.00
❑3, Oct 2005 ..... 2.99
❑4 2005 ..... 2.99

DC SPOTLIGHT
DC

❑1, Sep 1985; JL (c); Previews of Crisis on Infinite Earths, Who's Who, DC Challenge, Mask, Nathaniel Dusk, Outsiders, Hex, Legion of Super-Heroes, New Teen Titans, Swamp Thing, Omega Men, Super Powers, Batman: The Dark Knight, Watchmen, and others 1.00

DC SUPER-STARS
DC

❑1, Mar 1976, Double-size; NC (a); Teen Titans reprint 10.00
❑2, Apr 1976, Double-size; Space 5.00
❑3, May 1976, CS (a); A: Legion of Super-Heroes. Superman; Reprints Legion of Super-Heroes story from Adventure Comics #354 and #355 ..... 5.00
❑4, Jun 1976 ..... 2.00
❑5, Jul 1976, Flash; Bicentennial #33. ..... 10.00
❑6, Aug 1976 ..... 2.00
❑7, Sep 1976 ..... 2.00
❑8, Oct 1976, Reprints Showcase #15 ..... 4.00
❑9, Nov 1976, Man Behind the Gun 2.00
❑10, Dec 1976, A: Joker. Sports stories and Batman story 5.00
❑11, Jan 1977 ..... 7.00
❑12, Feb 1977 ..... 2.00
❑13, Mar 1977, SA (a) 2.00
❑14, May 1977, O: Doctor Light. O: Braniac. O: Two-Face. O: Gorilla Grodd. O: Shark 4.00
❑15, Jul 1977, war stories 4.00
❑16, Sep 1977, DN, BL (a); 1: Star Hunters. 3.00
❑17, Nov 1977, BL, JSa (w); BL, MGr, JSa (a); O: Green Arrow. O: The Huntress II (Helena Wayne). 1: The Huntress II (Helena Wayne). Secret Origins; Revealed that Earth-2 Batman had married Earth-2 Catwoman; Legion story 16.00
❑18, Jan 1978, Deadman, Phantom Stranger 2.00

DC: THE NEW FRONTIER
DC

❑1, Jan 2004 ..... 6.95
❑2, Apr 2004 ..... 6.95
❑3, May 2004 ..... 6.95
❑4, Jul 2004 ..... 6.95
❑5, Sep 2004 ..... 6.95
❑6 ..... 6.95

DC 2000
DC

❑1, 2000 ..... 6.95
❑2, 2000 ..... 6.95

DCU: BRAVE NEW WORLD
DC

❑1, Sep 2006 ..... 1.00

DCU HEROES SECRET FILES
DC

❑1, Feb 1999 ..... 4.95

DC UNIVERSE HOLIDAY BASH
DC

❑1, Jan 1997; Preview edition; JA, MWa (w); SB, KN (a); Holiday special for 1996 season 3.95
❑2, Jan 1998; prestige format; Holiday special for 1997 season 4.95
❑3, Jan 1999; Signed edition; Holiday special for 1998 season 4.95

DC UNIVERSE: TRINITY
DC

❑1, Aug 1993; foil cover 2.95
❑2, Sep 1993; foil cover 2.95

Other grades: Multiply price above by 5/6 for VF/NM • 2/3 for VERY FINE • 1/3 for FINE • 1/5 for VERY GOOD • 1/8 for GOOD

Deadenders

Haves and have-nots in post-apocalyptic future
©DC

Deadman (1st Series)

You can't keep a good man down
©DC

Dead of Night

Deservedly obscure horror series from Marvel
©Marvel

Deadpool

Wise-cracking mercenary gets own series
©Marvel

Deadworld (Vol. 1)

Zombies and worse walk the Earth
©Arrow

N-MINT

DCU VILLAINS SECRET FILES
DC

❑1, Apr 1999 .... 4.95

D-DAY
AVALON

❑1 .... 2.95

DEAD
ARROW

❑1 .... 2.95
❑1/A; alternate cover 2.95
❑2 .... 2.95
❑3 .... 2.95

DEAD (2ND SERIES)
ARROW

❑1 .... 2.95

DEAD AIR
SLAVE LABOR

❑1 .... 5.95

DEAD@17
VIPER

❑0 2003 .... 27.00
❑1 2003 .... 35.00
❑2 2003 .... 22.00
❑3 .... 10.00
❑4 2004 .... 7.00

DEAD@17: BLOOD OF SAINTS
VIPER

❑1 2004 .... 2.95
❑2 2004 .... 2.95
❑3 2004 .... 2.95
❑4 2004 .... 2.95

DEAD@17: PROTECTORATE
VIPER

❑1, Oct 2005 .... 2.95
❑2, Nov 2005 .... 2.95
❑3, Dec 2005 .... 2.95

DEAD@17: REVOLUTION
VIPER

❑1 2004 .... 4.00
❑2 2004 .... 2.95
❑3 2005 .... 2.95
❑4 2005 .... 2.95

DEAD@17: ROUGH CUT
VIPER

❑1 2004 .... 2.95

DEADBEATS
CLAYPOOL

❑1, Jun 1992, b&w RHo (w); RHo (a) 4.00
❑2, Jul 1992, b&w RHo (w); RHo (a) 3.00
❑3, Sep 1992, b&w RHo (w); RHo (a) 3.00
❑4, Oct 1992, b&w RHo (w); RHo (a). 3.00
❑5, Sep 1993, b&w RHo (w); RHo (a) 3.00
❑6, Mar 1994, b&w RHo (w); RHo (a) 2.50
❑7, Jun 1994, b&w RHo (w); RHo (a) 2.50
❑8, Aug 1994, b&w RHo (w); RHo (a) 2.50
❑9, Nov 1994, b&w 2.50
❑10, Jan 1995, b&w 2.50
❑11, Mar 1995, b&w 2.50
❑12, May 1995, b&w 2.50
❑13, Jul 1995, b&w 2.50
❑14, Sep 1995, b&w 2.50

N-MINT

❑15, Nov 1995, b&w 2.50
❑16, Jan 1996, b&w 2.50
❑17, Mar 1996, b&w 2.50
❑18, May 1996, b&w 2.50
❑19, Jul 1996, b&w 2.50
❑20, Sep 1996, b&w 2.50
❑21, Nov 1996, b&w 2.50
❑22, Jan 1997, b&w 2.50
❑23, Mar 1997, b&w 2.50
❑24, May 1997, b&w 2.50
❑25, Jul 1997, b&w 2.50
❑26, Sep 1997, b&w RHo (w) 2.50
❑27, Nov 1997, b&w RHo (w) 2.50
❑28, Jan 1998, b&w RHo (w); RHo (a) 2.50
❑29, Mar 1998, b&w 2.50
❑30, May 1998, b&w 2.50
❑31, Jul 1998, b&w 2.50
❑32, Oct 1998, b&w 2.50
❑33, Dec 1998, b&w 2.50
❑34, Feb 1999, b&w 2.50
❑35, Apr 1999, b&w 2.50
❑36, Jun 1999, b&w 2.50
❑37, Aug 1999, b&w 2.50
❑38, Oct 1999, b&w 2.50
❑39, Dec 1999, b&w 2.50
❑40, Feb 2000, b&w 2.50
❑41, Apr 2000, b&w 2.50
❑42, Jun 2000, b&w 2.50
❑43, Aug 2000, b&w RHo (w) 2.50
❑44, Oct 2000, b&w 2.50
❑45, Dec 2000, b&w 2.50
❑46, Feb 2001, b&w 2.50
❑47, Apr 2001, b&w 2.50
❑48, Jun 2001, b&w 2.50
❑49, Aug 2001, b&w 2.50
❑50, Oct 2001, b&w 2.50
❑51, Dec 2001, b&w 2.50
❑52, Feb 2002, b&w 2.50
❑53, Apr 2002, b&w 2.50
❑54, Jun 2002, b&w 2.50
❑55, Aug 2002, b&w 2.50
❑56, Oct 2002, b&w 2.50
❑57, Dec 2002, b&w 2.50
❑58, Feb 2003, b&w 2.50
❑59, Apr 2003, b&w 2.50
❑60, Jun 2003, b&w 2.50
❑61, Aug 2003, b&w 2.50
❑62, Oct 2003, b&w 2.50
❑63, Dec 2003, b&w 2.50
❑64, Feb 2004, b&w 2.50
❑65, Apr 2004, b&w 2.50
❑66, Jun 2004, b&w 2.50
❑67, Aug 2004, b&w 2.50
❑68 2004 .... 2.50

DEAD CLOWN
MALIBU

❑1, Oct 1996 .... 2.50
❑2 .... 2.50
❑3, Feb 1994 .... 2.50

DEAD CORPS(E)
DC / HELIX

❑1, Sep 1998 .... 2.50
❑2, Oct 1998 .... 2.50

N-MINT

❑3, Nov 1998 .... 2.50
❑4, Dec 1998 .... 2.50

DEADENDERS
DC / VERTIGO

❑1, Mar 2000 .... 2.50
❑2, Apr 2000 .... 2.50
❑3, May 2000 .... 2.50
❑4, Jun 2000 .... 2.50
❑5, Jul 2000 .... 2.50
❑6, Aug 2000 .... 2.50
❑7, Sep 2000 .... 2.50
❑8, Oct 2000 .... 2.50
❑9, Nov 2000 .... 2.50
❑10, Dec 2000 .... 2.50
❑11, Jan 2001 .... 2.50
❑12, Feb 2001 .... 2.50
❑13, Mar 2001 .... 2.50
❑14, Apr 2001 .... 2.50
❑15, May 2001 .... 2.50
❑16, Jun 2001 .... 2.50

DEAD EYES OPEN
SLAVE LABOR

❑1 2005, ... 2.95
❑2 2005, ... 2.95

DEADFACE
HARRIER

❑1, ca. 1987 .... 5.00
❑2, ca. 1987 .... 4.00
❑3, ca. 1987 .... 3.00
❑4, ca. 1987 .... 3.00
❑5, ca. 1987 .... 3.00
❑6, ca. 1987 .... 2.50
❑7, ca. 1987 .... 2.50
❑8, ca. 1987 .... 2.50

DEADFACE: DOING THE ISLANDS WITH BACCHUS
DARK HORSE

❑1, Jul 1991, b&w 2.95
❑2, Aug 1991, b&w 2.95
❑3, Sep 1991, b&w 2.95

DEADFACE: EARTH, WATER, AIR, AND FIRE
DARK HORSE

❑1 1992, b&w 2.50
❑2 1992, b&w 2.50
❑3 1992, b&w 2.50
❑4 1992, b&w 2.50

DEAD FOLKS (LANSDALES & TRUMAN'S)
AVATAR

❑1, Mar 2003 .... 3.50
❑1/A, Mar 2003; Wrap Cover 3.95
❑2, May 2003 .... 3.50
❑2/A, May 2003; Wrap Cover 3.95
❑3, Jul 2003 .... 3.50

DEADFORCE (STUDIONOIR)
STUDIO NOIR

❑1, Jul 1996, b&w 2.50

DEADFORCE (ANTARCTIC)
ANTARCTIC

❑1, May 1999, b&w 2.50

- ❑2, Jun 1999 ... 2.50
- ❑Ashcan 1 ... 1.00

DEAD GRRRL: DEAD AT 21
BONEYARD

- ❑1, Apr 1998 ... 2.95

DEAD IN THE WEST
DARK HORSE

- ❑1, Oct 1993, b&w ... 3.95
- ❑2, Mar 1994, b&w ... 3.95

DEAD KID ADVENTURES
KNIGHT

- ❑1, Jul 1998 ... 2.95

DEAD KILLER
CALIBER

- ❑1 ... 2.95

DEAD KING: BURNT
CHAOS

- ❑1, May 1998 ... 2.95
- ❑2, Jun 1998 ... 2.95
- ❑3, Jul 1998 ... 2.95
- ❑4, Aug 1998 ... 2.95

DEADLINE (MARVEL)
MARVEL

- ❑1, Jun 2002 ... 2.99
- ❑2, Jul 2002 ... 2.99
- ❑3, Aug 2002 ... 2.99
- ❑4, Sep 2002 ... 2.99

DEADLINE USA
DARK HORSE

- ❑1, Sep 1991, b&w; Reprints ... 3.95
- ❑2, b&w; Reprints ... 3.95
- ❑3, b&w; Reprints ... 3.95
- ❑4 ... 3.95
- ❑5 A: Gwar. ... 3.95
- ❑6 ... 3.95
- ❑7 ... 3.95
- ❑8 ... 3.95

DEADLY DUO
IMAGE

- ❑1, Nov 1994 ... 2.50
- ❑2, Dec 1994 ... 2.50
- ❑3, Jan 1995 ... 2.50

DEADLY DUO (2ND SERIES)
IMAGE

- ❑1, Jul 1995 ... 2.50
- ❑2, Aug 1995 ... 2.50
- ❑3, Sep 1995 ... 2.50
- ❑4, Oct 1995 ... 2.50

DEADLY FOES OF SPIDER-MAN
MARVEL

- ❑1, May 1991; AM, KGa (a); Punisher, Rhino, Kingpin, others appear ... 1.50
- ❑2, Jun 1991 AM, KGa (a) ... 1.50
- ❑3, Jul 1991 AM (a) ... 1.50
- ❑4, Aug 1991 AM (a) ... 1.50

DEADLY HANDS OF KUNG FU
MARVEL

- ❑1, Apr 1974 JSn (w) ... 30.00
- ❑2, Jun 1974 ... 8.00
- ❑3, Aug 1974 ... 6.00
- ❑4, Sep 1974 ... 6.00
- ❑5, Oct 1974 ... 6.00
- ❑6, Nov 1974 ... 5.00
- ❑7, Dec 1974 ... 5.00
- ❑8, Jan 1975 ... 5.00
- ❑9, Feb 1975 ... 5.00
- ❑10, Mar 1975 ... 5.00
- ❑11, Apr 1975 ... 4.00
- ❑12, May 1975 ... 4.00
- ❑13, Jun 1975 ... 4.00
- ❑14, Jul 1975 ... 4.00
- ❑15, Aug 1975 ... 4.00
- ❑16, Sep 1975 ... 4.00
- ❑17, Oct 1975 ... 4.00
- ❑18, Nov 1975 ... 4.00
- ❑19, Dec 1975 ... 4.00
- ❑20, Jan 1976 ... 4.00
- ❑21, Feb 1976 ... 3.00
- ❑22, Mar 1976 ... 3.00
- ❑23, Apr 1976 ... 3.00
- ❑24, May 1976 ... 3.00
- ❑25, Jun 1976 ... 3.00
- ❑26, Jul 1976 ... 3.00
- ❑27, Aug 1976 ... 3.00
- ❑28, Sep 1976 ... 3.00
- ❑29, Oct 1976 ... 3.00
- ❑30, Nov 1976 ... 3.00
- ❑31, Dec 1976 ... 3.00
- ❑32, Jan 1977 ... 3.00
- ❑33, Feb 1977 ... 3.00
- ❑Special 1 1974 ... 4.00

DEADMAN (1ST SERIES)
DC

- ❑1, May 1985 CI, NA (a) ... 2.50
- ❑2, Jun 1985 NA (a) ... 2.50
- ❑3, Jul 1985 NA (a) ... 2.50
- ❑4, Aug 1985 NA (a) ... 2.50
- ❑5, Sep 1985 NA (a) ... 2.50
- ❑6, Oct 1985 NA (a) ... 2.50
- ❑7, Nov 1985 NA (a) ... 2.50

DEADMAN (2ND SERIES)
DC

- ❑1, Mar 1986 JL (a) ... 2.00
- ❑2, Apr 1986 JL (a) ... 2.00
- ❑3, May 1986 JL (a) ... 2.00
- ❑4, Jun 1986 JL (a) ... 2.00

DEADMAN (3RD SERIES)
DC

- ❑1, Feb 2002 ... 2.50
- ❑2, Mar 2002 ... 2.50
- ❑3, Apr 2002 ... 2.50
- ❑4, May 2002 ... 2.50
- ❑5, Jun 2002 ... 2.50
- ❑6, Jul 2002 ... 2.50
- ❑7, Aug 2002 ... 2.50
- ❑8, Sep 2002 ... 2.50
- ❑9, Oct 2002 ... 2.50

DEADMAN: DEAD AGAIN
DC

- ❑1, Oct 2001 ... 2.50
- ❑2, Oct 2001 ... 2.50
- ❑3, Oct 2001 ... 2.50
- ❑4, Oct 2001 ... 2.50
- ❑5, Oct 2001 ... 2.50

DEADMAN: EXORCISM
DC

- ❑1, prestige format ... 4.95
- ❑2, prestige format ... 4.95

DEADMAN: LOVE AFTER DEATH
DC

- ❑1, Dec 1989; prestige format ... 3.95
- ❑2, Jan 1990; prestige format ... 3.95

DEAD OF NIGHT
MARVEL

- ❑1, Dec 1973, JSt (w); JSt (a); Reprints ... 35.00
- ❑2, Feb 1974, Reprints ... 12.00
- ❑3, Apr 1974, Reprints ... 8.00
- ❑4, Jun 1974, Reprints ... 8.00
- ❑5, Aug 1974, Reprints ... 8.00
- ❑6, Oct 1974, Reprints ... 8.00
- ❑7, Dec 1974, Reprints ... 8.00
- ❑8, Feb 1975, Reprints ... 8.00
- ❑9, Apr 1975, Reprints ... 8.00
- ❑10, Jun 1975, Reprints ... 8.00
- ❑11, Aug 1975 1: Scarecrow. ... 16.00

DEAD OR ALIVE: A CYBERPUNK WESTERN
DARK HORSE

- ❑1, Apr 1998 ... 2.50
- ❑2, May 1998 ... 2.50
- ❑3, Jun 1998 ... 2.50
- ❑4, Jul 1998 ... 2.50

DEADPAN
ICHOR

- ❑1, Mar 1995 ... 3.95

DEADPAN
SLAVE LABOR

- ❑1, Jan 2006 ... 2.95

DEADPOOL (LTD. SERIES)
MARVEL

- ❑1, Aug 1994 MWa (w) ... 3.00
- ❑2, Sep 1994 MWa (w) ... 2.50
- ❑3, Oct 1994 MWa (w) ... 2.50
- ❑4, Nov 1994 MWa (w) ... 2.50

DEADPOOL
MARVEL

- ❑-1, Jul 1997; O: Deadpool. Flashback ... 2.25
- ❑0; Included as giveaway with Wizard Magazine ... 1.50
- ❑1, Jan 1997; wraparound cover ... 4.00
- ❑2, Feb 1997 ... 3.00
- ❑3, Mar 1997 A: Siryn. ... 2.50
- ❑4, Apr 1997 A: Hulk. V: Hulk ... 2.50
- ❑5, May 1997 ... 2.00
- ❑6, Jun 1997 ... 2.00
- ❑7, Aug 1997; gatefold summary ... 2.00
- ❑8, Sep 1997; gatefold summary ... 2.00
- ❑9, Oct 1997; gatefold summary ... 2.00
- ❑10, Nov 1997; gatefold summary; A: Great Lakes Avengers. back-up feature on making of Deadpool #11 ... 2.00
- ❑11, Dec 1997; gatefold summary; A: Great Lakes Avengers. Deadpool and Blind Al interact with Amazing Spider-Man #47 ... 2.00
- ❑12, Jan 1998; gatefold summary; parody of Faces of the DC Universe month ... 2.00
- ❑13, Feb 1998; gatefold summary ... 2.00
- ❑14, Mar 1998; gatefold summary ... 2.00
- ❑15, Apr 1998; gatefold summary ... 2.00
- ❑16, May 1998; gatefold summary ... 2.00
- ❑17, Jun 1998; gatefold summary ... 2.00
- ❑18, Jul 1998; gatefold summary V: Ajax ... 2.00
- ❑19, Aug 1998; gatefold summary V: Ajax ... 2.00
- ❑20, Sep 1998; gatefold summary ... 2.00
- ❑21, Oct 1998; gatefold summary ... 2.00
- ❑22, Nov 1998; gatefold summary A: Cable. ... 2.00
- ❑23, Dec 1998; gatefold summary; wraparound cover ... 2.99
- ❑24, Jan 1999; gatefold summary A: Tiamat. A: Cosmic Messiah. ... 1.99
- ❑25, Feb 1999 A: Tiamat. A: Captain America. ... 2.99
- ❑26, Mar 1999 ... 1.99
- ❑27, Apr 1999 A: Wolverine. V: Doc Bong. ... 1.99
- ❑28, May 1999 ... 1.99
- ❑29, Jun 1999 ... 1.99
- ❑30, Jul 1999 ... 1.99
- ❑31, Aug 1999 ... 1.99
- ❑32, Sep 1999 ... 1.99
- ❑33, Oct 1999 ... 1.99
- ❑34, Nov 1999 ... 1.99
- ❑35, Dec 1999 ... 2.25
- ❑36, Jan 2000 ... 2.25
- ❑37, Feb 2000 ... 2.25
- ❑38, Mar 2000 ... 2.25
- ❑39, Apr 2000 ... 2.25
- ❑40, May 2000 ... 2.25
- ❑41, Jun 2000 ... 2.25
- ❑42, Jul 2000 ... 2.25
- ❑43, Aug 2000 ... 2.25
- ❑44, Sep 2000 ... 2.25
- ❑45, Oct 2000 ... 2.25
- ❑46, Nov 2000 ... 2.25
- ❑47, Dec 2000 ... 2.25
- ❑48, Jan 2001 ... 2.25
- ❑49, Feb 2001 ... 2.25
- ❑50, Mar 2001 ... 2.25
- ❑51, Apr 2001; A: Kid Deadpool. Detective Comics #39 cover homage ... 2.25
- ❑52, May 2001 ... 2.25
- ❑53, Jun 2001 ... 2.25
- ❑54, Jul 2001 ... 2.25
- ❑55, Aug 2001 ... 2.25
- ❑56, Sep 2001 ... 2.25
- ❑57, Oct 2001 ... 2.25
- ❑58, Nov 2001 ... 2.25
- ❑59, Dec 2001 ... 2.25
- ❑60, Jan 2002 ... 2.25
- ❑61, Feb 2002 ... 2.25
- ❑62, Mar 2002 ... 2.25
- ❑63, Apr 2002 ... 2.25
- ❑64, May 2002 ... 2.25
- ❑65, Jun 2002 ... 2.25
- ❑66, Jul 2002 ... 2.25
- ❑67, Aug 2002 ... 2.25
- ❑68, Sep 2002 ... 2.25
- ❑69, Oct 2002 ... 2.25

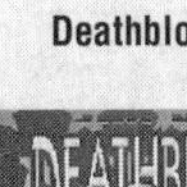

Deathblow

Human killing machine does dirty work
©Image

Deathlok (1st Series)

First mini-series for troubled cyborg soldier
©Marvel

Deathlok (2nd Series)

Cyborg finally lands ongoing series in 1991
©Marvel

Deathmate

Image/Valiant crossover plagued by delays
©Image

Deathstroke the Terminator

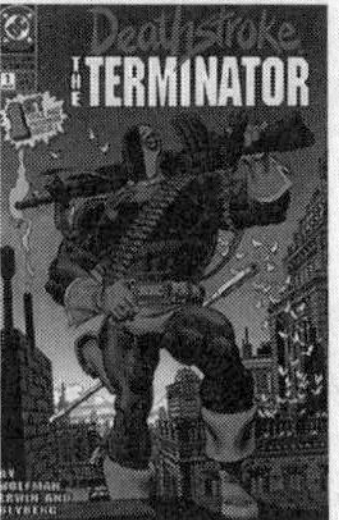

Bad-guy Slade Wilson gets own series
©DC

N-MINT

❑Annual 1998, ca. 1988; gatefold summary; Deadpool/Death '98; wraparound cover 2.99

DEADPOOL TEAM-UP
MARVEL

❑1, Dec 1998; gatefold summary; Secret Wars II tie-in 2.99

DEADPOOL: THE CIRCLE CHASE
MARVEL

❑1, Aug 1993; Embossed cover 2.50
❑2, Sep 1993 .... 2.00
❑3, Oct 1993 .... 2.00
❑4, Nov 1993 .... 2.00

DEADSHOT
DC

❑1, Nov 1988, O: Deadshot. 1.50
❑2, Dec 1988 .... 1.50
❑3, Win 1988 .... 1.50
❑4, Hol 1988 .... 1.50

DEADSHOT (2ND SERIES)
DC

❑1, Feb 2005 .... 2.95
❑2, Mar 2005 .... 2.95
❑3, Apr 2005 .... 2.95
❑4, May 2005 .... 2.99
❑5, Jun 2005 .... 2.99

DEADTIME STORIES
NEW COMICS

❑1, Oct 1987, b&w 1.75

DEADWALKERS
AIRCEL

❑1/A, Jan 1991, "gross" cover 2.50
❑1/B, Jan 1991, "not-so-gross" cover 2.50
❑2, Feb 1991 .... 2.50
❑3, Mar 1991 .... 2.50
❑4, Apr 1991 .... 2.50

DEADWORLD (VOL. 1)
ARROW

❑1, ca. 1986, b&w; Arrow publishes 5.00
❑2 .... 2.50
❑3 .... 2.50
❑4 .... 2.50
❑5 .... 2.50
❑6 .... 2.50
❑7 .... 2.50
❑8 .... 2.50
❑9 .... 2.50
❑10, b&w; Caliber begins as publisher 2.50
❑11, b&w 2.50
❑12, b&w 2.50
❑13, b&w 2.50
❑14, b&w 2.50
❑15, b&w 2.50
❑16, b&w 2.50
❑17, b&w 2.50
❑18, b&w 2.50
❑19, b&w 2.50
❑20, b&w 2.50
❑21, b&w 2.50
❑22, b&w 2.50
❑23, b&w 2.50
❑24, b&w 2.50
❑25, b&w 2.50
❑26, b&w 2.50

N-MINT

DEADWORLD (VOL. 2)
5
CALIBER

❑1, ca. 1993, b&w; Giant-size 3.50
❑2, b&w 3.00
❑3, b&w 3.00
❑4, b&w 3.00
❑5, b&w 3.00
❑6, b&w 3.00
❑7, b&w 2.95
❑8, b&w 2.95
❑9, b&w 2.95
❑10, b&w 2.95
❑11, b&w 2.95
❑12, b&w 2.95
❑13, b&w 2.95
❑14, b&w 2.95
❑15, b&w 2.95

DEADWORLD (3RD SERIES)
IMAGE

❑1, Apr 2005 .... 3.50
❑2 2005 .... 3.50
❑3, May 2006 .... 3.50
❑4, Jul 2006 .... 3.50

DEADWORLD ARCHIVES
CALIBER

❑1, b&w 2.50
❑2, b&w 2.50
❑3, b&w 2.50

DEADWORLD: BITS AND PIECES
CALIBER

❑1, b&w; Reprints 2.95

DEADWORLD CHRONICLES: PLAGUE
CALIBER

❑1 .... 2.95

DEADWORLD: DAEMONSTORM
CALIBER

❑1 .... 3.95

DEADWORLD: NECROPOLIS
CALIBER

❑1 .... 3.95

DEADWORLD: TO KILL A KING
CALIBER

❑1; Sinergy as flip-book 2.95
❑1/Ltd.; limited edition 5.95
❑2 .... 2.95
❑3 .... 2.95

DEAL WITH THE DEVIL
ALIAS

❑1 2005 .... 2.99
❑2 2005 .... 2.99
❑3, Jul 2005 .... 2.99
❑4, Sep 2005 .... 2.99
❑5, Nov 2005 ....

DEAR JULIA
BLACK EYE

❑1 .... 3.50
❑2 .... 3.50
❑3, Feb 1997 .... 3.50
❑4 .... 3.50

DEARS
TOKYOPOP

❑1, Jan 2005 .... 9.95

N-MINT

❑2, Apr 2005 .... 9.95
❑3, Jul 2005 .... 9.95
❑4, Oct 2005 .... 9.95
❑5, Jan 2006 .... 9.95

DEATH3
MARVEL

❑1, Sep 1993, Embossed cover 2.95
❑2, Oct 1993 .... 1.75
❑3, Nov 1993 .... 1.75
❑4, Dec 1993 .... 1.75

DEATH & CANDY
FANTAGRAPHICS

❑1, Win 1999 .... 3.95
❑2 .... 3.95
❑3 .... 3.95
❑4 2005 .... 4.95

DEATH & TAXES: THE REAL COSTS OF LIVING
PARODY

❑1, b&w 2.50

DEATHANGEL
LIGHTNING

❑1/A, Dec 1997 .... 2.95
❑1/B, Dec 1997; alternate cover 2.95

DEATHBLOW
IMAGE

❑0, Aug 1996 JLee (a); 2.50
❑1, Apr 1993; JLee (w); JLee (a); 1: Cybernary. Black varnish cover; Cybernary #1 as flip-book 3.00
❑2, Aug 1993; JLee (w); JLee (a); Cybernary #2 as flip-book 2.50
❑3, Feb 1994; 1: Cisco. Cybernary #3 as flip-book 3.00
❑4, Apr 1994; Cybernary #4 as flip-book 2.00
❑5, May 1994 .... 2.00
❑5/A, May 1994; Variant cover edition; alternate cover 2.00
❑6, Jun 1994 .... 1.95
❑7, Jul 1994 .... 1.95
❑8, Aug 1994 .... 1.95
❑9, Oct 1994 .... 1.95
❑10, Nov 1994; wraparound cover 2.50
❑11, Dec 1994 .... 2.50
❑12, Jan 1995 .... 2.50
❑13, Feb 1995 .... 2.50
❑14, Mar 1995 .... 2.50
❑15, Apr 1995 .... 2.50
❑16, May 1995; bound-in trading cards 1.95
❑16/Variant, May 1995 .... 4.00
❑17, Jun 1995 .... 2.50
❑17/A, Jun 1995; Chicago Comicon limited edition 4.00
❑18, Jul 1995 .... 2.50
❑19, Sep 1995 .... 2.50
❑20, Oct 1995 .... 2.50
❑21, Nov 1995 A: Gen13. .... 2.50
❑22, Dec 1995 .... 2.50
❑23, Jan 1996 .... 2.50
❑24, Feb 1996 A: Grifter. 2.50
❑25, Mar 1996 .... 2.50
❑26, Mar 1996 .... 2.50
❑27, Apr 1996 .... 2.50

❑28, Jul 1996 ... 2.50
❑28/Variant, Jul 1996; alternate cover 4.00
❑29, Aug 1996 ... 2.50

DEATHBLOW: BYBLOWS
WILDSTORM
❑1, Nov 1999 ... 2.95
❑2, Dec 1999 ... 2.95
❑3, Jan 2000 ... 2.95

DEATHBLOW/WOLVERINE
IMAGE
❑1, Sep 1996, crossover with Marvel. 2.50
❑2, Feb 1997, crossover with Marvel.. 2.50

DEATH BY CHOCOLATE
SLEEPING GIANT
❑1, Mar 1996, b&w ... 2.50

DEATH BY CHOCOLATE: SIR GEOFFREY AND THE CHOCOLATE CAR
SLEEPING GIANT
❑1, b&w ... 2.50

DEATH BY CHOCOLATE: THE METABOLATORS
SLEEPING GIANT
❑1, b&w ... 2.50

DEATH CRAZED TEENAGE SUPERHEROES
ARF! ARF!
❑1 ... 1.50
❑2 ... 1.50

DEATH DEALER
VEROTIK
❑1, Jul 1995, FF (c); FF (a); ... 6.00
❑2, May 1996 ... 6.95
❑3, Apr 1997 ... 6.95
❑4, Jul 1997 ... 6.95

DEATH DREAMS OF DRACULA
APPLE
❑1, b&w ... 2.50
❑2, b&w ... 2.50
❑3, b&w ... 2.50
❑4, b&w ... 2.50

DEATH GALLERY
DC / VERTIGO
❑1; portraits ... 3.00

DEATH HAWK
ADVENTURE
❑1, b&w ... 1.95
❑2, b&w ... 1.95
❑3, b&w ... 1.95

DEATH HUNT
ETERNITY
❑1, b&w ... 1.95

DEATH JR.
IMAGE
❑1 2005 ... 4.99
❑2 2005 ... 4.99
❑3, Oct 2005 ...

DEATH, JR.
IMAGE
❑1, May 2005 ... 4.99

DEATHLOK (1ST SERIES)
MARVEL
❑1, Jul 1990 ... 3.95
❑2, Aug 1990 ... 3.95
❑3, Sep 1990 ... 3.95
❑4, Oct 1990 ... 3.95

DEATHLOK (2ND SERIES)
MARVEL
❑1, Jul 1991; Silver ink cover ... 2.50
❑2, Aug 1991 A: Forge ... 2.00
❑3, Sep 1991 V: Doctor Doom ... 2.00
❑4, Oct 1991 ... 2.00
❑5, Nov 1991; X-Men & Fantastic Four crossover ... 2.00
❑6, Dec 1991; Punisher crossover ... 2.00
❑7, Jan 1992; Punisher crossover ... 2.00
❑8, Feb 1992; Punisher crossover ... 2.00
❑9, Mar 1992 A: Ghost Rider. V: Ghost Rider. ... 2.00
❑10, Apr 1992 A: Ghost Rider. V: Ghost Rider. ... 2.00
❑11, May 1992 1: High-Tech. ... 1.75
❑12, Jun 1992 ... 1.75
❑13, Jul 1992 ... 1.75
❑14, Aug 1992 O: Deathlok III (Luther Manning). ... 1.75
❑15, Sep 1992 ... 1.75
❑16, Oct 1992 ... 1.75
❑17, Nov 1992 ... 1.75
❑18, Dec 1992 ... 1.75
❑19, Jan 1993; O: Siege. 1: Siege. foil cover ... 2.25
❑20, Feb 1993 ... 1.75
❑21, Mar 1993 ... 1.75
❑22, Apr 1993 ... 1.75
❑23, May 1993 ... 1.75
❑24, Jun 1993 ... 1.75
❑25, Jul 1993; A: Black Panther. foil cover ... 1.75
❑26, Aug 1993 A: Hobgoblin. ... 1.75
❑27, Sep 1993 ... 1.75
❑28, Oct 1993; A: Timestream. A: Goddess. Infinity Crusade crossover 1.75
❑29, Nov 1993 ... 1.75
❑30, Dec 1993 ... 1.75
❑31, Jan 1994 ... 1.75
❑32, Feb 1994 ... 1.75
❑33, Mar 1994 ... 1.75
❑34, Apr 1994 ... 1.75
❑Annual 1, ca. 1992 BG (a) ... 2.50
❑Annual 2, ca. 1993; O: Tracer. 1: Tracer. Polybagged ... 2.95
❑Special 1, May 1991; BG (a); reprints Deathlok (1st series) #1 ... 2.00
❑Special 2, Jun 1991; BG (a); reprints Deathlok (1st series) #2 ... 2.00
❑Special 3, Jun 1991; reprints Deathlok (1st series) #3 ... 2.00
❑Special 4, Jun 1991; reprints Deathlok (1st series) #4 ... 2.00

DEATHLOK (3RD SERIES)
MARVEL
❑1, Sep 1999 ... 2.00
❑2, Oct 1999 ... 1.99
❑3, Nov 1999 ... 1.99
❑4, Nov 1999 ... 1.99
❑5, Dec 1999 ... 1.99

DEATHMARK
LIGHTNING
❑1, Dec 1994, b&w ... 2.95

DEATHMASK
FUTURE
❑1, Apr 2003 ... 2.99
❑2, Jun 2003 ... 2.99
❑3, Jul 2003 ... 2.99

DEATHMATE
IMAGE / VALIANT
❑1, Sep 1993; BL (w); crossover; prologue; silver cover ... 2.95
❑1/Gold, Sep 1993; Gold cover (limited promotional edition); BL (w); Gold cover (limited promotional edition); Prologue ... 4.00
❑2, Sep 1993; JLee (a); 1: Fairchild. 1: Burn-Out. 1: Gen13 (full). 1: Freefall. Black ... 3.00
❑2/Gold, Sep 1993; Gold edition 1: Gen13 (full). ... 6.00
❑3, Sep 1993; Yellow; cover says Oct, indicia says Sep ... 4.95
❑3/Gold, Sep 1993; Gold edition; Yellow ... 6.00
❑4, Oct 1993; Blue ... 4.95
❑4/Gold, Oct 1993; Gold edition; Blue 6.00
❑5, Nov 1993; Red ... 4.95
❑5/Gold, Nov 1993; Gold edition; Red 6.00
❑6, Feb 1994; BL (w); Epilogue; silver cover ... 2.95
❑6/Gold, Feb 1994; Gold edition ... 4.00
❑Ashcan 1, Aug 1993; ashcan edition 1.00

DEATH METAL
MARVEL
❑1, Jan 1994 ... 1.95
❑2, Feb 1994 ... 1.95
❑3, Mar 1994 ... 1.95
❑4, Apr 1994 ... 1.95

DEATH METAL VS. GENETIX
MARVEL
❑1, Dec 1993 ... 2.95
❑2, Jan 1994 ... 2.95

DEATH NOTE
VIZ
❑1, Oct 2005 ... 9.95
❑2, Dec 2005 ... 9.95

DEATH OF ANGEL GIRL
ANGEL
❑1 ... 2.95

DEATH OF ANTISOCIALMAN
NOT AVAILABLE
❑1 ... 0.50
❑2 ... 0.50
❑3 ... 0.50
❑4 ... 0.50
❑5 ... 0.50
❑6 ... 0.50
❑7 ... 0.50
❑8 ... 0.50
❑9 ... 0.50
❑10 ... 0.50

DEATH OF LADY VAMPRÉ
BLACKOUT
❑1, ... 2.95

DEATH OF STUPIDMAN
PARODY
❑1, ... 3.50

DEATH OF SUPERBABE
SPOOF
❑1, b&w ... 3.95

DEATH OF VAMPIRELLA
HARRIS
❑1, Feb 1997; Memorial Edition; Chromium cover; Green logo ... 15.00
❑1/Variant, Feb 1997; Holofoil chromium edition; 750 copies printed; Yellow logo ... 15.00

DEATH RACE 2020
COSMIC
❑1, Apr 1995; sequel to Corman film.. 2.50
❑2, May 1995 ... 2.50
❑5, Aug 1995 ... 2.50

DEATH RATTLE (VOL. 2)
KITCHEN SINK
❑1, Oct 1985 ... 2.00
❑2, Dec 1985 ... 2.00
❑3, Feb 1986 ... 2.00
❑4 ... 2.00
❑5 ... 2.00
❑6, b&w; Black and white; Listed as #5 in indicia ... 2.00
❑7, b&w ... 2.00
❑8, Dec 1986 ... 2.00
❑9, Jan 1987 ... 2.00
❑10, Mar 1987 ... 2.00
❑11, May 1987 ... 2.00
❑12, Jul 1987 ... 2.00
❑13, Nov 1987 ... 2.00
❑14, Jan 1988 ... 2.00
❑15, Mar 1988 ... 2.00
❑16, May 1988 ... 2.00
❑17, Jul 1988 ... 2.00
❑18, Oct 1988 ... 2.00

DEATH RATTLE (VOL. 3)
KITCHEN SINK
❑½, Nov 1995, b&w ... 1.00
❑1, Oct 1995, b&w ... 2.95
❑2, Dec 1995, b&w ... 2.95
❑3, Feb 1996 ... 2.95
❑4, Apr 1996 ... 2.95
❑5, Jun 1996, b&w ... 2.95
❑6 ... 2.95

DEATHROW
HEROIC / BLUE COMET
❑1, Sep 1993, b&w ... 2.50

DEATH'S HEAD
MARVEL
❑1, Dec 1988 ... 1.75
❑2, Jan 1989 ... 1.75
❑3, Feb 1989 ... 1.75
❑4, Mar 1989 ... 1.75
❑5, Apr 1989 ... 1.75
❑6, May 1989 ... 1.75
❑7, Jun 1989 ... 1.75
❑8, Jul 1989 ... 1.75

Other grades: Multiply price above by 5/6 for VF/NM • 2/3 for VERY FINE • 1/3 for FINE • 1/5 for VERY GOOD • 1/8 for GOOD

Death Talks About Life

AIDS-prevention giveaway comic
©DC

Death: The High Cost of Living

Acclaimed Neil Gaiman limited series
©DC

Decade of Dark Horse

All-new stories from Dark Horse creators
©Dark Horse

Decoy

Pudgy green alien helps policeman
©Penny-Farthing

Defenders

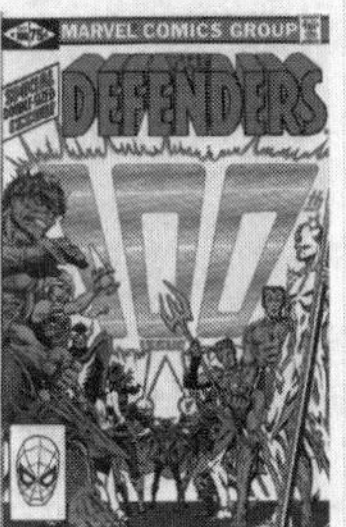

Often occult-themed super-hero "non-team"
©Marvel

N-MINT

❑9, Aug 1989 ... 1.75
❑10, Sep 1989 ... 1.75

DEATH'S HEAD II (VOL. 1)
MARVEL

❑1, Mar 1992 1: Death's Head II. D: Death's Head. ... 2.50
❑1/2nd, Mar 1992; 1: Death's Head II. D: Death's Head. Silver ink cover ... 1.75
❑2, Apr 1992 ... 2.00
❑2/2nd, Apr 1992; Silver ink cover ... 1.75
❑3, May 1992 1: Tuck. ... 2.00
❑4, Jun 1992 A: Wolverine. A: Captain America. ... 2.00

DEATH'S HEAD II (VOL. 2)
MARVEL

❑1, Dec 1992; A: X-Men. gatefold cover 2.00
❑2, Jan 1993 A: X-Men. ... 2.00
❑3, Feb 1993 A: X-Men. ... 2.00
❑4, Mar 1993 A: X-Men. ... 2.00
❑5, Apr 1993 ... 1.75
❑6, May 1993 ... 1.95
❑7, Jun 1993 ... 1.95
❑8, Jul 1993 ... 1.95
❑9, Aug 1993 ... 1.95
❑10, Sep 1993 ... 1.95
❑11, Oct 1993 1: Death's Head III. A: Doctor Necker. A: Charnel. ... 1.95
❑12, Nov 1993 ... 1.95
❑13, Dec 1993 ... 1.95
❑14, Jan 1994; Prelude to Death's Head Gold #1; foil cover ... 2.95
❑15, Feb 1994 ... 1.95
❑16, Mar 1994 ... 1.95

DEATH'S HEAD II & THE ORIGIN OF DIE-CUT
MARVEL

❑1, Aug 1993, foil cover ... 2.95
❑2, Sep 1993, ... 1.75

DEATH'S HEAD II GOLD
MARVEL

❑1; foil cover ... 3.95

DEATH SHRIKE
BRAINSTORM

❑1, Jul 1993, b&w ... 2.95

DEATHSNAKE
FANTAGRAPHICS / EROS

❑1, Aug 1994 ... 2.95
❑2, Oct 1994, b&w ... 2.95

DEATHSTROKE THE TERMINATOR
DC

❑0, Oct 1994; published between #40 and #41; Title changes to Deathstroke the Hunted ... 2.00
❑1, Aug 1991 O: Deathstroke the Terminator. ... 3.00
❑1/2nd O: Deathstroke the Terminator. 1.75
❑2, Sep 1991 ... 2.00
❑3, Oct 1991 ... 2.00
❑4, Nov 1991 V: Ravager. ... 2.00
❑5, Dec 1991 ... 2.00
❑6, Jan 1992 ... 2.00
❑7, Feb 1992; Batman ... 2.00
❑8, Mar 1992; Batman ... 2.00

N-MINT

❑9, Apr 1992; 1: Vigilante III (Pat Trayce). Batman ... 2.00
❑10, Jun 1992 ... 2.00
❑11, Jun 1992; Vigilante ... 2.00
❑12, Jul 1992 MG (a) ... 2.00
❑13, Aug 1992 ... 2.00
❑14, Sep 1992 ... 2.00
❑15, Oct 1992 ... 2.00
❑16, Nov 1992 D: Deathstroke the Terminator. ... 2.00
❑17, Dec 1992; Deathstroke the Terminator revived ... 2.00
❑18, Jan 1993 ... 2.00
❑19, Feb 1993; Quarac destroyed ... 2.00
❑20, Mar 1993 ... 1.75
❑21, Apr 1993 ... 1.75
❑22, May 1993 ... 1.75
❑23, May 1993 ... 1.75
❑24, Jun 1993 ... 1.75
❑25, Jun 1993 ... 1.75
❑26, Jul 1993 ... 1.75
❑27, Aug 1993 ... 1.75
❑28, Sep 1993 ... 1.75
❑29, Oct 1993 ... 1.75
❑30, Nov 1993 ... 1.75
❑31, Dec 1993 ... 1.75
❑32, Jan 1994 ... 1.75
❑33, Feb 1994 ... 1.75
❑34, Mar 1994 ... 1.75
❑35, Apr 1994 ... 1.75
❑36, May 1994 ... 1.75
❑37, Jun 1994 ... 1.75
❑38, Jul 1994 A: Vigilante III (Pat Trayce). A: Vigilante. ... 1.95
❑39, Aug 1994; A: Green Arrow. Title becomes "Deathstroke the Hunted" 1.95
❑40, Sep 1994 ... 1.95
❑41, Nov 1994 ... 1.95
❑42, Dec 1994 ... 1.95
❑43, Jan 1995 ... 1.95
❑44, Feb 1995 ... 1.95
❑45, Mar 1995 ... 1.95
❑46, Apr 1995 ... 1.95
❑47, May 1995 ... 1.95
❑48, Jun 1995 ... 2.25
❑49, Jul 1995 ... 2.25
❑50, Aug 1995; Giant-size; Title changes to Deathstroke ... 3.50
❑51, Sep 1995 ... 2.25
❑52, Oct 1995 GP (a); A: Hawkman. .. 2.25
❑53, Nov 1995 ... 2.25
❑54, Dec 1995 ... 2.25
❑55, Jan 1996 ... 2.25
❑56, Feb 1996 ... 2.25
❑57, Mar 1996 ... 2.25
❑58, Apr 1996 V: Joker. ... 2.25
❑59, May 1996 ... 2.25
❑60, Jun 1996 ... 2.25
❑Annual 1, ca. 1992 A: Vigilante. ... 3.50
❑Annual 2, ca. 1993 1: Gunfire. ... 3.50
❑Annual 3, ca. 1994; Elseworlds ... 3.95
❑Annual 4 1995; Year One. ... 3.95

DEATH TALKS ABOUT LIFE
DC / VERTIGO

❑1 NG (w) ... 1.50

N-MINT

DEATH: THE HIGH COST OF LIVING
DC / VERTIGO

❑1, Mar 1993 NG (w) ... 3.00
❑1/Platinum; Platinum edition NG (w) 6.00
❑2, Apr 1993 NG (w) ... 3.00
❑3, May 1993; regular edition NG (w) 3.00
❑3/A, May 1993; with error ... 4.00

DEATH: THE TIME OF YOUR LIFE
DC / VERTIGO

❑1, Apr 1996 NG (w) ... 3.50
❑2, May 1996 NG (w) ... 3.00
❑3, Jun 1996 NG (w) ... 3.00

DEATHWATCH
HARRIER

❑1, Jul 1987 ... 1.95

DEATHWISH
MILESTONE / DC

❑1, Dec 1994 ... 2.50
❑2, Jan 1995 ... 2.50
❑3, Feb 1995 ... 2.50
❑4, Mar 1995 ... 2.50

DEATHWORLD
ADVENTURE

❑1, Nov 1990, b&w ... 2.50
❑2, Dec 1990, b&w ... 2.50
❑3, Jan 1991, b&w ... 2.50
❑4, Feb 1991, b&w ... 2.50

DEATHWORLD BOOK II
ADVENTURE

❑1, Apr 1991, b&w ... 2.50
❑2, May 1991, b&w ... 2.50
❑3, Jun 1991, b&w ... 2.50
❑4, Jul 1991, b&w ... 2.50

DEATHWORLD BOOK III
ADVENTURE

❑1, Aug 1991, b&w ... 2.50
❑2, Sep 1991, b&w ... 2.50
❑3, Nov 1991, b&w ... 2.50
❑4, Dec 1991, b&w ... 2.50

DEATH WRECK
MARVEL

❑1, Jan 1994 ... 1.95
❑2, Feb 1994 ... 1.95
❑3, Mar 1994 ... 1.95
❑4, Apr 1994 ... 1.95

DEBBIE DOES COMICS
AIRCEL

❑1, b&w ... 2.95

DEBBIE DOES DALLAS
AIRCEL

❑1, Mar 1991 ... 2.50
❑1/3D ... 3.95
❑1/2nd ... 2.50
❑2, Apr 1991 ... 2.50
❑3, May 1991 ... 2.50
❑4, Jun 1991 ... 2.50
❑5, Jul 1991 ... 2.50
❑6 1991 ... 2.50
❑7, Oct 1991 ... 2.50
❑8, Nov 1991 ... 2.50
❑9, Dec 1991 ... 2.95
❑10 1992 ... 2.95

Other grades: Multiply price above by 5/6 for VF/NM • 2/3 for VERY FINE • 1/3 for FINE • 1/5 for VERY GOOD • 1/8 for GOOD

N-MINT

❑11 1992 2.95
❑12 1992 2.95
❑13 1992 2.95
❑14 1992 2.95
❑15 2.95
❑16 2.95
❑17 2.95
❑18 2.95

DEBBI'S DATES
DC

❑1, May 1969 30.00
❑2, Jul 1969 18.00
❑3, Sep 1969 18.00
❑4, Nov 1969 18.00
❑5, Jan 1970 18.00
❑6, Mar 1970 30.00
❑7, May 1970 18.00
❑8, Jul 1970 18.00
❑9, Sep 1970 18.00
❑10, Nov 1970 18.00
❑11, Jan 1971 18.00

DECADE OF DARK HORSE
DARK HORSE

❑1, Jul 1996; Sin City, Predator, Grendel stories 2.95
❑2, Aug 1996; Star Wars, Ghost, Trekker stories 2.95
❑3, Sep 1996; Aliens, Outlanders, Nexus, The Mask stories 2.95
❑4, Oct 1996; b&w and color, Concrete, Black Cross, Exon Depot, Godzilla stories, final issue 2.95

DECAPITATOR (RANDY BOWEN'S...)
DARK HORSE

❑1, Jun 1998 2.95
❑2, Jul 1998 2.95
❑3, Aug 1998 2.95
❑4, Sep 1998 2.95

DECEPTION
IMAGE

❑1, ca. 1999 2.95
❑2, ca. 1999 2.95
❑3, ca. 1999 2.95

DECIMATION: HOUSE OF M - THE DAY AFTER
MARVEL

❑1, Jan 2006, b&w 3.99

DECORATOR
FANTAGRAPHICS / EROS

❑1, b&w 2.50

DECOY
PENNY-FARTHING

❑1, Mar 1999 2.75
❑1/Autographed, Mar 1999 3.25
❑2, Apr 1999 2.75
❑3, May 1999 2.75
❑4, Jun 1999 2.75

HEROBEAR AND THE KID AND DECOY
ASTONISH

❑1, Jul 2002, 2.95
❑2, ca. 2002, Title changes to Decoy and Herobear and the Kid 2.95

DECOY: STORM OF THE CENTURY
PENNY-FARTHING

❑1, Jul 2002 0.00
❑2, Aug 2002 2.95
❑3, Sep 2002 2.95
❑4, Oct 2002 2.95

DEE DEE
FANTAGRAPHICS / EROS

❑1, Jul 1996, b&w 2.95

DEEP
MARVEL

❑1, Nov 1977 Cl (c); Cl (a); 1.50

DEEP BLACK
CHAOS!

❑1/A, Aug 1997; No cover price; b&w pencilled pin-ups 2.00
❑1/B, Aug 1997; b&w pencilled pin-ups; all-white cardstock cover 2.00

DEEPEST DIMENSION
REVOLUTIONARY

❑1, Jun 1993 2.50
❑2, Aug 1993 2.50

DEEP GIRL
ARIEL BORDEAUX

❑1 2.50
❑2 2.50
❑3 1.50
❑4 2.50
❑5 2.50

DEEP SLEEPER
ONI

❑1, Feb 2004 3.50
❑2, Apr 2004, Moves to Image with #3 3.50

DEEP SLEEPER (IMAGE)
IMAGE

❑3, Aug 2004 2.95
❑4, Sep 2004 2.95

DEEP TERROR
AVALON

❑1, b&w 2.95

DEE VEE
DEE VEE

❑1, Feb 1997 2.95
❑5, Feb 1998, b&w; wraparound cover 2.95
❑6, Apr 1998, b&w; wraparound cover 2.95
❑7, Jun 1998, b&w; wraparound cover 2.95

DEFCON 4
IMAGE

❑1/A, Feb 1996; wraparound cover 2.50
❑1/B, Feb 1996; alternate wraparound cover 2.50
❑2, Mar 1996 2.50
❑3, Jun 1996; cover says May, indicia says Jun 2.50
❑4, Sep 1996 2.50
❑5 1996 2.50

DEFENDERS (DELL)
DELL

❑1, Sep 1962 26.00
❑2, Feb 1963 16.00

DEFENDERS
MARVEL

❑1, Aug 1972, SB (c); SB (a); Team consists of Doctor Strange, Hulk, and Sub-Mariner 90.00
❑2, Oct 1972, SB (c); SB (a); A: Silver Surfer. Silver Surfer joins Defenders 35.00
❑3, Dec 1972, GK (c); SB, JM (a); A: . A: Black Knight. A: Silver Surfer. 50.00
❑4, Feb 1973, SB (c); FMc, SB (a); Valkyrie joins Defenders 26.00
❑5, Apr 1973, SB (c); FMc, SB (a); D: Omegatron. 26.00
❑6, Jun 1973,SB (c); FMc, SB (a) 16.00
❑7, Aug 1973, (c); SB (a); A: Hawkeye. 16.00
❑8, Sep 1973, SB (c); FMc, SB (a); A: Avengers. Avengers and Defenders vs. Loki and Dormammu, part 2 - continues in Avengers #116 (continued from Avengers #115) 30.00
❑9, Oct 1973, SB (c); FMc, SB (a); A: Avengers. Avengers and Defenders vs. Loki and Dormammu, part 4 - continues in Avengers #117 16.00
❑10, Nov 1973, SB (c); SB (a); A: Avengers. Avengers and Defenders vs. Loki and Dormammu, part 6 - continues in Avengers #118 65.00
❑11, Dec 1973, SB (c); SB (a); A: Avengers. Avengers and Defenders vs. Loki and Dormammu, part 8, continued from Avengers #118; Hawkeye, Silver Surfer and Sub-Mariner leave Defenders 15.00
❑12, Feb 1974, (c); SB, JAb (a); Hulk fights Xemnu the Titan 9.00
❑13, May 1974, SB, KJ (c); SB, KJ (a); 1: Nebulon. A: . A: Nighthawk. Marvel Value Stamp #86: Zemo 9.00
❑14, Jul 1974, (c); SB, DGr (a); Nighthawk joins Defenders 10.00
❑15, Sep 1974, SB (c); SB, KJ (a); A: . A: Professor X. A: Magneto. V: Magneto. Nighthawk gets new costume; Marvel Value Stamp #8: Captain America 10.00
❑16, Oct 1974, GK (c); SB (a); A: . A: Professor X. A: Magneto. Marvel Value Stamp #44: Absorbing Man 10.00
❑17, Nov 1974, (c); SB, DGr (a); 1: Bulldozer. A: . A: Luke Cage. Marvel Value Stamp #20: Brother Voodoo 6.50
❑18, Dec 1974, SB (c); SB, DGr (a); O: Bulldozer. A: . A: Luke Cage. V: Wrecking Crew. 6.50
❑19, Jan 1975, (c); SB, KJ (a); A: Luke Cage. Marvel Value Stamp #98: Puppet Master 6.50
❑20, Feb 1975, SB (c); SB (a); O: . O: Valkyrie. A: Thing. Marvel Value Stamp #31: Mordo 7.00
❑21, Mar 1975, SB, KJ (c); SB (a); 1: The Headmen. The Headmen introduced 6.00
❑22, Apr 1975, GK (c); SB (a); A: Sons of the Serpent. The Sons of the Serpent 6.00
❑23, May 1975, GK, KJ (c); SB (a); A: Yellowjacket. Marvel Value Stamp #78: Owl 6.00
❑24, Jun 1975, GK, KJ (c); SB, BMc (a); A: Yellowjacket. A: Daredevil. A: Luke Cage. A: Son of Satan. 6.00
❑25, Jul 1975, (c); SB, JAb (a); A: Yellowjacket. A: Yellowjacket. A: Daredevil. A: Luke Cage. A: Son of Satan. 6.50
❑26, Aug 1975, SB (c); SB (a); A: Guardians of the Galaxy. Continued from Giant-Size Defenders #5 7.00
❑27, Sep 1975, SB (c); SB (a); 1: Starhawk II (Aleta)-cameo. A: Guardians of the Galaxy. 7.00
❑28, Oct 1975, (c); SB (a); 1: Starhawk II (Aleta)-full. A: Guardians of the Galaxy. 7.00
❑29, Nov 1975, (c); SB (a); A: Guardians of the Galaxy. 7.00
❑30, Dec 1975, (c); JAb (a); 4.00
❑31, Jan 1976, GK (c); SB, JM (a); 4.00
❑32, Feb 1976, GK, KJ (c); SB, JM (a); O: Nighthawk II (Kyle Richmond). 4.00
❑33, Mar 1976, GK (c); SB, JM (a); 4.00
❑34, Apr 1976, RB, DA (c); SB, JM (a); V: Nebulon. 4.00
❑34/30 cent, Apr 1976, RB, DA (c); SB, JM (a); V: Nebulon. 30 cent regional price variant 20.00
❑35, May 1976, GK (c); SB, KJ (a); 1: Red Guardian II (Doctor Tanja Belinskya). 4.00
❑35/30 cent, May 1976, GK (c); SB, KJ (a); 1: Red Guardian II (Doctor Tanja Belinskya). 30 cent regional price variant 20.00
❑36, Jun 1976, GK (c); SB, KJ (a) 4.00
❑36/30 cent, Jun 1976, GK (c); SB, KJ (a); 30 cent regional price variant 20.00
❑37, Jul 1976, GK (c); SB, KJ (a) 4.00
❑37/30 cent, Jul 1976, GK (c); SB, KJ (a); 30 cent regional price variant 20.00
❑38, Aug 1976, SB (c); SB, KJ (a) 5.00
❑38/30 cent, Aug 1976,SB (c); SB, KJ (a); 30 cent regional price variant 5.00
❑39, Sep 1976, (c); SB, KJ (a) 4.00
❑40, Oct 1976, GK, KJ (c); SB, KJ (a). 4.00
❑41, Nov 1976, GK, KJ (c); SB, KJ (a) 4.00
❑42, Dec 1976, (c); KG, KJ (a) 4.00
❑43, Jan 1977, AM, JK (c); KG, KJ (a) 4.00
❑44, Feb 1977, (c); KG, KJ (a); Newsstand edition (distributed by Curtis); issue number in box; Hellcat joins Defenders 4.00
❑44/Whitman, Feb 1977, (c); KG, KJ (a); Special markets edition (usually sold in Whitman bagged prepacks); price appears in a diamond; UPC barcode appears; Hellcat joins Defenders 4.00
❑45, Mar 1977, JK (c); KG, KJ (a); Newsstand edition (distributed by Curtis); issue number in box 4.00
❑45/Whitman, Mar 1977, JK (c); KG, KJ (a); Special markets edition (usually sold in Whitman bagged prepacks); price appears in a diamond; UPC barcode appears 4.00
❑46, Apr 1977, (c); KG, KJ (a) 4.00
❑47, May 1977, (c); KG, KJ (a); A: Moon Knight. Newsstand edition (distributed by Curtis); issue number in box 4.00
❑47/Whitman, May 1977, (c); KG, KJ (a); A: Moon Knight. Special markets edition (usually sold in Whitman bagged prepacks); price appears in a diamond; UPC barcode appears 4.00
❑48, Jun 1977, (c); KG, DGr (a); O: Zodiac II. Newsstand edition (distributed by Curtis); issue number in box 5.00

N-MINT

❑48/Whitman, Jun 1977, (c); KG, DGr (a); O: Zodiac II. Special markets edition (usually sold in Whitman bagged prepacks); price appears in a diamond; UPC barcode appears ... 5.00
❑48/35 cent, Jun 1977, (c); KG, DGr (a); O: Zodiac II. Newsstand edition (distributed by Curtis); issue number in box; 35 cent regional price variant 15.00
❑49, Jul 1977, (c); KG (a); O: Zodiac II. 4.00
❑49/35 cent, Jul 1977, (c); KG (a); O: Zodiac II. 35 cent regional price variant 15.00
❑50, Aug 1977, KG (a); O: Zodiac II. Newsstand edition (distributed by Curtis); issue number in box 4.00
❑50/Whitman, Aug 1977, KG (a); O: Zodiac II. Special markets edition (usually sold in Whitman bagged prepacks); price appears in a diamond; UPC barcode appears 4.00
❑50/35 cent, Aug 1977, Newsstand edition (distributed by Curtis); issue number in box; 35 cent regional price variant 15.00
❑51, Sep 1977, GP (c); KG, KJ (a); 1: Ringer I (Anthony Davis). A: Moon Knight. Newsstand edition (distributed by Curtis); issue number in box; Moon Knight 4.00
❑51/Whitman, Sep 1977, GP (c); KG, KJ (a); 1: Ringer I (Anthony Davis). A: Moon Knight. Special markets edition (usually sold in Whitman bagged prepacks); price appears in a diamond; UPC barcode appears ... 4.00
❑51/35 cent, Sep 1977, GP (c); KG, KJ (a); 1: Ringer I (Anthony Davis). A: Moon Knight. Newsstand edition (distributed by Curtis); issue number in box; Moon Knight; 35 cent regional price variant 15.00
❑52, Oct 1977, GK (c); KG (a); O: Presence. 1: Presence. A: Hulk. V: Sub-Mariner. Newsstand edition (distributed by Curtis); issue number in box 4.00
❑52/Whitman, Oct 1977, GK (c); KG (a); O: Presence. 1: Presence. A: Hulk. V: Sub-Mariner. Special markets edition (usually sold in Whitman bagged prepacks); price appears in a diamond; no UPC barcode 4.00
❑52/35 cent, Oct 1977, GK (c); KG (a); O: Presence. 1: Presence. A: Hulk. V: Sub-Mariner. Newsstand edition (distributed by Curtis); issue number in box; 35 cent regional price variant 15.00
❑53, Nov 1977, GP, BWi (c); MG, KG, DC (a); 1: Lunatik. Newsstand edition (distributed by Curtis); issue number in box 4.00
❑53/Whitman, Nov 1977, GP, BWi (c); MG, KG, DC (a); 1: Lunatik. Special markets edition (usually sold in Whitman bagged prepacks); price appears in a diamond; no UPC barcode 4.00
❑54, Dec 1977, (c); MG, KG, BMc (a); 4.00
❑55, Jan 1978, GK (c); CI, KJ (a); O: Red Guardian II (Doctor Tanja Belinskya). 4.00
❑56, Feb 1978, (c); CI, KJ (a) 4.00
❑57, Mar 1978, (c); DGr, GT, DC (a) ... 4.00
❑58, Apr 1978, (c); DGr, KJ (a); 4.00
❑59, May 1978, (c); DGr (a) 4.00
❑60, Jun 1978, (c); DGr (a) 4.00
❑61, Jul 1978, (c) 4.00
❑62, Aug 1978, BL, JR2 (c); SB, JM (a); Newsstand edition (distributed by Curtis); issue number in box 4.00
❑62/Whitman, Aug 1978, BL, JR2 (c); SB, JM (a); Special markets edition (usually sold in Whitman bagged prepacks); price appears in a diamond; no UPC barcode 4.00
❑63, Sep 1978, JSt (c); SB, JM (a); Newsstand edition (distributed by Curtis); issue number in box 5.00
❑63/Whitman, Sep 1978, JSt (c); SB, JM (a); Special markets edition (usually sold in Whitman bagged prepacks); price appears in a diamond; UPC barcode appears 5.00
❑64, Oct 1978, SB (c); SB, DP (a); Newsstand edition (distributed by Curtis); issue number in box 4.00
❑64/Whitman, Oct 1978, SB (c); SB, DP (a); Special markets edition (usually sold in Whitman bagged prepacks); price appears in a diamond; no UPC barcode 4.00
❑65, Nov 1978, DP (a) 4.00
❑66, Dec 1978, SB (c) 4.00
❑67, Jan 1979, (c); Newsstand edition (distributed by Curtis); issue number in box 4.00
❑67/Whitman, Jan 1979, (c); Special markets edition (usually sold in Whitman bagged prepacks); price appears in a diamond; no UPC barcode 4.00
❑68, Feb 1979, (c); HT (a); Newsstand edition (distributed by Curtis); issue number in box 4.00
❑68/Whitman, Feb 1979, (c); HT (a); Special markets edition (usually sold in Whitman bagged prepacks); price appears in a diamond; no UPC barcode 4.00
❑69, Mar 1979, (c); AM, HT (a) 4.00
❑70, Apr 1979, (c); HT (a); A: Lunatik. V: Lunatik. 4.00
❑71, May 1979, HT (c); HT, JAb (a); O: Lunatik. 4.00
❑72, Jun 1979, HT (c); HT (a); A: Lunatik. 4.00
❑73, Jul 1979, HT (c); HT (a); A: Foolkiller II (Greg Salinger). 4.00
❑74, Aug 1979, HT (c); HT (a); A: Foolkiller II (Greg Salinger). Nighthawk II resigns from Defenders 4.00
❑75, Sep 1979, HT (c); HT (a); A: Foolkiller II (Greg Salinger). 4.00
❑76, Oct 1979, RB (c); HT (a); O: Omega. 4.00
❑77, Nov 1979, RB (c); AM, HT (a); D: James-Michael Starling (Omega the Unknown's counterpart). 4.00
❑78, Dec 1979, HT (a); m Original Defenders return 4.00
❑79, Jan 1980, RB (c); HT (a) 4.00
❑80, Feb 1980, RB (c); DGr, HT (a) 4.00
❑81, Mar 1980, RB (c); HT, JAb (a) 4.00
❑82, Apr 1980, RB (c); DP, JSt (a) 4.00
❑83, May 1980, RB (c); DP (a) 4.00
❑84, Jun 1980, RB (c); DP (a) 4.00
❑85, Jul 1980, RB (c); DP, JM (a) 4.00
❑86, Aug 1980, RB (c); DP (a) 4.00
❑87, Sep 1980, (c); DP (a) 4.00
❑88, Oct 1980, MN (c); DP (a) 4.00
❑89, Nov 1980, MN (c); DP (a) 4.00
❑90, Dec 1980, RB (c); DP (a); A: Daredevil. 4.00
❑91, Jan 1981, RB (c); DP (a); A: Daredevil. 4.00
❑92, Feb 1981, DP (a) 4.00
❑93, Mar 1981, DP, JSt (a) 2.50
❑94, Apr 1981, MG (c); DP, JSt (a); 1: Gargoyle. 2.50
❑95, May 1981, PB (c); DP, JSt (a); O: Gargoyle. A: Dracula. 2.50
❑96, Jun 1981, MG (c); DP, JSt (a); A: Ghost Rider. 2.50
❑97, Jul 1981, AM (c); DP, JSt (a) 2.50
❑98, Aug 1981, MR (c); DP, JSt (a) 2.50
❑99, Sep 1981, AM (c); DP, JSt (a) 2.50
❑100, Oct 1981, Giant-size; AM (c); DP, JSt (a); giant 2.50
❑101, Nov 1981, AM (c); DP, JSt (a); A: Silver Surfer. 2.00
❑102, Dec 1981, AM (c); DP, JSt, JAb (a) 2.00
❑103, Jan 1982, AM (c); DP, JSt (a); O: Null the Living Darkness. 1: Null the Living Darkness. 2.00
❑104, Feb 1982, AM (c); DP, JSt (a) 2.00
❑105, Mar 1982, AM (c); DP, JSt (a) 2.00
❑106, Apr 1982, AM (c); AM, DP, JAb (a); A: Daredevil. D: Nighthawk II (Kyle Richmond). 2.00
❑107, May 1982, AM (c); AM, DP (a); A: Enchantress. 2.00
❑108, Jun 1982, AM, DP (c); AM, DP, JSt (a) 2.00
❑109, Jul 1982, AM (c); DP, JSt (a) 2.00
❑110, Aug 1982, AM (c); DP (a) 2.00
❑111, Sep 1982, AM (c); DP (a) 2.00
❑112, Oct 1982, BA (c); DP, MGu (a); 1: Power Princess. 1: Nuke I (Albert Gaines). 2.00
❑113, Nov 1982, DP (c); DP (w); DP, MGu (a); 2.00
❑114, Dec 1982, AM, DP (c); DP (w); DP, MGu (a) 2.00
❑115, Jan 1983, DP (c); DP (a) 2.00
❑116, Feb 1983, DP (c); DP (a) 2.00
❑117, Mar 1983, DP, JAb (c); DP, JAb (a) 2.00
❑118, Apr 1983, AM, DP (c); DP (a) 2.00
❑119, May 1983, SB, JAb (a); 1: Yandroth II. 2.00
❑120, Jun 1983, DP, JAb (c); DP, JAb (a) 2.00
❑121, Jul 1983 DP (c); DP (w); DP, JAb (a) 2.00
❑122, Aug 1983 BA, DP (c); DP (a); 2.00
❑123, Sep 1983 BSz (c); DP (a); 1: Cloud. 2.00
❑124, Oct 1983 DP (a); 2.00
❑125, Nov 1983; double-sized; BSz (c); DP (a); 1: Mad-Dog. New team begins: Valkyrie, Beast, Iceman, Angel, Gargoyle, and Moondragon . 2.00
❑126, Dec 1983 MZ (c); O: Leviathan I (Edward Cobert). 1: Leviathan I (Edward Cobert). 2.00
❑127, Jan 1984 MZ (c); SB (a); 2.00
❑128, Feb 1984 KN (c); 2.00
❑129, Mar 1984 BG (c); DP (a); A: New Mutants. V: New Mutants. 2.00
❑130, Apr 1984 MZ (a); 2.00
❑131, May 1984 BSz (c); 1.50
❑132, Jun 1984 DP (a); 1.50
❑133, Jul 1984 KN (c); 1: Manslaughter (cameo). 1.50
❑134, Aug 1984 KN (c); DP (a); 1: Manslaughter (full appearance). 1.50
❑135, Sep 1984 BSz (c); DP (a); 1.50
❑136, Oct 1984 DP (a); 1.50
❑137, Nov 1984 KN (c); DP (a); 1.50
❑138, Dec 1984 DP (a); O: Moondragon. 1.50
❑139, Jan 1985; DP (a); Series continues as The New Defenders 1.50
❑140, Feb 1985 DP (a); 1.50
❑141, Mar 1985 DP (a); 1.50
❑142, Apr 1985 DP (a); 1.50
❑143, May 1985 BA (c); DP (a); O: Moondragon. 1: Runner. 1: Dragon of the Moon. 1: Andromeda. 1.50
❑144, Jun 1985 DP (a); 1.50
❑145, Jul 1985 DP (a); A: Johnny Blaze. 1.50
❑146, Aug 1985 LMc (a); 1.50
❑147, Sep 1985; DP (a); Sgt. Fury and His Howling Defenders on both cover and in indicia 1.50
❑148, Oct 1985 SB (a); 1.50
❑149, Nov 1985 KN (c); DP (a); O: Andromeda. 1.50
❑150, Dec 1985; double-sized DP (a); O: Cloud. 1.50
❑151, Jan 1986 KN (c); DP (a); 1.50
❑152, Feb 1986; double-sized; DP (a); O: Manslaughter. Secret Wars II 1.50
❑Annual 1, Nov 1976 (c); SB, KJ (a); O: Hulk. 12.00

DEFENDERS (VOL. 2)

MARVEL

❑1, Mar 2001 2.99
❑2, Apr 2001 2.25
❑2/Variant, Apr 2001 2.25
❑3, May 2001 2.25
❑4, Jun 2001 2.25
❑5, Jul 2001 2.25
❑6, Aug 2001 2.25
❑7, Sep 2001 2.25
❑8, Oct 2001, Cover quotes Comics International review: "Worst Comic Ever Published" 2.25
❑9, Nov 2001 2.25
❑10, Dec 2001 2.25
❑11, Jan 2002 2.25
❑12, Feb 2002 3.50

DEFENDERS (VOL. 3)

MARVEL

❑1, Sep 2005 5.00
❑2, Oct 2005 2.99
❑3 2005 2.99
❑4 2005 2.99
❑5, Mar 2006 2.99

DEFENDERS OF DYNATRON CITY

MARVEL

❑1, Feb 1992 1.25
❑2, Mar 1992 1.25

N-MINT

❑3, Apr 1992 ... 1.25
❑4, May 1992 ... 1.25
❑5, Jun 1992 ... 1.25
❑6, Jul 1992 ... 1.25

DEFENDERS OF THE EARTH
MARVEL / STAR

❑1, Jan 1987; Flash Gordon, Mandrake, Phantom ... 1.00
❑2, Mar 1987; Flash Gordon, Mandrake, Phantom ... 1.00
❑3, May 1987; Flash Gordon, Mandrake, Phantom ... 1.00
❑4, Jul 1987 ... 1.00

DEFENSELESS DEAD
ADVENTURE

❑1, Feb 1991, b&w; based on Larry Niven story ... 2.50
❑2, ca. 1991, b&w; based on Larry Niven story ... 2.50
❑3, ca. 1991, b&w; based on Larry Niven story ... 2.50

DEFEX
DEVIL'S DUE

❑1, Oct 2004 ... 5.00
❑1/Variant 2004 ... 1.48
❑2, Nov 2004 ... 2.95
❑3, Dec 2004 ... 2.95
❑4 2005 ... 2.95
❑5 2005 ... 2.95
❑6, Jun 2005 ... 2.95

DEFIANCE
IMAGE

❑1, Feb 2002 ... 3.50
❑2, Apr 2002 ... 2.95
❑3, Jun 2002 ... 2.95
❑4, Sep 2002 ... 2.95
❑5, Nov 2002; variant cover ... 2.95
❑6, Mar 2003; variant cover ... 2.95
❑7, Apr 2003; variant cover ... 2.95
❑8, Jul 2003 ... 2.95

DEFIANT GENESIS
DEFIANT

❑1, Oct 1993; no cover price ... 1.00

DEITY (VOL. 1)
IMAGE

❑0, May 1998; exclusive New Dimension Comics edition; Flip cover; Exclusive New Dimension Comics edition ... 6.00
❑0/A, May 1998 ... 3.00
❑1, Sep 1997; White background on cover ... 3.00
❑1/A, Sep 1997; variant cover ... 3.00
❑2, Oct 1997; Regular cover (power blasts) ... 3.00
❑2/A, Oct 1997; variant cover; Brandishing gun, sword ... 3.00
❑3, Nov 1997; Regular cover (brown background, bandages on face) ... 2.95
❑3/A, Nov 1997; variant cover; Cyborg girl ... 3.50
❑4, Dec 1997 ... 2.95
❑4/A, Dec 1997; variant cover ... 3.00
❑5, Feb 1998 ... 2.95
❑5/A, Feb 1998; variant cover ... 3.00
❑6, Apr 1998; Girl with backpack on cover ... 2.95
❑6/A, Apr 1998; variant cover ... 3.00

DEITY (VOL. 2)
IMAGE

❑1, Sep 1998; Flipbook preview of Catseye ... 2.95
❑1/A, Sep 1998; Variant cover with blue background, wielding sword ... 2.95
❑1/B, Sep 1998; Variant cover with monster threatening ... 2.95
❑1/C, Sep 1998; Variant cover with gratuitous bathing suit, cleavage ... 2.95
❑2, Nov 1998 ... 2.95
❑3, Jan 1999 ... 2.95
❑4, Jan 1999 ... 2.95
❑5, May 1999 ... 2.95
❑Ashcan 1, Jun 1998; Special Preview edition ... 2.95

DEITY: REQUIEM
IMAGE

❑1, May 2005 ... 6.95

DEITY: REVELATIONS
IMAGE

❑1, Jul 1999; Woman on floating skateboard, figures in background ... 2.95
❑1/A, Jul 1999; variant cover: woman holding her face on cover ... 2.95
❑1/B, Jul 1999; variant cover ... 2.95
❑2, Sep 1999; variant cover ... 2.95
❑3, Nov 1999 ... 2.95
❑4, Jan 2000 ... 2.95

DEJA VU
FANTACO

❑1, Flip cover ... 2.95

DEJA VU (RADIO COMIX)
RADIO

❑1, Nov 2000, Flip cover ... 2.95

DELIA CHARM
RED MENACE

❑1 ... 2.95
❑2 ... 2.95

DELIRIUM
METRO

❑1 ... 2.00

DELTA SQUADRON
ANDERPOL

❑1 ... 2.00

DELTA TENN
ENTERTAINMENT

❑1, Jul 1987 ... 1.50
❑2, Sep 1987 ... 1.50
❑3, Nov 1987 ... 1.50
❑4, Jan 1988 ... 1.50
❑5, Mar 1988 ... 1.50
❑6, May 1988 ... 1.50
❑7, Jul 1988 ... 1.50
❑8, Sep 1988 ... 1.50
❑9, b&w ... 1.50
❑10, b&w ... 1.50

DELTA, THE ULTIMATE DIFFERENCE
APEX ONE

❑1, Oct 1997, b&w; no cover price ... 2.00
❑2, Fal 1998, b&w; cardstock cover ... 2.95

DEMENTED: SCORPION CHILD
DMF

❑1, Nov 2000 ... 2.95
❑2, Dec 2000 ... 2.95
❑3, Jan 2001 ... 2.95
❑4, Feb 2001 ... 2.95
❑5, Mar 2001 ... 2.95

DEMI'S WILD KINGDOM ADVENTURE
OPUS

❑1, Mar 2000, b&w; squarebound ... 9.95

DEMI THE DEMONESS
RIP OFF

❑1, Mar 1993 ... 2.50
❑1/2nd, Rip-Off publishes ... 2.95
❑2, Nov 1993 ... 2.95
❑3, Mar 1995, flip-book with Kit-Ra back-up ... 2.95
❑4, ... 3.25
❑5, ... 2.95
❑6, Jun 2002, Carnal Comics publishes ... 5.95
❑Special 1, "Choose your own adventure"-style special ... 5.95

DEMOLITION MAN
DC

❑1, Nov 1993 ... 1.75
❑2, Dec 1993 ... 1.75
❑3, Jan 1994 ... 1.75
❑4, Feb 1994 ... 1.75

DEMON (1ST SERIES)
DC

❑1, Aug 1972, JK (a); O: Etrigan. 1: Jason Blood. 1: Etrigan. 1: Randu Singh. ... 30.00
❑2, Oct 1972, JK (a) ... 12.00
❑3, Nov 1972, JK (w); JK (a); A: Batman. ... 10.00
❑4, Dec 1972 JK (a) ... 10.00
❑5, Jan 1973 JK (a) ... 9.00
❑6, Feb 1973 JK (a) ... 9.00
❑7, Mar 1973, JK (a); 1: Klarion the Witch Boy. ... 9.00
❑8, Apr 1973, JK (a) ... 9.00
❑9, Jun 1973, JK (a) ... 9.00
❑10, Jul 1973, JK (a) ... 7.00
❑11, Aug 1973, JK (a) ... 7.00
❑12, Sep 1973, JK (a) ... 7.00
❑13, Oct 1973, JK (a) ... 7.00
❑14, Nov 1973, JK (a) ... 7.00
❑15, Dec 1973, JK (a) ... 7.00
❑16, Jan 1974, JK (a) ... 7.00

DEMON (2ND SERIES)
DC

❑1, Jan 1987 MW (w); MW (a) ... 2.00
❑2, Feb 1987 MW (a) ... 2.00
❑3, Mar 1987 MW (a) ... 2.00
❑4, Apr 1987 MW (w); MW (a) ... 2.00

DEMON (3RD SERIES)
DC

❑0, Oct 1994 O: Jason Blood. O: Etrigan. ... 2.00
❑1, Jul 1990 ... 4.00
❑2, Aug 1990 ... 2.50
❑3, Sep 1990; Batman ... 2.50
❑4, Oct 1990 ... 2.25
❑5, Nov 1990 ... 2.25
❑6, Dec 1990 ... 2.25
❑7, Jan 1991 ... 2.25
❑8, Feb 1991; Batman ... 2.25
❑9, Mar 1991 ... 2.25
❑10, Apr 1991 ... 2.25
❑11, May 1991 ... 3.00
❑12, Jun 1991 A: Lobo. ... 2.00
❑13, Jul 1991 A: Lobo. ... 2.00
❑14, Aug 1991 A: Lobo. ... 2.00
❑15, Sep 1991 A: Lobo. ... 2.00
❑16, Oct 1991 ... 2.00
❑17, Nov 1991; War of the Gods ... 2.00
❑18, Dec 1991 ... 2.00
❑19, Jan 1992; Double-size; Lobo poster ... 2.50
❑20, Feb 1992 ... 2.00
❑21, Mar 1992 ... 2.00
❑22, Apr 1992 ... 2.00
❑23, May 1992; Robin ... 2.00
❑24, Jun 1992; Robin ... 2.00
❑25, Jul 1992 ... 1.50
❑26, Aug 1992 ... 1.50
❑27, Sep 1992 ... 1.50
❑28, Oct 1992; Superman ... 1.50
❑29, Nov 1992 ... 1.75
❑30, Dec 1992 ... 1.75
❑31, Jan 1993 ... 1.75
❑32, Feb 1993 ... 1.75
❑33, Mar 1993 ... 1.75
❑34, Apr 1993; Lobo ... 1.75
❑35, May 1993; Lobo ... 1.75
❑36, Jun 1993 ... 1.75
❑37, Jul 1993 ... 1.75
❑38, Aug 1993 ... 1.75
❑39, Sep 1993 ... 1.75
❑40, Oct 1993 ... 1.75
❑41, Nov 1993 ... 1.75
❑42, Dec 1993 ... 1.75
❑43, Jan 1994 A: Hitman. ... 3.50
❑44, Feb 1994 A: Hitman. ... 3.00
❑45, Mar 1994 A: Hitman. ... 3.00
❑46, Apr 1994 A: Haunted Tank. ... 1.75
❑47, May 1994 A: Haunted Tank. ... 1.75
❑48, Jun 1994 ... 1.95
❑49, Jul 1994 ... 1.95
❑50, Aug 1994; Giant-size ... 2.95
❑51, Sep 1994 ... 1.95
❑52, Nov 1994 A: Hitman. ... 3.00
❑53, Dec 1994 A: Hitman. ... 3.00
❑54, Jan 1995 A: Hitman ... 3.00
❑55, Feb 1995 ... 1.95
❑56, Mar 1995 ... 1.95
❑57, Apr 1995 ... 1.95
❑58, May 1995 ... 1.95
❑Annual 1, ca. 1992 ... 3.00
❑Annual 2, ca. 1993 1: Hitman. ... 12.00

DEMON BEAST INVASION
CPM / BARE BEAR

❑1, Oct 1996, b&w; wraparound cover ... 2.95

DEMON BEAST INVASION: THE FALLEN
CPM / BARE BEAR

❑1, Sep 1998, b&w ... 2.95
❑2, Oct 1998, b&w ... 2.95

Other grades: Multiply price above by 5/6 for VF/NM • 2/3 for VERY FINE • 1/3 for FINE • 1/5 for VERY GOOD • 1/8 for GOOD

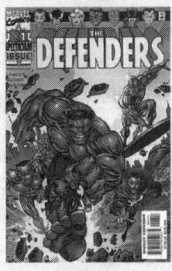

Defenders (Vol. 2)

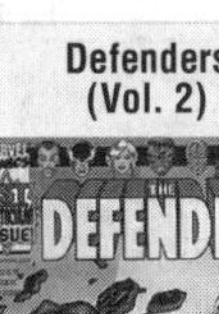

Short-lived series return from Kurt Busiek

Defenders of Dynatron City

Lucasarts' foray into all-ages comics

Delta Tenn

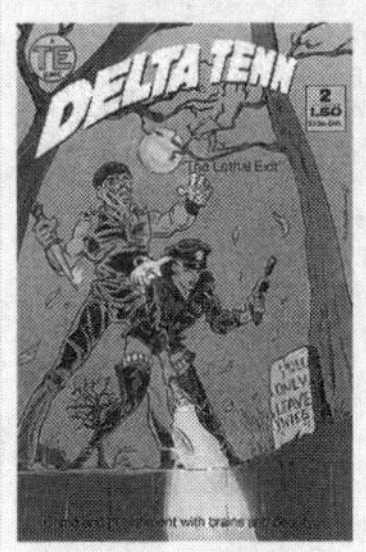

1980s glutcomic set in the scary world of 1997

Demolition Man

Adaptation of Sly Stallone/ Wesley Snipes film

Demon (1st Series)

The demon Etrigan is set free

N-MINT

DEMONBLADE
New Comics

❑1, b&w 1.95

DEMON DREAMS
Pacific

❑1, Feb 1984 .... 1.50
❑2, May 1984 .... 1.50

DEMON DRIVEN OUT
DC / Vertigo

❑1, Nov 2003 .... 2.50
❑2, Dec 2003 .... 2.50
❑3, Jan 2004 .... 2.50
❑4, Feb 2004 .... 2.50
❑5, Mar 2004 .... 2.50
❑6, Apr 2004 .... 2.50

DEMONGATE
Sirius

❑1, May 1996 .... 2.50
❑2, Jun 1996 .... 2.50
❑3, Jul 1996 .... 2.50
❑4 1996 .... 2.50
❑5, Oct 1996 .... 2.50
❑6, Nov 1996 .... 2.50
❑7, Dec 1996 .... 2.50
❑8, Jan 1997 .... 2.50
❑9, Feb 1997, b&w 2.50

DEMON GUN
Crusade

❑1, Jun 1996, b&w 2.95
❑2, Sep 1996, b&w 2.95
❑3, Jan 1997, b&w 2.95

DEMON-HUNTER
Atlas-Seaboard

❑1, Sep 1975 RB (w); RB (a); 1: Gideon Cross. 2.00

DEMON HUNTER (AIRCEL)
Aircel

❑1, Mar 1989, b&w 1.95
❑2, Apr 1989, b&w 1.95
❑3, May 1989, b&w 1.95
❑4, Jun 1989, b&w 1.95

DEMON HUNTER (DAVDEZ)
Davdez

❑1, Aug 1998 .... 2.50

DEMONIC TOYS
Eternity

❑1, Jan 1992 .... 2.50
❑2 .... 2.50
❑3 .... 2.50
❑4 .... 2.50

DEMONIQUE
London Night

❑1, Oct 1994, b&w 3.00
❑2 1995 .... 3.00
❑3 1995 .... 3.00
❑4 1995 .... 3.00

DEMONIQUE: ANGEL OF NIGHT
London Night

❑1, Jul 1997 .... 3.00

N-MINT

DEMON ORORON
Tokyopop

❑1, Apr 2004 .... 9.99

DEMON REALM
Medeia

❑0 .... 2.50

DEMONS & DARK ELVES
Weirdworx

❑1, b&w 2.95

DEMON'S BLOOD
Odyssey

❑1 .... 2.00

DEMONSLAYER
Image

❑1, Nov 1999 .... 2.95
❑2, Dec 1999 .... 2.95
❑3, Jan 2000 .... 2.95

DEMONSLAYER (NEXT)
Next

❑0; Tower Records cover 2.95

DEMONSLAYER (VOL. 2)
Image

❑1, Jun 2000 .... 2.95
❑2, Jul 2000 .... 2.95
❑3, Aug 2000 .... 2.95

DEMON'S TAILS
Adventure

❑1, b&w 2.50
❑2, b&w 2.50
❑3, b&w 2.50
❑4, b&w 2.50

DEMON WARRIOR
Eastern

❑1, Aug 1987, b&w 1.50
❑2 1987, b&w 1.50
❑3 1987, b&w 1.50
❑4 1988, b&w 1.50
❑5, b&w 1.50
❑6, b&w 1.50

DEMONWARS: EYE FOR AN EYE (RA SALVATORE'S)
CrossGen

❑1, Jun 2003 .... 2.95
❑2, Jul 2003 .... 2.95
❑3, Aug 2003 .... 2.95
❑4, Sep 2003 .... 2.95
❑5, Oct 2003 .... 2.95

DEMONWARS: TRIAL BY FIRE (R.A. SALVATORE'S...)
CrossGen

❑1, Jan 2003 .... 2.95
❑2, Feb 2003 .... 2.95
❑3, Mar 2003 .... 2.95
❑4, Apr 2003 .... 2.95
❑5, May 2003 .... 2.95

DEN
Fantagor

❑1 .... 3.00
❑2 .... 3.00
❑3 .... 3.00
❑4 .... 3.00

N-MINT

❑5 .... 3.00
❑6 .... 2.50
❑7 .... 2.50
❑8 .... 2.50
❑9 AN (a) 2.50
❑10 .... 2.50

DENIZENS OF DEEP CITY
Kitchen Sink

❑1, ca. 1988, b&w 2.00
❑2, ca. 1988, b&w 2.00
❑3, ca. 1988, b&w 2.00
❑4, ca. 1988, b&w 2.00
❑5, ca. 1988, b&w 2.00
❑6, ca. 1988, b&w 2.00
❑7, ca. 1988, b&w 2.00
❑8, ca. 1988, b&w 2.00
❑9, ca. 1988 .... 2.00

DENNIS THE MENACE
Fawcett

❑19, Nov 1956, Cover labeled with Boys Club endorsement by Herbert Hoover 45.00
❑20, Jan 1957, Cover labeled with Boys Club endorsement by Herbert Hoover 45.00
❑21, Mar 1957, Cover labeled with Boys Club endorsement by Herbert Hoover 35.00
❑22, May 1957, Cover labeled with Boys Club endorsement by Herbert Hoover; wrestling cover 35.00
❑23, Jul 1957, Cover labeled with Boys Club endorsement by Herbert Hoover 35.00
❑24, Sep 1957, Cover labeled with Boys Club endorsement by Herbert Hoover 35.00
❑25, Nov 1957, Cover labeled with Boys Club endorsement by Herbert Hoover 35.00
❑26, Jan 1958, Cover labeled with Boys Club endorsement by Herbert Hoover 35.00
❑27, Mar 1958, Cover labeled with Boys Club endorsement by Herbert Hoover 35.00
❑28, May 1958, Cover labeled with Boys Club endorsement by Herbert Hoover 35.00
❑29, Jul 1958, Cover labeled with Boys Club endorsement by Herbert Hoover 35.00
❑30, Sep 1958 .... 35.00
❑31, Nov 1958, Autumn cover 25.00
❑32 1959, Cats cover 25.00
❑33 1959, Hardware store cover 25.00
❑34 1959, Winter cover 25.00
❑35, May 1959, Golf cover 25.00
❑36 1959, Mud pies cover 25.00
❑37 1959 .... 25.00
❑38, Sep 1959 .... 25.00
❑39, Nov 1959 .... 25.00
❑40, Jan 1960 .... 25.00
❑41, Mar 1960 .... 18.00
❑42, May 1960 .... 18.00
❑43, Jun 1960 .... 18.00
❑44 1960 .... 18.00
❑45, Sep 1960 .... 18.00

Other grades: Multiply price above by 5/6 for VF/NM • 2/3 for VERY FINE • 1/3 for FINE • 1/5 for VERY GOOD • 1/8 for GOOD

	N-MINT
❑46 1960	18.00
❑47 1960	18.00
❑48 1961	18.00
❑49 1961	18.00
❑50 1961	18.00
❑51 1961	14.00
❑52 1961	14.00
❑53 1961	14.00
❑54 1961	14.00
❑55 1961	14.00
❑56 1962	14.00
❑57 1962	14.00
❑58 1962	14.00
❑59 1962	14.00
❑60, Jul 1962	14.00
❑61 1962	14.00
❑62 1962	14.00
❑63 1963	14.00
❑64, Jan 1963	14.00
❑65, Mar 1963	14.00
❑66, May 1963	14.00
❑67, Jul 1963	14.00
❑68, Sep 1963	14.00
❑69, Nov 1963	14.00
❑70, Jan 1964	14.00
❑71, Mar 1964	10.00
❑72, May 1964	10.00
❑73, Jul 1964	10.00
❑74, Sep 1964	10.00
❑75, Nov 1964	10.00
❑76, Jan 1965	10.00
❑77, Mar 1965	10.00
❑78, May 1965	10.00
❑79, Jul 1965	10.00
❑80, Sep 1965	10.00
❑81, Nov 1965	10.00
❑82, Jan 1966	10.00
❑83, Mar 1966	10.00
❑84, May 1966	10.00
❑85, Jul 1966	10.00
❑86, Sep 1966	10.00
❑87, Nov 1966	10.00
❑88, Jan 1967	10.00
❑89, Mar 1967	10.00
❑90, May 1967	10.00
❑91, Jul 1967	6.00
❑92, Sep 1967	6.00
❑93, Nov 1967	6.00
❑94, Jan 1968	6.00
❑95, Mar 1968	6.00
❑96, May 1968	6.00
❑97, Jul 1968	6.00
❑98, Sep 1968	6.00
❑99, Nov 1968	6.00
❑100, Jan 1969	6.00
❑101, Mar 1969	4.00
❑102, May 1969	4.00
❑103, Jul 1969	4.00
❑104, Sep 1969	4.00
❑105, Nov 1969	4.00
❑106, Jan 1970	4.00
❑107, Mar 1970	4.00
❑108, May 1970	4.00
❑109, Jul 1970	4.00
❑110, Sep 1970	4.00
❑111, Nov 1970	4.00
❑112, Jan 1971	4.00
❑113, Mar 1971	4.00
❑114, May 1971	4.00
❑115, Jul 1971	4.00
❑116, Sep 1971, anti-pollution issue	4.00
❑117, Nov 1971	4.00
❑118, Jan 1972	4.00
❑119, Mar 1972	4.00
❑120, May 1972	4.00
❑121, Jul 1972	3.00
❑122, Sep 1972, Spirit of '72	3.00
❑123, Nov 1972	3.00
❑124, Jan 1973	3.00
❑125, Mar 1973	3.00
❑126, May 1973, A: Gina.	3.00
❑127, Jul 1973	3.00
❑128, Sep 1973	3.00
❑129, Nov 1973	3.00
❑130, Jan 1974	3.00
❑131, Mar 1974	3.00
❑132, May 1974	3.00
❑133, Jul 1974	3.00
❑134, Sep 1974	3.00
❑135, Nov 1974, Dennis visits The Exploratorium at The Palace of Fine Arts in San Francisco	3.00
❑136, Jan 1975	3.00
❑137, Mar 1975	3.00
❑138, May 1975	3.00
❑139, Jul 1975	3.00
❑140, Sep 1975, at Winchester mansion	3.00
❑141, Nov 1975	2.00
❑142, Jan 1976	2.00
❑143, Mar 1976	2.00
❑144, May 1976	2.00
❑145, Jun 1976	2.00
❑146, Jul 1976	2.00
❑147, Sep 1976	2.00
❑148, Nov 1976	2.00
❑149, Jan 1977	2.00
❑150, Mar 1977	2.00
❑151, May 1977, Dennis visits Solvang	2.00
❑152, Jul 1977	2.00
❑153, Sep 1977	2.00
❑154, Nov 1977	2.00
❑155, Jan 1978	2.00
❑156, Mar 1978	2.00
❑157, May 1978	2.00
❑158, Jul 1978	2.00
❑159, Sep 1978	2.00
❑160, Nov 1978	2.00
❑161, Jan 1979	2.00
❑162, Mar 1979	2.00
❑163, May 1979	2.00
❑164, Jul 1979	2.00
❑165, Sep 1979	2.00
❑166, Nov 1979	2.00

DENNIS THE MENACE (GIANTS)

Fawcett

	N-MINT
❑Special 1, Sum 1955, Giant Vacation Special; first issue of this series	95.00
❑Special 2, ca. 1955, Christmas Special; actually, second issue of series	80.00
❑2, Sum 1956, Giant Vacation Special	60.00
❑3, Win 1956, Giant Christmas Issue.	60.00
❑4, Sum 1957, Giant Vacation Special; cover has Boys Club endorsement from Herbert Hoover	60.00
❑5, Win 1957, Giant Christmas Issue; cover has Boys Club endorsement from Herbert Hoover	60.00
❑6, Sum 1958, ...In Hawaii; reprinted several times; told a single 96-page story	60.00
❑6/A, Win 1958, Giant Christmas Issue; there are two #6s	60.00
❑7, ca. 1959, ...in Hollywood	50.00
❑8, Sum 1960, ...in Mexico	50.00
❑9, Sum 1961, ...Goes to Camp; includes Mark Trail pages	50.00
❑10, Win 1961, Giant Christmas issue	50.00
❑11, Win 1962, Giant Christmas issue	50.00
❑12, Win 1962, Three Books in One: ...and his Pal Joey; ...and Margaret; ...and Mr. Wilson	50.00
❑13, Spr 1963, The Best of Dennis the Menace	35.00
❑14, Sum 1963, ...and His Dog Ruff	35.00
❑15, Sum 1963, ...in Washington, D.C.; flag cover	35.00
❑16, Sum 1963, Vacation Special; reprints #9	35.00
❑17, Win 1963, ...and His Pal Joey; one date stamp has been seen on this issue for Oct. 17, 1963	35.00
❑18, Sum 1963, ...in Hawaii; reprints #6; cover says it's the sixth printing	35.00
❑19, Win 1963, ...in Christmas City	35.00
❑20, Spr 1964, Spring Special	35.00
❑21, Spr 1964, The Very Best of Dennis the Menace	22.00
❑22, Spr 1964, Television Special	22.00
❑23, Sum 1964, ...in Hollywood; reprints #7	22.00
❑24, Sum 1964, ...Goes to Camp; reprints #9	22.00
❑25, Sum 1964, ...in Mexico; reprints #8	22.00
❑26, Sum 1964, ...in Washington, D.C.; reprints #15	22.00
❑27, Win 1964, ...Christmas Special	22.00
❑28, Spr 1965, Triple Feature	22.00
❑29, Spr 1965, Best of Dennis the Menace (reprints)	22.00
❑30, Sum 1965, ...in Hawaii; reprints #6	18.00
❑31, Sum 1965, ...All Year 'Round	18.00
❑32, Sum 1965, ...and His Pal Joey; reprints #17	18.00
❑33, Sum 1965, ...in California	18.00
❑34, Sum 1965, ...and His Dog Ruff; reprints #14	18.00
❑35, Win 1965, gatefold summary; Christmas Special	18.00
❑36, Spr 1966, Spring Special	18.00
❑37, Spr 1966, Television Special; reprints #22	18.00
❑38, Sum 1966, ...in Mexico; reprints #8	18.00
❑39, Sum 1966, ...Goes to Camp; reprints #9	18.00
❑40, Sum 1966, ...Visits Washington D.C.; reprints #15	18.00
❑41, Sum 1966, ...From A to Z	15.00
❑42, Sum 1966, ...In Hollywood; reprints #7	15.00
❑43, Win 1966, Christmas Special	15.00
❑44, Spr 1967, ...Around the Clock	15.00
❑45, Spr 1967, ...and His Pal Joey; reprints #17	15.00
❑46, Sum 1967, ...Triple Feature; reprints #28	15.00
❑47, Sum 1967, ...in California; reprints #33	15.00
❑48, Sum 1967, ...Way Out Stories	15.00
❑49, Fal 1967, ...All Year 'Round; reprints #31	15.00
❑50, Sum 1967, ...at the Circus	15.00
❑51, Win 1967, Christmas Special	12.00
❑52, Spr 1968, Sports Special	12.00
❑53, Spr 1968, Spring Special; reprints part of #36	12.00
❑54, Sum 1968, ...and His Dog Ruff; reprints #14	12.00
❑55, Spr 1968, Television Special; reprints #22	12.00
❑56, Spr 1968, ...Tall Stories	12.00
❑57, Sum 1968, ...Pet Parade	12.00
❑58, Sum 1968, Best of Dennis the Menace (reprints from regular series)	12.00
❑59, Sum 1968, ...Day By Day	12.00
❑60, Fal 1968, ...in Hollywood; reprints #7	12.00
❑61, Win 1968, Christmas Favorites	10.00
❑62, Win 1968, ...Fun Book; partially reprints Dennis the Menace Fun Book #1	10.00
❑63, Win 1969, ...and His I-Wish-I-Was Book	10.00
❑64, Spr 1969, ...in Mexico; reprints #8	10.00
❑65, Spr 1969, ...Around the Clock; reprints #44	10.00
❑66, Sum 1969, ...Gags and Games	10.00
❑67, Sum 1969, ...Goes to Camp; reprints #9	10.00
❑68, Sum 1969, ...in Hawaii; reprints #6	10.00
❑69, Aug 1969, The Best of Dennis the Menace (reprints from regular series)	10.00
❑70, Aug 1969, ...Tangled Tales	10.00
❑71, Sep 1969, ...Highlights	10.00
❑72, Aug 1969, ...in Washington D.C.; reprints #15; date really is earlier than #71	10.00
❑73, Sep 1969, ...Way Out Stories; reprints #48	10.00
❑74, Dec 1969, ... and Mr. Wilson and His Gang at Christmas	10.00
❑75, Dec 1969, Series continued in Dennis the Menace Bonus Magazine Series #76; Christmas Special; numbering continues as Dennis the Menace Bonus Magazine Series	10.00

DENNIS THE MENACE (MARVEL)

Marvel

	N-MINT
❑1, Nov 1981	2.00
❑2, Dec 1981	1.50
❑3, Jan 1982	1.50
❑4, Feb 1982	1.50
❑5, Mar 1982	1.50
❑6, Apr 1982, Reuses dragon image on cover from Thor #277	1.50
❑7, May 1982	1.50
❑8, Jun 1982	1.50

Other grades: Multiply price above by 5/6 for VF/NM • 2/3 for VERY FINE • 1/3 for FINE • 1/5 for VERY GOOD • 1/8 for GOOD

Demon Hunter (Aircel)

Former cultist runs from assassins

©Aircel

Den

Richard Corben's fantasy continues

©Fantagor

Denizens of Deep City

Odd series about mundane urban travails

©Kitchen Sink

Dennis the Menace

Long-running series adapts Ketcham terror

©Fawcett

Dennis the Menace and his Friends

Reprint series later goes digest-size

©Fawcett

	N-MINT
❑9, Jul 1982	1.50
❑10, Aug 1982	1.50
❑11, Sep 1982	1.50
❑12, Oct 1982	1.50
❑13, Nov 1982	1.50

DENNIS THE MENACE AND HIS FRIENDS
FAWCETT

	N-MINT
❑1, ca. 1969, ...and Joey (#2 on cover)	12.00
❑2, ca. 1969, ...and Ruff (#2 on cover)	12.00
❑3, Oct 1969, ...and Mr. Wilson (#1 on cover)	12.00
❑4, ca. 1969, ...and Margaret (#1 on cover)	12.00
❑5, Jan 1970, ...and Margaret (#5 on cover)	8.00
❑6, Jun 1970, Joey	5.00
❑7, Aug 1970	5.00
❑8, Oct 1970	5.00
❑9, Jan 1971	5.00
❑10, Jun 1971	5.00
❑11, Aug 1971	4.00
❑12, Oct 1971, Mr. Wilson	4.00
❑13, Jan 1972, Margaret	4.00
❑14, Jun 1972	4.00
❑15, Aug 1972, Ruff	4.00
❑16, Oct 1972, Mr. Wilson	4.00
❑17, Jan 1973	4.00
❑18, Jun 1973, Joey	4.00
❑19, Aug 1973	4.00
❑20, Oct 1973	4.00
❑21, Jan 1974	3.00
❑22, Jun 1974, Joey	3.00
❑23, Aug 1974	3.00
❑24, Oct 1974	3.00
❑25, Jan 1975	3.00
❑26, Jun 1975	3.00
❑27, Aug 1975	3.00
❑28, Oct 1975	3.00
❑29, Jan 1976, ...and Margaret (#29)	3.00
❑30, Jun 1976	3.00
❑31, Aug 1976	3.00
❑32, Oct 1976	3.00
❑33, Jan 1977	3.00
❑34, Jun 1977	3.00
❑35, Aug 1977, Ruff	3.00
❑36, Oct 1977	3.00
❑37, Oct 1977	3.00
❑38, Apr 1978, digest size begins	2.50
❑39, Jun 1978	2.50
❑40, Aug 1978	2.50
❑41, Oct 1978, Reprints first Margaret story; Screamy Mimi story; Chub story	2.50
❑42, Apr 1979	2.50
❑43, Jun 1979, Reprints 24 of 26 Dennis Alphabet stories, omitting A and B	2.50
❑44, Jul 1979	2.50
❑45, Oct 1979	2.50
❑46, Apr 1980	2.50

DENNIS THE MENACE BIG BONUS SERIES
FAWCETT

	N-MINT
❑10, Feb 1980	3.00
❑11, Apr 1980	3.00

DENNIS THE MENACE BONUS MAGAZINE SERIES
FAWCETT

	N-MINT
❑76, Jan 1970, ...in the Caribbean, Jamaica, and Puerto Rico; series continued from Dennis the Menace (Giants) #75	8.00
❑77, Feb 1970, ...Sports Special	8.00
❑78, Mar 1970, Spring Special	8.00
❑79, Apr 1970, ...Tall Stories; reprints Dennis the Menace Giant #56	8.00
❑80, May 1970, ...Day by Day; reprints Dennis the Menace Giant #59	8.00
❑81, Jun 1970, ...Summer Funner	8.00
❑82, Jun 1970, ...In California; reprints Dennis the Menace Giant #33	8.00
❑83, Jul 1970, ...Mama Goose	8.00
❑84, Jul 1970, ...At the Circus; reprints Dennis the Menace Giant #50	8.00
❑85, Aug 1970, ...Fall-Ball	8.00
❑86, Oct 1970, ...and Mr. Wilson and His Gang at Christmas; reprints Dennis the Menace Giant #74	8.00
❑87, Oct 1970, Christmas Special	8.00
❑88, Jan 1971, ...in London	8.00
❑89, Feb 1971, Spring Fling	8.00
❑90, Mar 1971, ...Here's How	8.00
❑91, Apr 1971, ...Fun Book; reprints part of Dennis the Menace Fun Book #1	7.00
❑92, May 1971, ...in Hollywood; reprints Dennis the Menace Giant #7	7.00
❑93, Jun 1971, ...Visits Paris	7.00
❑94, Jun 1971, ...Jackpot	7.00
❑95, Jul 1971, ...That's Our Boy; there are two #95s and no #96	7.00
❑95/A, Jul 1971, ...Summer Games; there are two #95s and no #96	
❑97, Aug 1971, ...Comicapers	7.00
❑98, Oct 1971, Mr. Wilson and His Gang at Christmas; reprints Dennis the Menace Giant #74	7.00
❑99, Oct 1971, ...Fiesta	7.00
❑100, Jan 1972, Christmas Special	7.00
❑101, Feb 1972, ...Up in the Air	7.00
❑102, Mar 1972, ...Rise and Shine	7.00
❑103, Apr 1972, ...and His I-Wish-I-Was Book; reprints Dennis the Menace Giant #63	7.00
❑104, May 1972, ...Short Stuff Special	7.00
❑105, Jun 1972, ...in Mexico; reprints Dennis the Menace Giant #8	7.00
❑106, Jun 1972, ...Birthday Special	7.00
❑107, Jul 1972, ...Fast & Funny	7.00
❑108, Jul 1972, ...Around the Clock; reprints Dennis the Menace Giant #44	7.00
❑109, Aug 1972, ...Goes to Camp; reprints Dennis the Menace Giant #9	7.00
❑110, Oct 1972, ...Gags and Games; reprints Dennis the Menace Giant #66	7.00
❑111, Oct 1972, Christmas Special	7.00
❑112, Jan 1973, ...Go-Go Special	7.00
❑113, Feb 1973	7.00
❑114, Mar 1973	7.00
❑115, Apr 1973	7.00
❑116, May 1973	7.00
❑117, Jun 1973	7.00
❑118, Jun 1973	7.00
❑119, Jul 1973, Summer Number and state flags	7.00
❑120, Jul 1973	7.00
❑121, Aug 1973	6.00
❑122, Oct 1973	6.00
❑123, Oct 1973	6.00
❑124, Jan 1974	6.00
❑125, Feb 1974	6.00
❑126, Mar 1974	6.00
❑127, Apr 1974	6.00
❑128, May 1974	6.00
❑129, Jun 1974	6.00
❑130, Jun 1974	6.00
❑131, Jul 1974	6.00
❑132, Jul 1974	6.00
❑133, Aug 1974	6.00
❑134, Oct 1974, Christmas	6.00
❑135, Oct 1974	6.00
❑136, Jan 1975	6.00
❑137, Feb 1975	6.00
❑138, Mar 1975	6.00
❑139, Apr 1975	6.00
❑140, May 1975	6.00
❑141, Jun 1975	6.00
❑142, Jun 1975	6.00
❑143, Jul 1975	6.00
❑144, Jul 1975	6.00
❑145, Aug 1975	6.00
❑146, Oct 1975, Christmas	6.00
❑147, Oct 1975, ... and Mr. Wilson and His Gang at Christmas	6.00
❑148, Jan 1976	6.00
❑149, Feb 1976	6.00
❑150, Mar 1976	6.00
❑151, Apr 1976	4.00
❑152, May 1976	4.00
❑153, Jun 1976	4.00
❑154, Jun 1976	4.00
❑155, Jul 1976	4.00
❑156, Jul 1976	4.00
❑157, Aug 1976	4.00
❑158, Oct 1976	4.00
❑159, Oct 1976	4.00
❑160, Jan 1977	4.00
❑161, Feb 1977	4.00
❑162, Mar 1977	4.00
❑163, Apr 1977	4.00
❑164, May 1977	4.00
❑165, Jun 1977	4.00
❑166, Jun 1977	4.00
❑167, Jun 1977	4.00
❑168, Jul 1977	4.00
❑169, Aug 1977	4.00
❑170, Oct 1977	4.00
❑171, Oct 1977	3.00
❑172, Jan 1978	3.00
❑173, Feb 1978	3.00

❑174, Mar 1978 3.00
❑175, Apr 1978 3.00
❑176, May 1978 3.00
❑177, Jun 1978 3.00
❑178, Jun 1978 3.00
❑179, Jul 1978 3.00
❑180, Jul 1978 3.00
❑181, Aug 1978, San Diego tour 3.00
❑182, Oct 1978 3.00
❑183, Oct 1978 3.00
❑184, Jan 1979 3.00
❑185, Feb 1979 3.00
❑186, Mar 1979 3.00
❑187, Apr 1979 3.00
❑188, May 1979 3.00
❑189, Jun 1979 3.00
❑190, Jun 1979 3.00
❑191, Jul 1979 3.00
❑192, Jul 1979 3.00
❑193, Aug 1979 3.00
❑194, Oct 1979 3.00

DENNIS THE MENACE COMICS DIGEST
MARVEL

❑1, DC logo placed on cover in error by World Color Press; reprints 20.00
❑2, reprints 1.25
❑3, reprints 1.25

DENNIS THE MENACE POCKET FULL OF FUN
FAWCETT

❑1, Spr 1969 25.00
❑2, Win 1969; Christmas cover 20.00
❑3, Jan 1970 20.00
❑4, Apr 1970 20.00
❑5 1970 20.00
❑6 1970 20.00
❑7 1971 20.00
❑8 1971 20.00
❑9 1971 20.00
❑10 1971 20.00
❑11 1972 15.00
❑12 1972 15.00
❑13 1972 15.00
❑14 1972 15.00
❑15 1973 15.00
❑16 1973 15.00
❑17 1973 10.00
❑18 1973, Holiday cover 10.00
❑19 1974 10.00
❑20 1974 10.00
❑21, Jul 1974 10.00
❑22 1974 10.00
❑23, Jan 1975 10.00
❑24, Mar 1975 10.00
❑25 1975 10.00
❑26 1975 10.00
❑27 1976 10.00
❑28, Jun 1976 10.00
❑29 1976 10.00
❑30 1976 10.00
❑31, Jan 1977 10.00
❑32, Apr 1977 10.00
❑33 1977 10.00
❑34, Apr 1977 10.00
❑35, Jul 1977 10.00
❑36 1977 10.00
❑37, Jan 1978 10.00
❑38, Apr 1978 10.00
❑39, May 1978 10.00
❑40, Jun 1978 10.00
❑41, Aug 1978 10.00
❑42, Sep 1978 10.00
❑43, Jan 1979 10.00
❑44 1979 10.00
❑45, Oct 1979 10.00
❑46 1979 10.00
❑47, Jul 1979 10.00
❑48 1979 10.00
❑49, Jan 1980; Winter cover 10.00
❑50, Mar 1980 10.00

DEPUTY DAWG
GOLD KEY

❑1, Aug 1965 55.00

DEPUTY DAWG PRESENTS DINKY DUCK AND HASHIMOTO-SAN
GOLD KEY

❑1, Aug 1965 30.00

DER COUNTESS
AVALON COMMUNICATIONS / ACG

❑1, ca. 1996; reprints Scary Tales #1. 2.75

DER VANDALE
INNERVISION

❑1, b&w 2.50
❑1/Variant, b&w; alternate cover 2.50
❑2 2.50
❑3 2.50

DESCENDANTS OF TOSHIN
ARROW

❑1, Apr 1999, b&w 2.95

DESCENDING ANGELS
MILLENNIUM

❑1 2.95

DESERT PEACH
THOUGHTS & IMAGES

❑1, Jul 1988, b&w; Thoughts & Images publishes 10.00
❑2, Feb 1989, b&w 6.00
❑3, Jan 1990, b&w; Goes to Mu Press 4.00
❑4, Mar 1990, b&w; First Mu Issue 4.00
❑5, Jun 1990, b&w; MU Press begins publishing 4.00
❑6, Aug 1990, b&w 4.00
❑7, Sep 1990 3.00
❑8, Nov 1990 3.00
❑9, Dec 1990 3.00
❑10, Feb 1991 3.00
❑11, Jun 1991 3.00
❑12, Aug 1991 2.50
❑13, Oct 1991 2.50
❑14, Dec 1991 2.50
❑15, Feb 1992 2.50
❑16, Apr 1992 2.50
❑17, Aug 1992, b&w; Giant-size 3.95
❑18, Aug 1992, b&w; Last Mu Press issue 2.50
❑19, ca. 1993, b&w; aka Desert Peach: Self-Propelled Target; Aeon begins publishing 4.95
❑20, ca. 1993, b&w; aka Desert Peach: Fever Dream 4.95
❑21, Jun 1994, b&w 4.95
❑22, Nov 1994, b&w 4.95
❑23, Jun 1995, b&w; a.k.a. The Desert Peach: Visions 2.95
❑24, Sep 1995, b&w; a.k.a. The Desert Peach: Ups and Downs 2.95
❑25, ca. 1996; Last Aeon issue; moves to A Fine Line 2.95
❑26, ca. 1997, b&w; a.k.a. The Desert Peach: Miki; first issue from A Fine Line; cardstock cover 2.95
❑27, ca. 1997 2.95
❑28, Aug 1998 2.95
❑29, Apr 2000 2.95
❑30, Jun 2001 2.95

DESERT STORM JOURNAL
APPLE

❑1, Saddam Hussein on cover 2.75
❑1/A; Gen. Norman Schwartzkopf on cover 2.75
❑2, b&w 2.75
❑3, b&w 2.75
❑4, b&w 2.75
❑5, b&w 2.75
❑6, b&w 2.75
❑7, b&w 2.75
❑8, b&w 2.75

DESERT STORM: SEND HUSSEIN TO HELL!
INNOVATION

❑1, ca. 1991 2.95

DESERT STREAMS
DC / PIRANHA

❑1 5.95

DESOLATION JONES
DC

❑1, Jun 2005 2.99
❑2, Jul 2005 2.99
❑3, Oct 2005 2.99
❑4, Jan 2006 2.99
❑5, Mar 2006 2.99
❑6, Jun 2006 2.99

DESPAIR
PRINT MINT

❑1, ca. 1969 10.00

DESPERADOES
IMAGE

❑1, Sep 1997 2.50
❑1/2nd, Sep 1997 2.50
❑2, Oct 1997 2.95
❑3, Nov 1997 2.95
❑4, Dec 1997 2.95
❑5, Jun 1998 2.95

DESPERADOES: BANNERS OF GOLD
IDEA & DESIGN WORKS

❑1, ca. 2004 3.99
❑2, ca. 2004 3.99
❑3, ca. 2005 3.99
❑4, ca. 2005 3.99
❑5, ca. 2005 3.99

DESPERADOES: EPIDEMIC!
DC / WILDSTORM

❑1, Nov 1999; prestige format 5.95

DESPERADOES: QUIET OF THE GRAVE
DC / HOMAGE

❑1, Jul 2001 2.95
❑2, Aug 2001 2.95
❑3, Sep 2001 2.95
❑4, Oct 2001 2.95
❑5, Nov 2001 2.95

DESPERATE TIMES
IMAGE

❑0, Jan 2004 3.50
❑1, Jun 1998 2.95
❑2, Aug 1998 2.95
❑3, Oct 1998 2.95
❑4, Dec 1998 2.95

DESPERATE TIMES (VOL. 2)
IMAGE

❑1, Apr 2004 2.95

DESPERATE TIMES (AAAARGH)
AAARGH / WILDSTORM

❑1, Oct 2000, b&w 2.95
❑2, Jan 2001, b&w 2.95
❑3, Mar 2001, b&w 2.95
❑4, May 2001, b&w 2.35

DESSO-LETTE
FOLLIS BROTHERS

❑1, Jul 1997 2.95

DESTINY: A CHRONICLE OF DEATHS FORETOLD
DC / VERTIGO

❑1, ca. 1997, prestige format 5.95
❑2, ca. 1997, prestige format 5.95
❑3, ca. 1997, prestige format 5.95

DESTINY ANGEL
DARK FANTASY

❑1 3.95

DESTROY!!
ECLIPSE

❑1, Nov 1986, b&w; oversize 4.95
❑1/3D, 3-D 3.00

DESTROY ALL COMICS
SLAVE LABOR

❑1, Nov 1994; Oversized 3.50
❑2, Feb 1995; Oversized 3.50
❑3, Aug 1995; Oversized 3.50
❑4, Jan 1996; Oversized 3.50
❑5, Apr 1996; Oversized 3.50

DESTROYER DUCK
ECLIPSE

❑1, Feb 1982 ME (w); SA, VM, JK (a); 1&O: Destroyer Duck. 1: Groo. 4.00
❑2, Jan 1983 VM, JK (a) 1.50
❑3, Jun 1983 VM, JK (a) 1.50
❑4, Oct 1983 VM, JK (a) 1.50
❑5, Dec 1983 VM, JK (a) 1.50
❑6, Mar 1984 VM (a) 1.50
❑7, May 1984 FM (c); VM (a) 1.50

Desert Peach

Follows Rommel's grave-digging division

©Thoughts & Images

Desert Storm Journal

Don Lomax's Vietnam Journal follow-up

©Apple

Desperate Times

Humor series from Chris Eliopoulos

©Image

Destroyer Duck

Gerber's duck in exile during Howard fight

©Eclipse

Detective Comics

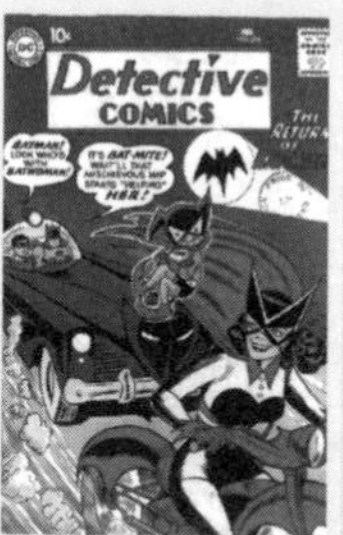

Batman series is world's longest-published comic

©DC

N-MINT

DESTROYER (MAGAZINE)
MARVEL

❑1, Nov 1989, b&w O: Remo Williams. 3.00
❑2, Dec 1989, b&w 2.50
❑3, Dec 1989, b&w 2.50
❑4, Jan 1990, b&w SD (a) 2.50
❑5, Feb 1990, b&w 2.50
❑6, Mar 1990, b&w 2.50
❑7, Apr 1990, b&w 2.50
❑8, May 1990, b&w 2.50

DESTROYER (VOL. 2)
MARVEL

❑1, Mar 1991 1.95

DESTROYER (VOL. 3)
MARVEL

❑1, Dec 1991 1.95
❑2, Jan 1992 1.95
❑3, Feb 1992 1.95
❑4, Mar 1992 1.95

DESTROYER (VALIANT)
VALIANT

❑0, Apr 1995 4.00
❑0/$2.50, Apr 1995 10.00

DESTRUCTOR
ATLAS-SEABOARD

❑1, Feb 1975, SD, WW (a); O: Destructor. 10.00
❑2, Apr 1975, SD, WW (a) 7.00
❑3, Jun 1975, SD (a) 5.00
❑4, Aug 1975 5.00

DETECTIVE, THE: CHRONICLES OF MAX FACCIONI
CALIBER

❑1 2.95

DETECTIVE COMICS
DC

❑0, Oct 1994 O: Batarangs. O: Batmobile. O: Batman. 2.50
❑236, Oct 1956 350.00
❑237, Nov 1956 300.00
❑238, Dec 1956 300.00
❑239, Jan 1957 300.00
❑240, Feb 1957 300.00
❑241, Mar 1957 250.00
❑242, Apr 1957 250.00
❑243, May 1957 250.00
❑244, Jun 1957 250.00
❑245, Jul 1957 250.00
❑246, Aug 1957, 1: Diane Meade (Martian Manhunter's girlfriend). 250.00
❑247, Sep 1957 1: Professor Ivo. 250.00
❑248, Oct 1957 250.00
❑249, Nov 1957 A: Batwoman. 250.00
❑250, Dec 1957 250.00
❑251, Jan 1958, Roy Raymond and John Jones/Manhunter from Mars back-ups 250.00
❑252, Feb 1958 250.00
❑253, Mar 1958 250.00
❑254, Apr 1958 250.00
❑255, May 1958 250.00
❑256, Jun 1958 250.00
❑257, Jul 1958 250.00
❑258, Aug 1958 250.00

N-MINT

❑259, Sep 1958; 1: Calendar Man. Roy Raymond and John Jones/ Manhunter from Mars back-ups 250.00
❑260, Oct 1958 250.00
❑261, Nov 1958 1: Doctor Double X. 200.00
❑262, Dec 1958 200.00
❑263, Jan 1959 200.00
❑264, Feb 1959 200.00
❑265, Mar 1959 O: Batman. A: Joker. 325.00
❑266, Apr 1959 200.00
❑267, May 1959, O: Bat-Mite. 1: Bat-Mite. 250.00
❑268, Jun 1959 200.00
❑269, Jul 1959 200.00
❑270, Aug 1959 200.00
❑271, Sep 1959 O: Martian Manhunter. 200.00
❑272, Oct 1959 175.00
❑273, Nov 1959; Martian Manhunter reveals his identity 200.00
❑274, Dec 1959 150.00
❑275, Jan 1960 150.00
❑276, Feb 1960 A: Bat-Mite. A: Batwoman. 150.00
❑277, Mar 1960 150.00
❑278, Apr 1960 150.00
❑279, May 1960 150.00
❑280, Jun 1960 150.00
❑281, Jul 1960 125.00
❑282, Aug 1960 125.00
❑283, Sep 1960 125.00
❑284, Oct 1960 125.00
❑285, Nov 1960 A: Batwoman. 125.00
❑286, Dec 1960 A: Batwoman. 125.00
❑287, Jan 1961 O: Martian Manhunter. 125.00
❑288, Feb 1961 125.00
❑289, Mar 1961 125.00
❑290, Apr 1961 125.00
❑291, May 1961 125.00
❑292, Jun 1961 A: Batwoman. 125.00
❑293, Jul 1961 125.00
❑294, Aug 1961 125.00
❑295, Sep 1961 125.00
❑296, Oct 1961 125.00
❑297, Nov 1961 125.00
❑298, Dec 1961, 1: Clayface II (Matt Hagen). 200.00
❑299, Jan 1962 100.00
❑300, Feb 1962 100.00
❑301, Mar 1962 100.00
❑302, Apr 1962, A: Batwoman. 100.00
❑303, May 1962 100.00
❑304, Jun 1962, 100.00
❑305, Jul 1962 100.00
❑306, Aug 1962 100.00
❑307, Sep 1962, A: Batwoman. 100.00
❑308, Oct 1962 100.00
❑309, Nov 1962, A: Batwoman. 100.00
❑310, Dec 1962 100.00
❑311, Jan 1963, 1: Cat-Man (DC). A: Batwoman. 125.00
❑312, Feb 1963 100.00
❑313, Mar 1963 100.00
❑314, Apr 1963 100.00
❑315, May 1963 100.00
❑316, Jun 1963 100.00

N-MINT

❑317, Jul 1963 100.00
❑318, Aug 1963, A: Batwoman. 100.00
❑319, Sep 1963 100.00
❑320, Oct 1963 100.00
❑321, Nov 1963, A: Batwoman. 100.00
❑322, Dec 1963 100.00
❑323, Jan 1964 100.00
❑324, Feb 1964 100.00
❑325, Mar 1964, A: Batwoman. 100.00
❑326, Apr 1964 100.00
❑327, May 1964, 25th anniversary; CI (a); symbol change; 300th Batman in Detective Comics 200.00
❑328, Jun 1964, D: Alfred. 175.00
❑329, Jul 1964 75.00
❑330, Aug 1964 75.00
❑331, Sep 1964 65.00
❑332, Oct 1964, A: Joker. 115.00
❑333, Nov 1964 60.00
❑334, Dec 1964, A: Joker. 60.00
❑335, Jan 1965 60.00
❑336, Feb 1965 60.00
❑337, Mar 1965 60.00
❑338, Apr 1965 60.00
❑339, May 1965 60.00
❑340, Jun 1965 60.00
❑341, Jul 1965, A: Joker. 75.00
❑342, Aug 1965 60.00
❑343, Sep 1965 60.00
❑344, Oct 1965 60.00
❑345, Nov 1965, 1: Blockbuster. 60.00
❑346, Dec 1965 60.00
❑347, Jan 1966 60.00
❑348, Feb 1966 60.00
❑349, Mar 1966 60.00
❑350, Apr 1966 60.00
❑351, May 1966, 1: Cluemaster. 60.00
❑352, Jun 1966, Elongated Man back-up 60.00
❑353, Jul 1966, 75.00
❑354, Aug 1966, 1: Doctor Tzin-Tzin. 75.00
❑355, Sep 1966 75.00
❑356, Oct 1966, Alfred returns 75.00
❑357, Nov 1966, 75.00
❑358, Dec 1966, 1: Spellbinder. 75.00
❑359, Jan 1967, 1: Batgirl (Barbara Gordon) 350.00
❑360, Feb 1967 65.00
❑361, Mar 1967 65.00
❑362, Apr 1967, A: Riddler. 65.00
❑363, May 1967, A: Batgirl (Barbara Gordon) 100.00
❑364, Jun 1967, A: Batgirl (Barbara Gordon) 60.00
❑365, Jul 1967, A: Joker. 90.00
❑366, Aug 1967 60.00
❑367, Sep 1967 60.00
❑368, Oct 1967 60.00
❑369, Nov 1967, NA (a); Robin teams with Batgirl; Elongated Man back-up 75.00
❑370, Dec 1967, GK, BK (a); Elongated Man 45.00
❑371, Jan 1968, A: Batgirl (Barbara Gordon) 80.00
❑372, Feb 1968 50.00

Other grades: Multiply price above by 5/6 for VF/NM • 2/3 for VERY FINE • 1/3 for FINE • 1/5 for VERY GOOD • 1/8 for GOOD

	N-MINT
❑373, Mar 1968, A: Riddler.	50.00
❑374, Apr 1968	50.00
❑375, May 1968	50.00
❑376, Jun 1968, Elongated Man back-up	50.00
❑377, Jul 1968	65.00
❑378, Aug 1968	50.00
❑379, Sep 1968	50.00
❑380, Oct 1968	50.00
❑381, Nov 1968	40.00
❑382, Dec 1968	40.00
❑383, Jan 1969	40.00
❑384, Feb 1969	40.00
❑385, Mar 1969	40.00
❑386, Apr 1969	40.00
❑387, May 1969, 1: Batman. Reprints Detective Comics #27	75.00
❑388, Jun 1969, A: Joker.	50.00
❑389, Jul 1969	35.00
❑390, Aug 1969	35.00
❑391, Sep 1969	25.00
❑392, Oct 1969, FR (w); MA, GK (a); 1: Jason Bard	25.00
❑393, Nov 1969	25.00
❑394, Dec 1969	35.00
❑395, Jan 1970, MA, DG, NA, GK (a)	125.00
❑396, Feb 1970, NA (c); GK (a); A: Batgirl.	35.00
❑397, Mar 1970, NA (a)	35.00
❑398, Apr 1970	30.00
❑399, May 1970	30.00
❑400, Jun 1970, GC, NA (a); O: Man-Bat. 1: Man-Bat.	150.00
❑401, Jul 1970	30.00
❑402, Aug 1970, NA (a);	55.00
❑403, Sep 1970, NA (c); GK (a); Robin	35.00
❑404, Oct 1970, DG, NA, GK (a); Batgirl	35.00
❑405, Nov 1970	30.00
❑406, Dec 1970	30.00
❑407, Jan 1971, NA (a); A: Man-Bat.	30.00
❑408, Feb 1971, NA (a)	40.00
❑409, Mar 1971, NA (c); DG, IN (a)	40.00
❑410, Apr 1971, DH, DG, NA (a); Batgirl	40.00
❑411, May 1971, 1: Talia.	25.00
❑412, Jun 1971	25.00
❑413, Jul 1971, DG (a);	25.00
❑414, Aug 1971, Giant-size	25.00
❑415, Sep 1971; Giant-size	25.00
❑416, Oct 1971; Giant-size	25.00
❑417, Nov 1971; Giant-size	25.00
❑418, Dec 1971; Giant-size	25.00
❑419, Jan 1972; Giant-size	25.00
❑420, Feb 1972; Giant-size	25.00
❑421, Mar 1972; Giant-size; DH (a); Batgirl story	25.00
❑422, Apr 1972; Giant-size	25.00
❑423, May 1972; Giant-size	25.00
❑424, Jun 1972; Giant-size	25.00
❑425, Jul 1972	20.00
❑426, Aug 1972	20.00
❑427, Sep 1972	20.00
❑428, Oct 1972, DD (a)	15.00
❑429, Nov 1972	15.00
❑430, Dec 1972	15.00
❑431, Jan 1973	15.00
❑432, Feb 1973	15.00
❑433, Mar 1973	15.00
❑434, Apr 1973, RB (a); 1: The Spook.	15.00
❑435, Jul 1973	15.00
❑436, Sep 1973	15.00
❑437, Nov 1973, JA (a); 1: Manhunter.	20.00
❑438, Jan 1974, Manhunter	28.00
❑439, Mar 1974, O: Manhunter. Manhunter	28.00
❑440, May 1974, Manhunter	28.00
❑441, Jul 1974, Manhunter	28.00
❑442, Sep 1974, Manhunter	28.00
❑443, Nov 1974, D: Manhunter.	28.00
❑444, Jan 1975	28.00
❑445, Mar 1975	28.00
❑446, Apr 1975; RB, JA (a); 1: Sterling Silversmith. Hawkman back-up	8.00
❑447, May 1975	8.00
❑448, Jun 1975	8.00
❑449, Jul 1975	8.00
❑450, Aug 1975	8.00
❑451, Sep 1975	6.00

	N-MINT
❑452, Oct 1975; JL (a); Hawkman back-up	6.00
❑453, Nov 1975	6.00
❑454, Dec 1975 JL (a)	6.00
❑455, Jan 1976 JL (a)	6.00
❑456, Feb 1976	6.00
❑457, Mar 1976, O: Batman. Elongated Man back-up	6.00
❑458, Apr 1976	6.00
❑459, May 1976	6.00
❑460, Jun 1976	6.00
❑461, Jul 1976, Bicentennial #29	6.00
❑462, Aug 1976	6.00
❑463, Sep 1976, 1: Black Spider. 1: the Calculator.	6.00
❑464, Oct 1976	6.00
❑465, Nov 1976, TD (a); A: Elongated Man.	6.00
❑466, Dec 1976, TD, MR (a)	9.00
❑467, Jan 1977, TD, MR (a)	9.00
❑468, Mar 1977, TD, MR (a)	9.00
❑469, May 1977, AM, MR (a); 1: Doctor Phosphorus.	5.00
❑470, Jun 1977, AM, MR (a); A: Hugo Strange	5.00
❑471, Aug 1977, MR (a); A: Hugo Strange	8.00
❑472, Sep 1977, MR (a)	8.00
❑473, Oct 1977, MR (a)	8.00
❑474, Dec 1977, MR (a)	8.00
❑475, Feb 1978, MR (a); A: Joker.	15.00
❑476, Mar 1978, MR (a); A: Joker.	15.00
❑477, May 1978, MR (a)	7.00
❑478, Jul 1978, MR (a); 1: Clayface III (Preston Payne)	7.00
❑479, Sep 1978, RB, MR (a); 1: The Fadeaway Man.	7.00
❑480, Nov 1978, DN, MA (a)	5.00
❑481, Dec 1978; Double-size DN, JSn, CR, MR, DA (a)	7.00
❑482, Feb 1979; Double-size JSn, HC, DG, CR (a)	5.00
❑483, Apr 1979; Double-size DN, MG, DG, DA (a); 1: Maxie Zeus.	7.00
❑484, Jun 1979; Double-size O: Robin I (Dick Grayson).	5.00
❑485, Aug 1979; Double-size	4.00
❑486, Oct 1979; Double-size	4.00
❑487, Dec 1979; Double-size	4.00
❑488, Feb 1980; Double-size	4.00
❑489, Apr 1980; Double-size; Batgirl forgets Batman and Robin's secret identities	4.00
❑490, May 1980; Double-size	4.00
❑491, Jun 1980; Double-size	4.00
❑492, Jul 1980; Double-size	4.00
❑493, Aug 1980; Double-size	4.00
❑494, Sep 1980; Double-size 1: Crime Doctor	4.00
❑495, Oct 1980; Double-size	4.00
❑496, Nov 1980	4.00
❑497, Dec 1980	4.00
❑498, Jan 1981	4.00
❑499, Feb 1981	4.00
❑500, Mar 1981; 500th anniversary issue CI, DG, TY, JKu (a); A: Deadman, Slam Bradley, Hawkman, Robin	5.00
❑501, Apr 1981	4.00
❑502, May 1981	4.00
❑503, Jun 1981, JSn (a)	4.00
❑504, Jul 1981, JSn (a); A: Joker.	6.00
❑505, Aug 1981	4.00
❑506, Sep 1981	4.00
❑507, Oct 1981	4.00
❑508, Nov 1981	4.00
❑509, Dec 1981	4.00
❑510, Jan 1982	4.00
❑511, Feb 1982, 1: Mirage (DC).	4.00
❑512, Mar 1982	4.00
❑513, Apr 1982	4.00
❑514, May 1982	4.00
❑515, Jun 1982	4.00
❑516, Jul 1982	4.00
❑517, Aug 1982	4.00
❑518, Sep 1982, 1: Velvet Tiger.	4.00
❑519, Oct 1982	4.00
❑520, Nov 1982	4.00
❑521, Dec 1982	4.00
❑522, Jan 1983	4.00

	N-MINT
❑523, Feb 1983	4.00
❑524, Mar 1983, 2: Jason Todd	5.00
❑525, Apr 1983	4.00
❑526, May 1983 DN, AA (a)	4.00
❑527, Jun 1983	4.00
❑528, Jul 1983	4.00
❑529, Aug 1983	4.00
❑530, Sep 1983	4.00
❑531, Oct 1983	4.00
❑532, Nov 1983, A: Joker.	4.00
❑533, Dec 1983	4.00
❑534, Jan 1984 V: Poison Ivy.	4.00
❑535, Feb 1984 2: Robin II (Jason Todd). V: Crazy Quilt.	5.00
❑536, Mar 1984 V: Deadshot.	4.00
❑537, Apr 1984	4.00
❑538, May 1984 V: Catman.	4.00
❑539, Jun 1984 V: Catman.	4.00
❑540, Jul 1984 V: Scarecrow.	4.00
❑541, Aug 1984	4.00
❑542, Sep 1984 V: Nocturna.	4.00
❑543, Oct 1984	4.00
❑544, Nov 1984	4.00
❑545, Dec 1984	4.00
❑546, Jan 1985	4.00
❑547, Feb 1985	4.00
❑548, Mar 1985	4.00
❑549, Apr 1985 AMo (w);	4.00
❑550, May 1985; AMo (w); Green Arrow back-up	4.00
❑551, Jun 1985 V: Calendar Man.	4.00
❑552, Jul 1985	4.00
❑553, Aug 1985 V: Black Mask.	4.00
❑554, Sep 1985	4.00
❑555, Oct 1985 V: Mirror Master. V: Captain Boomerang.	4.00
❑556, Nov 1985	4.00
❑557, Dec 1985	4.00
❑558, Jan 1986	4.00
❑559, Feb 1986 A: Catwoman. A: Green Arrow. A: Black Canary.	4.00
❑560, Mar 1986 1: Steelclaw.	4.00
❑561, Apr 1986	4.00
❑562, May 1986	4.00
❑563, Jun 1986 V: Two-Face.	4.00
❑564, Jul 1986 D: Steelclaw. V: Two-Face.	4.00
❑565, Aug 1986	3.00
❑566, Sep 1986 A: Joker.	3.00
❑567, Oct 1986 JSn (a);	3.00
❑568, Nov 1986; Legends	3.00
❑569, Dec 1986 A: Catwoman. A: Joker. V: Joker.	4.00
❑570, Jan 1987 A: Joker.	4.00
❑571, Feb 1987 V: Scarecrow.	3.00
❑572, Mar 1987; Giant-size A: Slam Bradley.	4.00
❑573, Apr 1987 V: Mad Hatter.	2.50
❑574, May 1987 O: Batman.	3.00
❑575, Jun 1987	3.50
❑576, Jul 1987 TMc (a);	3.00
❑577, Aug 1987 TMc (a);	3.00
❑578, Sep 1987 TMc (a);	3.00
❑579, Oct 1987 V: Two-Face.	2.00
❑580, Nov 1987 V: Two-Face.	2.00
❑581, Dec 1987 V: Two-Face.	2.00
❑582, Jan 1988; Millennium	2.00
❑583, Feb 1988 1: Ventriloquist.	2.00
❑584, Mar 1988	2.00
❑585, Apr 1988	2.00
❑586, May 1988 V: Rat-catcher.	2.00
❑587, Jun 1988	2.00
❑588, Jul 1988	2.00
❑589, Aug 1988; Bonus Book #5	2.00
❑590, Sep 1988	2.00
❑591, Oct 1988	2.00
❑592, Nov 1988	2.00
❑593, Dec 1988	2.00
❑594, Dec 1988 1: Joe Potato.	2.00
❑595, Jan 1989; Bonus Book; Invasion!	2.00
❑596, Jan 1989	2.00
❑597, Feb 1989	2.00
❑598, Mar 1989; Double-size	3.00
❑599, Apr 1989	2.50
❑600, May 1989; Double-size FM (a)	3.00
❑601, Jun 1989 A: Demon	2.00
❑602, Jul 1989 A: Demon	2.00

Other grades: Multiply price above by 5/6 for VF/NM • 2/3 for VERY FINE • 1/3 for FINE • 1/5 for VERY GOOD • 1/8 for GOOD

Detectives, Inc.: A Terror of Dying Dreams

Detective story drawn with sepia tones

©Eclipse

Detectives Inc. (Micro-Series)

Writer Don McGregor's modern noir series

©Eclipse

Detention Comics

One-shot with Superboy, Robin, Guy Gardner

©DC

Detonator

Human becomes explosive figure

©Chaos!

Detroit! Murder City Comix

Post-apocalyptic paean to rusted cars

©Kent Myers

	N-MINT
❑603, Aug 1989 A: Demon.	2.00
❑604, Sep 1989; poster	2.00
❑605, Sep 1989	2.00
❑606, Oct 1989	2.00
❑607, Oct 1989	2.00
❑608, Nov 1989 1: Anarky.	2.00
❑609, Dec 1989 2: Anarky.	2.00
❑610, Jan 1990; Penguin	2.00
❑611, Feb 1990; Penguin	1.50
❑612, Mar 1990; Catman, Catwoman .	1.50
❑613, Apr 1990	1.50
❑614, May 1990	1.50
❑615, Jun 1990; Penguin	1.50
❑616, Jun 1990	1.50
❑617, Jul 1990 A: Joker.	1.50
❑618, Jul 1990	1.50
❑619, Aug 1990	1.50
❑620, Aug 1990	1.50
❑621, Sep 1990	1.50
❑622, Oct 1990	1.50
❑623, Nov 1990	1.50
❑624, Dec 1990	1.50
❑625, Jan 1991	1.50
❑626, Feb 1991	1.50
❑627, Mar 1991; A: Batman's 600th. giant	3.00
❑628, Apr 1991	1.50
❑629, May 1991	1.50
❑630, Jun 1991	1.50
❑631, Jul 1991	1.50
❑632, Jul 1991	1.50
❑633, Aug 1991	1.50
❑634, Aug 1991	1.50
❑635, Sep 1991	1.50
❑636, Sep 1991	1.50
❑637, Oct 1991	1.50
❑638, Nov 1991 JA (a);	1.50
❑639, Dec 1991 JA (a);	1.50
❑640, Jan 1992 JA (a);	1.50
❑641, Feb 1992; JA (a); Anton Furst's Gotham City designs	1.50
❑642, Mar 1992 JA (a); V: Scarface.	1.50
❑643, Apr 1992 JA (a);	1.50
❑644, May 1992	1.50
❑645, Jun 1992	1.50
❑646, Jul 1992	1.50
❑647, Aug 1992	1.50
❑648, Aug 1992	1.50
❑649, Sep 1992	1.50
❑650, Sep 1992	1.50
❑651, Oct 1992	1.50
❑652, Oct 1992 A: The Huntress III (Helena Bertinelli).	1.50
❑653, Nov 1992 A: The Huntress III (Helena Bertinelli).	1.50
❑654, Dec 1992	1.50
❑655, Jan 1993 V: Ulysses.	1.50
❑656, Feb 1993 A: Bane.	2.50
❑657, Mar 1993	2.50
❑658, Apr 1993	2.50
❑659, May 1993	2.50
❑659/2nd, May 1993	1.25
❑660, May 1993	2.00
❑661, Jun 1993	2.00
❑662, Jun 1993	2.00

	N-MINT
❑663, Jul 1993	2.00
❑664, Aug 1993	2.00
❑665, Aug 1993	2.00
❑666, Sep 1993	2.00
❑667, Oct 1993	1.50
❑668, Nov 1993	1.50
❑669, Dec 1993	1.50
❑670, Jan 1994 V: Mr. Freeze.	1.50
❑671, Feb 1994	1.50
❑672, Mar 1994	1.50
❑673, Apr 1994 V: Joker.	1.50
❑674, May 1994	1.50
❑675, Jun 1994	1.50
❑675/Platinum, Jun 1994; Platinum edition; no cover price	5.00
❑675/Variant, Jun 1994; premium edition; Special cover	4.00
❑676, Jul 1994; Giant-size	2.50
❑677, Aug 1994 V: Nightwing.	1.50
❑678, Sep 1994; O: Batman. Zero Hour	1.50
❑679, Nov 1994 V: Ratcatcher.	1.50
❑680, Dec 1994 V: Two-Face.	1.50
❑681, Jan 1995	1.50
❑682, Feb 1995	1.50
❑682/Variant, Feb 1995; enhanced cover	2.50
❑683, Mar 1995 V: Penguin.	1.50
❑684, Apr 1995	1.50
❑685, May 1995	1.50
❑686, Jun 1995 A: Huntress. A: Nightwing	2.00
❑687, Jul 1995	2.00
❑688, Aug 1995	2.00
❑689, Sep 1995	2.00
❑690, Oct 1995 V: Firefly.	2.00
❑691, Nov 1995; V: Spellbinder. Underworld Unleashed	2.00
❑692, Dec 1995; Underworld Unleashed	2.00
❑693, Jan 1996 1: Allergent. A: Poison Ivy	2.00
❑694, Feb 1996 A: Poison Ivy. V: Allergent	2.00
❑695, Mar 1996	2.00
❑696, Apr 1996	2.00
❑697, Jun 1996 V: Two-Face.	2.00
❑698, Jul 1996 V: Two-Face.	2.00
❑699, Jul 1996	2.00
❑700, Aug 1996; Anniversary issue	3.50
❑700/Variant, Aug 1996; Anniversary issue; cardstock outer wrapper	5.00
❑701, Sep 1996 V: Bane.	2.00
❑702, Oct 1996	2.00
❑703, Nov 1996; Final Night	2.00
❑704, Dec 1996; self-contained story	2.00
❑705, Jan 1997 V: Riddler. V: Cluemaster.	2.00
❑706, Feb 1997 A: Riddler. V: Riddler.	2.00
❑707, Mar 1997 V: Riddler.	2.00
❑708, Apr 1997 BSz (a)	2.00
❑709, May 1997 BSz (a)	2.00
❑710, Jun 1997 BSz (a)	2.00
❑711, Jul 1997	2.00
❑712, Aug 1997	2.00
❑713, Sep 1997	2.00
❑714, Oct 1997 V: Firefly.	2.00

	N-MINT
❑715, Nov 1997 A: J'onn J'onzz.	2.00
❑716, Dec 1997; JA (a); Face cover	2.00
❑717, Jan 1998	2.00
❑718, Feb 1998 BMc (a); V: Finch.	2.00
❑719, Mar 1998 JA (a);	2.50
❑720, Apr 1998; continues in Catwoman #56	3.50
❑721, May 1998; continues in Catwoman #57	3.00
❑722, Jun 1998; JA (a); Aftershock	2.50
❑723, Jul 1998; continues in Robin #55	2.00
❑724, Aug 1998; Aftershock	2.00
❑725, Sep 1998; Aftershock	2.00
❑726, Oct 1998; A: Joker. Aftershock.	1.95
❑727, Dec 1998; A: Nightwing. A: Robin. Road to No Man's Land	1.99
❑728, Jan 1999; A: Nightwing. A: Robin. Road to No Man's Land	1.99
❑729, Feb 1999; A: Nightwing. A: Robin. A: Commissioner Gordan. Road to No Man; s Land	1.99
❑730, Mar 1999; A: Scarface. No Man; s Land	1.99
❑731, Apr 1999; A: Scarecrow. A: Huntress. No Man; s Land	1.99
❑732, May 1999; A: Batgirl. No Man; s Land	1.99
❑733, Jun 1999; No Man; s Land	1.99
❑734, Jul 1999; A: Batgirl. No Man; s Land	1.99
❑735, Aug 1999; BSz (a); A: Poison Ivy. V: Clayface. No Man; s Land	1.99
❑736, Sep 1999; No Man; s Land	1.99
❑737, Oct 1999; V: Joker. V: Harley Quinn. No Man; s Land	1.99
❑738, Nov 1999; No Man; s Land	1.99
❑739, Dec 1999; No Man; s Land	1.99
❑740, Jan 2000; No Man; s Land	1.99
❑741, Feb 2000 D: Sarah.	2.50
❑742, Mar 2000	1.99
❑743, Apr 2000	1.99
❑744, May 2000	1.99
❑745, Jun 2000	1.99
❑746, Jul 2000	1.99
❑747, Aug 2000	2.50
❑748, Sep 2000	2.50
❑749, Oct 2000	2.50
❑750, Nov 2000; Giant-size	4.95
❑751, Dec 2000	2.50
❑752, Jan 2001	2.50
❑753, Feb 2001	2.50
❑754, Mar 2001	2.50
❑755, Apr 2001	2.50
❑756, May 2001	2.50
❑757, Jun 2001	2.50
❑758, Jul 2001	2.50
❑759, Aug 2001	2.50
❑760, Sep 2001	2.50
❑761, Oct 2001	2.50
❑762, Nov 2001	2.50
❑763, Dec 2001; Joker: Last Laugh crossover	2.50
❑764, Jan 2002	2.50
❑765, Feb 2002	2.50
❑766, Mar 2002	2.50
❑767, Apr 2002	2.50

Other grades: Multiply price above by 5/6 for VF/NM • 2/3 for VERY FINE • 1/3 for FINE • 1/5 for VERY GOOD • 1/8 for GOOD

❑768, May 2002 2.50
❑769, Jun 2002 2.50
❑770, Jul 2002 2.50
❑771, Aug 2002 2.50
❑772, Sep 2002 2.50
❑773, Oct 2002 2.75
❑774, Nov 2002 2.75
❑775, Dec 2002 3.50
❑776, Jan 2003 2.75
❑777, Feb 2003 2.75
❑778, Mar 2003 2.75
❑779, Apr 2003 2.75
❑780, May 2003 2.75
❑781, Jun 2003 2.75
❑782, Jul 2003 2.75
❑783, Aug 2003 2.75
❑784, Sep 2003 2.75
❑785, Oct 2003 2.75
❑786, Nov 2003 2.75
❑787, Dec 2003 2.75
❑788, Jan 2004 2.75
❑789, Feb 2004 2.75
❑790, Mar 2004 2.75
❑791, Apr 2004 2.75
❑792, May 2004 2.75
❑793, Jun 2004 2.75
❑794, Jul 2004 2.75
❑795, Aug 2004 2.95
❑796, Sep 2004 2.95
❑797, Oct 2004 2.95
❑798, Nov 2004 2.95
❑799, Dec 2004 2.95
❑800, Jan 2005 3.50
❑801, Feb 2005 2.95
❑802, Mar 2005 2.95
❑803, Apr 2005 2.95
❑804, May 2005 2.99
❑805, Jun 2005 2.99
❑806, Jun 2005 2.99
❑807, Jul 2005 2.99
❑808, Aug 2005 2.99
❑809, Sep 2005 2.99
❑810, Oct 2005 2.99
❑811, Nov 2005 2.99
❑812, Dec 2005 2.99
❑813, Jan 2006 2.99
❑814, Jan 206 2.99
❑815, Mar 2006 2.99
❑816, Mar 2006 2.99
❑817, May 2006 2.99
❑818, Jun 2006 2.99
❑819, Jul 2006 2.99
❑820, Aug 2006 2.99
❑1000000, ca. 1998 4.00
❑1000000/Variant, ca. 1998; Signed 14.99
❑Annual 1, ca. 1988; TD, KJ (a); V: Penguin. ca. 1988; Fables 5.00
❑Annual 2, ca. 1989; Who's Who entries 4.00
❑Annual 3, ca. 1990 2.50
❑Annual 4, ca. 1991; Armageddon 2001 2.50
❑Annual 5, ca. 1992; V: Joker. Eclipso 2.75
❑Annual 6, ca. 1993; 1: Geist. 1993 Annual; Bloodlines 2.50
❑Annual 7, ca. 1994; Elseworlds 2.95
❑Annual 8, ca. 1995; O: Riddler. Year One 3.95
❑Annual 9, ca. 1996; Legends of the Dead Earth; 1996 annual 2.95
❑Annual 10, ca. 1997; SB (a); Pulp Heroes 3.95

DETECTIVES
Alpha Productions
❑1, Apr 1993, b&w 4.95

DETECTIVES, INC.: A TERROR OF DYING DREAMS
Eclipse
❑1, Jun 1987; GC (a); sepia 2.00
❑2, Sep 1987; GC (a); sepia 2.00
❑3, Dec 1987; GC (a); sepia 2.00

DETECTIVES INC. (MICRO-SERIES)
Eclipse
❑1, Apr 1985 MR (a); 2.00
❑2, Apr 1985 MR (a); 2.00

DETENTION COMICS
DC
❑1, Oct 1996; Robin, Superboy, and Warrior stories 3.50

DETONATOR
Chaos!
❑1, Dec 1994 2.75
❑2, Jan 1994 2.75

DETONATOR
Image
❑1, Jan 2005 2.50
❑2, Feb 2005 2.50
❑3, Mar 2005 2.50

DETOUR
Alternative
❑1, Oct 1997, b&w 2.95

DETROIT! MURDER CITY COMIX
Kent Myers
❑1 1993, b&w 3.00
❑2 1994, b&w 2.50
❑3 1994, b&w 2.50
❑4, Jun 1994, b&w 2.95
❑5, Aug 1994, b&w 2.95
❑6, Jan 1995, b&w A: Iggy Pop. 2.95
❑7, May 1995, b&w 2.95

DEVASTATOR
Image
❑1, ca. 1998, b&w 2.95
❑2, ca. 1998, b&w 2.95
❑3, ca. 1998 2.95

DEVIANT
Antarctic / Venus
❑1, Mar 1999, b&w 2.99

DEVIL CHEF
Dark Horse
❑1, Jul 1994, b&w 2.50

DEVIL DINOSAUR
Marvel
❑1, Apr 1978, JK (w); JK (a); O: Devil Dinosaur. 1: Devil Dinosaur. 1: Moon Boy. 5.00
❑2, May 1978, JK (a) 3.50
❑3, Jun 1978, JK (a) 2.50
❑4, Jul 1978, JK (a) 2.50
❑5, Aug 1978, JK (a) 2.50
❑6, Sep 1978, JK (a); Newsstand edition (distributed by Curtis); issue number in box 2.50
❑6/Whitman, Sep 1978, JK (a); Special markets edition (usually sold in Whitman bagged prepacks); price appears in a diamond; no UPC barcode 2.50
❑7, Oct 1978, JK (a) 2.50
❑8, Nov 1978, JK (a) 2.50
❑9, Dec 1978, JK (a) 2.50

DEVIL DINOSAUR SPRING FLING
Marvel
❑1, Jun 1997 2.99

DEVILINA
Atlas-Seaboard
❑1, Jan 1975, b&w; magazine 9.00
❑2, May 1975, b&w; magazine 12.00

DEVIL JACK
Doom Theater
❑1, Jul 1995 2.95
❑2 2.95

DEVIL KIDS
Harvey
❑1, Jul 1962 150.00
❑2, Sep 1962 75.00
❑3, Nov 1962 50.00
❑4, Jan 1963 25.00
❑5, Mar 1963 25.00
❑6, May 1963 20.00
❑7, Jul 1963 20.00
❑8, Sep 1963 20.00
❑9, Nov 1963 20.00
❑10, Jan 1964 20.00
❑11, Mar 1964 15.00
❑12, May 1964 15.00
❑13, Jul 1964 15.00
❑14, Sep 1964 15.00
❑15, Nov 1964 15.00
❑16, Jan 1965 15.00
❑17, Mar 1965 15.00
❑18, May 1965 10.00
❑19, Jul 1965 10.00
❑20, Sep 1965 10.00
❑21, Nov 1965 8.00
❑22, Jan 1966 8.00
❑23, Mar 1966 8.00
❑24, May 1966 8.00
❑25, Jul 1966 8.00
❑26, Sep 1966 8.00
❑27, Nov 1966 8.00
❑28, Jan 1967 8.00
❑29, Mar 1967 8.00
❑30, May 1967 8.00
❑31, Jul 1967 5.00
❑32, Sep 1967 5.00
❑33, Nov 1967 5.00
❑34 1968 5.00
❑35, Sep 1968 5.00
❑36, Nov 1968 5.00
❑37 1969 5.00
❑38 1969 5.00
❑39 1969 5.00
❑40, Jun 1969 5.00
❑41 1969 4.00
❑42 1969 4.00
❑43 1970 4.00
❑44 1970 4.00
❑45 1970 4.00
❑46 1970 4.00
❑47, Dec 1970 4.00
❑48 1971 4.00
❑49 1971 4.00
❑50 1971 4.00
❑51, Sep 1971 4.00
❑52 4.00
❑53, Mar 1972 4.00
❑54 1972 4.00
❑55 1972 4.00
❑56 1972 4.00
❑57, Dec 1972 4.00
❑58, Feb 1973 4.00
❑59, Apr 1973 4.00
❑60, Jun 1973 4.00
❑61, Aug 1973 3.00
❑62, Oct 1973 3.00
❑63, Dec 1973 3.00
❑64 1974 3.00
❑65 1974 3.00
❑66 1974 3.00
❑67 1974 3.00
❑68 1974 3.00
❑69, Apr 1975 3.00
❑70, Jun 1975 3.00
❑71, Aug 1975 3.00
❑72, Oct 1975 3.00
❑73, Dec 1975 3.00
❑74, Feb 1976 3.00
❑75, Apr 1976 3.00
❑76, Jun 1976 3.00
❑77, Aug 1976 3.00
❑78, Oct 1976 3.00
❑79, Dec 1976 3.00
❑80, Feb 1977 2.00
❑81, Apr 1977 2.00
❑82, Jun 1977 2.00
❑83, Aug 1977 2.00
❑84 1977 2.00
❑85 1977 2.00
❑86, Jan 1978 2.00
❑87, Mar 1978 2.00
❑88, May 1978 2.00
❑89, Jul 1978 2.00
❑90 1978 2.00
❑91, Dec 1978 2.00
❑92, Feb 1979 2.00
❑93 1979 2.00
❑94 1979 2.00
❑95, Sep 1979 2.00
❑96, Nov 1979 2.00
❑97, Feb 1980 2.00
❑98, Apr 1980 2.00
❑99, Jun 1980 2.00
❑100, Aug 1980 2.00
❑101, Oct 1980 2.00
❑102, Dec 1980 2.00

N-MINT

❑103, Feb 1981 .... 2.00
❑104, Apr 1981 .... 2.00
❑105, Jun 1981 .... 2.00
❑106, Aug 1981 .... 2.00
❑107, Oct 1981 .... 2.00

DEVILMAN
VEROTIK
❑1, Jun 1995 .... 3.50
❑2 .... 3.00
❑3 .... 3.00
❑4 .... 2.95
❑5 .... 2.95
❑6 .... 3.50

DEVIL MAY CRY
DREAMWAVE
❑1, Mar 2004 .... 3.95
❑1/2nd, Mar 2004; Reprints 3.95
❑2 2004 .... 3.95
❑3, Apr 2004 .... 3.95

DEVIL MAY CRY 3
TOKYOPOP
❑1, Oct 2005, ... 9.95

DEVIL'S ANGEL
FANTAGRAPHICS / EROS
❑1 .... 2.95

DEVIL'S BITE
BONEYARD
❑1 .... 2.95
❑2; Indicia lists as #1 .... 2.95

DEVIL'S DUE STUDIOS PREVIEWS 2003
IMAGE
❑1, Mar 2003 .... 1.00

DEVIL'S FOOTPRINTS
DARK HORSE
❑1, Mar 2003 .... 2.99
❑2, Apr 2003 .... 2.99
❑3, May 2003 .... 2.99
❑4, Jul 2003 .... 2.99

DEVIL'S KEEPER
ALIAS
❑1, Aug 2005 .... 1.00
❑2, Dec 2005 .... 2.99

DEVIL'S REIGN
IMAGE
❑½, ca. 1996; Wizard mail-in 3.00
❑½/Autographed, ca. 1996; Signed, limited edition 3.00
❑½/Platinum, ca. 1996; Platinum edition 3.00

DEVIL'S REJECTS
IDEA & DESIGN WORKS
❑0/Baby, Jul 2005; Based on 2005 Rob Zombie movie; given away with "Wanted" cards and pins at San Diego Comic-Con International 2005 .... 5.00
❑0/Otis, Jul 2005; Based on 2005 Rob Zombie movie; given away with "Wanted" cards and pins at San Diego Comic-Con International 2005 .... 6.00
❑0/Spaulding, Jul 2005 .... 5.00
❑1, Aug 2005 .... 3.99

DEVLIN
MAXIMUM
❑1, Apr 1996 .... 2.50

DEVLIN DEMON: NOT FOR NORMAL CHILDREN
DUBLIN
❑1 .... 2.95

DEWEY DESADE
ITEM
❑1 .... 3.50
❑2 .... 3.50
❑Ashcan 1; Promotional, mini-ashcan (4 x 2) 0.25

DEXTER'S LABORATORY
DC
❑1, Sep 1999 .... 2.50
❑2, Oct 1999 A: Mandark 2.00
❑3, Nov 1999; Dexter's robot takes his place 2.00
❑4, Dec 1999 .... 2.00
❑5, Jan 2000 .... 2.00
❑6, Feb 2000 .... 2.00
❑7, Mar 2000 .... 2.00
❑8, Apr 2000 .... 2.00
❑9, May 2000 .... 2.00
❑10, Jun 2000 .... 2.00
❑11, Jul 2000 .... 1.99
❑12, Aug 2000 .... 1.99
❑13, Sep 2000 .... 1.99
❑14, Oct 2000 .... 1.99
❑15, Nov 2000 .... 1.99
❑16, Dec 2000 .... 1.99
❑17, Jan 2001 .... 1.99
❑18, Feb 2001 .... 1.99
❑19, Mar 2001 .... 1.99
❑20, Apr 2001 .... 1.99
❑21, May 2001 .... 1.99
❑22, Jun 2001 .... 1.99
❑23, Jul 2001 .... 1.99
❑24, Aug 2001 .... 1.99
❑25, Sep 2001 .... 0.50
❑26, Oct 2001 .... 1.99
❑27, Nov 2001 .... 1.99
❑28, Dec 2001 .... 1.99
❑29, Jan 2002 .... 1.99
❑30, Aug 2002 .... 1.99
❑31, Oct 2002 .... 2.25
❑32, Dec 2002 .... 2.25
❑33, Feb 2004 .... 2.25
❑34, Apr 2004 .... 2.25

DHAMPIRE: STILLBORN
DC / VERTIGO
❑1, Sep 1996; prestige format 5.95

DIABLO: TALES OF SANCTUARY
DARK HORSE
❑1, Nov 2001; Several characters in profile on cover 5.95

DIA DE LOS MUERTOS (SERGIO ARAGONÉS')
DARK HORSE
❑nn, Oct 1998; Day of the Dead stories 2.95

DIATOM
PHOTOGRAPHICS
❑1, Apr 1995, b&w; prestige format; fumetti 4.95
❑2 .... 4.95
❑3 .... 4.95

DICK DANGER
OLSEN
❑1, Jan 1998 .... 2.95
❑2 .... 2.95
❑3 .... 2.95
❑4 .... 2.95
❑5 .... 2.95

DICK TRACY (BLACKTHORNE)
BLACKTHORNE
❑1, Jun 1986 .... 5.95
❑2, Jun 1986 .... 5.95
❑3, Jul 1986 .... 6.95
❑4, Aug 1986 .... 6.95
❑5, Oct 1986 .... 6.95
❑6, Oct 1986 .... 6.95
❑7, Dec 1986 .... 6.95
❑8, Jan 1987 .... 6.95
❑9, Jan 1987 .... 6.95
❑10, Feb 1987 .... 6.95
❑11, Mar 1987 .... 6.95
❑12, Apr 1987 .... 6.95
❑13, May 1987 .... 6.95
❑14, Jun 1987 .... 6.95
❑15, Jul 1987 .... 6.95
❑16, Aug 1987 .... 6.95
❑17, Sep 1987 .... 6.95
❑18, Sep 1987 .... 6.95
❑19, Oct 1987 .... 6.95
❑20, Oct 1987 .... 6.95
❑21, Nov 1987 .... 6.95
❑22, Nov 1987 .... 6.95
❑23, Nov 1987 .... 6.95
❑24, Dec 1987 .... 6.95

DICK TRACY (DISNEY)
DISNEY
❑1; newsstand format 2.95
❑1/Direct ed.; prestige format 4.95
❑2; newsstand format 2.95
❑2/Direct ed.; prestige format 5.95
❑3; newsstand format 2.95
❑3/Direct ed.; prestige format 5.95

DICK TRACY 3-D
BLACKTHORNE
❑1, Jul 1986 .... 2.50

DICK TRACY ADVENTURES (GLADSTONE)
GLADSTONE
❑1, Sep 1991 .... 4.95

DICK TRACY ADVENTURES (HAMILTON)
HAMILTON
❑1, b&w 3.95

DICK TRACY CRIMEBUSTER
AVALON
❑1 .... 2.95
❑2 .... 2.95
❑3 .... 2.95
❑4 .... 2.95

DICK TRACY DETECTIVE
AVALON
❑1 .... 2.95
❑2 .... 2.95
❑3 .... 2.95
❑4 .... 2.95

DICK TRACY MONTHLY (BLACKTHORNE)
BLACKTHORNE
❑1, May 1986 .... 2.50
❑2, Jun 1986 .... 2.00
❑3, Jul 1986 .... 2.00
❑4, Aug 1986 .... 2.00
❑5, Sep 1986 .... 2.00
❑6, Oct 1986 .... 2.00
❑7, Nov 1986 .... 2.00
❑8, Dec 1986 .... 2.00
❑9, Jan 1987 .... 2.00
❑10, Feb 1987 .... 2.00
❑11, Mar 1987 .... 2.00
❑12, Apr 1987; no month in indicia 2.00
❑13, May 1987 .... 2.00
❑14, Jun 1987 .... 2.00
❑15, Jul 1987 .... 2.00
❑16 1988 .... 2.00
❑17 1988 .... 2.00
❑18 1988 .... 2.00
❑19 1988 .... 2.00
❑20 1988 .... 2.00
❑21 1988 .... 2.00
❑22 1988 .... 2.00
❑23 1988 .... 2.00
❑24 1988 .... 2.00
❑25 1988; Series continues as Dick Tracy Weekly 2.00

DICK TRACY SPECIAL
BLACKTHORNE
❑1, Jan 1988 .... 2.95
❑2, Mar 1988 .... 2.95
❑3, May 1988 .... 2.95

DICK TRACY: THE EARLY YEARS
BLACKTHORNE
❑1, Aug 1987 .... 6.95
❑2, Oct 1987 .... 6.95
❑3, Apr 1988 .... 6.95
❑4 .... 2.95

DICK TRACY "UNPRINTED STORIES"
BLACKTHORNE
❑1, Sep 1987 .... 2.95
❑2, Nov 1987 .... 2.95
❑3, Jan 1988 .... 2.95
❑4, Jun 1988 .... 2.95

DICK TRACY WEEKLY
BLACKTHORNE
❑26, Jan 1988 .... 2.00
❑27, Jan 1988 .... 2.00
❑28, Jan 1988 .... 2.00
❑29, Jan 1988 .... 2.00
❑30, Feb 1988 .... 2.00
❑31, Feb 1988 .... 2.00
❑32, Feb 1988 .... 2.00
❑33, Feb 1988 .... 2.00
❑34, Mar 1988 .... 2.00
❑35, Mar 1988 .... 2.00
❑36, Mar 1988 .... 2.00

❑37, Mar 1988 2.00
❑38, Jun 1988 2.00
❑39, Jun 1988 2.00
❑40, Jun 1988 2.00
❑41, Jun 1988 2.00
❑42, Jul 1988 2.00
❑43, Jul 1988 2.00
❑44, Jul 1988 2.00
❑45, Jul 1988 2.00
❑46, Aug 1988 2.00
❑47, Aug 1988 2.00
❑48, Aug 1988 2.00
❑49, Aug 1988 2.00
❑50, Sep 1988 2.00
❑51, Sep 1988 2.00
❑52, Sep 1988 2.00
❑53, Sep 1988 2.00
❑54, Oct 1988 2.00
❑55, Oct 1988 2.00
❑56, Oct 1988 2.00
❑57, Oct 1988 2.00
❑58, Oct 1988 2.00
❑59, Oct 1988 2.00
❑60, Nov 1988 2.00
❑61, Nov 1988 2.00
❑62, Nov 1988 2.00
❑63, Nov 1988 2.00
❑64, Nov 1988 2.00
❑65, Nov 1988 2.00
❑66, Dec 1988 2.00
❑67, Dec 1988 2.00
❑68, Dec 1988 2.00
❑69, Dec 1988 2.00
❑70, Jan 1989 2.00
❑71, Jan 1989 2.00
❑72, Jan 1989 2.00
❑73, Jan 1989 2.00
❑74, Feb 1989 2.00
❑75, Feb 1989 2.00
❑76, Feb 1989 2.00
❑77, Feb 1989 2.00
❑78, Mar 1989 2.00
❑79, Mar 1989 2.00
❑80, Mar 1989 2.00
❑81, Mar 1989 2.00
❑82, Apr 1989 2.00
❑83, Apr 1989 2.00
❑84, Apr 1989 2.00
❑85, Apr 1989 2.00
❑86, May 1989 2.00
❑87, May 1989 2.00
❑88, May 1989 2.00
❑89, May 1989 2.00
❑90, Jun 1989 2.00
❑91, Jun 1989 2.00
❑92, Jun 1989 2.00
❑93, Jun 1989 2.00
❑94, Aug 1989 2.00
❑95, Aug 1989 2.00
❑96, Aug 1989 2.00
❑97, Aug 1989 2.00
❑98, Sep 1989 2.00
❑99, Sep 1989 2.00

DICK WAD
SLAVE LABOR

❑1, Sep 1993, b&w 2.50

DICTATORS OF THE TWENTIETH CENTURY: HITLER
ANTARCTIC

❑1, Apr 2004, 2.99
❑2, May 2004 2.99
❑3, Jun 2004 2.99
❑4, Jul 2004 2.99

DICTATORS OF THE TWENTIETH CENTURY: SADDAM HUSSEIN
ANTARCTIC

❑1, Aug 2004 3.95
❑2, Sep 2004 3.95

DIEBOLD
SILENT PARTNERS

❑1 1996, b&w 2.95
❑2 1996, b&w 2.95

DIE-CUT
MARVEL

❑1, Nov 1993; diecut cover 2.50
❑2, Dec 1993 1.75
❑3, Jan 1994 1.75
❑4, Feb 1994 1.75

DIE-CUT VS. G-FORCE
MARVEL

❑1, Nov 1993; Holo-Grafx cover 2.75
❑2, Dec 1993; foil cover 2.75

DIESEL
ANTARCTIC

❑1, Apr 1997 2.95

DIGIMON DIGITAL MONSTERS
DARK HORSE

❑1, May 2000 2.95
❑2, May 2000 2.95
❑3, May 2000 2.95
❑4, May 2000 2.95
❑5, Aug 2000 2.95
❑6, Sep 2000 2.95
❑7, Sep 2000 2.95
❑8, Sep 2000 2.95
❑9, Sep 2000 2.99
❑10, Oct 2000 2.99
❑11, Nov 2000 2.99
❑12, Nov 2000 2.99

DIGIMON TAMERS
TOKYOPOP

❑1, Apr 2004 9.99

DIGITAL DRAGON
PEREGRINE ENTERTAINMENT

❑1, Jan 1999, b&w 2.95
❑2, Apr 1999, b&w 2.95

DIGITAL WEBBING PRESENTS
DIGITAL WEBBING

❑1 2001, b&w 2.95
❑2 2001, b&w 2.95
❑3 2001, b&w 2.95
❑4, Aug 2001, b&w 2.95
❑5, Oct 2001, b&w 2.95
❑6, Dec 2001, b&w 2.95
❑7, Feb 2002, b&w 2.95
❑8, Apr 2002, b&w 2.95
❑9, Jun 2002, b&w 2.95
❑10, Aug 2002, b&w 2.95
❑11, Oct 2002, b&w 2.95
❑12 2003, b&w 2.95
❑13 2003, b&w 2.95
❑14 2003, b&w 2.95
❑15 2003, b&w 2.95
❑16 2004, b&w 2.95
❑17 2004, b&w 2.95
❑18 2004, b&w 2.95
❑19, ca. 2004, b&w 3.50
❑20, ca. 2005, b&w 2.95

DIGITEK
MARVEL

❑1, Dec 1992 2.00
❑2, Jan 1993 2.00
❑3, Feb 1993 2.00
❑4, Mar 1993 2.00

DIK SKYCAP
RIP OFF

❑1, Dec 1991, b&w 2.50
❑2, May 1992, b&w 2.50

DILEMMA PRESENTS
DILEMMA

❑1, Oct 1994, b&w 2.50
❑2, b&w; Flip-book 2.50
❑3, Apr 1995, b&w; Flip-book 2.50
❑4, b&w; Flip-book 2.50

DILTON'S STRANGE SCIENCE
ARCHIE

❑1, May 1989 2.00
❑2, Aug 1989 1.50
❑3, Nov 1989 1.50
❑4, Feb 1990 1.50
❑5, May 1990 1.50

DIMENSION 5
EDGE

❑1, Oct 1995, b&w 3.95

DIMENSION X
KARL ART

❑1, b&w 3.50

DIMENSION Z
PYRAMID

❑1 2.00
❑2 2.00

DIMM COMICS PRESENTS
DIMM

❑Ashcan 0, Jan 1996, b&w; ashcan promotional comic 1.00
❑Ashcan 1, May 1996, b&w; ashcan promotional comic 1.00

DIM-WITTED DARRYL
SLAVE LABOR

❑1, Jun 1998, b&w 2.95
❑2 2.95
❑3 2.95

DINGLEDORFS
SKYLIGHT

❑1, b&w 2.75

DINKY ON THE ROAD
BLIND BAT

❑1, Jun 1994, b&w 1.95

DINO ISLAND
MIRAGE

❑1, Feb 1993; covers form diptych 2.75
❑2, Mar 1993; covers form diptych 2.75

DINO-RIDERS
MARVEL

❑1, Mar 1989 1.50
❑2, Apr 1989 1.50
❑3, May 1989 1.50

DINOSAUR BOP
MONSTER

❑1, b&w 2.50
❑2, b&w 2.50

DINOSAUR ISLAND
MONSTER

❑1, b&w 2.50

DINOSAUR MANSION
EDGE

❑1, b&w; no indicia 2.95

DINOSAUR REX
UPSHOT

❑1 2.00
❑2, b&w 2.00
❑3, b&w 2.00

DINOSAURS
HOLLYWOOD

❑1; TV based 3.00
❑2; TV based 3.00

DINOSAURS ATTACK!
ECLIPSE

❑1, trading cards 3.95
❑2, 3.95
❑3, 3.95

DINOSAURS, A CELEBRATION
MARVEL / EPIC

❑1, ca. 1992; Horns and Heavy Armor 4.95
❑2, ca. 1992; Bone heads and Duck-bills 4.95
❑3, ca. 1992; Egg stealers and Earth shakers 4.95
❑4, ca. 1992; Terrible Claws and Tyrants 4.95

DINOSAURS FOR HIRE (ETERNITY)
ETERNITY

❑1, Mar 1988, b&w 2.00
❑1/3D; 3-D 2.95
❑1/2nd, Mar 1988 1.95
❑2, Jun 1988 1.95
❑3 1.95
❑4 1.95
❑5 1.95
❑6 1.95
❑7 1.95
❑8 1.95
❑9 1.95

DINOSAURS FOR HIRE (MALIBU)
MALIBU

❑1, Feb 1993 1.95
❑2, Mar 1993 1.95
❑3, Apr 1993 1.95

Devil Dinosaur

Silly Jack Kirby return trip to Marvel
©Marvel

Dexter's Laboratory

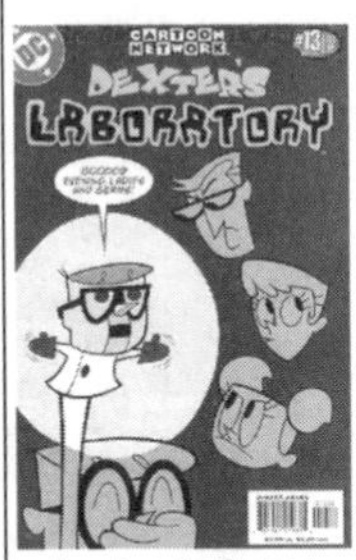

Based on the Cartoon Network series
©DC

Diablo: Tales of Sanctuary

Based on the computer game fantasy
©Dark Horse

Dia de los Muertos (Sergio Aragonés')

Sergio's take on Mexico's "Day of the Dead"
©Dark Horse

Dick Tracy (Blackthorne)

Reprinted stories from the classic comic strip
©Blackthorne

N-MINT

❑4, May 1993 .... 1.95
❑5, Jun 1993 .... 2.50
❑6, Jul 1993; Jurassic Park parody cover 2.50
❑7, Aug 1993 .... 2.50
❑8, Sep 1993 .... 2.50
❑9, Oct 1993 .... 2.50
❑10, Nov 1993; Comics' Greatest World parody cover 2.50
❑11, Dec 1993 .... 2.50
❑12, Feb 1994; Ultraverse parody cover 2.50

DINOSAURS FOR HIRE: DINOSAURS RULE!
Eternity

❑1; Dinosaurs Rule! 5.95

DINOSAURS FOR HIRE FALL CLASSIC
Eternity

❑1, Nov 1988, b&w; Fall Classic; Elvis 2.25

DINOSAURS FOR HIRE: GUNS 'N' LIZARDS
Eternity

❑1; Guns 'n' Lizards 5.95

DIORAMAS: LOVE STORY
Image

❑1, ca. 2004 .... 12.95

DIRECTORY TO A NONEXISTENT UNIVERSE
Eclipse

❑1, Dec 1987 .... 2.00

DIRE WOLVES: A CHRONICLE OF THE DEADWORLD
Caliber

❑1, b&w 3.95

DIRTBAG
Twist N Shout

❑1, ca. 1993 .... 2.95
❑2, ca. 1993 .... 2.95
❑3, Nov 1993 .... 2.95
❑4, Dec 1993 .... 2.95
❑5, ca. 1994 .... 2.95
❑6 .... 2.95
❑7 .... 2.95

DIRTY DOZEN
Dell

❑1, Oct 1967, 12-180-710 .... 25.00

DIRTY PAIR
Eclipse

❑1, Dec 1988, b&w 4.00
❑2, Jan 1989, b&w 3.00
❑3, Feb 1989, b&w 3.00
❑4, Mar 1989, b&w 3.00

DIRTY PAIR II
Eclipse

❑1, May 1989, b&w 2.50
❑2, Aug 1989, b&w 2.50
❑3, Nov 1989 .... 2.50
❑4, Feb 1990 .... 2.50
❑5, May 1990 .... 2.50

DIRTY PAIR III
Eclipse

❑1, Aug 1990, b&w 2.25
❑2, Nov 1990, b&w 2.25
❑3, Feb 1991 .... 2.25
❑4, May 1991 .... 2.25
❑5, Aug 1991 .... 2.25

DIRTY PAIR (4TH SERIES)
Viz

❑1 .... 4.95
❑2 .... 4.95
❑3 .... 4.95
❑4 .... 4.95
❑5 .... 4.95

DIRTY PAIR: DANGEROUS ACQUAINTANCES
Dark Horse / Manga

❑1, b&w 2.95
❑2, b&w 2.95
❑3, b&w 2.95
❑4, b&w 2.95
❑5, b&w 2.95

DIRTY PAIR, THE: FATAL BUT NOT SERIOUS
Dark Horse / Manga

❑1, Jul 1995 .... 2.95
❑2, Aug 1995 .... 2.95
❑3, Sep 1995 .... 2.95
❑4, Oct 1995 .... 2.95
❑5, Nov 1995 .... 2.95

DIRTY PAIR, THE: RUN FROM THE FUTURE
Dark Horse / Manga

❑1, Jan 2000 .... 2.95
❑1/A, Jan 2000; alternate cover 2.95
❑2, Feb 2000 .... 2.95
❑3, Mar 2000 .... 2.95
❑4, Apr 2000 .... 2.95

DIRTY PAIR, THE: SIM HELL
Dark Horse / Manga

❑1 1993, b&w 2.95
❑2 1993, b&w 2.95
❑3 1993, b&w 2.95
❑4 1993, b&w 2.95
❑5 1993 .... 2.95

DIRTY PAIR, THE: SIM HELL REMASTERED
Dark Horse / Manga

❑1, May 2001 .... 2.99
❑2, Jun 2001 .... 2.99
❑3, Jul 2001 .... 2.99
❑4, Aug 2001 .... 2.99

DIRTY PAIR, THE: START THE VIOLENCE
Dark Horse

❑1/A, Sep 1999 .... 2.95
❑1/B, Sep 1999; variant cover 2.95

DIRTY PICTURES
Aircel

❑1, Apr 1991, b&w 2.50
❑2, b&w 2.50
❑3, b&w 2.50

DIRTY PLOTTE
Drawn and Quarterly

❑1 .... 2.50
❑2 .... 2.50
❑3 .... 2.50
❑4 .... 2.50
❑5 .... 2.50
❑6 .... 2.50
❑7 .... 2.95
❑8 .... 2.95
❑9 .... 2.95
❑10, Nov 1996 .... 3.50

DISAVOWED
DC / Wildstorm

❑1, Mar 2000 .... 2.50
❑2, Apr 2000 .... 2.50
❑3, May 2000 .... 2.50
❑4, Jun 2000 .... 2.50
❑5, Jul 2000 .... 2.50
❑6, Aug 2000 .... 2.50

DISCIPLES
Image

❑1, Apr 2001 .... 2.95
❑2, Jun 2001 .... 2.95

DISHMAN
Eclipse

❑1, Sep 1988, b&w 2.50

DISNEY AFTERNOON
Marvel

❑1, Nov 1994; Darkwing Duck, Bonkers, Goof Troop, Tailspin 2.00
❑2, Dec 1994 .... 1.50
❑3, Jan 1995 .... 1.50
❑4, Feb 1995 .... 1.50
❑5, Mar 1995 .... 1.50
❑6, Apr 1995 .... 1.50
❑7, May 1995 .... 1.50
❑8, Jun 1995 .... 1.50
❑9, Jul 1995 .... 1.50
❑10, Aug 1995 .... 1.50

DISNEY COMIC HITS
Marvel

❑1, Oct 1995, Pocahontas 2.00
❑2, Nov 1995, Timon and Pumbaa 2.00
❑3, Dec 1995, A: Pocahontas. A: Captain John Smith. 2.00
❑4, Jan 1996, Adapts Toy Story 2.00
❑5, Feb 1996, Winter Wonderland 2.00
❑6, Mar 1996 .... 2.00
❑7, Apr 1996 .... 2.00
❑8, May 1996 .... 2.00
❑9, Jun 1996 .... 2.00
❑10, Jul 1996, adapts Hunchback of Notre Dame 2.00
❑11, Aug 1996, Hunchback of Notre Dame 2.00
❑12, Sep 1996, The Little Mermaid 2.00
❑13, Oct 1996, adapts Aladdin and the King of Thieves 2.00
❑14, Nov 1996, Timon & Pumbaa 2.00
❑15, Dec 1996, Toy Story adventures. 2.00
❑16, Jan 1997, adapts 101 Dalmations 2.00

Other grades: Multiply price above by 5/6 for VF/NM • 2/3 for VERY FINE • 1/3 for FINE • 1/5 for VERY GOOD • 1/8 for GOOD

DISNEY COMICS ALBUM
Disney

	N-MINT
❑1, Donald, Gyro	6.95
❑2, Uncle Scrooge	6.95
❑3, Donald Duck	7.95
❑4, Mickey Mouse vs. Phantom Blot	7.95
❑5, Chip 'n Dale	7.95
❑6, Uncle Scrooge	7.95
❑7, Donald Duck	6.95
❑8, Super Goof	7.95

DISNEYLAND BIRTHDAY PARTY (WALT DISNEY'S...)
Gladstone

	N-MINT
❑1, ca. 1985, CB (a); Reprints Disneyland Birthday Party (Giant), Uncle Scrooge Goes to Disneyland	10.00
❑1/A, digest	10.00

DISNEY'S ACTION CLUB
Acclaim

	N-MINT
❑1, digest; Hercules, Hunchback, Lion King, Aladdin, Toy Story, Mighty Ducks	4.50
❑2	4.50
❑3	4.50
❑4, digest; Mighty Ducks, Toy Story, Aladdin, Hercules stories	4.50
❑5	4.50
❑6	4.50
❑7, Jun 1997	4.50

DISNEY'S COLOSSAL COMICS
Disney

	N-MINT
❑1	2.00

DISNEY'S COLOSSAL COMICS COLLECTION
Disney

	N-MINT
❑1, digest	2.00
❑2, digest	2.00
❑3, digest	2.00
❑4, digest	2.00
❑5, digest	2.00
❑6, digest	2.00
❑7, digest	2.00
❑8, digest	2.00
❑9, digest	2.00
❑10, digest	2.00

DISNEY'S COMICS IN 3-D
Disney

	N-MINT
❑1	2.95

DISNEY'S ENCHANTING STORIES
Acclaim

	N-MINT
❑1	4.50
❑2, Pocahontas	4.50
❑3, Beauty & The Beast	4.50
❑4, 101 Dalmations	4.50

DISOBEDIENT DAISY
Fantagraphics / Eros

	N-MINT
❑1, Aug 1995, b&w	2.95
❑2, Oct 1995, b&w	2.95

DISTANT SOIL (1ST SERIES)
Warp

	N-MINT
❑1 1983	8.00
❑2 1984	5.00
❑3 1984	4.00
❑4 1984	4.00
❑5 1985	4.00
❑6, Jun 1985; Standard comic size 1: Panda Khan	3.00
❑7, Sep 1985	3.00
❑8, Dec 1985	3.00
❑9, Mar 1986	3.00

DISTANT SOIL, A (2ND SERIES)
Aria

	N-MINT
❑1 1991	5.00
❑1/2nd	3.00
❑1/3rd	2.00
❑1/4th	1.75
❑2	3.00
❑2/2nd	1.75
❑3 1992	3.00
❑3/2nd	1.75
❑4 1993	2.00
❑4/2nd	1.75
❑5 1993	1.75
❑6	1.75
❑7 1994	1.75
❑8, Jun 1994	1.75
❑9 1994	2.50
❑10	2.50
❑11, Apr 1995	2.50
❑12, Nov 1995	2.50
❑13, Jun 1996	2.95
❑14, Aug 1996	2.95
❑15, Aug 1996; Image begins as publisher	2.95
❑16, Oct 1996	2.95
❑17, Dec 1996	2.95
❑18, Feb 1997	2.95
❑19, Apr 1997	2.95
❑20, Jun 1997	2.95
❑21, Sep 1997	2.95
❑22, Dec 1997	2.95
❑23, Feb 1998	2.95
❑24, Apr 1998	2.95
❑25, Jun 1998; double-sized NG (w);	3.95
❑25/Ltd., Jun 1998; 15th anniversary issue NG (w);	8.00
❑26, Nov 1998; Christmas cover; not Christmas story	2.95
❑27, Apr 1999	2.95
❑28, Jul 1999	3.95
❑29, Dec 1999	3.95
❑30, Aug 2000	3.95
❑31, Jan 2001	3.95
❑32, May 2001	3.95
❑33, Aug 2001	3.95
❑34, Sep 2001; Giant-size	4.95
❑35	0.00
❑36, Oct 2003	4.50

DISTRICT X
Marvel

	N-MINT
❑1, Jul 2004	4.00
❑2, Aug 2004	2.99
❑3, Sep 2004	2.99
❑4, Oct 2004	2.99
❑5, Nov 2004	2.99
❑6, Dec 2004	2.99
❑7, Jan 2005	2.99
❑8, Feb 2005	2.99
❑9, Mar 2005	2.99
❑10, Apr 2005	2.99
❑11, May 2005	2.99
❑12, May 2005	2.99
❑13, Jun 2005	2.99

DIVA GRAFIX & STORIES
Starhead

	N-MINT
❑1, Nov 1993, b&w	3.95
❑2, b&w	3.95

DIVAS
Caliber

	N-MINT
❑1, b&w	2.50
❑2, b&w	2.50
❑3, b&w	2.50
❑4, b&w	2.50

DIVINE INTERVENTION/GEN13
DC / Wildstorm

	N-MINT
❑1, Nov 1999	2.50

DIVINE INTERVENTION/WILDCATS
DC / Wildstorm

	N-MINT
❑1, Nov 1999	2.50

DIVINE RIGHT
Image

	N-MINT
❑1, Sep 1997 JLee (w); JLee (a);	3.00
❑1/A, Sep 1997; JLee (w); JLee (a); variant cover	3.00
❑1/B, Sep 1997; JLee (c); JLee (w); JLee (a); American Entertainment variant; Christy Blaze with flag in background	3.00
❑1/C, Sep 1997; Bagged edition JLee (c); JLee (w); JLee (a);	3.00
❑1/D, Sep 1997; Spanish edition; alternate cover	2.50
❑1/E, Sep 1997; Voyager pack with preview of Stormwatch	2.50
❑2, Oct 1997; JLee (w); JLee (a); Sword battle scene on cover	3.00
❑2/Variant, Oct 1997; alternate cover; fight scene	2.50
❑3, Nov 1997 JLee (w); JLee (a); A: Fairchild	2.50
❑3/Variant, Nov 1997; no cover price on outer cover	2.50
❑4, Dec 1997; JLee (w); JLee (a); White cover w/blue figure (no Fairchild)	2.50
❑4/Variant, Dec 1997; JLee (w); JLee (a); Variant cover (Fairchild)	2.50
❑5, Feb 1998 JLee (w); JLee (a);	2.50
❑5/Variant, Feb 1998; Pacific Comicon variant cover edition; JLee (w); JLee (a); Pacific Comicon variant cover edition	2.50
❑6, Aug 1998 JLee (w); JLee (a);	2.50
❑7, Dec 1998 JLee (w); JLee (a);	2.50
❑8, Jan 1999 JLee (w); JLee (a);	2.50
❑8/Variant, Jan 1999; alternate cover	2.50
❑9, Jul 1999 JLee (w); JLee (a);	2.50
❑10, Oct 1999 JLee (w); JLee (a)	2.50
❑11, Nov 1999 JLee (w); JLee (a);	2.50
❑Ashcan 1, Jul 1997; JLee (w); JLee (a); 1: Divine Right. Team on cover.	3.00
❑Ashcan 1/A, Jul 1997; JLee (w); JLee (a); 1: Divine Right. variant cover: Faraday typing, woman's leg in foreground	3.00

DIVISION 13
Dark Horse

	N-MINT
❑1, Sep 1994	2.50
❑2, Oct 1994	2.50
❑3, Dec 1994	2.50
❑4, Jan 1995, b&w	2.50

DJANGO AND ANGEL
Caliber

	N-MINT
❑1, b&w	2.50
❑2, b&w	2.50
❑3, b&w	2.50
❑4, b&w	2.50
❑5, b&w	2.50

DMZ
DC / Vertigo

	N-MINT
❑1, Jan 2006,	2.99
❑2, Feb 2006	2.99
❑3, Mar 2006	2.99
❑4, Apr 2006	2.99
❑5, May 2006	2.99
❑6, Jun 2006	2.99
❑8, Aug 2006	2.99

DNAGENTS
Eclipse

	N-MINT
❑1, Mar 1983	2.50
❑2, Apr 1983 ME (w);	2.00
❑3, May 1983 ME (w);	2.00
❑4, Jul 1983	2.00
❑5, Aug 1983	2.00
❑6, Oct 1983	1.75
❑7, Nov 1983	1.75
❑8, Jan 1984	1.75
❑9, Feb 1984	1.75
❑10, Mar 1984	1.75
❑11, May 1984	1.75
❑12, May 1984	1.75
❑13, Jun 1984	1.75
❑14, Jul 1984	1.75
❑15, Aug 1984 EL (a);	1.75
❑16, Sep 1984	1.75
❑17, Dec 1984	1.75
❑18, Jan 1985	1.75
❑19, Feb 1985	1.75
❑20, Mar 1985	1.75
❑21, Apr 1985	1.75
❑22, May 1985	1.75
❑23, Jun 1985	1.75
❑24, Jul 1985 DSt (c);	1.75
❑3D 1, Jan 1986; 3-Dminensional DNAgents	2.50

DNAGENTS SUPER SPECIAL
Antarctic

	N-MINT
❑1, Apr 1994, b&w	3.50

D-N-ANGEL
Tokyopop

	N-MINT
❑1, Apr 2004	9.99
❑2, May 2004	9.99
❑3, Jul 2004	9.99
❑4, Oct 2004	9.99
❑5, Nov 2004	9.99
❑6, Feb 2005	9.99
❑7, Mar 2005	9.99
❑8, Jun 2005	9.99

Digitek

Series spinoff from Mys-TECH

©Marvel

Dim-Witted Darryl

Short stories from Michael Bresnahan

©Slave Labor

Dinosaurs For Hire (Eternity)

Series just missed Turtles popularity wave

©Eternity

Dirty Dozen

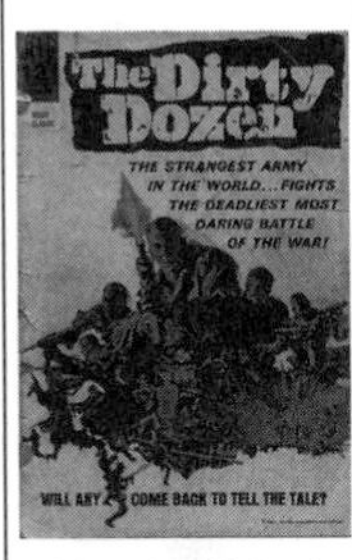

Adaptation of beloved 1967 war film

©Dell

Disney Afternoon

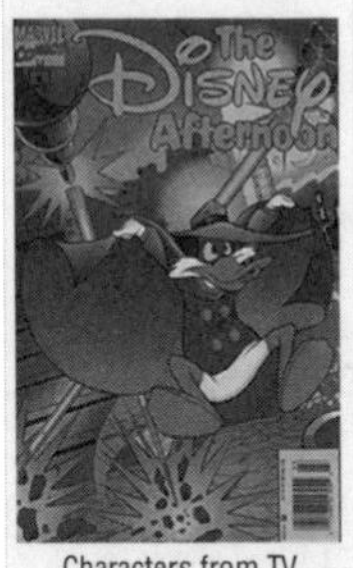

Characters from TV syndicated package

©Marvel

	N-MINT
❑9, Sep 2005	9.99
❑10, Dec 2005	9.99

D.O.A.
SAVING GRACE

❑1	1.00

DOC CHAOS: THE STRANGE ATTRACTOR
VORTEX

❑1, Apr 1990	3.00
❑2 1990	3.00
❑3 1990	3.00

DOC FRANKENSTEIN
BURLYMAN

❑1 2004	7.00
❑1/Darrow	10.00
❑2	3.50
❑2/Sketch 2004	5.00
❑3 2005	3.50
❑3/Variant 2005	5.00

DOC SAMSON
MARVEL

❑1, Jan 1996	1.95
❑2, Feb 1996	1.95
❑3, Mar 1996	1.95
❑4, Apr 1996	1.95

DOC SAMSON (2ND SERIES)
MARVEL

❑1, Feb 2006	2.99
❑2, Mar 2006	2.99
❑3, May 2006	2.99
❑4, Jun 2006	2.99
❑5, Jul 2006	2.99

DOC SAVAGE (GOLD KEY)
GOLD KEY

❑1, Nov 1966, 10192-611	38.00

DOC SAVAGE (MARVEL)
MARVEL

❑1, Oct 1972, RA, JM (a); adapts Man of Bronze	20.00
❑2, Dec 1972, adapts Man of Bronze	5.00
❑3, Feb 1973, adapts Death in Silver	3.00
❑4, Apr 1973, adapts Death in Silver	3.00
❑5, Jun 1973, adapts The Monsters	3.00
❑6, Aug 1973, GK (c); RA (a); adapts The Monsters	3.00
❑7, Oct 1973, adapts Brand of the Werewolf	3.00
❑8, Jan 1974, adapts Brand of the Werewolf	3.00

DOC SAVAGE (MARVEL MAGAZINE)
MARVEL

❑1, Aug 1975	6.00
❑2, Oct 1975	4.00
❑3, Jan 1976	4.00
❑4, Apr 1976	4.00
❑5, Jul 1976	4.00
❑6, Oct 1976	3.00
❑7, Jan 1977	3.00
❑8, Spr 1977	3.00

DOC SAVAGE (MINI-SERIES)
DC

	N-MINT
❑1, Nov 1987	2.00
❑2, Dec 1987	2.00
❑3, Jan 1988	2.00
❑4, Feb 1988	2.00

DOC SAVAGE (DC)
DC

❑1, Nov 1988	2.00
❑2, Dec 1988	2.00
❑3, Dec 1988	2.00
❑4, Jan 1989	2.00
❑5, Jan 1989	2.00
❑6, Mar 1989	2.00
❑7, Apr 1989	2.00
❑8, May 1989	2.00
❑9, Jun 1989	2.00
❑10, Jul 1989	2.00
❑11, Aug 1989 V: John Sunlight.	2.00
❑12, Sep 1989 V: John Sunlight.	2.00
❑13, Oct 1989 V: John Sunlight.	2.00
❑14, Nov 1989 V: John Sunlight.	2.00
❑15, Dec 1989	2.00
❑16, Jan 1990	2.00
❑17, Feb 1990; Shadow	2.00
❑18, Mar 1990; Shadow	2.00
❑19, May 1990	2.00
❑20, Jun 1990	2.00
❑21, Jul 1990	2.00
❑22, Aug 1990	2.00
❑23, Sep 1990	2.00
❑24, Oct 1990	2.00
❑Annual 1, ca. 1989	3.50

DOC SAVAGE: CURSE OF THE FIRE GOD
DARK HORSE

❑1, Sep 1995	2.95
❑2, Oct 1995	2.95
❑3, Nov 1995	2.95
❑4, Dec 1995	2.95

DOC SAVAGE: DEVIL'S THOUGHTS
MILLENNIUM

❑1	2.50
❑2	2.50
❑3	2.50

DOC SAVAGE: DOOM DYNASTY
MILLENNIUM

❑1	2.00
❑2	2.00

DOC SAVAGE: MANUAL OF BRONZE
MILLENNIUM

❑1, Aug 1992	2.50

DOC SAVAGE: REPEL
MILLENNIUM

❑1; only issue ever released	2.50

DOC SAVAGE: THE MAN OF BRONZE
MILLENNIUM

❑1	2.50
❑2	2.50
❑3	2.50
❑4	2.50

DOCTOR FATE (2ND MINI-SERIES)
DC

	N-MINT
❑1, Oct 2003	2.50
❑2, Nov 2003	2.50
❑3, Dec 2003	2.50
❑4, Jan 2004	2.50
❑5, Feb 2004	2.50

DR. ANDY
ALLIANCE

❑1, Aug 1994, b&w	2.50

DR. ATOMIC
LAST GASP

❑1	5.00
❑2	4.00
❑3	4.00
❑4	3.00
❑5	3.00
❑6	3.00

DOCTOR BANG
RIP OFF

❑1, Feb 1992, b&w	2.50

DOCTOR BOOGIE
MEDIA ARTS

❑1	1.75

DOCTOR CHAOS
TRIUMPHANT

❑1; Unleashed!	2.50
❑2; Unleashed!	2.50
❑3, Jan 1994	2.50
❑4, Feb 1994	2.50
❑5, Mar 1994	2.50
❑6, Mar 1994	2.50
❑7 1994	2.50
❑8 1994	2.50
❑9 1994	2.50
❑10 1994	2.50
❑11 1994	2.50
❑12 1994	2.50

DOCTOR CYBORG
ATTENTION!

❑1, b&w 1: Doctor Cyborg	2.95
❑1/Ashcan, b&w; Preview edition of Doctor Cyborg #1; 1: Doctor Cyborg. preview of series	1.00
❑2, b&w	2.95
❑3, b&w	2.95

DOCTOR DOOM'S REVENGE
MARVEL

❑1, ca. 1989, giveaway comic included with computer game from Paragon Software; Came with computer game by Paragon Software	1.00

DOCTOR FATE (1ST MINI-SERIES)
DC

❑1, Jul 1987 KG (a)	2.00
❑2, Aug 1987 KG (a)	2.00
❑3, Sep 1987 KG (a)	2.00
❑4, Oct 1987 KG (a); 1: Doctor Fate II (Eric Strauss & Linda Strauss). D: Doctor Fate I (Kent Nelson).	2.00

DOCTOR FATE
DC

❑1, Dec 1988 2.00
❑2, Jan 1989 1.25
❑3, Jan 1989 1.25
❑4, Feb 1989 1.25
❑5, Apr 1989 1.25
❑6, May 1989 1.75
❑7, Jun 1989 1.75
❑8, Jul 1989 1.75
❑9, Aug 1989 1.75
❑10, Sep 1989 1.75
❑11, Nov 1989 1.50
❑12, Dec 1989 1.50
❑13, Jan 1990 1.50
❑14, Feb 1990 1.50
❑15, Mar 1990 1.50
❑16, Apr 1990 1.50
❑17, May 1990 1.50
❑18, Jun 1990 1.50
❑19, Jul 1990 1.50
❑20, Aug 1990 1.50
❑21, Oct 1990 1.50
❑22, Nov 1990 1.50
❑23, Dec 1990 1.50
❑24, Jan 1991 1.50
❑25, Feb 1991 1.50
❑26, Mar 1991 1.50
❑27, Apr 1991 1.50
❑28, May 1991 1.50
❑29, Jun 1991 1.50
❑30, Jul 1991 1.50
❑31, Aug 1991 1.50
❑32, Sep 1991; War of the Gods 1.75
❑33, Oct 1991; War of the Gods 1.75
❑34, Nov 1991 1.75
❑35, Dec 1991 1.75
❑36, Jan 1992 1.75
❑37, Feb 1992 1.75
❑38, Mar 1992 1.75
❑39, Apr 1992 1.75
❑40, May 1992 1.75
❑41, Jun 1992 1.75
❑Annual 1, Nov 1989 2.95

DOCTOR FAUSTUS
ANARCHY

❑1, b&w 2.95
❑2 1994, b&w 2.95
❑Ashcan 1; ashcan, b&w 2.00

DOCTOR FRANKENSTEIN'S HOUSE OF 3-D
3-D ZONE

❑1, ca. 1992, Oversized; Oversized 4.00

DR. FU MANCHU
I.W.

❑1, ca. 1964 45.00

DR. GIGGLES
DARK HORSE

❑1 1992 2.50
❑2 1992 2.50

DOCTOR GORPON
ETERNITY

❑1, b&w 2.50
❑2, b&w 2.50
❑3, Aug 1991, b&w 2.50

DR. GOYLE SPECIAL
ARROW

❑1, b&w 2.95

DR. KILDARE
DELL

❑2 1962 50.00
❑3, Oct 1962 40.00
❑4, Dec 1962 40.00
❑5, Mar 1963 40.00
❑6, Jun 1963 40.00
❑7, Sep 1963 40.00
❑8, Oct 1964 40.00
❑9, Apr 1965 40.00

DOCTOR MID-NITE
DC

❑1, ca. 1999; D.O.A. 5.95
❑2, ca. 1999 5.95
❑3, ca. 1999 5.95
❑Book 1, ca. 1999; Collects series 19.95

DR. RADIUM AND THE GIZMOS OF BOOLA-BOOLA
SLAVE LABOR

❑1, Jan 1992, b&w 4.95

DR. RADIUM, MAN OF SCIENCE
SLAVE LABOR

❑1, Oct 1992, b&w 2.50
❑2, Jan 1993, b&w 2.50
❑3, Jul 1993 2.95
❑4, Jan 1994 2.95
❑5, Jan 1995, b&w 2.95

DR. ROBOT SPECIAL
DARK HORSE

❑1, Apr 2000, 2.95

DR. SLUMP
VIZ

❑1, May 2005 9.95
❑2, Jul 2005 9.95
❑3, Sep 2005 9.95
❑4, Nov 2005 9.95

DOCTOR SOLAR, MAN OF THE ATOM
GOLD KEY

❑1, Oct 1962, O: Doctor Solar. 1: Doctor Solar (out of costume). 1st Gold Key comic 150.00
❑2, Dec 1962, 1: Professor Harbinger. 80.00
❑3, Mar 1963 50.00
❑4, Jun 1963 60.00
❑5, Sep 1963, 1: Doctor Solar (in costume) 30.00
❑6, Nov 1963 25.00
❑7, Mar 1964, Painted cover 25.00
❑8, Jul 1964 25.00
❑9, Oct 1964 25.00
❑10, Jan 1965, 25.00
❑11, Mar 1965 16.00
❑12, May 1965, makes multiple versions of self 16.00
❑13, Jul 1965 16.00
❑14, Sep 1965, Painted cover 16.00
❑15, Dec 1965, O: Doctor Solar 20.00
❑16, Jun 1966, Painted cover 16.00
❑17, Sep 1966 16.00
❑18, Dec 1966 16.00
❑19, Apr 1967 16.00
❑20, Jul 1967 16.00
❑21, Oct 1967 12.00
❑22, Jan 1968 12.00
❑23, Apr 1968 12.00
❑24, Jul 1968 12.00
❑25, Oct 1968 12.00
❑26, Jan 1969, 12.00
❑27, Apr 1969, End of original series. 12.00
❑28, Apr 1981, Series begins again (1981) 3.50
❑29 1981 3.50
❑30, Feb 1982, A: Magnus, Robot Fighter (Gold Key). 3.50
❑31, Mar 1982, A: Magnus, Robot Fighter (Gold Key). 3.50

DR. SPECK
BUG BOOKS

❑1, b&w 2.95
❑2, b&w 2.95
❑3, b&w 2.95
❑4, b&w 2.95

DOCTOR SPECTRUM
MARVEL

❑1, Oct 2004 2.99
❑2, Nov 2004 2.99
❑3, Dec 2004 2.99
❑4, Jan 2005 2.99
❑5, Feb 2005 2.99
❑6, Mar 2005 2.99

DOCTOR STRANGE (1ST SERIES)
MARVEL

❑169, Jun 1968, DA (a); O: Doctor Strange. Series continued from Strange Tales #168 75.00
❑170, Jul 1968, DA (a); V: Nightmare. 30.00
❑171, Aug 1968, DA (a) 30.00
❑172, Sep 1968, GC (a); V: Dormammu. 27.00
❑173, Oct 1968, GC (a); V: Dormammu. 27.00
❑174, Nov 1968, GC (a); 1: Satannish. 20.00
❑175, Dec 1968, GC (a) 35.00
❑176, Jan 1969, GC (a) 27.00
❑177, Feb 1969, GC (a); 1: new costume 27.00
❑178, Mar 1969, GC (a); A: Black Knight. 27.00
❑179, Apr 1969, SD (a); A: Spider-Man. reprints Amazing Spider-Man Annual #2 27.00
❑180, May 1969, GC (a); A: Eternity. 27.00
❑181, Jun 1969, GC (a); 27.00
❑182, Sep 1969, GC (a); V: Juggernaut. 27.00
❑183, Nov 1969, GC (a) 27.00

DOCTOR STRANGE (2ND SERIES)
MARVEL

❑1, Jun 1974, FB, DG (a); Marvel Value Stamp #23: Sgt. Fury 25.00
❑2, Aug 1974, FB, DG (a); 1: Silver Dagger. A: Defenders. Marvel Value Stamp #5: Dracula 18.00
❑3, Sep 1974, FB, DG (a); V: Dormammu. reprints with changes Strange Tales #126 and 127; Marvel Value Stamp #14: Living Mummy 10.00
❑4, Oct 1974, FB, DG (a); Marvel Value Stamp #33: Invisible Girl 10.00
❑5, Nov 1974, FB, DG (a); O: Silver Dagger. Marvel Value Stamp #76: Dormammu 8.00
❑6, Dec 1974, GC (a); Marvel Value Stamp #37: Watcher 8.00
❑7, Apr 1975, GC (a); 7.00
❑8, Jun 1975, GC (a); O: Clea. 4.00
❑9, Aug 1975, GC (a); O: Clea. 4.00
❑10, Oct 1975, GC (a) 4.00
❑11, Dec 1975, GC (a) 4.00
❑12, Feb 1976, GC (a) 4.00
❑13, Apr 1976, GC (a) 4.00
❑13/30 cent, Apr 1976, 30 cent regional price variant 20.00
❑14, May 1976, GC (a) 3.00
❑14/30 cent, May 1976, 30 cent regional price variant 20.00
❑15, Jun 1976, GC (a) 3.00
❑15/30 cent, Jun 1976, 30 cent regional price variant 20.00
❑16, Jul 1976, GC (a) 3.00
❑16/30 cent, Jul 1976, 30 cent regional price variant 20.00
❑17, Aug 1976, GC (a) 3.00
❑17/30 cent, Aug 1976, 30 cent regional price variant 20.00
❑18, Sep 1976, GC (a); 3.00
❑19, Oct 1976, GC, AA (a); 1: Xander. 3.00
❑20, Dec 1976 3.00
❑21, Feb 1977, O: Doctor Strange. reprinted from Doctor Strange (1st series) #169 2.50
❑22, Apr 1977 2.50
❑23, Jun 1977 2.50
❑23/35 cent, Jun 1977, 35 cent regional price variant 15.00
❑24, Aug 1977 2.50
❑24/35 cent, Aug 1977, 35 cent regional price variant 15.00
❑25, Oct 1977 2.50
❑25/35 cent, Oct 1977, 35 cent regional price variant 15.00
❑26, Dec 1977 2.00
❑27, Feb 1978 2.00
❑28, Apr 1978 2.00
❑29, Jun 1978, TS (a) 2.00
❑30, Aug 1978, TS (a) 2.00
❑31, Oct 1978, TS (a) 2.00
❑32, Dec 1978 2.00
❑33, Feb 1979, Newsstand edition (distributed by Curtis); issue number in box 2.00
❑33/Whitman, Feb 1979, Special markets edition (usually sold in Whitman bagged prepacks); price appears in a diamond; no UPC barcode 2.00
❑34, Apr 1979 2.00
❑35, Jun 1979 2.00
❑36, Aug 1979, GC, DGr (a) 2.00
❑37, Oct 1979 2.00
❑38, Dec 1979, GC, DGr (a) 2.00
❑39, Feb 1980 2.00
❑40, Apr 1980 2.00
❑41, Jun 1980 2.00
❑42, Aug 1980 2.00
❑43, Oct 1980 2.00
❑44, Dec 1980 2.00

Distant Soil (1st Series)

Colleen Doran's long-running fantasy series

©Warp

Divine Right

Physics undergrad becomes powerful

©Image

DNAgents

More mutants, this time from Eclipse

©Eclipse

Doc Samson

Adventures of the super-hero psychiatrist

©Marvel

Doc Savage (Marvel)

Adapts "The Man of Bronze" and other tales

©Marvel

N-MINT

❑45, Feb 1981 .... 2.00
❑46, Apr 1981, FM (c); FM (a) 2.00
❑47, Jun 1981 .... 2.00
❑48, Aug 1981, A: Brother Voodoo 2.00
❑49, Oct 1981, A: Baron Mordo. 2.00
❑50, Dec 1981, A: Baron Mordo. 2.00
❑51, Feb 1982 .... 2.00
❑52, Apr 1982 .... 2.00
❑53, Jun 1982 .... 2.00
❑54, Aug 1982, PS, BA (a) 2.00
❑55, Oct 1982, MG (a) 2.00
❑56, Dec 1982, PS (a) 2.00
❑57, Feb 1983, KN (a) 2.00
❑58, Apr 1983, DGr (a) 2.00
❑59, Jun 1983, DGr (a) 2.00
❑60, Aug 1983, DGr (a); A: Dracula. 2.00
❑61, Oct 1983, cDGr (a); A: Dracula. 2.00
❑62, Dec 1983, A: Dracula. 2.00
❑63, Feb 1984 .... 2.00
❑64, Apr 1984 .... 2.00
❑65, Jun 1984, PS (a) 2.00
❑66, Aug 1984, PS (a) 2.00
❑67, Oct 1984 .... 2.00
❑68, Dec 1984, PS (a) 2.00
❑69, Feb 1985, PS (a) 2.00
❑70, Apr 1985 .... 2.00
❑71, Jun 1985, PS (a); O: Umar. 2.00
❑72, Aug 1985, PS (a) 2.00
❑73, Oct 1985, PS (a) 2.00
❑74, Dec 1985, 1: Ecstasy. Secret Wars II 2.00
❑75, Feb 1986, SB (a); O: Wong (Doctor Strange's manservant). 2.00
❑76, Apr 1986 .... 2.00
❑77, Jun 1986 .... 2.00
❑78, Aug 1986, New costume 2.00
❑79, Oct 1986 .... 2.00
❑80, Dec 1986 .... 2.00
❑81, Feb 1987 .... 2.00
❑Annual 1, ca. 1976 .... 6.00
❑Special 1, Mar 1983, FB (a) 3.00

DOCTOR STRANGE (3RD SERIES)
MARVEL

❑1, Feb 1999 .... 2.99
❑2, Mar 1999 .... 2.99
❑3, Apr 1999 .... 2.99
❑4, May 1999 .... 2.99

DOCTOR STRANGE CLASSICS
MARVEL

❑1, Mar 1984; SD (a); Reprints 2.00
❑2, Apr 1984; SD (a); Reprints 2.00
❑3, May 1984 .... 2.00
❑4, Jun 1984 .... 2.00

DOCTOR STRANGE/ GHOST RIDER SPECIAL
MARVEL

❑1, Apr 1991; reprints Doctor Strange #28; Continued from Ghost Rider # 12 .... 1.50

DOCTOR STRANGE: SHAMBALLA
MARVEL

❑1, ca. 1986 .... 5.95

DOCTOR STRANGE: SORCERER SUPREME
MARVEL

❑1, Nov 1988 .... 3.00
❑2, Jan 1989; Inferno 2.00
❑3, Mar 1989 .... 2.00
❑4, May 1989 .... 1.50
❑5, Jul 1989 .... 1.50
❑6, Aug 1989 .... 1.50
❑7, Sep 1989 .... 1.50
❑8, Oct 1989 O: Satannish. O: Mephisto. 1.50
❑9, Nov 1989 .... 1.50
❑10, Dec 1989 A: Morbius. 1.50
❑11, Dec 1989; A: Hobgoblin. Acts of Vengeance 1.50
❑12, Dec 1989; Acts of Vengeance 1.50
❑13, Jan 1990; Acts of Vengeance 1.50
❑14, Feb 1990; vampires 1.50
❑15, Mar 1990; Amy Grant cover (unauthorized, caused Marvel to be sued); vampires 3.00
❑16, Apr 1990; BG (a); vampires 1.50
❑17, May 1990; vampires 1.50
❑18, Jun 1990; vampires 1.50
❑19, Jul 1990 GC (a) 1.50
❑20, Aug 1990 .... 1.50
❑21, Sep 1990 .... 1.50
❑22, Oct 1990 O: Umar. 1.50
❑23, Nov 1990 .... 1.50
❑24, Dec 1990 .... 1.50
❑25, Jan 1991 .... 1.50
❑26, Feb 1991; werewolf 1.50
❑27, Mar 1991; werewolf 1.50
❑28, Apr 1991; Ghost Rider x-over 1.50
❑29, May 1991 .... 1.50
❑30, Jun 1991 .... 1.50
❑31, Jul 1991; Infinity Gauntlet 1.50
❑32, Aug 1991; Infinity Gauntlet 1.50
❑33, Sep 1991; Infinity Gauntlet 1.50
❑34, Oct 1991; Infinity Gauntlet 1.50
❑35, Nov 1991; Infinity Gauntlet 1.50
❑36, Dec 1991; Infinity Gauntlet; Prelude to Warlock & the Infinity Watch #1 .... 1.50
❑37, Jan 1992 A: Silver Surfer. 1.50
❑38, Feb 1992 .... 1.75
❑39, Mar 1992 .... 1.75
❑40, Apr 1992 .... 1.75
❑41, May 1992; Wolverine 1.75
❑42, Jun 1992; Galactus 1.75
❑43, Jul 1992 .... 1.75
❑44, Aug 1992 .... 1.75
❑45, Sep 1992 .... 1.75
❑46, Oct 1992 .... 1.75
❑47, Nov 1992 .... 1.75
❑48, Dec 1992 .... 1.75
❑49, Jan 1993 .... 1.75
❑50, Feb 1993; Prelude to Secret Defenders #1; Prism cover 2.95
❑51, Mar 1993 .... 1.75
❑52, Apr 1993 A: Morbius. 1.75
❑53, May 1993 .... 1.75
❑54, Jun 1993 .... 1.75
❑55, Jul 1993 .... 1.75
❑56, Aug 1993 .... 1.75
❑57, Sep 1993 .... 1.75
❑58, Oct 1993 A: Urthona 1.75
❑59, Nov 1993 .... 1.75
❑60, Dec 1993; Spot varnish cover 1.75
❑61, Jan 1994 .... 1.75
❑62, Feb 1994 .... 1.75
❑63, Mar 1994 .... 1.75
❑64, Apr 1994 .... 1.75
❑65, May 1994 .... 1.75
❑66, Jun 1994 .... 1.95
❑67, Jul 1994 .... 1.95
❑68, Aug 1994 .... 1.95
❑69, Sep 1994 .... 1.95
❑70, Oct 1994 A: Hulk. 1.95
❑71, Nov 1994 A: Hulk. 1.95
❑72, Dec 1994 .... 1.95
❑73, Jan 1995 .... 1.95
❑74, Feb 1995 .... 1.95
❑75, Mar 1995; Giant-size 2.50
❑75/Holo-grafix, Mar 1995; Giant-size; Holo-grafix cover 3.50
❑76, Apr 1995 .... 1.95
❑77, May 1995 .... 1.95
❑78, Jun 1995 .... 1.95
❑79, Jul 1995 .... 1.95
❑80, Aug 1995; indicia changes to Doctor Strange, Sorcerer Supreme for remainder of run 1.95
❑81, Sep 1995 .... 1.95
❑82, Oct 1995 .... 1.95
❑83, Nov 1995 .... 1.95
❑84, Dec 1995 A: Mordo. 1.95
❑85, Jan 1996 O: Mordo. 1.95
❑86, Feb 1996 .... 1.95
❑87, Mar 1996 D: Mordo. 1.95
❑88, Apr 1996 .... 1.95
❑89, May 1996 .... 1.95
❑90, Jun 1996 .... 1.95
❑Annual 1 .... 2.50
❑Annual 2, ca. 1992 .... 2.25
❑Annual 3, ca. 1993; trading card 2.95
❑Annual 4, ca. 1994 .... 2.95
❑Ashcan 1, ca. 1995, b&w; no indicia 0.75

DR. STRANGE VS. DRACULA
MARVEL

❑1, Mar 1994, Reprints 1.75

DOCTOR STRANGE: WHAT IS IT THAT DISTURBS YOU STEPHEN?
MARVEL

❑1, Oct 1997; squarebound 5.99

DOCTOR STRANGEFATE
DC / AMALGAM

❑1, Apr 1996 .... 1.95

DOCTOR TOM BRENT, YOUNG INTERN
CHARLTON

❑1, Feb 1963 .... 15.00
❑2, Apr 1963 .... 10.00
❑3, Jun 1963 .... 10.00
❑4, Aug 1963 .... 10.00
❑5, Oct 1963 .... 10.00

DR. TOMORROW
ACCLAIM

❑1, Sep 1997 .... 2.50

Other grades: Multiply price above by 5/6 for VF/NM • 2/3 for VERY FINE • 1/3 for FINE • 1/5 for VERY GOOD • 1/8 for GOOD

❑2, Oct 1997 .... 2.50
❑3, Nov 1997 .... 2.50
❑4, Dec 1997 .... 2.50
❑5, Jan 1998 .... 2.50
❑6, Feb 1998 .... 2.50
❑7, Mar 1998; Tomorrow and Mushroom Cloud go to Vietnam 2.50
❑8, Apr 1998 .... 2.50
❑9, May 1998; No cover date; indicia says Jan 98 .... 2.50
❑10, Jun 1998; No cover date; indicia says Jan 98 .... 2.50
❑11, Jul 1998 .... 2.50
❑12, Aug 1998 .... 2.50

DOCTOR WEIRD
CALIBER / BIG BANG
❑1, Oct 1994, b&w 2.95
❑2, May 1995, b&w 2.95
❑Special 1, Feb 1994, b&w 3.95

DR. WEIRD (VOL. 2)
OCTOBER
❑1, Oct 1997 .... 2.95
❑2, Jul 1998 .... 2.95

DOCTOR WHO
MARVEL
❑1, Oct 1984; DaG (a); BBC TV series; Reprint from Doctor Who Monthly (British) 3.00
❑2, Nov 1984; DaG (a); Reprint from Doctor Who Monthly (British) 2.00
❑3, Dec 1984; DaG (a); Reprint from Doctor Who Monthly (British) 2.00
❑4, Jan 1985; Reprint from Doctor Who Monthly (British) 2.00
❑5, Feb 1985; Reprint from Doctor Who Monthly (British) 2.00
❑6, Mar 1985; Reprint from Doctor Who Monthly (British) 2.00
❑7, Apr 1985; Reprint from Doctor Who Monthly (British) 2.00
❑8, May 1985; Reprint from Doctor Who Monthly (British) 2.00
❑9, Jun 1985; Reprint from Doctor Who Monthly (British) 2.00
❑10, Jul 1985; Reprint from Doctor Who Monthly (British) 2.00
❑11, Aug 1985; Reprint from Doctor Who Monthly (British) 1.50
❑12, Sep 1985; Reprint from Doctor Who Monthly (British) 1.50
❑13, Oct 1985; Reprint from Doctor Who Monthly (British) 1.50
❑14, Nov 1985; Reprint from Doctor Who Monthly (British) 1.50
❑15, Dec 1985; Reprint from Doctor Who Monthly (British) 1.50
❑16, Jan 1986; Reprint from Doctor Who Monthly (British) 1.50
❑17, Feb 1986; Reprint from Doctor Who Monthly (British) 1.50
❑18, Mar 1986; Reprint from Doctor Who Monthly (British) 1.50
❑19, Apr 1986; Reprint from Doctor Who Monthly (British) 1.50
❑20, May 1986; Reprint from Doctor Who Monthly (British) 1.50
❑21, Jun 1986; Reprint from Doctor Who Monthly (British) 1.50
❑22, Jul 1986; Reprint from Doctor Who Monthly (British) 1.50
❑23, Aug 1986; Reprint from Doctor Who Monthly (British) 1.50

DR. WONDER
OLD TOWN
❑1, Jun 1996, b&w 2.95
❑2, Jul 1996, b&w 2.95
❑3, Aug 1996, b&w 2.95
❑4, Oct 1996, b&w 2.95
❑5, Fal 1997, b&w; magazine-sized 2.95

DOCTOR ZERO
MARVEL / EPIC
❑1, Apr 1988, BSz (c); BSz (a) 1.50
❑2, Jun 1988, BSz (c) 1.50
❑3, Aug 1988 .... 1.50
❑4, Oct 1988 .... 1.50
❑5, Dec 1988 .... 1.50
❑6, Feb 1989 .... 1.50
❑7, Apr 1989, DS (a) 1.50
❑8, Jun 1989 .... 1.50

DOC WEIRD'S THRILL BOOK
PURE IMAGINATION
❑1 AW, ATh, FF (a) 2.00
❑2, WW (a); Jack Cole 2.00
❑3 WW (a) 2.00

DODEKAIN
ANTARCTIC
❑1, Nov 1994, b&w 2.95
❑2, Dec 1994, b&w 2.95
❑3, Jan 1995, b&w 2.95
❑4, Feb 1995, b&w 2.95
❑5, Mar 1995, b&w 2.95
❑6, Apr 1995, b&w 2.95
❑7, May 1995, b&w 2.95
❑8, Jun 1995, b&w 2.95

DO-DO MAN
EDGE
❑1 .... 2.99

DOG BOY
FANTAGRAPHICS
❑1 .... 2.00
❑2, Apr 1987 .... 1.75
❑3, May 1987 .... 1.75
❑4 .... 1.75
❑5 .... 1.75
❑6 .... 1.75
❑7, Sep 1987 .... 1.75
❑8 .... 1.75
❑9 .... 1.75

DOGS OF WAR
DEFIANT
❑1, Apr 1994 .... 2.50
❑2, May 1994 .... 2.50
❑3, Jun 1994 .... 2.50
❑4, Jul 1994 .... 2.50
❑5, Aug 1994 .... 2.50
❑6, Sep 1994 .... 2.50
❑7, Oct 1994 .... 2.50
❑8, Nov 1994 .... 2.50

DOG SOUP
DOG SOUP
❑1, b&w 2.50

DOGS-O-WAR
CRUSADE
❑1, Jun 1996, b&w 2.95
❑2, Jul 1996, b&w 2.95
❑3, Jan 1997, b&w 2.95

DOG T.A.G.S.: TRAINED ANIMAL GUN SQUADRON
BUGGED OUT
❑1, Jun 1993, b&w 1.95

DOGWITCH
SIRIUS
❑1 .... 6.00
❑2 .... 4.00
❑3 .... 4.00
❑4, Feb 2003 .... 4.00
❑5, May 2003 .... 4.00
❑6, Jul 2003 .... 4.00
❑7, Oct 2003 .... 2.95
❑8, Nov 2003 .... 2.95
❑9, Jan 2004 .... 2.95
❑10, Mar 2004 .... 2.95
❑11, May 2004 .... 2.95
❑12 2004 .... 2.95
❑13 2004 .... 2.95
❑14 2004 .... 2.95
❑15 2005 .... 2.95
❑16 2005 .... 2.95
❑17 2005 .... 2.95

DOIN' TIME WITH OJ
BONEYARD
❑1, Dec 1994, b&w 3.50

DOJINSHI
ANTARCTIC
❑1, Oct 1992, b&w 2.95
❑2, Dec 1992, b&w 2.95
❑3, Feb 1993, b&w 2.95
❑4, Apr 1993, b&w 2.95

DOLL
RIP OFF
❑1, Feb 1989, b&w 3.00
❑2, Mar 1989, b&w 2.50
❑3, May 1989, b&w 2.50
❑4, Feb 1990, b&w 2.50
❑5, Mar 1991, b&w 2.50
❑6, May 1991, b&w 2.50
❑7, Jun 1991, b&w 2.50
❑8, Sep 1992, b&w 2.95
❑Book 1 .... 9.95
❑Book 2 .... 15.95

DOLL AND CREATURE
IMAGE
❑1, Apr 2006 .... 2.95
❑2, Jun 2006 .... 2.95
❑3, Jul 2006 .... 2.95

DOLLMAN (MINI-SERIES)
ETERNITY
❑1, Nov 1991, movie tie-in 2.50
❑2 1992, movie tie-in 2.50
❑3 1992, movie tie-in 2.50
❑4 1992, movie tie-in 2.50

DOLL PARTS
SIRIUS
❑1, Oct 2000, b&w 2.95

DOLLS
SIRIUS
❑1, Jun 1996 .... 2.95

DOLL (TOKYOPOP)
TOKYOPOP
❑1, Aug 2004 .... 9.95
❑2, Oct 2004 .... 9.95
❑3, Jan 2005 .... 9.95
❑4, Apr 2005 .... 9.95
❑5, Jul 2005 .... 9.95
❑6, Oct 2005 .... 9.95

DOLLZ
IMAGE
❑1/A, Apr 2001; Two girls facing monster on cover 2.95
❑1/B, Apr 2001; Dynamic Forces cover: Girl posing with bunny, gun 2.95
❑1/C, Apr 2001; Alternate cover (figures include girl holding bunny) 2.95
❑1/D, Apr 2001; Girls posing with large face in background 2.95
❑1/E, Apr 2001; Nighttime fight scene on cover 2.95
❑2, Jun 2001 .... 2.95

DOME: GROUND ZERO
DC / HELIX
❑1; prestige format; computer-generated 7.95

DOMINATION FACTOR: AVENGERS
MARVEL
❑1, Nov 1999; says 1.2 on cover, 1 in indicia 2.50
❑2, Nov 1999; says 2.4 on cover, 2 in indicia 2.50

DOMINATION FACTOR: FANTASTIC FOUR
MARVEL
❑1, Dec 1999; cover forms diptych with Domination Factor: Avengers #1 .... 2.50
❑2, Dec 1999; says 2.3 on cover, 2 in indicia 2.50

DOMINION
ECLIPSE
❑1, ca. 1990, b&w; Japanese 3.00
❑2, ca. 1990, b&w; Japanese 2.50
❑3, ca. 1991, b&w; Japanese 2.50
❑4, ca. 1991, b&w; Japanese 2.00
❑5, ca. 1991, b&w; Japanese 2.00
❑6, ca. 1991, b&w; Japanese 2.00

DOMINION (DARK HORSE)
IMAGE
❑1, Feb 2003 .... 2.95
❑2, May 2003 .... 2.95

DOMINION: CONFLICT 1
DARK HORSE / MANGA
❑1, Mar 1996, b&w 2.95
❑2, Apr 1996, b&w 2.95
❑3, May 1996, b&w 2.95
❑4, Jun 1996, b&w 2.95
❑5, Jul 1996, b&w 2.95
❑6, Aug 1996, b&w 2.95

Other grades: Multiply price above by 5/6 for VF/NM • 2/3 for VERY FINE • 1/3 for FINE • 1/5 for VERY GOOD • 1/8 for GOOD

Doctor Fate

DC mystic uses Egyptian powers
©DC

Doctor Solar, Man of the Atom

Radioactivity turned researcher green
©Gold Key

Doctor Strange (1st Series)

Picks up numbering from Strange Tales
©Marvel

Doctor Strange (2nd Series)

Second longest-running Dr. Strange series
©Marvel

Doctor Strange: Sorcerer Supreme

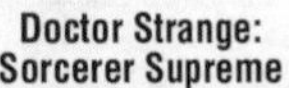

1990s version updated Doc's look
©Marvel

N-MINT

DOMINION: PHANTOM OF THE AUDIENCE
Dark Horse
❑1 2.50

DOMINIQUE: FAMILY MATTERS
Caliber
❑1, b&w 2.95

DOMINIQUE: KILLZONE
Caliber
❑1, ca. 1995, b&w 2.95

DOMINIQUE: PROTECT AND SERVE
Caliber
❑1, ca. 1995, b&w 2.95

DOMINIQUE: WHITE KNUCKLE DRIVE
Caliber
❑1, b&w 2.95

DOMINO
Marvel
❑1, Jan 1997 2.00
❑2, Feb 1997 V: Deathstrike 2.00
❑3, Mar 1997 2.00

DOMINO (2ND SERIES)
Marvel
❑1, Jun 2003 2.50
❑2, Jun 2003 2.50
❑3, Jul 2003 2.50
❑4, Aug 2003 2.50

DOMINO CHANCE
Chance
❑1, May 1982, b&w 2.50
❑1/2nd, b&w 1.50
❑2, Jul 1982, b&w 2.00
❑3, Sep 1982, b&w 2.00
❑4 1983, b&w 2.00
❑5, Jul 1983, b&w 2.00
❑6 1984, b&w 2.00
❑7 1984, b&w 1: Gizmo 2.00
❑8 1985, b&w 2: Gizmo 2.00
❑9 1985, b&w 2.00

DOMINO CHANCE: ROACH EXTRAORDINAIRE
Amazing
❑1 1.95

DOMINO LADY
Fantagraphics / Eros
❑1, Dec 1990, b&w 1.95
❑2, Jan 1991, b&w 1.95
❑3, Mar 1991, b&w 1.95

DOMINO LADY'S JUNGLE ADVENTURE
Fantagraphics / Eros
❑1, b&w 2.75
❑2, b&w 2.75
❑3, Nov 1992, b&w 2.75

DOMU: A CHILD'S DREAM
Dark Horse / Manga
❑1, Mar 1995, 5.95
❑2, Apr 1995, 5.95
❑3, May 1995, 5.95

N-MINT

DONALD AND MICKEY
Gladstone
❑19, Sep 1993; Reprints 1.50
❑20, Nov 1993 2.95
❑21, Jan 1994; Reprints 1.50
❑22, Mar 1994; Reprints 1.50
❑23, May 1994; Reprints 1.50
❑24, Jul 1994; Reprints 1.50
❑25, Sep 1994 2.95
❑26, Nov 1994; newsstand distribution by Marvel 1.50
❑27, Jan 1995 1.50
❑28, Mar 1995 1.50
❑29, May 1995 1.50
❑30, Jul 1995 1.50

DONALD AND SCROOGE
Disney
❑1, ca. 1992 1.75
❑2, ca. 1992 1.75
❑3, ca. 1992 1.75

DONALD DUCK (WALT DISNEY'S...)
Dell / Gold Key
❑50, Nov 1956 65.00
❑51, Jan 1967 65.00
❑52, Mar 1957, CB (a) 150.00
❑53, May 1957 65.00
❑54, Jul 1957 125.00
❑55, Sep 1957 50.00
❑56, Nov 1957 50.00
❑57, Jan 1958 50.00
❑58, Mar 1958 50.00
❑59, May 1958, CB (a) 125.00
❑60, Jul 1958, CB (a) 125.00
❑61, Sep 1958 40.00
❑62, Nov 1958 40.00
❑63, Jan 1959 40.00
❑64, Mar 1959 40.00
❑65, May 1959 40.00
❑66, Jul 1959 40.00
❑67, Sep 1959 40.00
❑68, Nov 1959, CB (a) 100.00
❑69, Jan 1960 40.00
❑70, Mar 1960 40.00
❑71, May 1960 30.00
❑72, Jul 1960 30.00
❑73, Sep 1960 30.00
❑74, Nov 1960 30.00
❑75, Jan 1961 30.00
❑76, Mar 1961 30.00
❑77, May 1961 30.00
❑78, Jul 1961 30.00
❑79, Sep 1961 30.00
❑80, Nov 1961 30.00
❑81, Jan 1962 30.00
❑82, Mar 1962 30.00
❑83, May 1962 30.00
❑84, Jul 1962 30.00
❑85, Sep 1962, Gold Key imprints begin 25.00
❑86, Nov 1962 25.00
❑87, Jan 1963 25.00
❑88, Mar 1963 25.00
❑89, May 1963 25.00
❑90, Jul 1963 25.00

N-MINT

❑91, Sep 1963 25.00
❑92, Nov 1963 25.00
❑93, Jan 1964 25.00
❑94, Mar 1964 25.00
❑95, May 1964 25.00
❑96, Jul 1964 25.00
❑97, Sep 1964 25.00
❑98, Nov 1964 25.00
❑99, Jan 1965, Reprints story from Donald Duck #46 25.00
❑100, Mar 1965 25.00
❑101, May 1965 25.00
❑102, Jul 1965 25.00
❑103, Sep 1965 25.00
❑104, Nov 1965 25.00
❑105, Jan 1966 25.00
❑106, Mar 1966 25.00
❑107, May 1966 25.00
❑108, Jul 1966 25.00
❑109, Sep 1966 25.00
❑110, Nov 1966 25.00
❑111, Jan 1967 25.00
❑112, Mar 1967 25.00
❑113, May 1967 25.00
❑114, Jul 1967 25.00
❑115, Sep 1967 25.00
❑116, Nov 1967 25.00
❑117, Jan 1968 25.00
❑118, Mar 1968 25.00
❑119, May 1968 25.00
❑120, Jul 1968 25.00
❑121, Sep 1968 20.00
❑122, Nov 1968 20.00
❑123, Jan 1969 20.00
❑124, Mar 1969 20.00
❑125, May 1969 20.00
❑126, Jul 1969 20.00
❑127, Sep 1969 20.00
❑128, Nov 1969 20.00
❑129, Jan 1970 20.00
❑130, Mar 1970 20.00
❑131, May 1970 20.00
❑132, Jul 1970 20.00
❑133, Sep 1970 20.00
❑134, Nov 1970, Reprints stories from Donald Duck #52 and Walt Disney's Comics #194 20.00
❑135, Jan 1971, Reprints stories from Uncle Scrooge #27 and Walt Disney's Comics #198 20.00
❑136, Mar 1971 15.00
❑137, May 1971 15.00
❑138, Jul 1971 15.00
❑139, Sep 1971 15.00
❑140, Nov 1971 15.00
❑141, Jan 1972 15.00
❑142, Mar 1972 15.00
❑143, May 1972 15.00
❑144, Jul 1972 15.00
❑145, Sep 1972 15.00
❑146, Nov 1972 15.00
❑147, Jan 1973 15.00
❑148, Mar 1973 15.00
❑149, May 1973 15.00
❑150, Jul 1973 15.00

Other grades: Multiply price above by 5/6 for VF/NM • 2/3 for VERY FINE • 1/3 for FINE • 1/5 for VERY GOOD • 1/8 for GOOD

	N-MINT
❑151, Sep 1973	10.00
❑152, Oct 1973	10.00
❑153, Nov 1973	10.00
❑154, Jan 1974, Reprints story from Donald Duck #46	10.00
❑155, Mar 1974	10.00
❑156, May 1974	10.00
❑157, Jul 1974, Reprints story from Donald Duck #45	10.00
❑158, Sep 1974	10.00
❑159, Oct 1974, Reprints story from Walt Disney's Comics #192	10.00
❑160, Nov 1974, Reprints story from Donald Duck #26	10.00
❑161, Jan 1975	10.00
❑162, Mar 1975	10.00
❑163, May 1975	10.00
❑164, Jul 1975	10.00
❑165, Sep 1975	10.00
❑166, Oct 1975	10.00
❑167, Nov 1975	10.00
❑168, Jan 1976	10.00
❑169, Mar 1976	10.00
❑170, Apr 1976	10.00
❑171, May 1976	10.00
❑172, Jun 1976	10.00
❑173, Jul 1976	10.00
❑174, Aug 1976	10.00
❑175, Sep 1976	10.00
❑176, Oct 1976	10.00
❑177, Nov 1976	10.00
❑178, Dec 1976	10.00
❑179, Jan 1977	10.00
❑180, Feb 1977	10.00
❑181, Mar 1977	10.00
❑182, Apr 1977	10.00
❑183, May 1977, Reprints story from Donald Duck #138	10.00
❑184, Jun 1977	10.00
❑185, Jul 1977	10.00
❑186, Aug 1977	10.00
❑187, Sep 1977	10.00
❑188, Oct 1977, Reprints story from Donald Duck #68	10.00
❑189, Nov 1977	10.00
❑190, Dec 1977	10.00
❑191, Jan 1978	5.00
❑192, Feb 1978, Reprints stories from Donald Duck #60 and Walt Disney's Comics #226 and 234	5.00
❑193, Mar 1978	5.00
❑194, Apr 1978	5.00
❑195, May 1978	5.00
❑196, Jun 1978	5.00
❑197, Jul 1978	5.00
❑198, Aug 1978	5.00
❑199, Sep 1978	5.00
❑200, Oct 1978	5.00
❑201, Nov 1978, Reprints story from Christmas Parade (Dell) #26	5.00
❑202, Dec 1978	5.00
❑203, Jan 1979	5.00
❑204, Feb 1979	5.00
❑205, Mar 1979	5.00
❑206, Apr 1979	5.00
❑207, May 1979	5.00
❑208, Jun 1979	5.00
❑209, Jul 1979	5.00
❑210, Aug 1979	5.00
❑211, Sep 1979	3.00
❑212, Oct 1979	3.00
❑213, Nov 1979	3.00
❑214, Dec 1979	3.00
❑215, Jan 1980	3.00
❑216, Feb 1980	3.00
❑217, Mar 1980, Whitman begins as publisher	5.00
❑218, Apr 1980	10.00
❑219, May 1980	10.00
❑220, Jun 1980	15.00
❑221, Aug 1980	30.00
❑222, Oct 1980	175.00
❑223, Nov 1980	30.00
❑224, Dec 1980	30.00
❑225, Feb 1981	15.00
❑226, Mar 1981	15.00
❑227, Apr 1981	15.00
❑228, May 1981	15.00
❑229, Jun 1981	8.00
❑230, Jul 1981	8.00
❑231, Aug 1981	8.00
❑232, Sep 1981	8.00
❑233, Oct 1981	8.00
❑234, Nov 1981	8.00
❑235, Dec 1981	8.00
❑236, Jan 1982	8.00
❑237, Feb 1982	8.00
❑238, Mar 1982	8.00
❑239, Apr 1982	8.00
❑240, May 1982	8.00
❑241, Mar 1983	15.00
❑242, May 1983	15.00
❑243, Mar 1984	15.00
❑244, Apr 1984	15.00
❑245, Jul 1984, Last issue of original run	15.00
❑246, Oct 1986, B (a); Series begins again (1986); Gladstone publishes	17.00
❑247, Nov 1986, CB (a)	5.00
❑248, Dec 1986, CB (a)	5.00
❑249, Jan 1987, CB (a)	5.00
❑250, Feb 1987, CB (a); reprints 1st Barks comic	8.00
❑251, Mar 1987, CB (a)	4.00
❑252, Apr 1987, CB (a)	4.00
❑253, May 1987, CB (a)	4.00
❑254, Jun 1987	4.00
❑255, Jul 1987	4.00
❑256, Aug 1987	4.00
❑257, Sep 1987, CB (a); forest fire	4.00
❑258, Oct 1987, CB (a)	4.00
❑259, Nov 1987, CB (a)	4.00
❑260, Dec 1987, CB (a)	4.00
❑261, Jan 1988, CB (a)	3.00
❑262, Mar 1988, CB (a)	3.00
❑263, Jun 1988, CB (a)	3.00
❑264, Jul 1988, CB (a)	3.00
❑265, Aug 1988	3.00
❑266, Sep 1988	3.00
❑267, Oct 1988	3.00
❑268, Nov 1988	3.00
❑269, Jan 1989	3.00
❑270, Mar 1989	3.00
❑271, Apr 1989, says Jun on cover, Apr in indicia	2.50
❑272, Jul 1989	2.50
❑273, Aug 1989	2.50
❑274, Sep 1989	2.50
❑275, Oct 1989, CB, WK (a); Donocchio	2.50
❑276, Nov 1989, CB (a)	2.50
❑277, Jan 1990, CB (a)	2.50
❑278, Mar 1990, CB, DR (a)	2.50
❑279, May 1990, CB (a); Series ends again (1990)	2.50
❑280, Sep 1993, Series begins again (1993)	1.50
❑281, Nov 1993	1.50
❑282, Jan 1994, CB (a); Reprints	1.50
❑283, Mar 1994 DR (a)	1.50
❑284, May 1994, CB (a); Reprints	1.50
❑285, Jul 1994, CB (a); Reprints	1.50
❑286, Sep 1994, Giant-size; Donald Duck's 60th	3.00
❑287, Nov 1994	1.50
❑288, Jan 1995, CB (a)	1.50
❑289, Mar 1995	1.50
❑290, May 1995	1.50
❑291, Jul 1995	1.50
❑292, Sep 1995	1.50
❑293, Nov 1995	1.50
❑294, Jan 1996, CB (a); Reprints	1.50
❑295, Mar 1996, newsprint covers begin	1.50
❑296, May 1996	1.50
❑297, Jul 1996	1.50
❑298, Sep 1996	1.50
❑299, Nov 1996	1.50
❑300, Jan 1997	1.50
❑301, Mar 1997, newsprint covers end	1.50
❑302, May 1997, CB (c); CB (a); Reprints	1.95
❑303, Jul 1997	1.95
❑304, Sep 1997, CB (a); Reprints	1.95
❑305, Nov 1997, CB (w); CB (a); Reprints	1.95
❑306, Jan 1998	1.95
❑307, Mar 1998	1.95

DONALD DUCK AND FRIENDS
GEMSTONE

	N-MINT
❑308, Sep 2003	2.95
❑309, Oct 2003	2.95
❑310, Nov 2003	2.95
❑311, Dec 2003	2.95
❑312, Jan 2004	2.95
❑313, Feb 2004	2.95
❑314, Mar 2004	2.95
❑315, Apr 2004	2.95
❑316, May 2004	2.95
❑317, Jun 2004	2.95
❑318, Jul 2004	2.95
❑319, Aug 2004	2.95
❑320, Sep 2004	2.95
❑321, Oct 2004	2.95
❑322, Nov 2004	2.95
❑323, Dec 2004	2.95
❑324, Jan 2005	2.95
❑325, Feb 2005	2.95
❑326, Mar 2005	2.95
❑327, Apr 2005	2.95
❑328, May 2005	2.95
❑329, Jun 2005	2.95
❑330, Jul 2005	2.95
❑331, Aug 2005	2.95
❑332, Sep 2005	2.95
❑333, Oct 2005	2.95
❑334, Nov 2005	2.95
❑335, Dec 2005	2.95

DONALD DUCK ADVENTURES (GEMSTONE)
GEMSTONE

	N-MINT
❑1, Jul 2003	7.95
❑2, Oct 2003	7.95
❑3, Dec 2003	7.95
❑4, Feb 2004	7.95
❑5, Mar 2004	7.95
❑6, Jun 2004	7.95
❑7, Jul 2004	7.95
❑8, Oct 2004	7.95
❑9, Dec 2004	7.95
❑10, Feb 2005	7.95
❑11, Mar 2005	7.95
❑12, Jun 2005	7.95
❑13, Jul 2005	7.95
❑14, Oct 2005	7.95

DONALD DUCK ADVENTURES (DISNEY)
DISNEY

	N-MINT
❑1, Jun 1990, DR (w); DR (a)	2.50
❑2, Jul 1990, CB (a)	2.00
❑3, Aug 1990	2.00
❑4, Sep 1990, CB (a)	2.00
❑5, Oct 1990	2.00
❑6, Nov 1990	2.00
❑7, Dec 1990	2.00
❑8, Jan 1991	2.00
❑9, Feb 1991, CB (a); reprint of 1: Uncle Scrooge	2.00
❑10, Mar 1991	2.00
❑11, Apr 1991, Mad #1 cover parody	2.00
❑12, May 1991	2.00
❑13, Jun 1991	2.00
❑14, Jul 1991, CB (a)	2.00
❑15, Aug 1991	2.00
❑16, Sep 1991	2.00
❑17, Oct 1991	2.00
❑18, Nov 1991	2.00
❑19, Dec 1991	2.00
❑20, Jan 1992	2.00
❑21, Feb 1992, CB (a); golden Christmas tree	1.50
❑22, Mar 1992, DR (a)	1.50
❑23, Apr 1992, CB (a)	1.50
❑24, May 1992, DR (a)	1.50
❑25, Jun 1992, map piece	1.50
❑26, Jul 1992, CB (a); map piece	1.50
❑27, Aug 1992, CB (a); map piece	1.50
❑28, Sep 1992, Olympics	1.50
❑29, Oct 1992	1.50
❑30, Nov 1992	1.50
❑31, Dec 1992	1.50
❑32, Jan 1993	1.50

Dr. Tomorrow

Super-hero gets help from future

©Acclaim

Doctor Who

Reprinted stories of time-traveling meddler

©Marvel

Domination Factor: Avengers

Weird numbering scheme caused confusion

©Marvel

Donald and Mickey

Was Mickey and Donald through #18

©Gladstone

Donald Duck (Walt Disney's...)

Includes many Carl Barks stories

©Dell

N-MINT

❑33, Feb 1993 .... 1.50
❑34, Mar 1993, DR (a); Return of Super-Duck 1.50
❑35, Apr 1993, CB (a); Reprints 1.50
❑36, May 1993, CB (a); Reprints 1.50
❑37, Jun 1993, CB, DR (a); Reprints 1.50
❑38, Jul 1993, Gladstone resumes publishing its series 1.50

DONALD DUCK ADVENTURES (GLADSTONE)
GLADSTONE

❑1, Nov 1987 CB (a) 2.50
❑2, Jan 1988 CB (a) 2.00
❑3, Mar 1988 CB (a) 2.00
❑4, May 1988 CB (a) 2.00
❑5, Jul 1988 CB, DR (a) 2.00
❑6, Aug 1988 CB (a) 1.50
❑7, Sep 1988 CB (a) 1.50
❑8, Oct 1988 CB, DR (a) 1.50
❑9, Nov 1988 CB (a) 1.50
❑10, Dec 1988 CB (a); 1.50
❑11, Feb 1989 CB (a) 1.50
❑12, May 1989 CB, DR (a) 1.50
❑13, Jul 1989 DR (c); CB (a) 1.50
❑14, Aug 1989 CB (a) 1.50
❑15, Sep 1989 CB (a) 1.50
❑16, Oct 1989 CB (a) 1.50
❑17, Nov 1989 CB (a) 1.50
❑18, Dec 1989 CB (a) 1.50
❑19, Feb 1990 CB (a) 1.50
❑20, Apr 1990; CB (a); series goes on hiatus during Disney run 1.50
❑21, Aug 1993; DR (c); CB (a); Reprints 1.50
❑22, Oct 1993; CB (a); Reprints 1.50
❑23, Dec 1993 DR (c 1.50
❑24, Feb 1994 .... 1.50
❑25, Apr 1994 .... 1.50
❑26, Jun 1994 CB (a) 2.95
❑27, Aug 1994 .... 1.50
❑28, Oct 1994; CB (a); cover uses portion of Barks painting 1.50
❑29, Dec 1994; newsstand distribution by Marvel 1.50
❑30, Feb 1995; CB (a); Reprints 2.95
❑31, Apr 1995 .... 1.50
❑32, Jun 1995 .... 1.50
❑33, Aug 1995; CB (a); Reprints 1.95
❑34, Oct 1995; newsprint covers begin 1.50
❑35, Dec 1995 .... 1.50
❑36, Feb 1996 .... 1.50
❑37, Apr 1996 .... 1.50
❑38, Jun 1996 .... 1.50
❑39, Aug 1996 .... 1.50
❑40, Oct 1996 .... 1.50
❑41, Dec 1996 .... 1.50
❑42, Feb 1997 .... 1.50
❑43, Apr 1997; newsprint covers end. 1.50
❑44, Jun 1997 .... 1.95
❑45, Aug 1997 .... 1.95
❑46, Oct 1997 .... 1.95
❑47, Dec 1997; CB (a); Reprints 1.95
❑48, Feb 1998 .... 1.95

N-MINT

DONALD DUCK ALBUM
GOLD KEY

❑1, Aug 1963 .... 50.00
❑2, Oct 1963 .... 40.00

DONALD DUCK & MICKEY MOUSE
GLADSTONE

❑1, Sep 1995 .... 1.50
❑2, Nov 1995 .... 1.50
❑3, Jan 1996 .... 1.50
❑4, Mar 1996 .... 1.50
❑5, May 1996 .... 1.50
❑6, Jul 1996 .... 1.50
❑7, Sep 1996 .... 1.50

DONALD DUCK BEACH PARTY
GOLD KEY

❑1, Sep 1965; reprints Walt Disney's Comics & Stories #45 .... 40.00

DONATELLO TEENAGE MUTANT NINJA TURTLE
MIRAGE

❑1, Aug 1986, b&w 2.00

DONIELLE: ENSLAVED AT SEA
RAGING RHINO

❑1, b&w 2.95
❑2, b&w 2.95
❑3, b&w 2.95
❑4, b&w 2.95
❑5 1993 .... 2.95
❑6 .... 2.95
❑7 .... 2.95
❑8 .... 2.95
❑9 .... 2.95

DONNA MATRIX
REACTOR

❑1, Aug 1993; O: Donna Matrix. 1: Donna Matrix. computer-generated 3.50

DONNA MIA
AVATAR

❑1, Dec 1996 .... 3.00
❑2, Jan 1997 .... 3.00
❑3, Feb 1997 .... 3.00

DONNA'S DAY
SLAB-O-CONCRETE

❑1; Postcard comic book 1.00

DOOFER
FANTAGRAPHICS

❑1, b&w 2.75

DOOFUS
FANTAGRAPHICS

❑1, Dec 1994, b&w 2.75
❑2, Spr 1997, b&w 2.75

DOOM
MARVEL

❑1, Oct 2000 .... 2.99
❑2, Nov 2000 .... 2.99
❑3, Dec 2000 .... 2.99

DOOM FORCE SPECIAL
DC

❑1, Jul 1992; X-Force parody 2.95

N-MINT

DOOM PATROL (1ST SERIES)
DC

❑86, Mar 1964; 1: Monsieur Mallah. 1: The Brain. 1: Madame Rouge. Series continued from My Greatest Adventure #85 .... 135.00
❑87, May 1964 .... 70.00
❑88, Jun 1964, O: The Chief. 50.00
❑89, Aug 1964 .... 50.00
❑90, Sep 1964 .... 50.00
❑91, Nov 1964, 1: Mento 40.00
❑92, Dec 1964 .... 40.00
❑93, Feb 1965 .... 40.00
❑94, Mar 1965 .... 40.00
❑95, May 1965 .... 40.00
❑96, Jun 1965 .... 40.00
❑97, Aug 1965, 1: Garguax 40.00
❑98, Sep 1965 .... 40.00
❑99, Nov 1965, 1: Changeling. 60.00
❑100, Dec 1965, O: Changeling 75.00
❑101, Feb 1966 .... 25.00
❑102, Mar 1966, A: Challengers of the Unknown. 25.00
❑103, May 1966 .... 25.00
❑104, Jun 1966 .... 25.00
❑105, Aug 1966 .... 25.00
❑106, Sep 1966, O: Negative Man. 25.00
❑107, Nov 1966 .... 25.00
❑108, Dec 1966 .... 25.00
❑109, Feb 1967 .... 25.00
❑110, Mar 1967 .... 25.00
❑111, May 1967 .... 25.00
❑112, Jun 1967 .... 25.00
❑113, Aug 1967 .... 25.00
❑114, Sep 1967 .... 25.00
❑115, Nov 1967 .... 25.00
❑116, Dec 1967 .... 25.00
❑117, Feb 1968, reprints story from Tales of the Unexpected #3 .... 25.00
❑118, Mar 1968 .... 25.00
❑119, May 1968 .... 25.00
❑120, Jun 1968 .... 25.00
❑121, Aug 1968, JO (a); D: The Doom Patrol. 45.00
❑122, Feb 1973, Reprints begin (1973); From DP #76 and 89 .... 2.00
❑123, Apr 1973, From DP #95; Premiani biography 2.00
❑124, Jul 1973, From DP #90 .... 2.00

DOOM PATROL (2ND SERIES)
DC

❑1, Oct 1987; The Doom Patrol returns from their supposed deaths 2.50
❑2, Nov 1987 .... 1.50
❑3, Dec 1987 1: Rhea Jones. 1: Lodestone. 1.50
❑4, Jan 1988 O: Lodestone. 1.50
❑5, Feb 1988 .... 1.50
❑6, Mar 1988 EL (a) 1.50
❑7, Apr 1988 1: Shrapnel. 1.50
❑8, May 1988 EL (a) 1.50
❑9, Jun 1988; Bonus Book 1.50
❑10, Jul 1988 A: Superman. 1.50
❑11, Aug 1988 .... 1.50
❑12, Sep 1988 .... 1.50

Other grades: Multiply price above by 5/6 for VF/NM • 2/3 for VERY FINE • 1/3 for FINE • 1/5 for VERY GOOD • 1/8 for GOOD

❑13, Oct 1988 .... 1.50
❑14, Nov 1988 1: Dorothy Spinner. A: Power Girl 1.50
❑15, Dec 1988 V: Animal-Vegetable-Mineral Man 1.50
❑16, Dec 1988 .... 1.50
❑17, Jan 1989; D: Celsius. Invasion! .. 1.50
❑18, Jan 1989; Invasion! 1.50
❑19, Feb 1989; 1: Crazy Jane. 1st Grant Morrison; New, very strange direction for The Doom Patrol 3.00
❑20, Mar 1989 1: The Scissormen. 2.00
❑21, Apr 1989 .... 2.00
❑22, May 1989 .... 2.00
❑23, Jun 1989 .... 2.00
❑24, Jul 1989 .... 2.00
❑25, Aug 1989 .... 2.00
❑26, Sep 1989 1: The Brotherhood of Dada. 2.00
❑27, Nov 1989 .... 2.00
❑28, Dec 1989 .... 2.00
❑29, Jan 1990; JL (a); Superman cover 2.00
❑30, Feb 1990 .... 2.00
❑31, Apr 1990 .... 2.00
❑32, May 1990 .... 2.00
❑33, Jun 1990 .... 2.00
❑34, Jul 1990 .... 2.00
❑35, Aug 1990 1: Danny the Street. 1: Flex Mentallo 2.00
❑36, Sep 1990 .... 2.00
❑37, Oct 1990 .... 2.00
❑38, Nov 1990 .... 2.00
❑39, Dec 1990 .... 2.00
❑40, Jan 1991 .... 2.00
❑41, Feb 1991 .... 2.00
❑42, Mar 1991 O: Flex Mentallo. 1: The Fact 2.00
❑43, Apr 1991 .... 2.00
❑44, May 1991 1: The Candlemaker. .. 2.00
❑45, Jul 1991 .... 2.00
❑46, Aug 1991 .... 2.00
❑47, Sep 1991 .... 2.00
❑48, Oct 1991 .... 2.00
❑49, Nov 1991 .... 2.00
❑50, Dec 1991; Giant-size BB (a) 2.50
❑51, Jan 1992 1: Yankee Doodle Dandy. 2.00
❑52, Feb 1992 .... 1.75
❑53, Mar 1992; Fantastic Four parody 1.75
❑54, Apr 1992 .... 1.75
❑55, May 1992 .... 1.75
❑56, Jun 1992 .... 1.75
❑57, Jul 1992; Giant-size 2.50
❑58, Aug 1992 .... 1.75
❑59, Sep 1992 .... 1.75
❑60, Oct 1992 .... 1.75
❑61, Nov 1992 .... 1.75
❑62, Dec 1992 .... 1.75
❑63, Jan 1993 .... 1.75
❑64, Mar 1993; Begins Vertigo line 1.75
❑65, Apr 1993 .... 1.75
❑66, May 1993 .... 1.95
❑67, Jun 1993 .... 1.95
❑68, Jul 1993 .... 1.95
❑69, Aug 1993 .... 1.95
❑70, Sep 1993; Partial photo cover 1.95
❑71, Oct 1993 .... 1.95
❑72, Nov 1993 .... 1.95
❑73, Dec 1993 .... 1.95
❑74, Jan 1994 .... 1.95
❑75, Feb 1994 .... 1.95
❑76, Mar 1994 .... 1.95
❑77, Apr 1994 .... 1.95
❑78, May 1994 .... 1.95
❑79, Jun 1994 .... 1.95
❑80, Jul 1994 .... 1.95
❑81, Aug 1994 .... 1.95
❑82, Sep 1994 .... 1.95
❑83, Oct 1994 .... 1.95
❑84, Nov 1994 .... 1.95
❑85, Dec 1994 .... 1.95
❑86, Jan 1995 .... 1.95
❑87, Feb 1995 .... 1.95
❑Annual 1, ca. 1988 .... 1.00
❑Annual 2, ca. 1994; Children's Crusade 3.95

DOOM PATROL (3RD SERIES)
DC

❑1, Dec 2001 .... 3.00
❑2, Jan 2002 .... 2.50
❑3, Feb 2002 .... 2.50
❑4, Mar 2002 .... 2.50
❑5, Apr 2002 .... 2.50
❑6, May 2002 .... 2.50
❑7, Jun 2002 .... 2.50
❑8, Jul 2002 .... 2.50
❑9, Aug 2002 .... 2.50
❑10, Sep 2002 .... 2.50
❑11, Oct 2002 .... 2.50
❑12, Nov 2002 .... 2.50
❑13, Dec 2002 .... 2.50
❑14, Jan 2003 .... 2.50
❑15, Feb 2003 .... 2.50
❑16, Mar 2003 .... 2.50
❑17, Apr 2003 .... 2.50
❑18, May 2003 .... 2.50
❑19, Jun 2003 .... 2.50
❑20, Jul 2003 .... 2.50
❑21, Aug 2003 .... 2.50
❑22, Sep 2003 .... 2.50

DOOM PATROL (4TH SERIES)
DC

❑1, Aug 2004 JBy (c); JBy (w); JBy (a) 2.95
❑2, Sep 2004 JBy (c); JBy (w); JBy (a) 2.50
❑3, Oct 2004 JBy (c); JBy (w); JBy (a) 2.50
❑4, Nov 2004 JBy (c); JBy (w); JBy (a) 2.50
❑5, Dec 2004 JBy (c); JBy (w); JBy (a) 2.50
❑6, Jan 2005 .... 2.50
❑7, Feb 2005 .... 2.50
❑8, Mar 2005 .... 2.50
❑9, Apr 2005 .... 2.50
❑10, May 2005 .... 2.50
❑11, Jun 2005 .... 2.50
❑12, Jul 2005 .... 2.50
❑13, Aug 2005 .... 2.50
❑14, Sep 2005 .... 2.50
❑15, Oct 2005 .... 2.50
❑16, Nov 2005 .... 2.50
❑17, Dec 2005 .... 2.50
❑18, Jan 2006 .... 2.50

DOOM PATROL AND SUICIDE SQUAD SPECIAL
DC

❑1, Feb 1988 EL (a) 2.00

DOOMSDAY + 1 (CHARLTON)
CHARLTON

❑1, Jul 1975 JBy (a) 8.00
❑2, Sep 1975 JBy (a) 5.00
❑3, Nov 1975 JBy (a) 4.00
❑4, Jan 1976 JBy (a) 4.00
❑5, Mar 1976 JBy (a) 4.00
❑6, May 1976 JBy (a) 4.00
❑7, Jun 1978, JBy (a); Reprints Doomsday + 1 #1 .... 3.00
❑8, Sep 1978, JBy (a); Reprints Doomsday + 1 #2 .... 3.00
❑9, Nov 1978, JBy (a); Reprints Doomsday + 1 #3 .... 3.00
❑10, Jan 1979; JBy (a); Reprints Doomsday + 1 #4 .... 3.00
❑11 1979; JBy (a); Reprints Doomsday + 1 #5 .... 3.00
❑12 1979; JBy (a); Reprints Doomsday + 1 #6 .... 3.00

DOOMSDAY + 1 (AVALON)
AVALON

❑1 .... 2.95
❑2 .... 2.95

DOOMSDAY ANNUAL
DC

❑1, ca. 1995 .... 3.95

DOOMSDAY SQUAD
FANTAGRAPHICS

❑1, Aug 1986 JBy (a) 2.00
❑2 JBy (a) 2.00
❑3 JBy (a); A: Usagi Yojimbo. 3.00
❑4 JBy (a) 2.00
❑5 JBy (a) 2.00
❑6 JBy (a) 2.00
❑7 JBy (a) 2.00

DOOM'S IV
IMAGE

❑½, Dec 1994; Preview promotional edition 2.50
❑1, Jul 1994 RL (w) 2.50
❑1/A, Jul 1994; RL (w); Alternate cover with left half of yellow two-part picture 2.50
❑1/B, Jul 1994; RL (w); Alternate cover with right half of yellow two-part picture 2.50
❑2, Aug 1994 .... 2.50
❑2/A, Aug 1994 .... 2.50
❑3, Sep 1994 .... 2.50
❑4, Oct 1994 .... 2.50

DOOM: THE EMPEROR RETURNS
MARVEL

❑1, Jan 2002 .... 2.50
❑2, Feb 2002 .... 2.50
❑3, Mar 2002 .... 2.50

DOOM 2099
MARVEL

❑1, Jan 1993; PB (a); 1: Doom 2099. Metallic ink cover 2.50
❑2, Feb 1993 PB (a) 1.75
❑3, Mar 1993 PB (a) 1.75
❑4, Apr 1993 PB (a) 1.75
❑5, May 1993 1: Fever. 1.75
❑6, Jun 1993 PB (a) 1.50
❑7, Jul 1993 PB (a) 1.50
❑8, Aug 1993 PB (a) 1.50
❑9, Sep 1993 .... 1.50
❑10, Oct 1993; PB (a); A: Xandra. Covers of #10-12 combine to form triptych 1.50
❑11, Nov 1993 PB (a) 1.25
❑12, Dec 1993 PB (a) 1.25
❑13, Jan 1994 .... 1.25
❑14, Feb 1994 PB (a) 1.25
❑15, Mar 1994 PB (a) 1.25
❑16, Apr 1994 .... 1.25
❑17, May 1994 PB (a) 1.25
❑18, May 1994; PB (a); D: Radian. poster 1.50
❑19, Jul 1994 PB (a) 1.50
❑20, Aug 1994 .... 1.50
❑21, Sep 1994 PB (a) 1.50
❑22, Oct 1994 PB (a) 1.50
❑23, Nov 1994 PB (a) 1.50
❑24, Dec 1994 PB (a) 1.50
❑25, Jan 1995; Giant-size; PB (a); regular cover 2.25
❑25/Variant, Jan 1995; Giant-size; PB (a); Embossed foil cover 2.95
❑26, Feb 1995 PB (a) 1.50
❑27, Mar 1995 PB (a) 1.50
❑28, Apr 1995 .... 1.95
❑29, May 1995 .... 1.95
❑29/Variant, May 1995; enhanced acetate overlay cover 3.50
❑30, Jun 1995 .... 1.95
❑31, Jul 1995 .... 1.95
❑32, Aug 1995 .... 1.95
❑33, Sep 1995 .... 1.95
❑34, Oct 1995 .... 1.95
❑35, Nov 1995 .... 1.95
❑36, Dec 1995 .... 1.95
❑37, Jan 1996 .... 1.95
❑38, Feb 1996 .... 1.95
❑39, Mar 1996 JB (a) 1.95
❑39/Variant, Mar 1996; Special cover. 3.50
❑40, Apr 1996; JB (a); Doom 2099 comes to present 1.95
❑41, May 1996 V: Namor. V: Daredevil. 1.95
❑42, Jun 1996 V: Fantastic Four. 1.95
❑43, Jul 1996; story continues in Fantastic Four 2099 #7 .... 1.95
❑44, Aug 1996; continues in 2099: World of Tomorrow 1.95

DOORMAN (CALIBER)
CALIBER

❑1 .... 2.95

DOORMAN (CULT)
CULT

❑1, b&w; Double-cover 2.95
❑2, b&w 2.50
❑3, b&w 2.50

Other grades: Multiply price above by 5/6 for VF/NM • 2/3 for VERY FINE • 1/3 for FINE • 1/5 for VERY GOOD • 1/8 for GOOD

Donald Duck Adventures (Gladstone)

Don Rosa sent Ducks on more outings
©Gladstone

Donna Matrix

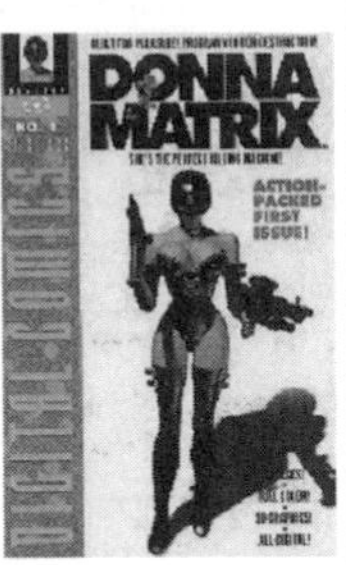

Only issue of computer-generated series
©Reactor

Doom

Latverian tyrant takes over Counter-Earth
©Marvel

Doom Patrol (1st Series)

Continues from My Greatest Adventure
©DC

Doom Patrol (2nd Series)

Revived team takes strange twist
©DC

N-MINT

❑4, b&w ... 2.95
❑Ashcan 1 ... 1.00

DOORMAN: FAMILY SECRETS
CALIBER

❑1 ... 2.95

DOORWAY TO NIGHTMARE
DC

❑1, Feb 1978 VM (a) ... 7.00
❑2, Apr 1978 ... 3.00
❑3, Jun 1978 ... 3.00
❑4, Aug 1978 ... 3.00
❑5, Oct 1978 ... 3.00

DOPE COMIX
KITCHEN SINK

❑1 ... 5.00
❑2 ... 3.00
❑3 ... 3.00
❑4 ... 3.00
❑5 ... 3.00

DOPIN' DAN
LAST GASP

❑1, Apr 1972 ... 5.00
❑2 ... 3.00
❑3 ... 3.00

DORIS NELSON: ATOMIC HOUSEWIFE
JAKE COMICS

❑1, Dec 1995, b&w ... 2.75

DORK
SLAVE LABOR

❑1, Jun 1993, b&w ... 3.00
❑1/2nd, Aug 1995, b&w ... 2.75
❑1/3rd, Mar 1997, b&w ... 2.75
❑2, May 1994, b&w ... 2.50
❑2/2nd, Jan 1996, b&w ... 2.75
❑3, Aug 1995, b&w ... 2.75
❑3/2nd, Sep 1996, b&w ... 2.75
❑4, Mar 1997, b&w ... 2.75
❑5, Jan 1998, b&w ... 2.95
❑6, May 1998, b&w ... 2.95
❑7, Aug 1999, b&w ... 2.95
❑8, Sep 2000, b&w ... 3.50
❑9, Aug 2001 ... 2.95

DORK HOUSE COMICS
PARODY

❑1 ... 2.50

DORKIER IMAGES
PARODY

❑1, Mar 1993; Standard edition ... 2.50
❑1/Variant; gold, silver, blue edition ... 3.00

DORK TOWER
DORK STORM

❑1, Jul 1998 ... 4.00
❑2, Oct 1998 ... 3.00
❑3, Jan 1999 ... 3.00
❑4, May 1999; Star Wars ... 3.00
❑5, Jul 1999; Babylon 5 ... 2.95
❑6 1999 ... 2.95
❑7, Jan 2000 ... 2.95
❑8, Mar 2000 ... 2.95
❑9, Aug 2000, b&w; switches to Dork Storm ... 2.95

N-MINT

❑10, Aug 2000 ... 2.95
❑11, Sep 2000 ... 2.95
❑12, Nov 2000 ... 2.95
❑13, Feb 2001 ... 2.95
❑14 2001 ... 2.95
❑15 2001 ... 2.95
❑16 2001 ... 2.99
❑17 2002 ... 2.99
❑18 2002 ... 2.99
❑19 2002 ... 2.99
❑20 2002 ... 2.99
❑21 2002 ... 2.99
❑22 2002 ... 2.99
❑23 2003 ... 2.99
❑24 2003 ... 2.99
❑25 2003 ... 2.99
❑26 2004 ... 2.99
❑27 2004 ... 2.99
❑28 2004 ... 2.99
❑29, Mar 2005 ... 2.99
❑30 2005 ... 2.99
❑31 2005 ... 2.99

DOUBLE DRAGON
MARVEL

❑1, Jul 1991 ... 1.00
❑2, Aug 1991 ... 1.00
❑3, Sep 1991 ... 1.00
❑4, Oct 1991 ... 1.00
❑5, Nov 1991 ... 1.00
❑6, Dec 1991 ... 1.00

DOUBLE EDGE: ALPHA
MARVEL

❑1, Aug 1995; Chromium cover; Punisher ... 4.95

DOUBLE EDGE: OMEGA
MARVEL

❑1, Oct 1995; enhanced wraparound cover; Punisher ... 4.95

DOUBLE IMAGE
IMAGE

❑1, Feb 2001; Flip-book ... 2.95
❑2, Mar 2001; Flip-book; Had two different front covers and was NOT a flipbook ... 2.95
❑3, Apr 2001; Flip-book ... 2.95
❑4, May 2001; Flip-book ... 2.95
❑5, Jun 2001; Flip-book ... 2.95

DOUBLE IMPACT
HIGH IMPACT

❑1, Mar 1995, No cover price; no indicia; gray polybag; preview of Double Impact #3 and 4; San Diego Comic-Con ed ... 3.95
❑1/Ltd., Mar 1995, No cover price; no indicia; black polybag; letters pages and pin-ups; limited to 5000 ... 3.95
❑2, May 1995 ... 3.00
❑3, Jul 1995 ... 3.00
❑5, Nov 1995 ... 3.00
❑4, Sep 1995 ... 3.00

DOUBLE IMPACT (VOL. 2)
HIGH IMPACT

❑0, Dec 1996 ... 2.95
❑1 1997; Chromium cover ... 4.00

N-MINT

❑2 1997 ... 3.00
❑3 1997 ... 3.00
❑4 1997 ... 3.00
❑5 1997 ... 3.00
❑6 1997 ... 3.00
❑7, May 1996 ... 3.00

DOUBLE IMPACT: ART ATTACK
ABC

❑1 ... 3.00
❑1/A; China & Jazz Nude Edition ... 4.00
❑1/B; Nude Jazz Edition ... 4.00

DOUBLE IMPACT: ASSASSINS FOR HIRE
HIGH IMPACT

❑1, Apr 1997, b&w; Hard Core! Edition; cardstock cover ... 2.95

DOUBLE IMPACT BIKINI SPECIAL
HIGH IMPACT

❑1, Sep 1998, b&w; pin-ups ... 3.00

DOUBLE IMPACT: FROM THE ASHES
HIGH IMPACT

❑1, b&w ... 3.00
❑2, b&w; says Swedish Erotika Vol. 5 on cover ... 5.95

DOUBLE IMPACT/HELLINA
ABC

❑1, Jan 1998, b&w; crossover with Lightning ... 3.00
❑1/Autographed, Mar 1996, b&w; Signed, limited edition nude cover; Signed, limited edition nude cover ... 4.00
❑1/Gold, Mar 1996, Gold nude cover ... 5.00
❑1/Nude, Jan 1998, Nude cover ... 3.00
❑1/Variant, Mar 1996, Nude cover ... 3.00

DOUBLE IMPACT: ONE STEP BEYOND
HIGH IMPACT

❑1, Sep 1998 ... 3.00
❑1/Variant; Leather cover ... 20.00

DOUBLE IMPACT: RAISING HELL
ABC

❑1, Sep 1997, b&w ... 2.95
❑1/Nude, Sep 1997, b&w; nude cover ... 3.50

DOUBLE IMPACT: RAW
ABC

❑1, Nov 1997; cardstock cover ... 2.95
❑1/A, Nov 1997; Eurotika Edition; no cover price ... 4.00
❑1/Nude, Nov 1997; Eurotika Edition; nude cover ... 4.00
❑1/2nd ... 3.50
❑2, ca. 1998 ... 3.00
❑2/Nude, ca. 1998; nude cover ... 3.00
❑3, ca. 1998 ... 3.00

DOUBLE IMPACT: RAW (VOL. 2)
ABC

❑1/Nude, Sep 1998; Nude cover ... 3.00

DOUBLE IMPACT: SUICIDE RUN
HIGH IMPACT

❑1, Jun 1997 ... 3.00
❑1/A, Jun 1997 ... 4.00
❑1/Leather, Jun 1997; no cover price ... 4.00
❑1/Nude, Jun 1997 ... 4.00

Other grades: Multiply price above by 5/6 for VF/NM • 2/3 for VERY FINE • 1/3 for FINE • 1/5 for VERY GOOD • 1/8 for GOOD

DOUBLE IMPACT: TRIGGER HAPPY
HIGH IMPACT

	N-MINT
❑1, ca. 1997	3.00
❑1/B, ca. 1997; Jazz Edition	3.00
❑1/Ltd., ca. 1997; Gold edition; No cover price; limited to 300 copies	4.00

DOWN
IMAGE

	N-MINT
❑1, Jan 2006	2.95
❑2, Jan 2006	2.95
❑3, Jan 2006	2.95
❑4, Apr 2006	2.95

D.P.7
MARVEL

	N-MINT
❑1, Nov 1986	1.00
❑2, Dec 1986	1.00
❑3, Jan 1987	1.00
❑4, Feb 1987	1.00
❑5, Mar 1987	1.00
❑6, Apr 1987	1.00
❑7, May 1987	1.00
❑8, Jun 1987	1.00
❑9, Jul 1987	1.00
❑10, Aug 1987	1.00
❑11, Sep 1987	1.00
❑12, Oct 1987	1.00
❑13, Nov 1987	1.00
❑14, Dec 1987	1.00
❑15, Jan 1988	1.00
❑16, Feb 1988	1.00
❑17, Mar 1988	1.00
❑18, Apr 1988	1.00
❑19, May 1988	1.00
❑20, Jun 1988	1.00
❑21, Jul 1988	1.00
❑22, Aug 1988	1.00
❑23, Sep 1988	1.00
❑24, Oct 1988	1.00
❑25, Nov 1988	1.00
❑26, Dec 1988	1.00
❑27, Jan 1989	1.00
❑28, Feb 1989	1.00
❑29, Mar 1989	1.00
❑30, Apr 1989	1.00
❑31, May 1989	1.00
❑32, Jun 1989	1.00
❑Annual 1, Nov 1987	1.00

DRACULA (ETERNITY)
ETERNITY

	N-MINT
❑1	2.50
❑1/2nd	2.50
❑2, b&w	2.50
❑3, b&w	2.50
❑4, b&w	2.50

DRACULA (BRAM STOKER'S...)
TOPPS

	N-MINT
❑1, Oct 1992	2.95
❑1/Variant, Oct 1992; no cover price	3.50
❑2, Nov 1992	2.95
❑3, Dec 1992	2.95
❑4, Jan 1993	2.95

DRACULA 3-D
3-D ZONE

	N-MINT
❑1	3.95

DRACULA CHRONICLES
TOPPS

	N-MINT
❑1	2.50
❑2	2.50
❑3	2.50

DRACULA IN HELL
APPLE

	N-MINT
❑1, Jan 1992, b&w	2.50
❑2, b&w	2.50

DRACULA LIVES! (MAGAZINE)
MARVEL

	N-MINT
❑1, Jun 1973, b&w	50.00
❑2, Aug 1973, b&w O: Dracula.	30.00
❑3, Oct 1973, b&w A: Soloman Kane.	30.00
❑4, Jan 1974, b&w; title changes to Dracula Lives!	25.00
❑5, Mar 1974, b&w; adapts Bram Stoker novel	25.00
❑6, May 1974, b&w	25.00
❑7, Jul 1974, b&w	20.00
❑8, Sep 1974, b&w	20.00
❑9, Nov 1974, b&w	20.00
❑10, Jan 1975, b&w	30.00
❑11, Mar 1975, b&w	25.00
❑12, May 1975, b&w	25.00
❑13, Jul 1975, b&w	25.00
❑Annual 1, ca. 1975, b&w; magazine	27.00

DRACULA: LORD OF THE UNDEAD
MARVEL

	N-MINT
❑1, Dec 1998; gatefold summary	2.99
❑2, Dec 1998; gatefold summary	2.99
❑3, Dec 1998; gatefold summary	2.99

DRACULA: RETURN OF THE IMPALER
SLAVE LABOR

	N-MINT
❑1, Jul 1993	2.95
❑2, Jan 1994	2.95
❑3, Mar 1994	2.95
❑4, Oct 1994	2.95

DRACULA'S DAUGHTER
FANTAGRAPHICS / EROS

	N-MINT
❑1, b&w	2.50

DRACULA'S REVENGE
IDEA & DESIGN WORKS

	N-MINT
❑1, May 2004	3.99
❑2, Jun 2004	3.99

DRACULA: THE LADY IN THE TOMB
ETERNITY

	N-MINT
❑1, b&w	2.50

DRACULA: THE SUICIDE CLUB
ADVENTURE

	N-MINT
❑1, Aug 1992	2.50
❑2, Sep 1992	2.50
❑3, Oct 1992	2.50
❑4, Nov 1992	2.50

DRACULA VERSUS ZORRO
TOPPS

	N-MINT
❑1, Oct 1993 TY (a)	4.00
❑2, Nov 1993 TY (a)	3.50

DRACULA VERSUS ZORRO (VOL. 2)
TOPPS

	N-MINT
❑1, Apr 1994	5.95

DRACULA VERSUS ZORRO (VOL. 3)
IMAGE

	N-MINT
❑1, Sep 1998	2.95
❑2, Oct 1998	2.95

DRACULA: VLAD THE IMPALER
TOPPS

	N-MINT
❑1, trading cards	2.95
❑2, trading cards	2.95
❑3, trading cards	2.95

DRACULINA (2ND SERIES)
DRACULINA

	N-MINT
❑1	2.50

DRACULINA'S COZY COFFIN
DRACULINA

	N-MINT
❑1, b&w; no indicia	2.50
❑2, b&w; no indicia	2.50

DRAFT
MARVEL

	N-MINT
❑1, Jul 1988; D.P.7, Nightmask	2.00

DRAG 'N' WHEELS
CHARLTON

	N-MINT
❑30, Sep 1968; Previous issues published as Top Eliminator	12.00
❑31, Nov 1968	12.00
❑32, Jan 1969	12.00
❑33, Mar 1969	12.00
❑34, May 1969	12.00
❑35, Jul 1969	12.00
❑36, Sep 1969	10.00
❑37, Nov 1969	10.00
❑38, Jan 1970	10.00
❑39, Feb 1970	10.00
❑40, Apr 1970	10.00
❑41, Jun 1970	10.00
❑42, Aug 1970	10.00
❑43, Oct 1970	10.00
❑44, Dec 1970	10.00
❑45, Feb 1971	10.00
❑46, Apr 1971	10.00
❑47, Jun 1971	10.00
❑48, Aug 1971	10.00
❑49, Oct 1971	10.00
❑50, Dec 1971	10.00
❑51, Feb 1972	10.00
❑52, Mar 1972	10.00
❑53 1972	10.00
❑54, Jul 1972	10.00
❑55, Sep 1972	10.00
❑56, Nov 1972	10.00
❑57, Jan 1973	10.00
❑58, Mar 1973	10.00
❑58/2nd, ca. 1978; Modern Comics reprint	10.00
❑59, May 1973	10.00

DRAGON
COMICS INTERVIEW

	N-MINT
❑1, Aug 1987; weekly	1.75
❑2, Aug 1987; weekly	1.75
❑3, Aug 1987; weekly	1.75
❑4, Aug 1987; weekly	1.75
❑Book 1	9.95

DRAGON (2ND SERIES)
IMAGE

	N-MINT
❑1, Mar 1996	2.00
❑2, Apr 1996	2.00
❑3, May 1996	2.00
❑4, Jun 1996	2.00
❑5, Jul 1996 A: Badrock.	2.00

DRAGON ARMS
ANTARCTIC

	N-MINT
❑1, Dec 2002	3.50
❑2, Jan 2003	3.50
❑3, Feb 2003	3.50
❑4, Mar 2003	3.50
❑5, Apr 2003	3.50
❑6, May 2003	3.50

DRAGON ARMS: CHAOS BLADE
ANTARCTIC

	N-MINT
❑1, Jan 2004	2.99
❑2 2004	2.99
❑3, May 2004	2.99
❑4 2004	2.99
❑5 2004	2.99
❑6 2004	2.99

DRAGONBALL
VIZ

	N-MINT
❑1, Mar 1998; 'Manga Style' Edition	4.00
❑2, Apr 1998; 'Manga Style' Edition	3.50
❑3, May 1998; 'Manga Style' Edition	3.50
❑4, Jun 1998; 'Manga Style' Edition	3.50
❑5, Jul 1998; 'Manga Style' Edition	3.50
❑6, Aug 1998; 'Manga Style' Edition	3.50
❑7, Sep 1998; 'Manga Style' Edition	3.50
❑8, Oct 1998	3.00
❑9, Nov 1998	3.00
❑10, Dec 1998	3.00
❑11, Jan 1999	3.00
❑12, Feb 1999	3.00

DRAGONBALL PART 2
VIZ

	N-MINT
❑1, Mar 1999	4.00
❑2, Apr 1999	3.00
❑3, May 1999	3.00
❑4, Jun 1999	3.00
❑5, Jul 1999	3.00
❑6, Aug 1999	3.00
❑7, Sep 1999	3.00
❑8, Oct 1999	3.00
❑9, Nov 1999	2.95
❑10, Dec 1999	2.95
❑11, Jan 2000	2.95
❑12, Feb 2000	2.95
❑13, Mar 2000	2.95
❑14, Apr 2000	2.95
❑15, May 2000	2.95

DRAGONBALL PART 3
VIZ

	N-MINT
❑1, Jun 2000	2.95
❑2, Jul 2000	2.95
❑3, Aug 2000	2.95
❑4, Sep 2000	2.95
❑5, Oct 2000	2.95
❑6, Nov 2000	2.95
❑7, Dec 2000	2.95
❑8, Jan 2001	2.95
❑9, Feb 2001	2.95
❑10, Mar 2001	2.95
❑11, Apr 2001	2.95

Doomsday + 1 (Charlton)

Early John Byrne work appears

©Charlton

Doom's IV

Series optioned for film in mid-1990s

©Image

Dork

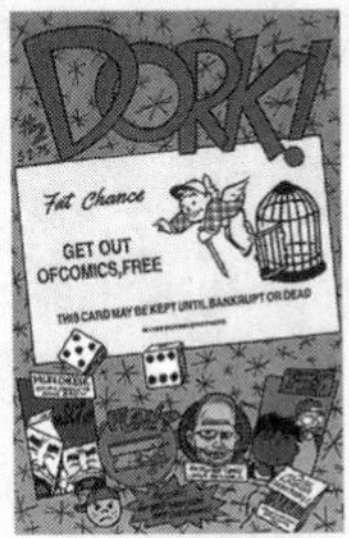

Evan Dorkin's humor anthology

©Slave Labor

Dork Tower

Gamer and cartoonist laughs with gamers

©Dork Storm

Double Dragon

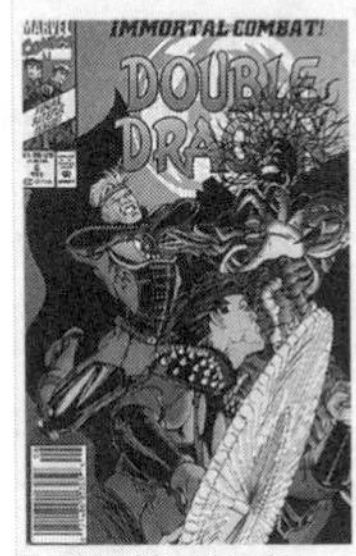

Fighting videogame features two brothers

©Marvel

	N-MINT
❑12, May 2001	2.95
❑13, Jun 2001	2.95
❑14, Jul 2001	2.95

DRAGONBALL PART 4
VIZ

	N-MINT
❑1, Aug 2001	2.95
❑2, Sep 2001	2.95
❑3, Oct 2001	2.95
❑4, Nov 2001	2.95
❑5, Dec 2001	2.95
❑6, Jan 2002	2.95
❑7, Feb 2002	2.95
❑8, Mar 2002	2.95
❑9, Apr 2002	2.95
❑10, May 2002	2.95

DRAGONBALL PART 5
VIZ

	N-MINT
❑1, Jun 2002	2.95
❑2, Jul 2002	2.95
❑3, Aug 2002	2.95
❑4, Sep 2002	2.95
❑5, Oct 2002	2.95
❑6, Nov 2002	2.95
❑7, Dec 2002	2.95

DRAGONBALL PART 6
VIZ

	N-MINT
❑1, Jan 2003	3.50
❑2, Feb 2003	3.50

DRAGONBALL Z
VIZ

	N-MINT
❑1, Mar 1998	4.00
❑2, Apr 1998	3.50
❑3, May 1998	3.50
❑4, Jun 1998	3.50
❑5, Jul 1998	3.50
❑6, Aug 1998	3.00
❑7, Sep 1998	3.00
❑8, Oct 1998	3.00
❑9, Nov 1998	3.00
❑10, ca. 1998	3.00

DRAGONBALL Z PART 2
VIZ

	N-MINT
❑1, Dec 1998; 'Manga Style' Edition	3.50
❑2, Jan 1999; 'Manga Style' Edition	3.00
❑3, Feb 1999; 'Manga Style' Edition	3.00
❑4, Mar 1999; 'Manga Style' Edition	3.00
❑5, Apr 1999; 'Manga Style' Edition	3.00
❑6, May 1999; 'Manga Style' Edition	2.95
❑7, Jun 1999; 'Manga Style' Edition	2.95
❑8, Jul 1999	2.95
❑9, Aug 1999	2.95
❑10, Sep 1999	2.95
❑11, Oct 1999	2.95
❑12, Nov 1999	2.95
❑13, Dec 1999	2.95
❑14, Jan 2000	2.95

DRAGONBALL Z PART 3
VIZ

	N-MINT
❑1, Feb 2000	2.95
❑2, Mar 2000	2.95
❑3, Apr 2000	2.95
❑4, May 2000	2.95
❑5, Jun 2000	2.95
❑6, Jul 2000	2.95
❑7, Aug 2000	2.95
❑8, Sep 2000	2.95
❑9, Oct 2000	2.95
❑10, Nov 2000	2.95

DRAGONBALL Z PART 4
VIZ

	N-MINT
❑1, Dec 2000	2.95
❑2, Jan 2001	2.95
❑3, Feb 2001	2.95
❑4, Mar 2001	2.95
❑5, Apr 2001	2.95
❑6, May 2001	2.95
❑7, Jun 2001	2.95
❑8, Jul 2001	2.95
❑9, Aug 2001	2.95
❑10, Sep 2001	2.95
❑11, Oct 2001	2.95
❑12, Nov 2001	2.95
❑13, Dec 2001	2.95

DRAGONBALL Z PART 5
VIZ

	N-MINT
❑1, Jan 2002	2.95
❑2, Feb 2002	2.95
❑3, Mar 2002	2.95
❑4, Apr 2002	2.95
❑5, May 2002	2.95
❑6, Jun 2002	2.95
❑7, Jul 2002	2.95
❑8, Aug 2002	2.95
❑9, Sep 2002	2.95
❑10, Oct 2002	2.95
❑11, Nov 2002	2.95
❑12, Dec 2002	2.95

DRAGON, THE: BLOOD & GUTS
IMAGE

	N-MINT
❑1, Mar 1995	2.50
❑2, Apr 1995	2.50
❑3, May 1995	2.50

DRAGON CHIANG
ECLIPSE

	N-MINT
❑1, ca. 1991, b&w; nn, cardstock cover	3.95

DRAGONFIRE (VOL. 1)
NIGHTWYND

	N-MINT
❑1, b&w	2.50
❑2, b&w	2.50
❑3, b&w	2.50
❑4, b&w	2.50

DRAGONFIRE (VOL. 2)
NIGHTWYND

	N-MINT
❑1, b&w	2.50
❑2, b&w	2.50
❑3, b&w	2.50
❑4, b&w	2.50

DRAGONFIRE: THE CLASSIFIED FILES
NIGHTWYND

	N-MINT
❑1, b&w	2.50
❑2, b&w	2.50
❑3, b&w	2.50
❑4, b&w	2.50

DRAGONFIRE: THE EARLY YEARS
NIGHT WYND

	N-MINT
❑1, b&w	2.50
❑2, b&w	2.50
❑3, b&w	2.50
❑4, b&w	2.50
❑5, b&w	2.50
❑6, b&w	2.50
❑7, b&w	2.50
❑8, b&w	2.50

DRAGONFIRE: UFO WARS
NIGHTWYND

	N-MINT
❑1, b&w	2.50
❑2, b&w	2.50
❑3, b&w	2.50

DRAGONFLIGHT
ECLIPSE

	N-MINT
❑1, Feb 1991	4.95
❑2 1991	4.95
❑3 1991; Anne McCaffrey	4.95

DRAGON FLUX
ANTARCTIC

	N-MINT
❑2, Jun 1996, b&w	2.95
❑3, Nov 1996, b&w	2.95

DRAGONFLY
AC

	N-MINT
❑1, Aug 1985	1.75
❑2	1.75
❑3	1.75
❑4	1.75
❑5	1.75
❑6, Feb 1987	1.75
❑7, Jul 1987	1.75
❑8	1.95

DRAGONFORCE
AIRCEL

	N-MINT
❑1, ca. 1988, b&w O: Dragonforce. O: Alloy. 1: Kohl. 1: Maire. 1: Dragonforce. 1: Alloy. 1: Kamikaze. 1: Sental	2.00
❑2, ca. 1988, b&w	2.00
❑3, ca. 1988, b&w	2.00
❑4, ca. 1988, b&w	2.00
❑5, ca. 1988, b&w	2.00
❑6, ca. 1988, b&w	2.00
❑7, ca. 1989, b&w	2.00
❑8, ca. 1989, b&w	2.00
❑9, ca. 1989, b&w	2.00
❑10, ca. 1989, b&w	2.00
❑11, ca. 1989, b&w	2.00
❑12, ca. 1989, b&w	2.00
❑13, ca. 1989, b&w	2.00

DRAGONFORCE CHRONICLES
AIRCEL

	N-MINT
❑1, ca. 1989, b&w; Reprints	2.95
❑2, ca. 1989, b&w; Reprints	2.95
❑3, ca. 1989, b&w; Reprints	2.95
❑4, ca. 1989, b&w; Reprints	2.95
❑5, ca. 1989, b&w; Reprints	2.95

DRAGON HEAD
TOKYOPOP

	N-MINT
❑1, Jan 2006	9.99

Other grades: Multiply price above by 5/6 for VF/NM • 2/3 for VERY FINE • 1/3 for FINE • 1/5 for VERY GOOD • 1/8 for GOOD

DRAGONHEART
TOPPS

- ❑1, May 1996 … 2.95
- ❑2, Jun 1996 … 4.95

DRAGON HUNTER
TOKYOPOP

- ❑1, Jun 2003, … 9.99
- ❑2, Aug 2005 … 9.99
- ❑3, Oct 2003 … 9.99
- ❑4, Jan 2004 … 9.99
- ❑5, Mar 2004 … 9.99
- ❑6, May 2004 … 9.99
- ❑7, Jul 2004 … 9.99
- ❑8, Sep 2004 … 9.99
- ❑9, Nov 2004 … 9.99
- ❑10, Jan 2005 … 9.99
- ❑11, Mar 2005 … 9.99
- ❑12, May 2005 … 9.99
- ❑13, Nov 2005 … 9.99

DRAGON KNIGHTS (SLAVE LABOR)
SLAVE LABOR / AMAZE INK

- ❑1, Aug 1998, b&w … 1.75
- ❑2 … 1.75
- ❑3 … 1.75

DRAGON KNIGHTS (TOKYOPOP)
TOKYOPOP

- ❑1, Apr 2002, b&w; printed in Japanese format … 9.99
- ❑2, Jun 2006 … 9.99
- ❑3, Aug 2002 … 9.99
- ❑4, Oct 2002 … 9.99
- ❑5, Dec 2002 … 9.99
- ❑6, Feb 2003 … 9.99
- ❑7, Apr 2003 … 9.99
- ❑8, Jun 2003 … 9.99
- ❑9, Aug 2003 … 9.99
- ❑10, Oct 2003 … 9.99
- ❑11, Dec 2003 … 9.99
- ❑12, Feb 2004 … 9.99
- ❑13, Apr 2004 … 9.99
- ❑14, Jun 2004 … 9.99
- ❑15, Aug 2004 … 9.99
- ❑16, Oct 2004 … 9.99
- ❑17, Dec 2004 … 9.99
- ❑18, Feb 2005 … 9.99
- ❑19, May 2005 … 9.99
- ❑20, Aug 2005 … 9.99
- ❑21, Nov 2005 … 9.99

DRAGON LADY
DRAGON LADY

- ❑1, King of Mounted … 6.95
- ❑2, Red Ryder … 6.95
- ❑3, Captain Easy … 5.95
- ❑4, Secret Agent X-9 … 5.95
- ❑5, Brick Bradford … 5.95
- ❑6, Secret Agent X-9 … 5.95
- ❑7, Captain Easy … 5.95
- ❑8, Terry … 5.95

DRAGONLANCE
DC

- ❑1, Dec 1988 … 2.00
- ❑2, Win 1988 … 1.50
- ❑3, Hol 1988 … 1.25
- ❑4, Jan 1989 … 1.25
- ❑5, Feb 1989 … 1.25
- ❑6, Mar 1989 … 1.50
- ❑7, Apr 1989 … 1.50
- ❑8, Jun 1989 … 1.50
- ❑9, Jul 1989 … 1.50
- ❑10, Aug 1989 … 1.50
- ❑11, Sep 1989 … 1.50
- ❑12, Oct 1989 … 1.50
- ❑13, Nov 1989 … 1.50
- ❑14, Dec 1989 … 1.50
- ❑15, Jan 1990 … 1.50
- ❑16, Feb 1990 … 1.50
- ❑17, Mar 1990 … 1.50
- ❑18, Apr 1990 … 1.50
- ❑19, May 1990 … 1.50
- ❑20, Jun 1990 … 1.50
- ❑21, Jul 1990 … 1.50
- ❑22, Aug 1990 … 1.50
- ❑23, Oct 1990 … 1.50
- ❑24, Nov 1990 … 1.75
- ❑25, Dec 1990 … 1.75
- ❑26, Jan 1991 … 1.75
- ❑27, Feb 1991 … 1.75
- ❑28, Mar 1991 … 1.75
- ❑29, Apr 1991 … 1.75
- ❑30, May 1991 … 1.75
- ❑31, Jun 1991 … 1.75
- ❑32, Jul 1991 … 1.75
- ❑33, Aug 1991 … 1.75
- ❑34, Sep 1991 … 1.75

DRAGONLANCE CHRONICLES
DEVIL'S DUE

- ❑1, Sep 2005 … 2.95
- ❑2 2005 … 2.95
- ❑2/Variant 2005 … 2.95
- ❑3, Dec 2005 … 2.95
- ❑3/Variant, Dec 2005 … 2.95
- ❑4, Nov 2005 … 2.95
- ❑4/Variant, Nov 2005 … 2.95
- ❑5, Jan 2006 … 2.95
- ❑5/Variant, Jan 2006 … 2.95
- ❑6, Feb 2006 … 2.95
- ❑6/Variant, Feb 2006 … 2.95
- ❑7, Mar 2006 … 2.95
- ❑7/Variant, Mar 2006 … 2.95
- ❑8, Apr 2006 … 2.95
- ❑8/Variant, Apr 2006 … 2.95

DRAGONLANCE COMIC BOOK
TSR

- ❑1 … 1.00

DRAGONLANCE SAGA
TSR

- ❑1 … 9.95
- ❑2 … 9.95
- ❑3 … 9.95
- ❑4 … 9.95
- ❑5 … 9.95

DRAGON LINES
MARVEL / EPIC

- ❑1, May 1993; Embossed cover … 2.50
- ❑2, Jun 1993 … 1.95
- ❑3, Jul 1993 … 1.95
- ❑4, Aug 1993 … 1.95

DRAGON LINES: WAY OF THE WARRIOR
MARVEL / EPIC

- ❑1, Nov 1993 … 2.25
- ❑2, Jan 1994 … 2.25

DRAGON OF THE VALKYR
RAK

- ❑1, b&w … 1.75
- ❑2 … 1.75
- ❑3 … 1.75

DRAGON QUEST
SILVERWOLF

- ❑1, b&w … 2.00
- ❑2 … 2.00

DRAGONRING
AIRCEL

- ❑1 1986, b&w … 2.00
- ❑2 1986, b&w … 2.00
- ❑3 1986, b&w … 2.00
- ❑4 1986, b&w … 2.00
- ❑5 1986, b&w … 2.00
- ❑6 1986, b&w … 2.00

DRAGONRING (VOL. 2)
AIRCEL

- ❑1 1986 … 2.00
- ❑2 1987 … 2.00
- ❑3 1987 … 2.00
- ❑4 1987 … 2.00
- ❑5 1987 … 2.00
- ❑6 1987 … 2.00
- ❑7 1987 … 2.00
- ❑8 1987 … 2.00
- ❑9 1987 … 2.00
- ❑10 1987 … 2.00
- ❑11 1987 … 2.00
- ❑12 1987 … 2.00
- ❑13 1987 … 2.00
- ❑14 1988 … 2.00
- ❑15 1988 … 2.00

DRAGONROK SAGA
HANTHERCRAFT

- ❑1 … 2.50
- ❑2 … 2.50
- ❑3 … 2.50
- ❑4 … 2.50
- ❑5 … 2.50
- ❑6 … 2.50
- ❑7 … 2.50
- ❑8 … 2.50
- ❑9 … 2.50
- ❑10 … 2.50

DRAGON'S BANE
HALL OF HEROES

- ❑1, … 2.50
- ❑Ashcan 1, Chicago Comic Con Ashcan limited to 100 copies … 4.95

DRAGON'S CLAWS
MARVEL

- ❑1, Jul 1988, 1: Dragon's Claws. … 1.50
- ❑2, Aug 1988 … 1.50
- ❑3, Sep 1988 … 1.50
- ❑4, Oct 1988 … 1.50
- ❑5, Nov 1988, 1: Death's Head I. … 2.00
- ❑6, Dec 1988 … 1.75
- ❑7, Jan 1989 … 1.75
- ❑8, Feb 1989 … 1.75
- ❑9, Mar 1989 … 1.75
- ❑10, Apr 1989 … 1.75

DRAGONS IN THE MOON
AIRCEL

- ❑1, Oct 1990, b&w … 2.50
- ❑2, Oct 1990, b&w … 2.50
- ❑3, Oct 1990, b&w … 2.50
- ❑4, Oct 1990, b&w … 2.50

DRAGON'S LAIR: SINGE'S REVENGE
CROSSGEN

- ❑1, Sep 2003 … 2.95
- ❑2, Nov 2003 … 2.95
- ❑3, Nov 2003 … 2.95

DRAGONSLAYER
MARVEL

- ❑1, Oct 1981 … 1.50
- ❑2, Nov 1981 … 1.50

DRAGON'S STAR
MATRIX

- ❑1, Dec 1986 … 2.00
- ❑2 1987 … 2.00
- ❑3 1987 … 2.00

DRAGON'S STAR 2
CALIBER

- ❑1 1994 … 2.95
- ❑2 1994 … 2.95
- ❑3 … 2.95

DRAGON'S TEETH
DRAGON'S TEETH

- ❑1, b&w … 2.95

DRAGON STRIKE
MARVEL

- ❑1, Feb 1994 … 1.50

DRAGONSTRIKE PRIME
ILLUSION

- ❑2, Dec 1996, b&w … 1.95

DRAGON VOICE
TOKYOPOP

- ❑1, Oct 2004 … 9.99
- ❑2, Dec 2004 … 9.99
- ❑3, Feb 2005 … 9.99
- ❑4, May 2005 … 9.99
- ❑5, Oct 2005 … 9.99
- ❑6, Apr 2006 … 9.99

DRAGON WARS
IRONCAT

- ❑1, Apr 1998 … 2.95
- ❑2, May 1998 … 2.95
- ❑3, Jun 1998 … 2.95
- ❑4, Jul 1998 … 2.95
- ❑5, Aug 1998 … 2.95
- ❑6, Sep 1998 … 2.95
- ❑7, Oct 1998 … 2.95

DRAG-STRIP HOTRODDERS
CHARLTON

- ❑1, Sum 1963 … 40.00
- ❑2, ca. 1964 … 25.00
- ❑3, ca. 1964 … 25.00
- ❑4, Jun 1965 … 25.00

Other grades: Multiply price above by 5/6 for VF/NM • 2/3 for VERY FINE • 1/3 for FINE • 1/5 for VERY GOOD • 1/8 for GOOD

D.P.7

New Universe title featuring EMT

©Marvel

Dragonball

Midget mystic quests for seven spheres

©Viz

Dragonball Z

Goku fights alien race for Dragonballs

©Viz

Dragonflight

Based on Anne McCaffrey fantasy series

©Eclipse

Dragonforce

Mercenaries in fantasy world join forces

©Aircel

N-MINT

❑5, Aug 1965 .... 25.00
❑6, Oct 1965 .... 25.00
❑7, Dec 1965 .... 25.00
❑8, Feb 1966 .... 25.00
❑9, Apr 1966 .... 25.00
❑10, Jun 1966 .... 25.00
❑11, Aug 1966 .... 25.00
❑12, Oct 1966 .... 25.00
❑13, Dec 1966 .... 25.00
❑14, Mar 1967 .... 25.00
❑15, Jun 1967 .... 25.00
❑16, Aug 1967, Later issues published as World of Wheels 25.00

DRAKE: DEMON BOX
IMAGE

❑1, Dec 2003 .... 2.50

DRAKKON WARS
REALM

❑0, Jul 1997; Battlestar Galactica story written by Richard Hatch 2.99

DRAKUUN
DARK HORSE / MANGA

❑1, Feb 1997 .... 2.95
❑2, Mar 1997 .... 2.95
❑3, Apr 1997 .... 2.95
❑4, May 1997 .... 2.95
❑5, Jun 1997 .... 2.95
❑6, Jul 1997 .... 2.95
❑7, Aug 1997 .... 2.95
❑8, Sep 1997 .... 2.95
❑9, Oct 1997 .... 2.95
❑10, Nov 1997 .... 2.95
❑11, Dec 1997 .... 2.95
❑12, Jan 1998 .... 2.95
❑13, Feb 1998 .... 2.95
❑14, Mar 1998 .... 2.95
❑15, Apr 1998 .... 2.95
❑16, May 1998 .... 2.95
❑17, Jun 1998 .... 2.95
❑18, Jul 1998 .... 2.95
❑19, Oct 1998 .... 2.95
❑20, Nov 1998 .... 2.95
❑21, Dec 1998 .... 2.95
❑22, Jan 1999 .... 2.95
❑23, Feb 1999 .... 2.95
❑24, Mar 1999 .... 2.95

DRAMA
SIRIUS ENTERTAINMENT

❑1, Jun 1994, Chronium Cover 4.00
❑1/Ltd., Chronium Cover; limited to 1400 copies; signed by Linsner; w/trading cards & Art Plate of Authenticity in an illustrated envelope 12.00

DRAMACON
TOKYOPOP

❑1, Oct 2005 .... 9.99

DRAWING ON YOUR NIGHTMARES: HALLOWEEN 2003 SPECIAL
DARK HORSE

❑1, Oct 2003 .... 2.99

N-MINT

DRAWN & QUARTERLY
DRAWN & QUARTERLY

❑1 1990, b&w 3.00
❑2 1990 .... 3.00
❑3, Jan 1991 .... 3.50
❑4, Mar 1991 .... 3.75
❑5 1991 .... 3.75
❑6 1991 .... 3.75
❑7 1992 .... 3.75
❑8, Apr 1992, b&w 3.75

DRAX THE DESTROYER
MARVEL

❑1 .... 2.99
❑2 2005 .... 2.99
❑3, Jan 2006 .... 2.99
❑4, Feb 2006 .... 2.99

DR. BLINK, SUPER-HERO SHRINK
DORK STORM

❑1 2005 .... 3.49
❑2 2005 .... 3.49

DREADLANDS
MARVEL / EPIC

❑1, ca. 1992 .... 3.95
❑2, ca. 1992 .... 3.95
❑3, ca. 1992 .... 3.95
❑4, ca. 1992 .... 3.95

DREAD OF NIGHT
HAMILTON

❑1, b&w 3.95
❑2, b&w 3.95

DREADSTAR
MARVEL / EPIC

❑1, Nov 1982; JSn (c); JSn (w); JSn (a); Story continued from Epic Illustrated #15 .... 2.50
❑2, Jan 1983; JSn (c); JSn (w); JSn (a); O: Willow. Willow 2.00
❑3, Mar 1983; JSn (c); JSn (w); JSn (a); Lord Papal 2.00
❑4, May 1983 JSn (c); JSn (w); JSn (a) 2.00
❑5, Jul 1983 JSn (c); JSn (w); JSn (a) 2.00
❑6, Sep 1983 JSn (c); JSn (w); JSn (a) 1.75
❑7, Nov 1983 JSn (c); JSn (w); JSn (a) 1.75
❑8, Jan 1984 JSn (c); JSn (w); JSn (a) 1.75
❑9, Mar 1984 JSn (c); JSn (w); JSn (a) 1.75
❑10, Apr 1984 JSn (c); JSn (w); JSn (a) 1.75
❑11, Jun 1984 JSn (c); JSn (w); JSn (a) 1.75
❑12, Jul 1984; JSn (c); JSn (w); JSn (a); New costume 1.75
❑13, Aug 1984 JSn (c); JSn (w); JSn (a) 1.75
❑14, Oct 1984; JSn (c); JSn (w); JSn (a); Fights Lord Papal 1.75
❑15, Nov 1984 JSn (c); JSn (w); JSn (a) 1.75
❑16, Dec 1984 JSn (c); JSn (w); JSn (a) 1.50
❑17, Feb 1985 JSn (c); JSn (w); JSn (a) 1.50
❑18, Apr 1985 JSn (c); JSn (w); JSn (a) 1.50
❑19, Jun 1985 JSn (c); JSn (w); JSn (a) 1.50
❑20, Aug 1985 JSn (c); JSn (w); JSn (a) 1.50
❑21, Oct 1985 JSn (c); JSn (w); JSn (a) 1.50
❑22, Dec 1985 JSn (c); JSn (w); JSn (a) 1.50
❑23, Feb 1986 JSn (c); JSn (w); JSn (a) 1.50
❑24, Apr 1986 JSn (c); JSn (w); JSn (a) 1.50
❑25, Jun 1986 JSn (c); JSn (w); JSn (a) 1.50
❑26, Aug 1986 JSn (c); JSn (w); JSn (a) 1.50

N-MINT

❑27, Nov 1986; JSn (c); JSn (w); JSn (a); First Comics begins publishing 1.75
❑28, Jan 1987 JSn (c); JSn (w); JSn (a); 1.75
❑29, Mar 1987 JSn (c); JSn (w); JSn (a) 1.75
❑30, May 1987 JSn (c); JSn (w); JSn (a) 1.75
❑31, Jul 1987 JSn (c); JSn (w); JSn (a) 1.75
❑32, Sep 1987 JSn (c); JSn (w); JSn (a) 1.75
❑33, Nov 1987 JSn (c); JSn (w); JSn (a) 1.75
❑34, Jan 1988 JSn (c); JSn (w); JSn (a) 1.75
❑35, Mar 1988 JSn (c); JSn (w); JSn (a) 1.75
❑36, May 1988 JSn (c); JSn (w); JSn (a) 1.75
❑37, Jul 1988 JSn (c); JSn (w); JSn (a) 1.75
❑38, Sep 1988 JSn (c); JSn (w); JSn (a) 1.75
❑39, Nov 1988 JSn (c); JSn (w); JSn (a) 1.95
❑40, Jan 1989 JSn (c); JSn (w); JSn (a) 1.95
❑41, Mar 1989; PD (w); Peter David writing starts 1.95
❑42, May 1989 PD (w) 1.95
❑43, Jun 1989 PD (w) 1.95
❑44, Jul 1989 PD (w) 1.95
❑45, Aug 1989 PD (w) 1.95
❑46, Sep 1989 PD (w) 1.95
❑47, Oct 1989 PD (w) 1.95
❑48, Nov 1989 PD (w) 1.95
❑49, Dec 1989 PD (w) 1.95
❑50, Jan 1990; Double-size; PD (w); Embossed cover 2.75
❑51, Feb 1990 PD (w) 1.95
❑52, Mar 1990 PD (w) 1.95
❑53, Apr 1990 PD (w) 1.95
❑54, May 1990 PD (w) 1.95
❑55, Jun 1990 PD (w) 2.25
❑56, Jul 1990 PD (w) 2.25
❑57, Aug 1990 PD (w) 2.25
❑58, Sep 1990 PD (w) 2.25
❑59, Oct 1990 PD (w) 2.25
❑60, Nov 1990 PD (w) 2.25
❑61, Dec 1990 PD (w) 2.25
❑62, Jan 1991 PD (w) 2.25
❑63, Feb 1991 PD (w) 2.25
❑64, Mar 1991 PD (w) 2.25
❑Annual 1, ca. 1983 JSn (a) 3.00

DREADSTAR (MALIBU)
MALIBU / BRAVURA

❑½, Mar 1994, Promotional edition included in Hero Illustrated 2.00
❑1/Gold, Mar 1994; sendaway with gold ink on cover ....
❑1, Apr 1994, PD (w) 2.50
❑2, May 1994, PD (w) 2.50
❑3, Jun 1994, PD (w) 2.50
❑4, Sep 1994, PD (w) 2.50
❑5, Oct 1994, PD (w); D: Dreadstar (Vanth) 2.50
❑6, Jan 1995, PD (w) 2.50

DREADSTAR & CO.
MARVEL / EPIC

❑1, Jul 1985; JSn (c); JSn (w); JSn (a); Reprints 1.00
❑2, Aug 1985; JSn (c); JSn (w); JSn (a); Reprints 1.00
❑3, Sep 1985; JSn (c); JSn (w); JSn (a); Reprints 1.00
❑4, Oct 1985; JSn (c); JSn (w); JSn (a); Reprints 1.00

Other grades: Multiply price above by 5/6 for VF/NM • 2/3 for VERY FINE • 1/3 for FINE • 1/5 for VERY GOOD • 1/8 for GOOD

N-MINT

❑5, Nov 1985; JSn (c); JSn (w); JSn (a); Reprints 1.00
❑6, Dec 1985; JSn (c); JSn (w); JSn (a); Reprints 1.00

DREAM ANGEL
ANGEL ENTERTAINMENT

❑0, Fal 1996, b&w 2.95

DREAM ANGEL AND ANGEL GIRL
ANGEL

❑1 3.00

DREAM ANGEL: THE QUANTUM DREAMER
ANGEL

❑0 2.95
❑1 2.95
❑2 2.95

DREAM CORRIDOR (HARLAN ELLISON'S...)
DARK HORSE

❑1, Mar 1995 JBy (a) 3.50
❑2, Apr 1995 JBy (a) 3.25
❑3, May 1995 JBy (a) 3.00
❑4, Jun 1995 JBy (a) 3.00
❑5, Aug 1995 3.00
❑Special 1, Jan 1995; prestige format 5.00
❑Special 1/2nd, Sep 1995; prestige format 4.95

DREAM CORRIDOR QUARTERLY (HARLAN ELLISON'S...)
DARK HORSE

❑1, Aug 1996; prestige format 5.95

DREAMER
DC

❑1, Jun 2000 7.95

DREAMERY
ECLIPSE

❑1, Dec 1986, b&w 2.00
❑2, Feb 1987, b&w; Lela Dowling bio 2.00
❑3, Apr 1987, b&w; Councilman Stinz story; Donna Barr bio 2.00
❑4, Jun 1987, b&w 2.00
❑5, Aug 1987, b&w 2.00
❑6, Oct 1987, b&w 2.00
❑7, Dec 1987, b&w 2.00
❑8, Feb 1988, b&w 2.00
❑9, Apr 1988, b&w; Young Stinz story 2.00
❑10, Jun 1988, b&w; Young Stinz story 2.00
❑11, Aug 1988, b&w; Young Stinz story 2.00
❑12, Oct 1988, b&w; Councilman Stinz story 2.00
❑13, Dec 1988, b&w; Councilman Stinz story 2.00
❑14, Feb 1989, b&w; Cover reads "The Ninjery" 2.00

DREAMING
DC / VERTIGO

❑1, Jun 1996 3.00
❑2, Jul 1996 2.50
❑3, Aug 1996 2.50
❑4, Sep 1996 2.50
❑5, Oct 1996 2.50
❑6, Nov 1996 2.50
❑7, Dec 1996 2.50
❑8, Jan 1997; self-contained story; cover says Nov 96, indicia says Jan 97 2.50
❑9, Feb 1997 2.50
❑10, Mar 1997 2.50
❑11, Apr 1997 2.50
❑12, May 1997 2.50
❑13, Jun 1997 2.50
❑14, Jul 1997 2.50
❑15, Aug 1997 2.50
❑16, Sep 1997 2.50
❑17, Oct 1997 2.50
❑18, Nov 1997 2.50
❑19, Dec 1997 2.50
❑20, Jan 1998 2.50
❑21, Feb 1998 2.50
❑22, Mar 1998 2.50
❑23, Apr 1998 2.50
❑24, May 1998 2.50
❑25, Jun 1998 2.50
❑26, Jul 1998 2.50
❑27, Aug 1998 2.50

N-MINT

❑28, Sep 1998; House of Mystery burns down 2.50
❑29, Oct 1998 2.50
❑30, Nov 1998 2.50
❑31, Dec 1998 2.50
❑32, Jan 1999 2.50
❑33, Feb 1999 2.50
❑34, Mar 1999 2.50
❑35, Apr 1999 2.50
❑36, May 1999 2.50
❑37, Jun 1999 2.50
❑38, Jul 1999 2.50
❑39, Aug 1999 2.50
❑40, Sep 1999 2.50
❑41, Oct 1999 2.50
❑42, Nov 1999 2.50
❑43, Dec 1999 2.50
❑44, Jan 2000 2.50
❑45, Feb 2000 2.50
❑46, Mar 2000 2.50
❑47, Apr 2000 2.50
❑48, May 2000 2.50
❑49, Jun 2000 2.50
❑50, Jul 2000 2.50
❑51, Aug 2000 2.50
❑52, Sep 2000 2.50
❑53, Oct 2000 2.50
❑54, Nov 2000 2.50
❑55, Dec 2000 2.50
❑56, Jan 2001 2.50
❑57, Feb 2001 2.50
❑58, Mar 2001 2.50
❑59, Apr 2001 2.50
❑60, May 2001 2.50
❑Special 1, Jul 1998; wraparound cover 5.95

DREAMING
TOKYOPOP

❑1, Dec 2005 9.99

DREAMLAND CHRONICLES
ASTONISH

❑1/Kunkel, Mar 2004 3.50
❑1/Sava, Mar 2004 3.50
❑1/Wieringo, Mar 2004 3.50
❑1/Yeagle, Mar 2004 3.50
❑2, Sep 2005; Published by Alias Comics 4.50
❑3, Oct 2005 4.50

DREAM POLICE
MARVEL / ICON

❑1, Jul 2005 3.99

DREAM-QUEST OF UNKNOWN KADATH, THE (H.P. LOVECRAFT'S...)

❑1 2.95
❑1/2nd, Mar 1998 2.95
❑2 2.95
❑3 2.95
❑4 2.95
❑5 2.95

DREAMS 'N' SCHEMES OF COL. KILGORE
SPECIAL STUDIO

❑1, Mar 1991, b&w 2.50
❑2, May 1991, b&w 2.50

DREAMS OF A DOG
RIP OFF

❑1, May 1990, b&w 2.00
❑2, Jun 1992, b&w 2.50

DREAMS OF EVERYMAN
RIP OFF

❑1, Jun 1992 2.50

DREAMS OF THE DARKCHYLDE
DARKCHYLDE

❑1, Oct 2000 3.50
❑1/A, Oct 2000, variant cover 3.50
❑1/B, Oct 2000, chromium cover 10.00
❑1/C, Oct 2000, Dynamic Forces cover 6.00
❑1/D, Oct 2000, DFE blue foil cover 7.00
❑1/E, Oct 2000, DFE chrome cover 10.00
❑1/F, Oct 2000, Tower Records cover 5.00
❑2, Nov 2000 3.00
❑3, Dec 2000 3.00
❑4, Mar 2001 2.95

N-MINT

❑5, ca. 2001 2.95
❑6, Sep 2001 2.95

DREAM TEAM
MALIBU

❑1, Jul 1995; Malibu/Marvel Pin-ups 4.95

DREAMTIME
BLIND BAT

❑1, May 1995, b&w 2.50
❑2, b&w; no indicia 2.50

DREAMWALKER (DREAMWALKER)
DREAMWALKER

❑1, ca. 1996, b&w 2.95
❑2, ca. 1996, b&w 2.95
❑3, ca. 1996, b&w 2.95
❑4, ca. 1996, b&w 2.95
❑5, ca. 1996, b&w 2.95

DREAMWALKER (CALIBER)
CALIBER / TAPESTRY

❑1, Dec 1996, b&w 2.95
❑2, Feb 1997, b&w 2.95
❑3 1997, b&w 2.95
❑4, Jul 1997, b&w 2.95
❑5, Sep 1997, b&w 2.95
❑6, Jul 1998, b&w 2.95

DREAMWALKER (AVATAR)
AVATAR

❑0, Nov 1998, b&w 3.00

DREAMWALKER (MARVEL)
MARVEL

❑1 6.95

DREAMWALKER: AUTUMN LEAVES
AVATAR

❑1, Sep 1999, b&w 3.00
❑2, Oct 1999, b&w 3.00

DREAMWALKER: CAROUSEL
AVATAR

❑1, Mar 1999, b&w 3.00
❑2, Apr 1999, b&w 3.00

DREAMWALKER: SUMMER RAIN
AVATAR

❑1, Jul 1999, b&w 3.00

DREAM WEAVER
ROBERT LANKFORD

❑1, Aug 1987 1.95

DREAM WEAVERS
GOLDEN REALM UNLIMITED

❑1 1.50
❑2 1.50

DREAM WOLVES
DRAMENON

❑1, b&w 3.00
❑2, Dec 1994, b&w; cardstock cover 3.00
❑3, Jan 1995, b&w; cardstock cover 3.00
❑4, Feb 1995, b&w 3.00

DREAM WOLVES SWIMSUIT BIZARRE
GOTHIC

❑0, Dec 1995 3.00

DREDD BY BISLEY
FLEETWAY-QUALITY

❑1 5.95

DREDD RULES!
FLEETWAY-QUALITY

❑1 3.50
❑2 3.00
❑3 3.00
❑4 3.00
❑5 3.00
❑6 2.95
❑7 2.95
❑8 2.95
❑9 2.95
❑10 2.95
❑11 2.95
❑12 2.95
❑13 2.95
❑14 V: Santa 2.95
❑15 2.95
❑16 2.95
❑17 2.95
❑18 2.95

Other grades: Multiply price above by 5/6 for VF/NM • 2/3 for VERY FINE • 1/3 for FINE • 1/5 for VERY GOOD • 1/8 for GOOD

Dragonheart

Adapts Sean Connery/ Dennis Quaid film

©Topps

Dragonlance

Based on Dungeons & Dragons setting

©DC

Dragonslayer

Adapts early 1980s fantasy film

©Marvel

Dreadstar

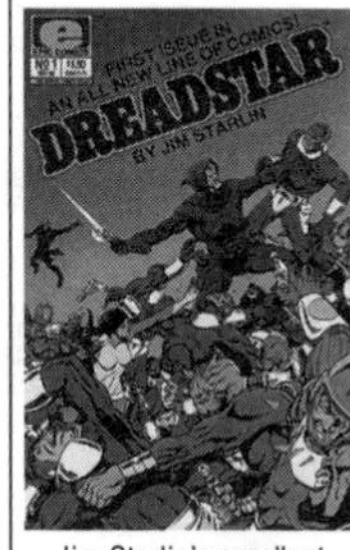

Jim Starlin's excellent space opera

©Marvel

Dream Corridor (Harlan Ellison's...)

Adaptation anthology of Ellison stories

©Dark Horse

N-MINT

❑19 .... 2.95
❑20 .... 2.95

DRIFTER
BRAINSTORM

❑1, b&w 2.95

DRIFTERS
INFINITY

❑1, Oct 1986 .... 2.00

DRIFTERS
CORNERSTONE

❑1, b&w 2.00

DRIVE-IN (JOE LANSDALE'S)
AVATAR

❑1, Nov 2003 .... 3.50
❑1/A, Nov 2003; Wrap Cover 3.95
❑2, Dec 2003 .... 3.50
❑3, Jan 2004 .... 3.95
❑3/A, Jan 2004; Wrap Cover 3.50
❑4, Mar 2004 .... 3.50

DROIDS
MARVEL / STAR

❑1, Apr 1986 .... 3.00
❑2, Jun 1986 JR (a) 2.00
❑3, Aug 1986 .... 2.00
❑4, Oct 1986 .... 2.00
❑5, Dec 1986 .... 2.00
❑6, Feb 1987; A New Hope told from droids' p.o.v. 2.00
❑7, Apr 1987; A New Hope told from droids' p.o.v. 2.00
❑8, Jun 1987; A New Hope told from droids' p.o.v. 2.00

DROOL MAGAZINE
CO. & SONS

❑1 .... 3.00

DROOPY
DARK HORSE

❑1, Oct 1995; Screwball Squirrel back-up 2.50
❑2, Nov 1995; Wolf and Red back-up . 2.50
❑3, Dec 1995; Screwball Squirrel back-up 2.50

DROPSIE AVENUE: THE NEIGHBORHOOD
KITCHEN SINK

❑1, Jun 1995, b&w 15.95

DRUID
MARVEL

❑1, May 1995 .... 2.50
❑2, Jun 1995 .... 1.95
❑3, Jul 1995 .... 1.95
❑4, Aug 1995 .... 1.95

DRUNKEN FIST
JADEMAN

❑1, Aug 1988 .... 1.95
❑2, Sep 1988 .... 1.95
❑3, Oct 1988 .... 1.95
❑4, Nov 1988 .... 1.95
❑5, Dec 1988 .... 1.95
❑6, Jan 1989 .... 1.95
❑7, Feb 1989 .... 1.95
❑8, Mar 1989 .... 1.95
❑9, Apr 1989 .... 1.95
❑10, May 1989 .... 1.95
❑11, Jun 1989 .... 1.95
❑12, Jul 1989 .... 1.95
❑13, Aug 1989 .... 1.95
❑14, Sep 1989 .... 1.95
❑15, Oct 1989 .... 1.95
❑16, Nov 1989 .... 1.95
❑17, Dec 1989 .... 1.95
❑18, Jan 1990 .... 1.95
❑19, Feb 1990 .... 1.95
❑20, Mar 1990 .... 1.95
❑21, Apr 1990 .... 1.95
❑22, May 1990 .... 1.95
❑23, Jun 1990 .... 1.95
❑24, Jul 1990 .... 1.95
❑25, Aug 1990 .... 1.95
❑26, Sep 1990 .... 1.95
❑27, Oct 1990 .... 1.95
❑28, Nov 1990 .... 1.95
❑29, Dec 1990 .... 1.95
❑30, Jan 1991 .... 1.95
❑31, Feb 1991 .... 1.95
❑32, Mar 1991 .... 1.95
❑33, Apr 1991 .... 1.95
❑34, May 1991 .... 1.95
❑35, Jun 1991 .... 1.95
❑36, Jul 1991 .... 1.95
❑37, Aug 1991 .... 1.95
❑38, Sep 1991 .... 1.95
❑39, Oct 1991 .... 1.95
❑40, Nov 1991 .... 1.95
❑41, Dec 1991 .... 1.95
❑42, Jan 1992 .... 1.95
❑43, Feb 1992 .... 1.95
❑44, Mar 1992 .... 1.95
❑45, Apr 1992 .... 1.95
❑46, May 1992 .... 1.95
❑47, Jun 1992 .... 1.95
❑48, Jul 1992 .... 1.95
❑49, Aug 1992 .... 1.95
❑50, Sep 1992 .... 1.95
❑51, Oct 1992 .... 1.95
❑52, Nov 1992 .... 1.95
❑53, Dec 1992 .... 1.95
❑54, Jan 1993 .... 1.95

DRY ROT
ZOLTON

❑1, b&w 2.95

DUCK AND COVER
CAT-HEAD

❑1, b&w 2.00
❑2, b&w 2.00

DUCKBOTS
BLACKTHORNE

❑1, Feb 1987 .... 2.00
❑2 .... 2.00

DUCKMAN
DARK HORSE

❑1, Sep 1990, b&w 1: Duckman. 2.00
❑2, b&w 2.00
❑Special 1, Apr 1990, b&w 2.00

DUCKMAN (TOPPS)
TOPPS

❑1, Nov 1994 .... 2.50
❑2, Dec 1994 .... 2.50
❑3, Mar 1995 .... 2.50
❑4, Mar 1995 .... 2.50
❑5, May 1995 .... 2.50
❑6 .... 2.50

DUCKMAN: THE MOB FROG SAGA
TOPPS

❑1, Nov 1994 .... 2.50
❑2, Dec 1994 .... 2.50
❑3, Feb 1995 .... 2.50

DUCKTALES (GLADSTONE)
GLADSTONE

❑1, Oct 1988 CB (a) 2.00
❑2, Nov 1988 .... 1.50
❑3, Jan 1989 .... 1.50
❑4, Feb 1989 .... 1.50
❑5, Apr 1989 .... 1.50
❑6, May 1989 .... 1.50
❑7, Jul 1989 .... 1.50
❑8, Aug 1989 .... 1.50
❑9, Oct 1989 CB (a) 1.50
❑10, Nov 1989 CB (a) 1.50
❑11, Jan 1990 CB (a) 1.50
❑12, Mar 1990 CB (a) 1.50
❑13, May 1990 CB (a) 1.50

DUCKTALES (DISNEY'S...)
DISNEY

❑1, Jun 1990 .... 2.00
❑2, Jul 1990 .... 1.50
❑3, Aug 1990 V: Magica de Spell 1.50
❑4, Sep 1990 .... 1.50
❑5, Oct 1990 .... 1.50
❑6, Nov 1990 .... 1.50
❑7, Dec 1990 .... 1.50
❑8, Jan 1991 .... 1.50
❑9, Feb 1991 .... 1.50
❑10, Mar 1991 .... 1.50
❑11, Apr 1991 .... 1.50
❑12, May 1991 .... 1.50
❑13, Jun 1991 .... 1.50
❑14, Jul 1991 .... 1.50
❑15, Aug 1991 .... 1.50
❑16, Sep 1991 .... 1.50
❑17, Oct 1991 .... 1.50
❑18, Nov 1991 .... 1.50

DUCKTALES: THE MOVIE
DISNEY

❑1; adaptation 5.95

DUDLEY DO-RIGHT
CHARLTON

❑1, Aug 1970 .... 45.00
❑2, Oct 1970 .... 18.00
❑3, Dec 1970 .... 12.00
❑4, Feb 1971 .... 10.00
❑5, Apr 1971 .... 10.00
❑6, Jun 1971 .... 10.00
❑7, Aug 1971 .... 10.00

Other grades: Multiply price above by 5/6 for VF/NM • 2/3 for VERY FINE • 1/3 for FINE • 1/5 for VERY GOOD • 1/8 for GOOD

DUEL MASTERS
DREAMWAVE

❑1, Nov 2003 2.95
❑1/Dynamic, Nov 2003; Holofoil Cover 5.95
❑1/A, Dec 2003 2.95
❑1/B, Nov 2003; no holo-foil on cover; packaged with cards 5.95
❑2, Dec 2003 2.95
❑3, Jan 2004 2.95
❑3/2nd, Mar 2004 2.95
❑4, Apr 2004 2.95
❑5, May 2004 3.95
❑6, Jun 2004 2.95
❑7, Aug 2004 2.95
❑8, Sep 2004 0.00

DUMB-ASS EXPRESS
MCMANN & TATE

❑1; slightly oversized 2.95

DUMM $2099
PARODY

❑1; Cover forms triptych with Rummage $2099, Pummeler $2099 2.95

DUNE
MARVEL

❑1, Apr 1985 BSz (a) 1.50
❑2, May 1985 BSz (a) 1.50
❑3, Jun 1985 BSz (a) 1.50

DUNG BOYS
KITCHEN SINK

❑1, Apr 1996, b&w 2.95
❑2, May 1996; nude cover with black bars 2.95
❑3, Jun 1996 2.95

DUNGEON
NBM

❑1, ca. 2002, Several characters in profile on cover 2.95

DUNGEONEERS
SILVERWOLF

❑1 1.50
❑2, Oct 1986 1.50
❑3, Nov 1986 1.50
❑4 1.50

DUNGEONS & DRAGONS: WHERE SHADOWS FALL
KENZER AND COMPANY

❑1, Aug 2003 3.50
❑2, Oct 2003 3.50
❑3, Dec 2003 3.50
❑4, Feb 2004 3.50
❑5, Jul 2004 3.50

DUPLEX PLANET ILLUSTRATED
FANTAGRAPHICS

❑1, Jan 1993, b&w 2.95
❑2 1993 2.50
❑3 1993 2.50
❑4 1993 2.50
❑5 1993 2.95
❑6 1994 2.95
❑7 1994, b&w 2.50
❑8, May 1994, b&w 2.50
❑9, Jul 1994, b&w 2.50
❑10, Sep 1994, b&w 2.50
❑11, Dec 1994 2.50
❑12 1995 2.50
❑13 1995 2.50
❑14 1995 2.50
❑15, Apr 1996, b&w 4.95

DURANGO KID
AC

❑1; some color 2.50
❑2, b&w 2.75
❑3 4.95

DUSK
DEADWOOD

❑1, b&w; cardstock cover 3.00

DUSTY STAR
IMAGE

❑0, Apr 1997, b&w; collects stories from Negative Burn #28 and #37 2.95
❑1, Jun 1997, b&w 2.95

DV8
DC / WILDSTORM

❑0, Dec 1998, 3.00
❑½, Jan 1997, Wizard 1/2 Promotional edition 3.00
❑½/A, Jan 1997, Wizard 1/2 Promotional edition; variant cover 3.00
❑½/Gold, Jan 1997, Wizard 1/2 "Authentic Gold" promotional edition 3.00
❑½/Platinum, Jan 1997, Wizard 1/2 Platinum promotional edition; Wizard promotional item; platinum version 3.00
❑1/A, Aug 1996, cover says Sep, indicia says Aug 3.00
❑1/B, Aug 1996, cover says Sep, indicia says Aug 3.00
❑1/C, Aug 1996, cover says Sep, indicia says Aug 3.00
❑1/D, Aug 1996, cover says Sep, indicia says Aug 3.00
❑1/E, Aug 1996, cover says Sep, indicia says Aug 3.00
❑1/F, Aug 1996, cover says Sep, indicia says Aug 3.00
❑1/G, Aug 1996, cover says Sep, indicia says Aug 3.00
❑1/H, Aug 1996, cover says Sep, indicia says Aug 3.00
❑2, Nov 1996 2.50
❑3, Dec 1996 2.50
❑4, Jan 1997 2.50
❑5, Feb 1997 2.50
❑6, Mar 1997 2.50
❑7, Apr 1997, cover says May, indicia says Apr 2.50
❑8, May 1997, cover says Jun, indicia says May 2.50
❑9, Jun 1997 2.50
❑10, Jul 1997 2.50
❑11, Sep 1997 2.50
❑12, Oct 1997 2.50
❑13, Nov 1997 2.50
❑14/A, Dec 1997, Has woman on cover 2.50
❑14/B, Dec 1997, Whole group on cover; white background 2.50
❑14/C, Dec 1997, Voyager pack with preview of Danger Girl 5.00
❑15, Jan 1998 2.50
❑16, Feb 1998 2.50
❑17, Apr 1998 2.50
❑18, May 1998 2.50
❑19, Jun 1998 2.50
❑20, Jul 1998 2.50
❑21, Aug 1998 2.50
❑22, Sep 1998 2.50
❑22/A, Sep 1998, alternate cover (white background) 2.50
❑23, Oct 1998 2.50
❑24, Nov 1998 2.50
❑25, Dec 1998 2.50
❑26, May 1999 2.50
❑27, Jun 1999 2.50
❑28, Jul 1999 2.50
❑29, Aug 1999 2.50
❑30, Sep 1999 2.50
❑31, Oct 1999 2.50
❑32, Nov 1999 2.50
❑Annual 1, Jan 1998 2.95
❑Annual 1999, Mar 1999, continued from Gen13 Annual 1999; wraparound cover 3.50

DV8 RAVE
IMAGE

❑1, Jul 1996 2.00

DV8 VS. BLACK OPS
IMAGE

❑1, Oct 1997 2.50
❑2, Nov 1997 2.50
❑3, Dec 1997 2.50

DYKE'S DELIGHT
FANNY

❑1 2.95
❑2 2.95

DYLAN DOG
DARK HORSE

❑1, Mar 1999 4.95
❑2, Apr 1999 4.95
❑3, May 1999 4.95
❑4, Jun 1999 4.95
❑5, Jul 1999 4.95
❑6, Aug 1999 4.95

DYNAMIC CLASSICS
DC

❑1, Sep 1978 2.50

DYNAMO
TOWER

❑1, Aug 1966 WW (a) 35.00
❑2, Oct 1966 WW (a) 25.00
❑3, Mar 1967 WW (a) 25.00
❑4, Jun 1967 WW (a) 25.00

DYNAMO JOE
FIRST

❑1, May 1986 1.50
❑2, Jun 1986 1.25
❑3, Jul 1986 1.25
❑4, Feb 1987 1.25
❑5, Mar 1987 1.25
❑6, Apr 1987 1.25
❑7, May 1987 1.25
❑8, Jun 1987 1.25
❑9, Jul 1987 1.25
❑10, Aug 1987 1.25
❑11, Sep 1987 1.25
❑12, Oct 1987 1.75
❑13, Nov 1987 1.75
❑14, Dec 1987 1.75
❑15, Jan 1988 1.75
❑Special 1, Jan 1987 1.25

DYNOMUTT
MARVEL

❑1, Nov 1977, Scooby Doo 10.00
❑2, Jan 1978, Scooby Doo 5.00
❑3, Mar 1978, Scooby Doo 3.00
❑4, May 1978, Scooby Doo 3.00
❑5, Jul 1978, Scooby Doo 3.00
❑6, Sep 1978, Scooby Doo 3.00

DYSTOPIK SNOMEN
SLAVE LABOR

❑1, Oct 1994; was college newspaper strip 4.95

DYSTOPIK SNOMEN (VOL. 2)
SLAVE LABOR

❑1, Sep 1995 1.50
❑2, Dec 1995 1.75

EAGLE (CRYSTAL)
CRYSTAL

❑1, Sep 1986 1.50
❑1/Ltd., Sep 1986; limited edition 1.50
❑2 1.50
❑3 1987 1.50
❑4, Apr 1987 1.50
❑5, May 1987 1.50
❑6, Jun 1987; Adam Hughes pin-up (his first major comics work) 1.50
❑7, Jul 1987 1.50
❑8, Aug 1987 1.50
❑9, Sep 1987 1.50
❑10, Oct 1987 1.50
❑11, Nov 1987 1.50
❑12, Dec 1987 1.50
❑13, Jan 1988 1.50
❑14, Feb 1988 1.50
❑15, Mar 1988 1.50
❑16, May 1988 1.50
❑17 1988, b&w 1.95
❑18, Sep 1988, b&w 1.95
❑19, Oct 1988, b&w 1.95
❑20, b&w 1.95
❑21 1989, b&w 1.95
❑22 1989, b&w 1.95
❑23 1989 2.25

EAGLE (COMIC ZONE)
COMIC ZONE

❑1, b&w 2.75
❑2, b&w 2.75
❑3, b&w 2.75

EAGLES DARE
AAGER

❑1 1.95
❑2, Sep 1994 1.95

EAGLE: THE DARK MIRROR SAGA
COMIC ZONE

❑1, Jan 1992 2.75
❑2 2.75
❑3 2.75

Dreaming

Uses characters from Neil Gaiman's Sandman
©DC

Dredd Rules!

More adventures of Mega City One lawman
©Fleetway-Quality

Droids

Solo outings of Star Wars favorites
©Marvel

Droopy

Tex Avery creation's misadventures
©Dark Horse

Duckman

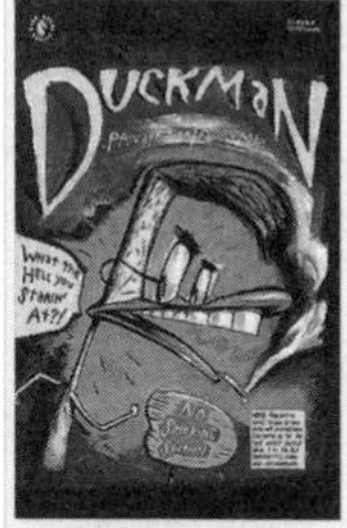

Animated series aired on USA
©Dark Horse

N-MINT

EARLY DAYS OF THE SOUTHERN KNIGHTS
Comics Interview

- ❑1 1986 .... 4.95
- ❑1/2nd 4.95
- ❑2, Feb 1987 .... 4.95
- ❑3, Jul 1987 .... 4.95
- ❑4 1987 .... 4.95
- ❑5 1988 .... 5.95
- ❑6, Nov 1988 .... 6.50
- ❑7, Jan 1989 .... 6.95
- ❑8, Mar 1989 .... 6.95

EARTH C.O.R.E.
Independent

- ❑1 .... 1.95

EARTH 4 (VOL. 2)
Continuity

- ❑1, Dec 1993; Previous series was spelled "Urth 4" 2.50
- ❑2, Dec 1993 .... 2.50
- ❑3, Dec 1993 .... 2.50
- ❑4, Jan 1994 .... 2.50

EARTH 4 DEATHWATCH 2000
Continuity

- ❑0, Apr 1993; Trading Cards 2.50
- ❑1, Apr 1993; trading cards; indicia says #0, a misprint 2.50
- ❑2, May 1993; trading card 2.50
- ❑3, Aug 1993; trading card; Deathwatch 2000 dropped from indicia 2.50

EARTHLORE
Eternity

- ❑1 .... 2.00
- ❑2 .... 2.00

EARTHWORM JIM
Marvel

- ❑1, Dec 1995; based on video game 2.25
- ❑2, Jan 1996 .... 2.25
- ❑3, Feb 1996 .... 2.25
- ❑4, Mar 1996 .... 2.25

EARTH X
Marvel

- ❑0, Mar 1999 ARo (c); ARo (w); ARo (a) 4.00
- ❑0/A, Mar 1999; ARo (c); ARo (w); ARo (a); A: X-51. A: Watcher. Covers of series form giant picture 5.00
- ❑0/B, Mar 1999; ARo (c); ARo (w); ARo (a); A: X-51. A: Watcher. Covers of series form giant picture 4.00
- ❑0/C, Mar 1999; ARo (c); ARo (w); ARo (a); A: X-51. A: Watcher. DFE alternate cover 5.00
- ❑1, Apr 1999; ARo (c); ARo (w); ARo (a); A: Inhumans. A: Hydra. Covers of series form giant picture 3.00
- ❑1/A, Apr 1999; ARo (c); ARo (w); ARo (a); A: Inhumans. A: Hydra. Covers of series form giant picture 5.00
- ❑1/B, Apr 1999; ARo (w); A: Inhumans. A: Hydra. DFE alternate cover 3.50
- ❑1/C, Apr 1999; ARo (w); A: Inhumans. A: Hydra. DFE alternate cover 5.00
- ❑2, May 1999 ARo (c); ARo (w); ARo (a) 2.99
- ❑3, Jun 1999 ARo (c); ARo (w); ARo (a) 2.99
- ❑4, Jul 1999 ARo (c); ARo (w); ARo (a); 2.99
- ❑5, Aug 1999 ARo (c); ARo (w); ARo (a) 2.99
- ❑6, Sep 1999 ARo (c); ARo (w); ARo (a) 2.99
- ❑7, Oct 1999 ARo (c); ARo (w); ARo (a); 2.99
- ❑8, Nov 1999 ARo (c); ARo (w); ARo (a) 2.99
- ❑9, Dec 1999 ARo (c); ARo (w); ARo (a) 2.99
- ❑10 2000 ARo (c); ARo (w); ARo (a); 2.99
- ❑11, Mar 2000 ARo (c); ARo (w); ARo (a) 2.99
- ❑12, Apr 2000 ARo (c); ARo (w); ARo (a) 2.99
- ❑13, Jun 2000; ARo (c); ARo (w); ARo (a); "X" issue 3.99

EARTH X SKETCHBOOK
Marvel

- ❑1, Mar 1999 .... 4.50

EAST MEETS WEST
Innovation

- ❑1, Apr 1990 .... 2.50

EASY WAY
Idea & Design Works

- ❑1, ca. 2005 .... 3.99
- ❑2 2005 .... 3.99
- ❑3 2005 .... 3.99
- ❑4, Sep 2005 .... 3.99

EAT-MAN
Viz

- ❑1, Aug 1997, b&w 2.95
- ❑2, Sep 1997, b&w 2.95
- ❑3, Oct 1997, b&w 2.95
- ❑4, Nov 1997, b&w 2.95
- ❑5, Dec 1997, b&w 2.95
- ❑6, Jan 1997, b&w 2.95

EAT-MAN SECOND COURSE
Viz

- ❑1, Feb 1998, b&w 2.95
- ❑2, Mar 1998, b&w 3.50
- ❑3, Apr 1998, b&w 3.50
- ❑4, May 1998, b&w 3.25
- ❑5, b&w 2.95

EB'NN
Now

- ❑3, Jun 1986 .... 1.50
- ❑4, Aug 1986 .... 1.50
- ❑5, Nov 1986 .... 1.50
- ❑6, Jan 1987 .... 1.50

EB'NN THE RAVEN
Crowquill

- ❑1 .... 3.00
- ❑2 .... 3.00

EBONY WARRIOR
Africa Rising

- ❑1, Apr 1993 .... 1.95

E.C. CLASSIC REPRINTS
East Coast Comix

- ❑1, May 1973; AF (w); GE, JO, GI (a); Reprints Crypt of Terror #1 (a series meant to have been launched when EC ceased publishing horror) 4.00
- ❑2, AF (w); AW, JO, WW, JKa (a); Reprints Weird Science #15 .... 3.00
- ❑3, Reprints Shock SuspenStories #12 3.00
- ❑4, Reprints Haunt of Fear #12 .... 3.00
- ❑5, Reprints Weird Fantasy #13 .... 3.00
- ❑6, GE, BK (a); Reprints Crime Suspen Stories #25 .... 3.00
- ❑7, Reprints Vault of Horror #26 .... 3.00
- ❑8, Reprints Shock SuspenStories #6 3.00
- ❑9, Reprints Two-Fisted Tales #34 .... 3.00
- ❑10, Reprints Haunt of Fear #23 .... 3.00
- ❑11, Reprints Weird Science #12 .... 3.00
- ❑12, ca. 1976; Reprints Shock SuspenStories #2 .... 3.00

EC CLASSICS
Cochran

- ❑1 .... 5.00
- ❑2 .... 5.00
- ❑3 .... 5.00
- ❑4 .... 5.00
- ❑5, AW (a); Reprints from Weird Fantasy #14, 15, 16, 17 .... 5.00
- ❑6 .... 5.00

ECHO
Image

- ❑0, Jul 2000 .... 2.50
- ❑1, Mar 2000 .... 2.95
- ❑2, Apr 2000 .... 2.50
- ❑3, May 2000 .... 2.50
- ❑4, Jun 2000 .... 2.50
- ❑5, Sep 2000 .... 2.50

ECHO OF FUTUREPAST
Continuity

- ❑1, May 1984 .... 2.95
- ❑2 1984 .... 2.95
- ❑3, Nov 1984 .... 2.95
- ❑4, Feb 1985 .... 2.95
- ❑5, Apr 1985 .... 2.95
- ❑6, Jul 1985 .... 2.95
- ❑7, Aug 1985 .... 2.95
- ❑8, Dec 1985 .... 2.95
- ❑9, Jan 1986 .... 2.95

ECLIPSE GRAPHIC ALBUM SERIES
Eclipse

- ❑1, Oct 1978; PG (a); Sabre 7.00
- ❑1/2nd; PG (a); Sabre 6.00
- ❑1/3rd; Sabre: 10th anniversary; PG (a); Sabre 5.95
- ❑2, Nov 1979; CR (w); CR (a); Night Music 5.00
- ❑3, May 1980; MR (a); Detectives, Inc. 6.95
- ❑4; GC (a); Stewart the Rat 5.95
- ❑5; JSn (w); JSn (a); The Price 7.00
- ❑6; MR (a); I am Coyote 6.00
- ❑7; DSt (w); DSt (a); The Rocketeer 8.00
- ❑7/HC; Hardcover edition; DSt (w); DSt (a); Hardcover; The Rocketeer 19.95
- ❑7/2nd; DSt (w); DSt (a); The Rocketeer 7.95
- ❑7/3rd; DSt (w); DSt (a); The Rocketeer 9.00
- ❑8; Zorro 6.00
- ❑9, Feb 1987; Somerset Holmes; The Sacred and the Profane 14.00
- ❑10, Mar 1987; BA (a); Sacred & Profane; Somerset Holmes 14.00
- ❑10/HC, Mar 1987; Hardcover edition; BA (a); Hardcover; Somerset Holmes 24.95
- ❑11 1987; Floyd Farland 25.00
- ❑12, Jul 1987; Silverheels 7.95
- ❑12/HC, Jul 1987, b&w; Hardcover edition; Silverheels; Hardcover Edition 14.95

	N-MINT
❑12/Ltd., Jul 1987; Signed hardcover; Silverheels	24.95
❑13; The Sisterhood of Steel	9.00
❑14; Samurai, Son of Death	5.00
❑15; Twisted Tales	3.95
❑16; Air Fighters Classics #1	4.50
❑17; PG (a); Valkyrie: Prisoner of the Past	6.95
❑18; Air Fighters Classics #2	4.50
❑19; Scout: Four Monsters; Collects Scout #1-7	14.95
❑20; Air Fighters Classics #3	4.50
❑21; XYR "choose your own adventure" game	3.95
❑22; Alien Worlds	5.00
❑23; Air Fighters Classics #4	4.50
❑24; Heartbreak Comics	5.00
❑25; ATh (w); ATh (a); Alex Toth's Zorro #1	9.00
❑26; ATh (w); ATh (a); Alex Toth's Zorro #2	9.00
❑27; She; Fast Fiction	6.00
❑28; AMo (w); DaG, BSz, TY (a); Brought to Light	9.00
❑29; JK (w); JK (a); Miracleman Book One	15.00
❑30; AMo (w); BSz, JK (a); Real Love: The Best of Simon & Kirby Romance Comics	9.00
❑30/HC, b&w; Hardcover edition; AMo (w); BSz (a); Hardcover Edition	30.00
❑31; Pigeons from Hell	7.00
❑31/Ltd.; Limited hardcover edition; Limited hardcover edition	30.00
❑32; HK, JK (w); HK, JK (a); Teenaged Dope Slaves & Reform School Girls	9.95
❑33; Bogie	9.95
❑34; Air Fighters Classics #5	3.95
❑35; Into the Shadow of the Sun; Rael	7.95
❑36; CR (a); Ariane & Bluebeard	4.95
❑37; Air Fighters Classics #6	3.95
❑38; Doctor Watchstop	8.95
❑39; MGr (a); James Bond 007: Permission to Die 1	4.95
❑40; MGr (a); James Bond 007: Permission to Die 2	4.95
❑41; MGr (a); James Bond 007: Permission to Die 3	4.95
❑42; MGr (a); James Bond 007: Licence to Kill	8.95
❑43; Tapping the Vein #1	7.95
❑44; Hobbit #1	5.95
❑45; Toadswart	10.95
❑46; Tapping the Vein #2	7.95
❑47; Scout: Mount Fire	14.95
❑48; Moderne Man Comics	9.95
❑49; Tapping the Vein #3	6.95
❑50; Miracleman Book Two	12.95
❑51; Tapping the Vein 4	7.95
❑52; James Bond 007: Permission to Die #3	4.95

ECLIPSE MAGAZINE
ECLIPSE

❑1, May 1981, b&w	2.95
❑2, Jul 1981	2.95
❑3, Nov 1981	2.95
❑4, Jan 1982	2.95
❑5, Mar 1982	2.95
❑6, Jul 1982	2.95
❑7, Nov 1982	2.95
❑8, Jan 1983	2.95

ECLIPSE MONTHLY
ECLIPSE

❑1, Aug 1983	2.00
❑2, Sep 1983	2.00
❑3, Oct 1983	2.00
❑4, Jan 1984	1.50
❑5, Feb 1984	1.50
❑6, Mar 1984	1.50
❑7, Apr 1984	1.50
❑8, May 1984	1.50
❑9, Jun 1984	1.50
❑10, Jul 1984	1.50

ECLIPSO
DC

	N-MINT
❑1, Nov 1992	2.00
❑2, Dec 1992 KG (a)	1.75
❑3, Jan 1993 KG (a)	1.75
❑4, Feb 1993 KG, LMc (a)	1.50
❑5, Mar 1993 KG, LMc (a)	1.50
❑6, Apr 1993 KG, LMc (a)	1.25
❑7, May 1993 KG (a)	1.25
❑8, Jun 1993	1.25
❑9, Jul 1993	1.25
❑10, Aug 1993	1.25
❑11, Sep 1993	1.25
❑12, Oct 1993	1.25
❑13, Nov 1993	1.25
❑14, Dec 1993	1.25
❑15, Jan 1994	1.50
❑16, Feb 1994	1.50
❑17, Mar 1994	1.50
❑18, Apr 1994 A: Spectre	1.50
❑Annual 1, ca. 1993 1: Prism	2.50

ECLIPSO: THE DARKNESS WITHIN
DC

❑1, Jul 1992; KG (w); KG (a); Without plastic gem (newsstand version)	2.50
❑1/Direct ed., Jul 1992; Direct Market edition; KG (w); KG (a); plastic diamond glued to cover	3.00
❑2, Jul 1992	2.50

ECTOKID
MARVEL

❑1, Sep 1993; Foil embossed cover	2.50
❑2, Oct 1993	1.75
❑3, Nov 1993	1.75
❑4, Dec 1993	1.75
❑5, Jan 1994	1.75
❑6, Feb 1994	1.75
❑7, Mar 1994	1.75
❑8, Apr 1994	1.75
❑9, May 1994	1.75

ECTOKID UNLEASHED!
MARVEL

❑1, Oct 1994	2.95

ED
3CG COMICS

❑1, Mar 1997, b&w	2.95

EDDY CURRENT
MAD DOG

❑1, Jul 1987	2.50
❑2, Sep 1987	2.50
❑3, Oct 1987	2.50
❑4, Nov 1987	2.50
❑5, Jan 1988	2.50
❑6, Feb 1988	2.50
❑7, Apr 1988 A: Amazing Broccoli.	2.50
❑8, Jun 1988	2.50
❑9, Jul 1988	2.50
❑10, Sep 1988	2.50
❑11, Nov 1988	2.50
❑12, Dec 1988	2.50

EDEN DESCENDANTS
QUESTER ENTERTAINMENT

❑1, b&w; cardstock cover	3.95

EDEN MATRIX
ADHESIVE

❑1/A	2.95
❑1/B	2.95

EDEN'S TRAIL
MARVEL

❑1, Jan 2003	2.99
❑2, Feb 2003	2.99
❑3, Mar 2003	2.99
❑4, Apr 2003	2.99
❑5, May 2003	2.99

EDGAR ALLAN POE
ETERNITY

❑1 1988, b&w; Black Cat	1.95
❑2 1988, b&w; Pit & Pendulum	1.95
❑3, Dec 1988, b&w; Red Death	1.95
❑4 1989, b&w; Rue Morgue	1.95
❑5 1989, b&w; Tell-Tale Heart	1.95

EDGE
MALIBU / BRAVURA

	N-MINT
❑1, Jul 1994, GK (a); 1: The Ultimates. 1: Intruder. 1: Edge. 1: Will Power. 1: Barricade. 1: Free Agent. 1: Winged Victory. 1: Phaseshifter.	2.50
❑1/Gold, Jul 1994; sendaway with gold ink on cover	
❑2, Aug 1994, GK (a)	2.50
❑3, Apr 1995, GK (a); story concludes in 'Books' The Last Heroes	2.95

EDGE OF CHAOS
PACIFIC

❑1, Jul 1983, GM (a);	1.00
❑2, Oct 1984, GM (a); Adam Kubert's first major comics work	1.00
❑3, Jan 1983, GM (a);	1.00

EEK! THE CAT
HAMILTON

❑1, Feb 1994; TV show	1.95
❑2, Mar 1994; TV show	1.95
❑3, Apr 1994; TV show	1.95

EERIE (I.W.)
I.W.

❑1	24.00
❑2	17.00

EERIE QUEERIE!
TOKYOPOP

❑1, Mar 2004	9.99
❑2 2004	9.99
❑3, Jun 2004	9.99
❑4, Sep 2004	9.99

EERIE TALES
SUPER

❑12, Reprints(?)	15.00

EGON
DARK HORSE

❑1, Jan 1998	2.95
❑2	2.95

EGYPT
DC / VERTIGO

❑1, Aug 1995	2.50
❑2, Sep 1995	2.50
❑3, Oct 1995	2.50
❑4, Nov 1995	2.50
❑5, Dec 1995	2.50
❑6, Jan 1996	2.50
❑7, Feb 1996	2.50

EHLISSA
HIGHLAND GRAPHICS

❑1, Nov 1992; Color on cover	2.00
❑1/2nd; Black & white cover	2.00
❑1/3rd; Black & white cover	2.00
❑2, Dec 1992; Color on cover	2.00
❑2/2nd; Black & white cover	2.00
❑3, Jan 1993; Color on cover	2.00
❑3/2nd; Black & white cover	2.00
❑4, Mar 1993; Color on cover	2.00
❑4/2nd; Black & white cover	2.00
❑5, Mar 1993; Color on cover	2.00
❑5/2nd; Black & white cover	2.00
❑6; Color on cover	2.00
❑6/2nd; Black & white cover	2.00
❑7; Color on cover	2.00
❑7/2nd; Black & white cover	2.00
❑8, May 1993; Color on cover	2.00
❑8/2nd; Black & white cover	2.00
❑9, Jul 1993; Color on cover	2.00
❑9/2nd; Black & white cover	2.00
❑10 1993; Color on cover	2.00
❑10/2nd; Black & white cover	2.00
❑11 1993; Color on cover	2.00
❑11/2nd; Black & white cover	2.00
❑12 1993; Color on cover	2.00
❑12/2nd; Black & white cover	2.00
❑13 1993; Color on cover	2.00
❑13/2nd; Black & white cover	2.00
❑14, Jan 1994; Color on cover	2.00
❑14/2nd; Black & white cover	2.00
❑15, Feb 1994; Color cover	2.00
❑15/2nd; Black & white cover	2.00
❑16, Mar 1994; Color on cover	2.00
❑16/2nd; Black & white cover	2.00
❑17, Apr 1994; Color on cover	2.00
❑17/2nd; Black & white cover	2.00
❑18, May 1994; Color on cover	2.00
❑18/2nd; Black & white cover	2.00
❑19, Jun 1994; Color on cover	2.00
❑19/2nd; Black & white cover	2.00
❑20, Jul 1994; Color on cover	2.00
❑20/2nd; Black & white cover	2.00
❑21, Aug 1994	2.00
❑22, Sep 1994	2.00

Other grades: Multiply price above by 5/6 for VF/NM • 2/3 for VERY FINE • 1/3 for FINE • 1/5 for VERY GOOD • 1/8 for GOOD

Dumm $2099

One of trio of Marvel 2099 parodies

©Parody

Dynamo

Super-belt powers T.H.U.N.D.E.R. agent

©Tower

Dynomutt

Blue Falcon sidekick's solo adventures

©Marvel

Earth X

Alex Ross covers form one large image

©Marvel

E.C. Classic Reprints

Early 1970s reprints from East Coast Comix

©East Coast Comix

N-MINT

❑23, Oct 1994 ... 2.00
❑24, Nov 1994 ... 2.00
❑25, Dec 1994 ... 2.00
❑26, Jan 1995 ... 2.00
❑27, Feb 1995 ... 2.00
❑28, Mar 1995 ... 2.00
❑29, Apr 1995 ... 2.00
❑30, May 1995 ... 2.00
❑31, Jun 1995; has #27's indicia ... 2.00
❑32 ... 2.00
❑33 ... 2.00

EIGHTBALL
FANTAGRAPHICS

❑1 ... 10.00
❑1/2nd ... 5.00
❑1/3rd ... 3.50
❑1/4th ... 3.00
❑2 ... 6.00
❑3 ... 5.00
❑4 ... 5.00
❑5 ... 4.00
❑6 ... 4.00
❑7 ... 4.00
❑8 ... 4.00
❑9 ... 3.00
❑10 ... 3.00
❑11 ... 3.00
❑12, Nov 1993 ... 3.00
❑13 ... 3.00
❑14 ... 3.00
❑15 ... 3.00
❑16, Nov 1995; cardstock cover ... 4.00
❑17 ... 2.95
❑18, Mar 1997 ... 2.95
❑19, May 1998 ... 3.95
❑20, Feb 1999; cardstock cover ... 4.50
❑21, Feb 2000 ... 4.95
❑22, Aug 2001 ... 2.95
❑23, Jul 2004 ... 2.95

EIGHTH WONDER
DARK HORSE

❑1, Nov 1997, b&w; cover says The 8th Wonder, indicia says The Eighth Wonder ... 2.95

EIGHT LEGGED FREAKS
WILDSTORM

❑1, Sep 2002, Several characters in profile on cover ... 6.95

80 PAGE GIANT MAGAZINE
DC

❑1, Aug 1964, Superman; Imaginary stories ... 295.00
❑2, Sep 1964, Jimmy Olsen ... 150.00
❑3, Sep 1964, Lois Lane ... 125.00
❑4, Oct 1964, CI (a); Flash ... 125.00
❑5, Nov 1964, Batman ... 125.00
❑6, Jan 1965, Superman ... 125.00
❑7, Feb 1965, Sgt. Rock ... 150.00
❑8, Mar 1965, Secret Origins ... 265.00
❑9, Apr 1965, CI (c); MA, CI (a); Flash; reprints stories from Showcase #14, and Flash #106, 108, 117, and 123. ... 125.00
❑10, May 1965, Superboy ... 125.00
❑11, Jun 1965, Superman ... 125.00

N-MINT

❑12, Jul 1965, Batman ... 80.00
❑13, Aug 1965, Jimmy Olsen ... 80.00
❑14, Sep 1965, Lois Lane ... 80.00
❑15, Oct 1965, Batman/Superman; reprints stories from World's Finest Comics #74, #81, #82, #88, #95, and #97 ... 80.00

86 VOLTZ: DEAD GIRL ONE-SHOT
IMAGE

❑1, ca. 2005 ... 5.95

EKOS PREVIEW
ASPEN

❑1, Jan 2004 ... 8.00

EL ARSENAL UNKNOWN ENEMY
ARCANA

❑1, Sep 2005 ... 2.95
❑2, Oct 2005 ...

EL CAZADOR
CROSSGEN

❑1, Oct 2003 ... 2.95
❑1/2nd, Nov 2003 ... 2.95
❑2, Nov 2003 ... 2.95
❑3, Dec 2003 ... 2.95
❑4, Jan 2004 ... 2.95
❑4/2nd, Feb 2004 ... 2.95
❑5, Mar 2004 ... 2.95
❑6, May 2004 ... 2.95

EL CAZADOR: BLACKJACK TOM
CROSSGEN

❑1, Apr 2004 ... 2.95

EL DIABLO
DC

❑1, Aug 1989; Double-size ... 2.50
❑2, Sep 1989 ... 1.50
❑3, Oct 1989 ... 1.50
❑4, Dec 1989 ... 1.50
❑5, Jan 1990 ... 1.50
❑6, Feb 1990 ... 1.50
❑7, Mar 1990 ... 1.75
❑8, Apr 1990 ... 1.75
❑9, May 1990 ... 1.75
❑10, Jun 1990 ... 1.75
❑11, Jul 1990 ... 1.75
❑12, Aug 1990; Golden Age Vigilante. ... 2.00
❑13, Sep 1990 ... 2.00
❑14, Oct 1990 ... 2.00
❑15, Dec 1990 ... 2.00
❑16, Jan 1991 ... 2.00

EL DIABLO (MINI-SERIES)
DC / VERTIGO

❑1, Mar 2001 ... 2.50
❑2, Apr 2001 ... 2.50
❑3, May 2001 ... 2.50
❑4, Jun 2001 ... 2.50

ELECTRIC FEAR
SPARKS

❑1, Win 1984 ... 1.50
❑2, Spr 1986 ... 1.50

ELECTRIC GIRL
MIGHTY GREMLIN

❑1, May 1998 ... 3.50

N-MINT

❑2, Spr 1999 ... 2.95
❑3, Sum 1999 ... 2.95

ELECTRIC WARRIOR
DC

❑1, May 1986 ... 1.50
❑2, Jun 1986 ... 1.50
❑3, Jul 1986 ... 1.50
❑4, Aug 1986 ... 1.50
❑5, Sep 1986 ... 1.50
❑6, Oct 1986 ... 1.50
❑7, Nov 1986 ... 1.50
❑8, Dec 1986 ... 1.50
❑9, Jan 1987 ... 1.50
❑10, Feb 1987 ... 1.50
❑11, Mar 1987 ... 1.50
❑12, Apr 1987 ... 1.50
❑13, May 1987 ... 1.50
❑14, Jun 1987 ... 1.50
❑15, Jul 1987 ... 1.50
❑16, Aug 1987 ... 1.50
❑17, Sep 1987 ... 1.50
❑18, Oct 1987 ... 1.50

ELECTROPOLIS
IMAGE

❑1, May 2001 ... 2.95
❑2, Jun 2001 ... 2.95
❑3, Dec 2001 ... 2.95

ELEKTRA (1ST SERIES)
MARVEL

❑1, Mar 1995; enhanced cover ... 4.00
❑2, Apr 1995; enhanced cover ... 3.25
❑3, May 1995; enhanced cover ... 3.25
❑4, Jun 1995; enhanced cover ... 3.25

ELEKTRA (2ND SERIES)
MARVEL

❑-1, Jul 1997, A: Daredevil. Flashback ... 2.25
❑1, Nov 1996 ... 4.00
❑1/A, Nov 1996, variant cover ... 3.00
❑2, Dec 1996, V: Bullseye ... 2.50
❑3, Jan 1997 ... 2.50
❑4, Feb 1997 ... 2.00
❑5, Mar 1997 ... 2.00
❑6, Apr 1997, V: Razorfist. ... 2.00
❑7, May 1997 ... 2.00
❑8, Jun 1997 ... 2.00
❑9, Aug 1997, gatefold summary ... 2.00
❑10, Sep 1997, gatefold summary ... 2.00
❑11, Oct 1997, gatefold summary A: Daredevil. ... 2.00
❑12, Nov 1997, gatefold summary A: Daredevil. ... 2.00
❑13, Dec 1997, gatefold summary A: Daredevil. ... 2.00
❑14, Jan 1998, gatefold summary ... 2.00
❑15, Feb 1998, gatefold summary ... 2.00
❑16, Mar 1998, gatefold summary A: Shang-Chi. ... 2.00
❑17, Apr 1998, gatefold summary ... 2.00
❑18, May 1998, gatefold summary ... 2.00
❑19, Jun 1998, gatefold summary ... 2.00

ELEKTRA (3RD SERIES)
MARVEL / MAX

❑1, Sep 2001 ... 3.50

Other grades: Multiply price above by 5/6 for VF/NM • 2/3 for VERY FINE • 1/3 for FINE • 1/5 for VERY GOOD • 1/8 for GOOD

	N-MINT
❑2, Oct 2001	2.99
❑2/A, Oct 2001	2.99
❑3, Nov 2001	2.99
❑3/Nude, Nov 2001, b&w; Recalled due to interior nudity	15.00
❑4, Dec 2001	2.99
❑5, Jan 2002	2.99
❑6, Feb 2002, Silent issue	2.99
❑7, Mar 2002	2.99
❑8, Apr 2002	2.99
❑9, May 2002	2.99
❑10, Jun 2002	2.99
❑11, Aug 2002	2.99
❑12, Sep 2002	2.99
❑13, Oct 2002	2.99
❑14, Nov 2002	2.99
❑15, Dec 2002	2.99
❑16, Jan 2003	2.99
❑17, Jan 2003	2.99
❑18, Feb 2003	2.99
❑19, Feb 2003	2.99
❑20, Mar 2003	2.99
❑21, Jun 2003	2.99
❑22, Jun 2003	2.99
❑23, Jul 2003, TP (a)	2.99
❑24, Aug 2003, TP (a)	2.99
❑25, Sep 2003, cardstock cover	2.99
❑26, Oct 2003	2.99
❑27, Nov 2003 (c)	2.99
❑28, Dec 2003	2.99
❑29, Jan 2004	2.99
❑30, Feb 2004	2.99
❑31, Mar 2004	2.99
❑32, Apr 2004	2.99
❑33, May 2004	2.99
❑34, May 2004	2.99
❑35, Jun 2004	2.99

ELEKTRA & WOLVERINE: THE REDEEMER
MARVEL

❑1, Jan 2002	5.95
❑2, Feb 2002	5.95
❑3, Mar 2002	5.95

ELEKTRA: ASSASSIN
MARVEL / EPIC

❑1, Aug 1986 BSz (c); FM (w); BSz (a)	3.00
❑2, Sep 1986 BSz (c); FM (w); BSz (a)	2.50
❑3, Oct 1986 BSz (c); FM (w); BSz (a)	2.50
❑4, Nov 1986 BSz (c); FM (w); BSz (a)	2.50
❑5, Dec 1986 BSz (c); FM (w); BSz (a)	2.50
❑6, Jan 1987 BSz (c); FM (w); BSz (a)	2.50
❑7, Feb 1987 BSz (c); FM (w); BSz (a)	2.50
❑8, Mar 1987; BSz (c); FM (w); BSz (a); Relatively scarce	3.00

ELEKTRA/CYBLADE
IMAGE

❑1, Mar 1997; crossover with Marvel; concludes in Silver Surfer/Weapon Zero	2.95
❑1/A, Mar 1997; Alternate cover; crossover with Marvel; concludes in Silver Surfer/Weapon Zero	2.95

ELEKTRA: GLIMPSE & ECHO
MARVEL

❑1, Sep 2002, Several characters in profile on cover	2.99
❑2, Oct 2002	2.99
❑3, Nov 2002	2.99
❑4, Dec 2002	2.99

ELEKTRA LIVES AGAIN
MARVEL / EPIC

❑1, Mar 1991; hardcover	24.95

ELEKTRA MEGAZINE
MARVEL

❑1, Nov 1996, Reprints Elektra stories from Daredevil	3.95
❑2, Nov 1996, Reprints Elektra stories from Daredevil	3.95

ELEKTRA SAGA
MARVEL

	N-MINT
❑1, Feb 1984; FM (w); FM (a); Daredevil reprint	4.00
❑2, Mar 1984; FM (w); FM (a); Daredevil reprint	3.50
❑3, Apr 1984; FM (w); FM (a); Daredevil reprint	3.50
❑4, May 1984; FM (w); FM (a); Daredevil reprint	3.50

ELEKTRA: THE HAND
MARVEL

❑1, Sep 2004	2.99
❑2, Oct 2004	2.99
❑3, Nov 2004	2.99
❑4, Dec 2004	2.99
❑5, Jan 2005	2.99

ELEKTRA: THE MOVIE
MARVEL

❑1,	5.99

ELEMENTALS (VOL. 1)
COMICO

❑1 1984	2.50
❑2 1985	2.00
❑3 1985	2.00
❑4, Jun 1985	2.00
❑5, Dec 1985	2.00
❑6, Feb 1986	1.50
❑7, Apr 1986	1.50
❑8, Jun 1986	1.50
❑9, Aug 1986	1.50
❑10, Oct 1986	1.50
❑11, Dec 1986	1.50
❑12, Feb 1987	1.50
❑13, Apr 1987	1.50
❑14, Jun 1987	1.50
❑15, Jul 1987	1.50
❑16, Aug 1987	1.50
❑17, Sep 1987	1.50
❑18, Oct 1987	1.50
❑19, Nov 1987	1.50
❑20, Dec 1987	1.50
❑21, Jan 1988	1.50
❑22, Feb 1988	1.50
❑23, Mar 1988	1.75
❑24, Apr 1988	1.75
❑25, May 1988	1.75
❑26, Jun 1988	1.75
❑27, Jul 1988	1.75
❑28, Aug 1988	1.75
❑29, Sep 1988	1.75
❑Special 1, Mar 1986; Child abuse special	3.00
❑Special 2, Jan 1989	1.95

ELEMENTALS (VOL. 2)
COMICO

❑1, Mar 1989	2.50
❑2, Apr 1989	2.00
❑3, May 1989	2.00
❑4, Jun 1989	2.50
❑5, Jul 1989	2.50
❑6, Aug 1989	2.50
❑7, Sep 1989	2.50
❑8, Oct 1989	2.50
❑9, Nov 1989	2.50
❑10, Dec 1989	2.50
❑11, Jan 1990	2.50
❑12, Feb 1990	2.50
❑13, Mar 1990	2.50
❑14, May 1990	2.50
❑15, Jul 1990	2.50
❑16, May 1991	2.50
❑17, May 1991	2.50
❑18, Jun 1991	2.50
❑19, Aug 1991	2.50
❑20, Oct 1991	2.50
❑21, Nov 1991	2.50
❑22, Mar 1992	2.50
❑23, May 1992, 1: New Monolith.	2.50
❑24, Aug 1992	2.50
❑25, Nov 1992	2.50
❑26, Apr 1993	2.50
❑27, Never published?	2.50
❑28, Never published?	2.50
❑29, Never published?	2.50
❑30, Never published?	2.50
❑31, Never published?	2.50
❑32, Never published?	2.50
❑33, Never published?	2.50
❑34, Never published?	2.50
❑35, Never published?	2.50
❑36, Never published?	2.50
❑37, Never published?	2.50
❑38, Never published?	2.50
❑39, Never published?	2.50
❑40, Never published?	2.50
❑41, Never published?	2.50

ELEMENTALS (VOL. 3)
COMICO

❑1, Dec 1995, Bagged w/ card	2.95
❑2, ca. 1996	2.95
❑3, May 1996	2.95

ELEMENTALS: GHOST OF A CHANCE
COMICO

❑1, Dec 1995	5.95

ELEMENTALS: HOW THE WAR WAS WON
COMICO

❑1, Jun 1996	2.95
❑2, Aug 1996	2.95

ELEMENTALS LINGERIE
COMICO

❑1, May 1996; pin-ups	2.95

ELEMENTALS SEX SPECIAL
COMICO

❑1/Gold, Oct 1991; Gold edition	3.50
❑1, Oct 1991	2.95
❑2, Jun 1992	2.95
❑3, Sep 1992	2.95
❑4, Feb 1993	2.95

ELEMENTALS SEX SPECIAL (2ND SERIES)
COMICO

❑1,	2.95

ELEMENTAL'S SEXY LINGERIE SPECIAL
COMICO

❑1/A, Jan 1993; without poster	2.95
❑1/B, Jan 1993	5.95

ELEMENTALS SWIMSUIT SPECTACULAR 1996
COMICO

❑1/Gold, Jun 1996; Gold edition; pin-ups	3.50
❑1, Jun 1996; pin-ups	2.95

ELEMENTALS: THE VAMPIRES' REVENGE
COMICO

❑1, Jun 1996	2.95
❑2, Jun 1996; Gold edition	3.00

ELEVEN OR ONE
SIRIUS ENTERTAINMENT

❑1, Apr 1995, reprints new story from Angry Christ Comics tpb	4.00
❑1/2nd,	3.00

ELFHEIM
NIGHTWYND

❑1 1991, b&w	2.50
❑2, b&w	2.50
❑3, b&w	2.50
❑4, b&w	2.50

ELFHEIM (VOL. 2)
NIGHTWYND

❑1, b&w	2.50
❑2, b&w	2.50
❑3, b&w	2.50
❑4, b&w	2.50

ELFHEIM (VOL. 3)
NIGHTWYND

❑1, b&w	2.50
❑2, b&w	2.50
❑3, b&w	2.50
❑4, b&w	2.50

ELFHEIM (VOL. 4)
NIGHTWYND

❑1, b&w	2.50
❑2, b&w	2.50

ELFHEIM: DRAGON DREAM (VOL. 5)
NIGHT WYND

❑1	2.50
❑2	2.50
❑3	2.50
❑4	2.50

Other grades: Multiply price above by 5/6 for VF/NM • 2/3 for VERY FINE • 1/3 for FINE • 1/5 for VERY GOOD • 1/8 for GOOD

Eclipso: The Darkness Within

First issue had plastic gem attached to cover

©DC

Ectokid

Part of the ill-fated Clive Barker Marvel line

©Marvel

Ehlissa

Fantasy had black-and-white cover variants

©Highland Graphics

80 Page Giant Magazine

Beloved giant-sized series from Silver Age

©DC

Elektra (1st Series)

Limited series for back-from-dead character

©Marvel

ELFIN ROMANCE
Mt. Wilson

	N-MINT
❑1, Feb 1994, b&w	1.50
❑2, Apr 1994, b&w	1.50
❑3, Apr 1994, b&w	1.50
❑4, Jun 1994, b&w	2.00
❑5, Aug 1994, b&w	2.00
❑6, Oct 1994, b&w	1.75
❑7, Dec 1996, b&w	3.25

ELFLORD
Aircel

	N-MINT
❑1, Feb 1986, b&w	2.00
❑1/2nd	2.00
❑2, Mar 1986	2.00
❑2/2nd	2.00
❑3, Apr 1986	2.00
❑4, May 1986	2.00
❑5, Jun 1986	2.00
❑6, Jul 1986	2.00
❑7, Aug 1986; Never published?	2.00
❑8, Sep 1986; Never published?	2.00

ELFLORD (2ND SERIES)
Aircel

	N-MINT
❑1, Oct 1986	2.00
❑2, Nov 1986	2.00
❑3, Dec 1986	2.00
❑4, Jan 1987	2.00
❑5, Feb 1987	2.00
❑6, Mar 1987	2.00
❑7, Apr 1987	2.00
❑8, May 1987	2.00
❑9, Jun 1987	2.00
❑10, Jul 1987	2.00
❑11, Aug 1987	2.00
❑12, Sep 1987	2.00
❑13, Oct 1987	2.00
❑14, Nov 1987	2.00
❑15, Dec 1987	2.00
❑15.5 1988; The Falcon Special	2.00
❑16, Jan 1988	2.00
❑17, Feb 1988	2.00
❑18, Mar 1988	2.00
❑19 1988	2.00
❑20 1988	2.00
❑21 1988; double-sized	4.95
❑22 1988	1.95
❑23 1988	1.95
❑24 1988	1.95
❑25 1988	1.95
❑26, Dec 1988	1.95
❑27, Jan 1989	1.95
❑28 1989	1.95
❑29 1989	1.95
❑30 1989	1.95
❑31 1989	1.95

ELFLORD (3RD SERIES)
Night Wynd

	N-MINT
❑1, b&w	2.50
❑2, b&w	2.50
❑3, b&w	2.50
❑4, b&w	2.50

ELFLORD (4TH SERIES)
Warp

	N-MINT
❑1, Jan 1997, b&w	2.95
❑2, Feb 1997, b&w	2.95
❑3, Mar 1997, b&w	2.95
❑4, Apr 1997, b&w	2.95

ELFLORD (5TH SERIES)
Warp

	N-MINT
❑1, Sep 1997, b&w	2.95
❑2, Oct 1997, b&w	2.95
❑3, Nov 1997, b&w	2.95
❑4, Dec 1997, b&w	2.95
❑5, Jan 1997	2.95
❑6, Feb 1997	2.95
❑7, Mar 1997	2.95

ELFLORD CHRONICLES
Aircel

	N-MINT
❑1, Oct 1990, b&w; Reprints	2.50
❑2, Oct 1990, b&w; Reprints	2.50
❑3, Nov 1990, b&w; Reprints	2.50
❑4, Dec 1990, b&w; Reprints	2.50
❑5, Jan 1991, b&w; Reprints	2.50
❑6, Feb 1991, b&w; Reprints	2.50
❑7, Mar 1991, b&w; Reprints	2.75
❑8, Apr 1991	2.75
❑9	2.75
❑10	2.75
❑11	2.75
❑12	2.75

ELFLORD: DRAGON'S EYE
Night Wynd

	N-MINT
❑1, ca. 1993	2.50
❑2, ca. 1993	2.50
❑3, ca. 1993	2.50

ELFLORD THE RETURN
Mad Monkey

	N-MINT
❑1, ca. 1996	6.96

ELFLORD: THE RETURN OF THE KING
Night Wynd

	N-MINT
❑1	2.50
❑2	2.50
❑3	2.50
❑4	2.50

ELFLORE
Nightwynd

	N-MINT
❑1, b&w	2.50
❑2, b&w	2.50
❑3, b&w	2.50
❑4, b&w	2.50

ELFLORE (VOL. 2)
Nightwynd

	N-MINT
❑1, b&w	2.50
❑2, b&w	2.50
❑3, b&w	2.50
❑4, b&w	2.50

ELFLORE: HIGH SEAS
Night Wynd

	N-MINT
❑1	2.50
❑2	2.50
❑3	2.50

ELFLORE (VOL. 3)
Nightwynd

	N-MINT
❑1, b&w	2.50
❑2, b&w	2.50
❑3, b&w	2.50
❑4, b&w	2.50

ELFQUEST
Warp

	N-MINT
❑1, Apr 1979 WP (w); WP (a)	32.00
❑1/2nd WP (w); WP (a)	12.00
❑1/3rd WP (w); WP (a)	8.00
❑1/4th WP (w); WP (a)	5.00
❑2, Aug 1978 WP (w); WP (a)	18.00
❑2/2nd WP (w); WP (a)	6.00
❑2/3rd WP (w); WP (a)	4.00
❑2/4th WP (w); WP (a)	3.00
❑3, Dec 1978 WP (w); WP (a)	18.00
❑3/2nd WP (w); WP (a)	3.00
❑3/3rd WP (w); WP (a)	3.00
❑3/4th WP (w); WP (a)	3.00
❑4, Apr 1979 WP (w); WP (a)	16.00
❑4/2nd WP (w); WP (a)	5.00
❑4/3rd WP (w); WP (a)	4.00
❑4/4th WP (w); WP (a)	2.50
❑5, Aug 1979 WP (w); WP (a)	16.00
❑5/2nd WP (w); WP (a)	3.00
❑5/3rd WP (w); WP (a)	3.00
❑6, Jan 1980 WP (w); WP (a)	13.00
❑6/2nd WP (w); WP (a)	4.00
❑6/3rd WP (w); WP (a)	3.00
❑7, May 1980 WP (w); WP (a)	10.00
❑7/2nd WP (w); WP (a)	4.00
❑7/3rd WP (w); WP (a)	3.00
❑8, Sep 1980 WP (w); WP (a)	10.00
❑8/2nd WP (w); WP (a)	4.00
❑8/3rd WP (w); WP (a)	3.00
❑9, Feb 1981 WP (w); WP (a)	10.00
❑9/2nd WP (w); WP (a)	4.00
❑9/3rd WP (w); WP (a)	3.00
❑10, Jun 1981 WP (w); WP (a)	7.50
❑11, Oct 1981 WP (w); WP (a)	7.50
❑12, Feb 1982 WP (w); WP (a)	7.50
❑13, Jun 1982 WP (w); WP (a)	7.50
❑14, Oct 1982 WP (w); WP (a)	7.50
❑15, Feb 1983 WP (w); WP (a)	7.50
❑16, Jun 1983 WP (w); WP (a)	10.00
❑17, Oct 1983; WP (w); WP (a); Elf orgy	7.00
❑18, Feb 1984 WP (w); WP (a)	7.00
❑19, Jun 1984 WP (w); WP (a)	7.00
❑20, Oct 1984 WP (w); WP (a)	7.00
❑21, Feb 1985; WP (w); WP (a); all letters issue	7.00

ELFQUEST (VOL. 2)
Warp

	N-MINT
❑1, May 1996	6.00
❑2, Jun 1996	5.00
❑3, Jul 1996	5.00
❑4, Aug 1996	5.00
❑5, Sep 1996	5.00
❑6, Nov 1996	5.00
❑7, Dec 1996	5.00
❑8, Jan 1997	5.00
❑9, Feb 1997 A: Mr. Beat.	5.00

Other grades: Multiply price above by 5/6 for VF/NM • 2/3 for VERY FINE • 1/3 for FINE • 1/5 for VERY GOOD • 1/8 for GOOD

❑10, Mar 1997 ... 5.00
❑11, Apr 1997 ... 4.95
❑12, May 1997 ... 4.95
❑13, Jun 1997 ... 4.95
❑14, Jul 1997 ... 4.95
❑15, Aug 1997 ... 4.95
❑16, Sep 1997 ... 4.95
❑17, Oct 1997 ... 4.95
❑18, Nov 1997 ... 4.95
❑19, Dec 1997 ... 4.95
❑20, Jan 1998 ... 4.95
❑21, Feb 1998 ... 4.95
❑22, Mar 1998 ... 4.95
❑23, Apr 1998 ... 4.95
❑24, May 1998 ... 4.95
❑25, Jun 1998; needlepoint style cover 4.95
❑26, Jul 1998 ... 4.95
❑27, Aug 1998 A: Mr. Beat. ... 4.95
❑28, Sep 1998 ... 4.95
❑29, Oct 1998 ... 4.95
❑30, Nov 1998 ... 4.95
❑31, Dec 1998; Christmas cover ... 4.95
❑32, Jan 1999 ... 2.95
❑33, Feb 1999 ... 2.95

ELFQUEST (EPIC)
Marvel / Epic

❑1, Aug 1985 WP (w); WP (a) ... 3.50
❑2, Sep 1985 WP (w); WP (a) ... 2.50
❑3, Oct 1985 WP (w); WP (a) ... 2.50
❑4, Nov 1985 WP (w); WP (a) ... 2.50
❑5, Dec 1985 WP (w); WP (a) ... 2.50
❑6, Jan 1986 WP (w); WP (a) ... 2.25
❑7, Feb 1986 WP (w); WP (a) ... 2.25
❑8, Mar 1986 WP (w); WP (a) ... 2.25
❑9, Apr 1986 WP (w); WP (a) ... 2.25
❑10, May 1986 WP (w); WP (a) ... 2.25
❑11, Jun 1986 WP (w); WP (a) ... 2.00
❑12, Jul 1986 WP (w); WP (a) ... 2.00
❑13, Aug 1986 WP (w); WP (a) ... 2.00
❑14, Sep 1986 WP (w); WP (a) ... 2.00
❑15, Oct 1986 WP (w); WP (a) ... 2.00
❑16, Nov 1986 WP (w); WP (a) ... 2.00
❑17, Dec 1986 WP (w); WP (a) ... 2.00
❑18, Jan 1987 WP (w); WP (a) ... 2.00
❑19, Feb 1987 WP (w); WP (a) ... 2.00
❑20, Mar 1987 WP (w); WP (a) ... 2.00
❑21, Apr 1987 WP (w); WP (a) ... 1.50
❑22, May 1987 WP (w); WP (a) ... 1.50
❑23, Jun 1987 WP (w); WP (a) ... 1.50
❑24, Jul 1987 WP (w); WP (a) ... 1.50
❑25, Aug 1987 WP (w); WP (a) ... 1.50
❑26, Sep 1987 WP (w); WP (a) ... 1.50
❑27, Oct 1987 WP (w); WP (a) ... 1.50
❑28, Nov 1987 WP (w); WP (a) ... 1.50
❑29, Dec 1987 WP (w); WP (a) ... 1.50
❑30, Jan 1988 WP (w); WP (a) ... 1.50
❑31, Feb 1988 WP (w); WP (a) ... 1.50
❑32, Mar 1988 WP (w); WP (a) ... 1.50

ELFQUEST (WARP REPRINTS)
Warp

❑1, May 1989 ... 2.00
❑2, Jun 1989 ... 2.00
❑3, Jul 1989 ... 2.00
❑4, Aug 1989 ... 2.00

ELFQUEST 25TH ANNIVERSARY EDITION
DC

❑1, Sep 2003 ... 2.95

ELFQUEST: BLOOD OF TEN CHIEFS
Warp

❑1, Aug 1993 ... 2.50
❑2, Sep 1993 ... 2.50
❑3, Nov 1993 ... 2.50
❑4, Jan 1994 ... 2.50
❑5, Mar 1994 ... 2.50
❑6, May 1994 ... 2.50
❑7, Jun 1994 ... 2.50
❑8, Jul 1994 ... 2.50
❑9, Aug 1994 ... 2.50
❑10, Sep 1994 ... 2.50
❑11, Oct 1994 ... 2.50
❑12, Nov 1994 ... 2.50
❑13, Dec 1994 ... 2.50
❑14, Jan 1995 ... 2.50
❑15, Feb 1995 ... 2.50
❑16, Apr 1995 ... 2.50
❑17, May 1995 ... 2.50
❑18, Jun 1995 ... 2.50
❑19, Aug 1995; contains Elfquest timeline ... 2.50
❑20, Sep 1995 ... 2.50

ELFQUEST: HIDDEN YEARS
Warp

❑1, May 1992 ... 3.00
❑2, Jul 1992 ... 2.50
❑3, Sep 1992; This story was previewed in Harbinger #11 (character reads it as in a comic book) ... 2.50
❑4, Nov 1992 ... 2.50
❑5, Jan 1993 ... 2.50
❑6, Mar 1993 ... 2.50
❑7, May 1993 ... 2.50
❑8, Jul 1993 ... 2.50
❑9, Sep 1993 ... 2.50
❑9.5, Nov 1993; double-sized JBy (a) 2.95
❑10, Jan 1994 ... 2.50
❑11, Mar 1994 ... 2.50
❑12, Apr 1994 ... 2.50
❑13, May 1994 ... 2.50
❑14, Jun 1994 WP (w) ... 2.50
❑15, Jul 1994 ... 2.50
❑16, Aug 1994 ... 2.50
❑17, Oct 1994 ... 2.50
❑18, Dec 1994 ... 2.50
❑19, Jan 1995 ... 2.50
❑20, Apr 1995 ... 2.50
❑21, May 1995 ... 2.50
❑22, Jul 1995 ... 2.50
❑23, Aug 1995; contains Elfquest timeline ... 2.50
❑24, Sep 1995 ... 2.50
❑25, Oct 1995, b&w ... 2.50
❑26, Dec 1995, b&w ... 2.50
❑27, Jan 1996, b&w ... 2.50
❑28, Feb 1996, b&w ... 2.50
❑29, Mar 1996, b&w ... 2.50

ELFQUEST: JINK
Warp

❑1, Nov 1994 ... 2.50
❑2, Dec 1994 ... 2.50
❑3, Jan 1995 WP (w) ... 2.50
❑4, Apr 1995 ... 2.50
❑5, May 1995 ... 2.50
❑6, Jul 1995; contains Elfquest world map ... 2.50
❑7, Aug 1995; contains Elfquest timeline ... 2.50
❑8, Oct 1995; b&w for remainder of series ... 2.50
❑9, Nov 1995 ... 2.50
❑10, Dec 1995 ... 2.50
❑11, Jan 1996 ... 2.50
❑12, Feb 1996 ... 2.50

ELFQUEST: KAHVI
Warp

❑1, Oct 1995 ... 2.25
❑2, Nov 1995 ... 2.25
❑3, Dec 1995 ... 2.25
❑4, Jan 1996 ... 2.25
❑5, Feb 1996 ... 2.25
❑6, Mar 1996 ... 2.25

ELFQUEST: KINGS CROSS
Warp

❑1, Nov 1997, b&w ... 2.95
❑2, Dec 1997, b&w ... 2.95

ELFQUEST: KINGS OF THE BROKEN WHEEL
Warp

❑1, Jun 1990 WP (a) ... 2.50
❑2, Aug 1990 WP (a) ... 2.00
❑3, Sep 1990 WP (a) ... 2.00
❑4, Dec 1990 WP (a) ... 2.00
❑5, Feb 1991 WP (a) ... 2.00
❑6, May 1991 WP (a) ... 2.00
❑7, Aug 1991 WP (a) ... 2.00
❑8, Nov 1991 WP (a) ... 2.00
❑9, Feb 1992 WP (a) ... 2.00

ELFQUEST: METAMORPHOSIS
Warp

❑1, Apr 1996 ... 2.95

ELFQUEST: NEW BLOOD
Warp

❑1, Aug 1992, gatefold summary; JBy (a); "Elfquest Summer Special" ... 5.00
❑2, Oct 1992 ... 2.50
❑3, Dec 1992 ... 2.50
❑4, Feb 1993 ... 2.50
❑5, Apr 1993 ... 2.50
❑6, Jun 1993 ... 2.50
❑7, Jul 1993 ... 2.50
❑8, Aug 1993 ... 2.50
❑9, Sep 1993 ... 2.50
❑10, Oct 1993 ... 2.50
❑11, Nov 1993 ... 2.25
❑12, Dec 1993 ... 2.25
❑13, Jan 1994 ... 2.25
❑14, Feb 1994 ... 2.25
❑15, Mar 1994 ... 2.25
❑16, Apr 1994 ... 2.25
❑17, May 1994 ... 2.25
❑18, Jun 1994 ... 2.25
❑19, Jul 1994 ... 2.25
❑20, Aug 1994 ... 2.25
❑21, Sep 1994 ... 2.25
❑22, Oct 1994 ... 2.25
❑23, Nov 1994 ... 2.25
❑24, Dec 1994 ... 2.25
❑25, Jan 1995 ... 2.25
❑26, Feb 1995 ... 2.25
❑27, Apr 1995 ... 2.50
❑28, May 1995 ... 2.50
❑29, Jul 1995 ... 2.50
❑30, Aug 1995; contains Elfquest timeline ... 2.50
❑31, Sep 1995 ... 2.50
❑32, Oct 1995 ... 2.50
❑33, Nov 1995 ... 2.50
❑34, Dec 1995 ... 2.25
❑35, Jan 1996 ... 2.25
❑Book 1 ... 25.00
❑Special 1, Jul 1993 JBy (a) ... 3.95

ELFQUEST: RECOGNITION SUMMER 2001 SPECIAL
Warp

❑2, Jul 2001, b&w; Previous issue was Elfquest: Wolfshadow ... 2.95

ELFQUEST: SHARDS
Warp

❑1, Aug 1994 WP (w) ... 2.50
❑2, Sep 1994 WP (w) ... 2.50
❑3, Oct 1994 WP (w) ... 2.50
❑4, Nov 1994 WP (w) ... 2.50
❑5, Dec 1994 WP (w) ... 2.50
❑6, Jan 1995 WP (w) ... 2.25
❑7, Mar 1995 WP (w) ... 2.25
❑8, May 1995 WP (w) ... 2.25
❑9, Jun 1995 WP (w) ... 2.50
❑10, Aug 1995; WP (w); contains Elfquest timeline ... 2.50
❑11, Sep 1995 WP (w) ... 2.50
❑12, Oct 1995 WP (w) ... 2.50
❑13, Dec 1995 ... 2.25
❑14, Feb 1996 ... 2.25
❑15, Apr 1996 ... 2.25
❑16, Jun 1996 ... 2.25
❑Ashcan 1, ashcan preview/ San Diego Comic-Con premium ... 1.00

ELFQUEST: SIEGE AT BLUE MOUNTAIN
Warp / Apple

❑1, Mar 1987, b&w WP (w); WP, JSa (a) 3.00
❑1/2nd, WP (w); WP (a) ... 2.50
❑2, May 1987, WP (w); WP, JSa (a) ... 3.00
❑2/2nd, WP (w); WP (a) ... 2.25
❑2/3rd, b&w ... 3.00
❑3, Jul 1987, WP (w); WP, JSa (a) ... 2.50
❑3/2nd, WP (w); WP (a) ... 2.00
❑4, Sep 1987, WP (w); WP, JSa (a) ... 2.50
❑5, Nov 1987, WP (w); WP, JSa (a) ... 2.50
❑6, Aug 1988, WP (w); WP, JSa (a) ... 2.50
❑7, Oct 1988, WP (w); WP, JSa (a) ... 2.50
❑8, Dec 1988, WP (w); WP, JSa (a) ... 2.50

ELFQUEST: THE DISCOVERY
DC

❑1, Mar 2006 ... 2.95

Elektra: Assassin

Clever Frank Miller series for Epic imprint
©Marvel

Elektra Saga

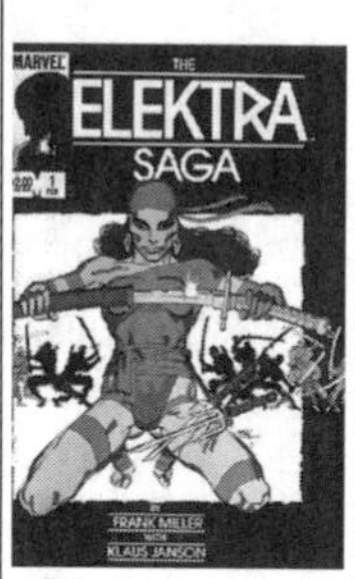

Reformatted reprint of Daredevil Elektra stories
©Marvel

Elementals (Vol. 1)

Band of super-heroes from Bill Willingham
©Comico

Elflord

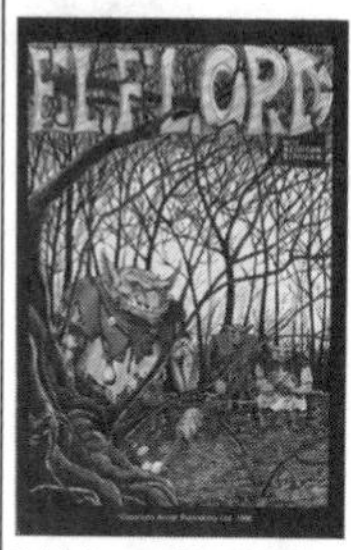

Elvish heroes in action from Barry Blair
©Aircel

Elfquest

Comics cultural phenomenon in 1980s
©Warp

N-MINT

❑2, May 2006 .... 2.95
❑3, Jul 2006 .... 2.95

ELFQUEST: THE REBELS
WARP

❑1, Nov 1994 .... 2.50
❑2, Dec 1994 .... 2.25
❑3, Jan 1995 .... 2.25
❑4, Mar 1995 .... 2.25
❑5, Apr 1995 .... 2.25
❑6, Jun 1995 .... 2.25
❑7, Jul 1995, contains Elfquest world map 2.25
❑8, Sep 1995 .... 2.25
❑9, Oct 1995 .... 2.25
❑10, Nov 1995 .... 2.25
❑11, Jan 1996 .... 2.25
❑12, Feb 1996 .... 2.25

ELFQUEST: TWO-SPEAR
WARP

❑1, Oct 1995 .... 2.25
❑2, Nov 1995 .... 2.25
❑3, Dec 1995 .... 2.25
❑4, Jan 1996 .... 2.25
❑5, Feb 1996 .... 2.25

ELFQUEST: WAVEDANCERS
WARP

❑1, Dec 1993 0: The Wavedancers. 2.25
❑2, Feb 1994 .... 2.25
❑3, Apr 1994 .... 2.25
❑4, Jun 1994 .... 2.25
❑5, Aug 1994 .... 2.25
❑6, Oct 1994 .... 2.25
❑Special 1 .... 2.25

ELFQUEST: WOLFSHADOW SUMMER 2001 SPECIAL
WARP

❑1, Jul 2001, b&w; Continued as Elfquest: Recognition 3.95

ELFQUEST: WORLDPOOL
WARP

❑1, Jul 1997, b&w 2.95

ELF-THING
ECLIPSE

❑1, Mar 1987, b&w 1.50

ELFTREK
DIMENSION

❑1, Jul 1986; parody of Star Trek, Elfquest 1.75
❑2, Oct 1986; parody of Star Trek, Elfquest 1.75

ELF WARRIOR
ADVENTURE

❑1, Feb 1987 .... 1.95
❑2 .... 1.95
❑3 .... 1.95
❑4; Published by Quadrant 1.95

EL GATO NEGRO
AZTECA

❑1, Oct 1993, b&w 2.00
❑2, Sum 1994, b&w 2.00
❑3, Fal 1995, b&w 2.00
❑4 .... 2.50

N-MINT

EL-HAZARD
VIZ

❑1, Apr 1997 .... 2.95

EL HAZARD: THE MAGNIFICENT WORLD PART 1
VIZ

❑1, Sep 2000 .... 2.95
❑2, Oct 2000 .... 2.95
❑3, Nov 2000 .... 2.95
❑4, Dec 2000 .... 2.95
❑5, Jan 2001 .... 2.95

EL HAZARD: THE MAGNIFICENT WORLD PART 2
VIZ

❑1, Feb 2001 .... 2.95
❑2, Mar 2001 .... 2.95
❑3, Apr 2001 .... 2.95
❑4, May 2001 .... 2.95
❑5, Jun 2001 .... 2.95

EL HAZARD: THE MAGNIFICENT WORLD PART 3
VIZ

❑1, Jul 2001 .... 2.95
❑2, Aug 2001 .... 2.95
❑3, Sep 2001 .... 2.95
❑4, Oct 2001 .... 2.95
❑5, Nov 2001 .... 2.95
❑6, Dec 2001 .... 2.95

ELIMINATOR
MALIBU / ULTRAVERSE

❑0, Apr 1995; Collects Eliminator appearances from Ultraverse Premiere 2.95
❑1, May 1995; 7th Infinity Gem revealed 2.50
❑1/Variant, May 1995; Black cover edition; Black cover edition; 7th Infinity Gem revealed 3.95
❑2, Jun 1995 .... 2.50
❑3, Jul 1995 .... 2.50

ELIMINATOR (ETERNITY)
ETERNITY

❑1, b&w 2.50
❑2, b&w 2.50
❑3, b&w 2.50

ELIMINATOR FULL COLOR SPECIAL
ETERNITY

❑1, Oct 1991, ... 2.95

ELONGATED MAN
DC

❑1, Jan 1992 .... 1.25
❑2, Feb 1992 .... 1.00
❑3, Mar 1992 .... 1.00
❑4, Apr 1992 .... 1.00

ELRIC
PACIFIC

❑1, Apr 1983 CR (a) 2.00
❑2, Aug 1983 CR (a) 1.75
❑3, Oct 1983 CR (a) 1.75
❑4, Dec 1983 CR (a) 1.75
❑5, Feb 1984 CR (a) 1.75
❑6, Apr 1984 CR (a) 1.75

N-MINT

ELRIC (TOPPS)
TOPPS

❑0, ca. 1996 NG (w); CR (a) 3.50
❑1, ca. 1996 .... 2.95
❑2, ca. 1996 .... 2.95
❑3, ca. 1996 .... 2.95
❑4, ca. 1996 CR (w); CR (a) 2.95

ELRIC: SAILOR ON THE SEAS OF FATE
FIRST

❑1, Jun 1985 .... 2.00
❑2, Aug 1985 .... 1.75
❑3, Oct 1985 .... 1.75
❑4, Dec 1985 .... 1.75
❑5, Feb 1986 .... 1.75
❑6, Apr 1986 .... 1.75
❑7, Jun 1986 .... 1.75

ELRIC: STORMBRINGER
DARK HORSE / TOPPS

❑1, ca. 1997 .... 2.95
❑2, ca. 1997 .... 2.95
❑3, ca. 1997 .... 2.95
❑4, ca. 1997 .... 2.95
❑5, ca. 1997 .... 2.95
❑6, ca. 1997 .... 2.95
❑7, ca. 1997 .... 2.95

ELRIC: THE BANE OF THE BLACK SWORD
FIRST

❑1, Aug 1988 .... 2.00
❑2, Oct 1988 .... 2.00
❑3, Dec 1988 .... 2.00
❑4, Feb 1989 .... 2.00
❑5, Apr 1989 .... 2.00
❑6, Jun 1989 .... 2.00

ELRIC: THE MAKING OF A SORCERER
DC

❑1 2004 .... 5.95
❑2 2005 .... 5.95
❑3, Aug 2006 ....

ELRIC: THE VANISHING TOWER
FIRST

❑1, Aug 1987 .... 1.75
❑2, Oct 1987 .... 1.75
❑3, Dec 1987 .... 1.75
❑4, Feb 1988 .... 1.75
❑5, Apr 1988 .... 1.75
❑6, Jun 1988 .... 1.75

ELRIC: WEIRD OF THE WHITE WOLF
FIRST

❑1, Oct 1986 .... 1.75
❑2, Dec 1986 .... 1.75
❑3, Feb 1987 .... 1.75
❑4, Apr 1987 .... 1.75
❑5, Jun 1987 .... 1.75

ELSEWHERE PRINCE
MARVEL / EPIC

❑1, May 1990 .... 1.95
❑2, Jun 1990 .... 1.95
❑3, Jul 1990 .... 1.95
❑4, Aug 1990 .... 1.95

Other grades: Multiply price above by 5/6 for VF/NM • 2/3 for VERY FINE • 1/3 for FINE • 1/5 for VERY GOOD • 1/8 for GOOD

N-MINT

❑5, Sep 1990 ... 1.95
❑6, Oct 1990 ... 1.95

ELSEWORLDS 80-PAGE GIANT
DC

❑1, Aug 1999; U.S. copies destroyed, only released in England; less than 700 copies estimated to exist ... 110.00

ELSEWORLD'S FINEST
DC

❑1, ca. 1997, prestige format; Superman and Batman in the 1920s; Elseworlds story ... 4.95
❑2, ca. 1997, prestige format; Superman and Batman in the 1920s ... 4.95

ELSEWORLD'S FINEST: SUPERGIRL & BATGIRL
DC

❑1, ca. 1998; prestige format ... 5.95
❑1/Ltd., ca. 1998; ca. 1998; Signed ... 18.95

ELSINORE
ALIAS

❑1 2005 ... 2.99
❑2, Jul 2005 ... 2.99
❑3, Oct 2005 ... 2.99

ELSINORE
DEVIL'S DUE

❑4, Mar 2006 ... 2.99
❑5, May 2006 ... 2.99

ELVEN
MALIBU / ULTRAVERSE

❑0, Oct 1994 1: Elven. ... 2.95
❑1, Feb 1995 A: Prime. ... 2.25
❑1/Ltd., Feb 1995; Limited foil edition A: Prime. ... 2.50
❑2, Mar 1995 ... 2.25
❑3, Apr 1995 ... 2.25
❑4, May 1995 ... 2.25

ELVIRA, MISTRESS OF THE DARK
CLAYPOOL

❑1, May 1993, b&w ... 4.00
❑2, Jun 1993, b&w KB (w) ... 3.00
❑3, Jul 1993, b&w KB (w) ... 3.00
❑4, Aug 1993, b&w ... 3.00
❑5, Sep 1993, b&w KB (w) ... 3.00
❑6, Oct 1993, b&w ... 3.00
❑7, Nov 1993, b&w KB (w) ... 3.00
❑8, Dec 1993, b&w ... 3.00
❑9, Jan 1994, b&w KB (w) ... 3.00
❑10, Feb 1994, b&w KB (w) ... 3.00
❑11, Mar 1994, b&w KB (w) ... 2.75
❑12, Apr 1994, b&w ... 2.75
❑13, May 1994, b&w ... 2.75
❑14, Jun 1994, b&w ... 2.75
❑15, Jul 1994, b&w ... 2.75
❑16, Aug 1994, b&w ... 2.75
❑17, Sep 1994, b&w ... 2.75
❑18, Oct 1994, b&w ... 2.75
❑19, Nov 1994, b&w ... 2.75
❑20, Dec 1994, b&w ... 2.75
❑21, Jan 1995, b&w ... 2.50
❑22, Feb 1995, b&w ... 2.50
❑23, Mar 1995, b&w ... 2.50
❑24, Apr 1995, b&w ... 2.50
❑25, May 1995, b&w KB (w) ... 2.50
❑26, Jun 1995, b&w ... 2.50
❑27, Jul 1995, b&w ... 2.50
❑28, Aug 1995, b&w ... 2.50
❑29, Sep 1995, b&w ... 2.50
❑30, Oct 1995, b&w ... 2.50
❑31, Nov 1995, b&w ... 2.50
❑32, Dec 1995, b&w ... 2.50
❑33, Jan 1996, b&w ... 2.50
❑34, Feb 1996, b&w ... 2.50
❑35, Mar 1996, b&w ... 2.50
❑36, Apr 1996, b&w ... 2.50
❑37, May 1996, b&w ... 2.50
❑38, Jun 1996, b&w ... 2.50
❑39, Jul 1996, b&w A: Portia Prinz. ... 2.50
❑40, Aug 1996, b&w ... 2.50
❑41, Sep 1996, b&w ... 2.50
❑42, Oct 1996, b&w ... 2.50
❑43, Nov 1996, b&w ... 2.50
❑44, Dec 1996, b&w ... 2.50
❑45, Jan 1997, b&w ... 2.50
❑46, Feb 1997, b&w ... 2.50
❑47, Mar 1997, b&w ... 2.50
❑48, Apr 1997, b&w ... 2.50
❑49, May 1997, b&w ... 2.50
❑50, Jun 1997, b&w ... 2.50
❑51, Jul 1997, b&w ... 2.50
❑52, Aug 1997, b&w ... 2.50
❑53, Sep 1997, b&w ... 2.50
❑54, Oct 1997, b&w ... 2.50
❑55, Nov 1997, b&w ... 2.50
❑56, Dec 1997, b&w ... 2.50
❑57, Jan 1998, b&w ... 2.50
❑58, Feb 1998, b&w ... 2.50
❑59, Mar 1998, b&w ... 2.50
❑60, Apr 1998, b&w ... 2.50
❑61, May 1998, b&w ... 2.50
❑62, Jun 1998, b&w ... 2.50
❑63, Jul 1998, b&w ... 2.50
❑64, Aug 1998, b&w ... 2.50
❑65, Sep 1998, b&w ... 2.50
❑66, Oct 1998, b&w ... 2.50
❑67, Nov 1998, b&w ... 2.50
❑68, Dec 1998, b&w ... 2.50
❑69, Jan 1999, b&w ... 2.50
❑70, Feb 1999, b&w ... 2.50
❑71, Mar 1999, b&w ... 2.50
❑72, Apr 1999, b&w ... 2.50
❑73, May 1999, b&w ... 2.50
❑74, Jun 1999, b&w ... 2.50
❑75, Jul 1999, b&w ... 2.50
❑76, Aug 1999, b&w ... 2.50
❑77, Sep 1999, b&w ... 2.50
❑78, Oct 1999, b&w ... 2.50
❑79, Nov 1999, b&w ... 2.50
❑80, Dec 1999, b&w ... 2.50
❑81, Jan 2000, b&w ... 2.50
❑82, Feb 2000, b&w ... 2.50
❑83, Mar 2000, b&w ... 2.50
❑84, Apr 2000, b&w ... 2.50
❑85, May 2000, b&w ... 2.50
❑86, Jun 2000, b&w ... 2.50
❑87, Jul 2000, b&w ... 2.50
❑88, Aug 2000, b&w RHo (w) ... 2.50
❑89, Sep 2000, b&w ... 2.50
❑90, Oct 2000, b&w RHo (w) ... 2.50
❑91, Nov 2000, b&w ... 2.50
❑92, Dec 2000, b&w ... 2.50
❑93, Jan 2001, b&w ... 2.50
❑94, Feb 2001, b&w ... 2.50
❑95, Mar 2001, b&w ... 2.50
❑96, Apr 2001, b&w ... 2.50
❑97, May 2001, b&w ... 2.50
❑98, Jun 2001, b&w ... 2.50
❑99, Jul 2001, b&w ... 2.50
❑100, Aug 2001, b&w ... 2.50
❑101, Sep 2001, b&w ... 2.50
❑102, Oct 2001, b&w ... 2.50
❑103, Nov 2001, b&w ... 2.50
❑104, Dec 2001, b&w ... 2.50
❑105, Jan 2002, b&w ... 2.50
❑106, Feb 2002, b&w ... 2.50
❑107, Mar 2002, b&w ... 2.50
❑108, Apr 2002, b&w ... 2.50
❑109, May 2002, b&w ... 2.50
❑110, Jun 2002, b&w ... 2.50
❑111, Jul 2002, b&w ... 2.50
❑112, Aug 2002, b&w ... 2.50
❑113, Sep 2002, b&w ... 2.50
❑114, Oct 2002, b&w ... 2.50
❑115, Nov 2002, b&w ... 2.50
❑116, Dec 2002, b&w ... 2.50
❑117, Jan 2003, b&w ... 2.50
❑118, Feb 2003, b&w ... 2.50
❑119, Mar 2003, b&w ... 2.50
❑120, Apr 2003, b&w ... 2.50
❑121, May 2003, b&w ... 2.50
❑122, Jun 2003, b&w ... 2.50
❑123, Jul 2003, b&w ... 2.50
❑124, Aug 2003, b&w ... 2.50
❑125, Sep 2003, b&w ... 2.50
❑126, Oct 2003, b&w ... 2.50
❑127, Nov 2003, b&w ... 2.50
❑128, Dec 2003, b&w ... 2.50
❑129, Jan 2004, b&w ... 2.50
❑130, Feb 2004, b&w ... 2.50
❑131, Mar 2004, b&w ... 2.50
❑132, Apr 2004, b&w ... 2.50
❑133, May 2004, b&w ... 2.50
❑134, Jun 2004, b&w ... 2.50
❑135, Jul 2004, b&w ... 2.50
❑136, Aug 2004, b&w ... 2.50
❑137, Sep 2004, b&w ... 2.50
❑138, Oct 2004, b&w ... 2.50
❑139, Nov 2004 ... 2.50
❑140, Dec 2004 ... 2.50
❑141, Feb 2005 ... 2.50

ELVIRA'S HOUSE OF MYSTERY
DC

❑1, Jan 1986; Double-size ... 2.50
❑2, Apr 1986 ... 2.00
❑3, May 1986 ... 2.00
❑4, Jun 1986 ... 2.00
❑5, Jul 1986 ... 2.00
❑6, Aug 1986; sideways issue ... 2.00
❑7, Sep 1986; science-fiction issue ... 2.00
❑8, Oct 1986 ... 2.00
❑9, Nov 1986 ... 2.00
❑10, Dec 1986 A: Cain. ... 2.00
❑11, Jan 1987; Double-size DSt (c) ... 2.50
❑Special 1, ca. 1987; Christmas stories ... 2.00

ELVIS MANDIBLE
DC / PIRANHA

❑1, ca. 1990, b&w ... 3.50

ELVIS PRESLEY EXPERIENCE
REVOLUTIONARY

❑1, Aug 1992, b&w ... 2.50
❑2, Oct 1992, b&w ... 2.50
❑3, Jan 1993, b&w ... 2.50
❑4, Feb 1993, b&w ... 2.50
❑5, Jul 1993, b&w ... 2.50
❑6, Aug 1993, b&w ... 2.50
❑7, Apr 1994, b&w ... 2.50

ELVIS SHRUGGED
REVOLUTIONARY

❑1, Feb 1992, b&w ... 2.50
❑2, Aug 1992, b&w ... 2.50
❑3, Apr 1992, b&w ... 3.95
❑Book 1, Dec 1993, b&w ... 9.95

EL ZOMBO
DARK HORSE

❑1, Apr 2004 ... 2.99
❑2, May 2004 ... 2.99
❑3, Aug 2004 ... 3.00

E-MAN (1ST SERIES)
CHARLTON

❑1, Oct 1973, O: E-Man. ... 4.00
❑2, Dec 1973 ... 2.50
❑3, Jun 1974 ... 2.50
❑4, Aug 1974 ... 2.50
❑5, Nov 1974 ... 2.50
❑6, Jan 1975, JBy (a) ... 2.50
❑7, Mar 1975 JBy (a) ... 2.50
❑8, May 1975, JBy (a); Nova becomes E-Man's partner ... 2.50
❑9, Jul 1975, JBy (a) ... 2.50
❑10, Sep 1975, JBy (a) ... 2.50

E-MAN (2ND SERIES)
FIRST

❑1, Apr 1983 JSa (a); O: E-Man. ... 2.00
❑2, Jun 1983; JSa (a); A: F-Men. X-Men parody ... 1.50
❑3, Jun 1983 JSa (a) ... 1.50
❑4, Jul 1983 JSa (a) ... 1.50
❑5, Aug 1983 JSa (a) ... 1.50
❑6, Sep 1983 JSa (a); O: E-Man. ... 1.25
❑7, Oct 1983 JSa (a) ... 1.25
❑8, Nov 1983 JSa (a) ... 1.25
❑9, Dec 1983 JSa (a) ... 1.25
❑10, Jan 1984 JSa (a); O: Nova Kane. ... 1.25
❑11, Feb 1984 JSa (a) ... 1.25
❑12, Mar 1984 JSa (a) ... 1.25
❑13, Apr 1984 JSa (a) ... 1.25
❑14, May 1984 JSa (a) ... 1.25
❑15, Jun 1984 JSa (a) ... 1.25
❑16, Jul 1984 JSa (a) ... 1.25
❑17, Aug 1984 JSa (a) ... 1.25
❑18, Sep 1984 JSa (a) ... 1.25
❑19, Oct 1984 JSa (a) ... 1.25
❑20, Nov 1984 JSa (a) ... 1.25
❑21, Dec 1984 JSa (a) ... 1.25
❑22, Feb 1985 JSa (a) ... 1.25
❑23, Apr 1985 JSa (a) ... 1.25

Elfquest (Epic)
Marvel reprints of the famous Warp series
©Marvel

Elfquest: Blood of Ten Chiefs
Tales from the wild side of Elfquest
©Warp

Elfquest: New Blood
Rotating teams of creators write the elves
©Warp

Elftrek
Simultaneous parody of Star Trek and Elfquest
©Dimension

Eliminator
Ultraverse resident with cybernetic arm
©Malibu

N-MINT

❑24, Jun 1985 JSa (a); O: Michael Mauser ... 1.25
❑25, Aug 1985 JSa (a) ... 1.25

E-MAN (3RD SERIES)
COMICO
❑1, Sep 1989 ... 2.75

E-MAN (4TH SERIES)
COMICO
❑1, Jan 1990 ... 2.50
❑2, Feb 1990 ... 2.50
❑3, Mar 1990 ... 2.50

E-MAN (5TH SERIES)
ALPHA
❑1, Oct 1993 ... 2.75

E-MAN RETURNS
ALPHA PRODUCTIONS
❑1, Mar 1994, b&w ... 2.75

EMBLEM
ANTARCTIC / VENUS
❑1, May 1994, b&w ... 3.50
❑2, Jun 1994, b&w ... 2.95
❑3, Jul 1994, b&w ... 2.95
❑5, Oct 1994, b&w ... 2.95
❑6, Nov 1994, b&w ... 2.95
❑7, Dec 1994, b&w ... 2.95
❑8, Feb 1995, b&w ... 2.95

EMBRACE
LONDON NIGHT
❑1, Jun 1997 ... 3.00
❑1/Ltd.; Signed, promotional edition .. 4.00

EMERALDAS
ETERNITY
❑1, Nov 1990, b&w ... 2.25
❑2, b&w ... 2.25
❑3, b&w ... 2.25
❑4, b&w ... 2.25

EMERGENCY!
CHARLTON
❑1, Jun 1976, JBy (a) ... 20.00
❑2, Aug 1976 ... 16.00
❑3, Oct 1976 ... 14.00
❑4, Dec 1976, Scarce ... 16.00

EMERGENCY! (MAGAZINE)
CHARLTON
❑1, Jun 1976, NA (c); NA (a) ... 30.00
❑2, Aug 1976 ... 25.00
❑3, Oct 1976 ... 22.00
❑4, Dec 1976 ... 22.00

EMIL AND THE DETECTIVES
GOLD KEY
❑1, Nov 1964; adapts Disney movie ... 16.00

EMILY THE STRANGE
DARK HORSE
❑1, Oct 2005 ... 2.95
❑2, Jan 2006 ... 2.95

EMISSARY
IMAGE
❑1, Jul 2006 ... 2.95

EMISSARY
STRATEIA
❑1, Jul 1998 ... 2.50

N-MINT

EMMA DAVENPORT
LOHMAN HILLS
❑1, Apr 1995, b&w ... 3.00
❑2, Jun 1995, b&w ... 2.75
❑3, Aug 1995, b&w ... 2.75
❑4, Oct 1995, b&w ... 2.75
❑5, Dec 1995, b&w ... 2.75
❑6, Feb 1996, b&w ... 2.75
❑7, Apr 1996, b&w ... 2.75
❑8, Feb 1996, b&w; crossover with Femforce ... 2.75

EMMA FROST
MARVEL
❑1, Aug 2003 ... 4.00
❑2, Sep 2003 ... 2.50
❑3, Oct 2003 ... 2.50
❑4, Dec 2003 ... 2.50
❑5, Jan 2004 ... 2.50
❑6, Feb 2004 ... 2.50
❑7, Mar 2004 ... 2.50
❑8, Apr 2004 ... 2.99
❑9, May 2004 ... 2.99
❑10, Jun 2004 ... 2.99
❑11, Jul 2004 ... 2.99
❑12, Aug 2004 ... 2.99
❑13, Sep 2004 ... 2.99
❑14, Oct 2004 ... 2.99
❑15, Nov 2004 ... 2.99
❑16, Dec 2004 ... 2.99
❑17, Jan 2005 ... 2.99
❑18, Feb 2005 ... 2.99

EMO BOY
SLAVE LABOR
❑1 2005 ... 2.95
❑2, Sep 2005 ... 2.95
❑3, Oct 2005 ... 2.95
❑4, Jan 2006 ... 2.95

EMPIRE
ETERNITY
❑1, Mar 1988 ... 1.95
❑2, Apr 1988 ... 1.95
❑3, May 1988 ... 1.95
❑4, Jun 1988 ... 1.95

EMPIRE (IMAGE)
IMAGE
❑1, May 2000 ... 2.50
❑2, Sep 2000 ... 2.50

EMPIRE (DC)
DC
❑0, Jul 2003 ... 4.95
❑1, Sep 2003 ... 2.50
❑2, Sep 2003 ... 2.50
❑3, Oct 2003 ... 2.50
❑4, Dec 2003 ... 2.50
❑5, Dec 2003 ... 2.50
❑6, Jan 2004 ... 2.50

EMPIRE LANES (NORTHERN LIGHTS)
NORTHERN LIGHTS
❑1, Dec 1986 ... 1.75
❑2 ... 1.75
❑3 ... 1.75
❑4 ... 1.75

N-MINT

EMPIRE LANES (KEYLINE)
KEYLINE
❑1 ... 1.75

EMPIRE LANES (VOL. 2)
KEYLINE
❑1 ... 2.95

EMPIRES OF NIGHT
REBEL
❑1, Dec 1993, b&w ... 2.25
❑2 ... 2.25
❑3 ... 2.25
❑4 ... 2.25

EMPTY LOVE STORIES
SLAVE LABOR
❑1, Nov 1994, b&w ... 2.95
❑2, Aug 1996, b&w ... 2.95

EMPTY LOVE STORIES (2ND SERIES)
FUNNY VALENTINE
❑1, Jul 1998, b&w; reprints Slave Labor issue ... 2.95
❑Special 1, Jan 1998, b&w ... 2.95

EMPTY SKULL COMICS
FANTAGRAPHICS
❑1, Apr 1996, b&w; Oversized; cardstock cover ... 4.95

EMPTY ZONE
SIRIUS
❑1 ... 2.50
❑2 ... 2.50
❑3 ... 2.50
❑4 ... 2.50

EMPTY ZONE (2ND SERIES)
SIRIUS
❑1, ca. 1998 ... 2.95
❑2, ca. 1998 ... 2.95
❑3, ca. 1998 ... 2.95
❑4, ca. 1998 ... 2.95
❑5, ca. 1998 ... 2.95
❑6, ca. 1998 ... 2.95
❑7, ca. 1998 ... 2.95
❑8, ca. 1998 ... 2.95

EMPTY ZONE: TRANCEMISSIONS
SIRIUS
❑1 ... 2.95

ENCHANTED
SIRIUS
❑1, ca. 1997 ... 2.95
❑2, ca. 1997 ... 2.95
❑3, ca. 1997 ... 2.95

ENCHANTED (VOL. 2)
SIRIUS
❑1 ... 2.95
❑2 ... 2.95
❑3 ... 2.95

ENCHANTED VALLEY
BLACKTHORNE
❑1, May 1997 ... 1.75
❑2 ... 1.75

ENCHANTED WORLDS
BLACKMORE
❑1, b&w ... 2.75

ENCHANTER
ECLIPSE
- ❑1, Oct 1985; Circulation reported in Comics Buyer's Guide #726 pg. 65 ... 2.00
- ❑2, Nov 1985 ... 2.00
- ❑3, Dec 1985 ... 2.00
- ❑4, Jan 1986 ... 2.00
- ❑5, Feb 1986 ... 2.00
- ❑6, Mar 1986 ... 2.00
- ❑7, Apr 1986 ... 2.00
- ❑8, May 1986 ... 2.00

ENCHANTER: APOCALYPSE MOON
EXPRESS / ENTITY
- ❑1, b&w; illustrated novella ... 2.95

ENCHANTER: PRELUDE TO APOCALYPSE
EXPRESS
- ❑1, b&w ... 2.50
- ❑2, b&w ... 2.50
- ❑3, b&w ... 2.50

ENCHANTERS
HIDDEN POET
- ❑1, Jun 1996 ... 2.50

ENCYCLOPÆDIA DEADPOOLICA
MARVEL
- ❑1, Dec 1998; Deadpool reference ... 2.99

END, THE: IN THE BEGINNING
AFC
- ❑1, Jun 2000, b&w ... 2.95

ENDLESS GALLERY
DC / VERTIGO
- ❑1; pin-ups; Introduction by Neil Gaiman ... 3.50

ENEMY
DARK HORSE
- ❑1, May 1994 ... 2.50
- ❑2, Jun 1994 ... 2.50
- ❑3, Jul 1994 ... 2.50
- ❑4, Aug 1994 ... 2.50
- ❑5, Sep 1994 ... 2.50

ENEMY ACE SPECIAL
DC
- ❑1, Oct 1990; JKu (a); reprints Showcase and Our Army at War ... 3.00

ENEMY ACE: WAR IN HEAVEN
DC
- ❑1, May 2001 ... 5.95
- ❑2, Jun 2001 ... 5.95

ENFORCE
REOCCURRING IMAGES
- ❑1 ... 2.95

ENGINEHEAD
DC
- ❑1, May 2004 ... 2.50
- ❑2, Jun 2004 ... 2.50
- ❑3, Aug 2004 ... 2.50
- ❑4, Oct 2004 ... 2.50
- ❑5, Nov 2004 ... 2.50
- ❑6, Jan 2005 ... 2.50

ENIGMA
DC / VERTIGO
- ❑1, Mar 1993 ... 2.50
- ❑2, Apr 1993 ... 2.50
- ❑3, May 1993 ... 2.50
- ❑4, Jun 1993 ... 2.50
- ❑5, Jul 1993 ... 2.50
- ❑6, Aug 1993 ... 2.50
- ❑7, Sep 1993 ... 2.50
- ❑8, Oct 1993 ... 2.50

ENO & PLUM
ONI
- ❑1, Mar 1998, b&w ... 2.95

ENTROPY TALES
ENTROPY
- ❑1 ... 1.50
- ❑2 ... 1.50
- ❑3 ... 1.50
- ❑4 ... 1.50

ENTS
MANIC
- ❑1, b&w ... 2.50
- ❑2, b&w ... 2.50
- ❑3, b&w ... 2.50

EO
REBEL
- ❑1 ... 3.00
- ❑1/Ltd.; Limited "Premier" edition ... 3.00
- ❑2 ... 3.00
- ❑2/Ltd.; limited edition ... 3.00
- ❑3 ... 3.00
- ❑4 ... 3.00

EPIC ANTHOLOGY
MARVEL / EPIC
- ❑1, Apr 2004, Sleepwalker, Young Ancient One, and Strange Magic stories ... 5.99

EPIC ILLUSTRATED
MARVEL / EPIC
- ❑1, Spr 1980, FF (c); WP, JSn, FF (a); 1: Dreadstar. A: Silver Surfer. ... 6.00
- ❑2, Sum 1980 ... 4.00
- ❑3, Aut 1980 ... 4.00
- ❑4, Win 1980 ... 4.00
- ❑5, Apr 1981 ... 3.00
- ❑6, Jun 1981 ... 3.00
- ❑7, Aug 1981 ... 3.00
- ❑8, Oct 1981 ... 3.00
- ❑9, Dec 1981 ... 3.00
- ❑10, Feb 1982 ... 3.00
- ❑11, Apr 1982 ... 3.00
- ❑12, Jun 1982 ... 3.00
- ❑13, Aug 1982 ... 3.00
- ❑14, Oct 1982 ... 3.00
- ❑15, Dec 1982 ... 3.00
- ❑16, Feb 1983 ... 3.00
- ❑17, Apr 1983 ... 3.00
- ❑18, Jun 1983 ... 3.00
- ❑19, Aug 1983 ... 3.00
- ❑20, Oct 1983 ... 3.00
- ❑21, Dec 1983 ... 3.00
- ❑22, Feb 1984 ... 3.00
- ❑23, Apr 1984 ... 3.00
- ❑24, Jun 1984 ... 3.00
- ❑25, Aug 1984 ... 3.00
- ❑26, Oct 1984 ... 3.00
- ❑27, Dec 1984 ... 3.00
- ❑28, Feb 1985 ... 3.00
- ❑29, Apr 1985 ... 3.00
- ❑30, Jun 1985 ... 3.00
- ❑31, Aug 1985 ... 3.00
- ❑32, Oct 1985 ... 3.00
- ❑33, Dec 1985 ... 3.00
- ❑34, Feb 1986 ... 3.00

EPIC LITE
MARVEL / EPIC
- ❑1, Sep 1991 ... 4.50

EPSILON WAVE
INDEPENDENT
- ❑1, Oct 1985; Independent Comics publishes ... 1.50
- ❑2, Dec 1985 ... 1.50
- ❑3, Feb 1986 ... 1.50
- ❑4, Apr 1986 ... 1.50
- ❑5, May 1986; Elite begins as publisher ... 1.75
- ❑6, Jun 1986 ... 1.75
- ❑7, Aug 1986 ... 1.75
- ❑8 1986 ... 1.75

EQUINE THE UNCIVILIZED
GRAPHXPRESS
- ❑1, b&w ... 2.00
- ❑2 ... 2.00
- ❑3 ... 2.00
- ❑4 ... 2.00
- ❑5 ... 2.00
- ❑6 ... 2.00

EQUINOX CHRONICLES
INNOVATION
- ❑1, b&w ... 2.25
- ❑2, b&w ... 2.25

ERADICATOR
DC
- ❑1, Aug 1996 ... 1.75
- ❑2, Sep 1996 ... 1.75
- ❑3, Oct 1996 ... 1.75

ERADICATORS
SILVERWOLF
- ❑1, May 1986 ... 1.50
- ❑2, Jul 1986 ... 1.50
- ❑3, Aug 1986 ... 1.50
- ❑4, Sep 1986 ... 1.50

ERADICATORS (VOL. 2)
SILVERWOLF
- ❑1, Aug 1989, b&w; Cover says September ... 2.00
- ❑2, Apr 1990, b&w ... 2.00

ERIC PRESTON IS THE FLAME
B-MOVIE
- ❑1 ... 1.00

ERIKA TELEKINETIKA
FANTAGRAPHICS
- ❑1 2004 ... 3.95
- ❑2 2004 ... 3.95
- ❑3 2005 ... 3.95

ERNIE
KITCHEN SINK
- ❑1; comics ... 2.00

EROS FORUM
FANTAGRAPHICS / EROS
- ❑1, b&w ... 2.50
- ❑3, b&w ... 2.95

EROS GRAPHIC ALBUM
FANTAGRAPHICS / EROS
- ❑1 ... 9.95
- ❑2 ... 12.95
- ❑3 ... 10.95
- ❑4 ... 10.95
- ❑5 ... 14.95
- ❑6 ... 16.95
- ❑7 ... 12.95
- ❑8 ... 12.95
- ❑9 ... 9.95
- ❑10 ... 12.95
- ❑11 ... 11.95
- ❑12 ... 12.95
- ❑13 ... 12.95
- ❑14 ... 14.95
- ❑15 ... 14.95
- ❑16 ... 14.95
- ❑17 ... 15.95
- ❑18 ... 12.95
- ❑19 ... 14.95
- ❑20 ... 12.95
- ❑21 ... 14.95
- ❑22 ... 14.95
- ❑23 ... 12.95
- ❑24 ... 12.95
- ❑25 ... 16.95
- ❑26 ... 13.95
- ❑27 ... 11.95
- ❑28 ... 16.95
- ❑29 ... 16.95
- ❑30 ... 13.95
- ❑31 ... 19.95
- ❑32 ... 16.95
- ❑33 ... 16.95
- ❑34; Buffy Collection ... 14.95
- ❑35 ... 14.95
- ❑36 ... 19.95
- ❑37 ... 19.95
- ❑38 ... 19.95
- ❑39 ... 19.95
- ❑40 ... 19.95
- ❑41 ... 19.95
- ❑42 ... 19.95
- ❑43 ... 16.95
- ❑44 ... 16.95

EROS HAWK
FANTAGRAPHICS / EROS
- ❑1 ... 2.75
- ❑2 ... 2.75
- ❑3 ... 2.75
- ❑4 ... 2.75

EROS HAWK III
FANTAGRAPHICS / EROS
- ❑1, Jul 1994, b&w ... 2.75

EROTIC FABLES & FAERIE TALES
FANTAGRAPHICS / EROS
- ❑1, b&w ... 2.50
- ❑2, b&w ... 2.50

EROTICOM
CALIBER
- ❑1 ... 2.50

ENCHANTER

Other grades: Multiply price above by 5/6 for VF/NM • 2/3 for VERY FINE • 1/3 for FINE • 1/5 for VERY GOOD • 1/8 for GOOD

Elvira, Mistress of the Dark

Horror hostess has satiric adventures

©Claypool

Elvira's House of Mystery

DC horror anthology gets new hostess

©DC

E-Man (1st series)

Joe Staton, Nicola Cuti super-hero series

©Charlton

Emma Davenport

Series began as strips in CBG

©Lohman Hills

Empire (Image)

Tyrant takes over Earth

©Image

N-MINT

EROTICOM II
CALIBER
❑1, ca. 1994, b&w; pin-ups, many swiped from Playboy's Book of Lingerie ... 2.95

EROTIC ORBITS
COMAX
❑1, b&w ... 2.95

EROTIC TALES
AIRCEL
❑1, b&w ... 2.95
❑2, b&w ... 2.95
❑3, b&w ... 2.95

EROTIC WORLDS OF FRANK THORNE
FANTAGRAPHICS / EROS
❑1, Oct 1990; FT (w); FT (a); sexy cover 2.95
❑1/A, Oct 1990; FT (w); FT (a); Violent cover ... 2.95
❑2 FT (w); FT (a) ... 2.95
❑3 FT (w); FT (a) ... 2.95
❑4 FT (w); FT (a) ... 2.95
❑5 FT (w); FT (a) ... 2.95
❑6 FT (w); FT (a) ... 2.95

EROTIQUE
AIRCEL
❑1, b&w ... 2.50

ERSATZ PEACH
AEON
❑1, Jul 1995; see also The Desert Peach; Charity fund-raiser; Desert Peach stories by various artists and writers ... 7.95

ESC
COMICO
❑1 1996 ... 2.95
❑2, Sep 1996 ... 2.95
❑3 1996 ... 2.95
❑4 1997 ... 2.95

ESCAPADE IN FLORENCE
GOLD KEY
❑1, Jan 1963 ... 40.00

ESCAPE TO THE STARS
SOLSON
❑1 ... 1.75

ESPERS
ECLIPSE
❑1, Jul 1986 ... 3.00
❑2, Sep 1986 ... 2.00
❑3, Nov 1986 BB (c); BB (a) ... 2.00
❑4, Feb 1987 ... 2.00
❑5, Apr 1987; Story continued in Interface #1 ... 2.00

ESPERS (VOL. 2)
HALLOWEEN
❑1 1996, b&w ... 3.50
❑2 1996, b&w ... 3.00
❑3 1997, b&w ... 3.00
❑4 1997, b&w ... 3.00
❑5 1997, b&w ... 3.00
❑6 1997 ... 3.00

N-MINT

ESPERS (VOL. 3)
IMAGE
❑1 1997, b&w ... 3.50
❑2 1997, b&w ... 3.00
❑3, Aug 1997, b&w ... 3.00
❑4 1997, b&w ... 3.00
❑5 1997, b&w ... 3.00
❑6 1997, b&w ... 3.00
❑7 1998, b&w ... 3.00
❑8 1998 ... 3.00
❑9 ... 3.00

ESPIONAGE
DELL
❑1 ... 18.00
❑2 ... 15.00

ESSENTIAL VERTIGO: SWAMP THING
DC / VERTIGO
❑1, Nov 1996; AMo (w); Reprints Saga of the Swamp Thing #21 ... 3.00
❑2, Dec 1996; AMo (w); Reprints Saga of the Swamp Thing #22 ... 2.50
❑3, Jan 1997; AMo (w); Reprints Saga of the Swamp Thing #23 ... 2.50
❑4, Feb 1997; AMo (w); Reprints Saga of the Swamp Thing #24 ... 2.50
❑5, Mar 1997; AMo (w); Reprints Saga of the Swamp Thing #25 ... 2.50
❑6, Apr 1997; Reprints Saga of the Swamp Thing #26 ... 2.00
❑7, May 1997; Reprints Saga of the Swamp Thing #27 ... 2.00
❑8, Jun 1997; Reprints Saga of the Swamp Thing #28 ... 2.00
❑9, Jul 1997; Reprints Saga of the Swamp Thing #29 ... 2.00
❑10, Aug 1997; AA (a); Reprints Saga of the Swamp Thing #30 ... 2.00
❑11, Sep 1997; Reprints Saga of the Swamp Thing #31 ... 2.00
❑12, Oct 1997; Reprints Saga of the Swamp Thing #32 ... 2.00
❑13, Nov 1997; AMo (w); Reprints Saga of the Swamp Thing #32 ... 2.00
❑14, Dec 1997; AMo (w); Reprints Saga of the Swamp Thing #34 ... 2.00
❑15, Jan 1998; Reprints Saga of the Swamp Thing #34 ... 2.00
❑16, Feb 1998; Reprints Saga of the Swamp Thing #35 ... 2.00
❑17, Mar 1998; Reprints Saga of the Swamp Thing #36 ... 2.00
❑18, Apr 1998; Reprints Saga of the Swamp Thing #37 ... 2.00
❑19, May 1998; Reprints Saga of the Swamp Thing #38 ... 2.00
❑20, Jun 1998; Reprints Saga of the Swamp Thing #39 ... 2.00
❑21, Jul 1998; Reprints Saga of the Swamp Thing #40 ... 2.00
❑22, Aug 1998; AA (a); Reprints Saga of the Swamp Thing #41 ... 2.00
❑23, Sep 1998; Reprints Saga of the Swamp Thing #42 ... 2.25
❑24, Oct 1998 ... 2.25

ESSENTIAL VERTIGO: THE SANDMAN
DC / VERTIGO
❑1, Aug 1996, NG (w); Reprints Sandman #1 ... 3.00

N-MINT

❑2, Sep 1996, NG (w); Reprints Sandman #2 ... 2.50
❑3, Oct 1996, NG (w); Reprints Sandman #3 ... 2.50
❑4, Oct 1996, NG (w); Reprints Sandman #4 ... 2.50
❑5, Dec 1996, NG (w); Reprints Sandman #5 ... 2.50
❑6, Jan 1997, NG (w); Reprints Sandman #6 ... 2.00
❑7, Feb 1997, NG (w); Reprints Sandman #7 ... 2.00
❑8, Mar 1997, NG (w); 1: Death (Sandman). Reprints Sandman #8.. 2.00
❑9, Apr 1997, NG (w); Reprints Sandman #9 ... 2.00
❑10, May 1997, NG (w); Reprints Sandman #10 ... 2.00
❑11, Jun 1997, NG (w); Reprints Sandman #11 ... 2.00
❑12, Jul 1997, NG (w); Reprints Sandman #12 ... 2.00
❑13, Aug 1997, NG (w); Reprints Sandman #13 ... 2.00
❑14, Sep 1997, NG (w); Reprints Sandman #14 ... 2.00
❑15, Oct 1997, NG (w); Reprints Sandman #15 ... 2.00
❑16, Nov 1997, NG (w); Reprints Sandman #16 ... 2.00
❑17, Dec 1997, NG (w); Reprints Sandman #17 ... 2.00
❑18, Jan 1998, NG (w); Reprints Sandman #18 ... 2.00
❑19, Feb 1998, NG (w); CV (a); Reprints Sandman #19 ... 2.00
❑20, Mar 1998, NG (w); Reprints Sandman #20 ... 2.00
❑21, Apr 1998, NG (w); Reprints Sandman #21 ... 1.95
❑22, May 1998, NG (w); Reprints Sandman #22 ... 1.95
❑23, Jun 1998, NG (w); Reprints Sandman #23 ... 1.95
❑24, Jul 1998, NG (w); Reprints Sandman #24 ... 1.95
❑25, Aug 1998, NG (w); Reprints Sandman #25 ... 1.95
❑26, Sep 1998, NG (w); Reprints Sandman #26 ... 2.25
❑27, Oct 1998, NG (w); Reprints Sandman #27 ... 2.25
❑28, Nov 1998, NG (w); Reprints Sandman #28 ... 2.25
❑29, Dec 1998, NG (w); Reprints Sandman #29 ... 2.25
❑30, Jan 1999, NG (w); Reprints Sandman #30 ... 2.25
❑31, Feb 1999, NG (w); Reprints Sandman #31 ... 2.25
❑32, Mar 1999, NG (w); BT (a); Reprints Sandman Special #1 ... 4.50

ESTABLISHMENT
DC / WILDSTORM
❑1, Nov 2001 ... 3.00
❑2, Dec 2001 ... 2.50
❑3, Jan 2002 ... 2.50
❑4, Feb 2002 ... 2.50
❑5, Mar 2002 ... 2.50

❑6, Apr 2002 .... 2.50
❑7, May 2002 .... 2.50
❑8, Jun 2002 .... 2.50
❑9, Jul 2002 .... 2.50
❑10, Aug 2002 .... 2.50
❑11, Sep 2002 .... 2.50
❑12, Oct 2002 .... 2.50
❑13, Nov 2002 .... 2.50

ETC
DC / Piranha

❑1 .... 2.50
❑2 .... 2.50
❑3 .... 2.50
❑4 .... 2.50
❑5 .... 2.50

ET CETERA
Tokyopop

❑1, Aug 2004, ... 9.95
❑2, Oct 2004 .... 9.95
❑3, Dec 2004 .... 9.95
❑4, Feb 2005 .... 9.95
❑5, May 2005 .... 9.95
❑6, Oct 2005 .... 9.95

ETERNAL
Marvel / MAX

❑1, Aug 2003 .... 2.99
❑2, Sep 2003 .... 2.99
❑3, Oct 2003 .... 2.99
❑4, Nov 2003 .... 2.99
❑5, Dec 2003 .... 2.99
❑6, Jan 2004 .... 2.99

ETERNAL ROMANCE
Best Destiny

❑1, Feb 1997, b&w 3.00
❑2, May 1997, b&w 2.50
❑3, Dec 1997 .... 2.50
❑4, Jul 1998 .... 2.50

ETERNAL ROMANCE LABOR OF LOVE SKETCHBOOK
Best Destiny

❑1; Labor of Love sketchbook. 250 printed 2.50

ETERNALS
Marvel

❑1, Jul 1976, JK (w); JK (a); O: Eternals. 1: Kro. 1: Margo Damian. 1: Brother Tode. 1: Ikaris. 1st appearance 10.00
❑1/30 cent, Jul 1976, JK (w); JK (a); O: Eternals. 1: Kro. 1: Margo Damian. 1: Brother Tode. 1: Ikaris. 30 cent regional price variant; 1st appearance 25.00
❑2, Aug 1976, JK (w); JK (a); 1: Ajak. 1: Arishem the Judge. 5.00
❑2/30 cent, Aug 1976, JK (w); JK (a); 1: Ajak. 1: Arishem the Judge. 30 cent regional price variant 20.00
❑3, Sep 1976, JK (w); JK (a); 1: Sersi. 2.50
❑4, Oct 1976, JK (w); JK (a); 1: Gammenon the Gatherer. 2.50
❑5, Nov 1976, JK (w); JK (a); 1: Makkari. 1: Zuras (Thena) 2.50
❑6, Dec 1976, JK (w); JK (a); 2.00
❑7, Jan 1977, JK (w); JK (a); 1: Nezarr. 2.00
❑8, Feb 1977, JK (w); JK (a); 1: Karkas. Newsstand edition (distributed by Curtis); issue number in box 2.00
❑8/Whitman, Feb 1977, JK (w); JK (a); 1: Karkas. Special markets edition (usually sold in Whitman bagged prepacks); price appears in a diamond; UPC barcode appears 2.00
❑9, Mar 1977, JK (w); JK (a); 1: Sprite I. Newsstand edition (distributed by Curtis); issue number in box 2.00
❑9/Whitman, Mar 1977, JK (w); JK (a); 1: Sprite I. Special markets edition (usually sold in Whitman bagged prepacks); price appears in a diamond; UPC barcode appears 2.00
❑10, Apr 1977, JK (w); JK (a); Newsstand edition (distributed by Curtis); issue number in box 2.00
❑10/Whitman, Apr 1977, JK (w); JK (a); Special markets edition (usually sold in Whitman bagged prepacks); price appears in a diamond; UPC barcode appears 2.00
❑11, May 1977, JK (w); JK (a); 1: Aginar. 2.00
❑12, Jun 1977, JK (w); JK (a); 1: Uni-Mind. Newsstand edition (distributed by Curtis); issue number in box 2.00
❑12/Whitman, Jun 1977, JK (w); JK (a); 1: Uni-Mind. Special markets edition (usually sold in Whitman bagged prepacks); price appears in a diamond; UPC barcode appears 2.00
❑12/35 cent, Jun 1977, JK (w); JK (a); 1: Uni-Mind. 35 cent regional price variant; newsstand edition (distributed by Curtis); issue number in box 15.00
❑13, Jul 1977, JK (w); JK (a); 1: Gilgamesh. 1: One Above All. Newsstand edition (distributed by Curtis); issue number in box 2.00
❑13/Whitman, Jul 1977, JK (w); JK (a); 1: Gilgamesh. 1: One Above All. Special markets edition (usually sold in Whitman bagged prepacks); price appears in a diamond; UPC barcode appears 2.00
❑13/35 cent, Jul 1977, JK (w); JK (a); 1: Gilgamesh. 1: One Above All. 35 cent regional price variant; newsstand edition (distributed by Curtis); issue number in box 15.00
❑14, Aug 1977, JK (w); JK (a); A: Hulk. Newsstand edition (distributed by Curtis); issue number in box 2.00
❑14/Whitman, Aug 1977, JK (w); JK (a); A: Hulk. Special markets edition (usually sold in Whitman bagged prepacks); price appears in a diamond; UPC barcode appears 2.00
❑14/35 cent, Aug 1977, JK (w); JK (a); A: Hulk. 35 cent regional price variant; newsstand edition (distributed by Curtis); issue number in box 15.00
❑15, Sep 1977, JK (w); JK (a); A: Hulk. Newsstand edition (distributed by Curtis); issue number in box 2.00
❑15/Whitman, Sep 1977, JK (w); JK (a); A: Hulk. Special markets edition (usually sold in Whitman bagged prepacks); price appears in a diamond; UPC barcode appears 2.00
❑15/35 cent, Sep 1977, JK (w); JK (a); A: Hulk. 35 cent regional price variant; newsstand edition (distributed by Curtis); issue number in box 15.00
❑16, Oct 1977, JK (w); JK (a); Newsstand edition (distributed by Curtis); issue number in box 2.00
❑16/Whitman, Oct 1977, JK (w); JK (a); Special markets edition (usually sold in Whitman bagged prepacks); price appears in a diamond; no UPC barcode 2.00
❑16/35 cent, Oct 1977, JK (w); JK (a); 35 cent regional price variant; newsstand edition (distributed by Curtis); issue number in box 15.00
❑17, Nov 1977, JK (w); JK (a); Newsstand edition (distributed by Curtis); issue number in box 2.00
❑17/Whitman, Nov 1977, JK (w); JK (a); Special markets edition (usually sold in Whitman bagged prepacks); price appears in a diamond; no UPC barcode 2.00
❑18, Dec 1977, JK (w); JK (a) 2.00
❑19, Jan 1978, JK (w); JK (a); 1: Ziran. 2.00
❑Annual 1, Oct 1977, JK (w); JK (a) ... 3.00

ETERNALS, THE (LTD. SERIES)
Marvel

❑1, Oct 1985; Giant-size 1: Khoryphos. 1.50
❑2, Nov 1985 1: Ghaur. 1.00
❑3, Dec 1985 .... 1.00
❑4, Jan 1986 .... 1.00
❑5, Feb 1986 .... 1.00
❑6, Mar 1986 .... 1.00
❑7, Apr 1986 .... 1.00
❑8, May 1986 .... 1.00
❑9, Jun 1986 .... 1.00
❑10, Jul 1986 O: Ghaur. D: Margo Damian. 1.00
❑11, Aug 1986 .... 1.00
❑12, Sep 1986; Giant-size 1.25

ETERNALS (2ND SERIES)
Marvel

❑1, Sep 2006 .... 2.99
❑1/Variant, Sep 2006 .... 2.99
❑1/2nd variant, Sep 2006 .... 2.99

ETERNALS SKETCHBOOK
Marvel

❑1, Aug 2006 .... 2.50

ETERNALS: THE HEROD FACTOR
Marvel

❑1, Nov 1991 .... 2.50

ETERNAL THIRST
Alpha Productions

❑3, b&w 1.95
❑4, b&w 1.95
❑5, b&w 1.95

ETERNAL WARRIOR
Valiant

❑1, Aug 1992; FM (c); Unity 4.00
❑1/GoldEmboss, Aug 1992, FM (c); ... 35.00
❑1/Gold, Aug 1992; FM (c); Gold logo (dealer promotion) 20.00
❑2, Sep 1992; Unity 3.00
❑3, Oct 1992 A: Armstrong. 2.00
❑4, Nov 1992 1: Bloodshot (cameo) ... 5.00
❑5, Dec 1992 A: Bloodshot 2.00
❑6, Jan 1993 V: Master Darque. 2.00
❑7, Feb 1993 .... 2.00
❑8, Mar 1993; Double-size; combined with Archer & Armstrong #8 .... 3.00
❑9, Apr 1993 .... 1.00
❑10, May 1993 .... 1.00
❑11, Jun 1993 .... 1.00
❑12, Jul 1993 .... 1.00
❑13, Aug 1993 V: Eternal Enemy. 1.00
❑14, Sep 1993 A: Bloodshot 1.00
❑15, Oct 1993 A: Bloodshot. 1.00
❑16, Nov 1993 .... 1.00
❑17, Dec 1993 .... 1.00
❑18, Jan 1994 .... 1.00
❑19, Feb 1994 A: Doctor Mirage 1.00
❑20, Mar 1994 .... 1.00
❑21, Apr 1994 .... 1.00
❑22, May 1994; trading card 2.00
❑23, Jun 1994 .... 1.00
❑24, Aug 1994 V: Immortal Enemy 1.00
❑25, Sep 1994 A: Archer & Armstrong. 1.00
❑26, Oct 1994; indicia says August; Flip-book with Archer & Armstrong #26; Chaos Effect Gamma 4 .... 4.00
❑27, Nov 1994 .... 1.00
❑27/VVSS, Nov 1994 .... 125.00
❑28, Dec 1994 .... 1.00
❑29, Jan 1995 .... 1.00
❑30, Feb 1995 .... 2.00
❑31, Mar 1995 .... 2.00
❑32, Apr 1995 .... 2.00
❑33, May 1995 PG (c) 2.00
❑34, Jun 1995 PG (c) 2.00
❑35, Jul 1995; PG (c); Birthquake; outer white cover with warning 2.00
❑36, Jul 1995; PG (a); Birthquake 2.00
❑37, Aug 1995 .... 2.00
❑38, Aug 1995 V: Spider Queen. 2.00
❑39, Sep 1995 PG (c) 2.00
❑40, Sep 1995 PG (c) 2.00
❑41, Oct 1995 .... 3.00
❑42, Oct 1995 .... 3.00
❑43, Nov 1995 .... 3.00
❑44, Nov 1995 .... 3.00
❑45, Dec 1995 .... 3.00
❑46, Dec 1995 .... 4.00
❑47, Jan 1996 .... 4.00
❑48, Jan 1996 .... 4.00
❑49, Feb 1996 .... 4.00
❑50, Mar 1996 A: Geomancer 7.00
❑Special 1, Feb 1996 .... 4.00
❑Yearbook 1, ca. 1993; Yearbook 1; cardstock cover 5.00
❑Yearbook 2, ca. 1994; Yearbook 2; PG (c); cardstock cover ....

ETERNAL WARRIOR: FIST AND STEEL
Acclaim / Valiant

❑1, May 1996, A: Geomancer. 5.00
❑2, Jun 1996, A: Geomancer. 6.00

ESTABLISHMENT

Other grades: Multiply price above by 5/6 for VF/NM • 2/3 for VERY FINE • 1/3 for FINE • 1/5 for VERY GOOD • 1/8 for GOOD

Encyclopédia Deadpoolica

Reveals background on Marvel mercenary
©Marvel

Endless Gallery

Pin-ups of Sandman and relatives
©DC

Enemy Ace Special

Reprints Showcase and Our Army at War
©DC

Ernie

Newspaper strip reprints
©Kitchen Sink

Espers (Vol. 2)

James Robinson's series about psychics
©Halloween

N-MINT

ETERNAL WARRIORS
ACCLAIM / VALIANT

❑1, Jun 1997 .... 3.95
❑1/Variant, Jun 1997; alternate painted cover 3.95
❑Ashcan 1, Feb 1997, b&w; No cover price; preview of Time and Treachery one-shot 1.00

ETERNAL WARRIORS: ARCHER & ARMSTRONG
ACCLAIM / VALIANT

❑1, Dec 1997; price stickered on cover 3.95

ETERNAL WARRIORS BLACKWORKS
ACCLAIM / VALIANT

❑1, Mar 1998 .... 3.95

ETERNAL WARRIORS: DIGITAL ALCHEMY
ACCLAIM / VALIANT

❑1, Sep 1997 .... 3.95

ETERNAL WARRIORS: MOG
ACCLAIM / VALIANT

❑1, Mar 1998 .... 3.95

ETERNAL WARRIOR SPECIAL
ACCLAIM / VALIANT

❑1, Feb 1996; Eternal Warrior in WW II 2.50

ETERNAL WARRIORS: THE IMMORTAL ENEMY
ACCLAIM / VALIANT

❑1; Final issue of VH-2 universe 3.95

ETERNAL WARRIORS: TIME AND TREACHERY
ACCLAIM / VALIANT

❑1, ca. 1997 .... 3.95

ETERNITY SMITH (VOL. 1)
RENEGADE

❑1, Sep 1986 .... 1.50
❑2, Nov 1986 .... 1.50
❑3, Jan 1987 .... 1.50
❑4, Mar 1987 .... 1.50
❑5, May 1987 .... 1.50

ETERNITY SMITH (VOL. 2)
HERO

❑1, Sep 1987 .... 1.95
❑2, Oct 1987 .... 1.95
❑3, Nov 1987 .... 1.95
❑4, Dec 1987 .... 1.95
❑5, Jan 1988 .... 1.95
❑6, Feb 1988 .... 1.95
❑7, Apr 1988 .... 1.95
❑8, Jun 1988 .... 1.95
❑9, Aug 1988 .... 1.95

ETERNITY TRIPLE ACTION
ETERNITY

❑1, b&w 2.50
❑2, b&w 2.50
❑3, b&w 2.50
❑4, b&w 2.50

EUDAEMON
DARK HORSE

❑1, Aug 1993 .... 2.50

N-MINT

❑2 .... 2.50
❑3 .... 2.50

EUGENUS
EUGENUS

❑1, b&w 3.50
❑2, b&w 3.50
❑3 .... 2.50

EUREKA
RADIO

❑1, Apr 2000, b&w 2.95
❑2, Jul 2000, b&w 2.95
❑3, Sep 2000, b&w 2.95

EUROPA AND THE PIRATE TWINS
POWDER MONKEY

❑1, Oct 1996, b&w 2.95
❑1/A, Oct 1996, b&w; no cover price . 2.95
❑Ashcan 1, Mar 1996, b&w; No cover price; smaller than normal comic ... 1.00

EVANGELINE SPECIAL
LODESTONE

❑1 .... 2.00

EVANGELINE (VOL. 1)
COMICO

❑1, ca. 1984, 1: Evangeline. 2.50
❑2, ca. 1984, ... 2.00

EVANGELINE (VOL. 2)
FIRST

❑1, May 1987 .... 2.50
❑2, Jul 1987 .... 2.00
❑3, Sep 1987 .... 2.00
❑4, Nov 1987 .... 2.00
❑5, Jan 1988 .... 2.00
❑6, Mar 1988 .... 2.00
❑7, May 1988 .... 2.00
❑8, Jul 1988 .... 2.00
❑9, Sep 1988 .... 2.00
❑10, Nov 1988 .... 2.00
❑11, Jan 1989 .... 2.00
❑12, Mar 1989 .... 2.00

EVEL KNIEVEL
MARVEL

❑1; giveaway 10.00

EVENFALL
SLAVE LABOR

❑1, Mar 2003, b&w; Title is actually The Fallen: Evenfall 2.95
❑2, May 2003, b&w 2.95
❑3, ca. 2003, b&w 2.95
❑4, ca. 2004, b&w 2.95
❑5, ca. 2004, b&w 2.95
❑6, ca. 2004, b&w 2.95
❑7, Feb 2005, b&w 2.95

EVEN MORE SECRET ORIGINS 80-PAGE GIANT
DC

❑1, ca. 2003 .... 6.95

E.V.E. PROTOMECHA
IMAGE

❑1 .... 2.50
❑1/A, Alternate Cover Finch 2.50
❑1/Gold; Gold Cover 2.50
❑1/Hologram; Holofield 2.50

N-MINT

❑2 .... 2.50
❑3, May 2000 .... 2.50
❑4, Nov 2000 .... 2.50
❑5 .... 2.50
❑6, Sep 2000 .... 2.50

EVERQUEST: THE RUINS OF KUNARK
DC / WILDSTORM

❑1, Feb 2002, Several characters in profile on cover 5.95

EVERQUEST: TRANSFORMATION
DC

❑1, Aug 2002, Several characters in profile on cover 5.95

EVERWINDS
SLAVE LABOR / AMAZE INK

❑1, Aug 1997, b&w 2.95
❑2, Oct 1997, b&w 2.95
❑3, Dec 1997, b&w 2.95
❑4, Mar 1998 .... 2.95

EVERY DOG HAS HIS DAY
SHIGA

❑1 .... 2.00

EVERYMAN
MARVEL / EPIC

❑1, Nov 1991 .... 4.50

EVERYTHING'S ARCHIE
ARCHIE

❑1, May 1969, Giant-size 48.00
❑2 1969 .... 26.00
❑3 1969 .... 20.00
❑4 1969 .... 20.00
❑5 .... 20.00
❑6 1970 .... 12.00
❑7 1970 .... 12.00
❑8 1970 .... 12.00
❑9 .... 12.00
❑10 1971 .... 12.00
❑11 1971 .... 7.00
❑12 1971 .... 7.00
❑13 1971 .... 7.00
❑14 1971 .... 7.00
❑15 1971 .... 7.00
❑16 .... 7.00
❑17 1972 .... 7.00
❑18 1972 .... 7.00
❑19 1972 .... 7.00
❑20 1972 .... 7.00
❑21, Aug 1972 .... 4.00
❑22, Oct 1972 .... 4.00
❑23, Dec 1972 .... 4.00
❑24, Feb 1973 .... 4.00
❑25, Apr 1973 .... 4.00
❑26, Jun 1973 .... 4.00
❑27, Aug 1973 .... 4.00
❑28, Sep 1973 .... 4.00
❑29, Oct 1973 .... 4.00
❑30, Dec 1973 .... 4.00
❑31, Feb 1974 .... 4.00
❑32, Apr 1974 .... 4.00
❑33, Jun 1974 .... 4.00
❑34, Aug 1974 .... 4.00
❑35, Sep 1974 .... 4.00
❑36, Oct 1974 .... 4.00

Other grades: Multiply price above by 5/6 for VF/NM • 2/3 for VERY FINE • 1/3 for FINE • 1/5 for VERY GOOD • 1/8 for GOOD

❑37, Dec 1974 .... 4.00
❑38, Feb 1975 .... 4.00
❑39, Apr 1975 .... 4.00
❑40, Jun 1975 .... 4.00
❑41, Aug 1975 .... 3.00
❑42, Sep 1975 .... 3.00
❑43, Oct 1975 .... 3.00
❑44, Dec 1975 .... 3.00
❑45, Feb 1976 .... 3.00
❑46, Apr 1976 .... 3.00
❑47, May 1976 .... 3.00
❑48, Jun 1976 .... 3.00
❑49, Jul 1976 .... 3.00
❑50, Aug 1976 .... 3.00
❑51, Sep 1976 .... 3.00
❑52, Oct 1976 .... 3.00
❑53, Dec 1976 .... 3.00
❑54, Feb 1977 .... 3.00
❑55, Apr 1977 .... 3.00
❑56, May 1977 .... 3.00
❑57, Jun 1977 .... 3.00
❑58, Jul 1977 .... 3.00
❑59, Aug 1977 .... 3.00
❑60, Sep 1977 .... 3.00
❑61, Oct 1977 .... 2.00
❑62, Dec 1977 .... 2.00
❑63, Feb 1978 .... 2.00
❑64, Apr 1978 .... 2.00
❑65, May 1978 .... 2.00
❑66, Jun 1978 .... 2.00
❑67, Jul 1978 .... 2.00
❑68, Aug 1978 .... 2.00
❑69, Sep 1978 .... 2.00
❑70, Oct 1978 .... 2.00
❑71, Dec 1978 .... 2.00
❑72, Feb 1979 .... 2.00
❑73, Apr 1979 .... 2.00
❑74, May 1979 .... 2.00
❑75, Jun 1979 .... 2.00
❑76, Jul 1979 .... 2.00
❑77, Aug 1979 .... 2.00
❑78, Sep 1979 .... 2.00
❑79, Oct 1979 .... 2.00
❑80, Dec 1979 .... 2.00
❑81, Feb 1980 .... 2.00
❑82, Apr 1980 .... 2.00
❑83, May 1980 .... 2.00
❑84, Jun 1980 .... 2.00
❑85, Jul 1980 .... 2.00
❑86, Aug 1980 .... 2.00
❑87, Sep 1980 .... 2.00
❑88, Oct 1980 .... 2.00
❑89, Dec 1980 .... 2.00
❑90, Feb 1981 .... 2.00
❑91, Apr 1981, (c) 2.00
❑92, May 1981 .... 2.00
❑93, Jun 1981 .... 2.00
❑94, Jul 1981 .... 2.00
❑95, Aug 1981, DDC (c) 2.00
❑96, Sep 1981 .... 2.00
❑97, Oct 1981 .... 2.00
❑98, Dec 1981, DDC (c) 2.00
❑99, Feb 1982 .... 2.00
❑100, Apr 1982 .... 2.00
❑101, Jun 1982 .... 1.50
❑102, Aug 1982 .... 1.50
❑103, Oct 1982 .... 1.50
❑104, Dec 1982 .... 1.50
❑105, Mar 1983 .... 1.50
❑106, Jun 1983, DDC (c) 1.50
❑107, Sep 1983, DDC (c) 1.50
❑108, Nov 1983, DDC (c) 1.50
❑109, Jan 1984, DDC (c) 1.50
❑110, Mar 1984, DDC (c) 1.50
❑111, May 1984 .... 1.50
❑112, Jul 1984 .... 1.50
❑113, Sep 1984, DDC (c) 1.50
❑114, Nov 1984, DDC (c); A: Reggie the Ruthless. A: Archie the Barbarian. A: Betty. A: Jughead. Veronica 1.50
❑115, Jan 1985, DDC (c) 1.50
❑116, Mar 1985, DDC (c) 1.50
❑117, May 1985, DDC (c) 1.50
❑118, Jul 1985, DDC (c) 1.50
❑119, Sep 1985, DDC (c) 1.50
❑120, Nov 1985, DDC (c) 1.50
❑121, Jan 1986, DDC (c) 1.50
❑122, Mar 1986, DDC (c) 1.50
❑123, May 1986, DDC (c) 1.50
❑124, Jul 1986, DDC (c) 1.50
❑125, Sep 1986, DDC (c) 1.50
❑126, Nov 1986, DDC (c) 1.50
❑127, Jan 1987, DDC (c) 1.50
❑128, Mar 1987, DDC (c) 1.50
❑129, May 1987, DDC (c) 1.50
❑130, Jul 1987, DDC (c) 1.50
❑131, Sep 1987, DDC (c) 1.50
❑132, Nov 1987, DDC (c) 1.50
❑133, Jan 1988, DDC (c) 1.50
❑134, Mar 1988, DDC (c) 1.50
❑135, May 1988, DDC (c) 1.50
❑136, Jul 1988, DDC (c) 1.50
❑137, Aug 1988, DDC (c) 1.50
❑138, Oct 1988, DDC (c) 1.50
❑139, Nov 1988, DDC (c) 1.50
❑140, Jan 1989 .... 1.50
❑141, Mar 1989, DDC (c) 1.50
❑142, May 1989, DDC (c) 1.50
❑143, Jul 1989, DDC (c) 1.50
❑144, Aug 1989, DDC (c) 1.50
❑145, Oct 1989, DDC (c) 1.50
❑146, Nov 1989, DDC (c) 1.50
❑147, Jan 1990, DDC (c) 1.50
❑148, Mar 1990, DDC (c) 1.50
❑149, May 1990, DDC (c) 1.50
❑150, Jul 1990, DDC (c) 1.50
❑151, Sep 1990, DDC (c) 1.50
❑152, Nov 1990, DDC (c) 1.50
❑153, Jan 1991, DDC (c) 1.50
❑154, Mar 1991, DDC (c) 1.50
❑155, May 1991, DDC (c) 1.50
❑156, Jul 1991, DDC (c) 1.50
❑157, Sep 1991, DDC (c) 1.50

EVIL ERNIE (ETERNITY)
ETERNITY

❑1, ca. 1991, b&w O: Evil Ernie. 1: Evil Ernie. 1: Lady Death. 12.00
❑1/Ltd.; Limited edition reprint (1992) O: Evil Ernie. 1: Evil Ernie. 1: Lady Death. 6.00
❑2, ca. 1992, b&w 5.00
❑3, ca. 1992, b&w 4.00
❑4, ca. 1992, b&w 4.00
❑5, ca. 1992, b&w 4.00

EVIL ERNIE (CHAOS!)
CHAOS!

❑0, ... 3.00
❑0/Platinum, Platinum edition 5.00
❑1, Jul 1998 .... 3.00
❑2, Aug 1998 .... 3.00
❑3, Sep 1998 .... 3.00
❑4, Oct 1998 .... 3.00
❑5, Nov 1998 .... 2.95
❑6, Dec 1998 .... 2.95
❑7, Jan 1999 .... 2.95
❑8, Feb 1999 .... 2.95
❑9, Mar 1999 .... 2.95
❑10, Apr 1999 .... 2.95

EVIL ERNIE: BADDEST BATTLES
CHAOS

❑1, Jan 1997 .... 1.50
❑1/Variant, Jan 1997; Splatterfest Premium Edition cover; Splatterfest Premium Edition cover 1.50

EVIL ERNIE: DEPRAVED
CHAOS!

❑1, Jul 1999 .... 2.95
❑2, Aug 1999 .... 2.95
❑3, Sep 1999 .... 2.95

EVIL ERNIE: DESTROYER
CHAOS!

❑1, Oct 1997 .... 2.95
❑2, Nov 1997 .... 2.95
❑3, Dec 1997 .... 2.95
❑4, Jan 1998 .... 2.95
❑5, Feb 1998 .... 2.95
❑6, Mar 1998 .... 2.95
❑7, Apr 1998 .... 2.95
❑8, May 1998 .... 2.95
❑9, Jun 1998 .... 2.95
❑Ashcan 1, Sep 1997 .... 2.50

EVIL ERNIE IN SANTA FE
DEVIL'S DUE / CHAOS

❑1, ... 2.99
❑2, Jan 2006 .... 2.99
❑2/Variant, Jan 2006 .... 2.99
❑3, Dec 2005 .... 2.99
❑4, Mar 2006 .... 2.99

EVIL ERNIE: NEW YEAR'S EVIL
CHAOS!

❑1 .... 5.00

EVIL ERNIE: PIECES OF ME
CHAOS!

❑1, Nov 2000, b&w 2.95
❑1/Variant, Nov 2000; Chromium Mega-Premium Edition; Limited to 2,500 .... 2.95

EVIL ERNIE: REVENGE
CHAOS!

❑0 .... 2.50
❑1, Oct 1994 .... 3.00
❑1/Deluxe, Oct 1994; Master of Annihilation premium edition 4.00
❑1/Ltd., Oct 1994; Glow-in-the-dark limited edition 4.00
❑2 1994 .... 3.00
❑3, Jan 1995 .... 2.50
❑4, Feb 1995 .... 2.50

EVIL ERNIE: STRAIGHT TO HELL
CHAOS!

❑1, Oct 1995; Coffin fold-out cover 3.00
❑1/A, Oct 1995; chromium cover 4.00
❑2, Dec 1995 .... 3.00
❑3, Feb 1996 .... 3.00
❑4, Apr 1996 .... 3.00
❑5, Jun 1996 .... 3.00

EVIL ERNIE: THE LOST SKETCHES
CHAOS

❑Ashcan 1, Jul 2001 .... 1.00

EVIL ERNIE: THE RESURRECTION
CHAOS!

❑1, ca. 1993, O: Evil Ernie. 4.00
❑1/Gold, ca. 1993, Gold promotional edition O: Evil Ernie. 5.00
❑2, ca. 1994, ... 3.50
❑3, ca. 1994, ... 3.50
❑4, ca. 1994, A: Lady Death. 3.00
❑Ashcan 1, ca. 1993, ... 5.00

EVIL ERNIE VS. THE MOVIE MONSTERS
CHAOS!

❑1/A, ca. 1997; TerrorVision cover 2.95
❑1, ca. 1997 .... 3.00

EVIL ERNIE VS. THE SUPER HEROES
CHAOS!

❑1, Aug 1995 O: Evil Ernie. 3.00
❑1/Variant, Aug 1995; premium edition (10, 000 copies); O: Evil Ernie. no cover price 3.00
❑2, Sep 1998 .... 2.95

EVIL ERNIE: WAR OF THE DEAD
CHAOS!

❑1, Nov 1999 .... 2.95
❑2, Dec 1999 .... 2.95
❑3, Jan 2000 .... 2.95

EVIL ERNIE: YOUTH GONE WILD
CHAOS!

❑1, Nov 1996, b&w; reprints Eternity's Evil Ernie 1.95
❑2, Dec 1996, b&w; reprints Eternity's Evil Ernie 1.95
❑3, Jan 1997, b&w; reprints Eternity's Evil Ernie 1.95
❑4, Feb 1997, b&w; reprints Eternity's Evil Ernie 1.95
❑5, Mar 1997, b&w; reprints Eternity's Evil Ernie 1.95
❑Special 1; "Director's Cut" #1 .... 4.95

EVIL EYE
FANTAGRAPHICS

❑1, Jun 1998 .... 2.95
❑2, Oct 1998 .... 2.95
❑3, Apr 1999 .... 2.95

EVILMAN SAVES THE WORLD
MOONSTONE

❑1, Jul 1996, b&w 2.95

Essential Vertigo: Swamp Thing

Black and white Alan Moore story reprints
©DC

Eternals

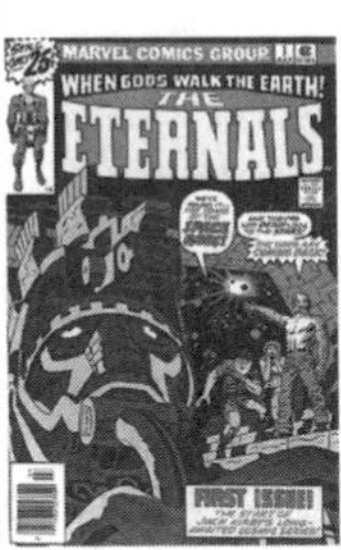

Jack Kirby's celestial series
©Marvel

Eternal Warrior

Armstrong's mercenary brother's adventures
©Valiant

Eternity Smith (Vol. 1)

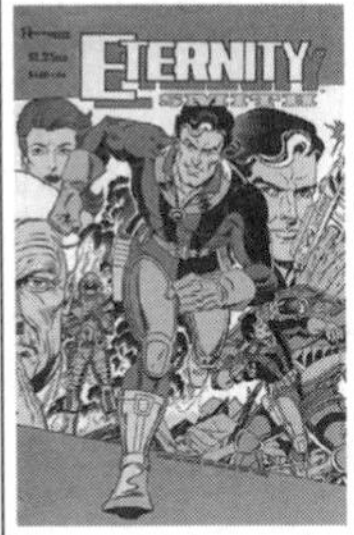

Super-powered companions thwart evil plots
©Renegade

Eudaemon

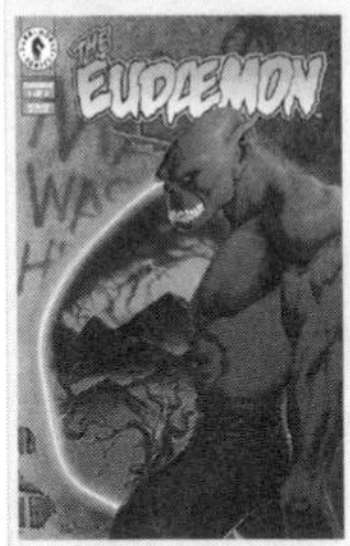

Friendly demon passes powers to son
©Dark Horse

N-MINT

EVIL'S RETURN
TOKYOPOP

- ❑1, Jul 2004, ... 9.95
- ❑2, Oct 2004 ... 9.95
- ❑3, Jan 2005 ... 9.95
- ❑4, Dec 2005 ... 9.95

EVO
IMAGE

- ❑1, Feb 2003 ... 2.99

EWOKS
MARVEL / STAR

- ❑1, May 1985 ... 3.00
- ❑2, Jul 1985 ... 2.00
- ❑3, Sep 1985 ... 2.00
- ❑4, Nov 1985 ... 2.00
- ❑5, Jan 1986 ... 2.00
- ❑6, Mar 1986 ... 2.00
- ❑7, May 1986 ... 2.00
- ❑8, Jul 1986 ... 2.00
- ❑9, Sep 1986 ... 2.00
- ❑10, Nov 1986 ... 2.00
- ❑11, Jan 1987 ... 2.00
- ❑12, Mar 1987 ... 2.00
- ❑13, May 1987 ... 2.00
- ❑14, Jul 1987 ... 2.00

EXCALIBUR
MARVEL

- ❑-1, Jul 1997; Flashback ... 2.00
- ❑1, Oct 1988 ... 2.50
- ❑2, Nov 1988 1: Tweedledope (in America). 1: Kylun. ... 2.00
- ❑3, Dec 1988 ... 2.00
- ❑4, Jan 1989 1: Jester (in America). 1: Red Queen (in America). 1: The Crazy Gang (in America). 1: Executioner (in America). 1: Knave (in America). 2.00
- ❑5, Feb 1989 ... 2.00
- ❑6, Mar 1989; Inferno ... 1.75
- ❑7, Apr 1989; Inferno ... 1.75
- ❑8, May 1989 ... 1.75
- ❑9, Jun 1989 ... 1.75
- ❑10, Jul 1989 ... 1.75
- ❑11, Aug 1989 ... 1.75
- ❑12, Sep 1989 ... 1.75
- ❑13, Oct 1989 ... 1.75
- ❑14, Nov 1989 ... 1.75
- ❑15, Nov 1989 ... 1.75
- ❑16, Dec 1989 ... 1.75
- ❑17, Dec 1989 ... 1.75
- ❑18, Jan 1990 ... 1.75
- ❑19, Feb 1990 ... 1.75
- ❑20, Mar 1990 ... 1.75
- ❑21, Apr 1990 ... 1.75
- ❑22, May 1990 ... 1.75
- ❑23, Jun 1990 ... 1.75
- ❑24, Jul 1990 ... 1.75
- ❑25, Aug 1990 ... 1.75
- ❑26, Aug 1990 ... 1.75
- ❑27, Aug 1990 A: Nth Man. ... 1.75
- ❑28, Sep 1990 ... 1.75
- ❑29, Sep 1990 ... 1.75
- ❑30, Oct 1990 ... 1.75
- ❑31, Nov 1990 ... 1.75
- ❑32, Dec 1990; with $1.75 price ... 1.75
- ❑32/A, Dec 1990; with $1.50 price ... 1.75
- ❑33, Jan 1991 ... 1.75
- ❑34, Feb 1991 ... 1.75
- ❑35, Mar 1991 ... 1.75
- ❑36, Apr 1991; Outlaws ... 1.75
- ❑37, May 1991 ... 1.75
- ❑38, Jun 1991 ... 1.75
- ❑39, Jul 1991 ... 1.75
- ❑40, Aug 1991 ... 1.75
- ❑41, Sep 1991 ... 1.75
- ❑42, Oct 1991 ... 1.75
- ❑43, Nov 1991 ... 1.75
- ❑44, Nov 1991 1: Micromax. ... 1.75
- ❑45, Dec 1991 1: Necrom. ... 1.75
- ❑46, Jan 1992 ... 1.75
- ❑47, Feb 1992 1: Cerise. ... 1.75
- ❑48, Mar 1992 1: Feron. ... 1.75
- ❑49, Apr 1992 ... 1.75
- ❑50, May 1992; Double-size; O: Feron. glow in the dark cover ... 2.75
- ❑51, Jun 1992 ... 1.75
- ❑52, Jul 1992 O: Phoenix III (Rachel Summers). A: X-Men ... 1.75
- ❑53, Aug 1992 A: Spider-Man. ... 1.75
- ❑54, Sep 1992 ... 1.75
- ❑55, Oct 1992 ... 1.75
- ❑56, Nov 1992 A: X-Men ... 1.75
- ❑57, Nov 1992 ... 1.75
- ❑58, Dec 1992 ... 1.75
- ❑59, Dec 1992 ... 1.75
- ❑60, Jan 1993 ... 1.75
- ❑61, Jan 1993 ... 1.75
- ❑62, Feb 1993 ... 1.75
- ❑63, Mar 1993 ... 1.75
- ❑64, Apr 1993 ... 1.75
- ❑65, May 1993 ... 1.75
- ❑66, Jun 1993 ... 1.75
- ❑67, Jul 1993 ... 1.75
- ❑68, Aug 1993 A: Starjammers. ... 1.75
- ❑69, Sep 1993 ... 1.75
- ❑70, Oct 1993 O: Cerise. A: Starjammers. A: Shi'Ar. ... 1.75
- ❑71, Nov 1993; Hologram cover; Fatal Attractions, Finale ... 3.50
- ❑72, Dec 1993 ... 1.75
- ❑73, Jan 1994 ... 1.75
- ❑74, Feb 1994 ... 1.75
- ❑75, Mar 1994; Giant-size 1: Britannic. 2.25
- ❑75/Variant, Mar 1994; Giant-size; 1: Britannic. Holo-grafix cover ... 3.50
- ❑76, Apr 1994 ... 1.75
- ❑77, May 1994 ... 1.95
- ❑78, Jun 1994 ... 1.95
- ❑79, Jul 1994 ... 1.95
- ❑80, Aug 1994 ... 1.95
- ❑81, Sep 1994 ... 1.95
- ❑82, Oct 1994; Giant-size ... 2.50
- ❑82/Variant, Oct 1994; Giant-size; foil cover ... 3.50
- ❑83, Nov 1994 ... 1.50
- ❑83/Deluxe, Nov 1994; Deluxe edition 1.95
- ❑84, Dec 1994 ... 1.50
- ❑84/Deluxe, Dec 1994; Deluxe edition 1.95
- ❑85, Jan 1995 ... 1.50
- ❑85/Deluxe, Jan 1995; Deluxe edition 1.95
- ❑86, Feb 1995 ... 1.95
- ❑86/Deluxe, Feb 1995; Deluxe edition 1.95
- ❑87, Jul 1995 ... 1.95
- ❑88, Aug 1995 ... 1.95
- ❑89, Sep 1995 ... 1.95
- ❑90, Oct 1995; OverPower cards inserted ... 1.95
- ❑91, Nov 1995 ... 1.95
- ❑92, Dec 1995 A: Colossus. A: Pete Wisdom. ... 1.95
- ❑93, Jan 1996; Rahne's past ... 1.95
- ❑94, Feb 1996 ... 1.95
- ❑95, Mar 1996 A: X-Man. ... 1.95
- ❑96, Apr 1996 ... 1.95
- ❑97, May 1996 ... 1.95
- ❑98, Jun 1996 ... 1.95
- ❑99, Jul 1996 ... 1.95
- ❑100, Aug 1996; Giant-size; wraparound cover ... 2.95
- ❑101, Sep 1996 ... 1.95
- ❑102, Oct 1996; bound-in trading cards 1.95
- ❑103, Nov 1996 ... 1.95
- ❑104, Dec 1996 ... 1.95
- ❑105, Jan 1997 KG (w) ... 1.95
- ❑106, Feb 1997 ... 1.95
- ❑107, Mar 1997 ... 1.95
- ❑108, Apr 1997 ... 1.95
- ❑109, May 1997 V: Spiral. ... 1.95
- ❑110, Jun 1997 ... 1.99
- ❑111, Aug 1997; gatefold summary ... 1.99
- ❑112, Sep 1997; gatefold summary ... 1.99
- ❑113, Oct 1997; gatefold summary A: High Evolutionary. ... 1.99
- ❑114, Nov 1997; gatefold summary ... 1.99
- ❑115, Dec 1997; gatefold summary ... 1.99
- ❑116, Jan 1998; gatefold summary ... 1.99
- ❑117, Feb 1998; gatefold summary ... 1.99
- ❑118, Mar 1998; gatefold summary ... 1.99
- ❑119, Apr 1998; gatefold summary V: Nightmare. ... 1.99
- ❑120, May 1998; gatefold summary ... 1.99
- ❑121, Jun 1998; gatefold summary ... 1.99
- ❑122, Jul 1998; gatefold summary V: Prime Sentinels. ... 1.99
- ❑123, Aug 1998; gatefold summary V: Mimic. ... 1.99
- ❑124, Sep 1998; gatefold summary; Captain Britain's bachelor party ... 1.99
- ❑125, Oct 1998; Giant-size; Wedding of Captain Britain, Meggan ... 3.00
- ❑Annual 1, ca. 1993; 1: Ghath. trading card ... 4.00
- ❑Annual 2, ca. 1994; 1994 Annual; ca. 1994 ... 2.95

EXCALIBUR (MINI-SERIES)
MARVEL

- ❑1, Feb 2001 ... 2.99
- ❑2, Mar 2001 ... 2.99
- ❑3, Apr 2001 ... 2.99
- ❑4, May 2001 ... 2.99

EXCALIBUR (2ND SERIES)
MARVEL

- ❑1, Jul 2004 ... 2.99
- ❑2, Aug 2004 ... 2.99
- ❑3, Sep 2004 ... 2.99

Other grades: Multiply price above by 5/6 for VF/NM • 2/3 for VERY FINE • 1/3 for FINE • 1/5 for VERY GOOD • 1/8 for GOOD

N-MINT

❑4, Oct 2004 .... 2.99
❑5, Nov 2004 .... 2.99
❑6, Dec 2004 .... 2.99
❑7, Jan 2005 .... 2.99
❑8, Feb 2005 .... 2.99
❑9, Mar 2005 .... 2.99
❑10, Apr 2005 .... 2.99
❑11, May 2005 .... 2.99
❑12, Jun 2005 .... 2.99
❑13, Jul 2005 .... 2.99

EXCALIBUR: AIR APPARENT
MARVEL

❑1, Dec 1991; Air Apparent Special Edition 4.95

EXCALIBUR: MOJO MAYHEM
MARVEL

❑1, Dec 1989 .... 4.50

EXCALIBUR: SWORD OF POWER
MARVEL

❑1, Feb 2002 .... 2.99
❑2, Mar 2002 .... 2.99
❑3, Apr 2002 .... 2.99
❑4, May 2002 .... 2.99

EXCALIBUR: THE POSSESSION
MARVEL

❑1, Jul 1991 .... 2.95

EXCALIBUR: THE SWORD IS DRAWN
MARVEL

❑1, ca. 1987; prestige format 0: Excalibur. 1: Excalibur. 4.00
❑1/2nd 1: Excalibur. 3.50
❑1/3rd 1: Excalibur. 3.50

EXCALIBUR: WEIRD WAR III
MARVEL

❑1, Dec 1990 .... 9.95

EXCALIBUR: XX CROSSING
MARVEL

❑1, May 1992; indicia says May, cover says Jul 2.50

EXCITING X-PATROL
MARVEL / AMALGAM

❑1, Jun 1997 .... 1.95

EXEC
COMICS CONSPIRACY

❑1, Feb 2001, Several characters in profile on cover 3.95

EXHIBITIONIST
FANTAGRAPHICS / EROS

❑1 .... 2.75
❑2, Aug 1994 .... 2.75

EXILE
EYEBALL SOUP DESIGNS

❑1, May 1996, b&w; cardstock cover. 2.95
❑2, Jul 1996, b&w; cardstock cover 2.95

EXILED
EXILED

❑1, Jan 1998 .... 2.75
❑2, Apr 1998 .... 2.75
❑3, Jun 1998; cover says 98, indicia says 97 .... 2.75

EXILE EARTH
RIVER CITY

❑1, ca. 1994 .... 1.95
❑2, ca. 1994 .... 1.95

EXILES (MALIBU)
MALIBU

❑1, Aug 1993, b&w 1: The Exiles. 2.00
❑1/Variant, Aug 1993, b&w; 1: The Exiles. Hologram cover 5.00
❑2, Sep 1993 .... 2.00
❑3, Oct 1993; Rune 2.50
❑4, Nov 1993 D: Exiles. 2.00

EXILES (MARVEL)
MARVEL

❑1, Aug 2001 .... 4.00
❑2, Sep 2001 .... 2.25
❑3, Oct 2001 .... 2.25
❑4, Nov 2001 .... 2.25
❑5, Dec 2001 .... 2.25
❑6, Jan 2002 .... 2.25
❑7, Feb 2002 .... 2.25
❑8, Mar 2002 .... 2.25
❑9, Apr 2002 .... 2.25
❑10, Apr 2002 .... 2.25
❑11, May 2002 .... 2.25
❑12, Jun 2002 .... 2.25
❑13, Jul 2002 .... 2.25
❑14, Aug 2002 .... 2.25
❑15, Sep 2002 .... 2.25
❑16, Oct 2002 .... 2.25
❑17, Nov 2002 .... 2.25
❑18, Dec 2002 .... 2.25
❑19, Jan 2003 .... 2.25
❑20, Feb 2003 .... 2.25
❑21, Mar 2003 .... 2.25
❑22, Apr 2003 .... 2.25
❑23, May 2003 .... 2.25
❑24, Jun 2003 .... 2.25
❑25, Jun 2003 .... 2.99
❑26, Jul 2003 .... 2.99
❑27, Jul 2003 .... 2.99
❑28, Aug 2003 .... 2.99
❑29, Sep 2003 .... 2.99
❑30, Sep 2003 .... 2.99
❑31, Oct 2003, Avengers turned into vampires 2.99
❑32, Oct 2003 .... 2.99
❑33, Nov 2003 .... 2.99
❑34, Nov 2003 .... 2.99
❑35, Dec 2003 .... 2.99
❑36, Dec 2003 .... 2.99
❑37, Jan 2004 .... 2.99
❑38, Feb 2004 .... 2.99
❑39, Feb 2004 .... 2.99
❑40, Mar 2004 .... 2.99
❑41, Apr 2004 .... 2.99
❑42, May 2004 .... 2.99
❑43, May 2004 .... 2.99
❑44, May 2004 .... 2.99
❑45, Jun 2004 .... 2.99
❑46, Jul 2004 .... 2.99
❑47, Jul 2004 .... 2.99
❑48, Aug 2004 .... 2.99
❑49, Sep 2004 .... 2.99
❑50, Oct 2004 .... 2.99
❑51, Oct 2004 .... 2.99
❑52, Nov 2004 .... 2.99
❑53, Dec 2004 .... 2.99
❑54, Jan 2005 .... 2.99
❑55, Jan 2005 .... 2.99
❑56, Feb 2005 .... 2.99
❑57, Mar 2005 .... 2.99
❑58, Mar 2005 .... 2.99
❑59, Apr 2005 .... 2.99
❑60, May 2005 .... 5.00
❑61, May 2005 .... 4.00
❑62, Jun 2005 .... 2.99
❑63, Jun 2005 .... 2.99
❑64, Jun 2005 .... 2.99
❑65, Jul 2005 .... 2.99
❑66, Aug 2005 .... 2.99
❑67, Sep 2005 .... 2.99
❑68, Oct 2005 .... 2.99
❑69, Nov 2005 .... 2.99
❑70 2005 .... 2.99
❑71 .... 2.99
❑72, Jan 2006 .... 2.99
❑73, Jan 2006 .... 2.99
❑74, Feb 2006 .... 2.99
❑75, Mar 2006 .... 2.99
❑76, Mar 2006 .... 2.99
❑77, May 2006 .... 2.99
❑78, Jun 2006 .... 2.99
❑79, Jun 2006 .... 2.99
❑80, Jul 2006 .... 2.99
❑81, Aug 2006 .... 2.99
❑82, Aug 2006 .... 2.99
❑83, Sep 2006 .... 2.99

EXILES (ALPHA)
ALPHA PRODUCTIONS

❑1, b&w 1.95

EXIT (VOL. 2)
CALIBER

❑1 .... 2.95
❑2 .... 2.95
❑3 .... 2.95
❑4 .... 2.95
❑5 .... 2.95

EXIT 6
PLASTIC SPOON

❑1, Aug 1998, b&w 2.95
❑2/Ashcan, Aug 1998; preview of upcoming issue 2.95
❑3, Jan 1999 .... 2.95
❑3/Ashcan, Aug 1998; preview of upcoming issue 2.95

EXIT FROM SHADOW
BRONZE MAN

❑4; indicia has name change, cover doesn't; was Secret Killers 2.95

EX MACHINA
DC

❑1, Aug 2004 .... 8.00
❑2, Sep 2004 .... 4.00
❑3, Oct 2004 .... 2.95
❑4, Nov 2004 .... 2.95
❑5, Dec 2004 .... 2.95
❑6, Jan 2005 .... 2.95
❑7, Feb 2005 .... 2.95
❑8, Mar 2005 .... 2.95
❑9, Apr 2005 .... 2.95
❑10, Jun 2005 .... 2.99
❑11, Jul 2005 .... 2.99
❑12, Aug 2005 .... 2.99
❑13, Sep 2005 .... 2.99
❑14, Oct 2005 .... 2.99
❑15 .... 2.99
❑16, Jan 2006 .... 2.99
❑17, Mar 2006 .... 2.99
❑18, May 2006 .... 2.99
❑19, Jun 2006 .... 2.99
❑20, Jul 2006 .... 2.99
❑21, Sep 2006 .... 2.99

EX MACHINA SPECIAL
DC

❑1, Jun 2006 .... 2.99
❑2, Aug 2006 .... 2.99

EX-MUTANTS (AMAZING)
PIED PIPER / AMAZING

❑1 .... 2.00
❑2 .... 2.00
❑3 .... 2.00
❑4 .... 2.00
❑5 A: New Humans 2.00
❑6, Jul 1987 .... 2.00
❑7 .... 2.00
❑8 .... 2.00
❑Special 1, Spr 1987, b&w 2.00

EX-MUTANTS (ETERNITY)
ETERNITY

❑1, ca. 1986 .... 2.00
❑2 .... 2.00
❑3 .... 2.00
❑4, Oct 1988, RL (c) 2.00
❑5 1988 .... 2.00
❑6 1988 .... 2.00
❑7 1988 .... 2.00
❑8, Jan 1989 .... 2.00
❑9, Feb 1989 .... 2.00
❑10 .... 2.00
❑11 .... 2.00
❑12 .... 2.00
❑13 .... 2.00
❑14 .... 2.00
❑15 .... 1.95
❑Annual 1, Mar 1998 .... 1.95

EX-MUTANTS (MALIBU)
MALIBU

❑1, Nov 1992 0: Ex-Mutants. 2.00
❑1/Variant, Nov 1992; 0: Ex-Mutants. shiny cover 2.50
❑2, Dec 1992 .... 1.95
❑3, Jan 1993 .... 1.95
❑4, Feb 1993 .... 1.95
❑5, Mar 1993 .... 1.95
❑6, Apr 1993 .... 1.95
❑7, May 1993 .... 1.95
❑8, Jun 1993 .... 1.95
❑9, Jul 1993 .... 1.95
❑10, Aug 1993 .... 1.95
❑11, Sep 1993; Crossover with Dinosaurs for Hire and Protectors 1.95
❑12, Oct 1993; Crossover with Dinosaurs for Hire and Protectors 2.25

Evel Knievel

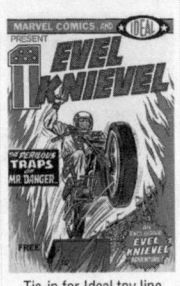

Tie-in for Ideal toy line
©Marvel

Evil Ernie (Eternity)

Lust for Lady Death sends Ernie on spree
©Eternity

Evil Ernie vs. the Super Heroes

Hellion takes out heroes
©Chaos!

Ewoks

Adventures of inhabitants of Endor moon
©Marvel

Excalibur

U.S. and British mutants join forces
©Marvel

N-MINT

❑13, Nov 1993; Genesis begins publishing 2.25
❑14, Dec 1993; Genesis 2.25
❑15, Jan 1994; Genesis 2.25
❑16, Feb 1994; Genesis 2.25
❑17, Mar 1994; Genesis 2.50
❑18, Apr 1994; Genesis 2.50

EX-MUTANTS MICROSERIES: ERIN (LAWRENCE & LIM'S...)
PIED PIPER

❑1, b&w 1.95

EX-MUTANTS PIN-UP BOOK
ETERNITY

❑1 .... 1.95

EXODUS REVELATION
EXODUS

❑1, Nov 1994, b&w; no cover price 1.00

EXOSQUAD
TOPPS

❑0, Jan 1994; cardstock cover 1.00

EXOTICA
CRY FOR DAWN

❑1, b&w 4.00
❑2, Nov 1993 .... 3.00

EXOTIC FANTASY
FANTAGRAPHICS / EROS

❑1, b&w; sketches 4.95
❑2, b&w; sketches 4.95
❑3, b&w; sketches 4.95

EXPATRIATE
IMAGE

❑1, May 2005 .... 2.95
❑2 2005 .... 2.95
❑3, Oct 2005 .... 2.95
❑4, Jan 2006 .... 2.95

EXPERIENCE
AIRCEL

❑1, b&w 3.25

EXPLORERS
EXPLORER

❑1, ca. 1996, b&w 2.95
❑2, ca. 1996, b&w 2.95
❑3, ca. 1996, b&w 2.95

EXPLORERS OF THE UNKNOWN
ARCHIE

❑1, Jun 1990 .... 1.00
❑2, Aug 1990 .... 1.00
❑3, Oct 1990 .... 1.00
❑4, Dec 1990 .... 1.00
❑5, Feb 1991 .... 1.00
❑6, Apr 1991 .... 1.00

EXPLORERS (VOL. 2)
CALIBER / TAPESTRY

❑1, ca. 1996, b&w 2.95
❑2, ca. 1996, b&w 2.95

EXPOSE
CRACKED PEPPER

❑1, Dec 1993, b&w 2.50

N-MINT

EXPOSURE
IMAGE

❑1, Nov 1999 .... 2.50
❑2, Dec 1999 .... 2.50
❑2/A, Dec 1999 .... 2.50
❑3, Jan 2000 .... 2.50
❑4, Feb 2000 .... 2.50
❑5, Mar 2000 .... 3.50
❑6, Apr 2000 .... 3.50

EXQUISITE CORPSE
DARK HORSE

❑1, Yellow issue 2.50
❑2, Red Issue 2.50
❑3, Green Issue 2.50

EXTERMINATORS
DC / VERTIGO

❑1, Feb 2006 .... 2.95
❑2, Mar 2006 .... 2.95
❑3, May 2006 .... 2.95
❑4, Jun 2006 .... 2.95
❑5, Jul 2006 .... 2.95
❑6, Aug 2006 .... 2.95

EXTINCT!
NEW ENGLAND

❑1, b&w; Reprints 3.50
❑2, b&w; Reprints 3.50

EXTINCTIONERS
SHANDA FANTASY ARTS

❑1, Apr 1999, b&w 2.95
❑2 .... 2.95

EXTINCTION EVENT
DC / WILDSTORM

❑1, Sep 2003 .... 2.50
❑2, Oct 2003 .... 2.50
❑3, Nov 2003 .... 2.50
❑4, Dec 2003 .... 2.50
❑5, Jan 2004 .... 2.50

EXTRA! (GEMSTONE)
GEMSTONE

❑1, Jan 2000 .... 2.50
❑2, Feb 2000 .... 2.50
❑3, Mar 2000 .... 2.50
❑4, Apr 2000 .... 2.50
❑5, May 2000 .... 2.50
❑Annual 1 .... 13.50

EXTRA TERRESTRIAL TRIO
SMILING FACE

❑1, ca. 1995, b&w 2.95

EXTREME (IMAGE)
IMAGE

❑0, Aug 1993 RL (w); RL (a) 2.50
❑0/A, Aug 1993 RL (w); RL (a) 2.50
❑0/B, Aug 1993; San Diego Con edition RL (w); RL (a) 2.50
❑0/Gold, Aug 1993; Gold edition RL (w); RL (a) 3.00
❑Holiday 1; "Extreme Hero" promotional edition from Hero Magazine; RL (w); RL (a); no cover price 1.00

N-MINT

EXTREME (CURTIS)
CURTIS

❑1 .... 2.95

EXTREME DESTROYER EPILOGUE
IMAGE

❑1, Jan 1996 .... 2.50

EXTREME DESTROYER PROLOGUE
IMAGE

❑1, Jan 1996; bagged with card 2.50

EXTREME JUSTICE
DC

❑0, Jan 1995 .... 2.00
❑1, Feb 1995 .... 1.75
❑2, Mar 1995 .... 1.75
❑3, Apr 1995 .... 1.75
❑4, May 1995 .... 1.75
❑5, Jun 1995 .... 1.75
❑6, Jul 1995 .... 1.75
❑7, Aug 1995 .... 1.75
❑8, Sep 1995 .... 1.75
❑9, Oct 1995 1: Zan and Jayna. 1.75
❑10, Nov 1995 .... 1.75
❑11, Dec 1995 .... 1.75
❑12, Jan 1996 .... 1.75
❑13, Feb 1996 V: Monarch. 1.75
❑14, Mar 1996 .... 1.75
❑15, Apr 1996 .... 1.75
❑16, May 1996 .... 1.75
❑17, Jun 1996 .... 1.75
❑18, Jul 1996 .... 1.75

EXTREMELY SILLY
ANTARCTIC

❑1 .... 3.00

EXTREMELY SILLY (VOL. 2)
ANTARCTIC

❑1, Nov 1996, b&w; Star Trek parody 1.25

EXTREMELY YOUNGBLOOD
IMAGE

❑1, Sep 1996 .... 3.50

EXTREME PREJUDICE
IMAGE

❑0, Nov 1994 .... 2.50

EXTREME PREVIEWS
IMAGE

❑1, Mar 1996 .... 1.00

EXTREME PREVIEWS 1997
IMAGE

❑1; No cover price; pin-ups 1.00

EXTREME SACRIFICE
IMAGE

❑1, Jan 1995, Prelude, polybagged with trading card 2.50
❑2, Jan 1995, Epilogue 2.50

EXTREMES OF VIOLET
BLACKOUT

❑0 .... 2.95
❑1 .... 2.95
❑2, Mar 1995 .... 2.95

Other grades: Multiply price above by 5/6 for VF/NM • 2/3 for VERY FINE • 1/3 for FINE • 1/5 for VERY GOOD • 1/8 for GOOD

EXTREME SUPER CHRISTMAS SPECIAL
IMAGE

❑1, Dec 1994 ... 2.95

EXTREME SUPER TOUR BOOK
IMAGE

❑1 ... 1.00
❑1/Gold; Gold edition ... 2.00

EXTREME TOUR BOOK
IMAGE

❑1; no cover price ... 2.50
❑1/Gold; Gold edition ... 2.50

EXTREMIST
DC / VERTIGO

❑1, Sep 1993 1: The Extremist. ... 2.50
❑1/Platinum, Sep 1993; Platinum edition 1: The Extremist. ... 4.00
❑2, Oct 1993 ... 2.50
❑3, Nov 1993 ... 2.50
❑4, Dec 1993 ... 2.50

EYE
HAMSTER

❑Special 1, Jun 1999; Special edition. 2.95

EYEBALL KID
DARK HORSE

❑1, b&w 1: Eyeball Kid (in comic books). 2.50
❑2, b&w ... 2.50
❑3, b&w ... 2.50

EYEBEAM
ADHESIVE

❑1, b&w; strip reprints ... 2.50
❑2, ca. 1994, b&w; strip reprints ... 2.50
❑3, ca. 1994, b&w; strip reprints ... 2.50
❑4, b&w; strip reprints ... 2.50
❑5, b&w; strip reprints ... 2.50

EYE OF MONGOMBO
FANTAGRAPHICS

❑1, b&w ... 2.00
❑2, b&w ... 2.00
❑3, b&w ... 2.00
❑4, b&w ... 2.00
❑5, b&w ... 2.00
❑6 1991, b&w ... 2.00
❑7, Dec 1991, b&w ... 2.25

EYE OF THE STORM
RIVAL

❑1, Dec 1994 ... 2.95

EYE OF THE STORM ANNUAL
DC / WILDSTORM

❑1, Sep 2003 ... 4.95

EYESHIELD 21
VIZ

❑1, Apr 2005 ... 9.95
❑2, May 2005 ... 9.95
❑3, Aug 2005 ... 9.95
❑4, Oct 2005 ... 9.95

EYES OF ASIA
DIGITAL WEBBING

❑1, Oct 2004, b&w ... 3.50
❑2, Dec 2004, b&w ... 3.50

FAANS
SIX HANDED

❑1, b&w ... 2.95

FABLES
DC / VERTIGO

❑1, Jul 2002 ... 3.50
❑2, Aug 2002 ... 3.00
❑3, Sep 2002 ... 3.00
❑4, Oct 2002 ... 2.75
❑5, Nov 2002 ... 2.50
❑6, Dec 2002 ... 2.50
❑6/Retailer ed., Dec 2002; Retailer Representative Program variant ... 15.00
❑7, Jan 2003 ... 2.50
❑8, Feb 2003 ... 2.50
❑9, Mar 2003 ... 2.50
❑10, Apr 2003 ... 2.50
❑11, May 2003 ... 2.50
❑12, Jun 2003 ... 2.50
❑13, Jul 2003 ... 2.50
❑14, Aug 2003 ... 2.50
❑15, Sep 2003 ... 2.50
❑16, Oct 2003 ... 2.50
❑17, Nov 2003 ... 2.50
❑18, Dec 2003 ... 2.50
❑19, Jan 2004 ... 2.50
❑20, Feb 2004 ... 2.50
❑21, Mar 2004 ... 2.50
❑22, Apr 2004 ... 2.50
❑23, May 2004 ... 2.50
❑24, Jun 2004 ... 2.50
❑25, Jul 2004 ... 2.50
❑26, Aug 2004 ... 2.50
❑27, Sep 2004 ... 2.50
❑28, Oct 2004 ... 2.50
❑29, Nov 2004 ... 2.50
❑30, Dec 2004 ... 2.50
❑31, Jan 2005 ... 2.50
❑32, Feb 2005 ... 2.50
❑33, Mar 2005 ... 2.50
❑34, Apr 2005 ... 2.50
❑35, May 2005 ... 2.50
❑36, Jun 2005 ... 2.50
❑37, Jun 2005 ... 2.50
❑38, Jul 2005 ... 2.75
❑39, Aug 2005 ... 2.75
❑40, Sep 2005 ... 2.75
❑41, Oct 2005 ... 2.79
❑42, b&w ... 2.99
❑43, Jan 2006 ... 2.99
❑44, Feb 2006 ... 2.99
❑45, Mar 2006 ... 2.99
❑46, Apr 2006 ... 2.99
❑47, May 2006 ... 2.99
❑48, Jun 2006 ... 2.99
❑49, Jul 2006 ... 2.99
❑50, Aug 2006 ... 2.99

FABLES BY THE BROTHERS DIMM
DIMM

❑1, Apr 1995, b&w ... 1.50

FABLES: LAST CASTLE
DC / VERTIGO

❑1, ca. 2003 ... 5.00

FABULOUS FURRY FREAK BROTHERS
RIP OFF

❑0; 1985 Compilation ... 2.95
❑1, b&w; Collected Adventures of the...; 1971 ... 55.00
❑1/2nd, Collected Adventures of the...; 1980 ... 2.95
❑1/3rd 2002; Collected Adventures of the... ... 3.95
❑2, b&w; Further Adventures of the... 35.00
❑2/2nd; Further Adventures of the...; 1989 ... 2.95
❑3, b&w; A Year Passes Like Nothing With... ... 15.00
❑4, ca. 1975, b&w; Brother Can You Spare 75¢ For... ... 13.00
❑5, ca. 1977, b&w; Fabulous Furry Freak Brothers ... 10.00
❑6, b&w; Six Snappy Sockeroos From the Archives Of... ... 4.00
❑7, b&w ... 2.00
❑8 ... 2.00
❑9 ... 2.00
❑10 ... 2.00
❑11 ... 2.95
❑12, b&w ... 2.95
❑13, b&w; reprints stories from High Times ... 2.95

FACE (PARADOX)
DC / VERTIGO

❑1, Jan 1995 ... 4.95

FACTION PARADOX
IMAGE

❑1, Aug 2003 ... 2.95
❑2, Nov 2003 ... 3.50

FACTOR-X
MARVEL

❑1, Mar 1995, AM (a); Age of Apocalypse ... 2.00
❑2, Apr 1995 ... 2.00
❑3, May 1995 ... 2.00
❑4, Jun 1995 ... 2.00

FACULTY FUNNIES
ARCHIE

❑1, Jun 1989 ... 4.00
❑2, Sep 1989 ... 2.50
❑3, Dec 1989 ... 2.50
❑4, Mar 1990 ... 2.50
❑5, May 1990 ... 2.50

FAERIE CODEX
RAVEN

❑1, b&w ... 2.95
❑2, b&w ... 2.95
❑3, Dec 1997, b&w ... 2.95

FAERIES' LANDING
TOKYOPOP

❑1, Jan 2004 ... 9.95
❑2, Mar 2004 ... 9.95
❑3, May 2004 ... 9.95
❑4, Jul 2004 ... 9.95
❑5, Sep 2004 ... 9.95
❑6, Nov 2004 ... 9.95
❑7, Jan 2005 ... 9.95
❑8, Mar 2005 ... 9.95
❑9, Jun 2005 ... 9.95
❑10, Sep 2005 ... 9.95
❑11, Dec 2005 ... 9.95

FAFHRD AND THE GRAY MOUSER
MARVEL / EPIC

❑1, Oct 1990 ... 4.50
❑2 ... 4.50
❑3 ... 4.50
❑4 ... 4.50

FAILED UNIVERSE
BLACKTHORNE

❑1, Dec 1986 ... 1.75

FAITH (LIGHTNING)
LIGHTNING

❑1/A, Jul 1997, b&w ... 2.95

FAITH
DC / VERTIGO

❑1, Nov 1999 ... 2.50
❑2, Dec 1999 ... 2.50
❑3, Jan 2000 ... 2.50
❑4, Feb 2000 ... 2.50
❑5, Mar 2000 ... 2.50

FAKE
TOKYOPOP

❑1, May 2003, b&w; printed in Japanese format ... 9.99

FALCON
MARVEL

❑1, Nov 1983, PS (a) ... 2.00
❑2, Dec 1983, PS (c); PS (a) ... 2.00
❑3, Jan 1984 ... 2.00
❑4, Feb 1984 ... 2.00

FALL, THE (BIG BAD WORLD)
BIG BAD WORLD

❑1, b&w ... 3.00

FALL (CALIBER)
CALIBER

❑1, b&w ... 2.95

FALLEN ANGEL
DC

❑1, Sep 2003 ... 2.50
❑2, Oct 2003 ... 2.50
❑3, Nov 2003 ... 2.50
❑4, Dec 2003 ... 2.50
❑5, Jan 2004 ... 2.50
❑6, Feb 2004 ... 2.50
❑7, Mar 2004 ... 2.50
❑8, Apr 2004 ... 2.50
❑9, May 2004 ... 2.50
❑10, Jun 2004 ... 2.50
❑11, Jul 2004 ... 2.95
❑12, Aug 2004 ... 2.95
❑13, Sep 2004 ... 2.95
❑14, Oct 2004 ... 2.95
❑15, Nov 2004 ... 2.95
❑16, Dec 2004 ... 2.95
❑17, Jan 2005 ... 2.95
❑18, Feb 2005 ... 2.95
❑19, Mar 2005 ... 2.99
❑20, Jun 2005 ... 2.99
❑Book 1, ca. 2004 ... 12.95

Ex Machina

Tech controller becomes NYC mayor

©DC

Ex-Mutants (Malibu)

Post-apocalyptic heroes fight to survive

©Malibu

Extra! (Gemstone)

Reprints short-lived E.C. New Direction title

©Gemstone

Extreme Justice

Darker version of Justice League

©DC

Fables

Fairy tale folks hide and survive in real world

©DC

N-MINT

FALLEN ANGEL (IDW)
IDEA & DESIGN WORKS

❑1, Jan 2006 .... 2.99
❑2, Feb 2006 .... 2.99
❑3, Mar 2006 .... 2.99
❑4, Apr 2006 .... 2.99
❑6, Jul 2006 .... 2.99

FALLEN ANGEL ON THE WORLD OF MAGIC: THE GATHERING
ACCLAIM / ARMADA

❑1, May 1996; prestige format; polybagged with Fallen Angel card.. 5.95

FALLEN ANGELS
MARVEL

❑1, Apr 1987 .... 2.00
❑2, May 1987 .... 1.50
❑3, Jun 1987 1: Chance II. 1.50
❑4, Jul 1987 .... 1.50
❑5, Aug 1987 D: Don. 1.50
❑6, Sep 1987 .... 1.50
❑7, Oct 1987 .... 1.50
❑8, Nov 1987 .... 1.50

FALLEN EMPIRES ON THE WORLD OF MAGIC: THE GATHERING
ACCLAIM / ARMADA

❑1, Sep 1995; polybagged with pack of Fallen Empires cards 2.75
❑2, Oct 1995; polybagged with sheet of creature tokens 2.75
❑Book 1; prestige format; collects mini-series; polybagged w/pack of Fallen Empires cards 4.95

FALLING MAN
IMAGE

❑1, Feb 1998, b&w 2.95

FALL OF THE ROMAN EMPIRE
GOLD KEY

❑1, Jul 1964 .... 25.00

FALLOUT 3000 (MIKE DEODATO'S...)
CALIBER

❑1 .... 2.95

FALLS THE GOTHAM RAIN
COMICO

❑1 .... 4.95

FAMILY AFFAIR
GOLD KEY

❑1, Jan 1970 .... 24.00
❑2, Apr 1970 .... 20.00
❑3, Jul 1970 .... 14.00
❑4, Oct 1970 .... 14.00

FAMILY MAN
DC / PARADOX

❑1, b&w; digest 4.95
❑2, b&w; digest 4.95
❑3, b&w; digest 4.95

FAMOUS FEATURES (JERRY IGER'S...)
PACIFIC

❑1, Jul 1984; Flamingo 2.50

N-MINT

FAMOUS FIRST EDITION
DC

❑F-4, Nov 1974; reprints Whiz Comics #2 .... 15.00
❑F-5, Jan 1975; reprints Batman #1... 13.00
❑F-6, May 1975; reprints Wonder Woman #1 .... 10.00
❑F-7, Jul 1975; reprints All-Star #3.... 12.00
❑F-8, Sep 1975; reprints Flash Comics #1 .... 9.00
❑C-26; 1: Superman. reprints Action Comics #1 .... 10.00
❑C-28; reprints Detective Comics #27 9.00
❑C-30; 1: Wonder Woman. reprints Sensation Comics #1 .... 10.00
❑C-61, Mar 1979; reprints Superman #1 .... 9.00
❑C-61/Whitman, Mar 1979; Whitman variant; reprints Superman #1........ 18.00

FANA
COMAX

❑1, b&w 2.95

FANA THE JUNGLE GIRL
COMAX

❑1, b&w 2.95

FANBOY
DC

❑1, Mar 1999, ... 2.50
❑2, Apr 1999, ... 2.50
❑3, May 1999, ... 2.50
❑4, Jun 1999, Our Army at War take-off 2.50
❑5, Jul 1999, ... 2.50
❑6, Aug 1999, ... 2.50

FANDOM CONFIDENTIAL
KITCHEN SINK

❑1 .... 2.95

FANG (SIRIUS)
SIRIUS ENTERTAINMENT

❑1, Feb 1995 .... 2.95
❑2, Apr 1995 .... 2.95
❑3, Jun 1995 .... 2.95

FANG (CONQUEST)
CONQUEST

❑1, b&w 2.95

FANG (TANGRAM)
TANGRAM

❑1, b&w 2.95

FANG: TESTAMENT
SIRIUS ENTERTAINMENT

❑1 .... 2.50
❑2 .... 2.50
❑3 .... 2.50
❑4 .... 2.50

FANGRAPHIX
FANGRAPHIX

❑1 .... 1.95
❑2 .... 1.95
❑3 .... 1.95

FANGS OF THE COBRA
MYTHIC

❑1, Win 1996; color and b&w 2.95

N-MINT

FANNY
FANNY

❑1 .... 3.00
❑2 .... 3.00
❑3, b&w 3.95

FANNY HILL
SHUNGA

❑1, b&w 2.50

FANTAESCAPE
ZINZINNATI

❑1, Jun 1988 .... 1.75

FANTAGOR
LAST GASP

❑1 .... 3.00
❑2 .... 3.00
❑3 .... 3.00

FANTASCI
APPLE

❑1, b&w 2.00
❑2, b&w 2.00
❑3, b&w; Apple Comics publisher Begins 2.00
❑4 .... 2.00
❑5 .... 1.75
❑6 .... 1.75
❑7 .... 1.75
❑8, Jul 1988 .... 1.75
❑9 .... 1.95

FANTASTIC ADVENTURES (ACE)
ACE

❑1, Mar 1987 .... 1.75
❑2, Jun 1987 .... 1.75
❑3, Oct 1987 .... 1.75

FANTASTIC FABLES (BASIL WOLVERTON'S...)
DARK HORSE

❑1, Oct 1993, b&w; Reprints 2.50
❑2 .... 2.50

FANTASTIC FANZINE
ARROW

❑1 .... 1.50
❑2 .... 1.50
❑3 .... 1.50

FANTASTIC FIVE
MARVEL

❑1, Oct 1999 .... 1.99
❑2, Nov 1999 .... 1.99
❑2/A, Nov 1999; variant cover 1.99
❑3, Dec 1999 .... 1.99

FANTASTIC FORCE
MARVEL

❑1, Nov 1994; O: Fantastic Force. 1: Fantastic Force. foil cover 2.50
❑2, Dec 1994 .... 2.00
❑3, Jan 1995 .... 2.00
❑4, Feb 1995 .... 1.75
❑5, Mar 1995 .... 1.75
❑6, Apr 1995 .... 1.75
❑7, May 1995 .... 1.75
❑8, Jun 1995 .... 1.75
❑9, Jul 1995 .... 1.75
❑10, Aug 1995 .... 1.75

N-MINT

❑11, Sep 1995 1.75
❑12, Oct 1995 1.75
❑13, Nov 1995; She-Hulk joins team 1.75
❑14, Dec 1995 A: She-Hulk. A: Black Panther. A: Human Torch. A: Wakanda. 1.75
❑15, Jan 1996; Team disbands; cover says Jan 95, indicia says Jan 96 1.75
❑16, Feb 1996 1.75
❑17, Mar 1996 1.75
❑18, Apr 1996 1.75

FANTASTIC ADVENTURES (ACE)
ACE

❑1, Mar 1987 1.75
❑2, Jun 1987 1.75
❑3, Oct 1987 1.75

FANTASTIC FABLES (BASIL WOLVERTON'S...)
DARK HORSE

❑1, Oct 1993, b&w; Reprints 2.50
❑2 2.50

FANTASTIC FANZINE
ARROW

❑1 1.50
❑2 1.50
❑3 1.50

FANTASTIC FIVE
MARVEL

❑1, Oct 1999 1.99
❑2, Nov 1999 1.99
❑2/A, Nov 1999; variant cover 1.99
❑3, Dec 1999 1.99

FANTASTIC FORCE
MARVEL

❑1, Nov 1994; O: Fantastic Force. 1: Fantastic Force. foil cover 2.50
❑2, Dec 1994 2.00
❑3, Jan 1995 2.00
❑4, Feb 1995 1.75
❑5, Mar 1995 1.75
❑6, Apr 1995 1.75
❑7, May 1995 1.75
❑8, Jun 1995 1.75
❑9, Jul 1995 1.75
❑10, Aug 1995 1.75
❑11, Sep 1995 1.75
❑12, Oct 1995 1.75
❑13, Nov 1995; She-Hulk joins team 1.75
❑14, Dec 1995 A: She-Hulk. A: Black Panther. A: Human Torch. A: Wakanda. 1.75
❑15, Jan 1996; Team disbands; cover says Jan 95, indicia says Jan 96 1.75
❑16, Feb 1996 1.75
❑17, Mar 1996 1.75
❑18, Apr 1996 1.75

FANTASTIC FOUR (VOL. 1)
MARVEL

❑1, Nov 1961, JK, SL (w); JK (a); O: Fantastic Four. O: Mole Man. 1: Fantastic Four. 1: Mole Man. 20000.00
❑1/Golden Record 1966, JK, SL (w); JK (a); Golden Record reprint 70.00
❑2, Jan 1962, JK, SL (w); JK (a); O: Fantastic Four. 1: Skrulls. 4500.00
❑3, Mar 1962, JK, SL (w); JK (a); 1: Fantasti-Copter. 1: The Miracle Man (Marvel). 1: Fantasti-Car. 1: Pogo Plane. 1: Baxter Building. Fantastic Four wear uniforms for first time 3000.00
❑4, May 1962, JK, SL (w); JK (a); 1: Sub-Mariner (in Silver Age). 1: Giganto. D: Giganto. 3500.00
❑5, Jul 1962, JK, SL (w); JK (a); O: Doctor Doom. 1: Doctor Doom 5000.00
❑6, Sep 1962, JK, SL (w); JK (a); 1: The Yancy Street Gang (name only). A: Doctor Doom. Doctor Doom & Sub-Mariner vs. Fantastic Four 2000.00
❑7, Oct 1962, JK, SL (w); JK (a); 1: Kurrgo. 1: The Xantha. 1250.00
❑8, Nov 1962, JK, SL (w); JK (a); 1: Puppet Master. 1: Alicia Masters. 1200.00
❑9, Dec 1962, JK, SL (w); JK (a); A: Sub-Mariner. 1150.00
❑10, Jan 1963, JK, SL (w); JK (a); 1: The Ovoids. 1: Jack Kirby (as character in story). 1: Stan Lee (as character in story). A: Doctor Doom. V: Doctor Doom. 1150.00
❑11, Feb 1963, JK, SL (w); JK (a); O: Fantastic Four. O: Impossible Man. 1: Willie Lumpkin (Fantastic Four's mailman)-Silver Age. 1: Impossible Man. 1: The Popuppians. 1000.00
❑12, Mar 1963, JK, SL (w); JK (a); 1: The Wrecker I (Dr. Karl Kort). V: Hulk. Thing fights Hulk for first time 2700.00
❑13, Apr 1963, JK, SL (w); JK (a); O: Red Ghost. 1: Red Ghost. 1: The Watcher. 600.00
❑14, May 1963, JK, SL (w); JK (a); A: Sub-Mariner. V: Puppet Master. 500.00
❑15, Jun 1963, JK, SL (w); JK (a); 1: Awesome Android. 1: Mad Thinker. 500.00
❑16, Jul 1963, SL (w); JK (a); A: Ant Man. A: Doctor Doom. A: The Wasp. V: Doctor Doom. 500.00
❑17, Aug 1963, SL (w); JK (a); A: Ant Man. A: Doctor Doom. V: Doctor Doom. 500.00
❑18, Sep 1963, SL (w); JK (a); O: Super-Skrull. 1: Super-Skrull. 500.00
❑19, Oct 1963, SL (w); JK (a); O: Rama-Tut. 1: Rama-Tut. 500.00
❑20, Nov 1963, SL (w); JK (a); O: Molecule Man. 1: Molecule Man. A: Watcher. 500.00
❑21, Dec 1963, SL (w); JK (a); O: Hate-Monger. 1: Hate-Monger. A: Nick Fury. 450.00
❑22, Jan 1964, SL (w); JK (a); V: Mole Man. 250.00
❑23, Feb 1964, SL (w); JK (a); A: Doctor Doom. V: Doctor Doom. 250.00
❑24, Mar 1964, SL (w); JK (a); 1: Moloids. 240.00
❑25, Apr 1964, SL (w); JK (a); A: Rick Jones. A: Avengers. V: Hulk. first mention of Thing's Aunt Petunia; Hulk Battles Thing 550.00
❑26, May 1964, SL (w); JK (a); A: Rick Jones. A: Avengers. V: Hulk. 550.00
❑27, Jun 1964, SL (w); JK (a); A: Doctor Strange. V: Sub-Mariner. 300.00
❑28, Jul 1964, SL (w); JK (a); A: X-Men. V: Puppet Master. V: Mad Thinker. 500.00
❑29, Aug 1964, SL (w); JK (a); A: Watcher. V: Red Ghost. 260.00
❑30, Sep 1964, JK (a); O: Diablo. 1: Diablo. 260.00
❑31, Oct 1964, JK (a); A: Avengers. V: Mole Man. 260.00
❑32, Nov 1964, JK (a); 1: Sue and Johnny's parents (Franklin and Mary). V: Super-Skrull. 250.00
❑33, Dec 1964, JK (a); 1: Attuma. A: Sub-Mariner. 250.00
❑34, Jan 1965, JK (a); 1: Thomas Gideon (later becomes Glorian) 250.00
❑35, Feb 1965, JK (a); O: Dragon Man. 1: Dragon Man. V: Diablo. 165.00
❑36, Mar 1965, JK (a); O: Frightful Four. 1: Frightful Four. 1: Medusa. 165.00
❑37, Apr 1965, JK (a) 165.00
❑38, May 1965, JK (a); 1: Trapster I (Peter Petruski). A: Frightful Four. Paste-Pot Pete becomes Trapster I. 165.00
❑39, Jun 1965, JK (a); A: Daredevil. A: Doctor Doom. V: Doctor Doom. 165.00
❑40, Jul 1965, JK (a); A: Daredevil. V: Doctor Doom 165.00
❑41, Aug 1965, JK (a); V: Frightful Four. 110.00
❑42, Sep 1965, JK (a); V: Frightful Four. 110.00
❑43, Oct 1965, JK (a); V: Frightful Four. V: Doctor Doom 110.00
❑44, Nov 1965, SL (w); JK (a); 1: Gorgon. A: Dragon Man. A: Medusa. 85.00
❑45, Dec 1965, JK (a); 1: Karnak. 1: Inhumans. 1: Crystal. 1: Triton. 1: Lockjaw. 1: Black Bolt. A: Trapster I. A: Sandman. V: Maximus. V: Dragon Man. 325.00
❑46, Jan 1966, JK, SL (w); JK (a); A: Inhumans. 140.00
❑47, Feb 1966, JK, SL (w); JK (a); 1: Maximus. A: Inhumans. V: Maximus. 100.00
❑48, Mar 1966, JK, SL (w); JK (a); 1: Galactus. 1: Silver Surfer. A: Inhumans. 460.00
❑49, Apr 1966, JK, SL (w); JK (a); A: Galactus. A: Silver Surfer. A: Watcher. V: Galactus. 350.00
❑50, May 1966, JK, SL (w); JK (a); 1: Wyatt Wingfoot. A: Galactus. A: Silver Surfer. A: Watcher. V: Galactus. Silver Surfer vs. Galactus 400.00
❑51, Jun 1966, JK, SL (w); JK (a); 1: Negative Zone. 150.00
❑52, Jul 1966, JK, SL (w); JK (a); 1: Black Panther. 300.00
❑53, Aug 1966, JK, SL (w); JK (a); O: Black Panther. O: Klaw. 1: Klaw. 2: Black Panther. 140.00
❑54, Sep 1966, JK, SL (w); JK (a); O: Prester John. 1: Prester John. A: Inhumans. A: Black Panther. 105.00
❑55, Oct 1966, JK, SL (w); JK, JSt (a); A: Silver Surfer. Thing vs. Silver Surfer 210.00
❑56, Nov 1966, JK, SL (w); JK (a); O: Klaw. V: Klaw. 100.00
❑57, Dec 1966, JK, SL (w); JK, JSt (a); A: Inhumans. A: Doctor Doom. V: Doctor Doom. V: Wizard. V: Sandman. 115.00
❑58, Jan 1967, JK, SL (w); JK, JSt (a); A: Doctor Doom. A: Lockjaw. A: Silver Surfer. V: Doctor Doom. 90.00
❑59, Feb 1967, JK, SL (w); JK, JSt (a); A: Inhumans. A: Silver Surfer. V: Doctor Doom. 60.00
❑60, Mar 1967, JK, SL (w); JK, JSt (a); A: Inhumans. A: Black Panther. A: Doctor Doom. A: Silver Surfer. A: Watcher. V: Doctor Doom. 65.00
❑61, Apr 1967, JK, SL (w); JK (a); A: Inhumans. A: Silver Surfer. V: Sandman. 70.00
❑62, May 1967, JK, SL (w); JK (a); 1: Blastaar. A: Sandman. 70.00
❑63, Jun 1967, JK, SL (w); JK (a); V: Blastaar. V: Sandman. 70.00
❑64, Jul 1967, JK, SL (w); JK (a); 1: Supreme Intelligence. 60.00
❑65, Aug 1967, JK, SL (w); JK (a); 1: Kree. 1: Kree Supreme Intelligence. 1: Ronan the Accuser. 55.00
❑66, Sep 1967, JK, SL (w); JK (a); O: The Enclave. O: Him (later Warlock). 1: Him (later Warlock). 1: The Enclave (unnamed). A: Crystal. 115.00
❑66/2nd, Sep 1967, JK (a) 2.00
❑67, Oct 1967, JK, SL (w); JK (a); O: Him (later Warlock). A: Him (later Warlock). 105.00
❑67/2nd, Oct 1967, JK (a) 2.00
❑68, Nov 1967, JK, SL (w); JK (a); V: Mad Thinker. 60.00
❑69, Dec 1967, JK, SL (w); JK (a); V: Mad Thinker. 60.00
❑70, Jan 1968, JK, SL (w); JK (a); V: Mad Thinker. 55.00
❑71, Feb 1968, JK, SL (w); JK (a); V: Mad Thinker. 45.00
❑72, Mar 1968, JK, SL (w); JK (a); A: Silver Surfer. 100.00
❑73, Apr 1968, JK, SL (w); JK (a); A: Daredevil. A: Spider-Man. A: Thor. V: Doctor Doom. 80.00
❑74, May 1968, JK, SL (w); JK (a); A: Galactus. A: Silver Surfer. V: Galactus. 85.00
❑75, Jun 1968, JK, SL (w); JK (a); A: Galactus. A: Silver Surfer. V: Galactus. 55.00
❑76, Jul 1968, JK, SL (w); JK (a); A: Silver Surfer. V: Galactus. V: Psycho-Man. 45.00
❑77, Aug 1968, JK, SL (w); JK (a); A: Silver Surfer. V: Galactus. V: Psycho-Man. 50.00
❑78, Sep 1968, JK, SL (w); JK (a); V: Wizard. 35.00
❑79, Oct 1968, JK, SL (w); JK (a); V: Mad Thinker. 50.00
❑80, Nov 1968, JK, SL (w); JK (a) 40.00
❑81, Dec 1968, JK, SL (w); JK (a); V: Wizard. Crystal joins Fantastic Four 40.00
❑82, Jan 1969, JK, SL (w); JK (a); A: Inhumans. V: Maximus. 40.00
❑83, Feb 1969, JK, SL (w); JK (a); A: Inhumans. V: Maximus. 40.00
❑84, Mar 1969, JK, SL (w); JK (a); A: Doctor Doom. V: Doctor Doom 40.00
❑85, Apr 1969, JK, SL (w); JK (a); A: Doctor Doom. V: Doctor Doom 40.00
❑86, May 1969, JK, SL (w); JK (a); A: Doctor Doom. V: Doctor Doom 50.00

Fabulous Furry Freak Brothers

Underground comic featuring hippie high jinks

©Rip Off

Fafhrd and the Gray Mouser

Adapts Fritz Leiber fantasy series

©Marvel

Fallen Angel

Peter David series with reluctant heroine

©DC

Fantastic Five

Potential future Richards' family super-team

©Marvel

Fantastic Four (Vol. 1)

Super-team launches Marvel Age of Comics

©Marvel

N-MINT

❑87, Jun 1969, JK, SL (w); JK (a); A: Doctor Doom. V: Doctor Doom... 40.00
❑88, Jul 1969, JK, SL (w); JK (a); V: Mole Man... 35.00
❑89, Aug 1969, JK, SL (w); JK (a); V: Mole Man... 35.00
❑90, Sep 1969, JK, SL (w); JK (a); V: Mole Man... 30.00
❑91, Oct 1969, JK, SL (w); JK (a); 1: Torgo... 30.00
❑92, Nov 1969, JK, SL (w); JK (a); 2: Torgo. V: Torgo... 30.00
❑93, Dec 1969, JK, SL (w); JK (a); A: Torgo. V: Torgo... 30.00
❑94, Jan 1970, JK, SL (w); JK (a); 1: Agatha Harkness. V: Trapster. V: Wizard. V: Sandman... 40.00
❑95, Feb 1970, JK, SL (w); JK (a); 1: The Monocle... 30.00
❑96, Mar 1970, JK, SL (w); JK (a); V: Mad Thinker... 30.00
❑97, Apr 1970, JK, SL (w); JK (a)... 25.00
❑98, May 1970, JK, SL (w); JK (a); A: Neil Armstrong... 25.00
❑99, Jun 1970, JK, SL (w); JK (a); A: Inhumans... 30.00
❑100, Jul 1970, anniversary JK, SL (w); JK (a); A: Puppet Master. A: Puppet Master. A: Sandman (Marvel). A: Doctor Doom. A: Sub-Mariner. A: Mad Thinker... 70.00
❑101, Aug 1970, JK, SL (w); JK (a); 1: Gimlet. 1: Top Man... 30.00
❑102, Sep 1970, JR (c); JK, SL (w); JK (a); A: Magneto. A: Sub-Mariner. V: Magneto... 30.00
❑103, Oct 1970, JR, SL (w); JR (a); 2: Agatha Harkness. A: Richard M. Nixon. A: Magneto. A: Sub-Mariner. V: Magneto... 30.00
❑104, Nov 1970, SL (w); JR (a); A: Richard M. Nixon. A: Magneto. A: Sub-Mariner. V: Magneto... 30.00
❑105, Dec 1970, SL (w); JR (a); 1: The "monster" (Larry Rambow). 1: Dr. Phillip Zolten Rambow... 30.00
❑106, Jan 1971, JR, SL (w); JR (a); 2: The "monster" (Larry Rambow). 2: Dr. Phillip Zolten Rambow... 22.00
❑107, Feb 1971, SL (w); JB (a); 1: Janus (the scientist)... 30.00
❑108, Mar 1971, JK, JR, SL (w); JB, JK (a); 2: Janus (the scientist)... 22.00
❑109, Apr 1971, SL (w); JB (a); A: Captain Marvel. D: Janus (the scientist). V: Annihilus... 20.00
❑110, May 1971, SL (w); JB (a); A: Joe Robertson. A: J. Jonah Jameson. V: Annihilus... 20.00
❑111, Jun 1971, SL (w); JB (a); 1: Collins (landlord of Baxter building). A: Joe Robertson. A: Peter Parker. A: Hulk. A: J. Jonah Jameson... 20.00
❑112, Jul 1971, SL (w); JB (a); 2: Collins. A: Bruce Banner. A: Hulk. A: J. Jonah Jameson. Thing vs. Hulk 175.00
❑113, Aug 1971, SL (w); JB (a); 1: Overmind. A: Bruce Banner. A: The Watcher... 25.00
❑114, Sep 1971, SL (w); JB (a); 2: Overmind. A: The Watcher. V: Overmind... 27.00
❑115, Oct 1971, SL (w); JB (a); O: Overmind. 1: The Eternals (a.k.a. Eternians). A: The Watcher... 25.00
❑116, Nov 1971, Giant-size JB (a); O: Stranger. A: The Stranger. A: The Watcher. A: Edwin Jarvis. A: Doctor Doom... 65.00
❑117, Dec 1971, JB (a); 1: Chiron. 1: Asmodeus. A: Crystal. A: Diablo. A: Kaliban. V: Diablo... 15.00
❑118, Jan 1972, JB (a); 1: Reed Richards of Earth-A. 1: Ben Grimm of Earth-A. 1: Sue Storm Grimm of Earth-A. A: Crystal. A: Diablo. A: Lockjaw. V: Diablo... 15.00
❑119, Feb 1972, JB (a); A: Black Panther. A: Klaw. V: Klaw... 15.00
❑120, Mar 1972, JB, SL (w); JB (a); 1: Air-Walker (robot form). A: General T. E. "Thunderbolt" Ross. V: Air-Walker Automaton... 15.00
❑121, Apr 1972, JB, SL (w); JB (a); 2: Air-Walker (robot form). A: Galactus. A: Silver Surfer. V: Air-Walker Automaton... 30.00
❑122, May 1972, SL (w); JB (a); A: Galactus. A: Silver Surfer. V: Galactus... 45.00
❑123, Jun 1972, SL (w); JB (a); A: General T. E. "Thunderbold" Ross. A: Galactus. A: Richard M. Nixon. A: Silver Surfer. V: Galactus... 27.00
❑124, Jul 1972, SL (w); JB (a)... 20.00
❑125, Aug 1972, SL (w); JB (a)... 20.00
❑126, Sep 1972, JB (a); O: Fantastic Four... 30.00
❑127, Oct 1972, JB (a); V: Mole Man. 35.00
❑128, Nov 1972, JB (a); V: Tyrannus. V: Mole Man... 30.00
❑129, Dec 1972, JB (a); 1: Thundra. A: Medusa... 25.00
❑130, Jan 1973, JB (a); 2: Thundra. A: Inhumans. V: Trapster. V: Thundra. V: Wizard. V: Sandman... 15.00
❑131, Feb 1973, JB (c); RA (a); 1: Omega (the ultimate Alpha Primitive). A: Inhumans. V: Maximus... 15.00
❑132, Mar 1973, JB (a); V: Maximus. Medusa Joins... 15.00
❑133, Apr 1973, JB (c); V: Trapster. V: Thundra. V: Wizard. V: Sandman. 12.00
❑134, May 1973, JB (a); V: Dragon Man... 12.00
❑135, Jun 1973, JB (a); V: Dragon Man. 12.00
❑136, Jul 1973, JB (a); V: Shaper of Worlds... 12.00
❑137, Aug 1973, JB (a); V: Shaper of Worlds... 12.00
❑138, Sep 1973, JB (a); V: Miracle Man. 12.00
❑139, Oct 1973, JB (a); V: Miracle Man. 12.00
❑140, Nov 1973, RB (c); JB (a); O: Annihilus. V: Annihilus... 12.00
❑141, Dec 1973, JR (c); JB (a); V: Annihilus... 12.00
❑142, Jan 1974, RB (a); 1: Darkoth the Death-Demon. V: Doctor Doom... 12.00
❑143, Feb 1974, GK (c); RB (a); V: Doctor Doom... 12.00
❑144, Mar 1974, RB (a); A: Doctor Doom. V: Doctor Doom. Marvel Value Stamp #39: Iron Fist... 12.00
❑145, Apr 1974, GK (c); RA (a); A: Doctor Doom. Marvel Value Stamp #9: Captain Marvel... 12.00
❑146, May 1974, GK (c); RA (a); Marvel Value Stamp #91: Hela... 10.00
❑147, Jun 1974, RB (a); A: Sub-Mariner. Marvel Value Stamp #82: Mary Jane... 15.00
❑148, Jul 1974, RB (a); V: Frightful Four... 10.00
❑149, Aug 1974, RB (a); Marvel Value Stamp #78: Owl... 10.00
❑150, Sep 1974, GK (c); RB (a); A: Inhumans. A: Avengers. Wedding of Crystal and Quicksilver; Marvel Value Stamp #27: Black Widow... 10.00
❑151, Oct 1974, RB (a); O: Thundra. 1: Mahkizmo. Marvel Value Stamp #21: Kull... 10.00
❑152, Nov 1974, RB (a); Marvel Value Stamp #23: Sgt. Fury... 10.00
❑153, Dec 1974, GK (c); RB (a); V: Mahkizmo. Marvel Value Stamp #62: Plunderer... 10.00
❑154, Jan 1975, GK (c); partial reprint of Strange Tales #127; Marvel Value Stamp #100: Galactus... 10.00
❑155, Feb 1975, RB (a); A: Silver Surfer. V: Doctor Doom. Marvel Value Stamp #16: Shang-Chi... 15.00
❑156, Mar 1975, RB (a); A: Doctor Doom. A: Silver Surfer. V: Doctor Doom... 12.00
❑157, Apr 1975, RB (a); A: Doctor Doom. A: Silver Surfer. V: Doctor Doom... 12.00
❑158, May 1975, RB (a); V: Xemu... 12.00
❑159, Jun 1975, RB (a); A: Inhumans. V: Xemu. Marvel Value Stamp #84: Dr. Doom... 10.00
❑160, Jul 1975, GK (c); JB (a); V: Arkon. Marvel Value Stamp #32: Red Skull 10.00
❑161, Aug 1975, RB (a); A: Valeria. A: Reed Richards of Earth-A. A: Sue Grimm of Earth-A. A: Ben Grimm of Earth-A. A: Lockjaw. A: Phineas... 10.00
❑162, Sep 1975, RB (a); A: Albert E. DeVoor. A: The "Old One". A: Valeria. A: Reed Richards of Earth-A. A: Gaard (Johnny Storm of Earth-A, reconstructed). A: Arkon. A: Ben Grimm of Earth-A. A: Phineas... 10.00
❑163, Oct 1975, RB (a); A: Albert E. DeVoor. A: Reed Richards of Earth-A. A: Gaard (Johnny Storm of Earth-A, reconstructed). A: Arkon... 10.00
❑164, Nov 1975, JK (c); GP (a); 1: Crusader (a.k.a. Marvel Boy). 1: Frankie Raye... 9.00
❑165, Dec 1975, GP (a); O: Crusader (a.k.a. Marvel Boy). D: Crusader... 7.00
❑166, Jan 1976, RB (c); GP (a); A: Hulk. A: Puppet Master. V: Hulk... 10.00
❑167, Feb 1976, JK (c); GP (a); A: Hulk. A: Puppet Master. V: Hulk... 15.00
❑168, Mar 1976, RB (a); A: Wreaker. Thing replaced by Luke Cage (Power Man)... 10.00
❑169, Apr 1976, RB (a); A: Luke Cage. 10.00

Other grades: Multiply price above by 5/6 for VF/NM • 2/3 for VERY FINE • 1/3 for FINE • 1/5 for VERY GOOD • 1/8 for GOOD

	N-MINT
❑169/30 cent, Apr 1976, RB (a); A: Luke Cage. 30 cent regional price variant	20.00
❑170, May 1976, GP (a); A: Luke Cage.	10.00
❑170/30 cent, May 1976, GP (a); A: Luke Cage. 30 cent regional price variant	20.00
❑171, Jun 1976, JK (c); RB, GP (a); 1: Gorr. V: Galactus.	6.00
❑171/30 cent, Jun 1976, JK (c); RB, GP (a); 1: Gorr. V: Galactus. 30 cent regional price variant	20.00
❑172, Jul 1976, JK (c); GP (a); 2: Gorr. A: Galactus. A: The High Evolutionary. A: The Destroyer. V: Galactus.	6.00
❑172/30 cent, Jul 1976, JK (c); GP (a); 2: Gorr. A: Galactus. A: The High Evolutionary. A: The Destroyer. V: Galactus. 30 cent regional price variant	20.00
❑173, Aug 1976, JK (c); JB (a); A: Galactus. A: Gorr. A: The High Evolutionary. A: Torgo. V: Galactus.	6.00
❑173/30 cent, Aug 1976, JK (c); JB (a); A: Galactus. A: Gorr. A: The High Evolutionary. A: Torgo. V: Galactus. 30 cent regional price variant	20.00
❑174, Sep 1976, JK (c); JB (a); A: Galactus. A: Gorr. A: The High Evolutionary. A: Torgo. V: Galactus.	6.00
❑175, Oct 1976 JK (c); JB (a); A: Galactus. A: The Impossible Man. A: Gorr. A: The High Evolutionary. V: Galactus.	6.00
❑176, Nov 1976, JK (c); GP (a); A: The Impossible Man. A: Roy Thomas. A: Stan Lee. A: Jack Kirby. V: Trapster. V: Wizard. V: Sandman.	6.00
❑177, Dec 1976, JK (c); GP (a); O: Texas Twister. 1: Texas Twister. 1: Captain Ultra. A: Tigra. A: Impossible Man. V: Trapster. V: Brute. V: Wizard. V: Sandman.	6.00
❑178, Jan 1977, JR (c); GP (a); A: The Impossible Man. A: Brute. V: Trapster. V: Brute. V: Wizard. V: Sandman.	6.00
❑179, Feb 1977, AM (c); 1: Metalloid. A: Tigra. A: Thundra. A: Reed Richards of Counter-Earth. A: Impossible Man. A: Annihilus. A: Mad Thinker. V: Annihilus. V: Mad Thinker. Newsstand edition (distributed by Curtis); issue number in box	6.00
❑179/Whitman, Feb 1977, AM (c); 1: Metalloid. A: Tigra. A: Thundra. A: Reed Richards of Counter-Earth. A: Impossible Man. A: Annihilus. A: Mad Thinker. V: Annihilus. V: Mad Thinker. Special markets edition (usually sold in Whitman bagged prepacks); price appears in a diamond; UPC barcode appears	6.00
❑180, Mar 1977, JK (c); JK, SL (w); JK (a); Reprints FF #101; newsstand edition (distributed by Curtis); issue number in box	6.00
❑180/Whitman, Mar 1977, JK (c); JK, SL (w); JK (a); Special markets edition (usually sold in Whitman bagged prepacks); price appears in a diamond; UPC barcode appears	6.00
❑181, Apr 1977, JK (c); A: Reed Richards of Counter-Earth. A: Annihilus. V: Reed Richards of Counter-Earth. V: Annihilus. V: Mad Thinker. Newsstand edition (distributed by Curtis); issue number in box	6.00
❑181/Whitman, Apr 1977, JK (c); A: Reed Richards of Counter-Earth. A: Annihilus. V: Reed Richards of Counter-Earth. V: Annihilus. V: Mad Thinker. Special markets edition (usually sold in Whitman bagged prepacks); price appears in a diamond; UPC barcode appears	6.00
❑182, May 1977, V: Reed Richards of Counter-Earth. V: Annihilus. V: Mad Thinker. Newsstand edition (distributed by Curtis); issue number in box	6.00
❑182/Whitman, May 1977, V: Reed Richards of Counter-Earth. V: Annihilus. V: Mad Thinker. Special markets edition (usually sold in Whitman bagged prepacks); price appears in a diamond; UPC barcode appears	6.00
❑183, Jun 1977, GP (c); SB (a); A: Tigra. A: Thundra. A: Impossible Man. A: Brute. A: Annihilus. A: Mad Thinker. V: Brute. V: Annihilus. V: Mad Thinker. Newsstand edition (distributed by Curtis); issue number in box	6.00
❑183/Whitman, Jun 1977, GP (c); SB (a); A: Tigra. A: Thundra. A: Impossible Man. A: Brute. A: Annihilus. A: Mad Thinker. V: Brute. V: Annihilus. V: Mad Thinker. Special markets edition (usually sold in Whitman bagged prepacks); price appears in a diamond; UPC barcode appears	6.00
❑183/35 cent, Jun 1977, 35 cent regional price variant; newsstand edition (distributed by Curtis); issue number in box	15.00
❑184, Jul 1977, GP (a); A: Tigra. A: Thundra. A: Impossible Man. Newsstand edition (distributed by Curtis); issue number in box	6.00
❑184/Whitman, Jul 1977, GP (a); A: Tigra. A: Thundra. A: Impossible Man. Special markets edition (usually sold in Whitman bagged prepacks); price appears in a diamond; UPC barcode appears	6.00
❑184/35 cent, Jul 1977, 35 cent regional price variant; newsstand edition (distributed by Curtis); issue number in box	15.00
❑185, Aug 1977, GP (a); 1: Nicholas Scratch. 2: New Salem's Witches. A: Impossible Man. Newsstand edition (distributed by Curtis); issue number in box	5.00
❑185/Whitman, Aug 1977, GP (a); 1: Nicholas Scratch. 2: New Salem's Witches. A: Impossible Man. Special markets edition (usually sold in Whitman bagged prepacks); price appears in a diamond; UPC barcode appears	5.00
❑185/35 cent, Aug 1977, 35 cent regional price variant; newsstand edition (distributed by Curtis); issue number in box	15.00
❑186, Sep 1977, GP (a); O: New Salem's Witches. 2: Nicholas Scratch. A: Impossible Man. Newsstand edition (distributed by Curtis); issue number in box	5.00
❑186/Whitman, Sep 1977, GP (a); O: New Salem's Witches. 2: Nicholas Scratch. A: Impossible Man. Special markets edition (usually sold in Whitman bagged prepacks); price appears in a diamond; no UPC barcode	5.00
❑186/35 cent, Sep 1977, GP (a); O: New Salem's Witches. 2: Nicholas Scratch. A: Impossible Man. 35 cent regional price variant; newsstand edition (distributed by Curtis); issue number in box	15.00
❑187, Oct 1977, GP (a); A: Molecule Man. A: Klaw. A: Impossible Man. V: Molecule Man. V: Klaw. Newsstand edition (distributed by Curtis); issue number in box	5.00
❑187/Whitman, Oct 1977, GP (a); A: Molecule Man. A: Klaw. A: Impossible Man. V: Molecule Man. V: Klaw. Special markets edition (usually sold in Whitman bagged prepacks); price appears in a diamond; no UPC barcode	5.00
❑187/35 cent, Oct 1977, GP (a); A: Molecule Man. A: Klaw. A: Impossible Man. V: Molecule Man. V: Klaw. 35 cent regional price variant; newsstand edition (distributed by Curtis); issue number in box	15.00
❑188, Nov 1977, GP (a); A: The Watcher. A: Molecule Man. A: Impossible Man. V: Molecule Man. V: Klaw. Newsstand edition (distributed by Curtis); issue number in box	5.00
❑188/Whitman, Nov 1977, GP (a); A: The Watcher. A: Molecule Man. A: Impossible Man. V: Molecule Man. V: Klaw. Special markets edition (usually sold in Whitman bagged prepacks); price appears in a diamond; no UPC barcode	5.00
❑189, Dec 1977, KP (c); JK, SL (w); JK (a); Reprints FF Annual #4; newsstand edition (distributed by Curtis); issue number in box	5.00
❑189/Whitman, Dec 1977, KP (c); JK, SL (w); JK (a); Special markets edition (usually sold in Whitman bagged prepacks); price appears in a diamond; no UPC barcode	5.00
❑190, Jan 1978, JK (c); SB (a); Thing recounts FF's career	5.00
❑191, Feb 1978, GP (a); A: Plunderer. A: Thundra. V: Plunderer. Fantastic Four resign	5.00
❑192, Mar 1978, GP (a); A: Texas Twister.	5.00
❑193, Apr 1978, KP (w); KP (a); O: Darketh the Death-Demon. 1: Victor Von Doom II (not face). A: Diablo. A: Impossible Man. V: Diablo. Newsstand edition (distributed by Curtis); issue number in box	5.00
❑193/Whitman, Apr 1978, KP (w); KP (a); O: Darketh the Death-Demon. 1: Victor Von Doom II (not face). A: Diablo. A: Impossible Man. V: Diablo. Special markets edition (usually sold in Whitman bagged prepacks); price appears in a diamond; no UPC barcode	5.00
❑194, May 1978, GP (c); KP (w); KP (a); A: Darketh. A: Diablo. A: Impossible Man. A: Sub-Mariner. V: Diablo. Newsstand edition (distributed by Curtis); issue number in box	5.00
❑194/Whitman, May 1978, GP (c); KP (w); KP (a); A: Darketh. A: Diablo. A: Impossible Man. A: Sub-Mariner. V: Diablo. Special markets edition (usually sold in Whitman bagged prepacks); price appears in a diamond; no UPC barcode	5.00
❑195, Jun 1978, GP (c); KP (a); 2: Victor Von Doom II (not face). A: Lord Vashti. A: Impossible Man. A: Sub-Mariner. Newsstand edition (distributed by Curtis); issue number in box	5.00
❑195/Whitman, Jun 1978, GP (c); KP (a); 2: Victor Von Doom II (not face). A: Lord Vashti. A: Impossible Man. A: Sub-Mariner. Special markets edition (usually sold in Whitman bagged prepacks); price appears in a diamond; no UPC barcode	5.00
❑196, Jul 1978, GP (c); KP (a); A: Victor Von Doom II. A: Doctor Doom.	5.00
❑197, Aug 1978, GP (c); KP (a); A: Red Ghost. A: Victor Von Doom II. A: Dr. Doom. A: Nick Fury. V: Red Ghost. V: Doctor Doom. Reed Richards gets powers back; newsstand edition (distributed by Curtis); issue number in box	5.00
❑197/Whitman, Aug 1978, GP (c); KP (a); A: Red Ghost. A: Victor Von Doom II. A: Dr. Doom. A: Nick Fury. V: Red Ghost. V: Doctor Doom. Special markets edition (usually sold in Whitman bagged prepacks); price appears in a diamond; UPC barcode appears	5.00
❑198, Sep 1978, JB (c); KP (a); A: Prince Zorba. A: Victor Von Doom II. A: Doctor Doom. V: Doctor Doom. Team gets together to fight Doctor Doom; newsstand edition (distributed by Curtis); issue number in box	5.00
❑198/Whitman, Sep 1978, JB (c); KP (a); A: Prince Zorba. A: Victor Von Doom II. A: Doctor Doom. V: Doctor Doom. Special markets edition (usually sold in Whitman bagged prepacks); price appears in a diamond; no UPC barcode	5.00
❑199, Oct 1978, KP (a); O: Victor Von Doom II. A: Prince Zorba. A: Doctor Doom. D: Victor Von Doom II. Newsstand edition (distributed by Curtis); issue number in box	5.00
❑199/Whitman, Oct 1978, KP (a); O: Victor Von Doom II. A: Prince Zorba. A: Doctor Doom. D: Victor Von Doom II. Special markets edition (usually sold in Whitman bagged prepacks); price appears in a diamond; no UPC barcode	5.00
❑200, Nov 1978, KP (a); A: Doctor Doom. V: Doctor Doom.	5.00

Other grades: Multiply price above by 5/6 for VF/NM • 2/3 for VERY FINE • 1/3 for FINE • 1/5 for VERY GOOD • 1/8 for GOOD

Fantastic Four (Vol. 2)

Jim Lee takes over during "Heroes Reborn"

©Marvel

Fantastic Four (Vol. 3)

Third series reverts to Volume 1 at end

©Marvel

Fantastic Four: Atlantis Rising

Giant-sized special kicked off summer event

©Marvel

Fantastic Four: Fireworks

Modernized retelling of classic stories

©Marvel

Fantastic Four: 1 2 3 4

Marvel Knights series from Grant Morrison

©Marvel

N-MINT

❑201, Dec 1978, KP (a); A: Prince Zorba. A: Quasimodo. Newsstand edition (distributed by Curtis); issue number in box 4.00
❑201/Whitman, Dec 1978, KP (a); A: Prince Zorba. A: Quasimodo. Special markets edition (usually sold in Whitman bagged prepacks); price appears in a diamond; no UPC barcode 4.00
❑202, Jan 1979, JB, KP (a); A: Iron Man. A: Quasimodo. A: Tony Stark. Newsstand edition (distributed by Curtis); issue number in box 4.00
❑202/Whitman, Jan 1979, JB, KP (a); A: Iron Man. A: Quasimodo. A: Tony Stark. Special markets edition (usually sold in Whitman bagged prepacks); price appears in a diamond; no UPC barcode 4.00
❑203, Feb 1979, KP (a); Newsstand edition (distributed by Curtis); issue number in box 4.00
❑203/Whitman, Feb 1979, KP (a); Special markets edition (usually sold in Whitman bagged prepacks); price appears in a diamond; no UPC barcode 4.00
❑204, Mar 1979, KP (a); 1: Queen Adora (of Xandar). 1: Skrull X. A: Man-Wolf. A: The Watcher. A: Monocle. A: Edwin Jarvis. A: Spider-Man. 4.00

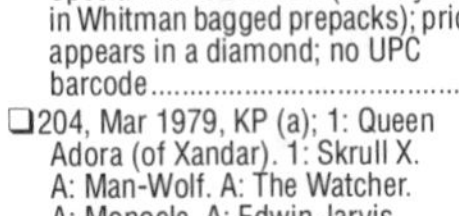

❑205, Apr 1979, KP (a); 1: Thoran Rul (Protector). 2: Queen Adora (of Xandar). A: The Watcher. A: Monocle. A: Emperor Dorrek. 4.00
❑206, May 1979, KP (a); Newsstand edition (distributed by Curtis); issue number in box 4.00
❑206/Whitman, May 1979, KP (a); Special markets edition (usually sold in Whitman bagged prepacks); price appears in a diamond; no UPC barcode 4.00

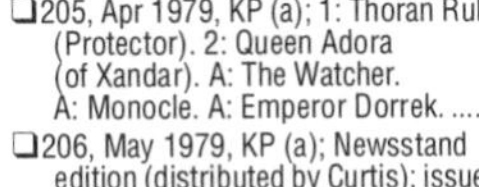

❑207, Jun 1979, SB (a); 1: The Enclave (identified). A: Barney Bushkin. A: Medusa. A: Monocle. A: Spider-Man. 4.00
❑208, Jul 1979, SB (a); O: Protector. A: Nova. A: Sphinx. A: Queen Adora. A: Comet. A: Diamondhead. A: Thoran Rul (Protector). A: Crimebuster. A: Doctor Sun. A: Powerhouse. 4.00
❑209, Aug 1979, JBy (a); 1: Herbie. ... 4.00
❑210, Sep 1979, JBy (a); 2: Herbie. A: Galactus. 4.00
❑211, Oct 1979, JBy (a); 1: Terrax the Tamer. A: Galactus. A: The Watcher. 4.00
❑212, Nov 1979, JBy (a); A: Galactus. A: Sphinx. A: The Watcher. A: Sayge. A: Skrull X. 4.00
❑213, Dec 1979, JBy (a); A: Galactus. A: Sphinx. A: The Watcher. A: Sayge. 4.00
❑214, Jan 1980, JBy (a); A: Queen Adora. A: Dum Dum Dugan. D: Skrull X. 4.00
❑215, Feb 1980, JBy (a) 4.00
❑216, Mar 1980, JBy (a) 4.00
❑217, Apr 1980, JBy (a); A: Dazzler. ... 4.00
❑218, May 1980, JBy, JSt (a); Continued from Peter Parker, the Spectacular Spider-Man #42 .... 4.00
❑219, Jun 1980 .... 4.00

N-MINT

❑220, Jul 1980, JBy (w); JBy (a); O: Fantastic Four. 4.00
❑221, Aug 1980, JBy (a) 4.00
❑222, Sep 1980, BSz, JSt (a) 4.00
❑223, Oct 1980 .... 4.00
❑224, Nov 1980 .... 4.00
❑225, Dec 1980, BSz (a); A: Thor. 4.00
❑226, Jan 1981, BSz (a) 4.00
❑227, Feb 1981, BSz (a) 4.00
❑228, Mar 1981, BSz, JSt (a) 4.00
❑229, Apr 1981, BSz, JSt (a) 4.00
❑230, May 1981, BSz, JSt (a) 4.00
❑231, Jun 1981, BSz, JSt (a) 4.00
❑232, Jul 1981, JBy (c); JBy (w); JBy (a) 4.00
❑233, Aug 1981, JBy (c); JBy (w); JBy (a) 4.00
❑234, Sep 1981, JBy (c); JBy (w); JBy (a) 4.00
❑235, Oct 1981, JBy (c); JBy (w); JBy (a); V: Ego. 4.00
❑236, Nov 1981, 20th Anniversary Issue JBy (c); JBy (w); JBy (a); O: Fantastic Four. V: Doctor Doom. 4.00
❑237, Dec 1981, JBy (c); JBy (w); JBy (a); 1: Julie Angel. 4.00
❑238, Jan 1982, JBy (c); JBy (w); JBy (a); O: Frankie Raye. A: Aunt Petunia. 4.00
❑239, Feb 1982, JBy (c); JBy (w); JBy (a) 4.00
❑240, Mar 1982, JBy (c); JBy (w); JBy (a); 1: Luna. 2.50
❑241, Apr 1982, JBy (c); JBy (w); JBy (a); A: Black Panther. 2.50
❑242, May 1982, JBy (c); JBy (w); JBy (a); A: Daredevil. 2.50
❑243, Jun 1982, JBy (c); JBy (w); JBy (a) 2.50
❑244, Jul 1982, JBy (c); JBy (w); JBy (a); 1: Nova II (Frankie Raye). Frankie Raye becomes herald of Galactus... 2.50
❑245, Aug 1982, JBy (c); JBy (w); JBy (a) 2.50
❑246, Sep 1982, JBy (c); JBy (w); JBy (a) 2.50
❑247, Oct 1982, JBy (c); JBy (w); JBy (a); 1: Kristoff Vernard. 2.50
❑248, Nov 1982, JBy (c); JBy (w); JBy (a) 2.50
❑249, Dec 1982, JBy (c); JBy (w); JBy (a); V: Gladiator. 4.00
❑250, Jan 1983, Double-size JBy (c); JBy (w); JBy (a); A: X-Men. A: Captain America. A: Spider-Man. 5.00
❑252, Mar 1983, JBy (c); JBy (w); JBy (a); sideways format 2.50
❑251, Feb 1983, JBy (c); JBy (w); JBy (a); Negative Zone 4.00
❑253, Apr 1983, JBy (c); JBy (w); JBy (a) 2.50
❑254, May 1983, JBy (c); JBy (w); JBy (a); A: She-Hulk. 2.50
❑255, Jun 1983, JBy (c); JBy (w); JBy (a) 2.50
❑256, Jul 1983, JBy (c); JBy (w); JBy (a) 4.00
❑257, Aug 1983, JBy (c); JBy (w); JBy (a) 2.50
❑258, Sep 1983, JBy (c); JBy (w); JBy (a) 2.50
❑259, Oct 1983, JBy (c); JBy (w); JBy (a) 2.50
❑260, Nov 1983, JBy (c); JBy (w); JBy (a); A: Doctor Doom. A: Silver Surfer. D: Terrax. Silver Surfer, Doctor Doom 5.00
❑261, Dec 1983, JBy (c); JBy (w); JBy (a); A: Silver Surfer. A: Watcher...... 4.00
❑262, Jan 1984, JBy (c); JBy (w); JBy (a); O: Galactus. Trial of Reed Richards; John Byrne appears in story........ 2.50

N-MINT

❑263, Feb 1984, JBy (a) 2.50
❑264, Mar 1984, JBy (w); JBy (a); V: Karisma. Cover swipe of Fantastic Four #1 .... 2.50
❑265, Apr 1984, JBy (a); 1: Lyja (as Alicia Masters). 1: Roberta the Receptionist. She-Hulk joins Fantastic Four (replaces Thing, who left in Secret Wars) 2.50
❑266, May 1984, JBy (w); JBy, KGa (a) 2.50
❑267, Jun 1984, JBy (a); Sue has a miscarriage 2.50
❑268, Jul 1984, JBy (a); A: Hulk. A: Doctor Octopus. 2.50
❑269, Aug 1984, JBy (w); JBy (a); 1: Terminus. 4.00
❑270, Sep 1984, JBy (w); JBy (a); V: Terminus. 2.50
❑271, Oct 1984, JBy (w); JBy (a) 4.00
❑272, Nov 1984, JBy (w); JBy (a); 1: Nathaniel Richards (Reed's father). 5.00
❑273, Dec 1984, JBy (w); JBy (a); O: Kang. 2.50
❑274, Jan 1985, JBy (w); JBy (a); Thing solo story; alien costume freed....... 2.50
❑275, Feb 1985, JBy (w); JBy (a) 2.50
❑276, Mar 1985, JBy (w); JBy (a) 2.50
❑277, Apr 1985, JBy (w); JBy (a) 2.50
❑278, May 1985, JBy (w); JBy (a); O: Doctor Doom. Kristoff becomes second Doctor Doom 2.50
❑279, Jun 1985, JBy (w); JBy (a)....... 2.50
❑280, Jul 1985, JBy (w); JBy (a); 1: Hate-Monger III ("H.M. Unger"). Sue becomes Malice 2.50
❑281, Aug 1985, JBy (w); JBy (a) 2.50
❑282, Sep 1985, JBy (w); JBy (a); Secret Wars II 2.50
❑283, Oct 1985, JBy (w); JBy (a) 2.50
❑284, Nov 1985, JBy (w); JBy (a); Invisible Girl becomes Invisible Woman 2.50
❑285, Dec 1985, JBy (w); JBy (a); Secret Wars II 2.50
❑286, Jan 1986, JBy (w); JBy (a); 2: X-Factor. A: X-Men. return of Jean Grey 3.00
❑287, Feb 1986, JBy (w); JBy (a); A: Doctor Doom. 2.00
❑288, Mar 1986, JBy (a); A: Doctor Doom. Secret Wars II; Doctor Doom vs. Beyonder 2.00
❑289, Apr 1986, JBy (a); D: Basilisk I (Basil Elks). 2.00
❑290, May 1986, JBy (w); JBy (a)...... 2.00
❑291, Jun 1986, JBy (w); JBy (a)....... 2.00
❑292, Jul 1986, JBy (w); JBy (a); A: Nick Fury. 2.00
❑293, Aug 1986, JBy (a) 2.00
❑294, Sep 1986, JOy (a) 2.00
❑295, Nov 1986, JOy (a) 2.00
❑296, Nov 1986, Double-size; Thing comes back. 2.50
❑297, Dec 1986, JB, SB (a) 2.00
❑298, Jan 1987, JB, SB (a) 2.00
❑299, Feb 1987 .... 2.00
❑300, Mar 1987, JB, SB (a); Wedding of Johnny Storm and Alicia; "Alicia" later revealed to be Lyja (a Skrull)... 2.50
❑301, Apr 1987, JB (a) 2.00

Other grades: Multiply price above by 5/6 for VF/NM • 2/3 for VERY FINE • 1/3 for FINE • 1/5 for VERY GOOD • 1/8 for GOOD

	N-MINT
❑302, May 1987, JB, SB (a)	2.00
❑303, Jun 1987, JB (a)	2.00
❑304, Jul 1987, JB, JSt (a); Reed and Sue take leave of absence	2.00
❑305, Aug 1987, JB, JSt (a)	2.00
❑306, Sep 1987, A: Ms. Marvel (Sharon Ventura).	2.00
❑307, Oct 1987, Crystal and new Ms. Marvel joins team	2.00
❑308, Nov 1987, JB, JSt (a); 1: Fasaud.	2.00
❑309, Dec 1987, JB, JSt (a)	2.00
❑310, Jan 1988, Ms. Marvel becomes She-Thing	2.00
❑311, Feb 1988	2.00
❑312, Mar 1988, A: Doctor Doom. Fall of Mutants	2.00
❑313, Apr 1988	2.00
❑314, May 1988, KP, JSt (a); V: Belasco.	2.00
❑315, Jun 1988, KP, JSt (a)	2.00
❑316, Jul 1988, KP, JSt (a)	2.00
❑317, Aug 1988	2.00
❑318, Sep 1988	2.00
❑319, Oct 1988, Giant-size; Doctor Doom vs. Beyonder; Beyonder returns, merges with Molecule Man	2.50
❑320, Nov 1988, Thing vs. Hulk	2.00
❑321, Dec 1988, 1: Aron the Rogue Watcher. Ms. Marvel vs. She-Hulk	1.50
❑322, Jan 1989, Inferno	1.50
❑323, Feb 1989, Inferno	1.50
❑324, Mar 1989, KP (a); Inferno	1.50
❑325, Apr 1989, RB (a)	1.50
❑326, May 1989, Reed and Sue return to team	1.50
❑327, Jun 1989, Thing reverts to human form	1.50
❑328, Jul 1989, KP (a)	1.50
❑329, Aug 1989, RB (a)	1.50
❑330, Sep 1989, RB (a); V: Doom.	1.50
❑331, Oct 1989, RB (a); V: Ultron.	1.50
❑332, Nov 1989, RB (a)	1.50
❑333, Nov 1989, RB (a)	1.50
❑334, Dec 1989, Acts of Vengeance	1.50
❑335, Dec 1989, RB (a); Acts of Vengeance	1.50
❑336, Jan 1990, Acts of Vengeance	1.50
❑337, Feb 1990	2.00
❑338, Mar 1990	2.00
❑339, Apr 1990	2.00
❑340, May 1990	2.00
❑341, Jun 1990	2.00
❑342, Jul 1990, A: Spider-Man.	2.00
❑343, Aug 1990	2.00
❑344, Sep 1990	2.00
❑345, Oct 1990	2.00
❑346, Nov 1990	2.00
❑347, Dec 1990, A: Hulk. A: Ghost Rider. A: Wolverine. A: Spider-Man.	2.50
❑347/2nd, Dec 1990, A: Hulk. A: Ghost Rider. A: Wolverine.	1.50
❑348, Jan 1991, A: Hulk. A: Ghost Rider. A: Wolverine. A: Spider-Man.	2.50
❑348/2nd, Jan 1991	1.50
❑349, Feb 1991, A: Punisher. A: Hulk. A: Ghost Rider. A: Wolverine. A: Spider-Man.	2.50
❑350, Mar 1991, Giant-size; A: Doctor Doom. Return of Thing	2.50
❑351, Apr 1991	2.00
❑352, May 1991, Reed and Doctor Doom battle through time	2.00
❑353, Jun 1991	2.00
❑354, Jul 1991	2.00
❑355, Aug 1991, AM (a)	2.00
❑356, Sep 1991, Alicia is Skrull; Fantastic Four vs. New Warriors	2.00
❑357, Oct 1991, 1: Lyja (in true form). Skrull's identity revealed as Lyja	2.00
❑358, Nov 1991, 30th Anniversary Issue; JBy (a); O: Paibok the Power Skrull. 1: Paibok the Power Skrull. Die-cut cover	2.50
❑359, Dec 1991, 1: Devos the Devastator. The real Alicia returns	1.50
❑360, Jan 1992	1.50
❑361, Feb 1992	1.50
❑362, Mar 1992	1.50
❑363, Apr 1992, O: Occulus. 1: Occulus.	1.50
❑364, May 1992	1.50
❑365, Jun 1992	1.50
❑366, Jul 1992	1.50
❑367, Aug 1992	1.50
❑368, Sep 1992	1.50
❑369, Oct 1992	1.50
❑370, Nov 1992, 1: Lyja the Lazerfist.	1.50
❑371, Dec 1992, All-white embossed cover	3.00
❑371/2nd, Dec 1992, red embossed cover	2.50
❑372, Jan 1993	1.25
❑373, Feb 1993, A: Silver Sable.	1.25
❑374, Mar 1993, Spider-Man, Hulk, Ghost Rider, Wolverine team up again; Secret Defenders crossover	1.25
❑375, Apr 1993, Prism cover	3.00
❑376, May 1993, Franklin returns from future as a young man	1.25
❑377, Jun 1993, 1: Huntara. Secret Defenders crossover	1.25
❑378, Jul 1993	1.25
❑379, Aug 1993	1.50
❑380, Sep 1993	1.50
❑381, Oct 1993, A: Hunger. D: Mister Fantastic (apparent death). D: Doctor Doom.	3.00
❑382, Nov 1993	2.00
❑383, Dec 1993	1.25
❑384, Jan 1994, A: Ant-Man (Scott Lang).	1.25
❑385, Feb 1994	1.25
❑386, Mar 1994, 1: Egg (Lyja's baby). Birth of Lyja's baby	1.25
❑387, Apr 1994	1.25
❑387/Variant, Apr 1994, diecut cover.	3.00
❑388, May 1994, A: Avengers. cards.	1.50
❑389, Jun 1994	1.50
❑390, Jun 1994, A: Galactus.	1.50
❑391, Aug 1994, A: Galactus.	1.50
❑392, Sep 1994	1.50
❑393, Oct 1994, A: Puppet Master. Nathaniel Richards takes over Latveria	1.50
❑394, Nov 1994	1.50
❑394/CS, Nov 1994, polybagged with 16-page Marvel Action Hour preview, acetate print, and other items	2.95
❑395, Dec 1994, A: Wolverine.	1.50
❑396, Jan 1995	1.50
❑397, Feb 1995, V: Aron.	1.50
❑398, Mar 1995	1.50
❑398/Variant, Mar 1995, foil cover	2.50
❑399, Apr 1995	1.50
❑399/Variant, Apr 1995, enhanced cardstock cover	2.50
❑400, May 1995, Giant-size; foil cover	3.95
❑401, Jun 1995	1.50
❑402, Jul 1995, A: Thor. Atlantis Rising	1.50
❑403, Aug 1995	1.50
❑404, Sep 1995	1.50
❑405, Oct 1995, A: Iron Man 2020. A: Conan. A: Red Raven. A: Young Allies. A: Zarko. A: Green Goblin. The Thing becomes human	1.50
❑406, Nov 1995, 1: Hyperstorm. Return of Doctor Doom	1.50
❑407, Dec 1995, Return of Reed Richards	1.50
❑408, Jan 1996, V: Hyperstorm.	1.50
❑409, Feb 1996, The Thing's face is healed	1.50
❑410, Mar 1996, O: Kristoff.	1.50
❑411, Apr 1996, A: Inhumans. V: Black Bolt.	1.50
❑412, May 1996	1.50
❑413, Jun 1996, Franklin Richards becomes a child again	1.50
❑414, Jul 1996, O: Hyperstorm.	1.50
❑415, Aug 1996, Franklin captured by Onslaught	2.00
❑416, Sep 1996, Giant-size; Series continues in Fantastic Four Vol. 2; wraparound cover	3.50
❑500, Sep 2003, numbering restarts at 500 adding in issues from Vol. 2 and Vol. 3	3.50
❑500/CS, Sep 2003	3.50
❑501, Oct 2003, MWa (w)	2.25
❑502, Oct 2003, MWa (w)	5.00
❑503, Nov 2003, MWa (w)	2.99
❑504, Nov 2003, MWa (w)	2.99
❑505, Dec 2003, MWa (w)	2.99
❑506, Jan 2003, MWa (w)	2.99
❑507, Jan 2004, MWa (w)	2.99
❑508, Feb 2004, MWa (w)	2.99
❑509, Mar 2004	2.25
❑510, Apr 2004, MWa (w)	2.99
❑511, May 2004, MWa (w); Reprints.	2.25
❑512, Jun 2004, MWa (w)	2.99
❑513, Jul 2004, MWa (w)	2.99
❑514, Aug 2004	2.25
❑515, Aug 2004	2.25
❑516, Sep 2004	2.25
❑517, Oct 2004	2.99
❑518, Nov 2004	2.99
❑519, Dec 2004	2.99
❑520, Jan 2005	2.99
❑521, Feb 2005	2.99
❑522, Mar 2005	2.99
❑523, Apr 2005	2.99
❑524, May 2005	2.99
❑525, Jun 2005	2.99
❑526, Jul 2005	2.99
❑527, Aug 2005	7.00
❑527/Variant, Aug 2005	4.00
❑527/DirCut, Aug 2005	5.00
❑527/Conv, Aug 2005, Wizard World Philadelphia	7.00
❑528, Sep 2005	2.99
❑529, Oct 2005	2.99
❑530, Oct 2005	2.99
❑531, Nov 2005	2.99
❑532, Jan 2006	2.99
❑533, Feb 2006	2.99
❑534, Mar 2006	2.99
❑535, May 2006	2.99
❑536, Jun 2006	2.99
❑537, Jul 2006	2.99
❑538, Sep 2006	2.99
❑Annual 1, ca. 1963, JK (a); O: Fantastic Four. O: Sub-Mariner. 1: Krang. A: Spider-Man. A: Doctor Doom. A: Sub-Mariner. V: Sub-Mariner. Spider-Man; reprints FF #1	900.00
❑Annual 2, ca. 1964, O: Doctor Doom. 1: Boris. reprints FF #5	500.00
❑Annual 3, ca. 1965, Wedding of Reed Richards and Susan Storm; Virtually all Marvel super-heroes appear; reprints FF #6 and 11	175.00
❑Annual 4, Nov 1966, JK, SL (w); JK (a); 1: Quasimodo. Return of Golden Age Human Torch; reprints FF #25 and 26	90.00
❑Annual 5, Nov 1967, JK, SL (w); JK (a); 1: Psycho-Man. A: Inhumans. A: Inhumans, Black Panther.	60.00
❑Annual 6, Nov 1968, JK, SL (w); JK (a); 1: Franklin Richards. 1: Annihilus.	40.00
❑Annual 7, Nov 1969, JK, SL (w); JK (a); reprints FF #1, FF Annual #2	18.00
❑Annual 8, Dec 1970, JK (a); reprints FF Annual #1	18.00
❑Annual 9, Dec 1971, JK, SL (w); JK (a); reprints stories from FF #43, Annual #3, and Strange Tales #131.	10.00
❑Annual 10, ca. 1973, JK, SL (w); JK (a); reprints stories from FF Annual #3 and 4; Reprints wedding of Reed and Sue Richards	8.00
❑Annual 11, ca. 1976, JK (c); JB (a); A: The Watcher. A: Invaders. V: Invaders.	6.00
❑Annual 12, ca. 1977, KP, BH (a); A: Karnak. A: Sphinx. A: Medusa. A: Crystal. A: Triton. A: Quicksilver. A: Lockjaw. A: Gorgon. A: Black Bolt.	5.00
❑Annual 13, ca. 1978, SB (a); A: Daredevil. A: Mole Man.	5.00
❑Annual 14, ca. 1979, GP (a)	5.00
❑Annual 15, ca. 1980, GP (a); Skrulls	3.00
❑Annual 16, ca. 1982, SD, JBy (a)	3.00
❑Annual 17, ca. 1983, JBy (w); JBy (a)	3.00
❑Annual 18, ca. 1984, JBy (w); Kree-Skrull War	3.00
❑Annual 19, ca. 1985, JBy (a); A: Avengers.	3.00
❑Annual 20, ca. 1986	3.00
❑Annual 21, ca. 1988	3.00
❑Annual 22, ca. 1989, RB (a); Atlantis Attacks	3.00
❑Annual 23, ca. 1990, 1: Kosmos.	3.00
❑Annual 24, ca. 1991, O: Fantastic Four. A: Guardians of Galaxy. Korvac Quest	2.50

Fantastic Four Roast

Hembeck book is one of funniest comics ever

©Marvel

Fantastic Four: The Legend

One-shot wraps up history before "Reborn"

©Marvel

Fantastic Four: The World's Greatest Comics Magazine

Series takes place between FF #100 and #101

©Marvel

Fantastic Four 2099

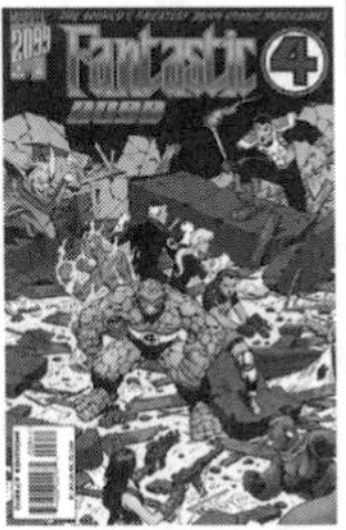

Future-universe variation of Fantastic Four

©Marvel

Fantastic Four Unlimited

Quarterly anthology series with short stories

©Marvel

N-MINT

❑Annual 25, ca. 1992, HT (a); 1: Temptress. Citizen Kang 2.50

❑Annual 26, ca. 1993, HT (a); 1: Wildstreak. Polybagged with trading card 3.00

❑Annual 27, ca. 1994, MGu (a); 1994 Annual 3.00

❑Special 1, JBy (a); Reprints Sub-Mariner vs. Fantastic Four from Annual #1 with added material 2.00

❑Ashcan 1, ashcan edition O: Fantastic Four 1.00

FANTASTIC FOUR (VOL. 2)

MARVEL

❑1 (417), Nov 1996; JLee (w); JLee (a); O: Fantastic Four (new origin). AKA Fantastic Four Vol. 1, #417 .... 4.00

❑1/Variant, Nov 1996; JLee (w); JLee (a); O: Fantastic Four (new origin). AKA Fantastic Four Vol. 1, #417; alternate cover 3.00

❑1/Gold, Nov 1996; JLee (w); JLee (a); AKA Fantastic Four Vol. 1, #417; Gold Signature Edition 3.50

❑2 (418), Dec 1996; JLee (w); JLee (a); V: Namor. AKA Fantastic Four Vol. 1, #418 .... 2.00

❑3 (419), Jan 1997; JLee (w); JLee (a); A: Avengers. V: Namor. AKA Fantastic Four Vol. 1, #419 .... 2.00

❑4 (420), Feb 1997; JLee (w); JLee (a); A: Black Panther. A: Doctor Doom. V: Doctor Doom. AKA Fantastic Four Vol. 1, #420 .... 2.00

❑4/Variant, Feb 1997; JLee (w); JLee (a); AKA Fantastic Four Vol. 1, #420 2.00

❑5 (421), Mar 1997; JLee (w); JLee (a); V: Doctor Doom. AKA Fantastic Four Vol. 1, #421 .... 2.00

❑6 (422), Apr 1997; JLee (w); JLee (a); A: Silver Surfer. V: Super Skrull. AKA Fantastic Four Vol. 1, #422; continues in Avengers #6 .... 2.00

❑7 (423), May 1997; JLee (w); A: Galactus. A: Wolverine. A: Blastaar. AKA Fantastic Four Vol. 1, #423 .... 2.00

❑8 (424), Jun 1997; JLee (w); A: Inhumans. AKA Fantastic Four Vol. 1, #424 .... 2.00

❑9 (425), Jul 1997; A: Inhumans. A: Firelord. AKA Fantastic Four Vol. 1, #425 .... 2.00

❑10 (426), Aug 1997; gatefold summary; A: Inhumans. AKA Fantastic Four Vol. 1, #426 .... 2.00

❑11 (427), Sep 1997; gatefold summary; V: Terrax. AKA Fantastic Four Vol. 1, #427 .... 2.00

❑12 (428), Oct 1997; gatefold summary; AKA Fantastic Four Vol. 1, #428; covers forms quadtych with Avengers #12, Iron Man #12, and Captain America #12 .... 2.99

❑13 (429), Nov 1997; gatefold summary; A: StormWatch. A: Wetworks. A: WildC.A.T.s. AKA Fantastic Four Vol. 1, #429; covers forms quadtych with Avengers #13, Iron Man #13, and Captain America #13 .... 2.00

N-MINT

FANTASTIC FOUR (VOL. 3)

MARVEL

❑1 (430), Jan 1998; Giant-size; AKA Fantastic Four Vol. 1, #430; Cover has green background with team facing forward 3.00

❑1/A, Jan 1998; gatefold summary; AKA Fantastic Four Vol. 1, #430; alternate cover 4.00

❑2 (431), Feb 1998; gatefold summary; AKA Fantastic Four Vol. 1, #431 .... 3.00

❑2/A, Feb 1998; gatefold summary; AKA Fantastic Four Vol. 1, #431; alternate cover 3.00

❑3 (432), Mar 1998; gatefold summary; 1: Crucible. AKA Fantastic Four Vol. 1, #432 .... 3.00

❑4 (433), Apr 1998; gatefold summary; 1: Billie the Postman. A: Silver Surfer. V: Terminus. AKA Fantastic Four Vol. 1, #433 .... 2.50

❑5 (434), May 1998; gatefold summary; V: Crucible. AKA Fantastic Four Vol. 1, #434 .... 2.50

❑6 (435), Jun 1998; gatefold summary; A: Iron Fist. AKA Fantastic Four Vol. 1, #435; Thing vs. Technet 2.25

❑7 (436), Jul 1998; gatefold summary; V: Warwolves. AKA Fantastic Four Vol. 1, #436 .... 2.25

❑8 (437), Aug 1998; gatefold summary; AKA Fantastic Four Vol. 1, #437 .... 2.25

❑9 (438), Sep 1998; gatefold summary; A: Spider-Man. AKA Fantastic Four Vol. 1, #438 .... 2.25

❑10 (439), Oct 1998; gatefold summary; V: Trapster. AKA Fantastic Four Vol. 1, #439 .... 2.25

❑11 (440), Nov 1998; gatefold summary; A: Her. AKA Fantastic Four Vol. 1, #440 .... 2.25

❑12 (441), Dec 1998; gatefold summary; V: Her. V: Crucible. AKA Fantastic Four Vol. 1, #441; wraparound cover 2.25

❑13 (442), Jan 1999; gatefold summary; V: Ronan. AKA Fantastic Four Vol. 1, #442 .... 2.25

❑14 (443), Feb 1999; gatefold summary; A: Ronan the Accuser. V: Ronan. AKA Fantastic Four Vol. 1, #443 .... 2.25

❑15 (444), Mar 1999; A: Kree. A: S.H.I.E.L.D.. A: Shi'Ar. A: Iron Man. A: Ronan the Accuser. A: Watcher. V: Ronan. AKA Fantastic Four Vol. 1, #444; Iron Man crossover, Part 1 ... 2.25

❑16 (445), Apr 1999; A: Kree. V: Kree. AKA Fantastic Four Vol. 1, #445 .... 2.25

❑17 (446), May 1999; AKA Fantastic Four Vol. 1, #446 .... 2.25

❑18 (447), Jun 1999; AKA Fantastic Four Vol. 1, #447 .... 2.25

❑19 (448), Jul 1999; V: Annihilus. AKA Fantastic Four Vol. 1, #448 .... 2.25

❑20 (449), Aug 1999; AKA Fantastic Four Vol. 1, #449 .... 2.25

❑21 (450), Sep 1999; AKA Fantastic Four Vol. 1, #450 .... 2.00

❑22 (451), Oct 1999; AKA Fantastic Four Vol. 1, #451 .... 2.00

N-MINT

❑23 (452), Nov 1999; AKA Fantastic Four Vol. 1, #452 .... 2.00

❑24 (453), Dec 1999; AKA Fantastic Four Vol. 1, #453 .... 2.00

❑25 (454), Jan 2000; Giant-size; AKA Fantastic Four Vol. 1, #454 .... 3.00

❑26 (455), Feb 2000; AKA Fantastic Four Vol. 1, #455 .... 2.25

❑27 (456), Mar 2000; AKA Fantastic Four Vol. 1, #456 .... 2.25

❑28 (457), Apr 2000; AKA Fantastic Four Vol. 1, #457 .... 2.25

❑29 (458), May 2000; AKA Fantastic Four Vol. 1, #458 .... 2.25

❑30 (459), Jun 2000; AKA Fantastic Four Vol. 1, #459 .... 2.25

❑31 (460), Jul 2000; AKA Fantastic Four Vol. 1, #460 .... 2.25

❑32 (461), Aug 2000; AKA Fantastic Four Vol. 1, #461 .... 2.25

❑33 (462), Sep 2000; AKA Fantastic Four Vol. 1, #462 .... 2.25

❑34 (463), Oct 2000; AKA Fantastic Four Vol. 1, #463 .... 2.25

❑35 (464), Nov 2000; AKA Fantastic Four Vol. 1, #464 .... 3.25

❑36 (465), Dec 2000; A: Daredevil. A: Spider-Man. A: Diablo. AKA Fantastic Four Vol. 1, #465 .... 2.25

❑37 (466), Jan 2001; AKA Fantastic Four Vol. 1, #466 .... 2.25

❑38 (467), Feb 2001; AKA Fantastic Four Vol. 1, #467 .... 2.25

❑39 (468), Mar 2001; A: Grey Gargoyle. A: Avengers. AKA Fantastic Four Vol. 1, #468; Thing can switch from rock form to human and back 2.25

❑40 (469), Apr 2001; AKA Fantastic Four Vol. 1, #469; Baxter Building reopens 2.25

❑41 (470), May 2001; JPH (w); A: First. AKA Fantastic Four Vol. 1, #470; First appearance of Hellscout 2.25

❑42 (471), Jun 2001; AKA Fantastic Four Vol. 1, #471 .... 2.25

❑43 (472), Jul 2001; AKA Fantastic Four Vol. 1, #472 .... 2.25

❑44 (473), Aug 2001; AKA Fantastic Four Vol. 1, #473 .... 2.25

❑45 (474), Sep 2001; AKA Fantastic Four Vol. 1, #474 .... 2.25

❑46 (475), Oct 2001; AKA Fantastic Four Vol. 1, #475 .... 2.25

❑47 (476), Nov 2001; AKA Fantastic Four Vol. 1, #476 .... 2.25

❑48 (477), Dec 2001; AKA Fantastic Four Vol. 1, #477 .... 2.25

❑49 (478), Jan 2002; AKA Fantastic Four Vol. 1, #478 .... 2.25

❑50 (479), Feb 2002; AKA Fantastic Four Vol. 1, #479 .... 3.99

❑51 (480), Mar 2002; AKA Fantastic Four Vol. 1, #480 .... 3.50

❑52 (481), Apr 2002; AKA Fantastic Four Vol. 1, #481 .... 2.25

❑53 (482), May 2002; AKA Fantastic Four Vol. 1, #482 .... 3.25

❑54 (483), Jun 2002; AKA Fantastic Four Vol. 1, #483 .... 3.50

❑55 (484), Jul 2002; AKA Fantastic Four Vol. 1, #484 .... 2.25

Other grades: Multiply price above by 5/6 for VF/NM • 2/3 for VERY FINE • 1/3 for FINE • 1/5 for VERY GOOD • 1/8 for GOOD

❑56 (485), Aug 2002; AKA Fantastic Four Vol. 1, #485 .... 2.25
❑57 (486), Aug 2002; AKA Fantastic Four Vol. 1, #486 .... 2.25
❑58 (487), Sep 2002; AKA Fantastic Four Vol. 1, #487 .... 2.25
❑59 (488), Oct 2002; AKA Fantastic Four Vol. 1, #488 .... 2.25
❑60 (489), Oct 2002; AKA Fantastic Four Vol. 1, #489 .... 1.00
❑61 (490), Nov 2002; AKA Fantastic Four Vol. 1, #490 .... 2.25
❑62 (491), Dec 2002; AKA Fantastic Four Vol. 1, #491 .... 2.25
❑63 (492), Jan 2003; AKA Fantastic Four Vol. 1, #492 .... 2.25
❑64 (493), Feb 2003; AKA Fantastic Four Vol. 1, #493 .... 2.25
❑65 (494), Mar 2003; AKA Fantastic Four Vol. 1, #494 .... 2.25
❑66 (495), Apr 2003; AKA Fantastic Four Vol. 1, #495 .... 2.25
❑67 (496), May 2003; AKA Fantastic Four Vol. 1, #496 .... 2.25
❑68 (497), Jun 2003; MWa (w); AKA Fantastic Four Vol. 1, #497 .... 2.25
❑69 (498), Jul 2003; MWa (w); AKA Fantastic Four Vol. 1, #498 .... 2.25
❑70 (499), Aug 2003, MWa (w); Numbering restarts at 500 under Vol. 1 .... 2.25
❑Annual 1998, ca. 1998; Fantastic Four/Fantastic 4 '98; alternate universe FF 5.00
❑Annual 1999, ca. 1999; Fantastic Four/Fantastic 4 '99 .... 3.50
❑Annual 2001, ca. 2001 .... 2.99

FANTASTIC FOUR: A DEATH IN THE FAMILY
MARVEL

❑1, Aug 2006 .... 4.99

FANTASTIC FOUR: ATLANTIS RISING
MARVEL

❑1, Jun 1995; Atlantis rises from sea; acetate outer cover 3.95
❑2, Jul 1995; acetate outer cover 3.95
❑Ashcan 1, May 1995; Collector's Preview 2.25

FANTASTIC FOUR: FIREWORKS
MARVEL

❑1, Jan 1999; Marvel Remix 2.99
❑2, Feb 1999; Marvel Remix 2.99
❑3, Mar 1999; Marvel Remix 2.99

FANTASTIC FOUR: FIRST FAMILY
MARVEL

❑1, May 2006 .... 2.99
❑2, Jun 2006 .... 2.99
❑3, Jul 2006 .... 2.99
❑4, Aug 2006 .... 2.99

FANTASTIC FOUR: FOES
MARVEL

❑1 .... 2.99
❑2, Apr 2005 .... 2.99
❑3, May 2005 .... 2.99
❑4, Jun 2005 .... 2.99
❑5, Jul 2005 .... 2.99
❑6, Aug 2005 .... 2.99

FANTASTIC FOUR: HOUSE OF M
MARVEL

❑1, Aug 2005 .... 5.00
❑1/Variant, Aug 2005 .... 4.00
❑2, Sep 2005 .... 2.99
❑3, Oct 2005 .... 2.99

FANTASTIC FOUR/IRON MAN: BIG IN JAPAN
MARVEL

❑1 .... 2.99
❑2, Jan 2006 .... 2.99
❑3, Feb 2006 .... 2.99
❑4, Mar 2006 .... 2.99

FANTASTIC FOUR: 1 2 3 4
MARVEL

❑1, Oct 2001 .... 2.99
❑2, Nov 2001 .... 2.99
❑3, Dec 2001 .... 2.99
❑4, Jan 2002 .... 2.99

FANTASTIC FOUR ROAST
MARVEL

❑1, May 1982; Celebrates 20th Anniversary of Fantastic Four FH (w); MA, FH, MG, JB, FM, TD (a) 2.00

FANTASTIC FOUR SPECIAL
MARVEL

❑1, May 1984; JBy (c); reprints FF Annual #1 .... 3.00

FANTASTIC FOUR SPECIAL (2006)
MARVEL

❑1, Feb 2006 .... 4.99

FANTASTIC FOUR: THE LEGEND
MARVEL

❑1, Oct 1996; highlights of group's history 3.95

FANTASTIC FOUR: THE MOVIE
MARVEL

❑1, Jul 2005 .... 4.99

FANTASTIC FOUR: THE WEDDING SPECIAL
MARVEL

❑1, Jan 2006, b&w 2.99

FANTASTIC FOUR: THE WORLD'S GREATEST COMICS MAGAZINE
MARVEL

❑1, Feb 2001; EL (c); EL (w); KG, EL (a); set after events of Fantastic Four (Vol. 1) #100 .... 3.00
❑2, Mar 2001 MG (c); EL (w); KG, EL (a) 2.99
❑3, Apr 2001 EL (w); KG, EL, ES (a) .. 2.99
❑4, May 2001 .... 2.99
❑5, Jun 2001 .... 2.99
❑6, Jul 2001 .... 2.99
❑7, Aug 2001 .... 2.99
❑8, Sep 2001 .... 2.99
❑9, Oct 2001 .... 2.99
❑10, Nov 2001 .... 2.99
❑11, Dec 2001 .... 2.99
❑12, Jan 2002 .... 2.99

FANTASTIC FOUR 2099
MARVEL

❑1, Jan 1996; enhanced wraparound cover 3.95
❑2, Feb 1996 JB (a) 2.00
❑3, Mar 1996 AW (a) 2.00
❑4, Apr 1996 AW (a); A: Spider-Man 2099 .... 2.00
❑5, May 1996; A: Doctor Strange. Joe Kelly's first major comics work 2.00
❑6, Jun 1996 A: Spider-Man 2099. A: Doctor Strange 2.00
❑7, Jul 1996 A: Doom 2099. V: Attuma. 2.00
❑8, Aug 1996 A: Doom 2099 .... 2.00

FANTASTIC FOUR UNLIMITED
MARVEL

❑1, Mar 1993 HT (a) 4.50
❑2, Jun 1993 HT (a) 4.00
❑3, Sep 1993 HT (a) 4.00
❑4, Dec 1993; HT (a); Thing vs. Hulk. 3.95
❑5, Mar 1994 HT (a) 3.95
❑6, Jun 1994 HT (a); V: Namor. 3.95
❑7, Sep 1994; HT (a); V: early Marvel monsters. wraparound cover 3.95
❑8, Dec 1994 V: Doom. 3.95
❑9, Mar 1995 HT (a) 3.95
❑10, Jul 1995 .... 3.95
❑11, Sep 1995 A: Inhumans 3.95
❑12, Dec 1995; HT (a); A: Hyperstorm. A: Doctor Doom. how Reed and Doom vanished; wraparound cover 3.95

FANTASTIC FOUR UNPLUGGED
MARVEL

❑1, Sep 1995 .... 1.25
❑2, Nov 1995; reading of Reed Richards' will 1.00
❑3, Jan 1996 .... 1.00
❑4, Mar 1996; Flip book with Untold Tales of Spider-Man #7 .... 1.00
❑5, May 1996 V: Blastaar. 1.00
❑6, Jul 1996 .... 1.00

FANTASTIC FOUR: UNSTABLE MOLECULES
MARVEL

❑1, Mar 2003 .... 2.99
❑2, Apr 2003 .... 2.99
❑3, May 2003 .... 2.99
❑4, Jun 2003 .... 2.99

FANTASTIC FOUR VS. X-MEN
MARVEL

❑1, Feb 1987 .... 2.50
❑2, Mar 1987 .... 2.50
❑3, Apr 1987 .... 2.50
❑4, May 1987 .... 2.50

FANTASTIC PANIC
ANTARCTIC

❑1, Aug 1993 .... 3.00
❑2, Oct 1993 .... 3.00
❑3, Dec 1993 .... 3.00
❑4, Feb 1994 .... 3.00
❑5, Apr 1994 .... 3.00
❑6, Jun 1994 .... 3.00
❑7, Aug 1994 .... 3.00
❑8, Oct 1994 .... 3.00

FANTASTIC PANIC (VOL. 2)
ANTARCTIC

❑1, Nov 1995 .... 2.95
❑2, Jan 1996 .... 2.95
❑3, Mar 1996 .... 2.95
❑4, May 1996 .... 2.95
❑5, Jul 1996 .... 2.95
❑6, Sep 1996 .... 2.95
❑7, Nov 1996 .... 2.95
❑8, Dec 1996 .... 2.95

FANTASTIC VOYAGE (MOVIE)
GOLD KEY

❑1, Feb 1967 .... 40.00

FANTASTIC VOYAGE (TV)
GOLD KEY

❑1, Aug 1969 .... 25.00
❑2, Dec 1969 .... 16.00

FANTASTIC VOYAGES OF SINDBAD
GOLD KEY

❑1, Oct 1965, pin-up on back cover ... 18.00
❑2, Jun 1967 .... 12.00

FANTASY FEATURES
AC

❑1 1987 .... 1.75
❑2 1987 .... 1.95

FANTASY GIRLS
COMAX

❑1, b&w 2.50

FANTASY MASTERPIECES (VOL. 1)
MARVEL

❑1, Feb 1966, SD, DH, JK (a); Golden Age reprints 75.00
❑2, Apr 1966, SD, DH, JK (a); Golden Age reprints; Fin Fang Foom reprinted from Strange Tales #89 ... 35.00
❑3, Jun 1966; Golden Age reprints; Captain America, other Golden Age super-heroes appear 30.00
❑4, Aug 1966; Golden Age reprints; Captain America, other Golden Age super-heroes appear 30.00
❑5, Oct 1966; Golden Age reprints; Captain America, other Golden Age super-heroes appear 30.00
❑6, Dec 1966; Golden Age reprints; Captain America, other Golden Age super-heroes appear 30.00
❑7, Feb 1967; Golden Age reprints; Captain America, other Golden Age super-heroes appear 30.00
❑8, Apr 1967; Golden Age reprints; Sub-Mariner vs. Human Torch (original) 30.00
❑9, Jun 1967; O: Human Torch (original). Golden Age reprints; Reprints from Marvel Comics #1 .... 30.00
❑10, Aug 1967; O: All Winners Squad. 1: All Winners Squad. Golden Age reprints; Reprints from All Winners #19 .... 35.00
❑11, Oct 1967; O: Toro. Series continues as Marvel Super-Heroes; Reprinted from Human Torch #1 .... 35.00

FANTASY MASTERPIECES (VOL. 2)
MARVEL

❑1, Dec 1979; SL (w); Reprints Silver Surfer (Vol. 1) #1 .... 6.00
❑2, Jan 1980; SL (w); Reprints Silver Surfer (Vol. 1) #2 .... 3.50

Fantastic Four Unplugged

Part of a low-price budget comics experiment

©Marvel

Fantastic Four vs. X-Men

Mutants tangle with super-hero family

©Marvel

Fantastic Voyage (TV)

Based on animated TV version of SF film

©Gold Key

Fantastic Voyages of Sindbad

Gold Key mythological adventures

©Gold Key

Fantasy Masterpieces (Vol. 1)

Series reprints Golden Age Marvel comics

©Marvel

N-MINT

❑3, Feb 1980; SL (w); Reprints Silver Surfer (Vol. 1) #3 ... 3.00
❑4, Mar 1980; SL (w); Reprints Silver Surfer (Vol. 1) #4 ... 3.00
❑5, Apr 1980; SL (w); Reprints Silver Surfer (Vol. 1) #5 ... 3.00
❑6, May 1980; SL (w); JB (a); Reprints Silver Surfer (Vol. 1) #6 ... 2.50
❑7, Jun 1980; SL (w); Reprints Silver Surfer (Vol. 1) #7 ... 2.50
❑8, Jul 1980; SL (w); Reprints Silver Surfer (Vol. 1) #8 ... 2.50
❑9, Aug 1980; SL (w); Reprints Silver Surfer (Vol. 1) #9 ... 2.50
❑10, Sep 1980; SL (w); JB (a); Reprints Silver Surfer (Vol. 1) #10 ... 2.50
❑11, Oct 1980; Reprints Silver Surfer (Vol. 1) #11 ... 2.00
❑12, Nov 1980; Reprints Silver Surfer (Vol. 1) #12 ... 2.00
❑13, Dec 1980; Reprints Silver Surfer (Vol. 1) #13 ... 2.00
❑14, Jan 1981, Reprints Silver Surfer (Vol. 1) #14 ... 2.00

FANTASY QUARTERLY
INDEPENDENT PUB. SYND.

❑1, Spr 1978, b&w; 1: Elfquest. back-up story with art by Sim ... 55.00

FARAWAY LOOKS
FARAWAY PRESS

❑nn, Fal 2002, b&w; "Fall Preview Edition" ... 9.95

FAREWELL, MOONSHADOW
DC / VERTIGO

❑1, Jan 1997; prestige format ... 7.95

FAREWELL TO WEAPONS
MARVEL / EPIC

❑1 ... 2.25

FARSCAPE: WAR TORN
DC / WILDSTORM

❑1, Apr 2002 ... 4.95
❑2, May 2002 ... 4.95

FAR WEST
ANTARCTIC

❑1, Nov 1998 ... 2.95
❑2, Jan 1999 ... 2.95
❑3, Mar 1999 ... 2.95
❑4, May 1999 ... 2.95

FASHION IN ACTION
ECLIPSE

❑Summer 1, Aug 1986; gatefold summary ... 2.00
❑WS 1; anniversary ... 2.00

FASHION POLICE
BRYCE ALAN

❑1 ... 2.50

FAST FORWARD
DC / PIRANHA

❑1, phobias ... 4.95
❑2, family ... 4.95
❑3, Storytellers ... 4.95

N-MINT

FASTLANE ILLUSTRATED
FASTLANE

❑½; Giveaway at 1994 San Diego Comicon ... 1.50
❑1, Sep 1994, b&w ... 2.50
❑2, Jun 1995, b&w ... 2.50
❑3, Jul 1996, b&w; wraparound cover ... 2.50

FAST WILLIE JACKSON
FITZGERALD PERIODICALS

❑1, Oct 1976 ... 24.00
❑2, Dec 1976 ... 16.00
❑3, Feb 1977 ... 16.00
❑4, Apr 1977 ... 16.00
❑5, Jun 1977 ... 16.00
❑6, Aug 1977 ... 16.00
❑7, Sep 1977, Last issue ... 16.00

FATAL BEAUTY
ILLUSTRATION

❑Ashcan 1/A, Jun 1996; Adult cover ... 3.95

FAT ALBERT
GOLD KEY

❑1, Mar 1974 ... 12.00
❑2, Jun 1974 ... 8.00
❑3, Sep 1974 ... 7.00
❑4, Dec 1974 ... 7.00
❑5, Feb 1975 ... 7.00
❑6, Apr 1975 ... 6.00
❑7, Jun 1975 ... 6.00
❑8, Aug 1975 ... 6.00
❑9, Oct 1975 ... 6.00
❑10, Dec 1975 ... 6.00
❑11, Feb 1976 ... 4.00
❑12, Apr 1976 ... 4.00
❑13, Jun 1976 ... 4.00
❑14, Aug 1976 ... 4.00
❑15, Oct 1976 ... 4.00
❑16, Dec 1976 ... 4.00
❑17, Feb 1977 ... 4.00
❑18, Apr 1977 ... 4.00
❑19, Jun 1977 ... 4.00
❑20, Aug 1977 ... 4.00
❑21, Oct 1977 ... 4.00
❑22, Dec 1977 ... 4.00
❑23, Feb 1978 ... 4.00
❑24, Apr 1978 ... 4.00
❑25, Jun 1978 ... 4.00
❑26, Aug 1978 ... 4.00
❑27, Oct 1978 ... 4.00
❑28, Dec 1978 ... 4.00
❑29, Feb 1979 ... 4.00

FATALE
BROADWAY

❑1, Jan 1996; Embossed cover ... 2.50
❑2, Feb 1996 ... 2.50
❑3, Mar 1996 ... 2.50
❑4, May 1996 ... 2.50
❑5, Jul 1996 ... 2.95
❑6, Oct 1996 ... 2.95
❑Ashcan 1, Sep 1995, b&w; giveaway preview edition ... 1.00

FAT DOG MENDOZA
DARK HORSE

❑1, Dec 1992, b&w ... 2.50

N-MINT

FATE
DC

❑0, Oct 1994 O: Doctor Fate IV (Jared Stevens). 1: Doctor Fate IV (Jared Stevens). D: Doctor Fate III (Kent & Inza Nelson) ... 2.50
❑1, Nov 1994 O: Doctor Fate IV (Jared Stevens) ... 2.50
❑2, Dec 1994 ... 2.00
❑3, Jan 1995 ... 2.00
❑4, Feb 1995 ... 2.00
❑5, Mar 1995 ... 2.00
❑6, Apr 1995 ... 2.00
❑7, May 1995 ... 2.00
❑8, Jun 1995 ... 2.25
❑9, Jul 1995 ... 2.25
❑10, Aug 1995 ... 2.25
❑11, Sep 1995 ... 2.25
❑12, Oct 1995 A: Sentinel ... 2.25
❑13, Nov 1995; Underworld Unleashed ... 2.25
❑14, Dec 1995 ... 2.25
❑15, Jan 1996 ... 2.25
❑16, Feb 1996 ... 2.25
❑17, Mar 1996 ... 2.25
❑18, May 1996 ... 2.25
❑19, Jun 1996 ... 2.25
❑20, Jul 1996 ... 2.25
❑21, Aug 1996 ... 2.25
❑22, Sep 1996; Kent and Inza Nelson go to heaven ... 2.25

FATE OF THE BLADE
DREAMWAVE

❑1, Aug 2002 ... 2.95
❑2, Oct 2002 ... 2.95
❑3, Nov 2002 ... 2.95
❑4, Jan 2003 ... 2.95
❑5, Feb 2003 ... 2.95

FATE'S FIVE
INNERVISION

❑1, b&w ... 2.50
❑2 ... 2.50
❑3 ... 2.50
❑4 ... 2.50

FAT FREDDY'S COMICS & STORIES
RIP OFF

❑1, Dec 1983 ... 3.00
❑2, Dec 1985 ... 2.50

FAT FURY SPECIAL
AVALON

❑1, b&w; reprints Herbie stories ... 2.95

FATHER & SON
KITCHEN SINK

❑1, Jul 1995, b&w ... 2.75
❑2, Sep 1995, b&w ... 2.75
❑3, Dec 1995, b&w ... 2.75
❑4, Jan 1996, b&w ... 2.75
❑Ashcan 1, Jul 1995; ashcan edition limited to 200, b&w ... 2.00
❑Special 1, b&w; "Like, Special #1" ... 3.95

FATHOM (MICHAEL TURNER'S ...)
ASPEN

❑1 2005 ... 5.00
❑1/A cover 2005 ... 4.00

❑1/B cover 2005 5.00
❑2 2005 2.99
❑3, Aug 2005 2.99

FATHOM (1ST SERIES)
COMICO

❑1, May 1987 1.50
❑2, Jun 1987 1.50
❑3, Jul 1987; wraparound cover 1.50

FATHOM (2ND SERIES)
COMICO

❑1, Nov 1992 2.50
❑2, Apr 1993 2.50
❑3, Jun 1993 2.50
❑Book 1 5.95

FATHOM (3RD SERIES)
IMAGE

❑0/Dynamic, 15.00
❑0/Conv, 2003 2003 10.00
❑0, Jan 2000; Wizard Promotional Edition: Given away with subsrciption to Wizard; Issue #0, with gold logo, had Jan. '00 in the indicia and Feb. on the cover 3.00
❑0/A, Jan 2000; Green holografix cover 0.00
❑0/B, Jan 2000; Wizard authentic edition 0.00
❑½, Feb 2003 3.00
❑½/A, Feb 2003; Gold foil variant 4.00
❑1/A, Aug 1998; Variant covers, some pages 3.00
❑1/B, Aug 1998, b&w; Fathom standing underwater; Variant covers, some pages, bubbles 3.00
❑1/C, Aug 1998; Fathom, dolphins on cover w/inset close-up 3.00
❑1/D, Aug 1998; Museum edition; Limited to 50 copies. 115.00
❑2, Sep 1998 3.00
❑2/A, Sep 1998; Museum edition 100.00
❑3, Oct 1998 3.00
❑3/Variant, Oct 1998; Monster Edition: No cover price; Monster Edition: No cover price 3.00
❑4, Mar 1999 2.50
❑5, May 1999 2.50
❑6, Jun 1999 2.50
❑7, Aug 1999 2.50
❑8, Sep 1999 2.50
❑9, Oct 1999 2.50
❑9/A, Oct 1999; Holofoil edition 8.00
❑9/B, Oct 1999; Platinum Holofoil edition 7.00
❑9/C, Oct 1999; Aspen on outcropping 5.00
❑9/D, Oct 1999; Green logo variant w/Aspen on rock outcropping 8.50
❑10, Jan 2000 2.50
❑10/A, Jan 2000; Perfect 10 DFE Alternate cover 4.00
❑10/B, Jan 2000; Perfect 10 DFE Alternate cover with Gold Stamp and certificate of authenticity 5.00
❑11, Apr 2000 2.50
❑12, Jul 2000; Witchblade in background, Fathom crawling on cover 2.50
❑12/A, Jul 2000 6.00
❑12/B, Jul 2000; Holofoil edition 6.00
❑12/C, Jul 2000; DF Alternate edition . 5.00
❑12/D, Jul 2000; DF Alternate edition with certificate of authenticity; Gold logo 8.00
❑13 2002 2.50
❑13/A 2002; Dynamic Forces variant with Certificate of Authenticity 5.00
❑13/B 2002; Dynamic Forces gold foil variant; Limited to 999 copies 15.00
❑13/C 2002; Dynamic Forces blue foil variant; Limited to 999 copies 15.00
❑14 2002 2.50
❑14/A 2002; Pittsburgh Convention exclusive 6.00
❑Deluxe 1; Collects Fathom #1-9 24.95
❑Book 1, Mar 1999; Collects Fathom (3rd Series) #1-2 6.50
❑Book 2, Mar 1999; Collects Fathom (3rd Series) #3-4 5.95
❑Book 3, Nov 1999; Collects Fathom (3rd Series) #5-6 5.95
❑Book 4; Collects Fathom (3rd Series) #7-8 5.95

FATHOM: BEGINNINGS
ASPEN

❑1, Jun 2003 3.00
❑1/Conv, Jun 2003 6.00

FATHOM: CANNON HAWKE
ASPEN

❑0, Jun 2004 6.00
❑0/Dynamic, Jun 2004 15.00
❑0/Conv, Jun 2004 10.00

FATHOM: CANNON HAWKE: BEGINNINGS
ASPEN

❑1, Jun 2004 5.00
❑1/Conv, Jun 2004 10.00

FATHOM: DAWN OF WAR
ASPEN

❑0 2004 5.00
❑1 2004 7.00
❑1/Jay 10.00
❑2 2004 4.00
❑2/Conv 10.00
❑3 2005 4.00

FATHOM: EAST & WEST COAST TOUR BOOKS
IMAGE

❑1, Jan 2004 3.00

FATHOM (MICHAEL TURNER'S...): KILLIAN'S TIDE
IMAGE

❑1, Apr 2001 3.00
❑2, Jun 2001 3.00
❑3/A, Sep 2001; Blue background on cover 3.00
❑3/B, Sep 2001; Dark background on cover, skull reflected in water 3.00
❑4/A, Nov 2001 3.00
❑4/B, Nov 2001 3.00

FATHOM PREVIEW SPECIAL
IMAGE

❑1, ca. 1998 3.00

FATHOM SWIMSUIT SPECIAL
IMAGE

❑1, May 1999 2.95
❑2000, Dec 2000 2.95
❑2002, 2002 San Diego giveaway; Sketch cover; 500 produced 8.00

FATMAN, THE HUMAN FLYING SAUCER
LIGHTNING

❑1, Apr 1967 35.00
❑2, Jun 1967 25.00
❑3, Sep 1967 25.00

FAT NINJA
SILVERWOLF

❑1, b&w 1.50
❑2, b&w 1.50
❑3, b&w 1.50
❑4, b&w 1.50
❑5, b&w 1.50

FATT FAMILY
SIDE SHOW

❑1, b&w 2.95

FAULTLINES
DC / VERTIGO

❑1, May 1997 2.50
❑2, Jun 1997 2.50
❑3, Jul 1997 2.50
❑4, Aug 1997 2.50
❑5, Sep 1997 2.50
❑6, Oct 1997 2.50

FAUNA REBELLION
FANTAGRAPHICS

❑1, Mar 1990, b&w 2.00
❑2, Apr 1990, b&w 2.00
❑3, b&w 2.00

FAUST
NORTHSTAR

❑1, ca. 1989 8.00
❑1/2nd 4.00
❑1/3rd 3.00
❑2, ca. 1989 6.00
❑2/2nd 4.00
❑2/3rd 3.00
❑3, ca. 1989 5.00
❑3/2nd 3.00
❑4 4.00
❑4/2nd 3.00
❑5, Aug 1989 4.00
❑5/2nd 3.00
❑6, Nov 1989; becomes Rebel title 3.50
❑6/2nd 2.50
❑7 3.50
❑7/2nd; gatefold cover 2.50
❑8 3.50
❑8/2nd 2.50
❑9 3.00
❑9/2nd 2.50
❑10 3.00
❑10/2nd 2.50
❑11 2.50
❑Special 1, ca. 1988 10.00

FAUST 777: THE WRATH
AVATAR

❑0, Dec 1998 3.00
❑1, ca. 1998 3.00
❑1/A, ca. 1998; wraparound cover 3.50
❑2, ca. 1998 3.00
❑3, ca. 1998 3.00

FAUST: THE BOOK OF M
AVATAR

❑1 3.00

F.B.I.
DELL

❑1, Apr 1965 60.00

FEAR
MARVEL

❑1, Nov 1970 95.00
❑2, Jan 1971 30.00
❑3, Mar 1971 15.00
❑4, Jul 1971 SD, JK, JSt (a) 15.00
❑5, Nov 1971 SD (a) 20.00
❑6, Feb 1972 SL (w); SD, DH (a) 15.00
❑7, May 1972 15.00
❑8, Jun 1972 15.00
❑9, Aug 1972 15.00
❑10, Oct 1972, HC (a); Man-Thing stories begin ("Adventures into Fear") 35.00
❑11, Dec 1972, Man-Thing 18.00
❑12, Feb 1973, Man-Thing 12.00
❑13, Apr 1973, Man-Thing 9.00
❑14, Jun 1973, Man-Thing 9.00
❑15, Aug 1973, Man-Thing 9.00
❑16, Sep 1973, Man-Thing 9.00
❑17, Oct 1973, V: Wundarr. Man-Thing 11.00
❑18, Nov 1973, Man-Thing 9.00
❑19, Dec 1973, 1: Howard the Duck. Man-Thing 25.00
❑20, Feb 1974, PG (a); Morbius stories begin; first Gulacy color work 18.00
❑21, Apr 1974, Morbius; Marvel Value Stamp #77: Swordsman 7.00
❑22, Jun 1974; Morbius; Marvel Value Stamp #49: Odin 7.00
❑23, Aug 1974; CR (a); A: Morbius. 1st Russell art; Marvel Value Stamp #86: Zemo 7.00
❑24, Oct 1974; A: Blade the Vampire Slayer. V: Blade. Morbius; Marvel Value Stamp #38: Red Sonja 12.00
❑25, Dec 1974; Morbius 8.00
❑26, Feb 1975; Morbius; Marvel Value Stamp #75: Morbius 7.00
❑27, Apr 1975; V: Simon Stroud. Morbius 7.00
❑28, Jun 1975; FR (a); Morbius 7.00
❑29, Aug 1975 DH (a); A: Helleyes. A: Simon Stroud. A: Morbius. 7.00
❑30, Oct 1975; Morbius 9.00
❑31, Dec 1975; Morbius; Marvel Value Stamp #75: Morbius 7.00

FEAR AGENT
IMAGE

❑1, Oct 2005 2.95
❑2, Jan 2006 2.95
❑3, Mar 2006 2.95
❑5, Jul 2006 2.95

FEAR EFFECT: RETRO HELIX
IMAGE

❑1, Mar 2002 2.95
❑1/Gold, Mar 2002 2.95

Other grades: Multiply price above by 5/6 for VF/NM • 2/3 for VERY FINE • 1/3 for FINE • 1/5 for VERY GOOD • 1/8 for GOOD

Fantasy Masterpieces (Vol. 2)

Reprints the original Silver Surfer series
©Marvel

Fat Albert

Fun with Bill Cosby's animated characters
©Gold Key

Fatale

Over-endowed heroine absorbs energy
©Broadway

Fathom (3rd Series)

First issue had variant story pages
©Image

Fatman, the Human Flying Saucer

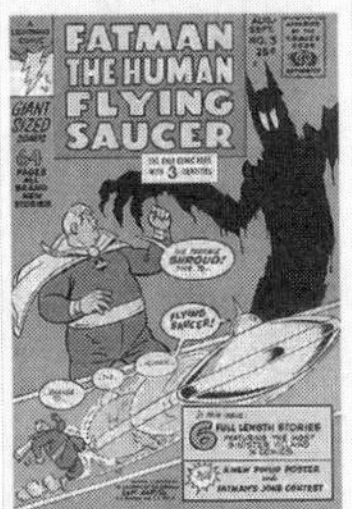

Parody of Silver Age comic stories
©Lightning

N-MINT

FEAR EFFECT SPECIAL
IMAGE

❑1, May 2000 ... 2.95

FEATHER
IMAGE

❑1, Aug 2003 ... 2.95
❑2, Oct 2003 ... 2.95
❑3, Dec 2003 ... 2.95
❑4, Feb 2004 ... 2.95
❑5, Jun 2004 ... 5.95

FEDS 'N' HEADS
PRINT MINT

❑1 ... 8.00

FEEDERS
DARK HORSE

❑1, Oct 1999 ... 2.95

FEELGOOD FUNNIES
RIP OFF

❑1 ... 3.00

FELICIA HARDY: THE BLACK CAT
MARVEL

❑1, Jul 1994 ... 1.50
❑2, Aug 1994 ... 1.50
❑3, Sep 1994 ... 1.50
❑4, Oct 1994 ... 1.50

FELIX THE CAT SILLY STORIES
FELIX

❑1, Aug 2005 ... 2.50

FELIX THE CAT (2ND SERIES)
DELL

❑1, ca. 1962 ... 35.00
❑2, Jan 1963 ... 24.00
❑3, Apr 1963 ... 24.00
❑4, Jul 1963 ... 24.00
❑5, Oct 1963 ... 24.00
❑6, Jan 1964 ... 24.00
❑7, Apr 1964 ... 24.00
❑8, Jul 1964 ... 24.00
❑9, Oct 1964 ... 24.00
❑10, Jan 1965 ... 24.00
❑11, Apr 1965 ... 24.00
❑12, Jul 1965 ... 24.00

FELIX THE CAT (3RD SERIES)
HARVEY

❑1, Sep 1991 ... 2.00
❑2, Nov 1991 ... 1.25
❑3, Jan 1992 ... 1.25
❑4, Mar 1992 ... 1.25
❑5, Jun 1992 ... 1.25
❑6, Sep 1992 ... 1.25
❑7, Jan 1993 ... 1.25
❑Book 1, Keeps on Walkin' ... 15.95

FELIX THE CAT AND FRIENDS
FELIX

❑1, ca. 1994 ... 1.95
❑2, ca. 1994 ... 1.95
❑3, ca. 1994 ... 1.95
❑4, ca. 1994 ... 1.95
❑5, ca. 1994 ... 1.95

N-MINT

FELIX THE CAT BIG BOOK (VOL. 2)
HARVEY

❑1, Sep 1992 ... 1.95

FELIX THE CAT BLACK & WHITE
FELIX

❑1 ... 1.95
❑2 ... 1.95
❑3 ... 1.95
❑4 ... 1.95
❑5 ... 1.95
❑6 ... 1.95
❑7 ... 2.25
❑8 ... 2.25

FELIX THE CAT DIGEST MAGAZINE
HARVEY

❑1 ... 1.75

FELL
IMAGE

❑1, Oct 2005 ... 2.95
❑2, 2005 ... 2.95
❑3, Jan 2006 ... 2.95
❑4, Apr 2006 ... 2.95

FELON
IMAGE

❑1, Nov 2001 ... 2.95
❑2, Jan 2002 ... 2.95
❑3, Feb 2002 ... 2.95
❑4, Apr 2002 ... 2.95

FELT: TRUE TALES OF UNDERGROUND HIP HOP
IMAGE

❑1, Apr 2005 ... 2.95

FEM 5
EXPRESS / PARODY

❑1/A; variant cover ... 2.95
❑1/B; variant cover ... 2.95
❑1/C; variant cover ... 2.95
❑1/D; variant cover ... 2.95
❑2 ... 2.95

FEMALE SEX PIRATES
FRIENDLY

❑1 ... 2.95

FEM FANTASTIQUE
AC

❑1, Jul 1988, b&w ... 1.95

FEMFORCE
AC

❑1, ca. 1985, O: Femforce ... 4.00
❑2 1986 ... 3.50
❑3 1986 ... 3.00
❑4 1986 ... 3.00
❑5 1986 ... 3.00
❑6, Feb 1987 ... 2.50
❑7, May 1987 ... 2.50
❑8, Jul 1987 ... 2.50
❑9, Aug 1987 ... 2.50
❑10 1987 ... 2.50
❑11, Mar 1988 ... 2.50
❑12, May 1988 ... 2.50
❑13, May 1988 ... 2.50
❑14 1988 ... 2.50

N-MINT

❑15, Aug 1988 ... 2.50
❑16 1988 ... 2.50
❑17, Jan 1989 ... 2.50
❑18 1989 ... 2.50
❑19, Apr 1989 ... 2.50
❑20 1989, b&w ... 2.50
❑21 1989, b&w ... 2.50
❑22 1989, b&w ... 2.50
❑23 1990, b&w ... 2.50
❑24, Apr 1990, b&w ... 2.50
❑25, May 1990, b&w ... 2.50
❑26, Jun 1990, b&w ... 2.50
❑27, Jul 1990, b&w ... 2.50
❑28, Aug 1990, b&w ... 2.50
❑29, Sep 1990, b&w ... 2.50
❑30, Oct 1990, b&w ... 2.50
❑31, Nov 1990 ... 2.75
❑32, Dec 1990 ... 2.75
❑33, Jan 1991 ... 2.75
❑34, Feb 1991 ... 2.75
❑35, Mar 1991 ... 2.75
❑36, Apr 1991 ... 2.75
❑37, May 1991 ... 2.75
❑38, Jun 1991 ... 2.75
❑39, Jul 1991 ... 2.75
❑40, Aug 1991 ... 2.75
❑41, Sep 1991 ... 2.75
❑42, Oct 1991 ... 2.75
❑43, Nov 1991; Includes pull-out comic, Rocketman and Jet Girl #0 ... 2.75
❑44, Dec 1991 ... 2.75
❑45, Jan 1992 ... 2.75
❑46, Feb 1992 ... 2.75
❑47, Mar 1992 ... 2.75
❑48, Apr 1992 ... 2.75
❑49, May 1992 ... 2.75
❑50, Jun 1992; Includes flexi-disc ... 2.95
❑51, Jul 1992 ... 2.75
❑52, Aug 1992 ... 2.75
❑53, ca. 1992 ... 2.75
❑54, ca. 1992 ... 2.75
❑55, ca. 1992 ... 2.75
❑56, ca. 1993 ... 2.75
❑57, ca. 1993 ... 2.75
❑58, ca. 1993 O: Microman ... 2.75
❑59, ca. 1993 ... 2.75
❑60, ca. 1993 ... 2.75
❑61, ca. 1993 ... 2.75
❑62, ca. 1993 ... 2.75
❑63, ca. 1993 ... 2.95
❑64, ca. 1993 ... 2.95
❑65, ca. 1993 ... 2.95
❑66, ca. 1993 ... 2.95
❑67, ca. 1994 ... 2.95
❑68, ca. 1994 ... 2.95
❑69, ca. 1994 ... 2.95
❑70, ca. 1994 ... 2.95
❑71, ca. 1994 ... 2.95
❑72, ca. 1994 ... 2.95
❑73, ca. 1994 ... 2.95
❑74, ca. 1994 ... 2.95
❑75, ca. 1994 ... 2.95
❑76, ca. 1994 ... 2.95
❑77, ca. 1994 ... 2.95

	N-MINT
❑78, ca. 1994	2.95
❑79, ca. 1994	2.95
❑80, ca. 1994 V: Iron Jaw.	2.95
❑81, ca. 1994	2.95
❑82, ca. 1995	2.95
❑83, ca. 1995	2.95
❑84, ca. 1995	2.95
❑85, ca. 1995	2.95
❑86, ca. 1995	2.95
❑87, ca. 1995; 10th anniversary issue; A: AC staff. 10th Anniversary	3.50
❑88, ca. 1995	2.95
❑89, ca. 1995	2.95
❑90, ca. 1995	2.95
❑91, ca. 1995	2.95
❑92, ca. 1995	2.95
❑93, ca. 1995	2.95
❑94, ca. 1996	2.95
❑95, ca. 1996	2.95
❑96, ca. 1996	2.95
❑97, ca. 1996, b&w	2.95
❑98, ca. 1996, b&w; subtitled in Spanish	2.95
❑99, ca. 1996, b&w	2.95
❑100, ca. 1996, b&w; photo back cover	3.95
❑100/CS, ca. 1996, b&w	6.90
❑101, ca. 1997, b&w	4.95
❑102, ca. 1997, b&w	4.95
❑103, ca. 1997, b&w	4.95
❑104, ca. 1997, b&w	4.95
❑105, ca. 1997, b&w	4.95
❑106, ca. 1997, b&w	4.95
❑107, ca. 1997, b&w	4.95
❑108, ca. 1998, b&w	4.95
❑109, ca. 2000, b&w	4.95
❑110/A, ca. 2000, b&w; Rayda on cover	2.95
❑110/B, ca. 2000, b&w; Femforce on cover	2.95
❑111, ca. 2001, b&w	2.95
❑112, ca. 2001, b&w	2.95
❑113, ca. 2001, b&w	2.95
❑114, ca. 2001, b&w	2.95
❑115, ca. 2002, b&w	5.95
❑116, ca. 2002, b&w	5.95
❑117, ca. 2002, b&w	5.95
❑118, ca. 2002, b&w; 20th anniversary special	5.95
❑119, ca. 2003, b&w	5.95
❑120, ca. 2003, b&w	5.95
❑121, ca. 2003, b&w	5.95
❑123, ca. 2003, b&w	5.95
❑122, Jan 2004, b&w	6.95
❑124, ca. 2003, b&w	6.95
❑125, ca. 2004, b&w	6.95
❑126, ca. 2004, b&w	6.95
❑127, ca. 2004, b&w	6.95
❑128, ca. 2004, b&w; Halloween special	6.95
❑Special 1, Nov 1984	1.50

FEMFORCE FRIGHTBOOK
AC

❑1, b&w	2.95

FEMFORCE IN THE HOUSE OF HORROR
AC

❑1, b&w	2.50

FEMFORCE: NIGHT OF THE DEMON
AC

❑1, b&w	2.75

FEMFORCE: OUT OF THE ASYLUM SPECIAL
AC

❑1, Aug 1987, b&w	2.50

FEMFORCE PIN UP PORTFOLIO
AC

❑1	2.50
❑2	2.50
❑3	2.50
❑4, Dec 1991	5.00
❑5	5.00

FEMFORCE UNCUT
AC

❑1	9.95

FEMFORCE UP CLOSE
AC

	N-MINT
❑1, Apr 1992, Nightveil	3.00
❑2, Jul 1992; Stardust	3.00
❑3; Dragonfly	3.00
❑4 O: She Cat.	2.95
❑5; Blue Bulleteer	2.95
❑6; Ms. Victory	2.95
❑7; Ms. Victory	2.95
❑8; Tara, Garganta	2.95
❑9; Synn	2.95
❑10, b&w; Yankee Girl	2.95
❑11, b&w; Nightveil	2.95

FEMME MACABRE
LONDON NIGHT

❑1	2.95

FEMME NOIRE
CAT-HEAD

❑1	1.75
❑2	1.75

FENRY
RAVEN

❑1	6.95

FERRET (1ST SERIES)
MALIBU

❑1, ca. 1992	1.95

FERRET (2ND SERIES)
MALIBU

❑1, May 1993	1.95
❑1/Variant, May 1993; die-cut	2.50
❑2, Jun 1993	2.50
❑3, Jul 1993	2.50
❑4, Aug 1993	2.50
❑5, Sep 1993	2.25
❑6, Oct 1993	2.25
❑7, Nov 1993	2.25
❑8, Dec 1993	2.25
❑9, Jan 1994	2.25
❑10, Feb 1994	2.25

FERRO CITY
IMAGE

❑1, Sep 2005	2.95
❑2, Oct 2005	2.95
❑3, Nov 2005	2.95
❑4, Jan 2006	2.95

FEUD
MARVEL / EPIC

❑1, Jul 1993; embossed cardstock cover	2.50
❑2, Aug 1993	1.95
❑3, Sep 1993	1.95
❑4, Oct 1993	1.95

FEVER
WONDER COMIX

❑1, b&w	1.95

FEVER DREAMS
KITCHEN SINK

❑1	3.00

FEVER IN URBICAND
NBM

❑1	12.95

F5
IMAGE

❑1, Apr 2000; Giant-size; Giant-size	2.95
❑2, Jun 2000	2.50
❑3, Aug 2000	2.50
❑4, Oct 2000	2.50
❑Ashcan 1, Jan 2000; Preview issue	2.50

F5 ORIGIN
DARK HORSE

❑1, Nov 2001, Several characters in profile on cover	2.99

15 MINUTES
SLAVE LABOR

❑1 2004	3.95
❑2	3.95
❑3, Jun 2005	3.95

FIFTH FORCE FEATURING HAWK AND ANIMAL
ANTARCTIC

❑1, Apr 1999	1.99
❑2, Jul 1999	2.50

FIFTIES TERROR
ETERNITY

	N-MINT
❑1, Oct 1988, b&w; Reprints	2.00
❑2, Nov 1988, b&w; Reprints	2.00
❑3, Dec 1988, b&w; Reprints	2.00
❑4, Jan 1989, b&w; Reprints	2.00
❑5, Feb 1989, b&w; Reprints	2.00
❑6, Mar 1989, b&w; Reprints	2.00

52
DC

❑1, Jul 2006	2.50
❑2, Jul 2006	2.50
❑3, Jul 2006	2.50
❑4, Aug 2006	2.50
❑5, Aug 2006	2.50
❑6, Aug 2006	2.50
❑7, Sep 2006	2.50
❑8, Sep 2006	2.50

FIGHT FOR TOMORROW
DC / VERTIGO

❑1, Nov 2002; Several characters in profile on cover	2.50
❑2, Dec 2002	2.50
❑3, Jan 2003	2.50
❑4, Feb 2003	2.50
❑5, Mar 2003	2.50
❑6, Apr 2003	2.50

FIGHTIN' 5
CHARLTON

❑28, Jul 1964, Continued from Space War (Vol. 2) #27	20.00
❑29, Oct 1964	10.00
❑30, Dec 1964	10.00
❑31, Feb 1965	9.00
❑32, May 1965	9.00
❑33, Jul 1965	9.00
❑34, Sep 1965	9.00
❑35, Nov 1965	9.00
❑36, Jan 1966	9.00
❑37, May 1966	9.00
❑38, Jul 1966	9.00
❑39, Sep 1966	9.00
❑40, Nov 1966, 1: The Peacemaker.	18.00
❑41, Jan 1967	10.00
❑42, Oct 1981, Reprints	3.00
❑43, Dec 1981, Reprints	3.00
❑44, Feb 1982, Reprints	3.00
❑45, Apr 1982, Reprints	3.00
❑46, Jun 1982, Reprints	3.00
❑47, Aug 1982, Reprints	3.00
❑48, Oct 1982, Reprints	3.00
❑49, Dec 1982, Reprints	3.00

FIGHTIN' AIR FORCE
CHARLTON

❑3, Feb 1956	32.00
❑4, Jun 1956, DG (c)	20.00
❑5, ca. 1956	20.00
❑6, ca. 1957	15.00
❑7, ca. 1957	15.00
❑8, ca. 1957	15.00
❑9, ca. 1957	15.00
❑10, Jan 1958	15.00
❑11, ca. 1958	12.00
❑12, ca. 1958	12.00
❑13, Dec 1958	12.00
❑14, ca. 1959	12.00
❑15, ca. 1959	12.00
❑16, ca. 1959	12.00
❑17, ca. 1959	12.00
❑18, ca. 1959	12.00
❑19, ca. 1960	12.00
❑20, ca. 1960	12.00
❑21, ca. 1960	8.00
❑22, Aug 1960	8.00
❑23, Oct 1960	8.00
❑24, Dec 1960	8.00
❑25, Feb 1961	8.00
❑26, Apr 1961	8.00
❑27, Jun 1961	8.00
❑28, Aug 1961	8.00
❑29, Oct 1961	8.00
❑30, Dec 1961	8.00
❑31, Mar 1962	8.00
❑32, May 1962	8.00
❑33, Jul 1962	8.00

Fear

Anthology reprinted Marvel monster tales
©Marvel

Felicia Hardy: The Black Cat

Teams with Spidey to fight Cardiac
©Marvel

Felix the Cat (3rd series)

Early animation icon returns in 1990s title
©Harvey

Femforce

Ms. Victory leads team of heroines
©AC

Ferret (2nd Series)

Protectors member gets solo series
©Malibu

N-MINT

❑34, Sep 1962 8.00
❑35, Nov 1962, DG (c) 8.00
❑36, Jan 1963 8.00
❑37, Mar 1963 8.00
❑38, May 1963 8.00
❑39, Jul 1963 8.00
❑40, Sep 1963 8.00
❑41, Nov 1963 8.00
❑42, Jan 1964 8.00
❑43, Mar 1964 8.00
❑44, Jun 1964 8.00
❑45, Sep 1964 8.00
❑46, Nov 1964 8.00
❑47, Jan 1965 8.00
❑48, ca. 1965 8.00
❑49, Jul 1965 8.00
❑50, Aug 1965, A: American Eagle. 8.00
❑51, Oct 1965, A: American Eagle. 8.00
❑52, Dec 1965, A: American Eagle. 8.00
❑53, Mar 1966, A: American Eagle. Series continues as War and Attack with #54 8.00

FIGHTIN' ARMY
CHARLTON

❑16, Jan 1956 24.00
❑17 1956 18.00
❑18 1956 18.00
❑19 1957 18.00
❑20 1957 18.00
❑21, Jul 1957 15.00
❑22, Oct 1957 15.00
❑23 1958 15.00
❑24 1958 15.00
❑25, Feb 1959 15.00
❑26, Apr 1959 15.00
❑27, Jun 1959 15.00
❑28, Aug 1959 15.00
❑29, Oct 1959 15.00
❑30, Dec 1959 15.00
❑31, Jan 1960 12.00
❑32, Feb 1960 12.00
❑33, Mar 1960 12.00
❑34, Apr 1960 12.00
❑35, May 1960 12.00
❑36, Jul 1960 12.00
❑37, Sep 1960 12.00
❑38, Nov 1960 12.00
❑39, Jan 1961 12.00
❑40, Mar 1961 12.00
❑41, May 1961 10.00
❑42, ca. 1961 10.00
❑43, ca. 1961 10.00
❑44, Dec 1961 10.00
❑45, ca. 1962 10.00
❑46, May 1962 10.00
❑47, ca. 1962 10.00
❑48, ca. 1962 10.00
❑49, Nov 1962 10.00
❑50, Jan 1963 10.00
❑51, ca. 1963 8.00
❑52, ca. 1963 8.00
❑53, Jul 1963 8.00
❑54, Sep 1963 8.00
❑55, Nov 1963 8.00

N-MINT

❑56 1964 8.00
❑57, Mar 1964 8.00
❑58, Jun 1964 8.00
❑59, ca. 1964 8.00
❑60 1964 8.00
❑61 1965 8.00
❑62, Mar 1965 8.00
❑63, Jun 1965 8.00
❑64, Aug 1965 8.00
❑65, Oct 1965 8.00
❑66 1965 8.00
❑67, Mar 1966 8.00
❑68, May 1966 8.00
❑69, Jul 1966 8.00
❑70, Sep 1966 8.00
❑71, Nov 1966 8.00
❑72, Jan 1967 8.00
❑73, Mar 1967 8.00
❑74, ca. 1967 8.00
❑75, Aug 1967 8.00
❑76, Oct 1967, Lonely War of Capt. Willy Schultz begins 10.00
❑77, Dec 1967 6.00
❑78, Feb 1968 6.00
❑79, May 1968 6.00
❑80, Jul 1968 6.00
❑81, Sep 1968 6.00
❑82, Nov 1968 6.00
❑83, Jan 1969 6.00
❑84, Mar 1969 6.00
❑85, May 1969 6.00
❑86, Jul 1969 6.00
❑87, Sep 1969 6.00
❑88, Nov 1969 6.00
❑89, Jan 1970 6.00
❑90, Mar 1970 6.00
❑91, May 1970 6.00
❑92, Jul 1970 6.00
❑93, Sep 1970 6.00
❑94, Nov 1970 6.00
❑95, Jan 1971 6.00
❑96, Mar 1971 6.00
❑97, May 1971 6.00
❑98, Jul 1971 6.00
❑99, Sep 1971 6.00
❑100, Nov 1971 6.00
❑101, Jan 1972 5.00
❑102, Mar 1972 5.00
❑103, May 1972 5.00
❑104, Jul 1972 5.00
❑105, Sep 1972 5.00
❑106, Nov 1972 5.00
❑107, Jan 1973 5.00
❑108, Mar 1973 5.00
❑109, May 1973 5.00
❑110, Jul 1973 5.00
❑111, Sep 1973 5.00
❑112, Nov 1973 5.00
❑113, May 1974 5.00
❑114, Jul 1974 5.00
❑115, Sep 1974 5.00
❑116, Nov 1974 5.00
❑117, Feb 1975 5.00
❑118, ca. 1975 5.00

N-MINT

❑119, Jun 1975 5.00
❑120, Sep 1975 5.00
❑121, Nov 1975 4.00
❑122 1976 4.00
❑123, ca. 1976 4.00
❑124, May 1976 4.00
❑125, ca. 1976 4.00
❑126, Oct 1976 4.00
❑127, Dec 1976 4.00
❑128, Sep 1977 4.00
❑129, Nov 1977 4.00
❑130, Feb 1978 4.00
❑131, Mar 1978 4.00
❑132, Apr 1978 4.00
❑133, Jun 1978 4.00
❑134, Sep 1978, has Iron Corporal story 4.00
❑135, Nov 1978 4.00
❑136 4.00
❑137, ca. 1979 4.00
❑138, May 1979 4.00
❑139, Jul 1979 4.00
❑140, Aug 1979 4.00
❑141, ca. 1979 4.00
❑142, Nov 1979 4.00
❑143 4.00
❑144, Feb 1980 4.00
❑145, Apr 1980 4.00
❑146, Jul 1980 4.00
❑147, Sep 1980 4.00
❑148, Nov 1980 4.00
❑149, Jan 1981 4.00
❑150, Mar 1981 4.00
❑151, Apr 1981 3.00
❑152, Jun 1981 3.00
❑153, Aug 1981 3.00
❑154, Oct 1981 3.00
❑155, Dec 1981 3.00
❑156, Feb 1982 3.00
❑157, Apr 1982 3.00
❑158, Jun 1982 3.00
❑159, Aug 1982 3.00
❑160, Oct 1982 3.00
❑161, Dec 1982 3.00
❑162, Feb 1983 3.00
❑163, Apr 1983 3.00
❑164, Jun 1983 3.00
❑165, Aug 1983 3.00
❑166, Oct 1983 3.00
❑167 3.00
❑168 3.00
❑169, May 1984 3.00
❑170, Jul 1984 3.00
❑171, Sep 1984 3.00
❑172, Nov 1984 3.00

FIGHTING AMERICAN (MINI-SERIES)
DC

❑1, Feb 1994 O: Fighting American. 2.00
❑2, Mar 1994 2.00
❑3, Apr 1994 2.00
❑4, May 1994 2.00
❑5, Jun 1994 2.00
❑6, Jul 1994 2.00

Other grades: Multiply price above by 5/6 for VF/NM • 2/3 for VERY FINE • 1/3 for FINE • 1/5 for VERY GOOD • 1/8 for GOOD

N-MINT

FIGHTING AMERICAN (AWESOME)
AWESOME

❑1/A, Aug 1997; Diving at guns, bayonets on cover 2.50
❑1/B, Aug 1997; Holding flag on cover 2.50
❑1/C, Aug 1997; Comics Cavalcade regular edition (two heroes diving toward a gun at lower left corner) ... 2.50
❑1/D, Aug 1997; Comics Cavalcade Liberty Gold Foil Edition 15.95
❑2, Oct 1997 .... 2.50
❑3, Dec 1997 .... 2.50

FIGHTING AMERICAN: DOGS OF WAR
AWESOME

❑1, Sep 1998, JSn (w) 2.50
❑1/A, Sep 1998, 98 Tour Edition cover; JSn (w); 98 Tour Edition cover 3.00

FIGHTING AMERICAN: RULES OF THE GAME
AWESOME

❑1, Nov 1997 .... 2.50
❑1/A, Nov 1997, Fighting American standing on cover 2.50
❑1/B, Nov 1997, Woman pointing gun on cover 2.50

FIGHTING AMERICAN SPECIAL COMICON EDITION
AWESOME

❑1, ca. 1997; No cover price; b&w preview of upcoming series given out at Comic-Con International: San Diego 1997 .... 1.00

FIGHTING FEM CLASSICS
FORBIDDEN FRUIT

❑1, b&w 3.50

FIGHTING FEMS
FORBIDDEN FRUIT

❑1, b&w 3.50
❑2, b&w 3.50

FIGHTIN' MARINES
CHARLTON

❑20 .... 16.00
❑21 .... 16.00
❑22 .... 16.00
❑23 .... 16.00
❑24, ca. 1957 .... 16.00
❑25, Mar 1958, Giant-size 36.00
❑26, ca. 1958, Giant-size 40.00
❑27, ca. 1958 .... 16.00
❑28 .... 16.00
❑29 .... 16.00
❑30, Jun 1959 .... 13.00
❑31, Aug 1959 .... 13.00
❑32, ca. 1959 .... 13.00
❑33, Jan 1960 .... 13.00
❑34, Mar 1960 .... 13.00
❑35, May 1960 .... 13.00
❑36, Jul 1960 .... 13.00
❑37, Sep 1960 .... 13.00
❑38, Nov 1960 .... 13.00
❑39, Jan 1961 .... 13.00
❑40, Mar 1961 .... 10.00
❑41, May 1961 .... 10.00
❑42, Jul 1961 .... 10.00
❑43, Sep 1961 .... 10.00
❑44, Nov 1961 .... 10.00
❑45, Feb 1962 .... 10.00
❑46, Apr 1962 .... 10.00
❑47, Jun 1962 .... 10.00
❑48, Aug 1962 .... 10.00
❑49, Oct 1962 .... 10.00
❑50, Dec 1962 .... 10.00
❑51, Feb 1963 .... 7.00
❑52, Apr 1963 .... 7.00
❑53, Jun 1963 .... 7.00
❑54, Aug 1963 .... 7.00
❑55 1963 .... 7.00
❑56 1963 .... 7.00
❑57 1964 .... 7.00
❑58, May 1964 .... 7.00
❑59, Jul 1964 .... 7.00
❑60, Oct 1964 .... 7.00
❑61 1964 .... 7.00
❑62, Feb 1965 .... 7.00
❑63, May 1965 .... 7.00
❑64, Jul 1965 .... 7.00

N-MINT

❑65, Sep 1965 .... 7.00
❑66, Nov 1965 .... 7.00
❑67, Jan 1966 .... 7.00
❑68, Mar 1966 .... 7.00
❑69, ca. 1966 .... 7.00
❑70, Aug 1966 .... 7.00
❑71 1966 .... 6.00
❑72 1966 .... 6.00
❑73 1967 .... 6.00
❑74 1967 .... 6.00
❑75, Jul 1967 .... 4.00
❑76, Sep 1967 .... 4.00
❑77, Nov 1967 .... 4.00
❑78, Jan 1968, 1: Shotgun Harker. 1: The Chicken 4.00
❑79, ca. 1968 .... 4.00
❑80, Jul 1968 .... 4.00
❑81, Sep 1968 .... 4.00
❑82, Nov 1968, Giant-size 6.00
❑83, Jan 1969 .... 4.00
❑84, Mar 1969 .... 4.00
❑85, May 1969 .... 4.00
❑86, Jul 1969 .... 4.00
❑87, Sep 1969 .... 4.00
❑88, Nov 1969 .... 4.00
❑89, Jan 1970 .... 4.00
❑90, Mar 1970 .... 4.00
❑91, May 1970 .... 3.50
❑92, Jul 1970 .... 3.50
❑93, Sep 1970 .... 3.50
❑94, Nov 1970 .... 3.50
❑95, Jan 1971 .... 3.50
❑96, Mar 1971 .... 3.50
❑97, May 1971 .... 3.50
❑98, Jul 1971 .... 3.50
❑99, Sep 1971 .... 3.50
❑100, Nov 1971 .... 3.50
❑101, Jan 1972 .... 3.00
❑102, Mar 1972 .... 3.00
❑103, Apr 1972 .... 3.00
❑104, Jun 1972 .... 3.00
❑105, Aug 1972, Don Perlin cover 3.00
❑106, Oct 1972 .... 3.00
❑107, Dec 1972, Nicolas A. Lascia cover 3.00
❑108, Jan 1973 .... 3.00
❑109, Mar 1973 .... 3.00
❑110, Apr 1973 .... 3.00
❑111, Jun 1973 .... 3.00
❑112, ca. 1973 .... 3.00
❑113, ca. 1973 .... 3.00
❑114, Oct 1973 .... 3.00
❑115 1973 .... 3.00
❑116, Jan 1974 .... 3.00
❑117, Jun 1974 .... 3.00
❑118, ca. 1974 .... 3.00
❑119, Nov 1974 .... 3.00
❑120, Jan 1975 .... 3.00
❑120/2nd, ca. 1975, reprints Charlton #120 .... 1.50
❑121, Mar 1975 .... 3.00
❑122, ca. 1975 .... 3.00
❑123, May 1975 .... 3.00
❑124, ca. 1975 .... 3.00
❑125, ca. 1975 .... 3.00
❑126, ca. 1975 .... 2.50
❑127, Jan 1976 .... 2.50
❑128, Mar 1976 .... 2.50
❑129, May 1976 .... 2.50
❑130, Jul 1976 .... 2.50
❑131, Sep 1976 .... 2.50
❑132, Nov 1976 .... 2.50
❑133, Oct 1977 .... 2.50
❑134, Dec 1977 .... 2.50
❑135, Feb 1978 .... 2.50
❑136, Apr 1978 .... 2.50
❑137, Jun 1978 .... 2.50
❑138, Aug 1978 .... 2.50
❑139, Oct 1978 .... 2.50
❑140 .... 2.50
❑141 .... 2.50
❑142, ca. 1979 .... 2.50
❑143, ca. 1979 .... 2.50
❑144, Jul 1979 .... 2.50
❑145, ca. 1979 .... 2.50
❑146, ca. 1979 .... 2.50
❑147, Dec 1979 .... 2.50

N-MINT

❑148, Jan 1980 .... 2.50
❑149, Mar 1980 .... 2.50
❑150, May 1980 .... 2.50
❑151, ca. 1980 .... 2.00
❑152, Oct 1980 .... 2.00
❑153, Dec 1980 .... 2.00
❑154, Jan 1981 .... 2.00
❑155, Mar 1981 .... 2.00
❑156, May 1981 .... 2.00
❑157, Jul 1981 .... 2.00
❑158, Sep 1981 .... 2.00
❑159, Oct 1981 .... 2.00
❑160, Dec 1981 .... 2.00
❑161, Feb 1982 .... 2.00
❑162, Apr 1982 .... 2.00
❑163, Jul 1982 .... 2.00
❑164, Sep 1982 .... 2.00
❑165, Nov 1982 .... 2.00
❑166, Jan 1983 .... 2.00
❑167, Mar 1983 .... 2.00
❑168, May 1983 .... 2.00
❑169, Jul 1983 .... 2.00
❑170, Sep 1983 .... 2.00
❑171, Nov 1983 .... 2.00
❑172, Jan 1984 .... 2.00
❑173, Mar 1984 .... 2.00
❑174, May 1984 .... 2.00
❑175, Jul 1984 .... 2.00
❑176, Sep 1984 .... 2.00

FIGHTIN' NAVY
CHARLTON

❑74, ca. 1956 .... 24.00
❑75 .... 18.00
❑76 .... 18.00
❑77 .... 18.00
❑78 .... 18.00
❑79 .... 18.00
❑80 .... 18.00
❑81 .... 15.00
❑82, Mar 1958 .... 15.00
❑83, Sep 1958 .... 15.00
❑84 .... 15.00
❑85 .... 15.00
❑86 .... 15.00
❑87, ca. 1959 .... 15.00
❑88, ca. 1959 .... 15.00
❑89, ca. 1959 .... 15.00
❑90, ca. 1959 .... 15.00
❑91, ca. 1959 .... 12.00
❑92, ca. 1959 .... 12.00
❑93, ca. 1959 .... 12.00
❑94, ca. 1959 .... 12.00
❑95, ca. 1959 .... 12.00
❑96, Jan 1960 .... 12.00
❑97 .... 12.00
❑98 .... 12.00
❑99, Jul 1961 .... 12.00
❑100, Sep 1961 .... 12.00
❑101, Nov 1961 .... 8.00
❑102, Jan 1962 .... 8.00
❑103, Apr 1962 .... 8.00
❑104, ca. 1962 .... 8.00
❑105, Aug 1962 .... 8.00
❑106, ca. 1962 .... 8.00
❑107, ca. 1962 .... 8.00
❑108, ca. 1963 .... 8.00
❑109, ca. 1963 .... 8.00
❑110, ca. 1963 .... 8.00
❑111, Aug 1963 .... 8.00
❑112, ca. 1963 .... 8.00
❑113, ca. 1963 .... 8.00
❑114, Feb 1964 .... 8.00
❑115, May 1964 .... 8.00
❑116, Jul 1964 .... 8.00
❑117, Sep 1964 .... 8.00
❑118, Nov 1964 .... 8.00
❑119, Feb 1965 .... 8.00
❑120, May 1965 .... 8.00
❑121, ca. 1965 .... 5.00
❑122, ca. 1965 .... 5.00
❑123, Dec 1965 .... 5.00
❑124, Jan 1966 .... 5.00
❑125, ca. 1966, Last issue of original run 5.00
❑126, Aug 1983, Series begins again 2.00
❑127, Oct 1983 .... 2.00

Other grades: Multiply price above by 5/6 for VF/NM • 2/3 for VERY FINE • 1/3 for FINE • 1/5 for VERY GOOD • 1/8 for GOOD

Fightin' Air Force

Charlton title featured specific military branch

©Charlton

Fightin' Army

Lonely War of Capt. Willy Schultz highlight

©Charlton

Fighting American (Awesome)

Attempted revival by Rob Liefeld

©Awesome

Fightin' Marines

Leatherneck adventures in various theaters

©Charlton

Fightin' Navy

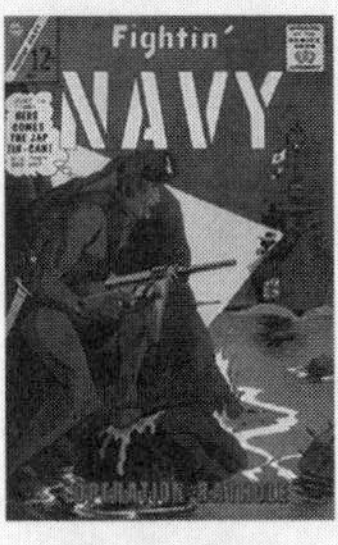

Battles above and beneath the waves

©Charlton

N-MINT

❑128, Dec 1983 .... 2.00
❑129, Feb 1984 .... 2.00
❑130, Apr 1984 .... 2.00
❑131, Jun 1984 .... 2.00
❑132, Aug 1984 .... 2.00
❑133, Oct 1984 .... 2.00

FIGHT MAN
MARVEL

❑1, Jun 1993 .... 2.00

FIGHT THE ENEMY
TOWER

❑1, Aug 1966 .... 22.00
❑2, Oct 1966 .... 16.00
❑3 .... 16.00

FIGMENTS
BLACKTHORNE

❑1 .... 1.75
❑2 .... 1.75

FIGMENTS UNLIMITED
GRAPHIK

❑1 .... 1.25
❑2 .... 1.25
❑3 .... 1.25

FILES OF MS. TREE
RENEGADE

❑1, Jun 1984, b&w 6.00
❑2, Sep 1985, b&w 6.00
❑3, b&w 6.00

FILIBUSTING COMICS
FANTAGRAPHICS

❑1, Jan 1995, b&w; Parody of Understanding Comics; b&w pin-ups, cardstock cover 2.75

FILTH
DC / VERTIGO

❑1, Aug 2002 .... 2.95
❑2, Sep 2002 .... 2.95
❑3, Oct 2002 .... 2.95
❑4, Nov 2002 .... 2.95
❑5, Dec 2002 .... 2.95
❑6, Jan 2003 .... 2.95
❑7, Feb 2003 .... 2.95
❑8, Mar 2003 .... 2.95
❑9, Apr 2003 .... 2.95
❑10, Jun 2003 .... 2.95
❑11, Jul 2003 .... 2.95
❑12, Aug 2003 .... 2.95
❑13, Sep 2003 .... 2.95

FILTHY ANIMALS
RADIO

❑1, Aug 1997 .... 2.95
❑2 1998 .... 2.95
❑3, Aug 1998 .... 2.95
❑4 .... 2.95

FILTHY HABITS
AEON

❑1, Jul 1996, b&w 2.95
❑2, Nov 1996, b&w 2.95
❑3, Feb 1997, b&w 2.95

FINAL CYCLE
DRAGON'S TEETH

❑1, b&w 1.75

N-MINT

❑2, b&w 1.75
❑3, b&w 1.75
❑4, b&w 1.75

FINAL MAN
C&T

❑1, b&w 1.50

FINAL NIGHT
DC

❑1, Nov 1996 .... 6.00
❑2, Nov 1996 .... 4.00
❑3, Nov 1996 .... 4.00
❑4, Nov 1996 D: Hal Jordan. 4.00

FINAL TABOO
AIRCEL

❑1, b&w 2.50
❑2, b&w 2.50

FINALS
DC / VERTIGO

❑1, Sep 1999 .... 2.95
❑2, Oct 1999 .... 2.95
❑3, Nov 1999 .... 2.95
❑4, Dec 1999 .... 2.95

FINDER
LIGHTSPEED

❑1, Nov 1996, b&w; wraparound cover 4.00
❑2, Jan 1997, b&w 3.50
❑3, Mar 1997, b&w 3.50
❑4, May 1997, b&w 3.50
❑5, Jul 1997, b&w 3.50
❑6, Sep 1997, b&w 3.50
❑7, Nov 1997, b&w 3.50
❑8 1998 .... 3.50
❑9 1998 .... 3.50
❑10 1998 .... 3.50
❑11 1998 .... 3.50
❑12 1999 .... 3.50
❑13 1999 .... 3.50
❑14 1999 .... 3.50
❑15, Dec 1999 .... 2.95
❑16, Feb 2000 .... 2.95
❑17, May 2000 .... 2.95
❑18 2000 .... 2.95
❑19 2000 .... 2.95
❑20 2000 .... 2.95
❑21 2001 .... 2.95
❑22, May 2001; Fight Scene 2.95
❑23, Jul 2001 .... 2.95
❑24, Nov 2001 .... 2.95
❑25, Jan 2002 .... 2.95
❑26, Mar 2002 .... 2.95
❑27, Jul 2002 .... 2.95
❑28, Sep 2002 .... 2.95
❑29, Nov 2002 .... 2.95
❑30, Jan 2003 .... 2.95
❑31 2003 .... 2.95
❑32 2003 .... 2.95
❑33 2004 .... 2.95
❑34 2004 .... 2.95
❑35 2004 .... 2.95
❑Ashcan 1 .... 1.00

N-MINT

FINDER FOOTNOTES
LIGHTSPEED

❑1 .... 6.00

FINIEOUS TREASURY
TSR

❑1; magazine-sized 3.00

FINK, INC.
FINK, INC.

❑1 .... 3.50

FIRE
CALIBER

❑1, b&w 2.95
❑2, b&w 2.95

FIREARM
MALIBU / ULTRAVERSE

❑0, Aug 1993, with videotape 14.95
❑1, Sep 1993 .... 2.25
❑1/Ltd., limited promotional edition; foil cover 3.00
❑2, Oct 1993, Rune 2.50
❑3, Nov 1993 .... 1.95
❑4, Dec 1993, Break-Thru 1.95
❑5, Jan 1994 .... 1.95
❑6, Feb 1994 .... 1.95
❑7, Mar 1994 .... 1.95
❑8, May 1994 .... 1.95
❑9, Jun 1994 .... 1.95
❑10, Jul 1994 .... 3.50
❑11, Aug 1994, Flipbook with Ultraverse Premiere #5 .... 1.95
❑12, Sep 1994 .... 1.95
❑13, Oct 1994 .... 1.95
❑14, Nov 1994 .... 1.95
❑15, Dec 1994 .... 1.95
❑16, Jan 1995 .... 1.95
❑17, Feb 1995 .... 1.95
❑18, Mar 1995 .... 1.95
❑19, Apr 1995 .... 1.95

FIREBIRDS ONE SHOT
IMAGE

❑1 .... 6.00

FIREBRAND
DC

❑1, Feb 1996, O: Firebrand III (Alex Sanchez). 1: Firebrand III (Alex Sanchez). 2.00
❑2, Mar 1996 .... 1.75
❑3, Apr 1996 .... 1.75
❑4, May 1996 .... 1.75
❑5, Jun 1996 .... 1.75
❑6, Jul 1996 .... 1.75
❑7, Aug 1996 .... 1.75
❑8, Sep 1996 .... 1.75
❑9, Oct 1996 .... 1.75

FIREBREATHER
IMAGE

❑1, Jan 2003 .... 2.95
❑2, Feb 2003 .... 2.95
❑3, Mar 2003 .... 2.95
❑4, Apr 2003 .... 2.95

Other grades: Multiply price above by 5/6 for VF/NM • 2/3 for VERY FINE • 1/3 for FINE • 1/5 for VERY GOOD • 1/8 for GOOD

N-MINT

FIREBREATHER: IRON SAINT ONE-SHOT
IMAGE

❑1 2005, 6.95

FIRE FROM HEAVEN
IMAGE

❑½ 1.00
❑1, Mar 1996; wraparound cover 2.50
❑2, Jul 1996 2.50

FIRE SALE
RIP OFF

❑1, Dec 1989, b&w; benefit 2.50

FIRESTAR
MARVEL

❑1, Mar 1986 O: Firestar. A: X-Men. A: New Mutants. 1.50
❑2, Apr 1986 A: Wolverine. 1.50
❑3, May 1986 1.00
❑4, Jun 1986 1.00

FIRESTORM
DC

❑1, Mar 1978, AM, JR (a); O: Firestorm. 1: Firestorm. 7.00
❑2, Apr 1978, AM (a) 2.00
❑3, Jun 1978, AM (a); 1: Killer Frost. 2.00
❑4, Aug 1978, AM (a) 2.00
❑5, Oct 1978, AM (a) 2.00

FIRESTORM (2ND SERIES)
DC

❑1, Jul 2004 5.00
❑2, Aug 2004 2.50
❑3, Sep 2004 2.50
❑4, Oct 2004 2.50
❑5, Nov 2004 2.50
❑6, Dec 2004 5.00
❑7, Jan 2005 2.50
❑8, Feb 2005 2.50
❑9, Mar 2005 2.50
❑10, Apr 2005 2.50
❑11, May 2005 2.50
❑12, Jun 2005 2.50
❑13, Jun 2005 2.50
❑14, Jul 2005 2.50
❑15, Aug 2005 2.50
❑16, Sep 2005 2.50
❑17, Oct 2005 2.50
❑18 2.50
❑19, Jan 2006 2.50
❑20, Feb 2006 2.50
❑21, Mar 2006 2.50
❑22, Apr 2006 2.50
❑23, May 2006 2.50
❑24, Jun 2006 2.50
❑25, Jul 2006 2.50
❑26, Aug 2006 2.50

FIRESTORM, THE NUCLEAR MAN
DC

❑65, Nov 1987; A: Green Lantern. A: new Firestorm. Series continued from Fury of Firestorm #64 1.00
❑66, Dec 1987 A: Green Lantern. 1.00
❑67, Jan 1988; Millennium 1.00
❑68, Feb 1988; Millennium 1.00
❑69, Mar 1988 1.00
❑70, Apr 1988 1.00
❑71, May 1988 1.00
❑72, Jun 1988 1.00
❑73, Jul 1988 A: Soyuz 1.00
❑74, Aug 1988 1.00
❑75, Sep 1988 1.00
❑76, Oct 1988 A: Firehawk. V: Brimstone. 1.00
❑77, Nov 1988 1.00
❑78, Dec 1988 1.00
❑79; no cover date 1.00
❑80; A: Firehawk, Power Girl. No cover date; Invasion! 1.00
❑81, Jan 1989; A: Soyuz. Invasion! Aftermath 1.00
❑82, Feb 1989 1.00
❑83, Mar 1989 1.00
❑84, Apr 1989 1.00
❑85, May 1989; new Firestorm 1.00
❑86, Jun 1989 1.00
❑87, Jul 1989 1.00
❑88, Aug 1989 1.00

N-MINT

❑89, Sep 1989 1.00
❑90, Oct 1989 1: Naiad. 1.00
❑91, Nov 1989 1.00
❑92, Dec 1989 1.00
❑93, Jan 1990 1.00
❑94, Feb 1990 1.00
❑95, Mar 1990 1.00
❑96, Apr 1990 1.00
❑97, May 1990 1.00
❑98, Jun 1990 1.00
❑99, Jul 1990 1.00
❑100, Aug 1990; Giant-size 2.95
❑Annual 5 1.25

FIRE TEAM
AIRCEL

❑1, b&w 2.50
❑2, Jan 1991, b&w 2.50
❑3, Feb 1991, b&w 2.50
❑4, b&w 2.50
❑5, b&w 2.50
❑6, b&w 2.50

FIRKIN
KNOCKABOUT

❑1 2.50
❑2 2.50
❑6, b&w 2.50

FIRST
CROSSGEN

❑1, Dec 2000 4.00
❑2, Jan 2001 3.00
❑3, Feb 2001 3.00
❑4, Mar 2001 3.00
❑5, Apr 2001 3.00
❑6, May 2001 2.95
❑7, Jun 2001 2.95
❑8, Jul 2001 2.95
❑9, Aug 2001 2.95
❑10, Sep 2001 2.95
❑11, Oct 2001 2.95
❑12, Nov 2001 2.95
❑13, Dec 2001 2.95
❑14, Jan 2002 2.95
❑15, Feb 2002 2.95
❑16, Mar 2002 2.95
❑17, Apr 2002 2.95
❑18, May 2002 2.95
❑19, Jun 2002 2.95
❑20, Jul 2002 2.95
❑21, Aug 2002 2.95
❑22, Sep 2002 2.95
❑23, Oct 2002 2.95
❑24, Nov 2002 2.95
❑25, Dec 2002 2.95
❑26, Jan 2003 2.95
❑27, Feb 2003 2.95
❑28, Mar 2003 2.95
❑29, Apr 2003 2.95
❑30, May 2003 2.95
❑31, Jun 2003 2.95
❑32, Jul 2003 2.95
❑33, Aug 2003 2.95
❑34, Sep 2003 2.95
❑35, Nov 2003 2.95
❑36, Dec 2003 2.95
❑37, Dec 2003 2.95

FIRST ADVENTURES
FIRST

❑1, Dec 1985 1.25
❑2, Jan 1986 1.25
❑3, Feb 1986 1.25
❑4, Mar 1986 1.25
❑5, Apr 1986 1.25

1ST FOLIO
PACIFIC

❑1, Mar 1984; Joe Kubert School 1.50

FIRST GRAPHIC NOVEL
FIRST

❑1, Jan 1984, Beowulf 6.00
❑2, Time Beavers 6.00
❑3, Jun 1985, American Flagg: Hard Times 11.95
❑4, Original Nexus 6.00
❑5 6.00
❑6, Elric of Melnibone 14.95
❑7, ca. 1986, 7.95

N-MINT

❑8, Time2 7.95
❑9, Teenage Mutant Ninja Turtles 9.95
❑10, Turtles Book II 9.95
❑11, Elric: Sailor on the Seas of Fate 14.95
❑12, Time2 Satisfaction of Black Mariah 7.95
❑13, American Flagg: Southern Comfort 11.95
❑14, Ice King of Oz 7.95
❑15, Turtles Book III 9.95
❑16, Badger: Hexbreaker 8.95
❑17 8.95
❑18, Turtles Book III 9.95
❑19, Mazinger 8.95
❑20, Team Yankee 12.95
❑21, Turtles Book IV 9.95
❑22, Lone Wolf and Cub 19.95
❑23, American Flagg: State of the Union 11.95
❑24, Grimjack: Demon Knight 8.95
❑25, Elric: Weird of the White Wolf 14.95

1ST ISSUE SPECIAL
DC

❑1, Apr 1975 JK (c); JK (w); JK (a); 1: Atlas. 7.00
❑2, May 1975; Green Team. 5.00
❑3, Jun 1975; Metamorpho 4.00
❑4, Jul 1975; (c); Lady Cop 4.00
❑5, Aug 1975 JK (c); JK (w); JK (a); 1: Manhunters. 1: Manhunter II (Mark Shaw). 4.00
❑6, Sep 1975; JK (c); JK (w); JK (a); Dingbats 4.00
❑7, Oct 1975 (c); SD (a); A: Creeper... 4.00
❑8, Nov 1975 MGr (c); MGr (w); MGr (a); O: Warlord. 1: Deimos. 1: Skartaris. 1: Warlord. 15.00
❑9, Dec 1975 JKu (c); A: Doctor Fate. 4.00
❑10, Jan 1976; (c); Outsiders 4.00
❑11, Feb 1976; MGr (c); AM (a); Code Name: Assassin 4.00
❑12, Mar 1976, JKu (c); O: Starman II (Mikaal Tomas). 1: Starman II (Mikaal Tomas). 4.00
❑13, Apr 1976, (c); Return of the New Gods 5.00

FIRST KINGDOM
BUD PLANT

❑1 3.00
❑2 2.50
❑3 2.50
❑4 2.50
❑5 2.50
❑6 2.00
❑7 2.00
❑8 2.00
❑9 2.00
❑10 2.00
❑11 2.00
❑12 2.00
❑13 2.00
❑14 2.00
❑15 2.00
❑16 2.00
❑17 2.00
❑18 2.00
❑19 2.00
❑20 2.00
❑21 2.00
❑22 2.00
❑23 2.00
❑24 2.00

FIRST KISS
CHARLTON

❑1, Dec 1957, DG (a) 45.00
❑2, Feb 1958 28.00
❑3, May 1958, DG (a) 22.00
❑4, ca. 1958 18.00
❑5, ca. 1958 18.00
❑6, ca. 1958, DG (a) 13.00
❑7, ca. 1959, DG (a) 13.00
❑8, ca. 1959 13.00
❑9, ca. 1959 13.00
❑10, Sep 1959 13.00
❑11, Nov 1959 12.00
❑12, Jan 1960, DG (a) 12.00
❑13, Mar 1960, DG (a) 12.00
❑14, May 1960, DG (a) 12.00
❑15, Jul 1960 12.00

Finals

Series delayed after Columbine, Colo., shooting
©DC

Firestorm

Short-lived first series led to later success
©DC

Firestorm, the Nuclear Man

Was Fury of Firestorm
©DC

1st Folio

Showcase of new artists' potential
©Pacific

1st Issue Special

Tryout title yielded Warlord
©DC

N-MINT

❑16, Sep 1960 .... 12.00
❑17, Nov 1960 .... 12.00
❑18, Jan 1961 .... 12.00
❑19, Mar 1961 .... 12.00
❑20, May 1961 .... 12.00
❑21, Jul 1961 .... 8.00
❑22, Sep 1961 .... 8.00
❑23, Nov 1961 .... 8.00
❑24, ca. 1962 .... 8.00
❑25, ca. 1962 .... 8.00
❑26, ca. 1962 .... 8.00
❑27, ca. 1962 .... 8.00
❑28, ca. 1962 .... 8.00
❑29, Dec 1962, DG (c) 8.00
❑30, Feb 1963, DG (a) 8.00
❑31, Apr 1963 .... 8.00
❑32, Jun 1963, DP (a) 8.00
❑33, Aug 1963 .... 8.00
❑34, Oct 1963 .... 8.00
❑35, Dec 1963, DG (c) 8.00
❑36, ca. 1964 .... 8.00
❑37, ca. 1964, DG (c) 8.00
❑38, ca. 1964, DG (c) 8.00
❑39, ca. 1964, DG (c) 8.00
❑40, ca. 1965, DG (c) 8.00

FIRST MAN
IMAGE

❑1, Jun 1997; cover says 1st Man, indicia says First Man 2.50

FIRST SIX PACK
FIRST

❑1, Jul 1987 .... 1.00
❑2, JSn, HC, MGr (w); PS, LMc (a) 1.00

FIRST TRIP TO THE MOON
AVALON

❑1, b&w; reprints Charlton story 2.50

FIRST WAVE
ANDROMEDA

❑1, Dec 2000 .... 2.99

FISHMASTERS
SLAVE LABOR

❑1, May 1994; adapts TV show 2.95

FISH POLICE (VOL. 1)
FISHWRAP

❑1, Dec 1985; Indicia title: Inspector Gill of the Fish Police 1.25
❑1/2nd; Indicia changed to "Fish Police" 1.25
❑2, Feb 1986 .... 1.25
❑3, Apr 1986 .... 1.25
❑4, Jun 1986 .... 1.50
❑5, Aug 1986 .... 1.50
❑6 1986 .... 1.50
❑7, Feb 1987; indicia says Feb 86 .... 1.50
❑8 1987 .... 1.50
❑9 1987 .... 1.50
❑10 1987 .... 1.50
❑11 1987 .... 1.50

FISH POLICE (VOL. 2)
COMICO

❑5 1987 .... 1.75
❑6 1987 .... 1.75
❑7 .... 1.75
❑8 .... 1.75
❑9 .... 1.75
❑10 1988 .... 1.75
❑11 1988 .... 1.75
❑12 1988 .... 1.75
❑13 1988 .... 1.75
❑14, Dec 1988 .... 1.75
❑15 .... 1.75
❑16 .... 1.75
❑17, Jun 1989 .... 2.50
❑18, Aug 1989, b&w; Black & white format begins, Apple Comics 2.25
❑19, Oct 1989, b&w 2.25
❑20, Mar 1990, b&w 2.25
❑21 1990, b&w 2.25
❑22 1990, b&w 2.25
❑23 1990, b&w 2.25
❑24 1990, b&w 2.25
❑25, Nov 1990, b&w 2.25
❑26, b&w 2.25
❑Special 1, ca. 1987 .... 2.25

FISH POLICE (MARVEL)
MARVEL

❑1, Oct 1992, b&w 1.25
❑2, Nov 1992, b&w 1.25
❑3, Dec 1992, b&w 1.25
❑4, Jan 1993, b&w 1.25
❑5, Feb 1993, b&w 1.25
❑6, Mar 1993 .... 1.25

FISH SHTICKS
APPLE

❑1, Nov 1991, b&w 2.00
❑2, b&w 2.00
❑3, May 1992, b&w 2.00
❑4, b&w 2.00
❑5, b&w 2.00
❑6, b&w 2.00

FISSION CHICKEN
FANTAGRAPHICS

❑1, ca. 1990, b&w 2.00
❑2, b&w 2.00
❑3, b&w 2.00
❑4, b&w 2.00

FISSION CHICKEN: PLAN NINE FROM VORTOX
MU

❑1, Jul 1994 .... 3.95

FIST OF GOD
ETERNITY

❑1, May 1988 .... 2.25
❑2, Jul 1988 .... 1.95
❑3, Sep 1988 .... 1.95
❑4, Nov 1988 .... 1.95

FIST OF THE NORTH STAR
VIZ

❑1 .... 2.95
❑2 .... 2.95
❑3 .... 2.95
❑4 .... 2.95
❑5 .... 2.95
❑6 .... 2.95
❑7 .... 2.95
❑8 .... 2.95

FIST OF THE NORTH STAR PART 2
VIZ

❑1 .... 2.75
❑2 .... 2.75
❑3 .... 2.95
❑4 .... 2.95
❑5 .... 2.95
❑6 .... 2.95
❑7 .... 2.95
❑8 .... 2.95

FIST OF THE NORTH STAR PART 3
VIZ

❑1 .... 2.95
❑2 .... 2.95
❑3, Sep 1996 .... 2.95
❑4, Oct 1996 .... 2.95
❑5, Nov 1996 .... 2.95

FIST OF THE NORTH STAR PART 4
VIZ

❑1, Dec 1996 .... 2.95
❑2, Jan 1997 .... 2.95
❑3, Feb 1997 .... 2.95
❑4, Mar 1997 .... 2.95
❑5 .... 2.95
❑6 .... 2.95
❑7 .... 2.95

FIVE FISTS OF SCIENCE
IMAGE

❑1, Jul 2006 .... 9.95

FIVE LITTLE COMICS
SCOTT MCCLOUD

❑1 .... 4.00

FIVE YEARS OF PAIN
BONEYARD

❑1, Jan 1997 .... 3.95

FLAG FIGHTERS
IRONCAT

❑1, Sep 1997, b&w 2.95
❑2 1997, b&w 2.95
❑3, Nov 1997, b&w 2.95
❑4 .... 2.95
❑5 .... 2.95

FLAMEHEAD
JNCO

❑0 .... 1.00

FLAME OF RECCA
VIZ

❑1, Aug 2003 .... 9.95
❑2, Oct 2003 .... 9.95
❑3, Dec 2003 .... 9.95
❑4, Feb 2004 .... 9.95
❑5, Apr 2004 .... 9.95
❑6, Jun 2004 .... 9.95
❑7, Aug 2004 .... 9.95
❑8, Oct 2004 .... 9.95
❑9, Dec 2004 .... 9.95
❑10, Feb 2005 .... 9.95
❑11, Apr 2005 .... 9.95
❑12, Jun 2005 .... 9.95

Other grades: Multiply price above by 5/6 for VF/NM • 2/3 for VERY FINE • 1/3 for FINE • 1/5 for VERY GOOD • 1/8 for GOOD

	N-MINT
❑13, Aug 2005	9.95
❑14, Oct 2005	9.95

FLAME (AJAX)
AJAX

	N-MINT
❑1; 1st appearance of Flame II	285.00
❑2	165.00
❑3	150.00

FLAME TWISTERS
BROWN STUDY

	N-MINT
❑1, Oct 1994, b&w	2.50
❑2, Mar 1995, b&w	2.50

FLAMING CARROT (KILIAN)
KILIAN

	N-MINT
❑1, Sum 1981, magazine	35.00

FLAMING CARROT (IMAGE)
IMAGE

	N-MINT
❑1, Dec 2004	2.95
❑2, Apr 2005	3.50
❑3, Jul 2005	3.50
❑4, Dec 2005	3.50

FLAMING CARROT COMICS
AARDVARK-VANAHEIM

	N-MINT
❑1, May 1984, b&w; 1: Flaming Carrot. Aardvark-Vanaheim publishes	26.00
❑2, Jul 1984, b&w	15.00
❑3, Sep 1984, b&w	12.00
❑4, Nov 1984, b&w	10.00
❑5, Jan 1985, b&w	8.00
❑6, Mar 1985, b&w; becomes Flaming Carrot Comics	8.00
❑7, May 1985, b&w; Renegade begins publishing	7.00
❑8, Aug 1985, b&w	5.00
❑9, Oct 1985, b&w	5.00
❑10, Dec 1985, b&w	4.00
❑11, Mar 1986, b&w	4.00
❑12, May 1986, b&w	4.00
❑13, Jul 1986, b&w	3.00
❑14, Oct 1986, b&w	3.00
❑15, Jan 1987, b&w	3.00
❑15/A, Jan 1987, b&w; no cover price	4.00
❑16, Jun 1987, b&w 1: Mystery Men.	4.00
❑17, Jul 1987, b&w A: Mystery Men.	3.00
❑18, Jun 2001, b&w; Dark Horse begins publishing	3.00
❑19, Jun 2001, b&w	3.00
❑20, Nov 1988, b&w	3.00
❑21, Spr 1989, b&w	3.00
❑22, Jun 1989, b&w	3.00
❑23, Nov 1989, b&w	3.00
❑24, Apr 1990, b&w	3.00
❑25, Apr 1991, b&w A: Teenage Mutant Ninja Turtles.	3.50
❑26, Jun 1991, b&w A: Teenage Mutant Ninja Turtles.	2.50
❑27, b&w; TMc (c); A: Mystery Men. A: Teenage Mutant Ninja Turtles. no indicia	2.50
❑28, Aug 1992, b&w	2.50
❑29, Oct 1992, b&w	2.50
❑30, Dec 1992, b&w; brown background	2.50
❑30/A, Dec 1992, b&w; blue background	2.50
❑32, Dec 2002, b&w; Reid Fleming guest appearance	3.95
❑31, Oct 1994, b&w; A: Herbie. Story originally scheduled for Herbie (Dark Horse) #3	2.50
❑Annual 1, Jan 1997, b&w; A: Mystery Men. 1997 Annual; cardstock cover	5.00

FLAMING CARROT STORIES
DARK HORSE

	N-MINT
❑1, "Version A"	5.00

FLARE
HERO

	N-MINT
❑1, Nov 1988	2.75
❑2, Dec 1988	2.75
❑3, Jan 1989	2.75

FLARE (VOL. 2)
HERO

	N-MINT
❑1	3.00
❑2	3.00
❑3, Jan 1989	3.00
❑4, Sum 1991	2.75
❑5; Eternity Smith	2.75
❑6, Sep 1991	2.75
❑7, Nov 1991	2.75
❑8, b&w	2.75
❑9, b&w	2.75
❑10, b&w	2.75
❑11, Apr 1993, b&w	2.75
❑12, Jun 1993, b&w	2.75
❑13, Aug 1993, b&w	2.75
❑14, Oct 1993, b&w	2.75
❑15, Jan 1994	2.75
❑16	2.75
❑Annual 1, b&w	4.50

FLARE (VOL. 3)
HEROIC

	N-MINT
❑1	3.95
❑2	3.95
❑3	3.95
❑4	3.95
❑5	3.95
❑25; Goes to whole numbering counting issues from first two Flare series	3.95
❑26	3.95
❑27	3.95
❑28	3.95
❑29	3.95

FLARE ADVENTURES
HEROIC

	N-MINT
❑1, Reprints	1.25
❑2, Flip-book format with Champions Classics #2	2.95
❑3, Flip-book format with Champions Classics #3	2.95
❑4, b&w; Flip-book format with Champions Classics #4	3.95
❑5, b&w; Flip-book format with Champions Classics #5	3.95
❑6, b&w; Flip-book format with Champions Classics #6	3.95
❑7, b&w; Flip-book format with Champions Classics #7	3.95
❑8, b&w; Flip-book format with Champions Classics #8	3.95
❑9, b&w; Flip-book format	3.95
❑10, b&w; Flip-book format	3.95
❑11, b&w; Flip-book format	3.95
❑12, b&w; Flip-book format	3.95
❑13, b&w; Flip-book format	3.95
❑14 2005, returns from hiatus; contains League of Champions story	3.95

FLARE FIRST EDITION
HERO

	N-MINT
❑1; contents will vary	3.50
❑2; contents will vary	3.50
❑3, b&w	3.50
❑4, b&w	4.50
❑5, b&w	4.50
❑6, b&w	3.95
❑7, b&w	3.95
❑8, b&w	3.95
❑9; Sparkplug	3.95
❑10	3.95
❑11, Oct 1993, b&w	3.95

FLASH (1ST SERIES)
DC

	N-MINT
❑105, Feb 1959, CI (a); O: Flash II (Barry Allen). 1: Mirror Master. numbering continued from Flash Comics	6500.00
❑106, May 1959 CI (a); O: Pied Piper. O: Gorilla Grodd. 1: Gorilla City. 1: Gorilla Grodd. 1: The Pied Piper.	2000.00
❑107, Jul 1959 CI (a); 2: Gorilla Grodd.	1000.00
❑108, Sep 1959 CI (a); A: Gorilla Grodd.	850.00
❑109, Nov 1959, CI (a)	650.00
❑110, Jan 1960, MA, CI (a); O: Kid Flash. 1: Weather Wizard. 1: Kid Flash.	1500.00
❑111, Mar 1960, CI (a); 2: Kid Flash.	450.00
❑112, May 1960, CI (a); O: Elongated Man. 1: Elongated Man.	600.00
❑113, Jul 1960, CI (a); O: Trickster. 1: Trickster.	550.00
❑114, Aug 1960 CI (a); O: Captain Cold.	275.00
❑115, Sep 1960, MA, CI (a)	350.00
❑116, Nov 1960, CI (a)	250.00
❑117, Dec 1960, MA, CI (a); O: Captain Boomerang. 1: Captain Boomerang.	300.00
❑118, Feb 1961, CI (a)	250.00
❑119, Mar 1961, CI (a); Wedding of Elongated Man and Sue Dearborn	250.00
❑120, May 1961, CI (a)	250.00
❑121, Jun 1961, CI (a)	200.00
❑122, Aug 1961, CI (a); O: Top, The. 1: Top, The.	200.00
❑123, Sep 1961, CI (a); O: Flash I (Jay Garrick). O: Flash II (Barry Allen). 1: Earth-2 (as an alternate Earth). A: Flash I (Jay Garrick). 1st meeting between Golden and Silver Age Flashes; First Alley Award winner: Best Cover, Best Single Issue of a Comic Book, Best Story	1500.00
❑124, Nov 1961, CI (a)	150.00
❑125, Dec 1961, CI (a); 1: cosmic treadmill	150.00
❑126, Feb 1962, CI (a)	150.00
❑127, Mar 1962, CI (a)	150.00
❑128, May 1962, CI (a); O: Abra Kadabra. 1: Abra Kadabra.	150.00
❑129, Jun 1962, CI (a); A: Flash I (Jay Garrick).	325.00
❑130, Aug 1962, CI (a)	150.00
❑131, Sep 1962, CI (a); A: Green Lantern.	125.00
❑132, Nov 1962, CI (a)	125.00
❑133, Dec 1962, CI (a)	125.00
❑134, Feb 1963, CI (a)	125.00
❑135, Mar 1963, CI (a)	125.00
❑136, May 1963, CI (a)	125.00
❑137, Jun 1963, CI (a); A: Flash I (Jay Garrick). Vandal Savage	475.00
❑138, Sep 1963, CI (a)	125.00
❑139, Sep 1963, CI (a); O: Professor Zoom. 1: Professor Zoom.	125.00
❑140, Nov 1963, CI (a); O: Heat Wave. 1: Heat Wave.	125.00
❑141, Dec 1963, CI (a)	150.00
❑142, Feb 1964, CI (a)	125.00
❑143, Mar 1964, CI (a)	125.00
❑144, May 1964, CI (a)	125.00
❑145, Jun 1964, CI (a)	125.00
❑146, Aug 1964, CI (a)	100.00
❑147, Sep 1964, CI (a)	100.00
❑148, Nov 1964, CI (a); V: Captain Boomerang.	100.00
❑149, Dec 1964, CI (a)	100.00
❑150, Feb 1965, CI (a)	100.00
❑151, Mar 1965, CI (a); A: Flash I (Jay Garrick).	80.00
❑152, May 1965, CI (a)	65.00
❑153, Jun 1965, CI (a)	65.00
❑154, Aug 1965, CI (a)	60.00
❑155, Sep 1965, CI (a)	60.00
❑156, Nov 1965, CI (a)	60.00
❑157, Dec 1965, CI (a)	60.00
❑158, Feb 1966, CI (a)	60.00
❑159, Mar 1966, CI (a)	75.00
❑160, Apr 1966; Giant-size; MA, CI (c); MM, CI (a); aka 80 Page Giant #G-21; reprints stories from Flash (1st series) #107, All-Flash #32, Flash (1st series) #113, Flash (1st series) #114, Flash (1st series) #124), and Adventure Comics #123	90.00
❑161, May 1966, CI (a)	50.00
❑162, Jun 1966, CI (a)	50.00
❑163, Aug 1966, CI (a)	50.00
❑164, Sep 1966, CI (a)	50.00
❑165, Nov 1966, CI (a); Wedding of Flash II (Barry Allen) and Iris West .	70.00
❑166, Dec 1966, CI (a)	50.00
❑167, Feb 1967, CI (a); O: Flash II (Barry Allen). 1: Mopee.	50.00
❑168, Mar 1967	95.00
❑169, May 1967; Giant-size; O: Flash II (Barry Allen). aka 80 Page Giant #G-34	70.00
❑170, Jun 1967	50.00
❑171, Jun 1967, V: Doctor Light.	50.00
❑172, Aug 1967	50.00
❑173, Sep 1967	50.00
❑174, Nov 1967, V: Rogue's Gallery. Flash II reveals identity to wife	50.00
❑175, Dec 1967, Flash II races Superman	175.00
❑176, Feb 1968	40.00
❑177, Mar 1968	40.00
❑178, May 1968; Giant-size; aka 80 Page Giant #G-46	40.00
❑179, May 1968, Flash visits DC Comics	40.00
❑180, Jun 1968	50.00

Other grades: Multiply price above by 5/6 for VF/NM • 2/3 for VERY FINE • 1/3 for FINE • 1/5 for VERY GOOD • 1/8 for GOOD

First Kiss

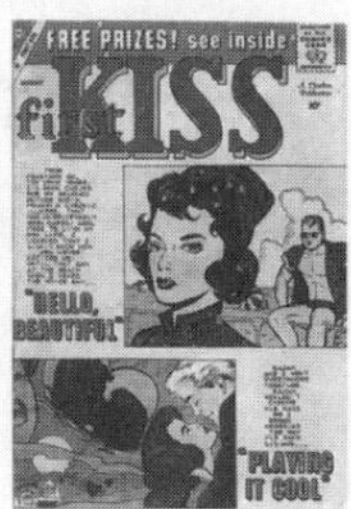

Romance title features early loves
©Charlton

Fish Police (Vol. 1)

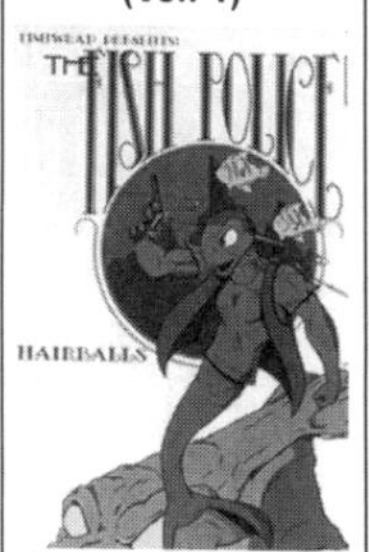

Spawned poor animated TV effort
©Fishwrap

Flaming Carrot Comics

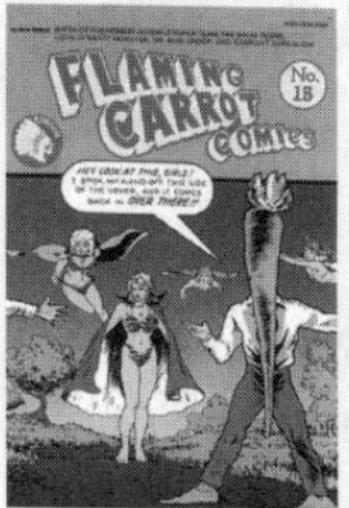

Mystery Men first appeared in Bob Burden title
©Aardvark-Vanaheim

Flare (Vol. 2)

Female heroine fights crime in leather jacket
©Hero

Flash (1st Series)

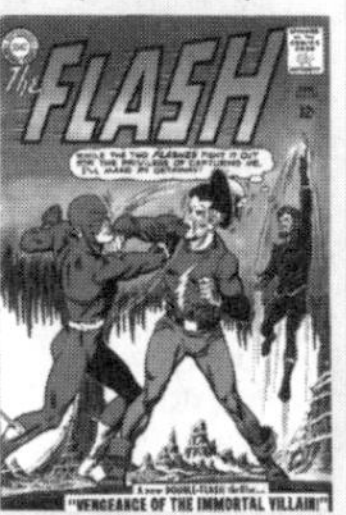

Picks up numbering of Flash Comics
©DC

	N-MINT
❑181, Aug 1968	35.00
❑182, Sep 1968	35.00
❑183, Nov 1968	35.00
❑184, Dec 1968	35.00
❑185, Feb 1969	35.00
❑186, Mar 1969	35.00
❑187, May 1969; Giant-size; aka Giant #G-58	40.00
❑188, May 1969	35.00
❑189, Jun 1969, cJKu (c)	35.00
❑190, Aug 1969	35.00
❑191, Sep 1969	35.00
❑192, Nov 1969	25.00
❑193, Dec 1969	25.00
❑194, Feb 1970	25.00
❑195, Mar 1970	25.00
❑196, May 1970; Giant-size; aka Giant #G-70	40.00
❑197, May 1970	25.00
❑198, Jun 1970	25.00
❑199, Aug 1970	25.00
❑200, Sep 1970	25.00
❑201, Nov 1970	20.00
❑202, Dec 1970	20.00
❑203, Feb 1971	20.00
❑204, Mar 1971	20.00
❑205, May 1971; Giant-size; aka Giant #G-82	20.00
❑206, May 1971	20.00
❑207, Jun 1971	17.00
❑208, Aug 1971; Giant-size; Elongated Man back-up	17.00
❑209, Sep 1971; Giant-size V: Captain Boomerang. V: Trickster.	17.00
❑210, Dec 1971; Giant-size; in future .	17.00
❑211, Dec 1971; Giant-size; Golden Age Flash back-up	17.00
❑212, Feb 1972	17.00
❑213, Mar 1972	17.00
❑214, Apr 1972, CI (a); O: Metal Men. a.k.a. DC 100-Page Super Spectacular #DC-11; ; wraparound cover; reprints O: Metal Men; Reprints Showcase #37	17.00
❑215, May 1972; A: Golden Age Flash. V: Vandal Savage. giant	17.00
❑216, Jun 1972	17.00
❑217, Sep 1972, FMc, DG, NA, IN (a); Green Lantern/Green Arrow back-up; Green Arrow back-up	17.00
❑218, Nov 1972, NA (a)	17.00
❑219, Jan 1973, NA (a); last Green Arrow back-up	17.00
❑220, Mar 1973	15.00
❑221, May 1973	15.00
❑222, Aug 1973	15.00
❑223, Oct 1973, NA (a); Green Lantern back-up	15.00
❑224, Dec 1973	15.00
❑225, Feb 1974	15.00
❑226, Apr 1974, NA (a); V: Captain Cold.	15.00
❑227, Jun 1974	15.00
❑228, Aug 1974	15.00
❑229, Oct 1974, 100 Page giant V: Rag Doll.	30.00
❑230, Dec 1974, V: Doctor Alchemy.	15.00
❑231, Feb 1975	15.00
❑232, Apr 1975, 100 Page giant	30.00
❑233, May 1975; 100 Page giant	10.00
❑234, Jun 1975	10.00
❑235, Aug 1975 A: Green Lantern. A: Golden Age Flash. V: Vandal Savage.	10.00
❑236, Sep 1975 A: Doctor Fate. A: Golden Age Flash.	10.00
❑237, Nov 1975 A: Green Lantern.	10.00
❑238, Dec 1975	7.00
❑239, Feb 1976	7.00
❑240, Mar 1976	7.00
❑241, May 1976	7.00
❑242, Jun 1976	7.00
❑243, Aug 1976	7.00
❑244, Sep 1976	7.00
❑245, Nov 1976	7.00
❑246, Jan 1977	7.00
❑247, Mar 1977	7.00
❑248, Apr 1977	7.00
❑249, May 1977	7.00
❑250, Jun 1977, 1: Golden Glider. V: Golden Glider.	7.00
❑251, Aug 1977	7.00
❑252, Sep 1977	7.00
❑253, Sep 1977	7.00
❑254, Oct 1977, V: Rogue's Gallery.	7.00
❑255, Nov 1977	7.00
❑256, Dec 1977, V: Rogue's Gallery.	7.00
❑257, Jan 1978	7.00
❑258, Feb 1978	7.00
❑259, Mar 1978	7.00
❑260, Apr 1978	7.00
❑261, May 1978	7.00
❑262, Jun 1978, V: Golden Glider.	7.00
❑263, Jul 1978, V: Golden Glider.	7.00
❑264, Aug 1978	7.00
❑265, Sep 1978	7.00
❑266, Oct 1978	7.00
❑267, Nov 1978	7.00
❑268, Dec 1978	7.00
❑268/Whitman, Dec 1978, Whitman variant	12.00
❑269, Jan 1979	7.00
❑270, Mar 1979	7.00
❑271, Mar 1979, RB (a)	3.50
❑272, Apr 1979, RB (a)	3.50
❑273, May 1979, RB (a)	3.50
❑273/Whitman, May 1979, RB (a); Whitman variant	7.00
❑274, Jun 1979, RB (a)	3.50
❑274/Whitman, Jun 1979, RB (a); Whitman variant	7.00
❑275, Jul 1979, D: Iris West Allen (Flash II's wife).	3.50
❑275/Whitman, Jul 1979, D: Iris West Allen (Flash II's wife). Whitman variant	7.00
❑276, Aug 1979, A: JLA.	3.50
❑276/Whitman, Aug 1979, A: JLA. Whitman variant	7.00
❑277, Sep 1979, A: JLA.	3.50
❑278, Oct 1979	3.50
❑278/Whitman, Oct 1979, Whitman variant	7.00
❑279, Nov 1979	3.50
❑280, Dec 1979	3.50
❑281, Jan 1980	3.50
❑282, Feb 1980	3.50
❑283, Mar 1980	3.50
❑283/Whitman, Mar 1980, Whitman variant	7.00
❑284, Apr 1980	3.50
❑285, May 1980	3.50
❑286, Jun 1980, 1: Rainbow Raider.	3.50
❑286/Whitman, Jun 1980, 1: Rainbow Raider. Whitman variant	7.00
❑287, Jul 1980	3.50
❑288, Aug 1980	3.50
❑289, Sep 1980, GP, DH (a); O: Firestorm. George Perez's first work at DC	5.00
❑290, Oct 1980, GP (a); A: Firestorm.	3.00
❑291, Nov 1980	3.00
❑292, Dec 1980	3.00
❑293, Jan 1981, A: Firestorm.	3.00
❑294, Feb 1981	3.00
❑295, Mar 1981, V: Gorilla Grodd	3.00
❑296, Apr 1981	3.00
❑297, May 1981	3.00
❑298, Jun 1981	3.00
❑299, Jul 1981	3.00
❑300, Aug 1981; Giant-size; CI (a); O: Flash. A: New Teen Titans. wraparound cover	5.00
❑301, Sep 1981, CI, DG (c)	3.00
❑302, Oct 1981	3.00
❑303, Nov 1981	3.00
❑304, Dec 1981, 1: Colonel Computron.	3.00
❑305, Jan 1982	3.50
❑306, Feb 1982, CI, KG (a)	3.50
❑307, Mar 1982, CI, KG (a); Doctor Fate back-up	2.50
❑308, Apr 1982, CI, KG (a)	2.50
❑309, May 1982, CI, KG (a)	2.50
❑310, Jun 1982, CI, KG (a)	2.50
❑311, Jul 1982, CI, KG (a)	2.50
❑312, Aug 1982, CI, KG (a); 1: Creed Phillips.	2.50
❑313, Sep 1982, CI, KG (a)	2.50
❑314, Oct 1982, 1: The Eradicator.	2.50
❑315, Nov 1982	2.50
❑316, Dec 1982	2.50
❑317, Jan 1983	2.50
❑318, Feb 1983, CI (a); 1: Big Sir.	2.50
❑319, Mar 1983	2.50
❑320, Apr 1983	2.50
❑321, May 1983	2.50
❑322, Jun 1983, V: Reverse Flash.	2.50
❑323, Jul 1983, V: Reverse Flash.	2.50
❑324, Aug 1983	2.50
❑325, Sep 1983	2.50
❑326, Oct 1983	2.50
❑327, Nov 1983	2.50
❑328, Dec 1983	2.50
❑329, Jan 1984 V: Gorilla Grodd.	2.50
❑330, Feb 1984	2.50
❑331, Mar 1984 CI (a); A: Gorilla Grodd.	2.50
❑332, Apr 1984 A: Green Lantern.	2.50
❑333, May 1984	2.50
❑334, Jun 1984	2.50

Other grades: Multiply price above by 5/6 for VF/NM • 2/3 for VERY FINE • 1/3 for FINE • 1/5 for VERY GOOD • 1/8 for GOOD

	N-MINT
❑335, Jul 1984	2.50
❑336, Aug 1984	2.50
❑337, Sep 1984 V: Pied Piper.	2.50
❑338, Oct 1984 V: Big Sir.	2.50
❑339, Nov 1984 V: Big Sir.	2.50
❑340, Dec 1984; Trial begins	2.50
❑341, Jan 1985	2.50
❑342, Feb 1985	2.50
❑343, Mar 1985	2.50
❑344, Apr 1985 O: Kid Flash.	2.50
❑345, May 1985	2.50
❑346, Jun 1985	2.50
❑347, Jul 1985	2.50
❑348, Aug 1985	2.50
❑349, Sep 1985 FMc, CI (a)	2.50
❑350, Oct 1985; Double-size	6.50
❑Annual 1, Dec 1963; O: Elongated Man. O: Kid Flash. Golden-Age Flash story	400.00
❑Annual 1/2nd, Nov 2001; Replica edition; O: Elongated Man. O: Kid Flash. 80 pages; Golden-Age Flash story	6.95

FLASH (2ND SERIES)
DC

	N-MINT
❑0, Oct 1994 O: Flash III (Wally West).	4.00
❑1, Jun 1987; BG (a); Wally West as Flash	5.00
❑2, Jul 1987 BG (a); V: Vandal Savage.	3.00
❑3, Aug 1987 1: Tina McGee. V: Kilg%re.	2.50
❑4, Sep 1987 V: Kilg%re.	2.50
❑5, Oct 1987	2.50
❑6, Nov 1987	2.50
❑7, Dec 1987 1: Red Trinity.	2.50
❑8, Jan 1988; Millennium	2.50
❑9, Feb 1988; 1: Chunk. Millennium	2.50
❑10, Mar 1988	2.50
❑11, Apr 1988	2.50
❑12, May 1988; Bonus Book #2	2.50
❑13, Jun 1988 V: Vandal Savage.	2.50
❑14, Jul 1988 V: Vandal Savage.	2.50
❑15, Aug 1988 GP (c)	2.50
❑16, Sep 1988 GP (c)	2.50
❑17, Oct 1988 GP (c)	2.50
❑18, Nov 1988	2.50
❑19, Dec 1988; Bonus Book #9	2.50
❑20	2.50
❑21; Invasion!	2.00
❑22, Jan 1989; A: Manhunter. Invasion!	2.00
❑23, Feb 1989	2.00
❑24, Mar 1989	2.00
❑25, Apr 1989	2.00
❑26, May 1989	2.00
❑27, Jun 1989	2.00
❑28, Jul 1989	2.00
❑29, Aug 1989 A: Phantom Lady.	2.00
❑30, Sep 1989	2.00
❑31, Oct 1989	1.50
❑32, Nov 1989	1.50
❑33, Dec 1989	1.50
❑34, Jan 1990	1.50
❑35, Feb 1990 V: Turtle.	1.50
❑36, Mar 1990	1.50
❑37, Apr 1990	1.50
❑38, May 1990	1.50
❑39, Jun 1990	1.50
❑40, Jul 1990	1.50
❑41, Aug 1990	1.50
❑42, Sep 1990	1.50
❑43, Oct 1990	1.50
❑44, Nov 1990 V: Gorilla Grodd.	1.50
❑45, Dec 1990 V: Gorilla Grodd.	1.50
❑46, Jan 1991 A: Vixen.	1.50
❑47, Feb 1991 A: Vixen. V: Gorilla Grodd.	1.50
❑48, Mar 1991	1.50
❑49, Apr 1991	1.50
❑50, May 1991; Giant size	2.50
❑51, Jun 1991	1.50
❑52, Jul 1991	1.50
❑53, Aug 1991; Superman	1.50
❑54, Sep 1991	1.50
❑55, Oct 1991; War of the Gods	1.50
❑56, Nov 1991; Icicle	1.50
❑57, Dec 1991; Icicle	1.50
❑58, Jan 1992	1.50

	N-MINT
❑59, Feb 1992 A: Power Girl.	1.50
❑60, Mar 1992 FMc (a)	1.50
❑61, Apr 1992	1.50
❑62, May 1992 MWa (w); O: Flash.	2.00
❑63, May 1992 O: Flash.	2.00
❑64, Jun 1992 O: Flash.	1.50
❑65, Jun 1992 O: Flash.	1.50
❑66, Jul 1992; Aquaman	1.50
❑67, Aug 1992 V: Abra Kadabra.	1.50
❑68, Sep 1992 V: Abra Kadabra.	1.50
❑69, Oct 1992 A: Green Lantern. V: Hector Hammond. V: Gorilla Grodd.	1.50
❑70, Nov 1992 A: Green Lantern. V: Hector Hammond. V: Gorilla Grodd.	1.50
❑71, Dec 1992 V: Doctor Alchemy.	1.50
❑72, Jan 1993	1.50
❑73, Feb 1993 A: Jay Garrick.	1.50
❑74, Mar 1993	1.50
❑75, Apr 1993	1.50
❑76, May 1993	1.50
❑77, Jun 1993	1.50
❑78, Jul 1993	1.50
❑79, Jul 1993; Giant-size MWa (w);	2.50
❑80, Aug 1993; regular cover	1.50
❑80/Variant, Aug 1993; foil cover	2.50
❑81, Sep 1993 A: Nightwing. A: Starfire.	1.50
❑82, Oct 1993 A: Nightwing. A: Starfire.	1.50
❑83, Oct 1993	1.50
❑84, Nov 1993 V: Razer.	1.50
❑85, Dec 1993 V: Razer.	1.50
❑86, Jan 1994	1.50
❑87, Feb 1994	1.50
❑88, Mar 1994 MWa (w)	2.00
❑89, Apr 1994 MWa (w)	2.00
❑90, May 1994 MWa (w)	2.00
❑91, Jun 1994 MWa (w)	4.00
❑92, Jul 1994 MWa (w); 1: Impulse.	8.00
❑93, Aug 1994 MWa (w); 2: Impulse.	5.00
❑94, Sep 1994; MWa (w); Zero Hour.	3.00
❑95, Nov 1994	3.00
❑96, Dec 1994	2.00
❑97, Jan 1995 MWa (w)	2.00
❑98, Feb 1995	2.00
❑99, Mar 1995	2.00
❑100, Apr 1995; Giant-size	3.00
❑100/Variant, Apr 1995; Giant-size; Holo-grafix cover	4.00
❑101, May 1995	2.00
❑102, Jun 1995 V: Mongul.	2.00
❑103, Jul 1995	2.00
❑104, Aug 1995	2.00
❑105, Sep 1995 V: Mirror Master.	2.00
❑106, Oct 1995; return of Frances Kane	2.00
❑107, Nov 1995; A: Captain Marvel. Underworld Unleashed	2.00
❑108, Dec 1995	2.00
❑109, Jan 1996; continues in Impulse #10	2.00
❑110, Feb 1996; MWa (w); continues in Impulse #11	2.00
❑111, Mar 1996 MWa (w)	2.00
❑112, Apr 1996 MWa (w); A: John Fox.	2.00
❑113, May 1996	2.00
❑114, Jun 1996 A: Don and Dawn Allen.	2.00
❑115, Jul 1996	2.00
❑116, Aug 1996	2.00
❑117, Sep 1996; Flash returns to present	2.00
❑118, Oct 1996 MWa (w)	2.00
❑119, Nov 1996; MWa (w); Final Night	2.00
❑120, Dec 1996; MWa (w); A: Trickster. Wally West asked to leave Keystone	2.00
❑121, Jan 1997 MWa (w); V: Top.	2.00
❑122, Feb 1997; MWa (w); Flash becomes a commuting super-hero.	2.00
❑123, Mar 1997 MWa (w)	2.00
❑124, Apr 1997 MWa (w); V: Major Disaster.	2.00
❑125, May 1997 V: Major Disaster.	2.00
❑126, Jun 1997; V: Major Disaster. return of Rogues Gallery	2.00
❑127, Jul 1997 A: Neron. A: Jay Garrick. V: Soulless Rogues Gallery.	2.00
❑128, Aug 1997 A: Wonder Woman. A: Superman. A: Martian Manhunter. A: Green Lantern. V: Soulless Rogues Gallery.	2.00
❑129, Sep 1997 V: Neron.	2.00

	N-MINT
❑130, Oct 1997; Wally has his legs broken	2.00
❑131, Nov 1997; Wally gets new costume	2.00
❑132, Dec 1997; A: Mirror Master. Face cover	1.95
❑133, Jan 1998 V: Mirror Master.	1.95
❑134, Feb 1998 A: Thinker. A: Wildcat. A: Johnny Thunder. A: Ted Knight. A: Sentinel. A: Jay Garrick.	1.95
❑135, Mar 1998; cover forms triptych with Green Arrow #130 and Green Lantern #96	1.95
❑136, Apr 1998 A: Krakkl.	1.95
❑137, May 1998	1.95
❑138, Jun 1998	1.95
❑139, Jul 1998 D: Linda Park.	1.95
❑140, Aug 1998; Linda's funeral.	1.95
❑141, Sep 1998 V: Black Flash.	1.95
❑142, Oct 1998; Wedding of Wally and Linda	1.95
❑143, Dec 1998 V: Cobalt Blue.	1.99
❑144, Jan 1999 O: Cobalt Blue.	1.99
❑145, Feb 1999 MWa (w); A: Cobalt Blue.	1.99
❑146, Mar 1999 MWa (w); A: Cobalt Blue.	1.99
❑147, Apr 1999 MWa (w); A: Reverse Flash. A: Cobalt Blue.	1.99
❑148, May 1999 MWa (w); A: Barry Allen.	1.99
❑149, Jun 1999; MWa (w); Crisis ending changed	1.99
❑150, Jul 1999; MWa (w); Wally vs. Anti-Monitor	2.95
❑151, Aug 1999; MWa (w); Teen Titans adventure	1.99
❑152, Sep 1999 MWa (w)	1.99
❑153, Oct 1999 MWa (w); V: Folded Man.	1.99
❑154, Nov 1999; new Flash reveals identity	1.99
❑155, Dec 1999 MWa (w)	1.99
❑156, Jan 2000 MWa (w)	1.99
❑157, Feb 2000	1.99
❑158, Mar 2000	1.99
❑159, Apr 2000 MWa (w)	1.99
❑160, May 2000	1.99
❑161, Jun 2000 A: JSA. A: Flash I (Jay Garrick).	1.99
❑162, Jul 2000	1.99
❑163, Aug 2000	2.25
❑164, Sep 2000	2.25
❑165, Oct 2000	2.25
❑166, Nov 2000	2.25
❑167, Dec 2000	2.25
❑168, Jan 2001	2.25
❑169, Feb 2001	2.25
❑170, Mar 2001	2.25
❑171, Apr 2001	2.25
❑172, May 2001	2.25
❑173, Jun 2001	2.25
❑174, Jul 2001; 1st appearance of Tar Pit	2.25
❑175, Aug 2001	2.25
❑176, Sep 2001	2.25
❑177, Oct 2001	2.25
❑178, Nov 2001	2.25
❑179, Dec 2001; Joker: Last Laugh crossover	2.25
❑180, Jan 2002	2.25
❑181, Feb 2002	2.25
❑182, Mar 2002	2.25
❑183, Apr 2002 1: Trickster II (Axel Walker).	2.25
❑184, May 2002	2.25
❑185, Jun 2002	2.25
❑186, Jul 2002	2.25
❑187, Aug 2002	2.25
❑188, Sep 2002	2.25
❑189, Oct 2002	2.25
❑190, Nov 2002	2.25
❑191, Dec 2002	2.25
❑192, Jan 2003	2.25
❑193, Feb 2003	2.25
❑194, Mar 2003	2.25
❑195, Apr 2003	2.25
❑196, May 2003	2.25
❑197, Jun 2003	2.25
❑198, Jul 2003	2.25
❑199, Aug 2003	2.25

Other grades: Multiply price above by 5/6 for VF/NM • 2/3 for VERY FINE • 1/3 for FINE • 1/5 for VERY GOOD • 1/8 for GOOD

Flash (2nd Series)

Wally West takes over as the new Flash

©DC

Flash & Green Lantern: The Brave and the Bold

Mark Waid and Tom Peyer power team-up

©DC

Flash/Green Lantern: Faster Friends

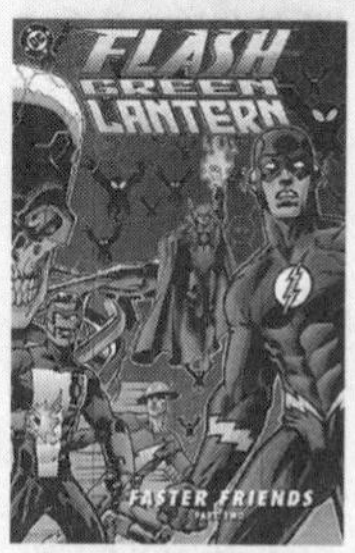

Continues from Green Lantern/Flash

©DC

Flash Plus

Flash and Nightwing take a road trip

©DC

Flash Secret Files

Encyclopedic info about the Flash's world

©DC

N-MINT

❑200, Sep 2003 ... 3.50
❑201, Oct 2003 ... 2.25
❑202, Nov 2003 ... 2.25
❑203, Dec 2003 ... 2.25
❑204, Jan 2004 ... 2.25
❑205, Feb 2004 ... 2.25
❑206, Mar 2004 ... 2.25
❑207, Apr 2004 ... 6.00
❑208, May 2004 ... 5.00
❑209, Jun 2004 ... 4.00
❑210, Jul 2004 ... 3.00
❑210/2nd, Aug 2004 ... 2.25
❑211, Aug 2004 ... 4.00
❑212, Sep 2004 ... 2.25
❑213, Oct 2004 ... 2.25
❑214, Nov 2004 ... 6.00
❑215, Dec 2004 ... 5.00
❑216, Jan 2005 ... 6.00
❑217, Feb 2005 ... 5.00
❑218, Mar 2005 ... 4.00
❑219, Apr 2005 ... 9.00
❑220, May 2005 ... 6.00
❑221, Jun 2005 ... 5.00
❑222, Jul 2005 ... 4.00
❑223, Aug 2005 ... 4.00
❑224, Sep 2005 ... 2.25
❑225, Oct 2005 ...
❑226, Nov 2005 ...
❑227, Dec 2005 ...
❑228, Jan 2006 ...
❑229, Feb 2006 ...
❑230, Mar 2006 ...
❑1000000, Nov 1998 MWa (w) ... 3.00
❑Annual 1, ca. 1987 BG (a ... 5.00
❑Annual 2; Private Lives ... 2.00
❑Annual 3; Who's Who entries ... 2.25
❑Annual 4 ... 2.25
❑Annual 5 ... 2.75
❑Annual 6 1: Argus. ... 2.50
❑Annual 7; Elseworlds ... 2.95
❑Annual 8, ca. 1995; Year One ... 3.50
❑Annual 9, ca. 1996; Legends of the Dead Earth ... 2.95
❑Annual 10, ca. 1997; DG (a); Pulp Heroes; 1997 Annual ... 3.95
❑Annual 11, ca. 1998; A: Johnny Quick. Ghosts; 1998 Annual ... 3.95
❑Annual 12, Oct 1999; JLApe; 1999 Annual ... 2.95
❑Annual 13, Sep 2000; 2000 Annual; Planet DC ... 3.50
❑Giant Size 1, Aug 1998 JBy, MWa (w); JBy (a); A: Flash II (Barry Allen). A: Lightning. A: Flash III (Wally West). A: Jesse Quick. A: Impulse. A: Flash I (Jay Garrick). A: Captain Boomerang. A: Flash IV (John Fox). ... 4.95
❑Giant Size 2, Apr 1999 ... 4.95
❑Special 1; 50th anniversary issue; JKu (c); CI (a); 1: John Fox. 3 Flashes ... 3.50
❑TV 1 1991; A: Kid Flash. TV Special; Stories about TV show Flash ... 3.95

FLASH & GREEN LANTERN: THE BRAVE AND THE BOLD
DC

❑1, Oct 1999 ... 2.50
❑2, Nov 1999 ... 2.50
❑3, Dec 1999 ... 2.50
❑4, Jan 2000 ... 2.50
❑5, Feb 2000 ... 2.50
❑6, Mar 2000 ... 2.50

FLASHBACK
SPECIAL

❑1 ... 3.00
❑2 ... 3.00
❑3, ca. 1974 ... 3.00
❑4 1974 ... 3.00
❑5 1974 ... 3.00
❑6 1974 ... 3.00
❑7 1974 ... 3.00
❑8 1974 ... 3.00
❑9 1974 ... 3.00
❑10, ca. 1974 ... 3.00
❑11 1974 ... 3.00
❑12 1974 ... 3.00
❑13 1974 ... 3.00
❑14, ca. 1974 ... 3.00
❑15 ... 3.00
❑16 ... 3.00
❑17 ... 3.00
❑18 ... 3.00
❑19 ... 3.00
❑20 ... 3.00
❑21 ... 3.00
❑22 ... 3.00
❑23 ... 3.00
❑24 ... 3.00
❑25 ... 3.00
❑26 ... 3.00
❑27 ... 3.00

FLASH GORDON (GOLD KEY ONE-SHOT)
GOLD KEY

❑1, Jun 1965, Dinosaur cover ... 26.00

FLASH GORDON (KING/CHARLTON/GOLD KEY/WHITMAN)
KING

❑1, Sep 1966, King begins publishing ... 50.00
❑2, Nov 1966 ... 30.00
❑3, Jan 1967 ... 24.00
❑4, Mar 1967 ... 24.00
❑5, May 1967 ... 24.00
❑6, Jul 1967 ... 24.00
❑7, Aug 1967 ... 24.00
❑8, Sep 1967 ... 24.00
❑9, Oct 1967, AR (a) ... 32.00
❑10, Nov 1967, AR (a) ... 32.00
❑11, Dec 1967 ... 20.00
❑12, Feb 1969, Charlton begins publishing ... 22.00
❑13, Apr 1969 ... 18.00
❑14, Jun 1969 ... 14.00
❑15, Aug 1969 ... 14.00
❑16, Oct 1969 ... 14.00
❑17, Nov 1969 ... 14.00
❑18, Jan 1969 ... 14.00
❑19, Sep 1978, Gold Key begins publishing ... 10.00
❑20, Nov 1978 ... 6.00
❑21, Jan 1979 ... 6.00
❑22, Mar 1979 ... 6.00
❑23, May 1979 ... 6.00
❑24, Jul 1979, Whitman begins publishing ... 5.00
❑25, Sep 1979 ... 4.00
❑26, Nov 1979 ... 4.00
❑27, Jan 1980 ... 4.00
❑28, Mar 1980 ... 4.00
❑29, May 1980 ... 4.00
❑30, Oct 1980, Released outside U.S. market ... 8.00
❑30/50 cent, ca. 1981; Later printing for U.S. market ... 4.00
❑31, Mar 1981, AW (a); The Movie Adaptation ... 3.00
❑32, Apr 1981, AW (a); The Movie Adaptation ... 3.00
❑33, May 1981, AW (a); The Movie Adaptation ... 3.00
❑34, Oct 1981 ... 3.00
❑35, Dec 1981 ... 3.00
❑36, Feb 1982 ... 3.00
❑37, ca. 1982 ... 3.00

FLASH GORDON (DC)
DC

❑1, Jun 1988 ... 2.00
❑2, Jul 1988 ... 1.50
❑3, Aug 1988 ... 1.50
❑4, Sep 1988 ... 1.50
❑5, Oct 1988 ... 1.50
❑6, Nov 1988 ... 1.50
❑7, Dec 1988 ... 1.50
❑8, Win 1988 ... 1.50
❑9, Hol 1988 ... 1.50

FLASH GORDON (MARVEL)
MARVEL

❑1, Jun 1995; wraparound cardstock cover ... 2.95
❑2, Jul 1995; wraparound cardstock cover ... 2.95

FLASH GORDON: THE MOVIE
GOLDEN PRESS

❑1 AW (a) ... 2.50

FLASH/GREEN LANTERN: FASTER FRIENDS
DC

Value: Cover or less

❑1; prestige format; continued from Green Lantern/Flash: Faster Friends ... 4.95

FLASH: OUR WORLDS AT WAR
DC

❑1, Oct 2001 ... 2.95

FLASH PLUS
DC

❑1, Jan 1997 ... 2.95

FLASH SECRET FILES
DC

❑1, Nov 1997; bios on major cast members and villains; timeline ... 4.95
❑2, Nov 1999; updates on cast ... 4.95
❑3, Nov 2001 ... 4.95

Other grades: Multiply price above by 5/6 for VF/NM • 2/3 for VERY FINE • 1/3 for FINE • 1/5 for VERY GOOD • 1/8 for GOOD

FLASH: THE FASTEST MAN ALIVE
DC

❑1, Sep 2006 2.99

FLASH, THE: IRON HEIGHTS
DC

❑1, Oct 2001 5.95

FLASH: TIME FLIES
DC

❑nn, ca. 2002 5.95

FLASHMARKS
FANTAGRAPHICS

❑1, b&w 2.95

FLASHPOINT
DC

❑1, Dec 1999; Elseworlds 2.95
❑2, Jan 2000 2.95
❑3, Feb 2000 2.95

FLATLINE COMICS PRESENTS...
FLATLINE

❑1, Dec 1993 2.50

FLAXEN
DARK HORSE

❑1; photo back cover 2.95

FLAXEN: ALTER EGO
CALIBER

❑1, Mar 1995 2.95

FLEENER
ZONGO

❑1, b&w 2.95
❑2, Dec 1996, b&w 2.95
❑3, b&w 2.95

FLESH
FLEETWAY-QUALITY

❑1 2.95
❑2 2.95
❑3 2.95
❑4 2.95

FLESH & BLOOD
BRAINSTORM

❑1; Partial foil cover 2.95
❑1/Ashcan; Ashcan preview from 1995 Philadelphia Comic Con 1.00

FLESH & BLOOD: PRE-EXISTING CONDITIONS
BLINDWOLF

❑1 2.95

FLESH AND BONES
UPSHOT

❑1 2.00
❑2 2.00
❑3 2.00
❑4 2.00

FLESH CRAWLERS
KITCHEN SINK

❑1, ca. 1994 2.50
❑2, Jan 1995 2.50
❑3, Feb 1995 2.50

FLESH GORDON
AIRCEL

❑1, Mar 1992 2.95
❑2, Apr 1992 2.95
❑3, May 1992 2.95
❑4, Jun 1992 2.95

FLESHPOT
FANTAGRAPHICS / EROS

❑1, Oct 1997 2.95

FLEX MENTALLO
DC / VERTIGO

❑1, Jun 1996 10.00
❑2, Jul 1996; EC parody cover 8.00
❑3, Aug 1996; Dark Knight parody cover 8.00
❑4, Sep 1996 8.00

FLICKERING FLESH
BONEYARD

❑1, Mar 1993 2.50

FLICKER'S FLEAS
FIFTH WHEEL

❑1 3.00

FLINCH
DC / VERTIGO

❑1, Jun 1999 JLee (a) 3.00
❑2, Jul 1999 BSz (a) 2.50
❑3, Aug 1999 2.50
❑4, Sep 1999 PG (a 2.50
❑5, Oct 1999 2.50
❑6, Nov 1999 2.50
❑7, Dec 1999 DGry (w) 2.50
❑8, Jan 2000 2.50
❑9, Feb 2000 2.50
❑10, Mar 2000 2.50
❑11, Apr 2000 2.50
❑12, May 2000 2.50
❑13 2000 2.50
❑14, Sep 2000 BWr (a) 2.50
❑15, Nov 2000 2.50
❑16, Jan 2001 2.50

FLINT ARMBUSTER JR. SPECIAL
ALCHEMY

❑1, b&w 2.95

FLINTSTONE KIDS
MARVEL / STAR

❑1, Aug 1987 2.00
❑2, Oct 1987 1.50
❑3, Dec 1987 1.50
❑4, Feb 1988 1.50
❑5, Apr 1988 1.50
❑6, Jun 1988 1.50
❑7, Aug 1988 1.50
❑8, Oct 1988 1.50
❑9, Dec 1988 1.50
❑10, Feb 1989 1.50
❑11, Apr 1989 1.50

FLINTSTONES (DELL/GOLD KEY)
DELL / GOLD KEY

❑1, a.k.a. Dell Giant #48 55.00
❑2, Dec 1961 38.00
❑3, Jan 1962 30.00
❑4, Mar 1962 30.00
❑5, May 1962 30.00
❑6, Jul 1962 24.00
❑7, Oct 1962, First Gold Key issue 24.00
❑8 20.00
❑9, Feb 1963 20.00
❑10, Apr 1963 20.00
❑11, Jun 1963 18.00
❑12, Jul 1963 18.00
❑13, Sep 1963 18.00
❑14, Oct 1963 18.00
❑15, Nov 1963 18.00
❑16, Jan 1964 18.00
❑17, Mar 1964 18.00
❑18, May 1964 18.00
❑19, Jul 1964 18.00
❑20, Aug 1964 18.00
❑21, Sep 1964 15.00
❑22, Oct 1964 15.00
❑23, Nov 1964 15.00
❑24, Jan 1965 15.00
❑25, Mar 1965 15.00
❑26, May 1965 15.00
❑27, Jul 1965 15.00
❑28, Aug 1965 15.00
❑29, Sep 1965 15.00
❑30, Oct 1965 15.00
❑31, Dec 1965 12.00
❑32, Feb 1966 12.00
❑33, Apr 1966 12.00
❑34, Jun 1966 12.00
❑35, Aug 1966 12.00
❑36, Oct 1966 12.00
❑37, Dec 1966 12.00
❑38, Feb 1967 12.00
❑39, Apr 1967 12.00
❑40, Jun 1967 12.00
❑41, Aug 1967 9.00
❑42, Oct 1967 9.00
❑43, Dec 1967 9.00
❑44, Feb 1968 9.00
❑45, Apr 1968 9.00
❑46, Jun 1968 9.00
❑47, Aug 1968 9.00
❑48, Oct 1968 9.00
❑49, Dec 1968 9.00
❑50, Feb 1969 9.00
❑51, Apr 1969 9.00
❑52, Jun 1969 9.00
❑53, Aug 1969 9.00
❑54, Oct 1969 9.00
❑55, Dec 1969 9.00
❑56, Feb 1970 9.00
❑57, Apr 1970 9.00
❑58, May 1970 9.00
❑59, Jul 1970 9.00
❑60, Sep 1970 9.00

FLINTSTONES (CHARLTON)
CHARLTON

❑1, Nov 1970 36.00
❑2, Jan 1971 22.00
❑3, Mar 1971 14.00
❑4, May 1971 14.00
❑5, Jul 1971 14.00
❑6, Sep 1971 9.00
❑7, Oct 1971 9.00
❑8, Nov 1971 9.00
❑9, Dec 1971 9.00
❑10, Jan 1972 9.00
❑11, Feb 1972 7.00
❑12, Mar 1972 7.00
❑13, May 1972 7.00
❑14, Jun 1972 7.00
❑15, Jul 1972 7.00
❑16, Aug 1972 7.00
❑17, Sep 1972 7.00
❑18, Nov 1972 7.00
❑19, Dec 1972 7.00
❑20, Jan 1973 7.00
❑21, Mar 1973 5.00
❑22, Apr 1973 5.00
❑23, ca. 1973 5.00
❑24, ca. 1973 5.00
❑25, ca. 1973 5.00
❑26, Oct 1973 5.00
❑27 1973 5.00
❑28 1974 5.00
❑29, May 1974 5.00
❑30, ca. 1974 5.00
❑31, ca. 1974 4.00
❑32, ca. 1974 4.00
❑33, Oct 1974 4.00
❑34, Nov 1974 4.00
❑35, Feb 1975 4.00
❑36, Mar 1975 4.00
❑37, May 1975 4.00
❑38, Jun 1975 4.00
❑39, ca. 1975 4.00
❑40, ca. 1975 4.00
❑41, ca. 1975 4.00
❑42 1975 4.00
❑43, Feb 1976 4.00
❑44, Mar 1976, Ray Dirgo, Jay Gill credits 4.00
❑45, ca. 1976 4.00
❑46, ca. 1976 4.00
❑47, Aug 1976, Ray Dirgo, Jay Gill credits 4.00
❑48, Oct 1976, Ray Dirgo credits 4.00
❑49, Dec 1976 4.00
❑50, Feb 1977 4.00

FLINTSTONES 3-D
BLACKTHORNE

❑1, Apr 1987; a.k.a. Blackthorne 3-D #19 2.50
❑2, Fal 1987; a.k.a. Blackthorne 3-D #22 2.50
❑3 2.50
❑4 2.50

FLINTSTONES (MARVEL)
MARVEL

❑1, Oct 1977 5.00
❑2, Dec 1977 3.00
❑3, Feb 1978 3.00
❑4, Apr 1978 3.00
❑5, Jun 1978 3.00
❑6, Aug 1978 3.00
❑7, Oct 1978 3.00
❑8, Dec 1978 3.00
❑9, Feb 1979 3.00

FLINTSTONES (HARVEY)
HARVEY

❑1, Sep 1992 2.50
❑2, Jan 1993 2.00
❑3, ca. 1993 2.00

Flash: Iron Heights

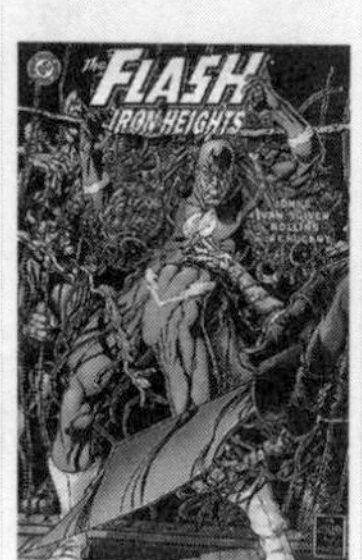

Viral outbreak hits Keystone City prison

©DC

Flashpoint

Elseworlds tale with Vandal Savage villainy

©DC

Flinch

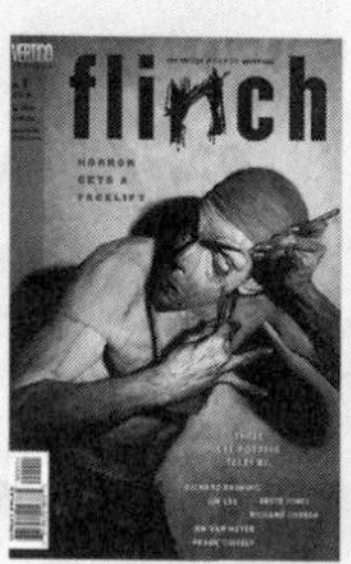

DC tries another horror anthology

©DC

Flintstones (Dell/Gold Key)

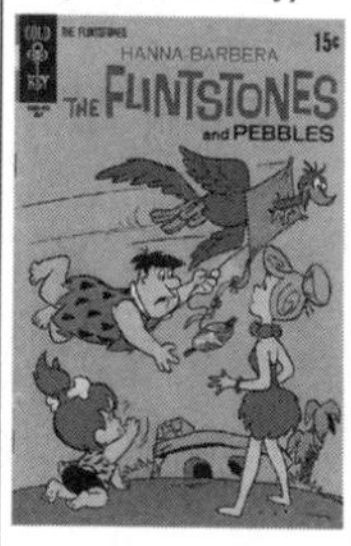

Prehistoric family hits comics early on

©Dell

Flintstones (Marvel)

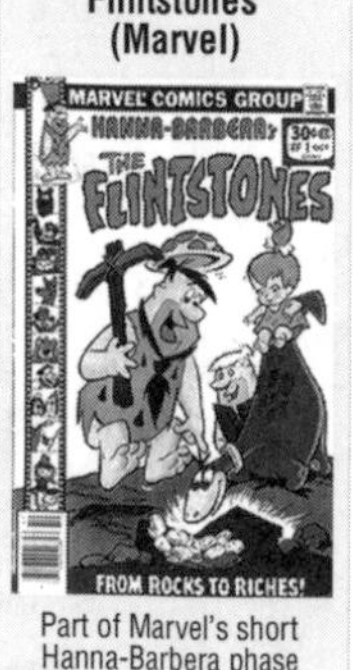

Part of Marvel's short Hanna-Barbera phase

©Marvel

	N-MINT
❑4, Sep 1993	2.00
❑5, Oct 1993	2.00
❑6, Nov 1993	2.00
❑7, Dec 1993	2.00
❑8, Jan 1994	2.00
❑9, Feb 1994	2.00
❑10, Mar 1994	2.00
❑11, Apr 1994	2.00
❑12, May 1994	2.00
❑13, Jun 1994	2.00

FLINTSTONES (ARCHIE)
ARCHIE

	N-MINT
❑1, Sep 1995	2.00
❑2, Oct 1995	1.50
❑3, Nov 1995	1.50
❑4, Dec 1995	1.50
❑5, Jan 1996	1.50
❑6, Feb 1996	1.50
❑7, Mar 1996	1.50
❑8, Apr 1996	1.50
❑9, May 1996	1.50
❑10, Jun 1996	1.50
❑12, Aug 1996	1.50
❑13, Sep 1996	1.50
❑14, Oct 1996	1.50
❑15, Nov 1996	1.50
❑16, Dec 1996	1.50
❑17, Jan 1997	1.50
❑18, Feb 1997, Fred becomes a cartoonist	1.50
❑19, Mar 1997, A: Great Gazoo.	1.50
❑20, Apr 1997	1.50
❑21, May 1997	1.50
❑22, Jun 1997, A: Gruesomes.	1.50

FLINTSTONES AND THE JETSONS
DC

	N-MINT
❑1, Aug 1997	2.00
❑2, Sep 1997	2.00
❑3, Oct 1997, Spacely turned into baby	2.00
❑4, Nov 1997, Gazoo turns Fred and Barney into women	2.00
❑5, Dec 1997, Judy and Elroy throw a party	2.00
❑6, Jan 1998,	2.00
❑7, Feb 1998, Spies issue	2.00
❑8, Mar 1998, Kung Fu issue	2.00
❑9, Apr 1998,	2.00
❑10, May 1998,	2.00
❑11, Jun 1998, Time travel	2.00
❑12, Jul 1998,	2.00
❑13, Aug 1998,	2.00
❑14, Oct 1998,	2.00
❑15, Nov 1998, Super-Fred	2.00
❑16, Dec 1998,	2.00
❑17, Jan 1999,	2.00
❑18, Feb 1999, A: Great Gazoo. It's A Wonderful Life homage	2.00
❑19, Mar 1999, Jetsons Bizarro story	2.00
❑20, Apr 1999,	2.00
❑21, May 1999, Fred and George switch places	1.99

FLINTSTONES AT THE NEW YORK WORLD'S FAIR
DELL

	N-MINT
❑1, ca. 1964	48.00

FLINTSTONES BIG BOOK
HARVEY

	N-MINT
❑1	1.95
❑2	1.95

FLINTSTONES BIGGER AND BOULDER
GOLD KEY

	N-MINT
❑1, Nov 1962	65.00
❑2, Jun 1966	45.00

FLINTSTONES DOUBLEVISION
HARVEY

	N-MINT
❑1, Sep 1994, polybagged with double vision glasses, adaptation of movie	2.95

FLINTSTONES GIANT SIZE
HARVEY

	N-MINT
❑2, ca. 1992	2.50
❑3, ca. 1993	2.50

FLINTSTONES WITH PEBBLES AND BAMM-BAMM
GOLD KEY

	N-MINT
❑1, Nov 1965, Regular paper (non-glossy) cover	50.00

FLIPPER
GOLD KEY

	N-MINT
❑1, Apr 1966	25.00
❑2, Nov 1966	18.00
❑3, Nov 1967	18.00

FLOATERS
DARK HORSE

	N-MINT
❑1, Sep 1993, b&w	2.50
❑2, Oct 1993, b&w	2.50
❑3, Nov 1993, b&w	2.50
❑4, Dec 1993, b&w	2.50
❑5, Jan 1994	2.50

FLOCK OF DREAMERS
KITCHEN SINK

	N-MINT
❑1, Nov 1997, b&w	12.95

FLOOD RELIEF
MALIBU

	N-MINT
❑1; Ultraverse Red Cross giveaway	5.00

FLOWERS
DRAWN AND QUARTERLY

	N-MINT
❑1	2.95

FLOWERS ON THE RAZORWIRE
BONEYARD

	N-MINT
❑1, b&w	2.95
❑2, b&w	2.95
❑3, b&w	2.95
❑4, Nov 1994, b&w	2.95
❑5, May 1995, b&w	2.95
❑6, May 1995, b&w	2.95
❑7, Oct 1995, b&w	2.95
❑8, b&w	2.95
❑9, b&w	2.95
❑10, Apr 1997, b&w	2.95

FLY (ARCHIE)
ARCHIE / RED CIRCLE

	N-MINT
❑1, May 1983	3.00
❑2, Jul 1983	1.50
❑3, Oct 1983	1.50
❑4, Dec 1983, SD (a)	1.50
❑5, Feb 1984	1.50
❑6, Apr 1984	1.50
❑7, Jun 1984	1.50
❑8, Aug 1984	1.50
❑9, Oct 1984	1.50

FLY (IMPACT)
DC / IMPACT

	N-MINT
❑1, Aug 1991	1.25
❑2, Sep 1991	1.00
❑3, Oct 1991	1.00
❑4, Nov 1991	1.00
❑5, Dec 1991	1.00
❑6, Jan 1992	1.00
❑7, Feb 1992	1.00
❑8, Mar 1992	1.00
❑9, Apr 1992	1.00
❑10, May 1992	1.00
❑11, Jun 1992	1.25
❑12, Jul 1992	1.25
❑13, Aug 1992	1.25
❑14, Sep 1992	1.25
❑15, Oct 1992	1.25
❑16, Nov 1992	1.25
❑17, Dec 1992	1.25
❑Annual 1; trading card	2.00

FLY MAN
ARCHIE / RADIO

	N-MINT
❑32, Jul 1965, Series continued from Adventures of the Fly #31	32.00
❑33, Sep 1965	20.00
❑34, Nov 1965	20.00
❑35, Jan 1966	16.00
❑36, Mar 1966, O: The Web.	16.00
❑37, May 1966	16.00
❑38, Jul 1966	16.00
❑39, Sep 1966, Series continued in Mighty Comics #40	16.00

FLYING COLORS 10TH ANNIVERSARY SPECIAL
FLYING COLORS

	N-MINT
❑1, Sep 1998	2.95

FLYING NUN
DELL

	N-MINT
❑1, Feb 1968	32.00
❑2, May 1968	20.00
❑3, Aug 1968	20.00
❑4	20.00

FLYING SAUCERS (DELL)
DELL

	N-MINT
❑1, Apr 1967, FS (a)	26.00
❑2, Jul 1967	15.00
❑3, Oct 1967, FS (a)	15.00
❑4, Nov 1967	15.00
❑5, Oct 1969	15.00

Other grades: Multiply price above by 5/6 for VF/NM • 2/3 for VERY FINE • 1/3 for FINE • 1/5 for VERY GOOD • 1/8 for GOOD

FOCUS
DC

❑1, Sum 1987; BSz, GP (a); no cover price 1.00

FOES
RAM

❑1 1.95

FOG CITY COMICS
STAMPART

❑1 1.00

FOODANG
CONTINUÜM

❑1, Jul 1994, b&w; foil cover 1.95
❑Ashcan 1; Ashcan promotional edition; 1: Foodang. Previews Foodang #1; Flip Book with The Dark Ashcan #1 1.00

FOODANG (2ND SERIES)
AUGUST HOUSE

❑1, Jan 1995; oversized trading card; enhanced cover 2.50

FOOD FIRST COMICS
IFDP

❑1 3.00
❑1/2nd, b&w 3.00
❑1/3rd, b&w

FOOFUR
MARVEL / STAR

❑1, Aug 1987 1.00
❑2, Oct 1987 1.00
❑3, Dec 1987 1.00
❑4, Feb 1988 1.00
❑5, Apr 1988 1.00
❑6, Jun 1988 1.00

FOOLKILLER
MARVEL

❑1, Oct 1990 O: FoolKiller III. 1: FoolKiller III (Kurt Gerhardt). A: Greg Salinger (FoolKiller II) 2.00
❑2, Nov 1990 2.00
❑3, Dec 1990; cover says Nov, indicia says Dec 2.00
❑4, Jan 1991 2.00
❑5, Feb 1991 TD (a) 2.00
❑6, Apr 1991 TD (a) 2.00
❑7 1991 2.00
❑8, Jul 1991 A: Spider-Man 2.00
❑9 1991 2.00
❑10 1991 2.00

FOOM MAGAZINE
MARVEL

❑1, Feb 1973 45.00
❑2, Sum 1973 30.00
❑3, Fal 1973; Spider-Man issue; Interview with Stan Lee 25.00
❑4, Win 1973 25.00
❑5, Spr 1974 20.00
❑6, Sum 1974 20.00
❑7, Fal 1974 20.00
❑8, Dec 1974 20.00
❑9, Mar 1975 20.00
❑10, Jun 1975 20.00
❑11, Sep 1975 20.00
❑12, Dec 1975 20.00
❑13, Mar 1976 20.00
❑14, Jun 1976 20.00
❑15, Sep 1976 20.00
❑16, Dec 1976 20.00
❑17, Mar 1977 20.00
❑18, Jun 1977 20.00
❑19, Fal 1977; Special Defenders Issue 20.00
❑20, Win 1977 20.00
❑21, Spr 1978; Science Fiction Special 25.00
❑22, Aut 1978; Mighty Marvel Media Special 40.00

FOOT SOLDIERS
DARK HORSE

❑1, Jan 1996 2.95
❑2, Feb 1996 2.95
❑3, Mar 1996 2.95
❑4, Apr 1996 2.95

FOOT SOLDIERS (VOL. 2)
IMAGE

❑1, Sep 1997, b&w 2.95
❑2, Nov 1997, b&w 2.95
❑3, Jan 1998, b&w 2.95
❑4, Mar 1998, b&w 2.95
❑5, May 1998, b&w 2.95

FOOZLE
ECLIPSE

❑1 1985 1.75
❑2 1985 1.75
❑3, Aug 1985; Reprints original Foozle Story in color 1.75

FORBIDDEN FRANKENSTEIN
FANTAGRAPHICS / EROS

❑1, b&w 2.25
❑2, b&w 2.50

FORBIDDEN KINGDOM
EASTERN

❑1, Nov 1987, b&w 1.95
❑2, Jan 1988, b&w 1.95
❑3, Mar 1988, b&w 1.95
❑4, May 1988, b&w 1.95
❑5, Jul 1988, b&w 1.95
❑6, b&w 1.95
❑7, b&w 1.95
❑8, b&w 1.95

FORBIDDEN KNOWLEDGE
LAST GASP

❑1 4.00

FORBIDDEN KNOWLEDGE: ADVENTURE BEYOND THE DOORWAY TO SOULS WITH RADICAL DREAMER
MARK'S GIANT ECONOMY SIZE

❑1, b&w; infinity cover 3.50

FORBIDDEN PLANET
INNOVATION

❑1, May 1992 2.50
❑2, Jul 1992 2.50
❑3, Sep 1992 2.50
❑4, Spr 1993 2.50

FORBIDDEN SUBJECTS
ANGEL

❑0 2.95
❑0/A; Nude edition A 3.95
❑0/B; Nude edition B 3.95

FORBIDDEN SUBJECTS: CANDY KISSES
ANGEL

❑1; Censored cover 3.00
❑1/B; Adult cover 3.00

FORBIDDEN TALES OF DARK MANSION
DC

❑5, Jun 1972; Series continued from The Dark Mansion of Forbidden Love #4 35.00
❑6, Aug 1972 17.00
❑7, Oct 1972, JO (w); HC, TD (a) 17.00
❑8, Dec 1972 12.00
❑9, Feb 1973 12.00
❑10, Apr 1973 10.00
❑11, Jul 1973 10.00
❑12, Sep 1973 10.00
❑13, Nov 1973 10.00
❑14, Jan 1974 10.00
❑15, Mar 1974 15.00

FORBIDDEN VAMPIRE
ANGEL

❑0 2.95

FORBIDDEN WORLDS
ACG

❑1, Jul 1951, AW, FF (a) 875.00
❑2, Sep 1951 500.00
❑3, Nov 1951, AW, WW (a) 465.00
❑4, Jan 1952 270.00
❑5, Mar 1952, AW (a) 290.00
❑6, May 1952, AW (a) 290.00
❑7, Jul 1952 190.00
❑8, Aug 1952 190.00
❑9, Sep 1952 190.00
❑10, Oct 1952 190.00
❑11, Nov 1952 135.00
❑12, Dec 1952 135.00
❑13, Jan 1953 135.00
❑14, Feb 1953 135.00
❑15, Mar 1953 135.00
❑16, Apr 1953 100.00
❑17, May 1953 100.00
❑18, Jun 1953 100.00
❑19, Jul 1953 100.00
❑20, Aug 1953 100.00
❑21, Sep 1953 85.00
❑22, Oct 1953 85.00
❑23, Nov 1953 85.00
❑24, Dec 1953 85.00
❑25, Jan 1954 85.00
❑26, Feb 1954 85.00
❑27, Mar 1954 85.00
❑28, Apr 1954 85.00
❑29, May 1954 85.00
❑30, Jun 1954 85.00
❑31, Jul 1954 75.00
❑32, Aug 1954 75.00
❑33, Sep 1954 75.00
❑34, Oct 1954 75.00
❑35, Aug 1955 75.00
❑36, Sep 1955 75.00
❑37, Oct 1955 75.00
❑38, Nov 1955 75.00
❑39, Dec 1955, KS (a) 75.00
❑40, Jan 1956 75.00
❑41, Feb 1956 54.00
❑42, Mar 1956 54.00
❑43, May 1956 54.00
❑44, Jul 1956 54.00
❑45, Aug 1956 54.00
❑46, Sep 1956 54.00
❑47, Oct 1956 54.00
❑48, Nov 1956 54.00
❑49, Dec 1956 54.00
❑50, Jan 1957 54.00
❑51, Feb 1957 45.00
❑52, Mar 1957 45.00
❑53, Apr 1957 45.00
❑54, May 1957 45.00
❑55, Jun 1957 45.00
❑56, Jul 1957 45.00
❑57, Aug 1957 45.00
❑58, Sep 1957 45.00
❑59, Oct 1957 45.00
❑60, Nov 1957 45.00
❑61, Dec 1957 40.00
❑62, Jan 1958 40.00
❑63, Feb 1958 40.00
❑64, Mar 1958 40.00
❑65, Apr 1958 40.00
❑66, May 1958 40.00
❑67, Jun 1958 40.00
❑68, Jul 1958 40.00
❑69, Aug 1958 40.00
❑70, Sep 1958 40.00
❑71, Oct 1958 35.00
❑72, Nov 1958 35.00
❑73, Dec 1958, 1: Herbie 275.00
❑74, Jan 1959 35.00
❑75, Feb 1959 35.00
❑76, Mar 1959 35.00
❑77, Apr 1959 35.00
❑78, May 1959 35.00
❑79, Jun 1959 35.00
❑80, Jul 1959 35.00
❑81, Aug 1959 24.00
❑82, Sep 1959 24.00
❑83, Oct 1959, reprints begin 24.00
❑84, Nov 1959 24.00
❑85, Jan 1960 24.00
❑86, Mar 1960, KS (c); Flying saucer cover 30.00
❑87, May 1960 24.00
❑88, Jul 1960 24.00
❑89, Aug 1960 24.00
❑90, Sep 1960 24.00
❑91, Oct 1960 20.00
❑92, Nov 1960 20.00
❑93, Jan 1961 20.00
❑94, Mar 1961, A: Herbie 55.00
❑95, May 1961 20.00
❑96, Jul 1961 20.00
❑97, Aug 1961 20.00
❑98, Sep 1961 20.00
❑99, Oct 1961 20.00
❑100, Nov 1961, CCB (a) 20.00
❑101, Jan 1962 16.00

Flipper

Beloved TV dolphin flopped in comics
©Gold Key

Forbidden Tales of Dark Mansion

Dark Mansion of Forbidden Love continues
©DC

Forbidden Worlds

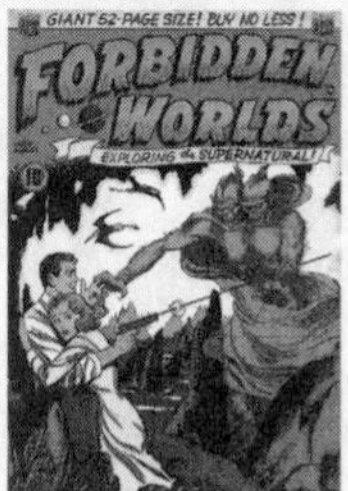

ACG's horror title spawned Herbie
©ACG

Force of Buddha's Palm

Hong Kong publisher tried American market
©Jademan

Force Works

Avengers task force featured Iron Man
©Marvel

	N-MINT
❑102, Mar 1962	16.00
❑103, May 1962	16.00
❑104, Jul 1962	16.00
❑105, Aug 1962	16.00
❑106, Sep 1962	16.00
❑107, Oct 1962	16.00
❑108, Nov 1962	16.00
❑109, Jan 1963	16.00
❑110, Mar 1963, A: Herbie.	35.00
❑111, May 1963	16.00
❑112, Jul 1963	16.00
❑113, Aug 1963	16.00
❑114, Sep 1963, A: Herbie.	35.00
❑115, Oct 1963	16.00
❑116, Nov 1963, A: Herbie.	30.00
❑117, Jan 1964	16.00
❑118, Mar 1964	16.00
❑119, May 1964	16.00
❑120, Jul 1964	16.00
❑121, Aug 1964	12.00
❑122, Sep 1964	12.00
❑123, Oct 1964	12.00
❑124, Nov 1964	12.00
❑125, Jan 1965, O: Magicman. 1: Magicman.	25.00
❑126, Mar 1965	12.00
❑127, May 1965	12.00
❑128, Jul 1965, A: Magicman.	14.00
❑129, Aug 1965	12.00
❑130, Sep 1965, A: Magicman.	14.00
❑131, Oct 1965	12.00
❑132, Nov 1965	12.00
❑133, Jan 1966	12.00
❑134, Mar 1966	12.00
❑135, May 1966	12.00
❑136, Jul 1966	12.00
❑137, Aug 1966	12.00
❑138, Sep 1966	12.00
❑139, Oct 1966	12.00
❑140, Nov 1966	12.00
❑141, Jan 1967	10.00
❑142, Mar 1967	10.00
❑143, May 1967	10.00
❑144, Jul 1967	10.00
❑145, Aug 1967	10.00

FORBIDDEN WORLDS (A+)
A-PLUS

❑1, b&w; Reprints	2.50

FORBIDDEN WORLDS (AVALON)
AVALON

❑1	2.95

FORBIDDEN X ANGEL
ANGEL

❑1	2.95

FORBIDDEN ZONE
GALAXY ENTERTAINMENT

❑1,	5.95

FORCE 10
CROW

❑1 1: Impel.	2.50
❑1/Ashcan; Ashcan preview edition 1: Flux. 1: Armadillos. 1: Spook. 1: Rukh. 1: Lodestar. 1: Teknik. 1: Leprechaun. 1: Force 10.	3.00

FORCE OF BUDDHA'S PALM
JADEMAN

	N-MINT
❑1, ca. 1988	2.00
❑2, ca. 1988	1.95
❑3, ca. 1988	1.95
❑4, ca. 1988	1.95
❑5, ca. 1988	1.95
❑6, ca. 1989	1.95
❑7, ca. 1989	1.95
❑8, ca. 1989	1.95
❑9, ca. 1989	1.95
❑10, ca. 1989	1.95
❑11, ca. 1989	1.95
❑12, ca. 1989	1.95
❑13, ca. 1989	1.95
❑14, ca. 1989	1.95
❑15, ca. 1989	1.95
❑16, ca. 1989	1.95
❑17, ca. 1989	1.95
❑18, ca. 1990	1.95
❑19, ca. 1990	1.95
❑20, ca. 1990	1.95
❑21, ca. 1990	1.95
❑22, ca. 1990	1.95
❑23, ca. 1990	1.95
❑24, ca. 1990	1.95
❑25, ca. 1990	1.95
❑26, ca. 1990	1.95
❑27, ca. 1990	1.95
❑28, ca. 1990	1.95
❑29, ca. 1990	1.95
❑30, ca. 1991	1.95
❑31, ca. 1991	1.95
❑32, ca. 1991	1.95
❑33, ca. 1991	1.95
❑34, ca. 1991	1.95
❑35, ca. 1991	1.95
❑36, ca. 1991	1.95
❑37, ca. 1991	1.95
❑38, ca. 1991	1.95
❑39, ca. 1991	1.95
❑40, ca. 1991	1.95
❑41, ca. 1991	1.95
❑42, ca. 1992	1.95
❑43, Feb 1992	1.95
❑44, Mar 1992	1.95
❑45	1.95
❑46, Apr 1992	1.95
❑47, May 1992	1.95
❑48, Jun 1992	1.95
❑49, Jul 1992	1.95
❑50, Sep 1992	1.95
❑51, Oct 1992	1.95
❑52, Nov 1992	1.95
❑53, Dec 1992	1.95
❑54, Jan 1993	1.95
❑55, Feb 1993	1.95

FORCE SEVEN
LONE STAR

❑1, Aug 1999	2.95
❑2, Sep 1999	2.95
❑3, Mar 2000	2.95

FORCE WORKS
MARVEL

	N-MINT
❑1, Jul 1994; Giant-size; Pop-up cover	3.95
❑2, Aug 1994	1.50
❑3, Sep 1994	1.50
❑4, Oct 1994	1.50
❑5, Nov 1994	1.50
❑5/CS, Nov 1994; with sericel	2.95
❑6, Dec 1994	1.50
❑7, Jan 1995	1.50
❑8, Feb 1995	1.50
❑9, Mar 1995	1.50
❑10, Apr 1995	1.50
❑11, May 1995	1.50
❑12, Jun 1995	2.50
❑13, Jul 1995	1.50
❑14, Aug 1995	1.50
❑15, Sep 1995	1.50
❑16, Oct 1995	1.50
❑17, Nov 1995	1.50
❑18, Dec 1995	1.50
❑19, Jan 1996	1.50
❑20, Feb 1996	1.50
❑21, Mar 1996	1.50
❑22, Apr 1996	1.50
❑Ashcan 1; ashcan edition	0.75

FORE/PUNK
PARODY

❑1/A; punk cover	2.50
❑1/B; fore cover	2.50

FORETERNITY
ANTARCTIC

❑1, Jul 1997, b&w	2.95
❑2, Sep 1997, b&w	2.95
❑3, Nov 1997, b&w	2.95
❑4, Jan 1998, b&w	2.95

FOREVER AMBER
IMAGE

❑1/A, Jul 1999	2.95
❑1/B, Jul 1999, alternate cover has white background	2.95
❑2, Aug 1999	2.95
❑3, Sep 1999	2.95
❑4, Oct 1999	2.95

FOREVER MAELSTROM
DC

❑1, Jan 2003	2.95
❑2, Feb 2003	2.95
❑3, Mar 2003	2.95
❑4, Apr 2003	2.95
❑5, May 2003	2.95
❑6, Jun 2003	2.95

FOREVER NOW
ENTERTAINMENT

❑1	1.50
❑2	1.50

FOREVER PEOPLE
DC

❑1, Mar 1971, JK (w); JK (a); O: Forever People. Darkseid	35.00
❑2, May 1971, JK (w); JK (a); 1: Desaad. 1: Mantis (DC). Darkseid	20.00

Other grades: Multiply price above by 5/6 for VF/NM • 2/3 for VERY FINE • 1/3 for FINE • 1/5 for VERY GOOD • 1/8 for GOOD

N-MINT

❑3, Jul 1971, JK (w); JK (a); 1: Glorious Godfrey. Darkseid.......... 18.00
❑4, Sep 1971; JK (w); JK (a); Darkseid 18.00
❑5, Nov 1971; Giant-size JK (w); JK (a) 18.00
❑6, Jan 1972; Giant-size; JK (w); JK (a); A: Sandy. A: Sandman. Darkseid..... 14.00
❑7, Mar 1972 JK (w); JK (a)........ 14.00
❑8, May 1972; JK (w); JK (a); Darkseid 14.00
❑9, Jul 1972 JK (w); JK (a)........ 14.00
❑10, Jul 1972, JK (w); JK (a)........ 14.00
❑11, Nov 1972, JK (w); JK (a); 1: The Pursuer.......... 14.00

FOREVER PEOPLE (MINI-SERIES)
DC

❑1, Feb 1988........ 2.00
❑2, Mar 1988........ 2.00
❑3, Apr 1988........ 2.00
❑4, May 1988........ 2.00
❑5, Jun 1988........ 2.00
❑6, Jul 1988........ 2.00

FOREVER WARRIORS
CFD

❑1, May 1997........ 2.95

FORGE
CROSSGEN

❑1, May 2002........ 9.95
❑2, Jun 2002........ 9.95
❑3, Jul 2002........ 9.95
❑4, Aug 2002........ 11.95
❑5, Sep 2002........ 11.95
❑6, Oct 2002........ 11.95
❑7, Nov 2002........ 11.95
❑8, Dec 2002........ 7.95
❑9, Jan 2003........ 7.95
❑10, Feb 2003........ 7.95
❑11, Mar 2003........ 7.95
❑12, Apr 2003........ 7.95
❑13, May 2003........ 7.95

FORGOTTEN REALMS (DC)
DC

❑1, Sep 1989........ 1.50
❑2, Oct 1989........ 1.00
❑3, Nov 1989........ 1.00
❑4, Dec 1989........ 1.00
❑5, Jan 1990........ 1.00
❑6, Feb 1990........ 1.00
❑7, Mar 1990........ 1.00
❑8, Apr 1990........ 1.00
❑9, May 1990........ 1.00
❑10, Jun 1990........ 1.00
❑11, Jul 1990........ 1.00
❑12, Aug 1990........ 1.00
❑13, Sep 1990........ 1.00
❑14, Oct 1990........ 1.00
❑15, Nov 1990........ 1.00
❑16, Dec 1990........ 1.00
❑17, Jan 1991........ 1.00
❑18, Feb 1991........ 1.00
❑19, Mar 1991........ 1.00
❑20, Apr 1991........ 1.00
❑21, May 1991........ 1.00
❑22, Jun 1991........ 1.00
❑23, Jul 1991........ 1.00
❑24, Aug 1991........ 1.00
❑25, Sep 1991........ 1.00
❑Annual 1, ca. 1990........ 1.50

FORGOTTEN REALMS: EXILE
DEVIL'S DUE

❑1, Nov 2005,........ 2.99
❑1/Special, Nov 2005........ 2.99
❑2, Jan 2006........ 2.99
❑2/Special, Jan 2006........ 2.99
❑3, Feb 2006........ 2.99
❑3/Special, Feb 2006........ 2.99

FORGOTTEN REALMS: HOMELAND
DEVIL'S DUE

❑1, Aug 2005........ 5.00
❑1/Variant, Aug 2005........ 9.00
❑1/Conv, Aug 2005, Available at San Diego 2005 ($10); 500 produced; Tyler Walpole cover........ 10.00
❑2, Sep 2005........ 4.95
❑2/Variant, Sep 2005........ 8.95
❑3, Oct 2005........ 4.95
❑3/Variant, Oct 2005........ 4.95

FORGOTTEN REALMS: SOJOURN
DEVIL'S DUE

❑1, Apr 2006........ 3.99
❑1/Variant, Apr 2006........ 3.99
❑2, May 2006........ 3.99
❑2/Special, May 2006........ 3.99
❑3, Jun 2006........ 3.99
❑3/Special, Jun 2006........ 3.99

FORGOTTEN REALMS: THE GRAND TOUR
TSR

❑1; no cover price........ 1.00

FOR LOVERS ONLY
CHARLTON

❑60, Aug 1971........ 20.00
❑61, Oct 1971........ 10.00
❑62, Dec 1971........ 10.00
❑63, Feb 1972........ 10.00
❑64, Apr 1972, Shirley Jones pin-up.. 10.00
❑65, Jun 1972........ 10.00
❑66, Aug 1972........ 10.00
❑67, Oct 1972, Bobby Sherman pictures........ 10.00
❑68, Dec 1972........ 10.00
❑69, Feb 1973........ 10.00
❑70, Apr 1973........ 10.00
❑71, Jun 1973........ 10.00
❑72, Aug 1973........ 10.00
❑73, Oct 1973........ 10.00
❑74, Dec 1973........ 10.00
❑75, Sep 1974........ 10.00
❑76, Nov 1974........ 10.00
❑77, ca. 1975........ 10.00
❑78, ca. 1975........ 10.00
❑79, Jun 1975........ 10.00
❑80, ca. 1975........ 10.00
❑81, Oct 1975........ 10.00
❑82, Dec 1975........ 10.00
❑83, ca. 1976........ 10.00
❑84, ca. 1976........ 10.00
❑85, ca. 1976........ 10.00
❑86, ca. 1976........ 10.00
❑87, Nov 1976........ 10.00

FORMERLY KNOWN AS THE JUSTICE LEAGUE
DC

❑1, Sep 2003........ 2.50
❑2, Oct 2003........ 2.50
❑3, Nov 2003........ 2.50
❑4, Dec 2003........ 2.50
❑5, Jan 2004........ 2.50
❑6, Feb 2004........ 2.50

FORSAKEN
IMAGE

❑1, Aug 2004........ 2.95
❑2, 2004........ 2.95
❑3, 2004........ 2.95

FORT: PROPHET OF THE UNEXPLAINED
DARK HORSE

❑1, Jun 2002........ 2.99
❑2, Jul 2002........ 2.99
❑3, Aug 2002........ 2.99
❑4, Sep 2002........ 2.99

FORTUNE AND GLORY
ONI

❑1, Dec 1999, b&w........ 4.95
❑2, Feb 2000, b&w........ 4.95
❑3, Apr 2000, b&w........ 4.95

FORTUNE'S FOOL, THE STORY OF JINXER
CRANIUM

❑0, Jul 1999........ 2.95

FORTUNE'S FRIENDS: HELL WEEK
ARIA

❑1; graphic novel........ 6.95

FORTY WINKS
ODD JOBS LIMITED

❑1, Nov 1997........ 2.95
❑2, Dec 1997........ 2.95
❑3, Mar 1998........ 2.95
❑4, Jun 1998........ 2.95

FORTY WINKS CHRISTMAS SPECIAL
PEREGRINE ENTERTAINMENT

❑1, Aug 1998, b&w........ 2.95

FORTY WINKS SUPER SPECIAL EDITION: TV PARTY TONITE!
PEREGRINE ENTERTAINMENT

❑1, Apr 1999, b&w........ 2.95

FOTON EFFECT
ACED

❑1, Oct 1986........ 1.50
❑2........ 1.50
❑3........ 1.50

FOUL!
TRAITORS GAIT

❑1........ 3.00

4
MARVEL

❑1, Oct 2000; Universe X tie-in; Sue Richards restored to life........ 3.99

4-D MONKEY
DR. LEUNG'S

❑1 1988........ 2.00
❑2 1988........ 2.00
❑3 1988........ 2.00
❑4 1989........ 2.00
❑5 1989........ 2.00
❑6 1989........ 2.00
❑7 1989........ 2.00
❑8 1989........ 2.00
❑9 1990........ 2.00
❑10 1990........ 2.00
❑11 1990........ 2.00
❑12 1990........ 2.00

FOUR HORSEMEN
DC / VERTIGO

❑1, Feb 2000........ 2.50
❑2, Mar 2000........ 2.50
❑3, Apr 2000........ 2.50
❑4, May 2000........ 2.50

FOUR KUNOICHI, THE: BLOODLUST
LIGHTNING

❑1, Dec 1996, b&w; Standard edition. 2.75
❑1/Nude; Nude cover........ 9.95
❑1/Platinum; Platinum edition........ 9.95
❑1/Platinum Nude; Platinum Nude edition........ 4.00

FOUR KUNOICHI: ENTER THE SINJA
LIGHTNING

❑1, Feb 1997, b&w........ 2.95

411
MARVEL

❑1, Jun 2003, cardstock cover........ 3.50
❑2, Jul 2003, cardstock cover........ 3.50

FOUR-STAR BATTLE TALES
DC

❑1, Feb 1973, Reprints........ 20.00
❑2, May 1973, Reprints........ 7.00
❑3, Aug 1973, Reprints........ 6.00
❑4, Oct 1973, Reprints........ 6.00
❑5, Nov 1973, Reprints........ 6.00

FOUR STAR SPECTACULAR
DC

❑1, Apr 1976, Giant-size........ 12.00
❑2, Jun 1976, Giant-size........ 7.00
❑3, Aug 1976, Giant-size; Bicentennial #15........ 7.00
❑4, Oct 1976, Giant-size........ 7.00
❑5, Dec 1976, Giant-size........ 7.00
❑6, Feb 1977, Giant-size........ 7.00

FOURTH WORLD (JACK KIRBY'S...)
DC

❑1, Mar 1997 JBy (w); JBy (a)........ 2.50
❑2, Apr 1997 JBy (w); JBy (a)........ 2.00
❑3, May 1997 JBy (w); JBy (a)........ 2.00
❑4, Jun 1997 JBy (w); JBy (a)........ 2.00
❑5, Jul 1997 JBy (w); JBy (a)........ 2.00
❑6, Aug 1997 JBy (w); JBy (a)........ 2.00
❑7, Sep 1997 JBy (w); JBy (a)........ 2.00
❑8, Oct 1997; JBy (w); JBy (a); Genesis 2.00
❑9, Nov 1997 JBy (w); JBy (a)........ 2.00
❑10, Dec 1997; JBy (w); JBy (a); Face cover........ 2.00
❑11, Jan 1998 JBy (w); JBy (a)........ 2.00
❑12, Feb 1998 JBy (w); JBy (a)........ 2.00

Other grades: Multiply price above by 5/6 for VF/NM • 2/3 for VERY FINE • 1/3 for FINE • 1/5 for VERY GOOD • 1/8 for GOOD

Forever People

Fourth World youngsters flee Darkseid
©DC

Four-Star Battle Tales

Reprints DC war stories
©DC

Fox and the Crow

Stanley and His Monster took over title
©DC

Fractured Fairy Tales

Bullwinkle feature s pawned one-shot
©Gold Key

Fraggle Rock (Star)

Muppet-like characters frolic underground
©Marvel

N-MINT

❑13, Mar 1998 JBy (w); JBy (a) 2.00
❑14, Apr 1998; JBy (w); JBy (a); Darkseid and Ares escape Source Wall 2.00
❑15, May 1998 JBy (w); JBy (a) 2.00
❑16, Jun 1998 JBy (w); JBy (a) 2.00
❑17, Jul 1998 JBy (w); JBy (a) 2.00
❑18, Aug 1998 JBy (w); JBy (a) 2.00
❑19, Sep 1998; JBy (w); JBy (a); Return of Supertown 2.25
❑20, Oct 1998 JBy (a); A: Superman. 2.25

FOURTH WORLD GALLERY
DC

❑1 1996; pin-ups based on Jack Kirby creations 3.50

FOUR WOMEN
DC / HOMAGE

❑1, Dec 2001 2.95
❑2, Jan 2002 2.95
❑3, Feb 2002 2.95
❑4, Mar 2002 2.95
❑5, Apr 2002 2.95

FOX AND THE CROW
DC

❑36, Oct 1956 85.00
❑37, Dec 1956 85.00
❑38, Feb 1957 85.00
❑39, Mar 1957 85.00
❑40, Apr 1957 85.00
❑41, Jun 1957 60.00
❑42, Aug 1957 60.00
❑43, Sep 1957 60.00
❑44, Oct 1957 60.00
❑45, Dec 1957 60.00
❑46, Feb 1958 60.00
❑47, Mar 1958 60.00
❑48, Apr 1958 60.00
❑49, Jun 1958 60.00
❑50, Aug 1958 60.00
❑51, Sep 1958 60.00
❑52, Oct 1958 60.00
❑53, Dec 1958 60.00
❑54, Mar 1959 60.00
❑55, May 1959 60.00
❑56, Jul 1959 60.00
❑57, Sep 1959 60.00
❑58, Nov 1959 60.00
❑59, Jan 1960 60.00
❑60, Mar 1960 60.00
❑61, May 1960 60.00
❑62, Jul 1960 42.00
❑63, Sep 1960 42.00
❑64, Nov 1960 42.00
❑65, Jan 1961 42.00
❑66, Mar 1961 42.00
❑67, May 1961 42.00
❑68, Jul 1961 42.00
❑69, Sep 1961 42.00
❑70, Nov 1961 42.00
❑71, Jan 1962 42.00
❑72, Mar 1962 42.00
❑73, May 1962 42.00
❑74, Jul 1962 42.00
❑75, Sep 1962 42.00

N-MINT

❑76, Nov 1962 42.00
❑77, Jan 1963 42.00
❑78, Mar 1963 42.00
❑79, May 1963 42.00
❑80, Jul 1963 42.00
❑81, Sep 1963 26.00
❑82, Nov 1963 26.00
❑83, Jan 1964 26.00
❑84, Mar 1964 26.00
❑85, May 1964 26.00
❑86, Jul 1964 26.00
❑87, Sep 1964 26.00
❑88, Nov 1964 26.00
❑89, Jan 1965 26.00
❑90, Feb 1965 26.00
❑91, May 1965 26.00
❑92, Jul 1965 26.00
❑93, Sep 1965 26.00
❑94, Nov 1965 26.00
❑95, Dec 1965, O: Stanley and His Monster. 1: Stanley and His Monster. 50.00
❑96, Mar 1966 22.00
❑97, May 1966 22.00
❑98, Jul 1966 22.00
❑99, Sep 1966 22.00
❑100, Nov 1966 22.00
❑101, Jan 1967 18.00
❑102, Mar 1967 18.00
❑103, May 1967 18.00
❑104, Jul 1967 18.00
❑105, Sep 1967, A: Stanley and His Monster. 18.00
❑106, Nov 1967 18.00
❑107, Jan 1968 18.00
❑108, Mar 1968, Series continued in Stanley and His Monster 18.00

FOX COMICS
FANTAGRAPHICS

❑24, b&w 2.95
❑25, b&w 2.95
❑26, b&w 2.95
❑Special 1, b&w; Australian; Special 2.95

FOX COMICS LEGENDS SERIES
FANTAGRAPHICS

❑1, Jul 1992, b&w; Three Stooges 2.50
❑2, b&w; Elvis 2.50

FOXFIRE (MALIBU)
MALIBU / ULTRAVERSE

❑1, Feb 1996 1.50
❑2, Mar 1996 1.50
❑3, Apr 1996 1.50
❑4, May 1996 1.50

FOXFIRE (NIGHT WYND)
NIGHTWYND

❑1, b&w 2.50
❑2, b&w 2.50
❑3, b&w 2.50

FOX KIDS FUNHOUSE
ACCLAIM

❑1, digest; The Tick, Life with Louie, Bobby's World 4.50
❑2, 4.50

N-MINT

FRACTION
DC / FOCUS

❑1, Jun 2004 2.50
❑2, Jul 2004 2.50
❑3, Aug 2004 2.50
❑4, Sep 2004 2.50
❑5, Oct 2004 2.50
❑6, Nov 2004 2.50

FRACTURED FAIRY TALES
GOLD KEY

❑1, Oct 1962 75.00

FRAGGLE ROCK (STAR)
MARVEL / STAR

❑1, Apr 1985 1.50
❑2, Jun 1985 1.25
❑3, Aug 1985 1.25
❑4, Oct 1985 1.25
❑5, Dec 1985 1.25
❑6, Feb 1986 1.25
❑7, Apr 1986 1.25
❑8, Jun 1986 1.25

FRAGGLE ROCK (MARVEL)
MARVEL

❑1, Apr 1988, Reprints 1.50
❑2, Jun 1988, Reprints 1.00
❑3, Jun 1988, Reprints 1.00
❑4, Jul 1988, Reprints 1.00
❑5, Aug 1988, Reprints 1.00

FRAGILE PROPHET
LOST IN THE DARK

❑1, Sep 2005 2.95

FRAGMENTS
SCREAMING CAT

❑1 2.50

FRANCIS, BROTHER OF THE UNIVERSE
MARVEL

❑1 1.50

FRANK (NEMESIS)
NEMESIS

❑1, Apr 1994; newsstand 1.75
❑1/Direct ed., Apr 1994; variant cover: direct sale 2.50
❑2, May 1994; newsstand 1.75
❑2/Direct ed., May 1994; direct sale 2.50
❑3, Jun 1994; newsstand 1.75
❑3/Direct ed., Jun 1994; direct sale 2.50
❑4, Jul 1994; newsstand 1.75
❑4/Direct ed., Jul 1994; direct sale 2.50

FRANK (FANTAGRAPHICS)
FANTAGRAPHICS

❑1, Sep 1996, b&w 2.95
❑2, Dec 1997, b&w 3.95

FRANK FRAZETTA FANTASY ILLUSTRATED
FRANK FRAZETTA FANTASY ILLUSTRATED

❑1, Spr 1998 7.00
❑1/Variant, Spr 1998; alternate cover 7.00
❑2, Sum 1998; Battle Chasers story 6.00
❑2/Variant, Sum 1998; alternate cover 6.00
❑3, Fal 1998 6.00

Other grades: Multiply price above by 5/6 for VF/NM • 2/3 for VERY FINE • 1/3 for FINE • 1/5 for VERY GOOD • 1/8 for GOOD

N-MINT

❑3/Variant, Fal 1998; alternate cover 6.00
❑4, Win 1998 5.99
❑4/Variant, Win 1998; alternate cover 6.00
❑5, Mar 1999 5.99
❑5/Variant, Mar 1999; alternate cover 7.50
❑6, May 1999 6.00
❑6/Variant, May 1999; alternate cover 6.00
❑7, Jul 1999 5.99
❑7/Variant, Jul 1999; alternate cover 5.99

FRANK IN THE RIVER
TUNDRA
❑1; "Tantalizing Stories Presents Frank in the River" 2.95

FRANK THE UNICORN
FRAGMENTS WEST
❑1, Sep 1986 2.00
❑2, Nov 1986 2.00
❑3, Jan 1987 2.00
❑4 2.00
❑5 2.00
❑6 2.00
❑7 2.00
❑8 2.00
❑9 2.00

FRANK ZAPPA: VIVA LA BIZARRE
REVOLUTIONARY
❑1, Feb 1994, b&w 3.00

FRANKENSTEIN (DELL)
DELL
❑1, Mar 1963 35.00
❑2, Sep 1966 25.00
❑3, Dec 1966 15.00
❑4, Mar 1967 15.00

FRANKENSTEIN (THE MONSTER OF...)
MARVEL
❑1, Jan 1973, MP (c); MP (a); O: Frankenstein's Monster 40.00
❑2, Mar 1973, MP (c); MP (w); MP (a); O: Bride of Frankenstein 15.00
❑3, May 1973, MP (c) 9.00
❑4, Jul 1973 9.00
❑5, Sep 1973 9.00
❑6, Oct 1973, Cover changes titles to "The Frankenstein Monster" 7.00
❑7, Nov 1973 7.00
❑8, Jan 1974, A: Dracula. Meets Dracula 18.00
❑9, Mar 1974, A: Dracula. Marvel Value Stamp #68: Son of Satan 20.00
❑10, May 1974, Marvel Value Stamp #69: Marvel Girl 6.00
❑11, Jul 1974, V: Ivan. Marvel Value Stamp #12: Daredevil 5.00
❑12, Sep 1974, The monster comes to the modern day; Marvel Value Stamp #59: Golem 5.00
❑13, Nov 1974, Marvel Value Stamp #60: Ka-Zar 5.00
❑14, Jan 1975, Marvel Value Stamp #90: Hercules 5.00
❑15, Mar 1975, VM, KJ (a); Back-up story reprinted from Tales of Suspense #10 5.00
❑16, May 1975, 1: Veronica Frankenstein. 1: Berserker. Marvel Value Stamp #8: Captain America 5.00
❑17, Jul 1975, V: Berserker. Monster regains speech 5.00
❑18, Sep 1975, 5.00

FRANKENSTEIN (ETERNITY)
ETERNITY
❑1, b&w 2.00
❑2, b&w 2.00
❑3, Aug 1989, b&w 2.00

FRANKENSTEIN (MARY SHELLEY'S...)
TOPPS
❑1, Oct 1994 2.95
❑2, 2.95
❑3, 2.95
❑4, 2.95

FRANKENSTEIN/DRACULA WAR
TOPPS
❑1, Feb 1995 2.50
❑2 2.50
❑3 2.50

FRANKENSTEIN JR.
GOLD KEY
❑1, Jan 1967 55.00

FRANKENSTEIN MOBSTER
IMAGE
❑0, Oct 2003 2.95
❑1, Dec 2003 2.95
❑2, Feb 2004 2.95
❑3, May 2004 2.95
❑4 2004 3.00
❑5 2004 3.00
❑6 2004 3.00
❑7/A, Dec 2004 2.95
❑7/B, Dec 2004 2.95

FRANKENSTEIN: OR THE MODERN PROMETHEUS
CALIBER
❑1 2.95

FRANK IRONWINE (WARREN ELLIS')
AVATAR
❑1 3.50
❑1/Foil 20.00

FRANKLIN RICHARDS, SON OF A GENIUS - EVERYBODY LOVES FRANKLIN
MARVEL
❑1, Apr 2006 3.99

FRAY
DARK HORSE
❑1, Jun 2001 3.00
❑2, Jul 2001 2.99
❑3, Aug 2001 2.99
❑4, Sep 2001 2.99
❑5, Oct 2001 2.99
❑6, Nov 2001 2.99
❑7, Apr 2003 2.99
❑8, ca. 2003 2.99
❑Book 1, ca. 2003 19.95

FREAK FORCE
IMAGE
❑1, Dec 1993 KG, EL (w); 1: Freak Force 2.00
❑2, Jan 1994 1.95
❑3, Feb 1994 1.95
❑4, Mar 1994 A: Vanguard 1.95
❑5, Apr 1994 1.95
❑6, Jun 1994; Identity of Mighty Man revealed 1.95
❑7, Jul 1994 1.95
❑8, Aug 1994 2.50
❑9, Sep 1994 A: Cyber Force 2.50
❑10, Oct 1994 2.50
❑11, Nov 1994 2.50
❑12, Dec 1994 2.50
❑13, Jan 1995; Jerry Ordway pin-up 2.50
❑13/A, Jan 1995; alternate cover 2.50
❑14, Feb 1995 2.50
❑15, Mar 1995 A: Maxx 2.50
❑16, Apr 1995 2.50
❑17, Jun 1995 2.50
❑18, Jul 1995 2.50

FREAK FORCE (MINI-SERIES)
IMAGE
❑1, Apr 1997 2.95
❑2, May 1997 2.95
❑3, Jul 1997 2.95

FREAK OUT ON INFANT EARTHS
BLACKTHORNE
❑1, Jan 1987 2.00
❑2 2.00

FREAKS
FANTAGRAPHICS / EROS
❑1 2.25
❑2 2.25
❑3 2.25

FREAKS' AMOUR
DARK HORSE
❑1 3.95
❑2 3.95
❑3 3.95

FREAKS OF THE HEARTLAND
DARK HORSE
❑1, Jan 2004 2.99
❑2, Mar 2004 2.99
❑3, May 2004 2.99
❑4 2004 2.99
❑5 2004 2.99
❑6 3.00

FRED & BIANCA CENSORSHIP SUCKS SPECIAL
COMICS INTERVIEW
❑1, b&w; Reprints 2.25

FRED & BIANCA MOTHER'S DAY MASSACRE
COMICS INTERVIEW
❑1, b&w; Reprints 2.25

FRED & BIANCA VALENTINE'S DAY MASSACRE
COMICS INTERVIEW
❑1, b&w; Reprints 2.25

FRED THE CLOWN
HOTEL FRED
❑1, Sep 2001 2.95
❑2, Jan 2002 2.95

FREDDY
DELL
❑1, Jul 1964 10.00
❑2, Sep 1964 8.00
❑3, Dec 1964 6.00

FREDDY KRUEGER'S NIGHTMARE ON ELM STREET
MARVEL
❑1, Oct 1989, b&w; magazine RB, AA, TD (a); O: Freddy Krueger. 4.50
❑2, Nov 1989, b&w; magazine AA, TD (a) 4.00

FREDDY'S DEAD: THE FINAL NIGHTMARE
INNOVATION
❑1 2.50
❑1/3D; part 3-D 2.50
❑2 2.50
❑3 2.50
❑3/3D; 3-D version of #3; Requires glasses provided at movie showings 2.50

FREDERIC REMINGTON: THE MAN WHO PAINTED THE WEST
TOME
❑1, b&w 2.95

FRED HEMBECK DESTROYS THE MARVEL UNIVERSE
MARVEL
❑1, Jul 1989 1.50

FRED HEMBECK SELLS THE MARVEL UNIVERSE
MARVEL
❑1, Oct 1990, FH (w); FH (a) 1.50

FRED THE POSSESSED FLOWER
HAPPY PREDATOR
❑1, b&w 2.95
❑2, b&w 2.95
❑3, b&w 2.95
❑4, b&w 2.95
❑5, b&w 2.95
❑6, b&w 2.95

FREE CEREBUS
AARDVARK-VANAHEIM
❑1, b&w; giveaway 1.00

FREE LAUGHS
DESCHAINE
❑1, b&w 1.00

FREE SPEECHES
ONI
❑1, Aug 1998; collects Nadine Strossen, Dave Sim, Neil Gaiman, and Frank Miller speeches; Fundraiser for Comic Book Legal Defense Fund 2.95

FREE-VIEW
ACCLAIM
❑1, Mar 1993 VM (a) 1.00

FREEBOOTERS/YOUNG GODS/ PARADOXMAN PREVIEW
DARK HORSE
❑1 1.00

Frankenstein Mobster

Lawman merges with gangsters he killed

©Image

Fred Hembeck Destroys the Marvel Universe

Every Marvel character dies

©Marvel

Free Speeches

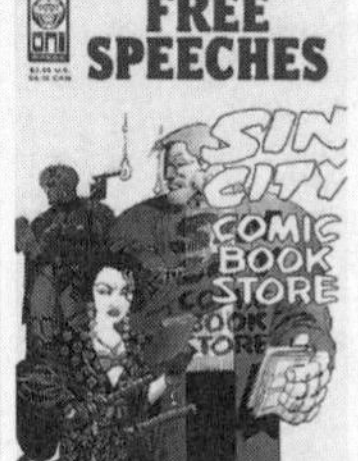

Comic Book Legal Defense Fund fundraiser

©Oni

French Ice

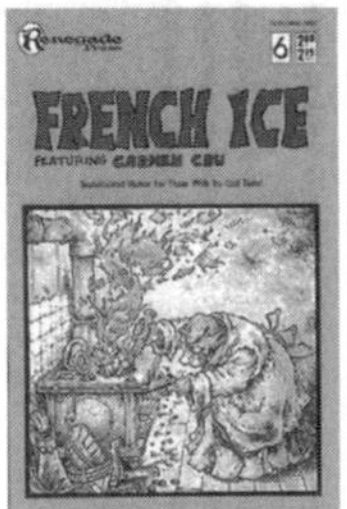

Crotchety old woman's tangles with authority

©Renegade

Friendly Ghost, Casper

Dyslexic title still confuses collectors

©Harvey

N-MINT

FREEDOM AGENT
Gold Key

❑1, Apr 1963 .... 24.00

FREEDOM FIGHTERS
DC

❑1, Apr 1976, RE (a); 1: Silver Ghost. V: Silver Ghost. Freedom Fighters arrive on Earth-1 .... 12.00
❑2, Jun 1976, V: Silver Ghost. 5.00
❑3, Aug 1976, A: Wonder Woman. Bicentennial #8 .... 5.00
❑4, Oct 1976, A: Wonder Woman. 4.00
❑5, Dec 1976 .... 4.00
❑6, Feb 1977 .... 4.00
❑7, Apr 1977 .... 4.00
❑8, Jun 1977, V: Crusaders. 4.00
❑9, Aug 1977, V: Crusaders. 4.00
❑10, Oct 1977, O: Doll Man. V: Cat-Man. 4.00
❑11, Dec 1977, O: Ray. 4.00
❑12, Feb 1978, O: Firebrand I (Rod Reilly). 4.00
❑13, Apr 1978, O: Black Condor. 4.00
❑14, Jun 1978, A: Batwoman. A: Batgirl. 4.00
❑15, Aug 1978, O: Phantom Lady. events continue in Secret Society of Super Villains #16 .... 4.00

FREEDOM FORCE
Image

❑1, Mar 2005 .... 2.95
❑2, Apr 2005 .... 2.95
❑3, May 2005 .... 2.95
❑4, Jun 2005 .... 2.95
❑5, Jul 2005 .... 2.95
❑6, Aug 2005 .... 2.95

FREEFLIGHT
Thinkblots

❑1, Apr 1994 .... 2.95

FREEJACK
Now

❑1, Apr 1992, newsstand 1.95
❑1/Direct ed., Apr 1992, direct-sale edition 2.50
❑2, May 1992, newsstand 1.95
❑2/Direct ed., May 1992, direct-sale 2.50
❑3, Jun 1992, newsstand 1.95
❑3/Direct ed., Jun 1992, direct-sale 2.50

FREEMIND
Future

❑1 2002 .... 3.50
❑2 2002 .... 3.50
❑3 2003 .... 3.50
❑4 2003 .... 3.50
❑5, Apr 2003 .... 3.50
❑6, May 2003 .... 3.50
❑7, Jul 2003 .... 2.99

FREEWAY NINJA HANZO
SleepyHouse

❑1; Heavyweight premiere issue 3.50

FREEX
Malibu / Ultraverse

❑1, Jul 1993 1: Freex. 1: Pressure. 2.00

N-MINT

❑1/Hologram, Jul 1993; 1: Freex. 1: Pressure. Hologram cover; "Ultra Limited" 5.00
❑2, Aug 1993 1: Rush. 2.00
❑3, Sep 1993 1: Bloodhounds. 2.00
❑4, Oct 1993; Rune 2.50
❑5, Nov 1993 .... 1.95
❑6, Dec 1993; Break-Thru 1.95
❑7, Jan 1994 O: Pressure. O: Hardcase. 1.95
❑8, Feb 1994 .... 1.95
❑9, Mar 1994 O: Sweetface. 1: Contrary. 1.95
❑10, Apr 1994 O: Boomboy. 1.95
❑11, May 1994 O: Plug. 1.95
❑12, Aug 1994 1: The Guardian. 1.95
❑13, Sep 1994 1: Prometheus. 1.95
❑14, Oct 1994 1: The Savior. 1.95
❑15, Jan 1995; 1: Eliminator. 1: Manic. 1: Oyabun. Flip-book with Ultraverse Premiere #9 .... 3.50
❑16, Jan 1995 .... 1.95
❑17, Feb 1995 A: Rune. 2.50
❑18, Feb 1995 1: A.J. Analla. 1: Tulath. 2.50
❑Giant Size 1; Giant-Size Freex #1 1: Pixx. 2.50

FRENCH ICE
Renegade

❑1, b&w 2.00
❑2, Apr 1987, b&w 2.00
❑3, May 1987, b&w 2.00
❑4, Jun 1987, b&w 2.00
❑5, Jul 1987, b&w 2.00
❑6, Sep 1987, b&w 2.00
❑7, Oct 1987, b&w 2.00
❑8, Nov 1987, b&w 2.00
❑9, Dec 1987, b&w 2.00
❑10, Jan 1988, b&w 2.00
❑11, Feb 1988, b&w 2.00
❑12, Mar 1988, b&w 2.00
❑13, Apr 1988, b&w 2.00

FRENCH TICKLERS
Kitchen Sink

❑1, Oct 1989, b&w 2.00
❑2, Oct 1989, b&w 2.00
❑3, Oct 1989, b&w 2.00

FRENZY
Independent

❑1 .... 1.00
❑1/A 1.00

FRESCAZIZIS
Last Gasp

❑1 .... 1.00

FRESH BLOOD FUNNY BOOK
Last Gasp

❑1 .... 1.25

FRESHMEN
Image

❑1/Preview, Jun 2005; Distributed at Wizard World Philadelphia 2005; 1,000 produced 7.00
❑1/Linsner, Aug 2005 .... 4.00
❑1/Migliari, Aug 2005 .... 2.99
❑1/Perez, Aug 2005 .... 4.00
❑2, Sep 2005 .... 2.99
❑3 2005 .... 2.99

N-MINT

❑4 2005 .... 2.99
❑5, Jan 2006 .... 2.99
❑6, Mar 2006 .... 2.99

FRESHMEN YEARBOOK ONE SHOT
Image

❑1, Jan 2006, ... 2.99

FRIENDLY GHOST, CASPER
Harvey

❑1, Aug 1958 .... 190.00
❑2, Sep 1958 .... 100.00
❑3, Oct 1958 .... 85.00
❑4, Nov 1958 .... 55.00
❑5, Jan 1959 .... 55.00
❑6, Feb 1959 .... 46.00
❑7, Mar 1959 .... 46.00
❑8, Apr 1959 .... 46.00
❑9, May 1959 .... 46.00
❑10, Jun 1959 .... 46.00
❑11, Jul 1959 .... 36.00
❑12, Aug 1959 .... 36.00
❑13, Sep 1959 .... 36.00
❑14, Oct 1959 .... 36.00
❑15, Nov 1959 .... 36.00
❑16, Dec 1959 .... 36.00
❑17, Jan 1960 .... 36.00
❑18, Feb 1960 .... 36.00
❑19, Mar 1960 .... 36.00
❑20, Apr 1960 .... 36.00
❑21, May 1960 .... 25.00
❑22, Jun 1960 .... 25.00
❑23, Jul 1960 .... 25.00
❑24, Aug 1960 .... 25.00
❑25, Sep 1960 .... 25.00
❑26, Oct 1960 .... 25.00
❑27, Nov 1960 .... 25.00
❑28, Dec 1960 .... 25.00
❑29, Jan 1961 .... 25.00
❑30, Feb 1961 .... 25.00
❑31, Mar 1961 .... 18.00
❑32, Apr 1961 .... 18.00
❑33, May 1961 .... 18.00
❑34, Jun 1961 .... 18.00
❑35, Jul 1961 .... 18.00
❑36, Aug 1961 .... 18.00
❑37, Sep 1961 .... 18.00
❑38, Oct 1961 .... 18.00
❑39, Nov 1961 .... 18.00
❑40, Dec 1961 .... 18.00
❑41, Jan 1962 .... 15.00
❑42, Feb 1962 .... 15.00
❑43, Mar 1962 .... 15.00
❑44, Apr 1962 .... 15.00
❑45, May 1962 .... 15.00
❑46, Jun 1962 .... 15.00
❑47, Jul 1962 .... 15.00
❑48, Aug 1962 .... 15.00
❑49, Sep 1962 .... 15.00
❑50, Oct 1962 .... 15.00
❑51, Nov 1962 .... 12.00
❑52, Dec 1962 .... 12.00
❑53, Jan 1963 .... 12.00
❑54, Feb 1963 .... 12.00
❑55, Mar 1963 .... 12.00

Other grades: Multiply price above by 5/6 for VF/NM • 2/3 for VERY FINE • 1/3 for FINE • 1/5 for VERY GOOD • 1/8 for GOOD

	N-MINT
❑56, Apr 1963	12.00
❑57, May 1963	12.00
❑58, Jun 1963	12.00
❑59, Jul 1963	12.00
❑60, Aug 1963	12.00
❑61, Sep 1963	10.00
❑62, Oct 1963	10.00
❑63, Nov 1963	10.00
❑64, Dec 1963	10.00
❑65, Jan 1964	10.00
❑66, Feb 1964	10.00
❑67, Mar 1964	10.00
❑68, Apr 1964	10.00
❑69, May 1964	10.00
❑70, Jun 1964	10.00
❑71, Jul 1964	8.00
❑72, Aug 1964	8.00
❑73, Sep 1964	8.00
❑74, Oct 1964	8.00
❑75, Nov 1964	8.00
❑76, Dec 1964	8.00
❑77, Jan 1965	8.00
❑78, Feb 1965	8.00
❑79, Mar 1965	8.00
❑80, Apr 1965	8.00
❑81, May 1965	7.00
❑82, Jun 1965	7.00
❑83, Jul 1965	7.00
❑84, Aug 1965	7.00
❑85, Sep 1965	7.00
❑86, Oct 1965	7.00
❑87, Nov 1965	7.00
❑88, Dec 1965	7.00
❑89, Jan 1966	7.00
❑90, Feb 1966	6.00
❑91, Mar 1966	6.00
❑92, Apr 1966	6.00
❑93, May 1966	6.00
❑94, Jun 1966	6.00
❑95, Jul 1966	6.00
❑96, Aug 1966	6.00
❑97, Sep 1966	6.00
❑98, Oct 1966	6.00
❑99, Nov 1966	6.00
❑100, Dec 1966	6.00
❑101, Jan 1967	5.00
❑102, Feb 1967	5.00
❑103, Mar 1967	5.00
❑104, Apr 1967	5.00
❑105, May 1967	5.00
❑106, Jun 1967	5.00
❑107, Jul 1967	5.00
❑108, Aug 1967	5.00
❑109, Sep 1967	5.00
❑110, Oct 1967	5.00
❑111, Nov 1967	5.00
❑112, Dec 1967	5.00
❑113, Jan 1968	5.00
❑114, Feb 1968	5.00
❑115, Mar 1968	5.00
❑116, Apr 1968	5.00
❑117, May 1968	5.00
❑118, Jun 1968	5.00
❑119, Jul 1968	5.00
❑120, Aug 1968	5.00
❑121, Sep 1968	4.00
❑122, Oct 1968	4.00
❑123, Nov 1968	4.00
❑124, Dec 1968	4.00
❑125, Jan 1969	4.00
❑126, Feb 1969	4.00
❑127, Mar 1969	4.00
❑128, Apr 1969	4.00
❑129, May 1969	4.00
❑130, Jun 1969	4.00
❑131, Jul 1969	4.00
❑132, Aug 1969	4.00
❑133, Sep 1969	4.00
❑134, Oct 1969	4.00
❑135, Nov 1969	4.00
❑136, Dec 1969	4.00
❑137, Jan 1970	4.00
❑138, Feb 1970	4.00
❑139, Mar 1970	4.00
❑140, Apr 1970	4.00
❑141, May 1970	3.00
❑142, Jun 1970	3.00
❑143, Jul 1970	3.00
❑144, Aug 1970	3.00
❑145, Sep 1970	3.00
❑146, Oct 1970	3.00
❑147, Nov 1970	3.00
❑148, Dec 1970	3.00
❑149, Jan 1971	3.00
❑150, Feb 1971	3.00
❑151, Mar 1971	3.00
❑152, Apr 1971	3.00
❑153, May 1971	3.00
❑154, Jun 1971	3.00
❑155, Jul 1971	3.00
❑156, Aug 1971	3.00
❑157, Sep 1971	3.00
❑158, Oct 1971	3.00
❑159, Nov 1971	3.00
❑160, Mar 1972	3.00
❑161, May 1972	3.00
❑162, Jul 1972	3.00
❑163, Sep 1972	3.00
❑164, Nov 1972	3.00
❑165, Jan 1973	3.00
❑166, Mar 1973	3.00
❑167, May 1973	3.00
❑168, Jul 1973	3.00
❑169, Sep 1973	3.00
❑170, Nov 1973	2.00
❑171, Jan 1974	2.00
❑172, Mar 1974	2.00
❑173, May 1974	2.00
❑174, Jul 1974	2.00
❑175, Sep 1974	2.00
❑176, Nov 1974	2.00
❑177, Jan 1975	2.00
❑178, Mar 1975	2.00
❑179, May 1975	2.00
❑180, Jul 1975	2.00
❑181, Sep 1975	2.00
❑182, Nov 1975	2.00
❑183, Jan 1976	2.00
❑184, Mar 1976	2.00
❑185, Apr 1976	2.00
❑186, Jun 1976	2.00
❑187, Aug 1976	2.00
❑188, Oct 1976, Richie Rich in Hostess ad ("Around the World")	2.00
❑189, Dec 1976	2.00
❑190, Feb 1977	2.00
❑191, Apr 1977	2.00
❑192, Jun 1977	2.00
❑193, Aug 1977	2.00
❑194, Oct 1977	2.00
❑195, Dec 1977	2.00
❑196, Feb 1978	2.00
❑197, Apr 1978	2.00
❑198, Jun 1978	2.00
❑199, Aug 1978	2.00
❑200, Oct 1978	2.00
❑201, Dec 1978	2.00
❑202, Feb 1979	2.00
❑203, Apr 1979	2.00
❑204, Jun 1979	2.00
❑205, Aug 1979	2.00
❑206, Oct 1979	2.00
❑207, Dec 1979	2.00
❑208, Feb 1980	2.00
❑209, Apr 1980	2.00
❑210, Jun 1980	2.00
❑211, Aug 1980	2.00
❑212, Oct 1980	2.00
❑213, Dec 1980	2.00
❑214, Feb 1981	2.00
❑215, Apr 1981	2.00
❑216, Jun 1981	2.00
❑217, Aug 1981	2.00
❑218, Oct 1981	2.00
❑219, Dec 1981	2.00
❑220, Feb 1982	2.00
❑221, Apr 1982	2.00
❑222, Jun 1982	2.00
❑223, Aug 1982	2.00
❑224, Oct 1982	2.00
❑225, Oct 1986	2.00
❑226, Nov 1986	2.00
❑227, Dec 1986	2.00
❑228, Jan 1987	2.00
❑229, Feb 1987	2.00
❑230, Mar 1987	2.00
❑231, Apr 1987	2.00
❑232, May 1987	2.00
❑233, Jun 1987	2.00
❑234, Jul 1987	2.00
❑235, Aug 1987	2.00
❑236, Sep 1987	2.00
❑237, Oct 1987	2.00
❑238, Jan 1988	2.00
❑239, Mar 1988	2.00
❑240, May 1988	2.00
❑241, Jul 1988	2.00
❑242, Sep 1988	2.00
❑243, Nov 1988	2.00
❑244, Jan 1989	2.00
❑245, Mar 1989	2.00
❑246, Jul 1989	2.00
❑247, Sep 1989	2.00
❑248, Oct 1989	2.00
❑249, Jan 1990	2.00
❑250, Mar 1990	2.00
❑251, Apr 1990	2.00
❑252, May 1990	2.00
❑253, Jun 1990, Series continued in Casper the Friendly Ghost (2nd series) #254	2.00

FRIENDLY NEIGHBORHOOD SPIDER-MAN
MARVEL

	N-MINT
❑1, Dec 2005	2.99
❑2, Jan 2006	2.99
❑3, Feb 2006	2.99
❑4, Mar 2006	2.99
❑5, May 2006	2.99
❑6, May 2006	2.99
❑7, Jun 2006	2.99
❑8, Jul 2006	2.99
❑9, Aug 2006	2.99

FRIENDS
RENEGADE

	N-MINT
❑1, May 1987, b&w	2.00
❑2, b&w	2.00
❑3, b&w	2.00

FRIENDS OF MAXX
IMAGE

	N-MINT
❑1, Apr 1996; Dude Japan	2.95
❑2, Nov 1996; Broadminded	2.95
❑3, Mar 1997	2.95

FRIGHT
ATLAS-SEABOARD

	N-MINT
❑1, Jun 1975 O: Son of Dracula.	6.00

FRIGHT (ETERNITY)
ETERNITY

	N-MINT
❑1,	2.00
❑2,	2.00
❑3,	2.00
❑4,	2.00
❑5,	2.00
❑6,	2.00
❑7,	2.00
❑8,	2.00
❑9, Apr 1989	2.00
❑10, May 1989	2.00
❑11, Jun 1989	2.00
❑12, Jul 1989	2.00

FRIGHT NIGHT
NOW

	N-MINT
❑1, Oct 1988; Adapts movie	2.50
❑2, Nov 1988; Adapts movie	2.00
❑3, Dec 1988	2.00
❑4, Feb 1989	2.00
❑5, Mar 1989	2.00
❑6, Apr 1989	2.00
❑7, May 1989	2.00
❑8, Jun 1989	2.00
❑9, Jul 1989	2.00
❑10, Aug 1989	2.00
❑11, Sep 1989	2.00
❑12, Oct 1989	2.00
❑13, Nov 1989	2.00
❑14, Dec 1989	2.00
❑15, Jan 1990	2.00

Friends of Maxx

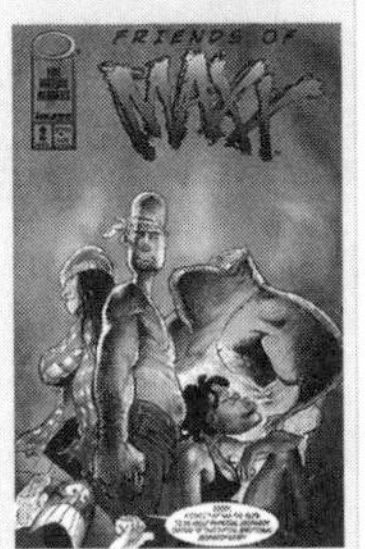

Sam Kieth's purple monster hosts anthology

©Image

Fright Night

Based on 1985 horror host homage

©Now

Frogmen

Underwater investigations began in Four Color

©Dell

From Beyond the Unknown

Science fiction anthology reprinted classics

©DC

From Hell

Jack the Ripper revelations from Alan Moore

©Tundra

N-MINT

❑16, Feb 1990 2.00
❑17, Mar 1990 2.00
❑18, Apr 1990 2.00
❑19, May 1990 2.00
❑20, Jun 1990 2.00
❑21, Jul 1990 2.00
❑22, Aug 1990 2.00

FRIGHT NIGHT 1993 HALLOWEEN ANNUAL
NOW

❑1, Oct 1993; 3-D 2.95

FRIGHT NIGHT 3-D
NOW

❑1, Jun 1992; with glasses 2.95
❑2, Fal 1992; Dracula 2.95

FRIGHT NIGHT 3-D WINTER SPECIAL
NOW

❑1, Win 1993; Brainbats 2.95

FRIGHT NIGHT II GRAPHIC NOVEL
NOW

❑1 3.95

FRINGE
CALIBER

❑1, b&w 2.50
❑2, b&w 2.50
❑3, b&w 2.50
❑4, b&w 2.50
❑5, b&w 2.50
❑6, b&w 2.50
❑7, b&w 2.50
❑8, b&w 2.50

FROGMEN
DELL

❑2, May 1962, Continued from Four Color Comics #1258 34.00
❑3, Sep 1962 26.00
❑4, Feb 1963 20.00
❑5, May 1963, ATh (a) 22.00
❑6, Aug 1963 20.00
❑7, Nov 1963 18.00
❑8, Feb 1964 18.00
❑9, May 1964 18.00
❑10, Aug 1964 18.00
❑11, Nov 1964 18.00

FROM BEYONDE
STUDIO INSIDIO

❑1, b&w 2.25

FROM BEYOND THE UNKNOWN
DC

❑1, Nov 1969 45.00
❑2, Jan 1970 20.00
❑3, Mar 1970 15.00
❑4, May 1970 15.00
❑5, Jul 1970 15.00
❑6, Sep 1970 15.00
❑7, Nov 1970 JKu (c) 12.00
❑8, Jan 1971 12.00
❑9, Mar 1971 12.00
❑10, May 1971 CS (c) 12.00
❑11, Jul 1971 10.00
❑12, Sep 1971 JKu (c) 10.00
❑13, Nov 1971 10.00

N-MINT

❑14, Jan 1972 JKu (c) 10.00
❑15, Mar 1972 10.00
❑16, May 1972 MA, CI (a) 10.00
❑17, Jul 1972 10.00
❑18, Sep 1972 8.00
❑19, Nov 1972 8.00
❑20, Jan 1973 8.00
❑21, Mar 1973, reprints from Strange Adventures #23, #149, and #159 8.00
❑22, May 1973 8.00
❑23, Aug 1973 8.00
❑24, Oct 1973 8.00
❑25, Dec 1973 8.00

FROM DUSK TILL DAWN
BIG

❑1/Deluxe 9.95
❑1 4.95

FROM FAR AWAY
VIZ

❑1, Nov 2004 9.95
❑2, Jan 2005 9.95
❑3, Mar 2005 9.95
❑4, May 2005 9.95
❑5, Jul 2005 9.95
❑6, Sep 2005 9.95
❑7, Nov 2005 9.95

FROM HELL
TUNDRA

❑1, Mar 1991 AMo (w) 6.00
❑1/2nd, Feb 1992 AMo (w) 5.00
❑1/3rd; AMo (w); 3rd printing (Kitchen Sink) 5.00
❑1/4th; 4th printing (Kitchen Sink) 4.95
❑2 AMo (w) 5.00
❑2/2nd; AMo (w); 2nd printing (Kitchen Sink) 5.00
❑2/3rd AMo (w) 5.00
❑3, Dec 1993 AMo (w) 5.00
❑3/2nd AMo (w) 5.00
❑3/3rd AMo (w) 5.00
❑4, Mar 1994 AMo (w) 5.00
❑4/2nd AMo (w) 5.00
❑4/3rd AMo (w) 5.00
❑5, Jun 1994 AMo (w) 4.95
❑6, Nov 1994 AMo (w) 4.95
❑7, Apr 1995 AMo (w) 4.95
❑8, Jul 1995 AMo (w) 4.95
❑9, Apr 1996 AMo (w) 4.95
❑10, Aug 1996; AMo (w); Eleventh issue published as From Hell: Dance of the Gull Catchers 4.95

FROM HELL: DANCE OF THE GULL CATCHERS
KITCHEN SINK

❑1, sequel to From Hell; #11 on spine 7.00

FROM THE DARKNESS
ADVENTURE

❑1 3.00
❑2 2.50
❑3, b&w 2.50
❑4, b&w 2.50

N-MINT

FROM THE DARKNESS BOOK II: BLOOD VOWS
CRY FOR DAWN

❑1 2.50
❑2 2.50
❑3 2.50

FRONTIER
SLAVE LABOR

❑1, Jul 1994 2.95

FRONTIERS '86 PRESENTS
FRONTIERS

❑1, Crusaders 1.50
❑2, Crusaders 1.50

FRONTLINE COMBAT (RCP)
GEMSTONE

❑1, Aug 1995; Reprints Frontline Combat (EC) #1 2.00
❑2, Nov 1995; Reprints Frontline Combat (EC) #2 2.00
❑3, Feb 1996; Reprints Frontline Combat (EC) #3 2.00
❑4, May 1996; Reprints Frontline Combat (EC) #4 2.00
❑5, Aug 1996; Reprints Frontline Combat (EC) #5 2.50
❑6, Nov 1996; Reprints Frontline Combat (EC) #6 2.50
❑7, Feb 1997; Reprints Frontline Combat (EC) #7 2.50
❑8, May 1997; Reprints Frontline Combat (EC) #8 2.50
❑9, Aug 1997; Reprints Frontline Combat (EC) #9 2.50
❑10, Nov 1997; Reprints Frontline Combat (EC) #10 2.50
❑11, Feb 1998; Reprints Frontline Combat (EC) #11 2.50
❑12, May 1998; Reprints Frontline Combat (EC) #12 2.50
❑13, Aug 1998; Reprints Frontline Combat (EC) #13 2.50
❑14, Nov 1998; Reprints Frontline Combat (EC) #14 2.50
❑15, Feb 1999; Reprints Frontline Combat (EC) #15 2.50
❑Annual 1; Collects Frontline Combat #1-5 10.95
❑Annual 2; Collects Frontline Combat #6-10 12.95

FROST
CALIBER

❑1, b&w 1.95

FROSTBITER: WRATH OF THE WENDIGO
CALIBER

❑1 2.95
❑2 2.95
❑3 2.95

FROST: THE DYING BREED
CALIBER

❑1, b&w 2.50
❑2, b&w 2.50
❑3, b&w 2.50

Other grades: Multiply price above by 5/6 for VF/NM • 2/3 for VERY FINE • 1/3 for FINE • 1/5 for VERY GOOD • 1/8 for GOOD

FROZEN EMBRYO
SLAVE LABOR

❑1, Dec 1992 ... 2.95

FRUITS BASKET
TOKYOPOP

❑1, Feb 2004 ... 9.95
❑2, Apr 2004 ... 9.95
❑3, Jun 2004 ... 9.95
❑4, Aug 2004 ... 9.95
❑5, Oct 2004 ... 9.95
❑6, Dec 2004 ... 9.95
❑7, Feb 2005 ... 9.95
❑8, Apr 2005 ... 9.95
❑9, Jun 2005 ... 9.95
❑10, Jul 2005 ... 9.95
❑11, Aug 2005 ... 9.95
❑12, Dec 2005 ... 9.95

F-3 BANDIT
ANTARCTIC

❑1, Jan 1995; mini-poster ... 2.95
❑2, Mar 1995; trading card ... 2.95
❑3, May 1995; trading card ... 2.95
❑4, Jul 1995; trading card ... 2.95
❑5, Sep 1995; trading card ... 2.95
❑6, Nov 1995 ... 2.95
❑7, Jan 1996 ... 2.95
❑8, Mar 1996 ... 2.95
❑9, May 1996, b&w ... 2.95
❑10, Jul 1996, b&w; trading card ... 2.95

F-TROOP
GOLD KEY

❑1, Aug 1966 ... 50.00
❑2, Nov 1966 ... 40.00
❑3, Feb 1967 ... 36.00
❑4, Apr 1967 ... 36.00
❑5, May 1967 ... 36.00
❑6, Jun 1967 ... 32.00
❑7, Aug 1967 ... 32.00

FUGITIVE
CALIBER

❑1, ca. 1989, b&w; No indicia ... 2.50

FUGITOID
MIRAGE

❑1 1985; Teenage Mutant Ninja Turtles tie-in; Continued from TMNT #4; continued in TMNT #5 ... 3.00

FULL FRONTAL NERDITY
DORK STORM

❑Annual 1, Jan 2005 ... 2.99

FULL METAL FICTION
LONDON NIGHT

❑1, Mar 1997 ... 3.95

FULL METAL PANIC
ADV MANGA

❑1, ca. 2003 ... 9.99
❑2, ca. 2003 ... 9.99

FULL METAL PANIC: OVERLOAD
ADV MANGA

❑1, ca. 2005 ... 9.99
❑2, ca. 2005 ... 9.99

FULL MOON
VIZ

❑1, Jul 2005 ... 9.95
❑2, Aug 2005 ... 9.95
❑3, Oct 2005 ... 9.95

FULL THROTTLE
AIRCEL

❑1, b&w ... 2.95
❑2, b&w ... 2.95

FUN BOYS SPRING SPECIAL
TUNDRA

❑1, b&w ... 1.95

FUN COMICS (BILL BLACK'S...)
AC

❑1, b&w; b&w magazine format ... 2.00
❑2, b&w; b&w magazine format ... 2.00
❑3; b&w magazine format ... 2.00
❑4, Mar 1983; Captain Paragon, Nightfall ... 2.00

FUN HOUSE
MN DESIGN

❑1, photos ... 6.50

FUN HOUSE (J.R. WILLIAMS'...)
STARHEAD

❑1, Nov 1993, b&w; Collections of Comics, Strips ... 3.95

FUN-IN
GOLD KEY

❑1, Feb 1970 ... 16.00
❑2 1970 ... 10.00
❑3 1970 ... 9.00
❑4, Nov 1970 ... 9.00
❑5, Jan 1971, Motormouse and Autocat, Dastardly and Muttley ... 8.00
❑6, Mar 1971, Dastardly and Muttley, It's the Wolf ... 8.00
❑7, May 1971, Motormouse and Autocat, Dastardly and Muttley, It's the Wolf ... 6.00
❑8, Jul 1971 ... 6.00
❑9, Oct 1971 ... 6.00
❑10, Jan 1972 ... 6.00
❑11, Apr 1974 ... 5.00
❑12, Jun 1974 ... 5.00
❑13, Aug 1974 ... 5.00
❑14, Oct 1974 ... 5.00
❑15 ... 5.00

FUNKY PHANTOM
GOLD KEY

❑1, Mar 1972 ... 24.00
❑2, Jun 1972 ... 15.00
❑3, Sep 1972 ... 10.00
❑4, Dec 1972 ... 10.00
❑5, Mar 1973 ... 10.00
❑6, Jun 1973 ... 8.00
❑7, Sep 1973 ... 8.00
❑8, Dec 1973, A: April. A: Skip. A: Augie. A: Elmo. A: Prissy Atwater. ... 8.00
❑9, Mar 1974 ... 8.00
❑10, Jun 1974 ... 8.00
❑11, Sep 1974 ... 6.00
❑12, Dec 1974 ... 6.00
❑13, Mar 1975 ... 6.00

FUNNY STUFF STOCKING STUFFER
DC

❑1, Mar 1985 ... 1.25

FUNNYTIME FEATURES
EENIEWEENIE

❑1, Jul 1994, b&w ... 2.50
❑1/2nd, b&w ... 2.50
❑2, ca. 1994, b&w ... 2.50
❑3, ca. 1994, b&w ... 2.50
❑4, ca. 1995, b&w ... 2.50
❑5, ca. 1995, b&w ... 2.50
❑6, ca. 1995, b&w ... 2.50
❑7, ca. 1995 ... 2.50
❑8, ca. 1995, b&w ... 2.50

FUNTASTIC WORLD OF HANNA-BARBERA
MARVEL

❑1, Dec 1977 ... 13.00
❑2, Mar 1978 ... 9.00
❑3, Jun 1978 ... 6.00

FUN WITH MILK & CHEESE
SLAVE LABOR

❑1, Apr 1994, b&w; collects stories; has pages 59 and 62 switched ... 9.95

FURIES (AVATAR)
AVATAR

❑0, Feb 1997 ... 3.00
❑0/Nude, Mar 1997; Nude cover ... 3.00

FURIES (CARBON-BASED)
CARBON-BASED

❑1, May 1996, b&w ... 2.75
❑2, Jul 1996, b&w ... 2.75
❑3, Sep 1996, b&w ... 2.75
❑4, Nov 1996, b&w ... 2.75
❑5, Jan 1997, b&w ... 2.75
❑6, Mar 1997, b&w ... 2.75
❑7, ca. 1997 ... 2.75
❑8, Sep 1997 ... 2.75

FURKINDRED
MU

❑1, Jan 1992, b&w ... 6.95
❑2, Nov 1992, b&w ... 7.95

FURRLOUGH
ANTARCTIC

❑1, Nov 1991 ... 4.00
❑2, Feb 1992 ... 3.50
❑3, May 1992 ... 3.50
❑4, Jul 1992 ... 3.00
❑5, Nov 1992 ... 3.00
❑6, Jan 1993 ... 3.00
❑7, Mar 1993 ... 3.00
❑8, May 1993 ... 3.00
❑9, Jul 1993 ... 3.00
❑10, Sep 1993 ... 3.00
❑11, Nov 1993 ... 2.75
❑12, Dec 1993 ... 2.75
❑13, Jan 1994 ... 2.75
❑14, Feb 1994 ... 2.75
❑15, Mar 1994 ... 2.75
❑16, Apr 1994 ... 2.75
❑17, May 1994 ... 2.75
❑18, Jun 1994 ... 2.75
❑19, Jul 1994 ... 2.75
❑20, Aug 1994 ... 2.75
❑21, Sep 1994 ... 2.75
❑22, Oct 1994 ... 2.75
❑23, Nov 1994; Giant-size ... 3.50
❑24, Dec 1994 ... 2.75
❑25, Jan 1995 ... 2.75
❑26, Feb 1995 ... 2.75
❑27, Mar 1995 ... 2.75
❑28, Apr 1995 ... 2.75
❑29, May 1995 ... 2.75
❑30, Jun 1995 ... 2.75
❑31, Jul 1995 ... 2.75
❑32, Aug 1995 ... 2.75
❑33, Sep 1995 ... 2.75
❑34, Oct 1995 ... 2.75
❑35, Nov 1995; fourth anniversary special ... 3.50
❑36, Dec 1995 ... 2.95
❑37, Jan 1996 ... 2.95
❑38, Feb 1996 ... 2.95
❑39, Mar 1996 ... 2.95
❑40, Apr 1996 ... 2.95
❑41, May 1996 ... 2.95
❑42, Jun 1996 ... 2.95
❑43, Jul 1996 ... 2.95
❑44, Aug 1996 ... 2.95
❑45, Sep 1996 ... 2.95
❑46, Oct 1996 ... 2.95
❑47, Nov 1996 ... 2.95
❑48, Dec 1996 ... 2.95
❑49, Jan 1997 ... 2.95
❑50, Feb 1997; Giant-size ... 3.95
❑51, Mar 1997 ... 2.95
❑52, Apr 1997 ... 2.95
❑53, May 1997 ... 2.95
❑54, Jun 1997 ... 2.95
❑55, Jul 1997 ... 2.95
❑56, Aug 1997 ... 2.95
❑57, Sep 1997 ... 2.95
❑58, Oct 1997 ... 2.95
❑59, Nov 1997 ... 2.95
❑60, Dec 1997 ... 2.95
❑61, Jan 1998 ... 2.95
❑62, Feb 1998 ... 2.95
❑63, Mar 1998 ... 2.95
❑64, Apr 1998 ... 2.95
❑65, May 1998 ... 2.95
❑66, Jun 1998 ... 2.95
❑67, Jul 1998 ... 2.95
❑68, Aug 1998 ... 2.95
❑69, Sep 1998 ... 2.95
❑70, Oct 1998 ... 2.95
❑71, Nov 1998 ... 2.95
❑72, Dec 1998 ... 2.95
❑73, Jan 1999 ... 2.95
❑79, Jul 1999 ... 2.95
❑80, Aug 1999 ... 2.95
❑81, Sep 1999 ... 2.95
❑82, Oct 1999 ... 2.95
❑83, Nov 1999 ... 2.95
❑84, Dec 1999 ... 2.95
❑85, Jan 2000 ... 2.95
❑86, Feb 2000 ... 2.95
❑87, Mar 2000 ... 2.95
❑88, Apr 2000 ... 2.95

F-Troop

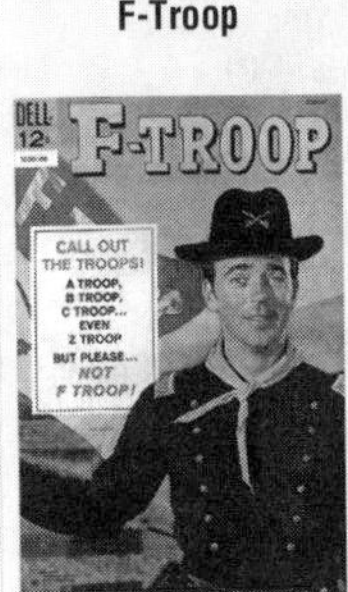

Ken Barry leads inept cavalry unit

©Gold Key

Fun-In

Hanna-Barbera character anthology

©Gold Key

Furrlough

Long-running anthropomorphic anthology

©Antarctic

Further Adventures of Indiana Jones

Follows Raiders of the Lost Ark adaptation

©Marvel

Fury (2nd series)

Nick Fury gets naughty while doing nasty job

©Marvel

N-MINT

❑89, May 2000 ... 2.95
❑90, Jun 2000 ... 2.95
❑91, Jul 2000 ... 2.95
❑92, Aug 2000 ... 2.95
❑93, Sep 2000 ... 2.95
❑94, Oct 2000 ... 2.95
❑95, Nov 2000 ... 2.95
❑96, Dec 2000 ... 2.95
❑97, Jan 2001 ... 2.95
❑98, Feb 2001 ... 2.95
❑99, Mar 2001 ... 2.95
❑100, Apr 2001 ... 2.95
❑101, May 2001 ... 2.95
❑102, Jun 2001 ... 2.95
❑103, Jul 2001 ... 2.99
❑104, Aug 2001 ... 2.99
❑105, Sep 2001 ... 2.99
❑106, Oct 2001 ... 2.99
❑107, Nov 2001 ... 2.99
❑108, Dec 2001 ... 2.99
❑109, Jan 2002 ... 2.99
❑110, Feb 2002 ... 2.99
❑111, Mar 2002 ... 2.99
❑112, Apr 2002 ... 2.99
❑113, May 2002 ... 2.99
❑114, Jun 2002 ... 2.99
❑115, Jul 2002 ... 2.99
❑116, Aug 2002 ... 2.99
❑117, Sep 2002 ... 2.99
❑118, Oct 2002 ... 2.99
❑119, Nov 2002 ... 2.99
❑120, Dec 2002 ... 2.99
❑121, Jan 2003 ... 2.99
❑122, Feb 2003 ... 2.99
❑123, Mar 2003 ... 2.99
❑124, Apr 2003 ... 2.99
❑125, 2003 ... 2.99
❑126, 2003 ... 2.99
❑127, 2003 ... 2.99
❑128, 2003 ... 2.99
❑129, 2003 ... 2.99
❑130, 2003 ... 2.99
❑131, 2003 ... 2.99
❑132, 2004 ... 2.99
❑133, 2004 ... 2.99
❑134, 2004 ... 2.99
❑135, 2004 ... 2.99
❑136, 2004 ... 2.99
❑137, 2004 ... 2.99
❑138, 2004 ... 2.99
❑139, 2004 ... 2.99
❑140 ... 0.00
❑141 ... 0.00
❑142 ... 0.00
❑143, 2005 ... 3.50
❑144, 2005 ... 3.50

FURTHER ADVENTURES OF CYCLOPS AND PHOENIX
MARVEL

❑1, Jun 1996 ... 1.95
❑2, Jul 1996 ... 1.95
❑3, Aug 1996 ... 1.95
❑4, Sep 1996 ... 1.95

N-MINT

FURTHER ADVENTURES OF INDIANA JONES
MARVEL

❑1, Jan 1983, JBy, TD (a) ... 2.50
❑2, Feb 1983, JBy, TD (a) ... 2.00
❑3, Mar 1983 ... 2.00
❑4, Apr 1983 ... 2.00
❑5, May 1983 ... 2.00
❑6, Jun 1983 ... 2.00
❑7, Jul 1983 ... 2.00
❑8, Aug 1983 ... 2.00
❑9, Sep 1983 ... 2.00
❑10, Oct 1983 ... 2.00
❑11, Nov 1983 ... 2.00
❑12, Dec 1983 ... 2.00
❑13, Jan 1984 ... 2.00
❑14, Feb 1984 ... 2.00
❑15, Mar 1984 ... 2.00
❑16, Apr 1984 ... 2.00
❑17, May 1984 ... 2.00
❑18, Jun 1984 ... 2.00
❑19, Jul 1984 ... 2.00
❑20, Aug 1984 ... 2.00
❑21, Sep 1984 ... 2.00
❑22, Oct 1984 ... 2.00
❑23, Nov 1984 ... 2.00
❑24, Dec 1984 ... 2.00
❑25, Jan 1985, SD (a) ... 2.00
❑26, Feb 1985, SD (a) ... 2.00
❑27, Mar 1985, SD (a) ... 2.00
❑28, Apr 1985, SD (a) ... 2.00
❑29, May 1985, SD (a) ... 2.00
❑30, Jul 1985, SD (a) ... 2.00
❑31, Sep 1985, SD (a) ... 2.00
❑32, Nov 1985, SD (a) ... 2.00
❑33, Jan 1986 ... 2.00
❑34, Mar 1986 ... 2.00

FURTHER ADVENTURES OF NYOKA THE JUNGLE GIRL
AC

❑1 ... 2.25
❑2 ... 2.25
❑3, b&w ... 2.25
❑4, b&w ... 2.25
❑5 ... 2.50

FURTHER ADVENTURES OF YOUNG JEFFY DAHMER
BONEYARD

❑1, b&w ... 3.00

FURTHER FATTENING ADVENTURES OF PUDGE, GIRL BLIMP
STAR*REACH

❑1; Comic size ... 4.00
❑1/A; large size ... 5.00
❑2; Comic size ... 4.00
❑3; Comic size ... 4.00

FURY (DELL)
DELL

❑1, Aug 1962 ... 25.00

FURY (1ST SERIES)
MARVEL

❑1, May 1994 O: S.H.I.E.L.D.. O: Hydra. O: Nick Fury. ... 3.00

N-MINT

FURY (2ND SERIES)
MARVEL / MAX

❑1, Nov 2001 ... 4.00
❑2, Dec 2001 ... 2.99
❑3, Jan 2002 ... 2.99
❑4, Feb 2002 ... 2.99
❑5, Mar 2002 ... 2.99
❑6, Apr 2002 ... 2.99

FURY/AGENT 13
MARVEL

❑1, Jun 1998; gatefold summary ... 2.99
❑2, Jul 1998; gatefold summary; Fury returns to Marvel universe ... 2.99

FURY/BLACK WIDOW: DEATH DUTY
MARVEL

❑1, Feb 1995; prestige format ... 5.95

FURY OF FIRESTORM
DC

❑1, Jun 1982, PB (a); O: Firestorm. 1: Lorraine Reilly. 1: Black Bison. ... 6.00
❑2, Jul 1982, PB (a) ... 1.75
❑3, Aug 1982, PB (a); A: Killer Frost ... 1.75
❑4, Sep 1982, PB (a); A: Justice League of America. A: Killer Frost. ... 1.75
❑5, Oct 1982, PB (a); A: Pied Piper ... 1.75
❑6, Nov 1982, PB (a); Master of the Universe preview insert ... 1.50
❑7, Dec 1982, PB (a); 1: Plastique ... 1.50
❑8, Jan 1983, A: Typhoon ... 1.50
❑9, Feb 1983, A: Typhoon ... 1.50
❑10, Mar 1983, PB (a); A: Hyena ... 1.50
❑11, Apr 1983, PB (a) ... 1.25
❑12, May 1983, PB (a) ... 1.25
❑13, Jun 1983, PB (a) ... 1.25
❑14, Jul 1983, PB (a); 1: Mica (Enforcer II). 1: Enforcer I (Leroy Merkyn). ... 1.25
❑15, Aug 1983, PB (a); A: Multiplex. ... 1.25
❑16, Sep 1983, PB (a) ... 1.25
❑17, Oct 1983, PB, GT (a); 1: Firehawk. ... 1.25
❑18, Nov 1983, GT (a); 1: Enforcer II (Mica) ... 1.25
❑19, Jan 1984 GC (a); V: Goldenrod ... 1.25
❑20, Feb 1984 1: Louise Lincoln. A: Firehawk. V: Killer Frost. ... 1.25
❑21, Mar 1984 D: Killer Frost I (Crystal Frost). V: Killer Frost ... 1.00
❑22, Apr 1984 PB (a); O: Firestorm. ... 1.00
❑23, May 1984 V: Byte. ... 1.00
❑24, Jun 1984 1: Bug. 1: Blue Devil. 1: Byte. ... 1.00
❑25, Jul 1984 1: Silver Deer. V: Black Bison. ... 1.00
❑26, Aug 1984 V: Black Bison. ... 1.00
❑27, Sep 1984 ... 1.00
❑28, Oct 1984 1: Slipknot. V: Slipknot. ... 1.00
❑29, Nov 1984 1: Mindboggler. 1: Breathtaker (villain). V: Stratos. ... 1.00
❑30, Dec 1984 GK (c); V: Mindboggler. ... 1.00
❑31, Jan 1985 V: Mindboggler. ... 1.00
❑32, Feb 1985 A: Phantom Stranger ... 1.00
❑33, Mar 1985 ... 1.00
❑34, Apr 1985 1: Killer Frost II (Louise Lincoln). V: Killer Frost ... 1.00
❑35, May 1985 V: Killer Frost. V: Plastique. ... 1.00

Other grades: Multiply price above by 5/6 for VF/NM • 2/3 for VERY FINE • 1/3 for FINE • 1/5 for VERY GOOD • 1/8 for GOOD

N-MINT

❑36, Jun 1985 V: Killer Frost. V: Plastique 1.00
❑37, Jul 1985 1.00
❑38, Aug 1985 1.00
❑39, Sep 1985 1.00
❑40, Oct 1985 1.00
❑41, Nov 1985; Crisis 1.00
❑42, Dec 1985; Crisis 1.00
❑43, Jan 1986 1.00
❑44, Feb 1986 V: Typhoon. 1.00
❑45, Mar 1986 1.00
❑46, Apr 1986 A: Blue Devil 1.00
❑47, May 1986 A: Blue Devil. V: Multiplex. 1.00
❑48, Jun 1986 1: Moonbow. 1.00
❑49, Jul 1986 1.00
❑50, Aug 1986 1.00
❑51, Sep 1986 1.00
❑52, Oct 1986 1.00
❑53, Nov 1986 1.00
❑54, Dec 1986 1.00
❑55, Jan 1987; A: Cosmic Boy. V: Brimstone. Legends 1.00
❑56, Feb 1987; A: Hawk. Legends 1.00
❑57, Mar 1987 1.00
❑58, Apr 1987 1: Parasite II. V: Parasite. 1.00
❑59, May 1987 A: Firehawk. V: Parasite. 1.00
❑60, Jun 1987 1.00
❑61, Jul 1987; V: Typhoon. regular cover 1.00
❑61/A, Jul 1987; V: Typhoon. Alternate cover (test cover) 4.00
❑62, Aug 1987 1.00
❑63, Sep 1987 A: Captain Atom. 1.00
❑64, Oct 1987; A: Suicide Squad. series continues as Firestorm, the Nuclear Man 1.00
❑Annual 1, ca. 1983 2.00
❑Annual 2, ca. 1984; text story 1.50
❑Annual 3, ca. 1985 1.50
❑Annual 4, ca. 1986 1.50

FURY OF HELLINA
LIGHTNING

❑1, Jan 1995, b&w 2.75

FURY OF S.H.I.E.L.D.
MARVEL

❑1, Apr 1995; HC (w); chromium cover 2.50
❑2, May 1995 HC (w); A: Iron Man. 2.00
❑3, Jun 1995 HC (w); A: Iron Man. 2.00
❑4, Jul 1995; HC (w); polybagged with decoder 2.50

FUSED
IMAGE

❑1, Mar 2002 2.95
❑2, Jul 2002 2.95
❑3, Oct 2002 2.95
❑4, Jan 2003 2.95

FUSED (DARK HORSE)
DARK HORSE

❑1, Jan 2004 2.99
❑2, Feb 2004 2.99
❑3, Feb 2004 2.99
❑4, Mar 2004 2.99

FUSHIGI YUGI
VIZ

❑1, Dec 2002 9.95
❑2, Feb 2003 9.95
❑3, Apr 2003 9.95
❑4, Jun 2003 9.95
❑5, Aug 2003 9.95
❑6, Oct 2003 9.95
❑7, Dec 2003 9.95
❑8, Feb 2004 9.95
❑9, Apr 2004 9.95
❑10, Jun 2004 9.95
❑11, Aug 2004 9.95
❑12, Oct 2004 9.95
❑13, Jan 2005 9.95
❑14, Apr 2005 9.95
❑15, Aug 2005 9.95
❑16, Oct 2005 9.95

FUSION
ECLIPSE

❑1, Jan 1987, b&w 2.00
❑2, Mar 1987, b&w 2.00
❑3, May 1987, b&w 2.00
❑4, Jul 1987, b&w 2.00
❑5, Sep 1987, b&w 2.00
❑6, Nov 1987, b&w 2.00
❑7, Jan 1988, b&w 2.00
❑8, Mar 1988, b&w 2.00
❑9, May 1988, b&w 2.00
❑10, Jul 1988, b&w 2.00
❑11, Sep 1988, b&w 2.00
❑12, Nov 1988, b&w 2.00
❑13, Jan 1989, b&w 2.00
❑14, Mar 1989, b&w 2.00
❑15, May 1989, b&w 2.00
❑16, Jul 1989, b&w 2.00
❑17, Sep 1989, b&w 2.00

FUTABA-KUN CHANGE
IRONCAT

❑1 2.95
❑2 2.95
❑3 2.95

FUTABA-KUN CHANGE (VOL. 3)
IRONCAT

❑1, Jul 1999 2.95
❑2 2.95
❑3 2.95
❑4 2.95

FUTURAMA
SLAVE LABOR

❑1, Apr 1989, b&w 2.00
❑2, Jun 1989, b&w 2.00
❑3, Aug 1989, b&w 2.00

FUTURAMA (BONGO)
BONGO

❑1, ca. 2000 5.00
❑1/2nd, ca. 2000 2.50
❑2 2001 2.50
❑3 2001 2.50
❑4 2001 2.50
❑5 2001 2.50
❑6 2001 2.50
❑7 2002 2.50
❑8 2002; Fake CGC cover 2.50
❑9 2002 2.50
❑10 2002 2.50
❑11 2003 2.50
❑12 2003 2.50
❑13 2003 2.50
❑14, Jul 2003 2.50
❑15, Oct 2003 2.99
❑16, Feb 2004 2.99
❑17, May 2004 2.99
❑18 2.99
❑19 2.99

FUTURAMA/SIMPSONS INFINITELY SECRET CROSSOVER CRISIS
BONGO

❑1, ca. 2002 2.50
❑2, ca. 2002 2.50

FUTURE BEAT
OASIS

❑1, Jul 1986 1.50
❑2 1.50

FUTURE COP: L.A.P.D.
DC / WILDSTORM

❑1, Jan 1999; magazine-sized 4.95
❑Ashcan 1 1998 1.00

FUTURE COURSE
REOCCURRING IMAGES

❑1 2.95

FUTURETECH
MUSHROOM

❑1, Feb 1995, b&w; 2nd Printing (first printing published by BlackLine Studios, Oct 94) 3.50

FUTURE WORLD COMIX
WARREN

❑1, Sep 1978 7.00

FUTURIANS BY DAVE COCKRUM
LODESTONE

❑1, Oct 1985, DC (w); DC (a); 1: Doctor Zeus. 1: Hammerhand. 2: The Futurians. Story continued from Marvel Graphic Novel #9 2.00
❑2, Dec 1985, DC (w); DC (a) 2.00
❑3, Apr 1986, DC (w); DC (a) 2.00

FUTURIANS (VOL. 2)
AARDWOLF

❑1, Aug 1995, b&w 2.95

FUZZY BUZZARD AND FRIENDS
HALL OF HEROES

❑1, Apr 1995 2.50

G-8 AND HIS BATTLE ACES
BLAZING

❑1, Oct 1966 1.50

GABRIEL
CALIBER

❑1, ca. 1995, b&w; prestige format; One-shot; prestige format; b&w 3.95

!GAG!
HARRIER

❑1 1987 3.50
❑2, Jul 1987 3.00
❑3 1987 3.00
❑4 1987; magazine 3.00
❑5 1988; magazine 3.00
❑6 1988; magazine 3.00
❑7 1988; magazine 3.00

GAG REFLEX (SKIP WILLIAMSON'S...)
WILLIAMSON

❑1, Jan 1994, b&w 2.95

GAIJIN (MATRIX)
MATRIX

❑1, Feb 1987 1.75

GAIJIN (CALIBER)
CALIBER

❑1, b&w 3.50

GAJIT GANG
AMAZING

❑1 1.95

GALACTIC
DARK HORSE

❑1, Aug 2003 2.99
❑2, Oct 2003 2.99
❑3, Oct 2003 2.99

GALACTICA: THE NEW MILLENNIUM
REALM

❑1, Sep 1999 2.99
❑1/Convention, Sep 1999; Convention edition 5.00

GALACTIC GLADIATORS
PLAYDIGM

❑1 2001 2.95
❑2 2001 2.95
❑3 2002 2.95
❑4 2002 2.95

GALACTIC GUARDIANS
MARVEL

❑1, Jul 1994 1.50
❑2, Aug 1994 1.50
❑3, Sep 1994 1.50
❑4, Oct 1994 1.50

GALACTIC PATROL
ETERNITY

❑1, Jul 1990, b&w 2.25
❑2, b&w 2.25
❑3, b&w 2.25
❑4, b&w 2.25
❑5, b&w 2.25

GALACTUS THE DEVOURER
MARVEL

❑1, Sep 1999 BSz (a) 3.50
❑2, Oct 1999 3.50
❑3, Nov 1999 3.50
❑4, Dec 1999 JB (a) 3.50
❑5, Jan 2000 3.50
❑6, Feb 2000 3.50

GALAXINA
AIRCEL

❑1 1991, b&w 2.95
❑2 1991, b&w 2.95
❑3 1991, b&w 2.95
❑4 1991 2.95

Futurama (Bongo)

Science fiction send-ups from Bongo

©Bongo

Galactic Guardians

Guardians of the Galaxy spin-off

©Marvel

Gambit (5th Series)

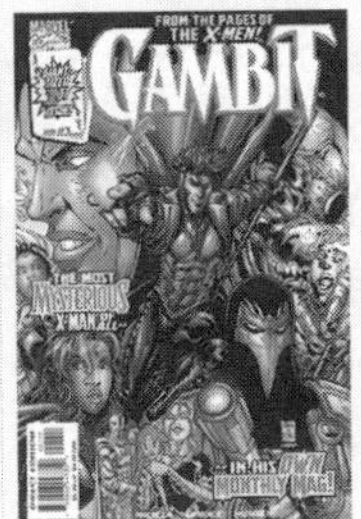

Reveals backstory of Cajun mutant

©Marvel

Game Boy

Pre-heroes Valiant comic book

©Valiant

Gargoyles

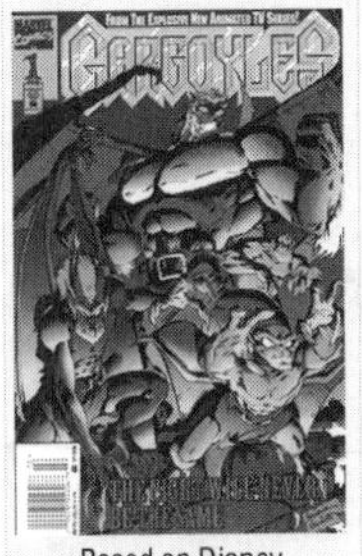

Based on Disney animated series

©Marvel

N-MINT

GALAXION
HELIKON

❑1, May 1997, b&w 2.75
❑2, Jul 1997, b&w 2.75
❑3, Sep 1997, b&w 2.75
❑4, Nov 1997, b&w 2.75
❑5, Jan 1998, b&w 2.75
❑6, Mar 1998, b&w 2.75
❑7 1998 2.75
❑8 1998 2.75
❑9 1999 2.75
❑10 1999 2.75
❑11, Nov 1999 2.75
❑Special 1, May 1998, b&w 1.00

GALAXY GIRL
DYNAMIC

❑1, b&w 2.50

GALLEGHER BOY REPORTER
GOLD KEY

❑1, May 1965 15.00

GALL FORCE: ETERNAL STORY
CPM

❑1, Mar 1995 2.95
❑2, May 1995 2.95
❑3, Jul 1995 2.95
❑4, Sep 1995 2.95

GAMBIT (1ST SERIES)
ETERNITY

❑1, Sep 1988, b&w 4.00

GAMBIT (2ND SERIES)
ORACLE

❑1, Sep 1986 1.50
❑2, Nov 1986 1.50

GAMBIT (3RD SERIES)
MARVEL

❑1, Dec 1993, foil cover 3.00
❑1/Gold, Dec 1993, Gold promotion edition 4.00
❑2, Jan 1994 2.50
❑3, Feb 1994 2.50
❑4, Mar 1994 2.50

GAMBIT (4TH SERIES)
MARVEL

❑1, Sep 1997, gatefold summary 2.50
❑2, Oct 1997, gatefold summary 2.50
❑3, Nov 1997 2.50
❑4, Dec 1997 2.50

GAMBIT (5TH SERIES)
MARVEL

❑1, Feb 1999, A: X-Men. A: X-Cutioner. 3.00
❑1/A, Feb 1999, A: X-Men. A: X-Cutioner. DFE alternate cover 4.00
❑1/B, Feb 1999, A: X-Men. A: X-Cutioner. DFE alternate cover 4.00
❑1/C, Feb 1999, A: X-Men. A: X-Cutioner. Marvel Authentix printed sketch cover; 600 printed 6.00
❑1/D, Feb 1999, White cover with sepiatone sketch art 4.00
❑2, Mar 1999, A: Storm. 2.50
❑3, Apr 1999, A: Courier. A: Mengo Brothers. 2.50
❑4, May 1999 2.50

N-MINT

❑5, Jun 1999 1.99
❑6, Jul 1999, early adventure 1.99
❑7, Aug 1999 1.99
❑8, Sep 1999 1.99
❑9, Oct 1999 1.99
❑10, Nov 1999 1.99
❑11, Dec 1999 1.99
❑12, Jan 2000 2.25
❑13, Feb 2000 2.25
❑14, Mar 2000 2.25
❑15, Apr 2000 2.25
❑16, May 2000 2.25
❑17, Jun 2000 2.25
❑18, Jul 2000 2.25
❑19, Aug 2000 2.25
❑20, Sep 2000 2.25
❑21, Oct 2000 2.25
❑22, Nov 2000 2.25
❑23, Dec 2000 2.25
❑24, Jan 2001 2.25
❑25, Feb 2001, double-sized 2.99
❑Annual 1999, Sep 1999 3.50
❑Annual 2000, ca. 2000 3.50
❑Giant Size 1, Dec 1998, Giant sized; Cover says Feb 99, indicia says Dec 98 5.00

GAMBIT (6TH SERIES)
MARVEL

❑1, Nov 2004 2.99
❑2, Nov 2004 2.99
❑3, Dec 2004 2.99
❑4, Jan 2005 2.99
❑5, Feb 2005 2.99
❑6, Mar 2005 2.99
❑7, Apr 2005 2.99
❑8, May 2005 2.99
❑9, May 2005 2.99
❑10, Jun 2005 2.99
❑11, Jul 2005 2.99
❑12, Aug 2005 2.99

GAMBIT AND BISHOP
MARVEL

❑1, Mar 2001 2.25
❑2, Apr 2001 2.25
❑3, May 2001 2.25
❑4, Jun 2001 2.25
❑5, May 2001 2.25
❑6, Jun 2001 2.25

GAMBIT AND BISHOP ALPHA
MARVEL

❑1, Feb 2001 2.25

GAMBIT AND BISHOP GENESIS
MARVEL

❑1, Mar 2001; reprints Uncanny X-Men #266, Uncanny X-Men #283, and X-Men (2nd series) #8 3.50

GAMBIT & THE X-TERNALS
MARVEL

❑1, Mar 1995 2.00
❑2, Apr 1995 2.00
❑3, May 1995 2.00
❑4, Jun 1995; AM (a); The Age of Apocalypse 2.00

N-MINT

GAME BOY
VALIANT

❑1 1.95
❑2 1.95
❑3 1.95
❑4 1.95

GAME GUYS!
WONDER

❑1 2.50

GAMERA
DARK HORSE

❑1, Aug 1996 2.95
❑2, Sep 1996 2.95
❑3, Oct 1996 2.95
❑4, Nov 1996 2.95

GAMMARAUDERS
DC

❑1, Jan 1989 1.25
❑2, Mar 1989 1.25
❑3, Apr 1989 1.25
❑4, May 1989 1.25
❑5, Jul 1989 1.25
❑6, Aug 1989 1.25
❑7, Sep 1989 2.00
❑8, Oct 1989 2.00
❑9, Nov 1989 2.00
❑10, Dec 1989 2.00

GAMORRA SWIMSUIT SPECIAL
IMAGE

❑1, Jun 1996; pin-ups 2.50

GANGLAND
DC / VERTIGO

❑1, Jun 1998; cover overlay 2.95
❑2, Jul 1998 2.95
❑3, Aug 1998 2.95
❑4, Sep 1998 2.95

GANTAR: THE LAST NABU
TARGET

❑1, Dec 1986 1.75
❑2, Feb 1987 1.75
❑3, Apr 1987, b&w 1.75
❑4 1.75
❑5 1.75
❑6 1.75
❑7 1.75

GARGOYLE
MARVEL

❑1, Jun 1985 BWr (c); BWr (a) 1.50
❑2, Jul 1985 1.50
❑3, Aug 1985 1.50
❑4, Sep 1985 1.50

GARGOYLES
MARVEL

❑1, Feb 1995; enhanced cover 2.50
❑2, Mar 1995 1.50
❑3, Apr 1995 1.50
❑4, May 1995 1.50
❑5, Jun 1995 1.50
❑6, Jul 1995 1.50
❑7, Aug 1995 1.50
❑8, Sep 1995 1.50
❑9, Oct 1995 1.50

N-MINT

❑10, Nov 1995 .... 1.50
❑11, Dec 1995 .... 1.50

GAROU: THE LONE WOLF
Bare Bones

❑1, Jul 1999 .... 2.00

GARRISON'S GORILLAS
Dell

❑1, Jan 1968 .... 21.00
❑2, Apr 1968 .... 14.00
❑3, Jul 1968 .... 14.00
❑4, Oct 1968 .... 14.00
❑5, Oct 1969, Reprints #1 .... 12.00

GASP!
Quebecor

❑1 1994; PF (w); PF (a); Previews Tyrant, Rare Bit Fiends, Wandering Star, and more. Contains new Buck Godot, Zap Gun for Hire story 1.00

GATECRASHER: RING OF FIRE
Black Bull

❑1, Mar 2000; Yellow cover with five figures 2.50
❑1/A, Mar 2000; Green cover with two figures 2.50
❑2, Apr 2000 .... 2.50
❑3, May 2000 .... 2.50
❑3/A, May 2000; variant cover 2.50
❑4, Jun 2000 .... 2.50
❑4/A, Jun 2000; Variant (woman in lingerie, shipped 1:4) 2.50

GATEKEEPER
Gatekeeper

❑1, b&w 2.50

GATES OF EDEN
Fantaco

❑1, ca. 1982, b&w 3.50

GATES OF PANDRAGON
Ianus

❑1, b&w 2.25

GATESVILLE COMPANY
Speakeasy Comics

❑1, Sep 2005 .... 2.99

GATEWAY TO HORROR (BASIL WOLVERTON'S...)
Dark Horse

Value: Cover or less

❑1, Aug 1987, b&w 1.75

GATHERING OF TRIBES
KC Arts

❑1; giveaway; no cover price 1.00

GAUNTLET
Aircel

❑1, Jul 1992 .... 3.00
❑2, Aug 1992 .... 3.00
❑3, Sep 1992 .... 3.00
❑4, Oct 1992 .... 3.00
❑5, Nov 1992 .... 3.00
❑6, Dec 1992 .... 3.00
❑7, Jan 1993 .... 3.00
❑8, Feb 1993 .... 3.00

GAY COMICS (BOB ROSS)
Bob Ross

❑1, "Gay Comix"; Published by Kitchen Sink 12.50
❑2, ca. 1981; "Gay Comix"; Published by Kitchen Sink 8.00
❑3; "Gay Comix"; Published by Kitchen Sink 6.00
❑4; "Gay Comix"; Published by Kitchen Sink 6.00
❑5; "Gay Comix"; Published by Kitchen Sink 6.00
❑6; Bob Ross begins as publisher 4.50
❑7 .... 4.50
❑8 .... 4.50
❑9, Win 1986 .... 4.50
❑10 .... 3.50
❑11, ca. 1987; Wee-Wee's Gayhouse 3.50
❑12, Spr 1988 .... 3.50
❑13, Sum 1991 .... 3.50
❑14, ca. 1991 .... 3.50
❑15; Title changes to 'Gay Comics' 3.50
❑16, Sum 1992; Desert Peach story 3.50
❑17, ca. 1992 .... 3.00
❑18 .... 3.00

N-MINT

❑19, Sum 1993; Alison Bechdel Special 3.00
❑20; super-heroes 3.00
❑21 .... 3.00
❑22, Sum 1994; Funny Animals Special with Omaha the Cat Dancer story 5.00
❑23, Sum 1996; Funny Animals Special 5.00
❑24, Fal 1996 A: The Maxx 5.00
❑25, ca. 1997 .... 3.50
❑Special 1 .... 3.00

GAZILLION
Image

❑1, Nov 1998 .... 2.50
❑1/Variant, Nov 1998; alternate cover; framed 2.50

GD MINUS 18
Antarctic

❑1, Feb 1998, b&w; Gold Digger Special 2.95

GEAR
Fireman

❑1, Nov 1998 .... 2.95
❑2, Dec 1998 .... 2.95
❑3, Jan 1999 .... 2.95
❑4, Feb 1999 .... 2.95
❑5, ca. 1999 .... 2.95
❑6, Apr 1999 .... 2.95

GEAR STATION
Image

❑1, Mar 2000 .... 2.50
❑2, Apr 2000 .... 2.50
❑3, Jun 2000 .... 2.50
❑4, Jul 2000 .... 2.50
❑5, Nov 2000 .... 2.95

GEEKSVILLE
3 Finger Prints

❑1, Aug 1999, b&w 3.00
❑2, Oct 1999, b&w 3.00
❑3, Dec 1999, b&w 2.75

GEEKSVILLE (VOL. 2)
Image

❑0, Mar 2000, b&w 3.00
❑1, May 2000, b&w 3.00
❑2, Jul 2000, b&w 2.95
❑3, Sep 2000, b&w 2.95
❑4, Nov 2000, b&w 2.95
❑5, Jan 2001, ... 2.95
❑6, Mar 2001, ... 2.95

GEISHA
Oni

❑1, Sep 1998 .... 2.95
❑2, Oct 1998 .... 2.95
❑3, Nov 1998 .... 2.95
❑4, Dec 1998 .... 2.95

GEMINAR
Image

❑Special 1, Jul 2000 .... 4.95

GEMINI BLOOD
DC / Helix

❑1, Sep 1996 .... 2.25
❑2, Oct 1996 .... 2.25
❑3, Nov 1996 .... 2.25
❑4, Dec 1996 .... 2.25
❑5, Jan 1997 .... 2.25
❑6, Feb 1997 .... 2.25
❑7, Mar 1997 .... 2.25
❑8, Apr 1997 .... 2.25
❑9, May 1997 .... 2.25

GEN-ACTIVE
WildStorm

❑1, May 2000, Superchick Smackdown cover 3.95
❑1/A, May 2000, Woman with knife on cover 3.95
❑2, Aug 2000, Group cover 3.95
❑2/A, Aug 2000, Woman kicking on cover 3.95
❑3, Nov 2000 .... 3.95
❑4, Feb 2001 .... 3.95
❑5, May 2001 .... 3.95
❑6, Aug 2001 .... 3.95

GENE DOGS
Marvel

❑1, Oct 1993, four trading cards; Polybagged 2.75
❑2, Nov 1993 .... 1.75

N-MINT

❑3, Dec 1993 .... 1.75
❑4, Jan 1994 .... 1.75

GENE POOL
Idea & Design Works

❑1, ca. 2003 .... 6.99

GENERATION HEX
DC / Amalgam

❑1, Jun 1997 .... 1.95

GENERATION M
Marvel

❑1, Jan 2006 .... 2.99
❑2, Feb 2006 .... 2.99
❑3, Mar 2006 .... 2.99
❑4, Apr 2006 .... 2.99
❑5, May 2006 .... 2.99

GENERATION NEXT
Marvel

❑1, Mar 1995 .... 1.95
❑2, Apr 1995 .... 1.95
❑3, May 1995, Age of Apocalypse 1.95
❑4, Jun 1995 .... 1.95

GENERATION X
Marvel

❑-1, Jul 1997, JRo (w); A: Stan Lee. Flashback 2.00
❑½, ca. 1998 .... 2.50
❑½/Ltd., ca. 1998 .... 3.00
❑1, Nov 1994, enhanced cover 4.00
❑2, Dec 1994 .... 1.75
❑2/Deluxe, Dec 1994; Deluxe edition 2.00
❑3, Jan 1995 .... 1.75
❑3/Deluxe, Jan 1995; Deluxe edition 2.00
❑4, Feb 1995, Holiday Spectacular 1.75
❑4/Deluxe, Feb 1995, Deluxe edition; Holiday Spectacular 2.00
❑5, Jul 1995 .... 2.00
❑6, Aug 1995 .... 2.00
❑7, Sep 1995 .... 2.00
❑8, Oct 1995 .... 2.00
❑9, Nov 1995, AM (a) 2.00
❑10, Dec 1995 AM (a); A: Wolverine. A: Omega Red. A: Banshee. V: Omega Red. 2.00
❑11, Jan 1996, AM (a) 2.00
❑12, Feb 1996 AM (a); V: Emplate 2.00
❑13, Mar 1996 V: Emplate. 2.00
❑14, Apr 1996 .... 2.00
❑15, May 1996, AM (a) 2.00
❑16, Jun 1996 .... 2.00
❑17, Jul 1996 .... 2.00
❑18, Aug 1996 .... 2.00
❑19, Sep 1996 .... 2.00
❑20, Oct 1996, A: Howard the Duck. 2.00
❑21, Nov 1996, A: Howard the Duck. 2.00
❑22, Dec 1996 A: Nightmare. 2.00
❑23, Jan 1997 .... 2.00
❑24, Feb 1997 .... 2.00
❑25, Mar 1997, Giant-size; wraparound cover 3.00
❑26, Apr 1997 .... 2.00
❑27, May 1997 .... 2.00
❑28, Jun 1997 .... 2.00
❑29, Aug 1997, gatefold summary; JRo (w); AM (a); Operation Zero Tolerance 2.00
❑30, Sep 1997, gatefold summary; Operation Zero Tolerance 2.00
❑31, Oct 1997, gatefold summary; JRo (w); Operation Zero Tolerance 2.00
❑32, Nov 1997, gatefold summary V: Circus of Crime. 2.00
❑33, Dec 1997; gatefold summary; gatefold summary 2.00
❑34, Jan 1998, gatefold summary; V: White Queen. gatefold summary 2.00
❑35, Feb 1998, gatefold summary; gatefold summary 2.00
❑36, Mar 1998; gatefold summary; gatefold summary 2.00
❑37, Apr 1998, gatefold summary; gatefold summary 2.00
❑38, May 1998, gatefold summary; gatefold summary 2.00
❑39, Jun 1998, gatefold summary; gatefold summary 2.00
❑40, Jul 1998, gatefold summary; gatefold summary 2.00
❑41, Aug 1998, gatefold summary; gatefold summary 2.00

Geeksville

Fuses "3 Geeks" with "Innocent Bystander"

©3 Finger Prints

Gemini Blood

Twins raised from birth to hunt humans

©DC

Generation X

The "new" new mutants, sort of...

©Marvel

Generic Comic

Contains one hero, one villain, and one plot

©Marvel

Gen13 (Mini-Series)

Jim Lee's super-team starts at Image

©Image

N-MINT

❑42, Sep 1998; gatefold summary; gatefold summary 2.00
❑43, Oct 1998; gatefold summary; White Queen powerless 2.00
❑44, Nov 1998, gatefold summary; gatefold summary 2.00
❑45, Dec 1998, gatefold summary; White Queen regains powers 2.00
❑46, Dec 1998, gatefold summary; gatefold summary 2.00
❑47, Jan 1999, gatefold summary; A: Forge. gatefold summary 2.00
❑48, Feb 1999 A: Jubilee. 2.00
❑49, Mar 1999, A: Maggott. 2.00
❑50, Apr 1999, A: Dark Beast. 3.00
❑50/Autographed, Apr 1999, A: Dark Beast. 3.00
❑51, May 1999 .... 2.00
❑52, Jun 1999 .... 2.00
❑53, Jul 1999 .... 2.00
❑54, Aug 1999 .... 2.00
❑55, Sep 1999 .... 2.00
❑56, Oct 1999 .... 2.00
❑57, Nov 1999 .... 2.99
❑58, Dec 1999 .... 1.99
❑59, Jan 2000 .... 1.99
❑60, Feb 2000 .... 2.25
❑61, Mar 2000 .... 2.25
❑62, Apr 2000 .... 2.25
❑63, May 2000 .... 2.25
❑64, Jun 2000 .... 2.25
❑65, Jul 2000 .... 2.25
❑66, Aug 2000 .... 2.25
❑67, Sep 2000 .... 2.25
❑68, Oct 2000 .... 2.25
❑69, Nov 2000 .... 2.25
❑70, Dec 2000 .... 2.25
❑71, Jan 2001 .... 2.25
❑72, Feb 2001 .... 2.25
❑73, Mar 2001 .... 2.25
❑74, Apr 2001 .... 2.25
❑75, May 2001 .... 2.99
❑Annual 1995, ca. 1995, wraparound cover 3.95
❑Annual 1996, ca. 1996; MG (w); Generation X '96; wraparound cover 2.99
❑Annual 1997, ca. 1997; gatefold summary; Generation X '97; wraparound cover 2.99
❑Annual 1998, ca. 1998, gatefold summary; Generation X/Dracula '98; wraparound cover 3.50
❑Annual 1999, ca. 1999 .... 3.50
❑Special 1, Feb 1998 A: Nanny. A: Orphan-Maker. 5.00
❑Ashcan 1; ashcan edition; 'Collector's Preview' 0.75
❑Holiday 1, Feb 1998; Giant-size; Holiday Special 3.50

GENERATION X/GEN13
MARVEL

❑1, ca. 1997; crossover with Image; wraparound cover 4.00
❑1/A, ca. 1997; variant cover 3.50

N-MINT

GENERATION X UNDERGROUND
MARVEL

❑1, May 1998, b&w; cardstock cover. 2.50

GENERIC COMIC
MARVEL

❑1, Apr 1984 .... 2.50

GENERIC COMIC (COMICS CONSPIRACY)
COMICS CONSPIRACY

❑1, Jan 2001 .... 1.95
❑2, May 2001 .... 1.95
❑3, ca. 2001 .... 1.95
❑4, ca. 2001 .... 1.95
❑5 .... 1.95
❑5/Variant; Special cover 5.95
❑6, Feb 2002 .... 1.95
❑7, Apr 2002 .... 1.95
❑8, Jun 2002 .... 1.95
❑9 .... 1.95

GENESIS (MALIBU)
MALIBU

❑0, Oct 1993; foil cover 3.50

GENESIS (DC)
DC

❑1, Oct 1997 .... 1.95
❑2, Oct 1997 .... 1.95
❑3, Oct 1997 .... 1.95
❑4, Oct 1997 .... 1.95

GENETIX
MARVEL

❑1, Oct 1993, wraparound cover 2.75
❑2, Nov 1993 .... 1.75
❑3, Dec 1993 .... 1.75
❑4, Jan 1994 .... 1.75
❑5, Feb 1994 .... 1.75
❑6, Mar 1994 .... 1.75

GENIE
FC9 PUBLISHING

❑1, Aug 2005 .... 2.95
❑2, Sep 2005 .... 2.95

GENOCIDE
RENEGADE TRIBE

❑1, Aug 1994 .... 2.95
❑1/2nd, Aug 1994 .... 2.95

GENOCYBER
VIZ

❑1 1993, b&w; Japanese 2.75
❑2 1993, b&w; Japanese 2.75
❑3, b&w; Japanese 2.75
❑4, b&w; Japanese 2.75
❑5, b&w; Japanese 2.75

GEN OF HIROSHIMA
EDUCOMICS

❑1, Jan 1980 .... 2.00
❑2, ca. 1981 .... 2.00

GENSAGA
EXPRESS / ENTITY

❑1 .... 2.50

N-MINT

GEN12
IMAGE

❑1, Feb 1998 .... 2.50
❑2, Mar 1998 .... 2.50
❑3, Apr 1998 .... 2.50
❑4, May 1998 .... 2.50
❑5, Jun 1998 .... 2.50

GEN13 (MINI-SERIES)
IMAGE

❑0, Sep 1994 .... 3.50
❑½, Mar 1994; Wizard promotional edition 2.00
❑½/A, Mar 1994 .... 5.00
❑1, Feb 1994; 1: Grunge (full appearance). 1: Burnout (full appearance). 1: Freefall (full appearance). first printing 4.00
❑1/A, Oct 1997; 3-D; 1: Grunge (full appearance). 1: Burnout (full appearance). 1: Freefall (full appearance). alternate cover; with glasses 4.95
❑1/B, Oct 1997; 3-D; 1: Grunge (full appearance). 1: Burnout (full appearance). 1: Freefall (full appearance). with glasses 5.00
❑1/C; 1: Grunge (full appearance). 1: Burnout (full appearance). 1: Freefall (full appearance). Fairchild flexing on cover 4.00
❑1/2nd, Jun 1994 1: Grunge (full appearance). 1: Burnout (full appearance). 3.00
❑2, Mar 1994 .... 3.00
❑3, Apr 1994 A: Pitt. 3.00
❑4, May 1994, b&w; A: Pitt. wraparound cover 2.50
❑5, Jul 1994 .... 3.00
❑5/A, Jul 1994; alternate cover 2.50
❑Ashcan 1; ashcan edition 4.00

GEN13
IMAGE

❑-1, Jan 1997, American Entertainment exclusive 3.00
❑0, Sep 1994, JLee (a) 3.00
❑1/3D, Feb 1998, 3D Edition; 1: Trance. 1: The Bounty Hunters. 1: Alex Fairchild. with glasses 4.95
❑1/A, Mar 1995, 1: Trance. 1: The Bounty Hunters. 1: Alex Fairchild. Cover 1 of 13: Charge!; ommon 3.00
❑1/B, Mar 1995, 1: Trance. 1: The Bounty Hunters. 1: Alex Fairchild. Cover 2 of 13: Thumbs Up; common 3.00
❑1/C, Mar 1995, 1: Trance. 1: The Bounty Hunters. 1: Alex Fairchild. Cover 3 of 13: Li'l GEN13 .... 3.00
❑1/D, Mar 1995, 1: Trance. 1: The Bounty Hunters. 1: Alex Fairchild. Cover 4 of 13: Barbari-GEN 3.00
❑1/E, Mar 1995, 1: Trance. 1: The Bounty Hunters. 1: Alex Fairchild. Cover 5 of 13: Your Friendly Neighborhood Grunge 3.00
❑1/F, Mar 1995, 1: Trance. 1: The Bounty Hunters. 1: Alex Fairchild. Cover 6 of 13: Gen13 Goes Madison Avenue 3.00

	N-MINT
❑1/G, Mar 1995, 1: Trance. 1: The Bounty Hunters. 1: Alex Fairchild. Cover 7 of 13: Lin-GEN-re	3.50
❑1/H, Mar 1995, 1: Trance. 1: The Bounty Hunters. 1: Alex Fairchild. Cover 8 of 13: GEN-et Jackson	3.50
❑1/I, Mar 1995, 1: Trance. 1: The Bounty Hunters. 1: Alex Fairchild. Cover 9 of 13: That's the Way We Became the GEN13	3.00
❑1/J, Mar 1995, 1: Trance. 1: The Bounty Hunters. 1: Alex Fairchild. Cover 10 of 13: All Dolled Up	3.00
❑1/K, Mar 1995, 1: Trance. 1: The Bounty Hunters. 1: Alex Fairchild. Cover 11 of 13: Verti-GEN	3.00
❑1/L, Mar 1995, 1: Trance. 1: The Bounty Hunters. 1: Alex Fairchild. Cover 12 of 13: Picto-Fiction	3.00
❑1/M, Mar 1995, 1: Trance. 1: The Bounty Hunters. 1: Alex Fairchild. Cover 13 of 13: Do-It-Yourself-Cover	3.00
❑1/N, 1: Trance. 1: The Bounty Hunters. 1: Alex Fairchild. Included all variant covers, plus new puzzle cover	39.95
❑1/2nd, Encore edition; Fairchild in French maid outfit on cover	2.50
❑2, May 1995, 1: Helmut. Flip cover	2.50
❑3, Jul 1995,	2.50
❑4, Jul 1995, 1: Lucius. indicia says Jul, cover says Aug	2.50
❑5, Oct 1995,	2.50
❑6, Nov 1995, 1: Frostbite. 1: The Order of the Cross.	2.50
❑7, Jan 1996, 1: Copycat. 1: Evo. indicia says Jan, cover says Dec	2.50
❑8, Feb 1996, 1: Powerhaus. 1: Sublime	2.50
❑9, Mar 1996, 1: Absolom	2.50
❑10, Apr 1996, 1: Sigma.	2.50
❑11, May 1996,	2.50
❑11/A, May 1996, European Tour Edition	3.00
❑12, Aug 1996	2.50
❑13/A, Nov 1996, A: Archie, Jughead, Betty, Veronica, Reggie	1.50
❑13/B, Nov 1996, A: TMNTs, Bone, Beanworld, Spawn, Madman. cover says Oct, indicia says Sep	1.50
❑13/C, Nov 1996, A: Madman, Maxx, Shi, Francine, Katchoo, Monkeyman, O'Brien, Hellboy.	1.50
❑13/CS, Nov 1996, Collected Edition of #13A, B, and C A: Maxx. A: Madman. A: Hellboy. A: Bone. A: Shi. A: Teenage Mutant Ninja Turtles. A: Spawn	6.95
❑13/D, Nov 1996, Collected Edition of #13A, B, and C; A: Maxx. A: Madman. A: Hellboy. A: Bone. A: Shi. A: Teenage Mutant Ninja Turtles. A: Spawn. Variant cover collected edition	6.95
❑14, Nov 1996	2.50
❑15, Dec 1996, JLee (w)	2.50
❑16, Jan 1997, JLee (w)	2.50
❑17, Feb 1997	2.50
❑18, Apr 1997	2.50
❑19, May 1997	2.50
❑20, Jun 1997	2.50
❑21, Aug 1997, in space	2.50
❑22, Sep 1997	2.50
❑23, Oct 1997	2.50
❑24, Nov 1997	2.50
❑25, Dec 1997	3.50
❑25/A, Dec 1997, Alternate cover; white background	3.50
❑25/B, Dec 1997, chromium cover	3.50
❑25/CS, Dec 1997, Voyager pack	4.00
❑26, Feb 1998	2.50
❑26/A, Feb 1998, Alternate cover; fight scene	2.50
❑27, Mar 1998	2.50
❑28, Apr 1998	2.50
❑29, May 1998	2.50
❑30, Jun 1998	2.50
❑30/A, Jun 1998, alternate swimsuit cover	2.50
❑31, Jul 1998	2.50
❑32, Aug 1998	2.50
❑33, Sep 1998, Planetary preview	2.50
❑34, Oct 1998,	2.50

	N-MINT
❑34/A, Oct 1998, Variant cover depicts Fairchild posing black background.	2.50
❑35, Nov 1998	2.50
❑36, Dec 1998	2.50
❑36/A, Dec 1998, KN (c); KN (a); Variant cover depicts corn dogs	2.50
❑37, Mar 1999	2.50
❑38, Apr 1999	2.50
❑38/Variant, Apr 1999, Variant cover depicts Grunge w/popcorn	2.50
❑39, May 1999	2.50
❑40, Jun 1999	2.50
❑40/Variant, Jun 1999, Variant cover depicts Roxy in shower	2.50
❑41, Jul 1999	2.50
❑42, Aug 1999	2.50
❑43, Sep 1999	2.50
❑44, Oct 1999, A: Mr. Majestic	2.50
❑45, Nov 1999	2.50
❑46, Dec 2000	2.50
❑47, Jan 2000	2.50
❑48, Feb 2000	2.50
❑49, Mar 2000	2.50
❑50, Apr 2000, Giant-size	3.95
❑51, May 2000	2.50
❑52, Jun 2000	2.50
❑53, Jul 2000	2.50
❑54, Aug 2000	2.50
❑55, Sep 2000	2.50
❑56, Oct 2000	2.50
❑57, Nov 2000	2.50
❑58, Dec 2000	2.50
❑59, Jan 2001	2.50
❑60, Feb 2001	2.50
❑61, Mar 2001	2.50
❑62, Apr 2001	2.50
❑63, May 2001	2.50
❑64, Jun 2001	2.50
❑65, Jul 2001	2.50
❑66, Aug 2001, JLee (a)	2.50
❑67, Sep 2001	2.50
❑68, Oct 2001	2.50
❑69, Nov 2001	2.50
❑70, Dec 2001	2.50
❑71, Jan 2002	2.50
❑72, Feb 2002	2.50
❑73, Mar 2002	2.50
❑74, Apr 2002	2.50
❑75, May 2002	2.50
❑76, Jun 2002	2.50
❑77, Jul 2002	2.50
❑3D 1, European Tour Edition	6.00
❑3D 1/A, double-sized; Fairchild holding open dinosaur mouth on cover	5.00
❑Annual 1, May 1997, 1997 Annual	2.95
❑Annual 1999, Mar 1999, wraparound cover; continues in DV8 Annual 1999	3.50
❑Annual 2000, Dec 2000,	3.50

GEN13 (WILDSTORM)
DC / WILDSTORM

❑0, Sep 2002	1.00
❑0/Variant, Sep 2002, b&w; Alternate art on cover	1.00
❑1, Nov 2002	2.95
❑2, Dec 2002	2.95
❑3, Jan 2003	2.95
❑4, Feb 2003	2.95
❑5, Mar 2003 JLee (c)	2.95
❑6, Apr 2003	2.95
❑7, May 2003	2.95
❑8, Jun 2003	2.95
❑9, Jul 2003	2.95
❑10, Aug 2003	2.95
❑11, Sep 2003	2.95
❑12, Oct 2003	2.95
❑13, Nov 2003	2.95
❑14, Dec 2003	2.95
❑15, Jan 2004	2.95
❑16, Feb 2004	2.95

GEN13: A CHRISTMAS CAPER
WILDSTORM

❑1, Jan 2000	5.95

GEN13: BACKLIST
IMAGE

❑1, Nov 1996; collects Gen13 #1/2, Gen13 #0, Gen13 #1, Gen13: The Unreal World, and WildStorm! #1	2.50

GEN13 BIKINI PIN-UP SPECIAL
IMAGE

	N-MINT
❑1, American Entertainment Exclusive	5.00

GEN13 BOOTLEG
IMAGE

❑1/A, Nov 1996, Team standing, Fairchild front on cover	3.00
❑1/B; Team falling	3.00
❑2, Dec 1996	2.50
❑3, Jan 1997	2.50
❑4, Feb 1997	2.50
❑5, Mar 1997	2.50
❑6, Apr 1997	2.50
❑7, May 1997, JRo (w)	2.50
❑8, Jun 1997, manga-style story	2.50
❑9, Jul 1997, manga-style story; action movie references	2.50
❑10, Aug 1997; manga-style story; video game references	2.50
❑11, Sep 1997	2.50
❑12, Oct 1997	2.50
❑13, Nov 1997	2.50
❑14, Dec 1997	2.50
❑15, Jan 1998	2.50
❑16, Feb 1998	2.50
❑17/A, Mar 1998, alternate cover; videogame	2.50
❑17/B, Mar 1998, alternate cover; videogame	2.50
❑18/A, May 1998, Surfing cover	2.50
❑18/B, May 1998; Beach cover	2.50
❑19, Jun 1998	2.50
❑20, Jul 1998	2.50
❑Annual 1, Feb 1998	2.95

GEN13: CARNY FOLK
WILDSTORM

❑1, Jan 2000	3.50

GEN13/FANTASTIC FOUR
WILDSTORM

❑1, Mar 2001	5.95

GEN13/GENERATION X
IMAGE

❑1/A, Jul 1997, crossover with Marvel	2.95
❑1/B, Jul 1997; alternate cover; crossover with Marvel	2.95
❑1/C, Jul 1997; 3D Edition; Limited cover	5.00
❑1/D, Jul 1997, 3D Edition; alternate cover; crossover with Marvel; with glasses	5.00
❑1/E, Jul 1997, San Diego Comic-Con edition	4.00

GEN13: GOING WEST
DC / WILDSTORM

❑1, Jun 1999	2.50

GEN13: GRUNGE SAVES THE WORLD
DC / WILDSTORM

❑1, May 1999, prestige format	5.95

GEN13 INTERACTIVE
IMAGE

❑1, Oct 1997	2.50
❑2, Nov 1997	2.50
❑3, Jan 1998, cover says Dec, indicia says Jan	2.50

GEN13: LONDON, NEW YORK, HELL
DC / WILDSTORM

❑1, Aug 2001, Collects Gen13 Anl #1, Gen13: Bootleg Anl #1	6.95

GEN13: MAGICAL DRAMA QUEEN ROXY
IMAGE

❑1, Oct 1998	3.50
❑1/A, Oct 1998; alternate cover	4.00
❑1/B, Oct 1998, DFE alternate cover	4.00
❑2, Nov 1998	3.50
❑2/A, Nov 1998, alternate cover	3.50
❑3, Dec 1998	3.50
❑3/A, Dec 1998; alternate cover	3.50

GEN13/MAXX
IMAGE

❑1, Dec 1995	3.50

GEN13: MEDICINE SONG
WILDSTORM

❑1	5.95

Other grades: Multiply price above by 5/6 for VF/NM • 2/3 for VERY FINE • 1/3 for FINE • 1/5 for VERY GOOD • 1/8 for GOOD

Gen13 Bootleg

Features creators new to the series

©Image

Gen13: Magical Drama Queen Roxy

Manga-ized version of familiar heroes

©Image

Gen13/Monkeyman & OíBrien

Good old-fashioned dimension-hopping

©Image

Genus

Long-running adults-only anthropomorphic title

©Antarctic

Geomancer

Magic-users who speak for Earth

©Valiant

N-MINT

GEN13/MONKEYMAN & O'BRIEN
IMAGE

- ❑1, Jun 1998 ... 2.50
- ❑1/A, Jun 1998, alternate cover ... 3.00
- ❑1/B, Jun 1998, Variant chromium cover ... 3.00
- ❑1/C, Jun 1998, Monkeyman holding team on cover, blue/gold background ... 3.00
- ❑2, Aug 1998 ... 2.50
- ❑2/A, Aug 1998; alternate cover ... 2.50

GEN13: ORDINARY HEROES
IMAGE

- ❑1, Feb 1996 ... 2.50
- ❑2, Jul 1996 ... 2.50

GEN13 RAVE
IMAGE

- ❑1, Mar 1995, wraparound cover ... 3.00

GEN13: SCIENCE FRICTION
WILDSTORM

- ❑1, Jun 2001 ... 5.95

GEN13: THE UNREAL WORLD
IMAGE

- ❑1, Jul 1996 ... 2.50

GEN13: WIRED
DC / WILDSTORM

- ❑1, Apr 1999 ... 2.50

GEN13 YEARBOOK '97
IMAGE

- ❑1, Jun 1997, Yearbook-style info on team ... 2.50

GEN13 'ZINE
IMAGE

- ❑1, Dec 1996, b&w; digest ... 2.00

GENTLE BEN
DELL

- ❑1, Feb 1968 ... 30.00
- ❑2, May 1968 ... 20.00
- ❑3, Aug 1968 ... 20.00
- ❑4, Nov 1968 ... 20.00
- ❑5, Oct 1969, Same cover as #1 ... 20.00

GENUS
ANTARCTIC / VENUS

- ❑1, May 1993; Antarctic publishes ... 3.50
- ❑2, Sep 1993 ... 3.00
- ❑3, Nov 1993 ... 3.00
- ❑4, Jan 1994 ... 3.00
- ❑5, Mar 1994 ... 3.00
- ❑6, May 1994 ... 3.00
- ❑7, Jul 1994 ... 3.00
- ❑8, Sep 1994 ... 3.00
- ❑9, Nov 1994 ... 3.00
- ❑10, Jan 1995 ... 3.00
- ❑11, Mar 1995 ... 2.95
- ❑12, May 1995 ... 2.95
- ❑13, Jul 1995 ... 2.95
- ❑14, Sep 1995 ... 2.95
- ❑15, Nov 1995 ... 2.95
- ❑16, Jan 1996 ... 2.95
- ❑17, Mar 1996 ... 2.95
- ❑18, May 1996 ... 2.95
- ❑19, Jul 1996 ... 2.95

N-MINT

- ❑20, Sep 1996 ... 2.95
- ❑21, Nov 1996 ... 2.95
- ❑22, Jan 1997 ... 2.95
- ❑23, Apr 1997; all-skunk issue; Radio Comix publishes ... 2.95
- ❑24, Jun 1997 ... 2.95
- ❑25, Aug 1997 ... 2.95
- ❑26, Oct 1997 ... 2.95
- ❑27, Dec 1997 ... 2.95
- ❑28, Feb 1998 ... 2.95
- ❑29, Apr 1998 ... 2.95
- ❑30, Jun 1998 ... 2.95
- ❑31, Aug 1998 ... 2.95
- ❑32, Oct 1998 ... 2.95
- ❑33, Dec 1998 ... 2.95
- ❑34, Feb 1999 ... 2.95
- ❑35, Apr 1999 ... 2.95
- ❑36, Jun 1999 ... 2.95
- ❑37, Aug 1999 ... 2.95
- ❑38, Oct 1999 ... 2.95
- ❑39, Dec 1999 ... 2.95
- ❑40, Feb 2000 ... 2.95
- ❑41, Apr 2000 ... 2.95
- ❑42, Jun 2000 ... 2.95
- ❑43, Aug 2000 ... 2.95
- ❑44, Oct 2000 ... 2.95
- ❑45, Dec 2000 ... 2.95
- ❑46, Feb 2001 ... 2.95
- ❑47, Apr 2001 ... 2.95
- ❑48, Jun 2001 ... 2.99
- ❑49, Aug 2001 ... 2.99
- ❑50, Oct 2001 ... 2.99
- ❑51, Dec 2001 ... 2.99
- ❑52, Feb 2002 ... 2.99
- ❑53, Apr 2002 ... 2.99
- ❑54, Jun 2002 ... 2.99
- ❑55, Aug 2002 ... 2.99
- ❑56, Oct 2002 ... 2.99
- ❑57, Dec 2002 ... 2.99
- ❑58, Feb 2003 ... 3.50

GENUS GREATEST HITS
ANTARCTIC

- ❑1, Apr 1996 ... 4.50
- ❑2, May 1997 ... 4.95

GENUS SPOTLIGHT
RADIO

- ❑1, Jul 1998; Skunkworks ... 2.95
- ❑2, Nov 1998; Skunkworks ... 2.95

GEOBREEDERS
CPM MANGA

- ❑1, Mar 1999 ... 2.95
- ❑2, Apr 1999 ... 2.95
- ❑3, May 1999 ... 2.95
- ❑4, Jun 1999 ... 2.95
- ❑5, Jul 1999 ... 2.95
- ❑6, Aug 1999 ... 2.95
- ❑7, Sep 1999 ... 2.95
- ❑8, Oct 1999 ... 2.95
- ❑9, Nov 1999 ... 2.95
- ❑10, Dec 1999 ... 2.95
- ❑11, Jan 2000 ... 2.95
- ❑12, Feb 2000 ... 2.95
- ❑13, Mar 2000 ... 2.95

N-MINT

- ❑14, Apr 2000 ... 2.95
- ❑15, May 2000 ... 2.95
- ❑16, Jun 2000 ... 2.95
- ❑17, Jul 2000 ... 2.95
- ❑18, Aug 2000 ... 2.95
- ❑19, Sep 2000 ... 2.95
- ❑20, Oct 2000 ... 2.95
- ❑21, Nov 2000 ... 2.95
- ❑22, Dec 2000 ... 2.95
- ❑23, Jan 2001 ... 2.95
- ❑24, Feb 2001 ... 2.95
- ❑25, Mar 2001 ... 2.95
- ❑26, Apr 2001 ... 2.95
- ❑27, May 2001 ... 2.95
- ❑28, Jun 2001 ... 2.95
- ❑29, Jul 2001 ... 2.95
- ❑30, Aug 2001 ... 2.95
- ❑31, Sep 2001 ... 2.95

GEOMANCER
VALIANT

- ❑1, Nov 1994; 1: Clay McHenry. A: Eternal Warrior. Chromium wraparound cover ... 2.00
- ❑1/VVSS, Nov 1994 ... 40.00
- ❑2, Dec 1994 A: Eternal Warrior. ... 1.00
- ❑3, Jan 1995 ... 1.00
- ❑4, Feb 1995 ... 2.00
- ❑5, Mar 1995 A: Turok. ... 2.00
- ❑6, Apr 1995 A: Turok. ... 2.00
- ❑7, May 1995 ... 2.00
- ❑8, Jun 1995 ... 4.00

GEORGE OF THE JUNGLE
GOLD KEY

- ❑1, Feb 1969, George, Tom Slick, and Super Chicken stories ... 35.00
- ❑2, Oct 1969, George, Tom Slick, and Super Chicken stories ... 24.00

GEORGE ROMERO'S LAND OF THE DEAD
IDEA & DESIGN WORKS

- ❑1 ... 3.99
- ❑2 2005 ... 3.99
- ❑3, Nov 2005 ... 3.99
- ❑4, Dec 2005 ... 3.99
- ❑5, Feb 2006 ... 3.99

GEPETTO FILES
QUICK TO FLY

- ❑1, Sep 1998 ... 3.00

GERIATRIC GANGRENE JUJITSU GERBILS
PLANET-X

- ❑1, b&w ... 1.50
- ❑2 ... 1.50

GERIATRICMAN
C&T

- ❑1, b&w ... 1.75

GE ROUGE
VEROTIK

- ❑½, Oct 1998 ... 2.95
- ❑1, Feb 1997 ... 2.95
- ❑2, Apr 1997 ... 2.95
- ❑3, Jul 1997 ... 2.95

GERTIE THE DINOSAUR COMICS
GERTIE THE DINOSAUR
- ❑1, Jul 2000 ... 2.95

GESTALT (NEC)
NEW ENGLAND
- ❑1, Apr 1993, b&w ... 1.95
- ❑2 ... 1.95

GESTALT (CALIBER)
CALIBER
- ❑0 ... 2.95

GET ALONG GANG
MARVEL / STAR
- ❑1, May 1985 ... 1.00
- ❑2, Jul 1985 ... 1.00
- ❑3, Sep 1985 ... 1.00
- ❑4, Nov 1985 ... 1.00
- ❑5, Jan 1986 ... 1.00
- ❑6, Mar 1986 ... 1.00

GETBACKERS
TOKYOPOP
- ❑1, Feb 2004 ... 9.95
- ❑2, Apr 2004 ... 9.95
- ❑3, Jun 2004 ... 9.95
- ❑4, Aug 2004 ... 9.95
- ❑5, Oct 2004 ... 9.95
- ❑6, Dec 2004 ... 9.95
- ❑7, Feb 2005 ... 9.95
- ❑8, Apr 2005 ... 9.95
- ❑9, Jun 2005 ... 9.95
- ❑10, Jul 2005 ... 9.95
- ❑11, Aug 2005 ... 9.95
- ❑12, Nov 2005 ... 9.95

GET BENT!
BEN T. STECKLER
- ❑1 ... 2.25
- ❑2, Dec 1998 ... 2.25
- ❑3 ... 2.25
- ❑4 ... 2.25
- ❑5 ... 2.25
- ❑6 ... 2.25
- ❑7; Mini-comic ... 2.25
- ❑8 ... 2.25
- ❑9 ... 2.25

GET LOST (VOL. 2)
NEW COMICS
- ❑1, Oct 1987, b&w; Reprints ... 1.95
- ❑2, ca. 1988, b&w; Reprints ... 1.95
- ❑3, ca. 1988, b&w; Reprints ... 1.95

GET REAL COMICS
TIDES CENTER
- ❑1 ... 1.95

GET SMART
DELL
- ❑1, Jun 1966 ... 45.00
- ❑2, Sep 1966 ... 30.00
- ❑3, Nov 1966 ... 22.00
- ❑4, Jan 1967 ... 22.00
- ❑5, Mar 1967 ... 22.00
- ❑6, Apr 1967 ... 20.00
- ❑7, Jun 1967 ... 20.00
- ❑8, Sep 1967, Cover from #1 reprinted ... 20.00

GHETTO BITCH
FANTAGRAPHICS / EROS
- ❑1, b&w ... 2.75

GHETTO BLASTERS
WHIPLASH
- ❑1, Sep 1997, b&w ... 2.50

GHOST
DARK HORSE
- ❑1, Apr 1995 ... 3.00
- ❑2, May 1995 ... 2.50
- ❑3, Jun 1995 ... 2.50
- ❑4, Jul 1995 ... 2.50
- ❑5, Aug 1995 ... 2.50
- ❑6, Sep 1995 ... 2.50
- ❑7, Oct 1995 ... 2.50
- ❑8, Nov 1995 ... 2.50
- ❑9, Dec 1995 ... 2.50
- ❑10, Jan 1996 ... 2.50
- ❑11, Feb 1996 ... 2.50
- ❑12, Mar 1996, preview of Ghost/Hellboy crossover ... 2.50
- ❑13, Apr 1996 ... 2.50
- ❑14, May 1996 ... 2.50
- ❑15, Jun 1996 ... 2.50
- ❑16, Jul 1996 ... 2.50
- ❑17, Aug 1996 ... 2.50
- ❑18, Sep 1996 ... 2.50
- ❑19, Nov 1996 ... 2.50
- ❑20, Dec 1996 ... 2.50
- ❑21, Jan 1997 ... 2.50
- ❑22, Feb 1997 ... 2.50
- ❑23, Mar 1997 ... 2.50
- ❑24, Apr 1997 ... 2.50
- ❑25, May 1997, Giant-size; 48-page special; photo front and back covers ... 3.95
- ❑26, Jun 1997 ... 2.95
- ❑27, Jul 1997 ... 2.95
- ❑28, Aug 1997 ... 2.95
- ❑29, Sep 1997, flip-book with Timecop story ... 2.95
- ❑30, Oct 1997 ... 2.95
- ❑31, Nov 1997 ... 2.95
- ❑32, Dec 1997 ... 2.95
- ❑33, Jan 1998 ... 2.95
- ❑34, Feb 1998 ... 2.95
- ❑35, Mar 1998 ... 2.95
- ❑36, Apr 1998 ... 2.95
- ❑Special 1, Jul 1994, Ghost Special ... 3.95
- ❑Special 2, Jun 1998, Immortal Coil ... 3.95
- ❑Special 3, Dec 1998, Scary Monsters ... 3.95

GHOST (VOL. 2)
DARK HORSE
- ❑1, Sep 1998 ... 3.50
- ❑2, Oct 1998 ... 3.00
- ❑3, Nov 1998 ... 3.00
- ❑4, Dec 1998 ... 3.00
- ❑5, Jan 1999 ... 3.00
- ❑6, Feb 1999 ... 2.95
- ❑7, Mar 1999 ... 2.95
- ❑8, Apr 1999 ... 2.95
- ❑9, May 1999 ... 2.95
- ❑10, Jun 1999, A: Vortex. ... 2.95
- ❑11, Jul 1999 ... 2.95
- ❑12, Sep 1999 ... 2.95
- ❑13, Oct 1999 ... 2.95
- ❑14, Nov 1999 ... 2.95
- ❑15, Dec 1999 ... 2.95
- ❑16, Jan 2000 ... 2.95
- ❑17, Feb 2000 ... 2.95
- ❑18, Mar 2000 ... 2.95
- ❑19, Apr 2000 ... 2.95
- ❑20, Jun 2000 ... 2.95
- ❑21, Jul 2000, A: X. ... 2.95
- ❑22, Aug 2000 ... 2.95

GHOST AND THE SHADOW
DARK HORSE
- ❑1, Dec 1995 ... 2.95

GHOST/BATGIRL
DARK HORSE
- ❑1, Aug 2000 ... 2.95
- ❑2, Oct 2000 ... 2.99
- ❑3, Nov 2000 ... 2.95
- ❑4, Dec 2000 ... 2.95

GHOSTBUSTERS
FIRST
- ❑1, Feb 1986 ... 1.50
- ❑2, Mar 1986 ... 1.50
- ❑3, May 1986 ... 1.50
- ❑4, Jun 1986 ... 1.50
- ❑5, Aug 1986 ... 1.50
- ❑6, Sep 1986 ... 1.50

GHOSTBUSTERS II
NOW
- ❑1, Oct 1989 ... 2.00
- ❑2, Nov 1989 ... 2.00
- ❑3, Dec 1989 ... 2.00

GHOSTDANCING
DC / VERTIGO
- ❑1, Mar 1995 ... 1.95
- ❑2, Apr 1995 ... 1.95
- ❑3, Jun 1995 ... 2.50
- ❑4, Jul 1995 ... 2.50
- ❑5, Aug 1995 ... 2.50
- ❑6, Sep 1995 ... 2.50

GHOST HANDBOOK
DARK HORSE
- ❑1, Aug 1999; background on characters ... 2.95

GHOST/HELLBOY SPECIAL
DARK HORSE
- ❑1, May 1996 ... 2.50
- ❑2, Jun 1996 ... 2.50

GHOST IN THE SHELL
DARK HORSE / MANGA
- ❑1, Mar 1995 ... 25.00
- ❑2, Apr 1995 ... 14.00
- ❑3, Apr 1995 ... 10.00
- ❑4, Jun 1995 ... 10.00
- ❑5, Jul 1995 ... 8.00
- ❑6, Aug 1995 ... 8.00
- ❑7, Sep 1995 ... 7.00
- ❑8, Oct 1995 ... 7.00

GHOST IN THE SHELL 2: MAN/MACHINE INTERFACE
DARK HORSE
- ❑1, Feb 2003 ... 3.99
- ❑1/Hologram, Feb 2003, Holo cover ... 10.00
- ❑2, Feb 2003 ... 3.50
- ❑2/A, Apr 2003, New cover painting ... 3.50
- ❑3, Apr 2003 ... 3.50
- ❑4, May 2003 ... 3.50
- ❑5, Jul 2003 ... 3.50
- ❑6, Aug 2003 ... 3.50
- ❑7, Sep 2003 ... 3.50
- ❑8, Oct 2003 ... 3.50
- ❑9, Nov 2003 ... 3.50
- ❑10, Dec 2003 ... 3.50
- ❑11, Dec 2003 ... 3.50

GHOSTLY HAUNTS
CHARLTON
- ❑20, Sep 1971, SD (a); Series continued from Ghost Manor (1st Series) #19 ... 6.00
- ❑21 1971 ... 5.00
- ❑22 1972 ... 5.00
- ❑23 1972 ... 5.00
- ❑24, Apr 1972 ... 5.00
- ❑25 1972 ... 5.00
- ❑26 1972 ... 5.00
- ❑27 1972 ... 5.00
- ❑28 1972 ... 5.00
- ❑29 1972 ... 5.00
- ❑30 1973 ... 5.00
- ❑31 1973 ... 4.00
- ❑32, May 1973 ... 4.00
- ❑33 1973 ... 4.00
- ❑34 1973 ... 4.00
- ❑35, Oct 1973 ... 4.00
- ❑36, Nov 1973 ... 4.00
- ❑37 1974 ... 4.00
- ❑38, May 1974 ... 4.00
- ❑39, Jul 1974 ... 4.00
- ❑40, Sep 1974 ... 4.00
- ❑41, Nov 1974 ... 3.00
- ❑42 1975 ... 3.00
- ❑43 1975 ... 3.00
- ❑44, May 1975 SD (a) ... 3.00
- ❑45 1975 ... 3.00
- ❑46 1975 ... 3.00
- ❑47, Dec 1975 ... 3.00
- ❑48 1976 ... 3.00
- ❑49 1976 ... 3.00
- ❑50 1976 ... 3.00
- ❑51 1976 ... 3.00
- ❑52 1976 ... 3.00
- ❑53, Dec 1976 ... 3.00
- ❑54 1977 ... 3.00
- ❑55 1977 ... 3.00
- ❑56, Jan 1978 ... 3.00
- ❑57, Mar 1978 ... 3.00
- ❑58, Apr 1978 ... 3.00

GHOST MANOR (1ST SERIES)
CHARLTON
- ❑1, Jul 1968 ... 12.00
- ❑2, Sep 1968 ... 7.00
- ❑3, Nov 1968 ... 7.00
- ❑4, Jan 1969 ... 7.00
- ❑5, Mar 1969 ... 7.00
- ❑6, May 1969 ... 6.00

Other grades: Multiply price above by 5/6 for VF/NM • 2/3 for VERY FINE • 1/3 for FINE • 1/5 for VERY GOOD • 1/8 for GOOD

George of the Jungle

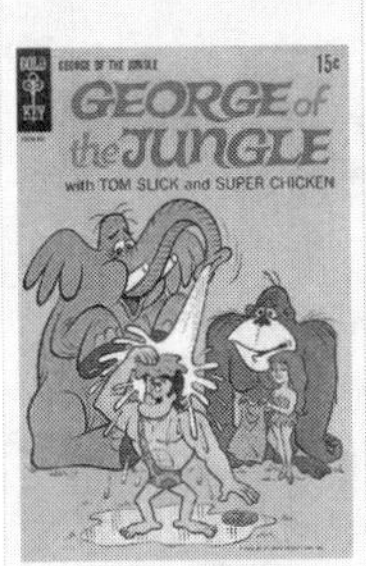

With Tom Slick and Super Chicken, no less

©Gold Key

Ghost Manor (1st Series)

More horror comics from Charlton

©Charlton

Ghost Manor (2nd Series)

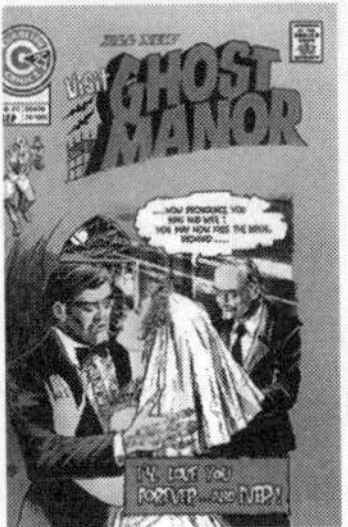

With your horrible host, Mr. Bones

©Charlton

Ghost Rider

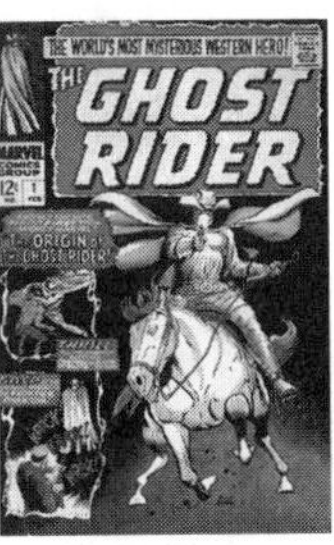

The Western version predated the biker

©Marvel

Ghost Rider (Vol. 1)

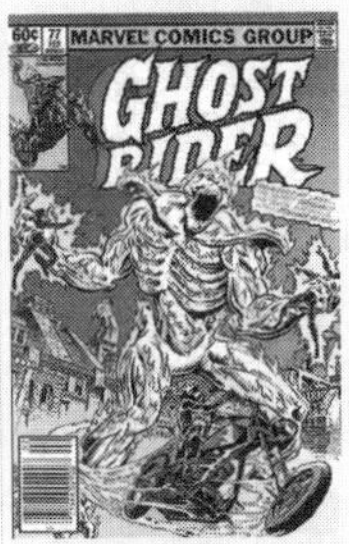

He's a Hell's Angel — literally

©Marvel

	N-MINT
❑7, Jul 1969	6.00
❑8, Sep 1969	6.00
❑9, Nov 1969	6.00
❑10, Jan 1970	6.00
❑11, Mar 1970	5.00
❑12, May 1970	5.00
❑13, Jul 1970	5.00
❑14, Sep 1970	5.00
❑15, Nov 1970	5.00
❑16, Jan 1971	5.00
❑17, Mar 1971	5.00
❑18, May 1971	5.00
❑19, Jul 1971, Series continued in Ghostly Haunts #20	5.00

GHOST MANOR (2ND SERIES)

CHARLTON

	N-MINT
❑1, Oct 1971, O: Ghost Manor.	10.00
❑2, Dec 1971	6.00
❑3, Feb 1972	6.00
❑4, Apr 1972	6.00
❑5, Jun 1972	6.00
❑6, Aug 1972	6.00
❑7, Oct 1972	6.00
❑8, Nov 1972, WW (a)	7.50
❑9, Feb 1973	5.00
❑10, Mar 1973	5.00
❑11, Apr 1973	4.00
❑12, Jun 1973	4.00
❑13, Jul 1973	4.00
❑14, Sep 1973	4.00
❑15, Oct 1973	4.00
❑16, Dec 1973	4.00
❑17, Jan 1974	4.00
❑18, May 1974	4.00
❑19, Jul 1974	4.00
❑20, Sep 1974	4.00
❑21, Nov 1974	4.00
❑22, Mar 1975	4.00
❑23, May 1975	4.00
❑24, Jul 1975	4.00
❑25, Sep 1975	4.00
❑26, Nov 1975	4.00
❑27, Jan 1976	4.00
❑28, Mar 1976	4.00
❑29, Jun 1976	4.00
❑30, Aug 1976	4.00
❑31, Oct 1976	3.00
❑32, Dec 1976	3.00
❑33, Sep 1977	3.00
❑34, Nov 1977	3.00
❑35, Feb 1978	3.00
❑36, Mar 1978	3.00
❑37, May 1978	3.00
❑38, Jun 1978	3.00
❑39, Oct 1978	3.00
❑40, Dec 1978, Warren Sattler credits	3.00
❑41, Feb 1979	3.00
❑42, Mar 1979	3.00
❑43, Jun 1979	3.00
❑44, Jul 1979	3.00
❑45, Sep 1979	3.00
❑46, Oct 1979	3.00
❑47, Nov 1979	3.00
❑48, Jan 1979	3.00
❑49, Mar 1980	3.00
❑50, May 1980	3.00
❑51, Jul 1980	3.00
❑52, Sep 1980	3.00
❑53, Nov 1980	3.00
❑54, Jan 1981	3.00
❑55, Mar 1981	3.00
❑56, May 1981	3.00
❑57, Jul 1981	3.00
❑58, Aug 1981	3.00
❑59, Oct 1981	3.00
❑60, Dec 1981	3.00
❑61, Feb 1982	3.00
❑62, Apr 1982	3.00
❑63, Jun 1982	3.00
❑64, Aug 1982	3.00
❑65, Oct 1982	3.00
❑66, Dec 1982	3.00
❑67, Feb 1983	3.00
❑68, Apr 1983	3.00
❑69, Jul 1983	3.00
❑70, Sep 1983	3.00
❑71, Nov 1983	3.00
❑72, Jan 1984	3.00
❑73, Mar 1984	3.00
❑74, May 1984	3.00
❑75, Jul 1984	3.00
❑76, Sep 1984	3.00
❑77, Nov 1984	3.00

GHOST RIDER

MARVEL

	N-MINT
❑1, Feb 1967, O: Ghost Rider. 1: Ghost Rider. Western; back-up reprints story from Kid Colt Outlaw #105	28.00
❑2, Apr 1967, V: Tarantula. Western; back-up reprints story from Kid Colt Outlaw #99	20.00
❑3, Jun 1967, Western; back-up reprints story from Kid Colt Outlaw #116	20.00
❑4, Aug 1967, A: Tarantula. V: Sting-Ray a.k.a. Scorpion. Western; back-up reprints story from Two-Gun Kid #69	12.50
❑5, Sep 1967, V: Tarantula. Western	12.50
❑6, Oct 1967, V: Towering Oak. Western	12.50
❑7, Nov 1967, Western	12.50

GHOST RIDER (VOL. 1)

MARVEL

	N-MINT
❑1, Aug 1973, GK (a); 1: Son of Satan (partially shown).	160.00
❑2, Oct 1973	37.00
❑3, Dec 1973, JM (a)	25.00
❑4, Feb 1974, JM (a)	30.00
❑5, Apr 1974, Marvel Value Stamp #24: Falcon	23.00
❑6, Jun 1974, Marvel Value Stamp #74: Stranger	20.00
❑7, Aug 1974, Marvel Value Stamp #20: Brother Voodoo	20.00
❑8, Oct 1974, JM (a); 1: Inferno. A: Roxanne. Marvel Value Stamp #48: Kraven	15.00
❑9, Dec 1974, Marvel Value Stamp #81: Rhino	15.00
❑10, Feb 1975, A: Hulk. Reprints Marvel Spotlight #5	15.00
❑11, Apr 1975, SB, GK, KJ (a); A: Hulk. Marvel Value Stamp #66: General Ross	15.00
❑12, Jun 1975, D: Phantom Eagle.	15.00
❑13, Aug 1975	15.00
❑14, Oct 1975	15.00
❑15, Dec 1975	12.00
❑16, Feb 1976	12.00
❑17, Apr 1976	12.00
❑17/30 cent, Apr 1976, 30 cent regional price variant	20.00
❑18, Jun 1976, A: Spider-Man	13.00
❑18/30 cent, Jun 1976, A: Spider-Man. 30 cent regional price variant	20.00
❑19, Aug 1976	12.00
❑19/30 cent, Aug 1976, 30 cent regional price variant	20.00
❑20, Oct 1976, JBy, GK, KJ (a); A: Daredevil.	9.00
❑21, Dec 1976, D: Eel I (Leopold Stryke).	7.00
❑22, Feb 1977, 1: Enforcer (Marvel)	7.00
❑23, Apr 1977, O: Water Wizard. 1: Water Wizard.	7.00
❑24, Jun 1977	7.00
❑24/35 cent, Jun 1977, 35 cent regional price variant	15.00
❑25, Aug 1977	7.00
❑25/35 cent, Aug 1977, 35 cent regional price variant	15.00
❑26, Oct 1977	7.00
❑26/35 cent, Oct 1977, 35 cent regional price variant	15.00
❑27, Dec 1977	7.00
❑28, Feb 1978	7.00
❑29, Apr 1978	7.00
❑30, Jun 1978	7.00
❑31, Aug 1978	6.00
❑32, Oct 1978	6.00
❑33, Dec 1978	6.00
❑34, Feb 1979	6.00
❑35, Apr 1979	6.00
❑36, Jun 1979	6.00
❑37, Aug 1979	6.00
❑38, Oct 1979	6.00
❑39, Dec 1979	6.00
❑40, Jan 1980	6.00
❑41, Feb 1980	6.00
❑42, Mar 1980	6.00
❑43, Apr 1980	6.00
❑44, May 1980	6.00
❑45, Jun 1980	6.00
❑46, Jul 1980	6.00
❑47, Aug 1980	6.00
❑48, Sep 1980	6.00
❑49, Oct 1980	6.00
❑50, Nov 1980, Giant-size DP (a); A: Night Rider.	12.00
❑51, Dec 1980	5.00
❑52, Jan 1981	5.00
❑53, Feb 1981	5.00
❑54, Mar 1981	5.00
❑55, Apr 1981	5.00

N-MINT

❑56, May 1981, 1: Night Rider II (Hamilton Slade). 5.00
❑57, Jun 1981 5.00
❑58, Jul 1981 5.00
❑59, Aug 1981 5.00
❑60, Sep 1981 5.00
❑61, Oct 1981 5.00
❑62, Nov 1981 5.00
❑63, Dec 1981 5.00
❑64, Jan 1982 5.00
❑65, Feb 1982 5.00
❑66, Mar 1982 5.00
❑67, Apr 1982 5.00
❑68, May 1982, O: Ghost Rider (Johnny Blaze). 5.00
❑69, Jun 1982 4.00
❑70, Jul 1982 4.00
❑71, Aug 1982 4.00
❑72, Sep 1982, 1: Fire-Eater. 4.00
❑73, Oct 1982 4.00
❑74, Nov 1982, 1: Centurius. 4.00
❑75, Dec 1982 4.00
❑76, Jan 1983 4.00
❑77, Feb 1983, O: Zarathos. O: Centurius. 4.00
❑78, Mar 1983 4.00
❑79, Apr 1983 4.00
❑80, May 1983, O: Centurius. 4.00
❑81, Jun 1983, D: Ghost Rider. Zarathos leaves Johnny Blaze-end of Ghost Rider I. 10.00

GHOST RIDER (VOL. 2)
MARVEL

❑-1, Jul 1997; Flashback 1.95
❑1, May 1990 O: Ghost Rider II (Dan Ketch). 1: Ghost Rider II (Dan Ketch). 1: Deathwatch. 4.00
❑1/2nd, Sep 1990; O: Ghost Rider II (Dan Ketch). 1: Ghost Rider II (Dan Ketch). 1: Deathwatch. 2nd Printing (gold) 2.25
❑2, Jun 1990 1: Blackout II. 3.00
❑3, Jul 1990 V: Blackout. V: Kingpin. V: Deathwatch. 3.00
❑4, Aug 1990; V: Mr. Hyde. Scarcer 3.00
❑5, Sep 1990 JLee (c); JLee (a); A: Punisher. 3.00
❑5/Variant, Jun 1994; JLee (c); JLee (a); A: Punisher. Die-cut cover 3.00
❑5/2nd, Sep 1990; JLee (c); JLee (a); A: Punisher. 2nd printing (gold) 1.50
❑6, Oct 1990 A: Punisher. 2.50
❑7, Nov 1990 V: Scarecrow. 2.00
❑8, Dec 1990 2.00
❑9, Jan 1991 A: X-Factor. 2.00
❑10, Feb 1991 2.00
❑11, Mar 1991 1.50
❑12, Apr 1991 A: Doctor Strange. 1.50
❑13, May 1991 1: Snowblind. A: Doctor Strange. 1.50
❑14, Jun 1991; Johnny Blaze; Ghost Rider vs. Johnny Blaze 1.50
❑15, Jul 1991; glow in the dark cover 5.00
❑15/2nd; 2nd Printing (gold); glow in the dark cover 2.00
❑16, Aug 1991 A: Hobgoblin. A: Spider-Man. A: Johnny Blaze. 1.75
❑17, Sep 1991 A: Hobgoblin. A: Spider-Man. 1.75
❑18, Oct 1991; Painted cover 1.75
❑19, Nov 1991 1.75
❑20, Dec 1991 1.75
❑21, Jan 1992 1.75
❑22, Feb 1992 1.75
❑23, Mar 1992 V: Deathwatch. 1.75
❑24, Apr 1992 D: Snowblind. V: Deathwatch. 1.75
❑25, May 1992; Pop-up centerfold, double-sized 2.00
❑26, Jun 1992 A: X-Men. 1.75
❑27, Jul 1992 A: X-Men. 1.75
❑28, Aug 1992 1: Lilith II. 2.50
❑29, Sep 1992 JKu (a); A: Wolverine. A: Beast 1.75
❑30, Oct 1992 JKu (a); V: Nightmare. 1.75
❑31, Nov 1992 JKu (a) 2.50
❑32, Dec 1992 1.75
❑33, Jan 1993 AW (a) 1.75
❑34, Feb 1993 1.75
❑35, Mar 1993 AW (a) 1.75
❑36, Apr 1993 1.75
❑37, May 1993 1.75
❑38, Jun 1993 1.75
❑39, Jul 1993 1.75
❑40, Aug 1993; black cover 2.25
❑41, Sep 1993 1.75
❑42, Oct 1993; A: Deathwatch. A: Centurius. A: Ghostie. A: John Blaze. Neon cover 1.75
❑43, Nov 1993 1.75
❑44, Dec 1993; Neon cover 1.75
❑45, Jan 1994; Spot-varnished cover 1.75
❑46, Feb 1994 1.75
❑47, Mar 1994 1.75
❑48, Apr 1994 A: Spider-Man. 1.75
❑49, May 1994 1.75
❑50, Jun 1994; Giant-size; foil cover 2.50
❑50/Variant, Jun 1994; Giant-size; Die-cut cover 4.00
❑51, Jul 1994 1.95
❑52, Aug 1994 1.95
❑53, Sep 1994 1.95
❑54, Oct 1994 1.95
❑55, Nov 1994 1.95
❑56, Dec 1994 1.95
❑57, Jan 1995 A: Wolverine. 1.95
❑58, Feb 1995 1.95
❑59, Mar 1995 1.95
❑60, Apr 1995 1.95
❑61, May 1995; Giant-size 2.50
❑62, Jun 1995 1.95
❑63, Jul 1995 1.95
❑64, Aug 1995 1.95
❑65, Sep 1995 1.95
❑66, Oct 1995 D: Blackout. 1.95
❑67, Nov 1995 A: Gambit. 1.95
❑68, Dec 1995 A: Gambit. A: Wolverine. 1.95
❑69, Jan 1996 1.95
❑70, Feb 1996 1.95
❑71, Mar 1996 1.95
❑72, Apr 1996 1.95
❑73, May 1996 V: Snowblind. 1.95
❑74, Jun 1996 1.95
❑75, Jul 1996 1.50
❑76, Aug 1996 1.50
❑77, Sep 1996 A: Doctor Strange. 1.50
❑78, Oct 1996 1.50
❑79, Nov 1996 1.50
❑80, Dec 1996 1.50
❑81, Jan 1997 A: Howard the Duck. 1.50
❑82, Feb 1997 A: Devil Dinosaur. A: Howard the Duck. A: Moonboy. 1.50
❑83, Mar 1997 1.95
❑84, Apr 1997 1.95
❑85, May 1997 A: Scarecrow. 1.95
❑86, Jun 1997 1.95
❑87, Aug 1997; gatefold summary 1.95
❑88, Sep 1997; gatefold summary 1.95
❑89, Oct 1997; gatefold summary 1.95
❑90, Nov 1997; gatefold summary 1.95
❑91, Dec 1997; gatefold summary 1.95
❑92, Jan 1998; gatefold summary 1.95
❑93, Feb 1998; Giant-size 2.99
❑Annual 1, ca. 1993; trading card 4.00
❑Annual 2, ca. 1994 V: Scarecrow. 2.95

GHOST RIDER (VOL. 3)
MARVEL

❑½, ca. 2001; Wizard promo 3.50
❑1, Aug 2001 2.99
❑2, Sep 2001 2.99
❑3, Oct 2001 2.99
❑4, Nov 2001 2.99
❑5, Dec 2001 2.99
❑6, Jan 2002 2.99

GHOST RIDER (VOL. 4)
MARVEL

❑1, Oct 2005 2.99
❑1/Ribic, Oct 2005; Incentive distributed one for every 20 copies ordered 2.99
❑1/DirCut, Oct 2005 2.99
❑1/RRP, Oct 2005, Distributed one per retail attendee at the 2005 Diamond seminar as part of the Retailer Rewards Program (RRP) 2.99
❑2, Nov 2005 2.99
❑3, Jan 2006 2.99
❑4, Feb 2006 2.99
❑5, Mar 2006 2.99
❑6, Apr 2006 2.99

GHOST RIDER & CABLE: SERVANTS OF THE DEAD
MARVEL

❑1, Sep 1991; cardstock cover; no indicia; Reprints Ghost Rider/Cable series from Marvel Comics Presents 3.95

GHOST RIDER AND THE MIDNIGHT SONS MAGAZINE
MARVEL

❑1 3.95

GHOST RIDER/BALLISTIC
MARVEL

❑1, Feb 1997; crossover with Top Cow; continues in Ballistic/Wolverine 2.95

GHOST RIDER/BLAZE: SPIRITS OF VENGEANCE
Value: Cover or less

❑1, Aug 1992; without poster 1.50
❑1/CS, Aug 1992 2.75
❑2, Sep 1992 1.75
❑3, Oct 1992 1.75
❑4, Nov 1992 1.75
❑5, Dec 1992; Venom 1.75
❑6, Jan 1993 1.75
❑7, Feb 1993 1.75
❑8, Mar 1993 1.75
❑9, Apr 1993 1.75
❑10, May 1993 1.75
❑11, Jun 1993 1.75
❑12, Jul 1993; Glow-in-the-dark cover 2.75
❑13, Aug 1993; black cover 2.25
❑14, Sep 1993 1.75
❑15, Oct 1993; Neon ink cover; Blaze's new costume and powers 1.75
❑16, Nov 1993 1.75
❑17, Dec 1993; Neon inks on cover 1.75
❑18, Jan 1994; Spot-varnished cover. 1.75
❑19, Feb 1994 1.75
❑20, Mar 1994 1.75
❑21, Apr 1994 1.75
❑22, May 1994 1.75
❑23, Jun 1994 1.95

GHOST RIDER/ CAPTAIN AMERICA: FEAR
MARVEL

❑1, Oct 1992; Fold-out cover 5.95

GHOST RIDER: CROSSROADS
MARVEL

❑1, Dec 1995; enhanced wraparound cardstock cover 3.95

GHOST RIDER: HIGHWAY TO HELL
MARVEL

❑1, Aug 2001 3.50

GHOST RIDER POSTER MAGAZINE
MARVEL

❑1 4.95

GHOST RIDER: THE HAMMER LANE
MARVEL

❑1, Aug 2001 2.99
❑2, Sep 2001 2.99
❑3, Oct 2001 2.99
❑4, Nov 2001 2.99
❑5, Dec 2001 2.99
❑6, Jan 2002 2.99

GHOST RIDER 2099
MARVEL

❑1, May 1994 O: Ghost Rider 2099. 1: Ghost Rider 2099. 2.00
❑1/CS, May 1994; Polybagged with trading card 2.50
❑2, Jun 1994; Polybagged with poster 1.50
❑3, Jul 1994 1.50
❑4, Aug 1994 1.50
❑5, Sep 1994 1.50
❑6, Oct 1994 1.50
❑7, Nov 1994 A: Spider-Man 2099. 1.50
❑8, Dec 1994 1.50
❑9, Jan 1995 1.50
❑10, Feb 1995 1.50
❑11, Mar 1995 1.50
❑12, Apr 1995 1.50
❑13, May 1995 1.95

Other grades: Multiply price above by 5/6 for VF/NM • 2/3 for VERY FINE • 1/3 for FINE • 1/5 for VERY GOOD • 1/8 for GOOD

Ghost Rider (Vol. 2)

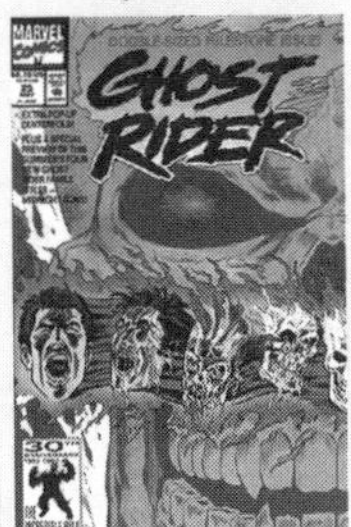

Spirit of Vengeance reborn for the 1990s

©Marvel

Ghost Rider 2099

Depressing character in depressing future

©Marvel

Ghosts

True tales of the supernatural, or so they say

©DC

Ghost Stories

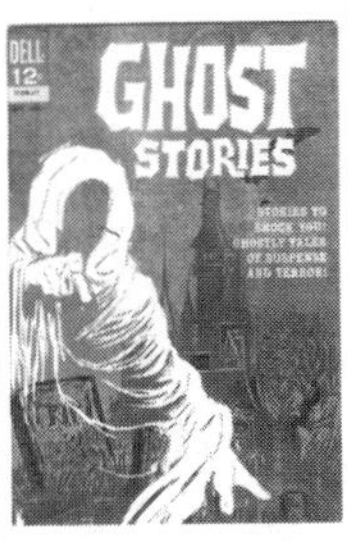

So much for the Dell "Pledge to Parents!"

©Dell

Giantkiller

Volcano plus monsters in Southern California

©DC

N-MINT

❑14, Jun 1995 ... 1.95
❑15, Jul 1995 1: Heartbreaker. ... 1.95
❑16, Aug 1995 ... 1.95
❑17, Sep 1995 ... 1.95
❑18, Oct 1995 ... 1.95
❑19, Nov 1995 ... 1.95
❑20, Dec 1995 A: L-Cypher. A: Heartbreaker. A: Archfiends. A: Zero Cochrane. ... 1.95
❑21, Jan 1996 ... 1.95
❑22, Feb 1996 ... 1.95
❑23, Mar 1996 ... 1.95
❑24, Apr 1996 ... 1.95
❑25, May 1996; double-sized; wraparound cover ... 2.50

GHOST RIDER; WOLVERINE; PUNISHER: THE DARK DESIGN
MARVEL

❑1, Dec 1991, squarebound; Double fold-out cover ... 5.95

GHOSTS
DC

❑1, Oct 1971 TD, JA (a) ... 100.00
❑2, Dec 1971 TD (a) ... 35.00
❑3, Feb 1972 TD (w) ... 17.00
❑4, Apr 1972 ... 17.00
❑5, Jun 1972 ... 17.00
❑6, Aug 1972 ... 12.00
❑7, Sep 1972 ... 12.00
❑8, Oct 1972 ... 12.00
❑9, Nov 1972 ... 12.00
❑10, Jan 1973 ... 12.00
❑11, Feb 1973 ... 10.00
❑12, Mar 1973 ... 10.00
❑13, Apr 1973 ... 10.00
❑14, May 1973 ... 10.00
❑15, Jun 1973 ... 10.00
❑16, Jul 1973 ... 10.00
❑17, Aug 1973 ... 10.00
❑18, Sep 1973 ... 10.00
❑19, Oct 1973 ... 10.00
❑20, Nov 1973 ... 10.00
❑21, Dec 1973 ... 6.00
❑22, Jan 1974 ... 6.00
❑23, Feb 1974 ... 6.00
❑24, Mar 1974 ... 6.00
❑25, Apr 1974 ... 6.00
❑26, May 1974 ... 6.00
❑27, Jun 1974 ... 6.00
❑28, Jul 1974 ... 6.00
❑29, Aug 1974 ... 6.00
❑30, Sep 1974 ... 6.00
❑31, Oct 1974 ... 5.00
❑32, Nov 1974 ... 5.00
❑33, Dec 1974 ... 5.00
❑34, Jan 1975 ... 5.00
❑35, Feb 1975 ... 5.00
❑36, Mar 1975 ... 5.00
❑37, Apr 1975 ... 5.00
❑38, May 1975 ... 5.00
❑39, Jun 1975 ... 5.00
❑40, Jul 1975, giant ... 6.00
❑41, Aug 1975 ... 5.00
❑42, Sep 1975 ... 5.00

N-MINT

❑43, Oct 1975 ... 5.00
❑44, Nov 1975 ... 5.00
❑45, Jan 1976 ... 5.00
❑46, Mar 1976 ... 5.00
❑47, Jun 1976 ... 5.00
❑48 1976, Bicentennial #2 ... 5.00
❑49 1976 ... 5.00
❑50, Nov 1976 ... 5.00
❑51, Jan 1977 ... 4.00
❑52 1977 ... 4.00
❑53 1977 ... 4.00
❑54, May 1977 ... 4.00
❑55 1977 ... 4.00
❑56, Sep 1977 ... 4.00
❑57, Oct 1977 ... 4.00
❑58, Nov 1977 ... 4.00
❑59, Dec 1977 ... 4.00
❑60, Jan 1978 ... 4.00
❑61, Feb 1978 ... 4.00
❑62, Mar 1978 ... 4.00
❑63, Apr 1978 ... 4.00
❑64, May 1978 ... 4.00
❑65, Jun 1978 ... 4.00
❑66, Jul 1978 ... 4.00
❑67, Aug 1978 ... 4.00
❑68, Sep 1978 ... 4.00
❑69, Oct 1978 ... 4.00
❑70, Nov 1978 ... 4.00
❑71, Dec 1978 ... 3.00
❑72, Jan 1979 ... 3.00
❑73, Feb 1979 ... 3.00
❑74, Mar 1979 ... 3.00
❑75, Apr 1979 ... 3.00
❑76, May 1979 ... 3.00
❑77, Jun 1979 ... 3.00
❑78, Jul 1979 ... 3.00
❑79, Aug 1979 ... 3.00
❑80, Sep 1979 ... 3.00
❑81, Oct 1979 ... 3.00
❑82, Nov 1979 ... 3.00
❑83, Dec 1979 ... 3.00
❑84, Jan 1980 ... 3.00
❑85, Feb 1980 ... 3.00
❑86, Mar 1980 ... 3.00
❑87, Apr 1980 ... 3.00
❑88, May 1980 ... 3.00
❑89, Jun 1980 ... 3.00
❑90, Jul 1980 ... 3.00
❑91, Aug 1980 ... 3.00
❑92, Sep 1980 ... 3.00
❑93, Oct 1980 ... 3.00
❑94, Nov 1980 ... 3.00
❑95, Dec 1980 ... 3.00
❑96, Jan 1981 ... 3.00
❑97, Feb 1981, A: Spectre ... 3.00
❑98, Mar 1981, A: Spectre ... 3.00
❑99, Apr 1981, A: Spectre ... 3.00
❑100, May 1981 ... 3.00
❑101, Jun 1981 ... 3.00
❑102, Jul 1981 ... 3.00
❑103, Aug 1981 ... 3.00
❑104, Sep 1981 ... 3.00
❑105, Oct 1981 ... 3.00
❑106, Nov 1981 ... 3.00

N-MINT

❑107, Dec 1981 ... 3.00
❑108, Jan 1982 ... 3.00
❑109, Feb 1982 ... 3.00
❑110, Mar 1982 ... 3.00
❑111, Apr 1982 ... 3.00
❑112, May 1982 ... 3.00

GHOST SHIP
SLAVE LABOR

❑1, Mar 1996, b&w; cardstock cover ... 3.50
❑2, Jun 1996, b&w; cardstock cover ... 2.95
❑3, Oct 1996, b&w; cardstock cover ... 2.95

GHOSTS OF DRACULA
ETERNITY

❑1, Sep 1991, b&w ... 2.50
❑2, b&w ... 2.50
❑3, b&w ... 2.50
❑4, b&w ... 2.50
❑5, b&w ... 2.50

GHOST SPY
IMAGE

❑1, Aug 2004 ... 2.95
❑2, Sep 2004 ... 2.95
❑3, Oct 2004 ... 2.95
❑4, Nov 2004 ... 2.95
❑5, Dec 2004 ... 2.95

GHOST STORIES
DELL

❑1, Sep 1962 ... 36.00
❑2, Apr 1963 ... 20.00
❑3, Jul 1963 ... 14.00
❑4, Oct 1963 ... 14.00
❑5, Jan 1964 ... 14.00
❑6, Apr 1964 ... 10.00
❑7, Jul 1964 ... 10.00
❑8, Oct 1964 ... 10.00
❑9, Jan 1965 ... 10.00
❑10, Apr 1965 ... 10.00
❑11, Aug 1965, FS (c); FS (a) ... 7.00
❑12, Dec 1965 ... 7.00
❑13, Mar 1966 ... 7.00
❑14, Jun 1966 ... 7.00
❑15, Sep 1966 ... 7.00
❑16, Dec 1966 ... 7.00
❑17, Mar 1967 ... 6.00
❑18, May 1967 ... 6.00
❑19, Aug 1967 ... 6.00
❑20, Nov 1967 ... 6.00
❑21, Oct 1968 ... 5.00
❑22, Oct 1969 ... 5.00
❑23, Jan 1970 ... 5.00
❑24, May 1970 ... 5.00
❑25, Jul 1970 ... 5.00
❑26, Oct 1970 ... 5.00
❑27, Jan 1971 ... 5.00
❑28, Apr 1971 ... 5.00
❑29, Jul 1971 ... 5.00
❑30, Oct 1971 ... 5.00
❑31, Jan 1972 ... 5.00
❑32, Apr 1972 ... 5.00
❑33, Jul 1972 ... 5.00
❑34, Oct 1972 ... 5.00
❑35, Jan 1973 ... 5.00

Other grades: Multiply price above by 5/6 for VF/NM • 2/3 for VERY FINE • 1/3 for FINE • 1/5 for VERY GOOD • 1/8 for GOOD

❑36, Jul 1973 .... 5.00
❑37, Oct 1973 .... 5.00

GHOULS
ETERNITY

❑1, b&w; Reprints 2.25

GIANTKILLER
DC

❑1, Aug 1999 .... 2.50
❑2, Sep 1999 .... 2.50
❑3, Oct 1999 .... 2.50
❑4, Nov 1999 .... 2.50
❑5, Dec 1999 .... 2.50
❑6, Jan 2000 .... 2.50

GIANTKILLER A TO Z
DC

❑1, Aug 1999; no indicia; biographical monster information 2.50

GIANT-SIZE AMAZING SPIDER-MAN
MARVEL

❑1, Aug 1999; cardstock cover; reprints stories from Spider-Man Adventures #6, #11, #12, and Marvel Tales #205 .... 4.50

GIANT-SIZE AVENGERS
MARVEL

❑1, Aug 1974, RB (a); 1: Whizzer I (Robert Frank). D: Miss America. Reprints 30.00
❑2, Nov 1974, DC (a); O: Rama-Tut. D: Swordsman. reprints Fantastic Four #19 (Rama-Tut) 25.00
❑3, Feb 1975, DC (a); O: Immortus. O: Kang. A: Wonder Man. A: Zemo. A: Human Torch. A: Frankenstein's Monster. continued from Avengers #132; reprints Avengers #2; Marvel Value Stamp #41: Gladiator 20.00
❑4, Jun 1975, DH (a); Wedding of Vision and Scarlet Witch 20.00
❑5, Dec 1975, Reprints 15.00

GIANT-SIZE CAPTAIN AMERICA
MARVEL

❑1 O: Captain America 20.00

GIANT-SIZE CAPTAIN MARVEL
MARVEL

❑1, A: Hulk. A: Captain America. Reprints 16.00

GIANT-SIZE CHILLERS (1ST SERIES)
MARVEL

❑1, Jun 1974, GC (a); 1: Lilith. Dracula 25.00

GIANT-SIZE CHILLERS (2ND SERIES)
MARVEL

❑1 1975 .... 20.00
❑2, Aug 1975 .... 15.00
❑3 1975 .... 15.00

GIANT-SIZE CONAN
MARVEL

❑1, Sep 1974, TS, BB, GK (a); 1: Belit. 1st appearance of Belit 16.00
❑2, Dec 1974, TS, GK (a) 10.00
❑3, Apr 1975, GK (a) 7.00
❑4, Jun 1975, GK (a) 6.00
❑5, Jun 1975 .... 6.00

GIANT-SIZE CREATURES
MARVEL

❑1, Jul 1974, DP (a); O: Tigra. 1: Tigra. Marvel Value Stamp A-34 (Mr. Fantastic) 25.00

GIANT-SIZE DAREDEVIL
MARVEL

❑1, ca. 1975 .... 15.00

GIANT-SIZE DEFENDERS
MARVEL

❑1, Jul 1974, JSn (a); A: Silver Surfer. Silver Surfer 20.00
❑2, Oct 1974, GK, KJ (a); Son of Satan 10.00
❑3, Jan 1975, DN, JSn, JM, DA (a); 1: Korvac. Marvel Value Stamp #48: Kraven 10.00
❑4, Apr 1975 DH (a) 7.00
❑5, Jul 1975 DH (a); A: Guardians of the Galaxy. 7.00

GIANT-SIZE DOC SAVAGE
MARVEL

❑1, Jan 1975, RA (a); reprints Doc Savage (Marvel) #1 and 2; adapts Man of Bronze 10.00

N-MINT

GIANT-SIZE DOCTOR STRANGE
MARVEL

❑1, ca. 1975, GT, DA (a); Reprints stories from Strange Tales #164, 165, 166, 167, 168 .... 15.00

GIANT-SIZE DRACULA
MARVEL

❑2, Sep 1974, Series continued from Giant-Size Chillers (1st Series) #1; SL (w); DH (a); Series continued from Giant-Size Chillers (1st Series) #1 .... 22.00
❑3, Dec 1974, DH (a) 15.00
❑4, Mar 1975, DH (a) 15.00
❑5, Jun 1975, JBy (a); Marvel Value Stamp #55: Medusa 20.00

GIANT-SIZE FANTASTIC FOUR
MARVEL

❑1, May 1974, published as Giant-Size Super-Stars; SL (w); RB, JK (a); A: Fantastic Four. A: Hulk. Thing battles Hulk 20.00
❑2, Aug 1974, Title changes to Giant-Size Fantastic Four; GK (c); JB (a); A: Willie Lumpkin. V: Tempus. also reprints Fantastic Four #13 .... 12.00
❑3, Nov 1974, RB (a); also reprints Fantastic Four #21 .... 10.00
❑4, Feb 1975, RB (c); JK, SL (w); JB, JK (a); O: Madrox the Multiple Man. 1: Madrox the Multiple Man. A: Professor X. A: Medusa. Marvel Value Stamp #2: Hulk 12.00
❑5, May 1975, reprints Fantastic Four Annual #5 and Fantastic Four #15 .. 10.00
❑6, Oct 1975, reprints Fantastic Four Annual #6 .... 10.00

GIANT-SIZE HULK
MARVEL

❑1, Jan 1975, reprints Hulk Annual #1 .... 23.00

GIANT-SIZE HULK (2ND SERIES)
MARVEL

❑1, Sep 2006 .... 4.99

GIANT-SIZE INVADERS
MARVEL

❑1, Jun 1975, O: the Sub-Mariner. O: Invaders. 1: Invaders 15.00

GIANT-SIZE IRON MAN
MARVEL

❑1, ca. 1975, Reprints 17.00

GIANT-SIZE KID COLT
MARVEL

❑1 A: Rawhide Kid 27.00
❑2 GK (c) 20.00
❑3, Jul 1975, GK (c); A: Night Rider ("Ghost Rider") 20.00

GIANT-SIZE MAN-THING
MARVEL

❑1, Aug 1974, SD, JK, MP (a); V: Glob. 15.00
❑2 .... 9.00
❑3, Feb 1975, Marvel Value Stamp #77: Swordsman 12.00
❑4, May 1975, FB (a); Howard the Duck; Marvel Value Stamp #36: Ancient One 10.00
❑5, Aug 1975, FB (a); Howard the Duck 12.00

GIANT-SIZE MARVEL TRIPLE ACTION
MARVEL

❑1, May 1975, Reprints 15.00
❑2, Jul 1975, Reprints 12.00

GIANT-SIZE MASTER OF KUNG FU
MARVEL

❑1, Sep 1974, PG, CR (a) 17.00
❑2, Dec 1974, PG (a) 12.00
❑3, Mar 1975, PG (a); Marvel Value Stamp #71: Vision 10.00
❑4, Jun 1975, JK (a); Yellow Claw 10.00

GIANT-SIZE MINI COMICS
ECLIPSE

❑1, Aug 1986, b&w 2.00
❑2, Oct 1986, b&w 2.00
❑3, Dec 1986, b&w 2.00
❑4, Feb 1987, b&w 2.00

GIANT SIZE MINI-MARVELS: STARRING SPIDEY
MARVEL

❑1, Feb 2002 .... 3.50

N-MINT

GIANT-SIZE MS. MARVEL
MARVEL

❑1, Apr 2006 .... 4.99

GIANT SIZE OFFICIAL PRINCE VALIANT
PIONEER

❑1, b&w; Hal Foster 3.95

GIANT-SIZE POWER MAN
MARVEL

❑1, ca. 1975 .... 20.00

GIANT-SIZE SPIDER-MAN
MARVEL

❑1, Jul 1974, JR (c); RA (a); A: Dracula. reprints story from Strange Tales Annual #2 .... 35.00
❑2, Oct 1974, JR (c); GK, RA (a); A: Shang-Chi. reprints story from Amazing Spider-Man Annual #3 .... 12.00
❑3, Jan 1975, GK (c); RA (a); A: Doc Savage. also reprints story from Amazing Spider-Man #16 .... 12.00
❑4, Apr 1975, GK (c); RA (a); 1: Moses Magnum (Magnum Force). A: Punisher. 45.00
❑5, Jul 1975 GK (c); RA (a); A: Man-Thing. V: Lizard. 12.00
❑6, Sep 1975, reprints Amazing Spider-Man Annual #4 .... 15.00

GIANT SIZE SPIDER-MAN (2ND SERIES)
MARVEL

❑1, Dec 1998; reprints stories from Marvel Team-Up 4.00

GIANT-SIZE SPIDER-WOMAN
MARVEL

❑1, Sep 2005 .... 4.99

GIANT-SIZE SUPER-HEROES
MARVEL

❑1, Jun 1974, GK (a); A: Man-Wolf. A: Spider-Man. A: Morbius. "How Stan'" reprinted from Amazing Spider-Man Annual #1 .... 25.00

GIANT-SIZE SUPER-STARS
MARVEL

❑1, May 1974 .... 20.00

GIANT-SIZE SUPER-VILLAIN TEAM-UP
MARVEL

❑1, Mar 1975 .... 17.00
❑2, Jun 1975, Doctor Doom, Sub-Mariner 10.00

GIANT-SIZE THOR
MARVEL

❑1, Jul 1975, GK (a); Reprints 20.00

GIANT-SIZE WEREWOLF BY NIGHT
MARVEL

❑2, Oct 1974, Title changes to Giant Size Werewolf by Night; SD (a); Frankenstein reprint 20.00
❑3, Jan 1975, GK (a) 15.00
❑4, Apr 1975, GK (a) 15.00
❑5, GK (a) 15.00

GIANT-SIZE X-MEN
MARVEL

❑1, Sum 1975, GK, DC (a); O: Storm. O: Nightcrawler. 1: X-Men (new). 1: Thunderbird. 1: Colossus. 1: Storm. 1: Nightcrawler. 1: Illyana Rasputin. 800.00
❑2, Nov 1975, GK, KJ (a); reprints X-Men #57-59 .... 80.00
❑3, Jul 2005 .... 4.99
❑4 2005 .... 4.99

GIANT THB PARADE
HORSE

❑1, b&w; over-sized 5.00

G.I. COMBAT (DC)
DC

❑44, Jan 1957, Previous issues published by Quality 500.00
❑45, Feb 1957 .... 300.00
❑46, Mar 1957 .... 250.00
❑47, Apr 1957 .... 225.00
❑48, May 1957 .... 100.00
❑49, Jun 1957 .... 100.00
❑50, Jul 1957, (c) 100.00
❑51, Aug 1957 .... 85.00
❑52, Sep 1957, (c) 85.00

Other grades: Multiply price above by 5/6 for VF/NM • 2/3 for VERY FINE • 1/3 for FINE • 1/5 for VERY GOOD • 1/8 for GOOD

Giant-Size Creatures

Origin and first appearance of Tigra

©Marvel

Giant-Size Doc Savage

Reprints the first two regular Marvel issues

©Marvel

Giant-Size Fantastic Four

First issue was "Giant-Size Super Stars"

©Marvel

Giant-Size X-Men

#1 's X-Men relaunch helped reinvent comics

©Marvel

G.I. Combat (DC)

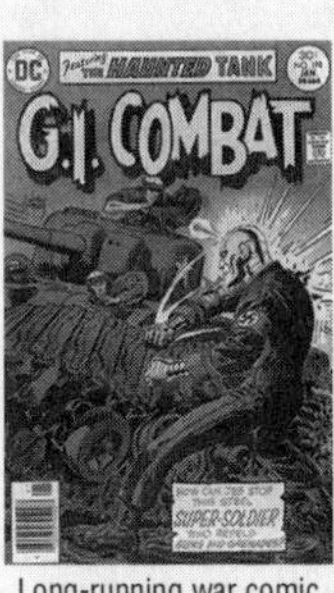

Long-running war comic with Joe Kubert art

©DC

	N-MINT
❑53, Oct 1957	85.00
❑54, Nov 1957	85.00
❑55, Dec 1957	125.00
❑56, Jan 1958, (c)	85.00
❑57, Feb 1958	85.00
❑58, Mar 1958	85.00
❑59, Apr 1958	85.00
❑60, May 1958	85.00
❑61, Jun 1958	70.00
❑62, Jul 1958	70.00
❑63, Aug 1958	70.00
❑64, Sep 1958	70.00
❑65, Oct 1958	70.00
❑66, Nov 1958	70.00
❑67, Dec 1958, 1: Tank Killer.	125.00
❑68, Jan 1959	400.00
❑69, Feb 1959	70.00
❑70, Mar 1959	70.00
❑71, Apr 1959	70.00
❑72, May 1959	70.00
❑73, Jun 1959	70.00
❑74, Jul 1959	70.00
❑75, Aug 1959	70.00
❑76, Sep 1959	70.00
❑77, Oct 1959	70.00
❑78, Nov 1959	70.00
❑79, Dec 1959	70.00
❑80, Mar 1960	70.00
❑81, May 1960	70.00
❑82, Jul 1960, JKu (a)	70.00
❑83, Sep 1960, RA (a); 1: Charlie Cigar. 1: Little Al. 1: Big Al.	70.00
❑84, Nov 1960	70.00
❑85, Jan 1961	70.00
❑86, Mar 1961	70.00
❑87, May 1961, 1: Haunted Tank.	300.00
❑88, Jul 1961	55.00
❑89, Sep 1961	55.00
❑90, Nov 1961	55.00
❑91, Jan 1962	55.00
❑92, Mar 1962	55.00
❑93, May 1962	55.00
❑94, Jul 1962	55.00
❑95, Sep 1962	55.00
❑96, Nov 1962	55.00
❑97, Jan 1963	55.00
❑98, Mar 1963	55.00
❑99, May 1963	55.00
❑100, Jul 1963	55.00
❑101, Sep 1963	45.00
❑102, Nov 1963	45.00
❑103, Jan 1964, RH (c); JKu (a); Painted cover	45.00
❑104, Mar 1964, Sgt. Mule back-up	45.00
❑105, May 1964, JKu (c)	45.00
❑106, Jul 1964, JKu (c)	45.00
❑107, Sep 1964, JKu (c); JKu (a)	45.00
❑108, Nov 1964, JKu (c)	45.00
❑109, Jan 1965, JKu (c)	45.00
❑110, Mar 1965, JKu (c); JKu (a)	45.00
❑111, May 1965, JKu (c)	38.00
❑112, Jul 1965, JKu (c)	38.00
❑113, Sep 1965, (c)	38.00
❑114, Nov 1965, RH (c); O: Haunted Tank.	75.00
❑115, Jan 1966, (c)	28.00
❑116, Mar 1966, JKu (c); A: Johnny Cloud.	28.00
❑117, May 1966, JKu (c)	28.00
❑118, Jul 1966, (c)	28.00
❑119, Sep 1966	28.00
❑120, Nov 1966, (c); A: Johnny Cloud. A: Sgt. Rock.	28.00
❑121, Jan 1967, (c)	22.00
❑122, Mar 1967, JKu (c); JAb (a)	22.00
❑123, May 1967, (c)	22.00
❑124, Jul 1967, RH (c); RH (a)	22.00
❑125, Sep 1967, RH (c)	22.00
❑126, Nov 1967, RH (c)	22.00
❑127, Jan 1968, JKu (c)	22.00
❑128, Mar 1968, (c)	22.00
❑129, May 1968, RH (c)	22.00
❑130, Jul 1968, RH (c); A: Attila the Hun's ghost.	22.00
❑131, Sep 1968	22.00
❑132, Nov 1968, JKu (c); JAb (a)	22.00
❑133, Jan 1969, JKu (c)	22.00
❑134, Mar 1969, JKu (c)	22.00
❑135, May 1969, JKu (c)	22.00
❑136, Jul 1969	22.00
❑137, Sep 1969, JKu (c)	22.00
❑138, Nov 1969, 1: Losers.	22.00
❑139, Jan 1970, JKu (c); RH (a)	22.00
❑140, Mar 1970	22.00
❑141, May 1970, JKu (c)	8.00
❑142, Jul 1970	8.00
❑143, Sep 1970, JKu (c)	8.00
❑144, Nov 1970, JKu (c)	8.00
❑145, Jan 1971	8.00
❑146, Mar 1971, Giant-size	10.00
❑147, May 1971, Giant-size (c)	10.00
❑148, Jul 1971, Giant-size	10.00
❑149, Sep 1971, JKu (c); Sgt. Rock back-up	10.00
❑150, Nov 1971, JKu (c); RH (a); 1: New Haunted Tank.	10.00
❑151, Jan 1972, JKu (c)	8.00
❑152, Mar 1972, JKu (c)	8.00
❑153, May 1972, JKu (c)	8.00
❑154, Jul 1972, JKu (c)	8.00
❑155, Sep 1972	8.00
❑156, Nov 1972	8.00
❑157, Jan 1973, JKu (c)	8.00
❑158, Feb 1973, (c)	8.00
❑159, Mar 1973, JKu (c); GM, RE (a)	8.00
❑160, May 1973	8.00
❑161, Jun 1973, JKu (c)	7.00
❑162, Jul 1973, JKu (c)	7.00
❑163, Aug 1973	7.00
❑164, Sep 1973, (c)	7.00
❑165, Oct 1973	7.00
❑166, Nov 1973, (c)	7.00
❑167, Dec 1973, (c)	7.00
❑168, Jan 1974, (c)	7.00
❑169, Feb 1974, Reprints	7.00
❑170, Mar 1974, (c)	7.00
❑171, Jun 1974, JKu (c)	7.00
❑172, Aug 1974, (c)	7.00
❑173, Oct 1974, JKu (c)	7.00
❑174, Dec 1974, JKu (c)	7.00
❑175, Feb 1975, JKu (c)	7.00
❑176, Mar 1975, JKu (c)	7.00
❑177, Apr 1975	7.00
❑178, May 1975, JKu (c)	7.00
❑179, Jun 1975, JKu (c)	7.00
❑180, Jul 1975, JKu (c)	7.00
❑181, Aug 1975	5.00
❑182, Sep 1975	5.00
❑183, Oct 1975, JKu (c)	5.00
❑184, Nov 1975, JKu (c)	5.00
❑185, Dec 1975	5.00
❑186, Jan 1976	5.00
❑187, Feb 1976, JKu (c)	5.00
❑188, Mar 1976, (c)	5.00
❑189, Apr 1976, (c)	5.00
❑190, May 1976	5.00
❑191, Jun 1976	5.00
❑192, Jul 1976, Bicentennial #27; O.S.S. stories begin	5.00
❑193, Aug 1976, JKu (c)	5.00
❑194, Sep 1976	5.00
❑195, Oct 1976, JKu (c)	5.00
❑196, Nov 1976, JKu (c)	5.00
❑197, Dec 1976, JKu (c)	5.00
❑198, Jan 1977, JKu (c)	5.00
❑199, Feb 1977, JKu (c)	5.00
❑200, Mar 1977, JKu (c)	5.00
❑201, Apr 1977, JKu (c)	3.50
❑202, Jun 1977, JKu (c)	3.50
❑203, Aug 1977, JKu (c)	3.50
❑204, Oct 1977, JKu (c)	3.50
❑205, Dec 1977, JKu (c)	3.50
❑206, Feb 1978	3.50
❑207, Apr 1978	3.50
❑208, Jun 1978	3.50
❑209, Aug 1978, JKu (c)	3.50
❑210, Oct 1978	3.50
❑211, Dec 1978, JKu (c)	3.50
❑212, Feb 1979, JKu (c)	3.50
❑213, Apr 1979, JKu (c)	3.50
❑214, Jun 1979	3.50
❑215, Aug 1979	3.50
❑216, Oct 1979	3.50
❑217, Dec 1979	3.50
❑218, Feb 1980	3.50
❑219, Apr 1980, JKu (c)	3.50
❑220, Jun 1980, JKu (c)	3.50
❑221, Aug 1980	3.50
❑222, Oct 1980, JKu (c)	3.50
❑223, Nov 1980, JKu (c)	3.50
❑224, Dec 1980, JKu (c)	3.50
❑225, Jan 1981	3.50
❑226, Feb 1981, JKu (c)	3.50
❑227, Mar 1981, JKu (c)	3.50
❑228, Apr 1981, JKu (c)	3.50
❑229, May 1981, JKu (c)	3.50
❑230, Jun 1981, JKu (c)	3.50
❑231, Jul 1981, JKu (c)	3.50
❑232, Aug 1981, JKu (c); 1: Kana.	3.50
❑233, Sep 1981, JKu (c)	3.50
❑234, Oct 1981, JKu (c)	3.50
❑235, Nov 1981, JKu (c)	3.50

Other grades: Multiply price above by 5/6 for VF/NM • 2/3 for VERY FINE • 1/3 for FINE • 1/5 for VERY GOOD • 1/8 for GOOD

❑236, Dec 1981, JKu (c) 3.50
❑237, Jan 1982, JKu (c) 3.50
❑238, Feb 1982, JKu (c) 3.50
❑239, Mar 1982, JKu (c) 3.50
❑240, Apr 1982, JKu (c) 3.50
❑241, May 1982, JKu (c) 3.50
❑242, Jun 1982, JKu (c); 1: The Mercenaries. 3.50
❑243, Jul 1982, JKu (c) 3.50
❑244, Aug 1982, JKu (c); A: Mercenaries. 3.50
❑245, Sep 1982, JKu (c) 3.50
❑246, Oct 1982, 30th anniversary JKu (c); A: Ninja. A: Johnny Cloud. A: Gunner & Sarge. A: Sgt. Rock. A: Captain Storm. A: Falcon. A: Haunted Tank. 3.50
❑247, Nov 1982, JKu (c) 3.50
❑248, Dec 1982, JKu (c) 3.50
❑249, Jan 1983, JKu (c) 3.50
❑250, Feb 1983, JKu (c) 3.50
❑251, Mar 1983, JKu (c) 2.50
❑252, Apr 1983, JKu (c) 2.50
❑253, May 1983, JKu (c) 2.50
❑254, Jun 1983, JKu (c) 2.50
❑255, Jul 1983, JKu (c) 2.50
❑256, Aug 1983, JKu (c) 2.50
❑257, Sep 1983, JKu (c) 2.50
❑258, Oct 1983, JKu (c) 2.50
❑259, Nov 1983, JKu (c) 2.50
❑260, Dec 1983, JKu (c) 2.50
❑261, Jan 1984, JKu (c) 2.50
❑262, Feb 1984, JKu (c) 2.50
❑263, Mar 1984, JKu (c) 2.50
❑264, Apr 1984, JKu (c) 2.50
❑265, May 1984, JKu (c) 2.50
❑266, Jun 1984, JKu (c) 2.50
❑267, Jul 1984, JKu (c); KG (a) 2.50
❑268, Aug 1984, JKu (c) 2.50
❑269, Sep 1984, JKu (c) 2.50
❑270, Oct 1984, JKu (c) 2.50
❑271, Nov 1984, JKu (c) 2.50
❑272, Dec 1984, JKu (c) 2.50
❑273, Jan 1985, JKu (c) 2.50
❑274, Feb 1985, JKu (c); A: Monitor. A: Attila 2.50
❑275, Mar 1985, JKu (c) 2.50
❑276, Apr 1985, JKu (c) 2.50
❑277, May 1985, JKu (c) 2.50
❑278, Jul 1985, JKu (c) 2.50
❑279, Sep 1985, JKu (c) 2.50
❑280, Nov 1985, JKu (c) 2.50
❑281, Jan 1986, JKu (c) 2.50
❑282, Mar 1986, JKu (c); Mercenaries 2.50
❑283, May 1986, JKu (c); Mercenaries 2.50
❑284, Jul 1986, JKu (c); Mercenaries. 2.50
❑285, Sep 1986, JKu (c); Mercenaries 2.50
❑286, Nov 1986, JKu (c); Mercenaries 2.50
❑287, Jan 1987, JKu (c); Haunted Tank 2.50
❑288, Mar 1987, JKu (c); Haunted Tank 2.50

GIDEON HAWK
BIG SHOT

❑1, Jan 1995, b&w 2.00
❑2, Mar 1995, b&w 2.00
❑3, Jun 1995, b&w 2.00

GIDGET
DELL

❑1, Apr 1966 100.00

GIFT
IMAGE

❑1, ca. 2004 2.99
❑1/DirCut, Apr 2005 3.99
❑2, ca. 2004 2.99
❑3, ca. 2004 2.99
❑4, ca. 2004 2.99
❑5, ca. 2004 2.99
❑6, ca. 2004 2.99
❑7, ca. 2004 2.99
❑8 2004 2.99
❑9, Nov 2004 2.99
❑10, Mar 2005 2.99
❑11, ca. 2005 2.99
❑12 2005 2.99
❑13 2005 2.99
❑14, Mar 2006 2.99

GIFT, THE: A FIRST PUBLISHING HOLIDAY SPECIAL
FIRST

❑1, Nov 1990 5.95

GIFTS OF THE NIGHT
DC / VERTIGO

❑1, Feb 1999 2.95
❑2, Mar 1999 2.95
❑3, Apr 1999 2.95
❑4, May 1999 2.95

GIGANTOR
ANTARCTIC / VERTIGO

❑1, Jan 2000 2.50

GIGOLO
FANTAGRAPHICS / EROS

❑1 2.95
❑2, Nov 1995 2.95

G.I. GOVERNMENT ISSUED
PARANOID

❑1, Aug 1994 2.00
❑2, Aug 1994 2.00

G.I. JACKRABBITS
EXCALIBUR

Value: Cover or less

❑1, Dec 1986, 1.50

GI JOE (VOL. 1)
DARK HORSE

❑1, Dec 1995 FM (c); FM (a); 1: Tall Sally. 1: Short Fuse. 2.00
❑2, Jan 1996 2.00
❑3, Mar 1996 2.00
❑4, Apr 1996 2.00

GI JOE (VOL. 2)
DARK HORSE

❑1, Jun 1996 2.50
❑2, Jul 1996 2.50
❑3, Aug 1996 2.50
❑4, Sep 1996 2.50

G.I. JOE (IMAGE)
IMAGE

❑1, Sep 2001 3.00
❑1/2nd, Sep 2001 2.95
❑2, ca. 2001 2.95
❑3, ca. 2002 2.95
❑4, ca. 2002 3.50
❑5, ca. 2002; Duke vs. Major Bludd 2.95
❑6, ca. 2002 2.95
❑7, ca. 2002 2.95
❑8, ca. 2002 2.95
❑9, ca. 2002 2.95
❑10, ca. 2002 2.95
❑11, ca. 2002 2.95
❑12, Nov 2002 2.95
❑13, Dec 2002 2.95
❑14, Jan 2003 2.95
❑15, Feb 2003 2.95
❑16, Mar 2003 2.95
❑17, Apr 2003 2.95
❑18, Jun 2003 2.95
❑19, Jul 2003 2.95
❑20, Aug 2003 2.95
❑21, Aug 2003 2.95
❑22, Nov 2003 2.95
❑22/Graham, Nov 2003; Michael Turner cover art. Produced exclusively for Graham Crackers Comics, Naperville, Ill. 12.00
❑23, Nov 2003 2.95
❑24, Nov 2003 2.95
❑25, Dec 2003 2.95

G.I. JOE (DEVIL'S DUE)
DEVIL'S DUE

❑26, Mar 2004 2.95
❑27, Apr 2004 2.95
❑28, May 2004 2.95
❑29, Jun 2004 2.95
❑30, Jul 2004 2.95
❑31, Aug 2004 2.95
❑32, Sep 2004 2.95
❑33, Oct 2004 2.95
❑34, Nov 2004 2.95
❑35, Dec 2004 2.95
❑35/Variant, Dec 2004 3.95
❑36, Jan 2005 2.95
❑37, Feb 2005 2.95
❑38, Mar 2005 2.95
❑39, Apr 2005 2.95
❑40, May 2005 2.95
❑41, Jun 2005 2.95
❑42, Jul 2005 2.95

G.I. JOE: AMERICA'S ELITE
DEVIL'S DUE

❑0, Jun 2005 2.95
❑1, Jul 2005 2.95
❑1/Conv, Jul 2005; San Diego Con exclusive; sold for $10; 500 produced. Cover by Sunder Raj. 10.00
❑1/Autographed, Jul 2005 14.95
❑2, Aug 2005 2.95
❑3, Sep 2005 2.95
❑4, Oct 2005 2.95
❑5, Nov 2005 2.95
❑6, Dec 2005 2.95
❑7, Jan 2006 2.95
❑9, Mar 2006 2.95
❑10, Apr 2006 2.95
❑11, May 2006 2.95
❑12, Jun 2006 2.95

G.I. JOE: AMERICA'S ELITE DATA DESK HANDBOOK
DEVIL'S DUE

❑1, Dec 2005 4.95

G.I. JOE: AMERICA'S ELITE - THE HUNT FOR COBRA COMMANDER
DEVIL'S DUE

❑1, May 2006 .25

G.I. JOE AND THE TRANSFORMERS
MARVEL

❑1, Jan 1987 HT (a) 1.00
❑2, Feb 1987 1.00
❑3, Mar 1987 1.00
❑4, Apr 1987 1.00

G.I. JOE: BATTLE FILES
IMAGE

❑1 2002 5.95
❑2 2002 5.95
❑3 2002 5.95

G.I. JOE BATTLE FILES ULTIMATE SOURCE BOOK
IMAGE

❑Book 1, ca. 2003 14.95

G.I. JOE COMICS MAGAZINE
MARVEL

❑1, Dec 1986; digest 3.00
❑2, Feb 1987; digest 2.00
❑3, Apr 1987; digest 2.00
❑4, Jun 1987; digest 2.00
❑5, Aug 1987; digest 2.00
❑6, Oct 1987; digest 2.00
❑7, Dec 1987; digest 2.00
❑8, Feb 1988; digest 2.00
❑9, Apr 1988; digest 2.00
❑10, Jun 1988; digest 2.00
❑11, Aug 1988; digest 2.00
❑12, Oct 1988; digest 2.00
❑13, Dec 1988; digest 2.00

G.I. JOE: DECLASSIFIED
DEVIL'S DUE

❑1, Jun 2006 3.95
❑1/Spaulding, Jun 2006 3.95

G.I. JOE EUROPEAN MISSIONS
MARVEL

❑1, Jun 1988 1.50
❑2, Jul 1988 1.50
❑3, Aug 1988 1.50
❑4, Sep 1988 1.50
❑5, Oct 1988 1.50
❑6, Nov 1988 1.50
❑7, Dec 1988 1.50
❑8, Jan 1989 1.50
❑9, Feb 1989 1.50
❑10, Mar 1989 1.50
❑11, Apr 1989 1.50
❑12, May 1989 1.75
❑13, Jun 1989 1.75
❑14, Jul 1989 1.75
❑15, Aug 1989 1.75

Gideon Hawk

High-tech bounty hunter in outer space

©Big Shot

Gifts of the Night

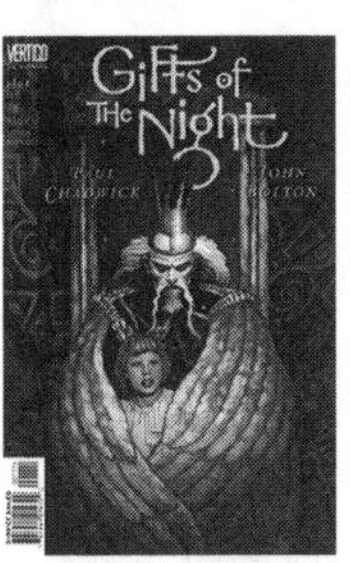

Paul Chadwick and John Bolton get medieval

©DC

G.I. Joe (Image)

Image relaunched the Joes for a new era

©Image

G.I. Joe European Missions

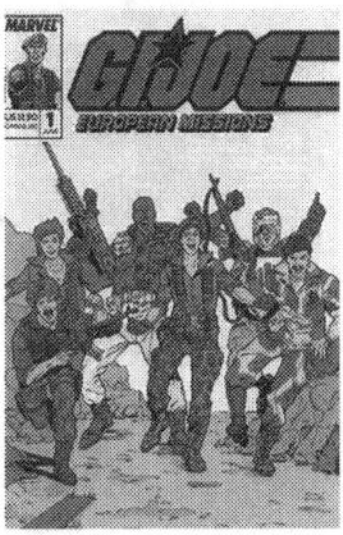

Reprints Action Force comics from Britain

©Marvel

G.I. Joe, A Real American Hero

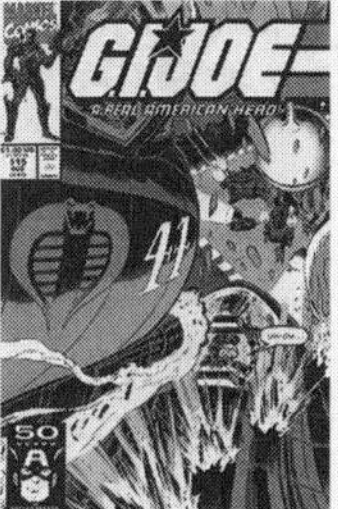

First series advertised on national TV

©Marvel

G.I. JOE: FRONTLINE
Image

	N-MINT
❑1, Oct 2002	2.95
❑1/Platinum, Oct 2002	5.00
❑2, Nov 2002	2.95
❑3, Dec 2002	2.95
❑4, Jan 2003	2.95
❑5, Feb 2003	2.95
❑6, Mar 2003	2.95
❑7, Apr 2003	2.95
❑8, Jul 2003	2.95
❑9, Jul 2003	2.95
❑10, Jul 2003	2.95
❑11, Aug 2003	2.95
❑12, Aug 2003	2.95
❑13, Aug 2003	2.95
❑14, Sep 2003	2.95
❑15, Oct 2003	2.95
❑16, Nov 2003	2.95
❑17, Nov 2003	2.95
❑18, Dec 2003	2.95

G.I. JOE IN 3-D
Blackthorne

	N-MINT
❑1, Jul 1987	3.00
❑2, Oct 1987	2.50
❑3, Jan 1988	2.50
❑4, Apr 1988	2.50
❑5, Jul 1988	2.50
❑6, Oct 1988	2.50

G.I. JOE: MASTER & APPRENTICE
Devil's Due

	N-MINT
❑1, Jun 2004	2.95
❑2, Jul 2004	2.95
❑3, Sep 2004	2.95
❑4, Oct 2004	2.95

G.I. JOE: MASTER & APPRENTICE VOL. II
Devil's Due

	N-MINT
❑1 2005	3.00
❑1/Variant 2005	4.00
❑2 2005	3.00
❑2/Variant 2005	4.00
❑3 2005	3.00
❑3/Variant 2005	4.00

G.I. JOE ORDER OF BATTLE
Marvel

	N-MINT
❑1, Dec 1986; The Official G.I. Joe Handbook	1.25
❑2, Jan 1987; Rocky Balboa	1.25
❑3, Feb 1987	1.25
❑4, Mar 1987	1.25

G.I. JOE, A REAL AMERICAN HERO
Marvel

	N-MINT
❑1, Jun 1982; Giant-size HT (a)	14.00
❑2, Aug 1982	8.00
❑2/2nd, Aug 1982	2.00
❑3, Sep 1982, HT, JAb (a)	4.00
❑3/2nd, Sep 1982	2.00
❑4, Oct 1982, BH (c); HT, JAb (a)	4.00
❑4/2nd, Oct 1982	2.00
❑5, Nov 1982, HT, JAb (a)	4.00
❑5/2nd, Nov 1982	2.00
❑6, Dec 1982, HT (a)	4.00
❑6/2nd, Dec 1982	1.00
❑7, Jan 1983, HT (a)	4.00
❑7/2nd, Jan 1983	1.00
❑8, Feb 1983, HT (a)	4.00
❑8/2nd, Feb 1983	1.00
❑9, Mar 1983	4.00
❑9/2nd, Mar 1983	1.00
❑10, Apr 1983	6.00
❑10/2nd, Apr 1983	1.00
❑11, May 1983	4.00
❑11/2nd, May 1983	1.00
❑12, Jun 1983	4.00
❑12/2nd, Jun 1983	1.00
❑13, Jul 1983	4.00
❑13/2nd, Jul 1983	1.00
❑14, Aug 1983	5.00
❑14/2nd, Aug 1983	1.00
❑15, Sep 1983	4.00
❑15/2nd, Sep 1983	1.00
❑16, Oct 1983	4.00
❑16/2nd, Oct 1983	1.00
❑17, Nov 1983	4.00
❑17/2nd, Nov 1983	1.00
❑18, Dec 1983	4.00
❑18/2nd, Dec 1983	1.00
❑19, Jan 1984	6.00
❑19/2nd, Jan 1984	1.00
❑20, Feb 1984	4.00
❑20/2nd, Feb 1984	1.00
❑21, Mar 1984, "silent" issue	15.00
❑21/2nd, Mar 1984	1.00
❑22, Apr 1984	4.00
❑22/2nd, Apr 1984	1.00
❑23, May 1984	4.00
❑23/2nd, May 1984	1.00
❑24, Jun 1984	4.00
❑24/2nd, Jun 1984	1.00
❑25, Jul 1984	4.00
❑25/2nd, Jul 1984	1.00
❑26, Aug 1984, O: Snake Eyes.	4.00
❑26/2nd, Aug 1984, O: Snake Eyes.	1.00
❑27, Sep 1984, O: Snake Eyes.	4.00
❑27/2nd, Sep 1984, O: Snake Eyes.	1.00
❑28, Oct 1984	4.00
❑28/2nd, Oct 1984	1.00
❑29, Nov 1984	4.00
❑29/2nd, Nov 1984	1.00
❑30, Dec 1984	4.00
❑30/2nd, Dec 1984	1.00
❑31, Jan 1985	4.00
❑31/2nd, Jan 1985	1.00
❑32, Feb 1985	4.00
❑32/2nd, Feb 1985	1.00
❑33, Mar 1985	4.00
❑33/2nd, Mar 1985	1.00
❑34, Apr 1985	4.00
❑34/2nd, Apr 1985	1.00
❑35, May 1985	4.00
❑35/2nd, May 1985	1.00
❑36, Jun 1985	4.00
❑36/2nd, Jun 1985	1.00
❑37, Jul 1985	4.00
❑38, Aug 1985	4.00
❑39, Sep 1985	4.00
❑40, Oct 1985	4.00
❑41, Nov 1985	4.00
❑42, Dec 1985	4.00
❑43, Jan 1986	4.00
❑44, Feb 1986	4.00
❑45, Mar 1986	4.00
❑46, Apr 1986	4.00
❑47, May 1986	4.00
❑48, Jun 1986	4.00
❑49, Jul 1986	4.00
❑50, Aug 1986; Double-size	4.00
❑51, Sep 1986	4.00
❑52, Oct 1986	4.00
❑53, Nov 1986	4.00
❑54, Dec 1986	4.00
❑55, Jan 1987	4.00
❑56, Feb 1987	5.00
❑57, Mar 1987	3.00
❑58, Apr 1987	4.00
❑59, May 1987	3.00
❑60, Jun 1987 TMc (a)	3.00
❑61, Jul 1987	3.00
❑62, Aug 1987	3.00
❑63, Sep 1987	3.00
❑64, Oct 1987	3.00
❑65, Nov 1987	3.00
❑66, Dec 1987	3.00
❑67, Jan 1988	3.00
❑68, Feb 1988	3.00
❑69, Mar 1988	3.00
❑70, Apr 1988	3.00
❑71, May 1988	3.00
❑72, Jun 1988	3.00
❑73, Jul 1988	3.00
❑74, Aug 1988	3.00
❑75, Sep 1988	3.00
❑76, Sep 1988	3.00
❑77, Oct 1988	3.00
❑78, Oct 1988	3.00
❑79, Nov 1988	3.00
❑80, Nov 1988	3.00
❑81, Dec 1988	3.00
❑82, Jan 1989	3.00
❑83, Feb 1989	3.00
❑84, Mar 1989	3.00
❑85, Apr 1989	3.00
❑86, May 1989	3.00
❑87, Jun 1989	3.00
❑88, Jul 1989	3.00
❑89, Aug 1989	3.00
❑90, Sep 1989	3.00
❑91, Oct 1989	3.00
❑92, Nov 1989	3.00
❑93, Nov 1989	3.00
❑94, Dec 1989	3.00
❑95, Dec 1989	3.00
❑96, Jan 1990	3.00
❑97, Feb 1990	3.00
❑98, Mar 1990	3.00
❑99, Apr 1990	3.00
❑100, May 1990; Giant size	3.00
❑101, Jun 1990	3.00
❑102, Jul 1990	3.00
❑103, Aug 1990	3.00

Other grades: Multiply price above by 5/6 for VF/NM • 2/3 for VERY FINE • 1/3 for FINE • 1/5 for VERY GOOD • 1/8 for GOOD

N-MINT

❑104, Sep 1990 .... 3.00
❑105, Oct 1990 .... 3.00
❑106, Nov 1990 .... 3.00
❑107, Dec 1990 .... 3.00
❑108, Jan 1991; Dossiers begin 3.00
❑109, Feb 1991 .... 3.00
❑110, Mar 1991 .... 3.00
❑111, Apr 1991 .... 3.00
❑112, May 1991 .... 3.00
❑113, Jun 1991 .... 3.00
❑114, Jul 1991 1: Metal-Head. 3.00
❑115, Aug 1991 .... 3.00
❑116, Sep 1991 .... 3.00
❑117, Oct 1991 .... 3.00
❑118, Nov 1991 .... 3.00
❑119, Dec 1991 HT (a) 3.00
❑120, Jan 1992 .... 3.00
❑121, Feb 1992 .... 3.00
❑122, Mar 1992 .... 3.00
❑123, Apr 1992 .... 3.00
❑124, May 1992 .... 3.00
❑125, Jun 1992 .... 3.00
❑126, Jul 1992 .... 3.00
❑127, Sep 1992 .... 3.00
❑128, Sep 1992 .... 3.00
❑129, Oct 1992 .... 3.00
❑130, Nov 1992 .... 3.00
❑131, Dec 1992 .... 3.00
❑132, Jan 1993 .... 3.00
❑133, Feb 1993 .... 3.00
❑134, Mar 1993 A: Snake Eyes. 3.00
❑135, Apr 1993; Polybagged with trading card; Team members are regrouped into three strike teams 3.00
❑136, May 1993; trading card 3.00
❑137, Jun 1993; trading card 3.00
❑138, Jul 1993; bagged with trading card 3.00
❑139, Aug 1993; Transformers 3.00
❑140, Sep 1993; Transformers 3.00
❑141, Oct 1993 A: Transformers: Generation 2. A: Megatron. A: Cobra Commander. 3.00
❑142, Nov 1993; Transformers 3.00
❑143, Dec 1993 .... 3.00
❑144, Jan 1994 .... 3.00
❑145, Feb 1994 .... 3.00
❑146, Mar 1994 .... 3.00
❑147, Apr 1994 .... 3.00
❑148, May 1994 .... 3.00
❑149, Jun 1994 .... 3.00
❑150, Jul 1994; Giant-size 3.00
❑151, Aug 1994 .... 3.00
❑152, Sep 1994 .... 7.00
❑153, Oct 1994 .... 7.00
❑154, Nov 1994 .... 7.00
❑155, Dec 1994 .... 16.00
❑Yearbook 1, Mar 1985; Yearbook (annual) #1 .... 2.50
❑Yearbook 2, Mar 1986; Yearbook (annual) #2 .... 2.50
❑Yearbook 3, Mar 1987; Yearbook (annual) #3 .... 2.50
❑Yearbook 4, Feb 1988; Yearbook (annual) #4 .... 2.50
❑Special 1, Feb 1995 TMc (c) 2.50

G.I. JOE: RELOADED
DEVIL'S DUE

❑1, May 2004 .... 5.00
❑2, Jun 2004 .... 3.00
❑3, Jul 2004 .... 3.00
❑4, Aug 2004 .... 2.95
❑5, Sep 2004 .... 2.95
❑6, Oct 2004 .... 2.95
❑7, Nov 2004 .... 2.95
❑8, Dec 2004 .... 2.95
❑9, Jan 2005 .... 2.95
❑10, Feb 2005 .... 2.95
❑11, Mar 2005 .... 2.95
❑12, Apr 2005 .... 2.95
❑13, May 2005 .... 2.95
❑14, Jun 2005 .... 2.95

G.I. JOE: SIGMA 6
DEVIL'S DUE

❑1, Jan 2006 .... 2.95
❑2, Jan 2006 .... 2.95
❑3, Mar 2006 .... 2.95
❑4, Mar 2006 .... 2.95
❑5, Apr 2006 .... 2.95
❑6, May 2006 .... 2.95

G.I. JOE: SNAKE EYES DECLASSIFIED
DEVIL'S DUE

❑1, Sep 2005 .... 2.95
❑2 2005 .... 2.95
❑3, Dec 2005 .... 2.95
❑4, Jan 2006 .... 2.95
❑5, Jan 2006 .... 2.95
❑6, Feb 2006 .... 2.95

G.I. JOE SPECIAL MISSIONS
MARVEL

❑1, Oct 1986 .... 1.50
❑2, Dec 1986 .... 1.00
❑3, Feb 1987 .... 1.00
❑4, Apr 1987 .... 1.00
❑5, Jun 1987 .... 1.00
❑6, Aug 1987 .... 1.00
❑7, Oct 1987 .... 1.00
❑8, Dec 1987 .... 1.00
❑9, Feb 1988 .... 1.00
❑10, Apr 1988 .... 1.00
❑11, Jun 1988 .... 1.00
❑12, Aug 1988 .... 1.00
❑13, Sep 1988 .... 1.00
❑14, Oct 1988 BMc (c); HT (a) 1.00
❑15, Nov 1988 .... 1.00
❑16, Dec 1988 BMc (c); HT (a) 1.00
❑17, Jan 1989 .... 1.00
❑18, Feb 1989 .... 1.00
❑19, Mar 1989 .... 1.00
❑20, Apr 1989 BMc (c); HT (a) 1.00
❑21, May 1989 .... 1.00
❑22, Jun 1989 .... 1.00
❑23, Jul 1989 .... 1.00
❑24, Aug 1989 .... 1.00
❑25, Sep 1989 .... 1.00
❑26, Oct 1989 HT (a) 1.00
❑27, Nov 1989 .... 1.00
❑28, Nov 1989 HT (a) 1.00
❑Book 1, Feb 1989 .... 6.95

G.I. JOE: SPECIAL MISSIONS - MANHATTAN
DEVIL'S DUE

❑1, Feb 2006 .... 2.95

G.I. JOE VS. TRANSFORMERS: THE ART OF WAR
DEVIL'S DUE

❑1, Mar 2006 .... 2.95
❑1/Variant, Mar 2006 .... 2.95
❑2, Apr 206 .... 2.95
❑2/Variant, Apr 2006 .... 2.95
❑3, May 2006 .... 2.95
❑3/Variant, May 2006 .... 2.95
❑4, Jun 2006 .... 2.95
❑4/Variant, Jun 2006 .... 2.95

G.I. JOE/TRANSFORMERS
IMAGE

❑1, Jul 2003 .... 4.00
❑1/Campbell, Jul 2003 .... 3.00
❑1/Foil, Jul 2003 .... 9.00
❑1/Graham, Jul 2003 .... 4.00
❑1/Graham foil, Jul 2003 .... 6.00
❑1/Miller, Jul 2003 .... 3.00
❑2, Aug 2003 .... 2.95
❑2/Sketch, Aug 2003 .... 12.00
❑3, Sep 2003 .... 2.95
❑3/Convention, Sep 2003 .... 4.00
❑3/Variant, Sep 2003 .... 3.00
❑4, Oct 2003 .... 2.00
❑4/Variant, Oct 2003 .... 3.00
❑5, Dec 2003 .... 2.00
❑5/Variant, Dec 2003 .... 3.00
❑6, Dec 2003 .... 2.00

G.I. JOE VS. THE TRANSFORMERS (2ND SERIES)
DEVIL'S DUE

❑1 2004 .... 4.00
❑1/Variant 2004 .... 4.00
❑2 2004 .... 2.95
❑2/Variant 2004 .... 2.95
❑3 2004 .... 2.95
❑3/Variant 2004 .... 2.95
❑4 2004 .... 2.95
❑4/Variant 2004 .... 2.95

GILGAMESH II
DC

❑1 1989; prestige format 3.95
❑2 1989; prestige format 3.95
❑3 1989; prestige format 3.95
❑4 1989; prestige format 3.95

GIMME
HEAD IMPORTS

❑1 .... 3.00

GIMOLES
ALIAS

❑1, Sep 2005 .... 1.00

G.I. MUTANTS
ETERNITY

❑1, ca. 1987 .... 1.95
❑2, ca. 1987 .... 1.95
❑3, ca. 1987 .... 1.95
❑4, ca. 1987 .... 1.95

GINGER FOX
COMICO

❑1, Sep 1988; Yellow 1.75
❑2, Oct 1988 .... 1.75
❑3, Nov 1988 .... 1.75
❑4, Dec 1988 .... 1.75

GIN-RYU
BELIEVE IN YOURSELF

❑1, Mar 1995 .... 2.75
❑2, May 1995 .... 2.75
❑3 .... 2.75
❑3/Ashcan 1.00
❑4, Oct 1995 .... 2.75

GIPSY
NBM

❑1 .... 10.95
❑2 .... 10.95

G.I. R.A.M.B.O.T.
WONDER COLOR

❑1, Apr 1987 .... 1.95

GIRL
RIP OFF

❑1, Feb 1991, b&w 2.50
❑1/2nd, Oct 1992, b&w 2.50
❑2, May 1991, b&w 2.50
❑3, Aug 1991, b&w 2.50
❑4, Dec 1991, b&w 2.50

GIRL
DC / VERTIGO

❑1, Jul 1996 .... 2.50
❑2, Aug 1996 .... 2.50
❑3, Sep 1996 .... 2.50

GIRL CALLED...WILLOW!
ANGEL

❑1, Fal 1996, b&w 2.95

GIRL CALLED...WILLOW! SKETCHBOOK
ANGEL

❑1, b&w; pin-ups and rough pencil sketches; wraparound cover 2.95

GIRL CRAZY
DARK HORSE

❑1, May 1996, b&w 2.95
❑2, Jul 1996, b&w 2.95
❑3, Jul 1996, b&w 2.95

GIRL FROM U.N.C.L.E.
GOLD KEY

❑1, Jan 1967, 10197-701; pin-up on back cover 36.00
❑2, Apr 1967 .... 24.00
❑3, Jun 1967 .... 20.00
❑4, Aug 1967 .... 15.00
❑5, Oct 1967 .... 15.00

GIRL GENIUS
STUDIO FOGLIO

❑Ashcan 1, Oct 2000, b&w; PF (c); PF (w); PF (a); No cover price; preview of upcoming series; smaller than normal comic book 1.00
❑1, Feb 2001, b&w; PF (c); PF (w); PF (a); cardstock cover 2.95
❑2, Apr 2001 PF (c); PF (w); PF (a) 2.95
❑3, Jun 2001 PF (c); PF (w); PF (a) 2.95

Other grades: Multiply price above by 5/6 for VF/NM • 2/3 for VERY FINE • 1/3 for FINE • 1/5 for VERY GOOD • 1/8 for GOOD

G.I. Joe Special Missions

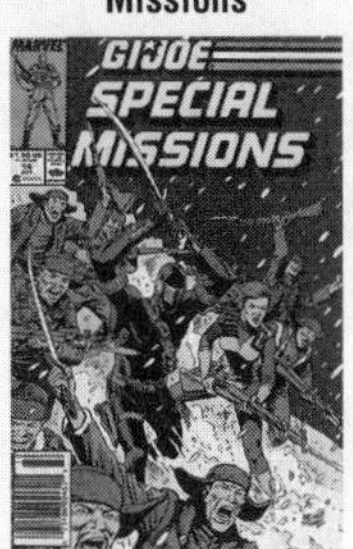

Spin-off title from the main Marvel series

©Marvel

Gilgamesh II

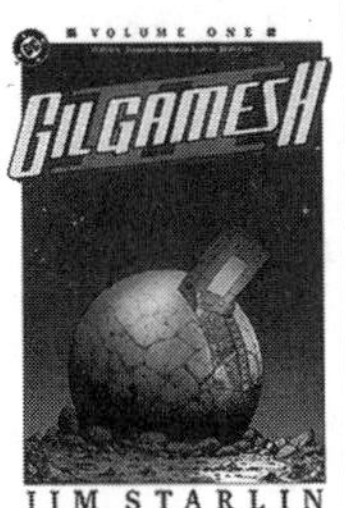

Fun tale of aliens from Jim Starlin

©DC

Girl from U.N.C.L.E.

Stephanie Powers swings in TV spinoff

©Gold Key

Girls' Love Stories

Long-running romance title survived to 1973

©DC

Give Me Liberty

Frank Miller's tale of a future civil war

©Dark Horse

N-MINT

❑4, Aug 2001 PF (c); PF (w); PF (a).... 3.95
❑5, Nov 2001 PF (c); PF (w); PF (a).... 3.95
❑6, May 2002; PF (c); PF (w); PF (a); Publisher name changes to Airship. 3.95
❑7, Jul 2002 PF (c); PF (w); PF (a) 3.95
❑8, Nov 2002 PF (c); PF (w); PF (a).... 3.95
❑9, ca. 2003 ..... 3.95
❑10, ca. 2004 ..... 3.95
❑11, ca. 2004 ..... 3.95

GIRLHERO
High Drive

❑1, Aug 1993, b&w 3.00
❑2, Feb 1994, b&w 3.00
❑3, Jul 1994, b&w 3.00

GIRL ON GIRL COLLEGE KINK: NEW YEAR'S BABES
Angel

❑1 ..... 3.00

GIRL ON GIRL: FEEDIN' TIME
Angel

❑1 ..... 3.00

GIRL ON GIRL: TICKLISH
Angel

❑1 ..... 3.00

GIRL + GIRL
Fantagraphics / Eros

❑1, Dec 2004, ... 3.95

GIRLS
Image

❑1, Jun 2005 ..... 6.00
❑1/Variant, Jun 2005, 2nd printing 4.00
❑1/Sketch, Jun 2005, Sketch version of 2nd print cover 5.00
❑2, Jul 2005 ..... 4.00
❑2/Variant, Jul 2005, 2nd printing 5.00
❑3, Aug 2005 ..... 2.95
❑4, Sep 2005 ..... 2.95
❑5, Oct 2005 ..... 2.95
❑6, Nov 2005 ..... 2.95
❑7, Dec 2006 ..... 2.95
❑8, Jan 2006 ..... 2.95
❑9, Jan 2006 ..... 2.95
❑10, Feb 2006 ..... 2.95
❑11, Apr 2006 ..... 2.95
❑12, May 2006 ..... 2.95
❑13, Jun 2006 ..... 2.95
❑14, Jul 2006 ..... 2.95

GIRLS BRAVO
Tokyopop

❑1, Sep 2005 ..... 9.95
❑2, Dec 2005 ..... 9.95

GIRLS' LOVE STORIES
DC

❑44, Nov 1956 ..... 38.00
❑45, Jan 1957 ..... 38.00
❑46, Mar 1957 ..... 38.00
❑47, May 1957 ..... 38.00
❑48, Jul 1957 ..... 38.00
❑49, Sep 1957 ..... 38.00
❑50, Nov 1957 ..... 30.00
❑51, Dec 1957 ..... 30.00
❑52, Feb 1958 ..... 30.00

N-MINT

❑53, Mar 1958 ..... 30.00
❑54, May 1958 ..... 30.00
❑55, Jun 1958 ..... 30.00
❑56, Aug 1958 ..... 30.00
❑57, Sep 1958 ..... 30.00
❑58, Nov 1958 ..... 30.00
❑59, Dec 1958 ..... 30.00
❑60, Feb 1959 ..... 30.00
❑61, Mar 1959 ..... 30.00
❑62, May 1959 ..... 30.00
❑63, Jun 1959 ..... 30.00
❑64, Aug 1959 ..... 30.00
❑65, Sep 1959 ..... 30.00
❑66, Nov 1959 ..... 30.00
❑67, Dec 1959 ..... 30.00
❑68, Feb 1960 ..... 30.00
❑69, Mar 1960 ..... 30.00
❑70, May 1960 ..... 30.00
❑71, Jun 1960 ..... 30.00
❑72, Aug 1960 ..... 25.00
❑73, Sep 1960 ..... 25.00
❑74, Oct 1960 ..... 25.00
❑75, Nov 1960 ..... 25.00
❑76, Feb 1961 ..... 25.00
❑77, Mar 1961 ..... 25.00
❑78, May 1961 ..... 25.00
❑79, Jun 1961 ..... 25.00
❑80, Jul 1961 ..... 25.00
❑81, Sep 1961 ..... 25.00
❑82, Oct 1961 ..... 25.00
❑83, Nov 1961 ..... 25.00
❑84, Jan 1962 ..... 25.00
❑85, Feb 1962 ..... 25.00
❑86, Apr 1962 ..... 25.00
❑87, May 1962 ..... 25.00
❑88, Jul 1962 ..... 25.00
❑89, Sep 1962 ..... 25.00
❑90, Oct 1962 ..... 25.00
❑91, Nov 1962 ..... 25.00
❑92, Jan 1963 ..... 25.00
❑93, Feb 1963 ..... 25.00
❑94, Apr 1963 ..... 25.00
❑95, May 1963 ..... 20.00
❑96, Jul 1963 ..... 20.00
❑97, Sep 1963 ..... 20.00
❑98, Oct 1963 ..... 20.00
❑99, Nov 1963 ..... 20.00
❑100, Jan 1964 ..... 20.00
❑101, Feb 1964 ..... 20.00
❑102, Apr 1964 ..... 20.00
❑103, May 1964 ..... 20.00
❑104, Jul 1964 ..... 20.00
❑105, Sep 1964 ..... 20.00
❑106, Oct 1964 ..... 17.00
❑107, Nov 1964 ..... 17.00
❑108, Jan 1965 ..... 17.00
❑109, Feb 1965 ..... 17.00
❑110, Apr 1965 ..... 17.00
❑111, May 1965 ..... 17.00
❑112, Jul 1965 ..... 15.00
❑113, Sep 1965 ..... 15.00
❑114, Oct 1965 ..... 15.00
❑115, Nov 1965 ..... 15.00
❑116, Jan 1966 ..... 15.00

N-MINT

❑117, Feb 1966 ..... 15.00
❑118, Apr 1966 ..... 15.00
❑119, May 1966 ..... 15.00
❑120, Jul 1966 ..... 15.00
❑121, Sep 1966 ..... 15.00
❑122, Oct 1966 ..... 15.00
❑123, Nov 1966 ..... 15.00
❑124, Jan 1967 ..... 14.00
❑125, Feb 1967 ..... 14.00
❑126, Apr 1967 ..... 14.00
❑127, May 1967 ..... 14.00
❑128, Jul 1967 ..... 14.00
❑129, Sep 1967 ..... 14.00
❑130, Oct 1967 ..... 14.00
❑131, Nov 1967 ..... 14.00
❑132, Jan 1968 ..... 14.00
❑133, Feb 1968 ..... 14.00
❑134, Apr 1968 ..... 14.00
❑135, May 1968 ..... 14.00
❑136, Jul 1968 ..... 14.00
❑137, Sep 1968 ..... 14.00
❑138, Oct 1968 ..... 14.00
❑139, Nov 1968 ..... 14.00
❑140, Jan 1969 ..... 14.00
❑141, Feb 1969 ..... 14.00
❑142, Apr 1969 ..... 14.00
❑143, May 1969 ..... 14.00
❑144, Jul 1969 ..... 9.00
❑145, Sep 1969 ..... 9.00
❑146, Oct 1969 ..... 9.00
❑147, Nov 1969 ..... 9.00
❑148, Jan 1970 ..... 9.00
❑149, Feb 1970 ..... 9.00
❑150, Apr 1970 ..... 9.00
❑151, May 1970 ..... 9.00
❑152, Jul 1970 ..... 9.00
❑153, Sep 1970 ..... 9.00
❑154, Oct 1970 ..... 9.00
❑155, Nov 1970 ..... 9.00
❑156, Jan 1971 ..... 9.00
❑157, May 1971 ..... 9.00
❑158, Jun 1971 ..... 9.00
❑159, Jul 1971 ..... 9.00
❑160, Aug 1971 ..... 9.00
❑161, Sep 1971 ..... 9.00
❑162, Oct 1971 ..... 9.00
❑163, Nov 1971 ..... 9.00
❑164, Dec 1971 ..... 9.00
❑165, Jan 1972 ..... 7.00
❑166, Feb 1972 ..... 7.00
❑167, Mar 1972 ..... 7.00
❑168, Apr 1972 ..... 7.00
❑169, May 1972 ..... 7.00
❑170, Jun 1972 ..... 7.00
❑171, Jul 1972 ..... 7.00
❑172, Aug 1972 ..... 7.00
❑173, Sep 1972 ..... 7.00
❑174, Oct 1972 ..... 7.00
❑175, Dec 1972 ..... 7.00
❑176, Feb 1973 ..... 7.00
❑177, May 1973 ..... 7.00
❑178, Aug 1973 ..... 7.00
❑179, Oct 1973 ..... 7.00
❑180, Dec 1973 ..... 7.00

Other grades: Multiply price above by 5/6 for VF/NM • 2/3 for VERY FINE • 1/3 for FINE • 1/5 for VERY GOOD • 1/8 for GOOD

GIRLS OF '95: GOOD, BAD & DEADLY
LOST CAUSE
❑1, Feb 1996 ... 3.95

GIRLS OF NINJA HIGH SCHOOL
ANTARCTIC
❑1, b&w ... 3.75
❑2, b&w ... 3.75
❑3, Apr 1993, b&w ... 3.75
❑4, Apr 1994, b&w; 1994 Annual ... 3.95
❑5, Apr 1995; 1995 Annual ... 4.50
❑6, ca. 1996; 1996 Annual ... 3.95
❑7, May 1997; 1997 Annual ... 3.95
❑8/A, May 1998; 1998 Annual ... 3.95
❑8/B, May 1998; 1998 Annual; alternate cover (manga-style) ... 3.95
❑9, Apr 1999; Nylon Menaces: Dandelion; Minerva: Blind Spot; back cover pin-up ... 2.99

GIRL SQUAD X
FANTACO
❑1, b&w ... 2.95

GIRL TALK
FANTAGRAPHICS
❑4, Sum 1996, b&w ... 3.50

GIRL: THE RULE OF DARKNESS
CRY FOR DAWN
❑1, b&w ... 2.50

GIRL WHO WOULD BE DEATH
DC / VERTIGO
❑1, Dec 1998 ... 2.50
❑2, Jan 1999 ... 2.50
❑3, Feb 1999 ... 2.50
❑4, Mar 1999 ... 2.50

GIVE ME LIBERTY! (RIP OFF)
RIP OFF
❑1, Jan 1976 ... 4.00

GIVE ME LIBERTY
DARK HORSE
❑1, Jun 1990; prestige format ... 5.00
❑2, Sep 1990; prestige format ... 5.00
❑3, Dec 1990; prestige format ... 5.00
❑4, Apr 1991; prestige format ... 5.00

G.I. WAR TALES
DC
❑1, Mar 1973 ... 12.00
❑2, Jun 1973, Reprints stories from Star Spangled War Stories #134, G.I. Combat #133 ... 7.00
❑3, Aug 1973, JKu, RH (a); Reprints stories from All American Men of War #55, 38 ... 6.00
❑4, Oct 1973 ... 6.00

GIZMO (MIRAGE)
MIRAGE
❑1, Feb 1986, b&w ... 1.50
❑2, Mar 1986, b&w ... 1.50
❑3, Apr 1986, b&w ... 1.50
❑4, May 1986, b&w ... 1.50
❑5, Mar 1987, b&w ... 1.50
❑6, Jul 1987, b&w ... 1.50
❑Book 1, Dec 1988, The Collected Gizmo 12.95

GIZMO (CHANCE)
CHANCE
❑1 ... 2.50

GIZMO AND THE FUGITOID
MIRAGE
❑1, Jun 1989, b&w ... 2.00
❑2, Jun 1989, b&w ... 2.00

G.L.A.
MARVEL
❑1, May 2005 ... 2.99
❑2, Jun 2005 ... 2.99

GLA
MARVEL
❑1, Jun 2005 ... 5.00
❑2, Jul 2005 ... 2.99
❑3, Aug 2005 ... 2.99
❑4, Sep 2005 ... 2.99

GLADIATOR/SUPREME
MARVEL
❑1, Mar 1997 ... 4.99

GLADSTONE COMIC ALBUM
GLADSTONE
❑1; Uncle Scrooge ... 5.95
❑2; Donald Duck ... 5.95
❑3; Mickey Mouse ... 5.95
❑4; Uncle Scrooge ... 5.95
❑5; Donald Duck ... 5.95
❑6; Uncle Scrooge ... 5.95
❑7; Donald Duck ... 5.95
❑8; Mickey Mouse ... 5.95
❑9; Bambi ... 5.95
❑10; Donald Duck ... 5.95
❑11; Uncle Scrooge ... 5.95
❑12; Donald & Daisy ... 5.95
❑13; Donald Duck ... 5.95
❑14; Uncle Scrooge ... 5.95
❑15; Donald & Gladstone ... 5.95
❑16; Donald Duck ... 5.95
❑17; Mickey Mouse ... 5.95
❑18; Junior Woodchucks ... 5.95
❑19; Uncle Scrooge ... 5.95
❑20; Uncle Scrooge ... 5.95
❑21; Duck Family ... 5.95
❑22; Mickey Mouse ... 5.95
❑23; Donald Duck; Halloween ... 5.95
❑24; Uncle Scrooge ... 5.95
❑25; Donald Duck; Xmas ... 5.95
❑26; Mickey & Donald ... 9.95
❑27; early Donald Duck ... 9.95
❑28; Uncle Scrooge & Donald Duck ... 9.95

GLADSTONE COMIC ALBUM SPECIAL
GLADSTONE
❑1 ... 8.95
❑2; Uncle Scrooge, Donald ... 8.95
❑3; Mickey Mouse ... 8.95
❑4; Uncle Scrooge ... 11.95
❑5; Donald ... 11.95
❑6; Uncle Scrooge ... 12.95
❑7; Mickey Mouse ... 13.95

GLAMOROUS GRAPHIX PRESENTS
GLAMOROUS GRAPHIX
❑1, Jan 1996, b&w; Becky Sunshine; pin-ups ... 3.95

GLASS JAW (VOL. 2)
CLAY HEELED
❑1; no date ... 2.95

GLOBAL FORCE
SILVERLINE
❑1 ... 1.95
❑2 ... 1.95

GLOBAL FREQUENCY
DC / WILDSTORM
❑1, Dec 2002 ... 2.95
❑2, Jan 2003 ... 2.95
❑3, Feb 2003 ... 2.95
❑4, Mar 2003 ... 2.95
❑5, Apr 2003 ... 2.95
❑6, May 2003 ... 2.95
❑7, Jun 2003 ... 2.95
❑8, Jul 2003 ... 2.95
❑9, Sep 2003 ... 2.95
❑10, Sep 2003 ... 2.95
❑11, Mar 2004 ... 2.95
❑12, Aug 2004 ... 2.95

GLOOMCOOKIE
SLAVE LABOR
❑1, Jun 1999 ... 4.00
❑2, Sep 1999 ... 3.50
❑3, Dec 1999 ... 3.00
❑4, Mar 2000 ... 2.95
❑5, Jun 2000 ... 2.95
❑6, Oct 2000 ... 2.95
❑7, Apr 2001 ... 2.95
❑8, Jun 2001 ... 2.95
❑9, Sep 2001 ... 2.95
❑10, Dec 2001 ... 2.95
❑11, Feb 2002 ... 2.95
❑12, Apr 2002 ... 2.95
❑13 2002 ... 2.95
❑14 2003 ... 2.95
❑15 2003 ... 2.95
❑16 2003 ... 2.95
❑17 2003 ... 2.95
❑18 2003 ... 2.95
❑19 2004 ... 2.95
❑20 2004 ... 2.95
❑21 2004 ... 2.95
❑22 2004 ... 2.95
❑23 2005 ... 2.95
❑24, Sep 2005 ... 2.95
❑25, Nov 2005 ... 2.95

GLOOM
APCOMICS
❑1, Jun 2005 ... 3.50
❑2, Sep 2005 ... 3.50

GLORIANNA
PRESS THIS
❑1, b&w ... 3.95

GLORY
IMAGE
❑0, Feb 1996 ... 2.50
❑1, Mar 1995 ... 2.50
❑1/A, Mar 1995; Image publishes; alternate cover ... 2.50
❑2, Apr 1995 ... 2.50
❑3, May 1995 ... 2.50
❑4, Jun 1995 ... 2.50
❑4/A, Jun 1995; Variant cover ... 2.50
❑5, Aug 1995; polybagged with trading card ... 2.50
❑6, Sep 1995 ... 2.50
❑7, Oct 1995 ... 2.50
❑8, Nov 1995; Babewatch ... 2.50
❑9, Jan 1996; polybagged with Glory card ... 2.50
❑10, Mar 1996 A: Angela ... 2.50
❑11, Apr 1996 ... 2.50
❑12, May 1996; double-sized anniversary issue ... 3.50
❑12/A, May 1996; double-sized anniversary issue; alternate cover ... 5.00
❑13, Jun 1996 ... 2.50
❑14, Jul 1996 ... 2.50
❑15, Sep 1996 ... 2.50
❑16, Oct 1996; Maximum begins as publisher ... 2.50
❑17, Nov 1996 ... 2.50
❑18, Dec 1996 ... 2.50
❑19, Jan 1997 ... 2.50
❑20, Feb 1997 ... 2.50
❑21, ca. 1997 ... 2.50
❑22, ca. 1997 ... 2.50
❑23, ca. 1997 ... 2.50

GLORY & FRIENDS BIKINI FEST
IMAGE
❑1, Sep 1995; pin-ups ... 2.50
❑1/Variant, Sep 1995; alternate cover; pin-ups ... 2.50

GLORY & FRIENDS CHRISTMAS SPECIAL
IMAGE
❑1, Dec 1995 ... 2.50

GLORY & FRIENDS LINGERIE SPECIAL
IMAGE
❑1, Sep 1995; pin-ups ... 2.95
❑1/Variant, Sep 1995; alternate cover; pin-ups ... 2.95

GLORY/ANGELA: ANGELS IN HELL
IMAGE
❑1, Apr 1996; flipbook with Darkchylde preview ... 2.50

GLORY/AVENGELYNE
IMAGE
❑1/A, Oct 1995; no title information on cover ... 3.95
❑1/B, Oct 1995; no title information on cover ... 3.95

GLORY/CELESTINE: DARK ANGEL
IMAGE
❑1, Sep 1996 ... 2.50
❑2, Oct 1996 ... 2.50

GLX-MAS SPECIAL
MARVEL
❑1, Feb 2006 ... 3.99

GLYPH
LABOR OF LOVE
❑1, b&w; magazine ... 4.95
❑2, b&w; magazine ... 4.95
❑3, b&w; magazine ... 4.95

Global Frequency

World-wide network of experts solves crises
©DC

Glory

Amazon warrior fights crime and injustice
©Image

God's Smuggler

Bibles penetrate The Iron Curtain
©Spire

Godzilla

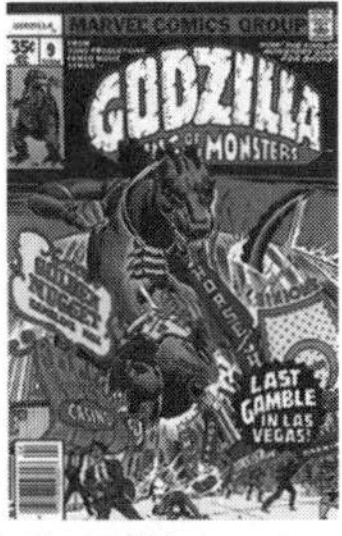

Fire-breathing monster faces S.H.I.E.L.D.
©Marvel

Gold Digger (2nd Series)

Female archaelogist and werecat seek artifacts
©Antarctic

N-MINT

G-MAN
IMAGE

❑1 2005; One-shot 5.95

G-MEN
CALIBER

❑1, b&w 2.50

GNATRAT: THE DARK GNAT RETURNS
PRELUDE

❑1 1986, b&w; Batman parody; continues in Darerat/Tadpole 1.95

GNATRAT: THE MOVIE
INNOVATION

❑1, b&w; Batman parody 2.25

GNOME-MOBILE
GOLD KEY

❑1, Oct 1967 25.00

GNOMES, FAIRIES, AND SEX KITTENS
FANTAGRAPHICS

❑1, Jan 2006 4.95

G'N'R'S GREATEST HITS
REVOLUTIONARY

❑1, Oct 1993, b&w 2.50

GO-GO
CHARLTON

❑1, Jun 1966 40.00
❑2, Aug 1966 30.00
❑3, Oct 1966 30.00
❑4, Dec 1966 30.00
❑5, Feb 1967 30.00
❑7, Jun 1967 30.00
❑8, Jun 1967 30.00
❑9, Oct 1967, A: Miss Bikini Luv 30.00

GOBBLEDYGOOK (1ST SERIES)
MIRAGE

❑1 1: The Teenage Mutant Ninja Turtles 110.00
❑2 70.00

GOBBLEDYGOOK (2ND SERIES)
MIRAGE

❑1, Dec 1986, b&w 5.00

GOBLIN LORD
GOBLIN

❑1, Oct 1996 2.50
❑2 2.50
❑3, Feb 1997 2.50

GOBLIN MAGAZINE
WARREN

❑1 8.50
❑2 5.00
❑3, Nov 1982 AN (a) 5.00
❑4 5.00

GOBLIN MARKET
TOME

❑1, b&w; poem 2.50

GOBLIN STUDIOS
GOBLIN

❑1 2.25
❑2 2.25
❑3 2.25

N-MINT

❑4 2.25
❑5, Aug 1995 2.25

GO BOY 7 HUMAN ACTION MACHINE
DARK HORSE

❑1, Jul 2003 2.99
❑2, Aug 2003 2.99
❑3, Oct 2003 2.99
❑4, Nov 2003 2.99
❑5, Mar 2004 2.99

GODDESS
DC / VERTIGO

❑1, Jun 1995 2.95
❑2, Jul 1995 2.95
❑3, Aug 1995 2.95
❑4, Sep 1995 2.95
❑5, Oct 1995 2.95
❑6, Nov 1995 2.95
❑7, Dec 1995 2.95
❑8, Jan 1996 2.95

GODDESS (TWILIGHT TWINS)
TWILIGHT TWINS

❑1, b&w; Zolastraya 2.00

GODHEAD
ANUBIS

❑1 4.00
❑1/Ltd.; limited edition 1: Jhatori. 4.00
❑2 6.00
❑2/Ltd.; Numbered, Limited edition (1500 printed) 6.00
❑3 6.00

GODLAND
IMAGE

❑1, Sep 2005 2.95
❑2, Oct 2005 2.95
❑3 2005 2.95
❑4 2005 2.95
❑5, Jan 2006 2.95
❑6, Jan 2006 2.95
❑7, Jan 2006 2.95
❑8, Mar 2006 2.95
❑9, May 2006 2.95
❑10, Jun 2006 2.95
❑11, Jul 2006 2.95

GODS & TULIPS
WESTHAMPTON

❑1 3.00

GODS FOR HIRE
HOT

❑1, Dec 1986 2.00
❑2, Jan 1987 2.00

GOD'S HAMMER
CALIBER

Value: Cover or less

❑1, b&w 2.50
❑2, b&w 2.50
❑3, b&w 2.50

GOD'S SMUGGLER
SPIRE

❑1; Based on the book "God's Smuggler" by Brother Andrew 6.00

N-MINT

GODWHEEL
MALIBU / ULTRAVERSE

❑0, Jan 1995, Flip cover 2.50
❑1, Jan 1995, Flip cover 2.50
❑1/Ashcan, Wizard ashcan edition; Flip cover; 1st appearance of Primevil 2.50
❑2, Feb 1995, Flip cover 2.50
❑3, Feb 1995, Flip cover; Marvel, Malibu universes cross 2.50

GODZILLA
MARVEL

❑1, Aug 1977, HT, JM (a) 12.00
❑1/35 cent, Aug 1977, HT, JM (a); 35 cent regional price variant 15.00
❑2, Sep 1977 6.00
❑2/35 cent, Sep 1977, 35 cent regional price variant 15.00
❑3, Oct 1977, A: Champions. Newsstand edition (distributed by Curtis); issue number in box 5.00
❑3/Whitman, Oct 1977, A: Champions. Special markets edition (usually sold in Whitman bagged prepacks); price appears in a diamond; no UPC barcode 5.00
❑3/35 cent, Oct 1977, A: Champions. 35 cent regional price variant; newsstand edition (distributed by Curtis); issue number in box 15.00
❑4, Nov 1977, 1: Doctor Demonicus. V: Batragon 5.00
❑5, Dec 1977, O: Doctor Demonicus 5.00
❑6, Jan 1978 4.00
❑7, Feb 1978, V: Red Ronin 4.00
❑8, Mar 1978, V: Red Ronin 4.00
❑9, Apr 1978 4.00
❑10, May 1978 4.00
❑11, Jun 1978, V: Red Ronin, Yetrigar 3.00
❑12, Jul 1978 3.00
❑13, Aug 1978 3.00
❑14, Sep 1978 3.00
❑15, Oct 1978 3.00
❑16, Nov 1978 3.00
❑17, Dec 1978, Godzilla shrunk by Henry Pym's gas 3.00
❑18, Jan 1979 3.00
❑19, Feb 1979, HT (a) 3.00
❑20, Mar 1979, A: Fantastic Four 3.00
❑21, Apr 1979, A: Devil Dinosaur 3.00
❑22, May 1979, A: Devil Dinosaur. Newsstand edition (distributed by Curtis); issue number in box 3.00
❑22/Whitman, May 1979, A: Devil Dinosaur. Special markets edition (usually sold in Whitman bagged prepacks); price appears in a diamond; no UPC barcode 3.00
❑23, Jun 1979, A: Avengers 3.00
❑24, Jul 1979, A: Spider-Man. V: Fantastic Four. V: Avengers 3.00

GODZILLA (MINI-SERIES)
DARK HORSE

❑1, Jul 1987, b&w; manga 4.00
❑2, Aug 1987, b&w; manga 3.00
❑3, Sep 1987, b&w; manga 3.00
❑4, Oct 1987, b&w; manga 3.00

Other grades: Multiply price above by 5/6 for VF/NM • 2/3 for VERY FINE • 1/3 for FINE • 1/5 for VERY GOOD • 1/8 for GOOD

❑5, Nov 1987, b&w; manga 3.00
❑6, Dec 1987, b&w; manga 3.00

GODZILLA (DARK HORSE)
DARK HORSE

❑0, May 1995, reprints and expands story from Dark Horse Comics #10 and 11 .... 4.00
❑1, Jun 1995, ... 3.00
❑2, Jul 1995, ... 3.00
❑3, Aug 1995, V: Bagorah, the Bat Monster 3.00
❑4, Sep 1995, V: Bagorah, the Bat Monster 3.00
❑5, Oct 1995, ... 3.00
❑6, Nov 1995, ... 2.95
❑7, Dec 1995, ... 2.95
❑8, Jan 1996, ... 2.95
❑9, Mar 1996, ... 2.95
❑10, Apr 1996, Godzilla vs. Spanish Armada 2.95
❑11, May 1996, Godzilla travels through time to sink the Titanic 2.95
❑12, Jun 1996, ... 2.95
❑13, Jun 1996, V: Burtannus. 2.95
❑14, Jul 1996, ... 2.95
❑15, Aug 1996, V: Lord Howe Monster. 2.95
❑16, Sep 1996, ... 2.95

GODZILLA COLOR SPECIAL
DARK HORSE

❑1, Aug 1992 .... 4.00

GODZILLA, KING OF THE MONSTERS SPECIAL
DARK HORSE

❑1/A, Aug 1987 .... 3.00
❑1/B; misprinted cover; fewer than 100 .... 3.00

GODZILLA VS. BARKLEY
DARK HORSE

❑1, ... 3.00

GODZILLA VERSUS HERO ZERO
DARK HORSE

❑1, Jul 1995 .... 2.50

GO GIRL!
IMAGE

❑1, Aug 2000 .... 3.50
❑2, Nov 2000 .... 3.50
❑3, Nov 2001 .... 3.50
❑4, Aug 2001 .... 3.50
❑5, Dec 2001 .... 3.50

GOG (VILLAINS)
DC

❑1, Feb 1998; New Year's Evil 1.95

GOING HOME
AARDVARK-VANAHEIM

❑1, b&w; no date 2.00

GOJIN
ANTARCTIC

❑1, Apr 1995 .... 2.95
❑2, Jun 1995 .... 2.95
❑3, Aug 1995 .... 2.95
❑3/A, Aug 1995; alternate cover 2.95
❑4, b&w 2.95
❑5, b&w 2.95
❑6, b&w 2.95
❑7, b&w 2.95
❑8, Jun 1996, b&w 2.95

GOLD DIGGER
ANTARCTIC

❑1, Sep 1992 .... 35.00
❑2, Nov 1992 .... 20.00
❑3, Jan 1993 .... 15.00
❑4, Mar 1993 .... 13.00

GOLD DIGGER (2ND SERIES)
ANTARCTIC

❑1, Jul 1993 .... 5.00
❑2, Aug 1993 .... 4.00
❑3, Sep 1993 .... 4.00
❑4, Oct 1993 .... 4.00
❑5, Nov 1993; has issue #0 on cover; production mistake 4.00
❑6, Dec 1993 .... 4.00
❑7, Jan 1994 .... 4.00
❑8, Feb 1994 .... 4.00
❑9, Mar 1994 .... 4.00
❑10, Apr 1994 .... 4.00
❑11, May 1994 .... 4.00
❑12, Jun 1994 .... 4.00
❑13, Jul 1994 .... 4.00
❑14, Aug 1994 .... 4.00
❑15, Sep 1994 .... 4.00
❑16, Oct 1994 .... 4.00
❑17, Nov 1994 .... 4.00
❑18, Dec 1994 .... 4.00
❑19, Feb 1995 .... 4.00
❑20, Apr 1995 .... 4.00
❑21, May 1995 .... 3.50
❑22, Jun 1995 .... 3.50
❑23, Jul 1995 .... 3.50
❑24, Aug 1995 .... 3.50
❑25, Oct 1995 .... 3.50
❑26, Nov 1995 .... 3.50
❑27, Dec 1995 .... 3.50
❑28, Feb 1996 .... 3.50
❑29, Apr 1996 .... 3.50
❑30, Jul 1996 .... 3.50
❑31, Aug 1996 .... 3.50
❑32, Oct 1996 .... 3.50
❑33, Dec 1996 .... 3.50
❑34, Feb 1997 .... 3.50
❑35, Apr 1997 .... 3.50
❑36, Jul 1997 .... 3.50
❑37, Aug 1997 .... 3.50
❑38, Jan 1998; cover says Nov 97, indicia says Jan 98 .... 3.50
❑39, Mar 1998 .... 3.50
❑40, May 1998 .... 3.50
❑41, Jun 1998 .... 3.50
❑42, Jul 1998 .... 3.50
❑43, Aug 1998 .... 3.50
❑44, Sep 1998 .... 3.50
❑45, Oct 1998 .... 3.50
❑46, Dec 1998 .... 3.50
❑47, Jan 1999 .... 3.50
❑48, Feb 1999 .... 3.50
❑49, Apr 1999 .... 3.50
❑50, Jun 1999 .... 3.50
❑50/CS, Jun 1999; poster edition 5.99
❑Annual 1, Sep 1995 .... 3.95
❑Annual 2, Sep 1996, b&w 3.95
❑Annual 3, Sep 1997, b&w; 1997 Annual 3.95
❑Annual 4, Sep 1998, b&w; 1998 Annual 3.95
❑GN 1; Graphic Novel 10.95
❑Special 1; Special edition; Reprints Gold Digger Vol. 1 #1 .... 3.00

GOLD DIGGER (3RD SERIES)
ANTARCTIC

❑1, Jul 1999; new color series 4.00
❑2, Aug 1999 .... 3.00
❑3, Sep 1999 .... 3.00
❑4, Oct 1999 .... 3.00
❑5, Nov 1999 .... 3.00
❑6, Dec 1999 .... 3.00
❑7, Jan 2000 .... 3.00
❑8, Feb 2000 .... 3.00
❑9, Mar 2000 .... 3.00
❑10, Apr 2000 .... 3.00
❑11, May 2000 .... 3.00
❑12, Jun 2000 .... 3.00
❑13, Jul 2000 .... 3.00
❑14, Aug 2000 .... 3.00
❑15, Oct 2000 .... 3.00
❑16, Nov 2000 .... 3.00
❑17, Dec 2000 .... 3.00
❑18, Jan 2000 .... 3.00
❑19, Feb 2001 .... 3.00
❑20, Mar 2001 .... 3.00
❑21, Apr 2001 .... 2.95
❑22, May 2001 .... 2.95
❑23, Jun 2001 .... 2.95
❑24, Jul 2001 .... 2.95
❑25, Aug 2001 .... 2.95
❑26, Nov 2001 .... 2.99
❑27, Dec 2001 .... 2.99
❑28, Jan 2002 .... 2.99
❑29, Feb 2002 .... 2.99
❑30, Mar 2002 .... 2.99
❑31, Apr 2002 .... 2.99
❑32, May 2002 .... 2.99
❑33, Jun 2002 .... 2.99
❑34, Jul 2002 .... 2.99
❑35, Aug 2002 .... 2.99
❑36, Oct 2002 .... 2.99
❑37, Nov 2002 .... 2.99
❑38, Dec 2002 .... 2.99
❑39, Jan 2003 .... 3.50
❑40, Feb 2003 .... 3.50
❑41, Mar 2003 .... 3.50
❑42, Apr 2003 .... 3.50
❑43, May 2003 .... 3.50
❑44, Jun 2003 .... 3.50
❑45, Oct 2003 .... 2.99
❑46, Oct 2003 .... 2.99
❑47, Nov 2003 .... 2.99
❑48, Dec 2003 .... 2.99
❑49, Jan 2004 .... 2.99
❑50, Feb 2004 .... 2.99
❑51, Mar 2004 .... 2.99
❑52, May 2004 .... 2.99
❑53, Jun 2004 .... 2.99
❑54, Jul 2004 .... 2.99
❑55, Aug 2004 .... 2.99
❑56, Sep 2004 .... 2.99
❑57, Oct 2004 .... 2.99
❑58, Nov 2004 .... 2.99
❑59, Dec 2004 .... 2.99
❑60, Jan 2005 .... 2.99
❑61, Feb 2005 .... 2.99
❑62, Mar 2005 .... 2.99
❑63, Apr 2005 .... 2.99
❑64, May 2005 .... 2.99
❑65, Jun 2005 .... 2.99
❑Annual 4, Sep 2003 .... 4.95
❑Annual 2004 .... 4.95

GOLD DIGGER: BETA
ANTARCTIC

❑1, Feb 1998 .... 2.95

GOLD DIGGER: EDGE GUARD
RADIO

❑1, Aug 2000 .... 2.95
❑2, Sep 2000 .... 2.95
❑3, Oct 2000 .... 2.95
❑4, Nov 2000 .... 2.95
❑5, Dec 2000 .... 2.95

GOLD DIGGER MANGAZINE
ANTARCTIC

❑1, Mar 1994 .... 2.99
❑1/2nd, Apr 1999 .... 2.99

GOLD DIGGER PERFECT MEMORY
ANTARCTIC

❑1, Jul 1996, b&w; story synopses, character profiles, and other material 4.50
❑2, Sep 2001 .... 6.95
❑3, Sep 2003 .... 6.95
❑4, Sep 2004 .... 6.95

GOLD DIGGER SWIMSUIT END OF SUMMER SPECIAL
ANTARCTIC

❑1, Jul 2003 .... 4.50

GOLD DIGGER SWIMSUIT SPECIAL
ANTARCTIC

❑1, May 2000 ....
❑2, May 2003; 2003 Swimsuit special 4.50
❑3, May 2004; 2004 Swimsuit special 4.50

GOLDEN AGE
DC

❑1, ca. 1993; JRo (w); PS (a); Elseworlds 5.50
❑2, Jan 1993; JRo (w); PS (a); O: Dynaman. Elseworlds 5.50
❑3, ca. 1993; JRo (w); PS (a); Elseworlds 5.50
❑4, ca. 1993; JRo (w); PS (a); D: Dynaman. D: Ultra-Humanite. D: Hawkman. D: Doll Man. D: Miss America. Elseworlds 5.50

GOLDEN-AGE GREATS
AC / PARAGON

❑1, Win 1994; Reprints Golden Age stories 9.95
❑2; Reprints Golden Age stories; Collects Phantom Lady #13-15, All-Top Comics #8 .... 9.95
❑3, b&w; Reprints Golden Age stories with The Flame, Espionage - Black X, Black Terror, Fighting Yank 9.95
❑4, b&w; reprints Golden Age stories. 9.95
❑5; Reprints Golden Age stories 9.95
❑6 .... 9.95

Other grades: Multiply price above by 5/6 for VF/NM • 2/3 for VERY FINE • 1/3 for FINE • 1/5 for VERY GOOD • 1/8 for GOOD

Golden Age

Elseworlds post-World War II story

©DC

Golden-Age Greats

Reprints popular 1940s stories

©AC

Gold Key Spotlight

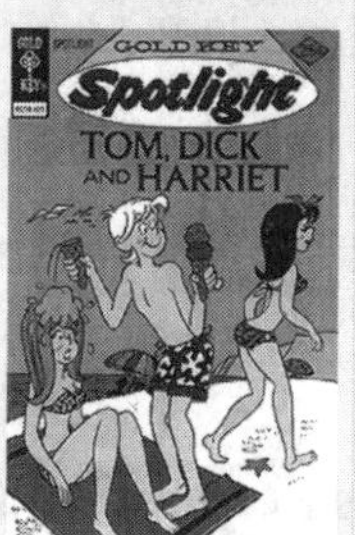

Anthology covered Gold Key genre gamut

©Gold Key

Gomer Pyle

Usage of Shazam didn't produce hero

©Gold Key

Goofy Adventures

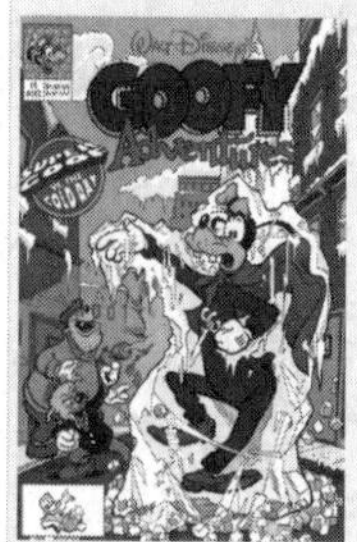

Goofy in more serious mode

©Disney

	N-MINT
❑7; Best of the West	9.95
❑8	9.95
❑9	9.95
❑10; Reprints Golden Age stories	9.95
❑11; Western reprints	11.95
❑12	9.95
❑13	9.95
❑14	11.95

GOLDEN AGE OF TRIPLE-X
REVISIONARY

❑1, b&w	3.50

GOLDEN AGE OF TRIPLE-X: JOHN HOLMES SPECIAL "JOHNNY DOES PARIS"
RE-VISIONARY

❑1	2.95

GOLDEN AGE SECRET FILES
DC

❑1, Feb 2001	4.95

GOLDEN AGE SHEENA
AC

❑1	9.95

GOLDEN COMICS DIGEST
GOLD KEY

❑1, May 1969, Looney Tunes/Woody Woodpecker/Tom and Jerry	20.00
❑2, Jun 1969, Hanna-Barbera TV Fun Favorites	20.00
❑3, Jul 1969, Looney Tunes/Woody Woodpecker/Tom and Jerry	20.00
❑4, Aug 1970, Tarzan	20.00
❑5, Sep 1969, Looney Tunes/Woody Woodpecker/Tom and Jerry	20.00
❑6, Oct 1969, Looney Tunes/Woody Woodpecker/Tom and Jerry	20.00
❑7, Nov 1969, Hanna-Barbera TV Fun Favorites	20.00
❑8, Jan 1970, Looney Tunes/Woody Woodpecker/Tom and Jerry	20.00
❑9, Mar 1970, Tarzan	20.00
❑10, May 1970, Looney Tunes	20.00
❑11, Jun 1970, Hanna-Barbera TV Fun Favorites	20.00
❑12 1970, Looney Tunes/Woody Woodpecker/Tom and Jerry	20.00
❑13 1970, Tom and Jerry	20.00
❑14, Oct 1970, Looney Tunes	20.00
❑15, Jan 1971, Looney Tunes/Woody Woodpecker/Tom and Jerry	20.00
❑16, Mar 1971, Woody Woodpecker	20.00
❑17, May 1971, Looney Tunes	20.00
❑18, Jul 1971, Tom and Jerry	20.00
❑19, Sep 1971, Little Lulu	20.00
❑20, Nov 1971, Woody Woodpecker	20.00
❑21, Jan 1972, Looney Tunes	20.00
❑22, Mar 1972, Tom and Jerry	20.00
❑23, May 1972, Little Lulu	20.00
❑24, Jul 1972, Woody Woodpecker	20.00
❑25, Sep 1972, Tom and Jerry	20.00
❑26, Nov 1972, Looney Tunes	20.00
❑27, Jan 1973, Little Lulu	20.00
❑28, Mar 1973, Tom and Jerry	20.00
❑29, May 1973, Little Lulu	20.00
❑30, Jul 1973, Looney Tunes	20.00

	N-MINT
❑31, Aug 1973, Turok	15.00
❑32, Sep 1973, Woody Woodpecker	15.00
❑33, Nov 1973, Little Lulu	15.00
❑34, Jan 1974, Looney Tunes	15.00
❑35, Mar 1974, Tom and Jerry	15.00
❑36, May 1974, Little Lulu	15.00
❑37, Jul 1974, Woody Woodpecker	15.00
❑38, Aug 1974, The Pink Panther	15.00
❑39, Sep 1974, Looney Tunes	15.00
❑40, Nov 1974, Little Lulu	15.00
❑41, Jan 1975, Tom and Jerry	15.00
❑42, Mar 1975, Looney Tunes	15.00
❑43, May 1975, Little Lulu	15.00
❑44, Jul 1975, Woody Woodpecker	15.00
❑45, Aug 1975, The Pink Panther	15.00
❑46, Sep 1975, Little Lulu	15.00
❑47, Nov 1975, Looney Tunes	15.00
❑48, Jan 1976, Lone Ranger	15.00

GOLDEN DRAGON
SYNCHRONICITY

❑1	1.50

GOLDEN FEATURES (JERRY IGER'S...)
BLACKTHORNE

❑1	2.00
❑2	2.00
❑3, Jun 1986	2.00
❑4, Aug 1986	2.00
❑5, Oct 1986	2.00
❑6	2.00

GOLDEN WARRIOR
INDUSTRIAL DESIGN

❑1, Mar 1997, b&w	2.95

GOLDEN WARRIOR ICZER ONE
ANTARCTIC

❑1, Apr 1994, b&w	2.95
❑2, May 1994, b&w	2.95
❑3, Jun 1994, b&w	2.95
❑4, Jul 1994, b&w	2.95
❑5, Aug 1994, b&w	2.95

GOLD KEY SPOTLIGHT
GOLD KEY

❑1, May 1976, Tom, Dick, and Harriet	6.00
❑2 1976	4.00
❑3 1976	4.00
❑4 1977	4.00
❑5 1977	4.00
❑6, Jun 1977, Dagar	4.00
❑7 1977	4.00
❑8 1977	4.00
❑9 1977	4.00
❑10 1977	4.00
❑11 1978	4.00

GOLDYN 3-D
BLACKTHORNE

❑1	2.00

GOLGOTHIKA
CALIBER

❑1, Nov 1996, b&w	2.95
❑2, ca. 1996, b&w	2.95
❑3, ca. 1996, b&w	2.95
❑4, b&w	2.95

N-MINT

GOLGO 13
LEAD

❑1, b&w	1.00
❑2	1.50

GOLGO 13 (2ND SERIES)
VIZ

❑1, b&w	4.95
❑2, b&w	4.95
❑3, b&w	4.95

GO-MAN!
CALIBER

❑1, Nov 1989, b&w	2.50
❑2, b&w	2.50
❑3, b&w	2.50
❑4, b&w	2.50

GOMER PYLE
GOLD KEY

❑1, Jul 1966	40.00
❑2, Oct 1966	25.00
❑3, Oct 1967	25.00

GON
DC / PARADOX PRESS

❑1, b&w; digest	5.95
❑2, b&w; digest	5.95
❑3, b&w; digest	5.95
❑4, b&w; digest	5.95
❑5, b&w; digest	6.95

GONAD THE BARBARIAN
ETERNITY

❑1	2.25

GON COLOR SPECTACULAR
DC / PARADOX PRESS

❑1; prestige format	5.95

GON UNDERGROUND
DC / PARADOX PRESS

❑1	7.95

GOOD GIRL ART QUARTERLY
AC

❑1, Jul 1990; new & reprints	3.95
❑2, Fal 1990	3.95
❑3, Win 1991	3.95
❑4, Spr 1991	3.95
❑5, Sum 1991	3.95
❑6, Fal 1991; Fall 1991	3.95
❑7, Win 1992	3.95
❑8, Spr 1992	3.95
❑9, Sum 1992	3.95
❑10, Fal 1992	3.95
❑11, Win 1993	3.95
❑12, Spr 1993	3.95
❑13, Sum 1993	3.95
❑14, Fal 1993	3.95
❑15, Win 1994	3.95
❑16, Spr 1994	3.95
❑17, Sum 1994	3.95
❑18, Fal 1994	3.95
❑19, Win 1995	6.95

GOOD GIRLS
FANTAGRAPHICS

❑1, Apr 1987, b&w	2.00
❑2, Oct 1987	2.00
❑3 1988	2.00

N-MINT | N-MINT | N-MINT

❑4, Feb 1989 .... 2.00
❑5, Jan 1991; Last Fantagraphics issue 2.00
❑6, Jun 1991, b&w; Published by Rip Off Press 2.00

GOOD GUYS
DEFIANT

❑1, Nov 1993; Giant-size 2.50
❑2, Dec 1993 .... 2.50
❑3, Jan 1994 .... 2.50
❑4, Feb 1994 .... 2.50
❑5, Mar 1994 .... 2.50
❑6, Apr 1994 .... 2.50
❑7, May 1994 .... 2.50
❑8, Jun 1994 .... 2.50
❑9, Jul 1994 .... 2.50
❑10, Aug 1994 .... 2.50
❑11, Sep 1994 .... 2.50
❑12, Oct 1994 .... 2.50

GOODY GOOD COMICS
FANTAGRAPHICS

❑1, Jun 2000 .... 2.95

GOOFY
DELL

❑-211, Nov 1962, (c); Cover code 12-308-211 .... 40.00

GOOFY ADVENTURES
DISNEY

❑1, Jun 1990 .... 2.50
❑2, Jul 1990 .... 1.50
❑3, Aug 1990 .... 1.50
❑4, Sep 1990 .... 1.50
❑5, Oct 1990 .... 1.50
❑6, Nov 1990 .... 1.50
❑7, Dec 1990; Three Musketeers 1.50
❑8, Jan 1991 .... 1.50
❑9, Feb 1991; FG (a); James Bond parody 1.50
❑10, Mar 1991 .... 1.50
❑11, Apr 1991 .... 1.50
❑12, May 1991 .... 1.50
❑13, Jun 1991 .... 1.50
❑14, Jul 1991 .... 1.50
❑15, Aug 1991; Super-Goof 1.50
❑16, Sep 1991; Sherlock Holmes parody 1.50
❑17, Oct 1991 GC (a) 1.50

GOON (1ST SERIES)
AVATAR

❑1, Mar 1999 .... 15.00
❑2, May 1999 .... 10.00
❑3, Jul 1999 .... 10.00

GOON (2ND SERIES)
ALBATROSS EXPLODING

❑1, ca. 2002, ... 10.00
❑1/Variant, ca. 2002, Sketch cover, limited convention edition 10.00
❑2, ca. 2002, ... 5.00
❑3, ca. 2002, Norman Rockwell tribute cover 5.00
❑4, ca. 2002, Says Vol. 2, #3 in indicia 5.00

GOON (3RD SERIES)
DARK HORSE

❑1 2003 .... 2.99
❑2 2003 .... 2.99
❑3, Oct 2003 .... 2.99
❑4, Dec 2003 .... 2.99
❑5, Feb 2004 .... 2.99
❑6, Apr 2004 .... 2.99
❑7, Aug 2004 .... 2.99
❑8 .... 3.00
❑9 .... 2.99
❑10 2005 .... 2.99
❑11 2005 .... 2.99
❑12 2005 .... 2.99
❑13, Aug 2005 .... 2.99
❑14 2005 .... 2.99
❑15, Jan 2006 .... 2.99
❑16, Mar 2006 .... 2.99
❑17, Apr 2006 .... 2.99

GOON PATROL
PINNACLE

❑1 .... 1.75

GOON: 25 CENT ISSUE
DARK HORSE

❑1 .... 0.25

GORDON YAMAMOTO AND THE KING OF THE GEEKS
HUMBLE

❑1, Oct 1997, b&w 2.95

GORE SHRIEK
FANTACO

❑1, ca. 1986, b&w; 1st Greg Capullo story 3.00
❑2, b&w 3.00
❑3, b&w 3.00
❑4, b&w 3.00
❑5 .... 3.50
❑6 .... 3.50
❑Annual 1, b&w 4.95

GORE SHRIEK (VOL. 2)
FANTACO

❑1, b&w 2.50
❑2, b&w 2.50
❑3, b&w 2.50

GORE SHRIEK DELECTUS
FANTACO

❑1 .... 8.95

GORGANA'S GHOUL GALLERY
AC

❑1, b&w; Reprints 2.95
❑2; Reprints 2.95

GORGO
CHARLTON

❑1, May 1961, SD (a) 200.00
❑2, Aug 1961 .... 100.00
❑3, Sep 1961, SD (a) 100.00
❑4, Nov 1961, SD (c) 75.00
❑5, Jan 1962 .... 50.00
❑6, Apr 1962 .... 40.00
❑7, Jun 1962 .... 40.00
❑8, Aug 1962 .... 40.00
❑9, Oct 1962 .... 40.00
❑10, Dec 1962 .... 40.00
❑11, Feb 1963 .... 30.00
❑12, Apr 1963 .... 30.00
❑13, Jun 1963, SD (a) 30.00
❑14, Aug 1963, SD (a) 30.00
❑15, Oct 1963, SD (a) 30.00
❑16, Dec 1963, SD (a) 30.00
❑17, Feb 1964 .... 20.00
❑18, May 1964 .... 20.00
❑19, Jul 1964 .... 20.00
❑20 1965 .... 20.00
❑21, Dec 1964 .... 20.00
❑22 1965 .... 20.00
❑23, Sep 1965 .... 20.00

GORGON
VENUS

❑1, Jun 1996 .... 2.95
❑2, Jun 1996 .... 2.95
❑3, Jun 1996 .... 2.95
❑4, Jun 1996 .... 2.95
❑5, Aug 1996 .... 2.95

GORILLA GUNSLINGER
MOJO

❑0, Sampler 1.00

GOTCHA!
RIP OFF

❑1, Sep 1991, b&w 2.50

G.O.T.H.
VEROTIK

❑1 .... 3.00
❑2, Mar 1996 .... 3.00
❑3, Jun 1996 .... 3.00
❑Book 1, Oct 1996; collects mini-series 9.95

GOTHAM CENTRAL
DC

❑1, Jan 2003 .... 2.50
❑2, Feb 2003 .... 2.50
❑3, Mar 2003 .... 2.50
❑4, Apr 2003 .... 2.50
❑5, May 2003 .... 2.50
❑6, Jun 2003 .... 2.50
❑7, Jul 2003 .... 2.50
❑8, Aug 2003 .... 2.50
❑9, Sep 2003 .... 2.50
❑10, Oct 2003 .... 2.50
❑11, Nov 2003 .... 2.50
❑12, Dec 2003 .... 2.50
❑13, Jan 2004 .... 2.50
❑14, Feb 2004 .... 2.50
❑15, Mar 2004 .... 2.50
❑16, Apr 2004 .... 2.50
❑17, May 2004 .... 2.50
❑18, Jun 2004 .... 2.50
❑19, Jul 2004 .... 2.50
❑20, Aug 2004 .... 2.50
❑21, Sep 2004 .... 2.50
❑22, Oct 2004 .... 2.50
❑23, Nov 2004 .... 2.50
❑24, Dec 2004 .... 2.50
❑25, Jan 2005 .... 2.50
❑26, Feb 2005 .... 2.50
❑27, Mar 2005 .... 2.50
❑28, Apr 2005 .... 2.50
❑29, May 2005 .... 2.50
❑30, Jun 2005 .... 2.50
❑31, Jun 2005 .... 2.50
❑32, Jul 2005 .... 2.50
❑33, Aug 2005 .... 2.50
❑34, Sep 2005 .... 2.50
❑35, Oct 2005 .... 2.50
❑36, Nov 2005 .... 2.50
❑37, Jan 2006 .... 2.50
❑38, Jan 2006 .... 2.50
❑39, Mar 2006 .... 2.50
❑40, Mar 2006 .... 2.50

GOTHAM GIRLS
DC

❑1, Oct 2002 .... 2.25
❑2, Nov 2002 .... 2.25
❑3, Dec 2002 .... 2.25
❑4, Jan 2003 .... 2.25
❑5, Feb 2003 .... 2.25

GOTHAM NIGHTS
DC

❑1, Mar 1992 .... 2.00
❑2, Apr 1992 .... 2.00
❑3, May 1992 .... 2.00
❑4, Jun 1992 .... 2.00

GOTHAM NIGHTS II
DC

❑1, Mar 1995 .... 2.00
❑2, Apr 1995 .... 2.00
❑3, May 1995 .... 2.00
❑4, Jun 1995 .... 2.00

GOTHIC
5TH PANEL

❑1, Apr 1997, b&w 2.50
❑2 .... 2.50

GOTHIC MOON
ANARCHY BRIDGEWORKS

❑1 .... 5.95

GOTHIC NIGHTS
REBEL

❑1, b&w 2.00
❑2 .... 2.00

GOTHIC RED
BONEYARD

❑1 .... 2.95
❑3, Mar 1997, b&w 2.95

GOTHIC SCROLLS, THE: DRAYVEN
DAVDEZ

❑1, Dec 1997 .... 2.95
❑2, Feb 1998 .... 2.50
❑3, Mar 1998 .... 2.50
❑Ashcan 1, Aug 1997; Preview edition; cover says Sep, indicia says Aug 1.50

GRACKLE
ACCLAIM

❑1, Jan 1997, b&w 2.95
❑2, Feb 1997, b&w 2.95
❑3, Mar 1997, b&w 2.95
❑4, Apr 1997, b&w 2.95

GRAFFITI KITCHEN
TUNDRA

❑1 .... 2.95

GRAFIK MUZIK
CALIBER

❑1, b&w A: Madman 15.00
❑2, ca. 1991 .... 10.00

Other grades: Multiply price above by 5/6 for VF/NM • 2/3 for VERY FINE • 1/3 for FINE • 1/5 for VERY GOOD • 1/8 for GOOD

Gotham Central

Police procedurals with hero cameos

©DC

Gotham Nights

Batman vignette focuses on common man

©DC

Grateful Dead Comix (Vol. 2)

Adapts songs fans already know by heart

©Kitchen Sink

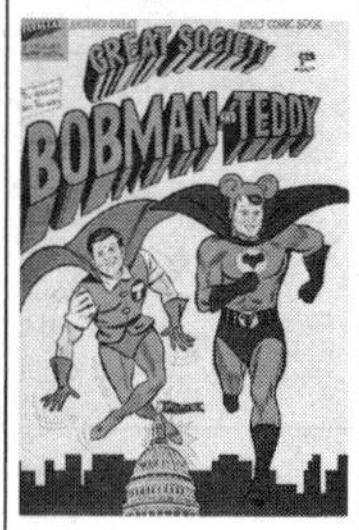

Great Society Comic Book

Political satire starring LBJ

©Parallax

Green Arrow

Character introduced in 1941, series in 1988

©DC

N-MINT

❑3 .... 6.00
❑4 .... 6.00

GRAMMAR PATROL
CASTEL

❑1 .... 2.00

GRAND PRIX
CHARLTON

❑16, Sep 1967, Previous issues published as Hot Rod Racers 14.00
❑17 1967 .... 8.00
❑18 1968 .... 8.00
❑19, May 1968 .... 8.00
❑20, Jul 1968 .... 8.00
❑21, Sep 1968 .... 5.00
❑22, Nov 1968 .... 5.00
❑23, Jan 1969 .... 5.00
❑24, Mar 1969 .... 5.00
❑25, May 1969, DP (a) 5.00
❑26, Jul 1969 .... 5.00
❑27, Sep 1969 .... 5.00
❑28, Nov 1969 .... 5.00
❑29, Jan 1970 .... 5.00
❑30, Mar 1970 .... 5.00
❑31, May 1970 .... 5.00

GRAPHIC
FANTACO

❑1 .... 3.95

GRAPHIC HEROES IN HOUSE OF CARDS
GRAPHIC STAFFING

❑1, personalized promotional piece for temporary graphics employees 1.00

GRAPHIC STORY MONTHLY
FANTAGRAPHICS

❑1, b&w 4.00
❑2, b&w 3.50
❑3, b&w 3.50
❑4, b&w 3.50
❑5, b&w 3.50
❑6, b&w 3.50
❑7 .... 3.50

GRAPHIQUE MUSIQUE
SLAVE LABOR

❑1, Dec 1989, b&w 8.00
❑2, Mar 1990, b&w 8.00
❑3, May 1990, b&w 8.00

GRATEFUL DEAD COMIX
KITCHEN SINK

❑1 .... 6.00
❑2 .... 5.00
❑3 .... 5.00
❑4 .... 5.00
❑5 .... 5.00
❑6 .... 5.00
❑7 .... 5.00

GRATEFUL DEAD COMIX (VOL. 2)
KITCHEN SINK

❑1; comic-book size 3.95
❑2, Apr 1994 .... 3.95

GRAVEDIGGERS
ACCLAIM

❑1, Nov 1996, b&w 2.95
❑2, Dec 1996, b&w 2.95
❑3, Jan 1997, b&w 2.95
❑4, Feb 1997, b&w 2.95

GRAVEDIGGER TALES
AVALON

❑1, b&w 2.95

GRAVE GRRRLS: DESTROYERS OF THE DEAD
MOONSTONE

❑1 2005 .... 3.50

GRAVESTONE
MALIBU

❑1 .... 2.25
❑2 .... 2.25
❑3, Sep 1993; Genesis 2.25
❑4 .... 2.25
❑5; Genesis 2.25
❑6; Genesis 2.25
❑7, Feb 1994; Genesis; last issue 2.25

GRAVESTOWN
ARIEL

❑1, Oct 1997 .... 2.95

GRAVE TALES
HAMILTON

❑1, Oct 1991, b&w 3.95
❑2, b&w 3.95
❑3, b&w 3.95

GRAVITY
MARVEL

❑1, Jul 2005 .... 2.99
❑2, Aug 2005 .... 2.99
❑3, Sep 2005 .... 2.99
❑4, Oct 2005 ....
❑5 ....

GRAY AREA
IMAGE

❑1, Aug 2004 .... 7.00
❑1/Incentive, Aug 2004 .... 8.00
❑1/SigSeries, Aug 2004 .... 20.00
❑1/Conv, Aug 2004 .... 15.00
❑2 2004 .... 5.95
❑3 2004 .... 5.95

GREASE MONKEY
KITCHEN SINK

❑1, Oct 1995 .... 3.50
❑2, Oct 1995 .... 3.50

GREASE MONKEY (IMAGE)
IMAGE

❑1, Jan 1998 .... 2.95
❑2, Mar 1998 .... 2.95

GREAT ACTION COMICS
I.W.

❑8, Reprints 70.00
❑9, Reprints 70.00

GREAT AMERICAN WESTERN
AC

❑1, ca. 1988 .... 2.00
❑2 1988 .... 2.95
❑3 .... 2.95
❑4 .... 3.50
❑5 .... 5.00

GREAT BIG BEEF
ERR

❑97, Jun 1996, b&w 2.00
❑98, Jan 1997, b&w; cover says Apr, indicia says Jan 2.00
❑99, Sep 1997, b&w 2.00

GREATEST AMERICAN COMIC BOOK
OCEAN

❑1; Spider-Man parody; Batman 2.55

GREATEST DIGGS OF ALL TIME!
RIP OFF

❑1, Feb 1991, b&w 2.00

GREATEST STARS OF THE NBA: ALLEN IVERSON
TOKYOPOP

❑1, Nov 2005, b&w 9.95

GREATEST STARS OF THE NBA: FUTURE GREATS
TOKYOPOP

❑1, Nov 2005, b&w 9.95

GREAT GALAXIES
ZUB

❑0, b&w 1: The Warp Patrol. 2.95
❑1, b&w 0: Captain Dean. 2.50
❑2, b&w 2.50
❑3, b&w 2.50
❑4, b&w 2.50
❑5, b&w 2.50
❑6/Ashcan; Flip book with Telluria Ashcan #6 .... 0.50

GREAT GAZOO
CHARLTON

❑1, Aug 1973 .... 20.00
❑2 1973 .... 12.00
❑3 1974 .... 10.00
❑4, Jun 1974 .... 10.00
❑5, Aug 1974 .... 10.00
❑6, Oct 1974 .... 10.00
❑7, Dec 1974 .... 10.00
❑8, Feb 1975 .... 10.00
❑9, Apr 1975 .... 10.00
❑10, Jun 1975 .... 10.00
❑11 1975 .... 10.00
❑12, Sep 1975 .... 10.00
❑13, Nov 1975 .... 10.00
❑14, Jan 1976 .... 10.00
❑15, Mar 1976 .... 10.00
❑16, May 1976 .... 10.00
❑17, Jul 1976 .... 10.00
❑18, Sep 1976 .... 10.00
❑19, Nov 1976 .... 10.00
❑20, Jan 1977 .... 10.00

GREAT MORONS IN HISTORY
REVOLUTIONARY

❑1, Oct 1993, b&w; Dan Quayle 2.50

GREAT SOCIETY COMIC BOOK
PARALLAX

❑1 .... 16.00
❑2 .... 12.00

GREEENLOCK
AIRCEL

❑1, b&w 2.50

Other grades: Multiply price above by 5/6 for VF/NM • 2/3 for VERY FINE • 1/3 for FINE • 1/5 for VERY GOOD • 1/8 for GOOD

N-MINT

GREEN ARROW
DC

❑0, Oct 1994 1: Connor Hawke (as adult) 3.00
❑1, Feb 1988; MGr (c); MGr (w); DG (a); Painted cover 4.00
❑2, Mar 1988; MGr (c); MGr (w); DG (a); Painted cover 2.00
❑3, Apr 1988; MGr (c); MGr (w); FMc, DG (a); Painted cover 2.00
❑4, May 1988 MGr (c); MGr (w) 2.00
❑5, Jun 1988 2.00
❑6, Jul 1988 2.00
❑7, Aug 1988 2.00
❑8, Sep 1988 2.00
❑9, Oct 1988 2.00
❑10, Nov 1988 MGr (c) 2.00
❑11, Dec 1988 MGr (c) 1.50
❑12, Dec 1988 MGr (c) 1.50
❑13, Jan 1989 1.50
❑14, Jan 1989 1.50
❑15, Feb 1989 1.50
❑16, Mar 1989 1.50
❑17, Apr 1989 1.50
❑18, May 1989 1.50
❑19, Jun 1989 1.50
❑20, Jul 1989 1.50
❑21, Aug 1989 1: Connor Hawke (baby) 2.50
❑22, Aug 1989 1.50
❑23, Sep 1989 1.50
❑24, Sep 1989 1.50
❑25, Oct 1989 1.50
❑26, Nov 1989 1.50
❑27, Dec 1989 A: Warlord 1.50
❑28, Jan 1990 A: Warlord 1.50
❑29, Feb 1990 1.50
❑30, Mar 1990 1.50
❑31, Apr 1990 1.50
❑32, May 1990 1.50
❑33, Jun 1990 1.50
❑34, Jul 1990 1.50
❑35, Aug 1990; Black Arrow 1.50
❑36, Sep 1990; Black Arrow 1.50
❑37, Sep 1990; Black Arrow 1.50
❑38, Oct 1990; Black Arrow 1.50
❑39, Nov 1990 1.50
❑40, Dec 1990 MGr (a) 1.50
❑41, Dec 1990 1.50
❑42, Jan 1991 1.50
❑43, Feb 1991 1.50
❑44, Mar 1991 1.50
❑45, Apr 1991 1.50
❑46, May 1991 1.50
❑47, Jun 1991 1.50
❑48, Jun 1991 1.50
❑49, Jul 1991 1.50
❑50, Aug 1991; Giant-size 2.50
❑51, Aug 1991 1.50
❑52, Sep 1991 1.50
❑53, Oct 1991 1.50
❑54, Nov 1991 1.50
❑55, Dec 1991 MGr (w) 1.50
❑56, Jan 1992 1.50
❑57, Feb 1992 1.50
❑58, Mar 1992 1.50
❑59, Apr 1992 1.50
❑60, May 1992 1.50
❑61, May 1992 FS (a) 1.50
❑62, Jun 1992 FS (a) 1.50
❑63, Jun 1992 1.50
❑64, Jul 1992 1.50
❑65, Aug 1992 1.50
❑66, Sep 1992 1.50
❑67, Oct 1992 1.50
❑68, Nov 1992 1.50
❑69, Dec 1992 MGr (w) 1.75
❑70, Jan 1993 1.75
❑71, Feb 1993 1.75
❑72, Mar 1993 1.75
❑73, Apr 1993 1.75
❑74, May 1993 1.75
❑75, Jun 1993; Giant-size 2.50
❑76, Jul 1993 O: Green Lantern and Green Arrow 1.75
❑77, Aug 1993 1.75
❑78, Sep 1993 1.75

N-MINT

❑79, Oct 1993 1.75
❑80, Nov 1993 MGr (w) 1.75
❑81, Dec 1993 JA (a) 1.75
❑82, Jan 1994 JA (a) 1.75
❑83, Feb 1994 JA (a) 1.75
❑84, Mar 1994 JA (a) 1.75
❑85, Apr 1994 JA (a); A: Deathstroke 1.75
❑86, May 1994; JA (a); Catwoman 1.75
❑87, Jun 1994 JA (a) 1.95
❑88, Jul 1994 JA (a); A: JLA 1.95
❑89, Aug 1994 1.95
❑90, Sep 1994; Zero Hour 2.25
❑91, Nov 1994 JA (a) 1.95
❑92, Dec 1994 JA (a) 1.95
❑93, Jan 1995 JA (a) 1.95
❑94, Feb 1995 JA (a) 1.95
❑95, Mar 1995 JA (a) 1.95
❑96, Apr 1995 3.00
❑97, Jun 1995 3.00
❑98, Jul 1995 JA (a) 3.00
❑99, Aug 1995 JA (a) 3.00
❑100, Sep 1995; Giant-size; enhanced cover 7.00
❑101, Oct 1995; D: Green Arrow I (Oliver Queen). Later disproved 18.00
❑102, Nov 1995; Underworld Unleashed 2.25
❑103, Dec 1995 A: Green Lantern 2.25
❑104, Jan 1996 2.25
❑105, Feb 1996 A: Robin 2.25
❑106, Mar 1996 2.25
❑107, Apr 1996 2.25
❑108, May 1996 A: Thorn 2.25
❑109, Jun 1996 JA (a) 2.25
❑110, Jul 1996 2.25
❑111, Aug 1996 2.25
❑112, Sep 1996 2.25
❑113, Oct 1996 2.25
❑114, Nov 1996; Final Night 2.25
❑115, Dec 1996 A: Shado, Black Canary 2.25
❑116, Jan 1997 A: Black Canary, Oracle, Shado 2.25
❑117, Feb 1997 A: Black Canary 2.25
❑118, Mar 1997 2.25
❑119, Apr 1997 A: Warlord 2.25
❑120, May 1997 A: Warlord 2.25
❑121, Jun 1997 2.25
❑122, Jul 1997 2.25
❑123, Aug 1997 JA (a) 2.25
❑124, Sep 1997 2.25
❑125, Oct 1997; Giant-size; continues in Green Lantern #92 3.50
❑126, Nov 1997 2.50
❑127, Dec 1997; Face cover 2.50
❑128, Jan 1998 2.50
❑129, Feb 1998 2.50
❑130, Mar 1998; cover forms triptych with Flash #135 and Green Lantern #96 2.50
❑131, Apr 1998 2.50
❑132, May 1998 2.50
❑133, Jun 1998 A: JLA 2.50
❑134, Jul 1998; A: Batman. continues in Detective Comics #723 2.50
❑135, Aug 1998 V: Lady Shiva 2.50
❑136, Sep 1998 A: Hal Jordan 2.50
❑137, Oct 1998 A: Superman 4.00
❑1000000, Nov 1998 3.00
❑Annual 1, Sep 1988 A: Batman 3.50
❑Annual 2, Aug 1989 A: Question 3.00
❑Annual 3, Dec 1990 A: Question 3.00
❑Annual 4, Jun 1991; 50th Anniversary; Robin Hood 3.00
❑Annual 5, ca. 1994 TVE, FS (a); A: Batman 3.00
❑Annual 6, ca. 1994 1: Hook 3.50
❑Annual 7, ca. 1994; Year One 3.95

GREEN ARROW (MINI-SERIES)
DC

❑1, May 1983, DG (a); O: Green Arrow 3.00
❑2, Jun 1983, DG, TVE (a) 2.50
❑3, Jul 1983, DG (a) 2.00
❑4, Aug 1983, DG (a) 2.00

GREEN ARROW (2ND SERIES)
DC

❑1, Apr 2001; MW (c); KSm (w); Return of Oliver Queen 6.00

N-MINT

❑2, May 2001 MW (c); KSm (w) 6.00
❑3, Jun 2001 MW (c); KSm (w) 3.00
❑4, Jul 2001 MW (c); KSm (w) 3.00
❑5, Aug 2001 MW (c); KSm (w) 3.00
❑6, Sep 2001 MW (c); KSm (w) 3.00
❑7, Oct 2001 MW (c); KSm (w) 2.50
❑8, Nov 2001 MW (c); KSm (w) 2.50
❑9, Dec 2001 MW (c); KSm (w) 2.50
❑10, Jan 2002 MW (c); KSm (w) 2.50
❑11, Feb 2002 MW (c); KSm (w) 2.50
❑12, Mar 2002 MW (c); KSm (w) 2.50
❑13, Apr 2002 MW (c); KSm (w) 2.50
❑14, Aug 2002 MW (c); KSm (w) 2.50
❑15, Sep 2002 MW (c); KSm (w) 2.50
❑16, Oct 2002 MW (c) 2.50
❑17, Nov 2002 MW (c) 2.50
❑18, Dec 2002 MW (c) 2.50
❑19, Jan 2003 MW (c) 2.50
❑20, Mar 2003 MW (c) 2.50
❑21, Apr 2003 MW (c) 2.50
❑22, May 2003 MW (c) 2.50
❑23, Jun 2003; MW (c); Continues in Green Lantern #162 2.50
❑24, Jun 2003; MW (c); Continues in Green Lantern #163 2.50
❑25, Jul 2003; MW (c); Continues in Green Lantern #164 2.50
❑26, Jul 2003 MW (c) 2.50
❑27, Aug 2003 2.50
❑28, Sep 2003 2.50
❑29, Oct 2003 2.50
❑30, Nov 2003 2.50
❑31, Dec 2003 2.50
❑32, Jan 2004 2.50
❑33, Feb 2004 2.50
❑34, Mar 2004 2.50
❑35, Apr 2004 2.50
❑36, May 2004 2.50
❑37, Jun 2004 2.50
❑38, Jul 2004 2.50
❑39, Aug 2004 2.50
❑40, Sep 2004 2.50
❑41, Oct 2004 2.50
❑42, Nov 2004 2.50
❑43, Dec 2004 7.00
❑44, Jan 2005 4.00
❑45, Feb 2005 2.50
❑46, Mar 2005 2.50
❑47, Apr 2005 2.50
❑48, May 2005 2.50
❑49, Jun 2005 2.50
❑50, Jun 2005 3.50
❑51, Jul 2005 2.50
❑52, Aug 2005 2.50
❑53, Sep 2005 2.50
❑54, Oct 2005 2.50
❑55 2.50
❑56, Jan 2006 2.50
❑57, Feb 2006 2.50
❑58, Mar 2006 2.50
❑59, Apr 2006 2.50
❑60, May 2006 2.50
❑61, Jun 2006 2.50
❑63, Aug 2006 2.50

GREEN ARROW BY JACK KIRBY
DC

❑nn, ca. 2001; Prestige one-shot reprinting stories from Adventure Comics and World's Finest 5.95

GREEN ARROW: THE LONGBOW HUNTERS
DC

❑1, Aug 1987 MGr (w); MGr (a); 1: Shado 3.50
❑1/2nd, Aug 1987 MGr (w); MGr (a); 1: Shado 3.00
❑1/3rd, Aug 1987 MGr (w); MGr (a); 1: Shado 3.00
❑2, Sep 1987 MGr (w); MGr (a) 3.00
❑3, Oct 1987 MGr (w); MGr (a) 3.00

GREEN ARROW: THE WONDER YEAR
DC

❑1, Feb 1993 MGr (w); GM, MGr (a) 2.00
❑2, Mar 1993 MGr (w); GM, MGr (a) 2.00
❑3, Apr 1993 MGr (w); GM, MGr (a) 2.00
❑4, May 1993 MGr (w); GM, MGr (a) 2.00

Green Arrow (2nd Series)

Slain archer gets better
©DC

Green Arrow: The Longbow Hunters

Mike Grell makes GA grow up
©DC

Green Goblin

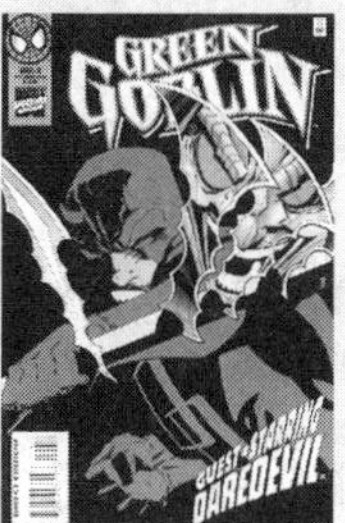

Not the villain, but a new hero
©Marvel

Green Hornet (Vol. 1)

Descendants of original take up mantle
©Now

Green Lantern (2nd Series)

Adventures of intergalactic lawman
©DC

N-MINT

GREEN CANDLES
DC / Paradox

❑1, ca. 1995, b&w; digest 5.95
❑2, ca. 1995, b&w; digest 5.95
❑3, ca. 1995, b&w; digest 5.95

GREENER PASTURES
Kronos

❑1 2.50
❑1/2nd, Jan 1997 2.50
❑2, Oct 1994 2.50
❑3, Feb 1995 2.50
❑4, Dec 1995 2.50
❑4.5, Feb 1996 1.95
❑5, Aug 1996 2.95
❑6, Nov 1996 2.95
❑7, Feb 1997 2.95

GREEN GOBLIN
Marvel

❑1, Oct 1995; enhanced cardstock cover 2.95
❑2, Nov 1995 1.95
❑3, Dec 1995; Story continued from Amazing Scarlet Spider #2 1.95
❑4, Jan 1996 1.95
❑5, Feb 1996 1.95
❑6, Mar 1996 1.95
❑7, Apr 1996 1.95
❑8, May 1996 1.95
❑9, Jun 1996 1.95
❑10, Jul 1996 1.95
❑11, Aug 1996 1.95
❑12, Sep 1996 1.95
❑13, Oct 1996 1.95

GREEN-GREY SPONGE-SUIT SUSHI TURTLES
Mirage

❑1, parody; cardstock cover 3.50

GREENHAVEN
Aircel

❑1 2.00
❑2 2.00
❑3, Continued in Elflord #21 2.00

GREEN HORNET (GOLD KEY)
Gold Key

❑1, Feb 1967 120.00
❑2, May 1967 80.00
❑3, Aug 1967 80.00

GREEN HORNET (VOL. 1)
Now

❑1, Nov 1989 JSo (c); JSo (a); O: Green Hornet I. O: 1940s Green Hornet 3.50
❑1/2nd, Apr 1990; prestige format; O: The Green Hornet. perfect bound 3.95
❑2, Dec 1989 2.50
❑3, Jan 1990 2.00
❑4, Feb 1990 SR (c) 2.00
❑5, Mar 1990 2.00
❑6, Apr 1990 2.00
❑7, May 1990; BSz (c); 1: new Kato. Mishi becomes new Kato 2.00
❑8, Jun 1990 2.00
❑9, Jul 1990 2.00
❑10, Aug 1990 2.00

N-MINT

❑11, Sep 1990 2.00
❑12, Oct 1990 2.00
❑13, Nov 1990 2.00
❑14, Feb 1991 2.00

GREEN HORNET (VOL. 2)
Now

❑1, Sep 1991 2.00
❑2, Oct 1991 2.00
❑3, Nov 1991 2.00
❑4, Dec 1991 2.00
❑5, Jan 1992 2.00
❑6, Feb 1992 2.00
❑7, Mar 1992 2.00
❑8, Apr 1992 2.00
❑9, May 1992 2.00
❑10, Jun 1992 2.00
❑11, Jul 1992 2.00
❑12, Aug 1992; bagged; with button 2.50
❑13, Sep 1992 1.95
❑14, Oct 1992 1.95
❑15, Nov 1992 1.95
❑16, Dec 1992 1.95
❑17, Jan 1993 1.95
❑18, Feb 1993 1.95
❑19, Mar 1993 1.95
❑20, Apr 1993 1.95
❑21, May 1993 1.95
❑22, Jun 1993; newsstand, trading card; newsstand; Has UPC, Comics Code seal 2.95
❑22/Direct ed., Jun 1993; alternate cover; direct sale; trading card; No Comics Code seal 2.95
❑23, Jul 1993 2.95
❑24, Aug 1993 1.95
❑25, Sep 1993 1.95
❑26, Oct 1993 1.95
❑27, Nov 1993 2.95
❑28, Dec 1993 1.95
❑29, Jan 1994 1.95
❑30, Feb 1994 1.95
❑31, Mar 1994 1.95
❑32, Apr 1994 1.95
❑33, May 1994 1.95
❑34, Jun 1994 1.95
❑35, Jul 1994 1.95
❑36, Aug 1994 1.95
❑37, Sep 1994 1.95
❑38, Nov 1994 2.50
❑39, Dec 1994 1.95
❑40, Jan 1995 2.50
❑Annual 1, Dec 1992 2.50
❑Annual 1994, Oct 1994 2.95

GREEN HORNET ANNIVERSARY SPECIAL
Now

❑1, Aug 1992; bagged; with button 2.50
❑2, Sep 1992 1.95
❑3, Oct 1992 1.95

GREEN HORNET, THE: DARK TOMORROW
Now

❑1, Jun 1993 2.50

N-MINT

❑2, Jul 1993 2.50
❑3, Aug 1993 2.50

GREEN HORNET, THE: SOLITARY SENTINEL
Now

❑1, Dec 1992 2.50
❑2, Jan 1993 2.50
❑3, Feb 1993 2.50

GREEN LANTERN (2ND SERIES)
DC

❑1, Aug 1960 GK (a); O: Green Lantern II (Hal Jordan). 1: the Guardians 4500.00
❑2, Oct 1960 GK (a); 1: Qward. 1: Pieface. 1000.00
❑3, Dec 1960 GK (a) 600.00
❑4, Feb 1961 GK (a) 450.00
❑5, Apr 1961 GK (a); 1: Hector Hammond. 450.00
❑6, Jun 1961 GK (a); 1: Tomar. 400.00
❑7, Aug 1961 GK (a); O: Sinestro. 1: Sinestro. 300.00
❑8, Oct 1961, GK (a) 300.00
❑9, Dec 1961 GK (a) 300.00
❑10, Jan 1962, GK (a) 300.00
❑11, Mar 1962, GK (a); 1: The Green Lantern Corps. 200.00
❑12, Apr 1962, GK (a); 1: Doctor Polaris. 200.00
❑13, Jun 1962, GK (a); A: Flash II (Barry Allen). 250.00
❑14, Jul 1962, GK (a); 1: Sonar. 175.00
❑15, Sep 1962, GK (a) 175.00
❑16, Oct 1962, GK (a); O: Star Sapphire. 1: Star Sapphire. 1: Zamarons. 175.00
❑17, Dec 1962, GK (a) 150.00
❑18, Jan 1963, GK (a) 150.00
❑19, Mar 1963, GK (a) 150.00
❑20, Apr 1963, GK (a); A: Flash II (Barry Allen). 150.00
❑21, Jun 1963, GK (a); O: Doctor Polaris. 125.00
❑22, Jul 1963, GK (a) 125.00
❑23, Sep 1963, GK (a); 1: Tattooed Man. 125.00
❑24, Oct 1963, GK (a); O: The Shark. 1: The Shark. 125.00
❑25, Dec 1963, GK (a) 125.00
❑26, Jan 1964, GK (a) 125.00
❑27, Mar 1964, GK (a) 125.00
❑28, Apr 1964, GK (a); 1: Goldface. 100.00
❑29, Jun 1964, GK (a); 1: Black Hand. A: Justice League of America. 100.00
❑30, Jul 1964, GK (a) 100.00
❑31, Sep 1964, GK (a) 75.00
❑32, Oct 1964, GK (a) 75.00
❑33, Dec 1964, GK (a) 75.00
❑34, Jan 1965, GK (a) 75.00
❑35, Mar 1965, GK (a) 75.00
❑36, Apr 1965, GK (a) 75.00
❑37, Jun 1965, GK (a); 1: Evil Star. 75.00
❑38, Jul 1965, GK (a) 75.00
❑39, Sep 1965, GK (a) 75.00
❑40, Oct 1965, O: the Guardians. 1: Krona. A: Green Lantern I (Alan Scott). 350.00

Other grades: Multiply price above by 5/6 for VF/NM • 2/3 for VERY FINE • 1/3 for FINE • 1/5 for VERY GOOD • 1/8 for GOOD

N-MINT | N-MINT | N-MINT

❑41, Dec 1965, GK (a); A: Star Sapphire. 75.00
❑42, Jan 1966, GK (a) 75.00
❑43, Mar 1966, GK (a); 1: Major Disaster. A: Flash II (Barry Allen). 75.00
❑44, Apr 1966, GK (a) 75.00
❑45, Jun 1966, GK (a); 1: Prince Peril. A: Green Lantern I (Alan Scott). 75.00
❑46, Jul 1966, GK (a) 75.00
❑47, Sep 1966, GK (a) 75.00
❑48, Oct 1966, GK (a) 75.00
❑49, Dec 1966, GK (a) 75.00
❑50, Jan 1967, GK (a) 60.00
❑51, Mar 1967 60.00
❑52, Apr 1967, A: Green Lantern I (Alan Scott) 80.00
❑53, Jun 1967 55.00
❑54, Jul 1967 55.00
❑55, Sep 1967 55.00
❑56, Oct 1967 55.00
❑57, Dec 1967 55.00
❑58, Jan 1968 55.00
❑59, Mar 1968, 1: Guy Gardner. 125.00
❑60, Apr 1968 50.00
❑61, Jun 1968, A: Green Lantern I (Alan Scott) 50.00
❑62, Jul 1968 50.00
❑63, Sep 1968 50.00
❑64, Oct 1968 50.00
❑65, Dec 1968 50.00
❑66, Jan 1969 50.00
❑67, Mar 1969 50.00
❑68, Apr 1969 50.00
❑69, Jun 1969 50.00
❑70, Jul 1969, GK (a) 50.00
❑71, Sep 1969, GK (a) 50.00
❑72, Oct 1969, GK (a) 50.00
❑73, Dec 1969, GK (a) 50.00
❑74, Jan 1970, GK (a) 50.00
❑75, Mar 1970, GK (a) 50.00
❑76, Apr 1970, NA (a); A: Green Arrow. Green Lantern/Green Arrow series 375.00
❑77, Jun 1970, NA (a); A: Green Arrow. Green Lantern/Green Arrow series 75.00
❑78, Jul 1970, NA (a); A: Green Arrow. Green Lantern/Green Arrow series 75.00
❑79, Sep 1970, NA (a); A: Green Arrow. Green Lantern/Green Arrow series 60.00
❑80, Oct 1970, NA (a); A: Green Arrow. Green Lantern/Green Arrow series 60.00
❑81, Dec 1970, NA (a); A: Green Arrow. Green Lantern/Green Arrow series 60.00
❑82, Mar 1971, NA (a); A: Green Arrow. Green Lantern/Green Arrow series 60.00
❑83, May 1971, NA (a); A: Green Arrow. Green Lantern/Green Arrow series; Anti-drug issue 60.00
❑84, Jul 1971, BWr, NA (a); Green Arrow; Green Lantern/Green Arrow series 60.00
❑85, Sep 1971; NA (a); Green Arrow; Anti-drug issue; Green Lantern/ Green Arrow series 50.00
❑86, Nov 1971; NA (a); Green Lantern/ Green Arrow series; Green Arrow; Anti-drug issue 60.00
❑87, Jan 1972; NA, GK (a); 1: John Stewart. A: Green Arrow. Guy Gardner cameo; Green Lantern/ Green Arrow series 50.00
❑88, Mar 1972 GK (a); A: Green Arrow. 30.00
❑89, May 1972; NA (a); A: Green Arrow. Green Lantern/Green Arrow series 45.00
❑90, Sep 1976, MGr (w); MGr (a); A: Green Arrow. Green Lantern/ Green Arrow series 10.00
❑91, Nov 1976, MGr (a) 10.00
❑92, Dec 1976, MGr (a) 10.00
❑93, Feb 1977, MGr (a) 9.00
❑94, Apr 1977, MGr (a) 9.00
❑95, Jun 1977, MGr (a) 9.00
❑96, Aug 1977, MGr (a) 9.00
❑97, Oct 1977, MGr (a) 9.00
❑98, Nov 1977, MGr (a) 9.00
❑99, Dec 1977, MGr (a) 9.00
❑100, Jan 1978, 100th anniversary issue MGr (a); 1: Air Wave II (Harry "Hal" Jordan). 10.00
❑101, Feb 1978, McGinty 9.00
❑102, Mar 1978, MGr (a); A: Green Arrow. 4.00
❑103, Apr 1978, MGr (a); A: Green Arrow 4.00
❑104, May 1978, MGr (a); A: Green Arrow 4.00
❑105, Jun 1978, MGr (a); A: Green Arrow 4.00
❑106, Jul 1978, MGr (a); A: Green Arrow 4.00
❑107, Aug 1978, MGr (a); A: Green Arrow 4.00
❑108, Sep 1978, MGr (a); A: Green Arrow. Golden Age Green Lantern back-up 4.00
❑109, Oct 1978, MGr (a); A: Green Arrow. Golden Age Green Lantern back-up 4.00
❑110, Nov 1978, MGr (a); A: Green Arrow 4.00
❑111, Dec 1978, MGr (a); A: Green Arrow 4.00
❑112, Jan 1979, O: Green Lantern I (Alan Scott). 8.00
❑113, Feb 1979 3.00
❑114, Mar 1979 3.00
❑115, Apr 1979 3.00
❑116, May 1979, Guy Gardner becomes a Green Lantern 8.00
❑116/Whitman, May 1979, Guy Gardner becomes a Green Lantern; Whitman variant 16.00
❑117, Jun 1979 3.00
❑117/Whitman, Jun 1979, Whitman variant 6.00
❑118, Jul 1979 3.00
❑118/Whitman, Jul 1979, Whitman variant 6.00
❑119, Aug 1979 2.50
❑119/Whitman, Aug 1979, Whitman variant 5.00
❑120, Sep 1979 2.50
❑120/Whitman, Sep 1979, Whitman variant 5.00
❑121, Oct 1979 2.50
❑121/Whitman, Oct 1979, Whitman variant 5.00
❑122, Nov 1979, A: Guy Gardner 3.50
❑123, Dec 1979, Guy Gardner as Green Lantern 6.00
❑124, Jan 1980 2.50
❑125, Feb 1980 2.50
❑126, Mar 1980 2.50
❑127, Apr 1980, JSa (a) 2.50
❑128, May 1980, JSa (a) 2.50
❑129, Jun 1980, JSa (a) 2.50
❑130, Jun 1980, JSa (a) 2.50
❑131, Aug 1980, JSa (a) 2.25
❑132, Sep 1980, JSa (a) 2.25
❑133, Oct 1980, JSa (a); A: Doctor Polaris. 2.25
❑134, Nov 1980, JSa (a); A: Doctor Polaris. 2.25
❑135, Dec 1980, JSa (a); A: Doctor Polaris. 2.25
❑136, Jan 1981, JSa (a) 2.50
❑137, Feb 1981, JSa (a); 1: Citadel. 2.50
❑138, Mar 1981, JSa (a) 2.50
❑139, Apr 1981, JSa (a) 2.50
❑140, May 1981, JSa (a) 2.00
❑141, Jun 1981, JSa (a); 1: Broot. 1: Harpis. 1: Omega Men. 1: Auron. 1: Kalista. 1: Demonia. 1: Primus. 5.00
❑142, Jul 1981, JSa (a); 1: The Gordanians. A: Omega Men. 2.50
❑143, Aug 1981, JSa (a); A: Omega Men. 2.50
❑144, Sep 1981, JSa (a); A: Omega Men. 2.50
❑145, Oct 1981, JSa (a) 2.00
❑146, Nov 1981, JSa (a) 2.00
❑147, Dec 1981, JSa (a) 2.00
❑148, Jan 1982, JSa (a) 2.00
❑149, Feb 1982, JSa (a) 2.00
❑150, Mar 1982; 150th anniversary issue JSa (a) 5.00
❑151, Apr 1982 2.00
❑152, May 1982 2.00
❑153, Jun 1982 2.00
❑154, Jul 1982 2.00
❑155, Aug 1982 2.00
❑156, Sep 1982 2.00
❑157, Oct 1982 2.00
❑158, Nov 1982 2.00
❑159, Dec 1982 2.00
❑160, Jan 1983, Omega Men 2.00
❑161, Feb 1983, Omega Men 1.50
❑162, Mar 1983, KB (w); KP (a); Back-up story is Kurt Busiek's first major comics work 1.50
❑163, Apr 1983, KP (a) 1.50
❑164, May 1983, KP (a); 1: The Green Man. 1.50
❑165, Jun 1983, KP (a) 1.50
❑166, Jul 1983 1.50
❑167, Aug 1983, DaG, GT (a); 1: Spider Guild. 1.50
❑168, Sep 1983 1.50
❑169, Oct 1983 1.50
❑170, Nov 1983, GK (c) 1.50
❑171, Dec 1983 1.50
❑172, Jan 1984 1.50
❑173, Feb 1984 DG (a); 1: Javelin. A: Monitor. V: Javelin. 1.50
❑174, Mar 1984 DG (a) 3.00
❑175, Apr 1984 DG (a); A: Flash. V: Shark. 1.50
❑176, May 1984 DG (a); 1: Demolition Team. V: Shark. 1.50
❑177, Jun 1984 GK (c); V: Hector Hammond. 1.50
❑178, Jul 1984 DG (a); 1: The Predator (Carol Ferris). A: Monitor. V: Demolition Team. 1.50
❑179, Aug 1984 DG (a); A: Predator. V: Demolition Team. 3.00
❑180, Sep 1984 DG (a); A: Superman. A: Green Arrow. A: Flash. 1.50
❑181, Oct 1984; DG (a); Hal Jordan quits as Green Lantern 1.50
❑182, Nov 1984; DG (a); John Stewart becomes new Green Lantern; retells origin 1.50
❑183, Dec 1984 1.50
❑184, Jan 1985; GK (a); reprints origin of Guy Gardner 1.50
❑185, Feb 1985 KB (w); DG (a) 1.50
❑186, Mar 1985 DG (a); V: Eclipso. 1.50
❑187, Apr 1985 1.50
❑188, May 1985; John Stewart reveals ID to public 1.50
❑189, Jun 1985 V: Sonar. 1.50
❑190, Jul 1985 V: Predator. 1.50
❑191, Aug 1985 1.50
❑192, Sep 1985 1.50
❑193, Oct 1985 1.50
❑194, Nov 1985; Crisis; Guy Gardner returns; Guy Gardner vs. Hal Jordan 2.50
❑195, Dec 1985; Crisis; Guy Gardner becomes new Green Lantern of Earth 4.00
❑196, Jan 1986; Crisis 1.50
❑197, Feb 1986; Crisis; Guy Gardner vs. John Stewart 1.50
❑198, Mar 1986; Crisis; giant; Hal Jordan returns as Green Lantern 1.50
❑199, Apr 1986; Crisis; Hal Jordan returns as GL 1.50
❑200, May 1986; Crisis; Guardians join Zamarons 2.00
❑201, Jun 1986; Crisis aftermath 1.50
❑202, Jul 1986 1.50
❑203, Aug 1986 O: Ch'p. 1.50
❑204, Sep 1986 1.50
❑205, Oct 1986; Series continues as Green Lantern Corps 1.50
❑Special 1, Dec 1988 2.50
❑Special 2, ca. 1989 2.50

GREEN LANTERN (3RD SERIES)
DC

❑0, Oct 1994; O: Green Lantern (Kyle Rayner). V: Hal Jordan. Oa destroyed 3.50
❑1, Jun 1990 PB (a) 7.00
❑2, Jul 1990 PB (a) 2.50
❑3, Aug 1990; Hal vs. Guy 2.00
❑4, Sep 1990 2.00
❑5, Oct 1990 2.00
❑6, Nov 1990 1.50
❑7, Dec 1990 1.50
❑8, Jan 1991 1.50
❑9, Feb 1991 A: G'Nort. 1.50
❑10, Mar 1991 A: G'Nort. 1.50
❑11, Apr 1991 A: G'Nort. 1.50
❑12, May 1991 A: G'Nort. 1.50

Other grades: Multiply price above by 5/6 for VF/NM • 2/3 for VERY FINE • 1/3 for FINE • 1/5 for VERY GOOD • 1/8 for GOOD

Green Lantern (3rd Series)

Hal goes crazy, Kyle takes over

©DC

Green Lantern/Atom

Part of GL: Circle of Fire mini-series

©DC

Green Lantern: Circle of Fire

Kyle's big crossover with galactic heroes

©DC

Green Lantern Corps

Picks up numbering from GL (2nd series)

©DC

Green Lantern Corps Quarterly

Anthology of intergalactic adventures

©DC

	N-MINT
❑13, Jun 1991; Giant-size	2.25
❑14, Jul 1991	1.50
❑15, Aug 1991	1.50
❑16, Sep 1991	1.50
❑17, Oct 1991	1.50
❑18, Nov 1991	1.50
❑19, Dec 1991; Giant-size; GK (c); PB, JSa, RT (a); 50th anniversary issue; Giant-size	2.00
❑20, Jan 1992 PB (a)	1.50
❑21, Feb 1992 PB (a)	1.50
❑22, Mar 1992 PB (a)	1.50
❑23, Apr 1992 PB (a)	1.50
❑24, May 1992 PB (a)	1.50
❑25, Jun 1992; Giant size; Hal Jordan vs. Guy Gardner	2.25
❑26, Jul 1992	1.50
❑27, Aug 1992	1.25
❑28, Sep 1992	1.25
❑29, Sep 1992	1.25
❑30, Oct 1992 A: Flash. V: Gorilla Grodd.	1.25
❑31, Oct 1992 A: Flash. V: Hector Hammond. V: Gorilla Grodd.	1.25
❑32, Nov 1992	1.25
❑33, Nov 1992	1.25
❑34, Dec 1992	1.25
❑35, Jan 1993	1.25
❑36, Feb 1993	1.25
❑37, Mar 1993	1.25
❑38, Apr 1993 A: Adam Strange.	1.25
❑39, May 1993 A: Adam Strange.	1.25
❑40, May 1993 A: Darkstar.	1.25
❑41, Jun 1993	1.25
❑42, Jun 1993	1.25
❑43, Jul 1993	1.25
❑44, Aug 1993 RT (c); RT (a)	1.25
❑45, Sep 1993	1.25
❑46, Oct 1993 A: Superman. V: Mongul.	4.00
❑47, Nov 1993 A: Green Arrow.	2.00
❑48, Jan 1994	5.00
❑49, Feb 1994	5.00
❑50, Mar 1994; Double-size; 1: Green Lantern IV (Kyle Rayner). D: Sinestro. D: Kilowog. Glow-in-the-dark cover..	5.00
❑51, May 1994; New costume	3.00
❑52, Jun 1994 V: Mongul.	2.00
❑53, Jul 1994 A: Superman.	2.00
❑54, Aug 1994 V: Major Force.	2.00
❑55, Sep 1994; A: Green Lantern I. A: Alan Scott. Zero Hour	2.00
❑56, Nov 1994	2.00
❑57, Dec 1994; A: New Titans. continues in New Titans #116	2.00
❑58, Jan 1995	2.00
❑59, Feb 1995 V: Doctor Polaris.	2.00
❑60, Mar 1995 A: Guy Gardner. V: Major Force.	2.00
❑61, Apr 1995 A: Darkstar. V: Kalibak.	2.00
❑62, May 1995	2.00
❑63, Jun 1995	2.00
❑64, Jul 1995	2.00
❑65, Aug 1995; continues in Darkstars #34	2.00
❑66, Sep 1995; teams with Flash	2.00
❑67, Oct 1995	2.00
❑68, Nov 1995; A: Donna Troy. Underworld Unleashed	2.00
❑69, Dec 1995; Underworld Unleashed	2.00
❑70, Jan 1996 A: John Stewart.	2.00
❑71, Feb 1996 A: Robin. A: Sentinel. A: Batman	2.00
❑72, Mar 1996 A: Captain Marvel.	2.00
❑73, Apr 1996 A: Wonder Woman.	2.00
❑74, Jun 1996	2.00
❑75, Jul 1996	2.00
❑76, Jul 1996	2.00
❑77, Aug 1996	2.00
❑78, Sep 1996	2.00
❑79, Oct 1996 V: Sonar.	2.00
❑80, Nov 1996; V: Doctor Light. Final Night	2.00
❑81, Dec 1996; Funeral of Hal Jordan; Memorial for Hal Jordan	3.00
❑81/Variant, Dec 1996; Embossed cover; Funeral of Hal Jordan; Kane back-up story; reprints origin; Memorial for Hal Jordan	4.00
❑82, Jan 1997	1.75
❑83, Feb 1997	1.75
❑84, Mar 1997	1.75
❑85, Apr 1997	1.75
❑86, May 1997 A: Jade. A: Obsidian.	1.75
❑87, Jun 1997 A: Martian Manhunter. A: Access.	1.75
❑88, Jul 1997	1.75
❑89, Aug 1997	1.75
❑90, Sep 1997	1.75
❑91, Oct 1997; V: Desaad. Genesis	1.75
❑92, Nov 1997; concludes in Green Arrow #126	1.75
❑93, Dec 1997; A: Deadman. Face cover	1.95
❑94, Jan 1998 A: Superboy.	1.95
❑95, Feb 1998	1.95
❑96, Mar 1998; cover forms triptych with Flash #135 and Green Arrow #130	1.95
❑97, Apr 1998 V: Grayven.	1.95
❑98, May 1998 1: Cary Wren as Green Lantern. A: Legion of Super-Heroes.	1.95
❑99, Jun 1998	1.95
❑100/A, Jul 1998; Hal Jordan cover (Kyle Rayner cover inside)	5.00
❑100/Autographed, Jul 1998	4.00
❑100/B, Jul 1998; Kyle Rayner cover (Hal Jordan cover inside)	2.95
❑101, Aug 1998	1.95
❑102, Aug 1998 V: Kalibak.	1.95
❑103, Sep 1998 A: JLA.	1.95
❑104, Sep 1998 A: Green Arrow.	1.95
❑105, Oct 1998 V: Parallax.	1.95
❑106, Oct 1998; Hal returned to past.	1.95
❑107, Dec 1998; Kyle gives a ring to Jade	1.99
❑108, Jan 1999; Wonder Woman	1.99
❑109, Feb 1999; Green Lantern IV (Jade)	1.99
❑110, Mar 1999 A: Green Lantern (Alan Scott). A: Green Arrow. A: Conner Hawke.	1.99
❑111, Apr 1999 A: Fatality. A: John Stewart. V: Fatality.	1.99
❑112, May 1999; Kyle returns	1.99
❑113, Jun 1999	1.99
❑114, Jul 1999	1.99
❑115, Aug 1999 A: Plastic Man. A: Booster Gold.	1.99
❑116, Sep 1999 A: Plastic Man. A: Booster Gold.	1.99
❑117, Oct 1999 V: Manhunter.	1.99
❑118, Nov 1999; A: Enchantress. Day of Judgment	1.99
❑119, Dec 1999 A: new Spectre	1.99
❑120, Jan 2000	1.99
❑121, Feb 2000	1.99
❑122, Mar 2000	1.99
❑123, Apr 2000	1.99
❑124, May 2000	1.99
❑125, Jun 2000	1.99
❑126, Jul 2000	1.99
❑127, Aug 2000	1.99
❑128, Sep 2000	2.25
❑129, Oct 2000	2.25
❑130, Nov 2000	2.25
❑131, Dec 2000	2.25
❑132, Jan 2001	2.25
❑133, Feb 2001	2.25
❑134, Mar 2001	2.25
❑135, Apr 2001	2.25
❑136, May 2001	2.25
❑137, Jun 2001	2.25
❑138, Jul 2001	2.25
❑139, Aug 2001	2.25
❑140, Sep 2001	2.25
❑141, Oct 2001	2.25
❑142, Nov 2001	2.25
❑143, Dec 2001; Joker: Last Laugh crossover	2.25
❑144, Jan 2002	2.25
❑145, Feb 2002	2.25
❑146, Mar 2002	2.25
❑147, Apr 2002	2.25
❑148, May 2002	2.25
❑149, Jun 2002	2.25
❑150, Jul 2002	3.50
❑151, Aug 2002	2.25
❑152, Sep 2002	2.25
❑153, Oct 2002	2.25
❑154, Nov 2002 JLee (c)	2.25
❑155, Dec 2002	2.25
❑156, Jan 2003	2.25
❑157, Feb 2003	2.25
❑158, Mar 2003	2.25
❑159, Apr 2003	2.25
❑160, May 2003	2.25
❑161, May 2003	2.25
❑162, Jun 2003; Continued from Green Arrow #23	2.25
❑163, Jun 2003; Continued from Green Arrow #24	2.25
❑164, Jul 2003; Continued from Green Arrow #25	2.25
❑165, Jul 2003	2.25
❑166, Aug 2003	2.25
❑167, Sep 2003	2.25
❑168, Oct 2003	2.25
❑169, Nov 2003	2.25

Other grades: Multiply price above by 5/6 for VF/NM • 2/3 for VERY FINE • 1/3 for FINE • 1/5 for VERY GOOD • 1/8 for GOOD

❑170, Dec 2003 2.25
❑171, Jan 2004 2.25
❑172, Feb 2004 2.25
❑173, Mar 2004 2.25
❑174, Apr 2004 2.25
❑175, May 2004 4.00
❑176, Jun 2004 8.00
❑177, Jul 2004 4.00
❑178, Aug 2004 2.25
❑179, Sep 2004 2.25
❑180, Oct 2004 2.25
❑181, Nov 2004 2.25
❑1000000, Nov 1998; One Million 3.00
❑Annual 1, ca. 1992 4.00
❑Annual 2, ca. 1993 O: Nightblade. 1: Nightblade 2.50
❑Annual 3, ca. 1994; Elseworlds 3.00
❑Annual 4, ca. 1995; Year One; Kyle and Hal switch places 3.50
❑Annual 5, ca. 1996; Legends of the Dead Earth 2.95
❑Annual 6, Oct 1997; Pulp Heroes; John Carter of Mars theme 3.95
❑Annual 7, Oct 1998; Ghosts 2.95
❑Annual 8, Oct 1999; KG (w); JLApe 2.95
❑Annual 9, Oct 2000; 1: Sala. Planet DC 3.50
❑Annual 1963; MA, ATh, GK (a); published in 1998 in style of 1963 annuals; cardstock cover 6.00
❑Giant Size 1, Dec 1998; 80-Page Giant A: G'Nort. 4.95
❑Giant Size 2, Jun 1999; 80-Page Giant MWa (w); A: Plastic Man. A: Guy Gardner. A: Deadman. A: Impulse. A: Zatanna. A: Big Barda. A: Aquaman. 4.95
❑Giant Size 3, Aug 2000 5.95
❑3D 1, Dec 1998 V: Doctor Light. 4.50
❑3D 1/Ltd., Dec 1998; V: Doctor Light. Signed 16.95

GREEN LANTERN (4TH SERIES)
DC

❑1, Jul 2005 6.00
❑2, Aug 2005 4.00
❑3, Sep 2005 2.99
❑4, Oct 2005 2.99
❑5, Jan 2006 2.99
❑7, Feb 2006 2.99
❑8, Mar 2006 2.99
❑9, May 2006 2.99
❑10, Jun 2006 2.99
❑11, Aug 2006 2.99

GREEN LANTERN/ADAM STRANGE
DC

❑1, Oct 2000 2.50

GREEN LANTERN/ATOM
DC

❑1, Oct 2000 2.50

GREEN LANTERN: BRIGHTEST DAY, BLACKEST NIGHT
DC

❑1, Aug 2002 5.95

GREEN LANTERN: CIRCLE OF FIRE
DC

❑1, Oct 2000 4.95
❑2, Oct 2000 4.95

GREEN LANTERN CORPS
DC

❑206, Nov 1986; Series continued from Green Lantern (2nd Series) #205 1.50
❑207, Dec 1986; Legends 1.50
❑208, Jan 1987 1.50
❑209, Feb 1987 1.50
❑210, Mar 1987 1.50
❑211, Apr 1987 1.50
❑212, May 1987 1.50
❑213, Jun 1987 1.50
❑214, Jul 1987 1.50
❑215, Aug 1987 1.50
❑216, Sep 1987 1.50
❑217, Oct 1987 1.50
❑218, Nov 1987 1.50
❑219, Dec 1987 1.50
❑220, Jan 1988; Millennium 1.50
❑221, Feb 1988; Millennium 1.50
❑222, Mar 1988 1.50
❑223, Apr 1988 1.50
❑224, May 1988; Giant-size GK (a) 1.50
❑Annual 1 1985 2.50
❑Annual 2 1986 2.25
❑Annual 3 1987 KB (w) 2.00

GREEN LANTERN CORPS (2ND SERIES)
DC

❑1, Aug 2006 2.99

GREEN LANTERN CORPS QUARTERLY
DC

❑1, Sum 1992 2.50
❑2, Aut 1992; Hector Hammond vs. Alan Scott 2.50
❑3, Win 1992 2.50
❑4, Spr 1993; Alan Scott vs. Solomon Grundy 2.50
❑5, Sum 1993 2.50
❑6, Aut 1993; Alan Scott vs. New Harlequin 2.95
❑7, Win 1993 2.95
❑8, Spr 1994; Jack Chance vs. Lobo 2.95

GREEN LANTERN CORPS: RECHARGE
DC

❑1 2.99
❑2, Dec 2005 2.99
❑3, Feb 2006 2.99
❑4, Mar 2006 2.99
❑5, May 2006 2.99

GREEN LANTERN: DRAGON LORD
DC

❑1, Jun 2001 4.95
❑2, Jul 2001 4.95
❑3, Aug 2001 4.95

GREEN LANTERN: EMERALD DAWN
DC

❑1, Dec 1989 KJ (c); RT (a); O: Green Lantern II (Hal Jordan). 2.00
❑2, Jan 1990 KJ (c); KG (w); RT (a) 1.50
❑3, Feb 1990 KJ (c); KG (w); RT (a) 1.50
❑4, Mar 1990 KJ (c); KG (w); RT (a) 1.50
❑5, Apr 1990 KJ (c); KG (w); RT (a) 1.50
❑6, May 1990 KJ (c); KG (w); RT (a) 1.50

GREEN LANTERN: EMERALD DAWN II
DC

❑1, Apr 1991 (c); KG (w); RT (a) 1.50
❑2, May 1991 (c); KG (w); RT (a) 1.00
❑3, Jun 1991 (c); KG (w); RT (a) 1.00
❑4, Jul 1991 (c); KG (w); RT (a) 1.00
❑5, Aug 1991 (c); KG (w); RT (a) 1.00
❑6, Sep 1991 (c); KG (w); RT (a) 1.00

GREEN LANTERN: EVIL'S MIGHT
DC

❑1, Oct 2002 5.95
❑2, Nov 2002 5.95
❑3, Dec 2002 5.95

GREEN LANTERN/FIRESTORM
DC

❑1, Oct 2000 2.50

GREEN LANTERN/FLASH: FASTER FRIENDS
DC

❑1; prestige format; concludes in Flash/Green Lantern: Faster Friends 4.95

GREEN LANTERN GALLERY
DC

❑1, Dec 1996; pin-ups 3.50

GREEN LANTERN: GANTHET'S TALE
DC

❑1 1992; prestige format; enhanced cover; Larry Niven 5.95

GREEN LANTERN/GREEN ARROW
DC

❑1, Oct 1983; DG, NA (a); Reprints 4.00
❑2, Nov 1983; DG, NA (a); Reprints 3.50
❑3, Dec 1983; DG, NA (a); Reprints 3.50
❑4, Jan 1984; DG, NA (a); Reprints 3.50
❑5, Feb 1984; BWr, DG, NA (a); Reprints 3.50
❑6, Mar 1984; DG, NA (a); Reprints 3.50
❑7, Apr 1984; DG, NA (a); Reprints 3.50

GREEN LANTERN/GREEN LANTERN
DC

❑1, Oct 2000 2.50

GREEN LANTERN: MOSAIC
DC

❑1, Jun 1992 1.25
❑2, Jul 1992 1.25
❑3, Aug 1992 1.25
❑4, Sep 1992 1.25
❑5, Oct 1992 1.25
❑6, Nov 1992 1.25
❑7, Dec 1992 1.25
❑8, Jan 1993 1.25
❑9, Feb 1993 1.25
❑10, Mar 1993 1.25
❑11, Apr 1993 1.25
❑12, May 1993 1.25
❑13, Jun 1993 1.25
❑14, Jul 1993 1.25
❑15, Aug 1993 1.25
❑16, Sep 1993 1.25
❑17, Oct 1993 1.25
❑18, Nov 1993 1.25

GREEN LANTERN: 1001 EMERALD NIGHTS
DC

❑1, May 2001, Elseworlds 6.95

GREEN LANTERN: OUR WORLDS AT WAR
DC

❑1, Aug 2001; hardcover 2.95

GREEN LANTERN PLUS
DC

❑1, Dec 1996 2.95

GREEN LANTERN/POWER GIRL
DC

❑1, Oct 2000 2.50

GREEN LANTERN: REBIRTH
DC

❑1, Dec 2004 10.00
❑1/2nd, Dec 2004 12.00
❑1/3rd, Dec 2004 5.00
❑2, Jan 2005 6.00
❑2/2nd, Jan 2005 3.00
❑3, Feb 2005 4.00
❑4, Mar 2005 2.95
❑5, Apr 2005 2.95
❑6, Jun 2005 2.99

GREEN LANTERN SECRET FILES
DC

❑1, Jul 1998; background on all Green Lanterns 4.95
❑2, Sep 1999; background on all Green Lanterns 4.95
❑3, Jul 2002 4.95

GREEN LANTERN/SENTINEL: HEART OF DARKNESS
DC

❑1, Mar 1998; covers form triptych 1.95
❑2, Apr 1998; covers form triptych 1.95
❑3, May 1998; covers form triptych 1.95

GREEN LANTERN/SILVER SURFER: UNHOLY ALLIANCES
DC

❑1 1995; prestige format; crossover with Marvel 4.95

GREEN LANTERN/SUPERMAN: LEGEND OF THE GREEN FLAME
DC

❑1 2000 5.95

GREEN LANTERN: THE NEW CORPS
DC

❑1, ca. 1999; prestige format 4.95
❑1/Autographed, ca. 1999 8.00
❑2, ca. 1999; prestige format 4.95

GREEN LANTERN VS. ALIENS
DC

❑1, Sep 2000 3.00
❑2, Oct 2000 3.00
❑3, Nov 2000 3.00
❑4, Dec 2000 3.00

GREENLEAF IN EXILE
CAT'S PAW

❑1 2.95
❑2 2.95
❑3 2.95

Green Lantern: Emerald Dawn

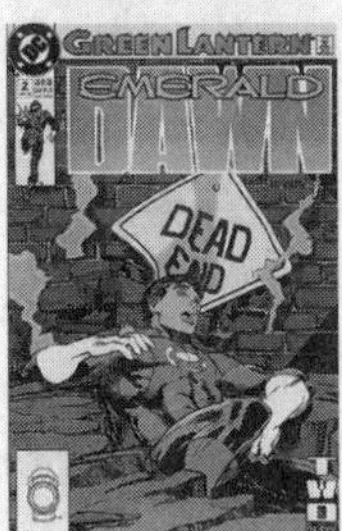

New origin gives Hal Jordan feet of clay

©DC

Green Lantern: Ganthet's Tale

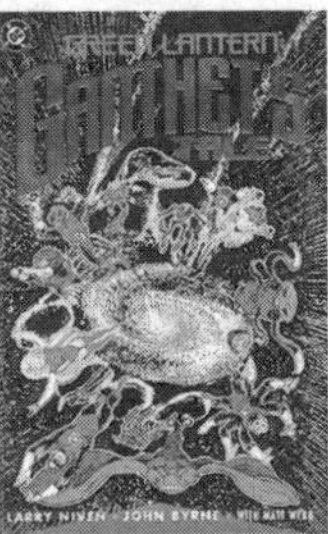

Larry Niven writes wandering Guardian tale

©DC

Grendel (1st Series)

Matt Wagner's generation-spanning vigilante

©Comico

Grendel: Black, White, & Red

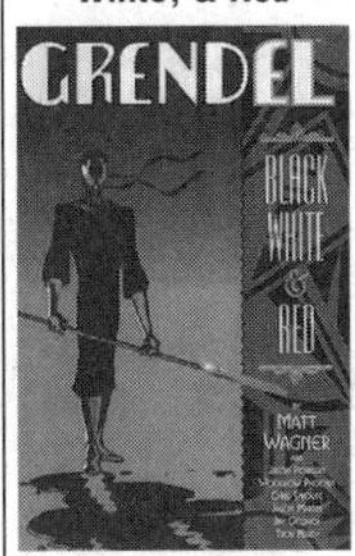

Other artists' takes on Wagner's creation

©Dark Horse

Grendel: The Devil Inside

Reprints of Comico issues

©Comico

N-MINT

❑4 .... 2.95
❑5 .... 2.95
❑6 .... 2.95

GREENLOCK
AIRCEL

❑1, Mar 1991, b&w 2.50

GREEN PLANET
CHARLTON

❑1, ca. 1962 .... 26.00

GREEN SKULL
KNOWN ASSOCIATES

❑1 .... 2.50

GREGORY
DC / PIRANHA

❑1, b&w 7.95
❑1/2nd 7.95
❑2; Herman Vermin's Very Own Best-selling & Critically Acclaimed Book with Gregory 4.95
❑3 .... 7.95
❑3/Gold; Gold logo edition (limited printing) 9.00
❑4, b&w; Fat Boy 4.95

GREMLIN TROUBLE
ANTI-BALLISTIC

❑1, b&w 3.50
❑2, b&w 3.00
❑3, b&w 3.00
❑4, b&w 3.00
❑5, b&w 3.00
❑6, b&w 2.95
❑7, b&w 2.95
❑8, b&w; Instigation of the Gremlin-Goblin War 2.95
❑9, b&w 2.95
❑10, b&w 2.95
❑11, b&w; Grommet cameo; Mr. Wingnut cameo; Xynophylyen 2.95
❑12, b&w 2.95
❑13, b&w; Dr. Brandy Schwarzchild ... 2.95
❑14, b&w 2.95
❑15, b&w 2.95
❑16, b&w 2.95
❑17, b&w 2.95
❑18, b&w 2.95
❑19, b&w 2.95
❑20, ca. 1999, b&w 2.95
❑21, ca. 2000, b&w 2.95
❑22, ca. 2000, b&w 2.95
❑23, ca. 2000, b&w 2.95
❑24, ca. 2000, b&w 2.95
❑25, ca. 2000, b&w 2.95
❑26, ca. 2001, b&w 2.95
❑27, ca. 2001, b&w 2.95
❑28, ca. 2001, b&w 2.95
❑29, ca. 2002, b&w 2.95
❑30, ca. 2002, b&w 4.95
❑Special 1, ca. 2003, b&w 0.00
❑Special 2, ca. 2004, b&w 0.00

GRENDEL (1ST SERIES)
COMICO

❑1, Mar 1983, b&w MW (a) 45.00
❑2, ca. 1983, b&w MW (a) 35.00
❑3, Feb 1984, b&w MW (a) 26.00

N-MINT

GRENDEL (2ND SERIES)
COMICO

❑1, Oct 1986, MW (w); MW (a) 5.00
❑1/2nd, MW (w); MW (a) 2.50
❑2, Nov 1986, MW (w); MW (a) 4.00
❑3, Dec 1986, MW (w); MW (a) 3.50
❑4, Jan 1987, DSt (c); MW (w) 3.50
❑5, Feb 1987, MW (w); MW (a) 3.50
❑6, Mar 1987, MW (w); MW (a) 3.00
❑7, Apr 1987, MW (w); MW (a) 3.00
❑8, May 1987, MW (w); MW (a) 3.00
❑9, Jun 1987, MW (w); MW (a) 3.00
❑10, Jul 1987, MW (w); MW (a) 3.00
❑11, Aug 1987, MW (w); MW (a) 3.00
❑12, Sep 1987, MW (w); MW (a); D: Grendel. 3.00
❑13, Oct 1987, MW (w); MW (a); new Grendel 3.00
❑14, Nov 1987, MW (w); MW (a); new Grendel 3.00
❑15, Dec 1987, MW (w); MW (a); new Grendel 3.00
❑16, Jan 1988, MW (w); MW (a); Mage begins 4.00
❑17, Feb 1988, MW (w); MW (a) 2.50
❑18, Apr 1988, MW (w); MW (a) 3.00
❑19, May 1988, MW (w); MW (a) 2.50
❑20, Jun 1988, MW (w); MW (a) 2.50
❑21, Jul 1988, MW (w); MW (a) 2.50
❑22, Aug 1988, MW (w); MW (a) 2.50
❑23, Sep 1988, MW (w); MW (a) 2.50
❑24, Oct 1988, MW (w); MW (a) 2.50
❑25, Nov 1988, MW (w); MW (a) 2.50
❑26, Dec 1988, MW (w); MW (a) 2.50
❑27, Jan 1989, MW (w); MW (a) 2.50
❑28, Feb 1989, MW (w); MW (a) 2.50
❑29, Mar 1989, MW (w); MW (a) 2.50
❑30, Apr 1989, MW (w); MW (a) 2.50
❑31, May 1989, MW (w); MW (a) 2.50
❑32, Jun 1989, MW (w); MW (a) 2.50
❑33, Jul 1989, Giant-size MW (w); MW (a) 3.75
❑34, Aug 1989, MW (w); MW (a) 2.50
❑35, Sep 1989, MW (w); MW (a) 2.50
❑36, Oct 1989, MW (w); MW (a) 2.50
❑37, Nov 1989, MW (w); MW (a) 2.50
❑38, Dec 1989, MW (w); MW (a) 2.50
❑39, Jan 1990, MW (w); MW (a) 2.50
❑40, Feb 1990, MW (w); MW (a); flip book with Grendel Tales Special Preview 3.50

GRENDEL: BLACK, WHITE, & RED
DARK HORSE

❑1, Nov 1998 MW (w) 4.00
❑2, Dec 1998 MW (w) 4.00
❑3, Jan 1999 MW (w) 4.00
❑4, Feb 1999 MW (w) 4.00

GRENDEL CLASSICS
DARK HORSE

❑1, Jul 1995; cardstock cover 3.95
❑2, Aug 1995; cardstock cover 3.95

N-MINT

GRENDEL CYCLE
DARK HORSE

❑1, Oct 1995; prestige format; background information on the various series including a timeline .. 5.95

GRENDEL: DEVIL BY THE DEED
COMICO

❑1; MW (a); graphic novel; reprints Comico one-shot; cardstock cover . 4.00
❑1/Ltd.; MW (a); Limited to 2000 .... 8.00
❑1/2nd, Jul 1993; MW (a); reprints Comico one-shot; cardstock cover . 3.95

GRENDEL: DEVIL CHILD
DARK HORSE

❑1, Jun 1999; cardstock cover 2.95
❑2, Aug 1999; cardstock cover 2.95

GRENDEL: DEVIL QUEST
DARK HORSE

❑1, Nov 1995; prestige format 4.95

GRENDEL: DEVIL'S LEGACY
COMICO

❑1, Mar 2000 .... 2.95
❑2, Apr 2000 .... 2.95
❑3, Apr 2000 .... 2.95
❑4, Jun 2000 .... 2.95
❑5, Jul 2000 .... 2.95
❑6, Aug 2000 .... 2.95
❑7, Sep 2000 .... 2.95
❑8, Oct 2000 .... 2.99
❑9, Nov 2000 .... 2.99
❑10, Dec 2000 .... 2.99
❑11, Jan 2001 .... 2.99
❑12, Feb 2001 .... 2.99

GRENDEL: DEVIL'S REIGN
DARK HORSE

❑1, May 2004 .... 3.50
❑2, Aug 2004 .... 3.50
❑3 2004 .... 3.50
❑4 2004 .... 3.50
❑5 2004 .... 3.50
❑6 .... 3.50
❑7 2005 .... 3.50

GRENDEL: DEVIL'S VAGARY
COMICO

❑1 .... 8.00

GRENDEL: GOD & THE DEVIL
DARK HORSE

❑1, Feb 2003 .... 3.50
❑2, Mar 2003 .... 3.50
❑3, Apr 2003 .... 3.50
❑4, May 2003 .... 3.50
❑5, Jun 2003 .... 3.50
❑6, Jul 2003 .... 3.50
❑7, Aug 2003 .... 3.50
❑8, Sep 2003 .... 3.50
❑9, Nov 2003 .... 3.50
❑10, Dec 2003 .... 4.99

GRENDEL: RED, WHITE & BLACK
DARK HORSE

❑1, Sep 2002 .... 4.99
❑2, Oct 2002 .... 4.99
❑3, Nov 2002 .... 4.99
❑4, Dec 2002 .... 4.99

GRENDEL TALES: DEVILS AND DEATHS
DARK HORSE

❑1, Oct 1994 ... 2.95
❑2, Nov 1994 ... 2.95

GRENDEL TALES: DEVIL'S CHOICES
DARK HORSE

❑1, Mar 1995 ... 2.95
❑2, Apr 1995 ... 2.95
❑3, May 1995 ... 2.95
❑4, Jun 1995 ... 2.95

GRENDEL TALES: DEVIL'S HAMMER
DARK HORSE

❑1, Feb 1994 ... 2.95
❑2, Mar 1994 ... 2.95
❑3, Apr 1994 ... 2.95

GRENDEL TALES: FOUR DEVILS, ONE HELL
DARK HORSE

❑1, Aug 1993, JRo (w); cardstock cover 3.00
❑2, Sep 1993, JRo (w); cardstock cover 3.00
❑3, Oct 1993, JRo (w); cardstock cover 3.00
❑4, Oct 1993, JRo (w); cardstock cover 3.00
❑5, Dec 1993, JRo (w); cardstock cover 3.00
❑6, Jan 1994, JRo (w); cardstock cover; Grendel-Prime returns ... 3.00

GRENDEL TALES: HOMECOMING
DARK HORSE

❑1, Dec 1994; cardstock cover ... 2.95
❑2, Jan 1995; cardstock cover ... 2.95
❑3, Feb 1995; cardstock cover ... 2.95

GRENDEL TALES: THE DEVIL IN OUR MIDST
DARK HORSE

❑1, May 1994 ... 2.95
❑2, Jun 1994 ... 2.95
❑3, Jul 1994 ... 2.95
❑4, Aug 1994 ... 2.95
❑5, Sep 1994 ... 2.95

GRENDEL TALES: THE DEVIL MAY CARE
DARK HORSE

❑1, Dec 1995; cardstock cover ... 2.95
❑2, Jan 1996; cardstock cover ... 2.95
❑3, Feb 1996; cardstock cover ... 2.95
❑4, Mar 1996; cardstock cover ... 2.95
❑5, Apr 1996; cardstock cover ... 2.95
❑6, May 1996; cardstock cover ... 2.95

GRENDEL TALES: THE DEVIL'S APPRENTICE
DARK HORSE

❑1, Sep 1997 ... 2.95
❑2, Oct 1997 ... 2.95
❑3, Nov 1997 ... 2.95

GRENDEL: THE DEVIL INSIDE
COMICO

❑1, Sep 2001; Dark Horse publishes; reprints of Comico Grendel issues #13-15 ... 2.95
❑2, Oct 2001 ... 2.95
❑3, Nov 2001 ... 2.95

GRENDEL: WAR CHILD
DARK HORSE

❑1, Aug 1992; MW (w); MW (a); Part 41 of Grendel total series ... 3.50
❑2, Sep 1992; MW (w); Part 42 of Grendel total series ... 3.00
❑3, Oct 1992; MW (w); Part 43 of Grendel total series ... 3.00
❑4, Nov 1992; MW (w); Part 44 of Grendel total series ... 3.00
❑5, Dec 1992; MW (w); Part 45 of Grendel total series ... 3.00
❑6, Jan 1993; MW (w); Part 46 of Grendel total series ... 2.50
❑7, Jan 1993; MW (w); Part 47 of Grendel total series ... 2.50
❑8, Mar 1993; MW (w); Part 48 of Grendel total series ... 2.50
❑9, Apr 1993; MW (w); Part 49 of Grendel total series ... 2.50
❑10, Jun 1993; Double-size; MW (w); Part 50 of Grendel total series ... 3.75

GRENUORD
FANTAGRAPHICS

❑1, Sep 2005 ... 9.95

GREY
VIZ

❑1, Oct 1989; Introduction by Harlan Ellison ... 4.00
❑2, Nov 1989 ... 3.50
❑3, Dec 1989 ... 3.50
❑4, Jan 1989 ... 3.50
❑5, Feb 1989 ... 3.50
❑6, Mar 1989 ... 3.25
❑7, Apr 1989 ... 3.25
❑8, May 1989 ... 3.25
❑9, Jun 1989 ... 3.25

GREY LEGACY
FRAGILE ELITE

❑1, b&w ... 2.75

GREYLORE
SIRIUS COMICS

❑1, Dec 1985 ... 1.50
❑2, Jan 1986 ... 1.50
❑3, Jan 1986 ... 1.50
❑4, Jan 1986 ... 1.50
❑5, Jan 1986 ... 1.50

GREYMATTER
ALAFFINITY

❑1, Oct 1993 ... 2.95
❑2, Nov 1993 ... 2.95
❑3, Dec 1993 ... 2.95
❑4, Jan 1994, b&w ... 2.95
❑5, Apr 1994, b&w ... 2.95
❑6, Sep 1994, b&w; cover forms diptych with #7 ... 2.95
❑7, Oct 1994, b&w; cover forms diptych with #6 ... 2.95
❑8, Mar 1995 ... 2.95
❑9, Dec 1995 ... 2.95
❑10, Mar 1996 ... 2.95
❑11, Jun 1996 ... 2.95

GREYSHIRT: INDIGO SUNSET
DC / AMERICA'S BEST COMICS

❑1, Dec 2001 ... 3.50
❑2, Jan 2002 ... 3.50
❑3, Feb 2002 ... 3.50
❑4, Apr 2002 ... 3.50
❑5, Jun 2002 ... 3.50
❑6, Aug 2002 ... 3.50

GRIFFIN (SLAVE LABOR)
SLAVE LABOR

❑1, Jul 1988, b&w ... 1.75
❑1/2nd, Apr 1989, b&w ... 1.75
❑2, Dec 1988 ... 1.75
❑3, Apr 1989 ... 1.75

GRIFFIN (DC)
DC

❑1, Nov 1991 ... 4.95
❑2, Dec 1991 ... 4.95
❑3, Jan 1991 ... 4.95
❑4, Feb 1991 ... 4.95
❑5, Mar 1991 ... 4.95
❑6, Apr 1991 ... 4.95

GRIFFIN (AMAZE INK)
SLAVE LABOR

❑1, May 1997 ... 2.95

GRIFFITH OBSERVATORY
FANTAGRAPHICS

❑1 ... 4.95

GRIFTER AND THE MASK
DARK HORSE

❑1, Sep 1996; crossover with Image ... 2.50
❑2, Oct 1996; crossover with Image ... 2.50

GRIFTER/BADROCK
IMAGE

❑1/A, Oct 1995 ... 2.50
❑1/B, Oct 1995; alternate cover ... 2.50
❑2/A, Nov 1995; flipbook with Badrock #2A ... 2.50
❑2/B, Nov 1995; flipbook with Badrock #2A ... 2.50

GRIFTER: ONE SHOT
IMAGE

❑1, Jan 1995 ... 4.95

GRIFTER/SHI
IMAGE

❑1, Apr 1996; cover says Mar, indicia says Apr; crossover with Crusade ... 2.95
❑2, May 1996; crossover with Crusade 2.95

GRIFTER (VOL. 1)
IMAGE

❑1, May 1995; bound-in trading cards 2.50
❑1/Direct ed., May 1995; Direct Market edition ... 4.00
❑2, Jun 1995 ... 2.00
❑3, Jul 1995; indicia says Jul, cover says Aug ... 2.00
❑4, Aug 1995 ... 2.00
❑5, Oct 1995; indicia says Oct, cover says Jun ... 2.00
❑6, Nov 1995 ... 2.00
❑7, Dec 1995 ... 2.00
❑8, Jan 1996 ... 2.00
❑9, Feb 1996 ... 2.00
❑10, Mar 1996 ... 2.00

GRIFTER (VOL. 2)
IMAGE

❑1, Jul 1996 ... 2.50
❑2, Aug 1996 ... 2.50
❑3, Sep 1996 ... 2.50
❑4, Oct 1996 ... 2.50
❑5, Nov 1996 ... 2.50
❑6, Dec 1996, cover says Nov, indicia says Dec ... 2.50
❑7, Jan 1997 ... 2.50
❑8, Feb 1997 ... 2.50
❑9, Mar 1997 ... 2.50
❑10, Apr 1997 ... 2.50
❑11, May 1997 ... 2.50
❑12, Jun 1997 ... 2.50
❑13, Jul 1997 ... 2.50
❑14, Aug 1997 ... 2.50

GRIM GHOST
ATLAS-SEABOARD

❑1, Jan 1975 O: Grim Ghost. 1: Grim Ghost. ... 10.00
❑2, Mar 1975 ... 5.00
❑3, Jul 1975 ... 5.00

GRIMJACK
FIRST

❑1, Aug 1984 ... 2.50
❑2, Sep 1984 ... 2.00
❑3, Oct 1984 ... 2.00
❑4, Nov 1984 ... 2.00
❑5, Dec 1984 ... 2.00
❑6, Jan 1985 ... 2.00
❑7, Feb 1985 ... 2.00
❑8, Mar 1985 ... 2.00
❑9, Apr 1985 ... 2.00
❑10, May 1985 ... 2.00
❑11, Jun 1985 ... 2.00
❑12, Jul 1985 ... 2.00
❑13, Aug 1985 ... 2.00
❑14, Sep 1985 ... 2.00
❑15, Oct 1985 ... 2.00
❑16, Nov 1985 ... 2.00
❑17, Dec 1985 ... 2.00
❑18, Jan 1986 ... 2.00
❑19, Feb 1986 ... 2.00
❑20, Mar 1986 ... 2.00
❑21, Apr 1986 ... 1.50
❑22, May 1986 ... 1.50
❑23, Jun 1986 ... 1.50
❑24, Jul 1986 ... 1.50
❑25, Aug 1986 ... 1.50
❑26, Sep 1986 TS (a); A: Teenage Mutant Ninja Turtles ... 3.00
❑27, Oct 1986 ... 1.50
❑28, Nov 1986 ... 1.50
❑29, Dec 1986 ... 1.50
❑30, Jan 1987; Dynamo Joe ... 1.50
❑31, Feb 1987 ... 1.50
❑32, Mar 1987 ... 1.50
❑33, Apr 1987 ... 1.50
❑34, May 1987 ... 1.50
❑35, Jun 1987 ... 1.50
❑36, Jul 1987 D: Grimjack. ... 1.50
❑37, Aug 1987 ... 1.50
❑38, Sep 1987 ... 1.50
❑39, Oct 1987 ... 1.50
❑40, Nov 1987 ... 1.95
❑41, Dec 1987 ... 1.95
❑42, Jan 1988 ... 1.95
❑43, Feb 1988 ... 1.95
❑44, Mar 1988 ... 1.95
❑45, Apr 1988 ... 1.95

Greyshirt: Indigo Sunset

Rick Veitch spin-off from Tomorrow Stories

©DC

Grifter (Vol. 1)

WildC.A.T.S member has solo outings

©Image

Grimjack

A bounty hunter in multiple dimensions

©First

Grimm's Ghost Stories

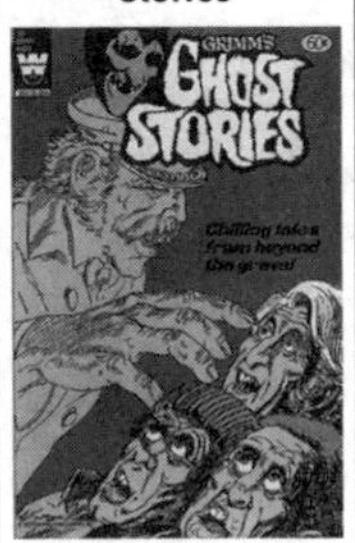

Gold Key horror series not too scary

©Gold Key

Groo (Image)

Wandering screw-up lands at Image for a time

©Image

	N-MINT
❑46, May 1988	1.95
❑47, Jun 1988	1.95
❑48, Jul 1988	1.95
❑49, Aug 1988	1.95
❑50, Sep 1988	1.95
❑51, Oct 1988	1.95
❑52, Nov 1988	1.95
❑53, Dec 1988	1.95
❑54, Jan 1989	1.95
❑55, Feb 1989; new Grimjack	1.95
❑56, Mar 1989	1.95
❑57, Apr 1989	1.95
❑58, May 1989	1.95
❑59, Jun 1989	1.95
❑60, Jul 1989	1.95
❑61, Aug 1989	1.95
❑62, Sep 1989	1.95
❑63, Oct 1989	1.95
❑64, Nov 1989	1.95
❑65, Dec 1989	1.95
❑66, Jan 1990	1.95
❑67, Feb 1990	1.95
❑68, Mar 1990	1.95
❑69, Apr 1990	1.95
❑70, May 1990	1.95
❑71, Jun 1990	2.00
❑72, Jul 1990	2.00
❑73, Aug 1990	2.00
❑74, Sep 1990	2.00
❑75, Oct 1990; Giant 75th issue	3.50
❑76, Nov 1990	2.00
❑77, Dec 1990	2.00
❑78, Jan 1991	2.00
❑79, Feb 1991	2.00
❑80, Mar 1991	2.00
❑81, Apr 1991	2.00

GRIMJACK CASEFILES
FIRST

❑1, Nov 1990, Reprints	1.95
❑2, Dec 1990, Reprints	1.95
❑3, Jan 1991, Reprints	1.95
❑4, Feb 1991, Reprints	1.95
❑5, Mar 1991, Reprints	1.95

GRIMJACK: KILLER INSTINCT
IDEA & DESIGN WORKS

❑1, ca. 2005	3.99
❑2, ca. 2005	3.99
❑3, ca. 2005	3.99
❑4, ca. 2005	3.99
❑5 2005	3.99
❑6, Sep 2005	3.99

GRIMLOCK
EMPYRE

❑1, Jan 1996, b&w	2.95
❑2, b&w; no cover date	2.95

GRIMMAX
DEFIANT

❑0, Aug 1994; DC (a); no cover price	1.00

GRIMM'S GHOST STORIES
GOLD KEY

	N-MINT
❑1, Jan 1972	14.00
❑2, Mar 1972	8.00
❑3, May 1972	8.00
❑4, Jul 1972	8.00
❑5, Sep 1972, AW (a)	8.00
❑6, Nov 1972, Misprinted editions duplicated stories	6.00
❑7, Jan 1973	6.00
❑8, Mar 1973, AW (a)	6.00
❑9, May 1973	6.00
❑10, Jul 1973	6.00
❑11, Aug 1973	4.00
❑12, Sep 1973	4.00
❑13, Nov 1973	4.00
❑14, Jan 1974	4.00
❑15, Mar 1974	4.00
❑16, May 1974	4.00
❑17, Jul 1974	4.00
❑18, Aug 1974	4.00
❑19, Sep 1974	4.00
❑20, Nov 1974	4.00
❑21, Jan 1975	4.00
❑22, Mar 1975	4.00
❑23, May 1975, (c)	4.00
❑24, Jul 1975	4.00
❑25, Aug 1975, (c)	4.00
❑26, Sep 1975	4.00
❑27, Nov 1975	4.00
❑28, Jan 1976	4.00
❑29, Mar 1976	4.00
❑30, May 1976 (c)	4.00
❑31, Jul 1976	3.00
❑32, Aug 1976	3.00
❑33, Sep 1976	3.00
❑34, Oct 1976	3.00
❑35, Nov 1976	3.00
❑36, Mar 1977	3.00
❑37, May 1977, (c)	3.00
❑38, Jul 1977	3.00
❑39, Aug 1977	3.00
❑40, Sep 1977, (c)	3.00
❑41, Oct 1977, (c); BMc (a)	3.00
❑42, Nov 1977, (c); DS (a)	3.00
❑43, Mar 1978	4.00
❑44, May 1978	4.00
❑45, Jul 1978	3.00
❑46, Sep 1978	3.00
❑47, Oct 1978	3.00
❑48, Nov 1978, (c)	3.00
❑49, Mar 1979, (c)	3.00
❑50, May 1979	3.00
❑51, Jul 1979	3.00
❑52, Sep 1979	3.00
❑53, Oct 1979	3.00
❑54, Nov 1979, Goes on hiatus	3.00
❑55, Apr 1981, Returns as Whitman	5.00
❑56, Oct 1981	5.00
❑57, Dec 1981, (c)	5.00
❑58, Feb 1982, (c)	5.00
❑59, May 1982, (c)	5.00
❑60 1982	5.00

GRIMOIRE
SPEAKEASY COMICS

	N-MINT
❑1 2005	2.99
❑2 2005	2.99
❑3 2005	2.99
❑4, Jul 2005	2.99
❑5, Oct 2005	2.99

GRINGO
CALIBER

❑1, b&w	1.95

GRIPS
SILVERWOLF

❑1, Sep 1986	3.00
❑1/Ltd.; Signed, Numbered edition (limited to 350)	9.95
❑2, Oct 1986	2.50
❑3, Nov 1986	2.50
❑4, Dec 1986	2.50

GRIPS (VOL. 2)
GREATER MERCURY

❑1	2.00
❑2, Apr 1990, b&w	2.00
❑3, Jun 1990	2.00
❑4, Aug 1990	2.00
❑5, Oct 1990, b&w	2.00
❑6, Nov 1990	2.00
❑7, Dec 1990, b&w	2.00
❑8, ca. 1991	1.95
❑9, ca. 1991	1.95
❑10, Dec 1991, b&w	2.50
❑11	2.50
❑12	2.50

GRIP: THE STRANGE WORLD OF MEN
DC / VERTIGO

❑1, Jan 2002	2.50
❑2, Feb 2002	2.50
❑3, Mar 2002	2.50
❑4, Apr 2002	2.50
❑5, May 2002	2.50

GRIT BATH
FANTAGRAPHICS

❑1, b&w	2.50
❑2; no cover price	2.50
❑3, Aug 1994; no cover price	2.50

GROO (IMAGE)
IMAGE

❑1, Dec 1994 SA (c); ME (w); SA (a)	4.00
❑2, Jan 1995; SA (c); ME (w); SA (a); indicia says issue #1	2.50
❑3, Feb 1995 SA (c); ME (w); SA (a)	2.50
❑4, Mar 1995 SA (c); ME (w); SA (a)	2.00
❑5, Apr 1995 SA (c); ME (w); SA (a)	2.00
❑6, May 1995 SA (c); ME (w); SA (a)	2.00
❑7, Jun 1995 SA (c); ME (w); SA (a)	2.00
❑8, Jul 1995 SA (c); ME (w); SA (a)	2.00
❑9, Aug 1995 SA (c); ME (w); SA (a)	2.25
❑10, Sep 1995 SA (c); ME (w); SA (a)	2.25
❑11, Oct 1995 SA (c); ME (w); SA (a)	2.25
❑12, Nov 1995 SA (c); ME (w); SA (a)	2.25

GROO (DARK HORSE)
DARK HORSE

❑1, Jan 1998	2.95
❑2, Feb 1998	2.95
❑3, Mar 1998	2.95
❑4, Apr 1998	2.95

Other grades: Multiply price above by 5/6 for VF/NM • 2/3 for VERY FINE • 1/3 for FINE • 1/5 for VERY GOOD • 1/8 for GOOD

GROO AND RUFFERTO (SERGIO ARAGONÉS')
DARK HORSE

- ❑1, Dec 1998; Rufferto sent through time 2.95
- ❑2, Jan 1999 2.95
- ❑3, Feb 1999 2.95
- ❑4, Mar 1999 2.95

GROO CHRONICLES
MARVEL / EPIC

- ❑1, Jun 1989, squarebound 3.50
- ❑2 1989, squarebound 3.50
- ❑3 1989, squarebound 3.50
- ❑4, squarebound 3.50
- ❑5, squarebound 3.50
- ❑6, Feb 1990, squarebound 3.50

GROO: DEATH & TAXES (SERGIO ARAGONÉS'...)
DARK HORSE

- ❑1, Dec 2001 2.99
- ❑2, Jan 2002 2.99
- ❑3, Feb 2002 2.99
- ❑4, Mar 2002 2.99

GROO: MIGHTIER THAN THE SWORD (SERGIO ARAGONÉS')
DARK HORSE

- ❑1, Jan 2000 2.95
- ❑2, Feb 2000 2.95
- ❑3, Mar 2000 2.95
- ❑4, Apr 2000 2.95

GROO SPECIAL
ECLIPSE

- ❑Special 1, Oct 1984 SA (c); ME (w); SA (a) 3.00

GROO THE WANDERER (SERGIO ARAGONÉS')
PACIFIC

- ❑1, Dec 1982 SA (c); ME (w); SA (a); 1: Groo. 1: Minstrel. 1: Sage. 6.50
- ❑2, Feb 1983 SA (c); ME (w); SA (a) 4.50
- ❑3, Apr 1983 SA (c); ME (w); SA (a) 3.75
- ❑4, Sep 1983 SA (c); ME (w); SA (a) 3.50
- ❑5, Oct 1983 SA (c); ME (w); SA (a) 3.00
- ❑6, Dec 1983 SA (c); ME (w); SA (a) 3.00
- ❑7, Feb 1984 SA (c); ME (w); SA (a) 3.00
- ❑8, Apr 1984 SA (c); ME (w); SA (a) 3.00

GROO THE WANDERER
MARVEL / EPIC

- ❑1, Mar 1985, SA (c); ME (w); SA (a); 1: Minstrel 5.00
- ❑2, Apr 1985, SA (c); ME (w); SA (a) 4.00
- ❑3, May 1985, SA (c); ME (w); SA (a) 3.50
- ❑4, Jun 1985, SA (c); ME (w); SA (a) 3.00
- ❑5, Jul 1985, SA (c); ME (w); SA (a) 3.00
- ❑6, Aug 1985, SA (c); ME (w); SA (a) 3.00
- ❑7, Sep 1985, SA (c); ME (w); SA (a) 3.00
- ❑8, Oct 1985, SA (c); ME (w); SA (a) 3.00
- ❑9, Nov 1985, SA (c); ME (w); SA (a) 3.00
- ❑10, Dec 1985, SA (c); ME (w); SA (a) 3.00
- ❑11, Jan 1986, SA (c); ME (w); SA (a) 2.50
- ❑12, Feb 1986, SA (c); ME (w); SA (a) 2.50
- ❑13, Mar 1986, SA (c); ME (w); SA (a) 2.50
- ❑14, Apr 1986, SA (c); ME (w); SA (a) 2.50
- ❑15, May 1986, SA (c); ME (w); SA (a) 2.50
- ❑16, Jun 1986, SA (c); ME (w); SA (a) 2.50
- ❑17, Jul 1986, SA (c); ME (w); SA (a) 2.50
- ❑18, Aug 1986, SA (c); ME (w); SA (a) 2.50
- ❑19, Sep 1986, SA (c); ME (w); SA (a) 2.50
- ❑20, Oct 1986, SA (c); ME (w); SA (a) 2.50
- ❑21, Nov 1986, SA (c); ME (w); SA (a) 2.50
- ❑22, Dec 1986, SA (c); ME (w); SA (a) 2.50
- ❑23, Jan 1987, SA (c); ME (w); SA (a) 2.50
- ❑24, Feb 1987, SA (c); ME (w); SA (a) 2.50
- ❑25, Mar 1987, SA (c); ME (w); SA (a) 2.50
- ❑26, Apr 1987, SA (c); ME (w); SA (a) 2.50
- ❑27, May 1987, SA (c); ME (w); SA (a) 2.50
- ❑28, Jun 1987, SA (c); ME (w); SA (a) 2.50
- ❑29, Jul 1987, SA (c); ME (w); SA (a) 2.50
- ❑30, Aug 1987, SA (c); ME (w); SA (a) 2.50
- ❑31, Sep 1987, SA (c); ME (w); SA (a) 2.00
- ❑32, Oct 1987, SA (c); ME (w); SA (a) 2.00
- ❑33, Nov 1987, SA (c); ME (w); SA (a) 2.00
- ❑34, Dec 1987, SA (c); ME (w); SA (a) 2.00
- ❑35, Jan 1988, SA (c); ME (w); SA (a) 2.00
- ❑36, Feb 1988, SA (c); ME (w); SA (a) 2.00
- ❑37, Mar 1988, SA (c); ME (w); SA (a) 2.00
- ❑38, Apr 1988, SA (c); ME (w); SA (a) 2.00
- ❑39, May 1988, SA (c); ME (w); SA (a) 2.00
- ❑40, Jun 1988, SA (c); ME (w); SA (a) 2.00
- ❑41, Jul 1988, SA (c); ME (w); SA (a) 2.00
- ❑42, Aug 1988, SA (c); ME (w); SA (a) 2.00
- ❑43, Sep 1988, SA (c); ME (w); SA (a) 2.00
- ❑44, Oct 1988, SA (c); ME (w); SA (a) 2.00
- ❑45, Nov 1988, SA (c); ME (w); SA (a) 2.00
- ❑46, Dec 1988, SA (c); ME (w); SA (a) 2.00
- ❑47, Jan 1989, SA (c); ME (w); SA (a) 2.00
- ❑48, Feb 1989, SA (c); ME (w); SA (a) 2.00
- ❑49, Mar 1989, SA (c); ME (w); SA (a); A: Chakaal 2.00
- ❑50, Apr 1989, Giant-size SA (c); ME (w); SA (a); A: Chakaal. 3.00
- ❑51, May 1989, SA (c); ME (w); SA (a); A: Chakaal 2.00
- ❑52, Jun 1989, SA (c); ME (w); SA (a); A: Chakaal 2.00
- ❑53, Jul 1989, SA (c); ME (w); SA (a); A: Chakaal 2.00
- ❑54, Aug 1989, SA (c); ME (w); SA (a) 2.00
- ❑55, Sep 1989, SA (c); ME (w); SA (a) 2.00
- ❑56, Oct 1989, SA (c); ME (w); SA (a) 2.00
- ❑57, Nov 1989, SA (c); ME (w); SA (a) 2.00
- ❑58, Nov 1989, SA (c); ME (w); SA (a) 2.00
- ❑59, Dec 1989, SA (c); ME (w); SA (a) 2.00
- ❑60, Dec 1989, SA (c); ME (w); SA (a) 2.00
- ❑61, Jan 1990, SA (c); ME (w); SA (a) 2.00
- ❑62, Feb 1990, SA (c); ME (w); SA (a) 2.00
- ❑63, Mar 1990, SA (c); ME (w); SA (a) 2.00
- ❑64, Apr 1990, SA (c); ME (w); SA (a) 2.00
- ❑65, May 1990, SA (c); ME (w); SA (a) 2.00
- ❑66, Jun 1990, SA (c); ME (w); SA (a) 2.00
- ❑67, Jul 1990, SA (c); ME (w); SA (a) 2.00
- ❑68, Aug 1990, SA (c); ME (w); SA (a) 2.00
- ❑69, Sep 1990, SA (c); ME (w); SA (a) 2.00
- ❑70, Oct 1990, SA (c); ME (w); SA (a) 2.00
- ❑71, Nov 1990, SA (c); ME (w); SA (a) 1.50
- ❑72, Dec 1990, SA (c); ME (w); SA (a) 1.50
- ❑73, Jan 1991, SA (c); ME (w); SA (a) 1.50
- ❑74, Feb 1991, SA (c); ME (w); SA (a) 1.50
- ❑75, Mar 1991, SA (c); ME (w); SA (a) 1.50
- ❑76, Apr 1991, SA (c); ME (w); SA (a) 1.50
- ❑77, May 1991, SA (c); ME (w); SA (a) 1.50
- ❑78, Jun 1991, SA (c); ME (w); SA (a); bookburners 1.50
- ❑79, Jul 1991, SA (c); ME (w); SA (a) 1.50
- ❑80, Aug 1991, SA (c); ME (w); SA (a) 1.50
- ❑81, Sep 1991, SA (c); ME (w); SA (a) 1.50
- ❑82, Oct 1991, SA (c); ME (w); SA (a) 1.50
- ❑83, Nov 1991, SA (c); ME (w); SA (a) 1.50
- ❑84, Dec 1991, SA (c); ME (w); SA (a) 1.50
- ❑85, Jan 1992, SA (c); ME (w); SA (a) 1.50
- ❑86, Feb 1992, SA (c); ME (w); SA (a) 1.50
- ❑87, Mar 1992, SA (c); ME (w); SA (a) 2.25
- ❑88, Apr 1992, SA (c); ME (w); SA (a) 2.25
- ❑89, May 1992, SA (c); ME (w); SA (a) 2.25
- ❑90, Jun 1992, SA (c); ME (w); SA (a) 2.25
- ❑91, Jul 1992, SA (c); ME (w); SA (a) 2.25
- ❑92, Aug 1992, SA (c); ME (w); SA (a); Groo finds fountain of youth 2.25
- ❑93, Sep 1992, SA (c); ME (w); SA (a); Groo finds fountain of youth 2.25
- ❑94, Oct 1992, SA (c); ME (w); SA (a) 2.25
- ❑95, Nov 1992, SA (c); ME (w); SA (a) 2.25
- ❑96, Dec 1992, SA (c); ME (w); SA (a) 2.25
- ❑97, Jan 1993, SA (c); ME (w); SA (a) 2.25
- ❑98, Feb 1993, SA (c); ME (w); SA (a) 2.25
- ❑99, Mar 1993, SA (c); ME (w); SA (a) 2.25
- ❑100, Apr 1993, 100th anniversary issue; SA (c); ME (w); SA (a); Groo learns to read 2.95
- ❑101, May 1993, SA (c); ME (w); SA (a) 2.25
- ❑102, Jun 1993, SA (c); ME (w); SA (a) 2.25
- ❑103, Aug 1993, SA (c); ME (w); SA (a) 2.25
- ❑104, Sep 1993, SA (c); ME (w); SA (a); O: Rufferto (Groo's Dog) 2.25
- ❑105, Oct 1993, SA (c); ME (w); SA (a) 2.25
- ❑106, Nov 1993, SA (c); ME (w); SA (a) 2.25
- ❑107, Dec 1993, SA (c); ME (w); SA (a) 2.25
- ❑108, Jan 1994, SA (c); ME (w); SA (a) 2.25
- ❑109, Feb 1994, SA (c); ME (w); SA (a) 2.25
- ❑110, Mar 1994, SA (c); ME (w); SA (a) 2.25
- ❑111, Apr 1994, SA (c); ME (w); SA (a) 2.25
- ❑112, May 1994, SA (c); ME (w); SA (a) 2.25
- ❑113, Jun 1994, SA (c); ME (w); SA (a) 2.25
- ❑114, Jul 1994, SA (c); ME (w); SA (a) 2.25
- ❑115, Aug 1994, SA (c); ME (w); SA (a) 2.25
- ❑116, Sep 1994, SA (c); ME (w); SA (a) 2.25
- ❑117, Oct 1994, SA (c); ME (w); SA (a) 2.25
- ❑118, Nov 1994, SA (c); ME (w); SA (a) 2.25
- ❑119, Dec 1994, SA (c); ME (w); SA (a) 2.25
- ❑120, Jan 1995, SA (c); ME (w); SA (a) 2.25
- ❑Book 4, SA (c); ME (w); SA (a); Reprints issues #21-24 10.95
- ❑Book 5, SA (c); ME (w); SA (a) 10.95

GROOTLORE
FANTAGRAPHICS

- ❑1, b&w 2.00
- ❑2, b&w 2.00

GROOTLORE (VOL. 2)
FANTAGRAPHICS

- ❑1, May 1991, b&w 2.00
- ❑2, b&w 2.00
- ❑3 2.25

GROOVY
MARVEL

- ❑1, Mar 1968, A: Monkees. 25.00
- ❑2, May 1968 16.00
- ❑3, Jul 1968, Marvel Comics Group Publisher 16.00

GROSS POINT
DC

- ❑1, Aug 1997 2.50
- ❑2, Sep 1997 2.50
- ❑3, Oct 1997 2.50
- ❑4, Nov 1997 2.50
- ❑5, Dec 1997 2.50
- ❑6, Dec 1997 2.50
- ❑7, Jan 1998 2.50
- ❑8, Feb 1998 2.50
- ❑9, Mar 1998 2.50
- ❑10, Apr 1998 2.50
- ❑11, May 1998 2.50
- ❑12, Jun 1998 2.50
- ❑13, Jul 1998 2.50
- ❑14, Aug 1998 2.50

GROUNDED
IMAGE

- ❑1, Sep 2005 2.95
- ❑1/Variant, Sep 2005 2.95
- ❑2, Oct 2005 2.95
- ❑3 2005 2.95
- ❑4, Dec 2005 2.95
- ❑5, Apr 2006 2.95

GROUND POUND! COMIX
BLACKTHORNE

- ❑1, Jan 1987 2.00

GROUND ZERO
ETERNITY

- ❑1, Oct 1991, b&w 2.50
- ❑2, b&w 2.50

GROUP LARUE (MIKE BARON'S...)
INNOVATION

- ❑1, Aug 1989 1.95
- ❑2 1.95
- ❑3 1.95
- ❑4 1.95

GROWING UP ENCHANTED
TOO HIP GOTTA GO

- ❑1, Jul 2002, b&w 2.95
- ❑2, Oct 2002, b&w 2.95
- ❑3, Mar 2003, b&w 2.95

GRRL SCOUTS (JIM MAHFOOD'S...)
ONI

- ❑1, Mar 1999, b&w 2.95
- ❑2, Jun 1999, b&w 2.95
- ❑3, Sep 1999, b&w 2.95

GRRL SCOUTS: WORK SUCKS
IMAGE

- ❑1, Feb 2003 2.95
- ❑2, Mar 2003 2.95
- ❑3, Apr 2003 2.95
- ❑4, Jun 2003 2.95

GRRRL SQUAD
AMAZING AARON

- ❑1, Mar 1999, b&w 2.95

Guardians of Metropolis

Aged Newsboy Legion reunites

©DC

Guardians of the Galaxy

Jim Valentino revives '70s space team

©Marvel

Gumby 3-D

Clay adventures that leap off the page

©Blackthorne

Gunfire

Short-lived "New Blood" spin-off

©DC

Gunhawks

Death of partner reduces plural title

©Marvel

	N-MINT

GRUMPY OLD MONSTERS
IDEA & DESIGN WORKS

❑1, Nov 2003	3.99
❑2, Jan 2004	3.99
❑3, Feb 2004	3.99

GRUN
HARRIER

❑1, Jun 1987	1.95
❑2, Aug 1987	1.95
❑3, Oct 1987	1.95
❑4	1.95

GRUNTS
MIRAGE

❑1, Nov 1987, b&w	2.00

GUARDIAN
SPECTRUM

❑1, Mar 1984	1.00
❑2, Jun 1984	1.00

GUARDIAN ANGEL
IMAGE

❑1, May 2002	2.95
❑2, Jul 2002	2.95

GUARDIAN KNIGHTS: DEMON'S KNIGHT
LIMELIGHT

❑1, b&w; no indicia	2.95
❑2, b&w; no indicia	2.95

GUARDIANS
MARVEL

❑1, Sep 2004	2.99
❑2, Oct 2004	2.99
❑3, Oct 2004	2.99
❑4, Nov 2004	2.99
❑5, Dec 2004	2.99

GUARDIANS OF METROPOLIS
DC

❑1, Nov 1994	1.50
❑2, Dec 1994	1.50
❑3, Jan 1995	1.50
❑4, Feb 1995	1.50

GUARDIANS OF THE GALAXY
MARVEL

❑1, Jun 1990	2.00
❑2, Jul 1990 V: The Stark.	2.00
❑3, Aug 1990	2.00
❑4, Sep 1990 A: Firelord.	2.00
❑5, Oct 1990 TMc (c); TMc (a); V: Force.	2.00
❑6, Nov 1990 A: Captain America's shield.	1.50
❑7, Dec 1990 1: Malevolence. V: Malevolence.	1.50
❑8, Jan 1991 1: Rancor.	1.50
❑9, Feb 1991 RL (c); RL (a); O: Rancor. 1: Replica. V: Rancor.	1.50
❑10, Mar 1991 JLee (c); JLee (a)	1.50
❑11, Apr 1991 1: Phoenix.	1.50
❑12, May 1991 V: Overkill.	1.50
❑13, Jun 1991 1: Spirit of Vengeance.	2.00
❑14, Jul 1991 A: Spirit of Vengeance..	2.00
❑15, Aug 1991 JSn (c); JSn (a); 1: Protege.	1.50
❑16, Sep 1991; Giant-size	1.75
❑17, Oct 1991; 1st appearance of Talon (Cameo)	1.50
❑18, Nov 1991; 1st appearance of Talon (Full appearance)	1.50
❑19, Dec 1991 1: Talon.	1.50
❑20, Jan 1992; A: Captain America's shield. Vance Astro becomes Major Victory	1.50
❑21, Feb 1992 V: Rancor.	1.50
❑22, Mar 1992	1.50
❑23, Apr 1992	1.50
❑24, May 1992 A: Silver Surfer.	1.50
❑25, Jun 1992; V: Galactus. regular cover	2.50
❑25/Variant, Jun 1992; V: Galactus. foil cover	2.50
❑26, Jul 1992 O: Guardians of the Galaxy.	1.50
❑27, Aug 1992 O: Talon.	1.50
❑28, Sep 1992; V: Doctor Octopus. Infinity War	1.50
❑29, Oct 1992; Infinity War	1.50
❑30, Nov 1992	1.25
❑31, Dec 1992	1.25
❑32, Jan 1993 A: Dr. Strange. A: Doctor Strange.	1.25
❑33, Feb 1993	1.25
❑34, Mar 1993; Yellowjacket joins team	1.25
❑35, Apr 1993; 1: Galactic Guardians. regular cover	1.25
❑35/Variant, Apr 1993; 1: Galactic Guardians. sculpted cover	2.95
❑36, May 1993 V: Dormammu.	1.25
❑37, Jun 1993 D: Doctor Strange.	1.25
❑38, Jul 1993 A: Beyonder.	1.25
❑39, Aug 1993; Holo-grafix cover; Rancor vs. Doom	2.95
❑40, Sep 1993 V: Composite.	1.25
❑41, Oct 1993 A: Inhumans. A: Starhawk. A: Composite. A: Loki. V: Loki.	1.25
❑42, Nov 1993	1.25
❑43, Dec 1993 1: Woden.	1.25
❑44, Jan 1994	1.25
❑45, Feb 1994	1.25
❑46, Mar 1994	1.25
❑47, Apr 1994; Protege vs. Beyonder	1.25
❑48, May 1994 V: Overkill.	1.50
❑49, Jun 1994 A: Celestial.	1.50
❑50, Jul 1994; Giant-size	2.00
❑50/Variant, Jul 1994; Giant-size; foil cover	2.95
❑51, Aug 1994	1.50
❑52, Sep 1994	1.50
❑53, Oct 1994; Drax vs. Wolfhound	1.50
❑54, Nov 1994; final fate of Spider-Man	1.50
❑55, Dec 1994 V: Ripjak.	1.50
❑56, Jan 1995 V: Ripjak.	1.50
❑57, Feb 1995 A: Bubonicus.	1.50
❑58, Mar 1995	1.50
❑59, Apr 1995 A: Silver Surfer.	1.50
❑60, May 1995 A: Silver Surfer.	1.50
❑61, Jun 1995	1.50
❑62, Jul 1995; Giant-size	2.50
❑Annual 1, Jul 1991, Korvac Quest	4.00
❑Annual 2, ca. 1992 HT, BWi (a)	2.50
❑Annual 3, ca. 1993, 1: Cuchulain. trading card	2.95
❑Annual 4, ca. 1994	2.95

GUERRILLA GROUNDHOG
ECLIPSE

❑1, Jan 1987, b&w	1.50
❑2, Mar 1987	1.50

GUERRILLA WAR
DELL

❑12, Series continued from Jungle War Stories #11	10.00
❑13	10.00
❑14, Mar 1966	10.00

GUFF!
DARK HORSE

❑1, Apr 1998, b&w; bound-in Meanie Babies card	1.95

GUMBY 3-D
BLACKTHORNE

❑1	2.50
❑2	2.50
❑3	2.50
❑4	2.50
❑5	2.50
❑6	2.50
❑7	2.50

GUMBY'S SUMMER FUN SPECIAL
COMICO

❑1, Jul 1987	2.50

GUMBY'S WINTER FUN SPECIAL
COMICO

❑1	2.50

GUNCANDY
IMAGE

❑1, Aug 2005	5.99
❑2, Mar 2006	5.99

GUNDAM SEED ASTRAY R
TOKYOPOP

❑1, Feb 2005, b&w	9.99
❑2, May 2005	9.99
❑3, Jul 2005	9.99
❑4, Nov 2005	9.99

GUNDAM: THE ORIGIN
VIZ

❑1, Apr 2002	7.95
❑2, Jul 2002	7.95

GUNDAM WING: BLIND TARGET
VIZ

❑1, Feb 2001	2.95
❑2, Mar 2001	2.95
❑3, Apr 2001	2.95
❑4, May 2001	2.95

GUNDAM WING: EPISODE ZERO
VIZ

❑1, Apr 2001	2.95
❑2, May 2001	2.95
❑3, Jun 2001	2.95
❑4, Jul 2001	2.95
❑5, Aug 2001	2.95
❑6, Sep 2001	2.95
❑7, Oct 2001	2.95
❑8, Nov 2001	2.95

Other grades: Multiply price above by 5/6 for VF/NM • 2/3 for VERY FINE • 1/3 for FINE • 1/5 for VERY GOOD • 1/8 for GOOD

N-MINT

GUN FIGHTERS IN HELL
REBEL

❑1 .... 2.25
❑2 .... 2.25
❑3, b&w 2.25
❑4 .... 2.25
❑5 .... 2.25

GUNFIRE
DC

❑0, Oct 1994; Continued in Gunfire #6 .... 2.00
❑1, May 1994 .... 2.00
❑2, Jun 1994 .... 2.00
❑3, Jul 1994 .... 2.00
❑4, Aug 1994 .... 2.00
❑5, Sep 1994; Continued in Gunfire #0 .... 2.00
❑6, Nov 1994 .... 2.00
❑7, Dec 1994 .... 2.00
❑8, Jan 1995 .... 2.00
❑9, Feb 1995 .... 2.00
❑10, Mar 1995 .... 2.00
❑11, Apr 1995 .... 2.00
❑12, May 1995 .... 2.00
❑13, Jun 1995 .... 2.25

GUN FURY
AIRCEL

❑1, Jan 1989, b&w 1.95
❑2, Feb 1989, b&w 1.95
❑3, Mar 1989, b&w 1.95
❑4, Apr 1989, b&w 1.95
❑5, May 1989, b&w 1.95
❑6, Jun 1989, b&w 1.95
❑7, Jul 1989, b&w 1.95
❑8, Aug 1989, b&w 1.95
❑9, Sep 1989, b&w 1.95
❑10, Oct 1989, b&w 1.95

GUN FURY RETURNS
AIRCEL

❑1, Sep 1990, b&w 2.25
❑2, Oct 1990, b&w 2.25
❑3, Nov 1990, b&w 2.25
❑4, Dec 1990, b&w 2.25

GUN FU: SHOWGIRLS ARE FOREVER
IMAGE

❑1, Apr 2006 .... 2.95

GUNG HO
AVALON

❑1, b&w; Reprints 2.95

GUNHAWKS
MARVEL

❑1, Oct 1972 1: Reno Jones and Kid Cassidy. 50.00
❑2, Dec 1972 .... 18.00
❑3, Feb 1973 .... 8.00
❑4, Apr 1973 .... 8.00
❑5, Jun 1973 V: Reverend Mr. Graves. 8.00
❑6, Aug 1973 D: Kid Cassidy. 8.00
❑7, Oct 1973, Title changes to Gunhawk 8.00

GUNHED
VIZ

❑1, Japanese 5.50
❑2, Japanese 5.50
❑3, Japanese 5.50

GUNNER
GUN DOG

❑1, Mar 1999 .... 2.95

GUN RUNNER
MARVEL

❑1, Oct 1993; four cards; Polybagged; wraparound cover 2.75
❑2, Nov 1993 .... 1.75
❑3, Dec 1993 .... 1.75
❑4, Jan 1994 .... 1.75
❑5, Feb 1994 .... 1.75
❑6, Mar 1994 .... 1.75

GUNSLINGERS
MARVEL

❑1, Feb 2000; One-shot reprinting Western stories 2.99

GUNSMITH CATS
DARK HORSE / MANGA

❑1, Sep 1995 .... 3.00
❑2, Sep 1995 .... 2.50
❑3, Sep 1995 .... 2.50
❑4, Sep 1995 .... 3.00
❑5, Sep 1995 .... 3.00
❑6, Oct 1995 .... 3.00
❑7, Nov 1995 .... 3.00
❑8, Dec 1995 .... 3.00
❑9, Jan 1996 .... 3.00
❑10, Feb 1996 .... 3.00

GUNSMITH CATS: BAD TRIP
DARK HORSE / MANGA

❑1, Jun 1998 .... 2.95
❑2, Jun 1998 .... 2.95
❑3, Aug 1998 .... 2.95
❑4, Sep 1998 .... 2.95
❑5, Oct 1998 .... 2.95
❑6, Nov 1998 .... 2.95

GUNSMITH CATS: BEAN BANDIT
DARK HORSE / MANGA

❑1, Jan 1999 .... 2.95
❑2, Feb 1999 .... 2.95
❑3, Mar 1999 .... 2.95
❑4, Apr 1999 .... 2.95
❑5, May 1999 .... 2.95
❑6, Jun 1999 .... 2.95
❑7, Jul 1999 .... 2.95
❑8, Aug 1999 .... 2.95
❑9, Sep 1999 .... 2.95

GUNSMITH CATS: GOLDIE VS. MISTY
DARK HORSE / MANGA

❑1, Nov 1997 .... 2.95
❑2, Dec 1997 .... 2.95
❑3, Jan 1998 .... 2.95
❑4, Feb 1998 .... 2.95
❑5, Mar 1998 .... 2.95
❑6, Apr 1998 .... 2.95
❑7, May 1998 .... 2.95

GUNSMITH CATS: KIDNAPPED
DARK HORSE / MANGA

❑1, Nov 1999 .... 2.95
❑2, Dec 1999 .... 2.95
❑3, Jan 2000 .... 2.95
❑4, Feb 2000 .... 2.95
❑5, Mar 2000 .... 2.95
❑6, Apr 2000 .... 2.95
❑7, May 2000 .... 2.95
❑8, Jun 2000 .... 2.95
❑9, Jul 2000 .... 2.95
❑10, Aug 2000 .... 2.95

GUNSMITH CATS: MISTER V
DARK HORSE / MANGA

❑1, Oct 2000 .... 3.50
❑2, Nov 2000 .... 3.50
❑3, Dec 2000 .... 3.50
❑4, Jan 2001 .... 3.50
❑5, Feb 2001 .... 3.50
❑6, Mar 2001 .... 3.50
❑7, Apr 2001 .... 3.50
❑8, May 2001 .... 3.50
❑9, Jun 2001 .... 3.50
❑10, Jul 2001 .... 3.50
❑11, Aug 2001 .... 3.50

GUNSMITH CATS: SHADES OF GRAY
DARK HORSE / MANGA

❑1, May 1997 .... 2.95
❑2, Jun 1997 .... 2.95
❑3, Jul 1997 .... 2.95
❑4, Aug 1997 .... 2.95
❑5, Sep 1997 .... 2.95

GUNSMITH CATS SPECIAL
DARK HORSE

❑1, Nov 2001 .... 2.99

GUNSMITH CATS: THE RETURN OF GRAY
DARK HORSE / MANGA

❑1, Aug 1996 .... 2.95
❑2, Sep 1996 .... 2.95
❑3, Oct 1996 .... 2.95
❑4, Nov 1996 .... 2.95
❑5, Dec 1996 .... 2.95
❑6, Jan 1997 .... 2.95
❑7, Feb 1997 .... 2.95

GUNSMOKE (GOLD KEY)
GOLD KEY

❑1, Feb 1969 .... 30.00
❑2, Apr 1969 .... 20.00
❑3, Jun 1969 .... 20.00
❑4, Aug 1969 .... 20.00
❑5, Nov 1969 .... 20.00
❑6, Feb 1970 .... 20.00

GUNS OF SHAR-PEI
CALIBER

❑1, b&w 2.95
❑2, b&w 2.95
❑3, b&w 2.95

GUNS OF THE DRAGON
DC

❑1, Oct 1998 .... 2.50
❑2, Nov 1998 .... 2.50
❑3, Dec 1998 .... 2.50
❑4, Jan 1999 .... 2.50

GUN THAT WON THE WEST
WINCHESTER

❑1; giveaway 24.00

GUN THEORY
MARVEL / EPIC

❑1, Oct 2003 .... 2.50
❑2, Nov 2003 .... 2.50

GUNWITCH, THE: OUTSKIRTS OF DOOM
ONI

❑1 2001 .... 2.95

GUTWALLOW
NUMBSKULL

❑1, Feb 1998, b&w 2.95
❑2, Apr 1998 .... 2.95
❑3, Jun 1998 .... 2.95
❑4, Aug 1998 .... 2.95
❑5, Oct 1998 .... 2.95
❑6, Feb 1999 .... 2.95
❑7, Apr 1999 .... 2.95
❑8, Jul 1999 .... 2.95
❑9, Sep 1999 .... 2.95
❑10, Dec 1999 .... 2.95
❑11, Mar 2000 .... 2.95
❑12, Jun 2000 .... 2.95

GUTWALLOW (VOL. 2)
NUMBSKULL

❑1, Nov 2000 .... 2.95
❑2, Feb 2001 .... 2.95
❑3, Jun 2001 .... 2.95

GUY GARDNER
DC

❑1, Oct 1992 JSa (a) 2.00
❑2, Nov 1992 JSa (a) 1.75
❑3, Dec 1992; JSa (a); (almost) wordless story 1.50
❑4, Jan 1993 JSa (a) 1.50
❑5, Feb 1993 JSa (a) 1.50
❑6, Mar 1993 JSa (a) 1.25
❑7, Apr 1993 JSa (a) 1.25
❑8, May 1993 JSa (a) 1.25
❑9, Jun 1993 JSa (a) 1.25
❑10, Jul 1993 JSa (a) 1.25
❑11, Aug 1993 JSa (a) 1.25
❑12, Sep 1993 JSa (a) 1.25
❑13, Oct 1993 JSa (a) 1.25
❑14, Nov 1993 JSa (a) 1.25
❑15, Dec 1993 .... 1.50
❑16, Jan 1994; Series continued in Guy Gardner: Warrior #17 .... 1.50

GUY GARDNER REBORN
DC

❑1, ca. 1992 .... 4.95
❑2, ca. 1992 .... 4.95
❑3, ca. 1992 .... 4.95

GUY GARDNER: WARRIOR
DC

❑0, Oct 1994 O: Guy Gardner's Warrior persona 1.75
❑17, Feb 1994; Title changes to Guy Gardner: Warrior; Series continued from Guy Gardner #16 .... 1.50
❑18, Mar 1994 .... 1.50
❑19, Apr 1994 .... 1.50
❑20, May 1994 .... 1.50
❑21, Jun 1994 V: Parallax 1.50
❑22, Jul 1994 .... 1.50
❑23, Aug 1994 .... 1.50
❑24, Sep 1994; Zero Hour 1.50
❑25, Nov 1994; Giant-size 2.50

Gunsmith Cats

Female investigators team in manga series

©Dark Horse

Gunsmoke (Gold Key)

Marshall Dillon cleans up Dodge

©Gold Key

Guy Gardner

Hot-headed GL with no finesse

©DC

Hair Bear Bunch

Trio of bruins scheme at zoo

©Gold Key

Halloween

Michael Myers makes comics debut

©Chaos

	N-MINT
❑26, Dec 1994	1.50
❑27, Jan 1995	1.50
❑28, Feb 1995	1.50
❑29, Mar 1995; Giant-size	1.50
❑29/Variant, May 1995; Giant-size; enhanced foldout cover	2.95
❑30, Apr 1995	1.50
❑31, Jun 1995	1.75
❑32, Jul 1995	1.75
❑33, Aug 1995	1.75
❑34, Sep 1995	1.75
❑35, Oct 1995	1.75
❑36, Nov 1995	1.75
❑37, Dec 1995; Underworld Unleashed	1.75
❑38, Jan 1996	1.75
❑39, Feb 1996; Christmas party at Warriors	1.75
❑40, Mar 1996	1.75
❑41, Apr 1996	1.75
❑42, May 1996; Guy becomes a woman	1.75
❑43, Jun 1996	1.75
❑44, Jul 1996 V: Major Force	1.75
❑Annual 1, ca. 1995; Year One	3.50
❑Annual 2, ca. 1996, JSa (a); Legends of the Dead Earth	2.95

GUY PUMPKINHEAD
SAINT GRAY

❑1	2.50

GUZZI LEMANS
ANTARCTIC

❑1, Aug 1996, b&w	2.95
❑2, Oct 1996, b&w	2.95

GYRE
ABACULUS

❑1, Dec 1997, b&w	3.50
❑2, Feb 1998, b&w	2.95
❑3, Apr 1998	2.95
❑Ashcan 1; Preview of Gyre #1	0.50
❑Special 1	4.50

GYRE: TRADITIONS & INTERRUPTIONS
ABACULUS

❑1, b&w; Promotional book for series	1.00

GYRO COMICS
RIP OFF

❑1, ca. 1988, b&w	2.00
❑2, ca. 1988, b&w	2.00
❑3, ca. 1988, b&w	2.00

GYRO GEARLOOSE
DELL

❑-207, Jul 1962; Cover code 01329-207	50.00

HACKER FILES
DC

❑1, Aug 1992, TS (a); 1: Jack Marshall.	2.25
❑2, Sep 1992, TS (a)	1.95
❑3, Oct 1992, TS (a)	1.95
❑4, Nov 1992, TS (a)	1.95
❑5, Dec 1992, TS (a)	1.95
❑6, Jan 1993, TS (a)	1.95
❑7, Feb 1993, TS (a)	1.95
❑8, Mar 1993, TS (a)	1.95
❑9, Apr 1993, TS (a)	1.95

	N-MINT
❑10, May 1993, TS (a)	1.95
❑11, Jun 1993, TS (a)	1.95
❑12, Jul 1993, TS (a)	1.95

HACKMASTERS OF EVERKNIGHT
KENZER AND COMPANY

❑1, May 2000, b&w; Knights of the Dinner Table back-up story	3.50
❑2, Jul 2000, b&w; Knights of the Dinner Table back-up story	2.95
❑3, Sep 2000, b&w; Knights of the Dinner Table back-up story	2.95
❑4, Nov 2000, b&w; Knights of the Dinner Table back-up story	2.95
❑5, Jan 2001, b&w; Knights of the Dinner Table back-up story	2.95
❑6, Mar 2001, b&w	2.95
❑7, May 2001, b&w	2.95
❑8, Jul 2001, b&w	2.95
❑9, Aug 2001	2.95
❑10, Sep 2001	2.95

HACK SLASH: LAND OF LOST TOYS
DEVIL'S DUE / CHAOS

❑1, Dec 2005	2.99
❑2, Dec 2005	2.99
❑3, Feb 2006	2.99
❑3/Variant, Feb 2006	2.99

HACK/SLASH: TRAILERS
DEVIL'S DUE

❑1, Mar 2006	2.99
❑1/Variant, Mar 2006	2.99
❑1/2nd variant, Mar 2006	2.99

HAIRBAT
SCREAMING RICE

❑1, b&w	2.50
❑2, b&w	2.50
❑3, b&w	2.50
❑4, b&w	2.50

HAIRBAT (VOL. 2)
SLAVE LABOR

❑1, Jul 1995, b&w	2.95

HAIR BEAR BUNCH
GOLD KEY

❑1, Feb 1972	10.00
❑2, May 1972	7.00
❑3, Aug 1972	6.00
❑4, Nov 1972	6.00
❑5, Feb 1973	6.00
❑6, May 1973	4.00
❑7, Aug 1973	4.00
❑8, Nov 1973	4.00
❑9, Feb 1974	4.00

HAIRBUTT THE HIPPO
RAT RACE

❑1, ca. 1992, b&w	2.95
❑2, ca. 1993, b&w	2.95
❑3, ca. 1993, b&w	2.95

HAIRBUTT THE HIPPO CRIME FILES
RAT RACE

❑1, Dec 1995, b&w	3.50
❑2, ca. 1996, b&w	3.50
❑3, ca. 1996, b&w	3.50
❑4, ca. 1996, b&w	3.50

	N-MINT
❑5, ca. 1996, b&w	3.50
❑6, ca. 1996, b&w	3.50

HAIRBUTT THE HIPPO: PRIVATE EYE
RATRACE

❑1, Spr 1997, b&w; no indicia	2.95
❑2, Sum 1997, b&w; no indicia	2.95
❑3, ca. 1997, b&w	2.95

HALIFAX EXPLOSION
HALIFAX

❑1, Apr 1997, b&w	2.50

HALL OF FAME
J.C.

❑1	1.50
❑2	1.50
❑3	1.50

HALL OF HEROES
HALL OF HEROES

❑1, May 1997, b&w	2.50
❑2	2.50
❑3	2.50

HALL OF HEROES HALLOWEEN SPECIAL
HALL OF HEROES

❑1, Oct 1997, b&w	2.50

HALL OF HEROES PRESENTS (1ST SERIES)
HALL OF HEROES

❑1, Aug 1993	2.50
❑2, Sep 1993	2.50
❑3, Nov 1993	2.50

HALL OF HEROES PRESENTS (2ND SERIES)
HALL OF HEROES

❑0/A, Mar 1997, b&w; Slingers cover	2.50
❑0/B, Mar 1997, b&w; Salamandroid cover	2.50
❑0/C, Mar 1997, b&w; The Fuzz cover	2.50
❑1, Jul 1996, b&w	2.50
❑2, Sep 1996, b&w	2.50
❑3/A, b&w; no indicia	2.50
❑3/B; alternate b cover with Nazi swastika in background	2.50
❑4, May 1997; Turaxx	2.50
❑5, Sep 1997; The Becoming; extra-wide	2.50

HALLOWED KNIGHT
SHEA

❑1, Apr 1997, b&w	2.95
❑2, Sep 1997, b&w	2.95
❑2/Autographed; Signed	2.95

HALLOWEEN
CHAOS

❑1, Nov 2000; based on movie	2.95

HALLOWEEN HORROR
ECLIPSE

❑1, Oct 1987; JD (a); a.k.a. Seduction of the Innocent #7	2.00

HALLOWEEN MEGAZINE
MARVEL

❑1, Dec 1996; reprints stories from Tomb of Dracula	2.99

Other grades: Multiply price above by 5/6 for VF/NM • 2/3 for VERY FINE • 1/3 for FINE • 1/5 for VERY GOOD • 1/8 for GOOD

HALLOWEEN TERROR
ETERNITY
❑1, b&w 2.50

HALLS OF HORROR (JOHN BOLTON'S...)
ECLIPSE
❑1, Jun 1985 .... 1.75
❑2, Jun 1985 .... 1.75
❑3 .... 1.75

HALO, AN ANGEL'S STORY
SIRIUS
❑1, Apr 1996 .... 2.95
❑2, May 1996 .... 2.95
❑3, Jun 1996 .... 2.95
❑4, Jul 1996 .... 2.95

HAMMER
DARK HORSE
❑1, Oct 1997 .... 2.95
❑2, Nov 1997 .... 2.95
❑3, Dec 1997 .... 2.95
❑4, Jan 1998 .... 2.95

HAMMERLOCKE
DC
❑1, Sep 1992 .... 1.75
❑2, Oct 1992 .... 1.75
❑3, Nov 1992 .... 1.75
❑4, Dec 1992 .... 1.75
❑5, Jan 1993 .... 1.75
❑6, Feb 1993 .... 1.75
❑7, Mar 1993 .... 1.75
❑8, Apr 1993 .... 1.75
❑9, May 1993 .... 1.75

HAMMER OF GOD
FIRST
❑1 .... 1.95
❑2 .... 1.95
❑3 .... 1.95
❑4 .... 1.95

HAMMER OF GOD: BUTCH
DARK HORSE
❑1, May 1994 .... 2.50
❑2, Jul 1994 .... 2.50
❑3, Aug 1994 .... 2.50

HAMMER OF GOD: PENTATHLON
DARK HORSE
❑1 .... 2.50

HAMMER OF GOD: SWORD OF JUSTICE
FIRST
❑1 .... 4.95
❑2 .... 4.95

HAMMER OF THE GODS
INSIGHT
❑1, ca. 2001, b&w 2.95
❑2, ca. 2001, b&w 2.95
❑3, ca. 2001, b&w 2.95
❑4, ca. 2001, b&w 2.95
❑5, ca. 2001, b&w; Contains extra material about the four-issue mini-series 2.95

HAMMER OF THE GODS COLOR SAGA
INSIGHT
❑nn, ca. 2001 .... 4.95

HAMMER OF THE GODS: HAMMER HITS CHINA
IMAGE
❑1, Feb 2003 .... 2.95
❑2, May 2003 .... 2.95
❑3, Oct 2003 .... 2.95

HAMMER, THE: THE OUTSIDER
DARK HORSE
❑1, Feb 1999 .... 2.95
❑2, Mar 1999 .... 2.95
❑3, Apr 1999 .... 2.95

HAMMER, THE: UNCLE ALEX
DARK HORSE
❑1, Aug 1998 .... 2.95

HAMSTER VICE (BLACKTHORNE)
BLACKTHORNE
❑1 .... 1.50
❑2 .... 1.50
❑3 .... 1.50
❑4 .... 1.50
❑5 .... 1.50
❑6 .... 1.50
❑7 .... 1.50
❑8, Jul 1987 .... 1.50
❑9 .... 1.50
❑3D 1, Nov 1986 .... 2.50
❑3D 2, Feb 1987; a.k.a. Blackthorne 3-D #15 .... 2.50

HAMSTER VICE (ETERNITY)
ETERNITY
❑1, Apr 1989, b&w 1.95
❑2, b&w 1.95

HANA-KIMI
VIZ
❑1, Sep 2004 .... 9.99
❑2, Nov 2004 .... 9.99
❑3, Jan 2005 .... 9.99
❑4, Feb 2005 .... 9.99
❑5, Apr 2005 .... 9.99
❑6, Jun 2005 .... 9.99
❑7, Aug 2005 .... 9.99
❑8, Oct 2005 .... 9.99

HAND SHADOWS
DOYAN
❑1 .... 1.50
❑2, Nov 1986 .... 1.50

HANDS OFF!
WARD SUTTON
❑1, b&w 2.95

HANDS OFF!
TOKYOPOP
❑1, Oct 2004 .... 9.99
❑2, Feb 2005 .... 9.99
❑3, May 2005 .... 9.99
❑4, Aug 2005 .... 9.99
❑5, Jan 2006 .... 9.99

HANDS OF THE DRAGON
ATLAS-SEABOARD
❑1, Jun 1975 .... 6.00

HANNA-BARBERA ALL-STARS
ARCHIE
❑1, Oct 1995 .... 2.00
❑2, Dec 1995 .... 2.00
❑3, Feb 1996 .... 2.00
❑4, Apr 1996 .... 2.00

HANNA-BARBERA BANDWAGON
GOLD KEY
❑1, Oct 1962 .... 70.00
❑2, Jan 1963 .... 50.00
❑3, Apr 1963 .... 50.00

HANNA-BARBERA BIG BOOK
HARVEY
❑1, Jun 1993 .... 1.95
❑3 .... 2.50

HANNA-BARBERA GIANT SIZE
HARVEY
❑2, Nov 1992 .... 2.25

HANNA-BARBERA PARADE
CHARLTON
❑1, Sep 1971 .... 35.00
❑2, Nov 1971 .... 18.00
❑3, Dec 1971 .... 15.00
❑4, Jan 1972 .... 13.00
❑5, Feb 1972 .... 14.00
❑6, Apr 1972, A: Wilma Flintstone. A: Fred Flintstone. A: Pebbles Flintstone. Dixie cameo; Pixie cameo 12.00
❑7, May 1972 .... 12.00
❑8, Jul 1972 .... 12.00
❑9, Oct 1972 .... 12.00
❑10, Dec 1972 .... 12.00

HANNA-BARBERA PRESENTS
ARCHIE
❑1, Nov 1995, Atom Ant and Secret Squirrel 1.50
❑2, Jan 1996, Wacky Races 1.50
❑3, Mar 1996, Yogi Bear 1.50
❑4, May 1996, Quick Draw McGraw and Magilla Gorilla 1.50
❑5, Jul 1996 .... 1.50
❑6, Aug 1996, Superstar Olympics 1.50
❑8, Oct 1996, Frankenstein Jr. and the Impossibles 1.50

HANNA-BARBERA PRESENTS ALL-NEW COMICS
HARVEY
❑1, giveaway promo 1.00

HANNA-BARBERA SUPER TV HEROES
GOLD KEY
❑1, Apr 1968, Herculoids 58.00
❑2, Jul 1968, Birdman 36.00
❑3, Oct 1968, Shazzan, Space Ghost, Moby Dick, Birdman, Young Samson and Goliath 36.00
❑4, Jan 1969, Herculoids, Birdman, Shazzan, Moby Dick, Mighty Mightor 30.00
❑5, Apr 1969 .... 30.00
❑6, Jul 1969, Space Ghost 35.00
❑7, Oct 1969, Space Ghost 35.00

HANSI, THE GIRL WHO LOVED THE SWASTIKA
SPIRE
❑1, ca. 1973 .... 28.00

HAP HAZARD
FANDOM HOUSE
❑1, b&w 2.00

HAPPENSTANCE JACK, III
-ISM
❑1, May 1998 .... 3.00

HAPPIEST MILLIONAIRE
GOLD KEY
❑1, Apr 1968 .... 25.00

HAPPY
WONDER COMICS
❑1, b&w 2.00

HAPPY BIRTHDAY GNATRAT!
DIMENSION
❑1 .... 1.95

HAPPY BIRTHDAY MARTHA WASHINGTON
DARK HORSE / LEGEND
❑1, Mar 1995; FM (w); DaG (a); cardstock cover 3.00

HAPPYDALE: DEVILS IN THE DESERT
DC / VERTIGO
❑1; prestige format 6.95
❑2; prestige format 6.95

HAPPY DAYS
GOLD KEY
❑1, Mar 1979 .... 20.00
❑2, May 1979 .... 10.00
❑3, Jul 1979 .... 10.00
❑4, Sep 1979 .... 10.00
❑5 1979 .... 10.00
❑6, Feb 1980 .... 10.00

HARBINGER
VALIANT
❑0, Feb 1993; O: Sting. sendaway; Special issue given as a premium from coupons in Harbinger #1-6 .... 4.00
❑0/Pink, Feb 1993; Pink variant 65.00
❑0/2nd, Feb 1993; O: Sting. Included with Harbinger trade paperback 2.00
❑1, Jan 1992 O: Harbinger. 1: Flamingo. 1: Zeppelin. 1: Sting. 1: Kris. 1: Torque. 1: Harbinger kids 30.00
❑2, Feb 1992 .... 8.00
❑3, Mar 1992 V: Ax 8.00
❑4, Apr 1992; Scarce 11.00
❑5, May 1992 A: Solar 10.00
❑6, Jun 1992 D: Torque 9.00
❑7, Jul 1992 .... 7.00
❑8, Aug 1992; FM (c); FM (a); Unity 4.00
❑9, Sep 1992; Unity; Birth of Magnus 4.00
❑10, Oct 1992 1: H.A.R.D Corps 4.00
❑11, Nov 1992 A: H.A.R.D Corps 2.00
❑12, Dec 1992 .... 1.00
❑13, Jan 1993; Dark Knight cover 1.00
❑14, Feb 1993 .... 1.00
❑15, Mar 1993 .... 1.00
❑16, Apr 1993 .... 1.00
❑17, May 1993 .... 1.00
❑18, Jun 1993 KN (c); 1: Screen 1.00
❑19, Jul 1993 .... 1.00
❑20, Aug 1993 .... 1.00
❑21, Sep 1993 .... 1.00
❑22, Oct 1993 A: Archer & Armstrong 1.00
❑23, Nov 1993 .... 1.00

Hamster Vice (Blackthorne)

Another artifact of the Turtles craze

©Blackthorne

Hansi, the Girl Who Loved the Swastika

Young German girl is saved by religion

©Spire

Harbinger

Valiant series got very hot, then very cold

©Valiant

Hard Rock Comics

More unauthorized rock biographies

©Revolutionary

Hardware

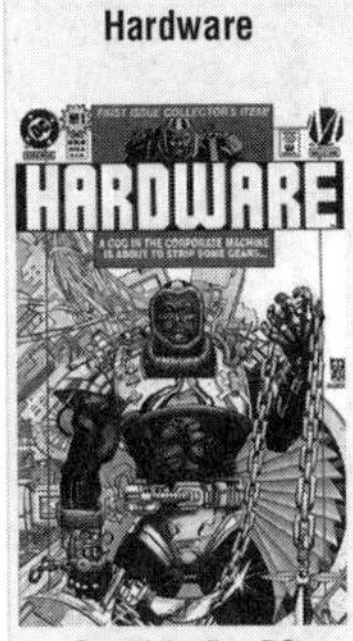

One of the first DC Milestone titles

©DC

N-MINT

❑24, Dec 1993 ... 1.00
❑25, Jan 1994; Giant-size; D: Rock. V: Harada. Sting vs. Harada; Harada put into coma; Sting loses powers ... 1.00
❑26, Feb 1994; 1: Sonix. 1: Anvil. 1: Amazon. 1: Microwave. 1: Jolt. new team; Zephyr rejoins Harbinger foundation ... 1.00
❑27, Mar 1994 ... 1.00
❑28, Apr 1994 ... 1.00
❑29, May 1994; trading card ... 2.00
❑30, Jun 1994 A: H.A.R.D.Corps. ... 1.00
❑31, Aug 1994 A: H.A.R.D.Corps. ... 1.00
❑32, Sep 1994 A: Eternal Warrior. ... 1.00
❑33, Oct 1994 A: Doctor Eclipse ... 1.00
❑34, Nov 1994; Chaos Effect Delta 1 .. 1.00
❑35, Dec 1994 ... 2.00
❑36, Jan 1995 A: Magnus ... 1.00
❑37, Feb 1995; Painted cover ... 1.00
❑38, Mar 1995 ... 1.00
❑39, Apr 1995 ... 3.00
❑40, May 1995 ... 4.00
❑41, Jun 1995 ... 5.00

HARBINGER: ACTS OF GOD
ACCLAIM

❑1 ... 3.95

HARBINGER FILES
VALIANT

❑1, Aug 1994, O: Toyo Harada. ... 2.00
❑2, Feb 1995, 1: The Harbinger. ... 4.00

HARDBALL
AIRCEL

❑1 1991 ... 2.95
❑2 1991 ... 2.95
❑3, Aug 1991 ... 2.95
❑4 1991 ... 2.95

HARD BOILED
DARK HORSE

❑1, Sep 1990 ... 4.95
❑2, Dec 1990 ... 5.95
❑3, Mar 1992 ... 5.95

HARDCASE
MALIBU / ULTRAVERSE

❑1, Jun 1993, 1: NM-E. 1: Nicholas Lone (Solitaire). 1: Hardcase ... 2.50
❑1/Hologram, Jun 1993, Holographic cover ... 5.00
❑1/Ltd., Jun 1993, Ultrafoil limited edition ... 3.00
❑2, Jul 1993, 1: Choice. trading card.. 2.00
❑3, Aug 1993, 1: The Needler. 1: Gun Nut. 1: Trouble. ... 2.00
❑4, Sep 1993, O: Hardcase. Fold-out cover ... 2.00
❑5, Oct 1993, Rune ... 2.00
❑6, Nov 1993 ... 1.95
❑7, Dec 1993, Break-Thru ... 1.95
❑8, Jan 1994, A: Solution. ... 1.95
❑9, Feb 1994, BA (a) ... 1.95
❑10, Mar 1994 ... 1.95
❑11, Apr 1994 ... 1.95
❑12, May 1994 ... 1.95
❑13, Jun 1994, 1: Karr. 1: Wynn. ... 1.95
❑14, Jul 1994 ... 1.95

N-MINT

❑15, Aug 1994 ... 1.95
❑16, Oct 1994, KB (w); Flip book with Ultraverse Premiere #7 ... 3.50
❑17, Nov 1994, 1: The Genius ... 1.95
❑18, Dec 1994 ... 1.95
❑19, Jan 1995, 1: Trauma. 1: Bismark. 1.95
❑20, Feb 1995 ... 2.50
❑21, Mar 1995 ... 2.50
❑22, Apr 1995, D: Trouble. ... 2.50
❑23, May 1995 ... 2.50
❑24, Jun 1995 ... 2.50
❑25, Jul 1995 ... 2.50
❑26, Aug 1995 ... 2.95

HARDCORE STATION
DC

❑1, Jul 1998 ... 2.50
❑2, Aug 1998 ... 2.50
❑3, Sep 1998 ... 2.50
❑4, Oct 1998 ... 2.50
❑5, Nov 1998 ... 2.50
❑6, Dec 1998 ... 2.50

H.A.R.D. CORPS
VALIANT

❑1, Dec 1992, Fold-out cover ... 1.00
❑1/Gold, Dec 1992, Gold (promotional) edition; Fold-out cover ... 12.00
❑2, Jan 1993 ... 1.00
❑3, Feb 1993 ... 1.00
❑4, Apr 1993 ... 1.00
❑5, Apr 1993 ... 1.00
❑5/ComicDef, Apr 1993 ... 5.00
❑6, May 1993 ... 1.00
❑7, Jun 1993 ... 1.00
❑8, Jul 1993 ... 1.00
❑9, Aug 1993 ... 1.00
❑10, Sep 1993 ... 1.00
❑11, Oct 1993 ... 1.00
❑12, Nov 1993 ... 1.00
❑13, Dec 1993 ... 1.00
❑14, Jan 1994 ... 1.00
❑15, Feb 1994 ... 1.00
❑16, Mar 1994 ... 1.00
❑17, Apr 1994 ... 1.00
❑18, May 1994, trading card ... 2.00
❑19, Jun 1994, Harada awakes from coma ... 1.00
❑20, Jul 1994 ... 1.00
❑21, Sep 1994 ... 1.00
❑22, Oct 1994 ... 1.00
❑23, Nov 1994, Chaos Effect Delta 4.. 1.00
❑24, Dec 1994 ... 1.00
❑25, Jan 1995 ... 1.00
❑26, Feb 1995 ... 2.00
❑27, Mar 1995 ... 2.00
❑28, Apr 1995 ... 2.00
❑29, May 1995 ... 3.00
❑30, Jun 1995 ... 5.00

HARDKORR
AIRCEL

❑1, Jun 1991, b&w ... 2.50
❑2, Jul 1991, b&w ... 2.50
❑3, Aug 1991, b&w ... 2.50
❑4, Sep 1991, b&w ... 2.50

N-MINT

HARD LOOKS
DARK HORSE

❑1 1992, b&w ... 2.50
❑2 1992, b&w ... 2.50
❑3 1992, b&w ... 2.50
❑4, b&w ... 2.50
❑5, b&w ... 2.50
❑6, b&w ... 2.95
❑7, b&w ... 2.95
❑8, b&w ... 2.95
❑9, b&w ... 2.95
❑10, b&w ... 3.50

HARD ROCK COMICS
REVOLUTIONARY

❑1, Mar 1992, b&w; Metallica; early ... 5.00
❑2, Apr 1992, b&w; Motley Crue ... 4.00
❑3, May 1992, b&w; Jane's Addiction 3.00
❑4, Jun 1992, b&w; Nirvana ... 4.00
❑5, Jul 1992, b&w; Kiss: Tales From the Tours ... 8.00
❑5/2nd, Jul 1992; Kiss: Tales From the Tours ... 5.00
❑6, Sep 1992, b&w; Def Leppard II 2.50
❑7, Oct 1992, b&w; Red Hot Chili Peppers ... 2.50
❑8, Nov 1992, b&w; Soundgarden, Pearl Jam ... 2.50
❑9, Dec 1992, b&w; Queen II ... 2.50
❑10, Jan 1993, b&w; Birth of Punk 2.50
❑11, Feb 1993, b&w; Pantera ... 2.50
❑12, Mar 1993, b&w; Hendrix ... 2.50
❑13, Apr 1993, b&w; Dead Kennedys. 3.00
❑14, May 1993, b&w; Van Halen II 2.50
❑15, Jun 1993, b&w; Megadeath, Motorhead; Dave Mustaine interview 2.50
❑16, Jul 1993, b&w; Joan Jett, Lita Ford 2.50
❑17; never published; British Metal 2.50
❑18, Sep 1993, b&w; Queensryche II. 2.50
❑19, Oct 1993, b&w; Tesla, Spirit, UKJ 2.50
❑20, Nov 1993, b&w; Ratt, P-Funk, Sweet ... 2.50

HARD TIME
DC / FOCUS

❑1, Apr 2004 ... 2.50
❑2, May 2004 ... 2.50
❑3, Jun 2004 ... 2.50
❑4, Jul 2004 ... 2.50
❑5, Aug 2004 ... 2.50
❑6, Sep 2004 ... 2.50
❑7, Oct 2004 ... 2.50
❑8, Nov 2004 ... 2.50
❑9, Dec 2004 ... 2.50
❑10, Jan 2005 ... 2.50
❑11, Feb 2005 ... 2.50
❑12, Mar 2005 ... 2.50

HARD TIME: SEASON TWO
DC

❑1, Jan 2006 ... 2.50
❑2, Mar 2006 ... 2.50
❑3, Mar 2006 ... 2.50
❑4, May 2006 ... 2.50
❑5, Jun 2006 ... 2.50
❑6, Jul 2006 ... 2.50
❑7, Aug 2006 ... 2.50

HARDWARE
DC / MILESTONE

❑1, Apr 1993; O: Hardware. 1: Reprise. 1: Edwin Alva. 1: Hardware. newsstand 1.50
❑1/CS, Apr 1993; O: Hardware. 1: Reprise. 1: Edwin Alva. 1: Hardware. bagged 2.95
❑1/Platinum, Apr 1993; Platinum (promotional) edition; O: Hardware. 1: Reprise. 1: Edwin Alva. 1: Hardware. no cover price; platinum 3.00
❑2, May 1993 1: Barraki Young. 1.50
❑3, May 1993 1: Systematic. 1.50
❑4, Jun 1993 1.50
❑5, Jul 1993 1: Deacon Stuart. 1: Deathwish. 1.50
❑6, Aug 1993 1.50
❑7, Sep 1993 O: Deathwish. 1.50
❑8, Oct 1993 1.50
❑9, Nov 1993 1: Technique. 1.50
❑10, Dec 1993 RB (a); 1: Harm. 1: Transit. 1.50
❑11, Jan 1994 1: Shadowspire. 1: Dharma. 1: The Star Chamber. 1.50
❑12, Feb 1994 RB (a) 1.50
❑13, Mar 1994 1.50
❑14, Apr 1994 1.50
❑15, May 1994 1.50
❑16, Jun 1994; Giant-size 1: Hardware Version 2.0. 2.50
❑16/Variant, Jun 1994; Giant-size; 1: Hardware Version 2.0. Fold-out cover 3.95
❑17, Jul 1994 A: Steel. 1.50
❑18, Aug 1994 A: Steel. 1.75
❑19, Sep 1994 1.75
❑20, Oct 1994 KP (a) 1.75
❑21, Nov 1994 1.75
❑22, Dec 1994 1.75
❑23, Jan 1995 1.75
❑24, Feb 1995 1.75
❑25, Mar 1995; Giant-size 2.95
❑26, Apr 1995 1.75
❑27, May 1995 1.75
❑28, Jun 1995 1.75
❑29, Jul 1995; cover has both .99 and 2.50 cover price 2.50
❑30, Aug 1995 2.50
❑31, Sep 1995 D: Edwin Alva. 2.50
❑32, Oct 1995 2.50
❑33, Nov 1995 HC (c) 2.50
❑34, Dec 1995 2.50
❑35, Jan 1996 2.50
❑36, Feb 1996 2.50
❑37, Mar 1996 2.50
❑38, Apr 1996 2.50
❑39, May 1996 2.50
❑40, Jun 1996 KP (a) 2.50
❑41, Jul 1996 2.50
❑42, Aug 1996 2.50
❑43, Sep 1996 2.50
❑44, Oct 1996 2.50
❑45, Nov 1996; return of Edwin Alva 2.50
❑46, Dec 1996 2.50
❑47, Jan 1997 2.50
❑48, Feb 1997 2.50
❑49, Mar 1997 2.50
❑50, Apr 1997; Giant-size 3.95

HARDWIRED
BANGTRO

❑1, May 1994 2.25

HARDY BOYS
GOLD KEY

❑1, Apr 1970 28.00
❑2, Jul 1970 18.00
❑3, Oct 1970 18.00
❑4, Jan 1971 18.00

HARI KARI
BLACK OUT

❑0; indicia says "#0 #1" 2.95
❑1 2.95

HARI KARI: LIVE & UNTAMED
BLACKOUT

❑0 2.95
❑0/Variant; variant cover 4.00
❑1 2.95

HARI KARI PRIVATE GALLERY
BLACKOUT

❑0; Pin-Ups 2.95

HARI KARI: REBIRTH
BLACK OUT

❑1 2.95

HARI KARI RESURRECTION
BLACKOUT

❑1 2.95

HARI KARI: THE BEGINNING
BLACK OUT

❑1 2.95

HARI KARI: THE DIARY OF KARI SUN
BLACKOUT

❑½; prose accompanied with pin-ups 2.95

HARI KARI: THE SILENCE OF EVIL
BLACK OUT

❑0 2.95

HARLEM GLOBETROTTERS
GOLD KEY

❑1, Apr 1972 13.00
❑2, Jul 1972 9.00
❑3, Oct 1972 A: Curly. A: Gip. A: Pabs. A: Geese. A: Granny. A: Dribbles. A: B.J.. A: Meadowlark. 7.00
❑4, Jan 1973 7.00
❑5, Apr 1973 7.00
❑6, Jul 1973 5.00
❑7, Oct 1973 5.00
❑8, Jan 1974 5.00
❑9, Apr 1974 5.00
❑10, Jul 1974 5.00
❑11, Oct 1974 5.00
❑12, Jan 1975 5.00

HARLEM HEROES
FLEETWAY-QUALITY

❑1, b&w 1.95
❑2, b&w 1.95
❑3, b&w 1.95
❑4, b&w 1.95
❑5, b&w 1.95
❑6, b&w 1.95

HARLEQUIN
CALIBER

❑1, May 1993, b&w 2.95

HARLEY & IVY: LOVE ON THE LAM
DC

❑1, Nov 2001, b&w 5.95

HARLEY QUINN
DC

❑1, Dec 2000 3.50
❑2, Jan 2001 3.00
❑3, Feb 2001 A: Catwoman. 3.00
❑4, Mar 2001 3.00
❑5, Apr 2001 3.00
❑6, May 2001 2.50
❑7, Jun 2001 2.50
❑8, Jul 2001 2.50
❑9, Aug 2001 2.50
❑10, Sep 2001 2.50
❑11, Oct 2001 2.25
❑12, Nov 2001 2.95
❑13, Dec 2001; Joker: Last Laugh crossover 2.25
❑14, Jan 2002 2.25
❑15, Feb 2002 2.25
❑16, Mar 2002 A: Poison Ivy. 2.25
❑17, Apr 2002 2.25
❑18, May 2002 2.25
❑19, Jun 2002 A: Superman. 2.25
❑20, Jul 2002 2.25
❑21, Aug 2002 2.25
❑22, Sep 2002 2.25
❑23, Oct 2002 2.50
❑24, Nov 2002 2.50
❑25, Dec 2002 2.50
❑26, Jan 2003 2.50
❑27, Feb 2003 2.50
❑28, Mar 2003 2.50
❑29, Apr 2003 2.50
❑30, May 2003 2.50
❑31, Jun 2003 2.50
❑32, Jul 2003 2.50
❑33, Aug 2003 2.50
❑34, Sep 2003 2.50
❑35, Oct 2003 2.50
❑36, Nov 2003 2.50
❑37, Dec 2003 2.50
❑38, Jan 2004 2.50

HARLEY QUINN: OUR WORLDS AT WAR
DC

❑1, Oct 2001, b&w 2.95

HARLEY RIDER
HUNGNESS

❑1 2.00

HAROLD HEDD (LAST GASP)
LAST GASP ECO-FUNNIES

❑1 8.00
❑2 4.00

HAROLD HEDD IN "HITLER'S COCAINE"
KITCHEN SINK

❑1 4.00
❑2 4.00

HARPY PIN-UP SPECIAL
PEREGRINE ENTERTAINMENT

❑1, May 1998, b&w 3.00

HARPY PREVIEW
GROUND ZERO

❑1, Oct 1996, b&w 3.00

HARPY: PRIZE OF THE OVERLORD
GROUND ZERO

❑1, Dec 1996, b&w 3.00
❑2, Feb 1997, b&w 3.00
❑3, Apr 1997, b&w; cover says Blood of the Demon 3.00
❑4 3.00
❑5 3.00
❑6 3.00

HARRIER PREVIEW
HARRIER

❑1 1.00

HARRIERS
EXPRESS / ENTITY

❑1; Foil stamped cover 2.95
❑2 2.95
❑3 2.95

HARROWERS (CLIVE BARKER'S)
MARVEL / EPIC

❑1, Dec 1993, glow in the dark cover. 2.95
❑2, Jan 1994 2.50
❑3, Feb 1994 2.50
❑4, Mar 1994 2.50
❑5, Apr 1994 2.50
❑6, May 1994 2.50

HARRY THE COP
SLAVE LABOR

❑1, Apr 1992, b&w 2.95
❑1/2nd, Oct 1992, b&w 2.95

HARSH REALM
HARRIS

❑1, Feb 1994 2.95
❑2, Mar 1994 2.95
❑3, Apr 1994 2.95
❑4, May 1994 2.95
❑5, Jun 1994 2.95
❑6, Jul 1994 2.95

HARTE OF DARKNESS
ETERNITY

❑1, b&w 2.50
❑2, b&w 2.50
❑3, b&w 2.50
❑4, b&w 2.50

HARVEY
MARVEL

❑1, Oct 1970, humor 50.00
❑2, Dec 1970, humor 18.00
❑3, Jun 1972, humor 8.00
❑4, Aug 1972, humor 6.00
❑5, Oct 1972, humor 6.00
❑6, Dec 1972, humor 6.00

HATE
FANTAGRAPHICS

❑1, Spr 1990, b&w 8.00
❑1/2nd 3.50

Hardy Boys

Live action version predated Shaun Cassidy
©Gold Key

Harlem Globetrotters

Based on the Hanna-Barbera animated series
©Gold Key

Harley Quinn

More with the Joker's wacky sidekick
©DC

Hate

You don't want Buddy Bradley's life...
©Fantagraphics

Hawk & the Dove (1st Series)

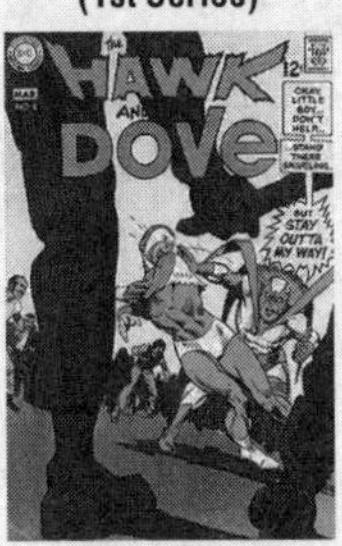

Brothers who become crimefighters
©DC

N-MINT

❑1/3rd 2.00
❑2, Sum 1990 5.00
❑2/2nd 3.00
❑2/3rd 2.50
❑3, Fal 1990 4.00
❑3/2nd 2.50
❑3/3rd 2.50
❑4, Spr 1991 4.00
❑4/2nd 2.00
❑5, Sum 1991 4.00
❑5/2nd 2.00
❑6, Fal 1991 4.00
❑7, Win 1991 3.00
❑8, Spr 1992 3.00
❑9, Sum 1992 3.00
❑10, Fal 1992 3.00
❑11, Win 1993 2.50
❑12, Spr 1993 2.50
❑13, Sum 1993 2.50
❑14, Fal 1993 2.50
❑15, Spr 1994 2.50
❑16, Fal 1994; color story 2.95
❑17, Win 1994 2.95
❑18, Apr 1995 2.95
❑19, Jun 1995 2.95
❑20, Aug 1995; color and b&w 2.95
❑21, Oct 1995 2.95
❑22, Dec 1995 2.95
❑23, ca. 1996 2.95
❑24, ca. 1996 2.95
❑25, ca. 1996 2.95
❑26, ca. 1996 2.95
❑27, May 1997 2.95
❑28, Jul 1997 2.95
❑29, ca. 1997 2.95
❑30, ca. 1997; color and b&w 2.95

HATEBALL
FANTAGRAPHICS

❑1; giveaway 1.00

HATE JAMBOREE!
FANTAGRAPHICS

❑1, Oct 1998, newsprint cover 3.95

HAUNTED
CHARLTON

❑1, Sep 1971, SD (w); SD (a) 12.00
❑2, Nov 1971, SD (c) 6.00
❑3, Jan 1972 6.00
❑4, Feb 1972, SD (c) 5.00
❑5, Apr 1972, SD (c) 5.00
❑6, Jun 1972, WH (a) 5.00
❑7, Aug 1972, SD (c) 4.00
❑8, Oct 1972, SD (c) 4.00
❑9, Dec 1972 4.00
❑10, Jan 1973, JAb (a) 4.00
❑11, Mar 1973 3.00
❑12, May 1973, PM (a) 3.00
❑13, Jul 1973, SD (a) 3.00
❑14, Sep 1973 3.00
❑15, Nov 1973, SD, JAb (a) 3.00
❑16, Jun 1974, SD, WH (a) 3.00
❑17, Jul 1974, PM (a) 3.00
❑18, Oct 1974, JSa (c); WH (w); WH (a) 3.00
❑19, Dec 1974, PM (a) 3.00
❑20, Feb 1975, TS (w); TS (a) 3.00
❑21, Apr 1975, TS (w); TS (a); Title becomes Baron Weirwulf's Haunted Library 3.00
❑22, Jun 1975, TS, JSa (a) 3.00
❑23, Sep 1975, TS (c); SD, PM (a) 3.00
❑24, Nov 1975, SD (a) 3.00
❑25, Jan 1976, TS (c) 3.00
❑26, Mar 1976 3.00
❑27, May 1976 3.00
❑28, Jul 1976, MZ (c) 3.00
❑29, Sep 1976 3.00
❑30, Nov 1976 3.00
❑31, Jan 1977, Cover says Sep 77 3.00
❑32, Oct 1977, WH (a) 3.00
❑33, Dec 1977, JSa, PM (a) 3.00
❑34, Feb 1978 3.00
❑35, Apr 1978, JSa (a); Cover reprinted from #12 3.00
❑36, May 1978, TS (a) 3.00
❑37, Jul 1978, TS (a); 'Fiendish Females' issue 3.00
❑38, Oct 1978 3.00
❑39, Dec 1978, SD (a); Cover reprinted from #10 3.00
❑40, Feb 1979, SD, JAb (a); Cover reprinted from #8 3.00
❑41, Apr 1979 3.00
❑42, Jun 1979, Cover reprinted from #15 3.00
❑43, Jul 1979, WH (a) 3.00
❑44, Sep 1979, Cover reprinted from #20 3.00
❑45, Oct 1979, DN, JSa, WH (a) 3.00
❑46, Dec 1979 3.00
❑47, Jan 1980, SD, MZ (a) 3.00
❑48, Mar 1980, SD (c); Cover reprinted from #3 3.00
❑49, May 1980 3.00
❑50, Jul 1980 3.00
❑51, Oct 1980 2.50
❑52, Dec 1980 2.50
❑53, Jan 1981, Doctor Graves issue 2.50
❑54, Mar 1981 2.50
❑55, May 1981, TS (w); TS, PM (a) 2.50
❑56, Jul 1981, SD (c) 2.50
❑57, Sep 1981, SD (c) 2.50
❑58, Oct 1981 2.50
❑59, Jan 1982, DN, JSa (a) 2.50
❑60, Mar 1982 2.50
❑61, Apr 1982 2.50
❑62, Jul 1982, Infinity cover 2.50
❑63, Sep 1982, WH (c); WH (w); JSa, WH (a) 2.50
❑64, Nov 1982 2.50
❑65, Jan 1983 2.50
❑66, Mar 1983, TS (c) 2.50
❑67, May 1983, TS, SD (a) 2.50
❑68, Jul 1983 2.50
❑69, Sep 1983, Cover reprinted from #5 2.50
❑70, Nov 1983 2.50
❑71, Jan 1984 2.50
❑72, Mar 1984 2.50
❑73, May 1984, TS (c) 2.50
❑74, Jul 1984 2.50
❑75, Sep 1984 2.50

HAUNTED
CHAOS

❑1, Jan 2002 2.95
❑1/Ltd.; premium edition; Limited to 3,000 copies 2.95
❑2, Feb 2002 2.95
❑3, Mar 2002 2.95
❑4, Apr 2002 2.95

HAUNTED MAN
DARK HORSE

❑1, Mar 2000 2.95
❑2 2.95
❑3 2.95

HAUNTED MANSION
SLAVE LABOR

❑1, Nov 2005 3.99

HAUNT OF FEAR (GLADSTONE)
GLADSTONE

❑1, May 1991 2.50
❑2, Jul 1991 2.50

HAUNT OF FEAR (RCP)
COCHRAN

❑1, Sep 1991; Giant-size; Reprints Haunt of Fear #14, Weird Fantasy #13 2.00
❑2, Nov 1991; Giant-size 2.00
❑3, Jan 1992; Giant-size 2.00
❑4, Mar 1992; Giant-size 2.00
❑5, May 1992; Giant-size 2.00

HAUNT OF FEAR (RCP)
GEMSTONE

❑1, Nov 1992; Reprints The Haunt of Fear (EC) #1 2.00
❑2, Feb 1993; Reprints The Haunt of Fear (EC) #2 2.00
❑3, May 1993; Reprints The Haunt of Fear (EC) #3 2.00
❑4, Aug 1993; Reprints The Haunt of Fear (EC) #4 2.00
❑5, Nov 1993; Reprints The Haunt of Fear (EC) #5 2.00
❑6, Feb 1994; Reprints The Haunt of Fear (EC) #6 2.00
❑7, May 1994; Reprints The Haunt of Fear (EC) #7 2.00
❑8, Aug 1994; Reprints The Haunt of Fear (EC) #8 2.00
❑9, Nov 1994; Reprints The Haunt of Fear (EC) #9 2.00
❑10, Feb 1995; Reprints The Haunt of Fear (EC) #10 2.00
❑11, May 1995; Reprints The Haunt of Fear (EC) #11 2.00
❑12, Aug 1995; Reprints The Haunt of Fear (EC) #12 2.00
❑13, Nov 1995; Reprints The Haunt of Fear (EC) #13 2.00
❑14, Feb 1996; O: The Old Witch. Reprints The Haunt of Fear (EC) #14 2.00
❑15, May 1996; Reprints The Haunt of Fear (EC) #15 2.00
❑16, Aug 1996; GE, JKa, GI (w); GE, JKa, GI (a); Ray Bradbury story; Reprints The Haunt of Fear (EC) #16; Ray Bradbury adaptation 2.50

Other grades: Multiply price above by 5/6 for VF/NM • 2/3 for VERY FINE • 1/3 for FINE • 1/5 for VERY GOOD • 1/8 for GOOD

❑17, Nov 1996; GE, JKa, GI (w); GE, JKa, GI (a); Reprints The Haunt of Fear (EC) #17 .... 2.50
❑18, Feb 1997; GE, JKa, GI (w); GE, JKa, GI (a); Ray Bradbury story; Reprints The Haunt of Fear (EC) #18 2.50
❑19, May 1997; GE, JKa, GI (w); GE, JKa, GI (a); Reprints The Haunt of Fear (EC) #19; Mentioned in Seduction of the Innocent 'A comic book baseball game' 2.50
❑20, Aug 1997; Reprints The Haunt of Fear (EC) #20 .... 2.50
❑21, Nov 1997; Reprints The Haunt of Fear (EC) #21 .... 2.50
❑22, Feb 1998; Reprints The Haunt of Fear (EC) #22 .... 2.50
❑23, May 1998; Reprints The Haunt of Fear (EC) #23 .... 2.50
❑24, Aug 1998; Reprints The Haunt of Fear (EC) #24 .... 2.50
❑25, Nov 1998; Reprints The Haunt of Fear (EC) #25 .... 2.50
❑26, Feb 1999; JKa, GI (w); JKa, GI (a); Reprints The Haunt of Fear (EC) #26 2.50
❑27, May 1999; GE, JKa, GI (w); Reprints The Haunt of Fear (EC) #27 2.50
❑28, Aug 1999; BK, JKa, GI (w); BK, JKa, GI (a); Reprints The Haunt of Fear (EC) #28 .... 2.50
❑Annual 1; Reprints The Haunt of Fear #1-5 .... 8.95
❑Annual 2; Reprints The Haunt of Fear #6-10 .... 9.95
❑Annual 3; Reprints The Haunt of Fear #11-15 .... 10.95
❑Annual 4; Reprints The Haunt of Fear #16-20 .... 10.50
❑Annual 5; Reprints The Haunt of Fear #21-25 .... 11.95
❑Annual 6; JKa, GI (w); JKa, GI (a); Reprints The Haunt of Fear #26-28. 8.95

HAUNT OF HORROR
MARVEL

❑1, May 1974 .... 8.00
❑2, Jul 1974 .... 6.00
❑3, Sep 1974 .... 5.00
❑4, Nov 1974 .... 5.00
❑5, Jan 1975 .... 5.00

HAUNT OF HORROR: EDGAR ALLAN POE
MARVEL

❑1, Aug 2006 .... 2.99
❑2, Sep 2006 .... 2.99

HAVEN: THE BROKEN CITY
DC

❑1, Feb 2002 .... 2.50
❑2, Mar 2002 .... 2.50
❑3, Apr 2002 .... 2.50
❑4, May 2002 .... 2.50
❑5, Jun 2002 .... 2.50
❑6, Jul 2002 .... 2.50
❑7, Aug 2002 .... 2.50
❑8, Sep 2002 .... 2.50
❑9, Oct 2002 .... 2.50

HAVOC, INC.
RADIO

❑1, Mar 1998 .... 2.95
❑2, Jun 1998 .... 2.95
❑3, Sep 1998 .... 2.95
❑4, Dec 1998 .... 2.95
❑5 1999 .... 2.95
❑6 1999 .... 2.95
❑7 .... 2.95
❑8, Jul 2000 .... 2.95
❑9 .... 2.95

HAVOK & WOLVERINE: MELTDOWN
MARVEL / EPIC

❑1, Mar 1989 .... 4.00
❑2, ca. 1989 .... 4.00
❑3, ca. 1989 .... 4.00
❑4, Oct 1989 .... 4.00

HAWAIIAN DICK
IMAGE

❑1, Dec 2002 .... 2.95
❑2, Jan 2003 .... 2.95
❑3, Feb 2003 .... 2.95

HAWAIIAN DICK: THE LAST RESORT
IMAGE

❑1, Aug 2004 .... 2.95
❑2, Dec 2004 .... 2.95

HAWK & THE DOVE (1ST SERIES)
DC

❑1, Aug 1968, SD (a) 60.00
❑2, Oct 1968, DG (w); SD (a) 40.00
❑3, Dec 1968, DG (w); GK (a) 40.00
❑4, Feb 1969, DG (w); GK (a) 40.00
❑5, Mar 1969, DG (w); GK (a); A: Teen Titans 40.00
❑6, Jun 1969, DG, GK (w); GK (a) 30.00

HAWK AND DOVE (2ND SERIES)
DC

❑1, Oct 1988 RL (a); 1: Dove II. 3.00
❑2, Nov 1988 RL (a) 2.50
❑3, Dec 1988 RL (a) 2.00
❑4, Win 1988 RL (a) 2.00
❑5, Hol 1989; RL (a); O: Dove. Hol 1989 2.00

HAWK AND DOVE (3RD SERIES)
DC

❑1, Jun 1989 .... 1.50
❑2, Jul 1989 .... 1.00
❑3, Aug 1989 .... 1.00
❑4, Sep 1989 .... 1.00
❑5, Oct 1989 .... 1.00
❑6, Nov 1989 .... 1.00
❑7, Dec 1989 .... 1.00
❑8, Jan 1990 .... 1.00
❑9, Feb 1990 .... 1.00
❑10, Mar 1990 .... 1.00
❑11, Apr 1990 .... 1.00
❑12, May 1990 A: New Titans. 1.00
❑13, Jun 1990 .... 1.00
❑14, Jul 1990 .... 1.00
❑15, Aug 1990 .... 1.00
❑16, Sep 1990 .... 1.00
❑17, Oct 1990 .... 1.00
❑18, Nov 1990 .... 1.00
❑19, Dec 1990 .... 1.00
❑20, Jan 1991 .... 1.00
❑21, Feb 1991 .... 1.00
❑22, Mar 1991 .... 1.00
❑23, Apr 1991 .... 1.00
❑24, May 1991 .... 1.00
❑25, Jun 1991; Giant-size 2.00
❑26, Aug 1992 O: Hawk and Dove. 1.25
❑27, Sep 1991 .... 1.25
❑28, Oct 1991; Giant-size; War of the Gods 2.00
❑Annual 1, Oct 1990; Titans West 3.00
❑Annual 2, Sep 1991; Armageddon 2001 .... 2.00

HAWK AND DOVE (4TH SERIES)
DC

❑1, Nov 1997 .... 2.50
❑2, Dec 1997 .... 2.50
❑3, Jan 1998 .... 2.50
❑4, Feb 1998 .... 2.50
❑5, Mar 1998 .... 2.50

HAWK & WINDBLADE
WARP

❑1, Aug 1997 .... 2.95
❑2, Sep 1997 .... 2.95

HAWKEYE (1ST SERIES)
MARVEL

❑1, Sep 1983, O: Hawkeye. 2.50
❑2, Oct 1983 .... 2.00
❑3, Nov 1983, 1: Oddball. 2.00
❑4, Dec 1983 .... 2.00

HAWKEYE (2ND SERIES)
MARVEL

❑1, Jan 1994 .... 1.75
❑2, Feb 1994 .... 1.75
❑3, Mar 1994 .... 1.75
❑4, Apr 1994 .... 1.75

HAWKEYE (3RD SERIES)
MARVEL

❑1, Dec 2003 .... 2.99
❑2, Jan 2004 .... 2.99
❑3, Feb 2004 .... 2.99
❑4, Mar 2004 .... 2.99
❑5, Apr 2004 .... 2.99
❑6, May 2004 .... 2.99
❑7, Jun 2004 .... 2.99
❑8, Aug 2004 .... 2.99

HAWKEYE: EARTH'S MIGHTIEST MARKSMAN
MARVEL

❑1, Oct 1998 .... 2.99

HAWKGIRL
DC

❑50, Jun 2006, Hawkman (4th series) 2.99
❑51, Jul 2006 .... 2.99
❑52, Aug 2006 .... 2.99
❑53, Sep 2006 .... 2.99

HAWKMAN (1ST SERIES)
DC

❑1, May 1964, MA (a) 475.00
❑2, Jul 1964, MA (a) 200.00
❑3, Sep 1964, MA (a) 75.00
❑4, Nov 1964, MA (a); O: Zatanna. 1: Zatanna. 200.00
❑5, Jan 1965, MA (a) 65.00
❑6, Mar 1965, MA (a) 65.00
❑7, May 1965, MA (a); reprint from Mystery in Space #87 .... 65.00
❑8, Jul 1965, MA (a) 65.00
❑9, Sep 1965, MA (a); A: Atom. Atom & Hawkman learn identities 65.00
❑10, Nov 1965, MA (a) 50.00
❑11, Jan 1966, MA (a) 50.00
❑12, Mar 1966, MA (a) 50.00
❑13, May 1966, MA (a) 40.00
❑14, Jul 1966, MA (a) 40.00
❑15, Sep 1966, MA (a) 40.00
❑16, Nov 1966, MA (a) 36.00
❑17, Jan 1967, MA (a) 36.00
❑18, Mar 1967, MA (a); A: Adam Strange. V: Manhawks. Part 1 .... 36.00
❑19, May 1967, MA (a); Part 2 .... 36.00
❑20, Jul 1967, MA (a) 32.00
❑21, Sep 1967, MA (a) 32.00
❑22, Nov 1967, DD (a) 32.00
❑23, Jan 1968, DD (a) 32.00
❑24, Mar 1968, DD (a); Reprint story. 32.00
❑25, May 1968, DD (a); Golden Age Hawkman reprint 32.00
❑26, Jul 1968, DD (a); reprints 2-page Kirby story 32.00
❑27, Sep 1968, DD (a) 32.00

HAWKMAN (2ND SERIES)
DC

❑1, Aug 1986 RHo (a) 2.50
❑2, Sep 1986 RHo (a); V: Shadow Thief. 2.00
❑3, Oct 1986 RHo (a); V: Shadow Thief. 2.00
❑4, Nov 1986 RHo (a); A: Zatanna. 1.50
❑5, Dec 1986 RHo (a); V: Lionmane... 1.50
❑6, Jan 1987 RHo (a); V: Lionmane. .. 1.50
❑7, Feb 1987 V: Darkwing. 1.50
❑8, Mar 1987 V: Darkwing. 1.50
❑9, Apr 1987 .... 1.50
❑10, May 1987 A: Superman. 1.50
❑11, Jun 1987 .... 1.50
❑12, Jul 1987 .... 1.50
❑13, Aug 1987 .... 1.50
❑14, Sep 1987 .... 1.50
❑15, Oct 1987 .... 1.50
❑16, Nov 1987 .... 1.50
❑17, Dec 1987 .... 1.50
❑Special 1, Mar 1986 RHo (w); RHo (a) 3.00

HAWKMAN (3RD SERIES)
DC

❑0, Oct 1994 O: Hawkman (new). 2.50
❑1, Sep 1993; JDu (a); foil cover 2.50
❑2, Oct 1993 JDu (a) 1.75
❑3, Nov 1993 JDu (a) 1.75
❑4, Dec 1993 JDu (a) 1.75
❑5, Jan 1994 .... 1.75
❑6, Feb 1994 .... 1.75
❑7, Mar 1994 LMc (a) 1.75
❑8, Apr 1994 LMc (a) 1.75
❑9, May 1994 .... 1.75
❑10, Jun 1994 .... 1.75
❑11, Jul 1994 A: Carter Hall. 1.75
❑12, Aug 1994 .... 1.95
❑13, Sep 1994; Zero Hour 1.95
❑14, Nov 1994 .... 1.95
❑15, Dec 1994 A: Aquaman. 1.95
❑16, Jan 1995 A: Wonder Woman 1.95

Hawkeye (1st Series)

Marvel's archer gets starring role, finally

©Marvel

Hawkman (1st Series)

Flier from The Brave and The Bold breaks out

©DC

Hawkworld (Mini-Series)

Mini-series remakes legend of Hawkman

©DC

Haywire

Stranger steals special super-suit

©DC

Heart Throbs

DC romance title inherited from Quality Comics

©DC

	N-MINT
❑17, Feb 1995	1.95
❑18, May 1995	1.95
❑19, Apr 1995	1.95
❑20, May 1995	1.95
❑21, Jun 1995 V: Shadow Thief. V: Gentleman Ghost.	2.25
❑22, Jul 1995	2.25
❑23, Aug 1995	2.25
❑24, Sep 1995	2.25
❑25, Oct 1995	2.25
❑26, Nov 1995; A: Scarecrow. Underworld Unleashed	2.25
❑27, Dec 1995; A: Neuron. A: Silent Knight. Underworld Unleashed	2.25
❑28, Jan 1996 V: Dr. Polaris. V: Doctor Polaris.	2.25
❑29, Feb 1996 A: Vandal Savage.	2.25
❑30, Mar 1996	2.25
❑31, Apr 1996	2.25
❑32, Jun 1996	2.25
❑33, Jul 1996 A: Arion. D: Hawkman.	2.25
❑Annual 1, ca. 1993 JDu (a); 1: Mongrel.	3.50
❑Annual 2, ca. 1995; BG (a); Year One	3.95

HAWKMAN (4TH SERIES)
DC

❑1, May 2002	3.00
❑2, Jun 2002	2.50
❑3, Jul 2002	2.50
❑4, Aug 2002	2.50
❑5, Sep 2002	2.50
❑6, Oct 2002 JRo (w)	2.50
❑7, Nov 2002 JRo (w)	2.50
❑8, Dec 2002	2.50
❑9, Jan 2003	2.50
❑10, Feb 2003	2.50
❑11, Mar 2003	2.50
❑12, Apr 2003	2.50
❑13, May 2003	2.50
❑14, Jun 2003	2.50
❑15, Jul 2003	2.50
❑16, Aug 2003	2.50
❑17, Sep 2003	2.50
❑18, Oct 2003	2.50
❑19, Nov 2003	2.50
❑20, Dec 2003	2.50
❑21, Jan 2004	2.50
❑22, Jan 2004	2.50
❑23, Feb 2004	2.50
❑24, Mar 2004	2.50
❑25, Apr 2004	2.50
❑26, May 2004	2.50
❑27, Jun 2004	2.50
❑28, Jul 2004	2.50
❑29, Aug 2004	2.50
❑30, Sep 2004	2.50
❑31, Oct 2004	2.50
❑32, Nov 2004	2.50
❑33, Dec 2004	2.50
❑34, Jan 2005	2.50
❑35, Feb 2005	2.50
❑36, Mar 2005	2.50
❑37, Apr 2005	2.50
❑38, May 2005	2.50
❑39, Jun 2005	2.50
❑40, Jul 2005	2.50
❑41, Aug 2005	5.00
❑42, Sep 2005	4.00
❑43, Oct 2005	2.50
❑44, Sep 2005	2.50
❑45	2.50
❑46, Jan 2006	2.50
❑47, Feb 2006	2.50
❑48, Mar 2006	2.50
❑49, Apr 2006, becomes Hawkgirl.	2.50

HAWKMAN SECRET FILES AND ORIGINS
DC

❑1, Oct 2002, b&w	4.95

HAWKMOON: THE JEWEL IN THE SKULL
FIRST

❑1, May 1986	1.75
❑2, Jul 1986	1.75
❑3, Sep 1986	1.75
❑4, Nov 1986	1.75

HAWKMOON: THE MAD GOD'S AMULET
FIRST

❑1, Jan 1987	1.75
❑2, Feb 1987	1.75
❑3, Mar 1987	1.75
❑4, Apr 1987	1.75

HAWKMOON: THE RUNESTAFF
FIRST

❑1, ca. 1988	2.00
❑2, ca. 1988	2.00
❑3, ca. 1988	2.00
❑4, ca. 1988	2.00

HAWKMOON: THE SWORD OF THE DAWN
FIRST

❑1, Sep 1987	1.75
❑2, Nov 1987	1.75
❑3, Jan 1988	1.75
❑4, Mar 1988	1.75

HAWKSHAWS
IMAGE

❑1, Mar 2000, b&w	2.95

HAWK, STREET AVENGER
TAURUS

❑1, Jun 1996, b&w	2.50

HAWKWORLD (MINI-SERIES)
DC

❑1, Aug 1989; O: Hawkman. New costume	4.00
❑2, Sep 1989	4.00
❑3, Oct 1989	4.00

HAWKWORLD
DC

❑1, Jun 1990	2.50
❑2, Jul 1990	2.00
❑3, Aug 1990	2.00
❑4, Sep 1990	2.00
❑5, Oct 1990	2.00
❑6, Dec 1990	2.00
❑7, Jan 1991	2.00
❑8, Feb 1991	2.00
❑9, Mar 1991	2.00
❑10, Apr 1991	2.00
❑11, May 1991	1.50
❑12, Jun 1991	1.50
❑13, Jul 1991	1.50
❑14, Aug 1991	1.50
❑15, Sep 1991; War of the Gods	1.50
❑16, Oct 1991; War of the Gods	1.50
❑17, Nov 1991	1.50
❑18, Dec 1991	1.50
❑19, Jan 1992	1.50
❑20, Feb 1992	1.50
❑21, Mar 1992	1.50
❑22, Apr 1992	1.50
❑23, May 1992	1.50
❑24, Jul 1992	1.50
❑25, Aug 1992	1.50
❑26, Sep 1992	1.50
❑27, Oct 1992 1: The White Dragon.	1.75
❑28, Nov 1992 JDu (a)	1.75
❑29, Dec 1992	1.75
❑30, Jan 1993 1: Count Viper. 1: The Netherworld.	1.75
❑31, Feb 1993	1.75
❑32, Mar 1993	1.75
❑Annual 1, Dec 1990 A: Flash	3.00
❑Annual 2, Aug 1991	2.95
❑Annual 2/2nd, Aug 1991; silver	2.95
❑Annual 3, ca. 1992; LMc (a); Eclipso	2.95

HAYWIRE
DC

❑1, Oct 1988	1.25
❑2, Nov 1988	1.25
❑3, Dec 1988	1.25
❑4, Dec 1988	1.25
❑5, Jan 1989	1.25
❑6, Jan 1989	1.25
❑7, Mar 1989	1.25
❑8, Apr 1989	1.25
❑9, May 1989	1.25
❑10, Jun 1989	1.25
❑11, Jul 1989	1.25
❑12, Aug 1989	1.25
❑13, Sep 1989	1.25

HAZARD
IMAGE

❑1, Jun 1996	1.75
❑2, Jul 1996, cover says Jun, indicia says Jul	1.75
❑3, Jul 1996	1.75
❑4, Aug 1996	1.75
❑5, Sep 1996	1.75
❑6, Oct 1996, cover says Sep, indicia says Oct	2.25
❑7, Nov 1996	2.25

HAZARD! (MOTION)
MOTION

❑1, b&w; Breakneck Blvd.	2.50

HAZARD! (RECKLESS VISION)
RECKLESS VISION

❑1, b&w; first Breakneck Blvd. Story..	2.50

N-MINT N-MINT N-MINT

H-BOMB
ANTARCTIC

❑1, Apr 1993, b&w 2.95

HEAD
FANTAGRAPHICS

❑1 2002 .... 7.00
❑2 .... 3.95
❑3 .... 3.95
❑4 .... 3.95
❑5 .... 3.95
❑6 .... 3.95
❑7 .... 3.95
❑8 .... 3.95
❑9 .... 3.95
❑10 .... 3.95
❑11, Aug 2005 .... 3.95
❑12 2005 .... 3.95
❑13, Dec 2005 .... 3.95

HEADBANGER
PARODY

❑1 .... 2.50

HEADBUSTER
ANTARCTIC

❑1, Sep 1998, b&w 2.95

HEADHUNTERS
IMAGE

❑1, Apr 1997, b&w; cover says Mar, indicia says Apr 2.95
❑2, May 1997, b&w 2.95
❑3, Jun 1997, b&w 2.95

HEADLESS HORSEMAN
ETERNITY

❑1, b&w 2.25
❑2, b&w 2.25

HEADMAN
INNOVATION

❑1 .... 2.50

HEALTH
DAVID TOMPKINS

❑1 .... 1.00
❑2 .... 1.50
❑3 .... 1.50
❑4 .... 2.00
❑5 .... 2.00
❑6 .... 5.00

HEAP
SKYWALD

❑1, Sep 1971 TS, JAb (a) 16.00

HEARTBREAK COMICS
ECLIPSE

❑1, b&w; magazine 3.95

HEARTBREAKERS
DARK HORSE

❑1, Apr 1996 .... 2.95
❑2, May 1996 .... 2.95
❑3, Jun 1996 .... 2.95
❑4, Jul 1996 .... 2.95

HEARTBREAKERS SUPERDIGEST: YEAR TEN
IMAGE

❑1, Dec 1999 .... 13.95

HEARTLAND
DC / VERTIGO

❑1, Mar 1997 .... 4.95

HEART OF DARKNESS
HARDLINE

❑1 .... 2.95

HEART OF EMPIRE
DARK HORSE

❑1, Apr 1999 .... 2.95
❑2, May 1999 .... 2.95
❑3, Jun 1999 .... 2.95
❑4, Jul 1999 .... 2.95
❑5, Aug 1999 .... 2.95
❑6, Sep 1999 .... 2.95
❑7, Oct 1999 .... 2.95
❑8, Nov 1999 .... 2.95
❑9, Dec 1999 .... 2.95

HEARTS OF DARKNESS
MARVEL

❑1, Dec 1991; Ghost Rider, Wolverine, and Punisher vs. Blackheart 4.95

HEART THROBS
DC

❑44 1956 .... 18.00
❑45 1957 .... 18.00
❑46 1957 .... 18.00
❑47, May 1957; DC begins as publisher 125.00
❑48, Jul 1957 .... 65.00
❑49, Sep 1957 .... 60.00
❑50, Nov 1957 .... 60.00
❑51, Jan 1958 .... 48.00
❑52, Mar 1958 .... 48.00
❑53, May 1958 .... 48.00
❑54, Jul 1958 .... 48.00
❑55, Sep 1958 .... 48.00
❑56, Nov 1958 .... 48.00
❑57, Jan 1959 .... 48.00
❑58, Feb 1959 .... 48.00
❑59, May 1959 .... 48.00
❑60, Jul 1959 .... 48.00
❑61, Sep 1959 .... 38.00
❑62, Nov 1959 .... 38.00
❑63, Jan 1960 .... 38.00
❑64, Mar 1960 .... 38.00
❑65, May 1960 .... 38.00
❑66, Jul 1960 .... 38.00
❑67, Sep 1960 .... 38.00
❑68, Nov 1960 .... 38.00
❑69, Jan 1961 .... 38.00
❑70, Mar 1961 .... 38.00
❑71, May 1961 .... 27.00
❑72, Jul 1961 .... 27.00
❑73, Sep 1961 .... 27.00
❑74, Nov 1961 .... 27.00
❑75, Jan 1962 .... 27.00
❑76, Mar 1962 .... 27.00
❑77, May 1962 .... 27.00
❑78, Jul 1962 .... 27.00
❑79, Sep 1962 .... 27.00
❑80, Nov 1962 .... 27.00
❑81, Jan 1963 .... 20.00
❑82, Mar 1963 .... 20.00
❑83, May 1963 .... 20.00
❑84, Jul 1963 .... 20.00
❑85, Sep 1963 .... 20.00
❑86, Nov 1963 .... 20.00
❑87, Jan 1964 .... 20.00
❑88, Mar 1964 .... 20.00
❑89, May 1964 .... 20.00
❑90, Jul 1964 .... 20.00
❑91, Sep 1964 .... 16.00
❑92, Nov 1964 .... 16.00
❑93, Jan 1965 .... 16.00
❑94, Mar 1965 .... 16.00
❑95, May 1965 .... 16.00
❑96, Jul 1965 .... 16.00
❑97, Sep 1965 .... 16.00
❑98, Nov 1965 .... 16.00
❑99, Jan 1966 .... 16.00
❑100, Mar 1966 .... 16.00
❑101, May 1966, A: The Beatles. Beauty column begins; Beatles mentioned on cover 60.00
❑102, Jul 1966 .... 13.00
❑103, Sep 1966, 3 Girls: Their Lives, Their Loves 13.00
❑104, Nov 1966 .... 13.00
❑105, Jan 1967, Mod fashion column debuts; 3 Girls: Their Lives, Their Loves 13.00
❑106, Mar 1967 .... 13.00
❑107, May 1967 .... 13.00
❑108, Jul 1967, 3 Girls: Their Lives, Their Loves 13.00
❑109, Sep 1967 .... 13.00
❑110, Nov 1967 .... 13.00
❑111, Jan 1968 .... 10.00
❑112, Mar 1968 .... 10.00
❑113, May 1968 .... 10.00
❑114, Jul 1968 .... 10.00
❑115, Sep 1968 .... 10.00
❑116, Nov 1968 .... 10.00
❑117, Jan 1969 .... 10.00
❑118, Mar 1969 .... 10.00
❑119, May 1969 .... 10.00
❑120, Jul 1969 .... 10.00
❑121, Sep 1969 .... 10.00
❑122, Nov 1969 .... 10.00
❑123, Jan 1970 .... 10.00
❑124, Mar 1970 .... 10.00
❑125, May 1970 .... 10.00
❑126, Jul 1970 .... 10.00
❑127, Sep 1970 .... 10.00
❑128, Nov 1970 .... 10.00
❑129, Jan 1971 .... 10.00
❑130, Mar 1971 .... 10.00
❑131, May 1971 .... 9.00
❑132, Jul 1971 .... 9.00
❑133, Sep 1971 .... 9.00
❑134, Oct 1971 .... 9.00
❑135, Nov 1971 .... 9.00
❑136, Dec 1971 .... 9.00
❑137, Jan 1972 .... 9.00
❑138, Feb 1972 .... 9.00
❑139, Mar 1972 .... 9.00
❑140, Apr 1972 .... 9.00
❑141, May 1972 .... 9.00
❑142, Jun 1972 .... 9.00
❑143, Jul 1972 .... 9.00
❑144, Aug 1972 .... 9.00
❑145, Sep 1972 .... 9.00
❑146, Oct 1972, Series continues as Love Stories 9.00

HEARTTHROBS (VERTIGO)
DC / VERTIGO

❑1, Jan 1999 .... 2.95
❑2, Feb 1999 .... 2.95
❑3, Mar 1999 .... 2.95
❑4, Apr 1999 .... 2.95

HEATHCLIFF
MARVEL / STAR

❑1, Apr 1985 .... 1.50
❑2, Jun 1985 .... 1.00
❑3, Aug 1985 .... 1.00
❑4, Oct 1985 .... 1.00
❑5, Dec 1985 .... 1.00
❑6, Feb 1986 .... 1.00
❑7, Apr 1986 .... 1.00
❑8, Jun 1986 .... 1.00
❑9, Aug 1986 .... 1.00
❑10, Sep 1986 .... 1.00
❑11, Oct 1986 .... 1.00
❑12, Nov 1986 .... 1.00
❑13, Dec 1986 .... 1.00
❑14, Feb 1987 .... 1.00
❑15, Apr 1987 .... 1.00
❑16, Jun 1987 .... 1.00
❑17, Aug 1987 .... 1.00
❑18, Sep 1987 .... 1.00
❑19, Oct 1987 .... 1.00
❑20, Nov 1987 .... 1.00
❑21, Dec 1987 .... 1.00
❑22, Feb 1988 .... 1.00
❑23, Apr 1988 .... 1.00
❑24, Jun 1988 .... 1.00
❑25, Aug 1988 .... 1.00
❑26, Sep 1988 .... 1.00
❑27, Oct 1988 .... 1.00
❑28, Nov 1988 .... 1.00
❑29, Dec 1988 .... 1.00
❑30, Feb 1989 .... 1.00
❑31, Mar 1989 .... 1.00
❑32, Apr 1989 .... 1.00
❑33, May 1989 .... 1.00
❑34, Jun 1989 .... 1.00
❑35, Jul 1989 .... 1.00
❑36, Aug 1989 .... 1.00
❑37, Sep 1989 .... 1.00
❑38, Oct 1989 .... 1.00
❑39, Nov 1989 .... 1.00
❑40, Nov 1989 .... 1.00
❑41, Dec 1989 .... 1.00
❑42, Dec 1989 .... 1.00
❑43, Jan 1990 .... 1.00
❑44, Feb 1990 .... 1.00
❑45, Mar 1990 .... 1.00
❑46, Apr 1990 .... 1.00
❑47, May 1990; Batman parody 1.00
❑48, Jun 1990 .... 1.00
❑49, Jul 1990 .... 1.00
❑50, Aug 1990; Giant-size; giant 1.50
❑51, Sep 1990 .... 1.00
❑52, Oct 1990 .... 1.00
❑53, Nov 1990 .... 1.00

Heathcliff

Comic-panel cat has longest-running Star title

©Marvel

Heckler

Villain from Hostess ad gets series

©DC

Hee Haw

"Doom, Despair, Agony, Oh Me..."

©Charlton

He is Just a Rat

Part of a wave of "rave-and-rant" comics

©Exclaim! Brand Comics

Hellblazer

The story of demon-foiler John Constantine

©DC

N-MINT

❑54, Dec 1990 — 1.00
❑55, Jan 1991 — 1.00
❑56, Feb 1991 — 1.00
❑Annual 1, ca. 1987 — 1.25

HEATHCLIFF'S FUNHOUSE
MARVEL / STAR

❑1, May 1987 — 1.25
❑2, Jun 1987 — 1.00
❑3, Jul 1987 — 1.00
❑4, Aug 1987 — 1.00
❑5, Sep 1987 — 1.00
❑6, Oct 1987 — 1.00
❑7, Nov 1987 — 1.00
❑8, Dec 1987 — 1.00
❑9, Jan 1988 — 1.00
❑10, Feb 1988 — 1.00

HEATSEEKER
FANTACO

❑1 — 5.95

HEAVEN ABOVE HEAVEN
TOKYOPOP

❑1, May 2005, b&w — 9.99
❑2, Aug 2005 — 9.99
❑3, Nov 2005 — 9.99

HEAVEN LLC
IMAGE

❑1, ca. 2004 — 12.95

HEAVEN'S DEVILS
IMAGE

❑1, Oct 2003 — 2.95
❑2, Nov 2003 — 3.50
❑3, Apr 2004 — 3.50
❑4, Sep 2004 — 3.50

HEAVEN SENT
ANTARCTIC

❑1, Jan 2004 — 2.99
❑2, Mar 2004 — 2.99
❑3, May 2004 — 2.99
❑4, Jul 2004 — 2.99
❑5, Sep 2004 — 2.99
❑6, Nov 2004 — 2.99

HEAVEN'S WAR
IMAGE

❑0, ca. 2003 — 12.95

HEAVY ARMOR
FANTASY GENERAL

❑1 — 1.70
❑2 — 1.70
❑3, b&w — 1.70

HEAVY HITTERS
MARVEL / EPIC

❑Annual 1 1993 — 3.75

HEAVY LIQUID
DC / VERTIGO

❑1, Oct 1999 — 5.95
❑2, Nov 1999 — 5.95
❑3, Dec 1999 — 5.95
❑4, Jan 2000 — 5.95
❑5, Feb 2000 — 5.95

N-MINT

HEAVY METAL MONSTERS
REVOLUTIONARY

❑1, Jan 1992, b&w — 3.00
❑2, ca. 1993; 3-D — 3.95

HECKLE AND JECKLE (GOLD KEY)
GOLD KEY

❑1, Nov 1962 — 36.00
❑2, Jan 1963 — 18.00
❑3, Dec 1962 — 16.00
❑4, Feb 1963 — 16.00

HECKLE AND JECKLE (DELL)
DELL

❑1, May 1966 — 25.00
❑2, Oct 1966 — 13.00
❑3, Aug 1967 — 13.00

HECKLER
DC

❑1, Sep 1992 — 1.25
❑2, Oct 1992; Generic issue — 1.25
❑3, Nov 1992 — 1.25
❑4, Dec 1992 — 1.25
❑5, Jan 1993 — 1.25
❑6, Feb 1993 — 1.25

HECTIC PLANET
SLAVE LABOR

❑6, Nov 1993, previously titled Pirate Corp$! — 2.50
❑6/2nd, Jan 1996 — 2.75

HECTOR PLASM
IMAGE

❑1, Jul 2006 — 2.99

HECTOR HEATHCOTE
GOLD KEY

❑1, Mar 1964, Based on Terrytoons cartoon series — 30.00

HEDGE KNIGHT
IMAGE

❑1, Aug 2003 — 2.95
❑2, Sep 2003 — 2.95
❑2/A, Sep 2003; Vallejo cover — 5.95
❑3, Feb 2004 — 2.95

HEE HAW
CHARLTON

❑1, Aug 1970 — 13.00
❑2, Oct 1970 — 8.00
❑3, Dec 1970 — 6.00
❑4, Feb 1971 — 6.00
❑5, Apr 1971 — 6.00
❑6, Jun 1971 — 6.00
❑7, Aug 1971 — 6.00

HEIRS OF ETERNITY
IMAGE

❑1, Apr 2003 — 2.95
❑2, Jun 2003 — 2.95
❑3, Jul 2003 — 2.95
❑4, Aug 2003 — 2.95
❑5, Sep 2003 — 2.95

HE IS JUST A RAT
EXCLAIM! BRAND COMICS

❑1, Spr 1995 — 2.75
❑2, Fal 1995 — 2.75
❑3, Spr 1996 — 2.75

N-MINT

❑4, Fal 1996 — 2.75
❑5, Spr 1997 — 2.75

HELL
DARK HORSE

❑1, Jul 2003 — 2.99
❑2, Sep 2003 — 2.99
❑3, Oct 2003 — 2.99
❑4, Mar 2004 — 2.99

HELLBENDER
ETERNITY

❑1, b&w; Shuriken — 2.25

HELLBLAZER
DC

❑1, Jan 1988 — 10.00
❑2, Feb 1988 — 5.00
❑3, Mar 1988 — 4.00
❑4, Apr 1988 — 4.00
❑5, May 1988 — 4.00
❑6, Jun 1988 — 4.00
❑7, Jul 1988 — 4.00
❑8, Aug 1988 AA (a) — 4.00
❑9, Sep 1988; AA (a); A: Swamp Thing. Continues in Swamp Thing #76 — 4.00
❑10, Oct 1988; A: Swamp Thing, Abby. Continues from Swamp Thing #76 — 4.00
❑11, Nov 1988 — 3.50
❑12, Dec 1988 — 3.50
❑13, Dec 1988; References to British comics — 3.50
❑14, Jan 1989 — 3.00
❑15, Jan 1989 — 3.00
❑16, Feb 1989 — 3.00
❑17, Apr 1989 — 3.00
❑18, May 1989 AA (a) — 3.00
❑19, Jun 1989 AA (a) — 3.00
❑20, Jul 1989 AA (a) — 3.00
❑21, Aug 1989 AA (a) — 2.50
❑22, Sep 1989 AA (a) — 2.50
❑23, Oct 1989 A: Sherlock Holmes — 2.50
❑24, Nov 1989 — 2.50
❑25, Jan 1990 — 2.50
❑26, Feb 1990 — 2.50
❑27, Mar 1990 NG (w) — 9.00
❑28, Apr 1990 D: Thomas Constantine — 3.00
❑29, May 1990 — 3.00
❑30, Jun 1990 — 3.00
❑31, Jul 1990 — 3.00
❑32, Aug 1990 — 3.00
❑33, Sep 1990 — 3.00
❑34, Oct 1990 — 3.00
❑35, Nov 1990 — 3.00
❑36, Dec 1990 — 3.00
❑37, Jan 1991 — 3.00
❑38, Feb 1991 — 3.00
❑39, Mar 1991 — 3.00
❑40, Apr 1991 — 3.50
❑41, May 1991; 1st Garth Ennis story — 6.00
❑42, Jun 1991 — 4.00
❑43, Jul 1991 — 4.00
❑44, Aug 1991 — 4.00
❑45, Sep 1991 — 4.00
❑46, Oct 1991 — 4.00
❑47, Nov 1991 — 3.00
❑48, Dec 1991 — 3.00

N-MINT

❑49, Jan 1992 ... 3.00
❑50, Feb 1992; Giant-size ... 4.00
❑51, Mar 1992 ... 3.00
❑52, Apr 1992 ... 3.00
❑53, May 1992 ... 3.00
❑54, Jun 1992 ... 3.00
❑55, Jul 1992 ... 3.00
❑56, Aug 1992 ... 3.00
❑57, Sep 1992 ... 3.00
❑58, Oct 1992 ... 3.00
❑59, Nov 1992 ... 3.00
❑60, Dec 1992 ... 3.00
❑61, Jan 1993 ... 3.00
❑62, Feb 1993; Death Talks About Life AIDS-awareness insert ... 3.00
❑63, Mar 1993 ... 3.00
❑64, Apr 1993 ... 3.00
❑65, May 1993 ... 3.00
❑66, Jun 1993 ... 3.00
❑67, Jul 1993 ... 3.00
❑68, Aug 1993 ... 3.00
❑69, Sep 1993 ... 3.00
❑70, Oct 1993 ... 3.00
❑71, Nov 1993 ... 3.00
❑72, Dec 1993 ... 3.00
❑73, Jan 1994 ... 3.00
❑74, Feb 1994 ... 3.00
❑75, Mar 1994; Double-size ... 3.50
❑76, Apr 1994 ... 3.00
❑77, May 1994 ... 3.00
❑78, Jun 1994 ... 3.00
❑79, Jul 1994 ... 3.00
❑80, Aug 1994 ... 3.00
❑81, Sep 1994 ... 3.00
❑82, Oct 1994 ... 3.00
❑83, Nov 1994 ... 3.00
❑84, Dec 1994 ... 3.00
❑85, Jan 1995 ... 3.00
❑86, Feb 1995 ... 3.00
❑87, Mar 1995 ... 3.00
❑88, Apr 1995 ... 3.00
❑89, May 1995 ... 3.00
❑90, Jun 1995 ... 3.00
❑91, Jul 1995 ... 3.00
❑92, Aug 1995 ... 3.00
❑93, Sep 1995 ... 3.00
❑94, Oct 1995 ... 3.00
❑95, Nov 1995 ... 3.00
❑96, Dec 1995 ... 3.00
❑97, Jan 1996 ... 3.00
❑98, Feb 1996 ... 3.00
❑99, Mar 1996 ... 3.00
❑100, Apr 1996 ... 3.00
❑101, May 1996 ... 2.50
❑102, Jun 1996 ... 2.50
❑103, Jul 1996 ... 2.50
❑104, Aug 1996 ... 2.50
❑105, Sep 1996 ... 2.50
❑106, Oct 1996 ... 2.50
❑107, Nov 1996 ... 2.50
❑108, Dec 1996 ... 2.50
❑109, Jan 1997 ... 2.50
❑110, Feb 1997 ... 2.50
❑111, Mar 1997 ... 2.50
❑112, Apr 1997 ... 2.50
❑113, May 1997 ... 2.50
❑114, Jun 1997 ... 2.50
❑115, Jul 1997 ... 2.50
❑116, Aug 1997 ... 2.50
❑117, Sep 1997 ... 2.50
❑118, Oct 1997 ... 2.50
❑119, Nov 1997 ... 2.50
❑120, Dec 1997; Giant-size A: Alan Moore. ... 2.50
❑121, Jan 1998 ... 2.50
❑122, Feb 1998 ... 2.50
❑123, Mar 1998 ... 2.50
❑124, Apr 1998 ... 2.50
❑125, May 1998 ... 2.50
❑126, Jun 1998 ... 2.50
❑127, Jul 1998 ... 2.50
❑128, Aug 1998 ... 2.50
❑129, Sep 1998 ... 2.50
❑130, Oct 1998 ... 2.50
❑131, Nov 1998 ... 2.50
❑132, Dec 1998 ... 2.50
❑133, Jan 1999 ... 2.50
❑134, Feb 1999 ... 2.50
❑135, Mar 1999 ... 2.50
❑136, Apr 1999 ... 2.50
❑137, May 1999 ... 2.50
❑138, Jun 1999 ... 2.50
❑139, Jul 1999 ... 2.50
❑140, Aug 1999 ... 2.50
❑141, Oct 1999 ... 2.50
❑142, Nov 1999 ... 2.50
❑143, Dec 1999 ... 2.50
❑144, Jan 2000 ... 2.50
❑145, Feb 2000 ... 2.50
❑146, Mar 2000 ... 2.50
❑147, Apr 2000 ... 2.50
❑148, May 2000 ... 2.50
❑149, Jun 2000 ... 2.50
❑150, Jul 2000 ... 2.50
❑151, Aug 2000 ... 2.50
❑152, Sep 2000 ... 2.50
❑153, Oct 2000 ... 2.50
❑154, Nov 2000 ... 2.50
❑155, Dec 2000 ... 2.50
❑156, Jan 2001 ... 2.50
❑157, Feb 2001 ... 2.50
❑158, Mar 2001 ... 2.50
❑159, Apr 2001 ... 2.50
❑160, May 2001 ... 2.50
❑161, Jun 2001 ... 2.50
❑162, Jul 2001 ... 2.50
❑163, Aug 2001 ... 2.50
❑164, Sep 2001 ... 2.50
❑165, Oct 2001 ... 2.50
❑166, Nov 2001 ... 2.50
❑167, Dec 2001 ... 2.50
❑168, Jan 2002 ... 2.50
❑169, Feb 2002 ... 2.50
❑170, Mar 2002 ... 2.50
❑171, Apr 2002 ... 2.50
❑172, May 2002 ... 2.50
❑173, Jun 2002 ... 2.50
❑174, Aug 2002 ... 2.50
❑175, Sep 2002 ... 2.50
❑176, Oct 2002 ... 2.75
❑177, Dec 2002 ... 2.75
❑178, Jan 2003 ... 2.75
❑179, Feb 2003 ... 2.75
❑180, Mar 2003 ... 2.75
❑181, Apr 2003 ... 2.75
❑182, May 2003 ... 2.75
❑183, Jun 2003 ... 2.75
❑184, Jul 2003 ... 2.75
❑185, Aug 2003 ... 2.75
❑186, Sep 2003 ... 2.75
❑187, Oct 2003 ... 2.75
❑188, Nov 2003 ... 2.75
❑189, Dec 2003 ... 2.75
❑190, Jan 2004 ... 2.75
❑191, Feb 2004 ... 2.75
❑192, Mar 2004 ... 2.75
❑193, Apr 2004 ... 2.75
❑194, May 2004 ... 2.75
❑195, Jun 2004 ... 2.75
❑196, Jul 2004 ... 2.75
❑197, Aug 2004 ... 2.75
❑198, Sep 2004 ... 2.75
❑199, Oct 2004 ... 2.75
❑200, Nov 2004 ... 4.50
❑201, Dec 2004 ... 2.75
❑202, Jan 2005 ... 2.75
❑203, Feb 2005 ... 2.75
❑204, Mar 2005 ... 2.75
❑205, Apr 2005 ... 2.75
❑206, May 2005 ... 2.75
❑207, Jun 2005 ... 2.75
❑208, Jul 2005 ... 2.75
❑209, Aug 2005 ... 2.75
❑210, Sep 2005 ... 2.75
❑211, Oct 2005 ... 2.75
❑212, Nov 2005 ... 2.75
❑213, Dec 2005 ... 2.75
❑214, Jan 2006 ... 2.75
❑215, Feb 2006 ... 2.75
❑216, Mar 2006 ... 2.75
❑217, Apr 2006 ... 2.75
❑218, Jun 2006 ... 2.75
❑219, Jun 2006 ... 2.75
❑220, Aug 2006 ... 2.75
❑221, Sep 2006 ... 2.75
❑Annual 1, Oct 1989 BT (a) ... 6.00
❑Special 1, Jan 1993 ... 5.00

HELLBLAZER SPECIAL: BAD BLOOD
DC / VERTIGO

❑1, Sep 2000 ... 2.95
❑2, Oct 2000 ... 2.95
❑3, Nov 2000 ... 2.95
❑4, Dec 2000 ... 2.95

HELLBLAZER SPECIAL: LADY CONSTANTINE
DC / VERTIGO

❑1, Feb 2003 ... 2.95
❑2, Mar 2003 ... 2.95
❑3, Apr 2003 ... 2.95
❑4, May 2003 ... 2.95

HELLBLAZER/THE BOOKS OF MAGIC
DC / VERTIGO

❑1, Dec 1997 ... 3.50
❑2, Jan 1998 ... 3.50

HELLBOY: ALMOST COLOSSUS
DARK HORSE / LEGEND

❑1, Jun 1997 ... 2.95
❑2, Jul 1997 ... 2.95

HELLBOY: ART OF THE MOVIE
DARK HORSE

❑1, ca. 2004 ... 24.95

HELLBOY: BOX FULL OF EVIL
DARK HORSE / MAVERICK

❑1, Aug 1999 ... 2.95
❑2, Sep 1999 ... 2.95

HELLBOY CHRISTMAS SPECIAL
DARK HORSE

❑1, Dec 1997 ... 4.00

HELLBOY: CONQUEROR WORM
DARK HORSE / MAVERICK

❑1, May 2001 ... 2.99
❑2, Jun 2001 ... 2.99
❑3, Jul 2001 ... 2.99
❑4, Aug 2001 ... 2.99

HELLBOY, THE CORPSE AND THE IRON SHOES
DARK HORSE / LEGEND

❑1; collects the story serialized in the distributor catalog Advance Comics #75-82 ... 3.50

HELLBOY: MAKOMA
DARK HORSE

❑1, Jan 2006 ... 2.99
❑2, May 2006 ... 2.99

HELLBOY: SEED OF DESTRUCTION
DARK HORSE / LEGEND

❑1, Mar 1994 O: Hellboy. 1: Monkeyman & O'Brien (in back-up story). ... 6.00
❑2, Apr 1994 ... 4.00
❑3, May 1994 ... 4.00
❑4, Jun 1994 ... 4.00

HELLBOY: THE ISLAND
DARK HORSE

❑1, Aug 2005 ... 2.99
❑2, Sep 2005 ... 2.99

HELLBOY: THE THIRD WISH
DARK HORSE

❑1, Jul 2002 ... 2.90
❑2, Aug 2002 ... 2.90

HELLBOY: THE WOLVES OF SAINT AUGUST
DARK HORSE / LEGEND

❑1; prestige format; collects the story from Dark Horse Presents #88-91 .. 4.95

HELLBOY: WAKE THE DEVIL
DARK HORSE / LEGEND

❑1, Jun 1996; Silent as the Grave back-up ... 4.00
❑2, Jul 1996; Silent as the Grave back-up ... 3.50
❑3, Aug 1996; Silent as the Grave back-up ... 3.50
❑4, Sep 1996; Silent as the Grave back-up ... 3.50
❑5, Oct 1996; Silent as the Grave back-up ... 3.50

Other grades: Multiply price above by 5/6 for VF/NM • 2/3 for VERY FINE • 1/3 for FINE • 1/5 for VERY GOOD • 1/8 for GOOD

Hellboy: Seed of Destruction

Nazi-summoned demon turns investigator
©Dark Horse

Hellcat

Patsy Walker for the new millennium
©Marvel

Hellina/Cynder

From the late, unlamented "Bad Girl" era
©Lightning

Hellshock

Caught between Heaven and Hell
©Image

Hellstorm: Prince of Lies

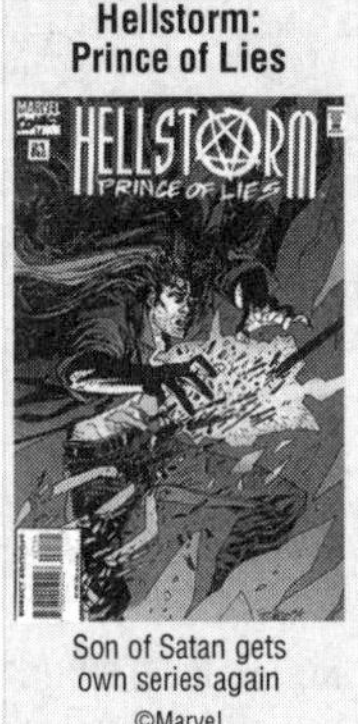

Son of Satan gets own series again
©Marvel

N-MINT

HELLBOY: WEIRD TALES
DARK HORSE

- ❑1, Feb 2003 ... 2.99
- ❑2, Apr 2003 ... 2.99
- ❑3, Jun 2003 ... 2.99
- ❑4, Aug 2003 ... 2.99
- ❑5, Oct 2003 ... 2.99
- ❑6, Dec 2003 ... 2.99
- ❑7, Feb 2004 ... 2.99
- ❑8, Apr 2004 ... 2.99

HELLBOY JR.
DARK HORSE

- ❑1, Oct 1999 ... 2.95
- ❑2, Nov 1999 ... 2.95

HELLBOY JR. HALLOWEEN SPECIAL
DARK HORSE

- ❑1, Oct 1997, Hellboy Jr. pinup; wraparound cover ... 3.95

HELL CAR COMIX
ALTERNATING CRIMES

- ❑1, Fal 1998 ... 2.95

HELLCAT
MARVEL

- ❑1, Sep 2000 ... 2.99
- ❑2 ... 2.99
- ❑3 ... 2.99

HELL CITY, HELL
DIABLO MUSICA

- ❑1; shrinkwrapped with CD-ROM ... 2.25

HELLCOP
IMAGE

- ❑1, Aug 1998; cover says Oct, indicia says Aug ... 2.50
- ❑1/A, Aug 1998; Alternate cover; Man kneeling with gun, woman, faces in background ... 2.50
- ❑2, Nov 1998 ... 2.50
- ❑2/A, Nov 1998; alternate cover ... 2.50
- ❑3, Jan 1999 ... 2.50
- ❑4, Mar 1999 ... 2.50

HELL ETERNAL
DC / VERTIGO

- ❑1; prestige format ... 6.95

HELLGIRL: DEMONSEED
KNIGHT

- ❑1, Mar 1995 ... 2.95

HELLHOLE
IMAGE

- ❑1, Jul 1999 ... 2.50
- ❑2, Oct 1999 ... 2.50
- ❑3, Dec 1999 ... 2.50

HELLHOUNDS
IMAGE

- ❑1, Aug 2003 ... 2.95
- ❑2, Sep 2003 ... 2.95
- ❑3, Oct 2003 ... 2.95
- ❑4, Feb 2004 ... 2.95

HELLHOUNDS: PANZER CORPS
DARK HORSE

- ❑1, b&w ... 2.50
- ❑2, b&w ... 2.50
- ❑3, Apr 1994, b&w ... 2.50

N-MINT

- ❑4, May 1994, b&w ... 2.50
- ❑5, Jun 1994, b&w ... 2.50
- ❑6, Jul 1994, b&w ... 2.50

HELLHOUND: THE REDEMPTION QUEST
MARVEL / EPIC

- ❑1, Dec 1993 ... 2.25
- ❑2, Jan 1994 ... 2.25
- ❑3, Feb 1994 ... 2.25
- ❑4, Mar 1994 ... 2.25

HELLINA
LIGHTNING

- ❑1, Sep 1994, b&w ... 2.75

HELLINA 1997 PIN-UP SPECIAL
LIGHTNING

- ❑1, Feb 1997; b&w pin-ups; cover version A ... 3.50

HELLINA/CATFIGHT
LIGHTNING

- ❑1, Oct 1995, b&w ... 3.00
- ❑1/A, Oct 1995; Olive metallic edition ... 3.00
- ❑1/2nd, Aug 1997, b&w; reprints Hellina, Catfight ... 2.95

HELLINA: CHRISTMAS IN HELL
LIGHTNING

- ❑1, Dec 1996, b&w ... 2.95
- ❑1/A, Dec 1996; nude cover A ... 4.00
- ❑1/B, Dec 1996; nude cover B ... 4.00

HELLINA/CYNDER
LIGHTNING

- ❑1, Sep 1997 ... 2.95

HELLINA/DOUBLE IMPACT
LIGHTNING

- ❑1, Feb 1996 ... 2.75
- ❑1/A, Feb 1996, crossover with High Impact ... 3.00
- ❑1/B, Feb 1996, alternate cover ... 3.00
- ❑1/Nude, Feb 1996, Nude edition with certificate of authenticity; polybagged nude cover ... 4.00
- ❑1/Platinum, Platinum edition ... 3.00

HELLINA: GENESIS
LIGHTNING

- ❑1, Apr 1996, b&w; bagged with Hellina poster ... 3.50

HELLINA: HEART OF THORNS
LIGHTNING

- ❑2, Sep 1996 ... 2.75
- ❑2/Nude, Sep 1996; nude cover edition; nude cover edition ... 4.00

HELLINA: HELLBORN
LIGHTNING

- ❑1, Dec 1997, b&w ... 2.95

HELLINA: HELL'S ANGEL
LIGHTNING

- ❑1, Nov 1996, b&w ... 2.75
- ❑2, Dec 1996, b&w ... 2.75

HELLINA: IN THE FLESH
LIGHTNING

- ❑1, Aug 1997, b&w ... 2.95

N-MINT

HELLINA: KISS OF DEATH
LIGHTNING

- ❑1, Jul 1995, b&w ... 2.75
- ❑1/Gold; Gold edition ... 3.00
- ❑1/Nude, Jul 1995, b&w; Nude edition ... 4.00
- ❑1/2nd, Mar 1997; Encore edition; alternate cover ... 2.95

HELLINA: NAKED DESIRE
LIGHTNING

- ❑1, May 1997 ... 2.95

HELLINA/NIRA X
LIGHTNING

- ❑1, Aug 1996; crossover with Entity ... 3.00

HELLINA: SKYBOLT TOYZ LIMITED EDITION
LIGHTNING

- ❑1/A, Aug 1997, b&w; reprints Hellina #1 ... 1.50
- ❑1/B, Aug 1997; alternate cover ... 1.50

HELLINA: TAKING BACK THE NIGHT
LIGHTNING

- ❑1 ... 4.50

HELLINA: WICKED WAYS
LIGHTNING

- ❑1/A, Nov 1995, b&w; alternate cover; polybagged ... 2.75
- ❑1/B, Nov 1995; polybagged ... 3.00
- ❑1/Nude, Nov 1995; polybagged; Cover C ... 9.95
- ❑1/Silver; silver edition ... 2.75

HELL MAGICIAN
FC9 PUBLISHING

- ❑1, Aug 2005 ... 2.95

HELL MICHIGAN
FC9 PUBLISHING

- ❑1, Aug 2005 ... 2.95
- ❑2, Sep 2005 ... 2.95
- ❑1/Ashcan, Aug 2005 ... 4.00

HELLRAISER (CLIVE BARKER'S)
MARVEL / EPIC

- ❑1, ca. 1989; prestige format ... 5.00
- ❑2; prestige format BSz (a) ... 5.00
- ❑3; prestige format ... 5.00
- ❑4; prestige format BSz (a) ... 5.00
- ❑5; prestige format ... 5.95
- ❑6; prestige format ... 5.95
- ❑7; prestige format TP (a) ... 5.95
- ❑8; prestige format ... 5.95
- ❑9; prestige format ... 5.95
- ❑10; prestige format MZ (a) ... 4.95
- ❑11; prestige format BG (a) ... 4.95
- ❑12; prestige format ... 4.95
- ❑13; prestige format ... 4.95
- ❑14; prestige format ... 4.95
- ❑15; prestige format ... 4.95
- ❑16 NG (w) ... 4.95
- ❑17, ca. 1992; ARo (a); 1st appearance of The Harrowers ... 4.95
- ❑18, ca. 1992 ARo (a) ... 4.95
- ❑19 ... 4.95
- ❑20, ca. 1993 NG (w) ... 4.95

Other grades: Multiply price above by 5/6 for VF/NM • 2/3 for VERY FINE • 1/3 for FINE • 1/5 for VERY GOOD • 1/8 for GOOD

❑Holiday 1; Nude edition with certificate of authenticity; Dark Holiday Special 4.95
❑Summer 1; Giant-size 5.95
❑Spring 1; Spring Special 6.95

HELLRAISER III: HELL ON EARTH
MARVEL / EPIC
❑1 .... 5.00

HELLRAISER NIGHTBREED: JIHAD
MARVEL / EPIC
❑1 .... 4.50
❑2 .... 4.50

HELLRAISER POSTERBOOK (CLIVE BARKER'S)
MARVEL / EPIC
❑1 .... 4.95

HELLRAISER: SPRING SLAUGHTER
MARVEL / EPIC
❑1 .... 6.95

HELLSAINT
BLACK DIAMOND
❑1, Mar 1998 .... 2.50

HELL'S ANGEL
MARVEL
❑1, Jul 1993 .... 1.75
❑2, Aug 1993 .... 1.75
❑3, Sep 1993 .... 1.75
❑4, Oct 1993 .... 1.75
❑5, Nov 1993; Series continued as Dark Angel #6 .... 1.75

HELLSHOCK (MINI-SERIES)
IMAGE
❑1, Jul 1994 .... 2.00
❑2, Aug 1994 .... 2.00
❑3, Oct 1994 O: Hellshock 2.00
❑4; Pin-up by Adam Kubert and Jae Lee 2.00
❑4/A, Nov 1994; variant cover 2.00
❑4/B, Nov 1994 BSz (c) 1.95
❑Ashcan 1; ashcan 1.00

HELLSHOCK
IMAGE
❑1, Jan 1997 .... 2.95
❑1/A, Jan 1997 .... 2.95
❑2, Feb 1997 .... 2.95
❑3, Mar 1997 .... 2.95
❑4, Never published? 2.95
❑5, Never published? 2.95
❑6, Never published? 2.95
❑7, Never published? 3.95

HELLSING
DARK HORSE
❑1, Dec 2003 .... 13.95
❑2, ca. 2004 .... 13.95
❑3, ca. 2004 .... 13.95

HELLSPAWN
IMAGE
❑1, Aug 2000 BMB (w) 3.00
❑2, Sep 2000 BMB (w) 2.50
❑3, Oct 2000 BMB (w) 2.50
❑4, Nov 2000 BMB (w) 2.50
❑5, Jan 2001 BMB (w) 2.50
❑6, Feb 2001 BMB (w) 2.50
❑7, Apr 2001 TMc (a) 2.50
❑8, May 2001 .... 2.50
❑9, Jun 2001 .... 2.50
❑10, Jul 2001 .... 2.50
❑11, Aug 2001 .... 2.50
❑12, Sep 2001 .... 2.50
❑13, May 2002 .... 2.50
❑14 2002 .... 2.50
❑15, Feb 2003 .... 2.50
❑16, Apr 2003 .... 2.50

HELLSPOCK
EXPRESS / PARODY
❑1, b&w 2.95

HELLSTALKER
REBEL CREATIONS
❑1 .... 2.25
❑2, Jul 1989 .... 2.25

HELLSTORM: PRINCE OF LIES
MARVEL
❑1, Apr 1993; parchment cover 2.95
❑2, May 1993 .... 2.00
❑3, Jun 1993 .... 2.00
❑4, Jul 1993 .... 2.00
❑5, Aug 1993 .... 2.00
❑6, Sep 1993 .... 2.00
❑7, Oct 1993; Book 1 .... 2.00
❑8, Nov 1993; Book 1 .... 2.00
❑9, Dec 1993; Book 1 .... 2.00
❑10, Jan 1994; Book 1 .... 2.00
❑11, Feb 1994 .... 2.00
❑12, Mar 1994 .... 2.00
❑13, Apr 1994 .... 2.00
❑14, May 1994 .... 2.00
❑15, Jun 1994 .... 2.00
❑16, Jul 1994 .... 2.00
❑17, Aug 1994 .... 2.00
❑18, Sep 1994 .... 2.00
❑19, Oct 1994 .... 2.00
❑20, Nov 1994 .... 2.00
❑21, Dec 1994 .... 2.00

HELM PREMIERE
HELM
❑1, Mar 1995, b&w; Preview edition .. 2.95

HELP
JEFF LEVINE
❑1 .... 2.00

HELP (VOL. 1)
WARREN
❑1, ca. 1964, HK (w) 45.00
❑2, ca. 1964, HK (w) 28.00
❑3, ca. 1964, HK (w) 20.00
❑4, ca. 1964, HK (w) 20.00
❑5, ca. 1964, HK (w) 20.00
❑6, ca. 1964, HK (w) 20.00
❑7, ca. 1964, HK (w) 20.00
❑8, ca. 1964, HK (w) 20.00
❑9, ca. 1964, HK (w) 20.00
❑10, ca. 1964, HK (w) 20.00
❑11, ca. 1964, HK (w) 20.00
❑12, HK (w) 20.00

HELP (VOL. 2)
WARREN
❑1 HK (w) 26.00
❑2 HK (w) 16.00
❑3 HK (w) 16.00

HELSING
CALIBER
❑1, b&w 2.95
❑1/A; cover has woman in black standing 2.95
❑2, b&w 2.95

HELTER SKELTER
ANTARCTIC
❑0, May 1997, b&w 2.95
❑1, Jun 1997, b&w 2.95
❑2, Sep 1997, b&w 2.95
❑3, Nov 1997, b&w 2.95
❑4, Dec 1997, b&w 2.95
❑6, Mar 1998 .... 2.95
❑5, Jan 1998, b&w 2.95

HELYUN: BONES OF THE BACKWOODS
SLAVE LABOR
❑1, Nov 1991, b&w 2.95

HELYUN BOOK 1
SLAVE LABOR
❑1, Aug 1990, b&w 6.95

HEMBECK
FANTACO
❑1; Best of Dateline: @!!?# 2.50
❑2, Feb 1980 FH (a) 2.50
❑3, Jun 1980 .... 1.50
❑4, Nov 1980 .... 1.50
❑5, Feb 1981 FH (a) 2.50
❑6, Sep 1981; Jimmy Olsen's Pal 2.25
❑7, Jan 1983; Dial H for Hembeck 1.95

HEMP FOR VICTORY
STARHEAD
❑1, Sep 1993, b&w; based on 1943 USDA film 2.50

HENRY V
CALIBER / TOME
❑1, b&w 2.95

HEPCATS
DOUBLE DIAMOND
❑1, May 1989 .... 5.00
❑2, Jul 1989 .... 4.00
❑3, Aug 1989 .... 3.00
❑4, Nov 1989 .... 3.00
❑5, Feb 1989 .... 3.00
❑6 .... 3.00
❑7 .... 3.00
❑8 .... 3.00
❑9 .... 3.00
❑10 .... 3.00
❑11, Jan 1994 .... 3.00
❑12, Jul 1994 .... 3.00
❑13 .... 3.00
❑14 .... 2.50
❑Special 1; Reprints 4.00
❑Special 2; Reprints 4.00

HEPCATS (ANTARCTIC)
ANTARCTIC
❑0, Nov 1996 .... 4.00
❑0/A; Comics Cavalcade Commemorative Edition 5.95
❑0/Deluxe, Nov 1996; Radio Hepcats edition; polybagged with compact disc 9.95
❑1, Dec 1996 .... 3.50
❑2, Jan 1997 .... 3.50
❑3, Feb 1997 .... 3.00
❑4, Mar 1997 .... 3.00
❑5, Apr 1997 .... 3.00
❑6, Jan 1998 .... 2.95
❑7, Mar 1998 .... 2.95
❑8 .... 2.95
❑9, Apr 1998 .... 2.95
❑10, May 1998 .... 2.95
❑11, May 1998 .... 2.95
❑12, Jun 1998 .... 2.95

HERBIE (DARK HORSE)
DARK HORSE
❑1, Oct 1992; Reprints 2.50
❑2, Nov 1992; Reprints 2.50

HERBIE (A+)
A-PLUS
❑1, Reprints (including part of Herbie #8) 2.50
❑2, Reprints 2.50
❑3, Reprints 2.50
❑4, Reprints 2.50
❑5, Reprints 2.50
❑6, Reprints 2.50

HERBIE (ACG)
ACG
❑1, Apr 1964, A: Castro. A: Lyndon Johnson. A: Sonny Liston. A: Khrushchev 95.00
❑2, Jun 1964, A: Marie Antoinette 60.00
❑3, Aug 1964, A: Churchill 48.00
❑4, Sep 1964, A: Doc Holliday. A: Clantons 48.00
❑5, Oct 1964, A: Frank Sinatra. A: Beatles. A: Dean Martin 48.00
❑6, Dec 1964, A: Gregory Peck. A: Ava Gardner 40.00
❑7, Feb 1965, A: Harry Truman. A: Mao. A: Khruschcev 40.00
❑8, Mar 1965, O: Fat Fury. A: George Washington. A: Barry Goldwater. A: Lyndon Johnson 50.00
❑9, Apr 1965 .... 38.00
❑10, Jun 1965 .... 38.00
❑11, Aug 1965, A: Adlai Stevenson. A: Queen Isabella. A: Columbus. A: Lyndon Johnson 30.00
❑12, Sep 1965, Fat Fury story 30.00
❑13, Oct 1965 .... 30.00
❑14, Dec 1965, A: Magicman. A: Fat Fury. A: Nemesis 30.00
❑15, Feb 1966, A: Josephine. A: Napoleon 30.00
❑16, Mar 1966, A: Mao Tse Tung. A: Fat Fury 30.00
❑17, Apr 1966 .... 30.00
❑18, Jun 1966 .... 30.00
❑19, Aug 1966 A: Cleopatra 30.00
❑20, Sep 1966, Fat Fury vs. Dracula 30.00
❑21, Oct 1966 .... 30.00

Hepcats

Relationship story abandoned by creator
©Double Diamond

Herbie (ACG)

"You want I should bop you with this lollipop?"
©ACG

Hercules (Vol. 1)

Layton's funny take on Hercules in space
©Marvel

Hercules Unbound

DC awakens Hercules after World War III
©DC

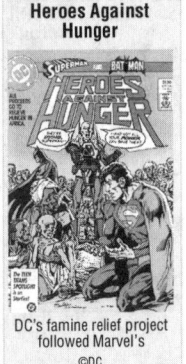

Heroes Against Hunger

DC's famine relief project followed Marvel's
©DC

N-MINT

❑22, Dec 1966, A: Charles de Gaulle. A: Queen Elizabeth. A: Ben Franklin. Fat Fury learns magic 30.00
❑23, Feb 1967 ..... 30.00

HERCULES (CHARLTON)
CHARLTON

❑1, Oct 1967, Thane of Bagarth by Steve Skeates and Jim Aparo; sell-through 46.6%, according to Charlton files 14.00
❑2, Dec 1967, Thane of Bagarth by Steve Skeates and Jim Aparo; sell-through 40.3%, according to Charlton files 9.00
❑3, Feb 1968, Sell-through 36.1%, according to Charlton files 6.00
❑4, Jun 1968, Sell-through 37.6%, according to Charlton files 6.00
❑5, Jul 1968, Sell-through 33.5%, according to Charlton files 6.00
❑6, Sep 1968, Sell-through 35.5%, according to Charlton files 5.00
❑7, Nov 1968 ..... 5.00
❑8, Dec 1968, JA (a); Thane of Bagarth by Steve Skeates and Jim Aparo; sell-through 47%, according to Charlton files 5.00
❑8/A, Dec 1968, Magazine-sized issue; Low distribution 10.00
❑9, Feb 1969, Sell-through 31.4%, according to Charlton files 5.00
❑10, Apr 1967, Sell-through 36.0%, according to Charlton files 5.00
❑11 1967, Sell-through 32.9%, according to Charlton files 5.00
❑12, Jul 1967, Sell-through 28%, according to Charlton files 5.00
❑13, Oct 1967 ..... 5.00

HERCULES (VOL. 1)
MARVEL

❑1, Sep 1982, BL (w); BL (a) 1.50
❑2, Oct 1982, BL (w); BL, LMc (a) 1.50
❑3, Nov 1982, BL (a) 1.50
❑4, Dec 1982, BL (w); BL (a) 1.50

HERCULES (VOL. 2)
MARVEL

❑1, Mar 1984, BL (w); BL (a) 1.50
❑2, Apr 1984, BL (w); BL (a) 1.25
❑3, May 1984, BL (w); BL (a) 1.25
❑4, Jun 1984, BL (w); BL (a) 1.25

HERCULES (VOL. 3)
MARVEL

❑1, Jun 2005 ..... 2.99
❑2, Jul 2005 ..... 2.99
❑3, Aug 2005 ..... 2.99
❑4, Sep 2005 ..... 2.99
❑5, Oct 2005 ..... 2.99

HERCULES (AVALON)
AVALON

❑1, Oct 2002, b&w; Reprints from Charlton series 5.95
❑2, Dec 2002; Reprints from Charlton series 5.95

HERCULES: HEART OF CHAOS
MARVEL

❑1, Aug 1997; gatefold summary 2.50
❑2, Sep 1997; gatefold summary 2.50
❑3, Oct 1997; gatefold summary 2.50

HERCULES: OFFICIAL COMICS MOVIE ADAPTATION
ACCLAIM

❑1; digest; adapts movie 4.50

HERCULES PROJECT
MONSTER

❑1, Aug 1991, b&w 1.95
❑2, b&w 1.95

HERCULES: THE LEGENDARY JOURNEYS
TOPPS

❑1, Jun 1996, wraparound cover 3.00
❑2, Jul 1996 ..... 3.00
❑3/A, Aug 1996, A: Xena. art cover 3.00
❑3/B, Aug 1996, A: Xena. 3.00
❑3/Gold, Aug 1996, 1: Xena. Gold logo variant 3.00
❑4, Sep 1996, 2: Xena. A: Xena. 3.00
❑5, Oct 1996, A: Xena. 3.00

HERCULES UNBOUND
DC

❑1, Nov 1975 WW, JL (a) 12.00
❑2, Jan 1976 ..... 7.00
❑3, Mar 1976 ..... 4.00
❑4, May 1976 ..... 3.00
❑5, Jul 1976 ..... 3.00
❑6, Sep 1976 ..... 2.50
❑7, Nov 1976 ..... 2.50
❑8, Jan 1977 ..... 2.50
❑9, Mar 1977 ..... 2.50
❑10, May 1977 ..... 2.50
❑11, Jul 1977 ..... 2.50
❑12, Sep 1977 ..... 2.50

HERE COME THE BIG PEOPLE
EVENT

❑1, Sep 1997 ..... 2.95
❑1/A, Sep 1997; Alternate cover (large woman burping man) 2.95

HERE COME THE LOVEJOYS AGAIN
FANTAGRAPHICS / EROS

❑1, Sep 2005 ..... 2.95
❑2, Jan 2006 ..... 2.95

HERE IS GREENWOOD
VIZ

❑1, Nov 2004 ..... 9.95
❑2, Jan 2005 ..... 9.95
❑3, Mar 2005 ..... 9.95
❑4, May 2005 ..... 9.95
❑5, Jul 2005 ..... 9.95
❑6, Sep 2005 ..... 9.95

HERETIC
DARK HORSE / BLANC NOIR

❑1, Nov 1996; Maximum Velocity back-up 2.95
❑2, Jan 1997; Maximum Velocity back-up 2.95
❑3, Feb 1997; Maximum Velocity back-up 2.95
❑4, Mar 1997; Maximum Velocity back-up 2.95

HERETICS
IGUANA

❑1, Nov 1993; Foil-embossed logo 2.95

HERMES VS. THE EYEBALL KID
DARK HORSE

❑1, Dec 1994, b&w 2.95
❑2, Jan 1995, b&w 2.95
❑3, Feb 1995, b&w 2.95

HERO
MARVEL

❑1, May 1990 ..... 1.50
❑2, Jun 1990 ..... 1.50
❑3, Jul 1990 ..... 1.50
❑4, Aug 1990 ..... 1.50
❑5, Sep 1990 ..... 1.50
❑6, Oct 1990 ..... 1.50

HERO ALLIANCE (WONDER COLOR)
WONDER COLOR

❑1, May 1987 ..... 1.95

HERO ALLIANCE (INNOVATION)
INNOVATION

❑1, Sep 1989 ..... 1.75
❑2, Oct 1989 ..... 1.75
❑3, Dec 1989 ..... 1.95
❑4, Feb 1990 ..... 1.95
❑5, Mar 1990 ..... 1.95
❑6, Apr 1990 ..... 1.95
❑7, May 1990 ..... 1.95
❑8, Jul 1990 ..... 1.95
❑9, Sep 1990 ..... 1.95
❑10, Oct 1990 ..... 1.95
❑11, Nov 1990 ..... 1.95
❑12, Dec 1990 ..... 1.95
❑13, Mar 1991 ..... 1.95
❑14, Apr 1991 ..... 1.95
❑15, May 1991 ..... 1.95
❑16, Jun 1991 ..... 1.95
❑17, Jul 1991 ..... 2.50
❑Annual 1, Sep 1990 ..... 2.75
❑Special 1 ..... 2.50

HERO ALLIANCE & JUSTICE MACHINE: IDENTITY CRISIS
INNOVATION

❑1, Oct 1990 ..... 2.75

HERO ALLIANCE: END OF THE GOLDEN AGE
INNOVATION

❑1/2nd, Jul 1989
❑1, Jul 1989 ..... 1.75
❑2, Jul 1989 ..... 1.75
❑3, Aug 1989 ..... 1.75

HERO ALLIANCE QUARTERLY
INNOVATION

❑1, Sep 1991 ..... 2.75
❑2, Dec 1991 ..... 2.75
❑3, Mar 1992 ..... 2.75
❑4 ..... 2.75

HERO AT LARGE
SPEAKEASY COMICS

❑1, Sep 2005 ..... 2.99

Other grades: Multiply price above by 5/6 for VF/NM • 2/3 for VERY FINE • 1/3 for FINE • 1/5 for VERY GOOD • 1/8 for GOOD

HEROBEAR AND THE KID
ASTONISH

	N-MINT
❑1, ca. 1999	2.95
❑1/2nd, ca. 2000, b&w	2.95
❑2, ca. 2000	2.95
❑2/2nd, ca. 2000, b&w	2.95
❑3, ca. 2001, b&w	3.50
❑4, ca. 2002, b&w	3.50
❑5, ca. 2002, b&w	3.50

HERO CAMP
IMAGE

	N-MINT
❑1, Jun 2005	2.95
❑2, Jul 2005	2.95
❑3, Aug 2005	2.95
❑4, Sep 2005	2.95

H-E-R-O (DC)
DC

	N-MINT
❑1, Apr 2003	2.50
❑1/2nd, Sep 2003	4.95
❑2, May 2003	2.50
❑3, Jun 2003	2.50
❑4, Jul 2003	2.50
❑5, Aug 2003	2.50
❑6, Sep 2003	2.50
❑7, Oct 2003	2.50
❑8, Nov 2003	2.50
❑9, Dec 2003	2.50
❑10, Jan 2004	2.50
❑11, Feb 2004	2.50
❑12, Mar 2004	2.50
❑13, Apr 2004	2.50
❑14, May 2004	2.50
❑15, Jun 2004	2.50
❑16, Jul 2004	2.50
❑17, Aug 2004	2.50
❑18, Sep 2004	2.50
❑19, Oct 2004	2.50
❑20, Nov 2004	2.50
❑21, Jan 2005	2.50
❑22, Feb 2005	2.50

HERO DOUBLE FEATURE
DC

	N-MINT
❑1, Jun 2003; Collects Hero (DC) #1 & #2	4.95

HEROES (BLACKBIRD)
BLACKBIRD

	N-MINT
❑1	3.00
❑2	1.75
❑3	1.75
❑4, Nov 1987	2.00
❑5	2.00
❑6	2.00

HEROES (MILESTONE)
DC / MILESTONE

	N-MINT
❑1, May 1996	2.50
❑2, Jun 1996	2.50
❑3, Jul 1996	2.50
❑4, Aug 1996	2.50
❑5, Sep 1996	2.50
❑6, Nov 1996	2.50

HEROES (MARVEL)
MARVEL

	N-MINT
❑1, Dec 2001	7.00
❑1/2nd, Dec 2001	3.50

HEROES AGAINST HUNGER
DC

	N-MINT
❑1, Aug 1986; JSn (w); DaG, CI, KG, JDu, GP, JK, JKu, RA, MR (a); Charity benefit comic for Ethiopian famine victims	3.00

HEROES ANONYMOUS
BONGO

	N-MINT
❑1, Jul 2003	2.99
❑2, Oct 2003	2.99
❑3, Dec 2003	2.99
❑4, Feb 2004	2.99
❑5, Jun 2004	2.99
❑6 2004	2.99

HEROES FOR HIRE
MARVEL

	N-MINT
❑1, Jul 1997; Hulk, Hercules, Iron Fist, Luke Cage, Black Knight, White Tiger; wraparound cover	2.99
❑2/A, Aug 1997; gatefold summary; Jim Hammond (original Human Torch) joins team	1.99
❑2/B, Aug 1997; gatefold summary; alternate cover; Jim Hammond (original Human Torch) joins team	1.99
❑3, Sep 1997; gatefold summary	1.99
❑4, Oct 1997; gatefold summary	1.99
❑5, Nov 1997; gatefold summary	1.99
❑6, Dec 1997; gatefold summary	1.99
❑7, Jan 1998; gatefold summary	1.99
❑8, Feb 1998; gatefold summary	1.99
❑9, Mar 1998; gatefold summary	1.99
❑10, Apr 1998; gatefold summary	1.99
❑11, May 1998; gatefold summary	1.99
❑12, Jun 1998; gatefold summary	2.99
❑13, Jul 1998; gatefold summary; Ant-Man inside Hammond's body	1.99
❑14, Aug 1998; gatefold summary; Black Knight vs. dragons	1.99
❑15, Sep 1998; gatefold summary	1.99
❑16, Oct 1998; gatefold summary	1.99
❑17, Nov 1998; gatefold summary	1.99
❑18, Dec 1998; gatefold summary	1.99
❑19, Jan 1999; gatefold summary	1.99
❑Annual 1998; gatefold summary; Heroes for Hire/Quicksilver '98; wraparound cover	2.99

HEROES FOR HOPE
MARVEL

	N-MINT
❑1, Dec 1985, MGr, SL, AMo (w); BWr, GM, JB, JBy, BG, JR2, SR, BB, FM, BA, CV (a); famine relief	5.00

HEROES FROM WORDSMITH
SPECIAL STUDIO

	N-MINT
❑1, b&w	2.50

HEROES INCORPORATED
DOUBLE EDGE

	N-MINT
❑1, Mar 1995	2.95

HEROES, INC. PRESENTS CANNON
ARMED SERVICES

	N-MINT
❑1 1969, WW (w); WW (a)	12.50
❑2	10.00

HEROES OF FAITH
CORETOONS

	N-MINT
❑1, Jun 1992	2.50

HEROES OF ROCK 'N FIRE
WONDER COMIX

	N-MINT
❑1, Apr 1987	1.95
❑2, Aug 1987, b&w	1.75

HEROES OF THE EQUINOX
FANTASY FLIGHT

	N-MINT
❑1	2.00

HEROES REBORN
MARVEL

	N-MINT
❑½ 1996; JPH (w); RL (a); With certificate of authenticity	3.00

HEROES REBORN: ASHEMA
MARVEL

	N-MINT
❑1, Jan 2000	1.99

HEROES REBORN: DOOM
MARVEL

	N-MINT
❑1, Jan 2000	1.99

HEROES REBORN: DOOMSDAY
MARVEL

	N-MINT
❑1, Jan 2000	1.99

HEROES REBORN: MASTERS OF EVIL
MARVEL

	N-MINT
❑1, Feb 1999	1.99

HEROES REBORN MINI COMIC
MARVEL

	N-MINT
❑1	1.00

HEROES REBORN: REBEL
MARVEL

	N-MINT
❑1, Jan 2000	1.99

HEROES REBORN: REMNANTS
MARVEL

	N-MINT
❑1, Jan 2000	1.99

HEROES REBORN: THE RETURN
MARVEL

	N-MINT
❑1, Dec 1997 PD (w)	2.50
❑1/Variant, Dec 1997; PD (w); Franklin Richards on cover	3.00
❑2, Dec 1997 PD (w)	2.50
❑2/Variant, Dec 1997; PD (w); Spider-Man/Hulk variant cover	3.00
❑3, Dec 1997 PD (w)	2.50
❑3/Variant, Dec 1997; PD (w); Iron Man variant cover	3.00
❑4, Dec 1997 PD (w)	2.50
❑4/Variant, Dec 1997; PD (w); Reed Richards variant cover	3.00
❑Ashcan 1, Dec 1997 RL, JLee (a)	1.00

HEROES REBORN: YOUNG ALLIES
MARVEL

	N-MINT
❑1, Jan 2000	1.99

HERO FOR HIRE
MARVEL

	N-MINT
❑1, Jun 1972 JR (c); GT, JR (a); O: Power Man II (Luke Cage). 1: Diamondback. 1: Power Man II (Luke Cage).	125.00
❑2, Aug 1972 JR (c); GT (a); V: Diamondback.	30.00
❑3, Oct 1972 GT (a); 1: Mace. V: Mace.	14.00
❑4, Dec 1972	12.00
❑5, Jan 1973	12.00
❑6, Feb 1973	12.00
❑7, Mar 1973 GT (a)	9.00
❑8, Apr 1973 GT (a); A: Doctor Doom.	9.00
❑9, May 1973 GT (a)	9.00
❑10, Jun 1973 GT (a); 1: Señor Muerte I (Ramon Garcia).	8.00
❑11, Jul 1973 GT (a); D: Señor Muerte I (Ramon Garcia).	9.00
❑12, Aug 1973 (c); GT (a); 1: Chemistro I (Curtis Carr)	9.00
❑13, Sep 1973 V: Lionfang.	9.00
❑14, Oct 1973 O: Luke Cage. V: Big Ben.	9.00
❑15, Nov 1973, Sub-Mariner back-up	9.00
❑16, Dec 1973, FMc (a); O: Stiletto. D: Rackham. V: Stiletto. series continues as Power Man	9.00

HERO HOTLINE
DC

	N-MINT
❑1, Apr 1989 KS (a)	2.00
❑2, May 1989	2.00
❑3, Jun 1989 1: Snafu.	2.00
❑4, Jul 1989	2.00
❑5, Aug 1989	2.00
❑6, Sep 1989	2.00

HEROIC
LIGHTNING

	N-MINT
❑1	1.75

HEROIC 17
PENNACLE

	N-MINT
❑1, Sep 1993	2.95

HEROIC TALES
LONE STAR

	N-MINT
❑1, Jun 1997, Amazon	2.50
❑2, Aug 1997, Amazon	2.50
❑3, Oct 1997	2.50
❑4, Dec 1997	2.50
❑5, Feb 1998	2.50
❑6, May 1998, Amazon and Blackheart	2.50
❑7, Jul 1998, Amazon and Gunslinger	2.50
❑8, Aug 1998, Atlas	2.50
❑9, Apr 2000	2.50
❑10, May 2000	2.50

HEROINES INC.
AVATAR

	N-MINT
❑1, Apr 1989, b&w	1.75

HEROMAN
DIMENSION

	N-MINT
❑1, Oct 1986	1.75

HERO ON A STICK
BIG-BABY

	N-MINT
❑1	2.95

HERO PREMIERE EDITION
WARRIOR

	N-MINT
❑1	2.00
❑2	2.00
❑3	2.00
❑4, 1963 #5 preview	2.00
❑5, Q-Unit	2.00
❑6	2.00

HEROS
OK

	N-MINT
❑1	2.50

Other grades: Multiply price above by 5/6 for VF/NM • 2/3 for VERY FINE • 1/3 for FINE • 1/5 for VERY GOOD • 1/8 for GOOD

Heroes Reborn: The Return

Peter David undoes what Liefeld and Lee did

©Marvel

Hero for Hire

The series that turns into Power Man

©Marvel

Hex

Western star is pulled forward into 2050

©DC

Hilly Rose

Investigative reporter proves her worth

©Astro

Hitman

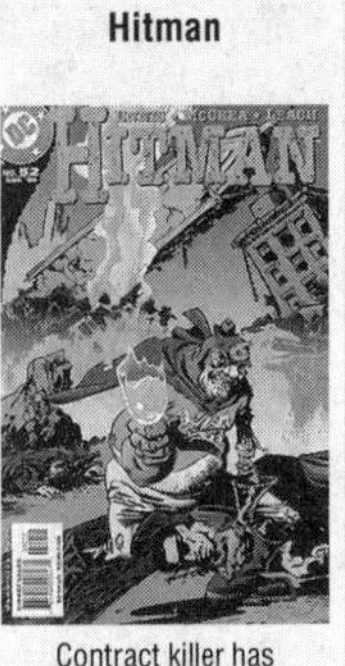

Contract killer has special skills

©DC

N-MINT

HERO SANDWICH
SLAVE LABOR

❑1, Feb 1987, b&w 2.00
❑2, May 1987, b&w 1.50
❑3, Aug 1987, b&w 1.50
❑4, Jan 1988, b&w 1.75
❑5, Oct 1988, b&w 1.75
❑6, Feb 1989, b&w 1.75
❑7, Mar 1990, b&w 2.25
❑8, Jun 1991, b&w 2.50
❑9, May 1992, b&w 2.50

HERO SQUARED
BOOM STUDIOS

❑1, Sep 2005 .... 3.99
❑1/Finger, Sep 2005 .... 3.99

HERO ZERO
DARK HORSE

❑0, Sep 1994 .... 2.50

HERU, SON OF AUSAR
ANIA

❑1, Apr 1993 .... 1.95

HE SAID/SHE SAID COMICS
FIRST AMENDMENT

❑1, Amy Fisher/Joey Buttafuoco 3.00
❑2, Woody Allen/Mia Farrow 3.00
❑3, Bill Clinton/Gennifer Flowers 3.00
❑4, Tonya Harding/Jeff Gillooly 3.00
❑5, O.J. Simpson/Nicole Brown 3.00

HEX
DC

❑1, Sep 1985; O: Hex (future Jonah Hex). 1: Hex (future Jonah Hex). 1: Stiletta. continued from Jonah Hex #92 .... 5.00
❑2, Oct 1985 .... 1.50
❑3, Nov 1985 .... 1.50
❑4, Dec 1985 .... 1.50
❑5, Jan 1986 .... 1.50
❑6, Feb 1986 .... 1.50
❑7, Mar 1986 .... 1.50
❑8, Apr 1986 .... 1.50
❑9, May 1986 .... 1.50
❑10, Jun 1986 A: Legion. 1.50
❑11, Jul 1986 A: Batman of future. 1.50
❑12, Aug 1986 A: Batman of future. 1.50
❑13, Sep 1986 1: Dogs of War. 1.50
❑14, Oct 1986 .... 1.50
❑15, Nov 1986 KG (a) 1.50
❑16, Dec 1986 KG (a) 1.50
❑17, Jan 1987 KG (a) 1.50
❑18, Feb 1987 KG (a) 1.50

HEXBREAKER: A BADGER GRAPHIC NOVEL
FIRST

❑1, Mar 1988 .... 8.95

HEX OF THE WICKED WITCH
ASYLUM

❑0/A, Aug 1999 .... 1.95
❑0/B, Aug 1999; Deluxe edition 3.95

HEY, BOSS!
VISIONARY

❑1 .... 2.00

N-MINT

HEY, MISTER
INSOMNIA

❑1, May 1997, b&w 2.50
❑2, Nov 1997, b&w 2.50
❑3, Aug 1998, b&w 2.95
❑4, Dec 1998, b&w 2.95

HEY MISTER: AFTER SCHOOL SPECIAL
TOP SHELF

❑1, b&w; digest; collects five-issue mini-comics series 4.95

HI-ADVENTURE HEROES
GOLD KEY

❑1, May 1969 .... 12.00
❑2, Aug 1969 .... 7.00

HIDEO LI FILES
RAGING RHINO

❑1, b&w 2.95

HIDING PLACE
DC / PIRANHA

❑1 .... 12.95

HIDING PLACE (SPIRE)
SPIRE

❑1, ca. 1973, adapts book by Carrie Ten Boom 5.00

HIEROGLYPH
DARK HORSE

❑1, Nov 1999 .... 2.95
❑2, Dec 1999 .... 2.95
❑3, Jan 2000 .... 2.95
❑4, Feb 2000 .... 2.95

HIGH ADVENTURE
RED TOP

❑1, Oct 1957 .... 40.00

HIGHBROW ENTERTAINMENT
IMAGE

❑Ashcan 1; Ascan promotional edition 1.00

HIGH CALIBER
CALIBER

❑1, b&w; Trade Paperback 9.95
❑2 .... 3.95
❑3 .... 3.95
❑4, Giant-size; flip book with Raven Chronicles #15 .... 3.95

HIGH CHAPARRAL
GOLD KEY

❑1, Aug 1968 .... 40.00

HIGH OCTANE THEATRE
INFINITI

❑1 .... 2.50

HIGH ROADS
DC / HOMAGE

❑1, Jun 2002 .... 2.95
❑2, Jul 2002 .... 2.95
❑3, Aug 2002 .... 2.95
❑4, Sep 2002 .... 2.95
❑5, Oct 2002 .... 2.95
❑6, Nov 2002 .... 2.95

HIGH SCHOOL AGENT
SUN

❑1 .... 2.50

N-MINT

HIGH SHINING BRASS
APPLE

❑1, b&w 2.75
❑2, b&w 2.75
❑3, b&w 2.75
❑4 .... 2.75

HIGH STAKES ADVENTURES
ANTARCTIC

❑1, Dec 1998 .... 2.95
❑1/Deluxe, Dec 1998; Deluxe edition 5.95

HIGHTOP NINJA
AUTHORITY

❑1 .... 2.95
❑2 .... 2.95
❑3 .... 2.95

HIGH VOLTAGE
BLACK OUT

❑0 .... 2.95

HI HI PUFFY AMIYUMI
DC

❑1, Apr 2006 .... 2.75
❑2, May 2006 .... 2.75
❑3, Jun 2006 .... 2.75

HIKARU NO GO
VIZ

❑1, Aug 2004 .... 9.95
❑2, Oct 2004 .... 9.95
❑3, Feb 2005 .... 9.95
❑4, May 2005 .... 9.95
❑5, Oct 2005 .... 9.95

HILLY ROSE
ASTRO

❑1, May 1995, b&w 3.00
❑1/A, b&w 3.00
❑2, Jul 1995, b&w 4.00
❑3, Oct 1995, b&w 3.00
❑4, Dec 1995, b&w 3.00
❑5, Feb 1996, b&w 3.00
❑6, Apr 1996, b&w 3.00
❑7, Aug 1996, b&w 3.00
❑8, Dec 1996, b&w 3.00
❑9, Apr 1997, b&w 3.00

HIP FLASK
COMICRAFT

❑½, Aug 1998, San Dego Comic-Con preview 2.95

HIP FLASK: ELEPHANTMEN
ACTIVE IMAGES

❑1/Desert, Jul 2003, Desert cover 6.00
❑1/Sushi, Jul 2003, Sushi bar cover 4.00
❑1/Street, Jul 2003, Alleyway cover 5.00
❑1/Townhouse, Jul 2003, Townhouse cover 6.00

HIS NAME IS... SAVAGE
ADVENTURE HOUSE

❑1, magazine GK (a) 24.00

HISTORY OF MARVELS COMICS
MARVEL

❑1, Jul 2000 .... 1.00

Other grades: Multiply price above by 5/6 for VF/NM • 2/3 for VERY FINE • 1/3 for FINE • 1/5 for VERY GOOD • 1/8 for GOOD

N-MINT N-MINT N-MINT

HISTORY OF THE DC UNIVERSE
DC

❑1, Sep 1986, GP (a) 3.25
❑2, Nov 1986, GP (a) 3.25

HISTORY OF VIOLENCE
DC / PARADOX

❑1, b&w 9.95

HITCHHIKER'S GUIDE TO THE GALAXY
DC

❑1 4.95
❑2, ca. 1993 4.95
❑3, ca. 1993 4.95

HITMAN
DC

❑1, Apr 1996 A: Batman. 3.00
❑2, Jun 1996 A: Joker. V: Joker. 3.00
❑3, Jul 1996 2.50
❑4, Aug 1996 2.50
❑5, Sep 1996 2.50
❑6, Oct 1996; cover says Part 4 of 4 2.50
❑7, Nov 1996 D: Nightfist. D: Johnny Navarone. 2.50
❑8, Dec 1996; O: Hitman. Final Night 2.50
❑9, Dec 1996 2.50
❑10, Jan 1997 2.50
❑11, Feb 1997 2.25
❑12, Mar 1997 A: Green Lantern. 2.25
❑13, Apr 1997 2.25
❑14, May 1997 2.25
❑15, Jun 1997 2.25
❑16, Jul 1997 A: Catwoman. 2.25
❑17, Aug 1997 2.25
❑18, Sep 1997 2.25
❑19, Oct 1997 2.25
❑20, Nov 1997 2.25
❑21, Dec 1997; Face cover 2.25
❑22, Jan 1998 2.25
❑23, Feb 1998 2.25
❑24, Mar 1998 2.25
❑25, Apr 1998 2.25
❑26, May 1998 2.25
❑27, Jun 1998 2.25
❑28, Jul 1998 2.25
❑29, Aug 1998 2.25
❑30, Sep 1998 2.50
❑31, Oct 1998 2.50
❑32, Dec 1998 2.50
❑33, Jan 1999 2.50
❑34, Feb 1999 A: Superman. 2.50
❑35, Mar 1999 1: Frances Monaghan. 2.50
❑36, Apr 1999 2: Frances Monaghan. D: Tommy's mother. 2.50
❑37, May 1999 2.50
❑38, Jun 1999 2.50
❑39, Jul 1999 2.50
❑40, Aug 1999 2.50
❑41, Sep 1999 2.50
❑42, Oct 1999 2.50
❑43, Nov 1999 2.50
❑44, Dec 1999 2.50
❑45, Jan 2000 2.50
❑46, Feb 2000 2.50
❑47, Mar 2000 2.50
❑48, Apr 2000 2.50
❑49, May 2000 2.50
❑50, Jun 2000 2.50
❑51, Jul 2000 2.50
❑52, Aug 2000 2.50
❑53, Sep 2000 2.50
❑54, Oct 2000 2.50
❑55, Nov 2000 2.50
❑56, Dec 2000 2.50
❑57, Jan 2001 2.50
❑58, Feb 2001 2.50
❑59, Mar 2001 2.50
❑60, Jun 2001 D: Hitman. 2.50
❑1000000, Nov 1998, b&w 3.00
❑Annual 1; Pulp Heroes; 1997 Annual 3.95

HITMAN/LOBO: THAT STUPID BASTICH
DC

❑1, Sep 2000 3.95

HITOMI 2
ANTARCTIC

❑1, Aug 1993, b&w 2.50
❑2, Oct 1993, b&w 2.75
❑3, Dec 1993, b&w 2.75
❑4, Feb 1994, b&w 2.75
❑5, Apr 1994, b&w 2.75
❑6, Jul 1994, b&w 2.75
❑7, Nov 1994, b&w 2.75
❑8, Mar 1995, b&w 2.75
❑9, May 1995, b&w 2.75
❑10, May 1997, b&w 3.95

HITOMI AND HER GIRL COMMANDOS
ANTARCTIC

❑1, Apr 1992, b&w 2.50
❑2, Jun 1992, b&w 2.50
❑3, Aug 1992, b&w 2.50
❑4, Oct 1992, b&w 2.50

HIT THE BEACH
ANTARCTIC

❑1, Jul 1993, b&w 2.95
❑1/Gold, Jul 1993; Deluxe edition; gold foil 4.95
❑2, Jul 1994, b&w 2.95
❑3, Jul 1995, b&w 2.95
❑4, Jul 1997, b&w 2.95
❑5, Jul 1998, b&w; regular edition 2.95
❑5/CS, Jul 1998, b&w; Special edition; polybagged with postcard 4.95
❑6, Jul 1999 3.95

HOBBIT (J.R.R. TOLKIEN'S...)
ECLIPSE

❑1/2nd 4.95
❑1, Aug 1989 4.95
❑2, ca. 1990 4.95
❑3, ca. 1990 4.95

HOCKEY MASTERS
REVOLUTIONARY

❑1, Dec 1993, b&w 2.95

HOE
THUNDERBALL

❑1 2.50

HOGAN'S HEROES
DELL

❑1, Jun 1966 50.00
❑2, Sep 1966, Photo still doctored for cover gag 40.00
❑3, Nov 1966, Photo still doctored for cover gag 32.00
❑4, Jan 1967 32.00
❑5, Mar 1967 32.00
❑6, May 1967 26.00
❑7, Jul 1967 26.00
❑8, Sep 1967 26.00
❑9, Oct 1969, Cover reprinted from #1 26.00

HOKUM & HEX
MARVEL

❑1, Sep 1993, Embossed cover 2.50
❑2, Oct 1993 1.75
❑3, Nov 1993 1.75
❑4, Dec 1993 1.75
❑5, Jan 1994 1.75
❑6, Feb 1994 1.75
❑7, Mar 1994 1.75
❑8, Apr 1994 1.75
❑9, May 1994 1.75

HOLED UP (RICH JOHNSON'S)
AVATAR

❑1, Apr 2004 3.50

HOLIDAY FOR SCREAMS
MALIBU

❑1, b&w 4.95

HOLIDAY OUT
RENEGADE

❑1, Mar 1987, b&w 2.00
❑2, b&w 2.00
❑3, b&w 2.00

HOLLOW EARTH
VISION

❑1, May 1996 2.50
❑2, ca. 1996 2.50
❑3, Jan 1997 2.50

HOLLOW GROUNDS
DC

❑1, ca. 2004 19.95

HOLLYWOOD SUPERSTARS
MARVEL / EPIC

❑1, Nov 1990 2.95
❑2, Jan 1991 2.25
❑3, Feb 1991 2.25
❑4, Mar 1991 2.25
❑5, Apr 1991 2.25

HOLO BROTHERS
MONSTER

❑1 1989, b&w 2.00
❑2, b&w 2.00
❑3 2.25
❑4 2.25
❑5 2.25
❑6 2.25
❑7 2.25
❑8 2.25
❑9 2.25
❑10 2.25
❑Special 1 O: Holo. Brothers. 2.25

HOLY AVENGER
SLAVE LABOR

❑1, Apr 1996 4.95

HOLY CROSS
FANTAGRAPHICS

❑0, b&w 4.95
❑1 2.95
❑2, Oct 1994, b&w 2.95

HOLY TERROR
IMAGE

❑1, Aug 2002, b&w 2.95

HOMAGE STUDIOS SWIMSUIT SPECIAL
IMAGE

❑1, Apr 1993; pin-ups 2.00

HOME GROWN FUNNIES
KITCHEN SINK

❑1, Jan 1971 55.00
❑1/2nd 22.00
❑1/3rd 10.00
❑1/4th 6.00
❑1/5th 4.00
❑1/6th 3.00
❑1/7th 3.00
❑1/8th 3.00
❑1/9th 3.00
❑1/10th 2.50
❑1/11th 2.50
❑1/12th 2.50
❑1/13th 2.50
❑1/14th 2.50
❑1/15th 2.50

HOMELANDS ON THE WORLD OF MAGIC: THE GATHERING
ACCLAIM / ARMADA

❑1; prestige format; polybagged with Homelands card 5.95

HOMER, THE HAPPY GHOST (2ND SERIES)
MARVEL

❑1, Nov 1969, DDC (c); SL (w); DDC (a) 40.00
❑2, Jan 1969, DDC (c); SL (w); DDC (a); Reprints cover from #21 of the Atlas series 30.00
❑3, Mar 1969, DDC (c); SL (w); DDC (a) 30.00
❑4, May 1970, DDC (c); SL (w); DDC (a) 30.00

HOMICIDE
DARK HORSE

❑1, Apr 1990, b&w 1.95

HOMICIDE: TEARS OF THE DEAD
CHAOS

❑1 2.95

HOMO PATROL
HELPLESS ANGER

❑1, b&w 3.50

HONEYMOONERS, (LODESTONE)
LODESTONE

❑1, Oct 1986 1.50

Other grades: Multiply price above by 5/6 for VF/NM • 2/3 for VERY FINE • 1/3 for FINE • 1/5 for VERY GOOD • 1/8 for GOOD

Hogan's Heroes

POW sitcom escapes into comics

©Dell

Hollywood Superstars

Stuntman, comedian, and actress fight crime

©Marvel

Honeymooners (Triad)

Ralph Kramden returns in 1980s relaunch

©Triad

Hot Rod Racers

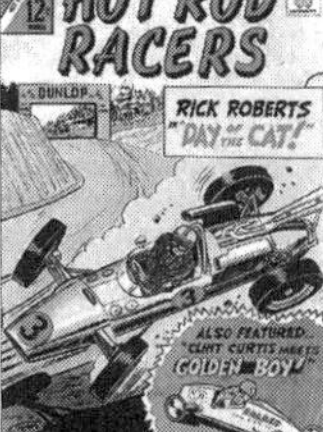

More racing comics from Charlton

©Charlton

Hot Shots: X-Men

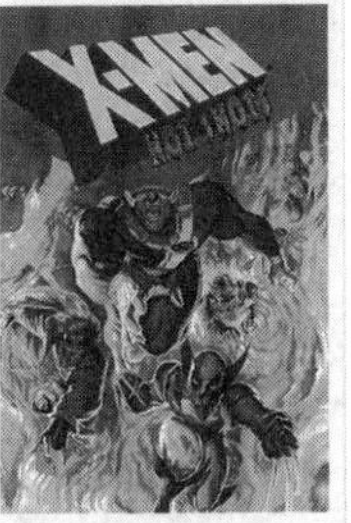

Pin-ups based on Fleer card series

©Marvel

N-MINT

HONEYMOONERS, (TRIAD)
Triad

- ❑1, Sep 1987 ... 2.00
- ❑2, Sep 1987; reprints #1's indicia; photo back cover ... 2.00
- ❑3, Dec 1987; Deluxe edition; squarebound; wraparound cover ... 3.50
- ❑4, Jan 1988; photo back cover ... 2.00
- ❑5, Feb 1988; wraparound cover ... 2.00
- ❑6, Mar 1988; photo back cover ... 2.00
- ❑7, Apr 1988; wraparound cover ... 2.00
- ❑8, May 1988; wraparound cover ... 2.00
- ❑9, Jul 1988; squarebound; wraparound cover ... 2.00
- ❑10, Apr 1989 ... 2.00
- ❑11, Jun 1989 ... 2.00
- ❑12, Aug 1989 ... 2.00
- ❑13 1989 ... 2.00

HONEY MUSTARD
Tokyopop

- ❑1, Aug 2005, b&w ... 9.95
- ❑2, Nov 2005 ... 9.95
- ❑3, Jan 2006 ... 9.95

HONEY WEST
Gold Key

- ❑1, Sep 1966 ... 25.00

HONG KONG PHOOEY
Charlton

- ❑1, May 1975 ... 40.00
- ❑2, Aug 1975 ... 20.00
- ❑3, Oct 1975 ... 10.00
- ❑4, Dec 1975 ... 10.00
- ❑5, Feb 1976 ... 10.00
- ❑6, May 1976 ... 10.00
- ❑7, Jul 1976 ... 10.00
- ❑8, Sep 1976 ... 10.00
- ❑9, Nov 1976 ... 10.00

HONG ON THE RANGE
Image

- ❑1, Dec 1997 ... 2.50
- ❑2, Jan 1998 ... 2.50
- ❑3, Feb 1998 ... 2.50

HONK!
Fantagraphics

- ❑1, Nov 1986, b&w ... 2.25
- ❑2, Jan 1987, b&w ... 2.25
- ❑3, Mar 1987, b&w ... 2.25
- ❑4, May 1987, b&w ... 2.25
- ❑5, Jul 1987, b&w ... 2.25

HONKO THE CLOWN
C&T

- ❑1, b&w ... 2.00

HONOR AMONG THIEVES
Gateway

- ❑1 ... 1.50

HOOD
South Central

- ❑1, b&w ... 2.75

HOOD (MARVEL)
Marvel

- ❑1, Jul 2002 ... 2.99
- ❑2, Aug 2002 ... 2.99

N-MINT

- ❑3, Sep 2002 ... 2.99
- ❑4, Oct 2002 ... 2.99
- ❑5, Nov 2002 ... 2.99
- ❑6, Dec 2002 ... 2.99

HOOD MAGAZINE
Oakland

- ❑1 ... 3.00
- ❑2 ... 3.00

HOODOO
3-D Zone

- ❑1, Nov 1988, b&w ... 2.50

HOOK
Marvel

- ❑1, Feb 1992, CV (w); GM (a) ... 1.25
- ❑2, Feb 1992, CV (w) ... 1.25
- ❑3, Mar 1992, CV (w) ... 1.25
- ❑4, Mar 1992, CV (w) ... 1.25

HOOK (MAGAZINE)
Marvel

- ❑1; magazine ... 2.95

HOON
Eenieweenie

- ❑1, Jun 1995, b&w ... 2.50
- ❑2, Aug 1995, b&w ... 2.50
- ❑3, Oct 1995, b&w ... 2.50
- ❑4, Dec 1995, b&w ... 2.50
- ❑5, Feb 1996, b&w ... 2.50
- ❑6, Apr 1996, b&w ... 2.50

HOON (VOL. 2)
Caliber / Tapestry

- ❑1, ca. 1996, b&w ... 2.95
- ❑2, ca. 1996, b&w ... 2.95

HOPELESS SAVAGES
Oni

- ❑1 2001, b&w ... 2.95
- ❑2 2001, b&w ... 2.95
- ❑3 2001, b&w ... 2.95
- ❑4 2001, b&w ... 2.95

HOPELESS SAVAGES: GROUND ZERO
Oni

- ❑1, Jul 2002, b&w ... 2.95
- ❑2, Aug 2002, b&w ... 2.95
- ❑3, Sep 2002, b&w ... 2.95
- ❑4, Oct 2002, b&w ... 2.95

HOPSTER'S TRACKS
Bongo

- ❑1, b&w ... 2.95
- ❑2, b&w ... 2.95

HORDE
Swing Shift

- ❑1, b&w ... 2.00

HORNY BIKER SLUTS
Last Gasp

- ❑1, b&w ... 2.95
- ❑2 ... 2.95
- ❑3 ... 2.95
- ❑4 1991 ... 2.95
- ❑5, b&w; b&w pin-ups, cardstock cover ... 2.95
- ❑6 ... 3.95
- ❑7 ... 3.95

N-MINT

- ❑8 ... 3.95
- ❑9 ... 3.95
- ❑10 ... 3.95
- ❑11 ... 3.95
- ❑12 ... 3.95
- ❑13 ... 3.95

HORNY COMIX & STORIES
Rip Off

- ❑1, Apr 1991, b&w ... 2.50
- ❑2, Jul 1991, b&w ... 2.50
- ❑3, Dec 1991, b&w ... 2.50
- ❑4, May 1992, b&w ... 2.50

HORNY TOADS (WALLACE WOOD'S...)
Fantagraphics / Eros

- ❑1, b&w ... 2.95

HOROBI PART 1
Viz

- ❑1, Mar 1990, b&w; Japanese ... 3.75
- ❑2, Apr 1990, b&w; Japanese ... 3.75
- ❑3, May 1990, b&w; Japanese ... 3.75
- ❑4, Jun 1990, b&w; Japanese ... 3.75
- ❑5, Jul 1990, b&w; Japanese ... 3.75
- ❑6, Aug 1990, b&w; Japanese ... 3.75
- ❑7, Sep 1990, b&w; Japanese ... 3.75
- ❑8, Oct 1990, b&w; Japanese ... 3.75

HOROBI PART 2
Viz

- ❑1, Nov 1990, b&w; Japanese ... 4.25
- ❑2, Dec 1990, b&w; Japanese ... 4.25
- ❑3, Jan 1991, b&w; Japanese ... 4.25
- ❑4, Feb 1991, b&w; Japanese ... 4.25
- ❑5, Mar 1991, b&w; Japanese ... 4.25
- ❑6, Apr 1991, b&w; Japanese ... 4.25
- ❑7, May 1991, b&w; Japanese ... 4.25

HORRIBLE TRUTH ABOUT COMICS
Alternative

- ❑1, Jan 1999, b&w ... 2.95

HORROR HOUSE
AC

- ❑1, ca. 1994 ... 2.95

HORROR, THE ILLUSTRATED BOOK OF FEARS
Northstar

- ❑1 ... 4.00
- ❑2, Feb 1990 ... 4.00

HORROR IN THE DARK
Fantagor

- ❑1, b&w ... 2.00
- ❑2, b&w ... 2.00
- ❑3, b&w ... 2.00
- ❑4, b&w ... 2.00

HORRORIST
DC / Vertigo

- ❑1, Dec 1995 ... 5.95
- ❑2, Jan 1996 ... 5.95

HORROR OF COLLIER COUNTY
Dark Horse

- ❑1, Oct 1999 ... 2.95
- ❑2 ... 2.95
- ❑3 ... 2.95

Other grades: Multiply price above by 5/6 for VF/NM • 2/3 for VERY FINE • 1/3 for FINE • 1/5 for VERY GOOD • 1/8 for GOOD

N-MINT

❑4 ... 2.95
❑5 ... 2.95

HORROR (ROBERT E. HOWARD'S...)
CROSS PLAINS

❑nn, Aug 2000 ... 5.95

HORRORS OF THE HAUNTER
AC

❑1, b&w; Reprints ... 2.95

HORSE
SLAVE LABOR

❑1, Sep 1989, b&w ... 2.95
❑2 ... 2.95
❑3 ... 2.95

HORSEMAN
KEVLAR

❑0, May 1996, b&w; Commemorative edition; no cover price; published after Crusade issue #1 ... 2.95
❑0/Gold, May 1996; gold foil-embossed cardstock cover; published after Crusade issue #1 ... 2.95
❑0/Silver; no cover price or indicia; published after Crusade issue #1 ... 2.95
❑0/A, May 1996; Woman holding sword facing forward on cover ... 2.95
❑1, Mar 1996 ... 2.95
❑1/A, Nov 1996; Kevlar edition ... 2.95
❑2, Jan 1997, b&w; no cover price or indicia ... 2.95

HOSIE'S HEROINES
SLAVE LABOR

❑1, Apr 1993 ... 2.95

HOSTILE TAKEOVER
MALIBU

❑Ashcan 1, Sep 1994; ashcan; Ultraverse Preview ... 1.00

HOTEL HARBOUR VIEW
VIZ

❑1, b&w; Japanese ... 9.95

HOTHEAD PAISAN: HOMICIDAL LESBIAN TERRORIST
GIANT ASS

❑13 ... 3.50

HOT LINE
FANTAGRAPHICS / EROS

❑1, Nov 1992 ... 2.50

HOT MEXICAN LOVE COMICS
HOT MEXICAN LOVE COMICS

❑1 ... 3.95
❑2 ... 3.95

HOT N' COLD HEROES
A-PLUS

❑1, b&w ... 2.50
❑2, Mar 1991, reprints O: Nemesis, Magicman ... 2.50

HOT NIGHTS IN RANGOON
FANTAGRAPHICS / EROS

❑1 ... 2.95
❑2 1994 ... 2.95
❑3, Nov 1994 ... 2.95

HOT ROD RACERS
CHARLTON

❑1 1965 ... 30.00
❑2 1965 ... 20.00
❑3, May 1965 ... 20.00
❑4, Jul 1965 ... 20.00
❑5, Sep 1965 ... 20.00
❑6, Nov 1965 ... 20.00
❑7 1966 ... 20.00
❑8 1966 ... 20.00
❑9 1966 ... 20.00
❑10 1966 ... 20.00
❑11 1966 ... 20.00
❑12 1967 ... 20.00
❑13 1967 ... 20.00
❑14 1967 ... 20.00
❑15 1967 ... 20.00

HOT RODS AND RACING CARS
CHARLTON

❑25 ... 28.00
❑26 ... 28.00
❑27 ... 28.00
❑28 ... 28.00
❑29 1957 ... 28.00
❑30 1957, DG (c) ... 28.00
❑31, Jul 1957 ... 24.00
❑32 1957 ... 24.00
❑33 1957 ... 24.00
❑34, Feb 1958 ... 24.00
❑35, Jun 1958 ... 24.00
❑36 1958 ... 24.00
❑37 1958 ... 24.00
❑38, Jan 1959 ... 24.00
❑39, Mar 1959 ... 24.00
❑40, May 1959 ... 24.00
❑41, Jul 1959 ... 24.00
❑42 1959 ... 24.00
❑43 1959 ... 24.00
❑44 1960 ... 24.00
❑45 1960 ... 24.00
❑46, Jun 1960 ... 24.00
❑47, Aug 1960 ... 24.00
❑48, Oct 1960 ... 24.00
❑49, Dec 1960 ... 24.00
❑50, Feb 1961, A: Road Knights. A: Clint Curtis ... 24.00
❑51, Apr 1961 ... 18.00
❑52, Jun 1961 ... 18.00
❑53, Aug 1961 ... 18.00
❑54 1961 ... 18.00
❑55 1961 ... 18.00
❑56, Mar 1962, A: Road Knights. A: Clint Curtis. ... 18.00
❑57, May 1962 ... 18.00
❑58, Jul 1962 ... 18.00
❑59, Sep 1962 ... 18.00
❑60, Nov 1962 ... 18.00
❑61, Jan 1963 ... 13.00
❑62, Mar 1963 ... 13.00
❑63, May 1963 ... 13.00
❑64, Jul 1963 ... 13.00
❑65, Sep 1963 ... 13.00
❑66, Nov 1963 ... 13.00
❑67, Jan 1964 ... 13.00
❑68, Mar 1964, A: Road Knights. A: Clint Curtis. ... 13.00
❑69, Jun 1964 ... 13.00
❑70, Sep 1964, 1: Ken King. ... 13.00
❑71 1964 ... 13.00
❑72 1965 ... 13.00
❑73 1965 ... 13.00
❑74 1965 ... 13.00
❑75, Aug 1965 ... 13.00
❑76, Oct 1965 ... 13.00
❑77 1965 ... 13.00
❑78, Mar 1966 ... 13.00
❑79, Jun 1966 ... 13.00
❑80, Aug 1966 ... 13.00
❑81, Oct 1966 ... 10.00
❑82, Dec 1966 ... 10.00
❑83, Feb 1967 ... 10.00
❑84, Apr 1967 ... 10.00
❑85, Jun 1967 ... 10.00
❑86, Aug 1967 ... 10.00
❑87, Oct 1967 ... 10.00
❑88 1967 ... 10.00
❑89 1968 ... 10.00
❑90, Jun 1968 ... 10.00
❑91, Aug 1968 ... 10.00
❑92, Oct 1968 ... 10.00
❑93, Dec 1968 ... 10.00
❑94, Feb 1969 ... 10.00
❑95, Apr 1969 ... 10.00
❑96, Jun 1969 ... 10.00
❑97, Aug 1969 ... 10.00
❑98, Oct 1969 ... 10.00
❑99, Dec 1969 ... 10.00
❑100, Feb 1970 ... 10.00
❑101, Apr 1970 ... 7.00
❑102, Jun 1970 ... 7.00
❑103, Aug 1970 ... 7.00
❑104, Oct 1970 ... 7.00
❑105, Dec 1970 ... 7.00
❑106, Feb 1971 ... 7.00
❑107, Apr 1971 ... 7.00
❑108, Jun 1971 ... 7.00
❑109, Aug 1971 ... 7.00
❑110, Oct 1971 ... 7.00
❑111, Dec 1971 ... 7.00
❑112, Feb 1972 ... 7.00
❑113, Apr 1972 ... 7.00
❑114, Jun 1972, A: Clint Curtis. A: Alex. ... 7.00
❑115, Aug 1972 ... 7.00
❑116, Oct 1972 ... 7.00
❑117, Dec 1972 ... 7.00
❑118, Feb 1973 ... 7.00
❑119, Apr 1973 ... 7.00
❑120, Jun 1973 ... 7.00

HOT SHOTS
HOT

❑1, Apr 1987 ... 2.00

HOT SHOTS: AVENGERS
MARVEL

❑1, Oct 1995; pin-ups ... 2.95

HOT SHOTS: SPIDER-MAN
MARVEL

❑1, Jan 1996; pin-ups ... 2.95

HOT SHOTS: X-MEN
MARVEL

❑1, Jan 1996; pin-ups; Introduction by Scott Lobdell ... 2.95

HOTSPUR
ECLIPSE

❑1, Jun 1987 ... 1.75
❑2 1987 ... 1.75
❑3 1987 ... 1.75

HOT STUF'
SAL QUARTUCCIO

❑1 ... 4.00
❑2 ... 3.00
❑3, Dec 1976 RCo (w); RCo (a) ... 3.00
❑4, Mar 1977 ATh, GM (w); ATh, GM, EC (a) ... 3.00
❑5, Fal 1977 ... 3.00
❑6, Dec 1977 MN, EC (w); MN, EC (a) ... 3.00
❑7 ... 3.00
❑8, ca. 1978 ... 3.00

HOT STUFF (VOL. 2)
HARVEY

❑1, Sep 1991 ... 1.50
❑2, Dec 1991 ... 1.25
❑3, Mar 1992 ... 1.25
❑4, Jun 1992 ... 1.25
❑5, Sep 1992 ... 1.25
❑6, Mar 1993 ... 1.25
❑7, May 1993 ... 1.25
❑8, Aug 1993 ... 1.25
❑9, Nov 1993 ... 1.50
❑10, Jan 1994 ... 1.50
❑11 1994 ... 1.50
❑12, Jun 1994 ... 1.50

HOT STUFF BIG BOOK
HARVEY

❑1, Nov 1992 ... 1.95
❑2 ... 1.95

HOT STUFF DIGEST
HARVEY

❑1 ... 2.25
❑2 ... 2.25
❑3 ... 1.75
❑4 ... 1.75
❑5 ... 1.75

HOT STUFF GIANT SIZE
HARVEY

❑1, Oct 1992 ... 2.25
❑2, Jul 1993 ... 2.25
❑3, Oct 1993 ... 2.25

HOT STUFF, THE LITTLE DEVIL
HARVEY

❑1, Oct 1957 ... 450.00
❑2, Dec 1957 ... 200.00
❑3, Feb 1958 ... 150.00
❑4, Apr 1958 ... 100.00
❑5, Jun 1958 ... 100.00
❑6, Aug 1958 ... 75.00
❑7, Sep 1958 ... 75.00
❑8, Dec 1958 ... 75.00
❑9, Feb 1959 ... 75.00
❑10, Apr 1959 ... 75.00
❑11, May 1959 ... 60.00
❑12, Jun 1959 ... 60.00
❑13, Jul 1959 ... 60.00
❑14, Aug 1959 ... 60.00
❑15, Sep 1959 ... 60.00
❑16, Oct 1959 ... 60.00

Hot Stuff, The Little Devil

Annoying demon tortures Enchanted Forest

Hot Wheels

DC gets license to drive in race series

Hourman

Series follows DC One Million story arc

House of M

Marvel universe upheaval from Bendis

House of Mystery

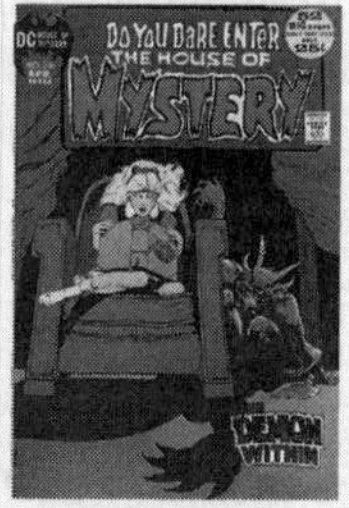

Horror series began back in 1951

	N-MINT
❑17, Nov 1959	60.00
❑18, Dec 1959	60.00
❑19, Jan 1960	60.00
❑20, Feb 1960	60.00
❑21, Mar 1960	40.00
❑22, Apr 1960	40.00
❑23, May 1960	40.00
❑24, Jun 1960	40.00
❑25, Jul 1960	40.00
❑26, Aug 1960	40.00
❑27, Sep 1960	40.00
❑28, Oct 1960	40.00
❑29, Nov 1960	40.00
❑30, Dec 1960	40.00
❑31, Jan 1961	25.00
❑32, Feb 1961	25.00
❑33, Mar 1961	25.00
❑34, Apr 1961	25.00
❑35, May 1961	25.00
❑36, Jun 1961	25.00
❑37, Jul 1961	25.00
❑38, Aug 1961	25.00
❑39, Sep 1961	25.00
❑40, Oct 1961	25.00
❑41, Nov 1961	20.00
❑42, Dec 1961	20.00
❑43, Jan 1962	20.00
❑44 1962	20.00
❑45 1962	20.00
❑46 1962	20.00
❑47 1962	20.00
❑48 1962	20.00
❑49 1962	20.00
❑50, Oct 1962	20.00
❑51, Dec 1962	15.00
❑52, Feb 1963	15.00
❑53, Apr 1963	15.00
❑54, Jun 1963	15.00
❑55, Aug 1963	15.00
❑56, Oct 1963	15.00
❑57, Dec 1963	15.00
❑58, Feb 1964	15.00
❑59, Apr 1964	15.00
❑60, Jun 1964	15.00
❑61, Aug 1964	15.00
❑62, Oct 1964	15.00
❑63, Dec 1964	15.00
❑64, Feb 1965	15.00
❑65, Apr 1965	15.00
❑66, Jun 1965	15.00
❑67, Aug 1965	15.00
❑68, Oct 1965	15.00
❑69, Dec 1965	15.00
❑70, Feb 1966	15.00
❑71, Apr 1966	10.00
❑72, Jun 1966	10.00
❑73, Aug 1966	10.00
❑74, Oct 1966	10.00
❑75, Dec 1966	10.00
❑76, Feb 1967	10.00
❑77, Apr 1967	10.00
❑78, Jun 1967	10.00
❑79, Aug 1967	10.00
❑80, Oct 1967	10.00

	N-MINT
❑81, Dec 1967	10.00
❑82, Feb 1968	10.00
❑83, Apr 1968	10.00
❑84, Jun 1968	10.00
❑85, Aug 1968	10.00
❑86, Oct 1968	10.00
❑87, Dec 1968	10.00
❑88, Feb 1969	10.00
❑89 1969	10.00
❑90, May 1969	10.00
❑91, Jul 1969	10.00
❑92 1969	10.00
❑93, Oct 1969	10.00
❑94 1969	10.00
❑95, Jan 1970	10.00
❑96, Mar 1970	10.00
❑97, May 1970	10.00
❑98 1970	10.00
❑99 1970	10.00
❑100 1970	10.00
❑101	7.00
❑102	7.00
❑103, Mar 1971	7.00
❑104, May 1971	7.00
❑105, Jul 1971	7.00
❑106, Sep 1971	7.00
❑107, Nov 1971	7.00
❑108, Jan 1972	7.00
❑109, Mar 1972	7.00
❑110, May 1972	7.00
❑111, Jul 1972	7.00
❑112, Sep 1972	7.00
❑113, Nov 1972	7.00
❑114, Jan 1973	7.00
❑115, Mar 1973	7.00
❑116, May 1973	7.00
❑117, Jul 1973	7.00
❑118, Sep 1973	7.00
❑119, Nov 1973	7.00
❑120, Jan 1974	7.00
❑121, Mar 1974	7.00
❑122, May 1974	5.00
❑123, Jul 1974	5.00
❑124, Sep 1974	5.00
❑125, Nov 1974	5.00
❑126, Jan 1975	5.00
❑127, Mar 1975	5.00
❑128, May 1975	5.00
❑129, Jul 1975	5.00
❑130, Sep 1975	5.00
❑131, Nov 1975	5.00
❑132, Jan 1976	5.00
❑133, Mar 1976	5.00
❑134, May 1976	5.00
❑135, Jul 1976	5.00
❑136, Sep 1976	5.00
❑137, Nov 1976	5.00
❑138, Jan 1977	5.00
❑139, Mar 1977	5.00
❑140, May 1977	5.00
❑141, Jul 1977	5.00
❑142, Feb 1978	5.00
❑143, Apr 1978	5.00
❑144, Jun 1978	5.00

	N-MINT
❑145, Sep 1978	5.00
❑146, Dec 1978	3.00
❑147, Feb 1979	3.00
❑148, Apr 1979	3.00
❑149, Jun 1979	3.00
❑150, Aug 1979	3.00
❑151, Oct 1979	3.00
❑152	3.00
❑153 1980	3.00
❑154, May 1980	3.00
❑155, Jul 1980	3.00
❑156, Sep 1980	3.00
❑157, Nov 1980	3.00
❑158, Jan 1981	3.00
❑159, Mar 1981	3.00
❑160, May 1981	3.00
❑161, Jul 1981	3.00
❑162, Sep 1981	3.00
❑163, Nov 1981	3.00
❑164	3.00
❑165, Oct 1986	3.00
❑166, Dec 1986	3.00
❑167, Feb 1987	3.00
❑168, Apr 1987	3.00
❑169, Jun 1987	3.00
❑170, Sep 1987	3.00
❑171	3.00
❑172	3.00
❑173, Sep 1990	3.00
❑174, Oct 1990	3.00
❑175, Nov 1990	3.00
❑176, Dec 1990	3.00
❑177, Jan 1991	3.00

HOT TAILS
Fantagraphics / Eros

	N-MINT
❑1	3.50

HOT WHEELS
DC

	N-MINT
❑1, Apr 1970	45.00
❑2, Jun 1970	30.00
❑3, Aug 1970, NA (c); NA (a)	24.00
❑4, Oct 1970	24.00
❑5, Dec 1970	24.00
❑6, Feb 1971, NA (c)	30.00

HOURMAN
DC

	N-MINT
❑1, Apr 1999 A: Amazo. A: Justice League of America. A: Snapper Carr. V: Amazo.	2.50
❑1/Autographed A: Amazo. A: Justice League of America. A: Snapper Carr.	15.95
❑2, May 1999 A: Tomorrow Woman	2.50
❑3, Jun 1999	2.50
❑4, Jul 1999 V: Lord of Time.	2.50
❑5, Aug 1999 A: Golden Age Hourman.	2.50
❑6, Sep 1999 V: Amazo.	2.50
❑7, Oct 1999 V: Amazo.	2.50
❑8, Nov 1999; Day of Judgment	2.50
❑9, Dec 1999	2.50
❑10, Jan 2000	2.50
❑11, Feb 2000	2.50
❑12, Mar 2000	2.50
❑13, Apr 2000	2.50
❑14, May 2000	2.50

Other grades: Multiply price above by 5/6 for VF/NM • 2/3 for VERY FINE • 1/3 for FINE • 1/5 for VERY GOOD • 1/8 for GOOD

N-MINT

❑15, Jun 2000 2.50
❑16, Jul 2000 2.50
❑17, Aug 2000 2.50
❑18, Sep 2000 2.50
❑19, Oct 2000 2.50
❑20, Nov 2000 2.50
❑21, Dec 2000 2.50
❑22, Jan 2001 2.50
❑23, Feb 2001 2.50
❑24, Mar 2001 2.50
❑25, Apr 2001 2.50

HOUSE II THE SECOND STORY
MARVEL

❑1, Oct 1987 2.00

HOUSE OF FRIGHTENSTEIN
AC

❑1, b&w; Reprints 2.95

HOUSE OF M
MARVEL

❑1, Jul 2005 5.00
❑1/Quesada, Jul 2005 30.00
❑1/DirCut, Jul 2005 4.00
❑1/Gatefold, Jul 2005 5.00
❑1/Madurera, Jul 2005
❑2 2005 2.99
❑2/Dodson 2005 25.00
❑3, Aug 2005 6.00
❑3/Cassaday, Aug 2005 20.00
❑4, Sep 2005 2.99
❑4/Peterson, Sep 2005 15.00
❑5, Oct 2005 5.00
❑5/McKone, Oct 2005 15.00
❑6, Nov 2005 2.99
❑6/Land, Nov 2005 2.99
❑7, Dec 2005 2.99
❑8, Jan 2006 2.99

HOUSE OF MYSTERY
DC

❑55, Oct 1956 95.00
❑56, Nov 1956 95.00
❑57, Dec 1956 95.00
❑58, Jan 1957 95.00
❑59, Feb 1957 95.00
❑60, Mar 1957 95.00
❑61, Apr 1957 JK (a) 95.00
❑62, May 1957 70.00
❑63, Jun 1957 JK (a) 85.00
❑64, Jul 1957 70.00
❑65, Aug 1957 JK (a) 85.00
❑66, Sep 1957 JK (a) 70.00
❑67, Oct 1957 70.00
❑68, Nov 1957 70.00
❑69, Dec 1957 70.00
❑70, Jan 1958 JK (a) 85.00
❑71, Feb 1958 65.00
❑72, Mar 1958 65.00
❑73, Apr 1958 65.00
❑74, May 1958 65.00
❑75, Jun 1958 65.00
❑76, Jul 1958 JK (a) 85.00
❑77, Aug 1958 RMo (a) 65.00
❑78, Sep 1958 65.00
❑79, Oct 1958 65.00
❑80, Nov 1958 54.00
❑81, Dec 1958 54.00
❑82, Jan 1959 54.00
❑83, Feb 1959 54.00
❑84, Mar 1959, JK (a) 85.00
❑85, Apr 1959 JK (a) 85.00
❑86, May 1959 54.00
❑87, Jun 1959 54.00
❑88, Jul 1959 54.00
❑89, Aug 1959 54.00
❑90, Sep 1959 54.00
❑91, Oct 1959 54.00
❑92, Nov 1959 54.00
❑93, Dec 1959 54.00
❑94, Jan 1960 54.00
❑95, Feb 1960 54.00
❑96, Mar 1960 54.00
❑97, Apr 1960 54.00
❑98, May 1960 54.00
❑99, Jun 1960 54.00
❑100, Jul 1960 65.00
❑101, Aug 1960 45.00

N-MINT

❑102, Sep 1960 45.00
❑103, Oct 1960 45.00
❑104, Nov 1960 45.00
❑105, Dec 1960 45.00
❑106, Jan 1961 45.00
❑107, Feb 1961 45.00
❑108, Mar 1961 45.00
❑109, Apr 1961 45.00
❑110, May 1961 45.00
❑111, Jun 1961 45.00
❑112, Jul 1961 45.00
❑113, Aug 1961 45.00
❑114, Sep 1961 45.00
❑115, Oct 1961 45.00
❑116, Nov 1961 45.00
❑117, Dec 1961 35.00
❑118, Jan 1962 35.00
❑119, Feb 1962 35.00
❑120, Mar 1962, ATh (a) 45.00
❑121, Apr 1962 28.00
❑122, May 1962 28.00
❑123, Jun 1962 28.00
❑124, Jul 1962 28.00
❑125, Aug 1962 28.00
❑126, Sep 1962 28.00
❑127, Oct 1962 28.00
❑128, Nov 1962 28.00
❑129, Dec 1962 28.00
❑130, Jan 1963 28.00
❑131, Feb 1963 22.00
❑132, Mar 1963 22.00
❑133, Apr 1963 22.00
❑134, May 1963 22.00
❑135, Jun 1963 22.00
❑136, Jul 1963 22.00
❑137, Sep 1963 22.00
❑138, Oct 1963 22.00
❑139, Dec 1963 22.00
❑140, Jan 1964 22.00
❑141, Mar 1964 22.00
❑142, Apr 1964 22.00
❑143, Jun 1964, MM (a); J'onn J'onzz; Martian Manhunter begins 175.00
❑144, Jul 1964 75.00
❑145, Sep 1964 50.00
❑146, Oct 1964 50.00
❑147, Dec 1964 50.00
❑148, Jan 1965 50.00
❑149, Mar 1965, ATh (a) 50.00
❑150, Apr 1965 50.00
❑151, Jun 1965 50.00
❑152, Jul 1965 50.00
❑153, Sep 1965, J'onn J'onzz 50.00
❑154, Oct 1965 50.00
❑155, Dec 1965 50.00
❑156, Jan 1966, O: Dial "H" For Hero. 1: Dial "H" For Hero. 1: Robby Reed. 75.00
❑157, Mar 1966 50.00
❑158, Apr 1966 50.00
❑159, Jun 1966 50.00
❑160, Jul 1966, Dial "H" for Hero; Robby Reed becomes Plastic Man. 90.00
❑161, Sep 1966, Dial "H" for Hero 35.00
❑162, Oct 1966 32.00
❑163, Dec 1966 32.00
❑164, Jan 1967 32.00
❑165, Mar 1967 32.00
❑166, Apr 1967 32.00
❑167, Jun 1967 32.00
❑168, Jul 1967 32.00
❑169, Sep 1967, 1: Gem Girl 32.00
❑170, Oct 1967 32.00
❑171, Dec 1967, Dial "H" for Hero 32.00
❑172, Feb 1968 32.00
❑173, Apr 1968 32.00
❑174, Jun 1968, NA (a); Mystery format begins 50.00
❑175, Aug 1968, NA (a); 1: Cain. 45.00
❑176, Oct 1968, NA (a) 24.00
❑177, Dec 1968, NA (a) 24.00
❑178, Feb 1969, NA (a) 45.00
❑179, Apr 1969, BWr, JO, NA (a); Bernie Wrightson's first professional work 60.00
❑180, Jun 1969, SA, BWr, NA, GK, WW (a) 25.00
❑181, Aug 1969, BWr, NA (a) 25.00
❑182, Oct 1969, NA, AT, WH (a) 18.00

N-MINT

❑183, Dec 1969, BWr, NA, WW (a) 25.00
❑184, Feb 1970, BWr, NA, GK, WW, AT (a) 18.00
❑185, Apr 1970, AW, BWr, NA, WW (a) 30.00
❑186, Jun 1970, BWr, NA (a) 75.00
❑187, Aug 1970, NA, AT, WH (a) 20.00
❑188, Oct 1970, BWr, NA (a) 30.00
❑189, Dec 1970, NA, AT (a) 20.00
❑190, Feb 1971, NA, AT (a) 20.00
❑191, Apr 1971, NA (a) 25.00
❑192, Jun 1971, GM, NA (a) 20.00
❑193, Jul 1971, BWr (a) 25.00
❑194, Sep 1971 BWr (a) 30.00
❑195, Oct 1971; BWr (a); Swamp Thing prototype? 45.00
❑196, Nov 1971 NA (a) 20.00
❑197, Dec 1971 NA (a) 20.00
❑198, Jan 1972 20.00
❑199, Feb 1972 JK, NA, WW (a) 20.00
❑200, Mar 1972 20.00
❑201, Apr 1972 SA, BWr (a) 20.00
❑202, May 1972 SA (a) 14.00
❑203, Jun 1972 14.00
❑204, Jul 1972, BWr, AN (a) 20.00
❑205, Aug 1972 12.00
❑206, Sep 1972 12.00
❑207, Oct 1972, JSn, BWr, NR, JSt (a) 40.00
❑208, Nov 1972 12.00
❑209, Dec 1972, BWr, AA (a) 10.00
❑210, Jan 1973 10.00
❑211, Feb 1973, BWr, NR, AA (a) 10.00
❑212, Mar 1973, AN (a) 10.00
❑213, Apr 1973, BWr (a) 10.00
❑214, May 1973, BWr (a) 6.00
❑215, Jun 1973 6.00
❑216, Jul 1973 6.00
❑217, Sep 1973, BWr (c) 6.00
❑218, Oct 1973 6.00
❑219, Nov 1973, BWr (a) 6.00
❑220, Dec 1973 6.00
❑221, Jan 1974, BWr (a) 12.00
❑222, Feb 1974 6.00
❑223, Mar 1974 6.00
❑224, Apr 1974, 100-page giant; BWr, NA, AN (a); A: Phantom Stranger. Phantom Stranger 35.00
❑225, Jun 1974, 100-page giant AN (a) 18.00
❑226, Aug 1974, 100-page giant BWr, NR, AA (a); A: Phantom Stranger. 18.00
❑227, Oct 1974, 100-page giant NR (a) 27.00
❑228, Dec 1974, 100-page giant NR, NA, AT (a) 18.00
❑229, Feb 1975, 100-page giant 18.00
❑230, Apr 1975 5.00
❑231, May 1975 5.00
❑232, Jun 1975 5.00
❑233, Jul 1975 5.00
❑234, Aug 1975 5.00
❑235, Sep 1975 5.00
❑236, Oct 1975 SD, BWr, NA (a) 5.00
❑237, Nov 1975 5.00
❑238, Dec 1975 5.00
❑239, Feb 1976 5.00
❑240, Apr 1976 5.00
❑241, May 1976 5.00
❑242, Jun 1976 5.00
❑243, Jul 1976, Bicentennial #10 5.00
❑244, Aug 1976 5.00
❑245, Sep 1976 5.00
❑246, Oct 1976 5.00
❑247, Nov 1976 5.00
❑248, Dec 1976 5.00
❑249, Jan 1977 5.00
❑250, Feb 1977 5.00
❑251, Mar 1977; NA, WW (a); giant 4.00
❑252, May 1977; NA, AN (a); giant 4.00
❑253, Jul 1977; NA, AN (a); giant 4.00
❑254, Sep 1977; SD, NA, WH (a); giant 4.00
❑255, Nov 1977; BWr (a); giant 4.00
❑256, Jan 1978; BWr (a); giant 4.00
❑257, Mar 1978; MG (a); giant 4.00
❑258, May 1978; SD (a); giant 4.00
❑259, Jul 1978; DN, MG (a); giant 4.00
❑260, Sep 1978 3.00
❑261, Oct 1978 3.00
❑262, Nov 1978 3.00
❑263, Dec 1978 3.00

House of Secrets

Witches, boogey men, and psychotics at large

©DC

Howard the Duck (Vol. 1)

Hip, hot comic from the 1970s

©Marvel

Howard the Duck: The Movie

Movie ruined all that was good in the world

©Marvel

How The West Was Won

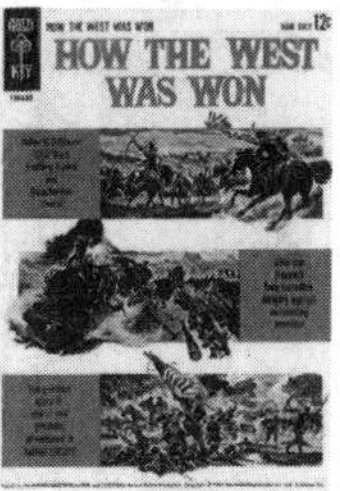

Wide-screen epic comes to comics

©Gold Key

H.R. Pufnstuf

Adapts costumed TV acid trip

©Gold Key

	N-MINT
❑264, Jan 1979	3.00
❑265, Feb 1979	3.00
❑266, Mar 1979	3.00
❑267, Apr 1979	3.00
❑268, May 1979	3.00
❑269, Jun 1979	3.00
❑270, Jul 1979	3.00
❑271, Aug 1979	3.00
❑272, Sep 1979	3.00
❑273, Oct 1979	3.00
❑274, Nov 1979, JO (a)	3.00
❑275, Dec 1979	3.00
❑276, Jan 1980	3.00
❑277, Feb 1980	3.00
❑278, Mar 1980	3.00
❑279, Apr 1980	3.00
❑280, May 1980	3.00
❑281, Jun 1980	3.00
❑282, Jul 1980 JSn (a)	3.00
❑283, Aug 1980	3.00
❑284, Sep 1980	3.00
❑285, Oct 1980	3.00
❑286, Nov 1980	3.00
❑287, Dec 1980	3.00
❑288, Jan 1981	3.00
❑289, Feb 1981, 1: I, Vampire.	3.00
❑290, Mar 1981, I, Vampire	3.00
❑291, Apr 1981, I, Vampire	3.00
❑292, May 1981	3.00
❑293, Jun 1981, I, Vampire	3.00
❑294, Jul 1981	3.00
❑295, Aug 1981	3.00
❑296, Sep 1981	3.00
❑297, Oct 1981	3.00
❑298, Nov 1981	3.00
❑299, Dec 1981, I, Vampire	3.00
❑300, Jan 1982	3.00
❑301, Feb 1982	3.00
❑302, Mar 1982, I, Vampire	3.00
❑303, Apr 1982, I, Vampire	3.00
❑304, May 1982, I, Vampire	3.00
❑305, Jun 1982, I, Vampire	3.00
❑306, Jul 1982, I, Vampire	3.00
❑307, Aug 1982, I, Vampire	3.00
❑308, Sep 1982, I, Vampire	3.00
❑309, Oct 1982, I, Vampire	3.00
❑310, Nov 1982, I, Vampire	3.00
❑311, Dec 1982, I, Vampire	3.00
❑312, Jan 1983, I, Vampire	3.00
❑313, Feb 1983	3.00
❑314, Mar 1983, I, Vampire	3.00
❑315, Apr 1983, I, Vampire	3.00
❑316, May 1983	3.00
❑317, Jun 1983	3.00
❑318, Jul 1983, I, Vampire	3.00
❑319, Aug 1983, D: I, Vampire.	3.00
❑320, Sep 1983	3.00
❑321, Oct 1983	3.00

HOUSE OF SECRETS
DC

	N-MINT
❑1, Nov 1956 RMo (c); MD (a)	1500.00
❑2, Jan 1957	550.00
❑3, Mar 1957, JK (c); JK (a)	450.00
❑4, May 1957 JK (a)	350.00
❑5, Jul 1957	200.00
❑6, Sep 1957	200.00
❑7, Nov 1957	200.00
❑8, Jan 1958, JK (a)	230.00
❑9, Mar 1958	200.00
❑10, Jun 1958	200.00
❑11, Aug 1958	200.00
❑12, Sep 1958 JK (c); JK (a)	200.00
❑13, Oct 1958	125.00
❑14, Nov 1958	125.00
❑15, Dec 1958	125.00
❑16, Jan 1959	110.00
❑17, Feb 1959	110.00
❑18, Mar 1959	110.00
❑19, Apr 1959	110.00
❑20, May 1959	110.00
❑21, Jun 1959	85.00
❑22, Jul 1959	80.00
❑23, Aug 1959 1: Mark Merlin.	100.00
❑24, Sep 1959 MM (a)	80.00
❑25, Oct 1959	80.00
❑26, Nov 1959 MM (a)	80.00
❑27, Dec 1959	80.00
❑28, Jan 1960	80.00
❑29, Feb 1960	80.00
❑30, Mar 1960	80.00
❑31, Apr 1960	65.00
❑32, May 1960	65.00
❑33, Jun 1960	65.00
❑34, Jul 1960	65.00
❑35, Aug 1960	65.00
❑36, Sep 1960 MM (a)	65.00
❑37, Oct 1960	65.00
❑38, Nov 1960	65.00
❑39, Dec 1960	65.00
❑40, Jan 1961	65.00
❑41, Feb 1961	65.00
❑42, Mar 1961	65.00
❑43, Apr 1961	65.00
❑44, May 1961	65.00
❑45, Jun 1961	65.00
❑46, Jul 1961	65.00
❑47, Aug 1961	65.00
❑48, Sep 1961 MM, ATh (a)	65.00
❑49, Oct 1961	65.00
❑50, Nov 1961	65.00
❑51, Dec 1961	52.00
❑52, Jan 1962	52.00
❑53, Mar 1962	52.00
❑54, May 1962	52.00
❑55, Jul 1962	52.00
❑56, Sep 1962	52.00
❑57, Nov 1962	52.00
❑58, Jan 1963	52.00
❑59, Mar 1963	52.00
❑60, May 1963	52.00
❑61, Jul 1963, 1: Eclipso.	125.00
❑62, Sep 1963	60.00
❑63, Nov 1963	50.00
❑64, Jan 1964	50.00
❑65, Mar 1964, ATh (a)	50.00
❑66, May 1964, ATh (a); Eclipso cover	65.00
❑67, Jul 1964, ATh (a); Eclipso cover	40.00
❑68, Sep 1964	36.00
❑69, Nov 1964	36.00
❑70, Jan 1965, Eclipso cover	36.00
❑71, Mar 1965	36.00
❑72, May 1965	36.00
❑73, Jul 1965, 1: Prince Ra-Man. Eclipso cover; Mark Merlin becomes Prince Ra-Man	36.00
❑74, Sep 1965	36.00
❑75, Nov 1965, Both Eclipso and Prince Ra-Man logos on cover	36.00
❑76, Jan 1966, Eclipso/Ra-Man crossover	36.00
❑77, Mar 1966	36.00
❑78, May 1966, Eclipso cover	36.00
❑79, Jul 1966, Eclipso/Ra-Man crossover	36.00
❑80, Sep 1966, Eclipso cover	45.00
❑81, Sep 1969, NA (c); 1: Abel. Mystery format begins	55.00
❑82, Nov 1969, NA (c); NA (a)	20.00
❑83, Jan 1970, ATh (a)	20.00
❑84, Mar 1970, NA (c)	20.00
❑85, May 1970, NA (c); NA, GK (a)	32.00
❑86, Jul 1970, NA (c); GM (a)	20.00
❑87, Sep 1970, NA (c); BWr (a)	45.00
❑88, Nov 1970, NA (c); DG, DD (a)	40.00
❑89, Jan 1971, GM (c); GM (a); Harlequin-esque cover	40.00
❑90, Mar 1971, RB, GM, NA (a); 1st Buckler DC art	40.00
❑91, May 1971, MA, NA, WW (a)	40.00
❑92, Jul 1971, BWr (c); DD, ME (w); BWr, DD, TD (a); 1: Swamp Thing.	450.00
❑93, Sep 1971 BWr (c); BWr, JA (a)	25.00
❑94, Nov 1971; BWr (c); SA, ATh, BWr, TD (a); Includes Abel's Fables by Aragones	25.00
❑95, Jan 1972	25.00
❑96, Mar 1972 BWr (c)	25.00
❑97, May 1972; JA (a); Includes Abel's Fables by Aragones	25.00
❑98, Jul 1972	25.00
❑99, Sep 1972	25.00
❑100, Oct 1972 BWr (c); TP (a)	27.00
❑101, Nov 1972 AN (a)	18.00
❑102, Dec 1972	18.00
❑103, Jan 1973 BWr (c)	18.00
❑104, Feb 1973	18.00
❑105, Mar 1973	18.00
❑106, Apr 1973, BWr (c)	18.00
❑107, May 1973, BWr (c)	18.00
❑108, Jun 1973	18.00
❑109, Jul 1973	18.00
❑110, Aug 1973	18.00
❑111, Sep 1973	18.00
❑112, Oct 1973	18.00
❑113, Nov 1973	10.00
❑114, Dec 1973	10.00
❑115, Jan 1974	10.00
❑116, Feb 1974	10.00
❑117, Mar 1974, AA, AN (a)	10.00
❑118, Apr 1974, This issue's Statement of Ownership was also accidentally printed in Our Fighting Forces #148	10.00
❑119, May 1974	10.00
❑120, Jun 1974	10.00

Other grades: Multiply price above by 5/6 for VF/NM • 2/3 for VERY FINE • 1/3 for FINE • 1/5 for VERY GOOD • 1/8 for GOOD

❑121, Jul 1974 .... 10.00
❑122, Aug 1974 .... 10.00
❑123, Sep 1974, FR (c); ATh (a) 10.00
❑124, Oct 1974 FR (c); RMo (a) 10.00
❑125, Nov 1974 .... 10.00
❑126, Dec 1974 .... 10.00
❑127, Jan 1975 .... 10.00
❑128, Feb 1975 .... 10.00
❑129, Mar 1975 .... 10.00
❑130, Apr 1975 SA, NR (a) 10.00
❑131, May 1975 .... 10.00
❑132, Jun 1975 .... 10.00
❑133, Jul 1975 .... 10.00
❑134, Aug 1975 .... 10.00
❑135, Sep 1975 BWr (c) 10.00
❑136, Nov 1975 BWr (c) 10.00
❑137, Jan 1976 .... 10.00
❑138, Mar 1976 .... 10.00
❑139, May 1976; BWr (c); Halloween cover 10.00
❑140, Jul 1976 O: Patchwork Man. 10.00
❑141, Sep 1976 .... 10.00
❑142, Nov 1976 .... 7.00
❑143, Jan 1977 .... 7.00
❑144, Mar 1977 .... 7.00
❑145, May 1977 .... 7.00
❑146, Jul 1977 GM (c) 7.00
❑147, Sep 1977 GM (c) 7.00
❑148, Nov 1977 .... 7.00
❑149, Jan 1978 .... 7.00
❑150, Mar 1978 JSn (c) 7.00
❑151, May 1978 MG (a) 7.00
❑152, Jul 1978 .... 7.00
❑153, Sep 1978 JA (c) 7.00
❑154, Nov 1978, Series merges with The Unexpected 7.00

HOUSE OF SECRETS (2ND SERIES)
DC / VERTIGO

❑1, Oct 1996 .... 3.00
❑2, Nov 1996 .... 3.00
❑3, Dec 1996 .... 3.00
❑4, Jan 1997 .... 3.00
❑5, Feb 1997 .... 3.00
❑6, Mar 1997 .... 3.00
❑7, Apr 1997 .... 3.00
❑8, May 1997 .... 3.00
❑9, Jun 1997 .... 3.00
❑10, Jul 1997 .... 3.00
❑11, Aug 1997 .... 3.00
❑12, Sep 1997 .... 3.00
❑13, Oct 1997 .... 3.00
❑14, Nov 1997 .... 3.00
❑15, Dec 1997 .... 3.00
❑16, Feb 1998 .... 3.00
❑17, Mar 1998; covers form triptych 3.00
❑18, Apr 1998; covers form triptych 3.00
❑19, May 1998; covers form triptych . 3.00
❑20, Jun 1998 .... 3.00
❑21, Jul 1998 .... 2.50
❑22, Aug 1998 .... 2.50
❑23, Sep 1998 .... 2.50
❑24, Nov 1998 .... 2.50
❑25, Dec 1998 .... 2.50

HOUSE OF SECRETS: FAÇADE
DC / VERTIGO

❑1, May 2001 .... 5.95
❑2, Jun 2001 .... 5.95

HOUSE OF YANG
CHARLTON

❑1, Jul 1975 .... 15.00
❑2, Oct 1975 .... 10.00
❑3, Dec 1975 .... 10.00
❑4, Feb 1976 .... 10.00
❑5, Apr 1976 .... 10.00
❑6, Jun 1976 .... 10.00

HOUSEWIVES AT PLAY
FANTAGRAPHICS / EROS

❑1 .... 2.95
❑2 .... 2.95
❑3 .... 2.95

HOWARD THE DUCK (VOL. 1)
MARVEL

❑1, Jan 1976, FB (c); FB (a); 1: Beverly. A: Spider-Man. 15.00
❑2, Mar 1976, FB (c); FB (a) 5.00
❑3, May 1976, RB (c); JB (a) 4.00
❑3/30 cent, May 1976, (c); JB (a); 30 cent regional price variant 20.00
❑4, Jul 1976, (c); GC (a) 2.00
❑4/30 cent, Jul 1976, (c); GC (a); 30 cent regional price variant 20.00
❑5, Sep 1976, (c); GC (a) 2.00
❑6, Nov 1976, (c); GC (a) 2.00
❑7, Dec 1976, (c); GC (a) 2.00
❑8, Jan 1977, (c); GC (a) 2.00
❑9, Feb 1977, (c); GC (a) 2.00
❑10, Mar 1977, GC (c); GC (a) 2.00
❑11, Apr 1977, GC (c); GC (a) 2.00
❑12, May 1977, (c); GC (a); 1: Kiss (rock group). 7.00
❑13, Jun 1977, (c); GC (a); A: Kiss (rock group). Newsstand edition (distributed by Curtis); issue number in box 5.00
❑13/Whitman, Jun 1977, (c); GC (a); A: Kiss (rock group). Special markets edition (usually sold in Whitman bagged prepacks); price appears in a diamond; UPC barcode appears 5.00
❑13/35 cent, Jun 1977, (c); GC (a); 35 cent regional price variant; newsstand edition (distributed by Curtis); issue number in box 15.00
❑14, Jul 1977, (c); GC, KJ (a) 2.00
❑14/35 cent, Jul 1977, (c); GC, KJ (a); 35 cent regional price variant 15.00
❑15, Aug 1977, (c); GC, KJ (a); 1: Doctor Bong. 2.00
❑15/35 cent, Aug 1977, (c); GC, KJ (a); 1: Doctor Bong. 35 cent regional price variant. 15.00
❑16, Sep 1977, (c); O: Doctor Bong. all-text issue 2.00
❑16/35 cent, Sep 1977, (c); O: Doctor Bong. 35 cent regional price variant; all-text issue 15.00
❑17, Oct 1977, (c); GC, KJ (a); O: Doctor Bong. 2.00
❑17/35 cent, Oct 1977, (c); GC, KJ (a); O: Doctor Bong. 35 cent regional price variant. 15.00
❑18, Nov 1977, (c); GC, KJ (a) 2.00
❑19, Dec 1977, (c); GC, KJ (a) 2.00
❑20, Jan 1978, (c); GC, KJ (a); V: Sudol. 2.00
❑21, Feb 1978, (c); Cl, KJ (a); V: Soofi. 2.00
❑22, Mar 1978, (c); VM (a) 2.00
❑23, Apr 1978, GC (c); VM (a) 2.00
❑24, May 1978, GC (c); GC, TP (a) 2.00
❑25, Jun 1978, GC, KJ (c); GC, KJ (a); A: Ringmaster. 2.00
❑26, Jul 1978, GC, KJ (c); GC, KJ (a); A: Ringmaster. 2.00
❑27, Sep 1978, (c); GC, KJ (a); A: Ringmaster. 2.00
❑28, Nov 1978, (c); Cl (a) 2.00
❑29, Jan 1979, GC (c); ME (w) 2.00
❑30, Mar 1979, AM, GC (c); AM, GC (a); V: Doctor Bong. 2.00
❑31, May 1979 AM, GC (c); AM, GC (a); V: Doctor Bong. 2.00
❑32, Jan 1986, PS (a); O: Howard the Duck. 2.00
❑33, Sep 1986, BB (c); VM (a) 2.50
❑Annual 1, Oct 1977, GC, TP (c); VM (a) 4.00

HOWARD THE DUCK (VOL. 2)
MARVEL / MAX

❑1, Mar 2002 .... 4.00
❑2, Apr 2002 .... 2.99
❑3, May 2002 .... 2.99
❑4, Jun 2002 .... 2.99
❑5, Jul 2002 .... 2.99
❑6, Aug 2002 .... 2.99

HOWARD THE DUCK (MAGAZINE)
MARVEL

❑1, Oct 1979, b&w; MG, KJ (a); contains nudity 4.00
❑2, Dec 1979, b&w VM (c); GC, KJ (a) 3.00
❑3, Feb 1980, b&w GC (a) 3.00
❑4, Mar 1980, b&w GC, JB (a); A: Kiss. A: Beatles. 4.00
❑5, May 1980, b&w MG, GC, BMc (a) 3.00
❑6, Jul 1980, b&w MG, BMc (a) 3.00
❑7, Sep 1980, b&w GC, AA, TP (a); A: Man-Thing. 3.00
❑8, Nov 1980, b&w; GC (a); Batman parody 3.00
❑9, Mar 1981, b&w GC (a) 3.00

HOWARD THE DUCK HOLIDAY SPECIAL
MARVEL

❑1, Feb 1997 .... 2.50

HOWARD THE DUCK: THE MOVIE
MARVEL

❑1, Dec 1986 O: Howard the Duck. 1.00
❑2, Jan 1987 .... 1.00
❑3, Feb 1987 .... 1.00

HOWL
ETERNITY

❑1, b&w; Reprints 2.25
❑2, b&w; Reprints 2.25

HOWL'S MOVING CASTLE FILM COMICS
VIZ

❑1, Aug 2005 .... 9.95
❑2, Sep 2005 .... 9.95
❑3, Oct 2005 .... 9.95
❑4, Nov 2005 .... 9.95

HOW THE WEST WAS WON
GOLD KEY

❑1, Jul 1963 .... 18.00

HOW TO DRAW COMICS COMIC
SOLSON

❑1, ca. 1985 .... 1.95

HOW TO DRAW FELIX THE CAT AND HIS FRIENDS
FELIX

❑1 1992, b&w 2.25

HOW TO DRAW MANGA
ANTARCTIC

❑1 .... 4.95
❑2 .... 4.95
❑3, Feb 2001 .... 4.95
❑4, Mar 2001 .... 4.95
❑5, Apr 2001 .... 4.95
❑6, Jun 2001 .... 4.95
❑7, Aug 2001 .... 4.95
❑8, Sep 2001 .... 4.95
❑9, Oct 2001 .... 4.95
❑10, Nov 2001 .... 4.95
❑11, Jan 2002 .... 4.95
❑12, Feb 2002 .... 4.95
❑13, Mar 2002 .... 4.95
❑14, Apr 2002 .... 4.95
❑15, May 2002 .... 4.95
❑16, Jun 2002 .... 4.95
❑17, Jul 2002 .... 4.95
❑18, Aug 2002 .... 4.95
❑19, Oct 2002 .... 4.95
❑20 2002 .... 4.95
❑21 2002 .... 4.95
❑22, Feb 2003 .... 4.95
❑23, Apr 2003 .... 4.95
❑24, May 2003 .... 4.95
❑25, Aug 2003 .... 4.95

HOW TO DRAW TEENAGE MUTANT NINJA TURTLES
SOLSON

❑1 .... 2.25

HOW TO PICK UP GIRLS IF YOU'RE A COMIC BOOK GEEK
3 FINGER PRINTS

❑1, Jul 1997; cardstock cover 3.95

HOW TO PUBLISH COMICS
SOLSON

❑1 .... 2.00

HOW TO SELF-PUBLISH COMICS ... NOT JUST CREATE THEM
DEVIL'S DUE

❑1, Mar 2006 .... 3.99
❑2 .... 3.99
❑3, Apr 2006 .... 3.99
❑4, Jun 2006 .... 3.99

H.R. PUFNSTUF
GOLD KEY

❑1, Oct 1970 .... 55.00
❑2, Jan 1971 .... 40.00
❑3, Apr 1971 .... 40.00
❑4, Jul 1971 .... 35.00
❑5, Oct 1971 .... 35.00
❑6, Jan 1972 .... 35.00

Huckleberry Hound (Gold Key)

Cornpone canine cracks wise

©Gold Key

Huey, Dewey, and Louie Junior Woodchucks

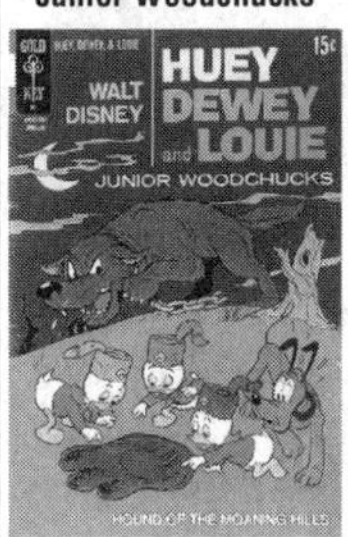

Carl Barks' diminutive trio solves problems

©Gold Key

Hulk

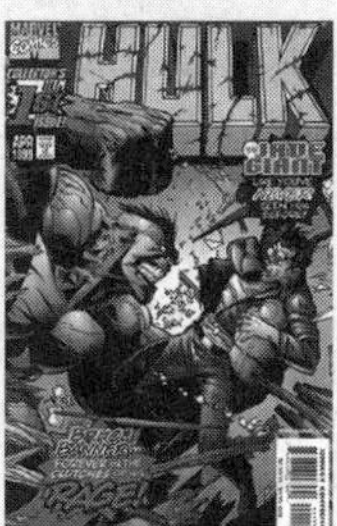

Became Incredible Hulk Vol. 2 after a year

©Marvel

Human Fly

Based on real-life Evel Knievel-type

©Marvel

Human Target

Mature-readers revival of 1970s character

©DC

	N-MINT
❑7, Apr 1972	25.00
❑8, Jul 1972	25.00

HSU AND CHAN
SLAVE LABOR

	N-MINT
❑1	2.95
❑2	2.95
❑3	2.95
❑4	2.95
❑5	2.95
❑6	2.95
❑7, Sep 2005	2.95

HUCKLEBERRY HOUND (GOLD KEY)
GOLD KEY

	N-MINT
❑3, Jan 1960, continues from Four Color	35.00
❑4, Mar 1960	35.00
❑5, May 1960	35.00
❑6, Jul 1960	30.00
❑7, Sep 1960	30.00
❑8, Nov 1960	30.00
❑9, Feb 1961	30.00
❑10, Apr 1961	30.00
❑11, Jun 1961	20.00
❑12, Aug 1961	20.00
❑13, Oct 1961	20.00
❑14	20.00
❑15 1962	20.00
❑16 1962	20.00
❑17 1962	20.00
❑18, Oct 1962, Giant-size	26.00
❑19, Jan 1963, Giant-size	26.00
❑20, Apr 1963	20.00
❑21, Jul 1963	15.00
❑22, Oct 1963	15.00
❑23, Jan 1964	15.00
❑24, May 1964	15.00
❑25, Aug 1964	15.00
❑26, Nov 1964	15.00
❑27, Jul 1965	15.00
❑28 1966	15.00
❑29, Apr 1967	15.00
❑30, Jul 1967	15.00
❑31, Oct 1967	9.00
❑32, Jan 1968	9.00
❑33, Apr 1968	9.00
❑34, Jul 1968	9.00
❑35, Oct 1968	9.00
❑36, Jan 1969	9.00
❑37, Apr 1969	9.00
❑38, Jul 1969	9.00
❑39, Oct 1969	9.00
❑40, Jan 1970	6.00
❑41, Apr 1970	6.00
❑42, Jul 1970	6.00
❑43, Oct 1970	6.00

HUCKLEBERRY HOUND & QUICK DRAW MCGRAW GIANT-SIZE FLIP BOOK
HARVEY

	N-MINT
❑1	2.25

HUEY, DEWEY, AND LOUIE JUNIOR WOODCHUCKS
GOLD KEY

	N-MINT
❑1, Aug 1966	36.00
❑2, Aug 1967	20.00
❑3 1968	16.00
❑4, Jan 1970, Reprinted from Walt Disney's Comics #181 and 227	12.00
❑5, Apr 1970, Reprinted from Walt Disney's Comics #125 and 132	12.00
❑6, Jul 1970	12.00
❑7, Oct 1970	12.00
❑8, Jan 1971	12.00
❑9, Apr 1971	12.00
❑10, Jul 1971	12.00
❑11, Oct 1971	10.00
❑12, Jan 1972, CB (w)	10.00
❑13, Mar 1972	10.00
❑14, May 1972	10.00
❑15, Jul 1972	10.00
❑16, Sep 1972	10.00
❑17, Nov 1972	10.00
❑18, Jan 1973	10.00
❑19, Mar 1973	10.00
❑20, May 1973	10.00
❑21, Jul 1973	8.00
❑22, Sep 1973	8.00
❑23, Nov 1973	8.00
❑24, Jan 1974	8.00
❑25, Mar 1974	8.00
❑26, May 1974, Reprinted from Walt Disney's Comics #232	8.00
❑27, Jul 1974	8.00
❑28, Sep 1974	8.00
❑29, Nov 1974	8.00
❑30, Jan 1975	8.00
❑31, Mar 1975	8.00
❑32, May 1975	8.00
❑33, Jul 1975	8.00
❑34, Sep 1975	8.00
❑35, Nov 1975, Reprinted from Huey, Dewey and Louie Junior Woodchucks #7	8.00
❑36, Jan 1976	8.00
❑37, Mar 1976	8.00
❑38, May 1976	8.00
❑39, Jul 1976	8.00
❑40 1976	8.00
❑41 1976, Reprinted from Huey, Dewey and Louie Junior Woodchucks #6	6.00
❑42, Mar 1977	6.00
❑43, Apr 1977	6.00
❑44, Jun 1977	6.00
❑45, Aug 1977	6.00
❑46, Sep 1977	6.00
❑47, Dec 1977	6.00
❑48, Feb 1978	6.00
❑49, Apr 1978	6.00
❑50, Jun 1978	6.00
❑51, Aug 1978	6.00
❑52, Sep 1978	6.00
❑53, Dec 1978	6.00
❑54, Feb 1979	6.00
❑55, Apr 1979	6.00
❑56, Jun 1979	6.00
❑57, Jul 1979	6.00
❑58, Aug 1979	6.00
❑59, Sep 1979	6.00
❑60, Dec 1979	6.00
❑61, Feb 1980	4.00
❑62, Mar 1980	4.00
❑63, ca. 1980	4.00
❑64, ca. 1980	4.00
❑65, Sep 1980	4.00
❑66, Nov 1980	4.00
❑67, Jan 1981	4.00
❑68, Jun 1981	4.00
❑69, Aug 1981	4.00
❑70, ca. 1981	4.00
❑71, Dec 1981	4.00
❑72, ca. 1982	4.00
❑73 1982	4.00
❑74 1982	4.00
❑75, Apr 1983	4.00
❑76, May 1983	4.00
❑77, Jul 1983	4.00
❑78, Aug 1983	4.00
❑79, ca. 1984	4.00
❑80, ca. 1984	4.00
❑81, ca. 1984	4.00

HUGGA BUNCH
MARVEL / STAR

	N-MINT
❑1, Oct 1986	1.00
❑2, Dec 1986	1.00
❑3, Feb 1986	1.00
❑4, Apr 1986	1.00
❑5, Jun 1986	1.00
❑6, Aug 1986	1.00

HUGO
FANTAGRAPHICS

	N-MINT
❑1	1.95
❑2	1.95
❑3, Jul 1985	1.95

HULK
MARVEL

	N-MINT
❑1, Apr 1999, JBy (w); DGr (a); wraparound cover	3.50
❑1/A, Apr 1999, JBy (w); DGr (a); Sunburst cover	5.00
❑1/Autographed, Apr 1999, JBy (w); DGr (a)	4.00
❑1/Gold, Apr 1999, JBy (w); DGr (a); DFE gold foil cover	4.00
❑2, May 1999, DGr (c); JBy (w); DGr (a)	2.50
❑3, Jun 1999, DGr (c); JBy (w); DGr (a)	2.50
❑4, Jul 1999, DGr (c); JBy (w); DGr (a)	2.50
❑5, Aug 1999, JBy (w); A: Avengers...	2.50
❑6, Sep 1999, DGr (c); JBy (w); DGr (a); A: Man-Thing.	2.50
❑7, Oct 1999, DGr (c); JBy (w); DGr (a); A: Man-Thing. A: Avengers.	2.50
❑8, Nov 1999, DGr (c); EL (w); SB (a); V: Wolverine	2.50
❑9, Dec 1999, DGr (c); JOy (w); SB (a)	2.50
❑10, Jan 2000, JOy (w); SB (a)	2.50
❑11, Feb 2000, SB (c); JOy (w); SB (a); becomes "Incredible Hulk (2nd series)"	2.50

HULK
MARVEL

	N-MINT
❑10, Aug 1978; format changes to color magazine; VM (c); Title changes to The Hulk	7.00
❑11, Oct 1978 GC, TD (a)	7.00

Other grades: Multiply price above by 5/6 for VF/NM • 2/3 for VERY FINE • 1/3 for FINE • 1/5 for VERY GOOD • 1/8 for GOOD

❑12, Dec 1978 KP (a) 7.00
❑13, Feb 1979 BSz, BMc (a) 7.00
❑14, Apr 1979 BSz, BMc (a) 7.00
❑15, Jun 1979 BSz, AA, BMc (a) 7.00
❑16, Aug 1979 MZ (a) 7.00
❑17, Oct 1979 BSz, AA, KJ (a) 7.00
❑18, Dec 1979 BSz, AA, KJ (a) 7.00
❑19, Feb 1980 GC, HT, AA, JSe, BWi (a) 7.00
❑20, Apr 1980 BSz, AA (a) 7.00
❑21, Jun 1980 HC, BMc (a) 7.00
❑22, Aug 1980 HC, AA (a) 5.00
❑23, Oct 1980 JB, HC, BA, AA (a) 5.00
❑24, Dec 1980 GC, HC, AA (a) 5.00
❑25, Feb 1981 GC, HC, AA (a) 5.00
❑26, Apr 1981 JB (c); GC, AA (a) 5.00
❑27, Jun 1981 GC (a) 5.00

HULK AND THING: HARD KNOCKS
MARVEL

❑1, Nov 2004 3.50
❑2, Dec 2004 3.50
❑3, Jan 2005 3.50
❑4, Feb 2005 3.50

HULK: DESTRUCTION
MARVEL

❑1, Sep 2005 2.99
❑2, Oct 2005 2.99
❑3 2005 2.99
❑4 2005 2.99

HULK: GAMMA GAMES
MARVEL

❑1, Feb 2004 2.99
❑2, Mar 2004 2.99
❑3, Apr 2004 2.99

HULK: GRAY
MARVEL

❑1, Nov 2003, JPH (w) 5.00
❑2, Dec 2003, JPH (w) 3.50
❑3, Jan 2004, JPH (w) 5.00
❑4, Feb 2004, JPH (w) 4.00
❑5, Mar 2004 5.00
❑6, Apr 2004, JPH (w) 3.50

HULK/PITT
MARVEL

❑1, Dec 1996 5.99

HULK: PROJECT H.I.D.E.
MARVEL

❑1, Aug 1998; No cover price; prototype for children's comic 2.00

HULK SMASH
MARVEL

❑1, Mar 2001 2.99
❑2, Apr 2001 2.99

HULK: THE MOVIE ADAPTATION
MARVEL

❑1, Aug 2003 3.50

HULK 2099
MARVEL

❑1, Dec 1994 2.50
❑2, Jan 1995 1.50
❑3, Feb 1995 1.50
❑4, Mar 1995 1.50
❑5, Apr 1995 1.50
❑6, May 1995 1.50
❑7, Jun 1995 1.95
❑8, Jul 1995 1.95
❑9, Aug 1995 1.95
❑10, Sep 1995; continued in 2099 A.D. Apocalypse #1 1.95

HULK: UNCHAINED
MARVEL

❑1, Feb 2004 2.99
❑2, Apr 2004 2.99
❑3, May 2004 2.99

HULK VERSUS THING
MARVEL

❑1, Dec 1999; Reprints Fantastic Four #24, 26, 112, Marvel Features #11 3.99

HULK/WOLVERINE: 6 HOURS
MARVEL

❑1, Feb 2003 2.99
❑2, Mar 2003 2.99
❑3, Apr 2003 2.99
❑4, May 2003 2.99

HUMAN DEFENSE CORPS
DC

❑1, Jul 2003 2.50
❑2, Aug 2003 2.50
❑3, Sep 2003 2.50
❑4, Oct 2003 2.50
❑5, Nov 2003 2.50
❑6, Dec 2003 2.50

HUMAN FLY
MARVEL

❑1, Sep 1977, O: Human Fly. 1: Human Fly. A: Spider-Man. 3.00
❑1/35 cent, Sep 1977, O: Human Fly. 1: Human Fly. A: Spider-Man. 35 cent regional price variant 15.00
❑2, Oct 1977, CI (a); A: Ghost Rider. Newsstand edition (distributed by Curtis); issue number in box 2.00
❑2/Whitman, Oct 1977, CI (a); A: Ghost Rider. Special markets edition (usually sold in Whitman bagged prepacks); price appears in a diamond; no UPC barcode 2.00
❑2/35 cent, Oct 1977, CI (a); A: Ghost Rider. 35 cent regional price variant; newsstand edition (distributed by Curtis); issue number in box 15.00
❑3, Nov 1977 1.50
❑4, Dec 1977 1.50
❑5, Jan 1978 1.50
❑6, Feb 1978 1.50
❑7, Mar 1978 1.50
❑8, Apr 1978 1.50
❑9, May 1978, A: Daredevil. 1.50
❑10, Jun 1978 1.50
❑11, Jul 1978 1.50
❑12, Aug 1978 1.50
❑12/Whitman, Aug 1978, Special markets edition (usually sold in Whitman bagged prepacks); price appears in a diamond; no UPC barcode 1.50
❑13, Sep 1978, Newsstand edition (distributed by Curtis); issue number in box 1.50
❑13/Whitman, Sep 1978, Special markets edition (usually sold in Whitman bagged prepacks); price appears in a diamond; UPC barcode appears 1.50
❑14, Oct 1978, Newsstand edition (distributed by Curtis); issue number in box 1.50
❑14/Whitman, Oct 1978, Special markets edition (usually sold in Whitman bagged prepacks); price appears in a diamond; no UPC barcode 1.50
❑15, Nov 1978, Newsstand edition (distributed by Curtis); issue number in box 1.50
❑15/Whitman, Nov 1978, Special markets edition (usually sold in Whitman bagged prepacks); price appears in a diamond; no UPC barcode 1.50
❑16, Dec 1978 1.50
❑17, Jan 1979 1.50
❑18, Feb 1979, Newsstand edition (distributed by Curtis); issue number in box 1.50
❑18/Whitman, Feb 1979, Special markets edition (usually sold in Whitman bagged prepacks); price appears in a diamond; no UPC barcode 1.50
❑19, Mar 1979 1.50

HUMAN GARGOYLES
ETERNITY

❑1, Jun 1988, b&w 1.95
❑2, Aug 1988, b&w 1.95
❑3, b&w 1.95
❑4, b&w 1.95

HUMAN HEAD COMIX
ICONOGRAFIX

❑1, b&w 2.50

HUMANKIND
IMAGE

❑1, Aug 2004 4.00
❑1/A, Aug 2004 2.00
❑2, Sep 2004 3.00
❑3, Oct 2004 3.00
❑4, Nov 2004 2.99
❑5, Jan 2005 2.99

HUMAN POWERHOUSE
PURE IMAGINATION

❑1, b&w 2.00

HUMAN RACE
DC

❑1, Apr 2005 2.99
❑2, Jun 2005 2.99
❑3, Jul 2005 2.99
❑4, Aug 2005 2.99
❑5, Sep 2005 2.99
❑6, Oct 2005 2.99
❑7, 2005 2.99

HUMAN REMAINS
BLACK EYE

❑1 3.50

HUMAN TARGET
DC / VERTIGO

❑1, Apr 1999 2.95
❑2, May 1999 2.95
❑3, Jun 1999 2.95
❑4, Jul 1999 2.95

HUMAN TARGET (2ND SERIES)
DC / VERTIGO

❑1, Oct 2003 2.95
❑2, Nov 2003 2.95
❑3, Dec 2003 2.95
❑4, Jan 2004 2.95
❑5, Feb 2004 2.95
❑6, Mar 2004 2.95
❑7, Apr 2004 2.95
❑8, May 2004 2.95
❑9, Jun 2004 2.95
❑10, Jul 2004 2.95
❑11, Aug 2004 2.95
❑12, Sep 2004 2.95
❑13, Oct 2004 2.95
❑14, Nov 2004 2.95
❑15, Dec 2004 2.95
❑16, Jan 2005 2.95
❑17, Feb 2005 2.95
❑18, Mar 2005 2.95
❑19, Apr 2005 2.95
❑20, May 2005 2.95
❑21, Jun 2005 2.99

HUMAN TARGET SPECIAL
DC

❑1, Nov 1991 2.00

HUMAN TORCH (2ND SERIES)
MARVEL

❑1, Sep 1974; JK (a); Torch vs. Torch reprinted from Strange Tales #101; Horror Hotel reprinted from The Human Torch (1st series) #33 9.00
❑2, Nov 1974; JK (a); Reprints Torch story from Strange Tales #102 and The Human Torch (1st series) #30 4.00
❑3, Jan 1975; SL (w); JK (a); Reprints Torch story from Strange Tales #103, Sub-Mariner #23 3.00
❑4, Mar 1975; Reprints Torch story from Strange Tales #104, The Human Torch (1st series) #38 3.00
❑5, May 1975; Reprints Torch story from Strange Tales #105, The Human Torch (1st series) #38 3.00
❑6, Jul 1975; Reprints Torch story from Strange Tales #106, The Human Torch (1st series) #38 3.00
❑7, Sep 1975; Reprints Torch story from Strange Tales #107, Sub-Mariner #35 3.00
❑8, Nov 1975; JK (a); Reprints Torch story from Strange Tales #108, Marvel Super-Heroes #16 3.00

HUMAN TORCH (3RD SERIES)
MARVEL

❑1, Jun 2003 2.50
❑2, Jul 2003 2.50
❑3, Aug 2003 2.50
❑4, Sep 2003 2.50
❑5, Oct 2003 2.50
❑6, Nov 2003 2.99
❑7, Jan 2004 2.50
❑8, Feb 2004 2.99
❑9, Mar 2004 2.99

Other grades: Multiply price above by 5/6 for VF/NM • 2/3 for VERY FINE • 1/3 for FINE • 1/5 for VERY GOOD • 1/8 for GOOD

Human Torch (3rd Series)

Johnny Storm gets another solo shot
©Marvel

Hunter: The Age of Magic

Continues the tales from Books of Magic
©DC

Hyperkind

Another artifact from the Clive Barker-verse
©Marvel

Iceman (1st Series)

Founding X-Man gets his own limited run
©Marvel

Icon

Alien visitor stars in Milestone series
©DC

N-MINT

❑10, Apr 2004 .... 2.99
❑11, May 2004 .... 2.99
❑12, Jun 2004 .... 2.99

HUMANTS
LEGACY

❑1 .... 2.45
❑2 .... 2.45

HUMMINGBIRD
SLAVE LABOR

❑1, Jun 1996 .... 4.95

HUMONGOUS MAN
ALTERNATIVE

❑1, Sep 1997, b&w 2.25
❑2, Nov 1997, b&w 2.25

HUMOR ON THE CUTTING...EDGE
EDGE

❑1, b&w 2.95
❑2, b&w 2.95
❑3, b&w 2.95
❑4, b&w 2.95

HUNCHBACK OF NOTRE DAME (DISNEY'S...)
MARVEL

❑1, Jul 1996; adapts movie; square binding; cardstock cover 4.95

HUNGER
SPEAKEASY COMICS

❑1 2005 .... 2.99
❑2, Jul 2005 .... 2.99
❑3, Sep 2005 .... 2.99
❑4, Oct 2005 .... 2.99

HUNTER-KILLER
IMAGE

❑0, Dec 2004 .... 1.00
❑0/Ltd., Dec 2004 .... 4.99
❑0/Autographed, Dec 2004 .... 19.99
❑0/Convention, Dec 2004; Sketch cover distributed at Wizard World Texas, 2004 .... 6.00
❑1/Campbell, ca. 2005 .... 3.00
❑1/Hairsine, ca. 2005, b&w 4.00
❑1/Silvestri, ca. 2005, b&w 5.00
❑2/Silvestri, ca. 2005 .... 2.99
❑2/Linsner 2005 .... 4.00
❑3 2005 .... 2.99
❑4 2005 .... 2.99
❑5, Jan 2006 .... 2.99

HUNTER-KILLER DOSSIER
IMAGE

❑0, Sep 2005 .... 2.99

HUNTER'S HEART
DC / PARADOX

❑1, b&w; digest 5.95
❑2, b&w; digest 5.95
❑3, b&w; digest 5.95

HUNTER: THE AGE OF MAGIC
DC / VERTIGO

❑1, Sep 2001 .... 3.50
❑2, Oct 2001 .... 3.00
❑3, Nov 2001 .... 3.00
❑4, Dec 2001 .... 3.00
❑5, Jan 2002 .... 3.00
❑6, Feb 2002 .... 3.00
❑7, Mar 2002 .... 3.00
❑8, Apr 2002 .... 3.00
❑9, May 2002 .... 3.00
❑10, Jun 2002 .... 3.00
❑11, Jul 2002 .... 2.50
❑12, Aug 2002 .... 2.50
❑13, Sep 2002 .... 2.50
❑14, Oct 2002 .... 2.75
❑15, Nov 2002 .... 2.75
❑16, Dec 2002 .... 2.75
❑17, Jan 2003 .... 2.75
❑18, Feb 2003 .... 2.75
❑19, Mar 2003 .... 2.75
❑20, Apr 2003 .... 2.75
❑21, May 2003 .... 2.75
❑22, Jun 2003 .... 2.75
❑23, Jul 2003 .... 2.75
❑24, Aug 2003 .... 2.75
❑25, Sep 2003 .... 2.75

HUNTER X HUNTER
VIZ

❑1, Apr 2005 .... 9.95
❑2, May 2005 .... 9.95
❑3, Jul 2005 .... 9.95
❑4, Sep 2005 .... 9.95
❑5, Nov 2005 .... 9.95

HUNT FOR BLACK WIDOW
FLEETWAY-QUALITY

❑1; Judge Dredd 2.95

HUNTING
NORTHSTAR

❑1, Nov 1993 .... 3.95

HUNTRESS
DC

❑1, Apr 1989 JSa (a); O: The Huntress III (Helena Bertinelli). 1: The Huntress III (Helena Bertinelli). 2.50
❑2, May 1989 JSa (a) 2.00
❑3, Jun 1989 .... 2.00
❑4, Jul 1989 .... 1.50
❑5, Aug 1989 .... 1.50
❑6, Sep 1989 .... 1.25
❑7, Oct 1989 .... 1.25
❑8, Nov 1989 .... 1.25
❑9, Dec 1989 .... 1.25
❑10, Jan 1990 .... 1.25
❑11, Feb 1990 .... 1.25
❑12, Mar 1990 .... 1.25
❑13, Apr 1990 .... 1.25
❑14, May 1990 JSa (a) 1.25
❑15, Jun 1990 .... 1.25
❑16, Jul 1990 .... 1.25
❑17, Aug 1990 A: Batman. 1.25
❑18, Sep 1990 A: Batman. 1.25
❑19, Oct 1990 A: Batman. 1.25

HUNTRESS (MINI-SERIES)
DC

❑1, Jun 1994 .... 2.00
❑2, Jul 1994 .... 2.00
❑3, Aug 1994 .... 2.00
❑4, Sep 1994 .... 2.00

HUP
LAST GASP

❑1, ca. 1986, b&w 3.00
❑2 .... 3.00
❑3 .... 3.00
❑4, ca. 1992 .... 3.00

HURRICANE GIRLS
ANTARCTIC

❑1, Jul 1995 .... 3.50
❑2, Sep 1995 .... 3.50
❑3, Nov 1995 .... 3.50
❑4 .... 3.50
❑5 .... 3.50
❑6 .... 3.50
❑7, Aug 1996 .... 3.50

HURRICANE LEROUX
INFERNO

❑1 .... 2.50

HUSTLER COMIX
L.F.P.

❑1, Spr 1997; magazine 4.99
❑2, Sum 1997; magazine 4.99
❑3, Fal 1997; magazine 4.99
❑4, Win 1997; magazine 4.99

HUSTLER COMIX (VOL. 2)
L.F.P.

❑1, Spr 1998; magazine 4.99
❑2, May 1998; magazine 4.99
❑3, Jul 1998; magazine 4.99
❑4, Sep 1998; magazine 4.99
❑5, Nov 1998; magazine 4.99

HUSTLER COMIX XXX
L.F.P.

❑1, Jan 1999; magazine 5.99

HUTCH OWEN'S WORKING HARD
NEW HAT

❑1, b&w 3.95

HY-BREED
DIVISION

❑1, ca. 1994, b&w 2.25
❑2, ca. 1994, b&w 2.25
❑3, ca. 1994, b&w 2.25
❑4, b&w 3.00
❑5, b&w 2.50
❑6, b&w 2.50
❑7, b&w 2.50
❑8 .... 2.50
❑9 .... 2.50

HYBRID: ETHERWORLDS
DIMENSION 5

❑1 .... 2.50
❑2 .... 2.50
❑3 .... 2.50

HYBRIDS (1ST SERIES)
CONTINUITY

❑0, Apr 1993, silver and red foil covers; title reads "Hybrids Deathwatch 2000" 1.00
❑1, Apr 1993, trading cards; diecut cardstock cover; title reads "Hybrids Deathwatch 2000" 2.50

Other grades: Multiply price above by 5/6 for VF/NM • 2/3 for VERY FINE • 1/3 for FINE • 1/5 for VERY GOOD • 1/8 for GOOD

❑2, Jun 1993, thermal cover; trading card; title reads "Hybrids Deathwatch 2000" 2.50
❑3, Aug 1993, trading card; Deathwatch 2000 dropped from indicia; Published out of sequence after #5 2.50
❑4, Published out of sequence after #5, #3 2.50
❑5 2.50

HYBRIDS (2ND SERIES)
CONTINUITY

❑1, Jan 1994; Embossed cover 2.50

HYBRIDS: THE ORIGIN
CONTINUITY

❑2, Jul 1993; "Revengers Special" on cover; #1 was actually Revengers: Hybrid Special 2.50
❑3, Sep 1993; "Revengers Special" on cover 2.50
❑4, Dec 1993 2.50
❑5, Jan 1994 2.50

HYDE-25
HARRIS

❑0, Apr 1995; Reprints Vampirella (Magazine) #1 in color; Reprints Vampirella (Magazine) #1 in color 2.95

HYDROGEN BOMB FUNNIES
RIP OFF

❑1 5.00

HYDROPHIDIAN
NBM

❑1 10.95

HYENA
TUNDRA

❑1, b&w 3.95
❑2, b&w 3.95
❑3, b&w 3.95
❑4 3.95

HYPERACTIVES
ALIAS

❑0, Jan 2006 2.00

HYPER COMIX
KITCHEN SINK

❑1 5.00

HYPER DOLLS
IRONCAT

❑1 2.95
❑2 2.95

HYPER DOLLS (VOL. 2)
IRONCAT

❑1 2.95
❑2 2.95
❑3 2.95
❑4 2.95
❑5 2.95
❑6, Jul 1999 2.95

HYPERKIND
MARVEL / RAZORLINE

❑1, Sep 1993, Foil embossed cover 2.50
❑2, Oct 1993 1.75
❑3, Nov 1993 1.75
❑4, Dec 1993 1.75
❑5, Jan 1994 1.75
❑6, Feb 1994 1.75
❑7, Mar 1994 1.75
❑8, Apr 1994 1.75
❑9, May 1994 1.75

HYPERKIND UNLEASHED!
MARVEL

❑1, Aug 1994 2.95

HYPER POLICE
TOKYOPOP

❑1, Jan 2005 9.95
❑2, Mar 2005 9.95
❑3, Jun 2005 9.95
❑4, Sep 2005 9.95
❑5, Jan 2006 9.95

HYPER RUNE
TOKYOPOP

❑1, Nov 2004 9.95
❑2, Jan 2005 9.95
❑3, Apr 2005 9.95
❑4, Oct 2005 9.95

HYPERSONIC
DARK HORSE

❑1, Nov 1997 2.95
❑2, Dec 1997 2.95
❑3, Jan 1998 2.95
❑4, Feb 1998 2.95

HYPER VIOLENTS
CFD

❑1, Jul 1996, b&w 2.95

HYPOTHETICAL LIZARD (ALAN MOORE'S)
AVATAR

❑1 2005 3.50
❑1/Wraparound 2005 5.00
❑1/Platinum 2005 12.00
❑1/Tarot, Jun 2005; 1,250 copies printed. "Queen of Cups" tarot cover fits with Nightjar tarot cover to create a set based on the worlds of Alan Moore. Painted by Lorenzo Lorente and Sebastian Fiumara. 3.99
❑2 2005 3.50
❑2/Wraparound 2005 5.00
❑3, Sep 2005 3.50
❑3/Foil, Sep 2005 6.00
❑3/Wraparound, Sep 2005 5.00

HYSTERIA: ONE MAN GANG
IMAGE

❑1, Apr 2006 2.99
❑2, May 2006 2.99

I 4 N I
MERMAID

❑1 1994 2.25
❑2, Feb 1995 2.25

I AM LEGEND
ECLIPSE

❑1, b&w 5.95
❑2 5.95
❑3 5.95
❑4 5.95

I AM LEGION: DANCING FAUN
DC

❑1, Oct 2004 6.95

I BEFORE E
FANTAGRAPHICS

❑1, b&w 3.95
❑1/2nd, May 1994 3.95
❑2, b&w 3.95

I-BOTS (ISAAC ASIMOV'S...) (1ST SERIES)
TEKNO

❑1, Dec 1995, HC (w); GP (a); 1: the I•Bots 2.00
❑2, Dec 1995, HC (w); GP (a) 2.00
❑3, Jan 1996, HC (w); GP (a) 2.25
❑4, Feb 1996, HC (w); GP (a) 2.25
❑5, Mar 1996, HC (w); GP (a) 2.25
❑6, Apr 1996, HC (w); GP (a) 2.25
❑7, May 1996, HC (w); GP (a); A: Lady Justice 2.25

I-BOTS (ISAAC ASIMOV'S...) (2ND SERIES)
BIG

❑1, Jun 1996 2.25
❑2, Jul 1996 2.25
❑3, Aug 1996 2.25
❑4, Sep 1996 2.25
❑5, Oct 1996 2.25
❑6, Nov 1996, E.C. tribute cover 2.25
❑7, Dec 1996, forms triptych 2.25
❑8, Jan 1997, forms triptych 2.25
❑9, Feb 1997, forms triptych 2.25

ICANDY
DC / VERTIGO

❑1 2.95
❑2 2.95
❑3 2.95
❑4 2.95
❑5 2.95
❑6 2.95

ICARUS (AIRCEL)
AIRCEL

❑1, 1987 2.00
❑2, Apr 1987 2.00
❑3, 1987 2.00
❑4, 1987 2.00
❑5, 1987 2.00

ICARUS (KARDIA)
KARDIA

❑1, Jun 1992 2.25

ICE AGE ON THE WORLD OF MAGIC: THE GATHERING
ACCLAIM / ARMADA

❑1, Jul 1995; bound-in Magic card (Chub Toad) 2.50
❑2, Aug 1995; bound-in Chub Toad card from Ice Age 2.50
❑3, Sep 1995; polybagged with sheet of creature tokens 2.50
❑4, Oct 1995; polybagged with sheet of creature tokens 2.50

ICEMAN (1ST SERIES)
MARVEL

❑1, Dec 1984, O: Iceman. 4.00
❑2, Feb 1985 2.50
❑3, Apr 1985 2.50
❑4, Jun 1985 2.50

ICEMAN (2ND SERIES)
MARVEL

❑1, Dec 2001 4.00
❑2, Jan 2002 2.50
❑3, Feb 2002 2.50
❑4, Mar 2002 2.50

ICICLE
HERO

❑1, Jul 1992, b&w 4.95
❑2, b&w 3.50
❑3, b&w 3.50
❑4, b&w 3.50
❑5, b&w 3.95

I COME IN PEACE
GREATER MERCURY

❑1 1.50

ICON
DC / MILESTONE

❑1, May 1993, O: Rocket. O: Icon. 1: S.H.R.E.D.. 1: Rocket. 1: Icon. 2.00
❑1/CS, May 1993, O: Rocket. O: Icon. poster; trading card 2.95
❑2, Jun 1993, 1: Payback. 1.50
❑3, Jul 1993 1.50
❑4, Aug 1993, A: Blood Syndicate. Rocket's pregnant 1.50
❑5, Sep 1993, V: Blood Syndicate. 1.50
❑6, Oct 1993, V: Blood Syndicate. 1.50
❑7, Nov 1993 1.50
❑8, Dec 1993, O: Icon. 1.50
❑9, Jan 1994 1.50
❑10, Feb 1994, V: Holocaust. 1.50
❑11, Mar 1994, KB (w); 1: Todd Loomis. 1.50
❑12, Apr 1994, 1: Gideon's Cord. 1.50
❑13, May 1994, 1: Buck Wild. 1.50
❑14, Jun 1994 1.50
❑15, Jul 1994, A: Superboy. 1.75
❑16, Aug 1994, A: Superman. 1.75
❑17, Sep 1994 1.75
❑18, Oct 1994 1.75
❑19, Nov 1994 1.75
❑20, Dec 1994, A: Static. A: Wise Son. A: Dharma. A: Hardware. 1.75
❑21, Jan 1995 1.75
❑22, Feb 1995, 1: New Rocket. A: Static. A: Hardware. A: DMZ. 1.75
❑23, Mar 1995 1.75
❑24, Apr 1995, Rocket's baby born 1.75
❑25, May 1995, Giant-size 2.95
❑26, Jun 1995, V: Oblivion. 1.75
❑27, Jul 1995, Icon returns from space 2.50
❑28, Aug 1995 2.50
❑29, Sep 1995 2.50
❑30, Oct 1995, Funeral of Buck Wild 2.50
❑31, Nov 1995 1.00
❑32, Dec 1995 2.50
❑33, Jan 1996 2.50
❑34, Feb 1996 2.50
❑35, Mar 1996 2.50
❑36, Apr 1996 2.50
❑37, Sep 1996, Icon in the 1920s 2.50
❑38, Oct 1996, V: Holocaust. 2.50

I Love Lucy

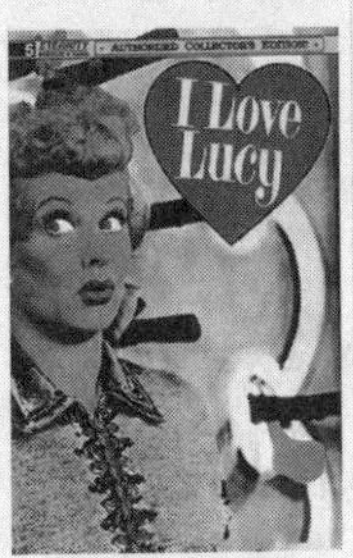

Reprints comic strip by Lawrence Nadel

©Eternity

I Love You (Charlton)

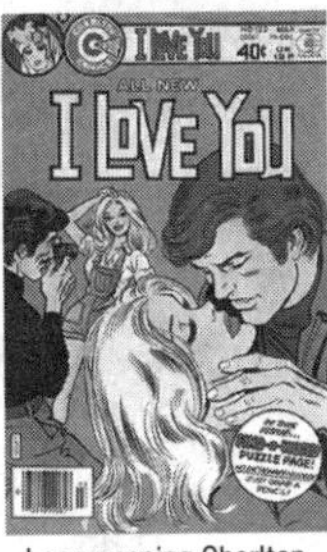

Long-running Charlton romance title

©Charlton

Images of Omaha

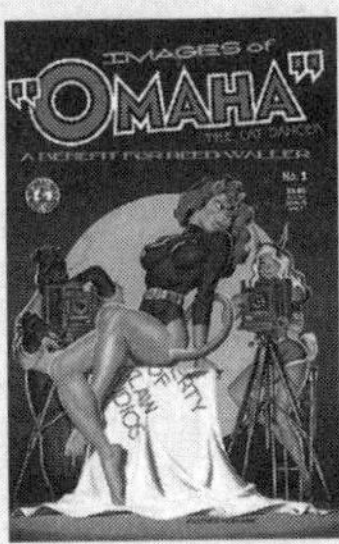

Benefit title for Omaha co-creator Reed Waller

©Kitchen Sink

Image Two-In-One

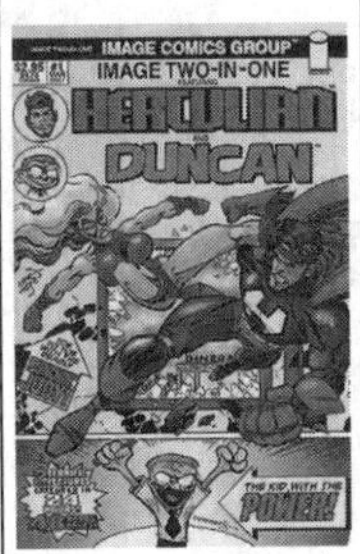

Cover styled like Marvel Two-in-One

©Image

Immortal Doctor Fate

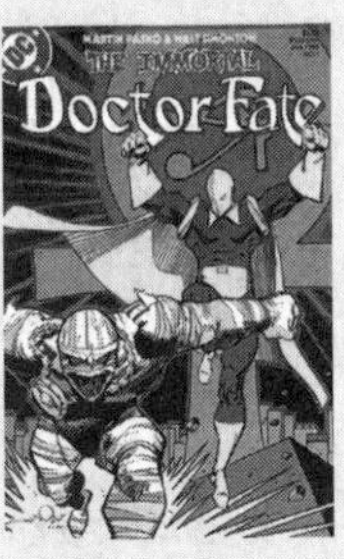

Retells tales of the original Doctor Fate

©DC

N-MINT

❑39, Nov 1996, V: Holocaust. 2.50
❑40, Dec 1996, V: Blood Syndicate. ... 2.50
❑41, Jan 1997 .... 2.50
❑42, Feb 1997 .... 2.50

ICON DEVIL
SPIDER

❑1 .... 1.50
❑2 .... 1.50

ICON DEVIL (VOL. 2)
SPIDER

❑2, b&w 2.25

ICONOGRAFIX SPECIAL
ICONOGRAFIX

❑1, b&w 2.50

ICZER 3
CPM

❑1, Sep 1996, b&w 2.95
❑2, Oct 1996, b&w 2.95

ID
FANTAGRAPHICS / EROS

❑1, b&w 2.50
❑2, b&w 2.50
❑3, b&w 2.50
❑3/2nd, Jun 1995, b&w 2.95

ID4: INDEPENDENCE DAY
MARVEL

❑0, Jun 1996; prequel to movie 2.50
❑1, Jul 1996; adapts movie 1.95
❑2, Aug 1996; adapts movie 1.95

ID_ENTITY
TOKYOPOP

❑1, May 2005 .... 9.95
❑2, Jul 2005 .... 9.95
❑3, Sep 2005 .... 9.95
❑4, Dec 2005 .... 9.95

IDENTITY CRISIS
DC

❑1, Aug 2004 .... 15.00
❑1/2nd, Aug 2004, Negative Sketch cover 6.00
❑1/3rd, Aug 2004, New Rags Morales cover 5.00
❑1/DF, Aug 2004 .... 15.00
❑1/Sketch, Aug 2004; Sketch cover variant from Diamond 2004 Retailer Summit 225.00
❑2, Sep 2004 .... 8.00
❑3, Oct 2004 .... 7.00
❑4, Nov 2004 .... 8.00
❑5, Dec 2004 .... 7.00
❑6, Jan 2005 .... 8.00
❑7, Feb 2005 .... 7.00
❑7/DF Morales, Feb 2005 .... 15.00
❑7/DF Turner, Feb 2005 .... 25.00

IDENTITY DISC
MARVEL

❑1, Aug 2004 .... 2.99
❑2, Sep 2004 .... 2.99
❑3, Oct 2004 .... 2.99
❑4, Nov 2004 .... 2.99
❑5, Dec 2004 .... 2.99

N-MINT

I DIE AT MIDNIGHT
DC / VERTIGO

❑1, ca. 2000 .... 2.95

IDIOTLAND
FANTAGRAPHICS

❑1, b&w 2.95
❑2, b&w 2.50
❑3, b&w 2.50
❑4, b&w 2.50
❑5, b&w 2.50
❑6, Aug 1994, b&w 2.50

IDLE WORSHIP
VISCERAL

❑1 .... 2.95

IDOL
MARVEL / EPIC

❑1 .... 2.95
❑2 .... 2.95
❑3 .... 2.95

I DREAM OF JEANNIE (DELL)
DELL

❑1, Apr 1966 .... 60.00
❑2, Dec 1966 .... 40.00

I DREAM OF JEANNIE (AIRWAVE)
AIRWAVE

❑1, Aug 2002, b&w 2.95
❑Annual 1, ca. 2002, b&w; Tricks and Treat Annual; cardstock cover 3.50

I FEEL SICK
SLAVE LABOR

❑1, Aug 1999 .... 3.95

IF THE DEVIL WOULD TALK (IMPACT)
IMPACT

❑1, ca. 1958 .... 450.00

IGRAT
VEROTIK

❑1, Nov 1995 .... 2.95

IGRAT ILLUSTRATIONS
VEROTIK

❑1, Apr 1997; pin-ups; embossed cardstock cover 3.95

I HAD A DREAM
KING INK EMPIRE

❑1, Jun 1995 .... 2.95

I (HEART) MARVEL: MARVEL AI
MARVEL

❑1, Apr 2006 .... 2.99

I (HEART) MARVEL: MASKED INTENTIONS
MARVEL

❑1, May 2006 .... 2.99

I (HEART) MARVEL: MY MUTANT HEART
MARVEL

❑1, Mar 2006 .... 2.99

I (HEART) MARVEL: OUTLAW LOVE
MARVEL

❑1, May 2006 .... 2.99

N-MINT

I (HEART) MARVEL: WEB OF ROMANCE
MARVEL

❑1, Apr 2006 .... 2.99

I HUNT MONSTERS
ANTARCTIC

❑1, Mar 2004 .... 2.99
❑2, Apr 2004 .... 2.99
❑3, May 2004 .... 2.99
❑4, Jun 2004 .... 2.99
❑5, Jul 2004 .... 2.99
❑6, Aug 2004 .... 2.99
❑7, Sep 2004 .... 2.99
❑8, Oct 2004 .... 2.99
❑9, Nov 2004 .... 2.99

I HUNT MONSTERS (VOL. 2)
ANTARCTIC

❑1, Jan 2005 .... 2.99
❑2, Feb 2005 .... 2.99
❑3, Mar 2005 .... 2.99
❑4, Apr 2005 .... 2.99
❑5, May 2005 .... 2.99
❑6, Jun 2005 .... 2.99
❑7, Jul 2005 .... 2.99

IKE AND KITZI
A CAPELLA

❑1 .... 2.50

ILIAD
SLAVE LABOR / AMAZE INK

❑1, Dec 1997, b&w 2.95
❑2, Jan 1998, b&w 2.95

ILIAD II
MICMAC

❑1, b&w 2.00
❑2, b&w 2.00
❑3, b&w 2.00

ILLEGAL ALIENS
ECLIPSE

❑1, Sep 1999, b&w 2.50

ILLUMINATIONS (VOL. 2)
MONOLITH

❑1 .... 2.50
❑2 .... 2.50
❑3 .... 2.50
❑4 .... 2.50
❑5 .... 2.50

ILLUMINATOR
MARVEL / NELSON

❑1, ca. 1993 .... 4.99
❑2, ca. 1993 .... 4.99
❑3, ca. 1993 .... 2.95

ILLUMINATUS (EYE-N-APPLE)
EYE-N-APPLE

❑1 .... 2.00
❑2 .... 2.00

ILLUMINATUS! (RIP OFF)
RIP OFF

❑1, Oct 1990, b&w 2.50
❑2, Dec 1990, b&w 2.50
❑3, Apr 1991, b&w 2.50

N-MINT

ILLUSTRATED CLASSEX
COMIC ZONE

❑1, b&w 2.75

ILLUSTRATED DORE: BOOK OF GENESIS
TOME

❑1, b&w 2.50

ILLUSTRATED DORE: BOOK OF THE APOCRYPHA
TOME

❑1, b&w 2.50

ILLUSTRATED EDITIONS
THWACK! POW!

❑1, Feb 1995 1.95

ILLUSTRATED KAMA SUTRA
NBM

❑1 12.95

ILLUSTRATED TALES (JAXON'S...)
FTR

❑1 1.95

I LOVE LUCY
ETERNITY

❑1, May 1990, b&w; strip reprint 2.95
❑2, Jun 1990, b&w; strip reprint 2.95
❑3, Jul 1990, b&w; strip reprint 2.95
❑4, Aug 1990, b&w; strip reprint 2.95
❑5, Sep 1990, b&w; strip reprint 2.95
❑6, Oct 1990, b&w; strip reprint 2.95

I LOVE LUCY BOOK TWO
ETERNITY

❑1, Nov 1990, b&w; strip reprints 2.95
❑2, Dec 1990, b&w; strip reprints 2.95
❑3, Jan 1991, b&w; strip reprints 2.95
❑4, Feb 1991, b&w; strip reprints 2.95
❑5, Mar 1991, b&w; strip reprints 2.95
❑6, Apr 1991, b&w; strip reprints 2.95

I LOVE LUCY IN 3-D
ETERNITY

❑1 3.95

I LOVE LUCY IN FULL COLOR
ETERNITY

❑1, comic book reprint; Collects I Love Lucy # 4,5,8,16 5.95

I LOVE NEW YORK
LINSNER.COM

❑1, ca. 2002; A: Dawn. 9/11 benefit issue; title appears on cover, spray painted on World Trade Center 10.00

I LOVE YOU (CHARLTON)
CHARLTON

❑7, Sep 1955, Continued from In Love #6 55.00
❑8 1955 16.00
❑9 16.00
❑10 1956 16.00
❑11 1956 14.00
❑12 1956 14.00
❑13 14.00
❑14 1957 14.00
❑15, Oct 1957 14.00
❑16 14.00
❑17 1958, Giant-size 18.00
❑18 1958 14.00
❑19 1958 14.00
❑20, Oct 1958 14.00
❑21, Jan 1959 12.00
❑22 1959 12.00
❑23 1959 12.00
❑24 1959 12.00
❑25 1959 12.00
❑26 1959 12.00
❑27 12.00
❑28 1960 12.00
❑29 1960 12.00
❑30 1960 12.00
❑31 10.00
❑32 10.00
❑33, Mar 1961 10.00
❑34, May 1961 10.00
❑35, Jul 1961 10.00
❑36, Sep 1961 10.00
❑37 1961 10.00
❑38 10.00
❑39 1962 10.00

N-MINT

❑40 1962 10.00
❑41 1962 10.00
❑42, Oct 1962 10.00
❑43, Dec 1963 10.00
❑44, Feb 1963 10.00
❑45, Apr 1963 10.00
❑46, Jun 1963 10.00
❑47, Aug 1963 10.00
❑48, Oct 1963 10.00
❑49, Feb 1964 10.00
❑50, Apr 1964 10.00
❑51, Jun 1964 8.00
❑52, Aug 1964 8.00
❑53, Oct 1964 8.00
❑54, Jan 1965 8.00
❑55, Mar 1965 8.00
❑56, May 1965 8.00
❑57, Jul 1965 8.00
❑58, Sep 1965 8.00
❑59, Nov 1965 8.00
❑60, Jan 1966, Elvis Presley story 60.00
❑61, Mar 1966 4.00
❑62, May 1966 4.00
❑63, Jul 1966 4.00
❑64, Sep 1966 4.00
❑65, Nov 1966 4.00
❑66, Feb 1967 4.00
❑67, Apr 1967 4.00
❑68, Jun 1967 4.00
❑69, Aug 1967 4.00
❑70, Oct 1967 3.00
❑71 3.00
❑72 3.00
❑73, Jun 1968 3.00
❑74, Aug 1968 3.00
❑75, Oct 1968 3.00
❑76, Dec 1968 3.00
❑77, Jan 1969 3.00
❑78, Mar 1969 3.00
❑79, May 1969 3.00
❑80, Jul 1969 3.00
❑81, Sep 1969 3.00
❑82, Nov 1969 3.00
❑83, Jan 1970 3.00
❑84, Mar 1970 3.00
❑85, May 1970 3.00
❑86, Jul 1970 3.00
❑87, Sep 1970 3.00
❑88, Nov 1970 3.00
❑89, Jan 1971 3.00
❑90, Mar 1971 3.00
❑91, May 1971 2.50
❑92, Jul 1971 2.50
❑93, Sep 1971 2.50
❑94, Nov 1971 2.50
❑95, Jan 1972 2.50
❑96, Mar 1972 2.50
❑97, May 1972 2.50
❑98, Jul 1972 2.50
❑99, Sep 1972 2.50
❑100, Dec 1972 2.50
❑101, Jan 1973 2.50
❑102, Mar 1973 2.50
❑103, May 1973 2.50
❑104, Jul 1973 2.50
❑105, Sep 1973 2.50
❑106, Nov 1973 2.50
❑107, Jun 1974 2.50
❑108, Sep 1974 2.50
❑109, Nov 1974 2.50
❑110, Jan 1975 2.50
❑111, Mar 1975 2.50
❑112, May 1975 2.50
❑113 1975 2.50
❑114, Oct 1975 2.50
❑115, Dec 1975 2.50
❑116, Feb 1976 2.50
❑117, Apr 1976 2.50
❑118, Jun 1976 2.50
❑119, Aug 1976 2.50
❑120, Oct 1976 2.50
❑121, Dec 1976, End of original run (1976) 2.50
❑122, Mar 1979, Series begins again (1979) 1.50
❑123, Jun 1979 1.50
❑124 1979 1.50

N-MINT

❑125 1979 1.50
❑126 1979 1.50
❑127 1.50
❑128, Feb 1980 1.50
❑129, Mar 1980 1.50
❑130, May 1980, Final issue 1.50

I LOVE YOU (AVALON)
AVALON

❑1 2.95

I LOVE YOU SPECIAL
AVALON

❑1, b&w 2.95

I, LUSIPHUR
MULEHIDE

❑1, b&w 20.00
❑2, b&w 12.00
❑3, b&w 15.00
❑4, b&w 12.00
❑5, b&w 10.00
❑6, b&w 8.00
❑7, b&w; series continues as Poison Elves 8.00

I LUV HALLOWEEN
TOKYOPOP

❑1, Oct 2005 9.95

IMAGE
IMAGE

❑0, ca. 1993; TMc, RL, JLee, EL (w); TMc, RL, JLee, EL (a); Mail-away coupon-redemption promo from coupons in early Image comics 4.00

IMAGE COMICS HOLIDAY SPECIAL 2005
IMAGE

❑1, Jan 2006 4.95

IMAGE INTRODUCES... BELIEVER
IMAGE

❑1, Dec 2001, b&w 2.95

IMAGE INTRODUCES... CRYPTOPIA
IMAGE

❑1, Apr 2002, b&w 2.95

IMAGE INTRODUCES... DOG SOLDIERS
IMAGE

❑1, Jun 2002, b&w 2.95

IMAGE INTRODUCES... LEGEND OF ISIS
IMAGE

❑1, Feb 2002, b&w 2.95

IMAGE INTRODUCES... PRIMATE
IMAGE

❑1/A, Sep 2001, b&w 2.95
❑1/B, Sep 2001 2.95

IMAGE OF THE BEAST
LAST GASP

❑1, ca. 1979 3.00

IMAGE PLUS
IMAGE

❑1, May 1993 2.25

IMAGES OF A DISTANT SOIL
IMAGE

❑1, Feb 1997, b&w; pin-ups by various artists 2.95

IMAGES OF OMAHA
KITCHEN SINK

❑1, ca. 1992, b&w; benefit comic; intro by Harlan Ellison; afterword by Neil Gaiman; cardstock cover 3.95
❑2, ca. 1992, b&w; benefit comic; cardstock cover 3.95

IMAGES OF SHADOWHAWK
IMAGE

❑1, Sep 1993 1.95
❑2, Oct 1993 1.95
❑3, Jan 1994 1.95

IMAGE TWO-IN-ONE
IMAGE

❑1, Dec 2001, b&w 2.95

IMAGI-MATION
IMAGI-MATION

❑1; Gnatman 1.75
❑2; Star Wreck 1.75

Other grades: Multiply price above by 5/6 for VF/NM • 2/3 for VERY FINE • 1/3 for FINE • 1/5 for VERY GOOD • 1/8 for GOOD

Imperial Guard

Adventures of the Shi'ar enforcers

©Marvel

Impossible Man Summer Vacation Spectacular

Generally silly stories of the alien imp

©Marvel

Impulse

Tales of a speedy and impulsive teen-ager

©DC

Incomplete Death's Head

Early cyborg stories from Marvel UK

©Marvel

Incredible Hulk

Title picks up Tales to Astonish numbering

©Marvel

N-MINT

IMAGINARIES
IMAGE

- ❑1, Apr 2005; Mike Miller cover 2.95
- ❑1/A, Apr 2005; Greg Titus cover 2.95
- ❑2/A cover 2005 .... 2.95
- ❑2/B cover 2005 .... 2.95
- ❑3/A cover, Sep 2005 .... 2.95
- ❑3/B cover, Sep 2005 .... 2.95
- ❑4, Dec 2005 .... 2.95

IMAGINE
STAR*REACH

- ❑1, May 1978, b&w NA, GD (w); NA, GD (a) 20.00
- ❑1/2nd, May 1978; NA, GD (w); NA, GD (a); Contains color centerspread 10.00
- ❑2, Jun 1978, b&w CR (c); CR (w); CR (a) 10.00
- ❑3, Aug 1978, b&w CR (c); CR (w); CR (a) 15.00
- ❑4, Nov 1978, Black & white with a color story 10.00
- ❑5, Apr 1979, b&w 6.00
- ❑6, Jul 1979, b&w CR (a) 6.00

I'M DICKENS... HE'S FENSTER
DELL

- ❑1, May 1963 .... 25.00
- ❑2, Aug 1963 .... 20.00

IMMORTAL COMBAT
EXPRESS / ENTITY

- ❑1, Feb 1995; Entity Illustrated Novella #5; cardstock cover......... 2.95

IMMORTAL DOCTOR FATE
DC

- ❑1, Jan 1985 MN, KG, JSa (a); O: Doctor Fate. 1.50
- ❑2, Feb 1985 KG (a) 1.50
- ❑3, Mar 1985 KG (a) 1.50

IMMORTAL II
IMAGE

- ❑1, Apr 1997, b&w; cover also says May, indicia says Apr 2.50
- ❑1/A, Apr 1997, b&w; cover says Immortal Two, indicia says Immortal II 2.50
- ❑2, Jun 1997, b&w; cover says Immortal Two, indicia says Immortal II 2.50
- ❑3, Aug 1997, b&w; cover says Immortal Two, indicia says Immortal II 2.50
- ❑4, Sep 1997, b&w; cover says Immortal Two, indicia says Immortal II 2.50
- ❑5, Feb 1998, b&w; cover says Immortal Two, indicia says Immortal II 2.50

IMMORTALS
COMICS BY DAY

- ❑1 .... 1.00

IMP
SLAVE LABOR

- ❑1, Jun 1994 .... 2.95

IMPACT (RCP)
RCP

- ❑1, Apr 1999 .... 2.50
- ❑2, May 1999 .... 2.50
- ❑3, Jun 1999 .... 2.50
- ❑4, Jul 1999 .... 2.50
- ❑5, Aug 1999 .... 2.50
- ❑Annual 1; Collects Impact (RCP) #1-5 13.50

N-MINT

IMPACT CHRISTMAS SPECIAL
DC / IMPACT

- ❑1 1991 .... 2.50

IMPACT COMICS WHO'S WHO
DC / IMPACT

- ❑1 .... 4.95
- ❑2 .... 4.95
- ❑3; trading cards 4.95

IMPERIAL DRAGONS
ALIAS

- ❑1, Sep 2005 .... 0.75

IMPERIAL GUARD
MARVEL

- ❑1, Jan 1997 .... 1.99
- ❑2, Feb 1997; wraparound cover 1.99
- ❑3, Mar 1997 .... 1.99

IMPOSSIBLE MAN SUMMER VACATION SPECTACULAR
MARVEL

- ❑1, Aug 1990 .... 2.00
- ❑2, Aug 1991 .... 2.00

IMPULSE
DC

- ❑1, Apr 1995, MWa (w); O: Impulse. . 4.00
- ❑2, May 1995, MWa (w) 3.50
- ❑3, Jun 1995, MWa (w) 2.50
- ❑4, Jul 1995, MWa (w); 1: White Lightning. 2.50
- ❑5, Aug 1995, MWa (w) 2.50
- ❑6, Sep 1995, MWa (w); Child abuse. 2.25
- ❑7, Oct 1995, MWa (w) 2.25
- ❑8, Nov 1995, MWa (w); V: Blockbuster. Underworld Unleashed 2.25
- ❑9, Dec 1995, MWa (w); A: Xs. 2.25
- ❑10, Jan 1996, MWa (w); continues in Flash #110 .... 2.00
- ❑11, Feb 1996, MWa (w); D: Johnny Quick. 2.00
- ❑12, Mar 1996, MWa (w) 2.00
- ❑13, May 1996, MWa (w) 2.00
- ❑14, Jun 1996, MWa (w); V: White Lightning. V: Trickster. 2.00
- ❑15, Jul 1996, MWa (w); V: White Lightning. V: Trickster. 2.00
- ❑16, Aug 1996, MWa (w); more of Max Mercury's past revealed 2.00
- ❑17, Sep 1996, MWa (w); A: Zatanna. 2.00
- ❑18, Oct 1996 .... 2.00
- ❑19, Nov 1996, MWa (w) 2.00
- ❑20, Dec 1996, MWa (w); Bart plays baseball 1.75
- ❑21, Jan 1997, MWa (w); A: Legion... 1.75
- ❑22, Feb 1997, MWa (w); A: Jesse Quick. 1.75
- ❑23, Mar 1997, MWa (w); Impulse's mother returns 1.75
- ❑24, Apr 1997, MWa (w); Impulse goes to 30th century 1.75
- ❑25, May 1997, MWa (w); Impulse in 30th century 1.75
- ❑26, Jun 1997, MWa (w); Impulse returns to 20th century 1.75
- ❑27, Jul 1997, MWa (w) 1.75
- ❑28, Aug 1997, 1: Arrowette. 1.75
- ❑29, Sep 1997 .... 1.75

N-MINT

- ❑30, Oct 1997, Genesis; Impulse gains new powers 1.75
- ❑31, Nov 1997 .... 1.75
- ❑32, Dec 1997, Face cover 1.95
- ❑33, Jan 1998, 1: Jasper Pierson. V: White Lightning. 1.95
- ❑34, Feb 1998, Max and Impulse travel in time 1.95
- ❑35, Mar 1998, Max and Impulse turned into apes 1.95
- ❑36, Apr 1998 .... 1.95
- ❑37, May 1998, 1: Glory Shredder...... 1.95
- ❑38, Jun 1998, Manchester floods..... 1.95
- ❑39, Jul 1998, A: Trickster. 1.95
- ❑40, Aug 1998 .... 1.95
- ❑41, Sep 1998, A: Arrowette. 2.25
- ❑42, Oct 1998, Virtual pets 2.25
- ❑43, Dec 1998 .... 2.25
- ❑44, Jan 1999, Halloween 2.25
- ❑45, Feb 1999, A: Bart's mother. Christmas 2.25
- ❑46, Mar 1999, A: Flash II (Barry Allen). 2.25
- ❑47, Apr 1999, A: Superman. Superboy cameo 2.25
- ❑48, May 1999, V: Riddler. 2.25
- ❑49, Jun 1999 .... 2.25
- ❑50, Jul 1999, A: Batman. V: Joker. ... 2.25
- ❑51, Aug 1999 .... 2.25
- ❑52, Sep 1999 .... 2.25
- ❑53, Oct 1999, V: Inertia. V: Kalibak.. 2.25
- ❑54, Nov 1999, Day of Judgment....... 2.25
- ❑55, Dec 1999 .... 2.25
- ❑56, Jan 2000, A: Young Justice. 2.25
- ❑57, Feb 2000, A: Plastic Man. 2.25
- ❑58, Mar 2000 .... 2.25
- ❑59, Apr 2000 .... 2.25
- ❑60, May 2000 .... 2.25
- ❑61, Jun 2000 .... 2.25
- ❑62, Jul 2000 .... 2.25
- ❑63, Aug 2000 .... 2.25
- ❑64, Sep 2000 .... 2.25
- ❑65, Oct 2000 .... 2.50
- ❑66, Nov 2000 .... 2.50
- ❑67, Dec 2000 .... 2.50
- ❑68, Jan 2001 .... 2.50
- ❑69, Feb 2001 .... 2.50
- ❑70, Mar 2001 .... 2.50
- ❑71, Apr 2001 .... 2.50
- ❑72, May 2001 .... 2.50
- ❑73, Jun 2001 .... 2.50
- ❑74, Jul 2001 .... 2.50
- ❑75, Aug 2001 .... 2.50
- ❑76, Sep 2001 .... 2.50
- ❑77, Oct 2001 .... 2.50
- ❑78, Nov 2001 .... 2.50
- ❑79, Dec 2001 .... 2.50
- ❑80, Jan 2002 .... 2.50
- ❑81, Feb 2002 .... 2.50
- ❑82, Mar 2002 .... 2.50
- ❑83, Apr 2002 .... 2.50
- ❑84, May 2002 .... 2.50
- ❑85, Jun 2002 .... 2.50
- ❑86, Jul 2002 .... 2.50
- ❑87, Aug 2002 .... 2.50
- ❑88, Sep 2002 .... 2.50

Other grades: Multiply price above by 5/6 for VF/NM • 2/3 for VERY FINE • 1/3 for FINE • 1/5 for VERY GOOD • 1/8 for GOOD

❑89, Oct 2002 ... 2.50
❑1000000, Nov 1998, A: John Fox. ... 4.00
❑Annual 1, ca. 1996, MWa (w); Legends of the Dead Earth ... 5.00
❑Annual 2, ca. 1997, A: Vigilante. Pulp Heroes ... 3.95

IMPULSE/ATOM DOUBLE-SHOT
DC

❑1, Feb 1998 ... 1.95

IMPULSE: BART SAVES THE UNIVERSE
DC

❑1, prestige format; Batman cameo; Flash I (Jay Garrick) cameo; Flash II (Barry Allen) cameo; Flash III (Wally West) cameo ... 5.95

IMPULSE PLUS
DC

❑1, Sep 1997, continues in Superboy Plus #2 ... 2.95

IMP-UNITY
SPOOF

❑1, b&w; parody ... 2.95

INCOMPLETE DEATH'S HEAD
MARVEL

❑1, Jan 1993; Giant-size; Die-cut cover 2.95
❑2, Feb 1993 ... 1.75
❑3, Mar 1993 ... 1.75
❑4, Apr 1993 ... 1.75
❑5, May 1993 ... 1.75
❑6, Jun 1993 ... 1.75
❑7, Jul 1993 ... 1.75
❑8, Aug 1993 ... 1.75
❑9, Sep 1993 ... 1.75
❑10, Oct 1993 ... 1.75
❑11, Nov 1993 ... 1.75
❑12, Dec 1993; double-sized ... 1.75

INCREDIBLE HULK
MARVEL

❑-1, Jul 1997, PD (w); O: Hulk. Flashback ... 2.25
❑1, May 1962, JK (c); SL (w); JK (a); O: Hulk. 1: General "Thunderbolt" Ross. 1: Hulk. 1: Rick Jones. 1: Betty Ross. Hulk's skin is gray (printing mistake) ... 13000.00
❑2, Jul 1962, JK (c); SL (w); SD, JK (a); O: Hulk. Hulk's skin is printed in green ... 3500.00
❑3, Sep 1962, (c); SL (w); JK (a); O: Hulk. 1: Ringmaster. 1: Cannonball (villain). 1: The Clown. 1: Teena the Fat Lady. 1: Bruto the Strongman. .. 2000.00
❑4, Nov 1962, JK (c); SL (w); JK (a); O: Hulk ... 1750.00
❑5, Jan 1963, JK (c); SL (w); JK (a); 1: Tyrannus. ... 1750.00
❑6, Mar 1963, SD (c); SL (w); SD (a); 1: Metal Master. 1: Teen Brigade. Moves to "Tales To Astonish" following this issue ... 2250.00
❑102, Apr 1968, GT (a); O: Hulk. Numbering continued from "Tales To Astonish" ... 150.00
❑103, May 1968, 1: Space Parasite. ... 100.00
❑104, Jun 1968, V: Rhino ... 75.00
❑105, Jul 1968, BEv (w); GT (a); 1: Missing Link. V: Gargoyle. ... 70.00
❑106, Aug 1968, HT, GT (a) ... 50.00
❑107, Sep 1968, HT (a); V: Mandarin. 50.00
❑108, Oct 1968, SL (w); HT, JSe (a); A: Nick Fury ... 50.00
❑109, Nov 1968, (c); SL (w); HT, JSe (a) 50.00
❑110, Dec 1968, HT (c); SL (w); HT, JSe (a) ... 50.00
❑111, Jan 1969, HT (c); SL (w); HT, DA (a) ... 50.00
❑112, Feb 1969, HT (c); SL (w); HT, DA (a) ... 50.00
❑113, Mar 1969, HT (c); SL (w); HT, DA (a); V: Sandman. ... 40.00
❑114, Apr 1969, HT (c); SL (w); HT, DA (a) ... 40.00
❑115, May 1969, HT (c); SL (w); HT, DA (a) ... 40.00
❑116, Jun 1969, HT (c); SL (w); HT, DA (a) ... 35.00
❑117, Jul 1969, HT (c); SL (w); HT, DA (a) ... 35.00
❑118, Aug 1969, HT (c); SL (w); HT (a); A: Sub-Mariner ... 35.00
❑119, Sep 1969, HT (c); SL (w); HT (a) 35.00
❑120, Oct 1969, HT (c); SL (w); HT (a) 35.00
❑121, Nov 1969, HT (c); HT (a) ... 35.00
❑122, Dec 1969, HT (c); HT (a); A: Thing. Hulk vs. Thing ... 55.00
❑123, Jan 1970, HT (c); HT (a) ... 30.00
❑124, Feb 1970, HT (c); SB, HT (a); V: Rhino ... 30.00
❑125, Mar 1970, HT (c); HT (a); V: Absorbing Man ... 30.00
❑126, Apr 1970, HT (c); HT (a) ... 25.00
❑127, May 1970, HT (c); HT (a); V: Mogol ... 25.00
❑128, Jun 1970, HT (c); HT (a) ... 25.00
❑129, Jul 1970, HT (c); HT (a) ... 25.00
❑130, Aug 1970, HT (c); HT (a) ... 25.00
❑131, Sep 1970, HT (c); HT, JSe (a); Iron Man ... 30.00
❑132, Oct 1970, HT (c); HT, JSe (a); V: Hydra ... 25.00
❑133, Nov 1970, HT (c); HT, JSe (a) .. 20.00
❑134, Dec 1970, HT (c); SB, HT (a) ... 16.00
❑135, Jan 1971, HT (c); SB, HT (a); V: Kang ... 16.00
❑136, Feb 1971, HT (c); SB, HT (a); 1: Xeron ... 16.00
❑137, Mar 1971, HT (c); HT (a) ... 20.00
❑138, Apr 1971, HT (c); HT (a) ... 20.00
❑139, May 1971, HT (c); HT (a) ... 20.00
❑140, Jun 1971, HT (c); HT (a); 1: Jarella. Written by Harlan Ellison ... 20.00
❑140/2nd, HT (c); HT (a); 1: Jarella. .. 2.50
❑141, Jul 1971, HT (c); HT, JSe (a); O: Doc Samson. 1: Doc Samson. .. 20.00
❑142, Aug 1971, HT (c); HT, JSe (a) .. 20.00
❑143, Sep 1971, HT (c); JSe (a); V: Doctor Doom ... 20.00
❑144, Oct 1971, HT (c); JSe (a); V: Doctor Doom ... 20.00
❑145, Nov 1971, Giant-size HT (c); HT, JSe (a); O: Hulk. ... 20.00
❑146, Dec 1971, HT (c); HT, JSe (a) .. 20.00
❑148, Feb 1972, HT (c); HT, JSe (a); 1: Peter Corbeau ... 20.00
❑147, Jan 1972, HT (c); HT, JSe (a) ... 20.00
❑149, Mar 1972, HT (c); HT, JSe (a); 1: Inheritor ... 20.00
❑150, Apr 1972, HT (c); HT, JSe (a); 1: Viking. A: Lorna Dane. A: Havoc. 20.00
❑151, May 1972, HT (c); HT, JSe (a) .. 20.00
❑152, Jun 1972, HT (c) ... 25.00
❑153, Jul 1972, HT (c); HT, JSe (a); A: Fantastic Four. A: Peter Parker. A: Matt Murdock ... 20.00
❑154, Aug 1972, HT (c); HT, JSe (a); A: Ant-Man. V: Chameleon ... 20.00
❑155, Sep 1972, HT (c); HT, JSe (a); 1: Shaper of Worlds. V: Captain Axis. 20.00
❑156, Oct 1972, HT (c); HT (a) ... 20.00
❑157, Nov 1972, HT (c); HT (a) ... 20.00
❑158, Dec 1972, HT (c); HT (a); A: Warlock. V: Rhino on Counter-Earth. 20.00
❑159, Jan 1973, V: Abomination. ... 20.00
❑160, Feb 1973, HT (c); HT (a) ... 20.00
❑161, Mar 1973, HT (c); HT (a); A: Mimic. D: Mimic. V: Beast ... 30.00
❑162, Apr 1973, HT (c); HT (a); 1: Wendigo. V: Wendigo. ... 55.00
❑163, May 1973, HT (a); 1: Gremlin... 15.00
❑164, Jun 1973, HT (c); HT (a); 1: Captain Omen. ... 15.00
❑165, Jul 1973, HT (c); HT (a); V: Aquon ... 15.00
❑166, Aug 1973, HT (a); 1: Zzzax. ... 15.00
❑167, Sep 1973, HT (c); HT, JAb (a); V: Modok. ... 15.00
❑168, Oct 1973, HT (c); HT, JAb (a); 1: Harpy. ... 15.00
❑169, Nov 1973, HT (c); HT, JAb (a); 1: Bi-Beast I. V: Bi-Beast I. ... 15.00
❑170, Dec 1973, HT (c); HT, JAb (a); D: Bi-Beast I. ... 15.00
❑171, Jan 1974, HT (c); HT, JAb (a); V: Abomination. V: Rhino. ... 15.00
❑172, Feb 1974, HT (c); HT, JAb (a); A: X-Men. ... 25.00
❑173, Mar 1974, HT (c); HT (a); V: Cobalt Man. ... 15.00
❑174, Apr 1974, HT (c); HT, JAb (a); V: Cobalt Man. Marvel Value Stamp #47: Green Goblin ... 15.00
❑175, May 1974, HT (c); HT, JAb (a); A: Inhumans. V: Inhumans. Marvel Value Stamp #56: Rawhide Kid ... 15.00
❑176, Jun 1974, HT (c); HT, JAb (a); A: Warlock. Marvel Value Stamp #67: Cyclops ... 15.00
❑177, Jul 1974, HT (c); HT, JAb (a); D: Warlock. Marvel Value Stamp #39: Iron Fist ... 17.00
❑178, Aug 1974, HT (c); HT, JAb (a); D: Warlock. Warlock returns ... 17.00
❑179, Sep 1974, HT (c); HT, JAb (a); Marvel Value Stamp #16: Shang-Chi ... 16.00
❑180, Oct 1974, HT (c); HT, JAb (a); 1: Wolverine (cameo). A: Wendigo. Marvel Value Stamp #67: Cyclops .. 180.00
❑181, Nov 1974, HT (c); HT, JAb (a); 1: Wolverine (full appearance). A: Wendigo. Marvel Value Stamp #54: Shanna the She-Devil ... 750.00
❑181/Ace, Wizard Ace Edition; acetate cover ... 5.00
❑182, Dec 1974, HT (c); HT (a); O: Hammer. O: Anvil. 1: Hammer. 1: Anvil. 1: Crackajack. A: Wolverine. V: Hammer. V: Anvil. Marvel Value Stamp #59: Golem ... 100.00
❑183, Jan 1975, V: Zzzax. Marvel Value Stamp #4: Thing ... 12.00
❑184, Feb 1975, HT (c); HT (a); Marvel Value Stamp #58: Mandarin ... 10.00
❑185, Mar 1975, HT (c); HT (a) ... 10.00
❑186, Apr 1975, HT (c); HT (a); 1: Devastator I (Kirov Petrovna). D: Devastator I (Kirov Petrovna). Marvel Value Stamp #11: Deathlok. 10.00
❑187, May 1975, HT (c); HT, JSa (a); V: Gremlin. ... 10.00
❑188, Jun 1975, HT (c); HT, JSa (a); V: Gremlin. ... 10.00
❑189, Jul 1975, HT (c); HT, JSa (a); V: Mole Man. ... 10.00
❑190, Aug 1975, HT (c); HT (a); 1: Glorian. V: Toad Men ... 10.00
❑191, Sep 1975, HT (c); HT, JSa (a); V: Shaper of Worlds. ... 8.00
❑192, Oct 1975, HT, JSa (a) ... 8.00
❑193, Nov 1975, GK (c); HT, JSa (a); V: Doc Samson. ... 8.00
❑194, Dec 1975, GK (c); SB, JSa (a) .. 8.00
❑195, Jan 1976, SB, JSa (a); V: Abomination. ... 8.00
❑196, Feb 1976, GK (c); SB, JSa (a); V: Abomination. ... 8.00
❑197, Mar 1976, BWr (c); SB, JSa (a); V: Man-Thing. V: Gardner. ... 8.00
❑198, Apr 1976, GK (c); SB, JSa (a); A: Man-Thing. ... 8.00
❑198/30 cent, Apr 1976, 30 cent regional variant ... 20.00
❑199, May 1976, RB (c); SB, JSa (a); V: Doc Samson. ... 8.00
❑199/30 cent, May 1976, 30 cent regional variant ... 20.00
❑200, Jun 1976, 200th anniversary issue RB (c); SB, JSa (a); A: Surfer and others. ... 11.00
❑200/30 cent, Jun 1976, 200th anniversary issue; RB (c); SB, JSa (a); A: Surfer and others. 30 cent regional variant ... 30.00
❑201, Jul 1976, RB, JR (c); SB, JSa (a) 7.00
❑201/30 cent, Jul 1976, 30 cent regional variant ... 20.00
❑202, Aug 1976, RB, JR (c); SB, JSa (a); A: Jarella. ... 7.00
❑202/30 cent, Aug 1976, RB (c); JSa (a); 30 cent regional variant ... 20.00
❑203, Sep 1976, JR (c); SB, JSa (a); V: Psyklop. ... 7.00
❑204, Oct 1976, HT (c); HT, JSa (a); O: Hulk. 1: Kronus. ... 7.00
❑205, Nov 1976, HT (c); SB, JSa (a) .. 7.00
❑206, Dec 1976, DC (c); SB, JSa (a) .. 7.00
❑207, Jan 1977, DC (c); SB, JSa (a); A: Defenders. ... 7.00
❑208, Feb 1977, SB, JSa (a); Newsstand edition (distributed by Curtis); issue number in box ... 7.00
❑208/Whitman, Feb 1977, SB, JSa (a); Special markets edition (usually sold in Whitman bagged prepacks); price appears in a diamond; UPC barcode appears ... 7.00

Incredible Hulk (2nd Series)

First 11 issue were simply titled "Hulk"

©Marvel

Incredible Hulk and Wolverine

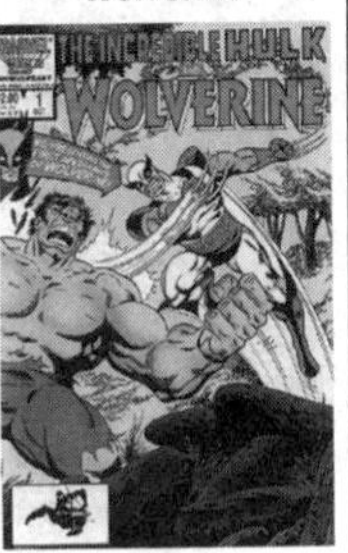

Reprints first Wolverine story

©Marvel

Incredible Hulk: Future Imperfect

Celebrated Peter David future tale

©Marvel

Incredible Hulk: Hercules Unleashed

Follow-up to the Onslaught storyline

©Marvel

Incredible Hulk Magazine

Giant-sized issue with plenty of reprints

©Marvel

	N-MINT
❑209, Mar 1977, SB, JSa (a); V: Absorbing Man. Newsstand edition (distributed by Curtis); issue number in box	7.00
❑209/Whitman, Mar 1977, SB, JSa (a); V: Absorbing Man. Special markets edition (usually sold in Whitman bagged prepacks); price appears in a diamond; UPC barcode appears	7.00
❑210, Apr 1977, SB (a); A: Doctor Druid. Newsstand edition (distributed by Curtis); issue number in box	7.00
❑210/Whitman, Apr 1977, SB (a); A: Doctor Druid. Special markets edition (usually sold in Whitman bagged prepacks); price appears in a diamond; UPC barcode appears	7.00
❑211, May 1977, SB (a); A: Doctor Druid. Newsstand edition (distributed by Curtis); issue number in box	7.00
❑211/Whitman, May 1977, SB (a); A: Doctor Druid. Special markets edition (usually sold in Whitman bagged prepacks); price appears in a diamond; UPC barcode appears	7.00
❑212, Jun 1977, RB (c); SB (a); 1: Constrictor. V: Constrictor. Newsstand edition (distributed by Curtis); issue number in box	7.00
❑212/Whitman, Jun 1977, RB (c); SB (a); 1: Constrictor. V: Constrictor. Special markets edition (usually sold in Whitman bagged prepacks); price appears in a diamond; UPC barcode appears	7.00
❑212/35 cent, Jun 1977, RB (c); SB (a); 1: Constrictor. V: Constrictor. 35 cent regional variant newsstand edition (distributed by Curtis); issue number in box	15.00
❑213, Jul 1977, SB, TP (a); V: Quintronic Man. Newsstand edition (distributed by Curtis); issue number in box	7.00
❑213/Whitman, Jul 1977, SB, TP (a); V: Quintronic Man. Special markets edition (usually sold in Whitman bagged prepacks); price appears in a diamond; UPC barcode appears	7.00
❑213/35 cent, Jul 1977, SB, TP (a); V: Quintronic Man. 35 cent regional variant newsstand edition (distributed by Curtis); issue number in box	15.00
❑214, Aug 1977, SB (a); Jack of Hearts; Newsstand edition (distributed by Curtis); issue number in box	7.00
❑214/Whitman, Aug 1977, SB (a); Special markets edition (usually sold in Whitman bagged prepacks); price appears in a diamond; UPC barcode appears	7.00
❑214/35 cent, Aug 1977, SB (a); Jack of Hearts; 35 cent regional variant newsstand edition (distributed by Curtis); issue number in box	15.00
❑215, Sep 1977, SB (a); 1: Bi-Beast II. Newsstand edition (distributed by Curtis); issue number in box	7.00
❑215/Whitman, Sep 1977, SB (a); 1: Bi-Beast II. Special markets edition (usually sold in Whitman bagged prepacks); price appears in a diamond; UPC barcode appears	7.00

	N-MINT
❑215/35 cent, Sep 1977, SB (a); 1: Bi-Beast II. 35 cent regional variant newsstand edition (distributed by Curtis); issue number in box	15.00
❑216, Oct 1977, SB (a); V: Bi-Beast II. Newsstand edition (distributed by Curtis); issue number in box	7.00
❑216/Whitman, Oct 1977, SB (a); V: Bi-Beast II. Special markets edition (usually sold in Whitman bagged prepacks); price appears in a diamond; no UPC barcode	7.00
❑216/35 cent, Oct 1977, SB (a); V: Bi-Beast II. 35 cent regional variant newsstand edition (distributed by Curtis); issue number in box	15.00
❑217, Nov 1977, JSn (c); SB (a); V: Circus of Crime. Newsstand edition (distributed by Curtis); issue number in box	7.00
❑217/Whitman, Nov 1977, JSn (c); SB (a); V: Circus of Crime. Special markets edition (usually sold in Whitman bagged prepacks); price appears in a diamond; no UPC barcode	7.00
❑218, Dec 1977, KP, GT (a); Doc Samson vs. Rhino; Newsstand edition (distributed by Curtis); issue number in box	7.00
❑218/Whitman, Dec 1977, KP, GT (a); Special markets edition (usually sold in Whitman bagged prepacks); price appears in a diamond; no UPC barcode	7.00
❑219, Jan 1978, SB (a)	5.00
❑220, Feb 1978, SB (a)	5.00
❑221, Mar 1978, SB, AA (a); A: Stingray.	5.00
❑222, Apr 1978, JSn, AA (a); Newsstand edition (distributed by Curtis); issue number in box	5.00
❑222/Whitman, Apr 1978, JSn, AA (a); Special markets edition (usually sold in Whitman bagged prepacks); price appears in a diamond; UPC barcode appears	5.00
❑223, May 1978, SB (a); Newsstand edition (distributed by Curtis); issue number in box	5.00
❑223/Whitman, May 1978, SB (a); Special markets edition (usually sold in Whitman bagged prepacks); price appears in a diamond; no UPC barcode	5.00
❑224, Jun 1978, SB (a); Newsstand edition (distributed by Curtis); issue number in box	5.00
❑224/Whitman, Jun 1978, SB (a); Special markets edition (usually sold in Whitman bagged prepacks); price appears in a diamond; no UPC barcode	5.00
❑225, Jul 1978, SB (a)	5.00
❑226, Aug 1978, SB, JSt (a); Newsstand edition (distributed by Curtis); issue number in box	5.00
❑226/Whitman, Aug 1978, SB, JSt (a); Special markets edition (usually sold in Whitman bagged prepacks); price appears in a diamond; UPC barcode appears	5.00
❑227, Sep 1978, HT (c); SB, KJ (a); Doc Samson; Newsstand edition (distributed by Curtis); issue number in box	5.00

	N-MINT
❑227/Whitman, Sep 1978, HT (c); SB, KJ (a); Special markets edition (usually sold in Whitman bagged prepacks); price appears in a diamond; no UPC barcode	5.00
❑228, Oct 1978, HT, BMc (c); SB, BMc (a); O: Moonstone. 1: Moonstone. Newsstand edition (distributed by Curtis); issue number in box	5.00
❑228/Whitman, Oct 1978, HT, BMc (c); SB, BMc (a); O: Moonstone. 1: Moonstone. Special markets edition (usually sold in Whitman bagged prepacks); price appears in a diamond; no UPC barcode	5.00
❑229, Nov 1978, BL, HT (c); SB (a); A: Moonstone. A: Doc Samson. Newsstand edition (distributed by Curtis); issue number in box	5.00
❑229/Whitman, Nov 1978, BL, HT (c); SB (a); A: Moonstone. A: Doc Samson. Special markets edition (usually sold in Whitman bagged prepacks); price appears in a diamond; no UPC barcode	5.00
❑230, Dec 1978, BL (c); BL, JM (a); Newsstand edition (distributed by Curtis); issue number in box	5.00
❑230/Whitman, Dec 1978, BL (c); BL, JM (a); Special markets edition (usually sold in Whitman bagged prepacks); price appears in a diamond; no UPC barcode	5.00
❑231, Jan 1979, HT (c); SB (a); Newsstand edition (distributed by Curtis); issue number in box	5.00
❑231/Whitman, Jan 1979, HT (c); SB (a); Special markets edition (usually sold in Whitman bagged prepacks); price appears in a diamond; no UPC barcode	5.00
❑232, Feb 1979, (c); SB (a); A: Captain America. Newsstand edition (distributed by Curtis); issue number in box	5.00
❑232/Whitman, Feb 1979, (c); SB (a); A: Captain America. Special markets edition (usually sold in Whitman bagged prepacks); price appears in a diamond; no UPC barcode	5.00
❑233, Mar 1979 AM (c); SB (a); A: Marvel Man (Quasar)	5.00
❑234, Apr 1979, AM (c); SB, JAb (a); 1: Quasar. (Marvel Man changed name to Quasar)	5.00
❑235, May 1979, AM (c); SB (a); A: Machine Man. Newsstand edition (distributed by Curtis); issue number in box	5.00
❑235/Whitman, May 1979, AM (c); SB (a); A: Machine Man. Special markets edition (usually sold in Whitman bagged prepacks); price appears in a diamond; no UPC barcode	5.00
❑236, Jun 1979, AM (c); SB (a); A: Machine Man.	5.00
❑237, Jul 1979, AM (c); SB, JAb (a)	5.00
❑238, Aug 1979, AM (c); SB, JAb (a).	5.00
❑239, Sep 1979, AM (c); SB (a)	5.00
❑240, Oct 1979, AM (c); SB, JSt (a)	5.00
❑241, Nov 1979, SB (a)	4.00
❑242, Dec 1979, BL (c); SB (a); V: Tyranus.	4.00

Other grades: Multiply price above by 5/6 for VF/NM • 2/3 for VERY FINE • 1/3 for FINE • 1/5 for VERY GOOD • 1/8 for GOOD

	N-MINT
❑243, Jan 1980, AM (c); SB (a); A: Power Man and Iron Fist.	4.00
❑244, Feb 1980, AM (c); CI (a); D: It, the Living Colossus.	4.00
❑245, Mar 1980, AM (c); SB (a)	4.00
❑246, Apr 1980, RB, JAb (c); SB (a); A: Captain Marvel.	4.00
❑247, May 1980, AM (c); SB (a); A: Jarella.	4.00
❑248, Jun 1980, MG (c); SB (a); V: Gardener.	4.00
❑249, Jul 1980, SD (c); SD (a); A: Jack Frost.	4.00
❑250, Aug 1980, Giant-sized AM (c); SB (a); 1: Sabra (cameo). A: Silver Surfer.	7.00
❑251, Sep 1980, MG (c); SB (a); A: 3-D Man.	2.50
❑252, Oct 1980, RB, FS (c); SB (a); A: Changelings.	2.50
❑253, Nov 1980, RB, FS (c); SB (a); A: Doc Samson. A: Changelings.	2.50
❑254, Dec 1980, AM (c); SB (a); O: X-Ray. O: Vector. O: U-Foes. O: Ironclad. 1: X-Ray. 1: Vector. 1: U-Foes. 1: Ironclad.	2.50
❑255, Jan 1981, AM, RB (c); SB (a); V: Thor.	2.50
❑256, Feb 1981, AM, RB (c); SB (a); O: Sabra. 1: Sabra (full).	2.50
❑257, Mar 1981, AM, TD (c); SB (a); O: Arabian Knight. 1: Arabian Knight.	2.50
❑258, Apr 1981, AM, FM (c); SB (a); O: Ursa Major. 1: Ursa Major. V: Soviet Super-Soldiers.	2.50
❑259, May 1981, AM, PB (c); AM, SB (a); O: Presence. O: Vanguard. A: Soviet Super-Soldiers.	2.50
❑260, Jun 1981, AM (c); SB (a)	2.50
❑261, Jul 1981, FM (c); SB (a); V: Absorbing Man.	2.50
❑262, Aug 1981, AM (c); SB (a)	2.50
❑263, Sep 1981, AM (c); SB (a); V: Landslide, Avalanche.	2.50
❑264, Oct 1981, FM (c); SB (a)	2.50
❑265, Nov 1981, AM (c); SB (a); 1: Shooting Star. 1: Firebird. V: Rangers.	2.50
❑266, Dec 1981, AM (c); SB (a); V: High Evolutionary.	2.50
❑267, Jan 1982, AM (c); SB (a); O: Glorian. V: Glorian.	2.50
❑268, Feb 1982, FM (c); SB (a); O: Rick Jones.	2.50
❑269, Mar 1982, AM (c); SB (a)	2.50
❑270, Apr 1982, AM (c); SB (a)	2.50
❑271, May 1982, 20th Anniversary Issue AM (c); SB (a); 1: Rocket Raccoon.	2.50
❑272, Jun 1982, SB (a); A: Alpha Flight.	2.50
❑273, Jul 1982, SB (a); A: Alpha Flight.	2.50
❑274, Aug 1982, SB (a)	2.50
❑275, Sep 1982, SB, JSt (a); V: Megalith.	2.50
❑276, Oct 1982, SB, JSt (a); V: U-Foes.	2.50
❑277, Nov 1982, SB (a); V: U-Foes.	2.50
❑278, Dec 1982, AM, SB (c); SB, JSt (a); Hulk granted amnesty	2.50
❑279, Jan 1983	2.50
❑280, Feb 1983, SB (a)	2.50
❑281, Mar 1983, SB, JSt (a)	2.50
❑282, Apr 1983, AM, JSt (c); SB, JSt (a); A: She-Hulk.	2.50
❑283, May 1983, AM (c); SB, JSt (a); A: Avengers.	2.50
❑284, Jun 1983, AM, JSt (c); SB, JSt (a); A: Avengers. V: Leader.	2.50
❑285, Jul 1983, JSt (c); SB (a)	2.50
❑286, Aug 1983, BA (c); SB (a)	4.00
❑287, Sep 1983, AM (c); SB (a)	2.50
❑288, Oct 1983, AM, JSt (c); SB, JM (a); V: Modok.	2.50
❑289, Nov 1983, AM (c); SB, JSt (a); V: A.I.M.	2.50
❑290, Dec 1983, AM (c); SB (a); V: Modok. V: Modame.	2.50
❑291, Jan 1984, SB (a); O: Thunderbolt Ross. Assistant Editor Month.	2.50
❑292, Feb 1984, KN (c); SB, JSt (a)	2.50
❑293, Mar 1984, SB (a); V: Fantastic Four.	2.50
❑294, Apr 1984, SB (a)	2.50
❑295, May 1984, BSz (c); SB (a); V: Boomerang. Secret Wars aftermath	2.50
❑296, Jun 1984, BSz (c); SB (a); V: ROM.	5.00
❑297, Jul 1984, BSz (c); SB (a)	4.00
❑298, Aug 1984, KN (c); SB (a); A: Nightmare.	2.50
❑299, Sep 1984, SB (a); A: Doctor Strange	2.50
❑300, Oct 1984, 300th anniversary edition; (c); SB (a); V: Everybody. Hulk banished to Crossroads.	4.00
❑301, Nov 1984, BSz (c); SB (a)	2.50
❑302, Dec 1984, SB (a)	2.50
❑303, Jan 1985, SB (a)	2.50
❑304, Feb 1985, SB (a)	2.50
❑305, Mar 1985, SB (a); V: U-Foes.	2.50
❑306, Apr 1985, SB (a)	2.50
❑307, May 1985, SB (a)	2.50
❑308, Jun 1985, SB (a)	2.50
❑309, Jul 1985, SB (a)	2.50
❑310, Aug 1985, AW (c); AW (a)	2.50
❑311, Sep 1985, AW (c)	2.50
❑312, Oct 1985, BSz (c); Secret Wars II	2.50
❑313, Nov 1985, A: Alpha Flight.	2.50
❑314, Dec 1985, JBy (c); JBy (w); JBy, BWi (a); A: Doc Samson.	2.50
❑315, Jan 1986, JBy (c); JBy (w); JBy (a); Hulk and Banner separated	3.00
❑316, Feb 1986, JBy (c); JBy (w); JBy (a); A: Avengers.	3.00
❑317, Mar 1986, JBy (c); JBy (w); JBy (a)	3.00
❑318, Apr 1986, JBy (c); JBy (w); JBy (a)	3.00
❑319, May 1986, JBy (c); JBy (w); JBy (a); Wedding of Bruce Banner and Betty Ross	3.00
❑320, Jun 1986, (c); AM (w); AM (a); V: Doc Samson	2.00
❑321, Jul 1986, AM, BWi (c); AM (w); AM (a); V: Avengers.	2.00
❑322, Aug 1986, AM (c); AM (w); AM (a)	2.00
❑323, Sep 1986, AM (c); AM (w); AM (a)	2.00
❑324, Oct 1986, AM (c); AM (w); AM (a); O: Hulk. 1: Grey Hulk (new).	5.00
❑325, Nov 1986, AM (c); AM (w); AM, BMc (a); 1: Rick Jones as green Hulk.	3.00
❑326, Dec 1986, BMc (c); AM (w); Green Hulk vs. Grey Hulk	3.50
❑327, Jan 1987, AM (c); AM (w); V: Zzzax.	2.50
❑328, Feb 1987, BMc (c); PD (w); TD (a); 1st Peter David writing	2.50
❑329, Mar 1987, AM (c); AM (w); AM (a)	2.00
❑330, Apr 1987, TMc (c); AM (w); AM, TMc (a); D: Thunderbolt Ross.	5.00
❑331, May 1987, PD (w); TMc (a); 2nd Peter David issue; gray Hulk revealed	5.00
❑332, Jun 1987, BMc (c); PD (w); TMc (a)	5.00
❑333, Jul 1987, (c); PD (w); TMc (a).	5.00
❑334, Aug 1987, (c); PD (w); TMc (a)	5.00
❑335, Sep 1987, BMc (c); PD (w)	2.00
❑336, Oct 1987, BMc (c); PD (w); TMc (a); A: X-Factor.	3.00
❑337, Nov 1987, BMc (c); PD (w); TMc (a); A: X-Factor.	3.00
❑338, Dec 1987, (c); PD (w); TMc (a); 1: Mercy	3.00
❑339, Jan 1988, BMc (c); PD (w); TMc (a); A: Ashcan, Leader.	3.00
❑340, Feb 1988, TMc, BWi (c); PD (w); TMc (a); V: Wolverine	14.00
❑341, Mar 1988, TMc (c); PD (w); TMc (a); V: Man-Bull.	4.00
❑342, Apr 1988, TMc (c); PD (w); TMc (a); A: Leader.	2.00
❑343, May 1988, TMc (c); PD (w); TMc (a)	2.00
❑344, Jun 1988, TMc, BWi (c); PD (w); TMc, BWi (a)	2.00
❑345, Jul 1988, Double-size TMc (c); PD (w); TMc (a)	2.00
❑346, Aug 1988, TMc, EL (c); PD (w); EL (a)	2.00
❑347, Sep 1988, PD (w); MGu (a); in Vegas	2.00
❑348, Oct 1988, MGu (c); PD (w); MGu (a); V: Absorbing Man.	2.00
❑349, Nov 1988, BMc (c); PD (w); A: Spider-Man.	2.00
❑350, Dec 1988, PD (w); Hulk vs. Thing	5.00
❑351, Jan 1989, PD (w); BWi (a)	2.00
❑352, Feb 1989, PD (w)	2.00
❑353, Mar 1989, PD (w)	2.00
❑354, Apr 1989, PD (w)	2.00
❑355, May 1989, PD (w); HT (a); A: Glorian.	2.00
❑356, Jun 1989, BMc (c); PD (w)	2.00
❑357, Jul 1989, BMc (c); PD (w)	2.00
❑358, Aug 1989, PD (w)	2.00
❑359, Sep 1989, JBy (c); PD (w)	2.00
❑360, Oct 1989, BMc (c); V: Nightmare.	2.00
❑361, Nov 1989, BMc (c); PD (w); Iron Man	2.00
❑362, Nov 1989, KN (c); PD (w); A: Werewolf by Night.	2.00
❑363, Dec 1989, GC (c); PD (w); V: Grey Gargoyle. Acts of Vengeance	2.00
❑364, Dec 1989, PD (w); V: Abomination.	2.00
❑365, Jan 1990, PD (w); V: Thing.	2.00
❑366, Feb 1990, PD (w); V: Leader.	2.00
❑367, Mar 1990, PD (w); V: Madman. 1st Dale Keown art	2.00
❑368, Apr 1990, PD (w); 1: Pantheon. V: Mr. Hyde.	2.00
❑369, May 1990, (c); PD (w); BMc (a); V: Freedom Force.	2.00
❑370, Jun 1990, BMc (c); PD (w); BMc (a); A: Doctor Strange. A: Sub-Mariner.	2.00
❑371, Jul 1990, BMc (c); PD (w); BMc (a); A: Doctor Strange. A: Sub-Mariner.	2.00
❑372, Aug 1990, PD (w); BMc (a); Green Hulk returns	3.00
❑373, Sep 1990, BMc (c); PD (w)	2.00
❑374, Oct 1990, BMc (c); PD (w); BMc (a); V: Super Skrull.	2.00
❑375, Nov 1990, BMc (c); PD (w); BMc (a); V: Super Skrull.	2.00
❑376, Dec 1990, BMc (c); PD (w); BMc (a); 1: Agamemnon (as hologram). Green Hulk vs. Grey Hulk	2.00
❑377, Jan 1991, BMc (c); PD (w); BMc (a); 1: Hulk (new, smart). Fluorescent inks on cover	2.50
❑377/2nd, Jan 1991, BMc (c); PD (w); BMc (a); 1: Hulk (new, smart). Fluorescent inks on cover; 2nd printing (gold)	2.00
❑377/3rd, Jan 1991, BMc (c); PD (w); BMc (a)	2.00
❑378, Feb 1991, BMc (c); PD (w); Rhino as Santa	3.00
❑379, Mar 1991, BMc (c); PD (w); A: Pantheon.	2.00
❑380, Apr 1991, PD (w); Doc Samson solo story	2.00
❑381, May 1991, PD (w); Hulk joins Pantheon	2.00
❑382, Jun 1991, BMc (c); PD (w)	2.00
❑383, Jul 1991, PD (w); V: Abomination.	2.00
❑384, Aug 1991, PD (w); V: Abomination. Infinity Gauntlet; tiny Hulk	2.00
❑385, Sep 1991, PD (w); Infinity Gauntlet	4.00
❑386, Oct 1991, PD (w); A: Sabra.	3.00
❑387, Nov 1991, PD (w); A: Sabra.	2.00
❑388, Dec 1991, PD (w); 1: Speedfreek.	2.00
❑389, Jan 1992, A: Man-Thing.	2.00
❑390, Feb 1992, PD (w)	2.00
❑391, Mar 1992, PD (w); A: X-Factor.	2.00
❑392, Apr 1992, PD (w); A: X-Factor.	3.00
❑393, May 1992, 30th Anniversary of the Hulk, Green Foil Cover PD (w); HT (a); A: X-Factor.	4.00
❑393/2nd, May 1992, 30th Anniversary of the Hulk; PD (w); HT (a); non-foil cover	2.50
❑394, Jun 1992, PD (w); 1: Trauma.	3.00
❑395, Jul 1992, PD (w); A: Punisher.	1.50
❑396, Aug 1992, PD (w); A: Punisher. V: Mr. Frost. V: Doctor Octopus.	1.50
❑397, Sep 1992, PD (w); V: U-Foes.	1.50
❑398, Oct 1992, PD (w); V: Leader.	1.50
❑399, Nov 1992, JDu (c); PD (w); JDu (a); D: Marlo.	1.50
❑400, Dec 1992, PD (w); JDu (a); D: Leader. Marlo revived; Prism cover.	3.00
❑400/2nd, Dec 1992, PD (w); JDu (a)	2.50
❑401, Jan 1993, PD (w); JDu (a); 1: Agamemnon (physical). V: U-Foes.	1.50

Other grades: Multiply price above by 5/6 for VF/NM • 2/3 for VERY FINE • 1/3 for FINE • 1/5 for VERY GOOD • 1/8 for GOOD

Incredible Hulk Versus Quasimodo

Based on Saturday morning cartoon episode
©Marvel

Indiana Jones and the Last Crusade

Marvel adaptation of third Indy film
©Marvel

Indiana Jones and the Spear of Destiny

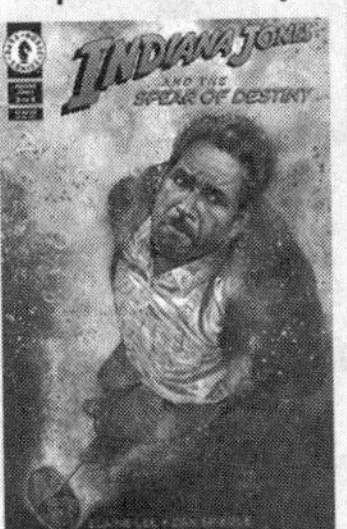

Original story picks up after Last Crusade
©Dark Horse

Indiana Jones and the Temple of Doom

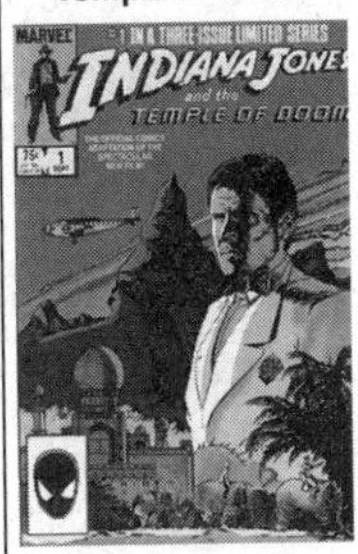

1984 film adaptation by Marvel
©Marvel

Inferior Five

Merryman, Dumb Bunny, and company
©DC

	N-MINT
❑402, Feb 1993, PD (w); JDu (a); A: Doc Samson. V: Juggernaut.	1.50
❑403, Mar 1993, PD (w); V: Juggernaut.	1.50
❑404, Apr 1993, PD (w); A: Avengers. V: Juggernaut.	1.50
❑405, May 1993, PD (w)	1.50
❑406, Jun 1993, PD (w); A: Doc Samson. A: Captain America	1.50
❑407, Jul 1993, PD (w); 1: Piecemeal.	1.50
❑408, Aug 1993, PD (w); D: Perseus. V: Madman.	1.50
❑409, Sep 1993, PD (w); A: Killpower. A: Motormouth.	1.50
❑410, Oct 1993, PD (w); A: Doctor Samson. A: S.H.I.E.L.D.. A: Nick Fury.	1.50
❑411, Nov 1993, PD (w); A: Nick Fury.	1.50
❑412, Dec 1993, PD (w); A: She-Hulk. V: Bi-Beast.	1.50
❑413, Jan 1994, PD (w)	1.50
❑414, Feb 1994, PD (w); A: Silver Surfer.	1.50
❑415, Mar 1994, PD (w); A: Starjammers.	1.50
❑416, Apr 1994, PD (w)	1.50
❑417, May 1994, PD (w); Rick's bachelor party	1.50
❑418, Jun 1994, PD (w); D: Sandman. Wedding of Rick Jones and Marlo; Peter David (writer) puts himself in script	2.00
❑418/Variant, Jun 1994, PD (w); D: Sandman. Die-cut cover; Wedding of Rick Jones and Marlo; Peter David (writer) puts himself in script	3.00
❑419, Jul 1994, PD (w); V: Talos the Tamed.	1.50
❑420, Aug 1994, PD (w); D: Jim Wilson.	1.50
❑421, Sep 1994, PD (w); V: Thor.	1.50
❑422, Oct 1994, PD (w)	1.50
❑423, Nov 1994, PD (w); A: Hel.	1.50
❑424, Dec 1994, PD (w)	1.50
❑425, Jan 1995, Giant-size PD (w)	2.25
❑425/Variant, Jan 1995, Giant-size; PD (w); Hologram cover	3.50
❑426, Feb 1995, PD (w); Hulk reverts to Banner	1.50
❑426/Deluxe, Feb 1995, Deluxe edition PD (w)	1.95
❑427, Mar 1995, PD (w); A: Man-Thing.	1.50
❑427/Deluxe, Mar 1995, PD (w)	1.95
❑428, Apr 1995 PD (w); A: Man-Thing.	1.50
❑428/Deluxe, Apr 1995, PD (w)	1.95
❑429, May 1995, (c); PD (w)	1.50
❑429/Deluxe, May 1995, (c); PD (w)	1.95
❑430, Jun 1995, PD (w); V: Speedfreek.	1.95
❑431, Jul 1995, (c); PD (w); V: Abomination.	1.95
❑432, Aug 1995, (c); PD (w); V: Abomination.	1.95
❑433, Sep 1995, PD (w); A: Punisher. A: Nick Fury	1.95
❑434, Oct 1995, (c); PD (w); AM (a); A: Howling Commandoes. Funeral of Nick Fury; OverPower cards inserted	1.95
❑435, Nov 1995, AM (c); PD (w); AM (a); V: Rhino. Casey at the Bat tribute	1.95

	N-MINT
❑436, Dec 1995, (c); PD (w); A: Maestro. continued in Cutting Edge #1	1.95
❑437, Jan 1996, AM (c); PD (w)	1.95
❑438, Feb 1996, (c); PD (w)	1.95
❑439, Mar 1996, (c); PD (w)	1.95
❑440, Apr 1996, (c); PD (w); V: Thor.	1.95
❑441, May 1996, (c); PD (w); A: She-Hulk. Pulp Fiction tribute cover	1.95
❑442, Jun 1996, (c); PD (w); A: She-Hulk. A: Doc Samson. A: Molecule Man. no Hulk	1.95
❑443, Jul 1996, (c); PD (w); A: Janis.	1.50
❑444, Aug 1996, PD (w); V: Cable.	1.50
❑445, Sep 1996, PD (w); A: Avengers.	1.50
❑446, Oct 1996, PD (w); post-Onslaught; Hulk turns savage and highly radioactive	1.50
❑447, Nov 1996, PD (w)	1.50
❑448, Dec 1996, PD (w); A: Pantheon.	1.50
❑449, Jan 1997, PD (w); 1: The Thunderbolts.	8.00
❑450, Feb 1997, Giant-size; PD (w); A: Doctor Strange. connection to Heroes Reborn universe revealed	5.00
❑451, Mar 1997, PD (w); Hulk takes over Duck Key	2.00
❑452, Apr 1997, PD (w); Hulk vs. Hurricane Betty	2.00
❑453, May 1997, PD (w); Hulk vs. Hulk	2.00
❑454, Jun 1997, PD (w)	2.00
❑455, Aug 1997, gatefold summary; PD (w); DGr (a); A: Apocalypse. V: X-Men. Thunderbolt Ross returns	2.00
❑456, Sep 1997, gatefold summary; PD (w); JKu (a); Apocalypse transforms Hulk into War	2.00
❑457, Oct 1997, gatefold summary PD (w); V: Juggernaut	2.00
❑458, Nov 1997, gatefold summary PD (w); A: Mercy. V: Mr. Hyde	2.00
❑459, Dec 1997, gatefold summary PD (w); A: Mercy. V: Abomination.	2.00
❑460, Jan 1998, gatefold summary; (c); PD (w); The Hulk and Bruce Banner are reunited; return of Maestro	2.00
❑461, Feb 1998, gatefold summary PD (w); V: Destroyer.	2.00
❑462, Mar 1998, gatefold summary PD (w)	2.00
❑463, Apr 1998, gatefold summary PD (w)	2.00
❑464, May 1998, gatefold summary JKu (c); PD (w); JKu (a); A: Silver Surfer.	2.00
❑465, Jun 1998, gatefold summary (c); PD (w); A: Reed Richards. A: Tony Stark	2.00
❑466, Jul 1998, gatefold summary PD (w); D: Betty Banner.	2.00
❑467, Aug 1998, gatefold summary; PD (w); final Peter David-written issue	2.00
❑468, Sep 1998, gatefold summary; 1st Joe Casey issue	2.00
❑469, Oct 1998, gatefold summary (c); V: Super-Adaptoid.	2.00
❑470, Nov 1998, gatefold summary (c); V: Circus of Crime.	2.00

	N-MINT
❑471, Dec 1998, gatefold summary V: Circus of Crime.	2.00
❑472, Jan 1999, gatefold summary (c); A: Xantarean.	2.00
❑473, Feb 1999, gatefold summary A: Xanterean. A: Watchers. A: Abomination. A: Xantarean.	1.99
❑474, Mar 1999, (c); A: Xanterean. A: Watchers. A: Abomination. A: Thunderbolt Ross.	1.99
❑Annual 1, Oct 1968, JSo (c)	115.00
❑Annual 2, Oct 1969, SD, JK (a); Reprints from Incredible Hulk #3 and Tales to Astonish #62-66	40.00
❑Annual 3, Jan 1971, Cover reads "King-Size Special"; JK (a); Cover reads King-Size Special; Reprints from Tales to Astonish #70-74	25.00
❑Annual 4, Jan 1972, HT (c); SL (w); JK, JR (a); Cover reads "Special"; Reprints from Tales to Astonish #75-77 and Not Brand Ecch #5	25.00
❑Annual 5, ca. 1976, (c); SB, JAb (a); V: Xemnu. V: Groot. V: Diablo. V: Diablo. V: Blip. V: Taboo. V: Goom.	9.00
❑Annual 6, ca. 1977, (c); HT (a); 1: Paragon. A: Warlock. A: Doctor Strange. Doctor Strange	7.00
❑Annual 7, ca. 1978, JBy, BL (c); JBy (w); JBy, BL (a); A: Iceman. A: Angel.	9.00
❑Annual 8, ca. 1979, (c); JBy (w); SB, AA (a); Alpha Flight	5.00
❑Annual 9, ca. 1980, (c); AM, SD (a)	3.00
❑Annual 10, ca. 1981, (c); AM (a); Captain Universe	4.00
❑Annual 11, ca. 1982, FM (a); First Frank Miller Marvel pencils	3.00
❑Annual 12, ca. 1983, BA (c); HT, BA (a)	2.50
❑Annual 13, ca. 1984	2.50
❑Annual 14, ca. 1985	2.50
❑Annual 15, ca. 1986, V: Abomination.	2.50
❑Annual 16, ca. 1990, PD (w); HT (a); Lifeform	2.50
❑Annual 17, ca. 1991	2.50
❑Annual 18, ca. 1992, PD (w); Return of Defenders	2.75
❑Annual 19, ca. 1993, 1: Lazarus. Polybagged with trading card	2.95
❑Annual 20, ca. 1994	4.00
❑Annual 1997, ca. 1997, Hulk vs. Gladiator; Incredible Hulk '97	2.99
❑Annual 1998, ca. 1998, gatefold summary; wraparound cover; Hulk/Sub-Mariner '98	2.99
❑Ashcan 1, Spr 1994, ashcan edition; Date is actually Spring/Summer	1.00

INCREDIBLE HULK (2ND SERIES)

MARVEL

❑12, Mar 2000; SB (c); SB (a) Was "Hulk"	2.50
❑13, Apr 2000 SB (c); SB (a)	2.50
❑14, May 2000 SB (c); SB (a)	2.50
❑15, Jun 2000 SB (c); SB (a)	2.50
❑16, Jul 2000 SB (c); SB (a)	2.50
❑17, Aug 2000 SB (c); SB (a)	2.50
❑18, Sep 2000 SB (c); SB (a)	2.50
❑19, Oct 2000 SB (a)	2.50
❑20, Nov 2000 SB (c); SB (a)	2.50
❑21, Dec 2000	2.25

Other grades: Multiply price above by 5/6 for VF/NM • 2/3 for VERY FINE • 1/3 for FINE • 1/5 for VERY GOOD • 1/8 for GOOD

N-MINT

❑22, Jan 2001 .... 2.25
❑23, Feb 2001 .... 2.25
❑24, Mar 2001; JR2 (c); JR2, DG (a); A: Abomination. A: Thunderbolt Ross. lower cover price; part of Marvel's Slashback program 2.00
❑25, Apr 2001; double-sized JR2 (c); JR2, TP (a); A: Abomination. 2.99
❑26, May 2001 .... 2.25
❑27, Jun 2001 JR2 (c); JR2, TP (a).... 2.25
❑28, Jul 2001 (c); JR2, TP (a) 2.25
❑29, Aug 2001 .... 2.25
❑30, Sep 2001 TP (a) 2.25
❑31, Oct 2001 TP (a) 2.25
❑32, Nov 2001 TP (a) 2.25
❑33, Dec 2001 .... 2.25
❑34, Jan 2002 JR2, TP (a)................. 12.50
❑35, Feb 2002 JR2, TP (a).................. 6.00
❑36, Mar 2002 JR2, TP (a) 5.00
❑37, Apr 2002 JR2, TP (a)................. 5.00
❑38, May 2002; JR2, TP (a); Norman Rockwell spoof cover..................... 5.00
❑39, Jun 2002; JR2, TP (a); wraparound cover........................ 4.00
❑40, Jul 2002; TP (a); wraparound cover... 4.00
❑41, Aug 2002; TP (a); wraparound cover... 4.00
❑42, Aug 2002; TP (a); wraparound cover... 3.00
❑43, Sep 2002; JR2 (a); wraparound cover... 3.00
❑44, Oct 2002; wraparound cover 3.00
❑45, Nov 2002; wraparound cover 3.00
❑46, Dec 2002; wraparound cover 2.50
❑47, Jan 2003; wraparound cover...... 2.25
❑48, Feb 2003; wraparound cover...... 2.25
❑49, Mar 2003; wraparound cover 2.25
❑50, Apr 2003; wraparound cover...... 5.00
❑51, May 2003 .... 4.00
❑52, Jun 2003 .... 3.00
❑53, Jun 2003 .... 3.00
❑54, Jul 2003 .... 3.00
❑55, Aug 2003 .... 2.00
❑56, Aug 2003 .... 2.25
❑57, Sep 2003 .... 2.25
❑58, Sep 2003 .... 2.25
❑59, Oct 2003 .... 2.25
❑60, Nov 2003 .... 2.25
❑61, Nov 2003 .... 2.25
❑62, Dec 2003 .... 2.25
❑63, Jan 2004 .... 2.25
❑64, Feb 2004 .... 2.99
❑65, Mar 2004 .... 2.25
❑66, Apr 2004 .... 2.25
❑67, Apr 2004 .... 2.99
❑68, May 2004 .... 2.99
❑69, May 2004 .... 2.99
❑70, Jun 2004 .... 2.99
❑71, Jun 2004, A: Tony Stark. 2.99
❑72, Jul 2004, A: Tony Stark. 2.99
❑73, Aug 2004 .... 2.25
❑74, Sep 2004 .... 2.25
❑75, Oct 2004 .... 3.50
❑76, Nov 2004 .... 3.50
❑77, Dec 2005 .... 2.99
❑78, Feb 2005 .... 2.99
❑79, Mar 2005 .... 2.99
❑80, Apr 2005 .... 2.99
❑81, May 2005 .... 2.99
❑82, Jun 2005 .... 2.99
❑83, Jul 2005 .... 5.00
❑83/Variant, Jul 2005 .... 4.00
❑84, Aug 2005 .... 2.99
❑84/Variant, Aug 2005....................... 2.99
❑85, Sep 2005 .... 2.99
❑86, Oct 2005 .... 2.99
❑87, Dec 2005 .... 2.99
❑88, Jan 2006 .... 2.99
❑89, Jan 2006 .... 2.99
❑90, Feb 2006 .... 2.99
❑91, Mar 2006 .... 2.99
❑92, Apr 2006 .... 2.99
❑92/2nd, Apr 2006 .... 2.99
❑93, Jun 2006 .... 2.99
❑94, Jul 2006 .... 2.99
❑95, Aug 2006 .... 2.99

N-MINT

❑Annual 1999, Oct 1999 DGr (c); JBy (w); DGr, KJ (a) 5.00
❑Annual 2000 A: She-Hulk. A: Avengers. 3.50
❑Annual 2001, Nov 2001 (c); EL (w).. 2.99

INCREDIBLE HULK AND WOLVERINE
MARVEL

❑1, Oct 1986; Reprints The Incredible Hulk #181-182, other story 7.00
❑1/2nd; Reprints The Incredible Hulk #181-182, other story 4.00

INCREDIBLE HULK, THE: FUTURE IMPERFECT
MARVEL

❑1, Jan 1993; prestige format; PD (w); GP (a); 1: The Maestro. Embossed cover; indicia lists date as Jan 93... 6.00
❑2, Feb 1993; prestige format; PD (w); GP (a); Embossed cover; indicia lists date as Dec 92.............................. 6.00

INCREDIBLE HULK: HERCULES UNLEASHED
MARVEL

❑1, Oct 1996; follows events of Onslaught...................................... 2.50

INCREDIBLE HULK MEGAZINE
MARVEL

❑1, Dec 1996; Reprints 3.95

INCREDIBLE HULK, THE: NIGHTMERICA
MARVEL

❑1, Aug 2003 .... 2.99
❑2, Sep 2003....................................... 2.99
❑3, Oct 2003 .... 2.99
❑4, Nov 2003 .... 2.99
❑5, Mar 2004 .... 2.99
❑6, May 2004 .... 2.99

INCREDIBLE HULK POSTER MAGAZINE
MARVEL

❑1/A; comics....................................... 3.95
❑1/B; TV show..................................... 2.00

INCREDIBLE HULK: THE END
MARVEL

❑1, Aug 2002 .... 5.95

INCREDIBLE HULK VERSUS QUASIMODO
MARVEL

❑1, Mar 1983, SB (a); Based on Saturday morning cartoon.............. 1.50

INCREDIBLE HULK VS. SUPERMAN
MARVEL

❑1, Jul 1999; prestige format............ 6.00

INCREDIBLE HULK VS. VENOM
MARVEL

❑1, Apr 1994 .... 3.00

INCREDIBLE MR. LIMPET
DELL

❑1, Jun 1964....................................... 25.00

INCREDIBLES
DARK HORSE

❑1, Nov 2004 .... 2.99
❑2, Dec 2004....................................... 2.99
❑3, Jan 2005....................................... 2.99
❑4, Feb 2005 .... 2.99

INCUBUS
PALLIARD

❑1, b&w 2.95
❑2, b&w 2.95

INDEPENDENT PUBLISHER'S GROUP SPOTLIGHT
HERO

❑0, Aug 1993, b&w; Bagged w/ card; no cover price or indicia 3.50

INDEPENDENT VOICES
PEREGRINE ENTERTAINMENT

❑1, Sep 1998, b&w; SPX '98 anthology 1.95
❑2/2nd, May 2000, b&w; CBLDF benefit comic book....................... 2.95
❑2, Sep 1999, b&w; CBLDF benefit comic book.. 2.95
❑3, Aug 2001, b&w 2.95

N-MINT

INDIANA JONES AND THE ARMS OF GOLD
DARK HORSE

❑1, Feb 1994 .... 2.50
❑2, Mar 1994....................................... 2.50
❑3, Apr 1994 .... 2.50
❑4, May 1994 .... 2.50
❑5.. 2.50
❑6.. 2.50

INDIANA JONES AND THE FATE OF ATLANTIS
DARK HORSE

❑1, Mar 1991; trading cards............. 2.50
❑1/2nd.. 2.50
❑2, May 1991; trading cards 2.50
❑3, Jul 1991 .... 2.50
❑4, Sep 1991 .... 2.50

INDIANA JONES AND THE GOLDEN FLEECE
DARK HORSE

❑1, Jun 1994....................................... 2.50
❑2, Jul 1994 .... 2.50

INDIANA JONES AND THE IRON PHOENIX
DARK HORSE

❑1, Dec 1994....................................... 2.50
❑2, Jan 1995 .... 2.50
❑3, Feb 1995 .... 2.50
❑4, Mar 1995....................................... 2.50

INDIANA JONES AND THE LAST CRUSADE
MARVEL

❑1, Oct 1989; comic book 1.00
❑2, Oct 1989; comic book................. 1.00
❑3, Nov 1989; comic book 1.00
❑4, Nov 1989; comic book 1.00

INDIANA JONES AND THE LAST CRUSADE (MAGAZINE)
MARVEL

❑1, Aug 1989, b&w; magazine 2.95

INDIANA JONES AND THE SARGASSO PIRATES
DARK HORSE

❑1, Dec 1995....................................... 2.50
❑2, Jan 1996 .... 2.50
❑3, Feb 1996 .... 2.50
❑4, Mar 1996....................................... 2.50

INDIANA JONES AND THE SHRINE OF THE SEA DEVIL
DARK HORSE

❑1, Sep 1994....................................... 2.50

INDIANA JONES AND THE SPEAR OF DESTINY
DARK HORSE

❑1, Apr 1995 .... 2.50
❑2, May 1995 .... 2.50
❑3, Jun 1995 .... 2.50
❑4, Jul 1995 .... 2.50

INDIANA JONES AND THE TEMPLE OF DOOM
MARVEL

❑1, Sep 1984 BG (a)........................... 2.00
❑2, Oct 1984 BG (a) 2.00
❑3, Nov 1984 BG (a)........................... 2.00

INDIANA JONES: THUNDER IN THE ORIENT
DARK HORSE

❑1, Sep 1993....................................... 2.50
❑2, Oct 1993....................................... 2.50
❑3, Nov 1993....................................... 2.50
❑4, Dec 1993....................................... 2.50
❑5, Mar 1994....................................... 2.50
❑6, Apr 1994 .... 2.50

INDIAN SUMMER
NBM

❑1.. 21.95

INDIGO VERTIGO ONE SHOT
IMAGE

❑1.. 2.95

Other grades: Multiply price above by 5/6 for VF/NM • 2/3 for VERY FINE • 1/3 for FINE • 1/5 for VERY GOOD • 1/8 for GOOD

Infinity, Inc.

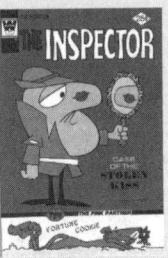

Formed by the kids and wards of the JSA

©DC

Inhumanoids

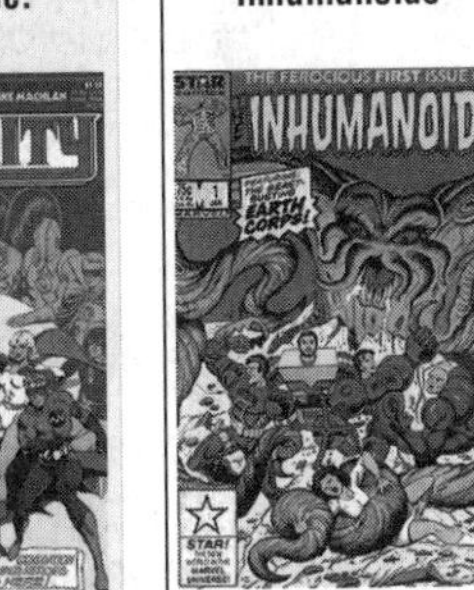

The Earth Corps battle plant monsters

©Marvel

Inhumans

Fantastic Four spinoff in its first series

©Marvel

Insane Clown Posse

Gross-out comic based on gross-out band

©Chaos!

Inspector

Includes some great Warren Tufts stories

©Gold Key

N-MINT

IN DREAM WORLD
TOKYOPOP

❑1, Apr 2005 .... 9.95
❑2, Jul 2005 .... 9.95
❑3, Oct 2005 .... 9.95

INDUSTRIAL GOTHIC
DC / VERTIGO

❑1, Dec 1995 .... 2.50
❑2, Jan 1996 .... 2.50
❑3, Feb 1996 .... 2.50
❑4, Mar 1996 .... 2.50
❑5, Apr 1996 .... 2.50

INDUSTRIAL STRENGTH PREVIEW
SILVER SKULL

❑1, b&w 1.50

INDUSTRY OF WAR ONE-SHOT
IMAGE

❑1, Jan 2006 .... 2.95

INDY BUZZ
BLINDWOLF

❑1, Mar 1999 .... 2.95

INEDIBLE ADVENTURES OF CLINT THE CARROT
HOT LEG

❑1, Mar 1994, b&w 2.50

INFANTRY
DEVIL'S DUE

❑1, Dec 2004 .... 3.00
❑1/Alternative, Dec 2004; "Team" cover, also known as B cover 4.00
❑1/Graham, Dec 2004; Graham Crackers exclusive; 1,000 printed. Skottie Young cover. Solicited December 2004 .... 7.00
❑2, Jan 2005 .... 2.95
❑3, Feb 2005 .... 2.95

INFECTIOUS
FANTACO

❑1 .... 3.95

INFERIOR FIVE
DC

❑1, Apr 1967 .... 24.00
❑2, Jun 1967 .... 16.00
❑3, Aug 1967 .... 14.00
❑4, Oct 1967 .... 14.00
❑5, Dec 1967 .... 14.00
❑6, Feb 1968, A: DC heroes 14.00
❑7, Apr 1968 .... 14.00
❑8, Jun 1968 .... 14.00
❑9, Aug 1968 .... 14.00
❑10, Oct 1968, A: other heroes. Final issue of original run (1968) 14.00
❑11, Sep 1972, reprints Showcase #62; Series begins again (1972) 10.00
❑12, Nov 1972, reprints Showcase #63 .... 10.00

INFERNO (AIRCEL)
AIRCEL

❑1, Oct 1990, b&w 2.50
❑2, Nov 1990, b&w 2.50
❑3, Dec 1990, b&w 2.50
❑4, Jan 1991, b&w 2.50
❑Book 1 .... 9.95

N-MINT

INFERNO (CALIBER)
CALIBER

❑1, Aug 1995, b&w 2.95

INFERNO (DC)
DC

❑1, Oct 1997, spin-off from Legion of Super-Heroes 2.50
❑2, Nov 1997 .... 2.50
❑3, Jan 1998 .... 2.50
❑4, Feb 1998 .... 2.50

INFERNO: HELLBOUND
IMAGE

❑0, Jul 2002 .... 2.50
❑1, Feb 2002 .... 2.50
❑2, Aug 2002 .... 2.50
❑3, Nov 2002 .... 2.99

INFINITE CRISIS
DC

❑1/Perez, Dec 2005, b&w 5.00
❑1/Lee, Dec 2005 .... 5.00
❑1/2nd, Dec 2005 .... 3.00
❑1/RRP, Dec 2005 .... 25.00
❑2/Perez, Jan 2006 .... 4.00
❑2/Lee, Jan 2006 .... 3.00
❑3/Perez, Feb 2006 .... 3.00
❑3/Lee, Feb 2006 .... 3.00
❑4/Perez, Mar 2006 .... 3.00
❑4/Lee, Mar 2006 .... 3.00
❑5/Perez, May 2006 .... 3.00
❑5/Lee, May 2006 .... 3.00
❑6, Jun 2006 .... 3.00
❑7, Jul 2006 .... 3.00

INFINITE CRISIS SECRET FILES 2006
DC

❑1, May 2006 .... 4.00

INFINITE KUNG FU
KAGAN MCLEOD

❑1, Aug 2000 .... 4.50
❑1/2nd; 2nd printing, 2002 .... 4.50

INFINITY ABYSS
MARVEL

❑1, Aug 2002 .... 2.99
❑2, Aug 2002 .... 2.99
❑3, Sep 2002 .... 2.99
❑4, Sep 2002 .... 2.99
❑5, Oct 2002 .... 2.99
❑6, Oct 2002 .... 3.50

INFINITY CHARADE
PARODY

❑1/A 2.50
❑1/B 2.50
❑1/Gold; Gold limited edition (1500 printed) 4.00

INFINITY CRUSADE
MARVEL

❑1, Jun 1993, Gold foil cover 3.50
❑2, Jul 1993 .... 2.50
❑3, Aug 1993 .... 2.50
❑4, Sep 1993 .... 2.50
❑5, Oct 1993 .... 2.50
❑6, Nov 1993 .... 2.50

N-MINT

INFINITY GAUNTLET
MARVEL

❑1, Jul 1991, JSn (w); GP (a); A: Thanos. A: Spider-Man. A: Avengers. A: Silver Surfer. 3.00
❑2, Aug 1991, JSn (w); GP (a); A: Thanos. A: Spider-Man. A: Avengers. A: Silver Surfer. 2.50
❑3, Sep 1991, JSn (w); GP (a); A: Thanos. A: Spider-Man. A: Avengers. A: Silver Surfer. 2.50
❑4, Oct 1991, JSn (w); GP (a); A: Thanos. A: Spider-Man. A: Avengers. A: Silver Surfer. 2.50
❑5, Nov 1991, GP (c); JSn (w) 2.50
❑6, Dec 1991, GP (c); JSn (w) 2.50

INFINITY, INC.
DC

❑1, Mar 1984 JOy (a); O: Infinity Inc. 2.50
❑2, May 1984 JOy (a); O: ends. V: Ultra-Humanite. 2.00
❑3, Jun 1984 JOy (a); V: Solomon Grundy. 2.00
❑4, Jul 1984 JOy (a) 2.00
❑5, Aug 1984 JOy (a) 2.00
❑6, Sep 1984 JOy (a) 1.50
❑7, Oct 1984 JOy (a); A: E-2 Superman. 1.50
❑8, Nov 1984 JOy (a) 1.50
❑9, Dec 1984 JOy (a) 1.50
❑10, Jan 1985 JOy (a) 1.50
❑11, Feb 1985; more on Infinity's origin 1.25
❑12, Mar 1985; 1: Yolanda Montez. Brainwave Junior's new powers 1.25
❑13, Apr 1985 V: Thorn. 1.25
❑14, May 1985 TMc (a); 1: Chroma. 1: Marcie Cooper. 3.50
❑15, Jun 1985 TMc (a); A: Chroma. 2.50
❑16, Jul 1985 TMc (a); 1: Mr. Bones. 2.50
❑17, Aug 1985 TMc (a); 1: Helix. 2.50
❑18, Sep 1985; TMc (a); V: Helix. Crisis 2.50
❑19, Oct 1985; TMc (a); 1: Mekanique. A: Steel. A: JLA. Crisis 2.50
❑20, Nov 1985; TMc (a); 1: Rick Tyler. Crisis 2.50
❑21, Dec 1985; TMc (a); 1: Doctor Midnight (new). 1: Hourman II (Rick Tyler). Crisis 2.50
❑22, Jan 1986; TMc (a); Crisis 2.50
❑23, Feb 1986; TMc (a); V: Solomon Grundy. Crisis 2.50
❑24, Mar 1986; TMc (a); Star Spangled Kid, Jonni Thunder vs. Last Criminal; Crisis 2.50
❑25, Apr 1986; TMc (a); Crisis aftermath; Hourman II joins team; Doctor Midnight joins team; Wildcat II joins team 2.50
❑26, May 1986 TMc (a); A: Helix. 2.50
❑27, Jun 1986; TMc (a); Lyta's memories erased 2.50
❑28, Jul 1986 TMc (a); V: Mr. Bones. 2.50
❑29, Jul 1986 TMc (a); V: Helix. 2.50
❑30, Sep 1986; TMc (a); JSA mourned 2.50
❑31, Oct 1986 TMc (a); 1: Skyman. A: Jonni Thunder. 2.50
❑32, Nov 1986 TMc (a); V: Psycho Pirate. 2.50
❑33, Dec 1986 TMc (a); O: Obsidian. 2.50

❑34, Jan 1987 TMc (a); V: Global Guardians 2.50
❑35, Feb 1987 TMc (a); V: Injustice Unlimited. 2.50
❑36, Mar 1987 TMc (a); V: Solomon Grundy. 2.50
❑37, Apr 1987 TMc (a); O: Northwing. 2.50
❑38, May 1987 1.25
❑39, Jun 1987 O: Solomon Grundy. 1.25
❑40, Jul 1987 1.25
❑41, Aug 1987 1.25
❑42, Sep 1987; Fury leaves team 1.25
❑43, Oct 1987 1.25
❑44, Nov 1987 1.25
❑45, Dec 1987 A: Titans. 1.25
❑46, Jan 1988; V: Floronic Man. Millennium 1.50
❑47, Feb 1988; V: Harlequin. Millennium 1.25
❑48, Mar 1988 O: Nuklon. 1.25
❑49, Apr 1988 A: Sandman. 1.25
❑50, May 1988; Giant-size 2.50
❑51, Jun 1988 D: Skyman. 1.25
❑52, Jul 1988 V: Helix. 1.25
❑53, Aug 1988 V: Injustice Unlimited. 1.75
❑Annual 1, Nov 1985; TMc (a); O: Jade and Obsidian. Crisis 2.50
❑Annual 2, Jul 1988; crossover with Young All-Stars Annual #1 2.50
❑Special 1, ca. 1987; cover forms diptych with Outsiders Special #1 1.50

INFINITY OF WARRIORS
OMINOUS

❑1, Oct 1994 1.95

INFINITY WAR
MARVEL

❑1, Jun 1992; gatefold cover 2.50
❑2, Jul 1992; gatefold cover 2.50
❑3, Aug 1992; gatefold cover 2.50
❑4, Sep 1992; gatefold cover 2.50
❑5, Oct 1992; gatefold cover 2.50
❑6, Nov 1992; gatefold cover 2.50

INFOCHAMELEON: COMPANY CULT
MEDIAWARP

❑1, Feb 1997, b&w 4.50

INHUMANOIDS
MARVEL / STAR

❑1, Jan 1987 1: Earth Corps. 1.00
❑2, Mar 1987 1.00
❑3, May 1987 1.00
❑4, Jul 1987 1.00

INHUMANS
MARVEL

❑1, Oct 1975, GP (a); V: Blastaar. 8.00
❑2, Dec 1976 4.00
❑3, Feb 1976 4.00
❑4, Apr 1976 3.50
❑4/30 cent, Apr 1976, 30 cent regional price variant 7.00
❑5, Jun 1976 3.50
❑6, Aug 1976 3.00
❑6/30 cent, Aug 1976, 30 cent regional price variant 20.00
❑7, Oct 1976 3.00
❑8, Dec 1976 3.00
❑9, Feb 1977 3.00
❑10, Apr 1977 3.00
❑11, Jun 1977 3.00
❑11/35 cent, Jun 1977, 35 cent regional price variant 15.00
❑12, Aug 1977, V: Hulk 3.00
❑12/35 cent, Aug 1977, V: Hulk. 35 cent regional price variant 15.00
❑Special 1, Apr 1990, RHo (a); O: Medusa. A: Fantastic Four. 4.00

INHUMANS (2ND SERIES)
MARVEL

❑1, Nov 1998, gatefold summary 4.00
❑1/Ltd., Nov 1998, DFE alternate cover signed 4.00
❑1/Variant, Nov 1998, DFE alternate cover 4.00
❑2/A, Dec 1998, gatefold summary; Woman in circle on cover 3.00
❑2/B, Dec 1998, gatefold summary 3.00
❑3, Jan 1999 3.00
❑4, Feb 1999 3.00
❑5, Mar 1999, Earth vs. Attilan war 3.00
❑6, Apr 1999 3.00
❑7, May 1999 3.00
❑8, Jun 1999 3.00
❑9, Jul 1999 3.00
❑10, Aug 1999 3.00
❑11, Sep 1999 3.00
❑12, Oct 1999 3.00

INHUMANS (3RD SERIES)
MARVEL

❑1, Jun 2000 2.99
❑2, Jul 2000 2.99
❑3, Aug 2000 2.99
❑4, Oct 2000 2.99

INHUMANS (4TH SERIES)
MARVEL

❑1, Jun 2003, Marvel called this Vol. 6, counting the specials 2.50
❑2, Jul 2003 2.50
❑3, Aug 2003 2.50
❑4, Oct 2003 2.99
❑5, Nov 2003 2.99
❑6, Dec 2003 2.99
❑7, Jan 2004 2.99
❑8, Feb 2004 2.99
❑9, Mar 2004 2.99
❑10, Apr 2004 2.99
❑11, May 2004 2.99
❑12, Jun 2004 2.99

INHUMANS, THE: THE GREAT REFUGE
MARVEL

❑1, May 1995 2.95

INHUMANS: THE UNTOLD SAGA
MARVEL

❑1, Apr 1990 1.50

INITIAL D
TOKYOPOP

❑1, May 2002, b&w 9.95
❑2, Jul 2002 9.95
❑3, Oct 2002 9.95
❑4, Jan 2003 9.95
❑5, Apr 2003 9.95
❑6, Jun 2003 9.95
❑7, Aug 2003 9.95
❑8, Oct 2003 9.95
❑9, Dec 2003 9.95
❑10, Feb 2004 9.95
❑11, Apr 2004 9.95
❑12, Jun 2004 9.95
❑13, Aug 2004 9.95
❑14, Oct 2004 9.95
❑15, Dec 2004 9.95
❑16, Feb 2005 9.95
❑17, Apr 2005 9.95
❑18, Jun 2005 9.95
❑19, Aug 2005 9.95
❑20, Oct 2005 9.95

INKPUNKS QUARTERLY
FUNK-O-TRON

❑1 2.95
❑2 2.95
❑3 2.95

INMATES PRISONERS OF SOCIETY
DELTA

❑1, Aug 1997 2.95
❑2, Mar 1998 2.95
❑3, Jul 1998 2.95
❑4, Nov 1998 2.95

INNERCIRCLE
MUSHROOM

❑0.1, Feb 1995 2.50

INNER-CITY PRODUCTS
HYPE

❑1, b&w 2.00

INNER CITY ROMANCE
LAST GASP

❑1 5.00
❑2 3.00
❑3 3.00
❑4 3.00
❑5 3.00

INNOCENT BYSTANDER
OLLIE OLLIE! OXEN FREE

❑1, 1: Lao Shan. 1: Balac-Soon. 2.95
❑2 2.95
❑3 2.95
❑4, Sum 1997 2.95
❑5, Win 1998 2.95
❑6, Fal 1998 2.95

INNOCENT ONES
FANTAGRAPHICS

❑1 2005 4.95

INNOVATION PREVIEW SPECIAL
INNOVATION

❑1, Jun 1989; sampler 1.00

INNOVATION SPECTACULAR
INNOVATION

❑1, Dec 1990 2.95
❑2, Jan 1991 2.95

INNOVATION SUMMER FUN SPECIAL
INNOVATION

❑1 3.50

INOVATORS
DARK MOON

❑1, Apr 1995; cardstock cover 2.50

IN RAGE
CFD

❑1, ca. 1994, b&w; no cover price or indicia 2.50

INSANE
DARK HORSE

❑1, Feb 1988 1.75
❑2 1.75

INSANE CLOWN POSSE
CHAOS!

❑1, Jun 1999 3.00
❑1/A, Jun 1999; Tower Reocrds variant 4.00
❑2, Aug 1999 3.00
❑2/CS, Aug 1999 4.00
❑3, Oct 1999 3.00
❑3/A, Oct 1999; Tower Reocrds variant 4.00
❑4, Jan 2000; Says #1 on cover with Pendulum below issue number; polybagged with first of 12 Pendulum CDs 3.00
❑4/CS, Jan 2000 4.00
❑5, ca. 2000 3.00
❑5/CS, ca. 2000 4.00
❑6, ca. 2000 3.00
❑6/CS, ca. 2000 4.00
❑7, ca. 2000 3.00
❑7/CS, ca. 2000 4.00
❑8, ca. 2001 3.00
❑8/CS, ca. 2001 4.00
❑9, ca. 2001 3.00
❑9/CS, ca. 2001 3.00
❑10, ca. 2001 3.00
❑10/CS, ca. 2001 3.00
❑11, ca. 2001 3.00
❑11/CS, ca. 2001 4.00
❑12, ca. 2001 3.00
❑12/CS, ca. 2001 3.00

IN SEARCH OF SHIRLEY
NBM

❑1 9.95

IN SEARCH OF THE CASTAWAYS
GOLD KEY

❑1, Mar 1963 20.00

INSECT MAN'S 25TH ANNIVERSARY SPECIAL
ENTERTAINMENT

❑1, Mar 1991 2.00

INSIDE OUT KING
FREE FALL

❑1 2.95
❑1/2nd 2.95

INSOMNIA
FANTAGRAPHICS

❑1 2.95

INSOMNIA (2ND SERIES)
FANTAGRAPHICS

❑1, Dec 2005 3.99

INSPECTOR
GOLD KEY

❑1, Jul 1974, (c); (w); (a); Cover code 90292-407 20.00

In the Presence of Mine Enemies

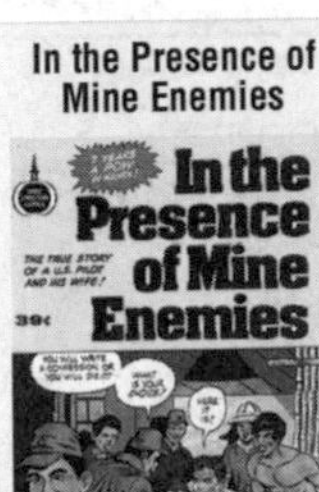

American POW in Vietnam tells spiritual story
©Spire

Inu-Yasha

Rumiko Takahashi's feudal fairy tale
©Viz

Invaders (Marvel, 1st Series)

Marvel's World War II super-team
©Marvel

Invaders from Mars

Based on the 1953 science-fiction film
©Eternity

Invincible

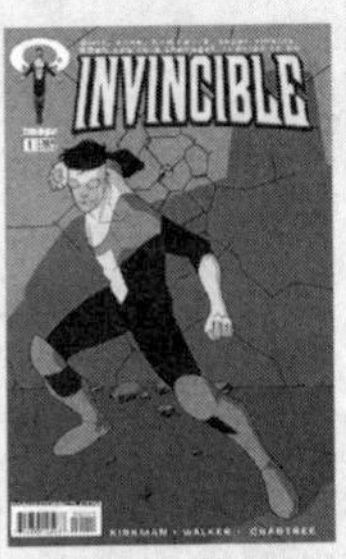

Son begins inheriting super-hero dad's power
©Image

N-MINT

❑2, Oct 1974, (c); (w); (a); Cover code 90292-410; unusual Pink Panther story without "Pink" in title; not Tufts art 10.00
❑3, Jan 1975, (c); (w); (a); Cover code 90292-501; includes 16-page toy catalog 5.00
❑4, Apr 1975, (c); (w); (a); Cover code 90292-504 .... 5.00
❑5, Jul 1975, (c); (w); (a); Cover code 90292-507 .... 5.00
❑6, Oct 1975, (c); (w); (a); Cover code 90292-510 .... 5.00
❑7, Jan 1976, (c); (w); Cover code 90292-601; includes Bugs Bunny in Hostess ad ("The Great Carrot Famine") 5.00
❑8, Mar 1976, (c); (w); (a); Cover code 90292-603 .... 5.00
❑9, May 1976, (c); (w); (a); Cover code 90292-605 .... 5.00
❑10, Jul 1976, (c); (w); Cover code 90292-607 .... 5.00
❑11, Sep 1976, (c); (w); Cover code 90292-609; includes Hulk in Hostess ad ("The Green Frog") 5.00
❑12, Nov 1976, (c); (w); (a); Cover code 90292-611 .... 5.00
❑13, Feb 1977, (c); (w); (a); Cover code 90292-702 .... 5.00
❑14, Apr 1977, (c); (w); Cover code 90292-704; includes Spider-Man in Hostess ad ("Will Power") 5.00
❑15, Jun 1977, (c); (w); Cover code 90292-706; includes Iron Man in Hostess ad ("A Dull Pain") 5.00
❑16, Aug 1977, (c); (w); (a); Cover code 90292-708 .... 5.00
❑17, Oct 1977, (c); (w); (a); Cover code 90292-710 .... 5.00
❑18, Dec 1977, (c); (w); (a); Cover code 90292-712; includes Daredevil in Hostess ad ("Because"); not Tufts art 5.00
❑19, Feb 1978, (c); (w); (a); Cover code 90292-802 .... 5.00

INSTANT PIANO
DARK HORSE

❑1, Aug 1994, b&w 3.95
❑2, Dec 1994, b&w 3.95
❑3, Feb 1995, b&w 3.95
❑4, Jun 1995, b&w 3.95

INTENSE!
PURE IMAGINATION

❑2, b&w; Reprints 3.00

INTERACTIVE COMICS
ADVENTURE

❑1 .... 4.95
❑2, b&w 4.95

INTERFACE
MARVEL / EPIC

❑1, Dec 1989 .... 5.00
❑2, Feb 1990 .... 4.00
❑3, Apr 1990 .... 4.00
❑4, Jun 1990 .... 4.00
❑5, Aug 1990 .... 4.00
❑6, Oct 1990 .... 9.00
❑7, Nov 1990 .... 9.00
❑8, Dec 1990 .... 9.00

N-MINT

INTERNAL FURY
FIERCE COMICS

❑1, Aug 2005 .... 2.00

INTERNATIONAL COWGIRL MAGAZINE
ICONOGRAFIX

❑1, b&w 2.95
❑2, b&w 2.95

INTERPLANETARY LIZARDS OF THE TEXAS PLAINS
LEADBELLY

❑0 .... 2.50
❑1, b&w 2.00
❑2, b&w 2.00
❑3 .... 2.00
❑8, b&w 2.50

INTERSTELLAR OVERDRIVE
LEONINE

❑1 1990 .... 1.25
❑2, Apr 1990 .... 1.25

INTERVIEW WITH THE VAMPIRE (ANNE RICE'S...)
INNOVATION

❑1, ca. 1991 .... 2.50
❑2, ca. 1991 .... 2.50
❑3, ca. 1991 .... 2.50
❑4, ca. 1991 .... 2.50
❑5, ca. 1992 .... 2.50
❑6, ca. 1992 .... 2.50
❑7, ca. 1992 .... 2.50
❑8, ca. 1993 .... 2.50
❑9, ca. 1993 .... 2.50
❑10, ca. 1993 .... 2.50
❑11, ca. 1993 .... 2.50
❑12, ca. 1993 .... 2.50

IN THE DAYS OF THE ACE ROCK 'N' ROLL CLUB
FANTAGRAPHICS

❑1, b&w 4.95

IN THE DAYS OF THE MOB
DC

❑1, Fal 1971 .... 50.00

IN THE PRESENCE OF MINE ENEMIES
SPIRE

❑1 .... 7.00

IN THIN AIR
TOME

❑1/A, b&w; With alternate ending #1 . 2.95
❑1/B, b&w; With alternate ending #2 . 2.95

INTIMATES
DC

❑1, Jan 2005 .... 2.95
❑2, Feb 2005 .... 2.95
❑3, Mar 2005 .... 2.95
❑4, Apr 2005 .... 2.95
❑5, May 2005 .... 2.95
❑6, Jun 2005 .... 2.95
❑7, Jun 2005 .... 2.99
❑8, Jul 2005 .... 2.99
❑9, Aug 2005 .... 2.99
❑10, Sep 2005 .... 2.99

N-MINT

❑11, Oct 2005 .... 2.99
❑12, Dec 2005 .... 2.99

INTIMIDATORS
IMAGE

❑1, Jan 2006 .... 2.99
❑2, Feb 2006 .... 2.99
❑3, Mar 2006 .... 2.99
❑4, Apr 2006 .... 2.99

INTRAZONE
BRAINSTORM

❑1, Mar 1993, b&w 2.95
❑1/Ltd., Mar 1993; limited edition 5.95
❑2, Apr 1993, b&w 2.95
❑2/Ltd., Apr 1993; limited edition 5.95

INTRIGUE
IMAGE

❑1/A, Aug 1999 .... 2.50
❑1/B, Aug 1999; alternate cover with woman firing directly at reader 2.50
❑2/A, Sep 1999; Woman posting next to target on cover 2.50
❑2/B, Sep 1999; alternate cover 2.50
❑3, Oct 1999 .... 2.95

INTRUDER COMICS MODULE
TSR

❑1 .... 2.95
❑2 .... 2.95
❑3 .... 2.95
❑4 .... 2.95
❑5; "Intruder II" on cover 2.95
❑6; "Intruder II" on cover 2.95
❑7; Intruder II 2.95
❑8; Intruder II 2.95
❑9; Intruder II 2.95

INU-YASHA
VIZ

❑1, Apr 1997 .... 3.00
❑2, May 1997 .... 2.95
❑3, Jun 1997 .... 2.95
❑4, Jul 1997 .... 2.95
❑5, Aug 1997 .... 2.95
❑6, Sep 1997 .... 3.25
❑7, Oct 1997 .... 3.25
❑8, Nov 1997 .... 3.25
❑9, Dec 1997 .... 3.25
❑10, Jan 1998 .... 3.25
❑11, Feb 1998 .... 3.25
❑12, Mar 1998 .... 3.25
❑13, Apr 1998 .... 3.25
❑14, May 1998 .... 3.25
❑15, Jun 1998 .... 3.25

INU-YASHA PART 2
VIZ

❑1, Jul 1998 .... 3.25
❑2, Aug 1998 .... 3.25
❑3, Sep 1998 .... 3.25
❑4, Oct 1998 .... 3.25
❑5, Nov 1998 .... 3.25
❑6, Dec 1998 .... 3.25
❑7, Jan 1999 .... 3.25
❑8, Feb 1999 .... 3.25
❑9, Mar 1999 .... 3.25

N-MINT N-MINT N-MINT

INU-YASHA PART 3
VIZ

❑1, Apr 1999 .... 3.25
❑2, May 1999 .... 3.25
❑3, Jun 1999 .... 3.25
❑4, Jul 1999 .... 3.25
❑5, Aug 1999 .... 3.25
❑6, Sep 1999 .... 3.25
❑7, Oct 1999 .... 3.25

INU-YASHA PART 4
VIZ

❑1, Nov 1999 .... 3.25
❑2, Dec 1999 .... 3.25
❑3, Jan 2000 .... 3.25
❑4, Feb 2000 .... 3.25
❑5, Mar 2000 .... 3.25
❑6, Apr 2000 .... 3.25
❑7, May 2000 .... 3.25

INU-YASHA PART 5
VIZ

❑1, Jun 2000 .... 2.95
❑2, Jul 2000 .... 2.95
❑3, Aug 2000 .... 2.95
❑4, Sep 2000 .... 2.95
❑5, Oct 2000 .... 2.95
❑6, Nov 2000 .... 2.95
❑7, Dec 2000 .... 2.95
❑8, Jan 2001 .... 2.95
❑9, Feb 2001 .... 2.95
❑10, Mar 2001 .... 2.95
❑11, Apr 2001 .... 2.95

INU-YASHA PART 6
VIZ

❑1, May 2001 .... 2.95
❑2, Jun 2001 .... 2.95
❑3, Jul 2001 .... 2.95
❑4, Aug 2001 .... 2.95
❑5, Sep 2001 .... 2.95
❑6, Oct 2001 .... 2.95
❑7, Nov 2001 .... 2.95
❑8, Dec 2001 .... 2.95
❑9, Jan 2002 .... 2.95
❑10, Feb 2002 .... 2.95
❑11, Mar 2002 .... 2.95
❑12, Apr 2002 .... 2.95
❑13, May 2002 .... 2.95
❑14, Jun 2002 .... 2.95
❑15, Jul 2002 .... 2.95

INU-YASHA PART 7
VIZ

❑1, Aug 2002 .... 2.95
❑2, Sep 2002 .... 2.95
❑3, Oct 2002 .... 2.95
❑4, Nov 2002 .... 2.95
❑5, Dec 2002 .... 2.95
❑6, Jan 2003 .... 2.95
❑7, Feb 2003 .... 2.95

INVADERS (GOLD KEY)
GOLD KEY

❑1, Oct 1967 .... 40.00
❑2, Jan 1968 .... 28.00
❑3, Jun 1968 .... 28.00
❑4, Oct 1968 .... 28.00

INVADERS (MARVEL, 1ST SERIES)
MARVEL

❑1, Aug 1975, continued from Giant-Size Invaders #1; FR (a); Marvel Value Stamp #37: Watcher 18.00
❑2, Oct 1975, 1: Mailbag. 1: Brain Drain. V: Donar 10.00
❑3, Nov 1975, 1: U-Man. Captain America vs. Namor vs. Torch; Marvel Value Stamp #97: Black Knight 6.00
❑4, Jan 1976, O: U-Man. V: U-Man 6.00
❑5, Mar 1976, 1: Fin. V: Red Skull 5.00
❑6, May 1976, A: Liberty Legion 5.00
❑6/30 cent, May 1976, 30 cent regional price variant 20.00
❑7, Jul 1976, V: Baron Blood 5.00
❑7/30 cent, Jul 1976, 30 cent regional price variant 20.00
❑8, Sep 1976, A: Union Jack 5.00
❑9, Oct 1976, O: Baron Blood. V: Baron Blood 5.00
❑10, Nov 1976, V: Reaper. reprints Captain America #22 .... 4.00
❑11, Dec 1976, O: Spitfire. 1: Blue Bullet. 1: Spitfire. V: Blue Bullet 4.00
❑12, Jan 1977, 1: Spitfire 4.00
❑13, Feb 1977, A: Golem. Newsstand edition (distributed by Curtis); issue number in box 4.00
❑13/Whitman, Feb 1977, A: Golem. Special markets edition (usually sold in Whitman bagged prepacks); price appears in a diamond; UPC barcode appears 4.00
❑14, Mar 1977, 1: Spirit of '76. 1: Dyna-Mite. 1: Crusaders. Newsstand edition (distributed by Curtis); issue number in box 4.00
❑14/Whitman, Mar 1977, 1: Spirit of '76. 1: Dyna-Mite. 1: Crusaders. Special markets edition (usually sold in Whitman bagged prepacks); price appears in a diamond; UPC barcode appears 4.00
❑15, Apr 1977, FR, FS (a); V: Crusaders. Newsstand edition (distributed by Curtis); issue number in box 4.00
❑15/Whitman, Apr 1977, FR, FS (a); V: Crusaders. Special markets edition (usually sold in Whitman bagged prepacks); price appears in a diamond; UPC barcode appears 4.00
❑16, May 1977, V: Master Man 4.00
❑17, Jun 1977, 1: Warrior Woman. V: Warrior Woman. Newsstand edition (distributed by Curtis); issue number in box 4.00
❑17/Whitman, Jun 1977, 1: Warrior Woman. V: Warrior Woman. Special markets edition (usually sold in Whitman bagged prepacks); price appears in a diamond; UPC barcode appears 4.00
❑17/35 cent, Jun 1977, 35 cent regional variant newsstand edition (distributed by Curtis); issue number in box 7.00
❑18, Jul 1977, 1: Mighty Destroyer. Newsstand edition (distributed by Curtis); issue number in box 4.00
❑18/Whitman, Jul 1977, 1: Mighty Destroyer. Special markets edition (usually sold in Whitman bagged prepacks); price appears in a diamond; UPC barcode appears 4.00
❑18/35 cent, Jul 1977, 35 cent regional variant newsstand edition (distributed by Curtis); issue number in box 7.00
❑19, Aug 1977, O: Union Jack II (Brian Falsworth). 1: the Sub-Mariner. 1: Union Jack II (Brian Falsworth). A: Hitler. Mighty Destroyer becomes Union Jack II; Reprints Motion Picture Funnies Weekly; Newsstand edition (distributed by Curtis); issue number in box 4.00
❑19/Whitman, Aug 1977, O: Union Jack II (Brian Falsworth). 1: the Sub-Mariner. 1: Union Jack II (Brian Falsworth). A: Hitler. Special markets edition (usually sold in Whitman bagged prepacks); price appears in a diamond; UPC barcode appears 4.00
❑19/35 cent, Aug 1977, 35 cent regional variant newsstand edition (distributed by Curtis); issue number in box 7.00
❑20, Sep 1977, O: Sub-Mariner. 1: Sub-Mariner. A: Spitfire. A: Union Jack. Reprints Sub-Mariner story from Motion Picture Funnies Weekly #1; Newsstand edition (distributed by Curtis); issue number in box 5.00
❑20/Whitman, Sep 1977, O: Sub-Mariner. 1: Sub-Mariner. A: Spitfire. A: Union Jack. Special markets edition (usually sold in Whitman bagged prepacks); price appears in a diamond; UPC barcode appears 5.00
❑20/35 cent, Sep 1977, 35 cent regional variant newsstand edition (distributed by Curtis); issue number in box 10.00
❑21, Oct 1977, FR, FS (a); Reprints Sub-Mariner story from Marvel Mystery Comics #10; Newsstand edition (distributed by Curtis); issue number in box 3.00
❑21/Whitman, Oct 1977, FR, FS (a); Special markets edition (usually sold in Whitman bagged prepacks); price appears in a diamond; no UPC barcode 3.00
❑21/35 cent, Oct 1977, 35 cent regional variant newsstand edition (distributed by Curtis); issue number in box 6.00
❑22, Nov 1977, O: Toro (new origin). V: Asbestos Lady 4.00
❑23, Dec 1977, 1: Scarlet Scarab. V: Scarlet Scarab 4.00
❑24, Jan 1978, reprints Marvel Mystery Comics #17 .... 4.00
❑25, Feb 1978, V: Scarlet Scarab 4.00
❑26, Mar 1978, 1: Destroyer II (Roger Aubrey). V: Agent Axis 4.00
❑27, Apr 1978 .... 4.00
❑28, May 1978, 1: Golden Girl. 1: Kid Commandos. 1: Human Top (David Mitchell) 4.00
❑29, Jun 1978, O: Invaders. 1: Teutonic Knight. V: Teutonic Knight 4.00
❑30, Jul 1978 .... 4.00
❑31, Aug 1978, V: Frankenstein. Newsstand edition (distributed by Curtis); issue number in box 3.00
❑31/Whitman, Aug 1978, V: Frankenstein. Special markets edition (usually sold in Whitman bagged prepacks); price appears in a diamond; no UPC barcode 3.00
❑32, Sep 1978, V: Thor 3.00
❑33, Oct 1978, V: Thor 4.00
❑34, Nov 1978, V: Destroyer 2.50
❑35, Dec 1978, A: Whizzer 2.50
❑36, Jan 1979, V: Iron Cross 2.50
❑37, Feb 1979, A: Liberty Legion. V: Iron Cross. Newsstand edition (distributed by Curtis); issue number in box 2.50
❑37/Whitman, Feb 1979, A: Liberty Legion. V: Iron Cross. Special markets edition (usually sold in Whitman bagged prepacks); price appears in a diamond; no UPC barcode 2.50
❑38, Mar 1979, 1: Lady Lotus. A: U-Man 2.50
❑39, Apr 1979 .... 2.50
❑40, May 1979, V: Baron Blood 2.50
❑41, Sep 1979, Double-size V: Super Axis (Baron Blood, U-Man, Warrior Woman, Master Man) 3.50
❑Annual 1, ca. 1977 .... 12.00

INVADERS (MARVEL, 2ND SERIES)
MARVEL

❑1, May 1993 .... 1.75
❑2, Jun 1993 .... 1.75
❑3, Jul 1993 .... 1.75
❑4, Aug 1993 .... 1.75

INVADERS (MARVEL, 3RD SERIES)
MARVEL

❑0, Sep 2004 .... 2.99
❑1, Oct 2004 .... 2.99
❑2, Nov 2004 .... 2.99
❑3, Dec 2004 .... 2.99
❑4, Jan 2005 .... 2.99
❑5, Feb 2005 .... 2.99
❑6, Mar 2005 .... 2.99
❑7, Apr 2005 .... 2.99
❑8, May 2005 .... 2.99
❑9, Jun 2005 .... 2.99

INVADERS FROM HOME
DC / PIRANHA

❑1 .... 2.50
❑2 .... 2.50
❑3 .... 2.50
❑4 .... 2.50
❑5 .... 2.50
❑6 .... 2.50

INVADERS FROM MARS
ETERNITY

❑1, Feb 1990, b&w 2.50
❑2, Mar 1990, b&w 2.50
❑3, Apr 1990, b&w 2.50

INVADERS FROM MARS (BOOK II)
ETERNITY

❑1, ca. 1990, b&w; sequel 2.50
❑2, ca. 1990, b&w; sequel 2.50
❑3, ca. 1990, b&w; sequel 2.50

INVASION!
DC

❑1, Jan 1989, 84 page giant KG (w); TMc (a); O: Blasters. 1: Garryn Bek. 1: Blasters. 1: Dominators. 1: Vril Dox II. 3.00

Other grades: Multiply price above by 5/6 for VF/NM • 2/3 for VERY FINE • 1/3 for FINE • 1/5 for VERY GOOD • 1/8 for GOOD

Invisibles

Secret society recruits problem kid

©DC

Invisibles (Vol. 3)

Issues released in reverse order, counting down

©DC

Iron Fist

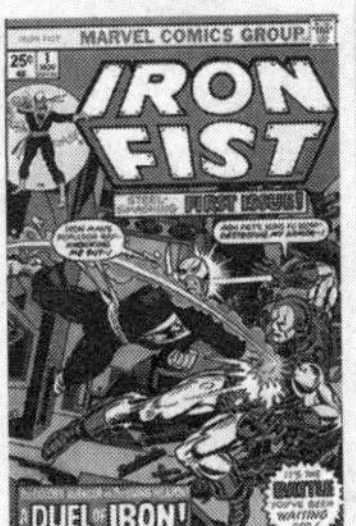

Short 1970s series introduced Sabretooth

©Marvel

Ironjaw

Metal-mandibled man from short-lived line

©Atlas-Seaboard

Iron Man (1st Series)

Billionaire inventor creates super suit

©Marvel

N-MINT

❑2, Feb 1989, 84 page giant TMc (a); 1: Strata. 1: L.E.G.I.O.N.. 1: Lyrissa Mallor. 3.00
❑3, Mar 1989, 84 page giant 3.00

INVASION (AVALON)
AVALON

❑1 2.95

INVASION '55
APPLE

❑1, Oct 1990, b&w 2.25
❑2, b&w 2.25
❑3, b&w 2.25

INVASION OF THE MIND SAPPERS
FANTAGRAPHICS

❑1, Jan 1996, b&w; cardstock cover 8.95

INVASION OF THE SPACE AMAZONS FROM THE PURPLE PLANET
GRIZMART

❑1, May 1997, b&w 2.25
❑2, Fal 1997, b&w 2.25
❑3, Win 1997, b&w 2.25

INVERT
CALIBER

❑1, b&w 2.50

INVINCIBLE
IMAGE

❑0, ca. 2005 1.00
❑1, Jan 2003 15.00
❑2, Feb 2003 10.00
❑3, Mar 2003 10.00
❑4, Apr 2003 10.00
❑5, Jun 2003 7.00
❑6, Oct 2003 7.00
❑7, Nov 2003 7.00
❑8, Jan 2004 7.00
❑9, Feb 2004 7.00
❑10, Mar 2004 7.00
❑11, Apr 2004 7.00
❑12, Apr 2004 5.00
❑13, Aug 2004 5.00
❑14, Sep 2004 5.00
❑15, Oct 2004 5.00
❑16, Nov 2004 2.95
❑17, Dec 2004 2.95
❑18, Jan 2005 2.95
❑19, Mar 2005 2.95
❑20, Apr 2005 2.95
❑21, May 2005 2.95
❑22, Jun 2005 2.95
❑23, Jul 2005 2.95
❑24, Aug 2005 2.99
❑25, Oct 2005 2.99
❑26 2005 2.99
❑27, Jan 2006 2.99
❑28, Mar 2006 2.99
❑29, Apr 2006 2.99
❑30, May 2006 2.99
❑31, Jun 2006 2.99
❑32, Jul 2006 2.99
❑33, Jul 2006 2.99

INVINCIBLE ED (SUMMERTIME)
SUMMERTIME

❑1 2002 3.50
❑2 2002 3.95

N-MINT

INVINCIBLE ED (DARK HORSE)
DARK HORSE

❑1 2003 2.99
❑2 2003 2.99
❑3, Jul 2003 2.99
❑4, Feb 2004 2.99

INVINCIBLE FOUR OF KUNG FU & NINJA
DR. LEUNG'S

❑1 2.00
❑2 2.00
❑3 2.00
❑4 2.00
❑5 2.00

INVINCIBLE MAN
JUNKO / DARK HORSE

❑1, Sum 1998, b&w; Glossy cover; 1500 printed 5.00
❑1/Ltd., b&w; has $100 cover price; 500 printed 8.00

INVINCIBLES
CFD

❑1, May 1997 2.95

INVINCIBLE SCRIPT BOOK
IMAGE

❑1, Mar 2006 4.95

INVISIBLE 9
FLYPAPER

❑1, May 1998 2.95

INVISIBLE DIRTY OLD MAN
RED GIANT

❑1 3.50

INVISIBLE PEOPLE
KITCHEN SINK

❑1 2.95
❑2 2.95
❑3 2.95

INVISIBLES
DC / VERTIGO

❑1, Sep 1994; Giant-size 1: King Mob. 3.50
❑2, Oct 1994 2.50
❑3, Nov 1994 2.50
❑4, Dec 1994 2.00
❑5, Jan 1995; There are at least four cover variants, denoted A through D. 2.00
❑6, Feb 1995 2.00
❑7, Mar 1995 2.00
❑8, Apr 1995 2.00
❑9, Jun 1995 2.50
❑10, Jul 1995 2.50
❑11, Aug 1995 2.50
❑12, Sep 1995 2.50
❑13, Oct 1995 2.50
❑14, Nov 1995 2.50
❑15, Dec 1995 2.50
❑16, Jan 1996 2.50
❑17, Feb 1996 2.50
❑18, Mar 1996 3.00
❑19, Apr 1996 3.00
❑20, May 1996 3.00
❑21, Jun 1996 3.00
❑22, Jul 1996 3.00
❑23, Aug 1996 3.00

N-MINT

❑24, Sep 1996 3.00
❑25, Oct 1996 4.00

INVISIBLES (VOL. 2)
DC / VERTIGO

❑1, Feb 1997 3.00
❑2, Mar 1997 2.50
❑3, Apr 1997 BB (c); BB (a) 2.50
❑4, May 1997 2.50
❑5, Jun 1997 BB (c); BB (a) 2.50
❑6, Jul 1997 2.50
❑7, Aug 1997 2.50
❑8, Sep 1997 2.50
❑9, Oct 1997 2.50
❑10, Nov 1997 BB (c); BB (a) 2.50
❑11, Dec 1997 2.50
❑12, Jan 1998 2.50
❑13, Feb 1998 2.50
❑14, Mar 1998 2.50
❑15, Apr 1998 2.50
❑16, May 1998 2.50
❑17, Aug 1998 2.50
❑18, Sep 1998 2.50
❑19, Oct 1998 2.50
❑20, Nov 1998 2.50
❑21, Jan 1999 2.50
❑22, Feb 1999 2.50

INVISIBLES (VOL. 3)
DC / VERTIGO

❑12, Apr 1999; Issues count from 12 to 1 2.95
❑11, May 1999; Issues count from 12 to 1 2.95
❑10, Jun 1999; Issues count from 12 to 1 2.95
❑9, Jul 1999; Issues count from 12 to 1 2.95
❑8, Aug 1999; Issues count from 12 to 1 2.95
❑7, Oct 1999; Issues count from 12 to 1 2.95
❑6, Dec 1999; Issues count from 12 to 1 2.95
❑5, Jan 2000; Issues count from 12 to 1 2.95
❑4, Mar 2000; Issues count from 12 to 1 2.95
❑3, Apr 2000; Issues count from 12 to 1 2.95
❑2, May 2000; Issues count from 12 to 1 2.95
❑1, Jun 2000; Issues count from 12 to 1 2.95

INVISOWORLD
ETERNITY

❑1 1.95

I.N.V.U.
TOKYOPOP

❑1, Feb 2003, b&w 9.99
❑2, Feb 2003, b&w 9.99

IO
INVICTUS

❑1, Oct 1994 2.25
❑3, Win 1995, b&w; ashcan 2.25

ION
DC

❑1, Jul 2006 2.99
❑2, Aug 2006 2.99
❑3, Sep 2006 2.99

IRONCAT
IRONCAT

❑1, Jul 1999 2.95
❑2, Aug 1999 2.95

	N-MINT

IRON CORPORAL (CHARLTON)
CHARLTON
- ❑23, Oct 1985, Continues From Army War Heroes 1.50
- ❑24, Dec 1985 .... 1.50
- ❑25, Feb 1985 .... 1.50

IRON CORPORAL (AVALON)
AVALON
- ❑1, b&w 2.95

IRON DEVIL
FANTAGRAPHICS / EROS
- ❑1, b&w 2.95
- ❑2, b&w 2.95
- ❑3, Mar 1994, b&w 2.95

IRON EMPIRES
DARK HORSE
- ❑Book 1, ca. 2004 .... 17.95
- ❑Book 2, ca. 2004; Sheva's War 17.95

IRON FIST
MARVEL
- ❑1, Nov 1975, JBy (a); A: Iron Man. Marvel Value Stamp #63: Sub-Mariner 35.00
- ❑2, Dec 1975, JBy (a) 12.00
- ❑3, Feb 1976, JBy (a) 10.00
- ❑4, Apr 1976, JBy (a) 8.00
- ❑4/30 cent, Apr 1976, JBy (a); 30 cent regional price variant 20.00
- ❑5, Jun 1976, JBy (a) 8.00
- ❑5/30 cent, Jun 1976, JBy (a); 30 cent regional price variant 20.00
- ❑6, Aug 1976, JBy (a) 8.00
- ❑6/30 cent, Aug 1976, JBy (a); 30 cent regional price variant 20.00
- ❑7, Sep 1976, JBy (a) 8.00
- ❑8, Oct 1976, JBy (a) 8.00
- ❑9, Nov 1976, JBy (a) 8.00
- ❑10, Dec 1976, JBy (a) 8.00
- ❑11, Feb 1977, JBy (a) 8.00
- ❑12, Apr 1977, JBy (a) 8.00
- ❑13, Jun 1977, JBy (a); V: Boomerang. 8.00
- ❑13/35 cent, Jun 1977, 35¢ cover price; Limited distribution 10.00
- ❑14, Aug 1977, JBy (a); 1: Sabretooth. 80.00
- ❑14/35 cent, Aug 1977, JBy (a); 1: Sabretooth. 35¢ cover price; Limited distribution 150.00
- ❑15, Sep 1977, JBy (a); A: X-Men. A: Wolverine 27.00
- ❑15/35 cent, Sep 1977, JBy (a); A: X-Men. 35¢ cover price; Limited distribution 75.00

IRON FIST (2ND SERIES)
MARVEL
- ❑1, Sep 1996 .... 2.00
- ❑2, Oct 1996 .... 1.50

IRON FIST (3RD SERIES)
MARVEL
- ❑1, Jul 1998; gatefold summary; gatefold summary 2.50
- ❑2, Aug 1998; gatefold summary; gatefold summary 2.50
- ❑3, Sep 1998; gatefold summary; gatefold summary 2.50

IRON FIST (4TH SERIES)
MARVEL
- ❑1, May 2004 .... 2.99
- ❑2, Jun 2004 .... 2.99
- ❑3, Jul 2004 .... 2.99
- ❑4, Aug 2004 .... 2.99
- ❑5, Sep 2004 .... 2.99
- ❑6, Oct 2004 .... 2.99

IRON FIST: WOLVERINE
MARVEL
- ❑1, Nov 2000 .... 2.99
- ❑2, Dec 2000 .... 2.99
- ❑3, Jan 2001 .... 2.99
- ❑4, Feb 2001 .... 2.99

IRON GHOST
IMAGE
- ❑1, Apr 2005 .... 2.95
- ❑2, Jul 2005 .... 2.95
- ❑3, Oct 2005 .... 2.95
- ❑4 2005 .... 2.95
- ❑5, Feb 2006 .... 2.95
- ❑6, Apr 2006 .... 2.95

IRONHAND OF ALMURIC
DARK HORSE
- ❑1, b&w 2.00
- ❑2, b&w 2.00
- ❑3, b&w 2.00
- ❑4, b&w 2.00

IRONJAW
ATLAS-SEABOARD
- ❑1, Jan 1975 NA (c) 9.00
- ❑2, Mar 1975 NA (c) 6.00
- ❑3, May 1975 .... 6.00
- ❑4, Jul 1975 O: Ironjaw 8.00

IRON LANTERN
MARVEL / AMALGAM
- ❑1, Jun 1997 .... 1.95

IRON MAN (1ST SERIES)
MARVEL
- ❑1, May 1968, GC, JCr (a); O: Iron Man. 250.00
- ❑2, Jun 1968, JCr (a); 1: Demolisher. 60.00
- ❑3, Jul 1968, JCr (a) 60.00
- ❑4, Aug 1968, JCr (a) 60.00
- ❑5, Sep 1968, JCr (a) 55.00
- ❑6, Oct 1968, JCr, GT (a) 50.00
- ❑7, Nov 1968, JCr, GT (a) 50.00
- ❑8, Dec 1968, JCr, GT (a) 40.00
- ❑9, Jan 1969, JCr, GT (a); V: Hulk (robot) 90.00
- ❑10, Feb 1969, JCr, GT (a) 42.00
- ❑11, Mar 1969, V: Mandarin. 35.00
- ❑12, Apr 1969, O: The Controller. 1: Janice Cord. 35.00
- ❑13, May 1969, V: Controller. 27.00
- ❑14, Jun 1969, V: Night Phantom 27.00
- ❑15, Jul 1969, V: Unicorn. 27.00
- ❑16, Aug 1969, V: Unicorn. 27.00
- ❑17, Sep 1969, 1: Madame Masque I (Whitney Frost). 27.00
- ❑18, Oct 1969, O: Madame Masque I. 25.00
- ❑19, Nov 1969, O: Madame Masque I. Tony Stark's heart repaired 25.00
- ❑20, Dec 1969, V: Lucifer. 25.00
- ❑21, Jan 1970, 1: Crimson Dynamo III (Alex Nevsky). Tony Stark quits as Iron Man 20.00
- ❑22, Feb 1970, D: Janice Cord. V: Crimson Dynamo. 20.00
- ❑23, Mar 1970 .... 20.00
- ❑24, Apr 1970, V: Minotaur. 20.00
- ❑25, May 1970, A: Sub-Mariner. V: Sub-Mariner. 20.00
- ❑26, Jun 1970, A: Val-Larr. 20.00
- ❑27, Jul 1970, 1: Firebrand (Marvel). V: Firebrand. 20.00
- ❑28, Aug 1970, V: Controller. 20.00
- ❑29, Sep 1970 .... 20.00
- ❑30, Oct 1970 .... 20.00
- ❑31, Nov 1970, 1: Kevin O'Brien (later Guardsman). V: Smashers. ... 15.00
- ❑32, Dec 1970, V: Mechanoid. 15.00
- ❑33, Jan 1971, 1: Spymaster. V: Spymaster. 15.00
- ❑34, Feb 1971, V: Spymaster. 15.00
- ❑35, Mar 1971, A: Daredevil. 15.00
- ❑36, Apr 1971, DH (a); V: Ramrod. ... 15.00
- ❑37, May 1971 .... 15.00
- ❑38, Jun 1971, V: Jonah. 15.00
- ❑39, Jul 1971, V: White Dragon. 15.00
- ❑40, Aug 1971, D: White Dragon I. 15.00
- ❑41, Sep 1971, V: Slasher. 12.00
- ❑42, Oct 1971 .... 12.00
- ❑43, Nov 1971, Giant-size GT, JM (a); 1: Guardsman. V: Mikas. 35.00
- ❑44, Jan 1972, GT (a); V: Night Phantom. 12.00
- ❑45, Mar 1972, GT (a) 15.00
- ❑46, May 1972, GT (a); 1: Marianne Rodgers. A: Guardsman. D: Guardsman. 15.00
- ❑47, Jun 1972, JM (a); O: Iron Man... 35.00
- ❑48, Jul 1972, V: Firebrand. 12.00
- ❑49, Aug 1972, V: Adaptoid. 12.00
- ❑50, Sep 1972, V: Princess Python. ... 12.00
- ❑51, Oct 1972 .... 17.00
- ❑52, Nov 1972, V: Raga. 10.00
- ❑53, Dec 1972, JSn (a); 1: Black Lama. V: Black Lama. 10.00
- ❑54, Jan 1973, 1: Moondragon (as Madame MacEvil). A: Sub-Mariner. V: Sub-Mariner. 16.00
- ❑55, Feb 1973, JSn (a); 1: Mentor. 1: Drax the Destroyer. 1: Thanos. 1: Kronos. 1: Blood Brothers. 1: Starfox. 110.00
- ❑56, Mar 1973, JSn (a); 1: Fangor...... 15.00
- ❑57, Apr 1973 .... 15.00
- ❑58, May 1973, V: Mandarin. 15.00
- ❑59, Jun 1973 .... 15.00
- ❑60, Jul 1973 .... 15.00
- ❑61, Aug 1973 .... 15.00
- ❑62, Sep 1973 .... 15.00
- ❑63, Oct 1973 .... 15.00
- ❑64, Nov 1973, survey 15.00
- ❑65, Dec 1973, O: Doctor Spectrum. . 15.00
- ❑66, Feb 1974, A: Thor. Marvel Value Stamp A80 .... 15.00
- ❑67, Apr 1974, A: Sunfire. Marvel Value Stamp #80: Ghost Rider 15.00
- ❑68, Jun 1974, GT (a); O: Iron Man. A: Sunfire. Marvel Value Stamp #29: Baron Mordo 10.00
- ❑69, Aug 1974, GT (a); V: Sunfire. V: Mandarin. V: Unicorn. V: Yellow Claw. Marvel Value Stamp #22: Man-Thing 10.00
- ❑70, Sep 1974, GT (a); Marvel Value Stamp #2: Hulk 10.00
- ❑71, Nov 1974, GT (a); Marvel Value Stamp #26: Mephisto 10.00
- ❑72, Jan 1975, GT, NA (a); comic con 10.00
- ❑73, Mar 1975 .... 10.00
- ❑74, May 1975, V: Modok. 10.00
- ❑75, Jun 1975 .... 10.00
- ❑76, Jul 1975, GT (a) 10.00
- ❑77, Aug 1975 .... 10.00
- ❑78, Sep 1975, in Vietnam 10.00
- ❑79, Oct 1975 .... 10.00
- ❑80, Nov 1975 .... 10.00
- ❑81, Dec 1975, Marvel Value Stamp .. 10.00
- ❑82, Jan 1976, repeats letter column from #81; Marvel Value Stamp B2 .. 10.00
- ❑83, Feb 1976, HT (a); V: Red Ghost. Marvel Value Stamp B16 .... 10.00
- ❑84, Mar 1976, HT (a); Marvel Value Stamp B56 .... 10.00
- ❑85, Apr 1976 .... 10.00
- ❑85/30 cent, Apr 1976 .... 20.00
- ❑86, May 1976, 1: Blizzard. V: Blizzard. Marvel Value Stamp B84 .... 10.00
- ❑86/30 cent, May 1976 .... 20.00
- ❑87, Jun 1976, Marvel Value Stamp... 10.00
- ❑87/30 cent, Jun 1976 .... 20.00
- ❑88, Jul 1976, GT (a); Marvel Value Stamp 66 .... 10.00
- ❑88/30 cent, Jul 1976 .... 20.00
- ❑89, Aug 1976, GT (a); A: Daredevil... 10.00
- ❑89/30 cent, Aug 1976 .... 20.00
- ❑90, Sep 1976 .... 10.00
- ❑91, Oct 1976, GT (a) 10.00
- ❑92, Nov 1976, GT (a); V: Melter. 10.00
- ❑93, Dec 1976 .... 10.00
- ❑94, Jan 1977, HT (a) 10.00
- ❑95, Feb 1977, Newsstand edition (distributed by Curtis); issue number in box 10.00
- ❑95/Whitman, Feb 1977, Special markets edition (usually sold in Whitman bagged prepacks); price appears in a diamond; UPC barcode appears 18.00
- ❑96, Mar 1977, GT (a); 1: New Guardsman. Michael O'Brien becomes New Guardsman; Newsstand edition (distributed by Curtis); issue number in box 10.00
- ❑96/Whitman, Mar 1977, GT (a); 1: New Guardsman. Special markets edition (usually sold in Whitman bagged prepacks); price appears in a diamond; UPC barcode appears ... 18.00
- ❑97, Apr 1977 .... 10.00
- ❑98, May 1977, Newsstand edition (distributed by Curtis); issue number in box 8.00
- ❑98/Whitman, May 1977, Special markets edition (usually sold in Whitman bagged prepacks); price appears in a diamond; UPC barcode appears 18.00
- ❑99, Jun 1977, GT (a); V: Mandarin. Newsstand edition (distributed by Curtis); issue number in box 8.00

Iron Man (2nd Series)

Jim Lee's "Heroes Reborn" take on Iron Man

©Marvel

Iron Man (3rd Series)

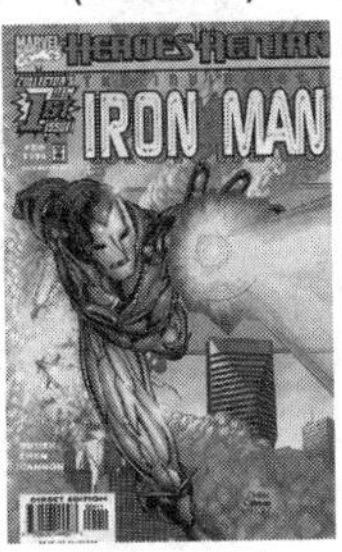

Series revealed Iron Man's identity

©Marvel

Iron Man & Sub-Mariner

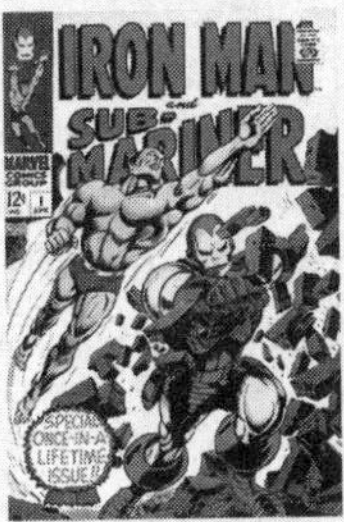

Single-issue prequel to solo series launches

©Marvel

Iron Man: Bad Blood

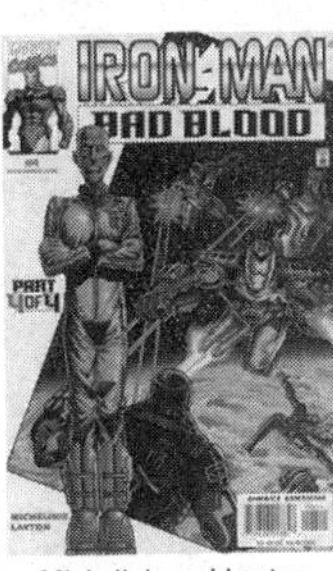

Michelinie and Layton reteam on Iron Man

©Marvel

Iron Man: The Iron Age

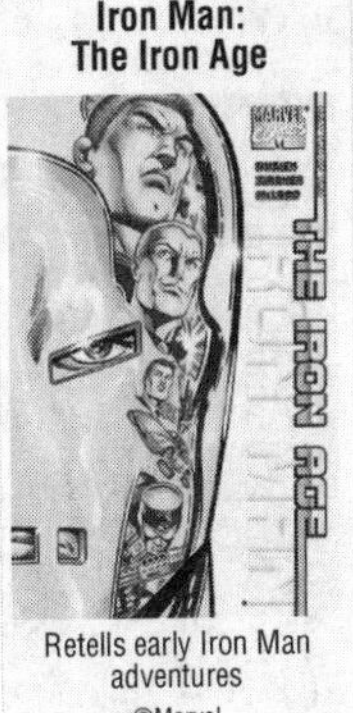

Retells early Iron Man adventures

©Marvel

	N-MINT
☐99/Whitman, Jun 1977, GT (a); V: Mandarin. Special markets edition (usually sold in Whitman bagged prepacks); price appears in a diamond; UPC barcode appears	18.00
☐99/35 cent, Jun 1977, GT (a); V: Mandarin. 35 cent regional variant newsstand edition (distributed by Curtis); issue number in box	15.00
☐100, Jul 1977, 100th anniversary issue; JSn (c); GT (a); Mandarin; Newsstand edition (distributed by Curtis); issue number in box	12.00
☐100/Whitman, Jul 1977, JSn (c); GT (a); Special markets edition (usually sold in Whitman bagged prepacks); price appears in a diamond; UPC barcode appears	20.00
☐100/35 cent, Jul 1977, 35 cent regional variant newsstand edition (distributed by Curtis); issue number in box	18.00
☐101, Aug 1977, GT (a); 1: Dreadknight. Newsstand edition (distributed by Curtis); issue number in box	7.00
☐101/Whitman, Aug 1977, GT (a); 1: Dreadknight. Special markets edition (usually sold in Whitman bagged prepacks); price appears in a diamond; UPC barcode appears	14.00
☐101/35 cent, Aug 1977, GT (a); 1: Dreadknight. 35 cent regional variant newsstand edition (distributed by Curtis); issue number in box	12.00
☐102, Sep 1977, O: Dreadknight. 1: Dreadknight. Newsstand edition (distributed by Curtis); issue number in box	7.00
☐102/Whitman, Sep 1977, O: Dreadknight. 1: Dreadknight. Special markets edition (usually sold in Whitman bagged prepacks); price appears in a diamond; no UPC barcode	14.00
☐102/35 cent, Sep 1977, O: Dreadknight. 1: Dreadknight. 35 cent regional variant newsstand edition (distributed by Curtis); issue number in box	12.00
☐103, Oct 1977, A: Jack of Hearts. Newsstand edition (distributed by Curtis); issue number in box	7.00
☐103/Whitman, Oct 1977, A: Jack of Hearts. Special markets edition (usually sold in Whitman bagged prepacks); price appears in a diamond; no UPC barcode	14.00
☐103/35 cent, Oct 1977, A: Jack of Hearts. 35 cent regional variant newsstand edition (distributed by Curtis); issue number in box	12.00
☐104, Nov 1977, Newsstand edition (distributed by Curtis); issue number in box	7.00
☐104/Whitman, Nov 1977, Special markets edition (usually sold in Whitman bagged prepacks); price appears in a diamond; no UPC barcode	14.00
☐105, Dec 1977, GT (a); A: Jack of Hearts.	7.00
☐106, Jan 1978	7.00
☐107, Feb 1978, KP (a); V: Midas.	7.00
☐108, Mar 1978, CI (a)	7.00
☐109, Apr 1978, 1: Vanguard. V: Darkstar. V: Vanguard	7.00
☐110, May 1978, KP (a); A: Jack of Hearts.	7.00
☐111, Jun 1978, Wundagore	7.00
☐112, Jul 1978, KP, AA (a)	7.00
☐113, Aug 1978, HT (a); Newsstand edition (distributed by Curtis); issue number in box	7.00
☐113/Whitman, Aug 1978, HT (a); Special markets edition (usually sold in Whitman bagged prepacks); price appears in a diamond; no UPC barcode	14.00
☐114, Sep 1978, Newsstand edition (distributed by Curtis); issue number in box	7.00
☐114/Whitman, Sep 1978, Special markets edition (usually sold in Whitman bagged prepacks); price appears in a diamond; no UPC barcode	14.00
☐115, Oct 1978, DGr (a); Newsstand edition (distributed by Curtis); issue number in box	7.00
☐115/Whitman, Oct 1978, DGr (a); Special markets edition (usually sold in Whitman bagged prepacks); price appears in a diamond; no UPC barcode	14.00
☐116, Nov 1978, BL, JR2 (a); D: Ape-Man I (Gordon Monk Keefer). D: Frog-Man I (Francois LeBlanc). D: Count Nefaria. D: Cat-Man I (Townshend Patane). D: Bird-Man I (Henry Hawk). 1st David Michelinie written issue; Newsstand edition (distributed by Curtis); issue number in box	7.00
☐116/Whitman, Nov 1978, BL, JR2 (a); D: Ape-Man I (Gordon Monk Keefer). D: Frog-Man I (Francois LeBlanc). D: Count Nefaria. D: Cat-Man I (Townshend Patane). D: Bird-Man I (Henry Hawk). Special markets edition (usually sold in Whitman bagged prepacks); price appears in a diamond; no UPC barcode	14.00
☐117, Dec 1978, BL, JR2 (a); 1: Beth Cabe. Newsstand edition (distributed by Curtis); issue number in box	7.00
☐117/Whitman, Dec 1978, BL, JR2 (a); 1: Beth Cabe. Special markets edition (usually sold in Whitman bagged prepacks); price appears in a diamond; no UPC barcode	14.00
☐118, Jan 1979, JBy, BL (a); 1: James Rhodes (Rhodey). 1: Mrs. Arbogast. Newsstand edition (distributed by Curtis); issue number in box	7.00
☐118/Whitman, Jan 1979, JBy, BL (a); 1: James Rhodes (Rhodey). 1: Mrs. Arbogast. Special markets edition (usually sold in Whitman bagged prepacks); price appears in a diamond; no UPC barcode	14.00
☐119, Feb 1979, BL, JR2 (a); Stark battles with alcohol; Newsstand edition (distributed by Curtis); issue number in box	7.00
☐119/Whitman, Feb 1979, BL, JR2 (a); Special markets edition (usually sold in Whitman bagged prepacks); price appears in a diamond; no UPC barcode	14.00
☐120, Mar 1979, 1: Justin Hammer. A: Sub-Mariner. Stark battles with alcohol	7.00
☐121, Apr 1979, A: Sub-Mariner. Stark battles with alcohol	7.00
☐122, May 1979, O: Iron Man. A: Sub-Mariner. Stark battles with alcohol; Newsstand edition (distributed by Curtis); issue number in box	7.00
☐122/Whitman, May 1979, O: Iron Man. A: Sub-Mariner. Special markets edition (usually sold in Whitman bagged prepacks); price appears in a diamond; no UPC barcode	14.00
☐123, Jun 1979, Stark battles with alcohol	7.00
☐124, Jul 1979, JR2 (a); Stark battles with alcohol	7.00
☐125, Aug 1979, JR2 (a); A: Scott Lang (Ant-Man). Stark battles with alcohol	7.00
☐126, Sep 1979, V: Justin Hammer. Stark battles with alcohol	7.00
☐127, Oct 1979, Stark battles with alcohol	7.00
☐128, Nov 1979, BL, JR2 (a); Stark begins recovery from alcohol	7.00
☐129, Dec 1979, SB (a); V: Dreadnought.	7.00
☐130, Jan 1980	5.00
☐131, Feb 1980, A: Hulk.	5.00
☐132, Mar 1980, A: Hulk.	5.00
☐133, Apr 1980, BL (a); A: Hulk. A: Ant-Man.	5.00
☐134, May 1980, BL (a)	5.00
☐135, Jun 1980, BL (a); V: Titanium Man.	5.00
☐136, Jul 1980, BWi (a)	5.00
☐137, Aug 1980, BL (a)	5.00
☐138, Sep 1980, BL, TP (a); 1: Dreadnought (silver).	5.00
☐139, Oct 1980, BL (a); Bethany Cabe knows Tony is Iron Man	5.00
☐140, Nov 1980, BL (a)	5.00
☐141, Dec 1980, BL, JR2 (a)	5.00
☐142, Jan 1981, BL, JR2 (a); 1: Space Armor.	5.00
☐143, Feb 1981, BL, JR2 (a); 1: Sunturion.	5.00
☐144, Mar 1981, BL, JR2 (a); O: James Rhodes (Rhodey)	5.00
☐145, Apr 1981, BL, JR2 (a)	5.00
☐146, May 1981, BL, JR2 (a); V: Blacklash.	5.00
☐147, Jun 1981, BL, JR2 (a)	5.00
☐148, Jul 1981, BL, JR2 (a)	5.00
☐149, Aug 1981, BL, JR2 (a); V: Doctor Doom.	5.00
☐150, Sep 1981, double-sized; BL, JR2 (a); V: Doctor Doom. In Camelot	7.00
☐151, Oct 1981, BL, LMc (a); A: Ant-Man.	5.00
☐152, Nov 1981, BL, JR2 (a); 1: Stealth Armor.	5.00
☐153, Dec 1981, BL, JR2 (a)	5.00
☐154, Jan 1982, BL, JR2 (a); D: Unicorn I (Milos Masaryk)	7.00
☐155, Feb 1982, BL, JR2 (a)	5.00
☐156, Mar 1982, JR2 (a)	5.00
☐157, Apr 1982	5.00
☐158, May 1982, CI (a)	5.00
☐159, Jun 1982, PS (a); Diablo	5.00
☐160, Jul 1982, SD (a); Serpent Squad	7.00

Other grades: Multiply price above by 5/6 for VF/NM • 2/3 for VERY FINE • 1/3 for FINE • 1/5 for VERY GOOD • 1/8 for GOOD

N-MINT

❑161, Aug 1982, LMc (a); Moon Knight 5.00
❑162, Sep 1982 5.00
❑163, Oct 1982, LMc (a); 1: Obadiah Stane (voice only). 1: Chessmen. 1: Indries Moomji. 1: Iron Monger (voice only) 5.00
❑164, Nov 1982, BA (c); LMc, BA (a). 5.00
❑165, Dec 1982, LMc (a) 5.00
❑166, Jan 1983, LMc (a); 1: Obadiah Stane (full appearance). 1: Iron Monger (full appearance) 5.00
❑167, Feb 1983, LMc (a); Alcohol problem returns 5.00
❑168, Mar 1983, LMc (a); Machine Man; Stark battles with alcohol 5.00
❑169, Apr 1983, LMc (a); Jim Rhodes takes over Stark's job as Iron Man; Stark battles with alcohol 5.00
❑170, May 1983, LMc (a); 1: Morley Erwin. 1: James Rhodes as Iron Man. Stark battles with alcohol 5.00
❑171, Jun 1983, LMc (a); 1: Clytemnestra Erwin. V: Thunderball. Stark battles with alcohol 2.50
❑172, Jul 1983, LMc (a); A: Captain America. Stark battles with alcohol. 2.50
❑173, Aug 1983, LMc (a); Stark International becomes Stane International; Stark battles with alcohol 2.50
❑174, Sep 1983, LMc (a); V: Chessmen. S.H.I.E.L.D. acquires armor; Stark battles with alcohol 2.50
❑175, Oct 1983, LMc (a); Stark battles with alcohol 2.50
❑176, Nov 1983, LMc (a); Stark battles with alcohol 2.50
❑177, Dec 1983, LMc (a); V: Flying Tiger. Stark battles with alcohol (alcohol storyline continues through next several issues) 2.50
❑178, Jan 1984, LMc (a) 2.50
❑179, Feb 1984, LMc (a); V: Mandarin. 2.50
❑180, Mar 1984, LMc (a); V: Mandarin. 2.50
❑181, Apr 1984, LMc (a); V: Mandarin. Erroneously reprints 1982 Statement of Ownership 2.50
❑182, May 1984, LMc (a); alcoholism cured again 4.00
❑183, Jun 1984, LMc (a); V: Taurus. 2.50
❑184, Jul 1984, LMc (a); Tony Stark founds new company in California 2.50
❑185, Aug 1984, LMc (a) 2.50
❑186, Sep 1984, LMc (a); O: Vibro. 1: Vibro. V: Vibro. 4.00
❑187, Oct 1984, LMc (a); V: Vibro. 2.50
❑188, Nov 1984, DP (a); 1: Circuits Maximus. V: Brothers Grimm. 2.50
❑189, Dec 1984, LMc (a); V: Termite. 2.50
❑190, Jan 1985, LMc (a); A: Scarlet Witch. V: Termite 2.50
❑191, Feb 1985, LMc (a); Tony Stark returns as Iron Man in original armor 2.50
❑192, Mar 1985, Iron Man (Stark) vs. Iron Man (Rhodey) 4.00
❑193, Apr 1985, LMc (a); West Coast Avengers learn Tony is Iron Man 2.50
❑194, May 1985, LMc (a); 1: Scourge. A: West Coast Avengers. D: Enforcer (Marvel) 2.50
❑195, Jun 1985, A: Shaman. 2.50
❑196, Jul 1985 2.50
❑197, Aug 1985, Secret Wars II 2.50
❑198, Sep 1985, SB (a); O: Obadiah Stane. O: Iron Monger. 2.50
❑199, Oct 1985, HT (a); D: Morley Erwin. James Rhodes crippled 2.50
❑200, Nov 1985, double-sized; 1: Red and white battlesuit. D: Obadiah Stane. D: Iron Monger. Tony Stark returns as Iron Man; New armor (red & white) 3.00
❑201, Dec 1985 2.00
❑202, Jan 1986, A: Ka-Zar. V: Fixer. 2.00
❑203, Feb 1986 2.00
❑204, Mar 1986 2.00
❑205, Apr 1986, V: Modok. 2.00
❑206, May 1986 2.00
❑207, Jun 1986 2.00
❑208, Jul 1986 2.00
❑209, Aug 1986 2.00
❑210, Sep 1986, A: Happy Hogan 2.00
❑211, Oct 1986 2.00
❑212, Nov 1986 2.00

N-MINT

❑213, Dec 1986, A: Dominic Fortune. 2.00
❑214, Jan 1987, Construction of Stark Enterprises begins 2.00
❑215, Feb 1987 2.00
❑216, Mar 1987, D: Clytemnestra Erwin. 2.00
❑217, Apr 1987, 1: undersea armor. 2.00
❑218, May 1987, BL (a); 1: Deep Sea armor. 2.00
❑219, Jun 1987, BL (a); 1: Ghost. V: Ghost 2.00
❑220, Jul 1987, D: Spymaster. 2.00
❑221, Aug 1987 2.00
❑222, Sep 1987 2.00
❑223, Oct 1987, 1: Rae LaCoste. 2.00
❑224, Nov 1987, BL (a) 2.00
❑225, Dec 1987, Giant-size 3.00
❑226, Jan 1988 2.50
❑227, Feb 1988 2.50
❑228, Mar 1988 2.50
❑229, Apr 1988, D: Gremlin a.k.a Titanium Man II. 3.00
❑230, May 1988, V: Firepower. apparent death of Iron Man 2.50
❑231, Jun 1988, V: Firepower. new armor 2.50
❑232, Jul 1988, offset 2.50
❑232/A, Jul 1988, Flexographic 2.50
❑233, Aug 1988, BG (a); 1: Kathy Dare. A: Ant-Man. 2.00
❑234, Sep 1988, BG (a); A: Spider-Man. 2.00
❑235, Oct 1988, BG (a) 1.50
❑236, Nov 1988, BG (a) 1.50
❑237, Dec 1988, BG (a) 1.50
❑238, Jan 1989, BG (a); 1: Madame Masque II. 1.50
❑239, Feb 1989, BG (a) 1.50
❑240, Mar 1989, BG (a) 1.50
❑241, Apr 1989 1.50
❑242, May 1989, Stark shot by Kathy Dare 1.50
❑243, Jun 1989, BL (a); Stark crippled 2.00
❑244, Jul 1989, Giant-size; Carl Walker a.k.a. Force becomes Iron Man; New armor to allow Stark to walk again. 3.00
❑245, Aug 1989, PS (a) 1.50
❑246, Sep 1989, BL (a) 1.50
❑247, Oct 1989, BL (a) 1.50
❑248, Nov 1989, BL (a); Stark cured by implanted bio-chip 1.50
❑249, Nov 1989, BL (a); Doctor Doom 1.50
❑250, Dec 1989, double-sized; BL (a); V: Doctor Doom. Acts of Vengeance 1.75
❑251, Dec 1989, HT (a); V: Wrecker. Acts of Vengeance 1.25
❑252, Jan 1990, HT (a); V: Chemistro. Acts of Vengeance 1.25
❑253, Feb 1990, JBy (c); GC (a) 1.25
❑254, Mar 1990, BL (w); BL (a) 1.25
❑255, Apr 1990, HT (a) 1.25
❑256, May 1990, BL (w); JR2 (a) 1.25
❑257, Jun 1990 1.25
❑258, Jul 1990, JBy (w); JR2 (a) 1.50
❑259, Aug 1990, JBy (w); JR2 (a) 1.50
❑260, Sep 1990, JBy (w); JR2 (a) 1.50
❑261, Oct 1990, JBy (w); JR2 (a) 1.50
❑262, Nov 1990, JBy (w); JR2 (a) 1.50
❑263, Dec 1990, JBy (w); JR2 (a) 1.50
❑264, Jan 1991, JBy (w); JR2 (a) 1.50
❑265, Feb 1991, JBy (w); JR2 (a) 1.50
❑266, Mar 1991, JR2 (a) 1.50
❑267, Apr 1991, JBy (w) 1.50
❑268, May 1991, JBy (w); O: Iron Man. 1.50
❑269, Jun 1991, JBy (w) 1.50
❑270, Jul 1991, JBy (w) 1.50
❑271, Aug 1991, JBy (w) 1.50
❑272, Sep 1991, JBy (w) 1.50
❑273, Oct 1991, JBy (w) 1.50
❑274, Nov 1991, JBy (w); O: Fin Fang Foom. V: Fin Fang Foom. 1.50
❑275, Dec 1991, Giant-size JBy (w); V: Fin Fang Foom. V: Mandarin. V: Dragon Lords. 1.50
❑276, Jan 1992, JBy (w) 1.50
❑277, Feb 1992, JBy (w) 1.50
❑278, Mar 1992, 1: new Space Armor. Galactic Storm 1.50
❑279, Apr 1992, V: Ronan the Accuser. Galactic Storm 1.50
❑280, May 1992, A: The Stark. 1.50

N-MINT

❑281, Jun 1992, 1: War Machine armor. 3.00
❑282, Jul 1992, 2: War Machine armor. 3.00
❑283, Aug 1992 1.50
❑284, Sep 1992, O: War Machine. 1: War Machine. D: Tony Stark 2.00
❑285, Oct 1992 1.25
❑286, Nov 1992 1.25
❑287, Dec 1992 1.25
❑288, Jan 1993, 30th anniversary special; Embossed cover; Tony Stark revived 2.50
❑289, Feb 1993 1.25
❑290, Mar 1993, Metallic ink cover; New Armor 3.50
❑291, Apr 1993, James Rhodes leaves to become War Machine 1.25
❑292, May 1993 1.25
❑293, Jun 1993 1.25
❑294, Jul 1993 1.25
❑295, Aug 1993 1.25
❑296, Sep 1993 1.25
❑297, Oct 1993, A: M.O.D.A.M. A: Omega Red 1.25
❑298, Nov 1993 1.25
❑299, Dec 1993, V: Ultimo. 1.25
❑300, Jan 1994, Giant size; A: Iron Legion (all substitute Iron Men). V: Ultimo. Stark dons new (modular) armor 2.50
❑300/Variant, Jan 1994, Giant size; Special (embossed foil) cover edition; Stark dons new (modular) armor 3.95
❑301, Feb 1994 1.25
❑302, Mar 1994, A: Venom. 1.25
❑303, Apr 1994 1.25
❑304, May 1994, 1: Hulkbuster Armor. 1.25
❑305, Jun 1994, A: Hulk 1.50
❑306, Jul 1994, Stark restructures company 1.50
❑307, Aug 1994 1.50
❑308, Sep 1994 1.50
❑309, Oct 1994 1.50
❑310, Nov 1994 1.50
❑310/CS, Nov 1994, polybagged with 16-page preview, acetate print, and other items 2.95
❑311, Dec 1994 1.50
❑312, Jan 1995 1.50
❑313, Feb 1995 1.50
❑314, Mar 1995 1.50
❑315, Apr 1995, V: Titanium Man 1.50
❑316, May 1995 1.50
❑317, Jun 1995, D: Titanium Man I. flip book with War Machine: Brothers in Arms part 3 back-up 2.50
❑318, Jul 1995 1.50
❑319, Aug 1995, O: Iron Man. 1.50
❑320, Sep 1995 1.50
❑321, Oct 1995, OverPower cards inserted 1.50
❑322, Nov 1995 1.50
❑323, Dec 1995, A: Avengers. A: Hawkeye. 1.50
❑324, Jan 1996 1.50
❑325, Feb 1996, Giant-size; wraparound cover; Tony Stark vs. young Tony Stark 3.00
❑326, Mar 1996 1.50
❑327, Apr 1996, V: Frostbite. reading of Tony Stark's will 1.50
❑328, May 1996 1.50
❑329, Jun 1996, Fujikawa International takes over Stark Enterprises 1.50
❑330, Jul 1996 1.50
❑331, Aug 1996 1.50
❑332, Sep 1996 1.50
❑Annual 1, Aug 1970, GC, DH, JK, WW, JAb (a); Reprints from Tales of Suspense #71, #79, and #80, and Tales to Astonish #82 27.00
❑Annual 2, Nov 1971, Reprints 20.00
❑Annual 3, ca. 1976 10.00
❑Annual 4, ca. 1977, Cover reads "King-Size Special"; Cover reads King-Size Special 4.00
❑Annual 5, ca. 1982 3.00
❑Annual 6, ca. 1983, LMc (a); A: Eternals. D: Zuras (spirit leaves body). New Iron Man appears 3.00
❑Annual 7, ca. 1984, LMc (a); 1: Goliath III (Erik Josten). A: . A: West Coast Avengers. West Coast Avengers 3.00

Other grades: Multiply price above by 5/6 for VF/NM • 2/3 for VERY FINE • 1/3 for FINE • 1/5 for VERY GOOD • 1/8 for GOOD

Iron Manual

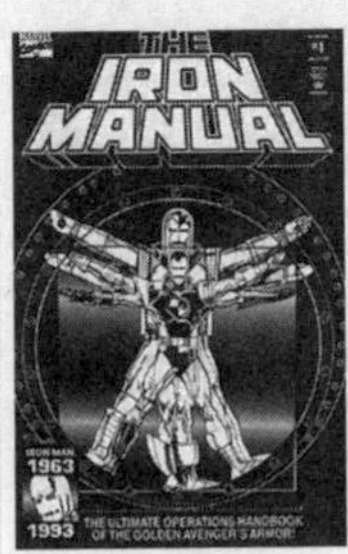

Shellhead's schematics with blueprint cover

©Marvel

Ironwolf

Collects Chaykin's Weird Worlds space opera

©DC

I Spy

Tennis player and secret agent team up

©Gold Key

J2

Juggernaut's son wants to be a hero

©Marvel

Jack of Hearts

Excess energy poses potential problem

©Marvel

N-MINT

❑Annual 8, ca. 1986 A: X-Factor. 3.00
❑Annual 9, ca. 1987 .... 3.00
❑Annual 10, ca. 1989, PS, DP (a); Atlantis Attacks 2.50
❑Annual 11, ca. 1990, A: Machine Man. 2.00
❑Annual 12, ca. 1991, 1: Trapster II.... 2.00
❑Annual 13, ca. 1992, GC (a); A: Darkhawk, Avengers West Coast. 2.00
❑Annual 14, ca. 1993, trading card..... 2.95
❑Annual 15, ca. 1994, GC (a); V: Controller. 2.95
❑Ashcan 1, Nov 1994, Collectors' Preview; "Iron Man & Force Works" on cover 1.95

IRON MAN (2ND SERIES)

MARVEL

❑1, Nov 1996; Giant-size JLee (w); O: Hulk (new). O: Iron Man (new)... 3.00
❑1/A, Nov 1996; Giant-size; JLee (w); O: Iron Man (new). variant cover 3.00
❑2, Dec 1996 JLee (w); V: Hulk. 2.00
❑3, Jan 1997 JLee (w); 1: Whirlwind. A: Fantastic Four. 2.00
❑4, Feb 1997 JLee (w); V: Living Laser. 2.00
❑4/A, Feb 1997; JLee (w); variant cover 2.00
❑5, Mar 1997 JLee (w); V: Whirlwind. 1.95
❑6, Apr 1997; JLee (a); A: Onslaught. concludes in Captain America #6.... 1.95
❑7, May 1997 JLee (w) 1.95
❑8, Jun 1997 .... 1.95
❑9, Jul 1997 .... 1.95
❑10, Aug 1997; gatefold summary 1.95
❑11, Sep 1997; gatefold summary A: Doctor Doom. 1.95
❑12, Oct 1997; gatefold summary; cover forms quadtych with Fantastic Four #12, Avengers #12, and Captain America #12 .... 3.50
❑13, Nov 1997; gatefold summary; cover forms quadtych with Fantastic Four #13, Avengers #13, and Captain America #13 .... 2.50

IRON MAN (3RD SERIES)

MARVEL

❑1, Feb 1998; Giant-size; KB (w); 1: Stark Solutions. wraparound cover. 3.50
❑1/A, Feb 1998; gatefold summary; KB (w); 1: Stark Solutions. wraparound cover 4.00
❑2, Mar 1998; gatefold summary KB (w) 2.00
❑2/Variant, Mar 1998; KB (w); variant cover 3.00
❑3, Apr 1998; gatefold summary KB (w) 2.00
❑4, May 1998; gatefold summary KB (w); V: Firebrand. 2.00
❑5, Jun 1998; gatefold summary KB (w); V: Firebrand 2.00
❑6, Jul 1998; gatefold summary KB (w); A: Black Widow. 2.00
❑7, Aug 1998; gatefold summary KB (w); A: Warbird. 2.00
❑8, Sep 1998; gatefold summary; KB (w); Tony beaten 2.00
❑9, Oct 1998; gatefold summary KB (w); A: Winter Guard. 2.00
❑10, Nov 1998; gatefold summary KB (w) 2.00
❑11, Dec 1998; gatefold summary; KB (w); A: Warbird. V: War Machine armor. new home 2.00

N-MINT

❑12, Jan 1999; gatefold summary KB (w); A: Warbird. V: War Machine armor. 2.00
❑13, Feb 1999; double-sized KB (w); A: Controller. V: Controller. 3.00
❑13/Autographed, Feb 1999 KB (w); A: Controller. 4.00
❑14, Mar 1999; KB (w); A: Fantastic Four. A: S.H.I.E.L.D.. A: Watcher. V: Ronan. Fantastic Four crossover, part 2 .... 1.99
❑15, Apr 1999 KB (w); V: Nitro. 1.99
❑16, May 1999 KB (w) 1.99
❑17, Jun 1999 KB (w); A: Fin Fang Foom. 1.99
❑18, Jul 1999 KB (w); A: Warbird. 1.99
❑19, Aug 1999 KB (w); V: War Machine. 1.99
❑20, Sep 1999 KB (w); V: War Machine. 1.99
❑21, Oct 1999; KB (w); 1: Inferno. continues in Thor #17 .... 1.99
❑22, Nov 1999; KB (w); 1: Carnivore. A: Thor. continues in Peter Parker, Spider-Man #11 .... 1.99
❑23, Dec 1999 KB (w); A: Ultimo. 1.99
❑24, Jan 2000 .... 1.99
❑25, Feb 2000; double-sized KB (w); A: Warbird. A: Ultimo 2.25
❑26, Mar 2000 .... 2.25
❑27, Apr 2000 .... 2.25
❑28, May 2000 .... 2.25
❑29, Jun 2000 .... 2.25
❑30, Jul 2000 .... 2.25
❑31, Aug 2000 .... 2.25
❑32, Sep 2000; A: Wong-Chu. concludes in Iron Man Annual 2000 2.25
❑33, Oct 2000 .... 2.25
❑34, Nov 2000 .... 2.25
❑35, Dec 2000 .... 2.25
❑36, Jan 2001 .... 2.25
❑37, Feb 2001 .... 2.25
❑38, Mar 2001 .... 2.25
❑39, Apr 2001 .... 2.25
❑40, May 2001 BL, JR, ES (a) 2.25
❑41, Jun 2001 .... 2.25
❑42, Jul 2001 .... 2.25
❑43, Aug 2001 .... 2.25
❑44, Sep 2001 .... 2.25
❑45, Oct 2001 .... 2.25
❑46, Nov 2001 .... 3.50
❑47, Dec 2001 .... 2.25
❑48, Jan 2002 .... 2.25
❑49, Feb 2002 .... 2.25
❑50, Mar 2002 MGr (w) 2.99
❑51, Apr 2002; MGr (w); wraparound cover 2.25
❑52, May 2002; MGr (w); wraparound cover 2.25
❑53, Jun 2002; MGr (w); wraparound cover 2.25
❑54, Jun 2002; MGr (w); wraparound cover 2.25
❑55, Jul 2002; MGr (w); wraparound cover 2.25
❑56, Aug 2002; MGr (w); wraparound cover 2.25
❑57, Sep 2002; MGr (w); wraparound cover 2.25

N-MINT

❑58, Oct 2002; MGr (w); wraparound cover 2.25
❑59, Nov 2002; MGr (w); wraparound cover 2.25
❑60, Dec 2002; MGr (w); wraparound cover 2.25
❑61, Jan 2003; MGr (w); wraparound cover 2.25
❑62, Feb 2003; MGr (w); wraparound cover 2.25
❑63, Feb 2003; MGr (w); wraparound cover 2.25
❑64, Mar 2003; MGr (w); wraparound cover 2.25
❑65, Apr 2003 .... 2.25
❑66, May 2003 .... 2.25
❑67, Jun 2003 .... 2.99
❑68, Jul 2003 .... 2.99
❑69, Aug 2003, (c) 2.99
❑70, Sep 2003 .... 2.99
❑71, Oct 2003 .... 2.99
❑72, Nov 2003 .... 2.99
❑73, Dec 2003, JJM (w); Stark seeks cabinet post 2.99
❑74, Jan 2004, JJM (w); Stark nomination announced 2.99
❑75, Feb 2004, JJM (w) 2.99
❑76, Mar 2004, JJM (w); A: Crimson Dynamo III (Alex Nevsky). Stark rejected by Senate subcommittee ... 2.99
❑77, Apr 2004, JJM (w) 2.99
❑78, May 2004, JJM (w); Stark named Secretary of Defense 2.99
❑79, Jun 2004, JJM (w) 2.99
❑80, Jun 2004, JJM (w); Stark visits Iraq 2.99
❑81, Jul 2004, JJM (w) 2.99
❑82, Jul 2004, JJM (w); Force reconciled with Stark 2.99
❑83, Jul 2004 JJM (w) 2.99
❑84, Aug 2004; JJM (w); Avengers Dissasemble Prologue 8.00
❑85, Aug 2004; JJM (w); Avengers Dissasemble Prologue 5.00
❑86, Sep 2004 .... 2.99
❑87, Oct 2004 .... 2.99
❑88, Nov 2004 .... 2.99
❑89, Dec 2004 .... 2.99
❑Annual 1998, ca. 1998; MWa (w); V: Modok. Iron Man/Captain America '98; wraparound cover 3.50
❑Annual 1999, Aug 1999; wraparound cover 3.50
❑Annual 2000, ca. 2000; D: Wong-Chu. wraparound cover 3.50
❑Annual 2001, ca. 2001 .... 2.99

IRON MAN (4TH SERIES)

MARVEL

❑1, Jan 2004 .... 3.50
❑2, Feb 2005 .... 2.99
❑3, May 2005 .... 2.99
❑4, Sep 2005 .... 2.99
❑5, Mar 2006 .... 2.99
❑6, Jun 2006 .... 2.99
❑7, Jul 2006 .... 2.99
❑8, Aug 2006 .... 2.99
❑9, Sep 2006 .... 2.99

Other grades: Multiply price above by 5/6 for VF/NM • 2/3 for VERY FINE • 1/3 for FINE • 1/5 for VERY GOOD • 1/8 for GOOD

IRON MAN & SUB-MARINER
MARVEL

❑1, Apr 1968, GC, JCr (a); O: Destiny. 100.00

IRON MAN: BAD BLOOD
MARVEL

❑1, Sep 2000 2.99
❑2, Oct 2000 2.99
❑3, Nov 2000 2.99
❑4, Dec 2000 2.99

IRON MAN: HOUSE OF M
MARVEL

❑1, Aug 2005 5.00
❑1/Variant, Aug 2005 4.00
❑2, Sep 2005 2.99
❑3, Oct 2005 2.99

IRON MAN: THE INEVITABLE
MARVEL

❑1, Feb 2006 2.99
❑2, Mar 2006 2.99
❑3, May 2006 2.99
❑4, Jun 2006 2.99
❑5, Jul 2006 2.99
❑6, Aug 2006 2.99

IRON MAN: THE IRON AGE
MARVEL

❑1, Aug 1998; prestige format; retells early Iron Man adventures 5.99
❑2, Sep 1998; prestige format; retells early Iron Man adventures 5.99

IRON MAN: THE LEGEND
MARVEL

❑1, Sep 1996; wraparound cover; summation of history of character 3.95

IRON MAN 2020
MARVEL

❑1 5.95

IRON MANUAL
MARVEL

❑1, ca. 1993; no cover date; background info on Iron Man's armor 2.00

IRON MAN/X-O MANOWAR: HEAVY METAL
MARVEL

❑1, Sep 1996, crossover with Acclaim 2.50

IRON MARSHAL
JADEMAN

❑1, Jul 1990 1.75
❑2, Aug 1990 1.75
❑3, Sep 1990 1.75
❑4, Oct 1990 1.75
❑5, Nov 1990 1.75
❑6, Dec 1990 1.75
❑7, Jan 1991 1.75
❑8, Feb 1991 1.75
❑9, Mar 1991 1.75
❑10, Apr 1991 1.75
❑11, May 1991 1.75
❑12, Jun 1991 1.75
❑13, Jul 1991 1.75
❑14, Aug 1991 1.75
❑15, Sep 1991 1.75
❑16, Oct 1991 1.75
❑17, Nov 1991 1.75
❑18, Dec 1991 1.75
❑19, Jan 1992 1.75
❑20, Feb 1992 1.75
❑21, Mar 1992 1.75
❑22, Apr 1992 1.75
❑23, May 1992 1.75
❑24, Jun 1992 1.75
❑25, Jul 1992 1.75
❑26, Aug 1992 1.75
❑27, Sep 1992 1.75
❑28, Oct 1992 1.75
❑29, Nov 1992 1.75
❑30, Dec 1992 1.75
❑31, Jan 1993 1.75
❑32, Feb 1993 1.75

IRON SAGA'S ANTHOLOGY
IRON SAGA

❑1, Jan 1987 1.75

IRON WINGS
ACTION

❑1, May 1999 2.50

IRON WINGS (VOL. 2)
IMAGE

❑1, Apr 2000 2.50

IRONWOLF
DC

❑1, ca. 1986; Reprints IronWolf adventures from Weird Worlds #8-10 2.00

IRONWOOD
FANTAGRAPHICS / EROS

❑1, b&w 4.00
❑2, b&w 2.25
❑3, b&w 2.25
❑4, b&w 2.25
❑5, b&w 2.25
❑6, ca. 1992, b&w 2.25
❑7, Mar 1992, b&w 2.50
❑8, ca. 1992, b&w 2.50
❑9, Aug 1993, b&w 2.50
❑10, Sep 1994, b&w 2.75

I SAW IT
EDUCOMICS

❑1, b&w; Hiroshima 2.00

ISIS
DC

❑1, Oct 1976 6.00
❑2, Dec 1976 4.00
❑3, Feb 1977 3.50
❑4, Apr 1977 3.50
❑5, Jun 1977 3.50
❑6, Aug 1977 3.50
❑7, Oct 1977, O: Isis. 4.00
❑8, Dec 1977 3.50

ISLAND OF DR. MOREAU
MARVEL

❑1, Oct 1977 3.00

ISMET
CANIS

❑1 1.25
❑2 1.25
❑3 1.25
❑4 1.25
❑5 1.25

I SPY
GOLD KEY

❑1, Aug 1966, based on TV series 55.00
❑2, Apr 1967, based on TV series 40.00
❑3, Nov 1967, based on TV series 33.00
❑4, Feb 1968, based on TV series 33.00
❑5, Jun 1968, based on TV series 33.00
❑6, Sep 1968, based on TV series 33.00

ITCHY & SCRATCHY COMICS
BONGO

❑1, ca. 1993 2.50
❑2, ca. 1994 2.00
❑3, ca. 1994 A: Bart Simpson. 2.25
❑Holiday 1, ca. 1994; Itchy & Scratchy Holiday Hi-Jinx Special 2.00

ITCHY PLANET
FANTAGRAPHICS

❑1, Spr 1988 2.25
❑2, Sum 1988 2.25
❑3, Fal 1988 2.25

IT'S ABOUT TIME
GOLD KEY

❑1, Jan 1967 25.00

IT'S ALL TRUE!
APESHOT

❑Book 1, Sum 1995; collects True Artist Tales strips 4.95

ITSI KITSI
FUNNY BOOK INSTITUTE

❑1, May 2000 3.00

IT'S ONLY A MATTER OF LIFE AND DEATH
FANTAGRAPHICS

❑1, b&w 3.95

IT'S SCIENCE WITH DR. RADIUM
SLAVE LABOR

❑1, Sep 1986 2.00
❑2, Jan 1987 2.00
❑3, Mar 1987 2.00
❑4, May 1987 2.00
❑5, Jul 1987 2.00
❑6, Oct 1987 2.00
❑7, Feb 1988 2.00
❑Special 1, Jan 1989, b&w 2.95

IT! THE TERROR FROM BEYOND SPACE
MILLENNIUM

❑1; Die-cut cover 2.50
❑2, Jan 1993 2.50
❑3 2.50
❑4 2.50

I WANT TO BE YOUR DOG
FANTAGRAPHICS / EROS

❑1, b&w 1.95
❑2, b&w 1.95
❑3, b&w 1.95
❑4, b&w 1.95
❑5, b&w 2.25

J2
MARVEL

❑1, Oct 1998; gatefold summary; son of Juggernaut 2.00
❑1/A, Oct 1998; gatefold summary; Alternate cover with J2 alone in foreground 2.00
❑2, Nov 1998; gatefold summary V: X-People. 2.00
❑3, Dec 1998 A: Hulk. A: Dr. Strange. A: Doctor Strange. A: Sub-Mariner.. 2.00
❑4, Jan 1999 1: Nemesus. A: Doc Magus. 2.00
❑5, Feb 1999 1: Wild Thing. A: Wolverine. A: Elektra. 2.00
❑6, Mar 1999; A: Magneta. Wild Thing story 2.00
❑7, Apr 1999; A: Cyclops. A: Uncanny X-People. A: Parody. Wild Thing story 2.00
❑8, May 1999 2.00
❑9, Jun 1999 1: Big Julie. 2.00
❑10, Jul 1999 A: Wolverine. 2.00
❑11, Aug 1999 A: Sons of the Tiger. A: Iron Fist. 2.00
❑12, Oct 1999 2.00

JAB
ADHESIVE

❑1 2.50
❑2 2.50
❑3, Spr 1993; bullet hole 2.50
❑4 2.50
❑5 2.50

JAB (FUNNY PAPERS)
FUNNY PAPERS

❑1, b&w 2.50
❑2, b&w 2.50

JAB (CUMMINGS DESIGN)
CUMMINGS DESIGN GROUP

❑3, Aut 1994, b&w 2.95

JACKAROO
ETERNITY

❑1, Feb 1990, b&w; Australian 2.25
❑2, Mar 1990, b&w; Australian 2.25
❑3, Apr 1990, b&w; Australian 2.25

JACK CROSS
DC

❑1, Oct 2005 2.99
❑2 2005 2.99
❑3 2.99
❑4, Jan 2006 2.99

JACK FROST
AMAZING

❑1, b&w 1.95
❑2, b&w 1.95

JACK HUNTER
BLACKTHORNE

❑1, Mar 1988 1.25
❑Book 1, b&w 3.50

JACKIE JOKERS
HARVEY

❑1, Mar 1973 12.00
❑2, May 1973, Richard Nixon appears on cover with Jackie 10.00
❑3, Jul 1973 10.00
❑4, Sep 1973 10.00

JACK OF HEARTS
MARVEL

❑1, Jan 1984 1.50

Jaguar

Brazilian student becomes were-creature

©DC

James Bond 007/ Goldeneye

Adapts Brosnan's first 007 outing

©Topps

Jason vs. Leatherface

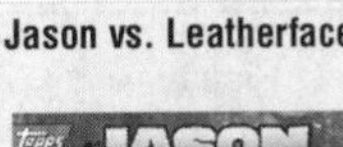

Horror icons don't play well together

©Topps

Jemm, Son of Saturn

Saturnian refugee seeks shelter on Earth

©DC

Jetsons (Gold Key)

First family of future's comic capers

©Gold Key

N-MINT

❑2, Feb 1984 .... 1.50
❑3, Mar 1984 .... 1.50
❑4, Apr 1984 .... 1.50

JACK'S LUCK RUNS OUT
Beekeeper Cartoon Amusements

❑1 .... 3.50

JACK STAFF
Image

❑1, Feb 2003 .... 0.00
❑2, Apr 2003 .... 2.95
❑3, Aug 2003 .... 2.95
❑4, Nov 2003 .... 2.95
❑5, Aug 2004 .... 3.50
❑6, Dec 2004 .... 3.50
❑7, ca. 2005 .... 3.50
❑8, ca. 2005 .... 3.50
❑9 2005 ....

JACK THE RIPPER (CALIBER)
Caliber / Tome

❑1 1998, b&w 2.95

JACK THE RIPPER
Eternity

❑1, b&w 2.25
❑2, b&w 2.25
❑3, b&w 2.25

JACQUELYN THE RIPPER
Fantagraphics

❑1, Oct 1994, b&w 2.95
❑2, Oct 1994, b&w 2.95

JACQUE'S VOICE OF DOOM
Doomed Comics

❑1, b&w; strip reprints 1.50

JADEMAN COLLECTION
Jademan

❑1 .... 2.50
❑2 .... 2.50
❑3, Feb 1990 .... 2.50

JADEMAN KUNG FU SPECIAL
Jademan

❑1; Previews of Jademan's Titles 1.50

JADE WARRIORS
Image

❑1 .... 2.50
❑1/A, Painted alternate cover 2.50
❑2, Jan 2000 .... 2.50

JAGUAR
DC / Impact

❑1, Aug 1991 O: Jaguar. 1: The Jaguar (Maria de Guzman). 1: Timon de Guzman. 1: Tracy Dickerson. 1: Maxim Ruiz. 1: Maxx-13. 1: Luiza Timmerman. 1.00
❑2, Sep 1991 .... 1.00
❑3, Oct 1991 V: Maxx-13. .... 1.00
❑4, Nov 1991 1: Victor Drago. A: Black Hood. 1.00
❑5, Dec 1991 1: Void. 1.00
❑6, Jan 1992 .... 1.00
❑7, Mar 1992 .... 1.00
❑8, Apr 1992 .... 1.00
❑9, May 1992; 1: Moonlighter. trading card 1.00
❑10, Jun 1992 .... 1.00
❑11, Jul 1992 .... 1.25
❑12, Aug 1992 .... 1.25
❑13, Sep 1992 .... 1.25
❑14, Oct 1992 .... 1.25
❑Annual 1, ca. 1992 .... 2.50

JAGUAR GOD
Verotik

❑0, Feb 1996 FF (c); FF (a) 4.00
❑1, Mar 1995 FF (c); FF (a) 4.00
❑2, Aug 1995 .... 4.00
❑3, Mar 1996 .... 3.50
❑4 1996 .... 3.50
❑5, Sep 1996 .... 3.50
❑6, Apr 1997 .... 2.95
❑7, Jun 1997 .... 2.95
❑8 1997 .... 2.95

JAGUAR GOD ILLUSTRATIONS
Verotik

❑nn, Nov 2000 .... 3.95

JAGUAR GOD: RETURN TO XIBALBA
Verotik

❑1, Feb 2003; Limited "Fan Club" edition 5.00

JAILBAIT
Fantagraphics / Eros

❑1, Dec 1998 .... 2.95

JAKE THRASH
Aircel

❑1 .... 2.00
❑2 .... 2.00

JAM
Slave Labor

❑1, Nov 1989, b&w 2.50
❑2, Jan 1990, b&w 2.00
❑3, Mar 1990, b&w 2.00
❑4, May 1990 .... 2.95
❑5, Mar 1991 .... 2.95
❑6 .... 2.50
❑7, Mar 1994, b&w 2.50
❑8, Feb 1995, b&w 2.95
❑9, Aug 1995, b&w 2.95
❑10, b&w 2.95
❑11, b&w 2.95
❑12 .... 2.95
❑13 .... 2.95

JAMAR CHRONICLES
Sweat Shop

❑1, b&w 2.00

JAMES BOND 007: A SILENT ARMAGEDDON
Dark Horse

❑1, Mar 1993; cardstock cover 2.95
❑2, May 1993; cardstock cover 2.95

JAMES BOND 007/GOLDENEYE
Topps

❑1, Jan 1996 .... 2.95
❑2, Feb 1996 .... 2.95
❑3, Mar 1996 .... 2.95

JAMES BOND 007: SERPENT'S TOOTH
Dark Horse

❑1, Jul 1992, prestige format 4.95
❑2, Aug 1992, prestige format 4.95
❑3, Feb 1993, prestige format 4.95

JAMES BOND 007: SHATTERED HELIX
Dark Horse

❑1, Jun 1994 .... 2.50
❑2, Jul 1994 .... 2.50

JAMES BOND 007: THE QUASIMODO GAMBIT
Dark Horse

❑1, Jan 1995; cardstock cover 3.95
❑2, Feb 1995; cardstock cover 3.95
❑3, May 1995; cardstock cover 3.95

JAMES BOND FOR YOUR EYES ONLY
Marvel

❑1, Oct 1981, HC (a) 1.50
❑2, Nov 1981, HC (a) 1.50

JAMES BOND JR.
Marvel

❑1, Jan 1992, TV cartoon 1.00
❑2, Feb 1992, TV cartoon 1.00
❑3, Mar 1992, TV cartoon 1.00
❑4, Apr 1992, TV cartoon 1.00
❑5, May 1992, TV cartoon 1.00
❑6, Jun 1992, TV cartoon 1.00
❑7, Jul 1992, TV cartoon 1.00
❑8, Aug 1992, TV cartoon 1.00
❑9, Sep 1992, TV cartoon 1.00
❑10, Oct 1992, TV cartoon 1.00
❑11, Nov 1992, TV cartoon 1.00
❑12, Dec 1992, TV cartoon 1.00

JAMES BOND: PERMISSION TO DIE
Eclipse

❑1, ca. 1989 MGr (w); MGr (a) 4.00
❑2, ca. 1989 MGr (w); MGr (a) 4.00
❑3, ca. 1991 MGr (w); MGr (a) 5.00

JAM QUACKY
JQ

❑1, b&w 2.00

JAM SPECIAL
Matrix

❑1 .... 2.50

JAM SUPER COOL COLOR-INJECTED TURBO ADVENTURE FROM HELL
Comico

❑1, May 1988 .... 2.50

JAM URBAN ADVENTURE
Tundra

❑1 .... 2.95
❑2 .... 2.95
❑3 .... 2.95

JANE BONDAGE
Fantagraphics / Eros

❑1 .... 2.95
❑2, Sep 1995 .... 2.95

JANE BOND: THUNDERBALLS
Fantagraphics / Eros

❑1, b&w 2.50

JANE DOE
Raging Rhino

❑1, b&w 2.95

Other grades: Multiply price above by 5/6 for VF/NM • 2/3 for VERY FINE • 1/3 for FINE • 1/5 for VERY GOOD • 1/8 for GOOD

❑2, b&w 2.95
❑3, b&w 2.95

JANE'S WORLD
Girl Twirl

❑1, 2003 2.95
❑2, 2003 2.95
❑3, 2003 2.95
❑4, 2003 2.95
❑5, 2003 2.95
❑6, 2003 2.95
❑7, 2003 2.95
❑8, 2003 2.95
❑9, 2004 5.95
❑10, 2004 5.95
❑11, 2004 5.95
❑12, 2004 5.95
❑13, 2004 5.95
❑14, 2004 5.95
❑15, 2004 5.95
❑16, 2004 5.95

JANX
Es Graphics

❑1 1.00
❑2 1.00

J.A.P.A.N.
Outerealm

❑1 1.80

JAR OF FOOLS PART ONE
Penny Dreadful

❑1, Jun 1994, b&w 5.95

JASON AND THE ARGONAUTS
Tome

❑1, b&w 2.50
❑2, b&w 2.50
❑3, b&w 2.50
❑4, b&w 2.50
❑5, b&w 2.50

JASON GOES TO HELL: THE FINAL FRIDAY
Topps

❑1, Jul 1993; glowing cover 2.95
❑2, Aug 1993 2.95
❑3, Sep 1993 2.95

JASON MONARCH
Oracle

❑1, b&w 2.00

JASON VS. LEATHERFACE
Topps

❑1, Oct 1995 2.95
❑2, Nov 1995 2.95
❑3, Dec 1995 2.95

JAVA TOWN
Slave Labor

❑1, May 1992, b&w 2.95
❑2, Nov 1993, b&w 2.95
❑3, Jul 1994, b&w 2.95
❑4, Jul 1995, b&w 2.95
❑5, Nov 1995, b&w 2.95
❑6, Jun 1996, b&w 2.95

JAVERTS
Firstlight

❑1, ca. 1997, b&w; no cover price or indicia 2.95

JAX AND THE HELL HOUND
Blackthorne

❑1, Nov 1986 1.75
❑2, Feb 1987 1.75
❑3 1987 1.75
❑4 1987 1.75

JAY ANACLETO SKETCHBOOK
Image

❑1, Apr 1999; no cover price 2.00
❑1/A, Apr 1999; Has cover price 2.00

JAY & SILENT BOB
Oni

❑1, Jul 1998 KSm (w) 4.00
❑1/Variant, Jul 1998 KSm (w) 5.00
❑1/2nd, Oct 1998 KSm (w) 2.95
❑2, Oct 1998 KSm (w) 3.00
❑3, Dec 1998 KSm (w) 3.00
❑4, Oct 1999 KSm (w) 3.00

JAZZ
High Impact

❑1 1996 2.95
❑2, May 1996 2.95

JAZZ AGE CHRONICLES (EF)
EF Graphics

❑1, Jan 1989 1.50
❑2, Mar 1989 1.50
❑3, May 1989 1.50

JAZZ AGE CHRONICLES (CALIBER)
Caliber

❑1, b&w 2.50
❑2, May 1990, b&w 2.50
❑3, b&w 2.50
❑4, b&w 2.50
❑5, b&w 2.50

JAZZBO COMICS THAT SWING
Slave Labor

❑1, Nov 1994 2.95
❑2, Apr 1995; Replacement God preview 2.95

JAZZ: SOLITAIRE
High Impact

❑1, May 1998 2.95
❑1/A, May 1998; wraparound cover 3.50
❑1/Gold, May 1998; gold foil logo; no cover price 3.50
❑2, May 1998 3.00
❑2/A; no cover price 5.00
❑2/B; nude cover (blue background) 5.00
❑3 3.00
❑3/A; Nude cover 5.00
❑3/B; wraparound nude cover 5.00

JCP FEATURES
J.C.

❑1, Feb 1981; DG, NA (a); THUNDER Agents 3.00

JEFFREY DAHMER: AN UNAUTHORIZED BIOGRAPHY OF A SERIAL KILLER
Boneyard

❑1, Mar 1992 4.00
❑1/2nd 3.00

JEFFREY DAHMER VS. JESUS CHRIST
Boneyard

❑1, Feb 1993; wraparound cover 4.00
❑1/Autographed 4.00

JEMM, SON OF SATURN
DC

❑1, Sep 1984 GC, KJ (a); 1: Jemm, Son of Saturn. 1.50
❑2, Oct 1984 1.00
❑3, Nov 1984 O: Jemm. 1.00
❑4, Dec 1984 1.00
❑5, Jan 1985 1.00
❑6, Feb 1985 1.00
❑7, Mar 1985 GC, KJ (a) 1.00
❑8, Apr 1985 1.00
❑9, May 1985 1.00
❑10, Jun 1985 1.00
❑11, Jul 1985 1.00
❑12, Aug 1985 1.00

JENNIFER DAYDREAMER: OLIVER
Top Shelf

❑1, ca. 2003, b&w; smaller than comic-book size 4.95

JENNY FINN
Oni

❑1, Jun 1999 2.95
❑2, Sep 1999 2.95
❑3, Nov 1999 2.95
❑4, Feb 2000 2.95

JENNY SPARKS: THE SECRET HISTORY OF THE AUTHORITY
DC / Wildstorm

❑1, Aug 2000 2.50
❑2, Sep 2000 2.50
❑3, Oct 2000 2.50
❑4, Nov 2000 2.50
❑5, Mar 2001 2.50

JEREMIAH: A FISTFUL OF SAND
Adventure

❑1, b&w 2.50
❑2, b&w 2.50

JEREMIAH: BIRDS OF PREY
Adventure

❑1, Apr 1991, b&w 2.50
❑2, Apr 1991, b&w 2.50

JEREMIAH: THE HEIRS
Adventure

❑1, b&w 2.50
❑2, b&w 2.50

JERSEY DEVIL
South Jersey Rebellion

❑1, 1992; no indicia 2.25
❑2 2.95
❑3 2.25
❑,4 1997 2.25
❑5, 1997 2.25
❑6, 1997 2.25
❑7, no indicia 2.25

JESSE JAMES
AC

❑1, b&w; Reprints 3.95

JESTER'S MOON
One Shot

❑1, Aug 1996, b&w 1.00

JESUS COMICS (FOOLBERT STURGEON'S...)
Rip Off

❑1 5.00
❑2 4.00
❑3 4.00

JET
Authority

❑1, Dec 1996 2.95

JET (WILDSTORM)
DC / Wildstorm

❑1, Nov 2000 2.50
❑2, Dec 2000 2.50
❑3, Jan 2001 2.50
❑4, Feb 2001 2.50

JET BLACK
Monolith

❑1, Sep 1997 2.50

JET COMICS
Slave Labor / Amaze Ink

❑1, Oct 1997, b&w 2.95
❑2, Feb 1998, b&w 2.95
❑3, Mar 1998 2.95

JET DREAM
Gold Key

❑1, Jun 1968, Painted cover 18.00

JETSONS (GOLD KEY)
Gold Key

❑1, Jan 1963 90.00
❑2, Apr 1963 65.00
❑3, Jun 1963 48.00
❑4, Jul 1963 48.00
❑5, Sep 1963 48.00
❑6, Nov 1963 40.00
❑7, Jan 1964 40.00
❑8, Mar 1964 40.00
❑9, May 1964 40.00
❑10, Jul 1964 40.00
❑11, Sep 1964 24.00
❑12, Nov 1964 24.00
❑13, Jan 1965 24.00
❑14, Mar 1965 24.00
❑15, May 1965 24.00
❑16, Jul 1965 24.00
❑17, Sep 1965 24.00
❑18, Nov 1965 24.00
❑19, Jan 1966 24.00
❑20, Mar 1966 24.00
❑21, Jun 1966 16.00
❑22, Sep 1966 16.00
❑23, Jul 1967 16.00
❑24, Oct 1967 16.00
❑25, Jan 1968 16.00
❑26, Apr 1968 16.00
❑27, Jul 1968 16.00
❑28, Oct 1968 16.00
❑29, Jan 1969 16.00
❑30, Apr 1969 16.00
❑31, Jul 1969 14.00
❑32, Oct 1969 14.00

Jingle Belle

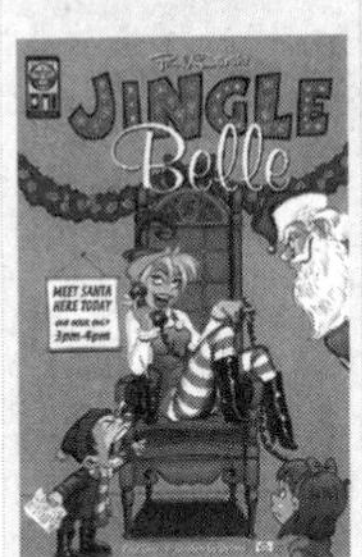

Santa's daughter's mischevious misadventures

©Oni

Jinx

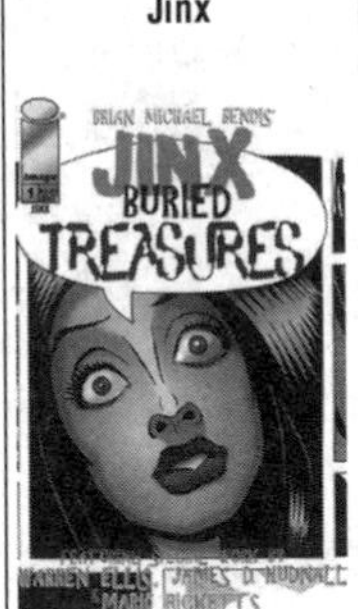

Brian Michael Bendis' crime compendium

©Caliber

JLA

Grant Morrison revives original team

©DC

JLA in Crisis Secret Files

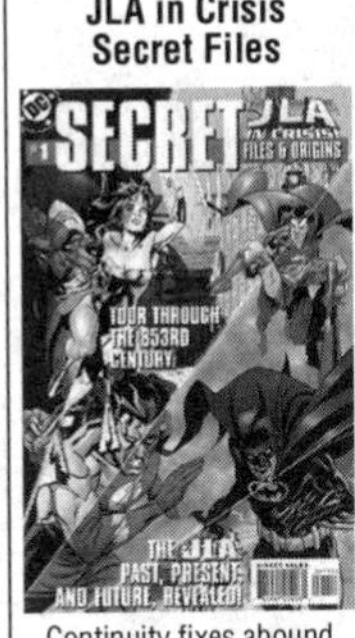

Continuity fixes abound with single Earth

©DC

JLA: Our Worlds At War

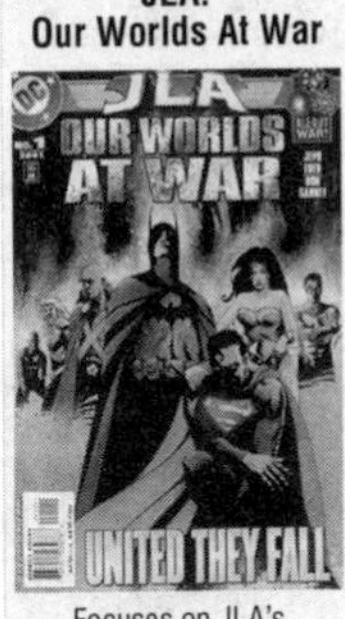

Focuses on JLA's involvement in conflict

©DC

N-MINT

❑33, Jan 1970 .... 14.00
❑34, Apr 1970 .... 14.00
❑35, Jul 1970 .... 14.00
❑36, Oct 1970 .... 14.00

JETSONS (CHARLTON)
CHARLTON

❑1, Nov 1970 .... 35.00
❑2, Jan 1971 .... 22.00
❑3, Mar 1971 .... 14.00
❑4, May 1971 .... 14.00
❑5, Jul 1971 .... 14.00
❑6, Sep 1971 .... 10.00
❑7, Nov 1971 .... 10.00
❑8, Jan 1972 .... 10.00
❑9, Mar 1972 .... 10.00
❑10, May 1972 .... 10.00
❑11, Jul 1972 .... 7.00
❑12, Sep 1972 .... 7.00
❑13, Nov 1972 .... 7.00
❑14, Jan 1973 .... 7.00
❑15, Feb 1973 .... 7.00
❑16, Apr 1973 .... 7.00
❑17, Jun 1973 .... 7.00
❑18, Aug 1973 .... 7.00
❑19, Oct 1973 .... 7.00
❑20, Dec 1973 .... 7.00

JETSONS (HARVEY)
HARVEY

❑1, Sep 1992 .... 1.50
❑2, Jan 1993 .... 1.50
❑3, May 1993 .... 1.50
❑4, Sep 1993 .... 1.50
❑5, Nov 1993 .... 1.50

JETSONS (ARCHIE)
ARCHIE

❑1, Sep 1995, A: The Flintstones. 2.00
❑2, Oct 1995 .... 1.50
❑3, Nov 1995 .... 1.50
❑4, Dec 1995 .... 1.50
❑5, Jan 1996 .... 1.50
❑6, Feb 1996 .... 1.50
❑7, Mar 1996 .... 1.50
❑8, Apr 1996 .... 1.50
❑9, May 1996 .... 1.50
❑10, Jun 1996 .... 1.50
❑11, Jul 1996 .... 1.50
❑12, Aug 1996 .... 1.50

JETSONS BIG BOOK
HARVEY

❑1, Nov 1992 .... 1.95
❑2, Apr 1993 .... 1.95
❑3, ca. 1993 .... 1.95

JETSONS GIANT SIZE
HARVEY

❑1, Oct 1992 .... 3.00
❑2, Mar 1993 .... 2.50
❑3, ca. 1993 .... 2.50

JEW IN COMMUNIST PRAGUE
NBM

❑1; oversized graphic novel 11.95
❑2; oversized graphic novel 11.95

N-MINT

JEZEBEL JADE
COMICO

❑1, Oct 1988; wraparound cover 2.00
❑2, Nov 1988; wraparound cover 2.00
❑3, Dec 1988; wraparound cover 2.00

JEZEBELLE
WILDSTORM

❑1/A, Mar 2001; Woman leaping backward on cover, two hands with energy glow 2.50
❑1/B, Mar 2001; Woman standing on cover, one hand in energy ball 2.50
❑2, Apr 2001 .... 2.50
❑3, May 2001 .... 2.50
❑4, Jun 2001 .... 2.50
❑5, Jul 2001 .... 2.50
❑6, Aug 2001 .... 2.50

JFK ASSASSINATION
ZONE

❑1 .... 3.50

JHEREG
MARVEL / EPIC

❑1 .... 8.95

JIGABOO DEVIL
MILLENNIUM

❑0, b&w 2.95

JIGSAW
HARVEY

❑1, Sep 1966, O: Jigsaw (Harvey). 1: Jigsaw (Harvey) 16.00
❑2 .... 10.00

JILL: PART-TIME LOVER
NBM

❑1 .... 11.95

JIM (VOL. 1)
FANTAGRAPHICS

❑1 .... 8.00
❑2 .... 6.00
❑3 .... 5.00
❑4 .... 5.00

JIM (VOL. 2)
FANTAGRAPHICS

❑1, Dec 1993, b&w 5.00
❑2, b&w 4.00
❑3, b&w 4.00
❑4, b&w 3.00
❑5, b&w 3.00
❑6, May 1996, b&w 3.00
❑Special 1; Frank's Real Pa Special Edition 4.00

JIMBO
BONGO / ZONGO

❑1, ca. 1995, b&w 2.95
❑2, ca. 1995, b&w 2.95
❑3, indicia says #2 .... 2.95
❑4, b&w; no indicia 2.95
❑5 .... 2.95
❑6 .... 2.95
❑7 .... 2.95

JIM HARDY (2ND SERIES)
UNITED FEATURE

❑1 .... 100.00
❑2, Jul 1947 .... 60.00

N-MINT

JIM LEE SKETCHBOOK
WILDSTORM

❑1 JLee (a) 40.00

JING: KING OF BANDITS
TOKYOPOP

❑1, Jun 2003 .... 9.95
❑2, Aug 2003 .... 9.95
❑3, Dec 2003 .... 9.95
❑4, Jan 2004 .... 9.95
❑5, Mar 2004 .... 9.95
❑6, May 2004 .... 9.95
❑7, Jul 2004 .... 9.95

JING: KING OF BANDITS - TWILIGHT TALES
TOKYOPOP

❑1, Sep 2004 .... 9.99
❑2, Dec 2004 .... 9.99
❑3, Mar 2005 .... 9.99
❑4, Jun 2005 .... 9.99
❑5, Sep 2005 .... 9.99
❑6, Dec 2005 .... 9.99

JINGLE BELLE
ONI

❑1, Nov 1999, b&w 2.95
❑2, Dec 1999, b&w 2.95

JINGLE BELLE (DARK HORSE)
DARK HORSE

❑1, Nov 2004 .... 2.99
❑2, Dec 2004 .... 2.99
❑3, Jan 2005 .... 2.99
❑4, Jun 2005 .... 3.00

JINGLE BELLE JUBILEE
ONI

❑nn, Nov 2001, b&w 2.95

JINGLE BELLE'S ALL-STAR HOLIDAY HULLABALOO
ONI

❑1, Nov 2000, b&w 4.95

JINGLE BELLE: THE FIGHT BEFORE CHRISTMAS
DARK HORSE

❑1, Jan 2006 ....

JINGLE BELLE WINTER WINGDING
ONI

❑nn, Nov 2002, b&w 2.95

JINN
IMAGE

❑1, Feb 2000 .... 2.95
❑2, May 2000 .... 2.95
❑3, Oct 2000 .... 2.95

JINX
CALIBER

❑1, b&w; BMB (w); BMB (a); Caliber publishes 3.50
❑2, b&w BMB (w); BMB (a) 3.00
❑3, b&w BMB (w); BMB (a) 3.00
❑4, b&w BMB (w); BMB (a) 3.00
❑5, Nov 1996, b&w BMB (w); BMB (a) 3.00
❑6, b&w; BMB (w); BMB (a); series moves to Image 3.00
❑7 BMB (w); BMB (a) 3.00
❑8; BMB (w); BMB (a); Charity Special 4.95

❑9; Homeless Edition BMB (w); BMB (a) 4.95
❑10, b&w; BMB (w); BMB (a); Image publishes 2.95
❑11, b&w BMB (w); BMB (a) 2.95
❑12 BMB (w); BMB (a) 3.95
❑13, b&w BMB (w); BMB (a) 3.95
❑14, b&w BMB (w); BMB (a) 3.95
❑15 BMB (w); BMB (a) 3.95
❑16; BMB (w); BMB (a); Torso 3.95
❑17; BMB (w); BMB (a); Torso 3.95
❑18; BMB (w); BMB (a); Fire 2.95
❑19; BMB (w); BMB (a); Buried Treasures 2.95
❑20, b&w; BMB (w); BMB (a); True Crime Confessions 3.95
❑21; BMB (w); BMB (a); Torso 3.95

JINX POP CULTURE HOO-HAH
IMAGE

❑1, b&w 3.95

JIZZ
FANTAGRAPHICS

❑1, b&w 2.00
❑2, b&w 2.00
❑3, b&w 2.00
❑4, b&w 2.00
❑5 2.25
❑6 2.25
❑7 2.25
❑8 2.50
❑9 2.95
❑10, b&w 2.50

JLA
DC

❑1, Jan 1997; Superman, Batman, Flash, Wonder Woman, Green Lantern, Martian Manhunter, Aquaman team 6.00
❑2, Feb 1997 4.00
❑3, Mar 1997 4.00
❑4, Apr 1997 4.00
❑5, May 1997; V: Prof. Ivo. V: T.O. Morrow. Membership drive 4.00
❑6, Jun 1997 1: Zauriel. A: Neron. A: Ghast. A: Abnegazar 4.00
❑7, Jul 1997 3.00
❑8, Aug 1997 V: Key. 3.00
❑9, Sep 1997 V: Key. 3.00
❑10, Oct 1997 V: New Injustice Gang. 3.00
❑11, Nov 1997 2.50
❑12, Dec 1997 2.50
❑13, Dec 1997; Face cover; Aquaman, Green Lantern, and Flash in future 2.50
❑14, Jan 1998 2.50
❑15, Feb 1998; Giant-size 2.95
❑16, Mar 1998; V: Prometheus. Watchtower blueprints 2.00
❑17, Apr 1998 V: Prometheus. 2.00
❑18, May 1998 1: Julian September. 2.00
❑19, Jun 1998 A: Atom 2.00
❑20, Jul 1998 V: Adam Strange. 2.00
❑21, Aug 1998 A: Aleaa. V: Adam Strange. 2.00
❑22, Sep 1998 A: Daniel (Sandman). 2.00
❑23, Oct 1998 A: Daniel. V: Star Conqueror. 2.00
❑24, Dec 1998 1: Ultramarine Corps. 2.00
❑25, Jan 1999 V: Ultramarine Corps 2.00
❑26, Feb 1999 A: Ultra-Marines. A: Shaggy Man. V: Shaggy Man 2.00
❑27, Mar 1999 A: Justice Society of America. V: Amazo 2.00
❑28, Apr 1999 A: Justice Society of America. A: Triumph. 2.00
❑29, May 1999 JSa (w); JSa (a); A: Justice Society of America. A: Captain Marvel 2.00
❑30, Jun 1999 A: Justice Society of America 2.00
❑31, Jul 1999 2.00
❑32, Aug 1999; DGry, MWa (w); JLA in No Man's Land 2.00
❑33, Sep 1999 MWa (w) 2.00
❑34, Oct 1999 2.00
❑35, Nov 1999; A: new Spectre. Day of Judgment 2.00
❑36, Dec 1999 2.00
❑37, Jan 2000 2.00
❑38, Feb 2000 2.00
❑39, Mar 2000 2.00
❑40, Apr 2000 2.00
❑41, May 2000; Giant-size 2.99
❑42, Jun 2000 1.99
❑43, Jul 2000 MWa (w) 1.99
❑44, Aug 2000 MWa (w) 2.25
❑45, Sep 2000 MWa (w) 2.25
❑46, Oct 2000 MWa (w) 2.25
❑47, Nov 2000 MWa (w) 2.25
❑48, Dec 2000 MWa (w) 2.25
❑49, Jan 2001 MWa (w) 2.25
❑50, Feb 2001; Giant-size MWa (w) 3.75
❑51, Apr 2001 MWa (w) 2.25
❑52, May 2001 MWa (w) 2.25
❑53, Jun 2001 2.25
❑54, Jul 2001 2.25
❑55, Aug 2001 2.25
❑56, Sep 2001 2.25
❑57, Oct 2001 2.25
❑58, Nov 2001 2.25
❑59, Dec 2001 2.25
❑60, Jan 2002 2.25
❑61, Feb 2002; Giant-size 2.25
❑62, Mar 2002 2.25
❑63, Apr 2002 2.25
❑64, May 2002 2.25
❑65, Jun 2002 2.25
❑66, Jul 2002 2.25
❑67, Aug 2002 2.25
❑68, Sep 2002 2.25
❑69, Oct 2002 2.25
❑70, Oct 2002 2.25
❑71, Nov 2002 2.25
❑72, Nov 2002 2.25
❑73, Dec 2002 2.25
❑74, Dec 2002 2.25
❑75, Jan 2003 3.95
❑76, Feb 2003 2.25
❑77, Mar 2003 2.25
❑78, Apr 2003 2.25
❑79, May 2003 2.25
❑80, Jun 2003 2.25
❑81, Jul 2003 2.25
❑82, Aug 2003 2.25
❑83, Sep 2003 2.25
❑84, Oct 2003 2.25
❑85, Oct 2003 2.25
❑86, Nov 2003 2.25
❑87, Nov 2003 2.25
❑88, Dec 2003 2.25
❑89, Dec 2003 2.25
❑90, Jan 2004 2.25
❑91, Feb 2004 2.25
❑92, Mar 2004 2.25
❑93, Apr 2004 2.25
❑94, May 2004, JOy, JBy (c); JBy (w); JOy, JBy (a) 2.25
❑95, May 2004 2.25
❑96, Jun 2004 2.25
❑97, Jun 2004 2.25
❑98, Jul 2004 2.25
❑99, Jul 2004 2.25
❑100, Aug 2004 3.50
❑101, Sep 2004 2.25
❑102, Sep 2004 2.25
❑103, Oct 2004 2.25
❑104, Oct 2004 2.25
❑105, Nov 2004 2.25
❑106, Nov 2004 2.25
❑107, Dec 2004 5.00
❑108, Jan 2005 5.00
❑109, Feb 2005 2.25
❑110, Mar 2005 2.25
❑111, Apr 2005 2.25
❑112, May 2005 2.25
❑113, Jun 2005 2.25
❑114, Jul 2005 2.25
❑115, Aug 2005 10.00
❑116, Sep 2005 2.50
❑117, Oct 2005 2.50
❑118, Nov 2005 2.50
❑119, Dec 2005 2.50
❑120 2.50
❑121 2.50
❑122, Jan 2006 2.50
❑123, Feb 2006 2.50
❑124, Mar 2006 2.50
❑125, Apr 2006 2.50
❑1000000, Nov 1998; One Million 2.00
❑Annual 1, ca. 1997; Pulp Heroes 6.00
❑Annual 2, Oct 1998; Ghosts 4.50
❑Annual 3, Sep 1999; JLApe 3.50
❑Giant Size 1, Jul 1998 4.95
❑Giant Size 2, Nov 1999 4.95
❑Giant Size 3, Oct 2000 5.95

JLA: ACT OF GOD
DC

❑1, Jan 2001 4.95
❑2, Feb 2001 4.95
❑3, Mar 2001 4.95

JLA: AGE OF WONDER
DC

❑1, Jun 2003 5.95
❑2, Jul 2003 5.95

JLA/AVENGERS
MARVEL

❑1, Nov 2003 7.00
❑3, Jan 2004 5.95
❑3/2nd, Apr 2004 7.00

JLA: BLACK BAPTISM
DC

❑1, May 2001 2.50
❑2, Jun 2001 2.50
❑3, Jul 2001 2.50
❑4, Aug 2001 2.50

JLA: CLASSIFIED
DC

❑1, Jan 2005 5.00
❑2, Feb 2005 2.95
❑3, Mar 2005 2.95
❑4, Apr 2005 2.95
❑5, May 2005 2.95
❑6, Jun 2005 2.99
❑7, Jul 2005 2.99
❑8, Aug 2005 2.99
❑9, Sep 2005 2.99
❑10, Oct 2005 2.99
❑11, Oct 2005 2.99
❑12 2005 2.99
❑13 2.99
❑14, Jan 2006 2.99
❑15, Feb 2006 2.99
❑17, May 2006 2.99
❑18, May 2006 2.99
❑19, Jun 2006 2.99
❑20, Jun 2006 2.99
❑21, Aug 2006 2.99
❑22, Aug 2006 2.99
❑23, Sep 2006 2.99

JLA CLASSIFIED: COLD STEEL
DC

❑1, Jan 2006 5.99
❑2, Mar 2006 5.99

JLA: CREATED EQUAL
DC

❑1, ca. 2000 5.95
❑2, ca. 2000 5.95

JLA/CYBERFORCE
DC

❑0, Oct 2005 5.99

JLA: DESTINY
DC

❑1, Aug 2002 5.95
❑2, Sep 2002 5.95
❑3, Oct 2002 5.95
❑4, Nov 2002 5.95

JLA: FOREIGN BODIES
DC

❑1 1999; prestige format 5.95

JLA GALLERY
DC

❑1, ca. 1997; pin-ups; wraparound cover 2.95

JLA: GATEKEEPER
DC

❑1, Dec 2001 4.95
❑2, Jan 2002 4.95
❑3, Feb 2002 4.95

JLA: GODS AND MONSTERS
DC

❑1, Aug 2001 6.95

JLA: World without Grown-Ups

Adult heroes become kids and vice versa

©DC

John Carter, Warlord of Mars

Adapts Burroughs' red planet adventures

©Marvel

John F. Kennedy

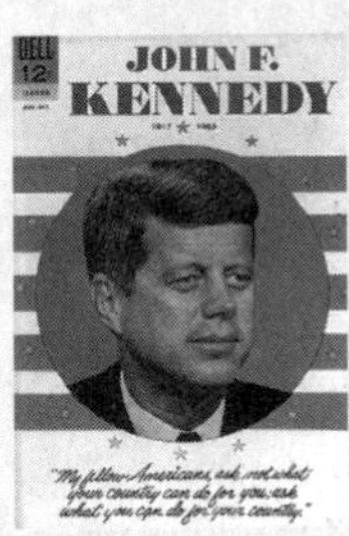

Tribute to slain leader

©Dell

Johnny the Homicidal Maniac

Jhonen Vasquez' pre-Invader Zim work

©Slave Labor

Jonah Hex

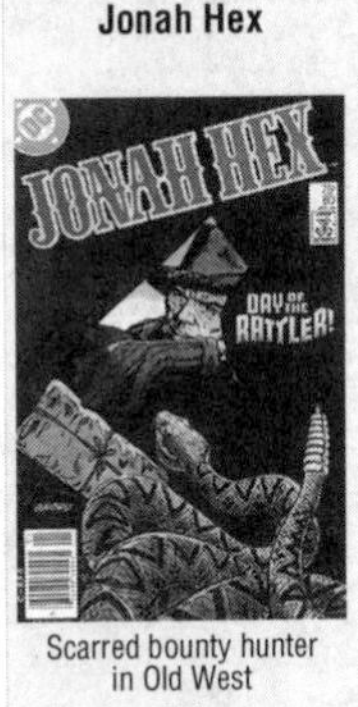

Scarred bounty hunter in Old West

©DC

N-MINT

JLA/HAVEN: ANATHEMA
DC

❑1, Nov 2002 .... 5.95

JLA/HAVEN: ARRIVAL
DC

❑1, Jan 2002 .... 5.95

JLA: HEAVEN'S LADDER
DC

❑1, ca. 2000; tabloid-sized one-shot .. 9.95

JLA: INCARNATIONS
DC

❑1, Jul 2001 .... 3.50
❑2, Aug 2001 .... 3.50
❑3, Sep 2001 .... 3.50
❑4, Oct 2001 .... 3.50
❑5, Nov 2001 .... 3.50
❑6, Dec 2001 .... 3.50
❑7, Feb 2002 .... 3.50

JLA IN CRISIS SECRET FILES
DC

❑1, Nov 1998; summaries of events from Crisis through One Million...... 4.95

JLA: OUR WORLDS AT WAR
DC

❑1, Sep 2001 .... 2.95

JLA: PARADISE LOST
DC

❑1, Jan 1998 .... 2.00
❑2, Feb 1998 .... 2.00
❑3, Mar 1998 .... 2.00

JLA: PRIMEVAL
DC

❑1, ca. 1999 .... 5.95

JLA: SCARY MONSTERS
DC

❑1, May 2003 .... 2.50
❑2, Jun 2003 .... 2.50
❑3, Jul 2003 .... 2.50
❑4, Aug 2003 .... 2.50
❑5, Aug 2003 .... 2.50
❑6, Sep 2003 .... 2.50

JLA SECRET FILES
DC

❑1, Sep 1997, bios of team members and key villains; timeline 4.95
❑2, Aug 1998, bios of team members and key villains 3.95
❑3, Dec 2000 .... 4.95

JLA SECRET FILES 2004
DC

❑1, Jan 2004 .... 5.00

JLA: SECRET SOCIETY OF SUPER-HEROES
DC

❑1, ca. 2000 .... 5.95
❑2 .... 5.95

JLA: SEVEN CASKETS
DC

❑1 .... 5.95

JLA: SHOGUN OF STEEL
DC

❑1, Apr 2002 .... 6.95

N-MINT

JLA SHOWCASE
DC

❑Giant Size 1, Feb 2000; 80-Page Giant 4.95

JLA/SPECTRE: SOUL WAR
DC

❑1, Mar 2003 .... 5.95
❑2, Apr 2003 .... 5.95

JLA: SUPERPOWER
DC

❑1, Nov 1999; prestige format 5.95

JLA: THE ISLAND OF DR. MOREAU
DC

❑1, Oct 2002 .... 6.95

JLA: THE NAIL
DC

❑1, Aug 1998; Elseworlds 5.50
❑2, Sep 1998; Elseworlds 5.00
❑3, Oct 1998; Elseworlds 5.00

JLA/TITANS
DC

❑1, Dec 1998 .... 3.00
❑1/Ltd., Dec 1998 .... 5.00
❑2, Jan 1999 .... 3.00
❑3, Feb 1999 .... 3.00

JLA: TOMORROW WOMAN
DC

❑1, Jun 1998; Girlfrenzy; set during events of JLA #5 .... 1.95

JLA VERSUS PREDATOR
DC

❑1, ca. 2000 .... 5.95

JLA: WELCOME TO WORKING WEEK
DC

❑1, ca. 2003 .... 6.95

JLA/WILDC.A.T.S
DC

❑1, ca. 1997; prestige format; crossover with Image; Crime Machine 5.95

JLA/WITCHBLADE
DC

❑1, ca. 2000 .... 5.95

JLA: WORLD WITHOUT GROWN-UPS
DC

❑1, Aug 1998; prestige format; wraparound cover 5.50
❑2, Sep 1998 .... 5.00

JLA: YEAR ONE
DC

❑1, Jan 1998 MWa (w) 3.50
❑2, Feb 1998 MWa (w) 3.00
❑3, Mar 1998 MWa (w) 3.00
❑4, Apr 1998 MWa (w) 3.00
❑5, May 1998 MWa (w); A: Doom Patrol 3.00
❑6, Jun 1998 MWa (w) 1.95
❑7, Jul 1998 MWa (w); A: Superman. 1.95
❑8, Aug 1998 MWa (w) 1.95
❑9, Sep 1998 MWa (w) 1.95
❑10, Oct 1998 MWa (w) 1.99

N-MINT

❑11, Nov 1998 JSa, MWa (w); JSa (a); A: Metal Men. A: Blackhawks. A: Freedom Fighters. A: Challengers. .. 1.99
❑12, Dec 1998 MWa (w) 2.95

JLA-Z
DC

❑1, Nov 2003 .... 2.50
❑2, Dec 2003 .... 2.50
❑3, Jan 2004 .... 2.50

JLX
DC / AMALGAM

❑1, Apr 1996 .... 1.95

JLX UNLEASHED
DC / AMALGAM

❑1, Jun 1997 .... 1.95

JOE DIMAGGIO
CELEBRITY

❑1; trading cards 6.95

JOEL BECK'S COMICS AND STORIES
KITCHEN SINK

❑1 ....

JOE PSYCHO & MOO FROG
GOBLIN

❑1 .... 3.50
❑2, ca. 1996 .... 3.00
❑3, Sep 1997 .... 3.00
❑4 .... 3.00
❑5 .... 3.00
❑Ashcan 1, b&w; Kinko's Ashcan Edition; no cover price 1.50

JOE PSYCHO FULL COLOR EXTRAVAGARBONZO
GOBLIN

❑1, ca. 1998 .... 2.95

JOE SINN
CALIBER

❑1, b&w 2.95
❑1/Ltd.; limited edition 3.00
❑2, b&w; Final issue (others never released) 2.95

JOHN CARTER OF MARS (EDGAR RICE BURROUGHS'...)
GOLD KEY

❑1, Apr 1964 .... 30.00
❑2, Jul 1964 .... 16.00
❑3, Oct 1964 .... 16.00

JOHN CARTER, WARLORD OF MARS
MARVEL

❑1, Jun 1977, GK, DC (a); O: John Carter, Warlord of Mars. 8.00
❑1/35 cent, Jun 1977, 35 cent regional price variant 15.00
❑2, Jul 1977, GK (a); V: White Apes. Newsstand edition (distributed by Curtis); issue number appears in box 4.00
❑2/35 cent, Jul 1977, 35 cent regional price variant; issue number appears in box 8.00
❑2/Whitman, Jul 1977, GK (a); V: White Apes. Special markets edition (usually sold in Whitman bagged prepacks); price appears in a diamond; UPC barcode appears...... 4.00

N-MINT

❑3, Aug 1977, GK, TD (a); V: White Apes 3.00
❑3/35 cent, Aug 1977, GK, TD (a); V: White Apes. 35 cent regional price variant 8.00
❑4, Sep 1977, GK (a) 3.00
❑4/35 cent, Sep 1977, GK (a); 35 cent regional price variant 8.00
❑5, Oct 1977, GK (a); V: Stara Kan. 3.00
❑5/35 cent, Oct 1977, GK (a); V: Stara Kan. 35 cent regional price variant 8.00
❑6, Nov 1977 2.50
❑7, Dec 1977 2.50
❑8, Jan 1978 2.50
❑9, Feb 1978 2.50
❑10, Mar 1978 2.50
❑11, Apr 1978, O: Dejah Thoris. 2.50
❑12, May 1978 2.50
❑13, Jun 1978 2.50
❑14, Jul 1978 2.50
❑15, Aug 1978 2.50
❑16, Sep 1978 2.50
❑17, Oct 1978 2.50
❑18, Nov 1978, FM (a) 2.50
❑19, Dec 1978 2.50
❑20, Jan 1979 2.50
❑21, Feb 1979 2.50
❑22, Mar 1979 2.50
❑23, Apr 1979 2.50
❑24, May 1979 2.50
❑25, Jul 1979, FM (c); FM (a) 2.50
❑26, Aug 1979, FM (c); FM (a) 2.50
❑27, Sep 1979 2.50
❑28, Oct 1979 2.50
❑Annual 1, ca. 1977 2.00
❑Annual 2, ca. 1978 2.00
❑Annual 3, ca. 1979 2.00

JOHN CONSTANTINE — HELLBLAZER: PAPA MIDNITE
DC / VERTIGO

❑1, Apr 2005 2.95
❑2, May 2005 2.95
❑3, Jun 2005 2.95
❑4, Jun 2005 2.99
❑5, Aug 2005 2.99

JOHN F. KENNEDY
DELL

❑1, Aug 1964, DG (a); 12-378-410; memorial comic book; Biography 45.00
❑1/2nd, ca. 1964, DG (a); Biography 30.00
❑1/3rd, ca. 1964, DG (a); Biography 22.00

JOHN LAW DETECTIVE
ECLIPSE

❑1, Apr 1983 WE (w); WE (a) 2.00

JOHNNY ATOMIC
ETERNITY

❑1, b&w 2.50
❑2, b&w 2.50
❑3, b&w 2.50

JOHNNY COMET
AVALON

❑1, Apr 1999 2.95
❑2 1999 2.95
❑3 1999 2.95
❑4 1999 2.95
❑5 1999 2.95

JOHNNY COSMIC
THORBY

❑1; Flip-book with Spacegal Comics #2 2.95

JOHNNY DYNAMITE
DARK HORSE

❑1, Sep 1994 2.95
❑2, Oct 1994 2.95
❑3, Nov 1994 2.95
❑4, Dec 1994 2.95

JOHNNY GAMBIT
HOT

❑1, Apr 1987 1.75

JOHNNY HAZARD (PIONEER)
PIONEER

❑1, Dec 1988, b&w 2.00

JOHNNY HAZARD QUARTERLY
DRAGON LADY

❑1 5.95
❑2 5.95
❑3 5.95
❑4 5.95

JOHNNY JASON, TEEN REPORTER
DELL

❑2, Aug 1962, First issue published as Dell's Four Color #1302 20.00

JOHNNY NEMO MAGAZINE
ECLIPSE

❑1, Sep 1995 2.75
❑2 2.75
❑3 2.75
❑4; Exists? 2.75
❑5; Exists? 2.75
❑6; Exists? 2.75

JOHNNY THE HOMICIDAL MANIAC
SLAVE LABOR

❑1, Aug 1995, b&w A: Squee. 13.00
❑1/2nd, Dec 1995, b&w 4.00
❑1/3rd, Aug 1996, b&w 3.00
❑1/4th, May 1997, b&w 3.00
❑2, Nov 1995, b&w 9.00
❑2/2nd, Jul 1996, b&w 3.00
❑3, Feb 1996, b&w 7.00
❑3/2nd, Jul 1996, b&w 3.00
❑4, May 1996, b&w 6.00
❑4/2nd, Apr 1997, b&w 3.00
❑5, Aug 1996, b&w 5.00
❑5/2nd, Apr 1997, b&w 3.00
❑6, Aug 1996, b&w 4.00
❑7, Aug 1996, b&w 4.00
❑Special 1; Limited to 2000; Reprints Johnny the Homicidal Maniac #1 with cardstock outer cover 20.00

JOHNNY THUNDER
DC

❑1, Mar 1973 12.00
❑2, May 1973 8.00
❑3, Aug 1973 8.00

JOHN STEELE, SECRET AGENT
GOLD KEY

❑1, Dec 1964 18.00

JOKER
DC

❑1, May 1975 DG, IN (a); A: Two-Face. 16.00
❑2, Jul 1975 12.00
❑3, Oct 1975 8.00
❑4, Dec 1975 V: Green Arrow. 8.00
❑5, Feb 1976 8.00
❑6, Apr 1976 7.00
❑7, Jun 1976 7.00
❑8, Aug 1976, Bicentennial #7 7.00
❑9, Sep 1976 A: Catwoman. 7.00

JOKER: LAST LAUGH
DC

❑1, Dec 2001 2.95
❑2, Dec 2001 2.95
❑3, Dec 2001 2.95
❑4, Dec 2001 2.95
❑5, Dec 2001 2.95
❑6, Jan 2002 2.95

JOKER: LAST LAUGH SECRET FILES
DC

❑1, Dec 2001 5.95

JOKER/MASK
DARK HORSE

❑1, May 2000 2.95
❑2, Jun 2000 2.95
❑3, Jul 2000 2.95
❑4, Aug 2000 2.95

JOLLY JACK STARJUMPER SUMMER OF '92 ONE-SHOT
CONQUEST

❑1, b&w 2.95

JONAH HEX
DC

❑1, Apr 1977 28.00
❑2, Jun 1977, 1: El Papagayo. V: El Papagayo. 10.00
❑3, Aug 1977 7.00
❑4, Sep 1977 7.00
❑5, Oct 1977 7.00
❑6, Nov 1977 6.00
❑7, Dec 1977, O: Jonah Hex. 7.00
❑8, Jan 1978, O: Jonah's facial scars. 7.00
❑9, Feb 1978 5.00
❑10, Mar 1978 5.00
❑11, Apr 1978 4.00
❑12, May 1978 4.00
❑13, Jun 1978 4.00
❑14, Jul 1978 4.00
❑15, Aug 1978 4.00
❑16, Sep 1978 4.00
❑17, Oct 1978 4.00
❑18, Nov 1978 4.00
❑19, Dec 1978 4.00
❑20, Jan 1979 4.00
❑21, Feb 1979 3.00
❑22, Mar 1979 3.00
❑23, Apr 1979 3.00
❑24, May 1979 3.00
❑25, Jun 1979 3.00
❑26, Jul 1979 3.00
❑27, Aug 1979 3.00
❑28, Sep 1979 3.00
❑29, Oct 1979 3.00
❑30, Nov 1979 3.00
❑31, Dec 1979 3.00
❑32, Jan 1980 3.00
❑33, Feb 1980 3.00
❑34, Mar 1980 3.00
❑35, Apr 1980 3.00
❑36, May 1980 3.00
❑37, Jun 1980, A: Stonewall Jackson. 3.00
❑38, Jul 1980 3.00
❑39, Aug 1980 3.00
❑40, Sep 1980 3.00
❑41, Oct 1980 3.00
❑42, Nov 1980 3.00
❑43, Dec 1980 3.00
❑44, Jan 1981 3.00
❑45, Feb 1981 3.00
❑46, Mar 1981 3.00
❑47, Apr 1981 3.00
❑48, May 1981 3.00
❑49, Jun 1981 3.00
❑50, Jul 1981 3.00
❑51, Aug 1981 2.50
❑52, Sep 1981 2.50
❑53, Oct 1981 2.50
❑54, Nov 1981 2.50
❑55, Dec 1981 2.50
❑56, Jan 1982 2.50
❑57, Feb 1982, El Diablo back-up 2.50
❑58, Mar 1982, El Diablo back-up 2.50
❑59, Apr 1982, El Diablo back-up 2.50
❑60, May 1982, El Diablo back-up 2.50
❑61, Jun 1982, in China 2.50
❑62, Jul 1982, in China 2.50
❑63, Aug 1982 2.50
❑64, Sep 1982 2.50
❑65, Oct 1982 2.50
❑66, Nov 1982 2.50
❑67, Dec 1982 2.50
❑68, Jan 1983 2.50
❑69, Feb 1983 2.50
❑70, Mar 1983 2.50
❑71, Apr 1983 2.50
❑72, May 1983 2.50
❑73, Jun 1983 2.50
❑74, Jul 1983 2.50
❑75, Aug 1983, TD (a) 2.50
❑76, Sep 1983, TD (a) 2.50
❑77, Oct 1983, TD (a) 2.50
❑78, Nov 1983, TD (a) 2.50
❑79, Dec 1983 2.50
❑80, Jan 1984 2.50
❑81, Feb 1984 2.50
❑82, Mar 1984 2.50
❑83, Apr 1984 2.50
❑84, May 1984 2.50
❑85, Jun 1984 V: Gray Ghost. 2.50
❑86, Aug 1984 2.50
❑87, Oct 1984 2.50
❑88, Dec 1984 2.50
❑89, Feb 1985 V: Gray Ghost 2.50
❑90, Apr 1985 2.50
❑91, Jun 1985 2.50
❑92, Aug 1985; events continue in Hex 2.50

Other grades: Multiply price above by 5/6 for VF/NM • 2/3 for VERY FINE • 1/3 for FINE • 1/5 for VERY GOOD • 1/8 for GOOD

Jonny Quest (Comico)

Son often extricates father from peril

©Comico

Jon Sable, Freelance

Mike Grell mercenary series

©First

Josie & the Pussycats

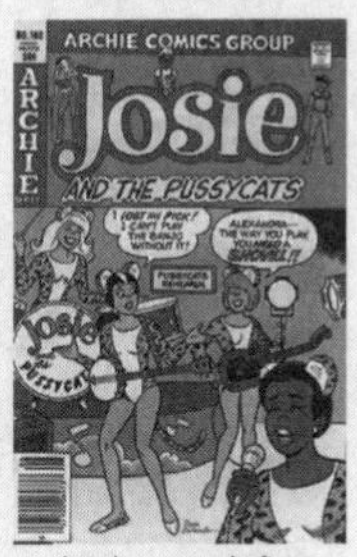

Leader named after co-creator DeCarlo's wife

©Archie

Journey

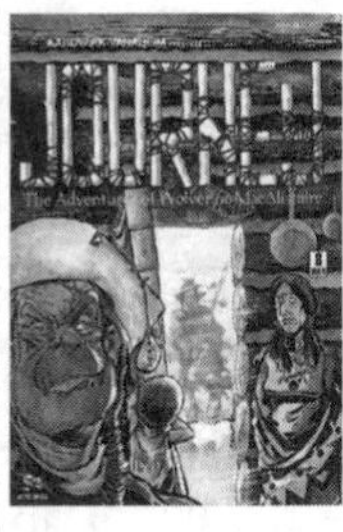

Frontier adventures from Wm. Messner-Loebs

©Aardvark-Vanaheim

Journey into Mystery (1st Series)

Moves from horror to Norse mythology at #83

©Marvel

N-MINT

JONAH HEX AND OTHER WESTERN TALES
DC

❑1, Oct 1979 ... 7.00
❑2, Dec 1979 ... 7.00
❑3, Feb 1980 ... 7.00

JONAH HEX: RIDERS OF THE WORM AND SUCH
DC / VERTIGO

❑1, Mar 1995 ... 3.00
❑2, Apr 1995 ... 3.00
❑3, May 1995 ... 3.00
❑4, Jun 1995 ... 3.00
❑5, Jul 1995 ... 3.00

JONAH HEX: SHADOWS WEST
DC / VERTIGO

❑1, Feb 1999 ... 2.95
❑2, Mar 1999 ... 2.95
❑3, Apr 1999 ... 2.95

JONAH HEX: TWO-GUN MOJO
DC / VERTIGO

❑1, Aug 1993 ... 3.50
❑1/Silver, Aug 1993; Silver (limited promotional) edition; platinum ... 6.00
❑2, Sep 1993 ... 3.00
❑3, Oct 1993 ... 3.00
❑4, Nov 1993 ... 3.00
❑5, Dec 1993 ... 3.00

JONAH HEX (VOLUME 2)
DC

❑1, Jan 2006 ... 2.99
❑2, Jan 2006 ... 2.99
❑3, Mar 2006 ... 2.99
❑4, Apr 2006 ... 2.99
❑5, May 2006 ... 2.99
❑6, Jun 2006 ... 2.99
❑7, Jul 2006 ... 2.99
❑8, Aug 2006 ... 2.99

JONAS! (MIKE DEODATO'S...)
CALIBER

❑1 ... 2.95

JONATHAN FOX
MARIAH GRAPHICS

❑1 ... 2.00

JONES TOUCH
FANTAGRAPHICS / EROS

❑1 ... 2.75

JONNI THUNDER
DC

❑1, Feb 1985 DG (a); O: Jonni Thunder. 1: Jonni Thunder. ... 1.25
❑2, Apr 1985 DG (a) ... 1.25
❑3, Jun 1985 DG (a) ... 1.25
❑4, Aug 1985 DG (a) ... 1.25

JONNY DEMON
DARK HORSE

❑1, May 1994 ... 2.50
❑2, Jun 1994 ... 2.50
❑3, Jul 1994 ... 2.50

JONNY DOUBLE
DC / VERTIGO

❑1, Sep 1998 ... 2.95

N-MINT

❑2, Oct 1998 ... 2.95
❑3, Nov 1998 ... 2.95
❑4, Dec 1998 ... 2.95

JONNY QUEST (GOLD KEY)
GOLD KEY

❑1, Dec 1964 ... 85.00

JONNY QUEST (COMICO)
COMICO

❑1, Jun 1986 ... 3.00
❑2, Jul 1986 ... 2.50
❑3, Aug 1986 DSt (c) ... 2.50
❑4, Sep 1986 TY (a) ... 2.50
❑5, Oct 1986 DSt (c) ... 2.50
❑6, Nov 1986 ... 2.00
❑7, Dec 1986 ... 2.00
❑8, Jan 1987 ... 2.00
❑9, Feb 1987 MA (a) ... 2.00
❑10, Mar 1987 ... 2.00
❑11, Apr 1987 BSz (c); BA (a) ... 1.50
❑12, May 1987 ... 1.50
❑13, Jun 1987 CI (a) ... 1.50
❑14, Jul 1987 ... 1.50
❑15, Aug 1987 ... 1.75
❑16, Sep 1987 ... 1.75
❑17, Oct 1987 ME (w); SR (a) ... 1.75
❑18, Nov 1987 ... 1.75
❑19, Dec 1987 ... 1.75
❑20, Jan 1988 ... 1.75
❑21, Feb 1988 ... 1.75
❑22, Mar 1988 ... 1.75
❑23, Apr 1988 ... 1.75
❑24, May 1988 ... 1.75
❑25, Jun 1988 ... 1.75
❑26, Jul 1988 ... 1.75
❑27, Aug 1988 ... 1.75
❑28, Sep 1988 ... 1.75
❑29, Oct 1988 ... 1.75
❑30, Nov 1988 ... 1.75
❑31, Dec 1988 ... 1.75
❑Special 1, Sep 1988 ... 1.75
❑Special 2, Oct 1988 ... 1.75

JONNY QUEST CLASSICS
COMICO

❑1, May 1987 ... 2.00
❑2, Jun 1987 ... 2.00
❑3, Jul 1987 ... 2.00

JON SABLE, FREELANCE
FIRST

❑1, Jun 1983 MGr (w); MGr (a); 1: Sable. ... 3.00
❑2, Jul 1983 MGr (w); MGr (a) ... 2.00
❑3, Aug 1983 MGr (w); MGr (a); O: Sable. ... 2.00
❑4, Sep 1983 MGr (w); MGr (a); O: Sable. ... 2.00
❑5, Oct 1983 MGr (w); MGr (a); O: Sable. ... 2.00
❑6, Nov 1983 MGr (w); MGr (a); O: Sable. ... 2.00
❑7, Dec 1983 MGr (w); MGr (a) ... 2.00
❑8, Jan 1984 MGr (w); MGr (a) ... 2.00
❑9, Feb 1984 MGr (w); MGr (a) ... 2.00
❑10, Mar 1984 MGr (w); MGr (a) ... 2.00
❑11, Apr 1984 MGr (w); MGr (a) ... 2.00

N-MINT

❑12, May 1984 MGr (w); MGr (a) ... 2.00
❑13, Jun 1984 MGr (w); MGr (a) ... 2.00
❑14, Jul 1984 MGr (w); MGr (a) ... 2.00
❑15, Aug 1984 MGr (w); MGr (a) ... 2.00
❑16, Sep 1984 MGr (w); MGr (a) ... 2.00
❑17, Oct 1984 MGr (w); MGr (a) ... 2.00
❑18, Oct 1984 MGr (w); MGr (a) ... 2.00
❑19, Dec 1984 MGr (w); MGr (a) ... 2.00
❑20, Jan 1985 MGr (w); MGr (a) ... 2.00
❑21, Feb 1985 MGr (w); MGr (a) ... 1.75
❑22, Mar 1985 MGr (w); MGr (a) ... 1.75
❑23, Apr 1985 MGr (w); MGr (a) ... 1.75
❑24, May 1985 MGr (w); MGr (a) ... 1.75
❑25, Jun 1985; MGr (w); MGr (a); Shatter back-up story ... 1.75
❑26, Jul 1985; MGr (w); MGr (a); Shatter back-up story ... 1.75
❑27, Aug 1985; MGr (w); MGr (a); Shatter back-up story ... 1.75
❑28, Sep 1985; MGr (w); MGr (a); Shatter back-up story ... 1.75
❑29, Oct 1985; MGr (w); MGr (a); Shatter back-up story ... 1.75
❑30, Nov 1985; MGr (w); MGr (a); Shatter back-up story ... 1.75
❑31, Dec 1985 MGr (w); MGr (a) ... 1.75
❑32, Jan 1986 MGr (w); MGr (a) ... 1.75
❑33, Feb 1986 MGr (w); MGr (a) ... 1.75
❑34, Mar 1986 MGr (w); MGr (a) ... 1.75
❑35, Apr 1986 MGr (w); MGr (a) ... 1.75
❑36, May 1986 MGr (w); MGr (a) ... 1.75
❑37, Jun 1986 MGr (w); MGr (a) ... 1.75
❑38, Jul 1986 MGr (w); MGr (a) ... 1.75
❑39, Aug 1986 MGr (w); MGr (a) ... 1.75
❑40, Sep 1986 MGr (w); MGr (a) ... 1.75
❑41, Oct 1986 MGr (w); MGr (a) ... 1.75
❑42, Nov 1986 MGr (w); MGr (a) ... 1.75
❑43, Dec 1986 MGr (w); MGr (a) ... 1.75
❑44, Jan 1987 MGr (c); MGr (w); MGr (a) ... 1.75
❑45, Mar 1987 MGr (c); MGr (w); MGr (a) ... 1.75
❑46, Apr 1987 MGr (c); MGr (w); MGr (a) ... 1.75
❑47, May 1987 MGr (c); MGr (w); MGr (a) ... 1.75
❑48, Jun 1987 MGr (c); MGr (w); MGr (a) ... 1.75
❑49, Jul 1987 MGr (c); MGr (w); MGr (a) ... 1.75
❑50, Aug 1987 MGr (c); MGr (w); MGr (a) ... 1.75
❑51, Sep 1987 MGr (c); MGr (w); MGr (a) ... 1.75
❑52, Oct 1987 MGr (c); MGr (w); MGr (a) ... 1.75
❑53, Nov 1987 MGr (c); MGr (w); MGr (a) ... 1.75
❑54, Dec 1987 MGr (c); MGr (w); MGr (a) ... 1.75
❑55, Jan 1988 MGr (c); MGr (w); MGr (a) ... 1.75
❑56, Feb 1988 MGr (c); MGr (w); MGr (a) ... 1.75

JON SABLE, FREELANCE: BLOODLINE
IDEA & DESIGN WORKS

❑1, ca. 2005 ... 3.99

Other grades: Multiply price above by 5/6 for VF/NM • 2/3 for VERY FINE • 1/3 for FINE • 1/5 for VERY GOOD • 1/8 for GOOD

❑2 2005 ... 3.99
❑3, Sep 2005 ... 3.99
❑4, Oct 2005 ... 3.99
❑5, Nov 2005 ... 3.99
❑6, Dec 2005 ... 3.99

JONTAR RETURNS
MILLER

❑1, b&w ... 2.00
❑2, b&w ... 2.00
❑3, b&w ... 2.00
❑4, b&w ... 2.00

JOSIE & THE PUSSYCATS
ARCHIE

❑45, Dec 1969 ... 12.00
❑46, Feb 1970 ... 6.00
❑47, Apr 1970 ... 6.00
❑48, Jun 1970 ... 6.00
❑49, Aug 1970 ... 6.00
❑50, Sep 1970 ... 6.00
❑51, Oct 1970 ... 6.00
❑52, Dec 1970 ... 6.00
❑53, Feb 1971 ... 6.00
❑54, Apr 1971 ... 6.00
❑55, Jun 1971, Giant-size ... 6.00
❑56, Aug 1971, Giant-size ... 6.00
❑57, Sep 1971, Giant-size ... 6.00
❑58, Oct 1971, Giant-size ... 6.00
❑59, Dec 1971, Giant-size ... 6.00
❑60, Feb 1972, Giant-size ... 6.00
❑61, Apr 1972, Giant-size ... 5.00
❑62, Jun 1972, Giant-size ... 5.00
❑63, Aug 1972, Giant-size ... 5.00
❑64, Sep 1972, Giant-size ... 5.00
❑65, Oct 1972, Giant-size ... 5.00
❑66, Dec 1972, Giant-size ... 5.00
❑67, Feb 1973 ... 5.00
❑68, Apr 1973 ... 5.00
❑69, Jun 1973 ... 5.00
❑70, Aug 1973 ... 5.00
❑71, Sep 1973 ... 4.00
❑72, Oct 1973 ... 4.00
❑73, Dec 1973 ... 4.00
❑74, Feb 1974 ... 4.00
❑75, Apr 1974 ... 4.00
❑76, Jun 1974 ... 4.00
❑77, Aug 1974 ... 4.00
❑78, Sep 1974 ... 4.00
❑79, Oct 1974 ... 4.00
❑80, Dec 1974 ... 4.00
❑81, Feb 1975 ... 4.00
❑82, Jun 1975 ... 4.00
❑83, Aug 1975 ... 4.00
❑84, Sep 1975 ... 4.00
❑85, Oct 1975 ... 4.00
❑86, Dec 1975 ... 4.00
❑87, Feb 1976 ... 4.00
❑88, Apr 1976 ... 4.00
❑89, Jun 1976 ... 4.00
❑90, Aug 1976 ... 4.00
❑91, Sep 1976 ... 3.00
❑92, Oct 1976 ... 3.00
❑93, Dec 1976 ... 3.00
❑94, Feb 1977 ... 3.00
❑95, Aug 1977 ... 3.00
❑96 ... 3.00
❑97 ... 3.00
❑98 ... 3.00
❑99, Aug 1979 ... 3.00
❑100, Oct 1979 ... 3.00
❑101, Aug 1980 ... 3.00
❑102 ... 3.00
❑103 ... 3.00
❑104 ... 3.00
❑105 ... 3.00
❑106, Oct 1982 ... 3.00

JOSIE & THE PUSSYCATS (2ND SERIES)
ARCHIE

❑1, ca. 1993 ... 2.00
❑2, ca. 1993 ... 2.00

JOURNEY
AARDVARK-VANAHEIM

❑1, Mar 1983, b&w ... 4.00
❑2 1983, b&w ... 3.00
❑3 1983, b&w ... 2.50
❑4 1983, b&w ... 2.50
❑5 1983, b&w ... 2.50
❑6, b&w ... 2.50
❑7, b&w ... 2.50
❑8, Mar 1984, b&w ... 2.50
❑9, Apr 1984, b&w ... 2.50
❑10, May 1984, b&w ... 2.50
❑11, Jun 1984, b&w ... 2.00
❑12, Jul 1984, b&w ... 2.00
❑13, Aug 1984, b&w ... 2.00
❑14, Sep 1984, b&w ... 2.00
❑15, Apr 1985, b&w ... 2.00
❑16, May 1985, b&w ... 2.00
❑17, Jun 1985, b&w ... 2.00
❑18, Jul 1985, b&w ... 2.00
❑19, Aug 1985, b&w ... 2.00
❑20, Sep 1985, b&w ... 2.00
❑21, Oct 1985, b&w ... 2.00
❑22, Nov 1985, b&w ... 2.00
❑23, Dec 1985, b&w ... 2.00
❑24, Jan 1986, b&w ... 2.00
❑25, Feb 1986, b&w ... 2.00
❑26, Mar 1986, b&w ... 2.00
❑27, Jul 1986, b&w ... 2.00

JOURNEY INTO MYSTERY (1ST SERIES)
MARVEL

❑-1, Jul 1997; Flashback ... 2.25
❑39, Oct 1956 ... 225.00
❑40, Nov 1956 ... 225.00
❑41, Dec 1956 ... 200.00
❑42, Jan 1957 ... 200.00
❑43, Feb 1957 ... 200.00
❑44, Mar 1957 ... 200.00
❑45, Apr 1957 ... 200.00
❑46, May 1957 ... 200.00
❑47, Jun 1957 ... 200.00
❑48, Sep 1957 ... 200.00
❑49, Oct 1957 ... 200.00
❑50, Nov 1957 ... 160.00
❑51, Mar 1959 ... 155.00
❑52, May 1959 ... 155.00
❑53, Jul 1959 ... 155.00
❑54, Sep 1959 ... 155.00
❑55, Nov 1959 ... 155.00
❑56, Jan 1960 ... 155.00
❑57, Mar 1960 ... 155.00
❑58, May 1960 ... 155.00
❑59, Jul 1960 ... 155.00
❑60, Sep 1960 ... 155.00
❑61, Oct 1960 ... 155.00
❑62, Nov 1960, 1: Xemnu: "Hulk" try-out? ... 250.00
❑63, Dec 1960 ... 145.00
❑64, Jan 1961 ... 145.00
❑65, Feb 1961 ... 145.00
❑66, Mar 1961 ... 145.00
❑67, Apr 1961 ... 145.00
❑68, May 1961 ... 145.00
❑69, Jun 1961 ... 145.00
❑70, Jul 1961 ... 145.00
❑71, Aug 1961 ... 145.00
❑72, Sep 1961 ... 140.00
❑73, Oct 1961 ... 200.00
❑74, Nov 1961 ... 140.00
❑75, Dec 1961 ... 140.00
❑76, Jan 1962 ... 140.00
❑77, Feb 1962 ... 140.00
❑78, Mar 1962, Doctor Strange prototype ... 140.00
❑79, Apr 1962 ... 140.00
❑80, May 1962 ... 140.00
❑81, Jun 1962 ... 140.00
❑82, Jul 1962 ... 160.00
❑83, Aug 1962, SL (w); SD, JK (a); O: Thor ... 4500.00
❑83/Golden Recor, ca. 1966; SL (w); SD, JK (a); O: Thor. 1: Thor. Golden Records reprint (with record) ... 60.00
❑84, Sep 1962, SL (w); SD, DH, JK (a); 1: Executioner. 1: Loki. 1: Jane Foster. 2: Thor. ... 725.00
❑85, Oct 1962, SL (w); SD, DH, JK (a); 1: Balder. 1: Loki. 1: Odin. 1: Tyr. 1: Heimdall. ... 450.00
❑86, Nov 1962, SL (w); SD, DH, JK (a); 1: Tomorrow Man. 1: Odin ... 400.00
❑87, Dec 1962, SL (w); SD, JK (a) ... 600.00
❑88, Jan 1963, SL (w); SD, DH, JK (a); A: Loki. ... 250.00
❑89, Feb 1963, SL (w); SD, JK (a); O: Thor. ... 300.00
❑90, Mar 1963, SL (w); SD, JSt (a); 1: Carbon-Copy. ... 150.00
❑91, Apr 1963, JK (c); SL (w); SD, JSt (a); 1: Sandu. ... 130.00
❑92, May 1963, SL (w); SD, JSt (a); 1: Frigga. A: Loki. ... 130.00
❑93, Jun 1963, SL (w); SD, JK (a); 1: Radioactive Man (Dr. Chen Lu)-Marvel ... 160.00
❑94, Jul 1963, JK (c); SL (w); SD, JSt (a); Loki ... 130.00
❑95, Aug 1963, JK (c); SL (w); SD, JSt (a) ... 130.00
❑96, Sep 1963, JK (c); SL (w); SD, JSt (a); Merlin ... 130.00
❑97, Oct 1963, SL (w); DH, JK (a); 1: Surtur. 1: Lava Men. V: Ymir. V: Molto. Tales of Asgard backup stories begin ... 325.00
❑98, Nov 1963, JK (c); SL (w); DH, JK (a) ... 120.00
❑99, Dec 1963, SL (w); DH, JK (a); 1: Mr. Hyde. ... 105.00
❑100, Jan 1964, JK (c); SL (w); DH, JK (a) ... 115.00
❑101, Feb 1964, SL (w); JK (a); A: Iron Man. A: Giant Man. ... 150.00
❑102, Mar 1964, SL (w); JK (a); 1: Hela. 1: Sif. 1: The Norns. ... 75.00
❑103, Apr 1964, SL (w); JK (a); 1: Enchantress. V: Executioner. ... 75.00
❑104, May 1964, SL (w); JK (a); giants 75.00
❑105, Jun 1964 SL (w); JK (a); V: Cobra. V: Hyde. ... 75.00
❑106, Jul 1964, JK (a); O: Balder. ... 75.00
❑107, Aug 1964, JK (a); O: Grey Gargoyle. 1: Grey Gargoyle. ... 75.00
❑108, Sep 1964, JK (a); A: Doctor Strange. ... 75.00
❑109, Oct 1964, JK (a); A: Magneto. .. 90.00
❑110, Nov 1964, JK (a); V: Loki. V: Cobra. V: Hyde. ... 75.00
❑111, Dec 1964, JK (a); V: Loki. V: Cobra. V: Hyde. ... 75.00
❑112, Jan 1965, JK (a); V: Hulk. ... 210.00
❑113, Feb 1965, JK (a); V: Grey Gargoyle. ... 75.00
❑114, Mar 1965, JK (a); O: Absorbing Man. 1: Absorbing Man. ... 75.00
❑115, Apr 1965, JK (a); O: Loki. ... 90.00
❑116, May 1965, JK (a); A: Daredevil. A: Loki. ... 75.00
❑117, Jun 1965, JK (a); A: Loki. ... 70.00
❑118, Jul 1965, JK (a); 1: The Destroyer. ... 70.00
❑119, Aug 1965, JK (a); 1: Warriors Three. 1: Hogun. 1: Fandrall. 1: Volstagg. ... 70.00
❑120, Sep 1965, JK (a) ... 70.00
❑121, Oct 1965, JK (a) ... 70.00
❑122, Nov 1965, JK (a) ... 70.00
❑123, Dec 1965, SL (w); JK (a) ... 70.00
❑124, Jan 1966, JK (a) ... 70.00
❑125, Feb 1966, JK (a); Series continues in Thor #126 ... 70.00
❑503, Nov 1996; A: Lost Gods. D: Red Norvell. Series continued from Thor #502 ... 1.50
❑504, Dec 1996 A: Ulik. ... 1.50
❑505, Jan 1997 A: Spider-Man. V: Wrecking Crew. ... 1.50
❑506, Feb 1997 ... 1.50
❑507, Mar 1997 ... 1.50
❑508, Apr 1997 V: Red Norvell. ... 1.50
❑509, May 1997; return of Loki ... 1.50
❑510, Jun 1997 V: Red Norvell. ... 1.50
❑511, Aug 1997; gatefold summary; Loki vs. Seth ... 1.99
❑512, Sep 1997; gatefold summary ... 1.99
❑513, Oct 1997; gatefold summary; SB (a); Asgardian storyline concludes.. 1.99
❑514, Nov 1997; gatefold summary; Shang-Chi ... 1.99
❑515, Dec 1997; gatefold summary; Shang-Chi ... 1.99
❑516, Jan 1998; gatefold summary; Shang-Chi ... 1.99
❑517, Feb 1998; gatefold summary; Black Widow ... 1.99

Other grades: Multiply price above by 5/6 for VF/NM • 2/3 for VERY FINE • 1/3 for FINE • 1/5 for VERY GOOD • 1/8 for GOOD

JSA

Golden Age team trains new generation

©DC

JSA: All Stars

Golden Age ties to modern day

©DC

Judge Dredd (Vol. 1)

Mega City One's chief lawman's solo title

©Eagle

Judge Dredd (DC)

Dredd brings the law to DC

©DC

Judge Dredd's Crime File (Eagle)

Reprints early 2000 A.D. Dredd doings

©Eagle

N-MINT

❑518, Mar 1998; gatefold summary; Black Widow 1.99
❑519, Apr 1998; gatefold summary; Black Widow 1.99
❑520, May 1998; gatefold summary; Hannibal King 1.99
❑521, Jun 1998; gatefold summary; Hannibal King 1.99
❑Annual 1, ca. 1965; King-Size Annual; JK (a); 1: Hercules. A: Zeus. 1st appearance of Hercules; New stories and reprints from JIM #85, 93 and 97; continues as Thor Annual 150.00

JOURNEY INTO MYSTERY (2ND SERIES)
MARVEL

❑1, Oct 1972, GK, TP (a); Robert Howard adaptation: "Dig Me No Grave" 17.00
❑2, Dec 1972 .... 7.00
❑3, Feb 1973 .... 7.00
❑4, Apr 1973, H.P. Lovecraft adaptation: "Haunter of the Dark" 6.00
❑5, Jun 1973, Robert Bloch adaptation: "Shadow From the Steeple" 6.00
❑6, Aug 1973 .... 5.00
❑7, Oct 1973 .... 5.00
❑8, Dec 1973 .... 5.00
❑9, Feb 1974 .... 5.00
❑10, Apr 1974 .... 5.00
❑11, Jun 1974 .... 5.00
❑12, Aug 1974 .... 5.00
❑13, Oct 1974 .... 5.00
❑14, Dec 1974 .... 5.00
❑15, Feb 1975 .... 5.00
❑16, Apr 1975 .... 5.00
❑17, Jun 1975 .... 5.00
❑18, Aug 1975 .... 5.00
❑19, Oct 1975 .... 5.00

JOURNEYMAN
IMAGE

❑1, Aug 1999 .... 2.95
❑2, Sep 1999 .... 2.95
❑3, Oct 1999 .... 2.95

JOURNEYMAN/DARK AGES
LUCID

❑1, Sum 1997, b&w; San Diego edition 3.00

JOURNEY: WARDRUMS
FANTAGRAPHICS

❑1, May 1987; sepia tones 2.00
❑1/2nd, Aug 1987, b&w; sepia dropped 1.75
❑2 .... 2.00

JR. CARROT PATROL
DARK HORSE

❑1, May 1989, b&w 2.00
❑2, b&w 2.00

JSA
DC

❑1, Aug 1999, JRo (w) 5.00
❑2, Sep 1999, JRo (w); V: Mordru. 2.50
❑3, Oct 1999, JRo (w); V: Mordru. 2.50
❑4, Nov 1999, JRo (w); V: Mordru. identity of new Doctor Fate revealed 2.50
❑5, Dec 1999, JRo (w) 2.50
❑6, Jan 2000 .... 2.50

N-MINT

❑7, Feb 2000 .... 2.50
❑8, Mar 2000 .... 2.50
❑9, Apr 2000 .... 2.50
❑10, May 2000 .... 2.50
❑11, Jun 2000 .... 2.50
❑12, Jul 2000 .... 2.50
❑13, Aug 2000 .... 2.50
❑14, Sep 2000 .... 2.50
❑15, Oct 2000 .... 2.50
❑16, Nov 2000 .... 2.50
❑17, Dec 2000 .... 2.50
❑18, Jan 2001 .... 2.50
❑19, Feb 2001 .... 2.50
❑20, Mar 2001 .... 2.50
❑21, Apr 2001 .... 2.50
❑22, May 2001 .... 2.50
❑23, Jun 2001 .... 2.50
❑24, Jul 2001 .... 2.50
❑25, Aug 2001 .... 2.50
❑26, Sep 2001 .... 2.50
❑27, Oct 2001 .... 2.50
❑28, Nov 2001 .... 2.50
❑29, Dec 2001 .... 2.50
❑30, Jan 2002 .... 2.50
❑31, Feb 2002 .... 2.50
❑32, Mar 2002 .... 2.50
❑33, Apr 2002, AM, KG (a) 2.50
❑34, May 2002 .... 2.50
❑35, Jun 2002 .... 2.50
❑36, Jul 2002 .... 2.50
❑37, Aug 2002 .... 3.50
❑38, Sep 2002 .... 2.50
❑39, Oct 2002 .... 2.50
❑40, Nov 2002 .... 2.50
❑41, Dec 2002 .... 2.50
❑42, Jan 2003 .... 2.50
❑43, Feb 2003 .... 2.50
❑44, Mar 2003 .... 2.50
❑45, Apr 2003 .... 2.50
❑46, May 2003 .... 2.50
❑47, Jun 2003 .... 2.50
❑48, Jul 2003 .... 2.50
❑49, Aug 2003 .... 2.50
❑50, Sep 2003 .... 3.95
❑51, Oct 2003 .... 2.50
❑52, Nov 2003 .... 2.50
❑53, Dec 2003 .... 2.50
❑54, Jan 2004 .... 2.50
❑55, Jan 2004 .... 2.50
❑56, Feb 2004 .... 2.50
❑57, Mar 2004 .... 2.50
❑58, Apr 2004 .... 4.00
❑59, May 2004 .... 2.50
❑60, Jun 2004 .... 2.50
❑61, Jul 2004 .... 2.50
❑62, Aug 2004 .... 2.50
❑63, Sep 2004, JOy (a) 2.50
❑64, Oct 2004, JOy (a) 2.50
❑65, Nov 2004 .... 2.50
❑66, Dec 2004 .... 2.50
❑67, Jan 2005, DaG (a) 7.00
❑68, Feb 2005, ARo (c) 5.00
❑69, Mar 2005 .... 4.00
❑70, Apr 2005 .... 4.00

N-MINT

❑71, May 2005 .... 2.50
❑72, Jun 2005 .... 4.00
❑73, Jun 2005 .... 5.00
❑74, Jul 2005 .... 4.00
❑75, Aug 2005 .... 2.50
❑76, Sep 2005 .... 2.50
❑77, Oct 2005 .... 2.50
❑78 2005 .... 2.50
❑79, Jan 2006 .... 2.50
❑80, Jan 2006 .... 2.50
❑81, Mar 2006 .... 2.50
❑82, Apr 2006 .... 2.50
❑83, May 2006 .... 2.50
❑84, Jun 2006 .... 2.50
❑85, Jul 2006 .... 2.50
❑86, Aug 2006 .... 2.50
❑Annual 1, Oct 2000; 1: Nemesis. Planet DC 5.00

JSA: ALL STARS
DC

❑1, Jul 2003 .... 2.50
❑2, Aug 2003 .... 2.50
❑3, Sep 2003 .... 2.50
❑4, Oct 2003 .... 2.50
❑5, Nov 2003 .... 2.50
❑6, Dec 2003 .... 2.50
❑7, Jan 2004 .... 3.50
❑8, Feb 2004 .... 2.50

JSA: CLASSIFIED
DC

❑1/Conner, Sep 2005 .... 7.00
❑1/Hughes, Sep 2005 .... 10.00
❑1/Sketch, Sep 2005; Sketch from Adam Hughes variant, 2nd print 5.00
❑2, Oct 2005 .... 2.99
❑2/Sketch, Oct 2005 .... 2.99
❑3 2005 .... 2.99
❑4 .... 2.99
❑5, Jan 2006 .... 2.99
❑6, Feb 2006 .... 2.99
❑8, Mar 2006 .... 2.99
❑9, Apr 2006 .... 2.99
❑10, Jun 2006 .... 2.99
❑11, Jun 2006 .... 2.99
❑12, Aug 2006 .... 2.99
❑13, Sep 2006 .... 2.99
❑16, Mar 2006 .... 2.99

JSA: OUR WORLDS AT WAR
DC

❑1, Sep 2001 .... 2.95

JSA SECRET FILES
DC

❑1, Aug 1999; background information on team's formation and members 4.95
❑2, Sep 1999 .... 4.95

JSA: STRANGE ADVENTURES
DC

❑1, Oct 2004 .... 3.50
❑2, Nov 2004 .... 3.50
❑3, Dec 2004 .... 3.50
❑4, Jan 2005 .... 3.50
❑5, Feb 2005 .... 3.50
❑6, Mar 2005 .... 3.50

Other grades: Multiply price above by 5/6 for VF/NM • 2/3 for VERY FINE • 1/3 for FINE • 1/5 for VERY GOOD • 1/8 for GOOD

JSA: THE LIBERTY FILE
DC

❑1, Feb 2000 ... 6.95
❑2, Mar 2000 ... 6.95

JSA: UNHOLY THREE
DC

❑1, Apr 2003 ... 6.95
❑2, May 2003 ... 6.95

JUBILEE
MARVEL

❑1 2004 ... 2.99
❑2 2004 ... 2.99
❑3 ... 2.99
❑4 ... 2.99
❑5, Feb 2005 ... 2.99
❑6, Mar 2005 ... 2.99

JUDGE DREDD VERSUS ALIENS: INCUBUS
DARK HORSE

❑1, Mar 2003 ... 2.99
❑2, Apr 2003 ... 2.99
❑3, May 2003 ... 2.99
❑4, Jun 2003 ... 2.99

JUDGE CHILD
EAGLE

❑1 BB (a) ... 2.00
❑2 ... 2.00
❑3 ... 2.00
❑4 ... 2.00
❑5 ... 2.00

JUDGE COLT
GOLD KEY

❑1, Oct 1969 ... 15.00
❑2, Feb 1970 ... 10.00
❑3, May 1970 O: Judge Colt. ... 10.00
❑4, Sep 1970 ... 10.00

JUDGE DREDD (VOL. 1)
EAGLE

❑1, Nov 1983 BB (a); 1: Judge Dredd (in U.S.). A: Judge Death. ... 4.00
❑2, Dec 1983 BB (a) ... 3.00
❑3, Jan 1984 BB (a); A: Judge Anderson. V: Judge Death ... 2.50
❑4, Feb 1984 BB (a) ... 2.50
❑5, Mar 1984 ... 2.50
❑6, Apr 1984 ... 2.50
❑7, May 1984 ... 2.50
❑8, Jun 1984 ... 2.50
❑9, Jul 1984 ... 2.50
❑10, Aug 1984 ... 2.50
❑11, Sep 1984 ... 2.00
❑12, Oct 1984 ... 2.00
❑13, Nov 1984 ... 2.00
❑14, Dec 1984 ... 2.00
❑15, Jan 1985; Umpty Candy ... 2.00
❑16, Feb 1985 V: Fink Angel. ... 2.00
❑17, Mar 1985 ... 2.00
❑18, Apr 1985 ... 2.00
❑19, May 1985 ... 2.00
❑20, Jun 1985 ... 2.00
❑21, Jul 1985 ... 2.00
❑22, Aug 1985 ... 2.00
❑23, Sep 1985 ... 2.00
❑24, Oct 1985 ... 2.00
❑25, Nov 1985 ... 2.00
❑26, Dec 1985 ... 2.00
❑27, Jan 1986 ... 2.00
❑28, Feb 1986 ... 2.00
❑29, Mar 1986 ... 2.00
❑30, Apr 1986 ... 2.00
❑31, May 1986 V: Judge Child. V: Mean Machine. ... 2.00
❑32, Jun 1986 V: Mean Machine. ... 2.00
❑33, Jul 1986; League of Fatties ... 2.00
❑34, Aug 1986 ... 2.00
❑35, Sep 1986 ... 2.00

JUDGE DREDD (VOL. 2)
FLEETWAY-QUALITY

❑1, Oct 1986 ... 3.00
❑2, Nov 1986 ... 2.50
❑3, Dec 1986 ... 2.00
❑4, Jan 1987 ... 2.00
❑5, Feb 1987, poster ... 2.00
❑6, Mar 1987, Christmas issue ... 2.00
❑7 1987 ... 2.00
❑8, Jul 1987, wraparound cover ... 2.00
❑9, Aug 1987 ... 2.00
❑10, Sep 1987 ... 2.00
❑11, Oct 1987 ... 2.00
❑12, dropped publication date from cover and indicia for rest of series . 2.00
❑13 ... 2.00
❑14, BB (a) ... 2.00
❑15 ... 2.00
❑16 ... 2.00
❑17 ... 2.00
❑18 ... 2.00
❑19 ... 2.00
❑20 ... 2.00
❑21, double issue #21, 22 ... 2.00
❑22 ... 2.00
❑23, double issue #23, 24 ... 2.00
❑24 ... 2.00
❑25 ... 2.00
❑26 ... 2.00
❑27 ... 2.00
❑28 ... 2.00
❑29 ... 2.00
❑30 ... 2.00
❑31 ... 2.00
❑32 ... 2.00
❑33 ... 2.00
❑34 ... 2.00
❑35 ... 2.00
❑36 ... 2.00
❑37 ... 2.00
❑38 ... 2.00
❑39 ... 2.00
❑40 ... 2.00
❑41, Reprints stories from 2000 A.D. #445, #447, and #449 ... 2.00
❑42, Reprints stories from 2000 A.D. #421, #422, and #434 ... 2.00
❑43, Reprints stories from 2000 A.D. #113-115 and #412 ... 2.00
❑44, Reprints stories from 2000 A.D. #60, #304, and #514 ... 2.00
❑45, BT (a); Reprints stories from 2000 A.D. #119, #457, #458, and #459... 2.00
❑46 ... 2.00
❑47 ... 2.00
❑48 ... 2.00
❑49, Reprints stories from 2000 A.D. #182, #490, #491, and #493 ... 2.00
❑50 ... 2.00
❑51 ... 2.00
❑52 ... 2.00
❑53, BB (a); Reprints stories from 2000 A.D. #25 and #519 ... 2.00
❑54, Reprints stories from 2000 A.D. #643-645 and 2000 A.D. 1990 Mega-Special ... 2.00
❑55 ... 2.00
❑56 ... 2.00
❑57 ... 2.00
❑58 ... 2.00
❑59 ... 1.95
❑60 ... 1.95
❑61, Series continued in Judge Dredd Classics #62 ... 1.95
❑Special 1 ... 2.50

JUDGE DREDD (DC)
DC

❑1, Aug 1994 ... 3.00
❑2, Sep 1994 ... 2.50
❑3, Oct 1994 ... 2.50
❑4, Nov 1994 ... 2.00
❑5, Dec 1994 ... 2.00
❑6, Jan 1995 ... 2.00
❑7, Feb 1995 ... 2.00
❑8, Mar 1995 ... 2.00
❑9, Apr 1995; homage to Judge Dredd #1 (first series) ... 2.00
❑10, May 1995 ... 2.00
❑11, Jun 1995 ... 2.25
❑12, Jul 1995 ... 2.25
❑13, Aug 1995 ... 2.25
❑14, Sep 1995 ... 2.25
❑15, Oct 1995 ... 2.25
❑16, Nov 1995 ... 2.25
❑17, Dec 1995 ... 2.25
❑18, Jan 1996 ... 2.25

JUDGE DREDD: AMERICA
FLEETWAY-QUALITY

❑1 ... 2.95
❑2 ... 2.95

JUDGE DREDD CLASSICS
FLEETWAY-QUALITY

❑62 ... 1.95
❑63 ... 1.95
❑64 ... 1.95
❑65 ... 1.95
❑66 ... 1.95
❑67 ... 1.95
❑68 ... 1.95
❑69 ... 1.95
❑70 ... 1.95
❑71 ... 1.95
❑72 ... 1.95
❑73 ... 1.95
❑74 ... 1.95
❑75 ... 1.95
❑76 ... 1.95
❑77 ... 1.95

JUDGE DREDD: EMERALD ISLE
FLEETWAY-QUALITY

❑1, ca. 1991 ... 4.95

JUDGE DREDD: LEGENDS OF THE LAW
DC

❑1, Dec 1994 BA (a) ... 2.50
❑2, Jan 1995 BA (a) ... 2.00
❑3, Feb 1995 BA (a) ... 2.00
❑4, Mar 1995 BA (a) ... 2.00
❑5, Apr 1995 ... 2.00
❑6, May 1995 ... 2.00
❑7, Jun 1995 ... 2.25
❑8, Jul 1995 JBy (a) ... 2.25
❑9, Aug 1995 JBy (a) ... 2.25
❑10, Sep 1995 JBy (a) ... 2.25
❑11, Oct 1995 JBy (c) ... 2.25
❑12, Nov 1995 ... 2.25
❑13, Dec 1995 ... 2.25

JUDGE DREDD: RAPTAUR
FLEETWAY-QUALITY

❑1; Judge Dredd ... 2.95
❑2; Judge Dredd ... 2.95

JUDGE DREDD'S CRIME FILE (EAGLE)
EAGLE

❑1 ... 3.00
❑2 ... 3.00
❑3 ... 3.00
❑4, Nov 1985 ... 3.00
❑5 ... 3.00
❑6 ... 3.00

JUDGE DREDD'S CRIME FILE (FLEETWAY)
FLEETWAY-QUALITY

❑1 ... 4.25
❑2 ... 4.25
❑3 ... 4.25
❑4 ... 4.25

JUDGE DREDD'S HARDCASE PAPERS
FLEETWAY-QUALITY

❑1 ... 5.95
❑2 ... 5.95
❑3 ... 5.95
❑4 ... 5.95

JUDGE DREDD THE MEGAZINE
FLEETWAY-QUALITY

❑1 ... 4.95
❑2 ... 4.95
❑3 ... 4.95

JUDGE DREDD: THE OFFICIAL MOVIE ADAPTATION
DC

❑1; prestige format ... 5.95

J.U.D.G.E.: SECRET RAGE
IMAGE

❑1, Mar 2000 ... 2.95

JUDGMENT DAY (LIGHTNING)
LIGHTNING

❑1/A, Sep 1993, Red prism border; red foil cover ... 3.50

Other grades: Multiply price above by 5/6 for VF/NM • 2/3 for VERY FINE • 1/3 for FINE • 1/5 for VERY GOOD • 1/8 for GOOD

Judgment Day

Liefeld heroes hold trial for one of their own
©Awesome

Judomaster

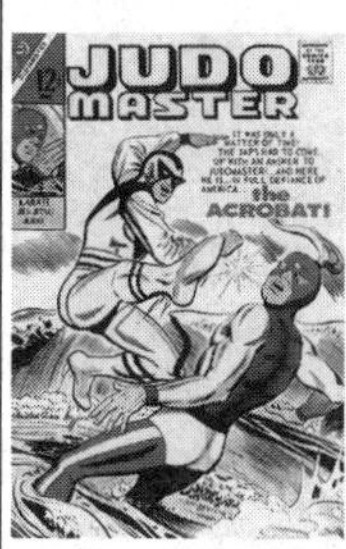

Charlton martial artist made Crisis appearance
©Charlton

Jughead (Vol. 2)

Archie's best pal's solo outings
©Archie

Jughead's Diner

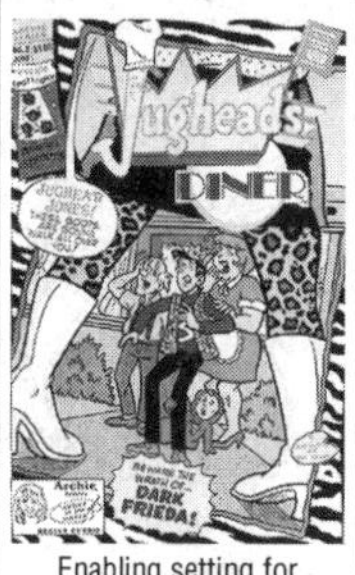

Enabling setting for food fanatic
©Archie

Jughead's Time Police

Jughead lusts for female Archie descendant
©Archie

N-MINT

❑1/B, Sep 1993, purple foil cover 3.50
❑1/C, Sep 1993, misprint 3.50
❑1/D, Aug 1993, promotional copy; metallic ink 3.50
❑1/Gold, Sep 1993, Gold prism border; Gold foil cover 3.50
❑1/Platinum, Aug 1993, promotional copy; platinum 3.50
❑2, Oct 1993, trading card 2.95
❑3, Nov 1993 .... 2.95
❑4, Dec 1993 .... 2.95
❑5, Jan 1994 .... 2.95
❑6, Feb 1994 .... 2.95
❑7, Mar 1994 .... 2.95
❑8, Apr 1994 .... 2.95

JUDGMENT DAY
AWESOME

❑1, Jun 1997; Alpha 2.50
❑1/A, Jun 1997; Alpha; variant cover.. 2.50
❑1/2nd; Alpha 2.50
❑2, Jul 1997; Omega 2.50
❑2/A, Jul 1997; Omega; variant cover. 2.50
❑3; Final Judgment 2.50
❑3/A; Final Judgment 2.50

JUDGMENT DAY: AFTERMATH
AWESOME

❑1, Jan 1998 .... 3.50
❑1/A; Purple cover by Evans 3.50

JUDGMENT DAY SOURCEBOOK
AWESOME

❑1; no cover price or indicia; American Entertainment exclusive preview of series 1.00

JUDGMENT PAWNS
ANTARCTIC

❑1, Feb 1997, b&w 2.95
❑2, Apr 1997, b&w 2.95
❑3, Jul 1997, b&w 2.95

JUDGMENTS
NBM

❑1 .... 14.95

JUDO GIRL
ALIAS

❑0/Conv 2005 .... 8.00
❑1/Balan 2005 .... 3.00
❑1/Taylor 2005 .... 4.00
❑2/Balan, Jul 2005 .... 3.00
❑2/Taylor, Jul 2005 .... 4.00
❑3/Balan, Aug 2005 .... 3.00
❑3/Taylor, Aug 2005 .... 4.00
❑4/Balan, Sep 2005 .... 3.00
❑4/Miller, Sep 2005 .... 4.00

JUDOMASTER
CHARLTON

❑89, Jun 1966, Series continued from Gun Master #89 .... 12.00
❑90, Aug 1966 .... 9.00
❑91, Oct 1966, A: Sarge Steel 9.00
❑92, Dec 1966 .... 9.00
❑93, Feb 1967 .... 9.00
❑94, Apr 1967 .... 9.00
❑95, Jun 1967, FMc (w); FMc, DG (a) 9.00
❑96, Aug 1967 .... 9.00

N-MINT

❑97, Oct 1967 .... 9.00
❑98, Dec 1967 .... 9.00

JUGGERNAUT
MARVEL

❑1, Apr 1997 .... 2.99

JUGGERNAUT (2ND SERIES)
MARVEL

❑1, Nov 1999 .... 2.99

JUGHEAD (VOL. 2)
ARCHIE

❑1, Aug 1987 .... 3.00
❑2, Oct 1987 .... 2.00
❑3, Dec 1987 .... 2.00
❑4, Feb 1988 .... 1.50
❑5, Apr 1988 .... 1.50
❑6, Jun 1988 .... 1.50
❑7, Aug 1988 .... 1.50
❑8, Oct 1988 .... 1.50
❑9, Dec 1988 .... 1.50
❑10, Feb 1989 .... 1.50
❑11, Apr 1989 .... 1.50
❑12, Jun 1989 .... 1.50
❑13, Aug 1989 .... 1.50
❑14, Oct 1989 .... 1.50
❑15, Dec 1989 .... 1.50
❑16, Feb 1990 .... 1.50
❑17, Apr 1990 .... 1.50
❑18, Jun 1990 .... 1.50
❑19, Aug 1990 .... 1.50
❑20, Oct 1990 .... 1.50
❑21, Dec 1990 .... 1.50
❑22, Feb 1991 .... 1.50
❑23, Apr 1991 .... 1.50
❑24, Jun 1991 .... 1.50
❑25, Aug 1991 .... 1.50
❑26, Oct 1991 .... 1.50
❑27, Nov 1991 .... 1.50
❑28, Dec 1991 .... 1.50
❑29, Jan 1992 .... 1.50
❑30, Feb 1992 .... 1.50
❑31, Mar 1992 .... 1.50
❑32, Apr 1992 .... 1.50
❑33, May 1992 .... 1.50
❑34, Jun 1992 .... 1.50
❑35, Jul 1992 .... 1.50
❑36, Aug 1992 .... 1.50
❑37, Sep 1992 .... 1.50
❑38, Oct 1992 .... 1.50
❑39, Nov 1992 .... 1.50
❑40, Dec 1992 .... 1.50
❑41, Jan 1993 .... 1.50
❑42, Feb 1993 .... 1.50
❑43, Mar 1993 .... 1.50
❑44, Apr 1993 .... 1.50
❑45, May 1993, Series continued in Archie's Pal Jughead #46 .... 1.50

JUGHEAD AND HIS FRIENDS DIGEST
ARCHIE

❑1, May 2005 .... 2.39
❑2, Jun 2005 .... 2.39
❑3, Aug 2005 .... 2.39
❑4, Sep 2005 .... 2.39
❑5, Jan 2006 .... 2.39

N-MINT

❑6, Nov 2005 .... 2.39
❑7, Feb 2006 .... 2.39
❑8, Mar 2006 .... 2.39
❑9, May 2006 .... 2.39
❑10, Jun 2006 .... 2.39
❑11, Aug 2006 .... 2.39

JUGHEAD AS CAPTAIN HERO
ARCHIE

❑1, Oct 1966 .... 28.00
❑2, Dec 1966 .... 15.00
❑3, Feb 1967 .... 10.00
❑4, Apr 1967 .... 7.00
❑5, Jun 1967 .... 7.00
❑6, Aug 1967 .... 7.00
❑7, Nov 1967 .... 7.00

JUGHEAD'S BABY TALES
ARCHIE

❑1, Spr 1994 .... 2.00
❑2, Win 1994, Continued from Baby Tales #1 .... 2.00

JUGHEAD'S DINER
ARCHIE

❑1, Apr 1990 .... 2.00
❑2, Jun 1990 .... 1.50
❑3, Aug 1990 .... 1.50
❑4, Oct 1990 .... 1.50
❑5, Dec 1990 .... 1.50
❑6, Feb 1991 .... 1.50
❑7, Apr 1991 .... 1.50

JUGHEAD'S DOUBLE DIGEST
ARCHIE

❑1, Oct 1989 .... 6.00
❑2, Jan 1990 .... 4.00
❑3, ca. 1990 .... 4.00
❑4, Aug 1990 .... 4.00
❑5, Nov 1990 .... 4.00
❑6, Feb 1991 .... 3.00
❑7, May 1991 .... 3.00
❑8, Aug 1991 .... 3.00
❑9, Nov 1991 .... 3.00
❑10, Feb 1992, DDC (c) 3.00
❑11, Apr 1992 .... 3.00
❑12, Jul 1992 .... 3.00
❑13, Oct 1992 .... 3.00
❑14, Dec 1992 .... 3.00
❑15, Feb 1993 .... 3.00
❑16, ca. 1993 .... 3.00
❑17, May 1993 .... 3.00
❑18 .... 3.00
❑19 .... 3.00
❑20 .... 3.00
❑21 .... 3.00
❑22, ca. 1993 .... 3.00
❑23 .... 3.00
❑24 .... 3.00
❑25 .... 3.00
❑26, ca. 1994 .... 3.00
❑27, Dec 1994 .... 3.00
❑28, Jan 1995 .... 3.00
❑29, Mar 1995 .... 3.00
❑30, May 1995 .... 3.00
❑31, Jul 1995 .... 2.75
❑32, Sep 1995 .... 2.75

Other grades: Multiply price above by 5/6 for VF/NM • 2/3 for VERY FINE • 1/3 for FINE • 1/5 for VERY GOOD • 1/8 for GOOD

	N-MINT
❑33, Nov 1995	2.75
❑34, Jan 1996	2.75
❑35, Feb 1996	2.75
❑36, Apr 1996	2.75
❑37, Jun 1996	2.75
❑38, Aug 1996	2.75
❑39, Sep 1996	2.75
❑40, Nov 1996, duplicate pages at front	2.75
❑41, Jan 1997	2.75
❑42, Feb 1997	2.75
❑43, Apr 1997	2.75
❑44, Jun 1997	2.75
❑45, Jul 1997	2.75
❑46, Sep 1997	2.79
❑47, Nov 1997	2.79
❑48, Dec 1997	2.79
❑49, Feb 1998	2.79
❑50, Apr 1998	2.79
❑51, Jun 1998	2.79
❑52, Jul 1998	2.79
❑53, Aug 1998	2.79
❑54, Oct 1998	2.79
❑55, Nov 1998, DDC (a)	2.95
❑56, Jan 1999	2.95
❑57, Feb 1999	2.95
❑58, Apr 1999	2.95
❑59, Jun 1999	2.99
❑60, Jul 1999	2.99
❑61, Aug 1999	2.99
❑62, Oct 1999	2.99
❑63, Nov 1999	2.99
❑64, Jan 2000	2.99
❑65, Feb 2000	2.99
❑66, Apr 2000	2.99
❑67, May 2000	2.99
❑68, Jul 2000	3.19
❑69, Aug 2000	3.19
❑70, Oct 2000	3.19
❑71, Nov 2000	3.19
❑72, Jan 2001	3.19
❑73, Feb 2001	3.19
❑74, Mar 2001	3.19
❑75, May 2001	3.29
❑76, Jun 2001	3.29
❑77, Aug 2001	3.29
❑78, Sep 2001	3.29
❑79, Oct 2001	3.29
❑80, Nov 2001	3.59
❑81, Jan 2002	3.59
❑82, Feb 2002	3.59
❑83, Mar 2002	3.59
❑84, May 2002	3.59
❑85, Jun 2002	3.59
❑86, Aug 2002	3.59
❑87, Sep 2002	3.59
❑88, Oct 2002	3.59
❑89, Nov 2002	3.59
❑90, Jan 2003	3.59
❑91, Feb 2003	3.59
❑92, Mar 2003	3.59
❑93, May 2003	3.59
❑94, Jun 2003	3.59
❑95, Aug 2003	3.59
❑96, Sep 2003	3.59
❑97, Oct 2003	3.59
❑98, Dec 2003	3.59
❑99, Jan 2004	3.59
❑100, Mar 2004, AM (a)	3.59
❑101, Apr 2004	3.59
❑102, May 2004	3.59
❑103, Jul 2004	3.59
❑104, Aug 2004	3.59
❑105, Sep 2004	3.59
❑106, Oct 2004	3.59
❑107, Nov 2004	3.59
❑108, Jan 2005	3.59
❑109, Feb 2005	3.59
❑110, Mar 2005	3.59
❑111, Apr 2005	3.59
❑112, May 2005	3.59
❑113 2005	3.59
❑114 2005	3.59
❑115 2005	3.59
❑116 2005	3.59
❑117, Dec 2005	3.59
❑118, Jan 2006	3.59
❑119, Feb 2006	3.59
❑120, May 2006	3.59
❑121, Jun 2006	3.59
❑122, Aug 2006	3.59

JUGHEAD'S JOKES
ARCHIE

	N-MINT
❑1, Aug 1967	60.00
❑2, Oct 1967	35.00
❑3, Jan 1968	25.00
❑4, Mar 1968	18.00
❑5, May 1968	18.00
❑6, Jul 1968	15.00
❑7, Sep 1968	15.00
❑8, Nov 1968	15.00
❑9, Jan 1969, Archie Giant	15.00
❑10, Mar 1969, Archie Giant	15.00
❑11, May 1969, Archie Giant	12.00
❑12, Jul 1969, Archie Giant	12.00
❑13, Sep 1969, Archie Giant	12.00
❑14, Nov 1969, Archie Giant	12.00
❑15, Jan 1970, Archie Giant	12.00
❑16, Mar 1970, Archie Giant	10.00
❑17, May 1970, Archie Giant	10.00
❑18, Jul 1970, Archie Giant	10.00
❑19, Sep 1970, Archie Giant	10.00
❑20, Nov 1970, Archie Giant	10.00
❑21, Jan 1971, Archie Giant	7.00
❑22, Mar 1971, Archie Giant	7.00
❑23, May 1971, Archie Giant	7.00
❑24, Jul 1971, Archie Giant	7.00
❑25, Sep 1971, Archie Giant	7.00
❑26, Oct 1971, Archie Giant	7.00
❑27, Jan 1972, Archie Giant	7.00
❑28, Apr 1972, Archie Giant	7.00
❑29, Jul 1972, Archie Giant	7.00
❑30, Sep 1972, Archie Giant	7.00
❑31, Oct 1972, Archie Giant	5.00
❑32, Jan 1973, Archie Giant	5.00
❑33, Apr 1973, Archie Giant	5.00
❑34, Jul 1973, Archie Giant	5.00
❑35, Sep 1973, Archie Giant	5.00
❑36, Oct 1973, Archie Giant	5.00
❑37, Jan 1974, Archie Giant	5.00
❑38, Apr 1974	5.00
❑39, Jul 1974	5.00
❑40, Sep 1974	5.00
❑41, Oct 1974	4.00
❑42, Jan 1975	4.00
❑43, Apr 1975	4.00
❑44, Jul 1975	4.00
❑45, Sep 1975	4.00
❑46, Oct 1975	4.00
❑47, Jan 1976	4.00
❑48, Apr 1976	4.00
❑49, Jul 1976	4.00
❑50, Sep 1976	4.00
❑51, Oct 1976	4.00
❑52, Jan 1977	4.00
❑53, Apr 1977	4.00
❑54, Jul 1977	4.00
❑55, Sep 1977	4.00
❑56, Oct 1977	4.00
❑57, Jan 1978	4.00
❑58, Apr 1978	4.00
❑59, Jul 1978	4.00
❑60, Sep 1978	4.00
❑61, Oct 1978	3.00
❑62, Jan 1979	3.00
❑63, Apr 1979	3.00
❑64, Jul 1979	3.00
❑65, Sep 1979	3.00
❑66, Oct 1979	3.00
❑67	3.00
❑68	3.00
❑69	3.00
❑70	3.00
❑71	3.00
❑72	3.00
❑73	3.00
❑74	3.00
❑75	3.00
❑76	3.00
❑77	3.00
❑78, Sep 1982	3.00

JUGHEAD'S PAL HOT DOG
ARCHIE

	N-MINT
❑1, Jan 1990	1.00
❑2, Jan 1990	1.00
❑3 1990	1.00
❑4 1990	1.00
❑5 1990	1.00

JUGHEAD'S TIME POLICE
ARCHIE

	N-MINT
❑1, Jul 1990	1.25
❑2, Sep 1990	1.00
❑3, Nov 1990	1.00
❑4, Jan 1991	1.00
❑5, Mar 1991, A: Abe Lincoln	1.00
❑6, May 1991, O: Time Beanie	1.00

JUGHEAD WITH ARCHIE DIGEST MAGAZINE
ARCHIE

	N-MINT
❑1, Mar 1974	12.00
❑2, May 1974	7.00
❑3, Jul 1974	7.00
❑4, Sep 1974	7.00
❑5, Nov 1974	7.00
❑6, Jan 1975	7.00
❑7, Mar 1975	7.00
❑8, May 1975	7.00
❑9, Jul 1975	7.00
❑10, Sep 1975	7.00
❑11, Nov 1975	4.00
❑12, Jan 1976	4.00
❑13, Mar 1976	4.00
❑14, May 1976	4.00
❑15, Jul 1976	4.00
❑16, Sep 1976	4.00
❑17, Nov 1976	4.00
❑18, Jan 1977	4.00
❑19, Mar 1977	4.00
❑20, May 1977	4.00
❑21, Jul 1977	2.50
❑22, Sep 1977	2.50
❑23, Nov 1977	2.50
❑24, Jan 1978	2.50
❑25, Mar 1978	2.50
❑26, May 1978	2.50
❑27, Jul 1978	2.50
❑28, Sep 1978	2.50
❑29, Nov 1978	2.50
❑30, Jan 1979	2.50
❑31, Mar 1979	2.50
❑32, May 1979	2.50
❑33, Jul 1979	2.50
❑34, Sep 1979	2.50
❑35, Nov 1979	2.50
❑36, Jan 1980	2.50
❑37, Mar 1980	2.50
❑38, May 1980	2.50
❑39, Jul 1980	2.50
❑40, Sep 1980	2.50
❑41, Nov 1980	2.50
❑42, Jan 1981, DDC (c)	2.50
❑43, Mar 1981	2.50
❑44, May 1981	2.50
❑45, Jul 1981	2.50
❑46, Sep 1981	2.50
❑47, Nov 1981	2.50
❑48, Jan 1982	2.50
❑49, Mar 1982	2.50
❑50, May 1982	2.50
❑51, Jul 1982	2.00
❑52, Sep 1982	2.00
❑53, Nov 1982	2.00
❑54, Jan 1983	2.00
❑55, Mar 1983	2.00
❑56, May 1983	2.00
❑57, Jul 1983	2.00
❑58, Sep 1983	2.00
❑59, Nov 1983	2.00
❑60, Jan 1984	2.00
❑61, Mar 1984	2.00
❑62, May 1984	2.00
❑63, Jul 1984	2.00
❑64, Sep 1984	2.00
❑65, Nov 1984, DDC (c)	2.00
❑66, Jan 1985	2.00
❑67, Mar 1985	2.00
❑68, May 1985	2.00

Jungle Action (Marvel)

Black Panther takes over with #5

©Marvel

Jungle Book (Gold Key)

Adapts Disney animated Kipling classic

©Gold Key

Jurassic Park

Simonson and Kane adapt Spielberg SF film

©Topps

Just a Pilgrim

Post-apocalyptic bounty hunter story

©Black Bull

Justice (Marvel)

New Universe hero wields energy sword

©Marvel

	N-MINT
❑69, Jul 1985	2.00
❑70, Sep 1985	2.00
❑71, Nov 1985	2.00
❑72, Jan 1986	2.00
❑73, Mar 1986	2.00
❑74, May 1986	2.00
❑75, Jul 1986	2.00
❑76, Sep 1986	2.00
❑77, Nov 1986	2.00
❑78, Jan 1987	2.00
❑79, Mar 1987, DDC (c)	2.00
❑80, May 1987	2.00
❑81, Jul 1987	2.00
❑82, Sep 1987	2.00
❑83, Nov 1987	2.00
❑84, Jan 1988	2.00
❑85, Mar 1988	2.00
❑86, May 1988	2.00
❑87, Jul 1988	2.00
❑88, Sep 1988	2.00
❑89, Nov 1988	2.00
❑90, Jan 1989	2.00
❑91, Mar 1989	2.00
❑92, May 1989	2.00
❑93, Jul 1989	2.00
❑94, Sep 1989	2.00
❑95, Nov 1989	2.00
❑96, Jan 1990	2.00
❑97, Mar 1990	2.00
❑98, May 1990	2.00
❑99, Jul 1990	2.00
❑100, Sep 1990	2.00
❑101, Nov 1990	1.75
❑102, Jan 1991	1.75
❑103, Mar 1991	1.75
❑104, May 1991	1.75
❑105, Jul 1991	1.75
❑106, Sep 1991	1.75
❑107, Nov 1991	1.75
❑108, Jan 1992, DDC (c); GC (a)	1.75
❑109, Feb 1992, DDC (c)	1.75
❑110, Apr 1992	1.75
❑111, Jun 1992	1.75
❑112, Aug 1992	1.75
❑113, Nov 1992	1.75
❑114, Feb 1993	1.75
❑115, May 1993	1.75
❑116, Aug 1993	1.75
❑117, Nov 1993	1.75
❑118, Mar 1994	1.75
❑119, May 1994	1.75
❑120, Aug 1994	1.75
❑121, Nov 1994	1.75
❑122, Jan 1995	1.75
❑123, May 1995	1.75
❑124, Aug 1995	1.75
❑125, Oct 1995	1.75
❑126, Jan 1996	1.75
❑127, ca. 1996	1.75
❑128, Sep 1996	1.79
❑129, Oct 1996	1.79
❑130, Dec 1997	1.79
❑131, Feb 1997	1.79
❑132, Mar 1997	1.79
❑133, May 1997	1.79
❑134, Jul 1997	1.79
❑135, Aug 1997	1.79
❑136, Oct 1997	1.79
❑137, Dec 1997	1.79
❑138, Jan 1998	1.95
❑139, Mar 1998	1.95
❑140, May 1998	1.95
❑141, Jun 1998	1.95
❑142, Aug 1998	1.95
❑143, Oct 1998, DDC (a)	1.95
❑144, Nov 1998	1.95
❑145, Dec 1998	1.95
❑146, Feb 1999	1.95
❑147, Apr 1999	1.95
❑148, May 1999	1.95
❑149, Jun 1999	1.99
❑150, Aug 1999	1.99
❑151, Sep 1999	1.99
❑152, Nov 1999	1.99
❑153, Dec 1999	1.99
❑154, Feb 2000	1.99
❑155, Mar 2000	1.99
❑156, May 2000	1.99
❑157, Jul 2000	2.19
❑158, Aug 2000	2.19
❑159, Sep 2000	2.19
❑160, Nov 2000	2.19
❑161, Dec 2000	2.19
❑162, Jan 2001	2.19
❑163, Feb 2001	2.19
❑164, Mar 2001	2.39
❑165, Jun 2001, Little Archie stories	2.39
❑166, Jul 2001	2.39
❑167, Aug 2001	2.39
❑168, Oct 2001	2.39
❑169, Nov 2001	2.39
❑170, Jan 2002	2.39
❑171, Feb 2002	2.39
❑172, Mar 2002	2.39
❑173, May 2002	2.39
❑174, Jul 2002	2.39
❑175, Aug 2002	2.39
❑176, Sep 2002	2.39
❑177, Nov 2002	2.39
❑178, Dec 2002	2.39
❑179, Jan 2003	2.39
❑180, Mar 2003	2.39
❑181, Apr 2003	2.39
❑182, May 2003	2.39
❑183, Jul 2003	2.39
❑184, Aug 2003	2.39
❑185, Sep 2003, Pop Tate's first name revealed as Leo	2.39
❑186, Oct 2003	2.39
❑187, Dec 2003	2.39
❑188, Jan 2004	2.39
❑189, Feb 2004	2.39
❑190, Apr 2004	2.39
❑191, May 2004	2.39
❑192, Jun 2004	2.39
❑193, Jul 2004	2.39
❑194, Aug 2004	2.39
❑195, Sep 2004	2.39
❑196, Oct 2004	2.39
❑197, Jan 2005	2.39
❑198, Feb 2005	2.39
❑199, Mar 2005	2.39

JUGULAR
BLACK OUT

	N-MINT
❑0	2.95

JUMPER
ZAV

	N-MINT
❑1, b&w	3.00
❑2, b&w	3.00

JUN
DISNEY

	N-MINT
❑1	1.50

JUNCTION 17
ANTARCTIC

	N-MINT
❑1, Aug 2003	3.50
❑2 2003	2.99
❑3 2003	2.99
❑4, Jan 2004	2.99

JUNGLE ACTION (MARVEL)
MARVEL

	N-MINT
❑1, Oct 1972, Reprints	15.00
❑2, Dec 1972, Reprints	7.00
❑3, Feb 1973, Reprints	7.00
❑4, Apr 1973, Reprints	7.00
❑5, Jul 1973, Black Panther begins	35.00
❑6, Sep 1973	12.00
❑7, Nov 1973	8.00
❑8, Jan 1974, RB, KJ (a); O: Black Panther.	15.00
❑9, May 1974, A: Black Panther. Marvel Value Stamp #31 Modok	7.00
❑10, Jul 1974, A: Black Panther. Marvel Value Stamp #38: Red Sonja	6.00
❑11, Sep 1974, A: Black Panther. Marvel Value Stamp #43: Enchantress	6.00
❑12, Nov 1974, A: Black Panther. Marvel Value Stamp #9: Captain Marvel	6.00
❑13, Jan 1975, A: Black Panther. Marvel Value Stamp #33: Invisible Girl	6.00
❑14, Mar 1975, A: Black Panther.	6.00
❑15, May 1975, A: Black Panther.	6.00
❑16, Jul 1975, A: Black Panther.	6.00
❑17, Sep 1975, A: Black Panther.	5.00
❑18, Nov 1975, A: Black Panther.	5.00
❑19, Jan 1976, 1: Baron Macabre. A: . A: Black Panther.	5.00
❑20, Mar 1976, A: Black Panther.	5.00
❑21, May 1976, A: Black Panther.	5.00
❑21/30 cent, May 1976, A: Black Panther. 30 cent regional variant	20.00
❑22, Jul 1976, A: Black Panther.	5.00
❑22/30 cent, Jul 1976, A: Black Panther. 30 cent regional variant	20.00
❑23, Sep 1976, A: Black Panther. reprints Daredevil #69	5.00
❑24, Nov 1976, 1: Wind Eagle. A: Black Panther.	5.00

JUNGLE BOOK (GOLD KEY)
GOLD KEY

	N-MINT
❑1, Mar 1968	25.00

JUNGLE BOOK
DISNEY

❑1/A; saddle-stitched 2.95
❑1/B; squarebound 5.95

JUNGLE BOOK (NBM)
NBM

❑1 .... 16.95

JUNGLE COMICS (A-LIST)
A-LIST

❑1, Spr 1997, gatefold summary; Sheena; Reprints Sheena 3-D special #1 in color 2.95
❑2, Fal 1997, Wambi 2.95
❑3, Win 1997 .... 2.95
❑4, Mar 1998 .... 2.95
❑5, Oct 1998, Sheena 2.95

JUNGLE FANTASY
AVATAR

❑1, Feb 2003 .... 3.50
❑2, Mar 2003 .... 3.50
❑3, Jul 2003 .... 3.50

JUNGLE GIRLS
AC

❑1, Aug 1988, b&w 2.00
❑2 .... 2.25
❑3 .... 2.75
❑4 .... 2.75
❑5 .... 2.75
❑6; MB (a); Reprints 2.95
❑7; MB (a); Reprints 2.95
❑8, b&w 2.95
❑9, b&w 2.95
❑10, ca. 1992, b&w 2.95
❑11, ca. 1992, b&w 2.95
❑12, b&w 2.95
❑13, ca. 1993, b&w 2.95
❑14, ca. 1993, b&w 2.95
❑15, ca. 1993, b&w 2.95
❑16, b&w 2.95

JUNGLE GIRLS! (ETERNITY)
ETERNITY

❑8 .... 2.95
❑Book 1, b&w; Reprints 9.95

JUNGLE JIM (KING)
KING

❑5, Dec 1967 .... 9.00

JUNGLE JIM (CHARLTON)
CHARLTON

❑22, Feb 1969, Series continued from Jungle Jim (Dell) 24.00
❑23, Apr 1969 .... 18.00
❑24, Jun 1969 .... 18.00
❑25, Aug 1969 .... 16.00
❑26, Oct 1969 .... 16.00
❑27, Dec 1969 .... 16.00
❑28, Feb 1970 .... 16.00

JUNGLE JIM (AVALON)
AVALON

❑1; published in 1998, indicia says 1995 .... 2.95

JUNGLE LOVE
AIRCEL

❑1, b&w 2.95
❑2, b&w 2.95
❑3, b&w 2.95

JUNGLE TALES OF CAVEWOMAN
BASEMENT

❑1 .... 2.95

JUNGLE TALES OF TARZAN
CHARLTON

❑1, Jan 1965 .... 45.00
❑2, Mar 1965 .... 35.00
❑3, May 1965 .... 35.00
❑4, Jul 1965 .... 35.00

JUNGLE TWINS
GOLD KEY

❑1, Apr 1972 .... 10.00
❑2, Jul 1972 .... 7.00
❑3, Oct 1972 .... 4.00
❑4, Jan 1972 .... 4.00
❑5, Apr 1972 .... 4.00
❑6, Jul 1973 .... 3.00
❑7, Oct 1973 .... 3.00
❑8, Jan 1974 .... 3.00
❑9, Apr 1974 .... 3.00
❑10, Jul 1974 .... 3.00
❑11, Oct 1974 .... 3.00
❑12, Jan 1975 .... 3.00
❑13, Mar 1975 .... 3.00
❑14, May 1975 .... 3.00
❑15, Jul 1975 .... 3.00
❑16, Sep 1975 .... 3.00
❑17, Nov 1975 .... 3.00
❑18, ca. 1982 .... 2.00

JUNIOR CARROT PATROL
DARK HORSE

❑1, May 1989, b&w; Flaming Carrot stories 2.00
❑2, ca. 1989 .... 2.00

JUNIOR JACKALOPE
NEVADA CITY

❑1, b&w 1.50
❑2, b&w 1.50

JUNIOR WOODCHUCKS (WALT DISNEY'S...)
DISNEY

❑1, Jul 1991, Reprints 1.50
❑2, Aug 1991 .... 1.50
❑3, Sep 1991 .... 1.50
❑4, Oct 1991 .... 1.50

JUNK CULTURE
DC / VERTIGO

❑1, Jul 1997 .... 2.50
❑2, Aug 1997 .... 2.50

JUNKER
FLEETWAY-QUALITY

❑1 .... 2.95
❑2 .... 2.95
❑3 .... 2.95
❑4 .... 2.95

JUNKFOOD NOIR
OKTOBER BLACK

❑1, Jun 1996, b&w 1.95

JUNK FORCE
COMICSONE

❑1, Jan 2004 .... 9.95

JUNKYARD ENFORCER
BOXCAR

❑1, Aug 1998, b&w 2.95

JUPITER
SANDBERG

❑1 .... 2.95
❑2 .... 2.95
❑3 .... 2.95

JURASSIC LARK DELUXE EDITION
PARODY

❑1, b&w 2.95

JURASSIC PARK
TOPPS

❑0, Nov 1993; GK (a); Polybagged with trade paperback; Flip book with two prequels to the movie 2.95
❑0/Direct ed., Nov 1993; GP (c); GK (a); trading cards (came packed with trade paperback) 3.00
❑1, Jun 1993 DC (c); GK (a) 3.00
❑1/Direct ed., Jun 1993; DC (c); GK (a); trading cards 3.00
❑2, Jul 1993 GK (a) 3.00
❑2/Direct ed., Jul 1993; GK (a); trading cards 3.00
❑3, Jul 1993 GK (a) 3.00
❑3/Direct ed., Jul 1993; GK (a); trading cards 3.00
❑4, Aug 1993 GK (a) 3.00
❑4/Direct ed., Aug 1993; GK (a); hologram card 3.00

JURASSIC PARK ADVENTURES
TOPPS

❑1, Jun 1994 .... 2.00
❑2, ca. 1994 .... 2.00
❑3, ca. 1994 .... 2.00
❑4, ca. 1994 .... 2.00
❑5, ca. 1994 .... 2.00
❑6, ca. 1994 .... 2.00
❑7, ca. 1994 .... 2.00
❑8, Dec 1994 .... 2.00
❑9 .... 2.00
❑10 .... 2.00

JURASSIC PARK: RAPTOR
TOPPS

❑1, Nov 1993; Zorro #0 .... 2.95
❑2, Dec 1993; cards 2.95

JURASSIC PARK: RAPTORS ATTACK
TOPPS

❑1, Mar 1994 .... 2.50
❑2, Apr 1994 .... 2.50
❑3, May 1994 .... 2.50
❑4, Jun 1994 .... 2.50

JURASSIC PARK: RAPTORS HIJACK
TOPPS

❑1 .... 2.50
❑2 .... 2.50
❑3 .... 2.50
❑4 .... 2.50

JUST A PILGRIM
BLACK BULL

❑1, May 2001 .... 4.00
❑2, Jun 2001 .... 2.99
❑3, Jul 2001 .... 2.99
❑4, Aug 2001 .... 2.99
❑5, Sep 2001 .... 2.99

JUSTICE (MARVEL)
MARVEL

❑1, Nov 1986 1: Justice 1.25
❑2, Dec 1986 .... 1.00
❑3, Jan 1987 .... 1.00
❑4, Feb 1987 .... 1.00
❑5, Mar 1987 .... 1.00
❑6, Apr 1987 .... 1.00
❑7, May 1987 .... 1.00
❑8, Jun 1987 .... 1.00
❑9, Jul 1987 .... 1.00
❑10, Aug 1987 .... 1.00
❑11, Sep 1987 .... 1.00
❑12, Oct 1987 .... 1.00
❑13, Nov 1987 .... 1.00
❑14, Dec 1987 .... 1.00
❑15, Jan 1988 .... 1.00
❑16, Feb 1988 .... 1.00
❑17, Mar 1988 .... 1.00
❑18, Apr 1988 .... 1.25
❑19, May 1988 .... 1.25
❑20, Jun 1988 .... 1.25
❑21, Jul 1988 .... 1.25
❑22, Aug 1988 .... 1.25
❑23, Sep 1988 .... 1.25
❑24, Oct 1988 .... 1.25
❑25, Nov 1988 .... 1.25
❑26, Dec 1988 .... 1.50
❑27, Jan 1989 .... 1.50
❑28, Feb 1989 .... 1.50
❑29, Mar 1989 .... 1.50
❑30, Apr 1989, PD (w); A: Psi-Force. . 1.50
❑31, May 1989 .... 1.50
❑32, Jun 1989 .... 1.50

JUSTICE (ANTARCTIC)
ANTARCTIC

❑1, May 1994, b&w 3.50

JUSTICE BRIGADE
TCB COMICS

❑1, b&w 1.50
❑2, b&w 1.50
❑3, b&w 1.50
❑4, b&w 1.50
❑5, b&w 1.50
❑6, b&w 1.50
❑7, b&w 1.50
❑8, b&w 1.50

JUSTICE (DC)
DC

❑1/Heroes, Sep 2005 .... 5.00
❑1/Villains, Sep 2005 .... 4.00
❑2, Dec 2005 .... 4.00
❑3, Feb 2006 .... 4.00
❑4, Apr 2006 .... 4.00
❑5, Jun 2006 .... 4.00
❑6, Sep 2006 .... 4.00

JUSTICE: FOUR BALANCE
MARVEL

❑1, Sep 1994 .... 1.75
❑2, Oct 1994 .... 1.75
❑3, Nov 1994 .... 1.75
❑4, Dec 1994 .... 1.75

Justice, Inc.

Pulp adventurer comes t o comics

©DC

Justice League

Bwah-ha-ha adventures begin

©DC

Justice League America

From Justice League to JL International to ...

©DC

Justice League Europe

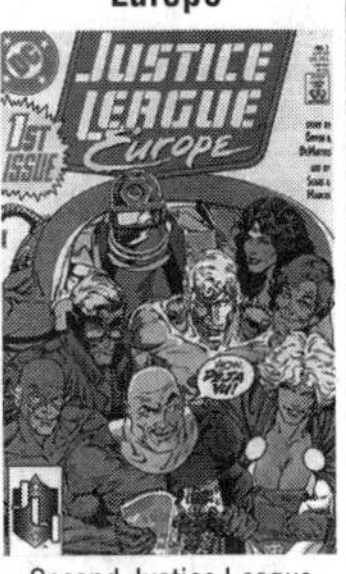

Second Justice League team big in France

©DC

Justice League of America

Silver Age DC heroes formed super-team

©DC

N-MINT

JUSTICE, INC.
DC

❑1, Jun 1975; O: The Avenger. adapts Justice Inc. novel 3.00
❑2, Aug 1975; JK (a); adapts The Skywalker 2.00
❑3, Oct 1975 JK (a); 1: Fergus MacMurdie 2.00
❑4, Dec 1975 JKu (c); JK (a) 2.00

JUSTICE, INC. (MINI-SERIES)
DC

❑1 1989; prestige format O: The Avenger 4.00
❑2 1989; prestige format 4.00

JUSTICE LEAGUE
DC

❑1, May 1987 1: Maxwell Lord. 6.00
❑2, Jun 1987 1: Silver Sorceress. 1: Bluejay. 1: Wandjina 2.50
❑3, Jul 1987 V: Rocket Reds. 2.50
❑3/Ltd., Jul 1987; Superman logo on cover (limited edition); alternate cover 10.00
❑4, Aug 1987; V: Royal Flush Gang. Booster Gold joins team 2.50
❑5, Sep 1987; Batman vs. Guy Gardner 2.00
❑6, Oct 1987; KG (w); KG (a); Series continues in Justice League International #7 ..... 2.00
❑Annual 1, ca. 1987, b&w; numbering continues with Justice League International Annual #2 ..... 3.00

JUSTICE LEAGUE ADVENTURES
DC

❑1, Jan 2002 ..... 2.50
❑2, Feb 2002 ..... 2.00
❑3, Mar 2002 ..... 2.00
❑4, Apr 2002 ..... 2.00
❑5, May 2002 ..... 2.00
❑6, Jun 2002 ..... 2.00
❑7, Jul 2002 ..... 2.00
❑8, Aug 2002 ..... 2.00
❑9, Sep 2002 ..... 2.00
❑10, Oct 2002 ..... 2.25
❑11, Nov 2002 ..... 2.25
❑12, Dec 2002 ..... 2.25
❑13, Jan 2003 ..... 2.25
❑14, Feb 2003 ..... 2.25
❑15, Mar 2003 ..... 2.25
❑16, Apr 2003 ..... 2.25
❑17, May 2003 ..... 2.25
❑18, Jun 2003 ..... 2.25
❑19, Jul 2003 ..... 2.25
❑20, Aug 2003 ..... 2.25
❑21, Sep 2003 ..... 2.25
❑22, Oct 2003 ..... 2.25
❑23, Nov 2003 ..... 2.25
❑24, Dec 2003 ..... 2.25
❑25, Jan 2004 ..... 2.25
❑26, Feb 2004 ..... 2.25
❑27, Mar 2004 ..... 2.25
❑28, Apr 2004 ..... 2.25
❑29, May 2004 ..... 2.25
❑30, Jun 2004 ..... 2.25
❑31, Jul 2004 ..... 2.25

N-MINT

❑32, Aug 2004 ..... 2.25
❑33, Sep 2004 ..... 2.25
❑34, Oct 2004 ..... 2.25

JUSTICE LEAGUE AMERICA
DC

❑0, Oct 1994; New team begins: Wonder Woman, Flash III (Wally West), Fire, Metamorpho, Crimson Fox, Hawkman, Obsidian, Nuklon 2.00
❑26, May 1989; A: Huntress. Continued from Justice League International 1.75
❑27, Jun 1989; Exorcist homage cover 1.75
❑28, Jul 1989 ..... 1.75
❑29, Aug 1989 ..... 1.75
❑30, Sep 1989 ..... 1.75
❑31, Oct 1989 A: Justice League Europe 1.75
❑32, Nov 1989 A: Justice League Europe 1.75
❑33, Dec 1989 A: Kilowog 1.75
❑34, Jan 1990 ..... 1.75
❑35, Feb 1990 ..... 1.75
❑36, Mar 1990 1: Mr. Nebula. 1: Scarlet Skier. A: G'Nort 1.75
❑37, Apr 1990 ..... 1.75
❑38, May 1990 V: Despero 1.75
❑39, Jun 1990 V: Despero 1.75
❑40, Jul 1990 V: Despero 1.75
❑41, Aug 1990 ..... 1.75
❑42, Sep 1990; membership drive; Return of Mr. Miracle; Orion joins team; Lightray joins team 1.75
❑43, Oct 1990 ..... 1.75
❑44, Nov 1990 ..... 1.75
❑45, Jan 1991 ..... 1.75
❑46, Jan 1991; 1: General Glory. Medley art begins 1.75
❑47, Feb 1991 ..... 1.75
❑48, Mar 1991 ..... 1.75
❑49, Apr 1991 ..... 1.75
❑50, May 1991; Double-size 1.75
❑51, Jun 1991 ..... 1.25
❑52, Jul 1991; Guy Gardner vs. Blue Beetle 1.25
❑53, Aug 1991 ..... 1.25
❑54, Sep 1991 ..... 1.25
❑55, Oct 1991 V: Global Guardians. 1.25
❑56, Nov 1991; back to Happy Harbor 1.25
❑57, Dec 1991 V: Extremists 1.25
❑58, Jan 1992 A: Lobo. V: Lobo. V: Despero 1.25
❑59, Feb 1992 ..... 1.25
❑60, Mar 1992 ..... 1.25
❑61, Apr 1992; 1: Bloodwynd. V: Weapons Master. new JLA 1.25
❑62, May 1992 BG (a); V: Weapons Master 1.25
❑63, Jun 1992; Bloodwynd joins team; Guy Gardner leaves team 1.25
❑64, Jul 1992 V: Starbreaker 1.25
❑65, Aug 1992 V: Starbreaker. 1.25
❑66, Sep 1992; Guy returns 1.25
❑67, Oct 1992 ..... 1.25
❑68, Nov 1992 ..... 1.25
❑69, Dec 1992; Doomsday 3.00
❑69/2nd, Dec 1992 ..... 1.75

N-MINT

❑70, Jan 1993; cover wrapper 2.00
❑70/2nd, Jan 1993; cover wrapper; Funeral for a Friend 1.75
❑71, Feb 1993; black cover wrapper; Wonder Woman joins team; Ray joins team; Agent Liberty joins team; Black Condor joins team 2.00
❑71/Variant, Feb 1993; New team begins; Split cover 2.00
❑72, Mar 1993 V: Doctor Destiny. 1.50
❑73, Apr 1993 V: Doctor Destiny. 1.50
❑74, May 1993 V: Doctor Destiny. 1.50
❑75, Jun 1993 V: Doctor Destiny. 1.50
❑76, Jul 1993 ..... 1.50
❑77, Jul 1993 ..... 1.50
❑78, Aug 1993 RT (a); A: Jay Garrick. 1.50
❑79, Aug 1993 V: new Extremists. 1.50
❑80, Sep 1993; Booster gets new armor 1.50
❑81, Oct 1993; Ray vs. Captain Atom. 1.50
❑82, Nov 1993 ..... 1.50
❑83, Dec 1993 ..... 1.50
❑84, Jan 1994 ..... 1.50
❑85, Feb 1994 ..... 1.50
❑86, Mar 1994 ..... 1.50
❑87, Apr 1994 ..... 1.50
❑88, May 1994 ..... 1.50
❑89, Jun 1994 ..... 1.50
❑90, Jul 1994 ..... 1.50
❑91, Aug 1994; Funeral of Ice 1.50
❑92, Sep 1994; A: Triumph. Zero Hour 1.50
❑93, Nov 1994 ..... 1.50
❑94, Dec 1994 ..... 1.50
❑95, Jan 1995 ..... 1.50
❑96, Feb 1995 ..... 1.50
❑97, Mar 1995 ..... 1.50
❑98, Apr 1995 ..... 1.50
❑99, May 1995 ..... 1.50
❑100, Jun 1995; Giant-size anniversary edition 2.95
❑100/Variant; Giant-size anniversary edition; Holo-grafix cover 3.95
❑101, Jul 1995 ..... 1.75
❑102, Aug 1995 ..... 1.75
❑103, Sep 1995 ..... 1.75
❑104, Oct 1995 ..... 1.75
❑105, Nov 1995 ..... 1.75
❑106, Dec 1995; Underworld Unleashed 1.75
❑107, Jan 1996 ..... 1.75
❑108, Feb 1996 1: Equinox 1.75
❑109, Mar 1996 A: Equinox 1.75
❑110, Apr 1996 A: El Diablo. 1.75
❑111, Jun 1996 ..... 1.75
❑112, Jul 1996 ..... 1.75
❑113, Aug 1996 ..... 1.75
❑Annual 4, ca. 1990; Justice League Antarctica 3.00
❑Annual 5, ca. 1989; Armageddon 2001 ..... 3.00
❑Annual 5/2nd, ca. 1990; Silver ink cover 2.50
❑Annual 6, ca. 1991; DC (a); Eclipso 2.50
❑Annual 7, ca. 1992; 1: Terrorsmith. Bloodlines 2.50
❑Annual 8, ca. 1993; Elseworlds 2.95

	N-MINT
❑Annual 9, ca. 1994; Year One	3.50
❑Annual 10, ca. 1996; Legends of the Dead Earth; events continue in Ray #26; 1996	2.95
❑Special 1, ca. 1990	1.50
❑Special 2, ca. 1991	2.95
❑SP 1/A, ca. 1992; Double-size; Justice League Spectacular; Green Lantern on cover	2.00
❑SP 1/B, ca. 1992; Double-size; Justice League Spectacular; Superman on cover	2.00

JUSTICE LEAGUE: A MIDSUMMER'S NIGHTMARE
DC

	N-MINT
❑1, Sep 1996; forms triptych with other two issues	2.95
❑2, Oct 1996; forms triptych with other two issues	2.95
❑3, Nov 1996; forms triptych with other two issues	2.95

JUSTICE LEAGUE ELITE
DC

	N-MINT
❑1, Sep 2004	4.00
❑2, Oct 2004	2.50
❑3, Nov 2004	2.50
❑4, Dec 2004	2.50
❑5, Jan 2005	2.50
❑6, Feb 2005	2.50
❑7, Mar 2005	2.50
❑8, Apr 2005	2.50
❑9, May 2005	2.50
❑10, Jun 2005	2.50
❑11, Jun 2005	2.50

JUSTICE LEAGUE EUROPE
DC

	N-MINT
❑1, Apr 1989 KG (w); KG (a); 1: Catherine Cobert.	2.00
❑2, May 1989	1.50
❑3, Jun 1989	1.50
❑4, Jul 1989 V: Queen Bee.	1.50
❑5, Aug 1989 A: Sapphire, Java.	1.50
❑6, Sep 1989 1: Crimson Fox.	1.50
❑7, Oct 1989 A: Justice League America.	1.50
❑8, Nov 1989 A: Justice League America.	1.50
❑9, Dec 1989 A: Superman.	1.50
❑10, Jan 1990	1.50
❑11, Feb 1990; Guy Gardner vs. Metamorpho	1.50
❑12, Mar 1990	1.50
❑13, Apr 1990	1.50
❑14, May 1990	1.50
❑15, Jun 1990 1: Extremists.	1.50
❑16, Jun 1990 V: Extremists.	1.50
❑17, Aug 1990 V: Extremists.	1.50
❑18, Sep 1990 V: Extremists.	1.50
❑19, Oct 1990 V: Extremists.	1.50
❑20, Nov 1990	1.50
❑21, Dec 1990	1.25
❑22, Jan 1991	1.25
❑23, Feb 1991	1.25
❑24, Mar 1991	1.25
❑25, Apr 1991	1.25
❑26, May 1991	1.25
❑27, Jun 1991	1.25
❑28, Jul 1991	1.25
❑29, Aug 1991	1.25
❑30, Sep 1991 V: Jack O'Lantern.	1.25
❑31, Oct 1991; evicted from JLI Embassy	1.25
❑32, Nov 1991	1.25
❑33, Dec 1991 A: Lobo. V: Lobo. V: Despero.	1.25
❑34, Jan 1992 A: Lobo. V: Lobo. V: Despero.	1.25
❑35, Feb 1992 V: Extremists.	1.25
❑36, Mar 1992	1.25
❑37, Apr 1992; new team	1.25
❑38, May 1992	1.25
❑39, Jun 1992	1.25
❑40, Jul 1992	1.25
❑41, Aug 1992	1.25
❑42, Sep 1992; Wonder Woman joins team	1.25
❑43, Oct 1992	1.25
❑44, Oct 1992	1.25
❑45, Dec 1992	1.25
❑46, Jan 1993	1.25
❑47, Feb 1993	1.25
❑48, Mar 1993 A: Justice Society of America.	1.25
❑49, Apr 1993	1.25
❑50, May 1993; Giant-size; A: Justice Society of America. V: Sonar. Series continues as Justice League International	2.50
❑Annual 1 A: Global Guardians.	2.00
❑Annual 2 A: Demon. A: Elongated Man. A: Anthro. A: Bat Lash. A: Hex. A: General Glory. A: Legion.	2.00
❑Annual 3; Eclipso; numbering continues as Justice League International Annual	2.50

JUSTICE LEAGUE INTERNATIONAL
DC

	N-MINT
❑7, Nov 1987; Title changes to Justice League International; Captain Marvel leaves team; Captain Atom joins team; Rocket Red joins team	2.00
❑8, Dec 1987	1.50
❑9, Jan 1988; Millennium	1.50
❑10, Feb 1988; 1: G'Nort. Millennium	1.50
❑11, Mar 1988	1.25
❑12, Apr 1988	1.25
❑13, May 1988 A: Suicide Squad.	1.25
❑14, Jun 1988	1.25
❑15, Jul 1988 1: Manga Khan. 1: L-Ron.	1.25
❑16, Aug 1988	1.25
❑17, Sep 1988	1.25
❑18, Oct 1988; A: Lobo. Bonus Book.	1.25
❑19, Nov 1988 A: Lobo.	1.25
❑20, Dec 1988 A: Lobo.	1.25
❑21; A: Lobo. no month of publication	1.25
❑22; Invasion!; no month of publication; Oberon solo story	1.25
❑23, Jan 1989; 1: Injustice League. V: Injustice League. Invasion!	1.25
❑24, Feb 1989; Giant-size; 1: JL Europe. Bonus Book	2.00
❑25, Apr 1989; becomes Justice League America	1.25
❑51, Jun 1993; was Justice League Europe	1.25
❑52, Jul 1993	1.25
❑53, Aug 1993	1.25
❑54, Sep 1993	1.25
❑55, Sep 1993	1.25
❑56, Oct 1993	1.25
❑57, Oct 1993	1.25
❑58, Nov 1993	1.25
❑59, Dec 1993	1.50
❑60, Jan 1994	1.50
❑61, Feb 1994	1.50
❑62, Mar 1994	1.50
❑63, Apr 1994	1.50
❑64, May 1994	1.50
❑65, Jun 1994	1.50
❑66, Jul 1994	1.50
❑67, Aug 1994	1.50
❑68, Sep 1994; A: Triumph. Zero Hour	1.50
❑Annual 2, ca. 1988; A: Joker. V: Joker. numbering continued from Justice League Annual #1	3.00
❑Annual 3, ca. 1989	3.00
❑Annual 4, ca. 1990 1: Lionheart.	2.50
❑Annual 5, ca. 1991; Elseworlds	2.95
❑Special 1; KG (w); KG (a); Mr. Miracle	1.50
❑Special 2; Huntress	2.95

JUSTICE LEAGUE OF AMERICA
DC

	N-MINT
❑1, Nov 1960; O: Despero. 1: Despero. Membership consists of Flash, Wonder Woman, J'onn J'onzz, Green Lantern, Superman, Batman and Aquaman	5000.00
❑2, Jan 1961 A: Merlin.	1250.00
❑3, Mar 1961 O: Kanjar Ro. 1: Kanjar Ro. 1: Hyathis.	1000.00
❑4, May 1961; Green Arrow joins team; Snapper Carr	700.00
❑5, Jul 1961 O: Doctor Destiny. 1: Doctor Destiny.	600.00
❑6, Sep 1961 1: Professor Amos Fortune.	400.00
❑7, Nov 1961	400.00
❑8, Jan 1962	400.00
❑9, Feb 1962, O: Justice League of America.	1000.00
❑10, Mar 1962, 1: Lord of Time. 1: Felix Faust.	400.00
❑11, May 1962	250.00
❑12, Jun 1962, O: Doctor Light I (Dr. Arthur Light). 1: Doctor Light I (Dr. Arthur Light).	250.00
❑13, Aug 1962	250.00
❑14, Sep 1962, Atom joins Justice League of America	250.00
❑15, Nov 1962	250.00
❑16, Dec 1962	225.00
❑17, Feb 1963, 1: Tornado Champion (Red Tornado)	225.00
❑18, Mar 1963	225.00
❑19, May 1963	225.00
❑20, Jun 1963	225.00
❑21, Aug 1963, 1: Earth-2 (named). Return of Justice Society of America; Justice League of America teams up with Justice Society of America	350.00
❑22, Sep 1963, Return of Justice Society of America; Justice League of America teams up with Justice Society of America	325.00
❑23, Nov 1963, 1: Queen Bee.	150.00
❑24, Dec 1963	150.00
❑25, Feb 1964	150.00
❑26, Mar 1964	150.00
❑27, May 1964	150.00
❑28, Jun 1964	150.00
❑29, Aug 1964, O: Crime Syndicate. 1: Earth-3. 1: Crime Syndicate. A: Justice Society of America.	150.00
❑30, Sep 1964, Justice League of America teams up with Justice Society of America against the Crime Syndicate of America	150.00
❑31, Nov 1964, Hawkman joins team.	100.00
❑32, Dec 1964, O: Brainstorm. 1: Brainstorm. V: Brain Storm	90.00
❑33, Feb 1965	90.00
❑34, Mar 1965, A: Joker. V: Doctor Destiny. V: Dr. Destiny	75.00
❑35, May 1965	75.00
❑36, Jun 1965	75.00
❑37, Aug 1965, 1: Earth-A. A: Justice Society of America.	125.00
❑38, Sep 1965, A: Justice Society of America.	125.00
❑39, Nov 1965; 80 page giant (#16); aka 80 Page Giant #G-16 (continuation of 80 Page Giant series' numbering as production codes); reprints Brave and the Bold #28, 30, and Justice League of America #5	125.00
❑40, Nov 1965, social issue	75.00
❑41, Dec 1965, MA (c); MA (a); 1: The Key. V: Key.	75.00
❑42, Feb 1966, MA (c); MA (a); A: Metamorpho.	60.00
❑43, Mar 1966, MA (c); MA (a); 1: Royal Flush Gang.	60.00
❑44, May 1966, MA (c); MA (a)	60.00
❑45, Jun 1966, MA (c); MA (a); 1: Shaggy Man. V: Shaggy Man.	60.00
❑46, Aug 1966, 1: Sandman I (in Silver Age). A: Justice Society of America. V: Solomon Grundy, Blockbuster.	110.00
❑47, Sep 1966, A: Justice Society of America. V: Anti-Matter Man.	95.00
❑48, Oct 1966; MA (c); MA (a); aka 80 Page Giant #G-29; reprints	140.00
❑49, Nov 1966, MA (c); MA (a)	60.00
❑50, Dec 1966, MA (c); MA (a)	60.00
❑51, Feb 1967, A: Elongated Man.	60.00
❑52, Mar 1967	60.00
❑53, May 1967	55.00
❑54, Jun 1967	55.00
❑55, Aug 1967, Justice League of America teams up with Justice Society of America	115.00
❑56, Sep 1967, Justice League of America teams up with Justice Society of America	100.00
❑57, Nov 1967	55.00
❑58, Dec 1967; Giant-size; aka 80 Page Giant #G-41	55.00
❑59, Dec 1968	55.00
❑60, Feb 1968	55.00
❑61, Mar 1968	55.00

Other grades: Multiply price above by 5/6 for VF/NM • 2/3 for VERY FINE • 1/3 for FINE • 1/5 for VERY GOOD • 1/8 for GOOD

	N-MINT
❑62, May 1968	55.00
❑63, Jun 1968	45.00
❑64, Aug 1968, DD (a); A: Justice Society of America. Return of Red Tornado	45.00
❑65, Sep 1968, DD (a); V: T.O.Morrow. Justice League of America teams up with Justice Society of America	45.00
❑66, Nov 1968, DD (a)	45.00
❑67, Dec 1968; DD (a); aka 80 Page Giant #G-53; reprints	60.00
❑68, Jan 1969, DD (a)	50.00
❑69, Feb 1969, DD (a); Wonder Woman leaves Justice League of America	45.00
❑70, Mar 1969, DD (a); A: Creeper.	45.00
❑71, May 1969, DD (a); 1: Blue Jay. Martian Manhunter leaves Justice League of America	45.00
❑72, Jun 1969, DD (a)	45.00
❑73, Aug 1969, DD (a); A: Justice Society of America.	35.00
❑74, Sep 1969, DD (a); A: Justice Society. D: Larry Lance. Black Canary goes to Earth-1	35.00
❑75, Nov 1969, DD (a); 1: Black Canary II (Dinah Lance).	35.00
❑76, Dec 1969; MA, DD (a); aka Giant #G-65; reprints #7 and #12; pin-ups of Justice Society of America and Seven Soldiers	35.00
❑77, Dec 1969, DD (a)	35.00
❑78, Feb 1970, DD (a)	35.00
❑79, Mar 1970, DD (a)	35.00
❑80, May 1970, DD (a)	35.00
❑81, Jun 1970, DD (a)	35.00
❑82, Aug 1970, DD (a)	45.00
❑83, Sep 1970, DD (a); A: Spectre.	30.00
❑84, Nov 1970, DD (a)	30.00
❑85, Dec 1970; Giant-size; aka Giant #G-77; reprints	40.00
❑86, Dec 1970, DD (a)	25.00
❑87, Feb 1971, DD (a); 1: Silver Sorceress.	25.00
❑88, Mar 1971, DD (a)	25.00
❑89, May 1971, DD (a)	25.00
❑90, Jun 1971, DD (a)	25.00
❑91, Aug 1971 DD (a)	35.00
❑92, Sep 1971 DD (a); 1: Starbreaker.	32.00
❑93, Nov 1971, Giant-size; aka Giant #G-89; reprints	25.00
❑94, Nov 1971; NA, DD (a); O: Sandman I (Wesley Dodds). 1: Merlyn. A: Deadman. Reprints Adventure Comics #40	60.00
❑95, Dec 1971; DD (a); O: Doctor Midnight. O: Doctor Fate. Reprints More Fun Comics #67 and All-American Comics #25	20.00
❑96, Feb 1972 DD (a); V: Cosmic Vampire.	20.00
❑97, Mar 1972 DD (a); O: Justice League of America.	20.00
❑98, May 1972 DD (a); A: Sargon.	20.00
❑99, Jun 1972 DD (a); A: Sargon.	20.00
❑100, Aug 1972, DD (a); Return of Seven Soldiers of Victory	65.00
❑101, Sep 1972, DD (a); Justice League of America teams up with Justice Society of America	20.00
❑102, Oct 1972, DD (a); D: Red Tornado. Justice League of America teams up with Justice Society of America	20.00
❑103, Dec 1972, DG, DD (a); A: Phantom Stranger	20.00
❑104, Feb 1973, DG, DD (a); V: Hector Hammond. V: Shaggy Man.	20.00
❑105, May 1973, DG, DD (a); Elongated Man joins the Justice League of America	20.00
❑106, Aug 1973, DG, DD (a); Red Tornado (new) joins the Justice League of America	20.00
❑107, Oct 1973, DG, DD (a); 1: Freedom Fighters. 1: Earth-X. A: Justice Society of America.	25.00
❑108, Dec 1973, DG, DD (a); A: Justice Society of America. A: Freedom Fighters.	25.00
❑109, Feb 1974, DG, DD (a); Hawkman resigns from Justice League of America	20.00
❑110, Apr 1974, DG, DD (a); Justice Society of America pin-up	25.00
❑111, Jun 1974, DG, DD (a); V: Libra.	25.00
❑112, Aug 1974, DG, DD (a); V: Amazo.	25.00
❑113, Oct 1974, DG, DD (a)	25.00
❑114, Dec 1974, DG, DD (a); V: Anakronus. Return of Snapper Carr	25.00
❑115, Feb 1975, DG, DD (a)	25.00
❑116, Mar 1975, DG, DD (a); V: Matter Master. Return of Hawkman	25.00
❑117, Apr 1975; FMc, DD (a); Hawkman rejoins JLA	15.00
❑118, May 1975 FMc, DD (a)	15.00
❑119, Jun 1975 FMc, DD (a)	15.00
❑120, Jul 1975 FMc, DD (a); A: Adam Strange. V: Kanjar Ro.	15.00
❑121, Aug 1975 FMc, DD (a)	15.00
❑122, Sep 1975 FMc, DD (a); V: Doctor Light. V: Dr. Light.	15.00
❑123, Oct 1975 FMc, DD (a); 1: Earth-Prime (named). A: Justice Society of America.	15.00
❑124, Nov 1975 FMc, DD (a); A: Justice Society of America.	15.00
❑125, Dec 1975 FMc, DD (a)	15.00
❑126, Jan 1976; FMc, DD (a); Joker	10.00
❑127, Feb 1976 FMc, DD (a)	10.00
❑128, Mar 1976; FMc, DD (a); Wonder Woman rejoins	10.00
❑129, Apr 1976, FMc, DD (a); D: Red Tornado (new).	10.00
❑130, May 1976, FMc, DD (a)	10.00
❑131, Jun 1976, FMc, DD (a)	10.00
❑132, Jul 1976, FMc, DD (a); Bicentennial #6	10.00
❑133, Aug 1976, FMc, DD (a)	10.00
❑134, Sep 1976, FMc, DD (a)	10.00
❑135, Oct 1976, FMc, DD (a); 1: Earth-S (named).	10.00
❑136, Nov 1976, FMc, DD (a)	10.00
❑137, Dec 1976, FMc, DD (a); A: Marvel Family. Superman vs. Captain Marvel (Golden Age)	20.00
❑138, Jan 1977, double-sized FMc, DD (a)	7.00
❑139, Feb 1977, double-sized FMc, DD (a)	7.00
❑140, Mar 1977, double-sized FMc, DD (a); A: Manhunters	7.00
❑141, Apr 1977, double-sized FMc, DD (a); A: Manhunters	7.00
❑142, May 1977, double-sized FMc, DD (a); 1: The Construct	7.00
❑143, Jun 1977, double-sized FMc, DD (a); 1: Privateer.	7.00
❑144, Jul 1977, double-sized FMc, DD (a); O: Justice League of America	7.00
❑145, Aug 1977, FMc, DD (a)	7.00
❑146, Sep 1977, FMc, DD (a)	7.00
❑147, Oct 1977, FMc, DD (a); A: Legion. V: Mordru.	7.00
❑148, Nov 1977, FMc, DD (a); A: Legion. V: Mordru.	7.00
❑149, Dec 1977, FMc, DD (a); 1: Star-Tsar.	7.00
❑150, Jan 1978, FMc, DD (a); V: Key.	7.00
❑151, Feb 1978, FMc, DD (a)	5.00
❑152, Mar 1978, FMc, DD (a)	5.00
❑153, Apr 1978, FMc, DD (a); 1: Ultraa.	5.00
❑154, May 1978, FMc, DD (a); V: Doctor Destiny. V: Dr. Destiny.	5.00
❑155, Jun 1978, FMc, DD (a)	5.00
❑156, Jul 1978 FMc, DD (a); A: Phantom Stranger.	5.00
❑157, Aug 1978, FMc, DD (a)	5.00
❑158, Sep 1978, FMc, DD (a)	5.00
❑158/Whitman, Sep 1978, FMc, DD (a); Whitman variant	10.00
❑159, Oct 1978, JSa (w); FMc, DD (a); A: Enemy Ace. A: Justice Society of America. A: Black Pirate. A: Viking Prince. A: Miss Liberty. A: Jonah Hex.	5.00
❑160, Nov 1978, JSa (w); FMc, DD (a); A: Enemy Ace. A: Justice Society of America. A: Black Pirate. A: Viking Prince. A: Miss Liberty. A: Jonah Hex.	5.00
❑160/Whitman, Nov 1978, JSa (w); FMc, DD (a); A: Enemy Ace. A: Justice Society of America. A: Black Pirate. A: Viking Prince. A: Miss Liberty. A: Jonah Hex. Whitman variant	10.00
❑161, Dec 1978, FMc, DD (a); Zatanna joins the Justice League of America	5.00
❑161/Whitman, Dec 1978, FMc, DD (a); Zatanna joins the Justice League of America; Whitman variant	10.00
❑162, Jan 1979, FMc, DD (a)	5.00
❑162/Whitman, Jan 1979, FMc, DD (a); Whitman variant	10.00
❑163, Feb 1979, FMc, DD (a)	5.00
❑164, Mar 1979, FMc, DD (a)	5.00
❑165, Apr 1979, FMc, DD (a)	5.00
❑166, May 1979, FMc, DD (a); V: Secret Society of Super-Villains.	5.00
❑166/Whitman, May 1979, FMc, DD (a); V: Secret Society of Super-Villains. Whitman variant	10.00
❑167, Jun 1979, FMc, DD (a)	5.00
❑167/Whitman, Jun 1979, FMc, DD (a); Whitman variant	10.00
❑168, Jul 1979, FMc, DD (a); V: Secret Society of Super-Villains.	5.00
❑168/Whitman, Jul 1979, FMc, DD (a); V: Secret Society of Super-Villains. Whitman variant	10.00
❑169, Aug 1979, FMc, DD (a)	5.00
❑169/Whitman, Aug 1979, FMc, DD (a); Whitman variant	10.00
❑170, Sep 1979, FMc, DD (a); A: Supergirl.	5.00
❑171, Oct 1979, FMc, DD (a); A: Justice Society of America. D: Mr. Terrific.	5.00
❑171/Whitman, Oct 1979, FMc, DD (a); A: Justice Society of America. D: Mr. Terrific. Whitman variant	10.00
❑172, Nov 1979, FMc, DD (a); A: Justice Society of America.	5.00
❑172/Whitman, Nov 1979, FMc, DD (a); A: Justice Society of America. Whitman variant	10.00
❑173, Dec 1979, FMc, DD (a); A: Black Lightning.	5.00
❑173/Whitman, Dec 1979, FMc, DD (a); A: Black Lightning. Whitman variant	10.00
❑174, Jan 1980, FMc, DD (a); A: Black Lightning.	5.00
❑175, Feb 1980, FMc, DD (a); V: Doctor Destiny. V: Dr. Destiny	5.00
❑176, Mar 1980, FMc, DD (a); V: Doctor Destiny. V: Dr. Destiny	5.00
❑176/Whitman, Mar 1980, FMc, DD (a); V: Doctor Destiny. V: Dr. Destiny. Whitman variant	10.00
❑177, Apr 1980, FMc, DD (a); A: J'onn J'onzz. V: Despero.	5.00
❑177/Whitman, Apr 1980; Whitman variant	10.00
❑178, May 1980, JSn (c); FMc, DD (a); V: Despero.	5.00
❑178/Whitman, May 1980; Whitman variant	10.00
❑179, Jun 1980, JSn (c); FMc, DD (a); Firestorm joins the Justice League of America	5.00
❑179/Whitman, Jun 1980; Whitman variant	10.00
❑180, Jul 1980, JSn (c); FMc, DD (a).	5.00
❑181, Aug 1980, FMc, DD (a); A: Snapper Carr. Green Arrow leaves team	5.00
❑181/Whitman, Aug 1980, FMc, DD (a); A: Snapper Carr. Green Arrow leaves team; Whitman variant	10.00
❑182, Sep 1980, DC (c); FMc, DD (a); A: Felix Faust. Elongated Man back-up.	5.00
❑183, Oct 1980, JSn (c); JSa (w); FMc, DD (a); A: Orion. A: Justice Society of America. A: Metron. A: Mr. Miracle. V: Icicle. V: Shade. V: Fiddler. V: Darkseid.	5.00
❑184, Nov 1980, GP (c); FMc, GP (a); A: Justice Society of America. A: New Gods. V: Darkseid. V: Injustice Society.	5.00
❑185, Dec 1980, JSn (c); FMc, GP (a); A: Justice Society of America. A: New Gods. V: Darkseid. V: Injustice Society.	5.00
❑186, Jan 1981, FMc, GP (a); V: Shaggy Man.	5.00
❑187, Feb 1981, DG (c); FMc, DH, RA (a)	5.00
❑188, Mar 1981, DG (c); FMc, DH, RA (a)	5.00
❑189, Apr 1981, BB (c); FMc, RB (a); V: Starro.	5.00
❑190, May 1981, BB (c); RB (a); V: Starro.	5.00

N-MINT

❑191, Jun 1981, DG (c); RB (a); V: Amazo. V: The Key. 5.00
❑192, Jul 1981, GP (a); O: Red Tornado. A: T.O. Morrow. 5.00
❑193, Aug 1981, GP (a); 1: Danette Reilly. 1: All-Star Squadron. 5.00
❑194, Sep 1981, GP (a) 5.00
❑195, Oct 1981, GP (a); A: Justice Society of America. V: Secret Society of Super-Villains 5.00
❑196, Nov 1981, GP (a); A: Justice Society of America. V: Secret Society of Super-Villains 5.00
❑197, Dec 1981, GP (a); A: Justice Society of America. V: Secret Society of Super-Villains 5.00
❑198, Jan 1982, RA (c); DH (a); A: Scalphunter. A: Bat Lash. A: Cinnamon. A: Jonah Hex. V: Lord of Time 5.00
❑199, Feb 1982, GP (c); DH (a); A: Scalphunter. A: Bat Lash. A: Cinnamon. A: Jonah Hex. V: Lord of Time 5.00
❑200, Mar 1982; Anniversary issue; CI, GP, DG, JKu, GK (a); O: JLA. A: Snapper Carr. Green Arrow rejoins 7.00
❑201, Apr 1982, GP (c); DH (a); V: Ultraa. 3.00
❑202, May 1982, GP (c); DH (a) 3.00
❑203, Jun 1982, GP (c); DH (a); V: Hector Hammond. V: New Royal Flush Gang. 3.00
❑204, Jul 1982, GP (c); DH (a); V: Hector Hammond. V: New Royal Flush Gang. 3.00
❑205, Aug 1982, GP (c); DH (a); V: Hector Hammond. V: New Royal Flush Gang. 3.00
❑206, Sep 1982, DC (c); DH, RT (a); V: Rath. V: Ghast. V: Abnegazar. 3.00
❑207, Oct 1982, GP (c); JSa (w); DH, RT (a); A: Justice Society of America. A: All-Star Squadron. V: Per Degaton. V: Crime Syndicate. Justice Society of America, Justice League of America, and All-Star Squadron team up 3.00
❑208, Nov 1982, GP (c); JSa (w); DH (a); A: Justice Society of America. A: All-Star Squadron. V: Per Degaton. V: Crime Syndicate. Justice Society of America, Justice League of America, and All-Star Squadron team up 3.00
❑209, Dec 1982, GP (c); JSa (w); DH (a); A: Justice Society of America. A: All-Star Squadron. V: Per Degaton. V: Crime Syndicate. Justice Society of America, Justice League of America, and All-Star Squadron team up 3.00
❑210, Jan 1983, RB (a); first publication of story slated for 1977 DC tabloid 3.00
❑211, Feb 1983, RB (a); first publication of story slated for 1977 DC tabloid 3.00
❑212, Mar 1983, GP (c); RB (a); concludes story slated for 1977 DC tabloid 3.00
❑213, Apr 1983, GP (c); DH, RT (a) 3.00
❑214, May 1983, GP (c); DH, RT (a) 3.00
❑215, Jun 1983, GP (c); DH, RT (a) 3.00
❑216, Jul 1983, DH (a) 3.00
❑217, Aug 1983, GP (c); D: Garn Daanuth. 3.00
❑218, Sep 1983, A: Amazo. V: Prof. Ivo. 4.00
❑219, Oct 1983, GP (c); JSa (w); JSa (a); A: Justice Society of America. A: Thunderbolt. 3.00
❑220, Nov 1983, GP (c); JSa (w); JSa (a); O: Black Canary. A: Justice Society of America. A: Sargon. 4.00
❑221, Dec 1983 3.00
❑222, Jan 1984 3.00
❑223, Feb 1984 3.00
❑224, Mar 1984 KB (w); V: Paragon 3.00
❑225, Apr 1984 3.00
❑226, May 1984 RA (c) 3.00
❑227, Jun 1984 4.00
❑228, Jul 1984; J'onn J'onzz returns 3.00
❑229, Aug 1984 3.00
❑230, Sep 1984 3.00
❑231, Oct 1984 JSa, KB (w); JSa (a); A: Justice Society of America. A: Supergirl. A: Phantom Stranger. 3.00
❑232, Nov 1984 JSa, KB (w); JSa (a); A: Justice Society of America. A: Supergirl. V: Crime Syndicate. 3.00

N-MINT

❑233, Dec 1984; A: Vibe. cover forms four-part poster with issues #234-236; New team begins 3.00
❑234, Jan 1985 A: Monitor. A: Vixen. 3.00
❑235, Feb 1985 O: Steel. 1: The Cadre. V: Overmaster. V: The Cadre. 3.00
❑236, Mar 1985 A: Gypsy. V: Overmaster. V: The Cadre. 3.00
❑237, Apr 1985 A: Wonder Woman. A: Superman. A: The Flash. V: Mad Maestro. 3.00
❑238, May 1985 D: Anton Allegro. 3.00
❑239, Jun 1985; D: General Mustapha Maksai. Wonder Woman leaves Justice League 3.00
❑240, Jul 1985 KB (w); 1: Doctor Anomaly. 3.00
❑241, Aug 1985 GT (a); V: Amazo 3.00
❑242, Sep 1985 GT (a); V: Amazo. 3.00
❑243, Oct 1985; GT (a); V: Amazo. Aquaman leaves the Justice League of America 3.00
❑244, Nov 1985; JSa (w); JSa (a); A: Justice Society of America. A: Infinity, Inc.. Crisis; Steel vs. Steel. 3.00
❑245, Dec 1985; LMc (a); A: Lord of Time. Crisis; Steel in future 3.00
❑246, Jan 1986; LMc (a); evicted from HQ 3.00
❑247, Feb 1986; LMc (a); back to Happy Harbor 3.00
❑248, Mar 1986; LMc (a); J'onn J'onzz solo story 3.00
❑249, Apr 1986 LMc (a) 3.00
❑250, May 1986; Giant-size; LMc (a); A: original JLA. Batman rejoins Justice League of America 3.00
❑251, Jun 1986 LMc (a); V: Despero. 3.00
❑252, Jul 1986 LMc (a); V: Despero. 3.00
❑253, Aug 1986 LMc (a); O: Despero. 3.00
❑254, Sep 1986 JO (w); LMc (a); V: Despero. 3.00
❑255, Oct 1986 LMc (a); O: Gypsy. 3.00
❑256, Nov 1986 LMc (a) 3.00
❑257, Dec 1986; LMc (a); Zatanna leaves Justice League. 3.00
❑258, Jan 1987 LMc (a); D: Vibe. 3.00
❑259, Feb 1987; LMc (a); Gypsy leaves team 3.00
❑260, Mar 1987 LMc (a); D: Steel. 3.00
❑261, Apr 1987; LMc (a); group disbands 4.00
❑Annual 1, Oct 1983 A: John Stewart. A: Sandman. V: Doctor Destiny. V: Dr. Destiny. 4.50
❑Annual 2, Oct 1984 O: New JLA (Vixen, Vibe, Gypsy, Steel). 1: Gypsy. 1: New JLA (Vixen, Vibe, Gypsy, Steel). 3.50
❑Annual 3, Nov 1985; 1: Red Tornado (in current form). Crisis. 3.50

JUSTICE LEAGUE OF AMERICA: ANOTHER NAIL
DC

❑1, Jul 2004 5.95
❑2, Aug 2004 5.95
❑3, Sep 2004 5.95

JUSTICE LEAGUE OF AMERICA INDEX
ECLIPSE / INDEPENDENT

❑1, Apr 1986 1.50
❑2, Apr 1986 1.50
❑3, May 1986 1.50
❑4, May 1986 1.50
❑5, Oct 1986 2.00
❑6, Nov 1986 2.00
❑7, Jan 1987 2.00
❑8; Title changes to Justice League of America Index 2.00

JUSTICE LEAGUE OF AMERICA SUPER SPECTACULAR
DC

❑1, ca. 1999; Reprints 5.95

JUSTICE LEAGUE QUARTERLY
DC

❑1, Win 1990 3.00
❑2, Spr 1991 3.00
❑3, Jun 1991; cover says Sum, indicia says Jun 3.00
❑4, Fal 1991 3.00
❑5, Win 1991 3.00
❑6, Spr 1992 3.00

N-MINT

❑7, Sum 1992 3.00
❑8, Sum 1992; cover says Aut, indicia says Sum; new Conglomerate 3.00
❑9, Win 1992 3.00
❑10, Spr 1993 3.00
❑11, Sum 1993 3.00
❑12, Sum 1993; covers says Aut, indicia says Sum; Conglomerate 3.00
❑13, Aut 1993; cover says Win, indicia says Aut 3.00
❑14, Spr 1994 3.00
❑15, Jun 1994; cover says Sum, indicia says Jun 3.00
❑16, Sep 1994 3.00
❑17, Win 1994 3.00

JUSTICE LEAGUES: JL?
DC

❑1, Mar 2001 2.50

JUSTICE LEAGUES: JLA
DC

❑1, Mar 2001 2.50

JUSTICE LEAGUES: JUSTICE LEAGUE OF ALIENS
DC

❑1, Mar 2001 2.50

JUSTICE LEAGUES: JUSTICE LEAGUE OF AMAZONS
DC

❑1, Mar 2001 2.50

JUSTICE LEAGUES: JUSTICE LEAGUE OF ARKHAM
DC

❑1, Mar 2001 2.50

JUSTICE LEAGUES: JUSTICE LEAGUE OF ATLANTIS
DC

❑1, Mar 2001 2.50

JUSTICE LEAGUE TASK FORCE
DC

❑0, Oct 1994 MWa (w); A: Triumph. 1.75
❑1, Jun 1993; membership card 2.00
❑2, Jul 1993 1.50
❑3, Aug 1993 1.50
❑4, Sep 1993 1.50
❑5, Oct 1993 1.50
❑6, Nov 1993 1.25
❑7, Dec 1993; transsexual J'onn J'onzz 1.50
❑8, Jan 1994; PD (w); transsexual J'onn J'onzz 1.50
❑9, Feb 1994 JPH (w); A: New Bloods. 1.50
❑10, Mar 1994 V: Aryan Brigade. 1.50
❑11, Apr 1994 V: Aryan Brigade. 1.50
❑12, May 1994 1.50
❑13, Jun 1994 MWa (w) 1.50
❑14, Jul 1994 1.50
❑15, Aug 1994 1.50
❑16, Sep 1994; A: Triumph. Zero Hour 1.50
❑17, Nov 1994 MWa (w) 1.50
❑18, Dec 1994 MWa (w) 1.50
❑19, Jan 1995 MWa (w); V: Vandal Savage. 1.50
❑20, Feb 1995 1.50
❑21, Mar 1995 1.50
❑22, Apr 1995 1.50
❑23, May 1995 1.50
❑24, Jun 1995 1.75
❑25, Jul 1995 1.75
❑26, Aug 1995 1.75
❑27, Sep 1995 1.75
❑28, Oct 1995 1.75
❑29, Nov 1995 1.75
❑30, Dec 1995; Underworld Unleashed 1.75
❑31, Jan 1996 1.75
❑32, Feb 1996 1.75
❑33, Mar 1996 1.75
❑34, May 1996 1.75
❑35, Jun 1996 A: Warlord. 1.75
❑36, Jul 1996 1.75
❑37, Aug 1996 1.75

JUSTICE LEAGUE UNLIMITED
DC

❑1, Nov 2004 2.25
❑2, Dec 2004 2.25
❑3, Jan 2005 2.25
❑4, Feb 2005 2.25

Justice League Quarterly

Anthology allows longer adventures

©DC

Justice Leagues: JL?

JLA founders form own teams

©DC

Justice League Task Force

Spin-off sanctions special super-teams

©DC

Justice Machine (Comico)

Super-powered police force in space

©Comico

Justice Society of America (Mini-Series)

Early 1950s adventure spells finis for JSA

©DC

N-MINT

❑5, Mar 2005 ... 2.25
❑6, Apr 2005 ... 2.25
❑7, May 2005 ... 2.25
❑8, Jun 2005 ... 2.25
❑9, Jun 2005 ... 2.25
❑10, Jul 2005 ... 2.25
❑11, Aug 2005 ... 2.25
❑12, Sep 2005 ... 2.25
❑13, Oct 2005 ... 2.25
❑14 2005 ... 2.25
❑15, Jan 2006 ... 2.25
❑16, Jan 2006 ... 2.25
❑17, Mar 2006 ... 2.25
❑18, Mar 2006 ... 2.25
❑19, May 2006 ... 2.25
❑20, Jun 2006 ... 2.25
❑21, Jul 2006 ... 2.25
❑22, Aug 2006 ... 2.25

JUSTICE MACHINE (NOBLE)
NOBLE

❑1 1981 JBy (c); MGu (a) ... 2.50
❑2 TD (c); MGu (a) ... 2.50
❑3 MGu (a) ... 2.50
❑4 MGu (a) ... 2.50
❑5, Nov 1983 MGu (a) ... 2.50
❑Annual 1, Jan 1984; 1: Elementals. THUNDER Agents ... 5.00

JUSTICE MACHINE (COMICO)
COMICO

❑1, Jan 1987 MGu (a) ... 2.50
❑2, Feb 1987 MGu (a) ... 2.00
❑3, Mar 1987 MGu (a) ... 1.75
❑4, Apr 1987 MGu (a) ... 1.75
❑5, May 1987 MGu (a) ... 1.75
❑6, Jun 1987 MGu (a) ... 1.75
❑7, Jul 1987 MGu (a) ... 1.75
❑8, Aug 1987 MGu (a); D: Demon. ... 1.75
❑9, Sep 1987 MGu (a) ... 1.75
❑10, Oct 1987 MGu (a) ... 1.75
❑11, Nov 1987 MGu (a) ... 1.75
❑12, Dec 1987 ... 1.75
❑13, Jan 1988 MGu (a) ... 1.75
❑14, Feb 1988 MGu (a) ... 1.75
❑15, Mar 1988 ... 1.75
❑16, Apr 1988 ... 1.75
❑17, May 1988 ... 1.75
❑18, Jun 1988 ... 1.75
❑19, Jul 1988 ... 1.75
❑20, Aug 1988 ... 1.75
❑21, Sep 1988 ... 1.75
❑22, Oct 1988 ... 1.75
❑23, Nov 1988 ... 1.75
❑24, Dec 1988 ... 1.75
❑25, Jan 1989 ... 1.75
❑26, Feb 1989 ... 1.75
❑27, Mar 1989 ... 1.75
❑28, Apr 1989 ... 1.95
❑29, May 1989 ... 1.95
❑Annual 1, Jun 1989 A: Elementals. ... 2.75

JUSTICE MACHINE (INNOVATION)
INNOVATION

❑1, Apr 1990 ... 1.95
❑2, May 1990 ... 1.95

N-MINT

❑3, Jul 1990 ... 1.95
❑4, Sep 1990 ... 1.95
❑5, Nov 1990 ... 1.95
❑6, Jan 1991 ... 2.25
❑7, Apr 1991 ... 2.25

JUSTICE MACHINE (MILLENNIUM)
MILLENNIUM

❑1, ca. 1992 ... 2.50
❑2, ca. 1992 ... 2.50

JUSTICE MACHINE FEATURING THE ELEMENTALS
COMICO

❑1, May 1986 ... 2.00
❑2, Jun 1986 ... 1.75
❑3, Jul 1986 ... 1.75
❑4, Aug 1986 ... 1.75

JUSTICE MACHINE SUMMER SPECTACULAR
INNOVATION

❑1 ... 2.75

JUSTICE RIDERS
DC

❑1 1997, prestige format; Elseworlds; Justice League in old West ... 5.95

JUSTICE SOCIETY OF AMERICA (MINI-SERIES)
DC

❑1, Apr 1991; Flash ... 2.00
❑2, May 1991; Black Canary ... 1.75
❑3, Jun 1991; Green Lantern ... 1.75
❑4, Jul 1991; FMc (a); Hawkman ... 1.50
❑5, Aug 1991; Flash, Hawkman ... 1.50
❑6, Sep 1991; FMc (a); Green Lantern, Black Canary ... 1.50
❑7, Oct 1991; Green Lantern, Black Canary, Hawkman, Flash, Starman ... 1.50
❑8, Nov 1991; Green Lantern, Black Canary, Hawkman, Flash, Starman ... 1.50

JUSTICE SOCIETY OF AMERICA
DC

❑1, Aug 1992 ... 1.50
❑2, Sep 1992 ... 1.50
❑3, Oct 1992 V: Ultra-Humanite. ... 1.50
❑4, Nov 1992 V: Ultra-Humanite. ... 1.50
❑5, Dec 1992 ... 1.50
❑6, Jan 1993 ... 1.25
❑7, Feb 1993; in Bahdnesia ... 1.25
❑8, Mar 1993 ... 1.25
❑9, Apr 1993; Alan Scott vs. Guy Gardner ... 1.25
❑10, May 1993 ... 1.25

JUSTICE SOCIETY OF AMERICA 100-PAGE SUPER SPECTACULAR
DC

❑1; 2000 facsimile of 1975 100-Page Super Spectacular; reprints The Flash #137 and #201, All Star Comics #57, The Brave and the Bold #62, and Adventure Comics #418 ... 6.95

JUSTICE SOCIETY RETURNS
DC

❑1, ca. 2003 ... 19.95

JUST IMAGINE COMICS AND STORIES
JUST IMAGINE

❑1 1982 ... 2.00

N-MINT

❑2 1982 ... 2.00
❑3 1982 ... 2.00
❑4 1982 ... 2.00
❑5 1983 ... 2.00
❑6 1983 ... 2.00
❑7 1983 ... 2.00
❑8 1983 ... 2.00
❑9 ... 2.00
❑10 1984 ... 2.00
❑11 1984 ... 2.00
❑Special 1 1983; gophers ... 2.00

JUST IMAGINE'S SPECIAL
JUST IMAGINE

❑1, Jul 1986; 1st appearance of The Mildly Microwaved Pre-Pubescent Kung-Fu Gophers! ... 1.50

JUST IMAGINE STAN LEE... SECRET FILES AND ORIGINS
DC

❑1, Mar 2002, DaG, JB, JOy, JBy, JKu, JLee (a) ... 4.95

JUST IMAGINE STAN LEE WITH CHRIS BACHALO CREATING CATWOMAN
DC

❑1, Jul 2002 ... 5.95

JUST IMAGINE STAN LEE WITH DAVE GIBBONS CREATING GREEN LANTERN
DC

❑1, Dec 2001 ... 5.95

JUST IMAGINE STAN LEE WITH GARY FRANK CREATING SHAZAM!
DC

❑1, May 2002 ... 5.95

JUST IMAGINE STAN LEE WITH JERRY ORDWAY CREATING JLA
DC

❑1, Feb 2002 ... 5.95

JUST IMAGINE STAN LEE WITH JIM LEE CREATING WONDER WOMAN
DC

❑1, Oct 2001 ... 5.95

JUST IMAGINE STAN LEE WITH JOE KUBERT CREATING BATMAN
DC

❑1, Sep 2001 ... 5.95

JUST IMAGINE STAN LEE WITH JOHN BUSCEMA CREATING SUPERMAN
DC

❑1, Nov 2001 ... 5.95

JUST IMAGINE STAN LEE WITH JOHN BYRNE CREATING ROBIN
DC

❑1, Apr 2002 ... 5.95

JUST IMAGINE STAN LEE WITH JOHN CASSADAY CREATING CRISIS
DC

❑1, Sep 2002 ... 5.95

Other grades: Multiply price above by 5/6 for VF/NM • 2/3 for VERY FINE • 1/3 for FINE • 1/5 for VERY GOOD • 1/8 for GOOD

JUST IMAGINE STAN LEE WITH KEVIN MAGUIRE CREATING THE FLASH
DC

❑1, Jan 2002 .... 5.95

JUST IMAGINE STAN LEE WITH SCOTT MCDANIEL CREATING AQUAMAN
DC

❑1, Jun 2002 .... 5.95

JUST IMAGINE STAN LEE WITH WALTER SIMONSON CREATING SANDMAN
DC

❑1, Aug 2002 .... 5.95

JUST TWISTED
NECROMICS

❑1 .... 2.00

JUSTY
VIZ

❑1, Dec 1988, b&w; Japanese 2.00
❑2, Dec 1988, b&w; Japanese 2.00
❑3, Jan 1989, b&w; Japanese 2.00
❑4, Jan 1989, b&w; Japanese 2.00
❑5, Feb 1989, b&w; Japanese 2.00
❑6, Feb 1989, b&w; Japanese 2.00
❑7, Mar 1989, b&w; Japanese 2.00
❑8, Mar 1989, b&w; Japanese 2.00
❑9, Apr 1989, b&w; Japanese 2.00

KABOOM
AWESOME

❑1, Sep 1997 JPH (w); 1: Kaboom. 2.50
❑1/A, Sep 1997; JPH (w); Dynamic Forces variant (marked as such); Purple Awesome logo 2.50
❑1/Gold, Sep 1997; Gold edition with silver logo JPH (w); 1: Kaboom. 2.50
❑2, Oct 1997 JPH (w) 2.50
❑2/Autographed, Oct 1997 JPH (w) 2.50
❑2/Gold, Oct 1997; Gold edition JPH (w) 2.50
❑3, Nov 1997 JPH (w) 2.50
❑4, Feb 1998 JPH (w) 2.50
❑5, Mar 1998 JPH (w) 2.50
❑Ashcan 1, Feb 1998; Preview edition JPH (w) 2.50
❑Ashcan 1/Gold, Feb 1998; Gold edition JPH (w) 2.50

KABUKI
IMAGE

❑½, Sep 2001; Speckle-foil Wizard variant 3.00
❑½/A; Image's reprinting of the Wizard variant 4.00
❑1, Oct 1997 .... 5.00
❑1/A, Oct 1997; alternate cover 5.00
❑2, Dec 1997 .... 4.00
❑3, Mar 1998 .... 4.00
❑4, Jun 1998 .... 3.50
❑5, Sep 1998 .... 2.95
❑6, Nov 1998 .... 2.95
❑7, Feb 1999 .... 2.95
❑7/Variant, Feb 1999; Alternate cover art 2.95
❑8, Jun 1999 .... 2.95
❑9, Mar 2000 .... 2.95

KABUKI AGENTS
IMAGE

❑1, Aug 1999; Scarab 2.95
❑1/A, Aug 1999; Scarab alternate cover 2.95
❑2, Oct 1999; Scarab 2.95
❑3, Nov 1999; Scarab 2.95
❑4, Apr 2000; Scarab 2.95
❑5, Nov 2000; Scarab 2.95
❑6, Jan 2001; Scarab 2.95
❑7, Mar 2001; Scarab 2.95
❑8, Aug 2001; Scarab 2.95

KABUKI: CIRCLE OF BLOOD
CALIBER

❑1, Jan 1995, b&w 4.00
❑1/Ltd., Jan 1995; Limited edition with new, painted cover 5.00
❑1/2nd, Jul 1995, b&w; enhanced cover 3.50
❑2, Mar 1995, b&w 3.50
❑3, May 1995, b&w; reprints #1's indicia 3.50
❑4, Jul 1995, b&w 3.00
❑5, Sep 1995, b&w 3.00
❑6, Nov 1995, b&w 3.00
❑6/Ltd., Nov 1995; New painted cover, signed 10.00

KABUKI CLASSICS
IMAGE

❑1, Feb 1999; Squarebound; Reprints Kabuki: Fear the Reaper 3.25
❑2, Mar 1999; Reprints Kabuki: Dance of Death 3.00
❑3, Mar 1999; Squarebound 4.95
❑4, Apr 1999 .... 3.25
❑5, Jul 1999 .... 3.25
❑6, Jul 1999 .... 3.25
❑7, Aug 1999 .... 3.25
❑8, Sep 1999 .... 3.25
❑9, Oct 1999 .... 3.25
❑10, Nov 1999 .... 3.25
❑11, Dec 1999 .... 3.25
❑12, Mar 2000 .... 3.25

KABUKI COLOR SPECIAL
CALIBER

❑1, Jan 1996 MGr (a) 3.50

KABUKI COMPILATION
CALIBER

❑1, Jul 1995; Collects Kabuki: Dance of Death and Kabuki: Fear the Reaper. 7.95

KABUKI: DANCE OF DEATH
LONDON NIGHT

❑1, Jan 1995, b&w; no cover price or indicia 3.50

KABUKI DREAMS
IMAGE

❑nn, Jan 1998, b&w; reprints Kabuki Color Special and Kabuki: Dreams of the Dead 5.00

KABUKI: DREAMS OF THE DEAD
CALIBER

❑1, Jul 1996 .... 2.95

KABUKI: FEAR THE REAPER
CALIBER

❑1, Nov 1994 .... 3.50

KABUKI GALLERY
CALIBER

❑1, Aug 1995; pin-ups 2.95
❑1/A, Aug 1995; Comic Cavalcade edition 15.00

KABUKI: THE GHOST PLAY
IMAGE

❑1, Nov 2002; No issue number in indicia 2.95

KABUKI-IMAGES
IMAGE

❑1, Jul 1998; prestige format; pin-ups and story; Reprints Kabuki (Image) #1 with new pin-ups 4.95
❑2, Jan 1999; prestige format; Reprints Kabuki (Image) #2-3 .... 4.95

KABUKI (MARVEL)
MARVEL

❑1, Sep 2004 .... 4.00
❑1/Variant, Sep 2004 .... 5.00
❑2, Oct 2004 .... 2.99
❑3, Nov 2004 .... 2.99
❑4, Dec 2004 .... 2.99
❑4/Hughes, Dec 2004 .... 4.00
❑5, Dec 2005 .... 2.99
❑6, May 2006 .... 2.99
❑6/Variant, May 2006 .... 2.99

KABUKI: MASKS OF THE NOH
IMAGE

❑1, May 1996, b&w 3.00
❑2, Jun 1996, b&w 3.00
❑3, Sep 1996, b&w 3.00
❑4, Jan 1997, b&w 3.00
❑Book 3/2nd, Apr 1998 .... 19.95

KABUKI REFLECTIONS
IMAGE

❑1, Jul 1998; prestige format; no number on cover or in indicia 4.95
❑2, Dec 1998; prestige format 4.95
❑3, Jan 2000 .... 4.95
❑4, May 2002 .... 4.95

KABUKI: SKIN DEEP
CALIBER

❑1, Oct 1996 .... 3.50
❑2, Feb 1997 .... 3.00
❑2/A, Feb 1997; alternate cover; white background 3.00
❑2/Ltd., Feb 1997; Wraparound cover by David Mack and Alex Ross 8.00
❑3, May 1997 .... 2.95

KAFKA
RENEGADE

❑1, Apr 1987, b&w 3.00
❑2, May 1987, b&w 2.50
❑3, Jun 1987, b&w 2.50
❑4, Jul 1987, b&w 2.50
❑5, Aug 1987, b&w 2.50
❑6, Sep 1987, b&w 2.50

KAFKA: THE EXECUTION
FANTAGRAPHICS

❑1, b&w; Duranona 2.95

KAKTUS
FANTAGRAPHICS

❑1, b&w 2.50

KALAMAZOO COMIX
DISCOUNT HOBBY

❑1 .... 1.95
❑2, Win 1996 .... 1.95
❑3, Win 1996 .... 1.95
❑4, Spr 1997 .... 2.95
❑5, Dec 1997 .... 2.95

KALGAN THE GOLDEN
HARRIER

❑1, Mar 1988 .... 1.95

KAMANDI: AT EARTH'S END
DC

❑1, Jun 1993 .... 1.75
❑2, Jul 1993 .... 1.75
❑3, Aug 1993 .... 1.75
❑4, Sep 1993 .... 1.75
❑5, Oct 1993 .... 1.75
❑6, Nov 1993 .... 1.75

KAMANDI, THE LAST BOY ON EARTH
DC

❑1, Nov 1972, JK (c); JK (w); JK (a); O: Kamandi. 1: Dr. Canus. 1: Ben Boxer. 20.00
❑2, Jan 1973, JK (c); JK (w); JK (a) 15.00
❑3, Feb 1973, JK (c); JK (w); JK (a); in Vegas 10.00
❑4, Mar 1973, JK (c); JK (w); JK (a); 1: Prince Tuftan. 8.00
❑5, Apr 1973, JK (c); JK (w); JK (a) 8.00
❑6, Jun 1973, JK (c); JK (w); JK (a) 8.00
❑7, Jul 1973, JK (c); JK (w); JK (a) 8.00
❑8, Aug 1973, JK (c); JK (w); JK (a); In Washington, D.C. 8.00
❑9, Sep 1973, JK (c); JK (w); JK (a) 8.00
❑10, Oct 1973, JK (c); JK (w); JK (a) 8.00
❑11, Nov 1973, JK (c); JK (w); JK (a) 7.00
❑12, Dec 1973, JK (c); JK (w); JK (a). 7.00
❑13, Jan 1974, JK (c); JK (w); JK (a) 7.00
❑14, Feb 1974, JK (c); JK (w); JK (a) 7.00
❑15, Mar 1974, JK (c); JK (w); JK (a) 7.00
❑16, Apr 1974, JK (c); JK (w); JK (a). 7.00
❑17, May 1974, JK (c); JK (w); JK (a) 7.00
❑18, Jun 1974, JK (c); JK (w); JK (a). 7.00
❑19, Jul 1974, JK (c); JK (w); JK (a); in Chicago 7.00
❑20, Aug 1974, JK (c); JK (w); JK (a); in Chicago 6.00
❑21, Sep 1974, JK (c); JK (w); JK (a). 6.00
❑22, Oct 1974, JK (c); JK (w); JK (a) 6.00
❑23, Nov 1974, JK (c); JK (w); JK (a) 6.00
❑24, Dec 1974, JK (c); JK (w); JK (a). 6.00
❑25, Jan 1975, JK (c); JK (w); JK (a) 6.00
❑26, Feb 1975, JK (c); JK (w); JK (a) 6.00
❑27, Mar 1975, JK (c); JK (w); JK (a) 6.00
❑28, Apr 1975, JK (c); JK (w); JK (a) 6.00
❑29, May 1975, JK (c); JK (w); JK (a); Superman's legend 6.00
❑30, Jun 1975, JK (c); JK (w); JK (a); 1: Pyra. 6.00
❑31, Jul 1975, JK (c); JK (w); JK (a) 6.00
❑32, Aug 1975, JK (c); JK (w); JK (a); O: Kamandi. giant; Jack Kirby interview; New story and reprints Kamandi #1 .... 6.00
❑33, Sep 1975, JK (c); JK (w); JK (a). 6.00

Other grades: Multiply price above by 5/6 for VF/NM • 2/3 for VERY FINE • 1/3 for FINE • 1/5 for VERY GOOD • 1/8 for GOOD

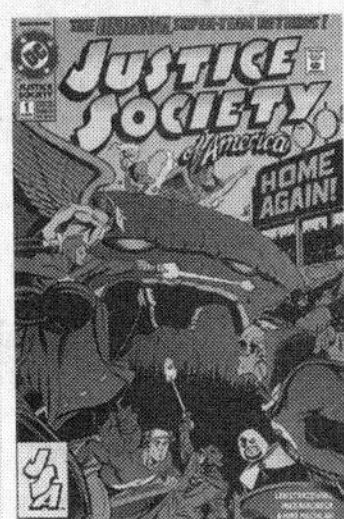
Justice Society of America

Short-lived series had animated look

©DC

Kaboom

Teen acquires e xplosive powers

©Awesome

Kabuki

Highly stylized martial arts series

©Image

Kabuki Agents

Kabuki's sidekicks mount rescue of leader

©Image

Kabuki Gallery

Mixed media pin-ups from creator David Mack

©Caliber

	N-MINT
❑34, Oct 1975, JKu (c); JK (w); JK (a)	6.00
❑35, Nov 1975, JKu (c); JK (w); JK (a)	6.00
❑36, Dec 1975, JKu (c); JK (w); JK (a)	6.00
❑37, Jan 1976, JKu (c); JK (w); JK (a)	6.00
❑38, Feb 1976, JKu (c); JK (w); JK (a)	6.00
❑39, Mar 1976, JKu (c); JK (w); JK (a)	5.00
❑40, Apr 1976, JKu (c); JK (w); JK (a)	5.00
❑41, May 1976, JKu (c)	4.00
❑42, Jun 1976, JL (c)	4.00
❑43, Jul 1976, Tales of the Great Disaster backup stories begin; Bicentennial #4	4.00
❑44, Aug 1976, KG (a)	4.00
❑45, Sep 1976, KG (a)	4.00
❑46, Oct 1976, KG, JAb (a); Tales of the Great Disaster backup stories end	4.00
❑47, Nov 1976, RB (c); KG, AA (a)	4.00
❑48, Jan 1977	4.00
❑49, Mar 1977, AA (a)	4.00
❑50, May 1977, RB, AA (c); AA (a); Kamandi reverts to OMAC	4.00
❑51, Jul 1977, RB, JAb (c); AA (a)	4.00
❑52, Sep 1977, RB, AA (c); AA (a)	4.00
❑53, Nov 1977, AM (c); AA (a)	4.00
❑54, Jan 1978, AM (c); AA (a)	4.00
❑55, Mar 1978, AM (c); V: Vortex Beast.	2.50
❑56, May 1978, RB, JAb (c)	2.50
❑57, Jul 1978, (c)	2.50
❑58, Sep 1978, (c); A: Karate Kid. Karate Kid	2.50
❑59, Oct 1978, JSn (c); JSn (w); JSn (a); OMAC back-up begins; continues in Warlord #37	4.00

KAMA SUTRA (MANARA'S...)
NBM

❑1	12.95

KAMA SUTRA (GIRL'S...)
BLACK LACE

❑1	2.95

KAMICHAMA KARIN
TOKYOPOP

❑1, Sep 2005	9.95
❑2, Dec 2005	9.95

KAMIKAZE
DC / CLIFFHANGER

❑1, Dec 2003	2.95
❑2, Jan 2004	2.95
❑3, Feb 2004	2.95
❑4, Mar 2004	2.95
❑5, Apr 2004	2.95
❑6, May 2004	2.95

KAMIKAZE CAT
PIED PIPER

❑1, Jul 1987	1.95

KANE
DANCING ELEPHANT

	N-MINT
❑1	3.50
❑2	3.50
❑3	3.50
❑4	3.50
❑5	3.50
❑6	3.50
❑7	3.50
❑8	3.50
❑9	3.50
❑10	3.50
❑11	3.50
❑12	3.50
❑13	3.50
❑14	3.50
❑15	3.50
❑16	3.50
❑17	3.50
❑18	3.50
❑19	3.50
❑20	3.50
❑21	3.50
❑22	3.50
❑23	2.95
❑24 1998	2.95
❑25, Jan 1999	2.95
❑26, Apr 1999	2.95
❑27, ca. 1999; Giant-size	5.00
❑28, ca. 2000	2.95
❑29, ca. 2000	2.95
❑30, Nov 2000	2.95
❑31, Apr 2001	2.95
❑32, Jul 2001	2.95

KANPAI!
TOKYOPOP

❑1, Sep 2005	9.95
❑2, Dec 2005	9.95

KANSAS THUNDER
RED MENACE

❑1, b&w	2.95

KAOS
TOMMY REGALADO

❑1, Aug 1994, b&w	2.00

KAOS MOON
CALIBER

❑1, ca. 1996, b&w	2.95
❑2, Nov 1996, b&w	2.95
❑3, Jul 1997	2.95
❑4, ca. 1997	2.95

KAPTAIN KEEN & KOMPANY
VORTEX

❑1, Dec 1986	1.75
❑2, ca. 1987	1.75
❑3, ca. 1987	1.75
❑4, ca. 1987	1.75
❑5, ca. 1987	1.75
❑6, Feb 1988	1.75

KARAS
DARK HORSE

❑1, Jan 2005	3.00

KARATE GIRL
FANTAGRAPHICS / EROS

❑1, ca. 1994, b&w	2.50
❑2, ca. 1994, b&w	2.50

KARATE GIRL TENGU WARS
FANTAGRAPHICS / EROS

❑1, ca. 1995	2.95
❑2, ca. 1995	2.95
❑3, Jun 1995	2.95

KARATE KID
DC

	N-MINT
❑1, Apr 1976 JSa, RE (a)	12.00
❑2, Jun 1976	7.00
❑3, Aug 1976	7.00
❑4, Oct 1976	5.00
❑5, Dec 1976	5.00
❑6, Feb 1977	5.00
❑7, Apr 1977, MGr (a)	5.00
❑8, Jun 1977, MGr, JSa, RE (a)	5.00
❑9, Aug 1977	5.00
❑10, Oct 1977	5.00
❑11, Dec 1977	5.00
❑12, Feb 1978	5.00
❑13, Apr 1978	5.00
❑14, Jun 1978	5.00
❑15, Aug 1978	5.00

KARATE KREATURES
MA

❑1, Sum 1989	2.00
❑2, ca. 1989	2.00

KARE KANO
TOKYOPOP

❑1, Jan 2003, b&w; printed in Japanese format	9.99
❑2, Mar 2003, b&w; printed in Japanese format	9.99
❑3, May 2003, b&w; printed in Japanese format	9.99
❑4, Jul 2003	9.99
❑5, Sep 2003	9.99
❑6, Nov 2003	9.99
❑7, Jan 2004	9.99
❑8, Mar 2004	9.99
❑9, May 2004	9.99
❑10, Jul 2004	9.99
❑11, Sep 2004	9.99
❑12, Nov 2004	9.99
❑13, Jan 2005	9.99
❑14, Mar 2005	9.99
❑15, May 2005	9.99
❑16, Jul 2005	9.99
❑17, Sep 2005	9.99
❑18, Dec 2005	9.99

KARMA INCORPORATED
VIPER

❑1, Sep 2005	2.95
❑2, Oct 2005	2.95

KARNEY
IDEA & DESIGN WORKS

❑1, ca. 2005	3.99
❑2 2005	3.99
❑3 2005	3.99
❑4, Sep 2005	3.99

KARZA
IMAGE

❑1, Feb 2003	2.95
❑2, Apr 2003	2.95
❑3, May 2003	2.95
❑4, May 2003	2.95

KATMANDU
ANTARCTIC

❑1, Nov 1993, b&w	2.75

Other grades: Multiply price above by 5/6 for VF/NM • 2/3 for VERY FINE • 1/3 for FINE • 1/5 for VERY GOOD • 1/8 for GOOD

	N-MINT
❑2, Jan 1994, b&w	2.95
❑3, Apr 1994, b&w	2.95
❑4, Mar 1995, b&w	2.75
❑5, May 1995, b&w	2.75
❑6, Aug 1995	2.75
❑7, ca. 1996	2.75
❑8, Jul 1996, b&w	1.95
❑9, ca. 1996, b&w	1.95
❑10, ca. 1996, b&w	1.95
❑11, ca. 1997, b&w	1.95
❑12, ca. 1997, b&w	1.95
❑13, Sep 1997, b&w	2.95
❑14, ca. 1998	2.95
❑15, ca. 1998	2.95
❑16, Apr 1999, b&w	2.95
❑17, ca. 1999	2.95
❑18, ca. 1999	2.95
❑19, ca. 2000	2.95
❑20, Apr 2000	2.95
❑21, Jul 2000	2.95
❑22, ca. 2000	2.95
❑23 2001	2.95
❑24 2001	2.95
❑25 2001	2.95
❑26, Jun 2002	4.99
❑27, Aug 2002	4.99
❑28, ca. 2002	4.99
❑Annual 1, ca. 1999	4.99
❑Annual 2, ca. 2000	4.99
❑Annual 3, Dec 2001	4.99
❑Annual 4, Dec 2002	4.99

KATO OF THE GREEN HORNET
Now

	N-MINT
❑1, Nov 1991	2.50
❑2, Dec 1991	2.50
❑3 1992	2.50
❑4 1992	2.50

KATO OF THE GREEN HORNET II
Now

	N-MINT
❑1, Nov 1992	2.50
❑2, Dec 1992	2.50

KA-ZAR (1ST SERIES)
Marvel

	N-MINT
❑1, Aug 1970, SL (w); GC, JK, FS (a); 1: Ka-Zar. 1: Zabu. A: X-Men. giant; reprints X-Men #10 (first series) and Daredevil #24; Hercules back-up	35.00
❑2, Dec 1970, SL (w); GT, JK, JR (a); O: Ka-Zar. A: Daredevil. giant; Angel back-up; reprints Daredevil #12 and 13	15.00
❑3, Mar 1971, giant; reprints Amazing Spider-Man #57 and Daredevil #14; Angel back-up continues in Marvel Tales #30	15.00

KA-ZAR (2ND SERIES)
Marvel

	N-MINT
❑1, Jan 1974, O: Savage Land.	17.00
❑2, Mar 1974, DH (a); Marvel Value Stamp #28: Hawkeye	7.00
❑3, May 1974, DH (a); Marvel Value Stamp #46: Mysterio	5.00
❑4, Jul 1974, DH (a); Marvel Value Stamp #9: Captain Marvel	5.00
❑5, Sep 1974, DH (a); Marvel Value Stamp #18: Volstagg	5.00
❑6, Nov 1974, JB (a); Marvel Value Stamp #17: Black Bolt	5.00
❑7, Jan 1975, JB (a)	5.00
❑8, Mar 1975, JB (a); Marvel Value Stamp #38: Red Sonja	3.00
❑9, Jun 1975, JB (a)	3.00
❑10, Aug 1975, JB (a); Marvel Value Stamp #72: Lizard	3.00
❑11, Oct 1975	3.00
❑12, Nov 1975, Marvel Value Stamp #95: Moleman	3.00
❑13, Dec 1975	3.00
❑14, Feb 1976, A: Klaw.	3.00
❑15, Apr 1976	3.00
❑15/30 cent, Apr 1976, 30 cent regional price variant	20.00
❑16, Jun 1976	3.00
❑16/30 cent, Jun 1976, 30 cent regional price variant	20.00
❑17, Aug 1976	3.00
❑17/30 cent, Aug 1976, 30 cent regional price variant	20.00
❑18, Oct 1976	3.00
❑19, Dec 1976	3.00
❑20, Feb 1977, A: Klaw.	3.00

KA-ZAR (3RD SERIES)
Marvel

	N-MINT
❑-1, Jul 1997, Flashback	2.00
❑1, May 1997	2.50
❑2, Jun 1997	2.00
❑2/A, Jun 1997, alternate cover	2.00
❑3, Jul 1997	2.00
❑4, Aug 1997, gatefold summary	2.00
❑5, Sep 1997, gatefold summary	2.00
❑6, Oct 1997, gatefold summary	2.00
❑7, Nov 1997, gatefold summary	2.00
❑8, Dec 1997, gatefold summary; Spider-Man CD-ROM inserted	2.00
❑9, Jan 1998, gatefold summary	2.00
❑10, Feb 1998, gatefold summary	2.00
❑11, Mar 1998, gatefold summary	1.99
❑12, Apr 1998, gatefold summary	1.99
❑13, May 1998, gatefold summary	1.99
❑14, Jun 1998, Flip-book	1.99
❑15, Jul 1998, gatefold summary; blinded	1.99
❑16, Aug 1998, gatefold summary	1.99
❑17, Sep 1998, gatefold summary	1.99
❑18, Oct 1998, gatefold summary	1.99
❑19, Nov 1998, gatefold summary	1.99
❑20, Dec 1998, gatefold summary	1.99
❑Annual 1997, ca. 1997, gatefold summary; wraparound cover	2.99

KAZAR OF THE SAVAGE LAND
Marvel

	N-MINT
❑1, Feb 1997; wraparound cover	2.50

KA-ZAR THE SAVAGE
Marvel

	N-MINT
❑1, Apr 1981, BA (a); O: Ka-Zar.	5.00
❑2, May 1981, BA (a)	2.00
❑3, Jun 1981, BA (a)	1.50
❑4, Jul 1981, BA (a)	1.50
❑5, Aug 1981, BA (a)	1.50
❑6, Sep 1981, BA (a)	1.50
❑7, Oct 1981, BA (a)	1.50
❑8, Nov 1981, BA (a)	1.50
❑9, Dec 1981, BA (a)	1.50
❑10, Jan 1982; BA (a); direct distribution	1.50
❑11, Feb 1982; BA (a); 1: Belasco. Zabu	1.50
❑12, Mar 1982; BA (a); panel missing	1.50
❑12/2nd; Reprints	1.00
❑13, Apr 1982 BA (a)	1.50
❑14, May 1982 BA (a)	1.50
❑15, Jun 1982 BA (a)	1.50
❑16, Jul 1982	1.50
❑17, Aug 1982	1.50
❑18, Sep 1982	1.50
❑19, Oct 1982 BA (a)	1.50
❑20, Nov 1982	1.50
❑21, Dec 1982	1.50
❑22, Jan 1983	1.50
❑23, Feb 1983 BH (a)	1.50
❑24, Mar 1983 BH (a)	1.50
❑25, Apr 1983	1.50
❑26, May 1983	1.50
❑27, Aug 1983	1.50
❑28, Oct 1983	1.50
❑29, Dec 1983; Double-size; Wedding of Ka-Zar, Shanna	1.50
❑30, Feb 1984	1.50
❑31, Apr 1984	1.50
❑32, Jun 1984	1.50
❑33, Aug 1984	1.50
❑34, Oct 1984	1.50

KEENSPOT SPOTLIGHT
Keenspot

	N-MINT
❑2002, Apr 2002	1.00
❑2003, May 2003, Free Comic Book Day edition	1.00

KEEP
Idea & Design Works

	N-MINT
❑1,	3.95
❑2, Dec 2005	3.95
❑3, Jan 2006	3.95
❑4, Feb 2006	3.95
❑5, Apr 2006	3.95

KEIF LLAMA
Oni

	N-MINT
❑1, Mar 1999	2.95

KEIF LLAMA XENO-TECH
Fantagraphics

	N-MINT
❑1, ca. 1987	2.00
❑2, ca. 1987	2.00
❑3, ca. 1987	2.00
❑4, ca. 1987	2.00
❑5, ca. 1987	2.00
❑6, ca. 1987	2.00

KEKKAISHI
Viz

	N-MINT
❑1, May 2005	9.95
❑2, Aug 2005	9.95
❑3, Nov 2005	9.95

KELLY BELLE POLICE DETECTIVE
Newcomers

	N-MINT
❑1	2.95
❑2	2.95
❑3	2.95

KELLY GREEN
Dargaud

	N-MINT
❑1	2.95
❑2	2.95

KELVIN MACE
Vortex

	N-MINT
❑1, ca. 1988	3.00
❑2, ca. 1988	1.75

KENDRA: LEGACY OF THE BLOOD
Perrydog

	N-MINT
❑1, Feb 1987, b&w	2.00
❑2, Apr 1987, b&w	2.00

KENTS
DC

	N-MINT
❑1, Aug 1997; Clark Kent's ancestors in frontier Kansas	3.00
❑2, Sep 1997	2.50
❑3, Oct 1997	2.50
❑4, Nov 1997 (c)	2.50
❑5, Dec 1997 (c)	2.50
❑6, Jan 1998 (c)	2.50
❑7, Feb 1998 (c)	2.50
❑8, Mar 1998	2.50
❑9, Apr 1998	2.50
❑10, May 1998	2.50
❑11, Jun 1998	2.50
❑12, Jul 1998	2.50

KERRY DRAKE
Blackthorne

	N-MINT
❑1, May 1986	6.95
❑2, Jul 1986	6.95
❑3, Dec 1986	6.95
❑4, Feb 1987	6.95
❑5, Jul 1987	6.95

KEYHOLE
Millennium

	N-MINT
❑1, Jun 1996	2.95
❑2, Oct 1996	2.95
❑3 1997	2.95
❑4, May 1997	2.95
❑5, Jun 1998	2.95

KHAN
Moonstone

	N-MINT
❑1, Sep 2005	3.95

KICKERS, INC.
Marvel

	N-MINT
❑1, Nov 1986	0.75
❑2, Dec 1986	0.75
❑3, Jan 1987	0.75
❑4, Feb 1987	0.75
❑5, Mar 1987	0.75
❑6, Apr 1987	0.75
❑7, May 1987	0.75
❑8, Jun 1987	0.75
❑9, Jul 1987	0.75
❑10, Aug 1987	0.75
❑11, Sep 1987	0.75
❑12, Oct 1987	0.75

KID ANARCHY
Fantagraphics

	N-MINT
❑1, ca. 1990, b&w	2.50
❑2, ca. 1990, b&w	2.75
❑3, ca. 1990, b&w	2.75

KID BLASTOFF
Slave Labor / Amaze Ink

	N-MINT
❑1, Jun 1996	2.75

Other grades: Multiply price above by 5/6 for VF/NM • 2/3 for VERY FINE • 1/3 for FINE • 1/5 for VERY GOOD • 1/8 for GOOD

Kamandi, the Last Boy on Earth

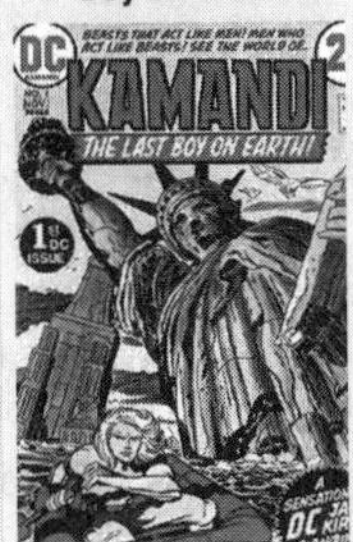

Apocalypse survivor's animal adventures

©DC

Kane

Anti-hero protects law and order in New Eden

©Dancing Elephant

Karate Kid

Not the movie with Arnold from Happy Days

©DC

Katmandu

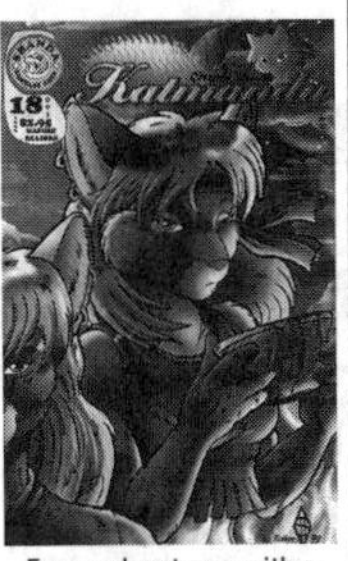

Furry adventures with a realistic bent

©Antarctic

Ka-Zar (2nd Series)

Tarzan-type battles dinos in Savage Land

©Marvel

N-MINT

KID CANNIBAL
Eternity

❑1, Oct 1991 .... 2.50
❑2 1991 .... 2.50
❑3 1992 .... 2.50
❑4 1992 .... 2.50

KID COLT OUTLAW
Marvel

❑65, Oct 1956 .... 48.00
❑66, Nov 1956 .... 48.00
❑67, Dec 1956 .... 48.00
❑68, Jan 1957 .... 48.00
❑69, Feb 1957 .... 48.00
❑70, Mar 1957 .... 48.00
❑71, Apr 1957 .... 40.00
❑72, May 1957, JSe (c); SL (w) 40.00
❑73, Jul 1957 .... 40.00
❑74, Sep 1957 .... 40.00
❑75, Nov 1957 .... 40.00
❑76, Jan 1958 .... 40.00
❑77, Mar 1958 .... 40.00
❑78, May 1958 .... 40.00
❑79, Jul 1958 .... 40.00
❑80, Sep 1958 .... 40.00
❑81, Nov 1958 .... 40.00
❑82, Jan 1959 .... 40.00
❑83, Mar 1959 .... 40.00
❑84, May 1959 .... 40.00
❑85, Jul 1959 .... 40.00
❑86, Sep 1959 .... 40.00
❑87, Nov 1959 .... 40.00
❑88, Jan 1960 .... 40.00
❑89, Mar 1960 .... 40.00
❑90, May 1960 .... 40.00
❑91, Jul 1960 .... 40.00
❑92, Sep 1960 .... 40.00
❑93, Oct 1960 .... 40.00
❑94, Nov 1960 .... 40.00
❑95, Dec 1960 .... 40.00
❑96, Jan 1961 .... 40.00
❑97, Mar 1961 .... 40.00
❑98, May 1961 .... 40.00
❑99, Jul 1961 .... 40.00
❑100, Sep 1961 .... 40.00
❑101, Nov 1961 .... 28.00
❑102, Jan 1962 .... 28.00
❑103, Mar 1962 .... 28.00
❑104, May 1962 .... 28.00
❑105, Jul 1962 .... 28.00
❑106, Sep 1962 .... 28.00
❑107, Nov 1962 .... 28.00
❑108, Jan 1963 .... 28.00
❑109, Mar 1963 .... 28.00
❑110, May 1963, SL (w) 28.00
❑111, Jul 1963 .... 18.00
❑112, Sep 1963, SL (w) 18.00
❑113, Nov 1963 .... 18.00
❑114, Jan 1964, V: Iron Mask. 18.00
❑115, Mar 1964 .... 18.00
❑116, May 1964 .... 18.00
❑117, Jul 1964 .... 18.00
❑118, Sep 1964, V: Scorpion. V: Bull Barton. V: Doctor Danger. 18.00
❑119, Nov 1964 .... 18.00

N-MINT

❑120, Jan 1965 .... 18.00
❑121, Mar 1965 .... 14.00
❑122, May 1965 .... 14.00
❑123, Jul 1965 .... 14.00
❑124, Sep 1965, V: Phantom Raider. . 14.00
❑125, Nov 1965, A: Two-Gun Kid. 14.00
❑126, Jan 1966 .... 14.00
❑127, Mar 1966, V: Iron Mask. V: Fat Man. V: Doctor Danger. 14.00
❑128, May 1966 .... 14.00
❑129, Jul 1966 .... 14.00
❑130, Sep 1966, SL (w); O: Kid Colt. giant 14.00
❑131, Nov 1966, SL (w); GC (a); giant 10.00
❑132, Jan 1967, giant 10.00
❑133, Mar 1967, V: Rammer Ramkin. 10.00
❑134, May 1967 .... 10.00
❑135, Jul 1967 .... 10.00
❑136, Sep 1967 .... 10.00
❑137, Nov 1967 .... 10.00
❑138, Jan 1968 .... 10.00
❑139, Mar 1968, series goes on hiatus 10.00
❑140, Nov 1969, Reprints begin 5.00
❑141, Dec 1969 .... 5.00
❑142, Jan 1970 .... 5.00
❑143, Feb 1970 .... 5.00
❑144, Mar 1970 .... 5.00
❑145, Apr 1970 .... 5.00
❑146, May 1970 .... 5.00
❑147, Jun 1970 .... 5.00
❑148, Jul 1970 .... 5.00
❑149, Aug 1970 .... 5.00
❑150, Oct 1970 .... 5.00
❑151, Dec 1970 .... 5.00
❑152, Feb 1971 .... 5.00
❑153, Apr 1971 .... 5.00
❑154, Jul 1971 .... 5.00
❑155, Sep 1971 .... 5.00
❑156, Nov 1971 .... 5.00
❑157, Jan 1972 .... 5.00
❑158, Mar 1972 .... 5.00
❑159, May 1972 .... 5.00
❑160, Jul 1972 .... 5.00
❑161, Aug 1972 .... 5.00
❑162, Sep 1972 .... 5.00
❑163, Oct 1972 .... 5.00
❑164, Nov 1972 .... 5.00
❑165, Dec 1972 .... 5.00
❑166, Jan 1973 .... 5.00
❑167, Feb 1973 .... 5.00
❑168, Mar 1973 .... 5.00
❑169, Apr 1973 .... 5.00
❑170, May 1973 .... 5.00
❑171, Jun 1973, A: Two-Gun Kid. 4.00
❑172, Jul 1973 .... 4.00
❑173, Aug 1973 .... 4.00
❑174, Sep 1973 .... 4.00
❑175, Oct 1973 .... 4.00
❑176, Nov 1973 .... 4.00
❑177, Dec 1973 .... 4.00
❑178, Jan 1974 .... 4.00
❑179, Feb 1974 .... 4.00
❑180, Mar 1974 .... 4.00
❑181, Apr 1974 .... 4.00

N-MINT

❑182, May 1974 .... 4.00
❑183, Jun 1974 .... 4.00
❑184, Jul 1974 .... 4.00
❑185, Aug 1974 .... 4.00
❑186, Sep 1974 .... 4.00
❑187, Oct 1974 .... 4.00
❑188, Nov 1974 .... 4.00
❑189, Dec 1974 .... 4.00
❑190, Jan 1975 .... 4.00
❑191, Feb 1975 .... 4.00
❑192, Mar 1975 .... 4.00
❑193, Apr 1975 .... 4.00
❑194, May 1975 .... 4.00
❑195, Jun 1975 .... 4.00
❑196, Jul 1975 .... 4.00
❑197, Aug 1975 .... 4.00
❑198, Sep 1975 .... 4.00
❑199, Oct 1975 .... 4.00
❑200, Nov 1975, GK (c); HT, JK (a); Jack Kirby pin-up 4.00
❑201, Dec 1975 .... 3.00
❑202, Jan 1976 .... 3.00
❑203, Feb 1976 .... 3.00
❑204, Mar 1976, Reprints Kid Colt Outlaw #72 .... 3.00
❑205, Apr 1976 .... 3.00
❑205/30 cent, Apr 1976, 30 cent regional price variant 20.00
❑206, May 1976 .... 3.00
❑206/30 cent, May 1976, 30 cent regional price variant 3.00
❑207, Jun 1976 .... 3.00
❑207/30 cent, Jun 1976, 30 cent regional price variant 3.00
❑208, Jul 1976 .... 3.00
❑208/30 cent, Jul 1976, 30 cent regional price variant 3.00
❑209, Aug 1976 .... 3.00
❑209/30 cent, Aug 1976, 30 cent regional price variant 3.00
❑210, Sep 1976 .... 3.00
❑211, Oct 1976 .... 3.00
❑212, Nov 1976 .... 3.00
❑213, Dec 1976 .... 3.00
❑214, Jan 1977 .... 3.00
❑215, Feb 1977 .... 3.00
❑216, Mar 1977 .... 3.00
❑217, Apr 1977 .... 3.00
❑218, Jun 1977 .... 3.00
❑219, Aug 1977 .... 3.00
❑219/35 cent, Aug 1977, 35 cent regional price variant 15.00
❑220, Oct 1977 .... 3.00
❑220/35 cent, Oct 1977, 35 cent regional price variant 15.00
❑221, Dec 1977 .... 3.00
❑222, Feb 1978 .... 3.00
❑223, Apr 1978 .... 3.00
❑224, Jun 1978 .... 3.00
❑225, Aug 1978 .... 3.00
❑226, Oct 1978 .... 3.00
❑227, Dec 1978 .... 3.00
❑228, Feb 1979 .... 3.00
❑229, Apr 1979 .... 3.00

Other grades: Multiply price above by 5/6 for VF/NM • 2/3 for VERY FINE • 1/3 for FINE • 1/5 for VERY GOOD • 1/8 for GOOD

KID DEATH & FLUFFY: HALLOWEEN SPECIAL
EVENT
- ❑1, Oct 1997 .... 2.95

KID DEATH & FLUFFY SPRING BREAK SPECIAL
EVENT
- ❑1, Jun 1996 .... 2.50

KID ETERNITY (MINI-SERIES)
DC / VERTIGO
- ❑1, May 1991 .... 4.95
- ❑2, Jul 1991 .... 4.95
- ❑3, Oct 1991 .... 4.95

KID ETERNITY
DC / VERTIGO
- ❑1, May 1993 .... 1.95
- ❑2, Jun 1993 .... 1.95
- ❑3, Jul 1993 .... 1.95
- ❑4, Aug 1993 .... 1.95
- ❑5, Sep 1993 .... 1.95
- ❑6, Oct 1993 .... 1.95
- ❑7, Nov 1993 .... 1.95
- ❑8, Dec 1993 .... 1.95
- ❑9, Jan 1994 .... 1.95
- ❑10, Feb 1994 .... 1.95
- ❑11, Mar 1994 .... 1.95
- ❑12, May 1994 .... 1.95
- ❑13, Jun 1994 .... 1.95
- ❑14, Jul 1994 .... 1.95
- ❑15, Aug 1994 .... 1.95
- ❑16, Sep 1994 .... 1.95

KID 'N PLAY
MARVEL
- ❑1, Feb 1992 .... 1.25
- ❑2, Mar 1992 .... 1.25
- ❑3, Apr 1992 .... 1.25
- ❑4, May 1992 .... 1.25
- ❑5, Jun 1992 .... 1.25
- ❑6, Jul 1992 .... 1.25
- ❑7, Aug 1992 .... 1.25
- ❑8, Sep 1992 .... 1.25
- ❑9, Oct 1992 .... 1.25

KID SUPREME
IMAGE
- ❑1, Mar 1996; Kid Supreme with fist outstretched on cover 2.50
- ❑1/A, Mar 1996; Kid Supreme surounded by girls on cover 2.50
- ❑2, Apr 1996 .... 2.50
- ❑3, Jul 1996 .... 2.50
- ❑3/A, Jul 1996; alternate cover (green background) 2.50

KID'S WB JAM PACKED ACTION
DC
- ❑1, ca. 2004 .... 7.99

KID TERRIFIC
IMAGE
- ❑1, Nov 1998, b&w 2.95

KIDZ OF THE KING
KING
- ❑1, Mar 1994 .... 2.95
- ❑2, May 1994 .... 2.95
- ❑3, Apr 1995 .... 2.95

KI-GORR THE KILLER
AC
- ❑1, Reprints 3.95

KIKU SAN
AIRCEL
- ❑1, Nov 1988 .... 1.95
- ❑2, Dec 1988 .... 1.95
- ❑3, Jan 1989 .... 1.95
- ❑4, Feb 1989 .... 1.95
- ❑5, Mar 1989 .... 1.95
- ❑6, Apr 1989 .... 1.95

KILGORE
RENEGADE
- ❑1, Nov 1987 .... 2.00
- ❑2, Jan 1988 .... 2.00
- ❑3, Mar 1988 .... 2.00
- ❑4, May 1988 .... 2.00

KILL BARNY
EXPRESS / PARODY
- ❑1, ca. 1992, b&w 2.50

KILL BARNY 3
EXPRESS / PARODY
- ❑1, ca. 1992, b&w 2.75

KILLBOX
ANTARCTIC
- ❑1, Dec 2002 .... 5.00
- ❑2, Jan 2003 .... 5.00
- ❑3, Feb 2003 .... 5.00

KILLER FLY
SLAVE LABOR
- ❑1, Mar 1995 .... 2.95
- ❑2, Jun 1995 .... 2.95
- ❑3, Sep 1995 .... 2.95

KILLER INSTINCT
ACCLAIM / ARMADA
- ❑1, Jun 1996, based on video game 2.50
- ❑2, Jul 1996, based on video game 2.50
- ❑3, Jul 1996, based on video game 2.50
- ❑4, Sep 1996, based on video game 2.50
- ❑5, Oct 1996, based on video game 2.50
- ❑6, Nov 1996, based on video game 2.50

KILLER INSTINCT TOUR BOOK
IMAGE
- ❑1/A; Embossed cover 3.00
- ❑1/B; Embossed cover 3.00
- ❑1/Gold; Gold edition 3.00

KILLER 7
DEVIL'S DUE
- ❑1, Feb 2006 .... 3.95
- ❑2, Apr 2006 .... 3.95
- ❑3, May 2006 .... 3.95
- ❑3/Special, May 2006 .... 3.95

KILLER STUNTS, INC.
ALIAS
- ❑1 2005 .... 2.99
- ❑2, Jul 2005 .... 2.99
- ❑3, Aug 2005 .... 2.99
- ❑4, Nov 2005 .... 2.99

KILLER...TALES BY TIMOTHY TRUMAN
ECLIPSE
- ❑1, Mar 1985 .... 1.75

KILL IMAGE
BONEYARD
- ❑1, b&w; foil cover 3.50

KILLING STROKE
ETERNITY
- ❑1, b&w 2.50
- ❑2, b&w 2.50
- ❑3, b&w 2.50
- ❑4, b&w 2.50

KILL MARVEL
BONEYARD
- ❑1/Ltd.; Special "Marvel Can..." edition 5.00

KILLPOWER: THE EARLY YEARS
MARVEL
- ❑1, Sep 1993; foil cover 1.75
- ❑2, Oct 1993 .... 1.75
- ❑3, Nov 1993 .... 1.75
- ❑4, Dec 1993 .... 1.75

KILLRAVEN
MARVEL
- ❑1, Feb 2001 .... 2.99

KILLRAVEN (2ND SERIES)
MARVEL
- ❑1, Dec 2002 .... 2.99
- ❑2, Jan 2003 .... 2.99
- ❑3, Feb 2003 .... 2.99
- ❑4, Mar 2003 .... 2.99
- ❑5, Apr 2003 .... 2.99
- ❑6, May 2003 .... 2.99

KILL RAZOR SPECIAL
IMAGE
- ❑1, Aug 1995 .... 2.50

KILL YOUR BOYFRIEND
DC / VERTIGO
- ❑1, Jun 1995 .... 4.95
- ❑1/2nd, May 1998; reprints 1995 one-shot with new afterword and other new material 5.95

KILROY IS HERE
CALIBER
- ❑0, ca. 1994, b&w 2.95
- ❑1, ca. 1995, b&w 2.95
- ❑2, ca. 1995, b&w 2.95
- ❑3, ca. 1995, b&w 2.95
- ❑4, ca. 1995, b&w 2.95
- ❑5, ca. 1995, #4 on cover 2.95

KILROY: REVELATIONS
CALIBER
- ❑1, ca. 1994, b&w; "Black light" cover 2.95

KILROYS (AVALON)
AVALON
- ❑1, ca. 2002 .... 2.95

KILROY: THE SHORT STORIES
CALIBER
- ❑1, ca. 1995, b&w; "Black light" cover 2.95

KILROY (VOL. 2)
CALIBER
- ❑1, Apr 1998 .... 2.95
- ❑1/A, ca. 1998 .... 2.95

KIMBER, PRINCE OF THE FEYLONS
ANTARCTIC
- ❑1, Apr 1992, b&w 2.50
- ❑2, Jun 1992, b&w 2.50

KIMURA
NIGHTWYND
- ❑1, ca. 1991, b&w 2.50
- ❑2, ca. 1991, b&w 2.50
- ❑3, ca. 1991, b&w 2.50
- ❑4, ca. 1991, b&w 2.50

KIN
IMAGE
- ❑1, Sep 1999 .... 2.95
- ❑2, Oct 1999 .... 2.95
- ❑3, Nov 1999 .... 2.95
- ❑4, Jul 2000 .... 2.95
- ❑5, Aug 2000 .... 2.95
- ❑6, Sep 2000 .... 3.95

KINDAICHI CASE FILES
TOKYOPOP
- ❑1 .... 9.95

KINDRED
IMAGE
- ❑1, Mar 1994 .... 2.50
- ❑2, Apr 1994 .... 1.95
- ❑3, May 1994 .... 1.95
- ❑3/A, May 1994; alternate cover 1.95
- ❑4, Jul 1994 .... 2.50

KINDRED II
DC / WILDSTORM
- ❑1, Mar 2002 .... 2.50
- ❑2, Apr 2002 .... 2.50
- ❑3, May 2002 .... 2.50
- ❑4, Jun 2002 .... 2.50

KINETIC
DC / FOCUS
- ❑1, May 2004 .... 2.50
- ❑2, Jun 2004 .... 2.50
- ❑3, Jul 2004 .... 2.50
- ❑4, Aug 2004 .... 2.50
- ❑5, Sep 2004 .... 2.50
- ❑6, Oct 2004 .... 2.50
- ❑7, Nov 2004 .... 2.50
- ❑8, Dec 2004 .... 2.50

KING ARTHUR AND THE KNIGHTS OF JUSTICE
MARVEL
- ❑1, Dec 1993 .... 1.25
- ❑2, Jan 1994 .... 1.25
- ❑3, Feb 1994 .... 1.25

KING COMICS PRESENTS
KING COMICS
- ❑1 .... 1.95

KING CONAN
MARVEL
- ❑1, Mar 1980; JB (a); V: Thoth-Amon, wife & son 5.00
- ❑2, Jun 1980 JB (a) 1.50
- ❑3, Sep 1980 JB (a) 1.50
- ❑4, Dec 1980 V: Thoth-Amon 1.50
- ❑5, Mar 1981 .... 1.50
- ❑6, Jun 1981 .... 1.50
- ❑7, Sep 1981 JB (a) 1.50
- ❑8, Dec 1981 .... 1.50
- ❑9, Mar 1982 .... 1.50

Other grades: Multiply price above by 5/6 for VF/NM • 2/3 for VERY FINE • 1/3 for FINE • 1/5 for VERY GOOD • 1/8 for GOOD

Kendra: Legacy of the Blood

Short-lived comic from height of b&w glut
©Perrydog

Kents

Adventures of Jonathan Kent's forebears
©DC

Kickers, Inc.

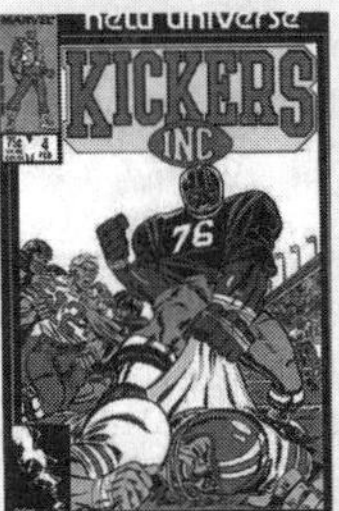

Enhanced football team from New Universe
©Marvel

Kid Colt Outlaw

Long-running western survived many others
©Marvel

Kid 'n Play

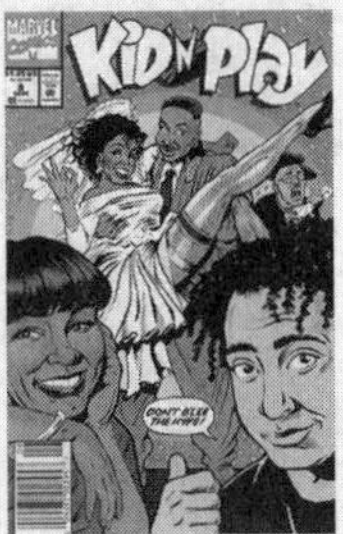

Based on stars of the House Party movie
©Marvel

N-MINT

❑10, May 1982 .... 1.50
❑11, Jul 1982 .... 1.25
❑12, Sep 1982 .... 1.25
❑13, Nov 1982 .... 1.25
❑14, Jan 1983 .... 1.25
❑15, Mar 1983 .... 1.25
❑16, May 1983 .... 1.25
❑17, Jul 1983 .... 1.25
❑18, Sep 1983 .... 1.25
❑19, Nov 1983; Series continued in Conan the King #20 .... 1.25

KING DAVID
DC / VERTIGO

❑1, May 2002 .... 19.95

KINGDOM
DC

❑1, Feb 1999; MWa (w); MZ (a); Elseworlds 2.95
❑1/Autographed, Feb 1999; MWa (w); Elseworlds 8.00
❑2, Feb 1999; MWa (w); MZ (a); Elseworlds 2.95
❑2/Autographed, Feb 1999; MWa (w); MZ (a); Elseworlds 12.00

KINGDOM COME
DC

❑1, ca. 1996; MWa (w); ARo (a); Elseworlds 5.00
❑1/2nd, ca. 1996 ARo (a) 4.95
❑2, ca. 1996; MWa (w); ARo (a); Elseworlds 5.00
❑3, ca. 1996; MWa (w); ARo (a); return of Captain Marvel; Elseworlds 5.00
❑4, ca. 1996; MWa (w); ARo (a); D: Captain Marvel. Elseworlds 5.00

KINGDOM HEARTS
TOKYOPOP

❑1, Oct 2005 .... 9.99

KINGDOM, THE: KID FLASH
DC

❑1, Feb 1999; Elseworlds 1.99

KINGDOM, THE: NIGHTSTAR
DC

❑1, Feb 1999; Elseworlds 1.99

KINGDOM, THE: OFFSPRING
DC

❑1, Feb 1999; Elseworlds 1.99

KINGDOM, THE: PLANET KRYPTON
DC

❑1, Feb 1999; Elseworlds 1.99

KINGDOM, THE: SON OF THE BAT
DC

❑1, Feb 1999; Elseworlds 1.99

KINGDOM OF THE DWARFS
COMICO

❑1 .... 4.95

KINGDOM OF THE WICKED
CALIBER

❑1, ca. 1996, b&w 2.95
❑2, ca. 1996, b&w 2.95
❑3, ca. 1996, b&w 2.95
❑4, ca. 1996, b&w 2.95

N-MINT

KING KONG (GOLD KEY)
GOLD KEY

❑1, Sep 1968, adapts 1932 film 12.00

KING KONG (MONSTER)
MONSTER

❑1, Feb 1991, b&w DSt (c); DSt (a) 2.50
❑2, ca. 1991 .... 2.50
❑3, ca. 1991 .... 2.50
❑4, ca. 1991 .... 2.50
❑5, Nov 1991, AW (c) 2.50
❑6, Mar 1992 .... 2.50

KING LEONARDO AND HIS SHORT SUBJECTS
GOLD KEY

❑1, May 1962 .... 35.00
❑2, Oct 1962 .... 25.00
❑3, Mar 1963 .... 25.00
❑4, ca. 1963 .... 25.00

KING LOUIE AND MOWGLI
GOLD KEY

❑1, May 1968 .... 20.00

KING OF DIAMONDS
DELL

❑1, Sep 1962, Based on TV show 30.00

KING OF HELL
TOKYOPOP

❑1, Jun 2003, b&w 9.95
❑2, Aug 2003 .... 9.95
❑3, Oct 2003 .... 9.95
❑4, Jan 2004 .... 9.95
❑5, Apr 2004 .... 9.95
❑6, Jul 2004 .... 9.95
❑7, Oct 2004 .... 9.95
❑8, Jan 2005 .... 9.95
❑9, Apr 2005 .... 9.95
❑10, Jul 2005 .... 9.95
❑11, Nov 2005 .... 9.95

KING OF THE DEAD
FANTACO

❑0, ca. 1988 .... 1.95
❑1, ca. 1988 .... 1.95
❑2, ca. 1988 .... 1.95
❑3, ca. 1988 .... 1.95
❑4, ca. 1988 .... 2.95

KINGPIN
MARVEL

❑1, Nov 1997; says "Spider-Man/ Kingpin: To the Death" on cover 5.99

KINGPIN (2ND SERIES)
MARVEL

❑1, Aug 2003 .... 2.50
❑2, Sep 2003 .... 2.50
❑3, Oct 2003 .... 2.99
❑4, Nov 2003 .... 2.99
❑5, Dec 2003 .... 2.99
❑6, Dec 2003 .... 2.99
❑7, Feb 2004 .... 2.99

KINGS IN DISGUISE
KITCHEN SINK

❑1, Mar 1988, b&w 2.00
❑2, May 1988 .... 2.00
❑3, Jul 1988 .... 2.00

N-MINT

❑4, Sep 1988 .... 2.00
❑5, Mar 1989 .... 2.00
❑6, Sep 1989 .... 2.00

KINGS OF THE NIGHT
DARK HORSE

❑1, ca. 1990 .... 2.25
❑2, ca. 1990 .... 2.25

KING TIGER & MOTORHEAD
DARK HORSE

❑1, Aug 1996 .... 2.95
❑2, Sep 1996 .... 2.95

KINKI KLITT KOMICS
RIP OFF

❑1, Apr 1992, b&w 2.95
❑2, Jun 1992, b&w 2.50

KINKY HOOK, THE
FANTAGRAPHICS / EROS

❑1, b&w 2.50

KIP
HAMMER & ANVIL

❑1, b&w 2.50

KIRBY KING OF THE SERIALS
BLACKTHORNE

❑1, Jan 1989, b&w 2.00

KISS
PERSONALITY

❑1, b&w 3.50
❑2 .... 3.00
❑3 .... 3.00

KISS (DARK HORSE)
DARK HORSE

❑1, Jun 2002 .... 2.99
❑1/Photo, Jun 2002 .... 2.99
❑2, Aug 2002, More Beast Now than Man cover 2.99
❑2/Photo, Aug 2002 .... 2.99
❑3, Sep 2002 .... 2.99
❑3/Photo, Sep 2002 .... 2.99
❑4, Nov 2002 .... 2.99
❑4/Photo, Nov 2002 .... 2.99
❑5, Nov 2002 .... 2.99
❑5/Photo, Nov 2002 .... 2.99
❑6, Jan 2003 .... 2.99
❑6/Photo, Jan 2003 .... 2.99
❑7, Feb 2003 .... 2.99
❑7/Photo, Feb 2003 .... 2.99
❑8, Mar 2003 .... 2.99
❑8/Photo, Mar 2003 .... 2.99
❑9, Apr 2003 .... 2.99
❑9/Photo, Apr 2003 .... 2.99
❑10, May 2003 .... 2.99
❑10/Photo, May 2003 .... 2.99
❑11, Jul 2003 .... 2.99
❑11/Photo, Jul 2003, Others appear in photo insets 2.99
❑12, Aug 2003 .... 2.99
❑12/Photo, Aug 2003, Others appear in photo insets 2.99
❑13, Sep 2003 .... 2.99
❑13/Photo, Sep 2003 .... 2.99

Other grades: Multiply price above by 5/6 for VF/NM • 2/3 for VERY FINE • 1/3 for FINE • 1/5 for VERY GOOD • 1/8 for GOOD

	N-MINT

KISS & TELL
PATRICIA BREEN

❑1, Dec 1995, b&w; magazine 2.75

KISS & TELL (VOL. 2)
SIRIUS

❑1, ca. 1996, b&w 2.50

KISS CLASSICS
MARVEL

❑1; Reprints Marvel Super Special #1, #5 .... 10.00

KISSES
SPOOF

❑1, b&w 2.95

KISSING CANVAS
MN DESIGN

❑1, photos 5.50

KISS KISS BANG BANG
CROSSGEN

❑1, Feb 2004 .... 4.00
❑1/2nd, Mar 2004 .... 2.95
❑2, Mar 2004 .... 2.95
❑3, Apr 2004 .... 2.95
❑4, Jun 2004 .... 2.95
❑4/2nd, Jun 2004 .... 2.95
❑5, Aug 2004 .... 2.95

KISSNATION
MARVEL

❑1; A: X-Men. Reprints Marvel Super Specials with new editorial 11.00

KISS OF DEATH
ACME

❑1, Apr 1987 .... 2.00

KISS OF THE VAMPIRE
BRAINSTORM

❑1, ca. 1996 .... 2.95

KISS PRE-HISTORY
REVOLUTIONARY

❑1, Apr 1993, b&w 3.00
❑2, May 1993, b&w 3.00
❑3, Jul 1993, b&w 3.00

KISS: PSYCHO CIRCUS
IMAGE

❑1, Aug 1997 .... 1.95
❑2, Sep 1997 .... 1.95
❑3, Oct 1997 .... 1.95
❑4, Nov 1997 .... 1.95
❑5, Dec 1997 .... 1.95
❑6, Jan 1998 .... 2.25
❑7, Mar 1998 .... 2.25
❑8, Apr 1998 .... 2.25
❑9, May 1998 .... 2.25
❑10, Jun 1998; covers of #10-12 form quadtych 2.25
❑11, Jul 1998 .... 2.25
❑12, Aug 1998 .... 2.25
❑13, Oct 1998 .... 2.25
❑14, Nov 1998 .... 2.25
❑15, Dec 1998 .... 2.25
❑16, Feb 1999 .... 2.25
❑17, Mar 1999 .... 2.25
❑18, Apr 1999 .... 2.25
❑19, May 1999 .... 2.25
❑20, Jun 1999 .... 2.25
❑21, Jul 1999 .... 2.25
❑22, Aug 1999 .... 2.25
❑23, Sep 1999 .... 2.25
❑24, Oct 1999 .... 2.25
❑25, Nov 1999 .... 2.25
❑26, Jan 2000 .... 2.25
❑27, Feb 2000 .... 2.25
❑28, Apr 2000 .... 2.25
❑29, Apr 2000 .... 2.50
❑30, May 2000 .... 2.50
❑31, Jun 2000 .... 2.50
❑Special 1, ca. 1999; Special Wizard Edition 2.00

KISS: SATAN'S MUSIC?
CELEBRITY

❑1; trading cards 4.00

KISSYFUR
DC

❑1, ca. 1989 .... 2.00

KISS: YOU WANTED THE BEST, YOU GOT THE BEST
WIZARD

❑1, Jun 1998 .... 1.00

KITCHEN SINK CLASSICS
KITCHEN SINK

❑1, Jan 1994, b&w; reprints Omaha #0 .... 4.50
❑2, b&w; reprints The People's Comics 3.00
❑3, b&w; reprints Death Rattle #8 .... 3.00

KITTY PRYDE & WOLVERINE
MARVEL

❑1, Nov 1984 AM (a) 3.00
❑2, Dec 1984 AM (a) 2.50
❑3, Jan 1985 AM (a) 2.50
❑4, Feb 1985 AM (a) 2.50
❑5, Mar 1985 AM (a) 2.50
❑6, Apr 1985 AM (a) 2.50

KITTY PRYDE, AGENT OF SHIELD
MARVEL

❑1, Dec 1997, gatefold summary 2.50
❑2, Jan 1998, gatefold summary 2.50
❑3, Feb 1998, gatefold summary 2.50

KITZ 'N' KATZ KOMIKS
PHANTASY

❑1, ca. 1986 .... 1.50
❑2, ca. 1986, b&w 1.50
❑3, ca. 1987, b&w 1.50
❑4, ca. 1987, b&w 1.50
❑5, ca. 1987 .... 1.50
❑6, ca. 1987 .... 1.50

KIWANNI: DAUGHTER OF THE DAWN
C&T

❑1, Feb 1988, b&w 2.25

KLOR
SIRIUS

❑1, ca. 1998 .... 2.95
❑2, ca. 1998 .... 2.95
❑3, ca. 1998 .... 2.95

KNEWTS OF THE ROUND TABLE
PAN

❑1, Jul 1998, b&w 2.50
❑2, Sep 1998, b&w 2.50
❑3, ca. 1998 .... 2.50
❑4, ca. 1999 .... 2.50
❑5, ca. 1999 .... 2.50

KNIGHT
BEAR CLAW

❑0, Oct 1993 .... 2.50

KNIGHTFOOL: THE FALL OF THE SPLATMAN
PARODY

❑1 .... 2.95

KNIGHTHAWK
ACCLAIM / WINDJAMMER

❑1, Sep 1995 .... 2.50
❑2, Sep 1995 .... 2.50
❑3, Oct 1995 .... 2.50
❑4, Oct 1995 .... 2.50
❑5, Nov 1995 .... 2.50
❑6, Nov 1995 .... 2.50

KNIGHTMARE (ANTARCTIC)
ANTARCTIC

❑1, Jul 1994, b&w 2.75
❑2, Sep 1994, b&w 2.75
❑3, Jan 1995, b&w 2.75
❑4, Mar 1995, b&w 2.75
❑5, Mar 1995, b&w 2.75
❑6, May 1995, b&w 2.75

KNIGHTMARE (IMAGE)
IMAGE

❑0, Aug 1995; chromium cover 3.50
❑1, Feb 1995 .... 2.50
❑2, Mar 1995 .... 2.50
❑3, Apr 1995 .... 2.50
❑4, May 1995 .... 2.50
❑4/A, May 1995; alternate cover 2.50
❑5, Jun 1995; Flip book with Warcry #1 .... 2.50
❑6, ca. 1995 .... 2.50
❑7, ca. 1995 .... 2.50
❑8, ca. 1995 .... 2.50

KNIGHTSHIFT
LONDON NIGHT

❑1, ca. 1996 .... 3.00
❑2, Dec 1996 .... 3.00

KNIGHTS' KINGDOM
LEGO

❑1 .... 4.99

KNIGHTS OF PENDRAGON (1ST SERIES)
MARVEL

❑1, Jul 1990 .... 2.50
❑2, Aug 1990 .... 2.00
❑3, Oct 1990 .... 2.00
❑4, Oct 1990 .... 2.00
❑5, Nov 1990 .... 2.00
❑6, Dec 1990 .... 2.00
❑7, Jan 1991 .... 2.00
❑8, Feb 1991 .... 2.00
❑9, Mar 1991 .... 2.00
❑10, Apr 1991 .... 2.00
❑11, May 1991, A: Iron Man 2.00
❑12, Jun 1991 .... 2.00
❑13, Jul 1991 .... 2.00
❑14, Aug 1991 .... 2.00
❑15, Sep 1991 .... 2.00
❑16, Oct 1991 .... 2.00
❑17, Nov 1991 .... 2.00
❑18, Dec 1991, A: Iron Man. 2.00

KNIGHTS OF PENDRAGON (2ND SERIES)
MARVEL

❑1, Jul 1992 A: Iron Man 2.00
❑2, Aug 1992 .... 1.75
❑3, Sep 1992 .... 1.75
❑4, Oct 1992 .... 1.75
❑5, Nov 1992; Title changes to The Knights of Pendragon; New armor.. 1.75
❑6, Dec 1992 .... 1.75
❑7, Jan 1993 A: Amazing Spider-Man. 1.75
❑8, Feb 1993 .... 1.75
❑9, Mar 1993; Spider-Man 1.75
❑10, Apr 1993 .... 1.75
❑11, May 1993 .... 1.75
❑12, Jun 1993 .... 1.75
❑13, Jul 1993 .... 1.75
❑14, Aug 1993 A: Death's Head II 1.75
❑15, Sep 1993 A: Death's Head II 1.75

KNIGHTS OF THE DINNER TABLE
KENZER

❑1, Jul 1994 .... 150.00
❑2, Jan 1995 .... 45.00
❑3, Apr 1995 .... 25.00
❑4, Nov 1995; Gary Con issue 30.00
❑4/2nd, Feb 1997 .... 25.00
❑5, Mar 1997 .... 25.00
❑6, Apr 1997 .... 18.00
❑7, May 1997 .... 18.00
❑8, Jun 1997 .... 18.00
❑9, Jul 1997 .... 18.00
❑10, Aug 1997 .... 18.00
❑11, Sep 1997 .... 14.00
❑12, Oct 1997 .... 14.00
❑13, Nov 1997 .... 14.00
❑14, Dec 1997 .... 14.00
❑15, Jan 1998 .... 14.00
❑16, Feb 1998 .... 10.00
❑17, Mar 1998 .... 10.00
❑18, Apr 1998 .... 10.00
❑19, May 1998 .... 10.00
❑20, Jun 1998 .... 10.00
❑21, Jul 1998; Gary Con issue 10.00
❑22, Aug 1998 .... 6.00
❑23, Sep 1998 .... 6.00
❑24, Oct 1998 .... 6.00
❑25, Nov 1998 .... 6.00
❑26, Dec 1998 .... 6.00
❑27, Jan 1999 .... 6.00
❑28, Feb 1999 .... 6.00
❑29, Mar 1999 .... 6.00
❑30, Apr 1999 .... 6.00
❑31, May 1999 .... 4.00
❑32, Jun 1999 .... 4.00
❑33, Jul 1999; Wild Wild Hack 3.00
❑34, Aug 1999 .... 2.95
❑35, Sep 1999 .... 2.95

Other grades: Multiply price above by 5/6 for VF/NM • 2/3 for VERY FINE • 1/3 for FINE • 1/5 for VERY GOOD • 1/8 for GOOD

King Conan

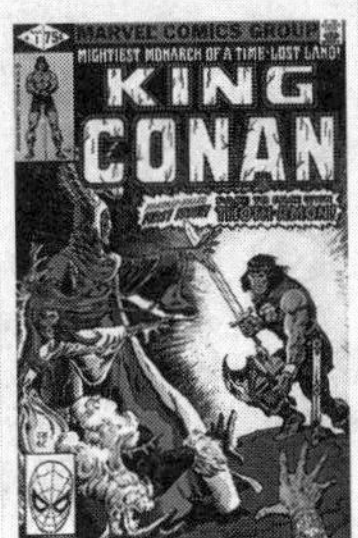

Series changes to "Conan the King" with #20

©Marvel

Kingdom Come

Lauded Mark Waid/Alex Ross Elseworlds

©DC

King Kong (Gold Key)

Gold Key version predates De Laurentiis

©Gold Key

Kiss: Psycho Circus

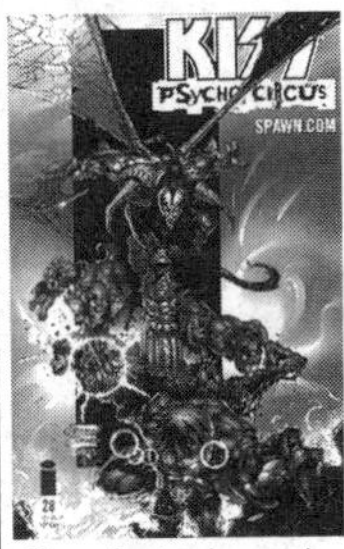

Circus freaks play music, make faces

©Image

Kitty Pryde & Wolverine

Series transforms Sprite into Shadowcat

©Marvel

N-MINT

❑36, Oct 1999 ... 2.95
❑37, Nov 1999 ... 2.95
❑38, Dec 1999 ... 2.95
❑39, Jan 2000 ... 2.95
❑40, Feb 2000 ... 2.95
❑41, Mar 2000 ... 2.95
❑42, Apr 2000 ... 2.95
❑43, May 2000 ... 2.95
❑44, Jun 2000 ... 2.95
❑45, Jul 2000 ... 2.95
❑46, Aug 2000 ... 2.95
❑47, Sep 2000 ... 2.95
❑48, Oct 2000 ... 2.95
❑49, Nov 2000 ... 2.95
❑50, Dec 2000; double-sized ... 4.95
❑51, Jan 2001 ... 2.95
❑52, Feb 2001 ... 2.95
❑53, Mar 2001 ... 2.95
❑54, Apr 2001 ... 2.95
❑55, May 2001 ... 2.95
❑56, Jun 2001 ... 2.95
❑57, Jul 2001 ... 2.95
❑58, Aug 2001 ... 2.95
❑59, Sep 2001 ... 2.95
❑60, Oct 2001 ... 2.99
❑61, Nov 2001 ... 2.99
❑62, Dec 2001 ... 2.99
❑63, Jan 2002 ... 2.99
❑64, Feb 2002 ... 2.99
❑65, Mar 2002 ... 2.99
❑66, Apr 2002 ... 2.99
❑67, May 2002 ... 2.99
❑68, Jun 2002 ... 2.99
❑69, Jul 2002 ... 2.99
❑70, Aug 2002 ... 3.99
❑71, Sep 2002 ... 3.99
❑72, Oct 2002 ... 3.99
❑73, Nov 2002 ... 3.99
❑74, Dec 2002 ... 3.99
❑75, Jan 2003 ... 3.99
❑76, Feb 2003 ... 3.99
❑77, Mar 2003 ... 3.99
❑78, Apr 2003 ... 3.99
❑79, May 2003 ... 3.99
❑80, Jun 2003 ... 3.99
❑81, Jul 2003 ... 3.99
❑82, Aug 2003 ... 3.99
❑83, Sep 2003 ... 3.99
❑84, Oct 2003 ... 3.99
❑85, Nov 2003 ... 3.99
❑86, Dec 2003 ... 3.99
❑87, Jan 2004 ... 3.99
❑88, Feb 2004 ... 3.99
❑89, Mar 2004 ... 3.99
❑90, Apr 2004 ... 3.99
❑91, May 2004 ... 3.99
❑92, Jun 2004 ... 3.99
❑93, Jul 2004 ... 3.99
❑94, Aug 2004 ... 3.99
❑95, Sep 2004 ... 3.99
❑96, Oct 2004 ... 3.99
❑97, Nov 2004 ... 3.99
❑98, Dec 2004 ... 3.99
❑99, Jan 2005 ... 3.99

N-MINT

❑100, Feb 2005 ... 7.99
❑101, Mar 2005, b&w ... 3.99
❑102, Apr 2005 ... 3.99
❑103, May 2005 ... 3.99
❑104, Jun 2005 ... 3.99
❑105, Jul 2005 ... 3.99
❑106, Aug 2005 ... 3.99
❑107, Sep 2005 ... 3.99
❑108, Oct 2005 ... 3.99
❑109, Dec 2005 ... 3.99

KNIGHTS OF THE DINNER TABLE: BLACK HANDS GAMING SOCIETY SPECIAL

KENZER AND COMPANY

❑1, ca. 2003 ... 2.99
❑2, ca. 2004 ... 2.99

KNIGHTS OF THE DINNER TABLE: EVERKNIGHTS

KENZER AND COMPANY

❑-5, Feb 2002 ... 2.99
❑-4, Mar 2002 ... 2.99
❑-3, Apr 2002 ... 2.99
❑-2, May 2002 ... 2.99
❑-1, Jun 2002 ... 2.99
❑1, Jul 2002 ... 2.99
❑2, Sep 2002 ... 2.99
❑3, Nov 2002 ... 2.99
❑4, Jan 2003 ... 2.99
❑5, Mar 2003 ... 2.99
❑6, May 2003 ... 2.99
❑7, Jul 2003 ... 2.99
❑8, Sep 2003 ... 2.99
❑9, Nov 2003 ... 2.99
❑10, Jan 2004 ... 2.99
❑11, Mar 2004 ... 2.99
❑12, May 2004 ... 2.99
❑13, Jul 2004 ... 2.99
❑14, Nov 2004 ... 2.99
❑Special 1, Jun 2004 ... 2.99

KNIGHTS OF THE DINNER TABLE/ FAANS CROSSOVER SPECIAL

SIX HANDED

❑1, Jul 1999, b&w ... 2.95

KNIGHTS OF THE DINNER TABLE ILLUSTRATED

KENZER

❑1, Jun 2000, b&w ... 2.95
❑2, Aug 2000, b&w ... 2.95
❑3, Oct 2000, b&w ... 2.95
❑4, Dec 2000, b&w; creative team switches from Aaron Williams to Brendan and Brian Fraim ... 2.95
❑5, Feb 2001 ... 2.95
❑6, Apr 2001 ... 2.95
❑7, Jun 2001 ... 2.95
❑8, Aug 2001 ... 2.95
❑9, Oct 2001 ... 2.95
❑10, Dec 2001; reprints of original KoDT strips end ... 2.99

N-MINT

❑11, Feb 2002; cover forms triptych with other parts of crossover, Travelers and Knights of the Dinner Table Illustrated vs. Tony Digerolamo's The Travelers Crossover Special; references to where original strips can be found begin ... 2.99
❑12, Apr 2002 ... 2.99
❑13, Jun 2002 ... 2.99
❑14, Aug 2002 ... 2.99
❑15, Oct 2002 ... 2.99
❑16, Nov 2002 ... 2.99
❑17, Dec 2002; full-page panels throughout ... 2.99
❑18, Jan 2003 ... 2.99
❑19, Feb 2003 ... 2.99
❑20, Mar 2003 ... 2.99
❑21, Apr 2003 ... 2.99
❑22, May 2003; cover forms diptych with #23 ... 2.99
❑23, Jun 2003; cover forms diptych with #22 ... 2.99
❑24, Jul 2003 ... 2.99
❑25, Aug 2003 ... 2.99
❑26, Sep 2003 ... 2.99
❑27, Oct 2003 ... 2.99
❑28, Nov 2003 ... 2.99
❑29, Dec 2003 ... 2.99
❑30, Jan 2004 ... 2.99
❑31, Feb 2004 ... 2.99
❑32, Mar 2004 ... 2.99
❑33, Apr 2004 ... 2.99
❑34, May 2004 ... 2.99
❑35, Jun 2004 ... 2.99
❑36, Jul 2004 ... 2.99
❑37, Aug 2004 ... 2.99
❑38, Sep 2004 ... 2.99
❑39, Oct 2004 ... 2.99
❑40, Nov 2004 ... 2.99
❑41, Dec 2004 ... 2.99

KNIGHTS OF THE JAGUAR SUPER LIMITED ONE SHOT

IMAGE

❑1, Jan 2004 ... 3.00

KNIGHTS OF THE ZODIAC

VIZ

❑1, Jan 2004 ... 9.95
❑2, Mar 2004 ... 9.95
❑3, May 2004 ... 9.95
❑4, Jul 8 ... 9.95
❑5, Sep 2004 ... 9.95
❑6, Nov 2004 ... 9.95
❑7, Jan 2005 ... 9.95
❑8, Mar 2005 ... 9.95
❑9, May 2005 ... 9.95
❑10, Jul 2005 ... 9.95
❑11, Sep 2005 ... 9.95
❑12, Nov 2005 ... 9.95

KNIGHTS ON BROADWAY

BROADWAY

❑1, Jul 1996 ... 2.95
❑2, Aug 1996 ... 2.95
❑3, Oct 1996 ... 2.95

Other grades: Multiply price above by 5/6 for VF/NM • 2/3 for VERY FINE • 1/3 for FINE • 1/5 for VERY GOOD • 1/8 for GOOD

KNIGHT'S ROUND TABLE
KNIGHT
❑1, Oct 1996, b&w 2.95
❑1/A, ca. 1996 2.95

KNIGHTSTRIKE
IMAGE
❑1, Dec 1995; polybagged with Sentinel card 2.50

KNIGHT WATCHMAN
IMAGE
❑1, Jun 1998; cover says May, indicia says Jun 2.95
❑2, Jul 1998 2.95
❑3, Aug 1998 2.95
❑4, Oct 1998 2.95

KNIGHT WATCHMAN: GRAVEYARD SHIFT
CALIBER
❑1, ca. 1994, b&w 2.95
❑2, ca. 1995 2.95

KNIGHT WOLF
FIVE STAR
❑1 2.50
❑2 2.50
❑3 2.50

KNUCKLES
ARCHIE
❑1, Apr 1997 4.00
❑2, May 1997 3.00
❑3, Jun 1997 3.00
❑4, Aug 1997 2.25
❑5, Sep 1997 2.25
❑6, Oct 1997 2.25
❑7, Dec 1997 2.25
❑8, Jan 1998 2.25
❑9, Feb 1998 2.25
❑10, Mar 1998 2.25
❑11, Apr 1998 2.25
❑12, May 1998 2.25
❑13, Jun 1998 2.25
❑14, Jul 1998 2.25
❑15, Aug 1998 2.25
❑16, Sep 1998 2.25
❑17, Oct 1998 2.25
❑18, Nov 1998 2.25
❑19, Dec 1998 2.25
❑20, Jan 1999 2.25
❑21, Feb 1999 2.25
❑22, Mar 1999, cover forms triptych with #23 and #24 2.25
❑23, Apr 1999, cover forms triptych with #22 and #24 2.25
❑24, May 1999, cover forms triptych with #22 and #23 2.25
❑25, Jun 1999 2.25
❑26, Jul 1999 2.25
❑27, Aug 1999 2.25
❑28, Sep 1999 2.25
❑29, Oct 1999, The Echidna 2.25

KNUCKLES' CHAOTIX
ARCHIE
❑1, Jan 1996 3.00

KNUCKLES THE MALEVOLENT NUN
FANTAGRAPHICS
❑1, ca. 1991, b&w 2.25
❑2, ca. 1991 2.25

KOBALT
DC / MILESTONE
❑1, Jun 1994 1.75
❑2, Jul 1994 1.75
❑3, Aug 1994 1.75
❑4, Sep 1994 1.75
❑5, Oct 1994 1.75
❑6, Nov 1994 1.75
❑7, Dec 1994 1.75
❑8, Jan 1995 1.75
❑9, Feb 1995 1.75
❑10, Mar 1995 1.75
❑11, Apr 1995 1.75
❑12, Jun 1995 1.75
❑13, Jul 1995 2.50
❑14, Jul 1995 2.50
❑15, Aug 1995 2.50
❑16, Sep 1995 2.50

KOBRA
DC
❑1, Mar 1976 JK (a); O: Kobra. 1: Kobra. 9.00
❑2, May 1976 3.00
❑3, Jul 1976, KG (a) 3.00
❑4, Sep 1976 3.00
❑5, Dec 1976 3.00
❑6, Feb 1977 3.00
❑7, Apr 1977 3.00

KODOCHA: SANA'S STAGE
TOKYOPOP
❑1, Jun 2002, b&w; printed in Japanese format 9.99
❑2, Jul 2002, b&w; printed in Japanese format 9.99
❑3, Sep 2002, b&w; printed in Japanese format 9.99

KOGARATSU: THE LOTUS OF BLOOD
ACME
❑1 5.95

KOLCHAK TALES: BLACK & WHITE & RED ALL OVER
MOONSTONE
❑1/A cover, Sep 2005 4.95
❑1/B cover, Sep 2005 4.95

KOLCHAK: TALES OF THE NIGHT STALKER
MOONSTONE
❑1/A, ca. 2004, Cover A 3.50
❑1/B, ca. 2004, Cover B 3.50
❑2/A, ca. 2004, Cover A 3.50
❑2/B, ca. 2004, Cover B 3.50
❑3/A, ca. 2004, Cover A 3.50
❑3/B, ca. 2004, Cover B 3.50
❑4/A, ca. 2004, Cover A 3.50
❑4/B, ca. 2004, Cover B 3.50
❑5/A 2005 3.50
❑5/B 2005 3.50
❑6/A, Jun 2005 3.50
❑6/B, Jun 2005 3.50

KOLCHAK: THE NIGHT STALKER: GET OF BELIAL
MOONSTONE
❑1, ca. 2002; Prestige format one-shot 6.95

KOLCHAK: THE NIGHT STALKER
MOONSTONE
❑1, ca. 2002; Prestige format one-shot 6.50

KOMODO AND THE DEFIANTS
VICTORY
❑1, ca. 1987 1.50
❑2, ca. 1987 1.50

KONA
DELL
❑2, Jul 1962, A: Numbering continued from. 18.00
❑3, Sep 1962 15.00
❑4, Oct 1962, O: Anak. 1: Anak. Anak stories begin as back-up 15.00
❑5, Jan 1963 15.00
❑6, Apr 1963 12.00
❑7, Jul 1963 12.00
❑8, Oct 1963 12.00
❑9, Jan 1964 12.00
❑10, Apr 1964 12.00
❑11, Jul 1964 12.00
❑12, Oct 1964 12.00
❑13, Jan 1965 12.00
❑14, Apr 1965 12.00
❑15, Jul 1965 10.00
❑16, Oct 1965 10.00
❑17, Jan 1966 10.00
❑18, Apr 1966 10.00
❑19, Jul 1966 10.00
❑20, Oct 1966 10.00
❑21, Jan 1967 10.00

KONGA
CHARLTON
❑1, ca. 1960 75.00
❑2, Aug 1961 50.00
❑3, Oct 1961 35.00
❑4, Dec 1961 35.00
❑5, Mar 1962 25.00
❑6, May 1962 25.00
❑7, Jul 1962 25.00
❑8, Sep 1962 25.00
❑9, Nov 1962 25.00
❑10, Jan 1963 25.00
❑11, Mar 1963 16.00
❑12, May 1963 16.00
❑13, Jul 1963 16.00
❑14, Sep 1963 16.00
❑15, Nov 1963 16.00
❑16, Jan 1964 16.00
❑17, Mar 1964 16.00
❑18, Jun 1964 16.00
❑19, Sep 1964 16.00
❑20, Dec 1965 16.00
❑21, Feb 1965 14.00
❑22, May 1965 14.00
❑23, Nov 1965 14.00

KONGA'S REVENGE
CHARLTON
❑1, ca. 1963, Reprints Konga's Revenge #3; Published out of sequence 10.00
❑2, ca. 1963 7.00
❑3, ca. 1963 7.00

KONG, 8TH WONDER OF THE WORLD - MOVIE ADAPTATION
DARK HORSE
❑1, Jan 2006 4.95

KONG THE UNTAMED
DC
❑1, Jul 1975 BWr (c); BWr, AA (a); O: Kong the Untamed 9.00
❑2, Sep 1975 3.00
❑3, Nov 1975 AA (a) 3.00
❑4, Jan 1976 3.00
❑5, Mar 1976 3.00

KONNY AND CZU
ANTARCTIC
❑1, Sep 1994, b&w 2.75
❑2, Nov 1994, b&w 2.75
❑3, Jan 1995, b&w 2.75
❑4, Mar 1995, b&w 2.75

KOOLAU THE LEPER (JACK LONDON'S...)
TOME
❑1, b&w 2.50

KOOSH KINS
ARCHIE
❑1, Oct 1991 1.00
❑2, Oct 1991 1.00
❑3, Dec 1991 1.00
❑4, Feb 1992 1.00

KORAK, SON OF TARZAN
GOLD KEY
❑1, Jan 1964, RM (a); Gold Key begins publishing 65.00
❑2, Mar 1964, RM (a) 45.00
❑3, May 1964, RM (a) 45.00
❑4, Aug 1964, RM (a) 45.00
❑5, Oct 1964, RM (a) 45.00
❑6, Dec 1964, RM (a) 30.00
❑7, Mar 1965, RM (a) 30.00
❑8, May 1965, RM (a) 30.00
❑9, Jul 1965, RM (a) 30.00
❑10, Sep 1965, RM (a) 30.00
❑11, Nov 1965, RM (a) 30.00
❑12, Mar 1966 25.00
❑13, Jun 1966 25.00
❑14, Sep 1966 25.00
❑15, Dec 1966 25.00
❑16, Mar 1967 25.00
❑17, Jun 1967 25.00
❑18, Aug 1967 25.00
❑19, Oct 1967 20.00
❑20, Dec 1967 20.00
❑21, Feb 1968, RM (a) 20.00
❑22, Apr 1968 20.00
❑23, Jun 1968 20.00
❑24, Aug 1968 20.00
❑25, Oct 1968 20.00
❑26, Dec 1968 20.00
❑27, Feb 1969 20.00
❑28, Apr 1969 20.00
❑29, Jun 1969 20.00
❑30, Aug 1969 20.00
❑31, Oct 1969 20.00
❑32, Dec 1969 20.00

Knights of the Dinner Table

Funny strip about role-playing gamers
©Kenzer

Knights of the Dinner Table Illustrated

Retells strip stories, with actual art
©Kenzer

Kobra

Twin brothers: one good, one evil
©DC

Kona

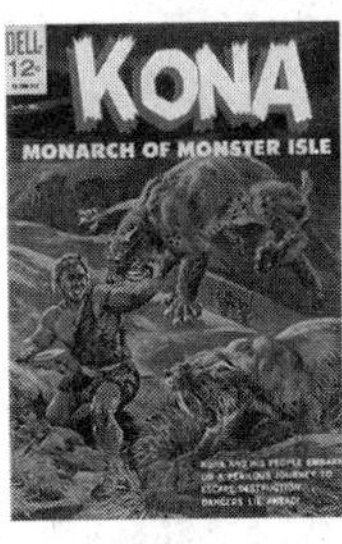

Caveman fights for survival on Monster Isle
©Dell

Konga

Steve Ditko adapts the 1961 monster film
©Charlton

N-MINT

❑33, Jan 1970 .... 20.00
❑34, Mar 1970 .... 20.00
❑35, May 1970 .... 20.00
❑36, Jul 1970 .... 20.00
❑37, Sep 1970 .... 20.00
❑38, Nov 1970 .... 17.00
❑39, Jan 1971 .... 17.00
❑40, Mar 1971 .... 17.00
❑41, May 1971 .... 17.00
❑42, Jul 1971 .... 17.00
❑43, Sep 1971 .... 17.00
❑44, Nov 1971 .... 17.00
❑45, Jan 1972 .... 17.00
❑46, May 1972, continues Gold Key numbering; DC begins publishing 17.00
❑47, Jul 1972 .... 15.00
❑48, Sep 1972 .... 15.00
❑49, Nov 1972 .... 15.00
❑50, Feb 1973 .... 15.00
❑51, Apr 1973, JKu (c); FT (a) 15.00
❑52, Jul 1973 .... 10.00
❑53, Sep 1973, JKu (c); Carson of Venus back-up 10.00
❑54, Nov 1973, JKu (c); Carson of Venus back-up 10.00
❑55, Jan 1974, JKu (c); Carson of Venus back-up 10.00
❑56, Mar 1974, JKu (c); Carson of Venus back-up 10.00
❑57, Jun 1975 .... 10.00
❑58, Aug 1975 .... 10.00
❑59, Oct 1975, Series continued in Tarzan Family #60 .... 10.00

KORE
IMAGE

❑1, Apr 2003 .... 2.95
❑2, Jun 2003 .... 2.95
❑3, Jul 2003 .... 2.95
❑4, Sep 2003 .... 2.95
❑5, Oct 2003 .... 2.95

KORG: 70,000 B.C.
CHARLTON

❑1, May 1975 .... 8.00
❑2, Aug 1975 .... 5.00
❑3, Oct 1975 .... 5.00
❑4, Dec 1975 .... 5.00
❑5, Feb 1976 .... 5.00
❑6, May 1976 .... 5.00
❑7, Jul 1976 .... 5.00
❑8, Sep 1976 .... 5.00
❑9, Nov 1976 .... 5.00

KORVUS
ARROW

❑0, Jul 1999; Flip book with Spank the Monkey #1 .... 2.95
❑1, ca. 1998 .... 2.95
❑2, ca. 1998 .... 2.95
❑3, Spr 1998 .... 2.95

KORVUS (VOL. 2)
ARROW

❑1, Fal 1998 .... 2.95
❑2, ca. 1998 .... 2.95

KOSMIC KAT
IMAGE

❑1, Aug 1999 .... 2.95

N-MINT

KOSMIC KAT ACTIVITY BOOK
IMAGE

❑1, Aug 1999 .... 2.95

KRAZY KAT
GOLD KEY

❑1, Jan 1964 .... 15.00

KREE-SKRULL WAR S TARRING THE AVENGERS
MARVEL

❑1, Sep 1983; JB, NA (a); Reprints 3.00
❑2, Oct 1983; JB, NA (a); Reprints 3.00

KREMEN
GREY PRODUCTIONS

❑1 .... 2.50
❑2 .... 2.50
❑3 .... 2.50

KREY
GAUNTLET

❑1, ca. 1992, b&w 2.50
❑2, ca. 1992, b&w 2.50
❑3, ca. 1992, b&w 2.50

KROFFT SUPERSHOW
GOLD KEY

❑1, Apr 1978 .... 6.00
❑2, May 1978 .... 4.00
❑3, Jun 1978 .... 4.00
❑4, Sep 1978 .... 4.00
❑5, Nov 1978 .... 4.00
❑6, Jan 1979 .... 4.00

KRULL
MARVEL

❑1, Nov 1983 .... 1.25
❑2, Dec 1983 .... 1.25

KRUSTY COMICS
BONGO

❑1, ca. 1995 .... 2.50
❑2, ca. 1995 .... 2.50
❑3, ca. 1995 .... 2.50

KRYPTON CHRONICLES
DC

❑1, Sep 1981, CS (a); A: Superman. .. 1.50
❑2, Oct 1981, CS (a); A: Black Flame. 1.50
❑3, Nov 1981, CS (a); O: name of Kal-El. 1.50

KULL AND THE BARBARIANS
MARVEL

❑1, May 1975, b&w; magazine; NA, GK, JSe, WW, RA (a); reprinted from Kull the Conqueror #1 and 2, Supernatural Thrillers #3 .... 16.00
❑2, Jul 1975, b&w; magazine HC, NA, GK (a) 4.00
❑3, Sep 1975, b&w; magazine O: Red Sonja. 5.00

KULL IN 3-D
BLACKTHORNE

❑1 .... 2.50
❑2 .... 2.50

KULL THE CONQUEROR (1ST SERIES)
MARVEL

❑1, Jun 1971, WW, RA (a); O: Kull. 1: Brule the Spear-Slayer. 20.00

N-MINT

❑2, Sep 1971, JSe (a) 12.00
❑3, Jul 1972, JSe (a); A: Thulsa Doom. 8.00
❑4, Sep 1972, JSe (a) 8.00
❑5, Nov 1972, JSe (a) 7.00
❑6, Jan 1973, JSe (a) 5.00
❑7, Mar 1973 .... 5.00
❑8, May 1973 .... 5.00
❑9, Jul 1973 .... 5.00
❑10, Sep 1973, Continued as "Kull the Destroyer" 5.00

KULL THE CONQUEROR (2ND SERIES)
MARVEL

❑1, Dec 1982; JB (a); Brule 5.00
❑2, Mar 1983; Misareena 3.00

KULL THE CONQUEROR (3RD SERIES)
MARVEL

❑1, May 1983; JB (a); Iraina 2.00
❑2, Jul 1983 JB (a) 1.75
❑3, Dec 1983 JB (a) 1.75
❑4, Feb 1984 JB (a) 1.50
❑5, Aug 1984 .... 1.50
❑6, Oct 1984 .... 1.25
❑7, Dec 1984 .... 1.25
❑8, Feb 1985 .... 1.25
❑9, Apr 1985 .... 1.25
❑10, Jun 1985 .... 1.25

KULL THE DESTROYER
MARVEL

❑11, Nov 1973, Continued from Kull the Conqueror (1st Series) #10 .... 2.00
❑12, Jan 1974, MP (a) 2.00
❑13, Mar 1974, MP (a); Marvel Value Stamp #73: Kingpin 2.00
❑14, May 1974, JSn, MP (a); Marvel Value Stamp #40: Loki 2.00
❑15, Aug 1974, SD, MP (a); series goes on hiatus; Marvel Value Stamp #42: Man Wolf 2.00
❑16, Aug 1976 .... 2.00
❑16/30 cent, Aug 1976, 30 cent regional price variant 20.00
❑17, Oct 1976, AA (a) 2.00
❑18, Dec 1976, AA (a) 2.00
❑19, Feb 1977, AA (a) 2.00
❑20, Apr 1977, AA (a) 2.00
❑21, Jun 1977 .... 2.00
❑21/35 cent, Jun 1977, 35 cent regional price variant 15.00
❑22, Aug 1977 .... 2.00
❑22/35 cent, Aug 1977, 35 cent regional price variant 15.00
❑23, Oct 1977, Newsstand edition (disrtributed by Curtis); issue number in box 2.00
❑23/Whitman, Oct 1977, Special markets edition (usually sold in Whitman bagged prepacks); price appears in a diamond; no UPC barcode 2.00
❑23/35 cent, Oct 1977, 35 cent regional price variant 15.00
❑24, Dec 1977 .... 2.00
❑25, Feb 1978 .... 2.00
❑26, Apr 1978 .... 2.00

Other grades: Multiply price above by 5/6 for VF/NM • 2/3 for VERY FINE • 1/3 for FINE • 1/5 for VERY GOOD • 1/8 for GOOD

N-MINT

- ❑27, Jun 1978 2.00
- ❑28, Aug 1978 2.00
- ❑29, Oct 1978, A: Thulsa Doom. 2.00

KUNOICHI
LIGHTNING

- ❑1, Sep 1996; also contains Sinja: Resurrection #1; indicia is for Sinja: Resurrection 3.00

KWAIDEN
DARK HORSE

- ❑1, ca. 2004 14.95

KYRA
ELSEWHERE

- ❑1, ca. 1985, b&w 2.00
- ❑2, Spr 1986, b&w 2.00
- ❑3, Sum 1986, b&w 2.00
- ❑4, Dec 1986 2.00
- ❑5, Jun 1987 2.00
- ❑6, ca. 1987 2.00

K-Z COMICS PRESENTS
K-Z

- ❑1, Jun 1985 1.50

LAB
ASTONISH

- ❑1, ca. 2001 3.50
- ❑2, ca. 2003 2.99

LA BLUE GIRL
CPM / BARE BEAR

- ❑1, Jul 1996, b&w; wraparound cover 2.95
- ❑2, Aug 1996, b&w 2.95
- ❑3, Sep 1996, b&w 2.95
- ❑4, Oct 1996, b&w 2.95
- ❑5, Nov 1996, b&w 2.95
- ❑6, Dec 1996 2.95
- ❑7, Jan 1997 2.95
- ❑8, Feb 1997 2.95
- ❑9, Mar 1997 2.95
- ❑10, Apr 1997 2.95
- ❑11, May 1997 2.95
- ❑12, Jun 1997 2.95

LABMAN
IMAGE

- ❑1, Nov 1996 3.50
- ❑1/A, Nov 1996; alternate cover 3.50
- ❑1/B, Nov 1996; alternate cover 3.50
- ❑1/C, Nov 1996; alternate cover 3.50
- ❑2, Dec 1996 2.95
- ❑3, Jan 1997 2.95

LABMAN SOURCEBOOK
IMAGE

- ❑1, Jun 1996; Limited edition giveaway from 1996 San Diego Comic-Con 1.00

LABOR FORCE
BLACKTHORNE

- ❑1, Sep 1986 1.50
- ❑2 1.50
- ❑3 1.50
- ❑4 1.75
- ❑5, Mar 1987 1.75
- ❑6 1.75
- ❑7 1.75
- ❑8 1.75

LABOURS OF HERCULES
MALAN CLASSICAL ENTERPRISES

- ❑1, b&w 2.95

LAB RATS
DC

- ❑1, Jun 2002 2.50
- ❑2, Jul 2002 2.50
- ❑3, Aug 2002 2.50
- ❑4, Sep 2002 2.50
- ❑5, Oct 2002 2.50
- ❑6, Nov 2002 2.50
- ❑7, Dec 2002 2.50

LABYRINTH OF MADNESS
TSR

- ❑1 1.00

LABYRINTH: THE MOVIE
MARVEL

- ❑1, Nov 1986 JB, RT (a) 1.50
- ❑2, Dec 1986 JB, RT (a) 1.50
- ❑3, Jan 1987 JB, RT (a) 1.50

N-MINT

LACKLUSTER WORLD
GEN: ERIC PUBLISHING

- ❑1 2005 3.95
- ❑2 2005 3.95
- ❑3, Aug 2005 3.95

L.A. COMICS
LOS ANGELES

- ❑1 3.00
- ❑2 3.00

LAD, A DOG
DELL

- ❑2, Sep 1962, First issue published as Dell's Four Color #1303; no photo cover on this issue 30.00

LADY AND THE TRAMP
DELL

- ❑1, Jun 1955 25.00

LADY AND THE TRAMP (GOLD KEY)
GOLD KEY

- ❑1, Jan 1963, adapts Disney animated film; reprints Four Color #629 25.00
- ❑1 (1973), Mar 1972, adapts Disney animated film; reissued for re-release of film; reprints Four Color #629 14.00

LADY AND THE VAMPIRE
NBM

- ❑1 10.95

LADY ARCANE
HERO GRAPHICS

- ❑1, Jul 1992 4.95
- ❑2, b&w 3.50
- ❑3, b&w 3.50
- ❑4, b&w 2.95

LADY CRIME
AC

- ❑1, ca. 1992, b&w; Bob Powell reprints 2.75

LADY DEATH (MINI-SERIES)
CHAOS!

- ❑0, Nov 1997 3.00
- ❑½ 1994; Wizard mail-in promotional edition 4.00
- ❑½/A 1994; Wizard mail-in promotional edition 6.00
- ❑½/Gold 1994; Gold edition 5.00
- ❑1, Jan 1994 8.00
- ❑1/Ltd., Jan 1994; Signed limited edition 12.00
- ❑1/2nd, Feb 1994; Commemorative edition 2.75
- ❑2, Feb 1994 8.00
- ❑3, Mar 1994 5.00

LADY DEATH
CHAOS!

- ❑1, Feb 1998 7.00
- ❑1/Ltd., Feb 1998; premium limited edition; no cover price 9.00
- ❑2, Mar 1998 2.95
- ❑3, Apr 1998; Signed edition 2.95
- ❑4, May 1998 2.95
- ❑5, Jun 1998 2.95
- ❑5/Variant, Jun 1998; variant cover 3.50
- ❑6, Jul 1998 2.95
- ❑7, Aug 1998 2.95
- ❑8, Sep 1998 2.95
- ❑9, Oct 1998 2.95
- ❑10, Nov 1998; cover says Oct, indicia says Nov 2.95
- ❑11, Dec 1998 2.95
- ❑12, Jan 1999 2.95
- ❑13, Feb 1999 2.95
- ❑14, Mar 1999 2.95
- ❑15, Apr 1999 2.95
- ❑16, May 1999 2.95

LADY DEATH (BRIAN PULIDO´S...): A MEDIEVAL TALE
CROSSGEN

- ❑1, Mar 2003 2.95
- ❑2, Apr 2003 2.95
- ❑3, May 2003 2.95
- ❑4, Jun 2003 2.95
- ❑5, Jul 2003 2.95
- ❑6, Sep 2003 2.95
- ❑7, Oct 2003 2.95
- ❑8, Oct 2003 2.95
- ❑9, Dec 2003 2.95

N-MINT

- ❑10, Feb 2004 2.95
- ❑11, Mar 2004 2.95
- ❑12, Apr 2004 2.95

LADY DEATH: ALIVE
CHAOS

- ❑1, May 2001 2.95
- ❑1/Ltd., May 2001 2.95
- ❑2, Jun 2001 2.95
- ❑3, Jul 2001 2.95
- ❑4, Aug 2001 2.95

LADY DEATH AND THE WOMEN OF CHAOS! GALLERY
CHAOS

- ❑1, Nov 1996 2.25

LADY DEATH/BAD KITTY
CHAOS

- ❑1, Sep 2001 2.99

LADY DEATH (BRIAN PULIDO´S...): WILD HUNT
CROSSGEN

- ❑1, Apr 2004 2.95
- ❑2, May 2004 2.95

LADY DEATH: DARK MILLENNIUM
CHAOS

- ❑1, Feb 2000 2.95
- ❑2, Mar 2000 2.95

LADY DEATH: DRAGON WARS
CHAOS

- ❑1, Apr 1998 2.95

LADY DEATH IV: THE CRUCIBLE
CHAOS!

- ❑½, Nov 1996; Wizard promotional edition 5.00
- ❑½/A; Wizard promotional edition; Cloth alternate cover 8.00
- ❑1, Nov 1996 3.00
- ❑1/A, Nov 1996; Leather edition 12.50
- ❑1/B, Nov 1996; All silver cover; Limited to 400; Comes with certificate of authenticity 16.00
- ❑1/Silver, Nov 1996; silver embossed cardstock wraparound cover 3.50
- ❑2, Jan 1997 2.95
- ❑3, Mar 1997 2.95
- ❑4, Apr 1997 2.95
- ❑5, Aug 1997 2.95
- ❑5/Variant, Aug 1997; Nightmare Premium Edition; no cover price 5.00
- ❑6, Oct 1997 2.95

LADY DEATH: HEARTBREAKER
CHAOS

- ❑1, Mar 2002 2.99
- ❑2 2.99
- ❑3 2.99
- ❑4 2.99
- ❑Ashcan 1; ashcan edition 1.00

LADY DEATH IN LINGERIE
CHAOS!

- ❑1, Aug 1995 2.95
- ❑1/Ltd., Aug 1995, foil-stamped leather premium edition; no cover price; limited to 10, 000 copies 10.00

LADY DEATH: JUDGEMENT WAR
CHAOS!

- ❑1, Nov 1999 2.95
- ❑2, Dec 1999 2.95
- ❑3, Jan 2000 2.95

LADY DEATH: JUDGEMENT WAR PRELUDE
CHAOS!

- ❑1, Oct 1999 2.95

LADY DEATH: RETRIBUTION
CHAOS!

- ❑1, Aug 1998 2.95
- ❑1/A, Aug 1998; Painted alternate cover 3.50
- ❑1/Ltd., Aug 1998; premium edition 4.00

LADY DEATH SWIMSUIT SPECIAL
CHAOS!

- ❑1, May 1994, b&w 2.50
- ❑1/Variant, May 1994; Red Velvet edition 8.00

LADY DEATH: THE GAUNTLET
CHAOS

- ❑1, Apr 2002 2.99
- ❑2, May 2002 2.99

Other grades: Multiply price above by 5/6 for VF/NM • 2/3 for VERY FINE • 1/3 for FINE • 1/5 for VERY GOOD • 1/8 for GOOD

Kong the Untamed

Kind of a 1970s version of Anthro
©DC

Korak, Son of Tarzan

A more youth-oriented version of Tarzan
©Gold Key

Kull the Conqueror (1st Series)

Barbarian series launched a year after Tarzan
©Marvel

Kyra

Woman wrestler in jungle comic
©Elsewhere

Lady Death (Mini-Series)

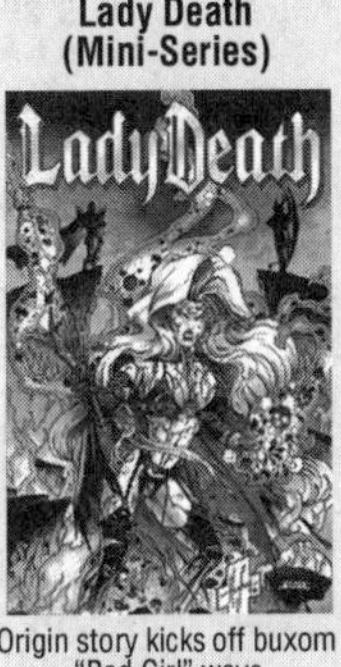

Origin story kicks off buxom "Bad Girl" wave
©Chaos!

N-MINT

LADY DEATH: THE RAPTURE
CHAOS!

- ❑1/Dynamic; Dynamic Forces cover ...
- ❑1/Ltd. ...
- ❑1, Jun 1999 ... 2.95
- ❑2, Jul 1999 ... 2.95
- ❑3, Aug 1999 ... 2.95
- ❑4, Sep 1999 ... 2.95

LADY DEATH III: THE ODYSSEY
CHAOS!

- ❑-1, Apr 1996; Sneak Peek Preview; promotional piece for mini-series ... 1.50
- ❑1, Apr 1996; Gold foil cover ... 3.50
- ❑1/Variant, Apr 1996; foil embossed cardstock wraparound cover ... 5.00
- ❑2, May 1996 ... 3.00
- ❑3, Jun 1996 ... 3.00
- ❑4, Aug 1996 ... 3.00
- ❑4/A, Aug 1996; alternate cover ... 8.00

LADY DEATH: TRIBULATION
CHAOS!

- ❑1, Dec 2000 ... 2.95
- ❑2, Jan 2001 ... 2.95

LADY DEATH II: BETWEEN HEAVEN & HELL
CHAOS!

- ❑1, Mar 1995, O: Lady Death. chromium cover ... 3.50
- ❑1/A, Mar 1995, Gold edition ... 4.00
- ❑1/B, Mar 1995, Black velvet limited edition ... 5.00
- ❑1/Ltd., Mar 1995 ... 5.00
- ❑1/2nd, Commemorative edition ... 2.75
- ❑2, Apr 1995 ... 3.00
- ❑3, May 1995 ... 3.00
- ❑4, Jun 1995 ... 3.00
- ❑4/Variant, Jun 1995, Lady Demon chase cover ... 5.00

LADY DEATH/VAMPIRELLA: DARK HEARTS
CHAOS!

- ❑1, Mar 1999; crossover with Harris .. 3.50
- ❑1/A, Mar 1999; Premium edition (5000 printed) ... 8.00

LADY DEATH VS. PURGATORI
CHAOS!

- ❑1/A, Dec 1999; Limited to 3,000 copies ...
- ❑1, Dec 1999; no cover price; red foil logo ... 3.00

LADY DEATH V. VAMPIRELLA
CHAOS

- ❑Ashcan 1, Feb 2000; Lady Death/ Vampirella II Preview Book ... 1.00
- ❑1/Ltd., Feb 2000 ...
- ❑1, Feb 2000 ...

LADY DEATH: WICKED WAYS
CHAOS!

- ❑1, Feb 1998 ... 2.95
- ❑1/Variant, Feb 1998; premium edition; white background cover ... 5.00

LADY DRACULA
FANTACO

- ❑1 ... 4.95
- ❑2 ... 4.95

N-MINT

LADY JUSTICE (VOL. 1) (NEIL GAIMAN'S...)
TEKNO

- ❑1, Sep 1995, 1: Lady Justice ... 2.00
- ❑2, Oct 1995 ... 2.00
- ❑3, Nov 1995 ... 2.00
- ❑4, Dec 1995, begins new story-arc with new Lady Justice ... 2.00
- ❑5, Dec 1995 ... 2.00
- ❑6, Jan 1996 ... 2.25
- ❑7, Jan 1996, stand-alone story ... 2.25
- ❑8, Feb 1996 ... 2.25
- ❑9, Mar 1996 ... 2.25
- ❑10, Apr 1996 ... 2.25
- ❑11, May 1996 ... 2.25

LADY JUSTICE (VOL. 2) (NEIL GAIMAN'S...)
BIG

- ❑1, Jun 1996 ... 2.25
- ❑2, Jul 1996 ... 2.25
- ❑3, Aug 1996 ... 2.25
- ❑4, Sep 1996 ... 2.25
- ❑5, Oct 1996 ... 2.25
- ❑6, Nov 1996 ... 2.25
- ❑7, Dec 1996 ... 2.25
- ❑8, Jan 1997 ... 2.25
- ❑9, Feb 1997 ... 2.25

LADY PENDRAGON GALLERY EDITION
IMAGE

- ❑1, Oct 1999 ... 2.95
- ❑1/A, Oct 1999; alternate cover ... 2.95

LADY PENDRAGON: MERLIN
IMAGE

- ❑1, Jan 2000 ... 2.95

LADY PENDRAGON/MORE THAN MORTAL
IMAGE

- ❑1, May 1999 ... 2.50
- ❑1/A, May 1999, alternate cover; white background ... 4.00
- ❑1/B, May 1999, DF alternate cover (holding spear facing forward) ... 5.00
- ❑Ashcan 1, Feb 1999, b&w; no cover price; preview of upcoming crossover ... 2.00

LADY PENDRAGON (VOL. 1)
MAXIMUM

- ❑1, Mar 1996 ... 2.50
- ❑1/A, Mar 1996; alternate cover ... 2.50
- ❑1/Autographed, Mar 1996 ... 6.00
- ❑1/2nd, Mar 1996; Remastered edition ... 2.50
- ❑Ashcan 1 ... 4.00
- ❑Ashcan 1/Autogr ... 6.00

LADY PENDRAGON (VOL. 2)
IMAGE

- ❑0, Mar 1999, flipbook with origin back-up ... 2.50
- ❑0/A ... 4.00
- ❑1, Nov 1998 ... 3.00
- ❑1/A, Nov 1998, alternate cover; castle ... 3.00
- ❑1/B, Nov 1998, Dynamic Forces alternate cover; Swordswoman amid city ruins with sword pointing at sky ... 3.00
- ❑1/2nd, Feb 1999, Lady Pendragon Remastered; reprints #1 with corrections ... 2.50
- ❑2, Dec 1998 ... 4.00
- ❑2/A, Dec 1998, alternate cover ... 3.00
- ❑3, Jan 1999, crucified on cover ... 2.50
- ❑3/A, Jan 1999, manga-style cover ... 2.50
- ❑Ashcan 1, Jun 1998, Convention Preview Edition; no cover price ... 2.00

N-MINT

LADY PENDRAGON (VOL. 3)
IMAGE

- ❑1, Mar 1999 ... 2.50
- ❑1/A, Apr 1999, "Stormkote"-covered flip book ... 2.50
- ❑1/B, Apr 1999, European Tour Edition 4.00
- ❑2, Apr 1999 ... 2.50
- ❑2/A, Apr 1999, alternate cover; Lady Pendragon vanquished ... 2.50
- ❑3, Jul 1999 ... 2.50
- ❑4, Aug 1999 ... 2.50
- ❑5, Sep 1999 ... 2.50
- ❑6, Oct 1999 ... 2.50
- ❑7, Dec 1999, Giant-size ... 3.95
- ❑8, Feb 2000 ... 2.50
- ❑9, Apr 2000 ... 2.50
- ❑10, Aug 2000 ... 2.50

LADY RAWHIDE
TOPPS

- ❑1, Jul 1995 ... 2.95
- ❑2, Sep 1995 ... 2.95
- ❑3, Nov 1995 ... 2.95
- ❑4, Jan 1996 ... 2.95
- ❑5, Mar 1996 ... 2.95

LADY RAWHIDE (VOL. 2)
TOPPS

- ❑½, ca. 1996 1: Star Wolf ... 5.00
- ❑1, Oct 1996 1: Scarlet Fever ... 2.95
- ❑2, Dec 1996 V: Scarlet Fever ... 2.95
- ❑3, Feb 1997 ... 2.95
- ❑4, Apr 1997, b&w ... 2.95
- ❑5, Jun 1997, b&w ... 2.95

LADY RAWHIDE MINI COMIC
TOPPS

- ❑1, Jul 1995; Wizard supplement; no cover price ... 1.00

LADY RAWHIDE: OTHER PEOPLE'S BLOOD
IMAGE

- ❑1, Mar 1999, b&w; Reprints Topps second series in b&w ... 2.95
- ❑2, Apr 1999, b&w; Reprints Topps second series in b&w ... 2.95
- ❑3, May 1999, b&w; Reprints Topps second series in b&w ... 2.95
- ❑4, Jun 1999, b&w; Reprints Topps second series in b&w ... 2.95
- ❑5, Jul 1999, b&w; Reprints Topps second series in b&w ... 2.95

LADY RAWHIDE SPECIAL EDITION
TOPPS

- ❑1, Jun 1995; reprints Zorro #2 and 3 3.95

Other grades: Multiply price above by 5/6 for VF/NM • 2/3 for VERY FINE • 1/3 for FINE • 1/5 for VERY GOOD • 1/8 for GOOD

LADY SPECTRA & SPARKY SPECIAL
J. KEVIN CARRIER
❑1, Jan 1995 .... 2.50

LADY SUPREME
IMAGE
❑1, May 1996; aquamarine background cover 2.50
❑1/A, May 1996; brown background cover 2.50
❑2, Aug 1996; flip-book with New Men Special Preview Edition 2.50

LADY VAMPRÉ
BLACK OUT
❑0 .... 2.95
❑1 .... 2.95

LADY VAMPRÉ: PLEASURES OF THE FLESH
BLACK OUT
❑1, b&w 2.95

LADY VAMPRÉ VS. BLACK LACE
BLACK OUT
❑1, Sep 1996, Flip-book 2.95

LAFF-A-LYMPICS
MARVEL
❑1, Mar 1978, based on Hanna-Barbera animated series 18.00
❑2, Apr 1978 .... 10.00
❑3, May 1978 .... 8.00
❑4, Jun 1978 .... 8.00
❑5, Jul 1978 .... 8.00
❑6, Aug 1978 .... 6.00
❑7, Sep 1978 .... 6.00
❑8, Oct 1978 .... 6.00
❑9, Nov 1978 .... 6.00
❑10, Dec 1978 .... 6.00
❑11, Jan 1979 .... 6.00
❑12, Feb 1979 .... 6.00
❑13, Mar 1979 .... 6.00

LAFFIN' GAS
BLACKTHORNE
❑1, Jun 1986 .... 2.00
❑2 1986 .... 2.00
❑3 1986 .... 2.00
❑4 1986 .... 2.00
❑5 .... 2.00
❑6; 3-D 2.00
❑7, Mar 1987 .... 2.00
❑8 1987 .... 2.00
❑9 1987 .... 2.00
❑10 1987 .... 2.00
❑11 .... 2.00
❑12 .... 2.00

LAMENT OF THE LAMB
TOKYOPOP
❑1, May 2004 .... 9.99

LANCE BARNES: POST NUKE DICK
MARVEL / EPIC
❑1, Apr 1993; Lance accidentally destroys the world 2.50
❑2, May 1993 .... 2.50
❑3, Jun 1993 .... 2.50
❑4, Jul 1993 .... 2.50

LANCELOT LINK, SECRET CHIMP
GOLD KEY
❑1, May 1971 .... 30.00
❑2, Aug 1971 .... 17.00
❑3, Nov 1971 .... 10.00
❑4, Feb 1972 .... 10.00
❑5, May 1972 .... 10.00
❑6, Aug 1972 .... 10.00
❑7, Nov 1972 .... 10.00
❑8, Feb 1973 .... 10.00

LANCELOT STRONG, THE SHIELD
ARCHIE / RED CIRCLE
❑1, Jun 1983, becomes Shield (Archie) 2.00

LANCER
GOLD KEY
❑1 1969 .... 25.00
❑2 1969 .... 20.00
❑3, Sep 1969 .... 20.00

LAND OF NOD
DARK HORSE
❑1, Jul 1997, b&w 2.95
❑2, Nov 1997, b&w 2.95
❑3, Feb 1998, b&w 2.95
❑4, Jun 1998, b&w 2.95

LAND OF OZ
ARROW
❑1, Nov 1998 .... 2.95
❑2, Jan 1999 .... 2.95
❑3, Mar 1999 .... 2.95
❑4, May 1999 .... 2.95
❑5, Jul 1999 .... 2.95
❑6, Sep 1999 .... 2.95
❑7, Nov 1999 .... 2.95
❑8, Mar 2000 .... 2.95
❑9, Apr 2000 .... 2.95

LAND OF THE GIANTS
GOLD KEY
❑1, Nov 1968 .... 30.00
❑2, Jan 1969 .... 18.00
❑3, Mar 1969 .... 15.00
❑4, Jun 1969 .... 15.00
❑5, Sep 1969 .... 15.00

LANDRA SPECIAL
ALCHEMY
❑1, b&w 2.00

LANN
FANTAGRAPHICS / EROS
❑1, b&w 2.50

LA PACIFICA
DC / PARADOX
❑1, b&w; digest 4.95
❑2, b&w; digest 4.95
❑3, b&w; digest 4.95

L.A. PHOENIX
DAVID G. BROWN
❑1, Jul 1994, b&w 2.00
❑2, Jul 1995, b&w 2.00
❑3, Jul 1996, b&w 2.00

L.A. RAPTOR
MORBID
❑1 .... 2.95

LARS OF MARS 3-D
ECLIPSE
❑1, Apr 1987 .... 2.50

LASER ERASER & PRESSBUTTON
ECLIPSE
❑1, Nov 1985 .... 1.50
❑2, Dec 1985 .... 1.50
❑3 .... 1.50
❑4 .... 1.50
❑5 .... 1.50
❑6 .... 1.50
❑3D 1 .... 2.00

LASH LARUE WESTERN
AC
❑1; some color 3.50
❑Annual 1, b&w; Reprints 2.95

LASSIE (GOLDEN PRESS)
GOLDEN PRESS
❑1, ca. 1978; Giant issue reprints stories from Lassie #19, 20, 21, 37, 38, 39, and 40; reprints painted cover from Lassie #30 .... 22.00

LAST AMERICAN
MARVEL / EPIC
❑1, Dec 1990 .... 2.25
❑2, Jan 1991 .... 2.25
❑3, Feb 1991 .... 2.25
❑4, Mar 1991 .... 2.25

LAST AVENGERS
MARVEL
❑1, Nov 1995; Alterniverse story 5.95
❑2, Dec 1995; Alterniverse story 5.95

LAST CHRISTMAS
IMAGE
❑1, Jun 2006 .... 3.95
❑2, Jul 2006 .... 3.95

LAST DANGEROUS CHRISTMAS
AEON
❑1, b&w; squarebound; benefit comic for neglected and abused children 5.95

LAST DAYS OF HOLLYWOOD, U.S.A.
MORGAN
❑1 .... 2.95
❑2 .... 2.95
❑3 .... 2.95
❑4 .... 2.95
❑5 .... 2.95

LAST DAYS OF THE JUSTICE SOCIETY SPECIAL
DC
❑1, ca. 1986; JSA to Ragnarok after Crisis 3.00

LAST DAZE OF THE BAT-GUY
MYTHIC
❑1, b&w 2.95

LAST DEFENDER OF CAMELOT
ZIM
❑1, b&w 1.95

LAST DITCH
EDGE
❑1, b&w 2.50

LAST GASP COMICS AND STORIES
LAST GASP ECO-FUNNIES
❑1, ca. 1994 .... 3.95
❑2 .... 3.95
❑3, b&w 3.95
❑4 .... 3.95

LAST GENERATION
BLACK TIE
❑1 1987 .... 1.95
❑2 .... 1.95
❑3 .... 1.95
❑4 .... 1.95
❑5 1989 .... 1.95

LAST HERO STANDING
MARVEL
❑1 2005 .... 2.99
❑2 2005 .... 2.99
❑3 2005 .... 2.99
❑4 2005 .... 2.99
❑5 2005 .... 2.99

LAST KISS
ECLIPSE
❑1, ca. 1990, b&w 3.95

LAST KISS (SHANDA)
SHANDA
❑1, Feb 2001 .... 4.95
❑2, Aug 2001 .... 4.95
❑3, Feb 2002 .... 4.95

LAST KNIGHT
NBM
❑1 .... 15.95

LAST OF THE DRAGONS
MARVEL / EPIC
❑1 .... 6.95

LAST OF THE VIKING HEROES
GENESIS WEST
❑1, Mar 1987 .... 1.50
❑2, Jun 1987 .... 2.00
❑3 .... 1.75
❑4 .... 1.75
❑5/A, Jun 1988 .... 1.95
❑5/B 1988 .... 1.95
❑6 1988 .... 1.95
❑7, Jan 1989 .... 1.95
❑8, Jul 1989 .... 1.95
❑9 .... 1.95
❑10 .... 2.50
❑11 .... 2.50
❑12 .... 2.50
❑Summer 1, Mar 1988 .... 2.50
❑Summer 2; Signed, numbered edition signed by authors 2.50
❑Summer 3, Apr 1991; Wizard mail-in promotional edition 2.50

LAST ONE
DC / VERTIGO
❑1, Jul 1993 .... 2.50
❑2, Aug 1993 .... 2.50
❑3, Sep 1993 .... 2.50
❑4, Oct 1993 .... 2.50
❑5, Nov 1993 .... 2.50
❑6, Dec 1993 .... 2.50

LAST PLANET
MBS
❑1 .... 2.50

LAST PLANET STANDING
MARVEL
❑1, Jul 2006 .... 2.99
❑2, Aug 2006 .... 2.99

Lady Justice (Vol. 1) (Neil Gaiman's...)

Spirit of Justice possesses, blinds females

©Tekno

Lady Pendragon (Vol. 1)

King Arthur's wife wields Excalibur

©Maximum

Lady Rawhide

Aptly named horse-riding Zorro gal pal

©Topps

Laff-a-Lympics

Battle of the Network Stars meets Olympics

©Marvel

Lancelot Link, Secret Chimp

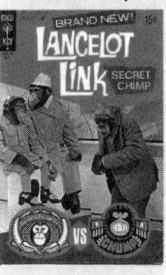

Simian secret agents oppose other apes

©Gold Key

	N-MINT
❑3, Aug 206	2.99
❑4, Sep 2006	2.99

LAST SHOT
IMAGE

❑1, Aug 2001	2.95
❑2, Oct 2001	2.95
❑3, Dec 2001	2.95
❑4, Mar 2002	2.95

LAST SHOT: FIRST DRAW
IMAGE

❑1, May 2001	2.95

LAST STARFIGHTER
MARVEL

❑1, Oct 1984	2.00
❑2, Nov 1984	2.00
❑3, Dec 1984	2.00

LAST TEMPTATION
MARVEL MUSIC

❑1, May 1994	4.95
❑1/A, May 1994; Variant cover with white background; came with the CD	4.95
❑2, Aug 1994	4.95
❑3, Dec 1994	4.95

LAST TRAIN TO DEADSVILLE, THE: A CAL MCDONALD MYSTERY
DARK HORSE

❑1, May 2004	2.99
❑2, Jun 2004	2.99
❑3, Jul 2004	2.99
❑4, Nov 2004	3.00

LATIGO KID WESTERN
AC

❑1, b&w	1.95

LAUGH (VOL. 2)
ARCHIE

❑1, Jun 1987	3.00
❑2, Aug 1987	2.00
❑3, Oct 1987	2.00
❑4, Dec 1987	2.00
❑5, Feb 1988	2.00
❑6, Apr 1988	1.00
❑7, Jun 1988	1.00
❑8, Jul 1988	1.00
❑9, Aug 1988	1.00
❑10, Oct 1988	1.00
❑11, Dec 1988	1.00
❑12, Feb 1989	1.00
❑13, Apr 1989	1.00
❑14, Jun 1989	1.00
❑15, Jul 1989	1.00
❑16, Aug 1989	1.00
❑17, Oct 1989	1.00
❑18, Dec 1989	1.00
❑19, Feb 1990	1.00
❑20, Apr 1990	1.00
❑21, Jun 1990	1.00
❑22, Jul 1990	1.00
❑23, Aug 1990	1.00
❑24, Oct 1990	1.00
❑25, Dec 1990	1.00
❑26, Feb 1991	1.00
❑27, Apr 1991	1.00
❑28, Jun 1991	1.00
❑29, Aug 1991	1.00

LAUGH COMICS
ARCHIE

❑77, Oct 1956	25.00
❑78, Dec 1956	25.00
❑79, Feb 1957	25.00
❑80, Apr 1957	25.00
❑81, Jun 1957	20.00
❑82, Aug 1957	20.00
❑83, Oct 1957	20.00
❑84, Dec 1957	20.00
❑85, Feb 1958	20.00
❑86, Apr 1958	20.00
❑87, Jun 1958	20.00
❑88, Jul 1958	20.00
❑89, Aug 1958	20.00
❑90, Sep 1958	20.00
❑91, Oct 1958	18.00
❑92, Nov 1958	18.00
❑93, Dec 1958	18.00
❑94, Jan 1959	18.00
❑95, Feb 1959	18.00
❑96, Mar 1959	18.00
❑97, Apr 1959	18.00
❑98, May 1959	18.00
❑99, Jun 1959	18.00
❑100, Jul 1959	18.00
❑101, Aug 1959	15.00
❑102, Sep 1959	15.00
❑103, Oct 1959	15.00
❑104, Nov 1959	15.00
❑105, Dec 1959	15.00
❑106, Jan 1960	15.00
❑107, Feb 1960	15.00
❑108, Mar 1960	15.00
❑109, Apr 1960	15.00
❑110, May 1960	15.00
❑111, Jun 1960	15.00
❑112, Jul 1960	15.00
❑113, Aug 1960	15.00
❑114, Sep 1960	15.00
❑115, Oct 1960	15.00
❑116, Nov 1960	15.00
❑117, Dec 1960	15.00
❑118, Jan 1961	15.00
❑119, Feb 1961	15.00
❑120, Mar 1961	15.00
❑121, Apr 1961	15.00
❑122, May 1961	15.00
❑123, Jun 1961	15.00
❑124, Jul 1961	15.00
❑125, Aug 1961	15.00
❑126, Sep 1961	15.00
❑127, Oct 1961	15.00
❑128, Nov 1961	15.00
❑129, Dec 1961	15.00
❑130, Jan 1962	15.00
❑131, Feb 1962	12.00
❑132, Mar 1962	12.00
❑133, Apr 1962	12.00
❑134, May 1962	12.00
❑135, Jun 1962	12.00
❑136, Jul 1962	12.00
❑137, Aug 1962	12.00
❑138, Sep 1962	12.00
❑139, Oct 1962	12.00
❑140, Nov 1962	12.00
❑141, Dec 1962	12.00
❑142, Jan 1963	12.00
❑143, Feb 1963	12.00
❑144, Mar 1963	12.00
❑145, Apr 1963	12.00
❑146, May 1963	12.00
❑147, Jun 1963	12.00
❑148, Jul 1963	12.00
❑149, Aug 1963	12.00
❑150, Sep 1963	12.00
❑151, Oct 1963	12.00
❑152, Nov 1963	12.00
❑153, Dec 1963	12.00
❑154, Jan 1964	12.00
❑155, Feb 1964	12.00
❑156, Mar 1964	12.00
❑157, Apr 1964	12.00
❑158, May 1964	12.00
❑159, Jun 1964	12.00
❑160, Jul 1964	12.00
❑161, Aug 1964	12.00
❑162, Sep 1964	12.00
❑163, Oct 1964	12.00
❑164, Nov 1964	12.00
❑165, Dec 1964	12.00
❑166, Jan 1965	12.00
❑167, Feb 1965	12.00
❑168, Mar 1965	12.00
❑169, Apr 1965	12.00
❑170, May 1965	12.00
❑171, Jun 1965	9.00
❑172, Jul 1965	9.00
❑173, Aug 1965	9.00
❑174, Sep 1965	9.00
❑175, Oct 1965	9.00
❑176, Nov 1965	9.00
❑177, Dec 1965	9.00
❑178, Jan 1966	9.00
❑179, Feb 1966	9.00
❑180, Mar 1966	9.00
❑181, Apr 1966	9.00
❑182, May 1966	9.00
❑183, Jun 1966	9.00
❑184, Jul 1966	9.00
❑185, Aug 1966	9.00
❑186, Sep 1966	9.00
❑187, Oct 1966	9.00
❑188, Nov 1966	9.00
❑189, Dec 1966	9.00
❑190, Jan 1967	8.00
❑191, Feb 1967	8.00
❑192, Mar 1967	8.00
❑193, Apr 1967	8.00
❑194, May 1967	8.00
❑195, Jun 1967	8.00
❑196, Jul 1967	8.00
❑197, Aug 1967	8.00
❑198, Sep 1967	8.00
❑199, Oct 1967	8.00
❑200, Nov 1967	8.00

Other grades: Multiply price above by 5/6 for VF/NM • 2/3 for VERY FINE • 1/3 for FINE • 1/5 for VERY GOOD • 1/8 for GOOD

	N-MINT
❑201, Dec 1967	6.00
❑202, Jan 1968	6.00
❑203, Feb 1968	6.00
❑204, Mar 1968	6.00
❑205, Apr 1968	6.00
❑206, May 1968	6.00
❑207, Jun 1968	6.00
❑208, Jul 1968	6.00
❑209, Aug 1968	6.00
❑210, Sep 1968	6.00
❑211, Oct 1968	6.00
❑212, Nov 1968	6.00
❑213, Dec 1968	6.00
❑214, Jan 1969	6.00
❑215, Feb 1969	6.00
❑216, Mar 1969	6.00
❑217, Apr 1969	6.00
❑218, May 1969	6.00
❑219, Jun 1969	6.00
❑220, Jul 1969	6.00
❑221, Aug 1969	6.00
❑222, Sep 1969	6.00
❑223, Oct 1969	6.00
❑224, Nov 1969	6.00
❑225, Dec 1969	6.00
❑226, Jan 1970, Title changes to Laugh	6.00
❑227, Feb 1970	6.00
❑228, Mar 1970	6.00
❑229, Apr 1970	6.00
❑230, May 1970	6.00
❑231, Jun 1970	6.00
❑232, Jul 1970	6.00
❑233, Aug 1970	6.00
❑234, Sep 1970	6.00
❑235, Oct 1970	6.00
❑236, Nov 1970	6.00
❑237, Dec 1970	6.00
❑238, Jan 1971	6.00
❑239, Feb 1971	6.00
❑240, Mar 1971	6.00
❑241, Apr 1971	6.00
❑242, May 1971	6.00
❑243, Jun 1971	6.00
❑244, Jul 1971	6.00
❑245, Aug 1971	6.00
❑246, Sep 1971	6.00
❑247, Oct 1971	6.00
❑248, Nov 1971	6.00
❑249, Dec 1971	6.00
❑250, Jan 1972	6.00
❑251, Feb 1972	4.00
❑252, Mar 1972	4.00
❑253, Apr 1972	4.00
❑254, May 1972	4.00
❑255, Jun 1972	4.00
❑256, Jul 1972	4.00
❑257, Aug 1972	4.00
❑258, Sep 1972	4.00
❑259, Oct 1972	4.00
❑260, Nov 1972	4.00
❑261, Dec 1972	4.00
❑262, Jan 1973	4.00
❑263, Feb 1973	4.00
❑264, Mar 1973	4.00
❑265, Apr 1973	4.00
❑266, May 1973	4.00
❑267, Jun 1973	4.00
❑268, Jul 1973	4.00
❑269, Aug 1973	4.00
❑270, Sep 1973	4.00
❑271, Oct 1973	4.00
❑272, Nov 1973	4.00
❑273, Dec 1973	4.00
❑274, Jan 1974	4.00
❑275, Feb 1974	4.00
❑276, Mar 1974	4.00
❑277, Apr 1974	4.00
❑278, May 1974	4.00
❑279, Jun 1974	4.00
❑280, Jul 1974	4.00
❑281, Aug 1974	4.00
❑282, Sep 1974	4.00
❑283, Oct 1974	4.00
❑284, Nov 1974	4.00
❑285, Dec 1974	4.00
❑286, Jan 1975	4.00

	N-MINT
❑287, Feb 1975	4.00
❑288, Mar 1975	4.00
❑289, Apr 1975	4.00
❑290, May 1975	4.00
❑291, Jun 1975	4.00
❑292, Jul 1975	4.00
❑293, Aug 1975	4.00
❑294, Sep 1975	4.00
❑295, Oct 1975	4.00
❑296, Nov 1975	4.00
❑297, Dec 1975	4.00
❑298, Jan 1976	4.00
❑299, Feb 1976	4.00
❑300, Mar 1976	4.00
❑301, Apr 1976	2.50
❑302, May 1976	2.50
❑303, Jun 1976	2.50
❑304, Jul 1976	2.50
❑305, Aug 1976	2.50
❑306, Sep 1976	2.50
❑307, Oct 1976	2.50
❑308, Nov 1976	2.50
❑309, Dec 1976	2.50
❑310, Jan 1977	2.50
❑311, Feb 1977	2.50
❑312, Mar 1977	2.50
❑313, Apr 1977	2.50
❑314, May 1977	2.50
❑315, Jun 1977	2.50
❑316, Jul 1977	2.50
❑317, Aug 1977	2.50
❑318, Sep 1977	2.50
❑319, Oct 1977	2.50
❑320, Nov 1977, A: Reggie. A: Betty. A: Li'l Jinx. A: Archie. A: Mr. Lodge. A: Jughead. A: Veronica. A: Moose. A: Fat Charley	2.50
❑321, Dec 1977	2.50
❑322, Jan 1978	2.50
❑323, Feb 1978	2.50
❑324, Mar 1978	2.50
❑325, Apr 1978	2.50
❑326, May 1978	2.50
❑327, Jun 1978	2.50
❑328, Jul 1978	2.50
❑329, Aug 1978	2.50
❑330, Sep 1978	2.50
❑331, Oct 1978	2.50
❑332, Nov 1978	2.50
❑333, Dec 1978	2.50
❑334, Jan 1979	2.50
❑335, Feb 1979	2.50
❑336, Mar 1979	2.50
❑337, Apr 1979	2.50
❑338, May 1979	2.50
❑339, Jun 1979	2.50
❑340, Jul 1979	2.50
❑341, Aug 1979	2.50
❑342, Sep 1979	2.50
❑343, Oct 1979	2.50
❑344, Nov 1979	2.50
❑345, Dec 1979	2.50
❑346, Jan 1980	2.50
❑347, Feb 1980	2.50
❑348, Mar 1980	2.50
❑349, Apr 1980	2.50
❑350, May 1980	2.50
❑351, Jun 1980	2.00
❑352, Jul 1980	2.00
❑353, Aug 1980	2.00
❑354, Sep 1980	2.00
❑355, Oct 1980	2.00
❑356, Nov 1980	2.00
❑357, Dec 1980	2.00
❑358, Jan 1981	2.00
❑359, Feb 1981	2.00
❑360, Mar 1981	2.00
❑361, Apr 1981	2.00
❑362, May 1981	2.00
❑363, Jun 1981	2.00
❑364, Jul 1981	2.00
❑365, Aug 1981	2.00
❑366, Sep 1981	2.00
❑367, Oct 1981	2.00
❑368, Nov 1981	2.00
❑369, Dec 1981	2.00
❑370, Jan 1982	2.00

	N-MINT
❑371, Feb 1982	2.00
❑372, May 1982	2.00
❑373, Jul 1982	2.00
❑374, Sep 1982	2.00
❑375, Nov 1982	2.00
❑376, Jan 1983	2.00
❑377, Apr 1983	2.00
❑378, Jul 1983	2.00
❑379, Oct 1983	2.00
❑380, Dec 1983	2.00
❑381, Feb 1984	2.00
❑382, Apr 1984	2.00
❑383, Jun 1984	2.00
❑384, Aug 1984	2.00
❑385, Oct 1984	2.00
❑386, Dec 1984	2.00
❑387, Feb 1985	2.00
❑388, Apr 1985	2.00
❑389, Jun 1985	2.00
❑390, Aug 1985	2.00
❑391, Oct 1985	2.00
❑392, Dec 1985	2.00
❑393, Feb 1986	2.00
❑394, Apr 1986	2.00
❑395, Jun 1986	2.00
❑396, Aug 1986	2.00
❑397, Oct 1986	2.00
❑398, Dec 1986	2.00
❑399, Feb 1987, Circ figs are provided in Laugh, Vol. 2	2.00
❑400, Apr 1987, Circ figs are provided in Laugh, Vol. 2	2.00

LAUGH DIGEST MAGAZINE

ARCHIE

	N-MINT
❑1, Aug 1974, NA (a)	10.00
❑2, Jan 1976	8.00
❑3, Mar 1976	8.00
❑4, May 1976	8.00
❑5, Jul 1976	8.00
❑6, Sep 1976	4.00
❑7, Nov 1976	4.00
❑8, Jan 1977	4.00
❑9, Mar 1977	4.00
❑10, May 1977	4.00
❑11, Jul 1977	3.00
❑12, Sep 1977	3.00
❑13, Nov 1977	3.00
❑14, Jan 1978	3.00
❑15, Mar 1978	3.00
❑16, May 1978	3.00
❑17, Jul 1978	3.00
❑18, Sep 1978	3.00
❑19, Nov 1978	3.00
❑20, Jan 1979	3.00
❑21, Mar 1979	2.00
❑22, May 1979	2.00
❑23, Jul 1979	2.00
❑24, Sep 1979	2.00
❑25, Nov 1979	2.00
❑26, Jan 1980	2.00
❑27, Mar 1980	2.00
❑28, May 1980	2.00
❑29, Jul 1980	2.00
❑30, Sep 1980	2.00
❑31, Nov 1980	2.00
❑32, Jan 1981	2.00
❑33, Mar 1981	2.00
❑34, May 1981	2.00
❑35, Jul 1981	2.00
❑36, Sep 1981	2.00
❑37, Nov 1981	2.00
❑38, Jan 1982	2.00
❑39, Mar 1982	2.00
❑40, May 1982	2.00
❑41, Jul 1982	1.50
❑42, Sep 1982	1.50
❑43, Nov 1982	1.50
❑44, Jan 1983	1.50
❑45, Mar 1983	1.50
❑46, May 1983	1.50
❑47, Jul 1983	1.50
❑48, Sep 1983	1.50
❑49, Nov 1983	1.50
❑50, Jan 1984	1.50
❑51, Mar 1984	1.50
❑52, May 1984	1.50

Other grades: Multiply price above by 5/6 for VF/NM • 2/3 for VERY FINE • 1/3 for FINE • 1/5 for VERY GOOD • 1/8 for GOOD

Last Days of the Justice Society Special

JSA fights Ragnarok over and over and ...

©DC

Last Kiss (Shanda)

John Lustig's redialogued romance comics

©Shanda

Last of the Viking Heroes

Conan Lite with more humor

©Genesis West

Last Starfighter

Videogame ranks potential defenders

©Marvel

Laugh Comics

More misadventures of Archie and the gang

©Archie

	N-MINT
❑53, Jul 1984	1.50
❑54, Sep 1984	1.50
❑55, Nov 1984	1.50
❑56, Jan 1985	1.50
❑57, Mar 1985	1.50
❑58, May 1985	1.50
❑59, Jul 1985	1.50
❑60, Sep 1985	1.50
❑61, Nov 1985	1.50
❑62, Jan 1986	1.50
❑63, Mar 1986	1.50
❑64, May 1986	1.50
❑65, Jul 1986	1.50
❑66, Sep 1986	1.50
❑67, Nov 1986	1.50
❑68, Jan 1987	1.50
❑69, Mar 1987	1.50
❑70, May 1987	1.50
❑71, Jul 1987	1.50
❑72, Sep 1987	1.50
❑73, Nov 1987	1.50
❑74, Jan 1988	1.50
❑75, Mar 1988	1.50
❑76, May 1988	1.50
❑77, Jul 1988	1.50
❑78, Sep 1988	1.50
❑79, Nov 1988	1.50
❑80, Jan 1989	1.50
❑81, Mar 1989	1.50
❑82, May 1989	1.50
❑83, Jul 1989	1.50
❑84, Sep 1989	1.50
❑85, Nov 1989	1.50
❑86, Jan 1990	1.50
❑87, Mar 1990	1.50
❑88, May 1990	1.50
❑89, Jul 1990	1.50
❑90, Sep 1990	1.50
❑91, Nov 1990	1.50
❑92, Jan 1991	1.50
❑93, Mar 1991	1.50
❑94, ca. 1991	1.50
❑95, ca. 1991	1.50
❑96, ca. 1991	1.50
❑97, ca. 1991	1.50
❑98	1.50
❑99, ca. 1992	1.50
❑100, ca. 1992	1.50
❑101, ca. 1992	1.50
❑102, ca. 1992	1.50
❑103, ca. 1992	1.50
❑104, ca. 1992	1.50
❑105, ca. 1992	1.50
❑106, ca. 1993	1.50
❑107, May 1993	1.50
❑108, Jul 1993	1.50
❑109, Sep 1993	1.50
❑110, Nov 1993	1.50
❑111, Dec 1994	1.50
❑112, Feb 1994	1.50
❑113, ca. 1994	1.50
❑114, ca. 1994	1.50
❑115, ca. 1994	1.50
❑116, ca. 1994	1.50
❑117, Nov 1994	1.75
❑118, Jan 1995	1.75
❑119, Mar 1995	1.75
❑120, May 1995	1.75
❑121, Jul 1995	1.75
❑122, Sep 1995	1.75
❑123, Nov 1995	1.75
❑124, Dec 1995	1.75
❑125, Feb 1996	1.75
❑126, Apr 1996	1.75
❑127, May 1996	1.75
❑128, Jul 1996	1.75
❑129, Sep 1996	1.79
❑130, Oct 1996	1.79
❑131, Dec 1996	1.79
❑132, Feb 1997	1.79
❑133, Apr 1997	1.79
❑134, May 1997	1.79
❑135, Jul 1997	1.79
❑136, Sep 1997	1.79
❑137, Oct 1997	1.79
❑138, Dec 1997	1.79
❑139, Jan 1998	1.95
❑140, Mar 1998	1.95
❑141, May 1998	1.95
❑142, Jul 1998	1.95
❑143, Aug 1998	1.95
❑144, Oct 1998	1.95
❑145, Nov 1998, DDC (a)	1.95
❑146, Jan 1999	1.95
❑147, Mar 1999	1.95
❑148, Apr 1999	1.99
❑149, May 1999	1.99
❑150, Jul 1999	1.99
❑151, Aug 1999	1.99
❑152, Oct 1999	1.99
❑153, Nov 1999	1.99
❑154, Jan 2000	1.99
❑155, Mar 2000	1.99
❑156, May 2000	1.99
❑157, Jul 2000	2.19
❑158, Aug 2000	2.19
❑159, Oct 2000	2.19
❑160, Nov 2000	2.19
❑161, Dec 2000	2.19
❑162, Jan 2001	2.19
❑163, Feb 2001	2.19
❑164, Apr 2001	2.19
❑165, May 2001	2.19
❑166, Jul 2001	2.19
❑167, Aug 2001	2.19
❑168, Oct 2001	2.19
❑169, Nov 2001	2.19
❑170, Dec 2001	2.19
❑171, Jan 2002	2.19
❑172, Mar 2002	2.19
❑173, May 2002	2.19
❑174, Jul 2002	2.19
❑175, Aug 2002	2.19
❑176, Sep 2002	2.19
❑177, Nov 2002	2.19
❑178, Dec 2002	2.19
❑179, Jan 2003	2.19
❑180, Feb 2003	2.39
❑181, Mar 2003	2.39
❑182, May 2003	2.39
❑183, Jun 2003	2.39
❑184, Jul 2003	2.39
❑185, Sep 2003	2.39
❑186, Oct 2003	2.39
❑187, Nov 2003	2.39
❑188, Dec 2003	2.39
❑189, Feb 2004	2.39
❑190, Mar 2004	2.39
❑191, May 2004	2.39
❑192, Jun 2004	2.39
❑193, Jul 2004	2.39
❑194, Aug 2004	2.39
❑195, Sep 2004	2.39
❑196, Oct 2004	2.39
❑197, Nov 2004	2.39
❑198, Dec 2004	2.39
❑199, Jan 2005	2.39
❑200, Feb 2005	2.39

LAUNCH!
ELSEWHERE

	N-MINT
❑1	1.75

LAUNDRYLAND
FANTAGRAPHICS

	N-MINT
❑1, b&w	2.25
❑2, Jun 1991, b&w	2.50
❑3, b&w	2.50
❑4, b&w	2.50

LAUREL AND HARDY (GOLD KEY)
GOLD KEY

	N-MINT
❑1, Jan 1967	24.00
❑2, Oct 1967	18.00

LAUREL AND HARDY (DC)
DC

	N-MINT
❑1, Aug 1972	40.00

LAUREL & HARDY IN 3-D
BLACKTHORNE

	N-MINT
❑1, Fal 1987; aka Blackthorne 3-D #23	2.50
❑2, Dec 1987; aka Blackthorne 3-D #34	2.50

LAVA
CROSSBREED

	N-MINT
❑1	2.95

LAW
ASYLUM GRAPHICS

	N-MINT
❑1, b&w; no publication date	1.75

LAW AND ORDER
MAXIMUM

	N-MINT
❑1, Sep 1995	2.50
❑1/A, Sep 1995; Alternate cover with women standing atop body	2.50
❑2, Oct 1995	2.50
❑3, Nov 1995	2.50

LAWDOG
MARVEL / EPIC

	N-MINT
❑1, May 1993, Embossed cover	2.50
❑2, Jun 1993	1.95
❑3, Jul 1993	1.95
❑4, Aug 1993	1.95
❑5, Sep 1993	1.95
❑6, Oct 1993	1.95
❑7, Nov 1993	1.95

❑8, Dec 1993, trading card 1.95
❑9, Jan 1994 .... 1.95
❑10, Feb 1994 .... 1.95

LAWDOG AND GRIMROD: TERROR AT THE CROSSROADS
MARVEL / EPIC

❑1, Sep 1993 .... 3.50

L.A.W. (LIVING ASSAULT WEAPONS)
DC

❑1, Sep 1999 .... 2.50
❑2, Oct 1999 .... 2.50
❑3, Nov 1999 .... 2.50
❑4, Dec 1999 .... 2.50
❑5, Jan 2000 .... 2.50
❑6, Feb 2000 .... 2.50

LAW OF DREDD
FLEETWAY-QUALITY

❑1; BB (a); Reprints Judge Dredd stories from 2000 A.D. #149- 1.50
❑2 .... 1.50
❑3 V: Judge Death. 1.50
❑4 .... 1.50
❑5 .... 1.50
❑6 .... 1.50
❑7 .... 1.50
❑8 .... 1.50
❑9 .... 1.75
❑10 .... 1.75
❑11 .... 1.75
❑12 .... 1.75
❑13 A: Judge Caligula. 1.75
❑14 .... 1.75
❑15 .... 1.75
❑16 .... 1.75
❑17 .... 1.75
❑18 .... 1.75
❑19 .... 1.75
❑20 .... 1.75
❑21 .... 1.75
❑22 .... 1.75
❑23 .... 1.75
❑24 .... 1.75
❑25 .... 1.75
❑26 .... 1.75
❑27 .... 1.75
❑28 .... 1.75
❑29 .... 1.75
❑30 .... 1.95
❑31 .... 1.95
❑32 .... 1.95
❑33 .... 1.95

LAZARUS CHURCHYARD
TUNDRA

❑1 .... 4.50
❑2 .... 4.50
❑3 .... 4.95

LAZARUS FIVE
DC

❑1, Jul 2000 .... 2.50
❑2, Aug 2000 .... 2.50
❑3, Sep 2000 .... 2.50
❑4, Oct 2000 .... 2.50
❑5, Nov 2000 .... 2.50

LAZARUS PITS
BONEYARD

❑1, Feb 1993, b&w; b&w pin-ups, cardstock cover 4.00

LEAF
NAB

❑1 .... 1.95
❑1/Deluxe; deluxe 4.95
❑2 .... 1.95

LEAGUE OF CHAMPIONS
HERO

❑1, Dec 1990 .... 3.00
❑2, Feb 1991 O: Malice (true origin) ... 3.00
❑3, Apr 1991 .... 3.00
❑4, b&w 3.50
❑5, b&w 3.50
❑6, b&w 3.50
❑7, Nov 1992, b&w A: the Southern Knights. 3.50
❑8, b&w 3.50
❑9, b&w 3.50

❑10, b&w 3.50
❑11, b&w 3.95
❑12, Jul 1993 .... 2.95

LEAGUE OF EXTRAORDINARY GENTLEMEN
DC / AMERICA'S BEST COMICS

❑1, Mar 1999 AMo (w) 8.00
❑1/A, Apr 1999; AMo (w); DF Alternate; 5000 copies 5.00
❑2, Apr 1999 AMo (w) 5.00
❑3, Jun 1999; AMo (w); Cover says May, indicia says June 4.00
❑4, Nov 1999 AMo (w) 4.00
❑5, Jun 2000 AMo (w) 4.00
❑5/A, Jun 2000; AMo (w); Contained fake ad for The Marvel; All but est. 200 destroyed by DC 65.00
❑6, Sep 2000 AMo (w) 4.00

LEAGUE OF EXTRAORDINARY GENTLEMEN, THE (VOL. 2)
AMERICA'S BEST

❑1, Sep 2002 .... 4.00
❑2, Oct 2002 .... 3.50
❑3, Nov 2002 .... 3.50
❑4, Feb 2003, AMo (w) 3.50
❑5, Jul 2003 .... 3.50
❑6, Nov 2003 .... 3.50

LEAGUE OF JUSTICE
DC

❑1, prestige format; Elseworlds 5.95
❑2, prestige format; Elseworlds 5.95

LEAGUE OF RATS
CALIBER / TOME

❑1, b&w 2.95

LEAGUE OF SUPER GROOVY CRIMEFIGHTERS
ANCIENT

❑1, Jun 2000 .... 2.95
❑2, Dec 2000, b&w 2.95
❑3 2001, b&w 2.95
❑4, May 2001, b&w; published after #3, but dated before 2.95
❑5 2001 .... 2.95

LEATHER & LACE
AIRCEL

❑1/A, Aug 1989, b&w; Adult version.. 2.50
❑1/B, Aug 1989, b&w; Tame version.. 1.95
❑2/A, Sep 1989, b&w; Adult version .. 2.50
❑2/B, Sep 1989, b&w; Tame version .. 1.95
❑3/A, Oct 1989, b&w; Adult version ... 2.50
❑3/B, Oct 1989, b&w; Tame version ... 1.95
❑4/A, Nov 1989, b&w; Adult version ... 2.50
❑4/B, Nov 1989, b&w; Tame version .. 1.95
❑5/A, Dec 1989, b&w; Adult version .. 2.50
❑5/B, Dec 1989, b&w; Tame version .. 1.95
❑6/A, Jan 1990, b&w; Adult version ... 2.50
❑6/B, Jan 1990, b&w; Tame version .. 1.95
❑7/A, Feb 1990, b&w; Adult version ... 2.50
❑7/B, Feb 1990, b&w; Tame version .. 1.95
❑8/A, Mar 1990, b&w; Adult version ... 2.50
❑8/B, Mar 1990, b&w; Tame version .. 1.95
❑9, Apr 1990, b&w 2.50
❑10, May 1990, b&w 2.50
❑11, Jun 1990, b&w 2.50
❑12, Jul 1990, b&w 2.50
❑13, Aug 1990, b&w 2.50
❑14, Sep 1990, b&w 2.50
❑15, Oct 1990, b&w 2.50
❑16, Nov 1990, b&w 2.50
❑17, Dec 1990, b&w 2.50
❑18, Jan 1991, b&w 2.50
❑19, Feb 1991, b&w 2.50
❑20, Mar 1991, b&w 2.50
❑21, Apr 1991, b&w 2.50
❑22, May 1991, b&w 2.95
❑23, Jun 1991, b&w 2.95
❑24, Jul 1991, b&w 2.95
❑25, Aug 1991, b&w 2.95

LEATHER & LACE: BLOOD, SEX, & TEARS
AIRCEL

❑1, Oct 1991, b&w 2.95
❑2, Nov 1991, b&w 2.95
❑3, Dec 1991, b&w 2.95
❑4, Jan 1992 .... 2.95

LEATHER & LACE SUMMER SPECIAL
AIRCEL

❑1, Jun 1990, b&w 2.50

LEATHERBOY
FANTAGRAPHICS / EROS

❑1, Jul 1994 .... 2.95
❑2, Oct 1994 .... 2.95
❑3, Nov 1994 .... 2.95

LEATHERFACE
ARPAD

❑1, Apr 1991 .... 2.75

LEATHER UNDERWEAR
FANTAGRAPHICS

❑1, b&w 2.50

LEAVE IT TO BEAVER
DELL

❑-207, Jul 1962, No number; cover says 01-428-207; previous issues appeared as Dell Four Color (2nd Series) #912, #999, #1103, #1191, and #1285 .... 100.00

LEAVE IT TO CHANCE
IMAGE

❑1, Sep 1996 JRo (w); PS (a) 3.00
❑1/2nd, Sep 1996 JRo (w); PS (a) 2.50
❑2, Oct 1996 JRo (w); PS (a) 3.00
❑3, Nov 1996 JRo (w); PS (a) 3.00
❑4, Feb 1997 JRo (w); PS (a) 3.00
❑5, May 1997 JRo (w); PS (a) 3.00
❑6, Jul 1997 JRo (w); PS (a) 2.50
❑7, Oct 1997 JRo (w); PS (a) 2.50
❑8, Feb 1998 JRo (w); PS (a) 2.50
❑9, Apr 1998 JRo (w); PS (a) 2.50
❑10, Jun 1998 JRo (w); PS (a) 2.50
❑11, Sep 1998 JRo (w); PS (a) 2.95
❑13, Jul 2002; JRo (w); PS (a); Published by Image 4.95
❑12, Jun 1999 JRo (w); PS (a) 2.95

LED ZEPPELIN
PERSONALITY

❑1, b&w 2.95
❑2, b&w 2.95
❑3, b&w 2.95
❑4, b&w 2.95

LED ZEPPELIN EXPERIENCE
REVOLUTIONARY

❑1, Aug 1992, b&w 2.50
❑2, Oct 1992, b&w 2.50
❑3, Dec 1992, b&w 2.50
❑4, Jan 1993, b&w 2.50
❑5, Feb 1993, b&w 2.50

LEFT-FIELD FUNNIES
APEX NOVELTIES

❑1 .... 4.00

LEGACY
MAJESTIC

❑0, Aug 1993 .... 2.25
❑0/Gold, Aug 1993, gold 2.25
❑1, Oct 1993 .... 2.25
❑2, Jan 1994 .... 2.25

LEGACY (FRED PERRY'S...)
ANTARCTIC

❑1, Aug 1999 .... 2.99

LEGACY (IMAGE)
IMAGE

❑1, May 2003 .... 2.95
❑2, Jul 2003 .... 2.95
❑3, Nov 2003 .... 2.95
❑4, Apr 2004 .... 2.95

LEGACY OF KAIN: DEFIANCE ONE SHOT
IMAGE

❑1, Jan 2004 .... 2.99

LEGACY OF KAIN: SOUL REAVER
TOP COW

❑1, Oct 1999 .... 2.00

LEGEND
DC

❑1, May 2005 .... 5.95
❑2, Jun 2005 .... 5.99
❑3, Jun 2005 .... 5.99

Other grades: Multiply price above by 5/6 for VF/NM • 2/3 for VERY FINE • 1/3 for FINE • 1/5 for VERY GOOD • 1/8 for GOOD

Laurel & Hardy in 3-D

Stan and Ollie's multi-dimensional adventures
©Blackthorne

L.A.W., The (Living Assault Weapons)

DC's Charlton heroes team again
©DC

League of Champions

Heroic heroes join forces
©Hero

League of Extraordinary Gentlemen

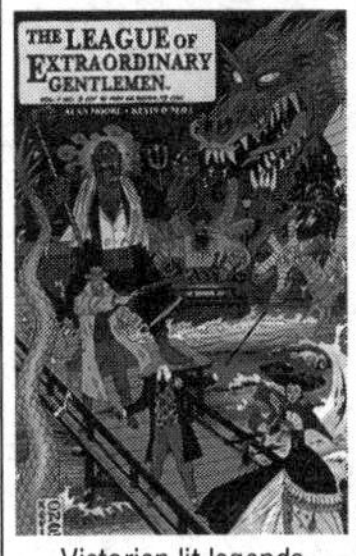

Victorian lit legends face threats
©DC

League of Super Groovy Crimefighters

1970s comics ad items give losers powers
©Ancient

N-MINT

LEGEND LORE (ARROW)
ARROW

❑1, b&w ... 2.00
❑2, b&w ... 2.00

LEGENDLORE (CALIBER)
CALIBER

❑1 ... 2.95
❑2 ... 2.95
❑3 ... 2.95
❑4 ... 2.95

LEGENDLORE: WRATH OF THE DRAGON
CALIBER

❑1; A.k.a. LegendLore #13 ... 2.95
❑2; A.k.a. LegendLore #14 ... 2.95

LEGEND OF ISIS
ALIAS

❑1, May 2005 ... 4.00
❑1/B cover, May 2005 ... 3.00
❑1/C cover, May 2005 ... 4.00
❑2, Jun 2005 ... 2.99
❑2/B cover, Jun 2005 ... 4.00
❑3, Sep 2005 ... 2.99
❑3/B cover, Sep 2005 ... 4.00
❑4, Nov 2005 ... 2.99
❑5, Dec 2005 ... 2.99
❑7, Jan 2006 ... 2.99

LEGEND OF JEDIT OJANEN ON THE WORLD OF MAGIC: THE GATHERING
ACCLAIM / ARMADA

❑1, Mar 1996; polybagged with card ... 2.50
❑2, Apr 1996 ... 2.50

LEGEND OF JESSE JAMES
GOLD KEY

❑1, Feb 1966 ... 24.00

LEGEND OF KAMUI
ECLIPSE / VIZ

❑1, May 1987, b&w; Japanese ... 3.00
❑1/2nd ... 1.50
❑2, Jun 1987 ... 2.00
❑2/2nd ... 1.50
❑3, Jun 1987 ... 2.00
❑3/2nd ... 1.50
❑4, Jul 1987 ... 1.50
❑5, Jul 1987 ... 1.50
❑6, Aug 1987 ... 1.50
❑7, Aug 1987 ... 1.50
❑8, Sep 1987 ... 1.50
❑9, Sep 1987 ... 1.50
❑10, Oct 1987 ... 1.50
❑11, Oct 1987 ... 1.50
❑12, Nov 1987 ... 1.50
❑13, Nov 1987 ... 1.50
❑14, Dec 1987 ... 1.50
❑15, Dec 1987 ... 1.50
❑16, Jan 1988 ... 1.50
❑17, Jan 1988 ... 1.50
❑18, Feb 1988 ... 1.50
❑19, Feb 1988 ... 1.50
❑20, Mar 1988 ... 1.50
❑21, Mar 1988 ... 1.50
❑22, Apr 1988 ... 1.50

N-MINT

❑23, Apr 1988 ... 1.50
❑24, May 1988 ... 1.50
❑25, May 1988 ... 1.50
❑26, Jun 1988 ... 1.50
❑27, Jun 1988 ... 1.50
❑28, Jul 1988 ... 1.50
❑29, Jul 1988 ... 1.50
❑30, Aug 1988 ... 1.50
❑31, Aug 1988 ... 1.50
❑32, Sep 1988 ... 1.50
❑33, Sep 1988 ... 1.50
❑34, Oct 1988 ... 1.50
❑35, Oct 1988 ... 1.50
❑36, Nov 1988 ... 1.50
❑37, Nov 1988 ... 1.50

LEGEND OF LEMNEAR
CPM

❑1, Jan 1998; wraparound cover ... 3.00
❑2, Feb 1998 ... 3.00
❑3, Mar 1998 ... 3.00
❑4, Apr 1998 ... 3.00
❑5, May 1998 ... 3.00
❑6, Jun 1998; wraparound cover ... 3.00
❑7, Jul 1998; wraparound cover ... 3.00
❑8, Aug 1998 ... 2.95
❑9, Sep 1998 ... 2.95
❑10, Oct 1998 ... 2.95
❑11, Nov 1998 ... 2.95
❑12, Dec 1998 ... 2.95
❑13, Jan 1999; wraparound cover ... 2.95
❑14, Feb 1999 ... 2.95

LEGEND OF LILITH
IMAGE

❑0; no date ... 4.95

LEGEND OF MOTHER SARAH
DARK HORSE / MANGA

❑1, Apr 1995, b&w ... 3.50
❑2, May 1995, b&w ... 3.00
❑3, Jun 1995, b&w ... 3.00
❑4, Jul 1995, b&w ... 2.50
❑5, Aug 1995, b&w ... 2.50
❑6, Sep 1995, b&w ... 2.50
❑7, Oct 1995, b&w ... 2.50
❑8, Nov 1995, b&w ... 2.50

LEGEND OF MOTHER SARAH, THE: CITY OF THE ANGELS
DARK HORSE / MANGA

❑1, Oct 1997 ... 3.95
❑2, Dec 1997 ... 3.95
❑3, Jan 1998 ... 3.95
❑4, Feb 1998 ... 3.95
❑5, Mar 1998 ... 3.95
❑6, Apr 1998 ... 3.95
❑7, May 1998 ... 3.95
❑8, Jun 1998 ... 3.95
❑9, Jul 1998 ... 3.95

LEGEND OF MOTHER SARAH, THE: CITY OF THE CHILDREN
DARK HORSE / MANGA

❑1, Jan 1996 ... 3.95
❑2, Feb 1996 ... 3.95
❑3, Mar 1996 ... 3.95
❑4, Apr 1996 ... 3.95

N-MINT

❑5, May 1996 ... 3.95
❑6, Jun 1996 ... 3.95
❑7, Jul 1996 ... 3.95

LEGEND OF SLEEPY HOLLOW
TUNDRA

❑1 ... 6.95

LEGEND OF SUPREME
IMAGE

❑1, Dec 1994 ... 2.50
❑2, Jan 1995 ... 2.50
❑3, Feb 1995 ... 2.50

LEGEND OF THE ELFLORD
DAVDEZ

❑1, Jul 1998 ... 2.95
❑2, Sep 1998 ... 2.95
❑3 ... 2.95

LEGEND OF THE HAWKMAN
DC

❑1 2000 ... 4.95
❑2 2000 ... 4.95
❑3 2000 ... 4.95

LEGEND OF THE SHIELD
DC / IMPACT

❑1, Jul 1991 ... 1.50
❑2, Aug 1991 ... 1.00
❑3, Sep 1991 ... 1.00
❑4, Oct 1991 ... 1.00
❑5, Nov 1991 ... 1.00
❑6, Dec 1991 ... 1.00
❑7, Jan 1992 ... 1.00
❑8, Feb 1992 ... 1.00
❑9, Mar 1992 ... 1.00
❑10, Apr 1992 ... 1.00
❑11, May 1992; trading card ... 1.00
❑12, Jun 1992 ... 1.00
❑13, Jul 1992 ... 1.00
❑14, Aug 1992 ... 1.00
❑15, Sep 1992 ... 1.00
❑16, Oct 1992 ... 1.00
❑Annual 1 ... 2.50

LEGEND OF WONDER WOMAN
DC

❑1, May 1986 KB (w) ... 1.50
❑2, Jun 1986 KB (w) ... 1.50
❑3, Jul 1986 KB (w) ... 1.50
❑4, Aug 1986 KB (w) ... 1.50

LEGEND OF YOUNG DICK TURPIN
GOLD KEY

❑1, May 1966 ... 16.00

LEGEND OF ZELDA
VALIANT

❑1, ca. 1990 ... 1.95
❑2, ca. 1990 ... 1.95
❑3, ca. 1990 ... 1.95
❑4, ca. 1990 ... 1.95
❑5, ca. 1990 ... 1.95

LEGEND OF ZELDA (2ND SERIES)
VALIANT

❑1, ca. 1990 ... 1.50
❑2, ca. 1990 ... 1.50
❑3, ca. 1990 ... 1.50
❑4, ca. 1990 ... 1.50
❑5, ca. 1990 ... 1.50

Other grades: Multiply price above by 5/6 for VF/NM • 2/3 for VERY FINE • 1/3 for FINE • 1/5 for VERY GOOD • 1/8 for GOOD

LEGENDS
DC

❑1, Nov 1986 JBy (a); 1: Amanda Waller.... 2.00
❑2, Dec 1986 JBy (a).... 1.50
❑3, Jan 1987 JBy (a); 1: Suicide Squad (modern).... 2.00
❑4, Feb 1987 JBy (a).... 1.50
❑5, Mar 1987 JBy (a).... 1.50
❑6, Apr 1987 JBy (a); 1: Justice League. 3.00

LEGENDS AND FOLKLORE
ZONE

❑1, b&w.... 2.95
❑2, ca. 1992, b&w.... 2.95

LEGENDS FROM DARKWOOD
ANTARCTIC

❑1, Nov 2003.... 3.50
❑2, Jan 2004.... 3.50
❑3, Feb 2004.... 3.50

LEGENDS FROM DARKWOOD: SUMMER FUN SPECIAL
ANTARCTIC

❑0, Jun 2005.... 2.99

LEGENDS OF ELFINWILD
WEHNER

❑1, b&w.... 1.75

LEGENDS OF KID DEATH & FLUFFY
EVENT

❑1, Feb 1997.... 2.95

LEGENDS OF LUXURA
BRAINSTORM

❑1, Feb 1996, b&w; collects Luxura stories.... 2.95
❑1/Ltd., Feb 1996; Special edition; no cover price; limited to 1000 copies. 4.00

LEGENDS OF NASCAR
VORTEX

❑1; Bill Elliott.... 3.50
❑1/2nd; Bill Elliott.... 2.00
❑1/3rd; Bill Elliott; Indicia marks it as 2nd Printing.... 3.00
❑2; Richard Petty; no indicia.... 2.00
❑2/Variant; hologram.... 3.00
❑3; Ken Shrader.... 2.00
❑4; Bobby Allison.... 2.00
❑5; Sterling Marlin.... 2.00
❑6.... 2.00
❑7.... 2.00
❑8; Benny Parsons.... 2.00
❑9; Rusty Wallace.... 2.00
❑10; Talladega Story.... 2.00
❑11; Morgan Shepherd.... 2.00
❑12.... 2.00
❑13.... 2.00
❑14.... 2.00
❑15.... 2.00
❑16; Final issue (?).... 2.00

LEGENDS OF THE DARK CLAW
DC / AMALGAM

❑1, Apr 1996 O: The Hyena. O: The Dark Claw.... 2.00

LEGENDS OF THE DCU: CRISIS ON INFINITE EARTHS
DC

❑1, Feb 1999; A: Flash II (Barry Allen). A: Supergirl. Takes place between Crisis on Infinite Earths #4 and #5.. 4.95
❑1/Autographed, Feb 1999; A: Flash II (Barry Allen). A: Supergirl. Takes place between Crisis on Infinite Earths #4 and #5.... 18.95

LEGENDS OF THE DC UNIVERSE
DC

❑1, Feb 1998; Superman.... 3.00
❑2, Mar 1998; Superman.... 2.50
❑3, Apr 1998; Superman.... 2.50
❑4, May 1998; Wonder Woman.... 2.50
❑5, Jun 1998; Wonder Woman.... 2.50
❑6, Jul 1998; KN (a); Robin, Superman 2.25
❑7, Aug 1998; Green Lantern/Green Arrow.... 2.25
❑8, Sep 1998; Green Lantern/Green Arrow.... 2.25
❑9, Oct 1998; Green Lantern/Green Arrow.... 2.25
❑10, Nov 1998; O: Oracle. Batgirl.... 2.25
❑11, Dec 1998; O: Oracle. Batgirl.... 2.25
❑12, Jan 1999; JLA.... 2.25
❑13, Feb 1999; JLA.... 2.25
❑14, Mar 1999 JK, ME (w); SR (a); A: Jimmy Olsen. A: Simyan. A: Superman. A: Darkseid. A: Guardian. A: Mokkari.... 2.25
❑15, Apr 1999 A: Flash II (Barry Allen). 2.25
❑16, May 1999 A: Flash II (Barry Allen). 2.25
❑17, Jun 1999 A: Flash II (Barry Allen). 2.25
❑18, Jul 1999; BG (a); Kid Flash, Raven 2.25
❑19, Aug 1999; Impulse; prelude to JLApe Annuals.... 2.25
❑20, Sep 1999; MZ (a); Green Lantern: Abin Sur.... 2.25
❑21, Oct 1999; MZ (a); Green Lantern: Abin Sur.... 1.99
❑22, Nov 1999.... 1.99
❑23, Dec 1999.... 1.99
❑24, Jan 2000.... 1.99
❑25, Feb 2000.... 1.99
❑26, Mar 2000.... 1.99
❑27, Apr 2000 TVE (a).... 1.99
❑28, May 2000 GK, KJ (a).... 1.99
❑29, Jun 2000 GK, KJ (a).... 1.99
❑30, Jul 2000.... 1.99
❑31, Aug 2000.... 2.50
❑32, Sep 2000.... 2.50
❑33, Oct 2000.... 2.50
❑34, Nov 2000.... 2.50
❑35, Dec 2000.... 2.50
❑36, Jan 2001.... 2.50
❑37, Feb 2001.... 2.50
❑38, Mar 2001.... 2.50
❑39, Apr 2001.... 2.50
❑40, May 2001.... 2.50
❑41, Jun 2001.... 2.50
❑Giant Size 1, Sep 1998; Spectre, Hawkman, Teen Titans, Adam Strange, Chronos, Doom Patrol, Rip Hunter, Linear Men.... 4.95
❑Giant Size 2, Jan 2000 KJ (a).... 4.95

LEGENDS OF THE DC UNIVERSE 3-D GALLERY
DC

❑1, Dec 1998; pin-ups.... 2.95

LEGENDS OF THE LEGION
DC

❑1, Feb 1998.... 2.25
❑2, Mar 1998.... 2.25
❑3, Apr 1998.... 2.25
❑4, May 1998.... 2.25

LEGENDS OF THE LIVING DEAD
FANTACO

❑1.... 3.95

LEGENDS OF THE STARGRAZERS
INNOVATION

❑1, Aug 1989.... 1.95
❑2.... 1.95
❑3.... 1.95
❑4.... 1.95
❑5.... 1.95
❑6.... 1.95

LEGENDS OF THE WORLD'S FINEST
DC

❑1, ca. 1994, Prestige format.... 6.00
❑2, ca. 1994, Prestige format.... 4.95
❑3, ca. 1994, Superman, Batman
❑Prestige format.... 4.95

LEGENDZ
VIZ

❑1, Mar 2005.... 9.95
❑2, Jun 2005.... 9.95
❑3, Nov 2005.... 9.95

L.E.G.I.O.N.
DC

❑1, Feb 1989; O: L.E.G.I.O.N.. 1: Stealth. L.E.G.I.O.N. '89 starts.... 2.50
❑2, Mar 1989.... 2.00
❑3, Apr 1989.... 2.00
❑4, May 1989 A: Lobo.... 2.00
❑5, Jun 1989; Lobo joins team.... 2.00
❑6, Jul 1989.... 1.75
❑7, Aug 1989.... 1.75
❑8, Sep 1989.... 1.75
❑9, Nov 1989 A: Phantom Girl.... 1.75
❑10, Dec 1989.... 1.75
❑11, Jan 1990; L.E.G.I.O.N. '90 starts 1.50
❑12, Feb 1990 A: Emerald Eye.... 1.50
❑13, Mar 1990.... 1.50
❑14, Apr 1990.... 1.50
❑15, May 1990.... 1.50
❑16, Jun 1990 A: Lar Gand.... 1.50
❑17, Jul 1990.... 1.50
❑18, Aug 1990.... 1.50
❑19, Sep 1990.... 1.50
❑20, Oct 1990.... 1.50
❑21, Nov 1990.... 1.50
❑22, Dec 1990 A: Lady Quark.... 1.50
❑23, Jan 1991; L.E.G.I.O.N. '91 starts 2.50
❑24, Feb 1991.... 1.50
❑25, Mar 1991.... 1.50
❑26, Apr 1991.... 1.50
❑27, May 1991.... 1.50
❑28, Jun 1991 KG (w).... 1.50
❑29, Jul 1991.... 1.50
❑30, Aug 1991 1: Ig'nea.... 1.50
❑31, Sep 1991; Painted cover; Lobo vs. Captain Marvel; Lobo vs. Capt. Marvel.... 1.50
❑32, Oct 1991 1: Ice Man.... 1.50
❑33, Nov 1991.... 1.50
❑34, Dec 1991.... 1.50
❑35, Jan 1992; L.E.G.I.O.N. '92 starts 1.50
❑36, Feb 1992.... 1.50
❑37, Mar 1992.... 1.50
❑38, Apr 1992.... 1.50
❑39, May 1992.... 1.50
❑40, Jun 1992.... 1.50
❑41, Jul 1992.... 1.50
❑42, Jul 1992.... 1.50
❑43, Aug 1992.... 1.50
❑44, Aug 1992.... 1.50
❑45, Sep 1992.... 1.50
❑46, Nov 1992.... 1.50
❑47, Dec 1992; Lobo vs. Green Lantern (Hal Jordan).... 1.50
❑48, Jan 1993; L.E.G.I.O.N. '93 starts 1.50
❑49, Feb 1993.... 1.75
❑50, Mar 1993; Double-size; L.E.G.I.O.N. '67 back-up.... 3.50
❑51, Apr 1993.... 1.75
❑52, May 1993.... 1.75
❑53, Jun 1993.... 1.75
❑54, Jun 1993 MWa (w).... 1.75
❑55, Jul 1993 MWa (w).... 1.75
❑56, Jul 1993.... 1.75
❑57, Aug 1993.... 1.75
❑58, Sep 1993.... 1.75
❑59, Oct 1993.... 1.75
❑60, Nov 1993.... 1.75
❑61, Dec 1993.... 1.75
❑62, Jan 1994; L.E.G.I.O.N. '94 starts 1.75
❑63, Feb 1994.... 1.75
❑64, Mar 1994.... 1.75
❑65, Apr 1994.... 1.75
❑66, May 1994.... 1.75
❑67, Jun 1994.... 1.75
❑68, Jul 1994.... 1.75
❑69, Aug 1994 A: Ultra Boy.... 1.75
❑70, Sep 1994; Giant-size; Zero Hour; story continues in R.E.B.E.L.S. '94 #0; L.E.G.I.O.N. goes renegade (becomes R.E.B.E.L.S.).... 2.50
❑Annual 1, ca. 1990; A: Superman. Vril Dox vs. Brainiac.... 4.00
❑Annual 2, ca. 1991; Armageddon 2001.... 2.95
❑Annual 3, ca. 1992.... 2.95
❑Annual 4, ca. 1993 1: Pax.... 3.50
❑Annual 5, ca. 1994; Elseworlds; L.E.G.I.O.N. 007.... 3.50

LEGION
DC

❑1, Dec 2001.... 3.00
❑2, Jan 2002.... 2.50
❑3, Feb 2002.... 2.50
❑4, Mar 2002.... 2.50
❑5, Apr 2002.... 2.50
❑6, May 2002.... 2.50
❑7, Jun 2002.... 2.50
❑8, Jul 2002.... 2.50
❑9, Aug 2002.... 2.50
❑10, Sep 2002.... 2.50
❑11, Oct 2002.... 2.50

Leave It to Chance

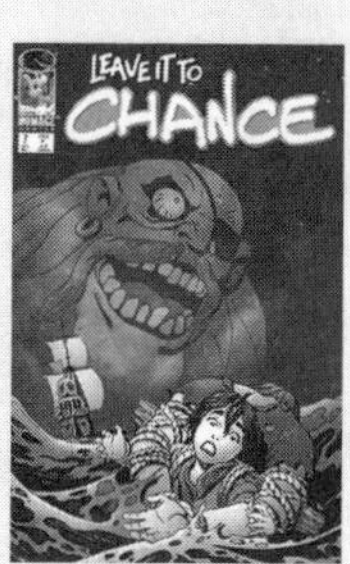

Monster hunter's daughter faces own perils

©Image

Led Zeppelin Experience

Unauthorized bio series of British rockers

©Revolutionary

Legend of the Shield

Early Archie super-hero gets revamp

©DC

Legends

Becomes unlawful for heroes to take action

©DC

Legends of the DC Universe

Rotates creative teams and characters

©DC

N-MINT

❑12, Nov 2002 ... 2.50
❑13, Dec 2002 ... 2.50
❑14, Jan 2003 ... 2.50
❑15, Feb 2003 ... 2.50
❑16, Mar 2003 ... 2.50
❑17, Apr 2003 ... 2.50
❑18, May 2003 ... 2.50
❑19, Jun 2003 ... 2.50
❑20, Jul 2003 ... 2.50
❑21, Aug 2003 ... 2.50
❑22, Sep 2003 ... 2.50
❑23, Oct 2003 ... 2.50
❑24, Nov 2003 ... 2.50
❑25, Dec 2003 ... 3.95
❑26, Jan 2004 ... 2.50
❑27, Jan 2004 ... 2.50
❑28, Feb 2004 ... 2.50
❑29, Mar 2004 ... 2.50
❑30, Apr 2004, (c) ... 2.50
❑31, May 2004 ... 2.50
❑32, Jun 2004 ... 2.50
❑33, Jul 2004 ... 2.50
❑34, Aug 2004 ... 2.50
❑35, Sep 2004 ... 2.50
❑36, Sep 2004 ... 2.50
❑37, Oct 2004 ... 2.50
❑38, Oct 2004 ... 2.50

LEGION ANTHOLOGY
LIMELIGHT

❑1, b&w; manga ... 2.95
❑2 ... 2.95

LEGION LOST
DC

❑1, May 2000 ... 2.50
❑2, Jun 2000 ... 2.50
❑3, Jul 2000 ... 2.50
❑4, Aug 2000 ... 2.50
❑5, Sep 2000 ... 2.50
❑6, Oct 2000 ... 2.50
❑7, Nov 2000 ... 2.50
❑8, Dec 2000 ... 2.50
❑9, Jan 2001 ... 2.50
❑10, Feb 2001 ... 2.50
❑11, Mar 2001 ... 2.50
❑12, Apr 2001 ... 2.50

LEGION MANGA ANTHOLOGY
LIMELIGHT

❑1 ... 2.95
❑2 ... 2.95
❑3 ... 2.95
❑4 ... 2.95

LEGIONNAIRES
DC

❑0, Oct 1994; MWa (w); revised Legion origin; continues in Legion of Super-Heroes #62 and Legionnaires #19 ... 2.25
❑1, Apr 1993; with trading card ... 3.00
❑2, May 1993; V: Fatal Five. covers of issues #2-6 form one image ... 2.00
❑3, Jun 1993 V: Fatal Five ... 2.00
❑4, Jul 1993 V: Fatal Five ... 2.00
❑5, Aug 1993 V: Fatal Five ... 2.00
❑6, Sep 1993 V: Fatal Five ... 1.50
❑7, Oct 1993 ... 1.50

N-MINT

❑8, Nov 1993; Brainiac 5 leaves team ... 1.50
❑9, Dec 1993 ... 1.50
❑10, Jan 1994 ... 1.50
❑11, Feb 1994; Kid Quantum joins team ... 1.50
❑12, Mar 1994 ... 1.50
❑13, Apr 1994; Matter-Eater Lad becomes a girl ... 1.50
❑14, May 1994 ... 1.50
❑15, Jun 1994 ... 1.50
❑16, Jul 1994; Return of Dream Girl ... 1.50
❑17, Aug 1994; End of an Era Conclusion ... 1.50
❑18, Sep 1994; Zero Hour ... 1.50
❑19, Nov 1994 ... 1.50
❑20, Dec 1994 V: Mano ... 1.50
❑21, Jan 1995 1: Work Force ... 1.50
❑22, Feb 1995 ... 1.50
❑23, Mar 1995 ... 1.50
❑24, Apr 1995 ... 1.50
❑25, May 1995 ... 1.50
❑26, Jun 1995 ... 1.75
❑27, Jul 1995 ... 2.25
❑28, Aug 1995 1: Legion Espionage Squad ... 2.25
❑29, Sep 1995 1: Dirk Morgna ... 2.25
❑30, Oct 1995; Lightning Lad turning point ... 2.25
❑31, Nov 1995; Future Tense, Part 3; Superboy made honorary member; Valor released into 30th century ... 2.25
❑32, Dec 1995; A: Chronos. Underworld Unleashed ... 2.25
❑33, Jan 1996; Kinetix finds Emerald Eye; [L1996-2] ... 2.25
❑34, Feb 1996; [L1996-4] ... 2.25
❑35, Mar 1996; XS returns to 30th century; [L1996-6] ... 2.25
❑36, May 1996; [L1996-8] ... 2.25
❑37, Jun 1996; O: M'onel. [L1996-10] ... 2.25
❑38, Jul 1996; [L1996-12] ... 2.25
❑39, Aug 1996; Triad's three personalities become distinct; [L1996-14] ... 2.25
❑40, Sep 1996; [L1996-16] ... 2.25
❑41, Oct 1996; [L1996-18] ... 2.25
❑42, Nov 1996; [L1996-20] ... 2.25
❑43, Dec 1996; Legion try-outs; Magno joins team; Umbra joins team; Sensor joins team; [L1996-22] ... 2.25
❑44, Jan 1997; [L1997-1] ... 2.25
❑45, Feb 1997; V: Mantis Morlo. [L1997-3] ... 2.25
❑46, Mar 1997; [L1997-5] ... 2.25
❑47, Apr 1997; [L1997-7] ... 2.25
❑48, May 1997; V: Mordru. [L1997-9] ... 2.25
❑49, Jun 1997; A: Workforce. A: Heroes of Xanthu. D: Atom'x. V: Mordru. [L1997-11] ... 2.25
❑50, Jul 1997; Giant-size; V: Mordru. Poster; Mysa becomes young; [L1997-13] ... 3.95
❑51, Aug 1997; [L1997-15] ... 2.25
❑52, Sep 1997; Vi's new powers manifest; [L1997-17] ... 2.25
❑53, Oct 1997; Monstress joins team; Magno leaves team; [L1997-19] ... 2.25
❑54, Nov 1997; Golden Age story; [L1997-21] ... 2.25

N-MINT

❑55, Dec 1997; V: Composite Man. Face cover; [L1997-23] ... 2.25
❑56, Jan 1998; M'onel returns to Daxam; [L1998-1] ... 2.25
❑57, Feb 1998; [L1998-3] ... 2.25
❑58, Mar 1998; [L1998-5] ... 2.25
❑59, Apr 1998; [L1998-7] ... 2.25
❑60, May 1998; Chameleon leaves team; Sensor leaves team; Karate Kid joins team; Kid Quantum joins team; [L1998-9] ... 2.25
❑61, Jun 1998; A: Superman (from Time and Time Again). Multiple time shifts; [L1998-11] ... 2.25
❑62, Jul 1998; Dark Circle Rising, Part 1: Crossfire!; [L1998-13] ... 2.25
❑63, Aug 1998; Dark Circle Rising, Part 3: Resignation!; [L1998-15] ... 2.25
❑64, Sep 1998; Dark Circle Rising, Part 5: Enlightenment!; [L1998-17] ... 2.25
❑65, Oct 1998; Dark Circle falls; [L1998-19] ... 2.50
❑66, Dec 1998; 1: Charma. [L1998-21] ... 2.50
❑67, Jan 1999; A: Kono. [L1999-1] ... 2.50
❑68, Feb 1999; Monstress changes color; [L1999-3] ... 2.50
❑69, Mar 1999; A: Plasma. [L1999-5] ... 2.50
❑70, Apr 1999; Cosmic Boy vs. Domain; [L1999-7] ... 2.50
❑71, May 1999; V: Elements of Disaster. [L1999-9] ... 2.50
❑72, Jun 1999; [L1999-11] ... 2.50
❑73, Jul 1999; Star Boy solo; [L1999-13] ... 2.50
❑74, Aug 1999; [L1999-15] ... 2.50
❑75, Sep 1999; [L1999-17] ... 2.50
❑76, Oct 1999; O: Wildfire. [L1999-19] ... 2.50
❑77, Nov 1999; [L1999-21] ... 2.50
❑78, Dec 2000; [L1999-23] ... 2.50
❑79, Jan 2000; [L2000-1] ... 2.50
❑80, Feb 2000; [L2000-3] ... 2.50
❑1000000, Nov 1998; set 1, 000 years after events of One Million ... 4.00
❑Annual 1, ca. 1994; Elseworlds; Futuristic Camelot ... 5.00
❑Annual 2, ca. 1995; D: Apparition. Andromeda leaves team ... 3.95
❑Annual 3, ca. 1996; A: Barry Allen. Legends of the Dead Earth; XS' travels in time; 1996 Annual ... 2.95

LEGIONNAIRES THREE
DC

❑1, Feb 1986 KG (w); V: Time Trapper. ... 1.25
❑2, Mar 1986 ... 1.00
❑3, Apr 1986 ... 1.00
❑4, May 1986 ... 1.00

LEGION OF MONSTERS
MARVEL

❑1, magazine, b&w ... 35.00

LEGION OF NIGHT
MARVEL

❑1, Nov 1991 ... 4.95
❑2, Dec 1991 ... 4.95

LEGION OF STUPID HEROES
ALTERNATE CONCEPTS

❑1, Jul 1997 ... 2.50
❑2, Sep 1997 ... 2.50

Other grades: Multiply price above by 5/6 for VF/NM • 2/3 for VERY FINE • 1/3 for FINE • 1/5 for VERY GOOD • 1/8 for GOOD

❑3 2.50
❑4, Mar 1998 2.50

LEGION OF STUPID KNIGHTS
ALTERNATE CONCEPTS

❑Special 1, Feb 1998, b&w 2.50

LEGION OF SUBSTITUTE HEROES SPECIAL
DC

❑1 KG (a) 2.00

LEGION OF SUPER-HEROES (1ST SERIES)
DC

❑1, Feb 1973, Tales of the Legion of Super-Heroes; Tommy Tomorrow reprint 15.00
❑2, Mar 1973, Tales of the Legion of Super-Heroes; Tommy Tomorrow reprint 8.00
❑3, May 1973, V: Computo. Tales of the Legion of Super-Heroes; Tommy Tomorrow reprint 7.00
❑4, Aug 1973, V: Computo. Tales of the Legion of Super-Heroes; Tommy Tomorrow reprint 7.00

LEGION OF SUPER-HEROES (2ND SERIES)
DC

❑259, Jan 1980, Superboy leaves team; Continued from "Superboy and the Legion of Super-Heroes" 3.50
❑260, Feb 1980, V: Circus of Crime. 2.75
❑261, Mar 1980, V: Circus of Crime. 2.50
❑261/Whitman, Mar 1980, V: Circus of Crime. Whitman variant 5.00
❑262, Apr 1980 2.50
❑262/Whitman, Apr 1980, Whitman variant 5.00
❑263, May 1980 2.50
❑263/Whitman, May 1980, Whitman variant 5.00
❑264, Jun 1980 2.50
❑264/Whitman, Jun 1980, Whitman variant 5.00
❑265, Jul 1980, O: Tyroc. bonus Superman story starring the TRS-80 Computer Whiz Kids (Radio Shack sponsored story) 2.50
❑265/Whitman, Jul 1980, O: Tyroc. bonus Superman story starring the TRS-80 Computer Whiz Kids (Radio Shack sponsored story); Whitman variant 5.00
❑266, Aug 1980, Return of Bouncing Boy; Return of Duo Damsel 2.50
❑266/Whitman, Aug 1980, Return of Bouncing Boy; Return of Duo Damsel; Whitman variant 5.00
❑267, Sep 1980, O: Legion Flight Rings. 2.50
❑268, Oct 1980, SD (a) 2.50
❑269, Nov 1980, V: Fatal Five. 2.50
❑270, Dec 1980, Dark Man's identity revealed 2.50
❑271, Jan 1981, O: Dark Man. 1.75
❑272, Feb 1981, O: Blok. 1: Dial 'H' for Hero (new). Blok joins Legion of Super-Heroes; Dial "H" For Hero preview story 1.75
❑273, Mar 1981 1.75
❑274, Apr 1981, SD (a); Ultra Boy becomes pirate 1.75
❑275, May 1981 1.75
❑276, Jun 1981 1.75
❑277, Jul 1981 1.75
❑278, Aug 1981, A: Reflecto. V: Grimbor 1.75
❑279, Sep 1981, Reflecto's identity revealed 1.75
❑280, Oct 1981, Superboy rejoins 1.75
❑281, Nov 1981, SD (a); V: Molecule Master 1.75
❑282, Dec 1981, O: Reflecto. Ultra Boy returns 1.75
❑283, Jan 1982, O: Wildfire. Wildfire story 1.75
❑284, Feb 1982 1.75
❑285, Mar 1982, PB (a) 2.50
❑286, Apr 1982, PB (a); V: Doctor Regulus. V: Dr. Regulus. 2.00
❑287, May 1982, KG (a); V: Kharlak. 2.00
❑288, Jun 1982, KG (a) 2.00
❑289, Jul 1982, KG (a) 2.00
❑290, Aug 1982, KG (a); Great Darkness Saga, Part 1 2.00
❑291, Sep 1982, KG (a); Great Darkness Saga, Part 2 2.00
❑292, Oct 1982, KG (a); Great Darkness Saga, Part 3 2.00
❑293, Nov 1982, KG (a); Great Darkness Saga, Part 4; Masters of the Universe preview story 2.00
❑294, Dec 1982; KG (a); Great Darkness Saga, Part 5; giant-size issue 2.00
❑295, Jan 1983, O: Universo (possible origin). A: Green Lantern Corps. 1.50
❑296, Feb 1983, KG (a) 1.50
❑297, Mar 1983, O: Legion of Super-Heroes. Cosmic Boy solo story 3.00
❑298, Apr 1983, 1: Gemworld. 1: Dark Opal. 1: Amethyst. Amethyst, Princess of Gemworld preview story 1.50
❑299, May 1983, Invisible Kid II meets Invisible Kid I 1.50
❑300, Jun 1983; Double-size; Tales of the Adult Legion; alternate futures 2.00
❑301, Jul 1983 1.50
❑302, Aug 1983, Lightning Lad vs. Lightning Lord 1.50
❑303, Sep 1983, V: Emerald Empress. 1.50
❑304, Oct 1983, Legion Academy 1.50
❑305, Nov 1983, Shrinking Violet revealed as Durlan; real Shrinking Violet returns 1.50
❑306, Dec 1983 O: Star Boy. 1.50
❑307, Jan 1984 V: Prophet. 1.50
❑308, Feb 1984 V: Prophet. 1.50
❑309, Mar 1984 V: Prophet. 1.50
❑310, Apr 1984 V: Omen 3.00
❑311, May 1984 1.50
❑312, Jun 1984 1.50
❑313, Jul 1984; series continues as Tales of the Legion of Super-Heroes 1.50
❑Annual 1, ca. 1982 KG (a); 1: Invisible Kid II (Jacques Foccart) 2.50
❑Annual 2, ca. 1983; DaG, KG (a); Wedding of Karate Kid and Princess Projectra; Karate Kid and Princess Projectra leave Legion of Super-Heroes 2.00
❑Annual 3, ca. 1984 CS (a); O: Validus. 2.00

LEGION OF SUPER-HEROES (3RD SERIES)
DC

❑1, Aug 1984; KG (w); KG (a); V: Legion of Super-Villains. Silver ink cover 5.00
❑2, Sep 1984 KG (a); 1: Kono. V: Legion of Super-Villains. 4.00
❑3, Oct 1984 V: Legion of Super-Villains. 4.00
❑4, Nov 1984 D: Karate Kid. V: Legion of Super-Villains. 4.00
❑5, Dec 1984 D: Nemesis Kid. 4.00
❑6, Jan 1985; 1: Laurel Gand. Spotlight on Lightning Lass 2.25
❑7, Feb 1985 2.25
❑8, Mar 1985 2.25
❑9, Apr 1985 2.25
❑10, May 1985 2.25
❑11, Jun 1985; Bouncing Boy back-up 2.00
❑12, Jul 1985 2.00
❑13, Aug 1985 2.00
❑14, Sep 1985; 1: Quislet. New members 2.00
❑15, Oct 1985 2.00
❑16, Nov 1985; Crisis 2.00
❑17, Dec 1985 2.00
❑18, Jan 1986; Crisis 2.00
❑19, Feb 1986 2.00
❑20, Mar 1986 V: Tyr. 2.00
❑21, Apr 1986 V: Emerald Empress. 2.00
❑22, May 1986 2.00
❑23, Jun 1986 2.00
❑24, Jul 1986 2.00
❑25, Aug 1986 2.00
❑26, Sep 1986 2.00
❑27, Oct 1986 V: Mordru. 2.00
❑28, Nov 1986 2.00
❑29, Dec 1986 V: Starfinger. 2.00
❑30, Jan 1987 2.00
❑31, Feb 1987; Karate Kid, Princess Projectra, Ferro Lad story 1.75
❑32, Mar 1987; Universo Project, Chapter 1 1.75
❑33, Apr 1987; Universo Project, Chapter 2 1.75
❑34, May 1987; Universo Project, Chapter 3 1.75
❑35, Jun 1987; Universo Project, Chapter 4 1.75
❑36, Jul 1987; Legion elections 1.75
❑37, Aug 1987; Fate of Superboy revealed; Return of Star Boy and Sun Girl 5.00
❑38, Sep 1987; D: Superboy. Death of Superboy 5.00
❑39, Oct 1987 CS (a); O: Colossal Boy. 1.75
❑40, Nov 1987 V: Starfinger. 1.75
❑41, Dec 1987 V: Starfinger. 1.75
❑42, Jan 1988; V: Laurel Kent. Millennium 1.75
❑43, Feb 1988; V: Laurel Kent. Millennium 1.75
❑44, Mar 1988 O: Quislet. 1.75
❑45, Apr 1988; Double-size; 30th Anniversary Issue 3.00
❑46, May 1988 1.75
❑47, Jun 1988 V: Starfinger. 1.75
❑48, Jul 1988 V: Starfinger. 1.75
❑49, Aug 1988 V: Starfinger. 1.75
❑50, Sep 1988; Giant-size; D: Duo Damsel (half). D: Time Trapper (possible death). D: Infinite Man. Mon-El wounded 2.00
❑51, Oct 1988 1.75
❑52, Nov 1988 1.75
❑53, Dec 1988 1.75
❑54, Win 1988; no month of publication; cover says Winter 1.75
❑55, Hol 1989; no month of publication; cover says Holiday 1.75
❑56, Jan 1989 1.75
❑57, Feb 1989 1.75
❑58, Mar 1989 D: Emerald Empress 1.75
❑59, Apr 1989 1.75
❑60, May 1989 KG (a) 1.75
❑61, Jun 1989 KG (a) 1.75
❑62, Jul 1989 KG (a); D: Magnetic Kid. 1.75
❑63, Aug 1989 KG (a) 1.75
❑Annual 1, Oct 1985 KG (a) 3.00
❑Annual 2, ca. 1986 V: Validus. 2.00
❑Annual 3, ca. 1987 O: new Legion of Substitute Heroes. 2.00
❑Annual 4, ca. 1988; O: Starfinger. 1988 annual 2.50

LEGION OF SUPER-HEROES (4TH SERIES)
DC

❑0, Oct 1994; KG (w); KG (a); O: Legion of Super-Heroes (revised). continues in Legion of Super-Heroes #62 and Legionnaires #19 2.00
❑1, Nov 1989; KG (w); KG (a); Begins five years after previous series 2.50
❑2, Dec 1989 2.00
❑3, Jan 1990 V: Roxxas. 2.00
❑4, Feb 1990 KG (w); KG (a); A: Mon-El. 2.00
❑5, Mar 1990 2.00
❑6, Apr 1990 2.00
❑7, May 1990 2.00
❑8, Jun 1990; origin 2.00
❑9, Jul 1990 2.00
❑10, Aug 1990 V: Roxxas. 2.00
❑11, Sep 1990 A: Matter-Eater Lad. 2.00
❑12, Oct 1990; Legion reformed 2.00
❑13, Nov 1990; poster 2.00
❑14, Jan 1991 2.00
❑15, Feb 1991 2.00
❑16, Mar 1991 2.00
❑17, Apr 1991 2.00
❑18, May 1991 V: Dark Circle. 2.00
❑19, Jun 1991 2.00
❑20, Jul 1991 2.00
❑21, Aug 1991 1.75
❑22, Sep 1991 1.75
❑23, Oct 1991 V: Lobo. 1.75
❑24, Dec 1991 KG (a) 1.75
❑25, Jan 1992 1.75
❑26, Feb 1992; contains map of Legion headquarters 1.75
❑27, Mar 1992 V: B.I.O.N.. 1.75
❑28, Apr 1992 KG (a); A: Sun Boy. 1.75
❑29, May 1992 1.75
❑30, Jun 1992; The Terra Mosaic 1.75
❑31, Jul 1992; The Terra Mosaic; romance cover 1.75

Other grades: Multiply price above by 5/6 for VF/NM • 2/3 for VERY FINE • 1/3 for FINE • 1/5 for VERY GOOD • 1/8 for GOOD

L.E.G.I.O.N.

Acronym title changed annually as year turned
©DC

Legion

Shortened title resulted in three-year run
©DC

Legionnaires

Futuristic teens defend domed cities
©DC

Legion of Super-Heroes (1st Series)

Quartet of reprint issues
©DC

Legion of Super-Heroes (2nd Series)

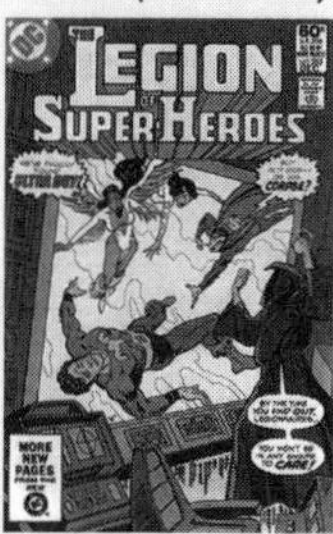

Superboy leaves team and title
©DC

	N-MINT
❑32, Aug 1992; The Terra Mosaic	1.75
❑33, Sep 1992; The Terra Mosaic; Fate of Kid Quantum	1.75
❑34, Oct 1992; The Terra Mosaic; Timber Wolf mini-series preview	1.75
❑35, Nov 1992; The Terra Mosaic; Sun Boy meets Sun Boy	1.75
❑36, Nov 1992; The Terra Mosaic conclusion	1.75
❑37, Dec 1992; Star Boy and Dream Girl return	1.75
❑38, Dec 1992; A: Death (Sandman). Earth destroyed	2.50
❑39, Jan 1993 KG (a)	1.75
❑40, Feb 1993	1.75
❑41, Mar 1993 1: Legionnaires	1.75
❑42, Apr 1993	1.75
❑43, May 1993; White Witch returns	1.75
❑44, Jun 1993	1.75
❑45, Jul 1993	1.75
❑46, Aug 1993	1.75
❑47, Sep 1993 V: dead heroes	1.75
❑48, Oct 1993 V: Mordru	1.75
❑49, Nov 1993	1.75
❑50, Nov 1993; Wedding of Matter-Eater Lad and Saturn Queen	3.50
❑51, Dec 1993	1.75
❑52, Dec 1993 O: Timber Wolf	1.75
❑53, Jan 1994 V: Glorith	1.75
❑54, Feb 1994; Die-cut cover	2.95
❑55, Mar 1994	1.75
❑56, Apr 1994	1.75
❑57, May 1994	1.75
❑58, Jun 1994	1.75
❑59, Jul 1994	1.95
❑60, Aug 1994; Crossover with Legionnaires and Valor	1.95
❑61, Sep 1994; Zero Hour; end of original Legion of Super-Heroes	1.95
❑62, Nov 1994	1.95
❑63, Dec 1994; 1: Athramites, new Legion headquarters. Tenzil Kem hired as chef	1.95
❑64, Jan 1995; MWa (w); Return of Ultra Boy	1.95
❑65, Feb 1995	1.95
❑66, Mar 1995; A: Laurel Gand. Andromeda, Shrinking Violet and Kinetix join team	1.95
❑67, Apr 1995	1.95
❑68, May 1995	1.95
❑69, Jun 1995	2.25
❑70, Jul 1995	2.25
❑71, Aug 1995; Trom destroyed	2.25
❑72, Sep 1995	2.25
❑73, Oct 1995 A: Mekt Ranz	2.25
❑74, Nov 1995; A: Superboy. A: Scavenger. Future Tense, Part 2; Concludes in Legionnaires #31	2.25
❑75, Dec 1995; A: Chronos. Underworld Unleashed	2.25
❑76, Jan 1996; Star Boy and Gates joins team; [L1996-1]	2.25
❑77, Feb 1996; O: Brainiac Five. [L1996-3]	2.25
❑78, Mar 1996; O: Fatal Five. 1: Fatal Five. [L1996-5]	2.25
❑79, Apr 1996; V: Fatal Five. [L1996-7]	2.25
❑80, May 1996; [L1996-9]	2.25
❑81, Jun 1996; Dirk Morgna becomes Sun Boy; Brainiac 5 quits; [L1996-11]	2.25
❑82, Jul 1996; Apparition returns; [L1996-13]	2.25
❑83, Aug 1996; D: Leviathan. Violet possessed by Emerald Eye; [L1996-15]	2.25
❑84, Sep 1996; [L1996-17]	2.25
❑85, Oct 1996; A: Superman. Seven Legionnaires, Inferno, and Shvaughn Erin in 20th century; [L1996-19]	2.25
❑86, Nov 1996; A: Ferro. Final Night; [L1996-21]	2.25
❑87, Dec 1996; A: Deadman. A: Phase. [L1996-23]	2.25
❑88, Jan 1997; A: Impulse. [L1997-2]	2.25
❑89, Feb 1997; A: Doctor Psycho. [L1997-4]	2.25
❑90, Mar 1997; V: Doctor Psycho. [L1997-6]	2.25
❑91, Apr 1997; Legion visits several DC eras; [L1997-8]	2.25
❑92, May 1997; 20th century group lands in 1958 Happy Harbor; [L1997-10]	2.25
❑93, Jun 1997; D: Douglas Nolan. [L1997-12]	2.25
❑94, Jul 1997; [L1997-14]	2.25
❑95, Aug 1997; A: Metal Men. [L1997-16]	2.25
❑96, Sep 1997; Wedding of Ultra Boy and Apparition; Cosmic Boy revives; [L1997-18]	2.25
❑97, Oct 1997; V: Mantis. Genesis; Spark gains gravity powers; [L1997-20]	2.25
❑98, Nov 1997; Phase meets Apparition; [L1997-22]	2.25
❑99, Dec 1997; Face cover; [L1997-24]	2.25
❑100, Jan 1998; Double-size; gatefold cover; Legionnaires return from 20th century; Pin-ups; [L1998-2]	5.95
❑101, Feb 1998; Spark gets her lightning powers back; [L1998-4]	2.25
❑102, Mar 1998; A: Heroes of Xanthu. [L1998-6]	2.25
❑103, Apr 1998; Karate Kid quits McCauley Industries; [L1998-8]	2.25
❑104, May 1998; A: Kono. time shifts to 2968; [L1998-10]	2.25
❑105, Jun 1998; V: Time Trapper. [L1998-12]	2.25
❑106, Jul 1998; Dark Circle Rising, Part 2: Assassination!; [L1998-14]	2.25
❑107, Aug 1998; Dark Circle Rising, Part 4: Duplicity!; [L1998-16]	2.25
❑108, Sep 1998; Dark Circle Rising, Part 6: Revelation!; [L1998-18]	2.25
❑109, Oct 1998; V: Emerald Eye. [L1998-20]	2.50
❑110, Dec 1998; Thunder joins team; [L1998-22]	2.50
❑111, Jan 1999; Karate Kid vs. M'onel; [L1999-2]	2.50
❑112, Feb 1999; [L1999-4]	2.50
❑113, Mar 1999; [L1999-6]	2.50
❑114, Apr 1999; 1: Bizarro Legion. [L1999-8]	2.50
❑115, May 1999; [L1999-10]	2.50
❑116, Jun 1999; Thunder vs. Pernisius; [L1999-12]	2.50
❑117, Jul 1999; [L1999-14]	2.50
❑118, Aug 1999; V: Pernisius. [L1999-16]	2.50
❑119, Sep 1999; M'Onel and Apparition tell a L.E.G.I.O.N. story; [L1999-18]	2.50
❑120, Oct 1999; V: Fatal Five. [L1999-20]	2.50
❑121, Nov 1999; [L1999-22]	2.50
❑122, Dec 1999; [L1999-24]	2.50
❑123, Jan 2000; [L2000-2]	2.50
❑1000000, Nov 1998; KG (a); set 1,000 years after events of One Million+E12681	4.00
❑Annual 1, ca. 1990 O: Glorith, Ultra Boy, Legion.	5.00
❑Annual 2, ca. 1991 O: Valor.	3.50
❑Annual 3, ca. 1992; Timber Wolf goes to 20th century	3.50
❑Annual 4, ca. 1993 O: Jamm. 1: Jamm	3.50
❑Annual 5, ca. 1994; CS (a); Elseworlds; Legion in Oz	3.50
❑Annual 6, ca. 1995; O: Leviathan. O: Kinetix. Year One; 0: XS; Legion Headquarters Map; Legion Equipment	3.95
❑Annual 7, ca. 1996; A: Wildfire. Legends of the Dead Earth; 1996 annual	2.95

LEGION OF SUPER-HEROES (5TH SERIES)
DC

	N-MINT
❑1, Mar 2005	4.00
❑2, Apr 2005	2.95
❑3, May 2005	2.95
❑4, Jun 2005	2.95
❑5, Jun 2005	2.99
❑6, Jul 2005	2.99
❑7, Aug 2005	2.99
❑8, Sep 2005	2.99
❑9, Oct 2005	2.99
❑10 2005	2.99
❑11	2.99
❑12, Jan 2006	2.99
❑13, Mar 2006	2.99
❑14, Mar 2006	2.99
❑15, May 2006, becomes Supergirl and the Legion of Super-Heroes.	2.99

LEGION OF SUPER-HEROES INDEX
ECLIPSE / INDEPENDENT

	N-MINT
❑1	2.00
❑2, Jan 1987	2.00
❑3, Feb 1987	2.00
❑4, Mar 1987	2.00
❑5, May 1987	2.00

LEGION OF SUPER-HEROES SECRET FILES
DC

	N-MINT
❑1, Jan 1998; bios on members and villains	4.95
❑2, Jun 1999; bios on members and villains; Legion constitution	4.95

Other grades: Multiply price above by 5/6 for VF/NM • 2/3 for VERY FINE • 1/3 for FINE • 1/5 for VERY GOOD • 1/8 for GOOD

LEGION OF THE STUPID-HEROES
BLACKTHORNE
❑1, b&w; parody 1.75

LEGION: SCIENCE POLICE
DC
❑1, Aug 1998 2.25
❑2, Sep 1998 2.25
❑3, Oct 1998 2.25
❑4, Nov 1998 2.25

LEGION SECRET FILES 3003
DC
❑1, Jan 2004 4.95

LEGIONS OF LUDICROUS HEROES
C&T
❑1, b&w 2.00

LEGION WORLDS
DC
❑1, Jun 2001 3.95
❑2, Jul 2001 3.95
❑3, Aug 2001 3.95
❑4, Sep 2001 3.95
❑5, Oct 2001 3.95
❑6, Nov 2001 3.95

LEGION X-1 (VOL. 2)
GREATER MERCURY
❑1, Aug 1989, b&w 2.00
❑2, Aug 1989, b&w; Cover says September 2.00
❑3, Jul 1990, b&w 2.00

LEJENTIA
OPUS
❑1 1.95
❑2 2.25

LEMONADE KID
AC
❑1, Powell reprints 2.50

LENA'S BAMBINAS
FANTAGRAPHICS
❑1 3.99

LENORE
SLAVE LABOR
❑1, Feb 1998 3.25
❑2, Jun 1998 3.00
❑3, Sep 1998 2.95
❑4, Jan 1999 2.95
❑5, Mar 1999 2.95
❑6, Jul 1999 2.95
❑7, Dec 1999 2.95
❑12, Oct 2005 2.95

LENSMAN
ETERNITY
❑1, Feb 1990, b&w 2.25
❑1/Variant, Feb 1990, b&w; Special edition; cardstock cover; Includes Episode Guide; History; Story Timeline; Cycroader info; Galactic Patrol & Eddore Organizational charts; Vital Statistics on characters, vehicles and weapons 3.95
❑2 2.25
❑3 2.25
❑4 2.25
❑5 2.25
❑6 2.25

LENSMAN: WAR OF THE GALAXIES
ETERNITY
❑1, Nov 1990, b&w 2.25
❑2 1991, b&w 2.25
❑3 1991, b&w 2.25
❑4 1991, b&w 2.25
❑5 1991, b&w 2.25
❑6, Jun 1991, b&w 2.25
❑7, Jul 1991, b&w 2.25

LEONARD NIMOY
CELEBRITY
❑1, b&w 5.95

LEONARDO TEENAGE MUTANT NINJA TURTLE
MIRAGE
❑1, Dec 1986; continues in Teenage Mutant Ninja Turtles #10 4.00

LEOPOLD AND BRINK
FAULTLINE
❑1, Jun 1997, b&w 2.50
❑2, Nov 1997, b&w 2.50
❑3, Jan 1998, b&w 2.95

LESTER GIRLS: THE LIZARD'S TRAIL
ETERNITY
❑1, b&w 2.50
❑2, b&w 2.50
❑3, b&w 2.50

LETHAL
IMAGE
❑1, Feb 1996 2.50

LETHAL FOES OF SPIDER-MAN
MARVEL
❑1, Sep 1993 2.00
❑2, Oct 1993 A: Answer. A: Hardshell. A: Doctor Octopus. A: Vulture 2.00
❑3, Nov 1993 KP (a) 2.00
❑4, Dec 1993 2.00

LETHAL INSTINCT
ALIAS
❑1, May 2005 2.99
❑2, Jun 2005 2.99
❑3, Sep 2005 2.99
❑4, Nov 2005
❑5, Jan 2006

LETHAL ORGASM
NBM
❑1 9.95

LETHAL STRIKE
LONDON NIGHT
❑0; Commemorative edition 5.95
❑½ 3.00
❑1, Jun 1995 3.00
❑2 3.00
❑3 3.00
❑Annual 1 3.00

LETHAL STRIKE/DOUBLE IMPACT: LETHAL IMPACT
LONDON NIGHT
❑1, May 1996; crossover with High Impact 3.00

LETHARGIC COMICS
ALPHA
❑1, b&w; Spawn/Cerebus parody cover 3.50
❑2, Feb 1994, b&w 3.00
❑3, Mar 1994, b&w 3.00
❑3.14, Apr 1994, b&w; Issue #pi 3.00
❑4, May 1994, b&w; Marvels #4 parody cover 3.00
❑5, Jul 1994, b&w; Dot-It-Yerself cover 3.00
❑6, b&w; Sin City parody cover 2.50
❑7, b&w; Spawn/Batman parody cover 2.50
❑8, b&w 2.50
❑9, Apr 1995, b&w; Bone 2.50
❑10, b&w; Sin City parody cover 2.50
❑11, Aug 1995, b&w; Milk & Cheese 2.50
❑12, b&w; A: Shi. Shi cover 2.50
❑13 2.50
❑14 2.50

LETHARGIC COMICS, WEAKLY
LETHARGIC
❑1, Jun 1991, b&w; 1: Guy with a Gun. 1: No Mutants. 1: Lethargic Lad. 1: Walrus Boy. 1: Him. 1: The Grad. 1: The Zit. Action Comics #601 parody cover 4.00
❑2, b&w; Detective Comics #27 parody cover 3.00
❑3, b&w; Spider-Man #1 parody cover 3.00
❑4, b&w; X-Men #1 parody cover 2.50
❑5, b&w; Dark Knight #1 parody cover 2.50
❑6, b&w; Dark Knight #4 parody cover 2.50
❑7; Crisis on Infinite Earths #12 parody cover 2.50
❑8; Avengers #4 parody cover 2.50
❑9; Spider-Man #16 parody cover; Issue reads sideways 2.50
❑10; Adventures of Captain America parody cover 2.50
❑11; Youngblood #1 parody cover 2.50
❑12, b&w; Alpha begins publishing; Superman #75 parody cover 2.50

LETHARGIC LAD (1ST SERIES)
CRUSADE
❑1, Jun 1996, b&w 2.95
❑2, Jul 1996, b&w 2.95
❑3, Sep 1996, b&w; wraparound cover; Kingdom Come parody 2.95

LETHARGIC LAD (2ND SERIES)
CRUSADE
❑1, Oct 1997; Team-up with Him 2.95
❑2, Dec 1997 2.95
❑3, Mar 1998; Thieves & Kings 2.95
❑4, Apr 1998; Starro'David, The Captain Company (Starro and Avengers parodies); Batman origin parody 2.95
❑5, Jun 1998 2.95
❑6, Sep 1998 2.95
❑7, Nov 1998 2.95
❑8, Jan 1999 2.95
❑9, Mar 1999 2.95

LEVEL X
CALIBER
❑1, b&w 3.95
❑2, b&w 3.95

LEVI'S WORLD
MOORDAM
❑1, Jan 1998 2.95
❑2, Mar 1998 2.95
❑3, May 1998 2.95
❑4, Aug 1998 2.95

LEWD MOANA
FANTAGRAPHICS / EROS
❑1 2.95

THE LEXIAN CHRONICLES: FULL CIRCLE
APCOMICS
❑1/Preview, May 2005 5.00
❑1, Jun 2005 3.50

LEX LUTHOR: MAN OF STEEL
DC
❑1, May 2005 2.99
❑2, Jun 2005 2.99
❑3, Jun 2005 2.99
❑4, Jul 2005 2.99
❑5, Aug 2005 2.99

LEX LUTHOR: THE UNAUTHORIZED BIOGRAPHY
DC
❑1, Jul 1989; O: Luthor. Painted cover 4.00

LEX TALIONIS: JUNGLE TALE ONE SHOT
IMAGE
❑1, Jan 2004 5.95

LIAISONS DELICIEUSES
FANTAGRAPHICS / EROS
❑1, b&w 1.95
❑2, b&w 1.95
❑3 2.25
❑4 2.25
❑5 2.25
❑6, Jun 1991 2.25

LIBBY ELLIS (ETERNITY)
ETERNITY
❑1, Jun 1988 1.95
❑2, Jul 1988 1.95
❑3, Aug 1988 1.95
❑4, Sep 1988 1.95

LIBBY ELLIS (MALIBU)
MALIBU
❑1 1.95
❑2 1.95
❑3 1.95
❑4 1.95

LIBERATOR
MALIBU
❑1, Dec 1987, b&w 1.95
❑2, Feb 1988 1.95
❑3, Mar 1988 1.95
❑4, Jun 1988 1.95
❑5, Oct 1988 1.95
❑6, Dec 1988 1.95

LIBERATOR (IMAGES & REALITIES)
IMAGES & REALITIES
❑1 2.00

LIBERTINE
FANTAGRAPHICS / EROS
❑1, b&w 2.25
❑2 2.50

Legion of Super-Heroes (4th Series)

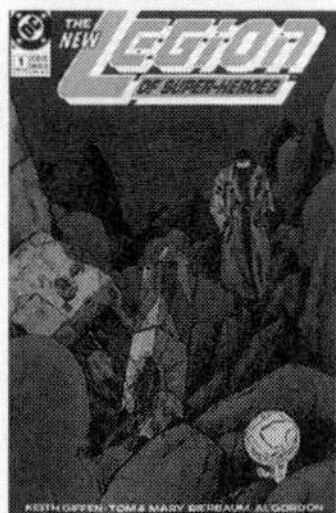

Keith Giffen shunts team five years ahead
©DC

Legion Worlds

Travelogue of United Planets
©DC

Lensman

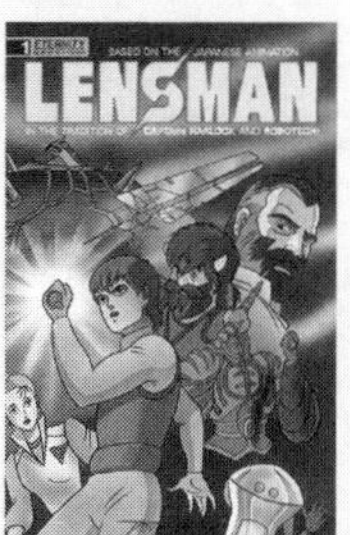

Manga version of E.E. Smith SF classic
©Eternity

Lethal Foes of Spider-Man

Doc Ock organizes new villainous group
©Marvel

Lethargic Comics

Simple-looking parodies have surprising depth
©Alpha

N-MINT

LIBERTY MEADOWS
INSIGHT

❑1, Jun 1999, Reprints first eight weeks of Liberty Meadows 18.00
❑1=2, Reprints first eight weeks of Liberty Meadows 6.00
❑1/2nd, Reprints first eight weeks of Liberty Meadows 2.95
❑2, Aug 1999, Reprints weeks 9-16 of Liberty Meadows strip 10.00
❑3, Oct 1999, Reprints weeks 17-24 of Liberty Meadows strip 6.00
❑4, Nov 1999, Reprints weeks 25-32 of Liberty Meadows strip 6.00
❑5, Dec 1999, 42 strips plus 3 Sunday strip reprints 5.00
❑6, Jan 2000 .... 4.00
❑7, Feb 2000 .... 4.00
❑8, Mar 2000 .... 4.00
❑9, Apr 2000 .... 4.00
❑10, May 2000 .... 4.00
❑11, Jun 2000 .... 3.00
❑12, Jul 2000 .... 3.00
❑13, Aug 2000 .... 3.00
❑14, Sep 2000 .... 3.00
❑15, Nov 2000, reader requests 3.00
❑16, Dec 2000, Wiener Dog Race 3.00
❑17, Jan 2001 .... 3.00
❑18, Feb 2001 .... 3.00
❑19, Mar 2001 .... 2.95
❑20, May 2001 .... 2.95
❑21, Jul 2001 .... 2.95
❑22 .... 2.95
❑23 .... 2.95
❑24 .... 2.95
❑25 .... 2.95
❑26 .... 2.95
❑27, Aug 2002, Image begins as publisher 2.95
❑28, Oct 2002 .... 2.95
❑29, Dec 2002 .... 2.95
❑30, Feb 2003 .... 2.95
❑31, Apr 2003 .... 2.95
❑32, Jul 2003 .... 2.95
❑33, Aug 2003 .... 2.95
❑34, Oct 2003 .... 2.95
❑35, Jan 2004 .... 2.95
❑36, Apr 2004 .... 2.95
❑37, Jul 2006 .... 2.95

LIBERTY MEADOWS SOURCE BOOK
IMAGE

❑1, Aug 2005 .... 4.95

LIBERTY MEADOWS WEDDING ALBUM
INSIGHT

❑nn, ca. 2001 .... 2.95

LIBERTY PROJECT
ECLIPSE

❑1, Jun 1987 KB (w); O: The Liberty Project. 1: Cimmaron. 1: Burnout. 1: Crackshot. 1: The Liberty Project. 1: Slick. 2.00
❑2, Jul 1987 KB (w) 1.75
❑3, Aug 1987 KB (w) 1.75
❑4, Sep 1987 KB (w) 1.75
❑5, Oct 1987 KB (w) 1.75
❑6, Nov 1987 KB (w); A: Valkyrie. 1.75
❑7, Dec 1987 KB (w) 1.75
❑8, May 1988 KB (w) 1.75

LIBRA
ETERNITY

❑1, Apr 1987 .... 1.95

LIBRARIAN
FANTAGRAPHICS

❑1, b&w 2.75

LICENSABLE BEAR
ABOUT

❑1, Nov 2003 .... 2.95

LICENSE TO KILL
ECLIPSE

❑1 .... 7.95

LIDSVILLE
GOLD KEY

❑1, Oct 1972 .... 20.00
❑2, Jan 1973 .... 14.00
❑3, Apr 1973 .... 12.00
❑4, Jul 1973 .... 12.00
❑5, Oct 1973 .... 12.00

LT. ROBIN CRUSOE, U.S.N.
GOLD KEY

❑1, Oct 1966, Cover code -601; later reprinted in Walt Disney Showcase #26 .... 20.00

LIFE AND ADVENTURES OF SANTA CLAUSE
TUNDRA

❑nn, ca. 1992 .... 24.95

L.I.F.E. BRIGADE
BLUE COMET

❑1 .... 2.00
❑1/2nd 2.00
❑2 .... 2.00
❑3; Title changes to New L.I.F.E. Brigade 2.00

LIFE EATERS
DC

❑1, ca. 2003 .... 29.95

LIFE OF CAPTAIN MARVEL
MARVEL

❑1, Aug 1985; JSn (w); JSn (a); Baxter reprint 3.00
❑2, Sep 1985; JSn (w); JSn (a); Baxter reprint 2.50
❑3, Oct 1985; JSn (a); Baxter reprint 2.50
❑4, Nov 1985; JSn (a); Baxter reprint 2.50
❑5, Dec 1985; JSn (a); Baxter reprint. 2.50

LIFE OF CHRIST
MARVEL / NELSON

❑1, Feb 1993 .... 3.00

LIFE OF CHRIST, THE: THE EASTER STORY
MARVEL / NELSON

❑1 .... 3.00

LIFE OF GROO
MARVEL / EPIC

❑Book 1, Mar 1993 .... 8.95
❑Book 1/2nd; reprints Marvel/Epic graphic novel 12.95

LIFE OF POPE JOHN PAUL II
MARVEL

❑1, Jan 1983 JSt (a) 2.50

LIFEQUEST
CALIBER

❑1 .... 2.95
❑2 .... 2.95

LIFE UNDER SANCTIONS
FANTAGRAPHICS

❑1, Feb 1994, b&w 2.95

LIFE, THE UNIVERSE AND EVERYTHING
DC

❑1, prestige format; adapts Douglas Adams book 6.95
❑2, prestige format; adapts Douglas Adams book 6.95
❑3, prestige format; adapts Douglas Adams book 6.95

LIFE WITH ARCHIE
ARCHIE

❑1, Sep 1958 .... 225.00
❑2, Sep 1959 .... 110.00
❑3, Jul 1960 .... 85.00
❑4, Sep 1960 .... 85.00
❑5, Nov 1960 .... 85.00
❑6, Jan 1961 .... 55.00
❑7, Mar 1961 .... 55.00
❑8, May 1961 .... 55.00
❑9, Jul 1961 .... 55.00
❑10, Sep 1961 .... 55.00
❑11, Nov 1961 .... 32.00
❑12, Jan 1962 .... 32.00
❑13, Mar 1962 .... 32.00
❑14, May 1962 .... 32.00
❑15, Jul 1962 .... 32.00
❑16, Sep 1962 .... 32.00
❑17, Nov 1962 .... 32.00
❑18, Jan 1963 .... 32.00
❑19, Mar 1963 .... 32.00
❑20, May 1963 .... 32.00
❑21, Jul 1963 .... 25.00
❑22, Aug 1963 .... 25.00
❑23 1963 .... 25.00
❑24 1963 .... 25.00
❑25 1964 .... 25.00
❑26, Mar 1964 .... 25.00
❑27, May 1964 .... 25.00
❑28, Jul 1964 .... 25.00
❑29 1964 .... 25.00
❑30, Oct 1964 .... 25.00
❑31, Nov 1964 .... 25.00
❑32, Dec 1964 .... 16.00
❑33, Jan 1965 .... 16.00
❑34, Feb 1965 .... 16.00
❑35, Mar 1965 .... 16.00
❑36, Apr 1965 .... 16.00
❑37, May 1965 .... 16.00
❑38, Jun 1965 .... 16.00
❑39, Jul 1965 .... 16.00
❑40, Aug 1965 .... 16.00

	N-MINT
❑41, Sep 1965	12.00
❑42, Oct 1965	12.00
❑43, Nov 1965	12.00
❑44, Dec 1965	12.00
❑45, Jan 1966	12.00
❑46, Feb 1966	12.00
❑47, Mar 1966	12.00
❑48, Apr 1966	12.00
❑49, May 1966	12.00
❑50, Jun 1966	12.00
❑51, Jul 1966	8.00
❑52, Aug 1966	8.00
❑53, Sep 1966	8.00
❑54, Oct 1966	8.00
❑55, Nov 1966	8.00
❑56, Dec 1966	8.00
❑57, Jan 1967	8.00
❑58, Feb 1967	8.00
❑59, Mar 1967	8.00
❑60, Apr 1967	8.00
❑61, May 1967	5.00
❑62, Jun 1967	5.00
❑63, Jul 1967	5.00
❑64, Aug 1967	5.00
❑65, Sep 1967	5.00
❑66, Oct 1967	5.00
❑67, Nov 1967	5.00
❑68, Dec 1967	5.00
❑69, Jan 1968	5.00
❑70, Feb 1968	5.00
❑71, Mar 1968	4.00
❑72, Apr 1968	4.00
❑73, May 1968	4.00
❑74, Jun 1968	4.00
❑75, Jul 1968	4.00
❑76, Aug 1968	4.00
❑77, Sep 1968	4.00
❑78, Oct 1968	4.00
❑79, Nov 1968	4.00
❑80, Dec 1968	4.00
❑81, Jan 1969	3.00
❑82, Feb 1969	3.00
❑83, Mar 1969	3.00
❑84, Apr 1969	3.00
❑85, May 1969	3.00
❑86, Jun 1969	3.00
❑87, Jul 1969	3.00
❑88, Aug 1969	3.00
❑89, Sep 1969	3.00
❑90, Oct 1969	3.00
❑91, Nov 1969	2.50
❑92, Dec 1969	3.00
❑93, Jan 1970	3.00
❑94, Feb 1970	3.00
❑95, Mar 1970	3.00
❑96, Apr 1970	3.00
❑97, May 1970	3.00
❑98, Jun 1970	3.00
❑99, Jul 1970	3.00
❑100, Aug 1970	3.00
❑101, Sep 1970	2.50
❑102, Oct 1970	2.50
❑103, Nov 1970	2.50
❑104, Dec 1970	2.50
❑105, Jan 1971	2.50
❑106, Feb 1971	2.50
❑107, Mar 1971	2.50
❑108, Apr 1971	2.50
❑109, May 1971	2.50
❑110, Jun 1971	2.50
❑111, Jul 1971	2.50
❑112, Aug 1971	2.50
❑113, Sep 1971	2.50
❑114, Oct 1971	2.50
❑115, Nov 1971	2.50
❑116, Dec 1971	2.50
❑117, Jan 1972	2.50
❑118, Feb 1972	2.50
❑119, Mar 1972	2.50
❑120, Apr 1972	2.50
❑121, May 1972	2.00
❑122, Jun 1972	2.00
❑123, Jul 1972	2.00
❑124, Aug 1972	2.00
❑125, Sep 1972	2.00
❑126, Oct 1972	2.00

	N-MINT
❑127, Nov 1972	2.00
❑128, Dec 1972	2.00
❑129, Jan 1973	2.00
❑130, Feb 1973	2.00
❑131, Mar 1973	2.00
❑132, Apr 1973	2.00
❑133, May 1973	2.00
❑134, Jun 1973	2.00
❑135, Jul 1973	2.00
❑136, Aug 1973	2.00
❑137, Sep 1973	2.00
❑138, Oct 1973	2.00
❑139, Nov 1973	2.00
❑140, Dec 1973	2.00
❑141, Jan 1974	2.00
❑142, Feb 1974	2.00
❑143, Mar 1974	2.00
❑144, Apr 1974	2.00
❑145, May 1974	2.00
❑146, Jun 1974	2.00
❑147, Jul 1974	2.00
❑148, Aug 1974	2.00
❑149, Sep 1974	2.00
❑150, Oct 1974	2.00
❑151, Nov 1974	1.75
❑152, Dec 1974	1.75
❑153, Jan 1975	1.75
❑154, Feb 1975	1.75
❑155, Mar 1975	1.75
❑156, Apr 1975	1.75
❑157, May 1975	1.75
❑158, Jun 1975	1.75
❑159, Jul 1975	1.75
❑160, Aug 1975	1.75
❑161, Sep 1975	1.75
❑162, Oct 1975	1.75
❑163, Nov 1975	1.75
❑164, Dec 1975	1.75
❑165, Jan 1976	1.75
❑166, Feb 1976	1.75
❑167, Mar 1976	1.75
❑168, Apr 1976	1.75
❑169, May 1976	1.75
❑170, Jun 1976	1.75
❑171, Jul 1976	1.50
❑172, Aug 1976	1.50
❑173, Sep 1976	1.50
❑174, Oct 1976	1.50
❑175, Nov 1976	1.50
❑176, Dec 1976	1.50
❑177, Jan 1977	1.50
❑178, Feb 1977	1.50
❑179, Mar 1977	1.50
❑180, Apr 1977	1.50
❑181, May 1977	1.50
❑182, Jun 1977	1.50
❑183, Jul 1977	1.50
❑184, Aug 1977	1.50
❑185, Sep 1977	1.50
❑186, Oct 1977	1.50
❑187, Nov 1977	1.50
❑188, Dec 1977	1.50
❑189, Jan 1978	1.50
❑190, Feb 1978	1.50
❑191, Mar 1978	1.50
❑192, Apr 1978	1.50
❑193, May 1978	1.50
❑194, Jun 1978	1.50
❑195, Jul 1978	1.50
❑196, Aug 1978	1.50
❑197, Sep 1978	1.50
❑198, Oct 1978	1.50
❑199, Nov 1978	1.50
❑200, Dec 1978	1.50
❑201, Jan 1979	1.50
❑202, Feb 1979	1.50
❑203, Mar 1979	1.50
❑204, Apr 1979	1.50
❑205, Jun 1979	1.50
❑206, Jul 1979	1.50
❑207, Aug 1979	1.50
❑208, Sep 1979	1.50
❑209, Nov 1979	1.50
❑210, Dec 1979	1.50
❑211, Feb 1980	1.50
❑212, Mar 1980	1.50

	N-MINT
❑213, Apr 1980	1.50
❑214, Jun 1980	1.50
❑215, Jul 1980	1.50
❑216, Aug 1980	1.50
❑217, Sep 1980	1.50
❑218, Nov 1980	1.50
❑219, Dec 1980	1.50
❑220, Feb 1981	1.50
❑221, Mar 1981	1.50
❑222, Apr 1981	1.50
❑223, Jun 1981	1.50
❑224, Jul 1981	1.50
❑225, Aug 1981	1.50
❑226, Sep 1981	1.50
❑227, Nov 1981	1.50
❑228, Dec 1981	1.50
❑229, Feb 1982	1.50
❑230, Mar 1982	1.50
❑231, May 1982	1.50
❑232, Jul 1982	1.50
❑233, Sep 1982	1.50
❑234, Nov 1982	1.50
❑235, Jan 1983	1.50
❑236, Apr 1983	1.50
❑237 1983	1.50
❑238 1983	1.50
❑239, Nov 1983	1.50
❑240, Jan 1984	1.50
❑241, Mar 1984	1.50
❑242, May 1984	1.50
❑243, Jul 1984	1.50
❑244, Sep 1984	1.50
❑245, Nov 1984	1.50
❑246, Jan 1985	1.50
❑247, Mar 1985	1.50
❑248, May 1985	1.50
❑249, Jul 1985	1.50
❑250, Sep 1985	1.50
❑251, Nov 1985	1.00
❑252, Jan 1986	1.00
❑253, Mar 1986	1.00
❑254, May 1986	1.00
❑255, Jul 1986	1.00
❑256, Sep 1986	1.00
❑257, Nov 1986	1.00
❑258, Jan 1987	1.00
❑259, Mar 1987	1.00
❑260, May 1987	1.00
❑261, Jul 1987	1.00
❑262, Sep 1987	1.00
❑263, Nov 1987	1.00
❑264, Jan 1988	1.00
❑265, Mar 1988	1.00
❑266, May 1988	1.00
❑267, Jul 1988	1.00
❑268, Sep 1988	1.00
❑269, Nov 1988	1.00
❑270, Jan 1989	1.00
❑271, Mar 1989	1.00
❑272, May 1989	1.00
❑273, Jul 1989	1.00
❑274, Sep 1989	1.00
❑275, Nov 1989	1.00
❑276, Jan 1990	1.00
❑277, Mar 1990	1.00
❑278, May 1990	1.00
❑279, Jul 1990	1.00
❑280, Sep 1990	1.00
❑281, Nov 1990	1.00
❑282, Jan 1991	1.00
❑283, Mar 1991	1.00
❑284, May 1991	1.00
❑285, Jul 1991, Final issue (?)	1.00

LIFE WITH MILLIE
ATLAS

	N-MINT
❑8, Dec 1960	35.00
❑9, Feb 1961	28.00
❑10, Apr 1961	28.00
❑11, Jun 1961	26.00
❑12, Aug 1961	26.00
❑13, Oct 1961	26.00
❑14, Dec 1961	26.00
❑15, Feb 1962	26.00
❑16, Apr 1962	26.00
❑17, Jun 1962	26.00
❑18, Aug 1962	26.00

Life, the Universe and Everything

Adaptation of the third Hitchhiker's novel

©DC

Life with Millie

More stories with Marvel's famous model

©Atlas

Lili

Brian Michael Bendis tale set in New Orleans

©Image

Limited Collectors' Edition

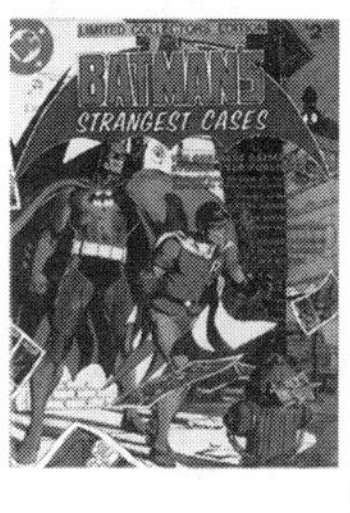

Oddly numbered treasury-sized comics

©DC

Linda Carter, Student Nurse

Clearly not the Wonder Woman actress

©Atlas

N-MINT

❑19, Oct 1962 .... 26.00
❑20, Dec 1962 .... 26.00

LIGHT AND DARKNESS WAR
MARVEL / EPIC

❑1, Oct 1988 .... 1.95
❑2, Nov 1988 .... 1.95
❑3, Jan 1989 .... 1.95
❑4, Feb 1989 .... 1.95
❑5, Apr 1989 .... 1.95
❑6, Sep 1989 .... 1.95

LIGHT BRIGADE
DC

❑1, Apr 2004 .... 5.95
❑2, May 2004 .... 5.95
❑3, Jun 2004 .... 5.95
❑4, Jun 2004 .... 5.95

LIGHT FANTASTIC (TERRY PRATCHETT'S...)
INNOVATION

❑0 .... 2.50
❑1, Jun 1992 .... 2.50
❑2 .... 2.50
❑3 .... 2.50
❑4 .... 2.50

LIGHTNING COMICS PRESENTS
LIGHTNING

❑1, May 1994 .... 3.50

LIGHTNING NUDE COLLECTION
LIGHTNING

❑Book 1, Jan 1997, b&w; reproduces nude covers 5.00

LIGHTS OUT
TOKYOPOP

❑1, Oct 2005 .... 9.95

LILI
IMAGE

❑0, ca. 1999 .... 4.95

LILING-PO
TOKYOPOP

❑1, Feb 2005 .... 9.95
❑2, May 2005 .... 9.95
❑3, Oct 2005 .... 9.95

LI'L KIDS
MARVEL

❑1, Jul 1970 .... 35.00
❑2, Oct 1970 .... 22.00
❑3, Nov 1971 .... 22.00
❑4, Feb 1972 .... 22.00
❑5, Apr 1972 .... 22.00
❑6, Jun 1972 .... 16.00
❑7, Aug 1972 .... 16.00
❑8, Oct 1972 .... 16.00
❑9 1973 .... 16.00
❑10, Feb 1973 .... 16.00
❑11, Apr 1973 .... 16.00
❑12, Jun 1973 .... 16.00

LILLITH: DEMON PRINCESS
ANTARCTIC

❑0, Mar 1998 .... 1.95
❑0/Variant, Mar 1998; Special limited cover (Lilith flying w/green swish) 5.00
❑1, Aug 1996 .... 5.00
❑2, Oct 1996 .... 5.00
❑3, Feb 1997 .... 5.00

N-MINT

LI'L PALS
MARVEL

❑1, Sep 1972 .... 25.00
❑2, Nov 1972 .... 20.00
❑3, Jan 1973 .... 20.00
❑4, Mar 1973 .... 20.00
❑5, May 1973 .... 20.00

LIMITED COLLECTORS' EDITION
DC

❑C-20; Rudolph the Red-Nosed Reindeer 32.00
❑C-21, Sum 1973; Shazam!; reprints Golden Age Marvel Family stories 16.00
❑C-22, Fal 1973; JK, JKu (a); Tarzan 14.00
❑C-23; House of Mystery 16.00
❑C-24; Rudolph the Red-Nosed Reindeer 26.00
❑C-25; NA (a); Batman 28.00
❑C-27; Shazam!; reprints Golden Age Marvel Family stories 16.00
❑C-29; JK (a); Tarzan 10.00
❑C-31, Nov 1974; Superman 15.00
❑C-32, Jan 1975; Ghosts 10.00
❑C-33, Feb 1975; Rudolph the Red-Nosed Reindeer 16.00
❑C-34, Mar 1975; Christmas With the Super-Heroes 12.00
❑C-35, May 1975; Shazam! 10.00
❑C-36, Jul 1975; NR, JK, JKu (a); The Bible 16.00
❑C-37, Sep 1975; Batman 20.00
❑C-38, Nov 1975; Superman 10.00
❑C-39, Nov 1975; CI, NA, DD, CCB (a); Secret Origins of Super Villains 10.00
❑C-40, Nov 1975; Dick Tracy 12.00
❑C-41, Jan 1976; ATh (a); Super Friends 10.00
❑C-42, Mar 1976; Rudolph the Red-Nosed Reindeer 10.00
❑C-43, Mar 1976; Christmas With the Super-Heroes 10.00
❑C-44, Jul 1976; Batman 12.00
❑C-45, Jul 1976; More Secret Origins of Super-Villains 10.00
❑C-46, Sep 1976; Justice League of America 10.00
❑C-47, Sep 1976; Superman Salutes the Bicentennial; reprints Tomahawk stories 10.00
❑C-48, Nov 1976; Superman vs. Flash 12.00
❑C-49, Nov 1976; Legion 10.00
❑C-50; Rudolph the Red-Nosed Reindeer; poster 10.00
❑C-51, Aug 1977; Batman vs. Ra's Al Ghul 12.00
❑C-52; NA (a); Best of DC 10.00
❑C-57; Welcome Back, Kotter 14.00
❑C-59; Series continued in All-New Collectors' Edition; Batman's Strangest Cases 14.00

LINCOLN-16
SKARWOOD

❑1, Aug 1997 .... 2.95
❑2, Oct 1997, b&w 2.95

LINDA CARTER, STUDENT NURSE
ATLAS

❑1, Sep 1961 .... 60.00
❑2, Nov 1961 .... 40.00

N-MINT

❑3, Jan 1962 .... 40.00
❑4, Mar 1962 .... 40.00
❑5, May 1962 .... 40.00
❑6, Jul 1962 .... 30.00
❑7, Sep 1962 .... 30.00
❑8, Nov 1962 .... 30.00
❑9, Jan 1963 .... 30.00

LINDA LARK
DELL

❑1, Oct 1961 .... 15.00
❑2, Jan 1962 .... 10.00
❑3, Apr 1962 .... 10.00
❑4, Jul 1962 .... 10.00
❑5, Sep 1962 .... 10.00
❑6, Dec 1962 .... 10.00
❑7, Mar 1963 .... 10.00
❑8, Aug 1963 .... 10.00

LINE THE DUSTBIN FUNNIES
EAST WILLIS

❑1, Sum 1997 .... 2.95

LIONHEART
AWESOME

❑1/A, Aug 1999, JPH (w); Dynamic Forces variant 3.50
❑1/B, Aug 1999, JPH (w); Women, treasure chest on cover 3.00
❑Ashcan 1, Jul 1999, Wizard World '99 preview edition JPH (w) 3.00

LION KING (DISNEY'S...)
MARVEL

❑1, Jul 1994 .... 2.50

LIONS, TIGERS & BEARS
IMAGE

❑1, Mar 2005 .... 2.95
❑2, Apr 2005 .... 2.95
❑3, May 2005 .... 2.95

LIONS, TIGERS & BEARS (VOL. 2)
IMAGE

❑1, May 2006 ....
❑1/Variant, May 2006 ....

LIPPY THE LION AND HARDY HAR HAR
GOLD KEY

❑1, Mar 1963 .... 60.00

LIPSTICK
RIP OFF

❑1, May 1992, b&w 2.50

LISA COMICS
BONGO

❑1 .... 2.25

LITA FORD: THE QUEEN OF HEAVY METAL
ROCK-IT COMICS

❑1 .... 5.00

LITTLE SCROWLIE
SLAVE LABOR

❑1 .... 2.95
❑2 .... 2.95
❑3 .... 2.95
❑4 .... 2.95
❑5 .... 2.95
❑6 .... 2.95

	N-MINT
❑7	2.95
❑8	2.95
❑9	2.95
❑10, Jul 2005	2.95
❑11, Aug 2005	2.95
❑12, Dec 2005	2.95

LITTLE ARCHIE

ARCHIE

	N-MINT
❑1, ca. 1956	525.00
❑2, Win 1956	210.00
❑3, ca. 1957	150.00
❑4, ca. 1957	115.00
❑5, ca. 1957	115.00
❑6, Spr 1958, Giant	80.00
❑7, Sum 1958, Giant	80.00
❑8, Fal 1958, Giant	80.00
❑9, Win 1958, Giant	80.00
❑10, Spr 1959, Giant	80.00
❑11, Sum 1959, Giant	52.00
❑12, Fal 1959, Giant	52.00
❑13, Win 1959, Giant	52.00
❑14, Spr 1960, Giant	52.00
❑15, Sum 1960, Giant	52.00
❑16, Fal 1960, Giant	52.00
❑17, Win 1960, Giant	52.00
❑18, Spr 1961, 1: Abercrombie and Stitch. Giant	52.00
❑19, Sum 1961, Giant	52.00
❑20, Fal 1961, Giant	52.00
❑21, Win 1961, Giant	32.00
❑22, Spr 1962, Giant	32.00
❑23, Sum 1962, Giant	32.00
❑24, Fal 1962, 1: Mad Doctor Doom. Giant	32.00
❑25, Win 1962, Giant	32.00
❑26, Spr 1963, Giant	32.00
❑27, Sum 1963, Giant	32.00
❑28, Fal 1963, Giant	32.00
❑29, Win 1963, Giant	32.00
❑30, Spr 1964, Giant	32.00
❑31, Sum 1964, Giant	32.00
❑32, Fal 1964, A: Mad Doctor Doom. Giant	32.00
❑33, Win 1964, Giant	32.00
❑34, Spr 1965, Giant	32.00
❑35, Sum 1965, Giant	32.00
❑36, Fal 1965, Giant	32.00
❑37, Win 1965, Giant	32.00
❑38, Spr 1966, Giant	32.00
❑39, Sum 1966, Giant	32.00
❑40, Fal 1966, Giant	32.00
❑41, Win 1966, Giant	22.00
❑42, Spr 1967, Giant	22.00
❑43, Sum 1967, Giant	22.00
❑44, Fal 1967, Giant	22.00
❑45, Win 1967, Giant	22.00
❑46, Spr 1968, Giant	22.00
❑47, Sum 1968, Giant	22.00
❑48, Jul 1968, Giant	22.00
❑49, Sep 1968, Giant	22.00
❑50, Nov 1968, Giant	22.00
❑51, Jan 1969, Giant	22.00
❑52, Mar 1969, Giant	22.00
❑53, May 1969, Giant	22.00
❑54, Jul 1969, Giant	22.00
❑55, Sep 1969, Giant	22.00
❑56, Nov 1969, Giant	22.00
❑57, Jan 1970, Giant	22.00
❑58, Mar 1970, Giant	22.00
❑59, May 1970, Giant	22.00
❑60, Jul 1970, Giant	22.00
❑61, Sep 1970, Giant	16.00
❑62, Nov 1970, Giant	16.00
❑63, Jan 1971, Giant	16.00
❑64, Mar 1971, Giant	16.00
❑65, May 1971, Giant	16.00
❑66, Jul 1971, Giant	16.00
❑67, Sep 1971, Giant	16.00
❑68, Nov 1971, Giant	16.00
❑69, Jan 1972, Giant	16.00
❑70, Mar 1972, Giant	16.00
❑71, May 1972, Giant	16.00
❑72, Jul 1972, Giant	16.00
❑73, Sep 1972, Giant	16.00
❑74, Oct 1972, Giant	16.00
❑75, Dec 1972, Giant	16.00
❑76, Feb 1973, Giant	16.00
❑77, Apr 1973, Giant	16.00
❑78, May 1973, Giant	16.00
❑79, Jul 1973, Giant	16.00
❑80, Aug 1973, Giant	16.00
❑81, Sep 1973, Giant	11.00
❑82, Oct 1973, Giant	11.00
❑83, Dec 1973, Giant	11.00
❑84, Feb 1974, Giant	11.00
❑85, Apr 1974	11.00
❑86, May 1974	11.00
❑87, Jul 1974	11.00
❑88, Aug 1974	11.00
❑89, Sep 1974	11.00
❑90, Oct 1974	11.00
❑91, Dec 1974	11.00
❑92, Feb 1975	11.00
❑93, Mar 1975	11.00
❑94, Apr 1975	11.00
❑95, May 1975	11.00
❑96, Jul 1975	11.00
❑97, Aug 1975	11.00
❑98, Sep 1975	11.00
❑99, Oct 1975	11.00
❑100, Nov 1975	11.00
❑101, Dec 1975	6.00
❑102, Jan 1976	6.00
❑103, Feb 1976	6.00
❑104, Mar 1976	6.00
❑105, Apr 1976	6.00
❑106, May 1976	6.00
❑107, Jun 1976	6.00
❑108, Jul 1976	6.00
❑109, Aug 1976	6.00
❑110, Sep 1976	6.00
❑111, Oct 1976	6.00
❑112, Nov 1976	6.00
❑113, Dec 1976	6.00
❑114, Jan 1977	6.00
❑115, Feb 1977	6.00
❑116, Mar 1977	6.00
❑117, Apr 1977	6.00
❑118, May 1977	6.00
❑119, Jun 1977	6.00
❑120, Jul 1977	6.00
❑121, Aug 1977	4.00
❑122, Sep 1977	4.00
❑123, Oct 1977	4.00
❑124, Nov 1977	4.00
❑125, Dec 1977	4.00
❑126, Jan 1978	4.00
❑127, Feb 1978	4.00
❑128, Mar 1978	4.00
❑129, Apr 1978	4.00
❑130, May 1978	4.00
❑131, Jun 1978	4.00
❑132, Jul 1978	4.00
❑133, Aug 1978	4.00
❑134, Sep 1978	4.00
❑135, Oct 1978	4.00
❑136, Nov 1978	4.00
❑137, Dec 1978	4.00
❑138, Jan 1979	4.00
❑139, Feb 1979	4.00
❑140, Mar 1979	4.00
❑141, Apr 1979	3.00
❑142, May 1979	3.00
❑143, Jun 1979	3.00
❑144, Jul 1979	3.00
❑145, Aug 1979	3.00
❑146, Sep 1979	3.00
❑147, Oct 1979	3.00
❑148, Nov 1979	3.00
❑149, Dec 1979	3.00
❑150, Jan 1980	3.00
❑151, Feb 1980	3.00
❑152, Mar 1980	3.00
❑153, Apr 1980	3.00
❑154, May 1980	3.00
❑155, Jun 1980	3.00
❑156, Jul 1980	3.00
❑157, Aug 1980	3.00
❑158, Sep 1980	3.00
❑159, Oct 1980	3.00
❑160, Nov 1980	3.00
❑161, Dec 1980	3.00
❑162, Jan 1981	3.00
❑163, Feb 1981	3.00
❑164, Mar 1981	3.00
❑165, Apr 1981	3.00
❑166, May 1981	3.00
❑167, Jun 1981	3.00
❑168, Jul 1981	3.00
❑169, Aug 1981	3.00
❑170, Sep 1981	3.00
❑171, Oct 1981	3.00
❑172, Nov 1981	3.00
❑173 1982	3.00
❑174 1982	3.00
❑175 1982	3.00
❑176 1982	3.00
❑177 1982	3.00
❑178 1982	3.00
❑179 1982	3.00
❑180, ca. 1983	3.00

LITTLE ARCHIE DIGEST MAGAZINE

ARCHIE

	N-MINT
❑1 1991	3.00
❑2 1991	2.00
❑3 1991	2.00
❑4 1991	2.00
❑5 1992	2.00
❑6 1992	2.00
❑7 1992	2.00
❑8 1992	2.00
❑9 1992	2.00
❑10	2.00
❑11	1.75
❑12	1.75
❑13	1.75
❑14, Aug 1995	1.75
❑15, Oct 1995	1.75
❑16, Jun 1996	1.75
❑17, Sep 1996	1.79
❑18, Mar 1997	1.79
❑19, Jun 1997	1.79
❑20, Sep 1997	1.79
❑21, Mar 1998	1.95
❑22	1.95
❑23	1.95
❑24	1.95
❑25	1.95

LITTLE ARCHIE MYSTERY

ARCHIE

	N-MINT
❑1, Aug 1963	60.00
❑2, Oct 1963	42.00

LITTLE AUDREY (2ND SERIES)

HARVEY

	N-MINT
❑1, Aug 1992	1.50
❑2 1992	1.25
❑3 1992	1.25
❑4 1992	1.25
❑5 1993	1.25
❑6 1993	1.25
❑7 1993	1.25
❑8 1993	1.25
❑9 1993	1.25

LITTLE AUDREY AND MELVIN

HARVEY

	N-MINT
❑1, May 1962	45.00
❑2, Jul 1962	25.00
❑3, Sep 1962	18.00
❑4, Nov 1962	18.00
❑5, Jan 1963	18.00
❑6, Mar 1963	14.00
❑7, May 1963	14.00
❑8, Jul 1963	14.00
❑9, Sep 1963	14.00
❑10 1964	14.00
❑11 1964	12.00
❑12 1964	12.00
❑13 1964	12.00
❑14, Sep 1964	12.00
❑15, Nov 1964	12.00
❑16, Jan 1965	12.00
❑17, Mar 1965	12.00
❑18, May 1965	12.00
❑19, Jul 1965	12.00
❑20, Sep 1965	12.00
❑21, Nov 1965	9.00
❑22, Jan 1966	9.00

Little Audrey TV Funtime

More antics from Harvey's irrepressible youth

©Harvey

Little Dot (Vol. 2)

Obsessive-compulsive child acts out

©Harvey

Little Dot's Uncles and Aunts

Child has amazingly large family

©Harvey

Little Lotta (Vol. 1)

Nothing politically correct about this series

©Harvey

Little Lotta Foodland

May be overkill to say this title was giant-sized

©Harvey

	N-MINT
❑23, Mar 1966	9.00
❑24, May 1966	9.00
❑25, Jul 1966	9.00
❑26, Sep 1966	9.00
❑27, Oct 1966	9.00
❑28, Jan 1967	9.00
❑29, Mar 1967	9.00
❑30, May 1967	9.00
❑31, Jul 1967	6.00
❑32, Sep 1967	6.00
❑33, Nov 1967	6.00
❑34, Jan 1968	6.00
❑35, Sep 1968	6.00
❑36, Nov 1968	6.00
❑37, Jan 1969	6.00
❑38, Mar 1969	6.00
❑39, Apr 1969	6.00
❑40, Jun 1969	6.00
❑41, Aug 1969	4.00
❑42, Oct 1969	4.00
❑43, Dec 1969	4.00
❑44, Feb 1970	4.00
❑45, Apr 1970	4.00
❑46, Aug 1970	4.00
❑47, Oct 1970	4.00
❑48, Nov 1970	4.00
❑49 1971	4.00
❑50, Aug 1971	4.00
❑51, Sep 1971	4.00
❑52, Nov 1971	4.00
❑53 1972	4.00
❑54, Sep 1972	4.00
❑55, Nov 1972	4.00
❑56, Feb 1973	4.00
❑57, Apr 1973	4.00
❑58, Jun 1973	4.00
❑59, Aug 1973	4.00
❑60, Oct 1973	4.00
❑61, Dec 1973	4.00

LITTLE AUDREY TV FUNTIME
HARVEY

	N-MINT
❑1, Sep 1962	45.00
❑2, Dec 1962	28.00
❑3, Mar 1963	24.00
❑4, Jun 1963	20.00
❑5, Sep 1963	20.00
❑6, Dec 1963	16.00
❑7, Mar 1964	16.00
❑8, Jun 1964	16.00
❑9, Sep 1964	16.00
❑10, Dec 1964	16.00
❑11, Mar 1965	12.00
❑12, Jun 1965	12.00
❑13, Sep 1965	12.00
❑14, Dec 1965	12.00
❑15, Mar 1966	12.00
❑16 1966	12.00
❑17, Nov 1966	12.00
❑18, Mar 1967	12.00
❑19 1967	12.00
❑20, Oct 1968	12.00
❑21, Dec 1968	9.00
❑22, May 1969	9.00
❑23, Jul 1969	9.00
❑24, Sep 1969	9.00
❑25, Nov 1969	9.00
❑26 1970	9.00
❑27, May 1970	9.00
❑28, Aug 1970	9.00
❑29 1970	9.00
❑30, Dec 1970	9.00
❑31 1971	9.00
❑32 1971	9.00
❑33 1971	9.00

LITTLE DOT (VOL. 1)
HARVEY

	N-MINT
❑20, Nov 1956	100.00
❑21, Jan 1957	60.00
❑22, Mar 1957	60.00
❑23, May 1957	60.00
❑24, Jul 1957	60.00
❑25, Sep 1957	60.00
❑26, Nov 1957	60.00
❑27, Dec 1957	60.00
❑28, Jan 1958	60.00
❑29, Feb 1958	60.00
❑30, Mar 1958	60.00
❑31, Apr 1958	45.00
❑32, May 1958	45.00
❑33, Jun 1958	45.00
❑34, Jul 1958	45.00
❑35, Aug 1958	45.00
❑36, Sep 1958	45.00
❑37, Oct 1958	45.00
❑38, Nov 1958	45.00
❑39, Dec 1958	45.00
❑40, Jan 1959	45.00
❑41, Feb 1959	25.00
❑42, Mar 1959	25.00
❑43, Apr 1959	25.00
❑44, May 1959	25.00
❑45, Jun 1959	25.00
❑46, Jul 1959	25.00
❑47, Aug 1959	25.00
❑48, Sep 1959	25.00
❑49, Oct 1959	25.00
❑50, Nov 1959	25.00
❑51, Dec 1959	20.00
❑52, Jan 1960	20.00
❑53, Feb 1960	20.00
❑54, Mar 1960	20.00
❑55, Apr 1960	20.00
❑56, May 1960	20.00
❑57, Jun 1960	20.00
❑58, Jul 1960	20.00
❑59, Aug 1960	20.00
❑60, Sep 1960	20.00
❑61, Oct 1960	15.00
❑62, Nov 1960	15.00
❑63, Dec 1960	15.00
❑64, Jan 1961	15.00
❑65, Feb 1961	15.00
❑66, Mar 1961	15.00
❑67, Apr 1961	15.00
❑68, May 1961	15.00
❑69, Jun 1961	15.00
❑70, Jul 1961	15.00
❑71, Aug 1961	15.00
❑72, Sep 1961	15.00
❑73, Oct 1961	15.00
❑74, Nov 1961	15.00
❑75, Dec 1961	15.00
❑76, Jan 1962	15.00
❑77, Feb 1962	15.00
❑78, Mar 1962	15.00
❑79, Apr 1962	15.00
❑80, May 1962	15.00
❑81, Jun 1962	10.00
❑82, Aug 1962	10.00
❑83, Oct 1962	10.00
❑84, Dec 1962	10.00
❑85, Feb 1963	10.00
❑86, Apr 1963	10.00
❑87, Jun 1963	10.00
❑88, Aug 1963	10.00
❑89, Oct 1963	10.00
❑90, Dec 1963	10.00
❑91, Feb 1964	10.00
❑92, Apr 1964	10.00
❑93, Jun 1964	10.00
❑94, Aug 1964	10.00
❑95, Oct 1964	10.00
❑96, Dec 1964	10.00
❑97, Feb 1965	10.00
❑98, Apr 1965	10.00
❑99, Jun 1965	10.00
❑100, Aug 1965	10.00
❑101, Oct 1965	7.00
❑102, Dec 1965	7.00
❑103, Feb 1966	7.00
❑104, Apr 1966	7.00
❑105, Jun 1966	7.00
❑106, Aug 1966	7.00
❑107, Oct 1966	7.00
❑108, Dec 1966	7.00
❑109, Feb 1967	7.00
❑110, Apr 1967	7.00
❑111, Jun 1967	7.00
❑112, Aug 1967	7.00
❑113, Oct 1967	7.00
❑114, Dec 1967	7.00
❑115, Feb 1968	7.00
❑116, Apr 1968	7.00
❑117, Jun 1968	7.00
❑118, Aug 1968	7.00
❑119, Oct 1968	7.00
❑120, Dec 1968	7.00
❑121, Feb 1969	7.00
❑122 1969	7.00
❑123, May 1969	7.00
❑124, Jul 1969	7.00
❑125 1969	7.00
❑126, Oct 1969	7.00
❑127, Dec 1969	7.00
❑128, Jan 1970	7.00
❑129, Mar 1970	7.00
❑130, May 1970	7.00
❑131, Jul 1970	7.00
❑132, Sep 1970	7.00
❑133, Oct 1970	7.00
❑134, Nov 1970	7.00
❑135, Jan 1971	7.00

Other grades: Multiply price above by 5/6 for VF/NM • 2/3 for VERY FINE • 1/3 for FINE • 1/5 for VERY GOOD • 1/8 for GOOD

Issue	N-MINT
❑136, Mar 1971	7.00
❑137, May 1971	7.00
❑138, Jul 1971	7.00
❑139, Sep 1971	7.00
❑140, Oct 1971	7.00
❑141, Nov 1971	7.00
❑142, Mar 1972, Giant-size	10.00
❑143, May 1972, Giant-size	10.00
❑144, Jul 1972, Giant-size	10.00
❑145, Sep 1972, Giant-size	10.00
❑146, Nov 1972	5.00
❑147, Jan 1973	5.00
❑148, Mar 1973	5.00
❑149, May 1973	5.00
❑150, Jul 1973	5.00
❑151, Sep 1973	5.00
❑152	5.00
❑153, Jun 1974	5.00
❑154, Aug 1974	5.00
❑155, Oct 1974	5.00
❑156, Dec 1974	5.00
❑157, Feb 1975	5.00
❑158, Apr 1975	5.00
❑159, Jun 1975	5.00
❑160, Aug 1975	5.00
❑161, Oct 1975	5.00
❑162, Dec 1975	5.00
❑163, Feb 1976	5.00
❑164, Apr 1976	5.00

LITTLE DOT (VOL. 2)
HARVEY

Issue	N-MINT
❑1, Sep 1992	1.50
❑2	1.50
❑3, Jun 1993	1.50
❑4 1993	1.50
❑5, Jan 1994	1.50
❑6, Apr 1994	1.50
❑7, Jun 1994	1.50

LITTLE DOT (VOL. 2)
HARVEY

Issue	N-MINT
❑1, Sep 1992	1.50
❑2	1.50
❑3, Jun 1993	1.50
❑4 1993	1.50
❑5, Jan 1994	1.50
❑6, Apr 1994	1.50
❑7, Jun 1994	1.50

LITTLE DOT DOTLAND
HARVEY

Issue	N-MINT
❑1, Jul 1962	75.00
❑2, Sep 1962	40.00
❑3, Nov 1962	40.00
❑4, Jan 1963	35.00
❑5, Mar 1963	35.00
❑6, May 1963	24.00
❑7, Jul 1963	24.00
❑8, Sep 1963	24.00
❑9, Nov 1963	24.00
❑10, Jan 1964	24.00
❑11, Mar 1964	20.00
❑12, May 1964	20.00
❑13, Jul 1964	20.00
❑14, Sep 1964	20.00
❑15, Nov 1964	20.00
❑16, Jan 1965	20.00
❑17, Mar 1965	20.00
❑18, May 1965	20.00
❑19, Jul 1965	20.00
❑20, Sep 1965	20.00
❑21, Nov 1965	16.00
❑22, Jan 1966	16.00
❑23, Mar 1966	16.00
❑24, May 1966	16.00
❑25, Jul 1966	16.00
❑26, Sep 1966	16.00
❑27, Oct 1966	16.00
❑28, Jan 1967	16.00
❑29, Mar 1967	16.00
❑30, May 1967	12.00
❑31, Jul 1967	12.00
❑32, Sep 1967	12.00
❑33, Nov 1967	12.00
❑34, Jan 1968	12.00
❑35, Sep 1968	12.00
❑36, Nov 1968	12.00
❑37, Jan 1969	12.00
❑38, Mar 1969	12.00
❑39, Apr 1969	12.00
❑40, Jun 1969	10.00
❑41, Aug 1969	10.00
❑42, Oct 1969	10.00
❑43, Dec 1969	10.00
❑44, Feb 1970	10.00
❑45, Apr 1970	10.00
❑46, Aug 1970	10.00
❑47, Oct 1970	10.00
❑48, Jan 1971	10.00
❑49, Apr 1971	10.00
❑50, Aug 1971	10.00
❑51, ca. 1971	10.00
❑52, ca. 1972	10.00
❑53, Jun 1972	10.00
❑54, Sep 1972	10.00
❑55, Nov 1972	8.00
❑56, Feb 1973	8.00
❑57, Apr 1973	8.00
❑58, Jun 1973	8.00
❑59, Aug 1973	8.00
❑60, Nov 1973	8.00
❑61, Dec 1973, becomes Dot Dotland	8.00
❑62, Sep 1974, was Little Dot Dotland	10.00
❑63, Nov 1974	10.00

LITTLE DOT IN 3-D
BLACKTHORNE

Issue	N-MINT
❑1	2.50

LITTLE DOT'S UNCLES AND AUNTS
HARVEY

Issue	N-MINT
❑1, ca. 1961	70.00
❑2, Aug 1962, A: Richie Rich	42.00
❑3, Nov 1962	42.00
❑4, Feb 1963	36.00
❑5, May 1963	36.00
❑6, Aug 1963	28.00
❑7, Nov 1963	28.00
❑8, Feb 1964	28.00
❑9, May 1964	28.00
❑10, Aug 1964	28.00
❑11, Nov 1964	22.00
❑12, Feb 1965	22.00
❑13, May 1965	22.00
❑14, Aug 1965	22.00
❑15	22.00
❑16	22.00
❑17 1966	22.00
❑18, Sep 1966	22.00
❑19, Nov 1966	22.00
❑20, Aug 1967	22.00
❑21, Nov 1967	22.00
❑22, Feb 1968	22.00
❑23, Jul 1968	22.00
❑24, Oct 1968	22.00
❑25, Dec 1968	22.00
❑26 1969	22.00
❑27, Jun 1969	22.00
❑28, Aug 1969	22.00
❑29, Oct 1969	22.00
❑30, Nov 1969	22.00
❑31, Mar 1970	22.00
❑32, Jun 1970	22.00
❑33, Aug 1970	22.00
❑34 1970	22.00
❑35, Nov 1970	22.00
❑36, Mar 1971	14.00
❑37 1971	14.00
❑38, Aug 1971	14.00
❑39, Oct 1971	14.00
❑40	14.00
❑41 1972	14.00
❑42, Jun 1972	14.00
❑43 1972	14.00
❑44, Dec 1972	14.00
❑45, Feb 1973	14.00
❑46, Apr 1973	14.00
❑47, Jun 1973	14.00
❑48, Aug 1973	14.00
❑49, Oct 1973	14.00
❑50, Dec 1973	14.00
❑51, Feb 1974	14.00
❑52, Apr 1974	14.00

LITTLE EGO
NBM

Issue	N-MINT
❑1	10.95

LITTLE ENDLESS STORYBOOK
DC / VERTIGO

Issue	N-MINT
❑1, Aug 2001	5.95

LITTLE GLOOMY
SLAVE LABOR

Issue	N-MINT
❑1, Oct 1999	2.95

LITTLE GLOOMY'S SUPER SCARY MONSTER SHOW
SLAVE LABOR

Issue	N-MINT
❑1 2005	2.95
❑2, Oct 2005	2.95

LITTLE GRETA GARBAGE
RIP OFF

Issue	N-MINT
❑1, Jul 1990, b&w	2.50
❑2, Jun 1991, b&w	2.50

LITTLE GREY MAN
IMAGE

Issue	N-MINT
❑1; graphic novel	6.95

LITTLE ITALY
FANTAGRAPHICS

Issue	N-MINT
❑1, b&w	3.95

LITTLE JIM-BOB BIG FOOT
JUMP BACK

Issue	N-MINT
❑1, b&w	2.95
❑2, Jan 1998, b&w	2.95

LITTLE LOTTA (VOL. 1)
HARVEY

Issue	N-MINT
❑1, Nov 1955	225.00
❑2, Jan 1956	90.00
❑3, Mar 1956	75.00
❑4, May 1956	55.00
❑5, Jul 1956	55.00
❑6, Sep 1956	40.00
❑7, Nov 1956	40.00
❑8, Jan 1957	40.00
❑9, Mar 1957	40.00
❑10, May 1957	40.00
❑11, Jul 1957	28.00
❑12, Sep 1957	28.00
❑13, Nov 1957	28.00
❑14, Jan 1958	28.00
❑15, Mar 1958	28.00
❑16, May 1958	28.00
❑17, Jul 1958	28.00
❑18, Sep 1958	28.00
❑19, Nov 1958	28.00
❑20, Feb 1959	28.00
❑21, Apr 1959	22.00
❑22, Jun 1959	22.00
❑23, Aug 1959	22.00
❑24, Oct 1959	22.00
❑25, Dec 1959	22.00
❑26, ca. 1960	22.00
❑27, ca. 1960	22.00
❑28, ca. 1960	22.00
❑29, ca. 1960	22.00
❑30, ca. 1960	22.00
❑31, ca. 1960	18.00
❑32, ca. 1961	18.00
❑33, ca. 1961	18.00
❑34, ca. 1961	18.00
❑35, ca. 1961	18.00
❑36, ca. 1961	18.00
❑37, Sep 1961	18.00
❑38, Nov 1961	18.00
❑39, Jan 1962	18.00
❑40, Mar 1962	18.00
❑41, May 1962	15.00
❑42, Jul 1962	15.00
❑43, Sep 1962	15.00
❑44, Nov 1962	15.00
❑45, Jan 1963	15.00
❑46, Mar 1963	15.00
❑47, May 1963	15.00
❑48, Jul 1963	15.00
❑49, Sep 1963	15.00
❑50, Nov 1963	15.00
❑51, Jan 1964	12.00
❑52, Mar 1964	12.00
❑53, May 1964	12.00
❑54, Jul 1964	12.00
❑55, Sep 1964	12.00
❑56, Nov 1964	12.00
❑57, Jan 1965	12.00
❑58, Mar 1965	12.00

Other grades: Multiply price above by 5/6 for VF/NM • 2/3 for VERY FINE • 1/3 for FINE • 1/5 for VERY GOOD • 1/8 for GOOD

Little Sad Sack

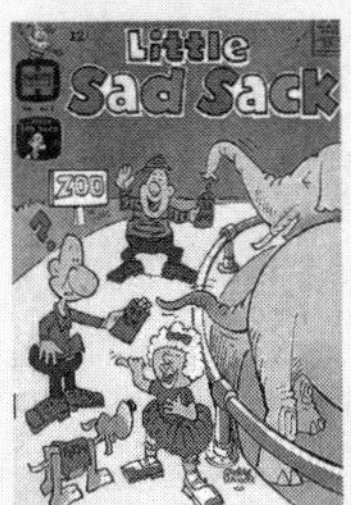

Adventures of a child before he's drafted
©Harvey

Little Stooges

The son of a stooge is a stooge as well
©Gold Key

Lobo

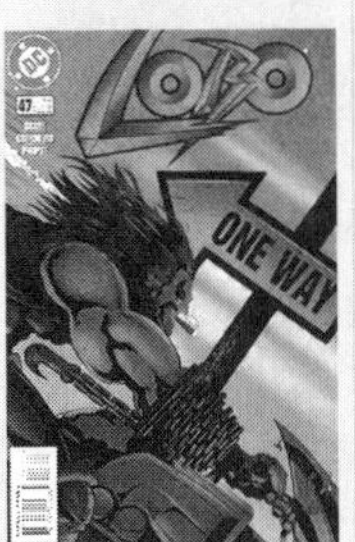

Hairy grouch gets title to himself
©DC

Logan's Run (Marvel)

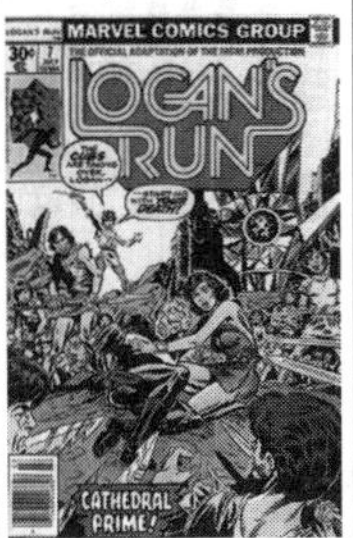

Film adaptation had Thanos back-up story
©Marvel

Lois Lane

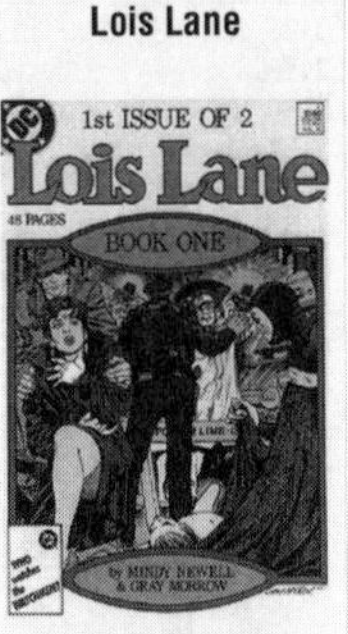

Main title was called "Superman's Girlfriend..."
©DC

	N-MINT
❑59, May 1965	12.00
❑60, Jul 1965	12.00
❑61, Sep 1965	12.00
❑62, Nov 1965	12.00
❑63, Jan 1966	12.00
❑64, Mar 1966	12.00
❑65, May 1966	12.00
❑66, Jul 1966	12.00
❑67, Sep 1966	12.00
❑68, Nov 1966	12.00
❑69, Jan 1967	12.00
❑70, Mar 1967	12.00
❑71, May 1967	8.00
❑72, Jul 1967	8.00
❑73, Sep 1967	8.00
❑74, Nov 1967	8.00
❑75, Jan 1968	8.00
❑76, Mar 1968	8.00
❑77, May 1968	8.00
❑78, Jul 1968	8.00
❑79, Sep 1968	8.00
❑80, Nov 1968	8.00
❑81, Jan 1969	8.00
❑82, Mar 1969	8.00
❑83, May 1969	8.00
❑84, Jul 1969	8.00
❑85 1969	8.00
❑86, Oct 1969	8.00
❑87, Dec 1969	8.00
❑88, Jan 1970	8.00
❑89, Apr 1970	8.00
❑90, Jul 1970	8.00
❑91 1970	5.00
❑92, Oct 1970	5.00
❑93, Nov 1970	5.00
❑94, Jan 1971	5.00
❑95, Mar 1971	5.00
❑96, May 1971	5.00
❑97, Jul 1971	5.00
❑98, Sep 1971	5.00
❑99, Nov 1971	6.00
❑100, Mar 1972	6.00
❑101, May 1972	6.00
❑102, Jul 1972	6.00
❑103, Sep 1972	3.00
❑104, Nov 1972	3.00
❑105, Jan 1973	3.00
❑106, Mar 1973	3.00
❑107, May 1973	3.00
❑108, Jul 1973	3.00
❑109, Sep 1973	3.00
❑110, Nov 1973	3.00
❑111, Sep 1974	3.00
❑112, Nov 1974	3.00
❑113, Jan 1975	3.00
❑114, Mar 1975	3.00
❑115, May 1975	3.00
❑116, Jul 1975	3.00
❑117, Sep 1975	3.00
❑118, Nov 1975	3.00
❑119, Jan 1976	3.00
❑120, Mar 1976	3.00

LITTLE LOTTA (VOL. 2)
Harvey

	N-MINT
❑1, Oct 1992	1.50
❑2, Jan 1993	1.50
❑3, Apr 1993	1.50
❑4, Jul 1993	1.50

LITTLE LOTTA FOODLAND
Harvey

	N-MINT
❑1, Sep 1963, Giant	45.00
❑2, Dec 1963, Giant	35.00
❑3, Mar 1964, Giant	35.00
❑4 1964, Giant	30.00
❑5 1964, Giant	30.00
❑6 1964, Giant	24.00
❑7 1965, Giant	24.00
❑8 1965, Giant	24.00
❑9 1965, Giant	24.00
❑10, Jan 1966, Giant	24.00
❑11, Apr 1966, Giant	16.00
❑12, Jul 1966, Giant	16.00
❑13, Oct 1966, Giant	16.00
❑14 1967, Giant	16.00
❑15, Oct 1968, Giant	16.00
❑16 1969, Giant	12.00
❑17 1969, Giant	12.00
❑18, Dec 1969, Giant	12.00
❑19, Sep 1970, Giant	12.00
❑20 1970, Giant	12.00
❑21, Feb 1971, Giant	8.00
❑22, May 1971, Giant	8.00
❑23, Aug 1971, Giant	8.00
❑24, Oct 1971, Giant	8.00
❑25, Dec 1971, Giant	8.00
❑26, Feb 1972, Giant	8.00
❑27, May 1972, Giant	8.00
❑28, Aug 1972, Giant	8.00
❑29, Oct 1972, Giant	8.00

LITTLE LULU (MARGE'S...)
Dell / Gold Key/Whitman

	N-MINT
❑100, Oct 1956	50.00
❑101, Nov 1956	30.00
❑102, Dec 1956	30.00
❑103, Jan 1957	30.00
❑104, Feb 1957	30.00
❑105, Mar 1957	30.00
❑106, Apr 1957	30.00
❑107, May 1957	30.00
❑108, Jun 1957	30.00
❑109, Jul 1957	30.00
❑110, Aug 1957	30.00
❑111, Sep 1957	30.00
❑112, Oct 1957	30.00
❑113, Nov 1957	30.00
❑114, Dec 1957	30.00
❑115, Jan 1958	30.00
❑116, Feb 1958	30.00
❑117, Mar 1958	30.00
❑118, Apr 1958	30.00
❑119, May 1958	30.00
❑120, Jun 1958	30.00
❑121, Jul 1958	28.00
❑122, Aug 1958	28.00
❑123, Sep 1958	28.00
❑124, Oct 1958	28.00
❑125, Nov 1958	28.00
❑126, Dec 1958	28.00
❑127, Jan 1959	28.00
❑128, Feb 1959	28.00
❑129, Mar 1959	28.00
❑130, Apr 1959	28.00
❑131, May 1959	28.00
❑132, Jun 1959	28.00
❑133, Jul 1959	28.00
❑134, Aug 1959	28.00
❑135, Sep 1959	28.00
❑136, Oct 1959	28.00
❑137, Nov 1959	28.00
❑138, Dec 1959	28.00
❑139, Jan 1960	28.00
❑140, Feb 1960	28.00
❑141, Mar 1960	25.00
❑142, Apr 1960	25.00
❑143, May 1960	25.00
❑144, Jun 1960	25.00
❑145, Jul 1960	25.00
❑146, Aug 1960	25.00
❑147, Sep 1960	25.00
❑148, Oct 1960	25.00
❑149, Nov 1960	25.00
❑150, Dec 1960	25.00
❑151, Jan 1961	25.00
❑152, Feb 1961	25.00
❑153, May 1961	25.00
❑154, Apr 1961	25.00
❑155, ca. 1961	25.00
❑156, ca. 1961	25.00
❑157, ca. 1961	25.00
❑158, ca. 1961	25.00
❑159, ca. 1961	25.00
❑160, ca. 1961	25.00
❑161, ca. 1962	20.00
❑162, ca. 1962	20.00
❑163, May 1962	20.00
❑164, Jul 1962	20.00
❑165, Oct 1962, Giant-size	70.00
❑166, Jan 1963, Giant-size	70.00
❑167, ca. 1963	20.00
❑168, ca. 1963	20.00
❑169, ca. 1963	20.00
❑170, Dec 1963	20.00
❑171, Mar 1964	20.00
❑172, Jun 1964	20.00
❑173, Sep 1964	20.00
❑174, Dec 1964	20.00
❑175, Mar 1965	20.00
❑176, Jun 1965	20.00
❑177, Sep 1965	20.00
❑178, Dec 1965	20.00
❑179, Mar 1966	20.00
❑180, Jun 1966	20.00
❑181, Sep 1966	15.00
❑182, Dec 1966	15.00
❑183, Mar 1967	15.00
❑184, Jun 1967	15.00
❑185, Sep 1967	15.00
❑186, Dec 1967	15.00
❑187, Mar 1968	15.00

Other grades: Multiply price above by 5/6 for VF/NM • 2/3 for VERY FINE • 1/3 for FINE • 1/5 for VERY GOOD • 1/8 for GOOD

N-MINT

❑188, Jun 1968 ... 15.00
❑189, Sep 1968 ... 15.00
❑190, Dec 1968 ... 15.00
❑191, Mar 1969 ... 15.00
❑192, Jun 1969 ... 15.00
❑193, Sep 1969 ... 15.00
❑194, Dec 1969 ... 15.00
❑195, Mar 1970 ... 15.00
❑196, Jun 1970 ... 15.00
❑197, Sep 1970 ... 15.00
❑198, Dec 1970 ... 15.00
❑199, Mar 1971 ... 15.00
❑200, Jun 1971 ... 15.00
❑201, Sep 1971 ... 9.00
❑202, Dec 1971 ... 9.00
❑203, Mar 1972 ... 9.00
❑204, May 1972 ... 9.00
❑205, Jul 1972 ... 9.00
❑206, Aug 1972 ... 9.00
❑207, Sep 1972 ... 9.00
❑208, Nov 1972 ... 9.00
❑209, Dec 1972 ... 9.00
❑210, Jan 1973 ... 9.00
❑211, Mar 1973 ... 9.00
❑212, May 1973 ... 9.00
❑213, Jul 1973 ... 9.00
❑214, Sep 1973 ... 9.00
❑215, Nov 1973 ... 9.00
❑216, Jan 1974 ... 9.00
❑217, Mar 1974 ... 9.00
❑218, May 1974 ... 9.00
❑219, Jul 1974 ... 9.00
❑220, Aug 1974 ... 9.00
❑221, Sep 1974 ... 6.00
❑222, Nov 1974 ... 6.00
❑223, Jan 1975 ... 6.00
❑224, Mar 1975 ... 6.00
❑225, May 1975 ... 6.00
❑226, Jul 1975 ... 6.00
❑227, Aug 1975 ... 6.00
❑228, Sep 1975 ... 6.00
❑229, Nov 1975 ... 6.00
❑230, Jan 1976 ... 6.00
❑231, Mar 1976 ... 6.00
❑232, May 1976 ... 6.00
❑233, ca. 1976 ... 6.00
❑234, ca. 1976 ... 6.00
❑235, ca. 1976 ... 6.00
❑236, Nov 1976 ... 6.00
❑237, Jan 1977 ... 6.00
❑238, Mar 1977 ... 6.00
❑239, May 1977 ... 6.00
❑240, Jul 1977 ... 6.00
❑241, Sep 1977 ... 4.00
❑242, Nov 1977 ... 4.00
❑243, ca. 1977 ... 4.00
❑244, ca. 1978 ... 4.00
❑245, ca. 1978 ... 4.00
❑246, ca. 1978 ... 4.00
❑247, ca. 1978 ... 4.00
❑248, Sep 1978 ... 4.00
❑249, Nov 1978 ... 4.00
❑250, Jan 1979 ... 4.00
❑251, Mar 1979 ... 3.00
❑252, May 1979 ... 3.00
❑253, Jul 1979 ... 3.00
❑254, Aug 1979 ... 3.00
❑255, ca. 1979 ... 3.00
❑256, Nov 1979 ... 3.00
❑257, Jan 1980 ... 3.00
❑258, Mar 1980 ... 12.00
❑259, May 1980 ... 12.00
❑260, Sep 1980, Sold only in packs; extremely low distribution ... 325.00
❑261, Nov 1980, Sold only in packs ... 45.00
❑262, ca. 1981, Sold only in packs ... 12.00
❑263, ca. 1981, Sold only in packs ... 12.00
❑264, Feb 1982, Sold only in packs ... 12.00
❑265, ca. 1982, Sold only in packs ... 12.00
❑266, Jul 1983, Sold only in packs ... 15.00
❑267, ca. 1983, Sold only in packs ... 15.00
❑268 1984, Sold only in packs ... 15.00

LITTLE MERMAID (DISNEY'S...)
MARVEL

❑1, Sep 1994 ... 2.50
❑2, Oct 1994 ... 2.00

N-MINT

❑3, Nov 1994 ... 2.00
❑4, Dec 1994 ... 2.00
❑5, Jan 1995 ... 2.00
❑6, Feb 1995 ... 2.00
❑7, Mar 1995 ... 2.00
❑8, Apr 1995 ... 2.00
❑9, May 1995 ... 2.00
❑10, Jun 1995 ... 2.00
❑11, Jul 1995 ... 2.00
❑12, Aug 1995 ... 2.00

LITTLE MERMAID LIMITED SERIES (DISNEY'S...)
DISNEY

❑1, Feb 1992 ... 2.00
❑2, Mar 1992 ... 2.00
❑3, May 1992 ... 2.00
❑4, Jun 1992 ... 2.00

LITTLE MERMAID (ONE-SHOT)
W.D.

❑1 ... 3.50

LITTLE MERMAID, THE: UNDERWATER ENGAGEMENTS (DISNEY'S...)
ACCLAIM

❑1; flip-book digest set before movie. 4.50

LITTLE MERMAID (WALT DISNEY'S...)
DISNEY

❑1, stapled ... 2.50
❑1/Direct ed., squarebound ... 5.95

LITTLE MISS STRANGE
MILLENNIUM

❑1 ... 2.95

LITTLE MISTER MAN
SLAVE LABOR

❑1, Nov 1995, b&w ... 2.95
❑2, Dec 1995, b&w ... 2.95
❑3, Feb 1996, b&w ... 2.95

LITTLE MONSTERS (GOLD KEY)
GOLD KEY

❑1, Nov 1964 ... 20.00
❑2, Feb 1965 ... 12.00
❑3, Nov 1965 ... 8.00
❑4 1966 ... 8.00
❑5, Jul 1966 ... 8.00
❑6, Oct 1966 ... 6.00
❑7, Dec 1966 ... 6.00
❑8, Feb 1967 ... 6.00
❑9, Apr 1967 ... 6.00
❑10, Jun 1967 ... 5.00
❑11 ... 5.00
❑12, Dec 1970 ... 5.00
❑13, ca. 1971 ... 5.00
❑14, Sep 1971 ... 5.00
❑15, Dec 1971 ... 5.00
❑16, Mar 1972 ... 5.00
❑17, Jun 1972 ... 5.00
❑18, Sep 1972 ... 5.00
❑19, Dec 1972 ... 5.00
❑20, Mar 1973 ... 5.00
❑21, Jun 1973 ... 4.00
❑22, Sep 1973 ... 4.00
❑23, Dec 1973 ... 4.00
❑24, Mar 1974 ... 4.00
❑25, Jun 1974 ... 4.00
❑26, Sep 1974 ... 4.00
❑27, Dec 1974 ... 4.00
❑28, Mar 1975 ... 4.00
❑29, Jun 1975 ... 4.00
❑30, Sep 1975 ... 4.00
❑31, Dec 1975 ... 4.00
❑32, Feb 1976 ... 4.00
❑33, Apr 1976 ... 4.00
❑34, Jun 1976 ... 4.00
❑35, Aug 1976 ... 4.00
❑36, Oct 1976 ... 4.00
❑37, Dec 1976 ... 4.00
❑38, Feb 1977 ... 4.00
❑39, Apr 1977 ... 4.00
❑40, Jun 1977 ... 4.00
❑41, Aug 1977 ... 4.00
❑42, Oct 1977 ... 4.00
❑43, Dec 1977 ... 4.00
❑44, Feb 1978 ... 4.00

N-MINT

LITTLE MONSTERS
NOW

❑1, Jan 1990 ... 1.50
❑2, Feb 1990 ... 1.50
❑3, Mar 1990 ... 1.50
❑4, Apr 1990 ... 1.50
❑5, May 1990 ... 1.50
❑6, Jun 1990 ... 1.50

LITTLE NEMO IN SLUMBERLAND 3-D
BLACKTHORNE

❑1 ... 2.50

LITTLE RED HOT: BOUND
IMAGE

❑1, Jul 2001 ... 2.95
❑2, Sep 2001 ... 2.95
❑3, Nov 2001 ... 2.95

LITTLE RED HOT: CHANE OF FOOLS
IMAGE

❑1, Feb 1999 ... 2.95
❑2, Mar 1999 ... 2.95
❑3, Apr 1999 ... 2.95

LITTLE RONZO IN SLUMBERLAND
SLAVE LABOR

❑1, Jul 1987 ... 1.75

LITTLE SAD SACK
HARVEY

❑1, Oct 1964 ... 7.00
❑2, Dec 1964 ... 4.00
❑3, Feb 1964 ... 4.00
❑4, Apr 1965 ... 4.00
❑5, Jun 1965 ... 4.00
❑6, Aug 1965 ... 3.00
❑7, Oct 1965 ... 3.00
❑8, Dec 1965 ... 3.00
❑9, Feb 1966 ... 3.00
❑10, Apr 1966 ... 3.00
❑11, Jun 1966 ... 3.00
❑12, Sep 1966 ... 3.00
❑13, Nov 1966 ... 3.00
❑14, Jan 1966 ... 3.00
❑15, Mar 1966 ... 3.00
❑16, May 1966 ... 3.00
❑17, Jul 1966 ... 3.00
❑18, Sep 1966 ... 3.00
❑19, Nov 1966 ... 3.00

LITTLE SHOP OF HORRORS
DC

❑1, Mar 1987 ... 2.00

LITTLE STAR
ONI

❑1 2005 ... 2.99
❑2, Jun 2005 ... 2.99
❑3 2005 ... 2.99
❑4, Oct 2005 ... 2.99
❑5, Nov 2005 ... 2.99

LITTLE STOOGES
GOLD KEY

❑1, Sep 1972 ... 16.00
❑2, Dec 1972 ... 12.00
❑3, Mar 1973 ... 12.00
❑4, Jun 1973 ... 9.00
❑5, Sep 1973 ... 9.00
❑6, Dec 1973 ... 9.00
❑7, Mar 1974 ... 9.00

LITTLE WHITE MOUSE
CALIBER

❑1, Nov 1997, b&w ... 2.95
❑2, Jan 1998, b&w ... 2.95
❑3 1998 ... 2.95
❑4, Jan 2001 ... 2.95

LIVEWIRES
MARVEL

❑1 2005 ... 2.99
❑2, May 2005 ... 2.99
❑3, Jun 2005 ... 2.99
❑4, Jul 2005 ... 2.99
❑5, Aug 2005 ... 2.99
❑6, Sep 2005 ... 2.99

LIVINGSTONE MOUNTAIN
ADVENTURE

❑1, Jul 1991, b&w ... 2.50
❑2, Aug 1991, b&w ... 2.50

Other grades: Multiply price above by 5/6 for VF/NM • 2/3 for VERY FINE • 1/3 for FINE • 1/5 for VERY GOOD • 1/8 for GOOD

Lone Ranger (Gold Key)

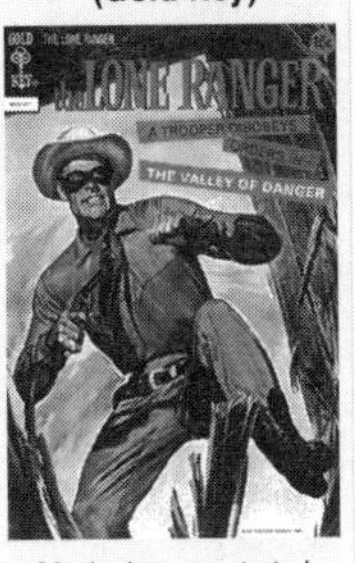

Masked man restarted from the Dell series

©Gold Key

Lone Wolf and Cub (First)

First (and first) U.S. printing of manga classic

©First

Longshot

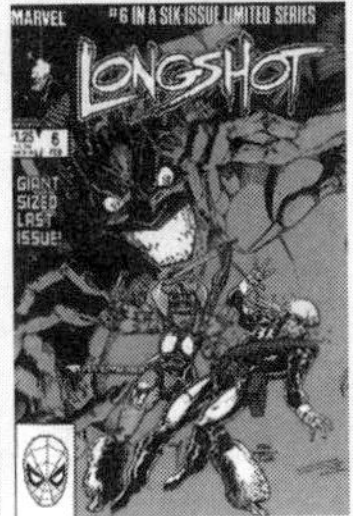

Tousle-haired person inhabits Mojo-world

©Marvel

Looney Tunes (Gold Key)

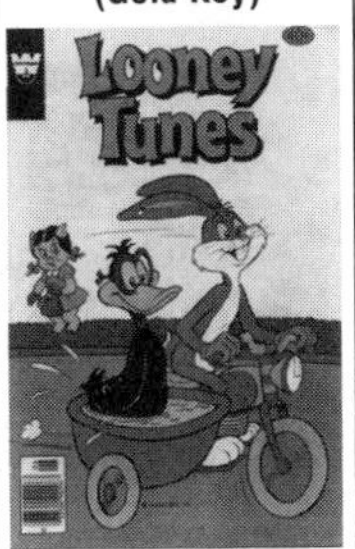

Gold Key version had some stories cross over

©Gold Key

Loose Cannon

Cop turns into gigantic blue behemoth

©DC

	N-MINT
❑3, Sep 1991, b&w	2.50
❑4, Oct 1991, b&w	2.50

LIVING WITH ZOMBIES
FRIGHTWORLD STUDIOS

	N-MINT
❑1 2005	2.50
❑2 2005	2.50
❑3, Aug 2005	2.50

LIZ AND BETH (VOL. 1)
FANTAGRAPHICS / EROS

	N-MINT
❑1, b&w	3.00
❑2, b&w	3.00
❑3, b&w	3.00
❑4	3.00

LIZ AND BETH (VOL. 2)
FANTAGRAPHICS / EROS

	N-MINT
❑1, b&w	2.50
❑2, b&w	2.50
❑3, b&w	2.50
❑4	2.50

LIZ AND BETH (VOL. 3)
FANTAGRAPHICS / EROS

	N-MINT
❑1, b&w	2.50
❑2, b&w	2.50
❑3, b&w	2.50
❑4, b&w	2.50
❑5, b&w	2.50
❑6, b&w	2.50
❑7, b&w	2.50

LIZARD LADY
AIRCEL

	N-MINT
❑1, b&w	2.95
❑2, b&w	2.95
❑3, b&w	2.95
❑4, b&w	2.95

LIZARDS SUMMER FUN SPECIAL
CALIBER

	N-MINT
❑1, b&w	3.50

LIZZIE MCGUIRE CINE-MANGA
TOKYOPOP

	N-MINT
❑1, May 2003, fumetti with photos from the TV show	7.99

LLISICA
NBM

	N-MINT
❑1	9.95

LLOYD LLEWELLYN
FANTAGRAPHICS

	N-MINT
❑1, Apr 1986	2.25
❑2, Jun 1986	2.25
❑3, Aug 1986	2.25
❑4, Oct 1986	2.25
❑5, Jan 1987	2.25
❑6, Jun 1987	2.25
❑Special 1	2.50
❑Special 1/2nd, Oct 1992	2.75

LOADED
INTERPLAY

	N-MINT
❑1	1.00

LOBO (MINI-SERIES)
DC

	N-MINT
❑1, Nov 1990, KG (a)	3.00
❑1/2nd, Nov 1990, KG (a)	2.00
❑2, Dec 1990, KG (a)	2.00
❑3, Jan 1991, KG (a)	2.00
❑4, Feb 1991, KG (a)	2.00

LOBO
DC

	N-MINT
❑0, Oct 1994; O: Lobo. 10/94	2.50
❑1, Dec 1993; foil cover	3.50
❑2, Feb 1994	2.50
❑3, Mar 1994	2.50
❑4, Apr 1994	2.50
❑5, May 1994	2.50
❑6, Jun 1994	2.50
❑7, Jul 1994	2.50
❑8, Aug 1994	2.50
❑9, Sep 1994	2.50
❑10, Nov 1994	2.50
❑11, Dec 1994	2.00
❑12, Jan 1995	2.00
❑13, Feb 1995	2.00
❑14, Mar 1995	2.00
❑15, Apr 1995	2.00
❑16, Jun 1995	2.25
❑17, Jul 1995	2.25
❑18, Aug 1995	2.25
❑19, Sep 1995	2.25
❑20, Oct 1995	2.25
❑21, Nov 1995 A: Space Cabby	2.25
❑22, Dec 1995; Underworld Unleashed	2.25
❑23, Jan 1996	2.25
❑24, Feb 1996	2.25
❑25, Mar 1996	2.25
❑26, Apr 1996	2.25
❑27, May 1996	2.25
❑28, Jun 1996	2.25
❑29, Jul 1996	2.25
❑30, Aug 1996	2.25
❑31, Sep 1996	2.25
❑32, Oct 1996; Lobo's body is destroyed	2.25
❑33, Nov 1996	2.25
❑34, Dec 1996	2.25
❑35, Jan 1997	2.25
❑36, Feb 1997 A: Hemingway. A: Poe. A: Mark Twain. A: Chaucer. A: Shakespeare	2.25
❑37, Mar 1997	2.25
❑38, Apr 1997	2.25
❑39, May 1997; Lobo as a pirate	2.25
❑40, Jun 1997; Lobo inside a whale	2.25
❑41, Jul 1997	2.25
❑42, Aug 1997	2.25
❑43, Sep 1997	2.25
❑44, Oct 1997; Genesis	2.25
❑45, Nov 1997 V: Jackie Chin	2.25
❑46, Dec 1997; Face cover	2.25
❑47, Jan 1998	2.25
❑48, Feb 1998	2.25
❑49, Mar 1998	2.25
❑50, Apr 1998 A: Keith Giffen. D: Everyone	2.25
❑51, May 1998	2.25
❑52, Jun 1998	2.25
❑53, Jul 1998	2.25
❑54, Aug 1998	2.25
❑55, Sep 1998	2.25
❑56, Oct 1998	2.50
❑57, Dec 1998; at police convention	2.50
❑58, Jan 1999 A: Orion. A: Superman	2.50
❑59, Feb 1999; A: Bad Wee Bastards. in miniature world	2.50
❑60, Mar 1999; 1: Superbo. Lobo reforms	2.50
❑61, Apr 1999 2: Superbo. A: Savage Six	2.50
❑62, May 1999	2.50
❑63, Jun 1999 A: Demon	2.50
❑64, Jul 1999 A: Demon	2.50
❑1000000, Nov 1998 1: Layla	4.00
❑Annual 1, ca. 1993	5.00
❑Annual 2, ca. 1994; SA (a); Elseworlds	3.50
❑Annual 3, ca. 1995; Year One	3.95

LOBO: A CONTRACT ON GAWD
DC

	N-MINT
❑1, Apr 1994	2.00
❑2, May 1994	2.00
❑3, Jun 1994	2.00
❑4, Jul 1994	2.00

LOBO: BLAZING CHAIN OF LOVE
DC

	N-MINT
❑1, Sep 1992	2.00

LOBO: BOUNTY HUNTING FOR FUN AND PROFIT
DC

	N-MINT
❑1; prestige format	4.95

LOBO: CHAINED
DC

	N-MINT
❑1, May 1997; Lobo goes to jail	2.50

LOBO CONVENTION SPECIAL
DC

	N-MINT
❑1; KG (w); Set at 1993 San Diego Comic Convention	2.00

LOBO/DEADMAN: THE BRAVE AND THE BALD
DC

	N-MINT
❑1, Feb 1995	3.50

LOBO: DEATH AND TAXES
DC

	N-MINT
❑1, Oct 1996	2.25
❑2, Nov 1996	2.25
❑3, Dec 1996	2.25
❑4, Jan 1997	2.25

LOBO/DEMON: HELLOWEEN
DC

	N-MINT
❑1, Dec 1996	2.25

LOBO: FRAGTASTIC VOYAGE
DC

	N-MINT
❑1, ca. 1998; prestige format	5.95

LOBO GALLERY, THE: PORTRAITS OF A BASTICH
DC

	N-MINT
❑1, Sep 1995; pin-ups	3.50

LOBO GOES TO HOLLYWOOD
DC

	N-MINT
❑1, Aug 1996	2.25

	N-MINT

LOBO: INFANTICIDE
DC
❑1, Oct 1992 KG (w); KG (a) 2.00
❑2, Nov 1992 KG (w); KG (a) 2.00
❑3, Dec 1992 KG (w); KG (a) 2.00
❑4, Jan 1993 KG (w); KG (a) 2.00

LOBO: IN THE CHAIR
DC
❑1, Aug 1994 .... 1.95

LOBO: I QUIT
DC
❑1, Dec 1995; Lobo stops smoking 2.75

LOBO/JUDGE DREDD: PSYCHO-BIKERS VS. THE MUTANTS FROM HELL
DC
❑1; prestige format 4.95

LOBO/MASK
DC
❑1, Feb 1997, prestige format crossover with Dark Horse 5.95
❑2, Mar 1997, prestige format crossover with Dark Horse 5.95

LOBO PARAMILITARY CHRISTMAS SPECIAL
DC
❑1, Jan 1991 KG (w); KG (a); D: Santa Claus 3.00

LOBO: PORTRAIT OF A VICTIM
DC
❑1, ca. 1993 .... 2.00

LOBO'S BACK
DC
❑1, May 1992, KG (a); 1: Ramona. Variant covers exist 2.00
❑2, Jun 1992, KG (a) 2.00
❑3, Oct 1992, KG (a) 2.00
❑4, Nov 1992, KG (a) 2.00

LOBO'S BIG BABE SPRING BREAK SPECIAL
DC
❑1, Spr 1995 .... 1.95

LOBO THE DUCK
DC / AMALGAM
❑1, Jun 1997 .... 1.95

LOBO: UN-AMERICAN GLADIATORS
DC
❑1, Jun 1993 .... 2.00
❑2, Jul 1993 .... 2.00
❑3, Aug 1993 .... 2.00
❑4, Sep 1993 .... 2.00

LOBO UNBOUND
DC
❑1, Aug 2003 .... 2.95
❑2, Sep 2003 .... 2.95
❑3, Nov 2003 .... 2.95
❑4, Jan 2004 .... 2.95
❑5, Mar 2004 .... 2.95
❑6, May 2004 .... 2.95

LOBOCOP
DC
❑1, Feb 1994 .... 2.00

LOCAL
ONI
❑1, Nov 2005 .... 2.99
❑2, Jan 2006 .... 2.99

LOCO VS. PULVERINE
ECLIPSE
❑1, Jul 1992, b&w; wraparound cover; parody 2.50

LOGAN: PATH OF THE WARLORD
MARVEL
❑1, Feb 1996 .... 6.00

LOGAN: SHADOW SOCIETY
MARVEL
❑1, Dec 1996 .... 6.00

LOGAN'S RUN (MARVEL)
MARVEL
❑1, Jan 1977, GP (a) 5.00
❑2, Feb 1977, GP (a) 2.00
❑3, Mar 1977, GP (a) 2.00
❑4, Apr 1977, GP (a) 2.00
❑5, May 1977, GP (a) 2.00
❑6, Jun 1977, PG (c); TS (a); A: Thanos. New stories begin; Back-up story is first solo story featuring Thanos 3.50
❑6/35 cent, Jun 1977, PG (c); TS (a); A: Thanos. New stories begin; Back-up story is first solo story featuring Thanos; 35 cent regional price variant 15.00
❑7, Jul 1977, GP (a) 2.00
❑7/35 cent, Jul 1977, GP (a); 35 cent regional price variant 15.00

LOGAN'S RUN (ADVENTURE)
ADVENTURE
❑1; PG (c); PG (a); Introduction by William F. Nolan 2.50
❑2, Jul 1990 .... 2.50
❑3 .... 2.50
❑4, Oct 1990 .... 2.50
❑5, Mar 1991 .... 2.50
❑6, Apr 1991 .... 2.50

LOGAN'S WORLD
ADVENTURE
❑1, May 1991, b&w 2.50
❑2, Aug 1991, b&w 2.50
❑3, Sep 1991, b&w 2.50
❑4, Nov 1991, b&w 2.50
❑5, Jan 1992, b&w 2.50
❑6, Mar 1992, b&w 2.50

LOIS LANE
DC
❑1, Aug 1986, GM (a) 2.00
❑2, Sep 1986, GM (a) 2.00

LOKI
MARVEL
❑1, Sep 2004 .... 12.00
❑2, Sep 2004 .... 6.00
❑3, Oct 2004 .... 3.50
❑4, Nov 2004 .... 3.50

LOLITA
NBM
❑1 .... 10.95
❑2 .... 10.95
❑3 .... 9.95
❑4 .... 9.95

LONE
DARK HORSE
❑1, Sep 2003 .... 2.99
❑2, Oct 2003 .... 2.99
❑3, Nov 2003 .... 2.99
❑4, Feb 2004 .... 2.99
❑5, Mar 2004 .... 2.99
❑6, Apr 2004 .... 2.99

LONE GUNMEN
DARK HORSE
❑Special 1, Jun 2001 .... 2.99

LONELY NIGHTS COMICS
LAST GASP
❑1 .... 2.00

LONELY TOMBSTONE ONE SHOT
IMAGE
❑1, Nov 2005 .... 4.99

LONELY WAR OF WILLY SCHULTZ
AVALON
❑1, b&w; Reprints 2.95
❑2 .... 2.95
❑3 .... 2.95
❑4 .... 2.95

LONE RANGER (DELL)
DELL
❑100, Oct 1956 .... 34.00
❑101, Nov 1956 .... 30.00
❑102, Dec 1956 .... 30.00
❑103, Jan 1957 .... 30.00
❑104, Feb 1957 .... 30.00
❑105, Mar 1957 .... 30.00
❑106, Apr 1957 .... 30.00
❑107, May 1957 .... 30.00
❑108, Jun 1957 .... 30.00
❑109, Jul 1957 .... 30.00
❑110, Aug 1957 .... 30.00
❑111, Sep 1957 .... 30.00
❑112, Oct 1957 .... 55.00
❑113, Nov 1957 .... 45.00
❑114, Dec 1957 .... 45.00
❑115, Jan 1958 .... 45.00
❑116, Feb 1958 .... 45.00
❑117, Mar 1958 .... 45.00
❑118, Apr 1958 O: Lone Ranger 50.00
❑119, May 1958 .... 45.00
❑120, Jun 1958 .... 45.00
❑121, Jul 1958 .... 45.00
❑122, Aug 1958 .... 45.00
❑123, Sep 1958 .... 45.00
❑124, Oct 1958 .... 45.00
❑125, Dec 1958 .... 45.00
❑126, Feb 1959 .... 45.00
❑127, Apr 1959 .... 45.00
❑128, Jun 1959 .... 45.00
❑129, Aug 1959 .... 45.00
❑130, Oct 1959 .... 45.00
❑131, Dec 1959 .... 45.00
❑132, Feb 1960 .... 45.00
❑133, Apr 1960 .... 45.00
❑134, Jun 1960 .... 45.00
❑135, Aug 1960 .... 45.00
❑136, Oct 1960 .... 45.00
❑137, Dec 1960 .... 45.00
❑138, Feb 1961 .... 45.00
❑139, Apr 1961 .... 45.00
❑140, Jun 1961 .... 45.00
❑141, Aug 1961 .... 45.00
❑142, Oct 1961 .... 45.00
❑143, Dec 1961 .... 45.00
❑144, Feb 1962 .... 45.00
❑145, May 1962 .... 45.00

LONE RANGER (GOLD KEY)
GOLD KEY
❑1, Sep 1964 .... 35.00
❑2, Sep 1965 .... 18.00
❑3, Mar 1966 .... 14.00
❑4, Aug 1966 .... 12.00
❑5, Jan 1967 .... 12.00
❑6, Apr 1967 .... 12.00
❑7, Jul 1967, Reprints 10.00
❑8, Oct 1967 .... 10.00
❑9, Jan 1968 .... 10.00
❑10, Apr 1968 .... 10.00
❑11, Jul 1968 .... 9.00
❑12, Oct 1968 .... 9.00
❑13, Mar 1969 .... 9.00
❑14, Jun 1969 .... 9.00
❑15, Sep 1969 .... 9.00
❑16, Dec 1969 .... 9.00
❑17, ca. 1972 .... 9.00
❑18, Sep 1974 .... 9.00
❑19, Dec 1974 .... 9.00
❑20, Mar 1975, Reprints 9.00
❑21, Jun 1975 .... 5.00
❑22, Sep 1975 .... 5.00
❑23, Dec 1975 .... 5.00
❑24, Mar 1976 .... 5.00
❑25, Jun 1976 .... 5.00
❑26, Sep 1976 .... 5.00
❑27, Dec 1976 .... 5.00
❑28, Mar 1977 .... 5.00

LONE RANGER (PURE IMAGINATION)
PURE IMAGINATION
❑1 1996, b&w; reprints newspaper strip 3.00

LONE RANGER AND TONTO
TOPPS
❑1, Aug 1994 .... 2.50
❑1/Variant, Aug 1994; foil edition 4.00
❑2, Sep 1994 .... 2.50
❑2/Variant, Sep 1994; limited edition 3.50
❑3, Oct 1994 .... 2.50
❑3/Variant, Oct 1994; limited edition 3.00
❑4, Nov 1994 .... 2.50
❑4/Variant, Nov 1994; limited edition 3.00

LONE RANGER GOLDEN WEST
GOLD KEY
❑1, ca. 1966 .... 45.00

LONE WOLF 2100: RED FILES
DARK HORSE
❑1, Feb 2003 .... 2.99

LONE WOLF AND CUB (FIRST)
FIRST
❑1, May 1987, FM (c); Introduction by Frank Miller 6.00
❑1/2nd, FM (c) 2.50

Lost Universe (Gene Roddenberry's...)

Producer creates comics series posthumously

©Tekno

Louder than Words (Sergio Aragonés')

Sergio series goes without saying... anything

©Dark Horse

Love & Rockets

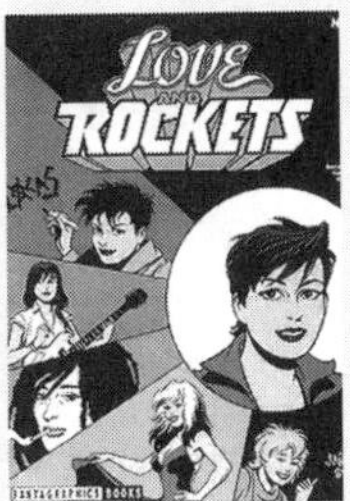

Celebrated title from Los Bros Hernandez

©Fantagraphics

Love and Romance

Charlton title tried to have hip 1970s feel

©Charlton

Lucifer (Vertigo)

Devilish Sandman character gets series

©DC

N-MINT

❑1/3rd, FM (c) 2.50
❑2, Jun 1987, FM (c) 4.00
❑2/2nd, Jun 1987, FM (c) 2.50
❑3, Jul 1987, FM (c) 4.00
❑3/2nd, FM (c) 2.50
❑4, Aug 1987, FM (c) 3.00
❑5, Sep 1987, FM (c) 3.00
❑6, Oct 1987, FM (c); O: Lone Wolf 3.00
❑7, Nov 1987, FM (c); O: Lone Wolf 3.00
❑8, Dec 1987, FM (c) 3.00
❑9, Jan 1988, FM (c) 3.00
❑10, Feb 1988, FM (c) 3.00
❑11, Mar 1988, FM (c) 2.50
❑12, Apr 1988, FM (c) 2.50
❑13, May 1988, BSz (c) 2.50
❑14, Jun 1988, BSz (c) 2.50
❑15, Jul 1988, BSz (c) 2.50
❑16, Aug 1988, BSz (c) 2.50
❑17, Sep 1988, BSz (c) 2.50
❑18, Oct 1988, BSz (c) 2.50
❑19, Nov 1988, BSz (c) 2.50
❑20, Dec 1988, BSz (c) 2.50
❑21, Jan 1989, BSz (c) 2.50
❑22, Feb 1989, BSz (c) 2.50
❑23, Mar 1989, BSz (c) 2.50
❑24, Apr 1989, BSz (c) 2.50
❑25, May 1989, MW (c) 2.50
❑26, Jun 1989, MW (c) 2.95
❑27, Jul 1989, MW (c) 3.00
❑28, Aug 1989, MW (c) 3.00
❑29, Sep 1989, MW (c) 3.00
❑30, Oct 1989, MW (c) 3.00
❑31, Jan 1990, MW (c) 3.00
❑32, Apr 1990, MW (c) 3.00
❑33, May 1990, MW (c) 3.00
❑34, Jun 1990, MW (c) 3.25
❑35, Jun 1990, MW (c) 3.25
❑36, Jul 1990, MW (c) 3.25
❑37, Aug 1990, MP (c) 3.25
❑38, Sep 1990, MP (c) 3.25
❑39, Oct 1990, Giant-size MP (c) 6.00
❑40, Nov 1990, MP (c) 3.25
❑41, Dec 1990, MP (c) 4.00
❑42, Jan 1991, MP (c) 4.00
❑43, Feb 1991, MP (c) 4.00
❑44, Mar 1991, MP (c) 4.00
❑45, Apr 1991, MP (c) 4.00
❑46, May 1991, MP (c) 4.00
❑47, Jun 1991, MP (c) 4.00
❑48, Jul 1991 4.00
❑49, Aug 1991 4.00

LONE WOLF AND CUB (DARK HORSE)
Dark Horse

❑1, Aug 2000; The Assassin's Road 9.99
❑2, Sep 2000; The Gateless Barrier 9.99
❑3, Nov 2000; The Flute of the Fallen Tiger 9.99
❑4, Dec 2000; The Bell Warden 9.99
❑5, Jan 2001; Black Wind; Samurai Executioner crossover 9.99
❑6, Feb 2001; Lanterns for the Dead 9.99
❑7, Mar 2001; Cloud Dragon, Wind Tiger 9.99
❑8, Apr 2001; Chains of Death 9.99

N-MINT

❑9, May 2001; Echo of the Assassin 9.99
❑10, Jun 2001; Hostage Child 9.99
❑11, Jul 2001; Talisman of Hades 9.99
❑12, Aug 2001; Shattered Stones 9.99
❑13, Sep 2001; The Moon in the East, The Sun in the West 9.99
❑14, Oct 2001; Day of the Demons 9.99
❑15, Nov 2001; Brothers of the Grass 9.99
❑16, Dec 2001; Gateway into Winter 9.99
❑17, Jan 2002; The Will of the Fang 9.99
❑18, Feb 2002; Twilight of the Kurokuwa 9.99
❑19, Mar 2002; The Moon in Our Hearts 9.99
❑20, Apr 2002; A Taste of Poison 9.99
❑21, May 2002; Fragrance of Death 9.99
❑22, Jun 2002; Heaven and Earth 9.99
❑23, Jul 2002; Tears of Ice 9.99
❑24, Aug 2002; In These Small Hands 9.99
❑25, Sep 2002; Perhaps in Death 9.99
❑26, Oct 2002; Struggle in the Dark 9.99
❑27, Nov 2002; Battle's Eve 9.99
❑28, Dec 2002; The Lotus Throne 9.99

LONE WOLF 2100
Dark Horse

❑1, May 2002 2.99
❑2, Jun 2002 2.99
❑3, Jul 2002 2.99
❑4, Aug 2002 2.99
❑5, Nov 2002 2.99
❑6, Dec 2002 2.99
❑7, Jan 2003 2.99
❑8, May 2003 2.99
❑9, Sep 2003 2.99
❑10, Oct 2003 2.99
❑11, Jan 2004 2.99

LONG, HOT SUMMER
DC / Milestone

❑1, Jul 1995; enhanced cover 2.95
❑2, Aug 1995 2.50
❑3, Sep 1995 2.50

LONGSHOT
Marvel

❑1, Sep 1985 1: Longshot 3.50
❑2, Oct 1985 1: Ricochet Rita 3.00
❑3, Nov 1985 1: Mojo. 1: Spiral 2.50
❑4, Dec 1985 A: Spider-Man 2.50
❑5, Jan 1986 2.00
❑6, Feb 1986; Double-size 2.50

LONGSHOT (2ND SERIES)
Marvel

❑1, Feb 1998; wraparound cover 3.99

LONGSHOT COMICS
Slave Labor

❑1, Jun 1995 2.95
❑1/2nd, Feb 1996 2.95
❑2, Jul 1997, b&w 2.95

LOOKERS
Avatar

❑1 3.00
❑2 3.00

LOOKERS: SLAVES OF ANUBIS
Avatar

❑1 3.50

N-MINT

LOOKING GLASS WARS: HATTER M
Image

❑1, Jan 2006 2.99
❑2, Apr 2006 2.99

LOONEY TUNES: BACK IN ACTION THE MOVIE
DC

❑1, ca. 2003 3.95

LOONEY TUNES (GOLD KEY)
Gold Key

❑1, Apr 1975 12.00
❑2, Jun 1975 7.00
❑3, Aug 1975 5.00
❑4, Oct 1975 5.00
❑5, Dec 1975 5.00
❑6, Feb 1976 3.50
❑7, Apr 1976 3.50
❑8, Jun 1976 3.50
❑9, Aug 1976 3.50
❑10, Oct 1976 3.50
❑11, Dec 1976 2.50
❑12, Feb 1977 2.50
❑13, Apr 1977, (c); (w); (a); Cover code 90296-704; Cracky in Hostess ad "Time on My Hands" 2.50
❑14, Jun 1977 2.50
❑15, Aug 1977 2.50
❑16, Oct 1977 2.50
❑17, Dec 1977 2.50
❑18, Feb 1978 2.50
❑19, Apr 1978 2.50
❑20, Jun 1978 2.50
❑21, Aug 1978 2.00
❑22, Oct 1978 2.00
❑23, Dec 1978 2.00
❑24, Feb 1979, (c); (w); (a) 2.00
❑25, Apr 1979 2.00
❑26, Jun 1979 2.00
❑27, Aug 1979 2.00
❑28, Oct 1979 2.00
❑29, Dec 1979 2.00
❑30, Feb 1980 2.00
❑31, Apr 1980 2.00
❑32, Jun 1980 2.00
❑33, Aug 1980 25.00
❑34, Oct 1980 40.00
❑35, Dec 1980 30.00
❑36, Feb 1981 2.00
❑37, Apr 1981 2.00
❑38, Jun 1981 2.00
❑39, Aug 1981 2.00
❑40, Oct 1981 2.00
❑41, Jan 1982 1.50
❑42, Feb 1982 1.50
❑43, Apr 1982 15.00
❑44, Jun 1982 15.00
❑45, Aug 1982 20.00
❑46, Mar 1984 20.00
❑47, Jun 1984 20.00

LOONEY TUNES (DC)
DC

❑1, Apr 1994 2.25
❑2, May 1994, Road Runner, Coyote 2.00

Other grades: Multiply price above by 5/6 for VF/NM • 2/3 for VERY FINE • 1/3 for FINE • 1/5 for VERY GOOD • 1/8 for GOOD

	N-MINT
❑3, Jun 1994, Baseball issue	2.00
❑4, Jul 1994	2.00
❑5, Aug 1994, Coyote, Martians	1.75
❑6, Sep 1994, Tazmanian Devil	1.50
❑7, Oct 1994	1.50
❑8, Nov 1994	1.50
❑9, Dec 1994	1.50
❑10, Jan 1995, Christmas issue	1.50
❑11, Feb 1995	1.50
❑12, Mar 1995	1.50
❑13, Apr 1995, Coyote	1.50
❑14, May 1995	1.50
❑15, Jun 1995	1.50
❑16, Jul 1995, Daffy, Speedy Gonzales	1.50
❑17, Aug 1995	1.50
❑18, Sep 1995, Duck Dodgers	1.50
❑19, Oct 1995	1.50
❑20, Nov 1995, Yosemite Sam	1.50
❑21, Feb 1996, Tazmanian Devil	1.50
❑22, Apr 1996	1.50
❑23, Jun 1996	1.75
❑24, Aug 1996	1.75
❑25, Oct 1996, Indiana Itz Mine	1.75
❑26, Nov 1996, indicia says Nov, cover says Dec	1.75
❑27, Jan 1997, indicia says Jan, cover says Feb	1.75
❑28, Feb 1997, cover says Apr 96, indicia says Feb 97; Valentine's issue	1.75
❑29, May 1997, Coyote	1.75
❑30, Jul 1997, Twilight Zone cover	1.75
❑31, Aug 1997	1.75
❑32, Sep 1997, Hercules parody	1.75
❑33, Oct 1997, Back to School issue	1.75
❑34, Nov 1997, Daffy versus Dinky Downunder	1.75
❑35, Dec 1997, Agent Daffy	1.95
❑36, Jan 1998, Sylvester, Tweety	1.95
❑37, Feb 1998	1.95
❑38, Mar 1998	1.95
❑39, Apr 1998, Foghorn Leghorn	1.95
❑40, May 1998, Sylvester	1.95
❑41, Jun 1998, Sylvester, Porky	1.95
❑42, Jul 1998, Speedy Gonzales, Sylvester	1.95
❑43, Aug 1998, Bugs and Daffy do Magic	1.95
❑44, Sep 1998, Tweety and Sylvester	1.99
❑45, Oct 1998, Marvin Martian	1.99
❑46, Nov 1998, Bugs and Taz	1.99
❑47, Dec 1998, Christmas issue	1.99
❑48, Jan 1999	1.99
❑49, Feb 1999, Pepe is stalked	1.99
❑50, Mar 1999	1.99
❑51, Apr 1999	1.99
❑52, May 1999	1.99
❑53, Jun 1999	1.99
❑54, Jul 1999	1.99
❑55, Aug 1999	1.99
❑56, Sep 1999	1.99
❑57, Oct 1999	1.99
❑58, Nov 1999	1.99
❑59, Dec 1999	1.99
❑60, Jan 2000	1.99
❑61, Feb 2000	1.99
❑62, Mar 2000	1.99
❑63, Apr 2000	1.99
❑64, May 2000	1.99
❑65, Jun 2000	1.99
❑66, Jul 2000	1.99
❑67, Aug 2000	1.99
❑68, Sep 2000	1.99
❑69, Oct 2000	1.99
❑70, Nov 2000	1.99
❑71, Dec 2000	1.99
❑72, Jan 2001	1.99
❑73, Feb 2001	1.99
❑74, Mar 2001	1.99
❑75, Apr 2001	1.99
❑76, May 2001	1.99
❑77, Jun 2001	1.99
❑78, Jul 2001	1.99
❑79, Aug 2001	1.99
❑80, Sep 2001	1.99
❑81, Oct 2001	1.99
❑82, Nov 2001	1.99
❑83, Dec 2001	1.99
❑84, Jan 2002	1.99
❑85, Feb 2002	1.99
❑86, Mar 2002	1.99
❑87, Apr 2002	1.99
❑88, May 2002	1.99
❑89, Jun 2002	1.99
❑90, Jul 2002	1.99
❑91, Aug 2002	1.99
❑92, Sep 2002	1.99
❑93, Oct 2002	2.25
❑94, Nov 2002	2.25
❑95, Dec 2002	2.25
❑96, Jan 2003	2.25
❑97, Feb 2003	2.25
❑98, Mar 2003	2.25
❑99, Apr 2003	2.25
❑100, May 2003	2.25
❑101, Jun 2003	2.25
❑102, Jul 2003	2.25
❑103, Aug 2003	2.25
❑104, Sep 2003	2.25
❑105, Oct 2003	2.25
❑106, Nov 2003	2.25
❑107, Dec 2003	2.25
❑108, Jan 2004	2.25
❑109, Feb 2004	2.25
❑110, Mar 2004	2.25
❑111, Apr 2004	2.25
❑112, May 2004	2.25
❑113, Jun 2004	2.25
❑114, Jul 2004	2.25
❑115, Aug 2004	2.25
❑116, Sep 2004	2.25
❑117, Oct 2004	2.25
❑118, Nov 2004	2.25
❑119, Dec 2004	2.25
❑120, Jan 2005	2.25
❑121, Feb 2005	2.25
❑122, Mar 2005	2.25
❑123, Apr 2005	2.25
❑124, May 2005	2.25
❑125, Jun 2005	2.25
❑126, Jul 2005	2.25
❑127, Aug 2005	2.25
❑128, Sep 2005	2.25
❑129, Oct 2005	2.25
❑130, Nov 2005	2.25
❑131, Dec 2005	2.25
❑132, Jan 2006	2.25
❑133, Jan 2006	2.25
❑134, Mar 2006	2.25
❑135, Mar 2006	2.25
❑136, May 2006	2.25
❑137, Jun 2006	2.25
❑138, Jul 2006	2.25
❑139, Aug 2006	2.25
❑140, Sep 2006	2.25

LOONEY TUNES AND MERRIE MELODIES COMICS
DELL

	N-MINT
❑180, Oct 1956	8.00
❑181, Nov 1956	8.00
❑182, Dec 1956	8.00
❑183, Jan 1957	8.00
❑184, Feb 1957	8.00
❑185, Mar 1957	8.00
❑186, Apr 1957	8.00
❑187, May 1957	8.00
❑188, Jun 1957	8.00
❑189, Jul 1957	8.00
❑190, Aug 1957	8.00
❑191, Sep 1957	8.00
❑192, Oct 1957	8.00
❑193, Nov 1957	8.00
❑194, Dec 1957	8.00
❑195, Jan 1958	8.00
❑196, Feb 1958	8.00
❑197, Mar 1958	8.00
❑198, Apr 1958	8.00
❑199, May 1958	8.00
❑200, Jun 1958	8.00
❑201, Jul 1958	6.00
❑202, Aug 1958	6.00
❑203, Sep 1958	6.00
❑204, Oct 1958	6.00
❑205, Nov 1958	6.00
❑206, Dec 1958	6.00
❑207, Jan 1959	6.00
❑208, Feb 1959	6.00
❑209, Mar 1959	6.00
❑210, Apr 1959	6.00
❑211, May 1959	6.00
❑212, Jun 1959	6.00
❑213, Jul 1959	6.00
❑214, Aug 1959	6.00
❑215, Sep 1959	6.00
❑216, Oct 1959	6.00
❑217, Nov 1959	6.00
❑218, Dec 1959	6.00
❑219, Jan 1960	6.00
❑220, Feb 1960	6.00
❑221, Mar 1960	6.00
❑222, Apr 1960	4.00
❑223, May 1960	4.00
❑224, Jun 1960	4.00
❑225, Jul 1960	4.00
❑226, Aug 1960	4.00
❑227, Sep 1960	4.00
❑228, Oct 1960	4.00
❑229, Nov 1960	4.00
❑230, Dec 1960	4.00
❑231, Jan 1961	4.00
❑232, Feb 1961	4.00
❑233, Mar 1961	4.00
❑234, Apr 1961	4.00
❑235, May 1961	4.00
❑236, Jun 1961	4.00
❑237, Jul 1961	4.00
❑238, Aug 1961	4.00
❑239, Sep 1961	4.00
❑240, Oct 1961	4.00
❑241, Nov 1961	4.00
❑242, Dec 1961	4.00
❑243 1962	4.00
❑244, May 1962	4.00
❑245, Jul 1962	4.00
❑246, Sep 1962	4.00

LOONEY TUNES MAGAZINE
DC

	N-MINT
❑1; Bugs Bunny	2.50
❑2; Batman parody	2.00
❑3	2.00
❑4	2.00
❑5	2.00
❑6	1.95
❑7	1.95
❑8	1.95
❑9	1.95
❑10	1.95
❑11; Title changes to Bugs Bunny & The Looney Tunes magazine	1.95
❑12	1.95
❑13	1.95
❑14	1.95
❑15	1.95
❑16; trading cards	1.95
❑17, Spr 1994	1.95
❑19, Fal 1994	1.50
❑20, Win 1995	1.95

LOOSE CANNON
DC

	N-MINT
❑1, Jun 1995	1.75
❑2, Jul 1995	1.75
❑3, Aug 1995	1.75
❑4, Sep 1995	1.75

LOOSE TEETH
FANTAGRAPHICS

	N-MINT
❑1, b&w	2.75
❑2, b&w	2.75
❑3, b&w	2.75

LORD FARRIS: SLAVEMASTER
FANTAGRAPHICS / EROS

	N-MINT
❑1, Feb 1996	2.95
❑2, May 1996	2.95

LORD JIM
GOLD KEY

	N-MINT
❑1, Sep 1965	18.00

LORD OF THE DEAD
CONQUEST

	N-MINT
❑1, b&w	2.95

LORD PUMPKIN
MALIBU / ULTRAVERSE
- ❑0, Oct 1994 ... 2.50

LORD PUMPKIN/NECROMANTRA
MALIBU / ULTRAVERSE
- ❑1, Apr 1995, b&w; Cover says Necromantra/Lord Pumpkin ... 2.95
- ❑2, May 1995, b&w; Cover says Necromantra/Lord Pumpkin ... 2.95
- ❑3, Jun 1995, b&w; Cover says Necromantra/Lord Pumpkin ... 2.95
- ❑4, Jul 1995, b&w; Cover says Necromantra/Lord Pumpkin ... 2.95

LORDS
LEGEND (NOT DARK HORSE IMPRINT)
- ❑1 ... 2.25

LORDS OF MISRULE (DARK HORSE)
DARK HORSE
- ❑1, Jan 1997, b&w ... 2.95
- ❑2, Feb 1997, b&w ... 2.95
- ❑3, Mar 1997, b&w ... 2.95
- ❑4, Apr 1997, b&w ... 2.95
- ❑5, May 1997, b&w ... 2.95
- ❑6, Jun 1997, b&w ... 2.95

LORDS OF MISRULE (ATOMEKA)
ATOMEKA
- ❑1 ... 6.95

LORDS OF THE ULTRA-REALM
DC
- ❑1, Jun 1987 ... 1.50
- ❑2, Jul 1986 ... 1.50
- ❑3, Aug 1986 ... 1.50
- ❑4, Sep 1986 ... 1.50
- ❑5, Oct 1986 ... 1.50
- ❑6, Nov 1986 ... 1.50
- ❑Special 1 ... 2.25

LORE
IDEA & DESIGN WORKS
- ❑1, Dec 2003 ... 5.99
- ❑2, Mar 2004 ... 3.99
- ❑3, Jun 2004 ... 3.99
- ❑4 2004 ... 5.99

LORELEI
STARWARP
- ❑1, b&w ... 2.50

LORELEI OF THE RED MIST
CONQUEST
- ❑1, b&w ... 2.95
- ❑2, b&w ... 2.95

LORI LOVECRAFT: MY FAVORITE REDHEAD
CALIBER
- ❑1, Feb 1997 ... 3.95

LORI LOVECRAFT: REPRESSION
A V
- ❑1, Jun 2002 ... 2.95

LORI LOVECRAFT: THE BIG COMEBACK
CALIBER
- ❑1 ... 2.95

LORI LOVECRAFT: THE DARK LADY
CALIBER
- ❑1 ... 2.95

LORTNOC
RADIO
- ❑1, Aug 1998, b&w ... 2.95

LOSERS
DC / VERTIGO
- ❑1, Aug 2003 ... 2.95
- ❑2, Sep 2003 ... 2.95
- ❑3, Oct 2003 ... 2.95
- ❑4, Nov 2003 ... 2.95
- ❑5, Dec 2003 ... 2.95
- ❑6, Jan 2004 ... 2.95
- ❑7, Feb 2004 ... 2.95
- ❑8, Mar 2004 ... 2.95
- ❑9, Apr 2004 ... 2.95
- ❑10, May 2004 ... 2.95
- ❑11, Jun 2004 ... 2.95
- ❑12, Jul 2004 ... 2.95
- ❑13, Aug 2004 ... 2.95
- ❑14, Sep 2004 ... 2.95
- ❑15, Oct 2004 ... 2.95
- ❑16, Nov 2004 ... 2.95
- ❑17, Jan 2005 ... 2.95
- ❑18, Feb 2005 ... 2.95
- ❑19, Mar 2005 ... 2.95
- ❑20, Apr 2005 ... 2.95
- ❑21, May 2005 ... 2.95
- ❑22, Jun 2005 ... 2.95
- ❑23, Jun 2005 ... 2.99
- ❑24, Jul 2005 ... 2.99
- ❑25, Aug 2005 ... 2.99
- ❑26, Sep 2005 ... 2.99
- ❑27, Oct 2005 ... 2.99
- ❑28 2005 ... 2.99
- ❑29 ... 2.99
- ❑30, Jan 2006 ... 2.99
- ❑31, Mar 2006 ... 2.99
- ❑32, Apr 2006 ... 2.99

LOSERS SPECIAL
DC
- ❑1, Sep 1985; O: Pooch (Gunner's Dog). O: Johnny Cloud. O: Captain Storm. D: The Losers. Crisis ... 2.50

LOST AND FOUND SEASON OF THE MOST POPEJOEY
ABANNE
- ❑1, Oct 2001 ... 2.95

LOST ANGEL
CALIBER
- ❑1, b&w ... 2.95

LOST (CALIBER)
CALIBER
- ❑1, Oct 1996, b&w ... 2.95
- ❑2 1996, b&w ... 2.95

LOST (CHAOS)
CHAOS
- ❑1, Dec 1997, b&w ... 2.95
- ❑2, Jan 1998, b&w ... 2.95
- ❑3, Feb 1998, b&w; cover says Feb 97; a misprint ... 2.95

LOST CONTINENT
ECLIPSE
- ❑1, b&w; Japanese ... 3.50
- ❑2, b&w; Japanese ... 3.50
- ❑3, b&w; Japanese ... 3.50
- ❑4, b&w; Japanese ... 3.50
- ❑5, b&w; Japanese ... 3.50
- ❑6, b&w; Japanese ... 3.50

LOST GIRLS
KITCHEN SINK
- ❑1, Nov 1995; Oversized; cardstock cover ... 5.95
- ❑2, Feb 1996; Oversized; cardstock cover ... 5.95

LOST HEROES
DAVDEZ
- ❑0, Mar 1998 ... 2.95
- ❑1, Apr 1998 ... 2.95
- ❑2, May 1998 ... 2.95
- ❑3, Jun 1998 ... 2.95
- ❑4, Aug 1998 ... 2.95

LOST IN SPACE (INNOVATION)
INNOVATION
- ❑1, Aug 1991 ... 3.00
- ❑2, Nov 1991 ... 2.75
- ❑3, Dec 1991 ... 2.75
- ❑4, Feb 1992 ... 2.50
- ❑5, Mar 1992 ... 2.50
- ❑6, May 1992 ... 2.50
- ❑7, Jun 1992 ... 2.50
- ❑8, Aug 1992 ... 2.50
- ❑9, Oct 1992 ... 2.50
- ❑10, Nov 1992 ... 2.50
- ❑11, Dec 1992; Judy's story ... 2.50
- ❑12 1993 ... 2.50
- ❑13, Aug 1993 ... 4.00
- ❑13/Gold, Aug 1993; Gold edition; enhanced cardstock cover ... 5.00
- ❑14, Sep 1993 ... 2.50
- ❑15, Aug 1993 ... 2.50
- ❑16, Sep 1993 ... 2.50
- ❑17, Oct 1993 ... 2.50
- ❑18, Nov 1993 ... 2.50
- ❑Annual 1, ca. 1991 ... 2.95
- ❑Annual 2, ca. 1992 PD (w); ... 2.95
- ❑Special 1; amended reprint of #1 ... 4.00
- ❑Special 2 ... 2.50

LOST IN SPACE (DARK HORSE)
DARK HORSE
- ❑1, Apr 1998 ... 2.95
- ❑2, May 1998 ... 2.95
- ❑3, Jul 1998 ... 2.95

LOST IN SPACE: PROJECT ROBINSON
INNOVATION
- ❑1, Nov 1993 ... 2.50

LOST IN THE ALPS
NBM
- ❑1 ... 13.95

LOST LAUGHTER
BAD HABIT
- ❑1, b&w ... 2.50
- ❑2, b&w ... 2.50
- ❑3, b&w ... 2.50
- ❑4, Apr 1994, b&w ... 2.50

LOST ONES
IMAGE
- ❑1 ... 2.95

LOST ONES, THE: FOR YOUR EYES ONLY
IMAGE
- ❑1, Mar 2000; special preview; no price ... 1.00

LOST PLANET
ECLIPSE
- ❑1, May 1987 ... 2.00
- ❑2, Jul 1987 ... 2.00
- ❑3, Sep 1987 ... 2.00
- ❑4, Dec 1987 ... 2.00
- ❑5, Feb 1988 ... 2.00
- ❑6, Mar 1989 ... 2.00

LOST SQUAD
DEVIL'S DUE
- ❑1 2005 ... 2.95
- ❑2, Dec 2005 ... 2.95
- ❑3, Mar 2006 ... 2.95
- ❑4, May 2006 ... 2.95

LOST UNIVERSE (GENE RODDENBERRY'S...)
TEKNO
- ❑0 ... 2.25
- ❑1, Apr 1995 ... 1.95
- ❑2, May 1995 ... 1.95
- ❑3, Jun 1995, trading card ... 1.95
- ❑3/A, Jun 1995, variant cover ... 1.95
- ❑4, Jul 1995, bound-in trading card ... 1.95
- ❑5, Aug 1995 ... 1.95
- ❑6, Sep 1995 ... 1.95
- ❑7, Oct 1995 ... 1.95

LOST WORLD
MILLENNIUM
- ❑1, Jan 1996; cover says Mar, indicia says Jan ... 2.95
- ❑2, Mar 1996 ... 2.95

LOST WORLD, THE: JURASSIC PARK
TOPPS
- ❑1, May 1997 ... 2.95
- ❑2, Jun 1997 ... 2.95
- ❑3, Jul 1997 ... 2.95

LOUD CANNOLI
CRAZYFISH / MJ-12
- ❑1 ... 2.95

LOUDER THAN WORDS (SERGIO ARAGONÉS')
DARK HORSE
- ❑1, Jul 1997 ... 2.95
- ❑2, Aug 1997 ... 2.95
- ❑3, Sep 1997 ... 2.95
- ❑4, Oct 1997 ... 2.95
- ❑5, Nov 1997 ... 2.95
- ❑6, Dec 1997 ... 2.95

LOUIE THE RUNE SOLDIER
ADV MANGA
- ❑1, Mar 2004 ... 9.99

LOUIS RIEL
DRAWN & QUARTERLY
- ❑1 ... 2.95
- ❑2 ... 2.95
- ❑3 ... 2.95
- ❑4 ... 2.95
- ❑5, Sep 2000 ... 2.95

LOUIS VS. ALI
REVOLUTIONARY

- ❑1, Dec 1993, b&w 2.95

LOVE & ROCKETS
FANTAGRAPHICS

- ❑1, Fal 1982 25.00
- ❑1/2nd 4.00
- ❑1/3rd 3.95
- ❑1/4th, May 1995 4.95
- ❑1/5th, May 1995 4.95
- ❑2, Spr 1983 12.00
- ❑2/2nd 3.95
- ❑2/3rd, May 1996 4.95
- ❑3, Fal 1983 9.00
- ❑3/2nd, Apr 1991 3.95
- ❑4, Fal 1983 8.00
- ❑4/2nd, Apr 1991 2.50
- ❑4/3rd 3.95
- ❑5, Mar 1984 7.00
- ❑5/2nd, May 1991 2.50
- ❑6, May 1984 5.00
- ❑6/2nd, May 1991 2.50
- ❑7, Jul 1984 5.00
- ❑7/2nd, May 1991 2.50
- ❑8, Sep 1984 5.00
- ❑8/2nd, Aug 1991 2.50
- ❑9, Nov 1984 5.00
- ❑9/2nd, Oct 1991 2.50
- ❑10, Jan 1985 5.00
- ❑10/2nd, Dec 1991 2.95
- ❑11, Apr 1985 4.00
- ❑11/2nd, Feb 1992 2.50
- ❑12, Jul 1985 4.00
- ❑12/2nd, Aug 1992 2.50
- ❑13, Sep 1985 4.00
- ❑13/2nd, Oct 1992 2.50
- ❑14, Nov 1985 4.00
- ❑14/2nd, Feb 1993 2.50
- ❑15, Jan 1986 4.00
- ❑15/2nd, Aug 1993 2.50
- ❑16, Mar 1986 3.00
- ❑16/2nd, Oct 1993 2.95
- ❑17, Jun 1986 3.00
- ❑18, Sep 1986 3.00
- ❑19, Jan 1987 3.00
- ❑20, Apr 1987 3.00
- ❑21, Jul 1987 2.25
- ❑22, Aug 1987 2.25
- ❑23, Oct 1987 2.25
- ❑24, Dec 1987 2.25
- ❑25, Mar 1988 2.25
- ❑26, Jun 1988 2.25
- ❑27, Aug 1988 2.25
- ❑28, Dec 1988 2.95
- ❑28/2nd, Apr 1995 2.95
- ❑29, Mar 1989 2.75
- ❑29/2nd, Mar 1992 2.25
- ❑30, Jul 1989 2.95
- ❑30/2nd, Mar 1992 2.95
- ❑31, Dec 1989 2.50
- ❑31/2nd, Apr 1992 2.50
- ❑32, May 1990 2.50
- ❑33, Aug 1990 2.50
- ❑34, Nov 1990 2.50
- ❑35, Mar 1991 2.75
- ❑36, Nov 1991 2.75
- ❑37, Feb 1992 2.75
- ❑38, Apr 1992 2.75
- ❑39, Aug 1992 2.75
- ❑40, Jan 1993 3.50
- ❑41, Apr 1993 2.95
- ❑42, Aug 1993 2.95
- ❑43, Nov 1993 2.95
- ❑44, Mar 1994 2.95
- ❑45, Jul 1994 2.95
- ❑46, Nov 1994 2.95
- ❑47, Apr 1995 2.95
- ❑48, Jul 1995 2.95
- ❑49, Nov 1995 2.95
- ❑50, Apr 1996, b&w 4.95

LOVE & ROCKETS (VOL. 2)
FANTAGRAPHICS

- ❑1, Spr 2001 6.00
- ❑2, Sum 2001 3.95
- ❑3, Fal 2001 3.95
- ❑4, Sum 2002 3.95
- ❑5, Sum 2002 3.95
- ❑6, ca. 2002 3.95
- ❑7, Spr 2003 3.95
- ❑8 3.95
- ❑9 3.95
- ❑10 5.95
- ❑11 4.50
- ❑12 4.50
- ❑13 4.50
- ❑14, Fal 2005 4.50
- ❑15, Jan 2006 4.50

LOVE & ROCKETS BONANZA
FANTAGRAPHICS

- ❑1, Mar 1989, b&w; Reprints 2.95
- ❑1/2nd, Feb 1992, b&w 2.95

LOVE AND ROMANCE
CHARLTON

- ❑1 1971 24.00
- ❑2 1971 16.00
- ❑3 1972 12.00
- ❑4 1972 12.00
- ❑5 1972 12.00
- ❑6 1972 8.00
- ❑7, Aug 1972 8.00
- ❑8, Oct 1972 8.00
- ❑9, Dec 1972 8.00
- ❑10, Feb 1973 8.00
- ❑11, Apr 1973 6.00
- ❑12 1973 6.00
- ❑13 1973 6.00
- ❑14 1973 6.00
- ❑15 1973 6.00
- ❑16, Jan 1974 6.00
- ❑17 1974 6.00
- ❑18 1974 6.00
- ❑19 1974 6.00
- ❑20 1974 6.00
- ❑21 1974 4.00
- ❑22 1975 4.00
- ❑23 1975 4.00
- ❑24 1975 4.00

LOVE AS A FOREIGN LANGUAGE
ONI

- ❑1 2005 9.95
- ❑2 2005 9.95
- ❑3 2005 9.95
- ❑4, Nov 2005 9.95

LOVE BITES
FANTAGRAPHICS / EROS

- ❑1, b&w 2.25
- ❑2 2.25

LOVE BITES (RADIO COMIX)
RADIO

- ❑1, Oct 2000 2.95

LOVE BOMB
ABACULUS

- ❑1 2.95
- ❑2 2.95

LOVE BUG
GOLD KEY

- ❑1, Jun 1969 24.00

LOVEBUNNY & MR. HELL: DAY IN THE LOVE LIFE
IMAGE

- ❑1, Feb 2003 2.95

LOVEBUNNY & MR. HELL: SAVAGE LOVE
IMAGE

- ❑1, Apr 2003 2.95

LOVECRAFT (DC)
DC

- ❑1, ca. 2004 24.95

LOVECRAFT
ADVENTURE

- ❑1 2.95
- ❑1/Ltd.; limited edition 3.00
- ❑2 2.95
- ❑3 2.95
- ❑4 2.95

LOVE DIARY (CHARLTON)
CHARLTON

- ❑1, Oct 1958, Swimsuit cover 45.00
- ❑2, Dec 1958 24.00
- ❑3, Feb 1959 16.00
- ❑4, Apr 1959 16.00
- ❑5, Jun 1959 14.00
- ❑6, Aug 1959 20.00
- ❑7, Oct 1959 14.00
- ❑8, Dec 1959 14.00
- ❑9, Mar 1960 14.00
- ❑10, Jun 1960 14.00
- ❑11, Aug 1960 12.00
- ❑12, Oct 1960 12.00
- ❑13, Dec 1960 12.00
- ❑14, Feb 1961 12.00
- ❑15, Apr 1961 12.00
- ❑16, Jun 1961 10.00
- ❑17, Aug 1961 10.00
- ❑18, Oct 1961 10.00
- ❑19, Dec 1961 10.00
- ❑20, Mar 1962 10.00
- ❑21, May 1962 7.00
- ❑22, Jul 1962 7.00
- ❑23, Sep 1962 7.00
- ❑24, Nov 1962, DG (c) 7.00
- ❑25, Jan 1963 7.00
- ❑26, Mar 1963 7.00
- ❑27, May 1963 7.00
- ❑28, Jul 1963 7.00
- ❑29, Sep 1963 7.00
- ❑30, Nov 1963 7.00
- ❑31, ca. 1964 5.00
- ❑32, ca. 1964 5.00
- ❑33, ca. 1964 5.00
- ❑34, ca. 1964 5.00
- ❑35, Nov 1964 5.00
- ❑36, Jan 1965, Swimsuit cover 5.00
- ❑37, Apr 1965 5.00
- ❑38, Jul 1965 5.00
- ❑39, ca. 1965 5.00
- ❑40, Oct 1965 5.00
- ❑41, Dec 1965 4.00
- ❑42, Feb 1966 4.00
- ❑43, Apr 1966 4.00
- ❑44, Jun 1966 4.00
- ❑45, Sep 1966 4.00
- ❑46, Nov 1966 4.00
- ❑47, Jan 1967 4.00
- ❑48, Mar 1967 4.00
- ❑49, Jun 1967 4.00
- ❑50, Aug 1967 4.00
- ❑51, Oct 1967 4.00
- ❑52, Dec 1967 4.00
- ❑53, Feb 1968 4.00
- ❑54, Jun 1968 4.00
- ❑55, Aug 1968 4.00
- ❑56, Oct 1968, JL (c) 4.00
- ❑57, Dec 1968 4.00
- ❑58, Feb 1969 4.00
- ❑59, Apr 1969 4.00
- ❑60, Jun 1969 4.00
- ❑61, Aug 1969 2.50
- ❑62, Oct 1969 2.50
- ❑63, Dec 1969 2.50
- ❑64, Feb 1970 2.50
- ❑65, Apr 1970 2.50
- ❑66, Jun 1970 2.50
- ❑67, Aug 1970 2.50
- ❑68, Oct 1970 2.50
- ❑69, Dec 1970 2.50
- ❑70, Jan 1971 2.50
- ❑71, Mar 1971 2.50
- ❑72, May 1971 2.50
- ❑73, Jul 1971 2.50
- ❑74, Sep 1971 2.50
- ❑75, Nov 1971 2.50
- ❑76, Jan 1972 2.50
- ❑77, Mar 1972 2.50
- ❑78, May 1972 2.50
- ❑79, Jul 1972, David Cassidy "poster" inside 2.50
- ❑80, Sep 1972, Bobby Sherman "poster" inside 2.50
- ❑81, Dec 1972, Bobby Sherman "poster" inside 2.50
- ❑82, Jan 1973 2.50
- ❑83, Mar 1973, Susan Dey "poster" inside 2.50
- ❑84, May 1973 2.50
- ❑85, Jul 1973 2.50

Lucy Show

Lucy"s 1960s series spawns comic spinoff

©Gold Key

Luftwaffe: 1946 (Vol. 1)

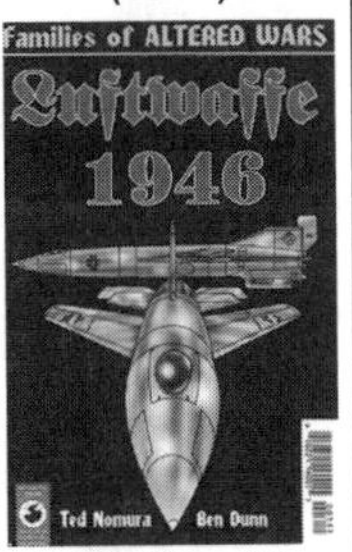

Set in the Tigers of Terra alternate universe

©Antarctic

Machine

Cyborg entry to the Comics' Greatest World line

©Dark Horse

Machine Man

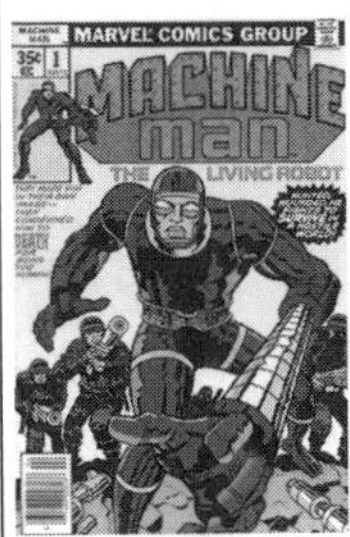

Kirby spinoff from 2001: A Space Odyssey

©Marvel

Machine Man (Ltd. Series)

Series transports Machine Man to 2020

©Marvel

N-MINT

❑86, Sep 1973 2.50
❑87, Nov 1973 2.50
❑88, Jun 1974 2.50
❑89, Sep 1974 2.50
❑90, Nov 1974 2.50
❑91, Jan 1975 2.50
❑92, Mar 1975 2.50
❑93, May 1975 2.50
❑94, Jul 1975 2.50
❑95, Sep 1975 2.50
❑96, Nov 1975 2.50
❑97, Feb 1976 2.50
❑98, Apr 1976 2.50
❑99, Jun 1976 2.50
❑100, Aug 1976 2.50
❑101, Oct 1976 2.50
❑102, Dec 1976 2.50

LOVE ETERNAL: A TORTURED SOUL
VLAD ENT.

❑1, b&w 2.00

LOVE FANTASY
RENEGADE

❑1, b&w 2.00

LOVE HINA
TOKYOPOP

❑1, 2002 2.95
❑2, 2002 2.95
❑3, 2002 2.95
❑4, 2002 2.95
❑5, 2002 2.95

LOVE IN TIGHTS
SLAVE LABOR

❑1, Nov 1998, b&w; First heart throbbin' issue 2.95

LOVELESS
DC / VERTIGO

❑1 2.99
❑2, Jan 2006 2.99
❑3, Feb 2006 2.99
❑4, Apr 2006 2.99
❑5, Jun 2006 2.99
❑6, Jun 2006 2.99
❑7, Aug 2006 2.99
❑8, Sep 2006 2.99

LOVE LETTERS IN THE HAND
FANTAGRAPHICS / EROS

❑1, b&w 2.25
❑2, b&w 2.25
❑3, b&w 2.50

LOVELY AS A LIE
ILLUSTRATION

❑1, Nov 1994 3.25

LOVELY LADIES
CALIBER

❑1, b&w; pin-ups 3.50

LOVELY PRUDENCE
ALL THE RAGE

❑1, ca. 1995 2.95
❑2, ca. 1995 2.95
❑3, ca. 1995, b&w 2.95

N-MINT

LOVE ME TENDERLOIN
DARK HORSE

❑1, Jan 2004, Cal McDonald Mystery One Shot 2.99

LOVE OR MONEY
TOKYOPOP

❑1, Dec 2004 9.95
❑2, Mar 2005 9.95
❑3, Jun 2005 9.95
❑4, Dec 2005 9.95

LOVE STORIES
DC

❑147, Nov 1972, Previous issues published as Heart Throbs 8.00
❑148, Jan 1973 8.00
❑149, Mar 1973 8.00
❑150, Jun 1973 8.00
❑151, Aug 1973 8.00
❑152, Oct 1973 8.00

LOVE SUCKS
ACE

❑1 2.95

LOWLIFE
CALIBER

❑1, b&w 2.50
❑2, b&w 2.50
❑3, b&w 2.50
❑4, Feb 1994, b&w 2.50

L.T. CAPER
SPOTLIGHT

❑1 1.75

LUBA
FANTAGRAPHICS

❑1, Feb 1998 2.95
❑2, Jul 1998 2.95
❑3, Dec 1998 2.95
❑4, Jan 2000 3.50
❑5, Oct 2000 3.50
❑6, Spr 2002 3.50
❑7, ca. 2002 3.50
❑8, ca. 2003 3.50
❑9, ca. 2004 3.50

LUCIFER (VERTIGO)
DC / VERTIGO

❑1, Jun 2000 3.50
❑2, Jul 2000 3.00
❑3, Aug 2000 3.00
❑4, Sep 2000 3.00
❑5, Oct 2000 3.00
❑6, Nov 2000 2.50
❑7, Dec 2000 2.50
❑8, Jan 2001 2.50
❑9, Feb 2001 2.50
❑10, Mar 2001 2.50
❑11, Apr 2001 2.50
❑12, May 2001 2.50
❑13, Jun 2001 2.50
❑14, Jul 2001 2.50
❑15, Aug 2001 2.50
❑16, Sep 2001 2.50
❑17, Oct 2001 2.50
❑18, Nov 2001 2.50
❑19, Dec 2001 2.50

N-MINT

❑20, Jan 2002 2.50
❑21, Feb 2002 2.50
❑22, Mar 2002 2.50
❑23, Apr 2002 2.50
❑24, May 2002 2.50
❑25, Jul 2002 A: Death (Sandman) 2.50
❑26, Jul 2002 2.50
❑27, Aug 2002 2.50
❑28, Sep 2002 2.50
❑29, Oct 2002 2.50
❑30, Nov 2002 2.50
❑31, Dec 2002 2.50
❑32, Jan 2003 2.50
❑33, Feb 2003 2.50
❑34, Mar 2003 2.50
❑35, Apr 2003 2.50
❑36, May 2003 2.50
❑37, Jun 2003 2.50
❑38, Jul 2003 2.50
❑39, Aug 2003 2.50
❑40, Sep 2003 2.50
❑41, Oct 2003 2.50
❑42, Nov 2003 2.50
❑43, Dec 2003 2.50
❑44, Jan 2004 2.50
❑45, Feb 2004 2.50
❑46, Mar 2004 2.50
❑47, Apr 2004 2.50
❑48, May 2004 2.50
❑49, Jun 2004 2.50
❑50, Jul 2004 3.50
❑51, Aug 2004 2.50
❑52, Sep 2004 2.50
❑53, Oct 2004 2.50
❑54, Nov 2004 2.50
❑55, Dec 2004 2.50
❑56, Jan 2005 2.50
❑57, Feb 2005 2.50
❑58, Mar 2005 2.50
❑59, Apr 2005 2.50
❑60, May 2005 2.50
❑61, Jun 2005 2.50
❑62, Jul 2005 2.50
❑63, Aug 2005 2.75
❑64, Sep 2005 2.75
❑65, Oct 2005 2.75
❑66 2005 2.75
❑67, Dec 2005 2.75
❑68, Jan 2006 2.75
❑69, Feb 2006 2.75
❑70, Mar 2006 2.75
❑71, May 2006 2.75
❑72, Jun 2006 2.75
❑73, Jul 2006 2.75
❑74, Aug 2006 2.75
❑75, Sep 2006 2.75

LUCIFER (TRIDENT)
TRIDENT

❑1, Jul 1990, b&w 1.95
❑2, b&w 1.95
❑3, b&w 1.95

LUCIFER: NIRVANA
DC / VERTIGO

❑1, Oct 2002, b&w 5.95

Other grades: Multiply price above by 5/6 for VF/NM • 2/3 for VERY FINE • 1/3 for FINE • 1/5 for VERY GOOD • 1/8 for GOOD

LUCIFER'S HAMMER
INNOVATION

❑1, Nov 1993 ... 2.50
❑2 ... 2.50
❑3 ... 2.50
❑4 ... 2.50
❑5 ... 2.50
❑6 ... 2.50

LUCK OF THE DRAW
RADIO

❑1, Jun 2000, b&w ... 3.95

LUCKY 7
RUNAWAY GRAPHICS

❑1, Apr 1993 ... 1.95

LUCKY LUKE: JESSE JAMES
FANTASY FLIGHT

❑1 ... 8.95

LUCKY LUKE: THE STAGE COACH
FANTASY FLIGHT

❑1 ... 8.95

LUCY SHOW
GOLD KEY

❑1, Jun 1963 ... 65.00
❑2, Sep 1963 ... 40.00
❑3, Dec 1963 ... 32.00
❑4, Mar 1964 ... 32.00
❑5, Jun 1964 ... 32.00

LUDWIG VON DRAKE (WALT DISNEY'S...)
DELL

❑1, Nov 1961 ... 16.00
❑2, Jan 1962 ... 10.00
❑3, Mar 1962 ... 8.00
❑4, Jun 1962 ... 8.00

LUFTWAFFE: 1946 TECHNICAL MANUAL
ANTARCTIC

❑1, Feb 1998; Projekt Saucer ... 4.00
❑2, Apr 1999; Hitler's Kamikazes ... 4.00

LUFTWAFFE: 1946 (VOL. 1)
ANTARCTIC

❑1, Jul 1996, b&w ... 5.00
❑2, Sep 1996, b&w ... 4.00
❑3, Nov 1996, b&w ... 4.00
❑4, Jan 1997, b&w ... 4.00
❑Annual 1, Apr 1998, b&w ... 4.00

LUFTWAFFE: 1946 (VOL. 2)
ANTARCTIC

❑1, Mar 1997 ... 4.00
❑2, Apr 1997; contains indicia for issue #1 ... 3.50
❑3, May 1997 ... 3.50
❑4, Jul 1997 ... 3.50
❑5, Aug 1997 ... 3.00
❑6, Oct 1997 ... 3.00
❑7, Nov 1997 ... 3.00
❑8, Feb 1998; 50th "Families of Altered Wars" issue ... 3.00
❑9, Apr 1998 ... 3.00
❑10, May 1998 ... 3.00
❑11, Jun 1998 ... 3.00
❑12, Jul 1998 ... 3.00
❑13, Aug 1998 ... 3.00
❑14, Oct 1998 ... 3.00
❑15, Feb 1999 ... 3.00
❑16, Mar 1999 ... 3.00
❑Annual 1, ca. 1998; 1998 Annual ... 3.00
❑Special 1, Apr 1998; Color Special ... 4.00
❑Special 2, Feb 1997, b&w; TriebflÉgel Special; German rocketry; Triebflngel Special ... 4.00

LUFTWAFFE: 1946 (VOL. 3)
ANTARCTIC

❑1, Aug 2002 ... 5.95
❑2, Oct 2002 ... 5.95
❑3, Oct 2002 ... 5.95
❑4, ca. 2002 ... 5.95
❑5, Jan 2003 ... 5.95
❑6, Feb 2003 ... 5.95
❑7, Mar 2003 ... 5.95
❑8, Apr 2003 ... 5.95
❑9, May 2003 ... 5.95
❑10, Jun 2003 ... 5.95
❑11, Jul 2003 ... 5.95
❑12, Aug 2003 ... 5.95
❑13, Nov 2003 ... 5.95
❑14, Dec 2003 ... 5.95
❑15, Dec 2003 ... 5.95
❑16, Jan 2004 ... 5.95
❑17, Feb 2004 ... 5.95

LUGER
ECLIPSE

❑1, Oct 1986 TY (a) ... 2.00
❑2, Dec 1986 TY (a) ... 2.00
❑3, Feb 1987 TY (a) ... 2.00

LUGH, LORD OF LIGHT
FLAGSHIP

❑1, Feb 1987 ... 1.75
❑2, Jun 1987 ... 1.75
❑3 ... 1.75
❑4 ... 1.75

LUGO
LOST BOYS

❑½; Promotional edition ... 1.00

LULLABY
ALIAS

❑1, Dec 2005 ... 2.99

LULLABY: WISDOM SEEKER
IMAGE

❑1, ca. 2005 ... 2.95
❑1/B cover 2005 ... 4.00
❑2, ca. 2005 ... 2.95
❑2/B cover 2005 ... 4.00
❑3 2005 ... 2.95
❑4, Sep 2005 ... 2.95

LUMENAGERIE
NBM

❑1 ... 11.95

LUM URUSEI*YATSURA
VIZ

❑1, b&w; Japanese ... 5.00
❑2, b&w; Japanese ... 4.00
❑3, b&w; Japanese ... 4.00
❑4, b&w; Japanese ... 4.00
❑5 ... 3.50
❑6 ... 3.50
❑7 ... 3.50
❑8 ... 3.50

LUNAR DONUT
LUNAR DONUT

❑0, b&w; says (Honey-Glazed); cardstock cover ... 2.50
❑1, b&w; Flip-book; cover says (With Sprinkles) ... 2.50
❑2, b&w; Flip-book; cover says (Cherry-Filled) ... 2.50
❑3, b&w; Flip-book; cover says (Jelly-Filled) ... 2.50

LUNATIC BINGE
ETERNITY

❑1 ... 3.95
❑2 ... 3.95

LUNATIC FRINGE
INNOVATION

❑1, Jul 1989 ... 1.75
❑2, Aug 1989 ... 1.75

LUNATIK
MARVEL

❑1, Dec 1995 ... 1.95
❑2, Jan 1996 ... 1.95
❑3, Feb 1996 ... 1.95

LURID
IDEA & DESIGN WORKS

❑1, Jan 2003 ... 2.99
❑2, Mar 2003 ... 2.99
❑3, Jun 2003 ... 2.99

LURID TALES
FANTAGRAPHICS / EROS

❑1, b&w ... 2.75

LUST
FANTAGRAPHICS / EROS

❑1, Apr 1997 ... 2.95
❑2, May 1997 ... 2.95
❑3, Jun 1997 ... 2.95
❑4, Jul 1997 ... 2.95
❑5, Aug 1997 ... 2.95
❑6, Sep 1997 ... 2.95

LUST FOR LIFE
SLAVE LABOR

❑1, Feb 1997, b&w ... 2.95
❑2, May 1997, b&w ... 2.95
❑3, Aug 1997, b&w ... 2.95
❑4, Jan 1998 ... 2.95

LUST OF THE NAZI WEASEL WOMEN
FANTAGRAPHICS

❑1, b&w ... 2.25
❑2, b&w ... 2.25
❑3, Jan 1991, b&w ... 2.25
❑4, b&w ... 2.25

LUX & ALBY SIGN ON AND SAVE THE UNIVERSE
DARK HORSE

❑1, b&w ... 2.50
❑2, May 1993, b&w ... 2.50
❑3, Jun 1993, b&w ... 2.50
❑4, Jul 1993 ... 2.50
❑5, Aug 1993 ... 2.50
❑6, Sep 1993 ... 2.50
❑7, Oct 1993 ... 2.50
❑8, Oct 1993 ... 2.50
❑9, Dec 1993 ... 2.50

LUXURA & VAMPFIRE
BRAINSTORM

❑1 ... 2.95

LUXURA COLLECTION (KIRK LINDO'S...)
BRAINSTORM

❑1, stories and pin-ups; cardstock cover ... 4.95

LUXURA LEATHER SPECIAL
BRAINSTORM

❑1, Mar 1996 ... 2.95

LYCANTHROPE LEO
VIZ

❑1, b&w ... 2.95
❑2, b&w ... 2.95
❑3, b&w ... 2.95
❑4, b&w ... 2.95
❑5, b&w ... 2.95
❑6, b&w ... 2.95
❑7, b&w ... 2.95

LYCEUM
HUNTER

❑1, Oct 1996, b&w ... 2.95
❑2, Aug 1997, b&w ... 2.95

LYCRA-WOMAN AND SPANDEX-GIRL
COMIC ZONE

❑1, Dec 1992, b&w ... 2.95

LYCRA WOMAN AND SPANDEX GIRL CHRISTMAS '77 SPECIAL
COMIC ZONE

❑1, b&w ... 2.95

LYCRA WOMAN AND SPANDEX GIRL HALLOWEEN SPECIAL
LOST CAUSE

❑1, b&w ... 2.95

LYCRA WOMAN AND SPANDEX GIRL JURASSIC DINOSAUR SPECIAL
COMIC ZONE

❑1, b&w ... 2.95

LYCRA WOMAN AND SPANDEX GIRL SUMMER VACATION SPECIAL
COMIC ZONE

❑1, b&w ... 2.95

LYCRA WOMAN AND SPANDEX GIRL TIME TRAVEL SPECIAL
COMIC ZONE

❑1, b&w ... 2.95

LYCRA WOMAN AND SPANDEX GIRL VALENTINE SPECIAL
COMIC ZONE

❑1, b&w ... 2.95

LYNCH
IMAGE

❑1, May 1997; no indicia ... 2.50

LYNCH MOB
CHAOS

❑1, Jun 1994 ... 2.50
❑2, Jul 1994 ... 2.50

Madballs

As thin a reed on which a title has been based

©Marvel

Mad-Dog

"Comic book" from a Bob Newhart series

©Marvel

Maelstrom

Executioner's life gets complicated

©Aircel

Mage

Mix of mythology and action-adventure

©Comico

Magical Mates

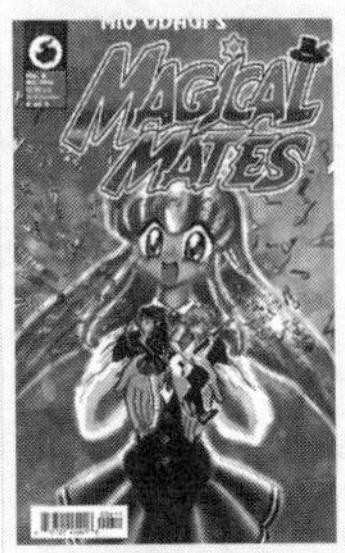

Manga story of three unusual girls

©Antarctic

N-MINT

❑3, Aug 1994 .... 2.50
❑4, Sep 1994 .... 2.50

LYNX: AN ELFLORD TALE
Peregrine Entertainment

❑1, Mar 1999, b&w 2.95

M
Eclipse

❑1, Jun 1990 .... 4.95
❑2 .... 4.95
❑3 .... 4.95
❑4 .... 5.95

MACABRE
Lighthouse

❑1 1989, b&w 2.50
❑2 1989, b&w 2.50
❑3 1989, b&w 2.50
❑4 1989 .... 2.50
❑5 1989 .... 2.50
❑6, Aug 1989 .... 2.50

MACABRE (VOL. 2)
Lighthouse

❑1 1989 .... 2.50
❑2 1989 .... 2.50

MACE: BOUNTY HUNTER
Image

❑1, Apr 2003 .... 2.99

M.A.C.H. 1
Fleetway-Quality

❑1, b&w 1: John Probe 2.00
❑2, b&w 2.00
❑3, b&w 2.00
❑4, b&w 2.00
❑5, b&w 2.00
❑6, b&w 2.00
❑7, b&w 2.00
❑8, b&w 2.00
❑9, b&w 2.00

MACHINE
Dark Horse

❑1, Nov 1994 .... 2.50
❑2, Dec 1994 .... 2.50
❑3, Jan 1995 .... 2.50
❑4, Feb 1995 .... 2.50

MACHINE MAN
Marvel

❑1, Apr 1978, JK (w); JK (a); 1: Machine Man 2.50
❑2, May 1978 .... 2.00
❑3, Jun 1978 .... 2.00
❑4, Jul 1978 .... 2.00
❑5, Aug 1978, Newsstand edition (distributed by Curtis); issue number in box 2.00
❑5/Whitman, Aug 1978, Special markets edition (usually sold in Whitman bagged prepacks); price appears in a diamond; UPC barcode appears 2.00
❑6, Sep 1978, Newsstand edition (distributed by Curtis); issue number in box 2.00

N-MINT

❑6/Whitman, Sep 1978, Special markets edition (usually sold in Whitman bagged prepacks); price appears in a diamond; UPC barcode appears 2.00
❑7, Oct 1978 .... 2.00
❑8, Nov 1978, Newsstand edition (distributed by Curtis); issue number in box 2.00
❑8/Whitman, Nov 1978, Special markets edition (usually sold in Whitman bagged prepacks); price appears in a diamond; no UPC barcode 2.00
❑9, Dec 1978, Storyline continues in Incredible Hulk, resuming eight months later 2.00
❑10, Aug 1979, Series resumes 2.00
❑11, Oct 1979 .... 2.00
❑12, Dec 1979 .... 2.00
❑13, Feb 1980 .... 2.00
❑14, Apr 1980 .... 2.00
❑15, Jun 1980, O: Ion. 1: Ion 2.00
❑16, Aug 1980, 1: Baron Brimstone 2.00
❑17, Oct 1980 .... 2.00
❑18, Dec 1980, A: Alpha Flight 2.00
❑19, Feb 1981, FM (c); 1: Jack O'Lantern I (Jason Macendale). Macendale becomes Hobgoblin II in Amazing Spider-Man #289 .... 12.50

MACHINE MAN (LTD. SERIES)
Marvel

❑1, Oct 1984, HT (a) 1.50
❑2, Nov 1984, HT (a); 1: Iron Man 2020 .... 1.50
❑3, Dec 1984, HT (a) 1.50
❑4, Jan 1985, HT (a) 1.50

MACHINE MAN/BASTION '98
Marvel

❑1, ca. 1998; gatefold summary; Marvel Annual; wraparound cover 2.99

MACHINE MAN 2020
Marvel

❑1, Aug 1994; Reprints 2.00
❑2, Sep 1994; Reprints 2.00

MACHINE TEEN
Marvel

❑1, Jul 2005 .... 2.99
❑2, Aug 2005 .... 2.99
❑3, Sep 2005 .... 2.99
❑4, Oct 2005 .... 2.99
❑5 2005 .... 2.99

MACK BOLAN: THE EXECUTIONER (DON PENDLETON'S...)
Innovation

❑1, Jul 1993, enhanced cardstock cover; adapts War Against the Mafia 2.95
❑1/A, Jul 1993, Indestructible Tyvek cover 3.95
❑1/B, Jul 1993, Double-cover edition; black outer cover with red X 3.50
❑2, Aug 1993, Adapts War Against the Mafia 2.50
❑3, Nov 1993, Adapts War Against the Mafia 2.50
❑4 .... 2.50

N-MINT

MACKENZIE QUEEN
Matrix

❑1 .... 1.50
❑2, b&w 1.50
❑3 .... 1.50
❑4 .... 1.50
❑5 .... 1.50

MACK THE KNIFE: MONOCHROME MEMORIES
Caliber

❑1, b&w 2.50

MACROSS II
Viz

❑1, ca. 1992 .... 3.00
❑2, ca. 1992 .... 2.75
❑3, ca. 1992 .... 2.75
❑4, ca. 1992 .... 2.75
❑5, ca. 1992 .... 2.75
❑6, ca. 1992 .... 2.75
❑7, ca. 1993 .... 2.75
❑8, ca. 1993 .... 2.75
❑9, ca. 1993 .... 2.75
❑10, ca. 1993 .... 2.75

MACROSS II: THE MICRON CONSPIRACY
Viz

❑1, b&w 3.00
❑2, b&w 2.75
❑3, b&w 2.75
❑4, b&w 2.75
❑5, b&w 2.75

MAD
E.C.

❑30, Dec 1956, b&w; Alfred E. Neuman cover 350.00
❑31, Feb 1957, b&w 200.00
❑32, Apr 1957, b&w 175.00
❑33, Jun 1957, b&w 165.00
❑34, Aug 1957, b&w 140.00
❑35, Oct 1957, b&w 140.00
❑36, Dec 1957, b&w 110.00
❑37, Jan 1958, b&w 110.00
❑38, Mar 1958, b&w 110.00
❑39, May 1958, b&w 110.00
❑40, Jul 1958, b&w 110.00
❑41, Sep 1958, b&w 80.00
❑42, Nov 1958, b&w 80.00
❑43, Dec 1958, b&w 80.00
❑44, Jan 1959, b&w 80.00
❑45, Mar 1959, b&w 80.00
❑46, Apr 1959, b&w 80.00
❑47, Jun 1959, b&w 80.00
❑48, Jul 1959, b&w 80.00
❑49, Sep 1959, b&w 80.00
❑50, Oct 1959, b&w 80.00
❑51, Dec 1959 .... 60.00
❑52, Jan 1960 .... 60.00
❑53, Mar 1960, b&w 60.00
❑54, Apr 1960, b&w 60.00
❑55, Jun 1960, b&w 60.00
❑56, Jul 1960, b&w 60.00
❑57, Sep 1960, b&w 60.00
❑58, Oct 1960, b&w 60.00

MAD

Issue	N-MINT
❑59, Dec 1960, b&w WW (a)	60.00
❑60, Jan 1961, b&w	60.00
❑61, Mar 1961, b&w	48.00
❑62, Apr 1961, b&w	48.00
❑63, Jun 1961, b&w	48.00
❑64, Jul 1961, b&w	48.00
❑65, Sep 1961, b&w	48.00
❑66, Oct 1961, b&w	48.00
❑67, Dec 1961, b&w	48.00
❑68, Jan 1962, b&w	48.00
❑69, Mar 1962, b&w	48.00
❑70, Apr 1962, b&w	48.00
❑71, Jun 1962, b&w	36.00
❑72, Jul 1962, b&w	36.00
❑73, Sep 1962, b&w	36.00
❑74, Oct 1962, b&w	36.00
❑75, Dec 1962, b&w	36.00
❑76, Jan 1963, b&w	36.00
❑77, Mar 1963, b&w JO, MD, WW (a)	36.00
❑78, Apr 1963, b&w	36.00
❑79, Jun 1963, b&w	36.00
❑80, Jul 1963, b&w	36.00
❑81, Sep 1963, b&w	32.00
❑82, Oct 1963, b&w	32.00
❑83, Dec 1963, b&w	32.00
❑84, Jan 1964, b&w SA, JO, MD, WW (a)	32.00
❑85, Mar 1964, b&w	32.00
❑86, Apr 1964, b&w; 1st fold-in	32.00
❑87, Jun 1964, b&w	32.00
❑88, Jul 1964, b&w	32.00
❑89, Sep 1964, b&w	32.00
❑90, Oct 1964, b&w	32.00
❑91, Dec 1964, b&w	32.00
❑92, Jan 1965, b&w	32.00
❑93, Mar 1965, b&w	32.00
❑94, Apr 1965, b&w	32.00
❑95, Jun 1965, b&w	32.00
❑96, Jul 1965, b&w JO, MD (a)	32.00
❑97, Sep 1965, b&w	32.00
❑98, Oct 1965, b&w	32.00
❑99, Dec 1965, b&w	32.00
❑100, Jan 1966, b&w	32.00
❑101, Mar 1966, b&w	18.00
❑102, Apr 1966, b&w	18.00
❑103, Jun 1966, b&w	18.00
❑104, Jul 1966, b&w	18.00
❑105, Sep 1966, b&w; Batman TV-show parody	18.00
❑106, Oct 1966, b&w	18.00
❑107, Dec 1966, b&w	18.00
❑108, Jan 1967, b&w	18.00
❑109, Mar 1967, b&w	18.00
❑110, Apr 1967, b&w	18.00
❑111, Jun 1967, b&w	18.00
❑112, Jul 1967, b&w	18.00
❑113, Sep 1967, b&w	18.00
❑114, Oct 1967, b&w	18.00
❑115, Dec 1967, b&w	18.00
❑116, Jan 1968, b&w	18.00
❑117, Mar 1968, b&w	18.00
❑118, Apr 1968, b&w	18.00
❑119, Jun 1968, b&w	18.00
❑120, Jul 1968, b&w	18.00
❑121, Sep 1968, b&w; Beatles parody	22.00
❑122, Oct 1968, b&w	18.00
❑123, Dec 1968, b&w	15.00
❑124, Jan 1969, b&w	15.00
❑125, Mar 1969, b&w	15.00
❑126, Apr 1969, b&w	15.00
❑127, Jun 1969, b&w	15.00
❑128, Jul 1969, b&w	15.00
❑129, Sep 1969, b&w	15.00
❑130, Oct 1969, b&w	15.00
❑131, Dec 1969, b&w	15.00
❑132, Jan 1970, b&w	15.00
❑133, Mar 1970, b&w	15.00
❑134, Apr 1970, b&w	15.00
❑135, Jun 1970, b&w	15.00
❑136, Jul 1970, b&w	15.00
❑137, Sep 1970, b&w	15.00
❑138, Oct 1970, b&w	15.00
❑139, Dec 1970, b&w	15.00
❑140, Jan 1971, b&w	15.00
❑141, Mar 1971, b&w	12.00
❑142, Apr 1971, b&w	12.00
❑143, Jun 1971, b&w	12.00
❑144, Jul 1971, b&w	12.00
❑145, Sep 1971, b&w	12.00
❑146, Oct 1971, b&w	12.00
❑147, Dec 1971, b&w	12.00
❑148, Jan 1972, b&w	12.00
❑149, Mar 1972, b&w	12.00
❑150, Apr 1972, b&w	12.00
❑151, Jun 1972, b&w	9.00
❑152, Jul 1972, b&w	9.00
❑153, Sep 1972, b&w	9.00
❑154, Oct 1972, b&w	9.00
❑155, Dec 1972, b&w	9.00
❑156, Jan 1973, b&w	9.00
❑157, Mar 1973, b&w	9.00
❑158, Apr 1973, b&w	9.00
❑159, Jun 1973, b&w	9.00
❑160, Jul 1973, b&w	9.00
❑161, Sep 1973, b&w	8.00
❑162, Oct 1973, b&w	8.00
❑163, Dec 1973, b&w	8.00
❑164, Jan 1974, b&w	8.00
❑165, Mar 1974, b&w	8.00
❑166, Apr 1974, b&w	8.00
❑167, Jun 1974, b&w	8.00
❑168, Jul 1974, b&w	8.00
❑169, Sep 1974, b&w	8.00
❑170, Oct 1974, b&w	8.00
❑171, Dec 1974, b&w	6.50
❑172, Jan 1975, b&w	6.50
❑173, Mar 1975, b&w	6.50
❑174, Apr 1975, b&w	6.50
❑175, Jun 1975, b&w	6.50
❑176, Jul 1975, b&w	6.50
❑177, Sep 1975, b&w	6.50
❑178, Oct 1975, b&w	6.50
❑179, Dec 1975, b&w	6.50
❑180, Jan 1976, b&w	6.50
❑181, Mar 1976, b&w	6.50
❑182, Apr 1976, b&w	6.50
❑183, Jun 1976, b&w	6.50
❑184, Jul 1976, b&w	6.50
❑185, Sep 1976, b&w	6.50
❑186, Oct 1976, b&w; Star Trek parody	6.50
❑187, Dec 1976, b&w	6.50
❑188, Jan 1977, b&w	6.50
❑189, Mar 1977, b&w	6.50
❑190, Apr 1977, b&w	5.00
❑191, Jun 1977, b&w	5.00
❑192, Jul 1977, b&w	5.00
❑193, Sep 1977, b&w	5.00
❑194, Oct 1977, b&w	5.00
❑195, Dec 1977, b&w	5.00
❑196, Jan 1978, b&w	5.00
❑197, Mar 1978, b&w	5.00
❑198, Apr 1978, b&w	5.00
❑199, Jun 1978, b&w	5.00
❑200, Jul 1978, b&w	5.00
❑201, Sep 1978, b&w	4.00
❑202, Oct 1978, b&w	4.00
❑203, Dec 1978, b&w	4.00
❑204, Jan 1979, b&w	4.00
❑205, Mar 1979, b&w	4.00
❑206, Apr 1979, b&w	4.00
❑207, Jun 1979, b&w	4.00
❑208, Jul 1979, b&w	4.00
❑209, Sep 1979, b&w	4.00
❑210, Oct 1979, b&w	4.00
❑211, Dec 1979, b&w	4.00
❑212, Jan 1980, b&w	4.00
❑213, Mar 1980, b&w	4.00
❑214, Apr 1980, b&w	4.00
❑215, Jun 1980, b&w	4.00
❑216, Jul 1980, b&w	4.00
❑217, Sep 1980, b&w	4.00
❑218, Oct 1980, b&w	4.00
❑219, Dec 1980, b&w	4.00
❑220, Jan 1981, b&w	4.00
❑221, Mar 1981, b&w	3.00
❑222, Apr 1981, b&w	3.00
❑223, Jun 1981, b&w	3.00
❑224, Jul 1981, b&w	3.00
❑225, Sep 1981, b&w	3.00
❑226, Oct 1981, b&w	3.00
❑227, Dec 1981, b&w	3.00
❑228, Jan 1982, b&w	3.00
❑229, Mar 1982, b&w	3.00
❑230, Apr 1982, b&w	3.00
❑231, Jun 1982, b&w	3.00
❑232, Jul 1982, b&w	3.00
❑233, Sep 1982, b&w	3.00
❑234, Oct 1982, b&w	3.00
❑235, Dec 1982, b&w	3.00
❑236, Jan 1983, b&w	3.00
❑237, Mar 1983, b&w	3.00
❑238, Apr 1983, b&w	3.00
❑239, Jun 1983, b&w	3.00
❑240, Jul 1983, b&w	3.00
❑241, Sep 1983, b&w	2.50
❑242, Oct 1983, b&w	2.50
❑243, Dec 1983, b&w	2.50
❑244, Jan 1984, b&w	2.50
❑245, Mar 1984, b&w	2.50
❑246, Apr 1984, b&w	2.50
❑247, Jun 1984, b&w	2.50
❑248, Jul 1984, b&w	2.50
❑249, Sep 1984, b&w	2.50
❑250, Oct 1984, b&w	2.50
❑251, Dec 1984, b&w	2.50
❑252, Jan 1985, b&w	2.50
❑253, Mar 1985, b&w	2.50
❑254, Apr 1985, b&w	2.50
❑255, Jun 1985, b&w	2.50
❑256, Jul 1985, b&w	2.50
❑257, Sep 1985, b&w	2.50
❑258, Oct 1985, b&w	2.50
❑259, Dec 1985, b&w	2.50
❑260, Jan 1986, b&w	2.50
❑261, Mar 1986, b&w	2.25
❑262, Apr 1986, b&w	2.25
❑263, Jun 1986, b&w	2.25
❑264, Jul 1986, b&w	2.25
❑265, Sep 1986, b&w	2.25
❑266, Oct 1986, b&w	2.25
❑267, Dec 1986, b&w	2.25
❑268, Jan 1987, b&w	2.25
❑269, Mar 1987, b&w	2.25
❑270, Apr 1987, b&w	2.25
❑271, Jun 1987, b&w	2.25
❑272, Jul 1987, b&w	2.25
❑273, Sep 1987, b&w	2.25
❑274, Oct 1987, b&w	2.25
❑275, Dec 1987, b&w	2.25
❑276, Jan 1988, b&w	2.25
❑277, Mar 1988, b&w	2.25
❑278, Apr 1988, b&w	2.25
❑279, Jun 1988, b&w	2.25
❑280, Jul 1988, b&w	2.25
❑281, Sep 1988, b&w	2.25
❑282, Oct 1988, b&w	2.25
❑283, Dec 1988, b&w	2.25
❑284, Jan 1989, b&w	2.25
❑285, Mar 1989, b&w	2.25
❑286, Apr 1989, b&w	2.25
❑287, Jun 1989, b&w	2.25
❑288, Jul 1989, b&w	2.25
❑289, Sep 1989, b&w; Batman parody	2.25
❑290, Oct 1989, b&w	2.25
❑291, Dec 1989, b&w; Teenage Mutant Ninja Turtles parody	2.25
❑292, Jan 1990, b&w	2.25
❑293, Mar 1990, b&w	2.25
❑294, Apr 1990, b&w	2.25
❑295, Jun 1990, b&w	2.25
❑296, Jul 1990, b&w	2.25
❑297, Sep 1990, b&w	2.25
❑298, Oct 1990, b&w	2.25
❑299, Dec 1990, b&w	2.25
❑300, Jan 1991, b&w	2.25
❑301, Mar 1991, b&w	2.00
❑302, Apr 1991, b&w	2.00
❑303, Jun 1991, b&w	2.00
❑304, Jul 1991, b&w	2.00
❑305, Sep 1991, b&w	2.00
❑306, Oct 1991, b&w	2.00
❑307, Dec 1991, b&w	2.00
❑308, Jan 1992, b&w	2.00
❑309, Mar 1992, b&w	2.00
❑310, Apr 1992, b&w	2.00
❑311, Jun 1992, b&w	2.00
❑312, Jul 1992, b&w	2.00
❑313, Sep 1992, b&w	2.00
❑314, Oct 1992, b&w	2.00

Other grades: Multiply price above by 5/6 for VF/NM • 2/3 for VERY FINE • 1/3 for FINE • 1/5 for VERY GOOD • 1/8 for GOOD

Magic: The Gathering: Antiquities War

Early comic based on trading-card game

©Acclaim

Magilla Gorilla (Gold Key)

Animated simian haunts pet store

©Gold Key

Magnus, Robot Fighter (Gold Key)

Robots gain free will and stage a revolution

©Gold Key

Magnus Robot Fighter (Valiant)

Valiant revives the old Gold Key series

©Valiant

Mai, the Psychic Girl

Wisdom Alliance pursues girl in manga import

©Eclipse

	N-MINT
❑315, Dec 1992, b&w	2.00
❑316, Jan 1993, b&w	2.00
❑317, Mar 1993, b&w	2.00
❑318, Apr 1993, b&w	2.00
❑319, Jun 1993, b&w	2.00
❑320, Jul 1993, b&w	2.00
❑321, Sep 1993, b&w; Star Trek: Deep Space Nine parody	2.00
❑322, Oct 1993, b&w	2.00
❑323, Dec 1993, b&w	2.00
❑324, Jan 1994, b&w	2.00
❑325, Feb 1994, b&w	2.00
❑326, Mar 1994, b&w	2.00
❑327, May 1994, b&w	2.00
❑328, Jun 1994, b&w	2.00
❑329, Jul 1994, b&w	2.00
❑330, Sep 1994, b&w	2.00
❑331, Oct 1994, b&w	1.75
❑332, Dec 1994, b&w	1.75
❑333, Jan 1995, b&w	1.75
❑334, Mar 1995, b&w	1.75
❑335, May 1995, b&w	1.75
❑336, Jun 1995, b&w	1.75
❑337, Jul 1995, b&w	1.75
❑338, Aug 1995, b&w	1.75
❑339, Sep 1995, b&w	1.75
❑340, Oct 1995, b&w	1.75
❑341, Dec 1995, b&w	1.75
❑342, Jan 1996, b&w	2.00
❑343, Mar 1996, b&w	2.50
❑344, Apr 1996, b&w	2.50
❑345, May 1996, b&w	2.50
❑346, Jun 1996, b&w	2.50
❑347, Jul 1996, b&w	2.50
❑348, Aug 1996, b&w	2.50
❑349, Sep 1996, b&w	2.50
❑350, Oct 1996, b&w	2.50
❑351, Nov 1996, b&w	2.50
❑352, Dec 1996, b&w	2.50
❑353, Jan 1997, b&w	2.50
❑354, Feb 1997, b&w	2.50
❑355, Mar 1997, b&w	2.50
❑356, Apr 1997, b&w	2.50
❑357, May 1997, b&w	2.50
❑358, Jun 1997, b&w	2.50
❑359, Jul 1997, b&w	2.50
❑360, Aug 1997, b&w	2.50
❑361, Sep 1997, b&w	2.50
❑362, Oct 1997, b&w	2.50
❑363, Nov 1997, b&w	2.50
❑364, Dec 1997, b&w	2.50
❑365, Jan 1998, b&w	2.50
❑366, Feb 1998, b&w	2.50
❑367, Mar 1998, b&w	2.50
❑368, Apr 1998, b&w	2.50
❑369, May 1998, b&w	2.50
❑370, Jun 1998, b&w	2.50
❑371, Jul 1998, b&w	2.50
❑372, Aug 1998, b&w	2.50
❑373, Sep 1998, b&w	2.50
❑374, Oct 1998, b&w	2.50
❑375, Nov 1998, b&w	2.50
❑376, Dec 1998, b&w	2.50
❑377, Jan 1999, b&w	2.95

	N-MINT
❑378, Feb 1999, b&w	2.50
❑379, Mar 1999, b&w	2.50
❑380, Apr 1999, b&w	2.75
❑381, May 1999, b&w	2.75
❑382, Jun 1999, b&w	2.75
❑383, Jul 1999, b&w	2.75
❑384, Aug 1999, b&w	2.75
❑385, Sep 1999, b&w	2.75
❑386, Oct 1999, b&w	2.75
❑387, Nov 1999, b&w	2.75
❑388, Dec 1999, b&w	2.75
❑389, Jan 2000, b&w	2.75
❑390, Feb 2000, b&w	2.75
❑391, Mar 2000, b&w	2.75
❑392, Apr 2000, b&w	2.75
❑393, May 2000, b&w	2.75
❑394, Jun 2000, b&w	2.99
❑395, Jul 2000, b&w	2.99
❑396, Aug 2000, b&w	2.99
❑397, Sep 2000, b&w	2.99
❑398, Oct 2000, b&w	2.99
❑399, Nov 2000, b&w	2.99
❑400, Dec 2000	2.99
❑401, Jan 2001	2.99
❑402, Feb 2001	2.99
❑403, Mar 2001	2.99
❑404, Apr 2001	2.99
❑405, May 2001	2.99
❑406, Jun 2001	2.99
❑407, Jul 2001	2.99
❑408, Aug 2001	2.99
❑409, Sep 2001	2.99
❑410, Oct 2001	2.99
❑411, Nov 2001	2.99
❑412, Dec 2001; MD (c); Special Harry Potter issue	2.99
❑413, Jan 2002	2.99
❑414, Feb 2002	2.99
❑415, Mar 2002	2.99
❑416, Apr 2002; Lord of the Rings	2.99
❑417, May 2002	2.99
❑418, Jun 2002; MD (c); Spider-Man	3.50
❑419, Jul 2002; Star Wars: Attack of the Clones	3.50
❑420, Aug 2002	3.50
❑421, Sep 2002	3.50
❑422, Oct 2002	3.50
❑423, Nov 2002; Golden (50th) Anniversary issue	3.50
❑424, Dec 2002	3.50
❑425, Jan 2003	3.50
❑426, Feb 2003	3.50
❑427, Mar 2003	3.50
❑428, Apr 2003	3.50
❑429, May 2003	3.50
❑430, Jun 2003	3.50
❑431, Jul 2003	3.50
❑432, Aug 2003	3.50
❑433, Sep 2003	3.50
❑434, Oct 2003	3.50
❑435, Nov 2003	3.50
❑436, Dec 2003	3.50
❑437, Jan 2004	3.50
❑438, Feb 2004	3.50

	N-MINT
❑439, Mar 2004	3.50
❑440, Apr 2004	3.50
❑441, May 2004	3.50
❑442, Jun 2004	3.50
❑443, Jul 2004	3.50
❑444, Aug 2004	3.50
❑445, Sep 2004	3.50
❑446, Oct 2004	3.50
❑447, Nov 2004	3.50
❑448, Dec 2004	3.50
❑449, Jan 2005	3.50
❑450, Feb 2005	3.50
❑451, Mar 2005	3.50
❑452, Apr 2005	3.50
❑453, May 2005	3.50
❑454, Jun 2005	3.99
❑455, Jul 2005	3.99
❑456, Aug 2005	3.99
❑457, Sep 2005	3.99
❑458, Oct 2005	3.99
❑459, Nov 2005	3.99
❑460, Dec 2005	3.99
❑461, Jan 2006	3.99
❑462, Mar 2006	3.99
❑463, Apr 2006	3.99
❑464, May 2006	3.99
❑465, Jun 2006	3.99
❑466, Jul 2006	3.99
❑467, Aug 2006	3.99
❑468, Sep 2006	3.99

MADAGASCAR
TOKYOPOP

❑1, Nov 2005	9.95

MADAME XANADU
DC

❑1, Jul 1981 BB, MR (a); O: Madame Xanadu	3.00

MADBALLS
MARVEL / STAR

❑1, Sep 1986 O: Madballs. 1: Madballs. 1: Colonel Corn	1.00
❑2, Oct 1986	1.00
❑3, Nov 1986	1.00
❑4, Jun 1987	1.00
❑5, Aug 1987	1.00
❑6, Oct 1987	1.00
❑7, Dec 1987	1.00
❑8, Feb 1988	1.00
❑9, Apr 1988	1.00
❑10, Jun 1988	1.00

MAD CLASSICS
DC

❑1, Jan 2005	4.95
❑2, Jan 2005	4.95
❑3, Feb 2006	4.95
❑4, Feb 2006	4.95
❑5, Mar 2006	4.95
❑6, May 2006	4.95
❑7, Jul 2006	4.95
❑8, Sep 2006	4.95

MAD-DOG
MARVEL

❑1, May 1993	1.25

Other grades: Multiply price above by 5/6 for VF/NM • 2/3 for VERY FINE • 1/3 for FINE • 1/5 for VERY GOOD • 1/8 for GOOD

❑2, Jun 1993 1.25
❑3, Jul 1993 1.25
❑4, Aug 1993 1.25
❑5, Sep 1993 1.25
❑6, Oct 1993 1.25

MAD DOG MAGAZINE
BLACKTHORNE

❑1, Nov 1986 1.75
❑2 1.75
❑3, Mar 1987 1.75

MAD DOGS
ECLIPSE

❑1 2.50
❑2 2.50
❑3 2.50

MAD FOLLIES
E.C.

❑1, ca. 1963 250.00
❑2, ca. 1964; Includes "Mad Mischief" Stickers 200.00
❑3, ca. 1965 150.00
❑4, ca. 1966; Includes Mad mobile 100.00
❑5, ca. 1967; Includes Mad stencils 100.00
❑6, ca. 1968; Includes "Mad Mischief" Stickers 100.00
❑7, ca. 1969; Includes "Nasty Cards" postcards 100.00

MADHOUSE GLADS
ARCHIE

❑73, May 1970, Previous issues published as Madhouse Ma-ad Freakout 3.00
❑74, Jul 1970 3.00
❑75, Sep 1970 3.00
❑76, Nov 1970 3.00
❑77, Feb 1971 3.00
❑78, May 1971 5.00
❑79, Aug 1971 5.00
❑80, Sep 1971 5.00
❑81, Nov 1971 5.00
❑82, Feb 1972 5.00
❑83, May 1972 5.00
❑84, Aug 1972 5.00
❑85, Oct 1972 5.00
❑86, Dec 1972 5.00
❑87, Feb 1973 5.00
❑88, May 1973 5.00
❑89, Aug 1973 5.00
❑90, Oct 1973 5.00
❑91, Dec 1973 5.00
❑92, Feb 1974 5.00
❑93, May 1974 3.00
❑94, Aug 1974, Later issues published as Madhouse 3.00

MADHOUSE MA-AD FREAKOUT
ARCHIE

❑71, ca. 1969, Earlier issues published as Madhouse Ma-ad Jokes 3.00
❑72, Jan 1970, Later issues published as Madhouse Glads 3.00

MADHOUSE MA-AD JOKES
ARCHIE

❑66, Feb 1969, Previous issues published as Archie's Madhouse 3.50
❑67, Apr 1969 3.50
❑68, Jun 1969 3.50
❑69, Aug 1969 3.50
❑70, Oct 1969, Series continues as Madhouse Ma-ad Freakout 3.50

MAD KIDS
DC

❑1, Dec 2005 3.99
❑2, Apr 2006 3.99
❑4, Jun 2006 3.99

MADMAN
TUNDRA

❑1/4th, Double-acetate cover 3.00
❑1, Mar 1992, b&w; prestige format; flip-action corners 8.00
❑1/2nd 5.00
❑1/3rd, Kitchen Sink publishes 4.00
❑2, Apr 1992 6.00
❑3, May 1992 6.00

MADMAN ADVENTURES
TUNDRA

❑1, ca. 1992 5.00
❑2, ca. 1993 4.00
❑3, ca. 1993 4.00

MADMAN BOOGALOO
DARK HORSE

❑Book 1, Jun 1999; Starring Nexus & The Jam 8.95

MADMAN COMICS
DARK HORSE

❑1, Apr 1994 FM (c); O: Madman 4.00
❑2, Jun 1994 3.50
❑3, Aug 1994 3.50
❑4, Oct 1994 3.00
❑5, Jan 1995 3.00
❑6, Mar 1995 3.00
❑7, May 1995 3.00
❑8, Jul 1995 3.00
❑9, Oct 1995 3.00
❑10, Jan 1996 ARo (c) 2.95
❑11, Oct 1996 2.95
❑12, Apr 1999; Doctor Robot back-up 2.95
❑13, May 1999; Doctor Robot back-up 2.95
❑14, Jun 1999; Doctor Robot back-up 2.95
❑15, Jul 1999; Doctor Robot back-up 2.95
❑16, Dec 1999 2.95
❑17, Aug 2000 2.95
❑18, Sep 2000 2.95
❑19, Oct 2000 2.99
❑20, Dec 2000 2.99

MADMAN PICTURE EXHIBITION
AAA POP

❑1, Apr 2002 3.95
❑2, May 2002 3.95
❑3, Jun 2002 3.95
❑4, Jul 2002 3.95

MADMAN/THE JAM
DARK HORSE

❑1, Jul 1998 2.95
❑2, Aug 1998 2.95

MAD MONSTER PARTY ADAPTATION
BLACK BEAR

❑1 2.95
❑2 2.95
❑3 2.95
❑4 2.95

MADONNA
PERSONALITY

❑1, b&w 2.95
❑1/Autographed, b&w 3.95
❑2, b&w 2.95
❑2/Autographed, b&w 3.95

MADONNA SEX GODDESS
FRIENDLY

❑1, ca. 1990 2.95
❑2, ca. 1991 2.95
❑3, ca. 1991 2.95

MADONNA SPECIAL
REVOLUTIONARY

❑1, Aug 1993, b&w 2.50

MADONNA VS. MARILYN
CELEBRITY

❑1 2.95

MAD RACCOONS
MU

❑1, Jul 1991 2.50
❑2, Sep 1992 2.50
❑3, Aug 1993 2.50
❑4, Aug 1994 2.95
❑5, Aug 1995; cardstock cover 2.95
❑6, Jul 1996; cardstock cover 2.95

MADRAVEN HALLOWEEN SPECIAL
HAMILTON

❑1, Oct 1995 2.95

MADROX
MARVEL

❑1, Nov 2004 2.99
❑2, Dec 2004 2.99
❑3, Jan 2005 2.99
❑4, Feb 2005 2.99
❑5, Mar 2005 2.99

MAD SUPER SPECIAL
E.C.

❑1, Fal 1970, b&w 90.00
❑2, Spr 1971, b&w 54.00
❑3 1971, b&w 44.00
❑4 1971, b&w 44.00
❑5 1971, b&w 44.00
❑6 1971, b&w 38.00
❑7 1972, b&w 38.00
❑8, b&w 38.00
❑9 1972, b&w 38.00
❑10 1973, b&w 38.00
❑11 1973, b&w 26.00
❑12 1974, b&w 26.00
❑13 1974, b&w 26.00
❑14 1974, b&w 26.00
❑15 1974, b&w 26.00
❑16 1975, b&w 20.00
❑17 1975, b&w 20.00
❑18 1975, b&w 20.00
❑19 1976, b&w 20.00
❑20 1976, b&w 20.00
❑21 1976, b&w 16.00
❑22 1977, b&w 16.00
❑23 1977, b&w 16.00
❑24 1977, b&w 16.00
❑25 1978, b&w 16.00
❑26 1978, b&w 12.00
❑27 1978, b&w 12.00
❑28, Fal 1979, b&w 12.00
❑29, Win 1979, b&w 12.00
❑30, Spr 1980, b&w 12.00
❑31, Sum 1980, b&w 10.00
❑32, Fal 1980, b&w 10.00
❑33, Win 1980, b&w 10.00
❑34, Spr 1981, b&w 10.00
❑35, Sum 1981, b&w 10.00
❑36, Fal 1981, b&w 10.00
❑37, Win 1981, b&w 10.00
❑38, Spr 1982, b&w 10.00
❑39, Sum 1982, b&w 10.00
❑40, Fal 1982, b&w 10.00
❑41, Win 1982, b&w 6.00
❑42, Win 1983, b&w 6.00
❑43, Spr 1983, b&w 6.00
❑44, Sum 1983, b&w 6.00
❑45, Fal 1983, b&w 6.00
❑46, Spr 1984, b&w 6.00
❑47, Sum 1984, b&w 6.00
❑48, Fal 1984, b&w 6.00
❑49, Win 1984, b&w 6.00
❑50, Spr 1985, b&w 6.00
❑51, Sum 1985, b&w 4.50
❑52, Fal 1985, b&w 4.50
❑53, Win 1985, b&w 4.50
❑54, Spr 1986, b&w 4.50
❑55, Sum 1986, b&w 4.50
❑56, Fal 1986, b&w 4.50
❑57, Win 1986, b&w 4.50
❑58, Spr 1987, b&w 4.50
❑59, Sum 1987, b&w 4.50
❑60, Fal 1987, b&w 4.50
❑61, Win 1987, b&w 4.00
❑62, Spr 1988, b&w 4.00
❑63, Sum 1988, b&w 4.00
❑64, Fal 1988, b&w 4.00
❑65, Win 1988, b&w 4.00
❑66, Spr 1989, b&w 4.00
❑67, Sum 1989, b&w 4.00
❑68, Fal 1989, b&w 4.00
❑69, Win 1989, b&w 4.00
❑70, Spr 1990, b&w 4.00
❑71, Sum 1990, b&w 3.50
❑72, Fal 1990, b&w 3.50
❑73, Win 1990, b&w 3.50
❑74, Spr 1991, b&w 3.50
❑75, Sum 1991, b&w 3.50
❑76, Fal 1991, b&w 3.50
❑77, Win 1991, b&w 3.50
❑78, Jan 1992, b&w 3.50
❑79, Feb 1992, b&w 3.50
❑80, Mar 1992, b&w 3.50
❑81, May 1992, b&w 3.50
❑82, Jul 1992, b&w 3.50
❑83, Sep 1992, b&w 3.50
❑84, Nov 1992, b&w 3.50
❑85, Jan 1993, b&w 3.50
❑86, Mar 1993, b&w 3.50
❑87, May 1993, b&w 3.50
❑88, Jul 1993, b&w 3.50

Maison Ikkoku Part 1

Rumiko Takahashi's long-running romance

©Viz

Major Bummer

Called by DC "The First Inaction Hero"

©DC

Man-Frog

Life in the carny in another book from the 1980s glut

©Mad Dog

Man from Atlantis

Bobby Ewing stars in so-so SF TV effort

©Marvel

Man from U.N.C.L.E.

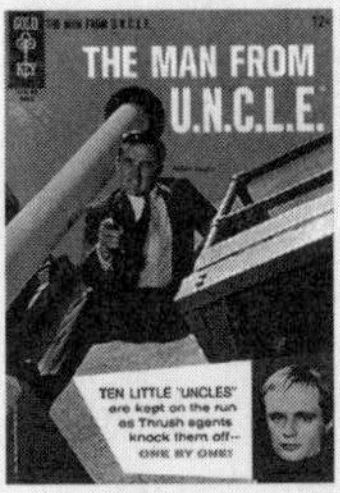

TV spy drama had a nice comics run

©Gold Key

	N-MINT
❑89, Sep 1993, b&w	3.50
❑90, Nov 1993, b&w	3.50
❑91, Jan 1994, b&w	3.50
❑92, Mar 1994, b&w	3.50
❑93, May 1994, b&w	3.50
❑94, Jul 1994, b&w	3.50
❑95, Sep 1994, b&w	3.50
❑96, Spr 1994, b&w	3.50
❑97, b&w	3.50
❑98, b&w	3.50
❑99, b&w	3.50
❑100, b&w	3.99
❑101, b&w	3.99
❑102, Spr 1995, b&w	3.99
❑103, Apr 1995, b&w	3.99
❑104, Jun 1995, b&w	3.99
❑105, Jul 1995, b&w	3.99
❑106 1995, b&w	3.99
❑107, Oct 1995, b&w	3.99
❑108 1995, b&w	3.99
❑109 1996, b&w	3.99
❑110 1996, b&w	3.99
❑111 1996, b&w	3.99
❑112 1996, b&w	3.99
❑113 1996, b&w	3.99
❑114, Jul 1996, b&w	3.99
❑115 1996, b&w	3.99
❑116, Oct 1996, b&w	3.99
❑117, Dec 1996, b&w	3.99
❑118, Feb 1997, b&w	3.99
❑119, Apr 1997, b&w	3.99
❑120 1997, b&w	3.99
❑121 1997, b&w	3.99
❑122 1997, b&w	3.99
❑123 1997, b&w	3.99
❑124 1997, b&w	3.99
❑125 1997, b&w	3.99
❑126, Jan 1998, b&w	3.99
❑127, Mar 1998, b&w	3.99
❑128, Jun 1998, b&w	3.99
❑129, Jul 1998, b&w	3.99
❑130, Aug 1998	3.99
❑131, Oct 1998	3.99
❑132, Nov 1998	3.99
❑133, Jan 1998	3.99
❑134, Mar 1999	3.99
❑135, Jun 1999	3.99

MAEL'S RAGE
OMINOUS

❑2, Aug 1994	2.50
❑2/Variant, Aug 1994; cardstock outer cover	2.50

MAELSTROM
AIRCEL

❑1, Jun 1987	1.70
❑2, Jul 1987	1.70
❑3, Aug 1987	1.70
❑4, Sep 1987	1.70
❑5, Oct 1987	1.50
❑6, Nov 1987	1.50
❑7, Dec 1987	1.50
❑8, Jan 1988	1.50
❑9, Feb 1988	1.50
❑10, Mar 1988	1.50

MAGDALENA
IMAGE

	N-MINT
❑1, Apr 2000	2.50
❑1/A, Apr 2000, 2000 Megacon Exclusive	2.50
❑1/B, Apr 2000, Alternate cover with Magdalena standing, cross at bottom center of design	2.50
❑2, Jun 2000	2.50
❑3, Jan 2001	2.50
❑3/A, Jan 2001, Alternate cover with Eruptor logo and foil additions	2.50

MAGDALENA (VOL. 2)
IMAGE

❑1, Jul 2003	2.99
❑1/A, Jul 2003	5.00
❑2, Aug 2003	2.99
❑3, Oct 2003	2.99
❑4, Dec 2003	2.99

MAGDALENA/ANGELUS
IMAGE

❑0	2.95
❑½, Nov 2001	2.95

MAGDALENA/VAMPIRELLA
IMAGE

❑1, Jun 2003	2.99

MAGE
COMICO

❑1, May 1984 MW (w); MW (a); 1: Kevin Matchstick	5.00
❑2, Jul 1984 MW (w); MW (a)	4.00
❑3, Sep 1984 MW (w); MW (a)	3.00
❑4, Nov 1984 MW (w); MW (a)	3.00
❑5, Jan 1985 MW (w); MW (a)	3.00
❑6, Mar 1985; MW (w); MW (a); 1: Grendel I (Hunter Rose) (in color). Grendel	15.00
❑7, May 1985 MW (w); MW (a); A: Grendel I (Hunter Rose)	8.00
❑8, Jul 1985 MW (w); MW (a); A: Grendel I (Hunter Rose)	4.00
❑9, Sep 1985 MW (w); MW (a); A: Grendel I (Hunter Rose)	3.00
❑10, Dec 1985 MW (w); MW (a); A: Grendel I (Hunter Rose)	3.00
❑11, Feb 1986 MW (w); MW (a); A: Grendel I (Hunter Rose)	3.00
❑12, Apr 1986 MW (w); MW (a); A: Grendel I (Hunter Rose)	3.00
❑13, Jun 1986 MW (w); MW (a); D: Grendel I (Hunter Rose). D: Edsel	4.00
❑14, Aug 1986 MW (w); MW (a); A: Grendel	3.00
❑15, Dec 1986; Giant-size MW (w); MW (a)	6.00

MAGE (IMAGE)
IMAGE

❑0, Jul 1997; MW (a); American Entertainment Exclusive	3.00
❑0/Autographed, Jul 1997 MW (a)	5.00
❑1, Jul 1997 MW (w); MW (a)	4.00
❑1/3D, Feb 1998; 3-D edition; MW (w); MW (a); with glasses	4.95
❑2, Aug 1997 MW (w); MW (a)	3.50
❑3, Sep 1997 MW (w); MW (a)	3.50
❑4, Nov 1997 MW (w); MW (a)	3.00

	N-MINT
❑5, Jan 1998 MW (w); MW (a)	3.00
❑6, Mar 1998 MW (w); MW (a)	2.50
❑7, Apr 1998 MW (w); MW (a)	2.50
❑8, Jun 1998 MW (w); MW (a)	2.50
❑9, Sep 1998 MW (w); MW (a)	2.50
❑10, Dec 1998 MW (w); MW (a)	2.50
❑11, Feb 1999 MW (w); MW (a)	2.50
❑12, Apr 1999 MW (w); MW (a)	2.50
❑13/A, Jun 1999; MW (a); covers form triptych	2.50
❑13/B, Jun 1999; MW (a); Mage cover	2.50
❑13/C, Jun 1999 MW (a)	2.50
❑14, Aug 1999 MW (w); MW (a)	2.50
❑15, Oct 1999 MW (w); MW (a)	2.50
❑15/Variant, Oct 1999; MW (w); MW (a); Special acetate double-cover	5.95

MAGEBOOK
COMICO

❑1 1985	8.95
❑2 1985	7.95

MAGE KNIGHT: STOLEN DESTINY
IDEA & DESIGN WORKS

❑1 2002	3.50
❑2 2002	3.50
❑3, Dec 2002	3.50
❑4, Feb 2003	3.50
❑5, Mar 2003	3.50

MAGE: THE HERO DISCOVERED
IMAGE

❑1, Oct 1998; Reprints #1-2 of the Comico series	4.95
❑2, Dec 1998; Reprints #3-4 of the Comico series	4.95
❑3, Feb 1999; Reprints #5-6 of the Comico series	4.95
❑4, Apr 1999; Reprints #7-8 of the Comico series	4.95
❑5, Jun 1999; Reprints #9-10 of the Comico series	4.95
❑6, Jul 1999; Reprints #11-12 of the Comico series	4.95
❑7, Aug 1999; Reprints #13-14 of the Comico series	4.95
❑8, Sep 1999; Reprints #15 of the Comico series plus other material	4.95

MAGGIE AND HOPEY COLOR SPECIAL
FANTAGRAPHICS

❑1, May 1997	3.50

MAGGIE THE CAT
IMAGE

❑1, Jan 1996	2.50
❑2, Mar 1996	2.50
❑3 1996, Exists?	2.50
❑4 1996, Exists?	2.50

MAGGOTS
HAMILTON

❑1, Nov 1991, b&w	3.95
❑2 1992, b&w	3.95
❑3 1992, b&w	3.95

MAGICAL MATES
ANTARCTIC

❑1, Feb 1996	2.95
❑2, Apr 1996	2.95
❑3, Jun 1996	2.95

N-MINT

❑4, Aug 1996 2.95
❑5, Oct 1996 2.95
❑6, Dec 1996 2.95
❑7 1997 2.95
❑8 1997 2.95
❑9 1997 2.95

MAGICAL NYMPHINI
RIP OFF

❑1, Feb 1991, b&w 2.50
❑1/2nd 2.50
❑2, Apr 1991, b&w 2.50
❑2/2nd 2.50
❑3, Aug 1991, b&w 2.50
❑3/2nd 2.50
❑4, Dec 1991, b&w 2.95
❑4/2nd 2.95
❑5, Aug 1992, b&w 2.95
❑5/2nd 2.95

MAGICAL TWILIGHT
GRAPHIC VISIONS

❑1 2.95

MAGIC BOY AND GIRLFRIEND
TOP SHELF

❑1, Jul 1998, b&w 8.95

MAGIC BOY & THE ROBOT ELF
SLAVE LABOR

❑1, May 1996 9.95

MAGIC CARPET
SHANDA FANTASY ARTS

❑1, Apr 1999, b&w 4.50

MAGIC FLUTE
ECLIPSE

❑1, ca. 1990; Part of Eclipse's Night Music series 4.95
❑2, ca. 1990 4.95
❑3, ca. 1990 4.95

MAGICIANS' VILLAGE
MAD MONKEY

❑1, ca. 1995 2.45

MAGIC INKWELL COMIC STRIP THEATRE
MOORDAM

❑1, Mar 1998 2.95

MAGIC KNIGHT RAYEARTH
MIXX

❑1 11.95
❑2 11.95
❑3 11.95
❑4 11.95
❑5 12.95
❑6 12.95

MAGICMAN
A-PLUS

❑1, b&w; Reprints 2.95

MAGIC PICKLE
ONI

❑1 2001 2.95
❑2 2001 2.95
❑3 2001 2.95
❑4 2.95

MAGIC PRIEST
ANTARCTIC

❑1, Jun 1998, b&w 2.95

MAGIC: THE GATHERING: ANTIQUITIES WAR
ACCLAIM / ARMADA

❑1, Nov 1995 2.50
❑2, Dec 1995 2.50
❑3, Jan 1996 2.50
❑4, Feb 1996 2.50

MAGIC: THE GATHERING: ELDER DRAGONS
ACCLAIM / ARMADA

❑1, Apr 1996 2.50
❑2, May 1996 2.50

MAGIC: THE GATHERING: GERARD'S QUEST
DARK HORSE

❑1, Mar 1998 2.95
❑2, Apr 1998 2.95
❑3, May 1998 2.95
❑4, Sep 1998 2.95

N-MINT

MAGIC: THE GATHERING: NIGHTMARE
ACCLAIM / ARMADA

❑1, ca. 1995 2.50

MAGIC: THE GATHERING: SHANDALAR
ACCLAIM / ARMADA

❑1, Mar 1996 2.50
❑2, Apr 1996 2.50

MAGIC: THE GATHERING: THE SHADOW MAGE
ACCLAIM / ARMADA

❑1, Jul 1995; bound-in Fireball card 2.50
❑2, Aug 1995; bound-in Blue Elemental card 2.50
❑3, Sep 1995; bagged with Magic: The Gathering tokens and counters 2.50
❑4, Oct 1995; polybagged with sheet of creature tokens 2.50

MAGIC: THE GATHERING: WAYFARER
ACCLAIM / ARMADA

❑1, Nov 1995 2.50
❑2, Dec 1995 2.50
❑3, Jan 1996 2.50
❑4, Feb 1996 2.50
❑5, Mar 1996 2.50

MAGIC WHISTLE
ALTERNATIVE

❑1, b&w 2.95
❑2, b&w 2.95

MAGIC WORDS (ALAN MOORE'S...)
AVATAR

❑1, Nov 2002, b&w 6.95

MAGIK
MARVEL

❑1, Dec 1983, TP (a) 2.25
❑2, Jan 1984, TP (a) 2.00
❑3, Feb 1984, TP (a) 2.00
❑4, Mar 1984, TP (a) 2.00

MAGIK (2ND SERIES)
MARVEL

❑1, Dec 2000 2.99
❑2, Jan 2001 2.99
❑3, Feb 2001 2.99
❑4, Mar 2001 2.99

MAGILLA GORILLA (GOLD KEY)
GOLD KEY

❑1, ca. 1964 30.00
❑2, ca. 1964 15.00
❑3, Dec 1964 12.00
❑4, ca. 1965 12.00
❑5, ca. 1965 12.00
❑6, Aug 1965 10.00
❑7, Nov 1965 10.00
❑8, Jul 1966 10.00
❑9 10.00
❑10, Dec 1968 10.00

MAGNA-MAN: THE LAST SUPERHERO
COMICS INTERVIEW

❑1, b&w 1.95
❑2, Sum 1988, b&w 1.95
❑3, Sum 1988, b&w 1.95

MAGNESIUM ARC
ICONOGRAFIX

❑1 3.50

MAGNETIC MEN FEATURING MAGNETO
MARVEL / AMALGAM

❑1, Jun 1997 1.95

MAGNETO
MARVEL

❑0, Sep 1993, retailer giveaway; JDu (a); O: Magneto. no cover price; Promotional give-away; Reprints "A Fire in the Sky" from X-Men Classic #19; Reprints "I Magneto" From X-Men Classic #12 3.00

MAGNETO (LTD. SERIES)
MARVEL

❑1, Nov 1996 2.00
❑2, Dec 1996 2.00
❑3, Jan 1997 2.00
❑4, Feb 1997 2.00

N-MINT

MAGNETO AND THE MAGNETIC MEN
MARVEL / AMALGAM

❑1, Apr 1996 1.95

MAGNETO ASCENDANT
MARVEL

❑1, Apr 1999; Reprints Magneto Stories from X-Men (1st Series) 3.99

MAGNETO: DARK SEDUCTION
MARVEL

❑1, Jun 2000 2.99
❑2, Jul 2000 2.99
❑3, Aug 2000 2.99
❑4, Sep 2000 2.99

MAGNETO REX
MARVEL

❑1, Apr 1999 2.50
❑2, Jun 1999 2.50
❑3, Jul 1999 2.50

MAGNETS: ROBOT DISMANTLER
PARODY

❑1, b&w; Foil-embossed cover 2.50

MAGNUS, ROBOT FIGHTER (GOLD KEY)
GOLD KEY

❑1, Feb 1963, O: Magnus. 1: Leeja Clane. 1: Magnus 200.00
❑2, May 1963 125.00
❑3, Aug 1963 125.00
❑4, Nov 1963 60.00
❑5, Feb 1964 60.00
❑6, May 1964, RM (a); Keys Of Knowledge: Atomic Energy #7: Atoms That Explode; Keys of Knowledge: Physical Fitness #11: Twisting and Bending 60.00
❑7, Aug 1964 60.00
❑8, Nov 1964 60.00
❑9, Feb 1965 60.00
❑10, May 1965 60.00
❑11, Aug 1965 35.00
❑12, Nov 1965 35.00
❑13, Feb 1966, 1: Doctor Noel 35.00
❑14, May 1966 35.00
❑15, Aug 1966 35.00
❑16, Nov 1966 35.00
❑17, Feb 1967 35.00
❑18, May 1967 35.00
❑19, Aug 1967 35.00
❑20, Nov 1967 35.00
❑21, Feb 1968 20.00
❑22, May 1968, O: Magnus. 1: Leeja Clane. 1: Magnus. Reprints Magnus, Robot Fighter (Gold Key) #1 20.00
❑23, Aug 1968, DS (a); Reprints 20.00
❑24, Nov 1968, Destruction of Malev-6 20.00
❑25, Feb 1969 20.00
❑26, May 1969 20.00
❑27, Aug 1969 20.00
❑28, Nov 1969, goes on hiatus 20.00
❑29, Nov 1971 10.00
❑30, Jan 1972 10.00
❑31, Apr 1972 10.00
❑32, Jul 1972 10.00
❑33, Oct 1972 10.00
❑34, Jan 1973 10.00
❑35, May 1974 10.00
❑36, Aug 1974 10.00
❑37, Nov 1974 10.00
❑38, Feb 1975 10.00
❑39, May 1975 10.00
❑40, Aug 1975 10.00
❑41, Nov 1975 10.00
❑42, Jan 1976 10.00
❑43, May 1976 10.00
❑44, Aug 1976 10.00
❑45, Oct 1976 10.00
❑45/Whitman, Oct 1976 18.00
❑46, Jan 1977 10.00

MAGNUS ROBOT FIGHTER (VALIANT)
VALIANT

❑0/card, ca. 1992 40.00
❑0/no card, ca. 1992 30.00
❑1, May 1991; O: Magnus. trading cards 10.00
❑2, Jul 1991 8.00
❑3, Aug 1991 1: Tekla 5.00

Other grades: Multiply price above by 5/6 for VF/NM • 2/3 for VERY FINE • 1/3 for FINE • 1/5 for VERY GOOD • 1/8 for GOOD

Man of Steel (Mini-Series)

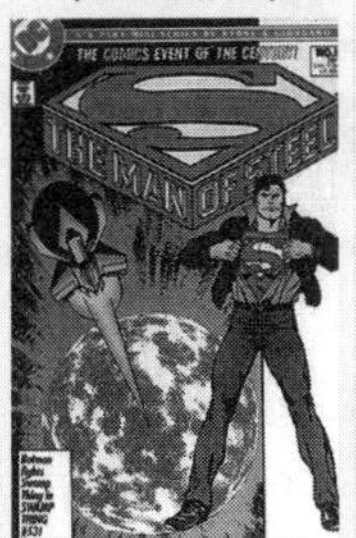

Byrne series rebooted Superman's history

©DC

Man-Thing (Vol. 1)

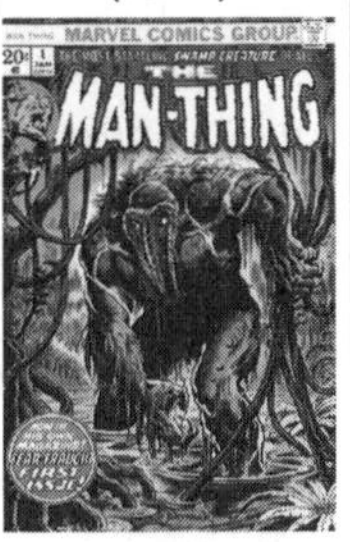

Swamp monster ruins lives, carpets

©Marvel

Mantra

Warrior's mind is transplanted into woman's body

©Malibu

Marc Spector: Moon Knight

Third comics series for man with many identities

©Marvel

Marines Attack

Interesting stories from veteran Sam Glanzman

©Charlton

	N-MINT
❑4, Sep 1991	5.00
❑5, Oct 1991; Flip-book; 1: Rai. Flip-book with Rai #1	6.00
❑6, Nov 1991; Flip-book A: Rai. A: Solar	6.00
❑7, Dec 1991; Flip-book A: Rai. V: Rai	4.00
❑8, Jan 1992; Flip-book A: Rai	4.00
❑9, Feb 1992	3.00
❑10, Mar 1992	3.00
❑11, Apr 1992	6.00
❑12, May 1992; Giant-size 1: Turok (Valiant). A: Turok	20.00
❑13, Jun 1992	3.00
❑14, Jul 1992	3.00
❑15, Aug 1992; FM (c); FM (a); Unity	3.00
❑16, Sep 1992; Unity	3.00
❑17, Nov 1992	2.00
❑18, Nov 1992 SD (w);	2.00
❑19, Dec 1992 SD (w);	2.00
❑20, Jan 1993	2.00
❑21, Feb 1993; New logo	2.00
❑21/Gold, Feb 1993; Gold edition; New logo	20.00
❑22, Mar 1993	2.00
❑23, Apr 1993	2.00
❑24, May 1993; Story leads into Rai and the Future Force #9	2.00
❑25, Jun 1993; BL (c); Silver embossed cover	2.00
❑25/VVSS, Jun 1993	15.00
❑26, Jul 1993	1.00
❑27, Aug 1993	1.00
❑28, Sep 1993	1.00
❑29, Oct 1993 A: Eternal Warrior	1.00
❑30, Nov 1993 A: X-O	1.00
❑31, Dec 1993	1.00
❑32, Jan 1994	1.00
❑33, Feb 1994 A: Timewalker	1.00
❑34, Mar 1994	1.00
❑35, Apr 1994	1.00
❑36, May 1994; trading card	2.00
❑37, Jun 1994 A: Starwatchers. A: Rai	1.00
❑38, Aug 1994	1.00
❑39, Sep 1994 A: Torque	1.00
❑40, Oct 1994	1.00
❑41, Nov 1994; Chaos Effect Epsilon 4	1.00
❑42, Dec 1994	1.00
❑43, Jan 1995	1.00
❑44, Feb 1995	3.00
❑45, Mar 1995	2.00
❑46, Apr 1995	2.00
❑47, May 1995	2.00
❑48, Jun 1995	2.00
❑49, Jul 1995	2.00
❑50, Jul 1995; Birthquake	2.00
❑51, Aug 1995; Birthquake	2.00
❑52, Aug 1995; Birthquake	2.00
❑53, Sep 1995	2.00
❑54, Sep 1995	2.00
❑55, Oct 1995	3.00
❑56, Oct 1995	3.00
❑57, Nov 1995	3.00
❑57/error, Nov 1995	10.00
❑58, Nov 1995	3.00
❑59, Dec 1995	3.00
❑60, Dec 1995	3.00
❑61, Jan 1996	4.00
❑62, Jan 1996; Torque becomes a Psi-Lord	4.00
❑63, Feb 1996	5.00
❑64, Feb 1996 D: Magnus, Robot Fighter (Valiant)	12.00
❑Yearbook 1, ca. 1994; cardstock cover	5.00

MAGNUS ROBOT FIGHTER (ACCLAIM)
ACCLAIM

	N-MINT
❑1, May 1997	2.50
❑1/Variant, May 1997, b&w; alternate painted cover	2.50
❑2, Jun 1997	2.50
❑3, Jul 1997	2.50
❑4, Aug 1997	2.50
❑5, Sep 1997	2.50
❑6, Oct 1997	2.50
❑7, Nov 1997; Gold Key homage cover	2.50
❑8, Dec 1997	2.50
❑9, Jan 1998	2.50
❑10, Feb 1998	2.50
❑11, Mar 1998	2.50
❑12, Apr 1998	2.50
❑13, Jan 1998; No cover date; indicia says Jan	2.50
❑14, Feb 1998; No cover date; indicia says Feb	2.50
❑15, Mar 1998	2.50
❑16, Apr 1998	2.50
❑17, May 1998	2.50
❑18, Jun 1998	2.50
❑Ashcan 1, Jan 1997, b&w; No cover price; preview of upcoming series	1.00

MAGNUS ROBOT FIGHTER/NEXUS
VALIANT / DARK HORSE

	N-MINT
❑0/Preview, ca. 1994	10.00
❑1, Dec 1993; covers says Mar, indicia says Dec	3.00
❑2, Apr 1994 SR (a)	3.00

MAGUS
CALIBER

	N-MINT
❑1	2.95
❑1/A; Variant cover of Girl praying in foreground, Magus behind	2.95
❑2	2.95

MAHOROMATIC: AUTOMATIC MAIDEN
TOKYOPOP

	N-MINT
❑1, May 2004	9.99
❑2, Jul 2004	9.99
❑3, Sep 2004	9.99
❑4, Dec 2004	9.99
❑5, Mar 2005	9.99
❑6, Jan 2005	9.99
❑7, Oct 2005	9.99

MAINE ZOMBIE LOBSTERMEN
MAINE STREAM COMICS

	N-MINT
❑1, b&w	2.50
❑2, b&w	2.50
❑3, b&w	3.50

MAI, THE PSYCHIC GIRL
ECLIPSE / VIZ

	N-MINT
❑1, May 1987, b&w; Japanese	3.50
❑1/2nd 1987	2.00
❑2, Jun 1987	2.50
❑2/2nd 1987	2.00
❑3, Jun 1987	2.50
❑4, Jul 1987	2.00
❑5, Jul 1987	2.00
❑6, Aug 1987	1.75
❑7, Aug 1987	1.75
❑8, Sep 1987	1.75
❑9, Sep 1987	1.75
❑10, Oct 1987	1.75
❑11, Oct 1987	1.75
❑12, Nov 1987	1.75
❑13, Nov 1987	1.75
❑14, Dec 1987	1.75
❑15, Dec 1987	1.75
❑16, Jan 1988	1.75
❑17, Jan 1988	1.75
❑18, Feb 1988	1.75
❑19, Feb 1988	1.75
❑20, Mar 1988	1.75
❑21, Mar 1988	1.75
❑22, Apr 1988	1.75
❑23, Apr 1988	1.75
❑24, May 1988	1.75
❑25, May 1988	1.75
❑26, Jun 1988	1.75
❑27, Jun 1988	1.75
❑28, Jul 1988	1.75

MAISON IKKOKU PART 1
VIZ

	N-MINT
❑1, Jun 1992	4.00
❑2, Jul 1992	3.50
❑3, Aug 1992	3.50
❑4, Sep 1992	3.50
❑5, Oct 1992	3.50
❑6, Nov 1992	3.50
❑7, Dec 1992	3.50

MAISON IKKOKU PART 2
VIZ

	N-MINT
❑1, Jan 1993	3.50
❑2, Feb 1993	3.00
❑3, Mar 1993	3.00
❑4, Apr 1993	3.00
❑5, May 1993	3.00
❑6, Jun 1993	3.00

MAISON IKKOKU PART 3
VIZ

	N-MINT
❑1, Jul 1993	3.00
❑2, Aug 1993	3.00
❑3, Sep 1993	3.00
❑4, Oct 1993	3.00
❑5, Nov 1993	3.00
❑6, Dec 1993	3.00

MAISON IKKOKU PART 4
VIZ

	N-MINT
❑1, Jan 1994	2.95
❑2, Feb 1994	2.95
❑3, Apr 1994	2.95
❑4, May 1994	2.95
❑5, Jun 1994	2.95
❑6, Jul 1994	2.95
❑7, Aug 1994	2.95

N-MINT

- ❑8, Sep 1994 ... 2.95
- ❑9, Oct 1994 ... 2.95
- ❑10, Nov 1994 ... 2.95

MAISON IKKOKU PART 5
VIZ

- ❑1, Nov 1995 ... 2.95
- ❑2, Dec 1995 ... 2.95
- ❑3, Jan 1996 ... 3.50
- ❑4, Feb 1996 ... 3.50
- ❑5, Mar 1996 ... 3.50
- ❑6, Apr 1996 ... 2.95
- ❑7, May 1996 ... 3.50
- ❑8, Jun 1996 ... 3.50
- ❑9, Jul 1996 ... 2.75

MAISON IKKOKU PART 6
VIZ

- ❑1, Aug 1996 ... 3.50
- ❑2, Sep 1996 ... 2.95
- ❑3, Oct 1996 ... 3.50
- ❑4, Nov 1996 ... 3.50
- ❑5, Dec 1996 ... 2.95
- ❑6, Jan 1997 ... 3.50
- ❑7, Feb 1997 ... 2.95
- ❑8, Mar 1997 ... 2.95
- ❑9, Apr 1997 ... 2.95
- ❑10, May 1997 ... 2.95
- ❑11, Jun 1997 ... 3.50

MAISON IKKOKU PART 7
VIZ

- ❑1, Jul 1997 ... 3.50
- ❑2, Aug 1997 ... 3.50
- ❑3, Sep 1997 ... 3.25
- ❑4, Oct 1997 ... 3.25
- ❑5, Nov 1997 ... 3.25
- ❑6, Dec 1997 ... 3.25
- ❑7, Jan 1998 ... 3.25
- ❑8, Feb 1998 ... 3.25
- ❑9, Mar 1998 ... 3.25
- ❑10, Apr 1998 ... 3.25
- ❑11, May 1998 ... 3.25
- ❑12, Jun 1998 ... 3.25
- ❑13, Jul 1998 ... 3.25

MAISON IKKOKU PART 8
VIZ

- ❑1, Aug 1998 ... 3.25
- ❑2, Sep 1998 ... 3.50
- ❑3, Oct 1998 ... 2.95
- ❑4, Nov 1998 ... 3.50
- ❑5, Dec 1998 ... 3.50
- ❑6, Jan 1999 ... 3.50
- ❑7, Feb 1999 ... 3.50
- ❑8, Mar 1999 ... 3.25

MAISON IKKOKU PART 9
VIZ

- ❑1, Apr 1999 ... 3.25
- ❑2, May 1999 ... 3.25
- ❑3, Jun 1999 ... 3.25
- ❑4, Jul 1999 ... 3.25
- ❑5, Aug 1999 ... 3.25
- ❑6, Sep 1999 ... 3.25
- ❑7, Oct 1999 ... 3.25
- ❑8, Nov 1999 ... 3.25
- ❑9, Dec 1999 ... 3.25
- ❑10, Jan 2000 ... 2.95

MAJCANS
P.S.

- ❑1 ... 1.00

MAJESTIC (1ST SERIES)
DC

- ❑1, Oct 2004 ... 2.95
- ❑2, Nov 2004 ... 2.95
- ❑3, Dec 2004 ... 2.95
- ❑4, Jan 2005 ... 2.95
- ❑5, Jun 2005 ... 2.99

MAJESTIC (2ND SERIES)
DC / WILDSTORM

- ❑1, Feb 2005 ... 2.95
- ❑2, Mar 2005 ... 2.95
- ❑3, Apr 2005 ... 2.95
- ❑4, May 2005 ... 2.95
- ❑5, Jun 2005 ... 2.95
- ❑6, Jul 2005 ... 2.99
- ❑7, Aug 2005 ... 2.99
- ❑8, Sep 2005 ... 2.99
- ❑9, Oct 2005 ... 2.99
- ❑10 ... 2.99
- ❑11, Jan 2006 ... 2.99
- ❑12, Feb 2006 ... 2.99
- ❑13, Mar 2006 ... 2.99
- ❑14, Apr 2006 ... 2.99
- ❑15, May 2006 ... 2.99
- ❑16, Jun 2006 ... 2.99

MAJOR BUMMER
DC

- ❑1, Aug 1997 O: Major Bummer. 1: The Gecko. 1: Major Bummer ... 3.00
- ❑2, Sep 1997 ... 2.50
- ❑3, Oct 1997 ... 2.50
- ❑4, Nov 1997 ... 2.50
- ❑5, Dec 1997; Face cover ... 2.50
- ❑6, Jan 1998 ... 2.50
- ❑7, Feb 1998 ... 2.50
- ❑8, Mar 1998 ... 2.50
- ❑9, Apr 1998 ... 2.50
- ❑10, May 1998 ... 2.50
- ❑11, Jun 1998 ... 2.50
- ❑12, Jul 1998 ... 2.50
- ❑13, Aug 1998 ... 2.50
- ❑14, Sep 1998 ... 2.50
- ❑15, Oct 1998 ... 2.50

MAJOR DAMAGE
INVICTUS

- ❑1, Oct 1994 ... 2.25
- ❑2 ... 2.25

MAJOR INAPAK THE SPACE ACE
MAGAZINE ENTERPRISES

- ❑1, ca. 1952 ... 8.00

MAJOR POWER AND SPUNKY
FANTAGRAPHICS / EROS

- ❑1, Oct 1994; one shot ... 3.50

MAKEBELIEVE
LIAR

- ❑1 ... 2.95

MALCOLM-10
ONLI

- ❑1, b&w ... 2.00

MALCOLM X (MILLENNIUM)
MILLENNIUM

- ❑1 ... 3.95

MALCOLM X, THE ANGRIEST MAN IN AMERICA
LONDON PUBLISHING

- ❑1, British ... 6.50

MALIBU ASHCAN: ULTRAFORCE
MALIBU / ULTRAVERSE

- ❑1, Jun 1994 ... 0.75

MALIBU SIGNATURE SERIES
MALIBU

- ❑1993; autograph book giveaway ... 0.25
- ❑1994; autograph book giveaway ... 0.25

MALICE IN WONDERLAND
FANTAGRAPHICS / EROS

- ❑1, Aug 1993, b&w ... 2.75

MALINKY ROBOT BICYCLE
SLAVE LABOR

- ❑1, Dec 2005 ... 3.95

MALLIMALOU
CHANCE

- ❑1 ... 1.50

MAN AGAINST TIME
IMAGE

- ❑1, May 1996 ... 2.25
- ❑1/A, May 1996 ... 2.25
- ❑2, Jun 1996 ... 2.25
- ❑3, Jul 1996 ... 2.25
- ❑4, Aug 1996 ... 2.25
- ❑5, Sep 1996 ... 2.25
- ❑6, Oct 1996 ... 2.25

MAN-BAT (1ST SERIES)
DC

- ❑1, Dec 1975, SD (a) ... 10.00
- ❑2, Feb 1976, SD (a) ... 4.00

MAN-BAT (2ND SERIES)
DC

- ❑1, Dec 1984; Reprints ... 2.50

MAN-BAT (MINI-SERIES)
DC

- ❑1, Feb 1996 ... 2.50
- ❑2, Mar 1996, A: Killer Croc ... 2.50
- ❑3, Apr 1996 ... 2.50

MAN-BAT (2ND MINI-SERIES)
DC

- ❑1, Jun 2006 ... 2.99
- ❑3, Sep 2006 ... 2.99
- ❑4, Sep 2006 ... 2.99

MAN CALLED A-X
MALIBU / BRAVURA

- ❑0, Feb 1995; Published between #3 and #4 ... 2.95
- ❑1, Nov 1994 ... 2.95
- ❑1/A, Nov 1994 ... 2.95
- ❑2, Dec 1994 ... 2.95
- ❑3, Jan 1995 ... 2.95
- ❑4, Feb 1995 ... 2.95
- ❑5, Mar 1995 ... 2.95

MAN CALLED A-X (DC)
DC

- ❑1, Oct 1997; follows events in Malibu/Bravura series ... 2.50
- ❑2, Nov 1997 ... 2.50
- ❑3, Dec 1997 ... 2.50
- ❑4, Jan 1998 ... 2.50
- ❑5, Feb 1998 ... 2.50
- ❑6, Mar 1998 ... 2.50
- ❑7, Apr 1998 ... 2.50
- ❑8, May 1998 ... 2.50

MAN CALLED LOCO
AVALON

- ❑1 ... 2.50

MANDRAKE THE MAGICIAN (KING)
KING

- ❑1, Sep 1966 ... 32.00
- ❑2, Nov 1966 ... 20.00
- ❑3, Jan 1967 ... 14.00
- ❑4, Mar 1967 ... 13.00
- ❑5, May 1967, Flying saucer story ... 13.00
- ❑6, Jul 1967 ... 10.00
- ❑7, Aug 1967 ... 10.00
- ❑8, Sep 1967, JJ (a) ... 16.00
- ❑9, Oct 1967 ... 9.00
- ❑10, Nov 1967, AR (a) ... 24.00

MANDRAKE THE MAGICIAN
MARVEL

- ❑1, Apr 1995; cardstock cover ... 2.95
- ❑2, May 1995; cardstock cover ... 2.95

MAN-EATING COW
NEC

- ❑1, Jul 1992 ... 4.50
- ❑2, Nov 1992 ... 3.50
- ❑3, Jan 1993 ... 3.50
- ❑4, Apr 1993; Scarcer ... 3.50
- ❑5, Jun 1993 ... 3.00
- ❑6, Aug 1993 ... 2.75
- ❑7, Nov 1993 ... 2.75
- ❑8, Jan 1994 ... 2.75
- ❑9 1994 A: The Tick ... 3.00
- ❑10 1994 A: The Tick ... 3.00

MAN-FROG
MAD DOG

- ❑1, Jul 1987, b&w ... 2.00
- ❑2, b&w ... 2.00

MAN FROM ATLANTIS
MARVEL

- ❑1, Feb 1978; Giant-size; TS (a); TV series; giant ... 3.00
- ❑2, Mar 1978, FR (a) ... 2.00
- ❑3, Apr 1978 ... 2.00
- ❑4, May 1978, FR (a) ... 2.00
- ❑5, Jun 1978 ... 2.00
- ❑6, Jul 1978 ... 2.00
- ❑7, Aug 1978, FR (a) ... 2.00

MAN FROM U.N.C.L.E.
GOLD KEY

- ❑1, Feb 1965, based on TV series ... 150.00
- ❑2, Oct 1965 ... 75.00
- ❑3, Nov 1965 ... 50.00
- ❑4, Jan 1966 ... 50.00
- ❑5, Mar 1966 ... 50.00
- ❑6, May 1966 ... 35.00
- ❑7, Jul 1966 ... 35.00

Mark of Charon

Negation spin-off features soulless hunter

©CrossGen

Married...With Children (Vol. 1)

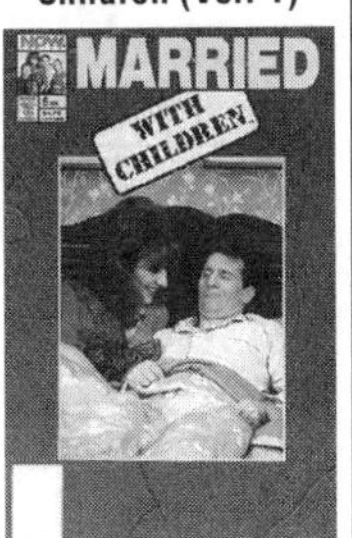

Fox's first dysfunctional family comes to comics

©Now

Mars Attacks (Vol. 1)

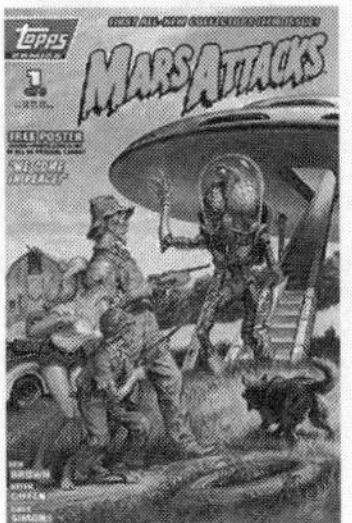

1950s card set inspires 1990s comic book

©Topps

Marshal Law

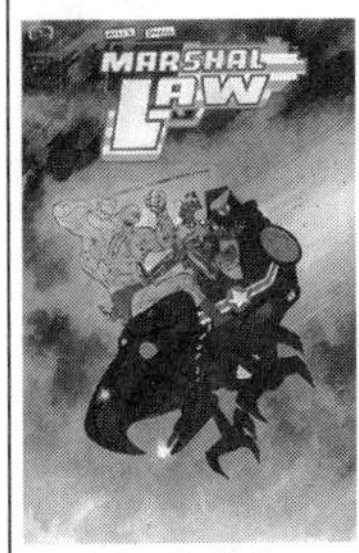

Judge Dredd-like hero hunter

©Marvel

Martian Manhunter

Early Silver Age hero finally gets series

©DC

N-MINT

❑8, Sep 1966, 10146-609 .... 35.00
❑9, Nov 1966 .... 35.00
❑10, Jan 1967 .... 35.00
❑11, Mar 1967 .... 35.00
❑12, May 1967 .... 35.00
❑13, Jul 1967 .... 35.00
❑14, Sep 1967 .... 35.00
❑15, Nov 1967 .... 35.00
❑16, Jan 1968 .... 35.00
❑17, Mar 1968 .... 35.00
❑18, May 1968 .... 35.00
❑19, Jul 1968 .... 35.00
❑20, Oct 1968 .... 35.00
❑21, Jan 1969, Reprints 25.00
❑22, Apr 1969, Reprints 25.00

MAN FROM U.N.C.L.E. (2ND SERIES)
ENTERTAINMENT

❑1, Jan 1987, b&w 2.00
❑2, Feb 1987 .... 2.00
❑3, Apr 1987 .... 2.00
❑4, Aug 1987 .... 2.00
❑5, Dec 1987 .... 2.00
❑6, Feb 1988 .... 2.00
❑7, May 1988 .... 2.00
❑8, Jul 1988 .... 2.00
❑9, Aug 1988 .... 2.00
❑10, Sep 1988 .... 2.00
❑11, Sep 1988 .... 2.00

MAN FROM U.N.C.L.E., THE: THE BIRDS OF PREY AFFAIR
MILLENNIUM

❑1, Mar 1993 .... 2.95
❑2, Sep 1993 .... 2.95

MANGA CALIENTE
FANTAGRAPHICS

❑1, ... 3.95
❑2, ... 3.95
❑3, ... 3.95

MANGA DARKCHYLDE
DARK HORSE

❑1 2005 .... 2.99
❑2, Jul 2005 .... 2.99

MANGA HORROR
AVALON

❑1, b&w; reprints Ghostly Tales 2.95

MANGAPHILE
RADIO

❑1, Aug 1999, b&w 2.95
❑2, Oct 1999, b&w 2.95
❑3, Dec 1999, b&w 2.95
❑4, Feb 2000, b&w 2.95
❑5, Apr 2000, b&w 2.95
❑6, Jun 2000, b&w 2.95
❑7, Aug 2000, b&w 2.95

MANGA SHI
CRUSADE

❑1, Aug 1996 .... 3.00

MANGA SHI: SHISEJI
CRUSADE

❑1 .... 2.95

N-MINT

MANGA SHI 2000
CRUSADE

❑1, Feb 1997; flip book with Shi: Heaven and Earth preview back-up; In the Killer Skies 2.95
❑1/A, Feb 1997; "Virgin" cover without price or logo 3.00
❑1/B; Rising Sun Edition 3.00
❑2, Apr 1997 .... 2.95
❑3, Jun 1997 .... 2.95

MANGA SURPRISE!
MORNING & AFTERNOON, KODANSHA LTD.

❑1, Jul 1996, b&w 2.00

MANGA VIZION
VIZ

❑1, Mar 1995 .... 5.00
❑2, Apr 1995 .... 5.00
❑3, May 1995 .... 5.00
❑4, Jun 1995 .... 5.00
❑5, Jul 1995 .... 5.00
❑6, Aug 1995 .... 5.00
❑7, Sep 1995 .... 5.00
❑8, Oct 1995 .... 5.00
❑9, Nov 1995 .... 5.00
❑10, Dec 1995 .... 5.00

MANGA VIZION (VOL. 2)
VIZ

❑1, Jan 1996 .... 5.00
❑2, Feb 1996 .... 5.00
❑3, Mar 1996 .... 5.00
❑4, Apr 1996 .... 5.00
❑5, May 1996 .... 5.00
❑6, Jun 1996 .... 5.00
❑7, Jul 1996 .... 5.00
❑8, Aug 1996 .... 5.00
❑9, Sep 1996 .... 5.00
❑10, Oct 1996 .... 5.00
❑11, Nov 1996 .... 5.00
❑12, Dec 1996 .... 5.00

MANGA VIZION (VOL. 3)
VIZ

❑1, Jan 1997 .... 4.95
❑2, Feb 1997 .... 4.95
❑3, Mar 1997 .... 4.95
❑4, Apr 1997 .... 4.95
❑5 1997 .... 4.95
❑6 1997 .... 4.95
❑7 1997 .... 4.95
❑8 1997 .... 4.95

MANGA VIZION (VOL. 4)
VIZ

❑1 .... 4.95
❑2 .... 4.95
❑3 .... 4.95
❑4 .... 4.95
❑5 .... 4.95
❑6 .... 4.95
❑7 .... 4.95
❑8 .... 4.95

MANGA ZEN
ZEN COMICS

❑1, b&w 2.50

N-MINT

MANGAZINE
ANTARCTIC

❑1, ca. 1985, b&w; first Antarctic publication; newsprint cover; company name misspelled throughout 4.00
❑1/2nd 2.00
❑2, ca. 1985 .... 3.50
❑3, ca. 1986 .... 1.75
❑4, ca. 1986 .... 3.50
❑5, ca. 1986 .... 3.50

MANGAZINE (VOL. 2)
ANTARCTIC

❑1, Jan 1989, b&w 3.50
❑2, Jun 1989, b&w 3.00
❑3 1989, b&w 2.00
❑4, b&w 2.00
❑5, ca. 1990, b&w 2.00
❑6 .... 3.00
❑7 .... 3.00
❑8 .... 3.00
❑9 .... 3.00
❑10, Jul 1991 .... 3.00
❑11, Sep 1991 .... 3.00
❑12, Nov 1991 .... 3.00
❑13, Jan 1992 .... 3.00
❑14, Mar 1992 .... 3.00
❑15, May 1992 .... 3.00
❑16, ca. 1992 .... 3.00
❑17, Nov 1992 .... 3.00
❑18, Nov 1992; Urusei Yatsura special issue 3.00
❑19, Jan 1993 .... 3.00
❑20, Feb 1993 .... 3.00
❑21, Mar 1993 .... 3.00
❑22, Apr 1993 .... 3.00
❑23, May 1993 .... 3.00
❑24, Jun 1993 .... 3.00
❑25, Jul 1993 .... 3.00
❑26, Aug 1993 .... 3.00
❑27, Sep 1993 .... 3.00
❑28, Oct 1993 .... 3.00
❑29, Nov 1993 .... 3.00
❑30, Dec 1993 .... 3.00
❑31, Jan 1994 .... 2.95
❑32, Feb 1994; Super Cat Nuku-Nuku 2.95
❑33, May 1994 .... 2.95
❑34, Jul 1994 .... 2.95
❑35, Sep 1994 .... 2.95
❑36, Nov 1994 .... 2.95
❑37, Jan 1995 .... 2.95
❑38, Mar 1995 .... 2.95
❑39, May 1995 .... 2.95
❑40, Sep 1995 .... 2.95
❑41, Sep 1995; Samurai Troopers 2.95
❑42, Sep 1995 .... 2.95
❑43, Sep 1995; Samurai Troopers Episode Guide, Part 2 .... 2.95
❑44, May 1996 .... 2.95

MANGLE TANGLE TALES
INNOVATION

❑1, Intro by Harlan Ellison 2.95

MANHUNTER (1ST SERIES)
DC

❑1, ca. 1984; Double-size; reprints serial from Detective Comics; Archie Goodwin 2.50

MANHUNTER (2ND SERIES)
DC

❑1, Jul 1988 O: Manhunter II (Mark Shaw) 1.50
❑2, Aug 1988 .... 1.25
❑3, Sep 1988 .... 1.25
❑4, Oct 1988 .... 1.25
❑5, Nov 1988 .... 1.25
❑6, Dec 1988 .... 1.25
❑7, Dec 1988 V: Count Vertigo 1.25
❑8, Jan 1989; A: Flash. Invasion! 1.25
❑9, Jan 1989; A: Flash. Invasion! 1.25
❑10, Feb 1989 A: Checkmate 1.25
❑11, Mar 1989 .... 1.25
❑12, Apr 1989 .... 1.25
❑13, May 1989 .... 1.25
❑14, Jun 1989 .... 1.25
❑15, Jul 1989 .... 1.25
❑16, Aug 1989 .... 1.25
❑17, Sep 1989 A: Batman 1.25
❑18, Oct 1989 .... 1.25
❑19, Nov 1989 .... 1.25
❑20, Dec 1989 .... 1.25
❑21, Jan 1990 .... 1.25
❑22, Feb 1990 .... 1.25
❑23, Mar 1990 .... 1.25
❑24, Apr 1990 .... 1.25

MANHUNTER (3RD SERIES)
DC

❑0, Oct 1994 1: Manhunter III (Chase Lawler) 2.25
❑1, Nov 1994 O: Manhunter III (Chase Lawler) 2.25
❑2, Dec 1994 O: Manhunter III (Chase Lawler) 2.00
❑3, Jan 1995 .... 2.00
❑4, Feb 1995 .... 2.00
❑5, Mar 1995 .... 2.00
❑6, Apr 1995 .... 2.00
❑7, Jun 1995 .... 2.00
❑8, Jul 1995 .... 2.25
❑9, Aug 1995 .... 2.25
❑10, Sep 1995 .... 2.25
❑11, Oct 1995 .... 2.25
❑12, Nov 1995; Underworld Unleashed 2.25

MANHUNTER (4TH SERIES)
DC

❑1, Oct 2004 .... 2.50
❑2, Nov 2004 .... 2.50
❑3, Dec 2004 .... 2.50
❑4, Jan 2005 .... 2.50
❑5, Feb 2005 .... 4.00
❑6, Mar 2005 .... 8.00
❑7, Apr 2005 .... 2.50
❑8, May 2005 .... 2.50
❑9, Jun 2005 .... 2.50
❑10, Jul 2005 .... 2.50
❑11, Aug 2005 .... 2.50
❑12, Sep 2005 .... 2.50
❑13, Oct 2005 .... 2.50
❑14 2005 .... 2.50
❑15, Dec 2005 .... 2.50
❑16, Jan 2006 .... 2.50
❑17, Feb 2006 .... 2.50
❑18, Mar 2006 .... 2.50
❑19, Apr 2006 .... 2.50
❑20, Jun 2006 .... 2.50
❑21, Jun 2006 .... 2.50
❑23, Sep 2006 .... 2.50

MANHUNTER: THE SPECIAL EDITION
DC

❑1, ca. 1999; collects serial from Detective Comics plus new story 9.95

MANIC ONE-SHOT
IMAGE

❑1, Feb 2004 .... 3.50

MANIFEST ETERNITY
DC / WILDSTORM

❑1, Aug 2006 .... 2.99
❑2, Sep 2006 .... 2.99

MANIK
MILLENNIUM

❑1, Sep 1995; foil cover 2.95
❑2 1995 .... 2.95
❑3 1996 .... 2.95

MANIMAL
RENEGADE

❑1, Jan 1986, b&w 1.70

MAN IN BLACK
RECOLLECTIONS

❑1, b&w 2.00
❑2, Jul 1991, b&w 2.00

MANKIND
CHAOS

❑1, Sep 1999 .... 2.95

MANN AND SUPERMAN
DC

❑1, ca. 2000 .... 5.95

MAN OF MANY FACES
TOKYOPOP

❑1, May 2003, b&w; printed in Japanese format 9.99

MAN OF RUST
BLACKTHORNE

❑1/A, Nov 1986 .... 1.50
❑1/B, Nov 1986 .... 1.50

MAN OF STEEL (MINI-SERIES)
DC

❑1, Oct 1986; JBy (w); JBy (a); newsstand 2.50
❑1/Variant, Oct 1986; JBy (w); JBy, DG (a); direct 2.50
❑1/Silver, Oct 1986; silver edition JBy (w); JBy (a) 2.50
❑2, Oct 1986 JBy (w); JBy (a) 2.50
❑2/Silver, Nov 1986; silver edition JBy (w); JBy (a) 2.50
❑3, Nov 1986 JBy (w); JBy (a); A: Batman 2.50
❑3/Silver, Nov 1986; silver edition JBy (w); JBy (a); A: Batman 2.50
❑4, Nov 1986 JBy (w); JBy (a) 2.50
❑4/Silver, Nov 1986; silver edition JBy (w); JBy (a) 2.50
❑5, Dec 1986 JBy (w); JBy (a) 2.50
❑5/Silver, Dec 1986; silver edition JBy (w); JBy (a) 2.50
❑6, Dec 1986 JBy (w); JBy (a) 2.50
❑6/Silver, Jan 1986; silver edition JBy (w); JBy (a) 2.50

MAN OF THE ATOM
ACCLAIM / VALIANT

❑1, Jan 1997; No cover price; preview of upcoming one-shot 1.00

MAN OF WAR (ECLIPSE)
ECLIPSE

❑1, Aug 1987 .... 1.75
❑2, Dec 1987 .... 1.75
❑3, Feb 1988 .... 1.75
❑4 .... 1.75
❑5 .... 1.75

MAN OF WAR (MALIBU)
MALIBU

❑1/Direct ed., Apr 1993; Direct Market edition with different cover, no UPC code 2.50
❑1, ca. 1993 .... 1.95
❑2, ca. 1993 .... 2.50
❑3, ca. 1993 .... 2.50
❑4, ca. 1993 .... 2.50
❑5, ca. 1993 .... 2.50
❑6, ca. 1993 .... 2.25
❑7, ca. 1994 .... 2.25
❑8, ca. 1994 .... 2.25

MANOSAURS
EXPRESS / ENTITY

❑1 .... 2.95
❑2 .... 2.95

MANTECH ROBOT WARRIORS
ARCHIE

❑1, Sep 1984, O: The Mantechs. 1: The Mantechs 1.00
❑2, Dec 1984 .... 1.00
❑3, Feb 1985 .... 1.00
❑4, May 1985 .... 1.00

MAN-THING (VOL. 1)
MARVEL

❑1, Jan 1974, FB, VM, JM (a); 2: Howard the Duck 30.00
❑2, Feb 1974, VM (a) 14.00
❑3, Mar 1974, VM, JAb (a); 1: FoolKiller I (Greg Everbest). Marvel Value Stamp #60: Ka-Zar 10.00
❑4, Apr 1974, VM, JAb (a); O: FoolKiller I (Greg Everbest). D: FoolKiller I (Greg Everbest). Marvel Value Stamp #17: Black Bolt 8.00
❑5, May 1974; MP (a); Marvel Value Stamp #83: Dragon Man 10.00
❑6, Jun 1974; MP (a); Marvel Value Stamp #55: Medusa 5.00
❑7, Jul 1974; MP (a); Marvel Value Stamp #19: Balder, Hogun, Fandral 5.00
❑8, Aug 1974; MP (a); Marvel Value Stamp #37: Watcher 5.00
❑9, Sep 1974; MP (a); Marvel Value Stamp #53: Grim Reaper 5.00
❑10, Oct 1974 MP (w); MP (a) 5.00
❑11, Nov 1974; MP (a); Marvel Value Stamp #28: Hawkeye 2.50
❑12, Dec 1974 JB, KJ (a) 2.50
❑13, Jan 1975; TS, JB (a); Marvel Value Stamp #54: Shanna 2.50
❑14, Feb 1975; AA (a); Marvel Value Stamp #64: Sif 2.50
❑15, Mar 1975 .... 2.50
❑16, Apr 1975 JB, TP (a) 2.50
❑17, May 1975 JM (a) 2.50
❑18, Jun 1975 JM (a) 2.50
❑19, Jul 1975 JM, FS (a); 1: Scavenger 2.50
❑20, Aug 1975 JM (a) 2.50
❑21, Sep 1975 JM (a); O: Scavenger.. 2.50
❑22, Oct 1975 JM (a); A: Howard the Duck 3.00

MAN-THING (VOL. 2)
MARVEL

❑1, Nov 1979, JM, BWi (a) 2.50
❑2, Jan 1980, VM (a) 2.00
❑3, Mar 1980, JM, BWi (a) 2.00
❑4, May 1980, DP, BWi (a); A: Dr. Strange 2.00
❑5, Jul 1980, DP, BWi (a) 2.00
❑6, Sep 1980, DP, BWi (a) 2.00
❑7, Nov 1980, DP, BWi (a) 2.00
❑8, Jan 1981 .... 2.00
❑9, Mar 1981 .... 2.00
❑10, May 1981 .... 2.00
❑11, Jul 1981 .... 2.00

MAN-THING (VOL. 3)
MARVEL

❑1, Dec 1997, gatefold summary; wraparound cover 2.99
❑2, Jan 1998, gatefold summary 2.99
❑3, Feb 1998, gatefold summary 2.99
❑4, Mar 1998, gatefold summary 2.99
❑5, Apr 1998, gatefold summary 2.99
❑6, May 1998, gatefold summary 2.99
❑7, Jun 1998, gatefold summary 2.99
❑8, Jul 1998, gatefold summary 2.99

MAN-THING (MINI-SERIES)
MARVEL

❑1, Sep 2004 .... 2.99
❑2, Oct 2004 .... 2.99
❑3, Nov 2004 .... 2.99

MANTRA
MALIBU / ULTRAVERSE

❑1, Jul 1993; O: Mantra I (Eden Blake). 1: Boneyard. 1: Warstrike. 1: Mantra I (Eden Blake). Ultraverse 2.50
❑1/Hologram, Jul 1993; O: Mantra I (Eden Blake). 1: Boneyard. 1: Warstrike. 1: Mantra I (Eden Blake). Hologram cover 6.00
❑1/Ltd., Jul 1993; Ultra Limited edition 3.00
❑2, Aug 1993 .... 2.25
❑3, Sep 1993 1: Kismet Deadly 2.25
❑4, Oct 1993; Rune 2.50
❑5, Nov 1993 .... 2.00
❑6, Dec 1993; Break-Thru 2.00
❑7, Jan 1994 .... 2.00
❑8, Feb 1994 .... 2.00
❑9, Mar 1994 .... 2.00
❑10, Apr 1994; Flip-book with Ultraverse Premiere #2 .... 3.50

Other grades: Multiply price above by 5/6 for VF/NM • 2/3 for VERY FINE • 1/3 for FINE • 1/5 for VERY GOOD • 1/8 for GOOD

Marvel Age

Fred Hembeck featured in house organ

©Marvel

Marvel Chillers

Modred the Mystic first featured

©Marvel

Marvel Classics Comics

Classics Illustrated for Marvel zombies

©Marvel

Marvel Collector's Edition

Mail-away from Charleston Chew

©Marvel

Marvel Collectors' Item Classics

Squarebound reprint title featured FF

©Marvel

N-MINT

❑11, May 1994 ... 1.95
❑12, Jun 1994 ... 1.95
❑13, Aug 1994; D: Boneyard's Wives. issue has two different covers ... 1.95
❑13/A; D: Boneyard's Wives. variant cover ... 1.95
❑14, Sep 1994 1: Mantra II (Lauren). D: Archimage ... 1.95
❑15, Oct 1994 A: Prime. D: Notch ... 1.95
❑16, Nov 1994 ... 1.95
❑17, Dec 1994 1: NecroMantra. V: Necro Mantra ... 1.95
❑18, Feb 1995 ... 1.95
❑19, Mar 1995 ... 1.95
❑20, Apr 1995 1: Overlord. D: Overlord ... 1.95
❑21, May 1995 ... 2.50
❑22, Jun 1995 ... 2.50
❑23, Jul 1995 ... 2.50
❑24, Aug 1995 ... 2.50
❑Giant Size 1, ca. 1994; Giant-Size Mantra #1 1: Topaz. 1: Opal Queen. 1: Sapphire Queen ... 3.50

MANTRA (VOL. 2)
MALIBU / ULTRAVERSE

❑0, Sep 1995; O: New Mantra. # Infinity ... 1.50
❑0/A, Sep 1995; O: New Mantra. alternate cover ... 1.50
❑1, Oct 1995 O: Coven. 1: Coven ... 2.00
❑2, Nov 1995 ... 1.50
❑3, Dec 1995 V: Necro Mantra ... 1.50
❑4, Jan 1996 ... 1.50
❑5, Feb 1996 V: N-ME ... 1.50
❑6, Mar 1996; A: Rush. Mantra gets new costume ... 1.50
❑7, Apr 1996 ... 1.50

MANTRA: SPEAR OF DESTINY
MALIBU / ULTRAVERSE

❑1, Apr 1995 ... 2.50
❑2, May 1995 ... 2.50

MANTUS FILES
ETERNITY

❑1, b&w ... 2.50
❑2, b&w ... 2.50
❑3, b&w ... 2.50
❑4, b&w ... 2.50

MAN WITH THE SCREAMING BRAIN
DARK HORSE

❑1/A cover, Jun 2005 ... 2.99
❑1/B cover, Jun 2005 ... 2.99
❑2/A cover, Jul 2005 ... 2.99
❑2/B cover, Jul 2005 ... 2.99
❑3/A cover, Aug 2005 ... 2.99
❑3/B cover, Aug 2005 ... 2.99
❑4/A cover, Sep 2005 ... 2.99
❑4/B cover, Sep 2005 ... 2.99

MANY REINCARNATIONS OF LAZARUS (VOL. 2)
FISHER

❑1, Dec 1998 ... 3.00
❑Ashcan 1, b&w; no cover price ... 1.00

MANY WORLDS OF TESLA STRONG
DC

❑1, May 2003 ... 3.99

N-MINT

MARA
AIRCEL

❑1, May 1991 ... 2.50
❑2 ... 2.50
❑3 ... 2.50
❑4, Jan 1992 ... 2.95

MARA CELTIC SHAMANESS
FANTAGRAPHICS / EROS

❑1 ... 2.95
❑2 ... 2.95
❑3 ... 2.95
❑4 ... 2.95
❑5 ... 2.95
❑6 ... 2.95

MARA OF THE CELTS BOOK 1
RIP OFF

❑Special 1, Sep 1993, b&w ... 2.95

MARA OF THE CELTS BOOK 2
FANTAGRAPHICS / EROS

❑1 ... 2.95

MARAUDER
SILVERLINE

❑1, Jan 1998 ... 2.95
❑2 1998 ... 2.95
❑3 1998 ... 2.95
❑4 1998 ... 2.95

MARCH HARE
LODESTONE

❑1, b&w ... 1.50

MARC SILVESTRI SKETCHBOOK
IMAGE

❑1, Jan 2004 ... 2.99

MARC SPECTOR: MOON KNIGHT
MARVEL

❑1, Jun 1989 ... 2.50
❑2, Jul 1989 ... 2.00
❑3, Mar 1989 ... 2.00
❑4, Sep 1989 ... 2.00
❑5, Oct 1989 ... 2.00
❑6, Nov 1989; Brother Voodoo ... 2.00
❑7, Nov 1989; Brother Voodoo ... 2.00
❑8, Dec 1989 A: Punisher ... 3.00
❑9, Dec 1989 A: Punisher ... 3.00
❑10, Jan 1990 1: Ringer II ... 2.00
❑11, Feb 1990 ... 2.00
❑12, Mar 1990 ... 2.00
❑13, Apr 1990 ... 2.00
❑14, May 1990 ... 2.00
❑15, Jun 1990 ... 2.00
❑16, Jul 1990 ... 2.00
❑17, Aug 1990 ... 2.00
❑18, Sep 1990 ... 2.00
❑19, Oct 1990 A: Punisher. A: Spider-Man ... 3.00
❑20, Nov 1990 A: Punisher. A: Spider-Man ... 3.00
❑21, Dec 1990 A: Punisher. A: Spider-Man ... 3.00
❑22, Jan 1991 ... 3.00
❑23, Feb 1991 ... 3.00
❑24, Mar 1991 ... 3.00
❑25, Apr 1991; Giant-size TP (a); A: Ghost Rider ... 2.50

N-MINT

❑26, May 1991 TP (a) ... 2.00
❑27, Jun 1991 ... 2.00
❑28, Jul 1991 ... 2.00
❑29, Aug 1991 ... 2.00
❑30, Sep 1991 ... 2.00
❑31, Oct 1991 ... 2.00
❑32, Nov 1991 A: Hobgoblin ... 3.00
❑33, Dec 1991 A: Hobgoblin ... 3.00
❑34, Jan 1992 ... 2.00
❑35, Feb 1992 A: Punisher ... 2.00
❑36, Mar 1992 A: Punisher ... 2.00
❑37, Apr 1992 A: Punisher ... 2.00
❑38, May 1992 A: Punisher ... 2.00
❑39, Jun 1992 V: Doctor Doom ... 2.00
❑40, Jul 1992 ... 2.00
❑41, Aug 1992 ... 2.00
❑42, Sep 1992 ... 2.00
❑43, Oct 1992 ... 2.00
❑44, Nov 1992 ... 2.00
❑45, Dec 1992 ... 2.00
❑46, Jan 1993 ... 2.00
❑47, Feb 1993 ... 2.00
❑48, Mar 1993 ... 2.00
❑49, Apr 1993 ... 2.00
❑50, May 1993; Die-cut cover ... 2.95
❑51, Jun 1993 ... 1.75
❑52, Jul 1993 ... 1.75
❑53, Aug 1993 ... 1.75
❑54, Sep 1993 ... 1.75
❑55, Oct 1993; 1: Sunstreak. 1st professional Stephen Platt art ... 2.50
❑56, Nov 1993 ... 2.50
❑57, Dec 1993 ... 2.50
❑58, Jan 1994 ... 2.00
❑59, Feb 1994 ... 2.00
❑60, Mar 1994 ... 2.00
❑Special 1, ca. 1992; Team-up with Shang-Chi, Master of Kung Fu ... 2.50

MARGIE
DELL

❑2, Sep 1962, First issue published as Dell's Four Color #1307 ... 25.00

MARIE-GABRIELLE
NBM

❑1 ... 15.95

MARILYN MONROE: SUICIDE OR MURDER?
REVOLUTIONARY

❑1, Sep 1993, b&w ... 2.50

MARINES ATTACK
CHARLTON

❑1 ... 16.00
❑2 ... 12.00
❑3 ... 9.00
❑4 ... 9.00
❑5 ... 9.00
❑6 ... 6.00
❑7 ... 6.00
❑8 ... 6.00
❑9 ... 6.00

MARIONETTE
RAVEN

❑1 1987, b&w ... 1.00
❑3, b&w ... 1.00

Other grades: Multiply price above by 5/6 for VF/NM • 2/3 for VERY FINE • 1/3 for FINE • 1/5 for VERY GOOD • 1/8 for GOOD

MARIONETTE
ALPHA PRODUCTIONS
- ❑1, b&w 2.50
- ❑2, b&w 2.50
- ❑3 2.50

MARK (1ST SERIES)
DARK HORSE
- ❑1, Sep 1987 2.00
- ❑2, Dec 1987 2.00
- ❑3, Aug 1988 2.00
- ❑4, Sep 1988 2.00
- ❑5, Nov 1988 2.00
- ❑6, Jan 1989 2.00

MARK (2ND SERIES)
DARK HORSE
- ❑1, Dec 1993 2.50
- ❑2, Jan 1994 2.50
- ❑3, Feb 1994 2.50
- ❑4, Mar 1994 2.50

MARKAM
GAUNTLET
- ❑1 2.50

MARK HAZZARD: MERC
MARVEL
- ❑1, Nov 1986, PD (w); GM (a); 1: Mark Hazzard 1.25
- ❑2, Dec 1986 1.00
- ❑3, Jan 1987 1.00
- ❑4, Feb 1987 1.00
- ❑5, Mar 1987 1.00
- ❑6, Apr 1987 1.00
- ❑7, May 1987 1.00
- ❑8, Jun 1987 1.00
- ❑9, Jul 1987 1.00
- ❑10, Aug 1987, GM (a) 1.00
- ❑11, Sep 1987 1.00
- ❑12, Oct 1987 1.00
- ❑Annual 1, Nov 1987, D: Hazzard 1.25

MARK OF CHARON
CROSSGEN
- ❑1, Apr 2003 2.95
- ❑2, May 2003 2.95
- ❑3, Jun 2003 2.95
- ❑4, Jul 2003 2.95
- ❑5, Sep 2003 2.95

MARK OF THE SUCCUBUS
TOKYOPOP
- ❑1, Nov 2005 9.95

MARKSMAN
HERO
- ❑1, Jan 1988 1.95
- ❑2, Feb 1988 1.95
- ❑3, Apr 1988 1.95
- ❑4, Jun 1988 1.95
- ❑5, Aug 1988 1.95
- ❑Annual 1, Dec 1988 2.75

MARMALADE BOY
TOKYOPOP
- ❑1 2001; printed in Japanese format 2.95
- ❑2 2001; printed in Japanese format 2.95
- ❑3 2001; printed in Japanese format 2.95

MAROONED!
FANTAGRAPHICS / EROS
- ❑1, b&w 1.95

MARQUIS, THE: DANSE MACABRE
ONI
- ❑1, b&w 2.95
- ❑2, Jul 2000, b&w 2.95
- ❑3, Oct 2000, b&w 2.95

MARRIAGE OF HERCULES AND XENA
TOPPS
- ❑1, Jul 1998 2.95

MARRIED...WITH CHILDREN (VOL. 1)
NOW
- ❑1, Jun 1990 2.50
- ❑1/2nd 2.00
- ❑2, Jul 1990 2.00
- ❑3, Aug 1990 2.00
- ❑4, Sep 1990 2.00
- ❑5, Oct 1990 2.00
- ❑6, Nov 1990 2.00
- ❑7, Feb 1991 2.00

MARRIED...WITH CHILDREN (VOL. 2)
NOW
- ❑1, Sep 1991 2.50
- ❑2, Oct 1991; Peggy invents bon-bon filling detector 2.25
- ❑3, Nov 1991; Al turns into Psychodad 2.25
- ❑4, Dec 1991 2.00
- ❑5, Jan 1992 2.00
- ❑6, Mar 1992 2.00
- ❑7, Apr 1992 2.00
- ❑Annual 1994, ca. 1994; Annual 2.50
- ❑Special 1, Jul 1992; Special; with poster 2.00

MARRIED...WITH CHILDREN: BUCK'S TALE
NOW
- ❑1, ca. 1994 O: Buck (the Bundy Family dog) 2.00

MARRIED...WITH CHILDREN: BUD BUNDY, FANBOY IN PARADISE
NOW
- ❑1 2.95

MARRIED...WITH CHILDREN: FLASHBACK SPECIAL
NOW
- ❑1, Jan 1993; Al & Peg's First Date 2.00
- ❑2, Feb 1993; Al & Peg's Wedding 2.00
- ❑3, Mar 1993 2.00

MARRIED...WITH CHILDREN: KELLY BUNDY
NOW
- ❑1, Aug 1992 2.25
- ❑2, Sep 1992 2.25
- ❑3, Oct 1992 2.25

MARRIED...WITH CHILDREN: KELLY GOES TO KOLLEGE
NOW
- ❑1 2.95
- ❑2 2.95
- ❑3 2.95

MARRIED...WITH CHILDREN: OFF BROADWAY
NOW
- ❑1, Sep 1993 2.00

MARRIED...WITH CHILDREN: QUANTUM QUARTET
NOW
- ❑1, Oct 1993; parody 2.00
- ❑2, Nov 1993; parody 2.00
- ❑3, Fal 1994; The Big Wrap-Up; combines issues #3 and 4 into flipbook; no indicia; parody 2.95

MARRIED...WITH CHILDREN 3-D SPECIAL
NOW
- ❑1, Jun 1993 2.95

MARRIED...WITH CHILDREN: 2099
NOW
- ❑1, Jun 1993; Terminator spoof 2.00
- ❑2, Jul 1993 2.00
- ❑3, Aug 1993 2.00

MARS (FIRST)
FIRST
- ❑1, Jan 1984 1.50
- ❑2, Feb 1984 1.25
- ❑3, Mar 1984 1.25
- ❑4, Apr 1984 1.25
- ❑5, May 1984 1.25
- ❑6, Jun 1984 1.25
- ❑7, Jul 1984 1.25
- ❑8, Aug 1984 1.25
- ❑9, Sep 1984 1.25
- ❑10, Oct 1984 1.25
- ❑11, Nov 1984 1.25
- ❑12, Dec 1984 1.25

MARS (TOKYOPOP)
TOKYOPOP
- ❑1, Mar 2002, b&w; printed in Japanese format 9.99
- ❑2, Jun 2002, b&w; printed in Japanese format 9.99
- ❑3, Aug 2002, b&w; printed in Japanese format 9.99

MARS ATTACKS (VOL. 1)
TOPPS
- ❑1, May 1994; KG (w); KG (a); Flip-book format 4.00
- ❑1/Ace, May 1994; Wizard Ace Edition #11; acetate overlay cover; sendaway from Wizard #65 4.00
- ❑1/Ltd., May 1994; Limited edition promotional edition (5,000 printed); Flip-book format 4.00
- ❑2, Jun 1994 3.00
- ❑3, Aug 1994 3.00
- ❑4, Sep 1994 3.00
- ❑5, Oct 1994 3.00

MARS ATTACKS (VOL. 2)
TOPPS
- ❑1, Aug 1995 KG (w) 3.50
- ❑2, Sep 1995 3.00
- ❑3, Oct 1995 3.00
- ❑4, Jan 1996 3.00
- ❑5, Jan 1996 3.00
- ❑6, Mar 1996 3.00
- ❑7, May 1996 3.00
- ❑8, Jul 1996 3.00

MARS ATTACKS BASEBALL SPECIAL
TOPPS
- ❑1, Jun 1996 2.95

MARS ATTACKS HIGH SCHOOL
TOPPS
- ❑1, May 1997 2.95
- ❑2, Sep 1997 2.95

MARS ATTACKS IMAGE
IMAGE
- ❑1, Dec 1996; crossover with Topps 2.50
- ❑2, Jan 1997 2.50
- ❑3, Mar 1997 2.50
- ❑4, Apr 1997 2.50

MARS ATTACKS THE SAVAGE DRAGON
TOPPS
- ❑1, Dec 1996; crossover with Image; trading cards 2.95
- ❑2, Jan 1997; crossover with Image 2.95
- ❑3, Feb 1997; crossover with Image 2.95
- ❑4, Mar 1997; crossover with Image 2.95

MARSHAL LAW
MARVEL / EPIC
- ❑1, Oct 1987 3.50
- ❑2, Feb 1988 2.50
- ❑3, Apr 1988 2.50
- ❑4, Aug 1988 2.50
- ❑5, Dec 1988 2.50
- ❑6, Apr 1989 2.50

MARSHAL LAW: KINGDOM OF THE BLIND
APOCALYPSE
- ❑1; newsstand 3.95
- ❑1/Direct ed.; squarebound 5.95

MARSHAL LAW: SECRET TRIBUNAL
DARK HORSE
- ❑1, Sep 1993; cardstock cover 2.95
- ❑2, Apr 1994; cardstock cover 2.95

MARSHAL LAW: SUPER BABYLON
DARK HORSE
- ❑1, May 1992; prestige format 4.95

MARSHAL LAW: THE HATEFUL DEAD
APOCALYPSE
- ❑1; prestige format 5.95

M.A.R.S. PATROL TOTAL WAR
GOLD KEY
- ❑3, Sep 1966, WW (a); Series continued from Total War #2 50.00
- ❑4, Oct 1967, back cover pin-up 35.00
- ❑5, May 1968 35.00
- ❑6, Aug 1968 25.00
- ❑7, Nov 1968 25.00
- ❑8, Feb 1969 25.00
- ❑9, May 1969 25.00
- ❑10, Aug 1969 25.00

MARTHA SPLATTERHEAD'S WEIRDEST STORIES EVER TOLD
MONSTER
- ❑1, b&w 3.50

Marvel Comics Presents

Biweekly serials featured Wolverine, others
©Marvel

Marvel Double Feature

Reprints of Tales of Suspense hero stories
©Marvel

Marvel Fanfare

Bimonthly deluxe outings from various creators
©Marvel

Marvel Feature (1st Series)

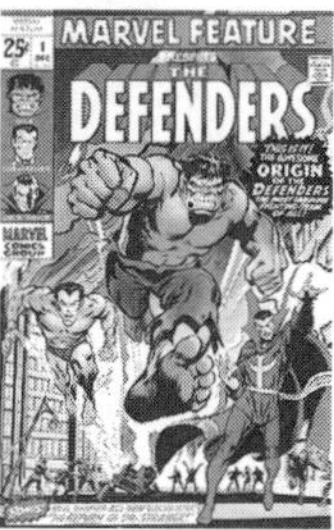

Test-bed for Defenders, Ant-Man
©Marvel

Marvel Feature (2nd Series)

Conan takes over series' second run
©Marvel

N-MINT

MARTHA WASHINGTON GOES TO WAR
DARK HORSE / LEGEND

- ❑1, May 1994; FM (w); DaG (a); cardstock cover.......... 3.00
- ❑2, Jun 1994; FM (w); DaG (a); cardstock cover.......... 3.00
- ❑3, Jul 1994; FM (w); DaG (a); cardstock cover.......... 3.00
- ❑4, Aug 1994; FM (w); DaG (a); cardstock cover.......... 3.00
- ❑5, Nov 1994; FM (w); DaG (a); cardstock cover.......... 3.00

MARTHA WASHINGTON SAVES THE WORLD
DARK HORSE

- ❑1, Dec 1997; FM (w); DaG (a); cardstock cover.......... 4.00
- ❑2, Jan 1998; FM (w); DaG (a); cardstock cover.......... 4.00
- ❑3, Feb 1998; FM (w); DaG (a); cardstock cover.......... 4.00

MARTHA WASHINGTON: STRANDED IN SPACE
DARK HORSE / LEGEND

- ❑1, Nov 1995; FM (w); DaG (a); A: The Big Guy. reprints story from Dark Horse Presents; cardstock cover 3.00

MARTIAN MANHUNTER (MINI-SERIES)
DC

- ❑1, May 1988 O: Martian Manhunter.. 1.50
- ❑2, Jun 1988.......... 1.50
- ❑3, Jul 1988.......... 1.50
- ❑4, Aug 1988.......... 1.50

MARTIAN MANHUNTER
DC

- ❑0, Oct 1998.......... 3.00
- ❑1, Dec 1998.......... 2.50
- ❑2, Jan 1999.......... 2.00
- ❑3, Feb 1999 A: Bette Noir.......... 2.00
- ❑4, Mar 1999 D: Karen Smith.......... 2.00
- ❑5, Apr 1999 JDu (a).......... 2.00
- ❑6, May 1999 V: JLA.......... 2.00
- ❑7, Jun 1999.......... 2.00
- ❑8, Jul 1999.......... 2.00
- ❑9, Aug 1999 A: JLA.......... 2.00
- ❑10, Sep 1999 A: Fire.......... 2.00
- ❑11, Oct 1999.......... 2.00
- ❑12, Nov 1999; A: Steel. A: Crimson Fox. A: Ice. A: Vibe. Day of Judgment 2.00
- ❑13, Dec 1999.......... 2.00
- ❑14, Jan 2000.......... 1.99
- ❑15, Feb 2000.......... 1.99
- ❑16, Mar 2000.......... 1.99
- ❑17, Apr 2000.......... 1.99
- ❑18, May 2000 A: JSA.......... 1.99
- ❑19, Jun 2000.......... 1.99
- ❑20, Jul 2000.......... 1.99
- ❑21, Aug 2000.......... 1.99
- ❑22, Sep 2000.......... 2.50
- ❑23, Oct 2000.......... 2.50
- ❑24, Nov 2000.......... 2.50
- ❑25, Dec 2000.......... 2.50
- ❑26, Jan 2001.......... 2.50

N-MINT

- ❑27, Feb 2001.......... 2.50
- ❑28, Mar 2001.......... 2.50
- ❑29, Apr 2001.......... 2.50
- ❑30, May 2001.......... 2.50
- ❑31, Jun 2001.......... 2.50
- ❑32, Jul 2001.......... 2.50
- ❑33, Aug 2001.......... 2.50
- ❑34, Sep 2001.......... 2.50
- ❑35, Oct 2001.......... 2.50
- ❑36, Nov 2001.......... 2.50
- ❑1000000, Nov 1998, b&w.......... 4.00
- ❑Annual 1, ca. 1998; Ghosts.......... 2.95
- ❑Annual 2, Oct 1999; JLApe.......... 2.95

MARTIAN MANHUNTER: AMERICAN SECRETS
DC

- ❑1, ca. 1992; prestige format.......... 4.95
- ❑2, ca. 1992; prestige format.......... 4.95
- ❑3, ca. 1992; prestige format.......... 4.95

MARTIAN MANHUNTER SPECIAL
DC

- ❑1, ca. 1996.......... 3.50

MARTIN MYSTERY
DARK HORSE

- ❑1, Mar 1999.......... 4.95
- ❑2, Apr 1999.......... 4.95
- ❑3, May 1999.......... 4.95
- ❑4, Jun 1999.......... 4.95
- ❑5, Jul 1999.......... 4.95
- ❑6, Aug 1999.......... 4.95

MARTIN THE SATANIC RACOON
GABE MARTINEZ

- ❑1.......... 1.00
- ❑2.......... 2.00

MARVEL ACTION HOUR, FEATURING IRON MAN
MARVEL

- ❑1, Nov 1994.......... 1.50
- ❑1/CS, Nov 1994; Collector's set: includes animation cel.......... 2.95
- ❑2, Dec 1994.......... 1.50
- ❑3, Jan 1995.......... 1.50
- ❑4, Feb 1995.......... 1.50
- ❑5, Mar 1995.......... 1.50
- ❑6, Apr 1995.......... 1.50
- ❑7, May 1995.......... 1.50
- ❑8, Jun 1995.......... 1.50

MARVEL ACTION HOUR, FEATURING THE FANTASTIC FOUR
MARVEL

- ❑1, Nov 1994.......... 1.50
- ❑1/CS, Nov 1994; Collector's set: includes animation cel.......... 2.95
- ❑2, Dec 1994.......... 1.50
- ❑3, Jan 1995.......... 1.50
- ❑4, Feb 1995.......... 1.50
- ❑5, Mar 1995.......... 1.50
- ❑6, Apr 1995.......... 1.50
- ❑7, May 1995.......... 1.50
- ❑8, Jun 1995.......... 1.50

N-MINT

MARVEL ACTION UNIVERSE
MARVEL

- ❑1, Jan 1989; Reprints Spider-Man and His Amazing Friends #1.......... 1.00

MARVEL ADVENTURE
MARVEL

- ❑1, Dec 1975, SL (w); GC (a); Reprints Daredevil #22.......... 8.00
- ❑2, Feb 1976, Reprints Daredevil #23 5.00
- ❑3, Apr 1976, Reprints Daredevil #24 5.00
- ❑3/30 cent, Apr 1976, 30 cent regional price variant; reprints Daredevil #24 20.00
- ❑4, Jun 1976, Reprints Daredevil #25 5.00
- ❑4/30 cent, Jun 1976, 30 cent regional price variant; reprints Daredevil #25 20.00
- ❑5, Aug 1976, Reprints Daredevil #26 4.00
- ❑5/30 cent, Aug 1976, 30 cent regional price variant; reprints Daredevil #26 20.00
- ❑6, Oct 1976, Reprints Daredevil #27. 4.00

MARVEL ADVENTURES
MARVEL

- ❑1, Apr 1997, A: Hulk. V: Leader. V: Abomination.......... 2.00
- ❑2, May 1997, A: Spider-Man. V: Scorpion.......... 1.50
- ❑3, Jun 1997, A: X-Men. V: Magneto.. 1.50
- ❑4, Jul 1997, A: Hulk. V: Brotherhood of Evil Mutants.......... 1.50
- ❑5, Aug 1997, A: X-Men. A: Spider-Man. V: Abomination. V: Magneto .. 1.50
- ❑6, Sep 1997, A: Torch. A: Spider-Man. V: Lava Men.......... 1.50
- ❑7, Oct 1997, A: Hulk. V: Tyrannus..... 1.50
- ❑8, Nov 1997, A: X-Men.......... 1.50
- ❑9, Dec 1997, A: Fantastic Four.......... 1.50
- ❑10, Jan 1998, A: Silver Surfer. V: Gladiator.......... 1.50
- ❑11, Feb 1998, A: Spider-Man. V: Sandman.......... 1.50
- ❑12, Mar 1998.......... 1.50
- ❑13, Apr 1998.......... 1.50
- ❑14, May 1998, A: Hulk. A: Doctor Strange. A: Juggernaut.......... 1.50
- ❑15, Jun 1998, A: Wolverine.......... 1.50
- ❑16, Jul 1998, A: Silver Surfer. V: Skrulls.......... 1.50
- ❑17, Aug 1998, A: Iron Man. A: Spider-Man. V: Grey Gargoyle.......... 1.50
- ❑18, Sep 1998.......... 1.50

MARVEL ADVENTURES: AVENGERS
MARVEL

- ❑1, Aug 2006.......... 2.50
- ❑2, Sep 2006.......... 2.50

MARVEL ADVENTURES: FANTASTIC FOUR
MARVEL

- ❑0, Jun 2005.......... 2.50
- ❑1, Jul 2005.......... 2.50
- ❑2, Aug 2005.......... 2.50
- ❑3, Sep 2005.......... 2.50
- ❑4, Oct 2005.......... 2.50
- ❑5, Nov 2005.......... 2.50
- ❑6, Jan 2006.......... 2.50
- ❑7, Feb 2006.......... 2.50
- ❑8, Mar 2006.......... 2.50

Other grades: Multiply price above by 5/6 for VF/NM • 2/3 for VERY FINE • 1/3 for FINE • 1/5 for VERY GOOD • 1/8 for GOOD

N-MINT

❑9, Apr 2006 2.50
❑10, May 2006 2.50
❑11, Jun 2006 2.50
❑12, Jul 2006 2.50
❑13, Aug 2006 2.50
❑14, Sep 2006 2.50

MARVEL ADVENTURES FLIP MAGAZINE
MARVEL

❑1, Jul 2005 3.99
❑2, Aug 2005 3.99
❑3, Sep 2005 3.99
❑4 2005 3.99
❑5 2005 3.99
❑6, Jan 2006 3.99
❑7, Feb 2006 3.99
❑8, Mar 2006 3.99
❑9, Apr 2006 3.99
❑10, May 2006 3.99
❑11, Jul 2006 3.99
❑13, Aug 2006 3.99

MARVEL ADVENTURES: SPIDER-MAN
MARVEL

❑1, Apr 2005 2.50
❑2, May 2005 2.50
❑3, Jun 2005 2.50
❑4, Jul 2005 2.50
❑5, Aug 2005 2.50
❑6, Sep 2005 2.50
❑7, Oct 2005 2.50
❑8 2005 2.50
❑9, Jan 2006 2.50
❑10, Feb 2006 2.50
❑11, Mar 2006 2.50
❑12, Mar 2006 2.50
❑13, May 2006 2.50
❑14, Jun 2006 2.50
❑15, Jul 2006 2.50
❑16, Aug 2006 2.50
❑17, Sep 2006 2.50

MARVEL ADVENTURES: THE THING
MARVEL

❑1, Apr 2005 2.25
❑2, May 2005 2.50
❑3, Jun 2005 2.50

MARVEL AGE
MARVEL

❑1, Apr 1983 2.00
❑2, May 1983 1.00
❑3, Jun 1983; Micronauts 1.00
❑4, Jul 1983; Return of the Jedi; Rock & Rule graphic novel 1.00
❑5, Aug 1983; Daredevil; The Hobgoblin 1.00
❑6, Sep 1983; Cloak & Dagger 1.00
❑7, Oct 1983; X-Men and Micronauts Ltd. Series 1.00
❑8, Nov 1983; Stan Lee, Jim Shooter interviews 1.00
❑9, Dec 1983; Super Boxers 1.00
❑10, Jan 1984; Star Wars cover 1.00
❑11, Feb 1984; Kitty Pryde & Wolverine 1.00
❑12, Mar 1984; Secret Wars 1.00
❑13, Apr 1984; Dreadstar; Feature on coloring comics 1.00
❑14, May 1984; FH (w); FH (a); John Byrne; Power Pack; Six From Sirius; Fred Hembeck strips begin 1.00
❑15, Jun 1984, FH (w); FH (a); Archie Goodwin on Epic Comics 1.00
❑16, Jul 1984, FH (w); FH (a) 1.00
❑17, Aug 1984, FH (w); FH (a); Muppets 1.00
❑18, Sep 1984, FH (w); FH (a); Questprobe 1.00
❑19, Oct 1984, FH (w); FH (a); Star Comics 1.00
❑20, Nov 1984, FH (w); FH (a); Letters to Marvel Super-Hero Secret Wars 1.00
❑21, Dec 1984, FH (w); FH (a); Void Indigo 1.00
❑22, Jan 1985, FH (w); FH (a); Sol Brodsky Remembered 1.00
❑23, Feb 1985, FH (w); FH (a); ROM 1.00
❑24, Mar 1985, FH (w); FH (a) 1.00
❑25, Apr 1985, FH (w); FH (a); Rocket Raccoon; Cloak & Dagger; Gargoyle 1.00

N-MINT

❑26, May 1985, FH (w); FH (a); Starstruck 1.00
❑27, Jun 1985, FH (w); FH (a); Secret Wars II 1.00
❑28, Jul 1985, FH (w); FH (a) 1.00
❑29, Aug 1985, FH (w); FH (a); Vision & Scarlet Witch; West Coast Avengers (Ltd. Series) 1.00
❑30, Sep 1985, FH (w); FH (a) 1.00
❑31, Oct 1985, FH (w); FH (a) 1.00
❑32, Nov 1985, FH (w); FH (a) 1.00
❑33, Dec 1985, FH (w); FH (a); X-Factor 1.00
❑34, Jan 1986, FH (w); FH (a); G.I. Joes 1.00
❑35, Feb 1986, FH (w); FH (a); A Day in the Life of Marvel Comics 1.00
❑36, Mar 1986, FH (w); FH (a) 1.00
❑37, Apr 1986, FH (w); FH (a) 1.00
❑38, May 1986, FH (w); FH (a); He-Man 1.00
❑39, Jun 1986, FH (w); FH (a) 1.00
❑40, Jul 1986, FH (w); FH (a) 1.00
❑41, Aug 1986, FH (w); FH (a) 1.00
❑42, Sep 1986, FH (w); FH (a) 1.00
❑43, Oct 1986, FH (w); FH (a) 1.00
❑44, Nov 1986, FH (w); FH (a) 1.00
❑45, Dec 1986, FH (w); FH (a) 1.00
❑46, Jan 1987, FH (w); FH (a) 1.00
❑47, Feb 1987, FH (w); FH (a) 1.00
❑48, Mar 1987, FH (w); FH (a) 1.00
❑49, Apr 1987, FH (w); FH (a) 1.00
❑50, May 1987, FH (w); FH (a) 1.00
❑51, Jun 1987, FH (w); FH (a) 1.00
❑52, Jul 1987, FH (w); FH (a) 1.00
❑53, Aug 1987, FH (w); FH (a) 1.00
❑54, Sep 1987, FH (w); FH (a); Spider-Man wedding 1.00
❑55, Oct 1987, FH (w); FH (a) 1.00
❑56, Nov 1987, FH (w); FH (a) 1.00
❑57, Dec 1987, FH (w); FH (a) 1.00
❑58, Jan 1988, FH (w); FH (a) 1.00
❑59, Feb 1988, FH (w); FH (a) 1.00
❑60, Mar 1988, FH (w); FH (a) 1.00
❑61, Apr 1988, FH (w); FH (a) 1.00
❑62, May 1988, FH (w); FH (a) 1.00
❑63, Jun 1988, FH (w); FH (a) 1.00
❑64, Jul 1988, FH (w); FH (a) 1.00
❑65, Aug 1988, FH (w); FH (a) 1.00
❑66, Sep 1988, FH (w); FH (a) 1.00
❑67, Oct 1988, FH (w); FH (a) 1.00
❑68, Nov 1988, FH (w); FH (a) 1.00
❑69, Dec 1988, FH (w); FH (a) 1.00
❑70, Jan 1989, FH (w); FH (a) 1.00
❑71, Feb 1989, FH (w); FH (a) 1.00
❑72, Mar 1989, FH (w); FH (a) 1.00
❑73, Apr 1989, FH (w); FH (a) 1.00
❑74, May 1989, FH (w); FH (a) 1.00
❑75, Jun 1989, FH (w); FH (a) 1.00
❑76, Jul 1989, FH (w); FH (a); Atlantis Attacks 1.00
❑77, Aug 1989, FH (w); FH (a) 1.00
❑78, Sep 1989, FH (w); FH (a) 1.00
❑79, Oct 1989 FH (w); FH (a) 1.00
❑80, Nov 1989 FH (w); FH (a) 1.00
❑81, Nov 1989 FH (w); FH (a) 1.00
❑82, Dec 1989; FH (w); FH (a); Squadron Supreme 1.00
❑83, Dec 1989 FH (w); FH (a) 1.00
❑84, Jan 1990 FH (w); FH (a) 1.00
❑85, Feb 1990 FH (w); FH (a) 1.00
❑86, Mar 1990 FH (w); FH (a) 1.00
❑87, Apr 1990 FH (w); FH (a) 1.00
❑88, May 1990; FH (w); FH (a); Guardians of the Galaxy 1.00
❑89, Jun 1990 FH (w); FH (a) 1.00
❑90, Jul 1990 FH (w); FH (a) 1.00
❑91, Aug 1990 FH (w); FH (a) 1.00
❑92, Sep 1990 FH (w); FH (a) 1.00
❑93, Oct 1990 FH (w); FH (a) 1.00
❑94, Nov 1990 FH (w); FH (a) 1.00
❑95, Dec 1990; FH (w); FH (a); Captain America issue 1.00
❑96, Jan 1991 FH (w); FH (a) 1.00
❑97, Feb 1991 FH (w); FH (a) 1.00
❑98, Mar 1991 FH (w); FH (a) 1.00
❑99, Apr 1991 FH (w); FH (a) 1.00
❑100, May 1991; 100th anniversary issue FH (w); FH (a) 1.00
❑101, Jun 1991 FH (w); FH (a) 1.00
❑102, Jul 1991 FH (w); FH (a) 1.00

N-MINT

❑103, Aug 1991 FH (w); FH (a) 1.00
❑104, Sep 1991 FH (w); FH (a) 1.00
❑105, Oct 1991 FH (w); FH (a) 1.00
❑106, Nov 1991; Daredevil 300th anniversary FH (w); FH (a) 1.00
❑107, Dec 1991 FH (w); FH (a) 1.00
❑108, Jan 1992 FH (w); FH (a) 1.00
❑109, Feb 1992 FH (w); FH (a) 1.00
❑110, Mar 1992 FH (w); FH (a) 1.00
❑111, Apr 1992 FH (w); FH (a) 1.00
❑112, May 1992; Captain America 400th Anniversary FH (w); FH (a) 1.00
❑113, Jun 1992 FH (w); FH (a) 1.00
❑114, Jul 1992; Spider-Man's 30th anniversary FH (w); FH (a) 1.00
❑115, Aug 1992 FH (w); FH (a) 1.00
❑116, Sep 1992; FH (w); FH (a); X-Men 1.00
❑117, Oct 1992; FH (w); FH (a); 2099 1.00
❑118, Nov 1992; FH (w); FH (a); with card 1.00
❑119, Dec 1992 FH (w); FH (a) 1.00
❑120, Jan 1993; Tenth anniversary special FH (w); FH (a) 1.00
❑121, Feb 1993; FH (w); FH (a); Ren & Stimpy 1.00
❑122, Mar 1993; X-Men 30th anniversary special FH (w); FH (a) 1.00
❑123, Apr 1993 FH (w); FH (a) 1.00
❑124, May 1993 FH (w); FH (a) 1.00
❑125, Jun 1993 FH (w); FH (a) 1.00
❑126, Jul 1993 FH (w); FH (a) 1.00
❑127, Aug 1993 FH (w); FH (a) 1.00
❑128, Sep 1993 FH (w); FH (a) 1.00
❑129, Oct 1993; Flip-book; GP (c); FH (w); FH, GP (a); 1/2 X-Men/Avengers crossover poster; Biker Mice from Mars preview; Hellraiser/Marshal Law preview; Heavy Hitters Preview 1.25
❑130, Nov 1993; FH (w); FH (a); Marvels; poster 1.25
❑131, Dec 1993; FH (w); FH (a); Excalibur 1.25
❑132, Jan 1994; FH (w); FH (a); Force Works, ClanDestine 1.25
❑133, Feb 1994; FH (w); FH (a); X-Wedding, War Machine 1.25
❑134, Mar 1994; FH (w); FH (a); Beavis & Butt-Head 1.50
❑135, Apr 1994; FH (w); FH (a); Ghost Rider 2099; Conan the Adventurer 1.25
❑136, May 1994 FH (w); FH (a) 1.25
❑137, Jun 1994 FH (w); FH (a) 1.50
❑138, Jul 1994; Giant-size; FH (w); FH (a); remembering Jack Kirby; Spider-Man Animated Series, Blaze 1.50
❑139, Aug 1994; FH (w); FH (a); Batman and the Punisher 1.25
❑140, Sep 1994; FH (w); FH (a); Marvel Action Hour 1.25
❑Annual 1, Sep 1985 1.00
❑Annual 2, Sep 1986 1.00
❑Annual 3, Sep 1987 FH, JB, TD, MR (a) 1.00
❑Annual 4, Sep 1988; Wolverine 1.00

MARVEL AGE: FANTASTIC FOUR
MARVEL

❑1, Jun 2004 2.99
❑2, Jul 2004 2.25
❑3, Aug 2004 2.25
❑4, Sep 2004 2.25
❑5, Oct 2004 2.25
❑6, Nov 2004 2.25
❑7, Dec 2004 2.25
❑8, Jan 2005 2.25
❑9, Feb 2005 2.25
❑10, Mar 2005 2.25
❑11, Mar 2005 2.25
❑12, Apr 2005 2.25

MARVEL AGE: FANTASTIC FOUR TALES - THE THING
MARVEL

❑1, Apr 2005 2.25

MARVEL AGE HULK
MARVEL

❑1, Nov 2004 1.75
❑2, Dec 2004 1.75
❑3, Jan 2005 1.75
❑4, Feb 2005 1.75

Marvel: Heroes & Legends

Major Marvel events told from different POV

©Marvel

Marvel Knights

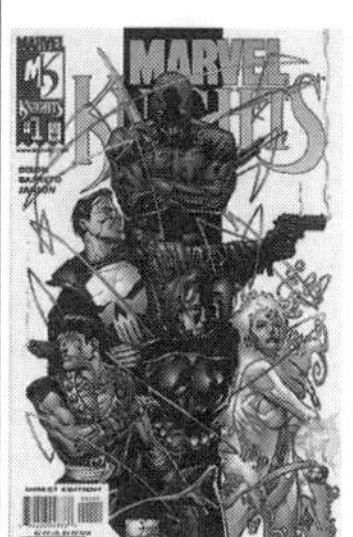

Marvel Knights characters cross over

©Marvel

Marvel Knights 4

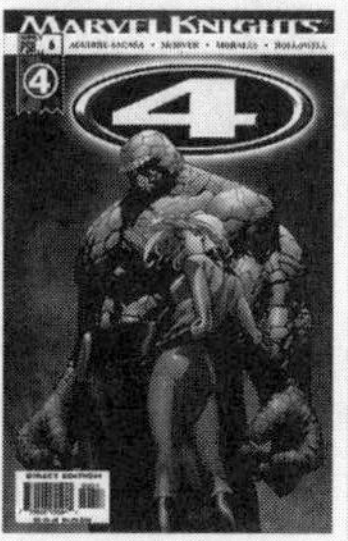

Fantastic adventures of Fantastic Four

©Marvel

Marvel Knights Spider-Man

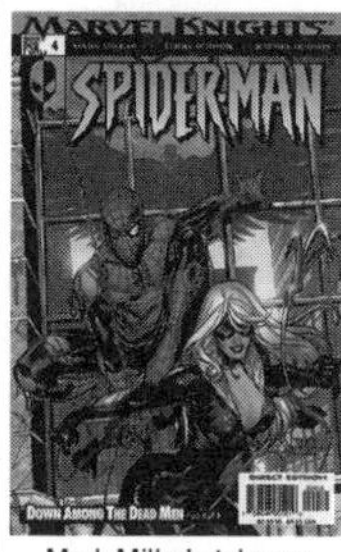

Mark Millar's take on the wallcrawler

©Marvel

Marvel Mangaverse

Manga-ized heroes failed to excite Marvelites

©Marvel

N-MINT

MARVEL AGE PREVIEW
MARVEL

❑1, Apr 1990 .... 1.50
❑2 .... 2.25

MARVEL AGE: RUNAWAYS
MARVEL

❑1, ca. 2004 .... 7.99

MARVEL AGE: SENTINEL
MARVEL

❑1, ca. 2004 .... 7.99

MARVEL AGE: SPIDER-GIRL
MARVEL

❑1, ca. 2004 .... 7.99

MARVEL AGE: SPIDER-MAN
MARVEL

❑1, May 2004, SD, SL (w) 2.99
❑1/FCBD, Aug 2004 .... 2.00
❑2, Jun 2004, SD, SL (w) 2.99
❑3, Jul 2004, SD, SL (w) 2.99
❑4, Jul 2004, SD, SL (w) 2.99
❑5, Aug 2004 .... 2.25
❑6, Aug 2004 .... 2.25
❑7, Sep 2004 .... 2.25
❑8, Sep 2004 .... 2.25
❑9, Oct 2004 .... 2.25
❑10, Oct 2004 .... 2.25
❑11, Nov 2004 .... 2.25
❑12, Nov 2004 .... 2.25
❑13, Dec 2004 .... 2.25
❑14, Dec 2004 .... 2.25
❑15, Jan 2005 .... 2.25
❑16, Jan 2005 .... 2.25
❑17, Feb 2005 .... 2.25
❑18, Feb 2005 .... 2.25
❑19, Mar 2005 .... 2.25
❑20, Apr 2005 .... 2.25

MARVEL AGE SPIDER-MAN TEAM UP
MARVEL

❑1, Nov 2004 .... 1.75
❑2, Dec 2004 .... 1.75
❑3, Jan 2005 .... 1.75
❑4, Mar 2005 .... 1.75
❑5, Apr 2005 .... 2.25

MARVEL AND DC PRESENT
MARVEL

❑1, Nov 1982; TD (a); X-Men & Titans; Early Marvel/DC crossover 12.00

MARVEL BOY (2ND SERIES)
MARVEL

❑1/A, Aug 2000; Dynamic Forces cover 5.00
❑1, Aug 2000 .... 2.99
❑2, Sep 2000 .... 2.99
❑3, Oct 2000 .... 2.99
❑4, Nov 2000 .... 2.99
❑5, Dec 2000 .... 2.99
❑6, Mar 2001 .... 2.99

MARVEL CHILLERS
MARVEL

❑1, Nov 1975, 1: The Other (Chthon). 1: Modred the Mystic 12.00
❑2, Jan 1976, A: Tigra. Modred 7.00

N-MINT

❑3, Mar 1976, O: Tigra. 1: The Darkhold. Tigra 10.00
❑4, May 1976, A: Tigra. A: Kraven 7.00
❑4/30 cent, May 1976, 30 cent regional price variant 20.00
❑5, Jun 1976, A: Tigra 7.00
❑5/30 cent, Jun 1976, 30 cent regional price variant 20.00
❑6, Aug 1976, JBy (a); A: Tigra 5.00
❑6/30 cent, Aug 1976, 30 cent regional price variant 20.00
❑7, Oct 1976, A: Tigra 5.00

MARVEL CHILLERS: SHADES OF GREEN MONSTERS
MARVEL

❑1, Mar 1997; mostly text story 2.99

MARVEL CHILLERS: THE THING IN THE GLASS CASE
MARVEL

❑1, Mar 1997; mostly text story 2.99

MARVEL CLASSICS COMICS
MARVEL

❑1, Jan 1976, NR (a) 7.00
❑2, Feb 1976 .... 5.00
❑3, Mar 1976 .... 5.00
❑4, Apr 1976 .... 5.00
❑5, May 1976 .... 5.00
❑6, Jun 1976 .... 4.00
❑7, Jul 1976 .... 4.00
❑8, Aug 1976 .... 4.00
❑9, Sep 1976 .... 4.00
❑10, Oct 1976 .... 4.00
❑11, Nov 1976 .... 4.00
❑12, Dec 1976 .... 4.00
❑13, Jan 1977 .... 4.00
❑14, Feb 1977 .... 4.00
❑15, Mar 1977 .... 4.00
❑16, Apr 1977 .... 4.00
❑17, May 1977 .... 4.00
❑18, Jun 1977 .... 4.00
❑19, Jul 1977 .... 4.00
❑20, Aug 1977 .... 4.00
❑21, Sep 1977 .... 4.00
❑22, Oct 1977 .... 4.00
❑23, Nov 1977 .... 4.00
❑24, Dec 1977 .... 4.00
❑25, Jan 1978 .... 4.00
❑26, Feb 1978, PG (a) 4.00
❑27, Mar 1978 .... 4.00
❑28, Apr 1978, MG (a); Mike Golden's first professional art 8.00
❑29, May 1978 .... 4.00
❑30, Jun 1978 .... 4.00
❑31, Jul 1978 .... 4.00
❑32, Aug 1978 .... 4.00
❑33, Sep 1978 .... 4.00
❑34, Oct 1978, AA (a) 4.00
❑35, Nov 1978 .... 4.00
❑36, Dec 1978, BH (c) 4.00

MARVEL COLLECTIBLE CLASSICS: AMAZING SPIDER-MAN
MARVEL

❑300, TMc (a); 1: Venom. Chromium wraparound cover; Reprints Amazing Spider-Man #300 .... 13.50

N-MINT

❑300/Autographed, TMc (a); 1: Venom. Chromium wraparound cover; Reprints Amazing Spider-Man #300 29.99

MARVEL COLLECTIBLE CLASSICS: AVENGERS (VOL. 3)
MARVEL

❑1, Nov 1998, Chromium wraparound cover 13.50

MARVEL COLLECTIBLE CLASSICS: X-MEN
MARVEL

❑1, Aug 1998, Chromium wraparound cover; Reprints X-Men #1 .... 13.50
❑Giant Size 1, Nov 1998, Reprints Giant Size X-Men #1; Chromium wraparound cover 13.50

MARVEL COLLECTIBLE CLASSICS: X-MEN (VOL. 2)
MARVEL

❑1, Oct 1998, JLee (a); Chromium wraparound cover 13.50
❑1/Autographed, Oct 1998, JLee (a); Chromium wraparound cover 29.99

MARVEL COLLECTOR'S EDITION
MARVEL

❑1 1992; RHo (w); Spider-Man, Wolverine, Ghost Rider; Charleston Chew promotion, $.50 and a candy bar wrapper; Flip-book format 2.50

MARVEL COLLECTORS' ITEM CLASSICS
MARVEL

❑1, Feb 1966 .... 125.00
❑2, Apr 1966 .... 70.00
❑3, Jun 1966; reprints Fantastic Four (Vol. 1) #4, Tales of Suspense #40, Incredible Hulk #3, Tales of Suspense #49, Strange Tales #110. 45.00
❑4, Aug 1966 .... 45.00
❑5, Oct 1966 .... 30.00
❑6, Dec 1966 .... 30.00
❑7, Feb 1967 .... 15.00
❑8, Apr 1967 .... 15.00
❑9, Jun 1967 .... 15.00
❑10, Aug 1967 .... 15.00
❑11, Oct 1967 .... 12.00
❑12, Dec 1967 .... 12.00
❑13, Feb 1968 .... 12.00
❑14, Apr 1968 .... 12.00
❑15, Jun 1968 .... 12.00
❑16, Aug 1968 .... 12.00
❑17, Oct 1968 .... 12.00
❑18, Dec 1968 .... 12.00
❑19, Feb 1969 SL (w); DH, JK (a) 12.00
❑20, Apr 1969 .... 12.00
❑21, Jun 1969 .... 15.00
❑22, Aug 1969; Series continued in Marvel's Greatest Comics #23 .... 17.00
❑23, Oct 1969 .... 20.00

MARVEL COMICS PRESENTS
MARVEL

❑1, Sep 1988; AM (w); AM, TS, JB, DC, KJ (a); Wolverine features begin 4.00
❑2, Sep 1988; KJ (c); AM (w); AM, TS, JB, DC, KJ (a); Wolverine 2.50

	N-MINT
❑3, Sep 1988; JR2, BWi (c); AM (w); AM, TS, JB, DC, KJ (a); Wolverine	2.50
❑4, Oct 1988; AM, CR (c); AM (w); AM, TS, JB, DC, KJ (a); Wolverine	2.50
❑5, Oct 1988; TS, JB, DC, MGu, KJ (a); Wolverine	2.50
❑6, Nov 1988; TS, JB (a); A: Sub-Mariner. Wolverine	2.00
❑7, Nov 1988; BL (c); SD (w); TS, SD, JB, DC, KJ (a); Wolverine	2.00
❑8, Dec 1988; TS, JB (a); Wolverine	2.00
❑9, Dec 1988; TS, JB, KJ (a); Wolverine	2.00
❑10, Jan 1989; SD (w); TS, SD, JB, CR, KJ (a); Wolverine; Colossus features begin	2.00
❑11, Jan 1989; TS, BL (a); Colossus	1.50
❑12, Feb 1989; TS, DH, FS (a); Colossus, Man-Thing	1.50
❑13, Feb 1989; GC (a); Colossus	1.50
❑14, Mar 1989; SD (w); GC (a); Colossus	1.50
❑15, Mar 1989; GC (a); Colossus	1.50
❑16, Mar 1989; GC (a); Colossus	1.50
❑17, Apr 1989; TS, GC (a); Cyclops features begin	1.50
❑18, Apr 1989; JBy (w); RHo, GC, JBy (a); She-Hulk, Cyclops	1.50
❑19, May 1989; GC (a); 1: Damage Control. Cyclops	1.50
❑20, May 1989; GC (a); Cyclops	1.50
❑21, Jun 1989; GC (a); Cyclops	1.50
❑22, Jun 1989; GC, DC (a); Cyclops	1.50
❑23, Jul 1989; GC, DC (a); Cyclops	1.50
❑24, Jul 1989; RB, GC (a); Cyclops, Havok	1.50
❑25, Aug 1989; RB, GC (a); O: Nth Man. 1: Nth Man. Havok	1.50
❑26, Aug 1989; RB, GC, PG (a); 1: Coldblood. Havok	1.50
❑27, Sep 1989; RB, GC, PG (a); Havok	1.50
❑28, Sep 1989; RB, GC, PG (a); Havok	1.50
❑29, Sep 1989; RB, GC, PG (a); Havok	1.50
❑30, Oct 1989; RB, GC, PG (a); A: Wolverine. Havok	1.50
❑31, Oct 1989; RB, GC, PG, EL (a); O: Coldblood. Havok, Excalibur	1.50
❑32, Nov 1989; TMc (c); GC, DH, PG, EL (a); Excalibur	1.50
❑33, Nov 1989; GC, PG, JLee, EL (a); Excalibur	1.50
❑34, Dec 1989; GC, PG, EL (a); Excalibur	1.50
❑35, Dec 1989; GC, PG, EL (a); 1: Starduster. Excalibur	1.50
❑36, Jan 1989; GC, EL (a); Excalibur	1.50
❑37, Jan 1989; GC, EL (a); Excalibur	1.50
❑38, Feb 1989; JB, EL, MR (a); Excalibur	2.00
❑39, Feb 1989; BL (w); JB, BL, EL (a); Wolverine	1.50
❑40, Mar 1989; BL (w); JB, BL, DH (a); Wolverine	1.50
❑41, Mar 1990; BL (w); JB, BL, DC (a); Wolverine	1.50
❑42, Mar 1990; JB (a); Wolverine	1.50
❑43, Apr 1990; JB (a); Wolverine	1.50
❑44, Apr 1990; JB (a); Wolverine	1.50
❑45, May 1990; JB (a); Wolverine	1.50
❑46, May 1990; JB (a); Wolverine	1.50
❑47, Apr 1990; JB (a); Wolverine; cover dates, which only appeared in the indicia or in Marvel's catalog copy, actually do go backwards for a while at this point	1.50
❑48, Apr 1990; Spider-Man, Wolverine	2.00
❑49, May 1990; 1: Whiplash II. Spider-Man, Wolverine	2.00
❑50, May 1990; O: Captain Ultra. Spider-Man, Wolverine	2.00
❑51, Jun 1990; PG (c); RL (a); Wolverine	2.00
❑52, Jun 1990; RL (a); Wolverine	2.00
❑53, Jul 1990; RL (a); Wolverine	2.00
❑54, Jul 1990; Wolverine & Hulk	2.50
❑55, Jul 1990; Wolverine & Hulk	2.50
❑56, Aug 1990; SD (w); Wolverine & Hulk	2.50
❑57, Aug 1990; Wolverine & Hulk	2.50
❑58, Sep 1990; SD (w); Wolverine & Hulk	2.50
❑59, Sep 1990; Wolverine & Hulk	2.50
❑60, Oct 1990; RHo (w); RHo (a); Wolverine & Hulk	2.50

	N-MINT
❑61, Oct 1990; RHo (w); RHo (a); Wolverine & Hulk	2.50
❑62, Nov 1990; RHo (w); RHo, BG (a); Wolverine	2.50
❑63, Nov 1990; RHo (w); RHo, DH (a); Wolverine	2.00
❑64, Dec 1990; Wolverine, Ghost Rider	2.00
❑65, Dec 1990; Wolverine, Ghost Rider	2.00
❑66, Dec 1990; Wolverine, Ghost Rider	2.00
❑67, Jan 1991; Wolverine, Ghost Rider	2.00
❑68, Jan 1991; PG (a); Wolverine, Ghost Rider	2.00
❑69, Feb 1991; PG (a); Wolverine, Ghost Rider	2.00
❑70, Feb 1991; PG (a); Wolverine, Ghost Rider	2.00
❑71, Mar 1991; PG (a); Wolverine, Ghost Rider	2.00
❑72, Mar 1991; PG (a); Weapon X	4.00
❑73, Mar 1991; PG, JM (a); Weapon X	3.00
❑74, Apr 1991; PG, JSa (a); Weapon X	3.00
❑75, Apr 1991; PG (a); Weapon X	3.00
❑76, May 1991; PG (a); Weapon X	3.00
❑77, May 1991; PG (a); Weapon X	3.00
❑78, Jun 1991; Weapon X	3.00
❑79, Jun 1991; JBy (a); Weapon X	3.00
❑80, Jul 1991; SD (w); SD (a); Weapon X	3.00
❑81, Jul 1991; SD (w); SD, MR (a); Weapon X; Daredevil	3.00
❑82, Aug 1991; Weapon X	3.00
❑83, Aug 1991; SD (w); EL (a); Weapon X	3.00
❑84, Sep 1991; Weapon X	3.00
❑85, Sep 1991; PD (w); RL (a); 1: Cyber. Wolverine; 1st Kieth art on Wolverine	3.00
❑86, Oct 1991; PD (w); RL (a); Wolverine	2.50
❑87, Oct 1991; PD (w); RL (a); Wolverine	2.00
❑88, Nov 1991; PD (w); Wolverine	2.00
❑89, Nov 1991; PD (w); Wolverine	2.00
❑90, Dec 1991; PD (w); A: Ghost Rider. A: Cable. Flip-book covers begin; Wolverine	2.00
❑91, Dec 1991; PD (w); A: Ghost Rider. A: Cable. Wolverine	1.50
❑92, Dec 1991; PD (w); A: Ghost Rider. A: Cable. Wolverine	1.50
❑93, Jan 1992; A: Ghost Rider. A: Cable. Wolverine	1.50
❑94, Jan 1992; A: Ghost Rider. A: Cable. Wolverine	1.50
❑95, Feb 1992; A: Ghost Rider. A: Cable. Wolverine	1.50
❑96, Feb 1992; A: Ghost Rider. A: Cable. Wolverine	1.50
❑97, Mar 1992; A: Ghost Rider. A: Cable. Wolverine	1.50
❑98, Mar 1992; Wolverine	1.50
❑99, Apr 1992; RL (w); Wolverine	1.50
❑100, Apr 1992; Anniversary issue; A: Ghost Rider. V: Doctor Doom. Wolverine	1.50
❑101, May 1992; TS, GC (a); Wolverine, Nightcrawler	1.50
❑102, May 1992; TS, GC (a); Wolverine, Nightcrawler	1.50
❑103, May 1992; TS, GC (a); Wolverine, Nightcrawler	1.50
❑104, Jun 1992; TS, GC (a); Wolverine, Nightcrawler	1.50
❑105, Jun 1992; TS, GC (a); Wolverine, Nightcrawler	1.50
❑106, Jul 1992; TS, GC (a); Wolverine, Nightcrawler	1.50
❑107, Jul 1992; TS, GC (a); Wolverine, Nightcrawler	1.50
❑108, Aug 1992; TS, GC (a); Wolverine, Ghost Rider	1.50
❑109, Aug 1992; JSn (w); A: Typhoid Mary. Wolverine, Ghost Rider	1.50
❑110, Sep 1992; JSn (w); A: Typhoid Mary. Wolverine, Ghost Rider	1.50
❑111, Sep 1992; JSn (w); A: Typhoid Mary. Infinity War; Wolverine, Ghost Rider	1.50
❑112, Oct 1992; JSn (w); GC (a); A: Typhoid Mary. Wolverine, Ghost Rider	1.50
❑113, Oct 1992; A: Typhoid Mary. Wolverine, Ghost Rider	1.50
❑114, Oct 1992; A: Typhoid Mary. Wolverine, Ghost Rider	1.50

	N-MINT
❑115, Nov 1992; A: Typhoid Mary. Wolverine, Ghost Rider	1.50
❑116, Nov 1992; GK (a); A: Typhoid Mary. Wolverine, Ghost Rider	1.50
❑117, Dec 1992; 1: Ravage 2099. A: Venom. Wolverine, Ghost Rider; Ravage 2099 preview	1.50
❑118, Dec 1992; 1: Doom 2099. A: Venom. Wolverine; Doom 2099 preview	1.50
❑119, Jan 1993; A: Venom. Wolverine	1.50
❑120, Jan 1993; A: Venom. Wolverine	1.50
❑121, Feb 1993; Wolverine	1.50
❑122, Feb 1993; Wolverine	1.50
❑123, Mar 1993; Wolverine	1.50
❑124, Mar 1993; Wolverine	1.50
❑125, Apr 1993; Wolverine	1.50
❑126, Apr 1993; Wolverine	1.50
❑127, May 1993; DP (a); Wolverine	1.50
❑128, May 1993; Wolverine	1.50
❑129, May 1993; Wolverine	1.50
❑130, Jun 1993; Wolverine	1.50
❑131, Jun 1993; Wolverine	1.50
❑132, Jul 1993; Wolverine	1.50
❑133, Jul 1993; Wolverine	1.50
❑134, Aug 1993; Wolverine	1.50
❑135, Aug 1993; Wolverine	1.50
❑136, Sep 1993; Wolverine	1.50
❑137, Sep 1993; Wolverine	1.50
❑138, Sep 1993 EL (w); A: Masters of Silence. A: Ghost Rider. A: Wolverine. A: Wusin. A: Spellbound. A: Nightcrawler	1.50
❑139, Oct 1993 EL (w); A: Masters of Silence. A: Ghost Rider. A: Wolverine. A: Wusin. A: Foreigner. A: Spellbound. A: Zxaxz	1.50
❑140, Oct 1993 EL (w); O: Captain Universe. A: Masters of Silence. A: Ghost Rider. A: Wolverine. A: Wusin. A: Captain Universe. A: Spellbound. A: Zxaxz	1.50
❑141, Nov 1993	1.50
❑142, Nov 1993	1.50
❑143, Dec 1993; Ghost Rider	1.75
❑144, Dec 1993; Ghost Rider	1.75
❑145, Jan 1994; Ghost Rider	1.75
❑146, Jan 1994	1.75
❑147, Feb 1994	1.75
❑148, Feb 1994	1.75
❑149, Mar 1994	1.75
❑150, Mar 1994	1.75
❑151, Apr 1994	1.75
❑152, Apr 1994	1.75
❑153, May 1994	1.75
❑154, May 1994	1.75
❑155, May 1994	1.75
❑156, Jun 1994	1.75
❑157, Jun 1994	1.75
❑158, Jul 1994	1.75
❑159, Jul 1994	1.75
❑160, Aug 1994	1.75
❑161, Aug 1994	1.75
❑162, Sep 1994	1.75
❑163, Sep 1994	1.75
❑164, Oct 1994	1.75
❑165, Oct 1994	1.75
❑166, Oct 1994	1.75
❑167, Nov 1994	1.75
❑168, Nov 1994	1.75
❑169, Dec 1994	1.75
❑170, Dec 1994	1.75
❑171, Jan 1995	1.75
❑172, Jan 1995	1.75
❑173, Feb 1995	1.75
❑174, Feb 1995 KG (a)	1.75
❑175, Mar 1995 KG (a)	1.75

MARVEL COMICS: 2001

Marvel

❑1, Jul 2001	1.00

MARVEL DOUBLE FEATURE

Marvel

❑1, Dec 1973	40.00
❑2, Feb 1974	20.00
❑3, Apr 1974	15.00
❑4, Jun 1974	10.00
❑5, Aug 1974	10.00
❑6, Oct 1974	10.00
❑7, Dec 1974	10.00

Marvel Premiere

Try-out title yielded Iron Fist, 3-D Man, others
©Marvel

Marvel Presents

Guardians of the Galaxy returned, expanded
©Marvel

Marvel Preview

Magazine-sized catch-all title
©Marvel

Marvel Riot

Aped Age of Apocalypse
©Marvel

Marvel Saga

Cohesive timeline applied to Marvel universe
©Marvel

	N-MINT
❑8, Feb 1975	10.00
❑9, Apr 1975	8.00
❑10, Jun 1975	8.00
❑11, Aug 1975	8.00
❑12, Oct 1975	8.00
❑13, Dec 1975	8.00
❑14, Feb 1976	8.00
❑15, Apr 1976	8.00
❑15/30 cent, Apr 1976, 30 cent regional price variant	20.00
❑16, Jun 1976	8.00
❑16/30 cent, Jun 1976, 30 cent regional price variant	20.00
❑17, Aug 1976, Reprints Iron Man vs. Sub-Mariner #1	8.00
❑17/30 cent, Aug 1976, Reprints Iron Man vs. Sub-Mariner #1; 30 cent regional price variant	20.00
❑18, Oct 1976, Reprints story from Iron Man #1	8.00
❑19, Dec 1976	6.00
❑20, Feb 1977	6.00
❑21, Apr 1977	6.00

MARVEL DOUBLE SHOT
MARVEL

	N-MINT
❑1, Jan 2003; Thor/Hulk	2.99
❑2, Feb 2003; Avengers/Doom	2.99
❑3, Mar 2003; Ant-Man/Fantastic Four	2.99
❑4, Apr 2003; Dr. Strange/Iron Man	2.99

MARVEL ENCYCLOPEDIA
MARVEL

	N-MINT
❑1, ca. 2003	29.99
❑2, ca. 2003	29.99
❑3, ca. 2003	19.99
❑4, ca. 2003	24.99
❑5, ca. 2004; Marvel Knights	29.99
❑6	29.99

MARVEL ENCYCLOPEDIA (MAGAZINE)
MARVEL

	N-MINT
❑1, ca. 2004; magazine-sized; compiles information from other Marvel Encyclopedias; sold in department stores	5.99

MARVEL FANFARE
MARVEL

	N-MINT
❑1, Mar 1982; FM (c); MG, PS, FM, TD (a); 1: Vertigo II. Spider-Man; Daredevil; Angel	4.50
❑2, May 1982; MG (a); Spider-Man; Angel; Ka-Zar; Fantastic Four	3.25
❑3, Jul 1982; DC (a); X-Men	3.25
❑4, Sep 1982; MG, PS, TD (a); X-Men; Deathlok	2.50
❑5, Nov 1982; CR, MR (a); Doctor Strange	2.50
❑6, Jan 1983; Spider-Man; Doctor Strange; Scarlet Witch	2.00
❑7, Mar 1983; DD (a); Hulk; Daredevil	2.00
❑8, May 1983; CI (a); Doctor Strange; Mowgli	2.00
❑9, Jul 1983; Man-Thing; Mowgli	2.00
❑10, Aug 1983; GP (c); GP (a); Black Widow; Mowgli	2.00
❑11, Nov 1983; GP (a); Black Widow	2.00
❑12, Jan 1984; GP (a); Black Widow	2.00
❑13, Mar 1984; GP (a); Black Widow	2.00
❑14, May 1984; Vision; Quicksilver	2.00
❑15, Jul 1984; Thing	2.00
❑16, Sep 1984; DC (a); Skywolf	2.00
❑17, Nov 1984; DC (a); Skywolf	2.00
❑18, Jan 1985; FM (a); Captain America	2.00
❑19, Mar 1985; JSn (a); Cloak & Dagger	2.00
❑20, May 1985; JSn (w); JSn (a); Thing; Hulk; Doctor Strange	2.00
❑21, Jul 1985; JSn (a); Thing; Hulk	2.00
❑22, Sep 1985; JSn (a); Thing; Hulk; Iron Man	2.00
❑23, Nov 1985; JSn (a); Thing; Hulk; Iron Man	2.00
❑24, Jan 1986; Weirdworld	2.00
❑25, Mar 1986; PB (a); Dave Sim pin-up section; Weirdworld	2.00
❑26, May 1986; PB (a); Weirdworld	2.00
❑27, Jul 1986; Weirdworld; Spider-Man; Daredevil	2.00
❑28, Sep 1986; Alpha Flight	2.00
❑29, Nov 1986; JBy (w); JBy (a); D: Hammer. D: Anvil. Hulk	2.00
❑30, Jan 1987; BA (a); Moon Knight; Painted cover	2.00
❑31, Mar 1987; KGa (a); Captain America	2.00
❑32, May 1987; Captain America	2.00
❑33, Jul 1987; Wolverine; X-Men	2.00
❑34, Sep 1987; Warriors Three	2.00
❑35, Nov 1987; Warriors Three	2.00
❑36, Jan 1988; Warriors Three	2.00
❑37, Mar 1988; Warriors Three	2.00
❑38, Apr 1988; Moon Knight	2.00
❑39, Aug 1988; Hawkeye; Moon Knight	2.00
❑40, Oct 1988; Angel; Storm	2.00
❑41, Dec 1988; DG (a); Doctor Strange	2.00
❑42, Feb 1989; BH (a); Spider-Man	2.00
❑43, Apr 1989; Sub-Mariner; Human Torch	2.00
❑44, Jun 1989; Iron Man; Iron Man vs. Doctor Doom	2.00
❑45, Aug 1989; JBy (c); all pin-ups	2.00
❑46, Oct 1989; Fantastic Four	2.00
❑47, Nov 1989; Spider-Man; Hulk	2.00
❑48, Dec 1989; She-Hulk	2.00
❑49, Feb 1990; Doctor Strange	2.00
❑50, Apr 1990; JSa (a); X-Factor	2.25
❑51, Jun 1990; Silver Surfer	2.95
❑52, Aug 1990; Black Knight; Fantastic Four	2.25
❑53, Oct 1990; Black Knight; Doctor Strange	2.25
❑54, Dec 1990; Black Knight; Wolverine	2.25
❑55, Feb 1991; Power Pack; Wolverine	2.25
❑56, Apr 1991; CI, DH (a); Shanna the She-Devil	2.25
❑57, Jun 1991; Captain Marvel; Shanna the She-Devil	2.25
❑58, Aug 1991; Shanna the She-Devil; Vision II (android); Scarlet Witch	2.25
❑59, Oct 1991; RHo, TD (a); Shanna the She-Devil	2.25
❑60, Jan 1992; PS (a); Black Panther; Rogue; Daredevil	2.25

MARVEL FANFARE (2ND SERIES)
MARVEL

	N-MINT
❑1, Sep 1996; A: Captain America. A: Deathlok. A: Falcon. Flipbook with Professor Xavier and the X-Men #11	1.50
❑2, Oct 1996 A: Wendigo. A: Hulk. A: Wolverine	1.00
❑3, Nov 1996 A: Ghost Rider. A: Spider-Man	1.00
❑4, Dec 1996 A: Longshot	1.00
❑5, Jan 1997 A: Dazzler. A: Longshot. V: Spiral	1.00
❑6, Feb 1997 A: Sabretooth. A: Power Man. A: Iron Fist. V: Sabretooth	1.00

MARVEL FEATURE (1ST SERIES)
MARVEL

	N-MINT
❑1, Dec 1971, NA (c); RA (a); O: Defenders. 1: Omegatron. 1: Defenders. D: Yandroth (physical body)	125.00
❑2, Mar 1972, BEv (a); 2: Defenders. Sub-Mariner reprint	60.00
❑3, Jun 1972, BEv (a); A: Defenders	30.00
❑4, Jul 1972, A: Peter Parker. A: Ant-Man	25.00
❑5, Sep 1972, A: Ant-Man	10.00
❑6, Nov 1972, A: Ant-Man	10.00
❑7, Jan 1973, GK (a); A: Ant-Man	10.00
❑8, Mar 1973, O: Wasp. A: Ant-Man	10.00
❑9, May 1973, CR (a); A: Iron Man. A: Ant-Man	10.00
❑10, Jul 1973, CR (a); A: Ant-Man	10.00
❑11, Sep 1973, Thing vs. Hulk	55.00
❑12, Nov 1973, A: Thing. A: Iron Man. A: Thanos	35.00

MARVEL FEATURE (2ND SERIES)
MARVEL

	N-MINT
❑1, Nov 1975, DG, NA (a); Red Sonja stories begin; Reprints Savage Sword of Conan #1	10.00
❑2, Jan 1976, FT (a)	3.00
❑3, Mar 1976	3.00
❑4, May 1976, FT (a)	3.00
❑4/30 cent, May 1976, 30 cent regional price variant	35.00
❑5, Jul 1976, FT (a)	3.00
❑5/30 cent, Jul 1976, 30 cent regional price variant	20.00
❑6, Sep 1976, A: Conan	3.00
❑7, Nov 1976, Red Sonja vs. Conan	3.00

MARVEL FRONTIER COMICS UNLIMITED
MARVEL

	N-MINT
❑1, Jan 1994	2.95

MARVEL FUMETTI BOOK
MARVEL

	N-MINT
❑1, Apr 1984, b&w; photos with balloon captions	2.00

MARVEL GRAPHIC NOVEL
MARVEL

	N-MINT
❑1, ca. 1982; JSn (w); JSn (a); D: Captain Marvel. Death of Captain Marvel	13.00
❑1/2nd; JSn (w); JSn (a); D: Captain Marvel. Death of Captain Marvel	6.00
❑1/3rd; JSn (w); JSn (a); D: Captain Marvel. Death of Captain Marvel	6.00

Other grades: Multiply price above by 5/6 for VF/NM • 2/3 for VERY FINE • 1/3 for FINE • 1/5 for VERY GOOD • 1/8 for GOOD

N-MINT | N-MINT | N-MINT

❑2, CR (a); Elric 7.00
❑3, JSn (w); JSn (a); Dreadstar 7.50
❑4, BMc (a); O: Sunspot. O: New Mutants. 1: Mirage II (Danielle "Dani" Moonstar). 1: New Mutants. New Mutants 12.00
❑4/2nd, BMc (a); O: Mirage II (Danielle "Dani" Moonstar). O: Sunspot. O: New Mutants. 1: Mirage II (Danielle "Dani" Moonstar). 1: Sunspot. 1: New Mutants. New Mutants 6.00
❑4/3rd, BMc (a); O: Mirage II (Danielle "Dani" Moonstar). O: Sunspot. O: New Mutants. 1: Mirage II (Danielle "Dani" Moonstar). 1: Sunspot. 1: New Mutants. New Mutants 5.00
❑5, BA (a); X-Men: God Loves, Man Kills 20.00
❑5/2nd; BA (a); X-Men: God Loves, Man Kills 7.00
❑5/3rd; BA (a); X-Men: God Loves, Man Kills 6.00
❑5/4th; BA (a); X-Men: God Loves, Man Kills 6.00
❑5/5th; BA (a); X-Men: God Loves, Man Kills 6.00
❑6; Star Slammers 6.00
❑7; CR (a); Killraven 6.00
❑8; JBy (a); Super Boxers 6.00
❑9; DC (w); DC (a); The Futurians 6.00
❑10; Heartburst 6.00
❑11; VM (a); Void Indigo 6.00
❑12; FS (a); Dazzler: The Movie 6.00
❑13; Starstruck 6.00
❑14; BG (a); Swords of the Swashbucklers 6.00
❑15; CV (a); Raven Banner 6.00
❑16; Aladdin Effect 6.00
❑17; Living Monolith 6.00
❑18; JBy (w); She-Hulk 7.00
❑19; Conan the Barbarian 7.00
❑20; Greenberg the Vampire 7.00
❑21; Marada the She-Wolf 7.00
❑22; BWr (a); Amazing Spider-Man 9.00
❑23; DGr (a); Dr. Strange 7.00
❑24; Daredevil 7.50
❑25; Dracula 7.00
❑26; Alien Legion 7.00
❑27; D: The Purple Man. Avengers 6.95
❑28; Conan the Reaver 6.95
❑29; Thing vs. Hulk 8.00
❑30, A Sailor's Story 5.95
❑31; O: Wolfpack. 1: Wolfpack. Wolfpack 6.95
❑32 D: Groo 10.00
❑33; Thor 6.95
❑34; Cloak & Dagger 6.95
❑35; Hardcover; Shadow 1941 .... 12.95
❑36; Willow 6.95
❑37; Hercules 7.00
❑38; Silver Surfer 16.00

MARVEL GRAPHIC NOVEL: ARENA
MARVEL

❑1 .... 5.95

MARVEL GRAPHIC NOVEL: CLOAK AND DAGGER AND POWER PACK: SHELTER FROM THE STORM
MARVEL

❑1 .... 7.95

MARVEL GRAPHIC NOVEL: EMPEROR DOOM: STARRING THE MIGHTY AVENGERS
MARVEL

❑1 .... 5.95

MARVEL GRAPHIC NOVEL: KA-ZAR: GUNS OF THE SAVAGE LAND
MARVEL

❑1 .... 8.95

MARVEL GRAPHIC NOVEL: RICK MASON, THE AGENT
MARVEL

❑1 1989 .... 9.95

MARVEL GRAPHIC NOVEL: ROGER RABBIT IN THE RESURRECTION OF DOOM
MARVEL

❑1 .... 8.95

MARVEL GRAPHIC NOVEL: WHO FRAMED ROGER RABBIT?
MARVEL

❑1 .... 6.95

MARVEL GUIDE TO COLLECTING COMICS
MARVEL

❑1, Sep 1982; no cover price 3.00

MARVEL HALLOWEEN: SUPERNATURALS TOUR BOOK
MARVEL

❑1, Nov 1998 .... 2.99

MARVEL: HEROES & LEGENDS
MARVEL

❑1, Oct 1996; backstory on Reed and Sue's wedding; wraparound cover.. 2.95
❑2, Nov 1997; untold Avengers story; Hawkeye, Quicksilver, Scarlet Witch joins team 2.99

MARVEL HEROES FLIP MAGAZINE
MARVEL

❑1, Jul 2005 .... 3.99
❑2, Aug 2005 .... 3.99
❑3, Sep 2005 .... 3.99
❑4 2005 .... 3.99
❑5 2005 .... 3.99
❑6, Jan 2006 .... 3.99
❑7, Feb 2006 .... 3.99
❑8, Mar 2006 .... 3.99
❑9, Apr 2006 .... 3.99
❑10, May 2006 .... 3.99
❑11, Jul 2006 .... 3.99
❑13, Aug 2006 .... 3.99
❑14, Sep 2006 .... 3.99

MARVEL HOLIDAY SPECIAL
MARVEL

❑1; SB, DC, KJ (a); no cover date or date in indicia 3.00
❑1992, Jan 1993; for 1992 holiday season 3.00
❑1993, Jan 1994; AM, MG (a); for 1993 holiday season 3.00
❑1994, Jan 1995; KB (w); GM, SB (a); for 1994 holiday season 3.00
❑1996, Jan 1997 .... 2.95

MARVEL HOLIDAY SPECIAL 2004
MARVEL

❑1, Dec 2004 .... 3.99

MARVEL HOLIDAY SPECIAL 2005
MARVEL

❑1, Jan 2006 .... 3.99

MARVEL ILLUSTRATED: SWIMSUIT ISSUE
MARVEL

❑1, Mar 1991 .... 3.95

MARVEL KNIGHTS
MARVEL

❑1, Jul 2000 .... 3.50
❑1/A, Jul 2000; Daredevil close-up cover 5.00
❑2/Barreto, Aug 2000, b&w; A: Ulik. Barreto cover; Cloak and Dagger 4.00
❑2/Quesada, Aug 2000, b&w; Variant cover by Joe Quesada; Dagger in foreground 5.00
❑3, Sep 2000 A: Ulik 2.99
❑4, Oct 2000 .... 2.99
❑5, Nov 2000 .... 2.99
❑6, Dec 2000 .... 2.99
❑7, Jan 2001 .... 2.99
❑8, Feb 2001 .... 2.99
❑9, Mar 2001 .... 2.99
❑10, Apr 2001 .... 2.99
❑11, May 2001 .... 2.99
❑12, Jun 2001 .... 2.99
❑13, Jul 2001 .... 2.99
❑14, Aug 2001 .... 2.99
❑15, Sep 2001 .... 2.99

MARVEL KNIGHTS (VOL. 2)
MARVEL

❑1, May 2002 .... 2.99
❑2, Jun 2002 .... 2.99
❑3, Jul 2002 .... 2.99
❑4, Aug 2002 .... 2.99
❑5, Sep 2002 .... 2.99
❑6, Oct 2002 .... 2.99

MARVEL KNIGHTS 4
MARVEL

❑1, Apr 2004 .... 4.00
❑2, Apr 2004 .... 2.99
❑3, May 2004 .... 2.99
❑4, May 2004 .... 2.99
❑5, Jun 2004 .... 2.99
❑6, Jun 2004 .... 2.99
❑7, Sep 2004 .... 2.99
❑8, Sep 2004 .... 2.99
❑9, Oct 2004 .... 2.99
❑10, Nov 2004 .... 2.99
❑11, Dec 2004 .... 2.99
❑12, Jan 2004 .... 2.99
❑13, Feb 2005 .... 2.99
❑14, Mar 2005 .... 2.99
❑15, Apr 2005 .... 2.99
❑16, May 2005 .... 2.99
❑17, Jun 2005 .... 2.99
❑18, Jul 2005 .... 2.99
❑19, Aug 2005 .... 2.99
❑20, Sep 2005 .... 2.99
❑21, Oct 2005 .... 2.99
❑22, Nov 2005 .... 2.99
❑23, Dec 2005 .... 2.99
❑24, Jan 2006 .... 2.99
❑25, Feb 2006 .... 2.99
❑26, Mar 2006 .... 2.99
❑27, Apr 2006 .... 2.99
❑28, May 2006 .... 2.99
❑29, Jul 2006 .... 2.99

MARVEL KNIGHTS DOUBLE-SHOT
MARVEL

❑1, Jun 2002 .... 2.99
❑2, Jul 2002 .... 2.99
❑3, Aug 2002 .... 2.99
❑4, Sep 2002 .... 2.99

MARVEL KNIGHTS MAGAZINE
MARVEL

❑1 .... 3.99
❑2 .... 3.99
❑3, Jul 2001 .... 3.99
❑4 .... 3.99
❑5 .... 3.99
❑6 .... 3.99

MARVEL KNIGHTS/MARVEL BOY GENESIS EDITION
MARVEL

❑1, Jun 2000; Polybagged with Punisher (5th Series) #3 .... 1.00

MARVEL KNIGHTS: MILLENNIAL VISIONS
MARVEL

❑1, Feb 2002 .... 3.99

MARVEL KNIGHTS SKETCHBOOK
MARVEL

❑1; BWr (a); Bundled with Wizard #84 1.00

MARVEL KNIGHTS SPIDER-MAN
MARVEL

❑1, Jun 2004 .... 5.00
❑2, Jul 2004 .... 4.00
❑3, Aug 2004 .... 2.99
❑4, Sep 2004 .... 2.99
❑5, Oct 2004 .... 2.25
❑6, Nov 2004 .... 2.99
❑7, Dec 2004 .... 2.99
❑8, Jan 2005 .... 2.99
❑9, Feb 2005 .... 2.99
❑10, Mar 2005 .... 2.99
❑11, Apr 2005 .... 2.99
❑12, May 2005 .... 2.99
❑13, Jun 2005 .... 2.99
❑14, Jul 2005 .... 2.99
❑15, Aug 2005 .... 2.99
❑16, Sep 2005 .... 2.99
❑17, Oct 2005 .... 2.99
❑18, Nov 2005 .... 2.99
❑19, Dec 2005 .... 2.99
❑20, Jan 2006 .... 2.99
❑21, Feb 2006 .... 2.99
❑22, Mar 2006 .... 2.99
❑24, May 2006 .... 2.99
❑25, Jun 2006 .... 2.99

Other grades: Multiply price above by 5/6 for VF/NM • 2/3 for VERY FINE • 1/3 for FINE • 1/5 for VERY GOOD • 1/8 for GOOD

Marvels Comics: Spider-Man

Comics as seen in the Marvel universe

©Marvel

Marvel's Greatest Comics

Continues Marvel Collector's Item Classics

©Marvel

Marvel: Shadows & Light

Black-and-white one-shot anthology

©Marvel

Marvel 1602

Neil Gaiman spins 17th century tale

©Marvel

Marvel Spectacular

Short-lived Thor reprint title

©Marvel

N-MINT

MARVEL KNIGHTS TOUR BOOK
MARVEL

❑1, Oct 1998; previews and interviews 2.99

MARVEL KNIGHTS 2099: BLACK PANTHER
MARVEL

❑1 2004 4.00

MARVEL KNIGHTS 2099: DAREDEVIL
MARVEL

❑1 2004 4.00

MARVEL KNIGHTS 2099: INHUMANS
MARVEL

❑1 2004 4.00

MARVEL KNIGHTS 2099: MUTANT
MARVEL

❑1 2004 4.00

MARVEL KNIGHTS 2099: PUNISHER
MARVEL

❑1 2004 4.00

MARVEL KNIGHTS WAVE 2 SKETCHBOOK
MARVEL

❑1; Special free edition from Marvel in Wizard #90; DGry (w); Sketchbook. 1.00

MARVEL LEGACY: THE 1960S HANDBOOK
MARVEL

❑1, Apr 2006 3.99

MARVEL MANGAVERSE
MARVEL

❑1, Jun 2002 2.25
❑2, Jul 2002 2.25
❑3, Aug 2002 2.25
❑4, Sep 2002 2.25
❑5, Oct 2002 2.25
❑6, Nov 2002 2.25

MARVEL MANGAVERSE: AVENGERS ASSEMBLE!
MARVEL

❑1, Mar 2002 2.25

MARVEL MANGAVERSE: ETERNITY TWILIGHT
MARVEL

❑1, Mar 2002 2.25
❑1/A 3.50

MARVEL MANGAVERSE: FANTASTIC FOUR
MARVEL

❑1, Mar 2002 2.25

MARVEL MANGAVERSE: GHOST RIDERS
MARVEL

❑1, Mar 2002 2.25

MARVEL MANGAVERSE: NEW DAWN
MARVEL

❑1, Mar 2002 3.50

MARVEL MANGAVERSE: PUNISHER
MARVEL

❑1, Mar 2002 2.25

N-MINT

MARVEL MANGAVERSE: SPIDER-MAN
MARVEL

❑1, Mar 2002 2.25

MARVEL MANGAVERSE: X-MEN
MARVEL

❑1, Mar 2002 2.25

MARVEL MASTERPIECES 2 COLLECTION
MARVEL

❑1, Jul 1994; Pin-ups 2.95
❑2, Aug 1994 2.95
❑3, Sep 1994 2.95

MARVEL MASTERPIECES COLLECTION
MARVEL

❑1, May 1993 2.95
❑2, Jun 1993 2.95
❑3, Jul 1993 2.95
❑4, Aug 1993 2.95

MARVEL MILESTONE EDITION: AMAZING FANTASY
MARVEL

❑15, Mar 1992, Reprints of Amazing Fantasy # 15: Spider-man's Origin.. 2.95

MARVEL MILESTONE EDITION: AMAZING SPIDER-MAN
MARVEL

❑1, Jan 1993; Reprints Amazing Spider-Man #1 2.95
❑3, Mar 1995; Reprints Amazing Spider-Man #3 2.95
❑129; Reprints Amazing Spider-Man #129 2.95
❑149, Nov 1994; indicia says Marvel Milestone Edition: Amazing Spider-Man #1; Reprints Amazing Spider-Man #149 2.95

MARVEL MILESTONE EDITION: AVENGERS
MARVEL

❑1, Sep 1993; Reprints The Avengers #1; Thor, Iron Man, Ant-man, Wasp, Hulk 2.95
❑4, Mar 1995; Reprints The Avengers #4; Captain America Joins 2.95
❑16; Reprints The Avengers #16; New team begins: Captain America, Hawkeye, Quicksilver, and Scarlet Witch 2.95

MARVEL MILESTONE EDITION: CAPTAIN AMERICA
MARVEL

❑1, Mar 1995; Reprints Captain America #1 3.95

MARVEL MILESTONE EDITION: FANTASTIC FOUR
MARVEL

❑1, Nov 1991 2.95
❑5, Nov 1992 2.95

MARVEL MILESTONE EDITION: GIANT-SIZE X-MEN
MARVEL

❑1 1991 3.95

N-MINT

MARVEL MILESTONE EDITION: INCREDIBLE HULK
MARVEL

❑1, Mar 1991; Reprints Incredible Hulk #1 2.95

MARVEL MILESTONE EDITION: IRON FIST
MARVEL

❑14 2.95

MARVEL MILESTONE EDITION: IRON MAN
MARVEL

❑55, Nov 1992, Reprints Iron Man #55 2.95

MARVEL MILESTONE EDITION: IRON MAN, ANT-MAN & CAPTAIN AMERICA
MARVEL

❑1, May 2005 3.99

MARVEL MILESTONE EDITION: TALES OF SUSPENSE
MARVEL

❑39, Nov 1994; Reprints Tales of Suspense #39 2.95

MARVEL MILESTONE EDITION: X-MEN
MARVEL

❑1 1991; reprint (first series) 2.95
❑9, Oct 1993; Reprints X-Men (1st Series) #9 2.95
❑28, Nov 1994; indicia says Marvel Milestone Edition: X-Men #1; Reprints X-Men (1st Series) #28 2.95

MARVEL MILESTONES: BEAST & KITTY
MARVEL

❑1, Jul 2006 3.99

MARVEL MILESTONES: BLACK PANTHER, STORM, AND KA-ZAR
MARVEL

❑1, Aug 2006 3.99

MARVEL MILESTONES: BLADE, MAN-THING & SATANA
MARVEL

❑1 3.99

MARVEL MILESTONES: BLOODSTONE, X-51, CAPTAIN MARVEL II
MARVEL

❑1, Mar 2006 3.99

MARVEL MILESTONES: CAPTAIN BRITAIN, PSYLOCKE, AND GOLDEN AGE SUB-MARINER
MARVEL

❑1, Oct 2005 3.99

MARVEL MILESTONES: DRAGON LORD, SPEEDBALL, AND MAN IN THE SKY
MARVEL

❑1, May 2006 3.99

MARVEL MILESTONES: DR. DOOM, SUB-MARINER, & RED SKULL
MARVEL

❑0, Jul 2005 3.99

Other grades: Multiply price above by 5/6 for VF/NM • 2/3 for VERY FINE • 1/3 for FINE • 1/5 for VERY GOOD • 1/8 for GOOD

MARVEL MILESTONES: DR. STRANGE, SILVER SURFER, SUB-MARINER, HULK
MARVEL
❑1, Sep 2005 ... 3.99

MARVEL MILESTONES: GHOST RIDER, BLACK WIDOW & ICEMAN
MARVEL
❑1 2005 ... 3.99

MARVEL MILESTONES: RAWHIDE KID AND TWO-GUN KID
MARVEL
❑1, Sep 2006 ... 3.99

MARVEL MILESTONES: STAR BRAND AND QUASAR
MARVEL
❑1, May 2006 ... 3.99

MARVEL MILESTONES: ULTIMATE SPIDER-MAN, ULTIMATE X-MEN, MICROMAN & MANTOR
MARVEL
❑1, Jan 2006 ... 3.99

MARVEL MONSTERS: DEVIL DINOSAUR
MARVEL
❑1 ... 3.99

MARVEL MONSTERS FIN FANG FOUR
MARVEL
❑1, Dec 2005, b&w ... 3.99

MARVEL MONSTERS: FROM THE FILES OF ULYSSES BLOODSTONE
MARVEL
❑1, Jan 2006 ... 3.99

MARVEL MONSTERS: MONSTERS ON THE PROWL
MARVEL
❑1, Dec 2005 ... 3.99

MARVEL MONSTERS: WHERE MONSTERS DWELL
MARVEL
❑1, Dec 2005 ... 3.99

MARVEL MOVIE PREMIERE
MARVEL
❑1, b&w; magazine ... 3.00

MARVEL MUST HAVES
MARVEL
❑1, Dec 2001, Reprints Wolverine: The Origin #1, Startling Stories: Banner #1, Cable #97, Spider-Man's Tangled Web #4 ... 3.99
❑2 ... 3.99

MARVEL MUST HAVES: AMAZING SPIDER-MAN #30-32
MARVEL
❑1, ca. 2003; Reprints Amazing Spider-Man (Vol. 2) #30-32 ... 3.99

MARVEL MUST HAVES: AVENGERS #500-502
MARVEL
❑1, ca. 2004 ... 3.99

MARVEL MUST HAVES: INCREDIBLE HULK #50-52
MARVEL
❑1, ca. 2003; Reprints Incredible Hulk (2nd series) #50-52 ... 3.99

MARVEL MUST HAVES: INCREDIBLE HULK #34-36
MARVEL
❑1, ca. 2003; Reprints Incredible Hulk (2nd series) #34-36 ... 3.99

MARVEL MUST HAVES: NEW AVENGERS #1-3
MARVEL
❑1 2005 ... 3.99

MARVEL MUST HAVES: NEW X-MEN #114-116
MARVEL
❑1, ca. 2003; Reprints New X-Men #114-116 ... 3.99

MARVEL MUST HAVES: NYX #4-5
MARVEL
❑0, Jul 2005 ... 3.99

MARVEL MUST HAVES: SENTINEL #1 & #2 AND RUNAWAYS #1 & #2
MARVEL
❑1, ca. 2003; Reprints Sentinel #1-2, Runaways #1-2 ... 3.99

MARVEL MUST HAVES: SPIDER-MAN & BLACK CAT #1-#3
MARVEL
❑1, Jan 2006 ... 3.99

MARVEL MUST HAVES: THE ULTIMATES #1-3
MARVEL
❑1, ca. 2003; Reprints The Ultimates #1-3 ... 3.99

MARVEL MUST HAVES: TRUTH: RED, WHITE AND BLACK
MARVEL
❑1, Apr 2003 ... 3.99

MARVEL MUST HAVES: ULTIMATE SPIDER-MAN #1-3
MARVEL
❑1, ca. 2003; Reprints Ultimate Spider-Man #1-3 ... 3.99

MARVEL MUST HAVES: ULTIMATE VENOM
MARVEL
❑1, May 2003 ... 3.99

MARVEL MUST HAVES: ULTIMATE WAR
MARVEL
❑1, May 2003 ... 3.99

MARVEL MUST HAVES: ULTIMATE X-MEN #1-3
MARVEL
❑1, ca. 2003; Reprints Ultimate X-Men #1-3 ... 3.99

MARVEL MUST HAVES: ULTIMATE X-MEN #34 & #35
MARVEL
❑1, ca. 2003; Reprints Ultimate X-Men #34-35 ... 2.99

MARVEL MUST HAVES: WOLVERINE #20-22
MARVEL
❑1 2005 ... 3.99

MARVEL MUST HAVES: WOLVERINE #1-3
MARVEL
❑1, ca. 2003; no indicia; reprints Wolverine (3rd series) #1-3 ... 3.99

MARVEL MYSTERY COMICS (2ND SERIES)
MARVEL
❑1, Dec 1999; Reprints ... 3.95

MARVEL NEMESIS: THE IMPERFECTS
MARVEL
❑1, Jun 2005 ... 4.00
❑2, Jul 2005 ... 2.99
❑3, Aug 2005 ... 2.99
❑4, Sep 2005 ... 2.99
❑5, Oct 2005 ... 2.99
❑6, Nov 2005 ... 2.99

MARVEL NO-PRIZE BOOK
MARVEL
❑1, Jan 1983; SL (w); JK (a); mistakes 3.00

MARVELOUS ADVENTURES OF GUS BEEZER AND SPIDER-MAN
MARVEL
❑1, Feb 2004 ... 2.99

MARVELOUS ADVENTURES OF GUS BEEZER: HULK
MARVEL
❑1, May 2003 ... 2.99

MARVELOUS ADVENTURES OF GUS BEEZER: SPIDER-MAN
MARVEL
❑1, May 2003 ... 2.99

MARVELOUS ADVENTURES OF GUS BEEZER: X-MEN
MARVEL
❑1, May 2003 ... 2.99

MARVELOUS DRAGON CLAN
LUNAR
❑1, Jul 1994, b&w ... 2.50
❑2, Sep 1994, b&w ... 2.50

MARVELOUS WIZARD OF OZ (MGM'S...)
MARVEL / DC
❑1, treasury-sized movie adaptation... 16.00

MARVEL: PORTRAITS OF A UNIVERSE
MARVEL
❑1, Mar 1995 ... 2.95
❑2, Apr 1995 ... 2.95
❑3, May 1995 ... 2.95
❑4, Jun 1995 ... 2.95

MARVEL POSTER BOOK
MARVEL
❑1, Jan 1991 ... 2.50

MARVEL POSTER MAGAZINE
MARVEL
❑2, Dec 2001, Winter 2001 ... 3.50

MARVEL PREMIERE
MARVEL
❑1, Apr 1972, GK (a); O: Counter-Earth. O: Warlock ... 35.00
❑2, May 1972, JK (a); A: Warlock. Yellow Claw ... 12.00
❑3, Jul 1972, A: Doctor Strange ... 30.00
❑4, Sep 1972, FB (a); A: Doctor Strange 10.00
❑5, Nov 1972, MP, CR (a); A: Doctor Strange ... 8.00
❑6, Jan 1973, FB, MP (a); A: Doctor Strange ... 8.00
❑7, Mar 1973, MP, CR (a); A: Doctor Strange ... 15.00
❑8, May 1973, JSn (a); A: Doctor Strange ... 10.00
❑9, Jul 1973, FB (a); A: Doctor Strange 6.00
❑10, Sep 1973, FB, NA (a); A: Doctor Strange. D: The Ancient One ... 9.00
❑11, Oct 1973, FB, NA (a); A: Doctor Strange ... 5.00
❑12, Nov 1973, FB, NA (a); A: Doctor Strange ... 5.00
❑13, Jan 1974, FB, NA (a); 1: Sise-Neg (as Cagliostro). A: Doctor Strange .. 8.00
❑14, Mar 1974, FB, NA (a); A: Sise-Neg. A: Doctor Strange ... 12.00
❑15, May 1974, GK (a); O: Iron Fist. 1: Iron Fist. Marvel Value Stamp #94: Electro ... 80.00
❑16, Jul 1974, 2: Iron Fist. 2: Iron Fist. Marvel Value Stamp #71: Vision ... 20.00
❑17, Sep 1974, A: Iron Fist. Marvel Value Stamp #32: Red Skull ... 12.00
❑18, Oct 1974, A: Iron Fist. Marvel Value Stamp #74: Stranger ... 12.00
❑19, Nov 1974, 1: Colleen Wing. A: Iron Fist. Marvel Value Stamp #6: Thor .. 10.00
❑20, Jan 1975, A: Iron Fist. Marvel Value Stamp #73: Kingpin ... 10.00
❑21, Mar 1975 A: Iron Fist ... 10.00
❑22, Jun 1975 A: Iron Fist ... 10.00
❑23, Aug 1975, PB (a); A: Iron Fist. Marvel Value Stamp #27: Black Widow ... 10.00
❑24, Sep 1975, PB (a); A: Iron Fist. Marvel Value Stamp #74: Stranger . 10.00
❑25, Oct 1975, JBy (a); A: Iron Fist. Marvel Value Stamp #6: Thor ... 15.00
❑26, Nov 1975, JK (a); A: Hercules 4.00
❑27, Dec 1975, A: Satana ... 10.00
❑28, Feb 1976, A: Werewolf. A: Man-Thing. A: Ghost Rider. A: Legion of Monsters. A: Morbius ... 13.00
❑29, Apr 1976, JK (a); O: Whizzer. O: Red Raven. O: Thin Man. O: Blue Diamond. O: Miss America. 1: Patriot. 1: Jack Frost I. 1: Thin Man. 1: Blue Diamond. A: Liberty Legion 3.00
❑29/30 cent, Apr 1976, JK (a); O: Whizzer. O: Red Raven. O: Thin Man. O: Blue Diamond. O: Miss America. 1: Patriot. 1: Jack Frost I. 1: Thin Man. 1: Blue Diamond. A: Liberty Legion. 30 cent regional price variant 20.00
❑30, Jun 1976, JK (a); A: Liberty Legion 2.50
❑30/30 cent, Jun 1976, JK (a); A: Liberty Legion. 30 cent regional price variant ... 20.00
❑31, Aug 1976, JK (a); O: Woodgod. 1: Woodgod ... 3.00

Other grades: Multiply price above by 5/6 for VF/NM • 2/3 for VERY FINE • 1/3 for FINE • 1/5 for VERY GOOD • 1/8 for GOOD

Marvel Super Action

Mostly Captain America reprints
©Marvel

Marvel Super Hero Contest of Champions

Wrong contender was handed victory
©Marvel

Marvel Super-Heroes (Vol. 1)

Introduces Kree Captain Mar-Vell
©Marvel

Marvel Super-Heroes (Vol. 2)

Seasonal super-hero anthology
©Marvel

Marvel Super-Heroes Megazine

Back to square-bound anthologies
©Marvel

N-MINT

- ❑31/30 cent, Aug 1976, JK (a); O: Woodgod. 1: Woodgod. 30 cent regional price variant 20.00
- ❑32, Oct 1976, HC (a); Monark Starstalker 3.00
- ❑33, Dec 1976, HC (a); A: Solomon Kane. Monark 3.00
- ❑34, Feb 1977, HC (a); A: Solomon Kane 3.00
- ❑35, Apr 1977, O: 3-D Man. 1: 3-D Man 3.00
- ❑36, Jun 1977, A: 3-D Man 3.00
- ❑36/35 cent, Jun 1977, A: 3-D Man. 35 cent regional price variant 15.00
- ❑37, Aug 1977, A: 3-D Man. Newsstand edition (distributed by Curtis); issue number in box 3.00
- ❑37/Whitman, Aug 1977, A: 3-D Man. Special markets edition (usually sold in Whitman bagged prepacks); price appears in a diamond; UPC barcode appears 3.00
- ❑37/35 cent, Aug 1977, A: 3-D Man. 35 cent regional price variant; newsstand edition (distributed by Curtis); issue number in box 15.00
- ❑38, Oct 1977, 1: Weirdworld. Newsstand edition (distributed by Curtis); issue number in box 3.00
- ❑38/Whitman, Oct 1977, 1: Weirdworld. Special markets edition (usually sold in Whitman bagged prepacks); price appears in a diamond; no UPC barcode 3.00
- ❑38/35 cent, Oct 1977, 1: Weirdworld. 35 cent regional price variant; newsstand edition (distributed by Curtis); issue number in box 15.00
- ❑39, Dec 1977, A: Torpedo 3.00
- ❑40, Feb 1978, 1: Bucky II (Fred Davis). A: Torpedo 3.00
- ❑41, Apr 1978, TS (a); A: Seeker 3000 3.00
- ❑42, Jun 1978, A: Tigra. Tigra 3.00
- ❑43, Aug 1978, TS (a); 1: Paladin 3.00
- ❑44, Oct 1978, KG (a); A: Jack of Hearts. Jack of Hearts 3.00
- ❑45, Dec 1978, A: Man-Wolf. Man-Wolf 3.00
- ❑46, Feb 1979, GP (a); A: Man-Wolf. War God 3.00
- ❑47, Apr 1979, JBy (a); 1: Ant-Man 3.00
- ❑48, Jun 1979, JBy, BL (a); A: Ant-Man 3.00
- ❑49, Aug 1979, FM (c); FM (a); A: The Falcon 3.00
- ❑50, Oct 1979, 1: Alice Cooper 12.50
- ❑51, Dec 1979, A: Black Panther 3.00
- ❑52, Feb 1980, A: Black Panther 3.00
- ❑53, Apr 1980, FM (c); FM (a); A: Black Panther 3.00
- ❑54, Jun 1980, GD (a); 1: Caleb Hammer 3.00
- ❑55, Aug 1980, A: Wonder Man 3.00
- ❑56, Oct 1980, HC, TD (a); A: Dominic Fortune 3.00
- ❑57, Dec 1980, DaG (a); 1: Doctor Who (in U.S.) 5.00
- ❑58, Feb 1981, DaG (a); A: Doctor Who 3.00
- ❑59, Apr 1981, A: Doctor Who 3.00
- ❑60, Jun 1981, DaG (a); A: Doctor Who 3.00
- ❑61, Aug 1981, TS (a); A: Star-Lord ... 3.00

N-MINT

MARVEL PRESENTS
MARVEL

- ❑1, Oct 1975, O: Bloodstone. 1: Bloodstone 11.00
- ❑2, Dec 1975, O: Bloodstone 5.00
- ❑3, Feb 1976, A: Guardians of the Galaxy 10.00
- ❑4, May 1976, O: Nikki. 1: Nikki. A: Guardians of the Galaxy 4.00
- ❑4/30 cent, May 1976, 30 cent regional price variant 20.00
- ❑5, Jun 1976, A: Guardians of the Galaxy 4.00
- ❑5/30 cent, Jun 1976, 30 cent regional price variant 20.00
- ❑6, Aug 1976, A: Guardians of the Galaxy. V: Planetary Man 3.50
- ❑6/30 cent, Aug 1976, 30 cent regional price variant 20.00
- ❑7, Nov 1976, A: Guardians of the Galaxy 3.50
- ❑8, Dec 1976, A: Guardians of the Galaxy. reprints Silver Surfer #2..... 3.50
- ❑9, Feb 1977, O: Starhawk II (Aleta). A: Guardians of the Galaxy 3.50
- ❑10, Apr 1977, O: Starhawk II (Aleta). A: Guardians of the Galaxy 3.50
- ❑11, Jun 1977, A: Guardians of the Galaxy 3.50
- ❑11/35 cent, Jun 1977, A: Guardians of the Galaxy. 35 cent regional price variant 15.00
- ❑12, Aug 1977, A: Guardians of the Galaxy 3.50
- ❑12/35 cent, Aug 1977, A: Guardians of the Galaxy. 35 cent regional price variant 15.00

MARVEL PREVIEW
MARVEL

- ❑1, Sum 1975; Man Gods From Beyond the Stars 15.00
- ❑2 1975 O: The Punisher. 1: Dominic Fortune 50.00
- ❑3, Sep 1975; Blade the Vampire Slayer 10.00
- ❑4, Jan 1976 O: Star-Lord. 1: Star-Lord 7.00
- ❑5; Sherlock Holmes 5.00
- ❑6; Sherlock Holmes 5.00
- ❑7, Sep 1976; 1: Rocket Raccoon. Satana 5.00
- ❑8, Fal 1976; A: Legion of Monsters. Morbius, Blade 5.00
- ❑9, Apr 1977; O: Star Hawk. Man-God 5.00
- ❑10, Jul 1977; JSn (a); Thor 5.00
- ❑11, Oct 1977; Star-Lord 5.00
- ❑12, Jan 1978; Haunt of Horror 5.00
- ❑13, Apr 1978; UFO 5.00
- ❑14, Aug 1978; Star-Lord 5.00
- ❑15, Oct 1978; Star-Lord; Joe Jusko's first major comics work 5.00
- ❑16, Mar 1979; Detectives 5.00
- ❑17, May 1979; Blackmark 5.00
- ❑18, Aug 1979; Star-Lord 5.00
- ❑19, Nov 1979 A: Kull 5.00
- ❑20, Mar 1980; Bizarre Adventures 5.00
- ❑21, May 1980 A: Moon Knight 5.00
- ❑22, Aug 1980; Merlin; King Arthur ... 5.00
- ❑23, Nov 1980; FM (a); Bizarre Adventures 5.00

N-MINT

- ❑24, Feb 1981; Paradox; Title continues as "Bizarre Adventures" with #25 ..... 5.00

MARVEL PREVIEW '93
MARVEL

- ❑1, ca. 1993 ...... 3.95

MARVEL RIOT
MARVEL

- ❑1, Dec 1995; parodies Age of Apocalypse; wraparound cover 1.95

MARVEL ROMANCE REDUX: BUT HE SAID HE LOVED ME
MARVEL

- ❑1, Mar 20006 ...... 3.99

MARVEL ROMANCE REDUX: GUYS & DOLLS
MARVEL

- ❑1, Jun 2006 ...... 3.99

MARVEL ROMANCE REDUX: I SHOULD HAVE BEEN A BLONDE
MARVEL

- ❑1, Jul 2006 ...... 3.99

MARVEL ROMANCE REDUX: LOVE IS A FOUR LETTER WORD
MARVEL

- ❑1, Aug 2006 ...... 3.99

MARVEL ROMANCE REDUX: RESTRAINING ORDERS ARE FOR OTHER GIRLS
MARVEL

- ❑1, Jun 2006 ...... 3.99

MARVELS
MARVEL

- ❑0, Aug 1994, KB (w); ARo (a); Collects promo art and Human Torch story from Marvel Age; Fully painted 4.00
- ❑1, Jan 1994, KB (w); ARo (a); wraparound acetate outer cover; Torch, Sub-Mariner, Captain America; Torch, Sub-Mariner, Capt. America; Fully painted 5.00
- ❑1/2nd, Apr 1996, KB (w); ARo (a) 2.95
- ❑2, Feb 1994, KB (w); ARo (a); Fully painted; wraparound acetate outer cover 5.00
- ❑2/2nd, May 1996, KB (w); ARo (a) ... 2.95
- ❑3, Mar 1994, KB (w); ARo (a); Coming of Galactus; Fully painted; wraparound acetate outer cover 5.00
- ❑3/2nd, May 1996, KB (w); ARo (a); wraparound cover 5.95
- ❑4, Apr 1994, KB (w); ARo (a); D: Gwen Stacy. Fully painted; wraparound acetate outer cover 5.00
- ❑4/2nd, Jun 1996, KB (w); ARo (a); wraparound cover 2.95
- ❑Book 1, ARo (a) 19.95
- ❑Book 1/HC, Hardcover edition; ARo (a); Hardcover; Collects Marvels #0-4 29.95
- ❑Book 1/Ltd., ARo (a); Signed, numbered hardcover edition; Collects Marvels #0-4 ...... 59.95

MARVELS 10TH ANNIVERSARY HARDCOVER
MARVEL

- ❑1, ca. 2004 ...... 49.99

N-MINT

MARVEL SAGA

MARVEL

- ❑1, Dec 1985 JBy, SL (w); SB, JBy, DH, JK, JSt (a); O: X-Men. O: Fantastic Four. O: Alpha Flight 2.50
- ❑2, Jan 1986 SL (w); SD, JK, BWi (a); O: Hulk. O: Spider-Man 2.00
- ❑3, Feb 1986 O: Sub-Mariner. O: Doom 2.00
- ❑4, Mar 1986 SL (w); ATh, JB, JBy, HT, JK, FM, BA, DC, BH, BWi (a); O: Thor 2.00
- ❑5, Apr 1986 O: Iceman. O: Angel 2.00
- ❑6, May 1986 SL (w); JB, DH, GT, JK, GK (a); O: Iron Man. O: Asgard. O: Odin 2.00
- ❑7, Jun 1986 SL (w); SD, BL, JR2, DH, JK, JM (a) 2.00
- ❑8, Jul 1986 SL (w); SD, DH, JK (a)... 2.00
- ❑9, Aug 1986 O: Vulture 2.00
- ❑10, Sep 1986 SL (w); SD, JB, BEv, JK (a); O: Marvel Girl. O: Beast. O: Avengers 2.00
- ❑11, Oct 1986 O: Molecule Man 1.50
- ❑12, Nov 1986; Captain America revived 1.50
- ❑13, Dec 1986 FM, SL (w); SD, GC, JB, BEv, DH, SR, JK, FM, TP, KJ (a); O: Daredevil 1.50
- ❑14, Jan 1987 SL (w); AM, SD, JBy, DGr, JR2, JK, JSt (a); O: Scarlet Witch. O: Quicksilver 1.50
- ❑15, Feb 1987 O: Wonder Man. O: Hawkeye 1.50
- ❑16, Mar 1987 SL (w); SD, GC, PS, DH, JK, GK, DA (a); O: Frightful Four. O: Dormammu 1.50
- ❑17, Apr 1987 SL (w); SD, VM, DH, JK, GK, JSt (a); O: Ka-Zar. O: Leader..... 1.50
- ❑18, May 1987 SD, SL (w); SD, DH, JK, JSo, JSt (a); O: S.H.I.E.L.D. 1.50
- ❑19, Jun 1987; new Avengers team ... 1.50
- ❑20, Jul 1987 .... 1.50
- ❑21, Aug 1987; X-Men 1.50
- ❑22, Sep 1987 O: Mary Jane 1.50
- ❑23, Oct 1987; Inhumans 1.50
- ❑24, Nov 1987 JK, SL (w); JB, JK, JSt (a); O: Galactus 1.50
- ❑25, Dec 1987 JK, SL (w); JB, JK, JSt (a); O: Silver Surfer 1.50

MARVELS COMICS: CAPTAIN AMERICA

MARVEL

- ❑1, Jul 2000 .... 2.25

MARVELS COMICS: DAREDEVIL

MARVEL

- ❑1, Jun 2000 .... 2.25

MARVELS COMICS: FANTASTIC FOUR

MARVEL

- ❑1, May 2000 .... 2.25

MARVELS COMICS: SPIDER-MAN

MARVEL

- ❑1, Jul 2000 .... 2.25

MARVELS COMICS: THOR

MARVEL

- ❑1, Jul 2000 .... 2.25

MARVELS COMICS: X-MEN

MARVEL

- ❑1, Jun 2000 .... 2.25

MARVEL SELECT FLIP MAGAZINE

MARVEL

- ❑1, Jul 2005 .... 3.99
- ❑2, Aug 2005 .... 3.99
- ❑3, Sep 2005 .... 3.99
- ❑4 2005 .... 3.99
- ❑5, Dec 2005 .... 3.99
- ❑6, Jan 2006 .... 3.99
- ❑7, Feb 2006 .... 3.99
- ❑8, Mar 2006 .... 3.99
- ❑9, Apr 2006 .... 3.99
- ❑10, May 2006 .... 3.99
- ❑11, Jun 2006 .... 3.99
- ❑12, Jul 2006 .... 3.99
- ❑13, Aug 2006 .... 3.99
- ❑14, Sep 2006 .... 3.99

MARVEL SELECTS: FANTASTIC FOUR

MARVEL

- ❑1, Jan 2000 .... 2.75

N-MINT

MARVEL SELECTS: SPIDER-MAN

MARVEL

- ❑1, Jan 2000; Reprints Amazing Spider-Man #100 .... 2.75
- ❑2, Feb 2000 .... 2.75
- ❑3, Mar 2000 .... 2.75

MARVEL'S GREATEST COMICS

MARVEL

- ❑23, Oct 1969, Giant-size; Title continued from "Marvel Collector's Item Classics" 15.00
- ❑24, Dec 1969, Giant-size 15.00
- ❑25, Feb 1970, Giant-size 15.00
- ❑26, Apr 1970, Giant-size 15.00
- ❑27, Jun 1970, Giant-size 15.00
- ❑28, Aug 1970, Giant-size 15.00
- ❑29, Dec 1970, Giant-size; Reprints Fantastic Four #12 and 31 .... 15.00
- ❑30, Mar 1971, Giant-size; Reprints Fantastic Four #37 and 38 .... 15.00
- ❑31, Jun 1971, Giant-size; Reprints Fantastic Four #39 and 40 .... 15.00
- ❑32, Sep 1971, Giant-size; Reprints Fantastic Four #41 and 42 .... 15.00
- ❑33, Dec 1971, Giant-size; Reprints Fantastic Four #44 and 45 .... 15.00
- ❑34, Mar 1972, Giant-size; Reprints Fantastic Four #46 and 47 .... 15.00
- ❑35, Jun 1972, A: Silver Surfer. Reprints Fantastic Four #48 .... 10.00
- ❑36, Jul 1972, Reprints Fantastic Four #49 .... 10.00
- ❑37, Sep 1972, Reprints Fantastic Four #50 .... 10.00
- ❑38, Oct 1972, Reprints Fantastic Four #51 .... 3.50
- ❑39, Nov 1972, Reprints Fantastic Four #52 .... 3.50
- ❑40, Jan 1973, Reprints Fantastic Four #53 .... 3.50
- ❑41, Mar 1973, Reprints Fantastic Four #54 .... 3.50
- ❑42, May 1973, Reprints Fantastic Four #55 .... 3.50
- ❑43, Jul 1973, Reprints Fantastic Four #56 .... 3.50
- ❑44, Sep 1973, Reprints Fantastic Four #61 .... 3.50
- ❑45, Oct 1973, Reprints Fantastic Four #62 .... 3.50
- ❑46, Nov 1973, Reprints Fantastic Four #63 .... 3.50
- ❑47, Jan 1974, Reprints Fantastic Four #64 .... 3.50
- ❑48, Mar 1974, Reprints Fantastic Four #65 .... 3.50
- ❑49, May 1974, Reprints Fantastic Four #66 .... 3.50
- ❑50, Jul 1974, JK, JSt (a); A: Warlock (Him). Reprints Fantastic Four #67 4.00
- ❑51, Sep 1974, Reprints Fantastic Four #68 .... 3.00
- ❑52, Oct 1974, Reprints Fantastic Four #69 .... 2.50
- ❑53, Nov 1974, Reprints Fantastic Four #70 .... 2.50
- ❑54, Jan 1975, Reprints Fantastic Four #71 .... 2.50
- ❑55, Mar 1975, Reprints Fantastic Four #73 .... 2.50
- ❑56, May 1975, Reprints Fantastic Four #74 .... 2.50
- ❑57, Jul 1975, Reprints Fantastic Four #75 .... 2.50
- ❑58, Sep 1975, Reprints Fantastic Four #76 .... 2.50
- ❑59, Oct 1975, Reprints Fantastic Four #77 .... 2.50
- ❑60, Nov 1975, Reprints Fantastic Four #78 .... 2.50
- ❑61, Jan 1976, Reprints Fantastic Four #79 .... 2.50
- ❑62, Mar 1976, Reprints Fantastic Four #80 .... 2.50
- ❑63, May 1976, Reprints Fantastic Four #81 .... 2.50
- ❑63/30 cent, May 1976, 30 cent regional price variant; Reprints Fantastic Four #81 .... 20.00
- ❑64, Jul 1976, Reprints Fantastic Four #82 .... 2.50
- ❑64/30 cent, Jul 1976, 30 cent regional price variant; Reprints Fantastic Four #82 .... 20.00

N-MINT

- ❑65, Sep 1976, Reprints Fantastic Four #83 .... 2.50
- ❑66, Oct 1976, Reprints Fantastic Four #84 .... 2.50
- ❑67, Nov 1976, Reprints Fantastic Four #85 .... 2.50
- ❑68, Jan 1977, Reprints Fantastic Four #86 .... 2.50
- ❑69, Mar 1977, Reprints Fantastic Four #87 .... 2.50
- ❑70, May 1977, Reprints Fantastic Four #88; newsstand edition (distributed by Curtis); issue number in box...... 2.50
- ❑70/Whitman, May 1977, Reprints Fantastic Four #88; special markets edition (usually sold in Whitman bagged prepacks); price appears in a diamond; UPC barcode appears... 2.50
- ❑71, Jul 1977, Reprints Fantastic Four #89; newsstand edition (distributed by Curtis); issue number in box...... 2.00
- ❑71/Whitman, Jul 1977, Reprints Fantastic Four #89; special markets edition (usually sold in Whitman bagged prepacks); price appears in a diamond; UPC barcode appears... 2.00
- ❑71/35 cent, Jul 1977, Reprints Fantastic Four #89; 35 cent regional price variant; newsstand edition (distributed by Curtis); issue number in box 15.00
- ❑72, Sep 1977, Reprints Fantastic Four #90; newsstand edition (distributed by Curtis); issue number in box...... 2.00
- ❑72/Whitman, Sep 1977, Reprints Fantastic Four #90; special markets edition (usually sold in Whitman bagged prepacks); price appears in a diamond; UPC barcode appears... 2.00
- ❑72/35 cent, Sep 1977, Reprints Fantastic Four #90; 35 cent regional price variant; newsstand edition (distributed by Curtis); issue number in box 15.00
- ❑73, Oct 1977, Reprints Fantastic Four #91; newsstand edition (distributed by Curtis); issue number in box...... 2.00
- ❑73/Whitman, Oct 1977, Reprints Fantastic Four #91; special markets edition (usually sold in Whitman bagged prepacks); price appears in a diamond; no UPC barcode 2.00
- ❑73/35 cent, Oct 1977, Reprints Fantastic Four #91; 35 cent regional price variant; newsstand edition (distributed by Curtis); issue number in box 15.00
- ❑74, Nov 1977, Reprints Fantastic Four #92; newsstand edition (distributed by Curtis); issue number in box...... 2.00
- ❑74/Whitman, Nov 1977, Reprints Fantastic Four #92; special markets edition (usually sold in Whitman bagged prepacks); price appears in a diamond; no UPC barcode 2.00
- ❑75, Jan 1978, Reprints Fantastic Four #93 .... 2.00
- ❑76, Mar 1978, Reprints Fantastic Four #95 .... 2.00
- ❑77, May 1978, Reprints Fantastic Four #96 .... 2.00
- ❑78, Jul 1978, Reprints Fantastic Four #97 .... 2.00
- ❑79, Sep 1978, Reprints Fantastic Four #98 .... 2.00
- ❑80, Nov 1978, Reprints Fantastic Four #99; newsstand edition (distributed by Curtis); issue number in box...... 2.00
- ❑80/Whitman, Nov 1978, Reprints Fantastic Four #99; special markets edition (usually sold in Whitman bagged prepacks); price appears in a diamond; no UPC barcode 2.00
- ❑81, Jan 1979, Reprints Fantastic Four #100 .... 2.00
- ❑82, Mar 1979, Reprints Fantastic Four #102 .... 2.00
- ❑83, Dec 1979, Reprints Fantastic Four #103 .... 2.00
- ❑84, Jan 1980, Reprints Fantastic Four #104 .... 2.00
- ❑85, Feb 1980, Reprints Fantastic Four #105 .... 2.00
- ❑86, Mar 1980, Reprints Fantastic Four #116 .... 2.00
- ❑87, Apr 1980, Reprints Fantastic Four #107 .... 2.00

Other grades: Multiply price above by 5/6 for VF/NM • 2/3 for VERY FINE • 1/3 for FINE • 1/5 for VERY GOOD • 1/8 for GOOD

Marvel Super Heroes Secret Wars

Event affected entire Marvel universe

©Marvel

Marvel Super Special

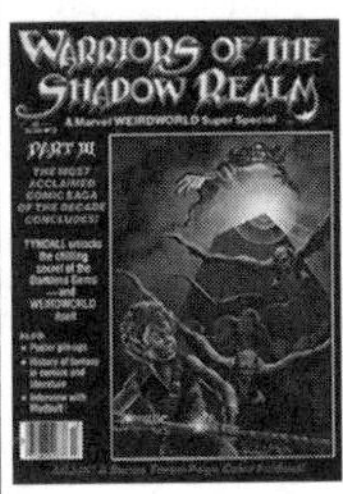

Movie adaptation magazine

©Marvel

Marvel Swimsuit Special

Characters in tighter, lesser outfits

©Marvel

Marvel Tails

Anthropomorphic version of arachnid hero

©Marvel

Marvel Tales (2nd Series)

Key Marvel moments reprints give way to Spidey

©Marvel

	N-MINT
❑88, May 1980, Reprints Fantastic Four #108	2.00
❑89, Jun 1980, Reprints Fantastic Four #109	2.00
❑90, Jul 1980, Reprints Fantastic Four #110	2.00
❑91, Aug 1980, Reprints Fantastic Four #111	2.00
❑92, Sep 1980, Reprints Fantastic Four #112	2.00
❑93, Oct 1980	2.00
❑94, Nov 1980	2.00
❑95, Dec 1980	2.00
❑96, Jan 1981	2.00

MARVEL'S GREATEST COMICS: FANTASTIC FOUR #52
MARVEL

❑1, Sep 2006	2.99

MARVEL: SHADOWS & LIGHT
MARVEL

❑1, Feb 1997, b&w; Wolverine, Dracula, Doctor Strange, Captain Marvel; wraparound cover	2.95

MARVEL 1602
MARVEL

❑1, Nov 2003, NG (w)	6.00
❑2, Nov 2003, NG (w)	5.00
❑3, Dec 2003, NG (w)	6.00
❑4, Jan 2004, NG (w)	5.00
❑5, Feb 2004, NG (w)	6.00
❑6, Mar 2004, NG (w)	5.00
❑7, Apr 2004, NG (w)	4.00
❑8, Jun 2004, NG (w)	5.00

MARVEL 1602: NEW WORLD
MARVEL

❑1, Sep 2005	3.50
❑2, Oct 2005	3.50
❑3, Nov 2005	3.50
❑4, Dec 2005	3.50
❑5, Jan 2006	3.50

MARVEL 65TH ANNIVERSARY SPECIAL
MARVEL

❑1, Sep 2004, reprints stories from Marvel Mystery Comics #8-10	4.99

MARVEL SPECIAL EDITION FEATURING CLOSE ENCOUNTERS OF THE THIRD KIND
MARVEL

❑3, ca. 1978; treasury-sized; adapts Close Encounters of the Third Kind	9.00

MARVEL SPECIAL EDITION FEATURING SPECTACULAR SPIDER-MAN
MARVEL

❑1, ca. 1975; treasury-sized	12.00

MARVEL SPECIAL EDITION FEATURING STAR WARS
MARVEL

❑1, ca. 1977; treasury-sized adaption of Star Wars	14.00
❑2, ca. 1977; treasury-sized adaption of Star Wars	12.00
❑3, ca. 1978; treasury-sized; collects previous two issues	14.00

MARVEL SPECTACULAR
MARVEL

❑1, Aug 1973, SL (w); JK (a); reprints Thor #128	5.00
❑2, Sep 1973, SL (w); JK (a); reprints Thor #129	3.00
❑3, Oct 1973, SL (w); JK (a); 1: Tana Nile (in real form). reprints Thor #130	3.00
❑4, Nov 1973, SL (w); JK (a); reprints Thor #133	3.00
❑5, Jan 1974, SL (w); JK (a); reprints Thor #134	3.00
❑6, Mar 1974, SL (w); JK (a); reprints Tales of Asgard from Journey Into Mystery #121 and Thor #135	3.00
❑7, May 1974; SL (w); JK (a); reprints Thor #136	3.00
❑8, Jul 1974; SL (w); JK (a); reprints Thor #137	3.00
❑9, Sep 1974; SL (w); JK (a); reprints Thor #138	3.00
❑10, Oct 1974; SL (w); JK (a); reprints Thor #139	3.00
❑11, Nov 1974; SL (w); JK (a); reprints Thor #140	2.50
❑12, Dec 1974; SL (w); JK (a); reprints Thor #141	2.50
❑13, Jan 1975; SL (w); JK (a); reprints Thor #142	2.50
❑14, Mar 1975; SL (w); JK (a); reprints Thor #143	2.50
❑15, Jun 1975; SL (w); JK (a); reprints Thor #144	2.50
❑16, Jul 1975; SL (w); JK (a); reprints Thor #145	2.50
❑17, Sep 1975; SL (w); JK (a); reprints Thor #146	2.50
❑18, Oct 1975; SL (w); JK (a); reprints Thor #147	2.50
❑19, Nov 1975; SL (w); JK (a); reprints Thor #148	2.50

MARVEL SPOTLIGHT (VOL. 1)
MARVEL

❑1, Nov 1971, NA, WW (a); O: Red Wolf. A: Red Wolf	25.00
❑2, Feb 1972, NA (c); FM (a); O: Werewolf. 1: Werewolf	130.00
❑3, May 1972, A: Werewolf	30.00
❑4, Jun 1972, A: Werewolf	30.00
❑5, Aug 1972, FM (c); SD, FM, MP (a); O: Ghost Rider I (Johnny Blaze). 1: Zarathos (Ghost Rider's Spirit of Vengeance)	275.00
❑6, Oct 1972, A: Ghost Rider	45.00
❑7, Dec 1972, FM (c); FM (a); A: Ghost Rider	35.00
❑8, Feb 1973, FM (a); A: Ghost Rider	25.00
❑9, Apr 1973, A: Ghost Rider	30.00
❑10, Jun 1973, A: Ghost Rider	35.00
❑11, Aug 1973, A: Ghost Rider	22.00
❑12, Oct 1973, SD (a); O: Son of Satan. 1: Son of Satan	22.00
❑13, Jan 1974, O: Satana. A: Son of Satan	12.00
❑14, Mar 1974, A: Son of Satan. Marvel Value Stamp #5: Dracula	10.00
❑15, May 1974, A: Son of Satan. Marvel Value Stamp #21: Kull	10.00
❑16, Jul 1974, A: Son of Satan. Marvel Value Stamp #83: Dragon Man	7.00
❑17, Sep 1974, A: Son of Satan. Marvel Value Stamp #45: Mantis	7.00
❑18, Oct 1974, A: Son of Satan. Marvel Value Stamp #81: Rhino	7.00
❑19, Dec 1974, A: Son of Satan. Marvel Value Stamp #14: Living Mummy	7.00
❑20, Feb 1975, A: Son of Satan. Marvel Value Stamp #26: Mephisto	5.00
❑21, Apr 1975, A: Son of Satan	5.00
❑22, Jun 1975, A: Ghost Rider. A: Son of Satan	6.00
❑23, Aug 1975, A: Son of Satan	5.00
❑24, Oct 1975, A: Son of Satan. Last Son of Satan in Marvel Spotlight	5.00
❑25, Dec 1975, A: Sinbad	3.00
❑26, Feb 1976, A: Scarecrow (Marvel)	3.00
❑27, Apr 1976, A: Sub-Mariner	3.00
❑27/30 cent, Apr 1976, 30 cent regional price variant	20.00
❑28, Jun 1976, A: Moon Knight. 1st solo story for Moon Knight	10.00
❑28/30 cent, Jun 1976, 30 cent regional price variant	18.00
❑29, Aug 1976, JK (a); A: Moon Knight	9.00
❑29/30 cent, Aug 1976, 30 cent regional price variant	15.00
❑30, Oct 1976, JB (a); A: Warriors Three	3.00
❑31, Dec 1976, HC (a); A: Nick Fury	3.00
❑32, Feb 1977, SB, JM (a); O: Spider-Woman I (Jessica Drew). 1: Spider-Woman I (Jessica Drew)	20.00
❑33, Apr 1977, 1: Devil-Slayer. A: Deathlok	3.00

MARVEL SPOTLIGHT (VOL. 2)
MARVEL

❑1, Jul 1979, PB (a); A: Captain Marvel	3.00
❑2, Sep 1979, FM (c); TD (a); A: Captain Marvel	2.00
❑3, Nov 1979, PB (a); A: Captain Marvel	2.00
❑4, Jan 1980, FM (c); SD (a); A: Dragon Lord	2.00
❑5, Mar 1980, FM (c); SD (a); A: Dragon Lord. A: Captain Marvel	2.00
❑6, May 1980, TS (a); O: Star-Lord	2.00
❑7, Jul 1980, TS (a); A: Star-Lord	2.00
❑8, Sep 1980, FM, TD (a); A: Captain Marvel	2.00
❑9, Nov 1980, SD (a); A: Captain Universe	2.00
❑10, Jan 1981, SD (a); A: Captain Universe	2.00
❑11, Mar 1981, SD (a); A: Captain Universe	2.00

MARVEL SPOTLIGHT: DANIEL WAY/OLIVER COIPEL
MARVEL

❑1, Jun 2006	3.99

MARVEL SPOTLIGHT: DAVID FINCH/ ROBERTO AGUIRRE-SACASA
MARVEL

❑1, Jun 2006	3.99

Other grades: Multiply price above by 5/6 for VF/NM • 2/3 for VERY FINE • 1/3 for FINE • 1/5 for VERY GOOD • 1/8 for GOOD

MARVEL SPOTLIGHT: JOHN CASSADAY/SEAN MCKEEVER
MARVEL

❑1, Feb 2006 .... 3.99

MARVEL SPOTLIGHT: JOSS WHEDON/MICHAEL LARK
MARVEL

❑1, May 2006 .... 3.99

MARVEL SPOTLIGHT: MARK MILLAR/ STEVE MCNIVEN
MARVEL

❑1, Aug 2006 .... 3.99

MARVEL SPOTLIGHT: NEIL GAIMAN/ SALVADOR LARROCA
MARVEL

❑1, Sep 2006 .... 3.99

MARVEL SPOTLIGHT: WARREN ELLIS/JIM CHEUNG
MARVEL

❑1, Mar 2006 .... 3.99

MARVEL SPRING SPECIAL
MARVEL

❑1, Nov 1988; Elvira 2.50

MARVEL SUPER ACTION
MARVEL

❑1, May 1977, JK (a); reprints Captain America #100; newsstand edition (distributed by Curtis); issue number in box 8.00
❑1/Whitman, May 1977, JK (a); Special markets edition (usually sold in Whitman bagged prepacks); price appears in a diamond; UPC barcode appears 8.00
❑2, Jul 1977, JK (a); Reprints Captain America #101 .... 2.50
❑2/35 cent, Jul 1977, JK (a); Reprints Captain America #101; 35 cent regional price variant 15.00
❑3, Sep 1977, JK (a); R eprints Captain America #102; newsstand edition (distributed by Curtis); issue number in box 2.50
❑3/Whitman, Sep 1977, JK (a); Special markets edition (usually sold in Whitman bagged prepacks); price appears in a diamond; UPC barcode appears 2.50
❑3/35 cent, Sep 1977, 35 cent regional price variant; reprints Captain America #102 .... 15.00
❑4, Nov 1977, JK (a); O: Marvel Boy. Reprints Marvel Boy #1; newsstand edition (distributed by Curtis); issue number in box 2.50
❑4/Whitman, Nov 1977, JK (a); O: Marvel Boy. Special markets edition (usually sold in Whitman bagged prepacks); price appears in a diamond; no UPC barcode 2.50
❑5, Jan 1978, JK (a); Reprints Captain America #103 .... 2.00
❑6, Mar 1978, JK (a); Reprints Captain America #104 .... 2.00
❑7, Apr 1978, JK (a); Reprints Captain America #105 .... 2.00
❑8, Jun 1978, JK (a); Reprints Captain America #106 .... 2.00
❑9, Aug 1978, JK (a); Reprints Captain America #107 .... 2.00
❑10, Oct 1978, JK (a); Reprints Captain America #108; newsstand edition (distributed by Curtis); issue number in box 2.00
❑10/Whitman, Oct 1978, JK (a); Special markets edition (usually sold in Whitman bagged prepacks); price appears in a diamond; no UPC barcode 2.00
❑11, Dec 1978, JK (a); Reprints Captain America #109; newsstand edition (distributed by Curtis); issue number in box 2.00
❑11/Whitman, Dec 1978, JK (a); Special markets edition (usually sold in Whitman bagged prepacks); price appears in a diamond; UPC barcode appears 2.00
❑12, Feb 1979, JSo (a); A: Hulk. Reprints Captain America #110 .... 2.00
❑13, Apr 1979, JSo (a); Reprints Captain America #111 .... 2.00
❑14, Dec 1979, reprints Avengers #55 .... 1.50
❑15, Jan 1980, reprints Avengers #56 .... 1.50
❑16, Feb 1980, reprints Avengers Annual #2 .... 1.50
❑17, Mar 1980, reprints Avengers Annual #2 .... 1.50
❑18, Apr 1980, reprints Avengers #57 .... 1.50
❑19, May 1980, reprints Avengers #58 .... 1.50
❑20, Jun 1980, reprints Avengers #59 .... 1.50
❑21, Jul 1980, reprints Avengers #60 .... 1.50
❑22, Aug 1980, reprints Avengers #61 .... 1.50
❑23, Sep 1980, reprints Avengers #62 .... 1.50
❑24, Oct 1980, reprints Avengers #63 .... 1.50
❑25, Nov 1980, reprints Avengers #64 .... 1.50
❑26, Dec 1980, reprints Avengers #65 .... 1.50
❑27, Jan 1981, reprints Avengers #66 .... 1.50
❑28, Feb 1981, reprints Avengers #67 .... 1.50
❑29, Mar 1981, reprints Avengers #68 .... 1.50
❑30, Apr 1981, reprints Avengers #69 .... 1.50
❑31, May 1981, reprints Avengers #70 .... 1.50
❑32, Jun 1981, reprints Avengers #71 .... 1.50
❑33, Jul 1981, reprints Avengers #72 .... 1.50
❑34, Aug 1981, reprints Avengers #73 .... 1.50
❑35, Sep 1981, reprints Avengers #74 .... 1.50
❑36, Oct 1981, reprints Avengers #75 .... 1.50
❑37, Nov 1981, reprints Avengers #76 .... 1.50

MARVEL SUPER ACTION (MAGAZINE)
MARVEL

❑1, Jan 1976, b&w; O: Dominic Fortune. 1: Mockingbird (as Huntress). Weird World and Punisher stories 35.00

MARVEL SUPER HERO CONTEST OF CHAMPIONS
MARVEL

❑1, Jun 1982, BL, JR2 (c); JR2 (a); 1: Shamrock. 1: Le Peregrine. 1: Blitzkrieg. 1: Talisman I. 1: Collective Man. Alpha Flight 4.00
❑2, Jul 1982, BL, JR2 (c); JR2 (a); X-Men 3.50
❑3, Aug 1982, AM (c); JR2 (a); X-Men 3.50

MARVEL SUPER-HEROES (VOL. 1)
MARVEL

❑12, Dec 1967, O: Captain Marvel. 1: Captain Marvel. Title continued from "Fantasy Masterpieces"; Captain Marvel original story; reprints 95.00
❑13, Mar 1968, 1: Carol Danvers. 2: Captain Marvel. Captain Marvel original story; reprints 50.00
❑14, May 1968, JK (a); A: Spider-Man. Spider-Man original story; reprints 1st Kirby art at Marvel 75.00
❑15, Jul 1968, GC (a); Medusa original story; reprints 42.00
❑16, Sep 1968, HT (a); O: Phantom Eagle. 1: Phantom Eagle. Phantom Eagle original story; reprints 25.00
❑17, Nov 1968, O: Black Knight III (Dane Whitman). D: Black Knight I (Sir Percy of Scandia). Black Knight original story; reprints All-Winners Squad #21 .... 30.00
❑18, Jan 1969, O: Vance Astro. O: Guardians of the Galaxy. 1: Vance Astro. 1: Yondu. 1: Guardians of the Galaxy. 1: Charlie-27. 1: Zarek. Guardians of the Galaxy original story; reprints 40.00
❑19, Mar 1969, GT (a); A: Ka-Zar. Ka-Zar original story; reprints 20.00
❑20, May 1969, A: Doctor Doom. Doctor Doom original story; reprints 35.00
❑21, Jul 1969, JK (a); Reprints Avengers #3 and X-Men #2; new cover from new design 12.00
❑22, Sep 1969, JO, JK (a); Reprints X-Men #3 and Daredevil #2; new cover based on design from X-Men #3 cover 12.00
❑23, Nov 1969, JO, JK (a); Reprints X-Men #4 and Daredevil #3; uses cover from X-Men #4, retouched with character moved 12.00
❑24, Jan 1970, JO, JK, JSt (a); Reprints X-Men #5 and Daredevil #4; uses cover from Daredevil #4, recolored and retouched 12.00
❑25, Mar 1970, SD, JK, WW (a); Reprints X-Men #6, Daredevil #5, and Tales to Astonish #60; uses cover from X-Men #6, recolored and retouched 12.00
❑26, May 1970, SD, JK, WW (a); Reprints X-Men #7, Daredevil #6, and Tales to Astonish #67; new cover adapts parts of Tales to Astonish #67 and Daredevil #6 covers 12.00
❑27, Jul 1970, JK, WW (a); Reprints X-Men #8, Daredevil #7, and Tales to Astonish #68; new cover from new design 12.00
❑28, Oct 1970, GC, WW (a); Reprints Daredevil #8, Tales of Suspense #73 and #74; new cover from new design 10.00
❑29, Jan 1971, SL (w); SD, GC, WW (a); Reprints Daredevil #9, Tales of Suspense #75 and #76; new cover from new design 10.00
❑30, Apr 1971, SD, GC, JR (a); Reprints Daredevil #15, Tales of Suspense #77 and #78; new cover from new design 10.00
❑31, Nov 1971, SD, GC, JR (a); Reprints Daredevil #19, Tales of Suspense #89 and #90; old cover, recolored with Iron Man added in inset 20.00
❑32, Sep 1972, GC, JK (a); Reprints from Tales to Astonish begin (#69 and #77); new cover from new design 6.00
❑33, Nov 1972, Reprints Tales to Astonish #78; new cover from new design 5.00
❑34, Jan 1973, Reprints Tales to Astonish #79; new cover from new design 5.00
❑35, Mar 1973, Reprints Tales to Astonish #80; new cover from new design 5.00
❑36, May 1973, Reprints Tales to Astonish #81; old cover, recolored . 5.00
❑37, Jul 1973, Reprints Tales to Astonish #82; old cover, recolored . 5.00
❑38, Sep 1973, Reprints Tales to Astonish #83; old cover, recolored . 5.00
❑39, Oct 1973, Reprints Tales to Astonish #84; old cover, recolored . 4.00
❑40, Nov 1973, Reprints Tales to Astonish #85; old cover, recolored . 4.00
❑41, Jan 1974, Reprints Tales to Astonish #86; new cover from new design 4.00
❑42, Mar 1974, Reprints Tales to Astonish #87; old cover, recolored . 4.00
❑43, May 1974, Reprints Tales to Astonish #88; new cover based on old design, with Hulk added 4.00
❑44, Jul 1974, Reprints Tales to Astonish #89; old cover, recolored . 4.00
❑45, Sep 1974, Reprints Tales to Astonish #90; new cover from new design 4.00
❑46, Oct 1974, Reprints Tales to Astonish #91; old cover, recolored . 3.00
❑47, Nov 1974, Reprints Tales to Astonish #92; new cover from new design 3.00
❑48, Jan 1975, Reprints Tales to Astonish #93; old cover, recolored . 3.00
❑49, Mar 1975, Reprints Tales to Astonish #94; new cover from new design 3.00
❑50, May 1975, Reprints Tales to Astonish #95; new cover based on the original 3.00
❑51, Jul 1975, Reprints Tales to Astonish #96; new cover from new design 3.00
❑52, Sep 1975, Reprints Tales to Astonish #97; old cover, recolored . 2.50
❑53, Oct 1975, Reprints Tales to Astonish #98; new cover from new design 2.50
❑54, Nov 1975, Reprints Tales to Astonish #99; new cover from new design 2.50
❑55, Jan 1976, Reprints Tales to Astonish #101; old cover, retouched and recolored 2.50
❑56, Mar 1976, Reprints Incredible Hulk #102; new cover, based on original 2.50
❑57, May 1976, Reprints Incredible Hulk #103; old cover, recolored 2.50
❑57/30 cent, May 1976, 30 cent regional price variant; reprints Incredible Hulk #103 .... 20.00
❑58, Jul 1976, Reprints Incredible Hulk #104; old cover, recolored 2.50
❑58/30 cent, Jul 1976, 30 cent regional price variant; reprints Incredible Hulk #104 .... 20.00

Marvel Team-Up

Mostly Spider-Man meetings

©Marvel

Marvel Team-Up (2nd Series)

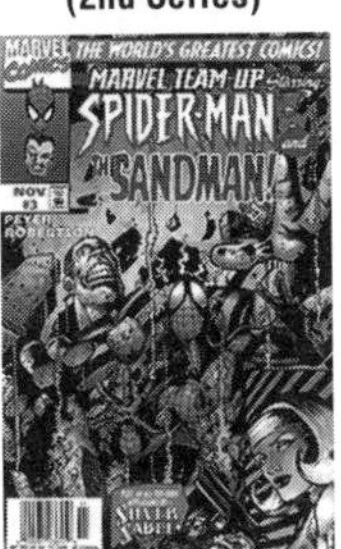

Spider-Man teams again

©Marvel

Marvel Team-Up (3rd series)

More Marvel-ous meetings

©Marvel

Marvel: The Lost Generation

Time-traveling series numbered backwards

©Marvel

Marvel Treasury Edition

Life-sized reprints hard to hold in small hands

©Marvel

N-MINT

❑59, Sep 1976, Reprints Incredible Hulk #105; old cover, recolored 2.50
❑60, Oct 1976, Reprints Incredible Hulk #106; old cover, recolored 2.50
❑61, Nov 1976, Reprints Incredible Hulk #107; old cover, partially redrawn 2.50
❑62, Jan 1977, Reprints Incredible Hulk #108; old cover, recolored 2.50
❑63, Mar 1977, Reprints Incredible Hulk #109; old cover, recolored 2.50
❑64, May 1977, Reprints Incredible Hulk #110; old cover, recolored; newsstand edition (distributed by Curtis); issue number in box........... 2.50
❑64/Whitman, May 1977, Special markets edition (usually sold in Whitman bagged prepacks); price appears in a diamond; UPC barcode appears.. 2.50
❑65, Jun 1977, Reprints Incredible Hulk #111; old cover, recolored; newsstand edition (distributed by Curtis); issue number in box........... 2.50
❑65/Whitman, Jun 1977, Special markets edition (usually sold in Whitman bagged prepacks); price appears in a diamond; UPC barcode appears.......... 2.50
❑65/35 cent, Jun 1977, 35 cent variant newsstand edition (distributed by Curtis); issue number in box........... 15.00
❑66, Sep 1977, Reprints Incredible Hulk #112; new cover, based on the original; newsstand edition (distributed by Curtis); issue number in box.. 2.50
❑66/Whitman, Sep 1977, Special markets edition (usually sold in Whitman bagged prepacks); price appears in a diamond; UPC barcode appears.. 2.50
❑66/35 cent, Sep 1977, 35 cent variant newsstand edition (distributed by Curtis); issue number in box........... 15.00
❑67, Oct 1977, Reprints Incredible Hulk #113; new cover, based on the original; newsstand edition (distributed by Curtis); issue number in box.. 2.50
❑67/Whitman, Oct 1977, Special markets edition (usually sold in Whitman bagged prepacks); price appears in a diamond; no UPC barcode.. 2.50
❑68, Nov 1977, Reprints Incredible Hulk #114; new cover, based on the original.. 2.50
❑69, Jan 1978, Reprints Incredible Hulk #115; new cover from new design..... 2.50
❑70, Mar 1978, Reprints Incredible Hulk #116; new cover, based on the original.. 2.50
❑71, May 1978, Reprints Incredible Hulk #117; new cover, based on the original.. 2.50
❑72, Jul 1978, Reprints Incredible Hulk #119; new cover, based on the original, also by Trimpe.................. 2.50
❑73, Aug 1978, Reprints Incredible Hulk #120; old cover, recolored 2.50
❑74, Sep 1978, Reprints Incredible Hulk #122; old cover, recolored; newsstand edition (distributed by Curtis); issue number in box........... 2.50

N-MINT

❑74/Whitman, Sep 1978, Special markets edition (usually sold in Whitman bagged prepacks); price appears in a diamond; UPC barcode appears.. 2.50
❑75, Oct 1978, Reprints Incredible Hulk #123; new cover from new design; newsstand edition (distributed by Curtis); issue number in box.......... 2.50
❑75/Whitman, Oct 1978, Special markets edition (usually sold in Whitman bagged prepacks); price appears in a diamond; UPC barcode appears.. 2.50
❑76, Nov 1978, Reprints Incredible Hulk #124; old cover, recolored; newsstand edition (distributed by Curtis); issue number in box.......... 2.50
❑76/Whitman, Nov 1978, Special markets edition (usually sold in Whitman bagged prepacks); price appears in a diamond; no UPC barcode.. 2.50
❑77, Dec 1978, Reprints Incredible Hulk #125; new cover, based on the original; newsstand edition (distributed by Curtis); issue number in box.. 2.50
❑77/Whitman, Dec 1978, Special markets edition (usually sold in Whitman bagged prepacks); price appears in a diamond; no UPC barcode.. 2.50
❑78, Jan 1979, Reprints Incredible Hulk #126; old cover, recolored; newsstand edition (distributed by Curtis); issue number in box.......... 2.50
❑78/Whitman, Jan 1979, Special markets edition (usually sold in Whitman bagged prepacks); price appears in a diamond; no UPC barcode.. 2.50
❑79, Mar 1979, Reprints Incredible Hulk #127; old cover, recolored...... 2.50
❑80, May 1979, Reprints Incredible Hulk #128; old cover, recolored; newsstand edition (distributed by Curtis); issue number in box.......... 2.50
❑80/Whitman, May 1979, Special markets edition (usually sold in Whitman bagged prepacks); price appears in a diamond; no UPC barcode 2.50
❑81, Jul 1979, Reprints Incredible Hulk #129; old cover, recolored............. 2.00
❑82, Aug 1979, Reprints Incredible Hulk #130; new cover from new design.. 2.00
❑83, Sep 1979, Reprints Incredible Hulk #131; old cover, recolored...... 2.00
❑84, Oct 1979, Reprints Incredible Hulk #132; old cover, recolored............. 2.00
❑85, Nov 1979, Reprints Incredible Hulk #133; old cover, recolored...... 2.00
❑86, Jan 1980, Reprints Incredible Hulk #134; old cover, recolored...... 2.00
❑87, Mar 1980, Reprints Incredible Hulk #135; old cover, recolored...... 2.00
❑88, May 1980, Reprints Incredible Hulk #138; old cover, recolored...... 2.00
❑89, Jul 1980, Reprints Incredible Hulk #139; old cover, recolored............. 2.00
❑90, Aug 1980, SB (a); Reprints Avengers #88; old cover, recolored 2.00

N-MINT

❑91, Sep 1980, Reprints Incredible Hulk #140; old cover, recolored 2.00
❑92, Oct 1980, Reprints Incredible Hulk #141; old cover, recolored 2.00
❑93, Nov 1980, Reprints Incredible Hulk #142; old cover, recolored and relettered 2.00
❑94, Jan 1981, Reprints Incredible Hulk #145; old cover, recolored 2.00
❑95, Mar 1981, Reprints Incredible Hulk #146; new cover, from new design 2.00
❑96, Apr 1981, Reprints Incredible Hulk #147; old cover, recolored 2.00
❑97, May 1981, Reprints Incredible Hulk #148; old cover, recolored 2.00
❑98, Jun 1981, Reprints Incredible Hulk #149; old cover, recolored 2.00
❑99, Jul 1981, Reprints Incredible Hulk #150; old cover, recolored 2.00
❑100, Aug 1981, Reprints Incredible Hulk #151-152; cover from #152, recolored and retouched 2.00
❑101, Sep 1981, Reprints Incredible Hulk #153; old cover, recolored 2.00
❑102, Oct 1981, Reprints Incredible Hulk #154; old cover, horizontally flipped and recolored 2.00
❑103, Nov 1981, Reprints Incredible Hulk #155; old cover, recolored 2.00
❑104, Dec 1981, Reprints Incredible Hulk #156; old cover, recolored 2.00
❑105, Jan 1982, Reprints Incredible Hulk #157; old cover, recolored 2.00
❑Special 1, Oct 1966; SL (w); BEv, JK (a); O: Daredevil. 1: Daredevil. One-shot from 1966; Reprints stories from Avengers #2, Daredevil #1, Marvel Mystery Comics #8; Human Torch meets Sub-Mariner 40.00

MARVEL SUPER-HEROES (VOL. 2)

MARVEL

❑1, May 1990; SD, FH, KP, MGu (a); O: Raptor. Spring Special............... 3.50
❑2, Jul 1990; Summer Special; Iron Man, Rogue, Falcon, Speeball, Tigra, Daredevil.. 3.25
❑3, Oct 1990; Fall Special; Captain America, Hulk, Wasp, Blue Shield, Speedball, Captain Marvel.............. 3.25
❑4, Dec 1990; Winter Special; Nick Fury, Daredevil, Spider-Man, Black Knight, Spitfire, Speedball 3.25
❑5, Apr 1991; SD (a); Spring Special; Thing, Thor, Dr. Strange, Speedball, She-Hulk.. 3.25
❑6, Jul 1991; RB (a); Summer Special; X-Men, Sabra, Speedball, Power Pack 3.25
❑7, Oct 1991; SD (a); Fall Special: X-Men, Shroud, Marvel Boy, Cloak and Dagger 3.25
❑8, Dec 1991; SD (a); Winter Special: X-Men, Namor, Iron Man 3.25
❑9, Apr 1992; KB (w); A: Cupid. Spring Special: Iron Man, West Coast Avengers, Thor 3.25
❑10, Jul 1992; Oversized format; A: Sabretooth. Summer Special: Ms. Marvel, Vision & Scarlet Witch, Namor.. 3.25

Other grades: Multiply price above by 5/6 for VF/NM • 2/3 for VERY FINE • 1/3 for FINE • 1/5 for VERY GOOD • 1/8 for GOOD

	N-MINT
❑11, Oct 1992; MGu (a); Fall Special: Giant Man, Ghost Rider, Ms. Marvel	3.00
❑12, Jan 1993; KB (w); Winter Special: Falcon, Dr. Strange, Iron Man	2.50
❑13, Apr 1993; KB (w); GC, DH (a); Spring Special: All-Iron Man issue	2.75
❑14, Jul 1993; BMc (a); Summer Special: Speedball, Dr. Strange, Iron Man	2.75
❑15, Oct 1993; KP, DH (a); A: Iron Man. A: Thor. Fall Special: Iron Man, Thor, Hulk	2.75

MARVEL SUPER-HEROES MEGAZINE

Marvel

	N-MINT
❑1, Oct 1994	2.95
❑2, Nov 1994	2.95
❑3, Dec 1994	2.95
❑4, Jan 1995	2.95
❑5, Feb 1995	2.95
❑6, Mar 1995	2.95

MARVEL SUPER HEROES SECRET WARS

Marvel

	N-MINT
❑1, May 1984; MZ (a); 1: Beyonder (voice only). X-Men, Avengers, Fantastic Four in all	4.00
❑2, Jun 1984 MZ (a)	2.00
❑3, Jul 1984 MZ (a); O: Volcana. 1: Volcana	3.00
❑4, Aug 1984 BL (a)	4.00
❑5, Sep 1984 BL (a)	3.00
❑6, Oct 1984 MZ (a); D: Wasp	4.00
❑7, Nov 1984 MZ (a); 1: Spider-Woman II (Julia Carpenter)	3.00
❑8, Dec 1984 MZ (a); O: Spider-Man's black costume. 1: Alien costume (later Venom)	15.00
❑9, Jan 1985 MZ (a)	2.00
❑10, Feb 1985 MZ (a)	2.00
❑11, Mar 1985 MZ (a)	3.00
❑12, Apr 1985; Giant-size; MZ (a); Conclusion	2.00
❑Book 1	19.95

MARVEL SUPER SPECIAL

Marvel

	N-MINT
❑1, Sep 1977; O: Kiss (rock group). Kiss; Group mixed drops of their blood into the printer's ink in publicity stunt; title begins as Marvel Comics Super Special	85.00
❑2, Mar 1978; Conan	8.00
❑3, Jun 1978; Close Encounters of the Third Kind	8.00
❑4, Aug 1978; The Beatles	30.00
❑5, Dec 1978; Title changes to Marvel Super Special; Kiss	55.00
❑6, Dec 1978; Jaws 2; #7, Marvel's adaptation of Sgt. Pepper's Lonely Hearts Club Band, was pulled from circulation	7.00
❑8, ca. 1979; Battlestar Galactica; tabloid	8.00
❑9, Feb 1979; Conan	7.00
❑10, Jun 1979; Star-Lord	6.00
❑11, Sep 1979; Warriors of Shadow Realm; Weirdworld	5.00
❑12, Nov 1979; Warriors of Shadow Realm; Weirdworld	5.00
❑13, Jan 1980; Warriors of Shadow Realm; Weirdworld	5.00
❑14, Feb 1980; GC, TP (a); Meteor	5.00
❑15, Mar 1980; Star Trek: The Motion Picture	5.00
❑16, Aug 1980; Empire Strikes Back	7.00
❑17, Nov 1980; Xanadu	3.50
❑18, Sep 1981; Raiders of the Lost Ark	3.50
❑19, Oct 1981; For Your Eyes Only	3.50
❑20, Oct 1981; Dragonslayer	3.50
❑21, Aug 1982; Conan movie	3.50
❑22, Sep 1982; Comic size; Blade Runner	3.50
❑23, Sep 1982; Annie	3.50
❑24, Mar 1983; Dark Crystal	3.50
❑25, Aug 1983; Comic size; Rock & Rule	3.50
❑26, Sep 1983; Octopussy	3.50
❑27, Sep 1983; Return of the Jedi	3.50
❑28, Oct 1983; Krull	3.50
❑29, Jul 1984; Tarzan of the Apes	3.50
❑30, Aug 1984; Indiana Jones and the Temple of Doom	3.50
❑31, Sep 1984; The Last Starfighter	3.50
❑32, Oct 1984; The Muppets Take Manhattan	3.50
❑33, Nov 1984; Buckaroo Banzai	3.50
❑34, Nov 1984; Sheena	3.50
❑35, Dec 1984; Conan the Destroyer	3.50
❑36, Apr 1985; Dune	3.50
❑37, Apr 1985; 2010	3.50
❑38, Nov 1985; Red Sonja	3.50
❑39, Mar 1985; Santa Claus: the Movie	3.50
❑40, Oct 1986; Labyrinth	3.50
❑41, Nov 1986; Howard the Duck movie adaptation	3.50

MARVEL SWIMSUIT SPECIAL

Marvel

	N-MINT
❑1, ca. 1992; 1992; in Wakanda	4.00
❑2, ca. 1993; 1993; on Monster Island	4.50
❑3, ca. 1994	4.50
❑4, ca. 1995	5.00

MARVEL TAILS

Marvel

	N-MINT
❑1, Nov 1983, 1: Peter Porker	1.50

MARVEL TALES (2ND SERIES)

Marvel

	N-MINT
❑1, ca. 1964, Giant-size; SL (w); SD, JK (a); O: Iron Man. O: Ant-Man. O: Spider-Man. O: The Hulk. O: Giant-Man. 1: Spider-Man. Reprints Amazing Fantasy #15; Listed as Marvel Tales Annual #1 in indicia	175.00
❑2, ca. 1965, Giant-size; O: X-Men. Reprints Uncanny X-Men #1, Incredible Hulk #3, Avengers #1	85.00
❑3, Jul 1966, Giant-size; reprints Amazing Spider-Man #6	45.00
❑4, Sep 1966, Giant-size; SD (a); Reprints Amazing Spider-Man #7	30.00
❑5, Nov 1966, Giant-size; SD (a); Reprints Amazing Spider-Man #8	30.00
❑6, Jan 1967, Giant-size; SD (a); Reprints Amazing Spider-Man #9	25.00
❑7, Mar 1967, Giant-size; SD (a); Reprints Amazing Spider-Man #10	25.00
❑8, May 1967, Giant-size; SD (a); Reprints Amazing Spider-Man #13	25.00
❑9, Jul 1967, Giant-size; SD (a); Reprints Amazing Spider-Man #14	25.00
❑10, Sep 1967, Giant-size; SD (a); Reprints Amazing Spider-Man #15	30.00
❑11, Nov 1967, Giant-size; SD (a); Reprints Amazing Spider-Man #16	25.00
❑12, Jan 1968, Giant-size; SL (w); SD, DH (a); 1: The Trapster (Paste-Pot Pete). Reprints stories from Amazing Spider-Man #17, Strange Tales #110, Tales to Astonish #58, Tales to Astonish #98	25.00
❑13, Mar 1968, Giant-size; SD (a); O: Marvel Boy. Reprints Amazing Spider-Man #18 and Marvel Boy #1	25.00
❑14, May 1968, Giant-size; SD (a); Marvel Boy; Reprints Amazing Spider-Man #19	25.00
❑15, Jul 1968, Giant-size; SD (a); Marvel Boy; Reprints Amazing Spider-Man #20	25.00
❑16, Sep 1968, Giant-size; SD (a); Marvel Boy; Reprints Amazing Spider-Man #21	25.00
❑17, Nov 1968, Giant-size; SD (a); Reprints Amazing Spider-Man #22	20.00
❑18, Jan 1969, Giant-size; SD (a); Reprints Amazing Spider-Man #23	20.00
❑19, Mar 1969, Giant-size; SD (a); Reprints Amazing Spider-Man #24	20.00
❑20, May 1969, Giant-size; SD (a); Reprints Amazing Spider-Man #25	20.00
❑21, Jul 1969, Giant-size; SD (a); Reprints Amazing Spider-Man #26	20.00
❑22, Sep 1969, Giant-size; SD (a); Reprints Amazing Spider-Man #27	15.00
❑23, Nov 1969, Giant-size	15.00
❑24, Jan 1970, Giant-size; SD (a); Reprints Amazing Spider-Man #31	15.00
❑25, Mar 1970, Giant-size; SD (a); Amazing Spider-Man #32	15.00
❑26, May 1970, Giant-size; SD (a); Reprints Amazing Spider-Man #33	15.00
❑27, Jul 1970, Giant-size; SD (a); Reprints Amazing Spider-Man #34	15.00
❑28, Oct 1970, Giant-size; SD (a); Reprints Amazing Spider-Man #35 and #36	15.00
❑29, Jan 1971, Giant-size; JR (a); O: Green Goblin. Reprints Amazing Spider-Man #39 and #40	15.00
❑30, Apr 1971, Giant-size; JR (a); Reprints Amazing Spider-Man #58 and #41; conclusion of Angel back-up from Ka-Zar #3	15.00
❑31, Jul 1971, Giant-size; SD, JR (a); Reprints Amazing Spider-Man #37 and #42	15.00
❑32, Nov 1971, Last giant-size issue JR (a)	15.00
❑33, Feb 1972, JR (a); Reprints Amazing Spider-Man #45 and #47	12.00
❑34, Apr 1972, JR (a); Reprints Amazing Spider-Man #48	12.00
❑35, Jun 1972, JR (a); Reprints Amazing Spider-Man #49	12.00
❑36, Aug 1972, JR (a); Reprints Amazing Spider-Man #51	12.00
❑37, Sep 1972, JR (a); Reprints Amazing Spider-Man #52	12.00
❑38, Oct 1972, JR (a); Reprints Amazing Spider-Man #53	12.00
❑39, Nov 1972, JR (a); Reprints Amazing Spider-Man #54	12.00
❑40, Dec 1972, JR (a); Reprints Amazing Spider-Man #55	12.00
❑41, Feb 1973, JR (a); Reprints Amazing Spider-Man #56	12.00
❑42, Apr 1973, JR (a); Reprints Amazing Spider-Man #59	12.00
❑43, Jun 1973, JR (a); Reprints Amazing Spider-Man #60	12.00
❑44, Aug 1973	12.00
❑45, Sep 1973	10.00
❑46, Oct 1973	10.00
❑47, Nov 1973	10.00
❑48, Dec 1973	10.00
❑49, Feb 1974	10.00
❑50, Apr 1974	10.00
❑51, Jun 1974	10.00
❑52, Aug 1974	10.00
❑53, Sep 1974	10.00
❑54, Oct 1974	10.00
❑55, Nov 1974	10.00
❑56, Dec 1974	10.00
❑57, Feb 1975	10.00
❑58, Apr 1975	10.00
❑59, Jun 1975	10.00
❑60, Aug 1975	10.00
❑61, Sep 1975	10.00
❑62, Oct 1975	10.00
❑63, Nov 1975	10.00
❑64, Jan 1976	10.00
❑65, Mar 1976	10.00
❑66, Apr 1976	10.00
❑66/30 cent, Apr 1976, 30 cent regional price variant	20.00
❑67, May 1976	10.00
❑67/30 cent, May 1976, 30 cent regional price variant	20.00
❑68, Jun 1976	10.00
❑68/30 cent, Jun 1976, 30 cent regional price variant	20.00
❑69, Jul 1976	10.00
❑69/30 cent, Jul 1976, 30 cent regional price variant	20.00
❑70, Aug 1976	10.00
❑70/30 cent, Aug 1976, 30 cent regional price variant	20.00
❑71, Sep 1976	10.00
❑72, Oct 1976	7.00
❑73, Nov 1976	7.00
❑74, Dec 1976	7.00
❑75, Jan 1977	7.00
❑76, Feb 1977	7.00
❑77, Mar 1977	7.00
❑78, Apr 1977	7.00
❑79, May 1977, Newsstand edition (distributed by Curtis); issue number in box	7.00
❑79/Whitman, May 1977, Special markets edition (usually sold in Whitman bagged prepacks); price appears in a diamond; UPC barcode appears	10.00
❑80, Jun 1977, Newsstand edition (distributed by Curtis); issue number in box	7.00

Other grades: Multiply price above by 5/6 for VF/NM • 2/3 for VERY FINE • 1/3 for FINE • 1/5 for VERY GOOD • 1/8 for GOOD

Marvel Treasury of Oz

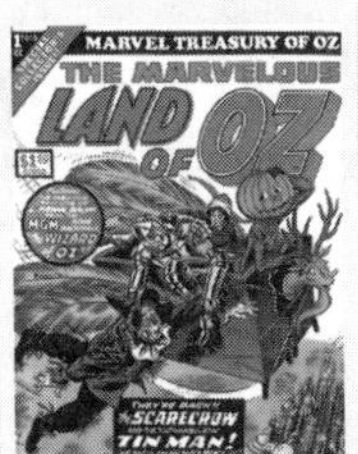

Adapts Baum's Land of Oz

©Marvel

Marvel Triple Action

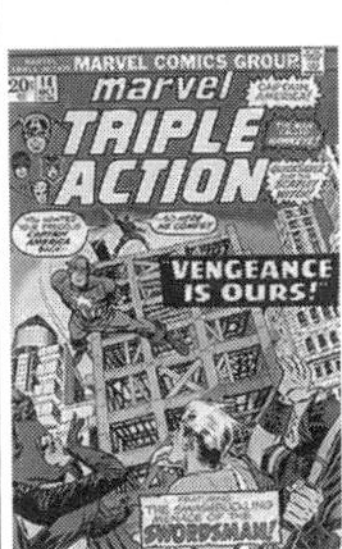

Fantastic Four and Avengers reprints

©Marvel

Marvel Two-In-One

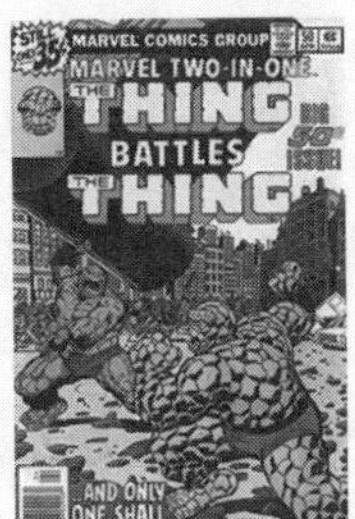

The Thing's team-up tour de force

©Marvel

Marvel Universe

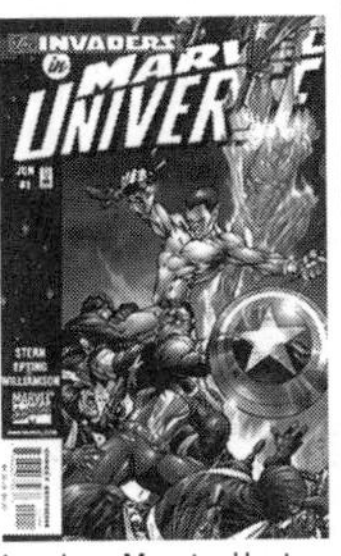

Invaders, Monster Hunters massacre series

©Marvel

Marvel Valentine Special

Romance blooms in Marvel universe

©Marvel

	N-MINT
❑80/Whitman, Jun 1977, Special markets edition (usually sold in Whitman bagged prepacks); price appears in a diamond; UPC barcode appears	10.00
❑80/35 cent, Jun 1977, 35 cent regional price variant; newsstand edition (distributed by Curtis); issue number in box	18.00
❑81, Jul 1977, Newsstand edition (distributed by Curtis); issue number in box	7.00
❑81/Whitman, Jul 1977, Special markets edition (usually sold in Whitman bagged prepacks); price appears in a diamond; UPC barcode appears	14.00
❑81/35 cent, Jul 1977, 35 cent regional price variant; newsstand edition (distributed by Curtis); issue number in box	15.00
❑82, Aug 1977, Newsstand edition (distributed by Curtis); issue number in box	7.00
❑82/Whitman, Aug 1977, Special markets edition (usually sold in Whitman bagged prepacks); price appears in a diamond; UPC barcode appears	14.00
❑82/35 cent, Aug 1977, 35 cent regional price variant; newsstand edition (distributed by Curtis); issue number in box	15.00
❑83, Sep 1977, Newsstand edition (distributed by Curtis); issue number in box	7.00
❑83/Whitman, Sep 1977, Special markets edition (usually sold in Whitman bagged prepacks); price appears in a diamond; UPC barcode appears	10.00
❑83/35 cent, Sep 1977, 35 cent regional price variant; newsstand edition (distributed by Curtis); issue number in box	15.00
❑84, Oct 1977, Newsstand edition (distributed by Curtis); issue number in box	7.00
❑84/Whitman, Oct 1977, Special markets edition (usually sold in Whitman bagged prepacks); price appears in a diamond; no UPC barcode	7.00
❑84/35 cent, Oct 1977, 35 cent regional price variant; newsstand edition (distributed by Curtis); issue number in box	15.00
❑85, Nov 1977, Newsstand edition (distributed by Curtis); issue number in box	7.00
❑85/Whitman, Nov 1977, Special markets edition (usually sold in Whitman bagged prepacks); price appears in a diamond; no UPC barcode	7.00
❑86, Dec 1977	5.00
❑87, Jan 1978	5.00
❑88, Feb 1978	5.00
❑89, Mar 1978	5.00
❑90, Apr 1978	5.00
❑91, May 1978, Newsstand edition (distributed by Curtis); issue number in box	5.00

	N-MINT
❑91/Whitman, May 1978, Special markets edition (usually sold in Whitman bagged prepacks); price appears in a diamond; no UPC barcode	5.00
❑92, Jun 1978	5.00
❑93, Jul 1978	5.00
❑94, Aug 1978, Newsstand edition (distributed by Curtis); issue number in box	5.00
❑94/Whitman, Aug 1978, Special markets edition (usually sold in Whitman bagged prepacks); price appears in a diamond; UPC barcode appears	5.00
❑95, Sep 1978, Newsstand edition (distributed by Curtis); issue number in box	5.00
❑95/Whitman, Sep 1978, Special markets edition (usually sold in Whitman bagged prepacks); price appears in a diamond; UPC barcode appears	5.00
❑96, Oct 1978, Newsstand edition (distributed by Curtis); issue number in box	5.00
❑96/Whitman, Oct 1978, Special markets edition (usually sold in Whitman bagged prepacks); price appears in a diamond; no UPC barcode	5.00
❑97, Nov 1978, Newsstand edition (distributed by Curtis); issue number in box	5.00
❑97/Whitman, Nov 1978, Special markets edition (usually sold in Whitman bagged prepacks); price appears in a diamond; no UPC barcode	5.00
❑98, Dec 1978, D: Gwen Stacy. Newsstand edition (distributed by Curtis); issue number in box	5.00
❑98/Whitman, Dec 1978, D: Gwen Stacy. Special markets edition (usually sold in Whitman bagged prepacks); price appears in a diamond; UPC barcode appears	5.00
❑99, Jan 1979, D: Green Goblin. Newsstand edition (distributed by Curtis); issue number in box	5.00
❑99/Whitman, Jan 1979, D: Green Goblin. Special markets edition (usually sold in Whitman bagged prepacks); price appears in a diamond; no UPC barcode	5.00
❑100, Feb 1979 MN, SD, GK, TD (a)	5.00
❑101, Mar 1979	5.00
❑102, Apr 1979	5.00
❑103, May 1979	5.00
❑104, Jun 1979	5.00
❑105, Jul 1979	5.00
❑106, Aug 1979, 1: Punisher. 1: Jackal. Reprints Amazing Spider-Man #129	5.00
❑107, Sep 1979	5.00
❑108, Oct 1979	5.00
❑109, Nov 1979	5.00
❑110, Dec 1979	5.00
❑111, Jan 1980, Punisher	5.00
❑112, Feb 1980, Punisher	5.00
❑113, Mar 1980	5.00
❑114, Apr 1980	5.00

	N-MINT
❑115, May 1980	5.00
❑116, Jun 1980	5.00
❑117, Jul 1980	5.00
❑118, Aug 1980	5.00
❑119, Sep 1980	5.00
❑120, Oct 1980	5.00
❑121, Nov 1980	5.00
❑122, Dec 1980	5.00
❑123, Jan 1981	4.00
❑124, Feb 1981	4.00
❑125, Mar 1981	4.00
❑126, Apr 1981	4.00
❑127, May 1981	4.00
❑128, Jun 1981	4.00
❑129, Jul 1981	4.00
❑130, Aug 1981	4.00
❑131, Sep 1981	4.00
❑132, Oct 1981	4.00
❑133, Nov 1981	4.00
❑134, Dec 1981	4.00
❑135, Jan 1982	4.00
❑136, Feb 1982	4.00
❑137, Mar 1982, O: Spider-Man. 1: Spider-Man. Reprints Amazing Fantasy #15	7.00
❑138, Apr 1982, Reprints Amazing Spider-Man #1	5.00
❑139, May 1982, Reprints Amazing Spider-Man #2	5.00
❑140, Jun 1982, Reprints Amazing Spider-Man #3	5.00
❑141, Jul 1982, Reprints Amazing Spider-Man #4	5.00
❑142, Aug 1982, Reprints Amazing Spider-Man #5	5.00
❑143, Sep 1982, Reprints Amazing Spider-Man #6	5.00
❑144, Oct 1982, Reprints Amazing Spider-Man #7	5.00
❑145, Nov 1982	4.00
❑146, Dec 1982	4.00
❑147, Jan 1983	4.00
❑148, Feb 1983	4.00
❑149, Mar 1983	4.00
❑150, Apr 1983, Giant-size	4.00
❑151, May 1983	4.00
❑152, Jun 1983	4.00
❑153, Jul 1983	4.00
❑154, Aug 1983	4.00
❑155, Sep 1983	4.00
❑156, Oct 1983	4.00
❑157, Nov 1983	4.00
❑158, Dec 1983	4.00
❑159, Jan 1984	4.00
❑160, Feb 1984	4.00
❑161, Mar 1984	4.00
❑162, Apr 1984	4.00
❑163, May 1984	4.00
❑164, Jun 1984	4.00
❑165, Jul 1984	4.00
❑166, Aug 1984	4.00
❑167, Sep 1984	4.00
❑168, Oct 1984	4.00
❑169, Nov 1984	4.00
❑170, Dec 1984	4.00

Other grades: Multiply price above by 5/6 for VF/NM • 2/3 for VERY FINE • 1/3 for FINE • 1/5 for VERY GOOD • 1/8 for GOOD

	N-MINT
❑171, Jan 1985	4.00
❑172, Feb 1985	4.00
❑173, Mar 1985	4.00
❑174, Apr 1985	4.00
❑175, May 1985	4.00
❑176, Jun 1985	4.00
❑177, Jul 1985	4.00
❑178, Aug 1985	4.00
❑179, Sep 1985	4.00
❑180, Oct 1985	4.00
❑181, Nov 1985	4.00
❑182, Dec 1985	4.00
❑183, Jan 1986	4.00
❑184, Feb 1986	2.00
❑185, Mar 1986	2.00
❑186, Apr 1986	2.00
❑187, May 1986	2.00
❑188, Jun 1986	2.00
❑189, Jul 1986	2.00
❑190, Aug 1986	2.00
❑191, Sep 1986	2.00
❑192, Oct 1986, Giant-size; Reprints Amazing Spider-Man #121-122	2.00
❑193, Nov 1986	2.00
❑194, Dec 1986	2.00
❑195, Jan 1987	2.00
❑196, Feb 1987	2.00
❑197, Mar 1987	2.00
❑198, Apr 1987	2.00
❑199, May 1987	2.00
❑200, Jun 1987, Giant-size; TMc, FM (c); FM (a); Reprints Amazing Spider-Man Annual #14	2.00
❑201, Jul 1987, TMc (c)	1.50
❑202, Aug 1987, TMc (c)	1.50
❑203, Sep 1987, TMc (c)	1.50
❑204, Oct 1987, TMc (c)	1.50
❑205, Nov 1987, TMc (c)	1.50
❑206, Dec 1987, TMc (c)	1.50
❑207, Jan 1988, TMc (c)	1.50
❑208, Feb 1988, TMc (c)	1.50
❑209, Mar 1988, TMc (c); 1: Punisher. 1: Jackal	2.00
❑210, Apr 1988, TMc (c); A: Punisher	2.00
❑211, May 1988, TMc (c); A: Punisher	1.50
❑212, Jun 1988, TMc (c); A: Punisher	1.50
❑213, Jul 1988, TMc (c); A: Punisher.	1.50
❑214, Aug 1988, TMc (c); A: Punisher	1.50
❑215, Sep 1988, TMc (c); A: Punisher	1.50
❑216, Oct 1988, TMc (c); A: Punisher	1.50
❑217, Nov 1988, TMc (c); A: Punisher	1.50
❑218, Dec 1988, TMc (c); A: Punisher	1.50
❑219, Jan 1989, TMc (c); A: Punisher	1.50
❑220, Feb 1989, TMc (c); A: Punisher	1.50
❑221, Mar 1989, TMc (c); A: Punisher	1.50
❑222, Apr 1989, TMc (c); A: Punisher	1.50
❑223, May 1989, TMc (c); TMc (a)	1.50
❑224, Jun 1989, TMc (c); TMc (a)	1.50
❑225, Jul 1989, TMc (c); TMc (a)	1.50
❑226, Aug 1989, TMc (c); TMc (a)	1.50
❑227, Sep 1989, TMc (c); TMc (a)	1.50
❑228, Oct 1989, TMc (c); TMc (a)	1.50
❑229, Nov 1989, TMc (c); TMc (a)	1.50
❑230, Nov 1989, TMc (c); TMc (a)	1.50
❑231, Dec 1989, TMc (c); TMc (a)	1.50
❑232, Dec 1989, TMc (c); TMc (a)	1.50
❑233, Jan 1990, TMc (c); TMc (a)	1.50
❑234, Feb 1990, TMc (c); TMc (a)	1.50
❑235, Mar 1990, TMc (c); TMc (a)	1.50
❑236, Apr 1990, TMc (c); TMc (a)	1.50
❑237, May 1990, TMc (c); TMc (a)	1.50
❑238, Jun 1990, TMc (c); TMc (a)	1.50
❑239, Jul 1990, TMc (c); TMc (a)	1.50
❑240, Aug 1990	1.50
❑241, Sep 1990	1.50
❑242, Oct 1990	1.50
❑243, Nov 1990	1.50
❑244, Dec 1990	1.50
❑245, Jan 1991	1.50
❑246, Feb 1991	1.50
❑247, Mar 1991	1.50
❑248, Apr 1991	1.50
❑249, May 1991, GK (a)	1.50
❑250, Jun 1991, Giant-size; FM (c); FM (a); O: Storm. Reprints Marvel Team-Up #100	1.50
❑251, Jul 1991, GK (a)	1.50
❑252, Aug 1991, GK, SL (w); GK (a); 1: Morbius. Reprints Amazing Spider-Man #101	1.50
❑253, Sep 1991, Giant-size; GK, SL (w); GK (a); O: Morbius. Reprints Amazing Spider-Man #102	1.50
❑254, Oct 1991, RA (a); A: Ghost Rider	1.50
❑255, Nov 1991, SB (a)	1.50
❑256, Dec 1991, PB (a); A: Ghost Rider	1.50
❑257, Jan 1992, JR2, JR (a)	1.50
❑258, Feb 1992, JR2 (a)	1.50
❑259, Mar 1992, JR2 (a)	1.50
❑260, Apr 1992, JR2, KJ (a)	1.50
❑261, May 1992, KJ (a)	1.50
❑262, Jun 1992, JBy (a); A: X-Men. X-Men	1.50
❑263, Jul 1992, JBy (a); O: Woodgod	1.50
❑264, Aug 1992, reprints Amazing Spider-Man Annual #5	1.50
❑265, Sep 1992, reprints Amazing Spider-Man Annual #6	1.50
❑266, Oct 1992	1.50
❑267, Nov 1992	1.50
❑268, Dec 1992	1.50
❑269, Jan 1993	1.50
❑270, Feb 1993	1.50
❑271, Mar 1993, Reprints Amazing Spider-Man #257	1.50
❑272, Apr 1993	1.50
❑273, May 1993	1.50
❑274, Jun 1993	1.50
❑275, Jul 1993	1.50
❑276, Aug 1993, A: Spider-Kid	1.50
❑277, Sep 1993, 1: Silver Sable	1.50
❑278, Oct 1993, A: Kingpin. A: Beyonder. Reprints Amazing Spider-Man #268	1.50
❑279, Nov 1993, A: Firelord	1.50
❑280, Dec 1993	1.50
❑281, Jan 1994	1.50
❑282, Feb 1994, SB (a)	1.50
❑283, Mar 1994, double-sized; O: Spider-Man. Reprints Amazing Spider-Man #275; Hobgoblin story	1.50
❑284, Apr 1994, A: Hobgoblin. D: Fly. Reprints Amazing Spider-Man #276	1.50
❑285, May 1994, Reprints Amazing Spider-Man #277	1.50
❑286, Jun 1994, PD (a); D: Wraith. Reprints Amazing Spider-Man #278	1.50
❑286/CS, Jun 1994, PD (a); Collector's Set; Reprints Amazing Spider-Man #278	2.95
❑286/2nd, Jun 1994, Collector's set; Includes animation cel, 16 page preview	2.95
❑287, Jul 1994, Jack O'Lantern cover/story; Reprints Amazing Spider-Man #279	1.50
❑288, Aug 1994, Reprints Amazing Spider-Man #280	1.50
❑289, Sep 1994, A: Jack O'Lantern. Reprints Amazing Spider-Man #281	1.50
❑290, Oct 1994, A: X-Factor. Reprints Amazing Spider-Man #282	1.50
❑291, Nov 1994, BL (a); Amazing Spider-Man #283	1.50

MARVEL TALES FLIP MAGAZINE
MARVEL

	N-MINT
❑1, Sep 2005	3.99
❑2, Oct 2005	3.99
❑3, Nov 2005	3.99
❑4, Dec 2005	3.99
❑6, Jan 2006	3.99
❑7, Mar 2006	3.99
❑8, Mar 2006	3.99
❑9, May 2006	3.99
❑10, Jun 2006	3.99
❑11, Jul 2006	3.99
❑12, Aug 2006	3.99
❑13, Sep 2006	3.99

MARVEL TEAM-UP
MARVEL

	N-MINT
❑1, Mar 1972, GK (c); RA (a); 1: Misty Knight. V: Sandman. Spider-Man; Human Torch	185.00
❑2, May 1972, GK (c); RA, JM (a); A: Human Torch. Spider-Man; Human Torch	30.00
❑3, Jul 1972, GK (c); RA (a); A: Morbius. Spider-Man; Human Torch	25.00
❑4, Sep 1972, GK (a); A: Morbius. Spider-Man; X-Men	45.00
❑5, Nov 1972, GK (a); 1: Ballox (The Monstroid). 1: Ballox ("The Monstroid"). Spider-Man; Vision	18.00
❑6, Jan 1973, GK (a); O: Puppet Master. Spider-Man; Thing	16.00
❑7, Mar 1973, GK (c); RA, JM (a); 1: Kryllk the Cruel. Spider-Man; Thor	16.00
❑8, Apr 1973, JM (a); 1: The Man-Killer. Spider-Man; The Cat	16.00
❑9, May 1973, JR (c); RA (a); A: Iron Man. Spider-Man; Iron Man	16.00
❑10, Jun 1973, JR (c); JM (a); A: Human Torch. Spider-Man; Human Torch	16.00
❑11, Jul 1973, JR (c); JM (a); A: The Inhumans. Spider-Man; Inhumans	13.00
❑12, Aug 1973, GK (c); DP, RA (a); 1: Moondark. Spider-Man; Werewolf	18.00
❑13, Sep 1973, GK (a); A: Captain America. Spider-Man; Captain America	13.00
❑14, Oct 1973, GK, WH (a); 1: The Aquanoids. Spider-Man; Sub-Mariner	13.00
❑15, Nov 1973, GK (c); DP, RA (a); O: Orb. 1: Orb. Spider-Man; Ghost Rider	13.00
❑16, Dec 1973, GK, JM (a); O: The Basilisk I (Basil Elks). 1: The Basilisk I (Basil Elks). Spider-Man; Captain Marvel	13.00
❑17, Jan 1974, GK (a); V: Basilisk. V: Mole Man. Spider-Man; Mr. Fantastic	13.00
❑18, Feb 1974, GK (a); A: The Hulk. Human Torch; Hulk	13.00
❑19, Mar 1974, GK (a); 1: Stegron, the Dinosaur Man. Spider-Man; Ka-Zar; Marvel Value Stamp #90: Hercules	13.00
❑20, Apr 1974, GK (c); SB (a); A: Black Panther. Spider-Man; Black Panther; Marvel Value Stamp #25: Torch	13.00
❑21, May 1974, GK (c); SB (a); A: Doctor Strange. Spider-Man; Doctor Strange; Marvel Value Stamp #33: Invisible Girl	8.00
❑22, Jun 1974, JR (c); SB (a); A: Hawkeye. Spider-Man; Hawkeye; Marvel Value Stamp #92: Byrrah	8.00
❑23, Jul 1974, GK (a); A: X-Men. Human Torch; Iceman; X-Men; Marvel Value Stamp #28: Hawkeye	8.00
❑24, Aug 1974, GK (c); JM (a); A: Brother Voodoo. Spider-Man; Brother Voodoo; Marvel Value Stamp #90: Hercules	8.00
❑25, Sep 1974, GK (c); JM (a); A: Daredevil. Spider-Man; Daredevil; Marvel Value Stamp #87: J. Jonah Jameson	8.00
❑26, Oct 1974, GK (c); JM (a); A: Thor. Human Torch; Thor; Marvel Value Stamp #56: Rawhide Kid	8.00
❑27, Nov 1974, JSn (c); JM (a); A: The Hulk. Spider-Man; Hulk; Marvel Value Stamp #68: Son of Satan	8.00
❑28, Dec 1974, GK (c); JM (a); A: Hercules. Spider-Man; Hercules; Marvel Value Stamp #43: Enchantress	8.00
❑29, Jan 1975, JR (c); JM (a); A: Iron Man. Human Torch; Iron Man; Marvel Value Stamp #11: Deathlok	8.00
❑30, Feb 1975, GK (c); JM (a); A: Falcon. Spider-Man; The Falcon; Marvel Value Stamp #89: Hammerhead	8.00
❑31, Mar 1975, GK (c); JM (a); A: Iron Fist. Spider-Man; Iron Fist	8.00
❑32, Apr 1975, GK (c); SB (a); A: Son of Satan. Human Torch; Son of Satan	5.00
❑33, May 1975, GK (c); SB (a); V: Meteor Man. Spider-Man; Nighthawk; Marvel Value Stamp #84: Dr. Doom	5.00
❑34, Jun 1975, GK (c); SB (a); V: Meteor Man. Spider-Man; Valkyrie	5.00
❑35, Jul 1975, GK (c); SB (a); A: Human Torch. A: Doctor Strange. Human Torch; Doctor Strange	5.00
❑36, Aug 1975, SB (a); A: Frankenstein. Spider-Man; Frankenstein	5.00
❑37, Sep 1975, SB (a); A: Man-Wolf. Spider-Man; Man-Wolf	5.00
❑38, Oct 1975, SB (a); A: Beast. Spider-Man; Beast	5.00
❑39, Nov 1975, SB (a); A: Human Torch. Spider-Man; Human Torch; Marvel Value Stamp #87: J. Jonah Jameson	5.00

Marville

Series ended with Epic invitation
©Marvel

Mary Poppins

Practically perfect adaptation
©Gold Key

Mask (1st Series)

Toy and cartoon tie-in featured teen drivers
©DC

Mask (Mini-Series)

Mischevious mayhem made by facial appliance
©Dark Horse

Master of Kung Fu

Shang-Chi fights father's fakery
©Marvel

	N-MINT
❑40, Dec 1975, SB (a); A: Sons of the Tiger. Spider-Man; Sons of Tiger; Human Torch	5.00
❑41, Jan 1976, GK (c); SB (a); A: Scarlet Witch. Spider-Man; Scarlet Witch	5.00
❑42, Feb 1976, SB (a); A: Vision. Spider-Man; Scarlet Witch; Vision	5.00
❑43, Mar 1976, GK (c); SB (a); A: Doctor Doom. Spider-Man; Doctor Doom	5.00
❑44, Apr 1976, GK (c); SB (a); A: Moondragon. Spider-Man; Moondragon	5.00
❑44/30 cent, Apr 1976, A: Moondragon. Spider-Man; Moondragon	20.00
❑45, May 1976, GK (c); SB (a); A: Killraven. Spider-Man; Killraven	5.00
❑45/30 cent, May 1976, A: Killraven. Spider-Man; Killraven	20.00
❑46, Jun 1976, RB (c); SB (a); A: Deathlok. Spider-Man; Deathlok	5.00
❑46/30 cent, Jun 1976, A: Deathlok. Spider-Man; Deathlok	20.00
❑47, Jul 1976, GK (c); V: Basilisk. Spider-Man; Thing	3.50
❑47/30 cent, Jul 1976, V: Basilisk. Spider-Man; Thing	20.00
❑48, Aug 1976, JR (c); SB (a); 1: Wraith. Spider-Man; Iron Man	3.50
❑48/30 cent, Aug 1976, 1: Wraith. Spider-Man; Iron Man	20.00
❑49, Sep 1976, JR (c); SB (a); O: Wraith. Spider-Man; Iron Man; Doctor Strange	3.50
❑50, Oct 1976, GK (c); SB (w); SB (a); A: Iron Man. Spider-Man; Doctor Strange; Iron Man	3.50
❑51, Nov 1976, GK (c); SB (a); A: Iron Man. Spider-Man; Iron Man	3.50
❑52, Dec 1976, SB (a); A: Batroc. Spider-Man; Captain America	3.50
❑53, Jan 1977, DC (c); JBy (a); A: X-Men. A: Woodgod. Spider-Man; Hulk; Woodgod; X-Men; 1st John Byrne art on X-Men	15.00
❑54, Feb 1977, GK (c); JBy (a); A: Woodgod. Spider-Man; Hulk; newsstand edition (distributed by Curtis); issue number in box	4.00
❑54/Whitman, Feb 1977, GK (c); JBy (a); A: Woodgod. Special markets edition (usually sold in Whitman bagged prepacks); price appears in a diamond; UPC barcode appears	4.00
❑55, Mar 1977, DC (c); JBy (a); 1: the Gardener. V: Gardener. Spider-Man; Warlock; newsstand edition (distributed by Curtis); issue number in box	4.00
❑55/Whitman, Mar 1977, DC (c); JBy (a); 1: the Gardener. V: Gardener. Special markets edition (usually sold in Whitman bagged prepacks); price appears in a diamond; UPC barcode appears	4.00
❑56, Apr 1977, JR2 (c); SB (a); V: Blizzard. V: Electro. Spider-Man; Daredevil; newsstand edition (distributed by Curtis); issue number in box	4.00

	N-MINT
❑56/Whitman, Apr 1977, JR2 (c); SB (a); V: Blizzard. V: Electro. Special markets edition (usually sold in Whitman bagged prepacks); price appears in a diamond; UPC barcode appears	4.00
❑57, May 1977, DC (c); SB (a); A: Black Widow. Spider-Man; Black Widow; newsstand edition (distributed by Curtis); issue number in box	4.00
❑57/Whitman, May 1977, DC (c); SB (a); A: Black Widow. Special markets edition (usually sold in Whitman bagged prepacks); price appears in a diamond; UPC barcode appears	4.00
❑58, Jun 1977, AM (c); SB (a); A: Ghost Rider. Spider-Man; Ghost Rider; newsstand edition (distributed by Curtis); issue number in box	4.00
❑58/Whitman, Jun 1977, AM (c); SB (a); A: Ghost Rider. Special markets edition (usually sold in Whitman bagged prepacks); price appears in a diamond; UPC barcode appears	4.00
❑58/35 cent, Jun 1977, AM (c); SB (a); A: Ghost Rider. 35 cent regional price variant newsstand edition (distributed by Curtis); issue number in box; Spider-Man; Ghost Rider	15.00
❑59, Jul 1977, DC (c); JBy (a); A: Wasp. Spider-Man; Yellowjacket; The Wasp; newsstand edition (distributed by Curtis); issue number in box	4.00
❑59/Whitman, Jul 1977, DC (c); JBy (a); A: Wasp. Special markets edition (usually sold in Whitman bagged prepacks); price appears in a diamond; UPC barcode appears	4.00
❑59/35 cent, Jul 1977, DC (c); JBy (a); A: Wasp. 35 cent regional price variant newsstand edition (distributed by Curtis); issue number in box; Spider-Man; Yellowjacket; The Wasp	15.00
❑60, Aug 1977, AM (c); JBy (a); A: Yellowjacket. Spider-Man; The Wasp; newsstand edition (distributed by Curtis); issue number in box	4.00
❑60/Whitman, Aug 1977, AM (c); JBy (a); A: Yellowjacket. Special markets edition (usually sold in Whitman bagged prepacks); price appears in a diamond; UPC barcode appears	4.00
❑60/35 cent, Aug 1977, AM (c); JBy (a); A: Yellowjacket. 35 cent regional price variant newsstand edition (distributed by Curtis); issue number in box; Spider-Man; The Wasp	15.00
❑61, Sep 1977, RA (c); JBy (a); V: Super-Skrull. Spider-Man; Human Torch; newsstand edition (distributed by Curtis); issue number in box	4.00
❑61/Whitman, Sep 1977, RA (c); JBy (a); V: Super-Skrull. Special markets edition (usually sold in Whitman bagged prepacks); price appears in a diamond; no UPC barcode	4.00
❑61/35 cent, Sep 1977, RA (c); JBy (a); V: Super-Skrull. 35 cent regional price variant newsstand edition (distributed by Curtis); issue number in box; Spider-Man; Human Torch	15.00

	N-MINT
❑62, Oct 1977, GK (c); JBy (a); V: Super-Skrull. Spider-Man; Ms. Marvel; newsstand edition (distributed by Curtis); issue number in box	4.00
❑62/Whitman, Oct 1977, GK (c); JBy (a); V: Super-Skrull. Special markets edition (usually sold in Whitman bagged prepacks); price appears in a diamond; no UPC barcode	4.00
❑62/35 cent, Oct 1977, GK (c); JBy (a); V: Super-Skrull. 35 cent regional price variant newsstand edition (distributed by Curtis); issue number in box; Spider-Man; Ms. Marvel	15.00
❑63, Nov 1977, DC (c); JBy (a); A: Iron Fist. Spider-Man; Iron Fist; newsstand edition (distributed by Curtis); issue number in box	4.00
❑63/Whitman, Nov 1977, DC (c); JBy (a); A: Iron Fist. Special markets edition (usually sold in Whitman bagged prepacks); price appears in a diamond; no UPC barcode	4.00
❑64, Dec 1977, DC (c); JBy (a); A: Daughters of Dragon. Spider-Man; Daughters of Dragon; newsstand edition (distributed by Curtis); issue number in box	4.00
❑64/Whitman, Dec 1977, DC (c); JBy (a); A: Daughters of Dragon. Special markets edition (usually sold in Whitman bagged prepacks); price appears in a diamond; UPC barcode appears	4.00
❑65, Jan 1978, GP (c); JBy (a); 1: Arcade. 1: Captain Britain (U.S.). Spider-Man; Captain Britain	4.00
❑66, Feb 1978, JBy (a); V: Arcade. Spider-Man; Captain Britain	7.00
❑67, Mar 1978, JBy (a); A: Tigra. V: Kraven. Spider-Man; Tigra	4.00
❑68, Apr 1978, JBy (a); 1: D'Spayre. A: Man-Thing. Spider-Man; Man-Thing	4.00
❑69, May 1978, DC (c); JBy (a); A: Havok. Spider-Man; Havok; newsstand edition (distributed by Curtis); issue number in box	4.00
❑69/Whitman, May 1978, DC (c); JBy (a); A: Havok. Special markets edition (usually sold in Whitman bagged prepacks); price appears in a diamond; no UPC barcode	4.00
❑70, Jun 1978, JBy (a); V: Living Monolith. Spider-Man; Thor	4.00
❑71, Jul 1978, A: The Falcon. Spider-Man; The Falcon	4.00
❑72, Aug 1978, JBy (c); JM (a); A: Iron Man. Spider-Man; Iron Man; newsstand edition (distributed by Curtis); issue number in box	4.00
❑72/Whitman, Aug 1978, JBy (c); JM (a); A: Iron Man. Special markets edition (usually sold in Whitman bagged prepacks); price appears in a diamond; UPC barcode appears	4.00
❑73, Sep 1978, KP (c); A: Daredevil. Spider-Man; Daredevil; newsstand edition (distributed by Curtis); issue number in box	4.00
❑73/Whitman, Sep 1978, KP (c); A: Daredevil. Special markets edition (usually sold in Whitman bagged prepacks); price appears in a diamond; no UPC barcode	4.00

N-MINT

❑74, Oct 1978, DC (c); BH (a); A: Not Ready For Prime Time Players (Saturday Night Live). Spider-Man; The Not-Ready-For-Prime-Time-Players (SNL) 4.00
❑75, Nov 1978, BH (c); JBy (a); A: Power Man. Spider-Man; Power Man; newsstand edition (distributed by Curtis); issue number in box 4.00
❑75/Whitman, Nov 1978, BH (c); JBy (a); A: Power Man. Special markets edition (usually sold in Whitman bagged prepacks); price appears in a diamond; no UPC barcode 4.00
❑76, Dec 1978, JBy (c); HC (a); A: Doctor Strange. Spider-Man; Doctor Strange; newsstand edition (distributed by Curtis); issue number in box 4.00
❑76/Whitman, Dec 1978, JBy (c); HC (a); A: Doctor Strange. Special markets edition (usually sold in Whitman bagged prepacks); price appears in a diamond; no UPC barcode 4.00
❑77, Jan 1979, JR2 (c); HC (a); A: Ms. Marvel. Spider-Man; Ms. Marvel; newsstand edition (distributed by Curtis); issue number in box 4.00
❑77/Whitman, Jan 1979, JR2 (c); HC (a); A: Ms. Marvel. Special markets edition (usually sold in Whitman bagged prepacks); price appears in a diamond; no UPC barcode 4.00
❑78, Feb 1979, AM (c); DP (a); A: Wonder Man. Spider-Man; Wonder Man; newsstand edition (distributed by Curtis); issue number in box 4.00
❑78/Whitman, Feb 1979, AM (c); DP (a); A: Wonder Man. Special markets edition (usually sold in Whitman bagged prepacks); price appears in a diamond; no UPC barcode 4.00
❑79, Mar 1979, JBy (a); A: Red Sonja. Spider-Man; Red Sonja 4.00
❑80, Apr 1979, RB (c); A: Clea. Spider-Man; Doctor Strange; Clea 4.00
❑81, May 1979, AM (c); D: Satana. Spider-Man; Satana; newsstand edition (distributed by Curtis); issue number in box 4.00
❑81/Whitman, May 1979, AM (c); D: Satana. Special markets edition (usually sold in Whitman bagged prepacks); price appears in a diamond; no UPC barcode 4.00
❑82, Jun 1979, RB (c); SB (a); A: Black Widow. Spider-Man; Black Widow 4.00
❑83, Jul 1979, RB (c); SB (a); A: Nick Fury. Spider-Man; Nick Fury 4.00
❑84, Aug 1979, SB (a); A: Shang-Chi. Spider-Man; Shang-Chi 4.00
❑85, Sep 1979, AM (c); SB (a); A: Nick Fury. Spider-Man; Shang-Chi; Nick Fury; Black Widow 4.00
❑86, Oct 1979, BMc (a); A: Guardians of the Galaxy. Spider-Man; Guardians of Galaxy 4.00
❑87, Nov 1979, AM (c); GC (a); 1: Hellrazor. Spider-Man; Black Panther 4.00
❑88, Dec 1979, RB (c); SB (a); A: Invisible Girl. Spider-Man; Invisible Girl 4.00
❑89, Jan 1980, MN, RB (a); 1: Cutthroat. Spider-Man; Nightcrawler 4.00
❑90, Feb 1980, AM (c); A: Beast. Spider-Man; Beast 4.00
❑91, Mar 1980, RB (c); PB (a); A: Ghost Rider. Spider-Man; Ghost Rider 4.00
❑92, Apr 1980, AM (c); CI (a); 1: Mister Fear IV (Alan Fagan). Spider-Man; Hawkeye 4.00
❑93, May 1980, DP (c); TS, CI (a); A: Werewolf. Spider-Man; Werewolf by Night 4.00
❑94, Jun 1980, AM (c); MZ (a); A: The Shroud. Spider-Man; Shroud 4.00
❑95, Jul 1980, FM (c); FM (a); 1: Mockingbird. 1: Huntress as Mockingbird. Spider-Man 3.00
❑96, Aug 1980, A: Howard the Duck. Spider-Man; Howard the Duck 3.00
❑97, Sep 1980, CI (a); A: Spider-Woman. Hulk; Spider-Woman 3.00
❑98, Oct 1980, AM (c); A: Black Widow. Spider-Man; Black Widow 3.00
❑99, Nov 1980, FM (c); FM (a); A: Machine Man. Spider-Man; Machine Man 3.00
❑100, Dec 1980, double-sized; FM (w); JBy, FM (a); O: Karma. O: Storm. 1: Karma. Spider-Man; Fantastic Four; Black Panther 6.00
❑101, Jan 1981, A: Nighthawk. Spider-Man; Nighthawk 3.00
❑102, Feb 1981, FM (c); FS (a); A: Doctor Samson. Spider-Man; Doc Samson 3.00
❑103, Mar 1981, A: Ant-Man. Spider-Man; Ant-Man 3.00
❑104, Apr 1981, AM (c); A: The Hulk. Hulk; Ka-Zar 3.00
❑105, May 1981, AM (c); CI (a); A: . A: Power Man and Iron Fist. Power Man; Iron Fist; Hulk 3.00
❑106, Jun 1981, FM (c); HT (a); V: Scorpion. Spider-Man; Captain America 3.00
❑107, Jul 1981, HT (a); A: She-Hulk. Spider-Man; She-Hulk 3.00
❑108, Aug 1981, HT (a); A: Paladin. Spider-Man; Paladin 3.00
❑109, Sep 1981, JR2 (c); HT (a); A: Dazzler. Spider-Man; Dazzler 3.00
❑110, Oct 1981, BL (c); HT (a); A: Iron Man. Spider-Man; Iron Man 3.00
❑111, Nov 1981, HT (a); A: Devil-Slayer. Spider-Man; Devil-Slayer 3.00
❑112, Dec 1981, HT (a); A: King Kull. Spider-Man; King Kull 3.00
❑113, Jan 1982, A: Quasar. Spider-Man; Quasar 3.00
❑114, Feb 1982, A: The Falcon. Spider-Man; The Falcon 3.00
❑115, Mar 1982, A: Thor. Spider-Man; Thor 3.00
❑116, Apr 1982, A: Valkyrie. Spider-Man; Valkyrie 3.00
❑117, May 1982, 1: Professor Power. Spider-Man; Wolverine 3.00
❑118, Jun 1982, HT (a); O: Professor Power. Spider-Man; Professor X 3.00
❑119, Jul 1982, KGa (a); A: Gargoyle. Spider-Man; Gargoyle 3.00
❑120, Aug 1982, KGa (a); A: Dominic Fortune. Spider-Man; Dominic Fortune 3.00
❑121, Sep 1982, KGa (a); 1: Frog-Man II. Spider-Man; Human Torch 3.00
❑122, Oct 1982, KGa (a); A: Man-Thing. Man-Thing 3.00
❑123, Nov 1982, KGa (a); A: Daredevil. Man-Thing; Daredevil 3.00
❑124, Dec 1982, KGa (a); O: Professor Power. Spider-Man; The Beast 3.00
❑125, Jan 1983, KGa (a); A: Tigra. Spider-Man; Tigra 3.00
❑126, Feb 1983, BH (a); A: Son of Satan. Spider-Man; Hulk; Power Man; Son of Satan 3.00
❑127, Mar 1983, KGa (a); A: The Watcher. Spider-Man; The Watcher 3.00
❑128, Apr 1983, A: Captain America. Spider-Man; Captain America 3.00
❑129, May 1983, KGa (a); A: Vision. Spider-Man; Vision; The Vision 3.00
❑130, Jun 1983, SB (a); A: Scarlet Witch. Spider-Man; Scarlet Witch; The Scarlet Witch 3.00
❑131, Jul 1983, KGa (a); A: Frogman. Spider-Man; Frogman 3.00
❑132, Aug 1983, A: Mr. Fantastic. Spider-Man; Mr. Fantastic 3.00
❑133, Sep 1983, SB (a); A: Fantastic Four. Spider-Man; Fantastic Four 3.00
❑134, Oct 1983, A: Jack of Hearts. Spider-Man; Jack of Hearts 3.00
❑135, Nov 1983, A: Kitty Pryde. Spider-Man; Kitty Pryde 3.00
❑136, Dec 1983, PS (c); A: Wonder Man. Spider-Man; Wonder Man 3.00
❑137, Jan 1984, O: Doctor Faustus. Spider-Man; Aunt May; Franklin Richards; Assistant Editor's Month. 4.00
❑138, Feb 1984, A: Sandman. Spider-Man; Sandman (Marvel); Nick Fury 3.00
❑139, Mar 1984, A: Nick Fury. Spider-Man; Sandman (Marvel); Nick Fury 3.00
❑140, Apr 1984, A: Black Widow. Spider-Man; Black Widow 3.00
❑141, May 1984, A: Daredevil. Spider-Man new costume; Daredevil 3.00
❑142, Jun 1984, A: Captain Marvel. Spider-Man; Captain Marvel (female, new) 3.00
❑143, Jul 1984, A: Starfox. Spider-Man; Starfox 3.00
❑144, Aug 1984, A: Moon Knight. Spider-Man; Moon Knight 4.00
❑145, Sep 1984, A: Iron Man. Spider-Man; Iron Man 3.00
❑146, Oct 1984, A: Nomad. Spider-Man; Nomad 3.00
❑147, Nov 1984, A: Human Torch. Spider-Man; Human Torch 3.00
❑148, Dec 1984, A: Thor. Spider-Man; Thor 3.00
❑149, Jan 1985, A: Cannonball. Spider-Man; Cannonball 3.00
❑150, Feb 1985, Giant-size; A: the X-Men. Spider-Man; X-Men 3.00
❑Annual 1, ca. 1976, DC (c); SB (a); Spider-Man; X-Men 30.00
❑Annual 2, ca. 1979, AM (c); SB (a); Spider-Man; Hulk 6.00
❑Annual 3, ca. 1980, FM (c); HT, FM (a); Hulk; Power Man; Iron Fist; Machine Man 4.00
❑Annual 4, ca. 1981, FM (c); FM (w); HT, FM (a); Spider-Man; Iron Fist; Power Man; Daredevil; Moon Knight 3.00
❑Annual 5, Nov 1981, Spider-Man; Thing; Scarlet Witch; Vision; Quasar 2.50
❑Annual 6, Oct 1983, New Mutants; Cloak & Dagger 2.50
❑Annual 7, Oct 1984, Alpha Flight 2.00

MARVEL TEAM-UP (2ND SERIES)

MARVEL

❑1, Sep 1997; gatefold summary; Spider-Man; Generation X; Story takes place before Generation X #32 ..... 2.00
❑2, Oct 1997; gatefold summary; AM (a); Spider-Man; Hercules 2.00
❑3, Nov 1997; gatefold summary; A: Silver Sable. Spider-Man; Sandman 2.00
❑4, Dec 1997; gatefold summary; Spider-Man; Man-Thing 2.00
❑5, Jan 1998; A: Authority. V: Authority. Spider-Man 2.00
❑6, Feb 1998; A: Wrecking Crew. V: Wrecking Crew. Spider-Man; Sub-Mariner 2.00
❑7, Mar 1998; Spider-Man; Blade 2.00
❑8, Apr 1998; Sub-Mariner; Doctor Strange 2.00
❑9, May 1998; Sub-Mariner; Captain America 2.00
❑10, Jun 1998; Sub-Mariner; Thing 2.00
❑11, Jul 1998; A: Wrecking Crew. V: Wrecking Crew. Sub-Mariner; Iron Man 2.00

MARVEL TEAM-UP (3RD SERIES)

MARVEL

❑1, Dec 2004 ..... 2.25
❑2, Jan 2005 ..... 2.25
❑3, Feb 2005 ..... 2.25
❑4, Mar 2005 ..... 2.25
❑5, Apr 2005 ..... 2.25
❑6, May 2005 ..... 2.25
❑7, Jun 2005 ..... 2.25
❑8, Jul 2005 ..... 2.25
❑9, Aug 2005 ..... 2.99
❑10, Sep 2005 ..... 2.99
❑11, Oct 2005 ..... 2.99
❑12, Nov 2005 ..... 2.99
❑13, Dec 2005 ..... 2.99
❑14, Jan 2006 ..... 2.99
❑15, Feb 2006 ..... 2.99
❑16, Mar 2006 ..... 2.99
❑17, Mar 2006 ..... 2.99
❑18, May 2006 ..... 2.99
❑19, Jun 2006 ..... 2.99
❑20, Jul 2006 ..... 2.99
❑21, Aug 2006 ..... 2.99
❑22, Sep 2006 ..... 2.99

MARVEL: THE LOST GENERATION

MARVEL

❑12, Mar 2000; #1 in sequence 2.95
❑11, Apr 2000; #2 in sequence 2.95
❑10, May 2000; #3 in sequence 2.95
❑9, Jun 2000; #4 in sequence 2.95
❑8, Jul 2000; #5 in sequence 2.95
❑7, Aug 2000; #6 in sequence 2.95
❑6, Sep 2000; #7 in sequence 2.95
❑5, Oct 2000; #8 in sequence 2.95
❑4, Nov 2000; #9 in sequence 2.95

Masters of the Universe (Mini-Series)

First comics based on somewhat silly TV show

©DC

Masters of the Universe

Marvel's kiddie comics version of TV series

©Marvel

Maverick (Dell)

Luck is his companion, gambling is his game

©Dell

Max the Magnificent

Jim Valentino's SF story was never completed

©Slave Labor

Maxx

It's just not easy being purple

©Image

N-MINT

❑3, Dec 2000; #10 in sequence 2.95
❑2, Jan 2001; #11 in sequence 2.95
❑1, Feb 2001; #12 in sequence 2.95

MARVEL TREASURY EDITION
MARVEL

❑1, ca. 1974; SD (a); The Spectacular Spider-Man 15.00
❑2, Dec 1974; SL (w); JK (a); 1: Galactus. 1: The Silver Surfer. A: Sub-Mariner. The Fabulous Fantastic Four; Reprints early Fantastic Four issues 10.00
❑3, ca. 1974; SL (w); JK (a); V: Hercules. The Mighty Thor; reprints Thor #125-130 .... 10.00
❑4, ca. 1975; Conan 10.00
❑5, ca. 1975; SL (w); JSn, HT, JSe, JSt, DA (a); reprints Hulk #3, 139, 141, Tales to Astonish #79, 100, and Marvel Feature #11 .... 10.00
❑6, ca. 1975; SL (w); SD, GC, FB, BEv, DA (a); O: The Ancient One. Doctor Strange 10.00
❑7, ca. 1975; Avengers 10.00
❑8, Hol 1975; SL (w); SD, GC, HT, GT, FS (a); Giant Super-Hero Holiday Grab Bag; The Incredible Hulk #147, Luke Cage, Hero for Hire #7 .... 10.00
❑9, ca. 1976; JB, SL (w); JB, JK (a); Giant Superhero Team-up; Reprints Prince Namor, the Sub-Mariner #8, Journey into Mystery #112, Silver Surfer (Vol. 1) #14, Daredevil #43; Namor vs. Human-Torch; Daredevil vs. Captain America; Thor vs. Hulk; Silver Surfer vs. Spider-Man 10.00
❑10, ca. 1976; SL (w); JK (a); The Mighty Thor; Reprints Thor #154-157 .... 10.00
❑11, ca. 1976; FF (a); Fantastic Four .. 10.00
❑12, ca. 1976; Reprints Howard the Duck #1, Giant-Size Man-Thing #4, 5, with new Defenders story; FB, VM, SB, TP, KJ (a); Howard the Duck..... 10.00
❑13, ca. 1976; Giant Super-Hero Holiday Grab-Bag 10.00
❑14, ca. 1977; Amazing Spider-Man; reprints Amazing Spider-Man #100-102 and Not Brand Echh #6 .... 10.00
❑15, ca. 1977; Conan; Red Sonja 10.00
❑16, ca. 1977; Defenders 10.00
❑17, ca. 1978; SB, HT, JSe (a); The Incredible Hulk; Reprints The Incredible Hulk #121, 134, 150 .... 10.00
❑18, ca. 1978; Spider-Man; X-Men..... 10.00
❑19, ca. 1978; Conan 10.00
❑20 1979; Hulk; reprints Incredible Hulk #136, 137, 143, 144; pin-up gallery 10.00
❑21, ca. 1979; FF (a); Fantastic Four .. 10.00
❑22, ca. 1979; Spider-Man 10.00
❑23, ca. 1979; Conan; newsstand edition (distributed by Curtis); issue number in box 10.00
❑23/Whitman, ca. 1979; Conan; special markets edition; price appears in a diamond; UPC barcode appears...... 10.00
❑24 1979; Incredible Hulk; reprints Incredible Hulk #167-170; Wolverine and Hercules new back-up story; newsstand edition (distributed by Curtis); issue number in box 10.00

N-MINT

❑24/Whitman 1979; Incredible Hulk; special markets edition; price appears in a diamond; UPC barcode appears 10.00
❑25, ca. 1980; Spider-Man and Hulk at Winter Olympics 10.00
❑26, ca. 1980; Hulk; Wolverine; Hercules 12.00
❑27, ca. 1980; Marvel Team-Up; reprints MTU #9-11 and 27; new Angel story. 10.00
❑28, Jul 1981; A: Wonder Woman. A: Hulk. V: Parasite. V: Doctor Doom. Spider-Man and Superman 25.00

MARVEL TREASURY OF OZ
MARVEL

❑1, ca. 1975; adapts Baum's Land of Oz 15.00

MARVEL TREASURY SPECIAL FEATURING CAPTAIN AMERICA'S BICENTENNIAL BATTLES
MARVEL

❑1, ca. 1976; JK (w); JK (a); Captain America's Bicentennial Battles........ 16.00

MARVEL TREASURY SPECIAL, GIANT SUPERHERO HOLIDAY GRAB-BAG
MARVEL

❑1, ca. 1974; SL (w); GC, JK, WW, RA (a); Giant Super-Hero Holiday Grab Bag; reprints Marvel Team-Up #1, Fantastic Four #25-26, Daredevil #7, and Amazing Adventures 10.00

MARVEL TRIPLE ACTION
MARVEL

❑1, Feb 1972, JK, JSt (a); reprints Fantastic Four #55 and #57 .... 20.00
❑2, Apr 1972, JK, JSt (a); reprints Fantastic Four #58 .... 12.00
❑3, Jun 1972, JK, JSt (a); reprints Fantastic Four #59 .... 12.00
❑4, Aug 1972, JK, JSt (a); reprints Fantastic Four #60 .... 12.00
❑5, Sep 1972 .... 12.00
❑6, Oct 1972, SL (w); DH (a) 8.00
❑7, Nov 1972 .... 8.00
❑8, Jan 1973 .... 8.00
❑9, Feb 1973 .... 8.00
❑10, Apr 1973 .... 8.00
❑11, Jun 1973 .... 8.00
❑12, Aug 1973 .... 8.00
❑13, Sep 1973 .... 8.00
❑14, Oct 1973, SL (w); DH (a) 8.00
❑15, Nov 1973 .... 8.00
❑16, Jan 1974 .... 8.00
❑17, Mar 1974 .... 8.00
❑18, May 1974 .... 8.00
❑19, Jul 1974 .... 8.00
❑20, Sep 1974 .... 8.00
❑21, Oct 1974 .... 8.00
❑22, Nov 1974, SL (w); DH (a); reprints Avengers #28 .... 8.00
❑23, Jan 1975 .... 8.00
❑24, Mar 1975 .... 8.00
❑25, Sep 1975 .... 8.00
❑26, Nov 1975 .... 8.00
❑27, Jan 1976 .... 8.00
❑28, Mar 1976 .... 8.00
❑29, May 1976 .... 8.00
❑29/30 cent, May 1976, 30 cent regional price variant 20.00

N-MINT

❑30, Jul 1976 .... 5.00
❑30/30 cent, Jul 1976, 30 cent regional price variant 20.00
❑31, Sep 1976 .... 5.00
❑32, Nov 1976 .... 5.00
❑33, Jan 1977 .... 5.00
❑34, Mar 1977 .... 5.00
❑35, May 1977, Newsstand edition (distributed by Curtis); issue number in box 5.00
❑35/Whitman, May 1977, Special markets edition (usually sold in Whitman bagged prepacks); price appears in a diamond; UPC barcode appears 5.00
❑36, Jul 1977 .... 5.00
❑36/35 cent, Jul 1977, 35 cent regional price variant 15.00
❑37, Sep 1977 .... 5.00
❑37/35 cent, Sep 1977, 35 cent regional price variant 15.00
❑38, Nov 1977, Newsstand edition (distributed by Curtis); issue number in box 5.00
❑38/Whitman, Nov 1977, Special markets edition (usually sold in Whitman bagged prepacks); price appears in a diamond; no UPC barcode 5.00
❑39, Jan 1978 .... 5.00
❑40, Mar 1978 .... 5.00
❑41, Apr 1978 .... 5.00
❑42, Jun 1978 .... 5.00
❑43, Aug 1978 .... 5.00
❑44, Oct 1978 .... 5.00
❑45, Dec 1978, A: X-Men 5.00
❑46, Feb 1979 .... 5.00
❑47, Apr 1979 .... 5.00
❑Giant Size 1, ca. 1975 .... 10.00
❑Giant Size 2, ca. 1975 .... 10.00

MARVEL TWO-IN-ONE
MARVEL

❑1, Jan 1974, Man-Thing 55.00
❑2, Mar 1974, Namor; Marvel Value Stamp #63: Sub-Mariner 15.00
❑3, May 1974, A: Black Widow. Daredevil; Marvel Value Stamp #89: Hammerhead 10.00
❑4, Jul 1974, Captain America; Marvel Value Stamp #88: Leader 7.00
❑5, Sep 1974, Guardians of the Galaxy; Marvel Value Stamp #93: Silver Surfer 8.00
❑6, Nov 1974, Doctor Strange; Marvel Value Stamp #47: Green Goblin...... 8.00
❑7, Jan 1975, A: Doctor Strange. Valkyrie; Marvel Value Stamp #45: Mantis 5.00
❑8, Mar 1975, Ghost Rider 5.00
❑9, May 1975, Thor 5.00
❑10, Jul 1975, Black Widow 5.00
❑11, Sep 1975, JAb (a); Golem 3.00
❑12, Nov 1975, JK (c); Iron Man; Marvel Value Stamp #45: Mantis 3.00
❑13, Jan 1976, Power Man 3.00
❑14, Mar 1976, HT (a); Son of Satan.. 3.00
❑15, May 1976, DG (a); Morbius........ 3.00
❑15/30 cent, May 1976, DG (a); 30 cent regional price variant 30.00

Other grades: Multiply price above by 5/6 for VF/NM • 2/3 for VERY FINE • 1/3 for FINE • 1/5 for VERY GOOD • 1/8 for GOOD

	N-MINT
❑16, Jun 1976, DA (a); Ka-Zar	3.00
❑16/30 cent, Jun 1976, DA (a); 30 cent regional price variant	30.00
❑17, Jul 1976, JSt (c); SB (a); A: Basilisk I (Basil Elks). Spider-Man	3.00
❑17/30 cent, Jul 1976, JSt (c); SB (a); 30 cent regional price variant	30.00
❑18, Aug 1976, JSt (c); JM, DA (a); Scarecrow; Spider-Man	3.00
❑18/30 cent, Aug 1976, JSt (c); JM, DA (a); 30 cent regional price variant; Scarecrow; Spider-Man	30.00
❑19, Sep 1976, Tigra	3.00
❑20, Oct 1976, Liberty Legion; continued from Marvel Two-In-One Annual #1	3.00
❑21, Nov 1976, A: Human Torch. Doc Savage	3.00
❑22, Dec 1976, Human Torch; Thor	3.00
❑23, Jan 1977, Human Torch; Thor	3.00
❑24, Feb 1977, SB (a); Black Goliath; newsstand editon (distributed by Curtis); issue number in box	3.00
❑24/Whitman, Feb 1977, SB (a); Special markets edition (usually sold in Whitman bagged prepacks); price appears in a diamond; UPC barcode appears	3.00
❑25, Mar 1977, Iron Fist; newsstand editon (distributed by Curtis); issue number in box	3.00
❑25/Whitman, Mar 1977, Special markets edition (usually sold in Whitman bagged prepacks); price appears in a diamond; UPC barcode appears	3.00
❑26, Apr 1977, Nick Fury; newsstand editon (distributed by Curtis); issue number in box	2.00
❑26/Whitman, Apr 1977, Special markets edition (usually sold in Whitman bagged prepacks); price appears in a diamond; UPC barcode appears	2.00
❑27, May 1977, JK, JSt (c); Deathlok	2.00
❑28, Jun 1977, GK (c); Sub-Mariner; newsstand editon (distributed by Curtis); issue number in box	2.00
❑28/Whitman, Jun 1977, GK (c); Special markets edition (usually sold in Whitman bagged prepacks); price appears in a diamond; UPC barcode appears	2.00
❑28/35 cent, Jun 1977, GK (c); 35 cent regional price variant newsstand editon (distributed by Curtis); issue number in box	20.00
❑29, Jul 1977, Shang-Chi; newsstand editon (distributed by Curtis); issue number in box	2.00
❑29/Whitman, Jul 1977, Special markets edition (usually sold in Whitman bagged prepacks); price appears in a diamond; UPC barcode appears	2.00
❑29/35 cent, Jul 1977, 35 cent regional price variant newsstand editon (distributed by Curtis); issue number in box	20.00
❑30, Aug 1977, AM, RB (c); JB (a); 2: Spider-Woman I (Jessica Drew). Spider-Woman I (Jessica Drew); newsstand editon (distributed by Curtis); issue number in box	2.00
❑30/Whitman, Aug 1977, AM, RB (c); JB (a); 2: Spider-Woman I (Jessica Drew). Special markets edition (usually sold in Whitman bagged prepacks); price appears in a diamond; UPC barcode appears	2.00
❑30/35 cent, Aug 1977, AM, RB (c); JB (a); 2: Spider-Woman I (Jessica Drew). 35 cent regional price variant newsstand editon (distributed by Curtis); issue number in box	20.00
❑31, Sep 1977, Spider-Woman I (Jessica Drew); newsstand editon (distributed by Curtis); issue number in box	2.00
❑31/Whitman, Sep 1977, Special markets edition (usually sold in Whitman bagged prepacks); price appears in a diamond; UPC barcode appears	2.00
❑31/35 cent, Sep 1977, 35 cent regional price variant newsstand editon (distributed by Curtis); issue number in box	20.00

	N-MINT
❑32, Oct 1977, GP (c); Invisible Girl; newsstand editon (distributed by Curtis); issue number in box	2.00
❑32/Whitman, Oct 1977, GP (c); Special markets edition (usually sold in Whitman bagged prepacks); price appears in a diamond; no UPC barcode	2.00
❑33, Nov 1977, Mordred; newsstand editon (distributed by Curtis); issue number in box	2.00
❑33/Whitman, Nov 1977, Special markets edition (usually sold in Whitman bagged prepacks); price appears in a diamond; no UPC barcode	2.00
❑34, Dec 1977, Nighthawk	2.00
❑35, Jan 1978, Skull the Slayer	2.00
❑36, Feb 1978, Mr. Fantastic	2.00
❑37, Mar 1978, JSt (c); Matt Murdock	2.00
❑38, Apr 1978, JM (a); Daredevil	2.00
❑39, May 1978, Vision; Daredevil; newsstand editon (distributed by Curtis); issue number in box	2.00
❑39/Whitman, May 1978, Special markets edition (usually sold in Whitman bagged prepacks); price appears in a diamond; no UPC barcode	2.00
❑40, Jun 1978, Black Panther	2.00
❑41, Jul 1978, Brother Voodoo	2.00
❑42, Aug 1978, GP (c); SB, AA (a); Captain America; newsstand editon (distributed by Curtis); issue number in box	2.00
❑42/Whitman, Aug 1978, GP (c); SB, AA (a); Special markets edition (usually sold in Whitman bagged prepacks); price appears in a diamond; UPC barcode appears	2.00
❑43, Sep 1978, JBy (c); JBy (a); Man-Thing; newsstand editon (distributed by Curtis); issue number in box	2.00
❑43/Whitman, Sep 1978, JBy (c); JBy (a); Special markets edition (usually sold in Whitman bagged prepacks); price appears in a diamond; no UPC barcode	2.00
❑44, Oct 1978, BH (c); BH (a); Hercules; newsstand editon (distributed by Curtis); issue number in box	2.00
❑44/Whitman, Oct 1978, BH (c); BH (a); Special markets edition (usually sold in Whitman bagged prepacks); price appears in a diamond; no UPC barcode	2.00
❑45, Nov 1978, Captain Marvel; newsstand editon (distributed by Curtis); issue number in box	2.00
❑45/Whitman, Nov 1978, Special markets edition (usually sold in Whitman bagged prepacks); price appears in a diamond; no UPC barcode	2.00
❑46, Dec 1978, Hulk; newsstand editon (distributed by Curtis); issue number in box	2.00
❑46/Whitman, Dec 1978, Special markets edition (usually sold in Whitman bagged prepacks); price appears in a diamond; no UPC barcode	2.00
❑47, Jan 1979, 1: Machinesmith. Yancy Street Gang; newsstand editon (distributed by Curtis); issue number in box	2.00
❑47/Whitman, Jan 1979, 1: Machinesmith. Special markets edition (usually sold in Whitman bagged prepacks); price appears in a diamond; no UPC barcode	2.00
❑48, Feb 1979, Jack of Hearts; newsstand editon (distributed by Curtis); issue number in box	2.00
❑48/Whitman, Feb 1979, Special markets edition (usually sold in Whitman bagged prepacks); price appears in a diamond; no UPC barcode	2.00
❑49, Mar 1979, AM (c); GD (a); Doctor Strange	2.00
❑50, Apr 1979, GP, JSt (c); JBy (w); JBy, JSt (a); Thing vs. Thing	2.00
❑51, May 1979, GP, JSt (c); FM, BMc (a); Beast; Wonder Man; Ms. Marvel; Nick Fury; newsstand editon (distributed by Curtis); issue number in box	3.00
❑51/Whitman, May 1979, GP, JSt (c); FM, BMc (a); Special markets edition (usually sold in Whitman bagged prepacks); price appears in a diamond; no UPC barcode	3.00

	N-MINT
❑52, Jun 1979, GP, JSt (c); Moon Knight	2.00
❑53, Jul 1979, JBy, JSt (c); JBy, JSt (a); Quasar	2.00
❑54, Aug 1979, JBy, JSt (a); 1: Screaming Mimi. 1: Poundcakes. D: Deathlok I (Luther Manning). Deathlok	3.50
❑55, Sep 1979, JBy, JSt (a); Giant Man II (Bill Foster)	2.00
❑56, Oct 1979, GP, GD (a); 1: Letha. Thundra	1.50
❑57, Nov 1979, AM, GP (c); GP, GD (a); Wundarr	1.50
❑58, Dec 1979, GP (c); GP, GD (a); Aquarian; Quasar	1.50
❑59, Jan 1980, Human Torch	1.50
❑60, Feb 1980, GP, GD (a); 1: Impossible Woman. Impossible Man	1.50
❑61, Mar 1980, GP (c); GD (a); 1: Her. Starhawk	1.50
❑62, Apr 1980, GP, JSt (c); GD (a); Moondragon	1.50
❑63, May 1980, GD (a); Warlock	1.50
❑64, Jun 1980, GP, GD (a); 1: Black Mamba. 1: Anaconda. 1: Death-Adder. Stingray	1.50
❑65, Jul 1980, GP, GD (a); Triton	1.50
❑66, Aug 1980, GD (a); A: Arcade. Scarlet Witch	1.50
❑67, Sep 1980, Hyperion; Thundra	1.50
❑68, Oct 1980, A: Arcade. Angel	1.50
❑69, Nov 1980, Guardians of the Galaxy	1.50
❑70, Dec 1980, Inhumans	1.50
❑71, Jan 1981, 1: Maelstrom. 1: Gronk. 1: Phobius. 1: Helio. Mr. Fantastic	1.50
❑72, Feb 1981, Stingray	1.50
❑73, Mar 1981, Quasar	1.50
❑74, Apr 1981, Puppet Master	1.50
❑75, May 1981, O: Blastaar. Avengers	1.50
❑76, Jun 1981, O: Ringmaster. Iceman	1.50
❑77, Jul 1981, Man-Thing	1.50
❑78, Aug 1981, Wonder Man	1.50
❑79, Sep 1981, 1: Star-Dancer. Blue Diamond	1.50
❑80, Oct 1981, Ghost Rider	1.50
❑81, Nov 1981, Sub-Mariner	1.50
❑82, Dec 1981, Captain America	1.50
❑83, Jan 1982, Sasquatch	1.50
❑84, Feb 1982, Alpha Flight	1.50
❑85, Mar 1982, Giant-Man; Spider-Woman	1.50
❑86, Apr 1982, Sandman (Marvel)	1.50
❑87, May 1982, Ant-Man	1.50
❑88, Jun 1982, She-Hulk	1.50
❑89, Jul 1982, Torch; Human Torch	1.50
❑90, Aug 1982, JM (a); Spider-Man	1.50
❑91, Sep 1982, Sphinx	1.50
❑92, Oct 1982, V: Ultron. Jocasta; Machine Man	1.50
❑93, Nov 1982, A: Machine Man. D: Jocasta. Machine Man	1.50
❑94, Dec 1982, Power Man; Iron Fist	1.50
❑95, Jan 1983, Living Mummy	1.50
❑96, Feb 1983, Marvel Heroes; Sandman (Marvel)	1.50
❑97, Mar 1983, Iron Man	1.50
❑98, Apr 1983, Franklin Richards	1.50
❑99, May 1983, BH (a); ROM	1.50
❑100, Jun 1983, Double-size; JSt (c); JBy (w); Ben Grimm	2.50
❑Annual 1, ca. 1976, JK (c); SB (a); Liberty Legion	4.00
❑Annual 2, Dec 1977, JSn (c); JSn (w); JSn (a); 1: Lord Chaos. 1: Champion of the Universe. 1: Master Order. D: Warlock. D: Thanos. Thanos transformed to stone; Spider-Man; Avengers; Captain Marvel	15.00
❑Annual 3, Aug 1978, SB (a); Nova	2.00
❑Annual 4, Oct 1979, Black Bolt	2.00
❑Annual 5, Sep 1980, Hulk	2.50
❑Annual 6, Oct 1981, 1: American Eagle. American Eagle	2.00
❑Annual 7, Oct 1982, 1: Champion of the Universe. Champion	2.00

MARVEL UNIVERSE

Marvel

❑1, Jun 1998; gatefold summary; Invaders	2.99
❑2, Jul 1998; gatefold summary; JBy (c); Invaders	1.99

Other grades: Multiply price above by 5/6 for VF/NM • 2/3 for VERY FINE • 1/3 for FINE • 1/5 for VERY GOOD • 1/8 for GOOD

'Mazing Man

Cutesy super-hero antics from DC
©DC

Mega Dragon & Tiger

Life after the asteroids devastate the earth
©Image

Megaton

Holiday Special had first mention Image series
©Megaton

Megaton Man

Don Simpson's super-hero parody
©Kitchen Sink

Mekanix

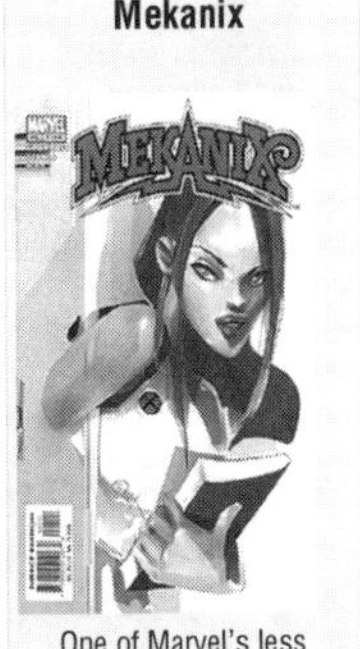

One of Marvel's less successful toy comics
©Marvel

N-MINT

❑2/A, Jul 1998; gatefold summary; JBy (c); alternate cover; Invaders 1.99
❑3, Aug 1998; gatefold summary; Invaders 1.99
❑4, Sep 1998; gatefold summary; Monster Hunters 1.99
❑5, Oct 1998; gatefold summary; Monster Hunters 1.99
❑6, Nov 1998; gatefold summary; Monster Hunters 1.99
❑7, Dec 1998; gatefold summary; O: Mole Man. Monster Hunters 1.99

MARVEL UNIVERSE: MILLENNIAL VISIONS
MARVEL

❑1, Feb 2002 .... 3.99

MARVEL UNIVERSE: THE END
MARVEL

❑1, May 2003 AM, JSn (c); JSn (w); AM, JSn (a) 3.50
❑2, May 2003 AM, JSn (c); JSn (w); AM, JSn (a) 3.50
❑3, Jun 2003 AM, JSn (c); JSn (w); AM, JSn (a) 3.50
❑4, Jun 2003 AM, JSn (c); JSn (w); AM, JSn (a) 3.50
❑5, Jul 2003 AM, JSn (c); JSn (w); AM, JSn (a) 3.50
❑6, Aug 2003, AM, JSn (c); JSn (w); AM, JSn (a) 3.50

MARVEL VALENTINE SPECIAL
MARVEL

❑1, Apr 1997; DDC (a); A: Cyclops. A: Venus. A: Daredevil. A: Spider-Man. A: Phoenix. A: Absorbing Man. romance anthology 2.00

MARVEL VERSUS DC/DC VERSUS MARVEL
DC / MARVEL

❑1, Mar 1996; 1: Access (out of costume). crossover with Marvel; continues in Marvel versus DC #2; cardstock cover 4.00
❑2, Mar 1996; PD (w); crossover with DC; cardstock cover 4.00
❑3, Apr 1996; 1: Access. cardstock cover; crossover with DC; voting results; Marvel and DC universes joined; Stories continued in Amalgam titles 4.00
❑4, Apr 1996; PD (w); continued from Marvel versus DC #3; cardstock cover 4.00
❑Ashcan 1; Consumer Preview; free preview of crossover series; with trading card and ballot 1.00

MARVEL WESTERNS: KID COLT AND ARIZONA GIRL
MARVEL

❑1 .... 3.99

MARVEL WESTERNS: OUTLAW FILES
MARVEL

❑1, Sep 2006 .... 3.99

MARVEL WESTERNS: TWO-GUN KID
MARVEL

❑1, Aug 2006 .... 3.99

N-MINT

MARVEL X-MEN COLLECTION
MARVEL

❑1, Jan 1994; Pin-Ups 2.95
❑2, Feb 1994 .... 2.95
❑3, Mar 1994 .... 2.95

MARVEL YEAR IN REVIEW
MARVEL

❑1, ca. 1989 .... 3.95
❑2, ca. 1990 .... 3.95
❑3, ca. 1991 .... 3.95
❑4, ca. 1992 .... 3.95
❑5, ca. 1993 .... 3.95
❑6, ca. 1994 .... 2.95

MARVEL ZOMBIES
MARVEL

❑1, Feb 2006, Amazing Fantasy #15 homage cover 2.99
❑1/2nd, Feb 2006, Spider-Man #1 homage cover 2.99
❑1/3rd, Feb 2006, Amazing Spider-Man #50 homage cover 2.99
❑2, Mar 2006, Avengers #4 homage cover 2.99
❑3, Apr 2006, Incredible Hulk #340 homage cover 2.99
❑3/2nd, Apr 2006, Daredevil #179 homage cover 2.99
❑4, May 2006, X-Men #1 homage cover 2.99
❑5, Jun 2006 .... 2.99

MARVILLE
MARVEL

❑1, Nov 2002 .... 2.25
❑2, Dec 2002 .... 2.25
❑3, Jan 2003 .... 2.25
❑4, Feb 2003 .... 2.25
❑5, Mar 2003 .... 2.25
❑6, May 2003 .... 2.25
❑7, Jul 2003; Introduction and submission guidelines to Marvel's Epic imprint 2.25

MARY JANE
MARVEL

❑1, Aug 2004 .... 2.25
❑2, Sep 2004 .... 2.25
❑3, Oct 2004 .... 2.25
❑4, Nov 2004 .... 2.25

MARY JANE: HOMECOMING
MARVEL

❑1, Apr 2005 .... 2.99
❑2, May 2005 .... 2.99
❑3, Jun 2005 .... 2.99

MARY POPPINS
GOLD KEY

❑1, Jan 1965 .... 28.00

MASK (1ST SERIES)
DC

❑1, Dec 1985 CS, KS (a) 1.00
❑2, Jan 1986 CS, KS (a) 1.00
❑3, Feb 1986 CS, KS (a) 1.00
❑4, Mar 1986 CS, KS (a) 1.00

MASK (2ND SERIES)
DC

❑1, Feb 1987 .... 1.00
❑2, Mar 1987 .... 1.00

N-MINT

❑3, Apr 1987 .... 1.00
❑4, May 1987 .... 1.00
❑5, Jun 1987 .... 1.00
❑6, Jul 1987 .... 1.00
❑7, Aug 1987 .... 1.00
❑8, Sep 1987 .... 1.00
❑9, Oct 1987 .... 1.00

MASK (MINI-SERIES)
DARK HORSE

❑0, ca. 1991; Reprints Mask stories from Mayhem 4.95
❑1, Aug 1991 .... 4.00
❑2, Sep 1991 .... 3.50
❑3, Oct 1991 .... 3.00
❑4, Nov 1991 .... 3.00

MASK
DARK HORSE

❑1, Feb 1995 .... 3.00
❑2, Mar 1995 .... 2.50
❑3, Apr 1995 .... 2.50
❑4, May 1995 .... 2.50
❑5, Jun 1995 .... 2.50
❑6, Jul 1995 .... 2.50
❑7, Aug 1995 .... 2.50
❑8, Sep 1995 .... 2.50
❑9, Oct 1995 .... 2.50
❑10, Dec 1995 A: Hero Zero, King Tiger 2.50
❑11, Jan 1996 A: Barb Wire, The Machine 2.50
❑12, Feb 1996 A: X, Ghost, King Tiger 2.50
❑13, Mar 1996 A: Warmaker, King Tiger, Vortex 2.50
❑14, Apr 1996 .... 2.50
❑15, May 1996 A: Lt. Kellaway 2.50
❑16, Jun 1996 .... 2.50
❑17, Jul 1996 .... 2.50

MASK, THE: OFFICIAL MOVIE ADAPTATION
DARK HORSE

❑1, Jul 1994 .... 2.50
❑2, Aug 1994 .... 2.50

MASK RETURNS
DARK HORSE

❑1, Dec 1992; with Mask mask 4.00
❑2, Jan 1993 .... 3.00
❑3, Feb 1993 .... 3.00
❑4, Mar 1993; Walter dons Mask 3.00

MASK, THE: TOYS IN THE ATTIC
DARK HORSE

❑1, Aug 1998 .... 2.95
❑2, Sep 1998 .... 2.95
❑3, Oct 1998 .... 2.95
❑4, Nov 1998 .... 2.95

MASK, THE: VIRTUAL SURREALITY
DARK HORSE

❑1, Jul 1997 .... 2.95

MASK CONSPIRACY
INK & FEATHERS

❑1 .... 6.95

MASKED MAN
ECLIPSE

❑1, Dec 1984, O: Masked Man 2.00
❑2, Feb 1985 .... 2.00

Other grades: Multiply price above by 5/6 for VF/NM • 2/3 for VERY FINE • 1/3 for FINE • 1/5 for VERY GOOD • 1/8 for GOOD

	N-MINT
❑3, Apr 1985	2.00
❑4, Jun 1985	2.00
❑5, Aug 1985	2.00
❑6, Oct 1985	2.00
❑7, Dec 1985	2.00
❑8, Feb 1986	2.00
❑9, Apr 1986	2.00
❑10, b&w	2.00
❑11, b&w	2.00
❑12, Apr 1988, b&w	2.00

MASKED RIDER
MARVEL

	N-MINT
❑1, Apr 1996, based on Saban television series, one-shot	2.95

MASKED WARRIOR X
ANTARCTIC

	N-MINT
❑1, Apr 1996, b&w	3.50
❑2, Jun 1996, b&w	2.95
❑3, Aug 1996, b&w	3.50
❑4, Oct 1996, b&w	2.95

MASK/MARSHAL LAW
DARK HORSE

	N-MINT
❑1, Feb 1998	2.95
❑2, Mar 1998; Law dons the Mask	2.95

MASK OF ZORRO
IMAGE

	N-MINT
❑1, Aug 1998	2.95
❑1/Variant, Sep 1998, alternate cover	2.95
❑2, Sep 1998	2.95
❑2/Variant, Sep 1998, alternate cover	2.95
❑3, Oct 1998, indicia says Oct	2.95
❑3/Variant, Oct 1998, alternate cover	2.95
❑4, Dec 1998, cover says Jan, indicia says Dec	2.95
❑4/Variant, Dec 1998	2.95

MASKS: TOO HOT FOR TV
DC

	N-MINT
❑1, ca. 2003	4.95

MASQUE OF THE RED DEATH
DELL

	N-MINT
❑1, Oct 1964	20.00

MASQUERADE
MAD MONKEY

	N-MINT
❑1	3.95
❑2	3.95
❑Ashcan 1	2.00

MASQUES (J.N. WILLIAMSON'S...)
INNOVATION

	N-MINT
❑1, Jul 1992	4.95
❑2	4.95

MASTER OF KUNG FU
MARVEL

	N-MINT
❑17, Apr 1974, Series continued from "Special Marvel Edition"; JSn (a); 1: Black Jack Tarr. Marvel Value Stamp #53: Grim Reaper	15.00
❑18, Jun 1974, PG (a); Marvel Value Stamp #62: Plunderer	7.00
❑19, Aug 1974, PG (a); A: Man-Thing. Man-Thing; Marvel Value Stamp #11: Deathlok	6.00
❑20, Sep 1974, PG (a)	6.00
❑21, Oct 1974, Marvel Value Stamp #62: Plunderer	5.00
❑22, Nov 1974, PG (a); Marvel Value Stamp #79: Kang	5.00
❑23, Dec 1974, Marvel Value Stamp #97: Black Knight	5.00
❑24, Jan 1975, JSn (a); Marvel Value Stamp #15: Iron Man	5.00
❑25, Feb 1975, PG (a); Marvel Value Stamp #41: Gladiator	5.00
❑26, Mar 1975	5.00
❑27, Apr 1975	5.00
❑28, May 1975	5.00
❑29, Jun 1975, PG (a); 1: Razor-Fist I. D: Razor-Fist I	5.00
❑30, Jul 1975, PG (a)	5.00
❑31, Aug 1975, PG (a); Marvel Value Stamp #85: Lilith	5.00
❑32, Sep 1975	4.00
❑33, Oct 1975, PG (a); 1: Leiko Wu	4.00
❑34, Nov 1975, PG (a)	4.00
❑35, Dec 1975, PG (a)	4.00
❑36, Jan 1976	4.00
❑37, Feb 1976	4.00
❑38, Mar 1976, PG (a)	4.00
❑39, Apr 1976, PG (a)	4.00
❑39/30 cent, Apr 1976, PG (a); 30 cent regional price variant	20.00
❑40, May 1976, PG (a)	3.00
❑40/30 cent, May 1976, PG (a); 30 cent regional price variant	20.00
❑41, Jun 1976	3.00
❑41/30 cent, Jun 1976, 30 cent regional price variant	20.00
❑42, Jul 1976, PG (a); 1: Shockwave	3.00
❑42/30 cent, Jul 1976, PG (a); 30 cent regional price variant	20.00
❑43, Aug 1976, PG (a)	3.00
❑43/30 cent, Aug 1976, 30 cent regional price variant	20.00
❑44, Sep 1976, PG (a)	3.00
❑45, Oct 1976, PG (a)	3.00
❑46, Nov 1976, PG (a)	3.00
❑47, Dec 1976, PG (a)	3.00
❑48, Jan 1977, PG (a)	3.00
❑49, Feb 1977, PG (a)	3.00
❑50, Mar 1977, PG (a)	3.00
❑51, Apr 1977, PG (c); PG (a)	3.00
❑52, May 1977	3.00
❑53, Jun 1977, PG (a); reprints Master of Kung Fu #20	3.00
❑53/35 cent, Jun 1977, PG (a); 35 cent regional price variant	15.00
❑54, Jul 1977	3.00
❑54/35 cent, Jul 1977, 35 cent regional price variant	15.00
❑55, Aug 1977, PG (c)	3.00
❑55/35 cent, Aug 1977, PG (c); 35 cent regional price variant	15.00
❑56, Sep 1977	3.00
❑56/35 cent, Sep 1977, 35 cent regional price variant	15.00
❑57, Oct 1977	3.00
❑57/35 cent, Oct 1977, 35 cent regional price variant	15.00
❑58, Nov 1977	3.00
❑59, Dec 1977	3.00
❑60, Jan 1978, V: Doctor Doom. Dr. Doom	3.00
❑61, Feb 1978	3.00
❑62, Mar 1978	3.00
❑63, Apr 1978	3.00
❑64, May 1978, PG (c)	3.00
❑65, Jun 1978	3.00
❑66, Jul 1978	3.00
❑67, Aug 1978, PG (c)	3.00
❑68, Sep 1978, V: The Cat	3.00
❑69, Oct 1978	3.00
❑70, Nov 1978	3.00
❑71, Dec 1978	3.00
❑72, Jan 1979	3.00
❑73, Feb 1979	3.00
❑74, Mar 1979	3.00
❑75, Apr 1979	3.00
❑76, May 1979	3.00
❑77, Jun 1979, O: Zaran. 1: Zaran	3.00
❑78, Jul 1979	3.00
❑79, Aug 1979	3.00
❑80, Sep 1979	3.00
❑81, Oct 1979	3.00
❑82, Nov 1979	3.00
❑83, Dec 1979, V: Fu Manchu	3.00
❑84, Jan 1980	3.00
❑85, Feb 1980	3.00
❑86, Mar 1980	3.00
❑87, Apr 1980	3.00
❑88, May 1980	3.00
❑89, Jun 1980, V: Fu Manchu	3.00
❑90, Jul 1980	3.00
❑91, Aug 1980, GD (a)	3.00
❑92, Sep 1980, GD (a)	3.00
❑93, Oct 1980, GD (a)	3.00
❑94, Nov 1980, GD (a)	3.00
❑95, Dec 1980, GD (a)	3.00
❑96, Jan 1981, GD (a)	3.00
❑97, Feb 1981, GD (a)	3.00
❑98, Mar 1981, GD (a)	3.00
❑99, Apr 1981, GD (a)	3.00
❑100, May 1981, Giant-size GD (a)	4.00
❑101, Jun 1981, GD (a)	2.00
❑102, Jul 1981, GD (a); 1: Day pencils	2.00
❑103, Aug 1981, GD (a)	2.00
❑104, Sep 1981	2.00
❑105, Oct 1981, 1: Razor-Fist II. 1: Razor-Fist III. D: Razor-Fist III	2.00
❑106, Nov 1981, GD (a); O: Razor-Fist II. O: Razor-Fist III. A: Velcro	2.00
❑107, Dec 1981, GD (a); A: Sata	2.00
❑108, Jan 1982, GD (a)	2.00
❑109, Feb 1982, GD (a)	2.00
❑110, Mar 1982, GD (a)	2.00
❑111, Apr 1982, GD (a)	2.00
❑112, May 1982, GD (a)	2.00
❑113, Jun 1982, GD (a)	2.00
❑114, Jul 1982	2.00
❑115, Aug 1982, GD (a)	2.00
❑116, Sep 1982, GD (a)	2.00
❑117, Oct 1982, GD (a)	2.00
❑118, Nov 1982, double-sized GD (a); D: Fu Manchu	2.00
❑119, Dec 1982, GD (a)	2.00
❑120, Jan 1983, GD (a)	2.00
❑121, Feb 1983	2.00
❑122, Mar 1983	2.00
❑123, Apr 1983	2.00
❑124, May 1983	2.00
❑125, Jun 1983; Double-size	3.00
❑Annual 1, ca. 1976, KP (a); 1976 Annual	20.00

MASTER OF KUNG FU: BLEEDING BLACK
MARVEL

	N-MINT
❑1, Feb 1991	3.00

MASTER OF MYSTICS: THE DEMONCRAFT
CHAKRA

	N-MINT
❑1	1.50
❑2	1.50

MASTER OF RAMPLING GATE (ANNE RICE'S...)
INNOVATION

	N-MINT
❑1, Jun 1991	6.95

MASTERS OF THE UNIVERSE: ICONS OF EVIL: BEAST MAN
IMAGE

	N-MINT
❑1, Jun 2003	4.95

MASTER OF THE VOID
IRON HAMMER

	N-MINT
❑1, Dec 1993	2.95

MASTERS OF HORROR
IDEA & DESIGN WORKS

	N-MINT
❑1, Dec 2005	3.99
❑1/Autographed, Dec 2005	3.99
❑3, Mar 2006	3.99
❑4, Apr 2006	3.99

MASTERS OF THE UNIVERSE (MINI-SERIES)
DC

	N-MINT
❑1, Dec 1982 GT, AA (a)	3.00
❑2, Jan 1983	2.00
❑3, Feb 1983	2.00

MASTERS OF THE UNIVERSE
MARVEL / STAR

	N-MINT
❑1, May 1986	4.00
❑2, Jul 1986	2.50
❑3, Sep 1986	2.50
❑4, Nov 1986	2.50
❑5, Jan 1987	2.50
❑6, Mar 1987	2.50
❑7, May 1987	2.50
❑8, Jul 1987	2.50
❑9, Sep 1987	2.50
❑10, Nov 1987	2.50
❑11, Jan 1988	2.50
❑12, Mar 1988	2.50
❑13, May 1988	3.00

MASTERS OF THE UNIVERSE
IMAGE

	N-MINT
❑1, Nov 2002, Cover A	2.95
❑1/B, Nov 2002, Cover B	2.95
❑1/Gold, Nov 2002, Gold foil logo on cover	5.95
❑2, Dec 2002, Cover A	2.95
❑2/B, Dec 2002, Cover B	2.95
❑3, Jan 2003, Cover A	2.95
❑3/B, Jan 2003, Cover B	2.95
❑4, Feb 2003, Cover A	2.95
❑4/B, Feb 2003, Cover B	2.95

Men in Black

Nearly forgotten comic later spawns movies
©Aircel

Men of War

War series focused on good writing
©DC

Meridian

One of four CrossGen flagship titles
©CrossGen

Merlin

Early years in the life of the fabled magician.
©Adventure

Metal Men

Robots from the Magnus that didn't fight robots
©DC

N-MINT

MASTERS OF THE UNIVERSE (VOL. 2)
IMAGE

❑1, Mar 2003 .... 5.95
❑1/A, Jun 2003 .... 2.95
❑2, Apr 2003 .... 2.95
❑3, May 2003 .... 2.95
❑4, Jun 2003 .... 2.95
❑4/A, Jun 2003, Edwards Holofoil cover 5.95
❑4/B, Jun 2003, Santalucia cover 2.95
❑4/C, Jun 2003, Vallejo Bell cover 5.95
❑5, Jul 2003 .... 2.95
❑6, Aug 2003 .... 2.95
❑7 .... 2.95
❑8 .... 2.95
❑8/Graham, Graham Crackers exclusive; 500 copies created. Wraparound Faker cover by Randy Green. Offered December 2004 for $7.99. .... 8.00

MASTER'S SERIES
AVALON

❑1; Wally Wood War 2.50

MASTERWORKS SERIES OF GREAT COMIC BOOK ARTISTS
DC / SEAGATE

❑1, Spr 1983, FF (a); Reprints Shining Knight stories from Adventure Comics (1950-1951) 2.50
❑2, Jul 1983, FF (a) 2.50
❑3, Oct 1983, BWr (a) 2.50

MATADOR
DC

❑1, Jun 2005 .... 2.99
❑2, Jul 2005 .... 2.99
❑3, Aug 2005 .... 2.99
❑4, Sep 2005 .... 2.99
❑5, Oct 2005 .... 2.99

MATT CHAMPION
METRO

❑1 .... 2.00

MATTERBABY
ANTARCTIC

❑1, Feb 1997, b&w 2.95
❑Annual 1 .... 2.95

MAVERICK (DELL)
DELL

❑7, Oct 1959 .... 50.00
❑8, Jan 1960 .... 50.00
❑9, Mar 1960 .... 50.00
❑10, May 1960 .... 50.00
❑11, Jul 1960 .... 40.00
❑12, Sep 1960 .... 40.00
❑13, Nov 1960 .... 40.00
❑14, Jan 1961 .... 40.00
❑15, Jun 1961 .... 40.00
❑16, Sep 1961 .... 30.00
❑17, Dec 1961 .... 30.00
❑18, Mar 1962 .... 30.00
❑19, Jun 1962 .... 30.00

MAVERICK (ONE-SHOT)
MARVEL

❑1, Jan 1997, Giant-size 2.95

N-MINT

MAVERICK
MARVEL

❑1, Sep 1997; gatefold summary; wraparound cover 3.00
❑2, Oct 1997; gatefold summary; wraparound cover 1.95
❑2/Variant, Oct 1997; variant cover 1.95
❑3, Nov 1997; gatefold summary; A: Alpha Flight. wraparound cover.. .... 1.99
❑4, Dec 1997; gatefold summary; A: Alpha Flight. wraparound cover.. .... 1.99
❑5, Jan 1998; gatefold summary A: Wolverine 1.99
❑6, Feb 1998; gatefold summary 1.99
❑7, Mar 1998; gatefold summary 1.99
❑8, Apr 1998; gatefold summary 1.99
❑9, May 1998; gatefold summary 1.99
❑10, Jun 1998; gatefold summary 1.99
❑11, Jul 1998; gatefold summary 1.99
❑12, Aug 1998; Giant-size 2.99

MAVERICKS (DAGGER)
DAGGER

❑1, Jan 1994 .... 2.50
❑2, Feb 1994 .... 2.50
❑3, Mar 1994 .... 2.50
❑4, Apr 1994 .... 2.50
❑5, May 1994 .... 2.50

MAVERICKS: THE NEW WAVE
DAGGER

❑1 .... 2.50
❑2 .... 2.50
❑3 .... 2.50

MAX BREWSTER: THE UNIVERSAL SOLDIER
FLEETWAY-QUALITY

❑1 .... 2.95
❑2 .... 2.95
❑3 .... 2.95

MAX BURGER PI
GRAPHIC IMAGE

❑1, b&w 2.00
❑2, b&w 2.50

MAX DAMAGE: PANIC!
HEAD

❑1, Jul 1995, b&w 2.75

MAXIMAGE
IMAGE

❑1, Dec 1995 .... 2.50
❑2, Jan 1996; polybagged with card 2.50
❑3, Feb 1996 .... 2.50
❑4, Mar 1996; continued from Glory #10 .... 2.50
❑5, Apr 1996 .... 2.50
❑6, May 1996 .... 2.50
❑7, Jun 1996 .... 2.50
❑8, Jul 1996 .... 2.50
❑9, Aug 1996 .... 2.50
❑10, Sep 1996 .... 2.50

MAXIMO ONE-SHOT
DREAMWAVE

❑1, Feb 2004 .... 3.95

MAXIMORTAL
TUNDRA

❑1, Aug 1992 .... 4.00

N-MINT

❑2, Oct 1992 .... 4.00
❑3, Dec 1992, A: Holmes 4.00
❑4, Mar 1993 .... 4.00
❑5, May 1993 .... 3.00
❑6, Jul 1993 .... 3.00
❑7, Dec 1993 .... 2.95

MAXIMUM SECURITY
MARVEL

❑1, Dec 2000 .... 2.99
❑2, Dec 2000 .... 2.99
❑3, Jan 2001 .... 2.99

MAXIMUM SECURITY DANGEROUS PLANET
MARVEL

❑1, Oct 2000, lead-in to Maximum Security 2.99

MAXIMUM SECURITY: THOR VS. EGO
MARVEL

❑1, Nov 2000; reprints Thor #133, #160, and #161 .... 2.99

MAXIMUM VOLUME
KITCHEN SINK

❑1 .... 14.95

MAXION
CPM MANGA

❑1, Dec 1999, b&w 2.95
❑2, Jan 2000, b&w 2.95
❑3, Feb 2000, b&w 2.95
❑4, Mar 2000, b&w 2.95
❑5, Apr 2000, b&w 2.95
❑6, May 2000, b&w 2.95
❑7, Jun 2000 .... 2.95
❑8, Jul 2000 .... 2.95
❑9, Aug 2000 .... 2.95
❑10, Sep 2000 .... 2.95
❑11, Oct 2000 .... 2.95
❑12, Nov 2000 .... 2.95
❑13, Dec 2000 .... 2.95
❑14, Jan 2001 .... 2.95
❑15, Feb 2001 .... 2.95
❑16, Mar 2001 .... 2.95
❑17, Apr 2001 .... 2.95
❑18, May 2001 .... 2.95
❑19, Jun 2001 .... 2.95
❑20, Jul 2001 .... 2.95

MAX OF THE REGULATORS
ATLANTIC

❑1 .... 1.50
❑2 .... 1.75
❑3 .... 1.75
❑4 .... 1.75

MAX REP IN THE AGE OF THE ASTROTITANS
DUMBBELL

❑1, Jun 1997, b&w 2.75
❑2, Mar 1998, b&w 2.75

MAX THE MAGNIFICENT
SLAVE LABOR

❑1, Jul 1987 .... 1.50
❑2 .... 1.50
❑3 .... 1.50

Other grades: Multiply price above by 5/6 for VF/NM • 2/3 for VERY FINE • 1/3 for FINE • 1/5 for VERY GOOD • 1/8 for GOOD

N-MINT

MAXWELL MOUSE FOLLIES
RENEGADE

❑1, Feb 1986, b&w 2.00
❑2, Apr 1986, b&w 2.00
❑3, Jun 1986, b&w 2.00
❑4, Sep 1986, b&w 2.00
❑5, Dec 1986 2.00
❑6, Mar 1987 2.00

MAXWELL THE MAGIC CAT
ACME

❑1 4.95
❑2 4.95
❑3 4.95
❑4 5.95

MAXX
IMAGE

❑½, Jun 1993; Wizard promotional edition 5.00
❑½/Gold, Jun 1993; Gold edition; Promotional edition in slipcover with certificate of authenticity 16.00
❑1, Mar 1993 3.00
❑1/3D, Jan 1998; 3-D edition; bound-in glasses 5.00
❑1/Variant, Mar 1993; Glow-in-the-dark promotional edition; glow in the dark cover 6.00
❑2, Apr 1993 3.00
❑3, May 1993 2.50
❑4, Aug 1993 2.50
❑5, Sep 1993 2.50
❑6, Nov 1993; cover says Oct, indicia says Nov 2.50
❑7, Mar 1994 A: Pitt 2.50
❑8, May 1994 A: Pitt 2.50
❑9, Jun 1994 2.50
❑10, Aug 1994 2.50
❑11, Oct 1994 2.00
❑12, Dec 1994 2.00
❑13, Jan 1995 2.00
❑14, Feb 1995 2.00
❑15, Apr 1995; cover says February, indicia says Apr 2.00
❑16, Jun 1995; cover says Feb, indicia says Jun 2.00
❑17, Jul 1995 2.00
❑18, Aug 1995 2.00
❑19, Sep 1995 2.00
❑20, Nov 1995 2.00
❑21, Jan 1996 2.00
❑22, Feb 1996 2.00
❑23, Mar 1996 2.00
❑24, May 1996 2.00
❑25, Jun 1996; cover says Jul, indicia says Jun 2.00
❑26, Aug 1996 O: Mr. Gone 2.00
❑27, Sep 1996 2.00
❑28, Jan 1997 2.00
❑29, Apr 1997 2.00
❑30, Jun 1997 2.00
❑31, Jul 1997 2.00
❑32, Sep 1997 2.00
❑33, Oct 1997 2.00
❑34, Dec 1997 2.00
❑35, Feb 1998 2.00

MAYHEM
DARK HORSE

❑1, May 1989, b&w 4.00
❑2, Jun 1989, b&w 3.50
❑3, Jul 1989, b&w 3.50
❑4, Aug 1989, b&w 3.50

MAYHEM (KELVA)
KELVA

❑1 1.25

MAZE
METAPHROG

❑1, Aug 1997, b&w; no indicia 3.75

MAZE AGENCY
IDEA & DESIGN WORKS

❑1, Jan 2006 3.99
❑2, Jan 2006 3.99
❑3, Mar 2006 3.99

MAZE AGENCY (COMICO)
COMICO

❑1, Dec 1988, 1: The Maze Agency 3.00
❑2, Jan 1989 2.50
❑3, Feb 1989 2.50
❑4, Mar 1989 2.00
❑5, Apr 1989 2.00
❑6, May 1989 2.00
❑7, Jun 1989 2.50
❑8, Dec 1989 2.00
❑9, Feb 1990, Ellery Queen 2.00
❑10, Apr 1990 2.00
❑11, Apr 1990 2.00
❑12, May 1990 2.00
❑13, Jun 1990 2.00
❑14, Jul 1990 2.00
❑15, Aug 1990 2.00
❑16, Oct 1990, RH (c) 2.50
❑17, Dec 1990 2.50
❑18, Feb 1991 2.50
❑19, Mar 1991 2.50
❑20, May 1991 2.50
❑21, Jun 1991 2.50
❑22, Jul 1991 2.50
❑23, Aug 1991 2.50
❑Annual 1, Aug 1990, MP (c); Spirit parody 3.00
❑Special 1, May 1990 3.00
❑Xmas 1, Special edition 3.00

MAZE AGENCY (CALIBER)
CALIBER

❑1, ca. 1997 2.00
❑2, ca. 1997 2.00
❑3, ca. 1997 2.00

'MAZING MAN
DC

❑1, Jan 1986, 1: 'mazing Man 1.00
❑2, Feb 1986 1.00
❑3, Mar 1986 1.00
❑4, Apr 1986 1.00
❑5, May 1986 1.00
❑6, Jun 1986 1.00
❑7, Jul 1986, 1: Zoot Sputnik 1.00
❑8, Aug 1986 1.00
❑9, Sep 1986 1.00
❑10, Oct 1986 1.00
❑11, Nov 1986 1.00
❑12, Dec 1986, FM (c) 1.00
❑Special 1, Jul 1987 2.00
❑Special 2, Apr 1988 2.00
❑Special 3, Sep 1990 2.00

MCHALE'S NAVY
DELL

❑1, May 1963 40.00
❑2, Aug 1963 32.00
❑3, Nov 1963 26.00

M.D. (GEMSTONE)
GEMSTONE

❑1, Sep 1999 2.50
❑2, Oct 1999 2.50
❑3, Nov 1999 2.50
❑4, Dec 1999 2.50
❑5, Jan 2000 2.50

M.D. GEIST
CPM

❑1, Jun 1995 2.95
❑2, Jul 1995 2.95
❑3, Aug 1995 2.95

M.D. GEIST: GROUND ZERO
CPM

❑1, Mar 1996; prequel to M.D. Geist, Armored Trooper Votoms preview back-up 2.95
❑2, Apr 1996; prequel to M.D. Geist, Armored Trooper Votoms preview back-up 2.95
❑3, May 1996; prequel to M.D. Geist, Armored Trooper Votoms preview back-up 2.95

MEA CULPA
FOUR WALLS EIGHT WINDOWS

❑1, Oct 1990 12.95

ME-A DAY WITH ELVIS
INVINCIBLE

❑1 0.50

MEADOWLARK
PARODY

❑1, b&w; Shadowhawk silver foil cover parody 2.95

ME AND HER
FANTAGRAPHICS / EROS

❑1, b&w 2.00
❑1/2nd 2.00
❑2, b&w 2.00
❑3 2.00
❑Special 1, b&w; Special edition 2.50

MEAN, GREEN BONDO MACHINE
MU

❑1, Jul 1992 2.50

MEAN MACHINE
FLEETWAY-QUALITY

❑1; Judge Dredd; no date of publication; Reprints Mean Machine stories from 2000 A.D. #730-736 4.95

MEANWHILE...
CROW

❑1, b&w 2.95
❑2, b&w 2.95

MEASLES
FANTAGRAPHICS

❑1 1998 2.95
❑2 1999 2.95
❑3, Sum 1999 2.95
❑4, Sum 1999 2.95
❑5, Win 2000 2.95
❑6, Spr 2000 2.95
❑7 2000 2.95
❑8, Aug 2001 2.95

MEAT CAKE (FANTAGRAPHICS)
FANTAGRAPHICS

❑1, b&w 2.50
❑2, b&w 2.50
❑3, b&w 2.50
❑4, b&w 2.50
❑5, Nov 1995, b&w 2.95
❑6, Jan 1996, b&w 2.95
❑7 1997, b&w 2.95
❑8, Jun 1998, b&w 2.95
❑9, Apr 1999 2.95
❑10 2.95
❑11 3.95

MEAT CAKE (ICONOGRAFIX)
ICONOGRAFIX

❑1, b&w 2.50

MEATFACE THE AMAZING FLESH
MONSTER

❑1, b&w 2.50

MECHA
DARK HORSE

❑1, Jun 1987 1.75
❑2, Aug 1987 1.75
❑3, Oct 1987, b&w 1.75
❑4, Dec 1987, b&w 1.75
❑5, Feb 1988, b&w 1.75
❑6, Apr 1988 1.75

MECHANIC
IMAGE

❑1 1998; prestige format 5.95

MECHANICAL MAN BLUES
RADIO

❑1, Dec 1998, b&w 2.95

MECHANICS
FANTAGRAPHICS

❑1 2.00
❑2 2.00
❑3 2.00

MECHANIMALS
NOVELLE

❑1, b&w 3.50
❑2, b&w 2.50

MECHANIMOIDS SPECIAL X ANNIVERSARY
MU

❑1, b&w; cardstock cover 3.50

MECHANOIDS
CALIBER

❑1, b&w 2.50
❑2 2.50
❑3 2.50

MECH DESTROYER
IMAGE

❑1, Mar 2001 2.95

Metamorpho

Man becomes freak, but he's not bitter

©DC

Meteor Man

Tie-in to forgotten super-hero movie

©Marvel

Miami Mice

Miami Mice, meet Hamster Vice. Oy...

©Rip Off

Mickey Mouse (Walt Disney's...)

Look for the Floyd Gottfredson reprints

©Dell

Microbots

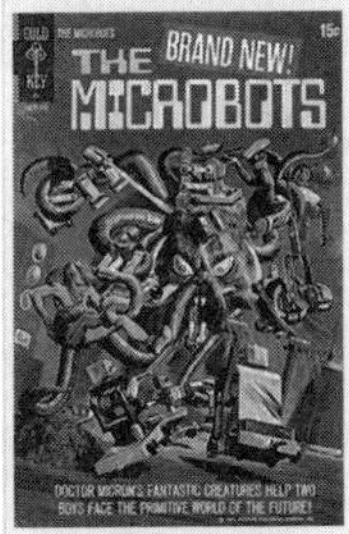

Doctor Micron's fantastic creatures

©Gold Key

N-MINT

❑2, Jun 2001; Indicia lists as March issue ... 2.95
❑3, Jul 2001 ... 2.95
❑4, Sep 2001 ... 2.95

MECHOVERSE
AIRBRUSH

❑1, Airbrushed ... 1.50
❑2, Airbrushed ... 1.50
❑3, Airbrushed ... 1.50

MECHTHINGS
RENEGADE

❑1, Jul 1987, b&w ... 2.00
❑2, Sep 1987, b&w ... 2.00
❑3, Nov 1987, b&w ... 2.00
❑4, Feb 1988, b&w ... 2.00

MEDABOTS PART 1
VIZ

❑1, Apr 2002, b&w ... 2.75
❑2, Apr 2002, b&w ... 2.75
❑3, May 2002, b&w ... 2.75
❑4, May 2002, b&w ... 2.75

MEDABOTS PART 2
VIZ

❑1, Jun 2002, b&w ... 2.75
❑2, Jun 2002, b&w ... 2.75
❑3, Jul 2002, b&w ... 2.75
❑4, Jul 2002, b&w ... 2.75

MEDABOTS PART 3
VIZ

❑1, Aug 2002, b&w ... 2.75
❑2, Aug 2002, b&w ... 2.75
❑3, Sep 2002, b&w ... 2.75
❑4, Sep 2002, b&w ... 2.75

MEDABOTS PART 4
VIZ

❑1, Oct 2002, b&w ... 2.75
❑2, Oct 2002, b&w ... 2.75
❑3, Nov 2002, b&w ... 2.75
❑4, Nov 2002, b&w ... 2.75

MEDAL OF HONOR
DARK HORSE

❑1, Oct 1994 ... 2.50
❑2, Nov 1994 ... 2.50
❑3, Dec 1994 ... 2.50
❑4, Jan 1995 ... 2.50
❑5 ... 2.50
❑Special 1, Apr 1994, Special edition . 2.50

MEDIA*STARR
INNOVATION

❑1, Jul 1989 ... 1.95
❑2, Aug 1989 ... 1.95
❑3, Sep 1989 ... 1.95

MEDIEVAL SPAWN
IMAGE

❑1; three-part story; polybagged with Fan 2.00
❑2; three-part story; polybagged with Fan 2.00
❑3; three-part story; polybagged with Fan 2.00

MEDIEVAL SPAWN/WITCHBLADE
IMAGE

❑1, May 1996 ... 3.00
❑1/American Ent; American Entertainment exclusive; Gold cover 4.00

N-MINT

❑1/Gold, May 1996; Gold edition ... 6.00
❑1/Platinum; Platinum edition ... 15.00
❑2, Jun 1996 ... 3.50
❑3, Jun 1996; cover says Jul, indicia says Jun ... 3.00

MEDIEVAL WITCHBLADE
IMAGE

❑1 ... 5.90
❑2 ... 5.90
❑3 ... 5.90

MEDORA
LOBSTER

❑1, Dec 1999 ... 2.95

MEDUSA COMICS
TRIANGLE

❑1 ... 1.50

MEGACITY 909
DEVIL'S DUE

❑1 ... 6.00
❑1/Variant ... 5.00
❑2 ... 3.00
❑2/Variant ... 4.00
❑3 ... 3.00
❑3/Variant ... 4.00
❑4 ... 3.00
❑4/Variant ... 4.00
❑5 ... 3.00
❑5/Variant ... 4.00
❑6 ... 3.00
❑6/Variant ... 4.00
❑7 ... 3.00
❑7/Variant ... 4.00
❑8, Oct 2005 ... 3.00
❑8/Variant, Oct 2005 ... 4.00

MEGA DRAGON & TIGER
IMAGE

❑1, Mar 1999 ... 2.95
❑2, Apr 1999 ... 2.95
❑3, May 1999 ... 2.95
❑4, Jun 1999 ... 2.95
❑5, Jul 1999 ... 2.95

MEGAHURTZ
IMAGE

❑1, Aug 1997, b&w ... 2.95
❑1/A, Aug 1997; no cover price ... 2.95
❑1/B, Aug 1997; no cover price ... 2.95
❑2, Sep 1997 ... 2.95
❑3, Oct 1997 ... 2.95

MEGALITH
CONTINUITY

❑1 1989 ... 2.00
❑2 1989 ... 2.00
❑3 1990 ... 2.00
❑4, Nov 1990 ... 2.00
❑5, Jan 1991; MN, NA, TVE (a); Rise of Magic storyline ... 2.50
❑6, Jun 1991 ... 2.50
❑7, Jul 1991 ... 2.50
❑8, Dec 1991 ... 2.50
❑9, Mar 1992 ... 2.50

MEGALITH (2ND SERIES)
CONTINUITY

❑0, Apr 1993; silver foil issue number; prelude to Deathwatch 2000 ... 1.00

N-MINT

❑0/A, Apr 1993; red foil cover ... 1.00
❑1, Apr 1993; trading cards ... 2.50
❑2, Jun 1993; trading cards ... 2.50
❑3, Aug 1993 ... 2.50
❑4, Oct 1993 ... 2.50
❑5, Dec 1993 ... 2.50
❑6, Dec 1993 ... 2.50
❑7, Jan 1994 ... 2.50

MEGALOMANIACAL SPIDER-MAN
MARVEL

❑1, Jun 2002 ... 2.99

MEGAMAN
DREAMWAVE

❑1, Sep 2003 ... 2.95
❑1/Dynamic, Sep 2003, Holofoil cover 5.95
❑2, Oct 2003 ... 2.95
❑3, Nov 2003 ... 2.95
❑4, Dec 2003 ... 2.95

MEGA MORPHS
MARVEL

❑1, Sep 2005 ... 2.99
❑2, Oct 2005 ... 2.99
❑3, Nov 2005 ... 2.99
❑4, Dec 2005 ... 2.99

MEGATOKYO
DARK HORSE

❑1, ca. 2004 ... 9.95
❑2, ca. 2004, b&w ... 9.95

MEGATON
MEGATON

❑1, Nov 1983 BG, MGu, GD, EL (a); 1: Megaton. A: Vanguard ... 3.00
❑2, Oct 1985; EL (a); One-page "Dragon" cameo by Erik Larsen ... 2.50
❑3, Feb 1986 EL (w); EL (a); 1: Savage Dragon ... 5.00
❑4, Apr 1986 ... 2.00
❑5, Jun 1986 ... 2.00
❑6, Dec 1986 ... 2.00
❑7, Apr 1987 ... 2.00
❑8, Aug 1987 ... 2.50
❑Holiday 1; says 1994 on cover, 1993 in indicia ... 4.00

MEGATON MAN
KITCHEN SINK

❑1, Nov 1984 O: Megaton Man ... 3.00
❑1/2nd ... 2.00
❑2, Feb 1985 ... 2.50
❑3, Apr 1985 ... 2.50
❑4, Jun 1985 ... 2.50
❑5, Aug 1985 ... 2.50
❑6, Oct 1985; Border Worlds storyline begins ... 2.50
❑7, Dec 1985 ... 2.50
❑8, Feb 1986; Border Worlds back-up 2.50
❑9, Apr 1986 ... 2.50
❑10, Jun 1986 ... 2.50

MEGATON MAN: BOMBSHELL
IMAGE

❑1, Jul 1999 ... 2.95

MEGATON MAN: HARDCOPY
IMAGE

❑1, Feb 1999, b&w; collects Internet strips ... 2.95

	N-MINT
❑2, Apr 1999, b&w; collects Internet strips	2.95

MEGATON MAN MEETS THE UNCATEGORIZABLE X+THEMS
KITCHEN SINK

❑1, Apr 1989, b&w; X-Men parody	2.00

MEGAZZAR DUDE
SLAVE LABOR

❑Special 1, Nov 1991, b&w	2.95

MEKANIX
MARVEL

❑1, Dec 2002	2.99
❑2, Jan 2003	2.99
❑3, Feb 2003	2.99
❑4, Mar 2003	2.99
❑5, Apr 2003	2.99
❑6, May 2003	2.99

MELISSA MOORE: BODYGUARD
DRACULINA

❑1, b&w	2.95

MELODY
KITCHEN SINK

❑1, b&w	2.50
❑2, b&w	2.25
❑3, b&w	2.00
❑4, b&w	2.00
❑5, b&w	2.00
❑6, b&w	2.00
❑7, b&w	2.25
❑8, b&w	2.25

MELONPOOL CHRONICLES
PARA-TROOP

❑1	2.95

MELTING POT
KITCHEN SINK

❑1, Dec 1993	3.50
❑2 1994	3.00
❑3 1994	3.00
❑4, Sep 1994	3.50

MELTY FEELING
ANTARCTIC / VENUS

❑1, Oct 1996, b&w	3.50
❑2, Dec 1996, b&w	3.50
❑3, Jan 1997, b&w	3.50
❑4, Feb 1997, b&w	3.50

MELVIN MONSTER (DELL)
DELL

❑1, Apr 1965, JS (c); JS (a)	60.00
❑2, Jul 1965, JS (c); JS (a)	45.00
❑3, Dec 1965, JS (c); JS (a)	40.00
❑4, Jul 1966, JS (c); JS (a)	32.00
❑5, Oct 1966, JS (c); JS (a)	32.00
❑6 1967, JS (c); JS (a)	26.00
❑7 1967, JS (c); JS (a)	26.00
❑8 1967, JS (c); JS (a)	26.00
❑9, Aug 1967, JS (c); JS (a)	26.00
❑10, Oct 1969, JS (c); JS (a)	26.00

MELVIS
CHAMELEON

❑1, Jul 1994; 2,500 copies	2.00
❑2 1994	2.00
❑3 1994	2.00
❑4 1994	2.00

MEMENTO MORI
MEMENTO MORI

❑1 1995	2.00
❑2, Mar 1995, b&w; no cover price	2.00

MEMORIES
MARVEL / EPIC

❑1, ca. 1992, b&w; Japanese	2.50

MEMORY
NBM

❑1	25.00

MEMORYMAN
DAVID MARKOFF

❑1/Ashcan; Ashcan edition given as promo at 1995 San Diego Comicon 1: Memoryman	0.50

MENAGERIE
CHROME TIGER

❑1, Nov 1987, b&w	1.95
❑2, Feb 1988, b&w	2.00

MENDY AND THE GOLEM
MENDY

	N-MINT
❑1, Sep 1981	2.50
❑2, Nov 1981	2.00
❑3 1982	2.00
❑4, Mar 1982	2.00
❑5 1982	2.00
❑6, Jul 1982	2.00
❑7, Sep 1982; Numbered Vol. 2 #1	2.00
❑8, Jan 1983; Numbered Vol. 2 #2	2.00
❑9, Mar 1983; Says Vol. 2 #3 in indicia only	2.00
❑10, May 1983	2.00
❑11, Jul 1983	2.00
❑12, Sep 1983	2.00
❑13, Nov 1983	2.00
❑14, Jan 1984	2.00
❑15, May 1984	2.00
❑16, Sep 1984	2.00
❑17, Feb 1985	2.00
❑18, Mar 1985	2.00
❑19, Apr 1985	2.00

MEN FROM EARTH
FUTURE-FUN

❑1	2.00

MEN IN BLACK
AIRCEL

❑1, Jan 1990, b&w	15.00
❑2, Feb 1990, b&w	10.00
❑3, Mar 1990, b&w	8.00

MEN IN BLACK (BOOK II)
AIRCEL

❑1, May 1991, b&w	14.00
❑2, Jun 1991, b&w	10.00
❑3, Jul 1991, b&w	8.00

MEN IN BLACK: FAR CRY
MARVEL

❑1, Aug 1997; Jay and Kay are reunited	3.99

MEN IN BLACK: RETRIBUTION
MARVEL

❑1, Dec 1997	3.99

MEN IN BLACK: THE MOVIE
MARVEL

❑1, Oct 1997; adapts movie	3.99
❑1/American Ent, ca. 1997, b&w; American Entertainment variant; reprints story from Aircel series	5.00

MEN OF WAR
DC

❑1, Aug 1977, O: Gravedigger. 1: Gravedigger. Enemy Ace back-up	15.00
❑2, Sep 1977, JKu (c); Enemy Ace back-up	6.00
❑3, Nov 1977, JKu (c); Enemy Ace back-up	6.00
❑4, Jan 1978, JKu (c); Dateline: Frontline back-up	6.00
❑5, Mar 1978	6.00
❑6, May 1978	6.00
❑7, Jul 1978	6.00
❑8, Sep 1978	6.00
❑9, Oct 1978	6.00
❑10, Nov 1978, JKu (c); Enemy Ace and Dateline: Frontline back-ups	6.00
❑11, Dec 1978	6.00
❑12, Jan 1979	6.00
❑13, Feb 1979, RT (a)	4.00
❑14, Mar 1979, JKu (c); Enemy Ace back-up	4.00
❑15, Apr 1979, JKu (c)	4.00
❑16, May 1979	4.00
❑17, Jun 1979	4.00
❑18, Jul 1979	4.00
❑19, Aug 1979	4.00
❑20, Sep 1979, JKu (c)	4.00
❑21, Oct 1979	4.00
❑22, Nov 1979	4.00
❑23, Dec 1979	4.00
❑24, Jan 1980	4.00
❑25, Feb 1980	4.00
❑26, Mar 1980	4.00

MEN'S ADVENTURE COMIX
PENTHOUSE INTERNATIONAL

❑1, May 1995; Comic-sized O: Miss Adventure. 1: Hericane. 1: Miss Adventure	6.00
❑2, Jul 1995	5.00

	N-MINT
❑3, Sep 1995	5.00
❑4, Nov 1995	5.00
❑5, Dec 1995	5.00
❑6, Feb 1996	5.00
❑7, Apr 1996	5.00

MENTHU
BLACK INC!

❑1, Jan 1998	2.95
❑2 1998	2.95
❑3 1998	2.95
❑4 1998	2.95

MENZ INSANA
DC / VERTIGO

❑1; prestige format	7.95

MEPHISTO VS.
MARVEL

❑1, Apr 1987, AM (w); JB (a); Fantastic Four	2.50
❑2, May 1987, AM (w); JB (a); X-Factor	2.00
❑3, Jun 1987, JB (a); X-Men	2.00
❑4, Jul 1987, JB (a); Avengers	2.00

MERCEDES
ANGUS

❑1 1995	2.95
❑2, Jan 1996	2.95
❑3, Feb 1996	2.95
❑4, Mar 1996	2.95
❑5, Apr 1996	2.95
❑6	2.95
❑7	2.95
❑8	2.95
❑9	2.95
❑10	2.95
❑11	2.95
❑12	2.95

MERCHANTS OF DEATH
ECLIPSE

❑1, Jul 1988, magazine	3.50
❑2, magazine	3.50
❑3, magazine	3.50
❑4, magazine	3.50

MERCHANTS OF VENUS
DC

❑1	6.00

MERCY
DC / VERTIGO

❑1	6.00

MERIDIAN
CROSSGEN

❑1, Jul 2000	3.50
❑2, Aug 2000	3.00
❑3, Sep 2000	3.00
❑4, Oct 2000	3.00
❑5, Nov 2000	3.00
❑6, Dec 2000	2.95
❑7, Jan 2001	2.95
❑8, Feb 2001	2.95
❑9, Mar 2001	2.95
❑10, Apr 2001	2.95
❑11, May 2001	2.95
❑12, Jun 2001	2.95
❑13, Jul 2001	2.95
❑14, Aug 2001	2.95
❑15, Sep 2001	2.95
❑16, Oct 2001	2.95
❑17, Nov 2001	2.95
❑18, Dec 2001	2.95
❑19, Jan 2002	2.95
❑20, Feb 2002	2.95
❑21, Mar 2002	2.95
❑22, Apr 2002	2.95
❑23, May 2002	2.95
❑24, Jun 2002	2.95
❑25, Jul 2002	2.95
❑26, Aug 2002	2.95
❑27, Sep 2002	2.95
❑28, Oct 2002	2.95
❑29, Nov 2002	2.95
❑30, Dec 2002	2.95
❑31, Jan 2003	2.95
❑32, Feb 2003	2.95
❑33, Mar 2003	2.95
❑34, Apr 2003	2.95
❑35, May 2003	2.95

Micronauts (Vol. 1)

Semi-popular toys launch popular comics

©Marvel

Mightyguy

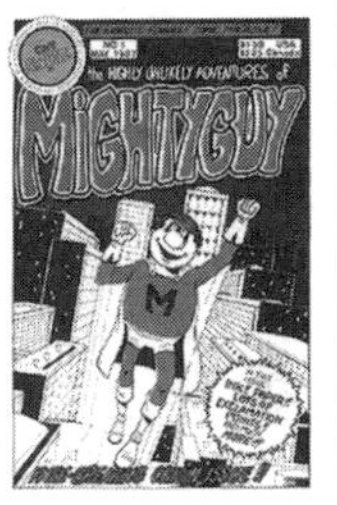

Tim Corrigan's minicomics character gets series

©C&T

Mighty Hercules

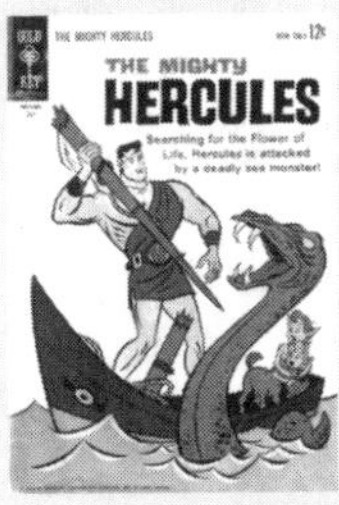

Stop saying "The Mighty Hercules"!

©Gold Key

Mighty Heroes (Marvel)

Based on long-ago Saturday morning cartoon

©Marvel

Mighty Marvel Western

Giant-sized reprint title for Marvel's westerns

©Marvel

	N-MINT
❑36, Jun 2003	2.95
❑37, Jul 2003	2.95
❑38, Sep 2003	2.95
❑39, Nov 2003	2.95
❑40, Dec 2003	2.95
❑41, Jan 2004	2.95
❑42, Jan 2004	2.95
❑43, Mar 2004	2.95
❑44, Apr 2004	2.95

MERLIN
ADVENTURE

❑1, Dec 1990, b&w	2.50
❑2, Jan 1991, b&w	2.50
❑3, Feb 1991, b&w	2.50
❑4, Mar 1991, b&w	2.50
❑5, Apr 1991, b&w	2.50
❑6, May 1991, b&w	2.50

MERLIN: IDYLLS OF THE KING
ADVENTURE

❑1, b&w	2.50
❑2, b&w	2.50

MERLINREALM 3-D
BLACKTHORNE

❑1, Oct 1985	2.25

MERMAID
ALTERNATIVE

❑1, May 1998, b&w	2.95

MERMAID FOREST
VIZ

❑1, b&w	2.75
❑2, b&w	2.75
❑3, b&w	2.75
❑4, b&w	2.75

MERMAID'S DREAM
VIZ

❑1, Oct 1985, b&w	2.75
❑2, b&w	2.75
❑3, b&w	2.75

MERMAID'S GAZE
VIZ

❑1, b&w	2.75
❑2, b&w	2.75
❑3, b&w	2.75
❑4, b&w	2.75

MERMAID'S MASK
VIZ

❑1, b&w	2.75
❑2, b&w	2.75
❑3, b&w	2.75
❑4	2.75

MERMAID'S PROMISE
VIZ

❑1, b&w	2.75
❑2, b&w	2.75
❑3, b&w	2.75
❑4, b&w	2.75

MERMAID'S SCAR
VIZ

❑1, ca. 1994, b&w	2.75
❑2, b&w	2.75
❑3, b&w	2.75
❑4, b&w	2.75

MERTON OF THE MOVEMENT
LAST GASP

	N-MINT
❑1	3.50

MERU PURI
VIZ

❑1, Jul 2005	9.95
❑2, Oct 2005	9.95

MERV PUMPKINHEAD, AGENT OF D.R.E.A.M.
DC / VERTIGO

❑nn, ca. 2000; Prestige one-shot; cover says Sandman Presents..., but not indicia	5.95

MESSENGER
IMAGE

❑1, Jul 2000	5.95

MESSENGER 29
SEPTEMBER

❑1, b&w	2.00

MESSIAH
PINNACLE

❑1, b&w	1.50

MESSOZOIC
KITCHEN SINK

❑1	2.95

META-4
FIRST

❑1, Feb 1991	3.95
❑2, Mar 1991	2.25
❑3, Apr 1991	2.25

METABARONS
HUMANOIDS

❑1, Jan 2000	4.00
❑2 2000	3.50
❑3 2000	3.50
❑4 2000	3.00
❑5, Jun 2000	3.00
❑6, Jul 2000	3.00
❑7, Aug 2000	3.00
❑8, Oct 2000	3.00
❑9, Dec 2000	3.00
❑10, Jan 2001	3.00
❑11, Feb 2001	2.95
❑12, Mar 2001	2.95
❑13, May 2001	2.95
❑14, May 2001	2.95

METACOPS
FANTAGRAPHICS / MONSTER

❑1, Feb 1991, b&w	1.95
❑2, Mar 1991, b&w	1.95
❑3, Jul 1991, b&w	1.95

METAL BIKINI
ETERNITY

❑1, Oct 1990, b&w	2.25
❑2 1990, b&w	2.25
❑3 1991, b&w	2.25
❑4 1991, b&w	2.25
❑5 1991, b&w	2.25
❑6 1991, b&w	2.25

METAL GEAR SOLID
IDEA & DESIGN WORKS

	N-MINT
❑1, Sep 2004	3.99
❑1/Silver, Sep 2004; Diamond 2004 Retailer Summit silver foil edition	7.00
❑1/2nd, Sep 2004; Woman with gun	3.99
❑1/Incentive, Sep 2004	35.00
❑2, Oct 2004	3.99
❑3, Nov 2004	3.99
❑4, Dec 2004	3.99
❑5, Jan 2005	3.99
❑6, Feb 2005	3.99
❑7, Mar 2005	3.99
❑8, Apr 2005	3.99
❑9, Jun 2005	3.99
❑10, Jul 2005	3.99
❑11, Aug 2005	3.99
❑12, Sep 2005	3.99
❑Ashcan 0, Jun 2004	1.00

METAL GEAR SOLID: SONS OF LIBERTY
IDEA & DESIGN WORKS

❑0 2005	3.95
❑2, Dec 2005	3.95
❑3, Feb 2006	3.95
❑4, Feb 2006	3.95
❑5, Apr 2006	3.95
❑6, Jun 2006	3.95

METAL GUARDIAN FAUST
VIZ

❑1, Mar 1997	2.95
❑2, Apr 1997	2.95
❑3, May 1997	2.95
❑4, Jun 1997	2.95
❑5, Jul 1997	2.95
❑6, Aug 1997	2.95
❑7, Sep 1997	2.95

METAL HURLANT
DC

❑1	8.00
❑2	8.00
❑3	8.00
❑4	7.00
❑5	7.00
❑6	7.00
❑7	5.00
❑8	5.00
❑9	4.00
❑10	4.00
❑11	4.00
❑12, Sep 2004	4.00
❑13, Oct 2004	3.95
❑14, Jan 2005	3.95

METALLICA (CELEBRITY)
CELEBRITY

❑1/A	2.95
❑1/B; trading cards	6.95

METALLICA (FORBIDDEN FRUIT)
FORBIDDEN FRUIT

❑1, b&w	2.95
❑2, b&w	2.95

METALLICA (ROCK-IT)
ROCK-IT COMICS

❑1	5.00

Other grades: Multiply price above by 5/6 for VF/NM • 2/3 for VERY FINE • 1/3 for FINE • 1/5 for VERY GOOD • 1/8 for GOOD

N-MINT

METALLICA'S GREATEST HITS
REVOLUTIONARY

❑1, Sep 1993, b&w ... 2.50

METALLIX
FUTURE

❑0, May 2003 ... 3.50
❑1 2002 ... 3.50
❑2 2003 ... 3.50
❑3 2003 ... 3.50
❑4, Apr 2003 ... 3.50
❑5, Jun 2003 ... 3.50
❑6, Jul 2003 ... 2.99

METAL MEN
DC

❑1, May 1963 ... 500.00
❑2, Jul 1963 ... 225.00
❑3, Sep 1963 ... 150.00
❑4, Nov 1963 ... 150.00
❑5, Jan 1964 ... 150.00
❑6, Mar 1964 ... 80.00
❑7, May 1964 ... 80.00
❑8, Jul 1964 ... 80.00
❑9, Sep 1964 ... 80.00
❑10, Nov 1964 ... 80.00
❑11, Jan 1965 ... 55.00
❑12, Mar 1965 ... 55.00
❑13, May 1965, 1: Tin's girlfriend. V: Skyscraper Robot ... 55.00
❑14, Jul 1965 ... 55.00
❑15, Sep 1965 ... 55.00
❑16, Nov 1965 ... 55.00
❑17, Jan 1966 ... 55.00
❑18, Mar 1966 ... 55.00
❑19, May 1966 ... 55.00
❑20, Jul 1966 ... 55.00
❑21, Sep 1966 ... 45.00
❑22, Nov 1966 ... 45.00
❑23, Jan 1967 ... 45.00
❑24, Mar 1967 ... 45.00
❑25, May 1967 ... 45.00
❑26, Jul 1967 ... 45.00
❑27, Sep 1967, O: Metal Men ... 80.00
❑28, Nov 1967 ... 42.00
❑29, Jan 1968 ... 42.00
❑30, Mar 1968 ... 42.00
❑31, May 1968 ... 24.00
❑32, Jul 1968 ... 24.00
❑33, Sep 1968 ... 24.00
❑34, Nov 1968 ... 24.00
❑35, Jan 1969 ... 24.00
❑36, Mar 1969 ... 24.00
❑37, May 1969 ... 24.00
❑38, Jul 1969 ... 24.00
❑39, Sep 1969 ... 24.00
❑40, Nov 1969 ... 24.00
❑41, Dec 1969, series put on hiatus ... 24.00
❑42, Mar 1973, Series begins again (1973); reprints ... 12.00
❑43, May 1973, Reprints ... 12.00
❑44, Jul 1973, V: Missile Men. back to hiatus; reprints ... 12.00
❑45, May 1976, Series begins again (1976) ... 6.00
❑46, Jul 1976 ... 6.00
❑47, Sep 1976, V: Plutonium Man ... 6.00
❑48, Nov 1976, V: Eclipso ... 6.00
❑49, Jan 1977, V: Eclipso ... 6.00
❑50, Mar 1977 ... 6.00
❑51, May 1977, V: Vox ... 6.00
❑52, Jul 1977 ... 6.00
❑53, Sep 1977 ... 6.00
❑54, Nov 1977, A: Green Lantern ... 6.00
❑55, Jan 1978, V: Missile Men ... 6.00
❑56, Mar 1978, V: Inheritor ... 6.00

METAL MEN (MINI-SERIES)
DC

❑1, Oct 1993; foil cover ... 2.50
❑2, Nov 1993 ... 1.50
❑3, Dec 1993 ... 1.50
❑4, Jan 1994 ... 1.50

METAL MEN OF MARS & OTHER IMPROBABLE TALES
SLAVE LABOR

❑1, Jan 1989, b&w A: Tasma. A: Captain Daring ... 2.00

N-MINT

METAL MILITIA
EXPRESS / ENTITY

❑1/Ashcan, ca. 1995, b&w; enhanced cover ... 1.00
❑1, Aug 1995 ... 2.50
❑1/A, Aug 1995, b&w; enhanced cover; came w/ PC game ... 6.95
❑2, Sep 1995 ... 2.50
❑3 1995 ... 2.50

METAMORPHO
DC

❑1, Aug 1965 ... 75.00
❑2, Oct 1965 ... 45.00
❑3, Dec 1965 ... 40.00
❑4, Feb 1966, Metamorpho in Mexico ... 30.00
❑5, Apr 1966, Metamorpho vs. Metamorpho ... 30.00
❑6, Jun 1966 ... 30.00
❑7, Aug 1966 ... 30.00
❑8, Oct 1966, V: Doc Dread ... 30.00
❑9, Dec 1966 ... 30.00
❑10, Feb 1967, 1: Element Girl ... 25.00
❑11, Apr 1967 ... 25.00
❑12, Jun 1967 ... 25.00
❑13, Aug 1967 ... 25.00
❑14, Oct 1967 ... 25.00
❑15, Dec 1967 ... 25.00
❑16, Feb 1968 ... 25.00
❑17, Apr 1968 ... 25.00

METAMORPHO (MINI-SERIES)
DC

❑1, Aug 1993 ... 1.50
❑2, Sep 1993 ... 1.50
❑3, Oct 1993 ... 1.50
❑4, Nov 1993 ... 1.50

METAPHYSIQUE (MALIBU)
MALIBU

❑1, Apr 1995 ... 2.95
❑2, May 1995 ... 2.95
❑3, Jun 1995 ... 2.95
❑4, Aug 1995 ... 2.95
❑5, ca. 1995 ... 2.95
❑6, ca. 1995 A: Superius ... 2.95
❑Ashcan 1 ... 1.00

METAPHYSIQUE
ECLIPSE

❑1 ... 2.50

METEOR MAN
MARVEL

❑1, Aug 1993; Movie tie-in ... 1.25
❑2, Sep 1993 ... 1.25
❑3, Oct 1993 ... 1.25
❑4, Nov 1993 ... 1.25
❑5, Dec 1993 ... 1.25
❑6, Jan 1994 ... 1.25

METEOR MAN: THE MOVIE
MARVEL

❑1, Apr 1993 ... 2.00

METROPOL A.D. (VOL. 2, TED MCKEEVER'S...)
MARVEL / EPIC

❑1, Oct 1992 ... 3.50
❑2, Nov 1992 ... 3.50
❑3, Dec 1992 ... 3.50

METROPOLIS
DARK HORSE

❑1, ca. 2003, b&w ... 13.95

METROPOLIS S.C.U.
DC

❑1, Nov 1994 ... 1.50
❑2, Dec 1994 ... 1.50
❑3, Jan 1995 ... 1.50
❑4, Feb 1995 ... 1.50

METROPOL (TED MCKEEVER'S...)
MARVEL / EPIC

❑1, ca. 1991 ... 2.95
❑2, ca. 1991 ... 2.95
❑3, ca. 1991 ... 2.95
❑4, ca. 1991 ... 2.95
❑5, ca. 1991 ... 2.95
❑6, ca. 1991 ... 2.95
❑7, ca. 1991 ... 2.95
❑8, ca. 1991 ... 2.95
❑9, ca. 1991 ... 2.95
❑10, ca. 1991 ... 2.95

N-MINT

❑11, ca. 1992 ... 2.95
❑12, ca. 1992 ... 2.95

MEZ
C.A.P.

❑1, May 1997, b&w; Canadian cover price only ... 2.00
❑2, Mar 1998, b&w; Canadian cover price only ... 2.00

MEZZ: GALACTIC TOUR 2494
DARK HORSE

❑1, May 1994, b&w ... 2.50

M FALLING
VAGABOND

❑1 ... 3.50

MFI: THE GHOSTS OF CHRISTMAS
IMAGE

❑1, Dec 1999 ... 3.95

MIAMI MICE
RIP OFF

❑1, Apr 1986 ... 2.00
❑1/2nd, May 1986 ... 2.00
❑1/3rd, May 1986 ... 2.00
❑2, Jul 1986, b&w ... 2.00
❑3, Oct 1986, b&w ... 2.00
❑3/A, Oct 1986, b&w; flexi-disc; w/ soundsheet ... 5.00
❑4, Jan 1987, b&w ... 2.00

MICHAELANGELO CHRISTMAS SPECIAL
MIRAGE

❑1, Dec 1990, b&w ... 2.00

MICHAELANGELO TEENAGE MUTANT NINJA TURTLE
MIRAGE

❑1 ... 2.50

MICHAEL JORDAN TRIBUTE
REVOLUTIONARY

❑1 ... 2.95

MICKEY AND DONALD (WALT DISNEY'S...)
GLADSTONE

❑1, Mar 1988, CB, DR (a) ... 2.00
❑2 1988, CB (a) ... 2.00
❑3, Jul 1988, CB (a) ... 2.00
❑4, Aug 1988, CB (a) ... 2.00
❑5, Sep 1988, WK (c); CB (a) ... 2.00
❑6, Oct 1988, CB (a) ... 2.00
❑7, Nov 1988, CB (a) ... 2.00
❑8, Dec 1988, CB (a) ... 2.00
❑9 1989, CB (a) ... 2.00
❑10 1989, CB (a) ... 2.00
❑11 1989, CB (a) ... 2.00
❑12, Aug 1989, CB (a) ... 2.00
❑13, Sep 1989, CB (a) ... 2.00
❑14, Oct 1989, CB (a) ... 2.00
❑15, Nov 1989, CB (a) ... 2.00
❑16, Jan 1990, CB (a) ... 2.00
❑17, Mar 1990, CB, FG, DR (a) ... 1.95
❑18, May 1990, WK (c); CB, FG (a); series continues as Donald and Mickey ... 1.95

MICKEY AND GOOFY EXPLORE ENERGY
DELL

❑1, ca. 1976; giveaway; no indicia or cover price ... 2.00

MICKEY & MINNIE
W.D.

❑1 ... 3.50

MICKEY MANTLE
MAGNUM

❑1, Dec 1991 JSt (a) ... 2.00
❑2 ... 2.00

MICKEY MOUSE (WALT DISNEY'S...)
DELL / GOLD KEY/WHITMAN

❑50, Oct 1956 ... 20.00
❑51, Dec 1956 ... 16.00
❑52, Feb 1957 ... 16.00
❑53, Apr 1957 ... 16.00
❑54, Jun 1957 ... 16.00
❑55, Aug 1957 ... 16.00
❑56, Oct 1957 ... 16.00
❑57, Dec 1957 ... 16.00
❑58, Feb 1958 ... 16.00

Other grades: Multiply price above by 5/6 for VF/NM • 2/3 for VERY FINE • 1/3 for FINE • 1/5 for VERY GOOD • 1/8 for GOOD

Mighty Samson

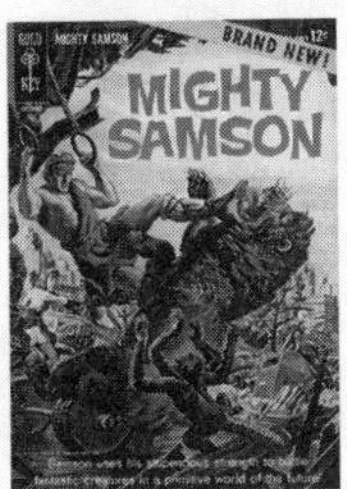

Gold Key hero didn't make it to Valiant

©Gold Key

Mike Danger (Vol. 1) (Mickey Spillane's...)

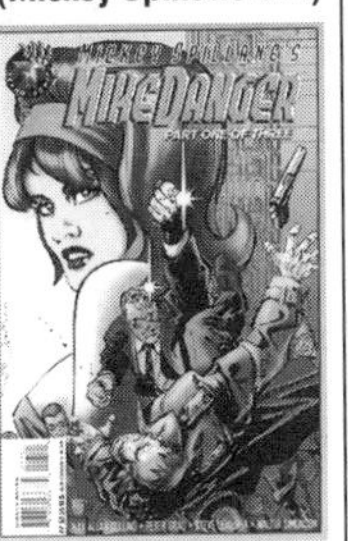

Mickey Spillane back in comics after 40 years

©Tekno

Milk & Cheese

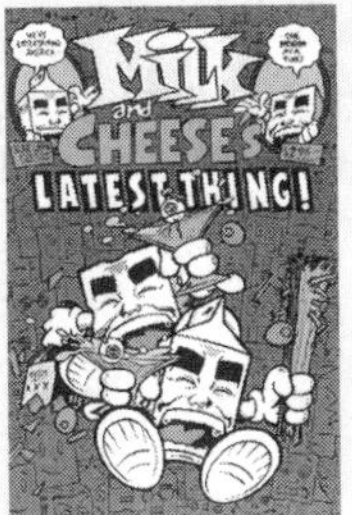

Foul-mouthed dairy products go bad

©Slave Labor

Millennium

DC's mega-crossover event of 1988

©DC

Millennium Edition: Action Comics

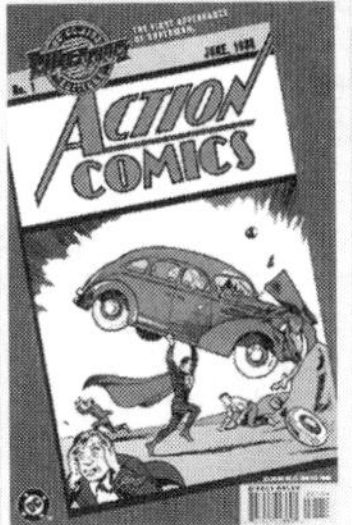

One of many reprints DC did in 2000

©DC

	N-MINT
❑59, Apr 1958	16.00
❑60, Jun 1958	16.00
❑61, Aug 1958	15.00
❑62, Oct 1958	15.00
❑63, Dec 1958	15.00
❑64, Feb 1959	15.00
❑65, Apr 1959	15.00
❑66, Jun 1959	15.00
❑67, Aug 1959	15.00
❑68, Oct 1959	15.00
❑69, Dec 1959	15.00
❑70, Feb 1960	15.00
❑71, Apr 1960	14.00
❑72, Jun 1960	14.00
❑73, Aug 1960	14.00
❑74, Oct 1960	14.00
❑75, Dec 1960	14.00
❑76, Mar 1961	14.00
❑77, ca. 1961	14.00
❑78, Jun 1961	14.00
❑79, ca. 1961	14.00
❑80, Nov 1961	14.00
❑81, Jan 1962	12.00
❑82, Mar 1962	12.00
❑83, Jun 1962	12.00
❑84, Sep 1962	12.00
❑85, Nov 1962	12.00
❑86, Feb 1963	12.00
❑87, May 1963	12.00
❑88, Jul 1963	12.00
❑89, Sep 1963	12.00
❑90, Nov 1963	12.00
❑91, Dec 1963	12.00
❑92, Feb 1964	12.00
❑93, ca. 1964	12.00
❑94, ca. 1964	12.00
❑95, Jul 1964	12.00
❑96, ca. 1964	12.00
❑97, Oct 1964	12.00
❑98, Nov 1964	12.00
❑99, Feb 1965	12.00
❑100, Apr 1965	12.00
❑101, Jun 1965	11.00
❑102, Aug 1965	11.00
❑103, Oct 1965	11.00
❑104, Dec 1965	11.00
❑105, Feb 1966	11.00
❑106, Apr 1966	11.00
❑107, Jun 1966	11.00
❑108, Aug 1966	11.00
❑109, Oct 1966	11.00
❑110, Dec 1966	11.00
❑111, Feb 1967	11.00
❑112, Apr 1967	11.00
❑113, Jun 1967	11.00
❑114, Aug 1967	11.00
❑115, Nov 1967	11.00
❑116, Feb 1968	11.00
❑117, May 1968	11.00
❑118, Aug 1968	11.00
❑119, Nov 1968	11.00
❑120, Feb 1969	11.00
❑121, May 1969	10.00
❑122, Aug 1969	10.00
❑123, Nov 1969	10.00
❑124, Feb 1970	10.00
❑125, May 1970	10.00
❑126, Aug 1970	10.00
❑127, Nov 1970	10.00
❑128, Feb 1971	10.00
❑129, Apr 1971	10.00
❑130, Jun 1971	10.00
❑131, Aug 1971	10.00
❑132, Oct 1971	10.00
❑133, Dec 1971	10.00
❑134, Feb 1972	10.00
❑135, Apr 1972	10.00
❑136, Jun 1972	10.00
❑137, Aug 1972	10.00
❑138, Oct 1972	10.00
❑139, Dec 1972	10.00
❑140, Feb 1973	10.00
❑141, Apr 1973	8.00
❑142, Jun 1973	8.00
❑143, Aug 1973	8.00
❑144, Sep 1973	8.00
❑145, Oct 1973	8.00
❑146, Dec 1973	8.00
❑147, Feb 1974	8.00
❑148, Apr 1974	8.00
❑149, Jun 1974	8.00
❑150, Aug 1974	8.00
❑151, Sep 1974	8.00
❑152, Oct 1974	8.00
❑153, Dec 1974	8.00
❑154, Feb 1975	8.00
❑155, Apr 1975	8.00
❑156, Jun 1975	8.00
❑157, Aug 1975	8.00
❑158, Sep 1975	8.00
❑159, Oct 1975	8.00
❑160, Nov 1975	8.00
❑161, Jan 1976	7.00
❑162, Apr 1976	7.00
❑163, Jun 1976	7.00
❑164, Aug 1976	7.00
❑165, Sep 1976	7.00
❑166, Oct 1976	7.00
❑167, Nov 1976	7.00
❑168, Dec 1976	7.00
❑169, Feb 1977	7.00
❑170, Apr 1977	7.00
❑171, May 1977	7.00
❑172, Jun 1977	7.00
❑173, Jul 1977	7.00
❑174, Aug 1977	7.00
❑175, Sep 1977	7.00
❑176, Oct 1977	7.00
❑177, Nov 1977	7.00
❑178, Dec 1977	7.00
❑179, Jan 1978	7.00
❑180, Feb 1978	7.00
❑181, Mar 1978	6.00
❑182, Apr 1978	6.00
❑183, May 1978	6.00
❑184, Jun 1978	6.00
❑185, Jul 1978	6.00
❑186, Aug 1978	6.00
❑187, Sep 1978	6.00
❑188, Oct 1978	6.00
❑189, Nov 1978	6.00
❑190, Dec 1978	6.00
❑191, Jan 1979	6.00
❑192, Feb 1979	6.00
❑193, Mar 1979	6.00
❑194, Apr 1979	6.00
❑195, May 1979	6.00
❑196, Jun 1979	6.00
❑197, Jul 1979	6.00
❑198, Aug 1979	6.00
❑199, Sep 1979	6.00
❑200, Oct 1979	6.00
❑201, Nov 1979	5.00
❑202, Dec 1979	5.00
❑203, Jan 1980	5.00
❑204, Feb 1980	8.00
❑205, Apr 1980	5.00
❑206, Jun 1980	5.00
❑207, Jul 1980	20.00
❑208, Aug 1980	50.00
❑209	20.00
❑210	7.00
❑211, Jun 1981	7.00
❑212, Aug 1981	7.00
❑213, Sep 1981	7.00
❑214, Dec 1981	7.00
❑215, Feb 1982	10.00
❑216	10.00
❑217	10.00
❑218	10.00
❑219, Oct 1986, FG (a)	12.00
❑220, Nov 1986, FG (a)	4.00
❑221, Dec 1986, FG (a)	3.00
❑222, Jan 1987, FG (a)	3.00
❑223, Feb 1987, FG (a)	3.00
❑224, Mar 1987, FG (a)	3.00
❑225, Apr 1987, FG (a)	3.00
❑226, May 1987, FG (a)	3.00
❑227, Jun 1987, FG (a)	3.00
❑228, Jul 1987, FG (a)	3.00
❑229, Aug 1987, FG (a)	3.00
❑230, Sep 1987, FG (a)	3.00
❑231, Oct 1987, FG (a)	3.00
❑232, Nov 1987, FG (a)	3.00
❑233, Dec 1987 FG (a)	3.00
❑234, Jan 1988, FG (a)	3.00
❑235, Mar 1988, FG (a)	3.00
❑236, Apr 1988, FG (a)	3.00
❑237, Jun 1988, FG (a)	3.00
❑238, Jul 1988, FG (a)	3.00
❑239, Aug 1988, FG (a)	3.00
❑240, Sep 1988, FG (a)	3.00
❑241, Oct 1988, FG (a)	2.00
❑242, Nov 1988, FG (a)	2.00
❑243, Dec 1988, FG (a)	2.00
❑244, Jan 1989, 60th anniversary, 100 pages; FG (a); Daily Strips compilation	2.00
❑245, Mar 1989, FG (a)	2.00
❑246, Apr 1989, FG (a)	2.00
❑247, Jun 1989, FG (a)	2.00
❑248, Jul 1989, FG (a)	2.00

Other grades: Multiply price above by 5/6 for VF/NM • 2/3 for VERY FINE • 1/3 for FINE • 1/5 for VERY GOOD • 1/8 for GOOD

N-MINT N-MINT N-MINT

❑249, Aug 1989, FG (a) 2.00
❑250, Sep 1989, FG (a) 2.00
❑251, Oct 1989, FG (a) 2.00
❑252, Nov 1989, FG (a) 2.00
❑253, Dec 1989, FG (a) 2.00
❑254, Jan 1990, FG (a) 2.00
❑255, Feb 1990 .... 2.00
❑256, Apr 1990 .... 2.00

MICKEY MOUSE AND FRIENDS
GEMSTONE

❑257, Sep 2003 .... 2.95
❑258, Oct 2003 .... 2.95
❑259, Nov 2003 .... 2.95
❑260, Dec 2003 .... 2.95
❑261, Jan 2004 .... 2.95
❑262, Feb 2004 .... 2.95
❑263, Mar 2004 .... 2.95
❑264, Apr 2004 .... 2.95
❑265, May 2004 .... 2.95
❑266, Jun 2004 .... 2.95
❑267, Jul 2004 .... 2.95
❑268, Aug 2004 .... 2.95
❑269, Sep 2004 .... 2.95
❑270, Oct 2004 .... 2.95
❑271, Nov 2004 .... 2.95
❑272, Dec 2004 .... 2.95
❑273, Jan 2005 .... 2.95
❑274, Feb 2005 .... 2.95
❑275, Mar 2005 .... 2.95
❑276, Apr 2005 .... 2.95
❑277, May 2005 .... 2.95
❑278, Jun 2005 .... 2.95
❑279, Jul 2005 .... 2.95
❑280, Aug 2005 .... 2.95
❑281, Sep 2005 .... 2.95
❑282, Oct 2005 .... 2.95
❑283, Nov 2005 .... 2.95
❑284, Dec 2005 .... 2.95

MICKEY MOUSE (ONE-SHOT)
DISNEY

❑1; in Russian 4.00

MICKEY MOUSE ADVENTURES
DISNEY

❑1, Jun 1990 .... 2.50
❑2, Jul 1990 .... 2.00
❑3, Aug 1990 V: Phantom Blot 2.00
❑4, Sep 1990 .... 2.00
❑5, Oct 1990 .... 2.00
❑6, Nov 1990 .... 2.00
❑7, Dec 1990 .... 2.00
❑8, Jan 1991 JBy (c) 2.00
❑9, Feb 1991; Fantasia 2.00
❑10, Mar 1991 .... 2.00
❑11, Apr 1991 .... 2.00
❑12, May 1991 .... 2.00
❑13, Jun 1991 .... 2.00
❑14, Jul 1991 .... 2.00
❑15, Aug 1991 .... 2.00
❑16, Sep 1991 KB (a) 2.00
❑17, Oct 1991; Dinosaur 2.00
❑18, Nov 1991; Dinosaur 2.00

MICKEY MOUSE ALBUM
GOLD KEY

❑-210, Oct 1962, Cover code 01-518-210; no number 25.00
❑1, Sep 1963, Cover code 10082-309 20.00

MICKEY MOUSE AND GOOFY EXPLORE ENERGY CONSERVATION
DELL

❑1, ca. 1978, giveaway; no indicia or cover price 2.00

MICKEY MOUSE CLUB
GOLD KEY

❑1, Jan 1964 .... 25.00

MICKEY MOUSE DIGEST
GLADSTONE

❑1, ca. 1986 .... 5.00
❑2, ca. 1986 .... 4.00
❑3, ca. 1986 .... 3.00
❑4, ca. 1986 .... 3.00
❑5, ca. 1987 .... 3.00

MICKEY MOUSE SURPRISE PARTY
GOLD KEY

❑1, Jan 1969 .... 18.00

MICKEY RAT
LOS ANGELES COMIC BOOK CO.

❑1, May 1972, b&w 25.00
❑2, Oct 1972, b&w 20.00
❑3, Jul 1980, b&w 15.00
❑4, ca. 1982, b&w 15.00

MICRA: MIND CONTROLLED REMOTE AUTOMATON
COMICS INTERVIEW

❑1, Nov 1986 .... 1.75
❑2, Jan 1987 .... 1.75
❑3, Feb 1987 .... 1.75
❑4 1987 .... 1.75
❑5 1987 .... 1.75
❑6 1987 .... 1.75
❑7 1987 .... 1.75

MICROBOTS
GOLD KEY

❑1, Dec 1971 .... 10.00

MICRONAUTS (VOL. 1)
MARVEL

❑1, Jan 1979, MG (a); O: Micronauts. 1: The Micronauts. 1: Baron Karza. 1: Space Glider. 1: Biotron. 1: Marionette. Newsstand edition (distributed by Curtis); issue number in box 4.00
❑1/Whitman, Jan 1979, MG (a); O: Micronauts. 1: The Micronauts. 1: Baron Karza. 1: Space Glider. 1: Biotron. 1: Marionette. Special markets edition (usually sold in Whitman bagged prepacks); price appears in a diamond; no UPC barcode 4.00
❑1/2nd, Jan 1979 .... 2.00
❑2, Feb 1979, MG (a); Newsstand edition (distributed by Curtis); issue number in box 3.00
❑2/Whitman, Feb 1979, MG (a); Special markets edition (usually sold in Whitman bagged prepacks); price appears in a diamond; no UPC barcode 3.00
❑3, Mar 1979, MG (a); Newsstand edition (distributed by Curtis); issue number in box 2.50
❑3/Whitman, Mar 1979, MG (a); Special markets edition (usually sold in Whitman bagged prepacks); price appears in a diamond; no UPC barcode 2.50
❑4, Apr 1979, MG (a) 2.50
❑5, May 1979, MG (a); Newsstand edition (distributed by Curtis); issue number in box 2.50
❑5/Whitman, May 1979, MG (a); Special markets edition (usually sold in Whitman bagged prepacks); price appears in a diamond; no UPC barcode 2.50
❑6, Jun 1979, MG (a) 2.00
❑7, Jul 1979, MG (a); A: Man-Thing... 2.00
❑8, Aug 1979, MG (a); 1: Captain Universe 2.25
❑9, Sep 1979, MG (a) 2.00
❑10, Oct 1979, MG (a) 2.00
❑11, Nov 1979, MG (a) 1.50
❑12, Dec 1979, MG (a) 1.50
❑13, Jan 1980 .... 1.50
❑14, Feb 1980 .... 1.50
❑15, Mar 1980, A: Fantastic Four. D: Microtron 1.50
❑16, Apr 1980, A: Fantastic Four 1.50
❑17, May 1980, A: Fantastic Four. D: Jasmine 1.50
❑18, Jun 1980 .... 1.50
❑19, Jul 1980 .... 1.50
❑20, Aug 1980, A: Ant-Man 1.50
❑21, Sep 1980 .... 1.50
❑22, Oct 1980 .... 1.50
❑23, Nov 1980, V: Molecule Man 1.50
❑24, Dec 1980 .... 1.50
❑25, Jan 1981, O: Baron Karza. V: Mentallo 1.50
❑26, Feb 1981, PB (a) 1.50
❑27, Mar 1981, PB (a); D: Biotron 1.50
❑28, Apr 1981, PB (a); A: Nick Fury 1.50
❑29, May 1981, PB (a); A: Nick Fury.. 1.50
❑30, Jun 1981, PB (a) 1.50
❑31, Jul 1981, FM (c); PB, FM (a); A: Doctor Strange 1.50
❑32, Aug 1981, PB (a); A: Doctor Strange 1.50
❑33, Sep 1981, PB (a); A: Doctor Strange 1.50
❑34, Oct 1981, PB (a); A: Doctor Strange 1.50
❑35, Nov 1981; double-sized O: Microverse. A: Doctor Strange ... 1.50
❑36, Dec 1981 .... 1.50
❑37, Jan 1982, A: X-Men. A: Nightcrawler 1.50
❑38, Feb 1982; Direct sales (only) begin 1.50
❑39, Mar 1982 .... 1.50
❑40, Apr 1982 A: Fantastic Four 1.50
❑41, May 1982 V: Dr. Doom. V: Doctor Doom 1.50
❑42, Jun 1982 .... 1.50
❑43, Jul 1982 .... 1.50
❑44, Aug 1982 .... 1.50
❑45, Sep 1982 .... 1.50
❑46, Oct 1982 .... 1.50
❑47, Nov 1982 .... 1.50
❑48, Dec 1982; BG (a); 1st Guice 1.50
❑49, Jan 1983 .... 1.50
❑50, Feb 1983 .... 1.50
❑51, Mar 1983 .... 1.50
❑52, May 1983 .... 1.50
❑53, Jul 1983 .... 1.50
❑54, Sep 1983 .... 1.50
❑55, Nov 1983 .... 1.50
❑56, Jan 1984 .... 1.50
❑57, Mar 1984; double-sized 1.50
❑58, May 1984 .... 1.50
❑59, Aug 1984 .... 3.00
❑Annual 1, Dec 1979 SD (a) 4.00
❑Annual 2, Oct 1980 SD (a); V: Toymaster 3.00
❑Special 1, Dec 1983 .... 2.00
❑Special 2, Jan 1984 .... 2.00
❑Special 3, Feb 1984 .... 2.00
❑Special 4, Mar 1984 .... 2.00
❑Special 5, Apr 1984 .... 2.00

MICRONAUTS (VOL. 2)
MARVEL

❑1, Oct 1984, Makers 3.00
❑2, Nov 1984 .... 1.50
❑3, Dec 1984 .... 1.50
❑4, Jan 1985 .... 1.50
❑5, Feb 1985 .... 1.50
❑6, Mar 1985 .... 1.50
❑7, Apr 1985 .... 1.50
❑8, May 1985 .... 1.50
❑9, Jun 1985 .... 1.50
❑10, Jul 1985 .... 1.50
❑11, Aug 1985 .... 1.50
❑12, Sep 1985 .... 1.50
❑13, Oct 1985 .... 1.50
❑14, Nov 1985 .... 1.50
❑15, Dec 1985 .... 1.50
❑16, Jan 1986, Secret Wars II 1.50
❑17, Feb 1986 .... 1.50
❑18, Mar 1986 .... 1.50
❑19, Apr 1986 .... 1.50
❑20, May 1986 .... 1.50

MICRONAUTS (IMAGE)
IMAGE

❑1, ca. 2002 .... 2.95
❑2, ca. 2002 .... 2.95
❑3, ca. 2002 .... 2.95
❑4, Dec 2002 .... 2.95
❑5, Feb 2003 .... 2.95
❑6, Mar 2003 .... 2.95
❑7, Apr 2003 .... 2.95
❑8, Jun 2003 .... 2.95
❑9, Jul 2003 .... 2.95
❑10, Aug 2003 .... 2.95
❑11, Oct 2003 .... 2.95

MIDDLE CLASS FANTASIES
CARTOONISTS CO-OP

❑1 .... 3.00
❑2 .... 3.00

MIDDLEMAN
VIPER

❑1, Aug 2005 .... 2.95
❑2, Sep 2005 .... 2.95
❑3, Oct 2005 .... 2.95
❑4, Nov 2005 .... 2.95

Other grades: Multiply price above by 5/6 for VF/NM • 2/3 for VERY FINE • 1/3 for FINE • 1/5 for VERY GOOD • 1/8 for GOOD

Minimum Wage

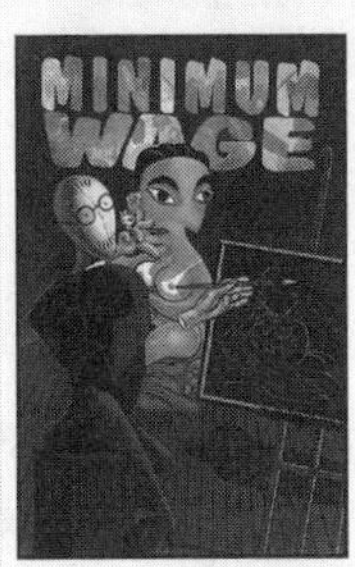

Struggling New York artist tries to make a living

©Fantagraphics

Minx

Imaginary childhood friend returns

©DC

Miracleman

Series had first Neil Gaiman work

©Eclipse

Mission: Impossible (Dell)

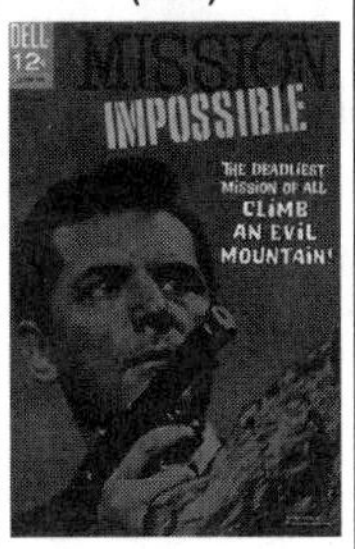

Your mission, should you choose to accept it...

©Dell

Mr. and Mrs. J. Evil Scientist

Based on the Hanna-Barbera cartoon

©Gold Key

N-MINT

MIDNIGHT
AJAX

❑1, Apr 1957 .... 54.00
❑2 1958 .... 38.00
❑3 .... 26.00
❑4 .... 26.00
❑5, Feb 1958 .... 26.00
❑6 .... 26.00

MIDNIGHT DAYS (NEIL GAIMAN'S...)
DC / VERTIGO

❑1, Jan 2000, Reprints Neil Gaiman stories from Swamp Thing, Hellblazer, Sandman Midnight Theatre........ 17.95

MIDNIGHT EYE GOKÜ
VIZ

❑1 .... 4.95
❑2 .... 4.95
❑3 .... 4.95
❑4 .... 4.95
❑5 .... 4.95
❑6 .... 4.95

MIDNIGHT MASS
DC / VERTIGO

❑1, Mar 2004 .... 2.95
❑2, Apr 2004 .... 2.95
❑3, May 2004 .... 2.50
❑4, Jun 2004 .... 2.50
❑5, Jul 2004 .... 2.95
❑6, Aug 2004 .... 2.95

MIDNIGHT, MASS
DC / VERTIGO

❑1, Jun 2002 .... 2.50
❑2, Jul 2002 .... 2.50
❑3, Aug 2002 .... 2.50
❑4, Sep 2002 .... 2.50
❑5, Oct 2002 .... 2.50
❑6, Nov 2002 .... 2.50
❑7, Dec 2002 .... 2.50
❑8, Jan 2003 .... 2.50

MIDNIGHT MEN
MARVEL / EPIC

❑1, Jun 1993; Embossed cover 2.50
❑2, Jul 1993 .... 1.95
❑3, Aug 1993 .... 1.95
❑4, Sep 1993 .... 1.95

MIDNIGHT NATION
IMAGE

❑½, Wizard send-away promotional edition........ 5.00
❑½/Gold, Gold edition........ 9.00
❑1/A, Oct 2000, Cover A........ 4.00
❑1/B, Oct 2000, Dynamic Forces Exclusive; Cover B........ 5.00
❑1/C, Oct 2000 .... 8.00
❑1/D, Oct 2000, Convention exclusive edition........ 4.50
❑2, Nov 2000 .... 3.00
❑3, Dec 2000 .... 3.00
❑4, Jan 2001 .... 3.00
❑5, Mar 2001 .... 3.00
❑6, Apr 2001 .... 2.50
❑7, May 2001 .... 2.50

N-MINT

❑8, Jun 2001 .... 2.50
❑9, Jul 2001 .... 2.50
❑10, Aug 2001 .... 2.50
❑11, Sep 2001 .... 2.50
❑12, Oct 2001 .... 2.95

MIDNIGHT PANTHER
CPM

❑1, Apr 1997 .... 2.95
❑2, May 1997 .... 2.95
❑3, Jun 1997 .... 2.95
❑4, Jul 1997 .... 2.95
❑5, Aug 1997 .... 2.95
❑6, Sep 1997 .... 2.95
❑7, Oct 1997 .... 2.95
❑8, Nov 1997 .... 2.95
❑9, Dec 1997 .... 2.95
❑10, Jan 1998 .... 2.95
❑11, Feb 1998 .... 2.95
❑12, Mar 1998 .... 2.95

MIDNIGHT PANTHER: FEUDAL FANTASY
CPM

❑1, Sep 1998; wraparound cover........ 2.95
❑2, Oct 1998 .... 2.95

MIDNIGHT PANTHER: SCHOOL DAZE
CPM

❑1, Apr 1998; wraparound cover 2.95
❑2, May 1998 .... 2.95
❑3, Jun 1998; wraparound cover 2.95
❑4, Jul 1998 .... 2.95
❑5, Aug 1998 .... 2.95

MIDNIGHT SCREAMS
MYSTERY GRAPHIX

❑1 .... 2.50
❑2 .... 2.50

MIDNIGHT SONS UNLIMITED
MARVEL

❑1, Apr 1993 KJ (a)........ 4.00
❑2, Jul 1993 .... 4.00
❑3, Oct 1993 JR2 (c); JR2 (a); A: Spider-Man 4.00
❑4, Jan 1994 .... 3.95
❑5, Apr 1994 .... 3.95
❑6, Jul 1994 .... 3.95
❑7, Oct 1994 .... 3.95
❑8, Jan 1995 .... 3.95
❑9, May 1995 ARo (c); A: Destroyer. A: Union Jack. A: Blazing Skull........ 3.95
❑Ashcan 1; Previews the Midnight Sons titles 0.75

MIDNITE
BLACKTHORNE

❑1, Nov 1986 .... 1.75
❑2, Jan 1987 .... 1.75
❑3, Mar 1987 .... 1.75

MIDNITE SKULKER
TARGET

❑1, Jun 1986 .... 1.75
❑2, Aug 1986, b&w 1.75
❑3, Oct 1986 .... 1.75
❑4, Dec 1986, b&w 1.75
❑5, Feb 1987 .... 1.75

N-MINT

❑6, Apr 1987 .... 1.75
❑7, Aug 1987 .... 1.75

MIDNITE'S QUICKIES
ONE SHOT

❑1, b&w........ 3.50
❑2, b&w........ 2.95
❑Special 1, Oct 1997, b&w; No cover price; no indicia; published in Oct 97 .... 3.00
❑Special 1/A, Jan 1998, b&w; No cover price; center color poster........ 3.00
❑Special 1/B, Oct 1997, b&w; foil variant cover........ 3.00

MIDORI DAYS
VIZ

❑1, Aug 2005........ 9.95
❑2, Oct 2005........ 9.95

MIDVALE
MU

❑1, b&w........ 2.50
❑2, Oct 1990, b&w 2.50

MIGHTILY MURDERED POWER RINGERS
EXPRESS / PARODY PRESS

❑1, b&w........ 2.50

MIGHTY ACE
OMEGA 7

❑1 .... 2.00
❑2; indicia indicates 1992 copyright, probably not year of publication 2.00

MIGHTY ATOM (2ND SERIES)
MAGAZINE ENTERPRISES

❑1, Nov 1957........ 22.00
❑2 .... 18.00
❑3, Mar 1958........ 18.00
❑4 .... 18.00
❑5 .... 18.00
❑6, Sep 1958........ 18.00

MIGHTY BOMB
ANTARCTIC

❑1, Jul 1997, b&w........ 2.95

MIGHTY BOMBSHELLS
ANTARCTIC

❑1, Sep 1993, b&w........ 2.75
❑2, Oct 1993, b&w........ 2.75

MIGHTY CARTOON HEROES
KARL ART

❑0 .... 2.95

MIGHTY COMICS
ARCHIE

❑40, Nov 1966, Series continued from Fly Man #39........ 15.00
❑41, Dec 1966........ 15.00
❑42, Jan 1967 .... 15.00
❑43, Feb 1967, 1: The Storm King. 1: The Stunner. A: The Web. A: The Shield. Black Hood appearace........ 15.00
❑44, Mar 1967........ 15.00
❑45, Apr 1967 .... 15.00
❑46, May 1967 .... 15.00
❑47, Jun 1967 .... 15.00
❑48, Jul 1967 .... 15.00
❑49 1967........ 15.00
❑50, Oct 1967........ 15.00

MIGHTY CRUSADERS (1ST SERIES)
ARCHIE

❑1, Nov 1965, O: The Shield ... 24.00
❑2 1966, O: The Comet ... 15.00
❑3, Mar 1966, O: Fly Man ... 12.00
❑4, Apr 1966, "Too Many Superheroes" 10.00
❑5, Jun 1966, 1: The Terrific Three ... 10.00
❑6, Aug 1966 ... 10.00
❑7, Oct 1966, O: Fly Girl ... 10.00

MIGHTY CRUSADERS (2ND SERIES)
ARCHIE / RED CIRCLE

❑4, Nov 1983, RB (w); RB (a); Previously titled All New Adventures of the Mighty Crusaders ... 1.25
❑5, Jan 1984 ... 1.25
❑6, Mar 1984 ... 1.25
❑7, May 1984 ... 1.25
❑8, Jul 1984 ... 1.25
❑9, Sep 1984 ... 1.25
❑10, Dec 1984 ... 1.25
❑11, Mar 1985 ... 1.25
❑12, Jun 1985 ... 1.25
❑13, Sep 1985 ... 1.25

MIGHTYGUY
C&T

❑1, May 1987 ... 1.50
❑2 1987 ... 1.50
❑3 1987 ... 1.50
❑4 1987 ... 1.50
❑5 1987 ... 1.50

MIGHTY HERCULES
GOLD KEY

❑1, Jul 1963 ... 40.00
❑2, Oct 1963 ... 40.00

MIGHTY HEROES (DELL)
DELL

❑1, Mar 1967, O: The Mighty Heroes. based on Terrytoons feature ... 125.00
❑2, ca. 1967 ... 60.00
❑3, ca. 1967 ... 60.00
❑4, ca. 1967 ... 60.00

MIGHTY HEROES (MARVEL)
MARVEL / PARAMOUNT

❑1, Jan 1998; based on Terrytoons feature ... 2.99

MIGHTY I
IMAGE

❑1, May 1995; Image Comics Fan Club ... 1.25
❑2, Jul 1995; Image Comics Fan Club ... 1.25

MIGHTY LOVE
DC

❑1, ca. 2005 ... 24.95
❑1/HC, ca. 2004 ... 24.65

MIGHTY MAGNOR
MALIBU

❑1, Apr 1993 ME (w); SA (a); 1: The Mighty Magnor ... 2.25
❑1/Variant, Apr 1993; ME (w); SA (a); 1: The Mighty Magnor. Pop-up cover 3.95
❑2, May 1993 ME (w); SA (a) ... 1.95
❑3, Jun 1993 ME (w); SA (a) ... 1.95
❑4, Jul 1993 ME (w); SA (a) ... 1.95
❑5, Dec 1993 ME (w); SA (a) ... 1.95
❑6, Apr 1994 ME (w); SA (a) ... 1.95

MIGHTY MAN
IMAGE

❑1, Mar 2005 ... 7.95

MIGHTY MARVEL MUST HAVES: ASTONISHING X-MEN #1-3
MARVEL

❑1 2004 ... 3.99

MIGHTY MARVEL WESTERN
MARVEL

❑1, Oct 1968, giant; Rawhide Kid, Kid Colt, Two-Gun Kid ... 45.00
❑2, Dec 1968, giant; Rawhide Kid, Kid Colt, Two-Gun Kid ... 30.00
❑3, Feb 1969, giant; Rawhide Kid, Kid Colt, Two-Gun Kid ... 25.00
❑4, Apr 1969, giant; Rawhide Kid, Kid Colt, Two-Gun Kid ... 25.00
❑5, Jun 1969, giant; Rawhide Kid, Kid Colt, Two-Gun Kid ... 25.00
❑6, Nov 1969 ... 20.00
❑7, Jan 1970 ... 20.00
❑8, May 1970 ... 20.00
❑9, Jul 1970 ... 20.00
❑10, Sep 1970 ... 20.00
❑11, Nov 1970 ... 20.00
❑12, Jan 1971 ... 20.00
❑13, May 1971 ... 20.00
❑14, Sep 1971 ... 20.00
❑15, Dec 1971 ... 20.00
❑16, Mar 1972 ... 15.00
❑17, Jun 1972 ... 15.00
❑18, Jul 1972 ... 15.00
❑19, Sep 1972 ... 15.00
❑20, Oct 1972 ... 15.00
❑21, Nov 1972, SL (w); JSe (a) ... 15.00
❑22, Jan 1973, SL (w) ... 10.00
❑23, Mar 1973 ... 10.00
❑24, May 1973, SL (w); JSe (a) ... 10.00
❑25, Jul 1973 ... 10.00
❑26, Sep 1973 ... 10.00
❑27, Oct 1973 ... 10.00
❑28, Dec 1973 ... 10.00
❑29, Jan 1974 ... 10.00
❑30, Mar 1974 ... 10.00
❑31, May 1974 ... 10.00
❑32, Jul 1974 ... 10.00
❑33, Aug 1974 ... 10.00
❑34, Sep 1974 ... 10.00
❑35, Oct 1974 ... 10.00
❑36, Dec 1974 ... 10.00
❑37, Jan 1975 ... 10.00
❑38, Mar 1975 ... 10.00
❑39, May 1975 ... 10.00
❑40, Jul 1975 ... 10.00
❑41, Sep 1975 ... 10.00
❑42, Oct 1975 ... 10.00
❑43, Dec 1975 ... 10.00
❑44, Mar 1976 ... 10.00
❑45, Jun 1976 ... 10.00
❑45/30 cent, Jun 1976, 30 cent regional price variant ... 20.00
❑46, Sep 1976 ... 10.00

MIGHTY MITES (VOL. 1)
ETERNITY

❑1, Oct 1986; X-Men parody ... 2.00
❑2/A, Jan 1987; Batman parody ... 2.00
❑2/B, Jan 1987; Batman parody ... 2.00
❑3, Mar 1987 ... 2.00

MIGHTY MITES (VOL. 2)
ETERNITY

❑1, May 1987 ... 1.95
❑2, Jul 1987 ... 1.95

MIGHTY MORPHIN POWER RANGERS (SABAN'S...)
MARVEL

❑1, Nov 1995 ... 2.50
❑2, Dec 1995 ... 2.00
❑3, Dec 1995, cover says Jan, indicia says Dec ... 2.00
❑4, Feb 1996 ... 2.00
❑5, Mar 1996 ... 2.00
❑6, Apr 1996 ... 2.00
❑7, May 1996 ... 2.00
❑8, Jun 1996 ... 2.00
❑9, Jul 1996 ... 2.00

MIGHTY MORPHIN POWER RANGERS: NINJA RANGERS/VR TROOPERS (SABAN'S...)
MARVEL

❑1, Dec 1995, flip book with VR Troopers back-up ... 2.50
❑2, Jan 1996, Power Rangers cover says Dec 95 ... 2.00
❑3, Feb 1996, flip book with VR Troopers back-up ... 2.00
❑4, Mar 1996, SD (a); flip book with VR Troopers back-up ... 2.00
❑5, Apr 1996, SD (a); flip book with VR Troopers back-up ... 2.00
❑6, May 1996 ... 2.00
❑7, Jun 1996 ... 2.00
❑8, Jul 1996 ... 2.00

MIGHTY MORPHIN POWER RANGERS SAGA (SABAN'S...)
HAMILTON

❑1, Dec 1994, O: the Power Rangers. 2.50
❑2, Jan 1995 ... 2.50
❑3, Feb 1995 ... 2.50

MIGHTY MORPHIN POWER RANGERS: THE MOVIE
MARVEL

❑1, Sep 1995 ... 2.95
❑1/Variant, Sep 1995; cardstock cover 3.95

MIGHTY MOUSE (GOLD KEY)
GOLD KEY

❑161, Oct 1964, Previous issues published as Adventures of Mighty Mouse (2nd Series) ... 30.00
❑162, Jan 1965 ... 30.00
❑163, Mar 1965 ... 30.00
❑164, Jul 1965 ... 30.00
❑165, Sep 1965, Series later revived with continued numbering as Adventures of Mighty Mouse (Gold Key) ... 30.00
❑167 ... 40.00
❑168, Sep 1966 ... 40.00
❑169, Dec 1966 ... 40.00

MIGHTY MOUSE (SPOTLIGHT)
SPOTLIGHT

❑1, ca. 1987 ... 2.00
❑2, ca. 1987 ... 2.00

MIGHTY MOUSE (MARVEL)
MARVEL / STAR

❑1, Oct 1990; Dark Knight parody cover 2.00
❑2, Nov 1990 ... 1.50
❑3, Dec 1990; 1: Bat-Bat. Sub-Mariner parody ... 1.50
❑4, Jan 1991; GP (c); Crisis parody ... 1.50
❑5, Feb 1991; Crisis parody ... 1.50
❑6, Mar 1991; McFarlane parody ... 1.50
❑7, Apr 1991; computer art ... 1.50
❑8, May 1991 ... 1.50
❑9, Jun 1991 ... 1.50
❑10, Jul 1991; Letterman parody ... 1.50

MIGHTY MOUSE ADVENTURE MAGAZINE
SPOTLIGHT

❑1, b&w ... 2.00

MIGHTY MOUSE AND FRIENDS HOLIDAY SPECIAL
SPOTLIGHT

❑1 ... 2.00

MIGHTY MUTANIMALS (MINI-SERIES)
ARCHIE

❑1, May 1991; TMNT spin-off ... 1.50
❑2 1991; TMNT spin-off ... 1.25
❑3 1991; TMNT spin-off ... 1.25

MIGHTY MUTANIMALS
ARCHIE

❑1, Apr 1992 ... 1.25
❑2, Jun 1992 ... 1.25
❑3, Aug 1992 ... 1.25
❑4, Sep 1992 ... 1.25
❑5, Oct 1992 ... 1.25
❑6, Dec 1992 ... 1.25
❑7, Feb 1993 ... 1.25
❑8, Apr 1993 ... 1.25

MIGHTY SAMSON
GOLD KEY

❑1, Jul 1964, O: Samson. 1: Samson. back cover pin-up ... 75.00
❑2, Jun 1965, 1: Terra of Jerz. back cover pin-up ... 45.00
❑3, Sep 1965, back cover pin-up ... 45.00
❑4, Dec 1965, back cover pin-up ... 45.00
❑5, Mar 1966, back cover pin-up ... 30.00
❑6, Jun 1966, back cover pin-up ... 30.00
❑7, Sep 1966, back cover pin-up ... 30.00
❑8, Dec 1966 ... 30.00
❑9, Mar 1967, In Washington, D.C. ... 30.00
❑10, Jun 1967 ... 30.00
❑11, Aug 1967 ... 20.00
❑12, Nov 1967 ... 20.00
❑13, Feb 1968 ... 20.00
❑14, May 1968 ... 20.00
❑15, Aug 1968 ... 20.00
❑16, Nov 1968 ... 20.00
❑17, Feb 1969 ... 20.00
❑18, May 1969 ... 20.00
❑19, Aug 1969, N'York floods ... 20.00
❑20, Nov 1969 ... 20.00
❑21, Aug 1972 ... 15.00

Mister Miracle (1st Series)

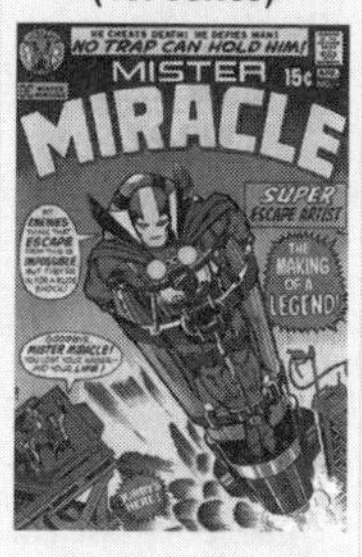

Son of the rulers of New Genesis
©DC

Mr. T and the T-Force

He pities da fools that mess with him
©Now

Mister X (Vol. 1)

Angst-ridden independent comic
©Vortex

Misty

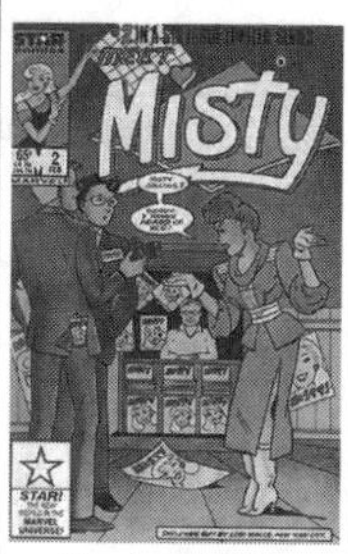

The niece of Millie the Model
©Marvel

Moby Duck

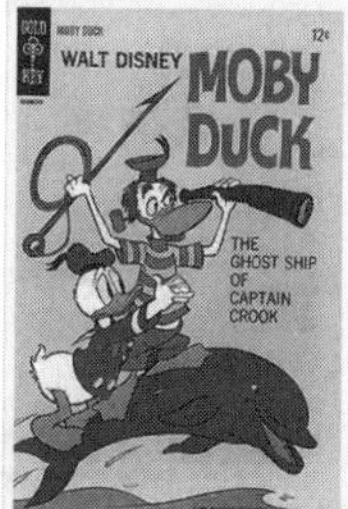

Crusty sea captain sails from Duckburg
©Gold Key

N-MINT

❑22, Dec 1973 .... 15.00
❑23, Mar 1974 .... 15.00
❑24, Jun 1974 .... 15.00
❑25, Sep 1974 .... 15.00
❑26, Dec 1974 .... 15.00
❑27, Mar 1975 .... 15.00
❑28, Jun 1975 .... 15.00
❑29, Sep 1975 .... 15.00
❑30, Dec 1975, In Macy's 15.00
❑31, Mar 1976, V: giant moths 15.00
❑32, Apr 1982, 1982 revival 10.00

MIGHTY THOR, THE: GODSTORM
MARVEL

❑1, Nov 2001 .... 3.50
❑2, Dec 2001; No indicia inside whatsoever 3.50
❑3, Jan 2002 .... 3.50

MIGHTY TINY
ANTARCTIC

❑1, b&w 2.00
❑2, b&w 2.00
❑3, b&w 2.00
❑4, b&w 2.00
❑5 .... 2.50

MIGHTY TINY: THE MOUSE MARINES
ANTARCTIC

❑1, b&w 2.50

MIKE DANGER (VOL. 1) (MICKEY SPILLANE'S...)
TEKNO

❑1, Sep 1995, FM (c) 1.95
❑2, Oct 1995 .... 1.95
❑3, Nov 1995 .... 1.95
❑4, Dec 1995 .... 1.95
❑5, Dec 1995 .... 2.25
❑6, Jan 1996 .... 2.25
❑7, Jan 1996 .... 2.25
❑8, Feb 1996 .... 2.25
❑9, Mar 1996 .... 2.25
❑10, Apr 1996 .... 2.25
❑11, May 1996 .... 2.25

MIKE DANGER (VOL. 2) (MICKEY SPILLANE'S...)
BIG

❑1, Jun 1996 .... 2.25
❑2, Jul 1996, Mike's head is separated from his body 2.25
❑3, Aug 1996 .... 2.25
❑4, Sep 1996 .... 2.25
❑5, Oct 1996 .... 2.25
❑6, Nov 1996 .... 2.25
❑7, Dec 1996 .... 2.25
❑8, Jan 1997 .... 2.25
❑9, Feb 1997 .... 2.25
❑10, Apr 1997 .... 2.25

MIKE MAUSER FILES
AVALON

❑1 1999 .... 2.95

MIKE MIGNOLA'S BPRD COLLECTION
DARK HORSE

❑1, ca. 2004 .... 17.95

MIKE MIST MINUTE MIST-ERIES
ECLIPSE

❑1, Apr 1981, b&w 1.50

N-MINT

MIKE REGAN
HARDBOILED

❑1, b&w 2.95

MIKE SHAYNE PRIVATE EYE
DELL

❑1, Nov 1962 .... 16.00
❑2, Feb 1962 .... 10.00
❑3, May 1962 .... 10.00

MILIKARDO KNIGHTS
MAD BADGER

❑1, Mar 1997, b&w 3.00
❑2, Jan 1998, b&w 3.00

MILK
RADIO

❑1, Sep 1997, b&w 2.95
❑2, Nov 1997, b&w 2.95
❑3, Jan 1998, b&w 2.95
❑4, Mar 1998, b&w 2.95
❑5, May 1998, b&w 2.95
❑6, Jul 1998, b&w 2.95
❑7, Sep 1998, b&w 2.95
❑8, Nov 1998, b&w 2.95
❑9, Jan 1999, b&w 2.95
❑10, Mar 1999, b&w 2.95
❑11, May 1999, b&w 2.95
❑12, Jul 1999, b&w 2.95
❑13, Sep 1999, b&w 2.95
❑14, Nov 1999, b&w 2.95
❑15, Jan 2000, b&w 2.95
❑16, Mar 2000, b&w 2.95
❑17, May 2000, b&w 2.95
❑18, Jul 2000, b&w 2.95
❑19, Sep 2000, b&w 2.95
❑20, Nov 2001 .... 2.95
❑21, Jan 2001 .... 2.99
❑22, Mar 2001 .... 2.99
❑23, May 2001 .... 2.99
❑24, Jul 2001 .... 2.99
❑25, Sep 2001 .... 2.99
❑26, Nov 2001 .... 2.99
❑27, Jan 2002 .... 2.99
❑28, Mar 2002 .... 2.99
❑29, May 2002 .... 2.99
❑30, Jul 2002 .... 2.99
❑31, Sep 2002 .... 2.99
❑32, Nov 2002 .... 2.99
❑33, Mar 2003 .... 2.99
❑34, May 2003 .... 2.99
❑35, Jul 2003 .... 2.99
❑36, Sep 2003 .... 2.99
❑37, Nov 2003 .... 2.99
❑38, Jan 2004 .... 0.00
❑39, Apr 2004 .... 0.00
❑40, May 2004 .... 0.00
❑41, Jul 2004 .... 0.00
❑42, Sep 2004 .... 3.50
❑43, Nov 2004 .... 3.50

MILK & CHEESE
SLAVE LABOR

❑1, Mar 1991, b&w 65.00
❑1/2nd, Sep 1991, b&w 6.00
❑1/3rd, Sep 1992, b&w 5.00
❑1/4th, Aug 1993, b&w 3.00

N-MINT

❑1/5th, Oct 1994, b&w 3.00
❑1/6th, Sep 1995, b&w 3.00
❑1/7th, Feb 1997, b&w 2.75
❑2, Mar 1992, b&w; Other Number One; has Doctor Radium ad on back cover 35.00
❑2/2nd, Jun 1993; has Fine Dairy Products ad on back cover 5.00
❑2/3rd, Oct 1994; has APE II ad on back cover 4.00
❑2/4th, Jan 1996 .... 2.75
❑2/5th 2.75
❑3, Aug 1992, b&w; Third #1; has Rats ad on back cover 28.00
❑3/2nd, May 1993; has Fine Dairy Products ad on back cover 4.00
❑3/3rd, Oct 1994; has APE II ad on back cover 3.00
❑3/4th, Feb 1996 .... 2.75
❑3/5th 2.75
❑4, Apr 1993, b&w; Fourth #1; has Fine Dairy Products ad on back cover 16.00
❑4/2nd, Mar 1995; has APE II ad on back cover 3.00
❑4/3rd, Aug 1996 .... 2.50
❑5, Apr 1994, b&w; First Second Issue; has APE ad on back cover 15.00
❑5/2nd, Nov 1994; has APE II ad on back cover 3.00
❑5/3rd, Feb 1996 .... 3.00
❑5/4th 2.75
❑6, Apr 1995, b&w; Six Six Six 8.00
❑6/2nd, Sep 1996 .... 2.75
❑7, Jun 1997, b&w; Latest Thing! 3.00

MILKMAN MURDERS
DARK HORSE

❑1 2004 .... 3.00
❑2 2004 .... 3.00
❑3 2004 .... 3.00
❑4 2004 .... 3.00

MILLENNIUM
DC

❑1, Jan 1988 JSa (a) 2.00
❑2, Jan 1988 .... 1.50
❑3, Jan 1988 .... 1.50
❑4, Jan 1988 .... 1.50
❑5, Feb 1988 .... 1.50
❑6, Feb 1988 .... 1.50
❑7, Feb 1988 .... 1.50
❑8, Feb 1988 .... 1.50

MILLENNIUM 2.5 A.D.
AVALON

❑1 .... 2.95

MILLENNIUM EDITION: ACTION COMICS
DC

❑1, Feb 2000 .... 3.95

MILLENNIUM EDITION: ADVENTURE COMICS
DC

❑61, Dec 2000 .... 3.95
❑247, Nov 2000 .... 2.50

MILLENNIUM EDITION: ALL STAR COMICS
DC

❑3, Jun 2000; 1: the Justice Society of America. Reprints 3.95

Other grades: Multiply price above by 5/6 for VF/NM • 2/3 for VERY FINE • 1/3 for FINE • 1/5 for VERY GOOD • 1/8 for GOOD

❑3/Variant, Jun 2000; 1: the Justice Society of America. chromium cover 10.00
❑8, Feb 2001 O: Wonder Woman. 1: Wonder Woman 3.95

MILLENNIUM EDITION: ALL-STAR WESTERN
DC

❑10, Apr 2000, Reprints All-Star Western #10 ..... 2.50

MILLENNIUM EDITION: BATMAN
DC

❑1, Feb 2001 ..... 3.95
❑1/Chrome, Feb 2001 ..... 5.00

MILLENNIUM EDITION: BATMAN: THE DARK KNIGHT RETURNS
DC

❑1, Oct 2000; Reprints Batman: The Dark Knight #1 ..... 5.95

MILLENNIUM EDITION: CRISIS ON INFINITE EARTHS
DC

❑1, Feb 2000; Reprints Crisis on Infinite Earths #1 ..... 2.50
❑1/Chrome, Feb 2000 ..... 5.00

MILLENNIUM EDITION: DETECTIVE COMICS
DC

❑1, Jan 2001; Reprints Detective Comics #1 ..... 3.95
❑27, Feb 2000 ..... 3.95
❑38, ca. 2000 ..... 3.95
❑225, Dec 2000 ..... 2.50
❑359, Oct 2000 ..... 3.95
❑327, Mar 2000 ..... 3.95

MILLENNIUM EDITION: FLASH COMICS
DC

❑1, Sep 2000; Reprints Flash Comics #1 ..... 3.95

MILLENNIUM EDITION: GEN13
WILDSTORM

❑1; Reprints Gen13 (Mini-Series) #1 ..... 2.50

MILLENNIUM EDITION: GREEN LANTERN
DC

❑76, ca. 2000 ..... 2.50

MILLENNIUM EDITION: HELLBLAZER
DC

❑1, Jul 2000; Reprints Hellblazer #1 ..... 2.95

MILLENNIUM EDITION: HOUSE OF MYSTERY
DC

❑1, Sep 2000; Reprints House of Mystery #1 ..... 2.50

MILLENNIUM EDITION: HOUSE OF SECRETS
DC

❑92, May 2000 ..... 2.50

MILLENNIUM EDITION: JLA
DC

❑1, ca. 2000 ..... 2.50

MILLENNIUM EDITION: JUSTICE LEAGUE
DC

❑1, Jul 2000; KG (w); KG (a); Reprints Justice League #1 ..... 2.50
❑1/Chrome, Jul 2000 ..... 5.00

MILLENNIUM EDITION: KINGDOM COME
DC

❑1, Aug 2000 ..... 5.95

MILLENNIUM EDITION: MAD
DC

❑1, Feb 2000 ..... 2.00
❑1/Recalled, Feb 2000 ..... 25.00

MILLENNIUM EDITION: MILITARY COMICS
DC

❑1, Oct 2000 ..... 3.95

MILLENNIUM EDITION: MORE FUN COMICS
DC

❑73, Jan 2001 ..... 3.95
❑101, Nov 2000 ..... 2.95

MILLENNIUM EDITION: MYSTERIOUS SUSPENSE
DC

❑1, Sep 2000; 1st appearance of The Question; Reprints Mysterious Suspense #1 ..... 2.50

MILLENNIUM EDITION: NEW GODS
DC

❑1, Jun 2000 ..... 2.50

MILLENNIUM EDITION: OUR ARMY AT WAR
DC

❑81, Jun 2000 ..... 2.50

MILLENNIUM EDITION: PLOP!
DC

❑1, Jul 2000; Reprints Plop! #1 ..... 2.50

MILLENNIUM EDITION: POLICE COMICS
DC

❑1, Sep 2000; Reprints Police Comics #1 ..... 3.95

MILLENNIUM EDITION: PREACHER
DC

❑1, Oct 2000 ..... 2.95

MILLENNIUM EDITION: SENSATION COMICS
DC

❑1, Oct 2000; Reprints Sensation Comics #1 ..... 3.95

MILLENNIUM EDITION: SHADOW
DC

❑

MILLENNIUM EDITION: SHOWCASE
DC

❑4, ca. 2000; Reprints Showcase #4 ..... 2.50
❑9, Jan 2001; Reprints Showcase #9 ..... 2.50
❑22, Dec 2000; Reprints Showcase #22 ..... 2.50

MILLENNIUM EDITION: SUPERBOY
DC

❑1, Feb 2001 ..... 2.95

MILLENNIUM EDITION: SUPERMAN (1ST SERIES)
DC

❑1, Dec 2000; Reprints Superman (1st Series) #1 ..... 2.95
❑1/Chrome, Dec 2000 ..... 2.95
❑76, ca. 2000 ..... 2.95
❑233, Jan 2001 ..... 2.50

MILLENNIUM EDITION: SUPERMAN (2ND SERIES)
DC

❑75, ca. 2000 ..... 2.95

MILLENNIUM EDITION: SUPERMAN'S PAL JIMMY OLSEN
DC

❑1, Apr 2000; Reprints Superman's Pal Jimmy Olsen #1 ..... 2.95

MILLENNIUM EDITION: TALES CALCULATED TO DRIVE YOU MAD
DC

❑1, ca. 2000 ..... 2.95

MILLENNIUM EDITION: THE BRAVE AND THE BOLD
DC

❑28, Feb 2000 ..... 2.50
❑85, Nov 2000 ..... 2.50

MILLENNIUM EDITION: THE FLASH
DC

❑123, May 2000; Reprints The Flash (1st Series) #123 ..... 2.50

MILLENNIUM EDITION: THE MAN OF STEEL
DC

❑1, ca. 2000 ..... 2.50

MILLENNIUM EDITION: THE NEW TEEN TITANS
DC

❑1, Dec 2000 ..... 2.50

MILLENNIUM EDITION: THE SAGA OF THE SWAMP THING
DC

❑21, Feb 2000 ..... 2.50

MILLENNIUM EDITION: THE SANDMAN
DC

❑1, Feb 2000; Reprints Sandman #1 ..... 2.95

MILLENNIUM EDITION: THE SPIRIT
DC

❑1, Jul 2000; Reprints The Spirit #1 ..... 2.95

MILLENNIUM EDITION: WATCHMEN
DC

❑1, ca. 2000; Reprints Watchmen #1 ..... 2.50

MILLENNIUM EDITION: WHIZ COMICS
DC

❑2, Mar 2000 ..... 3.95

MILLENNIUM EDITION: WILDC.A.T.S
DC

❑1, ca. 2000 ..... 2.50

MILLENNIUM EDITION: WONDER WOMAN (1ST SERIES)
DC

❑1, Aug 2000; Reprints Wonder Woman (1st Series) #1 ..... 3.95

MILLENNIUM EDITION: WONDER WOMAN (2ND SERIES)
DC

❑1, May 2000; Reprints Wonder Woman (2nd Series) #1 ..... 2.50

MILLENNIUM EDITION: WORLD'S FINEST
DC

❑71 ..... 2.50

MILLENNIUM EDITION: YOUNG ROMANCE COMICS
DC

❑1, Apr 2000; Reprints Young Romance (DC) #1; 1st romance comic 2.95

MILLENNIUM FEVER
DC / VERTIGO

❑1, Oct 1995 ..... 2.50
❑2, Nov 1995 ..... 2.50
❑3, Dec 1995 ..... 2.50
❑4, Jan 1996 ..... 2.50
❑Ashcan 1 ..... 0.75

MILLENNIUM INDEX
ECLIPSE

❑1, Mar 1988 ..... 2.00
❑2, Mar 1988 ..... 2.00

MILLIE THE MODEL COMICS
MARVEL

❑71 1956 ..... 25.00
❑72, Nov 1956 ..... 25.00
❑73, Dec 1956 ..... 25.00
❑74, Jan 1957 ..... 25.00
❑75, Feb 1957 ..... 25.00
❑76, Mar 1957 ..... 25.00
❑77, Apr 1957 ..... 25.00
❑78, May 1957 ..... 25.00
❑79 1957 ..... 25.00
❑80 1957 ..... 25.00
❑81, Nov 1957 ..... 25.00
❑82, Jan 1958 ..... 25.00
❑83, Mar 1958 ..... 25.00
❑84, May 1958 ..... 25.00
❑85, Jul 1958 ..... 25.00
❑86, Sep 1958 ..... 25.00
❑87, Nov 1958 ..... 25.00
❑88, Jan 1959 ..... 25.00
❑89, Mar 1959 ..... 25.00
❑90, May 1959 ..... 25.00
❑91, Jul 1959 ..... 25.00
❑92, Sep 1959 ..... 25.00
❑93, Nov 1959 ..... 25.00
❑94, Jan 1960 ..... 25.00
❑95, Mar 1960 ..... 25.00
❑96, May 1960 ..... 25.00
❑97, Jul 1960 ..... 25.00
❑98, Sep 1960 ..... 25.00
❑99, Nov 1960 ..... 25.00
❑100, Jan 1961 ..... 32.00
❑101, Mar 1961 ..... 15.00
❑102, May 1961 ..... 15.00
❑103, Jul 1961 ..... 15.00
❑104, Sep 1961 ..... 15.00

Mod Wheels

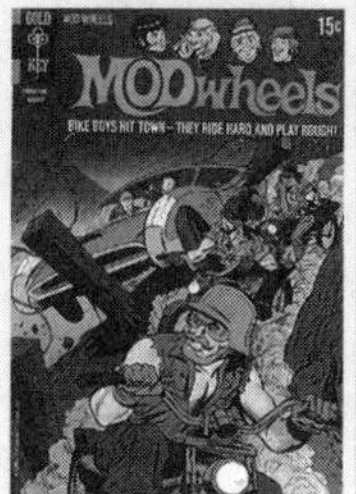

Mutton-chop sideburns and bell-bottom slacks

©Gold Key

Monarchy

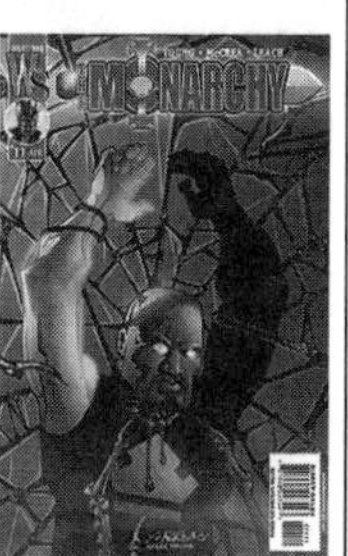

A new approach to changing the universe

©DC

Monkees

They may be coming to your town

©Gold Key

Monsters on the Prowl

Previously titled Chamber of Darkness

©Marvel

Moon Knight (1st Series)

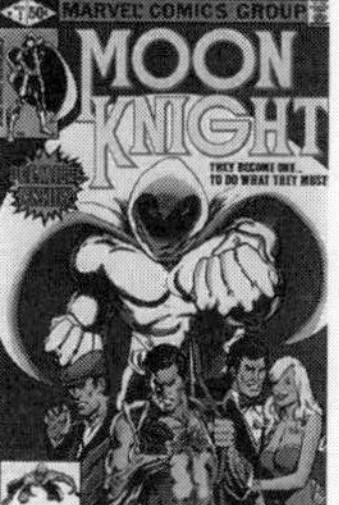

Batman variant has multiple identities

©Marvel

	N-MINT
❑105, Nov 1961	15.00
❑106, Jan 1962	15.00
❑107, Mar 1962	15.00
❑108, May 1962	15.00
❑109, Jul 1962	15.00
❑110, Sep 1962	15.00
❑111, Nov 1962	15.00
❑112, Jan 1963	15.00
❑113, Mar 1963	15.00
❑114, May 1963	15.00
❑115, Jul 1963	15.00
❑116, Sep 1963	15.00
❑117, Nov 1963	15.00
❑118, Jan 1964	15.00
❑119, Mar 1964	15.00
❑120, May 1964	15.00
❑121, Jul 1964	15.00
❑122, Sep 1964	15.00
❑123, Oct 1964	15.00
❑124, Nov 1964	15.00
❑125, Dec 1964	15.00
❑126, Jan 1965	15.00
❑127, Mar 1965	15.00
❑128, May 1965	15.00
❑129, Jul 1965	15.00
❑130, Sep 1965	15.00
❑131, Oct 1965	12.00
❑132, Nov 1965	12.00
❑133, Dec 1965	12.00
❑134, Jan 1966	12.00
❑135, Feb 1966	12.00
❑136, Apr 1966	12.00
❑137, May 1966	12.00
❑138, Jun 1966	12.00
❑139, Jul 1966	12.00
❑140, Aug 1966	12.00
❑141, Sep 1966	12.00
❑142, Oct 1966	12.00
❑143, Nov 1966	12.00
❑144, Dec 1966	12.00
❑145, Jan 1967	12.00
❑146, Feb 1967	12.00
❑147, Mar 1967	12.00
❑148, Apr 1967	12.00
❑149, May 1967	12.00
❑150, Jun 1967	12.00
❑151, Jul 1967	12.00
❑152, Aug 1967	12.00
❑153, Sep 1967	12.00
❑154, Oct 1967, New Millie begins	12.00
❑155, Nov 1967	10.00
❑156, Dec 1967	10.00
❑157, Feb 1968	10.00
❑158, Apr 1968	10.00
❑159, Jun 1968	10.00
❑160, Jul 1968	10.00
❑161, Aug 1968	10.00
❑162, Sep 1968	10.00
❑163, Oct 1968	10.00
❑164, Nov 1968	10.00
❑165, Dec 1968	10.00
❑166, Jan 1969	10.00
❑167, Feb 1969	10.00
❑168, Mar 1969	10.00
❑169, Apr 1969	10.00
❑170, May 1969	10.00
❑171, Jun 1969	10.00
❑172, Jul 1969	10.00
❑173, Aug 1969	10.00
❑174, Sep 1969	10.00
❑175, Oct 1969	10.00
❑176, Nov 1969	10.00
❑177, Dec 1969	10.00
❑178, Jan 1970	10.00
❑179, Feb 1970	10.00
❑180, Mar 1970	10.00
❑181, Apr 1970	8.50
❑182, May 1970	8.50
❑183, Jun 1970	8.50
❑184, Jul 1970	8.50
❑185, Aug 1970	8.50
❑186, Oct 1970	8.50
❑187, Dec 1970	8.50
❑188, Feb 1970	8.50
❑189, Apr 1970	8.50
❑190, Jun 1970	8.50
❑191, Aug 1970	8.50
❑192, Oct 1970	8.50
❑193, Dec 1970	8.50
❑194, Feb 1971	8.50
❑195, Apr 1971	8.50
❑196, Jun 1971	8.50
❑197, Aug 1971	8.50
❑198	8.50
❑199 1972	8.50
❑200 1972	8.50
❑201 1972	8.50
❑202	8.50
❑203, Aug 1973	8.50
❑204, Sep 1973	8.50
❑205, Oct 1973	8.50
❑206, Nov 1973	8.50
❑207, Dec 1973	8.50
❑Annual 1, ca. 1962	140.00
❑Annual 2, ca. 1963	95.00
❑Annual 3, ca. 1964	70.00
❑Annual 4, ca. 1965	70.00
❑Annual 5, Sep 1966	65.00
❑Annual 6, ca. 1967	45.00
❑Annual 7, ca. 1968	45.00
❑Annual 8, Sep 1969	45.00
❑Annual 9, ca. 1970	45.00
❑Annual 10, ca. 1971	45.00
❑Annual 11; "Queen-Size" #11	25.00
❑Annual 12; "Queen-Size" #12; 1975.	25.00

MILTON THE MONSTER AND FEARLESS FLY
Gold Key

	N-MINT
❑1, ca. 1966	60.00

MINDBENDERS
MBS

	N-MINT
❑1	2.50

MINDGAME GALLERY
Mindgame

	N-MINT
❑1, b&w	1.95

MIND PROBE
Rip Off

	N-MINT
❑1, b&w	3.25

MINERVA
NBM

	N-MINT
❑1	9.95

MINIMUM WAGE
Fantagraphics

	N-MINT
❑1, Oct 1995	2.95
❑2, Dec 1995	2.95
❑3, Mar 1996	2.95
❑4, Jun 1996; pin-ups	2.95
❑5, Nov 1996	2.95
❑6, Mar 1997	2.95
❑7, Aug 1997	2.95
❑8, Feb 1998	2.95
❑9, Jun 1998	2.95
❑10, Jan 1999	2.95

MINISTRY OF SPACE
Image

	N-MINT
❑1, Apr 2001	2.95
❑2, Sep 2001	2.95
❑3, May 2004	2.95

MINK
Tokyopop

	N-MINT
❑1, Apr 2004	9.99

MINKENSTEIN
Mu

	N-MINT
❑0, Aug 2005	2.95

MINOTAUR
Labyrinth

	N-MINT
❑1, Feb 1996, b&w	2.50
❑2, Apr 1996, b&w	2.50
❑3, Jun 1996, b&w; cover says Jul, indicia says Jun	2.50
❑4, Sep 1996, b&w	2.50

MINX
DC / Vertigo

	N-MINT
❑1, Oct 1998	2.50
❑2, Nov 1998	2.50
❑3, Dec 1998	2.50
❑4, Jan 1999	2.50
❑5, Feb 1999	2.50
❑6, Mar 1999	2.50
❑7, Apr 1999	2.50
❑8, May 1999	2.50

MIRACLE GIRLS
Tokyopop

	N-MINT
❑1, ca. 2000	2.95
❑2, ca. 2000	2.95
❑3	2.95
❑4	2.95
❑5, ca. 2001	2.95
❑6, ca. 2001	2.95
❑7, ca. 2001	2.95
❑8, ca. 2001	2.95
❑9, ca. 2001	2.95
❑10, ca. 2001	2.95
❑11, ca. 2001	2.95
❑12, ca. 2001	2.95
❑13, ca. 2001	2.95
❑14	2.95
❑15	2.95
❑16, ca. 2002	2.95
❑17, ca. 2002	2.95

Other grades: Multiply price above by 5/6 for VF/NM • 2/3 for VERY FINE • 1/3 for FINE • 1/5 for VERY GOOD • 1/8 for GOOD

❑18, ca. 2002 .... 2.95
❑19, ca. 2002 .... 2.95

MIRACLEMAN
ECLIPSE

❑1, Aug 1985 AMo (w) 10.00
❑2, Oct 1985 AMo (w) 8.00
❑3, Nov 1985 AMo (w) 8.00
❑4, Dec 1985 AMo (w) 8.00
❑4/Gold, Dec 1985........ 15.00
❑5, Jan 1986 PG (c); AMo (w)........ 8.00
❑5/Platinum, Jan 1986 .... 15.00
❑6, Feb 1986 AMo (w) 8.00
❑7, Apr 1986 PG (c); AMo (w); D: Gargunza........ 8.00
❑8, Jun 1986 AMo (w); 1: The New Wave........ 8.00
❑8/Gold, Jun 1986........ 15.00
❑9, Jul 1986; AMo (w); birth 10.00
❑10, Dec 1986 AMo (w) 10.00
❑11, May 1987 AMo (w)........ 14.00
❑12, Sep 1987 AMo (w) 14.00
❑13, Nov 1987 AMo (w) 18.00
❑14, Apr 1988 AMo (w)........ 24.00
❑15, Nov 1988; AMo (w); Scarce........ 35.00
❑16, Dec 1988; AMo (w); last Moore.. 16.00
❑17, Jun 1990; NG (w); 1st Neil Gaiman 25.00
❑17/Gold, Jun 1990........ 40.00
❑18, Aug 1990 NG (w)........ 20.00
❑19, Nov 1990; NG (w); cardstock cover........ 15.00
❑20, Mar 1991; NG (w); cardstock cover........ 15.00
❑21, Jul 1991 NG (w) 15.00
❑22, Aug 1991 NG (w)........ 15.00
❑23, Jun 1992 NG (w) 16.00
❑24, Aug 1993; scarcer 25.00
❑3D 1, Dec 1985; Giant-size; AMo (w); 3-D Special #1 .... 10.00
❑3D 1/Gold, Dec 1985 .... 18.00

MIRACLEMAN: APOCRYPHA
ECLIPSE

❑1, Nov 1991 JRo, MW, NG (w) 3.00
❑2, Jan 1992 KB, NG (w)........ 3.00
❑3, Apr 1991 NG (w) 3.00

MIRACLEMAN FAMILY
ECLIPSE

❑1, May 1988 O: Young Miracleman .. 3.00
❑2, Sep 1988 PG (c)........ 3.00

MIRACLE SQUAD
UPSHOT

❑1 .... 2.00
❑2 .... 2.00
❑3, b&w........ 2.00
❑4, b&w........ 2.00

MIRACLE SQUAD, THE: BLOOD AND DUST
APPLE

❑1, Jan 1989, b&w 2.00
❑2, Mar 1989, b&w 2.00
❑3, May 1989, b&w 2.00
❑4, Jul 1989, b&w........ 2.00

MIRRORWALKER
NOW

❑1, Oct 1990; semi-fumetti........ 2.95
❑2 .... 2.95

MIRRORWORLD: RAIN
NETCO

❑0, Apr 1997 .... 3.25
❑1, Feb 1997 .... 3.25

MISADVENTURES OF BREADMAN AND DOUGHBOY
HEMLOCK PARK

❑1, Oct 1999; no cover price 2.95
❑2 .... 2.95

MISEROTH: AMOK HELL
NORTHSTAR

❑1 .... 4.95
❑2 .... 4.95
❑3 .... 4.95

MISERY
IMAGE

❑1, Dec 1995 .... 2.95

MISPLACED
IMAGE

❑1, May 2003........ 2.95
❑2, Aug 2003 .... 2.95

MISS FURY (ADVENTURE)
ADVENTURE

❑1, Nov 1991 .... 2.50
❑1/Ltd.; limited edition........ 4.95
❑2, Dec 1991........ 2.50
❑3........ 2.50
❑4........ 2.50

MISS FURY (AVALON)
AVALON

❑1........ 2.95
❑2........ 2.95

MISSING BEINGS SPECIAL
COMICS INTERVIEW

❑1, b&w 2.25

MISSION: IMPOSSIBLE (DELL)
DELL

❑1, May 1967, Same cover as #5........ 24.00
❑2, Sep 1967........ 18.00
❑3, Dec 1967........ 18.00
❑4, Oct 1968 .... 18.00
❑5, Oct 1969, Same cover as #1; Reprints........ 12.00

MISSION IMPOSSIBLE (MARVEL)
MARVEL

❑1, May 1996; prequel to movie 2.95

MISSIONS IN TIBET
DIMENSION

❑1, Jul 1995........ 2.50

MISS PEACH
DELL

❑1, Oct 1963 .... 60.00

MISSPENT YOUTHS
BRAVE NEW WORDS

❑1........ 2.50
❑2........ 2.50
❑3, Jul 1991 .... 2.50

MISS VICTORY GOLDEN ANNIVERSARY SPECIAL
AC

❑1, Nov 1991, reprint 1: Miss Victory 5.00

MISTER AMERICA
ENDEAVOR

❑1........ 2.95
❑2, Apr 1994........ 2.95

MR. AND MRS. J. EVIL SCIENTIST
GOLD KEY

❑1, Nov 1963 .... 50.00
❑2, ca. 1964........ 30.00
❑3, ca. 1965........ 20.00
❑4, Sep 1966........ 20.00

MR. AVERAGE
B.S.

❑1........ 2.25
❑2........ 2.25
❑3........ 2.25

MR. BEAT ADVENTURES
MOORDAM

❑1, Jan 1997, b&w........ 2.95

MR. BEAT/CRAYBABY/WEIRDSVILLE POST HALLOWEEN LEFTOVER MONSTER THANKSGIVING SPECIAL
BLINDWOLF

❑1, Oct 1998 .... 2.95

MR. BEAT — EXISTENTIAL COOL
MOORDAM

❑0, Jun 1998; flip-book with Gyro-Man 2.95

MR. BEAT'S BABES AND BONGOS ANNUAL
MOORDAM

❑1/Blue, Oct 1998; Blue cover with Patty-Cake........ 2.95
❑1/Red, Oct 1998; Red cover with Betty Page 2.95

MR. BEAT'S HOUSE OF BURNING JAZZ LOVE
MOORDAM

❑1, Dec 1997, b&w 2.95

MR. BEAT'S TWO-FISTED ATOMIC ACTION SUPER SPECIAL
MOORDAM

❑1, Sep 1997, b&w........ 2.95

MR. BEAT SUPERSTAR
MOORDAM

❑1, Jun 1998........ 2.95

MISTER BLANK
SLAVE LABOR / AMAZE INK

❑0........ 2.95
❑1, May 1997 .... 2.95
❑2, May 1997 .... 2.95
❑3, Aug 1997........ 2.95
❑4, Nov 1997........ 2.95
❑5, Feb 1998........ 2.95

MR. CREAM PUFF
BLACKTHORNE

❑1 .... 1.75

MR. DAY & MR. NIGHT
SLAVE LABOR

❑1, Apr 1993 .... 3.95

MR. DOOM
PIED PIPER

❑1, Jul 1987 .... 1.95

MISTER E
DC

❑1, Jun 1991 .... 2.00
❑2, Jul 1991 .... 2.00
❑3, Aug 1991........ 2.00
❑4, Sep 1991........ 2.00

MR. FIXITT (APPLE)
APPLE

❑1, Jan 1989, b&w........ 1.95
❑2, Mar 1990........ 1.95

MR. FIXITT (HEROIC)
HEROIC

❑1, b&w; trading card........ 2.95

MR. HERO-THE NEWMATIC MAN (1ST SERIES) (NEIL GAIMAN'S...)
TEKNO

❑1, Mar 1995, game piece; trading card 1.95
❑2, Apr 1995, game piece; trading card 1.95
❑3, May 1995, game piece; trading card 1.95
❑4, Jun 1995, coupon 1.95
❑5, Jul 1995 .... 1.95
❑6, Aug 1995........ 1.95
❑7, Sep 1995........ 1.95
❑8, Oct 1995........ 1.95
❑9, Nov 1995........ 1.95
❑10, Dec 1995........ 1.95
❑11, Dec 1995........ 1.95
❑12, Jan 1996 .... 2.25
❑13, Jan 1996 .... 2.25
❑14, Feb 1996 .... 2.25
❑15, Mar 1996........ 2.25
❑16, Apr 1996 .... 2.25
❑17, May 1996 .... 2.25

MR. HERO-THE NEWMATIC MAN (2ND SERIES) (NEIL GAIMAN'S...)
BIG

❑1, Jun 1996 .... 2.25
❑2, Jul 1996 .... 2.25
❑3, Aug 1996........ 2.25
❑4, Sep 1996........ 2.25

MR. JIGSAW SPECIAL
OCEAN

❑1, Spr 1988; O: Mr. Jigsaw. blue paper 2.00

MR. LIZARD 3-D
NOW

❑1, May 1993; instant Mr. Lizard capsule 3.50

MR. LIZARD ANNUAL
NOW

❑1, Sep 1993; Ralph Snart capsule 2.95

MR. MAJESTIC
DC / WILDSTORM

❑1, Sep 1999........ 3.00
❑2, Oct 1999........ 2.50
❑3, Nov 1999........ 2.50
❑4, Dec 1999........ 2.50
❑5, Jan 2000........ 2.50
❑6, Feb 2000........ 2.50
❑7, Mar 2000........ 2.50

Other grades: Multiply price above by 5/6 for VF/NM • 2/3 for VERY FINE • 1/3 for FINE • 1/5 for VERY GOOD • 1/8 for GOOD

Moonshadow

A fairy tale for grown-ups
©Marvel

Morbius: The Living Vampire

Vampire got his start in Spider-Man
©Marvel

More Than Mortal

Fantasy had heat briefly in 1997
©Liar

Mort the Dead Teenager

More uplifting fare for our nation's youth
©Marvel

Mother Teresa of Calcutta

Companion to Marvel's Pope John Paul comic
©Marvel

N-MINT

❑8, Apr 2000 ... 2.50
❑9, May 2000 ... 2.50

MISTER MIRACLE (1ST SERIES)
DC

❑1, Apr 1971, JK (c); JK (w); JK (a); 1: Oberon. 1: Mister Miracle ... 50.00
❑2, Jun 1971, JK (c); JK (w); JK (a); 1: Doctor Bedlam. 1: Granny Goodness ... 25.00
❑3, Aug 1971, JK (c); JK (w); JK (a); V: Doctor Bedlam. Boy Commandos reprint ... 20.00
❑4, Oct 1971; Giant-size; JK (c); JK (w); JK (a); 1: Big Barda, Boy Commandos reprint. Boy Commandos reprint (Detective Comics #82) ... 25.00
❑5, Dec 1971; Giant-size; JK (c); JK (w); JK (a); Boy Commandos reprint (Detective Comics #76) ... 30.00
❑6, Feb 1972; Giant-size; JK (c); JK (w); JK (a); 1: Funky Flashman. 1: Lashina. 1: Female Furies. reprints Boy Commandos #1 ... 22.00
❑7, Apr 1972; Giant-size; JK (c); JK (w); JK (a); reprints Boy Commandos #3 ... 20.00
❑8, Jun 1972; Giant-size; JK (c); JK (w); JK (a); Boy Commandos reprint (Detective Comics #64) ... 20.00
❑9, Aug 1972, JK (c); JK (w); JK (a) ... 15.00
❑10, Oct 1972, JK (c); JK (w); JK (a) . 15.00
❑11, Dec 1972, JK (c); JK (w); JK (a) . 15.00
❑12, Feb 1973, JK (c); JK (w); JK (a) . 15.00
❑13, Apr 1973, JK (c); JK (w); JK (a) . 15.00
❑14, Jul 1973, JK (c); JK (w); JK (a); 1: Madame Evil Eye ... 15.00
❑15, Sep 1973, JK (c); JK (w); JK (a); 1: Mister Miracle II (Shilo Norman) ... 12.00
❑16, Nov 1973, JK (c); JK (w); JK (a) . 12.00
❑17, Jan 1974, JK (c); JK (w); JK (a) . 10.00
❑18, Mar 1974, JK (c); JK (w); JK (a); series goes on hiatus; Wedding of Mister Miracle and Barda ... 10.00
❑19, Sep 1977, MR (c); MR (a) ... 7.00
❑20, Oct 1977, MR (c); MR (a) ... 7.00
❑21, Dec 1977, MR (c); MR (a) ... 7.00
❑22, Feb 1978, MR (c); MR (a) ... 7.00
❑23, Apr 1978, MR (c); MG (a) ... 7.00
❑24, Jun 1978, MR (c); MG, RH (a) ... 7.00
❑25, Sep 1978, (c); MG, RH (a) ... 7.00
❑Special 1, ca. 1987 ... 3.50

MISTER MIRACLE (2ND SERIES)
DC

❑1, Jan 1989 O: Mister Miracle. A: Doctor Bedlam. A: Dr. Bedlam ... 2.50
❑2, Feb 1989 ... 1.50
❑3, Mar 1989 ... 1.50
❑4, Apr 1989 ... 1.50
❑5, Jun 1989 ... 1.50
❑6, Jul 1989 ... 1.25
❑7, Aug 1989 ... 1.25
❑8, Sep 1989 ... 1.25
❑9, Oct 1989 1: Maxi-Man ... 1.25
❑10, Nov 1989 ... 1.25
❑11, Dec 1989 ... 1.25
❑12, Jan 1990 ... 1.25
❑13, Mar 1990 A: Lobo ... 1.25
❑14, Apr 1990 A: Lobo ... 1.25
❑15, May 1990 ... 1.25
❑16, Jun 1990 ... 1.25
❑17, Jul 1990 ... 1.25
❑18, Aug 1990 ... 1.25
❑19, Sep 1990 ... 1.25
❑20, Oct 1990 ... 1.25
❑21, Nov 1990 ... 1.25
❑22, Dec 1990 ... 1.25
❑23, Jan 1991 ... 1.25
❑24, Feb 1991 ... 1.25
❑25, Mar 1991 ... 1.25
❑26, Apr 1991 ... 1.25
❑27, May 1991 ... 1.25
❑28, Jun 1991 ... 1.25

MISTER MIRACLE (3RD SERIES)
DC

❑1, Apr 1996 ... 1.95
❑2, May 1996 ... 1.95
❑3, Jun 1996 ... 1.95
❑4, Jul 1996 ... 1.95
❑5, Aug 1996 ... 1.95
❑6, Sep 1996 ... 1.95
❑7, Oct 1996 ... 1.95

MR. MONSTER
DARK HORSE

❑1, Feb 1988 O: Mr. Monster ... 2.00
❑2, Apr 1988 ... 2.00
❑3, Jun 1988 ... 2.00
❑4, Nov 1988 ... 2.00
❑5, Mar 1989 ... 2.00
❑6, Oct 1989; has indicia for #5 ... 2.00
❑7, Apr 1990 ... 2.00
❑8, Sep 1990; Giant-size D: Mr. Monster ... 5.00

MR. MONSTER ATTACKS!
TUNDRA

❑1, Aug 1992 ... 3.95
❑2, Sep 1992 ... 3.95
❑3, Oct 1992 ... 3.95

MR. MONSTER (DOC STEARN...)
ECLIPSE

❑1, Jan 1985; 1: Mr. Monster. Reprints Mr. Monster story from Vanguard Illustrated #7 ... 2.50
❑2, Aug 1985 DSt (c) ... 2.00
❑3, Oct 1985 BW, AMo (w); BW (a) ... 2.00
❑4, Dec 1985 ... 2.00
❑5, Feb 1986 ... 2.00
❑6, Jun 1986 ... 2.00
❑7, Dec 1986 ... 2.00
❑8, Mar 1987 ... 2.00
❑9, Apr 1987 A: Wolff & Byrd ... 2.00
❑10, Jun 1987; 6-D ... 2.00

MR. MONSTER PRESENTS (CRACK-A-BOOM!)
CALIBER

❑1, Jun 1997 ... 2.95
❑2 1997 ... 2.95
❑3, Sep 1997 ... 2.95

MR. MONSTER'S GAL FRIDAY... KELLY!
IMAGE

❑1, Jan 2000 ... 3.50
❑2, Mar 2002 ... 3.50
❑3, May 2002 ... 3.50

MR. MONSTER'S HIGH-OCTANE HORROR
ECLIPSE

❑1, May 1986; A.K.A. Super Duper Special #2 ... 2.00
❑3D 1, May 1986; A.K.A. Super Duper Special #1 ... 2.50

MR. MONSTER'S HI-SHOCK SCHLOCK
ECLIPSE

❑1, Mar 1987; A.K.A. Super Duper Special #6 ... 2.00
❑2, May 1987; A.K.A. Super Duper Special #7 ... 2.00

MR. MONSTER'S HI-VOLTAGE SUPER SCIENCE
ECLIPSE

❑1, Jan 1987; A.K.A. Super Duper Special #5 ... 2.00

MR. MONSTER'S TRIPLE THREAT 3-D
3-D ZONE

❑1, Jul 1993 ... 3.95

MR. MONSTER'S TRUE CRIME
ECLIPSE

❑1, Sep 1986; A.K.A. Super Duper Special #3 ... 2.00
❑2, Oct 1986; A.K.A. Super Duper Special #4 ... 2.00

MR. MONSTER'S WEIRD TALES OF THE FUTURE
ECLIPSE

❑1, BW (w); BW (a); A.K.A. Super Duper Special #8 ... 2.00

MR. MONSTER VS. GORZILLA
IMAGE

❑1, Jul 1998; red, white, and blue ... 2.95

MR. MXYZPTLK (VILLAINS)
DC

❑1, Feb 1998; New Year's Evil ... 1.95

MR. NATURAL
KITCHEN SINK

❑1 ... 90.00
❑1/2nd ... 40.00
❑1/3rd ... 25.00
❑1/4th, ca. 1970 ... 12.00
❑2, Oct 1971 ... 50.00
❑3, Jan 1977 ... 45.00
❑3/2nd ... 22.00
❑3/3rd ... 10.00
❑3/4th ... 4.50
❑3/5th, ca. 1980 ... 3.00
❑3/6th ... 2.50
❑3/7th ... 2.50
❑3/8th ... 2.50
❑3/9th ... 2.95
❑3/10th, Feb 1998 ... 3.50

MR. NIGHT
SLAVE LABOR

❑1, Nov 2005 ... 2.95

MR. NIGHTMARE'S WINTER SPECIAL
MOONSTONE

❑1, Dec 1995, b&w ... 3.50

MR. NIGHTMARE'S WONDERFUL WORLD
MOONSTONE

❑1, Jun 1995, b&w 2.95
❑2, Aug 1995, b&w 2.95
❑3, Oct 1995, b&w 2.95
❑4, Nov 1995, b&w 2.95
❑5, Feb 1996, b&w 2.95

MISTER PLANET
MR. PLANET

❑1, b&w 3.00
❑2, b&w 3.00

MISTER SIXX
IMAGINE NATION

❑1 .... 1.95

MR. T AND THE T-FORCE
NOW

❑1, Jun 1993; NA (w); NA (a); trading card 3.00
❑1/Gold; Gold logo promotional edition; NA (w); NA (a); gold, advance 4.00
❑2, Sep 1993; trading card 2.00
❑3, Oct 1993; trading card 2.00
❑4, Nov 1993; trading card 2.00
❑5, Dec 1993; trading card 2.00
❑6, Jan 1994; trading card 2.00
❑7, Feb 1994; trading card 2.00
❑8, Mar 1994; trading card 2.00
❑9, Apr 1994; trading card; cover says Aug, indicia says Apr 2.00
❑10, May 1994 .... 2.00

MISTER X (VOL. 1)
VORTEX

❑1, Jun 1984 1: Mister X 4.00
❑2, Aug 1984 .... 2.75
❑3 .... 2.75
❑4 .... 2.50
❑5 .... 2.50
❑6 .... 2.50
❑7 .... 2.50
❑8 .... 2.50
❑9 .... 2.50
❑10, Oct 1986 BSz (c) 2.50
❑11 .... 2.50
❑12, Jan 1988 .... 2.50
❑13, Mar 1988 .... 2.50
❑14 .... 2.50

MISTER X (VOL. 2)
VORTEX

❑1, b&w 3.00
❑2, b&w 2.50
❑3, b&w 2.50
❑4, b&w 2.50
❑5, b&w 2.50
❑6, b&w 2.25
❑7, b&w 2.25
❑8, b&w 2.25
❑9, b&w 2.25
❑10, b&w 2.25
❑11, b&w 2.25
❑12, b&w 2.50

MISTER X (VOL. 3)
CALIBER

❑1, ca. 1996, b&w 2.95
❑2, ca. 1996 .... 2.95
❑3, Sep 1996 .... 2.95
❑4, Dec 1996 .... 2.95

MISTRESS OF BONDAGE
FANTAGRAPHICS / EROS

❑1, b&w 2.95
❑2, b&w 2.95
❑3, b&w 2.95

MISTY
MARVEL / STAR

❑1, Dec 1985 .... 1.00
❑2, Feb 1986 .... 1.00
❑3, Apr 1986 .... 1.00
❑4, Jun 1986 .... 1.00
❑5, Aug 1986 .... 1.00
❑6, Oct 1986 .... 1.00

MISTY GIRL EXTREME
FANTAGRAPHICS / EROS

❑1, Jan 1997 .... 2.95
❑2, Feb 1997 .... 2.95

MITES
CONTINUÜM

❑1, b&w 1.50
❑2 .... 1.75

MIXXZINE
MIXX

❑1 .... 4.99
❑2 .... 4.99
❑3 .... 4.99
❑4 .... 4.99
❑5, Apr 1998 .... 4.99
❑6 .... 4.99

MNEMOVORE
DC / VERTIGO

❑1, May 2005 .... 2.99
❑2, Jun 2005 .... 2.99
❑3, Jul 2005 .... 2.99
❑4, Aug 2005 .... 2.99
❑5, Sep 2005 .... 2.99
❑6, Oct 2005 ....

MOBFIRE
DC / VERTIGO

❑1, Dec 1994 .... 2.50
❑2, Jan 1995 .... 2.50
❑3, Feb 1995 .... 2.50
❑4, Mar 1995 .... 2.50
❑5, Apr 1995, A: John Constantine 2.50
❑6, May 1995 .... 2.50
❑Ashcan 1, "Ashcan" preview given away by DC at shows 0.50

MOBILE POLICE PATLABOR PART 1
VIZ

❑1, Jul 1997, b&w 2.95
❑2, Aug 1997, b&w 2.95
❑3, Sep 1997, b&w 2.95
❑4, Oct 1997, b&w 2.95
❑5, Nov 1997, b&w 2.95
❑6, Dec 1997, b&w 2.95

MOBILE POLICE PATLABOR PART 2
VIZ

❑1, Jan 1998, b&w 2.95
❑2, Feb 1998, b&w 2.95
❑3, Mar 1998, b&w 2.95
❑4, Apr 1998, b&w 2.95
❑5, May 1998, b&w 2.95
❑6, Jun 1998, b&w 2.95

MOBILE SUIT GUNDAM 0079
VIZ

❑1, Mar 1999 .... 2.95
❑2, Apr 1999 .... 2.95
❑3, May 1999 .... 2.95
❑4, Jun 1999 .... 2.95
❑5, Jul 1999 .... 2.95
❑6, Aug 1999 .... 2.95
❑7, Sep 1999 .... 2.95
❑8, Oct 1999 .... 2.95

MOBILE SUIT GUNDAM 0083
VIZ

❑1, Nov 1999 .... 4.95
❑2, Dec 1999 .... 4.95
❑3, Jan 2000 .... 4.95
❑4, Feb 2000 .... 4.95
❑5, Mar 2000 .... 4.95
❑6, Apr 2000 .... 4.95
❑7, May 2000 .... 4.95
❑8, Jun 2000 .... 4.95
❑9, Jul 2000 .... 4.95
❑10, Aug 2000 .... 4.95
❑11, Sep 2000 .... 4.95
❑12, Oct 2000 .... 4.95
❑13, Nov 2000 .... 4.95

MOBILE SUIT GUNDAM SEED ASTRAY
TOKYOPOP

❑1, May 2004 .... 9.99

MOBILE SUIT GUNDAM WING: GROUND ZERO
VIZ

❑1, Jun 2000 .... 2.95
❑2, Jul 2000, b&w 2.95
❑3, Aug 2000, b&w 2.95
❑4, Sep 2000, b&w 2.95

MOBSTERS AND MONSTERS MAGAZINE
ORIGINAL SYNDICATE

❑1, Jul 1995 .... 3.00

MOBY DICK
NBM

❑1 .... 15.95

MOBY DUCK
GOLD KEY / WHITMAN

❑1, Oct 1967 .... 12.00
❑2, Jun 1968 .... 6.00
❑3, Sep 1968 .... 5.00
❑4, Dec 1968 .... 5.00
❑5, Mar 1969 .... 5.00
❑6 1969 .... 3.50
❑7, Oct 1969 .... 3.50
❑8, Jan 1970 .... 3.50
❑9, Apr 1970 .... 3.50
❑10, Jul 1970 .... 3.50
❑11, Oct 1970 .... 3.00
❑12, Jan 1974 .... 3.00
❑13, Apr 1974 .... 3.00
❑14, Jul 1974 .... 3.00
❑15, Oct 1974 .... 3.00
❑16 1975 .... 3.00
❑17 1975 .... 3.00
❑18 1975 .... 3.00
❑19, Aug 1975 .... 3.00
❑20, Oct 1975 .... 3.00
❑21, Jan 1976 .... 2.50
❑22, Apr 1976 .... 2.50
❑23, Jul 1976 .... 2.50
❑24, Oct 1976 .... 2.50
❑25, Jan 1977 .... 2.50
❑26, Apr 1977 .... 2.50
❑27, Jul 1977 .... 2.50
❑28, Oct 1977 .... 2.50
❑29, Jan 1978 .... 2.50
❑30, Mar 1978 .... 2.50

MOD
KITCHEN SINK

❑1, 1: Adventures in Limbo 5.00

MODEL
TOKYOPOP

❑1, May 2004 .... 9.99

MODEL
NBM

❑1, Oct 2002 .... 24.95

MODEL BY DAY
RIP OFF

❑1, Jul 1990, b&w 2.50
❑2, Oct 1990, b&w 2.50

MODELING WITH MILLIE
MARVEL

❑21, Feb 1963 .... 65.00
❑22, Apr 1963 .... 48.00
❑23, Jun 1963 .... 48.00
❑24, Aug 1963 .... 48.00
❑25 1963 .... 48.00
❑26 1963 .... 48.00
❑27, Nov 1963 .... 48.00
❑28 .... 48.00
❑29, ca. 1964 .... 48.00
❑30, ca. 1964 .... 48.00
❑31, ca. 1964 .... 36.00
❑32, Jul 1964 .... 36.00
❑33, ca. 1964 .... 36.00
❑34, ca. 1964 .... 36.00
❑35, ca. 1964 .... 36.00
❑36, Dec 1964 .... 36.00
❑37, Feb 1965 .... 36.00
❑38, Apr 1965 .... 36.00
❑39, Jun 1965 .... 36.00
❑40 1965 .... 36.00
❑41 1965 .... 30.00
❑42, Oct 1965 .... 30.00
❑43, Nov 1965 .... 30.00
❑44 .... 30.00
❑45, Feb 1966 .... 30.00
❑46, Apr 1966 .... 30.00
❑47, Jun 1966 .... 30.00
❑48, Aug 1966 .... 30.00
❑49, Sep 1966 .... 30.00
❑50, Oct 1966 .... 30.00
❑51, Nov 1966 .... 30.00

Ms. Marvel

Liberated heroine keeps changing her name
©Marvel

Ms. Mystic (Pacific)

One of a long line of delayed titles
©Pacific

Ms. Tree

Mysteries by Max Allan Collins and Terry Beatty
©Eclipse

Munsters (Gold Key)

TV family made seamless transition to comics
©Gold Key

Muppet Babies (Star/Marvel)

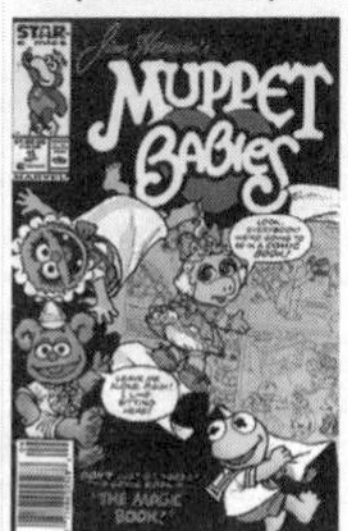

Apparently the real Muppets were too "mature"
©Marvel

N-MINT

❑52, Dec 1966 ... 30.00
❑53, Apr 1967 ... 30.00
❑54 ... 30.00

MODERN GRIMM
SYMPTOM

❑1, Dec 1996, b&w ... 2.75

MODERN PULP
SPECIAL STUDIO

❑1, b&w ... 2.75

MODERN ROMANS
FANTAGRAPHICS / EROS

❑1, b&w ... 2.25
❑2, b&w ... 2.25
❑3, b&w ... 2.25

MODEST PROPOSAL
TOME

❑1, b&w ... 2.50
❑2, b&w ... 2.50

MODNIKS
GOLD KEY

❑1, ca. 1967 ... 8.00
❑2 ... 4.00

MOD WHEELS
GOLD KEY

❑1, Feb 1971 ... 30.00
❑2, May 1971 ... 20.00
❑3, Aug 1971 A: Rick Bannon. A: Road Stompers. A: Digger. A: Cube. A: Bit Bannon. A: Big Al. A: 'Scot. A: Van Packard. A: Wheels Williams ... 20.00
❑4, Nov 1971 ... 20.00
❑5, Feb 1972 ... 20.00
❑6, Jun 1972 ... 20.00
❑7, Jan 1973 ... 20.00
❑8, Apr 1973 ... 20.00
❑9, Jul 1973, DS (a) ... 20.00
❑10, Oct 1973 ... 15.00
❑11, Jan 1974 ... 15.00
❑12, Apr 1974 ... 15.00
❑13, Jul 1974 ... 15.00
❑14, Oct 1974 ... 15.00
❑15, Jan 1975 ... 15.00
❑16, Apr 1975 ... 15.00
❑17, Jul 1975 ... 10.00
❑18, Oct 1976 ... 10.00
❑19, Jan 1976 ... 10.00

MOEBIUS COMICS
CALIBER

❑1, May 1996 ... 3.00
❑2, Jul 1996 ... 3.00
❑3, Sep 1996 ... 3.00
❑4, Nov 1996 ... 3.00
❑5, Jan 1997 ... 3.00
❑6, Mar 1997 ... 3.00

MOEBIUS: EXOTICS
DARK HORSE

❑1; prestige format ... 6.95

MOEBIUS: H.P.'S ROCK CITY
DARK HORSE

❑1 1996; smaller than a normal comic book; squarebound ... 7.95

N-MINT

MOEBIUS: MADWOMAN OF THE SACRED HEART
DARK HORSE

❑1 ... 12.95

MOEBIUS: THE MAN FROM THE CIGURI
DARK HORSE

❑1 1996, smaller than a normal comic book; squarebound ... 7.95

MOGOBI DESERT RATS
STUDIO 91

❑1, Jan 1991 ... 2.25

MOJO ACTION COMPANION UNIT
EXCLAIM

❑1, Spr 1997, b&w ... 2.75

MOJO MECHANICS
SYNDICATE

❑1, b&w ... 2.95
❑2 ... 2.95

MOMENT OF SILENCE
MARVEL

❑1, Feb 2002 ARo, JR2 (a) ... 4.00

MOMENT OF FREEDOM
CALIBER / TOME

❑nn, ca. 1997, b&w ... 4.95

MONA
KITCHEN SINK

❑1 ... 4.95

MONARCHY
DC / WILDSTORM

❑1, Apr 2001 ... 2.50
❑2, Jun 2001 ... 2.50
❑3, Jul 2001 ... 2.50
❑4, Aug 2001 ... 2.50
❑5, Sep 2001 ... 2.50
❑6, Sep 2001 ... 2.50
❑7, Oct 2001 ... 2.50
❑8, Nov 2001 ... 2.50
❑9, Dec 2001 ... 2.50
❑10, Jan 2002 ... 2.50
❑11, Feb 2002 ... 2.50
❑12, Mar 2002 ... 2.50

MONDO 3-D
3-D ZONE

❑1 ... 3.95

MONDO BONDO
LCD

❑1 ... 2.95

MONEY TALKS
SLAVE LABOR

❑1, Jun 1996 ... 3.50
❑2, Aug 1996 ... 2.95
❑3, Oct 1996 ... 2.95
❑4, Dec 1996 ... 2.95
❑5, Feb 1997 ... 2.95

MONGREL
NORTHSTAR

❑1/A, Dec 1994, b&w ... 3.95
❑2 ... 3.95
❑3 ... 3.95

N-MINT

MONICA'S STORY
ALTERNATIVE

❑1, Feb 1999, b&w ... 3.50

MONKEES
GOLD KEY

❑1, Mar 1967, based on TV series ... 45.00
❑2, May 1967 ... 30.00
❑3, Jul 1967 ... 24.00
❑4, Sep 1967 ... 20.00
❑5, Oct 1967 ... 20.00
❑6, Nov 1967 ... 18.00
❑7, Dec 1967 ... 18.00
❑8, Jan 1968 ... 18.00
❑9, Feb 1968 ... 18.00
❑10, Mar 1968 ... 18.00
❑11, May 1968 ... 12.00
❑12, Jun 1968 ... 12.00
❑13, Jul 1968 ... 12.00
❑14, Aug 1968 ... 12.00
❑15, Sep 1968 ... 12.00
❑16 1969 ... 12.00
❑17 1969 ... 12.00

MONKEY BUSINESS
PARODY

❑1, b&w ... 2.50
❑2; Ren & Stimpy parody ... 2.50

MONKEYMAN AND O'BRIEN
DARK HORSE / LEGEND

❑1, Jul 1996 V: Shrewmanoid ... 3.50
❑2, Aug 1996 V: Froglodytes ... 3.00
❑3, Sep 1996 A: Shrewmanoid. V: Quash ... 2.95
❑Special 1, Feb 1996 O: Monkeyman and O'Brien ... 2.95

MONKEY ON A WAGON VS. LEMUR ON A BIG WHEEL
ALIAS

❑1, Oct 2005 ... 4.00

MONNGA
DAIKAIJU

❑1, Aug 1995 ... 3.95

MONOLITH
COMICO

❑1, Oct 1991 ... 2.50
❑2, Nov 1991 ... 2.50
❑3 ... 2.50
❑4, Aug 1992 ... 2.50

MONOLITH (DC)
DC

❑1, Apr 2004 ... 4.00
❑2, May 2004 (c) ... 2.95
❑3, Jun 2004 ... 2.95
❑4, Jul 2004 ... 2.95
❑5, Aug 2004 ... 2.95
❑6, Sep 2004 ... 2.95
❑7, Oct 2004 ... 2.95
❑8, Nov 2004 ... 2.95
❑9, Dec 2004 ... 2.95
❑10, Jan 2005 ... 2.95
❑11, Feb 2005 ... 2.95
❑12, Mar 2005 ... 2.95

Other grades: Multiply price above by 5/6 for VF/NM • 2/3 for VERY FINE • 1/3 for FINE • 1/5 for VERY GOOD • 1/8 for GOOD

MONOLITH (LAST GASP)
Last Gasp
❑1 .... 3.00

MONROE
Conquest
❑1, b&w; poster; cards 4.95

MONSTER (BUTLER & HOGG'S...)
Slave Labor
❑1, b&w 2.95

MONSTER
Ring
❑1 .... 2.00

MONSTER BOY
Monster
❑1, b&w 2.50

MONSTER BOY COMICS
Slave Labor
❑1, Sep 1997, b&w 2.95
❑2, Dec 1997, b&w 2.95
❑3 .... 2.95

MONSTER CLUB
APComics
❑1, ca. 2002 .... 6.00
❑2 .... 5.00
❑3 .... 3.50
❑4 .... 3.50
❑5 .... 3.50
❑6 .... 3.50
❑7 .... 3.50
❑8 .... 3.50
❑9 .... 3.50

MONSTER CLUB (VOL. 2)
APComics
❑0, ca. 2004 .... 3.00
❑1, ca. 2004 .... 3.50
❑2 2004 .... 3.50
❑3 2004 .... 3.50
❑4 2004 .... 3.50
❑5 2004 .... 3.50

MONSTER FIGHTERS INC.
Image
❑1, Apr 1999 .... 3.50

MONSTER FIGHTERS INC.: THE BLACK BOOK
Image
❑1, Sep 2000 .... 3.50

MONSTER FIGHTERS INC.: THE GHOSTS OF CHRISTMAS
Image
❑1, Dec 1999 .... 3.95

MONSTER FRAT HOUSE
Eternity
❑1, Oct 1989, b&w 2.25

MONSTER HOUSE
Idea & Design Works
❑1, Jun 2006 .... 4.95

MONSTER IN MY POCKET
Harvey
❑1, Mar 1991 EC (a) 1.50
❑2, May 1991; The Exterminator 1.50
❑3, Jul 1991 GK (a) 1.50
❑4, Sep 1991 GK (a) 1.50

MONSTER ISLAND
Compass
❑1, Nov 1998, b&w; wraparound cover 3.95

MONSTER LOVE
Kitchen Sink
❑1 .... 2.50

MONSTERMAN
Image
❑1, Sep 1997, b&w 2.95

MONSTER MASSACRE
Atomeka
❑1 .... 7.95

MONSTER MASSACRE SPECIAL
Blackball
❑1 .... 2.50

MONSTER MATINEE
Chaos!
❑1, Oct 1997; monster pin-ups; commentary by Forrest J. Ackerman 2.50
❑1/Variant, Oct 1997; premium edition; alternate logoless cover; monster pin-ups; commentary by Forrest J. Ackerman 2.50
❑2, Oct 1997; monster pin-ups; commentary by Forrest J. Ackerman 2.50
❑3, Oct 1997; monster pin-ups; commentary by Forrest J. Ackerman 2.50

MONSTER MENACE
Marvel
❑1, Dec 1993; SL (w); SD (a); Reprints 1.50
❑2, Jan 1994; SD (a); Reprints 1.50
❑3, Feb 1994 SD (a) 1.50
❑4, Mar 1994 SD, JK (a) 1.50

MONSTERMEN (GARY GIANNI'S...)
Dark Horse
❑1, Aug 1999 .... 2.50

MONSTER POSSE
Adventure
❑1, b&w 2.50
❑2, Nov 1992 .... 2.50
❑3 .... 2.50

MONSTERS FROM OUTER SPACE
Adventure
❑1, Dec 1992, b&w 2.50
❑2, b&w 2.50
❑3, b&w 2.50

MONSTERS ON THE PROWL
Marvel
❑9, Feb 1971, Title changes to Monsters on the Prowl; Series continued from Chamber of Darkness #8 .... 25.00
❑10, Apr 1971, Reprints 15.00
❑11, Jun 1971, Reprints 15.00
❑12, Aug 1971, Reprints 15.00
❑13, Oct 1971 .... 15.00
❑14, Dec 1971 .... 15.00
❑15, Feb 1972 .... 15.00
❑16, Apr 1972, JSe (a); King Kull 18.00
❑17, Jun 1972 .... 12.00
❑18, Aug 1972 .... 12.00
❑19, Oct 1972 .... 12.00
❑20, Dec 1972, SD (a) 12.00
❑21, Feb 1973 .... 12.00
❑22, Apr 1973 .... 12.00
❑23, Jun 1973 .... 12.00
❑24, Aug 1973 .... 12.00
❑25, Sep 1973 .... 12.00
❑26, Oct 1973 .... 12.00
❑27, Nov 1974 .... 12.00
❑28, Jun 1975 .... 12.00
❑29, Aug 1975 .... 12.00
❑30, Oct 1975 .... 12.00

MONSTERS TO LAUGH WITH
Marvel
❑1, ca. 1964 .... 40.00
❑2, ca. 1964 .... 30.00
❑3, ca. 1965 .... 30.00

MONSTERS UNLEASHED
Marvel
❑1, Jul 1973, b&w; magazine 40.00
❑2, Sep 1973; Frankenstein 18.00
❑3, Nov 1973; Frankenstein, Man-Thing, Son of Satan 15.00
❑4, Jan 1974; Frankenstein 15.00
❑5, Mar 1974; Frankenstein, Man-Thing 15.00
❑6, May 1974; Frankenstein, Werewolf 10.00
❑7, Jul 1974; Frankenstein, Werewolf 10.00
❑8, Sep 1974; Frankenstein, Man-Thing 10.00
❑9, Nov 1974; Frankenstein, Man-Thing, Wendigo 7.00
❑10, Jan 1975; Frankenstein, Tigra 7.00
❑11, Mar 1975; Gabriel 7.00
❑Annual 1, ca. 1975; Reprints 12.00

MONSTER WAR: MAGDALENA VS. DRACULA
Image
❑1, ca. 2005 .... 2.99

MONSTER WAR: TOMB RAIDER VS. WOLF MEN
Image
❑2, Jul 2005 .... 2.99

MONSTER WAR: WITCHBLADE VS. FRANKENSTEIN
Image
❑3/A cover, Sep 2005; Joyce Chin cover 2.99
❑3/B cover, Sep 2005; Richard Ebas cover 2.99

MONSTER WAR: DARKNESS VS. MR. HYDE
Image
❑4/A, Oct 2005; Richard Ebas cover 2.99
❑4/B, Oct 2005; Joyce Chin cover 2.99

MONSTER WORLD
DC / Wildstorm
❑1, Jul 2001 .... 2.50
❑2, Aug 2001 .... 2.50
❑3, Sep 2001 .... 2.50
❑4, Oct 2001 .... 2.95

MONSTROSITY
Slap Happy
❑1, Oct 1998, b&w 4.95

MOON BEAST
Avalon
❑1 .... 2.95

MOONCHILD
Forbidden Fruit
❑1, b&w 2.95
❑2, b&w 2.95

MOON CHILD (VOL. 2)
Forbidden Fruit
❑1, b&w 3.50
❑2, b&w 3.50
❑3, b&w 3.50

MOONFIGHTING
Harrier
❑1, Mar 1988, b&w 1.95

MOON KNIGHT (1ST SERIES)
Marvel
❑1, Nov 1980, BSz (a); O: Moon Knight 10.00
❑2, Dec 1980, BSz (a) 7.00
❑3, Jan 1981, BSz (a) 5.00
❑4, Feb 1981, BSz (a) 5.00
❑5, Mar 1981, BSz (a) 2.50
❑6, Apr 1981, BSz (a) 2.50
❑7, May 1981, BSz (a) 2.50
❑8, Jun 1981, BSz (a); V: Moon Kings 2.50
❑9, Jul 1981, BSz, FM (a); V: Midnight Man 2.50
❑10, Aug 1981, BSz (a); V: Midnight Man 2.50
❑11, Sep 1981, BSz (a); V: Creed 2.50
❑12, Oct 1981, BSz, FM (a) 2.50
❑13, Nov 1981, BSz, FM (a); A: Daredevil 2.50
❑14, Dec 1981, BSz (a) 2.50
❑15, Jan 1982; FM (c); BSz, FM (a); A: Thing. direct 2.50
❑16, Feb 1982 BSz (c); BSz (a); V: Blacksmith 2.50
❑17, Mar 1982 BSz (a) 2.50
❑18, Apr 1982 BSz (a); V: Slayers Elite 2.50
❑19, May 1982 BSz (a); V: Arsenal 2.50
❑20, Jun 1982 BSz (a); V: Arsenal 2.50
❑21, Jul 1982 BSz (c); BSz (a) 2.00
❑22, Aug 1982 BSz (a) 2.00
❑23, Sep 1982 BSz (a) 2.00
❑24, Oct 1982 BSz (a) 2.00
❑25, Nov 1982; double-sized BSz (a) 2.50
❑26, Dec 1982 BSz (a) 2.00
❑27, Jan 1983 FM (c) 2.00
❑28, Feb 1983 BSz (a) 2.00
❑29, Mar 1983 BSz (a) 2.00
❑30, Apr 1983 BSz (a) 2.00
❑31, May 1983 BSz (c); BSz, KN (a) 2.00
❑32, Jul 1983 BSz (c); BSz, KN (a) 2.00
❑33, Sep 1983 BSz (c); BSz, KN (a) 2.00
❑34, Nov 1983 BSz (c); RHo, BSz (a) 2.00
❑35, Jan 1984; double-sized KN (a); A: X-Men 2.50
❑36, Mar 1984 .... 2.00
❑37, May 1984 BSz (a) 2.00
❑38, Jul 1984 .... 2.00

MOON KNIGHT (2ND SERIES)
Marvel
❑1, Jun 1985; Double-size O: Moon Knight 2.50
❑2, Aug 1985 .... 2.00

Mutant X (1st series)

It's just too complicated to explain
©Marvel

My Favorite Martian

1960s era's Mork, or ALF, or Third Rock
©Gold Key

My Greatest Adventure

Adventure title gives Doom Patrol its start
©DC

Mys-Tech Wars

Includes more characters than a keyboard
©Marvel

Mystery in Space

Infantino's Adam Strange was the draw
©DC

N-MINT

❑3, Sep 1985 .... 2.00
❑4, Oct 1985 .... 2.00
❑5, Nov 1985 .... 2.00
❑6, Dec 1985, Painted cover 2.00

MOON KNIGHT (3RD SERIES)
MARVEL

❑1, Jan 1998 .... 2.50
❑2, Feb 1998 .... 2.50
❑3, Mar 1998 .... 2.50
❑4, Apr 1998 .... 2.50

MOON KNIGHT (4TH SERIES)
MARVEL

❑1, Jan 1999; says Feb on cover, Jan in indicia 2.99
❑2, Feb 1999 .... 2.99
❑3, Feb 1999 .... 2.99
❑4, Feb 1999 .... 2.99

MOON KNIGHT: DIVIDED WE FALL
MARVEL

❑1, ca. 1992, b&w 4.95

MOON KNIGHT (5TH SERIES)
MARVEL

❑1, Jun 2006 .... 2.99
❑2, Jul 2006 .... 2.99
❑3, Sep 2006 .... 2.99

MOON KNIGHT SPECIAL
MARVEL

❑1; Shang-Chi 2.50

MOON KNIGHT SPECIAL EDITION
MARVEL

❑1, Nov 1983; Reprints from Hulk (magazine) BSz (a) 2.50
❑2, Dec 1983; BSz (a); Reprints 2.50
❑3, Jan 1984; BSz (a); Reprints 2.50

MOONSHADOW
MARVEL / EPIC

❑1, Mar 1985 O: Moonshadow 3.50
❑2, May 1985 .... 2.50
❑3, Jul 1985 .... 2.50
❑4, Sep 1985 .... 2.00
❑5, Nov 1985 .... 2.00
❑6, Jan 1986 .... 2.00
❑7, Mar 1986 .... 2.00
❑8, Jun 1986 .... 2.00
❑9, Aug 1986 .... 2.00
❑10, Oct 1986 .... 2.00
❑11, Jan 1987 O: Moonshadow 2.00
❑12, Feb 1987 .... 2.00

MOONSHADOW (VERTIGO)
DC / VERTIGO

❑1, Sep 1994, O: Moonshadow 3.00
❑2, Oct 1994 .... 2.50
❑3, Nov 1994 .... 2.50
❑4, Dec 1994 .... 2.50
❑5, Jan 1995 .... 2.50
❑6, Feb 1995 .... 2.25
❑7, Mar 1995 .... 2.25
❑8, Apr 1995 .... 2.25
❑9, May 1995 .... 2.25
❑10, Jun 1995 .... 2.25
❑11, Jul 1995, O: Moonshadow 2.25
❑12, Aug 1995 .... 2.95

N-MINT

MOON SHOT, THE FLIGHT OF APOLLO 12
PEPPER PIKE GRAPHIX

❑1, Jun 1994 .... 2.95

MOONSTONE MONSTERS: ZOMBIES
MOONSTONE

❑1, Jun 2005 .... 2.95

MOONSTRUCK
WHITE WOLF

❑1, May 1987 .... 2.00

MOONTRAP
CALIBER

❑1, b&w 2.00

MOONWALKER 3-D
BLACKTHORNE

❑1 .... 2.50

MOORDAM CHRISTMAS COMICS
MOORDAM

❑1, Dec 1999 .... 2.95

MORA
IMAGE

❑1, Mar 2005 .... 2.95
❑2, Apr 2005 .... 2.95
❑3 2005 .... 2.95
❑4, Dec 2005 ....

MORBID ANGEL
LONDON NIGHT

❑½, Jul 1996 .... 3.00
❑1 .... 3.00

MORBID ANGEL: PENANCE
LONDON NIGHT

❑1, Sep 1996 .... 3.95

MORBIUS REVISITED
MARVEL

❑1, Aug 1993; Reprints Fear #27 .... 2.00
❑2, Sep 1993; FR (a); Reprints Fear #28 .... 2.00
❑3, Oct 1993; DH (a); A: Helleyes. A: Simon Stroud. Reprints Fear #29 .... 2.00
❑4, Nov 1993; GE (a); Reprints Fear #30 .... 2.00
❑5, Dec 1993; Reprints Fear #31 .... 2.00

MORBIUS: THE LIVING VAMPIRE
MARVEL

❑1, Sep 1992; Without poster 1.50
❑1/CS, Sep 1992; Polybagged w/poster 3.00
❑2, Oct 1992 .... 2.00
❑3, Nov 1992 .... 2.00
❑4, Dec 1992 .... 2.00
❑5, Jan 1993 .... 2.00
❑6, Feb 1993 .... 1.75
❑7, Mar 1993 .... 1.75
❑8, Apr 1993 .... 1.75
❑9, May 1993 .... 1.75
❑10, Jun 1993 .... 1.75
❑11, Jul 1993 .... 1.75
❑12, Aug 1993; Double cover 2.25
❑13, Sep 1993 .... 1.75
❑14, Oct 1993 .... 1.75
❑15, Nov 1993 .... 1.75
❑16, Dec 1993; Neon ink/matte finish cover 1.75
❑17, Jan 1994; Spot-varnished cover 1.75
❑18, Feb 1994 .... 1.75

N-MINT

❑19, Mar 1994 .... 1.75
❑20, Apr 1994 .... 1.75
❑21, May 1994 .... 1.75
❑22, Jun 1994 .... 1.95
❑23, Jul 1994 .... 1.95
❑24, Aug 1994 .... 1.95
❑25, Sep 1994; Giant-size 2.50
❑26, Oct 1994 .... 1.95
❑27, Nov 1994 .... 1.95
❑28, Dec 1994 .... 1.95
❑29, Jan 1995 .... 1.95
❑30, Feb 1995 .... 1.95
❑31, Mar 1995 .... 1.95
❑32, Apr 1995 .... 1.95

MORE FETISH
BONEYARD

❑1, Nov 1993 .... 2.95

MORE SECRET ORIGINS REPLICA EDITION
DC

❑1, Dec 1999; reprints 80-Page Giant #8 .... 4.95

MORE TALES FROM GIMBLEY
HARRIER

❑1, Feb 1988 .... 1.95

MORE TALES FROM SLEAZE CASTLE
GRATUITOUS BUNNY

❑1 .... 4.00
❑2 .... 3.00
❑3 1990 .... 3.00
❑4, Jan 1991 .... 3.00
❑5, Jan 1992 .... 3.00
❑6, Jan 1993 .... 3.00

MORE THAN MORTAL
LIAR

❑1, Jun 1997 .... 3.00
❑1/2nd, Jun 1997 .... 2.95
❑2, Sep 1997 .... 3.00
❑2/Variant, Sep 1997; logoless cover 2.95
❑3, Dec 1997 .... 3.00
❑4, Apr 1998 .... 3.00
❑5, Dec 1999 .... 3.00
❑6, Mar 2000 .... 2.95

MORE THAN MORTAL/ LADY PENDRAGON
IMAGE

❑1, Jun 1999 .... 2.50
❑1/A, Jun 1999; alternate cover 3.00

MORE THAN MORTAL: OTHERWORLDS
IMAGE

❑1, Jul 1999 .... 3.00
❑1/A, Jul 1999; alternate cover 3.00
❑2, Aug 1999; Woman and man kneeling on cover, large figure standing behind 3.00
❑2/A, Aug 1999; alternate cover 3.00
❑3, Oct 1999; Woman holding sword on cover, red top left background 3.00
❑3/A, Oct 1999; alternate cover 3.00
❑4, Dec 1999 .... 3.00

MORE THAN MORTAL: SAGAS
LIAR

❑1, Aug 1998 O: Morlock. 1: Morlock 2.95

❑1/A, Aug 1998; variant cover for New Dimension Comics ... 3.00
❑2, Oct 1998 ... 2.95
❑3, Dec 1998 ... 2.95

MORE THAN MORTAL: TRUTHS & LEGENDS
LIAR

❑1, Jun 1998; Cover has man with glowing eye at bow of ship ... 2.95
❑1/A, Jun 1998; Variant edition ... 3.00
❑1/Ltd., Jun 1998; Variant edition ... 4.00
❑2, Aug 1998 ... 2.95
❑3, Oct 1998 ... 2.95
❑4, Jan 1999 ... 2.95
❑5, Apr 1999 ... 2.95

MORE TRASH FROM MAD
E.C.

❑1, ca. 1958, Magazine-sized; no number ... 275.00
❑2, ca. 1959, Magazine-sized; has Mad labels foldout ... 175.00
❑3, ca. 1960, Magazine-sized; has Mad textbook cover inserts ... 175.00
❑4, ca. 1961, Magazine-sized ... 175.00
❑5, ca. 1962, Magazine-sized; has window sticker inserts ... 175.00
❑6, ca. 1963, Magazine-sized; has color TV Guide parody insert ... 175.00
❑7, ca. 1964, Magazine-sized ... 150.00
❑8, ca. 1965, Magazine-sized ... 150.00
❑9, ca. 1966, Magazine-sized ... 150.00
❑10, ca. 1967, Magazine-sized ... 150.00
❑11, ca. 1968, Magazine-sized ... 150.00
❑12, ca. 1969, b&w; Magazine-sized; has "pocket medals" ... 150.00

MORLOCKS
MARVEL

❑1, Jun 2002 ... 2.50
❑2, Jul 2002 ... 2.50
❑3, Aug 2002 ... 2.50
❑4, Sep 2002 ... 2.50

MORLOCK 2001
ATLAS-SEABOARD

❑1, Feb 1975 AM (a); O: Morlock ... 9.00
❑2, Apr 1975 AM (a) ... 6.00
❑3, Jul 1975 AM, SD, BWr (a); O: Midnight Men ... 8.00

MORNING GLORY
RADIO

❑1, Nov 1998, b&w ... 2.95
❑2, Dec 1998, b&w ... 2.95
❑3, Jan 1999, b&w ... 2.95
❑4 ... 2.95
❑5, May 1999, b&w ... 2.95

MORNINGSTAR SPECIAL
TRIDENT

❑1, Apr 1990, b&w ... 2.50

MORPHING PERIOD
SHANDA

❑1 ... 4.95

MORPHOS THE SHAPECHANGER
DARK HORSE

❑1, Jul 1996; prestige format ... 4.95

MORPHS
GRAPHXPRESS

❑1 ... 2.00
❑2, Jul 1987 ... 2.00
❑3 ... 2.00
❑4 ... 2.00

MORRIGAN (DIMENSION X)
DIMENSION X

❑1, Aug 1993, b&w ... 2.75

MORRIGAN (SIRIUS)
SIRIUS

❑1, Jul 1997 ... 2.95

MORTAL COILS: BLOODLINES
RED EYE

❑1, Aug 2002 ... 2.50

MORTAL KOMBAT
MALIBU

❑1, Jul 1994, b&w; Blood and Thunder ... 3.00
❑1/A, Jul 1994, b&w; variant cover (Mortal Kombat logo) ... 3.00
❑2, Aug 1994, b&w; variant cover (Mortal Kombat logo); Blood and Thunder ... 3.00
❑3, Sep 1994, b&w; variant cover (Mortal Kombat logo); Blood and Thunder ... 3.00
❑4, Oct 1994, b&w; variant cover (Mortal Kombat logo); Blood and Thunder ... 3.00
❑5, Nov 1994, b&w; variant cover (Mortal Kombat logo); Blood and Thunder ... 3.00
❑6, Dec 1994, b&w; variant cover (Mortal Kombat logo) ... 3.00

MORTAL KOMBAT: BARAKA
MALIBU

❑1, ca. 1995 ... 2.95

MORTAL KOMBAT: BATTLEWAVE
MALIBU

❑1, ca. 1995 ... 3.00
❑2, Mar 1995 ... 3.00
❑3, ca. 1995 ... 3.00
❑4, ca. 1995 ... 3.00
❑5, ca. 1995 ... 3.00
❑6, ca. 1995 ... 3.00

MORTAL KOMBAT: GORO, PRINCE OF PAIN
MALIBU

❑1, Sep 1994 ... 2.95
❑2, Oct 1994 ... 2.95
❑3, Nov 1994 ... 2.95

MORTAL KOMBAT: KITANA & MILEENA
MALIBU

❑1, ca. 1995 ... 2.95

MORTAL KOMBAT: KUNG LAO
MALIBU

❑1, ca. 1995 ... 2.95

MORTAL KOMBAT: RAYDEN & KANO
MALIBU

❑1, ca. 1995 ... 2.95
❑2, Apr 1995 ... 2.95
❑3 ... 2.95

MORTAL KOMBAT SPECIAL EDITION
MALIBU

❑1, Nov 1994 ... 2.95
❑2 1994 ... 2.95

MORTAL KOMBAT: TOURNAMENT EDITION
MALIBU

❑1, Dec 1994 ... 2.25
❑2 1995 ... 2.25

MORTAL KOMBAT U.S. SPECIAL FORCES
MALIBU

❑1, Jan 1995 ... 3.50
❑2, Feb 1995 ... 3.50

MORTAL SOULS
AVATAR

❑1/A, Apr 2002 ... 3.50

MORTAR MAN
MARSHALL COMICS

❑1, May 1993, b&w ... 1.95
❑2, ca. 1993, b&w ... 1.95
❑3, ca. 1993 ... 1.95

MORTIGAN GOTH: IMMORTALIS
MARVEL

❑1, Sep 1993 ... 1.95
❑1/Variant, Sep 1993; foil cover ... 2.95
❑2, Oct 1993 ... 1.95
❑3, Jan 1994 ... 1.95
❑4, Mar 1994 ... 1.95

MORT THE DEAD TEENAGER
MARVEL

❑1, Nov 1992 ... 1.75
❑2, Dec 1992 ... 1.75
❑3, Feb 1993 ... 1.75
❑4, Mar 1993 ... 1.75

MORTY THE DOG (MU)
MU

❑1, b&w; digest ... 3.95
❑2, Spr 1991, b&w; digest ... 3.95

MORTY THE DOG (STARHEAD)
STARHEAD

❑1 ... 2.00

MOSAIC
SIRIUS

❑1/A, Mar 1999 ... 2.95
❑1/B, Mar 1999; alternate cover; smaller logos ... 2.95
❑2, Apr 1999 ... 2.95
❑3, May 1999 ... 2.95
❑4, Jun 1999 ... 2.95
❑5, Jul 1999 ... 2.95

MOSAIC: HELL CITY RIPPER
SIRIUS

❑1 ... 2.95
❑1/Variant; alternate cover ... 2.95

MOSTLY WANTED
WILDSTORM

❑1, Jul 2000 ... 2.50
❑2, Aug 2000 ... 2.50
❑3, Sep 2000 ... 2.50
❑4, Nov 2000 ... 2.50

MOTH (STEVE RUDE'S)
DARK HORSE

❑1, Apr 2004 ... 2.99
❑2, May 2004 ... 2.99
❑3, Aug 2004 ... 2.99
❑4, Oct 2004 ... 3.00

MOTHERLESS CHILD
KITCHEN SINK

❑1 ... 2.95

MOTHER'S OATS COMIX
RIP OFF

❑1 ... 5.00
❑2 ... 3.00

MOTHER SUPERION
ANTARCTIC

❑1, Jul 1997 ... 2.95

MOTHER TERESA OF CALCUTTA
MARVEL

❑1, ca. 1984 ... 1.50

MOTH, THE (STEVE RUDE'S) DOUBLE-SIZED SPECIAL
DARK HORSE

❑1, May 2004 ... 4.95

MOTLEY STORIES
DIVISION

❑1, b&w ... 2.75

MOTORBIKE PUPPIES
DARK ZULU LIES

❑1, Jun 1992 ... 2.50
❑2; Never published? ... 2.50

MOTORHEAD
DARK HORSE

❑1, Aug 1995 ... 2.50
❑2, Sep 1995 ... 2.50
❑3, Oct 1995 ... 2.50
❑4, Nov 1995 ... 2.50
❑5, Dec 1995 ... 2.50
❑6, Jan 1996 ... 2.50
❑Special 1, Mar 1994 ... 3.95

MOTORMOUTH
MARVEL

❑1, Jun 1992 1: Motormouth ... 2.00
❑2, Jul 1992 ... 1.75
❑3, Aug 1992; Punisher ... 1.75
❑4, Sep 1992 ... 1.75
❑5, Oct 1992 A: Punisher ... 1.75
❑6, Nov 1992; Title changes to Motormouth & Killpower ... 1.75
❑7, Dec 1992 A: Cable ... 1.75
❑8, Jan 1993 ... 1.75
❑9, Feb 1993 ... 1.75
❑10, Apr 1993 ... 1.75
❑11, Apr 1993 ... 1.75
❑12, May 1993 ... 1.75

MOUNTAIN
UNDERGROUND

❑1, Flipbook High School Funnies ... 3.00

MOUNTAIN WORLD
ICICLE RIDGE

❑1, b&w ... 2.00

MOUSE GUARD
ARCHAIA STUDIOS PRESS

❑1, Feb 2006 ... 100.00
❑1/2nd, Feb 2006 ... 25.00
❑2, Apr 2006 ... 55.00

Other grades: Multiply price above by 5/6 for VF/NM • 2/3 for VERY FINE • 1/3 for FINE • 1/5 for VERY GOOD • 1/8 for GOOD

Mystic (CrossGen)

Another of the first four CrossGen titles

©CrossGen

'Nam

Marvel's retelling of the Vietnam War

©Marvel

Names of Magic

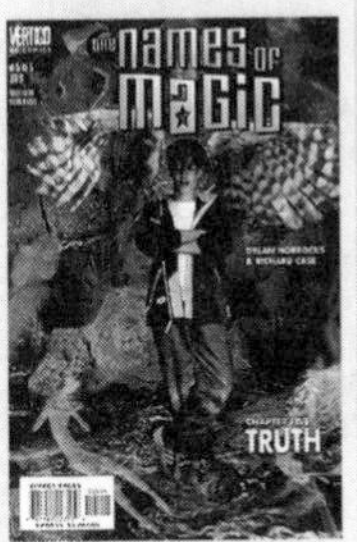

Continuing stories featuring Neil Gaiman characters

©DC

Namor

Bill Jemas' solo Subby title didn't last long

©Marvel

Namor, The Sub-Mariner

Old Fishface returns as a businessman

©Marvel

N-MINT

MOUSE ON THE MOON
DELL

❑1, Oct 1963 ... 15.00

MOVIE STAR NEWS
PURE IMAGINATION

❑1; DSt (c); Bettie Page photos ... 6.00

MOXI
LIGHTNING

❑1, Jul 1996 ... 3.00

MOXI'S FRIENDS: BOBBY JOE & NITRO
LIGHTNING

❑1, Sep 1996 ... 2.75

MOXI: STRANGE DAZE
LIGHTNING

❑1, Nov 1996, b&w ... 3.00

M. REX
IMAGE

❑1, Nov 1999 ... 2.95
❑1/A, Nov 1999; Alternate cover has large figure in background, boy, monkey on waterbike in foreground ... 2.95
❑2, Dec 1999 ... 2.95
❑Ashcan 1/A, Jul 1999; Flying car on cover ... 5.00
❑Ashcan 1/B, Jul 1999; Blue background on cover ... 5.00

MR. T
APCOMICS

❑1, Jun 2005 ... 3.50

MS. ANTI-SOCIAL
HELPLESS ANGER

❑1, b&w ... 1.75

MS. CYANIDE & ICE
BLACK OUT

❑0 ... 2.95
❑1; Sly & Furious preview ... 2.95

MS. FANTASTIC
CONQUEST

❑1, b&w ... 2.95
❑2, b&w ... 2.95
❑3, b&w ... 2.95
❑4, b&w ... 2.95

MS. FANTASTIC CLASSICS
CONQUEST

❑1, b&w ... 2.95

MS. FORTUNE
IMAGE

❑1, Jan 1998, b&w ... 2.95

MS. MARVEL
MARVEL

❑1, Jan 1977, JB (a); 1: Ms. Marvel ... 8.00
❑2, Feb 1977 ... 3.00
❑3, Mar 1977 ... 3.00
❑4, Apr 1977 ... 2.50
❑5, May 1977, A: Vision ... 2.50
❑6, Jun 1977 ... 2.50
❑6/35 cent, Jun 1977, 35 cent regional variant ... 15.00
❑7, Jul 1977 V: Modok. V: M.O.D.O.K. ... 2.50
❑7/35 cent, Jul 1977, 35 cent regional variant ... 15.00

N-MINT

❑8, Aug 1977 ... 2.50
❑8/35 cent, Aug 1977, 35 cent regional variant ... 15.00
❑9, Sep 1977, 1: Deathbird ... 2.50
❑9/35 cent, Sep 1977, 35 cent regional variant ... 15.00
❑10, Oct 1977 ... 2.50
❑10/35 cent, Oct 1977, 35 cent regional variant ... 15.00
❑11, Nov 1977 ... 2.00
❑12, Dec 1977, V: Hecate ... 2.00
❑13, Jan 1978 ... 2.00
❑14, Feb 1978, 1: Steeplejack II (Maxwell Plumm) ... 2.00
❑15, Mar 1978 ... 2.00
❑16, Apr 1978, 1: Mystique (cameo) . 15.00
❑17, May 1978 ... 8.00
❑18, Jun 1978, 1: Mystique (full appearance) ... 40.00
❑19, Aug 1978, A: Captain Marvel ... 2.50
❑20, Oct 1978, New costume ... 2.00
❑21, Dec 1978 ... 2.00
❑22, Feb 1979 ... 2.00
❑23, Apr 1979 ... 2.00

MS. MARVEL (2ND SERIES)
MARVEL

❑1, May 2006 ... 2.99
❑2, Jun 2006 ... 2.99
❑3, Jul 2006 ... 2.99
❑4, Aug 2006 ... 2.99
❑5, Sep 2006 ... 2.99

MS. MYSTIC (PACIFIC)
PACIFIC

❑1, Oct 1982; NA (w); NA (a); O: Ms. Mystic. origin ... 4.00
❑2, Feb 1984 NA (w); NA (a); O: Ayre. O: Fyre. O: Watr. O: Urth. 1: Ayre. 1: Fyre. 1: Watr. 1: Urth. 1: Urth 4 .. 3.00

MS. MYSTIC (CONTINUITY)
CONTINUITY

❑1, Mar 1988; reprints Ms. Mystic (Pacific) #1 ... 2.00
❑2, Jun 1988; reprints Ms. Mystic (Pacific) #2 ... 2.00
❑3, Jan 1989 ... 2.00
❑4, May 1989 ... 2.00
❑5, Aug 1990; Comics Code ... 2.00
❑6, Nov 1990; Comics Code ... 2.00
❑7, Aug 1991 ... 2.00
❑8, Mar 1992 ... 2.00
❑9, May 1992 ... 2.00

MS. MYSTIC (VOL. 2)
CONTINUITY

❑1, Oct 1993 ... 2.50
❑2, Nov 1993 ... 2.50
❑3, Dec 1993 ... 2.50
❑4, Jan 1994, b&w; Orders were taken for #5 and #6 but they never appeared ... 2.50

MS. MYSTIC DEATHWATCH 2000
CONTINUITY

❑1, May 1993; Stereo diffusion cover ... 2.50
❑2, Jun 1993; trading card ... 2.50
❑3, Aug 1993; trading card; drops Deathwatch 2000 from indicia ... 2.50

N-MINT

MS. PMS
AAAAHH!!

❑0, Mar 1992 ... 2.50
❑1 ... 2.50

MS. QUOTED TALES
CHANCE

❑1, Feb 1983 ... 1.50

MS. TREE
ECLIPSE

❑1, Apr 1983; Eclipse publishes ... 4.00
❑2, Jun 1983 ... 2.75
❑3, Aug 1983 ... 2.75
❑4, Oct 1983 ... 2.50
❑5, Nov 1983 ... 2.50
❑6, Feb 1984 ... 2.00
❑7, Apr 1984 ... 2.00
❑8, May 1984 ... 2.00
❑9, Jul 1984 ... 2.00
❑10, Aug 1984; Aardvark-Vanaheim begins as publisher ... 2.00
❑11, Sep 1984 ... 2.00
❑12, Oct 1984 ... 2.00
❑13, Nov 1984 ... 2.00
❑14, Dec 1984 ... 2.00
❑15, Jan 1985 ... 2.00
❑16, Feb 1985 ... 2.00
❑17, Apr 1985 ... 2.00
❑18, May 1985 ... 2.00
❑19, Jun 1985; Renegade Press begins as publisher ... 2.00
❑20, Jul 1985 ... 2.00
❑21, Sep 1985 ... 2.00
❑22, Oct 1985; Abortion story ... 2.00
❑23, Nov 1985; Abortion story ... 2.00
❑24, Dec 1985 ... 2.00
❑25, Jan 1986 ... 2.00
❑26, Feb 1986 ... 2.00
❑27, Mar 1986 ... 2.00
❑28, Apr 1986 ... 2.00
❑29, May 1986 ... 2.00
❑30, Jun 1986 ... 2.00
❑31, Jul 1986 ... 2.00
❑32, Sep 1986 ... 2.00
❑33, Oct 1986 ... 2.00
❑34, Nov 1986 ... 2.00
❑35, Dec 1986 ... 2.00
❑36, Feb 1987 ... 2.00
❑37, Mar 1987 ... 2.00
❑38, Apr 1987 ... 2.00
❑39, May 1987 ... 2.00
❑40, Jun 1987 ... 2.00
❑41, Oct 1987 ... 2.00
❑42, Nov 1987 ... 2.00
❑43, Dec 1987 ... 2.00
❑44, Feb 1988 ... 2.00
❑45, Apr 1988; Johnny Dynamite back-up ... 2.00
❑46, May 1988 ... 2.00
❑47, Aug 1988 ... 2.00
❑48, Nov 1988 ... 2.00
❑49, May 1989 ... 2.00
❑50, Jul 1989 JK (a) ... 2.75
❑3D 1, Aug 1985 ... 2.50
❑3D 2, Jul 1987; Ms. Tree's 1950's Three-Dimensional Crime ... 2.50

❑Summer 1, Aug 1986, b&w; Variant edition 2.00

MS. TREE QUARTERLY
DC

❑1, Sum 1990, MGr (a); Batman, Midnight 4.00
❑2, Aut 1990, Butcher 4.00
❑3, Spr 1991, Butcher 4.00
❑4, Sum 1991 4.00
❑5, Aut 1991 4.00
❑6, Win 1991 4.00
❑7, Spr 1992 4.00
❑8, Sum 1992 4.00
❑9, Fal 1992, Listed as Ms. Tree Special in indicia 4.00
❑10, Win 1992 3.50

MS. VICTORY SPECIAL
AC

❑1 2.00

MU
DEVIL'S DUE

❑1, Nov 2004 2.95
❑1/Ropie, Nov 2004 4.00
❑2, Dec 2004 2.95
❑2/Suh, Dec 2004 4.00
❑3, Jan 2005 2.95
❑3/MLim, Jan 2005 4.00
❑4, Aug 2005 2.95
❑4/Hyung, Aug 2005 4.00

MUCHA LUCHA
DC / VERTIGO

❑1, Jun 2003 2.25
❑2, Jul 2003 2.25
❑3, Aug 2003 2.25

MUKTUK WOLFSBREATH: HARD-BOILED SHAMAN
DC / VERTIGO

❑1, Aug 1998 2.50
❑2, Sep 1998 2.50
❑3, Oct 1998 2.50

MULLKON EMPIRE (JOHN JAKES'...)
TEKNO

❑1, Sep 1995 1.95
❑2, Oct 1995 1.95
❑3, Nov 1995 1.95
❑4, Dec 1995 1.95
❑5, Dec 1995 1.95
❑6, Jan 1996 1.95

MULTIVERSE (MICHAEL MOORCOCK'S...)
DC / HELIX

❑1, Nov 1997 2.50
❑2, Dec 1997 2.50
❑3, Jan 1998 2.50
❑4, Feb 1998 2.50
❑5, Mar 1998 2.50
❑6, Apr 1998 2.50
❑7, May 1998 2.50
❑8, Jun 1998 2.50
❑9, Jul 1998 2.50
❑10, Aug 1998 2.50
❑11, Sep 1998 2.50
❑12, Oct 1998 2.50

MUMMY (MONSTER)
MONSTER

❑1, b&w 2.00
❑2, b&w 2.00
❑3, b&w 2.00
❑4, b&w 2.00

MUMMY (DELL)
DELL

❑1 25.00

MUMMY ARCHIVES
MILLENNIUM

❑1, Jan 1992 2.50

MUMMY OR RAMSES THE DAMNED (ANNE RICE'S...)
MILLENNIUM

❑1, Oct 1990 3.00
❑2, Dec 1990 2.50
❑3, ca. 1992 2.50
❑4, ca. 1992 2.50
❑5, ca. 1992 2.50
❑6, ca. 1992 2.50
❑7, ca. 1992 2.50
❑8, ca. 1992 2.50
❑9, ca. 1992 2.50
❑10, ca. 1992 2.50
❑11, ca. 1992 2.50
❑12, ca. 1992 2.50

MUMMY'S CURSE
AIRCEL

❑1, Nov 1990, b&w 2.50
❑2, Dec 1990, b&w 2.50
❑3, Jan 1991, b&w 2.50
❑4, Feb 1991, b&w 2.50

MUMMY, THE: VALLEY OF THE GODS
CHAOS

❑1, May 2001 2.99
❑2 2001 2.99
❑3 2001 2.99

MUNDEN'S BAR
FIRST

❑Annual 1, Apr 1988; prestige format 2.95
❑Annual 2, Mar 1991; prestige format 5.95

MUNSTERS (GOLD KEY)
GOLD KEY

❑1, Jan 1965, (w); (a) 120.00
❑2, Apr 1965, (w); (a) 75.00
❑3, Jul 1965, (w); (a) 48.00
❑4, Oct 1965, (w); (a) 48.00
❑5, Jan 1966, (w); (a); back cover pin-up 48.00
❑6, Apr 1966, (w); (a) 34.00
❑7, Jun 1966, (w); (a) 34.00
❑8, Aug 1966, (w); (a) 34.00
❑9, Oct 1966, (w); (a) 34.00
❑10, Dec 1966, (w); (a) 34.00
❑11, Feb 1967, (w); (a) 30.00
❑12, Apr 1967, (w); (a) 30.00
❑13, Jun 1967, (w); (a) 30.00
❑14, Aug 1967, (w); (a); Cover reprints cover of #2, with green background rather than brown 30.00
❑15, Nov 1967, (w); (a); Cover the same image as #4, with yellow behind logo 30.00
❑16, Feb 1968, (w); (a) 30.00

MUNSTERS (TV COMICS!)
TV COMICS

❑1, Aug 1997 3.00
❑2/A, Oct 1997; blue background 3.00
❑2/B, Oct 1997; alternate cover (Marilyn); red background 3.00
❑3, Dec 1997 3.00
❑4, Mar 1998 3.00
❑4/Variant, Mar 1998; logoless 3.00
❑Special 1, Jul 1997; Comic Con 1997 Edition; Wraparound cover 3.00

MUPPET BABIES (STAR/MARVEL)
MARVEL / STAR

❑1, May 1985 1.50
❑2, Jul 1985 1.00
❑3, Sep 1985 1.00
❑4, Nov 1985 1.00
❑5, Jan 1986 1.00
❑6, Mar 1986 1.00
❑7, May 1986 1.00
❑8, Jul 1986 1.00
❑9, Sep 1986 1.00
❑10, Nov 1986 1.00
❑11, Jan 1987 1.00
❑12, Mar 1987 1.00
❑13, May 1987 1.00
❑14, Jul 1987 1.00
❑15, Sep 1987 1.00
❑16, Nov 1987 1.00
❑17, Jan 1988 1.00
❑18, Mar 1988; Marvel begins as publisher 1.00
❑19, May 1988 1.00
❑20, Jul 1988 1.00
❑21, Sep 1988 1.00
❑22, Nov 1988 1.00
❑23, Jan 1989 1.00
❑24, Mar 1989 1.00
❑25, May 1989 1.00
❑26, Jul 1989 1.00

MUPPET BABIES (HARVEY)
HARVEY

❑1, Jun 1993 1.50
❑2, Sep 1993 1.50
❑3, Dec 1993 1.50
❑4, Mar 1994 1.50
❑5, May 1994 1.50
❑6, Aug 1994 1.50

MUPPET BABIES ADVENTURES
HARVEY

❑1 1.25

MUPPET BABIES BIG BOOK
HARVEY

❑1 1.95

MUPPETS TAKE MANHATTAN
MARVEL / STAR

❑1, Nov 1984, Reprints Marvel Super Special #32 1.50
❑2, Dec 1984, Reprints Marvel Super Special #32 1.50
❑3, Jan 1985, Reprints Marvel Super Special #32 1.50

MURCIÉLAGA SHE-BAT
HEROIC

❑1, Jan 1993, b&w 1.50
❑2, Apr 1993, b&w 2.95
❑3, Jul 1993, b&w 2.95

MURDER
RENEGADE

❑1, Aug 1986, b&w; variant cover (Mortal Kombat logo) 2.00
❑2 2.00

MURDER CAN BE FUN
SLAVE LABOR

❑1, Feb 1996, b&w 4.00
❑2, May 1996, b&w 3.50
❑3, Aug 1996, b&w 3.50
❑4, Nov 1996, b&w 3.50
❑5, May 1997, b&w 3.00
❑6, Jul 1997, b&w 3.00
❑7, Sep 1997, b&w 2.95
❑8, Jan 1998, b&w 2.95
❑9, Apr 1998, b&w 2.95
❑10, Aug 1998, b&w 2.95
❑11, Nov 1998, b&w 2.95
❑12, Feb 1999, b&w 2.95

MURDER CITY
ETERNITY

❑1, b&w; Minute Movies 3.95

MURDER ME DEAD
EL CAPITÁN

❑1, Aug 2000 3.00
❑2, Oct 2000 3.00
❑3, Dec 2000 3.00
❑4, Feb 2001 3.00
❑5, Apr 2001 3.00
❑6, Jun 2001 3.00
❑7, Jul 2001 3.00

MUSIC COMICS
PERSONALITY

❑2 2.95
❑3 2.95
❑4, b&w 2.50

MUSIC COMICS ON TOUR
PERSONALITY

❑1, b&w; Beatles 2.95

MUTANT ALIENS
NBM

❑1 10.95

MUTANT BOOK OF THE DEAD
STARHEAD

❑1, b&w 2.50

MUTANT CHRONICLES
ACCLAIM / ARMADA

❑1, May 1996; polybagged with Doom Trooper card; cardstock cover 2.95
❑2, Jun 1996; polybagged with Doom Trooper card; cardstock cover 2.95
❑3, Jul 1996; polybagged with Doom Trooper card; cardstock cover 2.95
❑4, Aug 1996; polybagged with Doom Trooper card; cardstock cover 2.95

MUTANT CHRONICLES SOURCEBOOK
ACCLAIM / ARMADA

❑1, Sep 1996; polybagged with card; cardstock cover 2.95

MUTANT EARTH
IMAGE

❑1/A, Apr 2002; Flip book with Realm of the Claw #1 2.95

Nash

Adventures featuring the wrestling icon

©Image

National Velvet (Dell)

Based on the TV series, not the movie

©Dell

Navy War Heroes

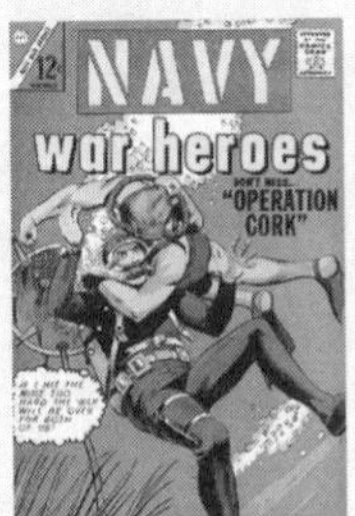

Yet another service-branch-centric war series

©Charlton

NBC Saturday Morning Comics

An NBC promo for its 1991 cartoon line-up

©Harvey

Negative Burn

Many new creators came from this anthology

©Caliber

N-MINT

❑1/B, Apr 2002; Flip book with Realm of the Claw #1 ... 2.95
❑2/A, Jun 2002, b&w; Flip book with Realm of the Claw #2 ... 2.95
❑2/B, Jun 2002, b&w; Flip book with Realm of the Claw #2 ... 2.95
❑3/A, Sep 2002, b&w; Flip book with Realm of the Claw #3 ... 2.95
❑3/B, Sep 2002, b&w; Flip book with Realm of the Claw #3 ... 2.95
❑4/A, ca. 2002, b&w ... 2.95
❑4/B, ca. 2002, b&w ... 2.95

MUTANT MISADVENTURES OF CLOAK & DAGGER
MARVEL

❑1, Oct 1988 A: X-Factor ... 2.00
❑2, Dec 1988 ... 1.50
❑3, Feb 1989 ... 1.50
❑4, Apr 1989; Inferno ... 1.50
❑5, Jun 1989 ... 1.50
❑6, Aug 1989 ... 1.50
❑7, Oct 1989 ... 1.50
❑8, Dec 1989 ... 1.50
❑9, Jan 1990; Avengers; Acts of Vengeance ... 2.50
❑10, Feb 1990 ... 1.50
❑11, Apr 1990 ... 1.50
❑12, Jun 1990 ... 1.50
❑13, Aug 1990 ... 1.50
❑14, Oct 1990; Title changes to Cloak & Dagger ... 1.50
❑15, Dec 1990 ... 1.50
❑16, Feb 1991 ... 1.50
❑17, Apr 1991; Spider-Man x-over ... 1.50
❑18, Jun 1991; Spider-Man, Ghost Rider ... 1.50
❑19, Aug 1991; Giant-size O: Cloak and Dagger ... 2.50

MUTANTS AND MISFITS
SILVERLINE

❑1 ... 2.00

MUTANTS VS. ULTRAS: FIRST ENCOUNTERS
MALIBU / ULTRAVERSE

❑1, Nov 1995; reprints Prime vs. Hulk, Night Man vs. Wolverine, and Exiles vs. X-Men ... 6.95

MUTANT, TEXAS: TALES OF SHERIFF IDA RED
ONI

❑1, May 2002, b&w ... 2.95
❑2, ca. 2002, b&w ... 2.95
❑3, Oct 2002, b&w ... 2.95
❑4, Nov 2002, b&w ... 2.95

MUTANT X (1ST SERIES)
MARVEL

❑1, Oct 1998; gatefold summary; Mutant X, Iceman, Marvel Woman standing on cover ... 3.00
❑1/A, Oct 1998; alternate cover ... 4.00
❑2, Nov 1998; gatefold summary ... 2.50
❑2/A, Nov 1998; gatefold summary; alternate cover ... 2.50
❑3, Dec 1998; gatefold summary ... 2.50
❑4, Jan 1999; gatefold summary ... 2.50

N-MINT

❑5, Feb 1999 A: Havok. A: Madelyne Pryor. A: Marvel Woman. A: Brute ... 2.50
❑6, Mar 1999 A: Madelyne Pryor. A: Man-Spider. A: Brute ... 2.00
❑7, Apr 1999 A: Havok. A: Man-Spider. A: Brute. A: Green Goblin ... 2.00
❑8, May 1999 ... 2.00
❑9, Jun 1999 A: Ben Grimm. A: Havok. A: Elektra. A: Mole Man ... 2.00
❑10, Jul 1999 A: X-Men. A: Magneto ... 1.99
❑11, Aug 1999 ... 1.99
❑12, Sep 1999; giant-size ... 2.99
❑14, Nov 1999 ... 1.99
❑13, Sep 1999 ... 1.99
❑15, Dec 1999 ... 1.99
❑16, Jan 2000 ... 1.99
❑17, Feb 2000 ... 2.25
❑18, Mar 2000 ... 2.25
❑19, Apr 2000 ... 2.25
❑20, May 2000 ... 2.25
❑21, Jun 2000 ... 2.25
❑22, Aug 2000 ... 2.25
❑23, Sep 2000 ... 2.25
❑24, Oct 2000 ... 2.25
❑25, Nov 2000 ... 2.99
❑26, Dec 2000 ... 2.25
❑27, Jan 2001 ... 2.25
❑29, Mar 2001 ... 2.25
❑28, Feb 2001 ... 2.25
❑30, Apr 2001 ... 2.25
❑31, May 2001 ... 2.25
❑32, Jun 2001 ... 2.25
❑Annual 2001, ca. 2001 A: Beyonder ... 2.99

MUTANT X (2ND SERIES)
MARVEL

❑1, Oct 2001 ... 2.99

MUTANT X: DANGEROUS DECISIONS
MARVEL

❑1, Jun 2002 ... 3.50

MUTANT X: ORIGIN
MARVEL

❑1, May 2002 ... 3.50

MUTANT ZONE
AIRCEL

❑1, Oct 1991, b&w ... 2.50
❑2, b&w ... 2.50
❑3, b&w ... 2.50

MUTATION
SPEAKEASY COMICS

❑1, Sep 2005 ... 2.99
❑2, Oct 2005

MUTATIS
MARVEL / EPIC

❑1, ca. 1992 ... 2.50
❑2, ca. 1992 ... 2.50
❑3, ca. 1992 ... 2.50

MUTATOR
CHECKER

❑1, Sum 1998 ... 1.95
❑2 1998 ... 1.95

MUTIES
MARVEL

❑1, Apr 2002 ... 2.50

N-MINT

❑2, May 2002 ... 2.50
❑3, Jun 2002 ... 2.50
❑4, Jul 2002 ... 2.50
❑5, Aug 2002 ... 2.50
❑6, Sep 2002 ... 2.50

MUTOPIA X
MARVEL

❑1, Aug 2005 ... 4.00
❑1/Variant, Aug 2005 ... 2.99
❑2, Sep 2005 ... 2.99
❑3, Oct 2005 ... 2.99
❑4, Nov 2005 ... 2.99
❑5, Jan 2006 ... 2.99

MUTT & JEFF
DC

❑90, Oct 1956 ... 24.00
❑91, ca. 1957 ... 18.00
❑92, ca. 1957 ... 18.00
❑93, Mar 1957 ... 18.00
❑94, Apr 1957 ... 18.00
❑95, May 1957 ... 18.00
❑96, Jun 1957 ... 18.00
❑97, Jul 1957 ... 18.00
❑98, Aug 1957 ... 18.00
❑99, Sep 1957 ... 18.00
❑100, Oct 1957 ... 18.00
❑101, Nov 1957 ... 15.00
❑102, Dec 1957 ... 15.00
❑103, Jan 1958 ... 15.00
❑104, Oct 1958; Dell begins as publisher ... 15.00
❑105, Nov 1958 ... 15.00
❑106, Dec 1958 ... 15.00
❑107, Jan 1959 ... 15.00
❑108, Feb 1959 ... 15.00
❑109, Mar 1959 ... 15.00
❑110, Apr 1959 ... 15.00
❑111, May 1959 ... 15.00
❑112, Jun 1959 ... 15.00
❑113, ca. 1959 ... 15.00
❑114, Sep 1959 ... 15.00
❑115, Oct 1959 ... 15.00
❑116, Feb 1960; Harvey begins as publisher ... 15.00
❑117, Apr 1960; Richie Rich story ... 15.00
❑118, Jun 1960 ... 15.00
❑119, Aug 1960 ... 15.00
❑120, Oct 1960 ... 15.00
❑121, Dec 1960 ... 12.00
❑122, Feb 1961 ... 12.00
❑123, Apr 1961 ... 12.00
❑124, Jun 1961 ... 12.00
❑125, Aug 1961 ... 12.00
❑126, Oct 1961 ... 12.00
❑127, Dec 1961 ... 12.00
❑128 1962 ... 12.00
❑129 1962 ... 12.00
❑130 1962 ... 12.00
❑131 1962 ... 12.00
❑132 1962 ... 12.00
❑133 1963 ... 12.00
❑134 1963 ... 12.00
❑135 1963 ... 12.00
❑136 1963 ... 12.00

N-MINT

❑137, Sep 1963 12.00
❑138, Nov 1963 12.00
❑139, Jan 1964 12.00
❑140, Mar 1964 12.00
❑141, ca. 1964 12.00
❑142, Nov 1964 12.00
❑143, Jan 1965 12.00
❑144, Mar 1965 12.00
❑145, May 1965 12.00
❑146, Jul 1965 12.00
❑147, Sep 1965 12.00
❑148, Nov 1965 12.00

MY FAITH IN FRANKIE
DC / VERTIGO

❑1, Mar 2004 2.95
❑2, Apr 2004 2.95
❑3, May 2004 2.95
❑4, Jun 2004 2.95

MY FAVORITE MARTIAN
GOLD KEY

❑1, Jan 1964 55.00
❑2, Jul 1964, Photo in small box; cover has art 35.00
❑3, Feb 1965 30.00
❑4, May 1965 30.00
❑5, Aug 1965 24.00
❑6 1966 24.00
❑7, Apr 1966 24.00
❑8, Jul 1966 24.00
❑9, Oct 1966 24.00

MY FLESH IS COOL (STEVEN GRANT'S)
AVATAR

❑1, Feb 2004 3.50

MY GREATEST ADVENTURE
DC

❑1, Jan 1955 1250.00
❑2, Mar 1955 600.00
❑3, May 1955 425.00
❑4, Jul 1955 425.00
❑5, Sep 1955 325.00
❑6, Nov 1955 325.00
❑7, Jan 1956 325.00
❑8, Mar 1956 325.00
❑9, May 1956 325.00
❑10, Jul 1956 325.00
❑11, Sep 1956 200.00
❑12, Nov 1956 200.00
❑13, Jan 1957 200.00
❑14, Mar 1957 200.00
❑15, May 1957 250.00
❑16, Jul 1957, JK (a) 250.00
❑17, Sep 1957 JK (a) 250.00
❑18, Nov 1957 JK (a) 300.00
❑19, Jan 1958 200.00
❑20, Mar 1958 JK (a) 225.00
❑21, May 1958 JK (a) 225.00
❑22, Jul 1958 175.00
❑23, Sep 1958 175.00
❑24, Oct 1958 175.00
❑25, Nov 1958 175.00
❑26, Dec 1958 175.00
❑27, Jan 1959 175.00
❑28, Feb 1959 JK (a) 200.00
❑29, Mar 1959 150.00
❑30, Apr 1959 150.00
❑31, May 1959 125.00
❑32, Jun 1959 125.00
❑33, Jul 1959 125.00
❑34, Aug 1959 125.00
❑35, Sep 1959 125.00
❑36, Oct 1959 125.00
❑37, Nov 1959 125.00
❑38, Dec 1959 125.00
❑39, Jan 1960 125.00
❑40, Feb 1960 125.00
❑41, Mar 1960 100.00
❑42, Apr 1960 100.00
❑43, May 1960 100.00
❑44, Jun 1960 100.00
❑45, Jul 1960 100.00
❑46, Aug 1960 100.00
❑47, Sep 1960 100.00
❑48, Oct 1960 100.00
❑49, Nov 1960 100.00
❑50, Dec 1960 100.00
❑51, Jan 1961 100.00
❑52, Feb 1961 100.00
❑53, Mar 1961 100.00
❑54, Apr 1961 100.00
❑55, May 1961 100.00
❑56, Jun 1961 100.00
❑57, Jul 1961 100.00
❑58, Aug 1961 ATh (a) 100.00
❑59, Sep 1961 100.00
❑60, Oct 1961 ATh (a) 100.00
❑61, Nov 1961 ATh (a) 100.00
❑62, Dec 1961 75.00
❑63, Jan 1962 75.00
❑64, Feb 1962 75.00
❑65, Mar 1962 75.00
❑66, Apr 1962 75.00
❑67, May 1962 75.00
❑68, Jun 1962 75.00
❑69, Jul 1962 75.00
❑70, Aug 1962 75.00
❑71, Sep 1962 75.00
❑72, Oct 1962 75.00
❑73, Nov 1962 75.00
❑74, Dec 1962 75.00
❑75, Jan 1963 75.00
❑76, Feb 1963 75.00
❑77, Mar 1963, ATh (a) 75.00
❑78, Apr 1963 75.00
❑79, May 1963 75.00
❑80, Jun 1963, O: The Doom Patrol. O: Elastic-Girl. O: Negative Man. O: Robotman. 1: The Doom Patrol. First Doom Patrol Story 425.00
❑81, Aug 1963, A: The Doom Patrol. Doom Patrol story 150.00
❑82, Sep 1963, A: The Doom Patrol. Doom Patrol story 150.00
❑83, Nov 1963, A: The Doom Patrol. Doom Patrol story 150.00
❑84, Dec 1963, A: The Doom Patrol. Doom Patrol story 150.00
❑85, Feb 1964, A: The Doom Patrol. Series continued in Doom Patrol (1st Series) #86 150.00

MY LITTLE MARGIE
CHARLTON

❑14, ca. 1956 26.00
❑15, ca. 1957 26.00
❑16, ca. 1957 26.00
❑17, Oct 1957 26.00
❑18, ca. 1958 26.00
❑19, ca. 1958 26.00
❑20, ca. 1958, Giant-sized issue 45.00
❑21, Oct 1958 20.00
❑22 20.00
❑23, ca. 1959 20.00
❑24, ca. 1959 20.00
❑25, ca. 1959 20.00
❑26 20.00
❑27 20.00
❑28, Mar 1960 20.00
❑29, ca. 1960 20.00
❑30, Jun 1960 20.00
❑31, ca. 1960 16.00
❑32, Oct 1960 16.00
❑33 16.00
❑34, ca. 1961 16.00
❑35, ca. 1961 16.00
❑36, ca. 1961 16.00
❑37, ca. 1961 16.00
❑38 16.00
❑39, ca. 1962 16.00
❑40, Mar 1962 12.00
❑41, ca. 1962 12.00
❑42, ca. 1962 12.00
❑43, ca. 1962 12.00
❑44 12.00
❑45 12.00
❑46, ca. 1963 12.00
❑47, ca. 1963 12.00
❑48, ca. 1963 12.00
❑49, ca. 1963 12.00
❑50 12.00
❑51, ca. 1964 9.00
❑52, ca. 1964 9.00
❑53, ca. 1964 9.00
❑54, ca. 1964, A: Beatles 40.00

MY MONKEY'S NAME IS JENNIFER
SLAVE LABOR

❑1, May 2002 2.95

MY NAME IS CHAOS
DC

❑1, ca. 1992 5.00
❑2, ca. 1992 5.00
❑3, ca. 1992 5.00
❑4, ca. 1992 5.00

MY NAME IS HOLOCAUST
DC / MILESTONE

❑1, May 1995 2.50
❑2, Jun 1995 2.50
❑3, Jul 1995 2.50
❑4, Aug 1995 2.50
❑5, Sep 1995 2.50

MY NAME IS MUD
INCOGNITO

❑1, Sum 1994 2.50

MY ONLY LOVE
CHARLTON

❑1, Jul 1975 10.00
❑2, Sep 1975 4.00
❑3, Nov 1975 3.00
❑4, Jan 1976 3.00
❑5, Mar 1976 3.00
❑6, May 1976 3.00
❑7, Jul 1976 3.00
❑8, Sep 1976 3.00
❑9, Nov 1976 3.00

MYRIAD
APPROBATION

❑1, ca. 2005, b&w 2.95
❑2, ca. 2005, b&w 2.95

MYRMIDON
RED HILLS

❑1, Jul 1998, b&w 2.95

MY ROMANTIC ADVENTURES? (AVALON)
AVALON

❑1 2.75

MYRON MOOSE FUNNIES
FANTAGRAPHICS

❑1 1.75
❑2 1.75
❑3 1.75

MYSFITS
BON-A-GRAM

❑1, Apr 1994 2.50

MYS-TECH WARS
MARVEL

❑1, Mar 1993; Virtually all X-Men, Marvel UK characters appear 1.75
❑2, Apr 1993; Virtually all X-Men, Marvel UK characters appear 1.75
❑3, May 1993; Virtually all X-Men, Marvel UK characters appear 1.75
❑4, Jun 1993; Virtually all X-Men, Marvel UK characters appear 1.75

MYSTERIES OF SCOTLAND YARD
MAGAZINE ENTERPRISES

❑1, ca. 1954, Reprinted from Manhunt (5 Stories) 50.00

MYSTERIOUS SUSPENSE
CHARLTON

❑1, Oct 1968, SD (a); Question 35.00

MYSTERY DATE
LIGHTSPEED

❑1, May 1999, b&w 2.95

MYSTERY IN SPACE
DC

❑34, Oct 1956 235.00
❑35, Dec 1956 235.00
❑36, Feb 1957 235.00
❑37, Apr 1957 235.00
❑38, Jun 1957 235.00
❑39, Aug 1957 235.00
❑40, Oct 1957 235.00
❑41, Dec 1957 195.00
❑42, Feb 1958 195.00
❑43, Apr 1958 195.00
❑44, Jun 1958 195.00
❑45, Aug 1958 195.00

Neil the Horse Comics and Stories

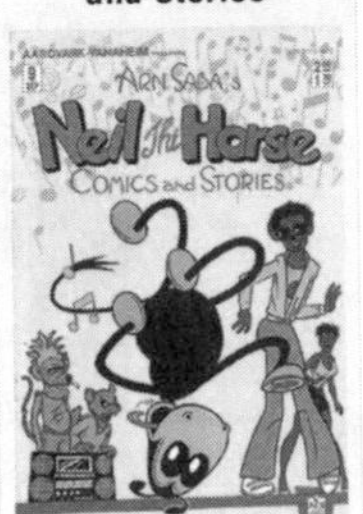

Happy-go-lucky horse usually comes out OK

©Aardvark-Vanaheim

Neon Genesis Evangelion Book 1

Giant robots fight aliens in manga import

©Viz

Nevada

Reuses showgirl and ostrich from "Howard"

©DC

New Adventures of Huck Finn

Adapts television series episodes

©Gold Key

New Adventures of Superboy

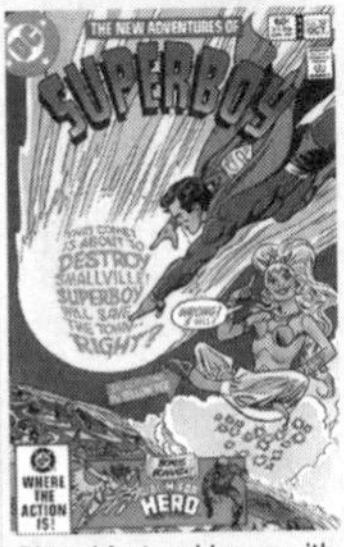

Played fast and loose with continuity

©DC

	N-MINT
❑46, Sep 1958	195.00
❑47, Oct 1958	195.00
❑48, Dec 1958	195.00
❑49, Feb 1959	195.00
❑50, Apr 1959	195.00
❑51, May 1959	195.00
❑52, Jun 1959	195.00
❑53, Aug 1959, CI (a); Adam Strange begins	1500.00
❑54, Sep 1959, CI (a)	425.00
❑55, Nov 1959, CI (a)	250.00
❑56, Dec 1959, CI (a)	175.00
❑57, Feb 1960, CI (a)	175.00
❑58, Mar 1960, GK (c); CI (a)	175.00
❑59, May 1960 CI (a)	175.00
❑60, Jun 1960, CI (a)	175.00
❑61, Aug 1960, CI (a); 1: Tornado Tyrant. Later becomes Red Tornado	125.00
❑62, Sep 1960, CI (a)	125.00
❑63, Nov 1960, CI (a)	125.00
❑64, Dec 1960, CI (a)	125.00
❑65, Feb 1961, CI (a)	125.00
❑66, Mar 1961, CI (a); 1: The Star Rovers	125.00
❑67, May 1961, CI (a)	125.00
❑68, Jun 1961, CI (a)	125.00
❑69, Aug 1961, CI (a)	125.00
❑70, Sep 1961, CI (a)	125.00
❑71, Nov 1961, CI (a)	125.00
❑72, Dec 1961, CI (a)	100.00
❑73, Feb 1962, CI (a)	100.00
❑74, Mar 1962, CI (a)	100.00
❑75, May 1962, CI (a); A: Justice League of America	225.00
❑76, Jun 1962, CI (a)	100.00
❑77, Aug 1962, CI (a)	100.00
❑78, Sep 1962, CI (a)	100.00
❑79, Nov 1962, CI (a)	100.00
❑80, Dec 1962, CI (a)	100.00
❑81, Feb 1963, CI (a)	75.00
❑82, Mar 1963, CI (a)	75.00
❑83, May 1963, CI (a)	75.00
❑84, Jun 1963, CI (a)	75.00
❑85, Aug 1963, MA, CI (a); A: Adam Strange	75.00
❑86, Sep 1963, CI (a)	75.00
❑87, Nov 1963, MA, CI (a); A: Hawkman	175.00
❑88, Dec 1963, MA, CI (a); A: Hawkman	90.00
❑89, Feb 1964, MA, CI (a); A: Hawkman	90.00
❑90, Mar 1964, MA, CI (a); A: Hawkman	90.00
❑91, May 1964, CI (a)	50.00
❑92, Jun 1964	50.00
❑93, Aug 1964	50.00
❑94, Sep 1964	40.00
❑95, Nov 1964	40.00
❑96, Dec 1964	40.00
❑97, Feb 1965	40.00
❑98, Mar 1965	40.00
❑99, May 1965	40.00
❑100, Jun 1965	40.00
❑101, Aug 1965	40.00
❑102, Sep 1965	40.00
❑103, Nov 1965	40.00
❑104, Dec 1965	30.00
❑105, Feb 1966	30.00
❑106, Mar 1966	30.00
❑107, May 1966	30.00
❑108, Jun 1966	30.00
❑109, Aug 1966	30.00
❑110, Sep 1966, Original series ends	30.00
❑111, Sep 1980, Series begins again	5.00
❑112, Oct 1980	5.00
❑113, Nov 1980	5.00
❑114, Dec 1980	5.00
❑115, Jan 1981	5.00
❑116, Feb 1981	5.00
❑117, Mar 1981	5.00

MYSTERY MAN
Slave Labor

❑1, Jul 1988, b&w	1.75
❑2, Nov 1988, b&w	1.75

MYSTERY MEN MOVIE ADAPTATION
Dark Horse

❑1, Jul 1999	2.95
❑2, Aug 1999	2.95

MYSTERYMEN STORIES
Bob Burden

❑1, Sum 1996, b&w; prose story with illustrations	5.00

MYSTERY OF WOOLVERINE WOO-BAIT
Fantagraphics

❑1, Dec 2004	4.95

MYSTIC (CROSSGEN)
CrossGen

❑1, Jul 2000	3.25
❑2, Aug 2000	3.00
❑3, Sep 2000	3.00
❑4, Oct 2000	3.00
❑5, Nov 2000	3.00
❑6, Dec 2000	2.95
❑7, Jan 2001	2.95
❑8, Feb 2001	2.95
❑9, Mar 2001	2.95
❑10, Apr 2001	2.95
❑11, May 2001	2.95
❑12, Jun 2001	2.95
❑13, Jul 2001	2.95
❑14, Aug 2001	2.95
❑15, Sep 2001	2.95
❑16, Oct 2001	2.95
❑17, Nov 2001	2.95
❑18, Dec 2001	2.95
❑19, Jan 2002	2.95
❑20, Feb 2002	2.95
❑21, Mar 2002	2.95
❑22, Apr 2002	2.95
❑23, May 2002	2.95
❑24, Jun 2002	2.95
❑25, Jul 2002	2.95
❑26, Aug 2002	2.95
❑27, Sep 2002	2.95
❑28, Oct 2002	2.95
❑29, Nov 2002	2.95
❑30, Dec 2002	2.95
❑31, Jan 2003	2.95
❑32, Feb 2003	2.95
❑33, Mar 2003	2.95
❑34, Apr 2003	2.95
❑35, May 2003	2.95
❑36, Jun 2003	2.95
❑37, Jul 2003	2.95
❑38, Aug 2003	2.95
❑39, Sep 2003	2.95
❑40, Nov 2003	2.95
❑41, Nov 2003	2.95
❑42, Dec 2003	2.95
❑43, Jan 2004	2.95

MYSTIC EDGE
Antarctic

❑1, Oct 1998	2.95

MYSTIC TRIGGER
Maelstrom

❑1; Tales of the Galactic Forces preview	3.25

MYSTIQUE
Marvel

❑1, Jun 2003	2.99
❑1/DF, Jun 2003	15.00
❑2, Jul 2003	2.99
❑3, Aug 2003	2.99
❑4, Sep 2003	2.99
❑5, Oct 2003	2.99
❑6, Nov 2003	2.99
❑7, Dec 2003	2.99
❑8, Jan 2004	2.99
❑9, Feb 2004	2.99
❑10, Mar 2004	2.99
❑11, Apr 2004	2.99
❑12, May 2004	2.99
❑13, Jun 2004	2.99
❑14, Jul 2004	2.99
❑15, Jul 2004	2.99
❑16, Aug 2004	2.99
❑17, Sep 2004	2.99
❑18, Oct 2004	2.99
❑19, Nov 2004	2.99
❑20, Dec 2004	2.99
❑21, Jan 2005	2.99
❑22, Feb 2005	2.99
❑23, Mar 2005	2.99
❑24, Apr 2005	2.99

MYSTIQUE & SABRETOOTH
Marvel

❑1, Dec 1996	1.95
❑2, Jan 1997	1.95
❑3, Feb 1997	1.95
❑4, Mar 1997	1.95

MYST: THE BOOK OF THE BLACK SHIPS
Dark Horse

❑0, ca. 1997; American Entertainment Exclusive Edition; No cover price; based on video game	1.50
❑1, Aug 1997; based on video game	2.95
❑2, Sep 1997	2.95
❑3, Oct 1997	2.95
❑4, Nov 1997	2.95

MY TERRIBLE ROMANCE
NEC

❑1	2.75

Other grades: Multiply price above by 5/6 for VF/NM • 2/3 for VERY FINE • 1/3 for FINE • 1/5 for VERY GOOD • 1/8 for GOOD

N-MINT

❑2, Jul 1994; Reprints from Hi-School Romance #9, My Desire #4, Voodoo #16, Romantic Love #8, All True Romance #17 2.75

MYTH
Fygmok

❑1, Dec 1996, b&w; wraparound cover 2.95
❑2, Feb 1997, b&w 2.95

MYTHADVENTURES
Warp

❑1, Mar 1984; Warp publishes 2.00
❑2, Jun 1984 1.50
❑3, Sep 1984 1.50
❑4, Dec 1984 1.50
❑5, Mar 1985 1.50
❑6, Jun 1985 1.50
❑7, Sep 1985 1.50
❑8, Dec 1985 PF (w); PF (a) 1.50
❑9, Mar 1986 1.50
❑10 1986; Apple begins as publisher 1.50
❑11 1986 1.50
❑12 1986 1.50

MYTH CONCEPTIONS
Apple

❑1, Nov 1987 2.00
❑2, Jan 1988 1.75
❑3, Mar 1988 1.75
❑4, May 1988 1.75
❑5, Jul 1988 1.75
❑6, Sep 1988 1.75
❑7, Nov 1988 1.75
❑8, Jan 1989 1.75

MYTHIC HEROES
Chapterhouse

❑1, Sep 1996, b&w 2.50

MYTH MAKER (ROBERT E. HOWARD'S...)
Cross Plains

❑1, Jun 1999 6.95

MYTHOGRAPHY
Bardic

❑1, Sep 1996 4.00
❑2, Feb 1997 4.00
❑3, Apr 1997 4.00
❑4, Jun 1997 4.00
❑5, Sep 1997 4.00
❑6, Nov 1997; Barr Girls story 4.00
❑7, Feb 1998 4.00
❑8, May 1998 4.00

MYTHOS
Wonder Comix

❑1, Jan 1987 2.00
❑2, Apr 1987 2.00
❑3, Aug 1987, b&w 2.00

MYTHOS: THE FINAL TOUR
DC / Vertigo

❑1, Dec 1996; prestige format 5.95
❑2, Jan 1997; prestige format 5.95
❑3, Feb 1997; prestige format 5.95

MYTHOS: X-MEN
Marvel

❑1, Mar 2006 3.99

MYTHSTALKERS
Image

❑1, Apr 2003 2.95
❑2, May 2003 2.95
❑3, Jun 2003 2.95
❑4, Sep 2003 2.95
❑5, Oct 2003 2.95
❑6, Dec 2003 2.95
❑7, Feb 2004 2.95
❑8, May 2004 2.95

MY UNCLE JEFF
Origin Comics

❑1, Feb 2003 3.95

MY WAR WITH BRIAN
NBM

❑1 16.95

NADESICO
CPM Manga

❑1, Jun 1999 2.95
❑2, Jul 1999 2.95
❑3, Aug 1999 2.95
❑4, Sep 1999 2.95
❑5, Oct 1999 2.95
❑6, Nov 1999 2.95
❑7, Dec 1999 2.95
❑8, Jan 2000 2.95
❑9, Feb 2000 2.95
❑10, Mar 2000 2.95
❑11, Apr 2000 2.95
❑12, May 2000 2.95
❑13, Jun 2000 2.95
❑14, Jul 2000 2.95
❑15, Aug 2000 2.95
❑16, Sep 2000 2.95
❑17, Oct 2000 2.95
❑18, Nov 2000 2.95
❑19, Dec 2000 2.95
❑20, Jan 2001 2.95
❑21, Feb 2001 2.95
❑22, Mar 2001 2.95
❑23, Apr 2001 2.95
❑24, May 2001 2.95
❑25, Jun 2001 2.95
❑26, Jul 2001 2.95

NAIL
Dark Horse

❑1, Aug 2004 2.99
❑2, Sep 2004 2.99
❑3, Oct 2004 2.99
❑4, Nov 2004 3.00

NAIVE INTER-DIMENSIONAL COMMANDO KOALAS
Eclipse

❑1, Oct 1986, b&w 1.50

NAKED ANGELS
Fantagraphics / Eros

❑1 1996 2.95
❑2, May 1996 2.95

NAKED EYE (S.A. KING'S...)
Antarctic

❑1, Dec 1994, b&w 2.75
❑2, Feb 1995, b&w 2.75
❑3, Apr 1995, b&w 2.75

'NAM
Marvel

❑1, Dec 1986, MG (a) 2.00
❑1/2nd, Dec 1986, MG (a) 1.00
❑2, Jan 1987, MG (a) 1.00
❑3, Feb 1987, MG (a) 1.00
❑4, Mar 1987 1.00
❑5, Apr 1987 1.00
❑6, May 1987, MG (a) 1.00
❑7, Jun 1987, MG (a) 1.00
❑8, Jul 1987, MG (a) 1.00
❑9, Aug 1987, D: Mike 1.00
❑10, Sep 1987 1.00
❑11, Oct 1987 1.00
❑12, Nov 1987 1.00
❑13, Dec 1987 1.00
❑14, Jan 1988 1.00
❑15, Feb 1988 1.00
❑16, Mar 1988 1.00
❑17, Apr 1988 1.00
❑18, May 1988 1.25
❑19, Jun 1988 1.25
❑20, Jul 1988 1.25
❑21, Aug 1988 1.25
❑22, Sep 1988 1.25
❑23, Oct 1988 1.25
❑24, Nov 1988 1.25
❑25, Dec 1988 1.25
❑26, Jan 1989 1.50
❑27, Feb 1989 1.50
❑28, Mar 1989 1.50
❑29, Apr 1989 1.50
❑30, May 1989 1.50
❑31, Jun 1989 1.50
❑32, Jul 1989 1.50
❑33, Aug 1989 1.50
❑34, Sep 1989 1.50
❑35, Oct 1989, A: Bob Hope. Christmas issue 1.50
❑36, Nov 1989 1.50
❑37, Nov 1989 1.50
❑38, Dec 1989 1.50
❑39, Dec 1989, A: Iron Man. A: Captain America. A: Thor 1.50
❑40, Jan 1990 1.50
❑41, Feb 1990, A: Iron Man. A: Captain America. A: Thor 1.50
❑42, Mar 1990 1.50
❑43, Apr 1990 1.50
❑44, May 1990 1.50
❑45, Jun 1990 1.50
❑46, Jul 1990 1.50
❑47, Aug 1990 1.50
❑48, Sep 1990 1.50
❑49, Oct 1990 1.50
❑50, Nov 1990 1.50
❑51, Dec 1990 1.50
❑52, Jan 1991, A: Frank Castle (Punisher) 1.50
❑52/2nd, Jan 1991, A: Frank Castle (Punisher) 1.50
❑53, Feb 1991, A: Frank Castle (Punisher) 1.50
❑53/2nd, Feb 1991, A: Frank Castle (Punisher) 1.50
❑54, Mar 1991, TD (a) 1.50
❑55, Apr 1991, TD (a) 1.50
❑56, May 1991 1.50
❑57, Jun 1991 1.50
❑58, Jul 1991 1.50
❑59, Aug 1991 1.50
❑60, Sep 1991 1.50
❑61, Oct 1991 1.50
❑62, Nov 1991 1.50
❑63, Dec 1991 1.50
❑64, Jan 1992 1.50
❑65, Feb 1992, RH (a) 1.75
❑66, Mar 1992 1.75
❑67, Apr 1992, A: Punisher 1.75
❑68, May 1992, A: Punisher 1.75
❑69, Jun 1992, A: Punisher 1.75
❑70, Jul 1992 1.75
❑71, Aug 1992 1.75
❑72, Sep 1992 1.75
❑73, Oct 1992 1.75
❑74, Nov 1992 1.75
❑75, Dec 1992, HT (a); Tells of Mai Lai Massacre from different points of view 2.25
❑76, Jan 1993 1.75
❑77, Feb 1993 1.75
❑78, Mar 1993 1.75
❑79, Apr 1993 1.75
❑80, May 1993 1.75
❑81, Jun 1993 1.75
❑82, Jul 1993 1.75
❑83, Aug 1993 1.75
❑84, Sep 1993, Told from Vietnamese point of view 1.75

NAMELESS
Image

❑1, May 1997 2.95
❑2, Jun 1997 2.95
❑3, Jul 1997, b&w 2.95
❑4, Aug 1997, b&w 2.95
❑5, Sep 1997, b&w 2.95

NAMES OF MAGIC
DC / Vertigo

❑1, Feb 2001 2.50
❑2, Mar 2001 2.50
❑3, Apr 2001 2.50
❑4, May 2001 2.50
❑5, Jun 2001 2.50

'NAM MAGAZINE
Marvel

❑1, Aug 1988, b&w; MG (a); Reprints 3.00
❑2, Sep 1988, b&w; Reprints 2.50
❑3, Oct 1988, b&w; Reprints 2.50
❑4, Nov 1988, b&w; Reprints 2.50
❑5, Dec 1988, b&w; Reprints 2.50
❑6, Dec 1988, b&w; Reprints 2.50
❑7, Jan 1989, b&w; Reprints 2.50
❑8, Feb 1989, b&w; Reprints 2.50
❑9, Mar 1989, b&w; Reprints 2.50
❑10, Apr 1989, b&w; Reprints 2.50

NAMOR
Marvel

❑1, Jun 2003 3.00
❑2, Jun 2003 2.25
❑3, Jul 2003 2.25
❑4, Aug 2003 2.25

New Adventures of the Phantom Blo t (Walt Disney's...)

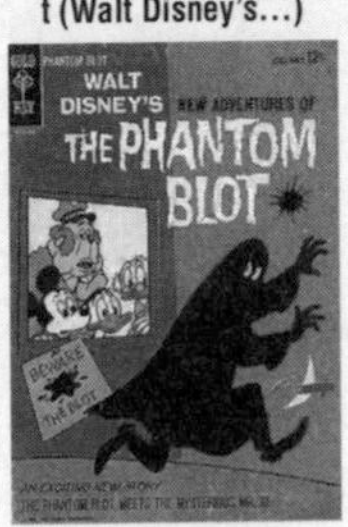

Short series gives birth to Super Goof
©Gold Key

New Archies

Portrays the gang as younger teen-agers
©Archie

New Avengers

Bendis restarts classic series from beginning
©Marvel

New Gods (1st series)

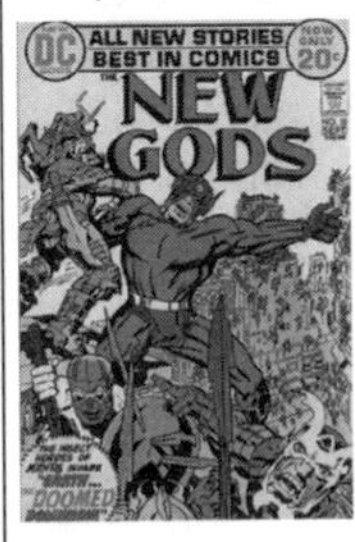

Jack Kirby's far-flung fantasy series
©DC

New Guardians

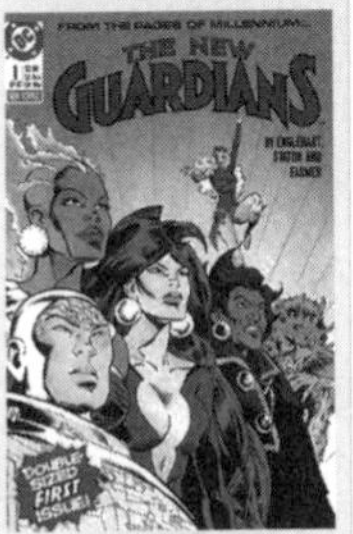

Series spinoff from Millennium event
©DC

	N-MINT
❑5, Oct 2003	2.99
❑6, Nov 2003	2.99
❑7, Dec 2003	2.99
❑8, Dec 2003	2.99
❑9, Jan 2004	2.99
❑10, Feb 2004	2.99
❑11, Mar 2004	2.99
❑12, Apr 2004	2.99

NAMOR, THE SUB-MARINER
MARVEL

	N-MINT
❑1, Apr 1990 JBy (w); JBy (a); O: Sub-Mariner	2.00
❑2, May 1990 JBy (w); JBy (a)	1.50
❑3, Jun 1990 JBy (a)	1.50
❑4, Jul 1990 JBy (a)	1.50
❑5, Aug 1990 JBy (a)	1.50
❑6, Sep 1990 JBy (a)	1.25
❑7, Oct 1990 JBy (a)	1.25
❑8, Nov 1990 JBy (a)	1.25
❑9, Dec 1990 JBy (a)	1.25
❑10, Jan 1991 JBy (a)	1.25
❑11, Feb 1991 JBy (a)	1.25
❑12, Mar 1991; Giant-size JBy (a); A: Human Torch. A: Captain America. A: Invaders	1.25
❑13, Apr 1991 JBy (a)	1.00
❑14, May 1991 JBy (a)	1.00
❑15, Jun 1991 JBy (a)	1.00
❑16, Jul 1991 JBy (a)	1.00
❑17, Aug 1991 JBy (a)	1.00
❑18, Sep 1991 JBy (a)	1.00
❑19, Oct 1991 JBy (a)	1.00
❑20, Nov 1991 JBy (a)	1.00
❑21, Dec 1991 JBy (a)	1.00
❑22, Jan 1992 JBy (a)	1.00
❑23, Feb 1992 JBy (a); A: Wolverine. A: Iron Fist	1.25
❑24, Mar 1992; JBy (a); A: Wolverine. Namor fights Wolverine	1.25
❑25, Apr 1992 JBy (a); A: Wolverine	1.25
❑26, May 1992; 1st Jae Lee art	1.25
❑27, Jun 1992	1.25
❑28, Jul 1992 A: Iron Fist	1.25
❑29, Aug 1992	1.25
❑30, Sep 1992	1.25
❑31, Oct 1992	1.25
❑32, Nov 1992	1.25
❑33, Dec 1992	1.25
❑34, Jan 1993	1.25
❑35, Feb 1993	1.25
❑36, Mar 1993	1.25
❑37, Apr 1993; foil cover	2.00
❑38, May 1993	1.25
❑39, Jun 1993	1.25
❑40, Jul 1993	1.25
❑41, Aug 1993	1.25
❑42, Sep 1993 A: Stingray	1.25
❑43, Oct 1993 A: Stingray	1.25
❑44, Nov 1993	1.25
❑45, Dec 1993	1.25
❑46, Jan 1994	1.25
❑47, Feb 1994	1.25
❑48, Mar 1994	1.25
❑49, Apr 1994	1.25
❑50, May 1994; Giant-size	1.75
❑50/Variant, May 1994; Giant-size; foil cover	2.95
❑51, Jun 1994	1.75
❑52, Jul 1994	1.50
❑53, Aug 1994	1.50
❑54, Sep 1994 1: Llyron	1.50
❑55, Oct 1994	1.50
❑56, Nov 1994	1.50
❑57, Dec 1994	1.50
❑58, Jan 1995 V: Avengers	1.50
❑59, Feb 1995	1.50
❑60, Mar 1995	1.50
❑61, Apr 1995	1.50
❑62, May 1995	1.50
❑Annual 1, ca. 1991 O: Namor	3.00
❑Annual 2, ca. 1992 A: The Defenders	2.25
❑Annual 3, ca. 1993 O: The Assassin	2.95
❑Annual 4, ca. 1994	2.95

NANCY AND SLUGGO (GOLD KEY)
GOLD KEY

	N-MINT
❑188 1962	10.00
❑189 1962	10.00
❑190 1963	10.00
❑191, Jul 1963	10.00
❑192 1963, Summer Camp	10.00

NANNY AND THE PROFESSOR
DELL

	N-MINT
❑1, Aug 1970, based on TV show	16.00
❑2, Oct 1970	10.00

NANOSOUP
MILLENNIUM

	N-MINT
❑1, ca. 1996, b&w; wraparound cover	2.95

NARCOLEPSY DREAMS
SLAVE LABOR

	N-MINT
❑1, Feb 1995	2.95
❑2, Aug 1995	2.95
❑4; Mini-comic	1.00

NARD N' PAT
CARTOONISTS CO-OP

	N-MINT
❑1, ca. 1974, b&w	3.00

NASCAR ADVENTURES
VORTEX

	N-MINT
❑1 1992; DH (a); Fred Lorenzen; regular cover	2.95
❑2 1992; Richard Petty	2.50
❑5 1992; Ernie Irvan	2.50
❑7 1992	2.50

NASCUB ADVENTURES
VORTEX

	N-MINT
❑1, Jun 1991	2.00

NASH
IMAGE

	N-MINT
❑1, Jul 1999; regular cover	2.95
❑1/A, Jul 1999	2.95
❑1/B, Jul 1999; no cover price	2.95
❑2, Jul 1999; regular cover	2.95
❑2/A, Jul 1999	2.95
❑Ashcan 1, Jul 1999; Preview Book; regular cover	2.50
❑Ashcan 1/Varian, Jul 1999	2.50

NASTI: MONSTER HUNTER
SCHISM

	N-MINT
❑1, b&w 1: Nasti	2.50
❑1/Autographed; Autographed, limited edition (250 printed) with certificate of authenticity 1: Nasti	3.00
❑2, b&w	2.50
❑3, b&w	2.50
❑Ashcan 1/Ltd., b&w; No cover price; preview of upcoming comic book on newsprint	1.00

NATHANIEL DUSK
DC

	N-MINT
❑1, Feb 1984, GC (a); 1: Nathaniel Dusk	1.50
❑2, Mar 1984, GC (a)	1.50
❑3, Apr 1984, GC (a)	1.50
❑4, May 1984, GC (a)	1.50

NATHANIEL DUSK II
DC

	N-MINT
❑1, Oct 1985	2.00
❑2, Nov 1985	2.00
❑3, Dec 1985	2.00
❑4, Jan 1986	2.00

NATHAN NEVER
DARK HORSE

	N-MINT
❑1, Mar 1999	4.95
❑2, Apr 1999	4.95
❑3, May 1999	4.95
❑4, Jun 1999	4.95
❑5, Jul 1999	4.95
❑6, Aug 1999	4.95

NATIONAL COMICS (2ND SERIES)
DC

	N-MINT
❑1, May 1999 MWa (w); A: Flash. A: Justice Society. A: Mr. Terrific	2.00

NATIONAL VELVET (DELL)
DELL

	N-MINT
❑1, Jul 1962, Code on cover ends in -207	30.00
❑2, Oct 1962, Code on cover ends in -210	30.00

NATION OF SNITCHES
DC / PIRANHA

	N-MINT
❑1	4.95

NAT TURNER
KYLE BAKER PUBLISHING

	N-MINT
❑1, Jul 2005	3.00

NATURAL INQUIRER
FANTAGRAPHICS

	N-MINT
❑1, Apr 1989, b&w	2.00

NATURAL SELECTION
ATOM

	N-MINT
❑1, Jan 1998, b&w	2.95
❑2, Feb 1998, b&w	2.95

NATURE OF THE BEAST
CALIBER

	N-MINT
❑1, b&w	2.95
❑2, b&w	2.95

NAUGHTY BITS
FANTAGRAPHICS

	N-MINT
❑1, Mar 1991, b&w	7.00
❑1/2nd, b&w	2.50
❑2, Jun 1991, b&w	5.00
❑3, Sep 1991, b&w	4.00
❑4, Dec 1991, b&w	3.75
❑5, Apr 1992, b&w	3.75

Other grades: Multiply price above by 5/6 for VF/NM • 2/3 for VERY FINE • 1/3 for FINE • 1/5 for VERY GOOD • 1/8 for GOOD

N-MINT

❑6, Aug 1992, b&w 3.00
❑7, Nov 1992, b&w 3.00
❑8, Feb 1993, b&w 3.00
❑9, Jun 1993, b&w 3.00
❑10, Oct 1993, b&w 3.00
❑11, Jan 1994, b&w 2.50
❑12, Apr 1994, b&w 2.50
❑13, Jul 1994, b&w 2.95
❑14, Oct 1994, b&w 2.95
❑15, Feb 1995, b&w 2.95
❑16, May 1995, b&w 2.95
❑17, Aug 1995, b&w 2.95
❑18, Jan 1996, b&w 2.95
❑19, Apr 1996, b&w 2.95
❑20, Aug 1996, b&w 2.95
❑21, Nov 1996, b&w 2.95
❑22, Mar 1997, b&w 2.95
❑23, Jun 1997, b&w 2.95
❑24, Oct 1997, b&w 2.95
❑25, b&w 2.95
❑26 2.95
❑27 2.95
❑28, ca. 1999 2.95
❑29, Jul 1999 2.95
❑30 2.95
❑31, Apr 2000 2.95
❑32 2.95
❑33 2.95
❑34, May 2001 2.95
❑35 2.95
❑36 2.95
❑37, Dec 2002 2.95
❑38 2.95

NAUSICAÄ OF THE VALLEY OF WIND PART 1
Viz

❑1 3.25
❑2 3.25
❑3 3.25
❑4 3.25
❑5 3.25
❑6 3.25
❑7 3.25

NAUSICAÄ OF THE VALLEY OF WIND PART 2
Viz

❑1 2.95
❑2 2.95
❑3 2.95
❑4 3.25

NAUSICAÄ OF THE VALLEY OF WIND PART 3
Viz

❑1 3.95
❑2 3.95
❑3 3.95

NAUSICAÄ OF THE VALLEY OF WIND PART 4
Viz

❑1 2.75
❑2 2.75
❑3 2.75
❑4 2.75
❑5 2.75
❑6 2.75

NAUSICAÄ OF THE VALLEY OF WIND PART 5
Viz

❑1 2.75
❑2 2.75
❑3 2.75
❑4 2.75
❑5 2.75
❑6 2.75
❑7 2.95
❑8 2.95

NAUTILUS
Shanda Fantasy Arts

❑1, May 1999, b&w 2.95

NAVY WAR HEROES
Charlton

❑1 12.00
❑2, Mar 1964 8.00
❑3 1964 6.00
❑4 1964 6.00

N-MINT

❑5, Nov 1964 6.00
❑6 6.00
❑7 6.00

NAZA
Dell

❑1, Jan 1964 15.00
❑2, Jun 1964 8.00
❑3, Sep 1964 8.00
❑4, Dec 1964 8.00
❑5, Mar 1965 8.00
❑6, Jun 1965 6.00
❑7, Sep 1965 6.00
❑8, Dec 1965 6.00
❑9, Mar 1966 6.00

NAZRAT
Imperial

❑1 2.00
❑2 2.00
❑3 2.00
❑4 2.00
❑5 2.00
❑6, Jun 1987, b&w 2.00

NAZZ
DC

❑1, Oct 1990 4.95
❑2, Nov 1990 4.95
❑3, Dec 1990 4.95
❑4, Jan 1991 4.95

NBC SATURDAY MORNING COMICS
Harvey

❑1, Sep 1991; Toys "R" Us giveaway A: Geoffrey Giraffe 1.50

NEAR MYTHS
Rip Off

❑1, Jul 1990, b&w 2.50

NEAR TO NOW
Fandom House

❑1, b&w 2.00
❑2, b&w 2.00

NEAT STUFF
Fantagraphics

❑1 5.00
❑1/2nd 2.50
❑2 4.00
❑2/2nd 2.50
❑3 3.50
❑3/2nd 2.50
❑4 3.00
❑4/2nd 2.50
❑5, Dec 1986 2.50
❑6, Apr 1987; all Bradley issue 2.50
❑7, Aug 1987 2.50
❑8, Dec 1987 2.50
❑9 1988 2.50
❑10 1988 2.50
❑11, Nov 1988 2.50
❑12 2.50
❑13 2.50
❑14 2.50
❑15 2.50

NECK AND NECK
Tokyopop

❑1, Dec 2004 9.95
❑2, Mar 2005 9.95
❑3, Jun 2005 9.95
❑4, Dec 2005 9.95

NECROMANCER
Anarchy

❑1, b&w 2.50
❑1/Deluxe; Deluxe edition 3.50
❑2, b&w 2.50
❑2/Deluxe; Deluxe edition 3.50
❑3, b&w 2.50
❑3/Deluxe; Deluxe edition 3.50
❑4, b&w 2.50
❑4/Deluxe; Deluxe edition 3.50

NECROMANCER (2ND SERIES)
Anarchy

❑1, b&w 2.50
❑2, b&w 2.50
❑3, b&w 2.50
❑4, b&w 2.50

N-MINT

NECROMANCER (IMAGE)
Image

❑1/Manapul, Sep 2005 2.99
❑1/Horn, Sep 2005 4.00
❑1/Bachalo, Sep 2005 3.00
❑2 2005 3.00
❑3, Jan 2006 3.00
❑4, Feb 2006 3.00
❑5, Jun 2006 3.00
❑6, Jul 2006 3.00

NECROPOLIS
Fleetway-Quality

❑1 2.95
❑2 2.95
❑3 2.95
❑4 2.95
❑5 2.95
❑6 2.95
❑7 2.95
❑8 2.95
❑9 2.95

NECROSCOPE
Malibu

❑1, Oct 1992 3.00
❑1/2nd, Dec 1992; Hologram cover 2.95
❑2, Dec 1992; bagged with tattoo 2.95
❑3, Feb 1993 2.95
❑4 2.95
❑5 2.95

NECROSCOPE BOOK II: WAMPHYRI
Malibu

❑1 2.95
❑2, Nov 1994 2.95
❑3, Jan 1994 2.95
❑4 2.95
❑5 2.95

NECROWAR
Dreamwave

❑1, Jul 2003 2.95
❑2, Aug 2003 2.95
❑3, Sep 2003 2.95

NEFARISMO
Fantagraphics / Eros

❑1 2.95
❑2 2.95
❑3 2.95
❑4 2.95
❑5, May 1995 2.95
❑6, Aug 1995 2.95
❑7, Sep 1995 2.95
❑8, Oct 1995 2.95

NEGATION
CrossGen

❑1, Jan 2002 2.95
❑2, Feb 2002 2.95
❑3, Mar 2002 2.95
❑4, Apr 2002 2.95
❑5, May 2002 2.95
❑6, Jun 2002 2.95
❑7, Jul 2002 2.95
❑8, Aug 2002 2.95
❑9, Sep 2002 2.95
❑10, Oct 2002 2.95
❑11, Nov 2002 2.95
❑12, Dec 2002 2.95
❑13, Jan 2003 2.95
❑14, Feb 2003 2.95
❑15, Mar 2003 2.95
❑16, Apr 2003 2.95
❑17, May 2003 2.95
❑18, Jun 2003 2.95
❑19, Jul 2003 2.95
❑20, Aug 2003 2.95
❑21, Oct 2003 2.95
❑22, Nov 2003 2.95
❑23, Nov 2003 2.95
❑24, Dec 2003 2.95
❑25, Jan 2004 2.95
❑26, Feb 2004 2.95
❑27, Mar 2004 2.95

NEGATION WAR
CrossGen

❑1, Apr 2004 2.95
❑1/2nd, May 2004 2.95
❑2, May 2004 2.95

New Mutants

X-Men farm team turned into X-Force

©Marvel

New Mutants (2nd series)

Relaunch didn't last nearly as long

©Marvel

New Talent Showcase

DC break-in title lasted longer than others

©DC

New Teen Titans (1st Series)

Brought X-Men approach to DC universe

©DC

New Teen Titans (2nd Series)

Restart was sold in comics shops only

©DC

NEGATION PREQUEL
CrossGen

	N-MINT
❑1, Dec 2001	2.95

NEGATIVE BURN
Image

	N-MINT
❑1, Jun 2006	4.95
❑2, Jul 2006	4.95

NEGATIVE BURN
Caliber

	N-MINT
❑1, ca. 1993, b&w BB (w); BB (a); A: Flaming Carrot	4.00
❑2, ca. 1993, b&w	4.00
❑3, Apr 1993, b&w A: Bone	4.00
❑4, ca. 1993, b&w	4.00
❑5, ca. 1993, b&w	4.00
❑6, ca. 1994, b&w	4.00
❑7, ca. 1994, b&w	4.00
❑8, ca. 1994, b&w	4.00
❑9, ca. 1994, b&w AMo (w);	4.00
❑10, ca. 1994, b&w AMo (w);	4.00
❑11, ca. 1994, b&w BB, NG (w);	4.00
❑12, ca. 1994, b&w	4.00
❑13, ca. 1994, b&w BMB, AMo, NG (w); A: Strangers in Paradise	6.50
❑14, ca. 1994, b&w	3.95
❑15, ca. 1994, b&w BB (w); BB (a)	3.95
❑16, ca. 1994, b&w	3.95
❑17, ca. 1994, b&w	3.95
❑18, ca. 1994, b&w	3.95
❑19, Jan 1995, b&w	3.95
❑20, Feb 1995, b&w	3.95
❑21, Mar 1995, b&w	3.95
❑22, Apr 1995, b&w	3.95
❑23, May 1995, b&w	3.95
❑24, Jun 1995, b&w	3.95
❑25, Jul 1995, b&w	3.95
❑26, Aug 1995, b&w	3.95
❑27, Sep 1995, b&w	3.95
❑28, Oct 1995, b&w; Dusty Star	3.95
❑29, Nov 1995, b&w	3.95
❑30, Dec 1995, b&w	3.95
❑31, Jan 1996, b&w	3.95
❑32, Feb 1996, b&w	3.95
❑33, Mar 1996, b&w	3.95
❑34, Apr 1996, b&w	3.95
❑35, May 1996, b&w	3.95
❑36, Jun 1996, b&w	3.95
❑37, Jul 1996, b&w BB, AMo (w); BMB, BB, CR (a); A: Dusty Star	3.95
❑38, Aug 1996	3.95
❑39, Sep 1996	3.95
❑40, Oct 1996	3.95
❑41, Nov 1996	3.95
❑42, Dec 1996	3.95
❑43, Jan 1997	3.95
❑44, Feb 1997	3.95
❑45 1997	3.95
❑46 1997	3.95
❑47 1997	3.95
❑48 1997	4.95
❑49 1997	4.95
❑50 1997	6.95

NEGATIVE BURN: SUMMER SPECIAL 2005
Image

	N-MINT
❑1, Dec 2005	4.95

NEGATIVE ONE
Eirich Olson

	N-MINT
❑1, Sep 1999	2.95

NEIL & BUZZ IN SPACE AND TIME
Fantagraphics

	N-MINT
❑1, Apr 1989, b&w	2.00

NEIL THE HORSE COMICS AND STORIES
Aardvark-Vanaheim

	N-MINT
❑1, Feb 1983, b&w	2.50
❑2, Apr 1983, b&w	2.00
❑3, Jun 1983, b&w	2.00
❑4, Aug 1983, b&w	2.00
❑5, Nov 1983, b&w	2.00
❑6, Feb 1984, b&w	2.00
❑7, Apr 1984, b&w	2.00
❑8, Jun 1984, b&w	2.00
❑9, Sep 1984, b&w	2.00
❑10, Dec 1984, b&w	2.00
❑11, Apr 1985, b&w; Title changes to Neil the Horse	2.00
❑12, Jun 1985, b&w	2.00
❑13, Dec 1986, b&w	2.00
❑14, Jul 1988, b&w; giant	3.00
❑15, Aug 1988, b&w; giant	3.00

NEMESISTER
Cheeky

	N-MINT
❑1, Apr 1997, b&w; cardstock cover	2.95
❑2, Jun 1997, b&w; cardstock cover	2.95
❑3, Sep 1997, b&w; cardstock cover	2.95
❑3/Ashcan; ashcan edition	0.50
❑4, Nov 1997, b&w; cardstock cover	2.95
❑5	2.95
❑6	2.95
❑7	2.95
❑8	2.95
❑9	2.95

NEMESIS THE WARLOCK (FLEETWAY/QUALITY)
Fleetway-Quality

	N-MINT
❑1 1989, b&w	2.00
❑2, b&w	2.00
❑3, b&w	2.00
❑4, b&w	2.00
❑5, b&w	2.00
❑6, b&w	2.00
❑7, b&w	2.00
❑8, b&w	2.00
❑9, b&w BT (a)	2.00
❑10, b&w	2.00
❑11, b&w	2.00
❑12, b&w	2.00
❑13, b&w	2.00
❑14, b&w O: Torquemada	2.00
❑15, b&w	2.00
❑16, b&w	2.00
❑17, b&w	2.00
❑18, b&w	2.00
❑19, b&w	2.00

NEO
Excalibur

	N-MINT
❑1, b&w	1.50

NEOMEN
Slave Labor

	N-MINT
❑1, Oct 1987; no indicia	1.75
❑2, Jan 1988	1.75

NEON CITY
Innovation

	N-MINT
❑1, b&w	2.25

NEON CITY: AFTER THE FALL
Innovation

	N-MINT
❑1, b&w	2.50

NEON CYBER
Image

	N-MINT
❑1, Aug 1999	2.50
❑1/Variant, Aug 1999; alternate cover	5.00
❑2, Sep 1999; Man facing giant on cover	2.50
❑2/Variant, Sep 1999; alternate cover.	2.50
❑3, Oct 1999; alternate cover	2.50
❑4, Dec 1999	2.50
❑5, Jan 2000	2.50
❑6, Mar 2000	2.50
❑7, May 2000	2.50
❑8, Jun 2000	2.50

NEON GENESIS EVANGELION BOOK 1
Viz

	N-MINT
❑1/A, Sep 1997	2.95
❑1/B, Sep 1997; Special collector's edition; printed in Japanese style (back to front)	2.95
❑2/A, Oct 1997	2.95
❑2/B, Oct 1997; Special collector's edition; printed in Japanese style (back to front)	2.95
❑3/A, Nov 1997	2.95
❑3/B, Nov 1997; Special collector's edition; printed in Japanese style (back to front)	2.95
❑4/A, Dec 1997	2.95
❑4/B, Dec 1997; Special collector's edition; printed in Japanese style (back to front)	2.95
❑5/A, Jan 1998	2.95
❑5/B, Jan 1998; Special collector's edition; printed in Japanese style (back to front)	2.95
❑6/A, Feb 1998	2.95
❑6/B, Feb 1998; Special collector's edition; printed in Japanese style (back to front)	2.95

NEON GENESIS EVANGELION BOOK 2
Viz

	N-MINT
❑1/A, Mar 1998	3.50
❑1/B, Mar 1998; Special collector's edition; printed in Japanese style (back to front)	3.50
❑2/A, Apr 1998	3.25
❑2/B, Apr 1998; Special collector's edition; printed in Japanese style (back to front)	3.25
❑3/A, May 1998	2.95
❑3/B, May 1998; Special collector's edition; printed in Japanese style (back to front)	2.95

Other grades: Multiply price above by 5/6 for VF/NM • 2/3 for VERY FINE • 1/3 for FINE • 1/5 for VERY GOOD • 1/8 for GOOD

❑4/A, Jun 1998 .... 2.95
❑4/B, Jun 1998; Special collector's edition; printed in Japanese style (back to front) 2.95
❑5/A, Jul 1998 .... 2.95
❑5/B, Jul 1998; Special collector's edition; printed in Japanese style (back to front) 2.95

NEON GENESIS EVANGELION BOOK 3
VIZ

❑1/A, Aug 1998 .... 2.95
❑1/B, Aug 1998; Special collector's edition; printed in Japanese style (back to front) 2.95
❑2/A, Sep 1998 .... 2.95
❑2/B, Sep 1998; Special collector's edition; printed in Japanese style (back to front) 2.95
❑3/A, Oct 1998 .... 2.95
❑3/B, Oct 1998; Special collector's edition; printed in Japanese style (back to front) 2.95
❑4/A, Nov 1998 .... 2.95
❑4/B, Nov 1998; Special collector's edition; printed in Japanese style (back to front) 2.95
❑5/A, Dec 1998 .... 2.95
❑5/B, Dec 1998; Special collector's edition; printed in Japanese style (back to front) 2.95
❑6/A, Jan 1999 .... 3.25
❑6/B, Jan 1999; Special collector's edition; printed in Japanese style (back to front) 3.25

NEON GENESIS EVANGELION BOOK 4
VIZ

❑1/A, Feb 1999 .... 2.95
❑1/B, Feb 1999; Special collector's edition; printed in Japanese style (back to front) 2.95
❑2/A, Mar 1999 .... 2.95
❑2/B, Mar 1999; Special collector's edition; printed in Japanese style (back to front) 2.95
❑3/A, Apr 1999 .... 2.95
❑3/B, Apr 1999; Special collector's edition; printed in Japanese style (back to front) 2.95
❑4/A, May 1999 .... 2.95
❑4/B, May 1999, Special collector's edition; printed in Japanese style (back to front) 2.95
❑5/A, Jun 1999 .... 2.95
❑5/B, Jun 1999; Special collector's edition; printed in Japanese style (back to front) 2.95
❑6/A, Jul 1999 .... 2.95
❑6/B, Jul 1999; printed in Japanese style (back to front) 2.95
❑7, Aug 1999 .... 2.95
❑7/B, Aug 1999; printed in Japanese style (back to front) 2.95

NEON GENESIS EVANGELION BOOK 5
VIZ

❑1, Oct 2000 .... 2.95
❑1/B, Oct 2000; printed in Japanese style (back to front) 2.95
❑2, Nov 2000 .... 2.95
❑2/B, Nov 2000; printed in Japanese style (back to front) 2.95
❑3, Dec 2000 .... 2.95
❑3/B, Dec 2000; printed in Japanese style (back to front) 2.95
❑4, Jan 2001 .... 2.95
❑4/B, Jan 2001; printed in Japanese style (back to front) 2.95
❑5, Feb 2001 .... 2.95
❑5/B, Feb 2001; printed in Japanese style (back to front) 2.95
❑6, Mar 2001 .... 2.95
❑6/B, Mar 2001; printed in Japanese style (back to front) 2.95
❑7, Apr 2001 .... 2.95
❑7/B, May 2001; printed in Japanese style (back to front) 2.95

NEON GENESIS EVANGELION BOOK 6
VIZ

❑1, Jul 2001 .... 3.50
❑1/B, Jul 2001; printed in Japanese style (back to front) 3.50
❑2, Aug 2001 .... 3.50
❑2/B, Aug 2001; printed in Japanese style (back to front) 3.50
❑3, Sep 2001 .... 3.50
❑3/B, Sep 2001; printed in Japanese style (back to front) 3.50
❑4, Oct 2001 .... 3.50
❑4/B, Oct 2001; printed in Japanese style (back to front) 3.50

NEON GENESIS EVANGELION BOOK 7
VIZ

❑1, May 2002 .... 2.95
❑1/B, May 2002; printed in Japanese style (back to front) 2.95
❑2, Jun 2002 .... 2.95
❑2/B, Jun 2002; printed in Japanese style (back to front) 2.95
❑3, Jul 2002 .... 2.95
❑3/B, Jul 2002; printed in Japanese style (back to front) 2.95
❑4, Aug 2002 .... 2.95
❑4/B, Aug 2002; printed in Japanese style (back to front) 2.95
❑5, Sep 2002 .... 2.95
❑5/B, Sep 2002; printed in Japanese style (back to front) 2.95
❑6, Oct 2002 .... 3.50
❑6/B, Oct 2002; printed in Japanese style (back to front) 3.50

NEOTOPIA
ANTARCTIC

❑1, Jan 2003 .... 3.95
❑2, Feb 2003 .... 3.95
❑3, Apr 2003 .... 3.95
❑4, May 2003 .... 3.95
❑5, Jun 2003 .... 3.95

NEOTOPIA (VOL. 2)
ANTARCTIC

❑1, Aug 2003 .... 2.99
❑2, Sep 2003 .... 2.99
❑3, Oct 2003 .... 2.99
❑4, Nov 2003 .... 2.99
❑5, Dec 2003 .... 2.99

NEOTOPIA (VOL. 3)
ANTARCTIC

❑1, Feb 2004 .... 2.99
❑2, Apr 2004 .... 2.99
❑3, May 2004 .... 2.99
❑4, Jun 2004 .... 2.99

NEOTOPIA (VOL. 4)
ANTARCTIC

❑1, Aug 2004 .... 2.99
❑2, Sep 2004 .... 2.99
❑3, Oct 2004 .... 2.99
❑4, 2004 .... 2.99

NERVE
NERVE

❑1 .... 2.00
❑2 .... 1.50
❑3 .... 1.50
❑4 .... 1.50
❑5, Apr 1987 .... 1.50
❑6 1987 .... 1.50
❑7, Jul 1987 .... 1.50
❑8, oversize 4.00

NERVOUS REX
BLACKTHORNE

❑1, Aug 1985 .... 2.00
❑2, Oct 1985 .... 2.00
❑3, Dec 1985 .... 2.00
❑4, Feb 1986 .... 2.00
❑5, Apr 1986 .... 2.00
❑6, Jun 1986 .... 2.00
❑7, Aug 1986 .... 2.00
❑8, Oct 1986 .... 2.00
❑9, Dec 1986 .... 2.00
❑10, Feb 1987 .... 2.00

NESTROBBER
BLUE SKY BLUE

❑1, Oct 1992, b&w 1.95
❑2, Jun 1994, b&w 1.95

NETHERWORLD
AMBITION

❑1, b&w 1.50

NETHERWORLDS
ADVENTURE

❑1, Aug 1988, b&w 1.95

NETMAN
INFORMATION NETWORKS

❑0, Aug 1992 .... 0.50

NEURO JACK
BIG

❑1, Aug 1996, all-digital art 2.25

NEUROMANCER: THE GRAPHIC NOVEL
MARVEL / EPIC

❑1 .... 8.95

NEVADA
DC / VERTIGO

❑1, May 1998 .... 2.50
❑2, Jun 1998 .... 2.50
❑3, Jul 1998 .... 2.50
❑4, Aug 1998 .... 2.50
❑5, Sep 1998 .... 2.50
❑6, Oct 1998 .... 2.50

NEVERMEN
DARK HORSE

❑1, May 2000 .... 2.95
❑2, Jun 2000 .... 2.95
❑3, Jul 2000 .... 2.95

NEVERMEN: STREETS OF BLOOD
DARK HORSE

❑1, Jan 2003 .... 2.99
❑2, Feb 2003 .... 2.99
❑3, May 2003 .... 2.99

NEVERWHERE (NEIL GAIMAN'S)
DC / VERTIGO

❑1, Aug 2005 .... 2.99
❑2, Sep 2005 .... 2.99
❑3, Oct 2005 .... 2.99
❑4 2005 .... 2.99
❑5, Jan 2006 .... 2.99
❑6, Apr 2006 .... 2.99
❑7, Jul 2006 .... 2.99

NEW ADVENTURES OF ABRAHAM LINCOLN
IMAGE

❑1 .... 19.95

NEW ADVENTURES OF BEAUTY AND THE BEAST (DISNEY'S...)
DISNEY

❑1 .... 1.50
❑1/Direct ed. 2.00
❑2 .... 1.50

NEW ADVENTURES OF CHOLLY AND FLYTRAP, THE: TILL DEATH DO US PART
MARVEL / EPIC

❑1, Dec 1990; prestige format 4.95
❑2, Jan 1991; prestige format 4.95
❑3, Feb 1991; prestige format 4.95

NEW ADVENTURES OF FELIX THE CAT
FELIX

❑1, Oct 1992 .... 2.25
❑2 1992 .... 2.25
❑3 1992 .... 2.25
❑4 .... 2.25
❑5 1993 .... 2.25
❑6 .... 2.25
❑7 1993; becomes New Adventures of Felix the Cat and Friends 2.25

NEW ADVENTURES OF HUCK FINN
GOLD KEY

❑1 .... 10.00

NEW ADVENTURES OF JESUS
RIP OFF

❑1 .... 4.50

NEW ADVENTURES OF JUDO JOE
ACE

❑1, Mar 1987, b&w; Reprints 1.75

NEW ADVENTURES OF PINOCCHIO
DELL

❑1, Oct 1962 .... 65.00
❑2 1963 .... 50.00
❑3 1963 .... 50.00

New Terrytoons (2nd Series)

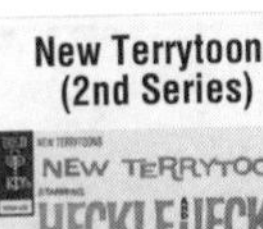

Your place to find Heckle and Jeckle

©Gold Key

New Titans

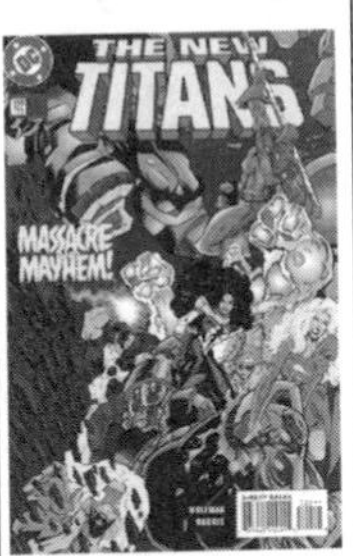

New Teen Titans without the "Teen"

©DC

New Vampire Miyu (Vol. 1)

Vampire princess and watcher of the dark

©Ironcat

New Warriors

New team for younger super-heroes

©Marvel

New Wave

Scientists break the barrier between worlds

©Eclipse

N-MINT

NEW ADVENTURES OF RICK O'SHAY AND HIPSHOT
COTTONWOOD

❑1 4.95
❑2 4.95

NEW ADVENTURES OF SHALOMAN
MARK 1

❑1, b&w 2.00
❑2 2.50
❑3 O: Shaloman 2.50
❑4, b&w 2.50
❑5; indicia says #4 2.95
❑8, b&w A: Y-Guys 2.50
❑Special 1, b&w 2.50

NEW ADVENTURES OF SPEED RACER
NOW

❑0, Nov 1993; multi-dimensional cover 3.95
❑1, Dec 1993 1.95
❑2, Jan 1994 1.95
❑3, Feb 1994 1.95

NEW ADVENTURES OF SUPERBOY
DC

❑1, Jan 1980, KS (a) 4.00
❑1/Whitman, Jan 1980; Whitman variant 8.00
❑2, Feb 1980, KS (a) 1.50
❑2/Whitman, Feb 1980, KS (a); Whitman variant 3.00
❑3, Mar 1980, KS (a) 1.50
❑4, Apr 1980, KS (a) 1.50
❑4/Whitman, Apr 1980, KS (a); Whitman variant 3.00
❑5, May 1980, KS (a) 1.50
❑5/Whitman, May 1980, KS (a); Whitman variant 3.00
❑6, Jun 1980, KS (a) 1.50
❑6/Whitman, Jun 1980; Whitman variant 3.00
❑7, Jul 1980, KS (a); bonus Superman story 1.50
❑8, Aug 1980, KS (a) 1.50
❑8/Whitman, Aug 1980, KS (a); Whitman variant 3.00
❑9, Sep 1980, KS (a); V: Phantom Zone villains 1.50
❑10, Oct 1980, KS (a); Krypto back-up 1.50
❑11, Nov 1980, KS (a); Superbaby back-up 1.50
❑12, Dec 1980, KS (a) 1.50
❑13, Jan 1981, KS (a) 1.50
❑14, Feb 1981, KS (a) 1.50
❑15, Mar 1981, KS (a) 1.50
❑16, Apr 1981, KS (a) 1.50
❑17, May 1981, KS (a); Krypto back-up 1.50
❑18, Jun 1981, KS (a) 1.50
❑19, Jul 1981, KS (a) 1.50
❑20, Aug 1981, KS (a) 1.50
❑21, Sep 1981, KS (a) 1.00
❑22, Oct 1981, KS (a) 1.00
❑23, Nov 1981, KS (a) 1.00
❑24, Dec 1981, KS (a) 1.00
❑25, Jan 1982, KS (a) 1.00
❑26, Feb 1982, KS (a) 1.00
❑27, Mar 1982, KS (a) 1.00
❑28, Apr 1982, KS (a); Dial H for Hero back-up 1.00
❑29, May 1982, KS (a); Dial H for Hero back-up 1.00
❑30, Jun 1982, KS (a); Dial H for Hero back-up 1.00
❑31, Jul 1982, KS (a); Dial H for Hero back-up 1.00
❑32, Aug 1982, KS (a); Dial H for Hero back-up 1.00
❑33, Sep 1982, KS (a); Dial H for Hero back-up 1.00
❑34, Oct 1982, KS (a); 1: The Yellow Peril. Dial H for Hero back-up 1.00
❑35, Nov 1982, KS (a); Dial H for Hero back-up 1.00
❑36, Dec 1982, KS (a); Dial H for Hero back-up 1.00
❑37, Jan 1983, KS (a); Dial H for Hero back-up 1.00
❑38, Feb 1983, KS (a); Dial H for Hero back-up 1.00
❑39, Mar 1983, KS (a); Dial H for Hero back-up 1.00
❑40, Apr 1983, KS (a); Dial H for Hero back-up 1.00
❑41, May 1983, GK (c); KS (a); Dial H for Hero back-up 1.00
❑42, Jun 1983, GK (c); KS (a); Dial H for Hero back-up 1.00
❑43, Jul 1983, GK (c); KS (a); Dial H for Hero back-up 1.00
❑44, Aug 1983, GK (c); KS (a); Dial H for Hero back-up 1.00
❑45, Sep 1983, GK (c); KS (a); 1: Sunburst. Dial H for Hero back-up 1.00
❑46, Oct 1983, KS (a); Dial H for Hero back-up 1.00
❑47, Nov 1983, KS (a); Dial H for Hero back-up 1.00
❑48, Dec 1983; KS (a); Dial H for Hero back-up 1.00
❑49, Jan 1984; KS (a); Dial H for Hero back-up 1.00
❑50, Feb 1984; Giant-size KG, KS (a); A: Legion of Super-Heroes 1.25
❑51, Mar 1984 FM (c); CS, KS (a) 1.00
❑52, Apr 1984 KS (a) 1.00
❑53, May 1984 KS (a) 1.00
❑54, Jun 1984 KS (a) 1.00

NEW ADVENTURES OF TERRY & THE PIRATES
AVALON

❑1, ca. 1998 2.95
❑2 2.95
❑3 2.95
❑4 2.95
❑5 2.95
❑6 2.95

NEW ADVENTURES OF THE PHANTOM BLOT (WALT DISNEY'S...)
GOLD KEY

❑1 22.00
❑2, 1st appearance of Super Goof 18.00
❑3 12.00
❑4 8.00
❑5 8.00
❑6 8.00
❑7 8.00

NEW AGE COMICS
FANTAGRAPHICS

❑1, ca. 1985, Independent comics sampler 1.50

NEW AMERICA
ECLIPSE

❑1, Nov 1987 TY (c) 2.00
❑2, Dec 1987 2.00
❑3, Jan 1988 TY (c) 2.00
❑4, Feb 1988 2.00

NEW ARCHIES
ARCHIE

❑1, Oct 1987 2.50
❑2, Jan 1988 1.50
❑3, Feb 1988 1.50
❑4, Apr 1988 1.50
❑5, May 1988 1.50
❑6, Jun 1988 1.00
❑7, Aug 1988 1.00
❑8, Sep 1988 1.00
❑9, Oct 1988 1.00
❑10, Dec 1988 1.00
❑11, Jan 1989 1.00
❑12, Feb 1989 1.00
❑13, Apr 1989 1.00
❑14, May 1989 1.00
❑15, Jun 1989 1.00
❑16, Aug 1989 1.00
❑17, Sep 1989 1.00
❑18, Oct 1989 1.00
❑19, Dec 1989 1.00
❑20, Jan 1990 1.00
❑21, Feb 1990 1.00
❑22, May 1990 1.00

NEW AVENGERS
MARVEL

❑0/Military 2005, Officially released on April 28th, 2005 at the Pentagon, this edition was made available only to the US Military. 10.00
❑1, Feb 2005 7.00
❑1/Retailer ed., Feb 2005, Spider-Man cover 70.00
❑1/DirCut, Feb 2005 5.00
❑1/Quesada, Feb 2005 12.00
❑1/Finch, Feb 2005, Third print cover. 9.00
❑1/2nd, Feb 2005 3.00
❑2, Mar 2005 2.25
❑2/Hairsine, Mar 2005 45.00
❑3, Apr 2005 2.25
❑3/Wolverine, Apr 2005 45.00
❑4, May 2005 3.00
❑4/Cheung, May 2005, Jim Cheung variant cover 15.00
❑4/DF, May 2005, Signed by John Romita Jr. 20.00
❑5, Jun 2005 2.25
❑5/Granov, Jun 2005 15.00
❑6, Jul 2005 2.25
❑6/Hitch, Jul 2005 15.00
❑7, Aug 2005 2.25
❑7/Adams, Aug 2005 25.00
❑8, Sep 2005 2.50
❑8/Romita, Sep 2005 20.00
❑9, Oct 2005 2.50

Other grades: Multiply price above by 5/6 for VF/NM • 2/3 for VERY FINE • 1/3 for FINE • 1/5 for VERY GOOD • 1/8 for GOOD

- ❑9/Trimpe, Oct 2005 2.50
- ❑10 2005 2.50
- ❑11 2005 2.50
- ❑12 2005 2.50
- ❑13, Jan 2006 2.50
- ❑14, Feb 2006 2.50
- ❑15, Mar 2006 2.50
- ❑16, Apr 2006 2.50
- ❑17, Jun 2006 2.50
- ❑18, Jun 2006 2.50
- ❑19, Aug 2006 2.50
- ❑20, Sep 2006 2.50
- ❑21, Sep 2006 2.50
- ❑Annual 1, Jul 2006 3.99

NEW AVENGERS/ILLUMINATI SPECIAL
MARVEL

- ❑1, Apr 2006 7.00

NEW AVENGERS: MOST WANTED FILES
MARVEL

- ❑1, Feb 2006 5.00

NEW BEGINNING
UNICORN

- ❑1, b&w 2.00
- ❑2, b&w 2.00
- ❑3, b&w 2.00

NEW BONDAGE FAIRIES
FANTAGRAPHICS / EROS

- ❑1, Nov 1996 2.95
- ❑2, Dec 1996 2.95
- ❑3, Jan 1997 2.95
- ❑4, Feb 1997 2.95
- ❑5, Mar 1997 2.95
- ❑6, Apr 1997 2.95
- ❑7, May 1997 2.95
- ❑8, Jun 1997 2.95
- ❑9, Jul 1997 2.95
- ❑10, Aug 1997 2.95
- ❑11, Sep 1997 2.95
- ❑12, Oct 1997 2.95

NEW CREW
PERSONALITY

- ❑1; Patrick Stewart 2.95
- ❑2; Jonathan Frakes 2.95
- ❑3 2.95
- ❑4 2.95
- ❑5 2.95
- ❑6 2.95
- ❑7 2.95
- ❑8 2.95
- ❑9 2.95
- ❑10 2.95

NEW CRIME FILES OF MICHAEL MAUSER, PRIVATE EYE
APPLE

- ❑1, b&w 2.50

NEW DNAGENTS
ECLIPSE

- ❑1, Oct 1985 ME (w); O: The DNAgents 1.50
- ❑2, Nov 1985 ME (w) 1.25
- ❑3, Nov 1985 ME (w) 1.25
- ❑4, Dec 1985 ME (w) 1.00
- ❑5, Jan 1986 ME (w) 1.00
- ❑6, Feb 1986 ME (w) 1.00
- ❑7, Apr 1986 ME (w) 1.00
- ❑8, Apr 1986 ME (w) 1.00
- ❑9, Jun 1986 ME (w) 1.00
- ❑10, Jun 1986 ME (w) 1.00
- ❑11, Aug 1986 ME (w) 1.00
- ❑12, Aug 1986 ME (w) 1.00
- ❑13, Oct 1986 ME (w) 1.00
- ❑14, Nov 1986 ME (w) 1.00
- ❑15, Dec 1986 ME (w) 1.00
- ❑16, Jan 1987 ME (w) 1.00
- ❑17, Mar 1987 ME (w) 1.00

NEW ENGLAND GOTHIC
VISIGOTH

- ❑1, Dec 1986 2.00
- ❑2, Jun 1987, b&w 2.00

NEW EXCALIBUR
MARVEL

- ❑1, Jan 2006 2.99
- ❑2, Feb 2006 2.99
- ❑3, Mar 2006 2.99
- ❑4, Mar 2006 2.99
- ❑5, May 2006 2.99
- ❑6, Jun 2006 2.99
- ❑7, Aug 2006 2.99
- ❑8, Sep 2006 2.99
- ❑9, Sep 2006 2.99

NEWFORCE
IMAGE

- ❑1, Jan 1996; polybagged with Kodiak card 2.50
- ❑2, Feb 1996 2.50
- ❑3, Mar 1996 2.50
- ❑4, Apr 1996 2.50

NEW FRONTIER
DARK HORSE

- ❑1, Oct 1992, b&w 2.75
- ❑2, Nov 1992, b&w 2.75
- ❑3, Dec 1992, b&w 2.75

NEW FRONTIERS
EVOLUTION

- ❑1, b&w 1.75
- ❑2, b&w 1.95

NEW GODS (1ST SERIES)
DC

- ❑1, Mar 1971, JK (c); JK (w); JK (a); 1: Orion. 1: Apokolips. 1: Metron. 1: Kalibak. 1: Highfather. 1: Lightray 35.00
- ❑2, May 1971, JK (c); JK (w); JK (a); 1: Deep Six 18.00
- ❑3, Jul 1971, JK (c); JK (w); JK (a); 1: Black Racer 12.00
- ❑4, Sep 1971; Giant-size JK (c); JK (w); JK (a) 12.00
- ❑5, Nov 1971; Giant-size JK (c); JK (w); JK (a) 12.00
- ❑6, Jan 1972; Giant-size JK (c); JK (w); JK (a); 1: Fastbak 12.00
- ❑7, Mar 1972; Giant-size JK (c); JK (w); JK (a); 1: Steppenwolf 12.00
- ❑8, May 1972; Giant-size JK (c); JK (w); JK (a) 12.00
- ❑9, Jul 1972; Giant-size JK (c); JK (w); JK (a); 1: Forager 12.00
- ❑10, Sep 1972, JK (c); JK (w); JK (a) 12.00
- ❑11, Nov 1972, JK (c); JK (w); JK (a) 12.00
- ❑12, Jul 1977, AM (c); DN, DA (a); Series begins again 6.00
- ❑13, Aug 1977, AM (c); DN, DA (a) 6.00
- ❑14, Oct 1977, AM, RB (c); DN, DA (a) 6.00
- ❑15, Dec 1977, RB (c); RB, BMc (a) 6.00
- ❑16, Feb 1978, AM (c); DN (a) 6.00
- ❑17, Apr 1978, JSn (c); DN, DA (a) 6.00
- ❑18, Jun 1978, AM (c); DN, DA (a) 6.00
- ❑19, Aug 1978, BL, JSa (c); DN, DA (a) 6.00

NEW GODS (2ND SERIES)
DC

- ❑1, Jun 1984; New Gods (Vol. 1) reprints 2.00
- ❑2, Jul 1984; New Gods (Vol. 1) reprints 2.00
- ❑3, Aug 1984; New Gods (Vol. 1) reprints 2.00
- ❑4, Sep 1984; New Gods (Vol. 1) reprints 2.00
- ❑5, Nov 1984; New Gods (Vol. 1) reprints 2.00
- ❑6, Dec 1984; reprints New Gods (Vol. 1) #11, plus new stories 2.00

NEW GODS (3RD SERIES)
DC

- ❑1, Feb 1989 ME (w) 2.25
- ❑2, Mar 1989 ME (w) 2.00
- ❑3, Apr 1989 ME (w) 2.00
- ❑4, May 1989 ME (w) 2.00
- ❑5, Jun 1989 ME (w) 2.00
- ❑6, Jul 1989 ME (w) 1.50
- ❑7, Aug 1989 ME (w) 1.50
- ❑8, Sep 1989 ME (w) 1.50
- ❑9, Oct 1989 ME (w) 1.50
- ❑10, Nov 1989 ME (w) 1.50
- ❑11, Dec 1989 ME (w) 1.50
- ❑12, Jan 1990 ME (w) 1.50
- ❑13, Feb 1990 1.50
- ❑14, Mar 1990 1.50
- ❑15, Apr 1990 1.50
- ❑16, May 1990 1.50
- ❑17, Jun 1990 1.50
- ❑18, Jul 1990 1.50
- ❑19, Aug 1990 1.50
- ❑20, Sep 1990 1.50
- ❑21, Dec 1990 1.50
- ❑22, Jan 1991 1.50
- ❑23, Feb 1991 1.50
- ❑24, Mar 1991 1.50
- ❑25, Apr 1991 1.50
- ❑26, May 1991 1.50
- ❑27, Jul 1991 1.50
- ❑28, Aug 1991 1.50

NEW GODS (4TH SERIES)
DC

- ❑1, Oct 1995 2.00
- ❑2, Nov 1995 2.00
- ❑3, Dec 1995 2.00
- ❑4, Jan 1996 2.00
- ❑5, Feb 1996 2.00
- ❑6, Mar 1996 2.00
- ❑7, Apr 1996 2.00
- ❑8, Jun 1996 2.00
- ❑9, Jul 1996 KG (a) 2.00
- ❑10, Aug 1996 A: Superman 2.00
- ❑11, Sep 1996 2.00
- ❑12, Nov 1996 JBy (w); JBy (a) 1.00
- ❑13, Dec 1996 JBy (w); JBy (a) 2.00
- ❑14, Jan 1997 JBy (w); JBy (a); A: Forever People 2.00
- ❑15, Feb 1997 JBy (w); JBy (a) 2.00

NEW GODS SECRET FILES
DC

- ❑1, Sep 1998 4.95

NEW GUARDIANS
DC

- ❑1, Sep 1988; Giant-size 2.00
- ❑2, Oct 1988 1.25
- ❑3, Nov 1988 1.25
- ❑4, Dec 1988 1.25
- ❑5, Dec 1988 1.25
- ❑6, Jan 1989; Invasion! 1.25
- ❑7, Feb 1989; Invasion! 1.25
- ❑8, Apr 1989 1.25
- ❑9, Jun 1989 1.25
- ❑10, Jul 1989 1.25
- ❑11, Aug 1989 1.25
- ❑12, Sep 1989 1.25

NEW HAT
BLACK EYE

- ❑1 1.00

NEW HERO COMICS
RED SPADE

- ❑1, b&w 1.00

NEW HORIZONS
SHANDA FANTASY ARTS

- ❑1, b&w 4.95
- ❑2, b&w 4.95
- ❑3, b&w 4.50
- ❑4, b&w 4.50
- ❑5, Apr 1999, b&w 4.50

NEW HUMANS (PIED PIPER)
PIED PIPER

- ❑1, Jul 1987, b&w 1.95
- ❑2 1987 1.95
- ❑3 1987 1.95

NEW HUMANS (ETERNITY)
ETERNITY

- ❑1, Dec 1987 1.95
- ❑2, Jan 1988 1.95
- ❑3, Feb 1988 1.95
- ❑4, Mar 1988; Nude cover 1.95
- ❑5 1988 1.95
- ❑6 1988 1.95
- ❑7 1988 1.95
- ❑8, Sep 1988 1.95
- ❑9 1988 1.95
- ❑10 1989 1.95
- ❑11 1.95
- ❑12, Mar 1989 1.95
- ❑13 1.95
- ❑14 1.95
- ❑15 1.95
- ❑16 1.95
- ❑17 1.95
- ❑Annual 1, b&w 2.95

Next Men (John Byrne's...)

Only survivors of a bio-engineering project
©Dark Horse

Nexus (Vol. 1)

Distant worlds with Mike Baron, Steve Rude
©Capital

NFL Superpro

Failed attempt to get comics fans into sports
©Marvel

Nick Fury, Agent of SHIELD (1st series)

Jim Steranko's celebrated and stylish series
©Marvel

Nick Fury vs. S.H.I.E.L.D.

Organization is invaded from within
©Marvel

N-MINT

NEW JUSTICE MACHINE
INNOVATION

❑1, Nov 1989 .... 2.00
❑2, Jan 1990 .... 2.00
❑3, Mar 1990 .... 2.00

NEW KIDS ON THE BLOCK, THE: BACKSTAGE PASS
HARVEY

❑1, ca. 1991 .... 1.25

NEW KIDS ON THE BLOCK: CHILLIN'
HARVEY

❑1, ca. 1990 .... 1.50
❑2, Jan 1991 .... 1.25
❑3, ca. 1991 .... 1.25
❑4, Apr 1991 .... 1.25
❑5, Jun 1991 .... 1.25
❑6, Oct 1991 .... 1.25
❑7, Dec 1991 .... 1.25

NEW KIDS ON THE BLOCK COMIC TOUR '90
HARVEY

❑1, ca. 1991 .... 1.25

NEW KIDS ON THE BLOCK MAGIC SUMMER TOUR
HARVEY

❑1, ca. 1991 .... 1.25
❑1/Ltd., ca. 1991; limited edition 3.95

NEW KIDS ON THE BLOCK, THE: NKOTB
HARVEY

❑1, Dec 1990 .... 1.25
❑2, Jan 1991 .... 1.25
❑3, Feb 1991 .... 1.25
❑4, Mar 1991 .... 1.25
❑5, May 1991 .... 1.25
❑6, Jul 1991 .... 1.25

NEW KIDS ON THE BLOCK STEP BY STEP
HARVEY

❑1, ca. 1991 .... 1.25

NEW KIDS ON THE BLOCK: VALENTINE GIRL
HARVEY

❑1, ca. 1991 .... 1.25

NEW LOVE
FANTAGRAPHICS

❑1, Aug 1996, b&w 2.95
❑2, Oct 1996, b&w 2.95
❑3, Mar 1997, b&w 2.95
❑4, Jun 1997, b&w 2.95
❑5, Sep 1997, b&w 2.95
❑6, Dec 1997, b&w 2.95

NEWMAN
IMAGE

❑1, Jan 1996; polybagged with card; Extreme Destroyer Part 3 .... 2.50
❑2, Feb 1996 .... 2.50
❑3, Apr 1996 .... 2.50
❑4, Apr 1996 .... 2.50

NEW MANGAVERSE
MARVEL

❑1, Mar 2006 .... 2.99
❑2, Apr 2006 .... 2.99

N-MINT

❑3, May 2006 .... 2.99
❑4, Jun 2006 .... 2.99

NEWMEN
IMAGE

❑1, Apr 1994 RL (w) 2.50
❑2, May 1994 .... 2.25
❑3, Jun 1994 .... 2.25
❑4, Jul 1994 .... 2.25
❑5, Aug 1994 .... 2.50
❑6, Sep 1994 .... 2.50
❑7, Oct 1994 .... 2.50
❑8, Nov 1994 .... 2.50
❑9, Dec 1994; Extreme Sacrifice 2.50
❑10, Jan 1995 .... 2.50
❑11, Feb 1995; polybagged 2.50
❑11/A, Feb 1995; Alternate cover; polybagged 2.50
❑12, Mar 1995 .... 2.50
❑13, Apr 1995 .... 2.50
❑14, May 1995 .... 2.50
❑15, Jun 1995; no indicia 2.50
❑16, Jul 1995 .... 2.50
❑16/A, Jul 1995; alternate cover 3.00
❑17, Aug 1995 .... 2.50
❑18, Sep 1995 .... 2.50
❑19, Oct 1995 .... 2.50
❑20, Nov 1995; Babewatch 2.50
❑20/A, Nov 1995; Babewatch 2.50
❑21, Aug 1996 .... 2.50
❑22, Nov 1996; becomes Adventures of the New Men 2.50
❑23, Mar 1997 .... 2.50
❑24, Apr 1997 .... 2.50
❑25, May 1997 .... 2.50

NEW MICKEY MOUSE CLUB FUN BOOK
GOLDEN PRESS

❑1, ca. 1977, Squarebound; has bio text piece on Lisa Whelchel 15.00

NEW MUTANTS
MARVEL

❑1, Mar 1983, BMc (a) 6.00
❑2, Apr 1983, BMc (a); V: Sentinels ... 2.00
❑3, May 1983, BMc (a); V: Brood 2.00
❑4, Jun 1983, SB (a) 1.50
❑5, Jul 1983, SB (a); A: Team America 1.50
❑6, Aug 1983, SB (a); A: Team America 1.50
❑7, Sep 1983, SB (a) 1.50
❑8, Oct 1983, BMc (a); O: Magma 1.50
❑9, Nov 1983, SB (a); 1: Selene 1.50
❑10, Dec 1983, SB (a); 1: Magma 1.50
❑11, Jan 1984, SB (a); Assistant Editor Month 1.50
❑12, Feb 1984, SB (a) 1.50
❑13, Mar 1984, SB (a); 1: Cypher. A: Kitty Pryde 1.50
❑14, Apr 1984, SB (a); A: X-Men. V: Sy'm 1.50
❑15, May 1984, SB (a); A: X-Men 1.50
❑16, Jun 1984, 1: Warpath. 1: Hellions 1.50
❑17, Jul 1984, SB (a); V: Hellions 1.50
❑18, Aug 1984, BSz (a); 1: Warlock (machine) 1.50
❑19, Sep 1984, BSz (a) 1.50
❑20, Oct 1984, BSz (a) 1.50

N-MINT

❑21, Nov 1984; Double-size BSz (a); O: Warlock (machine) 1.50
❑22, Dec 1984, BSz (a) 1.50
❑23, Jan 1985, BSz (a); A: Cloak & Dagger 1.50
❑24, Feb 1985, BSz (a); A: Cloak & Dagger 1.50
❑25, Mar 1985, BSz (c); BSz (a); 1: Legion (cameo). A: Cloak & Dagger 2.50
❑26, Apr 1985, BSz (c); BSz (a); 1: Legion (psychic) 2.50
❑27, May 1985, BSz (c); BSz (a); A: Legion. V: Legion 2.00
❑28, Jun 1985, BSz (a); A: Legion 2.00
❑29, Jul 1985, BSz (a); 1: Guido Carosella (Strong Guy) 2.00
❑30, Aug 1985, BSz (a) 1.50
❑31, Sep 1985, BSz (a) 1.50
❑32, Oct 1985 .... 1.50
❑33, Nov 1985 .... 1.50
❑34, Dec 1985 .... 1.50
❑35, Jan 1986; BSz (a); A: Magneto. Magneto begins as leader of New Mutants 1.50
❑36, Feb 1986 BSz (a) 1.50
❑37, Mar 1986 BSz (a) 1.50
❑38, Apr 1986 .... 1.50
❑39, May 1986 KP (a) 1.50
❑40, Jun 1986 A: Captain America 1.50
❑41, Jul 1986 .... 1.50
❑42, Aug 1986 .... 1.50
❑43, Sep 1986 .... 1.50
❑44, Oct 1986 BG (a); A: Legion 1.50
❑45, Nov 1986 BG (a) 1.50
❑46, Dec 1986 BG (a) 1.50
❑47, Jan 1987 .... 1.50
❑48, Feb 1987 BG (a) 1.50
❑49, Mar 1987 .... 1.50
❑50, Apr 1987; Double-size; BG (a); Professor X returns as headmaster 1.50
❑51, May 1987 KN (a); A: Star Jammers 1.50
❑52, Jun 1987 .... 1.50
❑53, Jul 1987 .... 1.50
❑54, Aug 1987 .... 1.50
❑55, Sep 1987 .... 1.50
❑56, Oct 1987 .... 1.50
❑57, Nov 1987 .... 1.50
❑58, Dec 1987; registration card 1.50
❑59, Jan 1988 .... 2.00
❑60, Feb 1988; double-sized D: Cypher 2.00
❑61, Mar 1988; new costumes; (conclusion) 2.00
❑62, Apr 1988 .... 1.50
❑63, May 1988 A: X-Men 2.00
❑64, Jun 1988 .... 1.50
❑65, Jul 1988 .... 1.50
❑66, Aug 1988 .... 1.50
❑67, Sep 1988 .... 1.50
❑68, Oct 1988 .... 1.50
❑69, Nov 1988 .... 1.50
❑70, Dec 1988; Inferno 1.50
❑71, Jan 1989; O: N'astirh. Inferno 1.50
❑72, Feb 1989; Inferno 1.50
❑73, Mar 1989; Giant-size; Inferno 2.00
❑74, Apr 1989 .... 1.50
❑75, May 1989 .... 1.50

Other grades: Multiply price above by 5/6 for VF/NM • 2/3 for VERY FINE • 1/3 for FINE • 1/5 for VERY GOOD • 1/8 for GOOD

N-MINT

❑76, Jun 1989 RB (a); A: X-Terminators. A: X-Factor. A: Sub-Mariner 1.50
❑77, Jul 1989 RB (a) 1.50
❑78, Aug 1989 1.50
❑79, Sep 1989 1.50
❑80, Oct 1989 1.50
❑81, Nov 1989 1.50
❑82, Nov 1989 1.50
❑83, Dec 1989 1.50
❑84, Dec 1989; Acts of Vengeance 1.50
❑85, Jan 1990; TMc (c); Acts of Vengeance 1.50
❑86, Feb 1990; TMc (c); 1: Zero. 1: Cable (cameo). Acts of Vengeance 3.00
❑87, Mar 1990 TMc (c); RL, BWi (a); 1: Stryfe. 1: Cable 6.00
❑87/2nd, Mar 1990; TMc (c); 1: Cable. 2nd printing (gold) 2.00
❑88, Apr 1990 TMc (c); RL (a); 2: Cable 2.50
❑89, May 1990 TMc (c) 2.00
❑90, Jun 1990 A: Sabretooth 2.00
❑91, Jul 1990 A: Sabretooth 2.00
❑92, Aug 1990 BH (a) 2.00
❑93, Sep 1990 TMc (c); A: Wolverine 2.00
❑94, Oct 1990 A: Wolverine 2.00
❑95, Nov 1990 D: Warlock (machine) 2.00
❑95/2nd, Nov 1990; D: Warlock (machine). 2nd printing (gold) 2.00
❑96, Dec 1990 2.00
❑97, Jan 1991 2.00
❑98, Feb 1991 RL (w); RL (a); 1: Deadpool. 1: Domino II. 1: Gideon 5.00
❑99, Mar 1991; RL (w); RL (a); 1: Feral. 1: Shatterstar (full appearance). A: Sunspot. Sunspot leaves 2.50
❑100, Apr 1991; Giant-size RL (w); RL (a); O: Shatterstar. 1: X-Force 2.00
❑100/2nd, Apr 1991; RL (w); RL (a); 1: X-Force. 2nd printing (gold) 2.00
❑100/3rd, Apr 1991; RL (w); RL (a); 1: X-Force. 3rd printing (silver) 2.00
❑Annual 1, ca. 1984 BMc (a); 1: Lila Cheney 3.00
❑Annual 2, Oct 1986 1: Meggan. 1: Psylocke 4.00
❑Annual 3, ca. 1987 A: Impossible Man 2.00
❑Annual 4, ca. 1988 2.00
❑Annual 5, ca. 1989 RL (a) 2.00
❑Annual 6, ca. 1990 1: Shatterstar (cameo) 2.50
❑Annual 7, ca. 1991 2.00
❑Special 1, Dec 1985 3.00
❑Summer 1; Giant-size 2.00

NEW MUTANTS (2ND SERIES)
MARVEL

❑1, Jul 2003 4.00
❑2, Aug 2003 2.50
❑3, Sep 2003 2.50
❑4, Oct 2003 2.99
❑5, Nov 2003 2.99
❑6, Dec 2003 2.99
❑7, Jan 2004 2.99
❑8, Apr 2004 2.99
❑9, Apr 2004 2.99
❑10, May 2004 2.99
❑11, May 2004 2.99
❑12, Jun 2004 2.99
❑13, Jun 2004 2.99

NEW MUTANTS, THE: TRUTH OR DEATH
MARVEL

❑1, Nov 1997; gatefold summary; original New Mutants travel through time and meet present-day counterparts 2.50
❑2, Dec 1997; gatefold summary 2.50
❑3, Jan 1998; gatefold summary 2.50

NEW NIGHT OF THE LIVING DEAD
FANTACO

❑0 2.00
❑1 3.95
❑2 3.95
❑3 3.95

NEW ORDER
CREATIVE FORCE

❑1, Nov 1994 2.95

NEW PALTZ COMIX
MOODS

❑1 1.50

N-MINT

❑2 1974 1.50
❑3 1.50

NEW PARTNERS IN PERIL
BLUE COMET

❑1, b&w 2.25

NEW PARTNERS IN PERIL (VOL. 2)
TAMI

❑1 2.25

NEW PEOPLE
DELL

❑1, Jan 1970 10.00
❑2, May 1970 8.00

NEW POWER STARS
BLUE COMET

❑1, b&w 2.00

NEW SHADOWHAWK
IMAGE

❑1, Jun 1995 2.50
❑2, Aug 1995 2.50
❑3, Sep 1995 2.50
❑4, Nov 1995 2.50
❑5, Dec 1995 2.50
❑6, Feb 1996 2.50
❑7, Mar 1996 2.50

NEW STATESMEN
FLEETWAY-QUALITY

❑1 4.00
❑2 4.00
❑3 4.00
❑4 4.00
❑5 4.00
❑Book 1 14.95

NEWSTIME
DC

❑1, May 1993; death of Superman magazine; Death of Superman Magazine 3.25

NEWSTRALIA
INNOVATION

❑1, Jul 1989 2.00
❑2 2.00
❑3 2.25
❑4 2.25
❑5, b&w 2.25

NEW TALENT SHOWCASE
DC

❑1, Jan 1984 1.50
❑2, Feb 1984 1.50
❑3, Mar 1984 1.50
❑4, Apr 1984 1.50
❑5, May 1984 1.50
❑6, Jun 1984 1.50
❑7, Jul 1984 1.50
❑8, Aug 1984 1.50
❑9, Sep 1984 1.50
❑10, Oct 1984 1.50
❑11, Nov 1984 1.25
❑12, Dec 1984 1.25
❑13, Jan 1985 1.25
❑14, Feb 1985 1.25
❑15, Mar 1985 1.25
❑16, Apr 1985; Title changes to Talent Showcase 1.25
❑17, May 1985 1.25
❑18, Jun 1985 1.25
❑19, Jul 1985 1.25

NEW TEEN TITANS (1ST SERIES)
DC

❑1, Nov 1980, GP, RT (a) 8.00
❑2, Dec 1980, GP, RT (a); 1: Trigon. 1: Wintergreen. 1: Deathstroke the Terminator. D: The Ravager 10.00
❑3, Jan 1981, GP (a); 1: Shimmer. 1: Gizmo. 1: Mammoth. 1: Fearsome Five. 1: Psimon. V: Doctor Light 3.00
❑4, Feb 1981, GP (a); A: Justice League 3.00
❑5, Mar 1981, CS, RT (a); O: Raven. 1: Trigon 3.00
❑6, Apr 1981, GP (w); GP (a); O: Raven. V: Trigon 3.00
❑7, May 1981, GP, RT (a); O: Cyborg. V: Fearsome Five 3.00
❑8, Jun 1981, GP (w); GP, RT (a); O: Kid Flash 3.00
❑9, Jul 1981, GP, RT (a) 3.00
❑10, Aug 1981, GP, RT (a); O: Changeling. A: Deathstroke the Terminator. V: Terminator 3.00

N-MINT

❑11, Sep 1981, GP, RT (a) 2.00
❑12, Oct 1981, GP, RT (a) 2.00
❑13, Nov 1981, GP, RT (a); A: Doom Patrol. A: Robotman 2.00
❑14, Dec 1981, GP, RT (a); 1: Houngan. 1: Plasmus. 1: Phobia. A: Doom Patrol 2.00
❑15, Jan 1982, GP, RT (a); A: Doom Patrol. V: Brotherhood of Evil 2.00
❑16, Feb 1982, GP, RA, RT (a); 1: Yankee Poodle. 1: Pig-Iron. 1: Fastback. 1: Captain Carrot. 1: Rubberduck. 1: Alley-Kat-Abra 2.00
❑17, Mar 1982, GP, RT (a); A: Francis Kane 2.00
❑18, Apr 1982, GP, RT (a); 1: Maladi Maranova. A: Starfire (later Red Star) 2.00
❑19, May 1982, GP, RT (a); A: Hawkman 2.00
❑20, Jun 1982, GP, RT (a); 1: The Disruptor 2.00
❑21, Jul 1982, GC, GP, RT (a); 1: Monitor. 1: Harbinger. 1: Brother Blood. 1: Night Force. 1: Baron Winters. V: Brother Blood 2.00
❑22, Aug 1982, GP, RT (a); V: Brother Blood 2.00
❑23, Sep 1982, GP, RT (a); 1: Komand'r (Blackfire) 2.00
❑24, Oct 1982, GP, RT (a); 1: X'Hal. A: Omega Men 2.00
❑25, Nov 1982, GP, CS, RT (a); 1: Masters of the Universe. A: Omega Men. Masters of the Universe preview 2.00
❑26, Dec 1982, GP, RT (a); 1: Terra 2.00
❑27, Jan 1983, GP, RT (a); 1: Howard Rondo. Atari Force preview 2.00
❑28, Feb 1983, GP, RT (a); A: Terra. V: Brotherhood of Evil 2.00
❑29, Mar 1983, GP, RT (a); A: Speedy. V: Brotherhood of Evil 2.00
❑30, Apr 1983, GP, RT (a); A: Terra 2.00
❑31, May 1983, GP, RT (a); V: Brotherhood of Evil 2.00
❑32, Jun 1983, GP, RT (a); O: Kid Flash. A: Thunder and Lightning 2.00
❑33, Jul 1983, GP, RT (a); D: Trident 2.00
❑34, Aug 1983, GP (a); A: Deathstroke the Terminator. V: Terminator 2.00
❑35, Oct 1983, GP, KP, RT (a) 2.00
❑36, Nov 1983, KP (a); A: Thunder and Lightning 2.00
❑37, Dec 1983 GP (a); A: Outsiders. V: Doctor Light. V: Shimmer. V: Gizmo. V: Mammoth. V: Psimon 2.00
❑38, Jan 1984 GP (w); GP (a); O: Wonder Girl 2.00
❑39, Feb 1984; GP (w); GP (a); Dick Grayson quits as Robin; Wally West retires as Kid Flash 2.50
❑40, Mar 1984; GP (w); GP (a); Series continued in Tales of the Teen Titans #41 2.00
❑Annual 1, ca. 1982 GP (a); A: Omega Men 3.00
❑Annual 2, ca. 1983 GP (a); 1: Lyla (Harbinger). 1: Vigilante. A: Monitor 2.00
❑Annual 3, ca. 1984; D: Terra. Published as Tales of the Teen Titans Annual 2.00

NEW TEEN TITANS (2ND SERIES)
DC

❑1, Aug 1984 GP (a) 3.00
❑2, Oct 1984 GP (a); A: Trigon 2.50
❑3, Nov 1984 GP (a); V: Trigon 2.50
❑4, Jan 1985 GP (a); V: Trigon 2.50
❑5, Feb 1985 GP (a); V: Trigon 2.50
❑6, Mar 1985 2.00
❑7, Apr 1985 JL (a); O: Lilith 2.00
❑8, May 1985 JL (a); A: Destiny 2.00
❑9, Jun 1985 JL (a); 1: Kole 2.00
❑10, Jul 1985 JL (a) 2.00
❑11, Aug 1985 JL (a) 2.00
❑12, Sep 1985 2.00
❑13, Oct 1985 2.00
❑14, Nov 1985 2.00
❑15, Dec 1985 2.00
❑16, Jan 1986 DG (a); A: Omega Men 2.00
❑17, Feb 1986; Wedding of Starfire 2.00
❑18, Mar 1986 2.00
❑19, Apr 1986 2.00
❑20, May 1986 A: original Titans. A: Robin II (Jason Todd) 2.00

Nightcrawler (Vol. 1)

Fanciful romp through alternate reality
©Marvel

Night Force

Wolfman and Colan's horror crew
©DC

Night Man

Short-lived comic spawns long-lived TV show
©Malibu

Night Music

Fantasy from P. Craig Russell
©Eclipse

Nightstalkers

Frank Drake, Hannibal King, and Blade
©Marvel

N-MINT

- ❑21, Jun 1986 A: Cheshire 1.50
- ❑22, Jul 1986 .... 1.50
- ❑23, Aug 1986 V: Hybrids 1.50
- ❑24, Oct 1986 V: Hybrids 1.50
- ❑25, Nov 1986 V: Hybrids 1.50
- ❑26, Dec 1986 KGa (a) 1.50
- ❑27, Jan 1987 KGa (a); V: Brotherhood of Evil 1.50
- ❑28, Feb 1987 V: Brother Blood 1.50
- ❑29, Mar 1987 V: Brother Blood 1.50
- ❑30, Apr 1987 V: Brother Blood 1.50
- ❑31, May 1987 A: Superman. A: Batman. V: Brother Blood 1.50
- ❑32, Jun 1987 .... 1.50
- ❑33, Jul 1987 EL (a) 1.50
- ❑34, Aug 1987 V: Hybrid 1.50
- ❑35, Sep 1987 PB (a) 1.50
- ❑36, Oct 1987 V: Wildebeest 1.50
- ❑37, Nov 1987 V: Wildebeest 1.75
- ❑38, Dec 1987 A: Infinity Inc.. V: Ultra-Humanite 1.75
- ❑39, Jan 1988 .... 1.75
- ❑40, Feb 1988 V: I.Q.. V: Silver Fog. V: The Gentleman Ghost 1.75
- ❑41, Mar 1988 V: Wildebeest 1.75
- ❑42, Apr 1988; Brother Blood's child born 1.75
- ❑43, May 1988 CS (a); V: Raven 1.75
- ❑44, Jun 1988 V: Godiva 1.75
- ❑45, Jul 1988 A: Dial H for Hero 1.75
- ❑46, Aug 1988 A: Dial H for Hero 1.75
- ❑47, Sep 1988 O: Titans 1.75
- ❑48, Oct 1988 V: Red Star 1.75
- ❑49, Nov 1988; V: Red Star. Series continued in New Titans #50 .... 1.75
- ❑Annual 1, ca. 1985 1: Vanguard. A: Superman. V: Vanguard 2.50
- ❑Annual 2, Aug 1986 JBy (a); O: Brother Blood. 1: Cheshire. A: Doctor Light 2.75
- ❑Annual 3, ca. 1987; 1: Godiva. 1: Danny Chase. A: King Faraday. cover indicates '87 Annual, indicia says '86 .... 2.50
- ❑Annual 4, ca. 1988; Private Lives 2.50

NEW TEEN TITANS (GIVEAWAYS AND PROMOS)
DC

- ❑1; Beverage; DC drug issue 1.00
- ❑2; IBM/DC drug issue 1.00
- ❑3; GP, DC (a); Keebler; drug issue 1.00
- ❑4; DC (a); Keebler; drug issue 1.00
- ❑5 .... 1.00

NEW TERRYTOONS (2ND SERIES)
GOLD KEY

- ❑1, Oct 1962 .... 35.00
- ❑2, Jan 1963, Summer Cruise 22.00
- ❑3 .... 12.00
- ❑4, Sep 1969 .... 8.00
- ❑5, Nov 1970 .... 8.00
- ❑6, Jan 1970 .... 6.00
- ❑7, Mar 1970 .... 6.00
- ❑8, May 1970 .... 6.00
- ❑9, Jul 1970 .... 6.00
- ❑10, Oct 1970 .... 6.00
- ❑11 1971 .... 5.00

N-MINT

- ❑12 1971 .... 5.00
- ❑13 1971 .... 5.00
- ❑14, Nov 1971 .... 5.00
- ❑15, Feb 1972 .... 5.00
- ❑16, May 1972 .... 5.00
- ❑17, Aug 1972 .... 5.00
- ❑18, Nov 1972 .... 5.00
- ❑19, Feb 1973 .... 5.00
- ❑20, May 1973 .... 5.00
- ❑21, Jul 1973 .... 3.50
- ❑22 1973 .... 3.50
- ❑23, Nov 1973 .... 3.50
- ❑24, Jan 1974 .... 3.50
- ❑25 .... 3.50
- ❑26, Jun 1974 .... 3.50
- ❑27, Aug 1974 .... 3.50
- ❑28, Oct 1974 .... 3.50
- ❑29, Dec 1974 .... 3.50
- ❑30, Feb 1975 .... 3.50
- ❑31, Apr 1976 .... 2.50
- ❑32, Jun 1975 .... 2.50
- ❑33, Aug 1975 .... 2.50
- ❑34, Oct 1975 .... 2.50
- ❑35, Dec 1975 .... 2.50
- ❑36, Feb 1976 .... 2.50
- ❑37, Apr 1976 .... 2.50
- ❑38, Jun 1976 .... 2.50
- ❑39, Aug 1976 .... 2.50
- ❑40, Sep 1976 .... 2.50
- ❑41, Nov 1976 .... 2.00
- ❑42, Jan 1977 .... 2.00
- ❑43, Mar 1977 .... 2.00
- ❑44, May 1977 .... 2.00
- ❑45, Jul 1977 .... 2.00
- ❑46, Sep 1977 .... 2.00
- ❑47, Nov 1977 .... 2.00
- ❑48, Jan 1978 .... 2.00
- ❑49, Mar 1978 .... 2.00
- ❑50, May 1978 .... 2.00
- ❑51, Jul 1979 .... 2.00
- ❑52, Sep 1979 .... 2.00
- ❑53, Nov 1979 .... 2.00
- ❑54, Jan 1979 .... 2.00

NEW THUNDERBOLTS
MARVEL

- ❑1, Dec 2004 .... 2.99
- ❑2, Jan 2005 .... 2.99
- ❑3, Feb 2005 .... 2.99
- ❑4, Mar 2005 .... 2.99
- ❑5, Apr 2005 .... 2.99
- ❑6, May 2005 .... 2.99
- ❑7, May 2005 .... 2.99
- ❑8, Jun 2005 .... 2.99
- ❑9, Jul 2005 .... 2.99
- ❑10, Aug 2005 .... 2.99
- ❑11, Sep 2005 .... 2.99
- ❑12, Oct 2005 .... 2.99
- ❑13, Nov 2005 .... 2.99
- ❑14, Dec 2005 .... 2.99
- ❑15, Jan 2006 .... 2.99
- ❑16, Feb 2006 .... 2.99
- ❑17, Mar 2006 .... 2.99
- ❑18, Apr 2006 .... 2.99

N-MINT

NEW TITANS
DC

- ❑0, Oct 1994; A: . A: Terra. A: Nightwing. A: Impulse. A: Mirage. A: Damage. Series continued in New Titans #115; Titans get new headquarters 1.95
- ❑50, Dec 1988; GP (a); O: Wonder Girl (new origin). Series continued from New Teen Titans #49 .... 2.00
- ❑51, Dec 1988 GP (a) 2.00
- ❑52, Jan 1989 GP (a) 2.00
- ❑53, Feb 1989 GP (a) 2.00
- ❑54, Mar 1989 GP (a) 2.00
- ❑55, Jun 1989 GP (w); GP (a); 1: Troia 2.00
- ❑56, Jul 1989 A: Gnaark 2.00
- ❑57, Aug 1989 GP (a); V: Wildebeest 2.00
- ❑58, Sep 1989 GP (a) 2.00
- ❑59, Oct 1989 GP (a); V: Wildebeest 2.00
- ❑60, Nov 1989 GP (w); GP (a); A: Tim Drake 2.50
- ❑61, Dec 1989 GP (w); GP (a) 2.50
- ❑62, Jan 1990 A: Deathstroke the Terminator 2.00
- ❑63, Feb 1990 A: Deathstroke the Terminator 2.00
- ❑64, Mar 1990 A: Deathstroke the Terminator 2.00
- ❑65, Apr 1990 A: Robin III. A: Deathstroke the Terminator 2.00
- ❑66, May 1990 GP (w); 2.00
- ❑67, Jul 1990 GP (w); 2.00
- ❑68, Jul 1990 V: Royal Flush Gang 2.00
- ❑69, Sep 1990 .... 2.00
- ❑70, Oct 1990 A: Deathstroke the Terminator 2.00
- ❑71, Nov 1990 .... 2.00
- ❑72, Jan 1991 A: Deathstroke the Terminator. D: Golden Eagle 2.00
- ❑73, Feb 1991 1: Phantasm. A: Deathstroke the Terminator 2.00
- ❑74, Mar 1991 1: Pantha. A: Deathstroke the Terminator 2.00
- ❑75, Apr 1991 A: Deathstroke the Terminator 2.00
- ❑76, Jun 1991; A: Deathstroke the Terminator. destruction of Titans Tower 2.00
- ❑77, Jul 1991; A: Deathstroke the Terminator. Cyborg rebuilt 2.00
- ❑78, Aug 1991 A: Deathstroke the Terminator 2.00
- ❑79, Sep 1991 A: Team Titans. A: Deathstroke the Terminator 2.00
- ❑80, Nov 1991 KGa (a); A: Team Titans 1.75
- ❑81, Dec 1991 CS (a); A: Pariah 1.75
- ❑82, Jan 1992 .... 1.75
- ❑83, Feb 1992 D: Jericho 1.75
- ❑84, Mar 1992 O: Phantasm. D: Raven 1.75
- ❑85, Apr 1992 1: baby Wildebeest. A: Team Titans 1.75
- ❑86, May 1992 V: Terminator 1.75
- ❑87, Jun 1992 .... 1.75
- ❑88, Jul 1992 .... 1.75
- ❑89, Aug 1992 .... 1.75
- ❑90, Sep 1992 .... 1.75
- ❑91, Oct 1992 A: Phantasm 1.75
- ❑92, Nov 1992 .... 1.75
- ❑93, Dec 1992; follow-up to Titans Sell-Out Special 1.75

Other grades: Multiply price above by 5/6 for VF/NM • 2/3 for VERY FINE • 1/3 for FINE • 1/5 for VERY GOOD • 1/8 for GOOD

❑94, Feb 1993; covers of #94-96 form triptych 1.75
❑95, Mar 1993 1.75
❑96, Apr 1993 1.75
❑97, May 1993 1.75
❑98, Jun 1993 1.75
❑99, Jul 1993 1: Arsenal 1.75
❑100, Aug 1993; Giant-size; V: Evil Raven. pin-ups; foil cover; wedding of Starfire II (Koriand'r) 3.00
❑101, Sep 1993 1.75
❑102, Oct 1993 1.75
❑103, Nov 1993 1.75
❑104, Dec 1993; final fate of Cyborg 1.75
❑105, Dec 1993 1.75
❑106, Jan 1994 1.75
❑107, Jan 1994 1.75
❑108, Feb 1994 1.75
❑109, Mar 1994 1.75
❑110, May 1994 1.75
❑111, Jun 1994 1.75
❑112, Jul 1994 1.95
❑113, Aug 1994 1.95
❑114, Sep 1994; new team; Series continued in The New Titans #0 1.95
❑115, Nov 1994 1.95
❑116, Dec 1994 A: Green Lantern. A: Psimon 1.95
❑117, Jan 1995 V: Psimon 1.95
❑118, Feb 1995 A: Thunder and Lightning 1.95
❑119, Mar 1995 V: Deathwing 1.95
❑120, Apr 1995 A: Supergirl 1.95
❑121, May 1995 1.95
❑122, Jun 1995 2.25
❑123, Jul 1995 2.25
❑124, Aug 1995 2.25
❑125, Sep 1995; Giant-size 3.50
❑126, Oct 1995 2.25
❑127, Nov 1995 2.25
❑128, Dec 1995 2.25
❑129, Jan 1996 2.25
❑130, Feb 1996 2.25
❑Annual 5, ca. 1989; See New Teen Titans Annual for previous issues; Who's Who entries 3.50
❑Annual 6, ca. 1990 CS (a); 1: Society of Sin. A: Starfire 3.50
❑Annual 7, ca. 1991 O: Team Titans. 1: Team Titans 3.50
❑Annual 8, ca. 1992 CS (a) 3.00
❑Annual 9, ca. 1993 O: Anima. 1: Anima 3.00
❑Annual 10, ca. 1994; Elseworlds 3.00
❑Annual 11, ca. 1995; Year One 3.95

NEW TRIUMPH FEATURING NORTHGUARD
Matrix

❑1 1.75
❑1/2nd 1.75
❑2, ca. 1985 1.50
❑3 1.50
❑4 1.50
❑5 1.50

NEW TWO-FISTED TALES
E.C. / Dark Horse

❑1 HK, WE (a) 5.50

NEW TWO-FISTED TALES (2ND SERIES)
Dark Horse

❑1, Oct 1993 4.95

NEW VAMPIRE MIYU (VOL. 1)
Ironcat

❑1, Sep 1997 3.00
❑2, Oct 1997 3.00
❑3, Nov 1997 3.00
❑4, Dec 1997 3.00
❑5, Jan 1998 3.00
❑6, Feb 1998 3.00

NEW VAMPIRE MIYU (VOL. 2)
Ironcat

❑1, Apr 1998 2.95
❑2, May 1998 2.95
❑3, Jun 1998 2.95
❑4, Jul 1998 2.95
❑5, Aug 1998 2.95
❑6, Sep 1998 2.95

NEW VAMPIRE MIYU (VOL. 3)
Ironcat

❑1, Oct 1998 2.95
❑2, Nov 1998 2.95
❑3, Dec 1998 2.95
❑4, Jan 1999 2.95
❑5, Feb 1999 2.95
❑6, Mar 1999 2.95
❑7, Apr 1999 2.95

NEW VAMPIRE MIYU (VOL. 4)
Ironcat

❑1, May 1999 2.95
❑2, Jun 1999 2.95
❑3, Jul 1999 2.95
❑4, Aug 1999 2.95
❑5, Sep 1999 2.95
❑6, Oct 1999 2.95

NEW WARRIORS
Marvel

❑1, Jul 1990 O: New Warriors 1.50
❑1/2nd, Jul 1990; O: New Warriors. 2nd Printing (gold) 1.00
❑2, Aug 1990 O: Night Thrasher. O: Silhouette. 1: Silhouette 1.25
❑3, Sep 1990 1.25
❑4, Oct 1990 1.25
❑5, Nov 1990 1.25
❑6, Dec 1990 1.25
❑7, Jan 1991 A: Punisher 1.25
❑8, Feb 1991 O: Bengal. A: Punisher 1.25
❑9, Mar 1991 A: Punisher 1.25
❑10, Apr 1991 1.25
❑11, May 1991 A: Wolverine 1.25
❑12, Jun 1991 1.25
❑13, Jul 1991 1.25
❑14, Aug 1991 A: Namor. A: Darkhawk 1.25
❑15, Sep 1991 1.25
❑16, Oct 1991 1.25
❑17, Nov 1991 A: Fantastic Four 1.25
❑18, Dec 1991 1.25
❑19, Jan 1992 1.25
❑20, Feb 1992 1.25
❑21, Mar 1992 1.25
❑22, Apr 1992 1.25
❑23, May 1992 O: Night Thrasher. O: Silhouette. O: Chord 1.25
❑24, Jun 1992 O: Silhouette. O: Chord 1.25
❑25, Jul 1992; O: Chord. Die-cut cover 2.50
❑26, Aug 1992 1.25
❑27, Sep 1992 1.25
❑28, Oct 1992 1: Cardinal. 1: Turbo I (Michiko "Mickey" Musashi) 1.25
❑29, Nov 1992 1.25
❑30, Dec 1992 1.25
❑31, Jan 1993 1.25
❑32, Feb 1993 1.25
❑33, Mar 1993 1: Turbo II (Mike Jeffries) 1.25
❑34, Apr 1993 1.25
❑35, May 1993 1.25
❑36, Jun 1993 1.25
❑37, Jul 1993 1.25
❑38, Aug 1993 1.25
❑39, Sep 1993 1.25
❑40, Oct 1993 A: Nova. A: Air-Walker. A: Super Nova. A: Firelord 1.25
❑40/Variant, Oct 1993; A: Nova. A: Air-Walker. A: Super Nova. A: Firelord. Gold foil on cover 2.25
❑41, Nov 1993 1.25
❑42, Dec 1993 1.25
❑43, Jan 1994 1.25
❑44, Feb 1994 1.25
❑45, Mar 1994 1.25
❑46, Apr 1994 1.25
❑47, May 1994 1.25
❑48, Jun 1994 1.50
❑49, Jul 1994 1.50
❑50, Aug 1994; Giant-size 2.00
❑50/Variant, Aug 1994; Giant-size; Glow-in-the-dark cover 2.95
❑51, Sep 1994 1.50
❑52, Oct 1994 1.50
❑53, Nov 1994 1.50
❑54, Dec 1994 1.50
❑55, Jan 1995 1.50
❑56, Feb 1995 1.50
❑57, Mar 1995 1.50
❑58, Apr 1995 1.50
❑59, May 1995 1.50
❑60, Jun 1995; Giant-size 2.50
❑61, Jul 1995; Maximum Clonage Prologue 1.50
❑62, Aug 1995 A: Scarlet Spider 1.50
❑63, Sep 1995 1.50
❑64, Oct 1995 A: Night Thrasher. A: Rage 1.50
❑65, Nov 1995 A: Namorita 1.50
❑66, Dec 1995 A: Scarlet Spider. A: Speedball 1.50
❑67, Jan 1996; concludes in Web of Scarlet Spider #3 1.50
❑68, Feb 1996 A: Guardians of the Galaxy 1.50
❑69, Mar 1996 D: Speedball 1.50
❑70, Apr 1996 1.50
❑71, May 1996 1.50
❑72, Jun 1996 A: Avengers 1.50
❑73, Jul 1996 1.50
❑74, Aug 1996 1.50
❑75, Sep 1996 1.50
❑Annual 1, ca. 1991 O: Night Thrasher 2.50
❑Annual 2, ca. 1992 2.25
❑Annual 3, ca. 1993 2.95
❑Annual 4, ca. 1994 2.95
❑Ashcan 1; "Ashcan" mini-comic 0.75

NEW WARRIORS (VOL. 3)
Marvel

❑1, Jul 2005 4.00
❑2, Aug 2005 2.99
❑3, Sep 2005 2.99
❑4 2005 2.99
❑5, Jan 2006 2.99
❑6, Feb 2006 2.99

NEW WARRIORS (VOL. 2)
Marvel

❑1, Oct 1999 2.99
❑2, Nov 1999 2.50
❑3, Dec 1999 2.50
❑4, Jan 2000 2.50
❑5, Feb 2000 2.50
❑6, Mar 2000 2.50
❑7, Apr 2000 2.50
❑8, May 2000 2.50
❑9, Jun 2000 2.50
❑10, Jul 2000 2.50

NEW WAVE
Eclipse

❑1, Jun 1986 2.00
❑1/A, misprint 2.00
❑2, Jul 1986 1.50
❑3, Jul 1986 1.50
❑4, Aug 1986 1.00
❑5, Aug 1986, PG (c) 1.00
❑6, Sep 1986 1.00
❑7, Sep 1986 1.00
❑8, Sep 1986 1.00
❑9, Oct 1986 1.50
❑10, Nov 1986 1.50
❑11, Dec 1986 1.50
❑12, Feb 1987 1.50
❑13, Mar 1987 1.50

NEW WAVE VERSUS THE VOLUNTEERS
Eclipse

❑1, Apr 1987 2.50
❑2, Jun 1987 2.50

NEW WORLD ORDER
Blazer

❑1, Nov 1992, b&w 3.00
❑2, b&w 2.75
❑3, b&w 2.75
❑4, Aug 1993, b&w 2.50
❑5, Jan 1994, b&w 2.50
❑6, May 1994, b&w 1: Skinhead 2.50
❑7, Aug 1994, b&w 1: Shining 2.50
❑8, Feb 1995, b&w 2.50

NEW WORLD ORDER (PIG'S EYE)
Pig's Eye

❑1 1.00

NEW WORLDS ANTHOLOGY
Caliber

❑1, ca. 1996, b&w 2.95
❑2, Jan 1996 3.95
❑3 3.95

Other grades: Multiply price above by 5/6 for VF/NM • 2/3 for VERY FINE • 1/3 for FINE • 1/5 for VERY GOOD • 1/8 for GOOD

Nightwatch

Scientist confronted by his future self

©Marvel

Nightwing

Original Robin breaks out on his own

©DC

1963

Image Comics' homage to the Silver Age

©Image

Nine Volt

Motley group defends Earth from aliens

©Image

Ninja High School

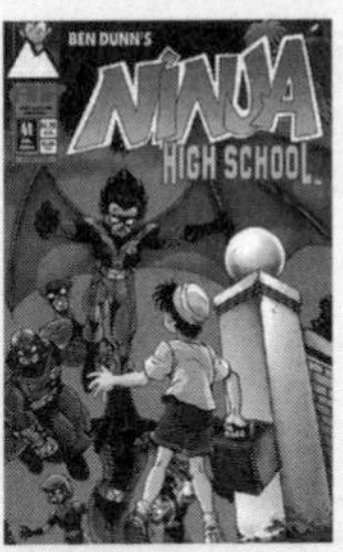

Long-running spoof of Japanese comics

©Antarctic

	N-MINT
❑4	3.95
❑5	3.95
❑6	3.95

NEW X-MEN (ACADEMY X)
MARVEL

	N-MINT
❑1, Jul 2004; Cover says New X-Men: Academy X; indicia says New X-Men	4.00
❑2, Aug 2004	2.99
❑3, Sep 2004	2.99
❑4, Oct 2004	2.99
❑5, Nov 2004	2.99
❑6, Dec 2004	2.99
❑7, Jan 2005	2.99
❑8, Feb 2005	2.99
❑9, Mar 2005	2.99
❑10, Apr 2005	2.99
❑11, May 2005	2.99
❑12, May 2005	2.99
❑13, Jun 2005	2.99
❑14, Jul 2005	2.99
❑15, Aug 2005	2.99
❑16, Sep 2005	2.99
❑16/Variant, Sep 2005; 2nd print	2.99
❑17, Oct 2005	2.99
❑18 2005	2.99
❑19, Dec 2005	2.99
❑20, Jan 2006	2.99
❑21, Feb 2006	2.99
❑22, Mar 2006	2.99
❑23, May 2006	2.99
❑24, May 2006	2.99
❑25, Jun 2006	2.99
❑26, Jul 2006	2.99
❑27, Aug 2006	2.99

NEW X-MEN: ACADEMY X YEARBOOK SPECIAL
MARVEL

	N-MINT
❑1, Dec 2005	3.99

NEW X-MEN: HELLIONS
MARVEL

	N-MINT
❑1, Jul 2005	4.00
❑2, Aug 2005	2.99
❑3, Sep 2005	2.99
❑4, Oct 2005	2.99

NEW YORK CITY OUTLAWS
OUTLAW

	N-MINT
❑1	2.00
❑2	2.00
❑3	2.00
❑4	2.00

NEW YORK: YEAR ZERO
ECLIPSE

	N-MINT
❑1, Aug 1988	2.00
❑2, Aug 1988	2.00
❑3, Sep 1988	2.00
❑4, Oct 1988	2.00

NEXT
DC

	N-MINT
❑1, Sep 2006	2.99

NEXT MAN
COMICO

	N-MINT
❑1, Mar 1985, O: Next Man. 1: Next Man	2.00
❑2, Apr 1985	2.00
❑3, Jun 1985	2.00
❑4, Aug 1985	2.00
❑5, Oct 1985	2.00

NEXT MEN (JOHN BYRNE'S...)
DARK HORSE

	N-MINT
❑0, Feb 1992; JBy (w); JBy (a); Reprints Next Men stories from Dark Horse Presents	3.00
❑1, Jan 1992; JBy (w); JBy (a); Embossed cover (silver logo)	3.00
❑1/2nd, Jan 1992; JBy (w); JBy (a); Embossed cover (gold logo)	2.50
❑2, Mar 1992 JBy (w); JBy (a); 1: Sathanus	3.00
❑3, Apr 1992 JBy (w); JBy (a)	2.50
❑4, May 1992 JBy (w); JBy (a)	2.50
❑5, Jun 1992 JBy (w); JBy (a)	2.50
❑6, Jul 1992 JBy (w); JBy (a)	2.50
❑7, Sep 1992; JBy (w); JBy (a); 1: M4. flipbook with M4 #1 back-up story.	2.50
❑8, Oct 1992; JBy (w); JBy (a); flipbook with M4 #2 back-up story	2.50
❑9, Nov 1992; JBy (w); JBy (a); flipbook with M4 #3 back-up story	2.50
❑10, Dec 1992; JBy (w); JBy (a); flipbook with M4 #4 back-up story.	2.50
❑11, Jan 1993; JBy (w); JBy (a); M4 back-up story	2.50
❑12, Feb 1993; JBy (w); JBy (a); M4 back-up story	2.50
❑13, Mar 1993; JBy (w); JBy (a); M4 back-up story	2.50
❑14, Apr 1993; JBy (w); JBy (a); M4 back-up story	2.50
❑15, Jun 1993; JBy (w); JBy (a); M4 back-up story	3.00
❑16, Jul 1993; JBy (w); JBy (a); M4 back-up story	2.50
❑17, Aug 1993; FM (c); JBy (w); JBy (a); M4 back-up story	2.50
❑18, Sep 1993; JBy (w); JBy (a); M4 back-up story	2.50
❑19, Oct 1993; JBy (w); JBy (a); M4 back-up story	2.50
❑20, Nov 1993; JBy (w); JBy (a); M4 back-up story	2.50
❑21, Dec 1993; JBy (w); JBy (a); A: Hellboy. M4 back-up story	30.00
❑22, Jan 1994; JBy (w); JBy (a); M4 back-up story	2.50
❑23, Mar 1994; JBy (w); JBy (a); M4 back-up story	2.50
❑24, Apr 1994; JBy (w); JBy (a); M4 back-up story	2.50
❑25, May 1994 JBy (w); JBy (a); A: Cutter and Skywise (Elfquest characters)	2.50
❑26, Jun 1994 JBy (w); JBy (a)	2.50
❑27, Aug 1994 JBy (w); JBy (a)	2.50
❑28, Sep 1994 JBy (w); JBy (a)	2.50
❑29, Oct 1994 JBy (w); JBy (a)	2.50
❑30, Dec 1994; JBy (w); JBy (a); series goes on hiatus	2.50

NEXT NEXUS
FIRST

	N-MINT
❑1, Jan 1989 SR (a)	2.00
❑2, Feb 1989 SR (a)	2.00
❑3, Mar 1989 SR (a)	2.00
❑4, Apr 1989 SR (a)	2.00

NEXT WAVE
OVERSTREET

	N-MINT
❑1; Sampling of Five Self-Published comics	2.00

NEXTWAVE
MARVEL

	N-MINT
❑1, Mar 2006	2.99
❑2, May 2006	2.99
❑3, Jun 2006	2.99
❑4, Jun 2006	2.99
❑5, Aug 2006	2.99
❑6, Sep 2006	2.99

NEXUS (VOL. 1)
CAPITAL

	N-MINT
❑1, b&w SR (a); 1: Nexus	15.00
❑2 SR (a)	10.00
❑3, Oct 1982 SR (a)	15.00

NEXUS (VOL. 2)
FIRST

	N-MINT
❑1 1983, SR (a); Nexus begins for first time in color	5.00
❑2, SR (a); O: Nexus	4.00
❑3, SR (a)	2.50
❑4, SR (a)	2.50
❑5, SR (a)	2.50
❑6, SR (a)	2.00
❑7, SR (a); First Comics begins publishing	2.00
❑8, SR (a)	2.00
❑9, SR (a)	1.50
❑10, SR (a)	1.75
❑11, SR (a)	1.75
❑12, SR (a)	1.75
❑13, SR (a)	1.75
❑14, SR (a)	1.75
❑15, SR (a)	1.75
❑16, SR (a)	1.75
❑17, ES (a)	1.75
❑18, SR (a)	1.75
❑19, SR (a)	1.75
❑20, SR (a)	1.75
❑21	1.75
❑22	1.75
❑23	1.75
❑24	1.75
❑25	1.75
❑26	1.75
❑27	1.75
❑28	1.75
❑29	1.75
❑30	1.75
❑31	1.75
❑32	1.75
❑33	1.75
❑34	1.75
❑35	1.75
❑36	1.75
❑37	1.75
❑38	1.75
❑39	1.75
❑40, SR (a)	1.75
❑41	1.75
❑42	1.75
❑43, SR (a)	1.75

Other grades: Multiply price above by 5/6 for VF/NM • 2/3 for VERY FINE • 1/3 for FINE • 1/5 for VERY GOOD • 1/8 for GOOD

N-MINT

❑44 .... 1.75
❑45, A: Badger 1.75
❑46, A: Badger 1.75
❑47, A: Badger 1.75
❑48, A: Badger 1.75
❑49, A: Badger 1.75
❑50, A: Badger. Crossroads 4.00
❑51 .... 1.95
❑52 .... 1.95
❑53 .... 1.95
❑54 .... 1.95
❑55, Apr 1989 .... 1.95
❑56, May 1989 .... 1.95
❑57, Jun 1989 .... 1.95
❑58, Jul 1989 .... 1.95
❑59, Aug 1989 .... 1.95
❑60, Sep 1989 .... 1.95
❑61, Oct 1989 .... 1.95
❑62, Nov 1989 .... 1.95
❑63, Dec 1989 .... 1.95
❑64, Jan 1990 .... 1.95
❑65, Feb 1990 .... 1.95
❑66, Mar 1990 .... 1.95
❑67, Apr 1990 .... 1.95
❑68, May 1990 .... 1.95
❑69, Jun 1990 .... 1.95
❑70, Jul 1990 .... 1.95
❑71, Aug 1990 .... 1.95
❑72, Sep 1990 .... 1.95
❑73, Oct 1990 .... 2.25
❑74, Nov 1990 .... 2.25
❑75, Dec 1990 .... 2.25
❑76, Jan 1991 .... 2.25
❑77, Feb 1991 .... 2.25
❑78, Mar 1991 .... 2.25
❑79, Apr 1991 .... 2.25
❑80, May 1991, Final issue of first series 2.25
❑81, Number not noted in indicia (was retroactive) 3.95
❑82, Number not noted in indicia (was retroactive) 3.95
❑83, Number not noted in indicia (was retroactive) 3.95
❑84, Number not noted in indicia (was retroactive) 3.95
❑85, Number not noted in indicia (was retroactive) 2.95
❑86, Number not noted in indicia (was retroactive) 2.95
❑87, Number not noted in indicia (was retroactive) 2.95
❑88, Number not noted in indicia (was retroactive) 2.95
❑89, Jun 1996, SR (a) 2.95
❑90, Jul 1996, SR (a) 2.95
❑91, Aug 1996, SR (a) 2.95
❑92, Sep 1996, SR (a) 2.95
❑93, Apr 1997, SR (a) 2.95
❑94, May 1997, SR (a) 2.95
❑95, Jul 1997, b&w SR (a) 2.95
❑96, Aug 1997, b&w SR (a) 2.95
❑97, Sep 1997, b&w SR (a) 2.95
❑98, Oct 1997, b&w SR (a) 2.95

NEXUS: ALIEN JUSTICE
DARK HORSE

❑1, Dec 1992 .... 3.95
❑2, Jan 1993 .... 3.95

NEXUS LEGENDS
FIRST

❑1, May 1989, SR (a); Reprints Nexus (Vol. 2) #1 with new cover 2.50
❑2, Jun 1989, SR (a); Reprints Nexus (Vol. 2) #2 with new cover 2.00
❑3, Jul 1989, SR (a); Reprints Nexus (Vol. 2) #3 with new cover 2.00
❑4, Aug 1989, SR (a); Reprints 2.00
❑5, Sep 1989, SR (a); Reprints 2.00
❑6, Oct 1989, SR (a); Reprints 2.00
❑7, Nov 1989, SR (a); Reprints 2.00
❑8, Dec 1989, SR (a); Reprints 2.00
❑9, Jan 1990, SR (a); Reprints 2.00
❑10, Feb 1990, SR (a); Reprints 2.00
❑11, Mar 1990, SR (a); Reprints 2.00
❑12, Apr 1990, SR (a); Reprints 2.00
❑13, May 1990, SR (a); Reprints 2.00
❑14, Jun 1990, SR (a); Reprints 2.00
❑15, Jul 1990, SR (a); Reprints 2.00

N-MINT

❑16, Aug 1990, SR (a); Reprints 2.00
❑17, Sep 1990, SR (a); Reprints 2.00
❑18, Oct 1990, SR (a); Reprints 2.00
❑19, Nov 1990, SR (a); Reprints 2.00
❑20, Dec 1990, SR (a); Reprints 2.00
❑21, Jan 1991, SR (a); Reprints 2.00
❑22, Feb 1991, SR (a); Reprints 2.00
❑23, Mar 1991, SR (a) 2.00

NEXUS MEETS MADMAN
DARK HORSE

❑1, May 1996 .... 2.95

NEXUS THE LIBERATOR
DARK HORSE

❑1, Aug 1992 .... 2.50
❑2, Sep 1992 .... 2.50
❑3, Oct 1992 .... 2.50
❑4, Nov 1992 .... 2.50

NEXUS: THE ORIGIN
DARK HORSE

❑1, ca. 1995 .... 3.95

NEXUS: THE WAGES OF SIN
DARK HORSE

❑1, Mar 1995; cardstock cover 2.95
❑2, Apr 1995; cardstock cover 2.95
❑3, May 1995; cardstock cover 2.95
❑4, Jun 1995 .... 2.95

NFL SUPERPRO
MARVEL

❑1, Oct 1991 .... 1.00
❑2, Nov 1991 .... 1.00
❑3, Dec 1991 .... 1.00
❑4, Jan 1992 .... 1.00
❑5, Feb 1992 .... 1.00
❑6, Mar 1992 .... 1.00
❑7, Apr 1992 .... 1.00
❑8, May 1992 .... 1.00
❑9, Jun 1992 .... 1.00
❑10, Jul 1992 .... 1.00
❑11, Aug 1992 .... 1.00
❑12, Sep 1992 .... 1.00
❑Special 1, Sep 1991; Special collector's edition; Says "Special Edition" on cover 2.00
❑Special 1/Prest, Sep 1991; Says "Super Bowl Special" on cover; prestige format 3.95

NICK FURY, AGENT OF SHIELD (1ST SERIES)
MARVEL

❑1, Jun 1968, JSo (w); JSo (a); 1: Scorpio 75.00
❑2, Jul 1968, JSo (a); O: Centurius. 1: Centurius 40.00
❑3, Aug 1968, JSo (w); JSo (a) 40.00
❑4, Sep 1968, O: Nick Fury. S.H.I.E.L.D. origin issue 40.00
❑5, Oct 1968, JSo (a) 40.00
❑6, Nov 1968, JSo (c); JSo, FS (a) 30.00
❑7, Dec 1968 .... 30.00
❑8, Jan 1969, HT (a); D: Supremus 30.00
❑9, Feb 1969, FS (a) 25.00
❑10, Mar 1969 .... 25.00
❑11, Apr 1969 .... 25.00
❑12, May 1969 .... 25.00
❑13, Jul 1969, HT (a) 25.00
❑14, Aug 1969, HT (a) 20.00
❑15, Nov 1969, 1: Bullseye 50.00
❑16, Nov 1969; Giant-size; JK (a); Reprints from Strange Tales #136-138 .... 20.00
❑17; Giant-size; Reprints from Strange Tales #139-141 .... 20.00
❑18, Mar 1971; Giant-size; Reprints from Strange Tales #142-144 .... 20.00

NICK FURY, AGENT OF SHIELD (2ND SERIES)
MARVEL

❑1, Dec 1983; BH (c); BH (a); Reprints from Nick Fury, Agent of SHIELD (1st series); wraparound cover 3.00
❑2, Jan 1984; Reprints from Nick Fury, Agent of SHIELD (1st series) 3.00

NICK FURY, AGENT OF S.H.I.E.L.D. (3RD SERIES)
MARVEL

❑1, Sep 1989 BH (a) 2.25
❑2, Oct 1989; KP (a); Death's Head 1.75

N-MINT

❑3, Nov 1989; KP (a); Death's Head 1.75
❑4, Nov 1989; KP (a); Sgt. Fury 1.50
❑5, Dec 1989 KP (a) 1.50
❑6, Dec 1989 KP (a) 1.50
❑7, Jan 1990 KP (a) 1.50
❑8, Feb 1990 .... 1.50
❑9, Mar 1990 KP (a) 1.50
❑10, Apr 1990 KP (a); A: Captain America 1.50
❑11, May 1990 .... 1.50
❑12, Jun 1990 .... 1.50
❑13, Jul 1990; KP (a); Return of Yellow Claw 1.50
❑14, Aug 1990 KP (a) 1.50
❑15, Sep 1990 A: Fantastic Four 1.50
❑16, Oct 1990 .... 1.50
❑17, Nov 1990 HT (a) 1.50
❑18, Dec 1990 .... 1.50
❑19, Jan 1991 HT (a) 1.50
❑20, Feb 1991 .... 1.50
❑21, Mar 1991; BG (a); Baron Strucker revived 1.50
❑22, Apr 1991 BG (a) 1.50
❑23, May 1991 BG (a) 1.50
❑24, Jun 1991 A: Fantastic Four. A: Captain America 1.50
❑25, Jul 1991 BG (a) 1.50
❑26, Aug 1991 BG (a); A: Fantastic Four. A: Avengers 1.50
❑27, Sep 1991 A: Wolverine 2.00
❑28, Oct 1991 A: Wolverine 2.00
❑29, Nov 1991 A: Wolverine 2.00
❑30, Dec 1991 A: Deathlok 1.50
❑31, Jan 1992 A: Deathlok 1.50
❑32, Feb 1992 A: Weapon Omega 1.75
❑33, Mar 1992 1: new agents (Psi-Borg, Violence, Knockabout, Ivory) 1.75
❑34, Apr 1992 V: Hydra. V: Baron Strucker 1.75
❑35, May 1992 .... 1.75
❑36, Jun 1992 O: Constrictor. A: Cage. V: Constrictor 1.75
❑37, Jul 1992 .... 1.75
❑38, Aug 1992 .... 1.75
❑39, Sep 1992 .... 1.75
❑40, Oct 1992 .... 1.75
❑41, Nov 1992 .... 1.75
❑42, Dec 1992 .... 1.75
❑43, Jan 1993 .... 1.75
❑44, Feb 1993 .... 1.75
❑45, Mar 1993 .... 1.75
❑46, Apr 1993 .... 1.75
❑47, May 1993 D: Kate Neville (Nick Fury's Girlfriend) 1.75

NICK FURY'S HOWLING COMMANDOS
MARVEL

❑1, Dec 2005, b&w 2.99
❑1/DirCut, Jan 2006 .... 2.99
❑2, Jan 2006 .... 2.99
❑3, Feb 2006 .... 2.99
❑4, Mar 2006 .... 2.99
❑5, May 2006 .... 2.99
❑6, Jun 2006 .... 2.99

NICK FURY VS. S.H.I.E.L.D.
MARVEL

❑1, Jun 1988 JSo (c) 4.00
❑2, Jul 1988 BSz (c) 3.50
❑3, Mar 1988 .... 3.50
❑4, Sep 1988 .... 3.50
❑5, Oct 1988 .... 3.50
❑6, Nov 1988 .... 3.50

NICK HAZARD
HARRIER

❑1, Jan 1988 .... 1.95

NICKI SHADOW
RELENTLESS

❑0, Jul 1997 .... 1.00
❑1, Nov 1997 .... 2.50

NICK NOYZ AND THE NUISANCE TOUR BOOK
RED BULLET

❑1, b&w 2.50

NICK RYAN THE SKULL
ANTARCTIC

❑1, Dec 1994, b&w 2.75

Ninjak

Kurt Busiek's Valiant enforcer
©Valiant

Nintendo Comics System (2nd Series)

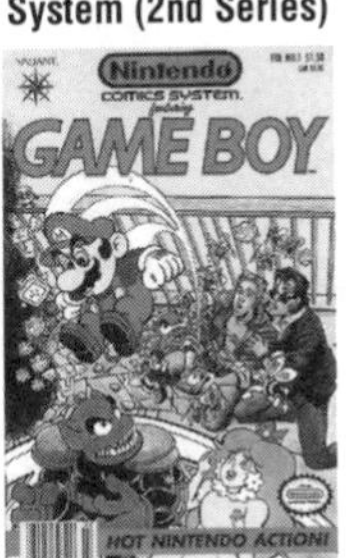

From Valiant's video-game beginnings
©Valiant

Noble Causes

A soap opera about super-heroes
©Image

Nobody

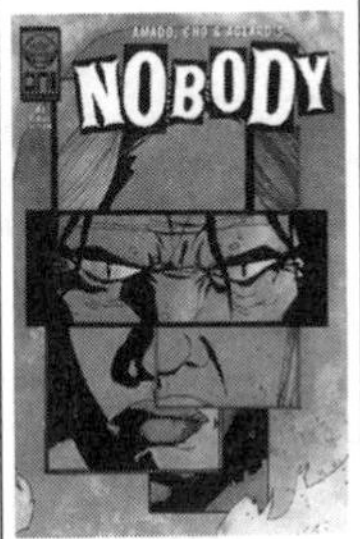

Nobody kills people like Nobody
©Oni

Nocturne (Aircel)

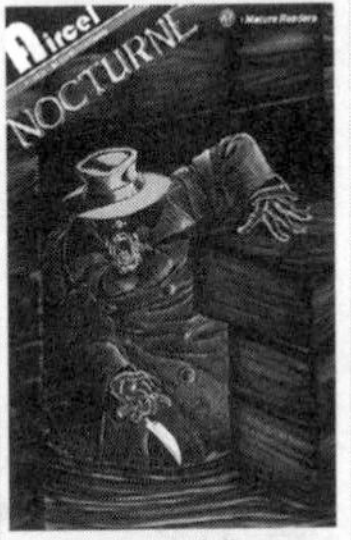

A hideous vigilante stalks the shadows
©Aircel

N-MINT

- ❑2, Jan 1995, b&w; El Gato Negro back-up feature 2.75
- ❑3, Feb 1995, b&w 2.75

NIGHT
SLAVE LABOR / AMAZE INK

- ❑0, Nov 1995 .... 1.50

NIGHTBIRD
HARRIER

- ❑1, May 1988, b&w 1.95
- ❑2 1988, b&w 1.95

NIGHT BREED (CLIVE BARKER'S)
MARVEL / EPIC

- ❑1, Apr 1990 .... 3.00
- ❑2, May 1990 .... 2.50
- ❑3, Jun 1990 .... 2.50
- ❑4, Jul 1990 .... 2.50
- ❑5, Sep 1990 .... 2.50
- ❑6, Nov 1990 .... 2.50
- ❑7, Jan 1991 .... 2.50
- ❑8, Mar 1991 .... 2.50
- ❑9, May 1991 .... 2.50
- ❑10, Jul 1991 .... 2.50
- ❑11, Sep 1991 .... 2.25
- ❑12, Nov 1991 .... 2.25
- ❑13, Jan 1992, Rawhead Rex 2.25
- ❑14, Mar 1992 .... 2.25
- ❑15, May 1992 .... 2.25
- ❑16, Jun 1992 .... 2.25
- ❑17, Jul 1992 .... 2.25
- ❑18, Aug 1992 .... 2.25
- ❑19, Sep 1992 .... 2.25
- ❑20, Oct 1992 .... 2.50
- ❑21, Nov 1992 .... 2.50
- ❑22, Dec 1992 .... 2.50
- ❑23, Jan 1993 .... 2.50
- ❑24, Feb 1993 .... 2.50
- ❑25, Mar 1993 .... 2.50

NIGHT BRIGADE
WONDER COMIX

- ❑1, Aug 1987, b&w 1.95

NIGHTCAT
MARVEL

- ❑1, Apr 1991 .... 3.95

NIGHT CITY
THORBY

- ❑1 .... 2.95

NIGHT CLUB
IMAGE

- ❑1, ca. 2005 .... 2.95
- ❑2, Jan 2006 .... 2.95
- ❑3, May 2006 .... 2.95

NIGHTCRAWLER (VOL. 1)
MARVEL

- ❑1, Nov 1985, DC (w); DC (a) 2.00
- ❑2, Dec 1985, DC (w); DC (a) 2.00
- ❑3, Jan 1986, DC (w); DC (a) 2.00
- ❑4, Feb 1986, DC (w); DC (a) 2.00

NIGHTCRAWLER (VOL. 2)
MARVEL

- ❑1, Jan 2002 .... 2.50
- ❑2, Feb 2002 .... 2.50
- ❑3, Mar 2002 .... 2.50
- ❑4, Apr 2002 .... 2.50

N-MINT

NIGHTCRAWLER (VOL. 3)
MARVEL

- ❑1 2004 .... 2.99
- ❑2 2004 .... 2.99
- ❑3 2005 .... 2.99
- ❑4, Feb 2005 .... 2.99
- ❑5 2005 .... 2.99
- ❑6 2005 .... 2.99
- ❑7 2005 .... 2.99
- ❑8, Sep 2005 .... 2.99
- ❑9, Oct 2005 .... 2.99
- ❑10 2005 .... 2.99
- ❑11, Jan 2006 .... 2.99
- ❑12, Jan 2006 .... 2.99

NIGHTCRY
CFD

- ❑1, b&w; cardstock cover 3.00
- ❑2, b&w; cardstock cover 3.00
- ❑3, b&w; cardstock cover 3.00
- ❑4, b&w; cardstock cover 3.00
- ❑5, b&w; cardstock cover 3.00
- ❑6, May 1996, b&w; cardstock cover. 3.00

NIGHTFALL: THE BLACK CHRONICLES
HOMAGE

- ❑1, Dec 1999 .... 2.95
- ❑2, Jan 2000 .... 2.95
- ❑3, Feb 2000 .... 2.95

NIGHT FISHER
FANTAGRAPHICS

- ❑1 2005 .... 5.00

NIGHT FORCE
DC

- ❑1, Aug 1982, GC (a); 1: Night Force . 2.50
- ❑2, Sep 1982, GC (a) 1.50
- ❑3, Oct 1982, GC (a) 1.50
- ❑4, Nov 1982, GC (a) 1.50
- ❑5, Dec 1982, GC (a) 1.50
- ❑6, Jan 1983, GC (a) 1.50
- ❑7, Feb 1983, GC (a) 1.50
- ❑8, Mar 1983, GC (a) 1.50
- ❑9, Apr 1983, GC (a) 1.50
- ❑10, May 1983, GC (a) 1.50
- ❑11, Jun 1983, GC (a) 1.50
- ❑12, Jul 1983, GC (a) 1.50
- ❑13, Aug 1983, GC (a) 1.50
- ❑14, Sep 1983, GC (a) 1.50

NIGHT FORCE (2ND SERIES)
DC

- ❑1, Dec 1996, BA (a) 2.50
- ❑2, Jan 1997, BA (a) 2.25
- ❑3, Feb 1997, BA (a) 2.25
- ❑4, Mar 1997 .... 2.25
- ❑5, Apr 1997 .... 2.25
- ❑6, May 1997 .... 2.25
- ❑7, Jun 1997 .... 2.25
- ❑8, Jul 1997, continues in Challengers of the Unknown #6 .... 2.25
- ❑9, Aug 1997 .... 2.25
- ❑10, Sep 1997 .... 2.25
- ❑11, Oct 1997 .... 2.25
- ❑12, Nov 1997 .... 2.50

N-MINT

NIGHT GLIDER
TOPPS

- ❑1, Apr 1993 .... 2.95

NIGHTHAWK
MARVEL

- ❑1, Sep 1998; gatefold summary 2.99
- ❑2, Oct 1998; gatefold summary 2.50
- ❑3, Nov 1998; gatefold summary 2.50

NIGHT IN A MOORISH HAREM
NBM

- ❑1 .... 11.95
- ❑2 .... 10.95

NIGHTJAR (ALAN MOORE'S)
AVATAR

- ❑1, Mar 2004 .... 3.00
- ❑1/Platinum 10.00
- ❑1/Wraparound 3.00
- ❑1/Tarot, Jun 2005; 1,250 copies printed. Tarot cover "Princess of Swords" fits with Hypothetical Lizard #1 Tarot cover. 3.99
- ❑2 .... 3.00
- ❑2/Platinum 10.00
- ❑2/Wraparound 4.00
- ❑3 .... 3.00
- ❑3/Platinum 10.00
- ❑3/Wraparound 4.00
- ❑4 .... 4.00
- ❑4/Tarot 5.00

NIGHTJAR: HOLLOW BONES
AVATAR

- ❑1 2004 .... 4.00
- ❑1/Platinum 2004 .... 10.00
- ❑1/Wraparound 2004 .... 4.00

NIGHT LIFE
STRAWBERRY JAM

- ❑1, b&w 1.50
- ❑2, b&w 1.50
- ❑3, Feb 1987, b&w 1.50
- ❑4, Mar 1987, b&w 1.50
- ❑5, Apr 1987, b&w 1.50
- ❑6, May 1987, b&w 1.50
- ❑7, b&w 1.50
- ❑8, Nov 1991, b&w 2.50

NIGHTLINGER
GAUNTLET

- ❑1, b&w 2.95
- ❑2, b&w 2.95

NIGHT MAN
MALIBU / ULTRAVERSE

- ❑1, Oct 1993 O: The Night Man. 1: The Night Man (in costume). 1: Death Mask 2.50
- ❑1/Ltd.; Ultra-limited edition O: The Night Man. 1: The Night Man (in costume). 1: Death Mask 25.00
- ❑2, Nov 1993 1: Mangle 2.00
- ❑3, Dec 1993 A: Freex 2.00
- ❑4, Jan 1994 O: Firearm 2.00
- ❑5, Feb 1994 .... 2.00
- ❑6, Mar 1994 .... 1.95
- ❑7, Apr 1994 .... 1.95
- ❑8, May 1994 .... 1.95
- ❑9, Jun 1994 D: Teknight I 1.95

N-MINT

❑10, Jul 1994 1: Silver Daggers. 1: Chalk ... 1.95
❑11, Aug 1994 1: Teknight II ... 1.95
❑12, Sep 1994 A: The Solution ... 1.95
❑13, Oct 1994; no indicia ... 1.95
❑14, Nov 1994 JRo (w); D: Torso ... 1.95
❑15, Dec 1994 ... 1.95
❑16, Feb 1995; MZ (a); flipbook with Ultraverse Premiere #11 ... 3.50
❑17, Feb 1995 1: BloodyFly ... 2.50
❑18, Mar 1995 ... 2.50
❑19, Apr 1995 D: Deathmask ... 2.50
❑20, May 1995 D: BloodyFly ... 2.50
❑21, Jun 1995 ... 2.50
❑22, Jul 1995 A: Loki ... 2.50
❑23, Aug 1995 ... 2.50
❑Annual 1, Jan 1995 ... 3.95

NIGHT MAN (VOL. 2)
MALIBU / ULTRAVERSE

❑0, Sep 1995; Listed as issue #Infinity ... 1.50
❑0/A, Sep 1995; alternate cover ... 1.50
❑1, Oct 1995 ... 1.50
❑2, Nov 1995 ... 1.50
❑3, Dec 1995 ... 1.50
❑4, Dec 1995 ... 1.50

NIGHT MAN/GAMBIT
MALIBU / ULTRAVERSE

❑1, Mar 1996 ... 1.95
❑2, Apr 1996 ... 1.95
❑3, May 1996 ... 1.95

NIGHT MAN VS. WOLVERINE
MALIBU / ULTRAVERSE

❑0, Aug 1995, no cover price ... 5.00

NIGHTMARE (ALEX NIÑO'S...)
INNOVATION

❑1, Dec 1989 ... 1.95

NIGHTMARE
MARVEL

❑1, Dec 1994 ... 1.95
❑2, Jan 1995 ... 1.95
❑3, Feb 1995 ... 1.95
❑4, Mar 1995 ... 1.95

NIGHTMARE & CASPER
HARVEY

❑1, Aug 1963 ... 60.00
❑2, Nov 1963 ... 35.00
❑3, Feb 1964 ... 35.00
❑4, May 1964 ... 35.00
❑5, Aug 1964; becomes Casper and Nightmare ... 35.00

NIGHTMARE ON ELM STREET (FREDDY KRUEGER'S...)
MARVEL

❑1 ... 3.00

NIGHTMARE ON ELM STREET: THE BEGINNING
INNOVATION

❑1 ... 2.50
❑2 ... 2.50

NIGHTMARES
ECLIPSE

❑1 PG (c); PG (a) ... 2.00
❑2 PG (c); PG (a) ... 2.00

NIGHTMARES & FAIRY TALES
SLAVE LABOR

❑1 2002 ... 8.00
❑2 ... 6.00
❑3 ... 5.00
❑4 ... 5.00
❑5 ... 5.00
❑6 ... 5.00
❑7 ... 2.95
❑8 ... 2.95
❑9 ... 2.95
❑10 ... 2.95
❑11 ... 2.95
❑12 ... 2.95
❑13, Aug 2005 ... 2.95
❑14, Dec 2005 ...

NIGHTMARES ON ELM STREET
INNOVATION

❑1, Sep 1991 ... 2.50
❑2 ... 2.50
❑3 ... 2.50

❑4 ... 2.50
❑5 ... 2.50
❑6 ... 2.50

NIGHTMARE THEATER
CHAOS!

❑1, Nov 1997; horror anthology ... 2.50
❑2, Nov 1997; horror anthology ... 2.50
❑3, Nov 1997; horror anthology ... 2.50
❑4, Nov 1997; horror anthology ... 2.50

NIGHTMARE WALKER
BONEYARD

❑1, Jul 1996, b&w ... 2.95

NIGHTMARK
ALPHA PRODUCTIONS

❑1, b&w ... 2.25

NIGHTMARK: BLOOD & HONOR
ALPHA

❑1, Apr 1994 ... 2.50
❑2 ... 2.50
❑3 ... 2.50

NIGHTMARK MYSTERY SPECIAL
ALPHA

❑1, b&w ... 2.50

NIGHT MARY
IDEA & DESIGN WORKS

❑1, Sep 2005 ... 3.99
❑2, Oct 2005 ... 3.99
❑3, Dec 2005 ... 3.99
❑4, Jan 2006 ... 3.99
❑5, Jan 2006 ... 3.99

NIGHTMASK
MARVEL

❑1, Nov 1986, O: Nightmask ... 1.00
❑2, Dec 1986 ... 1.00
❑3, Jan 1987 ... 1.00
❑4, Feb 1987 ... 1.00
❑5, Mar 1987 ... 1.00
❑6, Apr 1987 ... 1.00
❑7, May 1987 ... 1.00
❑8, Jun 1987 ... 1.00
❑9, Jul 1987, Mark Bagley's first major comics work ... 1.00
❑10, Aug 1987 ... 1.00
❑11, Sep 1987 ... 1.00
❑12, Oct 1987 ... 1.00

NIGHT MASTERS
CUSTOM PIC

❑1 1986 ... 1.50
❑2 1986 ... 1.50
❑3 1986 ... 1.50
❑4 1986 ... 1.50
❑5, Aug 1986 ... 1.50
❑6, Jan 1987 ... 1.50

NIGHT MUSIC
ECLIPSE

❑1, Dec 1984 CR (w); CR (a) ... 2.00
❑2, Feb 1985 CR (w); CR (a) ... 2.00
❑3, Mar 1985; CR (w); CR (a); Rudyard Kipling adaptation ... 2.00
❑4, Dec 1985 CR (a) ... 2.00
❑5, Dec 1985 CR (a) ... 2.00
❑6 CR (a) ... 2.00
❑7, Feb 1988 CR (w); CR (a) ... 2.00
❑8, ca. 1989 ... 3.95
❑9, ca. 1990 CR (a) ... 4.95
❑10, ca. 1990 CR (a) ... 4.95
❑11, ca. 1990 CR (a) ... 4.95

NIGHT NURSE
MARVEL

❑1, Nov 1972 ... 110.00
❑2, Jan 1973 ... 50.00
❑3, Mar 1973 ... 35.00
❑4, May 1973 ... 35.00

NIGHT OF THE LIVING DEAD
FANTACO

❑0, b&w ... 2.00
❑1, ca. 1991, b&w ... 4.95
❑2, b&w ... 4.95
❑3, b&w ... 5.95
❑4, b&w ... 5.95

NIGHT OF THE LIVING DEADLINE USA
DARK HORSE

❑1, Apr 1992, b&w ... 2.95

NIGHT OF THE LIVING DEAD: AFTERMATH
FANTACO

❑1 ... 1.95

NIGHT OF THE LIVING DEAD: LONDON
FANTACO

❑1 ... 5.95
❑2 ... 5.95

NIGHT OF THE LIVING DEAD: PRELUDE
FANTACO

❑1, ca. 1991, b&w ... 1.50

NIGHT RAVEN: HOUSE OF CARDS
MARVEL

❑1, Aug 1991 ... 5.95

NIGHT RIDER
MARVEL

❑1, Oct 1974, Reprints Ghost Rider (Western) #1 ... 25.00
❑2, Dec 1974, Reprints Ghost Rider (Western) #2 ... 10.00
❑3, Feb 1975, Reprints Ghost Rider (Western) #3 ... 10.00
❑4, Apr 1975, Reprints Ghost Rider (Western) #4 ... 10.00
❑5, Jun 1975, Reprints Ghost Rider (Western) #5 ... 10.00
❑6, Aug 1975, Reprints Ghost Rider (Western) #6 ... 10.00

NIGHT'S CHILDREN
FANTACO

❑1, b&w ... 3.50
❑2, b&w ... 3.50
❑3, b&w ... 3.50
❑4, b&w ... 3.50

NIGHT'S CHILDREN: DOUBLE INDEMNITY
FANTACO

❑1, b&w ... 7.95

NIGHT'S CHILDREN EROTIC FANTASIES
FANTACO

❑1 ... 4.50

NIGHT'S CHILDREN: FOREPLAY
FANTACO

❑1, b&w ... 4.95

NIGHT'S CHILDREN: THE VAMPIRE
MILLENNIUM

❑1 ... 2.95
❑2 ... 2.95

NIGHT'S CHILDREN: VAMPYR!
FANTACO

❑1, b&w ... 3.50
❑2, b&w ... 3.50
❑3, b&w ... 3.50

NIGHTSHADE
NO MERCY

❑1, Aug 1997 ... 2.50

NIGHTSHADES
LONDON NIGHT

❑1 ... 2.95

NIGHTSIDE
MARVEL

❑1, Dec 2001 ... 2.99
❑2, Jan 2002 ... 2.99
❑3, Feb 2002 ... 2.99
❑4, Mar 2002 ... 2.99

NIGHTS INTO DREAMS
ARCHIE

❑1, Feb 1998 ... 1.75
❑2, Mar 1998 ... 1.75
❑3, Apr 1998 ... 1.75
❑4, Aug 1998 ... 1.75
❑5, Sep 1998 ... 1.75
❑6, Oct 1998 ... 1.75

NIGHTSTALKERS
MARVEL

❑1, Nov 1992; Missing poster ... 1.00
❑1/CS ... 2.75
❑2, Dec 1992 ... 2.00
❑3, Jan 1993 ... 2.00
❑4, Feb 1993 ... 1.75

Other grades: Multiply price above by 5/6 for VF/NM • 2/3 for VERY FINE • 1/3 for FINE • 1/5 for VERY GOOD • 1/8 for GOOD

Nodwick

Henchman does the dirty work
©Henchman

Nomad

Spinoff series from Captain America
©Marvel

No Need for Tenchi! Part 1

Hitoshi Okuda's hit comedy anime series
©Viz

Normalman

Jim Valentino's hilarious parody title
©Aardvark-Vanaheim

Nova (1st Series)

1970s hero just can't keep a series going
©Marvel

N-MINT

❑5, Mar 1993 ... 1.75
❑6, Apr 1993 ... 1.75
❑7, May 1993 ... 1.75
❑8, Jun 1993 ... 1.75
❑9, Jul 1993 ... 1.75
❑10, Aug 1993; Double cover ... 2.25
❑11, Sep 1993 ... 1.75
❑12, Oct 1993; Gold cover ... 1.75
❑13, Nov 1993 ... 1.75
❑14, Dec 1993; Neon ink on cover ... 1.75
❑15, Jan 1994; Spot-varnish cover ... 1.75
❑16, Feb 1994 ... 1.75
❑17, Mar 1994 ... 1.75
❑18, Apr 1994 ... 1.75

NIGHTSTREETS (ARROW)
ARROW

❑1, Jul 1986 1: Mr. Katt ... 2.50
❑2, Oct 1986 ... 2.00
❑3, Jan 1987 ... 2.00
❑4, Apr 1987 ... 2.00
❑5, Jul 1987 ... 2.00

NIGHT TERRORS
CHANTING MONKS

❑1 BWr (a) ... 2.75

NIGHT THRASHER
MARVEL

❑1, Aug 1993; foil cover ... 2.95
❑2, Sep 1993 ... 1.75
❑3, Oct 1993 ... 1.75
❑4, Nov 1993 ... 1.75
❑5, Dec 1993 ... 1.75
❑6, Jan 1994 ... 1.75
❑7, Feb 1994 ... 1.75
❑8, Mar 1994 ... 1.75
❑9, Apr 1994 ... 1.75
❑10, May 1994 ... 1.95
❑11, Jun 1994 ... 1.95
❑12, Jul 1994 ... 1.95
❑13, Aug 1994 ... 1.95
❑14, Sep 1994 ... 1.95
❑15, Oct 1994 ... 1.95
❑16, Nov 1994 ... 1.95
❑17, Dec 1994 ... 1.95
❑18, Jan 1995 ... 1.95
❑19, Feb 1995 ... 1.95
❑20, Mar 1995 ... 1.95
❑21, Apr 1995 ... 1.95

NIGHT THRASHER: FOUR CONTROL
MARVEL

❑1, Oct 1992 ... 2.00
❑2, Nov 1992 ... 2.00
❑3, Dec 1992 ... 2.00
❑4, Jan 1993 ... 2.00

NIGHT TRIBES
DC / WILDSTORM

❑1, Jul 1999 ... 4.95

NIGHT TRIPPERS
IMAGE

❑1, Jul 2006 ... 2.95

NIGHTVEIL
AC

❑1, Feb 1984, PG (c) ... 2.00

N-MINT

❑2 ... 2.00
❑3 ... 2.00
❑4 ... 2.00
❑5 ... 2.00
❑6 ... 2.00
❑7, Mar 1987 ... 2.00
❑Special 1, Aug 1988 ... 2.00

NIGHTVEIL'S CAULDRON OF HORROR
AC

❑1, b&w; Reprints ... 2.50
❑2 ... 2.95
❑3, Sep 1991 ... 2.95

NIGHTVENGER
AXIS

❑Ashcan 1, May 1994 ... 2.00

NIGHTVISION
REBEL

❑1, Nov 1996 ... 3.00
❑2 1997 ... 2.50
❑3 1997 ... 2.50
❑4 1997 ... 2.50

NIGHTVISION: ALL ABOUT EVE
LONDON NIGHT

❑1 ... 3.00

NIGHTVISION (ATOMEKA)
ATOMEKA

❑1, b&w ... 2.95

NIGHT VIXEN
ABC

❑0/A, b&w ... 3.00
❑0/B; Eurotika Edition ... 4.00
❑0/C; Manga Flux Edition ... 4.00

NIGHT WALKER
FLEETWAY-QUALITY

❑1, Reprints Luke Kirby story from 2000 A.D. ... 2.95
❑2, Reprints Luke Kirby story from 2000 A.D. ... 2.95
❑3, Reprints Luke Kirby story from 2000 A.D. ... 2.95

NIGHT WARRIORS: DARKSTALKERS' REVENGE THE COMIC SERIES
VIZ

❑1, Nov 1998 ... 2.95
❑2, Dec 1998 ... 3.25
❑3, Jan 1999 ... 2.95
❑4, Feb 1999 ... 2.95
❑5, Mar 1999 ... 2.95
❑6, Apr 1999 ... 2.95

NIGHTWATCH
MARVEL

❑1, Apr 1994 ... 1.50
❑1/Variant, Apr 1994; foil cover ... 2.95
❑2, May 1994 ... 1.50
❑3, Jun 1994 ... 1.50
❑4, Jul 1994 ... 1.50
❑5, Aug 1994 ... 1.50
❑6, Sep 1994 ... 1.50
❑7, Oct 1994 ... 1.50
❑8, Nov 1994 ... 1.50
❑9, Dec 1994 ... 1.50

N-MINT

❑10, Jan 1995 ... 1.50
❑11, Feb 1995 ... 1.50
❑12, Mar 1995 ... 1.50

NIGHTWING (MINI-SERIES)
DC

❑1, Sep 1995 ... 3.50
❑2, Oct 1995 ... 2.50
❑3, Nov 1995 ... 2.50
❑4, Dec 1995 ... 2.50

NIGHTWING
DC

❑½ ... 4.00
❑½/Platinum; Platinum edition ... 7.00
❑1, Oct 1996 ... 11.00
❑2, Nov 1996 ... 6.00
❑3, Dec 1996 ... 4.00
❑4, Jan 1997 ... 3.50
❑5, Feb 1997 ... 3.50
❑6, Mar 1997 ... 3.00
❑7, Apr 1997 ... 3.00
❑8, May 1997 ... 3.00
❑9, Jun 1997 ... 3.00
❑10, Jul 1997 V: Scarecrow ... 3.00
❑11, Aug 1997 V: Scarecrow ... 2.50
❑12, Sep 1997 ... 2.50
❑13, Oct 1997 ... 2.50
❑14, Nov 1997 A: Batman ... 2.50
❑15, Dec 1997; A: Batman. V: Two-Face. Face cover ... 2.50
❑16, Jan 1998 ... 1.95
❑17, Feb 1998 ... 1.95
❑18, Mar 1998 ... 1.95
❑19, Apr 1998; continues in Batman #553 ... 1.95
❑20, May 1998; continues in Batman #554 ... 1.95
❑21, Jun 1998 1: Nitewing. A: Blockbuster ... 1.95
❑22, Jul 1998 V: Stallion. V: Brutale ... 1.95
❑23, Aug 1998; A: Lady Shiva. concludes in Green Arrow #135 ... 1.95
❑24, Sep 1998 ... 1.99
❑25, Oct 1998 ... 1.99
❑26, Dec 1998 A: Huntress ... 1.99
❑27, Jan 1999 A: Huntress ... 1.99
❑28, Feb 1999 1: Torque. A: Huntress ... 1.99
❑29, Mar 1999 A: Huntress ... 1.99
❑30, Apr 1999 A: Superman ... 1.99
❑31, May 1999; Dick joins the Bludhaven police force ... 1.99
❑32, Jun 1999 ... 1.99
❑33, Jul 1999 ... 1.99
❑34, Aug 1999 ... 1.99
❑35, Sep 1999; No Man's Land ... 1.99
❑36, Oct 1999; No Man's Land ... 1.99
❑37, Nov 1999; No Man's Land ... 1.99
❑38, Dec 2000; No Man's Land ... 1.99
❑39, Jan 2000 ... 1.99
❑40, Feb 2000 ... 1.99
❑41, Mar 2000 ... 1.99
❑42, Apr 2000 ... 1.99
❑43, May 2000 ... 1.99
❑44, Jun 2000 ... 1.99
❑45, Jul 2000 ... 1.99
❑46, Aug 2000 ... 1.99

Other grades: Multiply price above by 5/6 for VF/NM • 2/3 for VERY FINE • 1/3 for FINE • 1/5 for VERY GOOD • 1/8 for GOOD

- ❑47, Sep 2000 ... 1.99
- ❑48, Oct 2000 ... 2.25
- ❑49, Nov 2000 ... 2.25
- ❑50, Dec 2000 ... 3.50
- ❑51, Jan 2001 ... 2.25
- ❑52, Feb 2001 A: Catwoman ... 2.25
- ❑53, Mar 2001 DGry (w) ... 2.25
- ❑54, Apr 2001 ... 2.25
- ❑55, May 2001 ... 2.25
- ❑56, Jun 2001 ... 2.25
- ❑57, Jul 2001 ... 2.25
- ❑58, Aug 2001 ... 2.25
- ❑59, Sep 2001 ... 2.25
- ❑60, Oct 2001 ... 2.25
- ❑61, Nov 2001 ... 2.25
- ❑62, Dec 2001; Joker: Last Laugh crossover ... 2.25
- ❑63, Jan 2002 ... 2.25
- ❑64, Feb 2002 ... 2.25
- ❑65, Mar 2002 ... 2.25
- ❑66, Apr 2002 ... 2.00
- ❑67, May 2002 ... 2.00
- ❑68, Jun 2002 ... 2.25
- ❑69, Jul 2002 ... 2.25
- ❑70, Aug 2002 ... 2.25
- ❑71, Sep 2002 ... 2.25
- ❑72, Oct 2002 ... 2.25
- ❑73, Nov 2002 ... 2.25
- ❑74, Dec 2002 ... 2.25
- ❑75, Jan 2003 ... 2.00
- ❑76, Feb 2003 ... 2.25
- ❑77, Mar 2003 ... 2.25
- ❑78, Apr 2003 ... 2.25
- ❑79, May 2003 ... 2.25
- ❑80, Jun 2003 A: Deathstroke the Terminator ... 2.25
- ❑81, Jul 2003 A: Deathstroke the Terminator ... 2.25
- ❑82, Aug 2003 ... 2.25
- ❑83, Sep 2003 ... 2.25
- ❑84, Oct 2003 ... 2.25
- ❑85, Nov 2003 ... 2.25
- ❑86, Dec 2003 ... 2.25
- ❑87, Jan 2004 ... 2.25
- ❑88, Feb 2004 ... 2.25
- ❑89, Mar 2004 ... 2.25
- ❑90, Apr 2004 ... 2.25
- ❑91, May 2004, DGry (w) ... 2.25
- ❑92, Jun 2004 ... 2.25
- ❑93, Jul 2004 ... 2.25
- ❑94, Aug 2004 ... 2.25
- ❑95, Sep 2004 ... 2.25
- ❑96, Oct 2004 ... 2.25
- ❑97, Nov 2004 ... 2.25
- ❑98, Dec 2004 ... 2.25
- ❑99, Jan 2005 ... 3.00
- ❑100, Feb 2005 ... 4.00
- ❑101, Mar 2005 ... 6.00
- ❑102, Mar 2005 ... 5.00
- ❑103, Apr 2005 ... 6.00
- ❑104, May 2005 ... 6.00
- ❑105, Jun 2005 ... 5.00
- ❑106 2005 ... 6.00
- ❑107 2005 ... 2.25
- ❑108, Jun 2005 ... 2.25
- ❑109, Jul 2005 ... 2.50
- ❑110, Aug 2005 ... 2.50
- ❑111, Sep 2005 ... 2.50
- ❑112, Oct 2005 ... 2.50
- ❑113, Nov 2005 ... 2.50
- ❑114, Jan 2006 ... 2.50
- ❑115, Feb 2006 ... 2.50
- ❑116, Mar 2006 ... 2.50
- ❑117, Apr 2006 ... 2.50
- ❑118, May 2006 ... 2.50
- ❑119, Jun 2006 ... 2.50
- ❑120, Jul 2006 ... 2.50
- ❑121, Aug 2006 ... 2.50
- ❑1000000, Nov 1998 ... 2.00
- ❑Annual 1, ca. 1997; Pulp Heroes ... 5.00
- ❑Giant Size 1, Dec 2000 ... 5.95

NIGHTWING: ALFRED'S RETURN
DC

- ❑1, Jul 1995 ... 3.50

NIGHTWING AND HUNTRESS
DC

- ❑1, May 1998, DGry (w) ... 2.00
- ❑2, Jun 1998, DGry (w); BSz (a) ... 2.00
- ❑3, Jul 1998 ... 2.00
- ❑4, Aug 1998 ... 2.00

NIGHTWING: OUR WORLDS AT WAR
DC

- ❑1, Sep 2001 ... 2.95

NIGHTWING SECRET FILES
DC

- ❑1, Oct 1999; background information on series ... 4.95

NIGHTWING: THE TARGET
DC

- ❑1, Sep 2001 ... 5.95

NIGHTWOLF
DEVIL'S DUE

- ❑0, Jun 2006 ... 3.95

NIGHTWOLF
ENTROPY

- ❑1 ... 1.50
- ❑2 ... 1.50

NIGHT ZERO
FLEETWAY-QUALITY

- ❑1, b&w ... 1.95
- ❑2, b&w ... 1.95
- ❑3, b&w ... 1.95
- ❑4, b&w ... 1.95

NIKKI BLADE SUMMER FUN
ABC

- ❑1/A, b&w ... 3.00
- ❑1/B; solo figure on cover ... 3.00

NIMROD
FANTAGRAPHICS

- ❑1, Jun 1998, b&w ... 2.95
- ❑2, Aug 1998, b&w ... 2.95

NINA'S ALL-TIME GREATEST COLLECTORS' ITEM CLASSIC COMICS
DARK HORSE

- ❑1, Aug 1992, b&w ... 2.50

NINA'S NEW & IMPROVED ALL-TIME GREATEST COLLECTORS' ITEM CLASSIC COMICS
DARK HORSE

- ❑1, Feb 1994, b&w ... 2.50

9-11: EMERGENCY RELIEF
ALTERNATIVE

- ❑1 ... 14.95

NINE LIVES OF LEATHER CAT
FORBIDDEN FRUIT

- ❑1 ... 3.50
- ❑2 ... 3.50
- ❑3 ... 3.50
- ❑4 ... 3.50
- ❑5 ... 3.50
- ❑6 ... 3.50

NINE RINGS OF WU-TANG
IMAGE

- ❑0, Nov 1999; Giveaway bundled with Wizard Magazine ... 2.00
- ❑1/A, Nov 1999; Woman with bow reclining on cover with jungle cats ... 4.00
- ❑1/B, Nov 1999; Tower Records variant ... 5.00
- ❑2, Dec 1999 ... 2.95
- ❑3, Feb 2000 ... 2.95
- ❑4, Apr 2000 ... 2.95
- ❑5, Jul 2000 ... 2.95
- ❑Book 1; Collects series ... 19.95

1984 MAGAZINE
WARREN

- ❑1, Jun 1978 ... 6.00
- ❑2, Aug 1978 ... 4.00
- ❑3, Sep 1978 ... 4.00
- ❑4, Oct 1978 ... 4.00
- ❑5, Feb 1979 ... 4.00
- ❑6, Jun 1979 ... 4.00
- ❑7, Aug 1979 ... 4.00
- ❑8, Sep 1979 ... 4.00
- ❑9, Oct 1979 ... 4.00
- ❑10, Dec 1980; Series continued in 1994 #11 ... 4.00

1994 MAGAZINE
WARREN

- ❑11, Feb 1980; Series continued from 1984 #10 ... 3.00
- ❑12, Apr 1980 ... 3.00
- ❑13, Jun 1980 ... 3.00
- ❑14, Aug 1980 ... 3.00
- ❑15, Oct 1980 ... 3.00
- ❑16, Dec 1980 AN (a) ... 3.00
- ❑17, Feb 1981 ... 3.00
- ❑18, Apr 1981 FT (w); FT, AN (a) ... 3.00
- ❑19, Jun 1981 ... 3.00
- ❑20, Aug 1981 ... 3.00
- ❑21, Oct 1981 FT (w); FT, AN (a) ... 3.00
- ❑22, Dec 1981 ... 3.00
- ❑23, Feb 1982 ... 3.00
- ❑24, Apr 1982 ... 3.00
- ❑25, Jun 1982 ... 3.00
- ❑26, Aug 1982 ... 3.00
- ❑27, Oct 1982 ... 3.00
- ❑28, Dec 1982 ... 3.00
- ❑29, Feb 1983 ... 3.00

1963
IMAGE

- ❑1, Apr 1993, AMo (w); DaG (a); Mystery Incorporated ... 2.00
- ❑1/BR, Apr 1993, Promotional limited edition AMo (w); DaG (a) ... 3.00
- ❑1/Gold, Apr 1993, Gold edition; AMo (w); DaG (a); Profits donated to cancer research ... 5.00
- ❑1/Silver, Apr 1993, silver edition; AMo (w); DaG (a); Profits donated to cancer research ... 3.00
- ❑2, May 1993, AMo (w); No One Escapes...the Fury ... 2.00
- ❑3, Jun 1993, AMo (w); Tales of the Uncanny ... 2.00
- ❑4, Jul 1993, AMo (w); Tales From Beyond; Johnny Beyond ... 2.00
- ❑5, Aug 1993, AMo (w) ... 2.00
- ❑6, Oct 1993, AMo (w) ... 2.00

NINETY-NINE GIRLS
FANTAGRAPHICS / EROS

- ❑1, b&w ... 2.25

NINE VOLT
IMAGE

- ❑1, Jul 1997 ... 2.50
- ❑1/A, Jul 1997; alternate cover ... 2.50
- ❑2, Aug 1997 ... 2.50
- ❑3, Sep 1997 ... 2.50
- ❑4, Oct 1997 ... 2.50

NINJA
ETERNITY

- ❑1, 1986 ... 1.80
- ❑2, 1986 ... 1.80
- ❑3, 1986 ... 1.80
- ❑4, 1986 ... 1.80
- ❑5, 1986 ... 1.95
- ❑6, 1986 ... 1.95
- ❑7, 1987 ... 1.95
- ❑8, 1987 ... 1.95
- ❑9, 1987 ... 1.95
- ❑10, 1987 ... 1.95
- ❑11, 1988 ... 1.95
- ❑12, Sep 1988 ... 1.95
- ❑13, 1988 ... 1.95
- ❑Special 1, b&w ... 2.25

NINJA-BOTS SUPER SPECIAL
PIED PIPER

- ❑1 ... 1.95

NINJA BOY
DC / WILDSTORM

- ❑1, Oct 2001 ... 2.25
- ❑2, Nov 2001 ... 2.25
- ❑3, Dec 2001; Cover date says November, indicia says December ... 2.25
- ❑4, Jan 2002 ... 2.25
- ❑5, Feb 2002 ... 2.25
- ❑6, Mar 2002 ... 2.25
- ❑Ashcan 1; Ashcan preview; Flip book with Out There Ash #1 ... 0.50

NINJA ELITE
ADVENTURE

- ❑1; 7-1/2" x 8-1/2" version with black-and-white cover ... 1.50
- ❑1/2nd; 1st printing with color covers, full comic size; 1st printing with color covers, full comic size ... 1.50
- ❑2, Jul 1987 ... 1.50
- ❑3, ca. 1987 ... 1.50

Nth Man, the Ultimate Ninja

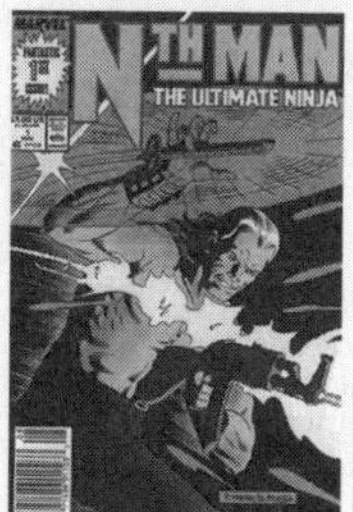

N = The number of readers who remember...

©Marvel

Occult Files of Dr. Spektor

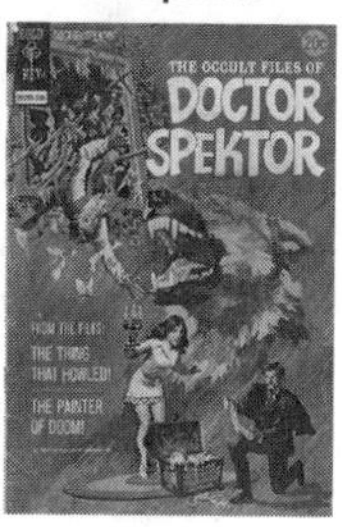

Supernatural researcher becomes horror host

©Gold Key

October Yen

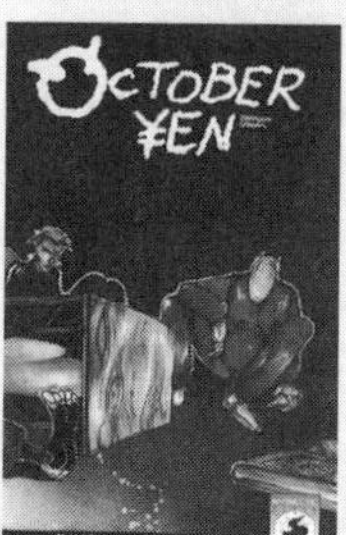

Juvenile artwork sullies SF story

©Antarctic

Odd Adventure-Zine

Delightfully surreal black-and-white title

©Zamboni

Official Handbook of the Marvel Universe (Vol. 1)

First encyclopedic work from the publisher

©Marvel

	N-MINT
❑4, Dec 1987	1.50
❑5, ca. 1988	1.50
❑6, May 1988, b&w	1.50
❑7, Jul 1988, b&w	1.50
❑8, Aug 1988, b&w	1.50

NINJA FUNNIES
ETERNITY

	N-MINT
❑1, Jan 1987	1.50
❑2	1.95
❑3	1.95
❑4	1.95
❑5	1.95

NINJA HIGH SCHOOL
ANTARCTIC

	N-MINT
❑0, May 1994, b&w; Antarctic publishes	3.00
❑0/Ltd., b&w; foil cover edition (500 made)	4.00
❑1	7.00
❑1/2nd	2.50
❑2	5.00
❑2/2nd	2.00
❑3	4.00
❑3/2nd	2.00
❑4	4.00
❑4/2nd	2.00
❑5, Jun 1988, b&w; Eternity begins publishing	4.00
❑6	3.50
❑6/2nd	2.00
❑7, Sep 1988	3.50
❑8, Dec 1988	3.50
❑9, Feb 1989	3.50
❑10, Mar 1989	3.50
❑11, May 1989	3.00
❑12, ca. 1989	3.00
❑13, ca. 1989	3.00
❑14, ca. 1989	3.00
❑15, ca. 1989	3.00
❑16, b&w	2.50
❑17, b&w	2.50
❑18, b&w	2.50
❑19, b&w	2.50
❑20, b&w	2.50
❑21, b&w	2.50
❑22, b&w	2.50
❑23	2.25
❑24, Apr 1991	2.25
❑25, ca. 1991	2.25
❑26, ca. 1991	2.25
❑27, ca. 1991	2.25
❑28, ca. 1991	2.25
❑29	2.25
❑30	2.25
❑31, ca. 1992	2.25
❑32, ca. 1992, b&w	2.50
❑33, May 1992, b&w	2.50
❑34, b&w	2.50
❑35, b&w	2.50
❑36, b&w	2.50
❑37, b&w	2.50
❑38, b&w	2.50
❑39, ca. 1993, b&w	2.50
❑40, Jun 1994, b&w	2.75
❑40/Ltd., Jun 1994, b&w; gold foil logo edition (500 made)	3.00
❑41, Jul 1994, b&w	2.75
❑42, Sep 1994, b&w	2.75
❑43, Nov 1994, b&w	2.75
❑44, Jan 1995, b&w	2.75
❑45, Mar 1995, b&w	2.75
❑46, May 1995, b&w	2.75
❑47, Jul 1995, b&w	2.75
❑48, Sep 1995, b&w	2.75
❑49, Nov 1995, b&w	2.75
❑50, Jan 1996, b&w	3.95
❑51, Apr 1996, b&w	2.95
❑52, Jun 1996, b&w	2.95
❑53, Sep 1996, b&w	2.95
❑54, Nov 1996, b&w	2.95
❑55, Jan 1997, b&w	2.95
❑56, Mar 1997, b&w	2.95
❑57, May 1997, b&w	2.95
❑58, Aug 1997, b&w	2.95
❑59, Oct 1997, b&w	2.95
❑60, Dec 1997, b&w	2.95
❑61, Feb 1998, b&w	2.95
❑62, Apr 1998, b&w	2.95
❑63, Jun 1998, b&w	2.95
❑64, Aug 1998, b&w	2.95
❑65, Oct 1998, b&w	2.95
❑66, Dec 1998, b&w	2.95
❑67, Mar 1999, b&w	2.95
❑68, Apr 1999, b&w	2.95
❑69, Jun 1999, b&w	2.95
❑70 1999	2.95
❑71 1999	2.95
❑72 1999	2.95
❑73 2000	2.95
❑74 2000	2.95
❑75 2000	2.95
❑76 2000	2.95
❑77 2000	2.95
❑78 2000	2.95
❑79 2000	2.95
❑80 2001	2.95
❑81 2001	2.95
❑82 2001	2.95
❑83 2001	2.95
❑84 2001	2.95
❑85 2001	2.95
❑86 2001	2.95
❑87 2001	2.95
❑88 2001	2.95
❑89 2001	2.95
❑90 2001	2.95
❑91 2002	2.95
❑92 2002	2.95
❑93 2002	2.95
❑94 2002	2.95
❑95 2002	2.95
❑96 2002	2.95
❑97 2002	2.95
❑98 2002	2.95
❑99 2002	2.95
❑100 2002	4.95
❑101 2002	3.50
❑102 2003	3.50
❑103 2003	3.50
❑104 2003	3.50
❑105 2003	3.50
❑106, Jun 2003	3.50
❑107, Jul 2003	3.50
❑108, Aug 2003	3.50
❑109, Sep 2003	3.50
❑110, Oct 2003	3.50
❑111, Dec 2003	3.50
❑112, Jan 2004	3.50
❑113, Feb 2004	3.50
❑114, Mar 2004	3.50
❑115, Apr 2004	3.50
❑116, May 2004	2.99
❑117, Jun 2004	2.99
❑118, Jul 2004	2.99
❑119, Aug 2004	2.99
❑120, Sep 2004	2.99
❑121, Oct 2004	2.99
❑122, Nov 2004	2.99
❑123, Dec 2004	2.99
❑124, Jan 2005	2.99
❑125, Feb 2005	2.99
❑126, Mar 2005	2.99
❑127, Apr 2005	2.99
❑128, May 2005	2.99
❑129, Jun 2005	2.99
❑130, Jul 2005	2.99
❑Yearbook 1, b&w	6.00
❑Yearbook 2, b&w; 1990 Yearbook	6.00
❑Yearbook 3, b&w; 1991 Yearbook	6.00
❑Yearbook 4; 1992 Yearbook	6.00
❑Yearbook 5, Oct 1993, b&w; 1993 Yearbook	6.00
❑Yearbook 6, Oct 1994, b&w; 1994 Yearbook	6.00
❑Yearbook 7, Oct 1995, b&w; 1995 Yearbook; cover says Oct 94, indicia says Oct 95	6.00
❑Yearbook 8, Oct 1996, b&w; 1996 Yearbook	6.00
❑Yearbook 9/A, Oct 1997, b&w; 1997 Yearbook	6.00
❑Yearbook 9/B, Oct 1997, b&w; 1997 Yearbook; alternate cover; Star Trek	6.00
❑Yearbook 10/A, Oct 1998, b&w; 1998 Yearbook	6.00
❑Yearbook 10/B, Oct 1998, b&w; 1998 Yearbook; "Titanic" themed cover	6.00
❑Summer 1, Jun 1999; Comic-sized; Summer Special (1999)	2.99
❑3D 1, Jul 1992; Trade Paperback	4.50

NINJA HIGH SCHOOL IN COLOR
ETERNITY

	N-MINT
❑1, Jul 1992	2.50
❑2	2.50
❑3	2.50
❑4	2.00
❑5	2.00
❑6	2.00
❑7	2.00
❑8, ca. 1993	2.00
❑9	2.00
❑10	2.00
❑11	2.00

	N-MINT
❑12	2.00
❑13	2.00

NINJA HIGH SCHOOL PERFECT MEMORY
ANTARCTIC

	N-MINT
❑1, b&w; sourcebook for series	5.00
❑1/2nd, Jun 1996	5.95
❑2, Nov 1993; 1996 version	5.95
❑2/Platinum, Nov 1993; platinum	5.00

NINJA HIGH SCHOOL SPOTLIGHT
ANTARCTIC

	N-MINT
❑1; Indicia says #29	3.50
❑2, Oct 1996	2.95
❑3, Dec 1996	3.50
❑4, May 1999; Indicia says #1	2.99

NINJA HIGH SCHOOL SWIMSUIT SPECIAL
ANTARCTIC

	N-MINT
❑1, Dec 1992; Gold edition; JDu, JSt, KJ (a); two different covers	4.00
❑2, Dec 1993	3.95
❑3, Dec 1994	3.95
❑4; Gold edition	3.95
❑1996, Dec 1996, b&w; Platinum edition; No cover price; pinups	3.95

NINJA HIGH SCHOOL TALKS ABOUT COMIC BOOK PRINTING
ANTARCTIC

	N-MINT
❑1, giveaway	1.00

NINJA HIGH SCHOOL TALKS ABOUT SEXUALLY TRANSMITTED DISEASES
ANTARCTIC

	N-MINT
❑1, giveaway	2.00

NINJA HIGH SCHOOL: THE PROM FORMULA
ETERNITY

	N-MINT
❑1, ca. 1989	2.95
❑2	2.95

NINJA HIGH SCHOOL: THE PROM FORMULA
ANTARCTIC

	N-MINT
❑1, Nov 2004	5.95

NINJA HIGH SCHOOL: THE SPECIAL EDITION
ETERNITY

	N-MINT
❑1, b&w	2.50
❑2, b&w	2.50
❑3, b&w	2.50
❑4	2.50

NINJA HIGH SCHOOL VERSION 2
ANTARCTIC

	N-MINT
❑1, Jul 1999	2.50
❑2, Aug 1999	2.50

NINJAK
VALIANT

	N-MINT
❑0, Jun 1995 O: Doctor Silk. O: Ninjak	3.00
❑0/A, Jun 1995; O: Doctor Silk. O: Ninjak. #00; cover forms diptych image with #0	4.00
❑1, Feb 1994; 1: Doctor Silk. chromium cover	2.00
❑1/Gold, Feb 1994; Gold edition; 1: Doctor Silk. wraparound chromium cover	20.00
❑2, Mar 1994	1.00
❑3, Apr 1994	1.00
❑4, May 1994; trading card	2.00
❑5, Jun 1994 A: X-O Manowar	1.00
❑6, Aug 1994 A: X-O Manowar	1.00
❑7, Sep 1994	1.00
❑8, Oct 1994; Chaos Effect Gamma 3	1.00
❑9, Nov 1994; new uniform	1.00
❑10, Dec 1994	1.00
❑11, Jan 1995	1.00
❑12, Feb 1995; trading card	2.00
❑13, Mar 1995; trading card	2.00
❑14, Apr 1995	1.00
❑15, May 1995	2.00
❑16, Jun 1995	2.00
❑17, Jul 1995	2.00
❑18, Jul 1995; Birthquake	2.00
❑19, Aug 1995	2.00
❑20, Aug 1995	2.00
❑21, Sep 1995	2.00
❑22, Sep 1995	2.00
❑23, Oct 1995	2.00
❑24, Oct 1995	2.00
❑25, Nov 1995	3.00
❑26, Nov 1995	5.00
❑Yearbook 1; cardstock cover	3.00

NINJAK (VOL. 2)
ACCLAIM / VALIANT

	N-MINT
❑1, Mar 1997, KB (w); O: Ninjak. 1: Ninjak II	2.50
❑1/Variant, Mar 1997, KB (w); O: Ninjak. 1: Ninjak II. alternate painted cover	2.50
❑2, Apr 1997, KB (w)	2.50
❑3, May 1997, KB (w)	2.50
❑4, Jun 1997, KB (w); A: Colin King. real origin of Ninjak	2.50
❑5, Jul 1997, KB (w)	2.50
❑6, Aug 1997, KB (w); A: X-O Manowar	2.50
❑7, Sep 1997, KB (w); A: X-O Manowar	2.50
❑8, Oct 1997, KB (w); A: Colin King	2.50
❑9, Nov 1997, KB (w)	2.50
❑10, Dec 1997, KB (w)	2.50
❑11, Jan 1998, KB (w)	2.50
❑12, Feb 1998, KB (w)	2.50
❑Ashcan 1, Nov 1996, b&w; No cover price; preview of upcoming series	1.00

NINJUTSU, ART OF THE NINJA
SOLSON

	N-MINT
❑1, b&w	2.00

NINTENDO COMICS SYSTEM
VALIANT

	N-MINT
❑1	4.95
❑2	4.95

NINTENDO COMICS SYSTEM (2ND SERIES)
VALIANT

	N-MINT
❑1, Game Boy	2.00
❑2, Game Boy	2.00
❑3, Game Boy	2.00
❑4, Game Boy	2.00
❑5, Game Boy	2.00
❑6, Game Boy	2.00
❑7, Zelda	2.00
❑8, Super Mario Bros.	2.00
❑9, Super Mario Bros.	2.00

N.I.O.
ACCLAIM / VERTIGO

	N-MINT
❑1, Nov 1998	2.50

NIRA X: ANIME
ENTITY

	N-MINT
❑0, Jan 1997	2.75

NIRA X: ANNUAL
EXPRESS / ENTITY

	N-MINT
❑1/A, Sep 1996, b&w; Snowman 1944 preview	2.75
❑1/B, Sep 1996, b&w; Snowman 1944 preview	9.95

NIRA X: CYBERANGEL (MINI-SERIES)
EXPRESS / ENTITY

	N-MINT
❑1, Dec 1994; cardstock cover	3.00
❑2, Feb 1995	2.50
❑3, Apr 1995	2.50
❑4, Jun 1995	2.50
❑Ashcan 1, Sum 1994, b&w; no cover price	1.00

NIRA X: CYBERANGEL
EXPRESS / ENTITY

	N-MINT
❑1, May 1996; 1: Delta-Void. 1: Millennia. 1: Paradoxx. 1: Quid. Gold foil logo	2.75
❑1/Ltd., May 1996; Limited commemorative edition; 1: Delta-Void. 1: Millennia. 1: Paradoxx. 1: Quid. 3000 printed	4.00
❑2, Jun 1996, b&w 1: Talon. 1: Vex. 1: Cyberhood. 1: Solace	2.50
❑3, Jul 1996, b&w	2.50
❑4, Aug 1996, b&w	2.50

NIRA X: CYBERANGEL (3RD SERIES)
EXPRESS / ENTITY

	N-MINT
❑1	2.50

NIRA X: CYBERANGEL - CYNDER: ENDANGERED SPECIES
EXPRESS / ENTITY

	N-MINT
❑1	2.95
❑1/Ltd.; Commemorative edition; limited to 1500 copies; cardstock cover	12.95

NIRA X: EXODUS
AVATAR / ENTITY

	N-MINT
❑1, Oct 1997	3.00

NIRA X: HEATWAVE
EXPRESS / ENTITY

	N-MINT
❑1, Jul 1995; enhanced wraparound cover	3.75
❑2, Aug 1995	2.50
❑3, Sep 1995	2.50

NIRA X: SOUL SKURGE
EXPRESS / ENTITY

	N-MINT
❑1, Nov 1996, b&w	2.75

NOBLE ARMOUR HALBERDER (JOHN AND JASON WALTRIP'S...)
ACADEMY

	N-MINT
❑1, Jan 1997	2.95

NOBLE CAUSES: EXTENDED FAMILY ONE SHOT
IMAGE

	N-MINT
❑1, Jun 2003	6.95

NOBLE CAUSES
IMAGE

	N-MINT
❑1/A 2002	5.00
❑1/B 2002	5.00
❑2/A, Mar 2002	2.95
❑2/B, Mar 2002	2.95
❑3/A 2002	2.95
❑3/B 2002	2.95
❑4/A, May 2002; Bueno cover	2.95
❑4/B, May 2002; Ponce cover	2.95
❑5	3.50

NOBLE CAUSES: DISTANT RELATIVES
IMAGE

	N-MINT
❑1, Aug 2003	2.95
❑2, Oct 2003	2.95
❑3, Oct 2003	2.95
❑4, Dec 2003	2.95

NOBLE CAUSES: FAMILY SECRETS
IMAGE

	N-MINT
❑1, Oct 2002	2.95
❑2/A, Dec 2002	2.95
❑2/B, Dec 2002	2.95
❑3/A 2003	2.95
❑3/B 2003	2.95
❑4/A 2003	2.95
❑4/B 2003	2.95

NOBLE CAUSES: FIRST IMPRESSIONS
IMAGE

	N-MINT
❑1, Sep 2001	2.95

NOBLE CAUSES (VOL. 2)
IMAGE

	N-MINT
❑1/A, Jul 2004	3.50
❑1/B, Jul 2004	3.50
❑2/A, Aug 2004	3.50
❑2/B, Aug 2004	3.50
❑3/A, Sep 2004	3.50
❑3/B, Sep 2004	3.50
❑4/A, Oct 2004	3.50
❑4/B, Oct 2004	3.50
❑5, Nov 2004	3.50
❑6, Dec 2004	3.50
❑7, Jan 2005	3.50
❑8, Feb 2005	3.50
❑9, Mar 2005	3.50
❑10 2005	3.50
❑11 2005	3.50
❑12, Sep 2005	3.50
❑13, Oct 2005	3.50
❑14, Nov 2005	3.50
❑15, Dec 2005	3.50
❑16, Jan 2006	3.50
❑17, Feb 2006	3.50
❑18, Apr 2006	3.50
❑19, May 2006	3.50
❑20, Jul 2006	3.50
❑21, Jul 2006	3.50

NOBODY
ONI

	N-MINT
❑1, Nov 1998	3.00
❑2, Dec 1998	3.00
❑3, Jan 1999	3.00
❑4, Feb 1999	3.00

Official Marvel Index to the X-Men

Marvel makes Olshevsky's index official

©Marvel

Official Secret Agent

Reprinting strips about G-Man Phil Corrigan

©Pioneer

Offworld

Science fiction anthology folded after one ish

©Graphic Image

Of Myths and Men

The lighter side of magic and super-heroics

©Blackthorne

O.G. Whiz

Boy owns his own toy company

©Gold Key

N-MINT

NO BUSINESS LIKE SHOW BUSINESS
3-D ZONE
❑1, b&w; not 3-D 2.50

NOCTURNAL EMISSIONS
VORTEX
❑1, b&w 2.50

NOCTURNALS
MALIBU / BRAVURA
❑1, Jan 1995, 1: The Nocturnals 3.50
❑2, Feb 1995 .... 3.00
❑3, Apr 1995 .... 3.00
❑4, Apr 1995 .... 3.00
❑5, Jun 1995 .... 3.00
❑6, Aug 1995 .... 3.00

NOCTURNALS: TROLL BRIDGE
ONI
❑1, Oct 2000; b&w and orange 4.95

NOCTURNALS, THE: WITCHING HOUR
DARK HORSE
❑1, May 1998 .... 4.95

NOCTURNE (AIRCEL)
AIRCEL
❑1, Jun 1991, b&w 2.50
❑2, Jul 1991, b&w 2.50
❑3, Aug 1991, b&w 2.50

NOCTURNE (MARVEL)
MARVEL
❑1, Jun 1995 .... 1.50
❑2, Jul 1995; indicia says Sep 95 .... 1.50
❑3, Aug 1995 .... 1.50
❑4, Sep 1995 .... 1.50

NODWICK
HENCHMAN
❑1, Feb 2000, b&w 2.95
❑2, Mar 2000, b&w 2.95
❑3 2000, b&w 2.95
❑4, Aug 2000, b&w 2.95
❑5, Oct 2000, b&w 2.95
❑6, Dec 2000, b&w 2.95
❑7, Feb 2001, b&w 2.95
❑8, Apr 2001, b&w; Action Comics #1 cover spoof 2.95
❑9, Jun 2001, b&w 2.95
❑10, Aug 2001, b&w 2.95
❑11, Oct 2001, b&w 2.95
❑12, Dec 2001, b&w 2.99
❑13, Feb 2002, b&w 2.99
❑14, Apr 2002, b&w 2.99
❑15, Jun 2002, b&w 2.99
❑16, Jul 2002, b&w 2.99
❑17, Sep 2002, b&w 2.99
❑18, Nov 2002, b&w 2.99
❑19, Jan 2003, b&w 2.99
❑20 .... 2.99
❑21 .... 2.99
❑22 .... 2.99
❑23 .... 2.99
❑24 .... 2.99
❑25 .... 2.99
❑26 .... 2.99
❑27 .... 2.99
❑28 .... 2.99
❑29 .... 2.99
❑30 .... 2.99

NO ESCAPE
MARVEL
❑1, Jun 1994 .... 1.50
❑2, Jul 1994 .... 1.50
❑3, Aug 1994 .... 1.50

NOG THE PROTECTOR OF THE PYRAMIDES
ONLI
❑1 .... 2.00

NO GUTS OR GLORY
FANTACO
❑1, ca. 1991, b&w 2.95

NO HONOR
IMAGE
❑0 .... 3.00
❑1, Feb 2001 .... 2.50
❑2, Mar 2001 .... 2.50
❑3, Apr 2001 .... 2.50
❑4, May 2002 .... 2.50

NO HOPE
SLAVE LABOR
❑1, Apr 1993 .... 2.95
❑1/2nd, Feb 1995 .... 2.95
❑2, Aug 1993 .... 2.95
❑2/2nd, Apr 1994 .... 2.95
❑3, Nov 1993 .... 2.95
❑3/2nd, Apr 1994 .... 2.95
❑4, Feb 1994 .... 2.95
❑4/2nd, Oct 1994 .... 2.95
❑5, Jun 1994 .... 2.95
❑6, Sep 1994 .... 2.95
❑7, Jan 1995 .... 2.95
❑8, Apr 1995 .... 2.95
❑9, Jul 1995 .... 2.95

NOID IN 3-D
BLACKTHORNE
❑1 .... 2.50
❑2 .... 2.50

NO ILLUSIONS
COMICS DEFENCE FUND
❑1; Benefit for Comics Defence Fund (UK) 1.00

NOIR (ALPHA)
ALPHA
❑1, Win 1994; text & comics 3.95

NOIR (CREATIVE FORCE)
CREATIVE FORCE
❑1, Apr 1995 .... 4.95

NO JUSTICE, NO PIECE!
HEAD
❑1, Oct 1997, b&w; benefit anthology for CBLDF 2.95
❑2, Jul 1998, b&w; benefit anthology for CBLDF 2.95

NOLAN RYAN
CELEBRITY
❑1 .... 2.95

NOLAN RYAN'S 7 NO-HITTERS
REVOLUTIONARY
❑1, Aug 1993, b&w 2.95

NOMAD (LTD. SERIES)
MARVEL
❑1, Nov 1990 .... 2.00
❑2, Dec 1990, O: Nomad 2.00
❑3, Mar 1991 .... 2.00
❑4, Feb 1991 .... 2.00

NOMAD
MARVEL
❑1, May 1992; gatefold cover 2.50
❑2, Jun 1992 .... 1.75
❑3, Jul 1992; Nomad vs. U.S.Agent 1.75
❑4, Aug 1992 .... 1.75
❑5, Sep 1992 .... 1.75
❑6, Oct 1992 .... 1.75
❑7, Nov 1992; Infinity War 1.75
❑8, Dec 1992; L.A riots 1.75
❑9, Jan 1993 .... 1.75
❑10, Feb 1993 A: Red Wolf 1.75
❑11, Mar 1993 .... 1.75
❑12, Apr 1993 A: Hate-Monger 1.75
❑13, May 1993 A: Hate-Monger 1.75
❑14, Jun 1993 A: Hate-Monger 1.75
❑15, Jul 1993 A: Hate-Monger 1.75
❑16, Aug 1993 A: Gambit 1.75
❑17, Sep 1993 .... 1.75
❑18, Oct 1993 A: Dr. Faustus 1.75
❑19, Nov 1993 .... 1.75
❑20, Dec 1993 .... 1.75
❑21, Jan 1994 A: Man-Thing 1.75
❑22, Feb 1994 .... 1.75
❑23, Mar 1994 .... 1.75
❑24, Apr 1994 .... 1.75
❑25, May 1994 .... 1.75

NOMAN
TOWER
❑1, Nov 1966 WW (c); WW (a) 40.00
❑2, Mar 1967 WW (c); WW (a) 28.00

NO MAN'S LAND
TUNDRA
❑1 .... 14.95

NON
RED INK
❑1 .... 3.00
❑2 .... 3.00
❑3 .... 3.00

NO NEED FOR TENCHI! PART 1
VIZ
❑1 .... 3.00
❑2 .... 3.00
❑3 .... 3.00
❑4 .... 3.00
❑5 .... 3.00
❑6 .... 3.00
❑7 .... 3.00

NO NEED FOR TENCHI! PART 2
VIZ
❑1 .... 3.00
❑2 .... 3.00
❑3 .... 3.00
❑4 .... 3.00
❑5 .... 3.00
❑6 .... 3.00
❑7 .... 3.00

Other grades: Multiply price above by 5/6 for VF/NM • 2/3 for VERY FINE • 1/3 for FINE • 1/5 for VERY GOOD • 1/8 for GOOD

NO NEED FOR TENCHI! PART 3
VIZ
- ❑1, Jun 1996 ... 2.95
- ❑2, Jul 1996 ... 2.95
- ❑3, Aug 1996 ... 2.95
- ❑4, Sep 1996 ... 2.95
- ❑5, Oct 1996 ... 2.95
- ❑6, Nov 1996 ... 2.95

NO NEED FOR TENCHI! PART 4
VIZ
- ❑1, Dec 1997 ... 2.95
- ❑2, Jan 1998 ... 2.95
- ❑3, Feb 1998 ... 2.95
- ❑4, Mar 1998 ... 2.95
- ❑5, Apr 1998 ... 2.95
- ❑6, May 1998 ... 2.95

NO NEED FOR TENCHI! PART 5
VIZ
- ❑1, Jun 1998 ... 3.25
- ❑2, Jul 1998 ... 2.95
- ❑3, Aug 1998 ... 2.95
- ❑4, Sep 1998 ... 2.95
- ❑5, Oct 1998 ... 2.95

NO NEED FOR TENCHI! PART 6
VIZ
- ❑1, Nov 1998 ... 3.25
- ❑2, Dec 1998 ... 2.95
- ❑3, Jan 1999 ... 3.25
- ❑4, Feb 1999 ... 3.25
- ❑5, Mar 1999 ... 3.25

NO NEED FOR TENCHI! PART 7
VIZ
- ❑1, Apr 1999 ... 2.95
- ❑2, May 1999 ... 2.95
- ❑3, Jun 1999 ... 2.95
- ❑4, Jul 1999 ... 2.95
- ❑5, Aug 1999 ... 2.95
- ❑6, Sep 1999 ... 2.95

NO NEED FOR TENCHI! PART 8
VIZ
- ❑1, Oct 1999 ... 3.25
- ❑2 ... 3.25
- ❑3 ... 3.25
- ❑4 ... 3.25
- ❑5 ... 3.25

NO NEED FOR TENCHI! PART 9
VIZ
- ❑1, Mar 2000 ... 2.95
- ❑2, Apr 2000 ... 2.95
- ❑3, May 2000 ... 2.95
- ❑4, Jun 2000 ... 2.95
- ❑5, Jul 2000 ... 2.95
- ❑6, Aug 2000 ... 2.95

NO NEED FOR TENCHI! PART 10
VIZ
- ❑1 ... 2.95
- ❑2 ... 2.95
- ❑3 ... 2.95
- ❑4 ... 2.95
- ❑5 2001 ... 2.95
- ❑6 2001 ... 2.95
- ❑7 2001 ... 2.95

NO NEED FOR TENCHI! PART 11
VIZ
- ❑1 2001 ... 3.50
- ❑2 2001 ... 3.50
- ❑3 2001 ... 3.50
- ❑4 2001 ... 3.50

NO NEED FOR TENCHI! PART 12
VIZ
- ❑1 2001 ... 2.95
- ❑2 2001 ... 2.95
- ❑3 2001 ... 2.95
- ❑4 ... 2.95
- ❑5 ... 2.95
- ❑6 2002 ... 2.95

NO NINJA MAN
CUSTOM PIC
- ❑1 ... 1.50
- ❑1/2nd ... 1.50

NO NO UFO
ANTARCTIC / VENUS
- ❑1, Aug 1996 ... 2.95
- ❑2, May 1997, b&w ... 2.95
- ❑3, Sep 1997, b&w ... 2.95
- ❑4, May 1998, b&w ... 2.95

NO PASARAN!
NBM
- ❑1 ... 13.95
- ❑2 ... 11.95

NO PROFIT FOR THE WISE
CFD
- ❑1, Jul 1996, b&w ... 2.95

NORB
MU
- ❑1, Jan 1992 ... 8.95

NORMALMAN
AARDVARK-VANAHEIM
- ❑1, Jan 1984; Aardvark-Vanaheim publishes ... 2.50
- ❑2, Apr 1984 O: Normalman ... 2.00
- ❑3, Jun 1984 ... 2.00
- ❑4, Aug 1984 ... 2.00
- ❑5, Oct 1984 ... 2.00
- ❑6, Dec 1984 ... 2.00
- ❑7, Feb 1985 ... 2.00
- ❑8, Apr 1985 ... 2.00
- ❑9, Jun 1985; Renegade begins as publisher ... 2.00
- ❑10, Aug 1985 ... 2.00
- ❑11, Oct 1985 ... 2.00
- ❑12, Dec 1985 ... 2.00
- ❑3D 1, Double-size ... 2.50

NORMALMAN 3-D
RENEGADE
- ❑1, Feb 1986 ... 2.25

NORMALMAN-MEGATON MAN SPECIAL
IMAGE
- ❑1, Aug 1994 ... 2.50

NORTHERN'S HEMISPHERE
NORTHERN'S HEMISPHERE
- ❑5, b&w ... 2.49
- ❑6, b&w ... 2.49
- ❑7, b&w ... 2.49

NORTHERN'S HEMISPHERE UNDISGUISED
NORTHERN'S HEMISPHERE
- ❑1 ... 2.50

NORTHGUARD: THE MANDES CONCLUSION
CALIBER
- ❑1, Sep 1989, b&w ... 1.95
- ❑2, Oct 1989, b&w ... 1.95
- ❑3, Nov 1989, b&w ... 1.95

NORTHSTAR
MARVEL
- ❑1, Apr 1994 ... 2.00
- ❑2, May 1994 ... 2.00
- ❑3, Jun 1994 ... 2.00
- ❑4, Jul 1994 ... 2.00

NORTHSTAR PRESENTS
NORTHSTAR
- ❑1, Oct 1994 ... 2.50
- ❑2 ... 2.50

NORTHWEST CARTOON COOKERY
STARHEAD
- ❑1, ca. 1995, b&w; recipes from Pacific Northwest cartoonists ... 2.75

NORTHWEST PASSAGE
NBM
- ❑1, Sep 2005 ... 5.95

NOSFERATU (DARK HORSE)
DARK HORSE
- ❑1, Mar 1991, b&w ... 3.95

NOSFERATU (CALIBER)
TOME
- ❑1, Jul 1991, b&w ... 2.75
- ❑2, Jul 1991, b&w ... 2.75
- ❑Book 1, Mar 1995; Deluxe edition; collects series ... 3.95

NOSFERATU, PLAGUE OF TERROR
MILLENNIUM
- ❑1, b&w; duotone ... 2.50
- ❑2, b&w; duotone ... 2.50
- ❑3, b&w; duotone ... 2.50
- ❑4, b&w; duotone ... 2.50

NOSFERATU: THE DEATH MASS
ANTARCTIC / VENUS
- ❑1, Dec 1997, b&w ... 2.95
- ❑2, Jan 1998, b&w ... 2.95
- ❑3, Feb 1998, b&w ... 2.95
- ❑4, Mar 1998, b&w ... 2.95

NOSTRADAMUS CHRONICLES 1559-1821
TOME / VENUS
- ❑1 ... 2.95

NOT APPROVED CRIME
AVALON
- ❑1 ... 2.95

NOT BRAND ECHH
MARVEL
- ❑1, Aug 1967, SL (w); BEv, JK, JSe, RA (a); 1: Forbush Man (on cover) ... 45.00
- ❑2, Sep 1967 ... 18.00
- ❑3, Oct 1967, O: Charlie America. O: Sore. O: Bulk ... 15.00
- ❑4, Nov 1967 ... 15.00
- ❑5, Dec 1967, GC (a); O: Forbush Man. 1: Forbush Man (full appearance) ... 15.00
- ❑6, Feb 1968 ... 10.00
- ❑7, Apr 1968, O: Stupor-Man. O: Fantastical Four ... 10.00
- ❑8, Jun 1968 ... 10.00
- ❑9, Aug 1968; Giant-size ... 25.00
- ❑10, Oct 1968; Giant-size ... 25.00
- ❑11, Dec 1968; Giant-size ... 25.00
- ❑12, Feb 1969; Giant-size ... 25.00
- ❑13, Apr 1969; Giant-size ... 25.00

NO TIME FOR SERGEANTS
DELL
- ❑1, Feb 1965, cover code -502; based on TV show ... 40.00
- ❑2, May 1965, cover code -505; a drawn cover, yet actors' names appear with their drawings ... 40.00
- ❑3, Aug 1965, cover code -510 ... 30.00

(NOT ONLY) THE BEST OF WONDER WART-HOG
PRINT MINT
- ❑1, ca. 1973, b&w ... 15.00
- ❑2, ca. 1973, b&w ... 12.00
- ❑3, ca. 1973, b&w ... 12.00

NOT QUITE DEAD
RIP OFF
- ❑1, Mar 1993, b&w ... 2.95
- ❑1/2nd ... 2.95
- ❑2, b&w ... 2.95
- ❑3 ... 2.95
- ❑4, ca. 1995 ... 2.95

NOVA (1ST SERIES)
MARVEL
- ❑1, Sep 1976, JB, JSt (a); O: Nova I (Richard Ryder). 1: Nova I (Richard Ryder) ... 8.00
- ❑2, Oct 1976, JB, JSt (a); 1: Powerhouse ... 4.00
- ❑3, Nov 1976, 1: Diamondhead ... 3.00
- ❑4, Dec 1976 ... 3.00
- ❑5, Jan 1977 ... 3.00
- ❑6, Feb 1977, 1: The Sphinx ... 3.00
- ❑7, Mar 1977, O: The Sphinx ... 3.00
- ❑8, Apr 1977 ... 3.00
- ❑9, May 1977 ... 3.00
- ❑10, Jun 1977 ... 3.00
- ❑10/35 cent, Jun 1977, 35 cent regional variant ... 15.00
- ❑11, Jul 1977 ... 3.00
- ❑11/35 cent, Jul 1977, 35 cent regional variant ... 15.00
- ❑12, Aug 1977, A: Spider-Man ... 3.00
- ❑12/35 cent, Aug 1977, 35 cent regional variant ... 15.00
- ❑13, Sep 1977, 1: Crimebuster ... 3.00
- ❑13/35 cent, Sep 1977, 35 cent regional variant ... 15.00
- ❑14, Oct 1977 ... 3.00
- ❑14/35 cent, Oct 1977, 35 cent regional variant ... 15.00
- ❑15, Nov 1977 ... 3.00
- ❑16, Dec 1977, V: Yellow Claw ... 3.00
- ❑17, Jan 1978 ... 3.00
- ❑18, Mar 1978 ... 3.00

Ohm's Law

"Mega-humans" brought back to life
©Imperial

Oh My Goddess!

Series numbering seems calculated to confuse
©Dark Horse

OMAC

One Man Army Corps serves world peace
©DC

Omaha The Cat Dancer (Kitchen Sink)

Cult favorite adults-only soap opera
©Kitchen Sink

Omega Men

Series guilty of the introduction of Lobo
©DC

	N-MINT
❑19, May 1978, O: Blackout I (Marcus Daniels). 1: Blackout I (Marcus Daniels)	3.00
❑20, Jul 1978	3.00
❑21, Sep 1978, 1: Harris Moore (Comet). Only appears as Harris Moore	3.00
❑22, Nov 1978, O: Comet (Harris Moore). 1: Comet (Harris Moore)	3.00
❑23, Jan 1979	3.00
❑24, Mar 1979, O: Crimebuster	3.00
❑25, May 1979	3.00

NOVA (2ND SERIES)
MARVEL

	N-MINT
❑1, Jan 1994	2.25
❑1/Variant, Jan 1994; Special cover	2.95
❑2, Feb 1994	2.00
❑3, Mar 1994 A: Spider-Man	1.75
❑4, Apr 1994	1.75
❑5, May 1994	1.75
❑6, Jun 1994	1.95
❑7, Jul 1994	1.95
❑8, Aug 1994	1.95
❑9, Sep 1994	1.95
❑10, Oct 1994	1.95
❑11, Nov 1994 V: new Fantastic Four	1.95
❑12, Dec 1994	1.95
❑13, Jan 1995	1.95
❑14, Feb 1995	1.95
❑15, Mar 1995	1.95
❑16, Apr 1995	1.95
❑17, May 1995	1.95
❑18, Jun 1995	1.95

NOVA (3RD SERIES)
MARVEL

	N-MINT
❑1, May 1999; wraparound cover	2.99
❑2, Jun 1999	1.99
❑2/Variant, Jun 1999	1.99
❑3, Jul 1999	1.99
❑4, Aug 1999	1.99
❑5, Sep 1999	1.99
❑6, Oct 1999	1.99
❑7, Nov 1999	1.99

NOVA HUNTER
RYAL

	N-MINT
❑1	2.50
❑1/Autographed; Autographed limited edition	4.00

NOVAVOLO
JUNGLE BOY

	N-MINT
❑1, ca. 2000, b&w	3.95
❑Annual 2001, ca. 2001, b&w	3.95

NOW COMICS PREVIEW
NOW

	N-MINT
❑1 1: Thunderstar. 1: Valor. 1: Vector. 1: Syphons. 1: Ralph Snart	1.00

NOWHERESVILLE
CALIBER

	N-MINT
❑1, ca. 1995, b&w	3.50

NOWHERESVILLE: DEATH BY STARLIGHT
CALIBER

	N-MINT
❑1, b&w	2.95
❑2, b&w	2.95
❑3, b&w; flip book with Wordsmith #7 back-up	2.95
❑4	2.95

NOWHERESVILLE: THE HISTORY OF COOL
CALIBER

	N-MINT
❑1	2.95

NOW, ON A MORE SERIOUS NOTE...
DAWN

	N-MINT
❑1, Sum 1994, b&w; no cover price	2.00

NOW WHAT?!
NOW

	N-MINT
❑1	3.00
❑2	2.00
❑3	2.00
❑4	2.00
❑5	2.00
❑6	2.00
❑7	2.00
❑8	2.00
❑9	2.00
❑10	2.00
❑11	2.00

NTH MAN, THE ULTIMATE NINJA
MARVEL

	N-MINT
❑1, Aug 1989	1.00
❑2, Sep 1989	1.00
❑3, Oct 1989	1.00
❑4, Nov 1989	1.00
❑5, Nov 1989	1.00
❑6, Dec 1989	1.00
❑7, Dec 1989	1.00
❑8, Jan 1990	1.00
❑9, Feb 1990	1.00
❑10, Mar 1990	1.00
❑11, Apr 1990	1.00
❑12, May 1990	1.00
❑13, Jun 1990	1.00
❑14, Jul 1990	1.00
❑15, Aug 1990	1.00
❑16, Sep 1990	1.00

NUANCE
MAGNETIC INK

	N-MINT
❑1, b&w	2.75
❑2, b&w	2.75
❑3, b&w	2.75

NUCLEAR WAR!
NEC

	N-MINT
❑1	3.50
❑2, Nov 2000	3.50

NULL PATROL
ESCAPE VELOCITY

	N-MINT
❑1	1.50
❑2	1.50

NUMIDIAN FORCE
KAMITE

	N-MINT
❑4	2.00

NURSES
GOLD KEY

	N-MINT
❑1, Apr 1963	50.00
❑2, Jul 1963	40.00
❑3, Oct 1963	30.00

NURTURE THE DEVIL
FANTAGRAPHICS

	N-MINT
❑2, Jul 1994, b&w	2.50
❑3, Dec 1994, b&w	2.50

NUT RUNNERS
RIP OFF

	N-MINT
❑1, Sep 1991, b&w	2.50
❑2, Jan 1992, b&w	2.50

NUTS & BOTS
EXCEL GRAPHICS

	N-MINT
❑1, Aug 1998, b&w; magazine	3.95

NYC MECH
IMAGE

	N-MINT
❑1, Apr 2004	2.95
❑2, Aug 2004	2.95
❑3 2004	2.95
❑4 2004	2.95
❑5 2004	2.95
❑6, Dec 2004	2.95

NYC MECH: BETA LOVE
IMAGE

	N-MINT
❑1, ca. 2005	3.50
❑2 2005	3.50
❑3, Oct 2005	3.50
❑4, Jan 2006	3.50
❑5, Mar 2006	3.50

NYGHT SCHOOL
BRAINSTORM

	N-MINT
❑2, b&w	2.95

NYX
MARVEL

	N-MINT
❑1, Dec 2003	9.00
❑1/Variant, Dec 2003	8.00
❑2, Jan 2004	7.00
❑2/Variant, Jan 2004	5.00
❑3, Feb 2004	45.00
❑4, Jul 2004	9.00
❑5, Aug 2004	4.00
❑6, Sep 2005	2.99
❑7 2005	

OBERGEIST: RAGNAROK HIGHWAY
IMAGE

	N-MINT
❑1, May 2001	2.95
❑2, Jun 2001	2.95
❑3, Jul 2001	2.95
❑4, Aug 2001	2.95
❑5, Sep 2001	2.95
❑6, Oct 2001	2.95

OBERGEIST: THE EMPTY LOCKET
DARK HORSE

	N-MINT
❑1, Mar 2002, b&w	2.95

OBJECTIVE FIVE
IMAGE

	N-MINT
❑1, Jul 2000	2.95
❑2, Aug 2000	2.95
❑3, Sep 2000	2.95
❑4, Nov 2000	2.95
❑5, Dec 2000	2.95
❑6, Jan 2001	2.95

OBLIVION
COMICO

	N-MINT
❑1, Jan 1996	2.50

❑2, Mar 1996 2.50
❑3, May 1996 2.50

OBLIVION CITY
SLAVE LABOR

❑1, Mar 1991, b&w 2.50
❑2, May 1991, b&w 2.50
❑3, Jun 1991, b&w 2.50
❑4, Jun 1991, b&w 2.50
❑5, Sep 1991, b&w 2.50
❑6, Jan 1992, b&w 2.50
❑7, Apr 1992 2.95
❑8, May 1992 2.95
❑9, Jun 1992 3.95

OBNOXIO THE CLOWN
MARVEL

❑1, Apr 1983, X-Men 2.00

OCCULT FILES OF DR. SPEKTOR
GOLD KEY

❑1, Apr 1973 32.00
❑2, Jun 1973 14.00
❑3, Aug 1973 14.00
❑4, Nov 1973 14.00
❑5, Dec 1973 14.00
❑6, Feb 1974 8.00
❑7, Apr 1974 8.00
❑8, Jun 1974 8.00
❑9, Aug 1974 8.00
❑10, Oct 1974 8.00
❑11, Dec 1974 5.00
❑12, Feb 1975, Fights werewolf 5.00
❑13, Apr 1975 5.00
❑14, Jun 1975 9.00
❑15, Aug 1975 5.00
❑16, Oct 1975 5.00
❑17, Dec 1975 5.00
❑18, Feb 1976, Rutland, Vermont story; Tom Fagan's name changed 7.00
❑19, Apr 1976 5.00
❑20, Jun 1976 5.00
❑21, Aug 1976 3.00
❑22, Oct 1976 3.00
❑23, Dec 1976 7.00
❑24, Feb 1977 3.00
❑25, May 1982, Whitman only 10.00

OCEAN
DC

❑1, Dec 2004 2.95
❑2, Jan 2005 2.95
❑3, Feb 2005 2.95
❑4, Mar 2005 2.95
❑5, Apr 2005 2.95
❑6 2005 2.95

OCEAN COMICS
OCEAN

❑1, b&w 1.75

OCELOT
FANTAGRAPHICS / EROS

❑1 2.75
❑2 2.75
❑3 2.75

OCTOBER YEN
ANTARCTIC

❑1, Jul 1996, b&w 3.50
❑2, Sep 1996, b&w 2.95
❑3, Nov 1996, b&w 2.95

OCTOBRIANA
REVOLUTION

❑1 3.50
❑2 2.95
❑3 2.95
❑4 2.95
❑5 2.95

OCTOBRIANA: FILLING IN THE BLANKS
ARTFUL SALAMANDER

❑1, Win 1998, b&w 2.95

ODD ADVENTURE-ZINE
ZAMBONI

❑1, Jan 1997 2.95
❑2, Apr 1997 2.95
❑3, Jul 1997 2.95
❑4, Dec 1997 2.95

ODDBALLS
NBM

❑1, ca. 2002, b&w 2.95
❑2, ca. 2002, b&w 2.95
❑3, ca. 2002, b&w 2.95
❑4, ca. 2002, b&w 2.95
❑5, ca. 2002, b&w 2.95
❑6, ca. 2002, b&w 2.95
❑7, ca. 2003, b&w 2.95

ODDBALLZ
NBM

❑1 2002 2.95
❑2 2002 2.95
❑3 2.95
❑4 2.95

ODDJOB
SLAVE LABOR

❑1, Spr 1999, b&w 2.95

ODDLY NORMAL
VIPER

❑1 2005 2.95
❑2, Jun 2005 2.95
❑3, Jul 2005 2.95
❑4, Sep 2005 2.95

OEMING SKETCHBOOK
MICHAEL AVON OEMING

❑1 5.00

OF BITTER SOULS
SPEAKEASY COMICS

❑1, Sep 2005 2.99
❑2, Oct 2005

OFFCASTES
MARVEL / EPIC

❑1; Embossed cover 2.50
❑2 1.95
❑3 1.95

OFFERINGS
CRY FOR DAWN

❑1, b&w 2.75
❑2, b&w 2.50

OFFICIAL, AUTHORIZED ZEN INTERGALACTIC NINJA SOURCEBOOK
EXPRESS / ENTITY

❑1, b&w 3.50
❑1/2nd; 94 revised edition 3.50

OFFICIAL BUZ SAWYER
PIONEER

❑1, Aug 1988, b&w 2.00
❑2, Sep 1988, b&w 2.00
❑3, Oct 1988, b&w 2.00
❑4, Nov 1988, b&w 2.00
❑5, Dec 1988, b&w 2.00

OFFICIAL HANDBOOK OF THE CONAN UNIVERSE
MARVEL

❑1 1.50
❑2, no price; sold with Conan Saga #75 1.00

OFFICIAL HANDBOOK OF THE MARVEL UNIVERSE (VOL. 1)
MARVEL

❑1, Jan 1983, Abomination to Avengers Quinjet 2.00
❑2, Feb 1983, Baron Mordo to The Collective Man 2.00
❑3, Mar 1983, The Collector to Dracula 2.00
❑4, Apr 1983, Dragon Man to Gypsy Moth 2.00
❑5, May 1983, Hangman to Juggernaut 2.00
❑6, Jun 1983, Kang to Man-Bull 2.00
❑7, Jul 1983, Mandarin to Mystique 2.00
❑8, Aug 1983, Namorita to Pyro 2.00
❑9, Sep 1983, Quasar to She-Hulk 2.00
❑10, Oct 1983, Shi'ar to Sub-Mariner 2.00
❑11, Nov 1983, Subterraneans to Ursa Major 2.00
❑12, Dec 1983, Valkyrie to Zzzax 2.00
❑13, Feb 1984, Book of the Dead: Air-Walker to Man-Wolf 2.00
❑14, Mar 1984, Book of the Dead: Marvel Boy to Zuras 2.00
❑15, May 1984, Weapons, Hardware, and Paraphernalia 2.00

OFFICIAL HANDBOOK OF THE MARVEL UNIVERSE (VOL. 2)
MARVEL

❑1, Dec 1985, Abomination to Batroc's Brigade 2.00
❑2, Jan 1986, Beast to Clea 2.00
❑3, Feb 1986, Cloak to Doctor Octopus 2.00
❑4, Mar 1986, Doctor Strange to Galactus 2.00
❑5, Apr 1986, Gardener to Hulk 2.00
❑6, May 1986, Human Torch to Ka-Zar 2.00
❑7, Jun 1986, Khoryphos to Magneto 2.00
❑8, Jul 1986, Magus to Mole Man 2.00
❑9, Aug 1986, Molecule Man to Owl 2.00
❑10, Sep 1986, Paladin to The Rhino 2.00
❑11, Oct 1986, Richard Rider to Sidewinder 2.00
❑12, Nov 1986, Sif to Sunspot 2.00
❑13, Dec 1986, Super-Adaptoid to Umar 2.00
❑14, Jan 1987, Unicorn to Wolverine 2.00
❑15, Mar 1987, Wonder Man to Zzzax and Alien Races 2.00
❑16, Jun 1987, Book of the Dead: Air-Walker to Death-Stalker 2.00
❑17, Aug 1987, Book of the Dead: Destiny to Hobgoblin 2.00
❑18, Oct 1987, Book of the Dead: Hyperion to Nighthawk; Book of the Dead: Hyperion II to Nighthawk II 2.00
❑19, Dec 1987, Book of the Dead: Nuke to Obadiah Stane 2.00
❑20, Feb 1988, Book of the Dead: Stick to Zuras 2.00

OFFICIAL HANDBOOK OF THE MARVEL UNIVERSE (VOL. 3)
MARVEL

❑1, Jul 1989, Adversary to Chameleon 2.00
❑2, Aug 1989, Champion of the Universe to Ecstasy 2.00
❑3, Sep 1989, Eon to Hulk 2.00
❑4, Oct 1989, Human Torch I to Manikin 2.00
❑5, Nov 1989, Marauders to Power Princess 2.00
❑6, Nov 1989, Prowler to Serpent Society 2.00
❑7, Dec 1989, Set to Tyrak 2.00
❑8, Dec 1989, U-Man to Madelyne Pryor 2.00

OFFICIAL HANDBOOK OF THE MARVEL UNIVERSE MASTER EDITION
MARVEL

❑1, Dec 1990, Three-hole punched looseleaf format 4.50
❑2, Jan 1991 4.50
❑3, Feb 1991 4.50
❑4, Mar 1991 4.50
❑5, Apr 1991 4.50
❑6, May 1991 3.95
❑7, Jun 1991 3.95
❑8, Jul 1991 3.95
❑9, Aug 1991 3.95
❑10, Sep 1991 3.95
❑11, Oct 1991 3.95
❑12, Nov 1991 3.95
❑13, Dec 1991 4.50
❑14, Jan 1992 4.50
❑15, Feb 1992 4.50
❑16, Mar 1992 4.50
❑17, Apr 1992 4.50
❑18, May 1992 4.50
❑19, Jun 1992 4.50
❑20, Jul 1992 4.50
❑21, Aug 1992 4.50
❑22, Sep 1992 4.50
❑23, Oct 1992 4.50
❑24, Nov 1992 4.50
❑25, Dec 1992 4.50
❑26, Jan 1993 4.50
❑27, Feb 1993 4.50
❑28, Mar 1993 4.95
❑29, Apr 1993 4.95
❑30, May 1993 4.95
❑31, Jun 1993 4.95
❑32, Jul 1993 4.95
❑33, Aug 1993 4.95
❑34, Sep 1993 4.95

Omega the Unknown

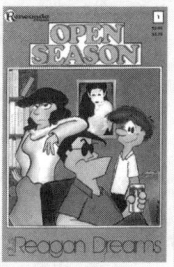

Storyline finally finished in The Defenders

©Marvel

100 Bullets

It"s the ammunition for revenge

©DC

Oni

Next, a title called "Dark Horse" from Oni Press

©Dark Horse

Oni Double Feature

Anthology flip-book from Oni Press

©Oni

Open Season

Jim Bricker's "slice of life" series

©Renegade

N-MINT

❑35, Oct 1993, KP (a) 4.95
❑36, Nov 1993 .... 4.95

OFFICIAL HANDBOOK OF THE MARVEL UNIVERSE: ALTERNATE UNIVERSES 2005
MARVEL

❑1 2005 .... 3.99

OFFICIAL HANDBOOK OF THE MARVEL UNIVERSE: AVENGERS 2005
MARVEL

❑0, Sep 2005 .... 3.99

OFFICIAL HANDBOOK OF THE MARVEL UNIVERSE: BOOK OF THE DEAD 2004
MARVEL

❑1 2004 .... 3.99

OFFICIAL HANDBOOK OF THE MARVEL UNIVERSE DAREDEVIL ELEKTRA 2004
MARVEL

❑1, Nov 2004 .... 3.50

OFFICIAL HANDBOOK OF THE MARVEL UNIVERSE: FANTASTIC FOUR 2005
MARVEL

❑0, Jul 2005 .... 3.99

OFFICIAL HANDBOOK OF THE MARVEL UNIVERSE: GOLDEN AGE MARVEL 2004
MARVEL

❑1, ca. 2004 .... 3.99

OFFICIAL HANDBOOK OF THE MARVEL UNIVERSE: HORROR 2005
MARVEL

❑1, Dec 2005, b&w 3.99

OFFICIAL HANDBOOK OF THE MARVEL UNIVERSE: HULK
MARVEL

❑1, ca. 2004 .... 3.99

OFFICIAL HANDBOOK OF THE MARVEL UNIVERSE: SPIDER-MAN 2004
MARVEL

❑1, ca. 2004 .... 3.99

OFFICIAL HANDBOOK OF THE MARVEL UNIVERSE: THE AVENGERS
MARVEL

❑1, ca. 2004 .... 3.99

OFFICIAL HANDBOOK OF THE MARVEL UNIVERSE: WOLVERINE 2004
MARVEL

❑1 2004 .... 3.99

OFFICIAL HANDBOOK OF THE MARVEL UNIVERSE: WOMEN OF MARVEL 2005
MARVEL

❑0 2005 .... 3.99

N-MINT

OFFICIAL HANDBOOK OF THE MARVEL UNIVERSE: X-MEN 2004
MARVEL

❑1, ca. 2004 .... 3.99

OFFICIAL HANDBOOK OF THE MARVEL UNIVERSE: X-MEN - AGE OF APOCALYPSE 2005
MARVEL

❑1, May 2005 .... 3.99

OFFICIAL HANDBOOK OF THE MARVEL UNIVERSE: X-MEN 2005
MARVEL

❑1, Jan 2006 .... 3.99

OFFICIAL HANDBOOK: ULTIMATE MARVEL UNIVERSE 2005
MARVEL

❑0, Oct 2005 .... 3.99

OFFICIAL HANDBOOK: ULTIMATE MARVEL UNIVERSE - ULTIMATES & X-MEN 2005
MARVEL

❑1, Feb 2006 .... 3.99

OFFICIAL HAWKMAN INDEX
ECLIPSE / INDEPENDENT

❑1, Nov 1986 .... 2.00
❑2, Dec 1986 .... 2.00

OFFICIAL HOW TO DRAW G.I. JOE
BLACKTHORNE

❑1, Nov 1987 .... 2.00
❑2, Jan 1988 .... 2.00
❑3, Mar 1988 .... 2.00

OFFICIAL HOW TO DRAW ROBOTECH
BLACKTHORNE

❑1, Feb 1987 .... 2.00
❑2, Mar 1987 .... 2.00
❑3, Apr 1987 .... 2.00
❑4, May 1987 .... 2.00
❑5, Jun 1987 .... 2.00
❑6, Jul 1987 .... 2.00
❑7, Aug 1987 .... 2.00
❑8, Sep 1987 .... 2.00
❑9, Oct 1987 .... 2.00
❑10, Nov 1987 .... 2.00
❑11, Dec 1987 .... 2.00
❑12, Jan 1988 .... 2.00
❑13, Feb 1988 .... 2.00
❑14, Mar 1988 .... 2.00

OFFICIAL HOW TO DRAW TRANSFORMERS
BLACKTHORNE

❑1, Sep 1987 .... 2.00
❑2, Nov 1987 .... 2.00
❑3, Jan 1988 .... 2.00
❑4, Mar 1988 .... 2.00

OFFICIAL JOHNNY HAZARD
PIONEER

❑1, Aug 1988, b&w; strips 2.00

OFFICIAL JUNGLE JIM
PIONEER

❑1, Jun 1988, b&w 2.00
❑2, Jul 1988, b&w 2.00

N-MINT

❑3, Aug 1988, b&w 2.00
❑4, Sep 1988, b&w 2.00
❑5, Oct 1988, b&w 2.00
❑6, Nov 1988, b&w 2.00
❑7, Dec 1988, b&w 2.00
❑8, Jan 1989, b&w 2.00
❑9, Feb 1989, b&w 2.00
❑10, Apr 1989 .... 2.50
❑11, Apr 1989 .... 2.50
❑12 .... 2.50
❑13 .... 2.50
❑14 .... 2.50
❑15 .... 2.50
❑16 .... 2.50
❑Annual 1, Jan 1989, b&w 3.95

OFFICIAL JUSTICE LEAGUE OF AMERICA INDEX
ICG

❑1 .... 2.00
❑2 .... 2.00
❑3 .... 2.00
❑4 .... 2.00
❑5 .... 2.00
❑6 .... 2.00
❑7 .... 2.00
❑8; Title changes to Justice League of America Index; Covers Justice League of America #238-261, other related titles 2.00

OFFICIAL MANDRAKE
PIONEER

❑1, Jun 1988, b&w 2.00
❑2, Jul 1988, b&w 2.00
❑3, Aug 1988, b&w 2.00
❑4, Sep 1988, b&w 2.00
❑5, Oct 1988, b&w 2.00
❑6, Nov 1988, b&w 2.00
❑7, Dec 1988, b&w 2.00
❑8, Jan 1989, b&w 2.00
❑9, Feb 1989, b&w 2.00
❑10, Apr 1989 .... 2.50
❑11, Apr 1989 .... 2.50
❑12 .... 2.50
❑13 .... 2.50
❑14 .... 2.50
❑15 .... 2.50

OFFICIAL MARVEL INDEX TO MARVEL TEAM-UP
MARVEL

❑1, Jan 1986 .... 1.25
❑2, Feb 1986 .... 1.25
❑3, May 1986 .... 1.25
❑4, Jul 1986 .... 1.25
❑5, Oct 1986 .... 1.25
❑6, Jul 1987; Indexes Marvel Team-Up #99 - 112, Annual 3 .... 1.25

OFFICIAL MARVEL INDEX TO THE AMAZING SPIDER-MAN
MARVEL

❑1, Apr 1985; Indexes Amazing Fantasy #15, Amazing Spider-Man #1-29 .... 1.25
❑2, May 1985 .... 1.25
❑3, Jun 1985; Indexes Amazing Spider-Man#59-84, King-Size Annual #5-6, Spectacular Spider-Man #1-2 .... 1.25

N-MINT

❑4, Jul 1985; Indexes Amazing Spider-Man#85-112, King-Size Annual #7-8 ... 1.25
❑5, Aug 1985; Indexes Amazing Spider-Man#114-137, King-Size Annual #9, Giant-Sized Super-Heroes #1 ... 1.25
❑6, Sep 1985; Indexes Amazing Spider-Man #138-155, Giant-Size Spider-Man #1-6 ... 1.25
❑7, Oct 1985; Indexes Amazing Spider-Man #156-174; Spider-Man Annual #10-11 ... 1.25
❑8, Nov 1985; Indexes issues #175-195, Annual #12 ... 1.25
❑9, Dec 1985; Indexes issues #196-215, Annual #13-14 ... 1.25

OFFICIAL MARVEL INDEX TO THE AVENGERS
MARVEL

❑1, Jun 1987 ... 2.95
❑2, Aug 1987 ... 2.95
❑3, Oct 1987 ... 2.95
❑4, Dec 1987 ... 2.95
❑5, Apr 1988 ... 2.95
❑6, Jun 1988 ... 2.95
❑7, Aug 1988 ... 2.95

OFFICIAL MARVEL INDEX TO THE AVENGERS (VOL. 2)
MARVEL

❑1, Oct 1994 ... 1.95
❑2, Nov 1994; Indexes issues #61-122 ... 1.95
❑3, Dec 1994 ... 1.95
❑4, Jan 1995; Indexes issues #177-230 ... 1.95
❑5, Feb 1995 ... 1.95
❑6, Mar 1995 ... 1.95

OFFICIAL MARVEL INDEX TO THE FANTASTIC FOUR
MARVEL

❑1, Dec 1985; Indexes Fantastic Four #1-15 ... 1.25
❑2, Jan 1986 ... 1.25
❑3, Feb 1986 ... 1.25
❑4, Mar 1986; Indexes Fantastic Four #46-65, Annual #4 ... 1.25
❑5, Apr 1986; Indexes Fantastic Four #66-84, Annual #5-6 ... 1.25
❑6, May 1986; Indexes issues #85-106, Annual #7-8 ... 1.25
❑7, Jun 1986; Indexes issues #107-125, Annual #9 ... 1.25
❑8, Jul 1986; Indexes issues #126-141, Annual #10, Giant-Size Super-Stars #1 ... 1.25
❑9, Aug 1986 ... 1.25
❑10, Sep 1986; Indexes issues #161-176, Annual #11, Giant-Size Fantastic Four #4-6 ... 1.25
❑11, Oct 1986; Indexes issues #177-198 ... 1.25
❑12, Jan 1987; Indexes issues #199-214, Annual # 12-13 ... 1.25

OFFICIAL MARVEL INDEX TO THE X-MEN
MARVEL

❑1, May 1987; squarebound; cardstock cover ... 2.95
❑2, Jul 1987 ... 2.95
❑3, Sep 1987 ... 2.95
❑4, Nov 1987 ... 2.95
❑5, Mar 1988 ... 2.95
❑6, May 1988 ... 2.95
❑7, Jul 1988 ... 2.95

OFFICIAL MARVEL INDEX TO THE X-MEN (VOL. 2)
MARVEL

❑1, Apr 1994 ... 1.95
❑2, May 1994 ... 1.95
❑3, Jun 1994 ... 1.95
❑4, Jul 1994 ... 1.95
❑5, Aug 1994 ... 1.95

OFFICIAL MODESTY BLAISE
PIONEER

❑1, Jul 1988, b&w ... 2.00
❑2, Aug 1988, b&w ... 2.00
❑3, Sep 1988, b&w ... 2.00
❑4, Oct 1988, b&w ... 2.00
❑5, Nov 1988, b&w ... 2.00
❑6, Dec 1988, b&w ... 2.00
❑7, Dec 1988, b&w ... 2.00

N-MINT

❑8, Jan 1989, b&w ... 2.00
❑Annual 1, Dec 1988, b&w ... 4.95

OFFICIAL PRINCE VALIANT
PIONEER

❑1, b&w ... 2.00
❑2, b&w ... 2.00
❑3, Aug 1988, b&w ... 2.00
❑4, Sep 1988, b&w ... 2.00
❑5, Oct 1988, b&w ... 2.00
❑6, Oct 1988, b&w ... 2.00
❑7, Nov 1988 ... 2.00
❑8, Dec 1988 ... 2.00
❑9, Jan 1989 ... 2.00
❑10, Feb 1989 ... 2.50
❑11, Mar 1989 ... 2.50
❑12, Apr 1989 ... 2.50
❑13 ... 2.50
❑14 ... 2.50
❑15 ... 2.50
❑16 ... 2.50
❑17 ... 2.50
❑18 ... 2.50
❑Annual 1, Win 1988, b&w ... 3.95
❑King Size 1, Apr 1989, b&w ... 3.95

OFFICIAL PRINCE VALIANT MONTHLY
PIONEER

❑1, Jun 1989, b&w ... 3.95
❑2, Jun 1989 ... 3.95
❑3, ca. 1989 ... 4.95
❑4, ca. 1989 ... 4.95
❑5, ca. 1989 ... 6.95
❑6 ... 6.95
❑7 ... 6.95
❑8 ... 6.95

OFFICIAL RIP KIRBY
PIONEER

❑1, Aug 1988, b&w ... 2.00
❑2, Sep 1988, b&w ... 2.00
❑3, Oct 1988, b&w ... 2.00
❑4, Nov 1988, b&w ... 2.00
❑5, Dec 1988, b&w ... 2.00
❑6, Jan 1989, b&w ... 2.00

OFFICIAL SECRET AGENT
PIONEER

❑1, Jun 1988, b&w ... 2.00
❑2, Jul 1988, b&w ... 2.00
❑3, Aug 1988, b&w ... 2.00
❑4, Sep 1988, b&w ... 2.00
❑5, Oct 1988, b&w ... 2.00
❑6, Nov 1988, b&w ... 2.00
❑7, Dec 1988, b&w ... 2.00

OFFICIAL TEEN TITANS INDEX
INDEPENDENT / ECLIPSE

❑1, Aug 1985 ... 1.50
❑2, Sep 1985; Indexes Teen Titans #23-53, DC Super-Stars #1, Showcase #75, The Hawk and the Dove #1-6 ... 1.50
❑3, Oct 1985; Indexes DC Comics Presents #26, New Teen Titans #1-25, Tales of the New Teen Titans #1-4, Marvel and DC Present #1 ... 1.50
❑4, Nov 1985 ... 1.50
❑5, Dec 1985 ... 1.50

OFFWORLD
GRAPHIC IMAGE

❑1 ... 3.95

OF MIND AND SOUL
RAGE

❑1, b&w ... 2.25

OF MYTHS AND MEN
BLACKTHORNE

❑1, b&w ... 1.75
❑2, Mar 1987, b&w ... 1.75

OGENKI CLINIC
AKITA

❑1, Sep 1997 ... 3.95
❑2, Oct 1997 ... 3.95
❑3, Nov 1997 ... 4.50
❑4, Dec 1997 ... 4.50
❑5, Jan 1998 ... 4.50
❑6, Feb 1998 ... 4.50

OGENKI CLINIC (VOL. 2)
AKITA

❑1, Mar 1998 ... 3.95

N-MINT

❑2, Apr 1998 ... 3.95
❑3, May 1998 ... 3.95
❑4, Jun 1998 ... 3.95
❑5, Jul 1998 ... 3.95
❑6, Aug 1998 ... 3.95

OGENKI CLINIC (VOL. 3)
SEXY FRUIT

❑1, Sep 1998, Antonio Honduras translation ... 3.95
❑2, Oct 1998 ... 3.95
❑3, Nov 1998 ... 3.95
❑4, Dec 1998 ... 3.95
❑5, Jan 1999 ... 3.95
❑6, Feb 1999 ... 3.95
❑7, Mar 1999 ... 3.95

OGENKI CLINIC (VOL. 4)
SEXY FRUIT

❑1, Apr 1999 ... 2.95
❑2, May 1999 ... 2.95
❑3, Jun 1999 ... 2.95
❑4, Jul 1999 ... 2.95
❑5, Aug 1999 ... 2.95
❑6, Sep 1999 ... 2.95

OGENKI CLINIC (VOL. 5)
SEXY FRUIT

❑1, Oct 1999 ... 2.95
❑2, Nov 1999 ... 2.95
❑3, Dec 1999 ... 2.95
❑4, Jan 2000 ... 2.95
❑5, Feb 2000 ... 2.95
❑6, Mar 2000 ... 2.95
❑7, Apr 2000 ... 2.95

OGENKI CLINIC (VOL. 6)
SEXY FRUIT

❑1, May 2000 ... 2.95
❑2, Jun 2000 ... 2.95
❑3, Jul 2000 ... 2.95
❑4, Aug 2000 ... 2.95
❑5, Sep 2000 ... 2.95
❑6, Oct 2000 ... 2.95
❑7, Nov 2000 ... 2.95

OGENKI CLINIC (VOL. 7)
IRONCAT

❑1, Dec 2000 ... 2.95
❑2, Jan 2001 ... 2.95
❑3, Feb 2001 ... 2.95
❑4, Mar 2001 ... 2.95
❑5, Apr 2001 ... 2.95
❑6, Jun 2001 ... 2.95
❑7, Jul 2001 ... 2.95

OGENKI CLINIC (VOL. 8)
IRONCAT

❑1, Aug 2001 ... 2.95
❑2, Sep 2001 ... 2.95
❑3, Oct 2001 ... 2.95
❑4, Nov 2001 ... 2.95
❑5, Dec 2001 ... 2.95
❑6, Jan 2002 ... 2.95
❑7, Feb 2002 ... 2.95
❑8, Mar 2002 ... 2.95

OGENKI CLINIC (VOL. 9)
IRONCAT

❑1, Apr 2002 ... 2.95
❑2, May 2002 ... 2.95
❑3, Jun 2002 ... 2.95
❑4, Jul 2002 ... 2.95
❑5, Aug 2002 ... 2.95
❑6, Sep 2002 ... 2.95
❑7, Oct 2002 ... 2.95
❑8, Nov 2002 ... 2.95

OGRE
BLACK DIAMOND

❑1, Jan 1994 ... 2.95
❑2, Mar 1994 ... 2.95
❑3, May 1994 ... 2.95
❑4, Jul 1994 ... 2.95

OGRE SLAYER
VIZ

❑Book 1, b&w; Japanese ... 15.95

O.G. WHIZ
GOLD KEY

❑1, Feb 1971 ... 25.00
❑2, May 1971 ... 15.00
❑3, Aug 1971 ... 10.00

Open Space

Short-lived science-fiction anthology

©Marvel

Oriental Heroes

Convoluted storyline with careless art

©Jademan

Original Astro Boy

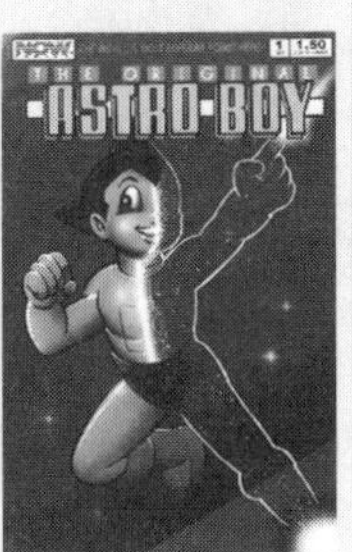

Child-sized robot with heart of gold

©Now

Orion (DC)

Walter Simonson's Jack Kirby tribute

©DC

Osborn Journals

Explains the Spider-Clone saga

©Marvel

	N-MINT
❏4, Nov 1971	10.00
❏5, Feb 1972	10.00
❏6, May 1972, Final issue of original run (1972)	10.00
❏7, May 1978, Series begins again (1978)	3.00
❏8, Jul 1978	3.00
❏9, Sep 1978, A: Tubby	3.00
❏10, Nov 1978	3.00
❏11, Jan 1979	3.00

OH.
B Publications

❏1; Magazine sized	2.95
❏2; Magazine sized	2.95
❏3; Magazine sized	2.95
❏4; Magazine sized	2.95
❏5; Magazine sized	2.95
❏6; Magazine sized	2.95
❏7; Magazine sized	2.95
❏8; Immola and the Luna Legion	2.95
❏9	2.95
❏10	2.95
❏11, Oct 1995	2.95
❏12	2.95
❏13	2.95
❏14	2.95
❏15	2.95
❏16	2.95
❏17	2.95
❏18	2.95
❏19	2.95
❏20	2.95
❏21	2.95
❏22	2.95

OHM'S LAW
Imperial

❏1	2.25
❏2, b&w; Black and White	1.95
❏3, b&w; Published out of sequence; Black and white	1.95

OH MY GODDESS!
Dark Horse

❏1, Aug 1994, b&w 1: Otaki. 1: Belldandy. 1: Tamiya. 1: Keiichi Morisato	5.00
❏2, Sep 1994, b&w 1: Urd	3.00
❏3, Oct 1994, b&w 1: Sayoko Aoshima. 1: Nekomi Motor Club. 1: Toshiyuki Aoshima	3.00
❏4, Nov 1994, b&w 1: Mara	3.00
❏5, Dec 1994, b&w	3.00
❏6, Jan 1995, b&w 1: Super-Deformed (SD) Urd	3.00
❏88, Jul 2002, b&w; Numbering continued from combined Oh My Goddess! Part II-XI series	3.50
❏89, Aug 2002, b&w	3.50
❏90, Sep 2002, b&w	3.50
❏91, Oct 2002, b&w	3.50
❏92, Nov 2002, b&w	3.50
❏93, Dec 2002, b&w	3.50
❏94, Jan 2003, b&w	3.50
❏95, Feb 2003, b&w	3.50
❏96, Apr 2003, b&w	2.99
❏97, May 2003, b&w	2.99
❏98, Jun 2003, b&w	2.99
❏99, Jul 2003, b&w	2.99
❏100, Aug 2003, b&w	2.99
❏101, Sep 2003, b&w	2.99
❏102, Oct 2003, b&w	2.99
❏103, Nov 2003, b&w	2.99
❏104, Dec 2003, b&w	2.99
❏105, Feb 2004, b&w	2.99
❏106, Mar 2004, b&w	3.50
❏107, Apr 2004, b&w	2.99
❏108, May 2004, b&w	2.99
❏109, Aug 2004, b&w	2.99
❏110, Sep 2004, b&w	3.99
❏111, Oct 2004, b&w	3.99
❏112, Nov 2004, b&w	3.99

OH MY GODDESS! PART II
Dark Horse

❏1, Feb 1995, 1: Skuld	3.00
❏2, Mar 1995	3.00
❏3, Apr 1995, Oh My Cartoonist! follow-up story	2.75
❏4, May 1995, 1: Megumi Morisato	2.75
❏5, Jun 1995	2.75
❏6, Jul 1995	2.75
❏7, Aug 1995	3.00
❏8, Sep 1995, The Adventures of Mini-Urd story	3.00

OH MY GODDESS! PART III
Dark Horse / Manga

❏1, Nov 1995, Cover reads "Oh My Goddess Special"	3.00
❏2, Dec 1995, Cover reads "Oh My Goddess Special"	3.00
❏3, Jan 1996, Cover reads "Oh My Goddess Special"	3.00
❏4, Feb 1996, Cover reads "Oh My Goddess Special"	3.00
❏5, Mar 1996, O: Sudaru. 1: Sudaru. Cover reads "Oh My Goddess Special"	3.00
❏6, Apr 1996, 1: Mao Za Haxon. Cover reads "Oh My Goddess! 1 of 6"	3.00
❏7, May 1996, Cover reads "Oh My Goddess! 2 of 6"	3.00
❏8, Jun 1996, Cover reads "Oh My Goddess! 3 of 6"	3.00
❏9, Jul 1996, 1: Fenrir. 1: Midgard Serpent. Cover reads "Oh My Goddess! 4 of 6"	3.00
❏10, Aug 1996, Cover reads "Oh My Goddess, part 5 of 6"	3.00
❏11, Sep 1996, Cover reads "Oh My Goddess! 6 of 6"	3.00

OH MY GODDESS! PART IV
Dark Horse / Manga

❏1, Dec 1996, Cover reads "Oh My Goddess Special"	2.95
❏2, Jan 1997, Cover reads "Oh My Goddess! 1 of 3"	2.95
❏3, Feb 1997, Cover reads "Oh My Goddess! 2 of 3"	2.95
❏4, Mar 1997, Cover reads "Oh My Goddess! 3 of 3"	2.95
❏5, Apr 1997, Cover reads "Oh My Goddess Special"	2.95
❏6, May 1997, Cover reads "Oh My Goddess! 1 of 3"	2.95
❏7, Jun 1997	2.95
❏8, Jul 1997, Cover reads "Oh My Goddess! 3 of 3"	2.95

OH MY GODDESS! PART V
Dark Horse / Manga

❏1, Sep 1997, Cover reads "Oh My Goddess Special"	2.95
❏2, Oct 1997, Cover reads "Oh My Goddess Special"	2.95
❏3, Nov 1997, Cover reads "Oh My Goddess Special"	3.95
❏4, Dec 1997, Cover reads "Oh My Goddess Special"	3.95
❏5, Jan 1998, 1: Kodama. Cover reads "Oh My Goddess! 1 of 2"	2.95
❏6, Feb 1998, 1: Hikari. Cover reads "Oh My Goddess! 2 of 2"; Alan Gleason and Toren Smith translation	3.95
❏7, Mar 1998, Cover reads "Oh My Goddess! 1 of 2"	3.95
❏8, Apr 1998, 1: Troubadour. Cover reads "Oh My Goddess! 2 of 2"	2.95
❏9, May 1998	3.50
❏10, Jun 1998, 1: Garm. 1: Shiho Sakakibara. Cover reads "Oh My Goddess! One-Shot"	3.95
❏11, Jul 1998, 1: Nekomi Tech Softball Club. 1: Nekomi Tech Baseball Club. Cover reads "Oh My Goddess! One-Shot"	3.95
❏12, Aug 1998, Cover reads "Oh My Goddess! One-Shot"	3.95

OH MY GODDESS! PART VI
Dark Horse / Manga

❏1, Oct 1998	3.50
❏2, Dec 1998	2.95
❏3, Jan 1999	2.95
❏4, Feb 1999	2.95
❏5, Mar 1999	2.95
❏6, Apr 1999	2.95

OH MY GODDESS! PART VII
Dark Horse / Manga

❏1, May 1999	2.95
❏2, Jun 1999	2.95
❏3, Jul 1999	2.95
❏4, Aug 1999	2.95
❏5, Sep 1999	2.95
❏6, Oct 1999	2.95
❏7, Nov 1999	2.95
❏8, Dec 1999	2.95

OH MY GODDESS! PART VIII
Dark Horse / Manga

❏1, Jan 2000	3.50
❏2, Feb 2000	3.50
❏3, Mar 2000	3.50
❏4, Apr 2000	3.50
❏5, May 2000	3.50
❏6, Jun 2000	3.50

OH MY GODDESS! PART IX
Dark Horse / Manga

❏1, Jul 2000	3.50
❏2, Aug 2000	3.50
❏3, Sep 2000	3.50
❏4, Oct 2000	3.50
❏5, Nov 2000	3.50

Other grades: Multiply price above by 5/6 for VF/NM • 2/3 for VERY FINE • 1/3 for FINE • 1/5 for VERY GOOD • 1/8 for GOOD

N-MINT

❑6, Dec 2000 3.50
❑7, Jan 2001 3.50

OH MY GODDESS! PART X
DARK HORSE / MANGA

❑1, Feb 2001 3.50
❑2, Mar 2001 3.50
❑3, Apr 2001 3.50
❑4, May 2001 3.50
❑5, Jun 2001 3.50

OH MY GODDESS! PART XI
DARK HORSE

❑1, Aug 2001 3.50
❑2, Sep 2001 3.50
❑3, Oct 2001 2.99
❑4, Nov 2001 2.99
❑5, Dec 2001 2.99
❑6, Feb 2002 2.99

OH MY GODDESS!: ADVENTURES OF THE MINI-GODDESSES
DARK HORSE / MANGA

❑1, May 2000 9.95

OH MY GOTH
SIRIUS / DOG STAR

❑1 1998 2.95
❑2, Oct 1998 2.95
❑3, Jan 1999 2.95
❑4, Apr 1999 2.95

OH MY GOTH: HUMANS SUCK!
SIRIUS

❑1, Jun 2000, b&w 2.95
❑2, Aug 2000, b&w 2.95

OINK: BLOOD AND CIRCUS
KITCHEN SINK

❑1 4.95
❑2 4.95
❑3 4.95
❑4, Jul 1998 4.95

OINK: HEAVEN'S BUTCHER
KITCHEN SINK

❑1, Dec 1995 4.95
❑2, Feb 1996 4.95
❑3, Apr 1996 4.95

OJ'S BIG BUST OUT
BONEYARD

❑1, Mar 1995, b&w 3.50

OKTANE
DARK HORSE

❑1, Aug 1995 2.50
❑2, Sep 1995 2.50
❑3, Oct 1995 2.50
❑4, Nov 1995 2.50

OLDBLOOD
PARODY

❑1 2.50
❑1/2nd 2.50

OLYMPIANS
MARVEL / EPIC

❑1 3.95
❑2, Jan 1992 3.95

OLYMPUS HEIGHTS
IDEA & DESIGN WORKS

❑1, Jul 2004 3.99
❑2 2004 3.99
❑3 2004 3.99

OMAC
DC

❑1, Oct 1974, JK (w); JK (a); O: Omac. 1: Omac 15.00
❑2, Dec 1974, JK (a); V: Mr. Big 10.00
❑3, Feb 1975, JK (a) 10.00
❑4, Apr 1975, JK (a) 10.00
❑5, Jun 1975 JK (w); JK (a) 7.00
❑6, Aug 1975 JK (a) 7.00
❑7, Oct 1975 JK (a) 7.00
❑8, Dec 1975 JKu (c); JK (a) 7.00

OMAC: ONE MAN ARMY CORPS
DC

❑1, b&w; prestige format JBy (w); JBy, JK (a) 4.00
❑2, b&w; prestige format JBy (w); JBy (a) 4.00
❑3, b&w; prestige format JBy (w); JBy (a) 4.00
❑4, b&w; prestige format JBy (w); JBy (a) 4.00

N-MINT

OMAC PROJECT
DC

❑1, Jun 2005 17.00
❑1/2nd, Jun 2005 5.00
❑1/3rd, Jun 2005 3.00
❑2, Jul 2005 6.00
❑2/2nd, Jul 2005 3.00
❑3, Aug 2005 4.00
❑4, Sep 2005 2.50
❑5, Oct 2005 2.50
❑6 2005 2.50

OMAC PROJECT: INFINITE CRISIS SPECIAL
DC

❑1, Jun 2006 3.99

OMAC (2ND SERIES)
DC

❑1, Sep 2006 2.99

OMAHA: CAT DANCER
STEELDRAGON

❑1, ca. 1984 12.00
❑1/Ashcan; preview 3.00
❑1/2nd 4.00
❑2, ca. 1985 8.00

OMAHA THE CAT DANCER (KITCHEN SINK)
KITCHEN SINK

❑0, Apr 1995, b&w; 1: Omaha the Cat Dancer. Reprints early Omaha stories from Vootie, Bizarre Sex #9 4.00
❑1, Oct 1986, b&w 10.00
❑1/2nd, b&w 4.00
❑1/3rd, b&w 3.00
❑2, Oct 1986, b&w 5.00
❑3, Oct 1986, b&w 4.00
❑4, Jan 1987, b&w 4.00
❑5, Mar 1987, b&w 4.00
❑6, May 1987, b&w 3.00
❑6/2nd, Sep 1988 2.50
❑7, Jul 1987, b&w 3.00
❑8, Oct 1987, b&w 3.00
❑9, Feb 1988, b&w 3.00
❑10, May 1988, b&w 3.00
❑11, Dec 1988, b&w 3.00
❑12, Jul 1989, b&w 3.00
❑12/2nd, b&w 2.95
❑13, Sep 1989, b&w 3.00
❑13/2nd, b&w 2.95
❑14, Mar 1990, b&w; Wendel back-up 3.00
❑15, Jan 1991, b&w 3.00
❑16, Nov 1991, b&w 2.50
❑17, Feb 1992, b&w 2.50
❑18, Jan 1993, b&w 2.95
❑19, Jun 1993, b&w 2.50
❑20, Jun 1994, b&w; Final Kitchen Sink issue 2.95

OMAHA THE CAT DANCER (FANTAGRAPHICS)
FANTAGRAPHICS

❑1, Jul 1994 3.00
❑2, Aug 1994 3.00
❑3, Nov 1994 3.00
❑4, Feb 1995 3.00

O'MALLEY AND THE ALLEY CATS
GOLD KEY

❑1, Apr 1971 8.00
❑2, Jul 1971 6.00
❑3, Jul 1972 6.00
❑4, Oct 1972 4.00
❑5, Jan 1973 4.00
❑6, Apr 1973 4.00
❑7, Jul 1973 4.00
❑8, Oct 1973 4.00
❑9, Jan 1974 4.00

OMAR LENNYX
MAGNECOM

❑1, b&w 2.95

OMEGA ELITE
BLACKTHORNE

❑1, b&w 3.50

OMEGA FORCE (SOUTH STAR)
SOUTH STAR

❑1, Aug 1992 2.00

N-MINT

OMEGA FORCE
ENTITY

❑1, ca. 1995 2.50

OMEGA KNIGHTS
UNDERGROUND

❑1 2.00
❑2 2.00
❑3 2.00
❑4 2.00
❑5 2.00
❑6, Oct 1992 2.00

OMEGA MAN
OMEGA 7

❑0 3.00
❑1, b&w; Simpson trial; no indicia 4.00
❑Ashcan 1, no cover price; no indicia; sideways format 1.00

OMEGA MEN
DC

❑1, Apr 1983 KG (a); O: Omega Men 4.00
❑2, May 1983 KG (a); O: Broot 3.00
❑3, Jun 1983 1: Lobo 2.00
❑4, Jul 1983 1: Felicity 1.50
❑5, Aug 1983 2: Lobo 2.00
❑6, Sep 1983 1.50
❑7, Oct 1983 O: Citadel 1.50
❑8, Nov 1983 1.50
❑9, Dec 1983 A: Lobo 2.00
❑10, Jan 1984; 1st Lobo Full Story 2.00
❑11, Feb 1984 1.25
❑12, Mar 1984 1.25
❑13, Apr 1984 1.25
❑14, May 1984 1.25
❑15, Jun 1984 1.25
❑16, Jul 1984 1.25
❑17, Aug 1984 1.25
❑18, Sep 1984 1.25
❑19, Oct 1984 A: Lobo 1.25
❑20, Nov 1984 A: Lobo 2.00
❑21, Dec 1984 1.25
❑22, Jan 1985 1.25
❑23, Feb 1985 1.25
❑24, Mar 1985 1.25
❑25, Apr 1985 1.25
❑26, May 1985 1: Elu 1.25
❑27, Jun 1985 1.25
❑28, Jul 1985 1.25
❑29, Aug 1985 1.25
❑30, Sep 1985 1.25
❑31, Oct 1985; Crisis 1.25
❑32, Nov 1985 1.25
❑33, Dec 1985 1.25
❑34, Jan 1986 1.25
❑35, Feb 1986 1.25
❑36, Mar 1986 1.25
❑37, Apr 1986 A: Lobo 1.25
❑38, May 1986 1.25
❑Annual 1, ca. 1984 2.00
❑Annual 2, ca. 1985 O: Primus 1.75

OMEGA THE UNKNOWN
MARVEL

❑1, Mar 1976, JM (a); 1: James-Michael Starling (Omega the Unknown's counterpart). 1: Omega the Unknown 9.00
❑2, May 1976, A: Hulk 6.00
❑2/30 cent, May 1976, 30 cent regional price variant 20.00
❑3, Jul 1976 3.00
❑3/30 cent, Jul 1976, 30 cent regional price variant 20.00
❑4, Sep 1976 2.00
❑5, Nov 1976 2.00
❑6, Jan 1977 2.00
❑7, Mar 1977 2.00
❑8, May 1977, 1: Foolkiller II (Greg Salinger)-cameo 2.00
❑9, Jul 1977, 1: Foolkiller II (Greg Salinger)-full 3.00
❑9/35 cent, Jul 1977, 1: Foolkiller II (Greg Salinger)-full. 35 cent regional price variant 15.00
❑10, Oct 1977, D: Omega the Unknown 2.00
❑10/35 cent, Oct 1977, D: Omega the Unknown. 35 cent regional price variant 15.00

Our Army at War

Longest-running war title becomes Sgt. Rock

©DC

Our Fighting Forces

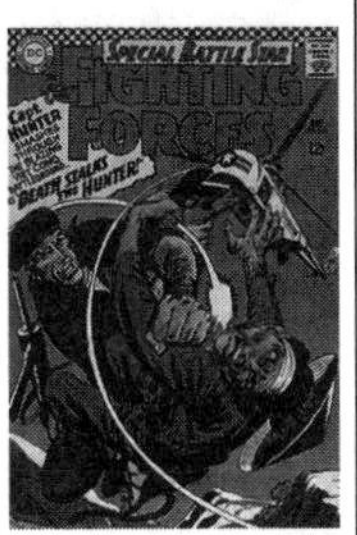

Launched Losers and Unknown Soldier

©DC

Outbreed 999

Prisoner subjected to experiments

©Blackout

Outcast

Brain-damaged man has alien consciousness

©Acclaim

Outcasts

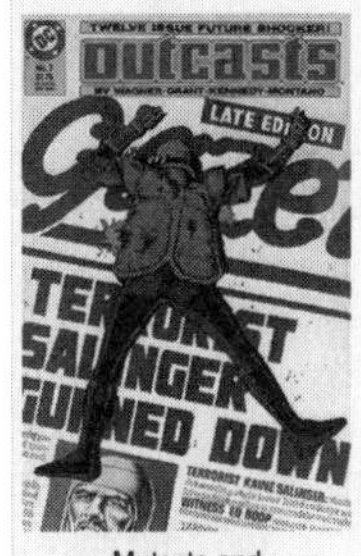

Mutants and undesireables rise up

©DC

N-MINT

OMEN (CHAOS)
CHAOS!

❑1, May 1998 .... 2.95
❑2, Jun 1998 .... 2.95
❑3, Jul 1998 .... 2.95
❑4, Aug 1998 .... 2.95
❑5, Sep 1998 .... 2.95

OMEN (NORTHSTAR)
NORTHSTAR

❑1, b&w 2.00
❑2, b&w 2.00

OMEN, THE: SAVE THE CHOSEN PREVIEW
CHAOS!

❑1, Sep 1997; preview of upcoming series 2.50

OMEN, THE: VEXED
CHAOS!

❑1, Oct 1998 .... 2.95

OMICRON: ASTONISHING ADVENTURES ON OTHER WORLDS
PYRAMID

❑1, b&w; flexi-disc 2.25
❑2, Sep 1987, b&w; flexi-disc 2.25

OMNIBUS: MODERN PERVERSITY
BLACKBIRD

❑1, b&w; squarebound 3.25

OMNI COMIX
OMNI

❑1, Mar 1995, magazine; BWi (a); Mar '95 issue of Omni inserted 4.00
❑2, Apr 1995, magazine; insert in Apr. '95 issue of Omni with Omni Comix #2 cover 4.00
❑3, Oct 1995, magazine; T.H.U.N.D.E.R. Agents story 4.95

OMNI MEN
BLACKTHORNE

❑1, Apr 1989, b&w 3.50

ON A PALE HORSE
INNOVATION

❑1; Adapts Piers Anthony story from his Incarnations of Immortality series 4.95
❑2 .... 4.95
❑3 .... 4.95
❑4, Oct 1993 .... 4.95
❑5, Dec 1993 .... 4.95

ONCE UPON A TIME IN THE FUTURE
PLATINUM

❑1 .... 9.95

ONE
TOKYOPOP

❑1, Apr 2004 .... 9.99
❑2, Jun 2004 .... 9.99
❑3, Aug 2004 .... 9.99
❑4, Oct 2004 .... 9.99
❑5, Dec 2004 .... 9.99
❑6, Feb 2005 .... 9.99
❑7, Apr 2005 .... 9.99
❑8, Oct 2005 .... 9.99

N-MINT

ONE (PACIFIC)
PACIFIC

❑1, b&w; 1st Pacific title 3.00

ONE, THE
MARVEL / EPIC

❑1, Jul 1985 BA (a) 2.00
❑2, Sep 1985 BA (a) 2.00
❑3, Nov 1985 BA (a) 2.00
❑4, Jan 1986 BA (a) 2.00
❑5, Mar 1986 BA (a) 2.00
❑6, May 1986 BA (a) 2.00

ONE-ARM SWORDSMAN
DR. LEUNG'S

❑1 .... 1.80
❑2 .... 1.80
❑3 .... 1.80
❑4 .... 1.80
❑5 .... 1.80
❑6 .... 1.80
❑7 .... 1.80

ONE-FISTED TALES
SLAVE LABOR

❑1, May 1990, b&w; brown paper wrapper 3.00
❑1/2nd, Nov 1990 .... 2.50
❑2, Sep 1990, b&w; brown paper wrapper (some wrappers printed red in error) 3.00
❑2/2nd, Apr 1993; no brown paper wrapper 2.95
❑3, Feb 1991, b&w; brown paper wrapper; Cherry cover and story 2.50
❑3/2nd, Apr 1993; no brown paper wrapper 2.50
❑3/3rd, Aug 1993; no brown paper wrapper 2.95
❑4, Jun 1991, b&w 2.50
❑4/2nd, Jan 1992 .... 2.95
❑4/3rd, Aug 1993; no brown paper wrapper 2.95
❑5, Sep 1991, b&w 3.95
❑5/2nd, Feb 1992 .... 2.95
❑6, Apr 1992 .... 2.95
❑7, Sep 1992, b&w 2.95
❑8, Mar 1993, b&w 2.95
❑9, Oct 1993, b&w 2.95
❑10, Feb 1994, b&w 2.95
❑11, Aug 1994, b&w 2.95

ONE HUNDRED AND ONE DALMATIANS (WALT DISNEY'S...)
DISNEY

❑1, ca. 1991 .... 2.50

100 BULLETS
DC / VERTIGO

❑1, Aug 1999 .... 10.00
❑2, Sep 1999 .... 6.50
❑3, Oct 1999 .... 5.00
❑4, Nov 1999 .... 5.00
❑5, Dec 1999 .... 5.00
❑6, Jan 2000 .... 4.00
❑7, Feb 2000 .... 4.00
❑8, Mar 2000 .... 4.00
❑9, Apr 2000 .... 4.00
❑10, May 2000 .... 4.00

N-MINT

❑11, Jun 2000 .... 3.00
❑12, Jul 2000 .... 3.00
❑13, Aug 2000 .... 3.00
❑14, Sep 2000 .... 3.00
❑15, Oct 2000 .... 3.00
❑16, Nov 2000 .... 3.00
❑17, Dec 2000 .... 3.00
❑18, Jan 2001 .... 3.00
❑19, Feb 2001 .... 3.00
❑20, Mar 2001 .... 3.00
❑21, Apr 2001 .... 3.00
❑22, May 2001 .... 3.00
❑23, Jun 2001 .... 3.00
❑24, Jul 2001 .... 3.00
❑25, Aug 2001 .... 3.00
❑26, Sep 2001, DaG, FM, JLee (a) 3.00
❑27, Oct 2001 .... 3.00
❑28, Nov 2001 .... 3.00
❑29, Dec 2001 .... 3.00
❑30, Jan 2002 .... 3.00
❑31, Feb 2002 .... 2.50
❑32, Mar 2002 .... 2.50
❑33, Apr 2002 .... 2.50
❑34, May 2002 .... 2.50
❑35, Jun 2002 .... 2.50
❑36, Jul 2002 .... 2.50
❑37, Sep 2002 .... 2.50
❑38, Oct 2002 .... 2.50
❑39, Nov 2002 .... 2.50
❑40, Jan 2003 .... 2.50
❑41, Feb 2003 .... 2.50
❑42, Mar 2003 .... 2.50
❑43, Apr 2003 .... 2.50
❑44, May 2003 .... 2.50
❑45, Jun 2003 .... 2.50
❑46, Jul 2003 .... 2.50
❑47, Oct 2003 .... 2.50
❑48, Dec 2003 .... 2.50
❑49, May 2004 .... 2.50
❑50, Aug 2004 .... 3.50
❑51, Sep 2004 .... 2.50
❑52, Oct 2004 .... 2.50
❑53, Nov 2004 .... 2.50
❑54, Dec 2004 .... 2.50
❑55, Jan 2005 .... 2.50
❑56, Feb 2005 .... 2.50
❑57, Mar 2005 .... 2.50
❑58, Apr 2005 .... 2.50
❑59, May 2005 .... 2.50
❑60, Jun 2005 .... 2.50
❑61, Jul 2005 .... 2.50
❑62, Aug 2005 .... 2.75
❑63, Sep 2005 .... 2.75
❑64, Oct 2005 .... 2.75
❑65 2005 .... 2.75
❑66, Jan 2006 .... 2.75
❑67, Feb 2006 .... 2.75
❑68, Mar 2006 .... 2.75
❑69, Apr 2006 .... 2.75
❑70, May 2006 .... 2.75
❑71, Jun 2006 .... 2.75
❑72, Jul 2006 .... 2.75
❑73, Aug 2006 .... 2.75
❑74, Sep 2006 .... 2.75

100 DEGREES IN THE SHADE
FANTAGRAPHICS / EROS

❑1, Feb 1992, b&w ... 2.50
❑2, May 1992, b&w ... 2.50
❑3, Jul 1992, b&w ... 2.50
❑4, Oct 1992, b&w ... 2.50

100 GIRLS
ARCANA

❑1 2004 ... 5.00
❑1/Variant ... 5.00
❑2 ... 2.95
❑3 ... 2.95
❑4 ... 2.95
❑5, Aug 2005 ... 2.95
❑6, Oct 2005 ... 2.95

100 GREATEST MARVELS OF ALL TIME
MARVEL

❑1, Dec 2001, reprints Uncanny X-Men #141, Fantastic Four (Vol. 1) #48, Amazing Spider-Man (Vol. 1) #1, Daredevil #181; cardstock cover ... 7.50
❑2, Dec 2001, reprints Avengers (Vol. 1) #1, Uncanny X-Men #350, Amazing Spider-Man (Vol. 1) #122, Captain America #109; cardstock cover ... 7.50
❑3, Dec 2001, reprints Incredible Hulk #181, X-Men #25, Amazing Spider-Man (Vol. 1) #33, Spider-Man #1; cardstock cover ... 7.50
❑4, Dec 2001, reprints Incredible Hulk (Vol. 1) #1, Ultimate X-Men #1, Daredevil #227, Wolverine #75; cardstock cover ... 7.50
❑5, Dec 2001, reprints Ultimate Spider-Man #1, X-Men (1st series) #1, Avengers (Vol. 1) #4, Amazing Spider-Man (Vol. 1) #121; cardstock cover ... 7.50
❑6, Dec 2001, reprints X-Men (2nd series) #1; cardstock cover ... 3.50
❑7, Dec 2001, reprints Giant-Size X-Men #1 ... 3.50
❑8, Dec 2001, reprints X-Men (1st series) #137; cardstock cover.. 3.50
❑9, Dec 2001, reprints Fantastic Four (Vol. 1) #1 ... 3.50
❑10, Dec 2001, reprints Amazing Fantasy #15 ... 3.50

101 OTHER USES FOR A CONDOM
APPLE

❑1, ca. 1991 ... 4.95

101 WAYS TO END THE CLONE SAGA
MARVEL

❑1, Jan 1997 ... 2.50

100%
DC / VERTIGO

❑1, Aug 2002 ... 5.95
❑2, Sep 2002 ... 5.95
❑3, Oct 2002 ... 5.95
❑4, Nov 2002 ... 5.95
❑5, Dec 2002 ... 5.95

100% TRUE?
DC / PARADOX PRESS

❑1, Sum 1996, b&w; magazine; excerpts from The Big Books of Death, Conspiracies, Weirdos, and Freaks ... 3.50
❑2, Win 1996, b&w; magazine; excerpts from The Big Books of Death, Conspiracies, Weirdos, and Freaks; Winter, 1996 issue ... 3.50

ONE MILE UP
ECLIPSE

❑1, b&w ... 2.50
❑2 ... 2.50

ONE MILLENNIUM
HUNTER

❑1, b&w ... 2.50
❑2, b&w ... 2.50
❑3, ca. 1997, b&w ... 2.50
❑4, ca. 1997, b&w ... 2.50
❑5, ca. 1997, b&w ... 2.50

ONE PIECE
VIZ

❑1, Feb 2004 ... 9.99
❑2, Apr 2004 ... 9.99
❑3, Jun 2004 ... 9.99
❑5, Nov 2004 ... 9.99
❑6, Mar 2005 ... 9.99
❑7, Jul 2005 ... 9.99
❑8, Oct 2005 ... 9.99

ONE-POUND GOSPEL
VIZ

❑1 ... 3.50
❑2 ... 3.50
❑3 ... 2.95
❑4 ... 2.95

ONE-POUND GOSPEL ROUND 2
VIZ

❑1, Jan 1997 ... 2.95
❑2, Feb 1997 ... 2.95
❑3, Mar 1997 ... 2.95
❑4 1997 ... 2.95
❑5 1997 ... 2.95
❑6 1997 ... 2.95

ONE-SHOT PARODY
MILKY WAY

❑1, ca. 1986, X-Men ... 1.50

ONE-SHOT WESTERN
CALIBER

❑1, b&w ... 2.50

1001 NIGHTS OF SHEHERAZADE
NBM

❑1 ... 12.95

1111
CRUSADE

❑1, Oct 1996, b&w; prose story with facing page illustrations; illustrated story ... 2.95

1,001 NIGHTS OF BACCHUS
DARK HORSE

❑1, May 1993, b&w ... 4.50

...ONE TO GO
ÄARDWOLF

❑1 ... 2.50

ONI
DARK HORSE

❑1, Feb 2001 ... 2.99
❑2, Feb 2001 ... 2.99
❑3, Feb 2001 ... 2.99

ONI DOUBLE FEATURE
ONI

❑1, Jan 1998; Flip-book; KSm (w); MW (a); 1: Silent Bob. 1: Jay. Jay & Silent Bob, Milk & Cheese, Secret Broadcast ... 6.00
❑1/2nd, Mar 1998 ... 2.95
❑2, Feb 1998; Too Much Coffee Man, Car Crash, Secret Broadcast ... 4.00
❑3, Mar 1998; Frumpy the Clown, Bacon, Car Crash ... 3.50
❑4, Apr 1998; BSz (c); Bacon, A River in Egypt, Cheetahman; Judd Winick's first major comics work ... 3.50
❑5, May 1998 ... 3.50
❑6, Jun 1998; CR, NG (w); Only The End of the World Again, Zombie Kid ... 4.00
❑7, Jul 1998 ... 2.95
❑8, Aug 1998; Only The End of the World Again, Satchel of Weltschmerz, Pip & Norton ... 2.95
❑9, Oct 1998 ... 2.95
❑10, Nov 1998; Sam & Max, Drive-By, Road Trip ... 2.95
❑11, Feb 1999; Usagi Yojimbo, Blue Monday, Drive-By ... 2.95
❑12, May 1999; The Harpooner, Bluntman & Chronic, The Honor Rollers ... 2.95

ONIGAMI
ANTARCTIC

❑1, Apr 1998 ... 2.95
❑2, Jun 1998 ... 2.95
❑3, Jul 1998 ... 2.95

ONI PRESS COLOR SPECIAL
ONI

❑2001, ca. 2001 ... 5.95
❑2002, ca. 2002 ... 5.95

ONI PRESS SUMMER VACATION SUPERCOLOR FUN SPECIAL
ONI

❑1, Jul 2000 ... 5.95

ONLY THE END OF THE WORLD AGAIN
ONI

❑1, May 2000 ... 6.95

ON OUR BUTTS
AEON

❑1, Apr 1995 ... 2.95

ON RAVEN'S WINGS
BONEYARD

❑1 ... 2.95
❑2, Sep 1994 ... 2.95

ONSLAUGHT: EPILOGUE
MARVEL

❑1, Feb 1997 ... 2.95

ONSLAUGHT: MARVEL
MARVEL

❑1, Oct 1996; MWa (w); DGr (a); wraparound cover ... 6.00
❑1/Gold, Oct 1996 ... 12.00

ONSLAUGHT: X-MEN
MARVEL

❑1, Aug 1996; MWa (w); DGr (a); wraparound cover; set-up for Onslaught crossover in Marvel titles ... 5.00
❑1/Gold, Aug 1996 ... 10.00
❑1/Variant, Aug 1996; MWa (w); DGr (a); variant cover ... 8.00

ON THE BUS
SLAVE LABOR

❑1, Aug 1994 ... 2.95

ON THE ROAD TO PERDITION
DC

❑1, May 2003 ... 7.95
❑2, Jan 2004 ... 7.95
❑3, Aug 2004; Detour ... 7.95

ONYX OVERLORD
MARVEL / EPIC

❑1, Oct 1992 ... 2.75
❑2, Nov 1992 ... 2.75
❑3, Dec 1992 ... 2.75
❑4, Jan 1993 ... 2.75

OOMBAH, JUNGLE MOON MAN
STRAWBERRY JAM

❑1, b&w ... 2.50

OPEN SEASON
RENEGADE

❑1 1987, b&w ... 2.00
❑2 1987, b&w ... 2.00
❑3 1987, b&w ... 2.00
❑4, Oct 1987, b&w ... 2.00
❑5, Dec 1987, b&w ... 2.00
❑6, Apr 1988, b&w; black issue ... 2.00
❑7, b&w ... 2.00

OPEN SORE FUNNIES
HOME-MADE EUTHANASIA

❑1 ... 1.25

OPEN SPACE
MARVEL

❑1, Dec 1989 KB (w) ... 5.00
❑2, Apr 1990 ... 5.00
❑3, Jun 1990 ... 5.00
❑4, Aug 1990 ... 5.00

OPERATION: KANSAS CITY
MOTION

❑1, Win 1993, b&w; Breakneck Blvd. Preview ... 2.50

OPERATION: KNIGHTSTRIKE
IMAGE

❑1, May 1995 ... 2.50
❑1/A, May 1995; Purple background on cover ... 2.50
❑2, Jun 1995 ... 2.50
❑2/A, Jun 1995 ... 2.50
❑3, Jul 1995 ... 2.50

OPERATION: STORMBREAKER
ACCLAIM / VALIANT

❑1, Aug 1997; cover says Jul, indicia says Aug ... 3.95

OPERATIVE: SCORPIO
BLACKTHORNE

❑1, Jan 1989, b&w ... 3.50

Other grades: Multiply price above by 5/6 for VF/NM • 2/3 for VERY FINE • 1/3 for FINE • 1/5 for VERY GOOD • 1/8 for GOOD

Outer Limits

Many stories based on the TV screenplays
©Dell

Outlanders

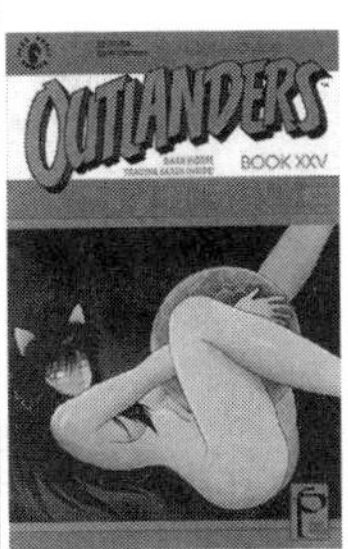

Romantic space humor from Johji Manabe
©Dark Horse

Outlaw Kid (2nd Series)

Attempted revival of the Atlas series
©Marvel

Outsiders (1st Series)

Team does without the Caped Crusader
©DC

Oz

Caliber's darker look at the fantasy world
©Caliber

N-MINT

OPPOSITE FORCES
FUNNYPAGES

❑1, ca. 2002 .... 2.95
❑2, ca. 2003 .... 2.95
❑3, ca. 2004 .... 2.95
❑4, ca. 2004 .... 2.95

OPPOSITE FORCES (VOL. 2)
ALIAS

❑1, Sep 2005 .... 1.00
❑2, Nov 2005 .... 2.95
❑3, Dec 2005 .... 2.95

OPTIC NERVE
DRAWN & QUARTERLY

❑1 .... 5.00
❑2 .... 3.00
❑3 .... 3.00
❑4, Mar 1997 .... 3.00
❑5, Feb 1998 .... 3.00
❑6, Jan 1999 .... 3.00
❑7, Jun 2000; Mini-Comic 3.00

OPTIMISM OF YOUTH
FANTAGRAPHICS

❑1, Oct 1991 .... 12.95

ORA
SON OF A TREEBOB

❑1, Mar 1999, b&w 2.95

ORACLE
ORACLE

❑1, b&w GP (a) 3.00

ORACLE - A TRESPASSERS MYSTERY
AMAZING MONTAGE

❑1, b&w 4.95

ORACLE PRESENTS
ORACLE

❑1, b&w; GP (a); reprint of Oracle #1 . 3.00
❑2, Aug 1986, b&w; Critter Corps 3.00

ORBIT
ECLIPSE

❑1 .... 4.95
❑2 .... 4.95
❑3 .... 4.95

ORB MAGAZINE
ORB

❑1 .... 1.25
❑2 .... 1.25
❑3 .... 1.25

ORDER
MARVEL

❑1, Apr 2002 .... 2.25
❑2, May 2002 .... 2.25
❑3, Jun 2002 .... 2.25
❑4, Jul 2002 .... 2.25
❑5, Aug 2002 .... 2.25
❑6, Sep 2002 .... 2.25

ORIENTAL HEROES
JADEMAN

❑1, Aug 1988 .... 1.95
❑2, Sep 1988 .... 1.95
❑3, Oct 1988 .... 1.95
❑4, Nov 1988 .... 1.95
❑5, Dec 1988 .... 1.95

N-MINT

❑6, Jan 1989 .... 1.95
❑7, Feb 1989 .... 1.95
❑8, Mar 1989 .... 1.95
❑9, Apr 1989 .... 1.95
❑10, May 1989 .... 1.95
❑11, Jun 1989 .... 1.95
❑12, Jul 1989 .... 1.95
❑13, Aug 1989 .... 1.95
❑14, Sep 1989 .... 1.95
❑15, Oct 1989 .... 1.95
❑16, Nov 1989 .... 1.95
❑17, Dec 1989 .... 1.95
❑18, Jan 1990 .... 1.95
❑19, Feb 1990 .... 1.95
❑20, Mar 1990 .... 1.95
❑21, Apr 1990 .... 1.95
❑22, May 1990 .... 1.95
❑23, Jun 1990 .... 1.95
❑24, Jul 1990 .... 1.95
❑25, Aug 1990 .... 1.95
❑26, Sep 1990 .... 1.95
❑27, Oct 1990 .... 1.95
❑28, Nov 1990 .... 1.95
❑29, Dec 1990 .... 1.95
❑30, Jan 1991 .... 1.95
❑31, Feb 1991 .... 1.95
❑32, Mar 1991 .... 1.95
❑33, Apr 1991 .... 1.95
❑34, May 1991 .... 1.95
❑35, Jun 1991 .... 1.95
❑36, Jul 1991 .... 1.95
❑37, Aug 1991 .... 1.95
❑38, Sep 1991 .... 1.95
❑39, Oct 1991 .... 1.95
❑40, Nov 1991 .... 1.95
❑41, Dec 1991 .... 1.95
❑42, Jan 1992 .... 1.95
❑43, Feb 1992 .... 1.95
❑44, Mar 1992 .... 1.95
❑45, Apr 1992 .... 1.95
❑46, May 1992 .... 1.95
❑47, Jun 1992 .... 1.95
❑48, Jul 1992 .... 1.95
❑49, Aug 1992 .... 1.95
❑50, Sep 1992 .... 1.95
❑51, Oct 1992 .... 1.95
❑52, Nov 1992 .... 1.95
❑53, Dec 1992 .... 1.95
❑54, Jan 1993 .... 1.95
❑55, Feb 1993 .... 1.95

ORIENT GATEWAY
NBM

❑1 .... 13.95

ORIGINAL ADVENTURES OF CHOLLY AND FLYTRAP
IMAGE

❑1, Mar 2006 .... 2.99

ORIGINAL ASTRO BOY
NOW

❑1, Sep 1987 .... 2.00
❑2, Oct 1987 .... 1.50
❑3, Nov 1987 .... 1.50
❑4, Dec 1987 .... 1.50

N-MINT

❑5, Jan 1988 .... 1.50
❑6, Feb 1988 .... 1.50
❑7, Mar 1988 .... 1.50
❑8, Apr 1988 .... 1.50
❑9, May 1988 .... 1.50
❑10, Jun 1988 .... 1.50
❑11, Aug 1988 .... 1.50
❑12, Sep 1988 .... 1.50
❑13, Oct 1988 .... 1.50
❑14, Nov 1988 .... 1.50
❑15, Jan 1989 .... 1.50
❑16, Feb 1989 .... 1.50
❑17, Mar 1989 .... 1.50
❑18, Apr 1989 .... 1.50
❑19, May 1989 .... 1.50
❑20, Jun 1989 .... 1.50

ORIGINAL BLACK CAT
RECOLLECTIONS

❑1 .... 2.00
❑2, Mar 1989; Reprints 2.00
❑3, Sep 1990 .... 2.00
❑4, Jun 1991 .... 2.00
❑5, Jul 1991 .... 2.00
❑6, Aug 1991; reprints first Black Cat story from Pocket Comics #1 .... 2.00
❑7, Nov 1991 .... 2.00
❑8; Title changes to Black Cat for one issue only 2.00
❑9; Title reverts to Original Black Cat.. 2.00
❑10; Title changes to Black Cat Comics for final issue 1.00

ORIGINAL BOY: DAY OF ATONEMENT
OMEGA 7

❑1; no cover price; no indicia; events deal with Million Man March on Washington 1.95

ORIGINAL CREW
PERSONALITY

❑1; William Shatner 3.00
❑2; Leonard Nimoy 3.00
❑3; DeForest Kelley 3.00
❑4 .... 2.95
❑5 .... 2.95
❑6 .... 2.95
❑7 .... 2.95
❑8 .... 2.95
❑9; Bruce Hyde 2.95
❑10 .... 2.95

ORIGINAL DICK TRACY
GLADSTONE

❑1, Sep 1990, Mrs. Pruneface 2.00
❑2, Nov 1990, Influence 2.00
❑3, Jan 1991, Gargles 2.00
❑4, Mar 1991, Itchy 2.00
❑5, May 1991, Shoulders 2.00

ORIGINAL DICK TRACY COMIC ALBUM
GLADSTONE

❑1, Jul 1990; Mumbles 5.95
❑2, Sep 1990 .... 5.95
❑3, Jan 1991; Mole 5.95

ORIGINAL DOCTOR SOLAR, MAN OF THE ATOM
VALIANT

❑1, Apr 1995 ..... 5.00

ORIGINAL E-MAN
FIRST

❑1, Oct 1985 ..... 2.00
❑2, Nov 1985 ..... 2.00
❑3, Dec 1985 ..... 2.00
❑4, Jan 1986 ..... 2.00
❑5, Feb 1986 ..... 2.00
❑6, Mar 1986 ..... 2.00
❑7, Apr 1986 ..... 2.00

ORIGINAL GHOST RIDER
MARVEL

❑1, Jul 1992 ..... 1.75
❑2, Aug 1992 ..... 1.75
❑3, Sep 1992 ..... 1.75
❑4, Oct 1992 ..... 1.75
❑5, Nov 1992 ..... 1.75
❑6, Dec 1992 ..... 1.75
❑7, Jan 1993 ..... 1.75
❑8, Feb 1993 ..... 1.75
❑9, Mar 1993 ..... 1.75
❑10, Apr 1993 ..... 1.75
❑11, May 1993 ..... 1.75
❑12, Jun 1993 ..... 1.75
❑13, Jul 1993 ..... 1.75
❑14, Aug 1993 ..... 1.75
❑15, Sep 1993 ..... 1.75
❑16, Oct 1993 ..... 1.75
❑17, Nov 1993 ..... 1.75
❑18, Dec 1993 ..... 1.75
❑19, Jan 1994; Reprints Marvel Two-In-One #8 ..... 1.75
❑20, Feb 1994 ..... 1.75

ORIGINAL GHOST RIDER RIDES AGAIN
MARVEL

❑1, Jul 1991; Reprinted from Ghost Rider #68 ..... 1.50
❑2, Aug 1991 ..... 1.50
❑3, Sep 1991 ..... 1.50
❑4, Oct 1991 ..... 1.50
❑5, Nov 1991 ..... 1.50
❑6, Dec 1991 ..... 1.50
❑7, Jan 1992 ..... 1.50

ORIGINAL MAGNUS ROBOT FIGHTER
VALIANT

❑1, Apr 1992, RM (w); RM (a); Reprints Magnus, Robot Fighter 4000 A.D. #2; cardstock cover 4.00

ORIGINAL MAN
OMEGA 7

❑1 ..... 3.50

ORIGINAL MAN: THE MOST POWERFUL MAN IN THE UNIVERSE
OMEGA 7

❑1; Darkforce #0 as flip-side support story 1.95

ORIGINAL MYSTERYMEN PRESENTS (BOB BURDEN'S...)
DARK HORSE

❑1, Jul 1999 ..... 2.95
❑2, Aug 1999 ..... 2.95
❑3, Sep 1999 ..... 2.95
❑4, Oct 1999 ..... 2.95

ORIGINAL SAD SACK
RECOLLECTIONS

❑1, b&w 2.00

ORIGINAL SHIELD
ARCHIE

❑1, Apr 1984 ..... 1.00
❑2, Jun 1984 ..... 1.00
❑3, Aug 1984 ..... 1.00
❑4, Oct 1984 ..... 1.00

ORIGINAL SIN
THWACK! POW!

❑1 ..... 1.00
❑2 ..... 1.00
❑3 ..... 1.00

ORIGINAL STREET FIGHTER
ALPHA

❑1, b&w 2.50

ORIGINAL TOM CORBETT
ETERNITY

❑1, Sep 1990, b&w; Reprinted from Field Enterprises strips Tom Corbett, Space Cadet; The Mercurian Invasion 2.95
❑2, Sep 1990, b&w; Reprinted from Field Enterprises strips Tom Corbett, Space Cadet; The Mercurian Invasion; Colonists on Titan 2.95
❑3, Oct 1990, b&w; Reprinted from Field Enterprises strips Tom Corbett, Space Cadet; Colonists on Titan 2.95
❑4, Nov 1990, b&w; Reprinted from Field Enterprises strips Tom Corbett, Space Cadet; The Revolt on Mars 2.95
❑5, Dec 1990, b&w; Reprinted from Field Enterprises strips Tom Corbett, Space Cadet; Slave Plantation of Venus; Issues #6-10 were planned but never published. 2.95

ORIGINAL TUROK, SON OF STONE
VALIANT

❑1, Apr 1995, cardstock cover 4.00
❑2, May 1995, Reprints of Turok, Son of Stone #24, #33; cardstock cover 7.00

ORIGINAL TZU, THE: SPIRITS OF DEATH
MURIM

❑1, Dec 1997, b&w; reprints manga series 2.95

ORIGIN OF GALACTUS
MARVEL

❑1, Feb 1996, reprints Super-Villain Classics #1 ..... 2.50

ORIGIN OF THE DEFIANT UNIVERSE
DEFIANT

❑1, Feb 1994 ..... 1.50

ORION
DARK HORSE

❑1, Feb 1993, b&w; manga 3.95
❑2, Mar 1993, b&w; manga 2.95
❑3, Apr 1993, b&w; manga 2.95
❑4, May 1993, b&w; manga 2.95
❑5, Jun 1993, b&w; manga 2.95
❑6, Jul 1993 ..... 3.95

ORION (DC)
DC

❑1, Jun 2000 ..... 2.50
❑2, Jul 2000 ..... 2.50
❑3, Aug 2000 ..... 2.50
❑4, Sep 2000 ..... 2.50
❑5, Oct 2000 ..... 2.50
❑6, Nov 2000 ..... 2.50
❑7, Dec 2000 ..... 2.50
❑8, Jan 2001 ..... 2.50
❑9, Feb 2001 ..... 2.50
❑10, Mar 2001 ..... 2.50
❑11, Apr 2001 ..... 2.50
❑12, May 2001 ..... 2.50
❑13, Jun 2001 ..... 2.50
❑14, Jul 2001 ..... 2.50
❑15, Aug 2001 ..... 2.50
❑16, Sep 2001 ..... 2.50
❑17, Sep 2001 ..... 2.50
❑18, Oct 2001 ..... 2.50
❑19, Nov 2001 ..... 2.50
❑20, Dec 2001 ..... 2.50
❑21, Jan 2002 ..... 2.50
❑22, Feb 2002 ..... 2.50
❑23, Mar 2002 ..... 2.50
❑24, Apr 2002 ..... 2.50
❑25, May 2002 ..... 2.50

ORLAK REDUX
CALIBER

❑1, b&w 3.95

ORORO: BEFORE THE STORM
MARVEL

❑1, Jul 2005 ..... 2.99
❑2, Aug 2005 ..... 2.99
❑3, Sep 2005 ..... 2.99
❑4, Oct 2005 ..... 2.99

ORPHEN
ADV MANGA

❑1, ca. 2005 ..... 9.99
❑2, ca. 2005 ..... 9.99
❑3, ca. 2005 ..... 9.99

OSBORN JOURNALS
MARVEL

❑1, Feb 1997; summation of Clone Saga and return of Norman Osborn as Green Goblin 2.95

OTHELLO
TOME

❑1, b&w 3.50

OTHER BIG THING (COLIN UPTON'S...)
FANTAGRAPHICS

❑1, b&w 2.50
❑2 ..... 2.25
❑3 ..... 2.25
❑4, Jul 1992 ..... 2.50

OTHERS (IMAGE)
IMAGE

❑0, Mar 1995 ..... 1.00
❑1, Apr 1995 ..... 2.50
❑2, May 1995 ..... 2.50
❑3, Jul 1995 ..... 2.50
❑4 ..... 2.50

OTHERS (CORMAC)
CORMAC

❑1 ..... 1.50

OTHERWORLD
DC / VERTIGO

❑1, May 2005 ..... 2.99
❑2, Jun 2005 ..... 2.99
❑3, Jul 2005 ..... 2.99
❑4, Aug 2005 ..... 2.99
❑5, Sep 2005 ..... 2.99
❑6, Oct 2005 ..... 2.99
❑7 2005 ..... 2.99

OTIS GOES HOLLYWOOD
DARK HORSE

❑1, Apr 1997, b&w 2.95
❑2, May 1997, b&w 2.95

OTTO SPACE!
MANIFEST DESTINY

❑1 ..... 2.00
❑2 ..... 2.00

OURAN HIGH SCHOOL HOST CLUB
VIZ

❑1, Jul 2005 ..... 9.99
❑2, Sep 2005 ..... 9.99
❑3, Nov 2005 ..... 9.99

OUR ARMY AT WAR
DC

❑51, Oct 1956 ..... 100.00
❑52, Nov 1956 ..... 100.00
❑53, Dec 1956 ..... 100.00
❑54, Jan 1957 ..... 100.00
❑55, Feb 1957 ..... 100.00
❑56, Mar 1957 ..... 100.00
❑57, Apr 1957 ..... 100.00
❑58, May 1957 ..... 100.00
❑59, Jun 1957 ..... 100.00
❑60, Jul 1957 ..... 100.00
❑61, Aug 1957 ..... 100.00
❑62, Sep 1957 ..... 100.00
❑63, Oct 1957 ..... 100.00
❑64, Nov 1957 ..... 100.00
❑65, Dec 1957, JKu, RH (a) 100.00
❑66, Jan 1958 ..... 100.00
❑67, Feb 1958 ..... 100.00
❑68, Mar 1958 ..... 100.00
❑69, Apr 1958 ..... 100.00
❑70, May 1958 ..... 100.00
❑71, Jun 1958 ..... 75.00
❑72, Jul 1958 ..... 75.00
❑73, Aug 1958 ..... 75.00
❑74, Sep 1958 ..... 75.00
❑75, Oct 1958 ..... 75.00
❑76, Nov 1958 ..... 75.00
❑77, Dec 1958 ..... 75.00
❑78, Jan 1959 ..... 75.00
❑79, Feb 1959 ..... 75.00
❑80, Mar 1959 ..... 75.00
❑81, Apr 1959 JKu, RA, RH, JAb (a); 1: Easy Co.. 1: Sgt. Rock 2500.00
❑82, May 1959 RA (a); 2: Sgt. Rock 650.00
❑83, Jun 1959; JKu (a); 1: Easy Company. 1st Kubert Sgt. Rock 1800.00
❑84, Jul 1959 ..... 300.00

	N-MINT
❑85, Aug 1959 O: The Ice Cream Soldier. 1: The Ice Cream Soldier	350.00
❑86, Sep 1959	300.00
❑87, Oct 1959	300.00
❑88, Nov 1959	325.00
❑89, Dec 1959	300.00
❑90, Jan 1960	300.00
❑91, Feb 1960; 1st full-length Sgt. Rock story; All-Rock issue	700.00
❑92, Mar 1960	175.00
❑93, Apr 1960	175.00
❑94, May 1960	175.00
❑95, Jun 1960	175.00
❑96, Jul 1960	175.00
❑97, Aug 1960	175.00
❑98, Sep 1960	175.00
❑99, Oct 1960	175.00
❑100, Nov 1960	175.00
❑101, Dec 1960	125.00
❑102, Jan 1961	125.00
❑103, Feb 1961	125.00
❑104, Mar 1961	125.00
❑105, Apr 1961	125.00
❑106, May 1961	125.00
❑107, Jun 1961	125.00
❑108, Jul 1961	125.00
❑109, Aug 1961	125.00
❑110, Sep 1961	125.00
❑111, Oct 1961	125.00
❑112, Nov 1961	125.00
❑113, Dec 1961	150.00
❑114, Jan 1962	150.00
❑115, Feb 1962	150.00
❑116, Mar 1962	150.00
❑117, Apr 1962	150.00
❑118, May 1962	150.00
❑119, Jun 1962	125.00
❑120, Jul 1962	80.00
❑121, Aug 1962	80.00
❑122, Sep 1962	75.00
❑123, Oct 1962	75.00
❑124, Nov 1962	75.00
❑125, Dec 1962	75.00
❑126, Jan 1963	100.00
❑127, Feb 1963	75.00
❑128, Mar 1963, O: Sgt. Rock	275.00
❑129, Apr 1963	75.00
❑130, May 1963	75.00
❑131, Jun 1963	75.00
❑132, Jul 1963	75.00
❑133, Aug 1963	75.00
❑134, Sep 1963	60.00
❑135, Oct 1963	60.00
❑136, Nov 1963	60.00
❑137, Dec 1963	60.00
❑138, Jan 1964, JKu (c); JKu, JAb (a)	50.00
❑139, Feb 1964	50.00
❑140, Mar 1964	50.00
❑141, Apr 1964	50.00
❑142, May 1964	50.00
❑143, Jun 1964	50.00
❑144, Jul 1964	50.00
❑145, Aug 1964	50.00
❑146, Sep 1964	50.00
❑147, Oct 1964, A: Sgt. Rock and Easy Co.	50.00
❑148, Nov 1964, A: Sgt. Rock and Easy Co.	50.00
❑149, Dec 1964	50.00
❑150, Jan 1965	50.00
❑151, Feb 1965, JKu (a); 1: Enemy Ace	350.00
❑152, Mar 1965	50.00
❑153, Apr 1965, JKu (a); 2: Enemy Ace	140.00
❑154, May 1965	40.00
❑155, Jun 1965, JKu (a); A: Enemy Ace (next appearance is in Showcase #57)	75.00
❑156, Jul 1965	40.00
❑157, Aug 1965, A: Enemy Ace	40.00
❑158, Sep 1965, JKu (c); JKu (a); 1: Iron Major	60.00
❑159, Oct 1965	40.00
❑160, Nov 1965	40.00
❑161, Dec 1965	40.00
❑162, Jan 1966, A: Viking Prince	40.00
❑163, Feb 1966, A: Viking Prince	40.00
❑164, Feb 1966; Giant-size (80-Page Giant #G-19); aka 80 Page Giant #G-19	80.00
❑165, Mar 1966, V: Iron Major	40.00
❑166, Apr 1966	40.00
❑167, May 1966	40.00
❑168, Jun 1966	90.00
❑169, Jul 1966, JKu (c); JKu (a)	30.00
❑170, Aug 1966	30.00
❑171, Sep 1966	30.00
❑172, Oct 1966	30.00
❑173, Nov 1966	30.00
❑174, Dec 1966	30.00
❑175, Jan 1967	30.00
❑176, Feb 1967	30.00
❑177, Feb 1967; Giant-size (80-Page Giant #G-32); aka 80 Page Giant #G-32	50.00
❑178, Mar 1967	30.00
❑179, Apr 1967	30.00
❑180, May 1967	30.00
❑181, Jun 1967	30.00
❑182, Jul 1967, RH (c); NA, RH (a)	40.00
❑183, Aug 1967, NA (a)	40.00
❑184, Sep 1967	30.00
❑185, Oct 1967	30.00
❑186, Nov 1967, NA (a)	40.00
❑187, Dec 1967	30.00
❑188, Jan 1968	30.00
❑189, Feb 1968	30.00
❑190, Feb 1968; aka 80 Page Giant #G-44	40.00
❑191, Mar 1968	25.00
❑192, Apr 1968	25.00
❑193, May 1968	25.00
❑194, Jun 1968, 1: Unit 3 (kid guerrillas)	25.00
❑195, Jul 1968	25.00
❑196, Aug 1968	25.00
❑197, Sep 1968	25.00
❑198, Oct 1968	25.00
❑199, Nov 1968	20.00
❑200, Dec 1968, 200th issue	20.00
❑201, Jan 1969	20.00
❑202, Feb 1969	20.00
❑203, Feb 1969; Giant-size; aka 80 Page Giant #G-56; last 80 Page Giant	35.00
❑204, Mar 1969	20.00
❑205, Apr 1969	20.00
❑206, May 1969	20.00
❑207, Jun 1969	20.00
❑208, Jul 1969	20.00
❑209, Aug 1969	20.00
❑210, Sep 1969	20.00
❑211, Oct 1969	20.00
❑212, Nov 1969	20.00
❑213, Dec 1969	20.00
❑214, Jan 1970	20.00
❑215, Feb 1970	20.00
❑216, Feb 1970, Giant-size (80-Page Giant #G-80); JKu (c); RH, RE (a); aka Giant #G-68	55.00
❑217, Mar 1970	15.00
❑218, Apr 1970	15.00
❑219, May 1970, JKu (c); MA, RH (a)	15.00
❑220, Jun 1970	15.00
❑221, Jul 1970, JKu (c); JKu, RH (a)	15.00
❑222, Aug 1970	15.00
❑223, Sep 1970	15.00
❑224, Oct 1970	15.00
❑225, Nov 1970	15.00
❑226, Dec 1970	15.00
❑227, Jan 1971	15.00
❑228, Feb 1971	15.00
❑229, Mar 1971; Giant-size; aka Giant #G-80	35.00
❑230, Mar 1971	15.00
❑231, Apr 1971	15.00
❑232, May 1971	15.00
❑233, Jun 1971	15.00
❑234, Jul 1971	15.00
❑235, Aug 1971	25.00
❑236, Sep 1971	25.00
❑237, Oct 1971	25.00
❑238, Nov 1971	25.00
❑239, Dec 1971	25.00
❑240, Jan 1972	25.00
❑241, Feb 1972	15.00
❑242, Feb 1972, JKu (c); a.k.a. DC 100-Page Super Spectacular #DC-9; wraparound cover	20.00
❑243, Mar 1972	15.00
❑244, Apr 1972	15.00
❑245, May 1972	15.00
❑246, Jun 1972	15.00
❑247, Jul 1972	15.00
❑248, Aug 1972	15.00
❑249, Sep 1972	15.00
❑250, Oct 1972	15.00
❑251, Nov 1972	15.00
❑252, Dec 1972	15.00
❑253, Jan 1973	15.00
❑254, Feb 1973	18.00
❑255, Mar 1973	15.00
❑256, Apr 1973	18.00
❑257, Jun 1973	15.00
❑258, Jul 1973	10.00
❑259, Aug 1973	10.00
❑260, Sep 1973	10.00
❑261, Oct 1973	10.00
❑262, Nov 1973	10.00
❑263, Dec 1973	10.00
❑264, Jan 1974	10.00
❑265, Feb 1974	10.00
❑266, Mar 1974	10.00
❑267, Apr 1974	10.00
❑268, May 1974	10.00
❑269, Jun 1974	10.00
❑270, Jul 1974	10.00
❑271, Aug 1974	10.00
❑272, Sep 1974	15.00
❑273, Oct 1974	10.00
❑274, Nov 1974	10.00
❑275, Dec 1974	10.00
❑276, Jan 1975	10.00
❑277, Feb 1975	10.00
❑278, Mar 1975	10.00
❑279, Apr 1975	10.00
❑280, May 1975	10.00
❑281, Jun 1975	10.00
❑282, Jul 1975	10.00
❑283, Aug 1975	10.00
❑284, Sep 1975	10.00
❑285, Oct 1975	10.00
❑286, Nov 1975	10.00
❑287, Dec 1975	10.00
❑288, Jan 1976	10.00
❑289, Feb 1976	10.00
❑290, Mar 1976	10.00
❑291, Apr 1976	10.00
❑292, May 1976	10.00
❑293, Jun 1976	10.00
❑294, Jul 1976	10.00
❑295, Aug 1976	10.00
❑296, Sep 1976	10.00
❑297, Oct 1976	10.00
❑298, Nov 1976	10.00
❑299, Dec 1976	10.00
❑300, Jan 1977	10.00
❑301, Feb 1977, JKu (c); RE (a); Series is continued as "Sgt. Rock"	10.00

OUR FIGHTING FORCES
DC

	N-MINT
❑14, Oct 1956	135.00
❑15, Nov 1956	135.00
❑16, Dec 1956	115.00
❑17, Jan 1957	115.00
❑18, Feb 1957	115.00
❑19, Mar 1957	115.00
❑20, Apr 1957	115.00
❑21, May 1957	90.00
❑22, Jun 1957	90.00
❑23, Jul 1957	90.00
❑24, Aug 1957	90.00
❑25, Sep 1957	90.00
❑26, Oct 1957	90.00
❑27, Nov 1957	90.00
❑28, Dec 1957	90.00
❑29, Jan 1958	90.00
❑30, Feb 1958	90.00
❑31, Mar 1958	75.00
❑32, Apr 1958	75.00
❑33, May 1958	75.00
❑34, Jun 1958	75.00
❑35, Jul 1958	75.00
❑36, Aug 1958	75.00
❑37, Sep 1958	75.00

	N-MINT
❑38, Oct 1958	75.00
❑39, Nov 1958	75.00
❑40, Dec 1958	75.00
❑41, Jan 1959; Unknown Soldier prototype	90.00
❑42, Feb 1959	70.00
❑43, Mar 1959	70.00
❑44, Apr 1959	70.00
❑45, May 1959 1: Gunner & Sarge	235.00
❑46, Jun 1959	95.00
❑47, Jul 1959	80.00
❑48, Aug 1959	60.00
❑49, Sep 1959	60.00
❑50, Oct 1959	60.00
❑51, Nov 1959	35.00
❑52, Dec 1959	35.00
❑53, Feb 1960	35.00
❑54, Apr 1960	35.00
❑55, Jun 1960	35.00
❑56, Aug 1960	35.00
❑57, Oct 1960	35.00
❑58, Dec 1960	35.00
❑59, Feb 1961	35.00
❑60, Apr 1961	35.00
❑61, Jun 1961	28.00
❑62, Aug 1961	28.00
❑63, Oct 1961	28.00
❑64, Dec 1961	28.00
❑65, Jan 1962	18.00
❑66, Feb 1962	18.00
❑67, Apr 1962	18.00
❑68, Jun 1962	18.00
❑69, Jul 1962	18.00
❑70, Aug 1962	18.00
❑71, Oct 1962	15.00
❑72, Nov 1962	15.00
❑73, Jan 1963	15.00
❑74, Feb 1963	15.00
❑75, Apr 1963	15.00
❑76, Jun 1963	15.00
❑77, Jul 1963	15.00
❑78, Aug 1963	15.00
❑79, Oct 1963	15.00
❑80, Nov 1963	15.00
❑81, Jan 1964	10.00
❑82, Feb 1964	10.00
❑83, Apr 1964	10.00
❑84, May 1964, Gunner & Sarge	10.00
❑85, Jul 1964	10.00
❑86, Aug 1964, JKu (c); GC, JAb (a)	10.00
❑87, Oct 1964	10.00
❑88, Nov 1964	10.00
❑89, Jan 1965	10.00
❑90, Feb 1965	10.00
❑91, Apr 1965, JAb (a)	7.00
❑92, May 1965	7.00
❑93, Jul 1965	7.00
❑94, Aug 1965	7.00
❑95, Oct 1965	7.00
❑96, Nov 1965	7.00
❑97, Dec 1965	7.00
❑98, Jan 1966	7.00
❑99, Feb 1966, 1: Captain Phil Hunter	7.00
❑100, Apr 1966, A: Captain Hunter	6.00
❑101, Jun 1966	6.00
❑102, Aug 1966	6.00
❑103, Oct 1966	6.00
❑104, Dec 1966	6.00
❑105, Feb 1967	6.00
❑106, Apr 1967, JAb (a); 1: Ben Hunter. 1: Hunter's Hellcats	6.00
❑107, Jul 1967	6.00
❑108, Aug 1967, A: Lt. Hunter's Hellcats	6.00
❑109, Oct 1967	6.00
❑110, Dec 1967	6.00
❑111, Feb 1968, JAb (a)	6.00
❑112, Apr 1968	6.00
❑113, Jul 1968, JAb (a)	6.00
❑114, Aug 1968	6.00
❑115, Sep 1968	6.00
❑116, Nov 1968	6.00
❑117, Jan 1969	6.00
❑118, Mar 1969, A: Lt. Hunter's Hellcats	6.00
❑119, May 1969	6.00
❑120, Jul 1969	6.00
❑121, Sep 1969, 1: Heller	5.00
❑122, Nov 1969	5.00
❑123, Jan 1970, Losers series begins	5.00
❑124, Mar 1970, JSe (a)	5.00
❑125, May 1970	5.00
❑126, Jul 1970	5.00
❑127, Sep 1970, RA (a); Losers	5.00
❑128, Nov 1970	5.00
❑129, Jan 1971	5.00
❑130, Mar 1971	5.00
❑131, May 1971	5.00
❑132, Jul 1971, Losers	5.00
❑133, Sep 1971	5.00
❑134, Nov 1971	5.00
❑135, Jan 1972	5.00
❑136, Mar 1972	5.00
❑137, May 1972; Giant-size; Losers	5.00
❑138, Jul 1972	5.00
❑139, Sep 1972	5.00
❑140, Nov 1972	5.00
❑141, Jan 1973	5.00
❑142, Mar 1973	5.00
❑143, May 1973	5.00
❑144, Jul 1973	5.00
❑145, Sep 1973	5.00
❑146, Nov 1973	5.00
❑147, Jan 1974	5.00
❑148, Mar 1974, Accidentally includes 1973 Statement of Ownership for House of Secrets	5.00
❑149, May 1974	5.00
❑150, Jul 1974	5.00
❑151, Sep 1974, Losers	4.00
❑152, Nov 1974, Losers	4.00
❑153, Feb 1975; Losers	4.00
❑154, Apr 1975; JK (a); Losers	4.00
❑155, May 1975; Losers	4.00
❑156, Jun 1975; Losers	4.00
❑157, Jul 1975; Losers	4.00
❑158, Aug 1975; JK (a); Losers	4.00
❑159, Sep 1975; JK (a); Losers	4.00
❑160, Oct 1975; JK (a); Losers	4.00
❑161, Nov 1975; Losers	4.00
❑162, Dec 1975; JK (a); Losers	4.00
❑163, Jan 1976	4.00
❑164, Feb 1976	4.00
❑165, Mar 1976	4.00
❑166, Apr 1976	4.00
❑167, Jun 1976	4.00
❑168, Aug 1976	4.00
❑169, Oct 1976	4.00
❑170, Dec 1976	4.00
❑171, Feb 1977	4.00
❑172, Apr 1977	4.00
❑173, Jun 1977	4.00
❑174, Aug 1977	4.00
❑175, Oct 1977	4.00
❑176, Dec 1977	4.00
❑177, Feb 1978	4.00
❑178, Apr 1978	4.00
❑179, Jun 1978	4.00
❑180, Aug 1978	4.00
❑181, Oct 1978	4.00

OUR LOVE STORY
Marvel

	N-MINT
❑1, Oct 1969, JR (a)	55.00
❑2, Dec 1969	25.00
❑3, Feb 1970	25.00
❑4, Apr 1970	25.00
❑5, Jun 1970, JSo (a)	75.00
❑6, Aug 1970	25.00
❑7, Oct 1970	25.00
❑8, Dec 1970	25.00
❑9, Feb 1971	35.00
❑10, Apr 1971	25.00
❑11, Jun 1971	25.00
❑12, Aug 1971	35.00
❑13, Oct 1971	20.00
❑14, Dec 1971	12.00
❑15, Feb 1972, JAb (a)	12.00
❑16, Apr 1972	12.00
❑17, Jun 1972	12.00
❑18, Aug 1972	12.00
❑19, Oct 1972	12.00
❑20, Dec 1972	12.00
❑21, Feb 1973	8.00
❑22, Apr 1973	8.00
❑23, Jun 1973	8.00
❑24, Aug 1973	8.00
❑25, Oct 1973	8.00
❑26, Dec 1973	8.00
❑27, Feb 1974	8.00
❑28, Jun 1974	8.00
❑29, Aug 1974	8.00
❑30, Oct 1974	8.00
❑31, Dec 1974	8.00
❑32, Feb 1975	8.00
❑33, Apr 1975	8.00
❑34, Jun 1975	8.00
❑35, Aug 1975	8.00
❑36, Oct 1975	8.00
❑37, Dec 1975	8.00
❑38, Feb 1976	15.00

OUTBREED 999
Blackout

	N-MINT
❑1, May 1994	2.95
❑2, Jul 1994	2.95
❑3, Aug 1994	2.95
❑4	2.95
❑5	2.95

OUTCAST
Acclaim / Valiant

	N-MINT
❑1, Dec 1995	5.00

OUTCASTS
DC

	N-MINT
❑1, Oct 1987	1.75
❑2, Nov 1987	1.75
❑3, Dec 1987	1.75
❑4, Jan 1988	1.75
❑5, Feb 1988	1.75
❑6, Mar 1988	1.75
❑7, Apr 1988	1.75
❑8, May 1988	1.75
❑9, Jun 1988	1.75
❑10, Jul 1988	1.75
❑11, Aug 1988	1.75
❑12, Sep 1988	1.75

OUTER EDGE
Innovation

	N-MINT
❑1, b&w	2.50

OUTER LIMITS
Dell

	N-MINT
❑1, Jan 1964	125.00
❑2, Apr 1964	65.00
❑3, Jul 1964	65.00
❑4, Dec 1964	65.00
❑5, Jan 1965	65.00
❑6, Apr 1965	50.00
❑7, Jul 1965	50.00
❑8, Dec 1965	50.00
❑9, Jul 1966	50.00
❑10, Oct 1966	50.00
❑11, Jan 1967	35.00
❑12, Apr 1967	35.00
❑13, May 1967	35.00
❑14, Jul 1967	35.00
❑15, Sep 1967	35.00
❑16 1968	35.00
❑17, Oct 1968	35.00
❑18, Oct 1969	35.00

OUTER SPACE (VOL. 2)
Charlton

	N-MINT
❑1	20.00

OUTER SPACE BABES (VOL. 3)
Silhouette

	N-MINT
❑1	2.95

OUT FOR BLOOD
Dark Horse

	N-MINT
❑1, Sep 1999	2.95
❑2, Oct 1999	2.95
❑3, Nov 1999	2.95
❑4, Dec 1999	2.95

OUTLANDER
Malibu

	N-MINT
❑1 1987	1.95
❑2 1987	1.95
❑3, Dec 1987, b&w	1.95
❑4, Jan 1988	1.95
❑5, Mar 1988	1.95
❑6 1988	1.95

Painkiller Jane

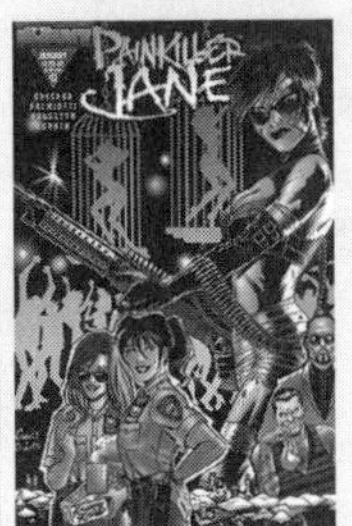

A supercop story with a voodoo touch

©Event

Painkiller Jane/ Darkchylde

Scantily clad women held captive

©Event

Paradise X

Alex Ross' follow-up to Universe X

©Marvel

Paranoia (Adventure)

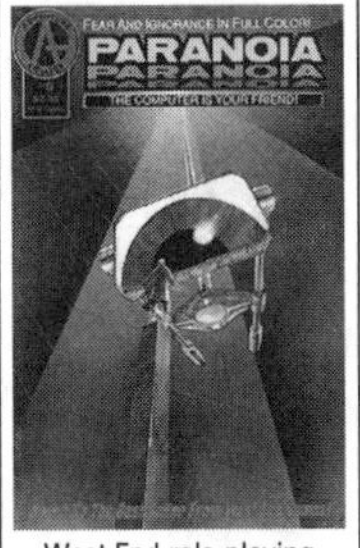

West End role-playing game comes to comics

©Adventure

Path

Set in a place very much like feudal Japan

©CrossGen

N-MINT

❑7 1988 .... 1.95

OUTLANDERS
DARK HORSE

❑0, Dec 1988 .... 3.00
❑1, Jan 1989 .... 2.50
❑2, Feb 1989 .... 2.00
❑3, Mar 1989 .... 2.00
❑4, Apr 1989 .... 2.00
❑5, May 1989 .... 2.00
❑6, Jun 1989 .... 2.00
❑7, Jul 1989 .... 2.00
❑8, Aug 1989 .... 2.00
❑9, Sep 1989 .... 2.25
❑10, Oct 1989 .... 2.25
❑11, Nov 1989 .... 2.25
❑12, Dec 1989 .... 2.25
❑13, Jan 1990 .... 2.25
❑14, Feb 1990 .... 2.25
❑15, Mar 1990 .... 2.25
❑16, Apr 1990 .... 2.25
❑17, May 1990 .... 2.25
❑18, Jun 1990 .... 2.25
❑19, Jul 1990 .... 2.25
❑20, Aug 1990 .... 2.25
❑21, Sep 1990 .... 2.25
❑22, Oct 1990 .... 2.50
❑23, Nov 1990 .... 2.50
❑24, Dec 1990 .... 2.50
❑25, Jan 1991 .... 2.50
❑26, Feb 1991 .... 2.50
❑27, Mar 1991; Giant-size special 2.95
❑28, Apr 1991 .... 2.50
❑29, May 1991 .... 2.50
❑30, Jun 1991 .... 2.50
❑31, Jul 1991 .... 2.50
❑32, Aug 1991 .... 2.50
❑33, Sep 1991 .... 2.50
❑Special 1, b&w; manga; Epilogue 2.50

OUTLANDERS EPILOGUE
DARK HORSE

❑1, Mar 1994, b&w 2.50

OUTLAW 7
DARK HORSE

❑1, Aug 2001 .... 2.99
❑2, Sep 2001 .... 2.99
❑3, Jan 2002 .... 2.99

OUTLAW KID (2ND SERIES)
MARVEL

❑1, Aug 1970 .... 25.00
❑2, Oct 1970 .... 10.00
❑3, Dec 1970 .... 10.00
❑4, Feb 1971 .... 10.00
❑5, Apr 1971 .... 10.00
❑6, Jun 1971 .... 10.00
❑7, Aug 1971 .... 10.00
❑8, Oct 1971, Giant-size 15.00
❑9, Dec 1971 .... 8.00
❑10, Jun 1972, O: Outlaw Kid. series goes on hiatus 20.00
❑11, Aug 1972 .... 8.00
❑12, Oct 1972 .... 8.00
❑13, Dec 1972 .... 8.00
❑14, Feb 1973 .... 8.00

N-MINT

❑15, Apr 1973 .... 8.00
❑16, Jun 1973 .... 8.00
❑17, Aug 1973 .... 8.00
❑18, Oct 1973 .... 8.00
❑19, Dec 1973 .... 8.00
❑20, Feb 1974 .... 8.00
❑21, Apr 1974 .... 5.00
❑22, Jun 1974 .... 5.00
❑23, Aug 1974 .... 5.00
❑24, Oct 1974 .... 5.00
❑25, Dec 1974 .... 5.00
❑26, Feb 1975 .... 5.00
❑27, Apr 1975 O: Outlaw Kid 5.00
❑28, Jun 1975 .... 5.00
❑29, Aug 1975 .... 5.00
❑30, Oct 1975 .... 5.00

OUTLAW NATION (VERTIGO)
DC / VERTIGO

❑1, Nov 2000 .... 2.50
❑2, Dec 2000 .... 2.50
❑3, Jan 2001 .... 2.50
❑4, Feb 2001 .... 2.50
❑5, Mar 2001 .... 2.50
❑6, Apr 2001 .... 2.50
❑7, May 2001 .... 2.50
❑8, Jun 2001 .... 2.50
❑9, Jul 2001 .... 2.50
❑10, Aug 2001 .... 2.50
❑11, Sep 2001 .... 2.50
❑12, Oct 2001 .... 2.50
❑13, Nov 2001 .... 2.50
❑14, Dec 2001 .... 2.50
❑15, Jan 2002 .... 2.50
❑16, Feb 2002 .... 2.50
❑17, Mar 2002 .... 2.50
❑18, Apr 2002 .... 2.50
❑19, May 2002 .... 2.50

OUTLAW NATION (VOL. 2)
BONEYARD

❑1 1994 .... 4.95
❑1/Platinum; Tim Bradstreet cover 5.00

OUTLAW OVERDRIVE
BLUE COMET

❑1, Red Edition 2.95

OUTLAWS (DC)
DC

❑1, Sep 1991 LMc (a) 2.00
❑2, Oct 1991 LMc (a) 2.00
❑3, Nov 1991 LMc (a) 2.00
❑4, Dec 1991 LMc (a) 2.00
❑5, Jan 1992 LMc (a) 2.00
❑6, Feb 1992 LMc (a) 2.00
❑7, Mar 1992 LMc (a) 2.00
❑8, Apr 1992 LMc (a) 2.00

OUT OF THE VORTEX (COMICS' GREATEST WORLD...)
DARK HORSE

❑5, Feb 1994, was Comics' Greatest World: Out of the Vortex 2.00
❑6, Mar 1994 .... 2.00
❑7, Apr 1994 .... 2.00
❑8, May 1994 .... 2.00
❑9, Jun 1994 .... 2.00

N-MINT

❑10, Jul 1994 .... 2.00
❑11, Sep 1994 .... 2.00
❑12, Oct 1994 .... 2.00

OUT OF THIS WORLD (ETERNITY)
ETERNITY

❑1, b&w; Reprints stories from Strange Worlds #9, Strange Planets #16, Tomb of Terror #6, and Weird Tales of the Future #1 .... 3.50

OUTPOSTS
BLACKTHORNE

❑1, Jun 1997 .... 1.50

OUTSIDERS (1ST SERIES)
DC

❑1, Nov 1985 .... 2.00
❑2, Dec 1985 .... 1.50
❑3, Jan 1986 .... 1.50
❑4, Feb 1986 .... 1.25
❑5, Mar 1986; Christmas Carol story . 1.25
❑6, Apr 1986 .... 1.25
❑7, May 1986 .... 1.25
❑8, Jun 1986 .... 1.25
❑9, Jul 1986 .... 1.25
❑10, Aug 1986 .... 1.25
❑11, Sep 1986 .... 1.00
❑12, Oct 1986 .... 1.00
❑13, Nov 1986 .... 1.00
❑14, Dec 1986 .... 1.00
❑15, Jan 1987 .... 1.00
❑16, Feb 1987 .... 1.00
❑17, Mar 1987; Batman returns 1.00
❑18, Apr 1987 .... 1.00
❑19, May 1987 .... 1.00
❑20, Jun 1987 .... 1.00
❑21, Jul 1987 .... 1.00
❑22, Aug 1987; EC parody back-up 1.00
❑23, Sep 1987 .... 1.00
❑24, Oct 1987 .... 1.00
❑25, Nov 1987 .... 1.00
❑26, Dec 1987 .... 1.00
❑27, Jan 1988; Millennium 1.00
❑28, Feb 1988; Millennium 1.00
❑Annual 1 .... 2.50
❑Special 1; Crossover continued in Infinity Inc. SE #1 .... 1.50

OUTSIDERS (2ND SERIES)
DC

❑0, Oct 1994; New team begins 2.50
❑1/A, Nov 1993; Alpha version 4.00
❑1/B, Nov 1993; Omega version 3.00
❑2, Dec 1993 .... 2.00
❑3, Jan 1994 A: Eradicator 2.00
❑4, Feb 1994 .... 2.00
❑5, Mar 1994 .... 2.00
❑6, Apr 1994 .... 2.00
❑7, May 1994 .... 2.00
❑8, Jun 1994 JA (a); A: Batman (Azrael) 2.00
❑9, Jul 1994 .... 2.00
❑10, Aug 1994 .... 2.00
❑11, Sep 1994 .... 2.00
❑12, Nov 1994 .... 2.00
❑13, Dec 1994 A: Superman 3.00
❑14, Jan 1995 .... 2.00
❑15, Feb 1995 .... 2.00

Other grades: Multiply price above by 5/6 for VF/NM • 2/3 for VERY FINE • 1/3 for FINE • 1/5 for VERY GOOD • 1/8 for GOOD

N-MINT N-MINT N-MINT

❑16, Mar 1995 2.00
❑17, Apr 1995 2.00
❑18, May 1995 2.00
❑19, Jun 1995 2.25
❑20, Jul 1995 2.25
❑21, Aug 1995 2.25
❑22, Sep 1995 2.25
❑23, Oct 1995 2.25
❑24, Nov 1995 2.25

OUTSIDERS (3RD SERIES)
DC

❑1, Aug 2003 2.50
❑2, Sep 2003 2.50
❑3, Oct 2003 2.50
❑4, Nov 2003 2.50
❑5, Dec 2003 2.50
❑6, Jan 2004 2.50
❑7, Feb 2004 2.50
❑8, Mar 2004 2.50
❑9, Apr 2004 2.50
❑10, May 2004 2.50
❑11, Jun 2004 2.50
❑12, Jul 2004 2.50
❑13, Aug 2004 2.50
❑14, Sep 2004 2.50
❑15, Oct 2004 2.50
❑16, Nov 2004 2.50
❑17, Dec 2004 2.50
❑18, Jan 2005 2.50
❑19, Feb 2005 2.50
❑20, Mar 2005 2.50
❑21, Apr 2005 4.00
❑22, May 2005 4.00
❑23, Jun 2005 4.00
❑24, Jul 2005 2.50
❑25, Aug 2005 2.50
❑26, Sep 2005 2.50
❑27, Oct 2005 2.50
❑28, Nov 2005 2.50
❑29 2005 2.50
❑30, Jan 2006 2.50
❑31, Jan 2006 2.50
❑32, Mar 2006 2.50
❑33, Mar 2006 2.50
❑35, Jun 2006 2.50
❑36, Jul 2006 2.50
❑37, Aug 2006 2.50
❑38, Sep 2006 2.50

OUTSIDERS DOUBLE FEATURE
DC

❑1, Oct 2003 4.95

OVERKILL: WITCHBLADE/ALIENS/ DARKNESS/PREDATOR
IMAGE

❑1, Dec 2000 5.95
❑2, Mar 2001 5.95

OVERLOAD MAGAZINE
ECLIPSE

❑1, Apr 1987, b&w 1.50

OVERMEN
EXCEL

❑1 2.95

OVER THE EDGE
MARVEL

❑1, Nov 1995, Daredevil 1.25
❑2, Dec 1995, A: Doctor Strange 1.00
❑3, Jan 1996, Hulk 1.00
❑4, Feb 1996, Ghost Rider 1.00
❑5, Mar 1996, Punisher 1.00
❑6, Apr 1996, Daredevil and Black Panther 1.00
❑7, May 1996, Doctor Strange vs. Nightmare 1.00
❑8, Jun 1996, Elektra 1.00
❑9, Jul 1996, Ghost Rider, John Blaze 1.00
❑10, Aug 1996, Daredevil 1.00

OVERTURE
INNOVATION / ALL-AMERICAN

❑1, Apr 1990, b&w 2.25
❑2, Jul 1990, b&w 2.25

OWL
GOLD KEY

❑1, Apr 1967 50.00
❑2, Apr 1968 40.00

OWLHOOTS
KITCHEN SINK

❑1 2.50
❑2 2.50

OX COW O' WAR
SPOOF

❑1, b&w; parody 2.95

OZ
CALIBER

❑0 4.00
❑1 6.00
❑2 4.00
❑3 4.00
❑4 4.00
❑5 3.50
❑6 3.50
❑7 3.50
❑8 3.50
❑9 3.50
❑10 3.50
❑11 3.00
❑12 3.00
❑13 3.00
❑14 3.00
❑15 1996 3.00
❑16 1996 3.00
❑17, Sep 1996 3.00
❑18, Nov 1996 2.95
❑19, Jan 1997 2.95
❑20, Mar 1997 2.95

OZ COLLECTION (BILL BRYAN'S...)
ARROW

❑1 2.95

OZ: DAEMONSTORM
CALIBER

❑1, ca. 1997, b&w; intracompany crossover 3.95

OZ: ROMANCE IN RAGS
CALIBER

❑1, ca. 1996, b&w 2.95
❑2, ca. 1996, b&w 2.95
❑3, ca. 1996, b&w 2.95

OZ SPECIAL: FREEDOM FIGHTERS
CALIBER

❑1, b&w 2.95

OZ SPECIAL: LION
CALIBER

❑1, b&w; continues in Oz Special: Tin Man 2.95

OZ SPECIAL: SCARECROW
CALIBER

❑1, b&w; continues in Oz Special: Lion 2.95

OZ SPECIAL: TIN MAN
CALIBER

❑1, b&w; continues in Oz Special: Freedom Fighters 2.95

OZ SQUAD (1ST SERIES)
BRAVE NEW WORDS

❑1, Oct 1991 3.00
❑2, Jan 1992 2.50
❑3 2.50
❑4 2.50

OZ SQUAD (2ND SERIES)
PATCHWORK

❑1 3.00
❑2 2.50
❑3 2.50
❑4, ca. 1994 2.75
❑5 2.75
❑6 2.95
❑7, Aug 1995 2.75
❑8, Oct 1995 2.75
❑9, Dec 1995 O: Tin Man 2.75
❑10 O: Tin Man 2.75

OZ: STRAW & SORCERY
CALIBER

❑1, Mar 1997, b&w 2.95
❑2 1997, b&w 2.95
❑3 1997, b&w 2.95

OZ-WONDERLAND WARS
DC

❑1, Jan 1986 2.50
❑2, Feb 1986 A: Hoppy the Marvel Bunny 2.50
❑3, Mar 1986 2.50

OZZY OSBOURNE
ROCK-IT COMICS

❑1 6.00

PACIFIC PRESENTS
PACIFIC

❑1, Oct 1982; SD, DSt (w); SD, DSt (a); Rocketeer; Missing Man 4.00
❑2, Apr 1983; SD, DSt (w); SD, DSt (a); Rocketeer; Missing Man 3.00
❑3, Mar 1984; SD (w); SD (a); Missing Man 1.50
❑4, Jun 1984 1.50

PAC (PRETER-HUMAN ASSAULT CORPS)
ARTIFACTS

❑1, Oct 1993 1.95

PACT
IMAGE

❑1, Feb 1994 1.95
❑2, Apr 1994 1.95
❑3, Jun 1994 1.95

PACT (VOL. 2)
IMAGE

❑1, ca. 2005 2.99
❑2 2005 2.99
❑3 2005 2.99
❑4, Jan 2006 2.99

PAGERS COMICS ANTHOLOGY
NO TALENT

❑1, Spr 1997 2.50
❑2, Sum 1997 2.50
❑3, Fal 1997 2.50
❑4, Win 1997 2.50
❑5, Spr 1998 2.50
❑6, Sum 1998 2.50

PAINKILLER JANE
EVENT

❑0, Nov 1998 O: Painkiller Jane 3.95
❑0/Ltd. O: Painkiller Jane 39.95
❑1, Jun 1997; MWa (w); wraparound cover 3.00
❑1/A, Jun 1997; MWa (w); variant cover 4.00
❑1/Red foil, Jun 1997; MWa (w); Red foil 25.00
❑2, Jul 1997; MWa (w); Standard cover: Jane in sunglasses close-up 3.00
❑2/A, Jul 1997; MWa (w); variant cover; Jane running 4.00
❑3, Aug 1997 MWa (w) 3.00
❑3/A, Aug 1997; MWa (w); variant cover 4.00
❑4, Sep 1997 MWa (w) 3.00
❑4/A, Sep 1997; MWa (w); variant cover 4.00
❑5, Oct 1997 MWa (w) 3.00
❑5/A 1997; MWa (w); variant cover 4.00

PAINKILLER JANE/DARKCHYLDE
EVENT

❑0; European Preview book 4.00
❑0/Autographed; European Preview book 29.95
❑1, Oct 1998 3.00
❑1/A, Oct 1998; DFE Omnichrome edition with COA 29.95
❑1/B, Oct 1998; DFE alternate cover 4.00
❑1/C, Oct 1998; Signed edition 39.95
❑Ashcan 1, Jul 1998; DF Exclusive; Sketches 5.00

PAINKILLER JANE/HELLBOY
EVENT

❑1, Aug 1998; Cover by Mike Mignola 2.95
❑1/Ltd., Aug 1998; Signed edition 29.95
❑1/A, Aug 1998; Cover by Quesada/ Palmiotti 2.95

PAINKILLER JANE VS. THE DARKNESS: STRIPPER
EVENT

❑1, Apr 1997; four alternate covers 2.95
❑1/A, Apr 1997; Jane facing forward, shooting on cover 3.00
❑1/B, Apr 1997 3.00
❑1/C, Apr 1997 3.00
❑1/Ltd., Apr 1997; Signed edition 20.00

PAINTBALL UNIVERSE 2000
SPLATTOONS

❑1 2.95

Other grades: Multiply price above by 5/6 for VF/NM • 2/3 for VERY FINE • 1/3 for FINE • 1/5 for VERY GOOD • 1/8 for GOOD

Patriots

WildStorm's elite force of super-agents

©WildStorm

Paul the Samurai (Mini-Series)

Samurai takes job as security guard

©NEC

Peanuts (Dell)

Snoopy and company visit comic books

©Dell

Pebbles and Bamm-Bamm

Uses teen-age versions from CBS cartoon

©Charlton

Pep

Long-running Archie series once had heroes

©Archie

N-MINT

PAJAMA CHRONICLES
BLACKTHORNE

❑1 .... 1.75

PAKKINS' LAND
CALIBER / TAPESTRY

❑0, Jun 1997 .... 1.95
❑1, Oct 1996 .... 2.95
❑1/2nd, ca. 1996, Labeled as "Special Edition" 2.95
❑2, Dec 1996 .... 2.95
❑2/2nd, ca. 1996, Labeled as "Special Edition" 2.95
❑3, Feb 1997 .... 2.95
❑4, May 1997 .... 2.95
❑5, Jun 1997 .... 2.95
❑6, Jul 1997 .... 2.95

PAKKINS' LAND (VOL. 2)
ALIAS

❑1 2005 .... 2.99
❑2 2005 .... 2.99
❑3 2005 .... 2.99
❑4, Sep 2005 .... 2.99
❑5 2005 .... 2.99

PAKKINS' LAND: FORGOTTEN DREAMS
CALIBER / TAPESTRY

❑1, Apr 1998 .... 2.95
❑2, ca. 1998 .... 2.95
❑3, ca. 1998 .... 2.95
❑4, Mar 2000, published by Image 2.95

PAKKINS' LAND: QUEST FOR KINGS
CALIBER / TAPESTRY

❑1 .... 2.95
❑1/A, Aug 1997 .... 2.95
❑2, Sep 1997 .... 2.95
❑2/A, Aug 1997, alternate cover 2.95
❑3, Nov 1997 .... 2.95
❑4, Dec 1997 .... 2.95
❑5, Jan 1998 .... 2.95
❑6, Mar 1998 .... 2.95

PALATINE
GRYPHON RAMPANT

❑1 .... 2.50
❑2, Oct 1994 .... 2.50
❑3, Jan 1995 .... 2.50
❑4 .... 2.50
❑5 .... 2.50

PALESTINE
FANTAGRAPHICS

❑1, b&w 2.50
❑2, b&w 2.50
❑3, b&w 2.50
❑4, b&w 2.95
❑5 .... 2.50
❑6 .... 2.50
❑7, Sep 1994 .... 2.95
❑9, Oct 1995, b&w 2.95

PAL-YAT-CHEE
ADHESIVE

❑1, b&w 2.50

PAMELA ANDERSON UNCOVERED
POP

❑1 .... 2.95

N-MINT

PANDA KHAN SPECIAL
ABACUS

❑1, b&w 3.00

PANDEMONIUM
CHAOS!

❑1, Sep 1998 .... 2.95

PANDORA PILL
ACID RAIN

❑1 .... 2.50

PANIC (RCP)
GEMSTONE

❑1, Mar 1997; Reprints Panic (EC) #1 .... 2.50
❑2, Jun 1997; Reprints Panic (EC) #2 .... 2.50
❑3, Sep 1997; Reprints Panic (EC) #3 .... 2.50
❑4, Dec 1997; Reprints Panic (EC) #4 .... 2.50
❑5, Mar 1998; Reprints Panic (EC) #5 .... 2.50
❑6, Jun 1998; Reprints Panic (EC) #6 .... 2.50
❑7, Sep 1998; Reprints Panic (EC) #7 .... 2.50
❑8, Dec 1998; Reprints Panic (EC) #8 .... 2.50
❑9, Mar 1999 .... 2.50
❑10, Jun 1999 .... 2.50
❑11, Sep 1999 .... 2.50
❑12, Dec 1999 .... 2.50
❑Annual 1; Collects issues #1-4 .... 10.95
❑Annual 2; Collects issues #5-8 .... 10.95

PANORAMA
ST.EVE PRODUCTIONS

❑1 .... 2.50
❑2, ca. 1991 .... 2.50

PANTERA
MALIBU / ROCK-IT

❑1, Aug 1994; magazine 4.00

PANTHA: HAUNTED PASSION
HARRIS / ROCK-IT

❑1 .... 2.95

PANTHEON (ARCHER)
ARCHER BOOKS & GAMES

❑1, Oct 1995, b&w 2.95
❑2, Jun 1997 ....

PANTHEON (LONE STAR)
LONE STAR

❑1, May 1998 .... 2.95
❑2, Jul 1998 .... 2.95
❑3, Sep 1998 .... 2.95
❑4, Jan 1999 .... 2.95
❑5, Jul 1999 .... 2.95
❑6, Aug 1999 .... 2.95

PANTHEON: ANCIENT HISTORY
LONE STAR

❑1, Aug 1999 .... 3.95

PANZER 1946
ANTARCTIC

❑1, Oct 2004 .... 5.95
❑2 .... 5.95

PAPER CINEMA: THE BOX
GREY BLOSSOM SEQUENTIALS

❑3, Dec 1998 .... 3.55

PAPER CINEMA: WAVES IN SPACE
GREY BLOSSOM SEQUENTIALS

❑2, Dec 1998 .... 3.55

N-MINT

PAPER DOLLS FROM THE CALIFORNIA GIRLS
ECLIPSE

❑1; paper dolls 5.95

PAPER MUSEUM
JUNGLE BOY

❑1, ca. 2002, b&w; magazine-sized 2.95

PAPER TALES
CLG COMICS

❑1, Sum 1993, b&w 2.50
❑2, Sum 1994, b&w 2.50

PARA-COPS
EXCEL

❑1 .... 2.95

PARADAX
VORTEX

❑1 .... 1.75
❑2, Aug 1987 .... 1.75

PARADIGM (IMAGE)
IMAGE

❑1, Sep 2002 .... 3.50
❑2, Oct 2002 .... 3.50
❑3, Nov 2002 .... 3.50
❑4, Dec 2002 .... 3.50
❑5, Jan 2003 .... 2.95
❑6, Feb 2003 .... 2.95
❑7, Mar 2003 .... 2.95
❑8, Apr 2003 .... 2.95
❑9, May 2003 .... 3.50
❑10, Jul 2003 .... 3.50
❑11, Oct 2003 .... 3.95
❑12, Dec 2003 .... 3.95

PARADIGM
GAUNTLET

❑1 .... 2.95

PARADISE KISS
TOKYOPOP

❑1, May 2002, b&w; printed in Japanese format 9.99

PARADISE TOO
ABSTRACT

❑nn, ca. 2000, b&w 2.75
❑2, ca. 2001, b&w 2.95
❑3, ca. 2001, b&w 2.95
❑4, ca. 2001, b&w 2.95
❑5, ca. 2002, b&w 2.95
❑6, ca. 2002, b&w 2.95
❑7, ca. 2002, b&w 2.95
❑8, ca. 2002, b&w 2.95
❑9, ca. 2002, b&w 2.95
❑10, ca. 2002, b&w 2.95
❑11, ca. 2003, b&w 2.95
❑12, Mar 2003, b&w 2.95
❑13, Jul 2003, b&w 2.95
❑14, Aug 2003, b&w 2.95

PARADISE X
MARVEL

❑0, Apr 2002 .... 4.50
❑1, May 2002 .... 2.99
❑2, Jun 2002 .... 2.99
❑3, Aug 2002 .... 2.99
❑4, Sep 2002 .... 2.99

Other grades: Multiply price above by 5/6 for VF/NM • 2/3 for VERY FINE • 1/3 for FINE • 1/5 for VERY GOOD • 1/8 for GOOD

N-MINT

❑5, Oct 2002 .... 2.99
❑6, Dec 2002 .... 2.99
❑7, ca. 2003 .... 2.99
❑8, ca. 2003 .... 2.99
❑9, ca. 2003 .... 2.99
❑10, Jun 2003 .... 2.99
❑11, Jul 2003 .... 2.99
❑12, Aug 2003 .... 2.99

PARADISE X: DEVILS
MARVEL
❑1, Nov 2002 .... 4.50

PARADISE X: HERALDS
MARVEL
❑1, Dec 2001 .... 3.50
❑2, Jan 2002 .... 3.50
❑3, Feb 2002 .... 3.50

PARADISE X: A
MARVEL
❑1, Oct 2003 .... 2.99

PARADISE X: X
MARVEL
❑1, Nov 2003 .... 2.99

PARADISE X: RAGNAROK
MARVEL
❑1, Mar 2003 .... 2.99
❑2, Apr 2003 .... 2.99

PARADISE X: XEN
MARVEL
❑1, Jul 2002 .... 4.50

PARADOX PROJECT: GENESIS
PARADOX PROJECT
❑1, Dec 1998, b&w 2.95

PARAGON: DARK APOCALYPSE
AC
❑1 .... 2.95
❑2 .... 2.95
❑3 .... 2.95
❑4 .... 2.95

PARALLAX: EMERALD NIGHT
DC
❑1, Nov 1996, D: Cyborg Superman. Final Night 15.00

PARANOIA (ADVENTURE)
ADVENTURE
❑1, Oct 1991 .... 2.95
❑2, Dec 1991 .... 2.95
❑3, Feb 1992 .... 2.95
❑4, Apr 1992 .... 2.95
❑5, Jun 1992 .... 2.95
❑6, Aug 1992 .... 2.95

PARANOIA (CO. & SONS)
CO. & SONS
❑1 .... 4.00

PARAPHERNALIA
GRAPHITTI
❑1; Ordering Catalogue 2.00

PARA TROOP
COMICS CONSPIRACY
❑0 .... 3.95
❑1 .... 2.95
❑2 .... 2.95
❑3, Oct 1998 .... 2.95
❑4, Dec 1998 .... 2.95
❑5, Feb 1999 .... 2.95
❑Ashcan 1; ashcan edition 2.95

PARDNERS
COTTONWOOD GRAPHICS
❑1, b&w 7.95
❑2, b&w 7.95

PARIS
SLAVE LABOR
❑1, Nov 2005 .... 2.95
❑2, Dec 2005 .... 2.95

PARIS THE MAN OF PLASTER
HARRIER
❑1, May 1987 .... 1.95
❑2 1987 .... 1.95
❑3 1987 .... 1.95
❑4 1987 .... 1.95
❑5 1987 .... 1.95
❑6 1987 .... 1.95

PARLIAMENT OF JUSTICE
IMAGE
❑1, Mar 2003, b&w 5.95

PARO-DEE
PARODY
❑1, b&w 2.50

PARODY PRESS ANNUAL SWIMSUIT SPECIAL '93
PARODY
❑1, Aug 1993 .... 2.50

PARTICLE DREAMS
FANTAGRAPHICS
❑1, Oct 1986 .... 2.25
❑2, Jan 1987 .... 2.25
❑3, Apr 1987 .... 2.25
❑4, Jun 1987 .... 2.25
❑5 1987 .... 2.25
❑6 1987 .... 2.25

PARTNERS IN PANDEMONIUM
CALIBER
❑1, b&w 2.50
❑2, b&w 2.50
❑3, b&w 2.50

PARTRIDGE FAMILY
CHARLTON
❑1, Mar 1971 .... 30.00
❑2, May 1971 .... 16.00
❑3, Jul 1971 .... 14.00
❑4, Sep 1971 .... 14.00
❑5, Sum 1971, Giant-size 20.00
❑6, Jan 1971 .... 12.00
❑7, Feb 1972 .... 12.00
❑8, Mar 1972 .... 12.00
❑9, Apr 1972 .... 12.00
❑10, May 1972 .... 12.00
❑11, Aug 1972 .... 12.00
❑12, Sep 1972 .... 12.00
❑13, Nov 1972 .... 12.00
❑14, Dec 1973 .... 12.00
❑15, Jan 1973 .... 10.00
❑16, ca. 1973 .... 10.00
❑17, ca. 1973 .... 10.00
❑18, ca. 1973 .... 10.00
❑19, Jul 1973 .... 10.00
❑20, Sep 1973 .... 10.00
❑21, ca. 1973 .... 10.00

PARTS OF A HOLE
CALIBER
❑1, b&w; Brian Michael Bendis' first major comics work 2.50

PARTS UNKNOWN
ECLIPSE
❑1, Aug 1995, b&w 2.50
❑2, Mar 1995, b&w 2.50
❑3, Jun 1995, b&w 2.50
❑4, Oct 1995, b&w 2.50

PARTS UNKNOWN: DARK INTENTIONS
KNIGHT
❑0, Aug 1995 .... 2.95
❑1, Mar 1995 .... 2.95
❑2, Jun 1995 .... 2.95
❑3, Oct 1995 .... 2.95
❑4 1995 .... 2.95

PARTS UNKNOWN: HOSTILE TAKEOVER
IMAGE
❑1, Jun 2000 .... 2.95
❑1/Ashcan, Jun 2000; Preview edition 4.95
❑2, Jul 2000 .... 2.95
❑2/Ashcan, Jul 2000; Preview edition 4.95
❑3, Aug 2000 .... 2.95
❑3/Ashcan, Aug 2000; Preview edition 4.95
❑4, Sep 2000 .... 2.95
❑4/Ashcan, Sep 2000; Preview edition 4.95

PARTS UNKNOWN II: THE NEXT INVASION
ECLIPSE
❑1, Dec 1993, b&w 2.95

PASSOVER
MAXIMUM
❑1, Dec 1996 .... 2.99

PATH
CROSSGEN
❑1, Apr 2002 .... 2.95
❑2, May 2002 .... 2.95
❑3, Jun 2002 .... 2.95
❑4, Jul 2002 .... 2.95
❑5, Aug 2002 .... 2.95
❑6, Sep 2002 .... 2.95
❑7, Oct 2002 .... 2.95
❑8, Nov 2002 .... 2.95
❑9, Dec 2002 .... 2.95
❑10, Jan 2003 .... 2.95
❑11, Feb 2003 .... 2.95
❑12, Mar 2003 .... 2.95
❑13, Apr 2003 .... 2.95
❑14, May 2003 .... 2.95
❑15, Jun 2003 .... 2.95
❑16, Jul 2003 .... 2.95
❑17, Sep 2003 .... 2.95
❑18, Oct 2003 .... 2.95
❑19, Nov 2003 .... 2.95
❑20, Dec 2003 .... 2.95
❑21, Jan 2004 .... 2.95
❑22, Mar 2004 .... 2.95
❑23, Apr 2004 .... 2.95

PATH PREQUEL
CROSSGEN
❑1, Mar 2002 .... 2.95

PATHWAYS TO FANTASY
PACIFIC
❑1, Jul 1984, JJ (a) 2.00

PATIENT ZERO
IMAGE
❑1, Apr 2004 .... 2.95
❑2, May 2004 .... 2.95
❑3, Aug 2004 .... 2.95
❑4, Sep 2004 .... 3.00

PATRICK RABBIT
FRAGMENTS WEST
❑1, Sum 1988 .... 2.00
❑2 .... 2.00
❑3 .... 2.00
❑4 .... 2.00
❑5 .... 2.00
❑6 .... 2.00
❑7 .... 2.00

PATRICK STEWART
CELEBRITY
❑1 .... 2.95

PATRICK STEWART VS. WILLIAM SHATNER
CELEBRITY
❑1, b&w 5.95

PATRIOTS
WILDSTORM
❑1, Jan 2000 .... 2.50
❑2, Feb 2000 .... 2.50
❑3, Mar 2000 .... 2.50
❑4, Apr 2000 .... 2.50
❑5, May 2000 .... 2.50
❑6, Jun 2000 .... 2.50
❑7, Jul 2000 .... 2.50
❑8, Aug 2000 .... 2.50
❑9, Sep 2000 .... 2.50
❑10, Oct 2000 .... 2.50

PAT SAVAGE: THE WOMAN OF BRONZE
MILLENNIUM
❑1, Oct 1992 .... 2.50

PATSY AND HEDY
MARVEL
❑46, ca. 1956 .... 23.00
❑47, ca. 1956 .... 23.00
❑48, ca. 1957 .... 23.00
❑49, ca. 1957 .... 23.00
❑50, ca. 1957 .... 23.00
❑51, ca. 1957 .... 15.00
❑52, ca. 1957 .... 15.00
❑53, ca. 1957 .... 15.00
❑54, ca. 1957 .... 15.00
❑55, ca. 1957 .... 15.00
❑56, Feb 1958 .... 15.00
❑57, Apr 1958 .... 15.00
❑58, Jun 1958 .... 15.00

Perry Mason

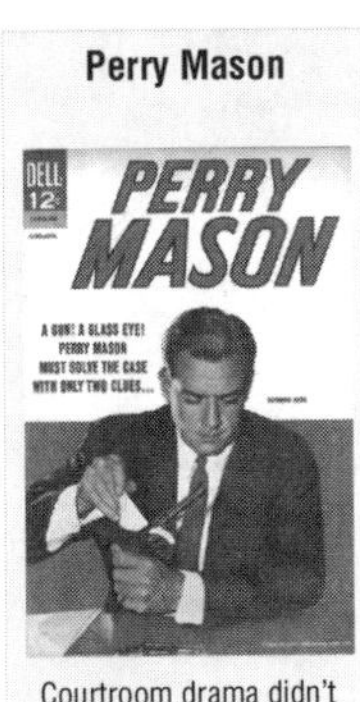

Courtroom drama didn't translate to comics page

©Dell

Peter Cannon-Thunderbolt

Tibetan-trained hero comes from Charlton

©DC

Peter Pan (Gold Key)

Perpetual pre-pubescents harass Hook

©Gold Key

Peter Parker: Spider-Man

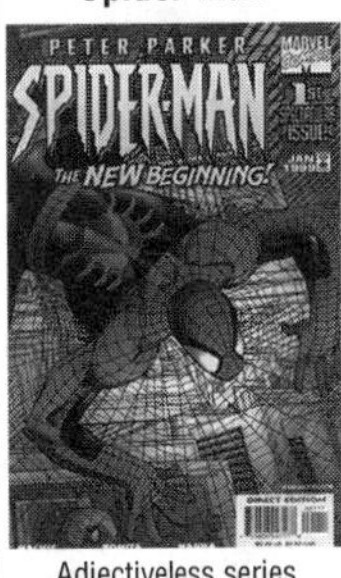

Adjectiveless series restarts, adds proper name

©Marvel

Pete the P.O.'d Postal Worker

The Punisher takes philatelic tact

©Sharkbait

N-MINT

❑59, Aug 1958 15.00
❑60, Oct 1958 15.00
❑61, Dec 1958 12.00
❑62, Feb 1959 12.00
❑63, Apr 1959 12.00
❑64, Jun 1959 12.00
❑65, Aug 1959 12.00
❑66, Oct 1959 12.00
❑67, Dec 1959 12.00
❑68, Feb 1960 12.00
❑69, Apr 1960 12.00
❑70, Jun 1960, SL (w) 12.00
❑71, Aug 1960 12.00
❑72, Oct 1960, SL (w) 12.00
❑73, Dec 1960 12.00
❑74, Feb 1961 12.00
❑75, Apr 1961 12.00
❑76, Jun 1961 12.00
❑77, Aug 1961 12.00
❑78, Oct 1961 12.00
❑79, Dec 1961, SL (w) 12.00
❑80, Feb 1962, SL (w) 12.00
❑81, Apr 1962 12.00
❑82, Jun 1962 12.00
❑83, Aug 1962 12.00
❑84, Oct 1962 12.00
❑85, Dec 1962 12.00
❑86, Feb 1963 12.00
❑87, Apr 1963 12.00
❑88, Jun 1963 12.00
❑89, Aug 1963 12.00
❑90, Oct 1963 12.00
❑91, Dec 1963 10.00
❑92, Feb 1964 10.00
❑93, Apr 1964 10.00
❑94, Jun 1964 10.00
❑95, Aug 1964, Graduation issue 10.00
❑96, Oct 1964, Patsy and Hedy "Career Girls" begins 10.00
❑97, Dec 1964 10.00
❑98, Feb 1965, SL (w); 10.00
❑99, Apr 1965, SL (w); 10.00
❑100, Jun 1965, SL (w); 10.00
❑101, Aug 1965 10.00
❑102, Oct 1965 10.00
❑103, Dec 1965 10.00
❑104, Feb 1966 10.00
❑105, Apr 1966 10.00
❑106, Jun 1966 10.00
❑107, Aug 1966 10.00
❑108, Oct 1966 10.00
❑109, Dec 1966 10.00
❑110, Feb 1967, "Girls on the Go-Go"; Peter and Gordon pin-up 10.00
❑Annual 1, ca. 1963 55.00

PATTY CAKE
PERMANENT PRESS

❑1, b&w 3.00
❑2, b&w 3.00
❑3, ca. 1995, b&w 3.00
❑4, ca. 1995, b&w 3.00
❑5, ca. 1996, b&w 3.00
❑6, ca. 1996, b&w 3.00
❑7, ca. 1996, b&w 3.00
❑8, ca. 1996, b&w 3.00
❑9, ca. 1996, b&w 3.00

PATTY CAKE (2ND SERIES)
CALIBER / TAPESTRY

❑1, ca. 1996, b&w 3.00
❑2, ca. 1997, b&w 3.00
❑3, ca. 1997, b&w 3.00
❑Holiday 1, Dec 1996, b&w 3.00

PATTY CAKE & FRIENDS
SLAVE LABOR

❑1, Nov 1997, b&w 3.00
❑2, Dec 1997, b&w 3.00
❑3, Jan 1998, b&w 3.00
❑4, Feb 1998, b&w 3.00
❑5, Mar 1998, b&w 3.00
❑6, Apr 1998, b&w 3.00
❑7, May 1998 2.95
❑8, Jun 1998 2.95
❑9, Aug 1998 2.95
❑10, Sep 1998 2.95
❑11, Nov 1998 2.95
❑12 2.95
❑Special 1, Oct 1997 3.95

PATTY CAKE & FRIENDS (VOL. 2)
SLAVE LABOR

❑1, Nov 2000, b&w; cardstock cover 4.95
❑2 4.95
❑3 4.95
❑4 4.95
❑5 4.95
❑6 4.95
❑7 4.95
❑8 4.95
❑9 4.95
❑10 4.95
❑11 4.95
❑12 4.95
❑13 2005 4.95
❑15, Jan 2006

PAUL THE SAMURAI
NEW ENGLAND

❑1, Jul 1992 4.00
❑2, Sep 1992 3.00
❑3, Nov 1992; Scarcer 6.00
❑4, Jan 1993 4.00
❑5, Mar 1993 2.75
❑6, May 1993 2.75
❑7, Jul 1993 2.75
❑8, Nov 1993 2.75
❑9, Mar 1994 A: The Tick 2.75
❑10, May 1994 A: The Tick 2.75

PAUL THE SAMURAI (MINI-SERIES)
NEC

❑1 A: The Tick 3.50
❑2 3.00
❑3 3.00

PAYNE
DREAM CATCHER

❑1, Sep 1995, b&w 2.50

PEACEMAKER
CHARLTON

❑1, Mar 1967 10.00
❑2, May 1967, Fightin' 5 back-up story 6.00
❑3, Jul 1967 6.00
❑4, Sep 1967, O: The Peacemaker 8.00
❑5, Nov 1967 6.00

PEACEMAKER (MINI-SERIES)
DC

❑1, Jan 1988 1.50
❑2, Feb 1988 1.50
❑3, Mar 1988 1.50
❑4, Apr 1988 1.50

PEACE PARTY
BLUE CORN

❑1 2.95

PEACE POSSE
MELLON BANK

❑1 2.95

PEANUT BUTTER AND JEREMY
ALTERNATIVE

❑1, Aug 2000, b&w 2.95
❑2 2001, b&w 2.95
❑3 2002, b&w 2.95
❑4/FCBD, May 2003, b&w 2.00

PEANUTS (DELL)
DELL

❑1, ca. 1954 125.00
❑4, Feb 1960 75.00
❑5, May 1960 55.00
❑6, Aug 1960 55.00
❑7, Nov 1960 55.00
❑8, Feb 1961 55.00
❑9, May 1961 55.00
❑10, Aug 1961 55.00
❑11, Nov 1961 55.00
❑12, Feb 1962 55.00
❑13, May 1962 55.00

PEANUTS (GOLD KEY)
GOLD KEY

❑1, May 1963 125.00
❑2, Aug 1963 75.00
❑3, Nov 1963 75.00
❑4, Feb 1964 75.00

PEBBLES AND BAMM-BAMM
CHARLTON

❑1, Jan 1972 18.00
❑2, Mar 1972 12.00
❑3, May 1972 9.00
❑4, Jul 1972 9.00
❑5, Aug 1972 9.00
❑6, Sep 1972 7.00
❑7, Oct 1972, No credits in issue 7.00
❑8, Nov 1972 7.00
❑9 7.00
❑10, ca. 1973 7.00
❑11, ca. 1973 5.00
❑12, ca. 1973 5.00
❑13, ca. 1973 5.00
❑14, ca. 1973 5.00
❑15, Aug 1973 5.00
❑16, Oct 1973 5.00
❑17, Nov 1973 5.00
❑18, Jan 1974 5.00
❑19, Feb 1974 5.00
❑20, Jun 1974 5.00

Other grades: Multiply price above by 5/6 for VF/NM • 2/3 for VERY FINE • 1/3 for FINE • 1/5 for VERY GOOD • 1/8 for GOOD

❑21, Aug 1974 — 4.00
❑22, Nov 1974 — 4.00
❑23, Jan 1975 — 4.00
❑24, Feb 1975 — 4.00
❑25, Mar 1975 — 4.00
❑26, ca. 1975 — 4.00
❑27, ca. 1975 — 4.00
❑28, ca. 1975 — 4.00
❑29, ca. 1975 — 4.00
❑30, Dec 1975 — 4.00
❑31, Feb 1976 — 3.00
❑32, Apr 1976 — 3.00
❑33, Jun 1976 — 3.00
❑34, Aug 1976, No credits listed — 3.00
❑35, Oct 1976 — 3.00
❑36, Dec 1976, No credits listed — 3.00

PEBBLES & BAMM-BAMM (HARVEY)
HARVEY

❑1, Nov 1993 — 1.50
❑2, Jan 1994 — 1.50
❑3, Mar 1994 — 1.50
❑Summer 1; first edition — 2.25

PEBBLES FLINTSTONE
GOLD KEY

❑1, Sep 1963 — 75.00

PEDESTRIAN VULGARITY
FANTAGRAPHICS

❑1, b&w — 2.50

PEEK-A-BOO 3-D
3-D ZONE

❑1 — 3.95

PEEPSHOW
DRAWN & QUARTERLY

❑1 — 2.50
❑2, May 1992 — 2.50
❑3 — 2.50
❑4 — 2.50
❑5, Oct 1993 — 2.95
❑6, Apr 1994 — 2.95
❑7 — 2.95
❑8 — 2.95
❑9 — 2.95

PEEP SHOW (KITCHEN SINK)
KITCHEN SINK

❑Book 1, b&w — 10.95

PELLESTAR
ETERNITY

❑1, Sep 1987 — 1.95
❑2 — 1.95

PENDRAGON (AIRCEL)
AIRCEL

❑1, Nov 1991, b&w — 2.95
❑2, Dec 1991, b&w — 2.95

PENDULUM
ADVENTURE

❑1, b&w — 2.50
❑2, b&w — 2.50
❑3, b&w — 2.50
❑4, b&w — 2.50

PENDULUM'S ILLUSTRATED STORIES
PENDULUM

❑1, Moby Dick; No apparent cover price — 4.95
❑2, Treasure Island — 4.95
❑3, Doctor Jekyll — 4.95
❑4, 20, 000 Leagues Under the Sea — 4.95
❑5, Midsummer Night's Dream — 4.95
❑6, Christmas Carol — 4.95

PENG ONE SHOT
ONI

❑1, Sep 2005 — 2.95

PENGUIN & PENCILGUIN
FRAGMENTS WEST

❑1, Jan 1987 — 2.00
❑2, Feb 1987 — 2.00
❑3, Mar 1987 — 2.00
❑4, Apr 1987 — 2.00
❑5, May 1987 — 2.00
❑6, Jun 1987 — 2.00

PENGUIN BROS.
LABYRINTH

❑1 — 2.50
❑2 — 2.50

PENNY & AGGIE
ALIAS

❑1, Jul 2005 — 2.99
❑2, Aug 2005 — 2.99
❑3, Sep 2005 — 2.99

PENNY ARCADE: 1X 25 CENTS
DARK HORSE

❑1, Nov 2005 — 0.25

PENNY CENTURY
FANTAGRAPHICS

❑1, Dec 1997, b&w — 2.95
❑2, Mar 1998, b&w — 2.95
❑3, Sep 1998, b&w — 2.95
❑4, Jan 1999, b&w — 2.95
❑5, Jun 1999, b&w — 2.95
❑6, Nov 1999, b&w — 2.95
❑7, Jul 2000, b&w — 2.95

PENTACLE: THE SIGN OF THE FIVE
ETERNITY

❑1, Feb 1991 — 2.25
❑2 1991 — 2.25
❑3 1991 — 2.25
❑4 1991 — 2.25

PENTHOUSE COMIX
PENTHOUSE INTERNATIONAL

❑1, Jun 1994 — 6.00
❑1/2nd, ca. 1995; subtitled Special Edition 1995 — 4.95
❑2, Jul 1994 — 4.95
❑3, Sep 1994 — 4.95
❑4, Nov 1994 — 4.95
❑5, Jan 1995 — 4.95
❑6, Mar 1995; Comic size — 4.95
❑6/A, Mar 1995; Magazine size — 4.95
❑7, May 1995; Comic size — 4.95
❑7/A, May 1995; Magazine size — 4.95
❑8, Jul 1995 — 4.95
❑9, Sep 1995 — 4.95
❑10, Nov 1995 — 4.95
❑11, Jan 1996 — 4.95
❑12, Mar 1996; second anniversary issue — 4.95
❑13, May 1996 — 4.95
❑14, Jul 1996 — 4.95
❑15, Sep 1996 — 4.95
❑16, Oct 1996 — 4.95
❑17, Nov 1996; reprints Manara's Hidden Camera — 4.95
❑18, Dec 1996 — 4.95
❑19, Jan 1997 — 4.95
❑20, Feb 1997 — 4.95
❑21, Apr 1997 — 4.95
❑22, May 1997 — 4.95
❑23, Jun 1997 — 4.95
❑24, Jul 1997 — 4.95
❑25, Sep 1997; Sweet Chastity reprints begin; pin-ups of Chastity by various artists — 4.95
❑26, Oct 1997 — 4.95
❑27, Nov 1997 — 4.95
❑28, Jan 1998 — 4.95
❑29, Feb 1998 — 4.95
❑30, Apr 1998 — 4.95
❑31, May 1998 — 4.95
❑32, Jun 1998 — 4.95
❑33, Jul 1998 — 4.95

PENTHOUSE MAX
PENTHOUSE INTERNATIONAL

❑1, Jul 1996 — 4.95
❑2, Nov 1996 — 4.95
❑3, Spr 1997 — 4.95

PENTHOUSE MEN'S ADVENTURE COMIX
PENTHOUSE

❑1, Apr 1995 — 4.95
❑2, Jun 1995 — 4.95
❑3, Aug 1995 — 4.95
❑4, Oct 1995 — 4.95
❑5, Dec 1995 — 4.95
❑6, Feb 1996 — 4.95
❑7, Apr 1996 — 4.95

PEOPLE ARE PHONY
SIEGEL AND SIMON

❑1 — 4.00

PEOPLE'S COMICS
GOLDEN GATE

❑1, Sep 1972 — 4.00

PEP
ARCHIE

❑118, Nov 1956 — 28.00
❑119, Jan 1957 — 28.00
❑120, Mar 1957 — 28.00
❑121, May 1957 — 23.00
❑122, Jul 1957 — 23.00
❑123, Sep 1957 — 23.00
❑124, Nov 1957 — 23.00
❑125, Jan 1958 — 23.00
❑126, Mar 1958 — 23.00
❑127, May 1958 — 23.00
❑128, Jul 1958 — 23.00
❑129, Sep 1958 — 23.00
❑130, Nov 1958 — 23.00
❑131, Feb 1959 — 19.00
❑132, Apr 1959 — 19.00
❑133, Jun 1959 — 19.00
❑134, Aug 1959 — 19.00
❑135, Oct 1959 — 19.00
❑136, Dec 1959 — 19.00
❑137, ca. 1960 — 19.00
❑138, ca. 1960 — 19.00
❑139, ca. 1960 — 19.00
❑140, ca. 1960 — 19.00
❑141, ca. 1960 — 15.00
❑142, ca. 1960 — 15.00
❑143, ca. 1960 — 15.00
❑144, Jan 1961 — 15.00
❑145, Mar 1961 — 15.00
❑146, May 1961 — 15.00
❑147, Jun 1961 — 15.00
❑148, Aug 1961 — 15.00
❑149, Sep 1961 — 15.00
❑150, Oct 1961 A: Jaguar — 15.00
❑151, ca. 1961 A: The Fly — 15.00
❑152, Jan 1962, A: Jaguar — 15.00
❑153, Mar 1962, A: Fly Girl — 15.00
❑154, May 1962, A: The Fly — 15.00
❑155, Jun 1962, A: Fly Girl — 15.00
❑156, Aug 1962, A: Fly Girl — 15.00
❑157, Sep 1962, 1: Kree-Nal. A: Jaguar — 15.00
❑158, Oct 1962, A: Fly Girl — 15.00
❑159, ca. 1962, A: Jaguar — 15.00
❑160, Jan 1963, A: The Fly — 15.00
❑161, Mar 1963 — 7.00
❑162, May 1963 — 7.00
❑163, Jun 1963 — 7.00
❑164, Aug 1963 — 7.00
❑165, Sep 1963 — 7.00
❑166, Oct 1963 — 7.00
❑167, ca. 1963 — 7.00
❑168, Jan 1964 — 7.00
❑169, Mar 1964 — 7.00
❑170, May 1964 — 7.00
❑171, Jun 1964 — 7.00
❑172, Aug 1964 — 7.00
❑173, Sep 1964 — 7.00
❑174, Oct 1964 — 7.00
❑175, Nov 1964 — 7.00
❑176, Dec 1964 — 7.00
❑177, Jan 1965 — 7.00
❑178, Feb 1965 — 6.00
❑179, Mar 1965 — 6.00
❑180, Apr 1965 — 6.00
❑181, May 1965 — 6.00
❑182, Jun 1965 — 6.00
❑183, Jul 1965 — 6.00
❑184, Aug 1965 — 6.00
❑185, Sep 1965 — 6.00
❑186, Oct 1965 — 6.00
❑187, Nov 1965 — 6.00
❑188, Dec 1965 — 6.00
❑189, Jan 1966 — 6.00
❑190, Feb 1966 — 6.00
❑191, Mar 1966 — 6.00
❑192, Apr 1966 — 6.00
❑193, May 1966 — 6.00
❑194, Jun 1966 — 6.00
❑195, Jul 1966 — 6.00
❑196, Aug 1966 — 6.00
❑197, Sep 1966 — 6.00
❑198, Oct 1966 — 6.00

Phantom (1st Series)

Ghost Who Walks' longest-running series

©Gold Key

Phantom Jack

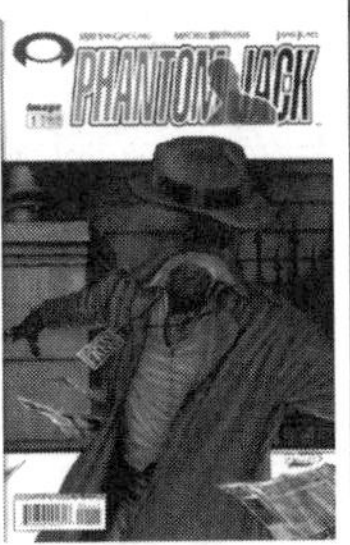

Pitched Epic series lands at Image

©Image

Phantom of Fear City

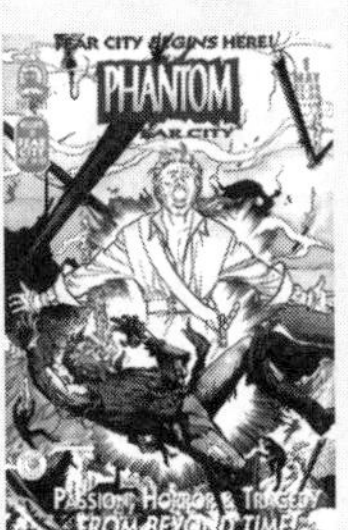

Fear City foundations established here

©Claypool

Phantom Stranger (2nd Series)

Angelic agent tussles with Dr. 13

©DC

Phantom Zone

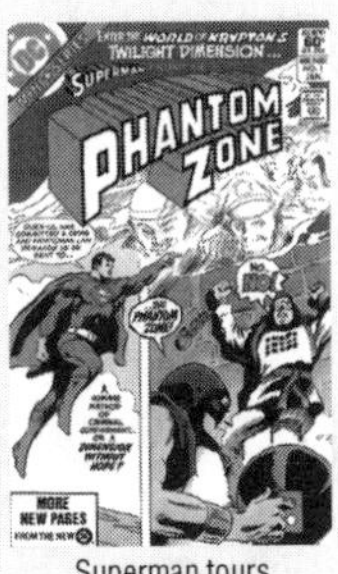

Superman tours spectral realm

©DC

	N-MINT
❑199, Nov 1966	6.00
❑200, Dec 1966	6.00
❑201, Jan 1967	5.00
❑202, Feb 1967	5.00
❑203, Mar 1967	5.00
❑204, Apr 1967	5.00
❑205, May 1967	5.00
❑206, Jun 1967	5.00
❑207, Jul 1967	5.00
❑208, Aug 1967	5.00
❑209, Sep 1967	5.00
❑210, Oct 1967	5.00
❑211, Nov 1967	5.00
❑212, Dec 1967	5.00
❑213, Jan 1968	5.00
❑214, Feb 1968	5.00
❑215, Mar 1968	5.00
❑216, Apr 1968	5.00
❑217, May 1968	5.00
❑218, Jun 1968	5.00
❑219, Jul 1968	5.00
❑220, Aug 1968	5.00
❑221, Sep 1968	4.00
❑222, Oct 1968	4.00
❑223, Nov 1968	4.00
❑224, Dec 1968	4.00
❑225, Jan 1969	4.00
❑226, Feb 1969	4.00
❑227, Mar 1969	4.00
❑228, Apr 1969	4.00
❑229, May 1969	4.00
❑230, Jun 1969	4.00
❑231, Jul 1969	4.00
❑232, Aug 1969	3.50
❑233, Sep 1969	3.50
❑234, Oct 1969	3.50
❑235, Nov 1969	3.50
❑236, Dec 1969	3.50
❑237, Jan 1970	3.50
❑238, Feb 1970	3.50
❑239, Mar 1970	3.50
❑240, Apr 1970	3.50
❑241, May 1970	3.50
❑242, Jun 1970	3.50
❑243, Jul 1970	3.50
❑244, Aug 1970	3.50
❑245, Sep 1970	3.50
❑246, Oct 1970	3.50
❑247, Nov 1970	3.50
❑248, Dec 1970	3.50
❑249, Jan 1971	3.50
❑250, Feb 1971	3.50
❑251, Mar 1971	1.75
❑252, Apr 1971	1.75
❑253, May 1971	1.75
❑254, Jun 1971	1.75
❑255, Jul 1971	1.75
❑256, Aug 1971	1.75
❑257, Sep 1971	1.75
❑258, Oct 1971	1.75
❑259, Nov 1971	1.75
❑260, Dec 1971	1.75
❑261, Jan 1972	1.75
❑262, Feb 1972	1.75

	N-MINT
❑263, Mar 1972	1.75
❑264, Apr 1972	1.75
❑265, May 1972	1.75
❑266, Jun 1972	1.75
❑267, Jul 1972	1.75
❑268, Aug 1972	1.75
❑269, Sep 1972	1.75
❑270, Oct 1972	1.75
❑271, Nov 1972	1.75
❑272, Dec 1972	1.75
❑273, Jan 1973	1.75
❑274, Feb 1973	1.75
❑275, Mar 1973	1.75
❑276, Apr 1973	1.75
❑277, May 1973	1.75
❑278, Jun 1973	1.75
❑279, Jul 1973	1.75
❑280, Aug 1973	1.75
❑281, Sep 1973	1.50
❑282, Oct 1973	1.50
❑283, Nov 1973	1.50
❑284, Dec 1973	1.50
❑285, Jan 1974	1.50
❑286, Feb 1974	1.50
❑287, Mar 1974	1.50
❑288, Apr 1974	1.50
❑289, May 1974	1.50
❑290, Jun 1974	1.50
❑291, Jul 1974	1.50
❑292, Aug 1974	1.50
❑293, Sep 1974	1.50
❑294, Oct 1974	1.50
❑295, Nov 1974	1.50
❑296, Dec 1974	1.50
❑297, Jan 1975	1.50
❑298, Feb 1975	1.50
❑299, Mar 1975	1.50
❑300, Apr 1975	1.50
❑301, May 1975	1.25
❑302, Jun 1975	1.25
❑303, Jul 1975	1.25
❑304, Aug 1975	1.25
❑305, Sep 1975	1.25
❑306, Oct 1975	1.25
❑307, Nov 1975	1.25
❑308, Dec 1975	1.25
❑309, Jan 1976	1.25
❑310, Feb 1976	1.25
❑311, Mar 1976	1.25
❑312, Apr 1976	1.25
❑313, May 1976	1.25
❑314, Jun 1976	1.25
❑315, Jul 1976	1.25
❑316, Aug 1976	1.25
❑317, Sep 1976	1.25
❑318, Oct 1976	1.25
❑319, Nov 1976	1.25
❑320, Dec 1976	1.25
❑321, Jan 1977	1.25
❑322, Feb 1977	1.25
❑323, Mar 1977	1.25
❑324, Apr 1977	1.25
❑325, May 1977	1.25
❑326, Jun 1977	1.25

	N-MINT
❑327, Jul 1977	1.25
❑328, Aug 1977	1.25
❑329, Sep 1977	1.25
❑330, Oct 1977	1.25
❑331, Nov 1977	1.25
❑332, Dec 1977	1.25
❑333, Jan 1978	1.25
❑334, Feb 1978	1.25
❑335, Mar 1978	1.25
❑336, Apr 1978	1.25
❑337, May 1978	1.25
❑338, Jun 1978	1.25
❑339, Jul 1978	1.25
❑340, Aug 1978	1.25
❑341, Sep 1978	1.25
❑342, Oct 1978	1.25
❑343, Nov 1978	1.25
❑344, Dec 1978	1.25
❑345, Jan 1979	1.25
❑346, Feb 1979	1.25
❑347, Mar 1979	1.25
❑348, Apr 1979	1.25
❑349, May 1979	1.25
❑350, Jun 1979	1.25
❑351, Jul 1979	1.25
❑352, Aug 1979	1.25
❑353, Sep 1979	1.25
❑354, Oct 1979	1.25
❑355, Nov 1979	1.25
❑356, Dec 1979	1.25
❑357, Jan 1980	1.25
❑358, Feb 1980	1.25
❑359, Mar 1980	1.25
❑360, Apr 1980	1.25
❑361, May 1980	1.25
❑362, Jun 1980	1.25
❑363, Jul 1980	1.25
❑364, Aug 1980	1.25
❑365, ca. 1980	1.25
❑366, ca. 1980	1.25
❑367, ca. 1980	1.25
❑368	1.25
❑369, ca. 1981	1.25
❑370, ca. 1981	1.25
❑371, ca. 1981	1.00
❑372, ca. 1981	1.00
❑373, ca. 1981	1.00
❑374, ca. 1981	1.00
❑375, ca. 1981	1.00
❑376, ca. 1981	1.00
❑377, ca. 1981	1.00
❑378, ca. 1981	1.00
❑379, ca. 1981	1.00
❑380	1.00
❑381, ca. 1982	1.00
❑382, ca. 1982	1.00
❑383, Apr 1982	1.00
❑384	1.00
❑385	1.00
❑386	1.00
❑387	1.00
❑388	1.00
❑389, ca. 1983	1.00
❑390, ca. 1983	1.00

Other grades: Multiply price above by 5/6 for VF/NM • 2/3 for VERY FINE • 1/3 for FINE • 1/5 for VERY GOOD • 1/8 for GOOD

	N-MINT
❑391, Nov 1983	1.00
❑392, Jan 1984	1.00
❑393, Mar 1984	1.00
❑394, May 1984	1.00
❑395, Jul 1984	1.00
❑396, Sep 1984	1.00
❑397, Nov 1984	1.00
❑398, Jan 1985	1.00
❑399, Mar 1985	1.00
❑400, May 1985	1.00
❑401, Jul 1985	1.00
❑402, Sep 1985	1.00
❑403, Nov 1985	1.00
❑404, Jan 1986	1.00
❑405, Mar 1986	1.00
❑406, May 1986	1.00
❑407, Jul 1986	1.00
❑408, Sep 1986	1.00
❑409, Nov 1986	1.00
❑410, Jan 1987	1.00
❑411, Mar 1987	1.00

PERAZIM
ANTARCTIC

❑1, Sep 1996, b&w ... 2.95
❑2 ... 2.95
❑3 ... 2.95

PERCEVAN: THE THREE STARS OF INGAAR
FANTASY FLIGHT

❑1 ... 8.95

PEREGRINE
ALLIANCE

❑1, Apr 1994, b&w ... 2.50
❑2, Aug 1994, b&w ... 2.50

PERG
LIGHTNING

❑1, Oct 1993, Glow-in the dark flip book ... 3.50
❑1/Gold, Oct 1993, Gold edition ... 3.50
❑1/Platinum, Oct 1993, Platinum edition ... 2.50
❑1/Variant, Oct 1993, glow cover ... 3.50
❑2, Nov 1993 ... 2.50
❑2/Platinum, Nov 1993, Platinum edition ... 2.50
❑3, Dec 1993 ... 2.50
❑3/Platinum, Dec 1993, Platinum edition ... 2.50
❑4, Jan 1994 ... 2.50
❑4/Platinum, Jan 1994, Platinum edition; platinum ... 2.50
❑5, Feb 1994 ... 2.50
❑6, Mar 1994 ... 2.50
❑7, Apr 1994 ... 2.50
❑8, May 1994 ... 2.50

PERHAPANAUTS
DARK HORSE

❑1, Nov 2005 ... 2.95
❑2, Dec 2005 ... 2.95
❑3, Jan 2006 ... 2.95
❑4, Apr 2006 ... 2.95

PERIPHERY
ARCH-TYPE

❑1 ... 2.95

PERRAMUS: ESCAPE FROM THE PAST
FANTAGRAPHICS

❑1, b&w ... 3.50
❑2, b&w ... 3.50
❑3, b&w ... 3.50
❑4, b&w ... 3.50

PERRY
LIGHTNING

❑1, Oct 1997 ... 2.95

PERRY MASON
DELL

❑1, Jun 1964 ... 40.00
❑2, Oct 1964 ... 40.00

PERSONALITY CLASSICS
PERSONALITY

❑1; John Wayne ... 2.95
❑2; Marilyn Monroe ... 2.95
❑3 ... 2.95
❑4 ... 2.95

PERSONALITY COMICS PRESENTS
PERSONALITY

❑1 1991; Paulina Porizkova ... 2.50
❑2, Apr 1991; Traci Lords ... 2.50
❑3 1991; Arnold Schwarzenegger ... 2.50
❑4 1991; Christina Applegate ... 2.50
❑5 1991; Patrick Swayze, Demi Moore ... 2.95
❑6 1991; Michael Jordan ... 2.95
❑7; Samantha Fox ... 2.95
❑8; Bettie Page, Jennifer Connelly ... 2.95
❑9; Kim Basinger, Michael Keaton ... 2.95
❑10; Gloria Estefan ... 2.95
❑11 ... 2.95
❑12 ... 2.95
❑13 ... 2.95
❑14 ... 2.95
❑15 ... 2.95
❑16 ... 2.95
❑17 ... 2.95
❑18 ... 2.95

PEST
PEST COMICS

❑1 ... 1.95
❑2 ... 1.95
❑3 ... 1.95
❑4 ... 1.95
❑5 ... 1.95
❑6, b&w ... 1.95
❑7 ... 1.95

PET
FANTAGRAPHICS / EROS

❑1, May 1997 ... 2.95

PETER CANNON-THUNDERBOLT
DC

❑1, Sep 1992 ... 1.50
❑2, Oct 1992 ... 1.50
❑3, Nov 1992 ... 1.50
❑4, Dec 1992 ... 1.25
❑5, Jan 1993 ... 1.25
❑6, Feb 1993 ... 1.25
❑7, Mar 1993 ... 1.25
❑8, Apr 1993 ... 1.25
❑9, May 1993 ... 1.25
❑10, May 1993 ... 1.25
❑11, Jul 1993 ... 1.25
❑12, Aug 1993 ... 1.25

PETER KOCK
FANTAGRAPHICS / EROS

❑1 1994, b&w ... 3.50
❑2 1994, b&w ... 2.75
❑3 1994, b&w ... 2.75
❑4, May 1994, b&w ... 2.75
❑5, Jul 1994, b&w ... 2.75
❑6, Aug 1994, b&w ... 2.75

PETER PAN (GOLD KEY)
GOLD KEY

❑1, Sep 1969, 10086-909 ... 20.00
❑2 ... 12.00

PETER PAN (TUNDRA)
TUNDRA

❑1 ... 14.95
❑2 ... 14.95

PETER PAN (WALT DISNEY'S...)
DISNEY

❑1, prestige format; Reprints ... 5.95

PETER PAN AND THE WARLORDS OF OZ
HAND OF DOOM

❑1 ... 2.95

PETER PAN & THE WARLORDS OF OZ: DEAD HEAD WATER
HAND OF DOOM

❑1 ... 2.95

PETER PAN: RETURN TO NEVER-NEVER LAND
ADVENTURE

❑1 ... 2.50
❑2 ... 2.50

PETER PARKER: SPIDER-MAN
MARVEL

❑1, Jan 1999; JR2 (a); V: Scorpion. wraparound cover ... 5.00
❑1/Sunburst, Jan 1999; JR2 (a); sunburst variant cover ... 6.00
❑1/Autographed, Jan 1999 JR2 (a) ... 10.00
❑1/Dynamic, Jan 1999; JR2 (a); DFE alternate cover ... 14.00
❑2/A, Feb 1999; JR2 (a); A: Tocketts. A: Thor. Cover A ... 2.00
❑2/B, Feb 1999; JR2 (a); A: Tocketts. A: Thor. Cover B by Arthur Suydam ... 2.00
❑3, Mar 1999; JR2 (a); A: Shadrac. A: Iceman. A: Mary Jane. V: Shadrac. Continued from Amazing Spider-Man #3 ... 4.00
❑4, Apr 1999 JR2 (a); A: Marrow ... 4.00
❑5, May 1999 A: Black Cat. V: Spider-Woman ... 4.00
❑6, Jun 1999 V: Kingpin. V: Bullseye ... 4.00
❑7, Jul 1999 A: Blade ... 4.00
❑8, Aug 1999 A: Kingpin. A: Blade. A: Morbius ... 4.00
❑9, Sep 1999 V: Venom ... 4.00
❑10, Oct 1999 V: Venom ... 4.00
❑11, Nov 1999; continues in Juggernaut #1 ... 4.00
❑12, Dec 1999 ... 4.00
❑13, Jan 2000 ... 4.00
❑14, Feb 2000 ... 4.00
❑15, Mar 2000 ... 4.00
❑16, Apr 2000 ... 4.00
❑17, May 2000 ... 4.00
❑18, Jun 2000 ... 4.00
❑19, Jul 2000 ... 4.00
❑20, Aug 2000 ... 4.00
❑21, Sep 2000 ... 4.00
❑25/Variant, Sep 2000 ... 6.00
❑22, Oct 2000 ... 4.00
❑23, Nov 2000 ... 4.00
❑24, Dec 2000 ... 4.00
❑25, Jan 2001 ... 4.00
❑26, Feb 2001 ... 4.00
❑27, Mar 2001 A: Mendel Stromm ... 4.00
❑28, Apr 2001 A: Mendel Stromm ... 4.00
❑29, May 2001; continues in Amazing Spider-Man Annual 2001 ... 4.00
❑30, Jun 2001 ... 3.00
❑31, Jul 2001 ... 3.00
❑32, Aug 2001 ... 3.00
❑33, Sep 2001 ... 3.00
❑34, Oct 2001 ... 3.00
❑35, Nov 2001 ... 3.00
❑36, Dec 2001 ... 3.00
❑37, Jan 2002 ... 3.00
❑38, Feb 2002 ... 3.00
❑39, Mar 2002 ... 3.00
❑40, Apr 2002 ... 3.00
❑41, May 2002 ... 3.00
❑42, Jun 2002 ... 3.00
❑43, Jun 2002 ... 3.00
❑44, Jul 2002 ... 3.00
❑45, Aug 2002 ... 3.00
❑46, Sep 2002 ... 3.00
❑47, Oct 2002 ... 3.00
❑48, Nov 2002 ... 3.00
❑49, Dec 2002 ... 3.00
❑50, Jan 2003 ... 3.00
❑51, Feb 2003 ... 3.00
❑52, Mar 2003 ... 3.00
❑53, Apr 2003 ... 3.00
❑54, May 2003 ... 3.00
❑55, Jun 2003 ... 3.00
❑56, Jul 2003 A: Sandman (Marvel) ... 3.00
❑57, Aug 2003 ... 3.00
❑Annual 1998, ca. 1998; gatefold summary; Peter Parker: Spider-Man/Elektra '98 ... 4.00
❑Annual 1999, Aug 1999 A: Man-Thing ... 3.50

PETER PORKER, THE SPECTACULAR SPIDER-HAM
MARVEL / STAR

❑1, May 1985, 1: Spider-Ham. 1: J. Jonah Jackal. 1: Peter Porker. 1: Duck Doom ... 1.00
❑2, Jul 1985 ... 1.00
❑3, Sep 1985 ... 1.00
❑4, Nov 1985 ... 1.00
❑5, Jan 1986 ... 1.00
❑6, Mar 1986 ... 1.00
❑7, May 1986 ... 1.00
❑8, Jul 1986 ... 1.00
❑9, Aug 1986 ... 1.00
❑10, Sep 1986 ... 1.00

Other grades: Multiply price above by 5/6 for VF/NM • 2/3 for VERY FINE • 1/3 for FINE • 1/5 for VERY GOOD • 1/8 for GOOD

Pink Panther (Gold Key)

Comics discarded main character's silence

©Gold Key

Pinky and the Brain

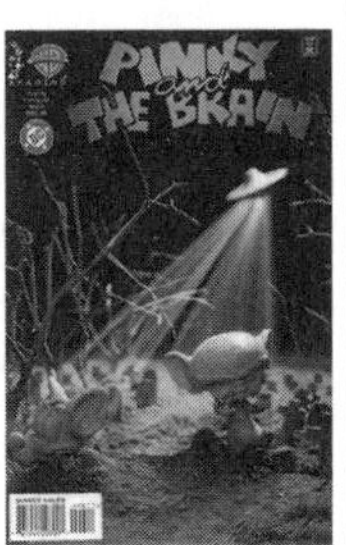

World domination plans derailed by dimwit

©DC

Pirates of Dark Water

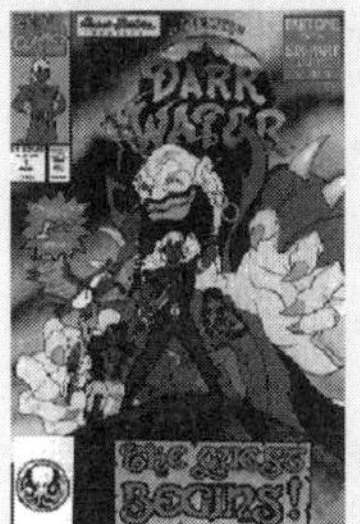

Adapts animated adventures on far-off world

©Marvel

Pitt

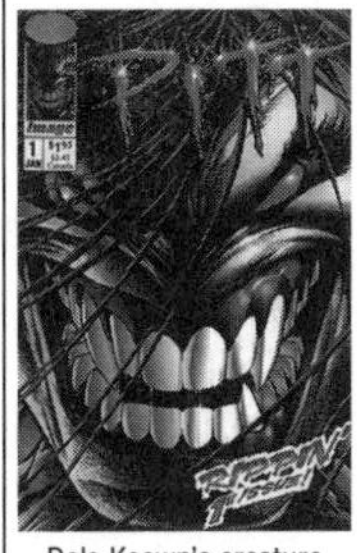

Dale Keown's creature seeks Earthly asylum

©Image

Planetary

Pulp, pop culture references abound

©DC

N-MINT

❑11, Oct 1986 .... 1.00
❑12, Nov 1986 .... 1.00
❑13, Jan 1987 .... 1.00
❑14, Mar 1987 .... 1.00
❑15, May 1987 .... 1.00
❑16, Jul 1987 .... 1.00
❑17, Sep 1987 .... 1.00

PETER RABBIT 3-D
ETERNITY

❑1; Reprints from Peter Rabbit (Avon) stories 2.95

PETER THE LITTLE PEST
MARVEL

❑1, Nov 1969, 1: Peter, The Little Pest. 1: Little Pixie 75.00
❑2, Jan 1970 .... 50.00
❑3, Mar 1970 .... 50.00
❑4, May 1970, titled Petey 50.00

PETE THE P.O.'D POSTAL WORKER
SHARKBAIT

❑1, Oct 1997 .... 3.50
❑2, Jan 1998 .... 3.00
❑3, Mar 1998 .... 3.00
❑4, Jun 1998 .... 3.00
❑5, Aug 1998; in England 3.00
❑6, Oct 1998 .... 2.95
❑7, Jan 1999 V: Teddy Cougar 2.95
❑8, Apr 1999 V: Teddy Cougar 2.95
❑9, Jun 1999; on Jerry Ringer Show 2.95
❑10, Aug 1999 V: Y2K 2.95

PETTICOAT JUNCTION
DELL

❑1, Oct 1964 .... 40.00
❑2, Jan 1965 .... 30.00
❑3, Apr 1965 .... 30.00
❑4, Jul 1965 .... 25.00
❑5, Oct 1965 .... 30.00

PETWORKS VS. WILDK.A.T.S.
PARODY

❑1 .... 2.50

PHAEDRA
EXPRESS / ENTITY

❑1, Sep 1994, b&w; cardstock cover; third in series of Entity illustrated novellas with Zen Intergalactic Ninja 2.95

PHAGE: SHADOWDEATH (NEIL GAIMAN'S...)
BIG

❑1, Jun 1996 .... 2.25
❑2, Aug 1996 .... 2.25
❑3, Sep 1996 .... 2.25
❑4, Sep 1996 .... 2.25
❑5, Oct 1996 .... 2.25
❑6, Nov 1996 .... 2.25

PHANTACEA: PHASE ONE
MCPHERSON

❑1 .... 5.00

PHANTASMAGORIA
TOME

❑1, b&w 2.50

PHANTASY AGAINST HUNGER
TIGER

❑1 BSz, JO, GC, BA, JR (a) 2.00

N-MINT

PHANTOM (1ST SERIES)
GOLD KEY

❑1, Nov 1962, Gold Key publishes 90.00
❑2, Feb 1963 .... 55.00
❑3, May 1963 .... 36.00
❑4, Aug 1963 .... 36.00
❑5, Nov 1963 .... 36.00
❑6, Feb 1964 .... 36.00
❑7, May 1964 .... 36.00
❑8, Aug 1964 .... 36.00
❑9, Nov 1964 .... 36.00
❑10, Feb 1965 .... 36.00
❑11, Apr 1965 .... 28.00
❑12, Jun 1965 .... 28.00
❑13, Aug 1965 .... 28.00
❑14, Oct 1965 .... 28.00
❑15, Dec 1965 .... 28.00
❑16, Apr 1966 .... 28.00
❑17, Jul 1966 .... 28.00
❑18, Sep 1966, King Features Syndicate begins publishing 32.00
❑19, Nov 1966 .... 24.00
❑20, Jan 1967 .... 24.00
❑21, Mar 1967 .... 24.00
❑22, May 1967 .... 24.00
❑23, Jul 1967 .... 24.00
❑24, Aug 1967 .... 24.00
❑25, Sep 1967 .... 24.00
❑26, Oct 1967 .... 24.00
❑27, Nov 1967 .... 24.00
❑28, Dec 1967 .... 24.00
❑30, Feb 1969, Charlton begins publishing (no issue #29) 15.00
❑31, Apr 1969 .... 15.00
❑32, Jun 1969 .... 15.00
❑33, Aug 1969 .... 15.00
❑34, Oct 1969 .... 15.00
❑35, Dec 1969 .... 15.00
❑36, Feb 1970 .... 15.00
❑37, Apr 1970 .... 15.00
❑38, Jun 1970 .... 15.00
❑39, Aug 1970 .... 15.00
❑40, Oct 1970 .... 15.00
❑41, Dec 1970 .... 12.00
❑42, Feb 1971 .... 12.00
❑43, Apr 1971 .... 12.00
❑44, Jun 1971 .... 12.00
❑45, Aug 1971 .... 12.00
❑46, Oct 1971, 1: Piranha 12.00
❑47, Dec 1971 .... 12.00
❑48, Feb 1972 .... 12.00
❑49, Apr 1972 .... 12.00
❑50, Jun 1972 .... 12.00
❑51, Aug 1972 .... 12.00
❑52, Oct 1972 .... 12.00
❑53, Nov 1972 .... 12.00
❑54, Feb 1973 .... 12.00
❑55, Apr 1973 .... 12.00
❑56, Jun 1973 .... 12.00
❑57, ca. 1973 .... 12.00
❑58, Oct 1973 .... 12.00
❑59, Dec 1973 .... 12.00
❑60, Jun 1974 .... 9.00
❑61, Aug 1974 .... 9.00

N-MINT

❑62, Nov 1974 .... 9.00
❑63, Jan 1975 .... 9.00
❑64, Mar 1975 .... 9.00
❑65, Jun 1975 .... 9.00
❑66, Aug 1975 .... 9.00
❑67, Oct 1975 .... 9.00
❑68, Dec 1975 .... 9.00
❑69, Feb 1976 .... 9.00
❑70, Apr 1976 .... 9.00
❑71, Jul 1976 .... 7.00
❑72, Aug 1976 .... 7.00
❑73, Oct 1976 .... 7.00
❑74, Jan 1977 .... 7.00

PHANTOM (2ND SERIES)
DC

❑1, May 1988 LMc (a); O: Phantom 2.00
❑2, Jun 1988 .... 2.00
❑3, Jul 1988 .... 2.00
❑4, Aug 1988 .... 2.00

PHANTOM (3RD SERIES)
DC

❑1, May 1989 .... 2.00
❑2, Jun 1989 .... 1.50
❑3, Jul 1989 .... 1.50
❑4, Aug 1989 .... 1.50
❑5, Sep 1989 .... 1.50
❑6, Oct 1989 .... 1.50
❑7, Nov 1989 .... 1.50
❑8, Dec 1989 .... 1.50
❑9, Jan 1989 .... 1.50
❑10, Feb 1989 .... 1.50
❑11, Mar 1990 .... 1.50
❑12, Apr 1990 .... 1.50
❑13, May 1990 .... 1.50

PHANTOM (4TH SERIES)
WOLF

❑0/Ltd.; limited edition subscribers' issue 3.50
❑1 1992 .... 2.50
❑2 1992 .... 2.25
❑3 1992 .... 2.25
❑4 1992 .... 2.25
❑5 1992 .... 2.25
❑6 1992 .... 2.25
❑7 1992 .... 1.95
❑8 1992 .... 1.95

PHANTOM (MOONSTONE)
MOONSTONE

❑1 2003 .... 3.50
❑2 .... 3.50
❑3 .... 3.50
❑4 .... 3.50
❑5 .... 3.50
❑6 .... 3.50
❑7 .... 3.50
❑8, Sep 2005 .... 3.50

PHANTOM FORCE
IMAGE

❑0, Mar 1994 .... 2.50
❑1, Dec 1993 .... 2.50
❑2, Apr 1994 .... 2.50
❑3, May 1994 .... 2.50
❑4, Jun 1994 .... 2.50

❑5, Jul 1994 .... 2.50
❑6, Aug 1994 .... 2.50
❑7, Sep 1994 .... 2.50
❑8, Oct 1994 .... 2.50
❑Ashcan 1; ashcan 2.50

PHANTOM FORCE (GENESIS WEST)
GENESIS WEST

❑0 .... 2.50

PHANTOM GUARD
IMAGE

❑1, Oct 1997 .... 2.50
❑1/A, Oct 1997; alternate cover (white background) 2.50
❑2, Oct 1997 .... 2.50
❑3, Dec 1997 .... 2.50
❑4, Jan 1998 .... 2.50
❑4/Variant, Jan 1998; chromium cover 2.50
❑5, Feb 1998 .... 2.50
❑6, Mar 1998 .... 2.50

PHANTOM JACK
IMAGE

❑1, Apr 2004 .... 2.95
❑2, May 2004 .... 2.95
❑3, Aug 2004 .... 2.95
❑4, Aug 2004 .... 2.95
❑4/Error, Aug 2004 .... 4.00
❑5 2004 .... 2.95

PHANTOM OF FEAR CITY
CLAYPOOL

❑1, May 1993 .... 2.50
❑2, Jul 1993 .... 2.50
❑3, Aug 1993 .... 2.50
❑4, Oct 1993 .... 2.50
❑5, Nov 1993 .... 2.50
❑6, Jan 1994 .... 2.50
❑7, Apr 1994 .... 2.50
❑8, Jul 1994 .... 2.50
❑9, Sep 1994 .... 2.50
❑10, Nov 1994 .... 2.50
❑11, Feb 1995 .... 2.50
❑12, May 1995 .... 2.50

PHANTOM OF THE OPERA (ETERNITY)
ETERNITY

❑1, b&w 2.00

PHANTOM OF THE OPERA (INNOVATION)
INNOVATION

❑1, Dec 1991 .... 6.95

PHANTOM QUEST CORP.
PIONEER

❑1, Mar 1997, b&w; wraparound cover 2.95

PHANTOM STRANGER (2ND SERIES)
DC

❑1, May 1969, A: Doctor 13 .... 125.00
❑2, Aug 1969, A: Doctor 13 .... 60.00
❑3, Oct 1969, A: Doctor 13 .... 60.00
❑4, Dec 1969, NA (a); 1: Tala. A: Doctor 13 .... 70.00
❑5, Feb 1970, A: Doctor 13 .... 50.00
❑6, Apr 1970, A: Doctor 13 .... 50.00
❑7, Jun 1970, NA (c); JA (a); A: Doctor 13 .... 50.00
❑8, Aug 1970, A: Doctor 13 .... 40.00
❑9, Oct 1970, A: Doctor 13 .... 40.00
❑10, Dec 1970, A: Doctor 13 .... 40.00
❑11, Feb 1971 .... 40.00
❑12, Apr 1971, A: Doctor 13 .... 40.00
❑13, Jun 1971, A: Doctor 13 .... 40.00
❑14, Aug 1971, A: Doctor 13 .... 35.00
❑15, Oct 1971; Giant-size A: Doctor 13 35.00
❑16, Dec 1971; Giant-size JA (a); A: Doctor 13. A: Mark Merlin 35.00
❑17, Feb 1972; Giant-size A: Doctor 13 35.00
❑18, Apr 1972; Giant-size 1: Cassandra Craft. A: Doctor 13. A: Mark Merlin. 25.00
❑19, Jun 1972; Giant-size A: Doctor 13. A: Mark Merlin 25.00
❑20, Aug 1972 .... 25.00
❑21, Oct 1972, A: Doctor 13 .... 25.00
❑22, Dec 1972, A: Doctor 13 .... 15.00
❑23, Feb 1973, 1: The Spawn of Frankenstein 15.00
❑24, Apr 1973, A: The Spawn of Frankenstein 15.00
❑25, Jul 1973, A: The Spawn of Frankenstein 15.00
❑26, Sep 1973, A: Doctor 13. A: The Spawn of Frankenstein 15.00
❑27, Nov 1973, A: The Spawn of Frankenstein 15.00
❑28, Jan 1974, A: The Spawn of Frankenstein 15.00
❑29, Mar 1974, A: The Spawn of Frankenstein 15.00
❑30, May 1974, A: The Spawn of Frankenstein 15.00
❑31, Jul 1974, A: Black Orchid 15.00
❑32, Sep 1974, A: Black Orchid 15.00
❑33, Nov 1974, A: Deadman 15.00
❑34, Jan 1975, A: Black Orchid. A: Doctor 13 .... 15.00
❑35, Mar 1975 A: Black Orchid 15.00
❑36, May 1975 A: Black Orchid 15.00
❑37, Jul 1975 .... 15.00
❑38, Sep 1975 A: Black Orchid 15.00
❑39, Nov 1975 A: Deadman 15.00
❑40, Jan 1976 A: Deadman 15.00
❑41, Mar 1976 A: Deadman 15.00

PHANTOM STRANGER (MINI-SERIES)
DC

❑1, Oct 1987 .... 3.00
❑2, Nov 1987 .... 2.50
❑3, Dec 1987 .... 2.50
❑4, Jan 1988 .... 2.50

PHANTOM: THE GHOST KILLER
MOONSTONE

❑nn, ca. 2002 .... 5.95

PHANTOM: THE HUNT
MOONSTONE

❑nn, ca. 2003 .... 6.95

PHANTOM: THE GHOST WHO WALKS (LEE FALK'S...)
MARVEL

❑1, Feb 1995, cardstock cover 2.95
❑2, Mar 1995, cardstock cover 2.95
❑3, Apr 1995, cardstock cover 2.95

PHANTOM: THE SINGH WEB
MOONSTONE

❑nn, ca. 2002 .... 6.95

PHANTOM: THE TREASURE OF BANGALLA
MOONSTONE

❑nn, ca. 2002; Cover erroneously reads "Bagalla" 6.95

PHANTOM 2040
MARVEL

❑1, May 1995 .... 1.50
❑2, Jun 1995 .... 1.50
❑3, Jul 1995; Poster 1.50
❑4, Aug 1995; Poster 1.50

PHANTOM ZONE
DC

❑1, Jan 1982, GC (a) 1.50
❑2, Feb 1982, GC (a) 1.25
❑3, Mar 1982, GC (a) 1.25
❑4, Apr 1982, GC (a) 1.25

PHASE ONE
VICTORY

❑1, Oct 1986 .... 1.50
❑2 .... 1.50
❑3 .... 1.50
❑4 .... 1.50
❑5 .... 1.50

PHATHOM
BLATANT

❑1 .... 2.95

PHATWARS
BON

❑1 .... 2.00

PHAZE
ECLIPSE

❑1, Apr 1988 .... 2.25
❑2, Oct 1988 .... 2.25

PHD: PHANTASY DEGREE
TOKYOPOP

❑1, Jan 2005 .... 9.99
❑2, Apr 2005 .... 9.99
❑3, Jul 2005 .... 9.99
❑4, Oct 2005 .... 9.99

PHENOMERAMA
CALIBER

❑1 .... 2.95

PHIGMENTS
AMAZING

❑1, b&w 1.95
❑2 .... 1.95

PHILBERT DESANEX' DREAMS
RIP OFF

❑1, b&w 2.95

PHILISTINE
ONE SHOT

❑1, Sep 1993, b&w 2.50
❑2, Apr 1994, b&w 2.50
❑3, Sep 1994, b&w 2.50
❑4 .... 2.50
❑5 .... 2.50
❑6 .... 2.50

PHINEUS: MAGICIAN FOR HIRE
PIFFLE

❑1, Oct 1994, b&w; wraparound cover 2.95

PHOBOS
FLASHPOINT

❑1, Jan 1994 .... 2.50

PHOEBE & THE PIGEON PEOPLE
KITCHEN SINK

❑1 .... 3.00

PHOEBE: ANGEL IN BLACK
ANGEL

❑1 .... 2.95

PHOEBE CHRONICLES
NBM

❑1 .... 9.95
❑2 .... 9.95

PHOENIX
ATLAS-SEABOARD

❑1, Mar 1975, O: Phoenix (Atlas character) 7.00
❑2, Jun 1975 .... 5.00
❑3, Oct 1975 .... 3.00
❑4 1975 .... 3.00

PHOENIX RESTAURANT
FANDOM HOUSE

❑1, b&w 3.50

PHOENIX RESURRECTION AFTERMATH
MALIBU / ULTRAVERSE

❑1, Jan 1996, continues in Foxfire #1 3.95

PHOENIX RESURRECTION GENESIS
MALIBU / ULTRAVERSE

❑1, Dec 1995; Giant-size; wraparound cover; continues in The Phoenix Resurrection: Revelations; Phoenix force returns 3.95
❑2 .... 3.95

PHOENIX RESURRECTION RED SHIFT
MALIBU / ULTRAVERSE

❑0, Mar 1996; collects the seven flipbook chapters plus one new chapter 2.50
❑0/Ltd., Dec 1995; American Entertainment Edition; no cover price 2.50

PHOENIX RESURRECTION REVELATIONS
MALIBU / ULTRAVERSE

❑1, Dec 1995, wraparound cover; continues in The Phoenix Resurrection: Aftermath 3.95

PHOENIX SQUARE
SLAVE LABOR

❑1, Aug 1997, b&w 2.95
❑2, Nov 1997 .... 2.95

PHOENIX: THE UNTOLD STORY
MARVEL

❑1, Apr 1984; JBy (a); X-Men #137 with unpublished alternate ending 8.00

PHONY PAGES (TERRY BEATTY'S...)
RENEGADE

❑1, Apr 1986, Parody of Famous Comic Strips 2.00
❑2, May 1986, Parody of Famous Comic Books 2.00

Other grades: Multiply price above by 5/6 for VF/NM • 2/3 for VERY FINE • 1/3 for FINE • 1/5 for VERY GOOD • 1/8 for GOOD

Planet of the Apes (1st Series)

Magazine adapts movies, adds new stories
©Marvel

Planet of the Apes (2nd Series)

First issue had pink, yellow, or green overlays
©Adventure

Plasmer

Title caused Defiant change
©Marvel

Plastic Man (DC, 1st Series)

Silver Age revival featured original's son
©DC

Plop!

DC horror hosts offered humorous helpings
©DC

N-MINT

PICTURE TAKER
Slave Labor
- ❑1, Jan 1998, b&w 2.95

PIE
Wow Cool
- ❑1, b&w 2.95

PIECE OF STEAK
Tome
- ❑1, b&w 2.50

PIECES
5th Panel
- ❑1, Apr 1997, b&w 2.50
- ❑2, Jul 1997, b&w 2.50
- ❑3 .... 2.50

PIED PIPER GRAPHIC ALBUM
Pied Piper
- ❑1; Hero Alliance 6.95
- ❑2; < Never Published > 6.95
- ❑3; Beast Warriors 6.95

PIED PIPER OF HAMELIN
Tome
- ❑1, b&w 2.95

PIGEONMAN
Above & Beyond
- ❑1 .... 2.95

PIGEON-MAN, THE BIRD-BRAIN
Ferry Tail
- ❑1, Apr 1993, b&w 2.50

PIGHEAD
Williamson
- ❑1, b&w 2.95

PIGTALE
Image
- ❑1, Mar 2005 .... 2.95
- ❑2, Apr 2005 .... 2.95
- ❑3, Sep 2005 .... 2.95
- ❑4, Jul 2006 .... 2.95

PILGRIM'S PROGRESS
Marvel / Nelson
- ❑1; adaptation 9.99

PINEAPPLE ARMY
Viz
- ❑1, Dec 1988 .... 1.75
- ❑2, Dec 1988 .... 1.75
- ❑3, Jan 1989 .... 1.75
- ❑4, Jan 1989 .... 1.75
- ❑5, Feb 1989 .... 1.75
- ❑6, Feb 1989 .... 1.75
- ❑7, Mar 1989 .... 1.75
- ❑8, Mar 1989 .... 1.75
- ❑9, Apr 1989 .... 1.75
- ❑10, Apr 1989 .... 1.75

PINHEAD
Marvel / Epic
- ❑1, Dec 1993; Embossed foil cover 2.95
- ❑2, Jan 1994 .... 2.50
- ❑3, Feb 1994 .... 2.50
- ❑4, Mar 1994 .... 2.50
- ❑5, Apr 1994 .... 2.50
- ❑6, May 1994 .... 2.50

N-MINT

PINHEAD VS. MARSHAL LAW: LAW IN HELL
Marvel / Epic
- ❑1, Nov 1993; foil cover 2.95
- ❑2, Dec 1993; foil cover 2.95

PINK DUST
Kitchen Sink
- ❑1, Aug 1998 .... 3.50

PINK FLOYD
Personality
- ❑1, b&w 2.95
- ❑2, b&w 2.95

PINK FLOYD EXPERIENCE
Revolutionary
- ❑1, Jun 1991, b&w 2.50
- ❑2, Aug 1991, b&w 2.50
- ❑3, Oct 1991, b&w 2.50
- ❑4, Dec 1991, b&w 2.50
- ❑5, Feb 1992, b&w 2.50

PINK PANTHER (GOLD KEY)
Gold Key
- ❑1, Apr 1971, (c); (w); (a); Cover code 10266-104 .... 40.00
- ❑2, Jul 1971, (c); (w); (a); Cover code 10266-107 .... 17.00
- ❑3, Oct 1971, (c); (w); (a); Cover code 90266-110; Inspector referred to as "Clouzot" in newspaper 15.00
- ❑4, Jan 1972, (c); (w); (a); Cover code 90266-201 .... 15.00
- ❑5, Mar 1972, (c); (w); (a); Cover code 90266-203 .... 15.00
- ❑6, May 1972, (c); (w); (a); Cover code 90266-205 .... 8.00
- ❑7, Jul 1972, (c); (w); (a); Cover code 90266-207; has uncommon Pink Panther stories without "Pink" in title; no Inspector story 8.00
- ❑8, Sep 1972, (c); (w); (a); Cover code 90266-209 .... 8.00
- ❑9, Nov 1972, (c); (w); (a); Cover code 90266-211 .... 8.00
- ❑10, Jan 1973, (c); (w); (a); Cover code 90266-301 .... 8.00
- ❑11, Mar 1973, (c); (w); (a); Cover code 90266-303; has uncommon Pink Panther story without "Pink" in title 6.00
- ❑12, May 1973, (c); (w); (a); Cover code 90266-305 .... 6.00
- ❑13, Jul 1973, (c); (w); (a); Cover code 90266-307 .... 6.00
- ❑14, Sep 1973, (c); (w); (a); Cover code 90266-309; has uncommon Pink Panther stories without "Pink" in title 6.00
- ❑15, Oct 1973, (c); (w); (a); Cover code 90266-310 .... 6.00
- ❑16, Nov 1973, (c); (w); Cover code 90266-311; has uncommon Pink Panther story without "Pink" in title; Warren Tufts art begins 6.00
- ❑17, Jan 1974, (c); (w); Cover code 90266-401 .... 6.00
- ❑18, Mar 1974, (c); (w); Cover code 90266-403 .... 6.00
- ❑19, May 1974, (c); (w); Cover code 90266-405 .... 6.00

N-MINT

- ❑20, Jul 1974, (c); (w); Cover code 90266-407; rare Panther/Inspector crossover 6.00
- ❑21, Sep 1974, (c); (w); Cover code 90266-409 .... 4.00
- ❑22, Oct 1974, (c); (w); (a); Cover code 90266-410 .... 4.00
- ❑23, Nov 1974, (c); (w); (a); Cover code 90266-411 .... 4.00
- ❑24, Jan 1975, (c); (w); Cover code 90266-501 .... 4.00
- ❑25, Mar 1975, (c); (w); (a); Cover code 90266-503; has uncommon Pink Panther story without "Pink" in the title 4.00
- ❑26, May 1975, (c); (w); (a); Cover code 90266-505 .... 4.00
- ❑27, Jul 1975, (c); (w); (a); Cover code 90266-507 .... 4.00
- ❑28, Sep 1975, (c); (w); (a); Cover code 90266-509 .... 4.00
- ❑29, Oct 1975, (c); (w); (a); Cover code 90266-510 .... 4.00
- ❑30, Nov 1975, (c); (w); Cover code 90266-511 .... 4.00
- ❑31, Jan 1976, (c); (w); Cover code 90266-601 .... 4.00
- ❑32, Mar 1976, (c); (w); Cover code 90266-603 .... 4.00
- ❑33, Apr 1976, (c); (w); (a); Cover code 90266-604 .... 4.00
- ❑34, May 1976, (c); (w); (a); Cover code 90266-605 .... 4.00
- ❑35, Jun 1976, (c); (w); Cover code 90266-606; Tweety and Sylvester in Hostess ad ("A Tasty Trap!") 4.00
- ❑36, Jul 1976, (c); (w); (a); Cover code 90266-607 .... 4.00
- ❑37, Sep 1976, (c); (w); (a); Cover code 90266-609 .... 4.00
- ❑38, Oct 1976, (c); (w); (a); Cover code 90266-610 .... 4.00
- ❑39, Nov 1976, (c); (w); (a); Cover code 90266-611 .... 4.00
- ❑40, Jan 1977, (c); (w); Cover code 90266-701; Captain America in Hostess ad ("When It Rains It Pours") 4.00
- ❑41, Mar 1977, (c); (w); Cover code 90266-703; Casper in Hostess ad ("The Boogy-Woogy Man") 3.00
- ❑42, Apr 1977, (c); (w); Cover code 90266-704; Spider-Man Hostess ad ("Will Power") 3.00
- ❑43, May 1977, (w); (a); Cover code 90266-705; reprints part of #1 .... 3.00
- ❑44, Jun 1977, (c); (w); Cover code 90266-706; Iron Man in Hostess ad ("A Dull Pain"); No Inspector story 3.00
- ❑45, Jul 1977, (c); (w); Cover code 90266-707; Iron Man in Hostess ad ("A Dull Pain") 3.00
- ❑46, Sep 1977, (c); (w); Cover code 90266-709; Sad Sack in Hostess ad ("Sarge is a Bully"); "Snoring Pink" based on script from "Rock-a-Bye Pink" in #5 .... 3.00
- ❑47, Oct 1977, (c); (w); Cover code 90266-710; Hulk in Hostess ad ("Up a Tree") 3.00
- ❑48, Nov 1977, (c); (w); Cover code 90266-711; Spider-Man in Hostess ad ("Break the Bank") 3.00

N-MINT

❑49, Jan 1978, (c); (w); Cover code 90266-801; Richie Rich in Hostess ad ("Brightens Up a Traffic Jam") ... 3.00
❑50, Mar 1978, (c); (w); Cover code 90266-803; Spider-Man in Hostess ad ("vs. the Chairman") ... 3.00
❑51, Apr 1978, (c); (w); Cover code 90266-804; Richie Rich Hostess ad ("A Real Treat") ... 3.00
❑52, May 1978, (c); (w); Cover code 90266-805; Captain America in Hostess ad "vs. the Aliens" ... 3.00
❑53, Jun 1978, (c); (w); Cover code 90266-806; Daredevil in Hostess ad ("The Peachy Keen Caper"); No Inspector story ... 3.00
❑54, Jul 1978, (c); (w); Cover code 90266-807; No Inspector story ... 3.00
❑55, Aug 1978, (c); (w); Cover code 90266-808; No Inspector story ... 3.00
❑56, Sep 1978, (c); (w); Cover code 90266-809; Captain America in Hostess ad "vs. the Aliens" ... 3.00
❑57, Oct 1978, (c); (w); Cover code 90266-810; Casper in Hostess ad ("A Real Oddball") ... 3.00
❑58, Nov 1978, (c); (w); Cover code 90266-811 ... 3.00
❑59, Dec 1978, (c); (w); Cover code 90266-812 ... 3.00
❑60, Jan 1979, (c); (w); (a); Cover code 90266-901; story directly adapts holiday cartoon special; Thor in Hostess ad ("The Storm Meets its Master") ... 3.00
❑61, Feb 1979, (c); (w); Cover code 90266-902 ... 3.00
❑62, Mar 1979, (c); (w); Cover code 90266-903; Spider-Man in Hostess ad ("Meets June Jitsui!") ... 3.00
❑63, Apr 1979, (c); (w); Cover code 90266-904; Captain America in Hostess ad ("An Invading Army!"); no Inspector story ... 3.00
❑64, May 1979, (c); (w); Cover code 90266-905; No Inspector story ... 3.00
❑65, Jun 1979, (c); (w); (a); Cover code 90266-906; Thor in Hostess ad "Good Overcomes Evil"; no Inspector story ... 3.00
❑66, Jul 1979, (c); (w); (a); Cover code 90266-907; No Inspector story ... 3.00
❑67, Aug 1979, (c); (w); (a); Cover code 90266-908 ... 3.00
❑68, Sep 1979, (c); (w); (a); Cover code 90266-909; Casper in Hostess ad "The Boo Keepers"; No Inspector story ... 3.00
❑69, Oct 1979, (c); (w); (a); Cover code 90266-910; Captain Marvel in Hostess ad "Returns to Earth!"; no inspector story ... 3.00
❑70, Nov 1979, (c); (w); (a); Cover code 90266-911 ... 3.00
❑71, Dec 1979, (c); (w); (a); Cover code 90266-912 ... 3.00
❑72, Jan 1980, (c); (w); (a); Cover code 90266-001; Reprints #5 in entirety, recoloring art from cover ... 3.00
❑73, Feb 1980, (c); (w); (a); Cover code 90266-002; Captain America in Hostess ad ("The Deserted City"); No Inspector story ... 3.00
❑74, Jul 1980, (c); (w); (a); Cover code 90266-007; Casper in Hostess ad ("In Outer Space"); No Inspector story ... 3.00
❑75, Aug 1980, (c); (w); (a); Cover code 90266-008; Casper in Hostess ad ("Ghosts in the House") ... 15.00
❑76, Oct 1981, (c); (w); (a); Cover code 90266-010; Spider-Man in Hostess ad ("Meets the Bikers!"); No Inspector story ... 15.00
❑77, Dec 1981, (c); (w); (a); Cover code 90266-012 ... 17.00
❑78, Jan 1981, (c); (w); (a); Cover code 90266-101; No Inspector Story ... 8.00
❑79, Jul 1981, (c); (w); (a); Cover code 90266-107 ... 8.00
❑80, Sep 1981, (c); (w); (a); Cover code 90266-109 ... 8.00
❑81, Feb 1982, (c); (w); (a); Cover code 90266-202; No Inspector story; "Pink in the Drink" reprinted from #1; "Pink on the Range" reprinted, probably from #4 ... 8.00

N-MINT

❑82, Mar 1982, (c); (w); (a); Cover code 90266-203; No Inspector story; Pink Shoelacer reprinted from #6; Mr. Zap (rare story without Pink in title) reprinted from #7 ... 8.00
❑83, Apr 1982, (c); (w); (a); Cover code 90266-204; "The Purloined Pink Lemonade" reprinted from #6 ... 8.00
❑84, Jun 1983, (c); (w); (a) ... 15.00
❑85, ca. 1983, (c); (w); (a) ... 15.00
❑86, ca. 1983, (c); (w); (a) ... 15.00
❑87, ca. 1983, (c); (w); (a); Cover code 90266; issue number listed ... 15.00

PINK PANTHER (HARVEY)
HARVEY

❑1, Nov 1993 ... 1.50
❑2, Dec 1993; Reprints Pink Panther (Gold Key) #50 ... 1.50
❑3, Jan 1994; Reprints Pink Panther (Gold Key) #51 ... 1.50
❑4, Feb 1994; Reprints Pink Panther (Gold Key) #52 ... 1.50
❑5, Mar 1994 ... 1.50
❑6, Apr 1994; Reprints Pink Panther (Gold Key) #53 ... 1.50
❑7, May 1994; Reprints Pink Panther (Gold Key) #54 ... 1.50
❑8, Jun 1994; Reprints Pink Panther (Gold Key) #55 ... 1.50
❑9, Jul 1994; Reprints Pink Panther (Gold Key) #56 ... 1.50
❑SS 1, ca. 1993; Super Special ... 2.25

PINKY AND THE BRAIN
DC

❑1, Jul 1996; based on animated series 2.50
❑2, Aug 1996 ... 2.00
❑3, Sep 1996 ... 2.00
❑4, Oct 1996; Oz parody ... 1.75
❑5, Nov 1996; Western parody issue . 1.75
❑6, Dec 1996; Ed Wood parody issue 1.75
❑7, Jan 1997; Faust parody ... 1.75
❑8, Feb 1997 ... 1.75
❑9, Mar 1997 ... 1.75
❑10, Apr 1997 ... 1.75
❑11, May 1997; Fantasia parody ... 1.75
❑12, Jun 1997; surfing parody ... 1.75
❑13, Jul 1997 ... 1.75
❑14, Aug 1997 ... 1.75
❑15, Sep 1997; Bikers ... 1.75
❑16, Oct 1997 ... 1.75
❑17, Nov 1997 ... 1.75
❑18, Dec 1997; Manga parody ... 1.95
❑19, Jan 1998; Brain plays Santa ... 1.95
❑20, Feb 1998 ... 1.95
❑21, Mar 1998 ... 1.95
❑22, May 1998 ... 1.95
❑23, Jun 1998; Jaws parody cover ... 1.95
❑24, Jul 1998; Zorro parody ... 1.95
❑25, Aug 1998 ... 1.95
❑26, Oct 1998; Demi Moore parody issue ... 1.95
❑27, Nov 1998 ... 1.99
❑Holiday 1, Jan 1996; Giant-size ... 3.00

PINOCCHIA
NBM

❑1 ... 11.95

PINOCCHIO AND THE EMPEROR OF THE NIGHT
MARVEL

❑1, Mar 1988 ... 1.25

PINOCCHIO SPECIAL (WALT DISNEY'S...)
GLADSTONE

❑1, Mar 1990 WK (a) ... 1.50

PINT-SIZED X-BABIES
MARVEL

❑1, Aug 1998; gatefold summary ... 2.99

PIPSQUEAK PAPERS (WALLACE WOOD'S...)
FANTAGRAPHICS / EROS

❑1, b&w ... 2.75

PIRACY (RCP)
GEMSTONE

❑1, Mar 1998; Reprints ... 2.50
❑2, Apr 1998; Reprints ... 2.50
❑3, May 1998; Reprints ... 2.50
❑4, Jun 1998; Reprints ... 2.50

N-MINT

❑5, Jul 1998; Reprints ... 2.50
❑6, Aug 1998; Reprints ... 2.50
❑7, Sep 1998 ... 2.50

PIRANHA IS LOOSE!
SPECIAL STUDIO

❑1, b&w ... 2.75
❑2, b&w ... 2.75

PIRATE CLUB
SLAVE LABOR

❑1 2004 ... 2.95
❑2 2004 ... 2.95
❑3 2004 ... 2.95
❑4 ... 2.95
❑5 2005 ... 2.95
❑6, Jun 2005 ... 2.95
❑8, Nov 2005 ... 2.95

PIRATE CORPS
ETERNITY

❑1 ... 2.50
❑2 ... 2.50
❑3, Dec 1987 ... 2.50
❑4, Feb 1988 ... 2.50

PIRATE CORP$! (2ND SERIES)
SLAVE LABOR

❑1, Jun 1989 ... 2.50
❑1/2nd, Aug 1993; has Fine Dairy Products ad on back cover ... 2.50
❑2, Sep 1989 ... 2.50
❑2/2nd, Feb 1993; has Fine Dairy Products ad on back cover ... 2.50
❑3, Feb 1991 ... 2.50
❑3/2nd, Feb 1993; has Fine Dairy Products ad on back cover ... 2.50
❑4, Apr 1992 ... 2.50
❑4/2nd, Sep 1993; has Fine Dairy Products ad on back cover ... 2.50
❑5, Dec 1992 ... 2.50
❑5/2nd, Apr 1994 ... 2.50
❑Special 1, Mar 1989, b&w; has Futurama ad on back cover ... 1.95
❑Special 1/2nd, Aug 1993; has Fine Dairy Products ad on back cover ... 2.95

PIRATE QUEEN, THE
COMAX

❑1, b&w ... 3.00

PIRATES OF DARK WATER
MARVEL / STAR

❑1, Nov 1991 ... 1.00
❑2, Dec 1991 ... 1.00
❑3, Jan 1992 ... 1.00
❑4, Feb 1992 ... 1.00
❑5, Mar 1992 ... 1.00
❑6, Apr 1992 ... 1.00
❑7, May 1992 ... 1.25
❑8, Jun 1992 ... 1.25
❑9, Jul 1992 ... 1.25

P.I.'S, THE: MICHAEL MAUSER AND MS. TREE
FIRST

❑1, Jan 1985; MGr, JSa (a); Ms. Tree, E-Man ... 1.50
❑2, Mar 1985 JSa (a) ... 1.50
❑3, May 1985 JSa (a) ... 1.50

PISTOLERO
ETERNITY

❑1, b&w ... 3.95

PITA TEN OFFICIAL FAN CLUB BOOK
TOKYOPOP

❑1, Nov 2005, b&w ... 9.95

PI: THE BOOK OF ANTS
ARTISAN ENTERTAINMENT

❑1, b&w; based on movie ... 2.95

PITT
IMAGE

❑½ ... 1.50
❑1, Jan 1993 1: Pitt ... 3.00
❑1/Gold, Jan 1993; Gold edition ... 4.00
❑2, Jul 1993 ... 1.95
❑3, Feb 1994 ... 1.95
❑4, Apr 1994 ... 1.95
❑5, Jun 1994 ... 1.95
❑6, Sep 1994 ... 1.95
❑7, Dec 1994 ... 1.95
❑8, Apr 1994 ... 1.95
❑9, Aug 1995 ... 1.95

Other grades: Multiply price above by 5/6 for VF/NM • 2/3 for VERY FINE • 1/3 for FINE • 1/5 for VERY GOOD • 1/8 for GOOD

Poison Elves (Mulehide)

I, Lusiphur changes to ambiguous title

©Mulehide

Poison Elves (Sirius)

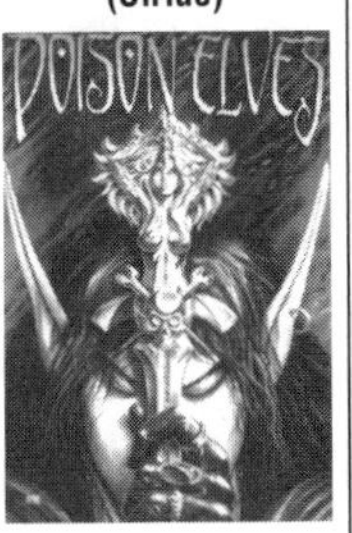

Sirius picks up odd fantasy series

©Sirius

Pokémon: The Electric Tale of Pikachu

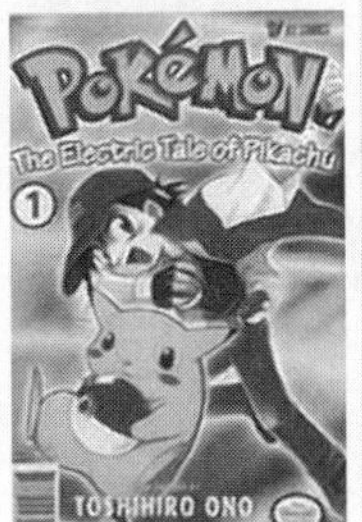

Catch 'em all creatures come to comics

©Viz

Popeye Special

Spinach addiction examined in origin story

©Ocean

Porky Pig (Gold Key)

Stuttering star shows stout heart

©Gold Key

N-MINT

❑10 1996 .... 1.95
❑11 1996 .... 1.95
❑12, Dec 1996 .... 1.95
❑13, Mar 1997 .... 1.95
❑14, Jun 1997 .... 2.50
❑15, Sep 1997 .... 2.50
❑16, Dec 1997 .... 2.50
❑17, Mar 1998 .... 2.50
❑18, Jun 1998 .... 2.50
❑19, Sep 1998 .... 2.50
❑20, Oct 1998; Published by Full Bleed Studios 2.50
❑Book 1 .... 9.95

PITT
MARVEL

❑1 .... 3.25

PITT CREW
FULL BLEED

❑1 .... 3.00

PITT: IN THE BLOOD
FULL BLEED

❑1, Aug 1996 .... 2.50

PIXY JUNKET
VIZ

❑1, b&w 2.75
❑2, b&w 2.75
❑3, b&w 2.75
❑4, b&w 2.75
❑5, b&w 2.75
❑6, b&w 2.75

P.J. WARLOCK
ECLIPSE

❑1, Nov 1986, b&w 2.00
❑2, Jan 1987, b&w 2.00
❑3, Mar 1987, b&w 2.00

PLACES THAT ARE GONE
AEON

❑1, Jul 1994 .... 2.75
❑2, Aug 1994 .... 2.75

PLAGUE
TOME

❑1, b&w 2.95

PLAN 9 FROM OUTER SPACE
ETERNITY

❑1, b&w 4.95
❑1/2nd 5.95

PLAN 9 FROM OUTER SPACE: THIRTY YEARS LATER
ETERNITY

❑1, Jan 1991, b&w 2.50
❑2, b&w 2.50
❑3, b&w 2.50

PLANET 29
CALIBER

❑1, b&w 2.50
❑2, b&w 2.50

PLANETARY
DC / WILDSTORM

❑1, Apr 1999 .... 8.00
❑2, May 1999 .... 3.00
❑3, Jun 1999 .... 3.00
❑4, Jul 1999 .... 2.50
❑5, Sep 1999 .... 2.50
❑6, Nov 1999 .... 2.50
❑7, Jan 2000 .... 2.50
❑8, Feb 2000 .... 2.50
❑9, Apr 2000 .... 2.50
❑10, Jun 2000 .... 2.50
❑11, Sep 2000 .... 2.50
❑12, Jan 2001 .... 2.50
❑13, Feb 2001 .... 2.50
❑14, Jun 2001 .... 2.50
❑15, Jul 2001 .... 2.50
❑16, Oct 2003 .... 2.95
❑17, Dec 2003 .... 2.95
❑18, Feb 2004 .... 2.95
❑19, May 2004 .... 2.95
❑20, Sep 2004 .... 2.95
❑21, Dec 2004 .... 2.95
❑22 2005 .... 2.95
❑23, Jul 2005 .... 2.99
❑24, Mar 2006 .... 2.99
❑25, Jun 2006 .... 2.99

PLANETARY/BATMAN: NIGHT ON EARTH
DC / WILDSTORM

❑1, ca. 2003 .... 5.95

PLANETARY/JLA: TERRA OCCULTA
WILDSTORM

❑1, Nov 2002 .... 5.95

PLANETARY/THE AUTHORITY: RULING THE WORLD
DC / WILDSTORM

❑nn, Aug 2000 .... 5.95

PLANET BLOOD
TOKYOPOP

❑1, Feb 2005 .... 9.95
❑2, Apr 2005 .... 9.95
❑3, Oct 2005 .... 9.95

PLANET COMICS (BLACKTHORNE)
BLACKTHORNE

❑1, Apr 1988 .... 2.00
❑2, Jun 1988 .... 2.00
❑3, Aug 1988 .... 2.00

PLANET COMICS (A-LIST)
A-LIST

❑1, Spr 1997 .... 2.95
❑2, Fal 1997, b&w 2.95
❑3, Win 1997 .... 2.95

PLANET COMICS (AVALON)
AVALON

❑1 .... 5.95

PLANET LADDER
TOKYOPOP

❑1, Mar 2002, b&w; printed in Japanese format 9.99
❑2, Jul 2002, b&w; printed in Japanese format 9.99

PLANET OF GEEKS
STARHEAD

❑1, b&w 2.75

PLANET OF TERROR (BASIL WOLVERTON'S...)
DARK HORSE

❑1, Jul 1987, BW (w); BW (a) 2.00

PLANET OF THE APES (1ST SERIES)
MARVEL

❑1, Aug 1974, b&w; magazine; adapts first movie plus new story 20.00
❑1/2nd; adapts first movie plus new story 5.00
❑2, Oct 1974, b&w; magazine; adapts first movie plus new story 10.00
❑3, Dec 1974, b&w; magazine; adapts first movie plus new stories 9.00
❑4, Jan 1975, b&w; magazine; adapts first movie plus new stories 8.00
❑5, Feb 1975, b&w; magazine; adapts first movie plus new stories 8.00
❑6, Mar 1975, b&w; magazine; concludes first movie adaptations plus new stories 6.00
❑7, Apr 1975, b&w; magazine 5.00
❑8, May 1975, b&w; magazine 5.00
❑9, Jun 1975 .... 5.00
❑10, Jul 1975 .... 5.00
❑11, Aug 1975 .... 5.00
❑12, Sep 1975 .... 5.00
❑13, Aug 1975 .... 5.00
❑14, Nov 1975 .... 5.00
❑15, Dec 1975 .... 5.00
❑16, Jan 1976 D: Zira. D: Cornelius 5.00
❑17, Feb 1976 .... 5.00
❑18, Mar 1976 .... 5.00
❑19, Apr 1976, b&w; magazine 5.00
❑20, May 1976, b&w; magazine 5.00
❑21, Jun 1976, b&w; magazine 5.00
❑22, Jul 1976, b&w; magazine 5.00
❑23, Aug 1976, b&w; magazine 5.00
❑24, Sep 1976, b&w; magazine 5.00
❑25, Oct 1976, b&w; magazine 5.00
❑26, Nov 1976, b&w; magazine 5.00
❑27, Dec 1976, b&w; magazine 5.00
❑28, Jan 1977, b&w; magazine 5.00
❑29, Feb 1977, b&w; magazine 5.00
❑Annual 1 .... 4.00

PLANET OF THE APES (2ND SERIES)
ADVENTURE

❑1, Apr 1990; extra cover in pink, yellow, or green 4.00
❑1/Ltd., Apr 1990; limited 4.00
❑1/2nd 2.50
❑2, Jun 1990 .... 3.00
❑3, Jul 1990 .... 3.00
❑4, Aug 1990 .... 3.00
❑5, Sep 1990 .... 3.00
❑6, Oct 1990 .... 3.00
❑7, Nov 1990 .... 3.00
❑8, Dec 1990; Christmas 3.00
❑9, Jan 1991 .... 3.00
❑10, Mar 1991 .... 3.00
❑11, Apr 1991 .... 2.50
❑12, May 1991; PG (c); Wedding of Alexander and Coure 2.50
❑13, Jun 1991 .... 2.50
❑14, Jul 1991 .... 2.50

❑15, Aug 1991 .... 2.50
❑16, Sep 1991 .... 2.50
❑17, Oct 1991 .... 2.50
❑18, Nov 1991 .... 2.50
❑19, Dec 1991 .... 2.50
❑20, Jan 1992 .... 2.50
❑21, Feb 1992 .... 2.50
❑22, Apr 1992; sequel to Conquest of the Planet of the Apes 2.50
❑23, May 1992 .... 2.50
❑24, Jul 1992 .... 2.50
❑Annual 1, b&w 3.50

PLANET OF THE APES (3RD SERIES)
DARK HORSE

❑1, Jun 2001 .... 2.99
❑1/Variant, Jun 2001 .... 2.99
❑2, Jul 2001 .... 2.99
❑2/Variant, Jul 2001 .... 2.99
❑3, Aug 2001 .... 2.99
❑3/Variant, Aug 2001 .... 2.99

PLANET OF THE APES (4TH SERIES)
DARK HORSE

❑1, Sep 2001 .... 2.99
❑1/Variant, Sep 2001 .... 2.99
❑2, Oct 2001 .... 2.99
❑2/Variant, Oct 2001 .... 2.99
❑3, Nov 2001 .... 2.99
❑3/Variant, Nov 2001 .... 2.99
❑4, Dec 2001 .... 2.99
❑4/Variant, Dec 2001 .... 2.99
❑5, Jan 2002 .... 2.99
❑5/Variant, Jan 2002 .... 2.99
❑6, Feb 2002 .... 2.99
❑6/Variant, Feb 2002 .... 2.99

PLANET OF THE APES: BLOOD OF THE APES
ADVENTURE

❑1, Nov 1991, b&w 2.50
❑2, Dec 1991, b&w 2.50
❑3, Jan 1992, b&w 2.50
❑4, Feb 1992, b&w 2.50

PLANET OF THE APES: FORBIDDEN ZONE
ADVENTURE

❑1 .... 2.50
❑2 .... 2.50
❑3 .... 2.50
❑4 .... 2.50

PLANET OF THE APES: SINS OF THE FATHER
ADVENTURE

❑1, Mar 1992, b&w 2.50

PLANET OF THE APES: URCHAK'S FOLLY
ADVENTURE

❑1, Jan 1991, b&w 2.50
❑2, Feb 1991, b&w 2.50
❑3, Mar 1991, b&w 2.50
❑4, Apr 1991, b&w 2.50

PLANET OF VAMPIRES
ATLAS-SEABOARD

❑1, Apr 1975 NA (c); PB (a) 12.00
❑2, Jul 1975 NA (c) 8.00
❑3, Jul 1975 .... 8.00

PLANET PATROL
EDGE / SEABOARD

❑1 .... 2.95

PLANET TERRY
MARVEL / STAR

❑1, Apr 1985, O: Planet Terry. 1: Planet Terry 1.00
❑2, May 1985 .... 1.00
❑3, Jun 1985 .... 1.00
❑4, Jul 1985 .... 1.00
❑5, Aug 1985 .... 1.00
❑6, Sep 1985 .... 1.00
❑7, Oct 1985 .... 1.00
❑8, Nov 1985 .... 1.00
❑9, Dec 1985 .... 1.00
❑10, Jan 1986 .... 1.00
❑11, Feb 1986 .... 1.00
❑12, Mar 1986 .... 1.00

PLANET-X
ETERNITY

❑1, b&w 2.50

PLANET X REPRINT COMIC
PLANET X

❑1, ca. 1987, reprints adaptation of The Man from Planet X; no cover price 2.00

PLAQUE X
AHOLATTAFUN

❑1, ca. 2004 .... 2.95

PLASM
DEFIANT

❑0; bound in Diamond Previews 1.00

PLASMA BABY
CALIBER

❑1, b&w 2.50
❑2, b&w 2.50
❑3, b&w 2.50

PLASMER
MARVEL

❑1, Nov 1993; four trading cards 2.50
❑2, Dec 1993 .... 1.95
❑3, Jan 1994 .... 1.95
❑4, Feb 1994 .... 1.95

PLASTIC FORKS
MARVEL / EPIC

❑1, ca. 1990 .... 4.95
❑2, ca. 1990 .... 4.95
❑3, ca. 1990 .... 4.95
❑4, ca. 1990 .... 4.95
❑5, ca. 1990 .... 4.95

PLASTIC LITTLE
CPM

❑Ashcan 1, Jun 1997 .... 3.00
❑1, Aug 1997 O: Captain Tita Mu Koshigaya. 1: Tita Mu Koshigay. 1: Mei Lin Jones. 1: Joshua Balboa. 1: Tita Mu Koshigaya. 1: Roger Rogers 2.95
❑2, Sep 1997 .... 2.95
❑3, Oct 1997 .... 2.95
❑4, Nov 1997 .... 2.95
❑5, Dec 1997 .... 2.95

PLASTIC MAN (DC, 1ST SERIES)
DC

❑1, Dec 1966, GK (a); O: Plastic Man. 150.00
❑2, Feb 1967 .... 50.00
❑3, Apr 1967 .... 30.00
❑4, Jun 1967 .... 20.00
❑5, Aug 1967 .... 20.00
❑6, Oct 1967 .... 15.00
❑7, Dec 1967, A: Plas' father (Plastic Man 1). A: Woozy Winks 15.00
❑8, Feb 1968 .... 15.00
❑9, Apr 1968 .... 15.00
❑10, Jun 1968, series goes on hiatus until 1976 .... 15.00
❑11, Mar 1976; Series begins again: 1976 .... 8.00
❑12, May 1976 .... 8.00
❑13, Jul 1976 .... 8.00
❑14, Sep 1976 .... 8.00
❑15, Nov 1976 .... 8.00
❑16, Mar 1977 .... 8.00
❑17, May 1977 .... 8.00
❑18, Jul 1977 .... 8.00
❑19, Sep 1977 .... 8.00
❑20, Nov 1977 .... 8.00

PLASTIC MAN (DC, 2ND SERIES)
DC

❑1, Feb 2004 .... 2.95
❑2, Mar 2004 .... 2.95
❑3, Apr 2004 .... 2.95
❑4, May 2004 .... 2.95
❑5, Jun 2004 .... 2.95
❑6, Jul 2004 .... 2.95
❑7, Aug 2004 .... 2.95
❑8, Sep 2004 .... 2.95
❑9, Oct 2004 .... 2.95
❑10, Nov 2004 .... 2.95
❑11, Dec 2004 .... 2.95
❑12, Jan 2005 .... 2.95
❑13, Feb 2005 .... 2.95
❑14, Mar 2005 .... 2.95
❑15, Apr 2005 .... 2.95
❑16 2005 .... 2.99
❑17, Sep 2005 .... 2.99
❑18 2005 .... 2.99
❑19, Jan 2006 .... 2.99
❑20, Mar 2006 .... 2.99

PLASTIC MAN (MINI-SERIES)
DC

❑1, Nov 1988 PF (w); O: Plastic Man 1.25
❑2, Dec 1988 PF (w) 1.25
❑3, Jan 1989 PF (w) 1.25
❑4, Feb 1989 PF (w) 1.25

PLASTIC MAN LOST ANNUAL
DC

❑1, Feb 2004 .... 6.95

PLASTIC MAN SPECIAL
DC

❑1, Aug 1999 .... 3.95

PLASTRON CAFÉ
MIRAGE

❑1, Dec 1992 .... 2.25
❑2, Feb 1993 .... 2.25
❑3, May 1993 .... 2.25
❑4, Jul 1993 .... 2.25

PLATINUM.44
COMAX

❑1, b&w 2.95

PLATINUM GRIT
DEAD NUMBAT

❑1 .... 3.50
❑2 .... 3.50
❑3 .... 3.50
❑4, Feb 1995, b&w 3.50
❑5 .... 3.50
❑6 .... 3.50

PLAYBEAR
FANTAGRAPHICS / EROS

❑1 .... 2.95
❑2, ca. 1995 .... 2.95
❑3, Aug 1995 .... 2.95

PLAYGROUND
CALIBER

❑1, b&w 2.50

PLAYGROUNDS
FANTAGRAPHICS

❑1, b&w 2.00

PLEASURE & PASSION (ALAZAR'S...)
BRAINSTORM

❑1, Oct 1997 .... 2.95

PLEASURE BOUND
FANTAGRAPHICS / EROS

❑1, Feb 1996 .... 2.95

PLOP!
DC

❑1, Oct 1973, BW (c); SA, BWr (a) 18.00
❑2, Dec 1973, SA (a) 8.00
❑3, Feb 1974, SA (a) 8.00
❑4, Apr 1974, SA, BW, FR (a) 7.00
❑5, Jun 1974, SA (a) 7.00
❑6, Aug 1974, SA (a) 6.00
❑7, Oct 1974, SA (a) 6.00
❑8, Dec 1974, SA (a) 6.00
❑9, Feb 1975 SA, BW, FR (a) 6.00
❑10, Mar 1975 JO (w); SA, BW, RE (a) 6.00
❑11, Apr 1975 SA (a) 5.00
❑12, May 1975 SA (a) 5.00
❑13, Jun 1975 SA (a) 5.00
❑14, Jul 1975 SA (a) 5.00
❑15, Aug 1975 SA (a) 5.00
❑16, Sep 1975 SA (a) 5.00
❑17, Oct 1975 SA (a) 5.00
❑18, Dec 1975 SA (a) 5.00
❑19, Feb 1976 SA (a) 5.00
❑20, Apr 1976 SA (a) 5.00
❑21, Jun 1976, Giant-size SA (a) 5.00
❑22, Aug 1976, Giant-size SA (a) 5.00
❑23, Oct 1976, Giant-size; Wally Wood's Lord of the Rings parody 5.00
❑24, Dec 1976, Giant-size SA (a) 8.00

POCAHONTAS (DISNEY'S...)
MARVEL

❑1, Jul 1995, prestige format one-shot 4.95

POE
CHEESE

❑1, Sep 1996 .... 2.50
❑2, Oct 1996 .... 2.50
❑3, Nov 1996 .... 2.50
❑4, Dec 1996 .... 2.50
❑5, Feb 1997, b&w 2.50

Power & Glory

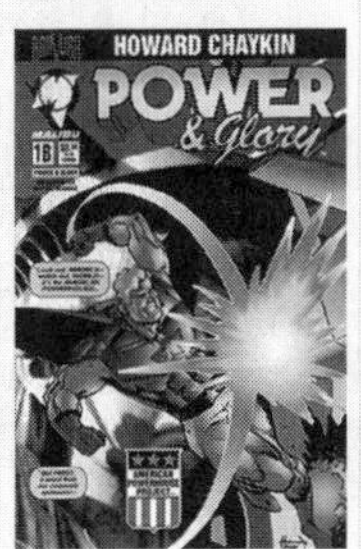

Chaykin makes corporate super-hero
©Malibu

Powerless

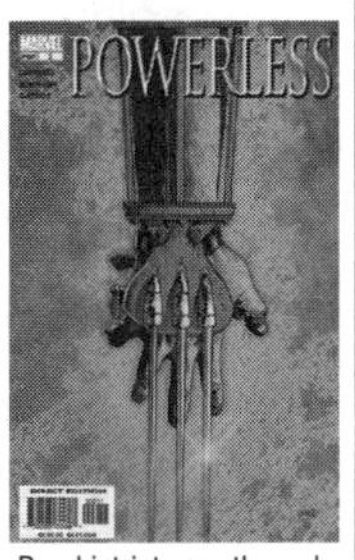

Psychiatrist sees through non-heroic world
©Marvel

Power Line

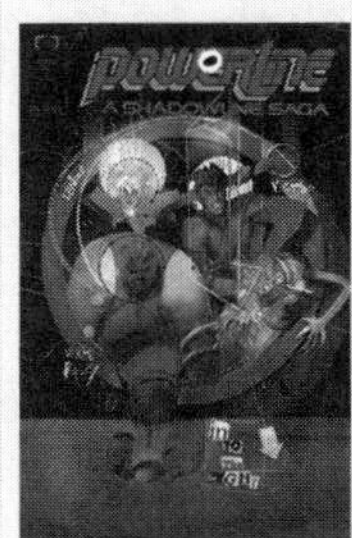

Shadow Dwellers tie Epic epics together
©Marvel

Power Man & Iron Fist

Hero for Hire gets a partner in Iron Fist
©Marvel

Power of Shazam

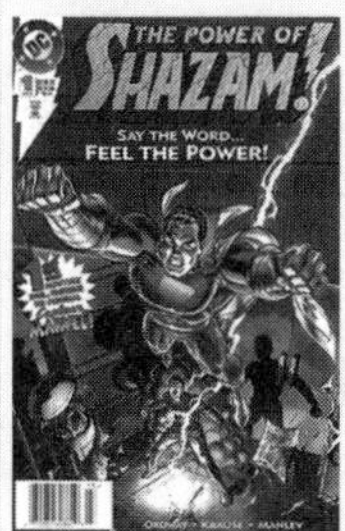

Jerry Ordway updates Captain Marvel
©DC

N-MINT

❑6, Apr 1997, b&w ... 2.50
❑7 ... 2.50
❑8 ... 2.50
❑9 ... 2.50
❑10 ... 2.50
❑11 ... 2.50

POE (VOL. 2)
SIRIUS

❑1, Oct 1997, b&w ... 2.50
❑2, Nov 1997, b&w ... 2.50
❑3, Dec 1997 ... 2.50
❑4, Jan 1998 ... 2.50
❑5, Feb 1998 ... 2.50
❑6, Mar 1998 ... 2.50
❑7, May 1998 ... 2.50
❑8, Jun 1998 ... 2.50
❑9, Jul 1998 ... 2.50
❑10, Aug 1998 ... 2.50
❑11, Sep 1998 ... 2.50
❑12, Oct 1998 ... 2.50
❑13, Nov 1998 ... 2.50
❑14, Jan 1999 ... 2.50
❑15, Feb 1999 ... 2.50
❑16, Mar 1999 ... 2.50
❑17, Apr 1999 ... 2.50
❑18, Aug 1999 ... 2.50
❑19 ... 2.50
❑20 ... 2.50
❑21, Jan 2000 ... 2.95
❑22, Mar 2000 ... 2.95
❑23, May 2000 ... 2.95
❑24, Jul 2000 ... 2.95
❑Special 1, Dec 1998; Color Special ... 2.95

POEMS FOR THE DEAD
BONEYARD

❑Book 1, Mar 1995, b&w ... 10.95

POETS PROSPER: RHYME & REVELRY
TOME

❑1 ... 3.50

POINT BLANK (WILDSTORM)
WILDSTORM

❑1, Oct 2002 ... 2.95
❑2, Nov 2002 ... 2.95
❑3, Dec 2002 ... 2.95
❑4, Jan 2003 ... 2.95
❑5, Feb 2003 ... 2.95

POINT-BLANK
ECLIPSE

❑1, b&w ... 2.95
❑2, b&w ... 2.95

POINT PLEASANT
APE ENTERTAINMENT

❑1, ca. 2004 ... 3.95

POISON ELVES (MULEHIDE)
MULEHIDE

❑8; magazine-sized; Series continued from I, Lusiphur #7 ... 15.00
❑9; magazine-sized ... 12.00
❑10; magazine-sized ... 12.00
❑11 ... 10.00
❑12, Oct 1993 ... 10.00

N-MINT

❑13, Dec 1993 ... 10.00
❑14, Feb 1994 ... 10.00
❑15, Apr 1994; Scarcer ... 10.00
❑15/2nd ... 2.50
❑16, Jun 1994 ... 8.00
❑17 ... 8.00
❑17/2nd ... 2.50
❑18 ... 5.00
❑19 ... 5.00
❑20 ... 5.00
❑Deluxe 1, ca. 2001; Poison Elves: The Mulehide Years ... 34.95

POISON ELVES (SIRIUS)
SIRIUS

❑1, May 1995, b&w ... 6.00
❑1/2nd ... 2.50
❑2, Jun 1995, b&w ... 4.00
❑3, Jul 1995, b&w ... 4.00
❑4, Aug 1995, b&w ... 3.00
❑5, Oct 1995 ... 3.00
❑6, Nov 1995 ... 3.00
❑7, Dec 1995 ... 2.50
❑8, Jan 1996 ... 2.50
❑9 1996 ... 2.50
❑10, Feb 1996 ... 2.50
❑11, Mar 1996 ... 2.50
❑12, Apr 1996 ... 2.50
❑13, May 1996 ... 2.50
❑14, Jun 1996 ... 2.50
❑15 1996 ... 2.50
❑16, Sep 1996 ... 2.50
❑17, Oct 1996 ... 2.50
❑18, Nov 1996 ... 2.50
❑19, Dec 1996 ... 2.50
❑20, Jan 1997 ... 2.50
❑21, Feb 1997 ... 2.50
❑22, Mar 1997 ... 2.50
❑23, Apr 1997 ... 2.50
❑24, May 1997 ... 2.50
❑25, Jul 1997 ... 2.50
❑26, Aug 1997 ... 2.50
❑27, Sep 1997 ... 2.50
❑28, Oct 1997 ... 2.50
❑29, Nov 1997 ... 2.50
❑30, Dec 1997 ... 2.50
❑31, Jan 1998 ... 2.50
❑32, Feb 1998 ... 2.50
❑33, Mar 1998 ... 2.50
❑34, Apr 1998 ... 2.50
❑35, May 1998 ... 2.50
❑36, Jun 1998 ... 2.50
❑37, Jul 1998 ... 2.50
❑38, Aug 1998 ... 2.50
❑39, Sep 1998 ... 2.50
❑40, Oct 1998 ... 2.50
❑41, Nov 1998 ... 2.50
❑42, Dec 1998 ... 2.50
❑43, Jan 1999 ... 2.50
❑44, Feb 1999 ... 2.50
❑45, Mar 1999 ... 2.50
❑46, Jun 1999 ... 2.95
❑47, Jul 1999 ... 2.50
❑48, Aug 1999 ... 2.50
❑49, Sep 1999 ... 2.50

N-MINT

❑50, Oct 1999 ... 2.50
❑51, Nov 1999 ... 2.50
❑52, Dec 1999 ... 2.50
❑53, Jan 2000 ... 2.95
❑54, Feb 2000 ... 2.95
❑55, Mar 2000 ... 2.95
❑56, Apr 2000 ... 2.95
❑57, May 2000 ... 2.95
❑58, Jun 2000 ... 2.95
❑59, Jul 2000 ... 2.95
❑60, Aug 2000 ... 2.95
❑61, Sep 2000 ... 2.95
❑62, Nov 2000 ... 2.95
❑63, Jan 2001 ... 2.95
❑64, Mar 2001 ... 2.95
❑65, May 2001 ... 2.95
❑66, Jul 2001 ... 2.95
❑67, Sep 2001 ... 2.95
❑68, Nov 2001 ... 2.95
❑69, Jan 2002 ... 2.95
❑70, Mar 2002 ... 2.95
❑71, Feb 2003 ... 2.95
❑72, Mar 2003 ... 2.95
❑73, May 2003 ... 2.95
❑74, Aug 2003 ... 2.95
❑75, Dec 2003 ... 2.95
❑76, Mar 2004 ... 2.95
❑77, Mar 2004 ... 2.95
❑79 2004 ... 2.95
❑78, May 2004 ... 2.95
❑Special 1, ca. 1998; Color Special ... 3.00

POISON ELVES: VENTURES
SIRIUS

❑1, Jul 2005 ... 3.50

POIZON
LONDON NIGHT

❑0 ... 3.00
❑0/Nude ... 3.50
❑½ ... 3.00
❑1, Feb 1996 ... 3.00
❑1/A; Green Death edition ... 15.00
❑1/Nude ... 5.00
❑2, Apr 1996 ... 3.00
❑3, Jun 1996 ... 3.00

POKÉMON: THE ELECTRIC TALE OF PIKACHU
VIZ

❑1, Nov 1998 1: Pikachu ... 3.50
❑1/2nd ... 3.25
❑1/3rd, Mar 1999 ... 3.25
❑2, Dec 1998 ... 3.25
❑2/2nd ... 3.25
❑3, Jan 1999 ... 3.25
❑4, Feb 1999 ... 3.25

POKÉMON PART 2
VIZ

❑1, Mar 1999 ... 3.25
❑2, Apr 1999 ... 3.25
❑3, May 1999 ... 3.25
❑4, Jun 1999 ... 2.95

POKÉMON PART 3
VIZ

❑1, Jul 1999 ... 3.50

❑2, Aug 1999 ... 3.50
❑3, Sep 1999 ... 3.50
❑4, Oct 1999 ... 3.50

POKÉMON ADVENTURES
VIZ

❑1, Sep 1999, Mysterious Mew ... 5.95
❑2, Oct 1999, Wanted: Pikachu ... 5.95
❑3, Nov 1999 ... 5.95
❑4, Dec 1999 ... 5.95
❑5, Jan 2000 ... 5.95

POKÉMON ADVENTURES PART 2
VIZ

❑1 2000 ... 2.95
❑2 2000 ... 2.95
❑3 2000 ... 2.95
❑4 2000 ... 2.95
❑5 2000 ... 2.95
❑6 2000 ... 2.95

POKÉMON ADVENTURES PART 3
VIZ

❑1 2000 ... 2.95
❑2 2000 ... 2.95
❑3 2000 ... 2.95
❑4 2000 ... 2.95
❑5 2000 ... 2.95
❑6, Jan 2001 ... 2.95
❑7, Feb 2001 ... 2.95

POKÉMON ADVENTURES PART 4
VIZ

❑1, Mar 2001 ... 2.95
❑2, Apr 2001 ... 2.95
❑3, May 2001 ... 4.95
❑4, Jun 2001 ... 4.95

POKÉMON ADVENTURES PART 5
VIZ

❑1, Jul 2001; Cover logo reads "Yellow Caballero" ... 4.95
❑2, Aug 2001; Cover logo reads "Yellow Caballero" ... 4.95
❑3, Sep 2001; Cover logo reads "Yellow Caballero" ... 4.95
❑4, Oct 2001; Cover logo reads "Yellow Caballero" ... 4.95
❑5, Nov 2001; Cover logo reads "Yellow Caballero" ... 4.95

POKÉMON ADVENTURES PART 6
VIZ

❑1, Dec 2001; Cover logo reads "Yellow Caballero" ... 4.95
❑2, Jan 2002; Cover logo reads "Yellow Caballero" ... 4.95
❑3, Feb 2002; Cover logo reads "Yellow Caballero" ... 4.95
❑4, Mar 2002; Cover logo reads "Yellow Caballero" ... 4.95

POKÉMON ADVENTURES PART 7
VIZ

❑1, Apr 2002; Cover logo reads "Yellow Caballero" ... 4.95
❑2, May 2002; Cover logo reads "Yellow Caballero" ... 4.95
❑3, Jun 2002; Cover logo reads "Yellow Caballero" ... 4.95
❑4, Jul 2002; Cover logo reads "Yellow Caballero" ... 4.95
❑5, Aug 2002; Cover logo reads "Yellow Caballero" ... 4.95

POLICE ACADEMY
MARVEL / STAR

❑1, Oct 1989 ... 1.00
❑2, Nov 1989 ... 1.00
❑3, Dec 1989 ... 1.00
❑4, Jan 1990 ... 1.00
❑5, Feb 1990 ... 1.00
❑6, Mar 1990 ... 1.00

POLICE ACTION (2ND SERIES)
ATLAS-SEABOARD

❑1, Feb 1975; MP (a); Includes Mike Ploog story/art ... 11.00
❑2, Apr 1975; MP, FS (a); Includes Mike Ploog story/art ... 5.00
❑3, Jun 1975; MP (a); Includes Mike Ploog story/art; Frank thorne cover ... 5.00

POLIS
BRAVE NEW WORDS

❑1, b&w ... 2.50
❑2, b&w ... 2.50

POLITICAL ACTION COMICS
COMICFIX

❑1, ca. 2004, John Kerry/John Edwards parody comic for 2004 election campaign ... 4.99

POLLY AND HER PALS
ETERNITY

❑1, Oct 1990, b&w; strip reprints ... 2.95
❑2 1990, b&w; strip reprints ... 2.95
❑3 1991, b&w; strip reprints ... 2.95
❑4 1991, b&w; strip reprints ... 2.95
❑5 1991, b&w; strip reprints ... 2.95

POLLY AND THE PIRATES
ONI

❑1, Sep 2005 ... 2.95
❑2, Nov 2005 ... 2.95

PONYTAIL
DELL

❑-209, Sep 1962, Counted as #1 of the ongoing series ... 12.00
❑2, Jun 1963 ... 8.00
❑3, Sep 1963 ... 8.00
❑4, Dec 1963 ... 8.00
❑5, Mar 1964 ... 8.00
❑6, Jun 1964 ... 8.00
❑7, Sep 1964 ... 8.00
❑8, Dec 1964 ... 8.00
❑9, Mar 1965 ... 8.00
❑10, Jun 1965 ... 8.00
❑11, Sep 1965 ... 8.00
❑12, Dec 1965, Last Dell issue; moves to Charlton ... 8.00

PONYTAIL (CHARLTON)
CHARLTON

❑13, Nov 1969, First Charlton issue ... 6.00
❑14, Jan 1970 ... 4.00
❑15, Mar 1970 ... 4.00
❑16, May 1970 ... 4.00
❑17, Jul 1970 ... 4.00
❑18, Sep 1970 ... 4.00
❑19, Nov 1970 ... 4.00
❑20, Jan 1971 ... 4.00

POOT
FANTAGRAPHICS

❑1, Win 1997 ... 2.95
❑2, Spr 1998 ... 2.95
❑3, Sum 1998 ... 2.95
❑4, Win 1998 ... 3.95

POPBOT
IDEA & DESIGN WORKS

❑1 2002 ... 7.99
❑2 2003 ... 7.99
❑3 2003 ... 7.99
❑4, Jun 2003 ... 7.99
❑5, Mar 2004 ... 9.99
❑7, May 2006 ...

POPCORN!
DISCOVERY

❑1, b&w; cardstock cover ... 3.95

POPCORN PIMPS
FANTAGRAPHICS

❑1, Jun 1996, b&w; squarebound ... 8.95

POPEYE
DELL

❑38, Oct 1956 ... 50.00
❑39, Jan 1957 ... 50.00
❑40, Apr 1957 ... 50.00
❑41, Jul 1957 ... 50.00
❑42, Oct 1957 ... 50.00
❑43, Jan 1958 ... 50.00
❑44, Apr 1958 ... 50.00
❑45, Jul 1958 ... 50.00
❑46, Oct 1958, O: Swee' Pea ... 50.00
❑47, Jan 1959 ... 50.00
❑48, Apr 1959 ... 50.00
❑49, Jul 1959 ... 50.00
❑50, Oct 1959 ... 50.00
❑51, Jan 1960 ... 40.00
❑52, Mar 1960 ... 40.00
❑53, May 1960 ... 40.00
❑54, Jul 1960 ... 40.00
❑55, Jun 1960 ... 40.00
❑56 1960 ... 40.00
❑57 1961 ... 40.00
❑58, Apr 1961 ... 40.00
❑59, Jun 1961 ... 40.00
❑60, Aug 1961 ... 40.00
❑61, Oct 1961 ... 40.00
❑62, Dec 1961 ... 40.00
❑63, Jan 1962 ... 40.00
❑64, Apr 1962 ... 40.00
❑65, Jul 1962, Last Dell issue ... 40.00
❑66, Oct 1962, First Gold Key issue ... 40.00
❑67, Jan 1963 ... 40.00
❑68, May 1963 ... 40.00
❑69, Jul 1963 ... 40.00
❑70, Nov 1963 ... 30.00
❑71, Jan 1964 ... 30.00
❑72, Apr 1964 ... 30.00
❑73, Jul 1964 ... 30.00
❑74, Nov 1964 ... 30.00
❑75, Feb 1965 ... 30.00
❑76, May 1965 ... 30.00
❑77, Aug 1965 ... 30.00
❑78, Nov 1965 ... 30.00
❑79, Feb 1966 ... 30.00
❑80, May 1966 ... 30.00
❑81, Aug 1966 ... 25.00
❑82, Oct 1966, Last Gold Key issue ... 25.00
❑83, Dec 1966, First King issue ... 25.00
❑84, Feb 1967 ... 25.00
❑85, Apr 1967 ... 25.00
❑86, Jun 1967 ... 25.00
❑87, Jul 1967 ... 25.00
❑88, Aug 1967 ... 25.00
❑89, Sep 1967 ... 25.00
❑90, Oct 1967 ... 25.00
❑91, Nov 1967 ... 25.00
❑92, Dec 1967, Last King issue ... 25.00
❑93 1968, First Charlton issue ... 20.00
❑94, Feb 1969 ... 20.00
❑95, Apr 1969 ... 20.00
❑96, Jun 1969 ... 20.00
❑97, Aug 1969 ... 20.00
❑98, Oct 1969 ... 20.00
❑99, Dec 1969 ... 20.00
❑100, Feb 1970 ... 20.00
❑101, Apr 1970 ... 15.00
❑102, Jun 1970 ... 15.00
❑103, Aug 1970 ... 15.00
❑104, Oct 1970 ... 15.00
❑105, Dec 1970 ... 15.00
❑106, Feb 1971, A: Sea Hag. A: Brutus. A: Junior Smith. A: Wimpy. A: Swee' Pea. A: Granny. A: Snuffy Smith. A: Pappy. A: Olive Oyl. A: Ma Smith ... 15.00
❑107, Apr 1971 ... 15.00
❑108, Jun 1971 ... 15.00
❑109, Aug 1971 ... 15.00
❑110, Oct 1971 ... 15.00
❑111, Dec 1971 ... 15.00
❑112, Jan 1972 ... 15.00
❑113, Mar 1972 ... 15.00
❑114, May 1972 ... 15.00
❑115, Jul 1972 ... 15.00
❑116, Sep 1972 ... 15.00
❑117, Nov 1972 ... 15.00
❑118, Feb 1973 ... 15.00
❑119, Apr 1973 ... 15.00
❑120, Jun 1973 ... 15.00
❑121, Aug 1973 ... 10.00
❑122, Oct 1973 ... 10.00
❑123, Nov 1973 ... 10.00
❑124, ca. 1974 ... 10.00
❑125, Sep 1974 ... 10.00
❑126, Dec 1974 ... 10.00
❑127, Feb 1975 ... 10.00
❑128, Apr 1975 ... 10.00
❑129, Jun 1975 ... 10.00
❑130, Aug 1975 ... 10.00
❑131, Oct 1975 ... 10.00
❑132 1976 ... 10.00
❑133 1976 ... 10.00
❑134, ca. 1976 ... 10.00
❑135, ca. 1976 ... 10.00
❑136, ca. 1976 ... 10.00
❑137, ca. 1976 ... 10.00
❑138, Jan 1977, Last Chalton issue ... 10.00
❑139, May 1978, First issue of second Gold Key run ... 7.00
❑140, Jul 1978 ... 7.00
❑141, Sep 1978 ... 7.00

Power Pack

Alien gives Powers children powers
©Marvel

Powerpuff Girls

Sugar and spice combine with Chemical X
©DC

Powers

Super-powered cop solves super-crimes
©Image

Powers That Be

Broadway's debut featured Fatale, Star Seed
©Broadway

Predator

Alien hunters pay New York a visit
©Dark Horse

N-MINT

❑142, Nov 1978 7.00
❑143, Jan 1979 7.00
❑144, Mar 1979 7.00
❑145, Apr 1979 7.00
❑146, May 1979 7.00
❑147, Jun 1979 7.00
❑148, Jul 1979 7.00
❑149, Aug 1979 7.00
❑150 1979 5.00
❑151 1979 5.00
❑152 1980 5.00
❑153 1980 5.00
❑154 1980 5.00
❑155 1980, Last GoldKey label issue 5.00
❑156, Mar 1980, First Whitman-label issue 10.00
❑157 1980 10.00
❑158, Sep 1980 35.00
❑159, Nov 1980 30.00
❑162, Mar 1981, #160-161 never printed 10.00
❑163 1981 10.00
❑164 1981 10.00
❑165 1981 10.00
❑166 1982 10.00
❑167 1982 10.00
❑168, Jun 1983 18.00
❑169 1983 18.00
❑170 1983 18.00
❑171, ca. 1984 18.00
❑Special 1, Bold Detergent giveaway; Reprints issue #94 2.00

POPEYE (HARVEY)
HARVEY

❑1 1.50
❑2 1.50
❑3, Mar 1994 1.50
❑4 1994 1.50
❑5, Jun 1994 1.50
❑6, Jul 1994 1.50
❑Summer 1 2.25

POPEYE SPECIAL
OCEAN

❑1, Sum 1987 O: Popeye 2.00
❑2, Sep 1988 2.00

POP LIFE
FANTAGRAPHICS

❑1, Oct 1998 3.95
❑2, Mar 1999 3.95

POPPLES
MARVEL / STAR

❑1, Dec 1986 1.00
❑2, Feb 1987 1.00
❑3, Apr 1987 1.00
❑4, Jun 1987 1.00

PORK KNIGHT: THIS LITTLE PIGGY
SILVER SNAIL

❑1 2.00

PORKY PIG (GOLD KEY)
GOLD KEY

❑1, Jan 1965, (c); (w); (a) 30.00
❑2, May 1965, (c); (w); (a) 14.00
❑3, Aug 1965, (c); (w); (a) 12.00

N-MINT

❑4, Nov 1965, (c); (w); (a) 12.00
❑5, Mar 1966, (c); (w); (a) 12.00
❑6, Jun 1966, (c); (w); (a) 8.00
❑7, Jul 1966, (c); (w); (a) 8.00
❑8, Sep 1966, (c); (w); (a) 8.00
❑9, Nov 1966, (c); (w); (a); Cover code 10140-611 8.00
❑10, Jan 1967, (c); (w); (a) 8.00
❑11, Mar 1967, (c); (w); (a) 5.00
❑12, May 1967, (c); (w); (a) 5.00
❑13, Jul 1967, (c); (w); (a) 5.00
❑14, Sep 1967, (c); (w); (a) 5.00
❑15, Nov 1967, (c); (w); (a) 5.00
❑16, Jan 1968, (c); (w); (a) 5.00
❑17, ca. 1968, (c); (w); (a) 5.00
❑18, Jun 1968, (c); (w); (a) 5.00
❑19, Aug 1968, (c); (w); (a) 5.00
❑20, Oct 1968, (c); (w); (a) 5.00
❑21, Dec 1968, (c); (w); (a) 4.00
❑22, Feb 1969, (c); (w); (a) 4.00
❑23, Apr 1969, (c); (w); (a) 4.00
❑24, Jun 1969, (c); (w); (a) 4.00
❑25, Aug 1969, (c); (w); (a) 4.00
❑26, Oct 1969, (c); (w); (a) 4.00
❑27, Dec 1969, (c); (w); (a) 4.00
❑28, Feb 1970, (w); (a) 4.00
❑29, Apr 1970, (c); (w); (a) 4.00
❑30, Jun 1970, (c); (w); (a) 4.00
❑31, Aug 1970 3.00
❑32, Oct 1970 3.00
❑33, Dec 1970 3.00
❑34, Feb 1971 3.00
❑35, Apr 1971 3.00
❑36, Jun 1971 3.00
❑37, Aug 1971 3.00
❑38, Oct 1971 3.00
❑39, Dec 1971 3.00
❑40, Feb 1972 3.00
❑41, Apr 1972, Cover code 90140-204 3.00
❑42, Jun 1972, Cover code 90140-206 3.00
❑43, Aug 1972, Cover code 90140-208 3.00
❑44, Oct 1972, Cover code 90140-210 3.00
❑45, Dec 1972, Cover code 90140-212 3.00
❑46, Feb 1973, Cover code 90140-302 3.00
❑47, Apr 1973, Cover code 90140-304 3.00
❑48, Jun 1973, Cover code 90140-306 3.00
❑49, Aug 1973, Cover code 90140-308 3.00
❑50, Oct 1973, Cover code 90140-310 3.00
❑51, Dec 1973, Cover code 90140-312 2.00
❑52, Feb 1974, Cover code 90140-402 2.00
❑53, Apr 1974, Cover code 90140-404 2.00
❑54, Jun 1974, Cover code 90140-406 2.00
❑55, Aug 1974, Cover code 90140-408 2.00
❑56, Oct 1974, Cover code 90140-410 2.00
❑57, Dec 1974, Cover code 90140-412 2.00
❑58, Feb 1975, Cover code 90140-502 2.00
❑59, Apr 1975, Cover code 90140-504 2.00
❑60, Jun 1975, Cover code 90140-506 2.00
❑61, Aug 1975 2.00
❑62, Sep 1975 2.00
❑63, Oct 1975 2.00
❑64, Nov 1975 2.00
❑65, Dec 1975 2.00
❑66, Apr 1976 2.00

N-MINT

❑67, Jun 1976 2.00
❑68, Jul 1976 2.00
❑69, Aug 1976 2.00
❑70, Sep 1976 2.00
❑71, Nov 1976 2.00
❑72, Jan 1977 2.00
❑73, Mar 1977 2.00
❑74, May 1977 2.00
❑75, Jul 1977 2.00
❑76, Aug 1977 2.00
❑77, Sep 1977 2.00
❑78, Nov 1977 2.00
❑79, Jan 1978 2.00
❑80, Mar 1978 2.00
❑81, May 1978 2.00
❑82, Jul 1978 2.00
❑83, Aug 1978 2.00
❑84, Sep 1978 2.00
❑85, Oct 1978 2.00
❑86, Nov 1978 2.00
❑87, Jan 1979 2.00
❑88, Mar 1979 2.00
❑89, May 1979 2.00
❑90, Jul 1979 2.00
❑91, Sep 1979 2.00
❑92, Nov 1979 2.00
❑93, Jan 1980 2.00
❑94, Mar 1980 2.00
❑95, May 1980 2.00
❑96, Jul 1980 2.00
❑97, Sep 1980 2.00
❑98, Nov 1980 2.00
❑99, Jan 1981 2.00
❑100, Mar 1981 2.00
❑101, ca. 1981 2.00
❑102, Sep 1981 2.00
❑103, Nov 1981 2.00
❑104, Feb 1982 2.00
❑105, Apr 1982 2.00
❑106 2.00
❑107 2.00
❑108 2.00
❑109, ca. 1984 2.00

PORNOTOPIA
RADIO

❑1, Aug 1999 2.95

PORT
SILVERWOLF

❑1, b&w 1.50
❑2, b&w 1.50

PORTABLE LOWLIFE
AEON

❑1, Jul 1993; prestige format 4.95

PORTALS OF ELONDAR
STORYBOOK

❑1, Jul 1996, b&w 2.95

PORTENT
IMAGE

❑1, Mar 2006 2.95
❑2, May 2006 2.95
❑3, Jul 2006 2.95

PORTIA PRINZ OF THE GLAMAZONS
ECLIPSE

❑1, Dec 1986, b&w 2.00

❑2, Feb 1987, b&w 2.00
❑3, Apr 1987, b&w 2.00
❑4, Jun 1987, b&w 2.00
❑5, Aug 1987, b&w 2.00
❑6, Oct 1987, b&w 2.00

PORTRAIT OF A YOUNG MAN AS A CARTOONIST
Hammer & Anvil

❑1, Oct 1996 2.95
❑2, Dec 1996 2.95
❑3, Feb 1997 2.95
❑4, Apr 1997 2.95
❑5, Jun 1997 2.95
❑6, Aug 1997 2.95
❑7, Oct 1997 2.95
❑8, Jan 1998 2.95

POSSESSED
DC / Cliffhanger

❑1, Sep 2003 2.95
❑2, Oct 2003 2.95
❑3, Nov 2003 2.95
❑4, Dec 2003 2.95
❑5, Jan 2004 2.95
❑6, Mar 2004 2.95

POSSIBLEMAN
Blackthorne

❑1, Jan 1987 1.75
❑2, Apr 1987 1.75

POST APOCALYPSE
Slave Labor

❑1, Dec 1994 2.95

(POST-ATOMIC) CYBORG GERBILS
Trigon

❑1, Aug 1986 2.50
❑2 2.50

POST BROTHERS
Rip Off

❑19, Apr 1991, b&w; Series continued from Those Annoying Post Brothers #18 2.50
❑20, Jun 1991, b&w 2.50
❑21, Aug 1991, b&w 2.50
❑22, Oct 1991, b&w 2.50
❑23, Oct 1991, b&w 2.50
❑24, Dec 1991, b&w 2.50
❑25, Feb 1992, b&w 2.50
❑26, Apr 1992, b&w 2.50
❑27, Jun 1992, b&w 2.50
❑28, Aug 1992, b&w 2.50
❑29, Oct 1992, b&w 2.50
❑30, Dec 1992, b&w 2.50
❑31, Feb 1993, b&w 2.50
❑32, Apr 1993, b&w 2.50
❑33, Jun 1993, b&w; Listed as "Those Annoying Post Brothers" 2.50
❑34, Aug 1993, b&w 2.50
❑35, Oct 1993, b&w 2.50
❑36, Dec 1993, b&w 2.50
❑37, Feb 1994, b&w 2.50
❑38, Apr 1994, b&w; series continues as Those Annoying Post Bros. 2.50

POTENTIAL
Slave Labor

❑1, Mar 1998, b&w; magazine-sized 3.50
❑2 3.50
❑3, Sep 1998 4.95
❑4, Feb 1999 3.50

POUND
Radio

❑1, Mar 2000, b&w 2.95

POUNDED
Oni

❑1 2002 2.95
❑2 2002 2.95
❑3 2002 2.95

POWDER BURN
Antarctic

❑1, Mar 1999, b&w 2.99
❑1/A, Mar 1999, b&w; wraparound cover 2.99
❑1/CS, Mar 1999; Collector's Set 5.99

POWER
Aircel

❑1, Mar 1991, b&w 2.25
❑2, Apr 1991, b&w 2.25
❑3, May 1991, b&w 2.25
❑4, Jun 1991, b&w 2.25

POWER & GLORY
Malibu / Bravura

❑1/A, Feb 1994, HC (w); HC (a); Alternate cover (marked) 2.50
❑1/B, Feb 1994, HC (w); HC (a); Alternate cover (marked) 2.50
❑1/Gold, Feb 1994, sendaway with gold ink on cover
❑1/Ltd., Feb 1994, serigraph cover 2.50
❑1/Variant, Feb 1994, blue foil 3.00
❑2, Mar 1994, HC (w); HC (a) 2.50
❑3, Apr 1994, HC (w); HC (a) 2.50
❑4, May 1994, HC (w); HC (a) 2.50
❑WS 1, Dec 1994, Giant-size; HC (w); HC (a); Winter Special #1 2.95

POWER BRIGADE
Moving Target / Malibu

❑1 1.75

POWER COMICS (POWER)
Power

❑1, Aug 1977; 1st Dave Sim aardvark 2.00
❑1/2nd 2.00
❑2, Sep 1977 2.00
❑3, Oct 1977 2.00
❑4, Nov 1977 2.00
❑5, Dec 1977 2.00

POWER COMICS (ECLIPSE)
Eclipse

❑1, Mar 1988, b&w 2.00
❑2, May 1988, b&w 2.00
❑3, Jul 1988, b&w 2.00
❑4, Sep 1988, b&w 2.00

POWER COMPANY
DC

❑1, Apr 2002 3.00
❑2, May 2002 2.50
❑3, Jun 2002 2.50
❑4, Jul 2002 2.50
❑5, Aug 2002 2.50
❑6, Sep 2002 2.50
❑7, Oct 2002 2.75
❑8, Nov 2002 2.75
❑9, Dec 2002 KB (w) 2.75
❑10, Jan 2003 KB (w) 2.75
❑11, Feb 2003 KB (w) 2.75
❑12, Mar 2003 KB (w) 2.75
❑13, Apr 2003 2.75
❑14, May 2003 2.75
❑15, Jun 2003 2.75
❑16, Jul 2003 2.75
❑17, Aug 2003 2.75
❑18, Sep 2003 2.75

POWER COMPANY: BORK
DC

❑1, Mar 2002 2.50

POWER COMPANY: JOSIAH POWER
DC

❑1, Mar 2002 2.50

POWER COMPANY: MANHUNTER
DC

❑1, Mar 2002 2.50

POWER COMPANY: SAPPHIRE
DC

❑1, Mar 2002 2.50

POWER COMPANY: SKYROCKET
DC

❑1, Mar 2002 2.50

POWER COMPANY: STRIKER Z
DC

❑1, Mar 2002 2.50

POWER COMPANY: WITCHFIRE
DC

❑1, Mar 2002 2.50

POWER DEFENSE
Miller

❑1, b&w 2.50

POWER FACTOR (1ST SERIES)
Wonder

❑1, May 1986; Wonder Color Publisher 1.95
❑2, Jun 1986; Pied Piper Publisher 1.95

POWER FACTOR (2ND SERIES)
Innovation

❑1, Oct 1990 1.95
❑2, Dec 1990 2.25
❑3, Feb 1991 2.25
❑Special 1, Jan 1991 2.75

POWER GIRL
DC

❑1, Jun 1988 1.00
❑2, Jul 1988 1.00
❑3, Aug 1988 1.00
❑4, Sep 1988 1.00

POWERLESS
Marvel

❑1, Aug 2004 2.99
❑2, Sep 2004 2.99
❑3, Oct 2004 2.99
❑4, Nov 2004 2.99
❑5, Dec 2004 2.99
❑6 2.99

POWER LINE
Marvel / Epic

❑1, May 1988 BSz (c); BSz (a) 1.50
❑2, Jul 1988 1.50
❑3, Sep 1988 1.50
❑4, Nov 1988 1.50
❑5, Jan 1989 1.50
❑6, Mar 1989 1.50
❑7, May 1989 GM (a) 1.50
❑8, Jul 1989 1.50

POWER LORDS
DC

❑1, Dec 1983 O: Power Lords. 1: Power Lords 1.00
❑2, Jan 1984 1.00
❑3, Feb 1985 1.00

POWER MAN & IRON FIST
Marvel

❑17, Feb 1974, GK (c); GT (a); A: Iron Man. Title continued from "Hero For Hire" 8.00
❑18, Apr 1974, GK (c); GT (a); Marvel Value Stamp #3: Conan 5.00
❑19, Jun 1974, GK (c); GT (a); Marvel Value Stamp #64: Sif 5.00
❑20, Aug 1974, GK (c); GT (a); Marvel Value Stamp #1: Spider-Man 5.00
❑21, Oct 1974, V: Power Man. Marvel Value Stamp #73: Kingpin 4.00
❑22, Dec 1974 4.00
❑23, Feb 1975, Marvel Value Stamp #3: Conan 4.00
❑24, Apr 1975, GK (c); GT (a); 1: Black Goliath. V: Circus of Crime. Marvel Value Stamp #27: Black Widow 4.00
❑25, Jun 1975, GK (c); V: Circus of Crime 4.00
❑26, Aug 1975, GK (c); GT (a) 4.00
❑27, Oct 1975, GP (a) 4.00
❑28, Dec 1975 4.00
❑29, Feb 1976 4.00
❑30, Apr 1976 4.00
❑30/30 cent, Apr 1976, 30 cent regional price variant 20.00
❑31, May 1976, NA (a) 4.00
❑31/30 cent, May 1976, NA (a); 30 cent regional price variant 20.00
❑32, Jun 1976 3.00
❑32/30 cent, Jun 1976, 30 cent regional price variant 20.00
❑33, Jul 1976 3.00
❑33/30 cent, Jul 1976, 30 cent regional price variant 20.00
❑34, Aug 1976 3.00
❑34/30 cent, Aug 1976, 30 cent regional price variant 20.00
❑35, Sep 1976 3.00
❑36, Oct 1976 3.00
❑37, Nov 1976, 1: Chemistro II (Archibald "Arch" Morton) 3.00
❑38, Dec 1976 3.00
❑39, Jan 1977 3.00
❑40, Feb 1977 3.00
❑41, Mar 1977, 1: Thunderbolt (William Carver as…) 3.00
❑42, Apr 1977 3.00
❑43, May 1977 3.00
❑44, Jun 1977 3.00

Pre-Teen Dirty-Gene Kung-Fu Kangaroos

Turtles rip-off has Turtles appearance

©Blackthorne

Prez

Keen teen becomes chief exec

©DC

Prime (Vol. 1)

Super shell turns to slime when done

©Malibu

Primer

Grendel premiered in Comico test title

©Comico

Primortals (Vol. 1) (Leonard Nimoy's...)

Tekno title featured actual celebrity input

©Tekno

	N-MINT
❑44/35 cent, Jun 1977, 35 cent regional price variant	15.00
❑45, Jul 1977, JSn (a); A: Mace	3.00
❑45/35 cent, Jul 1977, JSn (a); A: Mace. 35 cent regional price variant	15.00
❑46, Aug 1977, GT (a); 1: Zzax	3.00
❑46/35 cent, Aug 1977, GT (a); 1: Zzax. 35 cent regional price variant	15.00
❑47, Oct 1977, A: Iron Fist. Newsstand edition (distributed by Curtis); issue number in box	3.00
❑47/Whitman, Oct 1977, A: Iron Fist. Special markets edition (usually sold in Whitman bagged prepacks); price appears in a diamond; no UPC barcode	3.00
❑47/35 cent, Oct 1977, A: Iron Fist. 35 cent regional price variant; newsstand edition (distributed by Curtis); issue number in box	15.00
❑48, Dec 1977, JBy (a); 1: Power Man and Iron Fist	10.00
❑49, Feb 1978, JBy (a); A: Iron Fist. series continues as Power Man & Iron Fist	6.00
❑50, Apr 1978, JBy (a)	6.00
❑51, Jun 1978	3.00
❑52, Aug 1978	3.00
❑53, Oct 1978, O: Nightshade	4.00
❑54, Dec 1978, O: Iron Fist	4.00
❑55, Feb 1979	4.00
❑56, Apr 1979, O: Señor Suerte II (Jaime Garcia). 1: Señor Suerte II (Jaime Garcia)	3.00
❑57, Jun 1979, A: X-Men	12.00
❑58, Aug 1979, 1: El Aguila	3.00
❑59, Oct 1979, BL (a)	3.00
❑60, Dec 1979, BL (a)	3.00
❑61, Feb 1980, BL (a)	3.00
❑62, Apr 1980, BL (a); D: Thunderbolt	3.00
❑63, Jun 1980, BL (a)	3.00
❑64, Aug 1980, BL (a)	3.00
❑65, Oct 1980, BL (a); V: El Aguila	3.00
❑66, Dec 1980, FM (c); FM (a); 2: Sabretooth	20.00
❑67, Feb 1981, FM (c); FM (a)	2.00
❑68, Apr 1981, FM (c); FM (a)	2.00
❑69, May 1981	2.00
❑70, Jun 1981, FM (c); FM (a); O: Colleen Wing	2.00
❑71, Jul 1981, FM (c); FM (a)	2.00
❑72, Aug 1981, FM (c); FM (a)	2.00
❑73, Sep 1981, FM (c); FM (a); A: ROM	2.00
❑74, Oct 1981, FM (c)	2.00
❑75, Nov 1981, origins	2.00
❑76, Dec 1981, FM (a)	2.00
❑77, Jan 1982, A: Daredevil	2.00
❑78, Feb 1982, A: Sabretooth. V: El Aguila	5.00
❑79, Mar 1982	2.00
❑80, Apr 1982, FM (c); FM (a); V: Montenegro	2.00
❑81, May 1982	2.00
❑82, Jun 1982	2.00
❑83, Jul 1982	2.00
❑84, Aug 1982, A: Sabretooth	6.00
❑85, Sep 1982	2.00
❑86, Oct 1982, A: Moon Knight	2.00
❑87, Nov 1982, A: Moon Knight	2.00
❑88, Dec 1982	2.00
❑89, Jan 1983	2.00
❑90, Feb 1983, KB (w); A: Unus the Untouchable. V: Unus. Kurt Busiek's first Marvel work	2.00
❑91, Mar 1983	2.00
❑92, Apr 1983, KB (w); 1: Eel II (Edward Lavell). V: Hammerhead	2.00
❑93, May 1983, KB (w); V: Chemistro	2.00
❑94, Jun 1983, KB (w); 1: Chemistro III (Calvin Carr)	2.00
❑95, Jul 1983, KB (w)	2.00
❑96, Aug 1983, KB (w); V: Chemistro	2.00
❑97, Sep 1983, KB (w); V: Fera	2.00
❑98, Oct 1983, KB (w);	2.00
❑99, Nov 1983, KB (w); V: Fera	2.00
❑100, Dec 1983, Giant-size KB (w); V: Khan	2.00
❑101, Jan 1984	2.00
❑102, Feb 1984, KB (w)	2.00
❑103, Mar 1984	2.00
❑104, Apr 1984	2.00
❑105, May 1984, KB (w)	2.00
❑106, Jun 1984	2.00
❑107, Jul 1984	2.00
❑108, Aug 1984	2.00
❑109, Sep 1984, V: Reaper	2.00
❑110, Oct 1984	2.00
❑111, Nov 1984	2.00
❑112, Dec 1984	2.00
❑113, Jan 1985, D: Solarr	2.00
❑114, Feb 1985, JBy (c)	2.00
❑115, Mar 1985	2.00
❑116, Apr 1985	2.00
❑117, May 1985	2.00
❑118, Jul 1985	2.00
❑119, Sep 1985	2.00
❑120, Nov 1985	2.00
❑121, Jan 1986, Secret Wars II	2.00
❑122, Mar 1986	2.00
❑123, May 1986	2.00
❑124, Jul 1986	2.00
❑125, Sep 1986, D: Iron Fist (H'yithri double)	2.00
❑Annual 1, Jan 1976	3.50

POWER OF PRIME

MALIBU / ULTRAVERSE

	N-MINT
❑1, Jul 1995; story continues in Prime #25 and #26	2.50
❑2, Aug 1995	2.50
❑3, Sep 1995	2.50
❑4, Nov 1995	2.50

POWER OF SHAZAM

DC

	N-MINT
❑1, Mar 1995 JOy (w)	3.00
❑2, Apr 1995 JOy (w); V: Arson Fiend	2.00
❑3, May 1995 JOy (w)	2.00
❑4, Jun 1995; JOy (w); Return of Mary Marvel, Tawky Tawny	2.00
❑5, Jul 1995 JOy (w)	2.00
❑6, Aug 1995; JOy (w); Return of Captain Nazi; Freddy Freeman and grandfather injured	2.00
❑7, Sep 1995; JOy (w); Return of Captain Marvel Jr.	2.00
❑8, Oct 1995 JOy (w); CS (a); A: Minuteman. A: Bulletman. A: Spy Smasher	2.00
❑9, Nov 1995 JOy (w);	2.00
❑10, Dec 1995 JOy (w); O: Satanus. O: Blaze. O: Black Adam. O: Rock of Eternity. O: Shazam	2.00
❑11, Jan 1996; JOy (w); A: Bulletman. Return of Ibis; Return of Uncle Marvel; Return of Marvel Family	1.75
❑12, Feb 1996 JOy (w); O: Seven Deadly Foes of Man	1.75
❑13, Mar 1996 JOy (w);	1.75
❑14, Apr 1996; JOy (w); GK (a); 1: Chain Lightning. Captain Marvel Jr. solo story	1.75
❑15, Jun 1996 JOy (w)	1.75
❑16, Jul 1996 JOy (w)	1.75
❑17, Aug 1996 JOy (w)	1.75
❑18, Sep 1996 JOy (w)	1.75
❑19, Oct 1996; JOy (w); GK, JSa (a); A: Minuteman. Captain Marvel Jr. vs. Captain Nazi	1.75
❑20, Nov 1996; JOy (w); A: Superman. Final Night	1.75
❑21, Dec 1996 JOy (w); A: Plastic Man	1.75
❑22, Jan 1997 JOy (w); A: Batman	1.75
❑23, Feb 1997 JOy (w); V: Mr. Atom	1.75
❑24, Mar 1997 JOy (w); A: C.C. Batson. A: Baron Blitzkrieg. A: Spy Smasher	1.75
❑25, Apr 1997; V: Ibac. C.C. Batson as Captain Marvel	1.75
❑26, May 1997; Shazam attempts to set time right again	1.75
❑27, Jun 1997; A: Waverider. time is restored to proper course	1.75
❑28, Jul 1997 DG (a)	1.75
❑29, Aug 1997 A: Hoppy the Marvel Bunny	1.75
❑30, Sep 1997; V: Mr. Finish. Mary receives new costume	1.75
❑31, Oct 1997; Genesis; Billy and Mary reveal their identities to the Bromfields	1.95
❑32, Nov 1997 1: Windshear	1.95
❑33, Dec 1997; JOy (w); Face cover	1.95
❑34, Jan 1998 JOy (w); A: Gangbuster	1.95
❑35, Feb 1998; A: Starman. continues in Starman #40	1.95
❑36, Mar 1998 A: Starman	1.95
❑37, Apr 1998; JOy (w); CM3 vs. Doctor Morpheus; CM3 vs. Dr. Morpheus	1.95
❑38, May 1998	1.95
❑39, Jun 1998	1.95
❑40, Jul 1998	1.95
❑41, Aug 1998 D: Mr. Mind	1.95
❑42, Sep 1998 A: Chain Lightning	1.95
❑43, Oct 1998; kids on life support	2.50
❑44, Dec 1998 A: Black Adam. A: Thunder	2.50
❑45, Jan 1999 A: Justice League of America	2.50
❑46, Feb 1999 JOy (w); JOy (a); A: Superman. A: Black Adam. V: Superman	2.50
❑47, Mar 1999 JOy (w); JOy (a); A: Black Adam	2.50
❑1000000, Nov 1998 JOy (w); JOy (a)	4.00

Other grades: Multiply price above by 5/6 for VF/NM • 2/3 for VERY FINE • 1/3 for FINE • 1/5 for VERY GOOD • 1/8 for GOOD

N-MINT

❑Annual 1, ca. 1996; JOy (w); 1996; Legends of the Dead Earth 2.95

POWER OF STRONG MAN
AC

❑1, b&w; Reprints 2.50

POWER OF THE ATOM
DC

❑1, Aug 1988 ..... 1.00
❑2, Sep 1988 ..... 1.00
❑3, Oct 1988 ..... 1.00
❑4, Nov 1988; Bonus Book #8 ..... 1.00
❑5, Dec 1988 ..... 1.00
❑6, Win 1988 ..... 1.00
❑7, Hol 1988; Invasion! 1.00
❑8, Jan 1989; Invasion! 1.00
❑9, Feb 1989 ..... 1.00
❑10, Mar 1989 ..... 1.00
❑11, Apr 1989 ..... 1.00
❑12, May 1989 ..... 1.00
❑13, Jun 1989 ..... 1.00
❑14, Jul 1989 ..... 1.00
❑15, Aug 1989 ..... 1.00
❑16, Sep 1989 ..... 1.00
❑17, Oct 1989 ..... 1.00
❑18, Nov 1989 ..... 1.00

POWER PACHYDERMS
MARVEL

❑1, Sep 1989; one-shot parody 1.00

POWER PACK
MARVEL

❑1, Aug 1984; Giant-size O: Mass Master. O: Power Pack. O: Lightspeed. 1: Mass Master. 1: Power Pack. 1: Lightspeed. V: Snarks 2.00
❑2, Sep 1984 ..... 1.50
❑3, Oct 1984 ..... 1.00
❑4, Nov 1984 ..... 1.00
❑5, Dec 1984 ..... 1.00
❑6, Jan 1985, A: Spider-Man 1.00
❑7, Feb 1985, A: Cloak & Dagger 1.00
❑8, Mar 1985, A: Cloak & Dagger 1.00
❑9, Apr 1985, BA (a) 1.00
❑10, May 1985, BA (a) 2.00
❑11, Jun 1985 ..... 1.00
❑12, Jul 1985, A: X-Men 1.00
❑13, Aug 1985, BA, BWi (c); BA, BWi (a) 1.00
❑14, Sep 1985, BWi (c); BWi (a) 1.00
❑15, Oct 1985, BWi (c); BWi (a) 1.00
❑16, Nov 1985, 1: Kofi 1.00
❑17, Dec 1985 ..... 1.00
❑18, Jan 1986, BA (a) 1.00
❑19, Feb 1986; Giant-size BA (a); A: Wolverine 1.50
❑20, Mar 1986 A: New Mutants 1.00
❑21, Apr 1986 BA (a) 1.00
❑22, May 1986 ..... 1.00
❑23, Jun 1986 ..... 1.00
❑24, Jul 1986 ..... 1.00
❑25, Aug 1986 ..... 1.25
❑26, Oct 1986 A: Cloak & Dagger 1.00
❑27, Dec 1986 A: Wolverine. A: Sabretooth 4.00
❑28, Feb 1987 A: Fantastic Four. A: Avengers 1.00
❑29, Apr 1987; Giant-size DGr (c); DGr (a); A: Hobgoblin. A: Spider-Man 1.00
❑30, Jun 1987 VM (a) 1.00
❑31, Aug 1987 1: Trash 1.00
❑32, Oct 1987 ..... 1.00
❑33, Nov 1987 ..... 1.00
❑34, Jan 1988 ..... 1.00
❑35, Feb 1988; Fall of Mutants 1.00
❑36, Apr 1988 ..... 1.00
❑37, May 1988 ..... 1.00
❑38, Jul 1988 ..... 1.00
❑39, Aug 1988 ..... 1.00
❑40, Sep 1988 ..... 1.00
❑41, Nov 1988 ..... 1.00
❑42, Dec 1988 A: Inferno 1.00
❑43, Jan 1989 A: Inferno 1.00
❑44, Mar 1989 A: Inferno 1.50
❑45, Apr 1989 ..... 1.50
❑46, May 1989 A: Punisher 1.50
❑47, Jul 1989 ..... 1.50
❑48, Sep 1989 ..... 1.50
❑49, Oct 1989 ..... 1.50
❑50, Nov 1989; Giant-size 2.00
❑51, Dec 1989 1: Numinus 1.50
❑52, Dec 1989 ..... 1.50
❑53, Jan 1990 ..... 1.50
❑54, Feb 1990 ..... 1.50
❑55, Apr 1990 A: Mysterio 1.50
❑56, Jun 1990 ..... 1.50
❑57, Jul 1990 ..... 1.50
❑58, Sep 1990 A: Galactus 1.50
❑59, Oct 1990 ..... 1.50
❑60, Nov 1990 ..... 1.50
❑61, Dec 1990 ..... 1.50
❑62, Jan 1991 ..... 2.00
❑Holiday 1, Feb 1992; magazine-sized 2.50

POWER PACK (VOL. 2)
MARVEL

❑1, Aug 2000 ..... 2.99

POWER PACK (VOL. 3)
MARVEL

❑1, May 2005 ..... 2.99
❑2, Jun 2005 ..... 2.99
❑3, Jul 2005 ..... 2.99
❑4, Aug 2005 ..... 2.99

POWER PLAYS (MILLENNIUM)
MILLENNIUM

❑1, Feb 1995 ..... 2.95

POWER PLAYS (AC)
AC

❑1, b&w 1.75
❑2, Fal 1985, b&w 1.75

POWER PLAYS (EXTRAVA-GANDT)
EXTRAVA-GANDT

❑1, b&w 2.00
❑2 ..... 2.00
❑3, b&w 2.00

POWERPUFF GIRLS
DC

❑1, May 2000 ..... 5.00
❑2, Jun 2000 ..... 3.00
❑3, Jul 2000 ..... 2.50
❑4, Aug 2000 ..... 2.00
❑5, Sep 2000 ..... 1.99
❑6, Oct 2000 ..... 1.99
❑7, Nov 2000 ..... 1.99
❑8, Dec 2000 ..... 1.99
❑9, Jan 2001 ..... 1.99
❑10, Feb 2001 ..... 1.99
❑11, Mar 2001 ..... 1.99
❑12, Apr 2001 ..... 1.99
❑13, May 2001 ..... 1.99
❑14, Jun 2001 ..... 1.99
❑15, Jul 2001 ..... 1.99
❑16, Aug 2001 ..... 1.99
❑17, Sep 2001 ..... 1.99
❑18, Oct 2001 ..... 1.99
❑19, Nov 2001 ..... 1.99
❑20, Dec 2001 ..... 1.99
❑21, Jan 2002 ..... 1.99
❑22, Feb 2002 ..... 1.99
❑23, Mar 2002 ..... 1.99
❑24, Apr 2002 ..... 1.99
❑25, May 2002, JBy (a) 1.99
❑26, Jun 2002 ..... 1.99
❑27, Jul 2002 ..... 1.99
❑28, Aug 2002 ..... 1.99
❑29, Oct 2002 ..... 2.25
❑30, Nov 2002 ..... 2.25
❑31, Dec 2002 ..... 2.25
❑32, Jan 2003 ..... 2.25
❑33, Feb 2003 ..... 2.25
❑34, Mar 2003 ..... 2.25
❑35, Apr 2003 ..... 2.25
❑36, May 2003 ..... 2.25
❑37, Jun 2003 ..... 2.25
❑38, Jul 2003 ..... 2.25
❑39, Aug 2003 ..... 2.25
❑40, Sep 2003 ..... 2.25
❑41, Oct 2003 ..... 2.25
❑42, Nov 2003 ..... 2.25
❑43, Dec 2003 ..... 2.25
❑44, Jan 2004 ..... 2.25
❑45, Feb 2004 ..... 2.25
❑46, Mar 2004 ..... 2.25
❑47, Apr 2004 ..... 2.25
❑48, May 2004 ..... 2.25
❑49, Jun 2004 ..... 2.25
❑50, Jul 2004 ..... 2.25
❑51, Aug 2004 ..... 2.25
❑52, Sep 2004 ..... 2.25
❑53, Oct 2004 ..... 2.25
❑54, Nov 2004 ..... 2.25
❑55, Dec 2004 ..... 2.25
❑56, Jan 2005 ..... 2.25
❑57, Feb 2005 ..... 2.25
❑58, Mar 2005 ..... 2.25
❑59, Apr 2005 ..... 2.25
❑60, May 2005 ..... 2.25
❑61, Jun 2005 ..... 2.25
❑62, Jul 2005 ..... 2.25
❑63, Aug 2005 ..... 2.25
❑64, Sep 2005 ..... 2.25
❑65, Oct 2005 ..... 2.25
❑66 2005 ..... 2.25
❑67, Dec 2005 ..... 2.25
❑68, Jan 2006 ..... 2.25
❑69, Feb 2006 ..... 2.25
❑70, Mar 2006 ..... 2.25

POWERPUFF GIRLS DOUBLE WHAMMY
DC

❑1, Dec 2000; Collects stories from Powerpuff Girls #1-2, Dexter's Laboratory #7 ..... 5.00

POWER RANGERS TURBO: INTO THE FIRE
ACCLAIM

❑1 ..... 4.50

POWER RANGERS ZEO
IMAGE

❑1, Sep 1996 ..... 2.50
❑2, Oct 1996 ..... 2.50

POWERS
IMAGE

❑1, Apr 2000 BMB (w) 7.00
❑2, May 2000 BMB (w) 6.00
❑3, Jun 2000; BMB (w); #1 in indicia 5.00
❑4, Aug 2000 BMB (w) 3.50
❑5, Sep 2000 BMB (w) 4.00
❑6, Oct 2000 BMB (w) 4.00
❑7, Nov 2000 BMB (w) 4.00
❑8, Dec 2001 BMB (w) 4.00
❑9, Jan 2001 BMB (w) 4.00
❑10, Mar 2001 BMB (w) 4.00
❑11, Apr 2001 BMB (w) 2.95
❑12, Jun 2001 BMB (w) 2.95
❑13, Jun 2001 BMB (w) 2.95
❑14, Jul 2001 BMB (w) 2.95
❑15, Aug 2001 BMB (w) 2.95
❑16, Sep 2001 BMB (w) 2.95
❑17, Oct 2001 BMB (w) 2.95
❑18, Nov 2001 BMB (w) 2.95
❑19, Dec 2001 BMB (w) 2.95
❑20, Jan 2002 BMB (w) 2.95
❑21, ca. 2002 ..... 2.95
❑22, ca. 2002 ..... 2.95
❑23, ca. 2002 ..... 2.95
❑24, ca. 2002 ..... 2.95
❑25, ca. 2002 ..... 2.95
❑26, Dec 2002 ..... 2.95
❑27, Feb 2003 ..... 2.95
❑28, Jan 2003 ..... 2.95
❑29, Feb 2003 ..... 2.95
❑30, Mar 2003 ..... 2.95
❑31, Apr 2003 ..... 2.95
❑32, Jun 2003 ..... 2.95
❑33, Aug 2003 ..... 2.95
❑34, Oct 2003 ..... 2.95
❑35, Nov 2003 ..... 2.95
❑36, Jan 2004 ..... 2.95
❑37, Apr 2004 ..... 2.95
❑Annual 1, ca. 2001 BMB (w) 3.95

POWERS COLORING/ACTIVITY BOOK
IMAGE

❑1, Feb 2001 ..... 1.50

POWERS (MARVEL)
MARVEL

❑1, Sep 2004 ..... 2.95
❑2, Sep 2004 ..... 2.95
❑3, Oct 2004 ..... 2.95

Other grades: Multiply price above by 5/6 for VF/NM • 2/3 for VERY FINE • 1/3 for FINE • 1/5 for VERY GOOD • 1/8 for GOOD

Prisoner

Unnumbered issues denoted by letter
©DC

Professor Xavier and the X-Men

Modern-day updates of X-Men adventures
©Marvel

Promethea

A female hero from the world of myths
©DC

Prophet

Nazi science experiment awakes today
©Image

Prototype

Corporate armored hero goes solo
©Malibu

N-MINT

❑4, Oct 2004 .... 2.95
❑5, Nov 2004 .... 2.95
❑6, Dec 2004 .... 2.95
❑7, Jan 2005 .... 2.95
❑8, Feb 2005 .... 2.95
❑9, Mar 2005 .... 2.95
❑10, Apr 2005 .... 2.95
❑11 2005 .... 2.95
❑12/Bendis, Oct 2005 .... 2.95
❑12/Oeming, Oct 2005 .... 2.95
❑13 2005 .... 2.95
❑14, Jan 2006 .... 2.95
❑15, Feb 2006 .... 2.95
❑16, Mar 2006 .... 2.95
❑17, May 2006 .... 2.95
❑18, Aug 2006 .... 2.95

POWERS THAT BE
BROADWAY

❑1, Nov 1995; 1: Fatale. 1: Star Seed. Fatale and Star Seed; 1st comic from Broadway Comics 2.25
❑2, Dec 1995; Star Seed 2.50
❑2/Ashcan, Sep 1995, b&w; giveaway preview edition; Star Seed 1.00
❑3, Jan 1996; Star Seed 2.50
❑3/Ashcan, Oct 1995, b&w; giveaway preview edition; Star Seed 1.00
❑4, Feb 1996; Star Seed 2.50
❑5, Apr 1996; 1: Marnie. V: Gina and Charlotte. Star Seed 2.50
❑6, May 1996; 1: Ajax. Star Seed 2.95
❑7, Jul 1996; Title changes to Star Seed 2.95
❑8 1996 .... 2.95
❑9, Oct 1996 .... 2.95

PRAIRIE MOON AND OTHER STORIES
DARK HORSE

❑1, b&w; Rick Geary 2.25

PREACHER
DC / VERTIGO

❑1, Apr 1995 1: Jesse Custer 13.00
❑2, May 1995 1: The Saint of Killers 6.00
❑3, Jun 1995 .... 5.00
❑4, Jul 1995 .... 5.00
❑5, Aug 1995 .... 5.00
❑6, Sep 1995 .... 3.50
❑7, Oct 1995 .... 3.50
❑8, Nov 1995 .... 3.50
❑9, Dec 1995 .... 3.50
❑10, Jan 1996 .... 3.50
❑11, Feb 1996 .... 3.00
❑12, Mar 1996 .... 3.00
❑13, Apr 1996 .... 3.00
❑14, Jun 1996 .... 3.00
❑15, Jul 1996 .... 3.00
❑16, Aug 1996 .... 2.50
❑17, Sep 1996 .... 2.50
❑18, Oct 1996 .... 2.50
❑19, Nov 1996 .... 2.50
❑20, Dec 1996 .... 2.50
❑21, Jan 1997 .... 2.50
❑22, Feb 1997 .... 2.50
❑23, Mar 1997 .... 2.50
❑24, Apr 1997 .... 2.50
❑25, May 1997 O: Cassidy 2.50

N-MINT

❑26, Jun 1997 O: Cassidy 2.50
❑27, Jul 1997 .... 2.50
❑28, Aug 1997 .... 2.50
❑29, Sep 1997 A: You-Know-Who 2.50
❑30, Oct 1997 A: You-Know-Who 2.50
❑31, Nov 1997 .... 2.50
❑32, Dec 1997 .... 2.50
❑33, Jan 1998 .... 2.50
❑34, Feb 1998 .... 2.50
❑35, Mar 1998 .... 2.50
❑36, Apr 1998 .... 2.50
❑37, May 1998 .... 2.50
❑38, Jun 1998 A: You-Know-Who 2.50
❑39, Jul 1998; Jesse loses an eye; Starr loses a leg 2.50
❑40, Aug 1998 .... 2.50
❑41, Sep 1998; six months later; Jesse becomes sheriff of Salvation, Texas 2.50
❑42, Oct 1998 1: Odin Quincannon 2.50
❑43, Nov 1998; Jesse's mother's story 2.50
❑44, Dec 1998 .... 2.50
❑45, Jan 1999 .... 2.50
❑46, Feb 1999 .... 2.50
❑47, Mar 1999 .... 2.50
❑48, Apr 1999 D: Odin Quincannon 2.50
❑49, May 1999 .... 2.50
❑50, Jun 1999; Giant-size JLee (a) 3.75
❑51, Jul 1999; 100 Bullets preview 4.00
❑52, Aug 1999 .... 4.00
❑53, Sep 1999 .... 4.00
❑54, Oct 1999 .... 4.00
❑55, Nov 1999 .... 4.00
❑56, Dec 1999 .... 4.00
❑57, Jan 2000 .... 4.00
❑58, Feb 2000 .... 4.00
❑59, Mar 2000 .... 4.00
❑60, Apr 2000 .... 4.00
❑61, May 2000 .... 4.00
❑62, Jun 2000 .... 4.00
❑63, Jul 2000 .... 4.00
❑64, Aug 2000 .... 4.00
❑65, Sep 2000 .... 4.00
❑66, Oct 2000; Giant-size 3.75

PREACHER SPECIAL: CASSIDY: BLOOD & WHISKEY
DC / VERTIGO

❑1, Feb 1998, prestige format 5.95

PREACHER SPECIAL: ONE MAN'S WAR
DC / VERTIGO

❑1, Mar 1998, O: Starr 5.00

PREACHER SPECIAL: SAINT OF KILLERS
DC / VERTIGO

❑1, Aug 1996 .... 3.00
❑2, Sep 1996 .... 3.00
❑3, Oct 1996 .... 3.00
❑4, Nov 1996 .... 3.00

PREACHER SPECIAL: TALL IN THE SADDLE
DC / VERTIGO

❑1, Feb 2000 .... 4.95

N-MINT

PREACHER SPECIAL: THE GOOD OLD BOYS
DC / VERTIGO

❑1, Aug 1997 .... 4.95

PREACHER SPECIAL: THE STORY OF YOU-KNOW-WHO
DC / VERTIGO

❑1, Dec 1996 .... 4.95

PRECIOUS METAL
ARTS INDUSTRIA

❑1, b&w 2.50

PREDATOR
DARK HORSE

❑1, Jun 1989 .... 5.00
❑1/2nd 2.50
❑2, Sep 1989 .... 3.50
❑3, Dec 1989 .... 3.00
❑4, Mar 1990 .... 3.00

PREDATOR 2
DARK HORSE

❑1, Feb 1991 .... 3.00
❑2, Jun 1991 .... 3.00

PREDATOR: BAD BLOOD
DARK HORSE

❑1, Dec 1993 .... 2.50
❑2, Feb 1994 .... 2.50
❑3, May 1994 .... 2.50
❑4, Jun 1994 .... 2.50

PREDATOR: BIG GAME
DARK HORSE

❑1, Mar 1991; trading cards 2.50
❑2, Apr 1991; no trading cards despite cover advisory 2.50
❑3, May 1991; trading cards 2.50
❑4, Jun 1991 .... 2.50

PREDATOR: CAPTIVE
DARK HORSE

❑1, Apr 1998 .... 2.95

PREDATOR: COLD WAR
DARK HORSE

❑1, Sep 1991 .... 2.50
❑2, Oct 1991 .... 2.50
❑3, Nov 1991 .... 2.50
❑4, Dec 1991 .... 2.50

PREDATOR: DARK RIVER
DARK HORSE

❑1, Jul 1996 .... 2.95
❑2, Aug 1996 .... 2.95
❑3, Sep 1996 .... 2.95
❑4, Oct 1996 .... 2.95

PREDATOR: HELL & HOT WATER
DARK HORSE

❑1, Apr 1997; uninked pencils 2.95
❑2, May 1997; uninked pencils 2.95
❑3, Jun 1997; uninked pencils 2.95

PREDATOR: HELL COME A WALKIN'
DARK HORSE

❑1, Feb 1998; Predator in Civil War 2.95
❑2, Mar 1998; Predator in Civil War 2.95

PREDATOR: HOMEWORLD
DARK HORSE

❑1, Mar 1999 .... 2.95

❑2, Apr 1999 .... 2.95
❑3, May 1999 .... 2.95
❑4, Jun 1999 .... 2.95

PREDATOR: INVADERS FROM THE FOURTH DIMENSION
DARK HORSE

❑1, Jul 1994 .... 3.95

PREDATOR: JUNGLE TALES
DARK HORSE

❑1, Mar 1995; collects Predator: Rite of Passage from DHC #1 and 2; Predator: The Pride of Nghasa from DHC #10-12 .... 2.95

PREDATOR: KINDRED
DARK HORSE

❑1, Dec 1996 .... 2.50
❑2, Jan 1997 .... 2.50
❑3, Feb 1997 .... 2.50
❑4, Mar 1997 .... 2.50

PREDATOR: NEMESIS
DARK HORSE

❑1, Dec 1997 .... 2.95
❑2, Jan 1998 .... 2.95

PREDATOR: PRIMAL
DARK HORSE

❑1, Jul 1997, Predator vs. bears 2.95
❑2, Aug 1997, Predator vs. bears 2.95

PREDATOR: RACE WAR
DARK HORSE

❑0, Apr 1993 .... 2.50
❑1, Feb 1993 .... 2.50
❑2, Mar 1993 .... 2.50
❑3, Aug 1993 .... 2.50
❑4, Oct 1993 .... 2.50

PREDATOR: STRANGE ROUX
DARK HORSE

❑1, Nov 1996; recipe for Strange Roux in back 2.95

PREDATOR: THE BLOODY SANDS OF TIME
DARK HORSE

❑1, Feb 1992; Predator in WW I 2.75
❑2, Feb 1992; Predator in WW I 2.75

PREDATOR VERSUS JUDGE DREDD
DARK HORSE / EGMONT

❑1, Oct 1997 .... 2.50
❑2, Nov 1997 .... 2.50
❑3, Dec 1997 .... 2.50

PREDATOR VS. MAGNUS ROBOT FIGHTER
DARK HORSE / VALIANT

❑1, Nov 1992 .... 3.00
❑1/Platinum, Nov 1992; Platinum promotional edition 10.00
❑2, Dec 1993; trading cards 3.00

PREDATOR: XENOGENESIS
DARK HORSE

❑1, Aug 1999 .... 2.95
❑2, Sep 1999 .... 2.95
❑3, Oct 1999 .... 2.95
❑4, Nov 1999 .... 2.95

PREMIERE
DIVERSITY

❑1; 1500 printed 2.75
❑1/Gold; Gold limited edition (175 printed) 4.00
❑1/Ltd.; Limited edition (175 printed). 3.00
❑2 .... 2.75

PRESERVATION OF OBSCURITY, THE
LUMP OF SQUID

❑1 .... 2.75
❑2 .... 2.75

PRESIDENT DAD
TOKYOPOP

❑1, Dec 2004 .... 9.95
❑2, Mar 2005 .... 9.95
❑3, Jun 2005 .... 9.95
❑4, Oct 2005 .... 9.95

PRESSED TONGUE (DAVE COOPER'S...)
FANTAGRAPHICS

❑1, b&w 2.95
❑3, Dec 1994, b&w 2.95

PRESTO KID
AC

❑1, b&w; Reprints 2.50

PRE-TEEN DIRTY-GENE KUNG-FU KANGAROOS
BLACKTHORNE

❑1, Aug 1986 A: TMNT 2.00
❑2, Nov 1986 .... 2.00
❑3 1987 .... 2.00

PREY
MONSTER

❑1, b&w 2.25
❑2, b&w 2.25
❑3, b&w 2.25

PREY FOR US SINNERS
FANTACO

❑1 .... 4.95

PREZ
DC

❑1, Sep 1973 .... 12.00
❑2, Nov 1973 .... 6.00
❑3, Jan 1974 .... 5.00
❑4, Mar 1974 .... 5.00

PRIDE & JOY
DC / VERTIGO

❑1, Jul 1997 .... 2.50
❑2, Aug 1997 .... 2.50
❑3, Sep 1997 .... 2.50
❑4, Oct 1997 .... 2.50

PRIEST
MAXIMUM

❑1, Aug 1996 .... 2.99
❑2, Sep 1996 .... 2.99
❑3, Oct 1996 .... 2.99

PRIMAL
DARK HORSE

❑1 .... 2.50
❑2 .... 2.50

PRIMAL FORCE
DC

❑0, Oct 1994 .... 1.95
❑1, Nov 1994 .... 1.95
❑2, Dec 1994 .... 1.95
❑3, Jan 1995 .... 1.95
❑4, Feb 1995 .... 1.95
❑5, Mar 1995 .... 1.95
❑6, Apr 1995 .... 1.95
❑7, May 1995 .... 1.95
❑8, Jun 1995 .... 2.25
❑9, Jul 1995 .... 2.25
❑10, Aug 1995 .... 2.25
❑11, Sep 1995 .... 2.25
❑12, Oct 1995 .... 2.25
❑13, Nov 1995, Underworld Unleashed 2.25
❑14, Dec 1995 .... 2.25

PRIMAL RAGE
SIRIUS

❑1, Aug 1996, b&w 2.50
❑2, Oct 1996, b&w 2.50
❑3, Dec 1996, b&w 2.50
❑4, Feb 1997, b&w 2.50

PRIME (VOL. 1)
MALIBU / ULTRAVERSE

❑½; Wizard promotional edition 2.50
❑1, Jun 1993; 1: Prime. 1: Doctor Gross. Ultraverse 2.50
❑1/Hologram; Holographic promotional edition 1: Prime. 1: Doctor Gross 5.00
❑1/Ltd., Jun 1993; "Ultra-Limited" edition; 1: Prime. 1: Doctor Gross. foil stamped; $1.95 on cover 2.50
❑2, Jul 1993; Ultraverse; trading card 1.95
❑3, Aug 1993 O: Prime 1.95
❑4, Sep 1993; 1: Maxi-Man. A: Prototype II (Jimmy Ruiz). V: Prototype. two different covers .. 1.95
❑5, Oct 1993; Rune 1.95
❑6, Nov 1993 .... 1.95
❑7, Dec 1993; Break-Thru 1.95
❑8, Jan 1994 O: Freex. A: Mantra 1.95
❑9, Feb 1994 .... 1.95
❑10, Mar 1994 A: Firearm 1.95
❑11, Apr 1994 .... 1.95
❑12, May 1994; flip-book with Ultraverse Premiere #3 .... 3.50
❑13, Jul 1994; Freex preview; two different covers 1.95
❑13/A; variant cover 1.95
❑14, Sep 1994 1: Papa Verite 1.95
❑15, Oct 1994 GP (a) 1.95
❑16, Nov 1994 1: TurboCharge 1.95
❑17, Dec 1994 .... 1.95
❑18, Dec 1994 .... 1.95
❑19, Jan 1995 DC (a) 1.95
❑20, Mar 1995 1: Phade 1.95
❑21, Apr 1995 JSa (a); A: Chelsea Clinton 1.95
❑22, May 1995 .... 1.95
❑23, Jun 1995 .... 1.95
❑24, Jun 1995 .... 1.95
❑25, Jul 1995; O: Prime. continued from Power of Prime #1 .... 1.95
❑26, Aug 1995; O: Prime. continues in Power of Prime #2 .... 1.95
❑Annual 1, Oct 1994; 1: new Prime. A: Hardcase. Prime: Gross and Disgusting 3.95
❑Ashcan 1; ashcan edition 1.00

PRIME (VOL. 2)
MALIBU / ULTRAVERSE

❑0, Sep 1995; Black September; #Infinity 1.50
❑0/A, Sep 1995; Black September; alternate cover 1.50
❑1, Oct 1995; Spider-Prime 1.50
❑2, Nov 1995 .... 1.50
❑3, Dec 1995 .... 1.50
❑4, Jan 1996; Kevin rejoins Prime body 1.50
❑5, Feb 1996 .... 1.50
❑6, Mar 1996 .... 1.50
❑7, Apr 1996 .... 1.50
❑8, May 1996 .... 1.50
❑9, Jun 1996 .... 1.50
❑10, Jul 1996 .... 1.50
❑11, Aug 1996 .... 1.50
❑12, Sep 1996 .... 1.50
❑13, Oct 1996 .... 1.50
❑14, Nov 1996 .... 1.50
❑15, Dec 1996 .... 1.50

PRIME 8 CREATION
TWO MORROWS

❑1, Jul 2001, b&w 3.95

PRIME/CAPTAIN AMERICA
MALIBU / ULTRAVERSE

❑1, Mar 1996 .... 3.95

PRIME CUTS
FANTAGRAPHICS

❑1, Jan 1987 .... 3.50
❑2, Mar 1987 .... 3.50
❑3, May 1987 .... 3.50
❑4 1987 .... 3.50
❑5 1987 .... 3.50
❑6 1987 .... 3.50
❑7 1988 .... 3.95
❑8, Apr 1988 .... 3.95
❑9 1988 .... 3.95
❑10 1988 .... 3.95

PRIME CUTS (MIKE DEODATO'S...)
CALIBER

❑1 .... 2.95

PRIMER
COMICO

❑1, b&w 1: Slaughterman. 1: Skrog. 1: Az 5.00
❑2 1982 MW (w); MW (a); 1: Argent. 1: Grendel I (Hunter Rose) 55.00
❑3 .... 4.00
❑4 1982, b&w 1: Firebringer. 1: Laserman 4.00
❑5 1983; 1: The Maxx (original). 1st professional art by Sam Kieth 50.00
❑6 1: Evangeline 5.00

PRIMER (VOL. 2)
COMICO

❑1, May 1996 .... 2.95

PRIME SLIME TALES
MIRAGE

❑1 1986, b&w; Published By Mirage Studio 1.50
❑2; Published By Mirage Studio 1.50
❑3, Nov 1986; Published By Now Comics 1.50

Psi-Judge Anderson

Psychic Judge faces Death

©Fleetway-Quality

PS238

School days for super-hero offspring

©Dork Storm

Pulp (Vol. 1)

Large manga anthology with adult stories

©Viz

Pulse

Daily Bugle covers super-hero scene

©Marvel

Punisher (1st Series)

Mike Zeck draws Marvel merc's first mini

©Marvel

N-MINT

❑4, Jan 1987; Published By Now Comics ... 1.50

PRIME VS. THE INCREDIBLE HULK
MALIBU

❑0, Jul 1995; no cover price ... 5.00

PRIMITIVE CRETIN
FANTAGRAPHICS

❑Book 1, May 1996, b&w; oversized tpb ... 8.95

PRIMITIVES
SPARETIME

❑1, Jan 1995, b&w ... 2.50
❑2, May 1995, b&w ... 2.50
❑3, Oct 1995, b&w ... 2.50

PRIMORTALS (VOL. 1) (LEONARD NIMOY'S...)
TEKNO

❑1, Mar 1995 ... 1.95
❑2, Apr 1995 ... 1.95
❑3, May 1995 ... 1.95
❑4, Jun 1995 ... 1.95
❑5, Jul 1995 ... 1.95
❑6, Aug 1995 ... 1.95
❑7, Sep 1995 ... 1.95
❑8, Oct 1995 ... 1.95
❑9, Nov 1995 ... 1.95
❑10, Dec 1995 ... 1.95
❑11, Dec 1995 ... 1.95
❑12, Jan 1996 ... 2.25
❑13, Mar 1996 ... 2.25
❑14, Apr 1996 ... 2.25
❑15, May 1996 ... 2.25
❑16 ... 2.25

PRIMORTALS (VOL. 2) (LEONARD NIMOY'S...)
BIG

❑0, Jun 1996 ... 2.25
❑1, Jul 1996 ... 2.25
❑2, Aug 1996 ... 2.25
❑3, Sep 1996 ... 2.25
❑4, Oct 1996 ... 2.25
❑5, Nov 1996 ... 2.25
❑6, Dec 1996 ... 2.25
❑7, Jan 1997 ... 2.25
❑8, Feb 1997, b&w ... 2.25

PRIMORTALS ORIGINS (LEONARD NIMOY'S...)
TEKNO

❑1, Jun 1995 ... 2.25
❑2 ... 2.25

PRIMUS
CHARLTON

❑1, Feb 1972 ... 7.00
❑2 1972 ... 4.00
❑3 1972 ... 4.00
❑4, Jun 1972 ... 4.00
❑5 1972 ... 3.00
❑6 1972 ... 3.00
❑7, Oct 1972 ... 3.00

PRINCE: ALTER EGO
PIRANHA MUSIC

❑1, Dec 1991 ... 2.00

N-MINT

PRINCE AND THE NEW POWER GENERATION: THREE CHAINS OF GOLD
DC / PIRANHA

❑1 ... 3.50

PRINCE AND THE PAUPER
DELL

❑1, Jul 1962, 01-654-207 ... 15.00

PRINCE AND THE PAUPER (DISNEY'S...)
DISNEY

❑1, squarebound ... 5.95

PRINCE NAMOR, THE SUB-MARINER
MARVEL

❑1, Sep 1984 ... 1.50
❑2, Oct 1984 ... 1.50
❑3, Nov 1984 ... 1.50
❑4, Dec 1984 ... 1.50

PRINCE NIGHTMARE
AAAARGH!

❑1 ... 2.95

PRINCESS AND THE FROG
NBM

❑1 ... 15.95

PRINCESS KARANAM AND THE DJINN OF THE GREEN JUG
MU

❑1, b&w ... 2.50

PRINCESS NATASHA
DC

❑1, Sep 2006 ... 2.75

PRINCESS PRINCE
CPM MANGA

❑1, Oct 2000 ... 2.95
❑1/A, Oct 2000; alternate wraparound cover ... 2.95
❑2, Nov 2000 ... 2.95
❑3, Dec 2000 ... 2.95
❑4, Jan 2001 ... 2.95
❑5, Feb 2001 ... 2.95
❑6, Mar 2001 ... 2.95
❑7, Apr 2001 ... 2.95
❑8, May 2001 ... 2.95
❑9, Jun 2001 ... 2.95
❑10, Jul 2001 ... 2.95

PRINCESS SALLY
ARCHIE

❑1, Apr 1995 ... 1.50
❑2, May 1995 ... 1.50
❑3, Jun 1995 ... 1.50

PRINCESS TUTU
ADV MANGA

❑1, ca. 2005 ... 9.95
❑2, ca. 2005 ... 9.95

PRINCE VALIANT (MARVEL)
MARVEL

❑1, Dec 1994; cardstock cover ... 3.95
❑2, Jan 1995; cardstock cover ... 3.95
❑3, Feb 1995; cardstock cover ... 3.95
❑4, Mar 1995; cardstock cover ... 3.95

N-MINT

PRINCE VALIANT MONTHLY
PIONEER

❑1, b&w ... 4.95
❑2, b&w ... 4.95
❑3, b&w ... 4.95
❑4, b&w ... 4.95

PRINCE VANDAL
TRIUMPHANT

❑1; Unleashed! ... 2.50
❑2; Unleashed! ... 2.50
❑3 ... 2.50
❑4 ... 2.50
❑5 ... 2.50
❑6 ... 2.50

PRIORITY: WHITE HEAT
AC

❑1, Mar 1987 ... 1.75
❑2 ... 1.75

PRISONER
DC

❑1, Dec 1988; a ... 4.00
❑2, Jan 1989; b ... 4.00
❑3, Jan 1989; c ... 4.00
❑4, Feb 1989; d ... 4.00

PRISONER OF CHILLON
TOME

❑1, b&w ... 2.95

PRISONOPOLIS
MEDIAWARP

❑1, Feb 1997, b&w ... 2.75
❑2, Apr 1997, b&w ... 2.75
❑3, Jun 1997 ... 2.75
❑4, Aug 1997 ... 2.75

PRIVATE BEACH: FUN AND PERILS IN THE TRUDYVERSE
ANTARCTIC

❑1, Jan 1995, b&w ... 2.75
❑2, Mar 1995, b&w ... 2.75
❑3, May 1995, b&w ... 2.75

PRIVATE COMMISSIONS (GRAY MORROW'S...)
FORBIDDEN FRUIT

❑1, b&w ... 2.95
❑2, b&w ... 2.95

PRIVATEERS
VANGUARD

❑1 ... 1.50
❑2 ... 1.50

PRIVATE EYES
ETERNITY

❑1, Sep 1988, b&w; Saint reprints ... 1.95
❑2, Nov 1988, b&w; Saint reprints ... 1.95
❑3, Jan 1989, b&w; Saint reprints ... 1.95
❑4, May 1989 ... 2.95
❑5, Aug 1989 ... 3.50
❑6, Dec 1989 ... 3.95

PRO
IMAGE

❑1, Jul 2002 ... 5.95

PRO ACTION MAGAZINE (VOL. 2)
MARVEL / NFL PROPERTIES

❑1, Jul 1994 ... 2.95

Other grades: Multiply price above by 5/6 for VF/NM • 2/3 for VERY FINE • 1/3 for FINE • 1/5 for VERY GOOD • 1/8 for GOOD

❑2, Sep 1994 .... 2.95
❑3, Nov 1994; magazine with bound-in Spider-Man comic book 2.95

PROBE
IMPERIAL
❑1 .... 2.00
❑2 .... 2.00
❑3 .... 2.00

PROF. COFFIN
CHARLTON
❑19, Oct 1985, WH (w); JSa, JAb, WH (a) 2.00
❑20, Dec 1985 .... 2.00
❑21, Feb 1986, TS, JSa, WH (a) 2.00

PROFESSIONAL, THE: GOLGO 13
VIZ
❑1, Japanese 4.95
❑2, Japanese 4.95
❑3, Japanese 4.95

PROFESSOR OM
INNOVATION
❑1, May 1990 .... 2.50

PROFESSOR XAVIER AND THE X-MEN
MARVEL
❑1, Nov 1995; JDu (a); retells origin of team and first mission 1.50
❑2, Dec 1995; JDu (a); A: Vanisher. retells first Vanisher story 1.50
❑3, Jan 1996; retells first Blob story 1.50
❑4, Feb 1996; retells first meeting with Brotherhood of Evil Mutants 1.25
❑5, Mar 1996; retells first meeting with Brotherhood of Evil Mutants 1.25
❑6, Apr 1996 .... 1.25
❑7, May 1996; Sub-Mariner vs. Magneto 1.25
❑8, Jun 1996 .... 1.25
❑9, Jul 1996 .... 1.25
❑10, Aug 1996 V: Avengers 1.25
❑11, Sep 1996; A: Ka-Zar. Flipbook with Marvel Fanfare (2nd series) #1 .... 1.00
❑12, Oct 1996 V: Juggernaut 1.00
❑13, Nov 1996 V: Juggernaut 1.00
❑14, Dec 1996 .... 1.00
❑15, Jan 1997 V: Magneto. V: Stranger 1.00
❑16, Feb 1997 V: Sentinels 1.00
❑17, Mar 1997 .... 1.00
❑18, Apr 1997 V: Sentinels 1.00

PROFOLIO
ALCHEMY
❑1, b&w 1.50
❑2; some color 2.50
❑3, b&w 2.50

PROFOLIO (VOL. 3)
ALCHEMY
❑1 .... 5.95

PROGENY
CALIBER
❑1, b&w 4.95

PROGRAM ERROR: BATTLEBOT
PHANTASY
❑1 .... 2.00

PROJECT
DC / PARADOX PRESS
❑1, ca. 1997, b&w; digest; short story collection 5.95
❑2, ca. 1997, b&w; digest; short story collection 5.95

PROJECT A-KO
MALIBU
❑1, Mar 1994 .... 2.95
❑2, Mar 1994 .... 2.95
❑3, May 1994 .... 2.95
❑4, Jun 1994 .... 2.95

PROJECT A-KO 2
CPM
❑1, Apr 1995 .... 2.95
❑2, Jun 1995 .... 2.95
❑3, Aug 1995 .... 2.95

PROJECT A-KO VERSUS
CPM
❑1, Oct 1995 .... 2.95
❑2, Dec 1995 .... 2.95
❑3, Feb 1996 .... 2.95
❑4, Apr 1996 .... 2.95
❑5, Jun 1996 .... 2.95

PROJECT ARMS
VIZ
❑1, Sep 2002 .... 3.25
❑2, Oct 2002 .... 3.25
❑3, Nov 2002 .... 3.25
❑4, Dec 2002 .... 3.25
❑5, Jan 2003 .... 3.25

PROJECT: DARK MATTER
DIMM COMICS
❑1, Apr 1996, b&w 2.50
❑2, Jun 1996, b&w; cardstock cover . 2.50
❑3, b&w; cardstock cover 2.50
❑4, Sep 1997, b&w 2.50

PROJECT EON
IMAGE
❑1, Jul 2006 .... 2.99

PROJECT: GENERATION
TRUTH
❑1, Jun 2000, Distributed at San Diego Comic-Con 1.00
❑2, Sep 2000, Fall, 2000 .... 1.00

PROJECT: HERO
VANGUARD
❑1, Aug 1987 .... 1.50
❑2 .... 1.50

PROJECT SEX
FANTAGRAPHICS / EROS
❑1, b&w 2.50

PROJECT X
KITCHEN SINK
❑1; Eastman/Bisley; bagged Thump'n Guts; poster; trading card 2.95

PROMETHEA
DC / AMERICA'S BEST COMICS
❑1, Aug 1999 AMo (w); O: Promethea 6.00
❑1/Variant, Aug 1999 .... 7.00
❑2, Sep 1999 AMo (w) 4.00
❑3, Oct 1999 AMo (w) 2.95
❑4, Nov 1999 AMo (w) 2.95
❑5, Dec 1999 AMo (w) 2.95
❑6, Mar 2000 AMo (w) 2.95
❑7, Apr 2000 AMo (w) 2.95
❑8, May 2000 AMo (w) 2.95
❑9, Sep 2000 AMo (w) 2.95
❑10, Oct 2000 AMo (w) 2.95
❑11, Dec 2000 AMo (w) 2.95
❑12, Feb 2001 AMo (w) 2.95
❑13, Apr 2001 AMo (w) 2.95
❑14, May 2001 AMo (w) 2.95
❑15, Jun 2001 AMo (w) 2.95
❑16, Jul 2001 AMo (w) 2.95
❑17, Aug 2001 AMo (w) 2.95
❑18, Sep 2001 AMo (w) 2.95
❑19, Oct 2001 AMo (w) 2.95
❑20, Nov 2001 AMo (w) 2.95
❑21 2002 .... 2.95
❑22, Nov 2002 .... 2.95
❑23, Dec 2002 AMo (w) 3.50
❑24, ca. 2003 .... 2.95
❑25, May 2003 .... 2.95
❑26, Aug 2003 .... 2.95
❑27, Nov 2003 .... 2.95
❑28, Feb 2004 .... 2.95
❑29, May 2004, AMo (w) 2.95
❑30, Jul 2004 .... 2.95
❑31, Oct 2004 .... 2.95
❑32 2005 .... 4.00
❑32/Ltd 2005; Collects all 32 covers; signed by Alan Moore and J.H. Williams; 1,000 copies produced ... 125.00

PROMETHEUS' GIFT
CAT-HEAD
❑1, b&w 2.25

PROMETHEUS (VILLAINS)
DC
❑1, Feb 1998; New Year's Evil 1.95

PROMISE
VIZ
❑1, b&w; squarebound 5.95

PROPELLERMAN
DARK HORSE
❑1, ca. 1993 .... 2.95
❑2, ca. 1993 .... 2.95
❑3, ca. 1993 .... 2.95
❑4, ca. 1993 .... 2.95
❑5, ca. 1994 .... 2.95
❑6, ca. 1994 .... 2.95
❑7, ca. 1994 .... 2.95
❑8, ca. 1994 .... 2.95

PROPHECY OF THE SOUL SORCERER
ARCANE
❑1, May 1999 .... 2.95
❑2, Jul 1999 .... 2.95
❑3, Jul 1999 .... 2.95
❑Ashcan 1, Oct 1998 .... 2.00

PROPHECY OF THE SOUL SORCERER PREVIEW ISSUE
ARCANE
❑1 .... 2.00

PROPHECY OF THE SOUL SORCERER (VOL. 2)
ARCANE
❑1, Mar 2000 .... 2.95
❑2, Apr 2000 .... 2.95
❑3, May 2000 .... 2.95

PROPHET
IMAGE
❑0, Jul 1994 .... 3.00
❑0/A, Jul 1994; San Diego Comic-Con edition 3.00
❑1, Oct 1993 RL (w); O: Prophet 3.00
❑1/Gold, Oct 1993; Gold edition 3.00
❑2, Nov 1993 FM (c); FM (a) 2.50
❑3, Jan 1994 .... 2.50
❑4, Feb 1994 .... 2.50
❑4/Variant, Feb 1994; Variant cover by Platt 3.00
❑5, Apr 1994 .... 2.50
❑6, Jun 1994 .... 2.50
❑7, Sep 1994 .... 2.50
❑8, Nov 1994 .... 2.50
❑9, Dec 1994 .... 2.50
❑10, Jan 1995 .... 2.50

PROPHET (VOL. 2)
IMAGE
❑1, Aug 1995 .... 3.50
❑1/Chromium, Aug 1995; Chromium cover 5.00
❑1/Holochrome, Aug 1995; Holochrome wraparound cover 6.00
❑2, Sep 1995 FM (c) 2.50
❑2/Platt, Sep 1995; alternate cover 4.00
❑3, Nov 1995 .... 2.50
❑4, Feb 1996 A: NewMen 2.50
❑5, Feb 1996 .... 2.50
❑6, Apr 1996 .... 2.50
❑7, May 1996 A: Youngblood 2.50
❑8, Jul 1996 .... 2.50
❑Annual 1/A, Sep 1995; polybagged with PowerCardz 4.00
❑Annual 1/B, Sep 1995; polybagged with PowerCardz 4.00

PROPHET (VOL. 3)
AWESOME
❑1, Mar 2000; Flip cover (McFarlane cover on back side) 2.99
❑1/A, Mar 2000; Red background, woman standing with sword, large man in background 2.99

PROPHET BABEWATCH
IMAGE
❑1, Dec 1995; cover says #1, indicia says #2 .... 2.50

PROPHET/CABLE
MAXIMUM
❑1, Jan 1997; crossover with Marvel . 3.50
❑2, Mar 1997; cover says #1, indicia says #2; crossover with Marvel; #1 on cover, #2 in indicia 3.50

PROPHET/CHAPEL: SUPER SOLDIERS
IMAGE
❑1/A, May 1996 .... 2.50
❑1/B, May 1996; alternate cover (b&w) 2.50
❑2, Jun 1996 .... 2.50

PROPOSITION PLAYER
DC / VERTIGO
❑1, Dec 1999 .... 2.50
❑2, Jan 2000 .... 2.50
❑3, Feb 2000 .... 2.50

Other grades: Multiply price above by 5/6 for VF/NM • 2/3 for VERY FINE • 1/3 for FINE • 1/5 for VERY GOOD • 1/8 for GOOD

Punisher (4th Series)

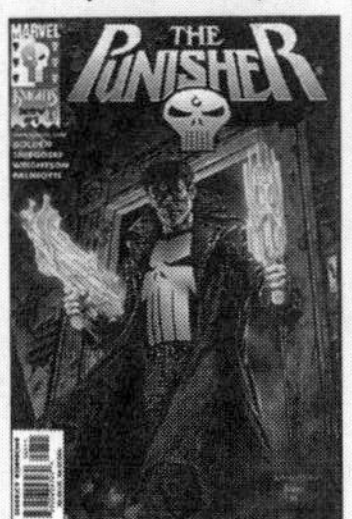

After-death adventure in afterlife

©Marvel

Punisher (5th Series)

Back from short supernatural outing

©Marvel

Punisher (7th series)

Move to MAX increases body count

©Marvel

Punisher 2099

Frank Castle's legacy carries to future

©Marvel

Punisher War Journal

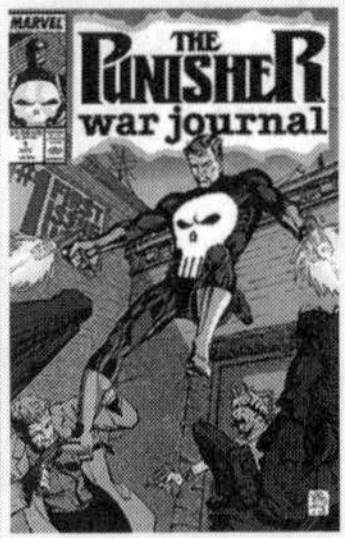

Narration creates own title

©Marvel

N-MINT

❑4, Mar 2000 .... 2.50
❑5, Apr 2000 .... 2.50
❑6, May 2000 .... 2.50

PROTECTORS HANDBOOK
MALIBU

❑1 .... 2.50

PROTECTORS, THE (MALIBU)
MALIBU

❑1, Sep 1992; Split cover (in various colors) 1.95
❑1/CS, Sep 1992; with poster and wrapper 2.50
❑2, Oct 1992; with poster 2.50
❑3, Nov 1992 .... 2.50
❑4, Dec 1992 .... 2.50
❑5/A, Jan 1993; bullet hole; bagged 2.50
❑5/B, Jan 1993; Embossed cover; bullet hole 2.50
❑5/C, Jan 1993; Die-cut cover; bullet hole 2.95
❑6, Feb 1993 .... 2.50
❑6/CS, Feb 1993; with poster 2.50
❑7, Mar 1993 .... 2.50
❑8, Apr 1993 .... 2.50
❑9, May 1993 .... 2.50
❑10, Jun 1993 .... 2.50
❑11, Jul 1993 .... 2.50
❑12, Aug 1993 .... 2.50
❑13, Sep 1993; Genesis 2.25
❑14, Oct 1993 .... 2.25
❑15, Nov 1993 .... 2.25
❑16, Dec 1993 .... 2.25
❑17, Jan 1994 .... 2.25
❑18, Feb 1994 .... 2.25
❑19, Mar 1994; Genesis 2.50
❑20 .... 2.50

PROTECTORS (NEW YORK)
NEW YORK

❑1 .... 1.70
❑2 .... 1.70

PROTHEUS (MIKE DEODATO'S...)
CALIBER

❑1 .... 2.95
❑2 .... 2.95

PROTISTA CHRONICLES
XULU

❑1; no cover price 2.00

PROTOTYKES HOLIDAY SPECIAL/ HERO ILLUSTRATED HOLIDAY SPECIAL
DARK HORSE

❑1 .... 1.00
❑2 JBy (w); JBy (a) 1.00

PROTOTYPE
MALIBU / ULTRAVERSE

❑0, Aug 1994; O: Prototype I (Bob Campbell). Reprints origin story from Malibu Sun plus new story 1.95
❑1, Aug 1993; 1: Prototype II (Jimmy Ruiz). 1: Prototype I (Bob Campbell). 1: Glare. 1: Veil. Ultraverse; 1st appear 2.50

N-MINT

❑1/Hologram; Hologram cover limited edition; 1: Prototype II (Jimmy Ruiz). 1: Prototype I (Bob Campbell). 1: Glare. 1: Veil. hologram 5.00
❑2, Sep 1993 1: Backstabber. A: Prime 1.95
❑3, Oct 1993; Giant-size; Rune 2.50
❑4, Nov 1993 1: Wrath 1.95
❑5, Dec 1993; A: Strangers. Break-Thru; Continued in Strangers #7 .... 1.95
❑6, Jan 1994 1: Arena 1.95
❑7, Feb 1994 .... 1.95
❑8, Mar 1994 .... 1.95
❑9, Apr 1994 .... 1.95
❑10, May 1994 .... 1.95
❑11, Jun 1994 .... 1.95
❑12, Jul 1994 .... 1.95
❑13, Aug 1994; KB (w); flipbook with Ultraverse Premiere #6 .... 3.50
❑14, Oct 1994 .... 1.95
❑15, Nov 1994 .... 1.95
❑16, Dec 1994 1: Wild Popes 1.95
❑17, Jan 1995 .... 1.95
❑18, Feb 1995 .... 2.50
❑Giant Size 1, ca. 1994; Giant-Size edition 2.50

PROWLER (ECLIPSE)
ECLIPSE

❑1, Jul 1987 .... 1.75
❑2, Aug 1987 .... 1.75
❑3, Sep 1987 .... 1.75
❑4, Oct 1987 .... 1.75

PROWLER (MARVEL)
MARVEL

❑1, Nov 1994 .... 1.75
❑2, Dec 1994 .... 1.75
❑3, Jan 1995 .... 1.75
❑4, Feb 1995 .... 1.75

PROWLER IN "WHITE ZOMBIE"
ECLIPSE

❑1, Oct 1988, b&w 2.00

PRO WRESTLING'S TRUE FACTS
DAN PETTIGLIO

❑1, Apr 1994, b&w 2.95

PROXIMITY EFFECT
IMAGE

❑1, ca. 2004 .... 9.99

PRUDENCE & CAUTION
DEFIANT

❑1, May 1994, Double-size; English and Spanish versions 3.25
❑2, Jun 1994 .... 2.50
❑3, Jul 1994 .... 2.50
❑4, Aug 1994 .... 2.50
❑5, Sep 1994 .... 2.50
❑6, Oct 1994 .... 2.50

PRYDE & WISDOM
MARVEL

❑1, Sep 1996 .... 1.95
❑2, Oct 1996 .... 1.95
❑3, Nov 1996 .... 1.95

PSCYTHE
IMAGE

❑1, Sep 2004, b&w 3.95
❑2, Oct 2004, b&w 3.95

N-MINT

PSI-FORCE
MARVEL

❑1, Nov 1986 .... 1.00
❑2, Dec 1986 .... 1.00
❑3, Jan 1987 .... 1.00
❑4, Feb 1987 .... 1.00
❑5, Mar 1987 .... 1.00
❑6, Apr 1987 .... 1.00
❑7, May 1987 BH (a) 1.00
❑8, Jun 1987 .... 1.00
❑9, Jul 1987 BH (a) 1.00
❑10, Aug 1987 .... 1.00
❑11, Sep 1987 BH (a) 1.00
❑12, Oct 1987 BH (a) 1.00
❑13, Nov 1987 .... 1.00
❑14, Dec 1987 BH (a) 1.00
❑15, Jan 1988 .... 1.00
❑16, Feb 1988 .... 1.00
❑17, Mar 1988 .... 1.00
❑18, Apr 1988 .... 1.00
❑19, May 1988 .... 1.25
❑20, Jun 1988 .... 1.25
❑21, Jul 1988 .... 1.25
❑22, Aug 1988 .... 1.25
❑23, Sep 1988 .... 1.25
❑24, Oct 1988 .... 1.25
❑25, Nov 1988 .... 1.25
❑26, Dec 1988 .... 1.25
❑27, Jan 1989 .... 1.25
❑28, Feb 1989 .... 1.25
❑29, Mar 1989 .... 1.25
❑30, Apr 1989 .... 1.25
❑31, May 1989 .... 1.25
❑32, Jun 1989 .... 1.25
❑Annual 1, ca. 1987 .... 1.25

PSI-JUDGE ANDERSON
FLEETWAY-QUALITY

❑1 .... 2.00
❑2 .... 2.00
❑3 .... 2.00
❑4 .... 2.00
❑5 .... 2.00
❑6 .... 2.00
❑7 .... 2.00
❑8 .... 2.00
❑9 .... 2.00
❑10 .... 2.00
❑11 .... 2.00
❑12 .... 2.00
❑13 .... 2.00
❑14 .... 2.00
❑15 .... 2.00

PSI-JUDGE ANDERSON: ENGRAMS
FLEETWAY-QUALITY

❑1, b&w 1.95
❑2, b&w 1.95

PSI-JUDGE ANDERSON: PSIFILES
FLEETWAY-QUALITY

❑1 .... 2.95

PSI-LORDS
VALIANT

❑1, Sep 1994; Valiant Vision; chromium wrap-around cover 3.50

Other grades: Multiply price above by 5/6 for VF/NM • 2/3 for VERY FINE • 1/3 for FINE • 1/5 for VERY GOOD • 1/8 for GOOD

N-MINT | N-MINT | N-MINT

❑1/VVSS, Sep 1994 .... 70.00
❑1/Gold, Sep 1994; Gold edition; no cover price 20.00
❑2, Oct 1994; Valiant Vision 1.00
❑3, Nov 1994; Valiant Vision; Chaos Effect Epsilon 3 .... 1.00
❑4, Dec 1994 .... 1.00
❑5, Jan 1995 .... 2.00
❑6, Feb 1995 .... 2.00
❑7, Mar 1995 .... 2.00
❑8, Apr 1995 V: Destroyer 2.00
❑9, May 1995 .... 3.00
❑10, Jun 1995 .... 5.00

PS238
DORK STORM

❑0, Nov 2002, b&w 2.95
❑1, Mar 2003, b&w 2.95
❑2, May 2003, b&w 2.95
❑3, Jul 2003, b&w 2.95
❑4, Sep 2003, b&w 2.95
❑5, Nov 2003, b&w 2.95
❑6, ca. 2004, b&w 2.95
❑7, ca. 2004, b&w 2.95
❑8, ca. 2004, b&w 2.95
❑9, Nov 2004, b&w 2.95

PSYBA-RATS
DC

❑1, Apr 1995 D: Channelman 2.50
❑2, May 1995 .... 2.50
❑3, Jun 1995 .... 2.50

PSYCHIC ACADEMY
TOKYOPOP

❑1, Mar 2004 .... 9.99
❑2, May 2004 .... 9.99
❑3, Jul 2004 .... 9.99
❑4, Sep 2004 .... 9.99
❑5, Nov 2004 .... 9.99
❑6, Jan 2005 .... 9.99
❑7, Mar 2005 .... 9.99
❑8, Jun 2005 .... 9.99
❑9, Sep 2005 .... 9.99
❑10, Dec 2005 .... 9.99

PSYCHO
DC

❑1, Sep 1991 .... 4.95
❑2, Oct 1991 .... 4.95
❑3, Dec 1991 .... 4.95

PSYCHO (ALFRED HITCHCOCK'S...)
INNOVATION

❑1 .... 2.50
❑2 .... 2.50
❑3 .... 2.50

PSYCHOANALYSIS (GEMSTONE)
GEMSTONE

❑1, Aug 1999 .... 2.50
❑2, Sep 1999 .... 2.50
❑3, Oct 1999 .... 2.50
❑4, Nov 1999 .... 2.50
❑Annual 1, Collects series 10.95

PSYCHOBLAST
FIRST

❑1, Nov 1987 .... 1.75
❑2, Dec 1987 .... 1.75
❑3, Jan 1988 .... 1.75
❑4, Feb 1988 .... 1.75
❑5, Mar 1988 .... 1.75
❑6, Apr 1988 .... 1.75
❑7, May 1988 .... 1.75
❑8, Jun 1988 .... 1.75
❑9, Jul 1988 .... 1.75

PSYCHO KILLERS
COMIC ZONE

❑1, b&w; Charles Manson 4.00
❑1/2nd; Charles Manson 3.00
❑2, b&w; David Berkowitz ("The Son of Sam") 3.50
❑2/2nd; David Berkowitz ("The Son of Sam") 3.00
❑3, b&w; Ed Gein 3.50
❑3/2nd; Ed Gein 2.95
❑4, Henry Lee Lucas 2.95
❑5, Jeffrey Dahmer 3.25
❑6, Richard Ramirez ("The Nightstalker") 2.95
❑7, Judias Buenoano 2.95
❑8, John Wayne Gacy 2.95
❑9, Ted Bundy 2.95
❑10, Dean Corll ("The Candy Man") 2.95
❑11, The Hillside Strangler; A lawsuit was filed and resulted in this book being taken off the market 3.50
❑12, The Boston Strangler 2.95
❑13, Andrei Chikatilo 2.95
❑14, Aileen Wuornos 2.95
❑15, Charles Starkweather 2.95

PSYCHO KILLERS PMS SPECIAL
ZONE

❑1 .... 3.25

PSYCHOMAN
REVOLUTIONARY

❑1 .... 2.50

PSYCHONAUT
FANTAGRAPHICS

❑1, Mar 1996, b&w 3.95
❑3, b&w; flipbook with The Pursuers 3.50

PSYCHONAUTS
MARVEL / EPIC

❑1 .... 4.95
❑2 .... 4.95
❑3 .... 4.95
❑4 .... 4.95

PSYCHO-PATH
VENUSIAN

❑1 .... 2.00
❑2, Sep 1990, b&w 2.00

PSYCHOTIC ADVENTURES ILLUSTRATED
LAST GASP

❑1 .... 3.00
❑2 .... 3.00
❑3 .... 3.00

PSY-COMM
TOKYOPOP

❑1, Nov 2005 .... 9.99

PSYENCE FICTION
ABACULUS

❑½, Sum 1998, b&w; Ashcan preview edition 1.00
❑1 .... 2.95

PSYLOCKE & ARCHANGEL: CRIMSON DAWN
MARVEL

❑1, Aug 1997; gatefold summary; gatefold cover 2.50
❑2, Sep 1997; gatefold summary 2.50
❑3, Oct 1997; gatefold summary 2.50
❑4, Nov 1997; gatefold summary 2.50

PTERANOMAN
KITCHEN SINK

❑1, Aug 1990 .... 2.00

PUBLIC ENEMIES (ETERNITY)
ETERNITY

❑1, b&w; Reprints 3.95
❑2, b&w; Reprints 3.95

PUBO
DARK HORSE

❑1, Nov 2002, b&w 3.50
❑2, Jan 2003, b&w 3.50
❑3, Mar 2003, b&w 3.50

PUFFED
IMAGE

❑1, Jul 2003 .... 2.95
❑2, Aug 2003 .... 2.95
❑3, Sep 2003 .... 2.95

PUKE & EXPLODE
NORTHSTAR

❑1 .... 2.50
❑2 .... 2.50

PULP (VOL. 1)
VIZ

❑1, Dec 1997 .... 5.95

PULP (VOL. 2)
VIZ

❑1, Jan 1998 .... 5.95
❑2, Feb 1998 .... 5.95
❑3, Mar 1998 .... 5.95
❑4, Apr 1998 .... 5.95
❑5, May 1998 .... 5.95
❑6, Jun 1998 .... 5.95
❑7, Jul 1998 .... 5.95
❑8, Aug 1998 .... 5.95
❑9, Sep 1998 .... 5.95
❑10, Oct 1998 .... 5.95
❑11, Nov 1998 .... 5.95
❑12, Dec 1998 .... 5.95

PULP (VOL. 3)
VIZ

❑1, Jan 1999 .... 5.95
❑2, Feb 1999 .... 5.95
❑3, Mar 1999 .... 5.95
❑4, Apr 1999 .... 5.95
❑5, May 1999 .... 5.95
❑6, Jun 1999 .... 5.95
❑7, Jul 1999 .... 5.95
❑8, Aug 1999 .... 5.95
❑9, Sep 1999 .... 5.95
❑10, Oct 1999 .... 5.95
❑11, Nov 1999 .... 5.95
❑12, Dec 1999 .... 5.95

PULP (VOL. 4)
VIZ

❑1, Jan 2000 .... 5.95
❑2, Feb 2000 .... 5.95
❑3, Mar 2000 .... 5.95
❑4, Apr 2000 .... 5.95
❑5, May 2000 .... 5.95
❑6, Jun 2000 .... 5.95

PULP (VOL. 5)
VIZ

❑1 .... 5.95
❑2 .... 5.95
❑3 .... 5.95
❑4 .... 5.95
❑5 .... 5.95
❑6 .... 5.95
❑7 .... 5.95
❑8 .... 5.95
❑9 .... 5.95
❑10 .... 5.95
❑11 .... 5.95
❑12 .... 5.95

PULP (VOL. 6)
VIZ

❑1 .... 5.95
❑2 .... 5.95
❑3 .... 5.95
❑4 .... 5.95
❑5 .... 5.95
❑6 .... 5.95
❑7 .... 5.95
❑8 .... 5.95

PULP ACTION
AVALON

❑1 .... 2.95
❑2 .... 2.95
❑3 .... 2.95
❑4 .... 2.95
❑5 .... 2.95
❑6 .... 2.95
❑7 .... 2.95
❑8 .... 2.95

PULP DREAMS
FANTAGRAPHICS / EROS

❑1, b&w 2.50

PULP FANTASTIC
DC / VERTIGO

❑1, Feb 2000 .... 2.50
❑2, Mar 2000 .... 2.50
❑3, Apr 2000 .... 2.50

PULP FICTION
A LIST

❑1, Spr 1997, b&w; reprints Golden Age material 2.50
❑2, Fal 1997, b&w; reprints Golden Age material 2.50
❑3, Win 1997, b&w; reprints Golden Age material 2.50
❑4 .... 2.50
❑5 .... 2.95
❑6 .... 2.95

PULP WESTERN
AVALON

❑1 .... 2.95

Other grades: Multiply price above by 5/6 for VF/NM • 2/3 for VERY FINE • 1/3 for FINE • 1/5 for VERY GOOD • 1/8 for GOOD

PvP

Pokes fun at popular culture

©Dork Storm

Quack!

Indy series had early Dave Sim work

©Star*Reach

Quantum & Woody

Semi-serious super-hero fare

©Acclaim

Quantum Leap

Adventures based on NBC's SF series

©Innovation

Quasar

Third-rate hero gives Marvel a title under Q

©Marvel

N-MINT

PULSE
BLACKJACK

❑1, Jun 1997, b&w; no cover price 2.00

PULSE
MARVEL

❑1, Apr 2004, BMB (w) 5.00
❑2, May 2004, BMB (w) 3.00
❑3, Jul 2004, BMB (w) 2.99
❑4, Sep 2004 .... 2.99
❑5, Oct 2004 .... 2.25
❑6 .... 2.99
❑7 2005 .... 2.99
❑8, May 2005 .... 2.99
❑9 2005 .... 2.99
❑10, Sep 2005 .... 6.00
❑10/Variant, Sep 2005 .... 6.00
❑11, Oct 2005 .... 2.99
❑12, Jan 2006 .... 2.99
❑13, Mar 2006 .... 2.99
❑14, May 2006 .... 2.99

PULSE: HOUSE OF M SPECIAL EDITION
MARVEL

❑1, Sep 2005 .... 1.00

PUMA BLUES
AARDVARK ONE

❑1, Jun 1986, b&w; 10,000 copies printed; Aardvark One International Publisher 2.00
❑1/2nd, b&w 2.00
❑2, Sep 1986, b&w; 10,000 copies printed 2.00
❑3, Dec 1986, b&w; 19,000 copies printed 2.00
❑4, Feb 1987, b&w; 13,000 copies printed 1.70
❑5, Mar 1987, b&w; 13,000 copies printed 1.70
❑6, Apr 1987, b&w; 13,000 copies printed 1.70
❑7, May 1987, b&w; 12,000 copies printed 1.70
❑8, May 1987, b&w 1.70
❑9, Jul 1987, b&w 1.70
❑10, Aug 1987, b&w 1.70
❑11, Sep 1987, b&w 1.70
❑12, Oct 1987, b&w 1.70
❑13, Nov 1987, b&w 1.70
❑14, Dec 1987, b&w 1.70
❑15, Jan 1988, b&w 1.70
❑16, Feb 1988, b&w 1.70
❑17, Mar 1988, b&w 1.70
❑18, Apr 1988, b&w; self-published 1.70
❑19 1988, b&w; self-published 1.70
❑20 1988, b&w; AMo (w); self-published 1.70
❑21 1988, b&w; Mirage Studio Publisher 1.70
❑22 1988, b&w 1.70
❑23, b&w 1.70

PUMMELER
PARODY

❑1, b&w; Foil embossed cover; Punisher parody 2.95

N-MINT

PUMMELER $2099
PARODY

❑1; Gold Trimmed Foil Cover 2.95

PUMPKINHEAD: THE RITES OF EXORCISM
DARK HORSE

❑1, ca. 1992 .... 2.50
❑2, ca. 1992 .... 2.50
❑3, ca. 1992 .... 2.50
❑4, ca. 1992 .... 2.50

PUNISHER (1ST SERIES)
MARVEL

❑1, Jan 1986; Double-size 13.00
❑2, Feb 1986 MZ (a) 7.00
❑3, Mar 1986 MZ (a) 7.00
❑4, Apr 1986 MZ (a) 6.00
❑5, May 1986 MZ (a) 6.00

PUNISHER (2ND SERIES)
MARVEL

❑1, Jul 1987 .... 7.00
❑2, Aug 1987 KJ (a) 4.00
❑3, Oct 1987 KJ (a) 4.00
❑4, Nov 1987 .... 3.00
❑5, Jan 1988 .... 3.00
❑6, Feb 1988 .... 3.00
❑7, Mar 1988 .... 3.00
❑8, May 1988 .... 3.00
❑9, Jun 1988 .... 3.00
❑10, Aug 1988 A: Daredevil 4.00
❑11, Sep 1988 .... 2.00
❑12, Oct 1988 .... 2.00
❑13, Nov 1988 .... 2.00
❑14, Dec 1988 A: Kingpin 2.00
❑15, Jan 1989 A: Kingpin 2.00
❑16, Feb 1989 A: Kingpin 2.00
❑17, Mar 1989 .... 2.00
❑18, Apr 1989 V: Kingpin 2.00
❑19, May 1989 .... 2.00
❑20, Jun 1989 .... 2.00
❑21, Jul 1989 EL (a) 2.00
❑22, Aug 1989 EL (a) 2.00
❑23, Sep 1989 EL (a) 2.00
❑24, Oct 1989 EL (a); 1: Shadowmasters 2.00
❑25, Nov 1989; Giant-sized EL (a); A: Shadowmasters 2.00
❑26, Nov 1989 RH (a) 2.00
❑27, Dec 1989 .... 2.00
❑28, Dec 1989; Acts of Vengeance 2.00
❑29, Jan 1990; Acts of Vengeance 2.00
❑30, Feb 1990 .... 2.00
❑31, Mar 1990 .... 2.00
❑32, Apr 1990 .... 2.00
❑33, May 1990 .... 2.00
❑34, Jun 1990 .... 2.00
❑35, Jul 1990; Jigsaw Puzzle 2.00
❑36, Aug 1990; Jigsaw Puzzle 2.00
❑37, Aug 1990; Jigsaw Puzzle 2.00
❑38, Sep 1990; Jigsaw Puzzle 2.00
❑39, Sep 1990; Jigsaw Puzzle 2.00
❑40, Oct 1990; Jigsaw Puzzle 2.00
❑41, Oct 1990 .... 1.50
❑42, Nov 1990 .... 1.50
❑43, Dec 1990 .... 1.50

N-MINT

❑44, Jan 1991 .... 1.50
❑45, Feb 1991 .... 1.50
❑46, Mar 1991 .... 1.50
❑47, Apr 1991 .... 1.50
❑48, May 1991 .... 1.50
❑49, Jun 1991 .... 1.50
❑50, Jul 1991; double-sized 2.00
❑51, Aug 1991 .... 1.50
❑52, Sep 1991 .... 1.50
❑53, Oct 1991 .... 1.50
❑54, Nov 1991 .... 1.50
❑55, Nov 1991 .... 1.50
❑56, Dec 1991 .... 1.50
❑57, Dec 1991; Two covers: outer wraparound cover, inner photo cover 2.00
❑58, Jan 1992 .... 1.50
❑59, Jan 1992; Punisher becomes black 1.50
❑60, Feb 1992 VM (a); A: Luke Cage 1.50
❑61, Mar 1992 VM (a); A: Luke Cage 1.50
❑62, Apr 1992; VM (a); Punisher becomes white again 1.50
❑63, May 1992 .... 1.25
❑64, Jun 1992 .... 1.25
❑65 1992 .... 1.25
❑66 1992 .... 1.25
❑67 1992 .... 1.25
❑68 1992 .... 1.25
❑69, Sep 1992 .... 1.25
❑70 1992 .... 1.25
❑71, Oct 1992 .... 1.25
❑72, Nov 1992 .... 1.25
❑73, Dec 1992 .... 1.25
❑74, Jan 1993 .... 1.25
❑75, Feb 1993; Embossed cover 2.75
❑76, Mar 1993 .... 1.50
❑77, Apr 1993 VM (a) 1.50
❑78, May 1993 VM (a) 1.50
❑79, Jun 1993 .... 1.50
❑80, Jul 1993 .... 1.50
❑81, Aug 1993 .... 1.25
❑82, Sep 1993 .... 1.25
❑83, Oct 1993 .... 1.25
❑84, Nov 1993 .... 1.25
❑85, Dec 1993 .... 1.25
❑86, Jan 1994; Giant-size 2.95
❑87, Feb 1994 .... 1.25
❑88, Mar 1994 .... 1.25
❑89, Apr 1994 RH (a) 1.25
❑90, May 1994 RH (a) 1.25
❑91, Jun 1994 RH (a) 1.50
❑92, Jul 1994 RH (a) 1.50
❑93, Aug 1994 .... 1.50
❑94, Sep 1994 .... 1.50
❑95, Oct 1994 .... 1.50
❑96, Nov 1994 .... 1.50
❑97, Dec 1994 .... 1.50
❑98, Jan 1995 .... 1.50
❑99, Feb 1995 .... 1.50
❑100, Mar 1995; Giant-size 2.95
❑100/Variant, Mar 1995; Giant-size; foil cover 3.95
❑101, Apr 1995 .... 4.00
❑102, May 1995 .... 1.50
❑103, Jun 1995 .... 1.50

❑104, Jul 1995 1.50
❑Annual 1, ca. 1988 3.50
❑Annual 2, ca. 1989; JLee (a); A: Moon Knight. V: Moon Knight. Atlantis Attacks 2.50
❑Annual 3, ca. 1990 2.50
❑Annual 4, ca. 1991 JLee (a) 2.00
❑Annual 5, ca. 1992; PD (w); VM (a); System Bytes 2.25
❑Annual 6 1993; 1993 Annual; Polybagged 2.95
❑Annual 7, ca. 1994 2.95

PUNISHER (3RD SERIES)
MARVEL

❑1, Nov 1995; foil cover 2.95
❑2, Dec 1995 A: Hatchetman 1.95
❑3, Dec 1995 1.95
❑4, Feb 1996 A: Daredevil. V: Jigsaw.. 1.95
❑5, Mar 1996 PB (a) 1.95
❑6, Apr 1996 PB (a) 1.95
❑7, May 1996 1.95
❑8, Jun 1996 1.95
❑9, Jul 1996 1.95
❑10, Aug 1996 V: Jigsaw 1.95
❑11, Sep 1996; S.H.I.E.L.D. helicarrier crashes 1.95
❑12, Oct 1996 V: X-Cutioner 1.95
❑13, Nov 1996 V: X-Cutioner 1.95
❑14, Dec 1996 V: X-Cutioner 1.50
❑15, Jan 1997 V: X-Cutioner 1.50
❑16, Feb 1997 V: X-Cutioner 1.50
❑17, Mar 1997 1.95
❑18, Apr 1997 1.95

PUNISHER (4TH SERIES)
MARVEL

❑1, Nov 1998; gatefold summary 3.00
❑1/Variant, Nov 1998; DFE alternate cover 6.00
❑2, Dec 1998; gatefold summary 2.99
❑3, Jan 1999 2.99
❑4, Feb 1999 2.99

PUNISHER (5TH SERIES)
MARVEL

❑1, Apr 2000 4.00
❑1/Variant, Apr 2000; White background on cover 8.50
❑2, May 2000 3.50
❑2/Variant, May 2000; White background on cover 6.00
❑3, Jun 2000; Polybagged with Marvel Knights/Marvel Boy Genesis Edition 3.50
❑4, Jul 2000 3.00
❑5, Aug 2000 3.00
❑6, Sep 2000 2.99
❑7, Oct 2000 2.99
❑8, Nov 2000 1: The Russian 2.99
❑9, Dec 2000 2.99
❑10, Jan 2001 2.99
❑11, Feb 2001 1: The Vigilante Squad. D: The Russian 2.99
❑12, Mar 2001 D: Ma Gnucci 2.99

PUNISHER (6TH SERIES)
MARVEL / MAX

❑1, Aug 2001 2.99
❑2, Sep 2001 2.99
❑3, Oct 2001 2.99
❑4, Nov 2001 2.99
❑5, Dec 2001 2.99
❑6, Jan 2002 2.99
❑7, Feb 2002; Silent issue 2.99
❑8, Mar 2002 2.99
❑9, Apr 2002 2.99
❑10, May 2002 2.99
❑11, Jun 2002 2.99
❑12, Jul 2002 2.99
❑13, Aug 2002 2.99
❑14, Sep 2002 2.99
❑15, Oct 2002 2.99
❑16, Nov 2002 2.99
❑17, Nov 2002 2.99
❑18, Dec 2002 2.99
❑19, Jan 2003 2.99
❑20, Feb 2003 2.99
❑21, Mar 2003 2.99
❑22, Apr 2003 2.99
❑23, May 2003 2.99
❑24, Jun 2003 2.99
❑25, Jun 2003 2.99
❑26, Jul 2003 2.99
❑27, Jul 2003 2.99
❑28, Aug 2003 2.99
❑29, Sep 2003 2.99
❑30, Oct 2003 2.99
❑31, Nov 2003 2.99
❑32, Nov 2003 2.99
❑33, Dec 2003 2.99
❑34, Dec 2003 2.99
❑35, Jan 2004 2.99
❑36, Jan 2004 2.99
❑37, Feb 2004 2.99

PUNISHER (7TH SERIES)
MARVEL / MAX

❑1, Mar 2004 5.00
❑1/DF, Mar 2004 15.00
❑2, Mar 2004 4.00
❑3, Apr 2004, TP (a) 2.99
❑4, May 2004, TP (a) 2.99
❑5, Jun 2004, TP (a) 2.99
❑6, Jul 2004 2.99
❑7, Aug 2004 2.99
❑8, Aug 2004 2.99
❑9, Sep 2004 2.99
❑10, Oct 2004 2.99
❑11, Oct 2004 2.99
❑12, Nov 2004 2.99
❑13, Dec 2004 2.99
❑14, Dec 2004 2.99
❑15, Jan 2005 2.99
❑16, Feb 2005 2.99
❑17, Mar 2005 2.99
❑18, Apr 2005 2.99
❑19, May 2005 2.99
❑20, Jun 2005 2.99
❑21, Jul 2005 2.99
❑22, Aug 2005 2.99
❑23, Sep 2005 2.99
❑24, Oct 2005 2.99
❑25, Nov 2005 2.99
❑26, Dec 2005 2.99
❑27, Jan 2006 2.99
❑28, Feb 2006 2.99
❑29, Mar 2006 2.99
❑30, Mar 2006 2.99
❑31, May 2006 2.99
❑32, Jun 2006 2.99
❑33, Jul 2006 2.99
❑34, Aug 2006 2.99
❑35, Sep 2006 2.99

PUNISHER, THE: A MAN NAMED FRANK
MARVEL

❑1, Jun 1994 6.95

PUNISHER ANNIVERSARY MAGAZINE
MARVEL

❑1 4.95

PUNISHER ARMORY
MARVEL

❑1, Jul 1990; weapons 2.00
❑2, Jun 1991 2.00
❑3, Apr 1991 2.00
❑4 2.00
❑5 1992 2.00
❑6 2.00
❑7, Sep 1993 2.00
❑8, Dec 1993 2.00
❑9 2.00
❑10, Nov 1994 2.00

PUNISHER BACK TO SCHOOL SPECIAL
MARVEL

❑1, Nov 1992; 1992 3.50
❑2, Oct 1993; BSz (c); BSz (a); 1993 . 3.00
❑3, Oct 1994; 1994 3.00

PUNISHER/BATMAN: DEADLY KNIGHTS
MARVEL

❑1, Oct 1994 4.95

PUNISHER/BLACK WIDOW: SPINNING DOOMSDAY'S WEB
MARVEL

❑1 9.95

PUNISHER: BLOODLINES
MARVEL

❑1, ca. 1991; prestige format 5.95

PUNISHER: BLOODY VALENTINE
MARVEL

❑1, Apr 2006 4.99

PUNISHER: DIE HARD IN THE BIG EASY
MARVEL

❑1, ca. 1992; prestige format one-shot 4.95

PUNISHER: EMPTY QUARTER
MARVEL

❑1, Nov 1994; prestige format one-shot 6.95

PUNISHER: G-FORCE
MARVEL

❑1, ca. 1992; squarebound with cardstock cover 4.95

PUNISHER HOLIDAY SPECIAL
MARVEL

❑1, Jan 1993; foil cover 3.00
❑2, Jan 1994 3.00
❑3, Jan 1995 3.00

PUNISHER: INTRUDER
MARVEL

❑1 9.95
❑1/HC 14.95

PUNISHER INVADES THE 'NAM: FINAL INVASION
MARVEL

❑1, Feb 1994 6.95

PUNISHER KILLS THE MARVEL UNIVERSE
MARVEL

❑1, Nov 1995 20.00
❑1/2nd, Mar 2000 5.95

PUNISHER, THE: KINGDOM GONE
MARVEL

❑1, Aug 1990 16.95

PUNISHER MAGAZINE
MARVEL

❑1, Sep 1989, b&w; Reprints Punisher (Ltd. Series) #1 in black & white 3.00
❑2, Oct 1989, b&w; Reprints Punisher (Ltd. Series) #2-3 in black & white . 2.50
❑3, Nov 1989, b&w; Reprints Punisher (Ltd. Series) #4-5 in black & white . 2.50
❑4, Dec 1989, b&w; Reprints Punisher #1-2 in black & white 2.50
❑5, Dec 1989, b&w; Reprints Punisher #3-4 in black & white 2.50
❑6, Jan 1990, b&w; Reprints Punisher #5-6 in black & white 2.50
❑7, Feb 1990, b&w; Reprints Punisher #7-8 in black & white 2.50
❑8, Mar 1990, b&w; Reprints 2.50
❑9, Apr 1990, b&w; Reprints 2.50
❑10, May 1990, b&w; Reprints 2.50
❑11, Jun 1990, b&w; Reprints 2.50
❑12, Jul 1990, b&w; Reprints 2.50
❑13, Aug 1990, b&w; Reprints 2.50
❑14, Sep 1990, b&w; Reprints Punisher War Journal #1-2 2.50
❑15, Oct 1990, b&w; Reprints 2.50
❑16, Nov 1990, b&w; Reprints 2.50

PUNISHER MEETS ARCHIE
MARVEL

❑1, Aug 1994; enhanced cover 4.00
❑1/Variant, Aug 1994; Die-cut cover... 4.50

PUNISHER MOVIE SPECIAL
MARVEL

❑1, Jun 1990 5.95

PUNISHER, THE: NO ESCAPE
MARVEL

❑1, ca. 1990, prestige format 4.95

PUNISHER, THE: OFFICIAL MOVIE ADAPTATION
MARVEL

❑1, May 2004 2.99
❑2, May 2004 2.99
❑3, May 2004 2.99

PUNISHER, THE: ORIGIN OF MICRO CHIP
MARVEL

❑1, Jul 1993 O: Micro Chip 2.00
❑2, Aug 1993 2.00

Queen & Country

British espionage adventures with Tara
©Oni

Question Quarterly

Only alliterative series beginning with Q
©DC

Quicksilver

Starring Scarlet Witch's speedster brother
©Marvel

Radioactive Man

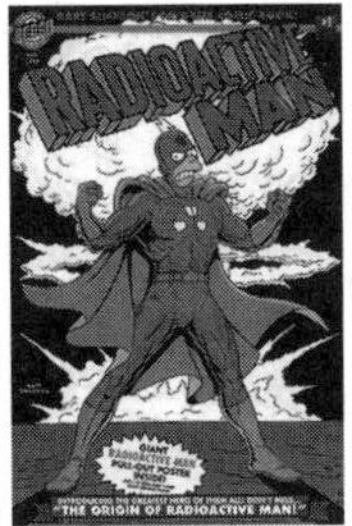

Bart Simpson's favorite super-hero
©Bongo

Ragman

Pawnbroker by day, crimefighter by night
©DC

N-MINT

PUNISHER/PAINKILLER JANE
MARVEL

❑1, Jan 2001; cardstock cover 3.50

PUNISHER: P.O.V.
MARVEL

❑1, ca. 1991 JSn (w); BWr, BW (a) 5.00
❑2, ca. 1991 JSn (w); BWr, BW (a) 5.00
❑3, ca. 1991 JSn (w); BWr, BW (a) 5.00
❑4, ca. 1991 JSn (w); BWr, BW (a) 5.00

PUNISHER: RED X-MAS
MARVEL

❑1, Jan 2004 .... 3.99

PUNISHER: SILENT NIGHT
MARVEL

❑1, Feb 2006 .... 4.99

PUNISHER SUMMER SPECIAL
MARVEL

❑1, Aug 1991 VM (a) 3.00
❑2, Aug 1992 .... 3.00
❑3 1993 .... 2.50
❑4, Jul 1994 .... 2.95

PUNISHER, THE: THE END
MARVEL / MAX

❑1, Jun 2004 .... 4.50

PUNISHER: THE GHOSTS OF INNOCENTS
MARVEL

❑1, ca. 1993 .... 5.95
❑2, ca. 1993 .... 5.95

PUNISHER: THE MOVIE
MARVEL

❑1, May 2004 .... 2.99
❑2, May 2004 .... 2.99
❑3, May 2004 .... 2.99

PUNISHER: THE PRIZE
MARVEL

❑1, ca. 1990; prestige format 4.95

PUNISHER: THE TYGER
MARVEL

❑1, Aug 2006 .... 3.99

PUNISHER 2099
MARVEL

❑1, Feb 1993; foil cover 1.75
❑2, Mar 1993 .... 1.25
❑3, Apr 1993 .... 1.25
❑4, May 1993 .... 1.25
❑5, Jun 1993 .... 1.25
❑6, Jul 1993 .... 1.25
❑7, Aug 1993 .... 1.25
❑8, Sep 1993 .... 1.25
❑9, Oct 1993 .... 1.25
❑10, Nov 1993 .... 1.25
❑11, Dec 1993 .... 1.25
❑12, Jan 1994 .... 1.25
❑13, Feb 1994 .... 1.25
❑14, Mar 1994 .... 1.25
❑15, Apr 1994 .... 1.25
❑16, May 1994 .... 1.50
❑17, Jun 1994 .... 1.50
❑18, Jul 1994 .... 1.50
❑19, Aug 1994 .... 1.50

N-MINT

❑20, Sep 1994 .... 1.50
❑21, Oct 1994 .... 1.50
❑22, Nov 1994 .... 1.50
❑23, Dec 1994 .... 1.50
❑24, Jan 1995 .... 1.50
❑25, Feb 1995; Giant-size 2.25
❑25/Variant, Feb 1995; Embossed cover 2.95
❑26, Mar 1995 .... 1.50
❑27, Apr 1995 .... 1.50
❑28, May 1995 .... 1.95
❑29, Jun 1995 .... 1.95
❑30, Jul 1995 .... 1.95
❑31, Aug 1995 .... 1.95
❑32, Sep 1995 .... 1.95
❑33, Oct 1995 .... 1.95
❑34, Nov 1995; continues in 2099 A.D. Apocalypse #1 .... 1.95

PUNISHER VS BULLSEYE
MARVEL

❑1, Jan 2006 .... 2.99
❑2, Feb 2006 .... 2.99
❑3, Mar 2006 .... 2.99
❑4, Apr 2006 .... 2.99
❑5, May 2006 .... 2.99

PUNISHER VS. DAREDEVIL
MARVEL

❑1, Jun 2000; Reprints 3.50

PUNISHER WAR JOURNAL
MARVEL

❑1, Nov 1988 JLee (a); O: Punisher ... 5.00
❑2, Dec 1988 JLee (a); A: Daredevil ... 3.00
❑3, Feb 1989 JLee (a); A: Daredevil ... 3.00
❑4, Mar 1989 JLee (a) 3.00
❑5, May 1989 JLee (a) 3.00
❑6, Jun 1989 JLee (a); A: Wolverine .. 3.00
❑7, Jul 1989 JLee (a); A: Wolverine ... 3.00
❑8, Sep 1989 JLee (a) 1.50
❑9, Oct 1989 JLee (a) 1.50
❑10, Nov 1989 JLee (a) 1.50
❑11, Dec 1989 JLee (a) 1.50
❑12, Dec 1989; JLee (a); Acts of Vengeance 1.50
❑13, Dec 1989; JLee (a); Acts of Vengeance 1.50
❑14, Jan 1990 RH (a); A: Spider-Man ... 1.50
❑15, Feb 1990 RH (a); A: Spider-Man ... 1.50
❑16, Mar 1990 .... 1.50
❑17, Apr 1990 JLee (a) 1.50
❑18, May 1990 JLee (a) 1.50
❑19, Jun 1990 JLee (a) 1.50
❑20, Jul 1990 .... 1.50
❑21, Aug 1990 .... 1.50
❑22, Sep 1990 .... 1.50
❑23, Oct 1990 .... 1.75
❑24, Nov 1990 .... 1.75
❑25, Dec 1990 .... 1.75
❑26, Jan 1991 .... 1.75
❑27, Feb 1991 .... 1.75
❑28, Mar 1991 .... 1.75
❑29, Apr 1991 A: Ghost Rider 1.75
❑30, May 1991 A: Ghost Rider 1.75
❑31, Jun 1991; Painted cover 1.75
❑32, Jul 1991 .... 1.75

N-MINT

❑33, Aug 1991 .... 1.75
❑34, Sep 1991 .... 1.75
❑35, Oct 1991 .... 1.75
❑36, Nov 1991 .... 1.75
❑37, Dec 1991 .... 1.75
❑38, Jan 1992 .... 1.75
❑39, Feb 1992 .... 1.75
❑40, Mar 1992 .... 1.75
❑41, Apr 1992 .... 1.75
❑42, May 1992 .... 1.75
❑43, Jun 1992 VM (a) 1.75
❑44, Jul 1992 VM (a) 1.75
❑45, Aug 1992 .... 1.75
❑46, Sep 1992 .... 1.75
❑47, Oct 1992 .... 1.75
❑48, Nov 1992 .... 1.75
❑49, Dec 1992 .... 1.75
❑50, Jan 1993; 1: Punisher 2099. Embossed cover; Punisher 2099 Preview 2.95
❑51, Feb 1993 .... 1.75
❑52, Mar 1993 .... 1.75
❑53, Apr 1993 .... 1.75
❑54, May 1993 .... 1.75
❑55, Jun 1993 .... 1.75
❑56, Jul 1993 .... 1.75
❑57, Aug 1993 A: Ghost Rider. A: Daredevil 1.75
❑58, Sep 1993 A: Ghost Rider. A: Daredevil 1.75
❑59, Oct 1993 A: Max 1.75
❑60, Nov 1993 A: Cage 1.75
❑61, Dec 1993; Giant-size; Embossed foil cover 2.95
❑62, Jan 1994 .... 1.75
❑63, Feb 1994 .... 1.75
❑64, Mar 1994; regular cover 2.25
❑64/Variant, Mar 1994; Die-cut cover. 2.00
❑65, Apr 1994 .... 3.00
❑66, May 1994 BA (a); A: Captain America 1.95
❑67, Jun 1994 .... 1.95
❑68, Jul 1994 .... 1.95
❑69, Aug 1994 .... 1.95
❑70, Sep 1994 .... 1.95
❑71, Oct 1994 .... 1.95
❑72, Nov 1994 .... 1.95
❑73, Dec 1994 .... 1.95
❑74, Jan 1995 .... 1.95
❑75, Feb 1995; Giant-size 4.00
❑76, Mar 1995; New Punisher (Lynn Michaels) begins 3.00
❑77, Apr 1995 .... 1.95
❑78, May 1995 .... 1.95
❑79, Jun 1995 D: Microchip 1.95
❑80, Jul 1995 D: Stone Cold 1.95

PUNISHER WAR ZONE
MARVEL

❑1, Mar 1992, JR2 (a); Die-cut cover. 2.50
❑2, Apr 1992, JR2 (a) 1.75
❑3, May 1992, JR2 (a) 1.75
❑4, Jun 1992, JR2 (a) 1.75
❑5, Jul 1992, JR2 (a) 1.75
❑6, Aug 1992, JR2 (a) 1.75
❑7, Sep 1992, JR2 (a) 1.75

Other grades: Multiply price above by 5/6 for VF/NM • 2/3 for VERY FINE • 1/3 for FINE • 1/5 for VERY GOOD • 1/8 for GOOD

❑8, Oct 1992, JR2 (a) 1.75
❑9, Nov 1992 1.75
❑10, Dec 1992 1.75
❑11, Jan 1993 1.75
❑12, Feb 1993 1.75
❑13, Mar 1993 1.75
❑14, Apr 1992 1.75
❑15, May 1993 1.75
❑16, Jun 1993 1.75
❑17, Jul 1993 1.75
❑18, Aug 1993 1.75
❑19, Sep 1993, A: Wolverine 1.75
❑20, Oct 1993 1.75
❑21, Nov 1993 1.75
❑22, Dec 1993 1.75
❑23, Jan 1994, Giant-size; VM (a); D: Rapido. Embossed foil cover 2.95
❑24, Feb 1994, JB, VM (a) 1.75
❑25, Mar 1994, JB, VM (a) 2.25
❑26, Apr 1994, JB (a) 1.75
❑27, May 1994, JB (a) 1.75
❑28, Jun 1994, JB (a) 1.95
❑29, Jul 1994, JB (a) 1.95
❑30, Aug 1994, JB (a) 1.95
❑31, Sep 1994, JKu (a) 1.95
❑32, Oct 1994, JKu (a) 1.95
❑33, Nov 1994, JKu (a) 1.95
❑34, Dec 1994, JKu (a) 1.95
❑35, Jan 1995, JKu (a) 1.95
❑36, Feb 1995, JKu (a) 1.95
❑37, Mar 1995, O: Max (The Punisher's dog) 1.95
❑38, Apr 1995 1.95
❑39, May 1995 1.95
❑40, Jun 1995 1.95
❑41, Jul 1995 1.95
❑Annual 1, ca. 1993, JB (a); trading card; pin-up gallery 2.95
❑Annual 2, ca. 1994, D: Roc 2.95

PUNISHER/WOLVERINE AFRICAN SAGA
MARVEL

❑1, ca. 1988 5.95

PUNISHER, THE: YEAR ONE
MARVEL

❑1, Dec 1994 2.50
❑2, Jan 1995 2.50
❑3, Feb 1995 2.50
❑4, Mar 1995 2.50

PUNX
ACCLAIM / VALIANT

❑1, Nov 1995 2.50
❑2, Dec 1995 2.50
❑3, Jan 1996 2.50

PUNX (MANGA) SPECIAL
ACCLAIM / VALIANT

❑1, Mar 1996, to be read from back to front 2.50

PUPPET MASTER
ETERNITY

❑1 2.50
❑2 2.50
❑3 2.50
❑4 2.50

PUPPET MASTER: CHILDREN OF THE PUPPET MASTER
ETERNITY

❑1 2.50
❑2 2.50

PURE IMAGES
PURE IMAGINATION

❑1, some color 2.50
❑2, some color 2.50
❑3, monsters; some color 2.50
❑4, monsters; some color 2.50

PURGATORI
CHAOS!

❑½, Dec 2000 2.95
❑1, Oct 1998 3.00
❑2, Nov 1998 V: Lady Death 2.95
❑3, Dec 1998 2.95
❑4, Jan 1999 2.95
❑5, Feb 1999 2.95
❑6, Mar 1999 2.95
❑7, Apr 1999 V: Dracula 2.95
❑Ashcan 1; ashcan preview; no cover price 3.00

PURGATORI
DEVIL'S DUE / CHAOS

❑1 2005 2.95
❑2, Dec 2005 2.95
❑3, Jan 2006 2.95
❑4, Feb 2006 2.95
❑5, Mar 2006 2.95
❑6, Sep 2006 2.95

PURGATORI: EMPIRE
CHAOS

❑1, May 2000 2.95
❑2, Jun 2000 2.95
❑3, Jul 2000 2.95

PURGATORI: GODDESS RISING
CHAOS!

❑1, Jul 1999 2.95
❑1/Ltd.; limited edition 2.95
❑2, Aug 1999 2.95
❑3, Sep 1999 2.95
❑4, Dec 1999 2.95

PURGATORI: THE DRACULA GAMBIT
CHAOS!

❑1, Aug 1997 2.95
❑1/Variant, Aug 1997; Centennial Premium Edition; no cover price 3.00

PURGATORI: THE DRACULA GAMBIT SKETCHBOOK
CHAOS!

❑1, Jul 1997; b&w preliminary sketches 2.95

PURGATORI: THE VAMPIRES MYTH
CHAOS!

❑-1, Aug 1996 1.50
❑1, Aug 1996; Red foil embossed 3.50
❑1/Ltd., Aug 1996; premium edition; limited to 10, 000 copies; wraparound acetate cover 5.00
❑1/Variant, Oct 1996; "Krome" edition (color) 8.00
❑2, Oct 1996 3.00
❑3, Dec 1996 2.95
❑4, Feb 1997 2.95
❑5, Apr 1997 2.95
❑6, Jun 1997 2.95

PURGATORI VS. VAMPIRELLA
CHAOS

❑nn, Apr 2000 2.95

PURGATORY USA
SLAVE LABOR

❑1, Mar 1989, b&w; Ed Brubaker's first published work 2.00

PURGE
ANIA

❑0 1.95
❑1, Aug 1993 1.95

PURGE (AMARA)
AMARA

❑0; Preview edition 1.50

PURPLE CLAW MYSTERIES
AC

❑1, b&w; Reprints 2.95

PURR
BLUE EYED DOG

❑1 8.00

PUSSYCAT
MARVEL

❑1, ca. 1968, b&w; magazine BWa, WW (a) 150.00

PVP
DORK STORM

❑1, Mar 2001 2.95

PVP (IMAGE)
IMAGE

❑1, Mar 2003, b&w; Printed sideways 5.00
❑2, May 2003, b&w; Printed sideways 2.95
❑3, Jul 2003, b&w; Printed sideways. 2.95
❑4, Oct 2003, b&w; Printed sideways 2.95
❑5, Dec 2003, b&w; Printed sideways 2.95
❑6, Jan 2004, b&w; Printed sideways 2.95
❑7, Apr 2004, b&w; Printed sideways 2.95
❑8, May 2004, b&w; Printed sideways 2.95
❑9, Jul 2004, b&w; Printed sideways. 2.95
❑10, Aug 2004, b&w; Printed sideways 2.95
❑11, Sep 2004, b&w; EL (c); Printed sideways 2.95
❑12, Oct 2004, b&w; Printed sideways 2.95
❑13, Nov 2004, b&w; Printed sideways 2.95
❑14, ca. 2005 2.95
❑15, ca. 2005 2.95
❑16, ca. 2005 2.95
❑17, ca. 2005 2.95
❑18, Oct 2005 2.95
❑19 2005 2.95
❑0, Sep 2005 1.00
❑20, Dec 2005 2.95
❑21, Jan 2006 2.95
❑22, Feb 2006 2.95
❑23, Mar 2006 2.95
❑24, Apr 2006 2.95
❑25, May 2006 2.95
❑26, Jun 2006 2.95
❑27, Jul 2006 2.95

Q-LOC
CHIASMUS

❑1, Aug 1994 2.50

QUACK!
STAR*REACH

❑1, Jul 1976, b&w FB, HC, ME (w); FB, HC, DSt, ME (a) 2.50
❑2, Jan 1977, b&w SA (w); SA (a) 2.50
❑3, Apr 1977, b&w 2.50
❑4, Jun 1977, b&w 2.50
❑5, Sep 1977, b&w 2.50
❑6, Dec 1977, b&w FB (w); FB (a) 2.50

QUADRANT
QUADRANT

❑1, ca. 1983, b&w 1.95
❑2, ca. 1984, b&w 1.95
❑3, ca. 1984, b&w 1.95
❑4, ca. 1985, b&w 1.95
❑5, ca. 1985, b&w 1.95
❑6, ca. 1985, b&w; no cover date 1.95
❑7, ca. 1986, b&w 1.95
❑8, ca. 1986, b&w 1.95

QUADRO GANG
NONSENSE UNLIMITED

❑1, b&w 1.25

QUAGMIRE
KITCHEN SINK

❑1, Sum 1970, b&w 3.00

QUAGMIRE U.S.A.
ANTARCTIC

❑1, Mar 1994, b&w 2.75
❑2, May 1994, b&w 2.75
❑3, Jul 1994, b&w 2.75

QUAGMIRE U.S.A. (VOL. 2)
ANTARCTIC

❑1, Feb 2004 2.99
❑2, Apr 2004 2.99
❑3, Jun 2004 2.99
❑4, Aug 2004 2.99
❑5, Oct 2004 2.99

QUALITY SPECIAL
FLEETWAY-QUALITY

❑1; Strontium Dog 2.00
❑2; Midnight Surfer 2.00

QUANTUM & WOODY
ACCLAIM / VALIANT

❑0/American Ent, ca. 1997, American Entertainment exclusive 3.00
❑1, Jun 1997 2.50
❑1/A, Jun 1997, Painted cover 2.50
❑2, Jul 1997 2.50
❑3, Aug 1997, 1: The Goat 2.50
❑4, Sep 1997 2.50
❑5, Oct 1997 2.50
❑6, Nov 1997 2.50
❑7, Dec 1997 2.50
❑8, Jan 1998 2.50
❑9, Feb 1998, A: Troublemakers 2.50
❑10, Mar 1998 2.50
❑11, Apr 1998 2.50
❑12, Jan 1998, indicia says Jan; no cover date 2.50
❑13, Feb 1998, indicia says Feb; no cover date 2.50
❑14, Mar 1998 2.50

Rai

Series name adds then drops "Future Force"

©Valiant

Rain

Memories of Germany after World War II

©Tundra

Ralph Snart Adventures (Vol. 1)

Fed-up man decides to go insane

©Now

Rampaging Hulk (Magazine)

Magazine becomes simply "Hulk!"

©Marvel

Ranma 1/2

Boy turns into girl, dad turns into panda

©Viz

N-MINT

❑15, Apr 1998 .... 2.50
❑16, May 1998 .... 2.50
❑17, Jun 1998 .... 2.50
❑Ashcan 1, Feb 1997, b&w preview of series; no cover price 1.00

QUANTUM CREEP
Parody

❑1, ca. 1992, b&w 2.50

QUANTUM LEAP
Innovation

❑1, Sep 1991 O: Doctor Sam Beckett (Quantum Leap). 1: Doctor Sam Beckett (Quantum Leap) 5.00
❑2, Dec 1991 .... 4.00
❑3, Mar 1992; Sam as Santa 4.00
❑4, Apr 1992; Sam on game show 4.00
❑5, May 1992; Superman theme cover 4.00
❑6, Sep 1992 .... 3.00
❑7, Oct 1992 .... 3.00
❑8, Dec 1992 .... 3.00
❑9, Feb 1993 .... 3.00
❑10, Apr 1993 .... 2.50
❑11, May 1993 .... 2.50
❑12, Jun 1993 .... 2.50
❑13, Aug 1993; Time and Space Special #1; foil-enhanced cardstock cover 2.95
❑Annual 1 1992 .... 4.00
❑Special 1, Oct 1992; reprints #1 .... 5.00

QUANTUM: ROCK OF AGES
Dreamchilde Press

❑1, ca. 2003 .... 2.99
❑2, ca. 2003 .... 2.99
❑3, Apr 2004 .... 2.99
❑4, Jun 2004 .... 2.99

QUASAR
Marvel

❑1, Oct 1989, O: Quasar 1.50
❑2, Nov 1989 .... 1.00
❑3, Nov 1989 .... 1.00
❑4, Dec 1989, O: Quantum 1.00
❑5, Dec 1989, V: Absorbing Man. Acts of Vengeance 1.00
❑6, Jan 1990, A: Venom. V: Red Ghost. V: Living Laser. V: Venom. Acts of Vengeance 1.00
❑7, Feb 1990, A: Spider-Man. Spider-Man has cosmic powers 1.00
❑8, Mar 1990 .... 1.00
❑9, Apr 1990, 1: Captain Atlas 1.00
❑10, May 1990, O: Captain Atlas 1.00
❑11, Jun 1990, Phoenix 1.00
❑12, Jul 1990 .... 1.00
❑13, Aug 1990 .... 1.00
❑14, Sep 1990, TMc (c) 1.00
❑15, Oct 1990 .... 1.00
❑16, Nov 1990 .... 1.00
❑17, Dec 1990 .... 1.00
❑18, Jan 1991 .... 1.00
❑19, Feb 1991, 1: Starlight 1.00
❑20, Mar 1991, Fantastic Four 1.00
❑21, Apr 1991 .... 1.00
❑22, May 1991, A: Ghost Rider 1.00
❑23, Jun 1991, A: Ghost Rider 1.00
❑24, Jul 1991, 1: Infinity (physical) 1.00

N-MINT

❑25, Aug 1991, new costume 1.00
❑26, Sep 1991, Infinity Gauntlet 1.00
❑27, Oct 1991, 1: Epoch. Infinity Gauntlet 1.00
❑28, Nov 1991 .... 1.00
❑29, Dec 1991 .... 1.00
❑30, Jan 1992, PB (a) 1.00
❑31, Feb 1992, A: D.P.7. New Universe 1.25
❑32, Mar 1992, 1: Korath the Pursuer. A: Imperial Guard. A: Starfox 1.25
❑33, Apr 1992 .... 1.25
❑34, May 1992, A: Binary 1.25
❑35, Jun 1992 .... 1.25
❑36, Jul 1992, A: Her. A: Makkari. V: Souleater 1.25
❑37, Aug 1992 .... 1.25
❑38, Sep 1992, Infinity War 1.25
❑39, Oct 1992, Infinity War 1.25
❑40, Nov 1992, Infinity War 1.25
❑41, Dec 1992, 1: Kismet 1.25
❑42, Jan 1993 .... 1.25
❑43, Feb 1993 .... 1.25
❑44, Mar 1993 .... 1.25
❑45, Apr 1993 .... 1.25
❑46, May 1993 .... 1.25
❑47, Jun 1993, 1: Thunderstrike 1.75
❑48, Jul 1993 .... 1.25
❑49, Aug 1993 .... 1.25
❑50, Sep 1993, Giant-size; A: Silver Surfer. Holo-grafix cover 2.95
❑51, Oct 1993, A: Squadron Supreme. A: Anglemen 1.25
❑52, Nov 1993 .... 1.25
❑53, Dec 1993 .... 1.25
❑54, Jan 1994 .... 1.25
❑55, Feb 1994 .... 1.25
❑56, Mar 1994 .... 1.25
❑57, Apr 1994 .... 1.25
❑58, May 1994 .... 1.25
❑59, Jun 1994 .... 1.25
❑60, Jul 1994 .... 1.25
❑Special 1, Mar 1992, reprints Quasar #32 for newsstand distribution 1.50
❑Special 2, Apr 1992, reprints Quasar #33 for newsstand distribution 1.50
❑Special 3, May 1992, reprints Quasar #34 for newsstand distribution 1.50

QUEEN & COUNTRY
Oni

❑1, Mar 2001, b&w 9.00
❑1/FCBD, Mar 2001 .... 1.00
❑2, May 2001, b&w 7.00
❑3, Jul 2001, b&w 6.00
❑4, Sep 2001, b&w 5.00
❑5, Nov 2001, b&w 5.00
❑6, Jan 2002, b&w 5.00
❑7, Mar 2002, b&w 5.00
❑8, May 2002, b&w 5.00
❑9, Jun 2002, b&w 5.00
❑10, Jul 2002, b&w 5.00
❑11, Aug 2002, b&w 5.00
❑12, Sep 2002, b&w 5.00
❑13, Jan 2003, b&w 5.00
❑14, Feb 2003, b&w 5.00
❑15, Apr 2003, b&w 5.00

N-MINT

❑16 2003, b&w 4.00
❑17 2003, b&w 4.00
❑18 2003, b&w 4.00
❑19 2003, b&w 4.00
❑20 2004, b&w 4.00
❑21 2004, b&w 2.99
❑22 2004, b&w 2.99
❑23 2004, b&w 2.99
❑24 2004, b&w 2.99
❑25 2004, b&w 2.99
❑26, Jul 2004, b&w 2.99
❑27 2004, b&w 2.99
❑28 2004 .... 2.99

QUEEN & COUNTRY: DECLASSIFIED
Oni

❑1, Nov 2002, b&w 2.95
❑2, Dec 2002, b&w 2.95
❑3, Jan 2003, b&w 2.95

QUEEN & COUNTRY: DECLASSIFIED (VOL. 2)
Oni

❑1 2005 .... 2.99

QUEEN & COUNTRY: DECLASSIFIED (VOL. 3)
Oni

❑1, Jun 2005 .... 2.99
❑2, Sep 2005 .... 2.99
❑3, Oct 2005 .... 2.99

QUEEN OF THE DAMNED (ANNE RICE'S...)
Innovation

❑1, ca. 1991 .... 2.50
❑2, ca. 1992 .... 2.50
❑3, ca. 1992 .... 2.50
❑4, ca. 1992 .... 2.50
❑5, ca. 1992 .... 2.50
❑6, ca. 1993 .... 2.50
❑7, ca. 1993 .... 2.50
❑8, Jul 1993 .... 2.50
❑9, Sep 1993 .... 2.50
❑10, Nov 1993 .... 2.50
❑11, Dec 1993 .... 2.50
❑12, Jan 1994 .... 2.50

QUEEN'S GREATEST HITS
Revolutionary

❑1, Nov 1993, b&w 2.50

QUEST FOR CAMELOT
DC

❑1, Jul 1998 .... 4.95

QUEST FOR DREAMS LOST
Literacy Volunteers

❑1, ca. 1987, b&w; The Realm story 2.00

QUESTION
DC

❑1, Feb 1987, Painted cover 2.00
❑2, Mar 1987 .... 1.75
❑3, Apr 1987 .... 1.75
❑4, May 1987 .... 1.50
❑5, Jun 1987 .... 1.50
❑6, Jul 1987 .... 1.50
❑7, Aug 1987 .... 1.50
❑8, Sep 1987 .... 1.50

N-MINT

❑9, Oct 1987 ... 1.50
❑10, Nov 1987 ... 1.50
❑11, Dec 1987 ... 1.50
❑12, Jan 1988 ... 1.50
❑13, Feb 1988 ... 1.50
❑14, Mar 1988 ... 1.50
❑15, Apr 1988 ... 1.50
❑16, May 1988 ... 1.50
❑17, Jun 1988, Rorschach, Green Arrow ... 1.50
❑18, Jul 1988, Green Arrow ... 1.50
❑19, Aug 1988 ... 1.50
❑20, Oct 1988 ... 1.50
❑21, Nov 1988 ... 1.50
❑22, Dec 1988 ... 1.50
❑23, Win 1988 ... 1.50
❑24, Jan 1989 ... 1.50
❑25, Feb 1989 ... 1.50
❑26, Mar 1989 ... 1.50
❑27, Jun 1989 ... 1.50
❑28, Jul 1989 ... 1.50
❑29, Aug 1989 ... 1.50
❑30, Sep 1989 ... 1.50
❑31, Oct 1989 ... 1.50
❑32, Nov 1989 ... 1.50
❑33, Dec 1989 ... 1.50
❑34, Jan 1990 ... 1.50
❑35, Mar 1990 ... 1.50
❑36, Apr 1990 ... 1.50
❑Annual 1, ca. 1988, Batman, Green Arrow ... 2.50
❑Annual 2, ca. 1989, Green Arrow ... 3.50

QUESTION (2ND SERIES)
DC

❑1, Jan 2005 ... 2.95
❑2, Feb 2005 ... 2.95
❑3, Mar 2005 ... 2.95
❑4, Apr 2005 ... 2.95
❑5, May 2005 ... 2.99
❑6, Jun 2005 ... 2.99

QUESTION QUARTERLY
DC

❑1, Aut 1990 ... 2.50
❑2, Sum 1991 ... 2.50
❑3, Aut 1991 ... 2.50
❑4, Win 1991 ... 2.95
❑5, Spr 1992 ... 2.95

QUESTION RETURNS
DC

❑1, Feb 1997 ... 3.50

QUEST OF THE TIGER WOMAN
MILLENNIUM

❑1 ... 2.95

QUEST PRESENTS
QUEST

❑1, Jul 1983 JD (a) ... 1.50
❑2, Sep 1983 JD (a) ... 1.50
❑3, Nov 1983 JD (a) ... 1.50

QUESTPROBE
MARVEL

❑1, Aug 1984, JR (a); O: Chief Examiner. 1: Chief Examiner. Hulk ... 1.50
❑2, Jan 1985, AM (w); AM, JM (a); Spider-Man ... 1.50
❑3, Nov 1985, Human Torch; Thing ... 1.50

QUICK DRAW MCGRAW (DELL)
DELL

❑2, Apr 1960 ... 15.00
❑3, Jul 1960 ... 10.00
❑4, Oct 1960 ... 10.00
❑5, Jan 1961 ... 10.00
❑6, Apr 1961 ... 10.00
❑7, Jul 1961 ... 10.00
❑8, Oct 1961 ... 8.00
❑9, Jan 1962 ... 8.00
❑10, Apr 1962 ... 8.00
❑11, Jul 1962 ... 8.00
❑12, Oct 1962 ... 8.00
❑13, Feb 1963 ... 6.00
❑14, ca. 1963 ... 6.00
❑15, Jun 1969 ... 10.00

QUICK DRAW MCGRAW (CHARLTON)
CHARLTON

❑1, Nov 1970 ... 10.00
❑2, Jan 1971 ... 7.00
❑3, Mar 1971 ... 5.00
❑4, May 1971 ... 5.00
❑5, Jul 1971 ... 5.00
❑6, Sep 1971 ... 4.00
❑7, Nov 1971 ... 4.00
❑8, Jan 1972 ... 4.00

QUICKEN FORBIDDEN
CRYPTIC

❑1, ca. 1996, b&w ... 3.25
❑2, ca. 1996, b&w ... 3.00
❑3, ca. 1997, b&w ... 3.00
❑4, ca. 1997, b&w ... 3.00
❑5, ca. 1998, b&w ... 3.00
❑6, ca. 1998, b&w ... 3.00
❑7, ca. 1999, b&w ... 3.00
❑8, ca. 1999, b&w ... 3.00
❑9, ca. 2000, b&w ... 3.00
❑10, ca. 2000, b&w ... 2.95
❑11 ... 2.95
❑12 ... 2.95
❑13, Oct 2005 ... 2.95

QUICKSILVER
MARVEL

❑1, Nov 1997, gatefold summary; wraparound cover ... 2.99
❑2, Dec 1997, gatefold summary ... 1.99
❑3, Jan 1998, gatefold summary ... 1.99
❑4, Feb 1998, gatefold summary ... 1.99
❑5, Mar 1998, gatefold summary ... 1.99
❑6, Apr 1998, gatefold summary ... 1.99
❑7, May 1998, gatefold summary ... 1.99
❑8, Jun 1998, gatefold summary; in Savage Land ... 1.99
❑9, Jul 1998, gatefold summary ... 1.99
❑10, Aug 1998, gatefold summary; concludes in Avengers #7 ... 1.99
❑11, Sep 1998, gatefold summary ... 1.99
❑12, Oct 1998, double-sized ... 1.99
❑13, Nov 1998, gatefold summary ... 1.99

QUINCY LOOKS INTO HIS FUTURE
GENERAL ELECTRIC

❑1; giveaway; King Features strip ... 2.00

QUIT CITY (WARREN ELLIS')
AVATAR

❑1, ca. 2004 ... 3.50
❑1/Foil, ca. 2004 ... 15.00

QUIT YOUR JOB
ALTERNATIVE

❑1, b&w ... 6.95

QUIVERS
CALIBER

❑1, ca. 1991, b&w ... 2.95
❑2, ca. 1991, b&w ... 2.95

Q-UNIT
HARRIS

❑1, Dec 1993; trading card; Polybagged with "layered reality cybercard" ... 2.95

QWAN
TOKYOPOP

❑1, Mar 2005 ... 9.99
❑2, Jul 2005 ... 9.99
❑3, Dec 2005 ... 9.99

RABBIT
SHARKBAIT

❑1 ... 2.50

RABID
FANTACO

❑1 ... 5.95

RABID ANIMAL KOMIX
KRANKIN' KOMIX

❑1 ... 2.95
❑2 ... 2.95

RABID RACHEL
MILLER

❑1, b&w ... 2.00

RACE AGAINST TIME
DARK ANGEL

❑1, Jun 1997 ... 2.50
❑2, Aug 1997 ... 2.50

RACE OF SCORPIONS (MINI-SERIES)
DARK HORSE

❑1, Mar 1990, b&w ... 4.50
❑2, Sep 1990, b&w ... 4.50

RACE OF SCORPIONS
DARK HORSE

❑1, Jul 1991, b&w ... 2.25
❑2, Aug 1991 ... 2.50
❑3, Sep 1992 ... 2.50
❑4, Oct 1991 ... 2.50

RACER X
NOW

❑1, Sep 1988 ... 2.00
❑2, Oct 1988 ... 1.75
❑3, Nov 1988 ... 1.75
❑4, Jan 1989 ... 1.75
❑5, Feb 1989 ... 1.75
❑6, Mar 1989 ... 1.75
❑7, Apr 1989 ... 1.75
❑8, May 1989; Comics Code ... 1.75
❑9, Jun 1989; Comics Code ... 1.75
❑10, Jul 1989; Comics Code ... 1.75
❑11, Aug 1989; Comics Code ... 1.75

RACER X (VOL. 2)
NOW

❑1, Sep 1989 ... 2.00
❑2, Oct 1989 ... 1.75
❑3, Nov 1989 ... 1.75
❑4, Dec 1989 ... 1.75
❑5, Jan 1990 ... 1.75
❑6, Feb 1990 ... 1.75
❑7, Mar 1990 ... 1.75
❑8, Apr 1990 ... 1.75
❑9, May 1990 ... 1.75
❑10, Jun 1990 ... 1.75

RACER X (3RD SERIES)
WILDSTORM

❑1, Oct 2000 ... 2.95
❑2, Nov 2000 ... 2.95
❑3, Dec 2000 ... 2.95

RACER X PREMIERE
NOW

❑1, Aug 1988 ... 3.50

RACK & PAIN
DARK HORSE

❑1, Mar 1994; Dark Horse ... 2.50
❑2, Apr 1994 ... 2.50
❑3, May 1994 ... 2.50
❑4, Jun 1994 ... 2.50

RACK & PAIN: KILLERS
CHAOS

❑1 1996; Chaos ... 2.95
❑2 1996 ... 2.95
❑3 1996 ... 2.95
❑4 1996 ... 2.95

RADICAL DREAMER
BLACKBALL

❑0, May 1994; poster comic ... 2.50
❑1, Jun 1994; poster comic ... 2.00
❑2, Jul 1994; poster comic ... 2.95
❑3, Sep 1994; poster comic ... 2.50
❑4, Nov 1994; foldout comic on cardstock ... 2.50

RADICAL DREAMER (VOL. 2)
MARK'S GIANT ECONOMY SIZE

❑1, Jun 1995, b&w ... 2.95
❑2, Jul 1995, b&w ... 2.95
❑3, Aug 1995, b&w ... 2.95
❑4, Sep 1995, b&w ... 2.95
❑5, Dec 1995, b&w ... 2.95

RADIOACTIVE MAN
BONGO

❑1, ca. 1993; O: Radioactive Man. glow cover ... 5.00
❑88; 2nd issue ... 5.00
❑216; 3rd issue ... 3.00
❑412, ca. 1994; 4th issue ... 3.00
❑679; 5th issue ... 3.00
❑1000, Jan 1995; 6th issue ... 3.00

RADIOACTIVE MAN (VOL. 2)
BONGO

❑1, ca. 2000, #100 on cover ... 2.50
❑2, Nov 2000, #222 on cover ... 2.50
❑3, ca. 2001, DDC (a); #136 on cover ... 3.00
❑4, ca. 2001, March 1953 on cover ... 3.00
❑5, ca. 2002, #575 on cover ... 3.00
❑6, ca. 2002 ... 3.00
❑7, ca. 2003 ... 3.00

Other grades: Multiply price above by 5/6 for VF/NM • 2/3 for VERY FINE • 1/3 for FINE • 1/5 for VERY GOOD • 1/8 for GOOD

Ravage 2099

Stan Lee creates character for future line

©Marvel

Raver

Guy occasionally visits parallel dimension

©Malibu

Rawhide Kid (1st Series)

Marvel's most successful Western character

©Marvel

Rawhide Kid (3rd Series)

Pilloried revamp packed with gay jokes

©Marvel

Ray (Mini-Series)

His dad was exposed to a "light bomb"

©DC

N-MINT

- ❑8, ca. 2003 ..... 2.99
- ❑9, ca. 2004 ..... 2.99

RADIOACTIVE MAN 80 PAGE COLOSSAL
BONGO

- ❑1, ca. 1995 ..... 4.95

RADIO BOY
ECLIPSE

- ❑1, b&w 1.50

RADISKULL & DEVIL DOLL: RADISKULL LOVE-HATE ONE SHOT
IMAGE

- ❑1, Apr 2003 ..... 2.95

RADIX
IMAGE

- ❑1, Dec 2001 ..... 2.95
- ❑2, Feb 2002 ..... 2.95

RADREX
BULLET

- ❑1, Jan 1990 ..... 2.25

RAGAMUFFINS
ECLIPSE

- ❑1, Jan 1985 GC (a) 2.00

RAGE
ANARCHY BRIDGEWORKS

- ❑1 ..... 2.95

RAGGEDY ANN AND ANDY (2ND SERIES)
DELL

- ❑1, Oct 1964 ..... 35.00
- ❑2 ..... 20.00
- ❑3 ..... 20.00
- ❑4, Mar 1966 ..... 20.00

RAGGEDY ANN AND ANDY (3RD SERIES)
GOLD KEY

- ❑1, Dec 1971 ..... 5.00
- ❑2, Mar 1972 ..... 3.50
- ❑3, Dec 1972 ..... 3.50
- ❑4 ..... 3.50
- ❑5 ..... 3.50
- ❑6 ..... 3.50

RAGGEDYMAN
CULT

- ❑1, b&w 2.50
- ❑1/Variant, b&w; Prism cover 2.75
- ❑2, b&w 1.95
- ❑3, b&w 1.95
- ❑4, b&w BT (c); BT (a) 2.50
- ❑5, Jul 1993, b&w 2.50
- ❑6 ..... 2.50

RAGING ANGELS
CLASSIC HIPPIE

- ❑1, b&w 2.50

RAGMAN
DC

- ❑1, Sep 1976, JKu (a); O: Ragman. 1: Ragman 5.00
- ❑2, Nov 1976, JKu (a) 3.00
- ❑3, Jan 1977, JKu (a) 3.00
- ❑4, Mar 1977, JKu (a) 3.00
- ❑5, Jul 1977, JKu (a) 3.00

N-MINT

RAGMAN (MINI-SERIES)
DC

- ❑1, Oct 1991, KG (w); PB (a) 2.00
- ❑2, Nov 1991, PB (a) 2.00
- ❑3, Dec 1991, PB (a); O: Ragman 2.00
- ❑4, Jan 1992, PB (a) 2.00
- ❑5, Feb 1992, PB (a) 2.00
- ❑6, Mar 1992, PB (a) 2.00
- ❑7, Apr 1992, KG (w); KG, PB, RT (a) 2.00
- ❑8, May 1992, RT (a); A: Batman 2.00

RAGMAN: CRY OF THE DEAD
DC

- ❑1, Aug 1993 ..... 2.00
- ❑2, Sep 1993 ..... 1.75
- ❑3, Oct 1993 ..... 1.75
- ❑4, Nov 1993 ..... 1.75
- ❑5, Dec 1993 ..... 1.75
- ❑6, Jan 1994 ..... 1.75

RAGMOP
PLANET LUCY

- ❑1 ..... 2.75
- ❑1/2nd, Dec 1995 ..... 3.10
- ❑2 ..... 2.75
- ❑2/2nd, Dec 1995 ..... 2.95
- ❑3, Oct 1995 ..... 2.95
- ❑4, Dec 1995 ..... 2.95
- ❑5, Feb 1996 ..... 2.95
- ❑6, Apr 1996 ..... 2.95
- ❑7, Jun 1996 ..... 2.95

RAGMOP (VOL. 2)
IMAGE

- ❑1, Sep 1997, b&w; synopsis of first series 2.95
- ❑2, Nov 1997, b&w 2.95
- ❑3, Feb 1998 ..... 2.95

RAGNAROK GUY
SUN

- ❑1 ..... 2.50

RAHRWL
NORTHSTAR

- ❑1; Limited edition original print (1988). 32 pages. 500 copies produced 2.50
- ❑1/2nd; New edition with redrawn art, 2 additional pages; Splash page identifies it as a new printing 2.25

RAI
VALIANT

- ❑0, Nov 1992; BL (w); O: Rai. 1: Bloodshot. 1: Rai (new). series continues as Rai and the Future Force; Foretells future of Valiant Universe 4.00
- ❑1, Mar 1992 ..... 8.00
- ❑1/Companion, Mar 1992 ..... 1.00
- ❑2, Apr 1992 ..... 6.00
- ❑3, May 1992 ..... 16.00
- ❑4, Jun 1992; Scarcer 15.00
- ❑5, Jul 1992 ..... 6.00
- ❑6, Aug 1992 FM (c) 3.00
- ❑7, Sep 1992; D: Rai (original). Unity 3.00
- ❑8, Oct 1992; Unity epilogue; Series continued in Rai and the Future Force #9 ..... 3.00
- ❑25, Oct 1994; Series continued from Rai and the Future Force #24 ..... 1.00
- ❑26, Nov 1994; Chaos Effect Epsilon 3 ..... 1.00
- ❑27, Dec 1994 ..... 1.00

N-MINT

- ❑28, Jan 1995 ..... 1.00
- ❑29, Feb 1995 ..... 2.00
- ❑30, Mar 1995 ..... 2.00
- ❑31, Apr 1995 ..... 2.00
- ❑32, May 1995 ..... 3.00
- ❑33, Jun 1995 ..... 5.00

RAI AND THE FUTURE FORCE
VALIANT

- ❑9, May 1993; BL (w); A: X-O Commando. A: Eternal Warrior. A: Magnus. Series continued from Rai #8; gatefold cover; first Sean Chen work 1.00
- ❑9/Gold, May 1993; BL (w); Gold 18.00
- ❑9/VVSS, May 1993 ..... 10.00
- ❑10, Jun 1993 ..... 1.00
- ❑11, Jul 1993 ..... 1.00
- ❑12, Aug 1993 ..... 1.00
- ❑13, Sep 1993 ..... 1.00
- ❑14, Oct 1993 A: X-O Manowar armor 1.00
- ❑15, Nov 1993 ..... 1.00
- ❑16, Dec 1993 ..... 1.00
- ❑17, Jan 1994 ..... 1.00
- ❑18, Feb 1994 ..... 1.00
- ❑19, Mar 1994 ..... 1.00
- ❑20, Apr 1994; Spylocke revealed as spider-alien 1.00
- ❑21, May 1994; trading card; series continues as Rai 2.00
- ❑21/VVSS, May 1994 ..... 60.00
- ❑22, Jun 1994 D: Rai 1.00
- ❑23, Aug 1994 ..... 1.00
- ❑24, Sep 1994; new Rai; Series continued in Rai #25 ..... 1.00

RAI COMPANION
VALIANT

- ❑1; no cover price 1.00

RAIDERS OF THE LOST ARK
MARVEL

- ❑1, Sep 1981, JB, KJ (a) 2.00
- ❑2, Oct 1981, JB, KJ (a) 2.00
- ❑3, Nov 1981, JB, KJ (a) 2.00

RAIDER 3000
GAUNTLET

- ❑1, b&w 2.95
- ❑2, b&w 2.95

RAIJIN COMICS
GUTSOON

- ❑1, Dec 2002 ..... 4.95
- ❑2, Dec 2002 ..... 4.95
- ❑3, Dec 2002 ..... 4.95
- ❑4, Dec 2002 ..... 4.95
- ❑5, Jan 2003 ..... 4.95
- ❑6, Jan 2003 ..... 4.95
- ❑7, Jan 2003 ..... 4.95
- ❑8, Jan 2003 ..... 4.95
- ❑9, Feb 2003 ..... 4.95
- ❑10, Feb 2003 ..... 4.95
- ❑11, Feb 2003 ..... 4.95
- ❑12, Feb 2003 ..... 4.95
- ❑13, Mar 2003 ..... 4.95
- ❑14, Mar 2003 ..... 4.95
- ❑15, Mar 2003 ..... 4.95
- ❑16, Mar 2003 ..... 4.95

N-MINT

❑17, Apr 2003 4.95
❑18, Apr 2003 4.95
❑19, Apr 2003 4.95
❑20, Apr 2003 4.95
❑21, May 2003 4.95
❑22, May 2003 4.95
❑23, May 2003 4.95
❑24, May 2003 4.95
❑25, Jun 2003 4.95
❑26, Jun 2003 4.95
❑27, Jun 2003 4.95
❑28, Jun 2003 4.95
❑29, Jul 2003 4.95
❑30, Jul 2003 4.95
❑31, Jul 2003 4.95
❑32, Jul 2003 4.95
❑33, Aug 2003 4.95
❑34, Aug 2003 4.95
❑35, Aug 2003 4.95
❑36, Aug 2003 4.95
❑37, Sep 2003 5.95
❑38, Oct 2003 5.95
❑39, Nov 2003 5.95
❑40, Dec 2003 5.95
❑41, Jan 2004 5.95

RAIKA
SUN

❑1 2.50
❑2 2.50
❑3 2.50
❑4 2.50
❑5 2.50
❑6 2.50
❑7 2.50
❑8 2.50
❑9 2.50
❑10 2.50
❑11 2.50
❑12 2.50
❑13 2.50
❑14 2.50
❑15 2.50
❑16 2.50
❑17 2.50
❑18 2.50
❑19 2.50
❑20 2.50

RAIN
TUNDRA

❑1; Introduction by Stephen R. Bissette 1.95
❑2 1.95
❑3 1.95
❑4 1.95
❑5 1.95
❑6 1.95

RAINBOW BRITE AND THE STAR STEALER
DC

❑1, ca. 1985, Official movie adaption 1.00

RAISIN PIE
FANTAGRAPHICS

❑1 4.95
❑2 4.95
❑3 4.95
❑4 4.95

RAK
RAK GRAPHICS

❑1, b&w 5.00

RAKEHELL
DRACULINA

❑1 2.50

RALFY ROACH
BUGGED OUT

❑1, Jun 1993 2.95

RALPH SNART ADVENTURES (VOL. 1)
NOW

❑1, Jun 1986, O: Ralph Snart. 1: Ralph Snart 3.00
❑2, Jul 1986 2.00
❑3, Aug 1986 2.00

RALPH SNART ADVENTURES (VOL. 2)
NOW

❑1, Nov 1986 2.00

N-MINT

❑2, Dec 1986 1.50
❑3, Jan 1987 1.50
❑4, Feb 1987 1.50
❑5, Mar 1987 1.50
❑6, Apr 1987 1.50
❑7, May 1987 1.50
❑8, Jun 1987 1.50
❑9, Jul 1987 1.50

RALPH SNART ADVENTURES (VOL. 3)
NOW

❑1, Sep 1988 2.00
❑1/3D, Nov 1992, bagged with no cards 2.95
❑1/CS, Nov 1992, 3-D; bagged with 12 cards 3.50
❑2, Oct 1988 1.75
❑3, Nov 1988 1.75
❑4, Jan 1989 1.75
❑5, Feb 1989 1.75
❑6, Mar 1989 1.75
❑7, Apr 1989 1.75
❑8, May 1989 1.75
❑9, Jun 1989 1.75
❑10, Jul 1989 1.75
❑11, Aug 1989 1.75
❑12, Sep 1989 1.75
❑13, Oct 1989 1.75
❑14, Nov 1989 1.75
❑15, Dec 1989 1.75
❑16, Jan 1990 1.75
❑17, Feb 1990 1.75
❑18, Mar 1990 1.75
❑19, Apr 1990 1.75
❑20, May 1990 1.75
❑21, Jun 1990 1.75
❑22, Jul 1990 1.75
❑23, Aug 1990, cover says May, indicia says Aug 1.75
❑24, Sep 1990, prestige format; with glasses 2.95
❑25, Oct 1990, The Early Years 1.75
❑26, Nov 1990 1.75

RALPH SNART ADVENTURES (VOL. 4)
NOW

❑1, May 1992 2.50
❑2, Jun 1992 2.50
❑3, Jul 1992 2.50

RALPH SNART ADVENTURES (VOL. 5)
NOW

❑1, Jul 1993 2.50
❑2, Aug 1993 2.50
❑3, Sep 1993 2.50
❑4, Oct 1993 2.50
❑5, Nov 1993 2.50

RALPH SNART: THE LOST ISSUES
NOW

❑1, Apr 1993 2.50
❑2, May 1993 2.50
❑3, Jun 1993 2.50

RAMBLIN' DAWG
EDGE

❑1, Jul 1994 2.95

RAMBO
BLACKTHORNE

❑1, Oct 1988, b&w 2.00

RAMBO III
BLACKTHORNE

❑1 2.00
❑3D 1 2.50

RAMM
MEGATON

❑1, May 1987 1.50
❑2 1.50

RAMPAGE
SLAP HAPPY

❑1, ca. 1997 9.95

RAMPAGING HULK
MARVEL

❑1, Aug 1998, b&w; Giant-size 1.99
❑2, Sep 1998; gatefold summary 1.99
❑2/A, Sep 1998; gatefold summary; variant cover 1.99

N-MINT

❑3, Oct 1998; gatefold summary 1.99
❑4, Nov 1998; gatefold summary 1.99
❑5, Dec 1998; gatefold summary 1.99
❑6, Jan 1999; gatefold summary 1.99

RAMPAGING HULK (MAGAZINE)
MARVEL

❑1, Jan 1977, b&w; JB, AA (a); Bloodstone back-up 35.00
❑2, Apr 1977, b&w; AA (a); O: the X-Men. Bloodstone back-up 14.00
❑3, Jun 1977, b&w; SB, AA (a); Bloodstone/Iron Man back-up story 5.00
❑4, Aug 1977, b&w; JSn (c); JSn, VM, AN (a); 1: Exo-Mind. Bloodstone/Iron Man back-up story 5.00
❑5, Oct 1977, b&w; JSn (c); VM, KP, AA, BWi (a); A: Sub-Mariner. Bloodstone back-up 5.00
❑6, Dec 1977, b&w; KP, TD (a); Bloodstone back-up 4.00
❑7, Feb 1978, b&w; JSn (c); JSn, KP, JM, BWi (a); A: Man-Thing. Man-Thing back-up 4.00
❑8, Apr 1978, b&w; HT, AA (a); A: Avengers. Bloodstone back-up 4.00
❑9, Jun 1978, b&w; SB, TD (a); Shanna back-up; later issues published as Hulk (magazine) 4.00

RANA 7
NGNG

❑1 2.95
❑2 2.95
❑3 2.95
❑4 2.95

RANA 7: WARRIORS OF VENGEANCE
NGNG

❑1, Dec 1995 2.50
❑2, Mar 1996 2.50

RANDOM ENCOUNTER
VIPER

❑1 2005 2.95
❑2, Jun 2005 2.95
❑3, Jul 2005 2.95
❑4, Sep 2005 2.95

RANDY O'DONNELL IS THE M@N
IMAGE

❑1, May 2001 2.95
❑2, Jul 2001 2.95
❑3, Sep 2001 2.95

RANGO
DELL

❑1, Aug 1967 25.00

RANK & STINKY
PARODY

❑1, b&w 2.50
❑1/2nd; Rank & Stinky Eencore Eedition 2.50
❑Special 1, b&w 2.75

RANMA 1/2
VIZ

❑1, ca. 1991; 1: Kasumi Tendo. 1: Nabiki. 1: Soun Tendo. Comic in color 25.00
❑2, ca. 1991 10.00
❑3, ca. 1991 8.00
❑4, ca. 1991; Comics become B&W 6.00
❑5, ca. 1991 6.00
❑6, ca. 1991 O: Ryoga Hibiki 5.00
❑7, ca. 1991 5.00

RANMA 1/2 PART 2
VIZ

❑1, Jan 1992 1: Ranma Saotome 7.00
❑2, Feb 1992 5.00
❑3, Mar 1992 4.00
❑4, Apr 1992 4.00
❑5, May 1992 1: Azusa Shiratori 4.00
❑6, Jun 1992 3.50
❑7, Jul 1992 3.50
❑8, Aug 1992 1: Shampoo 3.50
❑9, Sep 1992 O: Shampoo 3.50
❑10, Oct 1992 3.50
❑11, Nov 1992 3.50

RANMA 1/2 PART 3
VIZ

❑1, Dec 1992 1: Hikaru Gosunkugi 3.00
❑2, Jan 1993 3.00
❑3, Feb 1993 3.00

Razor

Razor-wearing woman avenges father

©London Night

Real Adventures of Jonny Quest

More with the TV cartoon hero

©Dark Horse

Real Ghostbusters (Vol. 1)

Based on cartoon version of film characters

©Now

Realm (Vol. 1)

Sword-and-sorcery themed series

©Arrow

Real Stuff

Critically acclaimed alternative comic

©Fantagraphics

	N-MINT
❑4, Mar 1993	3.00
❑5, Apr 1993	3.00
❑6, May 1993	3.00
❑7, Jun 1993	3.00
❑8, Jul 1993	3.00
❑9, Aug 1993	3.00
❑10, Sep 1993	3.00
❑11, Oct 1993	3.00
❑12, Nov 1993	3.00
❑13, Dec 1993	3.00

RANMA 1/2 PART 4
VIZ

❑1, Jan 1994 1: Happosai	3.00
❑2, Feb 1994	3.00
❑3, Mar 1994	3.00
❑4, Apr 1994	3.00
❑5, May 1994	3.00
❑6, Jun 1994	3.00
❑7, Jul 1994	3.00
❑8, Aug 1994	3.00
❑9, Sep 1994	3.00
❑10, Oct 1994	3.00
❑11, Nov 1994	3.00

RANMA 1/2 PART 5
VIZ

❑1, Dec 1994 1: Ukyo Kuonji	3.00
❑2, Jan 1995	3.00
❑3, Feb 1995	3.00
❑4, Mar 1995	3.00
❑5, Apr 1995	3.00
❑6, May 1995	3.00
❑7, Jun 1995	3.00
❑8, Jul 1995	3.00
❑9, Aug 1995	3.00
❑10, Sep 1995	3.00
❑11, Oct 1995	3.00
❑12, Nov 1995	3.00

RANMA 1/2 PART 6
VIZ

❑1, Dec 1996	2.95
❑2, Jan 1997	2.95
❑3, Feb 1997	2.95
❑4, Mar 1997	2.95
❑5, Apr 1997	2.95
❑6, May 1997	2.95
❑7, Jun 1997	2.95
❑8, Jul 1997	2.95
❑9, Aug 1997	2.95
❑10, Sep 1997	2.95
❑11, Oct 1997	2.95
❑12, Nov 1997	2.95
❑13, Dec 1997	2.95
❑14, Jan 1998	2.95

RANMA 1/2 PART 7
VIZ

❑1, Feb 1998	2.95
❑2, Mar 1998	2.95
❑3, Apr 1998	2.95
❑4, May 1998	2.95
❑5, Jun 1998	2.95
❑6, Jul 1998	2.95
❑7, Aug 1998	2.95
❑8, Sep 1998	2.95

	N-MINT
❑9, Oct 1998	2.95
❑10, Nov 1998	2.95
❑11, Dec 1998	2.95
❑12, Jan 1999	2.95
❑13, Feb 1999	2.95
❑14, Mar 1999	2.95

RANMA 1/2 PART 8
VIZ

❑1, Apr 1999	2.95
❑2, May 1999	2.95
❑3, Jun 1999	2.95
❑4, Jul 1999	2.95
❑5, Aug 1999	2.95
❑6, Sep 1999	2.95
❑7, Sep 1999	2.95
❑8, Oct 1999	2.95
❑9, Nov 1999	2.95
❑10, Dec 1999	2.95
❑11, Jan 2000	2.95
❑12, Feb 2000	2.95
❑13, Mar 2000	2.95

RANMA 1/2 PART 9
VIZ

❑1, May 2000	2.95
❑2, Jun 2000	2.95
❑3, Jul 2000	2.95
❑4, Aug 2000	2.95
❑5, Sep 2000	2.95
❑6, Oct 2000	2.95
❑7, Nov 2000	2.95
❑8, Dec 2000	2.95
❑9, Jan 2001	2.95
❑10, Feb 2001	2.95
❑11, Mar 2001	2.95

RANMA 1/2 PART 10
VIZ

❑1, Apr 2001	2.95
❑2, May 2001	2.95
❑3, Jun 2001	2.95
❑4, Jul 2001	2.95
❑5, Aug 2001	2.95
❑6, Sep 2001	2.95
❑7, Oct 2001	2.95
❑8, Nov 2001	2.95
❑9, Dec 2001	2.95
❑10, Jan 2002	2.95
❑11, Feb 2002	2.95

RANMA 1/2 PART 11
VIZ

❑1, Mar 2002	2.95
❑2, Apr 2002	2.95
❑3, May 2002	2.95
❑4, Jun 2002	2.95
❑5, Jul 2002	2.95
❑6, Aug 2002	2.95
❑7, Sep 2002	2.95
❑8, Oct 2002	2.95
❑9, Nov 2002	2.95
❑10, Dec 2002	2.95
❑11, Jan 2003	2.95

RANMA 1/2 PART 12
VIZ

❑1, Mar 2003	2.95

RANN-THANAGAR WAR
DC

	N-MINT
❑1, Jun 2005	8.00
❑1/Variant, Jun 2005	5.00
❑2, Jul 2005	4.00
❑3, Aug 2005	2.50
❑4, Sep 2005	2.50
❑5, Oct 2005	2.50
❑6 2005	2.50

RANN/THANAGAR WAR: INFINITE CRISIS SPECIAL
DC

❑1, Mar 2006	3.99

RANT
BONEYARD

❑1, Nov 1994, b&w JJ (a)	2.95
❑2, Feb 1995, b&w JJ (a)	2.95
❑3 JJ (a)	2.95
❑Ashcan 1; JJ (a); Ashcan version of issue #1. Black and white cover	2.50

RAPHAEL TEENAGE MUTANT NINJA TURTLE
MIRAGE

❑1, Nov 1987; Oversized	2.50
❑1/2nd	1.50

RAPTORS
NBM

❑1, Oct 1999	10.95

RARE BREED
CHRYSALIS

❑1, Nov 1995	2.50
❑2, Mar 1996	2.50

RASCALS IN PARADISE
DARK HORSE

❑1, Aug 1994; magazine	4.00
❑2, Oct 1994; magazine	4.00
❑3, Dec 1994; magazine	4.00

RAT BASTARD
CRUCIAL

❑1, Jun 1997	2.50
❑1/Ashcan, Jun 1997; Black and white ashcan edition	2.50
❑2, Nov 1997	2.00
❑3, Apr 1998	2.00
❑4, Jul 1998	2.00
❑5, Oct 1998	1.95
❑6, Jul 1999	1.95

RATED X
AIRCEL

❑1, Apr 1991, b&w	2.95
❑2, b&w	2.95
❑3, b&w	2.95
❑Special 1, b&w	2.95

RAT FINK COMICS
WORLD OF FANDOM

❑1, b&w	2.50
❑2, b&w	2.50
❑3, b&w	2.50

RAT FINK COMIX (ED "BIG DADDY" ROTH'S...)
STARHEAD

❑1	2.00

Other grades: Multiply price above by 5/6 for VF/NM • 2/3 for VERY FINE • 1/3 for FINE • 1/5 for VERY GOOD • 1/8 for GOOD

RATFOO
SPIT WAD

❑1, Sep 1997, b&w 2.95

RAT PATROL
DELL

❑1, Mar 1967 .... 40.00
❑2, Apr 1967 .... 40.00
❑3, May 1967 .... 40.00
❑4, Aug 1967 .... 40.00
❑5, Nov 1967 .... 40.00
❑6, Oct 1969, Same cover as #1, slightly recolored 25.00

RAT PREVIEW (JUSTIN HAMPTON'S...)
AEON / BACKBONE PRESS

❑1, May 1997, b&w; ashcan-sized; no cover price 1.00

RATS!
SLAVE LABOR

❑1, Aug 1992, b&w 2.50

RAVAGE 2099
MARVEL

❑1, Dec 1992; Metallic ink cover; foil cover 1.75
❑2, Jan 1993 .... 1.25
❑3, Feb 1993 .... 1.25
❑4, Mar 1993 .... 1.25
❑5, Apr 1993 .... 1.25
❑6, May 1993 .... 1.25
❑7, Jun 1993 .... 1.25
❑8, Jul 1993 .... 1.25
❑9, Aug 1993 .... 1.25
❑10, Sep 1993 .... 1.25
❑11, Oct 1993 .... 1.25
❑12, Nov 1993 .... 1.25
❑13, Dec 1993 .... 1.25
❑14, Jan 1994 .... 1.25
❑15, Feb 1994 .... 1.25
❑16, Mar 1994 .... 1.25
❑17, Apr 1994 .... 1.25
❑18, May 1994 .... 1.25
❑19, Jun 1994 .... 1.50
❑20, Jul 1994 .... 1.50
❑21, Aug 1994 .... 1.50
❑22, Sep 1994 .... 1.50
❑23, Oct 1994 .... 1.50
❑24, Nov 1994 .... 1.50
❑25, Dec 1994 .... 2.25
❑25/Variant, Dec 1994; enhanced cover 2.95
❑26, Jan 1995 .... 1.50
❑27, Feb 1995 .... 1.50
❑28, Mar 1995 .... 1.50
❑29, Apr 1995 .... 1.50
❑30, May 1995 .... 1.50
❑31, Jun 1995 .... 1.95
❑32, Jul 1995 .... 1.95
❑33, Aug 1995 .... 1.95

RAVE MASTER
TOKYOPOP

❑1, Feb 2003 .... 9.95
❑2, Apr 2003 .... 9.95
❑3, Jun 2003 .... 9.95
❑4, Aug 2003 .... 9.95
❑5, Oct 2003 .... 9.95
❑6, Dec 2003 .... 9.95
❑7, Feb 2004 .... 9.95
❑8, Apr 2004 .... 9.95
❑9, Jun 2004 .... 9.95
❑10, Apr 2004 .... 9.95
❑11, Oct 2004 .... 9.95
❑12, Dec 2004 .... 9.95
❑13, Feb 2005 .... 9.95
❑14, Apr 2005 .... 9.95
❑15, Jan 2005 .... 9.95
❑16, Aug 2005 .... 9.95
❑17, Oct 2005 .... 9.95
❑18, Dec 2005 .... 9.95

RAVEN
RENAISSANCE

❑1, Sep 1993 .... 2.50
❑2, Nov 1993 .... 2.50
❑3, Apr 1994 .... 2.50
❑4, Aug 1994 .... 2.75

RAVEN CHRONICLES
CALIBER

❑1, Jul 1995, b&w 2.95
❑2, b&w 2.95
❑3, b&w 2.95
❑4, b&w 2.95
❑5 .... 2.95
❑6 .... 2.95
❑7 .... 2.95
❑8 .... 2.95
❑9 .... 2.95
❑10 .... 2.95
❑11 .... 2.95
❑12 .... 2.95
❑13 .... 2.95
❑14 .... 2.95
❑15, Giant-size; flip book with High Caliber 3.95

RAVENS AND RAINBOWS
PACIFIC

❑1, Dec 1983 .... 1.50

RAVENWIND
PARIAH

❑1, Jun 1996, b&w 2.50

RAVER
MALIBU

❑1, Apr 1993; foil cover 2.95
❑2 1993 .... 1.95
❑3 1993 .... 1.95

RAW CITY
DRAMENON

❑1 .... 3.00

RAWHIDE (DELL)
DELL

❑1, Aug 1962, No issue number: Cover code ends in -208, indicating this issue is from August 1962 .... 200.00

RAWHIDE (GOLD KEY)
GOLD KEY

❑1, Jul 1963 .... 175.00
❑2, Jan 1964 .... 150.00

RAWHIDE KID (1ST SERIES)
MARVEL

❑1, Mar 1955 .... 800.00
❑2, May 1955 .... 350.00
❑3, Jul 1955 .... 185.00
❑4, Sep 1955 .... 185.00
❑5, Nov 1955 .... 185.00
❑6, Jan 1956 .... 140.00
❑7, Mar 1956 .... 140.00
❑8, May 1956 .... 140.00
❑9, Jul 1956 .... 140.00
❑10, Sep 1956 .... 140.00
❑11, Nov 1956 .... 110.00
❑12, Jan 1957 .... 110.00
❑13, Mar 1957 .... 110.00
❑14, May 1957 .... 110.00
❑15, Jul 1957 .... 110.00
❑16, Sep 1957, series goes on hiatus 110.00
❑17, Aug 1960, JK (a); O: Rawhide Kid 400.00
❑18, Oct 1960 .... 95.00
❑19, Dec 1960 .... 95.00
❑20, Feb 1961 .... 95.00
❑21, Apr 1961 .... 95.00
❑22, Jun 1961 .... 90.00
❑23, Aug 1961, JK (a); O: Rawhide Kid 200.00
❑24, Oct 1961 .... 90.00
❑25, Dec 1961 .... 90.00
❑26, Feb 1962 .... 90.00
❑27, Apr 1962 .... 90.00
❑28, Jun 1962 .... 90.00
❑29, Aug 1962 .... 90.00
❑30, Oct 1962 .... 90.00
❑31, Dec 1962 .... 75.00
❑32, Feb 1963 .... 75.00
❑33, Apr 1963 .... 75.00
❑34, Jun 1963 .... 75.00
❑35, Aug 1963 .... 75.00
❑36, Oct 1963 .... 75.00
❑37, Dec 1963 .... 75.00
❑38, Feb 1964 .... 75.00
❑39, Apr 1964 .... 75.00
❑40, Jun 1964, A: Two-Gun Kid 75.00
❑41, Aug 1964 .... 75.00
❑42, Oct 1964 .... 75.00
❑43, Dec 1964 .... 75.00
❑44, Feb 1965 .... 75.00
❑45, Apr 1965, JK (a); O: Rawhide Kid 90.00
❑46, Jun 1965 .... 60.00
❑47, Aug 1965 .... 35.00
❑48, Oct 1965, V: Marko the Manhunter 35.00
❑49, Dec 1965, V: Masquerader 35.00
❑50, Feb 1966, A: Kid Colt. V: Masquerader 35.00
❑51, Apr 1966, V: Aztecs 35.00
❑52, Jun 1966 .... 35.00
❑53, Aug 1966 .... 35.00
❑54, Oct 1966 .... 35.00
❑55, Dec 1966, V: Plunderers 35.00
❑56, Feb 1967, V: Peacemaker 35.00
❑57, Apr 1967, V: Enforcerers (not Spider-Man villains) 35.00
❑58, Jun 1967 .... 35.00
❑59, Aug 1967, V: Drako 35.00
❑60, Oct 1967 .... 35.00
❑61, Dec 1967, A: Wild Bill Hickock. A: Calamity Jane 25.00
❑62, Feb 1968, V: Drako 25.00
❑63, Apr 1968 .... 25.00
❑64, Jun 1968, Kid Colt back-up 25.00
❑65, Aug 1968 .... 25.00
❑66, Oct 1968, Two-Gun Kid back-up. 25.00
❑67, Dec 1968 .... 25.00
❑68, Feb 1969, V: Cougar 25.00
❑69, Apr 1969 .... 25.00
❑70, Jun 1969 .... 25.00
❑71, Aug 1969 .... 18.00
❑72, Oct 1969 .... 18.00
❑73, Dec 1969 .... 18.00
❑74, Feb 1970 .... 18.00
❑75, Apr 1970 .... 18.00
❑76, May 1970 .... 18.00
❑77, Jun 1970 .... 18.00
❑78, Jul 1970 .... 18.00
❑79, Aug 1970 .... 18.00
❑80, Oct 1970 .... 18.00
❑81, Nov 1970 .... 18.00
❑82, Dec 1970 .... 18.00
❑83, Jan 1971 .... 18.00
❑84, Feb 1971 .... 18.00
❑85, Mar 1971 .... 18.00
❑86, Apr 1971, JK (a); O: Rawhide Kid 18.00
❑87, May 1971 .... 15.00
❑88, Jun 1971 .... 15.00
❑89, Jul 1971 .... 15.00
❑90, Aug 1971 .... 15.00
❑91, Sep 1971 .... 15.00
❑92, Oct 1971 .... 15.00
❑93, Nov 1971 .... 12.00
❑94, Dec 1971 .... 12.00
❑95, Jan 1972 .... 12.00
❑96, Feb 1972 .... 12.00
❑97, Mar 1972 .... 12.00
❑98, Apr 1972 .... 12.00
❑99, May 1972 .... 12.00
❑100, Jun 1972, O: Rawhide Kid 18.00
❑101, Jul 1972 .... 12.00
❑102, Aug 1972 .... 12.00
❑103, Sep 1972 .... 12.00
❑104, Oct 1972 .... 12.00
❑105, Nov 1972, JR (a) 12.00
❑106, Dec 1972 .... 12.00
❑107, Jan 1973 .... 12.00
❑108, Feb 1973 .... 12.00
❑109, Mar 1973, SL (w); JK (a) 12.00
❑110, Apr 1973 .... 12.00
❑111, May 1973, JK (c); SL (w) 12.00
❑112, Jun 1973 .... 12.00
❑113, Jul 1973 .... 12.00
❑114, Aug 1973 .... 10.00
❑115, Sep 1973 .... 10.00
❑116, Oct 1973 .... 10.00
❑117, Nov 1973 .... 10.00
❑118, Jan 1974 .... 10.00
❑119, Mar 1974 .... 10.00
❑120, May 1974 .... 10.00
❑121, Jul 1974, reprints 7.00
❑122, Sep 1974, reprints 7.00
❑123, Nov 1974, reprints 7.00
❑124, Jan 1975, reprints 7.00
❑125, Mar 1975, reprints 7.00
❑126, May 1975, reprints 7.00

R.E.B.E.L.S.

Once they were known as L.E.G.I.O.N.
©DC

Redfox

Fantasy title momentarily hot in 1980s boom
©Harrier

Red Sonja (Vol. 1)

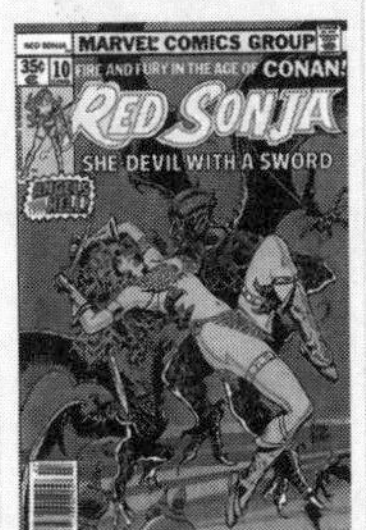

One of the early "hot" titles from the 1970s
©Marvel

Red Tornado

Hero's name sounds like bathroom cleanser
©DC

Red Wolf

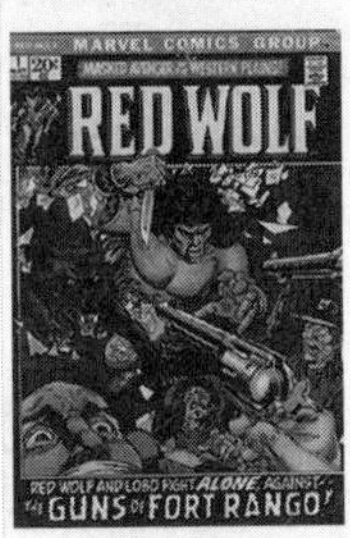

Billed as the first Native American super-hero
©Marvel

	N-MINT
❑127, Jul 1975, reprints	7.00
❑128, Sep 1975, reprints	7.00
❑129, Oct 1975, reprints	7.00
❑130, Nov 1975, reprints	7.00
❑131, Jan 1976, reprints	7.00
❑132, Mar 1976, reprints	7.00
❑133, May 1976, reprints	7.00
❑133/30 cent, May 1976, 30 cent regional price variant; reprints	20.00
❑134, Jul 1976, reprints	7.00
❑134/30 cent, Jul 1976, 30 cent regional price variant; reprints	20.00
❑135, Sep 1976, reprints	7.00
❑136, Nov 1976, reprints	7.00
❑137, Jan 1977, reprints	7.00
❑138, Mar 1977, reprints	7.00
❑139, May 1977, reprints	7.00
❑140, Jul 1977, reprints	7.00
❑140/35 cent, Jul 1977, reprints; 35 cent regional price variant	15.00
❑141, Sep 1977, reprints	6.00
❑142, Nov 1977, reprints	6.00
❑143, Jan 1978, reprints	6.00
❑144, Mar 1978, reprints	6.00
❑145, May 1978, reprints	6.00
❑146, Jul 1978, reprints	6.00
❑147, Sep 1978, PG (c); reprints	6.00
❑148, Nov 1978, reprints	6.00
❑149, Jan 1979, reprints	6.00
❑150, Mar 1979, reprints	6.00
❑151, May 1979, Reprints Rawhide Kid #99	6.00
❑Special 1, Sep 1971; Reprints	12.00

RAWHIDE KID (2ND SERIES)
MARVEL

❑1, Aug 1985 JBy (c); JBy, HT, JSe (a); O: Rawhide Kid	1.50
❑2, Sep 1985 KP (c); JBy, HT, JSe (a)	1.50
❑3, Oct 1985 KP (c); JBy, HT, JSe (a)	1.50
❑4, Nov 1985 KP (c); JBy, HT, JSe (a)	1.50

RAWHIDE KID (3RD SERIES)
MARVEL / MAX

❑1, Apr 2003 JSe (a)	5.00
❑2, May 2003 JSe (a)	4.00
❑3, May 2003 JSe (a)	3.00
❑4, Jun 2003 JSe (a)	3.00
❑5, Jun 2003 JSe (a)	2.99

RAW MEDIA ILLUSTRATED
ABC

❑1, May 1998; wet T-shirt cover	3.25
❑1/Nude, May 1998; nude cover	3.25

RAW MEDIA MAGS
REBEL

❑1, b&w	5.00
❑2, b&w	5.00
❑3, b&w	5.00
❑4, May 1994, b&w	5.00

RAW PERIPHERY
SLAVE LABOR

❑1, b&w	2.95

RAY (MINI-SERIES)
DC

	N-MINT
❑1, Feb 1992 O: The Ray II (Ray Terrill)	3.00
❑2, Mar 1992	2.00
❑3, Apr 1992	1.50
❑4, May 1992	1.50
❑5, Jun 1992	1.50
❑6, Jul 1992	1.50

RAY
DC

❑0, Oct 1994	1.95
❑1, May 1994	1.75
❑1/Variant, May 1994; foil cover	2.95
❑2, Jun 1994	1.75
❑3, Jul 1994	1.75
❑4, Aug 1994	1.95
❑5, Sep 1994	1.95
❑6, Nov 1994	1.95
❑7, Dec 1994	1.95
❑8, Jan 1995	1.95
❑9, Feb 1995	1.95
❑10, Mar 1995	1.95
❑11, Apr 1995	1.95
❑12, May 1995	1.95
❑13, Jun 1995	2.25
❑14, Jul 1995	2.25
❑15, Aug 1995	2.25
❑16, Sep 1995	2.25
❑17, Oct 1995	2.25
❑18, Nov 1995; Underworld Unleashed	2.25
❑19, Dec 1995; Underworld Unleashed	2.25
❑20, Jan 1996	2.25
❑21, Feb 1996	2.25
❑22, Mar 1996	2.25
❑23, May 1996	2.25
❑24, Jun 1996	2.25
❑25, Jul 1996; Ray in the future	3.50
❑26, Aug 1996; continued from events in JLA Annual #10	2.25
❑27, Sep 1996	2.25
❑28, Oct 1996; secrets of both Ray's pasts revealed	2.25
❑Annual 1, ca. 1995	3.95

RAY BRADBURY COMICS
TOPPS

❑1, Feb 1993 AW (w);	3.50
❑2, Apr 1993 MW, HK (w); MW, HK (a)	3.50
❑3, Jun 1993	3.50
❑4, Aug 1993	3.50
❑5, Oct 1993; Final issue (#6 canceled)	3.50
❑Special 1, ca. 1994; CR, JKa (w); Illustrated Man	3.50

RAY BRADBURY COMICS: MARTIAN CHRONICLES
TOPPS

❑1, Jun 1994	3.25

RAY BRADBURY COMICS: TRILOGY OF TERROR
TOPPS

❑1, May 1994 WW (a)	3.25

RAY BRADBURY SPECIAL: TALES OF HORROR
TOPPS

❑1, ca. 1994	2.50

RAY-MOND
DEEP-SEA

❑1	2.95
❑2	2.95

N-MINT

RAYNE
SHEET HAPPIES

❑1, Jul 1995, b&w	2.50
❑2, Apr 1996, b&w; cover says Mar, indicia says Apr	2.50
❑3, Aug 1996, b&w	2.50
❑4, Jul 1997, b&w	2.95

RAZOR
LONDON NIGHT

❑0	3.00
❑0/A; Direct Market edition	4.00
❑0/2nd	3.00
❑½; Promotional giveaway 1: Poizon .	3.00
❑1, Aug 1992	4.00
❑1/2nd	3.00
❑2	3.00
❑2/Platinum; Platinum edition	4.00
❑2/Variant	5.00
❑3	3.00
❑3/CS	4.00
❑4	3.00
❑4/Platinum	4.00
❑5	3.00
❑5/Platinum; Platinum edition	4.00
❑6	3.00
❑7	3.00
❑8	3.00
❑9	3.00
❑10 O: Stryke	3.00
❑11, Sep 1994, b&w	3.00
❑12, b&w; Series continued in Razor Uncut #13	3.00
❑Annual 1, ca. 1993 1: Shi	15.00
❑Annual 1/Gold; Gold limited edition 1: Shi	20.00
❑Annual 2, b&w	3.50

RAZOR (VOL. 2)
LONDON NIGHT

❑1, Oct 1996, chromium cover	3.00
❑2, Nov 1996	3.00
❑3, Dec 1996	3.00
❑4, Mar 1997	3.00
❑5, Apr 1997	3.00
❑6, May 1997	3.00
❑7, Jun 1997	3.00

RAZOR & SHI SPECIAL
LONDON NIGHT

❑1; Crossover with Crusade	3.00
❑1/Platinum; Platinum edition	4.00

RAZOR ARCHIVES
LONDON NIGHT

❑1, May 1997	3.95
❑2, Jun 1997	5.00
❑3	5.00
❑4, Jul 1997	5.00

RAZOR: BURN
LONDON NIGHT

❑1	3.00
❑2	3.00
❑3	3.00
❑4	3.00

RAZOR/CRY NO MORE
LONDON NIGHT

❑1 1995, b&w	3.95

Other grades: Multiply price above by 5/6 for VF/NM • 2/3 for VERY FINE • 1/3 for FINE • 1/5 for VERY GOOD • 1/8 for GOOD

RAZOR/DARK ANGEL: THE FINAL NAIL
LONDON NIGHT
❑1 ... 2.95

RAZORGUTS
MONSTER
❑1, b&w ... 2.25
❑2, Feb 1992, b&w ... 2.25
❑3, b&w ... 2.25
❑4, b&w ... 2.25

RAZORLINE: THE FIRST CUT
MARVEL
❑1, sampler; Previews Hokum & Hex, Hyperkind, Saint Sinner, and Ectokid ... 1.00

RAZOR/MORBID ANGEL
LONDON NIGHT
❑1, Aug 1996 ... 3.00
❑2, Nov 1996 ... 3.00
❑3, Dec 1996 ... 3.00

RAZOR'S EDGE
INNOVATION
❑1, b&w ... 2.50

RAZOR'S EDGE: WARBLADE
DC / WILDSTORM
❑1, Jan 2005 ... 2.95
❑2, Feb 2005 ... 2.95
❑3, Mar 2005 ... 2.95
❑4, Apr 2005 ... 2.95
❑5, May 2005 ... 2.95

RAZOR: THE SUFFERING
LONDON NIGHT
❑1 ... 3.00
❑1/A; "Director's Cut" ... 3.00
❑2 ... 3.00
❑2/A; "Director's Cut" ... 3.00
❑3 ... 3.00

RAZOR: TORTURE
LONDON NIGHT
❑0, Dec 1995; enhanced wraparound cover; polybagged with card and catalog ... 3.95
❑1 1996 ... 3.00
❑1/Variant 1996; alternate cover with no cover price ... 3.00
❑2 1996 ... 3.00
❑2/Variant 1996; no cover price ... 3.00
❑3, Apr 1996 ... 3.00
❑4, May 1996 ... 3.00
❑5, Jun 1996 ... 3.00
❑6, Jul 1996 ... 3.00

RAZOR: UNCUT
LONDON NIGHT
❑13 1995; Series continued from Razor #12 ... 3.00
❑14 1995 ... 3.00
❑15 1995 ... 3.00
❑16 1995 ... 3.00
❑17 1995 ... 3.00
❑18, Dec 1995 ... 3.00
❑19 1995 ... 3.00
❑20 1995, b&w ... 3.00
❑21, May 1996, b&w ... 3.00
❑22 1996, b&w ... 3.00
❑23 1996 ... 3.00
❑24 1996 ... 3.00
❑25 1996 ... 3.00
❑26, Sep 1996 ... 3.00
❑27, Oct 1996 ... 3.00
❑28, Oct 1996 ... 3.00
❑29, Nov 1996 ... 3.00
❑30, Dec 1996 ... 3.00
❑31, Jan 1997 ... 3.00
❑32, Feb 1997 ... 3.00
❑33, Feb 1997 ... 3.00
❑34, Mar 1997 ... 3.00
❑35, Apr 1997 ... 3.00
❑36, May 1997 ... 3.00
❑37, Jun 1997 ... 3.00
❑38, Jul 1997 ... 3.00
❑39, Aug 1997 ... 3.00
❑40, Sep 1997 ... 3.00
❑41, Oct 1997 ... 3.00
❑42, Nov 1997 ... 3.00
❑43, Dec 1997 ... 3.00
❑44 1998 ... 3.00
❑45 1998 ... 3.00
❑46 1998 ... 3.00
❑47 1998 ... 3.00
❑48 1998 ... 3.00
❑49 1998 ... 3.00
❑50 1999 ... 3.00
❑51, Mar 1999 ... 3.00

RAZOR/WARRIOR NUN AREALA: FAITH
LONDON NIGHT
❑1, May 1996; one-shot crossover with Antarctic ... 3.95

RAZORWIRE
5TH PANEL
❑1, Jun 1996, b&w ... 1.50
❑2, Jul 1997, b&w ... 1.50

REACTION: THE ULTIMATE MAN
STUDIO ARCHEIN
❑1 ... 2.95

REACTO-MAN
B-MOVIE
❑1 ... 1.50
❑2 ... 1.50
❑3 ... 1.50

REACTOR GIRL
TRAGEDY STRIKES
❑1, b&w ... 2.50
❑2 ... 2.95
❑3 ... 2.95
❑4 ... 2.95
❑5 ... 2.95

REAGAN'S RAIDERS
SOLSON
❑1, ca. 1986 ... 2.00
❑2, ca. 1986 ... 2.00
❑3, ca. 1987 ... 2.00

REAL ADVENTURES OF JONNY QUEST
DARK HORSE
❑1, Sep 1996; based on 1996 animated series ... 3.00
❑2, Oct 1996 ... 2.95
❑3, Nov 1996 ... 2.95
❑4, Dec 1996 ... 2.95
❑5, Jan 1997 ... 2.95
❑6, Feb 1997 ... 2.95
❑7, Mar 1997 ... 2.95
❑8, May 1997 ... 2.95
❑9, Jun 1997 ... 2.95
❑10, Jul 1997 ... 2.95
❑11, Aug 1997 ... 2.95
❑12, Sep 1997 ... 2.95

REAL AMERICANS ADMIT: "THE WORST THING I'VE EVER DONE!"
NBM
❑1 ... 8.95

REAL BOUT HIGH SCHOOL
TOKYOPOP
❑1, Mar 2002, b&w; printed in Japanese format ... 9.99
❑2, Jun 2002, b&w; printed in Japanese format ... 9.99

REAL DEAL MAGAZINE
REAL DEAL
❑5, b&w; magazine ... 2.00

REAL GHOSTBUSTERS SUMMER SPECIAL
NOW
❑1, Sum 1993 ... 2.95

REAL GHOSTBUSTERS 3-D SUMMER SPECIAL
NOW
❑1, Jul 1993; 3-D glasses included ... 2.95

REAL GHOSTBUSTERS (VOL. 1)
NOW
❑1, Aug 1988; Ghostbusters movie adaptation ... 2.00
❑2, Sep 1988 ... 1.75
❑3, Oct 1988 ... 1.75
❑4, Nov 1988 ... 1.75
❑5, Jan 1989 ... 1.75
❑6, Feb 1989 ... 1.75
❑7, Mar 1989 ... 1.75
❑8, Apr 1989 ... 1.75
❑9, May 1989 ... 1.75
❑10, Jun 1989 ... 1.75
❑11, Jul 1989 ... 1.75
❑12, Aug 1989 ... 1.75
❑13, Sep 1989 ... 1.75
❑14, Oct 1989 ... 1.75
❑15, Nov 1989 ... 1.75
❑16, Dec 1989 ... 1.75
❑17, Jan 1990 ... 1.75
❑18, Feb 1990 ... 1.75
❑19, Mar 1990 ... 1.75
❑20, Apr 1990 ... 1.75
❑21, May 1990 ... 1.75
❑22, Jun 1990 ... 1.75
❑23, Jul 1990 ... 1.75
❑24, Aug 1990 ... 1.75
❑25, Sep 1990 ... 1.75
❑26, Oct 1990 ... 1.75
❑27, Nov 1990 ... 1.75
❑28, Dec 1990; Final issue? ... 1.75
❑3D 1; gatefold summary ... 2.95

REAL GHOSTBUSTERS (VOL. 2)
NOW
❑1, Nov 1991 ... 1.75
❑1/3D, Oct 1991; polybagged; w/glasses ... 2.95
❑2, Dec 1991 ... 1.75
❑3, Jan 1992 ... 1.75
❑4, Feb 1992 ... 1.75
❑Annual 1992, Mar 1992 ... 1.00
❑Annual 1993, Dec 1992; 3-D ... 2.95

REAL GIRL
FANTAGRAPHICS
❑1, b&w; Magazine sized ... 2.50
❑2, b&w ... 2.50
❑3, b&w ... 2.95
❑4, b&w ... 2.95
❑5, b&w ... 3.50
❑6, b&w ... 3.50
❑7, Aug 1994, b&w ... 3.50

REAL LIFE
FANTAGRAPHICS
❑1, b&w ... 2.50

REALLY FANTASTIC ALIEN SEX FRENZY (CYNTHIA PETAL'S...)
FANTAGRAPHICS / EROS
❑1, b&w ... 3.95

REALM HANDBOOK
CALIBER
❑1 ... 2.95

REALM OF THE CLAW
IMAGE
❑0, Oct 2003 ... 5.95
❑1/A, Nov 2003; Flip book with Mutant Earth #1/A ... 2.95
❑1/B, Nov 2003, Flip book with Mutant Earth #1/B ... 2.95
❑1/C, Nov 2003 ... 2.95
❑2/A, Jan 2004 ... 2.95
❑2/B, Jan 2004, Flip book with Mutant Earth #2 ... 2.95

REALM OF THE DEAD
CALIBER
❑1 ... 2.95
❑2 ... 2.95
❑3 ... 2.95

REALM (VOL. 1)
ARROW
❑1, ca. 1986 ... 5.00
❑2, ca. 1986; repeats indicia for #1 ... 2.00
❑3, ca. 1986 ... 2.00
❑4, Sep 1986 1: Deadworld ... 4.00
❑5 ... 1.75
❑6 ... 1.75
❑7 ... 1.75
❑8 ... 1.75
❑9 ... 1.75
❑10 ... 1.75
❑11 ... 1.75
❑12 ... 1.75
❑13 ... 1.95
❑14, Feb 1989, b&w ... 1.95
❑15, Apr 1989, b&w ... 1.95
❑16, May 1989, b&w ... 2.50
❑17 ... 2.50

Ren & Stimpy Show

Tasteless show spawns many comics
©Marvel

Replacement God

Kid runs from troubling prophecy
©Slave Labor

Resurrection Man

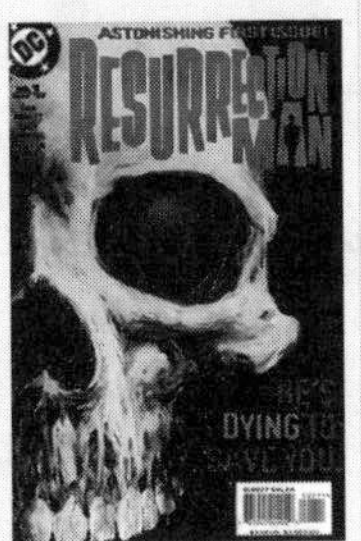

Amnesiac rediscovers bits of his past
©DC

Retaliator

Stranger intervenes on behalf of the abused
©Eclipse

Return of Lum Urusei*Yatsura

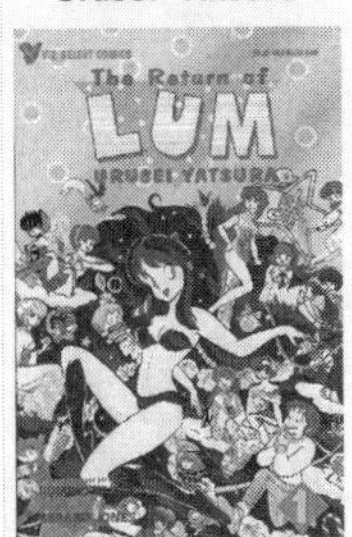

Alien princess with flying powers
©Viz

N-MINT

❑18 ... 2.50
❑19, no publication date ... 2.50
❑20, Dec 1990 ... 2.50
❑21, no publication date ... 2.50

REALM (VOL. 2)
CALIBER

❑1, b&w ... 2.95
❑2, b&w ... 2.95
❑3, b&w ... 2.95
❑4, b&w ... 2.95
❑5, b&w ... 2.95
❑6, b&w ... 2.95
❑7, b&w ... 2.95
❑8, b&w ... 2.95
❑9, b&w ... 2.95
❑10, b&w ... 2.95
❑11, b&w ... 2.95
❑12, b&w ... 2.95
❑13, b&w ... 2.95

REAL SCHMUCK
STARHEAD

❑1, b&w ... 2.95

REAL SMUT
FANTAGRAPHICS / EROS

❑1, b&w ... 2.50
❑2, b&w ... 2.50
❑3, b&w ... 2.50
❑4, b&w ... 2.75
❑5, b&w ... 2.75
❑6, b&w ... 2.50

REAL STUFF
FANTAGRAPHICS

❑1, b&w ... 3.00
❑2, b&w ... 2.75
❑3, b&w ... 2.50
❑4, b&w ... 2.50
❑5, b&w ... 2.50
❑6, b&w ... 2.50
❑7, b&w ... 2.50
❑8, b&w ... 2.50
❑9, b&w ... 2.50
❑10, b&w ... 2.95
❑11, b&w ... 2.50
❑12, b&w ... 2.50
❑13, b&w ... 2.50
❑14, b&w ... 2.50
❑15, b&w ... 2.50
❑16, b&w ... 2.50
❑17, b&w ... 2.50
❑18 ... 2.50
❑19, Jul 1994, b&w ... 2.50
❑20, Oct 1994, b&w ... 2.95

REAL WAR STORIES
ECLIPSE

❑1 ... 2.00
❑1/2nd, Feb 1988 ... 2.00
❑2, Jan 1991 ... 4.95

REAL WEIRD WAR
AVALON

❑1; "Real Weird War" on cover ... 2.95

REAL WEIRD WEST
AVALON

❑1 ... 2.95

N-MINT

REALWORLDS: BATMAN
DC

❑1 ... 5.95

REALWORLDS: JUSTICE LEAGUE OF AMERICA
DC

❑1, Jul 2000 ... 5.95

REALWORLDS: SUPERMAN
DC

❑1 ... 5.95

REALWORLDS: WONDER WOMAN
DC

❑1, Jun 2000 ... 5.95

RE-ANIMATOR (AIRCEL)
AIRCEL

❑1 ... 2.95
❑2 ... 2.95
❑3 ... 2.95

RE-ANIMATOR: DAWN OF THE RE-ANIMATOR
ADVENTURE

❑1, b&w ... 2.50
❑2, Apr 1992 ... 2.50
❑3, May 1992 ... 2.50
❑4 ... 2.50

RE-ANIMATOR IN FULL COLOR
ADVENTURE

❑1, Nov 1991 ... 2.95
❑2 ... 2.95
❑3, Apr 1992 ... 2.95

REAPER ONE SHOT
IMAGE

❑1, May 2004 ... 6.95

REAR ENTRY
FANTAGRAPHICS / EROS

❑1, ... 3.50
❑2, ... 3.50
❑3, ... 3.50
❑4, ... 3.50
❑5, ... 3.95
❑6, ... 3.95
❑7, ... 3.95
❑8, ... 3.95
❑9 2005 ... 3.95
❑10, Dec 2005 ... 3.95

R.E.B.E.L.S.
DC

❑0, Oct 1994, story continued from L.E.G.I.O.N. '94 #70 ... 1.95
❑1, Nov 1994 ... 1.95
❑2, Dec 1994 ... 1.95
❑3, Jan 1995 ... 1.95
❑4, Feb 1995 ... 1.95
❑5, Mar 1995 ... 1.95
❑6, Apr 1995 ... 1.95
❑7, May 1995 ... 1.95
❑8, Jun 1995 ... 2.25
❑9, Jul 1995 ... 2.25
❑10, Aug 1995 ... 2.25
❑11, Sep 1995, return of Captain Comet ... 2.25
❑12, Oct 1995 ... 2.25
❑13, Nov 1995, Underworld Unleashed ... 2.25

N-MINT

❑14, Dec 1995, Title changes to R.E.B.E.L.S. '96 ... 2.25
❑15, Jan 1996 ... 2.25
❑16, Feb 1996 ... 2.25
❑17, Mar 1996 ... 2.25

REBEL SWORD
DARK HORSE

❑1, Oct 1994, b&w ... 2.50
❑2, Nov 1994, b&w ... 2.50
❑3, Dec 1994, b&w ... 2.50
❑4, Jan 1995, b&w ... 2.50
❑5, Feb 1995, b&w ... 2.50

REBIRTH
TOKYOPOP

❑1, Mar 2003, b&w ... 9.95
❑2, Mar 2003 ... 9.95
❑3, Jul 2003 ... 9.95
❑4, Sep 2003 ... 9.95
❑5, Dec 2003 ... 9.95
❑6, Feb 2004 ... 9.95
❑7, Apr 2004 ... 9.95
❑8, Jun 2004 ... 9.95
❑9, Aug 2004 ... 9.95
❑10, Oct 2004 ... 9.95
❑11, Dec 2004 ... 9.95
❑12, Feb 2005 ... 9.95
❑13, Apr 2005 ... 9.95
❑14, Jun 2005 ... 9.95
❑15, Aug 2005 ... 9.95
❑16, Nov 2005 ... 9.95

RECIPE FOR DISASTER AND OTHER STORIES
FANTAGRAPHICS

❑1, Oct 1998, b&w ... 9.95

RECOLLECTIONS SAMPLER
RECOLLECTIONS

❑1, b&w; Reprints ... 1.00

RECORD OF LODOSS WAR: CHRONICLES OF THE HEROIC KNIGHT
CPM MANGA

❑1, Sep 2000, b&w ... 2.95
❑2, Oct 2000, b&w ... 2.95
❑3, Nov 2000 ... 2.95
❑4, Dec 2000 ... 2.95
❑5, Jan 2001 ... 2.95
❑6, Feb 2001 ... 2.95
❑7, Mar 2001 ... 2.95
❑8, Apr 2001 ... 2.95
❑9, May 2001 ... 2.95
❑10, Jun 2001 ... 2.95
❑11, Jul 2001 ... 2.95

RECORD OF LODOSS WAR: THE GREY WITCH
CPM

❑1, Nov 1998; wraparound cover ... 2.95
❑2, Dec 1998 ... 2.95
❑3, Jan 1999; wraparound cover ... 2.95
❑4, Feb 1999 ... 2.95
❑5, Mar 1999 ... 2.95
❑6, Apr 1999 ... 2.95
❑7, May 1999 ... 2.95

N-MINT

❑8, Jun 1999 ... 2.95
❑9, Jul 1999 ... 2.95
❑10, Aug 1999 ... 2.95
❑11, Sep 1999 ... 2.95
❑12, Oct 1999 ... 2.95
❑13, Nov 1999 ... 2.95
❑14, Dec 1999 ... 2.95
❑15, Jan 2000 ... 2.95
❑16, Feb 2000 ... 2.95
❑17, Mar 2000; wraparound cover ... 2.95
❑18, Apr 2000 ... 2.95
❑19, May 2000 ... 2.95
❑20, Jun 2000 ... 2.95
❑21, Jul 2000 ... 2.95
❑22, Aug 2000; wraparound cover ... 2.95

RECORD OF LODOSS WAR: THE LADY OF PHARIS
CPM

❑1 ... 2.95
❑2 ... 2.95
❑3 ... 2.95
❑4 ... 2.95
❑5 ... 2.95
❑6 ... 2.95
❑7 ... 2.95
❑8 ... 2.95

RECTUM ERRRECTUM
BONEYARD

❑1 ... 3.95

RED (DC)
DC / HOMAGE

❑1, Sep 2003 ... 2.95
❑2, Oct 2003 ... 2.95
❑3, Feb 2004 ... 2.95

REDBLADE
DARK HORSE

❑1; gatefold cover ... 2.50
❑2 ... 2.50
❑3 ... 2.50

RED CIRCLE SORCERY
RED CIRCLE

❑6, Apr 1974; Series continued from Chilling Adventures in Sorcery #5 ... 10.00
❑7, Jun 1974 ... 5.00
❑8, Aug 1974 GM, FT (a) ... 5.00
❑9, Oct 1974 ... 5.00
❑10, Dec 1974 WW, JAb (a) ... 5.00
❑11, Feb 1975 ... 5.00

REDDEVIL
AC

❑1, no indicia ... 2.95

RED DIARIES
CALIBER

❑1, ca. 1997 ... 3.95
❑2, ca. 1997 ... 3.95
❑3, ca. 1997 ... 3.95
❑4, ca. 1997 ... 3.95

RED DRAGON
COMICO

❑1, Jun 1996 ... 2.95

REDEEMER
IMAGES & REALITIES

❑1 ... 2.95

REDEEMERS
ANTARCTIC

❑1, Dec 1997, b&w ... 2.95

RED FLANNEL SQUIRREL
SIRIUS

❑1, Oct 1997, b&w ... 2.95

REDFOX
HARRIER

❑1, Jan 1986; 1: Redfox. Harrier publishes ... 4.00
❑1/2nd; 1: Redfox. Harrier publishes ... 1.75
❑2, Mar 1986 ... 3.00
❑3, May 1986 ... 2.50
❑4, Jul 1986 ... 1.75
❑5, Sep 1986 ... 1.75
❑6, Nov 1986 ... 1.75
❑7, Jan 1987 ... 1.75
❑8, Mar 1987 ... 1.75
❑9, May 1987 ... 1.75
❑10, Jul 1987; Last Harrier issue ... 1.75

N-MINT

❑11, Sep 1987; Valkyrie begins publishing ... 2.00
❑12, Nov 1987 ... 2.00
❑13, Jan 1988 ... 2.00
❑14, Mar 1988 ... 2.00
❑15, May 1988; Luther Arkwright cameo ... 2.00
❑16, Jun 1988 ... 2.00
❑17, Aug 1988 ... 2.00
❑18, Oct 1988 ... 2.00
❑19, Feb 1989 ... 2.00
❑20, Jun 1989 NG (w); ... 2.00

RED HEAT
BLACKTHORNE

❑1, Jul 1988, b&w ... 2.00
❑1/3D, Jul 1988 ... 2.50

REDMASK OF THE RIO GRANDE
AC

❑1, Reprints ... 2.95
❑2 ... 2.95
❑3, 3-D effects ... 2.95

RED MOON
MILLENNIUM

❑1, Mar 1995, b&w ... 2.95
❑2 ... 2.95

RED PLANET PIONEER
INESCO

❑1 ... 2.95

RED RAZORS: A DREDDWORLD ADVENTURE
FLEETWAY-QUALITY

❑1 ... 2.95
❑2 ... 2.95
❑3 ... 2.95

RED REVOLUTION
CALIBER / TOME

❑1, b&w ... 2.95

RED ROCKET 7
DARK HORSE / LEGEND

❑1, Aug 1997 ... 2.95
❑2, Sep 1997 ... 2.95
❑3, Oct 1997 ... 2.95
❑4, Nov 1997 ... 2.95
❑5, Jan 1998 ... 2.95
❑6, Mar 1998 ... 3.95
❑7, Jun 1998 ... 3.95

RED SONJA (VOL. 1)
MARVEL

❑1, Nov 1976, FT (a); O: Red Sonja ... 8.00
❑2, Jan 1977, FT (a) ... 3.00
❑3, May 1977, FT (a) ... 3.00
❑4, Jul 1977, FT (a) ... 3.00
❑4/35 cent, Jul 1977, 35 cent regional variant ... 20.00
❑5, Sep 1977, FT (a) ... 3.00
❑5/35 cent, Sep 1977, FT (a); 35 cent regional price variant ... 20.00
❑6, Nov 1977, WP (w); FT (a) ... 3.00
❑7, Jan 1978, FT (a) ... 1.50
❑8, Mar 1978, FT (a) ... 1.50
❑9, May 1978, FT (a) ... 1.50
❑10, Jul 1978, FT (a) ... 1.50
❑11, Sep 1978, FT (a) ... 1.50
❑12, Nov 1978 ... 1.50
❑13, Jan 1979 ... 1.50
❑14, Mar 1979 ... 1.50
❑15, May 1979 ... 1.50

RED SONJA (VOL. 2)
MARVEL

❑1, Feb 1983, TD (a) ... 1.00
❑2, Mar 1983 ... 1.00

RED SONJA (VOL. 3)
MARVEL

❑1, Aug 1983, giant ... 1.50
❑2, Oct 1983, giant ... 1.50
❑3, Dec 1983, giant ... 1.50
❑4, Feb 1984, giant ... 1.50
❑5, Jan 1985, PB (a) ... 1.50
❑6, Feb 1985, PB (a) ... 1.50
❑7, Mar 1985 ... 1.50
❑8, Apr 1985 ... 1.50
❑9, May 1985 ... 1.50
❑10, Aug 1985 ... 1.50
❑11, Nov 1985 ... 1.50

N-MINT

❑12, Feb 1986 ... 1.50
❑13, May 1986 ... 1.50

RED SONJA (VOL. 4)
DYNAMITE COMICS

❑0/Black 2005; Greg Land art. Promo comics priced at 25¢. Black background on cover. ... 3.00
❑0/White 2005; Greg Land art. Promo comics priced at 25¢. White background on cover. ... 3.00
❑0/Ross 2005; Alex Ross art. Retailer incentive provided 1 per 100 copies ordered. ... 30.00
❑0/Sketch 2005; Greg Land sketch cover. Retailer incentive provided 1 per 1,000 copies ordered. ... 150.00
❑0/Foil 2005 ... 10.00
❑0/Authentix 2005 ... 20.00
❑0/DF 2005 ... 25.00
❑1 2005 ... 20.00
❑1/Rivera 2005 ... 25.00
❑1/Adams 2005 ... 35.00
❑1/Linsner 2005 ... 125.00
❑1/Ross 2005 ... 40.00
❑1/Rubi 2005 ... 20.00
❑1/DF 2005 ... 35.00
❑2 2005 ... 2.99
❑3 2005 ... 2.99
❑4, Jan 2005 ... 2.99
❑5, Jan 2006 ... 2.99
❑6, Feb 2006 ... 2.99
❑7, Mar 2006 ... 2.99
❑8, Apr 2006 ... 2.99

RED SONJA/CLAW: DEVIL'S HANDS
DC

❑1, May 2006 ... 2.99
❑2, Jun 2006 ... 2.99
❑4, Aug 2006 ... 2.99

RED SONJA: SCAVENGER HUNT
MARVEL

❑1, Dec 1995 ... 2.95

RED SONJA: THE MOVIE
MARVEL

❑1, Nov 1985 ... 1.25
❑2, Dec 1985 ... 1.25

RED STAR
IMAGE

❑1, Jun 2000 ... 3.50
❑2, Jul 2000 ... 3.00
❑3, Oct 2000 ... 2.95
❑4, Jan 2001 ... 2.95
❑5, Feb 2001 ... 2.95
❑6, Mar 2001 ... 2.95
❑7, Apr 2001 ... 2.95
❑8/A ... 2.95
❑8/B ... 2.95
❑9, Jun 2002 ... 2.95

RED STAR, THE (VOL. 2)
CROSSGEN

❑1, Feb 2003 ... 2.95
❑2, Jun 2003 ... 2.95
❑3, Oct 2003 ... 2.99
❑4, Mar 2004 ... 2.99

RED TORNADO
DC

❑1, Jul 1985 KB (w); CI (a) ... 1.00
❑2, Aug 1985 KB (w); CI (a) ... 1.00
❑3, Sep 1985 KB (w); CI (a) ... 1.00
❑4, Oct 1985 KB (w); CI (a) ... 1.00

RED WOLF
MARVEL

❑1, May 1972, 1: Red Wolf. 1: Lobo (Marvel) ... 35.00
❑2, Jul 1972 ... 18.00
❑3, Sep 1972 ... 15.00
❑4, Nov 1972, V: Man-Bear ... 15.00
❑5, Jan 1973 ... 15.00
❑6, Mar 1973 ... 10.00
❑7, May 1973 ... 10.00
❑8, Jul 1973 ... 10.00
❑9, Sep 1973 ... 10.00

REESE'S PIECES
ECLIPSE

❑1, ca. 1986 ... 1.75
❑2, ca. 1986 ... 1.75

Revengers Featuring Armor and The Silverstreak

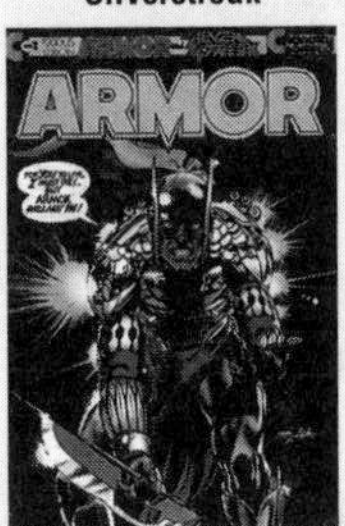

Cover title isn't actually the comic's name
©Continuity

Revolver

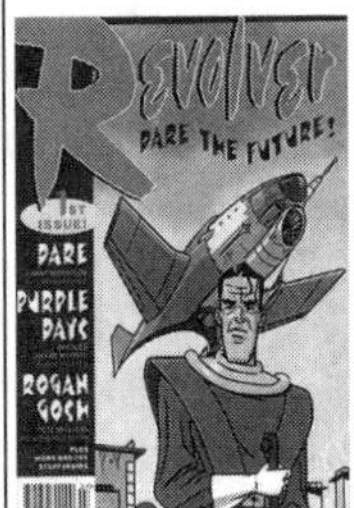

British anthology repackaged for America
©Fleetway-Quality

Rhudiprrt, Prince of Fur

Get reincarnated with your cats
©Mu

Richard Dragon, Kung-Fu Fighter

Sensei turns thief into good martial artist
©DC

Richie Rich (1st Series)

Poor little rich boy had many titles
©Harvey

N-MINT

RE:GEX
Awesome

- ❑0, Dec 1998; Woman with swords standing over figures ... 2.50
- ❑0/A, Jan 1999; Man with swords standing over figures ... 2.50
- ❑1 1998 ... 2.50
- ❑1/A; White background; Two women with swords on cover ... 2.50

REGGIE'S REVENGE
Archie

- ❑1, Spr 1994 ... 2.00
- ❑2, Fal 1994 ... 2.00
- ❑3, Spr 1995 ... 2.00

REGISTRY OF DEATH
Kitchen Sink

- ❑1, Nov 1996; oversized tpb ... 15.95

REGULATORS
Image

- ❑1, Jun 1995 ... 2.50
- ❑2, Jul 1995 ... 2.50
- ❑3, Aug 1995 ... 2.50
- ❑4 ... 2.50

REHD
Antarctic

- ❑0, Jun 2003 ... 2.50

REID FLEMING
Boswell

- ❑1 1: Reid Fleming ... 10.00
- ❑1/2nd ... 4.00

REID FLEMING, WORLD'S TOUGHEST MILKMAN
Eclipse

- ❑1, Oct 1986 ... 6.00
- ❑1/2nd ... 3.00
- ❑1/3rd ... 2.00
- ❑1/4th ... 2.00
- ❑1/5th ... 2.00
- ❑1/6th; 1996 ... 2.95
- ❑2, Mar 1987 ... 3.00
- ❑2/2nd ... 2.00
- ❑2/3rd, Mar 1989 ... 2.00
- ❑3, Dec 1988; Indicia says #2:3 ... 2.00
- ❑4, Nov 1989 ... 2.00
- ❑5, Nov 1990 ... 2.00
- ❑6 ... 2.00
- ❑7, Jan 1997 ... 2.95
- ❑8, Aug 1997 ... 2.95
- ❑9, Apr 1998 ... 2.95

REIGN OF THE DRAGONLORD
Eternity

- ❑1, Oct 1986 ... 1.80
- ❑2 ... 1.80

REIGN OF THE ZODIAC
DC / Homage

- ❑1, Oct 2003 ... 2.75
- ❑2, Nov 2003 ... 2.75
- ❑3, Dec 2003 ... 2.75
- ❑4, Jan 2004 ... 2.75
- ❑5, Feb 2004 ... 2.75
- ❑6, Mar 2004 ... 2.75
- ❑7, Apr 2004 ... 2.75
- ❑8, May 2004 ... 2.75

N-MINT

REIKI WARRIORS
Revolutionary

- ❑1, Aug 1993, b&w ... 2.95

RELATIVE HEROES
DC

- ❑1, Mar 2000 ... 2.50
- ❑2, Apr 2000 ... 2.50
- ❑3, May 2000 ... 2.50
- ❑4, Jun 2000 ... 2.50
- ❑5, Jul 2000 ... 2.50
- ❑6, Aug 2000 ... 2.50

RELENTLESS PURSUIT
Slave Labor

- ❑1, Jan 1989, b&w ... 1.75
- ❑2, May 1989, b&w ... 1.75
- ❑3, Sep 1989, b&w ... 2.95
- ❑4, Jan 1990, b&w ... 3.95

RELOAD
DC / Homage

- ❑1, May 2003 ... 2.95
- ❑2, Jul 2003 ... 2.95
- ❑3, Sep 2003 ... 2.95

REMAINS
Idea & Design Works

- ❑1, May 2004 ... 3.99
- ❑2, Jun 2004 ... 3.99
- ❑3, Jul 2004 ... 3.99
- ❑4, Aug 2004 ... 3.99
- ❑5, Sep 2004 ... 3.99

REMARKABLE WORLDS OF PHINEAS B. FUDDLE, THE
Paradox

- ❑1, Jul 2000 ... 5.95
- ❑2, Aug 2000 ... 5.95
- ❑3, Sep 2000 ... 5.95
- ❑4, Oct 2000 ... 5.95

REMOTE
Tokyopop

- ❑1, Jan 2004 ... 9.95
- ❑2, Aug 2004 ... 9.95
- ❑3, Oct 2004 ... 9.95
- ❑4, Jan 2005 ... 9.95
- ❑5, Apr 2005 ... 9.95
- ❑6, Jul 2005 ... 9.95
- ❑7, Oct 2005 ... 9.95

REN & STIMPY SHOW
Marvel

- ❑1/A, Dec 1992; Ren scratch&sniff card ... 2.50
- ❑1/B, Dec 1992; Stimpy scratch&sniff card ... 2.50
- ❑1/2nd; No air fouler ... 2.25
- ❑1/3rd; No air fouler ... 2.25
- ❑2, Jan 1993 ... 2.00
- ❑2/2nd ... 1.75
- ❑3, Feb 1993 ... 2.00
- ❑3/2nd ... 1.75
- ❑4, Mar 1993 A: Muddy Mudskipper ... 2.00
- ❑5, Apr 1993; in space ... 2.00
- ❑6, May 1993 A: Spider-Man ... 1.75
- ❑7, Jun 1993; Kid Stimpy ... 1.75
- ❑8, Jul 1993; Maltese Stimpy ... 1.75
- ❑9, Aug 1993 ... 1.75

N-MINT

- ❑10, Sep 1993 ... 1.75
- ❑11, Oct 1993 ... 1.75
- ❑12, Nov 1993; Stimpy cloned ... 1.75
- ❑13, Dec 1993; Halloween issue ... 1.75
- ❑14, Jan 1994 ... 1.75
- ❑15, Feb 1994; Christmas issue ... 1.75
- ❑16, Mar 1994; Elvis parody ... 1.75
- ❑17, Apr 1994 ... 1.75
- ❑18, May 1994; Powdered Toast Man ... 1.75
- ❑19, Jun 1994 ... 1.95
- ❑20, Jul 1994 A: Muddy Mudskipper ... 1.95
- ❑21, Aug 1994 ... 1.95
- ❑22, Sep 1994 ... 1.95
- ❑23, Oct 1994; wrestling ... 1.95
- ❑24, Nov 1994; box top collecting ... 1.95
- ❑25, Dec 1994 V: Dogzilla ... 1.95
- ❑25/Variant, Dec 1994; enhanced cover ... 2.95
- ❑26, Jan 1995 A: Sven Hoek ... 1.95
- ❑27, Feb 1995 ... 1.95
- ❑28, Mar 1995 A: Filthy the monkey ... 1.95
- ❑29, Apr 1995 ... 1.95
- ❑30, May 1995; Ren's birthday ... 1.95
- ❑31, Jun 1995 ... 1.95
- ❑32, Jul 1995 ... 1.95
- ❑33, Aug 1995 ... 1.95
- ❑34, Sep 1995 ... 1.95
- ❑35, Oct 1995 ... 1.95
- ❑36, Nov 1995 ... 1.95
- ❑37, Dec 1995; aliens ... 1.95
- ❑38, Jan 1996 ... 1.95
- ❑39, Feb 1996 ... 1.95
- ❑40, Mar 1996 ... 1.95
- ❑41, Apr 1996 ... 1.95
- ❑42, May 1996 ... 1.95
- ❑43, Jun 1996 ... 1.95
- ❑44, Jul 1996 ... 1.95
- ❑Special 1, Jul 1994 ... 2.95
- ❑Special 2, Oct 1994; Summer Jobs ... 3.00
- ❑Special 3, Oct 1994; Masters of Time and Space! ... 3.00
- ❑Holiday 1, Feb 1995 ... 2.95

REN & STIMPY SHOW: RADIO DAZE
Marvel

- ❑1, Nov 1995; based on audio release of same name ... 1.95

REN & STIMPY SHOW SPECIAL, THE: AROUND THE WORLD IN A DAZE
Marvel

- ❑1, Jan 1996 ... 2.95

REN & STIMPY SHOW SPECIAL: EENTERACTIVE
Marvel

- ❑1, Jul 1995 ... 2.95

REN & STIMPY SHOW SPECIAL: FOUR SWERKS
Marvel

- ❑1, Jan 1995 ... 2.95

REN & STIMPY SHOW SPECIAL: POWDERED TOAST MAN
Marvel

- ❑1, Apr 1994; O: Crusto. Powdered Toast Man ... 3.00

REN & STIMPY SHOW SPECIAL: POWDERED TOASTMAN'S CEREAL
MARVEL
❑1, Apr 1995 .... 2.95

REN & STIMPY SHOW SPECIAL: SPORTS
MARVEL
❑1, Oct 1995.......... 2.95

RENEGADE
RIP OFF
❑1, Aug 1991, b&w 2.50

RENEGADE!, THE (MAGNECOM)
MAGNECOM
❑1, Dec 1993.......... 2.95

RENEGADE RABBIT
PRINTED MATTER
❑1 .... 1.75
❑2 .... 1.75
❑3 .... 1.75
❑4 .... 1.75
❑5; Cerebus parody 1.75

RENEGADE ROMANCE
RENEGADE
❑1, b&w.......... 3.50
❑2, b&w.......... 3.50

RENEGADES
AGE OF HEROES
❑1 .... 1.00
❑2 .... 1.00

RENEGADES OF JUSTICE
BLUE MASQUE
❑1, ca. 1995, b&w 2.50
❑2, ca. 1995, b&w 2.50

RENFIELD
CALIBER
❑1, ca. 1994 .... 2.95
❑1/Ltd.; Limited "special edition" with second cover; Limited special edition with second cover 5.95
❑2, ca. 1994 .... 2.95
❑3, ca. 1995 .... 2.95
❑Ashcan 1, b&w; no cover price.......... 1.00

RENNIN COMICS (JIM CHADWICK'S...)
RESTLESS MUSE
❑1, Sum 1997, b&w 2.95

REPLACEMENT GOD
HANDICRAFT
❑6, Dec 1998 .... 6.95

REPLACEMENT GOD
SLAVE LABOR / AMAZE INK
❑1, Jun 1995, b&w.......... 6.00
❑1/2nd, Dec 1995, b&w.......... 3.00
❑2, Sep 1995, b&w.......... 3.50
❑3, Dec 1995, b&w.......... 3.00
❑4, Apr 1996, b&w 2.95
❑5, Jul 1996, b&w.......... 2.95
❑6, Sep 1996, b&w.......... 2.95
❑7, Dec 1996, b&w.......... 2.95
❑8, b&w.......... 2.95

REPLACEMENT GOD AND OTHER STORIES
IMAGE
❑1, May 1997, b&w; flip-book with Knute's Escapes back-up 2.95
❑2, Jul 1997, b&w; flip-book with Harris Thermidor back-up.......... 2.95
❑3, Sep 1997, b&w; flip-book with Knute's Escapes back-up 2.95
❑4, Nov 1997, b&w; flip-book with Knute's Escapes back-up 2.95
❑5, Jan 1998, b&w; flip-book with Knute's Escapes back-up 2.95

REPORTER
REPORTER
❑1 .... 3.00

REQUIEM FOR DRACULA
MARVEL
❑1; Reprints Tomb of Dracula #69, 70 .... 2.00

RESCUEMAN
BEST
❑1, b&w.......... 2.95

RESCUERS DOWN UNDER (DISNEY'S...)
DISNEY
❑1.......... 2.95

RESIDENT EVIL
IMAGE
❑1, Mar 1998 .... 5.50
❑2, Jun 1998 .... 5.00
❑3, Sep 1998.......... 5.00
❑4, Dec 1998.......... 5.00
❑5, Feb 1999 .... 5.00

RESIDENT EVIL: CODE VERONICA
DC / WILDSTORM
❑1, Aug 2002 .... 14.95
❑2, Oct 2002.......... 14.95
❑3, Dec 2002.......... 14.95

RESIDENT EVIL: FIRE AND ICE
WILDSTORM
❑1, Dec 2000.......... 2.50
❑2, Jan 2001 .... 2.50
❑3, Feb 2001 .... 2.50
❑4, May 2001 .... 2.50

RESISTANCE
WILDSTORM
❑1, Nov 2002 .... 2.95
❑2, Dec 2002.......... 2.95
❑3, Jan 2003.......... 2.95
❑4, Feb 2003.......... 2.95
❑5, Mar 2003 .... 2.95
❑6, Apr 2003 .... 2.95
❑7, May 2003 .... 2.95
❑8, Jun 2003.......... 2.95

RESTAURANT AT THE END OF THE UNIVERSE
DC
❑1 1994; prestige format 6.95
❑2 1994; prestige format 6.95
❑3 1994; prestige format 6.95

RESURRECTION MAN
DC
❑1, May 1997; Lenticular disc on cover 3.00
❑2, Jun 1997 A: Justice League of America.......... 2.50
❑3, Jul 1997.......... 2.50
❑4, Aug 1997 BG (a) 2.50
❑5, Sep 1997 BG (a) 2.50
❑6, Oct 1997; Genesis; Resurrection Man powerless 2.50
❑7, Nov 1997 BG (a); A: Batman 2.50
❑8, Dec 1997; BG (a); Face cover.......... 2.50
❑9, Jan 1998 BG (a); A: Hitman 2.50
❑10, Feb 1998 BG (a); A: Hitman 2.50
❑11, Mar 1998 BG (a); O: Resurrection Man.......... 2.50
❑12, Apr 1998 BG (a).......... 2.50
❑13, May 1998.......... 2.50
❑14, Jun 1998 BG (a).......... 2.50
❑15, Jul 1998.......... 2.50
❑16, Aug 1998 A: Supergirl.......... 2.50
❑17, Sep 1998 A: Supergirl.......... 2.50
❑18, Oct 1998 A: Deadman. A: Phantom Stranger.......... 2.50
❑19, Dec 1998.......... 2.50
❑20, Jan 1999 .... 2.50
❑21, Feb 1999 BG (a); A: Justice League of America. V: Major Force 2.50
❑22, Mar 1999 BG (a) 2.50
❑23, Apr 1999; BG (c); BG (a); Mitch as a woman.......... 2.50
❑24, May 1999 BG (a); A: Animal Man. A: Ray. A: Cave Carson. A: Ballistic. A: Vandal Savage. A: Vigilante 2.50
❑25, Jun 1999 BG (a); A: Forgotten Heroes.......... 2.50
❑26, Jul 1999 A: Immortal Man 2.50
❑27, Aug 1999 BG (a); D: Immortal Man 2.50
❑1000000, Nov 1998 BG (c); BG (a) .. 4.00

RETALIATOR
ECLIPSE
❑1, b&w 2.50
❑2, b&w 2.50
❑3, b&w 2.50
❑4, b&w 2.50
❑5.......... 2.50

RETIEF
ADVENTURE
❑1, b&w 2.25
❑2, b&w.......... 2.25
❑3, b&w.......... 2.25
❑4, b&w.......... 2.25
❑5, b&w.......... 2.25
❑6, b&w.......... 2.25

RETIEF AND THE WARLORDS
ADVENTURE
❑1, b&w.......... 2.50
❑2, b&w.......... 2.50
❑3, b&w.......... 2.50
❑4, b&w.......... 2.50

RETIEF: DIPLOMATIC IMMUNITY
ADVENTURE
❑1, b&w.......... 2.50
❑2, b&w.......... 2.50

RETIEF: GRIME AND PUNISHMENT
ADVENTURE
❑1, Nov 1991, b&w 2.50

RETIEF (KEITH LAUMER'S...)
MAD DOG
❑1, Apr 1987 .... 2.00
❑2, Jun 1987 .... 2.00
❑3, Aug 1987.......... 2.00
❑4, Oct 1987.......... 2.00
❑5, Jan 1988 .... 2.00
❑6, Mar 1988.......... 2.00

RETIEF OF THE C.D.T.
MAD DOG
❑1, b&w.......... 2.00

RETIEF: THE GARBAGE INVASION
ADVENTURE
❑1, b&w.......... 2.50

RETIEF: THE GIANT KILLER
ADVENTURE
❑1, b&w.......... 2.50

RETRO 50'S COMIX
EDGE
❑1, b&w.......... 2.95
❑2, b&w.......... 2.95
❑3, b&w; free fly.......... 3.50

RETRO COMICS
AC
❑0, b&w; Cardstock cover; Cat-Man... 5.95
❑1, b&w; Cardstock cover; Fighting Yank.......... 5.95
❑2, b&w; Cardstock cover; Miss Victory 5.95
❑3, Original Cat-Man and Kitten 5.95

RETRO-DEAD
BLAZER
❑1, Nov 1995, b&w.......... 2.95

RETROGRADE
ETERNITY
❑1 .... 1.95
❑2.......... 1.95
❑3.......... 1.95

RETRO ROCKET
IMAGE
❑1, Apr 2006 .... 2.99

RETURN OF DISNEY'S ALADDIN
DISNEY
❑1.......... 1.50
❑2.......... 1.50

RETURN OF GIRL SQUAD X
FANTACO
❑1 .... 4.95

RETURN OF GORGO
CHARLTON
❑2, Sum 1963.......... 75.00
❑3, Fal 1964 .... 75.00

RETURN OF HAPPY THE CLOWN
CALIBER
❑1, b&w.......... 3.50
❑2, ca. 1995, b&w.......... 2.95

RETURN OF HERBIE
AVALON
❑1, b&w; reprints and new story (originally scheduled for Dark Horse's Herbie #3) 2.50

RETURN OF LUM URUSEI*YATSURA
VIZ
❑1, Oct 1994, b&w 3.00
❑2, Nov 1994, b&w 3.00

Richie Rich (2nd Series)

1990s Harvey restart didn't last as long

©Harvey

Richie Rich & Casper

Richie went to the Enchanted Forest a lot

©Harvey

Richie Rich & Jackie Jokers

Stand-up comic appeared in many parodies

©Harvey

Richie Rich Big Book (Vol. 2)

1990s equivalent of the old 48-pagers

©Harvey

Richie Rich Cash

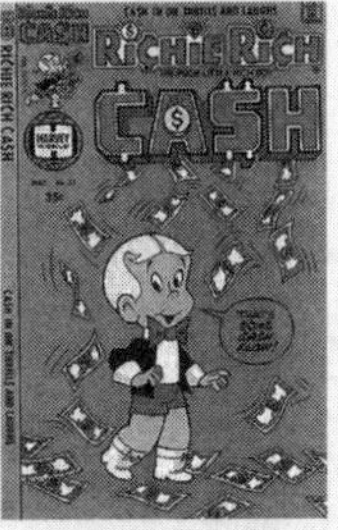

Cover gags usually involved currency

©Harvey

N-MINT

❑3, Dec 1994, b&w 3.00
❑4, Jan 1995, b&w 3.00
❑5, Feb 1995, b&w 3.00
❑6, Mar 1995, b&w 3.00
❑7, ca. 1995 .... 2.75
❑8, ca. 1995 .... 2.75

RETURN OF LUM URUSEI*YATSURA, PART 2
VIZ

❑1, Apr 1995, b&w 3.00
❑2, May 1995, b&w 3.00
❑3, Jun 1995, b&w 3.00
❑4, Jul 1995, b&w 3.00
❑5, Aug 1995, b&w 3.00
❑6, Sep 1995, b&w 3.00
❑7, Oct 1995, b&w 3.00
❑8, Nov 1995, b&w 3.00
❑9, Dec 1995, b&w 3.00
❑10, Jan 1996, b&w 3.00
❑11, Feb 1996, b&w 3.00
❑12, Mar 1996, b&w 3.00
❑13, Apr 1996, b&w 3.00

RETURN OF LUM URUSEI*YATSURA, PART 3
VIZ

❑1, May 1996, b&w 2.95
❑2, Jun 1996, b&w 2.95
❑3, Jul 1996, b&w 2.95
❑4, Aug 1996, b&w 2.95
❑5, Sep 1996, b&w 2.95
❑6, Oct 1996, b&w 2.95
❑7, Nov 1996, b&w 2.95
❑8, Dec 1996, b&w 2.95
❑9, Jan 1997, b&w 2.95
❑10, Feb 1997, b&w 2.95
❑11, Mar 1997, b&w 2.95

RETURN OF LUM URUSEI*YATSURA, PART 4
VIZ

❑1, Apr 1997, b&w 2.95
❑2, May 1997, b&w 2.95
❑3, Jun 1997, b&w 2.95
❑4, Jul 1997, b&w 2.95
❑5, Aug 1997, b&w 2.95
❑6, Sep 1997, b&w 2.95
❑7, Oct 1997, b&w 2.95
❑8, Nov 1997, b&w 2.95
❑9, Dec 1997, b&w 2.95
❑10, Jan 1998, b&w 2.95
❑11, Feb 1998, b&w 2.95

RETURN OF MEGATON MAN
KITCHEN SINK

❑1, Jul 1988 .... 2.50
❑2 .... 2.50
❑3 .... 2.50

RETURN OF SHADOWHAWK
IMAGE

❑1, Nov 2004; One-shot 2.99

RETURN OF TARZAN (EDGAR RICE BURROUGHS'...)
DARK HORSE

❑1, Apr 1997, adapts Burroughs novel 2.95

N-MINT

❑2, May 1997, adapts Burroughs novel 2.95
❑3, Jun 1997, back cover has reproductions of New Story Magazine covers; adapts Burroughs novel 2.95

RETURN OF THE SKYMAN
ACE

❑1, Sep 1987 .... 1.75

RETURN OF VALKYRIE
ECLIPSE

❑1 .... 9.95

RETURN TO JURASSIC PARK
TOPPS

❑1, Apr 1995 .... 2.50
❑2, May 1995 .... 2.50
❑3, Jun 1995 .... 2.95
❑4, Jul 1995 .... 2.95
❑5, Aug 1995 .... 2.95
❑6, Sep 1995 .... 2.95
❑7, Nov 1995 .... 2.95
❑8, Jan 1996 .... 2.95
❑9, Feb 1996 .... 2.95

RETURN TO THE EVE
MONOLITH

❑1 .... 2.50

REVEAL
DARK HORSE

❑1, Nov 2002; Squarebound anthology 6.95

REVELATIONS (DARK HORSE)
DARK HORSE

❑1/Ashcan, Mar 1995 KG (w); 1.00

REVELATIONS (GOLDEN REALM)
GOLDEN REALM UNLIMITED

❑1 .... 2.75

REVELATIONS (CLIVE BARKER'S)
ECLIPSE

❑1 .... 7.95

REVELATIONS (VOL. 2)
DARK HORSE

❑1, Aug 2005 .... 2.95
❑2, Sep 2005 .... 2.95
❑3, Oct 2005 .... 2.95
❑4, Nov 2005 .... 2.95
❑5, Dec 2005 .... 2.95
❑6, Jan 2006 .... 2.95

REVELATION: THE COMIC BOOK
DRAW NEAR

❑1, b&w; No cover price; based on Book of Revelation 3.56
❑2, b&w; based on Book of Revelation 3.56
❑3, b&w; based on Book of Revelation 3.56
❑4, b&w; based on Book of Revelation 3.56
❑5 .... 3.56
❑6 .... 3.56

REVELRY IN HELL
FANTAGRAPHICS / EROS

❑1, b&w 2.50

REVENGE OF THE PROWLER
ECLIPSE

❑1, Feb 1988 .... 2.00
❑2, Mar 1988 .... 2.50

N-MINT

❑3, Apr 1988 .... 2.00
❑4, Jun 1988 .... 2.00

REVENGERS FEATURING ARMOR AND THE SILVERSTREAK
CONTINUITY

❑1, Sep 1985 .... 2.00
❑2, Jun 1986; Origin of Armor 2.00
❑3, Feb 1987; Series continues as Armor (Continuity, 1st series) with #4; indicia for this issue accidentally reads "Revengers featuring Megalith"; who does not appear in the issue 2.00

REVENGERS FEATURING MEGALITH
CONTINUITY

❑1, Apr 1985; newsstand 2.00
❑1/Direct ed., Apr 1985 .... 2.00
❑2, Sep 1985; Revengers Featuring Megalith 2.00
❑3, Nov 1986 .... 2.00
❑4, Mar 1988 .... 2.00
❑5, Mar 1989 .... 2.00
❑6, ca. 1989 .... 2.00

REVENGERS: HYBRIDS SPECIAL
CONTINUITY

❑1, Jul 1992; continues in Hybrids: The Origin #2 .... 4.95

REVEREND ABLACK: ADVENTURES OF THE ANTICHRIST
CREATIVEFORCE DESIGNS

❑1 .... 2.50
❑2, Jul 1996, b&w 2.50

REVISIONARY
MOONSTONE

❑1, Sep 2005 .... 2.95

REVOLVER
FLEETWAY-QUALITY

❑1 .... 2.50
❑2 .... 2.50
❑3 .... 2.50
❑4 .... 2.50
❑5 .... 2.50
❑6 .... 2.50
❑7 .... 2.50

REVOLVER (ROBIN SNYDER'S...)
RENEGADE

❑1, Nov 1985, SD (a); Sci-Fi Adventure 2.00
❑2, Dec 1985, Sci-Fi Adventure 2.00
❑3, Jan 1986, SD (w); SD (a); Sci-Fi Adventure 2.00
❑4, Feb 1986, Fantastic Fables 2.00
❑5, Mar 1986, Fantastic Fables 2.00
❑6, Apr 1986, Fantastic Fables 2.00
❑7, May 1986 .... 2.00
❑8, Jun 1986 .... 2.00
❑9, Jul 1986 .... 2.00
❑10, Aug 1986, Murder 2.00
❑11, Sep 1986, Murder 2.00
❑12, Oct 1986, Murder 2.00
❑Annual 1, ca. 1986, b&w ATh (c) 2.00

REVOLVING DOORS
BLACKTHORNE

❑1, Oct 1986 .... 1.75

Other grades: Multiply price above by 5/6 for VF/NM • 2/3 for VERY FINE • 1/3 for FINE • 1/5 for VERY GOOD • 1/8 for GOOD

	N-MINT
❏2	1.75
❏3	1.75

REX LIBRIS
SLAVE LABOR

❏1, Aug 2005	2.95
❏2, Dec 2005	2.95

REX MUNDI
IMAGE

❏1, Feb 2003	2.95
❏2, Mar 2003	2.95
❏3, Apr 2003	2.95
❏4, Jun 2003	2.95
❏5, Sep 2003	2.95
❏6, Oct 2003	2.95
❏7, Dec 2003	2.95
❏8, Jan 2004	2.95
❏9, May 2004	2.95
❏10, Aug 2004	2.95
❏11 2004	2.95
❏12 2004	2.95
❏13, Apr 2005	2.95
❏14, Oct 2005	2.95
❏15, Dec 2005	2.95
❏16, Jan 2006	2.95
❏17, Apr 2006	2.95

RG VEDA
TOKYOPOP

❏1, Apr 2005	9.99
❏2, Jul 2005	9.99
❏3, Oct 2005	9.99

RHAJ
MU

❏1, b&w	2.00
❏2, b&w	2.00
❏3, b&w	2.00
❏4	2.25

RHANES OF TERROR
BUFFALO NICKEL

❏1, Oct 1999	2.99
❏2	2.99
❏3	2.99
❏4	2.99

RHUDIPRRT, PRINCE OF FUR
MU

❏1, b&w	2.00
❏2, b&w	2.00
❏3	2.00
❏4, Nov 1990	2.25
❏5, Jun 1991	2.50
❏6, Nov 1991	2.50
❏7, b&w	2.50
❏8, Jan 1994	2.50

RIB
DILEMMA

❏1, Apr 1996, b&w	1.95

RIBIT!
COMICO

❏1	1.95
❏2	1.95
❏3	1.95
❏4	1.95

RICHARD DRAGON
DC

❏1, Jul 2004	2.50
❏2, Aug 2004	2.50
❏3, Sep 2004	2.50
❏4, Oct 2004	2.50
❏5, Nov 2004	2.50
❏6, Dec 2004	2.50
❏7, Feb 2005	2.50
❏8, Mar 2005	2.50
❏9, Mar 2005	2.50
❏10, Apr 2005	2.50
❏11, May 2005	2.50
❏12, Jun 2005	2.50

RICHARD DRAGON, KUNG-FU FIGHTER
DC

❏1, Apr 1975, 1&O: Richard Dragon, Kung Fu Fighter	10.00
❏2, Jul 1975, JSn (a)	4.00
❏3, Sep 1975	4.00
❏4, Nov 1975	3.00
❏5, Jan 1976	3.00
❏6, Mar 1976	2.00
❏7, Apr 1976	2.00
❏8, May 1976	2.00
❏9, Jun 1976	2.00
❏10, Jul 1976	2.00
❏11, Sep 1976	1.50
❏12, Nov 1976	1.50
❏13, Feb 1977	1.50
❏14, Apr 1977	1.50
❏15, Jun 1977	1.50
❏16, Aug 1977	1.50
❏17, Oct 1977	1.50
❏18, Nov 1977	1.50

RICHARD SPECK
BONEYARD

❏1, Mar 1993	2.75

RICHIE RICH (1ST SERIES)
HARVEY

❏1, Nov 1960	3250.00
❏2, Jan 1961	950.00
❏3, Mar 1961	500.00
❏4, May 1961	375.00
❏5, Jul 1961	375.00
❏6, Sep 1961	250.00
❏7, Nov 1961	250.00
❏8, Jan 1962	250.00
❏9, Mar 1962	250.00
❏10, May 1962	175.00
❏11, Jul 1962	125.00
❏12, Sep 1962	125.00
❏13, Oct 1962	125.00
❏14, Nov 1962	125.00
❏15, Jan 1963	125.00
❏16, Mar 1963	90.00
❏17, May 1963	90.00
❏18, Jul 1963	90.00
❏19, Sep 1963	90.00
❏20, Nov 1963	90.00
❏21, Jan 1964	65.00
❏22, Mar 1964	65.00
❏23, May 1964	65.00
❏24, Jul 1964	65.00
❏25, Sep 1964	65.00
❏26, Oct 1964	65.00
❏27, Nov 1964	65.00
❏28, Dec 1964	65.00
❏29, Jan 1965	65.00
❏30, Feb 1965	65.00
❏31, Mar 1965	45.00
❏32, Apr 1965	45.00
❏33, May 1965	45.00
❏34, Jun 1965	45.00
❏35, Jul 1965	45.00
❏36, Aug 1965	45.00
❏37, Sep 1965	45.00
❏38, Oct 1965	45.00
❏39, Nov 1965	45.00
❏40, Dec 1965	45.00
❏41, Jan 1966	35.00
❏42, Feb 1966	35.00
❏43, Mar 1966	35.00
❏44, Apr 1966	35.00
❏45, May 1966	35.00
❏46, Jun 1966	35.00
❏47, Jul 1966	35.00
❏48, Aug 1966	35.00
❏49, Sep 1966	35.00
❏50, Oct 1966	25.00
❏51, Nov 1966	25.00
❏52, Dec 1966	25.00
❏53, Jan 1967	25.00
❏54, Feb 1967	25.00
❏55, Mar 1967	25.00
❏56, Apr 1967	25.00
❏57, May 1967	25.00
❏58, Jun 1967	25.00
❏59, Jul 1967	25.00
❏60, Aug 1967	25.00
❏61, Sep 1967	20.00
❏62, Oct 1967	20.00
❏63, Nov 1967	20.00
❏64, Dec 1967	20.00
❏65, Jan 1968	20.00
❏66, Feb 1968	20.00
❏67, Mar 1968	20.00
❏68, Apr 1968	20.00
❏69, May 1968	20.00
❏70, Jun 1968	20.00
❏71, Jul 1968	15.00
❏72, Aug 1968	15.00
❏73, Sep 1968	15.00
❏74, Oct 1968	15.00
❏75, Nov 1968	15.00
❏76, Dec 1968	15.00
❏77, Jan 1969	15.00
❏78, Feb 1969	15.00
❏79, Mar 1969	15.00
❏80, Apr 1969	15.00
❏81, May 1969	15.00
❏82, Jun 1969	15.00
❏83, Jul 1969	15.00
❏84, Aug 1969	15.00
❏85, Sep 1969	15.00
❏86, Oct 1969	15.00
❏87, Nov 1969	15.00
❏88, Dec 1969	15.00
❏89, Jan 1970	10.00
❏90, Feb 1970	10.00
❏91, Mar 1970	10.00
❏92, Apr 1970	10.00
❏93, May 1970	10.00
❏94, Jun 1970	10.00
❏95, Jul 1970	10.00
❏96, Aug 1970	10.00
❏97, Sep 1970	10.00
❏98, Oct 1970	10.00
❏99, Nov 1970	10.00
❏100, Dec 1970	10.00
❏101, Jan 1971	10.00
❏102, Feb 1971	10.00
❏103, Mar 1971	7.00
❏104, Apr 1971	7.00
❏105, May 1971	7.00
❏106, Jun 1971	7.00
❏107, Jul 1971	7.00
❏108, Aug 1971	7.00
❏109, Sep 1971	7.00
❏110, Oct 1971	7.00
❏111, Nov 1971	7.00
❏112, Jan 1972	7.00
❏113, Mar 1972	7.00
❏114, May 1972	7.00
❏115, Jul 1972	7.00
❏116, Sep 1972	7.00
❏117, Nov 1972	7.00
❏118, Jan 1973	7.00
❏119, Mar 1973	7.00
❏120, May 1973	7.00
❏121, Jul 1973	7.00
❏122, Sep 1973	7.00
❏123, Nov 1973	7.00
❏124, Jan 1974	7.00
❏125, Mar 1974	7.00
❏126, May 1974	7.00
❏127, Jul 1974	5.00
❏128, Sep 1974	5.00
❏129, Nov 1974	5.00
❏130, Jan 1975	5.00
❏131, Mar 1975	5.00
❏132, May 1975	5.00
❏133, Jul 1975	5.00
❏134, Sep 1975	5.00
❏135, Oct 1975	5.00
❏136, Nov 1975	5.00
❏137, Dec 1975	5.00
❏138, Jan 1976	5.00
❏139, Feb 1976	5.00
❏140, Mar 1976	5.00
❏141, Apr 1976	5.00
❏142, May 1976	5.00
❏143, Jun 1976	5.00
❏144, Jul 1976	5.00
❏145, Aug 1976	5.00
❏146, Sep 1976	5.00
❏147, Oct 1976, Casper in Hostess ad: "...and the Fog")	5.00
❏148, Nov 1976	5.00
❏149, Dec 1976	5.00
❏150, Jan 1977	5.00
❏151, Feb 1977	5.00
❏152, Mar 1977	5.00
❏153, Apr 1977	5.00
❏154, May 1977	5.00

Richie Rich Diamonds

Cover gags usually involved diamonds

©Harvey

Richie Rich Dollars & Cents

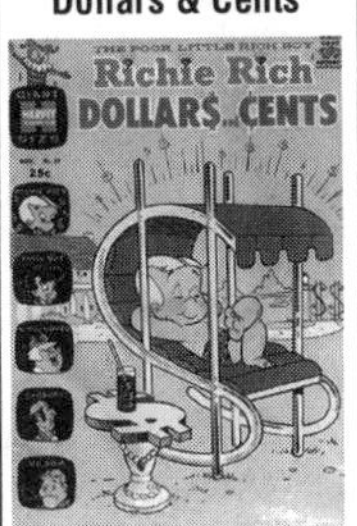

One of the earlier Richie Rich spinoffs

©Harvey

Richie Rich Fortunes

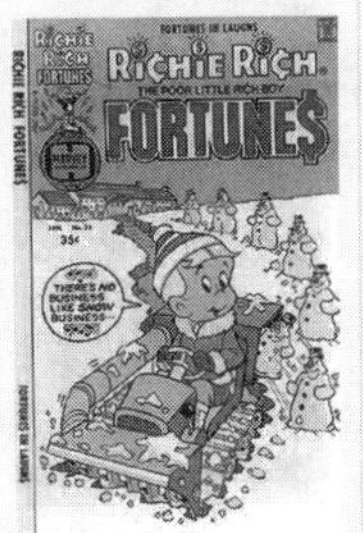

Series was bimonthly through the 1970s

©Harvey

Richie Rich Gold & Silver

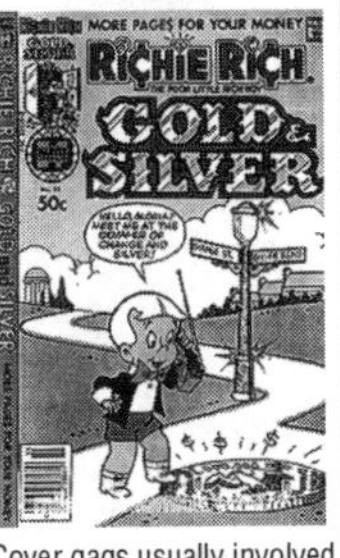

Cover gags usually involved precious metals

©Harvey

Richie Rich Jackpots

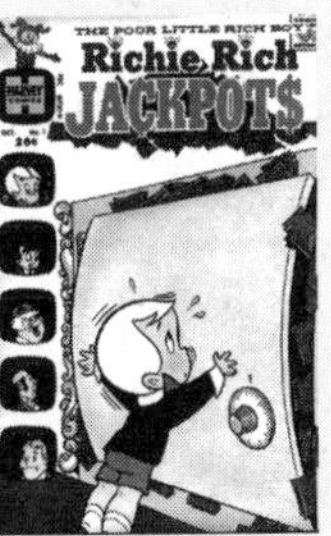

Issue #25 had Richie marrying Mayda Munny

©Harvey

	N-MINT
❑155, Jun 1977, Sad Sack in Hostess ad ("Oops")	5.00
❑156, Jul 1977	5.00
❑157, Aug 1977	5.00
❑158, Sep 1977	5.00
❑159, Oct 1977	5.00
❑160, Nov 1977	3.00
❑161, Dec 1977	3.00
❑162, Jan 1978, "Star Wars" reference on cover; Casper in Hostess ad ("Disguise")	3.00
❑163, Feb 1978	3.00
❑164, Mar 1978	3.00
❑165, Apr 1978	3.00
❑166, May 1978, Wendy in Hostess ad ("Give a Cheer")	3.00
❑167, Jun 1978	3.00
❑168, Jul 1978	3.00
❑169, Aug 1978	3.00
❑170, Sep 1978	3.00
❑171, Oct 1978	3.00
❑172, Nov 1978	3.00
❑173, Dec 1978	3.00
❑174, Jan 1979	3.00
❑175, Feb 1979	3.00
❑176, Mar 1979	3.00
❑177, Apr 1979, Hot Stuff in Hostess ad ("A Swell Party")	3.00
❑178, May 1979	3.00
❑179, Jun 1979	3.00
❑180, Jul 1979	3.00
❑181, Aug 1979	3.00
❑182, Sep 1979	3.00
❑183, Oct 1979	3.00
❑184, Nov 1979	3.00
❑185, Dec 1979	3.00
❑186, Jan 1980	3.00
❑187, Feb 1980, Holiday issue	3.00
❑188, Mar 1980	3.00
❑189, Apr 1980	3.00
❑190, May 1980	3.00
❑191, Jun 1980	3.00
❑192, Jul 1980	3.00
❑193, Aug 1980	3.00
❑194, Sep 1980	3.00
❑195, Oct 1980	3.00
❑196, Nov 1980	3.00
❑197, Dec 1980	3.00
❑198, Jan 1981	3.00
❑199, Feb 1981	3.00
❑200, Mar 1981	3.00
❑201, Apr 1981	1.75
❑202, May 1981	1.75
❑203, Jun 1981	1.75
❑204, Jul 1981	1.75
❑205, Aug 1981	1.75
❑206, Sep 1981	1.75
❑207, Oct 1981	1.75
❑208, Nov 1981	1.75
❑209, Dec 1981	1.75
❑210, Jan 1982	1.75
❑211, Feb 1982	1.75
❑212, Mar 1982	1.75
❑213, Apr 1982	1.75
❑214, May 1982	1.75

	N-MINT
❑215, Jun 1982	1.75
❑216, Jul 1982	1.75
❑217, Aug 1982	1.75
❑218, Oct 1982	1.75
❑219, Oct 1986	1.75
❑220, Nov 1986	1.75
❑221, Dec 1986	1.75
❑222, Jan 1987	1.75
❑223, Feb 1987	1.75
❑224, Mar 1987	1.75
❑225, Apr 1987	1.75
❑226, May 1987	1.75
❑227, Jun 1987	1.75
❑228, Jul 1987	1.75
❑229, Aug 1987	1.75
❑230, Sep 1987	1.75
❑231, Nov 1987	1.75
❑232 1988	1.75
❑233, Apr 1988	1.75
❑234, Jun 1988	1.75
❑235, Aug 1988	1.75
❑236 1988	1.75
❑237 1989	1.75
❑238 1989	1.75
❑239, Jul 1989	1.75
❑240, Sep 1989	1.75
❑241, Oct 1989	1.75
❑242, Dec 1989	1.75
❑243, Feb 1990	1.75
❑244, Mar 1990	1.75
❑245, Apr 1990	1.75
❑246, May 1990	1.75
❑247, Jun 1990	1.75
❑248, Jul 1990	1.75
❑249, Aug 1990	1.75
❑250, Sep 1990	1.75
❑251, Oct 1990	1.75
❑252, Nov 1990	1.75
❑253, Dec 1990	1.75
❑254, Jan 1991	1.75

RICHIE RICH (2ND SERIES)
HARVEY

	N-MINT
❑1, Mar 1991	5.00
❑2, May 1991	3.00
❑3, Jul 1991	1.50
❑4, Sep 1991	1.50
❑5, Nov 1991	1.50
❑6, Jan 1992	1.50
❑7, Mar 1992	1.50
❑8, May 1992	1.50
❑9, Jul 1992	1.50
❑10, Sep 1992	1.50
❑11, Nov 1992	1.00
❑12, Jan 1993	1.00
❑13, Mar 1993	1.00
❑14, May 1993	1.00
❑15, Jul 1993	1.00
❑16, Sep 1993	1.00
❑17, Nov 1993	1.00
❑18, Jan 1994	1.00
❑19, Feb 1994	1.00
❑20, Mar 1994	1.00
❑21, Apr 1994	1.00
❑22, May 1994	1.00
❑23, Jun 1994	1.00
❑24, Jul 1994	1.00
❑25, Aug 1994	1.00
❑26, Sep 1994	1.00
❑27, Oct 1994	1.00
❑28, Nov 1994	1.00

RICHIE RICH ADVENTURE DIGEST MAGAZINE
HARVEY

	N-MINT
❑1, May 1992	2.00
❑2, Feb 1993	1.75
❑3, Jun 1993	1.75
❑4, Oct 1993	1.75
❑5, Feb 1994	1.75
❑6, Jun 1994	1.75

RICHIE RICH AND BILLY BELLHOPS
HARVEY

	N-MINT
❑1, Oct 197	5.00

RICHIE RICH AND CADBURY
HARVEY

	N-MINT
❑1, Oct 1977	15.00
❑2, Sep 1978	10.00
❑3, Oct 1978	10.00
❑4	10.00
❑5, Jan 1979	10.00
❑6, Mar 1979	10.00
❑7, May 1979	10.00
❑8, Jul 1979	10.00
❑9, Sep 1979	10.00
❑10, Nov 1979	10.00
❑11, Jan 1980	5.00
❑12, Apr 1980	5.00
❑13, Jul 1980	4.00
❑14, Sep 1980	4.00
❑15, Nov 1980	4.00
❑16 1981	4.00
❑17 1981	4.00
❑18, Aug 1981	4.00
❑19 1981	4.00
❑20	3.00
❑21	3.00
❑22, May 1982	3.00
❑23, Jul 1982	3.00
❑24, Jul 1990	3.00
❑25, Sep 1990	3.00
❑26, Oct 1990	3.00
❑27, Nov 1990	3.00
❑28, Dec 1990	3.00
❑29, Jan 1991	3.00

RICHIE RICH & CASPER
HARVEY

	N-MINT
❑1, Aug 1974	12.00
❑2, Oct 1974	6.00
❑3, Dec 1974	4.00
❑4, Feb 1975	4.00
❑5, Apr 1975	4.00
❑6, Jun 1975	3.00
❑7, Aug 1975	3.00
❑8, Oct 1975	3.00
❑9, Dec 1975	3.00
❑10, Feb 1976	3.00
❑11, Apr 1976	2.00
❑12, Jun 1976	2.00

Other grades: Multiply price above by 5/6 for VF/NM • 2/3 for VERY FINE • 1/3 for FINE • 1/5 for VERY GOOD • 1/8 for GOOD

❑13, Aug 1976 2.00
❑14, Oct 1976 2.00
❑15, Dec 1977 2.00
❑16, Feb 1977 2.00
❑17, Apr 1977 2.00
❑18, Jun 1977 2.00
❑19, Aug 1977 2.00
❑20, Oct 1977 2.00
❑21, Dec 1977 2.00
❑22, Feb 1978 2.00
❑23, Apr 1978 2.00
❑24, Jul 1978 2.00
❑25, Sep 1978 2.00
❑26, Nov 1978 2.00
❑27 1979 2.00
❑28 1979 2.00
❑29 1979 2.00
❑30 1979 2.00
❑31 1979 2.00
❑32, Feb 1980, Has Wendy Hostess ad: "The Spell" 2.00
❑33, Apr 1980 2.00
❑34, Jun 1980 2.00
❑35, Sep 1980 2.00
❑36, Nov 1980 2.00
❑37, Dec 1980 2.00
❑38, Mar 1981 2.00
❑39 1981 2.00
❑40, Sep 1981 2.00
❑41, Nov 1981 2.00
❑42 1982 2.00
❑43 1982 2.00
❑44 1982 2.00
❑45, Sep 1982 2.00

RICHIE RICH AND CASPER IN 3-D
BLACKTHORNE

❑1/A 2.50
❑1/B, Spanish; Burger King 2.50

RICHIE RICH & DOLLAR, THE DOG
HARVEY

❑1, Sep 1977 5.00
❑2 3.00
❑3 1978 2.00
❑4 1978 2.00
❑5, Dec 1978 2.00
❑6, Feb 1979 1.50
❑7, Apr 1979 1.50
❑8, Jun 1979 1.50
❑9, Aug 1979 1.50
❑10, Oct 1979 1.50
❑11, Dec 1979 1.50
❑12 1980 1.50
❑13 1980 1.50
❑14 1980 1.50
❑15 1980 1.50
❑16, Nov 1980 1.50
❑17, Mar 1981 1.50
❑18, May 1981 1.50
❑19 1981 1.50
❑20 1.50
❑21 1.50
❑22 1982 1.50
❑23, Jun 1982 1.50
❑24, Aug 1982 1.50

RICHIE RICH AND DOT
HARVEY

❑1, Oct 1974, (c); (w); (a) 20.00

RICHIE RICH AND GLORIA
HARVEY

❑1, Sep 1977 10.00
❑2 1978 8.00
❑3, Aug 1978 8.00
❑4, Oct 1978 8.00
❑5 8.00
❑6 1979 8.00
❑7 1979 8.00
❑8 1979 8.00
❑9 1979 8.00
❑10 8.00
❑11, Nov 1979 5.00
❑12 5.00
❑13 1980 5.00
❑14 1980 5.00
❑15, Aug 1980 5.00
❑16, Oct 1980 5.00
❑17 5.00
❑18, Mar 1981 5.00
❑19, Jun 1981 5.00
❑20, Aug 1981 4.00
❑21, Oct 1981 4.00
❑22 4.00
❑23, Mar 1982 4.00
❑24 1982 4.00
❑25, Sep 1982 4.00

RICHIE RICH AND HIS GIRLFRIENDS
HARVEY

❑1, Apr 1979 10.00
❑2, Nov 1979 8.00
❑3 8.00
❑4 1980 8.00
❑5 1980 8.00
❑6, Oct 1980 8.00
❑7, Dec 1980 8.00
❑8 8.00
❑9 1981 8.00
❑10 1981 8.00
❑11 1981 5.00
❑12, Dec 1981 5.00
❑13 1982 5.00
❑14 1982 5.00
❑15 1982 5.00
❑16, Dec 1982 5.00

RICHIE RICH AND HIS MEAN COUSIN REGGIE
HARVEY

❑1, Apr 1979, (c); (w); (a) 10.00
❑2 1979, (c); (w); (a) 5.00
❑3, Jan 1980, (c); (w); (a) 5.00

RICHIE RICH & JACKIE JOKERS
HARVEY

❑1, Nov 1973 18.00
❑2, Jan 1974 10.00
❑3, Mar 1974 6.00
❑4, May 1974 6.00
❑5, Jul 1974 6.00
❑6, Sep 1974 4.00
❑7, Nov 1974 4.00
❑8, Jan 1975 4.00
❑9, Mar 1975 4.00
❑10, May 1975 4.00
❑11, Sep 1975 3.00
❑12, Nov 1975 3.00
❑13, Jan 1976 3.00
❑14, Mar 1976 3.00
❑15, May 1976 3.00
❑16, Jul 1976 3.00
❑17, Sep 1976 3.00
❑18, Nov 1976 3.00
❑19, Jan 1977, Welcome Back Kotter parody 3.00
❑20, Apr 1977 3.00
❑21, Jun 1977, Laverne and Shirley parody; Casper in Hostess ad ("Over the Rainboo") 3.00
❑22, Aug 1977 3.00
❑23, Oct 1977 3.00
❑24, Dec 1977 3.00
❑25, Feb 1978 3.00
❑26, Apr 1978 3.00
❑27, Jun 1978 3.00
❑28, Aug 1978 3.00
❑29, Oct 1978 3.00
❑30, Feb 1979 3.00
❑31, Apr 1979 2.00
❑32, Jun 1979 2.00
❑33, Aug 1979 2.00
❑34, Oct 1979 2.00
❑35, Dec 1979 2.00
❑36, Feb 1980 2.00
❑37, Apr 1980 2.00
❑38, Jul 1980 2.00
❑39, Sep 1980 2.00
❑40, Nov 1980 2.00
❑41, Jan 1981 2.00
❑42, Apr 1981 2.00
❑43, Jun 1981 2.00
❑44, Aug 1981 2.00
❑45, Nov 1981 2.00
❑46, Feb 1982 2.00
❑47, May 1982 2.00
❑48, Dec 1982 2.00

RICHIE RICH AND PROFESSOR KEENBEAN
HARVEY

❑1, Sep 1990 1.00
❑2, Nov 1990 1.00

RICHIE RICH AND THE NEW KIDS ON THE BLOCK
HARVEY

❑1, Feb 1991 1.50

RICHIE RICH AND TIMMY TIME
HARVEY

❑1, ca. 1977, (c); (w); (a) 8.00

RICHIE RICH BANK BOOKS
HARVEY

❑1, Oct 1972 24.00
❑2, Dec 1972 10.00
❑3, Feb 1973 6.00
❑4, Apr 1973 6.00
❑5, Jun 1973 6.00
❑6, Aug 1973 4.00
❑7, Oct 1973 4.00
❑8, Dec 1973 4.00
❑9, Feb 1974 4.00
❑10, Apr 1974 4.00
❑11, Jun 1974 3.00
❑12, Aug 1974 3.00
❑13, Oct 1974 3.00
❑14, Dec 1974 3.00
❑15, Feb 1975 3.00
❑16, Apr 1975 3.00
❑17, Jun 1975 3.00
❑18, Aug 1975 3.00
❑19, Oct 1975 3.00
❑20, Dec 1975 3.00
❑21, Feb 1976 2.00
❑22, Apr 1976 2.00
❑23, Jun 1976 2.00
❑24, Aug 1976 2.00
❑25, Oct 1976 2.00
❑26, Dec 1976 2.00
❑27, Feb 1977 2.00
❑28, Apr 1977 2.00
❑29, Jun 1977 2.00
❑30, Aug 1977 2.00
❑31, Sep 1977 2.00
❑32, Nov 1977 2.00
❑33, Jan 1978 2.00
❑34, Mar 1978 2.00
❑35, May 1978, Has Wendy Hostess ad: "Give a Cheer" 2.00
❑36, Aug 1978 2.00
❑37, Oct 1978 2.00
❑38, Jan 1979 2.00
❑39, Mar 1979 2.00
❑40, May 1979 2.00
❑41, Jul 1979 2.00
❑42 1979 2.00
❑43 1979 2.00
❑44, Dec 1979 2.00
❑45, Mar 1980 2.00
❑46, May 1980 2.00
❑47, Aug 1980 2.00
❑48, Oct 1980 2.00
❑49, Nov 1980 2.00
❑50 1981 2.00
❑51, Apr 1981 2.00
❑52, Jun 1981 2.00
❑53, Aug 1981 2.00
❑54, Oct 1981 2.00
❑55 1981 2.00
❑56 1982 2.00
❑57 1982 2.00
❑58, Jul 1982 2.00
❑59, Sep 1982 2.00

RICHIE RICH BEST OF THE YEARS
HARVEY

❑1, ca. 1977 10.00
❑2, ca. 1978 6.00
❑3, ca. 1979 6.00
❑4, ca. 1979 6.00
❑5, ca. 1980 6.00
❑6, ca. 1980 6.00

Other grades: Multiply price above by 5/6 for VF/NM • 2/3 for VERY FINE • 1/3 for FINE • 1/5 for VERY GOOD • 1/8 for GOOD

Richie Rich Millions

The earliest and longest-running Richie spinoff

©Harvey

Richie Rich Money World

Preteen plutocrat pitilessly shows off for poor

©Harvey

Richie Rich (Movie Adaptation)

Culkin looked like he was in his 30s in this movie

©Marvel

Richie Rich Profits

More lavish displays of wealth

©Harvey

Richie Rich Riches

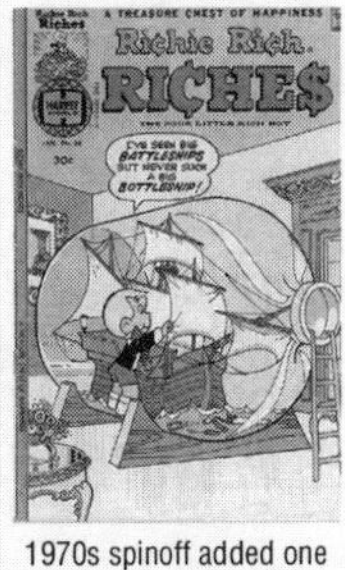

1970s spinoff added one more to the line

©Harvey

N-MINT

RICHIE RICH BIG BOOK (VOL. 2)
HARVEY

- ❑1, Nov 1992 .... 1.95
- ❑2, May 1993 .... 1.95

RICHIE RICH BIG BUCKS
HARVEY

- ❑1, Apr 1991 .... 2.00
- ❑2, Jun 1991 .... 1.25
- ❑3, Aug 1991 .... 1.25
- ❑4 1991 .... 1.25
- ❑5 1991 .... 1.25
- ❑6 1992 .... 1.25
- ❑7 1992 .... 1.25
- ❑8 1992 .... 1.25

RICHIE RICH BILLIONS
HARVEY

- ❑1, Oct 1974 .... 12.00
- ❑2 1974 .... 7.00
- ❑3 1975 .... 6.00
- ❑4 1975 .... 5.00
- ❑5 1975 .... 5.00
- ❑6 1975 .... 4.00
- ❑7 1975 .... 4.00
- ❑8 1976 .... 4.00
- ❑9 1976 .... 4.00
- ❑10 1976 .... 4.00
- ❑11 1976 .... 3.00
- ❑12, Sep 1976 .... 3.00
- ❑13 1976 .... 3.00
- ❑14 1977 .... 3.00
- ❑15 1977 .... 3.00
- ❑16 1977 .... 3.00
- ❑17 1977 .... 3.00
- ❑18 1977 .... 3.00
- ❑19, Oct 1977 .... 3.00
- ❑20 1977 .... 3.00
- ❑21 1978 .... 3.00
- ❑22 1978 .... 3.00
- ❑23, May 1978 .... 3.00
- ❑24, Jul 1978, Hot Stuff in Hostess ad ("Devilishly Good") 3.00
- ❑25, Sep 1978 .... 3.00
- ❑26, Nov 1978 .... 3.00
- ❑27, Jan 1979 .... 3.00
- ❑28, Feb 1979, Wendy in Hostess ad ("Wendy Puts Out the Fire") 3.00
- ❑29, Apr 1979 .... 3.00
- ❑30, Jun 1979 .... 3.00
- ❑31, Aug 1979 .... 2.00
- ❑32, Oct 1979 .... 2.00
- ❑33, Dec 1979 .... 2.00
- ❑34, Apr 1980 .... 2.00
- ❑35, Jun 1980 .... 2.00
- ❑36, Aug 1980 .... 2.00
- ❑37, Oct 1980 .... 2.00
- ❑38, Dec 1980, Wendy in Hostess ad ("...and the Cherry-Dactyl") 2.00
- ❑39, Feb 1981 .... 2.00
- ❑40, Apr 1981, Spooky in Hostess ad ("Pearl's Purse") 2.00
- ❑41, Jun 1981 .... 2.00
- ❑42, Aug 1981 .... 2.00
- ❑43, Oct 1981 .... 2.00
- ❑44, Dec 1981 .... 2.00

N-MINT

- ❑45 1982 .... 2.00
- ❑46, May 1982 .... 2.00
- ❑47 1982 .... 2.00
- ❑48 1982 .... 2.00

RICHIE RICH CASH
HARVEY

- ❑1, Sep 1974 .... 10.00
- ❑2, Nov 1974 .... 6.00
- ❑3, Jan 1975 .... 4.00
- ❑4, Mar 1975 .... 4.00
- ❑5, May 1975 .... 4.00
- ❑6, Jul 1975 .... 4.00
- ❑7, Sep 1975 .... 4.00
- ❑8, Nov 1975 .... 4.00
- ❑9, Jan 1976 .... 4.00
- ❑10, Mar 1976 .... 4.00
- ❑11 1976 .... 3.00
- ❑12 1976 .... 3.00
- ❑13, Aug 1976 .... 3.00
- ❑14, Oct 1976 .... 3.00
- ❑15, Dec 1976 .... 3.00
- ❑16, Feb 1977 .... 3.00
- ❑17, Apr 1977 .... 3.00
- ❑18, Jun 1977 .... 3.00
- ❑19, Aug 1977 .... 3.00
- ❑20 1977 .... 3.00
- ❑21 1977 .... 3.00
- ❑22, Mar 1978 .... 3.00
- ❑23, May 1978 .... 3.00
- ❑24, Jul 1978 .... 3.00
- ❑25, Sep 1978 .... 3.00
- ❑26, Dec 1978 .... 3.00
- ❑27 1979 .... 3.00
- ❑28 1979 .... 3.00
- ❑29 1979 .... 3.00
- ❑30 1979 .... 3.00
- ❑31, Sep 1979 .... 2.00
- ❑32 1979 .... 2.00
- ❑33, Jan 1980 .... 2.00
- ❑34, Apr 1980 .... 2.00
- ❑35, Jun 1980 .... 2.00
- ❑36, Sep 1980 .... 2.00
- ❑37, Nov 1980 .... 2.00
- ❑38, Jan 1981 .... 2.00
- ❑39, Mar 1981 .... 2.00
- ❑40, May 1981 .... 2.00
- ❑41, Jul 1981 .... 2.00
- ❑42, Sep 1981 .... 2.00
- ❑43, Nov 1981 .... 2.00
- ❑44 1982 .... 2.00
- ❑45, Apr 1982 .... 2.00
- ❑46, Jun 1982 .... 2.00
- ❑47, Aug 1982 .... 2.00

RICHIE RICH CASH MONEY
HARVEY

- ❑1, ca. 1992 .... 1.50
- ❑2, ca. 1992 .... 1.50

RICHIE RICH DIAMONDS
HARVEY

- ❑1, Aug 1972 .... 15.00
- ❑2, Oct 1972 .... 9.00
- ❑3, Dec 1972 .... 7.00
- ❑4, Feb 1973 .... 7.00

N-MINT

- ❑5, Apr 1973 .... 7.00
- ❑6, Jun 1973 .... 5.00
- ❑7, Aug 1973 .... 5.00
- ❑8, Oct 1973 .... 5.00
- ❑9, Dec 1973 .... 5.00
- ❑10, Feb 1974 .... 5.00
- ❑11, Apr 1974 .... 4.00
- ❑12, Jun 1974 .... 4.00
- ❑13, Aug 1974 .... 4.00
- ❑14, Oct 1974 .... 4.00
- ❑15, Dec 1974 .... 4.00
- ❑16, Feb 1975 .... 4.00
- ❑17, Apr 1975 .... 4.00
- ❑18, Jun 1975 .... 4.00
- ❑19, Aug 1975 .... 4.00
- ❑20, Oct 1975 .... 4.00
- ❑21, Dec 1975 .... 4.00
- ❑22, Feb 1976 .... 4.00
- ❑23, Apr 1976 .... 4.00
- ❑24, Jun 1976 .... 4.00
- ❑25, Aug 1976 .... 4.00
- ❑26, Oct 1976 .... 4.00
- ❑27, Dec 1976 .... 4.00
- ❑28, Feb 1977 .... 4.00
- ❑29, Mar 1977 .... 4.00
- ❑30, May 1977 .... 4.00
- ❑31, Jul 1977 .... 3.00
- ❑32, Sep 1977 .... 3.00
- ❑33, Nov 1977 .... 3.00
- ❑34, Jan 1978 .... 3.00
- ❑35, Mar 1978 .... 3.00
- ❑36, May 1978 .... 3.00
- ❑37, Jul 1978 .... 3.00
- ❑38, Sep 1978 .... 3.00
- ❑39, Nov 1978 .... 3.00
- ❑40, Jan 1979 .... 3.00
- ❑41, Mar 1979 .... 2.00
- ❑42, May 1979 .... 2.00
- ❑43, Jul 1979 .... 2.00
- ❑44, Sep 1979 .... 2.00
- ❑45, Oct 1979 .... 2.00
- ❑46, Feb 1980 .... 2.00
- ❑47, May 1980 .... 2.00
- ❑48, Jul 1980 .... 2.00
- ❑49, Sep 1980 .... 2.00
- ❑50, Nov 1980 .... 2.00
- ❑51, Feb 1981 .... 2.00
- ❑52, Apr 1981 .... 2.00
- ❑53, Jun 1981 .... 2.00
- ❑54, Sep 1981 .... 2.00
- ❑55, Nov 1981 .... 2.00
- ❑56, Jan 1982 .... 2.00
- ❑57, Mar 1982 .... 2.00
- ❑58, Jun 1982 .... 2.00
- ❑59, Aug 1982 .... 2.00

RICHIE RICH DIGEST MAGAZINE
HARVEY

- ❑1, Oct 1986 .... 4.00
- ❑2, Nov 1986 .... 3.00
- ❑3, Dec 1986 .... 3.00
- ❑4, Jan 1987 .... 3.00
- ❑5, Feb 1987 .... 3.00
- ❑6, Mar 1987 .... 3.00
- ❑7, Apr 1987 .... 3.00

Other grades: Multiply price above by 5/6 for VF/NM • 2/3 for VERY FINE • 1/3 for FINE • 1/5 for VERY GOOD • 1/8 for GOOD

	N-MINT
❑8	3.00
❑9	3.00
❑10	3.00
❑11	2.00
❑12	2.00
❑13	2.00
❑14	2.00
❑15	2.00
❑16	2.00
❑17	2.00
❑18	2.00
❑19	2.00
❑20, Apr 1990	2.00
❑21, Jun 1990	2.00
❑22, Aug 1990	2.00
❑23 1990	2.00
❑24 1990	2.00
❑25	2.00
❑26	2.00
❑27	2.00
❑28 1991	2.00
❑29, May 1991	2.00
❑30 1991	2.00
❑31	2.00
❑32	2.00
❑33, Feb 1992	2.00
❑34, Jun 1992	2.00
❑35, Sep 1992	2.00
❑36, Jan 1993	2.00
❑37, May 1993	2.00
❑38, Sep 1993	2.00
❑39	2.00
❑40	2.00
❑41, Jul 1994	2.00
❑42, Oct 1994	2.00

RICHIE RICH DIGEST STORIES
Harvey

	N-MINT
❑1	10.00
❑2	5.00
❑3	5.00
❑4	5.00
❑5	5.00
❑6	5.00
❑7	5.00
❑8	5.00
❑9	5.00
❑10	5.00
❑11	3.00
❑12	3.00
❑13	3.00
❑14	3.00
❑15	3.00
❑16	3.00
❑17	3.00

RICHIE RICH DIGEST WINNERS
Harvey

	N-MINT
❑1	10.00
❑2	5.00
❑3	5.00
❑4	5.00
❑5	5.00

RICHIE RICH DOLLARS & CENTS
Harvey

	N-MINT
❑1, Aug 1963	250.00
❑2	125.00
❑3	85.00
❑4	85.00
❑5	85.00
❑6	40.00
❑7	40.00
❑8	40.00
❑9	40.00
❑10	40.00
❑11	25.00
❑12	25.00
❑13	25.00
❑14, Aug 1966	25.00
❑15, Oct 1966	25.00
❑16, Dec 1966	25.00
❑17, Feb 1967	25.00
❑18, Apr 1967	25.00
❑19, Jun 1967	25.00
❑20, Oct 1967	25.00
❑21, Dec 1967	15.00
❑22, Feb 1968	15.00
❑23, Apr 1968	15.00
❑24, Jun 1968	15.00
❑25, Aug 1968	15.00
❑26, Oct 1968	15.00
❑27, Dec 1968	15.00
❑28, Feb 1969	15.00
❑29, Apr 1969	15.00
❑30, May 1969	15.00
❑31, Jul 1969	10.00
❑32, Sep 1969	10.00
❑33, Nov 1969	10.00
❑34, Jan 1970	10.00
❑35, Mar 1970	10.00
❑36, May 1970	10.00
❑37, Jul 1970	10.00
❑38, Sep 1970	10.00
❑39, Nov 1970	10.00
❑40, Jan 1971	10.00
❑41, Mar 1971	7.00
❑42, May 1971	7.00
❑43, Jul 1971	7.00
❑44, Sep 1971	7.00
❑45, Nov 1971	7.00
❑46, Jan 1972	7.00
❑47, Mar 1972	7.00
❑48, May 1972	7.00
❑49, Jun 1972	7.00
❑50, Aug 1972	7.00
❑51, Oct 1972	5.00
❑52, Dec 1972	5.00
❑53, Feb 1973	5.00
❑54, Apr 1973	5.00
❑55, Jun 1973	5.00
❑56, Aug 1973	5.00
❑57, Oct 1973	5.00
❑58, Dec 1973	5.00
❑59, Feb 1974	5.00
❑60, Apr 1974	5.00
❑61, Jun 1974	2.50
❑62, Aug 1974	2.50
❑63, Oct 1974	2.50
❑64, Dec 1974	2.50
❑65, Feb 1975	2.50
❑66, Apr 1975	2.50
❑67, Jun 1975	2.50
❑68, Aug 1975	2.50
❑69, Oct 1975	2.50
❑70, Dec 1975	2.50
❑71, Feb 1976	2.00
❑72, Apr 1976	2.00
❑73, Jun 1976	2.00
❑74, Aug 1976	2.00
❑75, Sep 1976	2.00
❑76, Nov 1976	2.00
❑77, Jan 1977	2.00
❑78, Mar 1977	2.00
❑79, May 1977	2.00
❑80, Jul 1977	2.00
❑81, Sep 1977	2.00
❑82, Oct 1977	2.00
❑83, Dec 1977	2.00
❑84, Feb 1978	2.00
❑85, Apr 1978	2.00
❑86, Jun 1978	2.00
❑87, Sep 1978	2.00
❑88, Oct 1978	2.00
❑89	2.00
❑90 1979	2.00
❑91 1979	1.25
❑92 1979	1.25
❑93 1979	1.25
❑94, Nov 1979	1.25
❑95, Feb 1980	1.25
❑96, Apr 1980	1.25
❑97, Jun 1980	1.25
❑98, Sep 1980	1.25
❑99, Nov 1980	1.25
❑100, Jan 1981	1.25
❑101, Mar 1981	1.25
❑102, May 1981	1.25
❑103 1981	1.25
❑104 1981	1.25
❑105 1981	1.25
❑106 1982	1.25
❑107, Apr 1982	1.25
❑108, Jun 1982	1.25
❑109, Aug 1982	1.25

RICHIE RICH FORTUNES
Harvey

	N-MINT
❑1, Sep 1971	25.00
❑2, Nov 1971	10.00
❑3, Jan 1972	7.00
❑4, Mar 1972	7.00
❑5, May 1972	7.00
❑6, Jul 1972	5.00
❑7, Sep 1972	5.00
❑8, Jan 1973	5.00
❑9, Mar 1973	5.00
❑10, May 1973	5.00
❑11, Jul 1973	4.00
❑12, Sep 1973	4.00
❑13, Nov 1973	4.00
❑14, Jan 1974	4.00
❑15, Mar 1974	4.00
❑16, May 1974	4.00
❑17, Jul 1974	4.00
❑18, Sep 1974	4.00
❑19, Nov 1974	4.00
❑20, Jan 1975	4.00
❑21, Mar 1975	3.00
❑22, May 1975	3.00
❑23, Jul 1975	3.00
❑24, Sep 1975	3.00
❑25, Nov 1975	3.00
❑26, Jan 1976	3.00
❑27, Mar 1976	3.00
❑28, May 1976	3.00
❑29, Jul 1976	3.00
❑30, Sep 1976	3.00
❑31, Nov 1976	3.00
❑32, Jan 1977	3.00
❑33, Mar 1977	3.00
❑34, May 1977	3.00
❑35, Jul 1977	3.00
❑36, Sep 1977	3.00
❑37, Nov 1977	3.00
❑38, Jan 1978	3.00
❑39, Mar 1978	3.00
❑40, May 1978	3.00
❑41, Jul 1978	2.00
❑42, Sep 1978	2.00
❑43, Dec 1978	2.00
❑44, Feb 1979	2.00
❑45, Apr 1979	2.00
❑46, Jun 1979	2.00
❑47, Aug 1979	2.00
❑48, Oct 1979	2.00
❑49, Dec 1979	2.00
❑50, Mar 1980	2.00
❑51, May 1980	2.00
❑52, Aug 1980	2.00
❑53, Oct 1980	2.00
❑54, Nov 1980	2.00
❑55, Mar 1981	2.00
❑56, May 1981	2.00
❑57, Jul 1981	2.00
❑58, Sep 1981	2.00
❑59, Nov 1981	2.00
❑60, Jan 1982	2.00
❑61, Mar 1982	2.00
❑62, Jun 1982	2.00
❑63, Aug 1982	2.00

RICHIE RICH GEMS
Harvey

	N-MINT
❑1, Sep 1974	10.00
❑2, Nov 1974	6.00
❑3, Jan 1975	4.00
❑4, Mar 1975	4.00
❑5, May 1975	4.00
❑6, Jul 1975	3.00
❑7, Sep 1975	3.00
❑8, Nov 1975	3.00
❑9, Jan 1976	3.00
❑10, Mar 1976	3.00
❑11, May 1976	2.00
❑12, Jul 1976	2.00
❑13, Sep 1976	2.00
❑14, Nov 1976	2.00
❑15, Jan 1977	2.00
❑16, Mar 1977	2.00
❑17, May 1977	2.00
❑18, Jul 1977	2.00
❑19, Sep 1977	2.00

Other grades: Multiply price above by 5/6 for VF/NM • 2/3 for VERY FINE • 1/3 for FINE • 1/5 for VERY GOOD • 1/8 for GOOD

Richie Rich Success Stories

Logo dropped "Stories" for much of run

©Harvey

Richie Rich Vaults of Mystery

Showcase for spooky-themed adventures

©Harvey

Richie Rich Zillionz

Once a 64-pager, page count soon dropped

©Harvey

Rima, the Jungle Girl

Intriguing jungle title by Nestor Redondo

©DC

Ripclaw (Vol. 1)

Native American hero from CyberForce

©Image

	N-MINT
❑20, Nov 1977	2.00
❑21, Jan 1978	2.00
❑22, Mar 1978	2.00
❑23 1978	2.00
❑24, Nov 1978, Has Hot Stuff Hostess ad: "Devilishly Good"	2.00
❑25, Jan 1979	2.00
❑26, Jul 1979	2.00
❑27, Sep 1979	2.00
❑28, Nov 1979	2.00
❑29, Feb 1980	2.00
❑30, May 1980	2.00
❑31, Jul 1980	2.00
❑32, Sep 1980	2.00
❑33, Nov 1980	2.00
❑34, Jan 1981	2.00
❑35, Mar 1981	2.00
❑36, May 1981	2.00
❑37, Aug 1981	2.00
❑38, Oct 1981	2.00
❑39, Dec 1981	2.00
❑40, Feb 1982	2.00
❑41, Apr 1982	2.00
❑42 1982	2.00
❑43, Sep 1982	2.00

RICHIE RICH GIANT SIZE
HARVEY

	N-MINT
❑1	2.25
❑2	2.25
❑3	2.25
❑4	2.25

RICHIE RICH GOLD & SILVER
HARVEY

	N-MINT
❑1, Sep 1975	10.00
❑2, Nov 1975	6.00
❑3, Jan 1976	4.00
❑4, Mar 1976	4.00
❑5, May 1976	4.00
❑6, Jul 1976	3.00
❑7, Aug 1976, Has Adam Awards promo panel	3.00
❑8, Oct 1976, Casper in Hostess ad ("Casper and the Fog")	3.00
❑9, Dec 1976	3.00
❑10, Feb 1977, Wendy in Hostess ad ("Which Witch is Which?")	3.00
❑11, Apr 1977	2.00
❑12, May 1977	2.00
❑13, Jul 1977	2.00
❑14, Sep 1977	2.00
❑15, Nov 1977	2.00
❑16, Jan 1978	2.00
❑17, Mar 1978	2.00
❑18, May 1978	2.00
❑19, Jul 1978	2.00
❑20, Sep 1978	2.00
❑21, Nov 1978	2.00
❑22, Jan 1979	2.00
❑23, Mar 1979	2.00
❑24, May 1979	2.00
❑25, Jul 1979	2.00
❑26, Sep 1979	2.00
❑27, Nov 1979	2.00
❑28, Feb 1980, Page count drops	2.00
❑29, Mar 1980	2.00
❑30, May 1980	2.00
❑31, Jul 1980	2.00
❑32, Sep 1980	2.00
❑33, Jan 1981	2.00
❑34, Mar 1981	2.00
❑35, May 1981, Burt Reynolds look-alike in story	2.00
❑36, Jul 1981	2.00
❑37, Sep 1981	2.00
❑38, Oct 1981	2.00
❑39, Dec 1981	2.00
❑40, May 1982	2.00
❑41, Jul 1982	2.00
❑42, Oct 1982	2.00

RICHIE RICH GOLD NUGGETS DIGEST MAGAZINE
HARVEY

	N-MINT
❑1 1990	2.50
❑2 1991	2.00
❑3, Apr 1991	2.00
❑4 1990	2.00

RICHIE RICH HOLIDAY DIGEST
HARVEY

	N-MINT
❑1	3.00
❑2	2.00
❑3	2.00
❑4	2.00
❑5	2.00

RICHIE RICH INVENTIONS
HARVEY

	N-MINT
❑1, Oct 1977	10.00
❑2, May 1978	6.00
❑3 1978	6.00
❑4 1978	6.00
❑5 1978	6.00
❑6 1979	6.00
❑7 1979	6.00
❑8 1979	6.00
❑9 1979	6.00
❑10, Sep 1979	6.00
❑11, Nov 1979	4.00
❑12, Mar 1980	4.00
❑13, May 1980	4.00
❑14 1980	4.00
❑15, Oct 1980	4.00
❑16, Dec 1980	4.00
❑17, Feb 1981	4.00
❑18, Apr 1981, Spooky in Hostess ad ("Pearl's Purse")	4.00
❑19, Jun 1981	4.00
❑20, Aug 1981	3.00
❑21, Oct 1981	3.00
❑22, Feb 1981	3.00
❑23, Apr 1982	3.00
❑24, Jun 1982	3.00
❑25, Aug 1982	3.00
❑26, Oct 1982	3.00

RICHIE RICH JACKPOTS
HARVEY

	N-MINT
❑1, Oct 1972	30.00
❑2, Dec 1972	12.00
❑3, Feb 1973	8.00
❑4, Apr 1973	8.00
❑5, Jun 1973	8.00
❑6, Aug 1973	6.00
❑7, Oct 1973	6.00
❑8, Dec 1973	6.00
❑9, Feb 1974	4.00
❑10, Apr 1974	4.00
❑11, Jun 1974	4.00
❑12, Aug 1974	4.00
❑13, Oct 1974	4.00
❑14, Dec 1974	4.00
❑15, Feb 1975	4.00
❑16, Apr 1975	4.00
❑17, Jun 1975	4.00
❑18, Aug 1975	4.00
❑19, Oct 1975	4.00
❑20, Dec 1975, Richie, Mayda legally married; Casper in Hostess ad (untitled, fights the No-Goodniks)	4.00
❑21, Feb 1976	3.00
❑22, Apr 1976	3.00
❑23, Jun 1976	3.00
❑24, Aug 1976	3.00
❑25, Oct 1976	3.00
❑26, Dec 1976	3.00
❑27, Feb 1977	3.00
❑28, Apr 1977	3.00
❑29, Jun 1977, Casper in Hostess ad ("Over the Rainboo")	3.00
❑30, Aug 1977	3.00
❑31, Oct 1977	3.00
❑32, Dec 1977	3.00
❑33, Feb 1978	3.00
❑34, Apr 1978	3.00
❑35, Jun 1978	3.00
❑36, Aug 1978	3.00
❑37, Oct 1978	3.00
❑38, Dec 1978	3.00
❑39, Feb 1979	3.00
❑40, Apr 1979	3.00
❑41, Jun 1979, Casper in Hostess ad ("Happy Boo-Day")	2.00
❑42, Aug 1979	2.00
❑43, Oct 1979	2.00
❑44, Dec 1980	2.00
❑45, Apr 1980	2.00
❑46, Jun 1980	2.00
❑47, Aug 1980	2.00
❑48, Oct 1980	2.00
❑49, Dec 1980, Casper in Hostess ad ("...Meets the Golden Ghost")	2.00
❑50, Feb 1981, Spooky in Hostess ad ("One Big Boo After Another")	2.00
❑51, Apr 1981, Spooky in Hostess ad ("Pearl's Purse")	2.00
❑52, Jun 1981, V: Leroy Blemish. Wendy in Hostess ad ("Catches the Good Taste Bandit")	2.00
❑53, Aug 1981	2.00
❑54, Oct 1981, Casper in Hostess ad ("Witches with a Heart of Gold"]	2.00
❑55 1982	2.00
❑56, Apr 1982	2.00
❑57, Jun 1982	2.00
❑58, Aug 1982	2.00

N-MINT

RICHIE RICH MILLION DOLLAR DIGEST (VOL. 1)
HARVEY

❑1, Oct 1980 10.00
❑2, Jan 1981 8.00
❑3, Apr 1981 6.00
❑4, Jul 1981 6.00
❑5, Nov 1981 6.00
❑6, Jan 1982 6.00
❑7, Mar 1982 5.00
❑8, Jun 1982 5.00
❑9, Aug 1982 5.00
❑10, Oct 1982 5.00

RICHIE RICH MILLION DOLLAR DIGEST (VOL. 2)
HARVEY

❑1, Nov 1986 5.00
❑2, Jan 1987 3.00
❑3, Mar 1987 3.00
❑4, May 1987 3.00
❑5, Jul 1987 3.00
❑6, Sep 1987 3.00
❑7, Nov 1987 3.00
❑8 1988 3.00
❑9 1988 3.00
❑10 1988 3.00
❑11, Oct 1988 2.00
❑12, Dec 1988 2.00
❑13, Aug 1989 2.00
❑14 1989 2.00
❑15 1990 2.00
❑16 1990 2.00
❑17 1990 2.00
❑18 1990 2.00
❑19 1990 2.00
❑20, Mar 1991 2.00
❑21 1991 2.00
❑22, Aug 1991 2.00
❑23, Oct 1991 2.00
❑24, Dec 1991 2.00
❑25, Mar 1992 2.00
❑26, Jul 1992 2.00
❑27, Nov 1992 2.00
❑28, Mar 1993 2.00
❑29, Jul 1993 2.00
❑30, Nov 1993 2.00
❑31, Mar 1994 2.00
❑32, May 1994 2.00
❑33, Aug 1994 2.00
❑34, Nov 1994 2.00

RICHIE RICH MILLIONS
HARVEY

❑1, Sep 1961 200.00
❑2, Sep 1962 100.00
❑3, Dec 1962 100.00
❑4, Mar 1963 75.00
❑5, Jun 1963 75.00
❑6, Sep 1963 75.00
❑7, Dec 1963 75.00
❑8, Mar 1964 75.00
❑9, Jun 1964 75.00
❑10, Sep 1964 75.00
❑11, Dec 1964 40.00
❑12, Mar 1965 40.00
❑13, Jun 1965 40.00
❑14, Sep 1965 40.00
❑15, Dec 1965 40.00
❑16, Mar 1966, V: Steve Rock. Story with Steve Rock, a James Bond send-up; Rocky and Bullwinkle in Cheerios ad 40.00
❑17, May 1966 40.00
❑18, Jul 1966 40.00
❑19, Sep 1966, V: Prof. Von Blitz. Rocky and Bullwinkle in Cheerios ad 40.00
❑20, Oct 1966 40.00
❑21, Jan 1967 25.00
❑22, Mar 1967 25.00
❑23, Jun 1967 25.00
❑24, Aug 1967 25.00
❑25, Oct 1967 25.00
❑26, Dec 1967 25.00
❑27, Feb 1968 25.00
❑28, Apr 1968 25.00
❑29, Jun 1968 25.00
❑30, Aug 1968 25.00

N-MINT

❑31, Oct 1968 15.00
❑32, Dec 1968, UFO cover 15.00
❑33, Feb 1969 15.00
❑34, Apr 1969 15.00
❑35, May 1969 15.00
❑36, Jul 1969 15.00
❑37, Sep 1969 15.00
❑38, Nov 1969 15.00
❑39, Jan 1970 15.00
❑40, Mar 1970 15.00
❑41, May 1970 15.00
❑42, Jul 1970 15.00
❑43, Sep 1970 10.00
❑44, Nov 1970 10.00
❑45, Jan 1971 10.00
❑46, Mar 1971 10.00
❑47, May 1971 10.00
❑48, Jul 1971 10.00
❑49, Sep 1971 10.00
❑50, Nov 1971 10.00
❑51, Jan 1972 7.00
❑52, Mar 1972 7.00
❑53, May 1972 7.00
❑54, Jul 1972 7.00
❑55, Sep 1972 7.00
❑56, Nov 1972 7.00
❑57, Jan 1973 7.00
❑58, Mar 1973 7.00
❑59, May 1973 7.00
❑60, Jul 1973 7.00
❑61, Sep 1973 7.00
❑62, Nov 1973 5.00
❑63, Jan 1974 5.00
❑64, Mar 1974 5.00
❑65, May 1974 5.00
❑66, Jul 1974 5.00
❑67, Sep 1974 5.00
❑68, Nov 1974 5.00
❑69, Jan 1975 5.00
❑70, Mar 1975 5.00
❑71, May 1975, Robot attacks 5.00
❑72, Jul 1975 5.00
❑73, Sep 1975 5.00
❑74, Nov 1975 5.00
❑75, Jan 1976, Winter cover 5.00
❑76, Mar 1976 5.00
❑77, May 1976 5.00
❑78, Jul 1976 5.00
❑79, Sep 1976 5.00
❑80, Nov 1976 5.00
❑81, Jan 1977 2.50
❑82, Mar 1977, Casper in Hostess ad ("Haunted House for Sale") 2.50
❑83, May 1977 2.50
❑84, Jul 1977 2.50
❑85, Sep 1977 2.50
❑86, Nov 1977 2.50
❑87, Jan 1978 2.50
❑88, Mar 1978 2.50
❑89, May 1978 2.50
❑90, Aug 1978 2.50
❑91, Oct 1978 2.00
❑92, Dec 1978 2.00
❑93, Feb 1979 2.00
❑94, Apr 1979, V: Leroy Blemish. Hot Stuff in Hostess ad ("A Swell Party"); Richie in Grit ad ("Father Knows Best") 2.00
❑95, Jun 1979, Casper in Hostess ad ("Happy Boo-Day"); Richie in Grit ad ("Father Knows Best") 2.00
❑96, Aug 1979 2.00
❑97, Oct 1979 2.00
❑98, Dec 1979 2.00
❑99, Mar 1980 2.00
❑100, May 1980, 100th Issue Spectacular 2.00
❑101, Aug 1980 1.50
❑102, Oct 1980 1.50
❑103, Dec 1981 1.50
❑104, Feb 1981 1.50
❑105, Apr 1981 1.50
❑106, Jun 1981 1.50
❑107, Aug 1981 1.50
❑108, Oct 1981 1.50
❑109 1981 1.50
❑110, Apr 1982 1.50

N-MINT

❑111, Jun 1982 1.00
❑112, Aug 1982, Accordion cover 1.00
❑113, Oct 1982 1.00

RICHIE RICH MONEY WORLD
HARVEY

❑1, Sep 1972 85.00
❑2, Nov 1972 35.00
❑3, Jan 1973 25.00
❑4, Mar 1973 20.00
❑5, May 1973 20.00
❑6, Jul 1973 15.00
❑7, Sep 1973 15.00
❑8, Nov 1973 15.00
❑9, Jan 1974 15.00
❑10, Mar 1974 15.00
❑11, May 1974 10.00
❑12, Jul 1974 10.00
❑13, Sep 1974 10.00
❑14, Nov 1974 10.00
❑15, Jan 1975 10.00
❑16, Mar 1975 10.00
❑17, May 1975 10.00
❑18, Jul 1975 10.00
❑19, Sep 1975 7.00
❑20, Nov 1975 7.00
❑21, Jan 1976 7.00
❑22, Mar 1976 7.00
❑23, May 1976 7.00
❑24, Jul 1976 7.00
❑25, Sep 1976 7.00
❑26, Nov 1976 7.00
❑27, Jan 1977 7.00
❑28, Mar 1977 7.00
❑29, May 1977 5.00
❑30, Jul 1977 5.00
❑31, Sep 1977 5.00
❑32, Nov 1977 5.00
❑33, Jan 1978 5.00
❑34, Mar 1978 5.00
❑35, May 1978 5.00
❑36, Aug 1978 5.00
❑37, Oct 1978 5.00
❑38, Jan 1979 5.00
❑39, Mar 1979 3.00
❑40, Jun 1979 3.00
❑41, Aug 1979 3.00
❑42, Sep 1979 3.00
❑43, Nov 1979 3.00
❑44, Jan 1980 3.00
❑45, Apr 1980 3.00
❑46, Jun 1980 3.00
❑47, Sep 1980 3.00
❑48, Oct 1980 3.00
❑49, Dec 1980 3.00
❑50, Feb 1981 3.00
❑51, Apr 1981 3.00
❑52, Jun 1981 3.00
❑53, Aug 1981 3.00
❑54, Oct 1981 3.00
❑55, Mar 1982 3.00
❑56 1982 3.00
❑57 1982 3.00
❑58 1982 3.00
❑59, Sep 1982 3.00

RICHIE RICH MONEY WORLD DIGEST
HARVEY

❑1, Apr 1991 2.00
❑2, Dec 1991 1.75
❑3, Apr 1992 1.75
❑4, Aug 1992 1.75
❑5, Dec 1992 1.75
❑6, Apr 1993 1.75
❑7, Aug 1993 1.75
❑8, Dec 1993 1.75

RICHIE RICH (MOVIE ADAPTATION)
MARVEL

❑1, Feb 1995 2.95

RICHIE RICH PROFITS
HARVEY

❑1, Oct 1974, A: Richie Rich 25.00
❑2, Dec 1974 15.00
❑3, Feb 1975 15.00
❑4, Apr 1975 (w); 10.00
❑5, Jun 1975 (w); 10.00
❑6, Aug 1975 (w); 10.00

Rip Hunter...Time Master

Rip and crew solve mysteries in time

©DC

Rip Off Comix

A classic salute to everything 1970s

©Rip Off

Rising Stars

Babylon 5 creator does super-heroes

©Image

Robin (Mini-Series)

Third Robin gets first Robin mini-series

©DC

Robin

Sidekick finally gets ongoing series

©DC

	N-MINT
❑7, Oct 1975 (w);	10.00
❑8, Dec 1975 (w);	10.00
❑9, Feb 1976 (w);	10.00
❑10, Apr 1976 (w);	10.00
❑11, Jun 1976 (w);	8.00
❑12, Aug 1976 (w);	8.00
❑13, Oct 1976 (w);	8.00
❑14, Dec 1976 (w);	8.00
❑15, Feb 1977 (w);	8.00
❑16, Apr 1977 (w);	8.00
❑17, Jun 1977 (w);	8.00
❑18, Aug 1977 (w);	8.00
❑19, Oct 1977 (w);	8.00
❑20, Dec 1977 (w);	6.00
❑21, Feb 1978 (w);	6.00
❑22, Apr 1978 (w);	6.00
❑23, Jun 1978 (w);	6.00
❑24, Aug 1978 (w);	6.00
❑25, Oct 1978 (w);	6.00
❑26, Jan 1979 (w);	6.00
❑27 1979 (w);	6.00
❑28 1979 (w);	6.00
❑29 1979 (w);	6.00
❑30 1979 (w);	5.00
❑31, Oct 1979	5.00
❑32, Dec 1979	5.00
❑33, Feb 1980	5.00
❑34, Apr 1980	5.00
❑35, Jul 1980	5.00
❑36, Sep 1980	5.00
❑37, Nov 1980	5.00
❑38, Jan 1981	5.00
❑39, Mar 1981	5.00
❑40, May 1981, Sad Sack in Hostess ad ("Down and Out")	4.00
❑41, Jul 1981	4.00
❑42, Sep 1981	4.00
❑43, Nov 1981	4.00
❑44, Feb 1982	4.00
❑45, Apr 1982	4.00
❑46, Jun 1982	4.00
❑47, Sep 1982	4.00

RICHIE RICH RELICS

HARVEY

	N-MINT
❑1, Jan 1988	2.50
❑2, May 1988	2.50
❑3, Sep 1988	2.50
❑4, Jan 1989	2.50

RICHIE RICH RICHES

HARVEY

	N-MINT
❑1, Jul 1972	28.00
❑2, Sep 1972	13.00
❑3, Nov 1972	8.00
❑4, Jan 1973	8.00
❑5, Mar 1973	8.00
❑6, May 1973	5.00
❑7, Jul 1973	5.00
❑8, Sep 1973	5.00
❑9, Nov 1973	5.00
❑10, Jan 1974	5.00
❑11, Mar 1974	4.00
❑12, May 1974	4.00
❑13, Jul 1974	4.00
❑14, Sep 1974	4.00
❑15, Nov 1974	4.00
❑16, Jan 1975	4.00
❑17, Mar 1975	4.00
❑18, May 1975	4.00
❑19, Jul 1975	4.00
❑20, Sep 1975	4.00
❑21, Nov 1975	3.00
❑22, Jan 1976	3.00
❑23, Mar 1976	3.00
❑24, May 1976	3.00
❑25, Jul 1976	3.00
❑26, Sep 1976	3.00
❑27, Nov 1976	3.00
❑28, Jan 1977, Casper in Hostess ad ("The Boohemians")	3.00
❑29, Mar 1977	3.00
❑30, May 1977	3.00
❑31, Jul 1977	2.00
❑32, Sep 1977	2.00
❑33, Nov 1977	2.00
❑34, Jan 1978	2.00
❑35, Mar 1978	2.00
❑36, May 1978	2.00
❑37, Jul 1978	2.00
❑38, Oct 1978	2.00
❑39, Dec 1978	2.00
❑40, Feb 1979	2.00
❑41, Apr 1979	2.00
❑42, Jun 1979	2.00
❑43, Aug 1979	2.00
❑44, Oct 1979	2.00
❑45, Dec 1979	2.00
❑46, Feb 1980	2.00
❑47, May 1980	2.00
❑48, Aug 1980	2.00
❑49, Oct 1980	2.00
❑50, Dec 1980	2.00
❑51, Feb 1981	2.00
❑52, Apr 1981	2.00
❑53, Jun 1981	2.00
❑54, Aug 1981	2.00
❑55, Oct 1981	2.00
❑56, Dec 1981	2.00
❑57, Mar 1982	2.00
❑58, Jun 1982	2.00
❑59, Aug 1982	2.00

RICHIE RICH SUCCESS STORIES

HARVEY

	N-MINT
❑1, Nov 1964	200.00
❑2, Feb 1965	100.00
❑3, May 1965	75.00
❑4, Aug 1965	75.00
❑5, Nov 1965	50.00
❑6, Feb 1966	50.00
❑7, May 1966	50.00
❑8, Jul 1966	50.00
❑9, Aug 1966	50.00
❑10, Oct 1966	50.00
❑11, Dec 1966	25.00
❑12, Feb 1967	25.00
❑13, Apr 1967	25.00
❑14, Jun 1967	25.00
❑15, Aug 1967	25.00
❑16, Nov 1967	25.00
❑17, Jan 1968	25.00
❑18, Mar 1968	25.00
❑19, May 1968	25.00
❑20, Jul 1968	25.00
❑21, Sep 1968	20.00
❑22, Nov 1968	20.00
❑23, Jan 1969	20.00
❑24, Mar 1969	20.00
❑25, Apr 1969	20.00
❑26, Jun 1969	15.00
❑27, Aug 1969	15.00
❑28, Oct 1969	15.00
❑29, Dec 1969	15.00
❑30, Feb 1970	15.00
❑31, Apr 1970	10.00
❑32, Jun 1970	10.00
❑33, Aug 1970	10.00
❑34, Oct 1970	10.00
❑35, Dec 1970	10.00
❑36, Feb 1971	10.00
❑37, Apr 1971	10.00
❑38, Jun 1971	10.00
❑39, Aug 1971	10.00
❑40, Oct 1971	10.00
❑41, Dec 1971	7.00
❑42, Feb 1972	7.00
❑43, Apr 1972	7.00
❑44, Jun 1972	7.00
❑45, Aug 1972	7.00
❑46, Oct 1972	7.00
❑47, Dec 1972	7.00
❑48, Feb 1973	7.00
❑49, Apr 1973	7.00
❑50, Jun 1973	7.00
❑51, Aug 1973	7.00
❑52, Oct 1973	7.00
❑53, Dec 1973	7.00
❑54, Feb 1974	7.00
❑55, Apr 1974	7.00
❑56, Jun 1974	7.00
❑57, Aug 1974	7.00
❑58, Oct 1974	7.00
❑59, Dec 1974	7.00
❑60, Feb 1975	7.00
❑61, Apr 1975	7.00
❑62, Jun 1975	7.00
❑63, Aug 1975	7.00
❑64, Oct 1975	7.00
❑65, Dec 1975	7.00
❑66, Feb 1976	7.00
❑67, Apr 1976	7.00
❑68, Jun 1976	7.00
❑69, Aug 1976	7.00
❑70, Oct 1976	7.00
❑71, Dec 1976	5.00
❑72, Feb 1977	5.00
❑73, Mar 1977	5.00
❑74, May 1977	5.00
❑75, Jul 1977	5.00
❑76, Sep 1977	5.00
❑77, Oct 1977	5.00
❑78, Dec 1977	5.00
❑79, Feb 1978	5.00
❑80, Apr 1978	5.00

Other grades: Multiply price above by 5/6 for VF/NM • 2/3 for VERY FINE • 1/3 for FINE • 1/5 for VERY GOOD • 1/8 for GOOD

❑81, Jun 1978 .... 5.00
❑82, Aug 1978 .... 5.00
❑83, Oct 1978 .... 5.00
❑84, Dec 1978 .... 5.00
❑85, Jan 1979 .... 5.00
❑86, Mar 1979 .... 5.00
❑87, May 1979 .... 5.00
❑88, Jul 1979 .... 5.00
❑89, Sep 1979 .... 5.00
❑90, Nov 1979, Wendy in Hostess ad ("Wendy Has a Visitor") 3.00
❑91, Jan 1980, Casper in Hostess ad ("Casper and the Ghnats") 3.00
❑92, Apr 1980, Casper in Hostess ad ("Casper Ends the Boo Hoos") 3.00
❑93, Jun 1980, Casper in Hostess ad ("Casper Plays Hide and Seek") 3.00
❑94, Sep 1980, Hot Stuff in Hostess ad ("Playing Cupid") 3.00
❑95, Nov 1980, Hot Stuff in Hostess ad ("Shut My Mouth!") 3.00
❑96, Jan 1981, Spooky in Hostess ad ("One Big Boo After Another") 3.00
❑97, Mar 1981, Hot Stuff in Hostess ad ("Too Much Mush!") 3.00
❑98, May 1981 .... 3.00
❑99, Jul 1981 .... 3.00
❑100, Sep 1981 .... 3.00
❑101, Dec 1981 .... 2.00
❑102, Feb 1982 .... 2.00
❑103, May 1982 .... 2.00
❑104, Jul 1982 .... 2.00
❑105, Sep 1982 .... 2.00

RICHIE RICH VACATION DIGEST
HARVEY

❑1992, Oct 1992, #1 on cover 1.75
❑1993, Oct 1993, #1 on cover 1.75

RICHIE RICH VACATIONS DIGEST
HARVEY

❑1, Oct 1980 .... 10.00
❑2, Dec 1980 .... 5.00
❑3, Feb 1981 .... 5.00
❑4, Apr 1981 .... 5.00
❑5, Jun 1981 .... 5.00
❑6, Aug 1981 .... 5.00
❑7, Oct 1981 .... 5.00
❑8, Dec 1981 .... 5.00

RICHIE RICH VAULTS OF MYSTERY
HARVEY

❑1, Nov 1974, Cover says "Vault" 10.00
❑2, Jan 1975, Cover says "Vault" 7.00
❑3, Mar 1975, Cover says "Vault" 5.00
❑4, May 1975, Cover says "Vault" 5.00
❑5, Jul 1975, Cover says "Vault" 5.00
❑6, Sep 1975, Cover title changes to "Vaults" 4.00
❑7, Nov 1975 .... 4.00
❑8, Jan 1976 .... 4.00
❑9, Mar 1976 .... 4.00
❑10, May 1976 .... 4.00
❑11, Jul 1976 .... 3.00
❑12, Sep 1976 .... 3.00
❑13, Nov 1976 .... 3.00
❑14, Jan 1977 .... 3.00
❑15, Mar 1977, Sad Sack in Hostess ad ("Sad vs. Merri") 3.00
❑16, May 1977 .... 3.00
❑17, Jul 1977 .... 3.00
❑18, Sep 1977 .... 3.00
❑19, Nov 1977 .... 3.00
❑20, Jan 1978 .... 3.00
❑21, Mar 1978 .... 2.00
❑22, May 1978 .... 2.00
❑23, Jul 1978 .... 2.00
❑24, Sep 1978 .... 2.00
❑25, Nov 1978 .... 2.00
❑26, Jan 1979 .... 2.00
❑27, Mar 1979 .... 2.00
❑28, May 1979 .... 2.00
❑29, Jul 1979, Ghosts 2.00
❑30, Sep 1979 .... 2.00
❑31, Nov 1979 .... 2.00
❑32, Jan 1980, Casper in Hostess ad ("Casper and the Ghnats") 2.00
❑33, Apr 1980, Casper in Hostess ad ("Casper Ends the Boo Hoos") 2.00
❑34, Jun 1980 .... 2.00
❑35, Aug 1980, Casper in Hostess ad ("Boo-tiful Endings") 2.00
❑36, Oct 1980, Hot Stuff in Hostess ad ("Mad, Mad, Mad World") 2.00
❑37, Dec 1980, Wendy in Hostess ad ("Cherry-Dactyl") 2.00
❑38, Feb 1981 .... 2.00
❑39, Apr 1981 .... 2.00
❑40, Jun 1981 .... 2.00
❑41, Aug 1981 .... 2.00
❑42, Oct 1981 .... 2.00
❑43, Dec 1981 .... 2.00
❑44, Feb 1982 .... 2.00
❑45, Apr 1982, Irona 2.00
❑46, Jun 1982 .... 2.00
❑47, Sep 1982 .... 2.00

RICHIE RICH ZILLIONZ
HARVEY

❑1, Oct 1976 .... 12.00
❑2, Jan 1977 .... 6.00
❑3, Apr 1977 .... 6.00
❑4, Jun 1977 .... 6.00
❑5, Aug 1977 .... 4.00
❑6, Oct 1977 .... 3.00
❑7, Dec 1977 .... 3.00
❑8, Feb 1978 .... 3.00
❑9, Apr 1978 .... 3.00
❑10, Jul 1978, Wendy in Hostess ad ("The Smart Wand") 3.00
❑11, Sep 1978 .... 2.00
❑12, Nov 1978 .... 2.00
❑13, Jan 1979 .... 2.00
❑14, Mar 1979 .... 2.00
❑15, May 1979 .... 2.00
❑16, Jul 1979 .... 2.00
❑17, Sep 1979 .... 2.00
❑18, Nov 1979, Sad Sack in Hostess ad ("What a Trip") 2.00
❑19, Dec 1979, Casper in Hostess ad ("Ends the Boo Hoos") 2.00
❑20, Mar 1980 .... 2.00
❑21, May 1980, Has Hostess ad (Wendy in "A Little Magic") 2.00
❑22, Jul 1980 .... 2.00
❑23, Oct 1980, Has Hostess ad (Hot Stuff in "Mad Mad, Mad World") 2.00
❑24, Nov 1980, Hot Stuff in Hostess ad ("Shut My Mouth!") 2.00
❑25 1981 .... 2.00
❑26 1981 .... 2.00
❑27 1981 .... 2.00
❑28, Sep 1981 .... 2.00
❑29, Nov 1981 .... 2.00
❑30, Jan 1982 .... 2.00
❑31, Mar 1982 .... 2.00
❑32, Jun 1982 .... 2.00
❑33, Sep 1982 .... 2.00

RIDE
IMAGE

❑1, Aug 2004 .... 2.95
❑2 2004 .... 2.95

RIDE, THE: 2 FOR THE ROAD ONE SHOT
IMAGE

❑1, Oct 2005, b&w 2.95

RIFLEMAN
DELL

❑2, Jan 1960 .... 85.00
❑3, Apr 1960 .... 85.00
❑4, Jul 1960 .... 70.00
❑5, Oct 1960 .... 70.00
❑6, Jan 1961 .... 70.00
❑7, Jun 1961 .... 70.00
❑8, Sep 1961 .... 70.00
❑9, Dec 1961 .... 70.00
❑10, Jan 1962 .... 70.00
❑11, Apr 1962 .... 55.00
❑12, Jul 1962 .... 55.00
❑13, Nov 1962 .... 55.00
❑14, Feb 1963 .... 55.00
❑15, May 1963 .... 55.00
❑16, Aug 1963 .... 55.00
❑17, Nov 1963 .... 55.00
❑18, Apr 1964 .... 55.00
❑19, Jul 1964 .... 55.00
❑20, Oct 1964 .... 55.00

RIMA, THE JUNGLE GIRL
DC

❑1, May 1974, O: Rima, the Jungle Girl 13.00
❑2, Jul 1974, JKu (c); NR, JKu, AN (a); O: Rima, the Jungle Girl 7.00
❑3, Sep 1974, JKu (c); NR, JKu, AN (a); O: Rima, the Jungle Girl 7.00
❑4, Nov 1974, O: Rima, the Jungle Girl 7.00
❑5, Jan 1975 .... 7.00
❑6, Mar 1975 .... 7.00
❑7, May 1975 .... 7.00

RIME OF THE ANCIENT MARINER (TOME)
TOME

❑1, b&w 3.95

RIMSHOT
RIP OFF

❑1, Jun 1990, b&w 2.00
❑2, Feb 1991, b&w 2.00
❑3, Jul 1991, b&w 2.50

RING
DARK HORSE

❑1, ca. 2003 .... 14.95
❑2, ca. 2004 .... 12.95

RING OF ROSES
DARK HORSE

❑1, b&w 2.50
❑2, b&w 2.50
❑3, b&w 2.50
❑4, b&w 2.50

RING OF THE NIBELUNG
DC

❑1, ca. 1989 .... 4.95
❑2 .... 4.95
❑3 .... 4.95
❑4 .... 4.95

RING OF THE NIBELUNG (DARK HORSE)
DARK HORSE

❑1, Feb 2000 .... 2.95
❑2, Mar 2000 .... 2.95
❑3, Apr 2000 .... 2.95
❑4, May 2000 .... 2.95

RING OF THE NIBELUNG (VOL. 2)
DARK HORSE

❑1, Aug 2000 .... 2.95
❑2, Sep 2000 .... 2.95
❑3, Oct 2000 .... 2.99

RING OF THE NIBELUNG (VOL. 3)
DARK HORSE

❑1, Dec 2000 .... 2.99
❑2, Jan 2001 .... 2.99
❑3, Feb 2001 .... 2.99

RING OF THE NIBELUNG (VOL. 4)
DARK HORSE

❑1, Jun 2001 .... 2.99
❑2, Jul 2001 .... 2.99
❑3, Aug 2001 .... 2.99
❑4, Sep 2001 .... 2.99

RINGO KID
MARVEL

❑1, Jan 1970, SL (w); AW (a); Reprint from Ringo Kid Western 20.00
❑2, Mar 1970, JSe (a) 8.00
❑3, May 1970 .... 5.00
❑4, Jul 1970 .... 5.00
❑5, Sep 1970 .... 5.00
❑6, Nov 1970 .... 5.00
❑7, Jan 1971 .... 5.00
❑8, Mar 1971 .... 5.00
❑9, May 1971 .... 5.00
❑10, Jul 1971 .... 5.00
❑11, Sep 1971 .... 4.00
❑12, Nov 1971 .... 10.00
❑13, Apr 1972 .... 4.00
❑14, May 1972 .... 4.00
❑15, Jul 1972 .... 4.00
❑16, Sep 1972 .... 4.00
❑17, Nov 1972 .... 4.00
❑18, Jan 1972, GK (c) 4.00
❑19, Mar 1973, SL (w) 4.00
❑20, May 1973 .... 4.00
❑21, Jul 1973 .... 4.00
❑22, Sep 1973 .... 4.00
❑23, Nov 1973 .... 4.00

Robin II

Second Robin mini has Joker on the loose
©DC

Robin Hood (Dell)

More adventures with the merry men
©Dell

Robocop (Marvel)

Marvel continues the movie's adventures
©Marvel

Robotech

Beverly Hills 90210 with fighter jets in this series
©Antarctic

Robotech Masters

Early series based on big robot warriors
©Comico

N-MINT

❑24, Nov 1975 .... 4.00
❑25, Jan 1976 .... 4.00
❑26, Mar 1976 .... 4.00
❑27, May 1976 .... 4.00
❑27/30 cent, May 1976, 30 cent regional price variant 20.00
❑28, Jul 1976 .... 4.00
❑28/30 cent, Jul 1976, 30 cent regional price variant 20.00
❑29, Sep 1976 .... 4.00
❑30, Nov 1976 .... 4.00

RIN TIN TIN & RUSTY
GOLD KEY

❑1, Nov 1963 .... 50.00

RIO AT BAY
DARK HORSE

❑1, Aug 1992 .... 2.95
❑2, Aug 1992 .... 2.95

RIO CONCHOS
GOLD KEY

❑1, Adapts film 22.00

RIO GRAPHIC NOVEL
COMICO

❑1, May 1987 .... 8.95

RIO KID
ETERNITY

❑1, b&w 2.50
❑2, b&w 2.50
❑3, b&w 2.50

RION 2990
RION

❑1, b&w 1.50
❑2, b&w 1.50
❑3 .... 1.50
❑4 .... 1.50

RIO RIDES AGAIN
MARVEL

❑1 .... 9.95

RIOT, ACT 1
VIZ

❑1, Oct 1995 .... 2.75
❑2, Nov 1995 .... 2.75
❑3, Dec 1995 .... 2.75
❑4, Jan 1996 .... 2.95
❑5, Feb 1996 .... 2.95
❑6, Mar 1996 .... 2.95

RIOT, ACT 2
VIZ

❑1, Apr 1996 .... 2.95
❑2, May 1996 .... 2.95
❑3, Jun 1996 .... 2.95
❑4, Jul 1996 .... 2.95
❑5, Aug 1996 .... 2.95
❑6, Sep 1996 .... 2.95
❑7, Oct 1996 .... 2.95

RIOT GEAR
TRIUMPHANT

❑1, Sep 1993 .... 2.50
❑1/Ashcan, Sep 1993; Ashcan edition (color) 2.50
❑2, Oct 1993 .... 2.50
❑3, Nov 1993 .... 2.50

N-MINT

❑4, Dec 1993; Unleashed! 2.50
❑5, Jan 1994 .... 2.50
❑6, Feb 1994 .... 2.50
❑7, Mar 1994 .... 2.50
❑8, Apr 1994 .... 2.50
❑9, May 1994 .... 2.50
❑10, Jun 1994 .... 2.50
❑11, Jul 1994; Final issue? 2.50
❑Ashcan 1, ashcan 2.50

RIOT GEAR: VIOLENT PAST
TRIUMPHANT

❑1, Feb 1994 .... 2.50
❑2, Feb 1994; 14,000 printed 2.50

RIPCLAW (VOL. 1)
IMAGE

❑½; Wizard promotional edition 2.00
❑½/Gold; Gold edition 2.50
❑1, Apr 1995 .... 2.50
❑2, Jun 1995 .... 2.50
❑3, Jul 1995 .... 2.50
❑4, Aug 1995 .... 2.50

RIPCLAW (VOL. 2)
IMAGE

❑1, Dec 1995 .... 2.50
❑2, Jan 1996 .... 2.50
❑3, Feb 1996 .... 2.50
❑4, Mar 1996 .... 2.50
❑5, Apr 1996 .... 2.50
❑6, Jun 1996 .... 2.50
❑Special 1, Oct 1995; Special Edition #1 .... 2.50

R.I.P. COMICS MODULE
TSR

❑1 .... 2.95
❑2 .... 2.95
❑3 .... 2.95
❑4 .... 2.95
❑5; Brasher 2.95
❑6; Brasher 2.95
❑7; Brasher 2.95
❑8; Brasher 2.95

R.I.P.D.
DARK HORSE

❑1, Oct 1999 .... 2.95
❑2, Nov 1999 .... 2.95
❑3, Dec 1999 .... 2.95
❑4, Jan 2000 .... 2.95

RIPFIRE
MALIBU

❑0, Jan 1995 .... 2.50

RIP HUNTER...TIME MASTER
DC

❑1, Mar 1961 .... 350.00
❑2, May 1961 .... 140.00
❑3, Jul 1961 .... 115.00
❑4, Sep 1961 .... 95.00
❑5, Nov 1961 .... 95.00
❑6, Jan 1962, ATh (a) 85.00
❑7, Mar 1962, ATh (a) 85.00
❑8, May 1962 .... 70.00
❑9, Jul 1962 .... 70.00
❑10, Sep 1962 .... 70.00

N-MINT

❑11, Nov 1962 .... 70.00
❑12, Jan 1963 .... 70.00
❑13, Mar 1963 .... 70.00
❑14, May 1963 .... 70.00
❑15, Jul 1963 .... 70.00
❑16, Sep 1963 .... 58.00
❑17, Nov 1963 .... 58.00
❑18, Jan 1964 .... 58.00
❑19, Mar 1964 .... 58.00
❑20, May 1964 .... 58.00
❑21, Jul 1964 .... 48.00
❑22, Sep 1964 .... 48.00
❑23, Nov 1964 .... 48.00
❑24, Jan 1965 .... 48.00
❑25, Mar 1965 .... 48.00
❑26, May 1965 .... 40.00
❑27, Jul 1965 .... 40.00
❑28, Sep 1965 .... 40.00
❑29, Nov 1965 .... 40.00

RIP IN TIME
FANTAGOR

❑1, b&w 2.00
❑2, b&w 2.00
❑3, b&w 2.00
❑4, b&w 2.00
❑5, b&w 2.00

RIPLEY'S BELIEVE IT OR NOT!
GOLD KEY

❑4, Apr 1967, Series continued from "Ripley's Believe it Or Not True War Stories" 26.00
❑5, Jun 1967 .... 16.00
❑6, Aug 1967 .... 16.00
❑7, Nov 1967 .... 16.00
❑8, Feb 1968 .... 16.00
❑9, May 1968 .... 16.00
❑10, Aug 1968 .... 16.00
❑11, Nov 1968, 10208-811 .... 12.00
❑12, Feb 1969 .... 12.00
❑13, Apr 1969 .... 12.00
❑14, Jun 1969 .... 12.00
❑15, Aug 1969 .... 12.00
❑16, Oct 1969 .... 10.00
❑17, Dec 1969 .... 10.00
❑18, Feb 1970 .... 10.00
❑19, Apr 1970 .... 10.00
❑20, Jun 1970 .... 10.00
❑21, Aug 1970 .... 8.00
❑22, Oct 1970 .... 8.00
❑23, Dec 1970 .... 8.00
❑24, Feb 1971 .... 8.00
❑25, Apr 1971 .... 8.00
❑26, Jun 1971 .... 8.00
❑27, Aug 1971 .... 8.00
❑28, Sep 1971 .... 8.00
❑29, Oct 1971 .... 8.00
❑30, Dec 1971 .... 8.00
❑31, Feb 1972 .... 5.00
❑32, Apr 1972 .... 5.00
❑33, Jun 1972 .... 5.00
❑34, Aug 1972, 90208-208 .... 5.00
❑35, Sep 1972 .... 5.00
❑36, Oct 1972 .... 5.00
❑37, Dec 1972, 90208-212 .... 5.00

N-MINT

❑38, Feb 1973 5.00
❑39, Apr 1973 5.50
❑40, Jun 1973 5.00
❑41, Aug 1973 5.00
❑42, Sep 1973 5.00
❑43, Oct 1973 5.00
❑44, Dec 1973 5.00
❑45, Feb 1974 5.00
❑46, Apr 1974 5.00
❑47, Jun 1974 5.00
❑48, Aug 1974 5.00
❑49, Sep 1974 5.00
❑50, Oct 1974 5.00
❑51, Dec 1974 4.00
❑52, Feb 1975 4.00
❑53, Apr 1975 4.00
❑54, Jun 1975 4.00
❑55, Jul 1975 4.00
❑56, Aug 1975 4.00
❑57, Sep 1975 4.00
❑58, Oct 1975 4.00
❑59, Dec 1975 4.00
❑60, Feb 1976 4.00
❑61, Apr 1976 4.00
❑62, Jun 1976 4.00
❑63, Jul 1976 4.00
❑64, Aug 1976 4.00
❑65, Oct 1976 4.00
❑66, Dec 1976 4.00
❑67, Jan 1977 4.00
❑68, Feb 1977 4.00
❑69, Apr 1977 4.00
❑70, Jun 1977 4.00
❑71, Jul 1977 3.00
❑72, Aug 1977 3.00
❑73, Oct 1977 3.00
❑74, Dec 1977 3.00
❑75, Jan 1978 3.00
❑76, Feb 1978 3.00
❑77, Apr 1978 3.00
❑78, Jun 1978 3.00
❑79, Jul 1977 3.00
❑80, Aug 1978 3.00
❑81, Sep 1978 3.00
❑82, Oct 1978 3.00
❑83, Nov 1978 3.00
❑84, Dec 1978 3.00
❑85, Jan 1979 3.00
❑86, Feb 1979 3.00
❑87, Apr 1979 3.00
❑88, May 1979 3.00
❑89, Jul 1979 3.00
❑90, Aug 1979 3.00
❑91, Sep 1979 3.00
❑92, Oct 1979 3.00
❑93, Nov 1979 3.00
❑94, Feb 1980 3.00

RIPLEY'S BELIEVE IT OR NOT! (DARK HORSE)
Dark Horse

❑1, May 2002 2.99
❑2, Oct 2002 2.99
❑3 2003 2.99
❑4 2003 2.99

RIPLEY'S BELIEVE IT OR NOT!: BEAUTY & GROOMING
Schanes

❑1 2.50

RIPLEY'S BELIEVE IT OR NOT!: CHILD PRODIGIES
Schanes

❑1 2.50

RIPLEY'S BELIEVE IT OR NOT!: CRUELTY
Schanes Products

❑1, Jun 1993, b&w; says Crime & Murder on cover; reprints newspaper cartoons 2.50
❑2, Jun 1993, b&w; says Crime & Murder on cover; reprints newspaper cartoons 2.50

RIPLEY'S BELIEVE IT OR NOT!: FAIRY TALES & LITERATURE
Schanes

❑1 2.50

RIPLEY'S BELIEVE IT OR NOT!: FEATS OF WONDER
Schanes

❑1 2.50

RIPLEY'S BELIEVE IT OR NOT!: SPORTS FEATS
Schanes Products

❑1, Jun 1993, b&w; reprints newspaper cartoons 2.50

RIPLEY'S BELIEVE IT OR NOT!: STRANGE DEATHS
Schanes Products

❑1, Jun 1993, b&w; reprints newspaper cartoons 2.50

RIPLEY'S BELIEVE IT OR NOT TRUE WAR STORIES
Gold Key

❑1, ca. 1966, #3 in overall series; Continued in Ripley's Believe It or Not #4 24.00

RIP OFF COMIX
Rip Off

❑1, Apr 1977 25.00
❑2, Jul 1977 16.00
❑3, Mar 1978 12.00
❑4, Nov 1978 8.00
❑5, Sep 1979 6.00
❑6, Mar 1980 6.00
❑6/2nd, Jan 1980; 2nd printing (1980) 2.50
❑7, Nov 1980 6.00
❑8, May 1981; 1981 5.00
❑9, Sep 1981; 1981 5.00
❑10, Mar 1982 5.00
❑11, Oct 1982 4.00
❑12, Apr 1983 4.00
❑13 4.00
❑14, Apr 1987 4.00
❑15, Jul 1987 4.00
❑16, Oct 1987 4.00
❑17, Jan 1988 4.00
❑18, Apr 1988 4.00
❑19, Jul 1988 4.00
❑20, Oct 1988 4.00
❑21, Jan 1989; 20th Anniversary 4.00
❑22, Apr 1989 4.00
❑23, Jul 1989 4.00
❑24, Oct 1989; San Diego Con 3.25
❑25, Jan 1990 3.25
❑26, Apr 1990 3.25
❑27, Jul 1990 3.95
❑28, Oct 1990 3.50
❑29, Jan 1991 3.50
❑30, Apr 1991 3.50
❑31, Mar 1992 3.50

RIPPER
Aircel

❑1 2.50
❑2 2.50
❑3 2.50
❑4 2.50
❑5 2.50
❑6 2.50

RIPPER LEGACY
Caliber

❑1 2.95
❑2 2.95
❑3 2.95

RIPTIDE
Image

❑1, Sep 1995 2.50
❑2, Oct 1995 2.50

RISE OF APOCALYPSE
Marvel

❑1, Oct 1996; wraparound cover 1.95
❑2, Nov 1996; wraparound cover 1.95
❑3, Dec 1996; wraparound cover 1.95
❑4, Jan 1997; wraparound cover 1.95

RISING STARS
Image

❑0, Apr 2000; Wizard promotional edition 5.00
❑0/Gold 1999; Gold logo variant from Wizard promotion 12.00
❑½, Jul 2001 2.95
❑1/Holofoil, Aug 1999; Holofoil edition 8.00
❑1/Chromium, Aug 1999; chromium cover 10.00
❑1/Kids, Aug 1999; Gold "Monster Edition"; Children running to house 7.00
❑1/Fighting, Aug 1999; Gold "Monster Edition"; Battle scene with blonde woman in foreground 6.00
❑1/Funeral, Aug 1999; Gold "Monster Edition"; Team standing over coffin 5.00
❑1/Wizard, Aug 1999; Another Universe/Wizard World variant (boy standing in foreground looking at large glowing sphere, Wizard World/AU markings) 3.50
❑2, Oct 1999 3.00
❑2/Dynamic, Dec 1999; Dynamic Forces variant cover 4.00
❑2/DF Gold, Dec 1999; Dynamic Forces gold variant cover (Dynamic Forces seal on cover) 7.00
❑3, Dec 1999 3.00
❑4 2000 3.00
❑5, Mar 2000 2.50
❑6, Apr 2000 2.50
❑7, May 2000 2.50
❑8 2000 2.50
❑9, Aug 2000 2.50
❑10, Oct 2000 2.50
❑11, Nov 2000 2.50
❑12, Jan 2001 2.50
❑13, Mar 2001 2.50
❑14, May 2001 2.50
❑15, Jun 2001; BA (a); Flip-book with Universe preview 2.50
❑16, Jul 2001 BA (a) 2.50
❑17, Jan 2002 BA (a) 2.50
❑18, Jan 2002 2.50
❑19, Sep 2002 BA (a) 2.50
❑20, Oct 2002 BA (a) 2.99
❑21, Jan 2003 2.99
❑22 2.99
❑23 2.99
❑24 2005 2.99
❑Ashcan 1/Conven, Oct 2000; Convention Exclusive preview 6.00
❑Ashcan 1, Mar 1999; Prelude edition 2.95

RISING STARS: BRIGHT
Image

❑1, Feb 2003 2.99
❑2, Mar 2003 2.99
❑3, Apr 2003 2.99

RISING STARS: UNTOUCHABLE
Image

❑1, Mar 2006 2.99
❑2, May 2006 2.99
❑3, May 2006 2.99
❑4, Jul 2006 2.99
❑5, Jul 2006 2.99

RISING STARS: VOICES OF THE DEAD
Image

❑1, Jun 2005 2.99
❑2, Jul 2005 2.99
❑3, Sep 2005 2.99
❑4, Oct 2005 2.99
❑5, Nov 2005 2.99
❑6, Dec 2005 2.99

RIVERDALE HIGH
Archie

❑1, Aug 1990 1.50
❑2, Oct 1990 1.00
❑3, Dec 1990 1.00
❑4, Feb 1990 1.00
❑5, Apr 1990 1.00

RIVETS & RUBY
Radio

❑1, Feb 1998 2.95
❑2, Apr 1998 2.95
❑3, Jul 1998 2.95
❑4 2.95

RIVIT
Blackthorne

❑1 1.75

ROACH KILLER
NBM

❑1 11.95

Other grades: Multiply price above by 5/6 for VF/NM • 2/3 for VERY FINE • 1/3 for FINE • 1/5 for VERY GOOD • 1/8 for GOOD

Robotech: The Macross Saga

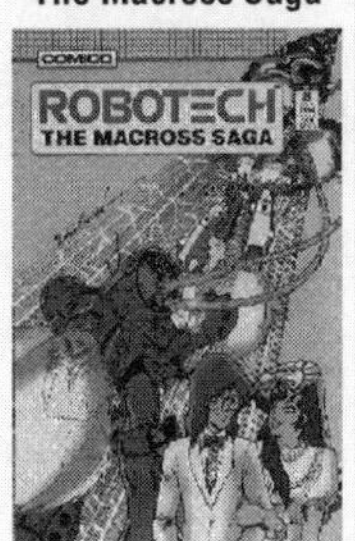

First issue is simply titled "Macross"
©Comico

Robotech Warriors

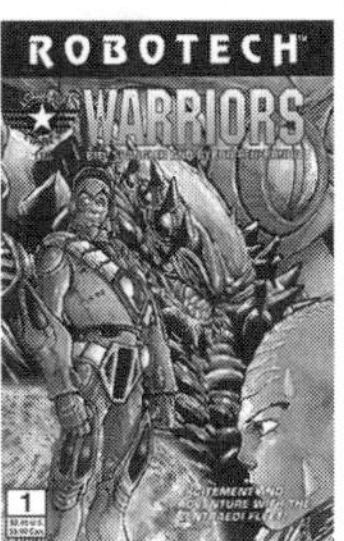

More with the Zentraedi race
©Academy

Rocketeer: The Official Movie Adaptation

Remarkably faithful movie adaptation
©Disney

Rocket Ranger

Lesser-known video game comic
©Adventure

Rock 'n' Roll Comics

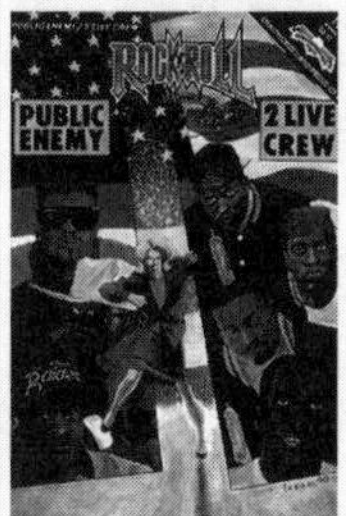

Bios from the Beatles to Public Enemy
©Revolutionary

N-MINT

ROACHMILL (BLACKTHORNE)
BLACKTHORNE

❑1, Dec 1986 ... 2.00
❑2, Feb 1987 ... 2.00
❑3, Apr 1987 ... 2.00
❑4, Jun 1987 ... 2.00
❑5, Sep 1987 ... 2.00
❑6, Oct 1987 ... 2.00

ROACHMILL (DARK HORSE)
DARK HORSE

❑1, May 1988 ... 2.00
❑2, Jun 1988 ... 1.75
❑3, Sep 1988 ... 1.75
❑4, Nov 1988 ... 1.75
❑5, Apr 1989 ... 1.75
❑6, Jun 1989 ... 1.75
❑7, Oct 1989 ... 1.75
❑8, Jan 1990; indicia says Jan 89; a misprint ... 1.75
❑9, Apr 1990 ... 1.95
❑10, Dec 1990; trading cards ... 1.95

ROADKILL
LIGHTHOUSE

❑1, b&w ... 2.00
❑2, b&w ... 2.00

ROADKILL: A CHRONICLE OF THE DEADWORLD
CALIBER

❑1, text ... 2.95

ROAD TO PERDITION
DC / PARADOX

❑1, Jun 1998, b&w ... 14.00
❑1/2nd, Jul 2002, b&w; includes new introduction by Collins ... 14.00

ROAD TRIP
ONI

❑1, Aug 2000, b&w; collects story from Oni Double Feature #9 and #10 ... 2.95

ROADWAYS
CULT

❑1, May 1994, b&w ... 2.75
❑2, Jun 1994, b&w ... 2.75
❑3 ... 2.75
❑4 ... 2.75

ROARIN' RICK'S RARE BIT FIENDS
KING HELL

❑1, Jul 1994; Dave Sim ... 2.95
❑2, Aug 1994; Neil Gaiman ... 2.95
❑3, Sep 1994; Neil Gaiman ... 2.95
❑4, Oct 1994 ... 2.95
❑5, Nov 1994 ... 2.95
❑6, Dec 1994 ... 2.95
❑7, Jan 1995 ... 2.95
❑8, Feb 1995 ... 2.95
❑9, Mar 1995 ... 2.95
❑10, Apr 1995 ... 2.95
❑11, May 1995 ... 2.95
❑12, Jun 1995 ... 2.95
❑13, Aug 1995 ... 2.95
❑14, Sep 1995 ... 2.95
❑15, Nov 1995 ... 2.95
❑16, Dec 1995 ... 2.95
❑17, Jan 1996 ... 2.95

N-MINT

❑18, Mar 1996 ... 2.95
❑19, ca. 1996 ... 2.95
❑20, ca. 1996 ... 2.95
❑21, ca. 1996; Subtleman ... 2.95

ROBBIN' $3000
PARODY

❑1, b&w ... 2.50

ROB HANES
WCG

❑1, Jan 1991, b&w ... 2.50

ROB HANES ADVENTURES
WCG

❑1, Oct 2000 ... 2.50
❑2 2001 ... 2.50
❑3 2002 ... 2.50
❑4 2003 ... 2.75
❑5 2004 ... 2.95
❑6 2004 ... 2.95

ROBIN (MINI-SERIES)
DC

❑1, Jan 1991; 1: King Snake. poster ... 3.00
❑1/2nd, Jan 1991; 1: King Snake. (no poster); (no poster) ... 1.50
❑1/3rd; 1: King Snake. (no poster); (no poster) ... 1.50
❑2, Feb 1991 ... 2.50
❑2/2nd, Feb 1991 ... 1.50
❑3, Mar 1991 ... 2.00
❑4, Apr 1991 V: Lady Shiva ... 2.00
❑5, May 1991 V: King Shark ... 2.00
❑Annual 1, ca. 1992; Eclipso ... 2.50
❑Annual 2, ca. 1993 1: Razorsharp ... 2.50

ROBIN
DC

❑0, Oct 1994 O: Robin I (Dick Grayson). O: Robin III (Timothy Drake). O: Robin II (Jason Todd) ... 2.00
❑1, Nov 1993 1: Shotgun Smith ... 4.00
❑1/Variant, Nov 1993; Embossed cover ... 3.50
❑2, Jan 1994 ... 2.00
❑3, Feb 1994 ... 2.00
❑4, Mar 1994 A: Spoiler ... 2.00
❑5, Apr 1994 ... 2.00
❑6, May 1994 A: Huntress ... 2.00
❑7, Jun 1994 ... 2.00
❑8, Jul 1994 ... 2.00
❑9, Aug 1994 ... 2.00
❑10, Sep 1994; Zero Hour; Tim Drake Robin teams with Dick Grayson Robin ... 2.00
❑11, Nov 1994 ... 1.75
❑12, Dec 1994 ... 1.75
❑13, Jan 1995 ... 1.75
❑14, Feb 1995 ... 1.75
❑14/Variant, Feb 1995; enhanced cardstock cover ... 2.50
❑15, Mar 1995 ... 1.75
❑16, Apr 1995 ... 1.75
❑17, Jun 1995 ... 2.00
❑18, Jul 1995 ... 2.00
❑19, Aug 1995 V: Ulysses ... 2.00
❑20, Sep 1995 V: Ulysses ... 2.00
❑21, Oct 1995; Ninja camp ... 2.00
❑22, Nov 1995; Ninja camp ... 2.00

N-MINT

❑23, Dec 1995; V: Killer Moth a.k.a. Charaxes. Underworld Unleashed ... 2.00
❑24, Jan 1996; V: Killer Moth a.k.a. Charaxes. Underworld Unleashed ... 2.00
❑25, Feb 1996; anti-guns issue ... 2.00
❑26, Mar 1996 ... 2.00
❑27, Mar 1996 ... 2.00
❑28, Apr 1996 ... 2.00
❑29, May 1996 ... 2.00
❑30, Jun 1996 ... 2.00
❑31, Jul 1996 A: Wildcat ... 2.00
❑32, Aug 1996 ... 2.00
❑33, Sep 1996 ... 2.00
❑34, Oct 1996; self-contained story ... 2.00
❑35, Nov 1996; A: Spoiler. Final Night ... 2.00
❑36, Dec 1996 V: Toyman. V: Ulysses ... 2.00
❑37, Jan 1997 V: Toyman. V: Ulysses ... 2.00
❑38, Feb 1997 ... 2.00
❑39, Mar 1997 ... 2.00
❑40, Apr 1997 ... 1.95
❑41, May 1997 ... 1.95
❑42, Jun 1997 ... 1.95
❑43, Jul 1997 ... 1.95
❑44, Aug 1997 A: Spoiler ... 1.95
❑45, Sep 1997; self-contained story ... 1.95
❑46, Oct 1997; self-contained story ... 1.95
❑47, Nov 1997 A: Nightwing. A: Batman. V: Ulysses ... 1.95
❑48, Dec 1997; Face cover ... 1.95
❑49, Jan 1998 A: King Snake ... 1.95
❑50, Feb 1998; Giant-size A: King Snake. A: Lady Shiva ... 2.95
❑51, Mar 1998 ... 1.95
❑52, Apr 1998; continues in Batman: Blackgate-Isle of Men #1 ... 1.95
❑53, May 1998 ... 1.95
❑54, Jun 1998; A: Spoiler. Aftershock ... 1.95
❑55, Jul 1998; continues in Nightwing #23 ... 1.95
❑56, Aug 1998; A: Spoiler. Tim breaks up with Ariana ... 1.95
❑57, Sep 1998; Spoiler and Robin date ... 1.99
❑58, Oct 1998 V: Steeljacket ... 1.99
❑59, Dec 1998 V: Steeljacket ... 1.99
❑60, Jan 1999 ... 1.99
❑61, Feb 1999 ... 1.99
❑62, Mar 1999; A: Flash III (Wally West). Tim relocates to Keystone City ... 1.99
❑63, Apr 1999 A: Riddler. A: Superman. A: Flash III (Wally West). A: Captain Boomerang ... 1.99
❑64, May 1999 A: Flash III (Wally West). V: Riddler. V: Captain Boomerang ... 1.99
❑65, Jun 1999; Spoiler's child is born ... 1.99
❑66, Jul 1999; Tim returns to Gotham ... 1.99
❑67, Aug 1999; A: Nightwing. No Man's Land ... 1.99
❑68, Sep 1999; V: Ratcatcher. No Man's Land ... 1.99
❑69, Oct 1999; V: Ratcatcher. No Man's Land ... 1.99
❑70, Nov 1999 ... 1.99
❑71, Dec 1999 ... 1.99
❑72, Jan 2000 ... 1.99
❑73, Feb 2000 ... 1.99

Other grades: Multiply price above by 5/6 for VF/NM • 2/3 for VERY FINE • 1/3 for FINE • 1/5 for VERY GOOD • 1/8 for GOOD

N-MINT N-MINT N-MINT

❑74, Mar 2000 1.99
❑75, Apr 2000; Giant-size 2.95
❑76, May 2000 1.99
❑77, Jun 2000 1.99
❑78, Jul 2000 1.99
❑79, Aug 2000 2.25
❑80, Sep 2000 2.25
❑81, Oct 2000 2.25
❑82, Nov 2000 2.25
❑83, Dec 2000 2.25
❑84, Jan 2001 2.25
❑85, Feb 2001 A: Joker 2.25
❑86, Mar 2001 2.25
❑87, Apr 2001 2.25
❑88, May 2001 2.25
❑89, Jun 2001 2.25
❑90, Jul 2001 2.25
❑91, Aug 2001 2.25
❑92, Sep 2001 2.25
❑93, Oct 2001 2.25
❑94, Nov 2001 2.25
❑95, Dec 2001 2.25
❑96, Jan 2002 2.25
❑97, Feb 2002 2.25
❑98, Mar 2002; Bruce Wayne, Murderer? Part 6 2.25
❑99, Apr 2002; Bruce Wayne, Murderer? Part 11 2.25
❑100, May 2002; Giant-size 3.50
❑101, Jun 2002 2.25
❑102, Jul 2002 2.25
❑103, Aug 2002 2.25
❑104, Sep 2002 2.25
❑105, Oct 2002 2.25
❑106, Nov 2002 2.25
❑107, Dec 2002 2.25
❑108, Jan 2003 2.25
❑109, Feb 2003 2.25
❑110, Mar 2003 2.25
❑111, Apr 2003 2.25
❑112, May 2003 2.25
❑113, Jun 2003 2.25
❑114, Jul 2003 2.25
❑115, Aug 2003 2.25
❑116, Sep 2003 2.25
❑117, Oct 2003 2.25
❑118, Nov 2003 2.25
❑119, Dec 2003 2.25
❑120, Jan 2004 2.25
❑121, Feb 2004 2.25
❑122, Mar 2004 2.25
❑123, Apr 2004 2.25
❑124, May 2004 2.25
❑125, Jun 2004 2.25
❑126, Jul 2004 5.00
❑127, Aug 2004 4.00
❑128, Sep 2004 3.00
❑129, Oct 2004 2.25
❑130, Nov 2004 2.25
❑131, Dec 2004 2.25
❑132, Jan 2005 2.25
❑133, Feb 2005 2.25
❑134, Mar 2005 2.25
❑135, Apr 2005 2.25
❑136, May 2005 2.25
❑137, Jun 2005 2.25
❑138, Jul 2005 2.25
❑139, Aug 2005 2.25
❑140, Sep 2005 2.50
❑141, Oct 2005 2.99
❑142, Nov 2005 2.99
❑143, Dec 2005 2.99
❑144, Jan 2006 2.99
❑145, Feb 2006 2.99
❑146, Mar 2006 2.99
❑147, Apr 2006 2.99
❑148, Jun 2006 2.99
❑149, Jun 2006 2.99
❑151, Sep 2006 2.99
❑1000000, Nov 1998 A: Robin the Toy Wonder 4.00
❑Annual 3, ca. 1994; Elseworlds 2.95
❑Annual 4, ca. 1995; Year One 3.95
❑Annual 5, ca. 1996; Legends of the Dead Earth 2.95
❑Annual 6, ca. 1997; Pulp Heroes 3.95

❑Giant Size 1, Sep 2000; Eighty Page Giant 5.95

ROBIN II
DC

❑1, Oct 1991; CR (a); newsstand; no hologram 1.00
❑1/A, Oct 1991; CR (a); Robin Hologram; Joker in straight jacket 1.75
❑1/B, Oct 1991; CR (a); Joker holding cover; Robin Hologram 1.75
❑1/C, Oct 1991; CR (a); Robin Hologram; Batman cover 1.75
❑1/CS, Oct 1991; set of all covers; extra hologram 10.00
❑1/D, Oct 1991; CR (a); Joker standing cover; Robin Hologram 1.75
❑2, Nov 1991; Normal cover; newsstand; no hologram 1.00
❑2/A, Nov 1991; Joker with mallet cover; Batman Hologram 1.75
❑2/B, Nov 1991; Joker with dart board cover; Batman Hologram 1.75
❑2/C, Nov 1991; Joker with dagger cover; Batman Hologram 1.75
❑2/CS, Nov 1991 9.00
❑3, Nov 1991; Normal cover; newsstand; no hologram 1.00
❑3/A, Nov 1991; Robin swinging cover; Joker Hologram 1.50
❑3/B, Nov 1991; Joker Hologram; Robin perched 1.50
❑3/CS, Nov 1991 6.00
❑4, Dec 1991; Normal cover; newsstand, no hologram 1.00
❑4/A, Dec 1991; Bat signal hologram 1.50
❑4/CS, Dec 1991 4.25
❑Deluxe 1; boxed with hologram cards (limited to 25, 000); Deluxe set; Contains all issues and variations in bookshelf binder 30.00

ROBIN PLUS
DC

❑1, Dec 1996 2.95
❑2, Dec 1997; continues in Scare Tactics #10 2.95

ROBIN 3000
DC

❑1, ca. 1992 4.95
❑2, ca. 1992 4.95

ROBIN: YEAR ONE
DC

❑1, Dec 2000 4.95
❑2, Jan 2001 4.95
❑3, Feb 2001 4.95
❑4, Mar 2001 4.95

ROBIN/ARGENT DOUBLE-SHOT
DC

❑1, Feb 1998 1.95

ROBIN III: CRY OF THE HUNTRESS
DC

❑1, Dec 1992; newsstand 1.25
❑1/Variant, Dec 1992; moving cover 2.50
❑2, Jan 1993; newsstand 1.25
❑2/Variant, Jan 1993; moving cover 2.50
❑3, Jan 1993; newsstand 1.25
❑3/Variant, Jan 1993; moving cover 2.50
❑4, Feb 1993; newsstand 1.25
❑4/Variant, Feb 1993; moving cover 2.50
❑5, Feb 1993; newsstand 1.25
❑5/Variant, Feb 1993; moving cover 2.50
❑6, Mar 1993; newsstand 1.25
❑6/Variant, Mar 1993; moving cover 2.50

ROBIN HOOD (DELL)
DELL

❑1, ca. 1963 20.00

ROBIN HOOD (ETERNITY)
ETERNITY

❑1, Aug 1989, b&w 2.25
❑2, Sep 1991, b&w 2.25
❑3, b&w 2.25
❑4, b&w 2.25

ROBIN HOOD (ECLIPSE)
ECLIPSE

❑1, Jul 1991 2.50
❑2, Sep 1991 2.50
❑3, Dec 1991 2.50

ROBIN RED AND THE LUTINS
ACE

❑1, Nov 1986 1.75
❑2, Jan 1987 1.75

ROBINSONIA
NBM

❑1 11.95

ROBOCOP (MAGAZINE)
MARVEL

❑1, Oct 1987 2.50

ROBOCOP (MARVEL)
MARVEL

❑1, Mar 1990 3.00
❑2, Apr 1990 2.00
❑3, May 1990 1.50
❑4, Jun 1990 1.50
❑5, Jul 1990 1.50
❑6, Aug 1990 1.50
❑7, Sep 1990 1.50
❑8, Oct 1990 1.50
❑9, Nov 1990 1.50
❑10, Dec 1990 1.50
❑11, Jan 1991 1.50
❑12, Feb 1991 1.50
❑13, Mar 1991 1.50
❑14, Apr 1991 1.50
❑15, May 1991 1.50
❑16, Jun 1991 1.50
❑17, Jul 1991 1.50
❑18, Aug 1991 1.50
❑19, Sep 1991 1.50
❑20, Oct 1991 1.50
❑21, Nov 1991 1.50
❑22, Dec 1991 1.50
❑23, Jan 1992 1.50

ROBOCOP (MOVIE ADAPTATION)
MARVEL

❑1, Jul 1990; prestige format 4.95

ROBOCOP 2
MARVEL

❑1, Aug 1990; comic book 1.50
❑2, Sep 1990; comic book 1.50
❑3, Sep 1990; comic book 1.50

ROBOCOP 2 (MAGAZINE)
MARVEL

❑1, Aug 1990, b&w; magazine 2.50

ROBOCOP 3
DARK HORSE

❑1, Jul 1993 2.50
❑2, Sep 1993 2.50
❑3, Nov 1993 2.50

ROBOCOP (FRANK MILLER'S)
AVATAR

❑1, Aug 2003 5.00
❑1/Platinum, Aug 2003 7.00
❑1/Wraparound 5.00
❑2, Oct 2003 3.50
❑2/Platinum 5.00
❑3, Nov 2003 3.50
❑3/Platinum, Nov 2003 6.00
❑3/Ryp 3.50
❑4, Dec 2003 3.50
❑4/Miller 6.00
❑4/Platinum 5.00
❑5, Feb 2004 3.50
❑5/Platinum 5.00
❑5/Wraparound 3.50
❑6 3.50
❑6/Miller 6.00
❑6/Platinum 5.00
❑7 3.50
❑7/Miller 6.00
❑7/Platinum 5.00
❑7/Wraparound 3.50
❑8 3.50
❑8/Miller 6.00
❑8/Platinum 5.00
❑8/Wraparound 3.50

ROBOCOP: KILLING MACHINE
AVATAR

❑1 5.99
❑1/Platinum 15.00
❑1/Wraparound 6.00

Other grades: Multiply price above by 5/6 for VF/NM • 2/3 for VERY FINE • 1/3 for FINE • 1/5 for VERY GOOD • 1/8 for GOOD

Roger Rabbit

Hit movie spawns comics title for Disney

©Disney

Rogue (1st Marvel Series)

First limited series with Marvel's mutant misfit

©Marvel

Rom

Forgotten toy results in long-running title

©Marvel

Ronald McDonald

Hamburger stand mascot comes to comics

©Charlton

Ronin

If you intend to die, you can do anything...

©DC

ROBOCOP: MORTAL COILS
Dark Horse

	N-MINT
❑1, Sep 1993	2.50
❑2, Oct 1993	2.50
❑3, Nov 1993	2.50
❑4, Dec 1993	2.50

ROBOCOP: PRIME SUSPECT
Dark Horse

	N-MINT
❑1, Oct 1992	2.50
❑2, Nov 1992	2.50
❑3, Dec 1992	2.50
❑4, Jan 1993	2.50

ROBOCOP: ROULETTE
Dark Horse

	N-MINT
❑1, Dec 1993	2.50
❑2, Jan 1994	2.50
❑3, Feb 1994	2.50
❑4, Mar 1994	2.50

ROBOCOP VERSUS THE TERMINATOR
Dark Horse

	N-MINT
❑1, ca. 1992 FM (w)	3.00
❑1/Platinum, ca. 1992; Platinum promotional edition FM (w)	4.00
❑2, ca. 1992 FM (w)	2.50
❑3, ca. 1992 FM (w)	2.50
❑4, ca. 1992 FM (w)	2.50

ROBOCOP: WILD CHILD
Avatar

	N-MINT
❑1 2005	2.99
❑1/Photo	4.00
❑1/Platinum	12.00
❑1/Rivalry	5.00
❑1/Wraparound	6.00

ROBOCOP: WILD CHILD - DETROIT'S FINEST
Avatar

	N-MINT
❑1 2005	5.99
❑1/Detroit 2005	7.00
❑1/Photo 2005	5.99
❑1/Platinum 2005	15.00
❑1/Rivalry 2005	7.00
❑1/Wraparound 2005	5.99

ROBO DOJO
DC / Wildstorm

	N-MINT
❑1, Apr 2002	2.95
❑2, May 2002	2.95
❑3, Jun 2002	2.95
❑4, Jul 2002	2.95
❑5, Aug 2002	2.95
❑6, Sep 2002	2.95

ROBO-HUNTER
Eagle

	N-MINT
❑1	1.50
❑2 DaG (a)	1.25
❑3 DaG (a)	1.25
❑4 DaG (a)	1.25
❑5	1.25

ROBOTECH
Antarctic

	N-MINT
❑1, Mar 1997	2.95
❑2, May 1997	2.95
❑3, Jul 1997	2.95
❑4, Sep 1997	2.95
❑5, Nov 1997	2.95
❑6, Jan 1998	2.95
❑7, Mar 1998	2.95
❑8, May 1998	2.95
❑9, Jul 1998	2.95
❑10, Sep 1998	2.95
❑11, Nov 1998	2.95
❑Annual 1, Apr 1998, b&w	2.95

ROBOTECH (WILDSTORM)
DC / Wildstorm

	N-MINT
❑0, Feb 2003	2.50
❑1, Feb 2003	2.95
❑2, Mar 2003	2.95
❑3, Apr 2003	2.95
❑4, May 2003	2.95
❑5, Jun 2003	2.95
❑6, Jul 2003	2.95

ROBOTECH: AMAZON WORLD-ESCAPE FROM PRAXIS
Academy

	N-MINT
❑1, Dec 1994	2.95

ROBOTECH: CLASS REUNION
Antarctic

	N-MINT
❑1, Dec 1998, b&w	3.95

ROBOTECH: CLONE
Academy

	N-MINT
❑0	2.95
❑1	2.95
❑2	2.95
❑3	2.95
❑4	2.95
❑5	2.95
❑Special 1	3.50

ROBOTECH: COVERT-OPS
Antarctic

	N-MINT
❑1, Aug 1998, b&w	2.95
❑2, Sep 1998, b&w	2.95

ROBOTECH: CYBER WORLD: SECRETS OF HAYDON IV
Academy

	N-MINT
❑1	2.95

ROBOTECH DEFENDERS
DC

	N-MINT
❑1, Jan 1985 MA (a)	2.00
❑2, Apr 1985; MA (a); three-issue series was finished in two issues	2.00

ROBOTECH: ESCAPE
Antarctic

	N-MINT
❑1, May 1998, b&w	2.95

ROBOTECH: FINAL FIRE
Antarctic

	N-MINT
❑1, Dec 1998, b&w	2.95

ROBOTECH: FIREWALKERS
Eternity

	N-MINT
❑1	2.50

ROBOTECH GENESIS
Eternity

	N-MINT
❑1, trading cards	2.50
❑1/Ltd.; limited	5.95
❑2	2.50
❑3	2.50
❑4, trading cards	2.50
❑5, trading cards	2.50
❑6	2.50

ROBOTECH IN 3-D
Comico

	N-MINT
❑1, Jul 1985	2.50

ROBOTECH: INVASION
DC / Wildstorm

	N-MINT
❑1, Mar 2004	2.95
❑2, Apr 2004	2.95
❑3, May 2004	2.95
❑4, Jun 2004	2.95
❑5, Jul 2004	2.95

ROBOTECH: INVID WAR
Eternity

	N-MINT
❑1, May 1992, b&w	2.50
❑2, b&w	2.50
❑3, b&w	2.50
❑4, b&w	2.50
❑5, b&w	2.50
❑6, b&w	2.50
❑7, b&w	2.50
❑8, b&w	2.50
❑9, b&w	2.50
❑10, b&w	1.25
❑11, b&w	1.25
❑12, b&w	1.25
❑13, b&w	1.25
❑14	2.50
❑15	2.50
❑16	2.50
❑17	2.50
❑18	2.50

ROBOTECH: INVID WAR AFTERMATH
Eternity

	N-MINT
❑1, b&w	2.50
❑2, b&w	2.50

ROBOTECH: LOVE & WAR
DC / Wildstorm

	N-MINT
❑1, Aug 2003	2.95
❑2, Sep 2003	2.95
❑3, Oct 2003	2.95
❑4, Nov 2003	2.95
❑5, Dec 2003	2.95
❑6, Jan 2004	2.95

ROBOTECH: MACROSS SAGA (DC)
DC / Wildstorm

	N-MINT
❑1, May 2003	14.95
❑2, Jul 2003	14.95
❑3, Sep 2003	14.95
❑4, Nov 2003	14.95

ROBOTECH MASTERS
Comico

	N-MINT
❑1, Jul 1985	2.00
❑2, Sep 1985	1.50
❑3, Nov 1985	1.50
❑4, Nov 1985	1.50
❑5	1.50
❑6, 1986	1.50
❑7, 1986	1.50

Other grades: Multiply price above by 5/6 for VF/NM • 2/3 for VERY FINE • 1/3 for FINE • 1/5 for VERY GOOD • 1/8 for GOOD

N-MINT

❑8, 1986 .... 1.50
❑9, 1986 .... 1.50
❑10, Aug 1986 .... 1.50
❑11 .... 1.50
❑12 .... 1.50
❑13 .... 1.50
❑14, 1987 .... 1.50
❑15, 1987 .... 1.50
❑16, 1987 .... 1.50
❑17, 1987 .... 1.50
❑18, 1987 .... 1.50
❑19, 1987 .... 1.50
❑20, 1987 .... 1.50
❑21 .... 1.50
❑22 .... 1.50
❑23, 1988 .... 1.50

ROBOTECH: MECHANGEL
ACADEMY

❑1 .... 2.95
❑2 .... 2.95
❑3 .... 2.95

ROBOTECH: MEGASTORM
ANTARCTIC

❑1, Aug 1998; wraparound cover 7.95

ROBOTECH: PRELUDE TO THE SHADOW CHRONICLES
DC

❑1 .... 2.99
❑2, Dec 2005 .... 2.99
❑3, Jan 2006 .... 2.99
❑4, Feb 2006 .... 2.99
❑5, Mar 2006 .... 2.99

ROBOTECH: RETURN TO MACROSS
ETERNITY

❑1, Mar 1993, b&w 3.00
❑2, b&w 2.50
❑3, b&w 2.50
❑4, b&w 2.50
❑5, b&w 2.50
❑6, b&w 2.50
❑7, b&w 2.50
❑8, b&w 2.50
❑9, b&w 2.50
❑10, Jan 1994, b&w 2.50
❑11 .... 2.50
❑12 .... 2.50
❑13 .... 2.50
❑14 .... 2.50
❑15 .... 2.50
❑16 .... 2.50
❑17 .... 2.50
❑18 .... 2.50
❑19 .... 2.50
❑20 .... 2.50
❑21 .... 2.50
❑22 .... 2.50
❑23 .... 2.50
❑24 .... 2.50
❑25 .... 2.50
❑26 .... 2.50
❑27 .... 2.50
❑28 .... 2.50
❑29 .... 2.50
❑30 .... 2.50
❑31 .... 2.50
❑32, May 1996 .... 2.95

ROBOTECH: SENTINELS - RUBICON
ANTARCTIC

❑1, Jun 1998, b&w 2.95
❑2 .... 2.95
❑3 .... 2.95
❑4 .... 2.95
❑5 .... 2.95
❑6 .... 2.95
❑7 .... 2.95

ROBOTECH SPECIAL
COMICO

❑1, May 1988 .... 2.50

ROBOTECH THE GRAPHIC NOVEL
COMICO

❑1 .... 5.95

ROBOTECH: THE MACROSS SAGA
COMICO

❑1, Dec 1984; "Macross" this issue 8.00
❑2, ca. 1985; Title changes to Robotech: The Macross Saga 4.00
❑3, ca. 1985 .... 3.00
❑4, ca. 1985 .... 3.00
❑5, ca. 1985 .... 3.00
❑6, Sep 1985 .... 2.00
❑7, Nov 1985 .... 2.00
❑8 .... 2.00
❑9, ca. 1986 .... 2.00
❑10, ca. 1986 .... 2.00
❑11, ca. 1986 .... 2.00
❑12, ca. 1986 .... 2.00
❑13, ca. 1986 .... 2.00
❑14, ca. 1986 .... 2.00
❑15, ca. 1986 .... 2.00
❑16, ca. 1986 .... 2.00
❑17, ca. 1986 .... 2.00
❑18 .... 2.00
❑19 .... 2.00
❑20 .... 2.00
❑21 .... 2.00
❑22, ca. 1987 .... 2.00
❑23, ca. 1987 .... 2.00
❑24, ca. 1987 .... 2.00
❑25, ca. 1987 .... 2.00
❑26, ca. 1987 .... 2.00
❑27, ca. 1987 .... 2.00
❑28 .... 2.00
❑29 .... 2.00
❑30 .... 2.00
❑31 .... 2.00
❑32 .... 2.00
❑33, ca. 1988 .... 2.00
❑34, ca. 1988 .... 2.00
❑35 .... 2.00
❑36, ca. 1989 .... 2.00

ROBOTECH: THE NEW GENERATION
COMICO

❑1, Jul 1985 .... 2.00
❑2, Sep 1985 .... 1.50
❑3, 1985 .... 1.50
❑4, 1985 .... 1.50
❑5, Jan 1986 .... 1.50
❑6, Mar 1986 .... 1.50
❑7, 1986 .... 1.50
❑8, 1986 .... 1.50
❑9, Jul 1986 .... 1.50
❑10 .... 1.50
❑11 .... 1.50
❑12 .... 1.50
❑13 .... 1.50
❑14 .... 1.50
❑15, 1987 .... 1.50
❑16, 1987 .... 1.50
❑17, 1987 .... 1.50
❑18, 1987 .... 1.50
❑19, 1987 .... 1.50
❑20 .... 1.50
❑21 .... 1.50
❑22 .... 1.50
❑23 .... 1.50
❑24 .... 1.50
❑25, 1988; last 1.50

ROBOTECH II: INVID WORLD, ASSAULT ON OPTERA
ACADEMY

❑1, Oct 1994 .... 2.95

ROBOTECH II: THE SENTINELS
ETERNITY

❑1, Nov 1988 .... 3.50
❑1/2nd 2.00
❑2, Dec 1988 .... 2.50
❑3, Jan 1989 .... 2.50
❑3/2nd, Feb 1989 .... 2.00
❑4, Mar 1989 .... 2.25
❑5, Apr 1989 .... 2.25
❑6, May 1989 .... 2.00
❑7, Jun 1989 .... 2.00
❑8, Jul 1989 .... 2.00
❑9, Sep 1989 .... 2.00
❑10, Oct 1989 .... 2.00
❑11, Oct 1989 .... 2.00
❑12, Nov 1989 .... 2.00
❑13, Dec 1989 .... 2.00
❑14, Jan 1990 .... 2.00
❑15 .... 2.00
❑16, Apr 1990 .... 1.95

ROBOTECH II: THE SENTINELS BOOK II
ETERNITY

❑1, May 1990 .... 2.25
❑2, Aug 1990 .... 2.25
❑3, Oct 1990 .... 2.25
❑4 .... 2.25
❑5, 1991 .... 2.25
❑6, 1991 .... 2.25
❑7, 1991 .... 2.25
❑8, 1991 .... 2.25
❑9, 1991 .... 2.25
❑10, 1991 .... 2.25
❑11 .... 2.25
❑12 .... 2.50
❑13, Mar 1992 .... 2.50
❑14 .... 2.50
❑15 .... 2.50
❑16 .... 2.50
❑17 .... 2.50
❑18 .... 2.50
❑19 .... 2.50
❑20 .... 2.50

ROBOTECH II: THE SENTINELS BOOK III
ETERNITY

❑1 .... 2.50
❑2 .... 2.50
❑3 .... 2.50
❑4 .... 2.50
❑5 .... 2.50
❑6 .... 2.50

ROBOTECH II: THE SENTINELS BOOK IV
ACADEMY

❑1 .... 2.95
❑2 .... 2.95
❑3 .... 2.95
❑4 .... 2.95
❑5 .... 2.95
❑6, May 1996 .... 2.95

ROBOTECH II: THE SENTINELS CYBERPIRATES
ETERNITY

❑1 .... 2.25
❑2 .... 2.25
❑3 .... 2.25
❑4 .... 2.25

ROBOTECH II: THE SENTINELS SPECIAL
ETERNITY

❑1, Apr 1989 .... 1.95
❑2 .... 1.95

ROBOTECH II: THE SENTINELS SWIMSUIT SPECTACULAR
ETERNITY

❑1 .... 2.95

ROBOTECH II: THE SENTINELS: THE ILLUSTRATED HANDBOOK
ETERNITY

❑1 .... 2.50
❑2 .... 2.50
❑3 .... 2.50

ROBOTECH II: THE SENTINELS THE MALCONTENT UPRISINGS
ETERNITY

❑9 .... 0.00
❑8 .... 0.00
❑7 .... 0.00
❑6 .... 0.00
❑5 .... 0.00
❑4, Dec 1989 .... 0.00
❑3 .... 0.00
❑2 .... 2.00
❑12 .... 0.00
❑11 .... 0.00
❑10 .... 0.00
❑1 .... 0.00

ROBOTECH II: THE SENTINELS THE MALCONTENT UPRISINGS
MALIBU / ETERNITY

❑1 .... 2.00

Route 666

Girl sees ghosts, seeks same

©CrossGen

Runaways

Acclaimed Marvel series got a second chance

©Marvel

Rune

One of Malibu's last major launches

©Malibu

Ruse

Victorian detective world has fantasy elements

©CrossGen

Sable

Dropped the first name after the TV series

©First

N-MINT

❑2 2.00
❑3 2.00
❑4 2.00
❑5 2.00
❑6 2.00
❑7 2.00
❑8 2.00
❑9 2.00
❑10 2.00
❑11 2.00
❑12 2.00

ROBOTECH II: THE SENTINELS: THE UNTOLD STORY
ETERNITY

❑1, b&w 2.50

ROBOTECH II: THE SENTINELS WEDDING SPECIAL
ETERNITY

❑1, Apr 1989 2.00
❑2, May 1989 2.00

ROBOTECH: VERMILION
ANTARCTIC

❑1, Aug 1997 2.95
❑2, Oct 1997 2.95
❑3, Dec 1997 2.95
❑4, Feb 1997 2.95

ROBOTECH WARRIORS
ACADEMY

❑1, Feb 1995 2.95

ROBOTECH: WINGS OF GIBRALTAR
ANTARCTIC

❑1, Aug 1998 2.95
❑2, Sep 1998 2.95

ROBOTIX
MARVEL

❑1, Feb 1986 HT (w); HT (a); 1: The Terrokors. 1: The Protectons 1.00

ROBO WARRIORS
CFW

❑1 1.75
❑2; 0: Citation; Origin of Citation 1.95
❑3 1.95
❑4 1.95
❑5 1.95
❑6 1.95
❑7 1.95
❑8; Reiki becomes Mister No 1.95

ROBYN OF SHERWOOD
CALIBER

❑1, Mar 1998, b&w 2.95

ROCKERS
RIP OFF

❑1, Jul 1988, b&w 2.00
❑2, Oct 1988, b&w 2.00
❑3, Jan 1989, b&w 2.00
❑4, Feb 1989, b&w 2.00
❑5, May 1989, b&w 2.00
❑6, Jun 1989, b&w 2.00
❑7, Sep 1989, b&w 2.00
❑8, Feb 1990, b&w 2.00

N-MINT

ROCKETEER 3-D COMIC
DISNEY

❑1, Jun 1991; with audiotape; Based on The Rocketeer movie 5.00

ROCKETEER ADVENTURE MAGAZINE
COMICO

❑1, Jul 1988; DSt (w); CV, DSt (a); Comico publishes 5.00
❑2, Jul 1989 DSt (w); DSt (a) 3.50
❑3, Jan 1995; DSt (w); DSt (a); Dark Horse publishes 3.00

ROCKETEER SPECIAL EDITION
ECLIPSE

❑1, Nov 1984 1.50

ROCKETEER, THE: THE OFFICIAL MOVIE ADAPTATION
DISNEY

❑1 1991; No cover date; stapled 2.95
❑1/Direct ed. 1991; No cover date; squarebound 5.95

ROCKETMAN: KING OF THE ROCKET MEN
INNOVATION

❑1 2.50
❑2 2.50
❑3 2.50
❑4 2.50

ROCKETO
SPEAKEASY COMICS

❑1, Sep 2005 2.99
❑2 2005 2.99
❑3 2005 2.99
❑4 2005 2.99
❑5 2005; Series moved to Image Comics with #6 2.99

ROCKETO: JOURNEY TO THE HIDDEN SEA
IMAGE

❑6, Apr 2006 2.99
❑7, Jun 2006 2.99
❑8, Jun 2006 2.99
❑9, Jul 2006 2.99

ROCKET RACCOON
MARVEL

❑1, May 1985 2.00
❑2, Jun 1985 1.00
❑3, Jul 1985 1.00
❑4, Aug 1985 1.00

ROCKET RANGER
ADVENTURE

❑1, Sep 1991 2.95
❑2, Dec 1991, b&w 2.95
❑3 1992, b&w 2.95
❑4 1992, b&w 2.95
❑5, Jul 1992, b&w 2.95
❑6 2.95

ROCK FANTASY
ROCK FANTASY

❑1; Pink Floyd 3.00
❑2; Rolling Stones 3.00
❑3; Led Zeppelin 3.00
❑4; New Kids on the Block; Stevie Nicks 3.00
❑5; Guns 'n Roses 3.00

N-MINT

❑6; Monstrosities of Rock 3.00
❑7; The Sex Pistols 3.00
❑8; Alice Cooper 3.00
❑9; Van Halen 3.00
❑10; Kiss 3.00
❑11; Jimi Hendrix 3.00
❑12; Def Leppard 3.00
❑13; David Bowie 3.00
❑14; The Doors 3.00
❑15; Pink Floyd II 3.00
❑16; Double-size; The Great Gig in the Sky 5.00
❑17; Rock Vixens 3.00

ROCKHEADS
SOLSON

❑1 1.95

ROCKIN' BONES
NEW ENGLAND

❑1, b&w 2.75
❑2, b&w 2.75
❑3, b&w 2.75
❑Holiday 1; Xmas Special 2.75

ROCKINFREAKAPOTAMUS PRESENTS THE RED HOT CHILI PEPPERS ILLUSTRATED LYRICS
TELLTALE

❑1, Jul 1997, b&w; magazine-sized 3.95

ROCKIN ROLLIN MINER ANTS
FATE

❑1, Oct 1991 2.25

ROCKMEEZ
JZINK COMICS

❑1, Oct 1992 2.50
❑2, Nov 1992 2.50
❑3 2.50
❑4 2.50

ROCK 'N' ROLL COMICS
REVOLUTIONARY

❑1, Jun 1989; Guns 'n' Roses 6.00
❑1/2nd, Jul 1989; Guns 'n' Roses 4.00
❑1/3rd, Aug 1989; Guns 'n' Roses 1.95
❑1/4th, Sep 1989; Guns 'n' Roses 1.95
❑1/5th, Oct 1989; Guns 'n' Roses 1.95
❑1/6th, Nov 1989; Guns 'n' Roses 1.95
❑1/7th, Dec 1989; Guns 'n' Roses; color; completely different than first six printings 1.95
❑2, Aug 1989; Metallica 3.00
❑2/2nd, Sep 1989; Metallica 1.95
❑2/3rd, Sep 1989; Metallica 1.95
❑2/4th, Sep 1989; Metallica 1.95
❑2/5th, Sep 1989; Metallica 1.95
❑2/6th, Metallica; 50% new material added 1.95
❑3, Sep 1989; Bon Jovi; Banned by Great Southern Co.; Rare 10.00
❑3/2nd, Oct 1989 1.95
❑4, Oct 1989; Motley Crue; Banned by Great Southern Co.; 15,000 copies burned by Great Southern 50.00
❑4/2nd, Oct 1989; 2nd printing (no Ace Backwords); Banned by Great Southern Co. 3.00
❑5, Nov 1989; Def Leppard 1.95

Other grades: Multiply price above by 5/6 for VF/NM • 2/3 for VERY FINE • 1/3 for FINE • 1/5 for VERY GOOD • 1/8 for GOOD

N-MINT

- ❑5/2nd, Nov 1989; Def Leppard 1.50
- ❑6, Dec 1989; Rolling Stones 1.95
- ❑6/2nd, Jan 1990; Rolling Stones 1.50
- ❑6/3rd, Jan 1990; Rolling Stones 1.50
- ❑6/4th, Feb 1990; Rolling Stones 1.50
- ❑7, Jan 1990; The Who 1.95
- ❑7/2nd, Feb 1990; The Who 1.50
- ❑7/3rd, Mar 1990; The Who 1.50
- ❑8, Feb 1990; Skid Row; Never published: banned by injunction from Great Southern Company 1.50
- ❑9, Mar 1990; Kiss 5.00
- ❑9/2nd, Apr 1990; Kiss 1.95
- ❑9/3rd, May 1990; Kiss 1.95
- ❑10, Apr 1990; Two different versions printed, one with Whitesnake on cover, one with Warrant 1.95
- ❑10/2nd, May 1990; Whitesnake only on cover 1.50
- ❑11, May 1990; Aerosmith 1.95
- ❑12, Jun 1990; New Kids on the Block 1.95
- ❑12/2nd, Aug 1990; New Kids On the Block 1.50
- ❑13, Jul 1990; Led Zeppelin 1.95
- ❑14, Aug 1990; Sex Pistols 1.95
- ❑15, Sep 1990, Poison 1.95
- ❑16, Oct 1990, Van Halen 1.95
- ❑17, Nov 1990, Madonna 3.00
- ❑18, Dec 1990; Alice Cooper; Full color 1.95
- ❑19, Apr 1991, b&w; Public Enemy, 2 Live Crew 2.50
- ❑20, Apr 1991, b&w; Queensryche 2.50
- ❑21, Jan 1991, b&w; Prince 2.50
- ❑22, Feb 1991, AC/DC 2.50
- ❑23, Mar 1991, b&w; Living Colour 2.50
- ❑24, Mar 1991; Anthrax b&w 2.50
- ❑25, May 1991, b&w; ZZ Top 2.50
- ❑26, May 1991; Doors 2.50
- ❑27, Jun 1991; Doors 2.50
- ❑28, Jun 1991; Ozzy Osbourne; Black Sabbath 2.50
- ❑29, Jul 1991; Ozzy Osbourne; Black Sabbath 2.50
- ❑30, Jul 1991; The Cure 2.50
- ❑31, Aug 1991; Vanilla Ice 2.50
- ❑32, Aug 1991; Frank Zappa 2.50
- ❑33, Sep 1991; Guns 'N' Roses II 2.50
- ❑34, Sep 1991; Black Crowes 2.50
- ❑35, Oct 1991; R.E.M. 2.50
- ❑36, Oct 1991; Michael Jackson 2.50
- ❑37, Nov 1991; Ice-T 2.50
- ❑38, Nov 1991; Rod Stewart 2.50
- ❑39, Dec 1991; The Fall of the New Kids 2.50
- ❑40, Dec 1991; NWA; Ice Cube 2.50
- ❑41, Jan 1992; Paula Abdul 2.50
- ❑42, Jan 1992; Metallica II 2.50
- ❑43, Feb 1992; Guns N' Roses: Tales from the Tour 2.50
- ❑44, Feb 1992; Scorpions 2.50
- ❑45, Mar 1992; Grateful Dead 2.50
- ❑46, Apr 1992; Grateful Dead II 2.50
- ❑47, May 1992; Grateful Dead III 2.50
- ❑48, Jun 1992; Queen 2.50
- ❑49, Jul 1992; Rush 2.50
- ❑50, Aug 1992; Bob Dylan 2.50
- ❑51, Sep 1992; Bob Dylan II 2.50
- ❑52, Oct 1992; Bob Dylan III 2.50
- ❑53, Nov 1992; Bruce Springsteen 2.50
- ❑54, Dec 1992; U2 2.50
- ❑55, Jan 1993; U2 II 2.50
- ❑56, Feb 1993; David Bowie 2.50
- ❑57, Mar 1993; Aerosmith 2.50
- ❑58, Apr 1993; Kate Bush 2.50
- ❑59, May 1993; Eric Clapton 2.50
- ❑60, Jun 1993; Genesis 2.50
- ❑61, Jul 1993; Yes 2.50
- ❑62, Aug 1993; Elton John 2.50
- ❑63, Sep 1993; Janis Joplin 2.50
- ❑64, Oct 1993; '60s San Francisco 2.50
- ❑65, Nov 1993; Sci-Fi Space Rockers 2.50

ROCK N' ROLL COMICS MAGAZINE
REVOLUTIONARY

- ❑1 2.95
- ❑2 2.95
- ❑3 2.95
- ❑4 2.95
- ❑5, Oct 1990; Aerosmith/Rolling Stones 2.95

N-MINT

ROCK 'N' ROLL (ONE-SHOT)
IMAGE

- ❑1, Jan 2006 2.99

ROCKOLA
MIRAGE

- ❑1 1.50

ROCKO'S MODERN LIFE
MARVEL

- ❑1, Jun 1994; TV cartoon 1.95
- ❑2, Jul 1994 1.95
- ❑3, Aug 1994 1.95
- ❑4, Sep 1994 1.95
- ❑5, Oct 1994 1.95
- ❑6, Nov 1994 1.95
- ❑7, Dec 1994 1.95

ROCKY AND HIS FIENDISH FRIENDS
GOLD KEY

- ❑1, Oct 1962 100.00
- ❑2, Dec 1962 75.00
- ❑3, Mar 1963 75.00
- ❑4, Jun 1963 60.00
- ❑5, Sep 1963 60.00

ROCKY HORROR PICTURE SHOW, THE: THE COMIC BOOK
CALIBER

- ❑1, Jul 1990 7.00
- ❑1/2nd; new cover 3.00
- ❑2, Aug 1990 4.00
- ❑3, Jan 1991 4.00

ROCKY LANE WESTERN (AC)
AC

- ❑1, b&w; Reprints 2.50
- ❑2, b&w; Reprints 5.95
- ❑Annual 1, b&w; Reprints 2.95

ROCKY: THE ONE AND ONLY
FANTAGRAPHICS

- ❑1, Jan 2006 4.99

ROEL
SIRIUS

- ❑1, Feb 1997, b&w; cardstock cover 2.95

ROGAN GOSH
DC / VERTIGO

- ❑1 6.95

ROGER FNORD
RIP OFF

- ❑1, Apr 1992, b&w 2.50

ROGER RABBIT
DISNEY

- ❑1, Jun 1990 1: Dick Flint 2.00
- ❑2, Jul 1990 1.75
- ❑3, Aug 1990 1.75
- ❑4, Sep 1990 1.75
- ❑5, Oct 1990 1.75
- ❑6, Nov 1990 1.50
- ❑7, Dec 1990 1.50
- ❑8, Jan 1991 1.50
- ❑9, Feb 1991 1.50
- ❑10, Mar 1991 1.50
- ❑11, Apr 1991 1.50
- ❑12, May 1991 1.50
- ❑13, Jun 1991 1.50
- ❑14, Jul 1991 1.50
- ❑15, Aug 1991 1.50
- ❑16, Sep 1991 1.50
- ❑17, Oct 1991 1.50
- ❑18, Nov 1991 1.50
- ❑Special 1 3.50

ROGER RABBIT IN 3-D
DISNEY

- ❑1; with glasses; 3-D Zone reprints 2.50

ROGER RABBIT'S TOONTOWN
DISNEY

- ❑1, Aug 1991 1.50
- ❑2, Sep 1991, Winsor McCay tribute 1.50
- ❑3, Oct 1991 1.50
- ❑4, Nov 1991 1.50
- ❑5, Dec 1991, Weasels solo story 1.50

ROGER WILCO
ADVENTURE

- ❑1 2.95
- ❑2, Apr 1992, b&w 2.95

N-MINT

ROG-2000
PACIFIC

- ❑1 2.00

ROGUE BATTLEBOOK
MARVEL

- ❑1 3.99

ROGUE (1ST MARVEL SERIES)
MARVEL

- ❑1, Jan 1995; enhanced cover 4.00
- ❑2, Feb 1995; enhanced cover 2.95
- ❑3, Mar 1995; enhanced cover 2.95
- ❑4, Apr 1995; enhanced cover 2.95

ROGUE (2ND MARVEL SERIES)
MARVEL

- ❑1, Sep 2001 2.50
- ❑2, Oct 2001 2.50
- ❑3, Nov 2001 2.50
- ❑4, Dec 2001 2.50

ROGUE (MARVEL 3RD SERIES)
MARVEL

- ❑1, Sep 2004 2.99
- ❑2, Oct 2004 2.99
- ❑3, Nov 2004 2.99
- ❑4, Dec 2004 2.99
- ❑5, Jan 2005 2.99
- ❑6, Feb 2005 2.99
- ❑7, Mar 2005 2.99
- ❑8, Apr 2005 2.99
- ❑9, May 2005 2.99
- ❑10, Jun 2005 2.99
- ❑11, Jul 2005 2.99
- ❑12, Aug 2005 2.99

ROGUE (MONSTER)
MONSTER

- ❑1, b&w 1.95

ROGUE SATELLITE COMICS
SLAVE LABOR

- ❑1, Aug 1996, b&w 2.95
- ❑2, b&w 2.95
- ❑3, Mar 1997, b&w 2.95
- ❑Special 1, b&w; Published by Modern; Flaming Carrot story 2.95

ROGUES GALLERY
DC

- ❑1, pin-ups 3.50

ROGUES, THE (VILLAINS)
DC

- ❑1, Feb 1998; New Year's Evil 1.95

ROGUE TROOPER (1ST SERIES)
FLEETWAY-QUALITY

- ❑1 DaG (a) 2.00
- ❑2 DaG (a) 2.00
- ❑3 DaG (a) 2.00
- ❑4 2.00
- ❑5 DaG (a) 2.00
- ❑6 1.75
- ❑7 AMo (w) 1.75
- ❑8 1.75
- ❑9 1.75
- ❑10 1.75
- ❑11 1.50
- ❑12 1.50
- ❑13 1.50
- ❑14 1.50
- ❑15 1.50
- ❑16 1.50
- ❑17 1.50
- ❑18 1.50
- ❑19 1.50
- ❑20 1.50
- ❑21, double issue #21/22 1.50
- ❑23, double issue #23/24 1.50
- ❑25 1.50
- ❑26 1.50
- ❑27 1.50
- ❑28 1.50
- ❑29 1.50
- ❑30 1.75
- ❑31 1.75
- ❑32 1.75
- ❑33 1.75
- ❑34 1.75
- ❑35 1.75
- ❑36 1.75

Sabre

Post-apocalyptic adventure from Gulacy

©Eclipse

Sabretooth

Logan's chief nemesis captured

©Marvel

Sabrina the Teenage Witch

Magical teen moves from Madhouse

©Archie

Sachs & Violens

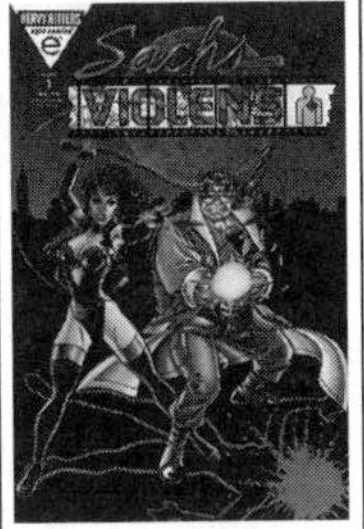

Photographer and model solve murder

©Marvel

Sad Sack

Reluctant draftee dodges responsibility

©Harvey

N-MINT

❑37 ... 1.75
❑38 ... 1.75
❑39 ... 1.75
❑40 ... 1.75
❑41 ... 1.75
❑42 ... 1.75
❑43 ... 1.75
❑44 ... 1.75
❑45 ... 1.75
❑46 ... 1.75
❑47 ... 1.75
❑48 ... 1.75
❑49 ... 1.75

ROGUE TROOPER (2ND SERIES)
FLEETWAY-QUALITY

❑1 ... 2.95
❑2 ... 2.95
❑3 ... 2.95
❑4 ... 2.95
❑5 ... 2.95
❑6 ... 2.95
❑7 ... 2.95
❑8 ... 2.95
❑9 ... 2.95

ROJA FUSION
ANTARCTIC

❑1, Apr 1995 ... 2.95

ROKKIN
DC

❑1, Sep 2006 ... 2.99

ROLAND: DAYS OF WRATH
TERRA MAJOR

❑1, Jul 1999 ... 2.95

ROLLERCOASTER
FANTAGRAPHICS

❑1, Sep 1996, b&w; magazine; cardstock cover ... 3.95

ROLLERCOASTERS SPECIAL EDITION
BLUE COMET

❑1 ... 2.00

ROLLING STONES
PERSONALITY

❑1, b&w ... 2.95
❑2, b&w ... 2.95
❑3, b&w ... 2.95

ROLLING STONES: VOODOO LOUNGE
MARVEL / MARVEL MUSIC

❑1, ca. 1995; prestige format one-shot ... 6.95

ROM
MARVEL

❑1, Dec 1979, SB (a); O: ROM. 1: ROM ... 8.00
❑2, Jan 1980, FM (c); SB, FM (a) ... 2.00
❑3, Feb 1980, FM (c); SB, FM (a); 1: Firefall ... 2.00
❑4, Mar 1980, SB (a) ... 1.50
❑5, Apr 1980, SB (a) ... 1.50
❑6, May 1980, SB (a) ... 1.50
❑7, Jun 1980, SB (a) ... 1.50
❑8, Jul 1980, SB (a) ... 1.50
❑9, Aug 1980, SB (a) ... 1.50
❑10, Sep 1980, SB (a) ... 1.50
❑11, Oct 1980, SB (a) ... 1.25

N-MINT

❑12, Nov 1980, SB (a) ... 1.25
❑13, Dec 1980, SB (a) ... 1.25
❑14, Jan 1981, SB (a) ... 1.25
❑15, Feb 1981, SB (a) ... 1.25
❑16, Mar 1981, SB (a) ... 1.25
❑17, Apr 1981, FM (c); SB, FM (a); A: X-Men ... 1.50
❑18, May 1981, FM (c); SB, FM (a); A: X-Men ... 1.50
❑19, Jun 1981, SB, JSt (a); A: X-Men ... 1.25
❑20, Jul 1981, SB, JSt (a) ... 1.25
❑21, Aug 1981, SB, JSt (a) ... 1.25
❑22, Sep 1981, SB, JSt (a) ... 1.25
❑23, Oct 1981, SB, JSt (a); A: Power Man ... 1.25
❑24, Nov 1981, SB, JSt (a); D: Crimebuster. D: Powerhouse. D: Nova-Prime. D: Comet (Harris Moore). D: Protector ... 1.50
❑25, Dec 1981; Giant-size SB, JSt (a) ... 1.50
❑26, Jan 1982 ... 1.25
❑27, Feb 1982 ... 1.25
❑28, Mar 1982 ... 1.25
❑29, Apr 1982 ... 1.25
❑30, May 1982 ... 1.25
❑31, Jun 1982 ... 1.25
❑32, Jul 1982 ... 1.25
❑33, Aug 1982 ... 1.25
❑34, Sep 1982 ... 1.25
❑35, Oct 1982 ... 1.25
❑36, Nov 1982 ... 1.25
❑37, Dec 1982 ... 1.25
❑38, Jan 1983 ... 1.25
❑39, Feb 1983 ... 1.25
❑40, Mar 1983 ... 1.25
❑41, Apr 1983 ... 1.25
❑42, May 1983 ... 1.25
❑43, Jun 1983 ... 1.25
❑44, Jul 1983, 1: Devastator II ... 1.25
❑45, Aug 1983 ... 1.25
❑46, Sep 1983 ... 1.25
❑47, Oct 1983 ... 1.25
❑48, Nov 1983 ... 1.25
❑49, Dec 1983 ... 1.25
❑50, Jan 1984; double-sized SB (a); A: Skrulls. D: Torpedo ... 1.25
❑51, Feb 1984 ... 1.25
❑52, Mar 1984 ... 1.25
❑53, Apr 1984 ... 1.25
❑54, May 1984 ... 3.00
❑55, Jun 1984 ... 1.25
❑56, Jul 1984, A: Alpha Flight ... 3.00
❑57, Aug 1984, A: Alpha Flight ... 1.25
❑58, Sep 1984, Dire Wraiths ... 1.25
❑59, Oct 1984, SD (a) ... 1.25
❑60, Nov 1984, SD (a) ... 1.25
❑61, Dec 1984, SD (a) ... 1.25
❑62, Jan 1985, SD (a) ... 1.25
❑63, Feb 1985, SD (a) ... 1.25
❑64, Mar 1985 ... 1.25
❑65, Apr 1985 ... 1.25
❑66, May 1985 ... 1.25
❑67, Jun 1985 ... 1.25
❑68, Jul 1985 ... 1.25
❑69, Aug 1985 ... 1.25

N-MINT

❑70, Sep 1985 ... 1.25
❑71, Oct 1985, D: The Unseen ... 1.25
❑72, Nov 1985, Secret Wars II ... 1.25
❑73, Dec 1985 ... 1.25
❑74, Jan 1986 D: Seeker ... 1.25
❑75, Feb 1986 D: Trapper. D: Scanner ... 2.00
❑Annual 1, ca. 1982; Stardust ... 1.00
❑Annual 2, ca. 1983 ... 1.00
❑Annual 3, ca. 1984 A: New Mutants . 1.00
❑Annual 4, ca. 1985 A: Gladiator. D: Pulsar ... 1.00

ROMANCER
MOONSTONE

❑1, Dec 1996, b&w ... 2.95

ROMAN HOLIDAYS
GOLD KEY

❑1, Feb 1973 ... 20.00
❑2, May 1973 ... 10.00
❑3, Aug 1973 ... 10.00

ROMANTIC TAILS
HEAD

❑1, Aug 1998, b&w ... 2.95

ROMP ONE SHOT
IMAGE

❑1, Jan 2004 ... 6.95

RONALD MCDONALD
CHARLTON

❑1, Sep 1970 ... 52.00
❑2, Nov 1970 ... 35.00
❑3, Jan 1971 ... 35.00
❑4, Mar 1971 ... 35.00

RONIN
DC

❑1, Jul 1983 FM (w); FM (a) ... 4.00
❑2, Sep 1983 FM (w); FM (a) ... 3.00
❑3, Nov 1983 FM (w); FM (a) ... 3.00
❑4, Jan 1984 FM (w); FM (a) ... 3.00
❑5, Jan 1984 FM (w); FM (a) ... 3.00
❑6, Aug 1984; FM (w); FM (a); Scarcer 5.00

ROOK
HARRIS

❑1, Jun 1995 ... 2.95
❑2 1995 ... 2.95

ROOK MAGAZINE
WARREN

❑1, Oct 1979 ... 4.00
❑2, Feb 1980 ... 2.50
❑3, Jun 1980 ... 2.50
❑4, Aug 1980 ... 2.50
❑5, Oct 1980 ... 2.50
❑6, Dec 1980 ... 2.50
❑7, Feb 1981 ... 2.50
❑8, Apr 1981 ... 2.50
❑9, Jun 1981 ... 2.50
❑10, Aug 1981 ... 2.50
❑11, Oct 1981 ... 2.00
❑12, Dec 1981 ... 2.00
❑13, Feb 1982 ... 2.00
❑14, Apr 1982 ... 2.00

ROOM 222
DELL

❑1, Jan 1970 ... 30.00

Other grades: Multiply price above by 5/6 for VF/NM • 2/3 for VERY FINE • 1/3 for FINE • 1/5 for VERY GOOD • 1/8 for GOOD

❑2, Mar 1970 ... 20.00
❑3, Jul 1970 ... 20.00
❑4, Jan 1971 ... 20.00

ROOTER
CUSTOM

❑1, Aug 1996 ... 2.95
❑2, Dec 1996 ... 2.95
❑3, Feb 1997 ... 2.95
❑4, May 1997 ... 2.95
❑5, Jul 1997 ... 2.95
❑6, Oct 1997 ... 2.95

ROOTER (VOL. 2)
CUSTOM

❑1, b&w ... 2.95
❑2, ca. 1998, b&w ... 2.95

ROOTS OF THE OPPRESSOR
NORTHSTAR

❑1, b&w ... 2.95

ROOTS OF THE SWAMP THING
DC

❑1, Jul 1986; Reprints ... 2.00
❑2, Aug 1986; Reprints ... 2.00
❑3, Sep 1986; reprints Swamp Thing #5 and #6 and House of Mystery #191 ... 2.00
❑4, Oct 1986; reprints Swamp Thing #7 and #8 and House of Mystery #221 2.00
❑5, Nov 1986; Reprints stories from Swamp Thing #9, #10, House of Mystery #92 ... 2.00

ROSCOE! THE DAWG, ACE DETECTIVE
RENEGADE

❑1, Jul 1987, b&w ... 2.00
❑2, Oct 1987, b&w ... 2.00
❑3, Nov 1987, b&w ... 2.00
❑4, Jan 1988, b&w ... 2.00

ROSE & THORN
DC / WILDSTORM

❑1, Feb 2004 ... 2.95
❑2, Mar 2004 ... 2.95
❑3, Apr 2004 ... 2.95
❑4, May 2004 ... 2.95
❑5, Jun 2004 ... 2.95
❑6, Jul 2004 ... 2.95

ROSE
HERO

❑1 ... 3.50
❑2 ... 2.95
❑3 ... 3.95
❑4 ... 3.95
❑5, Dec 1993 ... 2.95

ROSE (CARTOON BOOKS)
CARTOON BOOKS

❑1, Nov 2000 ... 5.95
❑2, Apr 2001 ... 5.95
❑3, Feb 2002 ... 5.95

ROSE & GUNN
BISHOP

❑3, May 1995, b&w ... 2.95
❑4, Jun 1995, b&w ... 2.95
❑5, Aug 1995, b&w ... 2.95

ROSE & GUNN CREATOR'S CHOICE
BISHOP

❑1, Sep 1995, b&w ... 2.95

ROSWELL: LITTLE GREEN MAN
BONGO

❑1, ca. 1996 ... 3.50
❑2, ca. 1996 ... 3.00
❑3, ca. 1996 V: Professor Von Sphinkter ... 3.00
❑4, ca. 1997 D: Shorty George ... 3.00
❑5, ca. 1998 ... 3.00
❑6, ca. 1999 ... 3.00

ROTOGIN JUNKBOTZ
IMAGE

❑0, Mar 2003 ... 2.50
❑1, May 2003 ... 2.95
❑2, Aug 2003 ... 2.95
❑3, Oct 2003 ... 2.95

ROUGH RAIDERS
BLUE COMET

❑1 ... 2.00
❑2 ... 2.00

❑3 ... 2.00
❑Annual 1 ... 2.50

ROULETTE
CALIBER

❑1, b&w ... 2.50

ROUTE 666
CROSSGEN

❑1, Jun 2002 ... 2.95
❑2, Jul 2002 ... 2.95
❑3, Aug 2002 ... 2.95
❑4, Sep 2002 ... 2.95
❑5, Oct 2002 ... 2.95
❑6, Nov 2002 ... 2.95
❑7, Dec 2002 ... 2.95
❑8, Jan 2003 ... 2.95
❑9, Feb 2003 ... 2.95
❑10, Mar 2003 ... 2.95
❑11, Apr 2003 ... 2.95
❑12, May 2003 ... 2.95
❑13, Jul 2003 ... 2.95
❑14, Aug 2003 ... 2.95
❑15, Oct 2003 ... 2.95
❑16, Nov 2003 ... 2.95
❑17, Dec 2003 ... 2.95
❑18, Dec 2003 ... 2.95
❑19, Jan 2004 ... 2.95
❑20, Mar 2004 ... 2.95
❑21, Apr 2004 ... 2.95
❑22, May 2004 ... 2.95

ROVERS
MALIBU

❑1, Sep 1987 ... 1.95
❑2 1987 ... 1.95
❑3 1987 ... 1.95
❑4 1988 ... 1.95
❑5 1988 ... 1.95
❑6 1988, b&w ... 1.95
❑7 1988, b&w ... 1.95

ROYAL ROY
MARVEL / STAR

❑1, May 1985 1: Royal Roy ... 1.00
❑2, Jul 1985 ... 1.00
❑3, Sep 1985 ... 1.00
❑4, Nov 1985 ... 1.00
❑5, Jan 1986 ... 1.00
❑6, Mar 1986 ... 1.00

ROY ROGERS WESTERN
AC

❑1, b&w; Reprints ... 4.95

ROY ROGERS WESTERN CLASSICS
AC

❑1, some color; reprints ... 2.95
❑2, some color; reprints ... 2.95
❑3, some color; reprints ... 3.95
❑4, some color; reprints ... 3.95
❑5, some color; reprints; photos ... 2.95

RTA: PERSONALITY CRISIS
IMAGE

❑0, Oct 2005 ... 2.99

RUBBER BLANKET
RUBBER BLANKET

❑1, b&w ... 5.75
❑2 ... 7.75
❑3 ... 7.95

RUBES REVUE
FRAGMENTS WEST

❑1, b&w ... 2.00

RUBY SHAFT'S TALES OF THE UNEXPURGATED
FANTAGRAPHICS / EROS

❑1, b&w ... 2.50

RUCK BUD WEBSTER AND HIS SCREECHING COMMANDOS
PYRAMID

❑1, b&w ... 1.60

RUDE AWAKENING
DENNIS MCMILLAN

❑1, Apr 1996, b&w ... 12.95

RUFF AND REDDY
DELL

❑4, Jan 1960, Previous issues appeared as Four Color #937, #981, and #1038 ... 40.00

❑5, Apr 1960 ... 40.00
❑6, Jul 1960 ... 40.00
❑7, Oct 1960 ... 40.00
❑8, Jan 1961 ... 40.00
❑9, Apr 1961 ... 30.00
❑10, Jul 1961 ... 30.00
❑11, Oct 1961 ... 30.00
❑12, Jan 1962 ... 30.00

RUGRATS COMIC ADVENTURES
NICKELODEON MAGAZINES

❑1, 1997 ... 3.50
❑2, 1997 ... 3.00
❑3, 1998 ... 3.00
❑4, 1998 ... 3.00
❑5, 1998 ... 3.00
❑6, 1998 ... 3.00
❑7, 1998 ... 3.00
❑8, Jun 1998; magazine; no cover price 3.00
❑9, 1998 ... 3.00
❑10, Aug 1998; magazine; no cover price ... 3.00

RUGRATS COMIC ADVENTURES (VOL. 2)
NICKELODEON MAGAZINES

❑1, Sep 1998; magazine; no cover price 3.00

RUINS
MARVEL

❑1, Aug 1995; Acetate cover overlaying cardstock inner cover ... 4.95
❑2, Sep 1995; Acetate cover overlaying cardstock inner cover ... 4.95

RUMBLE GIRLS: SILKY WARRIOR TANSIE
IMAGE

❑1, Apr 2000 ... 3.50
❑2, Jun 2000 ... 3.50
❑3, Jul 2000 ... 3.50
❑4, Aug 2000 ... 3.50
❑5, Nov 2000 ... 3.50
❑6, Jan 2001 ... 3.50

RUMIC WORLD
VIZ

❑1, b&w; Fire Tripper ... 3.25
❑2, b&w; Laughing Target ... 3.50

RUMMAGE $2099
PARODY

❑1, foil cover ... 2.95

RUNAWAY
DELL

❑1, Oct 1964 ... 16.00

RUNAWAY: A KNOWN ASSOCIATES MYSTERY
KNOWN ASSOCIATES

❑1, b&w ... 2.50

RUNAWAYS
MARVEL

❑1, Jul 2003 ... 4.00
❑2, Aug 2003 ... 2.50
❑3, Sep 2003 ... 2.50
❑4, Oct 2003 ... 2.50
❑5, Nov 2003 ... 2.99
❑6, Nov 2003 ... 2.99
❑7, Dec 2003, (c) ... 2.50
❑8, Jan 2004 ... 2.99
❑9, Feb 2004 ... 2.99
❑10, Mar 2004 ... 2.99
❑11, Apr 2004 ... 2.99
❑12, Apr 2004 ... 2.99
❑13, May 2004 ... 2.99
❑14, Jun 2004 ... 2.99
❑15, Jul 2004 ... 2.99
❑16, Aug 2004 ... 2.99
❑17, Oct 2004 ... 2.99
❑18, Nov 2004 ... 2.99

RUNAWAYS (VOL. 2)
MARVEL

❑1, Apr 2005 ... 2.99
❑1/Variant, Apr 2005 ... 4.00
❑2, May 2005 ... 2.99
❑3, Jun 2005 ... 2.99
❑4, Jul 2005 ... 2.99
❑5, Aug 2005 ... 2.99
❑6, Sep 2005 ... 2.99
❑7, Oct 2005 ... 2.99

Sad Sack & The Sarge

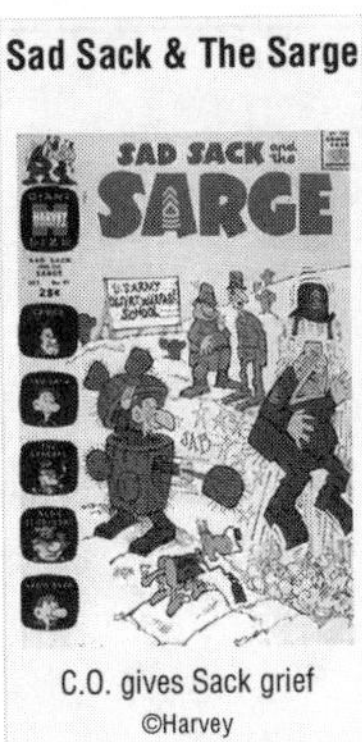

C.O. gives Sack grief
©Harvey

Sad Sack Army Life Parade

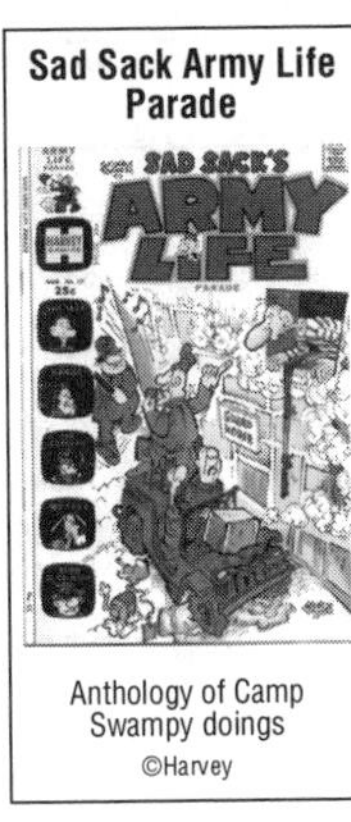

Anthology of Camp Swampy doings
©Harvey

Sad Sack Laugh Special

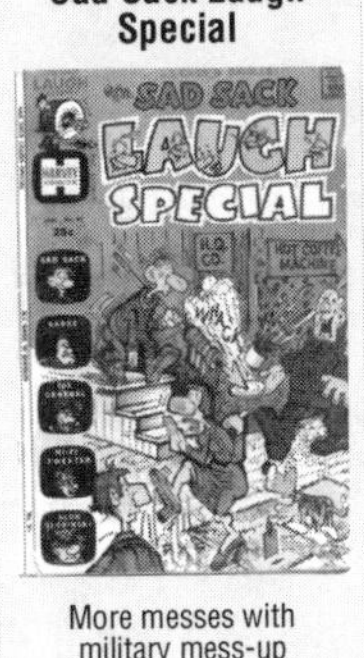

More messes with military mess-up
©Harvey

Sad Sack Navy, Gobs 'n' Gals

Sad Sack is all at sea in short-lived series
©Harvey

Sad Sack's Funny Friends

Solo spotlight shines on Sad Sack peers
©Harvey

N-MINT

❑8 2005 .... 2.99
❑9, Dec 2005 .... 2.99
❑10, Jan 2006 .... 2.99
❑11, Feb 2006 .... 2.99
❑12, Mar 2006 .... 2.99
❑13, Apr 2006 .... 2.99
❑14, May 2006 .... 2.99
❑15, Jul 2006 .... 2.99
❑16, Aug 2006 .... 2.99
❑17, Sep 2006 .... 2.99

RUN, BUDDY, RUN
GOLD KEY

❑1, Jun 1967 .... 15.00

RUNE
MALIBU / ULTRAVERSE

❑0, Jan 1994; Promotional edition (from redeeming coupons in early Ultraverse comics); no cover price . 3.00
❑1, Jan 1994 .... 2.00
❑1/Variant, Jan 1994; Foil limited edition; silver foil logo 2.00
❑2, Feb 1994 .... 1.95
❑3, Mar 1994; 1: Ripfire. 1: Elven. Flip-book with Ultraverse Premiere #1... 3.50
❑4, Jun 1994 .... 1.95
❑5, Sep 1994 .... 1.95
❑6, Dec 1994 .... 1.95
❑7, Feb 1995 .... 1.95
❑8, Feb 1995 .... 1.95
❑9, Apr 1995 D: Sybil. D: Master Oshi. D: Tantalus 1.95
❑Giant Size 1, Jan 1995; Giant-size Rune #1 O: Rune. 1: Sybil. 1: Master Oshi. 1: Tantalus. D: El Gato 2.50

RUNE (VOL. 2)
MALIBU / ULTRAVERSE

❑0, Sep 1995; Black September; Rune #Infinity; black cover 1.50
❑0/Variant, Sep 1995; alternate cover; Rune #Infinity 2.00
❑1, Oct 1995 A: Gemini. A: Adam Warlock. A: Annihilus 1.50
❑2, Nov 1995 .... 1.50
❑3, Dec 1995 .... 1.50
❑4, Jan 1996 .... 1.50
❑5, Feb 1996 .... 1.50
❑6, Mar 1996 .... 1.50
❑7, Apr 1996 .... 1.50

RUNE: HEARTS OF DARKNESS
MALIBU

❑1, Sep 1996; Flip-book 1.50
❑2, Oct 1996; Flip-book 1.50
❑3, Nov 1996; Flip-book 1.50

RUNE/SILVER SURFER
MARVEL

❑1, Apr 1995; newsstand edition; crossover 3.00
❑1/Direct ed., Apr 1995; Direct Market edition; crossover; Squarebound with glossier paper 6.00

RUNES OF RAGNAN
IMAGE

❑1, Dec 2005 .... 2.99
❑2, Jan 2006 .... 2.99
❑3, Mar 2006 .... 2.99
❑4, Apr 2006 .... 2.99

N-MINT

RUNE VS. VENOM
MALIBU / ULTRAVERSE

❑1, Dec 1995 .... 3.95

RUNE/WRATH
MALIBU / ULTRAVERSE

❑1; gold foil ashcan 1.00

RUNNERS: BAD GOODS
SERVE MAN PRESS

❑1, Jan 2003 .... 2.95
❑2, Sep 2003 .... 2.95
❑3, Jun 2004 .... 2.95
❑4, Aug 2004 .... 2.95
❑5, Feb 2005 .... 2.95

RUROUNI KENSHIN
VIZ

❑1, Oct 2003 .... 9.99
❑2, Dec 2003 .... 9.99
❑3, Feb 2004 .... 9.99
❑4, Apr 2004 .... 9.99
❑5, Jun 2004 .... 9.99
❑6, Aug 2004 .... 9.99
❑7, Oct 2004 .... 9.99
❑8, Nov 2004 .... 9.99
❑9, Dec 2004 .... 9.99
❑10, Jan 2005 .... 9.99
❑11, Feb 2005 .... 9.99
❑12, Mar 2005 .... 9.99
❑13, Apr 2005 .... 9.99
❑14, May 2005 .... 9.99
❑15, Jun 2005 .... 9.99
❑16, Jul 2005 .... 9.99
❑17, Aug 2005 .... 9.99
❑18, Sep 2005 .... 9.99
❑19, Oct 2005 .... 9.99

RUSE
CROSSGEN

❑1, Nov 2001 .... 2.95
❑2, Dec 2001 .... 2.95
❑3, Jan 2002 .... 2.95
❑4, Feb 2002 .... 2.95
❑5, Mar 2002 .... 2.95
❑6, Apr 2002 .... 2.95
❑7, May 2002 .... 2.95
❑8, Jun 2002 .... 2.95
❑9, Jul 2002 .... 2.95
❑10, Aug 2002 .... 2.95
❑11, Sep 2002 .... 2.95
❑12, Oct 2002 .... 2.95
❑13, Nov 2002 .... 2.95
❑14, Dec 2002 .... 2.95
❑15, Jan 2003 .... 2.95
❑16, Feb 2003 .... 2.95
❑17, Mar 2003 .... 2.95
❑18, Apr 2003 .... 2.95
❑19, May 2003 .... 2.95
❑20, Jun 2003 .... 2.95
❑21, Jul 2003 .... 2.95
❑22, Aug 2003 .... 2.95
❑23, Sep 2003 .... 2.95
❑24, Nov 2003 .... 2.95
❑25, Nov 2003 .... 2.95
❑26, Jan 2004 .... 2.95

N-MINT

RUSE: ARCHARD'S AGENTS: DEADLY DARE
CROSSGEN

❑1, Apr 2004 .... 2.95

RUSE: ARCHARD'S AGENTS: PUGILISTIC PETE
CROSSGEN

❑1, Nov 2003 .... 2.95

RUSH LIMBAUGH MUST DIE
BONEYARD

❑1, Nov 1993, b&w 5.00

RUST
NOW

❑1, Jul 1987 .... 2.00
❑2, Aug 1987 .... 2.00
❑3, Sep 1987 .... 2.00
❑4, Nov 1987 .... 2.00
❑5, Dec 1987 .... 2.00
❑6, Jan 1988 .... 2.00
❑7, Feb 1988 .... 2.00
❑8, Mar 1988 .... 2.00
❑9, Apr 1988 .... 2.00
❑10, May 1988 .... 2.00
❑11, Jul 1988 .... 2.00
❑12, Aug 1988; Terminator preview ... 2.00
❑13, Sep 1988 .... 2.00

RUST (2ND SERIES)
NOW

❑1, Feb 1989 .... 2.00
❑2, Mar 1989 .... 2.00
❑3, Apr 1989 .... 2.00
❑4, May 1989 .... 2.00
❑5, Jun 1989 .... 2.00
❑6, Aug 1989 .... 2.00
❑7, Sep 1989 .... 2.00

RUST (3RD SERIES)
ADVENTURE

❑1, Apr 1992, Adventure Comics 2.95
❑1/Ltd., Apr 1992; limited edition; Cardstock cover; rust-colored foil logo 4.95
❑2, Jun 1992 .... 2.95
❑3, Aug 1992 .... 2.95
❑4, Sep 1992 .... 2.95

RUST (4TH SERIES)
CALIBER

❑1 .... 2.95
❑2 .... 2.95

RUULE: GANGLORDS OF CHINATOWN
BECKETT

❑1, Nov 2003 .... 2.99
❑2, Dec 2003 .... 2.99
❑3, Jan 2004 .... 2.99
❑4, Feb 2004 .... 2.99
❑5, Mar 2004 .... 2.99

SABAN POWERHOUSE
ACCLAIM

❑1, ca. 1997; digest; Power Rangers Turbo, Masked Rider, Samurai Pizza Cats; no indicia 4.50
❑2, ca. 1997; digest; Power Rangers Turbo, Masked Rider, Samurai Pizza Cats, BettleBorgs 4.50

Other grades: Multiply price above by 5/6 for VF/NM • 2/3 for VERY FINE • 1/3 for FINE • 1/5 for VERY GOOD • 1/8 for GOOD

SABAN PRESENTS POWER RANGERS TURBO VS. BEETLEBORGS METALLIX
ACCLAIM
- ❑1, ca. 1997; digest ... 4.50

SABINA
FANTAGRAPHICS / EROS
- ❑1 ... 2.95
- ❑2 ... 2.95
- ❑3 ... 2.95
- ❑4 ... 2.95
- ❑5 ... 2.95
- ❑6 ... 2.95
- ❑7, Jul 1996 ... 2.95

SABLE
FIRST
- ❑1, Mar 1988 ... 2.00
- ❑2, Apr 1988 ... 2.00
- ❑3, May 1988 ... 2.00
- ❑4, Jun 1988 ... 2.00
- ❑5, Jul 1988 ... 2.00
- ❑6, Aug 1988 ... 2.00
- ❑7, Sep 1988 ... 2.00
- ❑8, Oct 1988 ... 2.00
- ❑9, Nov 1988 ... 2.00
- ❑10, Dec 1988 ... 2.00
- ❑11, Jan 1989 ... 2.00
- ❑12, Feb 1989 ... 2.00
- ❑13, Mar 1989 ... 2.00
- ❑14, Apr 1989 ... 2.00
- ❑15, May 1989 ... 2.00
- ❑16, Jun 1989 ... 2.00
- ❑17, Jul 1989 ... 2.00
- ❑18, Aug 1989 ... 2.00
- ❑19, Sep 1989 ... 2.00
- ❑20, Oct 1989 ... 2.00
- ❑21, Nov 1989 ... 2.00
- ❑22, Dec 1989 ... 2.00
- ❑23, Jan 1990 ... 2.00
- ❑24, Feb 1990 ... 2.00
- ❑25, Mar 1990 ... 2.00
- ❑26, Apr 1990 ... 2.00
- ❑27, May 1990 ... 2.00

SABLE & FORTUNE
MARVEL
- ❑1, Mar 2006 ... 2.99
- ❑2, Mar 2006 ... 2.99
- ❑3, Jun 2006 ... 2.99
- ❑4, Jun 2006 ... 2.99

SABLE (MIKE GRELL'S...)
FIRST
- ❑1, Mar 1990, MGr (w); MGr (a); Reprints Jon Sable, Freelance #1 ... 2.00
- ❑2, Apr 1990, MGr (w); MGr (a); Reprints ... 2.00
- ❑3, May 1990, MGr (w); MGr (a); Reprints ... 2.00
- ❑4, Jun 1990, MGr (w); MGr (a); Reprints ... 2.00
- ❑5, Jul 1990, MGr (w); MGr (a); Reprints ... 2.00
- ❑6, Aug 1990, MGr (w); MGr (a); Reprints ... 2.00
- ❑7, Sep 1990, MGr (w); MGr (a); Reprints ... 2.00
- ❑8, Oct 1990, MGr (w); MGr (a); Reprints ... 2.00
- ❑9, Nov 1990, MGr (w); MGr (a); Reprints ... 2.00
- ❑10, Dec 1990, MGr (w); MGr (a); Reprints ... 2.00

SABRA BLADE
DRACULINA
- ❑1, Dec 1994, b&w ... 2.50
- ❑1/Variant, Dec 1994, b&w; alternate two-color cover ... 2.50

SABRE
ECLIPSE
- ❑1, Aug 1982 PG (c); PG (a); 1: Sabre ... 2.50
- ❑2, Oct 1982 PG (c); PG (a) ... 2.00
- ❑3, Dec 1982 PG (a) ... 2.00
- ❑4, Mar 1983 ... 2.00
- ❑5, Jul 1983 ... 2.00
- ❑6, Oct 1983 ... 2.00
- ❑7, Dec 1983 ... 2.00
- ❑8, Feb 1984 ... 2.00
- ❑9, Apr 1984 ... 2.00
- ❑10, Jun 1984 ... 1.75
- ❑11, Aug 1984 ... 1.75
- ❑12, Jan 1985 ... 1.75
- ❑13, Apr 1985 ... 1.75
- ❑14, Aug 1985 ... 1.75

SABRETOOTH
MARVEL
- ❑1, Aug 1993; Die-cut cover ... 3.00
- ❑2, Sep 1993 ... 3.00
- ❑3, Oct 1993; A: Mystique. cardstock cover ... 3.00
- ❑4, Nov 1993 ... 3.00
- ❑Special 1, Jan 1995; Special edition; enhanced wraparound cover ... 4.95

SABRETOOTH (VOL. 2)
MARVEL
- ❑1, Jan 1998, Prestige format one-shot ... 5.99

SABRETOOTH (3RD SERIES)
MARVEL
- ❑1, 2004 ... 2.99
- ❑2 ... 2.99
- ❑3 ... 2.99
- ❑4, 2005 ... 2.99

SABRETOOTH CLASSIC
MARVEL
- ❑1, May 1994, reprints Power Man & Iron Fist #66 ... 2.00
- ❑2, Jun 1994, KGa (a); reprints Power Man & Iron Fist #78 ... 1.50
- ❑3, Jul 1994, reprints Power Man & Iron Fist #84 ... 1.50
- ❑4, Aug 1994, reprints Peter Parker, The Spectacular Spider-Man #116.. 1.50
- ❑5, Sep 1994, RB, BMc (a); reprints Peter Parker, The Spectacular Spider-Man #119 ... 1.50
- ❑6, Oct 1994, reprints X-Factor #10... 1.50
- ❑7, Nov 1994, SB (a); reprints The Mighty Thor #374 ... 1.50
- ❑8, Dec 1994, reprints Power Pack #27 1.50
- ❑9, Jan 1995, reprints Uncanny X-Men #212 ... 1.50
- ❑10, Feb 1995, reprints Uncanny X-Men #213 ... 1.50
- ❑11, Mar 1995, SB (a); reprints Daredevil #238 ... 1.50
- ❑12, Apr 1995, reprints back-up stories from Classic X-Men #10 and Marvel Super-Heroes (no issue given) ... 1.50
- ❑13, May 1995, reprints Uncanny X-Men #219 ... 1.50
- ❑14, Jun 1995, reprints Uncanny X-Men #221 ... 1.50
- ❑15, Jul 1995, reprints Uncanny X-Men #222 ... 1.50

SABRETOOTH: MARY SHELLEY OVERDRIVE
MARVEL
- ❑1, Aug 2002 ... 2.99
- ❑2, Sep 2002 ... 2.99
- ❑3, Oct 2002 ... 2.99
- ❑4, Nov 2002 ... 2.99

SABRINA
ARCHIE
- ❑1, May 1997, DDC (a); Photo worked into cover art ... 2.50
- ❑2, Jun 1997, Photo worked into cover art 2.00
- ❑3, Jul 1997, Photo worked into cover art 2.00
- ❑4, Aug 1997, Photo worked into cover art 1.50
- ❑5, Sep 1997, Photo worked into cover art 1.50
- ❑6, Oct 1997, Photo worked into cover art 1.50
- ❑7, Nov 1997, Photo worked into cover art 1.50
- ❑8, Dec 1997, Photo worked into cover art 1.50
- ❑9, Jan 1998, Photo worked into cover art 1.75
- ❑10, Feb 1998, Photo worked into cover art ... 1.75
- ❑11, Mar 1998, Photo worked into cover art ... 1.75
- ❑12, Apr 1998, Photo worked into cover art ... 1.75
- ❑13, May 1998, Photo worked into cover art ... 1.75
- ❑14, Jun 1998, Photo worked into cover art ... 1.75
- ❑15, Jul 1998, Photo worked into cover art ... 1.75
- ❑16, Aug 1998, Photo worked into cover art ... 1.75
- ❑17, Sep 1998, A: Josie & the Pussycats. Photo worked into cover art ... 1.75
- ❑18, Oct 1998, Photo worked into cover art ... 1.75
- ❑19, Nov 1998, DDC (a); Photo worked into cover art; back to the '60s ... 1.75
- ❑20, Dec 1998, Photo worked into cover art ... 1.75
- ❑21, Jan 1999, Photo worked into cover art ... 1.75
- ❑22, Feb 1999, Photo worked into cover art ... 1.75
- ❑23, Mar 1999, Photo worked into cover art (hidden in crowd) ... 1.75
- ❑24, Apr 1999, Photo is inset on cover 1.79
- ❑25, May 1999, Photo worked into cover art ... 1.79
- ❑26, Jun 1999, Photo is inset on cover 1.79
- ❑27, Jul 1999, Photo is inset on cover 1.79
- ❑28, Aug 1999, A: Sonic. Photo is inset on cover; continues in Sonic Super Special #10 ... 1.79
- ❑29, Sep 1999, Photo is inset on cover 1.79
- ❑30, Oct 1999, Photo is inset on cover 1.79
- ❑31, Nov 1999, Photo is inset on cover 1.79
- ❑32, Dec 1999, DDC (c); Photo appears in inset ... 1.79

SABRINA (VOL. 2)
ARCHIE
- ❑1, Jan 2000, based on the animated series ... 1.99
- ❑2, Feb 2000 ... 1.99
- ❑3, Mar 2000 ... 1.99
- ❑4, Apr 2000 ... 1.99
- ❑5, May 2000 ... 1.99
- ❑6, Jun 2000 ... 1.99
- ❑7, Jul 2000 ... 1.99
- ❑8, Aug 2000 ... 1.99
- ❑9, Sep 2000 ... 1.99
- ❑10, Oct 2000 ... 1.99
- ❑11, Nov 2000 ... 1.99
- ❑12, Dec 2000 ... 1.99
- ❑13, Jan 2001 ... 1.99
- ❑14, Feb 2001 ... 1.99
- ❑15, Mar 2001 ... 1.99
- ❑16, Apr 2001 ... 1.99
- ❑17, May 2001 ... 1.99
- ❑18, Jun 2001 ... 1.99
- ❑19, Jul 2001 ... 1.99
- ❑20, Aug 2001 ... 1.99
- ❑21, Sep 2001 ... 1.99
- ❑22, Oct 2001 ... 1.99
- ❑23, Nov 2001 ... 1.99
- ❑24, Dec 2001 ... 1.99
- ❑25, Jan 2002 ... 1.99
- ❑26, Jan 2002 ... 1.99
- ❑27, Feb 2002 ... 1.99
- ❑28, Mar 2002 ... 1.99
- ❑29, Apr 2002 ... 1.99
- ❑30, May 2002 ... 1.99
- ❑31, Jun 2002 ... 1.99
- ❑32, Jul 2002 ... 1.99
- ❑33, Aug 2002 ... 1.99
- ❑34, Sep 2002 ... 1.99
- ❑35, Oct 2002 ... 1.99
- ❑36, Nov 2002 ... 1.99
- ❑37, Dec 2002 ... 1.99
- ❑38, Jan 2003 ... 1.99
- ❑39, Jan 2003 ... 2.19
- ❑40, Feb 2003 ... 2.19
- ❑41, Mar 2003 ... 2.19
- ❑42, Apr 2003 ... 2.19
- ❑43, May 2003 ... 2.19
- ❑44, Jun 2003 ... 2.19
- ❑45, Jul 2003 ... 2.19
- ❑46, Aug 2003 ... 2.19
- ❑47, Sep 2003 ... 2.19
- ❑48, Oct 2003 ... 2.19
- ❑49, Nov 2003 ... 2.19
- ❑50, Dec 2003 ... 2.19
- ❑51, Dec 2003 ... 2.19
- ❑52, Jan 2004 ... 2.19
- ❑53, Feb 2004 ... 2.19
- ❑54, Mar 2004 ... 2.19
- ❑55, Apr 2004 ... 2.19
- ❑56, May 2004 ... 2.19
- ❑57, Jul 2004 ... 2.19
- ❑58, Aug 2004 ... 2.19
- ❑59, Sep 2004 ... 2.19
- ❑60, Oct 2004 ... 2.19

Safety-Belt Man

Crash-test dummy gains life

©Sirius

Saga of Ra's Al Ghul

Extreme conservationist's early appearances

©DC

Sailor Moon Comic

Manga series of cosmically-named heroines

©Mixxzine

Sam and Twitch

More cases for Spawn investigators

©Image

Sam Slade, Robo-Hunter

A rogue hunter of rogue robots

©Fleetway-Quality

	N-MINT
❑61, Nov 2004	2.19
❑62, Jan 2005	2.19
❑63, Feb 2005	2.19
❑64, Mar 2005	2.19
❑65, Apr 2005	2.19
❑66, May 2005	2.19
❑67 2005	2.39
❑68 2005	2.39
❑69 2005	2.39
❑70 2005	2.39
❑71, Dec 2005	2.39
❑72, Jan 2006	2.39
❑73, Feb 2006	2.39
❑74, May 2006	2.39
❑75, Jun 2006	2.39
❑76, Aug 2006	2.39
❑77, Aug 2006	2.39

SABRINA ONLINE
VISION

❑2	3.50

SABRINA THE TEENAGE WITCH
ARCHIE

❑1, Apr 1971, Giant-size	45.00
❑2, Jul 1971, Giant-size	20.00
❑3, Sep 1971, Giant-size	12.00
❑4, Dec 1971, Giant-size	12.00
❑5, Feb 1972, Giant-size	12.00
❑6, Jun 1972, Giant-size	10.00
❑7, Aug 1972, Giant-size	10.00
❑8, Sep 1972, Giant-size	10.00
❑9, Oct 1972, Giant-size	10.00
❑10, Feb 1973, Giant-size	10.00
❑11, Apr 1973, Giant-size	8.00
❑12, Jun 1973, Giant-size	8.00
❑13, Aug 1973, Giant-size	8.00
❑14, Sep 1973, Giant-size	8.00
❑15, Oct 1973, Giant-size	8.00
❑16, Dec 1973, Giant-size	8.00
❑17, Feb 1974, Giant-size	8.00
❑18, Apr 1974	6.00
❑19, Jun 1974	6.00
❑20, Aug 1974	6.00
❑21, Sep 1974	5.00
❑22, Oct 1974	5.00
❑23, Feb 1975	5.00
❑24, Apr 1975	5.00
❑25, Jun 1975	5.00
❑26, Aug 1975	5.00
❑27, Sep 1975	5.00
❑28, Oct 1975	5.00
❑29, Dec 1975	5.00
❑30, Feb 1976	5.00
❑31, Apr 1976	4.00
❑32, Jun 1976	4.00
❑33, Aug 1976	4.00
❑34, Sep 1976	4.00
❑35, Oct 1976, A: Betty. A: Ethel. A: Jughead. A: Veronica	4.00
❑36, Dec 1977	4.00
❑37, Feb 1977	4.00
❑38, May 1977	4.00
❑39, Jun 1977	4.00
❑40, Aug 1977	4.00
❑41, Sep 1977	4.00
❑42, Oct 1977	4.00
❑43, Dec 1977	4.00
❑44, Feb 1978	4.00
❑45, May 1978	4.00
❑46, Jun 1978	4.00
❑47, Aug 1978	4.00
❑48, Sep 1978	4.00
❑49, Oct 1978	4.00
❑50, Dec 1978	4.00
❑51, Feb 1979	3.00
❑52, May 1979	3.00
❑53, Jun 1979	3.00
❑54, Aug 1979	3.00
❑55, Sep 1979	3.00
❑56, Oct 1979	3.00
❑57, Dec 1979	3.00
❑58, Feb 1980	3.00
❑59, Apr 1980	3.00
❑60, Jun 1980	3.00
❑61, Aug 1980	2.00
❑62, Sep 1980	2.00
❑63, Oct 1980	2.00
❑64, Dec 1980	2.00
❑65, Feb 1981	2.00
❑66, Apr 1981	2.00
❑67, Jun 1981	2.00
❑68, Aug 1981	2.00
❑69, Oct 1981	2.00
❑70, Dec 1981	2.00
❑71, Feb 1982	2.00
❑72, Apr 1982	2.00
❑73, Jun 1982	2.00
❑74, Aug 1982	2.00
❑75, Oct 1982	2.00
❑76, Dec 1982	2.00
❑77, Feb 1983	2.00
❑Holiday 1, ca. 1993, "Sabrina's Halloween Spoook-Tacular"	3.00
❑Holiday 2, ca. 1994	2.00
❑Holiday 3, ca. 1995	2.00

SABRINA THE TEENAGE WITCH (2ND SERIES)
ARCHIE

❑1, ca. 1996	2.00

SACHS & VIOLENS
MARVEL / EPIC

❑1, Nov 1993; PD (w); GP (a); Embossed cover	3.00
❑1/Platinum, Nov 1993; Platinum promotional edition; PD (w); GP (a); Embossed cover	3.00
❑2, May 1994 PD (w); GP (a)	2.25
❑3, Jun 1994; PD (w); GP (a); Sex, nudity	2.25
❑4, Jul 1994 PD (w); GP (a)	2.25

SACRIFICED TREES
MANSION

❑1	3.00

SADE/RAZOR
LONDON NIGHT

❑1/2nd	3.00

SAD SACK
HARVEY

❑63, Oct 1956	10.00
❑64, Nov 1956	10.00
❑65, Dec 1956	10.00
❑66, Jan 1957	10.00
❑67, Feb 1957	10.00
❑68, Mar 1957	10.00
❑69, Apr 1957	10.00
❑70, May 1957	10.00
❑71, Jun 1957	8.00
❑72, Jul 1957	8.00
❑73, Aug 1957	8.00
❑74, Sep 1957	8.00
❑75, Oct 1957	8.00
❑76, Nov 1957	8.00
❑77, Dec 1957	8.00
❑78, Jan 1958	8.00
❑79, Feb 1958	8.00
❑80, Mar 1958	8.00
❑81, ca. 1958	8.00
❑82, ca. 1958	8.00
❑83, ca. 1958	8.00
❑84, ca. 1958	8.00
❑85, ca. 1958	8.00
❑86, ca. 1958	8.00
❑87, ca. 1958	8.00
❑88, Dec 1958	8.00
❑89, Jan 1959	8.00
❑90, Feb 1959	8.00
❑91, Mar 1959	5.00
❑92, Apr 1959	5.00
❑93, May 1959	5.00
❑94, Jun 1959	5.00
❑95, Jul 1959	5.00
❑96, Aug 1959	5.00
❑97, Sep 1959	5.00
❑98, Oct 1959	5.00
❑99, Nov 1959	5.00
❑100, Dec 1959	5.00
❑101, Jan 1960	2.50
❑102, Feb 1960	2.50
❑103, Mar 1960	2.50
❑104, Apr 1960	2.50
❑105, May 1960	2.50
❑106, Jun 1960	2.50
❑107, Jul 1960	2.50
❑108, Aug 1960	2.50
❑109, Sep 1960	2.50
❑110, Oct 1960	2.50
❑111, Nov 1960	2.50
❑112, Dec 1960	2.50
❑113, Jan 1961	2.50
❑114, Feb 1961	2.50
❑115, Mar 1961	2.50
❑116, Apr 1961	2.50
❑117, May 1961	2.50
❑118, Jun 1961	2.50
❑119, Jul 1961	2.50
❑120, Aug 1961	2.50
❑121, Sep 1961	2.50
❑122, Oct 1961	2.50
❑123, Nov 1961	2.50
❑124, Dec 1961	2.50
❑125, Jan 1962	2.50
❑126, Feb 1962	2.50
❑127, Mar 1962	2.50

	N-MINT
❑128, Apr 1962	2.50
❑129, May 1962	2.50
❑130, Jun 1962	2.50
❑131, Jul 1962	2.50
❑132, Aug 1962	2.50
❑133, Sep 1962	2.50
❑134, Oct 1962	2.50
❑135, Nov 1962	2.50
❑136, Dec 1962	2.50
❑137, Jan 1963	2.50
❑138, Feb 1963	2.50
❑139, Mar 1963	2.50
❑140, Apr 1963	2.50
❑141, May 1963	2.50
❑142, Jun 1963	2.50
❑143, Jul 1963	2.50
❑144, Aug 1963	2.50
❑145, Sep 1963	2.50
❑146, Oct 1963	2.50
❑147, Nov 1963	2.50
❑148, Dec 1963	2.50
❑149, Jan 1964	2.50
❑150, Feb 1964	2.50
❑151, Mar 1964	2.00
❑152, Apr 1964	2.00
❑153, May 1964	2.00
❑154, Jun 1964	2.00
❑155, Jul 1964	2.00
❑156, Aug 1964	2.00
❑157, Sep 1964	2.00
❑158, Oct 1964	2.00
❑159, Nov 1964	2.00
❑160, Dec 1964	2.00
❑161, Jan 1965	2.00
❑162, Feb 1965	2.00
❑163, Mar 1965	2.00
❑164, Apr 1965	2.00
❑165, May 1965	2.00
❑166, Jun 1965	2.00
❑167, Jul 1965	2.00
❑168, Aug 1965	2.00
❑169, Sep 1965	2.00
❑170, Oct 1965	2.00
❑171, Nov 1965	2.00
❑172, Dec 1965	2.00
❑173, Jan 1966	2.00
❑174, Feb 1966	2.00
❑175, Mar 1966	2.00
❑176, Apr 1966	2.00
❑177, May 1966	2.00
❑178, Jun 1966	2.00
❑179, Jul 1966	2.00
❑180, Aug 1966	2.00
❑181, Sep 1966	2.00
❑182, Oct 1966	2.00
❑183, Nov 1966	2.00
❑184, Dec 1966	2.00
❑185, Jan 1967	2.00
❑186, Feb 1967	2.00
❑187, Mar 1967	2.00
❑188, Apr 1967	2.00
❑189, May 1967	2.00
❑190, Jun 1967	2.00
❑191, Jul 1967	2.00
❑192, Aug 1967	2.00
❑193, Sep 1967	2.00
❑194, Oct 1967	2.00
❑195, Nov 1967	2.00
❑196, Dec 1967	2.00
❑197, Jan 1968	2.00
❑198, Mar 1968	2.00
❑199, May 1968	2.00
❑200, Jul 1968	2.00
❑201, Sep 1968	1.50
❑202, Oct 1968	1.50
❑203, Nov 1968	1.50
❑204, Jan 1969	1.50
❑205, Mar 1969	1.50
❑206, May 1969	1.50
❑207, Jul 1969	1.50
❑208, Sep 1969	1.50
❑209, Oct 1969	1.50
❑210, Nov 1969	1.50
❑211, Jan 1970	1.50
❑212, Mar 1970	1.50
❑213, May 1970	1.50

	N-MINT
❑214, Jul 1970	1.50
❑215, Sep 1970	1.50
❑216, Oct 1970	1.50
❑217, Nov 1970	1.50
❑218, Jan 1971	1.50
❑219, Mar 1971	1.50
❑220, May 1971	1.50
❑221, Jul 1971	1.50
❑222, Sep 1971	1.50
❑223, Nov 1971	1.50
❑224, Jan 1972	1.50
❑225, Mar 1972	1.50
❑226, May 1972	1.50
❑227, Jul 1972	1.50
❑228, Sep 1972	1.50
❑229, Nov 1972	1.50
❑230, Jan 1973	1.50
❑231, Mar 1973	1.50
❑232, May 1973	1.50
❑233, Jul 1973	1.50
❑234, Sep 1973	1.50
❑235, Nov 1973	1.50
❑236, Jan 1974	1.50
❑237, Mar 1974	1.50
❑238, May 1974	1.50
❑239, Jul 1974	1.50
❑240, Sep 1974	1.50
❑241, Nov 1974	1.50
❑242, Jan 1975	1.50
❑243, Mar 1975	1.50
❑244, May 1975	1.50
❑245, Jul 1975	1.50
❑246, Sep 1975	1.50
❑247, Nov 1975	1.50
❑248, Jan 1976	1.50
❑249, Mar 1976	1.50
❑250, May 1976	1.50
❑251, Jul 1976	1.50
❑252, Sep 1976	1.50
❑253, Nov 1976	1.50
❑254, Jan 1977	1.50
❑255, Mar 1977	1.50
❑256, May 1977	1.50
❑257, Jul 1977	1.50
❑258, Sep 1977	1.50
❑259, Nov 1977	1.50
❑260, Jan 1978	1.50
❑261, Mar 1978	1.50
❑262, May 1978	1.50
❑263, Jul 1978	1.50
❑264, Sep 1978	1.50
❑265, Nov 1978	1.50
❑266, Jan 1979	1.50
❑267, Mar 1979	1.50
❑268, May 1979	1.50
❑269, Jul 1979	1.50
❑270, Sep 1979	1.50
❑271, Nov 1979	1.50
❑272, Jan 1980	1.50
❑273, Mar 1980	1.50
❑274, May 1980	1.50
❑275, Jul 1980	1.50
❑276, Sep 1980	1.50
❑277, Nov 1980	1.50
❑278, Jan 1981	1.50
❑279, Mar 1981	1.50
❑280, May 1981	1.50
❑281, Jul 1981	1.50
❑282, Sep 1981	1.50
❑283, Nov 1981	1.50
❑284, Jan 1982	1.50
❑285, Mar 1982	1.50
❑286, May 1982	1.50
❑287, Jul 1982	1.50
❑288, ca. 1992	2.75
❑289, ca. 1992	2.75
❑290, ca. 1992, b&w	1.50
❑291, ca. 1993	1.50
❑292, ca. 1993	1.50
❑293, ca. 1993	1.50
❑3D 1, ca. 1954; Harvey 3-D Hits	125.00

SAD SACK & THE SARGE

HARVEY

	N-MINT
❑1, Sep 1957	80.00
❑2, Nov 1957	45.00
❑3, Jan 1958	30.00
❑4, Mar 1958	30.00
❑5 1958	30.00
❑6, Jun 1958	20.00
❑7 1958	20.00
❑8 1958	20.00
❑9, Oct 1958	20.00
❑10, Dec 1958	20.00
❑11, Feb 1959	16.00
❑12, Apr 1959	16.00
❑13, Jun 1959	16.00
❑14, Aug 1959; Substitute; From Bad to Worse; Good Example; Who's Who; Bad Deal; Rank (text story); Sad Sack Gets His Wires Crossed	16.00
❑15, Oct 1959	16.00
❑16, Dec 1959	16.00
❑17, Feb 1960	16.00
❑18, Apr 1960	16.00
❑19, Jun 1960	16.00
❑20, Aug 1960, New Interest; Who's in Charge; Modern Times; The Joker; Last Aid First; Big Change (text story); The Future	16.00
❑21, Oct 1960	12.00
❑22, Dec 1960	12.00
❑23, Feb 1961	12.00
❑24, Apr 1961	12.00
❑25, Jun 1961	12.00
❑26, Aug 1961	12.00
❑27, Oct 1961	12.00
❑28, Dec 1961	12.00
❑29, Feb 1962	12.00
❑30, Apr 1962	12.00
❑31, Jun 1962	9.00
❑32, Aug 1962	9.00
❑33, Oct 1962	9.00
❑34, Dec 1962	9.00
❑35, Feb 1963	9.00
❑36, Apr 1963	9.00
❑37, Jun 1963	9.00
❑38, Aug 1963	9.00
❑39, Oct 1963	9.00
❑40, Dec 1963	9.00
❑41, Feb 1964	7.00
❑42, Apr 1964	7.00
❑43, Jun 1964	7.00
❑44, Aug 1964	7.00
❑45, Oct 1964	7.00
❑46, Dec 1964	7.00
❑47, Feb 1965	7.00
❑48, Apr 1965	7.00
❑49, Jun 1965	7.00
❑50, Aug 1965	6.00
❑51, Oct 1965	6.00
❑52, Dec 1965	6.00
❑53, Feb 1966	6.00
❑54, Apr 1966	6.00
❑55, Jun 1966	6.00
❑56, Aug 1966	6.00
❑57, Sep 1966	6.00
❑58, Oct 1966	6.00
❑59, Dec 1966	6.00
❑60, Feb 1967	6.00
❑61, Apr 1967	5.00
❑62, Jun 1967	5.00
❑63, Aug 1967	5.00
❑64, Oct 1967	5.00
❑65, Dec 1967	5.00
❑66, Feb 1968	5.00
❑67, Apr 1968	5.00
❑68, Jun 1968	5.00
❑69, Aug 1968	5.00
❑70, Oct 1968	5.00
❑71, Dec 1968	5.00
❑72, Jan 1969	5.00
❑73 1969	5.00
❑74, May 1969	5.00
❑75, Jun 1969	5.00
❑76, Jul 1969	5.00
❑77, Sep 1969	5.00
❑78, Oct 1969	5.00
❑79, Dec 1969	5.00
❑80, Feb 1970	5.00
❑81, Apr 1970	3.00
❑82, Jun 1970	3.00
❑83, Aug 1970	3.00
❑84, Oct 1970	3.00

Samurai: Heaven and Earth

Swordsman seeks true love across world
©Dark Horse

Samuree (1st Series)

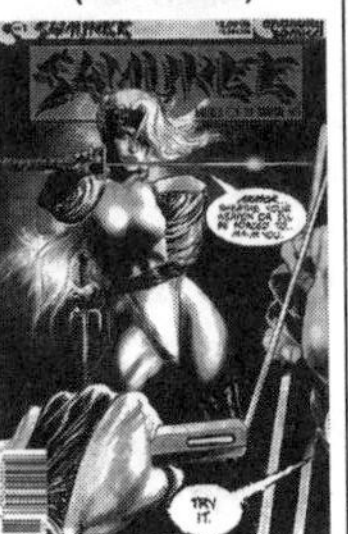

Teen martial artist meets Revengers
©Continuity

Sandman

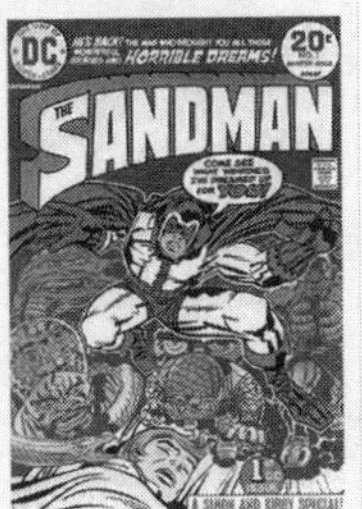

Short-lived Kirby creation
©DC

Sandman

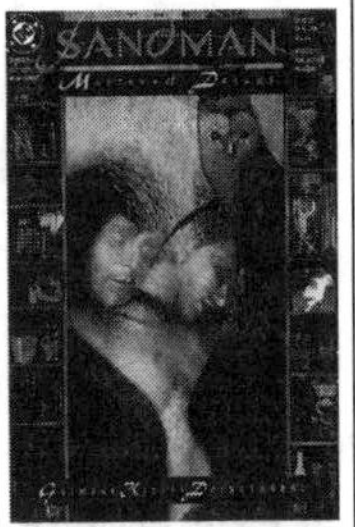

Lord of Dreams focus of fantasy series
©DC

Sandman Mystery Theatre

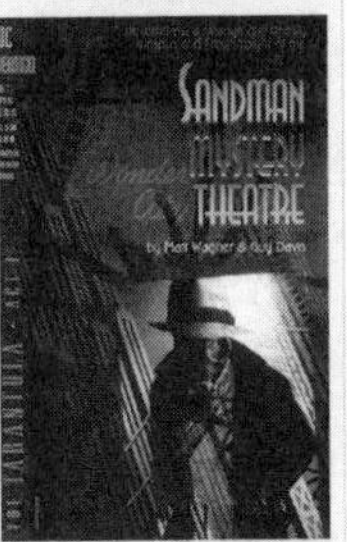

Darker stories of Golden Age hero
©DC

N-MINT

❑85, Nov 1970 .... 3.00
❑86, Jan 1971 .... 3.00
❑87, Feb 1971 .... 3.00
❑88, Apr 1971 .... 3.00
❑89, Jun 1971 .... 3.00
❑90, Aug 1971 .... 3.00
❑91, Oct 1971; Giant size A: The General. A: Slob Slobinski 4.00
❑92, Dec 1971; Giant size 4.00
❑93, Feb 1972; Giant size 4.00
❑94, Apr 1972; Giant size 4.00
❑95, Jun 1972; Giant size 4.00
❑96, Aug 1972; Giant size 4.00
❑97, Oct 1972 .... 3.00
❑98, Dec 1972 .... 3.00
❑99, Feb 1973 .... 3.00
❑100, Apr 1973 .... 3.00
❑101, Jun 1973 .... 2.00
❑102, Aug 1973 .... 2.00
❑103, Oct 1973 .... 2.00
❑104, Dec 1973 .... 2.00
❑105, Feb 1974 .... 2.00
❑106, Apr 1974 .... 2.00
❑107, Jun 1974 .... 2.00
❑108, Aug 1974 .... 2.00
❑109, Oct 1974 .... 2.00
❑110, Dec 1974 .... 2.00
❑111, Feb 1975 .... 2.00
❑112, Apr 1975 .... 2.00
❑113, Jun 1975 .... 2.00
❑114, Aug 1975 .... 2.00
❑115, Oct 1975 .... 2.00
❑116, Dec 1975 .... 2.00
❑117, Feb 1976 .... 2.00
❑118, Apr 1976 .... 2.00
❑119, Jun 1976 .... 2.00
❑120, Aug 1976 .... 2.00
❑121, Oct 1976 .... 2.00
❑122, Dec 1976 .... 2.00
❑123, Feb 1977 .... 2.00
❑124, Apr 1977 .... 2.00
❑125, Jun 1977 .... 2.00
❑126, Aug 1977 .... 2.00
❑127, Oct 1977 .... 2.00
❑128, Dec 1977 .... 2.00
❑129, Feb 1978 .... 2.00
❑130, Apr 1978 .... 2.00
❑131, Jun 1978 .... 2.00
❑132, Aug 1978 .... 2.00
❑133, Oct 1978 .... 2.00
❑134, Dec 1978 .... 2.00
❑135, Feb 1979 .... 2.00
❑136, Apr 1979 .... 2.00
❑137, Jun 1979 .... 2.00
❑138, Aug 1979 .... 2.00
❑139, Oct 1979 .... 2.00
❑140, Dec 1979 .... 2.00
❑141, Feb 1980 .... 2.00
❑142, Apr 1980 .... 2.00
❑143, Jun 1980 .... 2.00
❑144, Aug 1980 .... 2.00
❑145, Oct 1980 .... 2.00
❑146, Dec 1980 .... 2.00
❑147, Feb 1981 .... 2.00
❑148, Apr 1981 .... 2.00
❑149, Jun 1981 .... 2.00
❑150, Aug 1981 .... 2.00
❑151, Oct 1981 .... 2.00
❑152, Dec 1981 .... 2.00
❑153, Feb 1982 .... 2.00
❑154, Apr 1982 .... 2.00
❑155, Jun 1982 .... 2.00

SAD SACK ARMY LIFE PARADE
HARVEY

❑1, Oct 1963, Giant-size 35.00
❑2, Feb 1964, Giant-size 20.00
❑3, May 1964, Giant-size 15.00
❑4, Aug 1964, Giant-size 12.00
❑5, Nov 1964, Giant-size 12.00
❑6, Feb 1965, Giant-size 10.00
❑7, May 1965, Giant-size 10.00
❑8, Aug 1965, Giant-size 10.00
❑9, Nov 1965, Giant-size 10.00
❑10, Feb 1966, Giant-size 10.00
❑11, May 1966, Giant-size 8.00
❑12, Jul 1966, Giant-size 8.00
❑13, Sep 1966, Giant-size 8.00
❑14, Oct 1966, Giant-size 8.00
❑15, Jan 1967, Giant-size 8.00
❑16, Mar 1967, Giant-size 8.00
❑17 1967, Giant-size 8.00
❑18, Nov 1967, Giant-size 8.00
❑19, Feb 1968, Giant-size 8.00
❑20, May 1968, Giant-size 8.00
❑21, Aug 1968, Giant-size 6.00
❑22 1969, Giant-size 6.00
❑23, Feb 1969, Giant-size 6.00
❑24, Apr 1969, Giant-size 6.00
❑25, Aug 1969, Giant-size 6.00
❑26, Oct 1969, Giant-size 6.00
❑27, Dec 1969, Giant-size 6.00
❑28, Feb 1970, Giant-size 6.00
❑29, Apr 1970, Giant-size 6.00
❑30, Aug 1970, Giant-size 6.00
❑31, Oct 1970, Giant-size 5.00
❑32, Dec 1970, Giant-size 5.00
❑33, Feb 1971, Giant-size 5.00
❑34, Apr 1971, Giant-size 5.00
❑35, Aug 1971, Giant-size 5.00
❑36, Oct 1971, Giant-size 5.00
❑37, Dec 1971, Giant-size 5.00
❑38, Feb 1972, Giant-size 5.00
❑39, Apr 1972, Giant-size 5.00
❑40, Jun 1972, Giant-size 5.00
❑41, Aug 1972, Giant-size 4.00
❑42, Oct 1972, Giant-size 4.00
❑43, Dec 1972, Giant-size 4.00
❑44, Feb 1973, Giant-size 4.00
❑45, Apr 1973, Giant-size 4.00
❑46, Jun 1973, Giant-size 4.00
❑47, Aug 1973, Giant-size 4.00
❑48, Oct 1973, Giant-size 4.00
❑49, Dec 1973, Giant-size 4.00
❑50, Feb 1974, Giant-size 4.00
❑51, Apr 1974, Giant-size 2.50
❑52, Jun 1974, Giant-size 2.50
❑53, Aug 1974 .... 2.50
❑54, Oct 1974 .... 2.50
❑55, Dec 1974 .... 2.50
❑56, Feb 1975 .... 2.50
❑57, Apr 1975 .... 2.50
❑58, Jul 1975 .... 2.50
❑59 1975 .... 2.50
❑60, Nov 1975 .... 2.50
❑61, ca. 1976 .... 2.50

SAD SACK AT HOME FOR THE HOLIDAYS
LORNE-HARVEY

❑1, ca. 1992 .... 2.00

SAD SACK IN 3-D
BLACKTHORNE

❑1, ca. 1988 .... 2.00

SAD SACK LAUGH SPECIAL
HARVEY

❑1, Win 1958, Giant-size 90.00
❑2, Spr 1959, Giant-size 45.00
❑3, Sum 1959, Giant-size 25.00
❑4, ca. 1960, Giant-size 25.00
❑5, Jul 1960, Giant-size 25.00
❑6, ca. 1960, Giant-size 25.00
❑7, ca. 1960, Giant-size 25.00
❑8, ca. 1960, Giant-size 25.00
❑9, ca. 1961, Giant-size 25.00
❑10, ca. 1961, Giant-size 25.00
❑11, ca. 1962, Giant-size 20.00
❑12, ca. 1962, Giant-size 20.00
❑13, ca. 1962, Giant-size 20.00
❑14, ca. 1962, Giant-size 20.00
❑15, Jan 1963, Giant-size 20.00
❑16 1963, Giant-size 20.00
❑17 1963, Giant-size 20.00
❑18, Oct 1963, Giant-size 20.00
❑19, Giant-size 20.00
❑20, Apr 1964, Giant-size 20.00
❑21, Jul 1964, Giant-size 15.00
❑22, Sep 1964, Giant-size 15.00
❑23, Dec 1964, Giant-size 15.00
❑24, Mar 1965, Giant-size 15.00
❑25, Jun 1965, Giant-size 15.00
❑26, Sep 1965, Giant-size 15.00
❑27, Dec 1965, Giant-size 15.00
❑28, Mar 1966, Giant-size 15.00
❑29, Jun 1966, Giant-size 15.00
❑30, Aug 1966, Giant-size 15.00
❑31 1966, Giant-size 12.00
❑32, Oct 1966, Giant-size 12.00
❑33, Dec 1966, Giant-size 12.00
❑34, Feb 1967, Giant-size 12.00
❑35, Apr 1967, Giant-size 12.00
❑36, Jun 1967, Giant-size 12.00
❑37, Oct 1967, Giant-size 12.00
❑38, Nov 1967, Giant-size 12.00
❑39 1968, Giant-size 12.00
❑40, Apr 1968, Giant-size 12.00
❑41, Jun 1968, Giant-size 10.00
❑42, Aug 1968, Giant-size 10.00
❑43, Oct 1968, Giant-size 10.00
❑44, Dec 1968, Giant-size 10.00
❑45, Feb 1969, Giant-size 10.00
❑46, Apr 1969, Giant-size 10.00
❑47, May 1969, Giant-size 10.00

Other grades: Multiply price above by 5/6 for VF/NM • 2/3 for VERY FINE • 1/3 for FINE • 1/5 for VERY GOOD • 1/8 for GOOD

	N-MINT
❑48, Jul 1969, Giant-size	10.00
❑49, Sep 1969, Giant-size	10.00
❑50, Nov 1969, Giant-size	10.00
❑51, Jan 1970, Giant-size	10.00
❑52, Mar 1970, Giant-size	10.00
❑53, May 1970, Giant-size	10.00
❑54, Jul 1970, Giant-size	10.00
❑55, Sep 1970, Giant-size	10.00
❑56, Nov 1970, Giant-size	10.00
❑57, Jan 1971, Giant-size	10.00
❑58, Mar 1971, Giant-size	10.00
❑59, May 1971, Giant-size	10.00
❑60, Jul 1971, Giant-size	10.00
❑61, Sep 1971, Giant-size	8.00
❑62, Nov 1971, Giant-size	8.00
❑63, Jan 1972, Giant-size	8.00
❑64, Mar 1972, Giant-size	8.00
❑65, May 1972, Giant-size	8.00
❑66, Jul 1972, Giant-size	8.00
❑67, Sep 1972, Giant-size	8.00
❑68, Nov 1972, Giant-size	8.00
❑69, Jan 1973, Giant-size	8.00
❑70, Mar 1973, Giant-size	8.00
❑71, May 1973, Giant-size	8.00
❑72, Jul 1973, Giant-size	8.00
❑73, Sep 1973, Giant-size	8.00
❑74, Nov 1973, Giant-size	8.00
❑75, Jan 1974, Giant-size	8.00
❑76, Mar 1974, Giant-size	8.00
❑77, May 1974, Giant-size	8.00
❑78, Jul 1974	8.00
❑79, Sep 1974	8.00
❑80, Nov 1974	8.00
❑81, Jan 1975	6.00
❑82, Mar 1975	6.00
❑83, Jun 1975	6.00
❑84, Aug 1975	6.00
❑85, Oct 1975	6.00
❑86, Dec 1975	6.00
❑87, Feb 1976	6.00
❑88, Apr 1976	6.00
❑89, Jun 1976	6.00
❑90, Aug 1976	6.00
❑91, Oct 1976	6.00
❑92, Dec 1976	6.00
❑93, Feb 1977	6.00

SAD SACK NAVY, GOBS 'N' GALS

HARVEY

	N-MINT
❑1, Aug 1972	12.00
❑2, Oct 1972	8.00
❑3, Dec 1972	6.00
❑4, Feb 1973	6.00
❑5, Apr 1973	6.00
❑6, Jun 1973	4.00
❑7, Aug 1973	4.00
❑8, Oct 1973	4.00

SAD SACK'S FUNNY FRIENDS

HARVEY

	N-MINT
❑1, Dec 1955	50.00
❑2, Feb 1956	34.00
❑3, Apr 1956	22.00
❑4, Jun 1956	20.00
❑5, ca. 1957	20.00
❑6, ca. 1957	16.00
❑7, ca. 1957	16.00
❑8, ca. 1957	16.00
❑9, ca. 1957	16.00
❑10, ca. 1958	16.00
❑11, ca. 1958	12.00
❑12, ca. 1958	12.00
❑13, ca. 1958	12.00
❑14, ca. 1959	12.00
❑15, ca. 1959	12.00
❑16, ca. 1959	12.00
❑17, ca. 1959	12.00
❑18, ca. 1959	12.00
❑19, ca. 1960	12.00
❑20, ca. 1960	12.00
❑21, May 1960	10.00
❑22, Jul 1960	10.00
❑23, Sep 1960	10.00
❑24, Nov 1960	10.00
❑25, Jan 1961	10.00
❑26, Mar 1961	10.00
❑27, May 1961	10.00
❑28, Jul 1961	10.00
❑29, Sep 1961	10.00
❑30, Nov 1961	10.00
❑31, Jan 1962	8.00
❑32, Mar 1962	8.00
❑33, May 1962	8.00
❑34, Jul 1962	8.00
❑35, Sep 1962	8.00
❑36, Nov 1962	8.00
❑37, Jan 1963	8.00
❑38, Mar 1963	8.00
❑39, May 1963	8.00
❑40, Jul 1963	8.00
❑41, Sep 1963	5.00
❑42, Nov 1963	5.00
❑43, Jan 1964	5.00
❑44, Mar 1964	5.00
❑45, May 1964	5.00
❑46, Jul 1964	5.00
❑47, Sep 1964	5.00
❑48, Nov 1964	5.00
❑49, Jan 1965	5.00
❑50, Mar 1965	5.00
❑51, May 1965	3.00
❑52, Jul 1965	3.00
❑53, Sep 1965	3.00
❑54, Nov 1965	3.00
❑55, Jan 1966	3.00
❑56, Mar 1966	3.00
❑57, May 1966	3.00
❑58, Jul 1966	3.00
❑59, Sep 1966	3.00
❑60, Nov 1966	3.00
❑61, Jan 1967	3.00
❑62, Mar 1967	3.00
❑63, May 1967	3.00
❑64 1967	3.00
❑65, Aug 1967	3.00
❑66, Oct 1967	3.00
❑67, Jan 1968	3.00
❑68, Mar 1968	3.00
❑69, May 1968	3.00
❑70 1968	3.00
❑71 1968	3.00
❑72, Jan 1969	3.00
❑73, Apr 1969	3.00
❑74, Aug 1969	3.00
❑75, Oct 1969	3.00

SAD SAD SACK WORLD

HARVEY

	N-MINT
❑1, Oct 1964, Giant-size	45.00
❑2, ca. 1965, Giant-size	20.00
❑3, ca. 1965, Giant-size	20.00
❑4, ca. 1966, Giant-size	20.00
❑5, Oct 1966, Giant-size	20.00
❑6, Dec 1966, Giant-size	20.00
❑7, Apr 1967, Giant-size	20.00
❑8, Jun 1967, Giant-size	20.00
❑9, Aug 1967, Giant-size	20.00
❑10 1967, Giant-size	20.00
❑11, Dec 1967, Giant-size	15.00
❑12 1968, Giant-size	15.00
❑13 1968, Giant-size	15.00
❑14 1968, Giant-size	15.00
❑15, Nov 1968, Giant-size	15.00
❑16, Mar 1969, Giant-size	15.00
❑17, Jun 1969, Giant-size	15.00
❑18, Sep 1969, Giant-size	15.00
❑19, Nov 1969, Giant-size	15.00
❑20, Jan 1970, Giant-size	15.00
❑21 1970, Giant-size	15.00
❑22 1970, Giant-size	15.00
❑23, Oct 1970, Giant-size	15.00
❑24, ca. 1971, Giant-size	15.00
❑25, ca. 1971, Giant-size	15.00
❑26, ca. 1971, Giant-size	15.00
❑27, Sep 1971, Giant-size	15.00
❑28, ca. 1971, Giant-size	15.00
❑29, ca. 1972, Giant-size	15.00
❑30, Mar 1972, Giant-size	15.00
❑31, ca. 1972, Giant-size	12.00
❑32, ca. 1972, Giant-size	12.00
❑33, ca. 1972, Giant-size	12.00
❑34, ca. 1973, Giant-size	12.00
❑35, Mar 1973, Giant-size	12.00
❑36, ca. 1973, Giant-size	12.00
❑37, ca. 1973, Giant-size	12.00
❑38, ca. 1973, Giant-size	12.00
❑39, Oct 1973, Giant-size	12.00
❑40, Dec 1973	12.00
❑41, Feb 1973	10.00
❑42, Apr 1973	10.00
❑43, Jun 1973	10.00
❑44, Aug 1973	10.00
❑45, Oct 1973	10.00
❑46, Dec 1973	10.00

SAFE COMICS

GRAPHIC GRAPHICS

	N-MINT
❑1, ca. 1998	3.00
❑2, ca. 1999	3.00

SAFEST PLACE IN THE WORLD

DARK HORSE

	N-MINT
❑1, ca. 1993	2.50

SAFETY-BELT MAN

SIRIUS

	N-MINT
❑1, Jun 1994, b&w	2.50
❑2, Oct 1994, b&w	2.50
❑3, Feb 1995, b&w	2.50
❑4, Jun 1995, b&w; color centerfold; Linsner back-up story	2.50
❑5, Aug 1995, b&w	2.50
❑6, Oct 1995, b&w	2.50

SAFETY-BELT MAN: ALL HELL

SIRIUS

	N-MINT
❑1, Jun 1996	2.95
❑2, Jun 1996	2.95
❑3 1996	2.95
❑4, Sep 1996	2.95
❑5, Jan 1997	2.95
❑6, Aug 1997	2.95

SAFFIRE

IMAGE

	N-MINT
❑1, Apr 2000	2.95
❑2, Dec 2000	2.95
❑3, Feb 2001	2.95

SAGA

ODYSSEY

	N-MINT
❑1, b&w	1.95

SAGA OF CRYSTAR, THE CRYSTAL WARRIOR

MARVEL

	N-MINT
❑1, May 1983, O: Crystar. 1: Crystar	2.00
❑2, Jul 1983 1: Ika	1.00
❑3, Sep 1983, A: Doctor Strange	1.00
❑4, Nov 1983	1.00
❑5, Jan 1984	1.00
❑6, Mar 1984, A: Nightcrawler	1.00
❑7, May 1984	1.00
❑8, Jul 1984	1.00
❑9, Sep 1984	1.00
❑10, Nov 1984	1.00
❑11, Feb 1985, Double-size A: Alpha Flight	1.00

SAGA OF RA'S AL GHUL

DC

	N-MINT
❑1, Jan 1988	2.50
❑2, Feb 1988	2.50
❑3, Mar 1988	2.50
❑4, Apr 1988	2.50

SAGA OF THE MAN ELF

TRIDENT

	N-MINT
❑1, Aug 1989	2.25
❑2, 1989	2.25
❑3, 1989	2.25
❑4, 1990	2.25
❑5, 1990	2.25

SAGA OF THE ORIGINAL HUMAN TORCH

MARVEL

	N-MINT
❑1, Apr 1990	1.50
❑2, May 1990	1.50
❑3, Jun 1990	1.50
❑4, Jul 1990	1.50

SAGA OF THE SUB-MARINER

MARVEL

	N-MINT
❑1, Nov 1988 RB (a); O: Sub-Mariner	1.50
❑2, Dec 1988	1.50
❑3, Jan 1989	1.50
❑4, Feb 1989 A: Human Torch	1.50
❑5, Mar 1989 A: Human Torch. A: Captain America. A: Invaders	1.50

Other grades: Multiply price above by 5/6 for VF/NM • 2/3 for VERY FINE • 1/3 for FINE • 1/5 for VERY GOOD • 1/8 for GOOD

Sarge Snorkel

Beetle Bailey's C.O.'s solo stories
©Charlton

Sarge Steel

New meaning for iron hand in velvet glove
©Charlton

Satan's Six

Topps' heroic line featured demonic team
©Topps

Savage Dragon (Mini-Series)

Multi-colored logos made collectors nuts
©Image

Savage Dragon

Fin-headed hero joins Chicago P.D.
©Image

N-MINT

❑6, Apr 1989 A: Torch. A: Human Torch. A: Captain America. A: Invaders...... 1.50
❑7, May 1989 A: Fantastic Four.......... 1.50
❑8, Jun 1989 A: Fantastic Four. A: Avengers.................................... 1.50
❑9, Jul 1989 A: Fantastic Four. A: Avengers.................................... 1.50
❑10, Aug 1989.................................... 1.50
❑11, Sep 1989.................................... 1.50
❑12, Oct 1989.................................... 1.50

SAGA OF THE SWAMP THING
DC

❑1, May 1982, TY (a); O: Swamp Thing 3.00
❑2, Jun 1982, TY (a)........................... 2.00
❑3, Jul 1982, TY (a)........................... 2.00
❑4, Aug 1982, TY (a)........................... 2.00
❑5, Sep 1982, TY (a)........................... 2.00
❑6, Oct 1982, TY (a)........................... 2.00
❑7, Nov 1982, TY (a)........................... 2.00
❑8, Dec 1982, TY (a)........................... 2.00
❑9, Jan 1983, JDu (a)......................... 2.00
❑10, Feb 1983, TY (a)......................... 2.00
❑11, Mar 1983, TY (a)......................... 2.00
❑12, Apr 1983, TY (a)......................... 2.00
❑13, May 1983.................................... 2.00
❑14, Jun 1983.................................... 2.00
❑15, Jul 1983..................................... 2.00
❑16, Aug 1983.................................... 2.00
❑17, Oct 1983.................................... 2.00
❑18, Nov 1983, BWr (a)....................... 2.00
❑19, Dec 1983.................................... 2.00
❑20, Jan 1984; AMo (w); Alan Moore scripts begin.................................... 15.00
❑21, Feb 1984 AMo (w); O: Swamp Thing. O: Swamp Thing (new origin) 12.00
❑22, Mar 1984 AMo (w)....................... 6.00
❑23, Apr 1984 AMo (w)....................... 6.00
❑24, May 1984 AMo (w); A: Justice League.. 6.00
❑25, Jun 1984 AMo (w)....................... 6.00
❑26, Jul 1984 AMo (w)........................ 4.00
❑27, Aug 1984 AMo (w)....................... 4.00
❑28, Sep 1984 AMo (w)....................... 4.00
❑29, Oct 1984 AMo (w)....................... 4.00
❑30, Nov 1984 AMo (w); AA (a).......... 4.00
❑31, Dec 1984 AMo (w)....................... 4.00
❑32, Jan 1985 AMo (w)........................ 4.00
❑33, Feb 1985.................................... 3.00
❑34, Mar 1985 AMo (w)....................... 5.00
❑35, Apr 1985 AMo (w)....................... 3.00
❑36, May 1985 AMo (w); BWr (a)....... 3.00
❑37, Jun 1985 AMo (w); 1: John Constantine..................................... 55.00
❑38, Jul 1985; AMo (w); 2: John Constantine. Series continues as Swamp Thing.................................. 15.00
❑39, Aug 1985 AMo (w); A: John Constantine..................................... 9.00
❑40, Sep 1985 AMo (w); A: John Constantine..................................... 9.00
❑41, Oct 1985 AMo (w)....................... 4.00
❑42, Nov 1985 AMo (w)....................... 4.00
❑43, Dec 1985 AMo (w)....................... 4.00
❑44, Jan 1986 AMo (w)........................ 4.00

N-MINT

❑45, Feb 1986; AMo (w); AA (a); Series continued as "Swamp Thing (2nd Series) #46"......................... 4.00
❑Annual 1, ca. 1982 TD (a)................ 3.00
❑Annual 2, ca. 1985 AMo (w); A: Demon. A: Spectre. A: Deadman. A: Phantom Stranger..................... 4.00
❑Annual 3, ca. 1987 A: Congorilla...... 2.50

SAIGON CHRONICLES
AVALON

❑1... 2.95

SAIKANO
VIZ

❑1, Aug 2004...................................... 9.99
❑2, Oct 2004....................................... 9.99
❑3, Dec 2004....................................... 9.99
❑4, Apr 2005....................................... 9.99
❑5, Jul 2005.. 9.99
❑6, Oct 2005....................................... 9.99

SAILOR MOON COMIC
MIXXZINE

❑1, Oct 1998; Continued from MixxZine 15.00
❑1/A, Oct 1998; San Diego limited edition version............................... 12.00
❑2, Nov 1998....................................... 8.00
❑3, Dec 1998; D: Kunzite. Destruction of the Moon Kingdom (flashback).. 8.00
❑4, Jan 1999.. 8.00
❑5, Feb 1999.. 6.00
❑6, Mar 1999....................................... 6.00
❑7, Apr 1999.. 6.00
❑8, May 1999....................................... 5.00
❑9, Jun 1999.. 4.00
❑10, Jul 1999...................................... 3.00
❑11, Aug 1999..................................... 3.00
❑12, Sep 1999..................................... 3.00
❑13, Oct 1999..................................... 3.00
❑14, Nov 1999..................................... 3.00
❑15, Dec 1999..................................... 3.00
❑16, Jan 2000...................................... 3.00
❑17, Feb 2000...................................... 3.00
❑18, Mar 2000..................................... 3.00
❑19, Apr 2000...................................... 3.00
❑20, May 2000..................................... 3.00
❑21, Jun 2000...................................... 3.00
❑22, Jul 2000....................................... 3.00
❑23, Aug 2000...................................... 3.00
❑24, Sep 2000...................................... 3.00
❑25, Oct 2000...................................... 3.00
❑26, Nov 2000..................................... 3.00
❑27, Dec 2000...................................... 3.00
❑28, Jan 2001...................................... 3.00
❑29, Feb 2001...................................... 3.00
❑30, Mar 2001..................................... 3.00
❑31, Apr 2001...................................... 2.95
❑32, May 2001..................................... 2.95
❑33, Jun 2001...................................... 2.95

SAILOR'S STORY
MARVEL

❑1... 5.95

SAILOR'S STORY, A: WINDS, DREAMS, AND DRAGONS
MARVEL

❑1... 6.95

N-MINT

SAINT ANGEL
IMAGE

❑0, Mar 2000.. 2.95
❑1, Jun 2000.. 3.95
❑2, Oct 2000.. 3.95
❑3, Dec 2000.. 3.95
❑4, Mar 2001.. 3.95

ST. GEORGE
MARVEL / EPIC

❑1, Jun 1988, BSz (c); BSz, KJ (a)..... 1.50
❑2, Aug 1988.. 1.50
❑3, Oct 1988... 1.50
❑4, Dec 1988.. 1.50
❑5, Feb 1989.. 1.50
❑6, Apr 1989... 1.50
❑7, Jun 1989... 1.50
❑8, Aug 1989.. 1.50

SAINT GERMAINE
CALIBER

❑1, ca. 1997, b&w............................... 2.95
❑2... 2.95
❑3... 2.95
❑4... 2.95
❑5... 2.95

SAINTS
SATURN

❑0, Apr 1995, b&w............................... 2.50
❑1, Fal 1996, b&w................................ 2.50

SAINT SINNER
MARVEL

❑1, Oct 1993; foil cover....................... 2.50
❑2, Nov 1993.. 1.75
❑3, Dec 1993.. 1.75
❑4, Jan 1994... 1.75
❑5, Feb 1994... 1.75
❑6, Mar 1994.. 1.75
❑7, Apr 1994... 1.75
❑8, Apr 1994... 1.75

ST. SWITHIN'S DAY
TRIDENT

❑1, ca. 1990, b&w................................ 3.00
❑1/2nd, Mar 1998, b&w....................... 2.95

ST. SWITHIN'S DAY (ONI)
ONI

❑1, Mar 1998.. 2.95

SAIYUKI
TOKYOPOP

❑1, Mar 2004.. 9.99

SAIYUKI RELOAD
TOKYOPOP

❑1, Aug 2005.. 9.99
❑2, Dec 2005.. 9.99

SAKURA TAISEN
TOKYOPOP

❑1, Jul 2005... 9.99
❑2, Dec 2005.. 9.99

SALIMBA
BLACKTHORNE

❑1, b&w.. 3.50
❑3D 1, Aug 1986, b&w.......................... 2.50
❑3D 2, Sep 1986................................... 2.50

N-MINT

SALLY FORTH
FANTAGRAPHICS / EROS
❑1 2.95
❑1/2nd, Jun 1995 2.95
❑2, Oct 1993 2.95
❑3, Feb 1994 2.95
❑4, Apr 1994 2.95
❑5, Jul 1994 2.95
❑6, Sep 1994, b&w 2.95
❑7, Nov 1994 2.95
❑8, Jan 1995 2.95
❑15 1.50
❑16 1.50
❑17 DaG (a) 1.50
❑18 DaG (a) 1.50
❑19 1.50
❑20 1.50
❑21, double issue #21/22 1.50
❑22 1.50
❑23, double issue #23/24 1.50
❑24 1.50
❑25 1.50
❑26 1.50
❑27 1.50
❑28 1.50
❑29 1.50
❑30 1.50
❑31 1.50
❑32 1.50
❑33 1.50

SAM & MAX, FREELANCE POLICE
MARVEL / EPIC
❑1 2.25

SAM AND MAX, FREELANCE POLICE SPECIAL
FISHWRAP
❑1, ca. 1987, b&w 1.75

SAM & MAX FREELANCE POLICE SPECIAL
COMICO
❑1, ca. 1989 2.75

SAM & MAX FREELANCE POLICE SPECIAL COLOR COLLECTION
MARVEL / EPIC
❑1 4.95

SAM AND TWITCH
IMAGE
❑1, Aug 1999 2.50
❑2, Sep 1999 2.50
❑3, Oct 1999 2.50
❑4, Nov 1999 2.50
❑5, Dec 1999 2.50
❑6, Jan 2000 2.50
❑7, Feb 2000 2.50
❑8, Mar 2000 2.50
❑9, Apr 2000 2.50
❑10, May 2000 2.50
❑11, Jun 2000 2.50
❑12, Jul 2000 2.50
❑13, Aug 2000 2.50
❑14, Sep 2000 2.50
❑15, Oct 2000 2.50
❑16, Nov 2000 2.50
❑17, Dec 2000 2.50
❑18, Jan 2001 2.50
❑19, Feb 2001 2.50
❑20, Mar 2001 2.50
❑21, Apr 2001 2.50
❑22, May 2001 2.50
❑23, Jan 2002 2.50
❑24, Aug 2003 2.50
❑25, Oct 2003 2.50
❑26, Feb 2004 2.50

MBU GASSHO (A CHORUS IN THREE PARTS)
BODO GENKI
❑1, Aug 1994, b&w; no cover price 1.00

SAMMY: TOURIST TRAP
IMAGE
❑1, Feb 2003 2.95
❑2, Mar 2003 2.95
❑3, May 2003 2.95
❑4, May 2003 2.95

SAMMY VERY SAMMY DAY ONE SHOT
IMAGE
❑1, Aug 2004 5.95

SAM SLADE, ROBO-HUNTER
FLEETWAY-QUALITY
❑1 2.00
❑2 DaG (a) 1.50
❑3 DaG (a) 1.50
❑4 DaG (a) 1.50
❑5 DaG (a) 1.50
❑6 AMo (w) 1.50
❑7 1.50
❑8 DaG (a) 1.50
❑9 1.50
❑10 1.50
❑11, no year of publication 1.50
❑12 DaG (a) 1.50
❑13 DaG (a) 1.50
❑14 DaG (a) 1.50

SAMSON
SAMSON
❑½, Jan 1995; no indicia 2.50

SAM STORIES: LEGS
IMAGE / QUALITY
❑1, Dec 1999 2.50

SAMURAI
AIRCEL
❑1, Jan 1986 3.00
❑1/2nd 2.00
❑1/3rd 2.00
❑2, Feb 1986 2.00
❑3, Mar 1986 2.00
❑4, Apr 1986 2.00
❑5, May 1986 2.00
❑6, Jun 1986 2.00
❑7, Jul 1986 2.00
❑8, Aug 1986 2.00
❑9, Sep 1986 2.00
❑10, Oct 1986 2.00
❑11, Nov 1986 2.00
❑12, Dec 1986 2.00
❑13, Jan 1987, 1st Dale Keown art 3.00
❑14, Feb 1987 3.00
❑15, Mar 1987 3.00
❑16, Apr 1987 3.00
❑17, May 1987 2.00
❑18, Jun 1987 2.00
❑19, Jul 1987 2.00
❑20, Aug 1987 2.00
❑21, Sep 1987 2.00
❑22, Oct 1987 2.00
❑23, Nov 1987 2.00

SAMURAI CHAMPLOO
TOKYOPOP
❑1, Nov 2005 9.99

SAMURAI (VOL. 2)
AIRCEL
❑1, Dec 1987 2.00
❑2, Jan 1988 2.00
❑3, Feb 1988 2.00

SAMURAI (VOL. 3)
AIRCEL
❑1, 1988 1.95
❑2, 1988 1.95
❑3, 1988 1.95
❑4, 1988 1.95
❑5, 1988 1.95
❑6, Dec 1988 1.95
❑7, Jan 1989 1.95

SAMURAI (VOL. 4)
WARP
❑1, May 1997, b&w 2.95

SAMURAI 7
GAUNTLET
❑1, b&w 2.50
❑2, b&w 2.50
❑3, b&w 2.50

SAMURAI CAT
MARVEL / EPIC
❑1, Jun 1991 2.25
❑2, Aug 1991 2.25
❑3, Sep 1991 2.25

SAMURAI COMPILATION BOOK
AIRCEL
❑1, b&w 4.95
❑2, b&w 4.95

SAMURAI DEEPER KYO
TOKYOPOP
❑1, Jun 2003 9.99
❑2, Aug 2003 9.99
❑3, Oct 2003 9.99
❑4, Dec 2003 9.99
❑5, Feb 2004 9.99
❑6, Apr 2004 9.99
❑7, Jun 2004 9.99
❑8, Aug 2004 9.99
❑9, Oct 2004 9.99
❑10, Dec 2004 9.99
❑11, Feb 2005 9.99
❑12, Apr 2005 9.99
❑13, Jun 2005 9.99
❑14, Jul 2005 9.99
❑15, Aug 2005 9.99
❑16, Nov 2005 9.99

SAMURAI: DEMON SWORD
NIGHT WYND
❑1 2.50
❑2 2.50
❑3 2.50
❑4 2.50

SAMURAI EXECUTIONER
DARK HORSE
❑1, Jul 2004, When the Demon Knife Weeps 9.99
❑2, Dec 2004, Two Bodies, Two Minds 9.99
❑3, Jan 2005, The Hell Stick 9.99
❑4, Apr 2005, Portrait of Death 9.99
❑5, Aug 2005, Ten Fingers, One Life 9.99
❑6, Sep 2005, Shinko the Kappa 9.99
❑7, Dec 2005, The Bamboo Splitter 9.99
❑8, Jan 2006, The Death Sign of Spring 9.99
❑9, Mar 2006, Facing Life and Death 9.99

SAMURAI FUNNIES
SOLSON
❑1; Texas chainsaw 2.00
❑2; Samurai 13th 2.00

SAMURAI GUARD
COLBURN
❑1, Nov 1999 2.50
❑2, Jun 2000 2.50
❑Ashcan 1 1.00

SAMURAI: HEAVEN AND EARTH
DARK HORSE
❑1, Dec 2004 2.99
❑2, Jan 2005 2.99
❑3, Feb 2005 2.99
❑4, Sep 2005 2.99

SAMURAI JACK SPECIAL
DC
❑1, Sep 2002 3.95
❑1/2nd, Jul 2004; reprint 3.95

SAMURAI JAM
SLAVE LABOR
❑1, Jan 1994 2.95
❑2, Apr 1994 2.95
❑3, Jun 1994 2.95
❑4, Sep 1994 2.95

SAMURAI: MYSTIC CULT
NIGHTWYND
❑1, b&w 2.50
❑2, b&w 2.50
❑3, b&w 2.50
❑4, b&w 2.50

SAMURAI PENGUIN
SLAVE LABOR
❑1, Jun 1986, b&w 1.50
❑2, Aug 1986, b&w 1.50
❑3, Feb 1987, b&w; pink logo version also exist 1.50
❑4, May 1987, b&w 1.50
❑5, Sep 1987, b&w 1.50
❑6, Mar 1988 1.95
❑7, Jul 1988 1.75
❑8, May 1989 1.75

Savage Dragon: God War

Hero forgets advice from Almighty

©Image

Savage Hulk

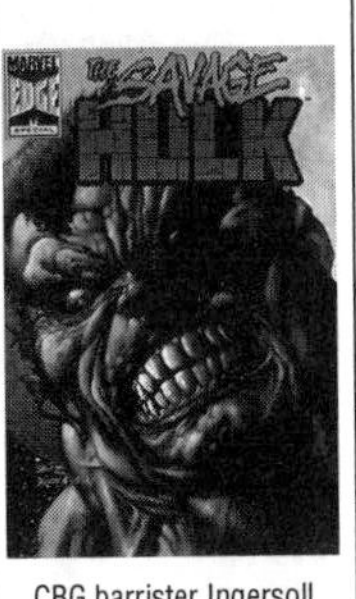

CBG barrister Ingersoll makes appearance

©Marvel

Savage She-Hulk

Banner's blood changes cousin considerably

©Marvel

Savage Sword of Conan

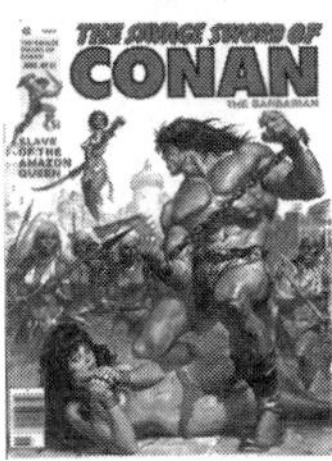

Black-and-white sword-wielding adventures

©Marvel

Savage Tales (1st Series)

Early Marvel black-and-white fantasy title

©Marvel

N-MINT

SAMURAI PENGUIN: FOOD CHAIN FOLLIES
SLAVE LABOR

❑1, Apr 1991 ... 5.95

SAMURAI SQUIRREL
SPOTLIGHT

❑1 ... 1.75
❑2 ... 1.75

SAMURAI: VAMPIRE'S HUNT
NIGHTWYND

❑1, b&w ... 2.50
❑2, b&w ... 2.50
❑3, b&w ... 2.50
❑4, b&w ... 2.50

SAMUREE (1ST SERIES)
CONTINUITY

❑1, May 1987 ... 2.00
❑2, Aug 1987 ... 2.00
❑3, May 1988 ... 2.00
❑4, Jan 1989 ... 2.00
❑5, Apr 1989 ... 2.00
❑6, Aug 1989 ... 2.00
❑7, Feb 1990 ... 2.00
❑8, Nov 1990 ... 2.00
❑9, Jan 1991 ... 2.00

SAMUREE (2ND SERIES)
CONTINUITY

❑1, May 1993 ... 2.50
❑2, Sep 1993 ... 2.50
❑3, Dec 1993 ... 2.50
❑4, Jan 1994 ... 2.50

SAMUREE (3RD SERIES)
ACCLAIM / WINDJAMMER

❑1, Oct 1995 ... 2.50
❑2, Nov 1995 ... 2.50

SANCTUARY PART 1
VIZ

❑1, Jun 1993, b&w ... 6.00
❑2, Jul 1993, b&w ... 5.00
❑3, Aug 1993 ... 5.00
❑4, Sep 1993 ... 5.00
❑5, Oct 1993 ... 5.00
❑6, Nov 1993 ... 5.00
❑7, Dec 1993 ... 5.00
❑8, Jan 1994 ... 5.00
❑9, Feb 1994 ... 5.00

SANCTUARY PART 2
VIZ

❑1, Mar 1994 ... 5.00
❑2, Apr 1994 ... 5.00
❑3, May 1994 ... 5.00
❑4, Jun 1994 ... 5.00
❑5, Jul 1994 ... 5.00
❑6, Aug 1994 ... 5.00
❑7, Sep 1994 ... 5.00
❑8, Oct 1994 ... 5.00
❑9, Nov 1994 ... 5.00

SANCTUARY PART 3
VIZ

❑1, Dec 1994, b&w ... 3.25
❑2, Jan 1995, b&w ... 3.25
❑3, Feb 1995, b&w ... 3.25

N-MINT

❑4, Mar 1995, b&w ... 3.25
❑5, Apr 1995, b&w ... 3.25
❑6, May 1995, b&w ... 3.25
❑7, Jun 1995, b&w ... 3.25
❑8, Jul 1995, b&w ... 3.25

SANCTUARY PART 4
VIZ

❑1, Aug 1995 ... 3.25
❑2, Sep 1995 ... 3.25
❑3, Oct 1995 ... 3.25
❑4, Nov 1995 ... 3.25
❑5, Dec 1995 ... 3.25
❑6, Jan 1996 ... 3.50
❑7, Feb 1996 ... 3.50

SANCTUARY PART 5
VIZ

❑1, Mar 1996 ... 3.50
❑2, Apr 1996 ... 3.50
❑3, May 1996 ... 3.50
❑4, Jun 1996 ... 3.50
❑5, Jul 1996 ... 3.50
❑6, Aug 1996 ... 3.50
❑7, Sep 1996 ... 3.50
❑8, Oct 1996 ... 3.50
❑9, Nov 1996 ... 3.50
❑10, Dec 1996 ... 3.50
❑11, Jan 1997 ... 3.50
❑12, Feb 1997 ... 3.50
❑13, Mar 1997 ... 3.50

SANCTUM
BLACKSHOE

❑1/Ltd.; Limited edition from 1999 San Diego Comic-Con ... 3.95

SAN DIEGO COMIC-CON COMICS
DARK HORSE

❑1, ca. 1992; con giveaway; 1992 Comic-Con ... 3.25
❑2, Aug 1993; con giveaway; 1993 Comic-Con ... 2.95
❑3, Aug 1994; con giveaway; 1994 Comic-Con ... 2.50
❑4, Aug 1995; 1995 Comic-Con ... 2.50

SANDMADAM
SPOOF

❑1, b&w ... 2.95

SANDMAN
DC

❑1, Win 1974, JK (a) ... 15.00
❑2, May 1975 JK (a) ... 7.00
❑3, Jul 1975 JK (a) ... 4.00
❑4, Sep 1975 JK (a); A: Demon ... 4.00
❑5, Nov 1975 JK (a) ... 4.00
❑6, Jan 1976 JK (a) ... 4.00

SANDMAN
DC

❑1, Jan 1989; Giant-size NG (w); 1: Sandman III (Morpheus) ... 25.00
❑2, Feb 1989 NG (w); A: Abel. A: Cain ... 12.00
❑3, Mar 1989 NG (w); A: John Constantine ... 12.00
❑4, Apr 1989 NG (w); A: Demon ... 3.50
❑5, May 1989 NG (w); ... 3.50
❑6, Jun 1989 NG (w); ... 3.50

N-MINT

❑7, Jul 1989 NG (w); ... 3.50
❑8, Aug 1989; Regular edition, no indicia in inside front cover; NG (w); 1: Death (Sandman). Regular edition, no indicia in inside front cover ... 15.00
❑8/Ltd., Aug 1989; limited edition; NG (w); 1: Death (Sandman). 1000 copies; Has indicia in inside front cover, editorial by Karen Berger ... 35.00
❑9, Sep 1989 NG (w) ... 3.50
❑10, Nov 1989 NG (w) ... 3.50
❑11, Dec 1989 NG (w) ... 3.50
❑12, Jan 1990 NG (w) ... 3.50
❑13, Feb 1990 NG (w) ... 3.50
❑14, Mar 1990 NG (w) ... 3.50
❑15, Apr 1990 NG (w) ... 2.50
❑16, Jun 1990 NG (w) ... 2.50
❑17, Jul 1990 NG (w) ... 2.50
❑18, Aug 1990 NG (w) ... 2.50
❑19, Sep 1990; NG (w); CV (a); properly printed; Midsummer Night's Dream ... 2.50
❑19/A, Sep 1990; NG (w); CV (a); pages out of order; Midsummer Night's Dream ... 2.50
❑20, Oct 1990 NG (w); D: Element Girl ... 2.50
❑21, Nov 1990 NG (w); ... 2.50
❑22, Jan 1991 NG (w); 1: Daniel (new Sandman) ... 3.50
❑23, Feb 1991 NG (w) ... 2.50
❑24, Mar 1991 NG (w) ... 2.50
❑25, Apr 1991 NG (w) ... 2.50
❑26, May 1991 NG (w) ... 2.50
❑27, Jun 1991 NG (w) ... 2.50
❑28, Jul 1991 NG (w) ... 2.50
❑29, Aug 1991 NG (w) ... 2.50
❑30, Sep 1991 NG (w) ... 2.50
❑31, Oct 1991 NG (w) ... 2.50
❑32, Nov 1991 NG (w) ... 2.50
❑33, Dec 1991 NG (w) ... 2.50
❑34, Jan 1992 NG (w) ... 2.50
❑35, Feb 1992 NG (w) ... 2.50
❑36, Apr 1992; Giant-size NG (w) ... 3.00
❑37, May 1992 NG (w) ... 2.50
❑38, Jun 1992 NG (w) ... 2.50
❑39, Jul 1992 NG (w) ... 2.50
❑40, Aug 1992 NG (w) ... 2.50
❑41, Sep 1992 NG (w) ... 2.50
❑42, Oct 1992 NG (w) ... 2.50
❑43, Nov 1992 NG (w) ... 2.50
❑44, Dec 1992 NG (w) ... 2.50
❑45, Jan 1993 NG (w) ... 2.50
❑46, Feb 1993; NG (w); Brief Lives ... 2.50
❑47, Mar 1993 NG (w) ... 2.50
❑48, Apr 1993 NG (w) ... 2.50
❑49, May 1993 NG (w) ... 2.50
❑50, Jun 1993; Double-size; NG (w); CR (a); Bronze ink ... 4.50
❑50/Gold, Jun 1993; Gold edition NG (w); CR (a) ... 20.00
❑51, Jul 1993 NG (w); BT, DG (a) ... 2.50
❑52, Aug 1993 NG (w); BT (a) ... 2.50
❑53, Sep 1993 NG (w); BT (a) ... 2.50
❑54, Oct 1993 NG (w); BT (a); O: Prez Rickard ... 2.50
❑55, Nov 1993 NG (w) ... 2.50

Other grades: Multiply price above by 5/6 for VF/NM • 2/3 for VERY FINE • 1/3 for FINE • 1/5 for VERY GOOD • 1/8 for GOOD

	N-MINT
❑56, Dec 1993 NG (w); BT (a)	2.50
❑57, Feb 1994 NG (w)	2.50
❑58, Mar 1994 NG (w)	2.50
❑59, Apr 1994 NG (w)	2.50
❑60, Jun 1994 NG (w)	2.50
❑61, Jul 1994 NG (w)	2.50
❑62, Aug 1994 NG (w); CV (a)	2.50
❑63, Sep 1994 NG (w)	2.50
❑64, Nov 1994 NG (w)	2.50
❑65, Dec 1994 NG (w)	2.50
❑66, Jan 1995 NG (w)	2.50
❑67, Mar 1995 NG (w)	2.50
❑68, May 1995 NG (w)	2.50
❑69, Jul 1995 NG (w); D: Sandman III (Morpheus)	3.00
❑70, Aug 1995 NG (w)	2.50
❑71, Sep 1995 NG (w)	2.50
❑72, Nov 1995; NG (w); burial of Dream	2.50
❑73, Dec 1995 NG (w); A: Hob Gadling	2.50
❑74, Jan 1996 NG (w);	2.50
❑75, Mar 1996; NG (w); CV (a); A: William Shakespeare. contains timeline	4.00
❑Special 1, ca. 1991; Orpheus special edition; NG (w); BT (a); Glow-in-the-dark cover	5.00

SANDMAN, THE: A GALLERY OF DREAMS
DC / VERTIGO

❑1, ca. 1994	5.00

SANDMAN MIDNIGHT THEATRE
DC / VERTIGO

❑1, Sep 1995; prestige format; Morpheus meets Wesley Dodds	6.95

SANDMAN MYSTERY THEATRE
DC / VERTIGO

❑1, Apr 1993 MW (w)	4.00
❑2, May 1993 MW (w)	3.00
❑3, Jun 1993 MW (w)	3.00
❑4, Jul 1993 MW (w)	3.00
❑5, Aug 1993 MW (w)	3.00
❑6, Sep 1993 MW (w)	3.00
❑7, Oct 1993 MW (w)	3.00
❑8, Nov 1993 MW (w)	3.00
❑9, Dec 1993 MW (w)	3.00
❑10, Jan 1994 MW (w)	3.00
❑11, Feb 1994 MW (w)	2.75
❑12, Mar 1994 MW (w)	2.75
❑13, Apr 1994 MW (w)	2.75
❑14, May 1994 MW (w)	2.75
❑15, Jun 1994 MW (w)	2.75
❑16, Jul 1994 MW (w)	2.75
❑17, Aug 1994 MW (w)	2.75
❑18, Sep 1994 MW (w)	2.75
❑19, Oct 1994 MW (w)	2.75
❑20, Nov 1994 MW (w)	2.75
❑21, Dec 1994 MW (w)	2.50
❑22, Jan 1995 MW (w)	2.50
❑23, Feb 1995 MW (w)	2.50
❑24, Mar 1995 MW (w)	2.50
❑25, Apr 1995 MW (w)	2.50
❑26, May 1995 MW (w)	2.50
❑27, Jun 1995 MW (w)	2.50
❑28, Jul 1995 MW (w)	2.50
❑29, Aug 1995 MW (w)	2.50
❑30, Sep 1995 MW (w)	2.50
❑31, Oct 1995 MW (w)	2.50
❑32, Nov 1995 MW (w)	2.50
❑33, Dec 1995 MW (w)	2.50
❑34, Jan 1996 MW (w)	2.50
❑35, Feb 1996 MW (w)	2.50
❑36, Mar 1996 MW (w)	2.50
❑37, Apr 1996 MW (w)	2.50
❑38, May 1996 MW (w)	2.50
❑39, Jun 1996 MW (w)	2.50
❑40, Jul 1996 MW (w)	2.50
❑41, Aug 1996 MW (w)	2.50
❑42, Sep 1996 MW (w)	2.50
❑43, Oct 1996 MW (w); A: Crimson Avenger	2.50
❑44, Nov 1996 MW (w)	2.50
❑45, Dec 1996 MW (w); A: Blackhawk	2.50
❑46, Jan 1997 MW (w)	2.50
❑47, Feb 1997 MW (w)	2.50
❑48, Mar 1997 MW (w)	2.50
❑49, Apr 1997 MW (w)	2.50
❑50, May 1997; Giant-size MW (w)	3.50
❑51, Jun 1997 MW (w)	2.50
❑52, Jul 1997 MW (w)	2.50
❑53, Aug 1997 MW (w)	2.50
❑54, Sep 1997 MW (w)	2.50
❑55, Oct 1997 MW (w)	2.50
❑56, Nov 1997 MW (w)	2.50
❑57, Dec 1997 MW (w)	2.50
❑58, Jan 1998 MW (w)	2.50
❑59, Feb 1998 MW (w)	2.50
❑60, Mar 1998 MW (w)	2.50
❑61, Apr 1998	2.50
❑62, May 1998	2.50
❑63, Jul 1998	2.50
❑64, Aug 1998	2.50
❑65, Sep 1998	2.50
❑66, Oct 1998	2.50
❑67, Nov 1998	2.50
❑68, Dec 1998	2.50
❑69, Jan 1999	2.50
❑70, Feb 1999	2.50
❑Annual 1 MW (w)	4.00

SANDMAN PRESENTS: BAST
DC / VERTIGO

❑1, Mar 2003	2.95
❑2, Apr 2003	2.95
❑3, May 2003	2.95

SANDMAN PRESENTS: LOVE STREET
DC / VERTIGO

❑1, Jul 1999; John Constantine in the '60s	2.95
❑2, Aug 1999	2.95
❑3, Sep 1999	2.95

SANDMAN PRESENTS: LUCIFER
DC / VERTIGO

❑1, Mar 1999	2.95
❑2, Apr 1999	2.95
❑3, May 1999	2.95

SANDMAN PRESENTS: PETREFAX
DC / VERTIGO

❑1, Mar 2000	2.95
❑2, Apr 2000	2.95
❑3, May 2000	2.95
❑4, Jun 2000	2.95

SANDMAN PRESENTS: DEADBOY DETECTIVES
DC / VERTIGO

❑1, Aug 2001	2.50
❑2, Sep 2001	2.50
❑3, Oct 2001	2.50
❑4, Nov 2001	2.50

SANDMAN PRESENTS, THE: EVERYTHING YOU ALWAYS WANTED TO KNOW ABOUT DREAMS...BUT WERE AFRAID TO ASK
DC / VERTIGO

❑1, Jul 2001	3.95

SANDMAN PRESENTS: THE FURIES
DC / WILDSTORM

❑1, ca. 2004	17.95

SANDMAN PRESENTS: THESSALY - WITCH FOR HIRE
DC / VERTIGO

❑1, Apr 2004	2.95
❑2, May 2004	2.95
❑3, Jun 2004	2.95
❑4, Jul 2004	2.95

SANDMAN PRESENTS: THE CORINTHIAN
DC / VERTIGO

❑1, Dec 2001	2.50
❑2, Jan 2002	2.50
❑3, Feb 2002	2.50

SANDMAN PRESENTS: THE THESSALIAD
DC / VERTIGO

❑1, Mar 2002	2.50
❑2, Apr 2002	2.50
❑3, May 2002	2.50
❑4, Jun 2002	2.50

SANDS
BLACK EYE

❑1, b&w; smaller than a normal comic book	2.50
❑2, b&w; smaller than a normal comic book	2.50
❑3, Feb 1997, b&w; smaller than a normal comic book	2.50

SANDSCAPE
DREAMWAVE

❑1, Jan 2003	2.95
❑2, Feb 2003	2.95
❑3, Apr 2003	2.95
❑4, Jun 2003	2.95

SAN FRANCISCO COMIC BOOK
SAN FRANCISCO COMIC BOOK CO.

❑1, Jan 1970	6.00
❑2	4.00
❑3	4.00
❑4	4.00
❑5	4.00
❑6	4.00
❑7	4.00

SANTA CLAUS ADVENTURES (WALT KELLY'S...)
INNOVATION

❑1, Reprints	6.95

SANTA CLAWS (ETERNITY)
ETERNITY

❑1, b&w	2.95

SANTA CLAWS (THORBY)
THORBY

❑1	2.95

SANTANA
MALIBU / ROCK-IT

❑1, May 1994; magazine TY (a)	5.00

SANTA THE BARBARIAN
MAXIMUM

❑1, Dec 1996	2.99

SAPPHIRE
AIRCEL

❑1, Feb 1990	2.95
❑2, Mar 1990	2.95
❑3, Apr 1990	2.50
❑4, May 1990	2.50
❑5, Jun 1990	2.50
❑6, Jul 1990	2.50
❑7, Aug 1990	2.50
❑8	2.50
❑9, Sep 1990	2.50

SAPPHIRE (NBM)
NBM

❑1	10.95
❑2	10.95

SAP TUNES
FANTAGRAPHICS

❑1, b&w	2.50
❑2, b&w	2.50

SARAH-JANE HAMILTON PRESENTS SUPERSTARS OF EROTICA
RE-VISIONARY

❑1	2.95

SARGE SNORKEL
CHARLTON

❑1, Oct 1973	8.00
❑2, Dec 1973	5.00
❑3, Jun 1974	4.00
❑4, Sep 1974	4.00
❑5, Nov 1974	4.00
❑6, Jan 1975	3.00
❑7, Mar 1975	3.00
❑8, May 1975	3.00
❑9, Jul 1975	3.00
❑10, Sep 1975	3.00
❑11, Nov 1975	3.00
❑12, Jan 1976	3.00
❑13, Mar 1976	3.00
❑14, May 1976	3.00
❑15, Aug 1976	3.00
❑16, Oct 1976	3.00
❑17, Dec 1976	3.00

SARGE STEEL
CHARLTON

❑1, Dec 1964	15.00
❑2, Feb 1965	10.00
❑3, May 1965	8.00
❑4, Jul 1965	8.00

Scamp (Walt Disney...)

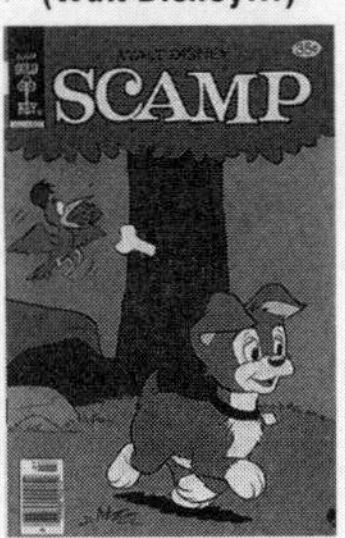

Lady and the Tramp's pup plays and plays
©Gold Key

Scarlett

Post-Buffy movie, pre-Buffy TV
©DC

Scary Godmother

Jill Thompson's tricky treat of a series
©Sirius

Scavengers (Fleetway/Quality)

Dinosaurs dumped in Dredd's domain
©Fleetway-Quality

Scene of the Crime

One-eyed P.I. seeks dame
©DC

	N-MINT
❑5, Sep 1965	8.00
❑6, Nov 1965	6.00
❑7, Apr 1966	6.00
❑8, Oct 1966	6.00
❑9	6.00

SATANIKA
VEROTIK

	N-MINT
❑0, ca. 1995	4.00
❑1, Jan 1995	5.00
❑2 1995	4.00
❑3 1995	4.00
❑4 1996	3.00
❑5, Oct 1996	3.00
❑6, Jan 1997	2.95
❑7, Apr 1997	2.95
❑8, Sep 1997	2.95
❑9, Mar 1998	2.95
❑10, Dec 1998	2.95
❑11, May 1999	3.95

SATANIKA ILLUSTRATIONS
VEROTIK

	N-MINT
❑1, Sep 1996; Cardstock cover; pin-ups	3.95

SATANIKA TALES
VEROTIK

	N-MINT
❑1 2005	3.95
❑2, Sep 2005	3.95

SATAN PLACE
THUNDERHILL

	N-MINT
❑1	3.50

SATAN'S SIX
TOPPS

	N-MINT
❑1, Apr 1993; trading card; Wolff and Byrd, Counselors of the Macabre backup story	2.95
❑2, May 1993; trading cards	2.95
❑3, Jun 1993; trading cards	2.95
❑4, Jul 1993; trading cards	2.95

SATAN'S SIX: HELLSPAWN
TOPPS

	N-MINT
❑1, Jun 1994; Inside index lists it as issue #2	2.50
❑2, Jun 1994	2.50
❑3, Jul 1994	2.50

SATURDAY MORNING: THE COMIC
MARVEL

	N-MINT
❑1, Apr 1996	1.95

SATURDAY NITE
ANSON JEW

	N-MINT
❑1, b&w	2.95

SAUCY LITTLE TART
FANTAGRAPHICS / EROS

	N-MINT
❑1, Dec 1995	2.95

SAURIANS: UNNATURAL SELECTION
CROSSGEN

	N-MINT
❑1, Feb 2002	2.95
❑2, Mar 2002	2.95

SAVAGE COMBAT TALES
ATLAS-SEABOARD

	N-MINT
❑1, Feb 1975; O: Sgt. Stryker's Death Squad. McWilliams cover/art; Archie Goodwin story, Goodwin/Sparling art	16.00
❑2, Apr 1975; Archie Goodwin story, Alex Toth art	10.00
❑3, Jul 1975; Rich Buckler cover. McWilliams art, Goodwin story, Sparling art	10.00

SAVAGE DRAGON (MINI-SERIES)
IMAGE

	N-MINT
❑1, Jul 1992; four cover logo variants (bottom of logo is white, blue, green, or yellow)	3.00
❑2, Oct 1992; Centerfold Savage Dragon poster	2.50
❑3, Dec 1992; Centerfold Savage Dragon poster	2.50

SAVAGE DRAGON
IMAGE

	N-MINT
❑½, ca. 1997 EL (w); EL (a)	3.00
❑½/Platinum, ca. 1997; Platinum edition EL (w); EL (a)	4.00
❑1, Jun 1993 EL (w); EL (a)	3.00
❑2, Jul 1993; EL (w); EL (a); A: Teenage Mutant Ninja Turtles. Flip book with Vanguard #0	3.00
❑3, Aug 1993; EL (w); EL (a); Mighty Man back-up feature	2.50
❑4, Sep 1993 EL (w); EL (a)	2.25
❑5, Oct 1993 EL (w); EL (a)	2.25
❑6, Nov 1993 EL (w); EL (a)	2.25
❑7, Jan 1994 EL (w); EL (a)	2.25
❑8, Mar 1994 EL (w); EL (a)	2.00
❑9, Apr 1994 EL (w); EL (a)	2.00
❑10, May 1994; EL (w); EL (a); alternate cover; newsstand version	2.00
❑10/Direct ed., May 1994 EL (w); EL (a)	2.00
❑11, Jul 1994 EL (w); EL (a)	2.00
❑12, Aug 1994; EL (w); EL (a); She Dragon	2.00
❑13, Jun 1995 EL (w); EL (a); 1: Condition Red	2.50
❑13/A, Jun 1995; JLee (w); JLee, EL (a); Image X month version	2.50
❑14, Oct 1994 EL (w); EL (a)	1.95
❑15, Dec 1994 EL (w); EL (a)	2.50
❑16, Jan 1995; EL (w); EL (a); Savage Dragon on cover	2.50
❑17/A, Feb 1995; EL (w); EL (a); One figure on cover; two different interior pages	2.50
❑17/B, Feb 1995 EL (w); EL (a)	2.50
❑18, Mar 1995 EL (w); EL (a)	2.50
❑19, Apr 1995 EL (w); EL (a)	2.50
❑20, Jul 1995 EL (w); EL (a)	2.50
❑21, Aug 1995 EL (w); EL (a)	2.50
❑22, Sep 1995 EL (w); EL (a); A: Teenage Mutant Ninja Turtles	2.50
❑23, Oct 1995 EL (w); EL (a)	2.50
❑24, Dec 1995 EL (w); EL (a)	2.50
❑25, Jan 1996; double-sized EL (w); EL (a)	3.95
❑25/A, Jan 1996; double-sized; EL (w); EL (a); alternate cover	3.95
❑26, Mar 1996 EL (w); EL (a)	2.50
❑27, Apr 1996 EL (w); EL (a)	2.50
❑27/A, Apr 1996; EL (w); EL (a); alternate cover only available at WonderCon	2.50
❑28, May 1996 EL (w); EL (a); A: Maxx	2.50
❑29, Jul 1996 EL (w); EL (a); A: Wildstar	2.50
❑30, Aug 1996 EL (w); EL (a); A: Spawn	2.50
❑31, Sep 1996; EL (w); EL (a); censored version says God is good inside Image logo on cover; God vs. The Devil	2.50
❑31/A, Sep 1996; EL (w); EL (a); God vs. The Devil; uncensored version	2.50
❑32, Oct 1996 EL (w); EL (a)	2.50
❑33, Nov 1996; EL (w); EL (a); Birth of Dragon's son	2.50
❑34, Dec 1996 EL (w); EL (a); A: Hellboy	2.50
❑35, Feb 1997 EL (w); EL (a); A: Hellboy	2.50
❑36, Mar 1997 EL (w); EL (a); 1: Zeek	2.50
❑37, Apr 1997 EL (w); EL (a)	2.50
❑38, May 1997 EL (w); EL (a)	2.50
❑39, Jun 1997 EL (w); EL (a)	2.50
❑40, Jul 1997 EL (w); EL (a)	2.50
❑40/A, Jul 1997 EL (w); EL (a)	2.50
❑41, Sep 1997 EL (w); EL (a); A: Wildstar. A: Monkeyman. A: Femforce. A: E-Man. A: Zot. A: Megaton. A: Madman. A: Vampirella. A: Hellboy. A: DNAgents	2.50
❑42, Oct 1997 EL (w); EL (a)	2.50
❑43, Nov 1997 EL (w); EL (a)	2.50
❑44, Dec 1997 EL (w); EL (a)	2.50
❑45, Jan 1998 EL (w); EL (a)	2.50
❑46, Feb 1998 EL (w); EL (a)	2.50
❑47, Mar 1998 EL (w); EL (a)	2.50
❑48, Apr 1998 EL (w); EL (a)	2.50
❑49, May 1998 EL (w); EL (a)	2.50
❑50, Jun 1998 JPH, EL (w); TMc, RL, EL (a)	5.95
❑51/A, Jul 1998; EL (w); EL (a); red logo	2.50
❑51/B, Jul 1998; EL (w); EL (a); yellow logo	2.50
❑52, Aug 1998 EL (w); EL (a)	2.50
❑53, Sep 1998 EL (w); EL (a)	2.50
❑54, Oct 1998 EL (w); EL (a)	2.50
❑55, Nov 1998 EL (w); EL (a)	2.50
❑56, Dec 1998 EL (w); EL (a)	2.50
❑57, Jan 1999 EL (w); EL (a)	2.50
❑58, Feb 1999 EL (w); EL (a)	2.50
❑59, Mar 1999 EL (w); EL (a)	2.50
❑60, Apr 1999 EL (w); EL (a)	2.50
❑61, May 1999 EL (w); EL (a)	2.50
❑62, Jun 1999 EL (w); EL (a)	2.50
❑63, Jun 1999 EL (w); EL (a)	2.50
❑64, Jul 1999 EL (w); EL (a)	2.50
❑65, Aug 1999 EL (w); EL (a)	2.50
❑66, Aug 1999 EL (w); EL (a)	2.50
❑67, Sep 1999 EL (w); EL (a)	2.50
❑68, Oct 1999 EL (w); EL (a)	2.50
❑69, Nov 1999 EL (w); EL (a)	2.50
❑70, Dec 1999 EL (w); EL (a)	2.50
❑71, Jan 2000 EL (w); EL (a)	2.50
❑72, Feb 2000 EL (w); EL (a); A: Mighty Man	2.95
❑73, Mar 2000 EL (w); EL (a)	2.95
❑74, Apr 2000 EL (w); EL (a)	2.95
❑75, May 2000; Giant-size EL (w); EL (a)	5.95
❑76, Jun 2000 EL (w); EL (a)	2.95
❑77, Jul 2000 EL (w); EL (a)	2.95
❑78, Aug 2000 EL (w); EL (a)	2.95
❑79, Sep 2000 EL (w); EL (a)	2.95

Other grades: Multiply price above by 5/6 for VF/NM • 2/3 for VERY FINE • 1/3 for FINE • 1/5 for VERY GOOD • 1/8 for GOOD

❑80, Oct 2000 EL (w); EL (a) 2.95
❑81, Nov 2000 EL (w); EL (a) 2.95
❑82, Dec 2000 EL (w); EL (a) 2.95
❑83, Jan 2001 EL (w); EL (a); A: Madman 2.95
❑84, Feb 2001 EL (w); EL (a)............ 2.95
❑85, Mar 2001 EL (w); EL (a); A: Madman 2.95
❑86, Apr 2001 EL (w); EL (a); A: Mighty Man............ 2.95
❑87, May 2001 EL (w); EL (a)............ 2.95
❑88, Jun 2001 EL (w); EL (a) 2.95
❑89, Jul 2001 EL (w); EL (a)............ 2.95
❑90, Aug 2001 EL (w); EL (a) 2.95
❑91, Sep 2001 EL (a)............ 2.95
❑92, Oct 2001 EL (w); EL (a) 2.95
❑93, Nov 2001 EL (a); A: SuperPatriot 2.95
❑94, Dec 2001 EL (w); EL (a) 2.95
❑95, Jan 2002 EL (w); EL (a)............ 2.95
❑96, Feb 2002 EL (w); EL (a)............ 2.95
❑97, Mar 2002 EL (w); EL (a) 2.95
❑98, Apr 2002 EL (w); EL (a)............ 2.95
❑99, May 2002 EL (w); EL (a)............ 2.95
❑100, Jun 2002 EL (w); JOy, EL (a).... 8.95
❑101, Jul 2002 EL (w); EL (a)............ 2.95
❑102, Aug 2002 EL (w); EL (a) 2.95
❑103, Sep 2002 EL (w); EL (a) 2.95
❑104, Oct 2002 EL (w); EL (a) 2.95
❑105, Nov 2002 EL (w); EL (a) 2.95
❑106, Dec 2002 EL (w); EL (a) 2.95
❑107, May 2003 EL (w); EL (a).......... 3.95
❑108, Jul 2003 .... 2.95
❑109, Jul 2003 .... 2.95
❑110, Sep 2003............ 2.95
❑111, Oct 2003............ 2.95
❑112, Nov 2003............ 2.95
❑113, Feb 2004 .... 2.95
❑114, May 2004 .... 2.95
❑115, Jun 2004 .... 2.95
❑116, Jul 2004 .... 2.95
❑117, Aug 2004............ 2.95
❑118, Sep 2004 .... 2.95
❑119, Oct 2004............ 2.95
❑120, ca. 2005 .... 2.95
❑121, ca. 2005 .... 2.95
❑122, Jan 2006 .... 2.95
❑123, Mar 2006............ 2.95
❑125, Jun 2006 .... 2.95
❑126, Jul 2006 .... 2.95
❑127, Jul 2006 .... 2.95

SAVAGE DRAGON ARCHIVES
IMAGE

❑1, Jun 1998 .... 2.95
❑2, Oct 1998; Reprints Graphic Fantasy #2 .... 2.95
❑3, Dec 1998............ 2.95
❑4, Jan 1999 .... 2.95

SAVAGE DRAGONBERT: FULL FRONTAL NERDITY
IMAGE

❑1, Oct 2002............ 5.95

SAVAGE DRAGON COMPANION
IMAGE

❑1, Jul 2002 .... 2.95

SAVAGE DRAGON/DESTROYER DUCK
IMAGE

❑1, Nov 1996............ 3.95

SAVAGE DRAGON: GOD WAR
IMAGE

❑1, Mar 2004............ 2.95
❑2............ 2.95
❑3, 2005 .... 2.95

SAVAGE DRAGON/HELLBOY
IMAGE

❑1, Oct 2002............ 5.95

SAVAGE DRAGON/MARSHAL LAW
IMAGE

❑1, Jul 1997, b&w; indicia says Savage Dragon/Marshall Law............ 2.95
❑2, Aug 1997, b&w 2.95

SAVAGE DRAGON: RED HORIZON
IMAGE

❑1, Feb 1997 .... 2.50
❑2, Apr 1997 .... 2.50
❑3, May 1997 .... 2.50

SAVAGE DRAGON: SEX & VIOLENCE
IMAGE

❑1, Aug 1997 .... 2.50
❑2, Sep 1997............ 2.50

SAVAGE DRAGON/TEENAGE MUTANT NINJA TURTLES CROSSOVER
MIRAGE

❑1, Sep 1993............ 2.75

SAVAGE DRAGON VS. THE SAVAGE MEGATON MAN
IMAGE

❑1, Mar 1993 EL (w); EL (a)............ 2.00
❑1/Gold, Mar 1993; EL (a); Gold foil cover 3.00

SAVAGE FISTS OF KUNG FU
MARVEL

❑1 AM, JSn, JB, HT, DG, DA (a); O: The Sons of the Dragon 8.00

SAVAGE FUNNIES
VISION

❑1, Jul 1996............ 1.95
❑2, Jul 1996............ 1.95

SAVAGE HENRY
VORTEX

❑1, Jan 1987 .... 2.00
❑2, Feb 1987 .... 2.00
❑3, Apr 1987 .... 2.00
❑4 1987............ 2.00
❑5 1987............ 2.00
❑6, Jul 1988 .... 2.00
❑7, Sep 1988, b&w 2.00
❑8, Dec 1988............ 2.00
❑9, Feb 1989 .... 2.00
❑10............ 2.00
❑11 1990............ 2.00
❑12 1990............ 2.00
❑13 1990; Last Vortex issue............ 2.00
❑14, Mar 1991, b&w; Rip Off begins as publisher 2.50
❑15, May 1991, b&w............ 2.50
❑16, Jul 1991, b&w............ 2.50
❑17, Sep 1991, b&w 2.50
❑18, Nov 1991, b&w 2.50
❑19, Jan 1992, b&w............ 2.50
❑20, Mar 1992, b&w 2.50
❑21, May 1992, b&w............ 2.50
❑22, Jul 1992, b&w............ 2.50
❑23, Sep 1992, b&w 2.50
❑24, Nov 1992, b&w 2.50
❑25, Jan 1993, b&w............ 2.50
❑26, Mar 1993, b&w............ 2.50
❑27, May 1993............ 2.50
❑28, Jul 1993, b&w............ 2.50
❑29, Sep 1993, b&w 2.50
❑30, Nov 1993, b&w; 1993............ 2.50

SAVAGE HENRY (ICONOGRAFIX)
CALIBER / ICONOGRAFIX

❑1, b&w 2.95
❑2, b&w 2.95
❑3, b&w 2.95

SAVAGE HENRY: HEADSTRONG
CALIBER

❑1, ca. 1995, b&w............ 2.95
❑2, ca. 1995, b&w............ 2.95
❑3, ca. 1995, b&w............ 2.95

SAVAGE HULK
MARVEL

❑1, Jan 1996; prestige format............ 6.95

SAVAGE NINJA
CADILLAC

❑1............ 1.00

SAVAGE RETURN OF DRACULA
MARVEL

❑1, ca. 1992; Reprints Tomb of Dracula #1, 2............ 2.00

SAVAGES (PEREGRINE)
PEREGRINE

❑1, ca. 2001 .... 2.95

SAVAGES
COMAX

❑1, b&w 2.50

SAVAGE SHE-HULK
MARVEL

❑1, Feb 1980, SL (w); JB (a); O: She-Hulk. 1: She-Hulk............ 8.00
❑2, Mar 1980, 1: Dan Zapper Ridge. 1: Morris Walters............ 5.00
❑3, Apr 1980 .... 2.50
❑4, May 1980 .... 2.50
❑5, Jun 1980 .... 2.50
❑6, Jul 1980, A: Iron Man............ 2.00
❑7, Aug 1980............ 2.00
❑8, Sep 1980, A: Man-Thing............ 2.00
❑9, Oct 1980............ 2.00
❑10, Nov 1980............ 2.00
❑11, Dec 1980............ 2.00
❑12, Jan 1981, V: Gemini 2.00
❑13, Feb 1981, FS (a); A: Man-Wolf... 2.00
❑14, Mar 1981, FS (a); A: Man-Wolf. A: Hellcat 2.00
❑15, Apr 1981, FS (a)............ 2.00
❑16, May 1981, FS (a)............ 2.00
❑17, Jun 1981, V: Man-Elephant 2.00
❑18, Jul 1981, V: Grappler............ 2.00
❑19, Aug 1981............ 2.00
❑20, Sep 1981............ 2.00
❑21, Oct 1981............ 2.00
❑22, Nov 1981, (c); FS (a); V: Radius. 2.00
❑23, Dec 1981, FS (a) 2.00
❑24, Jan 1982, AM (a)............ 2.00
❑25, Feb 1982; Giant-size............ 2.00

SAVAGE SWORD OF CONAN
MARVEL

❑1, Aug 1974, b&w GK (w); JB, NA, GK, RA, BS (a); O: Red Sonja. O: Blackmark 60.00
❑2, Oct 1974 HC (a); A: Kull 28.00
❑3, Dec 1974............ 16.00
❑4, Feb 1975 GK (w); JB, GK, AA (a).. 12.00
❑5, Apr 1975 JB (a) 12.00
❑6, Jun 1975 .... 12.00
❑7, Aug 1975............ 12.00
❑8, Oct 1975............ 12.00
❑9, Dec 1975............ 12.00
❑10, Feb 1976 .... 12.00
❑11, Apr 1976 .... 8.00
❑12, Jun 1976 .... 8.00
❑13, Aug 1976............ 8.00
❑14, Sep 1976............ 8.00
❑15, Oct 1976............ 8.00
❑16, Dec 1976............ 8.00
❑17, Feb 1977 .... 8.00
❑18, Apr 1977 .... 8.00
❑19, Jun 1977 .... 8.00
❑20, Jul 1977 .... 8.00
❑21, Aug 1977............ 6.00
❑22, Sep 1977............ 6.00
❑23, Oct 1977............ 6.00
❑24, Nov 1977............ 6.00
❑25, Dec 1977............ 6.00
❑26, Jan 1978 .... 6.00
❑27, Mar 1978; adapts Beyond the Black River............ 6.00
❑28, Apr 1978 .... 6.00
❑29, May 1978 .... 6.00
❑30, Jun 1978 .... 5.00
❑31, Jul 1978 .... 5.00
❑32, Aug 1978; adapts "The Flame Knife"............ 5.00
❑33, Sep 1978............ 5.00
❑34, Oct 1978; 1: Garth. 1st Appearance of Garth 5.00
❑35, Nov 1978............ 5.00
❑36, Dec 1978............ 5.00
❑37, Feb 1979 .... 5.00
❑38, Mar 1979 JB, TD (a)............ 5.00
❑39, Apr 1979 .... 5.00
❑40, May 1979 .... 5.00
❑41, Jun 1979 JB, TD (a) 5.00
❑42, Jul 1979 JB, TD (a) 5.00
❑43, Aug 1979............ 5.00
❑44, Sep 1979 SB, TD (a)............ 5.00
❑45, Oct 1979............ 5.00
❑46, Nov 1979 TD (a)............ 5.00
❑47, Dec 1979 JB, GK (a)............ 5.00
❑48, Jan 1980 JB, TD (a) 5.00
❑49, Feb 1980 .... 5.00
❑50, Mar 1980 JB, TD (a)............ 5.00
❑51, Apr 1980 .... 3.00
❑52, May 1980; JB, TD (a); Conan crowned King of Aquilonia............ 3.00
❑53, Jun 1980 JB (a)............ 3.00

Scion

Prince acquires power, incites war

©CrossGen

Scooby-Doo (DC)

Crimes crushed by darned kids and dog

©DC

Scorpion

Atlas hero, not Marvel villain

©Annruel

Scorpio Rose

Immortal gypsy fights mystic menaces

©Eclipse

Scout

Post-apocalyptic Apache fights to survive

©Eclipse

	N-MINT
❑54, Jul 1980 JB (a)	3.00
❑55, Aug 1980 JB, AA (a)	3.00
❑56, Sep 1980 JB, TD, GD (a)	3.00
❑57, Oct 1980 JB, TD (a)	3.00
❑58, Nov 1980 JB, TD, KGa (a)	3.00
❑59, Dec 1980 AA (a)	3.00
❑60, Jan 1981 JB (a)	3.00
❑61, Feb 1981 GD (w); JB (a)	3.00
❑62, Mar 1981 JB (a)	3.00
❑63, Apr 1981 GK (w); JB, GK, TP, BMc (a)	3.00
❑64, May 1981 ATh, GK (w); ATh, JB, GK (a)	3.00
❑65, Jun 1981 JB, GK (a)	3.00
❑66, Jul 1981 JB (a)	3.00
❑67, Aug 1981 GK (w); JB, GK, AA (a)	3.00
❑68, Sep 1981 GD (a)	3.00
❑69, Oct 1981 GD (a)	3.00
❑70, Nov 1981 JB (a)	3.00
❑71, Dec 1981 JB (a)	3.00
❑72, Jan 1982 JB (a)	3.00
❑73, Feb 1982 JB (a)	3.00
❑74, Mar 1982 JB, VM, GD (a)	3.00
❑75, Apr 1982 AA (a)	3.00
❑76, May 1982 JB, AA (a)	3.00
❑77, Jun 1982 JB (a)	3.00
❑78, Jul 1982 JB, DG (a)	3.00
❑79, Aug 1982 JB (a)	3.00
❑80, Sep 1982 JB, AA (a)	3.00
❑81, Oct 1982 JB (a)	3.00
❑82, Nov 1982 AA (a)	3.00
❑83, Dec 1982 NA, AA (a); A: Red Sonja	3.00
❑84, Jan 1983 VM (a)	3.00
❑85, Feb 1983 GK (a)	3.00
❑86, Mar 1983 GK (a)	3.00
❑87, Apr 1983 JB (a)	3.00
❑88, May 1983 JB (a)	3.00
❑89, Jun 1983 GK (w); NR, AA (a)	3.00
❑90, Jul 1983 NR, JB (a)	3.00
❑91, Aug 1983 JB, VM (a)	3.00
❑92, Sep 1983 JB (a)	3.00
❑93, Oct 1983 JB (a)	3.00
❑94, Nov 1983 VM (c); VM (a)	3.00
❑95, Dec 1983 JB (a)	3.00
❑96, Jan 1984 JB (a)	3.00
❑97, Feb 1984	3.00
❑98, Mar 1984 JB (a)	3.00
❑99, Apr 1984 JB (a)	3.00
❑100, May 1984 JB (a)	3.00
❑101, Jun 1984 MG (c); JB (a)	2.50
❑102, Jul 1984 BSz (c)	2.50
❑103, Aug 1984 GD (a)	2.50
❑104, Sep 1984 VM, GD (a)	2.50
❑105, Oct 1984	2.50
❑106, Nov 1984 MG (c); GD (a)	2.50
❑107, Dec 1984	2.50
❑108, Jan 1985	2.50
❑109, Feb 1985	2.50
❑110, Mar 1985	2.50
❑111, Apr 1985	2.50
❑112, May 1985	2.50
❑113, Jun 1985	2.50
❑114, Jul 1985	2.50
❑115, Aug 1985 VM (a)	2.50

	N-MINT
❑116, Sep 1985 SB (a)	2.50
❑117, Oct 1985 MG (c)	2.50
❑118, Nov 1985	2.50
❑119, Dec 1985	2.50
❑120, Jan 1986	2.50
❑121, Feb 1986	2.50
❑122, Mar 1986	2.50
❑123, Apr 1986	2.50
❑124, May 1986	2.50
❑125, Jun 1986	2.50
❑126, Jul 1986	2.50
❑127, Aug 1986	2.50
❑128, Sep 1986	2.50
❑129, Oct 1986	2.50
❑130, Nov 1986	2.50
❑131, Dec 1986	2.50
❑132, Jan 1987	2.50
❑133, Feb 1987	2.50
❑134, Mar 1987	2.50
❑135, Apr 1987	2.50
❑136, May 1987	2.50
❑137, Jun 1987	2.50
❑138, Jul 1987	2.50
❑139, Aug 1987	2.50
❑140, Sep 1987	2.50
❑141, Oct 1987	2.50
❑142, Nov 1987	2.50
❑143, Dec 1987	2.50
❑144, Jan 1988	2.50
❑145, Feb 1988 A: Red Sonja	2.50
❑146, Mar 1988	2.50
❑147, Apr 1988	2.50
❑148, May 1988	2.50
❑149, Jun 1988	2.50
❑150, Jul 1988	2.50
❑151, Aug 1988	2.50
❑152, Sep 1988	2.50
❑153, Oct 1988 LMc (a); A: Red Sonja	2.50
❑154, Nov 1988	2.50
❑155, Dec 1988	2.50
❑156, Jan 1989	2.50
❑157, Feb 1989	2.50
❑158, Mar 1989	2.50
❑159, Apr 1989	2.50
❑160, May 1989	2.50
❑161, Jun 1989	2.50
❑162, Jul 1989	2.50
❑163, Aug 1989	2.50
❑164, Sep 1989	2.50
❑165, Oct 1989	2.50
❑166, Nov 1989	2.50
❑167, Dec 1989	2.50
❑168, Dec 1989	2.50
❑169, Jan 1990	2.50
❑170, Feb 1990	2.50
❑171, Mar 1990	2.50
❑172, Apr 1990	2.50
❑173, May 1990	2.50
❑174, Jun 1990; Series continues as Savage Sword of Conan the Barbarian	2.25
❑175, Jul 1990	2.25
❑176, Aug 1990	2.25
❑177, Sep 1990	2.25
❑178, Oct 1990	2.25

	N-MINT
❑179, Nov 1990 A: Red Sonja	2.25
❑180, Dec 1990	2.25
❑181, Jan 1991	2.25
❑182, Feb 1991	2.25
❑183, Mar 1991	2.25
❑184, Apr 1991 AA (a)	2.25
❑185, May 1991	2.25
❑186, Jun 1991	2.25
❑187, Jul 1991 A: Red Sonja	2.25
❑188, Aug 1991 DC (a)	2.25
❑189, Sep 1991 AA (a)	2.25
❑190, Oct 1991 JB (a)	2.25
❑191, Nov 1991 JB (a)	2.25
❑192, Dec 1991 JB (a)	2.25
❑193, Jan 1992 JB (a)	2.25
❑194, Feb 1992 JB (a)	2.25
❑195, Mar 1992 JB (a)	2.25
❑196, Apr 1992 JB (a)	2.25
❑197, May 1992 JB (a)	2.25
❑198, Jun 1992 JB (a)	2.25
❑199, Jul 1992 JB (a)	2.25
❑200, Aug 1992; JB (a); Conan meets Robert E. Howard	2.25
❑201, Sep 1992	2.25
❑202, Oct 1992 JB (a)	2.25
❑203, Nov 1992 JB (a)	2.25
❑204, Dec 1992 JB (a)	2.25
❑205, Jan 1993	2.25
❑206, Feb 1993	2.25
❑207, Mar 1993 JB (a)	2.25
❑208, Apr 1993 JB (a)	2.25
❑209, May 1993 JB (a)	2.25
❑210, Jun 1993 JB (a)	2.25
❑211, Jul 1993	2.25
❑212, Aug 1993	2.25
❑213, Sep 1993	2.25
❑214, Oct 1993; Adapted from Robert E. Howard's "Red Nails"	2.25
❑215, Nov 1993	2.25
❑216, Dec 1993	2.25
❑217, Jan 1994	2.25
❑218, Feb 1994	2.25
❑219, Mar 1994; Conan and Solomon Kane meet	2.25
❑220, Apr 1994	2.25
❑221, May 1994, b&w	2.25
❑222, Jun 1994, b&w JB (a)	2.25
❑223, Jul 1994, b&w AA (a)	2.25
❑224, Aug 1994, b&w	2.25
❑225, Sep 1994, b&w JB (a)	2.25
❑226, Oct 1994, b&w	2.25
❑227, Nov 1994, b&w	2.25
❑228, Dec 1994, b&w AN (a)	2.25
❑229, Jan 1995, b&w	2.25
❑230, Feb 1995, b&w	2.25
❑231, Mar 1995, b&w	2.25
❑232, Apr 1995, b&w	2.25
❑233, May 1995, b&w	2.25
❑234, Jun 1995, b&w TS (c); JB (a)	2.25
❑235, Jul 1995, b&w JB (a)	2.25
❑Annual 1, ca. 1975, b&w; reprinted from Conan the Barbarian (1st series) #10 and 13; Kull the Conqueror #3; Monsters on the Prowl #16	17.00
❑Special 1, ca. 1975	6.00

Other grades: Multiply price above by 5/6 for VF/NM • 2/3 for VERY FINE • 1/3 for FINE • 1/5 for VERY GOOD • 1/8 for GOOD

N-MINT

SAVAGE SWORD OF MIKE
FANDOM HOUSE

❑1, b&w ... 2.00

SAVAGE TALES (1ST SERIES)
MARVEL

❑1, May 1971, b&w magazine SL (w); GM, GC, JB, JR, BS (a); O: Man-Thing. 1: Man-Thing. A: Conan ... 150.00
❑2, Oct 1973; JB (c); AW, BWr, GM, FB (a); "Crusader" reprinted from The Black Knight #1 ... 32.00
❑3, Feb 1974; AW, FB, JSt (a); Continues "Red Nails" story from issue #2 ... 20.00
❑4, May 1974 NA, GK (a) ... 20.00
❑5, Jul 1974 NA, GK (a) ... 12.00
❑6, Sep 1974 ... 10.00
❑7, Nov 1974 ... 10.00
❑8, Jan 1975 ... 10.00
❑9, Mar 1975 ... 10.00
❑10, May 1975 ... 10.00
❑11, Jul 1975 ... 10.00
❑12, Sum 1975 ... 8.00
❑Annual 1, ca. 1975, b&w; GK (a); O: Ka-Zar. Ka-Zar stories ... 25.00

SAVAGE TALES (2ND SERIES)
MARVEL

❑1, Oct 1985, b&w; magazine; MG (a); 1st 'Nam story ... 4.00
❑2, Dec 1985, JSe (a); 2nd 'Nam story 3.00
❑3, Feb 1986 ... 2.50
❑4, Apr 1986, 'Nam ... 2.50
❑5, Jun 1986, JSe (a) ... 2.50
❑6, Aug 1986 ... 2.00
❑7, Oct 1986 ... 2.00
❑8, Dec 1986 ... 2.00
❑9, Feb 1987 ... 2.00

SAVANT GARDE
IMAGE

❑1, Mar 1997 ... 2.50
❑2, Apr 1997 1: Innuendo ... 2.50
❑3, May 1997 ... 2.50
❑4, Jun 1997 ... 2.50
❑5, Jul 1997 ... 2.50
❑6, Aug 1997 ... 2.50
❑7, Sep 1997 ... 2.50
❑Fan ed. 1/A, Feb 1997 ... 1.00
❑Fan ed. 2/A, Mar 1997 ... 1.00
❑Fan ed. 3/A, Apr 1997 ... 1.00

SAVED BY THE BELL
HARVEY

❑1, May 1992 ... 1.25
❑2, Jun 1992 ... 1.25
❑3, Jul 1992 ... 1.25
❑4, Aug 1992 ... 1.25
❑5, Sep 1992 ... 1.25

SAVIOUR
TRIDENT

❑1 1989, b&w ... 4.00
❑2, Feb 1990, b&w ... 1.95
❑3 1990, b&w ... 2.50
❑4 1990, b&w ... 2.50
❑5 1990, b&w ... 2.50

SAW: REBIRTH
IDEA & DESIGN WORKS

❑1 ... 3.99

SB NINJA HIGH SCHOOL
ANTARCTIC

❑1/A, Aug 1992, b&w ... 2.50
❑1/B, Aug 1992, b&w; trading card ... 4.95
❑2/A, b&w ... 2.95
❑2/B, b&w; trading card ... 4.95
❑3/A, Sep 1994, b&w ... 2.75
❑3/B, Sep 1994, b&w; trading card ... 4.95
❑4, Feb 1995, b&w ... 2.75
❑5, May 1995, b&w ... 2.75
❑6, Aug 1995, b&w ... 2.75
❑7, Nov 1995, b&w ... 2.75

SCAB
FANTACO

❑1, b&w ... 3.50
❑2, b&w ... 3.50

SCALES OF THE DRAGON
SUNDRAGON

❑1, Mar 1997, b&w; Flip-book ... 1.95

N-MINT

SCAMP (WALT DISNEY...)
GOLD KEY / WHITMAN

❑1, ca. 1968 ... 8.00
❑2, Mar 1969 ... 4.00
❑3, ca. 1970 ... 4.00
❑4, Nov 1970 ... 4.00
❑5, Feb 1971 ... 4.00
❑6, Oct 1971 ... 3.00
❑7 1972 ... 3.00
❑8 1972 ... 3.00
❑9, Nov 1972 ... 3.00
❑10, Feb 1973 ... 3.00
❑11, Jun 1973 ... 2.50
❑12, Jul 1973 ... 2.50
❑13, Sep 1973 ... 2.50
❑14, Nov 1973 ... 2.50
❑15, Jan 1974 ... 2.50
❑16, Mar 1974 ... 2.50
❑17, May 1974 ... 2.50
❑18, Jul 1974 ... 2.50
❑19, Sep 1974 ... 2.50
❑20, Nov 1974 ... 2.50
❑21, Jan 1975 ... 2.00
❑22, Mar 1975 ... 2.00
❑23, May 1975 ... 2.00
❑24, Jul 1975 ... 2.00
❑25, Sep 1975 ... 2.00
❑26, Nov 1975 ... 2.00
❑27, Jan 1976 ... 2.00
❑28, Mar 1976 ... 2.00
❑29, May 1976 ... 2.00
❑30, Jul 1976 ... 2.00
❑31, Sep 1976 ... 2.00
❑32, Nov 1976 ... 2.00
❑33, Jan 1977 ... 2.00
❑34, Mar 1977 ... 2.00
❑35, May 1977 ... 2.00
❑36, Jul 1977 ... 2.00
❑37, Sep 1977 ... 2.00
❑38, Nov 1977 ... 2.00
❑39, Jan 1978 ... 2.00
❑40, Mar 1978 ... 2.00
❑41, May 1978 ... 2.00
❑42, Jul 1978 ... 2.00
❑43, Sep 1978 ... 2.00
❑44, Nov 1978, Aristokittens cross-over ... 2.00
❑45, Jan 1979 ... 2.00

SCAN
ICONOGRAFIX

❑1, b&w ... 2.95
❑2, b&w ... 2.95

SCANDALS
THORBY

❑1 ... 2.95

SCANDAL SHEET
ARRIBA

❑1, b&w ... 2.50

SCARAB
DC / VERTIGO

❑0, Mar 1994 ... 1.95
❑1, Nov 1993 ... 1.95
❑2, Dec 1993 ... 1.95
❑3, Jan 1994 ... 1.95
❑4, Feb 1994 ... 1.95
❑5, Mar 1994 ... 1.95
❑6, Apr 1994 ... 1.95
❑7, May 1994 ... 1.95
❑8, Jun 1994 ... 1.95

SCARAMOUCH
INNOVATION

❑1, b&w ... 2.25
❑2, b&w ... 2.25

SCARECROW OF ROMNEY MARSH
GOLD KEY

❑1, Apr 1964, No number; code on cover box ends in "404" ... 30.00
❑2, Jul 1965 ... 20.00
❑3, Oct 1965 ... 20.00

SCARECROW (VILLAINS)
DC

❑1, Feb 1998; New Year's Evil ... 1.95

SCARE TACTICS
DC

❑1, Dec 1996 ... 2.25

N-MINT

❑2, Jan 1997; Road Trip ... 2.25
❑3, Feb 1997 ... 2.25
❑4, Mar 1997 ... 2.25
❑5, Apr 1997; Valentine's Day Nightmare 2.25
❑6, May 1997 ... 2.25
❑7, Jun 1997 ... 2.25
❑8, Jul 1997 ... 2.25
❑9, Aug 1997; series goes on hiatus; story continues in Impulse Plus #1. 2.25
❑10, Jan 1998 ... 2.25
❑11, Feb 1998 ... 2.25
❑12, Mar 1998; Phil transforms ... 2.25

SCARLET CRUSH
AWESOME

❑1, Jan 1998 ... 2.50
❑2, Feb 1998 ... 2.50

SCARLET IN GASLIGHT
ETERNITY

❑1, Mar 1988, b&w; Sherlock Holmes vs. Dracula ... 1.95
❑2, Apr 1988 ... 1.95
❑3, May 1988 ... 1.95
❑4, Jun 1988 ... 1.95

SCARLET KISS: THE VAMPYRE
ALL AMERICAN

❑1, b&w ... 2.95

SCARLET SCORPION/DARKSHADE
AC

❑1, Jul 1995 ... 3.50
❑2 1995 ... 3.50

SCARLET SPIDER
MARVEL

❑1, Nov 1995, GK (a) ... 2.00
❑2, Dec 1995, JR2 (a); concludes in Spectacular Scarlet Spider #2 ... 2.00

SCARLET SPIDER UNLIMITED
MARVEL

❑1, Nov 1995 ... 3.95

SCARLETT
DC

❑1, Jan 1993 ... 3.00
❑2, Feb 1993 ... 2.00
❑3, Mar 1993 ... 2.00
❑4, Apr 1993 ... 1.75
❑5, May 1993 ... 1.75
❑6, Jun 1993 ... 1.75
❑7, Jul 1993 ... 1.75
❑8, Aug 1993 ... 1.75
❑9, Sep 1993 ... 1.75
❑10, Oct 1993 ... 1.75
❑11, Nov 1993 ... 1.75
❑12, Dec 1993 ... 1.75
❑13, Jan 1994 ... 1.75
❑14, Feb 1994 ... 1.75

SCARLET THUNDER
SLAVE LABOR / AMAZE INK

❑1, Nov 1995 ... 1.50
❑2, Feb 1996 ... 1.50
❑3, May 1996 ... 2.50
❑4, Dec 1996 ... 2.50

SCARLETT PILGRIM
LAST GASP

❑1 ... 1.00

SCARLET TRACES: THE GREAT GAME
DARK HORSE

❑1, Jul 2006 ... 2.99

SCARLET WITCH
MARVEL

❑1, Jan 1994 ... 1.75
❑2, Feb 1994 ... 1.75
❑3, Mar 1994 ... 1.75
❑4, Apr 1994 ... 1.75

SCARLET ZOMBIE
COMAX

❑1, b&w ... 2.95

SCARS (WARREN ELLIS')
AVATAR

❑1, Jan 2003 ... 3.50
❑2, Feb 2003 ... 3.50
❑2/A, Feb 2003; Wrap Cover ... 3.95
❑3, Mar 2003 ... 3.50
❑4, Apr 2003 ... 3.50
❑5, May 2003 ... 3.50
❑5/A, May 2003; Wrap Cover ... 3.95

Scud: The Disposable Assassin

Videogame suffered from limited marketing

©Fireman

Sea Devils

Quartet investigates underwater weirdness

©DC

Searchers

Descendants of lit characters form team

©Caliber

Second Life of Doctor Mirage

Slain psychic continues work after death

©Valiant

Secret Origins (2nd Series)

Precursor to Secret Files and Origins

©DC

N-MINT

❑6, Jun 2003 .... 3.50
❑6/A, Jun 2003; Wrap Cover 3.95

SCARY!
FANTAGRAPHICS

❑1, May 1997, b&w 12.95

SCARY BOOK
CALIBER

❑1, b&w 2.50
❑2, b&w 2.50

SCARY GODMOTHER
SIRIUS

❑1, May 2001 .... 2.95
❑2, ca. 2001 .... 2.95
❑3, ca. 2001 .... 2.95
❑4, ca. 2001 .... 2.95
❑5, ca. 2001 .... 2.95
❑6, ca. 2001 .... 2.95

SCARY GODMOTHER: BLOODY VALENTINE
SIRIUS

❑1, Feb 1998 .... 3.95

SCARY GODMOTHER HOLIDAY SPOOKTACULAR
SIRIUS

❑1, Nov 1998, b&w; wraparound cover 2.95

SCARY GODMOTHER: WILD ABOUT HARRY
SIRIUS

❑1, ca. 2000, b&w 2.95
❑2, ca. 2000, b&w 2.95
❑3, ca. 2000, b&w 2.95

SCARY TALES
CHARLTON

❑1, Aug 1975, O: Countess Von Bludd. 1: Countess Von Bludd 5.00
❑2, Oct 1975 .... 3.00
❑3, Dec 1975 .... 3.00
❑4, Feb 1976 .... 3.00
❑5, Apr 1976 .... 3.00
❑6, Jun 1976 .... 2.50
❑7, Sep 1976 .... 2.50
❑8, Nov 1976 .... 2.50
❑9, Jan 1977 .... 2.50
❑10, Sep 1977 .... 2.50
❑11, Jan 1978 .... 2.00
❑12, Mar 1978 .... 2.00
❑13, Apr 1978 .... 2.00
❑14, May 1978 .... 2.00
❑15, Jul 1978 .... 2.00
❑16, Oct 1978 .... 2.00
❑17, Dec 1978 .... 2.00
❑18, Feb 1979 .... 2.00
❑19, Apr 1979 .... 2.00
❑20, Jun 1979 .... 2.00
❑21, Aug 1980 .... 2.00
❑22, Oct 1980 .... 2.00
❑23, Dec 1980 .... 2.00
❑24, Feb 1981 .... 2.00
❑25, Apr 1981 .... 2.00
❑26, Jun 1981 .... 2.00
❑27, Aug 1981 .... 2.00
❑28, Oct 1981 .... 2.00
❑29, Dec 1981 .... 2.00

N-MINT

❑30, Feb 1982 .... 2.00
❑31, Apr 1982 .... 2.00
❑32, Jun 1982 .... 2.00
❑33, Aug 1982 .... 2.00
❑34, Oct 1982 .... 2.00
❑35, Dec 1982 .... 2.00
❑36, Feb 1983 .... 2.00
❑37, Apr 1983 .... 2.00
❑38, Jun 1983 .... 2.00
❑39, Aug 1983 .... 2.00
❑40, Oct 1983 .... 2.00
❑41, Dec 1983 .... 2.00
❑42, Feb 1984 .... 2.00
❑43, Apr 1984 .... 2.00
❑44, Jun 1984 .... 2.00
❑45, Aug 1984 .... 2.00
❑46, Oct 1984 .... 2.00

SCATTERBRAIN
DARK HORSE

❑1, Jun 1998 .... 2.95
❑2, Jul 1998 .... 2.95
❑3, Aug 1998 .... 2.95
❑4, Sep 1998 .... 2.95

SCAVENGERS (FLEETWAY/QUALITY)
FLEETWAY-QUALITY

❑1, Feb 1988; Judge Dredd 1.25
❑2, Mar 1988; Judge Dredd 1.25
❑3, Apr 1988; Judge Dredd 1.25
❑4, May 1988; Judge Dredd 1.25
❑5, Jun 1988 .... 1.25
❑6, Jul 1988 .... 1.50
❑7, Aug 1988 .... 1.50
❑8, Sep 1988 .... 1.50
❑9, Oct 1988 .... 1.50
❑10, Nov 1988 .... 1.50
❑11, Dec 1988 .... 1.50
❑12, Jan 1989 .... 1.50
❑13 1989 .... 1.50
❑14 1989 .... 1.50

SCAVENGERS (TRIUMPHANT)
TRIUMPHANT

❑0, Mar 1994; giveaway 1.00
❑0/A, Mar 1994; 18, 000-copy edition 2.50
❑0/B, Mar 1994; 5000-copy edition ... 2.50
❑1, Jul 1993 .... 2.50
❑1/Ashcan, Jul 1993; ashcan edition . 2.50
❑2, Aug 1993 .... 2.50
❑3, Sep 1993 .... 2.50
❑4, Oct 1993 .... 2.50
❑5, Nov 1993; D: Jack Hanal. Unleashed! 2.50
❑6, Dec 1993; Unleashed! 2.50
❑7, Jan 1994 .... 2.50
❑8, Feb 1994 .... 2.50
❑9, Mar 1994 .... 2.50
❑10, Apr 1994 .... 2.50
❑11, May 1994 .... 2.50

SCC CONVENTION SPECIAL
SUPER CREW

❑1, 1994 Convention Special 2.25

SCENARIO A
ANTARCTIC

❑1, Jul 1998, b&w 2.95
❑2, Sep 1998, b&w 2.95

N-MINT

SCENE OF THE CRIME
DC / VERTIGO

❑1, May 1999 .... 2.50
❑2, Jun 1999 .... 2.50
❑3, Jul 1999 .... 2.50
❑4, Aug 1999 .... 2.50

SCHIZO
ANTARCTIC

❑1, Dec 1994, b&w 3.50
❑2, Jan 1996, b&w 3.95
❑3, Mar 1998, b&w 3.95

SCIENCE AFFAIR
ANTARCTIC

❑1, Mar 1994, b&w 2.75
❑1/Gold, Mar 1994; Gold edition 3.00
❑2, May 1994, b&w 2.75

SCIENCE FICTION CLASSICS
DRAGON LADY

❑1; Twin Earths 5.95

SCI-FI
ROUGH COPY

❑1 .... 2.95

SCIMIDAR
ETERNITY

❑1, Jun 1988, b&w 2.50
❑2 1988, b&w 2.50
❑3 1988, b&w 2.50
❑4/A, Dec 1988; "mild" cover 2.00
❑4/B, Dec 1988; "hot" cover 2.00

SCIMIDAR BOOK II
ETERNITY

❑1, May 1989, b&w 3.00
❑1/2nd 3.00
❑2, b&w PG (c) 3.00
❑3, b&w 3.00
❑4, b&w 3.00

SCIMIDAR BOOK III
ETERNITY

❑1, b&w 3.00
❑1/2nd 3.00
❑2, b&w 3.00
❑3, b&w 3.00
❑4, b&w 3.00

SCIMIDAR BOOK IV: "WILD THING"
ETERNITY

❑1 .... 3.00
❑1/Nude; Nude cover 3.00
❑2, b&w 3.00
❑3, b&w 3.00
❑4, b&w 3.00

SCIMIDAR BOOK V: "LIVING COLOR"
ETERNITY

❑1, b&w 2.50
❑1/Nude, b&w; Nude cover 2.50
❑2, b&w 2.50
❑3, b&w 2.50
❑4, b&w 2.50

SCIMIDAR (CFD)
CFD

❑1, b&w 2.95
❑3 .... 2.75

Other grades: Multiply price above by 5/6 for VF/NM • 2/3 for VERY FINE • 1/3 for FINE • 1/5 for VERY GOOD • 1/8 for GOOD

SCIMIDAR PIN-UP BOOK
ETERNITY

	N-MINT
❑1, unstapled	3.75

SCION
CROSSGEN

	N-MINT
❑1, Jul 2000	2.95
❑2, Aug 2000	2.95
❑3, Sep 2000	2.95
❑4, Oct 2000	2.95
❑5, Nov 2000	2.95
❑6, Dec 2000	2.95
❑7, Jan 2001	2.95
❑8, Feb 2001	2.95
❑9, Mar 2001	2.95
❑10, Apr 2001	2.95
❑11, May 2001	2.95
❑12, Jun 2001	2.95
❑13, Jul 2001	2.95
❑14, Aug 2001	2.95
❑15, Sep 2001	2.95
❑16, Oct 2001	2.95
❑17, Nov 2001	2.95
❑18, Dec 2001	2.95
❑19, Jan 2002	2.95
❑20, Feb 2002	2.95
❑21, Mar 2002	2.95
❑22, Apr 2002	2.95
❑23, May 2002	2.95
❑24, Jun 2002	2.95
❑25, Jul 2002	2.95
❑26, Aug 2002	2.95
❑27, Sep 2002	2.95
❑28, Oct 2002	2.95
❑29, Nov 2002	2.95
❑30, Dec 2002	2.95
❑31, Jan 2003	2.95
❑32, Feb 2003	2.95
❑33, Mar 2003	2.95
❑34, Apr 2003	2.95
❑35, May 2003	2.95
❑36, Jun 2003	2.95
❑37, Jul 2003	2.95
❑38, Aug 2003	2.95
❑39, Oct 2003	2.95
❑40, Nov 2003	2.95
❑42, Jan 2004	2.95
❑41, Dec 2003	2.95
❑43, Apr 2004	2.95

SCI-SPY
DC / VERTIGO

	N-MINT
❑1, Apr 2002	2.50
❑2, May 2002	2.50
❑3, Jun 2002	2.50
❑4, Jul 2002	2.50
❑5, Aug 2002	2.50
❑6, Sep 2002	2.50

SCI-TECH
DC / WILDSTORM

	N-MINT
❑1, Sep 1999	2.50
❑2, Oct 1999	2.50
❑3, Nov 1999	2.50
❑4, Dec 1999	2.50

SCOOBY-DOO (MARVEL)
MARVEL

	N-MINT
❑1, Oct 1977	15.00
❑1/35 cent, Oct 1977, 35 cent regional price variant	20.00
❑2, Dec 1977	7.00
❑3, Feb 1978	7.00
❑4, Apr 1978	7.00
❑5, Jun 1978	4.00
❑6, Aug 1978	4.00
❑7, Oct 1978	4.00
❑8, Dec 1978	4.00
❑9, Feb 1979	4.00

SCOOBY-DOO (HARVEY)
HARVEY

	N-MINT
❑1, ca. 1992	1.50
❑2, ca. 1992	1.50
❑3, ca. 1992	1.50
❑Giant Size 1, ca. 1992	2.25
❑Giant Size 2, ca. 1992	2.25
❑Special 1	1.95
❑Special 2	1.95

SCOOBY-DOO (ARCHIE)
ARCHIE

	N-MINT
❑1, Oct 1995	1.50
❑2, Nov 1995	1.50
❑3, Dec 1995	1.50
❑4, Jan 1996	1.50
❑5, Feb 1996	1.50
❑6, Mar 1996	1.50
❑7, Apr 1996	1.50
❑8, May 1996	1.50
❑10, Jul 1996	1.50
❑11, Aug 1996	1.50
❑12, Sep 1996	1.50
❑14, Nov 1996	1.50
❑15, Dec 1996	1.50
❑16, Jan 1997	1.50
❑17, Feb 1997	1.50
❑18, Mar 1997	1.50
❑19, Apr 1997	1.50
❑20, May 1997	1.50
❑21, Jun 1997	1.50

SCOOBY-DOO (DC)
DC

	N-MINT
❑1, Aug 1997 JSa (a)	2.50
❑2, Sep 1997	2.00
❑3, Oct 1997 JSa (a)	2.00
❑4, Nov 1997	2.00
❑5, Dec 1997 JSa (a)	2.00
❑6, Jan 1998 A: Stetson Rogers (Shaggy's cousin)	2.00
❑7, Feb 1998	2.00
❑8, Mar 1998	2.00
❑9, Apr 1998	2.00
❑10, May 1998	2.00
❑11, Jun 1998	2.00
❑12, Jul 1998; JSa (a); mystery at a comic-book convention	2.00
❑13, Aug 1998	2.00
❑14, Sep 1998	2.00
❑15, Oct 1998	2.00
❑16, Nov 1998 A: Groovy Ghoulie	2.00
❑17, Dec 1998	2.00
❑18, Jan 1999	2.00
❑19, Feb 1999 JSa (a)	2.00
❑20, Mar 1999 JSa (a); A: Mystery, Inc.	2.00
❑21, Apr 1999 JSa (a); A: Mystery, Inc.	1.99
❑22, May 1999	1.99
❑23, Jun 1999 JSa (a)	1.99
❑24, Jul 1999 DP (a)	1.99
❑25, Aug 1999 DP (a)	1.99
❑26, Sep 1999 JSa (a)	1.99
❑27, Oct 1999 JSa (a)	1.99
❑28, Nov 1999 JSa (a)	1.99
❑29, Dec 1999 JSa, DP (a)	1.99
❑30, Jan 2000 JSa (a)	1.99
❑31, Feb 2000	1.99
❑32, Mar 2000	1.99
❑33, Apr 2000	1.99
❑34, May 2000 JSa (a)	1.99
❑35, Jun 2000 JSa (a)	1.99
❑36, Jul 2000	1.99
❑37, Aug 2000 JSa (a)	1.99
❑38, Sep 2000 JSa (a)	1.99
❑39, Oct 2000 JSa (a)	1.99
❑40, Nov 2000	1.99
❑41, Dec 2000 JSa (a)	1.99
❑42, Jan 2001 JSa (a)	1.99
❑43, Feb 2001 JSa (a)	1.99
❑44, Mar 2001 JSa (a)	1.99
❑45, Apr 2001 JSa (a)	1.99
❑46, May 2001 DDC (w); JSa (a)	1.99
❑47, Jun 2001 JSa (a)	1.99
❑48, Jul 2001 JSa (a)	1.99
❑49, Aug 2001	1.99
❑50, Sep 2001 JSa (a); A: Speed Buggy. A: Funky Phantom	1.99
❑51, Oct 2001 DDC (a)	1.99
❑52, Nov 2001 JSa (a)	1.99
❑53, Dec 2001 JSa (a)	1.99
❑54, Jan 2002 JSa (a)	1.99
❑55, Feb 2002 JSa (a)	1.99
❑56, Mar 2002 JSa (a)	1.99
❑57, Apr 2002 JSa (a)	1.99
❑58, May 2002	1.99
❑59, Jun 2002 JSa (a)	1.99
❑60, Jul 2002 JSa (a)	1.99
❑61, Aug 2002 JSa (a)	1.99
❑62, Sep 2002 JSa (a)	1.99
❑63, Oct 2002 JSa (a)	1.99
❑64, Nov 2002	1.99
❑65, Dec 2002 JSa (a)	2.25
❑66, Jan 2003	2.25
❑67, Feb 2003	2.25
❑68, Mar 2003	2.25
❑69, Apr 2003	2.25
❑70, May 2003	2.25
❑71, Jun 2003	2.25
❑72, Jul 2003	2.25
❑73, Aug 2003	2.25
❑74, Sep 2003	2.25
❑75, Oct 2003	2.25
❑76, Nov 2003	2.25
❑77, Dec 2003	2.25
❑78, Jan 2004	2.25
❑79, Feb 2004	2.25
❑80, Mar 2004	2.25
❑81, Apr 2004	2.25
❑82, May 2004	2.25
❑83, Jun 2004	2.25
❑84, Jul 2004	2.25
❑85, Aug 2004	2.25
❑86, Sep 2004	2.25
❑87, Oct 2004	2.25
❑88, Nov 2004	2.25
❑89, Dec 2004	2.25
❑90, Jan 2005	2.25
❑91, Feb 2005	2.25
❑92, Mar 2005	2.25
❑93, Apr 2005	2.25
❑94, May 2005	2.25
❑95, Jun 2005	2.25
❑96, Jun 2005	2.25
❑97, Jul 2005	2.25
❑98, Aug 2005	2.25
❑99, Sep 2005	2.25
❑100, Oct 2005	2.25
❑101, Nov 2005	2.25
❑102, Jan 2006	2.25
❑103, Feb 2006	2.25
❑104, Mar 2006	2.25
❑105, Apr 2006	2.25
❑106, May 2006	2.25
❑107, Jun 2006	2.25
❑109, Sep 2006	2.25
❑Summer 1, Aug 2001 JSa (a)	3.95
❑Special 1, Oct 1999; JSa, EC (a); Spooky Spectacular	3.00
❑Special 2, Oct 2000 JSa (a)	3.95

SCOOBY-DOO BIG BOOK
HARVEY

	N-MINT
❑1, 1992	1.95
❑2	1.95

SCOOBY-DOO DOLLAR COMIC
DC

	N-MINT
❑1, Oct 2003	1.00

SCOOBY-DOO SUPER SCAREFEST
DC

	N-MINT
❑1, Aug 2002	3.95

SCOOBY DOO, WHERE ARE YOU? (GOLD KEY)
GOLD KEY

	N-MINT
❑1, Mar 1970	100.00
❑2, Jun 1970	50.00
❑3, Sep 1970	50.00
❑4, Dec 1970	50.00
❑5, Mar 1971	50.00
❑6, Jun 1971	50.00
❑7, Aug 1971	50.00
❑8, Oct 1971	50.00
❑9, Dec 1971	25.00
❑10, Feb 1972	25.00
❑11, Apr 1972	25.00
❑12, Jun 1972	25.00
❑13, Aug 1972	25.00
❑14, Oct 1972	25.00
❑15, Dec 1972	25.00
❑16, ca. 1973	25.00
❑17, ca. 1973	25.00
❑18, ca. 1973	25.00
❑19, Jul 1973	25.00
❑20, Aug 1973	15.00
❑21, Oct 1973	15.00
❑22, Dec 1973	15.00

Secret Six

Cover of #1 is story's splash page
©DC

Secret Society of Super-Villains

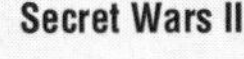

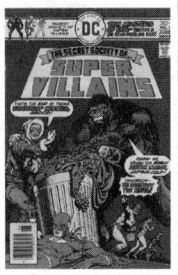

Super-villains form mutual aid group
©DC

Secret Wars II

Beyonder returns, seeking humanity
©Marvel

Seduction of the Innocent (Eclipse)

Horror reprints mock title of expose
©Eclipse

Sensational Spider-Man

Web of Spidey subscribers' substitution
©Marvel

N-MINT

❑23, Feb 1974 ... 15.00
❑24, Apr 1974 ... 15.00
❑25, Jun 1974 ... 15.00
❑26, ca. 1974 ... 15.00
❑27, ca. 1974 ... 15.00
❑28, ca. 1974 ... 15.00
❑29, Dec 1974 ... 15.00
❑30, ca. 1975 ... 15.00

SCOOBY DOO, WHERE ARE YOU? (CHARLTON)
CHARLTON

❑1, Apr 1975 ... 15.00
❑2, Jun 1975 ... 10.00
❑3, Aug 1975 ... 7.00
❑4, Oct 1975 ... 7.00
❑5, Dec 1975 ... 7.00
❑6, Feb 1976 ... 6.00
❑7, Apr 1976 ... 6.00
❑8, Jun 1976 ... 6.00
❑9, Aug 1976 ... 6.00
❑10, Oct 1976 ... 6.00
❑11, Dec 1976 ... 5.00

SCOOTERMAN
WELLZEE

❑1, Apr 1996, b&w ... 2.75
❑2, Dec 1996, b&w; poster ... 2.75
❑3, Jul 1997, b&w ... 2.75

SCORCHED EARTH
TUNDRA

❑1, Apr 1991 ... 2.95
❑2, Jun 1991 ... 2.95
❑3, Aug 1991 ... 2.95

SCORCHY
FORBIDDEN FRUIT

❑1, b&w ... 3.50

SCORE
DC / PIRANHA

❑1, ca. 1989 ... 4.95
❑2, ca. 1989 ... 4.95
❑3, ca. 1989 ... 4.95
❑4, ca. 1989 ... 4.95

SCORN: DEADLY REBELLION
SCC ENTERTAINMENT

❑0, Jul 1996, b&w ... 2.95

SCORN: HEATWAVE
SCC ENTERTAINMENT

❑1, Jan 1997, b&w; follows events in Scorn: Deadly Rebellion ... 3.95

SCORPIA
MILLER

❑1 ... 2.50
❑2 ... 2.50

SCORPION
ATLAS-SEABOARD

❑1, Feb 1975, HC (c); HC (w); HC (a); 1: The Scorpion I (Moro Frost). Chaykin cover, story, art. Scarce in high grade due to black cover ... 16.00
❑2, Apr 1975, BWr (a); Chaykin story/art. Assists from Wrightson, Kaluta, and Simonson. Ernie Colan cover. ... 16.00
❑3, Jul 1975, 1: The Scorpion II (David Harper). Golem cover and story; Jim Craig cover and art. Levy story. ... 10.00

N-MINT

SCORPION
ANNRUEL

❑1, b&w ... 2.50

SCORPION CORPS
DAGGER

❑1, Nov 1993 ... 2.50
❑2, Dec 1993 ... 2.50
❑3, Jan 1994 ... 2.50
❑4, Feb 1994 ... 2.50
❑5, Mar 1994 ... 2.50
❑6, Apr 1994 ... 2.50
❑7, May 1994 ... 2.50
❑8, Jun 1994 ... 2.50
❑9, Jul 1994 ... 2.50
❑10, Aug 1994 ... 2.50

SCORPION KING
DARK HORSE

❑1, Mar 2002 ... 2.99
❑2, Apr 2002 ... 2.99

SCORPION MOON
EXPRESS / ENTITY

❑1, Oct 1994, b&w; Cardstock cover; 4th in a series of Entity illustrated novellas with Zen Intergalactic Ninja ... 2.95

SCORPIO RISING
MARVEL

❑1, Oct 1994; prestige format one-shot ... 5.95

SCORPIO ROSE
ECLIPSE

❑1, Jan 1983 MR (a); O: Scorpio Rose. 1: Scorpio Rose. 1: Doctor Orient... 2.00
❑2, Oct 1983 MR (a) ... 2.00

SCOUT
ECLIPSE

❑1, Nov 1985; Fashion in Action back-up ... 2.00
❑2, Dec 1985; Fashion in Action back-up ... 2.00
❑3, Jan 1985; Fashion in Action back-up ... 2.00
❑4, Feb 1986; Fashion in Action back-up ... 2.00
❑5, Mar 1986; Fashion in Action back-up ... 2.00
❑6, Apr 1986; Fashion in Action back-up ... 2.00
❑7, May 1986; Fashion in Action back-up ... 2.00
❑8, Jun 1986; Fashion in Action back-up ... 2.00
❑9, Jul 1986; Airboy preview ... 2.00
❑10, Aug 1986; Scout: XQB portfolio ... 2.00
❑11, Sep 1986; Monday: The Eliminator back-up begins ... 1.75
❑12, Oct 1986; Monday: The Eliminator back-up ... 1.75
❑13, Nov 1986; Monday: The Eliminator back-up ... 1.75
❑14, Dec 1986; Monday: The Eliminator back-up ... 1.75
❑15, Jan 1987; Swords of Texas back-up ... 1.75
❑16, Feb 1987; 3-D; 3-D issue, glasses included ... 4.00
❑17, Mar 1987 A: Beanish ... 1.75
❑18, Apr 1987 ... 1.75
❑19, May 1987; Flexidisc record by Tim Truman included ... 4.00
❑20, Jun 1987 ... 1.75
❑21, Jul 1987 ... 1.75
❑22, Aug 1987 ... 1.75
❑23, Sep 1987 ... 1.75
❑24, Oct 1987 ... 1.75

N-MINT

SCOUT HANDBOOK
ECLIPSE

❑1, ca. 1987; Details about characters and locations found in Scout and Scout: War Shaman ... 1.75

SCOUT: WAR SHAMAN
ECLIPSE

❑1, Mar 1988 ... 2.00
❑2, May 1988 ... 2.00
❑3, Jun 1988 ... 2.00
❑4, Jul 1988 ... 2.00
❑5, Aug 1988 ... 2.00
❑6, Sep 1988 ... 2.00
❑7, Oct 1988 ... 2.00
❑8, Nov 1988 ... 2.00
❑9, Dec 1988 ... 2.00
❑10, Jan 1989 ... 2.00
❑11, Feb 1989 ... 2.00
❑12, Mar 1989 ... 2.00
❑13, Apr 1989 ... 2.00
❑14, May 1989 ... 2.00
❑15, Jun 1989 ... 2.00
❑16, Jul 1989 D: Scout ... 2.00

SCRAP CITY PACK RATS
OUT OF THE BLUE

❑1, b&w ... 1.50
❑2, b&w ... 1.50
❑3, b&w ... 1.50
❑4, b&w ... 1.75
❑5 1986, b&w ... 1.75

SCRATCH
OUTSIDE

❑1, 1986 ... 1.75
❑2, 1986 ... 1.75
❑3, 1987 ... 1.75
❑4, Apr 1987 ... 1.75
❑5, 1987 ... 1.75
❑6, 1987 ... 1.75

SCRATCH (DC)
DC

❑1, Aug 2004 ... 2.50
❑2, Sep 2004 ... 2.50
❑3, Oct 2004 ... 2.50
❑4, Nov 2004 ... 2.50
❑5, Dec 2004 ... 2.50

SCREAMERS
FANTAGRAPHICS / EROS

❑1, 1995 ... 2.95
❑2, 1995 ... 2.95
❑3, Oct 1995 ... 2.95

SCREEN MONSTERS
ZONE

❑1 ... 2.95

SCREENPLAY
SLAVE LABOR

❑1, Jun 1989, b&w ... 1.75

SCREWBALL SQUIRREL
DARK HORSE

❑1, Jul 1995, Wolf & Red back-up ... 2.50
❑2, Aug 1995, Droopy back-up ... 2.50
❑3, Sep 1995, Wolf & Red back-up ... 2.50

SCREW COMICS
FANTAGRAPHICS / EROS
- ❑1, b&w 3.50

SCRUBS IN SCRUBLAND: THE REFLEX
SCRUBLAND
- ❑1, b&w 2.50

SCUD: TALES FROM THE VENDING MACHINE
FIREMAN
- ❑1, Jan 1998 3.00
- ❑2, Mar 1998 2.50
- ❑3, May 1998 2.50
- ❑4, Jul 1998 2.50

SCUD: THE DISPOSABLE ASSASSIN
FIREMAN
- ❑1, Feb 1994, b&w 1: Scud 10.00
- ❑1/2nd 1: Scud 2.95
- ❑1/3rd 1997 1: Scud 2.95
- ❑2, May 1994, b&w 4.00
- ❑3, b&w 4.00
- ❑4, b&w 4.00
- ❑5, b&w 4.00
- ❑6, b&w 2.95
- ❑7, b&w 2.95
- ❑8 1995, b&w 2.95
- ❑9, b&w 2.95
- ❑10, b&w 2.95
- ❑11 2.95
- ❑12 2.95
- ❑13 2.95
- ❑14, Nov 1996 2.95
- ❑15, Apr 1997 2.95
- ❑16, Jun 1997 2.95
- ❑17, Aug 1997 2.95
- ❑18, Nov 1997 2.95
- ❑19, Dec 1997 2.95
- ❑20, Feb 1998 2.95

SCUM OF THE EARTH
AIRCEL
- ❑1, b&w 2.50
- ❑2, b&w 2.50

SEA DEVILS
DC
- ❑1, Oct 1961, RH (a) 500.00
- ❑2, Dec 1961 300.00
- ❑3, Feb 1962, RH (a) 200.00
- ❑4, Apr 1962 125.00
- ❑5, Jun 1962 125.00
- ❑6, Aug 1962 75.00
- ❑7, Oct 1962 75.00
- ❑8, Dec 1962 75.00
- ❑9, Feb 1963 75.00
- ❑10, Apr 1963 75.00
- ❑11, Jun 1963 75.00
- ❑12, Aug 1963 75.00
- ❑13, Oct 1963, GC, JKu (a) 75.00
- ❑14, Dec 1963 50.00
- ❑15, Feb 1964 50.00
- ❑16, Apr 1964 50.00
- ❑17, Jun 1964 50.00
- ❑18, Aug 1964 50.00
- ❑19, Oct 1964 50.00
- ❑20, Dec 1964 50.00
- ❑21, Feb 1965 35.00
- ❑22, Apr 1965 35.00
- ❑23, Jun 1965 35.00
- ❑24, Aug 1965 35.00
- ❑25, Oct 1965 35.00
- ❑26, Dec 1965 35.00
- ❑27, Feb 1966 35.00
- ❑28, Apr 1966 35.00
- ❑29, Jun 1966 35.00
- ❑30, Aug 1966 35.00
- ❑31, Oct 1966 35.00
- ❑32, Dec 1966 35.00
- ❑33, Feb 1967 35.00
- ❑34, Apr 1967 35.00
- ❑35, Jun 1967 35.00

SEADRAGON
ELITE
- ❑1, May 1986 1.75
- ❑2, Jun 1986 1.75
- ❑3, Aug 1986 1.75
- ❑4 1986 1.75
- ❑5 1986 1.75
- ❑6 1986 1.75

SEAGUY
DC
- ❑1, Jul 2004 2.95
- ❑2, Aug 2004 2.95
- ❑3, Sep 2004 2.95

SEA HUNT
DELL
- ❑4, Mar 1960, numbering continues from Dell Four Color 30.00
- ❑5, Jun 1960 30.00
- ❑6, Sep 1960 30.00
- ❑7, Dec 1960 25.00
- ❑8, Mar 1961; no cover price 25.00
- ❑9, Jun 1961 25.00
- ❑10, Sep 1961 20.00
- ❑11, Dec 1961 20.00
- ❑12, Mar 1962 20.00
- ❑13, Jun 1962 20.00

SEALS
STUDIO ARIES
- ❑Ashcan 1, May 2000, b&w; preview. 1.00

SEA OF RED
IMAGE
- ❑1, Apr 2005 2.95
- ❑2, May 2005 2.95
- ❑3, Jun 2005 2.95
- ❑4, Oct 2005 2.95
- ❑5 2005 2.95
- ❑6, Dec 2005 2.95
- ❑8, Jan 2006 2.95
- ❑9, Jun 2006 2.95
- ❑10, Jul 2006 2.95
- ❑11, Jul 2006 2.95

SEAQUEST
NEMESIS
- ❑1, Mar 1994; KP (a); cardstock cover; based on TV show 2.50
- ❑2 1994 2.25
- ❑3 1994 2.25

SEARCHERS
CALIBER
- ❑1 1996, b&w 2.95
- ❑2 1996, b&w 2.95
- ❑3, ca. 1996, b&w 2.95
- ❑4, ca. 1996, b&w 2.95

SEARCHERS, THE: APOSTLE OF MERCY
CALIBER
- ❑1, ca. 1997, b&w; Giant-size 2.95
- ❑2, ca. 1997, b&w 3.95

SEASON OF THE WITCH
IMAGE
- ❑0 2.99
- ❑1 2005 2.99
- ❑2, Jan 2006 2.99
- ❑3, Jan 2006 2.99
- ❑4, Jun 2006 2.99

SEBASTIAN O
DC / VERTIGO
- ❑1, May 1993 1: Sebastian O 2.00
- ❑2, Jun 1993 2.00
- ❑3, Jul 1993 2.00

SEBASTIAN (WALT DISNEY'S...)
DISNEY
- ❑1 2.00
- ❑2 2.00

SECOND CITY
HARRIER
- ❑1, Oct 1986 1.95
- ❑2, Dec 1986 1.95
- ❑3, Feb 1987 1.95
- ❑4, Apr 1987 1.95

SECOND LIFE OF DOCTOR MIRAGE
VALIANT
- ❑1, Nov 1993 1.00
- ❑1/Gold, Nov 1993; Gold edition 15.00
- ❑2, Dec 1993 1.00
- ❑3, Jan 1994 1.00
- ❑4, Feb 1994 1.00
- ❑5, Mar 1994 1.00
- ❑6, Apr 1994 1.00
- ❑7, May 1994; trading card 2.00
- ❑8, Jun 1994 1.00
- ❑9, Aug 1994 1.00
- ❑10, Sep 1994 1.00
- ❑11, Oct 1994; Chaos Effect Beta 2 1.00
- ❑12, Nov 1994 1.00
- ❑13, Dec 1994 1.00
- ❑14, Jan 1995 2.00
- ❑15, Feb 1995 2.00
- ❑16, Mar 1995 2.00
- ❑17, Apr 1995 2.00
- ❑18, May 1995 4.00

SECOND RATE HEROES
FOUNDATION
- ❑1, b&w 2.50
- ❑2, b&w 2.50

SECRET AGENT (CHARLTON)
CHARLTON
- ❑9, Oct 1966, 1: Mr. Ize!. Series continued from Sarge Steel #8 8.00
- ❑10, Oct 1967 6.00

SECRET AGENT (GOLD KEY)
GOLD KEY
- ❑1, Nov 1966 40.00
- ❑2, Jan 1968 25.00

SECRET AGENTS
PERSONALITY
- ❑1, b&w 2.95
- ❑2, b&w 2.95
- ❑3, b&w 2.95

SECRET CITY SAGA (JACK KIRBY'S...)
TOPPS
- ❑0, Apr 1993 2.95
- ❑1, May 1993, trading cards 2.95
- ❑2, Jun 1993, trading cards 2.95
- ❑3, Jul 1993, trading cards 2.95
- ❑4, Aug 1993, trading cards 2.95

SECRET DEFENDERS
MARVEL
- ❑1, Mar 1993; Story continued from Doctor Strange #50; foil cover 2.50
- ❑2, Apr 1993 1.75
- ❑3, May 1993 1.75
- ❑4, Jun 1993 1.75
- ❑5, Jul 1993 A: Punisher 1.75
- ❑6, Aug 1993 1.75
- ❑7, Sep 1993 1.75
- ❑8, Oct 1993, A: Captain America. A: Spider-Man. A: Scarlet Witch. A: Doctor Strange. A: Xanadu 1.75
- ❑9, Nov 1993 1.75
- ❑10, Dec 1993 1.75
- ❑11, Jan 1994 1.75
- ❑12, Feb 1994; foil cover 2.50
- ❑13, Mar 1994 1.75
- ❑14, Apr 1994 1.75
- ❑15, May 1994 1.75
- ❑16, Jun 1994 1.95
- ❑17, Jul 1994 1.95
- ❑18, Aug 1994 1.95
- ❑19, Sep 1994 1.95
- ❑20, Oct 1994 1.95
- ❑21, Nov 1994 1.95
- ❑22, Dec 1994 1.95
- ❑23, Jan 1995 1.95
- ❑24, Feb 1995 V: original Defenders 1.95
- ❑25, Mar 1995; Giant-size 2.50

SECRET DOORS
DIMENSION
- ❑1, b&w 1.50

SECRET FANTASIES
BULLSEYE
- ❑1, digest 2.25
- ❑2, b&w; normal-sized; cardstock cover 2.95

SECRET FILES
ANGEL
- ❑0, Jun 1996, b&w 2.95
- ❑0/Nude, Jun 1996, b&w; nude cover edition; cardstock cover 4.00
- ❑1, Fal 1996, b&w 2.95

SECRET FILES AND ORIGINS GUIDE TO THE DC UNIVERSE 2000
DC
- ❑1, Mar 2000 6.95

Other grades: Multiply price above by 5/6 for VF/NM • 2/3 for VERY FINE • 1/3 for FINE • 1/5 for VERY GOOD • 1/8 for GOOD

Sentry

Imaginary precursor to Fantastic Four

©Marvel

Serenity

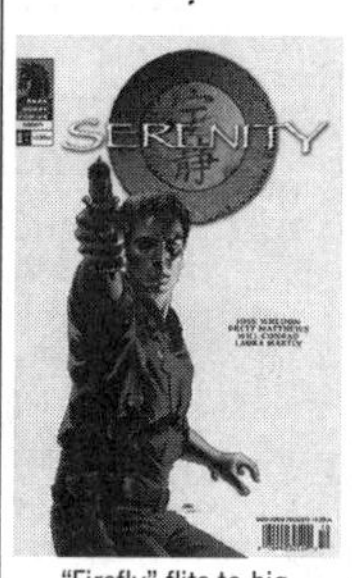

"Firefly" flits to big screen, comics

©Dark Horse

Sgt. Fury

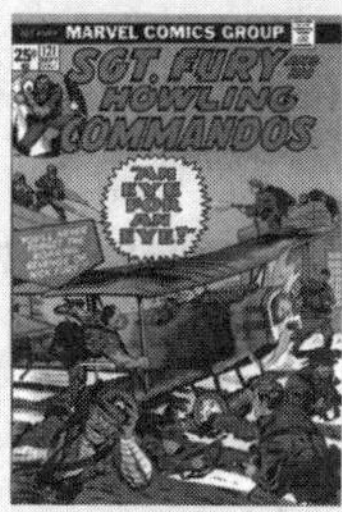

S.H.I.E.L.D. head in World War II

©Marvel

Sgt. Rock

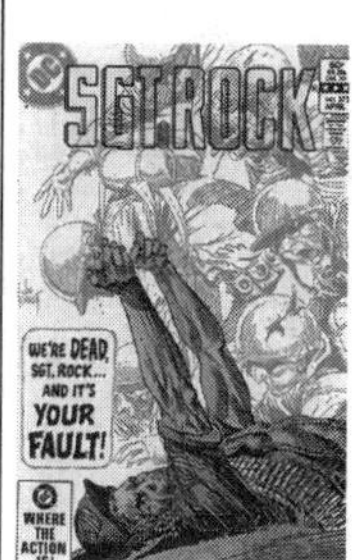

Our Army at War acknowledges star

©DC

Sgt. Rock (2nd Series)

Special reprints of Rock risks

©DC

N-MINT

SECRET FILES & ORIGINS GUIDE TO THE DC UNIVERSE 2001-2002
DC

❑1, Feb 2002 .... 4.95

SECRET FILES: INVASION DAY
ANGEL

❑1 .... 5.00
❑1/Nude 5.00
❑2 .... 5.00
❑2/Nude 5.00

SECRET FILES PRESIDENT LUTHOR
DC

❑1, Mar 2001 .... 4.95

SECRET FILES: THE STRANGE CASE
ANGEL

❑1 .... 2.95

SECRET KILLERS
BRONZE MAN

❑1, Oct 1997, b&w 2.95
❑2 1997, b&w 2.95
❑3 1998, b&w 2.95
❑4 1998, b&w; becomes Exit from Shadow; indicia indicates name change 2.95

SECRET MESSAGES
NBM

❑1 2001 .... 2.95
❑2 .... 2.95
❑3 .... 2.95
❑4 .... 2.95
❑5 .... 2.95

SECRET ORIGINS (1ST SERIES)
DC

❑Annual 1, Aug 1961, second issue published as 80 Page Giant #8; CI, JK (a); reprints Silver Age origins of the Superman/Batman team, Adam Strange, Green Lantern, Challengers of the Unknown, Green Arrow, Wonder Woman, Manhunter from Mars, and the Flash 400.00

SECRET ORIGINS (2ND SERIES)
DC

❑1, Mar 1973, CI, JKu (a); O: Superman. O: Flash. O: Batman.. 18.00
❑2, May 1973 .... 8.00
❑3, Aug 1973, O: Wonder Woman. O: Wildcat 7.00
❑4, Oct 1973, O: Kid Eternity. O: Vigilante 7.00
❑5, Dec 1973 .... 6.00
❑6, Feb 1974 .... 6.00
❑7, Oct 1974, O: Robin I (Dick Grayson). O: Aquaman........ 6.00

SECRET ORIGINS (3RD SERIES)
DC

❑1, Apr 1986 O: Superman........ 5.00
❑2, May 1986 O: Blue Beetle 2.00
❑3, Jun 1986 O: Captain Marvel 2.00
❑4, Jul 1986 O: Firestorm........ 2.00
❑5, Aug 1986 O: The Crimson Avenger 2.00
❑6, Sep 1986 O: Halo. O: Batman (Golden Age)........ 2.00
❑7, Oct 1986 O: Sandman II (Dr. Garrett Sanford). O: Green Lantern (Guy Gardner)........ 2.00

N-MINT

❑8, Nov 1986 O: Doll Man. O: Shadow Lass........ 2.00
❑9, Dec 1986 O: Flash I (Jay Garrick). O: Skyman. O: Stripsey........ 2.00
❑10, Jan 1987; O: Phantom Stranger. Legends........ 2.00
❑11, Feb 1987 JOy (c); O: Power Girl. O: Hawkman (Golden Age)........ 2.00
❑12, Mar 1987 O: The Fury (Golden Age). O: Challengers of the Unknown 2.00
❑13, Apr 1987 O: Johnny Thunder. O: Nightwing. O: Whip 2.00
❑14, May 1987; O: Suicide Squad. Legends........ 2.00
❑15, Jun 1987 O: Spectre. O: Deadman 2.00
❑16, Jul 1987 O: Hourman I (Rex Tyler). O: Warlord........ 2.00
❑17, Aug 1987 O: Adam Strange. O: Doctor Occult........ 2.00
❑18, Sep 1987 O: Creeper. O: Green Lantern I (Alan Scott)........ 2.00
❑19, Oct 1987 JK (c); MA (a); O: Uncle Sam. O: Guardian........ 2.00
❑20, Nov 1987 O: Doctor Mid-Nite (Golden Age). O: Batgirl........ 2.00
❑21, Dec 1987 O: Black Condor. O: Jonah Hex........ 2.00
❑22, Jan 1988; O: Manhunters. Millennium 2.00
❑23, Feb 1988; O: Floronic Man. O: Guardians of the Universe. Millennium 2.00
❑24, Mar 1988 O: Blue Devil. O: Doctor Fate........ 2.00
❑25, Apr 1988 O: The Atom (Golden Age). O: the Legion of Super-Heroes 2.00
❑26, May 1988 O: Miss America. O: Black Lightning........ 2.00
❑27, Jun 1988 O: Zatara. O: Zatanna.. 2.00
❑28, Jul 1988 O: Nightshade. O: Midnight........ 2.00
❑29, Aug 1988 O: The Atom (Silver Age). O: Red Tornado (Golden Age). O: Mr. America........ 2.00
❑30, Sep 1988 O: Plastic Man. O: Elongated Man........ 2.00
❑31, Oct 1988 O: Justice Society of America........ 2.00
❑32, Nov 1988 O: Justice League of America........ 2.00
❑33, Dec 1988 O: Icemaiden. O: Green Flame. O: Mr. Miracle........ 2.00
❑34, Dec 1988 O: Rocket Red. O: G'Nort. O: Captain Atom........ 2.00
❑35, Jan 1989 O: Booster Gold. O: Martian Manhunter. O: Max Lord 2.00
❑36, Jan 1989 O: Green Lantern (Silver Age). O: Poison Ivy 2.00
❑37, Feb 1989 O: Doctor Light. O: Legion of Substitute Heroes...... 2.00
❑38, Mar 1989 O: Speedy. O: Green Arrow 2.00
❑39, Apr 1989 O: Animal Man. O: Man-Bat 2.00
❑40, May 1989 O: Gorilla Grodd. O: Congorilla. O: Detective Chimp .. 2.00
❑41, Jun 1989 O: Flash's Rogue's Gallery........ 2.00
❑42, Jul 1989 O: Grim Ghost. O: Phantom Girl........ 2.00

N-MINT

❑43, Aug 1989 O: Chris KL-99. O: Hawk. O: Dove. O: Cave Carson.. 2.00
❑44, Sep 1989 O: Clayface III. O: Clayface I. O: Clayface IV. O: Clayface II........ 2.00
❑45, Oct 1989 O: Blackhawk. O: El Diablo 2.00
❑46, Dec 1989; Blueprints of Teen Titans Headquarters, Legion of Super-Heroes Headquarters........ 2.00
❑47, Feb 1990 O: Karate Kid. O: Chemical King. O: Ferro Lad 2.00
❑48, Apr 1990 O: Rex the Wonder Dog. O: Ambush Bug. O: Trigger Twins. O: Stanley and His Monster 2.00
❑49, Jun 1990 O: Newsboy Legion. O: Bouncing Boy. O: Silent Knight... 2.00
❑50, Aug 1990; 100 Page giant O: Robin I (Dick Grayson). O: Johnny Thunder (cowboy). O: Space Museum. O: Black Canary. O: Earth-2. O: Dolphin........ 2.00
❑Annual 1, ca. 1987 JBy (c); O: The Doom Patrol 3.00
❑Annual 2, ca. 1988 O: Flash III (Wally West). O: Flash II (Barry Allen) 2.00
❑Annual 3, ca. 1989 O: Teen Titans. 1: Flamebird........ 2.00
❑Giant Size 1, Dec 1998 O: Wonder Girl. O: Robin III (Tim Drake). O: Superboy. O: Impulse. O: Spoiler. O: Arrowette. O: Secret 4.95
❑Special 1, Oct 1989 O: Riddler. O: Two-Face. O: Penguin........ 2.00

SECRET ORIGINS OF KRANKIN' KOMIX
KRANKIN' KOMIX

❑1, Nov 1996........ 1.00

SECRET ORIGINS OF SUPER-VILLAINS
DC

❑Giant Size 1, Dec 1999 .... 4.95

SECRET ORIGINS OF THE WORLD'S GREATEST SUPER HEROES
DC

❑1, ca. 1989 .... 4.95

SECRET ORIGINS REPLICA EDITION
DC

❑1, Feb 2000; Cardstock fold-out cover; reprints Secret Origins #1 (1st series) 4.95

SECRET PLOT
FANTAGRAPHICS / EROS

❑1, Oct 1997........ 2.95
❑2, Nov 1997........ 2.95

SECRET SIX
DC

❑1, May 1968, O: The Secret Six. 1: The Secret Six. splash page is cover 45.00
❑2, Jul 1968 .... 15.00
❑3, Sep 1968........ 12.00
❑4, Nov 1968........ 12.00
❑5, Jan 1969 .... 12.00
❑6, Mar 1969........ 15.00
❑7, May 1969 .... 20.00

Other grades: Multiply price above by 5/6 for VF/NM • 2/3 for VERY FINE • 1/3 for FINE • 1/5 for VERY GOOD • 1/8 for GOOD

SECRET SIX (2ND SERIES)
DC

❑1, Aug 2006 .... 2.99
❑2, Sep 2006 .... 2.99

SECRET SOCIETY OF SUPER-VILLAINS
DC

❑1, Jun 1976, O: Secret Society 10.00
❑2, Aug 1976, DG (c); A: Captain Comet 5.00
❑3, Oct 1976 .... 5.00
❑4, Dec 1976 .... 5.00
❑5, Feb 1977, RB (a) 5.00
❑6, Apr 1977, RB (c); RB, BL (a) 5.00
❑7, Jun 1977, RB (c); RB, BL (a) 5.00
❑8, Aug 1977, RB, JAb (c); RB, BL (a) 5.00
❑9, Sep 1977, RB, JAb (c); RB, BMc (a) 2.50
❑10, Oct 1977, AM, JAb (c); JAb (a) .. 2.50
❑11, Dec 1977, RB (c); JO (a) 2.50
❑12, Jan 1978, RB, JAb (c); BMc (a) .. 2.50
❑13, Mar 1978, RB (c) 2.50
❑14, May 1978, RB, JAb (c) 2.50
❑15, Jul 1978, RB, DG (c) 2.50

SECRETS OF DRAWING COMICS (RICH BUCKLER'S...)
SHOWCASE

❑1, Jan 1994 .... 2.50
❑2 .... 2.50
❑3 .... 2.50
❑4 .... 2.50

SECRETS OF HAUNTED HOUSE
DC

❑1, Apr 1975 .... 35.00
❑2, Jun 1975 .... 12.00
❑3, Aug 1975 .... 12.00
❑4, Oct 1975 .... 12.00
❑5, Dec 1975 .... 18.00
❑6, Jun 1977 .... 10.00
❑7, Aug 1977 .... 10.00
❑8, Oct 1977 .... 10.00
❑9, Dec 1977 .... 10.00
❑10, Feb 1978 .... 10.00
❑11, Apr 1978 .... 10.00
❑12, Jun 1978 .... 10.00
❑13, Aug 1978 .... 10.00
❑14, Oct 1978 .... 10.00
❑15, Aug 1979 .... 10.00
❑16, Sep 1979 .... 6.00
❑17, Oct 1979 .... 6.00
❑18, Nov 1979 .... 6.00
❑19, Dec 1979 .... 6.00
❑20, Jan 1980 .... 6.00
❑21, Feb 1980 .... 3.00
❑22, Mar 1980 .... 3.00
❑23, Apr 1980 .... 3.00
❑24, May 1980 .... 3.00
❑25, Jun 1980 .... 3.00
❑26, Jul 1980 .... 3.00
❑27, Aug 1980 .... 3.00
❑28, Sep 1980 .... 3.00
❑29, Oct 1980 .... 3.00
❑30, Nov 1980 .... 3.00
❑31, Dec 1980, 1: Mister E 5.00
❑32, Jan 1981 .... 3.00
❑33, Feb 1981 .... 3.00
❑34, Mar 1981 .... 3.00
❑35, Apr 1981 .... 3.00
❑36, May 1981 .... 3.00
❑37, Jun 1981 .... 3.00
❑38, Jul 1981 .... 3.00
❑39, Aug 1981 .... 3.00
❑40, Sep 1981 .... 3.00
❑41, Oct 1981, JKu (c) 3.00
❑42, Nov 1981 .... 3.00
❑43, Dec 1981 .... 3.00
❑44, Jan 1982, BWr (c) 3.00
❑45, Feb 1982 .... 3.00
❑46, Mar 1982, DG (c) 3.00

SECRETS OF SINISTER HOUSE
DC

❑5, Jun 1972, Continues from Sinister House of Secret Love #4 .... 40.00
❑6, Aug 1972 .... 20.00
❑7, Nov 1972 .... 20.00
❑8, Dec 1972 .... 20.00
❑9, Feb 1973 .... 20.00
❑10, Mar 1973, NA (a) 25.00
❑11, Apr 1973 .... 15.00
❑12, Jun 1973 .... 15.00
❑13, Aug 1973 .... 15.00
❑14, Oct 1973 .... 15.00
❑15, Dec 1973 .... 15.00
❑16, Feb 1974 .... 12.00
❑17, Apr 1974 .... 12.00
❑18, Jun 1974, GK (a) 15.00

SECRETS OF THE HOUSE OF M
MARVEL

❑1, Sep 2005 .... 3.99

SECRETS OF THE LEGION OF SUPER-HEROES
DC

❑1, Jan 1981, O: the Legion of Super-Heroes 2.00
❑2, Feb 1981 .... 2.00
❑3, Mar 1981 .... 2.00

SECRETS OF THE VALIANT UNIVERSE
VALIANT

❑1, May 1994; Wizard Magazine promo; BL, BH (w); DP, BH (a); no price; bagged with Wizard Special .. 5.00
❑2, Oct 1994; BH (w); Chaos Effect Beta 4 .... 3.00
❑3, Oct 1995; BL (w); future Rai; indicia says Oct; cover says Feb 3.00

SECRETS OF YOUNG BRIDES
CHARLTON

❑5, ca. 1957 .... 25.00
❑6, ca. 1957 .... 20.00
❑7, ca. 1958 .... 20.00
❑8, ca. 1958 .... 20.00
❑9, ca. 1958 .... 20.00
❑10, ca. 1958 .... 20.00
❑11, ca. 1958 .... 20.00
❑12, ca. 1959 .... 20.00
❑13, ca. 1959 .... 20.00
❑14, ca. 1959 .... 20.00
❑15, ca. 1959 .... 20.00
❑16, ca. 1959 .... 20.00
❑17, ca. 1959 .... 20.00
❑18, Mar 1960 .... 20.00
❑19, May 1960 .... 20.00
❑20, Jul 1960 .... 20.00
❑21, Sep 1960 .... 20.00
❑22, Nov 1960 .... 20.00
❑23, Jan 1961 .... 20.00
❑24, ca. 1961 .... 15.00
❑25, ca. 1961 .... 15.00
❑26, ca. 1961 .... 15.00
❑27, ca. 1961 .... 15.00
❑28, ca. 1961 .... 15.00
❑29, ca. 1962 .... 15.00
❑30, ca. 1962 .... 15.00
❑31, ca. 1962 .... 15.00
❑32, ca. 1962 .... 15.00
❑33, ca. 1962 .... 15.00
❑34, ca. 1962 .... 15.00
❑35, ca. 1963 .... 10.00
❑36, ca. 1963 .... 10.00
❑37, ca. 1963 .... 10.00
❑38, ca. 1963 .... 10.00
❑39, ca. 1963 .... 10.00
❑40, ca. 1964 .... 10.00
❑41, ca. 1964 .... 10.00
❑42, ca. 1964 .... 10.00
❑43, ca. 1964 .... 10.00
❑44, Oct 1964 .... 10.00

SECRET TEACHINGS OF A COMIC BOOK MASTER: THE ART OF ALFREDO ALCALA
INT. HUMOR ADVISORY COUNCIL

❑Book 1, Spr 1994, b&w 11.95

SECRETUM SECRETORUM
TWILIGHT TWINS

❑0 .... 3.50

SECRET WAR
MARVEL

❑1, Apr 2004, (c); BMB (w) 10.00
❑1/2nd, Apr 2004; Commorative Edition 5.00
❑1/3rd, Apr 2004 .... 3.99
❑2, Jul 2004 .... 6.00
❑2/2nd 2004 .... 3.50
❑3, 2004 .... 5.00
❑4, Apr 2005 .... 3.99
❑5, Feb 2006 ....

SECRET WARS II
MARVEL

❑1, Jul 1985 A: X-Men. A: New Mutants 2.00
❑2, Aug 1985 A: Fantastic Four. A: Spider-Man. A: Power Man. A: Iron Fist. D: Hate-Monger III (H.M. Unger) 1.50
❑3, Sep 1985 .... 1.50
❑4, Oct 1985 O: Kurse. 1: Kurse. A: Kursei. V: Avengers 1.50
❑5, Nov 1985 O: Boomer (Boom Boom). 1: Boomer (Boom Boom). V: X-Men. V: Fantastic Four. V: New Mutants. V: Avengers 2.50
❑6, Dec 1985 .... 1.50
❑7, Jan 1986 V: All villains 1.50
❑8, Feb 1986 O: Beyonder 1.50
❑9, Mar 1986; double-sized D: Beyonder 1.50

SECRET WEAPONS
VALIANT

❑1, Sep 1993; O: Doctor Eclipse. 1: Doctor Eclipse. Serial number contest 1.00
❑2, Oct 1993 .... 1.00
❑3, Nov 1993 .... 1.00
❑4, Dec 1993 .... 1.00
❑5, Jan 1994 A: Ninjak 1.00
❑6, Feb 1994 .... 1.00
❑7, Mar 1994 A: X-O Manowar. A: Turok 1.00
❑8, Apr 1994 V: Harbinger 1.00
❑9, May 1994; A: Bloodshot. trading card 1.00
❑10, Jun 1994 .... 1.00
❑11, Aug 1994; A: Bloodshot. Enclosed in manila envelope "For Your Eyes Only" cover; bagged cover 1.00
❑11/VVSS, Aug 1994 .... 30.00
❑12, Sep 1994 A: Bloodshot 1.00
❑13, Oct 1994; Chaos Effect Gamma 2 .... 1.00
❑14, Nov 1994 .... 1.00
❑15, Dec 1994 .... 1.00
❑16, Jan 1995 .... 2.00
❑17, Feb 1995 .... 2.00
❑18, Mar 1995 A: Ninjak 2.00
❑19, Apr 1995 .... 2.00
❑20, May 1995; (see Bloodshot #28) . 4.00
❑21, May 1995 .... 5.00

SECTAURS
MARVEL / STAR

❑1, Jun 1985 .... 1.00
❑2, Aug 1985 .... 1.00
❑3, Oct 1985 .... 1.00
❑4, Dec 1985 .... 1.00
❑5, Mar 1986 .... 1.00
❑6, May 1986 .... 1.00
❑7, Jul 1986 .... 1.00
❑8, Sep 1986 .... 1.00

SECTION 12
MYTHIC

❑1, b&w 2.95

SECTION ZERO
IMAGE

❑1, Jun 2000 .... 2.50
❑2, Jul 2000 .... 2.50
❑3, Sep 2000 .... 2.50

SEDUCTION
ETERNITY

❑1, b&w 2.50

SEDUCTION OF THE INNOCENT (ECLIPSE)
ECLIPSE

❑1, Nov 1985; DSt (w); MM, ATh, TY (a); Reprints from Adventures into Darkness #6, Out of the Shadows #7, Fantastic Worlds #7, Out of the Shadows #9 .... 2.50
❑2, Dec 1985 MA, ATh, MB, NC, RMo (a) 2.00
❑3, Jan 1986 MA, ATh (w); ATh (a) 2.00
❑4, Feb 1986 ATh (w); ATh, NC (a) 2.00
❑5, Mar 1986 ATh (w); ATh, TY (a) 2.00
❑6, Apr 1986 ATh, GT, FF, RA (w); 2.00
❑3D 1, ca. 1985 DSt (c); DSt (w); MM (a) 2.50
❑3D 2, ca. 1986 BWr (c); ATh, MB, NC (a) 2.50

Other grades: Multiply price above by 5/6 for VF/NM • 2/3 for VERY FINE • 1/3 for FINE • 1/5 for VERY GOOD • 1/8 for GOOD

Shade, The Changing Man (1st Series)

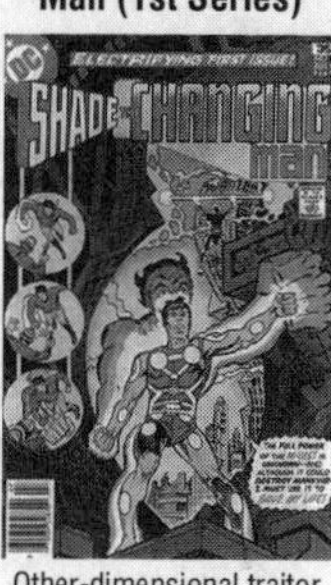

Other-dimensional traitor flees with M-vest

©DC

Shadow (1st Series)

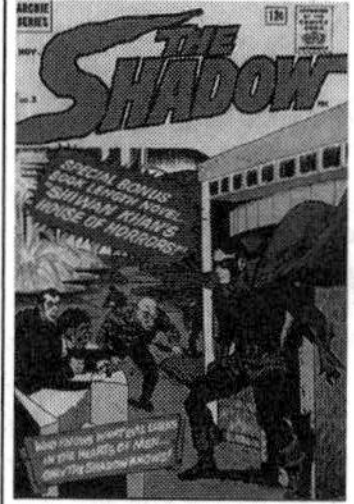

Archie series featured campy take

©Archie

Shadow (2nd Series)

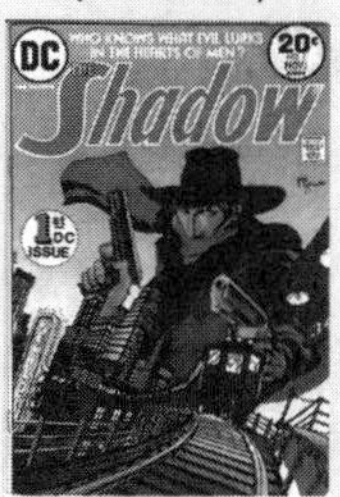

Kaluta returned Shadow to pulp roots

©DC

Shadow (3rd Series)

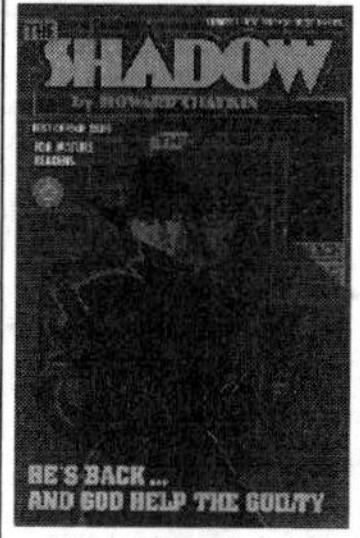

Chaykin brought pulp avenger to today

©DC

Shadow (4th Series)

Sienkiewicz sent Shadow on strange trips

©DC

N-MINT

SEEKER
CALIBER

- ❑1, Apr 1994, b&w 2.50
- ❑2 1994, b&w 2.95

SEEKERS INTO THE MYSTERY
DC / VERTIGO

- ❑1, Jan 1996 .... 2.50
- ❑2, Feb 1996 .... 2.50
- ❑3, Mar 1996 .... 2.50
- ❑4, Apr 1996 .... 2.50
- ❑5, Jun 1996 .... 2.50
- ❑6, Jul 1996 .... 2.50
- ❑7, Aug 1996 .... 2.50
- ❑8, Sep 1996 .... 2.50
- ❑9, Oct 1996 .... 2.50
- ❑10, Nov 1996 .... 2.50
- ❑11, Dec 1996 .... 2.50
- ❑12, Jan 1997 .... 2.50
- ❑13, Feb 1997 .... 2.50
- ❑14, Mar 1997 .... 2.50
- ❑15, Apr 1997 .... 2.95

SEEKER 3000
MARVEL

- ❑1, Jun 1998, wraparound cover 2.99
- ❑2, Jul 1998, wraparound cover 2.99
- ❑3, Aug 1998, wraparound cover 2.99
- ❑4, Sep 1998, wraparound cover 2.99

SEEKER 3000 PREMIERE
MARVEL

- ❑1, Jun 1998; reprints Marvel Premiere #41 .... 1.50

SEEKER: VENGEANCE
SKY

- ❑1, Nov 1993 .... 2.50
- ❑1/Gold, Nov 1993; Gold edition 3.00
- ❑2 1994 .... 2.50

SELF-LOATHING COMICS
FANTAGRAPHICS

- ❑1 1996 .... 2.95
- ❑2, May 1997 .... 2.95

SEMPER FI
MARVEL

- ❑1, Dec 1988 JSe (a) 1.25
- ❑2, Jan 1989 JSe (a) 1.25
- ❑3, Feb 1989 JSe (a) 1.25
- ❑4, Mar 1989 JSe (a) 1.25
- ❑5, Apr 1989 JSe (a) 1.25
- ❑6, May 1989 JSe (a) 1.25
- ❑7, Jun 1989 JSe (a) 1.25
- ❑8, Jul 1989 JSe (a) 1.25
- ❑9, Aug 1989 JSe (a) 1.25

SENSATIONAL SHE-HULK
MARVEL

- ❑1, May 1989 JBy (w); JBy (a) 2.50
- ❑2, Jun 1989 JBy (w); JBy (a); V: Toad Men 2.00
- ❑3, Jul 1989 JBy (w); JBy (a); A: Spider-Man 2.00
- ❑4, Aug 1989 JBy (w); JBy (a); O: Blonde Phantom. A: Blonde Phantom 2.00
- ❑5, Sep 1989 JBy (w); JBy (a) 2.00
- ❑6, Oct 1989 JBy (w); JBy (a); A: Razorback 2.00
- ❑7, Nov 1989 JBy (w); JBy (a); A: Razorback 2.00
- ❑8, Nov 1989 JBy (w); JBy (a); A: Nick St. Christopher 2.00
- ❑9, Dec 1989 V: Madcap 1.75
- ❑10, Dec 1989 .... 1.75
- ❑11, Jan 1990 .... 1.75
- ❑12, Feb 1990 .... 1.75
- ❑13, Mar 1990 .... 1.75
- ❑14, Apr 1990 A: Howard the Duck 1.75
- ❑15, May 1990 A: Howard the Duck 1.75
- ❑16, Jun 1990 A: Howard the Duck 1.75
- ❑17, Jul 1990 A: Howard the Duck 1.75
- ❑18, Aug 1990 .... 1.75
- ❑19, Sep 1990 A: Nosferata the She-Bat 1.75
- ❑20, Oct 1990 .... 1.75
- ❑21, Nov 1990; Blonde Phantom 1.75
- ❑22, Dec 1990; Blonde Phantom 1.75
- ❑23, Jan 1991; Blonde Phantom 1.75
- ❑24, Feb 1991; Death's Head 1.75
- ❑25, Mar 1991; Hercules 1.75
- ❑26, Apr 1991 .... 1.75
- ❑27, May 1991; white inside covers 1.75
- ❑28, Jun 1991 .... 1.75
- ❑29, Jul 1991 .... 1.75
- ❑30, Aug 1991 .... 1.75
- ❑31, Sep 1991 JBy (w); JBy (a) 1.75
- ❑32, Oct 1991 JBy (w); JBy (a) 1.75
- ❑33, Nov 1991 JBy (w); JBy (a) 1.75
- ❑34, Dec 1991 JBy (w); JBy (a) 1.75
- ❑35, Jan 1992 JBy (w); JBy (a) 1.75
- ❑36, Feb 1992 JBy (w); JBy (a); A: Wyatt Wingfoot 1.75
- ❑37, Mar 1992 JBy (w); JBy (a) 1.75
- ❑38, Apr 1992 JBy (w); JBy (a); V: Mahkizmo 1.75
- ❑39, May 1992 JBy (w); JBy (a); A: Thing. V: Mahkizmo 1.75
- ❑40, Jun 1992 JBy (w); JBy (a) 1.75
- ❑41, Jul 1992 JBy (w); JBy (a) 1.75
- ❑42, Aug 1992 JBy (w); JBy (a) 1.75
- ❑43, Sep 1992 JBy (w); JBy (a) 1.75
- ❑44, Oct 1992 JBy (w); JBy (a) 1.75
- ❑45, Nov 1992 JBy (w); JBy (a) 1.75
- ❑46, Dec 1992 JBy (w); JBy (a) 1.75
- ❑47, Jan 1993 .... 1.75
- ❑48, Feb 1993 JBy (w); JBy (a) 1.75
- ❑49, Mar 1993 JBy (w); JBy (a) 1.75
- ❑50, Apr 1993; Double-size; JBy, FM (w); WP, JBy, HC, DG, FM (a); Green foil cover 2.95
- ❑51, May 1993; Savage She-Hulk vs. Sensational She-Hulk 1.75
- ❑52, Jun 1993 .... 1.75
- ❑53, Jul 1993 .... 1.75
- ❑54, Aug 1993 DC (a) 1.75
- ❑55, Sep 1993 .... 1.75
- ❑56, Oct 1993 A: Hulk 1.75
- ❑57, Nov 1993 A: Hulk 1.75
- ❑58, Dec 1993 A: Tommy the Gopher. V: Electro 1.75
- ❑59, Jan 1994 .... 1.75
- ❑60, Feb 1994 A: Millie the Model 1.75

SENSATIONAL SHE-HULK IN CEREMONY
MARVEL

- ❑1, ca. 1989; leg shaving 3.95
- ❑2, ca. 1989 .... 3.95

SENSATIONAL SPIDER-MAN
MARVEL

- ❑-1, Jul 1997; Flashback 2.00
- ❑0, Jan 1996; O: Spider-Man. 1: Armada. enhanced wraparound cardstock cover with lenticular animation card attached; new costume 5.00
- ❑1, Feb 1996; Series picks up subscribers from Web of Spider-Man 2.00
- ❑1/CS, Feb 1996 .... 4.00
- ❑2, Mar 1996 .... 2.00
- ❑3, Apr 1996 .... 2.00
- ❑4, May 1996; Ben Reilly revealed as Spider-Man 2.00
- ❑5, Jun 1996 V: Molten Man 2.00
- ❑6, Jul 1996 .... 2.00
- ❑7, Aug 1996 .... 2.00
- ❑8, Sep 1996 V: Looter 2.00
- ❑9, Oct 1996 A: Swarm 2.00
- ❑10, Nov 1996 .... 2.00
- ❑11, Dec 1996 .... 2.00
- ❑11/CS, Dec 1996 .... 6.99
- ❑12, Jan 1997 V: Trapster 2.00
- ❑13, Feb 1997 A: Ka-Zar. A: Shanna 2.00
- ❑14, Mar 1997 A: Ka-Zar. A: Shanna. A: Hulk 2.00
- ❑15, Apr 1997 A: Ka-Zar. A: Shanna. A: Hulk 2.00
- ❑16, May 1997 V: Prowler 2.00
- ❑17, Jun 1997 V: Vulture 2.00
- ❑18, Aug 1997; gatefold summary 2.00
- ❑19, Sep 1997; gatefold summary V: Living Pharaoh 2.00
- ❑20, Oct 1997; gatefold summary 2.00
- ❑21, Nov 1997; gatefold summary 1.99
- ❑22, Dec 1997; gatefold summary A: Doctor Strange 1.99
- ❑23, Jan 1998; gatefold summary 1.99
- ❑24, Feb 1998; gatefold summary V: Hydro-Man 1.99
- ❑25, Mar 1998; double-sized 2.99
- ❑25/A, Mar 1998; double-sized; Wanted poster cover 2.99
- ❑26, Apr 1998; gatefold summary; V: Hydro-Man. V: Sandman. Identity Crisis 1.99
- ❑27, May 1998; gatefold summary 1.99
- ❑27/A, May 1998; gatefold summary; variant cover 1.99
- ❑28, Jun 1998; gatefold summary A: Hornet 1.99
- ❑29, Jul 1998; gatefold summary A: Black Cat 1.99
- ❑30, Aug 1998; gatefold summary 1.99
- ❑31, Sep 1998; gatefold summary V: Rhino 1.99
- ❑32, Oct 1998; gatefold summary 1.99
- ❑33, Nov 1998; gatefold summary V: Override 1.99
- ❑Annual 1996, ca. 1996 O: Kraven the Hunter 3.00

Other grades: Multiply price above by 5/6 for VF/NM • 2/3 for VERY FINE • 1/3 for FINE • 1/5 for VERY GOOD • 1/8 for GOOD

SENSATIONAL SPIDER-MAN (2ND SERIES)
MARVEL

❑23, May 2006 ... 2.99
❑24, Jun 2006 ... 2.99
❑25, Jul 2006 ... 2.99
❑26, Aug 2006 ... 2.99
❑28, Sep 2006 ... 2.99
❑27, Aug 2006 ... 2.99

SENSATION COMICS (2ND SERIES)
DC

❑1, May 1999; Justice Society Returns; Hawkgirl; Speed Saunders ... 1.99

SENSEI
FIRST

❑1, May 1989 ... 2.75
❑2 1989 ... 2.75
❑3 1989 ... 2.75
❑4, Dec 1989 ... 2.75

SENSUAL PHRASE
VIZ

❑1, Apr 2004 ... 9.99
❑2, Jun 2004 ... 9.99
❑3, Aug 2004 ... 9.99
❑4, Oct 2004 ... 9.99
❑5, Dec 2005 ... 9.99
❑6, Feb 2005 ... 9.99
❑7, Apr 2005 ... 9.99
❑8, Jun 2005 ... 9.99
❑9, Aug 2005 ... 9.99
❑10, Oct 2005 ... 9.99

SENTAI
ANTARCTIC

❑1, Feb 1994, b&w ... 2.95
❑2, Apr 1994, b&w ... 2.95
❑3, Jul 1994, b&w ... 2.95
❑4, Sep 1994, b&w ... 2.95
❑5, Nov 1994 ... 2.95
❑6, Feb 1995, b&w ... 2.95
❑7, Apr 1995, b&w ... 2.95

SENTINEL (HARRIER)
HARRIER

❑1, Dec 1986 ... 1.95
❑2, Feb 1987 ... 1.95
❑3, Apr 1987 ... 1.95
❑4, Jun 1987 ... 1.95

SENTINEL (MARVEL)
MARVEL

❑1, Jun 2003 ... 2.99
❑2, Jul 2003 ... 2.99
❑3, Aug 2003 ... 2.50
❑4, Sep 2003 ... 2.50
❑5, Oct 2003 ... 2.50
❑6, Nov 2003 ... 2.99
❑7, Dec 2003 ... 2.50
❑8, Dec 2003 ... 2.99
❑9, Jan 2004 ... 2.99
❑10, Feb 2004 ... 2.99
❑11, Mar 2004 ... 2.99
❑12, Apr 2004 ... 2.99

SENTINEL (2ND SERIES)
MARVEL

❑1, Jan 2006 ... 2.99
❑2, Feb 2006 ... 2.99
❑3, Mar 2006 ... 2.99
❑4, Mar 2006 ... 2.99
❑5, May 2006 ... 2.99

SENTINELS OF JUSTICE
AC

❑1, Avenger ... 4.00
❑2, Jet Girl ... 5.95
❑3, Yankee Girl ... 4.00

SENTINELS OF JUSTICE COMPACT
AC

❑1 ... 3.95
❑2 ... 3.95
❑3 ... 3.95

SENTINELS PRESENTS... CRYSTAL WORLD: PRISONERS OF SPHERIS
ACADEMY

❑1 ... 2.95

SENTINEL SQUAD O*N*E
MARVEL

❑1, Mar 2006 ... 2.99
❑2, Apr 2006 ... 2.99
❑3, May 2006 ... 2.99
❑4, Jun 2006 ... 2.99
❑5, Jul 2006 ... 2.99

SENTRY
MARVEL

❑1 ... 2.99
❑2 2005 ... 2.99
❑3, Jan 2006 ... 2.99
❑4, Feb 2006 ... 2.99
❑5, Mar 2006 ... 2.99
❑6, May 2006 ... 2.99
❑7, Jun 2006 ... 2.99
❑8, Jul 2006 ... 2.99

SENTRY
MARVEL

❑1, Sep 2000 ... 10.00
❑1/Variant, Sep 2000 ... 15.00
❑1/Conv, Sep 2000 ... 20.00
❑2, Oct 2000 ... 5.00
❑3, Nov 2000 A: Hulk. A: Spider-Man ... 2.99
❑4, Dec 2000 A: Doctor Strange ... 2.99
❑5, Jan 2001 A: Fantastic Four. A: Hulk. A: Spider-Man. A: Avengers ... 2.99

SENTRY/FANTASTIC FOUR
MARVEL

❑1, Feb 2001 ... 2.99

SENTRY/HULK
MARVEL

❑1, Feb 2001 ... 2.99

SENTRY: ROUGH CUT
MARVEL

❑1, Jan 2006 ... 3.99

SENTRY SPECIAL
INNOVATION

❑1, Jun 1991 ... 2.75

SENTRY/SPIDER-MAN
MARVEL

❑1, Feb 2001 ... 2.99

SENTRY/THE VOID
MARVEL

❑1, Feb 2001 ... 5.00

SENTRY/X-MEN
MARVEL

❑1, Feb 2001 ... 2.99

SEPULCHER
ILLUSTRATION

❑1, Mar 2000 ... 2.99
❑2, May 2000 ... 2.99

SEQUENTIAL
I DON'T GET IT

❑1 2000 ... 2.95
❑2 2000 ... 2.95
❑3, Jun 1999 ... 2.95

SERAPHIM
INNOVATION

❑1, May 1990 ... 2.50
❑2 1990 ... 2.50
❑3 1990 ... 2.50

SERENITY
DARK HORSE

❑1/Cassaday, Aug 2005; Cover: Mal by John Cassaday ... 8.00
❑1/Hitch, Aug 2005; Cover: Jayne by Brian Hitch ... 7.00
❑1/Jones, Aug 2005; Cover: Inara by J.G. Jones ... 8.00
❑2/Bradstreet, Sep 2005 ... 5.00
❑2/Chen, Sep 2005 ... 4.00
❑2/Quesada, Sep 2005 ... 5.00
❑2/DHP, Sep 2005 ... 10.00
❑3/Middleton, Oct 2005 ... 4.00
❑3/Phillips, Oct 2005 ... 4.00
❑3/Yu, Oct 2005 ... 4.00

SGT. FROG
TOKYOPOP

❑1, Mar 2004 ... 9.99
❑2, May 2004 ... 9.99
❑3, Jul 2004 ... 9.99
❑4, Sep 2004 ... 9.99
❑5, Nov 2004 ... 9.99
❑6, Jan 2005 ... 9.99
❑7, Mar 2005 ... 9.99
❑8, May 2005 ... 9.99
❑9, Jul 2005 ... 9.99
❑10, Dec 2005 ... 9.99

SGT. FURY
MARVEL

❑1, May 1963, 1: General Samuel Happy Sam Sawyer. 1: General Samuel "Happy Sam" Sawyer. 1: Dum Dum Dugan. 1: Sgt. Nick Fury ... 1500.00
❑2, Jul 1963 ... 400.00
❑3, Sep 1963, A: Reed Richards ... 225.00
❑4, Nov 1963, D: Junior Juniper ... 225.00
❑5, Jan 1964, SL (w); JK (a); 1: Baron Strucker ... 225.00
❑6, Mar 1964 ... 150.00
❑7, May 1964, SL (w); JK (a) ... 150.00
❑8, Jul 1964, 1: Percival Pinkerton. V: Doctor Zemo (later Baron Zemo) ... 150.00
❑9, Aug 1964 ... 150.00
❑10, Sep 1964, 1: Captain Savage ... 150.00
❑11, Oct 1964 ... 100.00
❑12, Nov 1964 ... 100.00
❑13, Dec 1964, SL (w); JK (a); A: Captain America ... 500.00
❑13/2nd, SL (w); JK (a); A: Captain America ... 2.00
❑14, Jan 1965, A: Baron Strucker ... 80.00
❑15, Feb 1965, 1: Hans Rooten ... 80.00
❑16, Mar 1965 ... 75.00
❑17, Apr 1965 ... 75.00
❑18, May 1965, D: Pamela Hawley ... 75.00
❑19, Jun 1965 ... 75.00
❑20, Jul 1965 ... 50.00
❑21, Aug 1965 ... 50.00
❑22, Sep 1965 ... 50.00
❑23, Oct 1965 ... 50.00
❑24, Nov 1965, SL (w) ... 30.00
❑25, Dec 1965 ... 50.00
❑26, Jan 1966 ... 50.00
❑27, Feb 1966, Explanation of Sgt. Fury's eye patch ... 50.00
❑28, Mar 1966, V: Baron Strucker ... 40.00
❑29, Apr 1966, V: Baron Strucker ... 40.00
❑30, May 1966 ... 40.00
❑31, Jun 1966 ... 40.00
❑32, Jul 1966 ... 25.00
❑33, Aug 1966 ... 25.00
❑34, Sep 1966, O: General Samuel Happy Sam Sawyer. O: Howling Commandos ... 25.00
❑35, Oct 1966, Eric Koenig joins Howling Commandos ... 25.00
❑36, Nov 1966 ... 25.00
❑37, Dec 1966 ... 25.00
❑38, Jan 1967 ... 25.00
❑39, Feb 1967 ... 20.00
❑40, Mar 1967 ... 20.00
❑41, Apr 1967 ... 15.00
❑42, May 1967 ... 15.00
❑43, Jun 1967 ... 15.00
❑44, Jul 1967, JSe (a) ... 15.00
❑45, Aug 1967 ... 15.00
❑46, Sep 1967 ... 15.00
❑47, Oct 1967, Fury on furlough ... 15.00
❑48, Nov 1967, JSe (a); return of Blitz Squad ... 15.00
❑49, Dec 1967, JSe (a); Howlers in Pacific ... 15.00
❑50, Jan 1968, JSe (a); Howlers in Pacific ... 15.00
❑51, Feb 1968 ... 15.00
❑52, Mar 1968, in Treblinka ... 15.00
❑53, Apr 1968 ... 15.00
❑54, May 1968 ... 15.00
❑55, Jun 1968 ... 15.00
❑56, Jul 1968 ... 15.00
❑57, Aug 1968, TS, JSe (a) ... 15.00
❑58, Sep 1968 ... 15.00
❑59, Oct 1968 ... 15.00
❑60, Nov 1968 ... 15.00
❑61, Dec 1968 ... 15.00
❑62, Jan 1969, O: Sgt. Fury ... 15.00
❑63, Feb 1969 ... 15.00
❑64, Mar 1969, Story continued from Captain Savage and his Leatherneck Raiders #11 ... 12.00
❑65, Apr 1969 ... 12.00
❑66, May 1969 ... 12.00
❑67, Jun 1969, JSe (c) ... 12.00
❑68, Jul 1969, Fury goes home on leave ... 12.00

ShadowHawk (Vol. 1)

Valentino vigilante contracted HIV

©Image

Shadowman

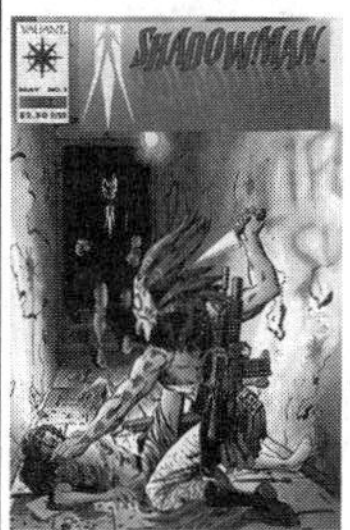

Big Easy jazz musician powered by voodoo

©Valiant

Shadow of the Batman

Reprints early 1970s Bat-stories

©DC

Shadow Strikes!

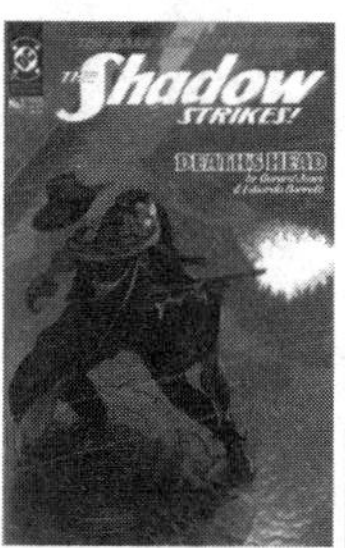

Shadow returns to 1930s adventures

©DC

Shadow War of Hawkman

Mistrust main focus of mini-series

©DC

N-MINT

❑69, Aug 1969, 1: Jacob Fury (later becomes Scorpio) 12.00
❑70, Sep 1969, 1: Missouri Marauders 12.00
❑71, Oct 1969 .... 12.00
❑72, Nov 1969 .... 12.00
❑73, Dec 1969 .... 12.00
❑74, Jan 1970 .... 12.00
❑75, Feb 1970 .... 12.00
❑76, Mar 1970, Fury's father vs. The Red Baron 12.00
❑77, Apr 1970 .... 12.00
❑78, May 1970 .... 12.00
❑79, Jun 1970 .... 12.00
❑80, Sep 1970 .... 12.00
❑81, Nov 1970 .... 12.00
❑82, Dec 1970 .... 12.00
❑83, Jan 1971, Dum-Dum Dugan vs. Man-Mountain McCoy 12.00
❑84, Feb 1971 .... 12.00
❑85, Mar 1971 .... 12.00
❑86, Apr 1971 .... 12.00
❑87, May 1971 .... 12.00
❑88, Jun 1971, A: Patton 12.00
❑89, Jul 1971 .... 12.00
❑90, Aug 1971 .... 12.00
❑91, Sep 1971 .... 12.00
❑92, Oct 1971, Giant-size 12.00
❑93, Dec 1971 .... 12.00
❑94, Jan 1972 .... 12.00
❑95, Feb 1972, JK (a); reprints Sgt. Fury #2 .... 12.00
❑96, Mar 1972 .... 12.00
❑97, Apr 1972 .... 12.00
❑98, May 1972, 1: Dugan's Deadly Dozen 12.00
❑99, Jun 1972 .... 12.00
❑100, Jul 1972, A: Gary Friedrich. A: Dick Ayers. A: Martin Goodman. A: Captain America. A: Stan Lee 25.00
❑101, Sep 1972, O: the Howling Commandos 12.00
❑102, Sep 1972 .... 10.00
❑103, Oct 1972 .... 8.00
❑104, Nov 1972, A: Combat Kelly and Deadly Dozen 8.00
❑105, Dec 1972 .... 8.00
❑106, Jan 1973 .... 8.00
❑107, Feb 1973 .... 8.00
❑108, Mar 1973 .... 8.00
❑109, Apr 1973 .... 8.00
❑110, May 1973 .... 8.00
❑111, Jun 1973 .... 6.00
❑112, Jul 1973, V: Baron Strucker 6.00
❑113, Aug 1973 .... 6.00
❑114, Sep 1973 .... 6.00
❑115, Oct 1973 .... 6.00
❑116, Nov 1973 .... 6.00
❑117, Jan 1974 .... 6.00
❑118, Mar 1974, V: Rommel. Marvel Value Stamp #93: Silver Surfer 6.00
❑119, May 1974, Marvel Value Stamp #79: Kang 6.00
❑120, Jul 1974, Marvel Value Stamp #98: Puppet Master 6.00
❑121, Sep 1974 .... 6.00
❑122, Oct 1974 .... 5.00

N-MINT

❑123, Nov 1974 .... 5.00
❑124, Jan 1975 .... 5.00
❑125, Mar 1975 .... 5.00
❑126, May 1975 .... 5.00
❑127, Jul 1975 .... 5.00
❑128, Sep 1975 .... 5.00
❑129, Oct 1975 .... 5.00
❑130, Nov 1975 .... 5.00
❑131, Jan 1976 .... 5.00
❑132, Mar 1976 .... 4.00
❑133, May 1976 .... 4.00
❑133/30 cent, May 1976, 30 cent regional price variant 20.00
❑134, Jul 1976 .... 4.00
❑134/30 cent, Jul 1976, 30 cent regional price variant 20.00
❑135, Sep 1976 .... 4.00
❑136, Oct 1976 .... 4.00
❑137, Nov 1976 .... 4.00
❑138, Jan 1977 .... 4.00
❑139, Mar 1977 .... 4.00
❑140, May 1977 .... 4.00
❑141, Jul 1977 .... 4.00
❑141/35 cent, Jul 1977, 35 cent regional price variant 15.00
❑142, Sep 1977 .... 4.00
❑142/35 cent, Sep 1977, 35 cent regional price variant 15.00
❑143, Nov 1977 .... 4.00
❑144, Jan 1978 .... 4.00
❑145, Mar 1978 .... 4.00
❑146, May 1978 .... 4.00
❑147, Jul 1978 .... 4.00
❑148, Sep 1978 .... 4.00
❑149, Nov 1978 .... 4.00
❑150, Jan 1979 .... 4.00
❑151, Mar 1979 .... 4.00
❑152, Jun 1979 .... 3.00
❑153, Aug 1979 .... 3.00
❑154, Oct 1979 .... 3.00
❑155, Dec 1979 .... 3.00
❑156, Feb 1980 .... 3.00
❑157, Apr 1980 .... 3.00
❑158, Jun 1980 .... 3.00
❑159, Aug 1980 .... 3.00
❑160, Oct 1980 .... 3.00
❑161, Dec 1980 .... 3.00
❑162, Feb 1981 .... 3.00
❑163, Apr 1981 .... 3.00
❑164, Jun 1981 .... 3.00
❑165, Aug 1981 .... 3.00
❑166, Oct 1981 .... 3.00
❑167, Dec 1981, Reprints Sgt. Fury #1 3.00
❑Annual 1, ca. 1965, Korea; reprints from Sgt. Fury #4 and 5 .... 125.00
❑Annual 2, Aug 1966, O: S.H.I.E.L.D.. D-Day 55.00
❑Annual 3, Aug 1966, Cover reads "King-Size Special"; Vietnam 30.00
❑Annual 4, Apr 1968, Cover reads "King-Size Special"; Battle of the Bulge 22.00
❑Annual 5, Aug 1969, Cover reads "King-Size Special"; Cover reads King Size Special; reprints from Sgt. Fury #6 and 7 .... 10.00

N-MINT

❑Annual 6, Aug 1970, Cover reads "King-Size Special"; Cover reads King-Size Special 9.00
❑Annual 7, ca. 1971, Cover reads "King-Size Special"; Cover reads King-Size Special 9.00

SGT. FURY: PEACEMAKER
MARVEL

❑1, Mar 2006 .... 3.50
❑2, May 2006 .... 3.50
❑3, Jul 2006 .... 3.50
❑4, Jul 2006 .... 3.50
❑5, Aug 2006 .... 3.50
❑6, Sep 2006 .... 3.50

SGT. ROCK
DC

❑302, Mar 1977, Series continued from "Our Army At War" 25.00
❑303, Apr 1977 .... 15.00
❑304, May 1977 .... 15.00
❑305, Jun 1977 .... 15.00
❑306, Jul 1977 .... 15.00
❑307, Aug 1977 .... 15.00
❑308, Sep 1977 .... 10.00
❑309, Oct 1977 .... 10.00
❑310, Nov 1977 .... 10.00
❑311, Dec 1977 .... 10.00
❑312, Jan 1978 .... 10.00
❑313, Feb 1978 .... 8.00
❑314, Mar 1978 .... 8.00
❑315, Apr 1978 .... 8.00
❑316, May 1978 .... 8.00
❑317, Jun 1978 .... 8.00
❑318, Jul 1978 .... 8.00
❑319, Aug 1978 .... 8.00
❑320, Sep 1978 .... 8.00
❑321, Oct 1978 .... 6.00
❑322, Nov 1978 .... 6.00
❑323, Dec 1978 .... 6.00
❑324, Jan 1979 .... 6.00
❑325, Feb 1979 .... 6.00
❑326, Mar 1979 .... 6.00
❑327, Apr 1979 .... 6.00
❑328, May 1979 .... 6.00
❑329, Jun 1979 .... 6.00
❑329/Whitman, Jun 1979, Whitman variant 15.00
❑330, Jul 1979 .... 6.00
❑331, Aug 1979 .... 5.00
❑332, Sep 1979 .... 5.00
❑333, Oct 1979 .... 5.00
❑334, Nov 1979 .... 5.00
❑335, Dec 1979 .... 5.00
❑336, Jan 1980 .... 5.00
❑337, Feb 1980 .... 5.00
❑338, Mar 1980 .... 5.00
❑339, Apr 1980 .... 5.00
❑340, May 1980 .... 5.00
❑341, Jun 1980 .... 5.00
❑342, Jul 1980 .... 4.00
❑343, Aug 1980 .... 4.00
❑344, Sep 1980 .... 4.00
❑345, Oct 1980 .... 4.00
❑346, Nov 1980 .... 4.00
❑347, Dec 1980 .... 4.00

Other grades: Multiply price above by 5/6 for VF/NM • 2/3 for VERY FINE • 1/3 for FINE • 1/5 for VERY GOOD • 1/8 for GOOD

❑348, Jan 1981 .... 4.00
❑349, Feb 1981 .... 4.00
❑350, Mar 1981 .... 4.00
❑351, Apr 1981 .... 3.00
❑352, May 1981 .... 3.00
❑353, Jun 1981 .... 3.00
❑354, Jul 1981 .... 3.00
❑355, Aug 1981 .... 3.00
❑356, Sep 1981 .... 3.00
❑357, Oct 1981 .... 3.00
❑358, Nov 1981 .... 3.00
❑359, Dec 1981 .... 3.00
❑360, Jan 1982 .... 3.00
❑361, Feb 1982 .... 3.00
❑362, Mar 1982 .... 3.00
❑363, Apr 1982 .... 3.00
❑364, May 1982 .... 3.00
❑365, Jun 1982 .... 3.00
❑366, Jul 1982 .... 3.00
❑367, Aug 1982 .... 3.00
❑368, Sep 1982, JKu (a) 3.00
❑369, Oct 1982 .... 3.00
❑370, Nov 1982 .... 3.00
❑371, Dec 1982 .... 2.50
❑372, Jan 1983 .... 2.50
❑373, Feb 1983 .... 2.50
❑374, Mar 1983 .... 2.50
❑375, Apr 1983 .... 2.50
❑376, May 1983 .... 2.50
❑377, Jun 1983, A: Worry Wart 2.50
❑378, Jul 1983, Christmas 2.50
❑379, Aug 1983 .... 2.50
❑380, Sep 1983 .... 2.50
❑381, Oct 1983 .... 2.50
❑382, Nov 1983 .... 2.50
❑383, Dec 1983 .... 2.50
❑384, Jan 1984 .... 2.50
❑385, Feb 1984 .... 2.50
❑386, Mar 1984 .... 2.50
❑387, Apr 1984 .... 2.50
❑388, May 1984 .... 2.50
❑389, Jun 1984 .... 2.50
❑390, Jul 1984 .... 2.50
❑391, Aug 1984 .... 2.00
❑392, Sep 1984 .... 2.00
❑393, Oct 1984 .... 2.00
❑394, Nov 1984 .... 2.00
❑395, Dec 1984 JKu (a) 2.00
❑396, Jan 1985; RH (a); children in war 2.00
❑397, Feb 1985 .... 2.00
❑398, Mar 1985 .... 2.00
❑399, Apr 1985 .... 2.00
❑400, May 1985 .... 2.00
❑401, Jun 1985 .... 2.00
❑402, Jul 1985 .... 2.00
❑403, Aug 1985 .... 2.00
❑404, Sep 1985 V: Iron Major 2.00
❑405, Oct 1985 .... 2.00
❑406, Nov 1985 .... 2.00
❑407, Dec 1985 .... 2.00
❑408, Feb 1986; Shelly Mayer tribute . 2.00
❑409, Apr 1986 .... 2.00
❑410, Jun 1986 .... 2.00
❑411, Aug 1986 .... 2.00
❑412, Oct 1986 .... 2.00
❑413, Dec 1986 .... 2.00
❑414, Feb 1987; Christmas 2.00
❑415, Apr 1987 .... 2.00
❑416, Jun 1987 .... 2.00
❑417, Aug 1987; looking into future ... 2.00
❑418, Oct 1987; looking into future 2.00
❑419, Dec 1987 .... 2.00
❑420, Feb 1988 .... 2.00
❑421, Apr 1988 .... 2.00
❑422, Jul 1988 .... 2.00
❑Annual 1 .... 4.00
❑Annual 2, Sep 1982 .... 4.00
❑Annual 3, Aug 1983 .... 3.00
❑Annual 4, Aug 1984 .... 3.00

SGT. ROCK (2ND SERIES)
DC

❑14, Jul 1991; Series continued from Sgt. Rock Special #13 .... 2.00
❑15, Aug 1991 .... 2.00
❑16, Sep 1991 .... 2.00
❑17, Oct 1991 .... 2.00
❑18, Nov 1991 .... 2.00
❑19, Dec 1991 .... 2.00
❑20, Jan 1992 .... 2.00
❑21, Feb 1992 .... 2.00
❑22, Mar 1992 .... 2.00
❑Special 1, Oct 1992; 1992 Special.... 2.95
❑Special 2, ca. 1994; Commemorates 50th anniversary of the Battle of the Bulge; 1994 Special 2.95

SGT. ROCK: BETWEEN HELL AND A HARD PLACE
DC

❑1, ca. 2003 .... 24.95

SGT. ROCK SPECIAL
DC

❑1, Sep 1988 A: Viking Prince 3.00
❑2, Dec 1988 .... 2.50
❑3, Mar 1989 .... 2.50
❑4, Jun 1989 .... 2.50
❑5, Sep 1989 .... 2.50
❑6, Dec 1989 .... 2.50
❑7, Mar 1990; reprints Our Fighting Forces #153 .... 2.50
❑8, Jun 1990 .... 2.50
❑9, Sep 1990 .... 2.50
❑10, Dec 1990 .... 2.50
❑11, Mar 1991 .... 2.50
❑12, May 1991 .... 2.50
❑13, Jun 1991 .... 2.50

SGT. ROCK'S PRIZE BATTLE TALES REPLICA EDITION
DC

❑1, ca. 2000 .... 5.95

SGT. ROCK: THE PROPHECY
DC

❑1, Mar 2006 .... 3.99
❑2, Apr 2006 .... 3.99
❑3, Jun 2006 .... 3.99
❑4, Jun 2006 .... 3.99
❑6, Sep 2006 .... 3.99

SERGIO ARAGONÉS DESTROYS DC
DC

❑1, Jun 1996 .... 3.50

SERGIO ARAGONÉS MASSACRES MARVEL
MARVEL

❑1, Jun 1996; wraparound cover 3.50

SERGIO ARAGONÉS STOMPS STAR WARS
DARK HORSE

❑1, Feb 2000 .... 2.95

SERINA
ANTARCTIC

❑1, Mar 1996, b&w 2.95
❑2, May 1996, b&w 2.95
❑3, Jul 1996 .... 2.95

SERIUS BOUNTY HUNTER
BLACKTHORNE

❑1, Nov 1987, b&w 1.75
❑2, Jan 1988, b&w 1.75
❑3, Mar 1988, b&w 1.75

SERPENTINA
LIGHTNING

❑1/A, Feb 1998, b&w 2.95
❑1/B, Feb 1998; Alternate cover 2.95

SERPENTYNE
NIGHTWYND

❑1, b&w 2.50
❑2, b&w 2.50
❑3, b&w 2.50

SERRA ANGEL ON THE WORLD OF MAGIC: THE GATHERING
ACCLAIM / ARMADA

❑1, Aug 1996; polybagged with oversized Serra Angel card 5.95

SETH THROB UNDERGROUND ARTIST
SLAVE LABOR

❑1, Mar 1994 .... 2.95
❑2, May 1994 .... 2.95
❑3, Aug 1994 .... 2.95
❑4, Dec 1994 .... 2.95
❑5, Mar 1995 .... 2.95
❑6, Jun 1995 .... 2.95
❑7, Sep 1995 .... 2.95

SETTEI
ANTARCTIC

❑1, Feb 1993, b&w 7.95
❑2, Apr 1993, b&w 7.95

SETTEI SUPER SPECIAL FEATURING: PROJECT A-KO
ANTARCTIC

❑1, Feb 1994 .... 2.95

SEVEN BLOCK
MARVEL / EPIC

❑1, ca. 1990, b&w; prestige format.... 4.50

SEVEN GUYS OF JUSTICE
FALSE IDOL

❑1, Apr 2000 .... 2.00
❑2, ca. 2000 .... 2.00
❑3, ca. 2000 .... 2.00
❑4, ca. 2000 .... 2.00
❑5, ca. 2000 .... 2.00
❑6, ca. 2001 .... 2.00
❑7, ca. 2001 .... 2.00
❑8, ca. 2001 .... 2.00
❑9, ca. 2001 .... 2.00
❑10, ca. 2001 .... 2.00

777: WRATH/FAUST FEARBOOK
REBEL

❑1 .... 14.20

SEVEN MILES A SECOND
DC / VERTIGO

❑1, ca. 1996; prestige format 7.95

SEVEN SOLDIERS
DC

❑0, Apr 2005 .... 5.00
❑0/Faces, Apr 2005; 2nd print. Cover by J.H. Williams features the faces of the new Seven Soldiers team...... 2.95

SEVEN SOLDIERS: FRANKENSTEIN
DC

❑1, Jan 2006 .... 2.99
❑2, Feb 2006 .... 2.99
❑3, May 2006 .... 2.99
❑4, Jul 2006 .... 2.99

SEVEN SOLDIERS: GUARDIAN
DC

❑1, Jun 2005 .... 2.99
❑2, Jul 2005 .... 2.99
❑3, Aug 2005 .... 2.99
❑4, Sep 2005 .... 2.99

SEVEN SOLDIERS: KLARION THE WITCH BOY
DC

❑1, Jun 2005 .... 4.00
❑2, Jul 2005 .... 2.99
❑3, Aug 2005 .... 2.99
❑4, Dec 2005 .... 2.99

SEVEN SOLDIERS: MISTER MIRACLE
DC

❑1 .... 2.99
❑2, Jan 2006 .... 2.99
❑3, Mar 2006 .... 2.99
❑4, May 2006 .... 2.99

SEVEN SOLDIERS: SHINING KNIGHT
DC

❑1, May 2005 .... 2.99
❑2, Jun 2005 .... 2.99
❑3, Jul 2005 .... 2.99
❑4, Oct 2005 .... 2.99

SEVEN SOLDIERS: THE BULLETEER
DC

❑1, Jan 2006 .... 2.99
❑2, Feb 2006 .... 2.99
❑3, Mar 2006 .... 2.99
❑4, May 2006 .... 2.99

SEVEN SOLDIERS: ZATANNA
DC

❑1 2005 .... 2.99
❑2 2005 .... 2.99
❑3, Sep 2005 .... 2.99
❑4, Jan 2006 .... 2.99

7TH MILLENNIUM
ALLIED

❑1 .... 2.50
❑2 .... 2.50
❑3 .... 2.50
❑4 .... 2.50

Shanda the Panda

Anthropomorphic soap opera rivals real life
©Mu

Shanna the She-Devil

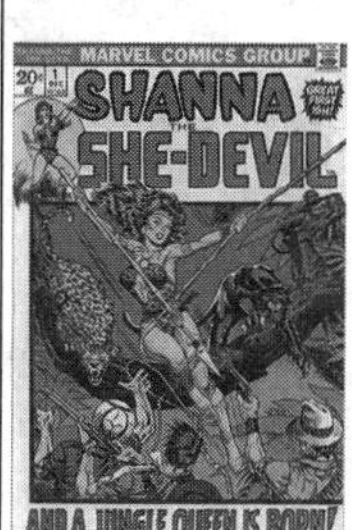

Ka-Zar's companion comes to jungle
©Marvel

Shatter (1st Series)

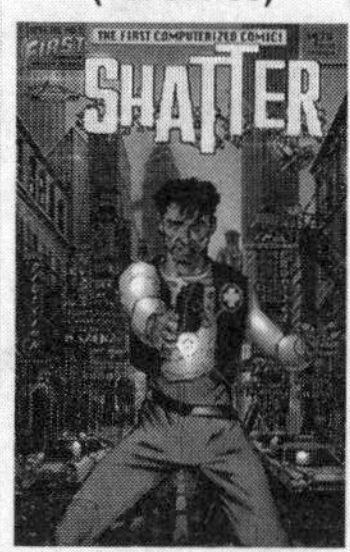

First computer-generated comic book
©First

Shazam!

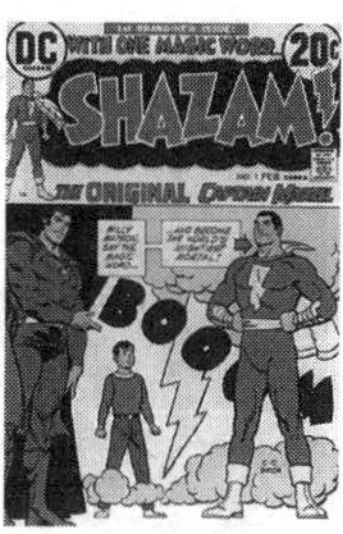

Marvel Family returns after two decades
©DC

She-Hulk

Brains favored over brawn
©Marvel

N-MINT

7TH SYSTEM
SIRIUS

❑1, Jan 1998, b&w 2.95
❑2, Feb 1998, b&w 2.95
❑3, Jul 1998, b&w 2.95
❑4, Dec 1998, b&w 2.95
❑6, Feb 1999, b&w 2.95
❑5, ca. 1999 2.95

77 SUNSET STRIP (DELL)
DELL

❑1, Jul 1962 150.00

77 SUNSET STRIP (GOLD KEY)
GOLD KEY

❑1, Nov 1962 100.00
❑2, Feb 1963 100.00

SEWAGE DRAGOON
PARODY

❑1 2.50
❑1/2nd 2.50

SEX & DEATH
ACID RAIN

❑1, b&w 3.95

SEX AND DEATH (ACID RAIN)
ACID RAIN

❑1 2.50

SEXCAPADES
FANTAGRAPHICS / EROS

❑1, Dec 1996 2.95
❑2, Jan 1997 2.95
❑3, Feb 1997 2.95

SEX DRIVE
M.A.I.N.

❑1 3.00

SEXECUTIONER
FANTAGRAPHICS / EROS

❑1, b&w 2.50
❑2, b&w 2.50
❑3, b&w 2.50

SEXHIBITION
FANTAGRAPHICS / EROS

❑1 2.95
❑2 2.95
❑3 2.95
❑4, Feb 1996 2.95

SEX IN THE SINEMA
COMIC ZONE

❑1, b&w 2.95
❑2, b&w 2.95
❑3, b&w 2.95
❑4, b&w 2.95

SEX, LIES AND MUTUAL FUNDS OF THE YUPPIES FROM HELL
MARVEL

❑1 2.95

SEX MACHINE
FANTAGRAPHICS / EROS

❑1, b&w 2.50
❑2, b&w 2.95
❑3, Dec 1997, b&w 2.95

N-MINT

SEXPLOITATION CINEMA: A CARTOON HISTORY
REVISIONARY

❑1, Nov 1998, b&w 3.50

SEX TREK: THE NEXT INFILTRATION
FRIENDLY

❑1, b&w 2.95

SEX WAD
FANTAGRAPHICS / EROS

❑1 2.95
❑2 2.95

SEX WARRIOR
DARK HORSE

❑1 2.50
❑2 2.50

SEX WARRIOR ISANE XXX
FANTAGRAPHICS

❑1 2.99
❑2 2.99
❑3 2.99
❑4 2.99
❑5 2.99
❑6 2.99
❑7 2.99
❑8, Nov 2005 2.99

SEXX WARS
IMMORTAL

❑1 2.95

SEXY STORIES FROM THE WORLD RELIGIONS
LAST GASP

❑1 2.50

SEXY SUPERSPY
FORBIDDEN FRUIT

❑1, b&w 2.95
❑2, b&w 2.95
❑3, b&w 2.95
❑4, b&w 2.95
❑5, b&w 2.95
❑6, b&w 2.95
❑7, b&w 2.95

SEXY WOMEN
CELEBRITY

❑1 2.95
❑2 2.95

SFA SPOTLIGHT
SHANDA FANTASY ARTS

❑1 2.95
❑2 2.95
❑3 2.95
❑4, May 1999, b&w 2.95
❑5, May 1999, b&w; Zebra Comics 4.50

SHADE
DC

❑1, Apr 1997, JRo (w) 2.50
❑2, May 1997, JRo (w) 2.50
❑3, Jun 1997, JRo (w); A: Jay Garrick 2.50
❑4, Jul 1997, JRo (w) 2.50

SHADE, THE CHANGING MAN (1ST SERIES)
DC

❑1, Jul 1977, SD (w); SD (a); O: Shade. 1: Shade 10.00

N-MINT

❑2, Sep 1977, SD (a) 4.00
❑3, Nov 1977, SD (a) 4.00
❑4, Jan 1978, SD (a) 4.00
❑5, Mar 1978, SD (a) 4.00
❑6, May 1978, SD (a); V: Khaos 4.00
❑7, Jul 1978, SD (a) 4.00
❑8, Sep 1978, SD (a) 4.00

SHADE, THE CHANGING MAN (2ND SERIES)
DC

❑1, Jul 1990 1: Kathy George. 1: American Scream 3.00
❑2, Aug 1990 2.00
❑3, Sep 1990 2.00
❑4, Oct 1990 2.00
❑5, Nov 1990 2.00
❑6, Dec 1990 2.00
❑7, Jan 1991 2.00
❑8, Feb 1991 2.00
❑9, Mar 1991 2.00
❑10, Apr 1991 2.00
❑11, May 1991 2.00
❑12, Jun 1991 2.00
❑13, Jul 1991 2.00
❑14, Aug 1991 2.00
❑15, Sep 1991 2.00
❑16, Oct 1991 2.00
❑17, Nov 1991 2.00
❑18, Dec 1991 2.00
❑19, Jan 1992 2.00
❑20, Jan 1992 2.00
❑21, Mar 1992 2.00
❑22, Apr 1992 2.00
❑23, May 1992 2.00
❑24, Jun 1992 2.00
❑25, Jul 1992 2.00
❑26, Aug 1992 2.00
❑27, Sep 1992 2.00
❑28, Oct 1992 2.00
❑29, Nov 1992 2.00
❑30, Dec 1992 2.00
❑31, Jan 1993 2.00
❑32, Feb 1993; Death Talks About Life AIDS insert 2.00
❑33, Mar 1993; Vertigo line starts 2.00
❑34, Apr 1993 2.00
❑35, May 1993 2.00
❑36, Jun 1993 2.00
❑37, Jul 1993 2.00
❑38, Aug 1993 2.00
❑39, Sep 1993 2.00
❑40, Oct 1993 2.00
❑41, Nov 1993 2.00
❑42, Dec 1993 2.00
❑43, Jan 1994 2.00
❑44, Feb 1994 2.00
❑45, Mar 1994 2.00
❑46, Apr 1994 2.00
❑47, May 1994 2.00
❑48, Jun 1994 2.00
❑49, Jul 1994 2.00
❑50, Aug 1994; Giant-size 3.00
❑51, Sep 1994 2.00
❑52, Oct 1994 2.00

❑53, Nov 1994 .... 2.00
❑54, Dec 1994 .... 2.00
❑55, Jan 1995 .... 2.00
❑56, Feb 1995 .... 2.00
❑57, Mar 1995 .... 2.00
❑58, Apr 1995 .... 2.00
❑59, May 1995 .... 2.25
❑60, Jun 1995 .... 2.25
❑61, Jul 1995 .... 2.25
❑62, Aug 1995 .... 2.25
❑63, Sep 1995 .... 2.25
❑64, Oct 1995 .... 2.25
❑65, Nov 1995 .... 2.25
❑66, Dec 1995 .... 2.25
❑67, Jan 1996 .... 2.25
❑68, Feb 1996 .... 2.25
❑69, Mar 1996 .... 2.25
❑70, Apr 1996 .... 2.25

SHADES AND ANGELS
CANDLE LIGHT
❑1, b&w 2.95

SHADES OF BLUE
AMP
❑1, Jul 1999, b&w 2.50
❑2 .... 2.50

SHADES OF GRAY
LADY LUCK
❑1, ca. 1994 .... 2.50
❑2 .... 2.50
❑3 .... 2.50
❑4 .... 2.50
❑5 .... 2.50
❑6 .... 2.50
❑7 .... 2.50
❑8 .... 2.50
❑9 .... 2.50
❑10 .... 2.50
❑11 .... 2.50

SHADES OF GRAY COMICS AND STORIES
TAPESTRY
❑1, ca. 1996 .... 2.95
❑2 .... 2.95
❑3 .... 2.95
❑4 .... 2.95

SHADE SPECIAL
AC
❑1, Oct 1984 .... 1.50

SHADO: SONG OF THE DRAGON
DC
❑1, ca. 1992, MGr (w) 5.00
❑2, ca. 1992, MGr (w) 5.00
❑3, ca. 1992, MGr (w) 5.00
❑4, ca. 1992, MGr (w) 5.00

SHADOW (1ST SERIES)
ARCHIE
❑1, Aug 1964 .... 30.00
❑2, Sep 1964 .... 18.00
❑3, Nov 1964 .... 18.00
❑4, Jan 1965 .... 18.00
❑5, Mar 1965, 1&O: Radiation Rogue 18.00
❑6, May 1965 .... 18.00
❑7, Jul 1965 .... 18.00
❑8, Sep 1965 .... 18.00

SHADOW (2ND SERIES)
DC
❑1, Nov 1973 .... 12.00
❑2, Jan 1974 .... 8.00
❑3, Mar 1974, BWr (a) 8.00
❑4, May 1974 .... 6.00
❑5, Jul 1974 .... 4.00
❑6, Sep 1974 .... 5.00
❑7, Nov 1974 .... 4.00
❑8, Jan 1975 .... 4.00
❑9, Mar 1975 FMc, FR (a) 4.00
❑10, May 1975 .... 4.00
❑11, Jul 1975 A: The Avenger 4.00
❑12, Sep 1975 .... 4.00

SHADOW (3RD SERIES)
DC
❑1, May 1986; HC (w); HC (a); The Shadow returns 3.00
❑2, Jun 1986 HC (w); HC (a) 2.00
❑3, Jul 1986 HC (w); HC (a) 2.00
❑4, Aug 1986 HC (w); HC (a) 2.00

SHADOW (4TH SERIES)
DC
❑1, Aug 1987 BSz (a) 2.50
❑2, Sep 1987 BSz (a) 2.00
❑3, Oct 1987 BSz (a) 2.00
❑4, Nov 1987 BSz (a) 2.00
❑5, Dec 1987 BSz (a) 2.00
❑6, Jan 1988 BSz (a) 2.00
❑7, Feb 1988 .... 2.00
❑8, Mar 1988 .... 2.00
❑9, Apr 1988 .... 2.00
❑10, May 1988 .... 2.00
❑11, Jun 1988 .... 2.00
❑12, Jul 1988 .... 2.00
❑13, Aug 1988 D: Shadow 2.00
❑14, Sep 1988 .... 2.00
❑15, Oct 1988 .... 2.00
❑16, Nov 1988 .... 2.00
❑17, Dec 1988 A: Avenger 2.00
❑18, Dec 1988 A: Avenger 2.00
❑19, Jan 1989; Shadow alive again 2.00
❑Annual 1, ca. 1987; EC parody 2.50
❑Annual 2, ca. 1988 .... 2.50

SHADOW (MOVIE ADAPTATION)
DARK HORSE
❑1, Jun 1994 .... 2.50
❑2, Jul 1994 .... 2.50

SHADOW AGENTS
ARMAGEDDON
❑1, May 1991 .... 2.50

SHADOW AND DOC SAVAGE
DARK HORSE
❑1, Jul 1995 .... 2.95
❑2, Aug 1995 .... 2.95

SHADOW AND THE MYSTERIOUS 3
DARK HORSE
❑1, Sep 1994 .... 2.95

SHADOWBLADE
HOT
❑1 .... 1.75

SHADOW CABINET
DC / MILESTONE
❑0, Jan 1994, Giant-size 2.50
❑1, Jun 1994 .... 1.75
❑2, Jul 1994 .... 1.75
❑3, Aug 1994 .... 1.75
❑4, Sep 1994 .... 1.75
❑5, Oct 1994 .... 1.75
❑6, Nov 1994 .... 1.75
❑7, Dec 1994 .... 1.75
❑8, Jan 1995 .... 1.75
❑9, Feb 1995 .... 1.75
❑10, Mar 1995 .... 1.75
❑11, Apr 1995 .... 1.75
❑12, May 1995 .... 1.75
❑13, Jun 1995 .... 2.50
❑14, Jul 1995 .... 2.50
❑15, Aug 1995 .... 2.50
❑16, Sep 1995 .... 2.50
❑17, Oct 1995 .... 2.50

SHADOW COMIX SHOWCASE
SHADOW COMIX
❑1, May 1996 .... 2.95

SHADOW CROSS
DARKSIDE
❑1, Oct 1995 .... 2.75

SHADOW EMPIRES: FAITH CONQUERS
DARK HORSE
❑1, Aug 1994 .... 3.25
❑2, Sep 1994 .... 3.00
❑3, Oct 1994 .... 3.00
❑4, Nov 1994 .... 3.00

SHADOWGEAR
ANTARCTIC
❑1, Feb 1999 .... 2.99
❑2, Mar 1999 .... 2.99
❑3, Apr 1999 .... 2.99

SHADOWHAWK (VOL. 1)
IMAGE
❑1, Aug 1992; 1: Shadowhawk. Embossed cover 3.00
❑1/A, Aug 1992; Newsstand edition (no gold stamp); 1: Shadowhawk. Embossed cover 2.00
❑2, Oct 1992 1: Arson. A: Spawn 2.50
❑3, Dec 1992; 1: The Others. 1: Liquefier. Glow-in-the-dark cover 2.50
❑4, Mar 1993 A: Savage Dragon 2.00

SHADOWHAWK (VOL. 2)
IMAGE
❑1, May 1993, diecut foil cover 3.50
❑1/Gold, May 1993, Gold 3.00
❑2, Jul 1993, 1: Hawk's Shadow. ShadowHawk's identity revealed; Foil-embossed cover 2.00
❑2/Gold, Jul 1993, Gold edition 3.00
❑3, Aug 1993, 1: The Pact. 1: J.P. Slaughter. Cover perforated to allow folding out into poster 2.95

SHADOWHAWK (VOL. 3)
IMAGE
❑0, Oct 1994, RL (w); RL (a); O: Shadowhawk. A: Mist. A: Bloodstrike. A: Mars Gunther. cover says September 2.50
❑1, Nov 1993, 1: Valentine. Foil-embossed cover 2.50
❑2, Dec 1993, 1: U.S. Male 2.00
❑3, Feb 1994, Fold-up cover 2.95
❑4, Mar 1994 .... 2.95
❑12, Aug 1994, (Numbering sequence follows from total of all ShadowHawk books published to this point) 1.95
❑13, Sep 1994, A: WildC.A.T.s 1.95
❑14, Oct 1994, A: 1963 heroes 2.50
❑15, Nov 1994, A: The Others 2.50
❑16, Jan 1995, A: Supreme 2.50
❑17, Mar 1995, A: Spawn 2.50
❑18, May 1995, D: Shadowhawk 2.50
❑Special 1, Dec 1994, Flip-book KB (w) 3.50

SHADOWHAWK (VOL. 4)
IMAGE
❑1, May 2005 .... 2.99
❑2, Jun 2005 .... 2.99
❑3, Jul 2005 .... 2.99
❑4, Sep 2005 .... 2.99
❑5 2005 .... 2.99
❑6 2005 .... 2.99
❑7, Jan 2006 .... 2.99
❑8, Jan 2006 .... 2.99
❑9, Mar 2006 .... 2.99
❑10, Apr 2006 .... 2.99
❑11, Jun 2006 .... 2.99
❑12, Jul 2006 .... 2.99
❑13, Jul 2006 .... 2.99

SHADOWHAWK GALLERY
IMAGE
❑1, Apr 1994 .... 2.00

SHADOWHAWK SAGA
IMAGE
❑1 .... 1.00

SHADOWHAWKS OF LEGEND
IMAGE
❑1, Nov 1995 .... 4.95

SHADOWHAWK-VAMPIRELLA
IMAGE / HARRIS
❑2, Feb 1995; crossover; continued from Vampirella - Shadowhawk #1 .... 4.95

SHADOW, THE: HELL'S HEAT WAVE
DARK HORSE
❑1, Apr 1995 .... 2.95
❑2, May 1995 .... 2.95
❑3, Jun 1995 .... 2.95

SHADOW HOUSE
SHADOW HOUSE
❑1, Aug 1997, b&w 2.95
❑2, Oct 1997, b&w 2.95
❑3, Dec 1997, b&w 2.95
❑4, Feb 1998, b&w 2.95

SHADOWHUNT SPECIAL
IMAGE
❑1/A, Apr 1996; Part 1 of five-part crossover 2.50
❑1/B, Apr 1996; alternate cover; Part 1 of five-part crossover 2.50

SHADOW, THE: IN THE COILS OF LEVIATHAN
DARK HORSE
❑1, Oct 1993 .... 2.95
❑2, Dec 1993 .... 2.95

Shi: The Way of the Warrior

Billy Tucci's female samurai seeks revenge

©Crusade

Shockrockets

Elite space squadron action from Kurt Busiek

©Image

Shock SuspenStories (RCP)

Reprints E.C. crime classics

©Gemstone

Shogun Warriors

Toy tie-in has Marvel character appearances

©Marvel

Shonen Jump

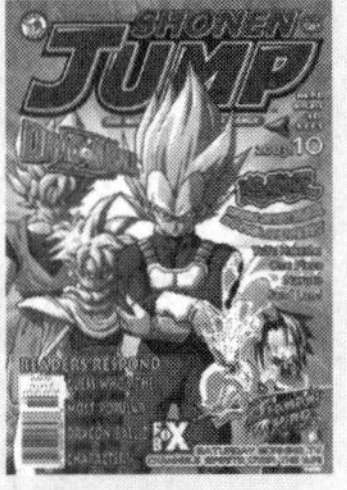

Viz anthology features Yu-Gi-Oh!

©Viz

N-MINT

❑3, Feb 1994 ... 2.95
❑4, Apr 1994 ... 2.95

SHADOW LADY (MASAKAZU KATSURA'S...)
DARK HORSE / MANGA

❑1, Oct 1998, 1: Shadow Lady ... 3.00
❑2, Nov 1998, 1: Bright Honda ... 2.50
❑3, Dec 1998 ... 2.50
❑4, Jan 1999 ... 2.50
❑5, Feb 1999 ... 2.50
❑6, Mar 1999 ... 2.50
❑7, Apr 1999 ... 2.50
❑8, May 1999 ... 2.50
❑9, Jun 1999 ... 2.50
❑10, Jul 1999 ... 2.50
❑11, Aug 1999 ... 2.50
❑12, Sep 1999 ... 2.50
❑13, Oct 1999 ... 2.50
❑14, Nov 1999 ... 2.50
❑15, Dec 1999 ... 2.50
❑16, Jan 2000 ... 2.50
❑17, Feb 2000 ... 2.50
❑18, Mar 2000 ... 2.50
❑19, Apr 2000 ... 2.50
❑20, May 2000 ... 2.50
❑21, Jun 2000 ... 2.50
❑22, Jul 2000 ... 2.50
❑23, Aug 2000 ... 2.50
❑24, Sep 2000 ... 2.50
❑Special 1, Oct 2000 ... 3.99

SHADOWLAND
FANTAGRAPHICS

❑1, b&w ... 2.25
❑2, b&w ... 2.25

SHADOWLINE SPECIAL
IMAGE

❑1 ... 1.00

SHADOWLORD/TRIUNE
JET CITY

❑1, Win 1986 ... 1.50

SHADOWMAN
VALIANT

❑0/Non-chromium ... 5.00
❑0/VVSS ... 45.00
❑0, Apr 1994; BH (c); BH (w); BH (a); O: Shadowman II (Jack Boniface). O: Shadowman I (Maxim St. James). Chromium cover ... 2.50
❑0/Gold, Apr 1994; Gold edition BH (a); O: Shadowman II (Jack Boniface). O: Shadowman I (Maxim St. James). ... 20.00
❑1, May 1992 O: Shadowman II (Jack Boniface). 1: Shadowman II (Jack Boniface). ... 8.00
❑2, Jun 1992 ... 5.00
❑3, Jul 1992 ... 5.00
❑4, Aug 1992; FM (c); FM (a); Unity ... 3.00
❑5, Sep 1992; BL (w); Unity ... 3.00
❑6, Oct 1992 BH (w) ... 3.00
❑7, Nov 1992 BH (w) ... 2.00
❑8, Dec 1992 BH (w); 1: Master Darque. V: Master Darque. ... 4.00
❑9, Jan 1993 ... 2.00
❑10, Feb 1993 BH (c); BH (w); BH (a) ... 1.00

N-MINT

❑11, Mar 1993 BH (c); BH (w); BH (a) ... 1.00
❑12, Apr 1993 BH (c); BH (w); BH (a); V: Master Darque ... 1.00
❑13, May 1993 (c); ... 1.00
❑14, Jun 1993 BH (c); BH (w); BH (a) ... 1.00
❑15, Jul 1993 BH (c); BH (w); BH (a). ... 1.00
❑16, Aug 1993 BH (c); BH (w); BH (a); 1: Doctor Mirage. ... 2.00
❑17, Sep 1993; BH (c); BH (w); BH (a); A: Archer & Armstrong. Serial number contest ... 1.00
❑18, Oct 1993 BH (c); BH (w); BH (a) ... 1.00
❑19, Nov 1993; BH (c); BH (w); BH (a); A: Aerosmith. Aerosmith ... 5.00
❑20, Dec 1993 BH (c); BH (w); BH (a) ... 1.00
❑21, Jan 1994 BH (c); BH (w); BH (a); V: Master Darque ... 1.00
❑22, Feb 1994 BH (c); BH (w); BH (a) ... 1.00
❑23, Mar 1994 BH (c); BH (w); BH (a); A: Doctor Mirage. ... 1.00
❑24, Apr 1994 BH (c); BH (w); BH (a) ... 1.00
❑25, Apr 1994; BH (c); BH (w); BH (a); trading card ... 2.00
❑26, Jun 1994 BH (c); BH (w); BH (a) ... 1.00
❑27, Aug 1994 BH (c); BH (w); BH (a) ... 1.00
❑28, Sep 1994 BH (c); BH (w); BH (a) ... 1.00
❑29, Oct 1994; BH (c); BH (w); BH (a); Chaos Effect Beta 1 ... 1.00
❑30, Nov 1994 BH (c); BH (w); BH (a) ... 1.00
❑31, Dec 1994 BH (c); BH (w); BH (a) ... 1.00
❑32, Jan 1994 BH (c); BH (w); BH (a) ... 2.00
❑33, Feb 1994 BH (c); BH (w); BH (a) ... 2.00
❑34, Mar 1994 BH (c); BH (w); BH (a) ... 2.00
❑35, Apr 1995 BH (c) ... 2.00
❑36, May 1995 BH (c) ... 2.00
❑37, Jun 1995 BH (a) ... 2.00
❑38, Jul 1995 BH (c); BH (w); BH (a). ... 2.00
❑39, Aug 1995 BH (w); BH (a) ... 2.00
❑40, Sep 1995 BH (w); BH (a) ... 3.00
❑41, Oct 1995 BH (w); BH (a) ... 3.00
❑42, Nov 1995 BH (c); BH (w); BH (a) ... 4.00
❑43, Dec 1995 BH (c); BH (w); BH (a) ... 7.00
❑Yearbook 1, Dec 1994; Yearbook 1 ... 3.95

SHADOWMAN (VOL. 2)
ACCLAIFM

❑1, Mar 1997 ... 2.50
❑1/Variant, Mar 1997, Painted cover ... 2.50
❑2, Apr 1997 ... 2.50
❑3, May 1997 ... 2.50
❑4, Jun 1997 ... 2.50
❑5, Jul 1997 ... 2.50
❑5/Ashcan, Mar 1997, b&w; No cover price; preview of upcoming issue ... 1.00
❑6, Aug 1997 ... 2.50
❑7, Sep 1997 ... 2.50
❑8, Oct 1997 ... 2.50
❑9, Nov 1997 ... 2.50
❑10, Dec 1997 ... 2.50
❑11, Jan 1998 ... 2.50
❑12, Feb 1998 ... 2.50
❑13, Mar 1998, Goat Month ... 2.50
❑14, Apr 1998 ... 2.50
❑15, Jan 1998, No cover date; indicia says Jan ... 2.50
❑16, Feb 1998, No cover date; indicia says Feb ... 2.50

N-MINT

❑Ashcan 1, Nov 1996, b&w; No cover price; preview of upcoming series ... 1.00

SHADOWMAN (VOL. 3)
ACCLAIM

❑1, Jul 1999 ... 3.95
❑2, Aug 1999 ... 3.95
❑3, Sep 1999 ... 3.95
❑4, Oct 1999 ... 3.95

SHADOW MASTER
PSYGNOSIS / MANGA

❑0; Preview ... 1.00

SHADOWMASTERS
MARVEL

❑1, Oct 1989 0: Shadowmasters. ... 4.00
❑2, Nov 1989 ... 4.00
❑3, Dec 1989 ... 4.00
❑4, Jan 1990 ... 4.00

SHADOWMEN
TRIDENT

❑1, b&w ... 2.25
❑2, b&w ... 2.25

SHADOW OF THE BATMAN
DC

❑1, Dec 1985 ... 3.00
❑2, Jan 1986 ... 2.00
❑3, Feb 1986 ... 2.00
❑4, Mar 1986 ... 2.00
❑5, Apr 1986 ... 2.00

SHADOW OF THE TORTURER (GENE WOLFE'S...)
INNOVATION

❑1, ca. 1991 ... 2.50
❑2, ca. 1991 ... 2.50
❑3, ca. 1991 ... 2.50
❑4, ca. 1992 ... 2.50
❑5, ca. 1992 ... 2.50
❑6, ca. 1992 ... 2.50

SHADOWPACT
DC

❑1, Aug 2006 ... 2.99
❑2, Sep 2006 ... 2.99

SHADOWPLAY
IDEA & DESIGN WORKS

❑1 2005 ... 3.99
❑2 2005 ... 3.99
❑3, Dec 2005 ... 3.99
❑4, Jan 2006 ... 3.99

SHADOW RAVEN
POC-IT

❑1, Jun 1995 ... 2.50

SHADOW REAVERS
BLACK BULL

❑1, Oct 2001 ... 2.99
❑2, Nov 2001 ... 2.99

SHADOW REIGNS
AIX C.C.

❑0, Dec 1997 ... 2.95

SHADOW RIDERS
MARVEL

❑1, Jun 1992; Embossed cover ... 2.50
❑2, Jul 1992 ... 1.75

Other grades: Multiply price above by 5/6 for VF/NM • 2/3 for VERY FINE • 1/3 for FINE • 1/5 for VERY GOOD • 1/8 for GOOD

❑3, Aug 1992 .... 1.75
❑4, Sep 1992 .... 1.75

SHADOWS
IMAGE

❑1, Mar 2003 .... 2.95
❑2, Apr 2003 .... 2.95
❑3, Aug 2003 .... 2.95
❑4, Dec 2003 .... 2.95

SHADOWS & LIGHT
MARVEL

❑1, Feb 1998, b&w 2.99
❑2, Apr 1998, b&w 2.99
❑3, Jul 1998, b&w 2.99

SHADOWS AND LIGHT (NBM)
NBM

❑1 .... 10.95
❑2 .... 10.95
❑3 .... 10.95
❑4 .... 10.95

SHADOW'S EDGE
LION

❑1 .... 3.95

SHADOWS FALL
DC / VERTIGO

❑1, Nov 1994 .... 2.95
❑2, Dec 1994 .... 2.95
❑3, Jan 1995 .... 2.95
❑4, Feb 1995 .... 2.95
❑5, Mar 1995 .... 2.95
❑6, Apr 1995 .... 2.95

SHADOWS FROM THE GRAVE
RENEGADE

❑1, b&w 2.00
❑2, Mar 1988, b&w 2.00

SHADOW SLASHER
POCKET CHANGE

❑1 .... 2.50

SHADOW SLAYER
ETERNITY

❑0 .... 1.95

SHADOWSTAR
SHADOWSTAR

❑1 .... 2.00
❑2, Nov 1985 .... 2.00
❑3, Dec 1985; first Slave Labor comic book 2.00

SHADOW STAR
DARK HORSE

❑1, ca. 2001 .... 15.95
❑2, ca. 2002 .... 14.95
❑3, ca. 2002 .... 13.95
❑4, ca. 2003 .... 14.95
❑5, ca. 2004 .... 15.95

SHADOW STATE
BROADWAY

❑1, Dec 1995, DC (a); 1: Blood S.C.R.E.A.M.. enhanced cardstock cover; BloodS.C.R.E.A.M., Fatale 2.50
❑2, Jan 1996, Till Death Do Us Part; Fatale 2.50
❑3, Mar 1996, Till Death Do Us Part 2.50
❑4, Apr 1996, Till Death Do Us Part 2.50
❑5, May 1996, Till Death Do Us Part 2.50
❑6, Jun 1996 .... 2.95
❑7, Jul 1996 .... 2.95
❑Ashcan 1, Sep 1995, b&w; giveaway preview edition; Till Death Do Us Part, Fatale 1.00

SHADOW STRIKES!
DC

❑1, Sep 1989 .... 2.50
❑2, Oct 1989 .... 2.25
❑3, Nov 1989 .... 2.00
❑4, Dec 1989 .... 2.00
❑5, Jan 1990 A: Doc Savage 2.00
❑6, Feb 1990 A: Doc Savage 2.00
❑7, Mar 1990 .... 2.00
❑8, Apr 1990 V: Shiwan Khan 2.00
❑9, May 1990 V: Shiwan Khan 2.00
❑10, Jun 1990 V: Shiwan Khan 2.00
❑11, Aug 1990 .... 2.00
❑12, Sep 1990 .... 2.00
❑13, Oct 1990 .... 2.00
❑14, Dec 1990 .... 2.00
❑15, Jan 1991 .... 2.00
❑16, Feb 1991 .... 2.00
❑17, Mar 1991 .... 2.00
❑18, Apr 1991 .... 2.00
❑19, May 1991 .... 2.00
❑20, Jun 1991 .... 2.00
❑21, Jul 1991 .... 2.00
❑22, Aug 1991 .... 2.00
❑23, Sep 1991 .... 2.00
❑24, Oct 1991 .... 2.00
❑25, Nov 1991 .... 2.00
❑26, Dec 1991 .... 2.00
❑27, Jan 1992 .... 2.00
❑28, Feb 1992 .... 2.00
❑29, Mar 1992 .... 2.00
❑30, Apr 1992 .... 2.00
❑31, May 1992 .... 2.00
❑Annual 1, Dec 1989 DS (a) 3.50

SHADOWTOWN
ICONOGRAFIX

❑1 .... 2.50

SHADOWTOWN: BLACK FIST RISING
MADHEART

❑1, b&w 2.50

SHADOW WAR OF HAWKMAN
DC

❑1, May 1985 RHo, AA (a) 1.50
❑2, Jun 1985 RHo (a) 1.25
❑3, Jul 1985 RHo (a); A: Elongated Man. A: Aquaman 1.25
❑4, Aug 1985 RHo (a) 1.25

SHADOW WARRIOR
GATEWAY

❑1, b&w 1.95

SHAIANA
EXPRESS / ENTITY

❑1, Jul 1995, b&w; enhanced cover 2.50
❑1/Chromium, Jul 1995 .... 10.00
❑1/Holochrome, Jul 1995 .... 15.00
❑2 .... 2.50
❑3 .... 2.50

SHALOMAN
MARK 1

❑1, b&w 1.75
❑2, b&w 1.75
❑3, b&w 1.75
❑4, b&w 1.75
❑5, b&w 1.75
❑6, b&w 1.75
❑7, b&w 1.75
❑8, b&w 1.75
❑9, b&w 1.75

SHAMAN
CONTINUITY

❑0, Jan 1994; NA, AN (a); Dealer incentive issue 2.00

SHAMAN'S TEARS
IMAGE

❑0, Dec 1995, MGr (w); MGr (a); says 1996 indicia; meant 1995 .... 2.50
❑1, May 1993, MGr (w); MGr (a); foil cover 2.50
❑1/Platinum, May 1993, Platinum edition MGr (a) 4.00
❑2, Jul 1993, MGr (w); MGr (a); cover says Aug; indicia says Jul 2.50
❑3, Nov 1994, MGr (w); MGr (a) 1.95
❑3/Ashcan, MGr (w); MGr (a); Limited "ashcan" run of Shaman's Tears #3 .... 3.00
❑4, Dec 1994, MGr (w); MGr (a); Title moves back to Image 1.95
❑5, Jan 1995, MGr (w); MGr (a) 1.95
❑6, Feb 1995, MGr (w); MGr (a) 1.95
❑7, May 1995, MGr (w); MGr (a) 1.95
❑8, May 1995, MGr (w); MGr (a) 1.95
❑9, Jun 1995, MGr (w); MGr (a) 1.95
❑10, Jul 1995, MGr (w); MGr (a) 1.95
❑11, Aug 1995, MGr (w); MGr (a) 1.95
❑12, Aug 1995, MGr (w); MGr (a) 1.95

SHANDA THE PANDA
MU

❑1, May 1992, b&w 2.50

SHANDA THE PANDA (2ND SERIES)
ANTARCTIC

❑1, Jun 1993 .... 2.50
❑2, Aug 1993 .... 2.50
❑3, Oct 1993 .... 2.75
❑4, Dec 1993 .... 2.75
❑5, Aug 1994 .... 2.75
❑6, Nov 1994 .... 2.75
❑7, Jan 1995 .... 2.75
❑8, Feb 1995 .... 2.75
❑9, May 1995 .... 2.75
❑10, Jul 1995 .... 2.75
❑11, Sep 1995 .... 2.75
❑12, Nov 1995 .... 2.75
❑13, Jan 1996 .... 2.75
❑14, Mar 1996 .... 2.75
❑15, May 1996 .... 2.75
❑16, Jul 1996 .... 1.95
❑17 .... 1.95
❑18 .... 1.95
❑19, May 1997 .... 1.95
❑20, Jul 1997 .... 1.95
❑21, Sep 1997; Demi Moore spoof cover 2.95
❑22 .... 2.95
❑23, Jan 1999 .... 2.95
❑24, Apr 1999 .... 2.95
❑25, Jul 1999; Giant-size 4.95
❑26, Nov 1999 .... 2.95
❑27, Feb 2000 .... 2.95
❑28, May 2000 .... 2.95
❑29, Aug 2000 .... 2.95
❑30, Nov 2000 .... 2.95
❑31, Feb 2001 .... 2.99
❑32, May 2001 .... 2.99
❑33, Aug 2001 .... 2.99
❑34, Nov 2001 .... 4.99
❑35, Aug 2002 .... 4.99
❑36, ca. 2002 .... 4.99
❑37, ca. 2003 .... 4.99
❑38, ca. 2003 .... 4.99
❑39, Dec 2003 .... 4.99
❑40, ca. 2004 .... 4.99
❑41, ca. 2004 .... 4.99
❑42, ca. 2004 .... 4.99
❑43, Mar 2005; Matrix-based cover 4.99
❑Annual 1 .... 4.00
❑Annual 2 .... 4.00
❑Annual 3 .... 4.50
❑Annual 4 .... 4.95

SHANG CHI: MASTER OF KUNG FU
MARVEL

❑1, Nov 2002 .... 2.99
❑2, Dec 2002 .... 2.99
❑3, Jan 2003 .... 2.99
❑4, Feb 2003 .... 2.99
❑5, Mar 2003 .... 2.99
❑6, Apr 2003 .... 2.99

SHANGHAI: BIG MACHINE
BRICK HOUSE DIGITAL

❑1, ca. 2000 .... 2.95

SHANGHAIED: THE SAGA OF THE BLACK KITE
ETERNITY

❑1 .... 2.00
❑2 .... 2.00
❑3 .... 2.00

SHANGRI LA
IMAGE

❑1, ca. 2004 .... 7.95

SHANNA THE SHE-DEVIL
MARVEL

❑1, Dec 1972, GT (a); 1: Shanna the She-Devil 27.00
❑2, Feb 1973, JSo (c); JSo (a) 6.00
❑3, Apr 1973 .... 3.50
❑4, Jun 1973 .... 3.50
❑5, Aug 1973 .... 3.50

SHANNA THE SHE-DEVIL (VOL. 2)
MARVEL

❑1, Mar 2005 .... 6.00
❑2, Apr 2005 .... 3.50
❑3, May 2005 .... 3.50
❑4, Jun 2005 .... 3.50
❑5, Jul 2005 .... 3.50
❑6, Aug 2005 .... 3.50
❑7, Sep 2005 .... 3.50

Shotgun Mary (1st Series)

Double-barreled action with gun-wielding woman

©Antarctic

Showcase

DC tryout title initiated Silver Age

©DC

Showcase '93

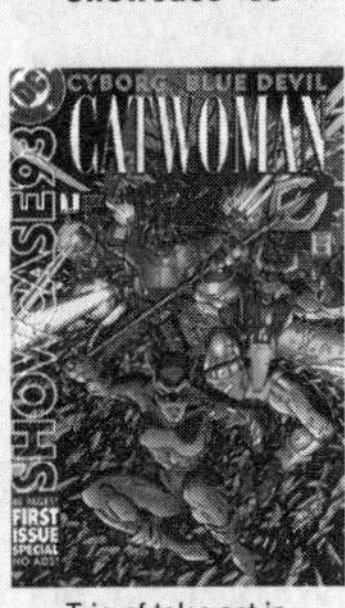

Trio of tales set in Gotham City

©DC

Showcase '95

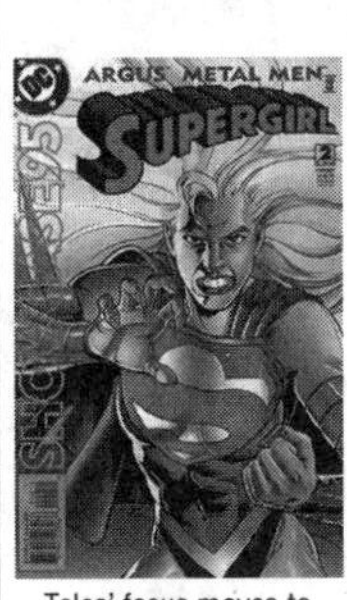

Tales' focus moves to Metropolis

©DC

Shrek

Animated adaptation definitely delayed

©Dark Horse

N-MINT

SHAOLIN
BLACK TIGER

❑1 ... 2.95
❑2 ... 2.95
❑3 ... 2.95
❑4 ... 2.95
❑5 ... 2.95

SHAOLIN COWBOY
BURLYMAN

❑1 2005 ... 3.50
❑1/Variant 2005 ... 5.00
❑2 2005 ... 3.50
❑2/Mignola 2005 ... 8.00
❑3 2005 ... 3.50

SHAOLIN SISTERS
TOKYOPOP

❑1, Feb 2003, b&w; printed in Japanese format ... 9.99
❑2, Apr 2003, b&w; printed in Japanese format ... 9.99

SHAOLIN SISTERS: REBORN
TOKYOPOP

❑1, May 2005, b&w ... 9.99
❑2, Aug 2005 ... 9.99
❑3, Nov 2005 ... 9.99

SHAQUILLE O'NEAL VS. MICHAEL JORDAN
PERSONALITY

❑1 ... 2.95
❑2 ... 2.95

SHARDS
ASCENSION

❑1, Feb 1994 ... 2.50

SHARKY
IMAGE

❑1/A, Feb 1998 ... 2.50
❑1/B, Feb 1998; back cover pin-up ... 2.50
❑1/C, Feb 1998; signing tour edition ... 2.50
❑1/D, Feb 1998; no cover price; The $1,000,000 variant ... 2.50
❑2/A, Apr 1998 ... 2.50
❑2/B, Apr 1998; alternate wraparound cover (with Savage Dragon) ... 2.50
❑3, May 1998 ... 2.50
❑4, Jul 1998; gives date of publication as Late; Group charging on cover, "The Bad Guy!" inset ... 2.50
❑4/A, Jul 1998 ... 2.50

SHATTER (1ST SERIES)
FIRST

❑1, Jun 1985; 1: Shatter. This is the first computer-generated comic book ... 2.50
❑1/2nd; 1: Shatter. This is the first computer-generated comic book ... 2.00

SHATTER (2ND SERIES)
FIRST

❑1, Dec 1985, first computer-drawn comic book; Continued from Shatter one-shot ... 2.50
❑2, Feb 1986 ... 2.00
❑3, Jun 1986 ... 2.00
❑4, Aug 1986 ... 2.00
❑5, Oct 1986 ... 2.00
❑6, Dec 1986 ... 2.00
❑7, Feb 1987 ... 2.00
❑8, Apr 1987 ... 2.00
❑9, Jun 1987 ... 2.00
❑10, Aug 1987 ... 2.00
❑11, Oct 1987 ... 2.00
❑12, Dec 1987 ... 2.00
❑13, Feb 1988 ... 2.00
❑14, Apr 1988 ... 2.00

SHATTERED EARTH
ETERNITY

❑1, Nov 1988 ... 1.95
❑2, Dec 1988 ... 1.95
❑3, Jan 1989 ... 1.95
❑4, Mar 1989 ... 1.95
❑5 1989 ... 1.95
❑6 1989 ... 1.95
❑7 1989 ... 1.95
❑8 1989 ... 1.95
❑9 1989 ... 1.95

SHATTERED IMAGE
IMAGE

❑1, Aug 1996 ... 2.50
❑2, Oct 1996; incorrect cover date ... 2.50
❑3, Nov 1996; cover says Oct, indicia says Nov ... 2.50
❑4, Dec 1996 ... 2.50

SHATTERPOINT
ETERNITY

❑1, b&w; Broid ... 2.25
❑2, b&w; Broid ... 2.25
❑3, b&w; Broid ... 2.25
❑4, b&w; Broid ... 2.25

SHAUN OF THE DEAD
IDEA & DESIGN WORKS

❑1, Jul 2005 ... 3.99
❑1/Autographed, Jul 2005 ... 19.99
❑2, Aug 2005 ... 3.99
❑3 2005 ... 3.99
❑4, Nov 2005 ... 3.99

SHAZAM!
DC

❑1, Feb 1973, CCB (a); O: Captain Marvel (Golden Age) ... 20.00
❑2, Apr 1973, CCB (a) ... 10.00
❑3, Jun 1973, CCB (a) ... 10.00
❑4, Jul 1973, CCB (a) ... 10.00
❑5, Sep 1973, CCB (a) ... 10.00
❑6, Oct 1973, CCB (a) ... 10.00
❑7, Nov 1973, CCB (a) ... 10.00
❑8, Dec 1973, 100 Page giant; CCB (a); scheduled as DC 100-Page Super-Spectacular #DC-23 ... 20.00
❑9, Jan 1974, CCB (a) ... 10.00
❑10, Feb 1974, BO (a); V: Aunt Minerva. Mary Marvel back-up ... 10.00
❑11, Mar 1974 ... 10.00
❑12, Jun 1974, 100 Page giant ... 10.00
❑13, Aug 1974, 100 Page giant ... 10.00
❑14, Oct 1974, 100 Page giant KS (a); A: Monster Society. ... 10.00
❑15, Dec 1974, 100 Page giant A: Lex Luthor. ... 10.00
❑16, Feb 1975, 100 Page giant V: Seven Deadly Sins. ... 10.00
❑17, Apr 1975, 100 Page giant ... 10.00
❑18, Jun 1975 ... 7.00
❑19, Aug 1975 ... 7.00
❑20, Oct 1975 ... 7.00
❑21, Dec 1975 CCB (w) ... 7.00
❑22, Feb 1976 V: King Kull. ... 7.00
❑23, Win 1976 ... 7.00
❑24, Spr 1976 ... 7.00
❑25, Oct 1976, O: Isis. 1: Isis. ... 7.00
❑26, Dec 1976 ... 7.00
❑27, Feb 1977 ... 7.00
❑28, Apr 1977, V: Black Adam ... 7.00
❑29, Jun 1977, V: Ibac. ... 7.00
❑30, Aug 1977 ... 7.00
❑31, Oct 1977, A: Minute Man ... 7.00
❑32, Dec 1977 ... 7.00
❑33, Feb 1978, V: Mr. Atom ... 7.00
❑34, Apr 1978, O: Captain Marvel Jr.. Captain Marvel Jr. vs. Captain Nazi 7.00
❑35, Jun 1978 ... 7.00

SHAZAM! AND THE SHAZAM FAMILY
DC

❑Annual 1, Sep 2002 ... 5.95

SHAZAM! POWER OF HOPE
DC

❑1, Nov 2000 ... 9.95
❑1/2nd, 2nd printing (2002) ... 9.95

SHAZAM: THE NEW BEGINNING
DC

❑1, Apr 1987 O: Captain Marvel (Golden Age)-new origin. ... 2.00
❑2, May 1987 V: Black Adam ... 2.00
❑3, Jun 1987 ... 2.00
❑4, Jul 1987 ... 2.00

SHEBA
SICK MIND

❑1, Jul 1996, b&w ... 2.50
❑2, Nov 1996, b&w ... 2.50
❑3, Feb 1997, b&w ... 2.50
❑4, Sep 1997, b&w ... 2.50

SHEBA (2ND SERIES)
SIRIUS

❑1, Dec 1997, b&w ... 2.50
❑2, Mar 1998, b&w ... 2.50
❑3, Jun 1998, b&w ... 2.50
❑4, Sep 1998, b&w ... 2.50
❑5 1999, b&w ... 2.50
❑6, May 1999, b&w ... 2.95
❑7 ... 2.95
❑8 ... 2.95

SHEBA PANTHEON
SIRIUS

❑1, Aug 1998, b&w; collects strips and character bios ... 2.50

SHE BUCCANEER
MONSTER

❑1, b&w ... 2.25
❑2, b&w ... 2.25

SHE-CAT
AC

❑1, Jun 1989, b&w ... 2.50
❑2, Apr 1990, b&w ... 2.50

N-MINT | N-MINT | N-MINT

❑3, May 1990, b&w 2.50
❑4, Jun 1990, b&w 2.50

SHEEDEVA
FANTAGRAPHICS / EROS

❑1, Aug 1994, b&w 2.95
❑2, Nov 1994, b&w 2.95

SHEENA
MARVEL

❑1, Dec 1984 GM (a) 2.00
❑2, Feb 1985 GM (a) 2.00

SHEENA 3-D SPECIAL
BLACKTHORNE

❑1, May 1985 .... 2.00

SHEENA-QUEEN OF THE JUNGLE
LONDON NIGHT

❑1/A, ca. 1998; Alligator cover 5.00
❑1/B, ca. 1998; Leopard cover 5.00
❑1/C, ca. 1998; Zebra cover 5.00
❑1/D, ca. 1998; Ministry Edition 3.00
❑1/Ltd., ca. 1998; White leather edition 15.00

SHEENA, QUEEN OF THE JUNGLE 3-D
BLACKTHORNE

❑1, May 1985, b&w DSt (a) 2.50

SHE-HULK
MARVEL

❑1, May 2004 .... 12.00
❑2, Jun 2004 .... 7.00
❑3, Jul 2004 .... 4.00
❑4, Aug 2004 .... 2.99
❑5, Sep 2004 .... 2.99
❑6, Oct 2004 .... 2.99
❑7, Nov 2004 .... 2.99
❑8, Dec 2004 .... 2.99
❑9, Jan 2005 .... 2.99
❑10, Feb 2005 .... 2.99
❑11, Mar 2005 .... 2.99
❑12, Apr 2005 .... 2.99

SHE HULK 2
MARVEL

❑1, Dec 2005, b&w 2.99
❑2, Jan 2006 .... 2.99
❑3, Feb 2006 .... 2.99
❑4, Mar 2006 .... 2.99
❑5, Apr 2006 .... 2.99
❑6, Jun 2006 .... 2.99
❑7, Jul 2006 .... 2.99
❑8, Aug 2006 .... 2.99

SHEILA TRENT: VAMPIRE HUNTER
DRACULINA

❑1 .... 2.50
❑2 .... 2.50

SHELL SHOCK
MIRAGE

❑1 .... 12.95

SHERLOCK HOLMES (DC)
DC

❑1, Oct 1975 .... 8.00

SHERLOCK HOLMES (ETERNITY)
ETERNITY

❑1, b&w; strip reprints 2.00
❑2 1988, b&w; strip reprints 2.00
❑3 1988, b&w; strip reprints 2.00
❑4 1988, b&w; strip reprints 2.00
❑5 1988, b&w; strip reprints 2.00
❑6 1988, b&w; strip reprints 2.00
❑7 1988, b&w; strip reprints 2.00
❑8, Jan 1989, b&w; strip reprints 2.00
❑9 1989, b&w; strip reprints 2.00
❑10 1989, b&w; strip reprints 2.00
❑11 1989, b&w; strip reprints 2.00
❑12 1989, b&w; strip reprints 2.00
❑13 1989, b&w; strip reprints 2.00
❑14 1989, b&w; strip reprints 2.00
❑15 1989, b&w; strip reprints 2.00
❑16 1989 .... 2.25
❑17 1989 .... 2.25
❑18 1990 .... 2.25
❑19 1990 .... 2.25
❑20 1990 .... 2.25
❑21 1990 .... 2.50
❑22 1990 .... 2.50
❑23 1990 .... 2.75

SHERLOCK HOLMES (AVALON)
AVALON

❑1, ca. 1997, b&w 2.95

SHERLOCK HOLMES: ADVENTURES OF THE OPERA GHOST
CALIBER

❑1 .... 2.95
❑2 .... 2.95

SHERLOCK HOLMES CASEBOOK
ETERNITY

❑1; Originally published as New Adventures of Sherlock Holmes 2.25
❑2; Originally published as New Adventures of Sherlock Holmes 2.25

SHERLOCK HOLMES: DR. JEKYLL & MR. HOLMES
CALIBER / TOME

❑1 1998, b&w 2.95

SHERLOCK HOLMES IN THE CASE OF THE MISSING MARTIAN
ETERNITY

❑1, Jul 1990, b&w 2.25
❑2, Aug 1990, b&w 2.25
❑3, Sep 1990, b&w 2.25
❑4, Oct 1990, b&w 2.25

SHERLOCK HOLMES IN THE CURIOUS CASE OF THE VANISHING VILLAIN
ATOMEKA

❑1 .... 4.50

SHERLOCK HOLMES MYSTERIES
MOONSTONE

❑1 .... 2.95

SHERLOCK HOLMES OF THE '30S
ETERNITY

❑1, b&w; strip reprints 2.95
❑2, b&w; strip reprints 2.95
❑3, b&w; strip reprints 2.95
❑4, b&w; strip reprints 2.95
❑5, b&w; strip reprints 2.95
❑6, b&w; strip reprints 2.95
❑7, b&w; strip reprints 2.95

SHERLOCK HOLMES READER
TOME

❑1, ca. 1998, b&w 3.95
❑2, ca. 1999, b&w 3.95
❑3, ca. 2000, b&w 3.95
❑4, ca. 2000, b&w 3.95

SHERLOCK HOLMES: RETURN OF THE DEVIL
ADVENTURE

❑1, Sep 1992, b&w 2.50
❑2 1992, b&w 2.50

SHERLOCK JR.
ETERNITY

❑1, b&w; strip reprints 2.50
❑2, Sep 1990, b&w; strip reprints 2.50
❑3, b&w; strip reprints 2.50

SHERMAN'S MARCH THROUGH ATLANTA TO THE SEA
HERITAGE COLLECTION

❑1; retells Civil War story; wraparound cover 3.50

SHEVA'S WAR
DC / VERTIGO

❑1, Oct 1998 .... 2.95
❑2, Nov 1998 .... 2.95
❑3, Dec 1998 .... 2.95
❑4, Jan 1999 .... 2.95
❑5, Feb 1999 .... 2.95

SHI
CRUSADE

❑0, ca. 1996; Flipbook with Wolverine/Shi Night of Justice Preview 2.99
❑½, ca. 1996; Wizard promotional edition with COA 3.00

SHI: ART OF WAR TOUR BOOK
CRUSADE

❑1, ca. 1998 .... 4.95

SHI: BLACK, WHITE, AND RED
CRUSADE

❑1, Mar 1998 .... 2.95
❑2, May 1998 .... 2.95

SHI/CYBLADE: THE BATTLE FOR INDEPENDENTS
CRUSADE

❑1, Sep 1995, 1: The Atomik Angels. A: Cerebus. A: Bone. crossover; concludes Image's Cyblade/Shi: The Battle for Independents #1; Numerous other independent characters appear 4.00
❑1/Variant, Sep 1995, alternate cover; crossover; concludes Image's Cyblade/Shi: The Battle for Independents #1 .... 5.00

SHI/DAREDEVIL: HONOR THY MOTHER
CRUSADE

❑1, Jan 1997; flipbook with TCB Sneak Attack Edition #1; crossover with Marvel 2.95
❑1/Ltd., Jan 1997; "Banzai" edition 6.00

SHIDIMA
IMAGE

❑0/A, Oct 2001 .... 2.95
❑0/B, Oct 2001 .... 2.95
❑1/A, Jan 2001; Many figures on cover, man center holding rope 2.95
❑1/B, Jan 2001; Four figures on cover, man front holding sword 2.95
❑2, Mar 2001 .... 2.95
❑3, May 2001 .... 2.95
❑4 2001 .... 2.95

SHI: EAST WIND RAIN
CRUSADE

❑1, Nov 1997; Painted cover 3.50
❑2, Feb 1998 .... 3.50
❑Ashcan 1, Jul 1997; No cover price; Sneak Teaser Preview 1.00

SHIELD
MARVEL

❑1, Feb 1973, SL (w); DH, JK (a); Nick Fury reprints from Strange Tales 15.00
❑2, Apr 1973, DH, JK (a); Nick Fury reprints from Strange Tales 5.00
❑3, Jun 1973, JB, JK (a); Nick Fury reprints from Strange Tales 5.00
❑4, Aug 1973, SL (w); JK (a); Nick Fury reprints from Strange Tales 5.00
❑5, Oct 1973, JSo (a); Nick Fury reprints from Strange Tales 5.00

SHIELD (ARCHIE)
ARCHIE / RED CIRCLE

❑2, Aug 1983, was Lancelot Strong, the Shield; becomes Shield — Steel Sterling 1.00

SHIELD, THE: SPOTLIGHT
IDEA & DESIGN WORKS

❑1, Jan 2004 .... 3.99
❑1/Photo, Jan 2004 .... 3.99
❑2, Feb 2004 .... 3.99
❑3, Mar 2004 .... 3.99
❑4, May 2004 .... 3.99
❑5, Jun 2004 .... 3.99

SHIELD — STEEL STERLING
ARCHIE / RED CIRCLE

❑3, Dec 1983, was Shield (Archie); becomes Steel Sterling 1.00

SHI: HEAVEN & EARTH
CRUSADE

❑1, Jul 1997 .... 2.95
❑1/A, Jul 1997; alternate cover 2.95
❑2, Nov 1997 .... 2.95
❑2/A, Nov 1997; logoless cover 2.95
❑3, Jan 1998 .... 2.95
❑4 .... 2.95
❑4/A, Apr 1998; alternate cover (Shi facing right) 2.95
❑Ashcan 1, ca. 1997; Special Teaser Preview 2.95

SHI: JU NEN
DARK HORSE

❑1 2004 .... 2.99
❑2 2004 .... 2.99
❑3 2005 .... 2.99

SHI: KAIDAN
CRUSADE

❑1, Oct 1996, b&w; Japanese ghost stories 2.95

Other grades: Multiply price above by 5/6 for VF/NM • 2/3 for VERY FINE • 1/3 for FINE • 1/5 for VERY GOOD • 1/8 for GOOD

Sigil

One of the first four CrossGen titles
©CrossGen

Silencers (Image)

Adventure series from Steve Ellis
©Image

Silly Daddy

Slice of life stories with Joe Chiappetta
©Joe Chiappetta

Silver Age

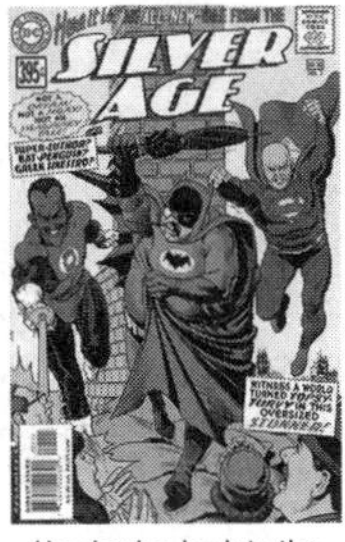

Hearkening back to the 80-page giants
©DC

Silverblade

Maltese Falcon rolls back the years
©DC

N-MINT

❑1/A, Oct 1996, b&w; alternate wraparound cover with no cover copy; Japanese ghost stories 3.00

SHILOH: THE DEVIL'S OWN DAY
HERITAGE COLLECTION

❑1, retells Civil War battle; wraparound cover 3.50

SHI: MASQUERADE
CRUSADE

❑1, Mar 1998; wraparound painted cover 3.50

SHIMMER
AVATAR

❑1 .... 3.50

SHI: NIGHTSTALKERS
CRUSADE

❑1, Sep 1997 .... 3.50

SHION: BLADE OF THE MINSTREL
VIZ

❑1, Sep 1990, b&w 9.95

SHI: PANDORA'S BOX
AVATAR

❑1, Apr 2003 .... 3.50

SHIP OF FOOLS (IMAGE)
IMAGE

❑0, Aug 1997, b&w 2.95
❑1, Oct 1997, b&w 2.95
❑2, Dec 1997, b&w 2.95
❑3, Feb 1998, b&w 2.95

SHIP OF FOOLS (CALIBER)
CALIBER

❑1, b&w 3.00
❑2 .... 3.00
❑3, b&w 3.00
❑4 .... 3.00
❑5 .... 3.00
❑6 .... 3.00

SHIP OF FOOLS (NBM)
NBM

❑1 .... 10.95

SHIPWRECKED!
DISNEY

❑1 .... 5.95

SHI: REKISHI
CRUSADE

❑1, Jan 1997; flipbook with Shi: East Wind Rain Sneak Attack Edition #1. 2.95
❑2, Apr 1997 .... 2.95

SHI: SEMPO
AVATAR

❑1, Aug 2003 .... 3.50
❑2, Oct 2003 .... 3.50

SHI: SENRYAKU
CRUSADE

❑1, Aug 1995 .... 3.25
❑1/Variant, Aug 1995; Variant "virgin" cover with no type 4.00
❑2, Oct 1995 .... 3.00
❑3, Dec 1995 .... 3.00

SHI: THE BLOOD OF SAINTS
CRUSADE

❑1, Nov 1996 .... 2.95

N-MINT

❑Fan ed. 1/A, Nov 1996; Promotional edition from FAN magazine 2.00

SHI: THE SERIES
CRUSADE

❑1, Aug 1997 .... 3.50
❑1/A, Aug 1997; Sneak preview edition with photo cover with Tia Carrera; Sneak preview edition 3.50
❑2, Sep 1997 .... 3.00
❑3, Oct 1997 .... 3.00
❑4, Nov 1997 .... 3.00
❑5, Dec 1997 .... 3.00
❑6, Jan 1998 .... 2.95
❑7, Feb 1998; manga-style cover 2.95
❑8, Mar 1998 .... 2.95
❑9, Apr 1998 .... 2.95
❑9/A, Apr 1998; alternate cover (full moon in background) 2.95
❑9/B, Apr 1998; alternate cover (Shi on her back) 2.95
❑9/C, Apr 1998; alternate cover (manga-style) 2.95
❑10, May 1998 .... 2.95
❑10/A, May 1998; alternate cover (in water) 2.95
❑10/B, May 1998; alternate cover (cherry blossoms) 2.95
❑10/C, May 1998; alternate cover (drawing sword) 2.95
❑11, Jun 1998, b&w 2.95
❑12, Jul 1998 .... 2.95
❑13, Aug 1998 .... 2.95
❑14, Aug 1998 .... 2.95
❑15, Sep 1998 .... 2.95
❑16, Sep 1998 .... 2.95

SHI: THE WAY OF THE WARRIOR
CRUSADE

❑½ 3.00
❑½/Platinum 4.00
❑1, Mar 1994 .... 6.00
❑1/A, Mar 1994 .... 5.00
❑1/B, Mar 1994; "Fan Appreciation Edition" #1 with no logo on cover; Fan Appreciation Edition #1 with no logo on cover 8.00
❑1/C, Mar 1994; Commemorative edition from the 1994 San Diego Comic Con; Gold logo on cover 8.00
❑2, Jun 1994 .... 5.00
❑2/A, Jun 1994; Fan appreciation edition #2 .... 3.00
❑2/B, Jun 1994; San Diego Comicon edition 6.00
❑2/Ashcan, Jun 1994; Ashcan promotional edition of Shi: The Way of the Warrior #2 .... 5.00
❑3, Oct 1994 .... 4.00
❑4 1995 .... 4.00
❑4/2nd; acetate cover 3.00
❑5, Apr 1995 1: Tomoe. 3.00
❑5/Variant, Apr 1995 1: Tomoe. 5.00
❑6 1995 .... 3.00
❑6/A 1995; Fan Appreciation Edition .. 3.00
❑6/Ashcan 1995; Commemorative edition from 1995 San Diego Comic Con 4.00

N-MINT

❑7, Mar 1996; back-up crossover with Lethargic Lad 3.00
❑7/Variant, Mar 1996; chromium edition; No cover price; back-up crossover with Lethargic Lad; limited to 5, 000 copies 4.00
❑8, Jun 1996 .... 3.00
❑8/A, Jun 1996; Combo Gold Club version; 5000 publisher; With certificate of Authenticity 5.00
❑9, Sep 1996 .... 3.00
❑10, Oct 1996; wraparound cover 3.00
❑11, Dec 1996 .... 3.00
❑12, Apr 1997; contains Angel Fire preview 3.00
❑Fan ed. 1/A, Jan 1995; Included with Fan magazine 1.00
❑Fan ed. 2/A; Overstreet Fan promotional edition #2 .... 1.00
❑Fan ed. 3/A; Overstreet Fan promotional edition #3 .... 1.00

SHI/VAMPIRELLA
CRUSADE

❑1, Oct 1997; crossover with Harris... 2.95

SHI VS. TOMOE
CRUSADE

❑1, Aug 1996; Foil wrap-around cover 3.95
❑1/Ltd., Aug 1996; Preview sold at San Diego Comic Con, black and white.. 5.00

SHI: YEAR OF THE DRAGON
CRUSADE

❑1, Sep 2000 .... 2.99

SHOCK & SPANK THE MONKEYBOYS SPECIAL
ARROW

❑1, b&w 2.50

SHOCKROCKETS
IMAGE

❑1, Apr 2000 .... 2.50
❑2, May 2000 .... 2.50
❑3, Jun 2000 .... 2.50
❑4, Jul 2000 .... 2.50
❑5, Aug 2000 .... 2.50
❑6, Oct 2000 .... 2.50

SHOCK SUSPENSTORIES (RCP)
GEMSTONE

❑1, Sep 1992; JO, JKa, GI (a); Reprints Shock SuspenStories #1; Ray Bradbury adaptation; Electrocution cover 2.00
❑2, Dec 1992; Reprints Shock SuspenStories #2 .... 2.00
❑3, Mar 1993; Reprints Shock SuspenStories #3 .... 2.00
❑4, Jun 1993; JO, WW, JKa (a); Reprints Shock SuspenStories #4 .. 2.00
❑5, Sep 1993; JO, WW, JKa (a); Reprints Shock SuspenStories #5 .. 2.00
❑6, Dec 1993; JO, WW, JKa, GI (w); JO, WW, JKa, GI (a); Reprints Shock SuspenStories #6 .... 2.00
❑7, Mar 1994; AF (c); JO, WW, JKa, GI (w); GE, JO, JK, WW, JKa, GI (a); Reprints Shock SuspenStories #7 .. 2.00
❑8, Jun 1994; AF (c); GE, AW, WW, JKa (w); GE, AW, WW, JKa (a); Reprints Shock SuspenStories #8 .... 2.00

❑9, Sep 1994; JO, WW, JKa (w); JO, WW, JKa (a); Reprints Shock SuspenStories #9 .... 2.00
❑10, Dec 1994; JO, WW, JKa (w); JO, WW, JKa (a); Reprints Shock SuspenStories #10 .... 2.00
❑11, Mar 1995; Reprints Shock SuspenStories #11 .... 2.00
❑12, Jun 1995; Reprints Shock SuspenStories #12 .... 2.00
❑13, Sep 1995; Reprints Shock SuspenStories #13 .... 2.00
❑14, Dec 1995; Reprints Shock SuspenStories #14 .... 2.00
❑15, Mar 1996; GE, WW, JKa (w); GE, WW, JKa (a); Reprints Shock SuspenStories #15; Cannibalism story 2.00
❑16, Jun 1996; GE, JO, JKa (w); GE, JO, JKa (a); Reprints Shock SuspenStories #16 .... 2.00
❑17, Sep 1996; GE, JO, JKa (w); GE, JO, JKa (a); Reprints Shock SuspenStories #17 .... 2.50
❑18, Dec 1996; GE, BK, JKa (w); GE, BK, JKa (a); Reprints Shock SuspenStories #18 .... 2.50
❑Annual 1; Reprints Shock SuspenStories #1-5 .... 8.95
❑Annual 2; JO, WW, JKa, GI (w); JO, WW, JKa, GI (a); Reprints Shock SuspenStories #6-10 .... 9.95
❑Annual 3; Reprints Shock SuspenStories #11-14 .... 8.95
❑Annual 4; GE, BK, JKa (w); GE, BK, JKa (a); Reprints Shock SuspenStories #15-18 .... 9.95

SHOCK THE MONKEY
Millennium

❑1 .... 2.95
❑2, b&w 3.95

SHOCK THERAPY
Harrier

❑1, Nov 1986 .... 1.95
❑2, Dec 1986 .... 1.95
❑3, Jan 1987 .... 1.95
❑4, Feb 1987 .... 1.95
❑5, Mar 1987 .... 1.95

SHOGUN WARRIORS
Marvel

❑1, Feb 1979, HT (a); 1: Shogun Warriors. Newsstand edition (distributed by Curtis); issue number in box 5.00
❑1/Whitman, Feb 1979, HT (a); 1: Shogun Warriors. Special markets edition (usually sold in Whitman bagged prepacks); price appears in a diamond; no UPC barcode 5.00
❑2, Mar 1979, Newsstand edition (distributed by Curtis); issue number in box 2.00
❑2/Whitman, Mar 1979, Special markets edition (usually sold in Whitman bagged prepacks); price appears in a diamond; no UPC barcode 2.00
❑3, Apr 1979, Newsstand edition (distributed by Curtis); issue number in box 2.00
❑3/Whitman, Apr 1979, Special markets edition (usually sold in Whitman bagged prepacks); price appears in a diamond; no UPC barcode 2.00
❑4, May 1979, Newsstand edition (distributed by Curtis); issue number in box 2.00
❑4/Whitman, May 1979, Special markets edition (usually sold in Whitman bagged prepacks); price appears in a diamond; no UPC barcode 2.00
❑5, Jun 1979 .... 2.00
❑6, Jul 1979 .... 2.00
❑7, Aug 1979 .... 2.00
❑8, Sep 1979 .... 2.00
❑9, Oct 1979 .... 2.00
❑10, Nov 1979 .... 2.00
❑11, Dec 1979 .... 1.50
❑12, Jan 1980 .... 1.50
❑13, Feb 1980 .... 1.50
❑14, Mar 1980 .... 1.50
❑15, Apr 1980 .... 1.50
❑16, May 1980, D: Followers. 1.50
❑17, Jun 1980 .... 1.50
❑18, Jul 1980 .... 1.50
❑19, Aug 1980, A: Fantastic Four. 1.50
❑20, Sep 1980, A: Fantastic Four. 1.50

SHOJO ZEN
Zen

❑1 .... 2.50

SHONEN JUMP
Viz

❑0, Aug 2002; Promo give-away preview; Translated by Andy Nakatani and Bill Flanagan 5.00
❑1, Jan 2003; Giant anthology, reads back to front. Includes Polybagged with YYG ultra-rare Blue-Eyes White Dragon promo card. Feature: Akira Toriyama. Q&A: Kazuki Takahashi, Yoshiro Togashi, Eiichiro Oda. All comics come from Japan's Shonen Jump magazine. 4.95
❑2, Feb 2003; Reads back to front; feature: Game Master interview with Kazuki Takahashi 4.95
❑3, Mar 2003; Reads back to front. Features: Interview with Eiichiro Oda; Shonen Jump Live in New York; Toriyami/Yasutoko interview; interview with top Japanese inline skaters and X Games winners; interview with Yuji Horii 4.95
❑4, Apr 2003; Reads back to front. Features: Live from Jump Festa, Manga Artists on Stage, Enter the Shueisha, See Japan 4.95
❑5, May 2003; Reads back to front. Features: The Art of Yoshihiro Togashi, All About YuYu Kakusho Anime 4.95
❑6, Jun 2003; Reads back to front. Features: Ninja Master Masashi Kishimoto, Sports Manga 4.95
❑7, Jul 2003; Reads back to front. Features: Yu-Gi-Oh! Universe, Rurouni Kenshin, Martial Arts Manga 4.95
❑8, Aug 2003; Reads back to front. Features: Hiroyuki Takei interview, Yu-Gi-Oh! Power of Chaos CD-ROM preview 4.95
❑9, Sep 2003; Polybagged with Yu-Gi-Oh! Power of Chaos CD-ROM and three cards. Reads back to front. Hiroyuki Takei interview. 4.95
❑10, Oct 2003; Reads back to front. Includes card game strategies, anime, and popular characters. 4.95
❑11, Nov 2003; Reads back to front. Rurouni Kenshin starts. Sand Land ends. 4.95
❑12, Dec 2003; Reads back to front. Knights of the Zodiac preview. 4.95
❑13, Jan 2004; Reads back to front. Polybagged with bound-in YYG card [Red-Eyes B. Dragon]. Hiraku No Go begins. Features: Shonen Jump anniversary; Heian Period culture, Shaman King profile. 4.95
❑14, Feb 2004; Reads back to front. Features: Eiichiro Oda interview 4.95
❑15, Mar 2004; Reads back to front. Yugi vs. Kaiba. 4.95
❑16, Apr 2004; Reads back to front. Ultimate Muscle preview 4.95
❑17, May 2004; Reads back to front. 60+ pages of Yu-Gi-Oh! Polybagged with Dragon Ball Z pinup and bound-in promo card (Erratic Energy Drill). 4.95
❑18, Jun 2004; Reads back to front. Bleach preview. 60+ pages of YGO. 4.95
❑19, Jul 2004; Reads back to front 4.95
❑20, Aug 2004; Reads back to front. Features: Takahashi interview. 70+ pages of Yu-Gi-Oh! 4.95
❑21, Sep 2004; Reads back to front. Kazuki Takahashi interview. Whistle preview. 60+ pages of Dragon Ball Z. 4.95
❑22, Oct 2004; Reads back to front 4.95
❑23, Nov 2004; Reads back to front. Koji Inada and Riku Sanjo (Beet the Vandel Buster) interview. 60+ pages each of One Piece and Dragon Ball Z. 4.95
❑24, Dec 2004; Reads back to front 4.95
❑25, Jan 2005; Reads back to front. Polybagged with Yu-Gi-Oh! card (Archfiend of Gilfer). No Yu-Gi-Oh! story. 4.95
❑26, Feb 2005 .... 4.95
❑27, Mar 2005 .... 4.95
❑28, Apr 2005 .... 4.95
❑29, May 2005 .... 4.95
❑30, Jun 2005 .... 4.95
❑31, Jul 2005 .... 4.95
❑32, Aug 2005 .... 4.95
❑33, Sep 2005 .... 4.95
❑34, Oct 2005 .... 4.95
❑35, Nov 2005 .... 4.95
❑36, Dec 2005 .... 4.95

SHONEY BEAR AND HIS FRIENDS
Golden Press

❑1, ca. 1986, Promotional comic book for Shoney's restaurant chain in the Southeast; possibly last comic book to come from Western/Golden's Racine, Wis. office? 2.00

SHONEY'S FUN AND ADVENTURE MAGAZINE
Paragon

❑1, Jul 1983, Follow-up to Big Boy (Paragon) from Shoney's, a southeastern restaurant chain 1.00
❑2, Aug 1983 .... 1.00
❑3, Sep 1983 .... 1.00
❑4, Oct 1983 .... 1.00
❑5, Nov 1983 .... 1.00
❑6, Dec 1983, Christmas cover; Opryland feature; Muppets crossword 1.00
❑7, Jan 1984 .... 1.00
❑8, Feb 1984, "Pak-Man" video game characters in story 1.00

SHOOTY BEAGLE
Fantagraphics / Eros

❑1, b&w 2.25
❑2, b&w 2.25
❑3, b&w 2.25

SHORT ON PLOT!
Mu

❑1, b&w 2.50

SHORT ORDER
Head

❑1 .... 20.00
❑2, Jan 1974 .... 15.00

SHORTS (PAT KELLEY'S...)
Antarctic

❑1, Oct 1997 .... 2.95
❑2 .... 2.95

SHORTSTOP SQUAD
Ultimate Sports Force

❑1, ca. 1999; Barry Larkin apperance. 3.95

SHOTGUN MARY (1ST SERIES)
Antarctic

❑1, Sep 1995 .... 4.00
❑1/CS, Sep 1995; CD edition 9.95
❑1/Variant, Sep 1995; alternate cover. 2.95
❑2 1995 .... 3.00
❑3 1995; Exists? 3.00
❑Ashcan 1, Sep 1995; ashcan edition. 2.95

SHOTGUN MARY (2ND SERIES)
Antarctic

❑1, Mar 1998 .... 2.95
❑1/Variant, Mar 1998; Limited edition cover (purple); Limited edition cover (purple) 4.00
❑2, May 1998 .... 2.95
❑3, Jul 1998 .... 2.95

SHOTGUN MARY: BLOOD LORE
Antarctic

❑1, Feb 1997 .... 2.95
❑2, Apr 1997 .... 2.95
❑3, Jun 1997 .... 2.95
❑4, Aug 1997 .... 2.95

SHOTGUN MARY: DEVILTOWN
Antarctic

❑1, Jul 1996 .... 2.95
❑1/Ltd., ca. 1996; Commemorative edition 5.40

SHOTGUN MARY SHOOTING GALLERY
Antarctic

❑1, Jun 1996 .... 2.95

Silver Sable

Female gun-for-hire spinoff from Spider-Man

©Marvel

Silver Surfer (Vol. 1)

Stan Lee and Jack Kirby's hip series

©Marvel

Silver Surfer (Vol. 3)

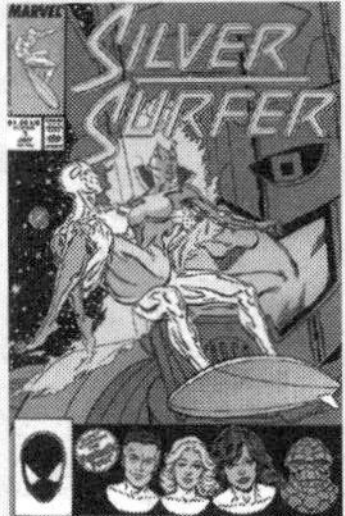

1987 relaunch lasted more than a decade

©Marvel

Silver Surfer (Vol. 4)

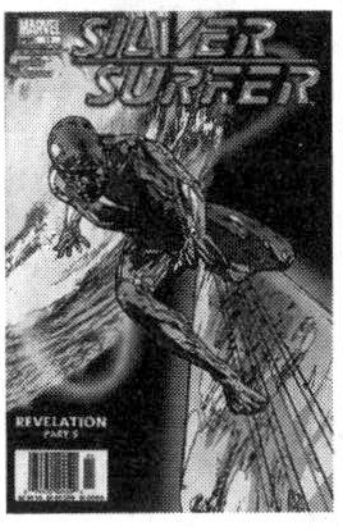

Surfer series had a short ride

©Marvel

Simpsons Comics

TV's favorite dysfunctional cartoon family

©Bongo

N-MINT

SHOTGUN MARY: SON OF THE BEAST
ANTARCTIC

❑1, Oct 1997 ... 2.95

SHOUJO
ANTARCTIC

❑1, Jun 2003 ... 5.95
❑2, Aug 2003 ... 5.95
❑3, Oct 2003 ... 5.95

SHOWCASE
DC

❑1, Apr 1956, Fire Fighters ... 3500.00
❑2, Jun 1956, JKu, RH (a); Kings of Wild ... 1000.00
❑3, Aug 1956; RH (a); Frogmen ... 1000.00
❑4, Oct 1956, CI, JKu (a); O: Flash II (Barry Allen). 1: Flash II (Barry Allen). Begins DC Silver Age revival of heroes ... 27500.00
❑5, Dec 1956 MM (a); A: Manhunters. 1000.00
❑6, Feb 1957 JK (c); JK (a); O: Challengers of the Unknown. 1: Challengers of the Unknown. ... 4000.00
❑7, Apr 1957 JK (c); JK (a); 2: Challengers of the Unknown. ... 2000.00
❑8, Jun 1957, CI (a); O: Captain Cold. 1: Captain Cold. 2: Flash II (Barry Allen) ... 11500.00
❑9, Aug 1957 RMo (a); A: Lois Lane. . 7500.00
❑10, Oct 1957, A: Lois Lane. ... 3000.00
❑11, Dec 1957 JK (c); JK (a); A: Challengers of the Unknown. ... 1750.00
❑12, Feb 1958, JK (c); JK (a); A: Challengers of the Unknown. ... 1750.00
❑13, Apr 1958, CI (a); O: Mr. Element. 1: Mr. Element. A: Flash II (Barry Allen). ... 4500.00
❑14, Jun 1958, CI (a); O: Doctor Alchemy. 1: Doctor Alchemy. A: Flash II (Barry Allen). ... 4500.00
❑15, Aug 1958, 1: Space Ranger. ... 2000.00
❑16, Oct 1958 2: Space Ranger. ... 1000.00
❑17, Dec 1958, GK (c); O: Adam Strange. 1: Adam Strange. ... 2750.00
❑18, Feb 1959 GK (c); 1: Rann. ... 1200.00
❑19, Apr 1959 GK (c); A: Adam Strange. ... 1500.00
❑20, Jun 1959, 1: Rip Hunter. ... 1000.00
❑21, Aug 1959 2: Rip Hunter. ... 500.00
❑22, Oct 1959 GK (a); O: Green Lantern II (Hal Jordan). 1: Green Lantern II (Hal Jordan). 1: Carol Ferris. ... 5600.00
❑23, Dec 1959 GK (a); 1: Invisible Destroyer. ... 1750.00
❑24, Feb 1960 GK (a); A: Green Lantern II. ... 1750.00
❑25, Apr 1960 JKu (a); A: Rip Hunter. 350.00
❑26, Jun 1960, JKu (a); A: Rip Hunter. 350.00
❑27, Aug 1960 RH (a); 1: Sea Devils. . 900.00
❑28, Oct 1960, RH (a); 2: Sea Devils. . 400.00
❑29, Dec 1960 RH (a); A: Sea Devils. . 400.00
❑30, Feb 1961 O: Aquaman. ... 800.00
❑31, Apr 1961, A: Aquaman. ... 400.00
❑32, Jun 1961 A: Aquaman. ... 400.00
❑33, Aug 1961 A: Aquaman. ... 375.00
❑34, Oct 1961, GK (a); O: Atom II (Ray Palmer). 1: Atom II (Ray Palmer).... 1250.00
❑35, Dec 1961, MA, GK (a); 2: Atom II (Ray Palmer). ... 700.00
❑36, Feb 1962, MA, GK (a); A: Atom II (Ray Palmer). ... 525.00
❑37, Apr 1962, 1: Metal Men. ... 700.00
❑38, Jun 1962, A: Metal Men. ... 400.00
❑39, Aug 1962, 1: Chemo. A: Metal Men. ... 350.00
❑40, Oct 1962, A: Metal Men. ... 300.00
❑41, Dec 1962, O: Tommy Tomorrow. 150.00
❑42, Feb 1963, A: Tommy Tomorrow. 150.00
❑43, Apr 1963, James Bond, Agent 007; movie adaptation ... 450.00
❑44, Jun 1963, A: Tommy Tomorrow. 100.00
❑45, Aug 1963, JKu (a); O: Sgt. Rock. 325.00
❑46, Oct 1963, A: Tommy Tomorrow. 100.00
❑47, Dec 1963, A: Tommy Tomorrow. 100.00
❑48, Feb 1964, A: Cave Carson. ... 80.00
❑49, Apr 1964, A: Cave Carson. ... 80.00
❑50, Jun 1964, MA, CI (a); A: King Faraday. ... 80.00
❑51, Aug 1964, MA, CI (a); A: King Faraday. ... 80.00
❑52, Oct 1964, A: Cave Carson. ... 80.00
❑53, Dec 1964, JKu, RH (a); A: G.I. Joe. 100.00
❑54, Feb 1965, JKu, RH (a); A: G.I. Joe. 100.00
❑55, Apr 1965, MA (a); O: Doctor Fate. Hourman ... 275.00
❑56, Jun 1965, MA (a); 1: Psycho-Pirate II (Roger Hayden). Doctor Fate, Hourman ... 125.00
❑57, Aug 1965, JKu (a); A: Enemy Ace. 225.00
❑58, Oct 1965, JKu (a); A: Enemy Ace. 150.00
❑59, Dec 1965, NC (c); NC (a); A: Teen Titans. ... 125.00
❑60, Feb 1966, MA (a); O: The Spectre. 225.00
❑61, Apr 1966, MA (a); A: Spectre. ... 100.00
❑62, Jun 1966, JO (a); O: Inferior Five. 1: Earth-12. 1: Dumb Bunny. 1: Merryman. 1: Awkwardman. 1: Blimp. 1: White Feather. 1: Inferior Five. ... 80.00
❑63, Aug 1966, JO (a); A: Inferior Five. 50.00
❑64, Oct 1966, MA (a); A: Spectre. ... 100.00
❑65, Dec 1966, A: Inferior Five. X-Men parody ... 50.00
❑66, Feb 1967, 1: B'wana Beast. ... 30.00
❑67, Apr 1967, A: B'wana Beast. ... 30.00
❑68, Jun 1967, A: Maniaks. ... 30.00
❑69, Aug 1967, A: Maniaks. ... 30.00
❑70, Oct 1967, A: Binky. ... 30.00
❑71, Dec 1967, A: Maniaks. ... 30.00
❑72, Feb 1968, ATh, JKu (a); A: Johnny Thunder. Trigger Twins, Texas Rangers ... 30.00
❑73, Apr 1968, SD (a); O: Creeper. 1: Creeper. Profiles of Don Segall and Steve Ditko ... 85.00
❑74, May 1968, 1: Anthro. Profile of Howie Post ... 45.00
❑75, Jun 1968, SD, DG (w); SD (a); O: Dove I (Don Hall). O: Hawk I (Hank Hall). 1: Dove I (Don Hall). 1: Hawk I (Hank Hall) ... 75.00
❑76, Aug 1968, 1: Bat Lash. ... 50.00
❑77, Sep 1968, 1: Angel & Ape. ... 50.00
❑78, Nov 1968, 1: Jonny Double. ... 35.00
❑79, Dec 1968, 1: Dolphin. ... 45.00
❑80, Feb 1969, NA (c); A: Phantom Stranger. ... 45.00
❑81, Mar 1969, Windy & Willy ... 45.00
❑82, May 1969, 1: Nightmaster. ... 40.00
❑83, Jun 1969, BWr (a); A: Nightmaster. ... 40.00
❑84, Aug 1969, BWr (a); A: Nightmaster. ... 40.00
❑85, Sep 1969, JKu (a); A: Firehair.... 20.00
❑86, Nov 1969, JKu (a); A: Firehair.... 20.00
❑87, Dec 1969, JKu (a); A: Firehair.... 20.00
❑88, Feb 1970, Jason's Quest ... 15.00
❑89, Mar 1970, Jason's Quest ... 15.00
❑90, May 1970, A: Manhunter 2070... 15.00
❑91, Jun 1970, A: Manhunter 2070.... 15.00
❑92, Aug 1970, A: Manhunter 2070. .. 15.00
❑93, Sep 1970, A: Manhunter 2070.... 15.00
❑94, Aug 1977, JSa, JA (a); O: Doom Patrol II. 1: Celsius. 1: Doom Patrol II. ... 20.00
❑95, Oct 1977, JSa, JA (a); A: The Doom Patrol. ... 8.00
❑96, Dec 1977, JSa, JA (a); A: The Doom Patrol. ... 8.00
❑97, Feb 1978, A: Power Girl. ... 6.00
❑98, Mar 1978, JSa (a); O: Power Girl. 6.00
❑99, Apr 1978, A: Power Girl. ... 6.00
❑100, May 1978, Double-size; JSa (a); all-star issue ... 6.00
❑101, Jun 1978, JK (c); AM, MA (a); A: Hawkman. ... 6.00
❑102, Jul 1978, JK (c); AM, MA (a); A: Hawkman. ... 6.00
❑103, Aug 1978, JK (c); AM, MA (a); A: Hawkman. ... 6.00
❑104, Sep 1978, OSS Spies ... 5.00

SHOWCASE '93
DC

❑1, Jan 1993; Catwoman, Cyborg, Blue Devil ... 2.25
❑2, Feb 1993; Catwoman, Cyborg, Blue Devil ... 2.25
❑3, Mar 1993; Catwoman, Flash, Blue Devil ... 2.25
❑4, Apr 1993; Catwoman, Geo-Force, Blue Devil ... 2.00
❑5, May 1993; Robin, Peacemaker, Blue Devil ... 2.00
❑6, Jun 1993; Robin, Peacemaker, Blue Devil ... 2.00
❑7, Jul 1993; Two-Face, Deathstroke, Jade, Obsidian, Peacemaker ... 2.50
❑8, Aug 1993; KJ (a); Two-Face, Batman, Deadshot, Fire and Ice ... 2.50
❑9, Sep 1993; JRo (w); Huntress, Peacemaker, Shining Knight ... 2.00
❑10, Oct 1993; PG (c); Huntress, Deathstroke, Katana ... 2.00
❑11, Nov 1993; BMc (a); Nightwing, Robin, Kobra Kronicles ... 2.00
❑12, Dec 1993; KG, BMc (a); Nightwing, Robin, Green Lantern, Creeper ... 2.00

SHOWCASE '94
DC

❑1, Jan 1994; Joker, New Gods, Gunfire 1.95
❑2, Feb 1994; Joker ... 1.95
❑3, Mar 1994; Arkham Asylum, Blue Beetle, Psyba-Rats ... 1.95
❑4, Apr 1994; Arkham Asylum, Blue Beetle, Psyba-Rats ... 1.95

	N-MINT
❑5, May 1994; Huntress, Loose Cannon, Bloodwynd	1.95
❑6, Jun 1994; Robin	1.95
❑7, Jul 1994; Penguin, Arsenal, Terrorsmith	1.95
❑8, Aug 1994; Scarface, Zero Hour Prelude	1.95
❑9, Sep 1994; Scarface, Zero Hour Prelude	1.95
❑10, Oct 1994; Azrael, Zero Hour, Black Condor	1.95
❑11, Nov 1994; Man-Bat, Starfire, Black Condor	1.95
❑12, Dec 1994	1.95

SHOWCASE '95
DC

❑1, Jan 1995; Supergirl, Alan Scott, Argus	2.50
❑2, Feb 1995; Supergirl, Metal Men, Argus	2.50
❑3, Mar 1995; Eradicator, Claw, The Question	2.50
❑4, Apr 1995	2.50
❑5, Jun 1995	2.50
❑6, Jul 1995; Bibbo, Lobo, Science Police, Legionnaires	2.95
❑7, Aug 1995; Mongul, Arion, New Gods	2.95
❑8, Sep 1995; Mongul, Spectre, Arsenal	2.95
❑9, Oct 1995; Lois Lane, Lobo, Martian Manhunter	2.95
❑10, Nov 1995; Gangbuster, Ferrin Colos, Hi-Tech	2.95
❑11, Nov 1995; Agent Liberty; Arkham Asylum; Hi-Tech	2.95
❑12, Dec 1995; Supergirl, Maitresse, The Shade	2.95

SHOWCASE '96
DC

❑1, Jan 1996; Steel and Guy Gardner: Warrior, Aqualad, Metropolis S.C.U.	2.95
❑2, Feb 1996; Steel and Guy Gardner: Warrior, Circe, Metallo	2.95
❑3, Mar 1996; Lois Lane and Black Canary, Doctor Fate and The Shade, Lightray	2.95
❑4, Apr 1996; Guardian and Firebrand, Doctor Fate and The Shade, The Demon	2.95
❑5, Jun 1996; Green Arrow and Thorn, Doctor Fate and The Shade, New Gods	2.95
❑6, Jul 1996; Superboy and The Demon, Firestorm, The Atom	2.95
❑7, Aug 1996; Gangbuster and The Power of Shazam!, Fire, Firestorm	2.95
❑8, Sep 1996; Superboy and Superman, Legionnaires, Supergirl	2.95
❑9, Oct 1996; Shadowdragon and Lady Shiva, Doctor Light, Martian Manhunter	2.95
❑10, Nov 1996; Bibbo, Ultra Boy, Captain Comet	2.95
❑11, Dec 1996; Brainiac vs. Legion, Wildcat, Scare Tactics	2.95
❑12, Win 1996; Brainiac vs. Legion, Jesse Quick, King Faraday	2.95

SHRED
CFW

❑1	2.25
❑2	2.25
❑3	2.25
❑4	2.25
❑5	2.25
❑6	2.25
❑7	2.25
❑8	2.25

SHREK
DARK HORSE

❑1, Sep 2003	2.99
❑2, Dec 2003	2.99
❑3, Dec 2003	2.99

SHRIEK
FANTACO

❑1, b&w	4.95
❑2, b&w	4.95
❑Special 1, b&w	3.50
❑Special 2, b&w; Dangerbrain	3.50
❑Special 3, b&w	3.50

SHRIKE
VICTORY

	N-MINT
❑1, May 1987, b&w	1.50
❑2	1.50

SHROUD
MARVEL

❑1, Mar 1994	1.75
❑2, Apr 1994	1.75
❑3, May 1994	1.75
❑4, Jun 1994	1.75

SHUGGA
FANTAGRAPHICS / EROS

❑1, b&w	2.50
❑2, b&w	2.50

SHURIKEN (VICTORY)
VICTORY

❑1, Win 1985; Win-85	1.50
❑2, Fal 1985; Fal-85	1.50
❑3	1.50
❑4, Nov 1986	1.50
❑5 1987	1.50
❑6, Feb 1987	1.50
❑7, Mar 1987	1.50
❑8, Apr 1987	1.50

SHURIKEN (ETERNITY)
ETERNITY

❑1, Jun 1991, b&w	2.50
❑2, ca. 1991, b&w	2.50
❑3, ca. 1991, b&w	2.50
❑4, ca. 1991, b&w	2.50
❑5, ca. 1991, b&w	2.50
❑6, ca. 1992, b&w	2.50

SHURIKEN (BLACKTHORNE)
BLACKTHORNE

❑1	7.95

SHURIKEN: COLD STEEL
ETERNITY

❑1, Jul 1989, b&w; 16 pgs.	1.50
❑2, Aug 1989	1.95
❑3, Sep 1989	1.95
❑4, Oct 1989	1.95
❑5, Nov 1989	1.95
❑6, Dec 1989	1.95

SHURIKEN TEAM-UP
ETERNITY

❑1, ca. 1989, b&w; Shuriken, Libra, Kokutai	1.95

SHUT UP AND DIE!
IMAGE

❑1, Jan 1998	2.95
❑2, Mar 1998	2.95
❑3, May 1998	2.95
❑4, Aug 1998	2.95
❑5, ca. 1999	2.95

SICK SMILES
AIIIE!

❑1, Jun 1994	2.50
❑2, Jul 1994	2.50
❑3, ca. 1994	2.50
❑4, ca. 1994	2.50
❑5, ca. 1994	2.50
❑6, ca. 1995	2.50
❑7, ca. 1995	2.50
❑8, Apr 1995	2.95

SIDEKICK
IMAGE

❑1, Jul 2006	2.99

SIDEKICKS
FANBOY

❑1, Jun 2000	2.75

SIDEKICKS: THE SUBSTITUTE
ONI

❑1, Jul 2002	2.95

SIDE SHOW
MATURE MAGIC

❑1	1.75

SIDESHOW COMICS
PAN GRAPHICS

❑1, b&w BT (a)	1.75
❑2, b&w	1.75
❑3	1.75
❑4	1.75
❑5	1.75

SIDETRACK CITY AND OTHER TALES
FANTAGRAPHICS

	N-MINT
❑1, Feb 1996; oversized squarebound collection of b&w stories	9.95

SIEGE
IMAGE

❑1, Jan 1997	2.50
❑2, Feb 1997	2.50
❑3, Mar 1997	2.50
❑4, Apr 1997	2.50

SIEGEL AND SHUSTER: DATELINE 1930S
ECLIPSE

❑1, Nov 1984	1.75
❑2, Sep 1985	1.75

SIEGE OF THE ALAMO
TOME

❑1, Jul 1991, b&w	2.50

SIGHT UNSEEN
FANTAGRAPHICS

❑1, Apr 1997, b&w; collects story from The Stranger and The Philadelphia Weekly; wraparound cover	2.95

SIGIL
CROSSGEN

❑1, Jul 2000	4.00
❑2, Aug 2000	3.00
❑3, Sep 2000	3.00
❑4, Oct 2000	3.00
❑5, Nov 2000	3.00
❑6, Dec 2000	2.95
❑7, Jan 2001	2.95
❑8, Feb 2001	2.95
❑9, Mar 2001	2.95
❑10, Apr 2001	2.95
❑11, May 2001	2.95
❑12, Jun 2001	2.95
❑13, Jul 2001	2.95
❑14, Aug 2001	2.95
❑15, Sep 2001	2.95
❑16, Oct 2001	2.95
❑17, Nov 2001	2.95
❑18, Dec 2001	2.95
❑19, Jan 2002	2.95
❑20, Feb 2002	2.95
❑21, Mar 2002	2.95
❑22, Apr 2002	2.95
❑23, May 2002	2.95
❑24, Jun 2002	2.95
❑25, Jul 2002	2.95
❑26, Aug 2002	2.95
❑27, Sep 2002	2.95
❑28, Oct 2002	2.95
❑29, Nov 2002	2.95
❑30, Dec 2002	2.95
❑31, Jan 2003	2.95
❑32, Feb 2003	2.95
❑33, Mar 2003	2.95
❑34, Apr 2003	2.95
❑35, May 2003	2.95
❑36, Jun 2003	2.95
❑37, Jul 2003	2.95
❑38, Aug 2003	2.95
❑39, Oct 2003	2.95
❑40, Nov 2003	2.95
❑41, Nov 2003	2.95
❑42, Dec 2003	2.95

SIGMA
IMAGE

❑1, Apr 1996	2.50
❑2, May 1996	2.50
❑3, Jun 1996	2.50

SILBUSTER
ANTARCTIC

❑1, Jan 1994	2.95
❑2, Feb 1994	2.95
❑3, Mar 1994	2.95
❑4, Apr 1994	2.95
❑5, Oct 1994	2.95
❑6, Nov 1994	2.95
❑7, Dec 1994	2.95
❑8, Jan 1995	2.95
❑9, Feb 1995	2.95
❑10, Aug 1995	2.95
❑11, Oct 1995	2.95

Other grades: Multiply price above by 5/6 for VF/NM • 2/3 for VERY FINE • 1/3 for FINE • 1/5 for VERY GOOD • 1/8 for GOOD

Simpsons Comics Presents Bart Simpson

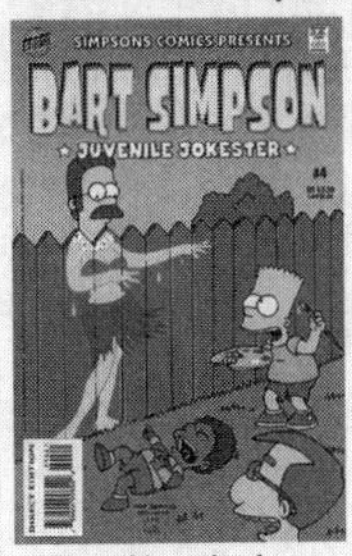

Bimonhly antics from television terror
©Bongo

Sinbad

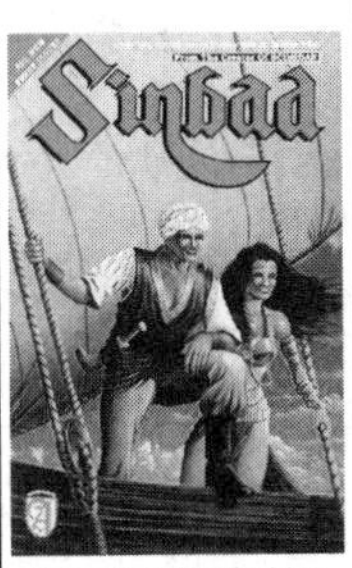

Sailor from the Arabian Nights gets series
©Adventure

Sin City: A Dame to Kill For

Frank Miller continues his noir epic
©Dark Horse

Sinja: Deadly Sins

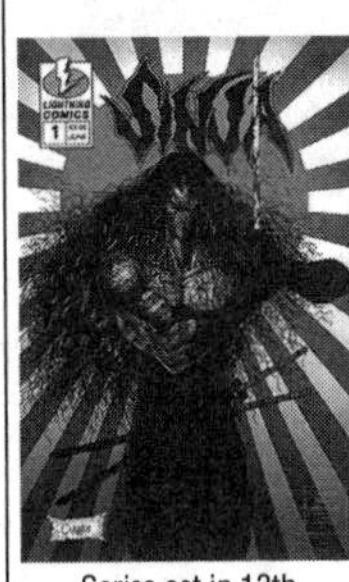

Series set in 13th century Japan
©Lightning

Sins of Youth: Wonder Girls

Wonder Woman and Wonder Girl switch ages
©DC

N-MINT

❑12, Oct 1995 .... 2.95
❑13, Oct 1995 .... 2.95
❑14, Oct 1995 .... 2.95
❑15, May 1996 .... 2.95
❑16, Jul 1996 .... 2.95
❑17, Sep 1996 .... 2.95
❑18, Sep 1996 .... 2.95
❑19, Jan 1997 .... 2.95

SILENCERS (CALIBER)
CALIBER

❑1, Jul 1991, b&w 2.50
❑2 1991, b&w 2.50
❑3 1991, b&w 2.50
❑4 1991, b&w 2.50

SILENCERS (MOONSTONE)
MOONSTONE

❑1 2003 .... 3.50
❑2 2003 .... 3.50

SILENCERS (IMAGE)
IMAGE

❑1, Sep 2005 .... 2.95

SILENT HILL: PAINT IT BLACK
IDEA & DESIGN WORKS

❑0 2005 .... 7.49

SILENT CITY
KITCHEN SINK

❑1, Oct 1995, b&w; oversized graphic novel 24.95

SILENT DRAGON
DC / WILDSTORM

❑1, Sep 2005 .... 2.99
❑2, Oct 2005 .... 2.99
❑3 2005 .... 2.99
❑4 .... 2.99
❑5, Jan 2006 .... 2.99
❑6, Feb 2006 .... 2.99

SILENT HILL: DEAD/ALIVE
IDEA & DESIGN WORKS

❑1, Dec 2005 .... 3.99
❑2, Feb 2006 .... 3.99
❑3, Mar 2006 .... 3.99
❑4, Apr 2006 .... 3.99

SILENT HILL: DYING INSIDE
IDEA & DESIGN WORKS

❑1, Apr 2004 .... 3.99
❑2, Mar 2004 .... 3.99
❑3, Apr 2004 .... 3.99
❑3/Variant 0.00
❑4, May 2004 .... 3.99
❑5, Jun 2004 .... 3.99

SILENT INVASION
RENEGADE

❑1, Apr 1986, b&w 2.00
❑2, Jun 1986, b&w 2.00
❑3, Aug 1986, b&w 2.75
❑4, Oct 1986, b&w 2.75
❑5, Dec 1986, b&w 2.75
❑6, Feb 1987, b&w 2.75
❑7, May 1987, b&w 2.75
❑8, Jul 1987, b&w 2.75
❑9, Sep 1987, b&w 2.75
❑10, Nov 1987, b&w 2.75

N-MINT

❑11, Jan 1988, b&w 2.75
❑12, Mar 1988, b&w 2.75

SILENT INVASION, THE: ABDUCTIONS
CALIBER

❑1, May 1998, b&w 2.95

SILENT MOBIUS PART 1
VIZ

❑1, ca. 1991 .... 4.95
❑2, ca. 1991 .... 4.95
❑3, ca. 1991 .... 4.95
❑4, ca. 1991 .... 4.95
❑5, ca. 1991 .... 4.95
❑6, ca. 1991 .... 4.95

SILENT MOBIUS PART 2
VIZ

❑1, ca. 1992 .... 4.95
❑2, ca. 1992 .... 4.95
❑3, ca. 1992 .... 4.95
❑4, ca. 1992 .... 4.95
❑5, ca. 1992 .... 4.95

SILENT MOBIUS PART 3
VIZ

❑1, ca. 1992 .... 2.75
❑2, ca. 1992 .... 2.75
❑3, ca. 1992 .... 2.75
❑4, ca. 1992 .... 2.75
❑5, ca. 1992 .... 2.75

SILENT MOBIUS PART 4
VIZ

❑1, ca. 1992 .... 2.75
❑2, ca. 1992 .... 2.75
❑3, ca. 1992 .... 2.75
❑4, ca. 1992 .... 2.75
❑5, ca. 1992 .... 2.75

SILENT MOBIUS PART 5: INTO THE LABYRINTH
VIZ

❑1, May 1999 .... 2.95
❑2, Jun 1999 .... 2.95
❑3, Jul 1999 .... 2.95
❑4, Aug 1999 .... 2.95
❑5, Sep 1999 .... 2.95
❑6, Oct 1999 .... 2.95

SILENT MOBIUS PART 6: KARMA
VIZ

❑1, Nov 1999 .... 3.25
❑2, Dec 1999 .... 3.25
❑3, Jan 2000 .... 3.25
❑4, Feb 2000 .... 3.25
❑5, Mar 2000 .... 3.25
❑6, Apr 2000 .... 3.25
❑7, May 2000 .... 3.25

SILENT MOBIUS PART 7: CATASTROPHE
VIZ

❑1, Jun 2000 .... 2.95
❑2, Jul 2000 .... 2.95
❑3, Aug 2000 .... 2.95
❑4, Sep 2000 .... 2.95
❑5, Oct 2000 .... 2.95
❑6, Nov 2000 .... 2.95

N-MINT

SILENT MOBIUS PART 8: LOVE & CHAOS
VIZ

❑1, Dec 2000 .... 2.95
❑2, Jan 2000 .... 2.95
❑3, Feb 2000 .... 2.95
❑4, Mar 2001 .... 2.95
❑5, Apr 2001 .... 2.95
❑6, May 2001 .... 2.95
❑7, Jun 2001 .... 2.95

SILENT MOBIUS PART 9: ADVENT
VIZ

❑1, Jul 2001 .... 2.95
❑2, Aug 2001 .... 2.95
❑3, Sep 2001 .... 2.95
❑4, Oct 2001 .... 2.95
❑5, Nov 2001 .... 2.95
❑6, Dec 2001 .... 2.95

SILENT MOBIUS PART 10: TURNABOUT
VIZ

❑1, Jan 2002 .... 2.95
❑2, Feb 2002 .... 2.95
❑3, Mar 2002 .... 2.95
❑4, Apr 2002 .... 2.95
❑5, May 2002 .... 2.95
❑6, Jun 2002 .... 2.95

SILENT MOBIUS PART 11: BLOOD
VIZ

❑1, Jul 2002 .... 2.95
❑2, Aug 2002 .... 2.95
❑3, Sep 2002 .... 2.95
❑4, Oct 2002 .... 2.95
❑5, Nov 2002 .... 2.95

SILENT MOBIUS PART 12: HELL
VIZ

❑1, Dec 2002 .... 2.95
❑2, Jan 2003 .... 2.95

SILENT RAPTURE
AVATAR

❑1, ca. 1997 .... 3.00
❑2, ca. 1997 .... 3.00

SILENT SCREAMERS: NOSFERATU
IMAGE

❑1, Oct 2000 .... 4.95

SILENT WINTER/PINEAPPLEMAN
LIMELIGHT

❑1 .... 2.95

SILKE
DARK HORSE

❑1, Jan 2001 .... 2.95
❑2, Feb 2001 .... 2.99
❑3, Mar 2001 .... 2.99
❑4, Apr 2001 .... 2.99

SILKEN GHOST
CROSSGEN

❑1, Jun 2003 .... 2.95
❑2, Jul 2003 .... 2.95
❑3, Aug 2003 .... 2.95
❑4, Oct 2003 .... 2.95
❑5, Oct 2003 .... 2.95

SILLY-CAT
JOE CHIAPPETTA

- ❑1, Dec 1997 ... 1.00

SILLY DADDY
JOE CHIAPPETTA

- ❑1 ... 2.75
- ❑2, Sep 1995, b&w; flipbook with King Cat back-up ... 2.75
- ❑3 ... 2.75
- ❑4 ... 2.75
- ❑5 ... 2.75
- ❑6 ... 2.75
- ❑7 ... 2.75
- ❑8 ... 2.75
- ❑9 ... 2.75
- ❑10, Mar 1996, b&w ... 2.75
- ❑11 1996, b&w ... 2.75
- ❑12, b&w ... 2.75
- ❑13, b&w ... 2.75
- ❑14, b&w; no cover price ... 2.75
- ❑15 ... 2.75
- ❑16 ... 2.75
- ❑17 ... 2.75
- ❑18 ... 2.75

SILVER
COMICOLOR

- ❑1, Oct 1996 ... 2.00

SILVER AGE
DC

- ❑1, Jul 2000 ... 2.50
- ❑Giant Size 1, Jul 2000 ... 5.95

SILVER AGE: CHALLENGERS OF THE UNKNOWN
DC

- ❑1, Jul 2000 ... 2.50

SILVER AGE: DIAL H FOR HERO
DC

- ❑1, Jul 2000 ... 2.50

SILVER AGE: DOOM PATROL
DC

- ❑1, Jul 2000 ... 2.50

SILVER AGE: FLASH
DC

- ❑1, Jul 2000 ... 2.50

SILVER AGE: GREEN LANTERN
DC

- ❑1, Jul 2000 ... 2.50

SILVER AGE: JUSTICE LEAGUE OF AMERICA
DC

- ❑1, Jul 2000 ... 2.50

SILVER AGE SECRET FILES
DC

- ❑1, Jul 2000 ... 4.95

SILVER AGE: SHOWCASE
DC

- ❑1, Jul 2000 ... 2.50

SILVER AGE: TEEN TITANS
DC

- ❑1, Jul 2000 ... 2.50

SILVER AGE: THE BRAVE AND THE BOLD
DC

- ❑1, Jul 2000 ... 2.50

SILVERBACK
COMICO

- ❑1, Oct 1989 ... 2.50
- ❑2, Nov 1989 ... 2.50
- ❑3, Dec 1989 ... 2.50

SILVERBLADE
DC

- ❑1, Sep 1987 ... 1.25
- ❑2, Oct 1987 ... 1.25
- ❑3, Nov 1987 ... 1.25
- ❑4, Dec 1987 ... 1.25
- ❑5, Jan 1988 ... 1.25
- ❑6, Feb 1988 ... 1.25
- ❑7, Mar 1988 ... 1.25
- ❑8, May 1988 ... 1.25
- ❑9, Jun 1988 ... 1.25
- ❑10, Jul 1988 ... 1.25
- ❑11, Aug 1988 ... 1.25
- ❑12, Sep 1988 ... 1.25

SILVER CROSS
ANTARCTIC

- ❑1, Nov 1997 ... 2.95
- ❑2, Jan 1998 ... 2.95
- ❑3, Mar 1998 ... 2.95

SILVERFAWN
CALIBER

- ❑1 ... 1.95

SILVERHAWKS
MARVEL / STAR

- ❑1, Aug 1987 ... 1.00
- ❑2, Oct 1987 ... 1.00
- ❑3, Dec 1987 ... 1.00
- ❑4, Feb 1988 ... 1.00
- ❑5, Apr 1988 ... 1.00
- ❑6, Jun 1988 ... 1.00
- ❑7, Jul 1988 ... 1.00

SILVERHEELS
PACIFIC

- ❑1, Dec 1983 ... 1.50
- ❑2, Mar 1984 ... 1.50
- ❑3, May 1984 ... 1.50

SILVER SABLE
MARVEL

- ❑1, Jun 1992; Embossed cover ... 2.00
- ❑2, Jul 1992 ... 1.50
- ❑3, Aug 1992 ... 1.50
- ❑4, Sep 1992 ... 1.50
- ❑5, Oct 1992 ... 1.25
- ❑6, Nov 1992 A: Deathlok. ... 1.25
- ❑7, Dec 1992 A: Deathlok. ... 1.25
- ❑8, Jan 1993 ... 1.25
- ❑9, Feb 1993 O: Wild Pack. ... 1.25
- ❑10, Mar 1993 A: Punisher. ... 1.25
- ❑11, Apr 1993 ... 1.25
- ❑12, May 1993 ... 1.25
- ❑13, Jun 1993 ... 1.25
- ❑14, Jul 1993 ... 1.25
- ❑15, Aug 1993 ... 1.25
- ❑16, Sep 1993 ... 1.25
- ❑17, Oct 1993; A: New Outlaws. A: Baron Von Strucker. A: Crippler. Infinity Crusade crossover ... 1.25
- ❑18, Nov 1993 ... 1.25
- ❑19, Dec 1993 ... 1.25
- ❑20, Jan 1994 ... 1.25
- ❑21, Feb 1994 ... 1.25
- ❑22, Mar 1994 ... 1.25
- ❑23, Apr 1994 A: Daredevil. V: Deadpool. ... 1.25
- ❑24, May 1994 ... 1.50
- ❑25, Jun 1994; Giant-size ... 2.00
- ❑26, Jul 1994 ... 1.50
- ❑27, Aug 1994 ... 1.50
- ❑28, Sep 1994 ... 1.50
- ❑29, Oct 1994 ... 1.50
- ❑30, Nov 1994 ... 1.50
- ❑31, Dec 1994 ... 1.50
- ❑32, Jan 1995 ... 1.50
- ❑33, Feb 1995 ... 1.50
- ❑34, Mar 1995 ... 1.50
- ❑35, Apr 1995 ... 1.50

SILVER SCREAM
RECOLLECTIONS

- ❑1, b&w; Reprints ... 2.00
- ❑2, b&w; Reprints ... 2.00
- ❑3, b&w; Reprints ... 2.00

SILVER STAR
PACIFIC

- ❑1, Feb 1983 ... 1.00
- ❑2, Apr 1983 ... 1.00
- ❑3, Jun 1983 ... 1.00
- ❑4, Aug 1983 ... 1.00
- ❑5, Nov 1983 ... 1.00
- ❑6, Jan 1984 ... 1.00

SILVER STAR (JACK KIRBY'S...)
TOPPS

- ❑1, Oct 1993, trading cards; bagged; later planned issues do not exist ... 2.95

SILVERSTORM (AIRCEL)
AIRCEL

- ❑1 1990, b&w ... 2.25
- ❑2 1990, b&w ... 2.25
- ❑3, Jul 1990, b&w ... 2.25
- ❑4 1990, b&w ... 2.25

SILVERSTORM (SILVERLINE)
SILVERLINE

- ❑1, Oct 1998 ... 2.95
- ❑2 1999 ... 2.95
- ❑3 1999 ... 2.95
- ❑4 1999 ... 2.95

SILVER SURFER (VOL. 1)
MARVEL

- ❑1, Aug 1968; Giant-size; SL (w); GC, JB (a); O: Silver Surfer. adaptation from Tales of Suspense #53 ... 375.00
- ❑2, Oct 1968; Giant-size; SL (w); JB (a); adaptation from Amazing Adult Fantasy #8 ... 160.00
- ❑3, Dec 1968; Giant-size; SL (w); JB (a); 1: Mephisto. A: Thor. adaptation from Amazing Adult Fantasy #7 ... 135.00
- ❑4, Feb 1969; Giant-size; SL (w); JB (a); Scarce; adaptation from Amazing Adult Fantasy #9 ... 265.00
- ❑5, Apr 1969; Giant-size; SL (w); JB (a); adaptation from Tales to Astonish #26 ... 75.00
- ❑6, Jun 1969; Giant-size; SL (w); FB, JB (a); adaptation from Amazing Adult Fantasy #13 ... 75.00
- ❑7, Aug 1969; Giant-size; SL (w); JB (a); adaptation from Amazing Adult Fantasy #12 ... 90.00
- ❑8, Sep 1969, SL (w); JB (a) ... 95.00
- ❑9, Oct 1969, SL (w); JB (a) ... 60.00
- ❑10, Nov 1969, SL (w); JB (a) ... 60.00
- ❑11, Dec 1969, SL (w); JB (a) ... 65.00
- ❑12, Jan 1970, SL (w); JB (a) ... 50.00
- ❑13, Feb 1970, SL (w); JB (a) ... 70.00
- ❑14, Mar 1970, SL (w); JB (a); A: Spider-Man. ... 125.00
- ❑15, Apr 1970, SL (w); JB (a) ... 55.00
- ❑16, May 1970, SL (w); JB (a) ... 55.00
- ❑17, Jun 1970, SL (w); JB (a) ... 55.00
- ❑18, Sep 1970, SL (w); JK (a); A: Inhumans. Inhumans ... 55.00

SILVER SURFER (VOL. 2)
MARVEL / EPIC

- ❑1, Dec 1988 SL (w) ... 3.00
- ❑2, Jan 1989 SL (w) ... 2.50

SILVER SURFER (VOL. 3)
MARVEL

- ❑-1, Jul 1997; A: Stan Lee. Flashback ... 3.00
- ❑½, ca. 1998; Wizard promotional edition (mail-in) ... 3.00
- ❑½/Platinum, ca. 1998; Wizard promotional edition (mail-in) ... 6.00
- ❑1, Jul 1987; Double-size MR (a) ... 7.00
- ❑2, Aug 1987 ... 6.00
- ❑3, Sep 1987 ... 4.00
- ❑4, Oct 1987 A: Mantis. ... 4.00
- ❑5, Nov 1987 O: Skrulls. A: Mantis. ... 4.00
- ❑6, Dec 1987 ... 3.50
- ❑7, Jan 1988 ... 3.50
- ❑8, Feb 1988 ... 3.50
- ❑9, Mar 1988 ... 3.50
- ❑10, Apr 1988 ... 3.50
- ❑11, May 1988 JSa (a); 1: Reptyl. ... 3.00
- ❑12, Jun 1988 ... 3.00
- ❑13, Jul 1988 ... 3.00
- ❑14, Aug 1988 ... 3.00
- ❑15, Sep 1988 ... 4.00
- ❑16, Oct 1988 A: Fantastic Four. ... 3.00
- ❑17, Nov 1988 ... 3.00
- ❑18, Dec 1988 ... 3.00
- ❑19, Jan 1989 ... 3.00
- ❑20, Feb 1989 ... 3.00
- ❑21, Mar 1989 ... 3.00
- ❑22, Apr 1989 ... 3.00
- ❑23, May 1989 ... 3.00
- ❑24, Jun 1989 ... 3.00
- ❑25, Jul 1989; Giant-size V: new Super-Skrull. ... 3.50
- ❑26, Aug 1989 ... 2.50
- ❑27, Sep 1989 ... 2.50
- ❑28, Oct 1989 ... 2.50
- ❑29, Nov 1989 ... 2.50
- ❑30, Nov 1989 ... 2.50
- ❑31, Dec 1989; Giant-size ... 3.00
- ❑32, Dec 1989 ... 2.00
- ❑33, Jan 1990 ... 2.00
- ❑34, Feb 1990 A: Thanos. ... 5.00
- ❑35, Mar 1990; A: Thanos. Drax the Destroyer resurrected ... 3.50

Other grades: Multiply price above by 5/6 for VF/NM • 2/3 for VERY FINE • 1/3 for FINE • 1/5 for VERY GOOD • 1/8 for GOOD

Sisterhood of Steel

Life in the age of the longsword and crossbow
©Marvel

Six From Sirius

Moench and Gulacy's space opera
©Marvel

Six Million Dollar Man

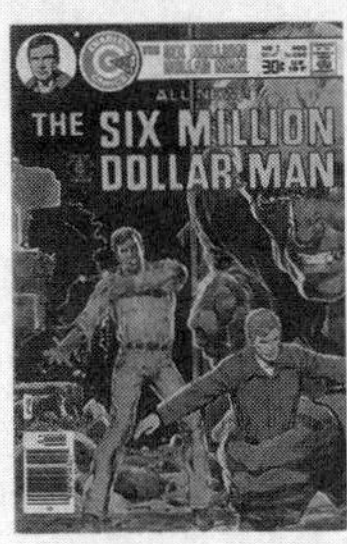

1970s TV hit was a good get for Charlton
©Charlton

Skull the Slayer

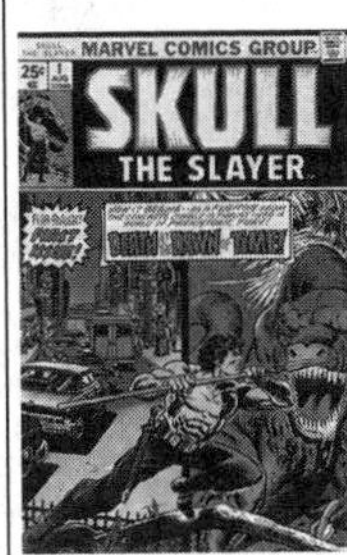

Dinosaurs and cavemen roam the earth
©Marvel

Slacker Comics

A tribute to high-school life and outcasts
©Slave Labor

N-MINT

❑36, Apr 1990 A: Thanos. 3.00
❑37, May 1990 A: Thanos. 3.00
❑38, Jun 1990 A: Thanos. A: Silver Surfer vs. Thanos 3.00
❑39, Jul 1990 A: Thanos. 2.00
❑40, Aug 1990 2.00
❑41, Sep 1990 2.00
❑42, Oct 1990 2.00
❑43, Nov 1990 2.00
❑44, Dec 1990 2.00
❑45, Jan 1991 2.00
❑46, Feb 1991; A: Adam Warlock. Return of Adam Warlock 2.50
❑47, Mar 1991 A: Warlock. 2.50
❑48, Apr 1991 2.00
❑49, May 1991 2.00
❑50, Jun 1991; JSn (w); O: Silver Surfer. Silver embossed cover 5.00
❑50/2nd, Jun 1991; JSn (w); O: Silver Surfer. Silver embossed cover 2.00
❑50/3rd, Jun 1991; JSn (w); O: Silver Surfer. Silver embossed cover 2.00
❑51, Jul 1991 2.00
❑52, Aug 1991 A: Firelord. A: Drax. 2.00
❑53, Aug 1991 2.00
❑54, Sep 1991 2.00
❑55, Sep 1991 2.00
❑56, Oct 1991 2.00
❑57, Oct 1991 A: Thanos. 2.00
❑58, Nov 1991 2.00
❑59, Nov 1991 2.00
❑60, Dec 1991 2.00
❑61, Jan 1992 2.00
❑62, Feb 1992 2.00
❑63, Mar 1992 2.00
❑64, Apr 1992 2.00
❑65, May 1992 2.00
❑66, Jun 1992 1: Avatar. 2.00
❑67, Jul 1992 2.00
❑68, Aug 1992 2.00
❑69, Aug 1992 1: Morg. 2.00
❑70, Sep 1992 O: Morg. 2.00
❑71, Sep 1992 2.00
❑72, Oct 1992 2.00
❑73, Oct 1992 2.00
❑74, Nov 1992 2.00
❑75, Nov 1992; D: Nova (female). silver foil cover 3.50
❑76, Dec 1992 1.50
❑77, Jan 1993 1.50
❑78, Feb 1993 1.50
❑79, Mar 1993 1.50
❑80, Apr 1993 1.50
❑81, May 1993 1.50
❑82, Jun 1993 1.75
❑83, Jul 1993 1.50
❑84, Aug 1993 1.50
❑85, Sep 1993; A: Wonder Man. A: Storm. A: Goddess. Infinity Crusade 1.50
❑85/CS, Sep 1993; A: Wonder Man. A: Storm. A: Goddess. "Dirtbag special"; Polybagged with Dirt #4; Infinity Crusade crossover 2.95
❑86, Oct 1993 1.50
❑87, Nov 1993 1.50
❑88, Jan 1994 1.50

N-MINT

❑89, Feb 1994 1.50
❑90, Mar 1994; Giant-size 1.95
❑91, Apr 1994 1.25
❑92, May 1994 1.50
❑93, Jun 1994 1.50
❑94, Jul 1994 1.50
❑95, Aug 1994 A: Fantastic Four. 1.50
❑96, Sep 1994 A: Fantastic Four. A: Hulk. 1.50
❑97, Oct 1994 1.50
❑98, Nov 1994 1.50
❑99, Dec 1994 1.50
❑100, Jan 1995; Giant-size 2.50
❑100/Variant, Jan 1995; Giant-size; enhanced cover 3.95
❑101, Feb 1995 1.50
❑102, Mar 1995 1.50
❑103, Apr 1995 1.50
❑104, May 1995 1.50
❑105, Jun 1995 V: Super-Skrull. 1.50
❑106, Jul 1995; Relinquishes Power Cosmic 1.50
❑107, Aug 1995 1.50
❑108, Sep 1995; Regains Power Cosmic 1.50
❑109, Oct 1995 1.50
❑110, Nov 1995 1.50
❑111, Dec 1995 GP (w) 1.50
❑112, Jan 1996 1.95
❑113, Feb 1996 1.95
❑114, Mar 1996 GP (w) 1.95
❑115, Apr 1996 1.95
❑116, May 1996 1.95
❑117, Jun 1996 1.95
❑118, Jul 1996 1.95
❑119, Aug 1996 1.95
❑120, Sep 1996 1.95
❑121, Oct 1996 1.95
❑122, Nov 1996 GP (w); V: Captain Marvel. 1.95
❑123, Dec 1996; Surfer returns to Earth 1.95
❑124, Jan 1997 A: Kymaera. 1.50
❑125, Feb 1997; Giant-size; V: Hulk. wraparound cover 2.99
❑126, Mar 1997 A: Doctor Strange. 1.99
❑127, Apr 1997 1.95
❑128, May 1997 A: Spider-Man, Daredevil. 1.99
❑129, Jun 1997 1.99
❑130, Aug 1997; gatefold summary 1.99
❑131, Sep 1997; gatefold summary 1.99
❑132, Oct 1997; gatefold summary 1.99
❑133, Nov 1997; gatefold summary A: Puppet Master. 1.99
❑134, Dec 1997; gatefold summary 1.99
❑135, Jan 1998; gatefold summary A: Agatha Harkness. 1.99
❑136, Feb 1998; gatefold summary 1.99
❑137, Mar 1998; gatefold summary A: Agatha Harkness. 1.99
❑138, Apr 1998; gatefold summary A: Thing. 1.99
❑139, May 1998; gatefold summary 1.99
❑140, Jun 1998; gatefold summary 1.99
❑141, Jul 1998; gatefold summary 1.99
❑142, Aug 1998; gatefold summary 1.99

N-MINT

❑143, Sep 1998; gatefold summary V: Psycho-Man. 1.99
❑144, Oct 1998; gatefold summary 1.99
❑145, Oct 1998; gatefold summary 1.99
❑146, Nov 1998; gatefold summary 1.99
❑Annual 1, ca. 1988 4.00
❑Annual 2, ca. 1989 3.00
❑Annual 3, ca. 1990 2.50
❑Annual 4, ca. 1991 O: The Silver Surfer. 2.50
❑Annual 5, ca. 1992 O: Nebula. 2.50
❑Annual 6, ca. 1993; 1: Legacy. A: Terrax. A: Jack of Hearts. A: Ronan the Accuser. A: Ganymede. trading card; Polybagged 2.95
❑Annual 7, ca. 1994 2.95
❑Annual 1997, ca. 1997; wraparound cover 4.00
❑Annual 1998, ca. 1998; gatefold summary; V: Millennius. Silver Surfer/Thor '98; wraparound cover. 2.99

SILVER SURFER (VOL. 4)
MARVEL

❑1, Sep 2003 2.25
❑2, Dec 2003 2.99
❑3, Jan 2004 2.99
❑4, Feb 2004 2.99
❑5, Mar 2004 2.25
❑6, Apr 2004 2.25
❑7, May 2004 2.99
❑8, Jun 2004 2.99
❑9, Jul 2004 2.99
❑10, Aug 2004 2.99
❑11, Sep 2004 2.99
❑12, Oct 2004 2.99
❑13, Nov 2004 2.99
❑14, Dec 2004 2.99

SILVER SURFER (ONE-SHOT)
MARVEL

❑1, Jun 1982 JBy, SL (w); JBy (a) 12.00

SILVER SURFER: DANGEROUS ARTIFACTS
MARVEL

❑1, Jun 1996 3.95

SILVER SURFER: INNER DEMONS
MARVEL

❑1, Apr 1998; collects Silver Surfer #123, 125, 126 3.50

SILVER SURFER: JUDGMENT DAY
MARVEL

❑1, Oct 1988; hardcover 14.95

SILVER SURFER: LOFTIER THAN MORTALS
MARVEL

❑1, Oct 1999 2.50
❑2, Nov 1999 2.50

SILVER SURFER/SUPERMAN
MARVEL

❑1, Nov 1996; prestige format; crossover with DC 5.95

SILVER SURFER VS. DRACULA
MARVEL

❑1, ca. 1994; Reprints Tomb of Dracula #50 1.75

Other grades: Multiply price above by 5/6 for VF/NM • 2/3 for VERY FINE • 1/3 for FINE • 1/5 for VERY GOOD • 1/8 for GOOD

SILVER SURFER/WARLOCK: RESURRECTION
MARVEL

❑1, Mar 1993 ... 2.50
❑2, Apr 1993 ... 2.50
❑3, May 1993 ... 2.50
❑4, Jun 1993 ... 2.50

SILVER SURFER/WEAPON ZERO
MARVEL

❑1, Apr 1997; crossover with Image .. 2.95

SILVER SWEETIE
SPOOF

❑1, b&w ... 2.95

SILVERWING SPECIAL
NOW

❑1, Jan 1987 ... 1.00

SIMON AND KIRBY CLASSICS
PURE IMAGINATION

❑1, Nov 1986; new Vagabond Prince and reprints from Stuntman #1, All-New #13 and Green Hornet #39 ... 2.00

SIMON CAT IN TAXI
SLAB-O-CONCRETE

❑1; Post card comics ... 1.50

SIMON SPECTOR (WARREN ELLIS'...)
AVATAR

❑1 2005 ... 3.50

SIMPSONS COMICS
BONGO

❑1, ca. 1993; Fantastic Four #1 homage cover; Bart Simpsons' Creepy Crawly Tales back-up ... 5.00
❑2, ca. 1994; V: Sideshow Bob. Patty & Selma's Ill-Fated Romance Comics back-up ... 4.00
❑3, ca. 1994; Krusty, Agent of K.L.O.W.N. back-up ... 3.00
❑4, ca. 1994; infinity cover; trading card; Gnarly Adventures of Busman back-up ... 3.00
❑5, ca. 1994; wraparound cover ... 3.00
❑6, ca. 1994; Chief Wiggum's Pre-Code Crime Comics back-up ... 2.50
❑7, ca. 1994; McBain Comics back-up 2.50
❑8, ca. 1995; Edna; Queen of the Jungle back-up ... 2.50
❑9, ca. 1995; Lisa's diary; Barney Gumble back-up ... 2.50
❑10, ca. 1995; Apu's Kwik-E Comics back-up ... 2.50
❑11, ca. 1995; evil Flanders; Homer on the Range back-up ... 2.25
❑12, ca. 1995; White-Knuckled War Stories back-up ... 2.25
❑13, ca. 1995; Jimbo Jones' Wedgie Comics back-up ... 2.25
❑14, ca. 1995; Cantankerous Coot Classics back-up ... 2.25
❑15, ca. 1995; Heinous Funnies back-up 2.25
❑16, ca. 1996; Bongo Grab Bag back-up 2.25
❑17, ca. 1996; Headlight Comics back-up 2.25
❑18, ca. 1996; Milhouse Comics back-up 2.25
❑19, ca. 1996; Roswell back-up ... 2.25
❑20, ca. 1996; Roswell back-up; Bad homage cover ... 2.25
❑21, ca. 1996; Roswell back-up ... 2.25
❑22, ca. 1996; Burns and Apu team up; Roswell back-up ... 2.25
❑23, ca. 1996; Reverend Lovejoy's Hellfire Comics back-up ... 2.25
❑24, ca. 1996; Li'l Homey back-up ... 2.25
❑25, ca. 1996; Marge gets her own talk show; Itchy & Scratchy back-up ... 2.25
❑26, ca. 1996; Speed parody ... 2.25
❑27, ca. 1996; Homer gets smart ... 2.25
❑28, ca. 1997; Krusty founds his own country ... 2.25
❑29, ca. 1997; Homer becomes a pro wrestler ... 2.25
❑30, ca. 1997; Burns clones Smithers 2.25
❑31, ca. 1997; Homer thinks he's Radioactive Man ... 2.25
❑32, ca. 1997; Krusty's coffee bar ... 2.95
❑33, ca. 1997; Alternate Springfield ... 2.25
❑34, ca. 1997; Burns sponsors Bart as a snowboarder ... 2.25
❑35, ca. 1998; Marge opens a daycare 2.25
❑36, ca. 1998; The return of the geeks 2.25
❑37, ca. 1998; El Grampo ... 2.25
❑38, ca. 1998; Burns makes addictive donuts ... 2.25
❑39, ca. 1998; Homer and Comic Book Guy on trial ... 2.25
❑40, ca. 1998; Krusty does live show from Simpsons house; Lard Lad back-up ... 2.50
❑41, ca. 1999 ... 2.50
❑42, ca. 1999; The Homer Show; Slobberwacky back-up ... 2.50
❑43, ca. 1999; story told backwards; Poochie back-up ... 2.50
❑44, ca. 1999; Lisa substitutes; Bartman back-up ... 2.50
❑45, ca. 1999; Hot Dog On A Schtick. 2.50
❑46, ca. 1999 A: Sideshow Bob. ... 2.50
❑47, ca. 2000 ... 2.50
❑48, ca. 2000 ... 2.50
❑49, ca. 2000 ... 2.50
❑50, ca. 2000; Giant-size ... 2.50
❑51, ca. 2000; Cletus back-up ... 2.50
❑52, ca. 2000 ... 2.50
❑53, ca. 2000; Ned Flanders back-up . 2.50
❑54, ca. 2000 ... 2.50
❑55, ca. 2001 ... 2.50
❑55/2nd, ca. 2001 ... 2.50
❑56, ca. 2001 ... 2.50
❑56/2nd, ca. 1992 ... 2.50
❑57, ca. 2001 ... 2.50
❑58, ca. 2001 ... 2.50
❑59, ca. 2001 ... 2.50
❑60, ca. 2001 ... 2.50
❑61, ca. 2001 ... 2.50
❑62, ca. 2001 ... 2.50
❑63, ca. 2001 ... 2.50
❑64, ca. 2001 ... 2.50
❑65 ... 2.50
❑66, ca. 2002 ... 2.50
❑67, ca. 2002 ... 2.50
❑68, ca. 2002 ... 2.50
❑69, ca. 2002 ... 2.50
❑70, ca. 2002 ... 2.50
❑71, ca. 2002 ... 2.50
❑72, ca. 2002 ... 2.50
❑73, ca. 2002 ... 2.50
❑74, ca. 2002 ... 2.50
❑75, ca. 2002 ... 2.50
❑76, ca. 2002 ... 2.50
❑77 ... 2.50
❑78, ca. 2003 ... 2.50
❑79, ca. 2003 ... 2.50
❑80, ca. 2003 ... 2.50
❑81, ca. 2003 ... 2.50
❑82, ca. 2003 ... 2.50
❑83, Jun 2003 ... 2.50
❑84, Jul 2003 ... 2.50
❑85, Aug 2003 ... 2.99
❑86, Sep 2003 ... 2.99
❑87, Oct 2003 ... 2.99
❑88, Nov 2003 ... 2.99
❑89, Dec 2003 ... 2.99
❑90, Jan 2004 ... 2.99
❑91, Feb 2004 ... 2.99
❑92, Mar 2004 ... 2.99
❑93, Apr 2004 ... 2.99
❑94, May 2004 ... 2.99
❑95, Jun 2004 ... 2.99
❑96, Jul 2004 ... 2.99
❑97, Aug 2004 ... 2.99
❑98, Sep 2004 ... 2.99
❑99, Oct 2004 ... 2.99
❑100, Nov 2004 ... 2.99
❑101, Dec 2004 ... 2.99
❑102, Jan 2005 ... 2.99
❑103, Feb 2005 ... 2.99
❑104, Mar 2005 ... 2.99
❑105, Apr 2005 ... 2.99
❑106, May 2005 ... 2.99
❑107, Jun 2005 ... 2.99
❑108, Jul 2005 ... 2.99
❑109, Sep 2005 ... 2.99

SIMPSONS COMICS AND STORIES
WELSH

❑1, ca. 1993; O: Bartman. 1: The Simpsons. with poster ... 4.00

SIMPSONS COMICS (MAGAZINE)
BONGO

❑1, Mar 1997 ... 4.00
❑2, Apr 1997 ... 3.25
❑3, May 1997 ... 3.25
❑4, Jun 1997 ... 3.25
❑5, Jul 1997 ... 3.25
❑6, Aug 1997 ... 3.25
❑7, Sep 1997 ... 3.25
❑8, Oct 1997 ... 3.25
❑9, Nov 1997 ... 3.25
❑10, Dec 1997 ... 3.25
❑11, Jan 1998 ... 3.25
❑12, Feb 1998 ... 3.25
❑13, Mar 1998 ... 3.25
❑14, Apr 1998 ... 3.25
❑15, May 1998 ... 3.25
❑16, Jun 1998 ... 3.25
❑17, Jul 1998 ... 3.25
❑18, Aug 1998 ... 3.25
❑19, Sep 1998 ... 3.25
❑20, Oct 1998 ... 3.25
❑21, Nov 1998 ... 3.25
❑22, Dec 1998 ... 3.25
❑23, Jan 1999 ... 3.25
❑24, Feb 1999 ... 3.25
❑25, Mar 1999; Reprints Bartman #1 . 3.25

SIMPSONS COMICS PRESENTS BART SIMPSON
BONGO

❑1 2000 ... 2.50
❑2 2000 ... 2.50
❑3 2001 ... 2.50
❑4 2001 ... 2.50
❑5 2001 ... 2.50
❑6 2001 ... 2.50
❑7 2002 ... 2.50
❑8 2002 ... 2.50
❑9 2002 ... 2.50
❑10 2002 ... 2.50
❑11 2003 ... 2.50
❑12 2003 ... 2.50
❑13, Sep 2003 ... 2.99
❑14, Oct 2003 ... 2.99
❑15, Dec 2003 ... 2.99
❑16, Feb 2004 ... 2.99
❑17, Apr 2004 ... 2.99
❑18, Jun 2004 ... 2.99
❑19, Aug 2004 ... 2.99
❑20, ca. 2004 ... 2.99
❑21 2005 ... 2.99
❑22 2005 ... 2.99
❑23 2005 ... 2.99
❑24 2005 ... 2.99
❑25, Oct 2005; Cover reads "Prince of Pranks" ... 2.99
❑26 2005; Cover reads "Big Spender" 2.99

SIMPSONS/FUTURAMA CROSSOVER CRISIS PART 2
BONGO

❑1, Jan 2005 ... 2.99

SIMPSONS SUPER SPECTACULAR
BONGO

❑1, Oct 2005 ... 4.99

SIMULATORS
NEATLY CHISELED FEATURES

❑1 ... 2.50

SIN
TRAGEDY STRIKES

❑1, b&w ... 2.95
❑2, b&w ... 2.95
❑3, b&w ... 2.95

SINBAD
ADVENTURE

❑1, Nov 1989, b&w; cardstock cover . 2.25
❑2, Dec 1989, b&w; cardstock cover .. 2.25
❑3, Jan 1990, b&w; cardstock cover .. 2.25
❑4, Mar 1990, b&w ... 2.25

SINBAD BOOK II
ADVENTURE

❑1, Mar 1991, b&w ... 2.50
❑2, Apr 1991, b&w ... 2.50
❑3, May 1991, b&w ... 2.50
❑4, Jun 1991, b&w ... 2.50

Other grades: Multiply price above by 5/6 for VF/NM • 2/3 for VERY FINE • 1/3 for FINE • 1/5 for VERY GOOD • 1/8 for GOOD

Slash Maraud

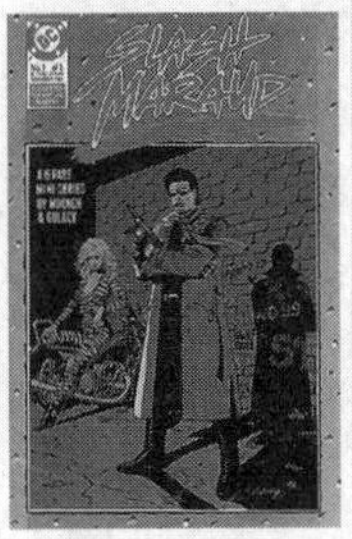

Earth is overrun by aliens in the future

©DC

Sliders

TV series was a modest SF hit

©Acclaim

Slimer!

Uses the "pet" ghost from Ghostbusters

©Now

Slingers

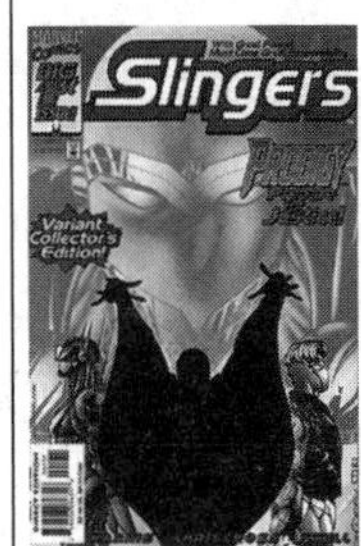

Characters based on aspects of Spider-Man

©Marvel

Smith Brown Jones

Goofy send-up of 1990s X-Files culture

©Kiwi

	N-MINT

SIN CITY (DARK HORSE)
Dark Horse

❑1, Jan 1993	15.00
❑1/HC, Dec 1994	30.00
❑1/Ltd.	100.00
❑1/2nd	15.00
❑1/3rd	15.00
❑1/4th	15.00
❑1/5th	15.00
❑1/6th	15.00
❑Deluxe 1; 1st edition in slipcase	30.00

SIN CITY (COZMIC)
Cozmic

❑1	1.50

SIN CITY: A DAME TO KILL FOR
Dark Horse

❑1/2nd, Jul 1994	2.95
❑1, Nov 1993, b&w FM (w); FM (a)	3.50
❑2, Jan 1994, b&w FM (w); FM (a)	3.25
❑3, Feb 1994, b&w FM (w); FM (a)	3.00
❑4, Mar 1994, b&w FM (w); FM (a)	3.00
❑5, Apr 1994, b&w FM (w); FM (a)	3.00
❑6, May 1994, b&w FM (w); FM (a)	3.00

SIN CITY ANGELS
Fantagraphics

❑1, Dec 2004	3.95

SIN CITY: FAMILY VALUES
Dark Horse

❑1, Oct 1997, b&w FM (w); FM (a)	15.00
❑1/A, Oct 1997, FM (w); FM (a); Cover has Roller-skating girl	18.00
❑1/Ltd., Oct 1997, Limited edition hardcover FM (w); FM (a)	75.00

SIN CITY: HELL AND BACK
Dark Horse / Maverick

❑1, Jul 1999, b&w; cardstock cover	2.95
❑2, Aug 1999, b&w; cardstock cover	2.95
❑3, Sep 1999, b&w; cardstock cover	2.95
❑4, Oct 1999, b&w; cardstock cover	2.95
❑5, Nov 1999, b&w; cardstock cover	2.95
❑6, Dec 1999, b&w; cardstock cover	2.95
❑7, Jan 2000, b&w; cardstock cover	2.95
❑8, b&w; cardstock cover	2.95
❑9, Apr 2000, b&w; cardstock cover	2.95

SIN CITY: JUST ANOTHER SATURDAY NIGHT
Dark Horse

❑½, Aug 1997, Wizard promotional edition FM (w); FM (a)	3.00
❑1, Oct 1998, b&w FM (w); FM (a)	2.50

SIN CITY: LOST, LONELY, & LETHAL
Dark Horse / Legend

❑1, Dec 1996, Cardstock cover; b&w and blue	2.95

SIN CITY: SEX & VIOLENCE
Dark Horse

❑1, Mar 1997, b&w; cardstock cover	2.95

SIN CITY: SILENT NIGHT
Dark Horse / Legend

❑1, Nov 1995, b&w; cardstock cover	2.95

	N-MINT

SIN CITY: THAT YELLOW BASTARD
Dark Horse / Legend

❑1, Feb 1996	2.95
❑2, Mar 1996	2.95
❑3, Apr 1996	2.95
❑4, May 1996	2.95
❑5, Jun 1996	2.95
❑6, Jul 1996	3.50

SIN CITY: THE BABE WORE RED AND OTHER STORIES
Dark Horse

❑1, Nov 1994	2.95

SIN CITY: THE BIG FAT KILL
Dark Horse

❑1, Nov 1994, b&w	2.95
❑2, Dec 1994, b&w; cardstock cover	2.95
❑3, Jan 1995, b&w; cardstock cover	2.95
❑4, Feb 1995, b&w; cardstock cover	2.95
❑5, Mar 1995, b&w; cardstock cover	2.95

SINDY
Forbidden Fruit

❑1, b&w	2.95
❑2, b&w	2.95
❑3, b&w	2.95
❑4, b&w	2.95
❑5, b&w	2.95

SINERGY
Caliber

❑1, ca. 1994, b&w	2.95
❑1/Ltd., ca. 1994; limited edition	5.95
❑2, ca. 1994, b&w	2.95
❑2/Ltd., ca. 1994; limited edition	5.95
❑3, ca. 1994, b&w	2.95
❑3/Ltd., ca. 1994; limited edition	5.95
❑4, ca. 1994, b&w	2.95
❑4/Ltd., ca. 1994; limited edition	5.95
❑5, ca. 1994, b&w	2.95
❑5/Ltd., ca. 1994; limited edition	5.95

SINGULARITY 7
Idea & Design Works

❑1 2004	3.99
❑2 2004	3.99
❑3 2004	3.99
❑4 2004	3.99

SINISTER HOUSE OF SECRET LOVE
DC

❑1, Oct 1971	125.00
❑2, Dec 1971 JO (w); TD (a)	75.00
❑3, Feb 1972	75.00
❑4, Apr 1972; TD (a); Series continued in Secrets of Sinister House #5	75.00

SINISTER ROMANCE
Harrier

❑1, b&w	2.00
❑2, b&w	2.00
❑3, b&w	1.95
❑4, b&w	1.95

SINJA: DEADLY SINS
Lightning

❑1	3.00
❑1/A; Commemorative edition	5.95
❑1/B; Nude edition	9.95

	N-MINT

SINJA: RESURRECTION
Lightning

❑1, Aug 1996; flipbook with Kunoichi #1; indicia says Sinja: Resurrection; cover says Kunoichi	3.00

SINNAMON (VOL. 1)
Catfish

❑1, Dec 1995	2.50

SINNAMON (VOL. 2)
Catfish

❑1 1996	2.75
❑2 1996	2.75
❑3 1996	2.75
❑4 1996	2.75
❑4/Variant 1996; Variant cover edition (500 printed)	5.00
❑5 1996	2.75
❑5/Variant 1996; Variant cover edition (500 printed)	4.00
❑6 1996	2.75
❑7 1996	2.75
❑8 1996; Sinnamon vs. Aerobica	2.75

SINNER
Fantagraphics

❑1	2.95
❑2	2.95
❑3	2.95
❑4	2.95
❑5	2.95

SINNERS
DC / Piranha

❑1	9.95

SINNIN!
Fantagraphics / Eros

❑1, b&w	2.25
❑2, b&w	2.25

SIN OF THE MUMMY
Fantagraphics / Eros

❑1, b&w	2.50

SINS OF YOUTH: AQUABOY/ LAGOON MAN
DC

❑1, May 2000	2.50

SINS OF YOUTH: BATBOY AND ROBIN
DC

❑1, May 2000	2.50

SINS OF YOUTH: JLA, JR.
DC

❑1, May 2000	2.50

SINS OF YOUTH: KID FLASH/IMPULSE
DC

❑1, May 2000	2.50

SINS OF YOUTH SECRET FILES
DC

❑1, May 2000	4.95

SINS OF YOUTH: STARWOMAN AND THE JSA (JUNIOR SOCIETY)
DC

❑1, May 2000	2.50

SINS OF YOUTH: SUPERMAN, JR./ SUPERBOY, SR.
DC
❑1, May 2000 .... 2.50

SINS OF YOUTH: THE SECRET/DEADBOY
DC
❑1, May 2000 .... 2.50

SINS OF YOUTH: WONDER GIRLS
DC
❑1, May 2000 .... 2.50

SINTHIA
LIGHTNING
❑1/A, Oct 1997 .... 2.95
❑1/B, Oct 1997; alternate cover 2.95
❑1/Platinum, Oct 1997; Platinum edition 4.00
❑2/A, Jan 1998 .... 3.00
❑2/B, Jan 1998 .... 3.00

SIR CHARLES BARKLEY AND THE REFEREE MURDERS
HAMILTON
❑1, ca. 1993 .... 9.95

SIREN (MALIBU)
MALIBU / ULTRAVERSE
❑0, Sep 1995; Black September; #Infinity 1.50
❑0/A, Sep 1995; alternate cover 1.50
❑1, Oct 1995 .... 1.50
❑2, Nov 1995 .... 1.50
❑3, Dec 1995; continues in Siren Special #1 .... 1.50
❑Special 1, Feb 1996 .... 1.95

SIREN: SHAPES
IMAGE
❑1, May 1998 .... 2.95
❑2, Sep 1998 .... 2.95

SIRENS OF THE LOST WORLD
COMAX
❑1, b&w 2.95

SIRIUS GALLERY
SIRIUS
❑1, ca. 1997 .... 3.00
❑2, Apr 1999; cardstock cover; pin-ups 3.00
❑3, Jun 2000; no cover price; pin-ups 3.00

SISTER ARMAGEDDON
DRACULINA
❑1, 1: Sister Armageddon 2.75
❑2, b&w 2.75
❑3, b&w 3.00
❑4 .... 3.00

SISTERHOOD OF STEEL
MARVEL / EPIC
❑1, Dec 1984 .... 2.00
❑2, Feb 1985 .... 2.00
❑3, Apr 1985 .... 2.00
❑4, Jun 1985 .... 2.00
❑5, Aug 1985 .... 2.00
❑6, Oct 1985 .... 2.00
❑7, Dec 1985 .... 2.00
❑8, Feb 1986 .... 2.00

SISTER RED
COMICSONE
❑1, Feb 2004 .... 9.95
❑2, Apr 2004 .... 9.95

SISTERS OF DARKNESS
ILLUSTRATION
❑1/A 1997; Adult cover 3.25
❑1/B 1997; tame cover 3.25
❑2/A 1997; Adult cover 3.25
❑2/B 1997; tame cover 3.25
❑3, Aug 1997 .... 3.25

SISTERS OF MERCY
MAXIMUM
❑1, Dec 1995 .... 2.50
❑1/A, Dec 1995; alternate cover 2.50
❑2 1996 .... 2.50
❑3 1996 .... 2.50
❑4 1996 .... 2.50
❑5 1996 .... 2.50

SISTERS OF MERCY (VOL. 2)
LONDON NIGHT
❑0, Mar 1997 .... 1.50

SISTERS OF MERCY: WHEN RAZORS CRY CRIMSON TEARS
NO MERCY
❑1, Oct 1996 .... 2.50

SISTER VAMPIRE
ANGEL
❑1 .... 2.95

6, THE
VIRTUAL
❑1, Oct 1996 .... 2.50
❑2, Nov 1996 .... 2.50
❑3, Dec 1996 .... 2.50

SIX
IMAGE
❑0 2005 .... 5.99

6, THE: LETHAL ORIGINS
VIRTUAL
❑1, May 1996, digest 3.99

SIX DEGREES
HERETIC
❑1, b&w 3.50
❑1/Autographed 6.00
❑2, b&w 2.95
❑3, b&w 2.95
❑4, b&w 2.95
❑5, b&w 2.95

SIX FROM SIRIUS
MARVEL / EPIC
❑1, Jul 1984 PG (c); PG (a) 2.00
❑2, Aug 1984 PG (c); PG (a) 2.00
❑3, Sep 1984 PG (c); PG (a) 2.00
❑4, Oct 1984 PG (c); PG (a) 2.00

SIX FROM SIRIUS 2
MARVEL / EPIC
❑1, Feb 1986 PG (c); PG (a) 2.00
❑2, Mar 1986 PG (c); PG (a) 2.00
❑3, Apr 1986 PG (c); PG (a) 2.00
❑4, May 1986 PG (c); PG (a) 2.00

SIX-GUN HEROES (CHARLTON)
CHARLTON
❑40, ca. 1956 .... 55.00
❑41, ca. 1956 .... 48.00
❑42, ca. 1957 .... 48.00
❑43, ca. 1957 .... 48.00
❑44, ca. 1957 .... 48.00
❑45, ca. 1957 .... 48.00
❑46, ca. 1957 .... 48.00
❑47, Jul 1958 .... 48.00
❑48, Sep 1958 .... 48.00
❑49, Nov 1958 .... 48.00
❑50, Feb 1959 .... 48.00
❑51, ca. 1959 .... 32.00
❑52, Jul 1959 .... 32.00
❑53, Sep 1959 .... 32.00
❑54, Nov 1959 .... 32.00
❑55, Jan 1959 .... 32.00
❑56, Mar 1960 .... 32.00
❑57, May 1960 .... 32.00
❑58, Jul 1960 .... 32.00
❑59, Sep 1960 .... 32.00
❑60, Nov 1960 .... 32.00
❑61, Jan 1961 .... 22.00
❑62, Mar 1961 .... 22.00
❑63, May 1961 .... 22.00
❑64, Jul 1961 .... 22.00
❑65, Sep 1961 .... 22.00
❑66, Dec 1961 .... 22.00
❑67, ca. 1962 .... 22.00
❑68, ca. 1962 .... 22.00
❑69, Jul 1962, Gunmaster, Wyatt Earp, and Annie Oakley 22.00
❑70, Sep 1962 .... 22.00
❑71, Nov 1962 .... 16.00
❑72, Jan 1963 .... 16.00
❑73, Mar 1963 .... 16.00
❑74, May 1963 .... 16.00
❑75, Jul 1963 .... 16.00
❑76, Sep 1963 .... 16.00
❑77, Nov 1963, Gunmaster, Wyatt Earp, and Annie Oakley 16.00
❑78, Jan 1964 .... 16.00
❑79, Mar 1964 .... 16.00
❑80, Sep 1964 .... 16.00
❑81, Nov 1964 .... 16.00
❑82, Jan 1965 .... 16.00
❑83, Mar 1965 .... 16.00

SIX-GUN SAMURAI
ALIAS
❑1, Sep 2005 .... 0.75
❑2, Nov 2005 ....

SIX MILLION DOLLAR MAN
CHARLTON
❑1, Jun 1976, JSa (a); O: The Six Million Dollar Man. 1: The Six Million Dollar Man (in comics) 12.00
❑2, Aug 1976, JSa (a); Nicola Cuti, Joe Staton credits; Action figure tie-in .. 6.00
❑3, Oct 1976, JSa (a); Nicola Cuti, Joe Staton credits 5.00
❑4, Dec 1977 .... 5.00
❑5, Oct 1977 .... 5.00
❑6, Feb 1978 .... 4.00
❑7, Mar 1978, Boyette and Himes credits 4.00
❑8, May 1978 .... 4.00
❑9, Jun 1978 .... 4.00

SIX MILLION DOLLAR MAN (MAGAZINE)
CHARLTON
❑1 .... 10.00
❑2 .... 8.00
❑3 .... 5.00
❑4 .... 5.00
❑5 .... 5.00
❑6 .... 5.00
❑7 .... 5.00

666: THE MARK OF THE BEAST
FLEETWAY-QUALITY
❑1, ca. 1986 .... 2.50
❑2, ca. 1986 .... 2.00
❑3, ca. 1986 .... 2.00
❑4, ca. 1986 .... 2.00
❑5, ca. 1986 .... 2.00
❑6, ca. 1986 .... 2.00
❑7, ca. 1986 .... 2.00
❑8, ca. 1986 .... 2.00
❑9, ca. 1986 .... 2.00
❑10, ca. 1987 .... 2.00
❑11, ca. 1987 .... 2.00
❑12, ca. 1987; AMo (w); Alan Moore special 2.00
❑13, ca. 1987 .... 2.00
❑14, ca. 1987 .... 2.00
❑15, ca. 1987 .... 2.00
❑16, ca. 1987 .... 2.00
❑17, ca. 1987 .... 2.00
❑18, ca. 1987 .... 2.00

SIX STRING SAMURAI
AWESOME
❑1, Sep 1998 .... 2.95

SIXTY NINE
FANTAGRAPHICS / EROS
❑1, ca. 1993 .... 2.75
❑2 .... 2.75
❑3 .... 2.75
❑4, Jul 1994, b&w 2.75

67 SECONDS
MARVEL / EPIC
❑1 .... 15.95

SIZZLE THEATRE
SLAVE LABOR
❑1, Aug 1991, b&w 2.50

SIZZLIN' SISTERS
FANTAGRAPHICS / EROS
❑1 1997 .... 2.95
❑2, Aug 1997 .... 2.95

SKATEMAN
PACIFIC
❑1, Nov 1983 .... 1.50

SKELETON GIRL
SLAVE LABOR
❑1, Dec 1995 .... 2.95
❑2, Apr 1996 .... 2.95
❑3, Sep 1996 .... 2.95

SKELETON HAND (2ND SERIES)
AVALON
❑1 .... 2.99

Other grades: Multiply price above by 5/6 for VF/NM • 2/3 for VERY FINE • 1/3 for FINE • 1/5 for VERY GOOD • 1/8 for GOOD

Smurfs

Relic from a long-dead period of madness

©Marvel

Snarf

Short black-and-white stories by top talent

©Kitchen Sink

Sock Monkey

Tony Millionaire's odd adventurer

©Dark Horse

Sojourn (CrossGen)

Popular addition to the CrossGen universe

©CrossGen

Solar, Man of the Atom

Popular relaunch of old Gold Key character

©Valiant

N-MINT

SKELETON KEY
AMAZE INK

❑1, Jul 1995 .... 2.00
❑2, Aug 1995 .... 2.00
❑3, Sep 1995 .... 2.00
❑4, Oct 1995 .... 2.00
❑5, Nov 1995 .... 2.00
❑6, Dec 1995 .... 2.00
❑7, Jan 1996 .... 2.00
❑8, Feb 1996 .... 2.00
❑9, Mar 1996 .... 2.00
❑10, Apr 1996 .... 2.00
❑11, May 1996 .... 1.75
❑12, Jun 1996 .... 1.75
❑13, Jul 1996 .... 1.75
❑14, Aug 1996 .... 1.75
❑15, Sep 1996, cover says Aug, indicia says Sep 1.75
❑16, Oct 1996 .... 1.75
❑17, Nov 1996 .... 1.75
❑18, Dec 1996 .... 1.75
❑19, Jan 1997 .... 1.75
❑20, Feb 1997 .... 1.75
❑21, Mar 1997 .... 1.75
❑22, Apr 1997 .... 1.75
❑23, May 1997 .... 1.75
❑24, Jun 1997 .... 1.75
❑25, Jul 1997 .... 1.75
❑26, Aug 1997 .... 1.75
❑27, Sep 1997 .... 1.75
❑28, Oct 1997 .... 1.75
❑29, Nov 1997 .... 1.75
❑30, Dec 1997 .... 1.75

SKELETON WARRIORS
MARVEL

❑1, Apr 1995 .... 1.50
❑2, May 1995 .... 1.50
❑3, Jun 1995 .... 1.50
❑4, Jul 1995 .... 1.50

SKETCHBOOK SERIES
TUNDRA

❑1, Melting Pot 3.95
❑2, Totleben 3.95
❑3, Zulli 3.95
❑4 .... 3.95
❑5 .... 3.95
❑6, Screaming Masks 3.95
❑7 .... 3.95
❑8, Forg 3.95
❑9 .... 3.95
❑10 .... 4.95

SKIDMARKS
TUNDRA

❑0, b&w 2.95
❑1, b&w 2.95
❑2, b&w 2.95
❑3, b&w 2.95

SKID ROZE
LONDON NIGHT

❑1, Jul 1998 .... 2.00

SKIM LIZARD
PUPPY TOSS

❑1 .... 2.95

N-MINT

SKIN
TUNDRA

❑1 .... 8.95

SKIN GRAFT
ICONOGRAFIX

❑1, b&w 3.50

SKIN GRAFT: THE ADVENTURES OF A TATTOOED MAN
DC / VERTIGO

❑1, Jul 1993 .... 2.50
❑2, Aug 1993 .... 2.50
❑3, Sep 1993 .... 2.50
❑4, Oct 1993 .... 2.50

SKINHEADS IN LOVE
FANTAGRAPHICS / EROS

❑1, b&w 2.25

SKINNERS
IMAGE

❑1/A 2.95
❑1/B 2.95
❑1/C 2.95

SKIN13
EXPRESS / PARODY

❑½/A, Oct 1995, b&w; Amazing SKIN Thir-Teen; reprints Skin13 #1 .... 2.50
❑½/B, Oct 1995, b&w; Barbari-SKIN; reprints Skin13 #1 .... 2.50
❑½/C, Oct 1995, b&w; SKIN-et Jackson; reprints Skin13 #1 .... 2.50
❑½/A/2nd 2.50
❑½/B/2nd 2.50
❑½/C/2nd 2.50
❑1/A, b&w 2.50
❑1/B, b&w; Heavy Metal-style cover .. 2.50
❑1/C, b&w; Spider-Man #1-style cover 2.50

SKIZZ
FLEETWAY-QUALITY

❑1 .... 1.95
❑2 .... 1.95
❑3 .... 1.95

SKREEMER
DC

❑1, May 1989 .... 2.00
❑2, Jun 1989 .... 2.00
❑3, Jul 1989 .... 2.00
❑4, Aug 1989 .... 2.00
❑5, Sep 1989 .... 2.00
❑6, Oct 1989 .... 2.00

SKROG
COMICO

❑1, b&w 1.50

SKROG (YIP, YIP, YAY) SPECIAL
CRYSTAL

❑1, b&w 2.50

SKRULL KILL KREW
MARVEL

❑1, Sep 1995; cardstock cover 2.95
❑2, Oct 1995; cardstock cover 2.95
❑3, Nov 1995; cardstock cover 2.95
❑4, Dec 1995; cardstock cover 2.95
❑5, Jan 1996; cardstock cover 2.95

N-MINT

SKULKER
THORBY

❑1 .... 2.95

SKULL & BONES
DC

❑1, ca. 1992 .... 4.95
❑2, ca. 1992 .... 4.95
❑3, ca. 1992 .... 4.95

SKULL COMICS
LAST GASP

❑1 .... 18.00
❑2, Jan 1970 .... 10.00
❑3 .... 6.00
❑4 .... 6.00
❑5, Jan 1972 .... 6.00
❑6, Jun 1972 .... 6.00

SKULL THE SLAYER
MARVEL

❑1, Aug 1975, GK (c); GK (a); O: Skull the Slayer. 12.00
❑2, Nov 1975 .... 5.00
❑3, Jan 1976 .... 1.50
❑4, Mar 1976 .... 4.00
❑5, May 1976 .... 4.00
❑5/30 cent, May 1976, 30 cent regional price variant 20.00
❑6, Jul 1976 .... 3.00
❑6/30 cent, Jul 1976, 30 cent regional price variant 20.00
❑7, Sep 1976 .... 3.00
❑8, Nov 1976 .... 3.00

SKUNK
MU

❑1, Dec 1993, b&w 2.50

SKUNK
EXPRESS / ENTITY

❑1, ca. 1996 .... 2.75
❑2, ca. 1996 .... 2.75
❑3, Jul 1996, b&w; cover says #tree .. 2.75
❑4, Sep 1996, b&w 2.75
❑5, Sep 1996, b&w; cover says Cinco de Mayo 2.75
❑6, Oct 1996, b&w; cover says #sick . 2.75
❑GN 1, ca. 1996, Collects issues #1-3 4.75

SKY APE (LES ADVENTURES)
SLAVE LABOR

❑1, Jun 1997, b&w 2.95
❑2, Sep 1997, b&w 2.95
❑3, Jan 1998, b&w 2.95

SKY COMICS PRESENTS MONTHLY
SKY COMICS

❑1, b&w 2.50

SKYE BLUE
MU

❑1, b&w 2.50
❑2, b&w 2.50
❑3 .... 2.50

SKYE RUNNER
DC

❑1, Jul 2006 .... 2.99
❑2, Aug 2006 .... 2.99

SKY GAL
AC

❑1; some reprint; Reprints Sky Gal stories from Jumbo Comics #68, others plus new story ... 3.95
❑2; some color; some reprint; Reprints Sky Gal stories from Jumbo Comics plus new story ... 3.95
❑3; some color; some reprint; Reprints Sky Gal stories from Jumbo Comics plus new story ... 3.95

SKY MASTERS
PURE IMAGINATION

❑1, ca. 1991, b&w; strip reprints ... 7.95

SKYNN & BONES
BRAINSTORM

❑1 ... 2.95

SKYNN & BONES: DEADLY ANGELS
BRAINSTORM

❑1 ... 2.95

SKYWOLF
ECLIPSE

❑1, Mar 1988 ... 2.00
❑2, May 1988 ... 2.00
❑3, Oct 1988 ... 2.00

SLACKER COMICS
SLAVE LABOR

❑1, Aug 1994 ... 3.00
❑1/2nd, Apr 1995 ... 2.95
❑2, Nov 1994 ... 2.95
❑3, Feb 1995 ... 2.95
❑4, May 1995 ... 2.95
❑5, Sep 1995 ... 2.95
❑6, Dec 1995 ... 2.95
❑7, Feb 1996 ... 2.95
❑8, May 1996 ... 2.95
❑9, Aug 1996 ... 2.95
❑10 1996 ... 2.95
❑11, Jan 1997 ... 2.95
❑12 1997 ... 2.95
❑13, Apr 1997 ... 2.95
❑14, May 1997; Slacker Annual; Also titled "Annual #1" ... 2.95
❑15 1997; no indicia ... 2.95
❑16, Apr 1998 ... 2.95
❑17, Jul 1998 ... 2.95
❑18, Oct 1998 ... 2.95

SLÁINE THE BERSERKER
FLEETWAY-QUALITY

❑1, Jul 1987 ... 1.50
❑2, Aug 1987 ... 1.50
❑3, Sep 1987 ... 1.50
❑4, Oct 1987 ... 1.50
❑5, Nov 1987 ... 1.50
❑6, Dec 1987 ... 1.50
❑7, Jan 1988 ... 1.50
❑8, Feb 1988 ... 1.50
❑9, Mar 1988 ... 1.50
❑10, Apr 1988 ... 1.50
❑11, May 1988 ... 1.50
❑12, Jun 1988 ... 1.50
❑13, Jul 1988 ... 1.50
❑14, Aug 1988; double issue #14/15 ... 1.50
❑16, Sep 1988; double issue #16/17 ... 1.50
❑18, Oct 1988 ... 1.50
❑19, Nov 1988 ... 1.50
❑20, Dec 1988 ... 1.50

SLÁINE THE HORNED GOD
FLEETWAY-QUALITY

❑1, ca. 1990 ... 3.50
❑2 ... 3.00
❑3 ... 3.00
❑4 ... 3.00
❑5 ... 3.00
❑6 ... 3.00

SLÁINE THE KING
FLEETWAY-QUALITY

❑21, Jan 1989 ... 1.50
❑22, Feb 1989 ... 1.50
❑23 1989 ... 1.50
❑24 1989 ... 1.50
❑25 1989 ... 1.50
❑26 1989 ... 1.50
❑27 1989 ... 1.50
❑28 1989 ... 1.50

SLAM DUNK KINGS
PERSONALITY

❑1, Mar 1992, b&w; Michael Jordan ... 2.95
❑2 1992, b&w ... 2.95
❑3 1992, b&w ... 2.95
❑4 1992, b&w ... 2.95

SLAPSTICK
MARVEL

❑1, Nov 1992 ... 1.25
❑2, Dec 1992 ... 1.25
❑3, Jan 1993 ... 1.25
❑4, Feb 1993 ... 1.25

SLASH
NORTHSTAR

❑1, Aug 1993, b&w ... 2.75
❑1/Special, Aug 1993 ... 4.95
❑2 1993, b&w ... 2.95
❑3 1993, b&w ... 2.95
❑4 1993, b&w ... 2.95
❑5, Oct 1993 ... 2.95

SLASH MARAUD
DC

❑1, Nov 1987 PG (c); PG (a) ... 2.25
❑2, Dec 1987 PG (c); PG (a) ... 2.00
❑3, Jan 1988 PG (c); PG (a) ... 2.00
❑4, Feb 1988 PG (c); PG (a) ... 2.00
❑5, Mar 1988 PG (c); PG (a) ... 2.00
❑6, Apr 1988 PG (c); PG (a) ... 2.00

SLAUGHTERMAN
COMICO

❑1, b&w ... 3.50
❑2, b&w ... 3.50

SLAVE GIRL
ETERNITY

❑1, Mar 1989, b&w; Reprints ... 2.25

SLAVE LABOR STORIES
SLAVE LABOR

❑1, Feb 1992, b&w; Doctor Radium ... 2.95
❑2, Apr 1992, b&w; Milk & Cheese ... 2.95
❑3, Jul 1992, b&w; Bill the Clown ... 2.95
❑4, Nov 1992, b&w; Samurai Penguin 2.95

SLAVE PIT FUNNIES
SLAVE PIT

❑1 ... 4.95

SLAYERS
CPM MANGA

❑1, Oct 1998 ... 2.95
❑2, Nov 1998 ... 2.95
❑3, Dec 1998 ... 2.95
❑4, Jan 1999 ... 2.95
❑5, Feb 1999 ... 2.95

SLAYERS
TOKYOPOP

❑1, Sep 2004 ... 9.99
❑2, Dec 2004 ... 9.99
❑3, Mar 2005 ... 9.99
❑4, Jun 2005 ... 9.99
❑5, Sep 2005 ... 9.99
❑6, Dec 2005 ... 9.99

SLEAZY SCANDALS OF THE SILVER SCREEN
KITCHEN SINK

❑1, Apr 1993, b&w; b&w pin-ups, cardstock cover ... 2.50

SLEDGE HAMMER
MARVEL

❑1, Feb 1988; TV tie-in ... 1.00
❑2, Mar 1988; TV tie-in ... 1.00

SLEEPER
DC / WILDSTORM

❑1, Mar 2003 ... 2.95
❑2, Apr 2003 ... 2.95
❑3, May 2003 ... 2.95
❑4, Jun 2003 ... 2.95
❑5, Jul 2003 ... 2.95
❑6, Aug 2003 ... 2.95
❑7, Oct 2003 ... 2.95
❑8, Oct 2003 ... 2.95
❑9, Nov 2003 ... 2.95
❑10, Jan 2004 ... 2.95
❑11, Feb 2004 ... 2.95
❑12, Mar 2004 ... 2.95

SLEEPER: SEASON 2
DC / WILDSTORM

❑1, Aug 2004 ... 2.95
❑2, Sep 2004 ... 2.95
❑3, Oct 2004 ... 2.95
❑4, Nov 2004 ... 2.95
❑5, Dec 2004 ... 2.95
❑6, Jan 2005 ... 2.95
❑7, Feb 2005 ... 2.95
❑8, Mar 2005 ... 2.95
❑9, Apr 2005 ... 2.95
❑10, May 2005 ... 2.95
❑11, Jun 2005 ... 2.99

SLEEPING DRAGONS
SLAVE LABOR / AMAZE INK

❑1 2000 ... 2.95
❑2 2000 ... 2.95
❑3, Mar 2001 ... 2.95
❑4, Jul 2001 ... 2.95

SLEEPWALKER
MARVEL

❑1, Jun 1991, 1: Sleepwalker ... 1.50
❑2, Jul 1991, 1: 8-Ball ... 1.00
❑3, Aug 1991 ... 1.00
❑4, Sep 1991 ... 1.00
❑5, Oct 1991, A: Spider-Man ... 1.00
❑6, Nov 1991, A: Spider-Man ... 1.00
❑7, Dec 1991, Infinity Gauntlet ... 1.00
❑8, Jan 1992, A: Deathlok ... 1.25
❑9, Feb 1992 ... 1.25
❑10, Mar 1992 ... 1.25
❑11, Apr 1992, A: Ghost Rider ... 1.25
❑12, May 1992 ... 1.25
❑13, Jun 1992, 1: Spectra ... 1.25
❑14, Jul 1992 ... 1.25
❑15, Aug 1992 ... 1.25
❑16, Sep 1992 ... 1.25
❑17, Oct 1992 ... 1.25
❑18, Nov 1992 ... 1.25
❑19, Dec 1992, Die-cut cover ... 2.00
❑20, Jan 1993 ... 1.25
❑21, Feb 1993 ... 1.25
❑22, Mar 1993 ... 1.25
❑23, Apr 1993 ... 1.25
❑24, May 1993 ... 1.25
❑25, Jun 1993, Holo-grafix cover ... 2.95
❑26, Jul 1993 ... 1.25
❑27, Aug 1993 ... 1.25
❑28, Sep 1993 ... 1.25
❑29, Oct 1993, A: Spectra ... 1.25
❑30, Nov 1993 ... 1.25
❑31, Dec 1993 ... 1.25
❑32, Jan 1994 ... 1.25
❑33, Feb 1994 ... 1.25
❑Holiday 1, Jan 1993 ... 2.00

SLEEPWALKING
HALL OF HEROES

❑1, Jan 1996, b&w ... 2.50
❑1/Variant, Jan 1996, b&w; Black Magic edition; alternate logoless cover ... 9.95
❑2, Jun 1997, b&w ... 2.50
❑2/Variant, Jun 1997, b&w; alternate logoless cover ... 2.50
❑3, b&w ... 2.50

SLEEPY HOLLOW
DC / VERTIGO

❑1, Jan 2000 ... 7.95

SLEEZE BROTHERS
MARVEL / EPIC

❑1, Aug 1989 ... 1.75
❑2, Sep 1989 ... 1.75
❑3, Oct 1989 ... 1.75
❑4, Nov 1989 ... 1.75
❑5, Dec 1989 ... 1.75
❑6, Jan 1990 ... 1.75

SLEEZE BROTHERS (2ND SERIES)
MARVEL / EPIC

❑1, ca. 1991 ... 3.95

SLICE
EXPRESS / ENTITY

❑1, Oct 1996, b&w ... 2.75

SLIDERS
ACCLAIM / ARMADA

❑1, Jun 1996; DG (a); based on TV series ... 3.00

Solution

Quartet of ultra-powered heroes for hire

©Malibu

Somerset Holmes

Amnesiac actress makes an escape

©Pacific

Sonic Disruptors

Uncompleted Baron title has pirate deejay

©DC

Sonic the Hedgehog

Long-running series based on Sega game

©Archie

Son of Ambush Bug

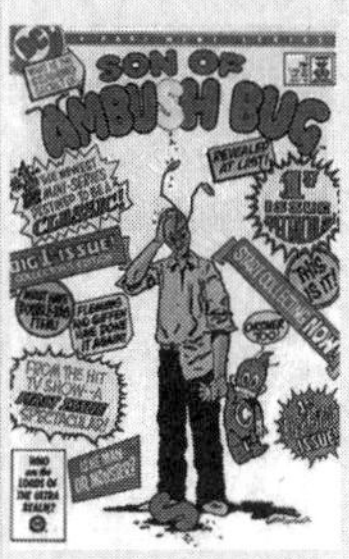

Ambush Bug in a variety of goofy vignettes

©DC

N-MINT

❑2, Jul 1996; DG (a); b ased on TV series 2.50
❑3, Sep 1996 .... 2.50
❑4, Sep 1996 .... 2.50
❑5, Oct 1996 VM (a) 2.50
❑6, Nov 1996 VM (a) 2.50
❑7, Dec 1996 VM (a) 2.50
❑Special 1, Nov 1996; Narcotica 3.95
❑Special 2, Jan 1997 .... 3.95
❑Special 3, Mar 1997; Deadly Secrets 3.95

SLIGHTLY BENT COMICS
SLIGHTLY BENT

❑1, Fal 1998, b&w 3.00
❑2, Win 1999, b&w 3.00

SLIMER!
NOW

❑1, May 1989 .... 2.00
❑2, Jun 1989 .... 2.00
❑3, Jul 1989 .... 2.00
❑4, Aug 1989 .... 1.75
❑5, Sep 1989 .... 1.75
❑6, Oct 1989 .... 1.75
❑7, Nov 1989 .... 1.75
❑8, Dec 1989 .... 1.75
❑9, Jan 1990 .... 1.75
❑10, Feb 1990 .... 1.75
❑11, Mar 1990 .... 1.75
❑12, Apr 1990 .... 1.75
❑13, May 1990 .... 1.75
❑14, Jun 1990 .... 1.75
❑15, Jul 1990 .... 1.75
❑16, Aug 1990 .... 1.75
❑17, Sep 1990 .... 1.75
❑18, Oct 1990 .... 1.75
❑19, Nov 1990 .... 1.75

SLINGERS
MARVEL

❑0; Wizard promotional edition 1.00
❑1/A, Dec 1998; gatefold summary; A: Ricochet. A: Dusk. A: Hornet. A: Prodigy. A: Black Marvel. variant cover with caption "Prodigy: Prepare for Justice!" 2.99
❑1/B, Dec 1998; gatefold summary; A: Ricochet. A: Dusk. A: Hornet. A: Prodigy. A: Black Marvel. Caption "Dusk Falls Over Manhattan" on cover 2.99
❑1/C, Dec 1998; gatefold summary; variant cover with caption "Hornet: Feel the Sting!" 2.99
❑1/D, Dec 1998; gatefold summary; variant cover with caption "Ricochet Springs into Action!" 2.99
❑2, Jan 1999; gatefold summary; Cover A 2.00
❑2/Variant, Jan 1999; Cover B 2.00
❑3, Feb 1999 A: Spider-Man. A: Prodigy. 1.99
❑4, Mar 1999 A: Prodigy. 1.99
❑5, Apr 1999 A: Black Marvel. 1.99
❑6, May 1999 .... 1.99
❑7, Jun 1999 V: Griz. 1.99
❑8, Jul 1999 .... 1.99
❑9, Aug 1999; Ricochet vs. Nanny and Orphanmaker 1.99
❑10, Sep 1999 .... 1.99
❑12, Nov 1999 .... 1.99

N-MINT

SLOTH PARK
BLATANT

❑1, Jun 1998 .... 2.95

SLOW BURN
FANTAGRAPHICS / EROS

❑1 .... 2.95

SLOW DEATH
LAST GASP

❑1, Apr 1970 .... 20.00
❑1/Silver, Apr 1970 .... 25.00
❑2, Jan 1970 .... 12.00
❑3 .... 10.00
❑4, Jan 1972 .... 10.00
❑5, Jan 1973 .... 10.00
❑6 .... 6.00
❑7, Dec 1976 .... 6.00
❑8, Jul 1977; Greenpeace issue 6.00
❑9 .... 6.00
❑10 .... 6.00
❑11 .... 6.00

SLOWPOKE COMIX
ALTERNATIVE

❑1, Nov 1998, b&w 2.95

SLUDGE
MALIBU / ULTRAVERSE

❑1, Oct 1993, Rune 2.50
❑1/Ltd., Oct 1993, Ultra Ltd. 3.00
❑2, Nov 1993 .... 2.00
❑3, Dec 1993, Break-Thru 2.00
❑4, Jan 1994 .... 2.00
❑5, Feb 1994 .... 2.00
❑6, Mar 1994 .... 1.95
❑7, Jun 1994 .... 1.95
❑8, Jul 1994 .... 1.95
❑9, Sep 1994 .... 1.95
❑10, Oct 1994 .... 1.95
❑11, Nov 1994 .... 1.95
❑12, Dec 1994, flipbook with Ultraverse Premiere #8 .... 3.50
❑13, Jan 1995 .... 1.95

SLUDGE: RED X-MAS
MALIBU / ULTRAVERSE

❑1, Dec 1994 .... 2.50

SLUG 'N' GINGER
FANTAGRAPHICS / EROS

❑1, b&w 2.25

SLUTBURGER STORIES
RIP OFF

❑1/2nd, Oct 1992, b&w 2.50
❑1, Jul 1990, b&w 2.50
❑2, Jul 1991, b&w 2.50

SMALL FAVORS
FANTAGRAPHICS / EROS

❑1, Nov 2000 .... 3.50
❑2 .... 3.50
❑3 .... 3.50
❑4 .... 3.50

SMALL GODS
IMAGE

❑1, b&w 4.00
❑2, b&w 2.95
❑3, b&w 2.95

N-MINT

❑4, Sep 2004, b&w 2.95
❑5, Nov 2004, b&w 2.95
❑6, Feb 2005 .... 2.95
❑7, Mar 2005 .... 2.95
❑8, May 2005 .... 2.95
❑9, Jun 2005 .... 2.95
❑10, Sep 2005 .... 2.95
❑11 2005 .... 2.95
❑12, Feb 2006 .... 2.95

SMALL GODS SPECIAL
IMAGE

❑0, Aug 2005 .... 2.99

SMALL PRESS EXPO
INSIGHT

❑1995, ca. 1995; Benefit Comic for American Cancer Society 2.95
❑1996, ca. 1996 .... 2.95
❑1997, ca. 1997; Benefit comic for Comic Legal Defense Fund 2.95

SMALL PRESS SWIMSUIT SPECTACULAR
ALLIED

❑1, Jun 1995, b&w; pin-ups; benefit comic for American Cancer Society 2.95

SMALLVILLE
DC

❑1, May 2003 .... 3.50
❑2, Jul 2003 .... 3.50
❑3, Sep 2003 .... 3.95
❑4, Nov 2003 .... 3.95
❑5, Jan 2004 .... 3.95
❑6, Mar 2004 .... 3.95
❑7, May 2004 .... 3.95
❑8, Jul 2004 .... 3.95
❑9, Sep 2004 .... 3.95
❑10, Oct 2004 .... 3.95
❑11, Jan 2005 .... 3.95

SMASH COMICS (2ND SERIES)
DC

❑1, May 1999; Justice Society Returns 1.99

SMAX
DC / AMERICA'S BEST COMICS

❑1, Oct 2003 .... 2.95
❑2, Nov 2003 .... 2.95
❑3, Dec 2003 .... 2.95
❑4, Feb 2004 .... 2.95
❑5, May 2004 .... 2.95

SMILE (MIXX)
MIXX

❑1, Dec 1998; Sailor Moon 3.99
❑2 1999 .... 3.99
❑3 1999 .... 3.99
❑4 1999 .... 3.99
❑5 1999 .... 3.99
❑6 1999 .... 3.99
❑7, Dec 1999 .... 3.99
❑8 .... 3.99
❑9 .... 3.99
❑10 .... 3.99
❑11 .... 3.99
❑12 .... 3.99
❑13 .... 4.99
❑14 .... 4.99

N-MINT

❑15 ... 4.99
❑16 ... 4.99
❑17 ... 4.99
❑18 ... 4.99
❑19 ... 4.99
❑20 ... 4.99
❑21 ... 4.99
❑22 ... 4.99
❑23 ... 4.99
❑24, Nov 2001 ... 4.99
❑25, Dec 2001 ... 4.99
❑26, Jan 2002 ... 4.99
❑27, Feb 2002 ... 4.99
❑28, Mar 2002 ... 4.99
❑29, Apr 2002 ... 4.99

SMILE (KITCHEN SINK)
KITCHEN SINK

❑1 ... 3.00

SMILEY
CHAOS

❑1, Jun 1998 ... 2.95

SMILEY ANTI-HOLIDAY SPECIAL
CHAOS!

❑1, Jan 1999 ... 2.95

SMILEY'S SPRING BREAK
CHAOS!

❑1, Apr 1999 ... 2.95

SMILEY WRESTLING SPECIAL
CHAOS!

❑1, May 1999 ... 2.95

SMILIN' ED
FANTACO

❑1, 1982, b&w ... 1.25
❑2, 1982, b&w ... 1.25
❑3, 1982, b&w ... 1.25
❑4, 1982, b&w ... 1.25

SMITH BROWN JONES
KIWI

❑1, 1997 ... 4.00
❑2, 1997 ... 2.95
❑3, 1997 ... 2.95
❑4, 1998 ... 2.95
❑5, 1998 ... 2.95

SMITH BROWN JONES: ALIEN ACCOUNTANT
SLAVE LABOR

❑1, May 1998 ... 2.95
❑2, Aug 1998 ... 2.95
❑3, Nov 1998 ... 2.95
❑4, Feb 1999 ... 2.95

SMITH BROWN JONES: HALLOWEEN SPECIAL
SLAVE LABOR

❑1, Oct 1998, b&w ... 2.95

SMOKE
IDEA & DESIGN WORKS

❑1, Jul 2005 ... 10.00
❑2, Aug 2005 ... 7.49
❑3, Sep 2005 ... 7.49

SMOKE AND MIRRORS
SPEAKEASY COMICS

❑1, Oct 2005 ... 3.00

SMOKEY BEAR
GOLD KEY

❑1, Feb 1970 ... 8.00
❑2, May 1970 ... 5.00
❑3, Sep 1970 ... 4.00
❑4, Dec 1970 ... 3.00
❑5, Mar 1971 ... 3.00
❑6, Jun 1971 ... 3.00
❑7, Sep 1971 ... 3.00
❑8, Dec 1971 ... 3.00
❑9, Mar 1972 ... 3.00
❑10, Jun 1972 ... 3.00
❑11, Sep 1972 ... 3.00
❑12, Dec 1972 ... 3.00
❑13, Mar 1973 ... 3.00

SMOOT
SKIP WILLIAMSON

❑1 ... 2.95

SMURFS
MARVEL

❑1, Dec 1982 ... 4.00

N-MINT

❑2, Jan 1983 ... 4.00
❑3, Feb 1983 ... 4.00

SMUT THE ALTERNATIVE COMIC
WILTSHIRE

❑1 ... 3.00

SNACK BAR
BIG TOWN

❑1 ... 2.95

SNAGGLEPUSS
GOLD KEY

❑1, Oct 1962 ... 45.00
❑2, Dec 1962 ... 30.00
❑3, Mar 1963 ... 30.00
❑4, Jun 1963 ... 30.00

SNAKE
SPECIAL STUDIO

❑1, Dec 1989, b&w ... 3.50

SNAKE EYES
FANTAGRAPHICS

❑1, b&w ... 7.95
❑2, b&w ... 7.95
❑3, b&w ... 7.95

SNAKE PLISSKEN CHRONICLES (JOHN CARPENTER'S...)
CROSSGEN

❑1/A, Jun 2003 ... 2.99
❑1/B, Jun 2003 ... 2.99
❑2, Sep 2003 ... 2.99

SNAK POSSE
HCOM

❑1, Jun 1994 ... 1.95
❑2, Jul 1994 ... 1.95

SNAP DRAGONS
DORK STORM

❑1, Aug 2002 ... 2.95
❑1/Variant, Aug 2002 ... 2.95
❑2, Oct 2002 ... 2.95
❑3, May 2003 ... 2.95

SNAP THE PUNK TURTLE
SUPER CREW

❑½ ... 2.25

SNARF
KITCHEN SINK

❑1, Feb 1972 ... 10.00
❑2, Aug 1972 ... 8.00
❑3, Nov 1972, WE (c); WE (a) ... 8.00
❑4, Mar 1973 ... 8.00
❑5, Mar 1974, HK (c) ... 6.00
❑6, Feb 1976 ... 6.00
❑7, Feb 1977 ... 6.00
❑8, Oct 1978 ... 6.00
❑9, Feb 1981 ... 6.00
❑10, Feb 1987 A: Omaha the Cat Dancer ... 6.00
❑11, Feb 1989 ... 4.00
❑12, ca. 1989 ... 4.00
❑13, Dec 1989 ... 4.00
❑14, Mar 1990 ... 4.00
❑15, Oct 1990 ... 5.00

SNARL
CALIBER

❑1, b&w ... 2.50
❑2, b&w ... 2.50
❑3, b&w ... 2.50

SNOID COMICS
KITCHEN SINK

❑1, Dec 1979 ... 2.00

SNOOPER AND BLABBER DETECTIVES
GOLD KEY

❑1, Nov 1962 ... 100.00
❑2, Feb 1963 ... 75.00
❑3, May 1963 ... 75.00

S'NOT FOR KIDS
VORTEX

❑1, b&w ... 6.95

SNOWBUNI
MU

❑1, Jan 1991 ... 3.25

SNOW DROP
TOKYOPOP

❑1, Jan 2004, b&w ... 9.99

N-MINT

❑2, Mar 2004 ... 9.99
❑3, May 2004 ... 9.99
❑4, Jul 2004 ... 9.99
❑5, Sep 2004 ... 9.99
❑6, Nov 2004 ... 9.99
❑7, Jan 2005 ... 9.99
❑8, Mar 2005 ... 9.99
❑9, May 2005 ... 9.99
❑10, Aug 2005 ... 9.99
❑11, Nov 2005 ... 9.99

SNOWMAN
EXPRESS / ENTITY

❑1, Nov 1996 1: Snowman ... 5.00
❑1/A 1996; 1: Snowman. variant cover 6.00
❑1/2nd, Jul 1996, b&w; 1: Snowman. no cover price; given out at 1996 Comic Con International: San Diego 2.50
❑2 1996 ... 4.00
❑2/A 1996; variant cover ... 5.00
❑2/2nd 1996 ... 2.50
❑3 1996 ... 3.00
❑3/A 1996; variant cover ... 3.00

SNOWMAN: 1944
ENTITY

❑1, Oct 1996 ... 2.75

SNOW WHITE
MARVEL

❑1, Jan 1995; lead story is reprint of Dell Four Color #49 ... 2.00

SNOW WHITE AND THE SEVEN DWARFS (WALT DISNEY'S...)
GLADSTONE

❑1 ... 3.50

SNUFF
BONEYARD

❑1, May 1997, b&w ... 2.95

SOAP OPERA LOVE
CHARLTON

❑1, Feb 1983 ... 25.00
❑2, Mar 1983 ... 15.00
❑3, Jun 1983 ... 15.00

SOAP OPERA ROMANCES
CHARLTON

❑1, Jul 1982, Nurse Betsy Crane ... 12.00
❑2, Sep 1982, Nurse Betsy Crane ... 8.00
❑3, Dec 1983, Nurse Betsy Crane ... 8.00
❑4, Jan 1983, Nurse Betsy Crane ... 8.00
❑5, Mar 1983, Nurse Betsy Crane ... 8.00

SOB: SPECIAL OPERATIONS BRANCH
PROMETHEAN

❑1, May 1994, b&w ... 2.25

SOCKETEER
KARDIA

❑1, b&w; parody ... 2.25

SOCK MONKEY
DARK HORSE

❑1, Sep 1998, b&w ... 2.95
❑2, Oct 1998, b&w ... 2.95

SOCK MONKEY (TONY MILLIONAIRE'S...)
DARK HORSE / MAVERICK

❑1, Jul 1999, b&w ... 2.95
❑2, Aug 1999, b&w ... 2.95

SOCK MONKEY (VOL. 3) (TONY MILLIONAIRE'S...)
DARK HORSE / MAVERICK

❑1, Nov 2000 ... 2.99
❑2, Dec 2000 ... 2.99

SOCK MONKEY (VOL. 4) (TONY MILLIONAIRE'S)
DARK HORSE

❑1, May 2003 ... 2.99
❑2, Aug 2003 ... 2.99

SOCRATES IN LOVE
VIZ

❑1, Oct 2005 ... 9.95

SO DARK THE ROSE
CFD

❑1, Oct 1995 ... 2.95

SOFA JET CITY CRISIS
VISUAL ASSAULT

❑1, b&w ... 6.95

Other grades: Multiply price above by 5/6 for VF/NM • 2/3 for VERY FINE • 1/3 for FINE • 1/5 for VERY GOOD • 1/8 for GOOD

Soulsearchers and Company

Peter David's group of paranormal researchers

©Claypool

Southern Knights

Long-running regional super-hero group

©Guild

Sovereign Seven

Claremont's less successful X-Men follow-up

©DC

Space Adventures

Science fiction tales and Steve Ditko

©Charlton

Space Family Robinson

The inspiration for "Lost in Space"

©Gold Key

N-MINT

S.O.F.T. CORPS
SPOOF

❑1 .... 2.95

SOJOURN
DREAMER

❑1, May 1998 .... 2.10
❑2 .... 2.10
❑3 .... 2.10
❑4 .... 2.10
❑5 .... 2.10
❑6 .... 3.15
❑7 .... 3.15
❑8 .... 3.15
❑9 .... 3.15
❑10 .... 3.15

SOJOURN (CROSSGEN)
CROSSGEN

❑1, Aug 2001 .... 5.00
❑2, Sep 2001 .... 2.95
❑3, Oct 2001 .... 2.95
❑4, Nov 2001 .... 2.95
❑5, Dec 2001 .... 2.95
❑6, Jan 2002 .... 2.95
❑7, Feb 2002 .... 2.95
❑8, Mar 2002 .... 2.95
❑9, Apr 2002 .... 2.95
❑10, May 2002 .... 2.95
❑11, Jun 2002 .... 2.95
❑12, Jul 2002 .... 2.95
❑13, Aug 2002 .... 2.95
❑14, Sep 2002 .... 2.95
❑15, Oct 2002 .... 2.95
❑16, Nov 2002 .... 2.95
❑17, Dec 2002 .... 2.95
❑18, Jan 2003 .... 2.95
❑19, Feb 2003 .... 2.95
❑20, Mar 2003 .... 2.95
❑21, Apr 2003 .... 2.95
❑22, May 2003 .... 2.95
❑23, Jun 2003 .... 2.95
❑24, Jul 2003 .... 2.95
❑25, Sep 2003 .... 1.00
❑26, Sep 2003 .... 2.95
❑27, Oct 2003 .... 2.95
❑28, Nov 2003 .... 2.95
❑29, Dec 2003 .... 2.95
❑30, Jan 2004 .... 2.95
❑31, Feb 2004 .... 2.95
❑32, Mar 2004 .... 2.95
❑33, Apr 2004 .... 2.95
❑34, May 2004 .... 2.95
❑34/2nd, Apr 2004 .... 2.95
❑Special 1, Sep 2001; Collects Prequel and #1 .... 3.95

SOJOURN PREQUEL
CROSSGEN

❑1, Jul 2001 .... 5.00

SOLAR LORD
IMAGE

❑1, Mar 1999 .... 2.50
❑2, Apr 1999 .... 2.50
❑3, May 1999 .... 2.50
❑4, Jun 1999 .... 2.50
❑5, Jul 1999 .... 2.50
❑6, Aug 1999 .... 2.50
❑7, Sep 1999 .... 2.50

SOLARMAN
MARVEL

❑1, Jan 1989 .... 1.00
❑2, May 1990 .... 1.00

SOLAR, MAN OF THE ATOM
VALIANT

❑1, Sep 1991 O: Solar. 7.00
❑2, Oct 1991 DP (a); O: Solar. 5.00
❑3, Nov 1991 O: Solar. 1: Toyo Harada. 1: Harbinger Foundation. 5.00
❑4, Dec 1991 O: Solar. 5.00
❑5, Jan 1992 EC (a) 5.00
❑6, Feb 1992 DP (a); V: Spider-Aliens. 5.00
❑7, Mar 1992 DP (a); V: X-O armor. 5.00
❑8, Apr 1992 .... 6.00
❑9, May 1992 .... 6.00
❑10, Jun 1992; 1: Eternal Warrior (cameo). All-black embossed cover 16.00
❑10/2nd 3.00
❑11, Jul 1992 1: Eternal Warrior (full appearance). 5.00
❑12, Aug 1992; FM (c); DP (a); Unity. 4.00
❑13, Sep 1992; Unity 2.00
❑14, Oct 1992 1: Fred Bender. 4.00
❑15, Nov 1992 .... 2.00
❑16, Dec 1992 D: Lyja (Valiant). 2.00
❑17, Jan 1993 A: X-O Manowar. 1.00
❑18, Feb 1993 .... 1.00
❑19, Mar 1993 .... 1.00
❑20, Apr 1993 .... 1.00
❑21, May 1993 V: Master Darque. 1.00
❑22, Jun 1993 V: Master Darque. 1.00
❑23, Jul 1993 1: Solar the Destroyer. 1.00
❑24, Aug 1993 .... 1.00
❑25, Sep 1993; V: Doctor Eclipse. Secret Weapons x-over 1.00
❑26, Oct 1993 .... 1.00
❑27, Nov 1993 .... 1.00
❑28, Dec 1993; Solar the Destroyer vs. spiders 1.00
❑29, Jan 1994; Valiant Vision 1.00
❑30, Feb 1994 .... 1.00
❑31, Mar 1994 .... 1.00
❑32, Apr 1994 .... 1.00
❑33, May 1994; Valiant Vision; trading card 2.00
❑34, Jun 1994; Valiant Vision 1.00
❑35, Aug 1994; Valiant Vision 1.00
❑36, Sep 1994 V: Ravenus. V: Doctor Eclipse. 1.00
❑37, Oct 1994 V: Ravenus. V: Doctor Eclipse. 1.00
❑38, Nov 1994; Chaos Effect Epsilon 1 .... 1.00
❑39, Dec 1994 .... 1.00
❑40, Jan 1995 .... 1.00
❑41, Feb 1995 .... 1.00
❑42, Mar 1995 .... 2.00
❑43, Apr 1995 .... 2.00
❑44, May 1995 .... 2.00
❑45, Jun 1995 .... 2.00
❑46, Jul 1995 DG (a) 2.00
❑47, Aug 1995 DG (a) 2.00
❑48, Sep 1995 DG (a) 2.00
❑49, Sep 1995 DG (a) 2.00
❑50, Oct 1995 DG (a) 2.00
❑51, Nov 1995 DG (a) 3.00
❑52, Nov 1995 DG (a) 3.00
❑53, Dec 1995 DG (a) 3.00
❑54, Dec 1995 DG (a) 3.00
❑55, Jan 1996 .... 3.00
❑56, Jan 1996 .... 3.00
❑57, Feb 1996 .... 4.00
❑58, Feb 1996 .... 4.00
❑59, Mar 1996; Texas destroyed 5.00
❑60, Apr 1996 .... 10.00

SOLAR, MAN OF THE ATOM (VOL. 2)
ACCLAIM / VALIANT

❑1, May 1997; lays groundwork for second Valiant universe 3.95

SOLAR, MAN OF THE ATOM: HELL ON EARTH
ACCLAIM

❑1, Jan 1998 .... 2.50
❑2, Feb 1998 .... 2.50
❑3, Mar 1998 .... 2.50
❑4, Apr 1998 .... 2.50

SOLAR, MAN OF THE ATOM: REVELATIONS
ACCLAIM

❑1, Nov 1997 .... 3.95

SOLAR STELLA
SIRIUS

❑1, Aug 2000, b&w 2.95

SOLDIERS OF FREEDOM
AC

❑1, Jul 1987 .... 1.75
❑2, Aug 1987 .... 1.95

SOLDIER X
MARVEL

❑1, Sep 2002 .... 2.99
❑2, Oct 2002 .... 2.25
❑3, Nov 2002 .... 2.25
❑4, Dec 2002 .... 2.25
❑5, Jan 2003 .... 2.25
❑6, Feb 2003 .... 2.25
❑7, Mar 2003 .... 2.99
❑8, Apr 2003 .... 2.99
❑9, May 2003 .... 2.99
❑10, Jun 2003 .... 2.99
❑11, Jul 2003 .... 2.99
❑12, Aug 2003 .... 2.99

SOLD OUT
FANTACO

❑1, ca. 1986 .... 1.50
❑2, ca. 1987 .... 1.50

SOLITAIRE
MALIBU / ULTRAVERSE

❑1, Nov 1993; 1: Solitaire. Comes polybagged with one of 4 "ace" trading cards 2.00
❑1/CS, Nov 1993; trading card 2.50
❑2, Dec 1993; Break-Thru 2.00
❑3, Feb 1994 O: Night Man. 2.00
❑4, Mar 1994 O: Solitaire. 2.00
❑5, Apr 1994 .... 2.00

Other grades: Multiply price above by 5/6 for VF/NM • 2/3 for VERY FINE • 1/3 for FINE • 1/5 for VERY GOOD • 1/8 for GOOD

	N-MINT
❑6, May 1994	1.95
❑7, Sep 1994 1: Double Edge.	1.95
❑8, Sep 1994 1: The Degenerate.	1.95
❑9, Sep 1994 D: The Degenerate.	1.95
❑10, Oct 1994	1.95
❑11, Nov 1994	1.95
❑12, Dec 1994 D: Jinn. D: Anton Lone.	1.95

SOLO (MARVEL)
MARVEL

❑1, Sep 1994	1.75
❑2, Oct 1994	1.75
❑3, Nov 1994	1.75
❑4, Dec 1994	1.75

SOLO (DARK HORSE)
DARK HORSE

❑1, Jul 1996	2.50
❑2, Aug 1996	2.50

SOLO (DC)
DC

❑1, Jan 2005	4.95
❑2, Feb 2005	4.95
❑3, Mar 2005	4.95
❑4, Jun 2005	4.99
❑5, Jul 2005	4.99
❑6, Oct 2005	4.99
❑7	4.99
❑8, Feb 2006	4.99
❑9, May 2006	4.99
❑10, Jul 2006	4.99
❑11, Sep 2006	4.99

SOLO AVENGERS
MARVEL

❑1, Dec 1987; I.D. card; 1st solo Mockingbird story	1.00
❑2, Jan 1988; Captain Marvel	1.00
❑3, Feb 1988; BH (c); BH (a); V: Batroc. Moon Knight vs. Shroud	1.00
❑4, Mar 1988; Black Knight	1.00
❑5, Apr 1988; Scarlet Witch	1.00
❑6, May 1988; Falcon	1.00
❑7, Jun 1988; Black Widow	1.00
❑8, Jul 1988; Hank Pym	1.00
❑9, Aug 1988; Hellcat	1.00
❑10, Sep 1988; Doctor Druid	1.00
❑11, Oct 1988; Hercules	1.00
❑12, Nov 1988	1.00
❑13, Dec 1988; Wonder Man	1.00
❑14, Jan 1989; Black Widow	1.00
❑15, Feb 1989	1.00
❑16, Mar 1989; Moondragon	1.00
❑17, Apr 1989; Sub-Mariner	1.00
❑18, May 1989; Moondragon	1.00
❑19, Jun 1989; Black Panther	1.00
❑20, Jul 1989; Moondragon; series continues as Avengers Spotlight	1.00

SOLO EX-MUTANTS
ETERNITY

❑1 1987	2.00
❑2, Feb 1988	2.00
❑3, Apr 1988	2.00
❑4 1988	2.00
❑5 1988	2.00
❑6, Jan 1989	2.00

SOLOMON KANE
MARVEL

❑1, Sep 1985; Double-size	1.50
❑2, Nov 1985	1.25
❑3, Jan 1986	1.25
❑4, Mar 1986	1.25
❑5, May 1986	1.25
❑6, Jul 1986 AW (a)	1.25

SOLOMON KANE IN 3-D
BLACKTHORNE

❑1	2.50

SOLSON CHRISTMAS SPECIAL
SOLSON

❑1, ca. 1986; JLee (a); Samurai Santa; 1st Jim Lee art	3.00

SOLSON'S COMIC TALENT STARSEARCH
SOLSON

❑1	1.50
❑2	1.50

SOLUS
CROSSGEN

❑1, Apr 2003	2.95
❑2, May 2003	2.95
❑3, Jun 2003	2.95
❑4, Jul 2003	2.95
❑5, Aug 2003	2.95
❑6, Oct 2003	2.95
❑7, Nov 2003	2.95
❑8, Dec 2003	2.95

SOLUTION
MALIBU / ULTRAVERSE

❑0, Jan 1994; Promotional (coupon redemption) edition; no cover price	2.50
❑1, Sep 1993; 1: Quattro. 1: The Solution. 1: Outrage. 1: Dropkick. 1: Tech. 1: Shadowmage	2.00
❑1/Ltd., Sep 1993; Ultra-Limited foil edition; 1: Quattro. 1: The Solution. 1: Outrage. 1: Dropkick. 1: Tech. 1: Shadowmage	3.00
❑2, Oct 1993; Rune	2.50
❑3, Nov 1993	2.00
❑4, Dec 1993; Break-Thru	2.00
❑5, Jan 1994; O: The Strangers. Dropkick solo story	1.95
❑6, Feb 1994 O: The Solution. O: Tech.	1.95
❑7, Mar 1994 O: The Solution.	1.95
❑8, Apr 1994 O: The Solution.	1.95
❑9, Jun 1994	1.95
❑10, Jul 1994	1.95
❑11, Aug 1994	1.95
❑12, Oct 1994	1.95
❑13, Oct 1994	1.95
❑14, Dec 1994	1.95
❑15, Jan 1995	1.95
❑16, Jan 1995; MZ (a); flipbook with Ultraverse Premiere #10	3.50
❑17, Feb 1995	2.50

SOMEPLACE STRANGE
MARVEL / EPIC

❑1	6.95

SOMERSET HOLMES
PACIFIC

❑1, Sep 1983 BA (a)	2.50
❑2, Nov 1983 BA (a)	2.00
❑3, Feb 1984 BA (a)	2.00
❑4, Apr 1984 BA (a)	2.00
❑5, Nov 1984 BA (a)	2.00
❑6, Dec 1984 BA (a)	2.00

SOME TALES FROM GIMBLEY
HARRIER

❑1, Jun 1987	1.95

SOMETHING
STRICTLY UNDERGROUND

❑1	2.95

SOMETHING AT THE WINDOW IS SCRATCHING
SLAVE LABOR

❑1	9.95

SOMETHING DIFFERENT
WOOGA CENTRAL

❑1, b&w	2.00
❑2, Spr 1992	2.00
❑3, Win 1993, flexidisc	2.00

SOMETHING WICKED
IMAGE

❑1, Nov 2003	2.95
❑2, Dec 2003	2.95
❑3, Apr 2004	2.95

SOME TROUBLE OF A SERRIOUS NATURE
CRUSADE

❑1, Nov 2001	3.50

SOMNAMBULO: SLEEP OF THE JUST
9TH CIRCLE

❑1, Aug 1996, b&w	2.95

SON OF VULCAN
DC

❑1, Jul 2005	2.99
❑2, Aug 2005	2.99
❑3, Sep 2005	2.99
❑4, Oct 2005	2.99
❑5 2005	2.99
❑6, Jan 2006	2.99

SONGBOOK (ALAN MOORE'S...)
CALIBER

❑1, Collected from issues of Negative Burn	5.95

SONG OF MYKAL, THE: ATLANTIS FANTASYWORLD 25TH ANNIVERSARY COMIC
ATLANTIS FANTASYWORLD

❑1, Nov 2001	2.99

SONG OF THE CID
TOME

❑1, b&w	2.95
❑2, b&w	2.95

SONG OF THE SIRENS
MILLENNIUM

❑1, b&w	2.95
❑2, b&w	2.95

SONGS OF BASTARDS
CONQUEST

❑1, b&w	2.95

SONIC & KNUCKLES: MECHA MADNESS SPECIAL
ARCHIE

❑1 1995	2.00

SONIC & KNUCKLES SPECIAL
ARCHIE

❑1, Aug 1995	2.00

SONIC BLAST SPECIAL
ARCHIE

❑1, Oct 1996	2.00

SONIC DISRUPTORS
DC

❑1, Dec 1987	1.00
❑2, Jan 1988	1.00
❑3, Feb 1988	1.00
❑4, Mar 1988	1.00
❑5, May 1988	1.00
❑6, Jun 1988	1.00
❑7, Jul 1988; series goes on hiatus with unresolved storyline; Series cancelled	1.00

SONIC LIVE SPECIAL
ARCHIE

❑1, Knuckles back-up continues in Sonic the Hedgehog #45	2.00

SONIC QUEST - THE DEATH EGG SAGA
ARCHIE

❑2, Jan 1997	1.50

SONIC'S FRIENDLY NEMESIS KNUCKLES
ARCHIE

❑1, Jul 1996	3.00
❑2, Aug 1996	2.00
❑3, Sep 1996	2.00

SONIC THE HEDGEHOG (MINI-SERIES)
ARCHIE

❑1, ca. 1993	20.00
❑2, ca. 1993	10.00
❑3, ca. 1993	10.00

SONIC THE HEDGEHOG
ARCHIE

❑0, Feb 1993	9.00
❑1, Jul 1993	12.00
❑2, Sep 1993	9.00
❑3, Oct 1993	9.00
❑4, Nov 1993	7.00
❑5, Dec 1993	7.00
❑6, Jan 1994	6.00
❑7, Feb 1994	6.00
❑8, Mar 1994	6.00
❑9, Apr 1994	6.00
❑10, May 1994	6.00
❑11, Jun 1994	4.00
❑12, Jul 1994	4.00
❑13, Aug 1994	4.00
❑14, Sep 1994	4.00
❑15, Oct 1994	4.00
❑16, Nov 1994	4.00
❑17, Dec 1994	4.00
❑18, Jan 1995	4.00
❑19, Feb 1995	4.00
❑20, Mar 1995	4.00
❑21, Apr 1995	3.00
❑22, May 1995	3.00
❑23, Jun 1995	3.00
❑24, Jul 1995	3.00

Other grades: Multiply price above by 5/6 for VF/NM • 2/3 for VERY FINE • 1/3 for FINE • 1/5 for VERY GOOD • 1/8 for GOOD

Spacehawk

Basil Wolverton reprints plus new material
©Dark Horse

Space War

Ditko worked on science-fiction anthology
©Charlton

Space Wolf

Dan Flahive's anthropomorphic adventure
©Antarctic

Spanner's Galaxy

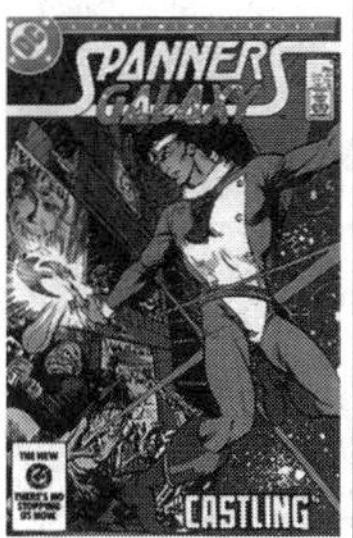

Wanted man doesn't know why he's wanted
©DC

Spawn

Todd McFarlane's flagship Image title
©Image

	N-MINT
❑25, Aug 1995	3.00
❑26, Sep 1995	3.00
❑27, Oct 1995	3.00
❑28, Nov 1995	3.00
❑29, Dec 1995	3.00
❑30, Jan 1996	3.00
❑31, Feb 1996	3.00
❑32, Mar 1996	3.00
❑33, Apr 1996	3.00
❑34, May 1996	3.00
❑35, Jun 1996	3.00
❑36, Jul 1996	3.00
❑37, Aug 1996, Bunnie Rabbot back-up story	3.00
❑38, Sep 1996, Tails solo story	3.00
❑39, Oct 1996	3.00
❑40, Nov 1996	3.00
❑41, Dec 1996	3.00
❑42, Jan 1997	3.00
❑43, Feb 1997	3.00
❑44, Mar 1997	3.00
❑45, Apr 1997	3.00
❑46, May 1997	3.00
❑47, Jun 1997	3.00
❑48, Jul 1997	3.00
❑49, Aug 1997	3.00
❑50, Sep 1997	3.00
❑51, Oct 1997	1.50
❑52, Nov 1997, noir issue	1.50
❑53, Dec 1997	1.50
❑54, Jan 1998	1.50
❑55, Feb 1998	1.50
❑56, Mar 1998	1.50
❑57, Apr 1998	1.50
❑58, May 1998	1.50
❑59, Jun 1998	1.50
❑60, Jul 1998	1.50
❑61, Aug 1998	1.50
❑62, Sep 1998	1.50
❑63, Oct 1998	1.50
❑64, Nov 1998	1.75
❑65, Dec 1998	1.75
❑66, Jan 1999	1.75
❑67, Feb 1999	1.75
❑68, Mar 1999	1.75
❑69, Apr 1999	1.79
❑70, May 1999	1.79
❑71, Jun 1999	1.79
❑72, Jul 1999	1.79
❑73, Aug 1999	1.79
❑74, Sep 1999	1.79
❑75, Oct 1999	1.79
❑76, Nov 1999	1.79
❑77, Dec 1999	1.79
❑78, Jan 2000	1.79
❑79, Feb 2000	1.79
❑80, Mar 2000	1.79
❑81, Apr 2000	1.79
❑82, May 2000	1.79
❑83, Jun 2000	1.99
❑84, Jul 2000	1.99
❑85, Aug 2000	1.99
❑86, Sep 2000	1.99
❑87, Oct 2000	1.99
❑88, Nov 2000	1.99
❑89, Dec 2000	1.99
❑90, Jan 2001	1.99
❑91, Feb 2001	1.99
❑92, Mar 2001	1.99
❑93, Apr 2001	1.99
❑94, May 2001	1.99
❑95, Jun 2001	1.99
❑96, Jul 2001	1.99
❑97, Aug 2001	1.99
❑98, Sep 2001	1.99
❑99, Oct 2001	1.99
❑100, Nov 2001	1.99
❑101, Nov 2001	1.99
❑102, Dec 2001	1.99
❑103, Jan 2002	1.99
❑104, Feb 2002	1.99
❑105, Mar 2002	1.99
❑106, Apr 2002	1.99
❑107, May 2002	1.99
❑108, May 2002	1.99
❑109, Jun 2002	1.99
❑110, Jul 2002	1.99
❑111, Aug 2002	1.99
❑112, Sep 2002	1.99
❑113, Oct 2002	1.99
❑114, Nov 2002	1.99
❑115, Dec 2002	1.99
❑116, Jan 2003	2.19
❑117, Feb 2003	2.19
❑118, ca. 2003	2.19
❑119, Mar 2003	2.19
❑120, Apr 2003	2.19
❑121, May 2003	2.19
❑122, Jun 2003	2.19
❑123, Jul 2003	2.19
❑124, Aug 2003	2.19
❑125, Sep 2003	2.19
❑126, Oct 2003	2.19
❑127, Nov 2003	2.19
❑128, Dec 2003	2.19
❑129, Jan 2004	2.19
❑130, Feb 2004	2.19
❑131, Mar 2004	2.19
❑132, Mar 2004	2.19
❑133, Apr 2004	2.19
❑134, May 2004	2.19
❑135, Jun 2004	2.19
❑136, Jul 2004	2.19
❑137, Aug 2004	2.19
❑138, Sep 2004	2.19
❑139, Oct 2004	2.19
❑140, Nov 2004	2.19
❑141, Dec 2004	2.19
❑142, Jan 2005	2.19
❑143, Feb 2005	2.19
❑144, Feb 2005	2.19
❑145, Mar 2005	2.19
❑146, Apr 2005	2.19
❑147, May 2005	2.19
❑148, Jun 2005	2.19
❑149, Jul 2005	2.39
❑150, Aug 2005	2.39
❑151, Sep 2005	2.39
❑152, Oct 2005	2.39
❑153, Nov 2005	2.39
❑154, Dec 2005	2.39
❑155, Jan 2006	2.39
❑156, Feb 2006	2.39
❑157, Feb 2006	2.39
❑158, Mar 2006	2.39
❑159, Apr 2006	2.39
❑160, May 2006	2.39
❑161, Jun 2006	2.39
❑163, Aug 2006	2.39
❑Special 1, Nov 1997	3.00
❑Special 2, ca. 1997, Brave New World	2.00
❑Special 3, Jan 1998, Firsts	2.25
❑Special 4, Mar 1998	2.25
❑Special 5, Jun 1998, Sonic Kids	2.25
❑Special 6, Sep 1998, Director's Cut; expanded version of Sonic #50	2.25
❑Special 7, Dec 1998, crossover with Image	2.25
❑Special 8, Mar 1999	2.25
❑Special 9, Jun 1999	2.29
❑Special 10, Sep 1999, A: Sabrina.	2.29
❑Special 11, Dec 1999	2.29
❑Special 12, Apr 2000	2.29
❑Special 13, Jun 2000	2.29
❑Special 14, Sep 2000	2.29
❑Special 15, Feb 2001	2.49

SONIC THE HEDGEHOG IN YOUR FACE SPECIAL
ARCHIE

❑1	2.00

SONIC THE HEDGEHOG TRIPLE TROUBLE SPECIAL
ARCHIE

❑1, Oct 1995	2.00

SONIC VS. KNUCKLES BATTLE ROYAL SPECIAL
ARCHIE

❑1, ca. 1997	2.00

SONIC X
ARCHIE

❑1	2.39
❑2, Nov 2005	2.39
❑3, Dec 2005	2.39
❑4, Jan 2006	2.39
❑5, Apr 2006	2.39
❑6, May 2006	2.39
❑7, May 2006	2.39
❑8, Jul 2006	2.39
❑9, Aug 2006	2.39
❑10, Aug 2006	2.39

SON OF AMBUSH BUG
DC

❑1, Jul 1986 KG (a)	1.50
❑2, Aug 1986 KG (a)	1.50
❑3, Sep 1986 KG (a)	1.50
❑4, Oct 1986 KG (a)	1.50
❑5, Nov 1986 KG (a)	1.50
❑6, Dec 1986 KG (a)	1.50

SON OF M
MARVEL

❑1, Feb 2006	2.99

Other grades: Multiply price above by 5/6 for VF/NM • 2/3 for VERY FINE • 1/3 for FINE • 1/5 for VERY GOOD • 1/8 for GOOD

❑2, Mar 2006 2.99
❑3, Apr 2006 2.99
❑4, May 2006 2.99
❑5, Jun 2006 2.99
❑6, Aug 2006 2.99

SON OF MUTANT WORLD
FANTAGOR

❑1 3.00
❑2 2.50
❑3, b&w; Black and white issues begin 2.00
❑4, b&w 2.00
❑5, ca. 1990, b&w 2.00

SON OF RAMPAGE
SLAP HAPPY

❑2, ca. 1998 13.95

SON OF SATAN
MARVEL

❑1, Dec 1975, Marvel Value Stamp #13: Dr. Strange 20.00
❑2, Feb 1976 15.00
❑3, Apr 1976 10.00
❑3/30 cent, Apr 1976, 30 cent regional variant 15.00
❑4, Jun 1976, CR (a) 10.00
❑4/30 cent, Jun 1976, CR (a); 30 cent regional variant 15.00
❑5, Aug 1976 10.00
❑5/30 cent, Aug 1976, 30 cent regional variant 15.00
❑6, Oct 1976 10.00
❑7, Dec 1976 10.00
❑8, Feb 1977 10.00

SON OF SUPERMAN
DC

❑Book 1/HC, ca. 1999 14.95
❑Book 1, ca. 1999 14.95

SON OF YUPPIES FROM HELL
MARVEL

❑1 3.50

SONS OF KATIE ELDER
DELL

❑1, Sep 1965 125.00

SOPHISTIKATS KATCH-UP KOLLECTION
SILK PURRS

❑1, Jul 1995, b&w 5.95

SORCERER'S CHILDREN
SILLWILL

❑1, Dec 1998 2.95
❑2, Feb 1999 2.95
❑3, Apr 1999 2.95
❑4, Jul 1999 2.95

S.O.S.
FANTAGRAPHICS

❑1, b&w 2.75

SOUL
FLASHPOINT

❑1, Mar 1994 2.50
❑1/Gold, Mar 1994; Gold edition 3.00

SOULFIRE (MICHAEL TURNER'S ...)
ASPEN

❑0, May 2004 5.00
❑0/Conv, May 2004 7.00
❑0/Dynamic, May 2004 15.00
❑1/Diamond, May 2004 5.00
❑1, May 2004 7.00
❑1/DF, May 2004 15.00
❑1/Jay, May 2004 6.00
❑1/Virgin, May 2004 8.00
❑1/Wizard, May 2004 5.00
❑2 6.00
❑2/Rupps 10.00
❑3 5.00
❑4 2005 2.99
❑4/Variant 4.00
❑4/Campbell 3.00
❑4/Lee 4.00
❑4/Conv 2005; Wizard World Los Angeles (March 2004) convention. 3,500 created 10.00

SOULFIRE: BEGINNINGS
ASPEN

❑1, Jun 2003 4.00
❑1/Conv, Jun 2003 10.00

SOULFIRE: DYING OF THE LIGHT
ASPEN

❑0, Aug 2005 2.50
❑0/Conv, Aug 2005 15.00
❑1, Sep 2005
❑2, Oct 2005

SOULFIRE PREVIEW
ASPEN

❑1, Jun 2003 4.00
❑1/Conv, Jun 2003; Pittsburgh Comic Con Edition 8.00

SOUL OF A SAMURAI
IMAGE

❑1, Jun 2003 5.95
❑2, Jul 2003 5.95
❑3, Jan 2004 5.95
❑4, Aug 2004 5.95

SOULQUEST
INNOVATION

❑1, Apr 1989 3.95

SOUL SAGA
TOP COW

❑1, Feb 2000 2.50
❑2, Apr 2000 2.50
❑3, Aug 2000 2.50
❑4, Oct 2000 2.95
❑5, Apr 2001 2.95

SOULSEARCHERS AND COMPANY
CLAYPOOL

❑1 1993, b&w RHo, PD (w) 4.00
❑2 1993, b&w PD (w) 3.00
❑3, Aug 1993, b&w; PD (w); Sandman parody 3.00
❑4, Sep 1993, b&w PD (w) 3.00
❑5, Oct 1993, b&w PD (w) 3.00
❑6, Feb 1994, b&w PD (w) 2.50
❑7, May 1994, b&w PD (w) 2.50
❑8, Jul 1994, b&w PD (w) 2.50
❑9 1995, b&w PD (w) 2.50
❑10, Jan 1995, b&w PD (w) 2.50
❑11, Feb 1995, b&w PD (w); RHo (a) 2.50
❑12, May 1995, b&w PD (w) 2.50
❑13, Jul 1995, b&w PD (w) 2.50
❑14, Oct 1995, b&w PD (w) 2.50
❑15, Dec 1995, b&w PD (w) 2.50
❑16, Feb 1996, b&w PD (w) 2.50
❑17, Apr 1996, b&w PD (w) 2.50
❑18, Jun 1996, b&w PD (w) 2.50
❑19, Aug 1996, b&w PD (w) 2.50
❑20, Oct 1996, b&w PD (w) 2.50
❑21, Dec 1996, b&w PD (w) 2.50
❑22, Feb 1997, b&w PD (w) 2.50
❑23, Apr 1997, b&w PD (w) 2.50
❑24, Jun 1997, b&w PD (w) 2.50
❑25, Aug 1997, b&w PD (w) 2.50
❑26, Oct 1997, b&w PD (w) 2.50
❑27, Dec 1997, b&w PD (w) 2.50
❑28, Feb 1998, b&w PD (w) 2.50
❑29, Apr 1998, b&w PD (w); DC, JM (a) 2.50
❑30, Jun 1998, b&w PD (w) 2.50
❑31, Aug 1998, b&w; PD (w); Li'l Soulsearchers 2.50
❑32, Sep 1998, b&w PD (w) 2.50
❑33, Nov 1998, b&w PD (w) 2.50
❑34, Jan 1999, b&w PD (w) 2.50
❑35, Mar 1999, b&w PD (w) 2.50
❑36, May 1999, b&w PD (w) 2.50
❑37, Jul 1999, b&w PD (w) 2.50
❑38, Sep 1999, b&w PD (w) 2.50
❑39, Nov 1999, b&w PD (w) 2.50
❑40, Jan 2000, b&w PD (w) 2.50
❑41, Mar 2000, b&w PD (w) 2.50
❑42, May 2000, b&w PD (w) 2.50
❑43, Jul 2000, b&w PD (w); DC (a) ... 2.50
❑44, Sep 2000, b&w PD (w); DC (a) .. 2.50
❑45, Nov 2000, b&w 2.50
❑46, Jan 2001, b&w 2.50
❑47, Mar 2001, b&w 2.50
❑48, May 2001, b&w 2.50
❑49, Jul 2001, b&w 2.50
❑50, Sep 2001, b&w 2.50
❑51, Nov 2001, b&w 2.50
❑52, Jan 2002, b&w 2.50
❑53, Mar 2002, b&w 2.50
❑54, May 2002, b&w 2.50
❑55, Jul 2002, b&w 2.50
❑56, Sep 2002, b&w 2.50
❑57, Nov 2002, b&w 2.50
❑58, Jan 2003, b&w 2.50
❑59, Mar 2003, b&w 2.50
❑60, May 2003, b&w 2.50
❑61, Jul 2003, b&w 2.50
❑62, Sep 2003, b&w 2.50
❑63, Nov 2003, b&w 2.50
❑64, Jan 2004, b&w 2.50
❑65, Mar 2004, b&w 2.50
❑66, May 2004, b&w 2.50
❑67, Jul 2004, b&w 2.50
❑68, ca. 2004 2.50
❑69 2004 2.50

SOUL TO SEOUL
TOKYOPOP

❑1, Jan 2005 9.99
❑2, Apr 2005 9.99
❑3, Oct 2005 9.99

SOUL TREK
SPOOF

❑1, b&w; parody 2.95
❑2, b&w; parody 2.95

SOULWIND
IMAGE

❑1, Mar 1997, b&w 2.95
❑2, Apr 1997, b&w 2.95
❑3, May 1997, b&w 2.95
❑4, Jun 1997, b&w 2.95
❑5, Oct 1997, b&w 2.95
❑6, Dec 1997, b&w 2.95
❑7, Feb 1998, b&w 2.95
❑8, Apr 1998, b&w 2.95

SOUPY SALES COMIC BOOK
ARCHIE

❑1, Jan 1965 80.00

SOUTHERN BLOOD
JM COMICS

❑1, b&w 2.50
❑2, b&w 2.50

SOUTHERN CUMFORT
FANTAGRAPHICS / EROS

❑1 2.95

SOUTHERN-FRIED HOMICIDE
CREMO / SHEL-TONE

❑1, b&w; cardstock cover 7.95

SOUTHERN KNIGHTS
GUILD

❑2, Apr 1983; Title changes to Southern Knights 2.00
❑3, Jul 1983 2.00
❑4 1983 2.00
❑5 1984 2.00
❑6, Jun 1984 2.00
❑7, Sep 1984 2.00
❑8, Apr 1985 2.00
❑9, Jun 1985 2.00
❑10, Aug 1985 2.00
❑11, Oct 1985 2.00
❑12, Dec 1985 2.00
❑13, Feb 1986 2.00
❑14, Apr 1986 2.00
❑15, Jun 1986 2.00
❑16, Aug 1986 2.00
❑17, Oct 1986 2.00
❑18, Dec 1986 2.00
❑19, Feb 1987 2.00
❑20, Apr 1987 2.00
❑21, Jun 1987 2.00
❑22, Aug 1987 2.00
❑23, Dec 1987 2.00
❑24, Dec 1987 2.00
❑25, Feb 1988 2.00
❑26, Apr 1988 2.00
❑27, Jun 1988 2.00
❑28, Aug 1988 2.00
❑29, Aug 1988 2.00
❑30, Sep 1988 2.00
❑31, Oct 1988 2.00
❑32, Jan 1989 2.00
❑33, Sep 1989 2.00
❑34 2.25
❑35, b&w GP (c); 3.50

Spawn: The Dark Ages

Spawn series set in medieval times

©Image

Special Marvel Edition

Gave birth to Master of Kung Fu

©Marvel

Spectacular Spider-Man (Magazine)

Two-issue 1968 attempt at magazine format

©Marvel

Spectacular Spider-Man

Title had "Peter Parker" in name for part of run

©Marvel

Spectacular Spider-Man (2nd Series)

Relaunch opened with Venom storyline

©Marvel

N-MINT

❑36, b&w 3.50
❑Holiday 1, Oct 1988; Wizard promotional edition; Dread Halloween Special; b&w Reprint 2.25
❑Special 1, Apr 1989, b&w; Reprints 2.25

SOUTHERN KNIGHTS PRIMER
COMICS INTERVIEW

❑1, b&w; Reprints 2.25

SOUTHERN SQUADRON (AIRCEL)
AIRCEL

❑1, Aug 1990 2.25
❑2, Sep 1990 2.25
❑3, Sep 1990 2.25
❑4, Nov 1990 2.25

SOUTHERN SQUADRON (2ND SERIES)
ETERNITY

❑1, 1991 2.50
❑2, 1991 2.50
❑3, 1991 2.50
❑4, 1991 2.50

SOUTHERN SQUADRON: THE FREEDOM OF INFORMATION ACT
ETERNITY

❑1, Jan 1992; Fantastic Four #1 homage cover 2.50
❑2, Feb 1992 2.50
❑3, Mar 1992 2.50

SOVEREIGN SEVEN
DC

❑1, Jul 1995 2.50
❑1/Variant, Jul 1995; foil edition; no cover price 4.00
❑2, Aug 1995 2.00
❑3, Sep 1995 2.00
❑4, Oct 1995 2.00
❑5, Nov 1995 2.00
❑6, Dec 1995 2.00
❑7, Jan 1996 2.00
❑8, Feb 1996 2.00
❑9, Mar 1996 2.00
❑10, Apr 1996 2.00
❑11, Jun 1996 1.95
❑12, Jul 1996 1.95
❑13, Aug 1996 1.95
❑14, Sep 1996 1.95
❑15, Oct 1996 1.95
❑16, Nov 1996; Final Night 1.95
❑17, Dec 1996 1.95
❑18, Jan 1997; Cascade quits 1.95
❑19, Feb 1997 1.95
❑20, Mar 1997 1.95
❑21, Apr 1997 1.95
❑22, May 1997 1.95
❑23, Jun 1997 1.95
❑24, Jul 1997 1.95
❑25, Aug 1997 1.95
❑26, Sep 1997 2.25
❑27, Oct 1997; Genesis 2.25
❑28, Nov 1997 2.25
❑29, Dec 1997; Face cover 2.25
❑30, Jan 1998 2.25
❑31, Feb 1998 2.25
❑32, Mar 1998 2.25

N-MINT

❑33, Apr 1998 2.25
❑34, May 1998 2.25
❑35, Jun 1998 2.25
❑36, Jul 1998 2.25
❑Annual 1, ca. 1995; Year One; Big Barda 3.95
❑Annual 2, ca. 1996; Legends of the Dead Earth; 1996 Annual 2.95

SOVEREIGN SEVEN PLUS
DC

❑1, Feb 1997 2.95

SOVIET SUPER SOLDIERS
MARVEL

❑1, Nov 1992 2.00

SPACE: 1999
CHARLTON

❑1, Nov 1975, JSa (c); JSa (a); O: Moonbase Alpha. 10.00
❑2, Jan 1976, JSa (c); JSa (a) 7.00
❑3, Mar 1976, JBy (c); JBy (a) 7.00
❑4, May 1976, JBy (c); JBy (a) 7.00
❑5, Jul 1976, JBy (c); JBy (a) 5.00
❑6, Sep 1976, JBy (c); JBy (a) 5.00
❑7, Nov 1976 5.00

SPACE: 34-24-34
MN DESIGN

❑1, b&w; photos 4.50

SPACE: ABOVE AND BEYOND
TOPPS

❑1, Jan 1996 2.95
❑2, Feb 1996 2.95
❑3, Mar 1996 2.95

SPACE: ABOVE AND BEYOND: THE GAUNTLET
TOPPS

❑1, May 1996 2.95
❑2, Jun 1996 2.95

SPACE ADVENTURES
CHARLTON

❑23, May 1958, Series continued from Nyoka, the Jungle Girl #22 100.00
❑24, Jul 1958 70.00
❑25, Sep 1958 70.00
❑26, Nov 1958 70.00
❑27, Feb 1959 70.00
❑28 1959 70.00
❑29, Jul 1959 70.00
❑30, Sep 1959 70.00
❑31, Dec 1959 70.00
❑32, Jan 1960 70.00
❑33, Mar 1960, SD (a); O: Captain Atom. 1: Captain Atom. 325.00
❑34, Jun 1960, SD (a); 2: Captain Atom. 150.00
❑35, Aug 1960, SD (a); A: Captain Atom 125.00
❑36, Oct 1960, SD (a); A: Captain Atom. 125.00
❑37, Dec 1960, SD (a); A: Captain Atom 125.00
❑38, Feb 1961, SD (a); A: Captain Atom. 125.00
❑39, Apr 1961, SD (a); A: Captain Atom. 125.00
❑40, Jun 1961, SD (a); A: Captain Atom. 125.00
❑41, Aug 1961 25.00
❑42, Oct 1961, SD (a); A: Captain Atom. 75.00
❑43, Dec 1961 25.00

N-MINT

❑44, Feb 1962 25.00
❑45, May 1962 25.00
❑46, Jul 1962 25.00
❑47, Sep 1962 25.00
❑48, Nov 1962 25.00
❑49, Jan 1963 25.00
❑50, Mar 1963 25.00
❑51, May 1963 18.00
❑52, Jul 1963 18.00
❑53, Sep 1963 18.00
❑54, Nov 1963 18.00
❑55, Mar 1964 18.00
❑56, May 1964 18.00
❑57, Jul 1964 18.00
❑58, Sep 1964 18.00
❑59, Nov 1964 18.00
❑60, Oct 1967, JA (a) 18.00
❑61, Jul 1968 12.00
❑62, Sep 1968 12.00
❑63, Nov 1968 12.00
❑64, Jan 1969 12.00
❑65, Mar 1969 12.00
❑66, May 1969 12.00
❑67, Jul 1969 12.00
❑68, May 1978 12.00
❑69 1978 12.00
❑70 1978 12.00
❑71, Jan 1979 12.00
❑72, Mar 1979 12.00

SPACE ARK
AC

❑1 1.75
❑2 1.75
❑3, b&w 1.75
❑4, b&w 1.75
❑5, b&w 1.75

SPACE BANANAS
KARL ART

❑0 1.95

SPACE BEAVER
TEN-BUCK

❑1, Oct 1986 1.50
❑2 1.50
❑3, Feb 1987 1.50
❑4 1987 1.50
❑5 1987 1.50
❑6, Sep 1987 1.50
❑7, Oct 1987 1.50
❑8, Nov 1987 1.50
❑9, Dec 1987 1.50
❑10, Jan 1988 1.50
❑11, Feb 1988 1.50

SPACE CIRCUS
DARK HORSE

❑1, Jul 2000 2.95
❑2, Aug 2000 2.95
❑3, Sep 2000 2.95
❑4, Oct 2000 2.95

SPACE COWBOY ANNUAL 2001
VANGUARD

❑1/Frazetta, Dec 2001, Variant Frazetta cover 4.95
❑1/Williamson, Dec 2001, Variant Williamson cover 4.95

SPACED
Unbridled Ambition

- ❑1 .... 2.00
- ❑2 .... 2.00
- ❑3 .... 2.00
- ❑4 .... 2.00
- ❑5 .... 2.00
- ❑6 .... 2.00
- ❑7 .... 2.00
- ❑8 .... 2.00
- ❑9 .... 2.00
- ❑10, b&w; Eclipse publisher 2.00
- ❑11, b&w 2.00
- ❑12, b&w 2.00
- ❑13, b&w 2.00

SPACED (COMICS AND COMIX)
Comics and Comix

- ❑1 .... 4.00

SPACED OUT (FORBIDDEN FRUIT)
Forbidden Fruit

- ❑1, Jul 1992 .... 2.95

SPACED OUT (PRINT MINT)
Print Mint

- ❑1 .... 3.00

SPACE FAMILY ROBINSON
Gold Key

- ❑1, Dec 1962, Low circulation 225.00
- ❑2, Mar 1963, Robinson's become lost in space 100.00
- ❑3, Jun 1963 .... 75.00
- ❑4, Sep 1963 .... 75.00
- ❑5, Dec 1963 .... 75.00
- ❑6, Feb 1964 .... 50.00
- ❑7, Apr 1964 .... 50.00
- ❑8, Jun 1964 .... 50.00
- ❑9, Aug 1964 .... 50.00
- ❑10, Oct 1964 .... 50.00
- ❑11, Dec 1964 .... 35.00
- ❑12, Apr 1965 .... 35.00
- ❑13, Jul 1965 .... 35.00
- ❑14, Oct 1965 .... 35.00
- ❑15, Jan 1966, Title changes to "Space Family Robinson Lost in Space" 35.00
- ❑16, Apr 1966 .... 25.00
- ❑17, Jul 1966 .... 25.00
- ❑18, Oct 1966 .... 25.00
- ❑19, Dec 1966 .... 25.00
- ❑20, Feb 1967 .... 25.00
- ❑21, Apr 1967 .... 20.00
- ❑22, Jun 1967 .... 20.00
- ❑23, Aug 1967 .... 20.00
- ❑24, Oct 1967 .... 20.00
- ❑25, Dec 1967 .... 20.00
- ❑26, Feb 1968 .... 20.00
- ❑27, Apr 1968 .... 20.00
- ❑28, Jun 1968 .... 20.00
- ❑29, Aug 1968 .... 20.00
- ❑30, Oct 1968 .... 20.00
- ❑31, Dec 1968 .... 20.00
- ❑32, Feb 1969 .... 20.00
- ❑33, Apr 1969 .... 20.00
- ❑34, Jun 1969 .... 20.00
- ❑35, Aug 1969 .... 20.00
- ❑36, Oct 1969, Final issue of original run 20.00
- ❑37, Oct 1973, Series begins again 20.00
- ❑38, Jan 1974, Title changes to "Space Family Robinson, Lost in Space on Space Station One" 20.00
- ❑39, Apr 1974 .... 20.00
- ❑40, Jul 1974 .... 20.00
- ❑41, Oct 1974 .... 20.00
- ❑42, Jan 1975 .... 20.00
- ❑43, Apr 1975 .... 20.00
- ❑44, Aug 1975 .... 20.00
- ❑45, Oct 1975 .... 10.00
- ❑46, Jan 1976 .... 10.00
- ❑47, Apr 1976 .... 10.00
- ❑48, Aug 1976 .... 10.00
- ❑49 .... 10.00
- ❑50 .... 10.00
- ❑51 .... 10.00
- ❑52, ca. 1977 .... 10.00
- ❑53, ca. 1977 .... 10.00
- ❑54, Dec 1977 .... 10.00
- ❑55, ca. 1981, Series begins again 6.00
- ❑56, Jul 1981 .... 6.00
- ❑57, Oct 1981 .... 6.00
- ❑58, Feb 1982 .... 6.00
- ❑59, May 1982 .... 6.00

SPACE FUNNIES
Archival

- ❑1 .... 5.95

SPACEGAL COMICS
Thorby

- ❑1 .... 2.95
- ❑2; Flip-Book with Johnny Cosmic #1 .... 2.95

SPACE GHOST (GOLD KEY)
Gold Key

- ❑1, Mar 1967 .... 150.00

SPACE GHOST (COMICO)
Comico

- ❑1, Dec 1987 .... 3.50

SPACE GHOST (DC)
DC

- ❑1, Feb 2005 .... 22.00
- ❑2, Mar 2005 .... 10.00
- ❑3, Apr 2005 .... 2.95
- ❑4, May 2005 .... 2.95
- ❑5, Jun 2005 .... 2.95
- ❑6, Jun 2005 .... 2.99

SPACE GIANTS
Boneyard

- ❑1 .... 2.75

SPACEGIRL COMICS
Bill Jones Graphics

- ❑1, Nov 1995, b&w 2.50
- ❑2, Nov 1995, b&w 2.50

SPACEHAWK
Dark Horse

- ❑1, ca. 1989 BW (w); BW (a) 2.00
- ❑2, ca. 1989 BW (w); BW (a) 2.00
- ❑3, ca. 1989 BW (w); BW (a) 2.25
- ❑4, ca. 1989 BW (w); BW (a) 2.25
- ❑5, Jan 1993 BW (w); BW (a) 2.50

SPACE HUSTLERS
Slave Labor

- ❑1, Mar 1997, b&w 2.95

SPACE JAM
DC

- ❑1, Oct 1996; prestige format 5.95

SPACEKNIGHTS
Marvel

- ❑1, Oct 2000 .... 2.99
- ❑2, Nov 2000 .... 2.99
- ❑3, Dec 2000 .... 2.99
- ❑4, Jan 2001 .... 2.99
- ❑5, Feb 2001 .... 2.99

SPACEMAN
Dell

- ❑2, Jun 1962 .... 40.00
- ❑3, Sep 1962 .... 32.00
- ❑4 1963 .... 24.00
- ❑5, Jun 1963 .... 24.00
- ❑6, Sep 1963 .... 24.00
- ❑7, Dec 1964 .... 22.00
- ❑8, Mar 1964 .... 22.00
- ❑9, ca. 1972, Reprints Space Man #1 .... 5.00
- ❑10, ca. 1972, Reprints Space Man #2 .... 5.00

SPACEMAN (ONI)
Oni

- ❑nn, Jul 2002 .... 2.95

SPACE: 1999 (MAGAZINE)
Charlton

- ❑1, Nov 1975, b&w GM (c) 30.00
- ❑2, Jan 1976, b&w GM (c); GM (a) 20.00
- ❑3, Mar 1976, b&w GM (c); GM (a) 20.00
- ❑4, May 1976, b&w GM (c) 20.00
- ❑5, Jul 1976, b&w 20.00
- ❑6, Aug 1976, b&w 20.00
- ❑7, Sep 1976, b&w 20.00
- ❑8, Oct 1976, b&w 20.00

SPACE PATROL (ADVENTURE)
Adventure

- ❑1 .... 2.50
- ❑2, b&w 2.50
- ❑3 .... 2.50

SPACE SLUTZ
Comic Zone

- ❑1, b&w 3.95

SPACE TIME SHUFFLE A TRILOGY
Alpha Productions

- ❑1, b&w 1.95
- ❑2, b&w 1.95

SPACE TRIP TO THE MOON
Avalon

- ❑1, ca. 1999, b&w; adapts Destination: Moon 2.95

SPACE USAGI
Mirage

- ❑1, Jun 1992, b&w 3.00
- ❑2, Jul 1992, b&w 3.00
- ❑3, Aug 1992, b&w 3.00

SPACE USAGI (VOL. 2)
Mirage

- ❑1, Nov 1993 .... 3.00
- ❑2, Jan 1994 .... 3.00
- ❑3, Mar 1994 .... 3.00

SPACE USAGI (VOL. 3)
Dark Horse

- ❑1, Jan 1996, b&w 2.95
- ❑2, Feb 1996, b&w 2.95
- ❑3, Mar 1996, b&w 2.95

SPACE WAR
Charlton

- ❑1, Oct 1959 .... 95.00
- ❑2, Dec 1959 .... 55.00
- ❑3, Feb 1960 .... 55.00
- ❑4, Apr 1960, SD (a) 100.00
- ❑5, Jun 1960, SD (a) 100.00
- ❑6, Aug 1960, SD (a) 100.00
- ❑7, Oct 1960 .... 30.00
- ❑8, Dec 1960, SD (a) 100.00
- ❑9, Feb 1961 .... 30.00
- ❑10, Apr 1961, SD (a) 100.00
- ❑11, Jun 1961 .... 30.00
- ❑12, Aug 1961 .... 30.00
- ❑13, Oct 1961 .... 30.00
- ❑14, Dec 1961 .... 30.00
- ❑15 1962 .... 30.00
- ❑16 1962 .... 16.00
- ❑17 1962 .... 16.00
- ❑18 1962 .... 16.00
- ❑19 1962 .... 16.00
- ❑20, Jan 1963 .... 16.00
- ❑21, Mar 1963 .... 16.00
- ❑22, May 1963 .... 16.00
- ❑23, Jul 1963 .... 16.00
- ❑24, Sep 1963 .... 16.00
- ❑25, Nov 1963 .... 16.00
- ❑26, Jan 1964 .... 16.00
- ❑27, Mar 1964, Series continued in Fightin' 5 #28 .... 16.00
- ❑28, Mar 1978, Series begins again (1978) 4.00
- ❑29, May 1978 .... 4.00
- ❑30, Jun 1978 .... 4.00
- ❑31, Oct 1978 .... 4.00
- ❑32, ca. 1979 .... 4.00

SPACE WAR CLASSICS
Avalon

- ❑1, b&w 2.95

SPACE WOLF
Antarctic

- ❑1, b&w 2.50
- ❑2, b&w 2.50

SPAM
Alpha Productions

- ❑1, b&w 1.50
- ❑2, b&w 1.50

SPANDEX TIGHTS
Lost Cause

- ❑1, Sep 1994, b&w 2.50
- ❑2, Nov 1994, b&w 2.25
- ❑3, b&w 2.25
- ❑4, Mar 1995, b&w 2.25
- ❑5, May 1995, b&w 2.25
- ❑6, Jul 1995, b&w; V: Mighty Awful Sour Rangers. false cover for Mighty Awful Sour Rangers #1 .... 2.50

Other grades: Multiply price above by 5/6 for VF/NM • 2/3 for VERY FINE • 1/3 for FINE • 1/5 for VERY GOOD • 1/8 for GOOD

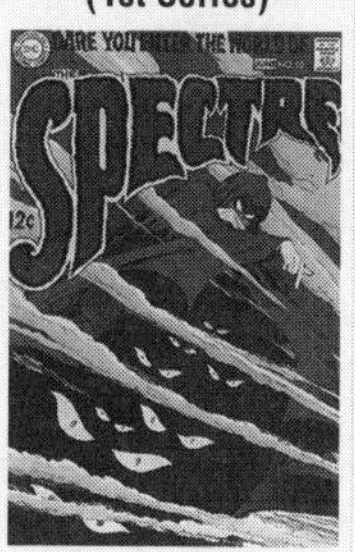
Spectre (1st Series)
Some of Neal Adams' earliest work
©DC

Spectre (2nd Series)
Spectre given a second chance
©DC

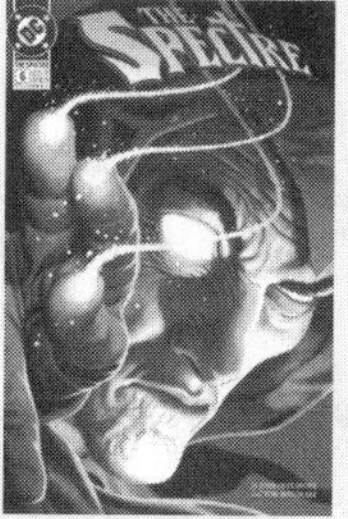
Spectre (3rd Series)
Character remains compelling in third series
©DC

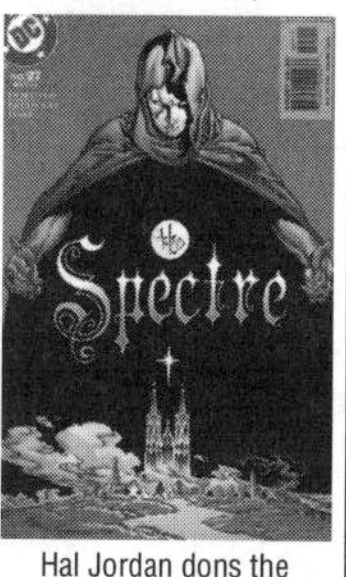
Spectre (4th Series)
Hal Jordan dons the Spectre's cape
©DC

Speedball
Ditko's wacky teen-age speedster
©Marvel

N-MINT

SPANDEX TIGHTS (VOL. 2)
Lost Cause

- ❑1, Jan 1997, b&w ... 2.95
- ❑2, Mar 1997, b&w ... 2.95
- ❑3, May 1997, b&w ... 2.95

SPANISH FLY
Fantagraphics / Eros

- ❑1 ... 2.95
- ❑2 ... 2.95
- ❑3 ... 2.95
- ❑4 ... 2.95
- ❑5, May 1996 ... 2.95

SPANK
Fantagraphics / Eros

- ❑2, b&w ... 2.25
- ❑3, b&w ... 2.25
- ❑4, b&w ... 2.25

SPANK THE MONKEY
Arrow

- ❑1, Jul 1999, b&w ... 2.95

SPANNER'S GALAXY
DC

- ❑1, Dec 1984; mini-series ... 1.00
- ❑2, Jan 1985 ... 1.00
- ❑3, Feb 1985 ... 1.00
- ❑4, Mar 1985 ... 1.00
- ❑5, Apr 1985 ... 1.00
- ❑6, May 1985 ... 1.00

SPARK GENERATORS
Slave Labor

- ❑1, ca. 2002, b&w; anthology ... 13.95

SPARKPLUG
Heroic

- ❑1, b&w ... 2.95
- ❑2, b&w; trading card ... 2.95
- ❑3 ... 2.95

SPARKY & TIM
Aaron Warner

- ❑1, Feb 1999 ... 5.95

SPARROW (MILLENNIUM)
Millennium

- ❑1 1995, b&w ... 2.95
- ❑2, Apr 1995, b&w ... 2.95
- ❑3, May 1995, b&w ... 2.95
- ❑4, Jul 1995, b&w ... 2.95

SPARROW (DC/PIRANHA)
DC / Piranha

- ❑1, b&w; paperback ... 9.95

SPARTAN: WARRIOR SPIRIT
Image

- ❑1, Jul 1995 ... 2.50
- ❑2, Sep 1995 ... 2.50
- ❑3, Oct 1995 ... 2.50
- ❑4, Nov 1995 ... 2.50

SPARTAN X: HELL-BENT-HERO-FOR-HIRE (JACKIE CHAN'S...)
Image

- ❑1, Mar 1998 ... 2.95
- ❑2, Apr 1998 ... 2.95
- ❑3, May 1998, cover says Jun, indicia says May ... 2.95
- ❑4, Jul 1998, cover says Aug, indicia says Jul ... 2.95

N-MINT

SPARTAN X: THE ARMOUR OF HEAVEN (JACKIE CHAN'S...)
Topps

- ❑1, May 1997 ... 2.95

SPASM (PARODY PRESS)
Parody

- ❑1 ... 9.95

SPASM (ROUGH COPY)
Rough Copy

- ❑1 ... 2.95
- ❑2 ... 2.95
- ❑3 ... 2.95
- ❑4 ... 2.95
- ❑5 ... 2.95

SPAWN
Image

- ❑1, May 1992 TMc (c); TMc (w); TMc (a); 1: Spawn. ... 5.00
- ❑1/A, Sep 1997; TMc (w); TMc (a); promo with Spawn #65 ... 2.95
- ❑2, Jul 1992; TMc (c); TMc (w); TMc (a); 1: Violator. cover says Jun, indicia says Jul ... 4.00
- ❑3, Aug 1992 TMc (c); TMc (w); TMc (a) 2.50
- ❑4, Sep 1992; TMc (c); TMc (w); TMc (a); with coupon ... 2.50
- ❑5, Oct 1992 TMc (c); TMc (w); TMc (a) 2.50
- ❑6, Nov 1992 TMc (c); TMc (w); TMc (a); 1: Overt-Kill. ... 2.50
- ❑7, Jan 1993 TMc (c); TMc (w); TMc (a) 4.00
- ❑8, Mar 1993; TMc (c); AMo (w); TMc (a); cover says Feb, indicia says Mar 4.00
- ❑9, Mar 1993 TMc (c); NG (w); TMc (a); 1: Angela. ... 4.00
- ❑10, May 1993 TMc (c); TMc (a); A: Cerebus. ... 2.75
- ❑11, Jun 1993 TMc (c); FM (w); TMc (a) 2.50
- ❑12, Jul 1993 TMc (c); TMc (w); TMc (a) 2.50
- ❑13, Aug 1993; TMc (c); TMc (w); TMc (a); Spawn vs. Chapel ... 2.50
- ❑14, Sep 1993 TMc (c); TMc (w); TMc (a); A: Violator. ... 2.50
- ❑15, Nov 1993 TMc (c); TMc (w); TMc (a) 2.50
- ❑16, Dec 1993 1: Anti-Spawn. ... 2.50
- ❑17, Jan 1994; 1: Anti-Spawn. Spawn vs. Anti-Spawn ... 3.00
- ❑18, Feb 1994 ... 3.00
- ❑19, Oct 1994; Published out of sequence with fill-in art ... 3.00
- ❑20, Nov 1994; TMc (a); Published out of sequence with fill-in art ... 3.00
- ❑21, May 1994 TMc (c); TMc (w); TMc (a) 3.00
- ❑22, Jun 1994 TMc (c); TMc (w); TMc (a) 3.00
- ❑23, Aug 1994 TMc (c); TMc (w); TMc (a) 3.00
- ❑24, Sep 1994 TMc (c); TMc (w); TMc (a) 3.00
- ❑25, Oct 1994 TMc (w) ... 3.00
- ❑26, Dec 1994 TMc (c); TMc (w); TMc (a) 3.00
- ❑27, Jan 1995 TMc (c); TMc (w); TMc (a) 3.00
- ❑28, Feb 1995 TMc (c); TMc (w); TMc (a) 3.00
- ❑29, Mar 1995 TMc (c); TMc (w); TMc (a) 3.00
- ❑30, Apr 1995 TMc (c); TMc (w); TMc (a) 3.00
- ❑31, May 1995 TMc (c); TMc (w); TMc (a) 3.00
- ❑32, Jun 1995 TMc (c); TMc (w); TMc (a) 3.00

N-MINT

- ❑33, Jul 1995 TMc (c); TMc (w); TMc (a) 3.00
- ❑34, Aug 1995 TMc (c); TMc (w); TMc (a) 3.00
- ❑35, Sep 1995 TMc (c); TMc (w); TMc (a) 3.00
- ❑36, Oct 1995 TMc (c); TMc (w); TMc (a) 3.00
- ❑37, Nov 1995 TMc (c); TMc, AMo (w); TMc (a) ... 3.00
- ❑38, Dec 1995; TMc (w); 1: Cy-Gor. cover says Aug, indicia says Dec ... 3.00
- ❑39, Dec 1995; TMc (c); TMc (w); TMc (a); Christmas story ... 3.00
- ❑40, Jan 1996 TMc (w) ... 3.00
- ❑41, Jan 1996 TMc (c); TMc (w); TMc (a) 3.00
- ❑42, Feb 1996 TMc (w) ... 3.00
- ❑43, Feb 1996 TMc (c); TMc (w); TMc (a) 3.00
- ❑44, Mar 1996 TMc (w) ... 3.00
- ❑45, Mar 1996 TMc (c); TMc (w); TMc (a) 3.00
- ❑46, Apr 1996 TMc (w) ... 3.00
- ❑47, Apr 1996 TMc (c); TMc (w); TMc (a) 3.00
- ❑48, May 1996 TMc (w) ... 3.00
- ❑49, May 1996 TMc (w); TMc (a) ... 3.00
- ❑50, Jun 1996 TMc (c); TMc (w); TMc (a) 2.95
- ❑51, Aug 1996; TMc (c); TMc (w); TMc (a); cover says Jul, indicia says Aug 1.95
- ❑52, Aug 1996 TMc (c); TMc (w); TMc (a) 1.95
- ❑53, Sep 1996 TMc (c); TMc (w); TMc (a) 1.95
- ❑54, Oct 1996 TMc (c); TMc (w); TMc (a) 1.95
- ❑55, Nov 1996 TMc (w); TMc (a) ... 1.95
- ❑56, Dec 1996 TMc (c); TMc (w); TMc (a) 1.95
- ❑57, Jan 1997 TMc (c); TMc (w); TMc (a) 1.95
- ❑58, Feb 1997 TMc (c); TMc (w); TMc (a) 1.95
- ❑59, Mar 1997 TMc (c); TMc (w); TMc (a) 1.95
- ❑60, Apr 1997 TMc (c); TMc (w); TMc (a) 1.95
- ❑61, May 1997 TMc (c); TMc (w); TMc (a) 1.95
- ❑62, Jun 1997 TMc (c); TMc (w); TMc (a); A: Angela. ... 1.95
- ❑63, Jul 1997 TMc (c); TMc (w); TMc (a) 1.95
- ❑64, Aug 1997; TMc (c); TMc (w); TMc (a); polybagged with McFarlane Toys catalog ... 1.95
- ❑65, Sep 1997 TMc (w); TMc (a) ... 1.95
- ❑66, Oct 1997 TMc (c); TMc (w); TMc (a) 1.95
- ❑67, Nov 1997 TMc (c); TMc (w); TMc (a) 1.95
- ❑68, Jan 1998 TMc (c); TMc (w); TMc (a) 1.95
- ❑69, Jan 1998 TMc (c); TMc (w); TMc (a) 1.95
- ❑70, Feb 1998 TMc (w); TMc (a) ... 1.95
- ❑71, Apr 1998 TMc (w); TMc (a) ... 1.95
- ❑72, May 1998 TMc (c); TMc (w); TMc (a) 1.95
- ❑73, Jun 1998 TMc (w); TMc (a) ... 1.95
- ❑74, Jul 1998 TMc (c); TMc (w) ... 1.95
- ❑75, Aug 1998 TMc (c); TMc (w) ... 1.95
- ❑76, Sep 1998 TMc (w) ... 1.95
- ❑77, Oct 1998 TMc (c); TMc (w) ... 1.95
- ❑78, Nov 1998 TMc (w) ... 1.95
- ❑79, Jan 1999 TMc (w) ... 1.95
- ❑80, Feb 1999 TMc (w) ... 1.95
- ❑81, Mar 1999 TMc (c); TMc (w) ... 1.95
- ❑82, Apr 1999 TMc (c); TMc (w) ... 1.95
- ❑83, May 1999 TMc (c); TMc (w) ... 1.95
- ❑84, Jun 1999 TMc (c); TMc (w) ... 1.95
- ❑85, Jul 1999 TMc (w) ... 1.95
- ❑86, Aug 1999 TMc (c); TMc (w) ... 1.95
- ❑87, Sep 1999 TMc (w) ... 1.95
- ❑88, Oct 1999 TMc (c); TMc (w) ... 1.95
- ❑89, Nov 1999 TMc (c); TMc (w) ... 1.95
- ❑90, Dec 1999 TMc (c); TMc (w) ... 1.95

- ❑91, Jan 2000 TMc (c); TMc (w) 1.95
- ❑92, Feb 2000 TMc (c); TMc (w) 1.95
- ❑93, Mar 2000 TMc (c); TMc (w) 1.95
- ❑94, Apr 2000 TMc (c); TMc (w) 1.95
- ❑95, May 2000 TMc (c); TMc (w) 1.95
- ❑96, Jun 2000 TMc (c); TMc (w) 1.95
- ❑97, Jul 2000 TMc (c); TMc (w) 1.95
- ❑98, Aug 2000 TMc (c); TMc (w) 2.50
- ❑99, Sep 2000 TMc (w) 2.50
- ❑100/A, Nov 2000; Giant-size TMc (c); TMc (w) 6.00
- ❑100/B, Nov 2000; Giant-size TMc (w) 4.95
- ❑100/C, Nov 2000; Giant-size FM (c); TMc (w) 4.95
- ❑100/D, Nov 2000; Giant-size TMc (w) 4.95
- ❑100/E, Nov 2000; Giant-size ARo (c); TMc (w) 4.95
- ❑100/F, Nov 2000; Giant-size TMc (w) 4.95
- ❑101, Dec 2000 TMc (w) 2.50
- ❑102, Jan 2001 TMc (c); TMc (w) 2.50
- ❑103, Feb 2001 TMc (w) 2.50
- ❑104, Feb 2001 TMc (c); TMc (w) 2.50
- ❑105, Feb 2001 TMc (c); TMc (w) 2.50
- ❑106, Mar 2001 TMc (c); TMc (w) 2.50
- ❑107, Apr 2001 TMc (c); TMc (w) 2.50
- ❑108, May 2001 TMc (w); TMc (a) 2.50
- ❑109, Jun 2001 TMc (w) 2.50
- ❑110, Jul 2001 TMc (c); TMc (w) 2.50
- ❑111, Aug 2001 TMc (c); TMc (w) 2.50
- ❑112, Sep 2001 TMc (c); TMc (w) 2.50
- ❑113, Oct 2001 TMc (c); TMc (w) 2.50
- ❑114, Nov 2001 TMc (c); TMc (w) 2.50
- ❑115, Dec 2001 TMc (c); TMc (w) 2.50
- ❑116, Jan 2002 TMc (c); TMc (w) 2.50
- ❑117, May 2002 TMc (c); TMc (w) 2.50
- ❑118, Jun 2002 TMc (c); TMc (w) 2.50
- ❑119, Aug 2002 TMc (c); TMc (w) 2.50
- ❑120, Sep 2002 TMc (c); TMc (w) 2.50
- ❑121, Dec 2002 TMc (w) 2.50
- ❑122, Feb 2003 TMc (w) 2.50
- ❑123, Mar 2003 TMc (w) 2.50
- ❑124, Apr 2003 TMc (w) 2.50
- ❑125, May 2003 TMc (w) 2.50
- ❑126, Jul 2003 TMc (w) 2.50
- ❑127, Aug 2003 TMc (w) 2.50
- ❑128, Sep 2003 TMc (w) 2.50
- ❑129, Oct 2003 TMc (w) 2.50
- ❑130, Nov 2003 TMc (w) 2.50
- ❑131, Dec 2003 TMc (c); TMc (w) 2.50
- ❑132, Feb 2004 TMc (w) 2.50
- ❑133, Apr 2004 TMc (w) 2.50
- ❑134, May 2004 TMc (w) 2.50
- ❑135, Aug 2004 TMc (w) 2.50
- ❑136, Sep 2004 TMc (w) 2.50
- ❑137, Oct 2004 TMc (w) 2.50
- ❑138, Nov 2004 TMc (w) 2.50
- ❑139, Dec 2004 TMc (w) 2.50
- ❑140, Jan 2004, TMc (w) 2.50
- ❑141, Feb 2005 TMc (w) 2.50
- ❑142, Mar 2005 2.50
- ❑143, Apr 2005 2.50
- ❑144, May 2005 2.50
- ❑145, Jun 2005 2.50
- ❑146, Jul 2005 2.50
- ❑147, Aug 2005 2.50
- ❑148, Sep 2005 2.50
- ❑149, Oct 2005 2.50
- ❑150, Nov 2005 2.50
- ❑151, Dec 2005 2.50
- ❑152, Jan 2006 2.50
- ❑153, Mar 2006 2.50
- ❑154, Apr 2006 2.50
- ❑155, May 2006 2.50
- ❑156, Jun 2006 2.50
- ❑157, Jul 2006 2.50
- ❑Annual 1, May 1999; squarebound 4.95
- ❑Fan ed. 1/A, Aug 1996, Promotional edition included in Overstreet Fan 1.00
- ❑Fan ed. 1/B, Aug 1996 1.00
- ❑Fan ed. 2/A, Sep 1996, Promotional edition included in Overstreet Fan 1.00
- ❑Fan ed. 2/B, Sep 1996 1.00
- ❑Fan ed. 3/A, Oct 1996, Promotional edition included in Overstreet Fan 1.00
- ❑Fan ed. 3/B, Oct 1996 1.00
- ❑Book 11; TMc (w); TMc (a); Collects Spawn #48-50 10.95
- ❑Book 12; TMc (w); TMc (a); Collects Spawn #51-54 10.95

SPAWN: ANGELA'S HUNT
IMAGE

- ❑Book 1 9.95
- ❑Book 1/2nd 7.95

SPAWN-BATMAN
IMAGE

- ❑1, ca. 1994 FM (w); TMc (a) 4.00

SPAWN BIBLE
IMAGE

- ❑1, Aug 1996; background on series 1.95

SPAWN BLOOD AND SALVATION
IMAGE

- ❑1, Nov 1999 4.95

SPAWN BLOOD FEUD
IMAGE

- ❑1, Jun 1995 2.25
- ❑2, Jul 1995 2.25
- ❑3, Aug 1995 2.25
- ❑4, Sep 1995 2.25

SPAWN MOVIE ADAPTATION
IMAGE

- ❑1, Dec 1997; prestige format 4.95

SPAWN #1 IN 3-D
IMAGE

- ❑1, May 2006 4.95

SPAWN: SIMONY ONE-SHOT
IMAGE

- ❑1, Apr 2004 7.95

SPAWN: THE DARK AGES
IMAGE

- ❑1, Mar 1999 3.00
- ❑1/Variant, Mar 1999 TMc (c); TMc (a) 2.50
- ❑2, Apr 1999 TMc (c); TMc (a) 2.50
- ❑3, May 1999 2.50
- ❑4, Jun 1999 2.50
- ❑5, Jul 1999 2.50
- ❑6, Aug 1999 2.50
- ❑7, Sep 1999 2.50
- ❑8, Oct 1999 2.50
- ❑9, Nov 1999 2.50
- ❑10, Dec 1999 2.50
- ❑11, Jan 2000 2.50
- ❑12, Feb 2000 2.50
- ❑13, Mar 2000 2.50
- ❑14, Apr 2000 2.50
- ❑15, May 2000 2.50
- ❑16, Jun 2000 2.50
- ❑17, Jul 2000 2.50
- ❑18, Aug 2000 2.50
- ❑19, Sep 2000 2.50
- ❑20, Oct 2000 2.50
- ❑21, Nov 2000 2.50
- ❑22, Jan 2001 2.50
- ❑23, Feb 2001 2.50
- ❑24, Mar 2001 2.50
- ❑25, Apr 2001 2.50
- ❑26, May 2001 2.50
- ❑27, Jun 2001 2.50
- ❑28, Jul 2001 2.50

SPAWN THE IMPALER
IMAGE

- ❑1, Oct 1996 2.95
- ❑2, Nov 1996 2.95
- ❑3, Dec 1996 2.95

SPAWN THE UNDEAD
IMAGE

- ❑1, Jun 1999 2.00
- ❑2, Jul 1999 1.95
- ❑3, Aug 1999 1.95
- ❑4, Sep 1999 1.95
- ❑5, Oct 1999 1.95
- ❑6, Nov 1999 1.95
- ❑7, Dec 1999 1.95
- ❑8, Jan 2000 2.25
- ❑9, Feb 2000 2.25

SPAWN/WILDC.A.T.S
IMAGE

- ❑1, Jan 1996, AMo (w) 3.00
- ❑2, Feb 1996, AMo (w) 2.50
- ❑3, Mar 1996, AMo (w) 2.50
- ❑4, Apr 1996, AMo (w) 2.50

SPECIAL HUGGING AND OTHER CHILDHOOD TALES
SLAVE LABOR

- ❑1, Apr 1989, b&w 1.95

SPECIAL MARVEL EDITION
MARVEL

- ❑1, Jan 1971; SL (w); JK (a); reprints Thor stories from Journey into Mystery #117-119; Thor reprints begin 20.00
- ❑2 1971; reprints Thor stories from Journey into Mystery #120-122 15.00
- ❑3, Sep 1971; reprints Thor stories from Journey into Mystery #123-125 15.00
- ❑4, Feb 1972; reprints Thor #126 and #127; Thor reprints end 15.00
- ❑5, Jul 1972, Sgt. Fury reprints begin 7.00
- ❑6, Sep 1972 7.00
- ❑7, Nov 1972, Sgt. Fury 7.00
- ❑8, Jan 1973 7.00
- ❑9, Mar 1973 7.00
- ❑10, May 1973 7.00
- ❑11, Jul 1973, A: Captain America. 7.00
- ❑12, Sep 1973 7.00
- ❑13, Oct 1973, SD (a) 7.00
- ❑14, Nov 1973, Sgt. Fury reprints end 7.00
- ❑15, Dec 1973, JSn (a); 1: Shang-Chi, Master of Kung Fu. 1: Nayland Smith. Master of Kung Fu 45.00
- ❑16, Feb 1974, JSn (a); O: Midnight. 1: Midnight. 2: Shang-Chi, Master of Kung Fu. series continues as Master of Kung Fu 18.00

SPECIAL WAR SERIES
CHARLTON

- ❑1, Aug 1965 10.00
- ❑2, Sep 1965, Attack! 8.00
- ❑3, Oct 1965, War and Attack 8.00
- ❑4, Nov 1965, O: Judomaster. 1: Judomaster. 16.00

SPECIES
DARK HORSE

- ❑1, Jun 1995 2.50
- ❑2, Jul 1995 2.50
- ❑3, Aug 1995 2.50
- ❑4, Sep 1995 2.50

SPECIES: HUMAN RACE
DARK HORSE

- ❑1, Nov 1996 2.95
- ❑2, Dec 1996 2.95
- ❑3, Jan 1997 2.95
- ❑4, Feb 1997 2.95

SPECTACLES
ALTERNATIVE

- ❑1, Feb 1997, b&w 2.95
- ❑2, May 1997, b&w 2.95
- ❑3, Sep 1997, b&w 2.95
- ❑4, Jan 1998, b&w 2.95

SPECTACULAR SCARLET SPIDER
MARVEL

- ❑1, Nov 1995 1.95
- ❑2, Dec 1995 1.95

SPECTACULAR SPIDER-MAN (MAGAZINE)
MARVEL

- ❑1, Jul 1968, b&w; magazine JR (a); 1: Richard Raleigh, Man Monster 90.00
- ❑2, Nov 1968, magazine JR (a); V: Green Goblin 75.00

SPECTACULAR SPIDER-MAN
MARVEL

- ❑-1, Jul 1997; Flashback 2.00
- ❑1, Dec 1976, JR, SL (w); SB, JR (a); Tarantula 25.00
- ❑3, Feb 1977, SB (a); O: Lightmaster. 1: Lightmaster. Newsstand edition (distributed by Curtis); issue number in box 8.00
- ❑2, Jan 1977, JR, SL (w); SB, JR, JM (a); Kraven 15.00
- ❑3/Whitman, Feb 1977, SB (a); O: Lightmaster. 1: Lightmaster. Special markets edition (usually sold in Whitman bagged prepacks); price appears in a diamond; UPC barcode appears 8.00
- ❑4, Mar 1977, SB (a); V: Vulture. Newsstand edition (distributed by Curtis); issue number in box 5.00

Speed Racer (1st Series)	Spellbound (Marvel)	Spelljammer	Spider-Girl	Spider-Man

Anime liked by some, loathed by others ©Now	Rival spellbinders in a mystical universe ©Marvel	Melds Dungeons & Dragons with science fiction ©DC	Spider-Man's daughter from alternate future ©Marvel	"Adjectiveless" series created for McFarlane ©Marvel

	N-MINT
❑4/Whitman, Mar 1977, SB (a); V: Vulture. Special markets edition (usually sold in Whitman bagged prepacks); price appears in a diamond; UPC barcode appears	5.00
❑5, Apr 1977 SB (a); V: Vulture.	5.00
❑6, May 1977, A: Morbius. V: Morbius. Newsstand edition (distributed by Curtis); issue number in box	5.00
❑6/Whitman, May 1977, A: Morbius. V: Morbius. Special markets edition (usually sold in Whitman bagged prepacks); price appears in a diamond; UPC barcode appears	5.00
❑7, Jun 1977, A: Morbius. V: Morbius. Newsstand edition (distributed by Curtis); issue number in box	5.00
❑7/Whitman, Jun 1977, A: Morbius. V: Morbius. Special markets edition (usually sold in Whitman bagged prepacks); price appears in a diamond; UPC barcode appears	5.00
❑7/35 cent, Jun 1977, A: Morbius. V: Morbius. 35 cent regional price variant newsstand edition (distributed by Curtis); issue number in box	15.00
❑8, Jul 1977, PG (c); A: Morbius. V: Morbius. Newsstand edition (distributed by Curtis); issue number in box	5.00
❑8/Whitman, Jul 1977, PG (c); A: Morbius. V: Morbius. Special markets edition (usually sold in Whitman bagged prepacks); price appears in a diamond; UPC barcode appears	5.00
❑8/35 cent, Jul 1977, PG (c); A: Morbius. V: Morbius. 35 cent regional price variant newsstand edition (distributed by Curtis); issue number in box	15.00
❑9, Aug 1977, A: White Tiger. Newsstand edition (distributed by Curtis); issue number in box	5.00
❑9/Whitman, Aug 1977, A: White Tiger. Special markets edition (usually sold in Whitman bagged prepacks); price appears in a diamond; UPC barcode appears	5.00
❑9/35 cent, Aug 1977, 35 cent regional price variant newsstand edition (distributed by Curtis); issue number in box	15.00
❑10, Sep 1977, A: White Tiger. Newsstand edition (distributed by Curtis); issue number in box	3.50
❑10/Whitman, Sep 1977, A: White Tiger. Special markets edition (usually sold in Whitman bagged prepacks); price appears in a diamond; no UPC barcode	3.50
❑10/35 cent, Sep 1977, A: White Tiger. 35 cent regional price variant newsstand edition (distributed by Curtis); issue number in box	15.00
❑11, Oct 1977, JM (a); Newsstand edition (distributed by Curtis); issue number in box	3.50
❑11/Whitman, Oct 1977, JM (a); Special markets edition (usually sold in Whitman bagged prepacks); price appears in a diamond; no UPC barcode	3.50

	N-MINT
❑11/35 cent, Oct 1977, JM (a); 35 cent regional price variant newsstand edition (distributed by Curtis); issue number in box	15.00
❑12, Nov 1977, SB (a); 1: Razorback (partial). A: Brother Power. Newsstand edition (distributed by Curtis); issue number in box	3.50
❑12/Whitman, Nov 1977, SB (a); 1: Razorback (partial). A: Brother Power. Special markets edition (usually sold in Whitman bagged prepacks); price appears in a diamond; no UPC barcode	3.50
❑13, Dec 1977, SB (a); O: Razorback. 1: Razorback (full)	3.50
❑14, Jan 1978, SB (a); V: Hatemonger.	3.50
❑15, Feb 1978, SB (a); A: Razorback.	3.50
❑16, Mar 1978, SB (a); V: Beetle.	3.50
❑17, Apr 1978, A: Iceman. A: Angel.	3.50
❑18, May 1978, A: Iceman. A: Angel. Newsstand edition (distributed by Curtis); issue number in box	3.50
❑18/Whitman, May 1978, A: Iceman. A: Angel. Special markets edition (usually sold in Whitman bagged prepacks); price appears in a diamond; no UPC barcode	3.50
❑19, Jun 1978, V: Enforcers	3.50
❑20, Jul 1978, V: Light Master.	3.50
❑21, Aug 1978, A: Moon Knight. Newsstand edition (distributed by Curtis); issue number in box	2.75
❑21/Whitman, Aug 1978, A: Moon Knight. Special markets edition (usually sold in Whitman bagged prepacks); price appears in a diamond; UPC barcode appears	2.75
❑22, Sep 1978, A: Moon Knight. Newsstand edition (distributed by Curtis); issue number in box	2.75
❑22/Whitman, Sep 1978, A: Moon Knight. Special markets edition (usually sold in Whitman bagged prepacks); price appears in a diamond; no UPC barcode	2.75
❑23, Oct 1978, A: Moon Knight.	2.75
❑24, Nov 1978, Newsstand edition (distributed by Curtis); issue number in box	2.75
❑24/Whitman, Nov 1978, Special markets edition (usually sold in Whitman bagged prepacks); price appears in a diamond; no UPC barcode	2.75
❑25, Dec 1978, 1: Carrion I. Newsstand edition (distributed by Curtis); issue number in box	2.75
❑25/Whitman, Dec 1978, 1: Carrion I. Special markets edition (usually sold in Whitman bagged prepacks); price appears in a diamond; no UPC barcode	2.75
❑26, Jan 1979, A: Daredevil. Newsstand edition (distributed by Curtis); issue number in box	2.75
❑26/Whitman, Jan 1979, A: Daredevil. Special markets edition (usually sold in Whitman bagged prepacks); price appears in a diamond; no UPC barcode	2.75

	N-MINT
❑27, Feb 1979, FM, DC (a); A: Daredevil. Frank Miller's first Daredevil art; newsstand edition (distributed by Curtis); issue number in box	15.00
❑27/Whitman, Feb 1979, FM, DC (a); A: Daredevil. Frank Miller's first Daredevil art; special markets edition (usually sold in Whitman bagged prepacks); price appears in a diamond; no UPC barcode	15.00
❑28, Mar 1979, FM (a); A: Daredevil.	15.00
❑29, Apr 1979, V: Carrion	2.75
❑30, May 1979, V: Carrion. Newsstand edition (distributed by Curtis); issue number in box	2.75
❑30/Whitman, May 1979, V: Carrion. Special markets edition (usually sold in Whitman bagged prepacks); price appears in a diamond; no UPC barcode	2.75
❑31, Jun 1979, O: Carrion I. D: Carrion I.	2.75
❑32, Jul 1979	2.75
❑33, Aug 1979, O: Iguana	2.75
❑34, Sep 1979, V: Lizard.	2.75
❑35, Oct 1979	2.75
❑36, Nov 1979, V: Swarm.	2.75
❑37, Dec 1979, V: Swarm	2.75
❑38, Jan 1980, A: Morbius. V: Morbius.	2.75
❑39, Feb 1980, V: Schizoid Man	2.75
❑40, Mar 1980, V: Lizard.	2.75
❑41, Apr 1980, V: Meteor Man.	2.75
❑42, May 1980, A: Human Torch.	2.75
❑43, Jun 1980, 1: Belladonna	2.75
❑44, Jul 1980	2.75
❑45, Aug 1980, Vulture	2.75
❑46, Sep 1980, FM (c); MZ (a); Cobra	2.75
❑47, Oct 1980	2.75
❑48, Nov 1980, FM (c);	2.75
❑49, Dec 1980, JM (a); A: Prowler. Title changes to Peter Parker, The Spectacular Spider-Man	2.75
❑50, Jan 1981, FM (c); JR2, JM (a); Smuggler	2.75
❑51, Feb 1981, FM (c); JM (a); V: Mysterio.	2.75
❑52, Mar 1981, FM (c); A: White Tiger.	2.75
❑53, Apr 1981, JM (a); V: Tinkerer.	2.75
❑54, May 1981, FM (c);	2.75
❑55, Jun 1981, FM (c); LMc (a); V: Nitro.	2.75
❑56, Jul 1981, FM (c); JM (a); 2: Jack O'Lantern II. V: Jack O'Lantern II.	5.00
❑57, Aug 1981, FM (c); JM (a)	2.75
❑58, Sep 1981, JBy (a); V: Ringer.	2.75
❑59, Oct 1981, JM (a)	2.75
❑60, Nov 1981; Giant-size FM, JM (c); JM (a); O: Spider-Man. V: Beetle.	2.75
❑61, Dec 1981, JM (a); A: Moonstone.	2.75
❑62, Jan 1982, FM (c); FM (a); V: Gold Bug.	2.75
❑63, Feb 1982, V: Molten Man.	2.75
❑64, Mar 1982, 1: Cloak & Dagger.	5.00
❑65, Apr 1982, BH (a); V: Kraven.	3.00
❑66, May 1982, V: Electro.	3.00
❑67, Jun 1982, V: Kingpin.	3.00
❑68, Jul 1982, V: Robot Master.	3.00
❑69, Aug 1982, A: Cloak & Dagger.	3.00

Other grades: Multiply price above by 5/6 for VF/NM • 2/3 for VERY FINE • 1/3 for FINE • 1/5 for VERY GOOD • 1/8 for GOOD

	N-MINT
❏70, Sep 1982, A: Cloak & Dagger.	3.00
❏71, Oct 1982, Gun control story	3.00
❏72, Nov 1982, V: Doctor Octopus.	3.00
❏73, Dec 1982, V: Owl.	3.00
❏74, Jan 1983, BH (c); BH (a); A: Black Cat.	3.00
❏75, Feb 1983; Giant-size A: Black Cat.	2.75
❏76, Mar 1983, A: Black Cat.	3.00
❏77, Apr 1983, A: Gladiator.	3.00
❏78, May 1983, V: Doctor Octopus.	3.00
❏79, Jun 1983, V: Doctor Octopus.	3.00
❏80, Jul 1983, J. Jonah Jameson solo story	3.00
❏81, Aug 1983, AM, JM (a); A: Punisher. A: Cloak & Dagger.	3.00
❏82, Sep 1983, A: Punisher. A: Cloak & Dagger.	2.75
❏83, Oct 1983, A: Punisher.	7.00
❏84, Nov 1983	3.00
❏85, Dec 1983, A: Hobgoblin (Ned Leeds). V: Hobgoblin.	5.00
❏86, Jan 1984, A: Fred Hembeck. Asst. Editor Month	3.00
❏87, Feb 1984, AM (a); reveals identity	3.00
❏88, Mar 1984, A: Black Cat. V: Mr. Hyde. V: Cobra.	3.00
❏89, Apr 1984, A: Fantastic Four. A: Kingpin. Fantastic Four apperance	3.00
❏90, May 1984, AM (a); new costume; Black Cat's new powers	3.00
❏91, Jun 1984, V: Blob.	3.00
❏92, Jul 1984, 1: The Answer. V: Answer.	3.00
❏93, Aug 1984, V: Answer.	3.00
❏94, Sep 1984, A: Cloak & Dagger. V: Silvermane.	3.00
❏95, Oct 1984, A: Cloak & Dagger. V: Silvermane.	3.00
❏96, Nov 1984, A: Cloak & Dagger. V: Silvermane.	3.00
❏97, Dec 1984, V: Hermit.	3.00
❏98, Jan 1985, 1: Spot. V: Kingpin.	3.00
❏99, Feb 1985, V: Spot.	3.00
❏100, Mar 1985; Giant-size V: Spot.	5.00
❏101, Apr 1985, V: Blacklash.	3.00
❏102, May 1985, V: Killer Shrike.	2.25
❏103, Jun 1985	2.25
❏104, Jul 1985, O: Rocket Racer. V: Rocket Racer.	2.25
❏105, Aug 1985, A: Wasp.	2.25
❏106, Sep 1985, A: Wasp.	2.25
❏107, Oct 1985, D: Jean DeWolff.	2.25
❏108, Nov 1985	2.25
❏109, Dec 1985	2.25
❏110, Jan 1986, A: Daredevil.	2.25
❏111, Feb 1986; Secret Wars II	2.25
❏112, Mar 1986; Christmas story	2.25
❏113, Apr 1986	2.25
❏114, May 1986	2.25
❏115, Jun 1986 A: Doctor Strange.	2.25
❏116, Jul 1986 A: Sabretooth.	3.00
❏117, Aug 1986 A: Doctor Strange.	2.00
❏118, Sep 1986	2.00
❏119, Oct 1986 A: Sabretooth.	2.00
❏120, Nov 1986	2.00
❏121, Dec 1986	2.00
❏122, Jan 1987	2.00
❏123, Feb 1987 PD (w); V: Blaze.	2.00
❏124, Mar 1987 BH (c); V: Doctor Octopus.	2.00
❏125, Apr 1987 A: Spider Woman.	2.00
❏126, May 1987 A: Spider Woman.	2.00
❏127, Jun 1987 V: Lizard.	2.00
❏128, Jul 1987 A: Silver Sable.	2.00
❏129, Aug 1987 V: Foreigner.	2.00
❏130, Sep 1987 A: Hobgoblin. V: Hobgoblin.	3.00
❏131, Oct 1987; MZ (a); Kraven	5.00
❏132, Nov 1987; Kraven	4.00
❏133, Dec 1987 BSz (a)	3.00
❏134, Jan 1988 V: Sin Eater.	2.00
❏135, Feb 1988; V: Sin Eater. V: Electro. Title returns to The Spectacular Spider-Man	2.00
❏136, Mar 1988 V: Sin Eater.	2.00
❏137, Apr 1988 V: Tarantula.	2.00
❏138, May 1988 A: Captain America. V: Tarantula.	2.00
❏139, Jun 1988 O: Tombstone.	2.00
❏140, Jul 1988 A: Punisher.	2.00
❏141, Aug 1988 A: Punisher.	2.00
❏142, Sep 1988 A: Punisher.	2.00
❏143, Oct 1988 A: Punisher.	4.00
❏144, Nov 1988; V: Boomerang. in San Diego	2.00
❏145, Dec 1988	2.00
❏146, Jan 1989; SB (a); Inferno	2.00
❏147, Feb 1989; 1: Hobgoblin III. Inferno	8.00
❏148, Mar 1989; Inferno	2.00
❏149, Apr 1989 O: Carrion II (Malcolm McBride). 1: Carrion II (Malcolm McBride)	3.00
❏150, May 1989 V: Tombstone.	2.00
❏151, Jun 1989 V: Tombstone.	2.00
❏152, Jul 1989 SB (a); V: Lobo Brothers.	2.00
❏153, Aug 1989 V: Tombstone.	2.00
❏154, Sep 1989 V: Puma.	2.00
❏155, Oct 1989 V: Tombstone.	2.00
❏156, Nov 1989 V: Banjo.	2.00
❏157, Nov 1989 V: Electro.	2.00
❏158, Dec 1989; V: Trapster. Acts of Vengeance; Spider-Man gets cosmic powers	5.00
❏159, Dec 1989; V: Brothers Grimm. Acts of Vengeance; Cosmic-powered Spider-Man	4.00
❏160, Jan 1990; V: Doctor Doom. Acts of Vengeance; Cosmic-powered Spider-Man	1.50
❏161, Feb 1990 A: Hobgoblin III. V: Hobgoblin III.	1.50
❏162, Mar 1990 A: Hobgoblin III. V: Carrion.	1.50
❏163, Apr 1990 A: Hobgoblin III. V: Hobgoblin III. V: Carrion.	1.50
❏164, May 1990 V: Beetle.	1.50
❏165, Jun 1990 D: Arranger.	1.50
❏166, Jul 1990 SB (a)	1.50
❏167, Aug 1990 SB (a)	1.50
❏168, Sep 1990; Avengers	1.50
❏169, Oct 1990; Avengers	1.50
❏170, Nov 1990; Avengers	1.50
❏171, Dec 1990 SB (a); V: Puma.	1.50
❏172, Jan 1991 V: Puma.	1.50
❏173, Feb 1991; SB (a); Doctor Octopus	1.50
❏174, Mar 1991; SB (a); Doctor Octopus	1.50
❏175, Apr 1991; SB (a); Doctor Octopus	1.50
❏176, May 1991 KB (w); SB (a); O: Corona. 1: Corona.	1.50
❏177, Jun 1991 KB (w); SB (a)	1.50
❏178, Jul 1991 SB (a); V: Vermin.	1.50
❏179, Aug 1991 SB (a); V: Vermin.	1.50
❏180, Sep 1991 SB (a); A: Green Goblin. V: Green Goblin.	1.50
❏181, Oct 1991 SB (a); A: Green Goblin. V: Green Goblin.	1.50
❏182, Nov 1991 SB (a); O: Vermin. A: Green Goblin. V: Green Goblin.	1.50
❏183, Dec 1991 SB (a); A: Green Goblin. V: Green Goblin.	1.50
❏184, Jan 1992 SB (a); A: Green Goblin.	1.50
❏185, Feb 1992 SB (a); A: Frogman.	1.50
❏186, Mar 1992 SB (a); V: Vulture.	1.50
❏187, Apr 1992 SB (a); V: Vulture.	1.50
❏188, May 1992 SB (a); V: Vulture.	1.50
❏189, Jun 1992; 30th Anniversary Issue; SB (a); O: Spider-Man. Silver hologram cover; Gatefold painted poster	4.00
❏189/2nd, Jun 1992; 30th Anniversary Issue SB (a); O: Spider-Man.	3.00
❏190, Jul 1992 SB (a)	1.50
❏191, Aug 1992 SB (a)	1.50
❏192, Sep 1992 SB (a)	1.50
❏193, Oct 1992 SB (a); V: Puma.	1.50
❏194, Nov 1992 SB (a); V: Vermin.	1.50
❏195, Dec 1992 SB (a); V: Vermin.	1.50
❏195/CS, Dec 1992; Polybagged with Dirt Magazine #2, cassette sampler tape; SB (a); "Dirtbag Special"	2.50
❏196, Jan 1993 SB (a); D: Vermin.	1.50
❏197, Feb 1993 SB (a); A: Spider-Man.	1.50
❏198, Mar 1993 SB (a); A: X-Men.	1.50
❏199, Apr 1993 SB (a); A: X-Men.	1.50
❏200, May 1993; SB (a); A: Green Goblin. D: Green Goblin. foil cover.	4.00
❏201, Jun 1993 SB (a); A: Carnage. A: Venom.	1.50
❏202, Jul 1993 SB (a); A: Carnage. A: Venom.	1.50
❏203, Aug 1993 SB (a); A: Carnage. A: Venom.	1.50
❏204, Sep 1993 SB (a); A: Tombstone. V: Tombstone.	1.50
❏205, Oct 1993 SB (a); A: Tombstone. V: Tombstone.	1.50
❏206, Nov 1993 SB (a); V: Tombstone.	1.50
❏207, Dec 1993 SB (a); V: Shroud.	1.50
❏208, Jan 1994 SB (a); V: Shroud.	1.50
❏209, Feb 1994 SB (a); A: Punisher. V: Foreigner.	1.50
❏210, Mar 1994 SB (a); V: Foreigner.	1.50
❏211, Apr 1994 SB (a)	1.50
❏212, May 1994 SB (a)	1.50
❏213, Jun 1994 V: Typhoid Mary.	1.50
❏213/CS, Jun 1994; V: Typhoid Mary. TV preview; print	2.95
❏214, Jul 1994 V: Bloody Mary.	1.50
❏215, Aug 1994 SB (a)	1.50
❏216, Sep 1994 SB (a); V: Scorpion.	1.50
❏217, Oct 1994 A: Ben Reilly.	1.50
❏217/Variant, Oct 1994; Giant-size; O: Ben Reilly. A: Ben Reilly. flip-book with back-up story; enhanced cover	2.95
❏218, Nov 1994 SB (a); V: Puma	1.50
❏219, Dec 1994 SB (a); A: Daredevil.	1.50
❏220, Jan 1995; Giant-size; flip book with illustrated story from The Ultimate Spider-Man back-up	2.50
❏221, Feb 1995 BSz, SB (a); D: Doctor Octopus.	3.00
❏222, Mar 1995 BSz, SB (a)	1.50
❏223, Apr 1995; Giant-size	2.50
❏223/Variant, Apr 1995; Giant-size; enhanced cover	2.95
❏224, May 1995	1.50
❏225, Jun 1995; Giant-size SB (a); 1: Green Goblin IV.	5.00
❏225/Variant, Jun 1995; Hologram on cover	3.95
❏226, Jul 1995; identity of clone revealed	1.50
❏227, Aug 1995	1.50
❏228, Sep 1995; continues in Web of Spider-Man #129	1.50
❏229, Oct 1995; Giant-size; BSz, SB (a); the clone retires; wraparound cover	2.50
❏229/Variant, Oct 1995; enhanced acetate outer cover; the clone retires	3.95
❏230, Jan 1996; Giant-size; V: D.K.. Special cover	3.95
❏231, Feb 1996 SB (a)	1.50
❏232, Mar 1996; SB (a); New Doctor Octopus returns	1.50
❏233, Apr 1996 SB (a)	1.50
❏234, May 1996	1.50
❏235, Jun 1996; return of Will o' the Wisp	1.50
❏236, Jul 1996 V: Dragon-Man.	1.50
❏237, Aug 1996 V: Lizard.	1.50
❏238, Sep 1996 O: second Lizard	1.50
❏239, Oct 1996 V: Lizard.	1.50
❏240, Nov 1996	1.50
❏240/A, Nov 1996; Variant cover showing pregnant Mary Jane	1.50
❏241, Dec 1996	1.50
❏242, Jan 1997 V: Chameleon	1.50
❏243, Feb 1997 V: Chameleon	1.50
❏244, Mar 1997 1: Kangaroo II. V: Kraven.	1.99
❏245, Apr 1997 V: Chameleon	1.99
❏246, May 1997 V: Legion of Losers (Gibbon, Spot, Kangaroo, Grizzly).	1.99
❏247, Jun 1997	1.99
❏248, Aug 1997; gatefold summary	1.99
❏249, Sep 1997; gatefold summary; Norman Osborn buys Daily Bugle	1.99
❏250, Oct 1997; Giant-size; wraparound cover	2.99
❏251, Nov 1997; gatefold summary V: Kraven.	1.99
❏252, Dec 1997; gatefold summary V: Kraven.	1.99
❏253, Jan 1998; gatefold summary V: Kraven. V: Calypso.	1.99
❏254, Feb 1998; gatefold summary	1.99
❏255, Mar 1998; gatefold summary	1.99
❏255/Variant, Mar 1998; Variant "Wanted Dead or Alive" cover	

Spider-Man & Wolverine

Popular characters in 2003 team-up

©Marvel

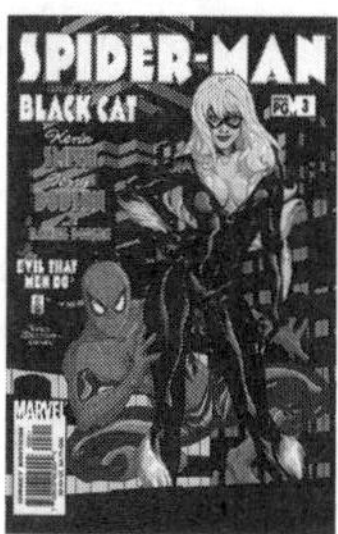

Spider-Man/Black Cat: The Evil That Men Do

Kevin Smith agrees to do series, forgets

©Marvel

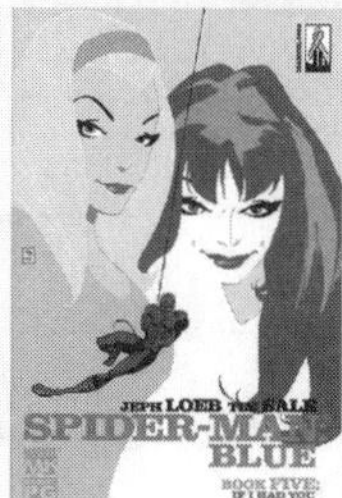

Spider-Man: Blue

Jeph Loeb and Tim Sale's take on Spidey

©Marvel

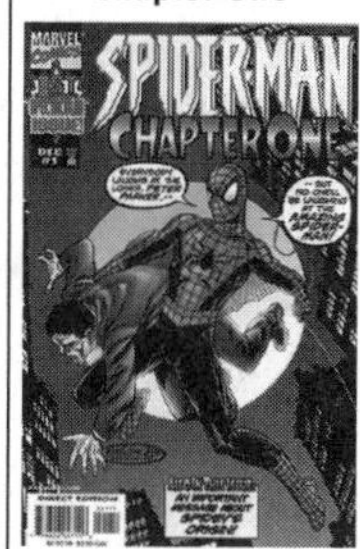

Spider-Man: Chapter One

John Byrne tries to reboot Spider-Man

©Marvel

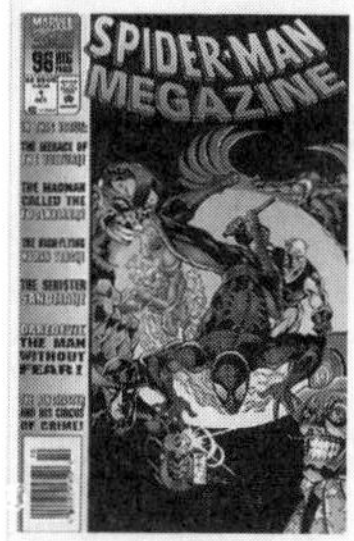

Spider-Man Megazine

Fun 96-page Spider-Man reprint series

©Marvel

	N-MINT
❑256, Apr 1998; gatefold summary V: White Rabbit.	1.99
❑257, May 1998; gatefold summary; Identity Crisis; has second cover with The Spectacular Prodigy #1	1.99
❑258, Jun 1998; gatefold summary	1.99
❑259, Jul 1998; gatefold summary	1.99
❑260, Aug 1998; gatefold summary	1.99
❑261, Sep 1998; gatefold summary	1.99
❑262, Oct 1998; gatefold summary	1.99
❑263, Nov 1998; gatefold summary JBy (c);	1.99
❑Annual 1, Dec 1979; RB, JM (a); Doctor Octopus	5.00
❑Annual 2, Sep 1980 JM (a); O: Rapier. 1: Rapier	4.00
❑Annual 3, Nov 1981	3.00
❑Annual 4, Nov 1984; O: Ben Parker ("Uncle Ben"). Title changes to Peter Parker, The Spectacular Spider-Man Annual	3.00
❑Annual 5, Oct 1985	3.00
❑Annual 6, Oct 1986; series continues as Spectacular Spider-Man Annual .	3.00
❑Annual 7, ca. 1987; V: Puma. Title returns to Spectacular Spider-Man Annual	3.00
❑Annual 8, ca. 1988	4.00
❑Annual 9, ca. 1989; Atlantis Attacks .	2.50
❑Annual 10, ca. 1990; SL (w); RB, TMc, RA (a); tiny Spider-Man	2.50
❑Annual 11, ca. 1991 FH (w); FH (a) ..	2.50
❑Annual 12, ca. 1992; A: New Warriors. Venom back-up story	2.50
❑Annual 13, ca. 1993; AM, JR (a); trading card	2.95
❑Annual 14, ca. 1994 SB (a); V: Green Goblin.	2.95
❑Annual 1997, ca. 1997; Peter Parker Spider-Man '97	2.99
❑Special 1, ca. 1995; Flip-book; A: Scarlet Spider. A: The Lizard. A: Carnage. A: Venom. Super special	3.95

SPECTACULAR SPIDER-MAN (2ND SERIES)
MARVEL

	N-MINT
❑1, Sep 2003, A: Venom.	4.00
❑1/CanExpo, Sep 2003	6.00
❑2, Sep 2003, A: Venom.	3.00
❑3, Oct 2003, A: Venom.	2.99
❑4, Nov 2003, A: Venom	4.00
❑5, Dec 2003, A: Venom.	2.99
❑6, Jan 2004, A: Doctor Octopus.	2.99
❑7, Jan 2004	2.99
❑8, Feb 2004	2.25
❑9, Mar 2004	2.25
❑10, Apr 2004	2.25
❑11, May 2004	2.25
❑12, May 2005	2.25
❑13, Jun 2004	2.25
❑14, Jul 2004	2.99
❑15, Aug 2004	7.00
❑16, Aug 2004	5.00
❑17, Sep 2004	2.25
❑18, Oct 2004	2.25
❑19, Nov 2004	2.25
❑20, Dec 2004	3.00
❑21, Jan 2005	2.25
❑22, Feb 2005	2.25
❑23, Mar 2005	2.25
❑24, Apr 2005	2.25
❑25, May 2005	2.25
❑26, Jun 2005	2.25
❑27, Jul 2005	2.25

SPECTACULAR SPIDER-MAN SUPER SPECIAL
MARVEL

	N-MINT
❑1, Sep 1995; Flip-book; two of the stories conclude in Web of Spider-Man Super Special #1	3.95

SPECTRE (1ST SERIES)
DC

	N-MINT
❑1, Dec 1967, MA, GC (a)	150.00
❑2, Feb 1968, NA (a)	60.00
❑3, Apr 1968, NA (a)	50.00
❑4, Jun 1968, NA (a)	50.00
❑5, Aug 1968, NA (a)	50.00
❑6, Oct 1968, MA (a)	40.00
❑7, Dec 1968, MA (a)	40.00
❑8, Feb 1969, MA (a)	40.00
❑9, Apr 1969, BWr (a)	40.00
❑10, Jun 1969	40.00

SPECTRE (2ND SERIES)
DC

	N-MINT
❑1, Apr 1987 GC (a)	3.00
❑2, May 1987	2.50
❑3, Jun 1987	2.50
❑4, Jul 1987	2.50
❑5, Aug 1987	2.50
❑6, Sep 1987 GC (a)	2.25
❑7, Oct 1987 A: Zatanna.	2.25
❑8, Nov 1987	2.25
❑9, Dec 1987	2.25
❑10, Jan 1988; Millennium	2.25
❑11, Feb 1988; Millennium	2.00
❑12, Mar 1988	2.00
❑13, Apr 1988	2.00
❑14, May 1988	2.00
❑15, Jun 1988	2.00
❑16, Jul 1988	2.00
❑17, Aug 1988	1.75
❑18, Sep 1988	1.75
❑19, Oct 1988	1.75
❑20, Nov 1988	1.75
❑21, Dec 1988	1.50
❑22, Dec 1988	1.50
❑23, Jan 1989; Invasion!	1.50
❑24, Feb 1989	1.50
❑25, Apr 1989	1.50
❑26, May 1989	1.50
❑27, Jun 1989	1.50
❑28, Aug 1989	1.50
❑29, Sep 1989	1.50
❑30, Oct 1989	1.50
❑31, Nov 1989	1.50
❑Annual 1, ca. 1988 A: Deadman.	2.50

SPECTRE (3RD SERIES)
DC

	N-MINT
❑0, Oct 1994 O: The Spectre.	2.50
❑1, Dec 1992; O: The Spectre. Glow-in-the-dark cover	6.00
❑2, Jan 1993	5.00
❑3, Feb 1993	4.00
❑4, Mar 1993	3.00
❑5, Apr 1993 CV (c)	3.00
❑6, May 1993	3.00
❑7, Jun 1993	3.00
❑8, Jul 1993; Glow-in-the-dark cover.	3.50
❑9, Aug 1993	3.00
❑10, Sep 1993	3.00
❑11, Oct 1993	3.00
❑12, Nov 1993	3.00
❑13, Dec 1993; Glow-in-the-dark cover	3.00
❑14, Jan 1994	2.50
❑15, Feb 1994	2.50
❑16, Mar 1994 JA (a)	2.50
❑17, Apr 1994	2.50
❑18, May 1994	2.50
❑19, Jun 1994	2.50
❑20, Jul 1994	2.50
❑21, Aug 1994	2.00
❑22, Sep 1994 A: Spear of Destiny. V: Superman.	2.00
❑23, Nov 1994	2.00
❑24, Dec 1994	2.00
❑25, Jan 1995	2.00
❑26, Feb 1995	2.00
❑27, Mar 1995	2.00
❑28, Apr 1995	2.00
❑29, May 1995	2.00
❑30, Jun 1995	2.25
❑31, Jul 1995	2.25
❑32, Aug 1995	2.25
❑33, Sep 1995	2.25
❑34, Oct 1995	2.25
❑35, Nov 1995; Underworld Unleashed	2.25
❑36, Dec 1995; Underworld Unleashed	2.25
❑37, Jan 1996	2.50
❑38, Feb 1996 O: Uncle Sam.	2.50
❑39, Mar 1996 O: Shadrach.	2.50
❑40, Apr 1996 O: Captain Fear.	2.50
❑41, May 1996	2.50
❑42, Jun 1996	2.50
❑43, Jul 1996	2.50
❑44, Aug 1996	2.50
❑45, Sep 1996; homosexuality issues	2.50
❑46, Oct 1996; National Interest acquires Spear of Destiny	2.50
❑47, Nov 1996; Final Night	2.50
❑48, Dec 1996	2.50
❑49, Jan 1997	2.50
❑50, Feb 1997	2.50
❑51, Mar 1997	2.50
❑52, Apr 1997	2.50
❑53, May 1997	2.50
❑54, Jun 1997	2.50
❑55, Jul 1997	2.50
❑56, Aug 1997	2.50
❑57, Sep 1997	2.50
❑58, Oct 1997	2.50
❑59, Nov 1997	2.50
❑60, Dec 1997; Face cover	2.50
❑61, Jan 1998	2.50
❑62, Feb 1998; funeral of Jim Corrigan	2.50
❑Annual 1, ca. 1995; A: Doctor Fate. Year One	3.95

Other grades: Multiply price above by 5/6 for VF/NM • 2/3 for VERY FINE • 1/3 for FINE • 1/5 for VERY GOOD • 1/8 for GOOD

SPECTRE (4TH SERIES)
DC

❑1, Mar 2001 ... 3.00
❑2, Apr 2001 ... 2.50
❑3, May 2001 ... 2.50
❑4, Jun 2001 ... 2.50
❑5, Jul 2001 A: Two-Face ... 2.50
❑6, Aug 2001 ... 2.50
❑7, Sep 2001 ... 2.50
❑8, Oct 2001 ... 2.50
❑9, Nov 2001 ... 2.50
❑10, Dec 2001 ... 2.50
❑11, Jan 2002 ... 2.50
❑12, Feb 2002 ... 2.50
❑13, Mar 2002 ... 2.50
❑14, Apr 2002 ... 2.50
❑15, May 2002 ... 2.50
❑16, Jun 2002 ... 2.50
❑17, Jul 2002 ... 2.50
❑18, Aug 2002 ... 2.50
❑19, Sep 2002 ... 2.50
❑20, Oct 2002 ... 2.75
❑21, Nov 2002 ... 2.75
❑22, Dec 2002 ... 2.75
❑23, Jan 2003 ... 2.75
❑24, Feb 2003 ... 2.75
❑25, Mar 2003 ... 2.75
❑26, Apr 2003 ... 2.75
❑27, May 2003 ... 2.75

SPECTRESCOPE
SPECTRE

❑1, Mar 1994; giveaway; no cover price 1.00

SPECTRUM
NEW HORIZONS

❑1, Jul 1987, b&w ... 1.50

SPECTRUM COMICS PREVIEWS
SPECTRUM

❑1, Feb 1983 ... 3.00

SPEEDBALL
MARVEL

❑1, Sep 1988 SD (w); SD (a); O: Speedball ... 1.00
❑2, Oct 1988 SD (w); SD (a) ... 1.00
❑3, Nov 1988 SD (a) ... 1.00
❑4, Dec 1988 SD (a) ... 1.00
❑5, Jan 1989 SD (a) ... 1.00
❑6, Feb 1989 SD (a) ... 1.00
❑7, Mar 1989 SD (a) ... 1.00
❑8, Apr 1989 SD (a) ... 1.00
❑9, May 1989 SD (a) ... 1.00
❑10, Jun 1989 SD (a) ... 1.00

SPEED BUGGY
CHARLTON

❑1, May 1975 ... 12.00
❑2, Sep 1975 ... 8.00
❑3, Nov 1975 ... 8.00
❑4, Jan 1976 ... 8.00
❑5, Mar 1976 ... 8.00
❑6, May 1976 ... 8.00
❑7, Jul 1976 ... 8.00
❑8, Sep 1976 ... 8.00
❑9, Nov 1976 ... 8.00

SPEED DEMON
MARVEL / AMALGAM

❑1, Apr 1996, AM (a) ... 2.00

SPEED FORCE
DC

❑1, Nov 1997; anthology series with stories of the various Flashes ... 3.95

SPEED RACER (1ST SERIES)
NOW

❑1, Aug 1987 O: Speed Racer ... 2.50
❑1/2nd O: Speed Racer ... 1.50
❑2, Sep 1987 ... 2.00
❑3, Oct 1987 ... 2.00
❑4, Nov 1987 ... 1.75
❑5, Dec 1987 ... 1.75
❑6, Jan 1988 ... 1.75
❑7, Mar 1988 ... 1.75
❑8, Apr 1988 ... 1.75
❑9, May 1988 ... 1.75
❑10, Jun 1988 ... 1.75
❑11, Jul 1988 ... 1.75
❑12, Aug 1988 ... 1.75
❑13, Sep 1988 ... 1.75
❑14, Oct 1988 ... 1.75
❑15, Nov 1988 ... 1.75
❑16, Dec 1988 ... 1.75
❑17, Jan 1989 ... 1.75
❑18, Mar 1989 ... 1.75
❑19, Apr 1989 ... 1.75
❑20, May 1989 ... 1.75
❑21, Jun 1989 ... 1.75
❑22, Jul 1989 ... 1.75
❑23, Aug 1989 ... 1.75
❑24, Sep 1989 ... 1.75
❑25, Oct 1989 ... 1.75
❑26, Nov 1989 ... 1.75
❑27, Dec 1989 ... 1.75
❑28, Jan 1990 ... 1.75
❑29, Feb 1990 ... 1.75
❑30, Mar 1990 ... 1.75
❑31, Apr 1990 ... 1.75
❑32, May 1990 ... 1.75
❑33, Jun 1990 ... 1.75
❑34, Jul 1990 ... 1.75
❑35, Aug 1990 ... 1.75
❑36, Sep 1990 ... 1.75
❑37, Oct 1990 ... 1.75
❑38, Nov 1990 ... 1.75
❑Special 1, Mar 1988 O: The Mach 5 (Speed Racer's car) ... 2.50
❑Special 1/2nd, Sep 1988 O: The Mach 5 (Speed Racer's car) ... 1.75

SPEED RACER (2ND SERIES)
DC / WILDSTORM

❑1, Oct 1999 ... 2.50
❑2, Nov 1999 ... 2.50
❑3, Dec 1999 ... 2.50

SPEED RACER 3-D SPECIAL
NOW

❑1, Jan 1993 ... 2.95

SPEED RACER CLASSICS
NOW

❑1, Oct 1988, b&w ... 3.75
❑2, Feb 1989, b&w ... 3.95

SPEED RACER FEATURING NINJA HIGH SCHOOL
NOW / ETERNITY

❑1, Aug 1993; trading card ... 2.50
❑2, Sep 1993; two trading cards ... 2.50

SPEED RACER: RETURN OF THE GRX
NOW

❑1, Mar 1994 ... 1.95
❑2, Apr 1994 ... 1.95

SPEED RACER: THE ORIGINAL MANGA
DC / WILDSTORM

❑1 ... 9.95

SPEED TRIBES
NEMICRON

❑1, Aug 1998 ... 2.95

SPELLBINDERS
FLEETWAY-QUALITY

❑1, Dec 1986 ... 1.50
❑2, Jan 1986 ... 1.50
❑3, Feb 1986 ... 1.50
❑4, Mar 1986 ... 1.50
❑5, Apr 1986 ... 1.50
❑6, May 1986 ... 1.50
❑7, Jun 1986 ... 1.50
❑8, Jul 1986 ... 1.50
❑9, Aug 1986 ... 1.50
❑10, Sep 1986 ... 1.50
❑11, Oct 1986 ... 1.50
❑12, Nov 1986 ... 1.50

SPELLBINDERS
MARVEL

❑1, May 2005 ... 2.99
❑2, Jun 2005 ... 2.99
❑3, Jul 2005 ... 2.99
❑4, Aug 2005 ... 2.99
❑5, Sep 2005 ... 2.99
❑6, Oct 2005 ... 2.99

SPELLBOUND (MARVEL)
MARVEL

❑1, Jan 1988 ... 1.50
❑2, Feb 1988 ... 1.50
❑3, Feb 1988 ... 1.50
❑4, Mar 1988 ... 1.50
❑5, Apr 1988 ... 1.50
❑6, Apr 1988; Double Size ... 2.25

SPELLCASTER
MEDUSA

❑1 ... 2.95
❑2 ... 2.95
❑3 ... 2.95

SPELLJAMMER
DC

❑1, Sep 1990 ... 1.75
❑2, Oct 1990 ... 1.75
❑3, Nov 1990 ... 1.75
❑4, Dec 1990 ... 1.75
❑5, Jan 1991 ... 1.75
❑6, Feb 1991 ... 1.75
❑7, Mar 1991 ... 1.75
❑8, Apr 1991 ... 1.75
❑9, May 1991 ... 1.75
❑10, Jun 1991 ... 1.75
❑11, Jul 1991 ... 1.75
❑12, Aug 1991 ... 1.75
❑13, Sep 1991 ... 1.75
❑14, Oct 1991 ... 1.75
❑15, Nov 1991 ... 1.75
❑16, Dec 1991 ... 1.75
❑17, Jan 1992 ... 1.75
❑18, Feb 1992 ... 1.75

SPEX-7
SHADOW SHOCK

❑1, Sum 1994, b&w ... 1.50

SPICECAPADES
FANTAGRAPHICS

❑1, Spr 1999; magazine-sized; wraparound cover; Spice Girls parody ... 4.95

SPICY ADULT STORIES
AIRCEL

❑1, Mar 1991; pulp reprints ... 2.50
❑2, Apr 1991; pulp reprints ... 2.50
❑3, May 1991; pulp reprints ... 2.50
❑4; pulp reprints ... 2.50

SPICY TALES
ETERNITY

❑1, Apr 1988, b&w; Reprints ... 1.95
❑2, Jun 1988, b&w; Reprints ... 1.95
❑3, Aug 1988, b&w; Reprints ... 1.95
❑4, Oct 1988, b&w; Reprints ... 1.95
❑5, Dec 1988, b&w; Reprints ... 1.95
❑6, Feb 1989, b&w; Reprints ... 1.95
❑7, b&w; Reprints ... 1.95
❑8, b&w; Reprints ... 1.95
❑9, b&w; Reprints ... 1.95
❑10 ... 1.95
❑11 ... 1.95
❑12 ... 1.95
❑13 ... 1.95
❑14 ... 2.25
❑15 ... 2.25
❑16 ... 2.25
❑17 ... 2.25
❑18 ... 2.95
❑19 ... 2.95
❑20 ... 2.95
❑Special 1, Feb 1989, b&w; Reprints ... 2.25
❑Special 2, b&w; Reprints ... 2.25

SPIDER
ECLIPSE

❑1, Jun 1991 ... 4.95
❑2, Aug 1991 ... 4.95
❑3, Oct 1991 ... 4.95

SPIDERBABY COMIX (S.R. BISSETTE'S...)
SPIDERBABY

❑1, Nov 1996 ... 3.95

SPIDER-BOY
MARVEL / AMALGAM

❑1, Apr 1996 ... 2.50

SPIDER-BOY TEAM-UP
MARVEL / AMALGAM

❑1, Jun 1997 ... 1.95

SPIDER-FEMME
SPOOF

❑1; parody ... 2.50

Spider-Man: The Clone Journal

Special edition explains the Clone Saga

©Marvel

Spider-Man: The Manga

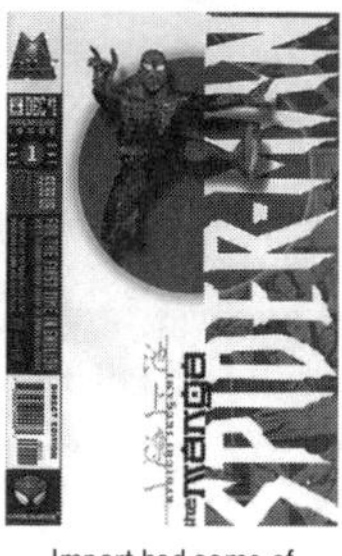

Import had some of Marvel's lowest sales ever

©Marvel

Spider-Man 2099

Flagship title of the futuristic 2099 line

©Marvel

Spider-Woman

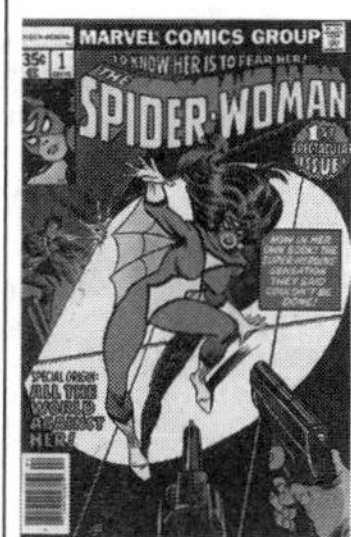

Female version didn't fare so well

©Marvel

Spidey Super Stories

Educational series with The Electric Company

©Marvel

SPIDER GARDEN
NBM

	N-MINT
❑1	12.95

SPIDER-GIRL
MARVEL

	N-MINT
❑0, Oct 1998; O: Spider-Girl. reprints What If? #105	2.00
❑½; Wizard promotional edition	3.00
❑1, Oct 1998, White cover with Spider-Girl facing forward	4.00
❑1/A, Oct 1998, variant cover	4.00
❑2, Nov 1998, gatefold summary A: Darkdevil.	3.00
❑3, Dec 1998, gatefold summary A: Fantastic Five.	3.00
❑4, Jan 1999, V: Dragon King.	3.00
❑5, Feb 1999, 1: Spider-Venom. A: Venom.	3.00
❑6, Mar 1999, A: Ladyhawk. A: Green Goblin.	1.99
❑7, Apr 1999, A: Nova. A: Mary Jane Parker.	1.99
❑8, May 1999, A: Kingpin. V: Mr. Nobody. V: Crazy Eight.	1.99
❑9, Jun 1999, V: Killer Watt.	1.99
❑10, Jul 1999, A: Spider-Man.	1.99
❑11, Aug 1999, A: Human Torch. A: Spider-Man. V: Spider-Slayer.	1.99
❑12, Sep 1999	1.99
❑13, Oct 1999	1.99
❑14, Nov 1999	1.99
❑15, Dec 1999	1.99
❑16, Jan 2000	2.25
❑17, Feb 2000	2.25
❑18, Mar 2000	2.25
❑19, Apr 2000	2.25
❑20, May 2000	2.25
❑21, Jun 2000	2.25
❑22, Jul 2000	2.25
❑23, Aug 2000	2.25
❑24, Sep 2000	2.25
❑25, Oct 2000	2.99
❑26, Nov 2000	2.25
❑27, Dec 2000	2.25
❑28, Jan 2001	2.25
❑29, Feb 2001	2.25
❑30, Mar 2001	2.25
❑31, Apr 2001	2.25
❑32, May 2001	2.25
❑33, Jun 2001	2.25
❑34, Jul 2001	2.25
❑35, Aug 2001	2.25
❑36, Sep 2001	2.25
❑37, Oct 2001	2.25
❑38, Nov 2001	2.25
❑39, Dec 2001	2.25
❑40, Jan 2002	2.25
❑41, Feb 2002	2.25
❑42, Mar 2002	2.25
❑43, Mar 2002	2.25
❑44, Apr 2002	2.25
❑45, May 2002, wraparound cover	2.25
❑46, Jun 2002	2.25
❑47, Jul 2002	2.25
❑48, Aug 2002	2.25
❑49, Sep 2002	2.25
❑50, Oct 2002	2.25
❑51, Nov 2002	2.25
❑52, Dec 2002	2.25
❑53, Jan 2003	2.25
❑54, Feb 2003	2.25
❑55, Mar 2003	2.25
❑56, Apr 2003	2.25
❑57, May 2003	2.25
❑58, Jun 2003	2.25
❑59, Jun 2003	2.99
❑60, Jul 2003, AW (c); AW (a)	2.99
❑61, Aug 2003, AW (c); AW (a)	2.99
❑62, Sep 2003, SB (a)	2.99
❑63, Oct 2003, SB (a)	2.99
❑64, Nov 2003, KJ (c); SB (a)	2.99
❑65, Dec 2003, KJ (c); SB (a)	2.99
❑66, Jan 2004, SB (c); SB (a)	2.99
❑67, Feb 2004, SB (c); SB (a)	2.99
❑68, Mar 2004, SB (c); SB (a)	2.99
❑69, Mar 2004	2.99
❑70, Apr 2004, SB (a)	2.99
❑71, May 2004, SB (a)	2.99
❑72, Jun 2004, SB (a)	2.99
❑73, Jul 2004, SB (a)	2.99
❑74, Aug 2004, SB (a)	2.99
❑75, Sep 2004	8.00
❑76, Sep 2004	2.99
❑77, Oct 2004	2.99
❑78, Oct 2004	2.99
❑79, Nov 2004	2.99
❑80, Dec 2004	2.99
❑81, Jan 2005	2.99
❑82, Feb 2005	2.99
❑83, Mar 2005	2.99
❑84, Apr 2005	2.99
❑85, May 2005	2.99
❑86, Jun 2005	2.99
❑87, Jul 2005	2.99
❑88, Aug 2005	2.99
❑89, Sep 2005	2.99
❑90, Oct 2005	2.99
❑91, Nov 2005	2.99
❑92, Jan 2006	2.99
❑93, Feb 2006	2.99
❑94, Mar 2006	2.99
❑95, Mar 2006	2.99
❑96, May 2006	2.99
❑97, Jun 2006	2.99
❑98, Jul 2006	2.99
❑99, Aug 2006	2.99
❑Annual 1999, ca. 1999	3.99

SPIDER-MAN
MARVEL

	N-MINT
❑-1, Jul 1997; Flashback	2.00
❑½, ca. 1999	4.00
❑½/Platinum, ca. 1999; Platinum edition	6.00
❑1, Aug 1990; TMc (c); TMc (w); TMc (a); Green cover (newsstand)	5.00
❑1/CG, Aug 1990; TMc (c); TMc (w); TMc (a); bagged newsstand (green)	5.00
❑1/CS, Aug 1990; TMc (c); TMc (w); TMc (a); bagged silver cover	5.00
❑1/Platinum, Aug 1990; giveaway TMc (c); TMc (w); TMc (a)	42.00
❑1/Silver, Aug 1990; TMc (c); TMc (w); TMc (a); silver cover	5.00
❑1/2nd; TMc (c); TMc (w); TMc (a); Gold cover; UPC box	50.00
❑1/Direct ed./2n, Aug 1990; TMc (c); TMc (w); TMc (a); Gold cover; direct sale	5.00
❑2, Sep 1990; TMc (w); TMc (a); Lizard	3.00
❑3, Oct 1990; TMc (w); TMc (a); Lizard	3.00
❑4, Nov 1990; TMc (w); TMc (a); Lizard	3.00
❑5, Dec 1990; TMc (w); TMc (a); Lizard	3.00
❑6, Jan 1991 TMc (w); TMc (a); A: Hobgoblin. A: Ghost Rider. V: Hobgoblin.	3.00
❑7, Feb 1991 TMc (w); TMc (a); A: Hobgoblin. A: Ghost Rider. V: Hobgoblin.	3.00
❑8, Mar 1991 TMc (w); TMc (a); A: Wolverine. V: Wendigo.	2.50
❑9, Apr 1991 TMc (w); TMc (a); A: Wolverine. V: Wendigo.	6.00
❑10, May 1991 TMc (w); TMc (a); A: Wolverine. V: Wendigo.	4.00
❑11, Jun 1991 TMc (w); TMc (a); A: Wolverine. V: Wendigo.	2.50
❑12, Jul 1991 TMc (w); TMc (a); A: Wolverine. V: Wendigo.	2.50
❑13, Aug 1991; TMc (w); TMc (a); Spider-Man wears black costume	5.00
❑14, Sep 1991 TMc (w); TMc (a)	2.50
❑15, Oct 1991 EL (w); EL (a); A: Beast.	2.00
❑16, Nov 1991; TMc (w); TMc (a); X-Force; Sideways printing	2.00
❑17, Dec 1991 AW (a); A: Thanos. V: Thanos.	2.00
❑18, Jan 1992; EL (w); EL (a); Ghost Rider	2.00
❑19, Feb 1992 EL (w); EL (a); A: Hulk.	2.00
❑20, Mar 1992 EL (w); EL (a); A: Nova. A: Hulk. A: Solo. A: Deathlok.	2.00
❑21, Apr 1992; EL (w); EL (a); A: Solo. A: Deathlok. Deathlok appearnace	2.00
❑22, May 1992 EL (w); EL (a); A: Sleepwalker. A: Hulk. A: Ghost Rider. A: Deathlok.	2.00
❑23, Jun 1992 EL (w); EL (a); A: Fantastic Four. A: Hulk. A: Ghost Rider. A: Deathlok.	2.00
❑24, Jul 1992; Infinity War	2.00
❑25, Aug 1992 A: Phoenix.	2.00
❑26, Sep 1992; 30th Anniversary Edition; O: Spider-Man. Gatefold poster; Hologram cover	4.00
❑27, Oct 1992 MR (a)	2.00
❑28, Nov 1992	2.00
❑29, Dec 1992	2.00
❑30, Jan 1993	2.00
❑31, Feb 1993	2.00
❑32, Mar 1993 BMc (a)	2.00
❑33, Apr 1993 BMc (a); A: Punisher.	2.00
❑34, May 1993 BMc (a); A: Punisher.	2.00
❑35, Jun 1993 A: Carnage. A: Venom.	2.00
❑36, Jul 1993 A: Carnage. A: Venom.	2.00
❑37, Aug 1993 AM (a); A: Carnage. A: Venom.	2.00
❑38, Sep 1993 KJ (a)	2.00
❑39, Oct 1993 KJ (a); A: Electro	2.00

❑40, Nov 1993 KJ (a); V: Electro 2.00
❑41, Dec 1993 .... 2.00
❑42, Jan 1994 .... 2.00
❑43, Feb 1994 .... 2.00
❑44, Mar 1994.................................... 2.00
❑45, Apr 1994 .... 2.00
❑46, May 1994 .... 2.00
❑46/CS, May 1994; with print............. 3.00
❑47, Jun 1994 V: Hobgoblin................ 2.00
❑48, Jul 1994 V: Hobgoblin 2.00
❑49, Aug 1994.................................... 2.00
❑50, Sep 1994 .... 2.50
❑50/Variant, Sep 1994; Holo-grafix cover.. 3.95
❑51, Oct 1994 A: Ben Reilly. 2.50
❑51/Variant, Oct 1994; Giant-size; O: Ben Reilly. A: Ben Reilly. flip-book with back-up; enhanced cover 2.95
❑52, Nov 1994; The clone vs. Venom . 2.00
❑53, Dec 1994; The clone defeats Venom 2.00
❑54, Jan 1995; flip book with illustrated story from The Ultimate Spider-Man back-up.. 2.00
❑55, Feb 1995 .... 2.00
❑56, Mar 1995 .... 2.00
❑57, Apr 1995; Giant-size JR2 (a) 2.50
❑57/Variant, Apr 1995; Giant-size; enhanced cardstock cover 2.95
❑58, May 1995 .... 2.00
❑59, Jun 1995 .... 2.00
❑60, Jul 1995; Kaine's identity revealed 2.00
❑61, Aug 1995.................................... 2.00
❑62, Sep 1995 .... 2.00
❑63, Oct 1995; OverPower game cards bound-in... 2.00
❑64, Jan 1996 V: Poison. 2.00
❑65, Feb 1996 .... 2.00
❑66, Mar 1996 JR2 (a) 2.00
❑67, Apr 1996 JR2 (w); AM, AW, JR2 (a).. 2.00
❑68, May 1996 .... 2.00
❑69, Jun 1996 .... 2.00
❑70, Jul 1996 A: Hammerhead. 2.00
❑71, Aug 1996 JR2 (a); V: Hammerhead. 2.00
❑72, Sep 1996 JR2 (a); V: Sentinels... 2.00
❑73, Oct 1996 JR2 (a) 2.00
❑74, Nov 1996 JR2 (a); A: Daredevil. . 2.00
❑75, Dec 1996; Giant-size; JR2 (a); D: Ben Reilly. wraparound cover; return of original Green Goblin........ 3.50
❑76, Jan 1997 JR2 (a); A: S.H.O.C.. V: S.H.O.C.. .... 2.00
❑77, Feb 1997 V: Morbius. 2.00
❑78, Mar 1997 JR2 (a); V: Morbius.... 2.00
❑79, Apr 1997 JR2 (a); A: Morbius. V: S.H.O.C.. .... 2.00
❑80, May 1997 JR2 (a); A: Morbius. V: Hammerhead. 2.00
❑81, Jun 1997 JR2 (a) 2.00
❑82, Aug 1997; gatefold summary JR2 (a)... 2.00
❑83, Sep 1997; gatefold summary JR2 (a)... 2.00
❑84, Oct 1997; gatefold summary JR2 (a); V: Juggernaut. 2.00
❑85, Nov 1997; gatefold summary V: Shocker.. 2.00
❑86, Dec 1997; gatefold summary JR2 (a); A: Trapster. V: Shocker............. 2.00
❑87, Jan 1998; gatefold summary JR2 (a); V: Shocker. 2.00
❑88, Feb 1998; gatefold summary...... 2.00
❑89, Mar 1998; gatefold summary JR2 (a); V: Punisher. V: Shotgun............ 2.00
❑90, Apr 1998; gatefold summary 1: Spidey as Dusk. V: Blastaar......... 2.00
❑91, May 1998; gatefold summary; Identity Crisis................................. 2.00
❑92, Jun 1998; gatefold summary; JR2 (a); Identity Crisis 2.00
❑93, Jul 1998; gatefold summary A: Ghost Rider................................. 2.00
❑94, Aug 1998; gatefold summary 2.00
❑95, Sep 1998; gatefold summary V: Nitro.. 2.00
❑96, Oct 1998; gatefold summary A: Madame Web............................. 2.00
❑97, Nov 1998; gatefold summary JBy (c);.. 2.00
❑98/A, Nov 1998; gatefold summary . 2.00
❑98/B, Nov 1998; gatefold summary; JBy (c); Alternate cover; series begins again as Peter Parker: Spider-Man.. 2.00
❑Annual 1997, ca. 1997; 1997 Annual 2.99
❑Annual 1998, ca. 1998; gatefold summary; A: Devil Dinosaur. A: Moon Boy. wraparound cover 2.99
❑Giant Size 1, Dec 1998; Giant-Sized Spider-Man.. 3.99
❑Holiday 1995, Hol 1995; Trade Paperback; A: Human Torch. A: Venom. 1995 Holiday Special......... 2.95

SPIDER-MAN ADVENTURES
MARVEL

❑1, Dec 1994; adapts animated series 1.50
❑1/Variant, Dec 1994; Adapts animated series; enhanced cover.................. 2.95
❑2, Jan 1995; adapts animated series 1.50
❑3, Feb 1995; adapts animated series 1.50
❑4, Mar 1995; adapts animated series 1.50
❑5, Apr 1995; adapts animated series 1.50
❑6, May 1995; adapts animated series 1.50
❑7, Jun 1995; adapts animated series 1.50
❑8, Jul 1995; Adapts animated series 1.50
❑9, Aug 1995; Adapts animated series 1.50
❑10, Sep 1995; Adapts animated series 1.50
❑11, Oct 1995; Adapts animated series 1.50
❑12, Nov 1995; Adapts animated series 1.50
❑13, Dec 1995; Adapts animated series 1.50
❑14, Jan 1996; Adapts animated series 1.50
❑15, Feb 1996; Adapts animated series; Continues in Adventures of Spider-Man #1 .... 1.50

SPIDER-MAN AND ARANA SPECIAL
MARVEL

❑1, Jun 2006..................................... 2.99

SPIDER-MAN AND BATMAN
MARVEL

❑1, Sep 1995; prestige format 5.95

SPIDER-MAN AND DAREDEVIL SPECIAL EDITION
MARVEL

❑1, Mar 1984 .... 2.00

SPIDER-MAN AND DOCTOR OCTOPUS: NEGATIVE EXPOSURE
MARVEL

❑1, Dec 2003...................................... 2.99
❑2, Jan 2004 .... 2.99
❑3, Feb 2004, Negative Exposure....... 2.99
❑4, Mar 2004 .... 2.99
❑5, Apr 2004....................................... 0.00

SPIDER-MAN AND HIS AMAZING FRIENDS
MARVEL

❑1, Dec 1981, DS (a); 1: Firestar. A: Iceman. A: Green Goblin. Adapted from television show 10.00

SPIDER-MAN AND MYSTERIO
MARVEL

❑1, Jan 2001; says Spider-Man: The Mysterio Manifesto on the cover.... 2.99
❑2, Feb 2001; says Spider-Man: The Mysterio Manifesto on the cover.... 2.99
❑3, Mar 2001; says Spider-Man: The Mysterio Manifesto on the cover.... 2.99

SPIDER-MAN AND THE DALLAS COWBOYS
MARVEL

❑1, Sep 1983; Danger in Dallas giveaway... 10.00

SPIDER-MAN AND THE INCREDIBLE HULK
MARVEL

❑1, Sep 1981; Chaos in Kansas City giveaway... 10.00

SPIDER-MAN & THE NEW MUTANTS
MARVEL

❑1, giveaway; child abuse 3.00

SPIDER-MAN & WOLVERINE
MARVEL

❑1, Aug 2003 .... 2.99
❑2, Sep 2003...................................... 2.99
❑3, Oct 2003 .... 2.99
❑4, Nov 2003 .... 2.99

SPIDER-MAN AND X-FACTOR: SHADOWGAMES
MARVEL

❑1, May 1994 KB (w); PB (a); O: Shadow Force. 1: Shadow Force. 2.25
❑2, Jun 1994 KB (w); PB (a) 2.25
❑3, Jul 1994 KB (w); PB (a)............... 2.25

SPIDER-MAN/BADROCK
MAXIMUM

❑1/A, Mar 1997; first part of story...... 2.99
❑1/B, Mar 1997; second part of story. 2.99

SPIDER-MAN/BLACK CAT: THE EVIL THAT MEN DO
MARVEL

❑1, Aug 2002 KSm (w)....................... 5.00
❑1/Dynamic, Aug 2002....................... 7.00
❑2, Sep 2002 KSm (w)........................ 3.00
❑3, Oct 2002 KSm (w)........................ 2.00
❑4, Feb 2006 .... 2.99
❑5, Feb 2006 .... 2.99
❑6, Mar 2006...................................... 2.99

SPIDER-MAN: BLUE
MARVEL

❑1, Jul 2002 .... 6.00
❑2, Aug 2002...................................... 5.00
❑3, Sep 2002 .... 3.50
❑4, Oct 2002....................................... 3.50
❑5, Nov 2002...................................... 3.50
❑6, Apr 2003 .... 3.50

SPIDER-MAN: BREAKOUT
MARVEL

❑1, Jun 2005 .... 2.99
❑2, Jul 2005 .... 2.99
❑3, Aug 2005...................................... 2.99
❑4, Sep 2005 .... 2.99
❑5, Oct 2005....................................... 2.99

SPIDER-MAN: CHAPTER ONE
MARVEL

❑0, May 1999 .... 2.50
❑1, Dec 1998 .... 2.50
❑1/A, Dec 1998; DFE alternate cover .. 4.00
❑1/B, Dec 1998; Signed edition 14.00
❑1/C, Dec 1998; DFE alternate cover, signed 14.00
❑2/A, Dec 1998; Cover A 2.50
❑2/B, Dec 1998; Cover B 2.50
❑2/C, Dec 1998; Cover forms diptych with issue #1 DFE cover.................. 4.00
❑3, Jan 1999 .... 2.50
❑4, Feb 1999 .... 2.50
❑5, Mar 1999....................................... 2.50
❑6, Apr 1999 .... 2.50
❑7, May 1999 .... 2.50
❑8, Jun 1999 .... 2.50
❑9, Jul 1999 .... 2.50
❑10, Aug 1999..................................... 2.50
❑11, Sep 1999..................................... 2.50
❑12, Oct 1999...................................... 2.50
❑Deluxe 1 .... 29.95
❑Deluxe 1/Ltd.; #1 & #2 Pack, DFE alternate cover signed..................... 29.95

SPIDER-MAN: CHRISTMAS IN DALLAS
MARVEL

❑1, Dec 1983; giveaway 10.00

SPIDER-MAN CLASSICS
MARVEL

❑1, Apr 1993; SL (w); SD (a); O: Spider-Man. O: Doctor Strange. 1: Spider-Man. Reprints Amazing Fantasy #15 & Strange Tales #115........................ 2.00
❑2, May 1993; SD, SL (w); SD (a); O: Spider-Man. 1: J. Jonah Jameson. 1: Chameleon. A: Fantastic Four. Reprints Amazing Spider-Man #1 ... 1.50
❑3, Jun 1993; SD, SL (w); SD (a); 1: Mysterio (as alien). 1: Mysterio (as "alien"). 1: Tinkerer. 1: Vulture. Reprints Amazing Spider-Man #2 ... 1.50
❑4, Jul 1993; SD, SL (w); SD (a); O: Doctor Octopus. 1: Doctor Octopus. Reprints Amazing Spider-Man #3 ... 1.50
❑5, Aug 1993; SD, SL (w); SD (a); O: Sandman (Marvel). 1: Betty Brant. 1: Sandman (Marvel). Reprints Amazing Spider-Man #4................. 1.50

Spirit (Magazine)	Spirit of the Tao	Spirit: The New Adventures	Splitting Image	Spooky (Vol. 1)
		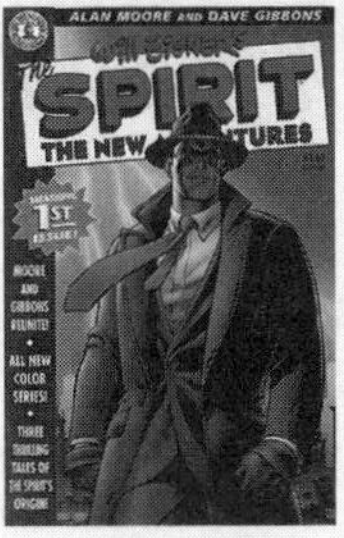	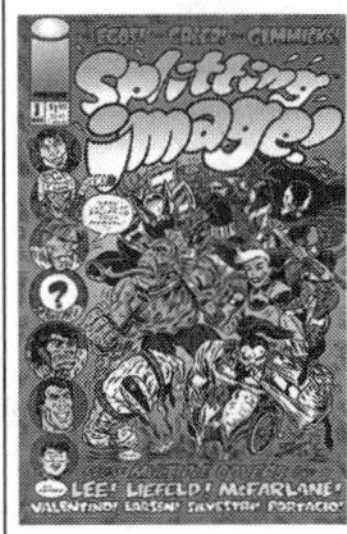	
Kitchen Sink takes over from Warren at #17	D-Tron brings his style from Witchblade	Final ongoing title from Kitchen Sink	Image decides to lampoon itself	"Tuff Little Ghost" haunts, smokes
©Warren	©Image	©Kitchen Sink	©Image	©Harvey

N-MINT

❑6, Sep 1993; SD, SL (w); SD (a); A: Doctor Doom. Reprints Amazing Spider-Man #5 ... 1.50
❑7, Oct 1993; SD, SL (w); SD (a); O: The Lizard. 1: The Lizard. Reprints Amazing Spider-Man #6 ... 1.50
❑8, Nov 1993; SD, SL (w); SD (a); 2: The Vulture. Reprints Amazing Spider-Man #7 ... 1.50
❑9, Dec 1993; SD, SL (w); SD (a); 1: The Living Brain. A: Human Torch. Reprints Amazing Spider-Man #8 ... 1.50
❑10, Jan 1994; SD, SL (w); SD (a); O: Electro. 1: Electro. Reprints Amazing Spider-Man #9 ... 1.50
❑11, Feb 1994; SD, SL (w); SD (a); 1: Big Man. 1: Enforcers. Reprints Amazing Spider-Man #10 ... 1.50
❑12, Mar 1994; SD, SL (w); SD (a); 2: Doctor Octopus. Reprints Amazing Spider-Man #11 ... 1.50
❑13, Apr 1994 ... 1.25
❑14, May 1994 ... 1.25
❑15, Jun 1994 1: Green Goblin I (Norman Osborn) ... 1.25
❑15/CS, Jun 1994; 1: Green Goblin I (Norman Osborn). polybagged with animation print ... 2.95
❑16, Jul 1994 ... 1.25

SPIDER-MAN COLLECTORS' PREVIEW
MARVEL

❑1, Dec 1994 ... 1.50

SPIDER-MAN COMICS MAGAZINE
MARVEL

❑1, Jan 1987, digest ... 1.50
❑2, Mar 1987, digest ... 1.50
❑3, May 1987, digest ... 1.50
❑4, Jul 1987, digest ... 1.50
❑5, Sep 1987, digest ... 1.50
❑6, Nov 1987, digest ... 1.50
❑7, Jan 1988, digest ... 1.50
❑8, Mar 1988, digest ... 1.50
❑9, May 1988, digest ... 1.50
❑10, Jul 1988, digest ... 1.50
❑11, Sep 1988, digest ... 1.50
❑12, Nov 1988, digest ... 1.50
❑13, Jan 1989, digest ... 1.50

SPIDER-MAN/DAREDEVIL
MARVEL

❑1, Oct 2002 ... 2.99

SPIDER-MAN: DEAD MAN'S HAND
MARVEL

❑1, Apr 1997, wraparound cover ... 2.99

SPIDER-MAN: DEATH AND DESTINY
MARVEL

❑1, Aug 2000 ... 2.99
❑2, Sep 2000 ... 2.99
❑3, Oct 2000 ... 2.99

SPIDER-MAN/DOCTOR OCTOPUS: OUT OF REACH
MARVEL

❑1, Jan 2004 ... 4.00
❑2, Feb 2004 ... 2.99
❑3, Mar 2004 ... 2.99
❑4, Apr 2004 ... 2.99
❑5, May 2004 ... 2.99

SPIDER-MAN/DOCTOR OCTOPUS: YEAR ONE
MARVEL

❑1, Aug 2004 ... 2.99
❑2, Aug 2004 ... 2.99
❑3 ... 2.99
❑4 ... 2.99
❑5 ... 2.99

SPIDER-MAN/DR. STRANGE: THE WAY TO DUSTY DEATH
MARVEL

❑1, ca. 1992, No cover price; graphic novel ... 6.95

SPIDER-MAN FAMILY
MARVEL

❑1, Dec 2005, b&w ... 4.99

SPIDER-MAN: FEAR ITSELF
MARVEL

❑1, Feb 1992 ... 12.95

SPIDER-MAN: FRIENDS & ENEMIES
MARVEL

❑1, Jan 1995 ... 1.95
❑2, Feb 1995 ... 1.95
❑3, Mar 1995 ... 1.95
❑4, Apr 1995 ... 1.95

SPIDER-MAN: FUNERAL FOR AN OCTOPUS
MARVEL

❑1, Mar 1995 ... 1.50
❑2, Apr 1995 ... 1.50
❑3, May 1995 ... 1.50
❑4, Jun 1995 ... 1.50

SPIDER-MAN/GEN13
MARVEL

❑1, Nov 1996; prestige format ... 4.95

SPIDER-MAN: GET KRAVEN
MARVEL

❑1, Aug 2002 ... 2.25
❑2, Sep 2002 ... 2.25
❑3, Oct 2002 ... 2.25
❑4, Nov 2002 ... 2.25
❑5, Dec 2002 ... 2.25
❑6, Jan 2003 ... 2.25

SPIDER-MAN: HOBGOBLIN LIVES
MARVEL

❑1, Jan 1997; wraparound cover ... 2.50
❑2, Feb 1997; wraparound cover ... 2.50
❑3, Apr 1997; identity of Hobgoblin revealed; wraparound cover; True identity of Hobgoblin I revealed ... 2.50

SPIDER-MAN: HOUSE OF M
MARVEL

❑1, Jul 2005 ... 4.00
❑1/Conv, Jul 2005 ... 15.00
❑2, Aug 2005 ... 2.99
❑2/Variant, Aug 2005 ... 2.99
❑3, Sep 2005 ... 2.99
❑4 2005 ... 2.99
❑5, Jan 2006 ... 2.99

SPIDER-MAN/HUMAN TORCH
MARVEL

❑1, Apr 2005 ... 2.99
❑2, May 2005 ... 2.99
❑3, Jun 2005 ... 2.99
❑4, Jul 2005 ... 2.99
❑5, Aug 2005 ... 2.99

SPIDER-MAN: INDIA
MARVEL

❑1, Dec 2004 ... 2.99
❑2, Jan 2005 ... 2.99
❑3, Feb 2005 ... 2.99
❑4, Mar 2005 ... 2.99

SPIDER-MAN: LEGACY OF EVIL
MARVEL

❑1, Jun 1996; retells history of Green Goblin ... 3.95

SPIDER-MAN: LIFELINE
MARVEL

❑1, Apr 2001 ... 2.99
❑2, May 2001 ... 2.99
❑3, Jun 2001 ... 2.99

SPIDER-MAN LOVES MARY JANE
MARVEL

❑1, Feb 2006 ... 2.99
❑2, Mar 2006 ... 2.99
❑3, May 2006 ... 2.99
❑4, Jun 2006 ... 2.99
❑5, Jul 2006 ... 2.99
❑6, Aug 2006 ... 2.99
❑7, Sep 2006 ... 2.99

SPIDER-MAN: MADE MEN
MARVEL

❑1, Aug 1999 ... 5.99

SPIDER-MAN MAGAZINE
MARVEL

❑1, Win 1994 ... 2.00
❑2, Jun 1994 ... 2.00
❑3, Jul 1994 ... 2.00
❑4, Aug 1994; X-Men ... 2.00
❑5, Sep 1994 ... 2.00
❑6, Oct 1994; X-Men ... 2.00
❑7, Nov 1994 ... 2.00
❑8, Dec 1994 ... 2.00
❑9, Jan 1995; flip book with Iron Man back-up ... 2.00
❑10, Feb 1995; flip book with X-Men back-up ... 2.00

SPIDER-MAN MAGAZINE (2ND SERIES)
MARVEL

❑1, Spr 1995 ... 2.50

SPIDER-MAN: MAXIMUM CLONAGE ALPHA
MARVEL

❑1, Aug 1995; Acetate wraparound cover overlay ... 10.00

SPIDER-MAN: MAXIMUM CLONAGE OMEGA
MARVEL

❑1, Aug 1995; D: The Jackal. enhanced wraparound cover ... 10.00

Other grades: Multiply price above by 5/6 for VF/NM • 2/3 for VERY FINE • 1/3 for FINE • 1/5 for VERY GOOD • 1/8 for GOOD

SPIDER-MAN MEGAZINE
MARVEL
- ❑1, Oct 1994 ... 2.50
- ❑2, Nov 1994 ... 2.95
- ❑3, Dec 1994 ... 2.95
- ❑4, Jan 1995 ... 2.95
- ❑5, Feb 1995 ... 2.95
- ❑6, Mar 1995 ... 2.95

SPIDER-MAN 2 MOVIE ADAPTATION
MARVEL
- ❑1, Aug 2004 ... 3.50

SPIDER-MAN 2 MOVIE TPB
MARVEL
- ❑1, ca. 2004 ... 12.99

SPIDER-MAN MYSTERIES
MARVEL
- ❑1, Aug 1998; No cover price; prototype for children's comic ... 1.00

SPIDER-MAN: POWER OF TERROR
MARVEL
- ❑1, Jan 1995 ... 1.95
- ❑2, Feb 1995 ... 1.95
- ❑3, Mar 1995 ... 1.95
- ❑4, Apr 1995 ... 1.95

SPIDER-MAN, POWER PACK
MARVEL
- ❑1, Aug 1984; Giveaway from the National Committee for Prevention of Child Abuse; JM (a); No cover price; sexual abuse ... 1.00

SPIDER-MAN/PUNISHER: FAMILY PLOT
MARVEL
- ❑1, Feb 1996 ... 2.95
- ❑2, Feb 1996 ... 2.95

SPIDER-MAN, PUNISHER, SABRETOOTH: DESIGNER GENES
MARVEL
- ❑1, ca. 1993; no cover price ... 8.95

SPIDER-MAN: QUALITY OF LIFE
MARVEL
- ❑1, Jul 2002 ... 2.99
- ❑2, Aug 2002 ... 2.99
- ❑3, Sep 2002 ... 2.99
- ❑4, Oct 2002 ... 2.99

SPIDER-MAN: REDEMPTION
MARVEL
- ❑1, Sep 1996, no ads ... 1.50
- ❑2, Oct 1996 ... 1.50
- ❑3, Nov 1996 ... 1.50
- ❑4, Dec 1996 ... 1.50

SPIDER-MAN: REVENGE OF THE GREEN GOBLIN
MARVEL
- ❑1, Oct 2000 ... 2.99
- ❑2, Nov 2000 ... 2.99
- ❑3, Dec 2000; events lead in to Amazing Spider-Man #25 and Peter Parker, Spider-Man #25 ... 2.99

SPIDER-MAN SAGA
MARVEL
- ❑1, Nov 1991 ... 2.95
- ❑2, Dec 1991 ... 2.95
- ❑3, Jan 1992 ... 2.95
- ❑4, Feb 1992 ... 2.95

SPIDER-MAN: SON OF THE GOBLIN
MARVEL
- ❑1, ca. 2004 ... 15.99

SPIDER-MAN SPECIAL EDITION
MARVEL
- ❑1, Nov 1992; "The Trial of Venom" special edition to benefit Unicef; PD (w); A: Venom. Embossed cover ... 7.00

SPIDER-MAN, STORM AND POWER MAN
MARVEL
- ❑1, Apr 1982; Smokescreen giveaway ... 2.00

SPIDER-MAN SUPER SPECIAL
MARVEL
- ❑1, Jul 1995; Flip-book; two of the stories continue in Venom Super Special #1 ... 3.95

SPIDER-MAN: SWEET CHARITY
MARVEL
- ❑1, Aug 2002 ... 4.99

SPIDER-MAN TEAM-UP
MARVEL
- ❑1, Dec 1995, MWa (w); A: X-Men. A: Cyclops. A: Archangel. A: Hellfire Club. A: Beast. A: Phoenix. A: Psylocke ... 3.00
- ❑2, Mar 1996, GP (w); A: Silver Surfer ... 3.00
- ❑3, Jun 1996, A: Fantastic Four ... 3.00
- ❑4, Sep 1996, A: Avengers ... 3.00
- ❑5, Dec 1996, A: Howard the Duck. A: Gambit ... 3.00
- ❑6, Mar 1997, TP, BMc (a); A: Dracula. A: Aquarian. A: Hulk. A: Doctor Strange ... 3.00
- ❑7, Jun 1997, KB (w); SB, DG (a); A: Thunderbolts ... 3.00

SPIDER-MAN TEAM-UP SPECIAL
MARVEL
- ❑0 2005 ... 2.99

SPIDER-MAN: THE ARACHNIS PROJECT
MARVEL
- ❑1, Aug 1994 ... 2.00
- ❑2, Sep 1994 ... 2.00
- ❑3, Oct 1994 ... 2.00
- ❑4, Nov 1994 ... 2.00
- ❑5, Dec 1994 ... 2.00
- ❑6, Jan 1995 ... 2.00

SPIDER-MAN: THE CLONE JOURNAL
MARVEL
- ❑1, Mar 1995 SB (a); O: Ben Reilly ... 3.00

SPIDER-MAN: THE DEATH OF CAPTAIN STACY
MARVEL
- ❑1, Aug 2000, Reprints Amazing Spider-Man #88-90 ... 3.50

SPIDER-MAN: THE FINAL ADVENTURE
MARVEL
- ❑1, Dec 1995, enhanced cardstock cover; clone returns to action one last time ... 3.00
- ❑2, Jan 1996, enhanced cardstock cover ... 3.00
- ❑3, Feb 1996, enhanced cardstock cover ... 3.00
- ❑4, Mar 1996, enhanced cardstock cover; Peter loses his powers ... 3.00

SPIDER-MAN: THE JACKAL FILES
MARVEL
- ❑1, Aug 1995, files on main Spider-Man characters and equipment ... 1.95

SPIDER-MAN: THE LOST YEARS
MARVEL
- ❑0, Jan 1996, JR2 (a); collects clone origin back-up stories; Collects prologue chapters to series ... 3.95
- ❑1, Aug 1995,; JR2 (a); enhanced cardstock cover ... 3.00
- ❑2, Sep 1995, JR2 (a); enhanced cardstock cover ... 3.00
- ❑3, Oct 1995, JR2 (a); enhanced cardstock cover ... 3.00

SPIDER-MAN: THE MANGA
MARVEL
- ❑1, Dec 1997 ... 3.99
- ❑2, Jan 1998 ... 2.99
- ❑3, Feb 1998 ... 2.99
- ❑4, Feb 1998 ... 2.99
- ❑5, Mar 1998 ... 2.99
- ❑6, Mar 1998 ... 2.99
- ❑7 1998 ... 2.99
- ❑8, Apr 1998 ... 2.99
- ❑9, Apr 1998 ... 2.99
- ❑10, May 1998 ... 2.99
- ❑11, May 1998 ... 2.99
- ❑12, Jun 1998 ... 2.99
- ❑13, Jun 1998 ... 2.99
- ❑14, Jul 1998 ... 2.99
- ❑15, Jul 1998 ... 2.99
- ❑16, Aug 1998 ... 2.99
- ❑17, Aug 1998 ... 2.99
- ❑18, Sep 1998 ... 2.99
- ❑19, Sep 1998 ... 2.99
- ❑20, Oct 1998 ... 2.99
- ❑21, Oct 1998 ... 2.99
- ❑22, ca. 1998 ... 2.99
- ❑23, ca. 1998 ... 2.99
- ❑24, ca. 1998 ... 2.99
- ❑25, ca. 1998 ... 2.99
- ❑26, ca. 1999 ... 2.99
- ❑27, ca. 1999 ... 2.99
- ❑28, ca. 1999 ... 2.99
- ❑29, ca. 1999 ... 2.99
- ❑30, ca. 1999 ... 2.99
- ❑31, ca. 1999 ... 2.99

SPIDER-MAN: THE MUTANT AGENDA
MARVEL
- ❑0, Mar 1994; strip reprints; Spaces to paste in newspaper strip; cover says Feb, indicia says Mar ... 1.25
- ❑1, Mar 1994; Ties in with daily Spider-Man newspaper strip ... 1.75
- ❑2, Apr 1994 ... 1.75
- ❑3, May 1994 ... 1.75

SPIDER-MAN: THE OFFICIAL MOVIE ADAPTATION
MARVEL
- ❑1, Jun 2002 ... 5.95

SPIDER-MAN: THE OTHER SKETCHBOOK
MARVEL
- ❑1 2005 ... 1.00

SPIDER-MAN: THE PARKER YEARS
MARVEL
- ❑1, Nov 1995; retells events in the clone's life from Amazing Spider-Man #150 to the present ... 2.50

SPIDER-MAN 2099
MARVEL
- ❑1, Nov 1992; PD (w); O: Spider-Man 2099. 1: Tyler Stone. foil cover ... 3.00
- ❑1/Autographed, Nov 1992; AW (a); foil cover with certificate of authenticity ... 1.75
- ❑2, Dec 1992 PD (w); O: Spider-Man 2099. ... 1.25
- ❑3, Jan 1993 PD (w); O: Spider-Man 2099. ... 1.25
- ❑4, Feb 1993 PD (w); 1: The Specialist. ... 1.25
- ❑5, Mar 1993 PD (w) ... 1.25
- ❑6, Apr 1993 PD (w); 1: Vulture 2099. ... 1.25
- ❑7, May 1993 PD (w) ... 1.25
- ❑8, Jun 1993 PD (w) ... 1.25
- ❑9, Jul 1993 PD (w) ... 1.25
- ❑10, Aug 1993 PD (w) ... 1.25
- ❑11, Sep 1993 PD (w) ... 1.25
- ❑12, Oct 1993 PD (w) ... 1.25
- ❑13, Nov 1993 PD (w) ... 1.25
- ❑14, Dec 1993 PD (w) ... 1.25
- ❑15, Jan 1994 PD (w) ... 1.25
- ❑16, Feb 1994 PD (w) ... 1.25
- ❑17, Mar 1994 PD (w) ... 1.25
- ❑18, Apr 1994 PD (w) ... 1.25
- ❑19, May 1994 PD (w) ... 1.50
- ❑20, Jun 1994 PD (w) ... 1.50
- ❑21, Jul 1994 PD (w) ... 1.50
- ❑22, Aug 1994 PD (w) ... 1.50
- ❑23, Sep 1994 PD (w) ... 1.50
- ❑24, Oct 1994 PD (w) ... 1.50
- ❑25, Nov 1994; Giant-size PD (w) ... 2.25
- ❑25/Variant, Nov 1994; Giant-size; PD (w); enhanced cover ... 2.95
- ❑26, Dec 1994 PD (w) ... 1.50
- ❑27, Jan 1995 PD (w) ... 1.50
- ❑28, Feb 1995 PD (w) ... 1.50
- ❑29, Mar 1995 PD (w) ... 1.50
- ❑30, Apr 1995 PD (w) ... 1.50
- ❑31, May 1995 PD (w) ... 1.50
- ❑32, Jun 1995 PD (w) ... 1.95
- ❑33, Jul 1995 PD (w); A: Strange 2099. ... 1.95
- ❑34, Aug 1995 PD (w) ... 1.95
- ❑35, Sep 1995 PD (w) ... 1.95
- ❑35/Variant, Sep 1995; PD (w); alternate cover ... 1.95
- ❑36, Oct 1995; PD (w); Spiderman 2099 on cover ... 1.95
- ❑36/Variant, Oct 1995; PD (w); alternate cover; says Venom 2099; forms diptych ... 1.95
- ❑37, Nov 1995 PD (w) ... 1.95
- ❑37/Variant, Nov 1995; alternate cover; says Venom 2099 ... 1.95
- ❑38, Dec 1995; PD (w); Spiderman 2099 on cover ... 1.95
- ❑38/Variant, Dec 1995; PD (w); alternate cover; says Venom 2099; forms diptych ... 1.95

Other grades: Multiply price above by 5/6 for VF/NM • 2/3 for VERY FINE • 1/3 for FINE • 1/5 for VERY GOOD • 1/8 for GOOD

Spooky Spooktown

Series' name would not go over well today

©Harvey

Spring Break Comics

Beach humor from AC Comics

©AC

SpyBoy

Peter David series had three 13th issues

©Dark Horse

Squadron Supreme

Mark Gruenwald's look at an alternate Earth

©Marvel

Squee!

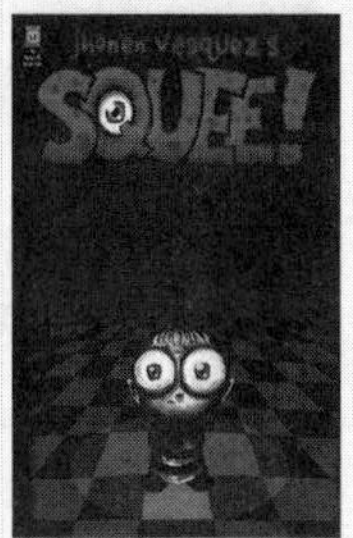

Jhnoen Vazquez is the Tim Burton of comics

©Slave Labor

	N-MINT
❑39, Jan 1996 PD (w)	1.95
❑40, Feb 1996 PD (w); V: Goblin 2099.	1.95
❑41, Mar 1996 PD (w)	1.95
❑42, Apr 1996 PD (w); BSz (a)	1.95
❑43, May 1996 PD (w)	1.95
❑44, Jun 1996	1.95
❑45, Jul 1996 V: Goblin 2099.	1.95
❑46, Aug 1996; V: Vulture 2099. story continues in Fantastic Four 2099 #8	1.95
❑Annual 1, ca. 1994; 1994 Annual	2.95
❑Special 1, Nov 1995	3.95

SPIDER-MAN 2099 MEETS SPIDER-MAN
MARVEL

❑1, Nov 1995	5.95

SPIDER-MAN UNIVERSE
MARVEL

❑1, Mar 2000; Reprints Peter Parker: Spider-Man #13, Webspinners #13, Spider-Woman (2nd Series) #8	4.99
❑2	4.99
❑3	4.99
❑4	4.99
❑5	4.99
❑6	3.99
❑7	3.99

SPIDER-MAN UNLIMITED
MARVEL

❑1, May 1993	4.00
❑2, Aug 1993	4.00
❑3, Nov 1993; Doctor Octopus	4.00
❑4, Feb 1994; Mysterio	4.00
❑5, May 1994; Human Torch	4.00
❑6, Aug 1994	4.00
❑7, Nov 1994; Spider-Man and clone	4.00
❑8, Feb 1995; Spider-Man and clone	4.00
❑9, May 1995	4.00
❑10, Sep 1995	4.00
❑11, Jan 1996	4.00
❑12, May 1996	4.00
❑13, Aug 1996	2.95
❑14, Dec 1996	2.99
❑15, Feb 1997	2.99
❑16, May 1997	2.99
❑17, Aug 1997; gatefold summary	2.99
❑18, Nov 1997; gatefold summary	2.99
❑19, Feb 1998; gatefold summary	2.99
❑20, May 1998; gatefold summary	2.99
❑21, Aug 1998; gatefold summary	2.99
❑22, Nov 1998; gatefold summary	2.99

SPIDER-MAN UNLIMITED (2ND SERIES)
MARVEL

❑1, Dec 1999; based on animated television show	2.99

SPIDER-MAN UNLIMITED (3RD SERIES)
MARVEL

❑1, Mar 2004	2.99
❑2, May 2004	2.99
❑3, Jul 2004	2.99
❑4, Sep 2004	2.99
❑5, Oct 2004	2.99
❑6, Nov 2004	2.99
❑7, Dec 2004	2.99
❑8, Jan 2005	2.99
❑9 2005	2.99
❑10 2005	2.99
❑11, Oct 2005	2.99
❑12, Jan 2006	2.99
❑13, Mar 2006	2.99
❑14, May 2006	2.99
❑15, Jul 2006	2.99

SPIDER-MAN UNMASKED
MARVEL

❑1, Nov 1996	5.95

SPIDER-MAN: VENOM AGENDA
MARVEL

❑1, Jan 1998; gatefold summary	2.99

SPIDER-MAN VS. DRACULA
MARVEL

❑1; RA (a); Reprints	2.00

SPIDER-MAN VS. PUNISHER
MARVEL

❑1, Jul 2000	2.99

SPIDER-MAN VS. THE HULK
MARVEL

❑1, ca. 1979; giveaway	7.00

SPIDER-MAN VS. WOLVERINE
MARVEL

❑1, Feb 1987 D: Ned Leeds.	6.00
❑1/2nd, Aug 1990; D: Ned Leeds. cardstock cover	4.95

SPIDER-MAN: WEB OF DOOM
MARVEL

❑1, Aug 1994	2.00
❑2, Sep 1994	2.00
❑3, Oct 1994	2.00

SPIDER: REIGN OF THE VAMPIRE KING
ECLIPSE

❑1, ca. 1992	4.95
❑2, ca. 1992	4.95
❑3, ca. 1992	4.95

SPIDER SNEAK PREVIEW
ARGOSY

❑1, ca. 2001, b&w; prestige format one-shot	5.00

SPIDER'S WEB
BLAZING

❑1; Flip-book	1.50

SPIDER-WOMAN
MARVEL

❑1, Apr 1978, Cl (a); O: Spider-Woman I (Jessica Drew).	6.00
❑2, May 1978, 1: Morgan LeFay. Newsstand edition (distributed by Curtis); issue number appears in box	3.00
❑2/Whitman, May 1978, 1: Morgan LeFay. Special markets edition (usually sold in Whitman bagged prepacks); price appears in a diamond; no UPC barcode	3.00
❑3, Jun 1978, 1: Brothers Grimm.	2.50
❑4, Jul 1978	2.00
❑5, Aug 1978, Newsstand edition (distributed by Curtis); issue number appears in box	2.00
❑5/Whitman, Aug 1978, Special markets edition (usually sold in Whitman bagged prepacks); price appears in a diamond; no UPC barcode	2.00
❑6, Sep 1978, Newsstand edition (distributed by Curtis); issue number appears in box	1.75
❑6/Whitman, Sep 1978, Special markets edition (usually sold in Whitman bagged prepacks); price appears in a diamond; no UPC barcode	1.75
❑7, Oct 1978	1.75
❑8, Nov 1978	1.75
❑9, Dec 1978, O: Needle. 1: Needle.	1.75
❑10, Jan 1979	1.75
❑11, Feb 1979, Newsstand edition (distributed by Curtis); issue number appears in box	1.50
❑11/Whitman, Feb 1979, Special markets edition (usually sold in Whitman bagged prepacks); price appears in a diamond; no UPC barcode	1.50
❑12, Mar 1979, D: Brothers Grimm.	1.50
❑13, Apr 1979	1.50
❑14, May 1979	1.50
❑15, Jun 1979	1.50
❑16, Jul 1979	1.50
❑17, Aug 1979	1.50
❑18, Sep 1979	1.50
❑19, Oct 1979, V: Werewolf	1.50
❑20, Nov 1979, A: Spider-Man.	1.50
❑21, Dec 1979	1.50
❑22, Jan 1980	1.50
❑23, Feb 1980	1.50
❑24, Mar 1980, TVE (a)	1.50
❑25, Apr 1980	1.50
❑26, May 1980, JBy (c)	1.50
❑27, Jun 1980	1.50
❑28, Jul 1980, A: Spider-Man	1.50
❑29, Aug 1980, A: Spider-Man.	1.50
❑30, Sep 1980, 1: Doctor Karl Malus.	1.50
❑31, Oct 1980, FM (c); FM (a)	1.50
❑32, Nov 1980, FM (c); FM (a)	1.50
❑33, Dec 1980, O: Turner D. Century. 1: Turner D. Century.	1.50
❑34, Jan 1981	1.50
❑35, Feb 1981	1.50
❑36, Mar 1981	1.50
❑37, Apr 1981, 1: Siryn. A: X-Men.	4.00
❑38, Jun 1981, A: X-Men.	4.00
❑39, Aug 1981	1.25
❑40, Oct 1981	1.25
❑41, Dec 1981	1.25
❑42, Feb 1982	1.25
❑43, Apr 1982	1.25
❑44, Jun 1982	1.25
❑45, Aug 1982	1.25
❑46, Oct 1982	1.25
❑47, Dec 1982	1.25
❑48, Feb 1983	1.25
❑49, Apr 1983	1.25

Other grades: Multiply price above by 5/6 for VF/NM • 2/3 for VERY FINE • 1/3 for FINE • 1/5 for VERY GOOD • 1/8 for GOOD

❑50, Jun 1983; Giant-size D: Spider-Woman I (Jessica Drew)................. 4.00

SPIDER-WOMAN (2ND SERIES)
MARVEL

❑1, Nov 1993 ..... 1.75
❑2, Dec 1993 ..... 1.75
❑3, Jan 1994 ..... 1.75
❑4, Feb 1994 ..... 1.75

SPIDER-WOMAN (3RD SERIES)
MARVEL

❑1, Jul 1999 JBy (w) 2.99
❑2, Aug 1999 ..... 2.99
❑3, Sep 1999 ..... 1.99
❑4, Oct 1999 ..... 1.99
❑5, Nov 1999 ..... 1.99
❑6, Dec 1999 ..... 1.99
❑7, Jan 2000 ..... 1.99
❑8, Feb 2000 ..... 1.99
❑9, Mar 2000 ..... 1.99
❑10, Apr 2000 ..... 2.25
❑11, May 2000 ..... 2.25
❑12, Jun 2000 ..... 2.25
❑13, Jul 2000 ..... 2.25
❑14, Aug 2000 ..... 2.25
❑15, Sep 2000 ..... 2.25
❑16, Oct 2000 ..... 2.25
❑17, Nov 2000 ..... 2.25
❑18, Dec 2000 JBy (w) 2.25

SPIDER-WOMAN: ORIGIN
MARVEL

❑1, Feb 2006 ..... 2.99
❑2, Mar 2006 ..... 2.99
❑3, Apr 2006 ..... 2.99
❑4, May 2006 ..... 2.99
❑5, Jun 2006 ..... 2.99

SPIDERY-MON: MAXIMUM CARCASS
PARODY

❑1/A, b&w; Variant edition A; Covers of the three variants join together to form a mural 3.25
❑1/B, b&w; Variant edition B; Covers of the three variants join together to form a mural 3.25
❑1/C, b&w; Variant edition C; Covers of the three variants join together to form a mural 3.25

SPIDEY AND THE MINI-MARVELS
MARVEL

❑1, May 2003 ..... 3.50

SPIDEY SUPER STORIES
MARVEL

❑1, Oct 1974, O: Spider-Man. 20.00
❑2, Nov 1974 ..... 6.00
❑3, Dec 1974, V: Circus of Crime. 5.00
❑4, Jan 1975 ..... 5.00
❑5, Feb 1975 ..... 5.00
❑6, Mar 1975 ..... 5.00
❑7, Apr 1975 ..... 5.00
❑8, May 1975 ..... 5.00
❑9, Jun 1975, V: Dr. Doom. V: Doctor Doom. Hulk 5.00
❑10, Jul 1975 ..... 5.00
❑11, Aug 1975 ..... 5.00
❑12, Sep 1975 ..... 5.00
❑13, Oct 1975 ..... 5.00
❑14, Dec 1975, A: Shanna. 5.00
❑15, Feb 1976, A: Storm. 5.00
❑16, Apr 1976 ..... 5.00
❑17, Jun 1976 ..... 5.00
❑18, Aug 1976 ..... 5.00
❑19, Oct 1976 ..... 5.00
❑20, Dec 1976 ..... 5.00
❑21, Feb 1977 ..... 5.00
❑22, Apr 1977 ..... 5.00
❑23, Jun 1977 ..... 5.00
❑24, Jul 1977, A: Thundra. 5.00
❑25, Aug 1977 ..... 5.00
❑26, Sep 1977 ..... 5.00
❑27, Oct 1977 ..... 5.00
❑28, Nov 1977 ..... 5.00
❑29, Dec 1977, V: Kingpin. 5.00
❑30, Jan 1978, V: Kang the Conqueror. 5.00
❑31, Feb 1978 ..... 5.00
❑32, Mar 1978 ..... 5.00
❑33, Apr 1978 A: Hulk. 5.00
❑34, May 1978 ..... 5.00
❑35, Jul 1978, A: Shanna. 5.00
❑36, Sep 1978 ..... 5.00
❑37, Nov 1978, Newsstand edition (distributed by Curtis); issue number in box 5.00
❑37/Whitman, Nov 1978, Special markets edition (usually sold in Whitman bagged prepacks); price appears in a diamond; no UPC barcode 5.00
❑38, Jan 1979, Newsstand edition (distributed by Curtis); issue number in box 5.00
❑38/Whitman, Jan 1979, Special markets edition (usually sold in Whitman bagged prepacks); price appears in a diamond; no UPC barcode 5.00
❑39, Mar 1979, A: Thanos. A: Hellcat. 5.00
❑40, May 1979, Newsstand edition (distributed by Curtis); issue number in box 5.00
❑40/Whitman, May 1979, Special markets edition (usually sold in Whitman bagged prepacks); price appears in a diamond; no UPC barcode 5.00
❑41, Jul 1979 ..... 5.00
❑42, Sep 1979 ..... 5.00
❑43, Nov 1979 ..... 5.00
❑44, Jan 1980 ..... 5.00
❑45, Mar 1980, A: Doctor Doom. A: Silver Surfer. 5.00
❑46, May 1980 ..... 5.00
❑47, Jul 1980 ..... 5.00
❑48, Sep 1980 ..... 5.00
❑49, Nov 1980 ..... 5.00
❑50, Jan 1981 ..... 5.00
❑51, Mar 1981 ..... 5.00
❑52, May 1981 ..... 5.00
❑53, Jul 1981 ..... 5.00
❑54, Sep 1981 ..... 5.00
❑55, Nov 1981, V: Kingpin. 5.00
❑56, Jan 1982 ..... 5.00
❑57, Mar 1982 ..... 5.00

SPIKE: LOST AND FOUND
IDEA & DESIGN WORKS

❑1, May 2006 ..... 3.99

SPIKE: OLD TIMES
IDEA & DESIGN WORKS

❑0, Sep 2005 ..... 3.99

SPIKE: OLD WOUNDS
IDEA & DESIGN WORKS

❑1, Feb 2006 ..... 3.99

SPIKE VS. DRACULA
IDEA & DESIGN WORKS

❑1, Mar 2006 ..... 3.99
❑2, Apr 2006 ..... 3.99
❑3, May 2006 ..... 3.99

SPINELESS-MAN $2099
PARODY

❑1 ..... 2.50

SPINE-TINGLING TALES (DR. SPEKTOR PRESENTS...)
GOLD KEY

❑1, May 1975 ..... 20.00
❑2, Aug 1975 ..... 8.00
❑3, Nov 1975 ..... 8.00
❑4, Feb 1976 ..... 8.00

SPINWORLD
SLAVE LABOR / AMAZE INK

❑1, Jul 1997, b&w 2.95
❑2, Aug 1997, b&w 2.95
❑3, Oct 1997, b&w 2.95
❑4, Jan 1998, b&w 2.95

SPIRAL PATH
ECLIPSE

❑1, ca. 1986 ..... 1.75
❑2, ca. 1986 ..... 1.75

SPIRAL ZONE
DC

❑1, Feb 1988 ..... 1.00
❑2, Mar 1988 ..... 1.00
❑3, Apr 1988 ..... 1.00
❑4, May 1988 ..... 1.00

SPIRIT (5TH SERIES)
HARVEY

❑1, Oct 1966; WE (c); WE (w); WE (a); O: The Spirit. Harvey 50.00
❑2, Mar 1967 WE (c); WE (w); WE (a) 42.00

SPIRIT (6TH SERIES)
KITCHEN SINK

❑1, Jan 1973, b&w; WE (c); WE (w); WE (a); Krupp/Kitchen Sink publishes 14.00
❑2, Sep 1973, WE (c); WE (w); WE (a) 14.00

SPIRIT, THE (7TH SERIES)
KEN PIERCE

❑1 WE (c); WE (w); WE (a) 18.00
❑2 WE (c); WE (w); WE (a) 18.00
❑3 WE (c); WE (w); WE (a) 18.00
❑4 WE (c); WE (w); WE (a) 18.00

SPIRIT, THE (8TH SERIES)
KITCHEN SINK

❑1, Oct 1983, WE (w); WE (a); O: The Spirit. Kitchen Sink publishes; reprints #291-294 ..... 5.00
❑2, Dec 1983, WE (w); WE (a); reprints #295-298 ..... 4.00
❑3, Feb 1984, WE (w); WE (a); reprints #299-302 ..... 4.00
❑4, Mar 1984, WE (w); WE (a); Reprints #303, 304, and Spirit story from Police Comics #98 ..... 3.50
❑5, Jun 1984, WE (w); WE (a) 3.50
❑6, Aug 1984, WE (w); WE (a) 3.50
❑7, Oct 1984, WE (w); WE (a) 3.50
❑8, Feb 1985, WE (w); WE (a) 3.50
❑9, Apr 1985, WE (w); WE (a) 3.50
❑10, Jun 1985, WE (w); WE (a) 2.95
❑11, Aug 1985, WE (w); WE (a) 2.95
❑12, Oct 1985, b&w WE (w); WE (a) 2.00
❑13, Nov 1985, b&w WE (w); WE (a) 2.00
❑14, Dec 1985, b&w WE (w); WE (a) 2.00
❑15, Jan 1986, b&w; WE (w); WE (a); reprints #356-359 ..... 2.00
❑16, Feb 1986, b&w WE (w); WE (a) 2.00
❑17, Mar 1986, b&w WE (w); WE (a) 2.00
❑18, Apr 1986, b&w WE (w); WE (a) 2.00
❑19, May 1986, b&w WE (w); WE (a) 2.00
❑20, Jun 1986, b&w WE (w); WE (a) 2.00
❑21, Jul 1986, b&w WE (w); WE (a) 2.00
❑22, Aug 1986, b&w WE (w); WE (a) 2.00
❑23, Sep 1986, b&w WE (w); WE (a) 2.00
❑24, Oct 1986, b&w WE (w); WE (a) 2.00
❑25, Nov 1986, b&w WE (w); WE (a) 2.00
❑26, Dec 1986, b&w WE (w); WE (a) 2.00
❑27, Jan 1987, b&w WE (w); WE (a) 2.00
❑28, Feb 1987, b&w WE (w); WE (a) 2.00
❑29, Mar 1987, b&w WE (w); WE (a) 2.00
❑30, Apr 1987, b&w WE (w); WE (a) 2.00
❑31, May 1987, b&w WE (w); WE (a) 2.00
❑32, Jun 1987, b&w WE (w); WE (a) 2.00
❑33, Jul 1987, b&w WE (w); WE (a) 2.00
❑34, Aug 1987, b&w WE (w); WE (a) 2.00
❑35, Sep 1987, b&w WE (w); WE (a) 2.00
❑36, Oct 1987, b&w WE (w); WE (a) 2.00
❑37, Nov 1987, b&w WE (w); WE (a) 2.00
❑38, Dec 1988, b&w WE (w); WE (a) 2.00
❑39, Jan 1988, b&w WE (w); WE (a) 2.00
❑40, Feb 1988, b&w WE (w); WE (a) 2.00
❑41, Mar 1988, b&w; WE (w); WE (a); Wertham parody 2.00
❑42, Apr 1988, b&w WE (w); WE (a) 2.00
❑43, May 1988, b&w WE (w); WE (a) 2.00
❑44, Jun 1988, b&w WE (w); WE (a) 2.00
❑45, Jul 1988, b&w WE (w); WE (a) 2.00
❑46, Aug 1988, b&w WE (w); WE (a) 2.00
❑47, Sep 1988, b&w WE (w); WE (a) 2.00
❑48, Oct 1988, b&w WE (w); WE (a) 2.00
❑49, Nov 1988, b&w WE (w); WE (a) 2.00
❑50, Dec 1988, b&w WE (w); WE (a) 2.00
❑51, Jan 1989, b&w WE (w); WE (a) 2.00
❑52, Feb 1989, b&w WE (w); WE (a) 2.00
❑53, Mar 1989, b&w WE (w); WE (a) 2.00
❑54, Apr 1989, b&w WE (w); WE (a) 2.00
❑55, May 1989, b&w WE (w); WE (a) 2.00
❑56, Jun 1989, b&w WE (w); WE (a) 2.00
❑57, Jul 1989, b&w WE (w); WE (a) 2.00
❑58, Aug 1989, b&w WE (w); WE (a) 2.00
❑59, Sep 1989, b&w WE (w); WE (a) 2.00
❑60, Oct 1989, b&w; WE (w); WE (a); Reprints #532-535 ..... 2.00
❑61, Nov 1989, b&w; WE (w); WE (a); Reprints #536-539 ..... 2.00
❑62, Dec 1989, b&w WE (w); WE (a) 2.00
❑63, Jan 1990, b&w WE (w); WE (a) 2.00
❑64, Feb 1990, b&w WE (w); WE (a) 2.00

Stanley and His Monster (2nd Series)

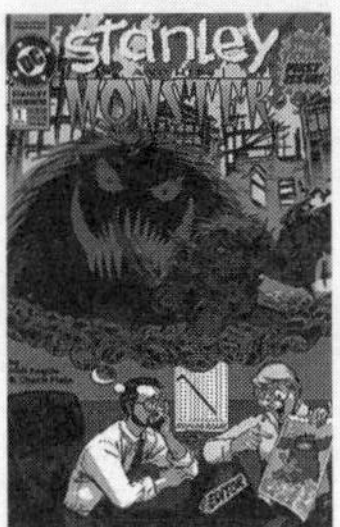

Phil Foglio's version of the 1960s silliness

©DC

Star Brand

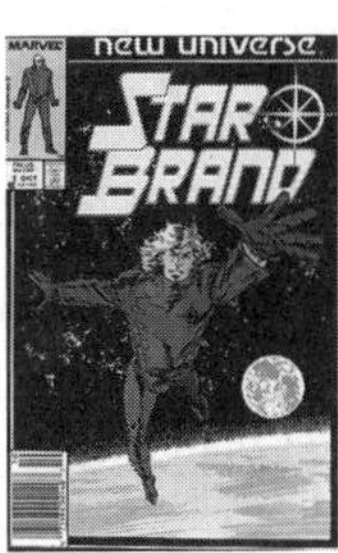

Flagship title of ill-fated New Universe

©Marvel

Starjammers (Vol. 2)

Kevin Anderson's version failed to connect

©Marvel

Starman (1st Series)

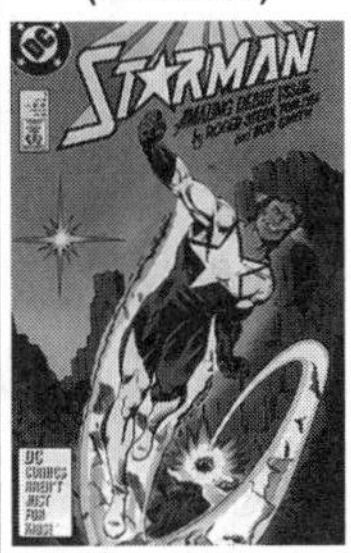

Actually the fourth person to use the name

©DC

Starman (2nd Series)

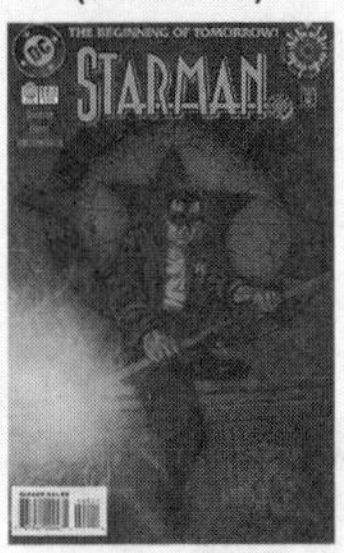

James Robinson delved into Golden Age lore

©DC

	N-MINT
❑65, Mar 1990, b&w WE (w); WE (a)	2.00
❑66, Apr 1990, b&w WE (w); WE (a)	2.00
❑67, May 1990, b&w WE (w); WE (a)	2.00
❑68, Jun 1990, b&w WE (w); WE (a)	2.00
❑69, Jul 1990, b&w WE (w); WE (a)	2.00
❑70, Aug 1990, b&w WE (w); WE (a)	2.00
❑71, Sep 1990, b&w WE (w); WE (a)	2.00
❑72, Oct 1990, b&w WE (w); WE (a)	2.00
❑73, Nov 1990, b&w	2.00
❑74, Dec 1990, b&w	2.00
❑75, Jan 1991, b&w	2.00
❑76, Feb 1991, b&w	2.00
❑77, Mar 1991, b&w	2.00
❑78, Apr 1991, b&w	2.00
❑79, May 1991, b&w; reprints #608-611	2.00
❑80, Jun 1991, b&w; reprints #612-615	2.00
❑81, Jul 1991, b&w; reprints #616-619	2.00
❑82, Aug 1991, b&w; reprints #620-623	2.00
❑83, Sep 1991, b&w; reprints #625-628	2.00
❑84, Oct 1991, b&w; reprints #629-631	2.00
❑85, Nov 1991, b&w; reprints #632-635	2.00
❑86, Dec 1991, b&w	2.00
❑87, Jan 1992, b&w	2.00

SPIRIT JAM
KITCHEN SINK

❑1	5.95

SPIRIT (MAGAZINE)
WARREN

❑1, Apr 1974, b&w WE (w); WE (a)	22.00
❑2, Jun 1974, b&w WE (w); WE (a)	10.00
❑3, Aug 1974, b&w WE (w); WE (a)	7.00
❑4, Oct 1974, b&w WE (w); WE (a)	6.00
❑5, Dec 1974, b&w WE (w); WE (a)	6.00
❑6, Feb 1975, b&w WE (w); WE (a)	6.00
❑7, Apr 1975, b&w WE (w); WE (a)	6.00
❑8, Jun 1975, b&w WE (w); WE (a)	6.00
❑9, Aug 1975, b&w WE (w); WE (a)	6.00
❑10, Oct 1975, b&w WE (w); WE (a)	6.00
❑11, Dec 1975, b&w WE (w); WE (a)	6.00
❑12, Feb 1976, b&w WE (w); WE (a)	6.00
❑13, Apr 1976, b&w WE (w); WE (a)	5.00
❑14, Jun 1976, b&w WE (w); WE (a)	5.00
❑15, Aug 1976, b&w WE (w); WE (a)	5.00
❑16, Oct 1976, b&w WE (w); WE (a)	7.00
❑17, Nov 1977, b&w; WE (w); WE (a); Kitchen Sink begins as publisher; wraparound covers begin	4.00
❑18, May 1978, b&w; WE (w); WE (a); Wraparound cover	4.00
❑19, Oct 1978, b&w; WE (w); WE (a); Wraparound cover	4.00
❑20, Mar 1979, b&w; WE (w); WE (a); Wraparound cover	4.00
❑21, Jul 1979, b&w; WE (w); WE (a); Wraparound cover	4.00
❑22, Dec 1979, b&w; WE (w); WE (a); Wraparound cover	4.00
❑23, Feb 1980, b&w; WE (w); WE (a); Wraparound cover	4.00
❑24, May 1980, b&w; WE (w); WE (a); Wraparound cover	4.00
❑25, Aug 1980, b&w; WE (w); WE (a); Wraparound cover	4.00
❑26, Dec 1980, b&w; WE, WW (w); WE, WW (a); Wraparound cover	4.00
❑27, Feb 1981, b&w; WE (w); WE (a); Wraparound cover	4.00
❑28, Apr 1981, b&w; WE (w); WE (a); Wraparound cover	4.00
❑29, Jun 1981, b&w; WE (w); WE (a); Wraparound cover	4.00
❑30, Jul 1981, b&w; WE (w); WE (a); Featuring more than 50 artists; Wraparound cover	4.00
❑31, Oct 1981, b&w; WE (w); WE (a); Wraparound cover	4.00
❑32, Dec 1981, b&w; WE (w); WE (a); No wraparound cover	4.00
❑33, Feb 1982, b&w; WE (w); WE (a); Wraparound cover	4.00
❑34, Apr 1982, b&w; WE (w); WE (a); No wrapraround cover	4.00
❑35, Jun 1982, b&w; WE (w); WE (a); No wraparound cover	4.00
❑36, Aug 1982, b&w; WE (w); WE (a); Wraparound cover	4.00
❑37, Oct 1982, b&w; WE (w); WE (a); Wraparound cover	4.00
❑38, Dec 1982, b&w; WE (w); WE (a); Wraparound cover	4.00
❑39, Feb 1983, b&w; WE (w); WE (a); Wraparound cover	4.00
❑40, Apr 1983, b&w; WE (w); WE (a); Wraparound cover	4.00
❑41, Jun 1983, b&w; WE (w); WE (a); Wraparound cover	4.00
❑Special 1 1975, b&w	35.00

SPIRIT OF THE TAO
IMAGE

❑1, Jun 1998	2.50
❑2, Jul 1998	2.50
❑3, Aug 1998	2.50
❑4, Sep 1998	2.50
❑5, Nov 1998	2.50
❑6, Dec 1998	2.50
❑7, Feb 1999	2.50
❑8, Apr 1999	2.50
❑9, May 1999	2.50
❑10, Jun 1999	2.50
❑11, Aug 1999	2.50
❑12, Oct 1999	2.50
❑13, Nov 1999	2.50
❑Ashcan 1, 1: Jasmine. 1: Lance	5.00

SPIRIT OF THE WIND
CHOCOLATE MOUSE

❑1, b&w	2.00

SPIRIT OF WONDER
DARK HORSE / MANGA

❑1, Apr 1996, b&w	2.95
❑2, May 1996, b&w	2.95
❑3, Jun 1996, b&w	2.95
❑4, Jul 1996, b&w	2.95
❑5, Aug 1996, b&w	2.95

SPIRITS
MIND WALKER

❑3, Sep 1995, b&w	2.95

SPIRITS OF VENOM
MARVEL

❑1	9.95

SPIRIT: THE NEW ADVENTURES
KITCHEN SINK

❑1, Mar 1998	3.50
❑2, Apr 1998	3.50
❑3, May 1998	3.50
❑4, Jun 1998	3.50
❑5, Jul 1998	3.50
❑6, Sep 1998	3.50
❑7, Oct 1998	3.50
❑8, Nov 1998	3.50

SPIRIT: THE ORIGIN YEARS
KITCHEN SINK

❑1, May 1992	2.95
❑2, Jul 1992	2.95
❑3, Sep 1992	2.95
❑4, Nov 1992	2.95
❑5, Jan 1993	2.95
❑6, Mar 1993	2.95
❑7, May 1993	2.95
❑8, Jul 1993	2.95
❑9, Sep 1993	2.95
❑10, Dec 1993	2.95

SPIRIT WORLD
DC

❑1, Jul 1971 JK (w); JK (a)	35.00

SPIROU & FANTASIO: Z IS FOR ZORGLUB
FANTASY FLIGHT

❑1; graphic novel	8.95

SPITFIRE AND THE TROUBLESHOOTERS
MARVEL

❑1, Oct 1986, HT (a)	1.00
❑2, Nov 1986	1.00
❑3, Dec 1986	1.00
❑4, Jan 1987, TMc (a)	1.00
❑5, Feb 1987	1.00
❑6, Mar 1987	1.00
❑7, Apr 1987	1.00
❑8, May 1987	1.00
❑9, Jun 1987, Series continued in "Code Name: Spitfire"	1.00

SPITTIN' IMAGE
ECLIPSE

❑1; b&w parody	2.50

SPIT WAD COMICS
SPIT WAD

❑1, Jun 1983, b&w	2.50

SPLAT!
MAD DOG

❑1, b&w	2.00
❑2, Mar 1987	2.00
❑3	2.00

SPLATTER (ARPAD)
ARPAD

❑1, b&w	2.50

SPLATTER (NORTHSTAR)
NORTHSTAR

❑1, b&w	4.95

Other grades: Multiply price above by 5/6 for VF/NM • 2/3 for VERY FINE • 1/3 for FINE • 1/5 for VERY GOOD • 1/8 for GOOD

	N-MINT
❑2, b&w	2.75
❑3, b&w	2.75
❑4, b&w	2.75
❑5, b&w	2.75
❑6, b&w	2.75
❑7, b&w	2.75
❑8	2.75
❑Annual 1	4.95

SPLITTING IMAGE
IMAGE

❑1, Mar 1993; parody	1.95
❑2, Apr 1993; parody	1.95

SPOOF
MARVEL

❑1, ca. 1970, Infinity cover	15.00
❑2, Nov 1972	7.00
❑3, Jan 1973	8.00
❑4, Mar 1973	7.00
❑5, May 1973, HT, JSe (c)	7.00

SPOOF COMICS
SPOOF

❑0 1992, b&w; Imp-Unity	2.50
❑1 1992, b&w; Spider-Femme	2.50
❑1/2nd 1992, Spider-Femme	2.50
❑2 1992, b&w; Batbabe	2.50
❑2/2nd 1992, Batbabe	2.50
❑3, Aug 1992, b&w; Wolverbroad	2.95
❑4, Sep 1992, b&w; Superbabe	2.95
❑5, Oct 1992, b&w; Daredame	2.95
❑6 1992, b&w; X-Babes	2.95
❑7 1993, b&w; Justice Broads	2.95
❑8 1993, b&w; Fantastic Femmes	2.95
❑9 1993, b&w; Hobo	2.95
❑10 1993, b&w	2.95
❑11 1993, b&w	2.95
❑12, Mar 1993, b&w; Deathlocks	2.95

SPOOK CITY
MYTHIC

❑1, Nov 1997, b&w	2.95

SPOOKGIRL
SLAVE LABOR

❑1, ca. 2000	2.95

SPOOKY (VOL. 1)
HARVEY

❑1, Nov 1955	200.00
❑2, Jan 1956	110.00
❑3, Mar 1956	65.00
❑4, May 1956	50.00
❑5, Jul 1956	50.00
❑6, Sep 1956	35.00
❑7, Nov 1956	35.00
❑8, Jan 1957	35.00
❑9, Mar 1957	35.00
❑10, May 1957	35.00
❑11, Jul 1957	24.00
❑12, Sep 1957	24.00
❑13, Oct 1957	24.00
❑14, Nov 1957	24.00
❑15, Dec 1957	24.00
❑16, Jan 1958	24.00
❑17, Feb 1958	24.00
❑18, Mar 1958	24.00
❑19, May 1958	24.00
❑20, Jun 1958	24.00
❑21, Jul 1958	20.00
❑22, Aug 1958	20.00
❑23, Sep 1958	20.00
❑24, Oct 1958	20.00
❑25, Nov 1958	20.00
❑26, Dec 1958	20.00
❑27, Jan 1959	20.00
❑28, Feb 1959	20.00
❑29, Mar 1959	20.00
❑30, Apr 1959	18.00
❑31, May 1959	18.00
❑32, Jun 1959	18.00
❑33, Jul 1959	18.00
❑34, Aug 1959	18.00
❑35, Sep 1959	18.00
❑36, Oct 1959	18.00
❑37, Nov 1959	18.00
❑38, Dec 1959	18.00
❑39, Jan 1960	18.00
❑40, Feb 1960	15.00
❑41, Mar 1960	15.00
❑42, Apr 1960	15.00
❑43, May 1960	15.00
❑44, Jun 1960	15.00
❑45, Jul 1960	15.00
❑46, Aug 1960	15.00
❑47, Sep 1960	15.00
❑48, Oct 1960	15.00
❑49, Nov 1960	15.00
❑50, Dec 1960	15.00
❑51, Jan 1961	12.00
❑52, Feb 1961	12.00
❑53, Mar 1961	12.00
❑54, Apr 1961	12.00
❑55, May 1961	12.00
❑56, Jun 1961	12.00
❑57, Jul 1961	12.00
❑58, Aug 1961	12.00
❑59, Sep 1961	12.00
❑60, Oct 1961	12.00
❑61, Nov 1961	12.00
❑62, Dec 1961	12.00
❑63, Jan 1962	12.00
❑64, Feb 1962	12.00
❑65, Mar 1962	12.00
❑66, Apr 1962	12.00
❑67, May 1962	12.00
❑68, Jun 1962	12.00
❑69, Aug 1962	12.00
❑70, Oct 1962	12.00
❑71, Dec 1962	8.00
❑72, Feb 1963	8.00
❑73, Apr 1963	8.00
❑74, Jun 1963	8.00
❑75, Aug 1963	8.00
❑76, Oct 1963	8.00
❑77, Dec 1963	8.00
❑78, Feb 1964	8.00
❑79, Apr 1964	8.00
❑80, Jun 1964	8.00
❑81, Aug 1964	8.00
❑82, Oct 1964	8.00
❑83, Dec 1964	8.00
❑84, Feb 1965	8.00
❑85, Apr 1965	8.00
❑86, Jun 1965	8.00
❑87, Aug 1965	8.00
❑88, Oct 1965	8.00
❑89, Dec 1965	8.00
❑90, Feb 1966	8.00
❑91, Apr 1966	6.00
❑92, Jun 1966	6.00
❑93, Aug 1966	6.00
❑94, Oct 1966	6.00
❑95, Dec 1966	6.00
❑96, Feb 1967	6.00
❑97, Apr 1967	6.00
❑98, Jun 1967	6.00
❑99, Aug 1967	6.00
❑100, Oct 1967	6.00
❑101, Dec 1967	6.00
❑102, Feb 1968	6.00
❑103, Apr 1968	6.00
❑104, Jun 1968	6.00
❑105, Aug 1968	6.00
❑106, Oct 1968	6.00
❑107, Dec 1968	6.00
❑108, Feb 1969	6.00
❑109 1969	6.00
❑110, May 1969	6.00
❑111 1969	5.00
❑112 1969	5.00
❑113, Oct 1969	5.00
❑114 1969	5.00
❑115, Jan 1970	5.00
❑116, Mar 1970	5.00
❑117, May 1970	5.00
❑118, Jul 1970	5.00
❑119, Sep 1970	5.00
❑120, Nov 1970	5.00
❑121, Dec 1970	5.00
❑122, Feb 1971	5.00
❑123 1971	5.00
❑124, Jun 1971	5.00
❑125 1971	5.00
❑126, Sep 1971	5.00
❑127, Oct 1971	5.00
❑128, Dec 1971	5.00
❑129	5.00
❑130, May 1972	5.00
❑131, Jul 1972	4.00
❑132, Sep 1972	4.00
❑133, Nov 1972	4.00
❑134, Jan 1973	4.00
❑135, Mar 1973	4.00
❑136, May 1973	4.00
❑137, Jul 1973	4.00
❑138, Sep 1973	4.00
❑139, Nov 1973	4.00
❑140, Jul 1974	4.00
❑141, Sep 1974	4.00
❑142, Nov 1974	4.00
❑143, Jan 1975	4.00
❑144, Mar 1975	4.00
❑145, May 1975	4.00
❑146, Jul 1975	4.00
❑147, Sep 1975	4.00
❑148, Nov 1975	4.00
❑149, Jan 1976	4.00
❑150, Mar 1976	4.00
❑151, May 1976	4.00
❑152, Jul 1976	4.00
❑153, Sep 1976	4.00
❑154, Nov 1976	4.00
❑155, Jan 1977	4.00
❑156, Dec 1977	4.00
❑157, Feb 1978	4.00
❑158, Apr 1978	4.00
❑159, Sep 1978	4.00
❑160, Oct 1979, Casper in Hostess ad ("Meets a Robot")	4.00
❑161, Sep 1980	4.00

SPOOKY (VOL. 2)
HARVEY

❑1, ca. 1991	1.25
❑2, ca. 1991	1.25
❑3, ca. 1991	1.25
❑4, ca. 1991	1.25

SPOOKY DIGEST
HARVEY

❑1	2.00
❑2	2.00

SPOOKY HAUNTED HOUSE
HARVEY

❑1, Oct 1972	15.00
❑2, Dec 1972	10.00
❑3, Feb 1973	10.00
❑4, Apr 1973	10.00
❑5, Jun 1973	10.00
❑6, Aug 1973	10.00
❑7, Oct 1973	10.00
❑8, Dec 1973	10.00
❑9, Feb 1974	10.00
❑10, Apr 1974	10.00
❑11, Jun 1974	10.00

SPOOKY SPOOKTOWN
HARVEY

❑1, Sep 1961	85.00
❑2, Sep 1962	45.00
❑3, Dec 1962	30.00
❑4, ca. 1963	30.00
❑5, ca. 1963	30.00
❑6, ca. 1963	22.00
❑7, ca. 1963	22.00
❑8, ca. 1964	22.00
❑9, ca. 1964	22.00
❑10, ca. 1964	22.00
❑11, ca. 1964	15.00
❑12, ca. 1964	15.00
❑13, ca. 1965	15.00
❑14, ca. 1965	15.00
❑15, Sep 1965	15.00
❑16, Mar 1966	15.00
❑17, Sep 1966	15.00
❑18, ca. 1967	15.00
❑19, ca. 1967	15.00
❑20, May 1967	15.00
❑21, Sep 1967	8.00
❑22, Nov 1967	8.00
❑23, ca. 1968	8.00
❑24, ca. 1968	8.00
❑25, Jul 1968	8.00

Other grades: Multiply price above by 5/6 for VF/NM • 2/3 for VERY FINE • 1/3 for FINE • 1/5 for VERY GOOD • 1/8 for GOOD

Star Rangers

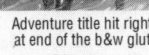

Adventure title hit right at end of the b&w glut

©Adventure

Stars and S.T.R.I.P.E.

Stepfather and stepdaughter hero team

©DC

Star Slammers (Malibu)

Simonson tale began as Marvel Graphic Novel

©Malibu

Starslayer

Celtic barbarian whisked away to future

©Pacific

Star Spangled War Stories

Home to Enemy Ace and Unknown Soldier

©DC

N-MINT

❑26, ca. 1968 ..... 8.00
❑27, Dec 1968 ..... 8.00
❑28, ca. 1969 ..... 8.00
❑29, ca. 1969 ..... 8.00
❑30, ca. 1969 ..... 5.00
❑31, Oct 1969 ..... 5.00
❑32, ca. 1970 ..... 5.00
❑33, ca. 1970 ..... 5.00
❑34, ca. 1970 ..... 5.00
❑35, ca. 1970 ..... 5.00
❑36, Oct 1970 ..... 5.00
❑37, ca. 1971 ..... 5.00
❑38, ca. 1971 ..... 5.00
❑39, ca. 1971 ..... 5.00
❑40, ca. 1971 ..... 5.00
❑41, ca. 1971 ..... 3.00
❑42, Dec 1971 ..... 3.00
❑43, Mar 1972 ..... 3.00
❑44, Jun 1972 ..... 3.00
❑45, Sep 1972 ..... 3.00
❑46, Dec 1972 ..... 3.00
❑47, Feb 1973 ..... 3.00
❑48, Apr 1973 ..... 3.00
❑49, Jun 1973 ..... 3.00
❑50, Aug 1973 ..... 3.00
❑51, Oct 1973 ..... 3.00
❑52, Dec 1973 ..... 3.00
❑53, Oct 1974 ..... 3.00
❑54, Dec 1974 ..... 3.00
❑55, Feb 1975 ..... 3.00
❑56, Apr 1975 ..... 3.00
❑57, Jun 1975 ..... 3.00
❑58, Aug 1975 ..... 3.00
❑59, Oct 1975 ..... 3.00
❑60, Dec 1975 ..... 3.00
❑61, Feb 1976 ..... 3.00
❑62, Apr 1976, A: Casper. A: Nightmare. 3.00
❑63, Jun 1976 ..... 3.00
❑64, Aug 1976 ..... 3.00
❑65, Oct 1976 ..... 3.00
❑66, Dec 1976 ..... 3.00

SPOOKY THE DOG CATCHER
PAW PRINTS

❑1, Oct 1994, b&w 2.50
❑2, Jan 1995, b&w 2.50
❑3, May 1995, b&w 2.50

SPORTS CLASSICS
PERSONALITY

❑1 ..... 2.95
❑1/Ltd.; limited edition 5.95
❑2 ..... 2.95
❑3 ..... 2.95
❑4 ..... 2.95
❑5 ..... 2.95

SPORTS COMICS
PERSONALITY

❑1 ..... 2.50
❑2 ..... 2.50
❑3 ..... 2.50
❑4 ..... 2.50

SPORTS HALL OF SHAME IN 3-D
BLACKTHORNE

❑1; baseball 2.50

N-MINT

SPORTS LEGENDS
REVOLUTIONARY

❑1, Sep 1992, b&w; Joe Namath 2.50
❑2, Oct 1992, b&w; Gordie Howe 2.50
❑3, Nov 1992, b&w; Arthur Ashe 2.50
❑4, Dec 1992, Muhammad Ali 2.50
❑5, Jan 1993, O.J. Simpson 2.50
❑6, Feb 1993, K.A. Jabbar 2.50
❑7, Mar 1993, b&w; Walter Payton 2.95
❑8, Apr 1993, b&w; Wilt Chamberlain 2.95
❑9, May 1993, b&w; Joe Louis 2.95

SPORTS LEGENDS SPECIAL - BREAKING THE COLOR BARRIER
REVOLUTIONARY

❑1, Oct 1993, b&w 2.95

SPORTS PERSONALITIES
PERSONALITY

❑1, Bo Jackson 2.95
❑2, Nolan Ryan 2.95
❑3, Rickey Henderson 2.95
❑4, Magic Johnson 2.95
❑5 ..... 2.95
❑6 ..... 2.95
❑7 ..... 2.95
❑8 ..... 2.95
❑9 ..... 2.95
❑10 ..... 2.95
❑11 ..... 2.95
❑12 ..... 2.95
❑13 ..... 2.95

SPORTS SUPERSTARS
REVOLUTIONARY

❑1, Apr 1992, b&w; Michael Jordan 2.50
❑2, May 1992, b&w; Wayne Gretzsky 2.50
❑3, Jun 1992, b&w; Magic Johnson 2.50
❑4, Jul 1992, b&w; Joe Montana 2.50
❑5, Aug 1992, b&w; Mike Tyson 2.50
❑6, Sep 1992, b&w; Larry Bird 2.50
❑7, Oct 1992, b&w; John Elway 2.50
❑8, Nov 1992, b&w; Julius Erving 2.50
❑9, Dec 1992, Barry Sanders 2.75
❑10, Jan 1993, Isiah Thomas 2.75
❑11, Feb 1992, Mario Lemieux 2.95
❑12, Mar 1993, b&w; Dan Marino 2.95
❑13, Apr 1993, b&w; Deion Sanders 2.95
❑14, May 1993, b&w; Patrick Ewing 2.95
❑15, Jun 1993, b&w; Charles Barkley 2.95
❑16, Aug 1993, b&w; Shaquille O'neal, Christian Laettner 2.95
❑Annual 1, Feb 1993, Michael Jordan II 2.75

SPOTLIGHT
MARVEL

❑1, Sep 1978, Huckleberry Hound 8.00
❑2, Nov 1978 ..... 6.00
❑3, Jan 1979 ..... 6.00
❑4, Mar 1979 ..... 6.00

SPOTLIGHT ON THE GENIUS THAT IS JOE SACCO
FANTAGRAPHICS

❑1, b&w 4.95

SPRING BREAK COMICS
AC

❑1, Mar 1987, b&w 1.50

N-MINT

SPRING-HEEL JACK
REBEL

❑1, b&w 2.25
❑2, b&w 2.25

SPRINGTIME TALES (WALT KELLY'S...)
ECLIPSE

❑1, Peter Wheat 2.50

SPUD
SPUD

❑1, Sum 1996, b&w 3.50

SPUNGIFEEL PRIMER
SPUNGIFEEL

❑Book 1, b&w 11.95

SPUNKY KNIGHT
FANTAGRAPHICS / EROS

❑1, May 1996 ..... 2.95
❑2, Jun 1996 ..... 2.95
❑3, Jul 1996 ..... 2.95

SPUNKY KNIGHT EXTREME
FANTAGRAPHICS / EROS

❑1, Dec 2004 ..... 3.95
❑2, Dec 2004 ..... 3.95
❑3, Dec 2004 ..... 3.95
❑4, Dec 2004 ..... 3.95

SPUNKY TODD: THE PSYCHIC BOY
CALIBER

❑1, b&w 2.95

SPYBOY
DARK HORSE

❑1, Oct 1999 PD (w) 3.00
❑2, Nov 1999 PD (w) 2.75
❑3, Dec 1999 PD (w) 2.75
❑4, Jan 2000 PD (w) 2.75
❑5, Feb 2000 PD (w) 2.75
❑6, Mar 2000 PD (w) 2.50
❑7, Apr 2000 PD (w) 2.50
❑8, May 2000 PD (w) 2.50
❑9, Jun 2000 PD (w) 2.50
❑10, Jul 2000 PD (w) 2.50
❑11, Aug 2000 PD (w) 2.50
❑12, Sep 2000, b&w; PD (w); #13 skipped; story for that issue published as SpyBoy 13 miniseries 2.95
❑14, Nov 2000 PD (w) 2.99
❑15, Jan 2001 PD (w) 2.99
❑16, Mar 2001 PD (w) 2.99
❑17, May 2001 PD (w) 2.99
❑Special 1, May 2002 ..... 4.99

SPYBOY 13: MANGA AFFAIR
DARK HORSE

❑1, Apr 2003; Series took the place of the 13th issue of SpyBoy 2.99
❑2, Jun 2003 ..... 2.99
❑3, Aug 2003 ..... 2.99

SPYBOY: FINAL EXAM
DARK HORSE

❑1, May 2004 ..... 2.99
❑2, Aug 2004 ..... 2.99
❑3, Sep 2004 ..... 2.99
❑4, Oct 2004 ..... 2.99

SPYBOY/YOUNG JUSTICE
DARK HORSE
- ❑1, Feb 2002 ... 2.99
- ❑2, Mar 2002 ... 2.99
- ❑3, Apr 2002 ... 2.99

SPYKE
MARVEL / EPIC
- ❑1, Jul 1993; Embossed cover ... 2.50
- ❑2, Aug 1993 ... 1.95
- ❑3, Sep 1993 ... 1.95
- ❑4, Oct 1993 ... 1.95

SPYMAN
HARVEY
- ❑1 ... 30.00
- ❑2 ... 24.00
- ❑3, Feb 1967 ... 24.00

SQUADRON SUPREME
MARVEL
- ❑1, Sep 1985 BH (c); BH (a) ... 1.50
- ❑2, Oct 1985 BH (c); BH (a); V: Scarlet Centurion. ... 1.00
- ❑3, Nov 1985 BH (c); BH (a) ... 1.00
- ❑4, Dec 1985 BH (c); BH (a) ... 1.00
- ❑5, Jan 1986 BH (c); BH (a); V: Institute of Evil ... 1.00
- ❑6, Feb 1986 ... 1.00
- ❑7, Mar 1986 ... 1.00
- ❑8, Apr 1986 BH (c); BH (a) ... 1.00
- ❑9, May 1986 D: Tom Thumb. ... 1.00
- ❑10, Jun 1986 ... 1.00
- ❑11, Jul 1986 ... 1.00
- ❑12, Aug 1986 ... 1.25

SQUADRON SUPREME: NEW WORLD ORDER
MARVEL
- ❑1, Sep 1998 ... 5.99

SQUADRON SUPREME (2ND SERIES)
MARVEL
- ❑1, Jun 2006 ... 2.99
- ❑2, Jun 2006 ... 2.99
- ❑3, Aug 2006 ... 2.99
- ❑4, Aug 2006 ... 2.99

SQUALOR
FIRST
- ❑1, Dec 1989; 1st comics work by Stefan Petrucha ... 2.75
- ❑2, Jun 1990 ... 2.75
- ❑3, Jul 1990 ... 2.75
- ❑4, Aug 1990 ... 2.75

SQUEE!
SLAVE LABOR
- ❑1, Apr 1997 ... 7.00
- ❑1/2nd 1997 ... 2.95
- ❑2, Jul 1997 ... 5.00
- ❑3, Nov 1997 ... 3.50
- ❑4, Feb 1998 ... 3.50

SRI KRISHNA
CHAKRA
- ❑1 ... 3.50

STACIA STORIES
KITCHEN SINK
- ❑1, Jun 1995, b&w ... 2.95

STAGGER LEE
IMAGE
- ❑1, Jul 2006 ... 2.99

STAIN
FATHOM
- ❑1 ... 2.95

STAINLESS STEEL ARMADILLO
ANTARCTIC
- ❑1, Feb 1995, b&w ... 2.95
- ❑2, Apr 1995, b&w ... 2.95
- ❑3, Jun 1995, b&w ... 2.95
- ❑4, Aug 1995, b&w ... 2.95
- ❑5, Oct 1995, b&w ... 2.95

STAINLESS STEEL RAT
EAGLE
- ❑1, Oct 1985; Reprinted from 2000 A.D. #140-145 ... 2.50
- ❑2, Nov 1985; Reprinted from 2000 A.D. #146-151 ... 2.50
- ❑3, Dec 1985 ... 2.50
- ❑4, Jan 1986 ... 2.50
- ❑5, Feb 1986 ... 2.50
- ❑6, Mar 1986 ... 2.50

STALKER
DC
- ❑1, Jul 1975 SD, WW (a); 1&O: Stalker ... 7.00
- ❑2, Sep 1975 ... 4.00
- ❑3, Nov 1975 ... 4.00
- ❑4, Jan 1976 ... 4.00

STALKERS
MARVEL / EPIC
- ❑1, Apr 1990 ... 1.50
- ❑2, May 1990 ... 1.50
- ❑3, Jun 1990 ... 1.50
- ❑4, Jul 1990 ... 1.50
- ❑5, Aug 1990 ... 1.50
- ❑6, Sep 1990 ... 1.50
- ❑7, Oct 1990 ... 1.50
- ❑8, Nov 1990 ... 1.50
- ❑9, Dec 1990 ... 1.50
- ❑10, Jan 1991 ... 1.50
- ❑11, Feb 1991 ... 1.50
- ❑12, Mar 1991 ... 1.50

STALKING RALPH
AEON
- ❑1, Oct 1995; cardstock cover ... 4.95

STAND UP COMIX (BOB RUMBA'S...)
GREY
- ❑1, b&w ... 2.50

STANLEY & HIS MONSTER
DC
- ❑109, May 1968 ... 20.00
- ❑110, Jul 1968 ... 15.00
- ❑111, Sep 1968 ... 15.00
- ❑112, Nov 1968 ... 15.00

STANLEY AND HIS MONSTER (2ND SERIES)
DC
- ❑1, Feb 1993 PF (w); PF (a) ... 2.50
- ❑2, Mar 1993 PF (w); PF (a) ... 2.00
- ❑3, Apr 1993 PF (w); PF (a) ... 2.00
- ❑4, May 1993 PF (w); PF (a) ... 2.00

STANLEY THE SNAKE WITH THE OVERACTIVE IMAGINATION
EMERALD
- ❑1, b&w ... 1.50
- ❑2, b&w ... 1.50

STAR
IMAGE
- ❑1, Jun 1995 ... 2.50
- ❑2, Jul 1995 ... 2.50
- ❑3, Aug 1995 ... 2.50
- ❑4, Oct 1995; cover says Aug, indicia says Oct ... 2.50

STARBIKERS
RENEGADE
- ❑1, b&w ... 2.00

STARBLAST
MARVEL
- ❑1, Jan 1994 ... 2.00
- ❑2, Feb 1994 ... 1.75
- ❑3, Mar 1994 ... 1.75
- ❑4, Apr 1994 ... 1.75

STAR BLAZERS
COMICO
- ❑1, Apr 1987 ... 2.00
- ❑2, ca. 1987 ... 2.00
- ❑3, ca. 1987 ... 2.00
- ❑4, ca. 1987 ... 2.00

STAR BLAZERS (VOL. 2)
COMICO
- ❑1, ca. 1989 ... 2.00
- ❑2, Jun 1989 ... 2.00
- ❑3, 1989 ... 2.50
- ❑4, 1989 ... 2.50
- ❑5, 1989 ... 2.50

STAR BLAZERS: THE MAGAZINE OF SPACE BATTLESHIP YAMATO
ARGO
- ❑0, 1995 ... 2.95
- ❑1, Mar 1995 ... 2.95

STAR BLECCH: DEEP SPACE DINER
PARODY
- ❑1/A; Star Blecch: Deep Space Diner cover ... 2.50
- ❑1/B; Star Blecch: The Degeneration cover ... 2.50

STAR BLECCH: GENERATION GAP
PARODY
- ❑1, ca. 1995 ... 3.95

STAR BRAND
MARVEL
- ❑1, Oct 1986 JR2 (a); 1&O: Star Brand ... 1.00
- ❑2, Nov 1986 ... 1.00
- ❑3, Dec 1986 ... 1.00
- ❑4, Jan 1987 ... 1.00
- ❑5, Feb 1987 ... 1.00
- ❑6, Mar 1987 ... 1.00
- ❑7, Apr 1987 ... 1.00
- ❑8, May 1987 ... 1.00
- ❑9, Jun 1987 ... 1.00
- ❑10, Jul 1987 ... 1.00
- ❑11, Jan 1988; JBy (a); Title changes to The Star Brand ... 1.00
- ❑12, Mar 1988; JBy (a); O: Star Brand. O: New Universe (explains "White Event"). Prelude to The Pitt ... 1.00
- ❑13, May 1988 JBy (a) ... 1.00
- ❑14, Jul 1988 JBy (a) ... 1.00
- ❑15, Sep 1988 JBy (a) ... 1.00
- ❑16, Nov 1988 JBy (a) ... 1.00
- ❑17, Jan 1989 JBy (a) ... 1.00
- ❑18, Mar 1989 JBy (a) ... 1.00
- ❑19, May 1989 JBy (a) ... 1.00
- ❑Annual 1, ca. 1987 ... 1.25

STARCHILD
TALIESEN
- ❑0, Apr 1993, b&w ... 4.00
- ❑1, b&w; wraparound cover ... 4.00
- ❑1/2nd ... 2.25
- ❑2 1993, b&w; wraparound cover ... 4.00
- ❑2/2nd, Feb 1994, b&w; wraparound cover ... 2.50
- ❑2/3rd, Feb 1994, b&w; wraparound cover ... 2.50
- ❑3 1993, b&w; wraparound cover ... 3.00
- ❑4 1993, b&w; wraparound cover ... 3.00
- ❑5, Jan 1994, b&w; wraparound cover ... 3.00
- ❑6, Feb 1994, b&w; wraparound cover ... 3.00
- ❑7, Mar 1994, b&w; wraparound cover ... 2.50
- ❑8, Apr 1994, b&w; wraparound cover ... 2.50
- ❑9, May 1994, b&w; wraparound cover ... 2.50
- ❑10, Aug 1994, b&w; wraparound cover ... 2.50
- ❑11, Dec 1994, b&w; wraparound cover ... 2.50
- ❑12, Jun 1995, b&w; wraparound cover ... 2.50
- ❑13 ... 2.50
- ❑14 ... 2.50

STARCHILD: CROSSROADS
COPPERVALE
- ❑1, Nov 1995, b&w ... 2.95
- ❑2, Jan 1996, b&w ... 2.95
- ❑3, Mar 1996, b&w ... 2.95

STARCHILD: MYTHOPOLIS
IMAGE
- ❑0, Jul 1997, b&w ... 2.95
- ❑1, Sep 1997, b&w ... 2.95
- ❑2, Nov 1997, b&w ... 2.95
- ❑3, Jan 1998, b&w ... 2.95
- ❑4, Apr 1998, b&w ... 2.95
- ❑5 ... 2.95
- ❑6 ... 2.95

STARCHY
EXCEL
- ❑1 ... 1.95

STAR COMICS MAGAZINE
MARVEL / STAR
- ❑1, Dec 1986; digest; Reprints ... 3.00
- ❑2, Feb 1987; digest; Reprints ... 2.00
- ❑3, Apr 1987; digest; Reprints ... 2.00
- ❑4, Jun 1987; digest; Reprints ... 2.00
- ❑5, Aug 1987; digest; Reprints ... 2.00
- ❑6, Oct 1987; digest; Reprints ... 2.00
- ❑7, Dec 1987; digest; Reprints ... 2.00
- ❑8, Feb 1988; digest; Reprints ... 2.00
- ❑9, Apr 1988; digest; Reprints ... 2.00
- ❑10, Jun 1988; digest; Reprints ... 2.00
- ❑11, Aug 1988; digest; Reprints ... 2.00
- ❑12, Oct 1988; digest; Reprints ... 2.00
- ❑13, Dec 1988; digest; Reprints ... 2.00

Other grades: Multiply price above by 5/6 for VF/NM • 2/3 for VERY FINE • 1/3 for FINE • 1/5 for VERY GOOD • 1/8 for GOOD

Starstruck (Epic)
Tale of mystery, love, and cybernetics
©Marvel

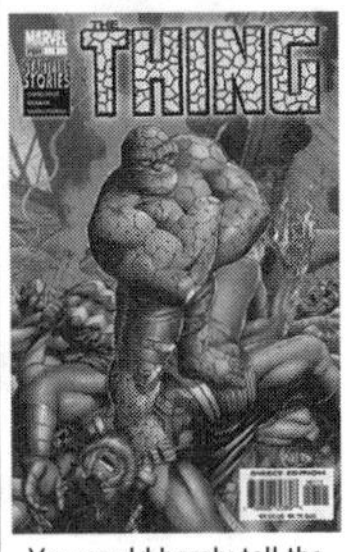
Startling Stories: The Thing
You could barely tell the real name of this title
©Marvel

Star Trek (1st Series)
Overseas artist hadn't seen the TV show
©Gold Key

Star Trek (2nd Series)
Marvel series followed the motionless picture
©Marvel

Star Trek (4th Series)
Peter David wrote many of the early issues
©DC

N-MINT

S.T.A.R. CORPS
DC

	N-MINT
❑1, Nov 1993	1.50
❑2, Dec 1993	1.50
❑3, Jan 1994	1.50
❑4, Feb 1994	1.50
❑5, Mar 1994	1.50
❑6, Apr 1994	1.50

STAR CROSSED
DC / HELIX

❑1, Jun 1997	2.50
❑2, Jul 1997	2.50
❑3, Aug 1997	2.50

STARDUST (NEIL GAIMAN AND CHARLES VESS'...)
DC / VERTIGO

❑1, prestige format	6.50
❑2, prestige format	6.00
❑3, prestige format	6.00
❑4, prestige format	6.00

STARDUSTERS
NIGHTWYND

❑1, b&w	2.50
❑2, b&w	2.50
❑3, b&w	2.50
❑4, b&w	2.50

STARDUST KID
IMAGE

❑1, 2005	2.99
❑2, Oct 2005	2.99
❑3, 2005	2.99

STARFIRE
DC

❑1, Sep 1976, O: Starfire I. 1: Starfire I.	7.00
❑2, Nov 1976	3.00
❑3, Jan 1977	3.00
❑4, Mar 1977	3.00
❑5, May 1977	3.00
❑6, Jul 1977	3.00
❑7, Sep 1977	3.00
❑8, Nov 1977	3.00

STAR FORCES
THE OTHER FACULTY / HELIX

❑1	3.00

STARFORCE SIX SPECIAL
AC

❑1, Nov 1984	1.50

STARGATE
EXPRESS / ENTITY

❑1, Jul 1996	2.95
❑1/Variant, Jul 1996	3.50
❑2, Aug 1996; photo section back-up	2.95
❑2/Variant, Aug 1996; photo section back-up	3.50
❑3, Sep 1996; photo section back-up	2.95
❑3/Variant, Sep 1996; photo section back-up	3.50
❑4, Oct 1996; photo section back-up	2.95
❑4/Variant, Oct 1996; photo section back-up	3.50

STARGATE DOOMSDAY WORLD
ENTITY

❑1, Nov 1996	2.95
❑2, Dec 1996	2.95
❑3, Jan 1997	2.95

STARGATE SG1 CON SPECIAL 2003
AVATAR

❑1, Sep 2003	3.95

STARGATE SG1 CON SPECIAL 2004
AVATAR

❑1, Apr 2004	2.99
❑1/A, Apr 2004; Wrap/Photo Cover	3.99

STARGATE SG-1: DANIEL'S SONG
AVATAR

❑1 2005	2.99
❑1/Photo	4.00
❑1/Wraparound	3.00
❑1/Glow, 1,000 copies printed.	20.00
❑1/Gold Foil; Retailer incentive. 500 copies printed	6.00
❑1/PlatFoil; Retailer incentive. 700 copies printed	10.00
❑1/Adversary	5.99

STARGATE SG1: FALL OF ROME
AVATAR

❑0/Preview	6.00
❑1	3.99
❑1/Foil	3.99
❑1/Platinum	10.00
❑2	3.99
❑2/Painted	5.99
❑2/Photo	3.99
❑2/Platinum	10.00
❑3	3.99
❑3/Painted	5.99
❑3/Platinum	10.00
❑3/Photo	3.99

STARGATE SG1: P.O.W.
AVATAR

❑1, Feb 2004	3.50
❑2, Mar 2004	3.50
❑3, May 2004	3.50

STARGATE UNDERWORLD
ENTITY

❑1, ca. 1997	2.95

STARGODS
ANTARCTIC

❑1, Jul 1998	2.95
❑1/CS, Jul 1998; poster; alternate cover	5.95
❑2, Sep 1998	2.95
❑2/CS, Sep 1998; poster; alternate cover	5.95

STARGODS: VISIONS
ANTARCTIC

❑1, Dec 1998; pin-ups	2.95

STARHEAD PRESENTS
STARHEAD

❑1	1.00
❑2, Apr 1987	1.00
❑3	1.00

STAR HUNTERS
DC

❑1, Nov 1977	1.00
❑2, Jan 1978, BL (a)	1.00
❑3, Mar 1978, MN, BL (a)	1.00
❑4, May 1978	1.00
❑5, Jul 1978	1.00
❑6, Sep 1978	1.00
❑7, Nov 1978	1.00

STAR JACKS
ANTARCTIC

❑1, Jun 1994, b&w	2.75

STAR JAM COMICS
REVOLUTIONARY

❑1, Apr 1992, b&w; M.C. Hammer story	2.50
❑2, Jun 1992, b&w; Janet Jackson story	2.50
❑3, Aug 1992, b&w; Beverly Hills 90210 story	2.50
❑4, Sep 1992, b&w; Beverly Hills 90210 story	2.50
❑5, Oct 1992, b&w; Beverly Hills 90210 story	2.50
❑6, Nov 1992, b&w; Kriss Kross story	2.50
❑7, Dec 1992, b&w; Marky Mark story	2.50
❑8, Jan 1993, b&w; Madonna story	2.50
❑9, Feb 1993, b&w; Jennie Garth story	2.50
❑10, Mar 1993, b&w; Melrose Place story	2.50

STARJAMMERS
MARVEL

❑1, Oct 1995; OverPower cards bound-in; enhanced cardstock cover	2.95
❑2, Nov 1995; enhanced cardstock cover	2.95
❑3, Dec 1995; enhanced cardstock cover	2.95
❑4, Jan 1996; enhanced cardstock cover	2.95

STARJAMMERS (VOL. 2)
MARVEL

❑1, Sep 2004	2.99
❑2, Sep 2004	2.99
❑3, Oct 2004	2.99
❑4, Oct 2004	2.99
❑5, Nov 2004	2.99
❑6, Nov 2004	2.99

STARJONGLEUR
TRYLVERTEL

❑1, Aug 1986, b&w	2.00
❑2, Win 1987, b&w	2.00

STARKID
DARK HORSE

❑1, Jan 1998; prequel to movie	2.95

STARK RAVEN
ENDLESS HORIZONS

❑1, Sep 2000	2.95

STARKWEATHER
ARCANA

❑1, 2004	2.95
❑1/Ltd. 2004	2.95
❑2, 2004	2.95
❑3, 2005	2.95
❑4, 2005	2.95
❑5, Oct 2005	2.95

Other grades: Multiply price above by 5/6 for VF/NM • 2/3 for VERY FINE • 1/3 for FINE • 1/5 for VERY GOOD • 1/8 for GOOD

STARLIGHT
ETERNITY

❑1, Oct 1987 .... 1.95

STARLIGHT AGENCY
ANTARCTIC

❑1, Jun 1991, b&w 2.50
❑2, Aug 1991, b&w 2.50
❑3, Sep 1991, b&w 2.50

STARLION: A PAWN'S GAME
STORM

❑1, Feb 1993 .... 2.25

STARLORD
MARVEL

❑1, Dec 1996 .... 2.50
❑2, Jan 1997 .... 2.50
❑3, Feb 1997 .... 2.50

STARLORD MEGAZINE
MARVEL

❑1, Nov 1996, Reprints Star-Lord, The Special Edition #1; back cover pin-up 2.95

STAR-LORD, THE SPECIAL EDITION
MARVEL

❑1, Feb 1982 MG, JBy (a) 2.00

STARLOVE
FORBIDDEN FRUIT

❑1, b&w 2.95
❑2, b&w 3.50

STARMAN (1ST SERIES)
DC

❑1, Oct 1988 O: Starman IV (William Payton). 1: Starman IV (William Payton). 2.00
❑2, Nov 1988 .... 1.50
❑3, Dec 1988 V: Bolt. 1.50
❑4, Win 1988 V: Power Elite. 1.50
❑5, Hol 1989; Invasion! 1.50
❑6, Jan 1989; Invasion! 1.50
❑7, Feb 1989 .... 1.50
❑8, Mar 1989 A: Lady Quark. 1.50
❑9, Apr 1989 O: Blockbuster. A: Batman. 1.50
❑10, May 1989 O: Blockbuster. A: Batman. 1.50
❑11, Jun 1989 .... 1.25
❑12, Jul 1989 .... 1.25
❑13, Aug 1989 .... 1.25
❑14, Sep 1989; Superman 1.25
❑15, Oct 1989 1: Deadline. 1.25
❑16, Nov 1989 .... 1.25
❑17, Dec 1989; Power Girl 1.25
❑18, Jan 1990 .... 1.25
❑19, Feb 1990 .... 1.25
❑20, Mar 1990 .... 1.25
❑21, Apr 1990 .... 1.25
❑22, May 1990 V: Deadline. 1.25
❑23, Jun 1990 .... 1.25
❑24, Jul 1990 .... 1.25
❑25, Aug 1990 .... 1.25
❑26, Sep 1990 1: David Knight. 2.00
❑27, Oct 1990 O: Starman III (David Knight) 1.25
❑28, Nov 1990; Superman 1.25
❑29, Dec 1990 .... 1.25
❑30, Jan 1991 .... 1.25
❑31, Feb 1991 .... 1.25
❑32, Mar 1991 .... 1.25
❑33, Apr 1991 .... 1.25
❑34, May 1991 .... 1.25
❑35, Jun 1991 .... 1.25
❑36, Jul 1991 .... 1.25
❑37, Aug 1991 .... 1.25
❑38, Sep 1991, War of the Gods 1.25
❑39, Oct 1991 .... 1.25
❑40, Nov 1991 .... 1.25
❑41, Dec 1991 .... 1.25
❑42, Jan 1992 .... 1.25
❑43, Feb 1992 .... 1.25
❑44, Mar 1992, Lobo 1.25
❑45, Apr 1992, Lobo 1.25

STARMAN (2ND SERIES)
DC

❑0, Oct 1994 JRo (w) 5.00
❑1, Nov 1994 JRo (w) 5.00
❑2, Dec 1994 JRo (w) 4.00
❑3, Jan 1995 JRo (w) 4.00
❑4, Feb 1995 JRo (w) 3.00
❑5, Mar 1995 JRo (w) 3.00
❑6, Apr 1995 JRo (w) 3.00
❑7, May 1995 JRo (w) 3.00
❑8, Jun 1995 JRo (w) 3.00
❑9, Jul 1995 JRo (w) 3.00
❑10, Aug 1995 JRo (w); V: Solomon Grundy. 3.00
❑11, Sep 1995 JRo (w) 2.50
❑12, Oct 1995 JRo (w) 2.50
❑13, Nov 1995; JRo (w); Underworld Unleashed 2.50
❑14, Dec 1995 JRo (w) 2.50
❑15, Jan 1996 JRo (w) 2.50
❑16, Feb 1996 JRo (w) 2.50
❑17, Mar 1996 JRo (w) 2.50
❑18, Apr 1996; JRo (w); Original Starman versus The Mist 2.50
❑19, Jun 1996; JRo (w); Times Past.. .... 2.50
❑20, Jul 1996 JRo (w); A: Wesley Dodds. A: Dian Belmont. 2.50
❑21, Aug 1996 JRo (w) 2.50
❑22, Sep 1996 JRo (w) 2.50
❑23, Oct 1996 JRo (w) 2.50
❑24, Nov 1996 JRo (w) 2.50
❑25, Dec 1996 JRo (w) 2.50
❑26, Jan 1997 JRo (w) 2.50
❑27, Feb 1997 JRo (w) 2.50
❑28, Mar 1997 JRo (w) 2.50
❑29, Apr 1997 JRo (w) 2.50
❑30, May 1997 JRo (w) 2.50
❑31, Jun 1997 JRo (w) 2.50
❑32, Jul 1997 JRo (w) 2.50
❑33, Aug 1997 JRo (w); A: Solomon Grundy. A: Sentinel. A: Batman 2.50
❑34, Sep 1997 JRo (w); A: Ted Knight. A: Solomon Grundy. A: Sentinel. A: Batman. A: Jason Woodrue. 2.50
❑35, Oct 1997; JRo (w); Genesis 2.50
❑36, Nov 1997 JRo (w); A: Will Payton. 2.50
❑37, Dec 1997; JRo (w); Face cover 2.50
❑38, Jan 1998; JRo (w); 1: Baby Starman. Mist vs. Justice League Europe 2.50
❑39, Feb 1998; JRo (w); continues in Power of Shazam! #35; cover forms diptych with Starman #40 .... 2.50
❑40, Mar 1998; JRo (w); cover forms diptych with Starman #39 .... 2.50
❑41, Apr 1998 JRo (w); V: Doctor Phosphorus 2.25
❑42, May 1998 JRo (w); A: Demon. 2.25
❑43, Jun 1998 JRo (w); A: Justice League of America 2.25
❑44, Jul 1998 JRo (w); A: Phantom Lady. 2.25
❑45, Aug 1998 JRo (w) 2.25
❑46, Sep 1998 JRo (w) 2.25
❑47, Oct 1998 JRo (w) 2.50
❑48, Dec 1998 JRo (w); A: Solomon Grundy 2.50
❑49, Jan 1999 JRo (w) 2.50
❑50, Feb 1999 JRo (w); A: Legion 3.95
❑51, Mar 1999; JRo (w); A: Jor-El. on Krypton 2.50
❑52, Apr 1999; JRo (w); A: Turran Kha. A: Adam Strange. on Rann 2.50
❑53, May 1999; JRo (w); A: Adam Strange. on Rann 2.50
❑54, Jun 1999; JRo (w); Times Past 2.50
❑55, Jul 1999 JRo (w); A: Space Cabbie. 2.50
❑56, Aug 1999 JRo (w) 2.50
❑57, Sep 1999; JRo (w); A: Fastbak. A: Tigorr. on Throneworld 2.50
❑58, Oct 1999 JRo (w); A: Will Payton. 2.50
❑59, Nov 1999 JRo (w) 2.50
❑60, Dec 1999; Jack returns to Earth. 2.50
❑61, Jan 2000 JRo (w) 2.50
❑62, Feb 2000 JRo (w) 2.50
❑63, Mar 2000 JRo (w) 2.50
❑64, Apr 2000 JRo (w) 2.50
❑65, May 2000 JRo (w) 2.50
❑66, Jun 2000 JRo (w) 2.50
❑67, Jul 2000 JRo (w) 2.50
❑68, Aug 2000 JRo (w) 2.50
❑69, Sep 2000 JRo (w) 2.50
❑70, Oct 2000 JRo (w) 2.50
❑71, Nov 2000 JRo (w) 2.50
❑72, Dec 2000 JRo (w) 2.50
❑73, Jan 2001 JRo (w) 2.50
❑74, Feb 2001; JRo (w); RH (a); Times Past 2.50
❑75, Mar 2001 JRo (w) 2.50
❑76, Apr 2001 JRo (w) 2.50
❑77, May 2001 JRo (w) 2.50
❑78, Jun 2001 JRo (w) 2.50
❑79, Jul 2001 .... 2.50
❑80, Aug 2001 .... 2.50
❑1000000, Nov 1998 JRo (w) 3.50
❑Annual 1, ca. 1996; JRo (w); Legends of the Dead Earth; Shade tells stories of Ted Knight and Gavyn; 1996 Annual 5.00
❑Annual 2, ca. 1997; JRo (w); Pulp Heroes; 1997 annual 3.95
❑Giant Size 1, Jan 1999; 80 page giant JRo (w) 4.95

STARMAN: SECRET FILES
DC

❑1, Apr 1998; background on series 4.95

STARMAN: THE MIST
DC

❑1, Jun 1998; Girlfrenzy 1.95

STAR MASTERS (MARVEL)
MARVEL

❑1, Dec 1995 .... 1.95
❑2, Jan 1996 .... 1.95
❑3, Feb 1996; continues in Cosmic Powers Unlimited #4 .... 1.95

STARMASTERS (AC)
AC

❑1 .... 1.50

STAR RANGERS
ADVENTURE

❑1, Oct 1987 .... 1.95
❑2, Nov 1987 .... 1.95
❑3, Dec 1987 .... 1.95

STAR*REACH
STAR*REACH

❑1, ca. 1974 JSn, HC (w); JSn, HC (a) 2.00
❑2, ca. 1975 NA (c); JSn (w); JSn, DG (a) 2.00
❑3, ca. 1975 .... 2.00
❑4, ca. 1976 .... 2.00
❑5, ca. 1976 FB, HC, JSa (a) 1.50
❑6, Oct 1976 JSa, GD, AN (a) 1.50
❑7, ca. 1977 JSa (a) 1.50
❑8, ca. 1977; CR (c); CR (a); Adapts Wagner's Parsifal 1.50
❑9, ca. 1977 .... 1.50
❑10, ca. 1977 .... 1.50
❑11, ca. 1977 .... 1.50
❑12, ca. 1978 .... 1.50
❑13, ca. 1978 .... 1.50
❑14, ca. 1978 .... 1.50
❑15, ca. 1978 .... 1.50
❑16, ca. 1979 .... 1.50
❑17, ca. 1979 .... 1.50
❑18, ca. 1979 .... 1.50

STAR*REACH CLASSICS
ECLIPSE

❑1, Mar 1984 DG (a) 2.00
❑2, Apr 1984 .... 2.00
❑3, May 1984 .... 2.00
❑4, Jun 1984 .... 2.00
❑5, Jul 1984 HC (a) 2.00
❑6, Aug 1984 CR (a) 2.00

STARRIORS
MARVEL / STAR

❑1, Nov 1984 .... 1.00
❑2, Dec 1984 .... 1.00
❑3, Jan 1985 .... 1.00
❑4, Feb 1985 .... 1.00

STAR ROVERS
COMAX

❑1, b&w 2.95

STARS AND S.T.R.I.P.E.
DC

❑0, Jul 1999; JRo (w); A: Starman. 1st Geoff Johns work 2.95
❑1, Aug 1999 .... 2.50
❑2, Sep 1999 .... 2.50
❑3, Oct 1999 1: Skeeter. 2.50
❑4, Nov 1999; A: Captain Marvel. Day of Judgment 2.50

Star Trek: Deep Space Nine (Malibu)

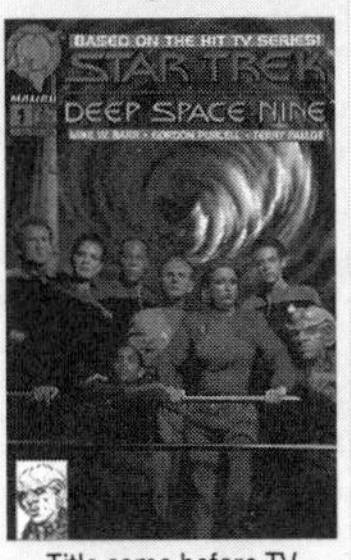

Title came before TV series got really good
©Malibu

Star Trek: Early Voyages

Captain Pike thinks outside the box
©Marvel

Star Trek: Starfleet Academy

They almost did a TV show like this
©Marvel

Star Trek: The Next Generation

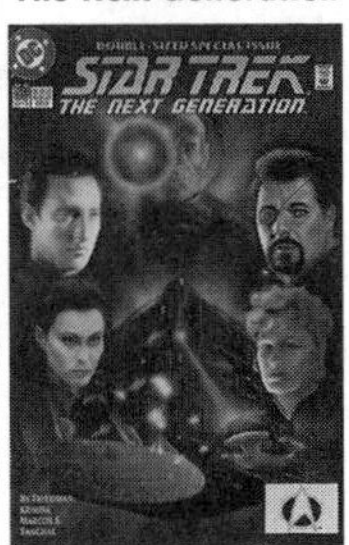

Jean-Luc Picard sips wine, gives orders
©DC

Star Trek Unlimited

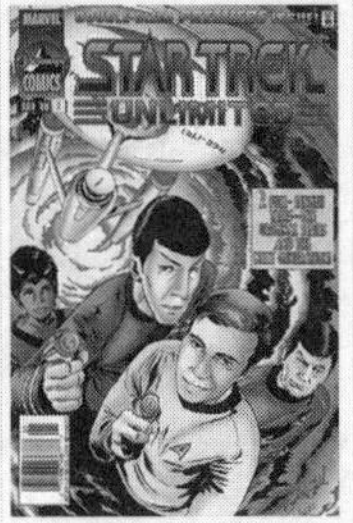

Stories not restricted to one cast of characters
©Marvel

N-MINT

- ❑5, Dec 1999 A: Young Justice 2.95
- ❑6, Jan 2000 2.95
- ❑7, Feb 2000 2.95
- ❑8, Mar 2000 2.95
- ❑9, Apr 2000 2.95
- ❑10, May 2000 2.50
- ❑12, Jul 2000 2.50
- ❑11, Jun 2000 2.50
- ❑13, Aug 2000 2.50
- ❑14, Sep 2000 2.50

STAR SEED
BROADWAY

- ❑7, Jul 1996; Series continued from Powers That Be #6 2.95
- ❑8, Aug 1996 2.95
- ❑9, Sep 1996 2.95

STARSHIP TROOPERS
DARK HORSE

- ❑1, Oct 1997 2.95
- ❑2, Nov 1997 2.95

STARSHIP TROOPERS: BRUTE CREATIONS
DARK HORSE

- ❑1, Sep 1997 2.95

STARSHIP TROOPERS: DOMINANT SPECIES
DARK HORSE

- ❑1, Aug 1998 2.95
- ❑2, Sep 1998 2.95
- ❑3, Oct 1998 2.95
- ❑4, Nov 1998 2.95

STARSHIP TROOPERS: INSECT TOUCH
DARK HORSE

- ❑1, May 1997, cardstock cover 2.95
- ❑2, Jun 1997, cardstock cover 2.95
- ❑3, Jul 1997, cardstock cover 2.95

STAR SLAMMERS (MALIBU)
MALIBU / BRAVURA

- ❑1, May 1994 2.50
- ❑1/Gold, May 1994
- ❑2, Jun 1994 2.50
- ❑3, Aug 1994 2.50
- ❑4, Feb 1995 2.50

STAR SLAMMERS SPECIAL
DARK HORSE / LEGEND

- ❑1, Jun 1996; finishes Malibu/Bravura series 2.95

STARSLAYER
PACIFIC

- ❑1, Feb 1982 MGr (w); MGr (a); O: Starslayer. 1: Rocketeer (cameo). 2.00
- ❑2, Apr 1982; MGr (w); SA, MGr, DSt (a); O: Rocketeer. 1: Rocketeer (full appearance). Rocketeer backup story 4.00
- ❑3, Jun 1982; MGr (w); MGr, DSt (a); A: Rocketeer. Rocketeer backup story 2.00
- ❑4, Aug 1982 MGr (w); MGr (a) 1.00
- ❑5, Nov 1982 MGr, ME (w); SA, MGr (a); A: Groo. 2.00
- ❑6, Apr 1983 MGr (w); MGr (a) 1.00
- ❑7, Aug 1983; First Comics begins publishing 1.00
- ❑8, Sep 1983 1.00
- ❑9, Oct 1983 1.00
- ❑10, Nov 1983 1: Grimjack. 1.50
- ❑11, Dec 1983 A: Grimjack. 1.00
- ❑12, Jan 1984 A: Grimjack. 1.00
- ❑13, Feb 1984 A: Grimjack. 1.00
- ❑14, Mar 1984 A: Grimjack. 1.00
- ❑15, Apr 1984 A: Grimjack. 1.00
- ❑16, May 1984 A: Grimjack. 1.00
- ❑17, Jun 1984 A: Grimjack. 1.00
- ❑18, Jul 1984 A: Grimjack. 1.00
- ❑19, Aug 1984 1.00
- ❑20, Sep 1984 1.00
- ❑21, Oct 1984 1.00
- ❑22, Nov 1984 1.25
- ❑23, Dec 1984 1.25
- ❑24, Jan 1985 1.25
- ❑25, Feb 1985; The Black Flame back-up story 1.25
- ❑26, Mar 1985 1.25
- ❑27, Apr 1985 TS (a) 1.25
- ❑28, May 1985 1.25
- ❑29, Jun 1985 1.25
- ❑30, Jul 1985 1.25
- ❑31, Aug 1985 1.25
- ❑32, Sep 1985 1.25
- ❑33, Oct 1985 1.25
- ❑34, Nov 1985 1.25

STARSLAYER: THE DIRECTOR'S CUT
ACCLAIM / WINDJAMMER

- ❑1, Jun 1995; New story and artwork 2.50
- ❑2, Jun 1995; Reprints Starslayer #1. 2.50
- ❑3, Jul 1995; Reprints Starslayer #2 2.50
- ❑4, Jul 1995; Reprints Starslayer #3 2.50
- ❑5, Aug 1995; Reprints Starslayer #4 2.50
- ❑6, Sep 1995; cover says Aug, indicia says Sep; Reprints Starslayer #5 2.50
- ❑7, Sep 1995; Reprints Starslayer #6 2.50
- ❑8, Dec 1995; New story and artwork 2.50

STAR SPANGLED COMICS (2ND SERIES)
DC

- ❑1, May 1999; A: Star Spangled Kid. A: Sandman. Justice Society Returns. 2.00

STAR SPANGLED WAR STORIES
DC

- ❑50, Oct 1956 70.00
- ❑51, Nov 1956 60.00
- ❑52, Dec 1956 60.00
- ❑53, Jan 1957 60.00
- ❑54, Feb 1957 60.00
- ❑55, Mar 1957 60.00
- ❑56, Apr 1957 60.00
- ❑57, May 1957 60.00
- ❑58, Jun 1957 60.00
- ❑59, Jul 1957 60.00
- ❑60, Aug 1957 60.00
- ❑61, Sep 1957 60.00
- ❑62, Oct 1957 60.00
- ❑63, Nov 1957 60.00
- ❑64, Dec 1957 60.00
- ❑65, Jan 1958 60.00
- ❑66, Feb 1958 60.00
- ❑67, Mar 1958 60.00
- ❑68, Apr 1958 60.00
- ❑69, May 1958 60.00
- ❑70, Jun 1958 60.00
- ❑71, Jul 1958 55.00
- ❑72, Aug 1958 55.00
- ❑73, Sep 1958 55.00
- ❑74, Oct 1958 55.00
- ❑75, Nov 1958 55.00
- ❑76, Dec 1958 55.00
- ❑77, Jan 1959 55.00
- ❑78, Feb 1959 55.00
- ❑79, Mar 1959 55.00
- ❑80, Apr 1959 55.00
- ❑81, May 1959 55.00
- ❑82, Jun 1959 55.00
- ❑83, Jul 1959 55.00
- ❑84, Aug 1959 1&O: Mademoiselle Marie 125.00
- ❑85, Sep 1959 A: Mademoiselle Marie. 80.00
- ❑86, Oct 1959 A: Mademoiselle Marie. 80.00
- ❑87, Nov 1959 JKu (a); A: Mademoiselle Marie. 80.00
- ❑88, Jan 1960 65.00
- ❑89, Mar 1960 65.00
- ❑90, May 1960; RA (a); 1: Dinosaur Island. 1st Dinosaur Island, War That Time Forgot story 325.00
- ❑91, Jul 1960 45.00
- ❑92, Sep 1960; Dinosaurs; War That Time Forgot 110.00
- ❑93, Nov 1960 45.00
- ❑94, Jan 1961; Dinosaurs; War That Time Forgot 110.00
- ❑95, Mar 1961; RA, RH (a); Dinosaurs; War That Time Forgot 110.00
- ❑96, May 1961; RA (a); Dinosaurs; War That Time Forgot 110.00
- ❑97, Jul 1961; RA, RH (a); Dinosaurs; War That Time Forgot 110.00
- ❑98, Sep 1961; JKu, RA (a); Dinosaurs; War That Time Forgot 110.00
- ❑99, Nov 1961; RA, RH (a); Dinosaurs; War That Time Forgot 110.00
- ❑100, Jan 1962, RA (a); Dinosaurs; War That Time Forgot 145.00
- ❑101, Mar 1962, Dinosaurs; War That Time Forgot 60.00
- ❑102, May 1962, Dinosaurs; War That Time Forgot 60.00
- ❑103, Jul 1962, Dinosaurs; War That Time Forgot 60.00
- ❑104, Sep 1962, Dinosaurs; War That Time Forgot 60.00
- ❑105, Nov 1962, Dinosaurs; War That Time Forgot 60.00
- ❑106, Jan 1963, RA (a); Dinosaurs; War That Time Forgot 60.00
- ❑107, Mar 1963, RA (a); Dinosaurs; War That Time Forgot 60.00
- ❑108, May 1963, Dinosaurs; War That Time Forgot 60.00
- ❑109, Jul 1963, Dinosaurs; War That Time Forgot 60.00
- ❑110, Sep 1963, Dinosaurs; War That Time Forgot 60.00

Other grades: Multiply price above by 5/6 for VF/NM • 2/3 for VERY FINE • 1/3 for FINE • 1/5 for VERY GOOD • 1/8 for GOOD

N-MINT

❑111, Nov 1963, Dinosaurs; War That Time Forgot 60.00
❑112, Jan 1964, Dinosaurs; War That Time Forgot 60.00
❑113, Mar 1964, Dinosaurs; War That Time Forgot 60.00
❑114, May 1964, Dinosaurs; War That Time Forgot 60.00
❑115, Jul 1964, Dinosaurs; War That Time Forgot 60.00
❑116, Sep 1964, RA (a); Dinosaurs; War That Time Forgot 60.00
❑117, Nov 1964, Dinosaurs; War That Time Forgot 60.00
❑118, Jan 1965, Dinosaurs; War That Time Forgot 60.00
❑119, Mar 1965, Dinosaurs; War That Time Forgot 60.00
❑120, Apr 1965, Dinosaurs; War That Time Forgot 60.00
❑121, Jun 1965, Dinosaurs; War That Time Forgot 60.00
❑122, Aug 1965, Dinosaurs; War That Time Forgot 60.00
❑123, Oct 1965, Dinosaurs; War That Time Forgot 60.00
❑124, Dec 1965, Dinosaurs; War That Time Forgot 60.00
❑125, Feb 1966, JKu (a); Dinosaurs; War That Time Forgot 60.00
❑126, Apr 1966, JKu (c); JKu, JAb (a); 1: Sgt. Gorilla. 60.00
❑127, Jun 1966, Dinosaurs; War That Time Forgot 60.00
❑128, Aug 1966, Dinosaurs; War That Time Forgot 60.00
❑129, Oct 1966, Dinosaurs; War That Time Forgot 60.00
❑130, Dec 1966, JAb (a); Dinosaurs... 60.00
❑131, Mar 1967, JAb (a); Dinosaurs; War That Time Forgot 60.00
❑132, May 1967, Dinosaurs; War That Time Forgot 60.00
❑133, Jul 1967, Dinosaurs; War That Time Forgot 60.00
❑134, Sep 1967, RH (c); NA, JAb (a); Dinosaurs 65.00
❑135, Nov 1967, RH (c); RH, JAb (a); Dinosaurs 60.00
❑136, Jan 1968, Dinosaurs 60.00
❑137, Mar 1968, RH (c); JKu (a); Dinosaurs 60.00
❑138, May 1968, JKu (a); Enemy Ace stories begin 60.00
❑139, Jul 1968, JKu (a); O: Enemy Ace. 50.00
❑140, Sep 1968, JKu (c); JKu (a); Enemy Ace 24.00
❑141, Nov 1968, JKu (c); JKu (a); Enemy Ace 24.00
❑142, Jan 1969, JKu (c); JKu (a); Enemy Ace 24.00
❑143, Mar 1969, Enemy Ace 24.00
❑144, May 1969, JKu, NA (a); Enemy Ace 27.00
❑145, Jul 1969, Enemy Ace 35.00
❑146, Sep 1969, Enemy Ace 20.00
❑147, Nov 1969, JKu (c); JKu (a); Enemy Ace 20.00
❑148, Jan 1970, Enemy Ace 20.00
❑149, Mar 1970, JKu (c); JKu, RE (a) 20.00
❑150, May 1970, JKu (c); JKu (a); Enemy Ace, Viking Prince 20.00
❑151, Jul 1970, JKu (a); 1: Unknown Soldier. 125.00
❑152, Sep 1970, 2: The Unknown Soldier. 20.00
❑153, Nov 1970, JKu (a) 20.00
❑154, Jan 1971, JKu (c); JKu (a); O: Unknown Soldier. Unknown Soldier; Enemy Ace 55.00
❑155, Mar 1971, JKu (c); JKu (a); reprints Enemy Ace story 16.00
❑156, May 1971, JKu (c); JKu (a); Unknown Soldier; Enemy Ace back-up 14.00
❑157, Jul 1971, JKu (c); JKu (a); Unknown Soldier meets Easy Co.; Enemy Ace back-up 14.00
❑158, Sep 1971 JKu (c); JKu (a) 14.00
❑159, Nov 1971 JKu (a) 14.00
❑160, Jan 1972 14.00
❑161, Mar 1972; Regular Enemy Ace stories end 14.00
❑162, May 1972 JKu (c); JSe (a) 6.00
❑163, Jul 1972 CI, JKu, DS (a) 6.00
❑164, Sep 1972, ATh (a) 6.00
❑165, Nov 1972 6.00
❑166, Jan 1973 6.00
❑167, Feb 1973 6.00
❑168, Mar 1973, TS (w); TS (a) 6.00
❑169, Apr 1973, JKu (c); JKu (a) 6.00
❑170, Jun 1973, JKu (c); 6.00
❑171, Jul 1973, JKu (c); JKu (a); O: The Unknown Soldier. 6.00
❑172, Aug 1973 6.00
❑173, Sep 1973, JKu (c); FR (w) 6.00
❑174, Oct 1973, JKu (c); FR (w); JKu (a) 6.00
❑175, Nov 1973, JKu (c); FR (w); RE (a) 6.00
❑176, Dec 1973, FR (w); FT (a) 6.00
❑177, Jan 1974 6.00
❑178, Feb 1974 6.00
❑179, Mar 1974, JKu (c); FR (w); RE (a) 6.00
❑180, Jun 1974, JKu (c); FR (w) 6.00
❑181, Aug 1974, FR (w); FT (a) 5.00
❑182, Oct 1974, FR (w) 5.00
❑183, Dec 1974 5.00
❑184, Feb 1975 SA (w); SA (a) 5.00
❑185, Mar 1975 5.00
❑186, Apr 1975 JKu (c); 5.00
❑187, May 1975 5.00
❑188, Jun 1975 5.00
❑189, Jul 1975 JKu (c); JKu (a) 5.00
❑190, Aug 1975 JKu (c); JKu (a) 5.00
❑191, Sep 1975 5.00
❑192, Oct 1975 JKu (c); JKu (a) 5.00
❑193, Nov 1975 5.00
❑194, Dec 1975 5.00
❑195, Jan 1976 5.00
❑196, Feb 1976 5.00
❑197, Mar 1976 5.00
❑198, Apr 1976 5.00
❑199, May 1976 5.00
❑200, Jul 1976, JKu (a); A: Mademoiselle Marie. 5.00
❑201, Sep 1976, JKu (c); JKu (a) 5.00
❑202, Nov 1976 5.00
❑203, Jan 1977, JKu (c); JKu (a) 5.00
❑204, Mar 1977, JKu (c); BMc (a); Series continues as Unknown Soldier 5.00

STARSTONE
Aircel

❑1, b&w 1.70
❑2, b&w 1.70
❑3, b&w 1.70

STARSTREAM
Gold Key / Whitman

❑1, ca. 1976 3.00
❑2, 1976, Stories by Science-Fiction writers 3.00
❑3 1976 3.00
❑4 1976, JAb (a) 3.00

STARSTRUCK (EPIC)
Marvel / Epic

❑1, Feb 1985 2.50
❑2, Apr 1985 2.00
❑3, Jun 1985 2.00
❑4, Aug 1985 2.00
❑5, Oct 1985 2.00
❑6, Feb 1986 2.00

STARSTRUCK (DARK HORSE)
Dark Horse

❑1, Aug 1990, b&w 2.95
❑2 1990, b&w 2.95
❑3, Jan 1991, b&w 2.95
❑4, Mar 1991; trading cards 2.95

STARTLING CRIME ILLUSTRATED
Caliber

❑1, b&w 2.95

STARTLING STORIES: BANNER
Marvel

❑1, Sep 2001 2.99
❑2, Oct 2001 2.99
❑3, Nov 2001 2.99
❑4, Dec 2001 2.99

STARTLING STORIES: THE THING
Marvel

❑1, ca. 2003 3.50

STARTLING STORIES: THE THING -- NIGHT FALLS ON YANCY STREET
Marvel

❑1, Jun 2003 3.50
❑2, Jul 2003 3.50
❑3, Aug 2003 3.50
❑4, Sep 2003 3.50

STAR TREK (1ST SERIES)
Gold Key

❑1, Oct 1967, wraparound photo cover 350.00
❑2, Jun 1968 125.00
❑3, Dec 1968 100.00
❑4, Jun 1969 90.00
❑5, Sep 1969 75.00
❑6, Dec 1969, cover photo shows Spock from "Amok Time" 75.00
❑7, Mar 1970 60.00
❑8, Sep 1970 50.00
❑9, Feb 1971, last photo cover 50.00
❑10, May 1971, William Shatner and Leonard Nimoy photos in small boxes on cover 40.00
❑11, Aug 1971, William Shatner and Leonard Nimoy photos in small boxes on cover 30.00
❑12, Nov 1971, William Shatner and Leonard Nimoy photos in small boxes on cover 30.00
❑13, Feb 1972, William Shatner and Leonard Nimoy photos in small boxes on cover 30.00
❑14, May 1972, William Shatner and Leonard Nimoy photos in small boxes on cover 30.00
❑15, Aug 1972, William Shatner and Leonard Nimoy photos in small boxes on cover 30.00
❑16, Nov 1972, William Shatner and Leonard Nimoy photos in small boxes on cover 30.00
❑17, Feb 1973, William Shatner and Leonard Nimoy photos in small boxes on cover 30.00
❑18, May 1973, William Shatner and Leonard Nimoy photos in small boxes on cover 30.00
❑19, Jul 1973, William Shatner and Leonard Nimoy photos in small boxes on cover 30.00
❑20, Sep 1973, William Shatner and Leonard Nimoy photos in small boxes on cover 30.00
❑20/Whitman, Sep 1973, William Shatner and Leonard Nimoy photos in small boxes on cover 50.00
❑21, Nov 1973, William Shatner and Leonard Nimoy photos in small boxes on cover 30.00
❑22, Jan 1974, William Shatner and Leonard Nimoy photos in small boxes on cover 30.00
❑23, Mar 1974, William Shatner and Leonard Nimoy photos in small boxes on cover 30.00
❑23/Whitman, Mar 1974, William Shatner and Leonard Nimoy photos in small boxes on cover 50.00
❑24, May 1974, William Shatner and Leonard Nimoy photos in small boxes on cover 25.00
❑24/Whitman, May 1974, William Shatner and Leonard Nimoy photos in small boxes on cover 45.00
❑25, Jul 1974, William Shatner and Leonard Nimoy photos in small boxes on cover 25.00
❑25/Whitman, Jul 1974, William Shatner and Leonard Nimoy photos in small boxes on cover 45.00
❑26, Sep 1974, William Shatner and Leonard Nimoy photos in small boxes on cover 25.00
❑26/Whitman, Sep 1974, William Shatner and Leonard Nimoy photos in small boxes on cover 45.00
❑27, Nov 1974, William Shatner and Leonard Nimoy photos in small boxes on cover 20.00
❑27/Whitman, Nov 1974, William Shatner and Leonard Nimoy photos in small boxes on cover 45.00
❑28, Jan 1975, William Shatner and Leonard Nimoy photos in small boxes on cover 20.00

Star Wars

First issue was best-selling comic of the 1970s

©Marvel

Star Wars (Dark Horse)

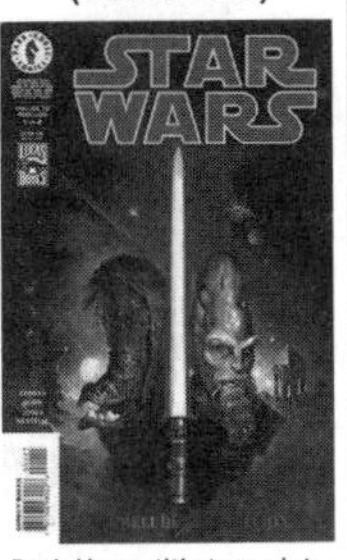

Dark Horse title turns into Star Wars: Republic

©Dark Horse

Star Wars: Dark Empire

Could be the basis of Episodes VII-IX

©Dark Horse

Star Wars: Dark Force Rising

Timothy Zahn novel comes to comics

©Dark Horse

Star Wars: Darth Maul

Short-lived Sith proved popular

©Dark Horse

	N-MINT
❑29, Mar 1975, William Shatner and Leonard Nimoy photos in small boxes on cover; reprints #1	20.00
❑29/Whitman, Mar 1975, William Shatner and Leonard Nimoy photos in small boxes on cover; reprints #1	40.00
❑30, May 1975, William Shatner and Leonard Nimoy photos in small boxes on cover	20.00
❑31, Jul 1975, William Shatner and Leonard Nimoy photos in small boxes on cover	20.00
❑31/Whitman, Jul 1975, William Shatner and Leonard Nimoy photos in small boxes on cover	40.00
❑32, Aug 1975, William Shatner and Leonard Nimoy photos in small boxes on cover	20.00
❑32/Whitman, Aug 1975, William Shatner and Leonard Nimoy photos in small boxes on cover	40.00
❑33, Sep 1975, William Shatner and Leonard Nimoy photos in small boxes on cover	20.00
❑33/Whitman, Sep 1975, William Shatner and Leonard Nimoy photos in small boxes on cover	40.00
❑34, Oct 1975, William Shatner and Leonard Nimoy photos in small boxes on cover	20.00
❑34/Whitman, Oct 1975, William Shatner and Leonard Nimoy photos in small boxes on cover	40.00
❑35, Nov 1975, William Shatner and Leonard Nimoy photos in small boxes on cover; reprints #4	20.00
❑35/Whitman, Nov 1975, William Shatner and Leonard Nimoy photos in small boxes on cover; reprints #4	40.00
❑36, Mar 1976, William Shatner and Leonard Nimoy photos in small boxes on cover	20.00
❑36/Whitman, Mar 1976, William Shatner and Leonard Nimoy photos in small boxes on cover	40.00
❑37, May 1976, William Shatner and Leonard Nimoy photos in small boxes on cover; reprints #5	20.00
❑38, Jul 1976, William Shatner and Leonard Nimoy photos in small boxes on cover	20.00
❑38/Whitman, Jul 1976, William Shatner and Leonard Nimoy photos in small boxes on cover	40.00
❑39, Aug 1976, William Shatner and Leonard Nimoy photos in small boxes on cover	20.00
❑39/Whitman, Aug 1976, William Shatner and Leonard Nimoy photos in small boxes on cover	40.00
❑40, Sep 1976, William Shatner and Leonard Nimoy photos in small boxes on cover	20.00
❑40/Whitman, Sep 1976, William Shatner and Leonard Nimoy photos in small boxes on cover	40.00
❑41, Nov 1976, William Shatner and Leonard Nimoy photos in small boxes on cover	15.00
❑41/Whitman, Nov 1976, William Shatner and Leonard Nimoy photos in small boxes on cover	30.00

	N-MINT
❑42, Jan 1977, William Shatner and Leonard Nimoy photos in small boxes on cover	15.00
❑43, Feb 1977, William Shatner and Leonard Nimoy photos in small boxes on cover	15.00
❑44, May 1977, William Shatner and Leonard Nimoy photos in small boxes on cover	15.00
❑44/Whitman, May 1977, William Shatner and Leonard Nimoy photos in small boxes on cover	30.00
❑45, Jul 1977, reprints #7, including photo cover	15.00
❑45/Whitman, Jul 1977, reprints #7, including photo cover	30.00
❑46, Aug 1977	15.00
❑46/Whitman, Aug 1977	30.00
❑47, Sep 1977	15.00
❑47/Whitman, Sep 1977	30.00
❑48, Oct 1977	15.00
❑48/Whitman, Oct 1977	30.00
❑49, Nov 1977, William Shatner and Leonard Nimoy photo in small box on cover	15.00
❑50, Jan 1978, William Shatner and Leonard Nimoy photo in small box on cover	15.00
❑51, Mar 1978, A: Professor Whipple. William Shatner and Leonard Nimoy photo in small box on cover	15.00
❑51/Whitman, Mar 1978, A: Professor Whipple. William Shatner and Leonard Nimoy photo in small box on cover	30.00
❑52, May 1978, William Shatner and Leonard Nimoy photo in small box on cover	15.00
❑52/Whitman, May 1978, William Shatner and Leonard Nimoy photo in small box on cover	30.00
❑53, Jul 1978, William Shatner and Leonard Nimoy photo in small box on cover	15.00
❑53/Whitman, Jul 1978, William Shatner and Leonard Nimoy photo in small box on cover	30.00
❑54, Aug 1978, William Shatner and Leonard Nimoy photo in small box on cover	15.00
❑54/Whitman, Aug 1978, William Shatner and Leonard Nimoy photo in small box on cover	30.00
❑55, Sep 1978, William Shatner and Leonard Nimoy photo in small box on cover	15.00
❑55/Whitman, Sep 1978, William Shatner and Leonard Nimoy photo in small box on cover	30.00
❑56, Oct 1978, William Shatner and Leonard Nimoy photo in small box on cover	15.00
❑56/Whitman, Oct 1978, William Shatner and Leonard Nimoy photo in small box on cover	30.00
❑57, Nov 1978, William Shatner and Leonard Nimoy photo in small box on cover	15.00
❑57/Whitman, Nov 1978, William Shatner and Leonard Nimoy photo in small box on cover	30.00

	N-MINT
❑58, Dec 1978, William Shatner and Leonard Nimoy photo in small box on cover	15.00
❑58/Whitman, Dec 1978, William Shatner and Leonard Nimoy photo in small box on cover	30.00
❑59, Jan 1979, William Shatner and Leonard Nimoy photo in small box on cover	15.00
❑59/Whitman, Jan 1979, William Shatner and Leonard Nimoy photo in small box on cover	30.00
❑60, Feb 1979	12.00
❑60/Whitman, Feb 1979	30.00
❑61, Mar 1979, A: Klingons. A: Harry Mudd.	12.00

STAR TREK (2ND SERIES)

MARVEL

❑1, Apr 1980, DC, KJ (a); adapts Star Trek: The Motion Picture	5.00
❑2, May 1980, DC, KJ (c); DC, KJ (a); adapts Star Trek: The Motion Picture	3.00
❑3, Jun 1980, BWi (c); DC, KJ (a); adapts Star Trek: The Motion Picture	2.00
❑4, Jul 1980, DC, KJ (c); DC, KJ (a)	2.00
❑5, Aug 1980, FM, KJ (c); DC, KJ (a)	2.00
❑6, Sep 1980, DC, KJ (c); DC, KJ (a)	2.00
❑7, Oct 1980, MN (c); MN, KJ (a)	2.00
❑8, Nov 1980, DC (c); DC (a)	2.00
❑9, Dec 1980, DC (c); DC, FS (a)	2.00
❑10, Jan 1981, FM (c); KJ (a); Starfleet files	2.00
❑11, Feb 1981, TP (c); TP (a)	2.00
❑12, Mar 1981, LMc, TP (a)	2.00
❑13, Apr 1981, TP (a); A: McCoy's daughter	2.00
❑14, Jun 1981, LMc, GD (a)	2.00
❑15, Aug 1981, DC (c); GK (a)	2.00
❑16, Oct 1981, AM, LMc (c); LMc, GD (a)	2.00
❑17, Dec 1981, TP (a)	2.00
❑18, Feb 1982	2.00

STAR TREK (3RD SERIES)

DC

❑1, Feb 1984; TS (a); 1: Nancy Bryce. 1: Konom. 1: Bearclaw. Kirk regains captaincy of Enterprise	4.00
❑2, Mar 1984; TS (a); Klingon Emperor Kahless IV declares war on Federation	3.00
❑3, Apr 1984 TS (a); A: Excalbians	3.00
❑4, May 1984 TS (c); TS (a); A: Organians.	3.00
❑5, Jun 1984 TS (c); TS (a)	3.00
❑6, Jul 1984 TS (c); TS (a); A: Ambassador Robert Fox.	2.50
❑7, Aug 1984; DG (c); O: Saavik. hints of Star Trek III dropped	2.50
❑8, Nov 1984; TS, JO (c); TS (a); V: Romulans. David Marcus and Saavik transfer to U.S.S. Grissom	2.50
❑9, Dec 1984; TS (c); TS (a); A: Mirror Universe Spock. A: Mirror Universe Kirk. A: Spock. Return of Mirror Universe; story set after events of Star Trek III: The Search for Spock.	2.50
❑10, Jan 1985; TS (c); TS (a); A: U.S.S. Excelsior. A: Captain Styles. U.S.S. Excelsior vs. I.S.S. Enterprise	2.50

Other grades: Multiply price above by 5/6 for VF/NM • 2/3 for VERY FINE • 1/3 for FINE • 1/5 for VERY GOOD • 1/8 for GOOD

❑11, Feb 1985; TS (c); TS (a); A: Mirror Universe Spock. The two Spocks mind-meld 2.00
❑12, Mar 1985; TS (a); A: Mirror Universe Spock. Mirror Universe Enterprise's engineering hull destroyed 2.00
❑13, Apr 1985 TS (c); TS (a); 1: Mirror Universe David Marcus. 2.00
❑14, May 1985; TS (c); TS (a); A: Mirror Universe Romulans. A: Mirror Universe Klingons. Spocks visit Mirror Universe Klingons 2.00
❑15, Jun 1985 TS (c); TS (a); 1: Mirror Universe U.S.S. Excelsior. 2.00
❑16, Jul 1985; TS, KJ (c); TS (a); Kirk receives command of U.S.S. Excelsior 2.00
❑17, Aug 1985; TS, KJ (c); TS (a); Sulu, Uhura, and Bearclaw on shoreleave 2.00
❑18, Sep 1985; TS, KJ (c); TS (a); Scotty solo story 2.00
❑19, Oct 1985; TS (c); DS (a); Written by Walter Koenig 2.00
❑20, Nov 1985 TS (c); TS (a) 2.00
❑21, Dec 1985 TS (c); TS (a) 2.00
❑22, Jan 1986; TS (c); TS (a); return of Redjac 2.00
❑23, Feb 1986; KJ (c); TS (a); return of Redjac 2.00
❑24, Mar 1986 JSn (c); TS (a) 2.00
❑25, Apr 1986; JSn (c); TS (a); Ajir vs. Grond 2.00
❑26, May 1986 DG (c); TS (a) 2.00
❑27, Jun 1986 TS (a) 2.00
❑28, Jul 1986 GM (a) 2.00
❑29, Aug 1986 TS (a) 2.00
❑30, Sep 1986; KJ (c); CI (a); Uhura's early days on the Enterprise 2.00
❑31, Oct 1986 TS (a) 2.00
❑32, Nov 1986 TS (a) 2.00
❑33, Dec 1986; 20th Anniversary of Star Trek issue; TS (a); original Enterprise meets Excelsior 2.00
❑34, Jan 1987 TS (a) 2.00
❑35, Feb 1987 GM (a) 2.00
❑36, Mar 1987; GM (a); Kirk and company return to Vulcan; leads into Star Trek IV: The Voyage Home 2.00
❑37, Apr 1987; CS (a); Follows events of Star Trek IV: The Voyage Home .. 2.00
❑38, May 1987 .... 2.00
❑39, Jun 1987; TS (a); return of Harry Mudd 2.00
❑40, Jul 1987 TS (a); A: Harry Mudd.. 2.00
❑41, Aug 1987 TS (a); V: Orion pirates. 2.00
❑42, Sep 1987 TS (a) 2.00
❑43, Oct 1987 TS (a) 2.00
❑44, Nov 1987 TS (a) 2.00
❑45, Dec 1987 TS (a) 2.00
❑46, Jan 1988 TS (a) 2.00
❑47, Feb 1988 TS (a) 2.00
❑48, Mar 1988; PD (w); TS (a); 1: Moron. first Peter David script 2.00
❑49, Apr 1988 PD (w); TS (a) 2.00
❑50, May 1988; Giant-size; PD (w); TS (a); Konom and Nancy marry 2.00
❑51, Jun 1988 PD (w); TS (a) 2.00
❑52, Jul 1988; PD (w); TS (a); Dante's Inferno 2.00
❑53, Aug 1988 PD (w) 2.00
❑54, Sep 1988; PD (w); A: Sean Finnegan. Return of Finnegan 2.00
❑55, Oct 1988; PD (w); TS (a); Trial of Bearclaw 2.00
❑56, Nov 1988; GM (a); set during first five-year mission 2.00
❑Annual 1, ca. 1985; A: Captain Pike. Kirk's first mission on The Enterprise 3.00
❑Annual 2, ca. 1986; A: Captain Pike. The final mission of the first five-year mission 3.00
❑Annual 3, ca. 1988; GM (c); PD (w); CS (a); Scotty's romances 3.00

STAR TREK (4TH SERIES)
DC

❑1, Oct 1989; PD (w); 1: Salla. 1: M'yra. Set after the events of Star Trek V: The Final Frontier; Klingons place bounty on Kirk 5.00
❑2, Nov 1989 PD (w) 4.00
❑3, Dec 1989 PD (w) 3.00
❑4, Jan 1990 PD (w); 1: R.J. Blaise. ... 3.00
❑5, Feb 1990 PD (w) 2.50
❑6, Mar 1990 PD (w) 2.50
❑7, Apr 1990 PD (w); 1: Sweeney. 2.50
❑8, May 1990 PD (w); V: Sweeney. 2.50
❑9, Jun 1990 PD (w); V: Sweeney. 2.50
❑10, Jul 1990 PD (w); A: Areel Shaw. A: Samuel Cogsley 2.50
❑11, Aug 1990 PD (w); A: Bella Oxmyx. A: Leonard James Akaar. 2.00
❑12, Sep 1990 PD (w) 2.00
❑13, Oct 1990; PD (w); Lost in Space homage 2.00
❑14, Dec 1990; PD (w); Lost in Space homage 2.00
❑15, Jan 1991; PD (w); Lost in Space homage 2.00
❑16, Feb 1991; Written by J. Michael Straczynski 2.00
❑17, Mar 1991 .... 2.00
❑18, Apr 1991 .... 2.00
❑19, May 1991; PD (w); final Peter David issue 2.00
❑20, Jun 1991 .... 2.00
❑21, Jul 1991 .... 2.00
❑22, Aug 1991 A: Harry Mudd. 2.00
❑23, Sep 1991 A: Harry Mudd. 2.00
❑24, Oct 1991; 25th anniversary of Star Trek; PD (w); BA, DC (a); A: Harry Mudd. Star Trek's 25th anniversary issue; Text pieces by Chris Claremont, Michael Jan Friedman, Peter David, and Howard Weinstein 3.00
❑25, Nov 1991 A: Saavik. A: Captain Styles. 2.00
❑26, Dec 1991 .... 2.00
❑27, Jan 1992 .... 2.00
❑28, Feb 1992 .... 2.00
❑29, Mar 1992 .... 2.00
❑30, Apr 1992 .... 2.00
❑31, May 1992 .... 2.00
❑32, Jun 1992 .... 2.00
❑33, Jul 1992 .... 2.00
❑34, Aug 1992; JDu (a); Dream sequence 2.00
❑35, Sep 1992; Series goes biweekly; Sulu takes command of U.S.S. Excelsior 2.00
❑36, Sep 1992 .... 2.00
❑37, Oct 1992 .... 2.00
❑38, Oct 1992 .... 2.00
❑39, Nov 1992 .... 2.00
❑40, Nov 1992; Biweekly run ends..... 2.00
❑41, Dec 1992 .... 2.00
❑42, Jan 1993 .... 2.00
❑43, Feb 1993 .... 2.00
❑44, Mar 1993 .... 2.00
❑45, Apr 1993; A: Trelane. Return of Trelane 2.00
❑46, May 1993; Back to biweekly status 2.00
❑47, May 1993 .... 2.00
❑48, Jun 1993 .... 2.00
❑49, Jun 1993; RT (a); last biweekly issue 2.00
❑50, Jul 1993; Giant-size anniversary special; A: Gary Seven. Double-sized issue 3.50
❑51, Aug 1993; Saavik on secret mission 2.00
❑52, Sep 1993 .... 2.00
❑53, Oct 1993 A: Lt. Worf. 2.00
❑54, Nov 1993 .... 2.00
❑55, Dec 1993 .... 2.00
❑56, Jan 1994 .... 2.00
❑57, Feb 1994 .... 2.00
❑58, Mar 1994; Chekov's first days on the Enterprise; cover forms triptych with issues #59 and 60 .... 2.00
❑59, Apr 1994; Chekov's first days on the Enterprise; cover forms triptych with issues #57 and 58 .... 2.00
❑60, Jun 1994; Chekov's first days on the Enterprise; cover forms triptych with issues #57 and 58 .... 2.00
❑61, Jul 1994; return to Talos IV 2.00
❑62, Aug 1994; set near end of first five-year mission 2.00
❑63, Sep 1994 .... 2.00
❑64, Oct 1994; follows events of Where No Man Has Gone Before 2.00
❑65, Nov 1994 .... 2.00
❑66, Dec 1994 .... 2.00
❑67, Jan 1995 .... 2.00
❑68, Feb 1995 .... 2.00
❑69, Mar 1995 .... 2.00
❑70, Apr 1995 .... 2.00
❑71, May 1995 .... 2.50
❑72, Jun 1995 .... 2.50
❑73, Jul 1995 .... 2.50
❑74, Aug 1995 .... 2.50
❑75, Sep 1995 .... 3.95
❑76, Oct 1995 .... 2.50
❑77, Nov 1995 .... 2.50
❑78, Dec 1995 .... 2.50
❑79, Jan 1996 .... 2.50
❑80, Feb 1996 .... 2.50
❑Annual 1, ca. 1990; PD (w); GM (a); Story by George Takei 3.50
❑Annual 2, ca. 1991; PD (w); CS (a); Kirk at Starfleet Academy 3.25
❑Annual 3, ca. 1992 .... 3.50
❑Annual 4, ca. 1993; Spock on Enterprise with Captain Pike 3.50
❑Annual 5, ca. 1994 .... 3.95
❑Annual 6, ca. 1995; D: Gary Seven. Convergence, Part 1; continues in Star Trek: The Next Generation Annual #6 .... 3.95
❑Special 1, Spr 1994 BSz (c); PD (w). 3.50
❑Special 2, Win 1994 .... 3.50
❑Special 3, Win 1995 .... 3.95

STAR TREK: DEBT OF HONOR
DC

❑1 .... 14.95

STAR TREK: DEEP SPACE NINE (MALIBU)
MALIBU

❑0, Jan 1995; premium limited edition; QVC offer 3.00
❑1/A, Aug 1993; Newsstand cover 3.00
❑1/B, Aug 1993; line-drawing cover ... 3.00
❑1/C, Aug 1993; deluxe edition (black/foil) 4.00
❑2, Sep 1993; trading card 2.50
❑3, Oct 1993 .... 2.50
❑4, Nov 1993; Part 1 .... 2.50
❑5, Dec 1993; Part 2 .... 2.50
❑6, Jan 1994 .... 2.50
❑7, Feb 1994 .... 2.50
❑8, May 1994; Part 1 .... 2.50
❑9, Jun 1994; Part 2 .... 2.50
❑10, Jun 1994 .... 2.50
❑11, Jul 1994 .... 2.50
❑12, Jul 1994 .... 2.50
❑13, Aug 1994 .... 2.50
❑14, Sep 1994; Part 1 .... 2.50
❑15, Sep 1994; Part 2 .... 2.50
❑16, Nov 1994 .... 2.50
❑17, Dec 1994 .... 2.50
❑18, Jan 1995 .... 2.50
❑19, Feb 1995 .... 2.50
❑20, Mar 1995 .... 2.50
❑21, Apr 1995 .... 2.50
❑22, May 1995 .... 2.50
❑23, May 1995; The Secret of the Lost Orb, Part 1 .... 2.50
❑24, Jun 1995; The Secret of the Lost Orb, Part 2 .... 2.50
❑25, Jul 1995; The Secret of the Lost Orb, Part 3; Double-sized issue 3.50
❑26, Jul 1995; Part 1 .... 2.50
❑27, Aug 1995; Part 2 .... 2.50
❑28, Sep 1995 .... 2.50
❑29, Oct 1995; Part 1; Commander Riker; Mirror Tuvok 2.50
❑30, Nov 1995 .... 2.50
❑31, Dec 1995 .... 3.95
❑32, Jan 1996 .... 3.50
❑Annual 1, ca. 1995 .... 3.95
❑Ashcan 1; limited edition ashcan 5.00
❑Special 1, ca. 1995 .... 3.50

STAR TREK: DEEP SPACE NINE (MARVEL)
MARVEL / PARAMOUNT

❑1, Nov 1996; Part 1; DS9 is drawn into the wormhole 2.00
❑2, Dec 1996; Part 2 .... 2.00
❑3, Jan 1997; Part 1 .... 2.00
❑4, Feb 1997; Part 1 .... 2.00
❑5, Mar 1997 .... 2.00
❑6, Apr 1997 .... 2.00

Star Wars: Droids (Vol. 1)

Robotic Laurel and Hardy provided laughs

©Dark Horse

Star Wars: Episode I The Phantom Menace

In the comics, you can't hear Jar Jar

©Dark Horse

Star Wars Handbook

Guide to Stackpole's Rogue Squadron series

©Dark Horse

Star Wars: Infinities: A New Hope

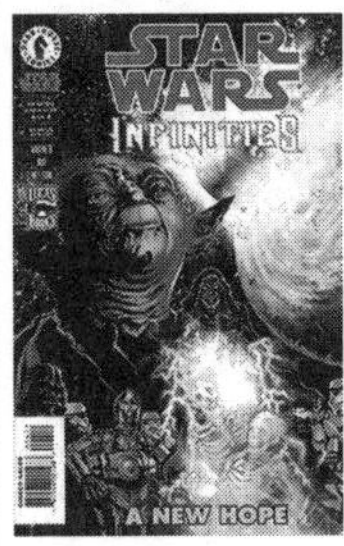

How one tiny change can affect a universe

©Dark Horse

Star Wars: Jabba the Hutt

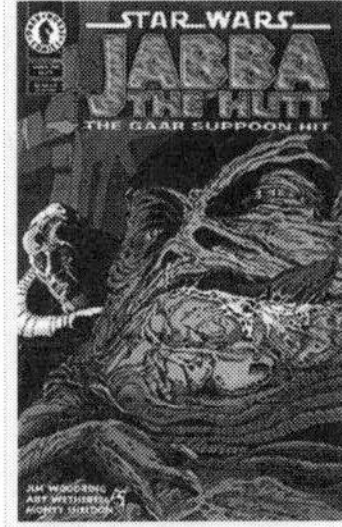

Should have had extra widescreen version

©Dark Horse

N-MINT

❑7, May 1997 .... 2.00
❑8, Aug 1997 .... 2.00
❑9, Sep 1997 .... 2.00
❑10, Oct 1997 .... 2.00
❑11, Nov 1997; gatefold summary; Telepathy War, Part 1; Crossover with ST: Starfleet Academy, ST: Telepathy War one-shot, ST Unlimited and ST: Voyager; 2.00
❑12, Dec 1997; gatefold summary; Telepathy War, Part 2; Crossover with ST: Starfleet Academy, ST: Telepathy War one-shot, ST Unlimited and ST: Voyager 2.00
❑13, Jan 1998; gatefold summary 2.00
❑14, Feb 1998; gatefold summary A: Tribbles. 2.00
❑15, Mar 1998; gatefold summary 2.00

STAR TREK: DEEP SPACE NINE, THE CELEBRITY SERIES: BLOOD AND HONOR
MALIBU

❑1, May 1995; Written by Mark Lenard 2.95

STAR TREK: DEEP SPACE NINE HEARTS AND MINDS
MALIBU

❑1, Jun 1994; an original Deep Space Nine mini series 2.50
❑2, Jul 1994 .... 2.50
❑3, Aug 1994 .... 2.50
❑4, Sep 1994 .... 2.50

STAR TREK: DEEP SPACE NINE: LIGHTSTORM
MALIBU

❑1, Dec 1994 .... 3.50

STAR TREK: DEEP SPACE NINE: N-VECTOR
DC / WILDSTORM

❑1, Aug 2000 .... 2.50
❑2, Sep 2000 .... 2.50
❑3, Oct 2000 .... 2.50
❑4, Nov 2000 .... 2.50

STAR TREK: DEEP SPACE NINE: RULES OF DIPLOMACY
MALIBU

❑1, Aug 1995; Co-Author Aron Eisenberg plays "Nog" in series 2.95

STAR TREK: DEEP SPACE NINE/STAR TREK: THE NEXT GENERATION
MALIBU

❑1, Oct 1994; part two of a four-part crossover with DC; Deep Space Nine/ The Next Generation crossover, Part 2; Continued from Star Trek: The Next Generation/Star Trek: Deep Space Nine #1; Continues in Star Trek: The Next Generation/Star Trek: Deep Space Nine #2 .... 2.50
❑2, Nov 1994; part three of a four-part crossover with DC; Deep Space Nine/ The Next Generation crossover, Part 4; Continued from Star Trek: The Next Generation/Star Trek: Deep Space Nine #2 .... 2.50
❑Ashcan 1; No cover price; Ashcan preview; flip-book with DC's Star Trek: The Next Generation/Star Trek: Deep Space Nine Ashcan 1.00

N-MINT

STAR TREK: DEEP SPACE NINE: TEROK NOR
MALIBU

❑0, Jan 1995 .... 2.95

STAR TREK: DEEP SPACE NINE, THE MAQUIS
MALIBU

❑1, Feb 1995; Soldier of Peace, Part 1 2.50
❑2, Mar 1995; Soldier of Peace, Part 2 2.50
❑3, Apr 1995; Soldier of Peace, Part 3 2.50

STAR TREK: DEEP SPACE NINE, ULTIMATE ANNUAL
MALIBU

❑1, ca. 1995 .... 5.95

STAR TREK: DEEP SPACE NINE, WORF SPECIAL
MALIBU

❑0, Dec 1995 .... 3.95

STAR TREK: DIVIDED WE FALL
DC

❑1, Jul 2001 .... 2.95
❑2, Aug 2001 .... 2.95
❑3, Sep 2001 .... 2.95
❑4, Oct 2001 .... 2.95

STAR TREK: EARLY VOYAGES
MARVEL / PARAMOUNT

❑1, Feb 1997; Christopher Pike as Enterprise captain 2.99
❑2, Mar 1997; Battle with the Klingons 1.99
❑3, Apr 1997; prequel to The Cage 1.99
❑4, May 1997; Yeoman Colt's POV on The Cage 1.99
❑5, Jun 1997 .... 1.99
❑6, Jul 1997 .... 1.99
❑7, Aug 1997; gatefold summary; Pike vs. Kaaj 1.99
❑8, Sep 1997; gatefold summary 1.99
❑9, Oct 1997; gatefold summary 1.99
❑10, Nov 1997; gatefold summary 1.99
❑11, Dec 1997; gatefold summary 1.99
❑12, Jan 1998; gatefold summary 1.99
❑13, Feb 1998; gatefold summary 1.99
❑14, Mar 1998; gatefold summary; Pike vs. Kirk 1.99
❑15, Apr 1998; gatefold summary 1.99
❑16, May 1998; gatefold summary; Pike goes undercover 1.99
❑17, Jun 1998; gatefold summary 1.99

STAR TREK: ENTER THE WOLVES
WILDSTORM / PARAMOUNT

❑1, ca. 2001 .... 5.99

STAR TREK: FIRST CONTACT
MARVEL / PARAMOUNT

❑1, Nov 1996; prestige format; Movie adaptation; cardstock cover 5.95

STAR TREK GENERATIONS
DC

❑1; Movie adaptation; Newstand edition 3.95
❑1/Prestige; Movie adaptation; Prestige format one-shot 5.95

STAR TREKKER
ANTARCTIC

❑1, Dec 1992, b&w; parody (never distributed) 2.95

N-MINT

STAR TREK: MIRROR MIRROR
MARVEL / PARAMOUNT

❑1, Feb 1997; one-shot sequel to original series episode 3.99

STAR TREK MOVIE SPECIAL
DC

❑3, ca. 1984; Movie adaptation 2.00
❑4, ca. 1987; Movie adaptation 2.00
❑5, ca. 1989; Movie adaptation 2.00

STAR TREK: NEW FRONTIER: DOUBLE TIME
DC / WILDSTORM

❑1, Nov 2000, Captain Calhoun on the USS Excalibur 5.95

STAR TREK: OPERATION ASSIMILATION
MARVEL / PARAMOUNT

❑1, Apr 1997, Romulans as Borg 2.99

STAR TREK VI: THE UNDISCOVERED COUNTRY
DC

❑1, ca. 1992; The Undiscovered Country Movie adaptation; Newsstand edition 2.95
❑1/Direct ed., ca. 1992; prestige format; The Undiscovered Country Movie adaptation 5.95

STAR TREK SPECIAL
WILDSTORM

❑1 2001; Prestige format; stories for Star Trek, Next Generation, Deep Space Nine and Voyager 6.95

STAR TREK: STARFLEET ACADEMY
MARVEL / PARAMOUNT

❑1, Dec 1996 A: Nog. 2.00
❑2, Jan 1997 .... 2.00
❑3, Feb 1997 .... 2.00
❑4, Mar 1997; Part 1 .... 2.00
❑5, Apr 1997 D: Kamilah. 2.00
❑6, May 1997 .... 2.00
❑7, Jun 1997 .... 2.00
❑8, Jul 1997; return of Charlie X 2.00
❑9, Aug 1997; gatefold summary; A: Pike. on Talos IV 2.00
❑10, Sep 1997; gatefold summary 2.00
❑11, Oct 1997; gatefold summary; cadets on trial for going to Talos IV 2.00
❑12, Nov 1997; gatefold summary; Part 1; Crossover with ST: Deep Space Nine, ST: Telepathy War one-shot; ST Unlimited and ST: Voyager 2.00
❑13, Dec 1997; gatefold summary 2.00
❑14, Jan 1998; gatefold summary; Part 1 .... 2.00
❑15, Feb 1998; gatefold summary; Part 2 .... 2.00
❑16, Mar 1998; gatefold summary; Part 3 .... 2.00
❑17, Apr 1998; gatefold summary 2.00
❑18/A, May 1998; English language edition; English language edition 2.00
❑18/B, May 1998; Klingon language edition; Klingon language edition 2.00
❑19, Jun 1998; gatefold summary 2.00

Other grades: Multiply price above by 5/6 for VF/NM • 2/3 for VERY FINE • 1/3 for FINE • 1/5 for VERY GOOD • 1/8 for GOOD

STAR TREK: TELEPATHY WAR
MARVEL / PARAMOUNT

❑1, Nov 1997; concludes crossover between ST: Deep Space Nine, ST: Starfleet Academy; ST Unlimited and ST: Voyager 2.99

STAR TREK: THE MODALA IMPERATIVE
DC

❑1, Jul 1991 .... 2.50
❑2, Aug 1991 .... 2.00
❑3, Aug 1991 .... 2.00
❑4, Sep 1991 .... 2.00

STAR TREK: THE NEXT GENERATION (MINI-SERIES)
DC

❑1, Feb 1988 .... 3.00
❑2, Mar 1988 .... 2.00
❑3, Apr 1988 .... 2.00
❑4, May 1988 .... 2.00
❑5, Jun 1988 D: Geordi. 2.00
❑6, Jul 1988 .... 2.00

STAR TREK: THE NEXT GENERATION
DC

❑1, Oct 1989 .... 5.00
❑2, Nov 1989 .... 4.00
❑3, Dec 1989 .... 3.00
❑4, Jan 1990 .... 3.00
❑5, Feb 1990 .... 3.00
❑6, Mar 1990 .... 2.50
❑7, Apr 1990 .... 2.50
❑8, May 1990 .... 2.50
❑9, Jun 1990 .... 2.50
❑10, Jul 1990 .... 2.50
❑11, Aug 1990 .... 2.50
❑12, Sep 1990 .... 2.50
❑13, Oct 1990 .... 2.50
❑14, Dec 1990 .... 2.50
❑15, Jan 1991 V: Ferengi. 2.50
❑16, Feb 1991 .... 2.50
❑17, Mar 1991 .... 2.50
❑18, Apr 1991 .... 2.50
❑19, May 1991 .... 2.50
❑20, Jun 1991 .... 2.50
❑21, Jul 1991 .... 2.00
❑22, Aug 1991 .... 2.00
❑23, Sep 1991 .... 2.00
❑24, Oct 1991; double-sized; Double-sized 25th Anniversary issue 2.00
❑25, Nov 1991; Giant-size 2.00
❑26, Dec 1991 .... 2.00
❑27, Jan 1992 .... 2.00
❑28, Feb 1992; Return of K'ehleyr 2.00
❑29, Mar 1992 .... 2.00
❑30, Apr 1992 .... 2.00
❑31, May 1992 .... 2.00
❑32, Jun 1992 .... 2.00
❑33, Jul 1992; Q turns the crew into Klingons 2.00
❑34, Jul 1992 .... 2.00
❑35, Aug 1992 .... 2.00
❑36, Aug 1992; Part 1 .... 2.00
❑37, Sep 1992; Part 2 .... 2.00
❑38, Sep 1992; Part 3 .... 2.00
❑39, Oct 1992 .... 2.00
❑40, Nov 1992; Part 1 .... 2.00
❑41, Dec 1992; Part 2 .... 2.00
❑42, Jan 1993; Part 3 .... 2.00
❑43, Feb 1993; Part 4 .... 2.00
❑44, Mar 1993; Part 5 .... 2.00
❑45, Apr 1993 .... 2.00
❑46, May 1993 .... 2.00
❑47, Jun 1993; Worst of Both Worlds, Part 1 .... 2.00
❑48, Jul 1993; Worst of Both Worlds, Part 2 .... 2.00
❑49, Aug 1993; Worst of Both Worlds, Part 3 .... 2.00
❑50, Sep 1993; Giant-size; Worst of Both Worlds, Part 4; Double-sized issue 3.50
❑51, Oct 1993 .... 2.00
❑52, Oct 1993; Part 1; Dixon Hill story 2.00
❑53, Nov 1993; Part 2 .... 2.00
❑54, Nov 1993; Part 3 .... 2.00
❑55, Dec 1993 .... 2.00
❑56, Jan 1994 .... 2.00
❑57, Mar 1994 .... 2.00
❑58, Apr 1994 .... 2.00
❑59, May 1994 .... 2.00
❑60, Jun 1994 .... 2.00
❑61, Jul 1994 .... 2.00
❑62, Aug 1994 .... 2.00
❑63, Sep 1994 .... 2.00
❑64, Oct 1994 .... 2.00
❑65, Nov 1994 .... 2.00
❑66, Dec 1994 .... 2.00
❑67, Jan 1995; Part 1 .... 2.00
❑68, Feb 1995; Part 2 .... 2.00
❑69, Mar 1995; Part 3 .... 2.00
❑70, Apr 1995; Part 4 .... 2.00
❑71, May 1995 .... 2.00
❑72, Jun 1995; War and Madness, Part 1 .... 2.50
❑73, Jul 1995; War and Madness, Part 2 .... 2.50
❑74, Aug 1995; War and Madness, Part 3 .... 2.50
❑75, Sep 1995; Giant-size; V: Borg. War and Madness, Part 4; Double-sized issue 3.95
❑76, Oct 1995 .... 2.50
❑77, Nov 1995 .... 2.50
❑78, Dec 1995 .... 2.50
❑79, Jan 1996; Q transforms the crew into androids 2.50
❑80, Feb 1996 .... 2.50
❑Annual 1, ca. 1990; Q story written by deLancie; Stardate back-up feature (puts comics & books in conjunction with TV series); 1990 Annual 3.50
❑Annual 2, ca. 1991; 1991 Annual 3.50
❑Annual 3, ca. 1992; 1992 Annual 3.50
❑Annual 4, ca. 1993; 1993 Annual 3.50
❑Annual 5, ca. 1994; 1994 Annual 3.50
❑Annual 6, ca. 1995; Part 2; continued from Star Trek Annual #6; 1995 Annual 3.95
❑Special 1, ca. 1993; 1993 Special 4.50
❑Special 2, Sum 1994; Captain Bateson of the Bozeman; 1994 Special 4.50
❑Special 3, Win 1995; 1995 Special 4.50

STAR TREK: THE NEXT GENERATION/ DEEP SPACE NINE
DC

❑1, Dec 1994; crossover with Malibu; Deep Space Nine/The Next Generation crossover, Part 1; Continues in Star Trek: Deep Space Nine/The Next Generation #1 .... 2.50
❑2, Jan 1995; crossover with Malibu; Deep Space Nine/The Next Generation crossover, Part 4; Continued from Star Trek: Deep Space Nine/The Next Generation #1; Continues in Star Trek: Deep Space Nine/The Next Generation #2 .... 2.50
❑Ashcan 1; No cover price; flip-book with Malibu's Deep Space Nine/Star Trek: The Next Generation Ashcan 1.00

STAR TREK: THE NEXT GENERATION: FORGIVENESS
DC

❑1, ca. 2002 .... 17.95
❑1/HC, ca. 2001 .... 24.95

STAR TREK: THE NEXT GENERATION: ILL WIND
DC

❑1, Nov 1995 .... 2.50
❑2, Dec 1995 .... 2.50
❑3, Jan 1996 .... 2.50
❑4, Feb 1996 .... 2.50

STAR TREK: THE NEXT GENERATION: PERCHANCE TO DREAM
DC / WILDSTORM

❑1, Feb 2000 .... 2.50
❑2, Mar 2000 .... 2.50
❑3, Apr 2000 .... 2.50
❑4, May 2000 .... 2.50

STAR TREK: THE NEXT GENERATION: RIKER
MARVEL / PARAMOUNT

❑1, Jul 1998 .... 3.50

STAR TREK:THE NEXT GENERATION: SHADOWHEART
DC

❑1, Dec 1994 .... 1.95
❑2, Jan 1995 .... 1.95
❑3, Feb 1995 .... 1.95
❑4, Mar 1995 .... 1.95

STAR TREK: THE NEXT GENERATION: THE GORN CRISIS
DC / WILDSTORM

❑1, ca. 2002 .... 17.95
❑1/HC 29.95

STAR TREK: THE NEXT GENERATION: THE KILLING SHADOWS
DC / WILDSTORM

❑1, Nov 2000 .... 2.50
❑2, Dec 2000 .... 2.50
❑3, Jan 2001 .... 2.50
❑4, Feb 2001 .... 2.50

STAR TREK: THE NEXT GENERATION: THE MODALA IMPERATIVE
DC

❑1, Sep 1991; Incorrect date in indicia 1.75
❑2, Aug 1991 .... 1.75
❑3, Aug 1991 .... 1.75
❑4, Oct 1991 .... 1.75

STAR TREK: THE NEXT GENERATION: THE SERIES FINALE
DC

❑1, ca. 1994; adapts final TV episode. 3.95

STAR TREK UNLIMITED
MARVEL / PARAMOUNT

❑1, Nov 1996; Original crew story; Next Generation story 3.00
❑2, Jan 1997; Original crew story; Next Generation story 3.00
❑3, Apr 1997; Original crew story; Next Generation story 3.00
❑4, May 1997; Original crew story; Next Generation story; Original series and Next Generation stories crossover 3.00
❑5, Sep 1997; Original series and Next Generation stories crossover; Original crew story; Next Generation story 3.00
❑6, Nov 1997; Part 4; Crossover with ST: Deep Space Nine, ST: Starfleet Academy, ST: Telepathy War one-shot and ST: Voyager; 3.00
❑7, Jan 1998 .... 3.00
❑8, Mar 1998; Kang vs. Sulu 3.00
❑9, May 1998; Chekov wins a Klingon cruiser 3.00
❑10, Jul 1998 .... 3.00

STAR TREK: UNTOLD VOYAGES
MARVEL / PARAMOUNT

❑1, Mar 1998 .... 2.50
❑2, Apr 1998 .... 2.50
❑3, May 1998 .... 2.50
❑4, Jun 1998; Sulu takes command 2.50
❑5, Jul 1998 .... 3.50

STAR TREK: VOYAGER
MARVEL / PARAMOUNT

❑1, Nov 1996 .... 2.00
❑2, Dec 1996 .... 2.00
❑3, Jan 1997 .... 2.00
❑4, Feb 1997; Part 1 .... 2.00
❑5, Mar 1997; Part 2 .... 2.00
❑6, Apr 1997; Part 1 .... 2.00
❑7, May 1997; Part 2 .... 2.00
❑8, Jun 1997 .... 2.00
❑9, Sep 1997; gatefold summary 2.00
❑10, Oct 1997; gatefold summary; replays events at Wolf 359 .... 2.00
❑11, Nov 1997; gatefold summary V: Leviathan. 2.00
❑12, Dec 1997; gatefold summary 2.00
❑13, Jan 1998; gatefold summary; Part 5; Crossover with ST: Deep Space Nine, ST: Starfleet Academy, ST: Telepathy War one-shot and ST Unlimited 2.00
❑14, Feb 1998; gatefold summary 1: Seven of Nine 2.00
❑15, Mar 1998; gatefold summary 2.00

STAR TREK: VOYAGER: AVALON RISING
DC

❑1, Sep 2000 .... 5.95

Star Wars: Jedi - Mace Windu

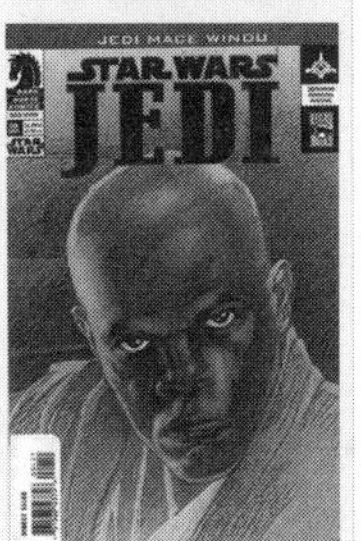

Polished, poised Jedi proves himself
©Dark Horse

Star Wars Tales

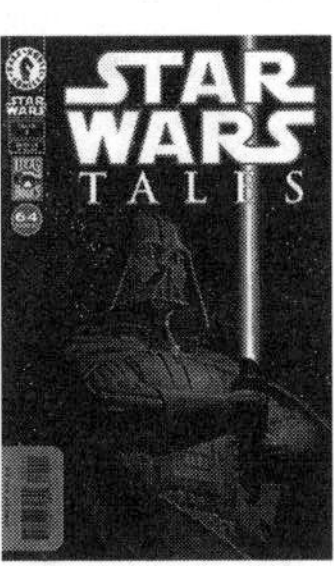

Anthology covered stories from different eras
©Dark Horse

Star Wars: X-Wing Rogue Squadron

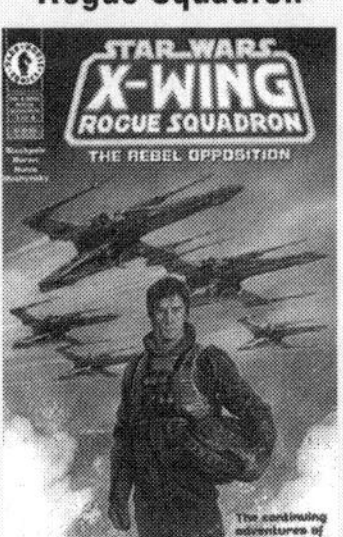

Carries over characters from the prose novels
©Dark Horse

Star Western

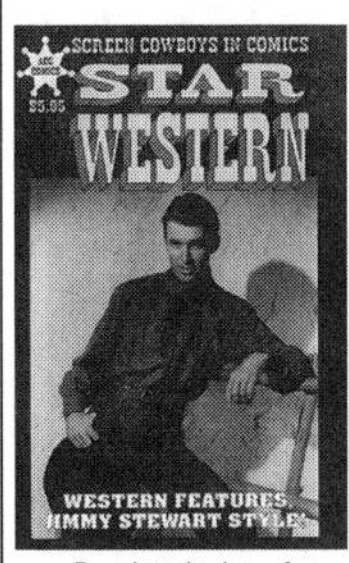

Reprinted tales of western hero greats
©Avalon

Static

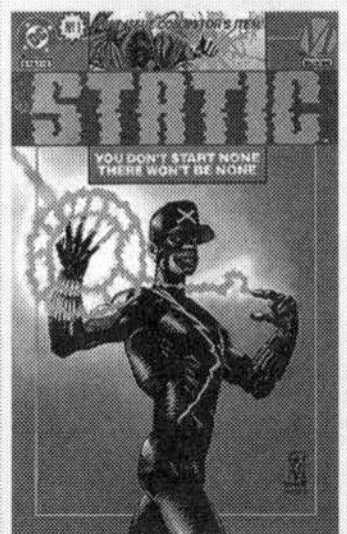

Most successful Milestone title
©DC

N-MINT

STAR TREK: VOYAGER: FALSE COLORS
DC / WILDSTORM

❑1, Jan 2000 .... 5.95

STAR TREK: VOYAGER: SPLASHDOWN
MARVEL / PARAMOUNT

❑1, Apr 1998; gatefold summary 2.50
❑2, May 1998; gatefold summary 2.50
❑3, Jun 1998; gatefold summary 2.50
❑4, Jul 1998; gatefold summary; final Marvel Star Trek comic book 2.50

STAR TREK: VOYAGER: THE PLANET KILLER
DC / WILDSTORM

❑1, Mar 2001 .... 2.95
❑2, Apr 2001 .... 2.95
❑3, May 2001 .... 2.95

STAR TREK/X-MEN
MARVEL / PARAMOUNT

❑1, Dec 1996; X-Men meet original Enterprise crew 5.00

STAR TREK/X-MEN: SECOND CONTACT
MARVEL / PARAMOUNT

❑1, May 1998, A: Kang. X-Men meet Next Generation crew; Sentinels; continues in Star Trek: The Next Generation/X-Men: Planet X novel .. 5.00
❑1/Variant, May 1998 .... 4.99

STAR WARS
MARVEL

❑1, Jul 1977, HC (a); Newsstand edition (distributed by Curtis); issue number in box 20.00
❑1/35 cent, Jul 1977, HC (a); 35 cent regional price variant; Rare variation; Price is in a square area, and UPC code appears with no line drawn through it 800.00
❑1/2nd 1977, HC (a); Newsstand reprint (distributed by Curtis); "reprint" in upper-left corner box and inside; price and issue number in square with Curtis Circulation (CC) logo 4.00
❑1/Whitman 2nd 1977; Special markets edition (usually sold in Whitman bagged prepacks); price appears in a diamond; no UPC barcode; 35¢ cover price; reprint on cover 4.00
❑1/Whitman 3rd 1977; Special markets edition (usually sold in Whitman bagged prepacks); price appears in a diamond; no UPC barcode; 35¢ cover price; reprint on cover 4.00
❑2, Aug 1977, HC (a); Newsstand edition (distributed by Curtis); issue number in box 10.00
❑2/35 cent, Aug 1977, HC (a); 35 cent regional price variant; newsstand edition (distributed by Curtis); issue number in box 150.00
❑2/2nd 1977, HC (a); Newsstand reprint (distributed by Curtis); "reprint" in upper-left corner box and inside; price and issue number in square with Curtis Circulation (CC) logo 3.50
❑2/Whitman, Aug 1977, HC (a); Special markets edition (usually sold in Whitman bagged prepacks); price appears in a diamond; UPC barcode appears; 30¢ cover price 10.00
❑2/Whitman 2nd, Aug 1977, HC (a); Special markets edition (usually sold in Whitman bagged prepacks); price appears in a diamond; no UPC barcode; 35¢ cover price; reprint in indicia only 10.00
❑2/Whitman 3rd, Aug 1977, HC (a); Special markets edition (usually sold in Whitman bagged prepacks); price appears in a diamond; no UPC barcode; 35¢ cover price; reprint on cover 10.00
❑3, Sep 1977, HC (a); Newsstand edition (distributed by Curtis); issue number in box 8.00
❑3/35 cent, Sep 1977, HC (a); 35 cent regional price variant; newsstand edition (distributed by Curtis); issue number in box 150.00
❑3/2nd 1977, HC (a); Newsstand reprint (distributed by Curtis); "reprint" in upper-left corner box and inside; price and issue number in square with Curtis Circulation (CC) logo 3.50
❑3/Whitman, Sep 1977, HC (a); Special markets edition (usually sold in Whitman bagged prepacks); price appears in a diamond; UPC barcode appears; 30¢ cover price 8.00
❑3/Whitman 2nd, Sep 1977, HC (a); Special markets edition (usually sold in Whitman bagged prepacks); price appears in a diamond; no UPC barcode; 35¢ cover price; reprint in indicia only 8.00
❑3/Whitman 3rd, Sep 1977, HC (a); Special markets edition (usually sold in Whitman bagged prepacks); price appears in a diamond; no UPC barcode; 35¢ cover price; reprint on cover 8.00
❑4, Oct 1977, HC (a); Newsstand edition (distributed by Curtis); issue number in box; low distribution 7.00
❑4/35 cent, Oct 1977, HC (a); 35 cent regional price variant; newsstand edition (distributed by Curtis); issue number in box 150.00
❑4/2nd 1977, HC (a); Newsstand reprint (distributed by Curtis); "reprint" in upper-left corner box and inside; price and issue number in square with Curtis Circulation (CC) logo 3.50
❑4/Whitman, Oct 1977, HC (a); Special markets edition (usually sold in Whitman bagged prepacks); price appears in a diamond; no UPC barcode; 30¢ cover price 7.00
❑4/Whitman 2nd, Oct 1977, HC (a); Special markets edition (usually sold in Whitman bagged prepacks); price appears in a diamond; no UPC barcode; 35¢ cover price; reprint in indicia only 7.00
❑4/Whitman 3rd, Oct 1977, HC (a); Special markets edition (usually sold in Whitman bagged prepacks); price appears in a diamond; no UPC barcode; 35¢ cover price; reprint on cover 7.00
❑5, Nov 1977, HC (a); Newsstand edition (distributed by Curtis); issue number in box 7.00
❑5/2nd, Nov 1977, HC (a); Newsstand reprint (distributed by Curtis); "reprint" in upper-left corner box; price and issue number in square with Curtis Circulation (CC) logo 7.00
❑5/Whitman 1977, HC (a); Special markets edition (usually sold in Whitman bagged prepacks); price appears in a diamond; no UPC barcode 3.50
❑5/Whitman 2nd 1977, HC (a); Special markets reprint (usually sold in Whitman bagged prepacks); price appears in a diamond; no UPC barcode; reprint on cover 3.50
❑6, Dec 1977, HC (a); Newsstand edition (distributed by Curtis); issue number in box 7.00
❑6/2nd, Dec 1977, HC (a); Newsstand reprint (distributed by Curtis); "reprint" in upper-left corner box; price and issue number in square with Curtis Circulation (CC) logo 7.00
❑6/Whitman 1977, HC (a); Special markets edition (usually sold in Whitman bagged prepacks); price appears in a diamond; no UPC barcode 3.50
❑6/Whitman 2nd 1977, HC (a); Special markets reprint (usually sold in Whitman bagged prepacks); price appears in a diamond; no UPC barcode; reprint on cover 3.50
❑7, Jan 1978, HC (a); Newsstand edition (distributed by Curtis); issue number in box 7.00
❑7/Whitman 1978, HC (a); Special markets edition (usually sold in Whitman bagged prepacks); price appears in a diamond; no UPC barcode
❑8, Feb 1978, HC, TP (a); Newsstand edition (distributed by Curtis); issue number in box 7.00
❑8/Whitman 1978, HC, TP (a); Special markets edition (usually sold in Whitman bagged prepacks); price appears in a diamond; no UPC barcode 3.00
❑9, Mar 1978, HC, TP (a); Newsstand edition (distributed by Curtis); issue number in box 7.00
❑9/Whitman 1978, HC, TP (a); Special markets edition (usually sold in Whitman bagged prepacks); price appears in a diamond; no UPC barcode 3.00
❑10, Apr 1978, HC, TP (a); Newsstand edition (distributed by Curtis); issue number in box 7.00
❑10/Whitman, Apr 1978, HC, TP (a); Special markets edition (usually sold in Whitman bagged prepacks); price appears in a diamond; no UPC barcode 7.00
❑11, May 1978, CI (a); Newsstand edition (distributed by Curtis); issue number in box 7.00
❑11/Whitman, May 1978, CI (a); Special markets edition (usually sold in Whitman bagged prepacks); price appears in a diamond; UPC barcode appears 7.00
❑11/Whitman B, May 1978, CI (a); Special markets edition (usually sold in Whitman bagged prepacks); price appears in a diamond; no UPC barcode 7.00

	N-MINT
❑12, Jun 1978, CI (a); Newsstand edition (distributed by Curtis); issue number in box	7.00
❑12/Whitman, Jun 1978, CI (a); Special markets edition (usually sold in Whitman bagged prepacks); price appears in a diamond; no UPC barcode	7.00
❑13, Jul 1978, CI (a); Newsstand edition (distributed by Curtis); issue number in box	7.00
❑13/Whitman, Jul 1978, CI (a); Special markets edition (usually sold in Whitman bagged prepacks); price appears in a diamond; no UPC barcode	7.00
❑14, Aug 1978, CI (a); Newsstand edition (distributed by Curtis); issue number in box	7.00
❑14/Whitman, Aug 1978, CI (a); Special markets edition (usually sold in Whitman bagged prepacks); price appears in a diamond; UPC barcode appears	7.00
❑15, Sep 1978, CI (a); D: Crimson Jack. Newsstand edition (distributed by Curtis); issue number in box	7.00
❑15/Whitman, Sep 1978, CI (a); D: Crimson Jack. Special markets edition (usually sold in Whitman bagged prepacks); price appears in a diamond; no UPC barcode	7.00
❑16, Oct 1978, BWi (a); 1: Valance the bounty hunter. Newsstand edition (distributed by Curtis); issue number in box	7.00
❑16/Whitman, Oct 1978, BWi (a); 1: Valance the bounty hunter. Special markets edition (usually sold in Whitman bagged prepacks); price appears in a diamond; no UPC barcode	7.00
❑17, Nov 1978, AM, HT (a); Newsstand edition (distributed by Curtis); issue number in box; low distribution; Tatooine adventure set before first movie	7.00
❑17/Whitman, Nov 1978, AM, HT (a); Special markets edition (usually sold in Whitman bagged prepacks); price appears in a diamond; no UPC barcode	7.00
❑18, Dec 1978, Newsstand edition (distributed by Curtis); issue number in box; low distribution	7.00
❑18/Whitman, Dec 1978, Special markets edition (usually sold in Whitman bagged prepacks); price appears in a diamond; no UPC barcode	7.00
❑19, Jan 1979, CI, BWi (a); low distribution	7.00
❑20, Feb 1979, CI, BWi (a)	6.00
❑21, Mar 1979, CI, GD (a)	6.00
❑22, Apr 1979, CI, BWi (a)	5.00
❑23, May 1979, CI, BWi (a); Newsstand edition (distributed by Curtis); issue number in box	5.00
❑23/Whitman, May 1979, CI, BWi (a); Special markets edition (usually sold in Whitman bagged prepacks); price appears in a diamond; no UPC barcode	5.00
❑24, Jun 1979, CI, BWi (a); flashback to before first movie	4.00
❑25, Jul 1979, CI, GD (a)	4.00
❑26, Aug 1979, CI, GD (a)	4.00
❑27, Sep 1979, CI, BWi (a)	4.00
❑28, Oct 1979, CI, BWi (a); A: Jabba the Hutt (not movie version)	4.00
❑29, Nov 1979, CI, BWi (c); CI, BWi (a); A: Darth Vader	4.00
❑30, Dec 1979, CI, GD (a)	4.00
❑31, Jan 1980, CI, BWi (c); CI, BWi (a); return to Tatooine	4.00
❑32, Feb 1980, CI, BWi (a)	4.00
❑33, Mar 1980, CI, GD (a)	4.00
❑34, Apr 1980, CI, BWi (a); D: Baron Tagge	4.00
❑35, May 1980, CI, GD (a); A: Darth Vader. A: Luke Skywalker	4.00
❑36, Jun 1980, CI, GD (a)	4.00
❑37, Jul 1980, CI, GD (a); 1st Vader/Luke duel	4.00
❑38, Aug 1980, MG (w); MG (a); living spaceship	4.00
❑39, Sep 1980, AW (a); Empire Strikes Back adaptation	4.00
❑40, Oct 1980, AW (a); Empire Strikes Back adaptation	4.00
❑41, Nov 1980, AW (a); Empire Strikes Back adaptation	4.00
❑42, Dec 1980, AW (a); Empire Strikes Back adaptation	4.00
❑43, Jan 1981, AW (a); Empire Strikes Back adaptation	4.00
❑44, Feb 1981, AW (a); Empire Strikes Back adaptation	4.00
❑45, Mar 1981, CI, GD (a); first post-Empire Strikes Back story	4.00
❑46, Apr 1981, CI, TP (a)	4.00
❑47, May 1981, FM (c); CI, GD (a)	4.00
❑48, Jun 1981, CI, BWi (c); CI (a)	4.00
❑49, Jul 1981, TP (a); low distribution	5.00
❑50, Aug 1981; double-sized AW, TP (a)	4.00
❑51, Sep 1981, TP (a); A: Death of Star II. A: Tarkin. A: Star II appearance. D: Death of Star II	4.00
❑52, Oct 1981, TP (a); A: Death of Star II. A: Tarkin. A: Star II appearance. D: Death of Star II	4.00
❑53, Nov 1981, CI, TP (a)	4.00
❑54, Dec 1981, AM, CI, TP (a)	4.00
❑55, Jan 1982, TP (a)	4.00
❑56, Feb 1982, TP (a)	4.00
❑57, Mar 1982, TP (a)	4.00
❑58, Apr 1982, TP (a); Return to Cloud City	4.00
❑59, May 1982, TP (a)	4.00
❑60, Jun 1982, TP (a)	4.00
❑61, Jul 1982, TP (a)	4.00
❑62, Aug 1982, TP (a); Luke kicked out of Alliance	4.00
❑63, Sep 1982, TP (a)	4.00
❑64, Oct 1982, BA (c)	4.00
❑65, Nov 1982, TP (a)	4.00
❑66, Dec 1982, TP (a)	4.00
❑67, Jan 1983, TP (a)	4.00
❑68, Feb 1983, TP, GD (a)	4.00
❑69, Mar 1983, TP, GD (a)	4.00
❑70, Apr 1983, TP, KGa (a)	4.00
❑71, May 1983, TP (a)	4.00
❑72, Jun 1983, TP (a)	4.00
❑73, Jul 1983, TP (a)	4.00
❑74, Aug 1983, TP (a)	4.00
❑75, Sep 1983, TP (a)	4.00
❑76, Oct 1983, TP (a)	4.00
❑77, Nov 1983, TP (a)	4.00
❑78, Dec 1983, BL, LMc (a)	4.00
❑79, Jan 1984, TP (a)	4.00
❑80, Feb 1984, TP (a)	4.00
❑81, Mar 1984, TP (a); first post-Return of the Jedi story	4.00
❑82, Apr 1984	4.00
❑83, May 1984, BMc (a)	4.00
❑84, Jun 1984, TP (a)	4.00
❑85, Jul 1984, TP, BMc (a)	4.00
❑86, Aug 1984, TP, BMc (a)	4.00
❑87, Sep 1984, TP (a)	4.00
❑88, Oct 1984, TP, BMc (a)	4.00
❑89, Nov 1984	4.00
❑90, Dec 1984, TP, BMc (a)	4.00
❑91, Jan 1985, TP (a)	4.00
❑92, Feb 1985; Giant-size JDu (a)	4.00
❑93, Mar 1985, SB, TP (a)	4.00
❑94, Apr 1985, TP (a)	4.00
❑95, May 1985	4.00
❑96, Jun 1985, BWi (a)	4.00
❑97, Jul 1985	4.00
❑98, Aug 1985, AW (a)	4.00
❑99, Sep 1985	4.00
❑100, Oct 1985; Giant-size	4.00
❑101, Nov 1985	4.00
❑102, Dec 1985, SB (a)	4.00
❑103, Jan 1986	4.00
❑104, Mar 1986	4.00
❑105, May 1986	4.00
❑106, Jul 1986	4.00
❑107, Sep 1986	25.00
❑Annual 1, Dec 1979	8.00
❑Annual 2, ca. 1982 CI (a)	5.00
❑Annual 3, ca. 1983 KJ (a)	5.00

STAR WARS (MAGAZINE)

DARK HORSE

	N-MINT
❑1, Oct 1992	5.00
❑2	4.00
❑3	3.00
❑4	3.00
❑5	3.00
❑6	3.00
❑7	3.00
❑8	3.00
❑9	3.00
❑10	3.00

STAR WARS (DARK HORSE)

DARK HORSE

	N-MINT
❑0, Jun 1999; HC (a); American Entertainment exclusive	10.00
❑1, Dec 1998	4.00
❑2, Jan 1999	3.00
❑3, Feb 1999	3.00
❑4, Mar 1999	3.00
❑5, Apr 1999	3.00
❑6, May 1999	3.00
❑7, Jun 1999	2.50
❑8, Jul 1999	2.50
❑9, Aug 1999	2.50
❑10, Sep 1999	2.50
❑11, Oct 1999	2.50
❑12, Nov 1999	2.50
❑13, Dec 1999	2.50
❑14, Jan 2000	2.50
❑15, Feb 2000	2.50
❑16, Mar 2000	2.50
❑17, Apr 2000	2.50
❑18, May 2000	2.50
❑19, Jun 2000 JDu (a)	2.50
❑20, Jul 2000 JDu (a)	2.50
❑21, Aug 2000 JDu (a)	2.50
❑22, Sep 2000 JDu (a)	2.50
❑23, Oct 2000	2.50
❑24, Nov 2000	2.50
❑25, Dec 2000	2.50
❑26, Jan 2001	2.50
❑27, Feb 2001	2.99
❑28, Mar 2001	2.99
❑29, Apr 2001	2.99
❑30, May 2001	2.99
❑31, Jun 2001	2.99
❑32, Jul 2001 JDu (a)	2.99
❑33, Aug 2001 JDu (a)	2.99
❑34, Sep 2001 JDu (a)	2.99
❑35, Oct 2001	2.99
❑36, Nov 2001	2.99
❑37, Dec 2001	2.99
❑38, Jan 2002	2.99
❑39, Feb 2002	2.99
❑40, Mar 2002	2.99
❑41, Apr 2002	2.99
❑42, May 2002	2.99
❑43, Jun 2002	2.99
❑44, Jul 2002 JDu (a)	2.99
❑45, Aug 2002	2.99
❑46, Sep 2002	2.99
❑47, Oct 2002	2.99
❑48, Nov 2002	2.99
❑49, Dec 2002	2.99
❑50, Jan 2003	5.99
❑51 2003	2.99
❑52 2003	2.99
❑53 2003	2.99
❑54, Jun 2003	2.99
❑55, Jul 2003	2.99
❑56, Jul 2003	2.99
❑57, Sep 2003	2.99
❑58, Dec 2003	2.99
❑59, Dec 2003	2.99
❑60, Jan 2004	2.99
❑61, Feb 2004	2.99
❑62, Mar 2004	2.99
❑63, Apr 2004	2.99
❑64, May 2004	2.99
❑65, Jun 2004	2.99
❑66, Jul 2004	2.99
❑67, Aug 2004	2.99
❑68, Sep 2004	2.99
❑69, Oct 2004	2.99
❑70, Nov 2004	2.99
❑71, Dec 2004; Republic	2.99
❑72, Jan 2005; Republic	2.99
❑73, Feb 2005	2.99
❑74, Mar 2005	2.99
❑75, May 2005	2.99
❑76 2005	2.99

Static Shock!: Rebirth of the Cool

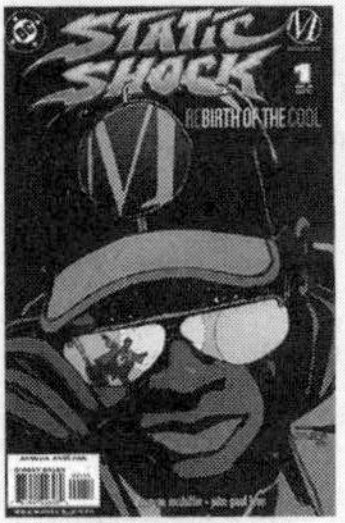

Milestone book resurrected in TV cartoon

©DC

Stealth Force

Operatives are killed... and then revived

©Malibu

Steampunk

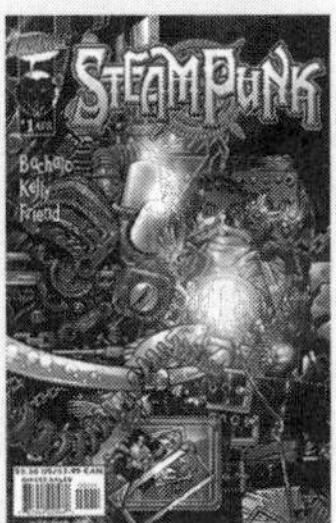

Nightmare techno-Victorian world

©DC

Steel

Steelworker filled in for Superman

©DC

Stinz (1st Series)

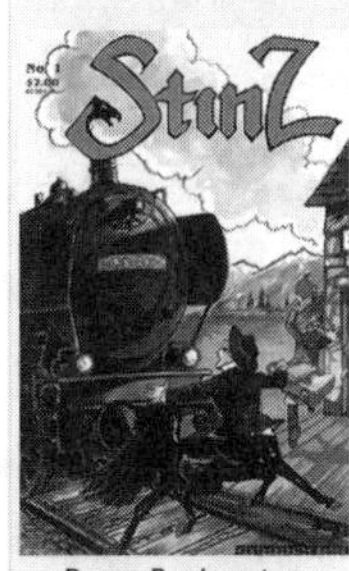

Donna Barr's gutsy, macho farmer centaurs

©Fantagraphics

	N-MINT
❑77, Sep 2005	2.99
❑78, Oct 2005	2.99
❑79, Nov 2005	2.99
❑80, Dec 2005	2.99
❑81, Jan 2006	2.99
❑82, Feb 2006	2.99
❑83, Mar 2006	2.99

STAR WARS: A NEW HOPE MANGA
DARK HORSE

❑1, Jul 1998	9.95
❑2, Jul 1998	9.95
❑3, Sep 1998	9.95
❑4, Oct 1998	9.95

STAR WARS: A NEW HOPE: THE SPECIAL EDITION
DARK HORSE

❑1, Jan 1997	2.95
❑2, Feb 1997	2.50
❑3, Mar 1997	2.50
❑4, Apr 1997	2.50

STAR WARS: BOBA FETT
DARK HORSE

❑½, Dec 1997, Wizard mail-in edition	3.00
❑½/Gold, Dec 1997, Gold edition	5.00
❑1, Dec 1995, cardstock cover	3.95
❑2, Sep 1996, cardstock cover	3.95
❑3, Aug 1997, cardstock cover	3.95

STAR WARS: BOBA FETT: AGENT OF DOOM
DARK HORSE

❑1, Nov 2000	2.99

STAR WARS: BOBA FETT: ENEMY OF THE EMPIRE
DARK HORSE

❑1, Jan 1999	2.95
❑2, Feb 1999	2.95
❑3, Mar 1999	2.95
❑4, Apr 1999	2.95

STAR WARS: BOBA FETT ONE-SHOT
DARK HORSE

❑1, May 2006	2.99

STAR WARS: BOBA FETT: TWIN ENGINES OF DESTRUCTION
DARK HORSE

❑1, Jan 1997	2.95

STAR WARS: CHEWBACCA
DARK HORSE

❑1, Jan 2000	2.95
❑2, Feb 2000	2.95
❑3, Mar 2000	2.95
❑4, Apr 2000	2.95

STAR WARS: CLONE WARS
DARK HORSE

❑Book 1, ca. 2003	14.95
❑Book 1/2nd, ca. 2004; re-print	14.95
❑Book 2, ca. 2003	14.95
❑Book 3, ca. 2004	14.95
❑Book 4, ca. 2004	16.95

STAR WARS: CRIMSON EMPIRE
DARK HORSE

	N-MINT
❑1, Dec 1997 PG (a)	6.00
❑2, Jan 1998 PG (a)	5.00
❑3, Feb 1998 PG (a)	5.00
❑4, Mar 1998 PG (a)	5.00
❑5, Apr 1998 PG (a)	5.00
❑6, May 1998 PG (a)	5.00

STAR WARS: CRIMSON EMPIRE II: COUNCIL OF BLOOD
DARK HORSE

❑1, Nov 1998 PG (a)	4.00
❑2, Dec 1998 PG (a)	2.95
❑3, Jan 1999 PG (a)	2.95
❑4, Feb 1999 PG (a)	2.95
❑5, Mar 1999 PG (a)	2.95
❑6, Apr 1999 PG (a)	2.95

STAR WARS: DARK EMPIRE
DARK HORSE

❑1, Dec 1993; cardstock cover	6.00
❑1/2nd, Aug 1993	3.00
❑1/Gold 1993	5.00
❑1/Platinum 1993	6.00
❑2, Feb 1993; cardstock cover	4.00
❑2/2nd, Aug 1993	3.00
❑2/Gold 1993	4.00
❑2/Platinum 1993	5.00
❑3, Apr 1993; cardstock cover	4.00
❑3/2nd 1993	3.00
❑3/Gold 1993	4.00
❑3/Platinum 1993	5.00
❑4, Apr 1993; cardstock cover	4.00
❑4/Gold 1993	4.00
❑4/Platinum 1993	5.00
❑5, Aug 1993; cardstock cover	3.00
❑5/Gold 1993	4.00
❑5/Platinum 1993	5.00
❑6, Oct 1993; cardstock cover	3.00
❑6/Gold 1993	4.00
❑6/Platinum 1993	5.00
❑Ashcan 1, Mar 1996; newsprint preview of trade paperback collection of mini-series; wraparound cover	1.00

STAR WARS: DARK EMPIRE II
DARK HORSE

❑1, Dec 1994; cardstock cover	2.95
❑1/Gold, Dec 1994	4.00
❑2, Jan 1995; cardstock cover	2.95
❑2/Gold, Jan 1995	4.00
❑3, Feb 1995; cardstock cover	2.95
❑3/Gold, Feb 1995	4.00
❑4, Mar 1995; cardstock cover	2.95
❑4/Gold, Mar 1995	4.00
❑5, Apr 1995; cardstock cover	2.95
❑5/Gold, Apr 1995	4.00
❑6, May 1995; cardstock cover	2.95
❑6/Gold, May 1995	4.00

STAR WARS: DARK FORCE RISING
DARK HORSE

	N-MINT
❑1, May 1997; adapts Timothy Zahn novel; cardstock cover	2.95
❑2, Jun 1997; adapts Timothy Zahn novel; cardstock cover	2.95
❑3, Jul 1997; adapts Timothy Zahn novel; cardstock cover	2.95
❑4, Aug 1997; adapts Timothy Zahn novel; cardstock cover	2.95
❑5, Sep 1997; adapts Timothy Zahn novel; cardstock cover	2.95
❑6, Oct 1997; adapts Timothy Zahn novel; cardstock cover	2.95

STAR WARS: DARTH MAUL
DARK HORSE

❑1, Sep 2000	2.95
❑1/Variant, Sep 2000	2.95
❑2, Oct 2000	2.99
❑2/Variant, Oct 2000	2.99
❑3, Nov 2000	2.99
❑3/Variant, Nov 2000	2.99
❑4, Dec 2000	2.99
❑4/Variant, Dec 2000	2.99

STAR WARS: DROIDS (VOL. 1)
DARK HORSE

❑1, Apr 1994; enhanced cover	3.00
❑2, May 1994	2.75
❑3, Jun 1994	2.75
❑4, Jul 1994	2.50
❑5, Aug 1994	2.50
❑6, Sep 1994	2.50
❑Special 1, Jan 1995; Special edition; Reprints serial from Dark Horse Comics	2.50

STAR WARS: DROIDS (VOL. 2)
DARK HORSE

❑1, Apr 1995	2.50
❑2, May 1995	2.50
❑3, Jun 1995	2.50
❑4, Jul 1995	2.50
❑5, Sep 1995	2.50
❑6, Oct 1995	2.50
❑7, Nov 1995	2.50
❑8, Dec 1995	2.50

STAR WARS: EMPIRE
DARK HORSE

❑1, Sep 2002	2.99
❑2, Oct 2002	2.99
❑3, Nov 2002	2.99
❑4, Dec 2002	2.99
❑5, Jan 2003	2.99
❑6 2003	2.99
❑7 2003	2.99
❑8 2003	2.99
❑9, Jul 2003	2.99
❑10, Jul 2003	2.99
❑11, Aug 2003	2.99
❑12, Sep 2003	2.99
❑13, Oct 2003	2.99
❑14, Nov 2003	2.99
❑15, Dec 2003	2.99
❑16, Jan 2004	2.99
❑17, Feb 2004	2.99
❑18, Mar 2004	2.99
❑19, Apr 2004	2.99
❑20, May 2004	2.99
❑21, Jun 2004	2.99
❑22, Jul 2004	2.99
❑23, Aug 2004	2.99
❑24, Sep 2004	2.99
❑25, Oct 2004	2.99

❑26, Nov 2004 .... 2.99
❑27, Dec 2004 .... 2.99
❑28, Jan 2005 .... 2.99
❑29, Feb 2005 .... 2.99
❑30, Jun 2005 .... 3.00
❑31, Jul 2005 .... 2.99
❑32, Aug 2005 .... 2.99
❑33, Sep 2005 .... 2.99
❑34, Oct 2005 .... 2.99
❑35 2005 JJM (w) 2.99
❑36 .... 2.99
❑37, Nov 2005 .... 2.99
❑38, Jan 2006 .... 2.99
❑39, Mar 2006 .... 2.99
❑40, Mar 2006 .... 2.99

STAR WARS: EMPIRE'S END
Dark Horse
❑1, Oct 1995; cardstock cover 2.95
❑2, Nov 1995; cardstock cover 2.95

STAR WARS: EPISODE I ANAKIN SKYWALKER
Dark Horse
❑1, May 1999; cardstock cover 2.95
❑1/Variant, May 1999 .... 2.95

STAR WARS: EPISODE III: REVENGE OF THE SITH
Dark Horse
❑1, 2005 .... 2.99
❑2, 2005 .... 2.99
❑3, May 2005 .... 3.00
❑4, May 2005 .... 3.00

STAR WARS: EPISODE I OBI-WAN KENOBI
Dark Horse
❑1, May 1999; cardstock cover 2.95
❑1/Variant, May 1999 .... 2.95

STAR WARS: EPISODE I QUEEN AMIDALA
Dark Horse
❑1, Jun 1999; cardstock cover 2.95
❑1/Variant, Jun 1999 .... 2.95

STAR WARS: EPISODE I QUI-GON JINN
Dark Horse
❑1, Jun 1999; cardstock cover 2.95
❑1/Variant, Jun 1999 .... 2.95

STAR WARS: EPISODE I THE PHANTOM MENACE
Dark Horse
❑1, May 1999; cardstock cover 2.95
❑1/Variant, May 1999 .... 2.95
❑2, May 1999; cardstock cover 2.95
❑2/Variant, May 1999 .... 2.95
❑3, May 1999; cardstock cover 2.95
❑3/Variant, May 1999 .... 2.95
❑4, May 1999; cardstock cover 2.95
❑4/Variant, May 1999 .... 2.95

STAR WARS: EPISODE II: ATTACK OF THE CLONES
Dark Horse
❑1 .... 3.99
❑1/Variant 3.99
❑2 .... 3.99
❑2/Variant 3.99
❑3 .... 3.99
❑3/Variant 3.99
❑4 .... 3.99
❑4/Variant 3.99

STAR WARS: GENERAL GRIEVOUS
Dark Horse
❑1 2005 .... 2.99
❑2, May 2005 .... 2.99
❑3 2005 .... 2.99
❑4, Sep 2005 .... 2.99

STAR WARS HANDBOOK
Dark Horse
❑1, Jul 1998; X-Wing Rogue Squadron profiles 2.95
❑2, Jul 1999; Crimson Empire profiles 2.95

STAR WARS: HEIR TO THE EMPIRE
Dark Horse
❑1, Oct 1995 .... 2.95
❑2, Nov 1995 .... 2.95
❑3, Dec 1995 .... 2.95
❑4, Jan 1996 .... 2.95
❑5, Mar 1996 .... 2.95
❑6, Apr 1996 .... 2.95

STAR WARS IN 3-D
Blackthorne
❑1, Dec 1987; a.k.a. Blackthorne in 3-D #30 .... 2.50

STAR WARS: INFINITIES: A NEW HOPE
Dark Horse
❑1, May 2001 .... 2.99
❑2, Jun 2001 .... 2.99
❑3, Jul 2001 .... 2.99
❑4, Aug 2001 .... 2.99

STAR WARS: INFINITIES: RETURN OF THE JEDI
Dark Horse
❑1, Dec 2003 .... 2.99
❑2, Jan 2004 .... 2.99
❑3, Mar 2004 .... 2.99
❑4, Mar 2004 .... 2.99

STAR WARS: INFINITIES: THE EMPIRE STRIKES BACK
Dark Horse
❑1, Jul 2002 .... 2.99
❑2, Aug 2002 .... 2.99
❑3, Sep 2002 .... 2.99
❑4, Oct 2002 .... 2.99

STAR WARS: JABBA THE HUTT
Dark Horse
❑1, Apr 1995 .... 2.50
❑2, Jun 1995 .... 2.50
❑3, Aug 1995 .... 2.50
❑4, Feb 1996 .... 2.50

STAR WARS: JANGO FETT: OPEN SEASONS
Dark Horse
❑1, Apr 2002 .... 2.99
❑2, May 2002 .... 2.99
❑3, Jun 2002 .... 2.99
❑4, Jul 2002 .... 2.99

STAR WARS: JEDI - AAYLA SECURA
Dark Horse
❑1, Aug 2003 .... 4.99

STAR WARS: JEDI ACADEMY: LEVIATHAN
Dark Horse
❑1, Oct 1998 .... 2.95
❑2, Nov 1998 .... 2.95
❑3, Dec 1998 .... 2.95
❑4, Jan 1999 .... 2.95

STAR WARS: JEDI COUNCIL: ACTS OF WAR
Dark Horse
❑1, Jun 2000 .... 2.95
❑2, Jul 2000 .... 2.95
❑3, Aug 2000 .... 2.95
❑4, Sep 2000 .... 2.95

STAR WARS: JEDI - DOOKU CLONE WARS
Dark Horse
❑1, Dec 2003 .... 4.99

STAR WARS: JEDI - MACE WINDU
Dark Horse
❑1, Feb 2003 .... 4.99

STAR WARS: JEDI QUEST
Dark Horse
❑1, Sep 2001 .... 2.99
❑2, Oct 2001 .... 2.99
❑3, Nov 2001 .... 2.99
❑4, Dec 2001 .... 2.99

STAR WARS: JEDI - SHAAK TI
Dark Horse
❑1, May 2003 .... 4.99

STAR WARS: JEDI VS. SITH
Dark Horse
❑1, Apr 2001 .... 2.99
❑2, May 2001 .... 2.99
❑3, Jun 2001 .... 2.99
❑4, Jul 2001 .... 2.99
❑5, Aug 2001 .... 2.99
❑6, Sep 2001 .... 2.99

STAR WARS: JEDI - YODA
Dark Horse
❑1, Aug 2004 .... 5.00

STAR WARS: KNIGHTS OF THE OLD REPUBLIC
Dark Horse
❑1, Mar 2006 .... 2.99
❑2, Apr 2006 .... 2.99
❑3, May 2006 .... 2.99
❑4, Jun 2006 .... 2.99
❑5, Jul 2006 .... 2.99
❑6, Aug 2006 .... 2.99

STAR WARS: KNIGHTS OF THE OLD REPUBLIC 25¢ FLIP BOOK
Dark Horse
❑1, Mar 2006 .... 0.25

STAR WARS: LEGACY
Dark Horse
❑0, Jul 2006 .... 2.99
❑1, Jun 2006 .... 2.99

STAR WARS: MARA JADE
Dark Horse
❑1, Aug 1998 .... 3.00
❑2, Sep 1998 2: Mara Jade 2.95
❑3, Oct 1998 .... 2.95
❑4, Nov 1998; Darth Vader cameo; Luke Skywalker cameo; Emperor Palpatine cameo 2.95
❑5, Dec 1998 .... 2.95
❑6, Jan 1999 .... 2.95

STAR WARS: OBSESSION
Dark Horse
❑1, Nov 2004 .... 8.00
❑2, Dec 2004 .... 4.00
❑3, Jan 2005 .... 2.99
❑4, Feb 2005 .... 2.99
❑5 2005 .... 2.99

STAR WARS: PURGE
Dark Horse
❑1, Dec 2005 .... 2.99

STAR WARS: QUI-GON & OBI-WAN: LAST STAND ON ORD MANTELL
Dark Horse
❑1/A, Dec 2000; Obi-Wan leaping on cover, Qui-Gon standing 2.99
❑1/B, Dec 2000; Qui-gon and Obi-Wan standing on cover, Obi-Wan has light sabre out 2.99
❑1/C, Dec 2000 .... 2.99
❑2/A, Feb 2001; Drawn cover 2.99
❑2/B, Feb 2001 .... 2.99
❑3/A, Mar 2001; Drawn cover 2.99
❑3/B, Mar 2001 .... 2.99

STAR WARS: QUI-GON & OBI-WAN: THE AURORIENT EXPRESS
Dark Horse
❑1, Feb 2002 .... 2.99
❑2, May 2002 .... 2.99

STAR WARS: REBELLION
Dark Horse
❑1, May 2006 .... 2.99
❑3, Jun 2006 .... 2.99

STAR WARS: RETURN OF THE JEDI
Marvel
❑1, Oct 1983, AW (a); Reprints Marvel Super Special #27 .... 4.00
❑2, Nov 1983, AW (a); Reprints Marvel Super Special #27 .... 4.00
❑3, Dec 1983, AW (a); Reprints Marvel Super Special #27 .... 4.00
❑4, Jan 1984, AW (a); Reprints Marvel Super Special #27 .... 4.00

STAR WARS: RETURN OF THE JEDI - MANGA
Dark Horse
❑1, Jul 1999 .... 9.95
❑2, Aug 1999 .... 9.95
❑3, Sep 1999 .... 9.95
❑4, Oct 1999 .... 9.95

STAR WARS: RIVER OF CHAOS
Dark Horse
❑1, Jun 1995 .... 2.50
❑2, Jul 1995 .... 2.50
❑3, Sep 1995 .... 2.50
❑4, Nov 1995 .... 2.50

Other grades: Multiply price above by 5/6 for VF/NM • 2/3 for VERY FINE • 1/3 for FINE • 1/5 for VERY GOOD • 1/8 for GOOD

Storm

X-Men star Ororo gets limited series

Stormwatch

Sort of a super-powered U.N. task force

Stormwatch (2nd Series)

Laid groundwork for The Authority

Strange Adventures

Animal Man and Deadman got their start here

Strange Attractors

Curator finds mysterious amulet

N-MINT

STAR WARS: SHADOWS OF EMPIRE: EVOLUTION
DARK HORSE

❑1, Feb 1998 ... 2.95
❑2, Mar 1998 ... 2.95
❑3, Apr 1998 ... 2.95
❑4, May 1998 ... 2.95
❑5, Jun 1998 ... 2.95

STAR WARS: SHADOWS OF THE EMPIRE
DARK HORSE

❑1, May 1996 ... 2.95
❑2, Jun 1996 ... 2.95
❑3, Jul 1996 ... 2.95
❑4, Aug 1996 ... 2.95
❑5, Sep 1996 ... 2.95
❑6, Oct 1996 ... 2.95

STAR WARS: SHADOW STALKER
DARK HORSE

❑1, Sep 1997 ... 2.95

STAR WARS: SPLINTER OF THE MIND'S EYE
DARK HORSE

❑1, Dec 1995 ... 2.50
❑2, Feb 1996 ... 2.50
❑3, Apr 1996 ... 2.50
❑4, Jun 1996 ... 2.50

STAR WARS: STARFIGHTER: CROSSBONES
DARK HORSE

❑1, Jan 2002 ... 2.99
❑2, Feb 2002 ... 2.99
❑3, Mar 2002 ... 2.99

STAR WARS: TAG & BINK ARE DEAD
DARK HORSE

❑1, Oct 2001 ... 2.99
❑2, Nov 2001 ... 2.99

STAR WARS: TAG & BINK EPISODE I - REVENGE OF THE CLONE MENACE
DARK HORSE

❑1, May 2006 ... 3.99

STAR WARS TALES
DARK HORSE

❑1, Sep 1999 PD (w) ... 4.95
❑2, Dec 1999 ... 4.95
❑3, Mar 2000 ... 4.95
❑4, Jun 2000 ... 4.95
❑5, Sep 2000 ... 5.95
❑5/PH, Sep 2000 ... 5.95
❑6, Dec 2000 ... 5.95
❑7, Mar 2001 ... 5.99
❑8, Jun 2001 ... 5.99
❑9, Sep 2001 ... 5.99
❑10, Dec 2001 ... 5.99
❑11, Mar 2002 ... 5.99
❑12, Jun 2002 ... 5.99
❑13, Sep 2002 ... 5.99
❑14, Dec 2002 ... 5.99
❑15, Mar 2003 ... 5.99
❑16, Jun 2003 ... 5.99
❑17, Oct 2003 ... 5.99
❑18, Dec 2003 ... 5.99

N-MINT

❑19, Apr 2004 ... 5.99
❑20, Aug 2004 ... 5.99
❑21 2005 ... 5.99
❑22/Art 2005 ... 7.00
❑22/Photo 2005 ... 5.99
❑23/Art 2005 ... 7.00
❑23/Photo 2005 ... 5.99
❑24/Art, Aug 2005 ... 7.00
❑24/Photo, Aug 2005 ... 5.99

STAR WARS TALES- A JEDI'S WEAPON
DARK HORSE

❑1 ... 1.00

STAR WARS: TALES: A JEDI'S WEAPON
DARK HORSE

❑1, May 2002 ... 2.00

STAR WARS: TALES FROM MOS EISLEY
DARK HORSE

❑1, Mar 1996 ... 2.95

STAR WARS: TALES OF THE JEDI
DARK HORSE

❑1, Oct 1993 ... 4.00
❑1/Special, Oct 1993 ... 6.00
❑2, Nov 1993 ... 3.50
❑2/Special, Nov 1993 ... 5.00
❑3, Dec 1993 ... 3.25
❑3/Special, Dec 1993 ... 5.00
❑4, Jan 1994 ... 2.50
❑4/Special, Jan 1994 ... 5.00
❑5, Feb 1994 ... 2.50
❑5/Special, Feb 1994 ... 5.00

STAR WARS: TALES OF THE JEDI: DARK LORDS OF THE SITH
DARK HORSE

❑1, Oct 1994 ... 3.00
❑2, Nov 1994 ... 3.00
❑3, Dec 1994 ... 3.00
❑4, Jan 1995 ... 3.00
❑5, Feb 1995 ... 3.00
❑6, Mar 1995 ... 3.00

STAR WARS: TALES OF THE JEDI: FALL OF THE SITH EMPIRE
DARK HORSE

❑1, Jun 1997; Man with marionettes on cover ... 2.95
❑1/A, Jun 1997; Variant cover, flame in background ... 2.95
❑2, Jul 1997 ... 2.95
❑3, Aug 1997 ... 2.95
❑4, Sep 1997 ... 2.95
❑5, Oct 1997 ... 2.95

STAR WARS: TALES OF THE JEDI: REDEMPTION
DARK HORSE

❑1, Jul 1998 ... 2.95
❑2, Aug 1998 ... 2.95
❑3, Sep 1998 ... 2.95
❑4, Oct 1998 ... 2.95
❑5, Nov 1998 ... 2.95

N-MINT

STAR WARS: TALES OF THE JEDI: THE FREEDON NADD UPRISING
DARK HORSE

❑1, Aug 1994 ... 2.50
❑2, Sep 1994 ... 2.50

STAR WARS: TALES OF THE JEDI: THE GOLDEN AGE OF THE SITH
DARK HORSE

❑0, ca. 1996 ... 0.99
❑1, Oct 1996 ... 2.95
❑2, Nov 1996 ... 2.95
❑3, Dec 1996 ... 2.95
❑4, Jan 1997 ... 2.95
❑5, Feb 1997 ... 2.95

STAR WARS: TALES OF THE JEDI: THE SITH WAR
DARK HORSE

❑1, Aug 1995 ... 2.50
❑2, Sep 1995 ... 2.50
❑3, Oct 1995 ... 2.50
❑4, Nov 1995 ... 2.50
❑5, Dec 1995 ... 2.50
❑6, Jan 1996 ... 2.50

STAR WARS: THE BOUNTY HUNTERS: AURRA SING
DARK HORSE

❑1, Jul 1999 ... 2.95

STAR WARS: THE BOUNTY HUNTERS: KENIX KIL
DARK HORSE

❑1, Oct 1999; one shot ... 2.95

STAR WARS: THE BOUNTY HUNTERS: SCOUNDREL'S WAGES
DARK HORSE

❑1, Aug 1999 ... 2.95

STAR WARS: THE EMPIRE STRIKES BACK: MANGA
DARK HORSE

❑1, Jan 1999 ... 9.95
❑2, Feb 1999 ... 9.95
❑3, Mar 1999 ... 9.95
❑4, Apr 1999 ... 9.95

STAR WARS: THE JABBA TAPE
DARK HORSE

❑1, Dec 1998 ... 2.95

STAR WARS: THE LAST COMMAND
DARK HORSE

❑1, Nov 1997 ... 3.50
❑2, Dec 1997 ... 3.00
❑3, Feb 1998 ... 3.00
❑4, Mar 1998 ... 3.00
❑5, Apr 1998 ... 3.00
❑6, Jul 1998 ... 2.95

STAR WARS: THE PROTOCOL OFFENSIVE
DARK HORSE

❑1, Sep 1997; prestige format; Co-written by Anthony Daniels, the actor who played C-3PO ... 4.95

STAR WARS: THE RETURN OF TAG & BINK SPECIAL EDITION
DARK HORSE

❑1, May 2006 ... 3.99

STAR WARS: UNDERWORLD: THE YAVIN VASSILIKA
DARK HORSE

❑1/A, Dec 2000; Drawn cover with Han Solo, Lando Calrisian, and Boba Fett ... 2.99
❑1/B, Dec 2000; Painted cover with Jabba the Hutt ... 2.99
❑2/A, Jan 2001 ... 2.99
❑2/B, Jan 2001 ... 2.99
❑3/A, Feb 2001; Drawn cover with Han Solo, Lando Calrisian, and Boba Fett ... 2.99
❑3/B, Feb 2001 ... 2.99
❑4/A, Mar 2001 ... 2.99
❑4/B, Mar 2001 ... 2.99
❑5/A, Apr 2001 ... 2.99
❑5/B, Apr 2001 ... 2.99

STAR WARS: UNION
DARK HORSE

❑1, Nov 1999 ... 14.00
❑2, Dec 1999 ... 10.00
❑3, Jan 2000 ... 7.00
❑4, Feb 2000; Wedding of Luke Skywalker & Mara Jade ... 5.00

STAR WARS: VADER'S QUEST
DARK HORSE

❑1, Feb 1999 ... 2.95
❑2, Mar 1999 ... 2.95
❑3, Apr 1999 ... 2.95
❑4, May 1999 ... 2.95

STAR WARS: VALENTINES STORY
DARK HORSE

❑1, Feb 2003 ... 3.50

STAR WARS: X-WING ROGUE LEADER
DARK HORSE

❑1 ... 2.99
❑2, Oct 2005 ... 2.99
❑3, Dec 2005 ... 2.99

STAR WARS: X-WING ROGUE SQUADRON
DARK HORSE

❑½, Feb 1997; Wizard mail-in edition ... 3.00
❑½/Platinum, Feb 1997; Platinum edition ... 5.00
❑1, Jul 1995 ... 4.00
❑2, Aug 1995 ... 3.50
❑3, Sep 1995 ... 3.50
❑4, Oct 1995 ... 3.50
❑5, Feb 1996 ... 3.00
❑6, Mar 1996 ... 3.00
❑7, Apr 1996 ... 3.00
❑8, Jun 1996 ... 3.00
❑9, Jul 1996 ... 3.00
❑10, Jul 1996 ... 3.00
❑11, Aug 1996 ... 3.00
❑12, Sep 1996 ... 3.00
❑13, Oct 1996 ... 3.00
❑14, Dec 1996 ... 3.00
❑15, Jan 1997 ... 3.00
❑16, Feb 1997 ... 3.00
❑17, Mar 1997 ... 3.00
❑18, Apr 1997 ... 3.00
❑19, May 1997 ... 3.00
❑20, Jun 1997 ... 3.00
❑21, Aug 1997 ... 3.00
❑22, Sep 1997 ... 3.00
❑23, Oct 1997 ... 3.00
❑24, Nov 1997 ... 3.00
❑25, Dec 1997; Giant-size O: Baron Fel. ... 4.00
❑26, Jan 1998 ... 2.95
❑27, Feb 1998 ... 2.95
❑28, Mar 1998 ... 2.95
❑29, Apr 1998 ... 2.95
❑30, May 1998 ... 2.95
❑31, Jun 1998 ... 2.95
❑32, Jul 1998 ... 2.95
❑33, Aug 1998 ... 2.95
❑34, Sep 1998 ... 2.95
❑35, Nov 1998 ... 2.95
❑Special 1, Aug 1995; promotional giveaway with Kellogg's Apple Jacks; Promotional giveaway with Kellogg's Apple Jacks ... 1.00

STAR WEEVILS
RIP OFF

❑1 ... 1.00

STAR WESTERN
AVALON

❑1 ... 5.95
❑2; John Wayne feature ... 5.95
❑3; Clint Eastwood feature ... 5.95
❑4 ... 5.95
❑5 ... 5.95

S.T.A.T.
MAJESTIC

❑1, Dec 1993 ... 2.25
❑1/Variant, Dec 1993; foil cover ... 2.25

STATIC
DC / MILESTONE

❑1, Jun 1993 1: Hotstreak. 1: Frieda Goren. 1: Static ... 2.00
❑1/CS, Jun 1993; 1: Hotstreak. 1: Frieda Goren. 1: Static. poster; trading card; Collector's Set ... 3.00
❑1/Silver, Jun 1993; Silver (limited promotional) edition 1: Hotstreak. 1: Frieda Goren. 1: Static. ... 3.00
❑2, Jul 1993 O: Static. 1: Tarmack. ... 1.50
❑3, Aug 1993 ... 1.50
❑4, Sep 1993 1: Don Giacomo Cornelius. ... 1.50
❑5, Oct 1993 1: Commando X. ... 1.50
❑6, Nov 1993 ... 1.50
❑7, Dec 1993 ... 1.50
❑8, Jan 1994; Shadow War ... 1.50
❑9, Feb 1994 1: Virus. ... 1.50
❑10, Mar 1994 1: Puff. 1: Coil. ... 1.50
❑11, Apr 1994 ... 1.50
❑12, May 1994 1: Snakefinger. ... 1.50
❑13, Jun 1994 ... 1.50
❑14, Aug 1994; Giant-size ... 2.50
❑15, Sep 1994 ... 1.75
❑16, Oct 1994 1: Joyride. ... 1.75
❑17, Nov 1994 ... 1.75
❑18, Dec 1994 ... 1.75
❑19, Jan 1995 ... 1.75
❑20, Feb 1995 ... 1.75
❑21, Mar 1995 A: Blood Syndicate. ... 1.75
❑22, Apr 1995 ... 1.75
❑23, Jun 1995 ... 1.75
❑24, Jul 1995 ... 1.75
❑25, Jul 1995; Double-size ... 3.95
❑26, Aug 1995 ... 2.50
❑27, Sep 1995 ... 2.50
❑28, Oct 1995 ... 2.50
❑29, Nov 1995 ... 2.50
❑30, Dec 1995 D: Larry. ... 2.50
❑31, Jan 1996 GK (a) ... 0.99
❑32, Feb 1996 ... 2.50
❑33, Mar 1996 ... 2.50
❑34, Apr 1996 ... 2.50
❑35, May 1996 ... 2.50
❑36, Jun 1996 ... 2.50
❑37, Jul 1996 ... 2.50
❑38, Aug 1996 ... 2.50
❑39, Sep 1996 ... 2.50
❑40, Oct 1996 KP (a) ... 2.50
❑41, Nov 1996 ... 2.50
❑42, Dec 1996 ... 2.50
❑43, Jan 1997 ... 2.50
❑44, Feb 1997 ... 2.50
❑45, Mar 1997 ... 2.50
❑46, Apr 1997 ... 2.50
❑47, May 1997 ... 2.50

STATIC SHOCK!: REBIRTH OF THE COOL
DC / MILESTONE

❑1, Jan 2001 ... 2.50
❑2, Feb 2001 ... 2.50
❑3, May 2001 ... 2.50
❑4, Sep 2001 ... 2.50

STAY PUFFED
IMAGE

❑1, Jan 2004 ... 3.50

STEADY BEAT
TOKYOPOP

❑1, Oct 2005 ... 9.99

STEALTH FORCE
MALIBU

❑1, Jul 1987 ... 1.95
❑2, Aug 1987 ... 1.95
❑3, Sep 1987 ... 1.95
❑4, Oct 1987 ... 1.95
❑5, Nov 1987 ... 1.95
❑6, Dec 1987 ... 1.95
❑7, Jan 1988 ... 1.95
❑8, Feb 1988; Eternity begins as publisher ... 1.95

STEALTH SQUAD
PETRA

❑0 ... 2.50
❑1 ... 2.50
❑2 ... 2.50
❑3 ... 2.50
❑4 ... 2.50

STEAM DETECTIVES
VIZ

❑1, Aug 1998, b&w ... 15.95

STEAMPUNK
DC / WILDSTORM

❑1, Apr 2000 ... 2.50
❑2, May 2000 ... 2.50
❑3, Jun 2000 ... 2.50
❑4, Jul 2000 ... 2.50
❑5, Oct 2000 ... 2.50
❑6, Jan 2001 ... 2.50
❑7, Apr 2001 ... 2.50
❑8, Jun 2001 ... 2.50
❑9, Sep 2001 ... 2.50
❑10, Jan 2002 ... 2.50
❑11, Apr 2002 ... 2.50
❑12, Jul 2002 ... 3.50
❑Book 2, ca. 2003 ... 14.95

STEAMPUNK: CATECHISM
DC / WILDSTORM

❑1, Jan 2000 ... 2.50

STECH
SILVERWOLF

❑1, Dec 1986, b&w ... 1.50

STEED AND MRS. PEEL
ECLIPSE

❑1, Dec 1990 ... 5.00
❑2, May 1991 ... 5.00
❑3 ... 5.00

STEEL
DC

❑0, Oct 1994 ... 1.50
❑1, Feb 1994 ... 1.50
❑2, Mar 1994 ... 1.50
❑3, Apr 1994 ... 1.50
❑4, May 1994 ... 1.50
❑5, Jun 1994 ... 1.50
❑6, Jul 1994 A: Hardware. ... 1.50
❑7, Aug 1994 A: Icon. A: Hardware. ... 1.50
❑8, Sep 1994 ... 1.50
❑9, Nov 1994 ... 1.50
❑10, Dec 1994 ... 1.50
❑11, Jan 1995 ... 1.50
❑12, Feb 1995 ... 1.50
❑13, Mar 1995 ... 1.50
❑14, Apr 1995 ... 1.50
❑15, May 1995 ... 1.50
❑16, Jun 1995 ... 1.95
❑17, Jul 1995 ... 1.95
❑18, Aug 1995 ... 1.95
❑19, Sep 1995 ... 1.95
❑20, Oct 1995 ... 1.95
❑21, Nov 1995; Underworld Unleashed ... 1.95
❑22, Dec 1995 A: Supergirl. A: Eradicator. ... 1.95
❑23, Jan 1996 ... 1.95
❑24, Feb 1996 ... 1.95
❑25, Mar 1996 ... 1.95
❑26, May 1996 ... 1.95
❑27, Jun 1996 ... 1.95
❑28, Jul 1996 V: Plasmus ... 1.95
❑29, Aug 1996 ... 1.95
❑30, Sep 1996 ... 1.95
❑31, Oct 1996 ... 1.95
❑32, Nov 1996 V: Blockbuster. ... 1.95
❑33, Dec 1996 ... 1.95
❑34, Jan 1997; TP (a); A: Margot. new armor ... 1.95
❑35, Feb 1997 TP (a) ... 1.95
❑36, Mar 1997 TP (a) ... 1.95
❑37, Apr 1997 ... 1.95
❑38, May 1997 ... 1.95

Other grades: Multiply price above by 5/6 for VF/NM • 2/3 for VERY FINE • 1/3 for FINE • 1/5 for VERY GOOD • 1/8 for GOOD

Strangehaven	Strangers	Strangers in Paradise	Strange Sports Stories	Strange Sports Stories (Adventure)
				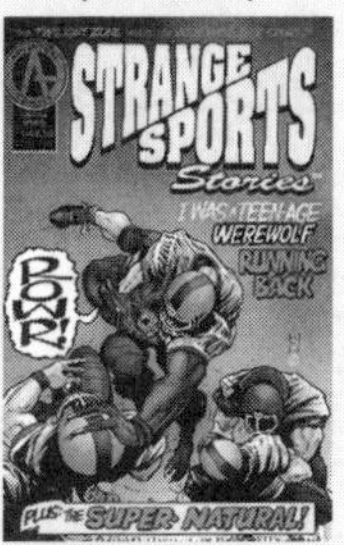
Acclaimed title from Gary Spencer Millidge ©Abiogenesis	Cable car struck by energy, mutates riders ©Malibu	Long-running relationship title by Terry Moore ©Antarctic	Mixed fantasy elements with sports themes ©DC	They might have seen the movie "Teen Wolf" ©Adventure

N-MINT

❑39, Jun 1997 TP (a) 1.95
❑40, Jul 1997 1: new hammer. 2.25
❑41, Aug 1997 1.95
❑42, Sep 1997 TP (a) 1.95
❑43, Oct 1997; TP (a); A: Superman. Genesis 1.95
❑44, Nov 1997 1.95
❑45, Dec 1997; TP (a); Face cover 1.95
❑46, Jan 1998 TP (a); A: Superboy. 1.95
❑47, Feb 1998 2.50
❑48, Mar 1998 BSz (a) 2.50
❑49, Apr 1998 TP (a) 2.50
❑50, May 1998; TP (a); A: Superman. Millennium Giants 2.50
❑51, Jun 1998 2.50
❑52, Jul 1998 TP (a) 2.50
❑Annual 1, ca. 1994; Elseworlds 4.00
❑Annual 2, ca. 1995; Year One 3.95

STEEL ANGEL
GAUNTLET

❑1 2.50

STEEL CLAW
FLEETWAY-QUALITY

❑1, Dec 1986 1.50
❑2, Jan 1987 1.50
❑3, Feb 1987 1.50
❑4, Mar 1987 1.50
❑5, Apr 1987 1.50

STEELDRAGON STORIES
STEELDRAGON

❑1 1.50

STEELE DESTINIES
NIGHTSCAPES

❑1, Apr 1995, b&w 2.95
❑2, Jun 1995, b&w 2.95
❑3, Sep 1995, b&w 2.95

STEELGRIP STARKEY
MARVEL / EPIC

❑1, Jun 1986 1.75
❑2, Aug 1986 1.75
❑3, Nov 1986 1.75
❑4, Dec 1986 1.75
❑5, Jan 1987 1.75
❑6, May 1987 1.75

STEEL PULSE
TRUE FICTION

❑1, Mar 1986, b&w 2.00
❑2, b&w 2.00
❑3, b&w 2.00
❑4 3.50

STEEL STERLING
ARCHIE / RED CIRCLE

❑4, Jan 1984; Red Circle publishes; was Shield - Steel Sterling 1.00
❑5, Mar 1984, Archie publishes 1.00
❑6, May 1984 1.00
❑7, Jul 1984 1.00

STEEL, THE INDESTRUCTIBLE MAN
DC

❑1, Mar 1978, DH (a); 1&O: Steel 5.00
❑2, Apr 1978 2.00
❑3, Jun 1978 2.00

N-MINT

❑4, Sep 1978 2.00
❑5, Nov 1978 2.00

STEEL: THE OFFICIAL COMIC ADAPTATION OF THE WARNER BROS. MOTION PICTURE
DC

❑1, Sep 1997; prestige format 4.95

STEELTOWN ROCKERS
MARVEL

❑1, Apr 1990 1.00
❑2, May 1990 1.00
❑3, Jun 1990 1.00
❑4, Jul 1990 1.00
❑5, Aug 1990 1.00
❑6, Sep 1990 1.00

STELLAR COMICS
STELLAR

❑1 2.50

STELLAR LOSERS
ANTARCTIC

❑1, Feb 1993, b&w 2.50
❑2, Apr 1993, b&w 2.50
❑3, Jun 1993, b&w 2.50

STEPHEN DARKLORD
RAK

❑1, b&w 1.75
❑2, b&w 1.75
❑3, b&w 1.75

STEPS TO A DRUG FREE LIFE
DAVID G. BROWN

❑1, Feb 1998; promotional comic done for the Alcohol and Drug Council of Greater L.A. and Share Inc. 1.00

STERN WHEELER
SPOTLIGHT

❑1 1.75

STEVEN
KITCHEN SINK

❑1, b&w 3.00
❑2, b&w 3.00
❑3, May 1999, b&w 3.00
❑4, b&w 3.00
❑5 3.50
❑6, b&w 3.50
❑7 3.50
❑8, Dec 1996, b&w; over-sized; cardstock cover 3.50

STEVEN PRESENTS DUMPY
FANTAGRAPHICS

❑1, May 1999, b&w 2.95

STEVEN'S COMICS
DK PRESS / YELL COMICS

❑3, b&w 3.00
❑1 1.00
❑2 2.00
❑4 3.50

STEVE ZODIAK AND THE FIREBALL XL-5
GOLD KEY

❑1, Jan 1964 65.00

N-MINT

STEWART THE RAT
ABOUT

❑1, Feb 2003 3.95

STICKBOY (FANTAGRAPHICS)
FANTAGRAPHICS

❑1, b&w 2.50
❑1/2nd 2.75
❑2, b&w 2.50
❑3, b&w 2.50
❑4, Nov 1990, b&w 2.95
❑5, Feb 1992, b&w 2.50

STICKBOY (REVOLUTIONARY)
REVOLUTIONARY

❑1 2.95
❑2 2.95
❑3 2.95
❑4, Nov 1990 2.95

STICKBOY (STARHEAD)
STARHEAD

❑1, b&w 2.50
❑2, b&w 2.50
❑3, b&w 2.50
❑4, b&w 2.50
❑5, b&w 2.50
❑6, b&w 2.50

STIG'S INFERNO
VORTEX

❑1, ca. 1989 2.00
❑2 1989 2.00
❑3 1989 3.50
❑4 1989 3.50
❑5 1989 1.75
❑6 1989, b&w 1.50
❑7 1989, b&w 1.50

STIMULATOR
FANTAGRAPHICS / EROS

❑1, b&w 2.50

STING
ARTLINE

❑1; flip book with Killer Synthetic Toads 2.50

STING OF THE GREEN HORNET
NOW

❑1, Jun 1992, bagged with poster 2.50
❑1/CS, Jun 1992 2.75
❑2, Jul 1992 2.50
❑2/CS, Jul 1992, bagged with poster . 2.75
❑3, Aug 1992 2.50
❑3/CS, Aug 1992, bagged with poster 2.75
❑4, Sep 1992 2.50
❑4/CS, Sep 1992, stitched with poster 2.75

STINKTOOTH
STINKTOOTH

❑1, Nov 1991 1.00

STINZ (1ST SERIES)
FANTAGRAPHICS

❑1, Aug 1989, b&w 4.00
❑2, Oct 1989, b&w 3.00
❑3, ca. 1989, b&w 3.00
❑4, Feb 1990, b&w; Moves to Brave New Words 2.50
❑5, ca. 1990; Published by Brave New Words 2.50

Other grades: Multiply price above by 5/6 for VF/NM • 2/3 for VERY FINE • 1/3 for FINE • 1/5 for VERY GOOD • 1/8 for GOOD

STINZ (2ND SERIES)
Brave New Words

- ❑1, ca. 1990, b&w 2.50
- ❑3, ca. 1991 ..... 2.50
- ❑2, ca. 1991, b&w 2.50

STINZ (3RD SERIES)
Mu

- ❑1, Oct 1994 ..... 2.50
- ❑2, Oct 1994 ..... 2.50
- ❑3, Feb 1995 ..... 2.50
- ❑4, Oct 1995 ..... 2.95
- ❑5, Jan 1997; Last Mu issue; moves to A Fine Line 4.95
- ❑6, Jun 1998; First A Fine Line Press issue 5.50
- ❑7, Aug 1998 ..... 4.95

STINZ: WARHORSE
Mu

- ❑1, Mar 1993 ..... 9.95

STOKER'S DRACULA
Marvel

- ❑1, 2004 ..... 3.99
- ❑2, ca. 2004 ..... 3.99
- ❑3, 2005 ..... 3.99
- ❑4, 2005 ..... 3.99

STONE
Image

- ❑1, Aug 1998 ..... 2.50
- ❑1/A, Aug 1998; Variant cover with white background 2.50
- ❑1/B, Aug 1998; Variant cover with side view of Stone, jewel showing in armband 2.50
- ❑2, Sep 1998 ..... 2.50
- ❑2/A, Sep 1998; DFE chrome cover; reprints indicia from #1 ..... 6.00
- ❑2/B, Sep 1998; alternate cover (white border) 4.00
- ❑3, Nov 1998 ..... 2.50
- ❑4, Apr 1999 ..... 2.50

STONE (VOL. 2)
Image

- ❑1, Aug 1999 ..... 2.50
- ❑1/Variant, Aug 1999; Chrome cover 6.95
- ❑2, Sep 1999 ..... 2.50
- ❑3, Dec 1999 ..... 2.50

STONE COLD STEVE AUSTIN
Chaos

- ❑1, Oct 1999; cover says Nov, indicia says Oct 2.95
- ❑2, Nov 1999 ..... 2.95
- ❑3, Dec 1999 ..... 2.95
- ❑4, Jan 2000 ..... 2.95

STONE PROTECTORS
Harvey

- ❑1, May 1994 ..... 1.50
- ❑2 ..... 1.50
- ❑3, Sep 1994 ..... 1.50

STONEWALL IN THE SHENANDOAH
Heritage Collection

- ❑1, wraparound cover 3.50

STONEY BURKE
Dell

- ❑1, Jun 1963 ..... 25.00
- ❑2, Sep 1963 ..... 20.00

STORIES FROM BOSNIA
Drawn and Quarterly

- ❑1, b&w; Oversized; cardstock cover 3.95

STORM
Marvel

- ❑1, Feb 1996; enhanced cardstock cover 2.95
- ❑2, Mar 1996; enhanced cardstock cover 2.95
- ❑3, Apr 1996; enhanced cardstock cover 2.95
- ❑4, May 1996; enhanced cardstock cover 2.95

STORMBREAKER: THE SAGA OF BETA RAY BILL
Marvel

- ❑1, Mar 2005 ..... 2.99
- ❑2, Apr 2005 ..... 2.99
- ❑3, May 2005 ..... 2.99
- ❑4, Jun 2005 ..... 2.99
- ❑5, Jul 2005 ..... 2.99
- ❑6, Aug 2005 ..... 2.99

STORM (MINI-SERIES)
Marvel

- ❑1, May 2006 ..... 2.99
- ❑2, Jun 2006 ..... 2.99
- ❑3, Jul 2006 ..... 2.99
- ❑4, Aug 2006 ..... 2.99
- ❑5, Sep 2006 ..... 2.99

STORMQUEST
Caliber / Sky

- ❑1, Nov 1994 ..... 1.95
- ❑2, Dec 1994 ..... 1.95
- ❑3, ca. 1995 ..... 1.95
- ❑4, ca. 1995 ..... 1.95
- ❑5, ca. 1995 ..... 1.95
- ❑6, ca. 1955 ..... 1.95

STORMWATCH
Image

- ❑0, Aug 1993; JLee (w); 1: Backlash. 1: Flashpoint. 1: Nautica. 1: Warguard. Polybagged 2.50
- ❑1, Mar 1993 1: Hellstrike. 1: Battalion. 1: Diva. 1: Winter. 1: Strafe. 1: StormWatch. 1: Synergy. 1: Deathtrap. 1: Fuji. 2.50
- ❑1/Gold, Mar 1993; Gold foil cover 3.00
- ❑2, May 1993 1: Regent. 1: Cannon. 1: Fahrenheit. 1: Ion & Lance. 1.95
- ❑3, Jul 1993 1: LaSalle. A: Backlash. 1.95
- ❑4, Aug 1993; V: Warguard. cover says Oct 1.95
- ❑5, Nov 1993 ..... 1.95
- ❑6, Dec 1993 ..... 1.95
- ❑7, Feb 1994 1: Sunburst 1.95
- ❑8, Mar 1994 1: Rainmaker 1.95
- ❑9, Apr 1994 ..... 2.50
- ❑10, Jun 1994 ..... 1.95
- ❑10/A, Jun 1994; Variant edition cover; Variant edition cover 3.00
- ❑10/B, Jun 1994; variant cover 3.00
- ❑11, Aug 1994 ..... 1.95
- ❑12, Aug 1994 ..... 1.95
- ❑13, Sep 1994 ..... 1.95
- ❑14, Sep 1994 ..... 1.95
- ❑15, Oct 1994 ..... 1.95
- ❑16, Nov 1994 ..... 1.95
- ❑17, Dec 1994 ..... 2.50
- ❑18, Jan 1995 ..... 2.50
- ❑19, Feb 1995 ..... 2.50
- ❑20, Mar 1995 ..... 2.50
- ❑21, Apr 1995; 1: Tao. cover says #1. ..... 2.50
- ❑22, May 1995; bound-in trading cards 2.50
- ❑23, Jun 1995 ..... 2.50
- ❑24, Jul 1995 ..... 2.50
- ❑25, May 1994; cover says Jun 95; Images of Tomorrow; Shipped out of sequence as preview to future events (after #9) 2.50
- ❑25/2nd, Aug 1995 ..... 2.50
- ❑26, Aug 1995 ..... 2.50
- ❑27, Aug 1995 ..... 2.50
- ❑28, Sep 1995; 1: Swift. 1: Storm Force. 1: Flint. cover forms right half of diptych with issue #29 ..... 2.50
- ❑29, Oct 1995; indicia says Oct, cover says Nov 2.50
- ❑30, Nov 1995 ..... 2.50
- ❑31, Dec 1995 ..... 2.50
- ❑32, Jan 1996 ..... 2.50
- ❑33, Feb 1996 ..... 2.50
- ❑34, Mar 1996 ..... 2.50
- ❑35, Apr 1996 ..... 2.50
- ❑36, Jun 1996 ..... 2.50
- ❑37, Jul 1996; Giant-size 1: Hawksmoor. 1: Jenny Sparks 3.50
- ❑38, Aug 1996 ..... 2.50
- ❑39, Aug 1996 ..... 2.50
- ❑40, Oct 1996 ..... 2.50
- ❑41, Oct 1996 ..... 2.50
- ❑42, Nov 1996 ..... 2.50
- ❑43, Dec 1996 ..... 2.50
- ❑44/A, Jan 1997; O: Jenny Sparks. Torrid Tales cover; homages to various comics eras 2.50
- ❑44/B, Jan 1997; GK (c); O: Jenny Sparks. Pop Art Masterpiece cover 2.50
- ❑44/C, Jan 1997; O: Jenny Sparks. Who Watches The Weathermen cover 2.50
- ❑45, Feb 1997 ..... 2.50
- ❑46, Mar 1997 ..... 2.50
- ❑47, Apr 1997 ..... 2.50
- ❑48, May 1997 ..... 2.50
- ❑49, Jun 1997 ..... 2.50
- ❑50, Jul 1997; Giant-size 4.50
- ❑Special 1, Jan 1994 1: Argos 3.50
- ❑Special 2, May 1995 ..... 2.50

STORMWATCH (2ND SERIES)
Image

- ❑1, Oct 1997 ..... 2.50
- ❑1/A, Oct 1997; alternate cover (white background) 2.50
- ❑1/B, Oct 1997; Voyager pack 2.50
- ❑2, Nov 1997 ..... 2.50
- ❑3, Dec 1997 ..... 2.50
- ❑4, Feb 1998 ..... 2.50
- ❑5, Mar 1998 ..... 2.50
- ❑5/A, Mar 1998; alternate cover; group flying 2.50
- ❑6, Apr 1998 ..... 2.50
- ❑7, May 1998 ..... 2.50
- ❑8, Jun 1998 ..... 2.50
- ❑9, Jul 1998 ..... 2.50
- ❑10, Aug 1998 ..... 2.50
- ❑11, Sep 1998 ..... 2.50
- ❑12, Oct 1998 ..... 2.50

STORMWATCHER
Eclipse

- ❑1, Apr 1989, b&w 2.00
- ❑2, May 1989, b&w 2.00
- ❑3, b&w 2.00
- ❑4, b&w 2.00

STORMWATCH SOURCEBOOK
Image

- ❑1, Jan 1994 ..... 2.50

STORMWATCH: TEAM ACHILLES
WildStorm

- ❑1, Aug 2002 ..... 2.95
- ❑2, Oct 2002 ..... 2.95
- ❑3, Nov 2002 ..... 2.95
- ❑4, Dec 2002 ..... 2.95
- ❑5, Jan 2003 ..... 2.95
- ❑6, Feb 2003 ..... 2.95
- ❑7, Mar 2003 ..... 2.95
- ❑8, Apr 2003 ..... 2.95
- ❑9, May 2003 ..... 2.95
- ❑10, Jun 2003 ..... 2.95
- ❑11, Jul 2003 ..... 2.95
- ❑12, Aug 2003 ..... 2.95
- ❑13, Sep 2003 ..... 2.95
- ❑14, Oct 2003 ..... 2.95
- ❑15, Nov 2003 ..... 2.95
- ❑16, Dec 2003 ..... 2.95
- ❑17, Jan 2004 ..... 2.95
- ❑18, Feb 2004 ..... 2.95
- ❑19, Mar 2004 ..... 2.95
- ❑20, May 2004 ..... 2.95
- ❑21, Jun 2004 ..... 2.95
- ❑22, Jul 2004 ..... 2.95
- ❑23, Aug 2004 ..... 2.95

STORY OF ELECTRONICS: THE DISCOVERY THAT CHANGED THE WORLD!
Radio Shack

- ❑1, Sep 1980 ..... 2.50

STRAITJACKET STUDIOS PRESENTS
Straitjacket

- ❑0 ..... 2.95

STRAND
Trident

- ❑1, Nov 1990, b&w 2.50
- ❑2, b&w 2.50

STRANDED ON PLANET X
Radio

- ❑1, Jun 1999 ..... 2.95

STRANGE
Marvel

- ❑1, 2004 ..... 3.50
- ❑2, 2004 ..... 3.50
- ❑3, Dec 2004 ..... 3.50
- ❑4, 2005 ..... 3.50
- ❑5, 2005 ..... 3.50
- ❑6, Jul 2005 ..... 3.50

Other grades: Multiply price above by 5/6 for VF/NM • 2/3 for VERY FINE • 1/3 for FINE • 1/5 for VERY GOOD • 1/8 for GOOD

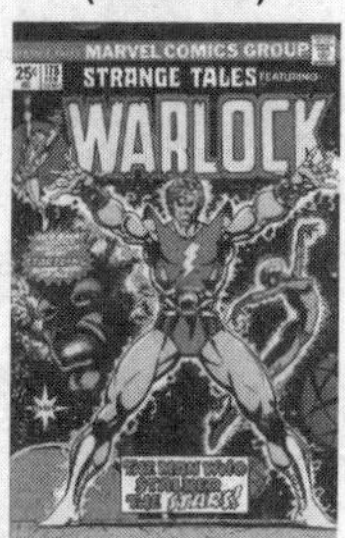

Strange Tales (1st Series)

Title gave birth to Dr. Strange and S.H.I.E.L.D.

©Marvel

Strange Tales (2nd Series)

Half Dr. Strange, half Cloak and Dagger

©Marvel

Strange Tales (3rd Series)

Acetate-covered graphic novel

©Marvel

Strange Tales (4th Series)

Stars Werewolf by Night and Man-Thing

©Marvel

Stray Bullets

David Lapham's irregularly published crime hit

©El Capitan

STRANGE ADVENTURES
DC

	N-MINT
❑73, Oct 1956	100.00
❑74, Nov 1956	100.00
❑75, Dec 1956	75.00
❑76, Jan 1957	100.00
❑77, Feb 1957	100.00
❑78, Mar 1957	100.00
❑79, Apr 1957	150.00
❑80, May 1957	100.00
❑81, Jun 1957	100.00
❑82, Jul 1957	100.00
❑83, Aug 1957	100.00
❑84, Sep 1957	125.00
❑85, Oct 1957	100.00
❑86, Nov 1957	100.00
❑87, Dec 1957	100.00
❑88, Jan 1958	100.00
❑89, Feb 1958	100.00
❑90, Mar 1958	100.00
❑91, Apr 1958	90.00
❑92, May 1958	80.00
❑93, Jun 1958	80.00
❑94, Jul 1958	75.00
❑95, Aug 1958	90.00
❑96, Sep 1958	65.00
❑97, Oct 1958	90.00
❑98, Nov 1958	75.00
❑99, Dec 1958	90.00
❑100, Jan 1959; 100th anniversary issue	125.00
❑101, Feb 1959	65.00
❑102, Mar 1959	90.00
❑103, Apr 1959	90.00
❑104, May 1959 1: Space Museum.	65.00
❑105, Jun 1959	65.00
❑106, Jul 1959	65.00
❑107, Aug 1959	75.00
❑108, Sep 1959, Water (PSA)	65.00
❑109, Oct 1959	65.00
❑110, Nov 1959	75.00
❑111, Dec 1959	65.00
❑112, Jan 1960	60.00
❑113, Feb 1960 GK (c);	90.00
❑114, Mar 1960 RH (a); 1: Star Hawkins.	125.00
❑115, Apr 1960	60.00
❑116, May 1960 GK (c); RH (a)	60.00
❑117, Jun 1960 1: The Atomic Knights.	550.00
❑118, Jul 1960	75.00
❑119, Aug 1960	90.00
❑120, Sep 1960 2: The Atomic Knights.	200.00
❑121, Oct 1960	75.00
❑122, Nov 1960	75.00
❑123, Dec 1960	75.00
❑124, Jan 1961	90.00
❑125, Feb 1961	75.00
❑126, Mar 1961	75.00
❑127, Apr 1961	50.00
❑128, May 1961	75.00
❑129, Jun 1961	90.00
❑130, Jul 1961	50.00
❑131, Aug 1961	50.00
❑132, Sep 1961	75.00

	N-MINT
❑133, Oct 1961	65.00
❑134, Nov 1961	65.00
❑135, Dec 1961	65.00
❑136, Jan 1962	50.00
❑137, Feb 1962	50.00
❑138, Mar 1962 A: The Atomic Knights.	55.00
❑139, Apr 1962	50.00
❑140, May 1962	50.00
❑141, Jun 1962	55.00
❑142, Jul 1962	50.00
❑143, Aug 1962	50.00
❑144, Sep 1962 A: The Atomic Knights.	50.00
❑145, Oct 1962	50.00
❑146, Nov 1962	40.00
❑147, Dec 1962 A: The Atomic Knights.	50.00
❑148, Jan 1963	50.00
❑149, Feb 1963	40.00
❑150, Mar 1963 A: The Atomic Knights.	50.00
❑151, Apr 1963	50.00
❑152, May 1963	50.00
❑153, Jun 1963 A: The Atomic Knights.	50.00
❑154, Jul 1963	50.00
❑155, Aug 1963	50.00
❑156, Sep 1963 A: The Atomic Knights.	50.00
❑157, Oct 1963	50.00
❑158, Nov 1963	50.00
❑159, Dec 1963	50.00
❑160, Jan 1964 A: The Atomic Knights.	50.00
❑161, Feb 1964	35.00
❑162, Mar 1964	35.00
❑163, Apr 1964	35.00
❑164, May 1964	35.00
❑165, Jun 1964	35.00
❑166, Jul 1964	35.00
❑167, Aug 1964	35.00
❑168, Sep 1964	30.00
❑169, Oct 1964	35.00
❑170, Nov 1964	50.00
❑171, Dec 1964	30.00
❑172, Jan 1965	30.00
❑173, Feb 1965	40.00
❑174, Mar 1965	30.00
❑175, Apr 1965	40.00
❑176, May 1965	30.00
❑177, Jun 1965 O: Immortal Man. 1: Immortal Man	30.00
❑178, Jul 1965	25.00
❑179, Aug 1965	30.00
❑180, Sep 1965 O: Animal Man (no costume). 1: Animal Man (no costume)	150.00
❑181, Oct 1965	25.00
❑182, Nov 1965	30.00
❑183, Dec 1965	30.00
❑184, Jan 1966 A: Animal Man.	60.00
❑185, Feb 1966 A: Immortal Man. A: Star Hawkins.	25.00
❑186, Mar 1966	25.00
❑187, Apr 1966 O: The Enchantress. 1: The Enchantress.	20.00
❑188, May 1966	25.00
❑189, Jun 1966	30.00
❑190, Jul 1966 1: Animal Man (in costume)	100.00
❑191, Aug 1966	20.00

	N-MINT
❑192, Sep 1966	25.00
❑193, Oct 1966	25.00
❑194, Nov 1966	20.00
❑195, Dec 1966 A: Animal Man.	35.00
❑196, Jan 1967	25.00
❑197, Feb 1967	25.00
❑198, Mar 1967	20.00
❑199, Apr 1967	30.00
❑200, May 1967	25.00
❑201, Jun 1967 A: Animal Man.	40.00
❑202, Jul 1967	20.00
❑203, Aug 1967	20.00
❑204, Sep 1967	20.00
❑205, Oct 1967 O: Deadman. 1: Deadman.	125.00
❑206, Nov 1967 NA (a); 2: Deadman.	60.00
❑207, Dec 1967, NA (a); Deadman	50.00
❑208, Jan 1968, NA (a); Deadman	60.00
❑209, Feb 1968, NA (a); Deadman	60.00
❑210, Mar 1968, NA (a); Deadman	60.00
❑211, Apr 1968, NA (a); Deadman	60.00
❑212, Jun 1968, NA (a); Deadman	60.00
❑213, Aug 1968, NA (a); Deadman	40.00
❑214, Oct 1968, NA (a); Deadman	60.00
❑215, Dec 1968, NA (a); 1: League of Assassins. 1: Sensei. Deadman	45.00
❑216, Feb 1969, NA (a); Deadman	40.00
❑217, Apr 1969	20.00
❑218, Jun 1969	20.00
❑219, Aug 1969	20.00
❑220, Oct 1969	25.00
❑221, Dec 1969	20.00
❑222, Feb 1970, NA (a); New Adam Strange story	20.00
❑223, Apr 1970	20.00
❑224, Jun 1970	15.00
❑225, Aug 1970	15.00
❑226, Oct 1970; giant series begins	15.00
❑227, Dec 1970 JKu (c)	15.00
❑228, Feb 1971	15.00
❑229, Apr 1971	15.00
❑230, Jun 1971	15.00
❑231, Aug 1971; reprints from Strange Adventures #67, #83, #125, and #160, and Adam Strange from Mystery in Space #71	10.00
❑232, Oct 1971	10.00
❑233, Dec 1971	10.00
❑234, Feb 1972	10.00
❑235, Apr 1972	10.00
❑236, Jun 1972	10.00
❑237, Jun 1972	10.00
❑238, Oct 1972 MA, CI (a)	10.00
❑239, Dec 1972	10.00
❑240, Feb 1973	10.00
❑241, Apr 1973, Reprints Adam Strange from Mystery in Space #81	10.00
❑242, Jul 1973, Reprints Adam Strange from Mystery in Space #82	10.00
❑243, Sep 1973, reprints from Strange Adventures #131 and Adam Strange from Mystery in Space #83	10.00
❑244, Nov 1973	10.00

Other grades: Multiply price above by 5/6 for VF/NM • 2/3 for VERY FINE • 1/3 for FINE • 1/5 for VERY GOOD • 1/8 for GOOD

STRANGE ADVENTURES (MINI-SERIES)
DC / VERTIGO
- ❑1, Nov 1999 ... 2.50
- ❑2, Dec 1999 ... 2.50
- ❑3, Jan 2000 ... 2.50
- ❑4, Feb 2000 ... 2.50

STRANGE ATTRACTORS
RETROGRAFIX
- ❑1, May 1993 ... 4.00
- ❑1/2nd, Jul 1994 ... 2.75
- ❑2, Aug 1993 ... 3.50
- ❑2/2nd, Jul 1993 ... 2.75
- ❑3, Nov 1993 ... 3.50
- ❑3/2nd, Jun 1993 ... 2.75
- ❑4, Feb 1994 ... 3.00
- ❑4/2nd, Jun 1994 ... 2.75
- ❑5, May 1994 ... 3.00
- ❑6, Aug 1994 ... 2.50
- ❑7, Nov 1994 ... 2.50
- ❑8, Jan 1995 ... 2.50
- ❑9, Apr 1995 ... 2.50
- ❑10, Jun 1995 ... 2.50
- ❑11, Sep 1995 ... 2.50
- ❑12, Nov 1995 ... 2.50
- ❑13, Feb 1996 ... 2.50
- ❑14, Jul 1996 ... 2.50
- ❑15, Feb 1997 ... 2.50

STRANGE ATTRACTORS: MOON FEVER
CALIBER
- ❑1, Feb 1997, b&w ... 2.95
- ❑2, 1997 ... 2.95
- ❑3, 1997 ... 2.95

STRANGE AVENGING TALES (STEVE DITKO'S...)
FANTAGRAPHICS
- ❑1, Feb 1997 ... 2.95

STRANGE BEDFELLOWS
HIPPY
- ❑1, 2002 ... 5.95
- ❑2, Jun 2002 ... 5.95

STRANGE BREW
AARDVARK-VANAHEIM
- ❑1, b&w ... 3.00

STRANGE COMBAT TALES
MARVEL / EPIC
- ❑1, Oct 1993 ... 2.50
- ❑2, Nov 1993 ... 2.50
- ❑3, Dec 1993 ... 2.50
- ❑4, Jan 1984 ... 2.50

STRANGE DAYS
ECLIPSE
- ❑1 ... 1.50
- ❑2 ... 1.50
- ❑3 ... 1.50

STRANGE DETECTIVE TALES: DEAD LOVE
ODDGOD PRESS
- ❑1, Aug 2005 ... 3.95

STRANGE EMBRACE
ATOMEKA
- ❑1, b&w ... 3.95
- ❑2, b&w ... 3.95
- ❑3, b&w ... 3.95

STRANGE GIRL
IMAGE
- ❑1, 2005 ... 2.95
- ❑2, 2005 ... 2.95
- ❑3, Oct 2005 ... 2.95
- ❑4, 2005 ... 2.95
- ❑5, Jan 2006 ... 2.95
- ❑6, Feb 2006 ... 2.95
- ❑7, May 2006 ... 2.95
- ❑8, Jun 2006 ... 2.95

STRANGEHAVEN
ABIOGENESIS
- ❑1, Jun 1995 ... 5.00
- ❑1/2nd ... 3.00
- ❑2 ... 4.00
- ❑2/2nd ... 3.00
- ❑3, Dec 1995 ... 4.00
- ❑3/2nd ... 3.00
- ❑4, Jun 1996 ... 2.95
- ❑5, Nov 1996 ... 2.95
- ❑6, May 1997 ... 2.95
- ❑7 ... 2.95
- ❑8, 1997 ... 2.95
- ❑9, Jun 1998 ... 2.95
- ❑10, Nov 1998 ... 2.95
- ❑11, Apr 1999 ... 2.95
- ❑12, Oct 1999 ... 2.95
- ❑13, ... 2.95
- ❑14 ... 2.95
- ❑15, May 2003 ... 2.95
- ❑16, ca. 2004 ... 2.95
- ❑17, Apr 2005 ... 2.95
- ❑18, ca. 2005 ... 2.95

STRANGE HEROES
LONE STAR
- ❑1, Jun 2000 ... 2.95
- ❑2 ... 2.95

STRANGE KILLINGS: BODY ORCHARD (WARREN ELLIS')
AVATAR
- ❑1 2002 ... 3.50
- ❑2 2002 ... 3.50
- ❑3 2002 ... 3.50
- ❑4 2002 ... 3.50
- ❑5 ... 3.50
- ❑6, Feb 2003 ... 3.50

STRANGE KILLINGS: NECROMANCER (WARREN EILIS')
AVATAR
- ❑1, Mar 2004 ... 3.50
- ❑2, Apr 2004 ... 3.50

STRANGE KILLINGS: STRONG MEDICINE (WARREN ELLIS')
AVATAR
- ❑1, Jul 2003 ... 3.50
- ❑2, Aug 2003 ... 3.50
- ❑2/A, Aug 2003; Wrap Cover ... 3.95
- ❑3, Oct 2003 ... 3.50

STRANGE LOOKING EXILE
ROBERT KIRBY
- ❑1 ... 2.00
- ❑2 ... 2.00
- ❑3 ... 2.00

STRANGELOVE
EXPRESS / ENTITY
- ❑1, b&w ... 2.50
- ❑2, b&w ... 2.50

STRANGER IN A STRANGE LAND
RIP OFF
- ❑1, Jun 1989, b&w ... 2.00
- ❑2, May 1990, b&w ... 2.00
- ❑3, Sep 1991, b&w ... 2.50

STRANGERS
MALIBU / ULTRAVERSE
- ❑1, Jun 1993 O: The Strangers. 1: The Strangers. 1: The Night Man (out of costume) ... 2.00
- ❑1/Hologram, Jun 1993; hologram edition ... 5.00
- ❑1/Ltd., Jun 1993; Ultra-limited edition ... 4.00
- ❑2, Jul 1993; card ... 2.00
- ❑3, Aug 1993 1: TNTNT ... 2.00
- ❑4, Sep 1993 A: Hardcase ... 2.00
- ❑5, Oct 1993; Rune ... 2.50
- ❑6, Nov 1993 ... 1.95
- ❑7, Dec 1993; Break-Thru ... 1.95
- ❑8, Jan 1994 O: The Solution ... 1.95
- ❑9, Feb 1994 ... 1.95
- ❑10, Mar 1994 ... 1.95
- ❑11, Apr 1994 ... 1.95
- ❑12, May 1994 ... 1.95
- ❑13, Jun 1994; KB (w); MGu (a); 1: Pilgrim. contains Ultraverse Premiere #4 ... 3.50
- ❑14, Jul 1994 1: Byter ... 1.95
- ❑15, Aug 1994 1: Lightshow. 1: Generator X. 1: Rodent ... 1.95
- ❑16, Sep 1994 ... 1.95
- ❑17, Oct 1994 A: Rafferty ... 1.95
- ❑18, Nov 1994 ... 1.95
- ❑19, Dec 1994 ... 1.95
- ❑20, Jan 1995 1: Beater. 1: M.C. Zed. ... 1.95
- ❑21, Feb 1995 ... 1.95
- ❑22, Mar 1995 ... 1.95
- ❑23, Apr 1995 ... 1.95
- ❑24, May 1995 ... 1.95
- ❑Annual 1, Dec 1994 ... 3.95

STRANGERS (IMAGE)
IMAGE
- ❑1, Mar 2003 ... 2.95
- ❑2, Apr 2003 ... 2.95
- ❑3, May 2003 ... 2.95
- ❑4, Jul 2003 ... 2.95
- ❑5, Aug 2003 ... 2.95
- ❑6, Sep 2003 ... 2.95

STRANGERS IN PARADISE
ANTARCTIC
- ❑0, b&w ... 75.00
- ❑1, Nov 1993, b&w ... 65.00
- ❑1/2nd, Mar 1994, b&w ... 5.00
- ❑1/3rd, Apr 1994, b&w ... 3.00
- ❑2, Dec 1993, b&w ... 24.00
- ❑3, Feb 1994, b&w ... 18.00

STRANGERS IN PARADISE (2ND SERIES)
ABSTRACT
- ❑1, Sep 1994, b&w ... 30.00
- ❑1/Gold, Gold logo edition; Gold logo edition ... 4.00
- ❑1/2nd, Apr 1995, b&w ... 2.75
- ❑2, Nov 1994, b&w ... 15.00
- ❑2/Gold, Gold logo edition; Gold logo edition ... 3.00
- ❑3, Jan 1995, b&w ... 12.00
- ❑3/Gold, Gold logo edition; Gold logo edition ... 3.00
- ❑4, Mar 1995, b&w ... 10.00
- ❑4/Gold, Gold logo edition; Gold logo edition ... 2.75
- ❑5, Jun 1995, b&w ... 10.00
- ❑5/Gold, Gold logo edition; Gold logo edition ... 2.75
- ❑6, Jul 1995, b&w ... 8.00
- ❑6/Gold, Gold logo edition; Gold logo edition ... 2.75
- ❑7, Sep 1995, b&w ... 8.00
- ❑7/Gold, Gold logo edition; Gold logo edition ... 2.75
- ❑8, Nov 1995, b&w ... 8.00
- ❑8/Gold, Gold logo edition; Gold logo edition ... 2.75
- ❑9, Jan 1996, b&w ... 8.00
- ❑9/Gold, Gold logo edition; Gold logo edition ... 2.75
- ❑10, Feb 1996, b&w ... 8.00
- ❑10/Gold, Gold logo edition; Gold logo edition ... 2.75
- ❑11 1996, b&w ... 5.00
- ❑11/Gold, Gold logo edition; Gold logo edition ... 2.75
- ❑12, May 1996, b&w ... 5.00
- ❑12/Gold, Gold logo edition; Gold logo edition ... 2.75
- ❑13, Jun 1996, b&w ... 4.00
- ❑13/Gold 1998; Gold logo edition ... 2.75
- ❑14, Jul 1996, b&w; continues in 3rd series (Image); Titled: Terry Moore's Strangers in Paradise; no gold logo edition ... 2.75

STRANGERS IN PARADISE (3RD SERIES)
HOMAGE
- ❑1, Oct 1996 ... 4.00
- ❑2, Dec 1996 ... 3.00
- ❑3, Jan 1997 ... 3.00
- ❑4, Feb 1997 ... 3.00
- ❑5, Apr 1997, cover says Mar, indicia says Apr ... 3.00
- ❑6, May 1997, b&w ... 3.00
- ❑7, Jul 1997, b&w ... 3.00
- ❑8, Aug 1997, b&w ... 3.00
- ❑9, Sep 1997, b&w; returns to Abstract ... 3.00
- ❑10, Dec 1997, b&w ... 3.00
- ❑11, Dec 1997, b&w ... 3.00
- ❑12, Jan 1998, b&w ... 3.00
- ❑13, Mar 1998, b&w ... 3.00
- ❑14, Apr 1998, b&w ... 3.00
- ❑15, Jun 1998, b&w ... 3.00
- ❑16, Jul 1998, b&w ... 3.00
- ❑17, Sep 1998, b&w ... 3.00

Street Poet Ray (Marvel)

Marvel's worst-selling comic book ever

©Marvel

Strontium Dog

Irradiated Johnny Alpha seeks bounties

©Fleetway-Quality

Stupid Comics (Image)

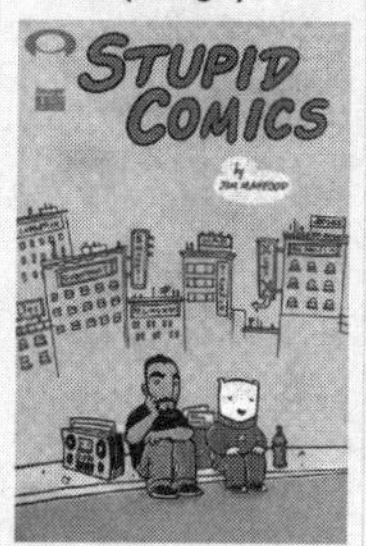

Mahfood's musings meander to Image

©Image

Stupid, Stupid Rat Tails

Bone prequel features Big Johnson Bone

©Cartoon Books

Sub-Mariner (Vol. 2)

Angry Atlantean has control issues

©Marvel

	N-MINT
❑18, Oct 1998, b&w	3.00
❑19, Nov 1998, b&w	3.00
❑20, Dec 1998, b&w	3.00
❑21, Feb 1999, b&w	3.00
❑22, Mar 1999, b&w	3.00
❑23, Mar 1999, b&w	3.00
❑24, Jun 1999, b&w	3.00
❑25, Jul 1999, b&w	3.00
❑26, Aug 1999, b&w	3.00
❑27, Sep 1999	3.00
❑28, Nov 1999	3.00
❑29, Dec 1999	3.00
❑30, Feb 2000, b&w	3.00
❑31, Mar 2000	2.95
❑32, May 2000	2.95
❑33, May 2000	2.95
❑34, Aug 2000	2.95
❑35, Sep 2000	2.95
❑36, Nov 2000	2.95
❑37, Dec 2000	2.95
❑38, Jan 2001	2.95
❑39, Mar 2001	2.95
❑40, Apr 2001	2.95
❑41, Jun 2001	2.95
❑42, Jul 2001	2.95
❑43, Aug 2001	2.95
❑44, Oct 2001	2.95
❑45, Nov 2001	2.95
❑46, Dec 2001	2.95
❑47, Feb 2002	2.95
❑48, Mar 2002	2.95
❑49, Apr 2002	2.95
❑50, May 2002	2.95
❑51, Jun 2002	2.95
❑52, Aug 2002	2.95
❑53, Sep 2002	2.95
❑54, Nov 2002	2.95
❑55, Dec 2002	2.95
❑56, Feb 2003	2.95
❑57, Mar 2003	2.95
❑58, May 2003	3.00
❑59, Jul 2003	3.00
❑60, Sep 2003	3.00
❑61, Dec 2003	3.00
❑62, Jan 2004	3.00
❑63, Feb 2004	3.00
❑64, May 2004	3.00
❑65, Jun 2004	2.95
❑66, Aug 2004	2.95
❑67, Sep 2004	2.95
❑68, Nov 2004	2.95
❑69 2005	2.95
❑70 2005	2.95
❑71 2005	2.95
❑72 2005	2.95
❑73 2005	2.95
❑74 2005	2.95
❑75 2005	2.95
❑76 2005	2.95
❑77 2005	2.95
❑78, Jan 2006	2.95
❑Special 1, Feb 1999; Lyrics and Poems	4.00

STRANGERS IN PARADISE SOURCEBOOK
Abstract

	N-MINT
❑1, Oct 2003	2.95

STRANGER'S TALE
Vineyard

	N-MINT
❑1, b&w; cardstock cover	2.00

STRANGER THAN FICTION
Impact

	N-MINT
❑1 1998, b&w	1.99
❑2, Jul 1998, b&w	1.99
❑3 1998	1.99
❑4 1998	1.99

STRANGE SPORTS STORIES
DC

	N-MINT
❑1, Oct 1973 FR (w); BO, DG, CS (a)	18.00
❑2, Dec 1973 FR (w); MA, DG, CS, IN (a)	9.00
❑3, Feb 1974 FR (w); DG, CS (a)	7.00
❑4, Apr 1974 DG, IN (a)	7.00
❑5, Jun 1974	7.00
❑6, Aug 1974	7.00

STRANGE SPORTS STORIES (ADVENTURE)
Adventure

	N-MINT
❑1	2.50
❑2	2.50
❑3	2.50

STRANGE STORIES
Avalon

	N-MINT
❑1, b&w; reprints John Force and Magic Man stories	2.95

STRANGE TALES (1ST SERIES)
Marvel

	N-MINT
❑51, Oct 1956 BEv (c)	200.00
❑52, Nov 1956 BEv (c)	200.00
❑53, Dec 1956 BEv (c)	200.00
❑54, Jan 1957 BEv (c)	200.00
❑55, Feb 1957 BEv (c)	200.00
❑56, Mar 1957 BEv (c)	200.00
❑57, Apr 1957 BEv (c)	200.00
❑58, May 1957 BEv (c); AW (a)	200.00
❑59, Jul 1957 BK (a)	225.00
❑60, Dec 1957 BEv (c)	200.00
❑61, Feb 1958 BK (a)	225.00
❑62, Apr 1958	175.00
❑63, Jun 1958 BEv (c)	175.00
❑64, Aug 1958 AW (a)	200.00
❑65, Oct 1958	175.00
❑66, Dec 1958	175.00
❑67, Feb 1959, Quicksilver prototype?	200.00
❑68, Apr 1959	200.00
❑69, Jun 1959, Professor X prototype?	200.00
❑70, Aug 1959	200.00
❑71, Oct 1959	200.00
❑72, Dec 1959	200.00
❑73, Feb 1960 BEv, JK (a)	200.00
❑74, Apr 1960	200.00
❑75, Jun 1960	200.00
❑76, Aug 1960	200.00
❑77, Oct 1960	200.00
❑78, Nov 1960 JK (a)	200.00
❑79, Dec 1960, Doctor Strange try-out character	250.00
❑80, Jan 1961	200.00
❑81, Feb 1961 SD, JK (a)	175.00
❑82, Mar 1961	175.00
❑83, Apr 1961	175.00
❑84, May 1961, Magneto prototype character (?)	200.00
❑85, Jun 1961	175.00
❑86, Jul 1961 JK (c); SD, JK (a)	175.00
❑87, Aug 1961 JK (c); SD, DH, JK (a)	175.00
❑88, Sep 1961 JK (c); SD, DH, JK (a)	175.00
❑89, Oct 1961 JK (c); SD, JK (a); O: Fin Fang Foom. 1: Fin Fang Foom	400.00
❑90, Nov 1961 JK (c); SD, JK (a)	175.00
❑91, Dec 1961 JK (c); SD, JK (a)	175.00
❑92, Jan 1962 JK (c); SD, JK (a)	175.00
❑93, Feb 1962 SD (c); SD, JK (a)	150.00
❑94, Mar 1962 JK (c); SD, JK (a)	150.00
❑95, Apr 1962 JK (c); SD, DH, JK (a)	150.00
❑96, May 1962	150.00
❑97, Jun 1962, Aunt May & Uncle Ben prototype characters (?)	350.00
❑98, Jul 1962	150.00
❑99, Aug 1962 JK (c); SD, DH, JK (a)	150.00
❑100, Sep 1962 JK (c); SD, DH, JK (a)	150.00
❑101, Oct 1962, JK (c); SD, JK (a); A: Human Torch. Human Torch features begin	900.00
❑102, Nov 1962 JK (c); SD, JK (a); A: Human Torch. A: Wizard.	425.00
❑103, Dec 1962 JK (c); SD, JK (a); A: Human Torch.	300.00
❑104, Jan 1963 JK (c); SD, JK (a); O: Paste-Pot Pete. 1: Paste-Pot Pete. A: Human Torch.	300.00
❑105, Feb 1963 JK (c); SD, JK (a); A: Human Torch. V: Wizard.	300.00
❑106, Mar 1963 SD (a); A: Fantastic Four. A: Human Torch. V: Acrobat.	225.00
❑107, Apr 1963, SD (a); A: Human Torch. A: Sub-Mariner. Human Torch vs. Sub-Mariner	250.00
❑108, May 1963 SD, JK (a); A: Fantastic Four. A: Human Torch.	225.00
❑109, Jun 1963 SD, JK (a); 1: Circe (later becomes Sersi). A: Human Torch.	225.00
❑110, Jul 1963 SL (w); SD (a); 1: The Ancient One. 1: Doctor Strange. 1: Wong (Doctor Strange's manservant). A: Human Torch.	1250.00
❑111, Aug 1963 SL (w); SD (a); 1: Asbestos. 1: Baron Mordo. 1: Eel I (Leopold Stryke). 2: Doctor Strange. A: Human Torch.	350.00
❑112, Sep 1963 SL (w); SD (a); A: Fantastic Four. A: Human Torch.	150.00
❑113, Oct 1963 SL (w); SD (a); 1: Plantman. A: Human Torch.	150.00
❑114, Nov 1963, SL (w); SD, JK (a); A: Human Torch. A: Baron Mordo. A: Doctor Strange. V: Acrobat. Villain (The Acrobat) appears, dressed as Captain America	350.00
❑115, Dec 1963 SL (w); SD (a); O: Doctor Strange. A: Human Torch. A: Sandman (Marvel).	450.00
❑116, Jan 1964, SL (w); SD (a); A: Thing. A: Human Torch. A: Doctor Strange. V: Puppet Master. Human Torch vs. Thing	125.00

Other grades: Multiply price above by 5/6 for VF/NM • 2/3 for VERY FINE • 1/3 for FINE • 1/5 for VERY GOOD • 1/8 for GOOD

❑117, Feb 1964 SL (w); SD (a); A: Fantastic Four. A: Human Torch. A: Doctor Strange. V: Baron Mordo. 100.00
❑118, Mar 1964 SL (w); SD (a); A: Fantastic Four. A: Human Torch. A: Doctor Strange. V: Wizard. 100.00
❑119, Apr 1964 SL (w); SD (a); A: Human Torch. A: Spider-Man. A: Doctor Strange. 125.00
❑120, May 1964 SL (w); SD (a); A: X-Men. A: Fantastic Four. A: Human Torch. A: Iceman. A: Doctor Strange. 125.00
❑121, Jun 1964 SL (w); SD (a); A: Human Torch. A: Doctor Strange. V: Plantman. 125.00
❑122, Jul 1964 SL (w); SD (a); A: Human Torch. A: Doctor Strange. A: Doctor Doom. 125.00
❑123, Aug 1964 SL (w); SD (a); O: The Beetle. 1: The Beetle. A: Thing. A: Human Torch. A: Thor. 125.00
❑124, Sep 1964 SL (w); SD (a); A: Thing. A: Human Torch. 75.00
❑125, Oct 1964 SL (w); SD (a); A: Human Torch. 75.00
❑126, Nov 1964 JK (c); SL (w); SD (a); 1: Dormammu. 1: Clea. A: Human Torch. 90.00
❑127, Dec 1964 SL (w); SD (a); A: Human Torch. 75.00
❑128, Jan 1965 SL (w); SD (a); A: Human Torch. 75.00
❑129, Feb 1965 SD (a); A: Human Torch. 75.00
❑130, Mar 1965 SL (w); SD (a); A: Human Torch. A: Beatles. 90.00
❑131, Apr 1965 SL (w); SD (a); A: Thing. A: Human Torch. 75.00
❑132, May 1965 SL (w); SD (a); A: Thing. A: Human Torch. 75.00
❑133, Jun 1965 SL (w); SD (a); A: Thing. A: Human Torch. 75.00
❑134, Jul 1965, SL (w); SD (a); A: Torch. A: Human Torch. A: Watcher. Last Human Torch issue 75.00
❑135, Aug 1965 SL (w); SD, JK (a); O: Nick Fury, Agent of SHIELD. 1: S.H.I.E.L.D.. 1: Nick Fury, Agent of SHIELD. 1: Hydra. A: Doctor Strange. 125.00
❑136, Sep 1965 SL (w); SD, JK (a); A: Doctor Strange. A: Nick Fury 75.00
❑137, Oct 1965 SL (w); SD (a) 50.00
❑138, Nov 1965 SL (w); SD (a); 1: Eternity 50.00
❑139, Dec 1965 SL (w); SD (a) 50.00
❑140, Jan 1966 SL (w); SD (a) 50.00
❑141, Feb 1966 SL (w); SD (a); 1: The Fixer. 1: Mentallo 50.00
❑142, Mar 1966 SL (w); SD (a) 50.00
❑143, Apr 1966 SD (a) 50.00
❑144, May 1966 SD (a); 1: The Druid. 1: Jasper Sitwell (SHIELD agent). 50.00
❑145, Jun 1966 SD (a) 50.00
❑146, Jul 1966 SD (a); 1: Advanced Idea Mechanics (A.I.M.) 50.00
❑147, Aug 1966 SL (w); BEv (a); O: Kaluu. 1: Kaluu. 50.00
❑148, Sep 1966 BEv (c); BEv, JK (a); O: The Ancient One. 75.00
❑149, Oct 1966 BEv, JK (a) 50.00
❑150, Nov 1966, BEv (c); SL (w); JB, BEv, JK (a); 1: Umar. 1st John Buscema art at Marvel 50.00
❑151, Dec 1966, JK, JSo (c); SL (w); BEv, JK, JSo (a); 1st Jim Steranko art at Marvel 75.00
❑152, Jan 1967 BEv (c); SL (w); BEv, JSo (a) 50.00
❑153, Feb 1967 JSo (c); SL (w); JK, JSo (a) 50.00
❑154, Mar 1967 JSo, SL (w); JSo (a); 1: Dreadnought (original) 50.00
❑155, Apr 1967 JSo (c); JSo, SL (w); JSo (a) 50.00
❑156, May 1967 JSo, SL (w); JSo (a); A: Daredevil 50.00
❑157, Jun 1967 JSo (c); JSo, SL (w); HT, JSo (a); 1: Living Tribunal 50.00
❑158, Jul 1967 BEv (c); JSo (w); HT, JSo (a); D: Baron Strucker. 50.00
❑159, Aug 1967 JSo (c); JSo (w); HT, JSo (a); O: Nick Fury, Agent of SHIELD. O: Fury. 1: Val Fontaine. A: Captain America. 60.00
❑160, Sep 1967 JSo (w); HT, JSo (a); A: Captain America. 50.00
❑161, Oct 1967 JSo (c); JSo (w); JSo, DA (a); A: Captain America. 50.00
❑162, Nov 1967 JSo (w); JSo, DA (a); A: Captain America. 50.00
❑163, Dec 1967 JSo (c); JSo (w); JSo, DA (a) 50.00
❑164, Jan 1968 JSo (w); BEv, JSo, DA (a); 1: Yandroth. 50.00
❑165, Feb 1968 JSo (c); JSo (w); DA (a) 50.00
❑166, Mar 1968 JSo (w); GT, JSo, JSt, DA (a) 50.00
❑167, Apr 1968 JSo (c); JSo (w); JSo, DA (a) 50.00
❑168, May 1968, JSo (w); JSo, DA (a); original series continues as Doctor Strange; Nick Fury, Agent of SHIELD series ends 50.00
❑169, Jun 1973, O: Brother Voodoo. 1: Brother Voodoo. second series begins 15.00
❑170, Aug 1973 10.00
❑171, Oct 1973 1: Baron Samedi. 7.00
❑172, Dec 1973 7.00
❑173, Feb 1974, GC (a); 1: Black Talon I (Desmond Drew). Marvel Value Stamp #45: Mantis 7.00
❑174, Jun 1974, JB, JM (a); O: Golem. Marvel Value Stamp #44: Absorbing Man 7.00
❑175, Aug 1974, SD (a); reprints Amazing Adventures #1; Marvel Value Stamp #10: Power Man 7.00
❑176, Oct 1974, Marvel Value Stamp #94: Electro 7.00
❑177, Dec 1974 TD (a) 7.00
❑178, Feb 1975 JSn (a); O: Warlock. 1: Magus. 15.00
❑179, Apr 1975 JSn (a); 1: Pip. A: Warlock. 10.00
❑180, Jun 1975 JSn (a); 1: Gamora. A: Warlock. 10.00
❑181, Aug 1975 JSn (a); A: Warlock. 10.00
❑182, Oct 1975, reprinted from Strange Tales #123 and 124 3.00
❑183, Dec 1975, reprinted from Strange Tales #130 and 131 3.00
❑184, Feb 1976, reprinted from Strange Tales #132 and 133 3.00
❑185, Apr 1976, reprinted from Strange Tales #134 and 135 3.00
❑185/30 cent, Apr 1976, 30 cent regional price variant; reprinted from Strange Tales #134 and 135 20.00
❑186, Jun 1976, reprinted from Strange Tales #136 and 137 3.00
❑186/30 cent, Jun 1976, 30 cent regional price variant; reprinted from Strange Tales #136 and 137 20.00
❑187, Aug 1976, reprinted from Strange Tales #138 and 139 3.00
❑188, Oct 1976, reprinted from Strange Tales #140 and 141 3.00
❑Annual 1, ca. 1962, reprinted from Journey Into Mystery #53, 55 and 59; Strange Tales #73, 76 and 78; Tales of Suspense #7 and 9; Tales to Astonish #1,6 and 7 325.00
❑Annual 2, ca. 1963, A: Human Torch. A: Spider-Man. Spider-Man new, all others reprinted from Strange Tales #67; Strange Worlds #1,2 and 3; World of Fantasy #16 350.00

STRANGE TALES (2ND SERIES)
MARVEL

❑1, Apr 1987; Doctor Strange, Cloak & Dagger 1.50
❑2, May 1987 1.25
❑3, Jun 1987 1.25
❑4, Jul 1987 1.25
❑5, Aug 1987 1.25
❑6, Sep 1987 1.25
❑7, Oct 1987; Defenders 1.25
❑8, Nov 1987 1.25
❑9, Dec 1987 1.25
❑10, Jan 1988 1.25
❑11, Feb 1988 1.25
❑12, Mar 1988; Black Cat 1.25
❑13, Apr 1988 A: Punisher. 1.75
❑14, May 1988 A: Punisher. 1.75
❑15, Jun 1988 1.25
❑16, Jul 1988 1.25
❑17, Aug 1988 1.50
❑18, Sep 1988 A: X-Factor. 1.25
❑19, Oct 1988 1.25

STRANGE TALES (3RD SERIES)
MARVEL

❑1, Nov 1994; prestige format; acetate overlay cover 6.95

STRANGE TALES (4TH SERIES)
MARVEL

❑1, Sep 1998; gatefold summary A: Werewolf. A: Man-Thing. 4.99
❑2, Oct 1998; gatefold summary A: Werewolf. A: Man-Thing. 4.99
❑3, Jan 1999 4.99
❑4, Dec 1998 4.99

STRANGE TALES: DARK CORNERS
MARVEL

❑1, May 1998; gatefold summary 3.99

STRANGE WEATHER LATELY
METAPHROG

❑1 1997 3.50
❑2, Dec 1997 3.50
❑3, Feb 1998 3.50
❑4 1998 3.50
❑5, Jun 1998 3.50
❑6, Aug 1998 3.50
❑7, Oct 1998 3.00
❑8 1999 3.00
❑9 1999 3.00
❑10, May 1999 3.50

STRANGE WINK (JOHN BOLTON'S...)
DARK HORSE

❑1, Mar 1998, b&w 2.95
❑2, Apr 1998, b&w 2.95
❑3, May 1998, b&w 2.95

STRANGE WORLDS (ETERNITY)
ETERNITY

❑1, b&w; Reprints 3.95

STRANGE WORLDS (NORTH COAST)
NORTH COAST

❑1, b&w; magazine; cardstock cover 4.00

STRANGLING DESDEMONA
NINGEN MANGA

❑1, b&w 2.95

STRAPPED (DERRECK WAYNE JACKSON'S...)
GOTHIC IMAGES

❑1 2.00
❑2 2.00
❑3 2.00
❑4 2.00

STRATA
RENEGADE

❑1, Jan 1986, b&w 2.00
❑2, Mar 1986, b&w 2.00
❑3 1986 2.00
❑4 1986 2.00
❑5 2.00

STRATONAUT
NIGHTWYND

❑1, b&w 2.50
❑2, b&w 2.50
❑3, b&w 2.50
❑4, b&w 2.50

STRATOSFEAR
CALIBER

❑1 2.95

STRAWBERRY SHORTCAKE
MARVEL / STAR

❑1, Apr 1985 1.00
❑2, Jun 1985 1.00
❑3, Aug 1985 1.00
❑4, Oct 1985 1.00
❑5, Dec 1985 1.00
❑6, Feb 1986 1.00

STRAW MEN
ALL AMERICAN

❑1, 1989, b&w 1.95
❑2, 1989, b&w 1.95
❑3, 1989, b&w 1.95
❑4, Jan 1990, b&w 1.95
❑5, 1990, b&w 1.95
❑6, 1990, b&w 1.95
❑7, 1990, b&w 1.95
❑8, 1990, b&w 1.95

Superboy (2nd Series)

TV series inspired second comics series
©DC

Superboy and the Legion of Super-Heroes

Star shares series with futuristic team
©DC

Super DC Giant

Add an S before issue numbers for this one
©DC

Super Friends

Alex Toth also designed animated series
©DC

Supergirl (1st Series)

Short-lived series spun out of Adventure
©DC

N-MINT

SUBMARINE ATTACK
CHARLTON

- ❑11, May 1958 ... 24.00
- ❑12 1958 ... 16.00
- ❑13, Oct 1958, Below the Storm; Fire Ships of Antwerp (text story); Gestapo's Prize; Hidden Menace; The World Below ... 16.00
- ❑14 ... 16.00
- ❑15 ... 16.00
- ❑16 1959 ... 16.00
- ❑17 1959 ... 16.00
- ❑18 ... 16.00
- ❑19 ... 16.00
- ❑20 ... 16.00
- ❑21, Apr 1960, Disneyland TWA contest ad on back ... 12.00
- ❑22 1960 ... 12.00
- ❑23 1960 ... 12.00
- ❑24, Oct 1960, Ran contest for winning a car ... 12.00
- ❑25, Dec 1960 ... 12.00
- ❑26, Feb 1961 ... 12.00
- ❑27, Apr 1961 ... 12.00
- ❑28, Jun 1961 ... 12.00
- ❑29, Aug 1961, Contains contest for readers to win a swimming pool ... 12.00
- ❑30 1961 ... 12.00
- ❑31 1962 ... 9.00
- ❑32, Mar 1962 ... 9.00
- ❑33 1962 ... 9.00
- ❑34 1962 ... 9.00
- ❑35 1962 ... 9.00
- ❑36 1962 ... 9.00
- ❑37, Jan 1963 ... 9.00
- ❑38 1963 ... 9.00
- ❑39 1963 ... 9.00
- ❑40 1963 ... 9.00
- ❑41, Sep 1963 ... 7.00
- ❑42 1963 ... 7.00
- ❑43 1964 ... 7.00
- ❑44, Mar 1964 ... 7.00
- ❑45, Jun 1964 ... 7.00
- ❑46 1964 ... 7.00
- ❑47 1964 ... 7.00
- ❑48, Jan 1965 ... 7.00
- ❑49, Mar 1965 ... 7.00
- ❑50 1965 ... 7.00
- ❑51, Aug 1965 ... 7.00
- ❑52 1965 ... 7.00
- ❑53, Dec 1965 ... 7.00
- ❑54, Feb 1966 ... 7.00

SUB-MARINER
MARVEL

- ❑1, May 1968 JB (a); O: Sub-Mariner. 125.00
- ❑2, Jun 1968 JB (a); A: Triton ... 45.00
- ❑3, Jul 1968 JB (a); A: Triton ... 35.00
- ❑4, Aug 1968 JB (a) ... 35.00
- ❑5, Sep 1968 JB (a); O: Tiger Shark. 1: Tiger Shark ... 30.00
- ❑6, Oct 1968 JB (a) ... 25.00
- ❑7, Nov 1968, JB (a); 1: Ikthon. Cover is black-and-white photo of New York parade; drawing of Namor superimposed ... 25.00
- ❑8, Dec 1968 JB (a); V: Thing ... 75.00
- ❑8/2nd JB (a); V: The Thing ... 1.50
- ❑9, Jan 1969 1: Lemuria. 1: Naga ... 30.00
- ❑10, Feb 1969 O: Naga ... 25.00
- ❑11, Mar 1969 ... 20.00
- ❑12, Apr 1969 ... 20.00
- ❑13, May 1969 ... 20.00
- ❑14, Jun 1969 A: Human Torch. D: Toro ... 50.00
- ❑15, Jul 1969 ... 20.00
- ❑16, Aug 1969 1: Thakos ... 20.00
- ❑17, Sep 1969 1: Kormok ... 20.00
- ❑18, Oct 1969 ... 20.00
- ❑19, Nov 1969 O: Stingray. 1: Stingray. 20.00
- ❑20, Dec 1969 ... 20.00
- ❑21, Jan 1970 ... 20.00
- ❑22, Feb 1970 A: Doctor Strange ... 20.00
- ❑23, Mar 1970 O: Orka. 1: Orka ... 20.00
- ❑24, Apr 1970 ... 20.00
- ❑25, May 1970 O: Atlantis ... 20.00
- ❑26, Jun 1970 A: Red Raven. D: Red Raven ... 20.00
- ❑27, Jul 1970 SB (a); 1: Commander Kraken ... 20.00
- ❑28, Aug 1970 ... 20.00
- ❑29, Sep 1970 SB (a); V: Hercules ... 20.00
- ❑30, Oct 1970 SB (a); A: Captain Marvel ... 20.00
- ❑31, Nov 1970 ... 15.00
- ❑32, Dec 1970 O: Llyra. 1: Llyra ... 15.00
- ❑33, Jan 1971 SB, JM (a); 1: Namora. 15.00
- ❑34, Feb 1971, SB, JM (a); A: Hulk. A: Silver Surfer. Leads into Defenders #1 ... 70.00
- ❑35, Mar 1971 SB, JM (a); A: Hulk. A: Silver Surfer ... 35.00
- ❑36, Apr 1971, BWr, SB (a); 1: The Octo-Meks. Wedding of Lady Dorma 15.00
- ❑37, May 1971 RA (a); D: Lady Dorma. 15.00
- ❑38, Jun 1971 JSe, RA (a); O: Sub-Mariner ... 15.00
- ❑39, Jul 1971 RA, JM (a) ... 15.00
- ❑40, Aug 1971 A: Spider-Man ... 15.00
- ❑41, Sep 1971 GT (a) ... 10.00
- ❑42, Oct 1971 GT (a) ... 10.00
- ❑43, Nov 1971; Giant-size ... 10.00
- ❑44, Dec 1971 A: Human Torch ... 10.00
- ❑45, Jan 1972 ... 10.00
- ❑46, Feb 1972 GC (a) ... 10.00
- ❑47, Mar 1972 GC (a) ... 10.00
- ❑48, Apr 1972 GC (a) ... 10.00
- ❑49, May 1972 GC (a) ... 10.00
- ❑50, Jun 1972 BEv (a); 1: Namorita ... 10.00
- ❑51, Jul 1972 BEv (a) ... 10.00
- ❑52, Aug 1972, BEv (a); Marvel Value Stamp # ... 10.00
- ❑53, Sep 1972, BEv (a); Reprinted from Sub-Mariner (Vol. 1) #41 ... 10.00
- ❑54, Oct 1972, BEv (a); 1: Lorvex. Reprinted from Sub-Mariner (Vol. 1) #39 ... 10.00
- ❑55, Nov 1972 BEv (a) ... 10.00
- ❑56, Dec 1972 1: Tamara Rahn ... 10.00
- ❑57, Jan 1973 ... 10.00
- ❑58, Feb 1973 BEv (a) ... 10.00
- ❑59, Mar 1973 BEv (a) ... 10.00
- ❑60, Apr 1973 BEv (a) ... 10.00
- ❑61, May 1973 ... 10.00
- ❑62, Jun 1973, Tales of Atlantis ... 10.00
- ❑63, Jul 1973, 1: Arkus. 1: Volpan. Tales of Atlantis ... 10.00
- ❑64, Aug 1973, 1: Madoxx. Tales of Atlantis ... 10.00
- ❑65, Sep 1973, Tales of Atlantis ... 10.00
- ❑66, Oct 1973, 1: Raman. Tales of Atlantis ... 10.00
- ❑67, Nov 1973 ... 10.00
- ❑68, Jan 1974 ... 10.00
- ❑69, Mar 1974, Marvel Value Stamp #20: Brother Voodoo ... 10.00
- ❑70, May 1974; Marvel Value Stamp #98: Puppet Master ... 10.00
- ❑71, Jul 1974; Marvel Value Stamp #52: Quicksilver ... 10.00
- ❑72, Sep 1974; DA (a); Marvel Value Stamp #100: Galactus ... 10.00
- ❑Special 1, ca. 1971; Sub-Mariner Special Edition #1; SB (a); Reprinted from Tales to Astonish #70-73 ... 10.00
- ❑Special 2, ca. 1972; Sub-Mariner Special Edition #2; BEv (a); Reprinted from Tales to Astonish #74-76 ... 15.00

SUBMISSIVE SUZANNE
FANTAGRAPHICS / EROS

- ❑1, b&w ... 2.50
- ❑2, b&w ... 2.50
- ❑3, b&w ... 2.95
- ❑4, b&w ... 2.95
- ❑5, b&w ... 2.95
- ❑6, Aug 1998, b&w ... 2.95

SUBSPECIES
ETERNITY

- ❑1, May 1991 ... 2.50
- ❑2, 1991 ... 2.50
- ❑3, 1991 ... 2.50
- ❑4, 1991 ... 2.50

SUBSTANCE AFFECT
CRAZYFISH

- ❑1 ... 2.95

SUBSTANCE QUARTERLY
SUBSTANCE

- ❑1, Spr 1994, b&w ... 3.00
- ❑2, Sum 1994, b&w ... 3.00
- ❑3, Fal 1994, b&w ... 3.00

SUBTLE VIOLENTS
CRY FOR DAWN

- ❑1, ca. 1991 ... 15.00
- ❑1/A, ca. 1991; San Diego Comic-Con edition ... 160.00

SUBURBAN HIGH LIFE
SLAVE LABOR

- ❑1, Jun 1987 ... 1.75
- ❑1/2nd, Feb 1988 ... 1.75
- ❑2, Aug 1987 ... 1.75
- ❑3, Oct 1987 ... 1.75

SUBURBAN HIGH LIFE (VOL. 2)
SLAVE LABOR

- ❑1, May 1988; Oversized ... 5.95

SUBURBAN NIGHTMARES
RENEGADE

- ❑1, Jul 1988, b&w ... 2.00

	N-MINT
❑2, Jul 1988, b&w	2.00
❑3, Aug 1988, b&w	2.00
❑4, Aug 1988, b&w	2.00

SUBURBAN SHE-DEVILS
MARVEL

	N-MINT
❑1, Cover reads Suburban Jersey Ninja She-Devils	1.50

SUBURBAN VOODOO
FANTAGRAPHICS

	N-MINT
❑1, b&w	2.50

SUCCUBUS
FANTAGRAPHICS / EROS

	N-MINT
❑1, b&w	2.50

SUCKER THE COMIC
TROMA

	N-MINT
❑1	2.50

SUCKLE
FANTAGRAPHICS

	N-MINT
❑1, Jan 1996, b&w; digest	14.95

SUGAR & SPIKE
DC

	N-MINT
❑1, May 1956 O: Spike. O: Sugar.	1700.00
❑1/2nd, Mar 2002; Facsimile Edition	2.95
❑2, Jul 1956	700.00
❑3, Sep 1956	500.00
❑4, Nov 1956	500.00
❑5, Jan 1957	500.00
❑6, Mar 1957	350.00
❑7, May 1957	350.00
❑8, Jun 1957	350.00
❑9, Aug 1957	350.00
❑10, Sep 1957	350.00
❑11, Oct 1957	250.00
❑12, Dec 1957	250.00
❑13, Feb 1958	250.00
❑14, Mar 1958	250.00
❑15, Apr 1958; left-handedness	250.00
❑16, Jun 1958	250.00
❑17, Aug 1958	250.00
❑18, Sep 1958	250.00
❑19, Oct 1958	250.00
❑20, Dec 1958	250.00
❑21, Mar 1959	150.00
❑22, May 1959	150.00
❑23, Jul 1959	150.00
❑24, Sep 1959	150.00
❑25, Nov 1959; Halloween issue	150.00
❑26, Jan 1960; Christmas issue	150.00
❑27, Mar 1960; Valentine's issue	150.00
❑28, May 1960	150.00
❑29, Jul 1960	150.00
❑30, Sep 1960	150.00
❑31, Nov 1960; Halloween issue	125.00
❑32, Jan 1961; Christmas issue	125.00
❑33, Mar 1961	125.00
❑34, May 1961	125.00
❑35, Jul 1961 A: Grampa Plumm.	125.00
❑36, Sep 1961	125.00
❑37, Nov 1961; Halloween issue	125.00
❑38, Jan 1962, Christmas issue with Christmas cards	125.00
❑39, Mar 1962, Valentine's issue with valentines	125.00
❑40, May 1962 1: Space Sprout.	125.00
❑41, Jul 1962	75.00
❑42, Sep 1962, Vacation issue	75.00
❑43, Nov 1962, Halloween issue	75.00
❑44, Jan 1963, Christmas issue with Christmas cards	75.00
❑45, Mar 1963, Valentine's issue with valentines	75.00
❑46, May 1963, Wedding cover	75.00
❑47, Jul 1963	75.00
❑48, Sep 1963	75.00
❑49, Nov 1963, Halloween issue	75.00
❑50, Jan 1964, Christmas issue with Christmas cards	75.00
❑51, Mar 1964, Valentine's issue with valentines	55.00
❑52, May 1964	55.00
❑53, Jul 1964	55.00
❑54, Sep 1964	55.00
❑55, Nov 1964, Halloween issue	55.00
❑56, Jan 1965, Christmas issue with Christmas cards	55.00
❑57, Mar 1965, Valentine's issue with valentines	55.00
❑58, May 1965	55.00
❑59, Jul 1965	55.00
❑60, Sep 1965	55.00
❑61, Nov 1965, A: Uncle Charley. Halloween issue	50.00
❑62, Jan 1966, Christmas issue with Christmas cards	50.00
❑63, Mar 1966, Valentine's issue with valentines	50.00
❑64, May 1966	50.00
❑65, Jul 1966, Summer issue	50.00
❑66, Sep 1966	50.00
❑67, Nov 1966, Halloween issue	50.00
❑68, Jan 1967, Christmas issue	50.00
❑69, Mar 1967 1: Tornado Tot.	50.00
❑70, May 1967, Sugar & Spike become giants	50.00
❑71, Jul 1967	50.00
❑72, Sep 1967 1: Bernie the Brain.	50.00
❑73, Nov 1967	50.00
❑74, Jan 1968	50.00
❑75, Mar 1968 1: M.C.P. pellet.	50.00
❑76, May 1968	50.00
❑77, Jul 1968 A: Bernie the Brain.	50.00
❑78, Sep 1968	50.00
❑79, Nov 1968	50.00
❑80, Jan 1969 A: Bernie the Brain.	50.00
❑81, Mar 1969	35.00
❑82, May 1969, Sugar & Spike as grown-ups	35.00
❑83, Jul 1969, super-powers	35.00
❑84, Sep 1969	35.00
❑85, Oct 1969	35.00
❑86, Nov 1969	35.00
❑87, Jan 1970 1: Marvin the Midget.	35.00
❑88, Mar 1970	35.00
❑89, May 1970	35.00
❑90, Jul 1970 1: Flumsh.	35.00
❑91, Sep 1970	35.00
❑92, Nov 1970	35.00
❑93, Jan 1971	35.00
❑94, Mar 1971 1: Raymond.	35.00
❑95, May 1971	35.00
❑96, Jul 1971	35.00
❑97, Sep 1971	35.00
❑98, Nov 1971	35.00

SUGAR BUZZ
SLAVE LABOR

	N-MINT
❑1, Jan 1998, b&w	2.95
❑2 1998	2.95
❑3 1998	2.95
❑4 1998	2.95

SUGAR RAY FINHEAD
WOLF

	N-MINT
❑1	2.50
❑2	2.95
❑3	2.95
❑4	2.95
❑5, Publisher changes to Jump Back Productions	2.95
❑6, Jul 1994	2.95
❑7, Nov 1994, b&w	2.95
❑8, Feb 1995, b&w	2.95
❑9, Aug 1995, b&w	2.95
❑10, Sep 1997	2.95
❑11, Oct 1998	2.95

SUGARVIRUS
ATOMEKA

	N-MINT
❑1, b&w	3.95

SUICIDE SQUAD
DC

	N-MINT
❑1, May 1987 HC (c)	1.25
❑2, Jun 1987	1.00
❑3, Jul 1987 D: Mindboggler. V: Female Furies.	1.00
❑4, Aug 1987	1.00
❑5, Sep 1987	1.00
❑6, Oct 1987	1.00
❑7, Nov 1987	1.00
❑8, Dec 1987	1.00
❑9, Jan 1988; 1: Duchess. Millennium Week 4	1.00
❑10, Feb 1988 A: Batman.	1.00
❑11, Mar 1988 A: Speedy, Vixen.	1.00
❑12, Apr 1988	1.00
❑13, May 1988; A: Justice League International. continued from Justice League International #13; Suicide Squad view of Justice League	1.00
❑14, Jun 1988	1.00
❑15, Jul 1988	1.00
❑16, Aug 1988 A: Shade, the Changing Man.	1.00
❑17, Sep 1988 V: Jihad.	1.00
❑18, Oct 1988; Ravan vs. Bronze Tiger	1.00
❑19, Nov 1988	1.00
❑20, Dec 1988	1.00
❑21, Dec 1988	1.00
❑22, Jan 1989	1.00
❑23, Jan 1989	1.00
❑24, Feb 1989	1.00
❑25, Mar 1989	1.00
❑26, Apr 1989	1.00
❑27, May 1989	1.00
❑28, May 1989 V: Force of July.	1.00
❑29, Jun 1989	1.00
❑30, Jun 1989	1.00
❑31, Jul 1989	1.00
❑32, Aug 1989	1.00
❑33, Sep 1989	1.00
❑34, Oct 1989	1.00
❑35, Nov 1989	1.00
❑36, Dec 1989	1.00
❑37, Jan 1990	1.00
❑38, Feb 1990	1.00
❑39, Mar 1990	1.00
❑40, Apr 1990	1.00
❑41, May 1990	1.00
❑42, Jun 1990	1.00
❑43, Jul 1990	1.00
❑44, Aug 1990; Flash	1.00
❑45, Sep 1990	1.00
❑46, Oct 1990	1.00
❑47, Nov 1990	1.00
❑48, Dec 1990; Joker	1.00
❑49, Jan 1991	1.00
❑50, Feb 1991	1.50
❑51, Mar 1991	1.00
❑52, Apr 1991	1.00
❑53, May 1991	1.00
❑54, Jun 1991	1.00
❑55, Jul 1991	1.00
❑56, Aug 1991	1.00
❑57, Sep 1991	1.00
❑58, Oct 1991 A: Black Adam.	1.00
❑59, Nov 1991	1.00
❑60, Dec 1991	1.00
❑61, Jan 1992	1.00
❑62, Feb 1992	1.00
❑63, Mar 1992	1.00
❑64, Apr 1992	1.25
❑65, May 1992	1.25
❑66, Jun 1992	1.25
❑Annual 1; A: Manhunter. secret of Argent revealed	1.50

SUICIDE SQUAD (2ND SERIES)
DC

	N-MINT
❑1, Nov 2001	2.50
❑2, Dec 2001	2.50
❑3, Jan 2002	2.50
❑4, Feb 2002	2.50
❑5, Mar 2002	2.50
❑6, Apr 2002	2.50
❑7, May 2002	2.50
❑8, Jun 2002	2.50
❑9, Jul 2002	2.50
❑10, Aug 2002	2.50
❑11, Oct 2002	2.50
❑12, Nov 2002	2.50

SUIKODEN III: THE SUCCESSOR OF FATE
TOKYOPOP

	N-MINT
❑1, May 2004	9.99
❑2, Jul 2004	9.99
❑3, Sep 2004	9.99
❑4, Nov 2004	9.99
❑5, Feb 2005	9.99
❑6, May 2005	9.99
❑7, Aug 2005	9.99
❑8, Nov 2005	9.99

Other grades: Multiply price above by 5/6 for VF/NM • 2/3 for VERY FINE • 1/3 for FINE • 1/5 for VERY GOOD • 1/8 for GOOD

Supergirl (3rd Series)

Pocket universe heroine merges with delinquent

©DC

Supergirl (Mini-Series)

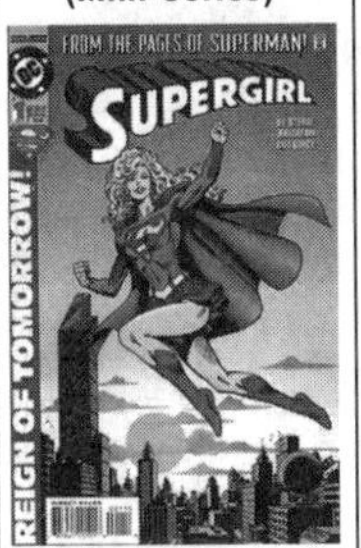

Betrayed by Luthor, Matrix seeks revenge

©DC

Super Goof (Walt Disney...)

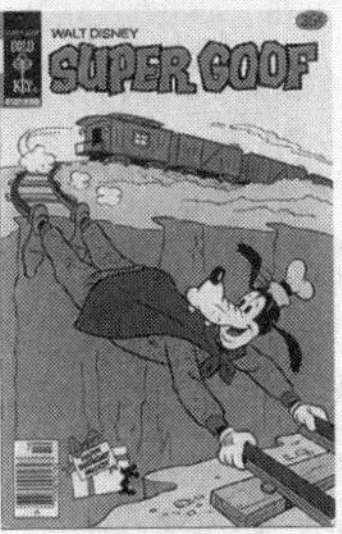

Ta-da! Powerful peanuts provide punch

©Gold Key

Super Heroes Stamp Album

DC does deal with Postal Service

©USPS

Super Information Hijinks: Reality Check

Reality didn't need checking, title did

©Tavicat

N-MINT

SUIT
VIRTUAL

- ❑1/A, May 1996 .... 3.99
- ❑1, May 1996 .... 2.50
- ❑2/A, Jun 1997 .... 3.99
- ❑2, Jun 1997 .... 3.99

SULTRY TEENAGE SUPER FOXES
SOLSON

- ❑1, b&w 2.00
- ❑2, b&w 2.00

SUMMER LOVE
CHARLTON

- ❑46, ca. 1965 .... 95.00
- ❑47, Oct 1966, Beatles cover drawings in ad for Help! and Hard Days Night 70.00
- ❑48, ca. 1967 .... 15.00

SUNBURN
ALTERNATIVE

- ❑1, Aug 2000, b&w; smaller than normal comic book 2.95

SUN DEVILS
DC

- ❑1, Jul 1984 .... 1.50
- ❑2, Aug 1984 .... 1.50
- ❑3, Sep 1984 .... 1.50
- ❑4, Oct 1984 .... 1.50
- ❑5, Nov 1984 .... 1.50
- ❑6, Dec 1984 .... 1.50
- ❑7, Jan 1985 .... 1.50
- ❑8, Feb 1985 .... 1.50
- ❑9, Mar 1985 .... 1.50
- ❑10, Apr 1985 .... 1.50
- ❑11, May 1985 .... 1.50
- ❑12, Jun 1985 .... 1.50

SUNDIATA: A LEGEND OF AFRICA
NBM

- ❑1 .... 15.95

SUNFIRE & BIG HERO SIX
MARVEL

- ❑1, Sep 1998 .... 2.50
- ❑2, Oct 1998 .... 2.50
- ❑3, Nov 1998 .... 2.50

SUNGLASSES AFTER DARK
VEROTIK

- ❑1, Nov 1995 .... 2.95
- ❑2, Jan 1996 .... 2.95
- ❑3, Mar 1996 .... 2.95
- ❑4, Aug 1996 .... 2.95
- ❑5, Oct 1996 .... 2.95
- ❑6, Nov 1996 .... 3.95

SUNRISE
HARRIER

- ❑1, Dec 1986 .... 1.95
- ❑2, May 1987 .... 1.95

SUN-RUNNERS
PACIFIC

- ❑1, Feb 1984 .... 1.50
- ❑2, Mar 1984 .... 1.50
- ❑3, May 1984 .... 1.50
- ❑4 1984 .... 1.50
- ❑5 1984 .... 1.75
- ❑6 1984 .... 1.75

N-MINT

- ❑7 1984 .... 1.75
- ❑Holiday 1, Double-size 1.95
- ❑Special 1, Special edition 1.95

SUPER BAD JAMES DYNOMITE
IDEA & DESIGN WORKS

- ❑1, Jan 2006 .... 3.99
- ❑2, Apr 2006 .... 3.99

SUPERBOY (1ST SERIES)
DC

- ❑52, Oct 1956 .... 175.00
- ❑53, Dec 1956 .... 175.00
- ❑54, Jan 1957 .... 175.00
- ❑55, Mar 1957 .... 175.00
- ❑56, Apr 1957 .... 175.00
- ❑57, Jun 1957 .... 175.00
- ❑58, Jul 1957 .... 175.00
- ❑59, Sep 1957 .... 175.00
- ❑60, Oct 1957 .... 175.00
- ❑61, Dec 1957 .... 125.00
- ❑62, Jan 1958 .... 125.00
- ❑63, Mar 1958 .... 125.00
- ❑64, Apr 1958 .... 125.00
- ❑65, Jun 1958 .... 125.00
- ❑66, Jul 1958 .... 125.00
- ❑67, Sep 1958 O: Klax-Ar. 1: Klax-Ar. 125.00
- ❑68, Oct 1958 O: Bizarro. 1: Bizarro 500.00
- ❑69, Dec 1958 .... 100.00
- ❑70, Jan 1959 O: Mr. Mxyzptlk. 100.00
- ❑71, Mar 1959 .... 100.00
- ❑72, Apr 1959 CS (a) 100.00
- ❑73, Jun 1959 .... 100.00
- ❑74, Jul 1959 .... 100.00
- ❑75, Sep 1959 .... 100.00
- ❑76, Oct 1959 1: Supermonkey. 100.00
- ❑77, Dec 1959 .... 100.00
- ❑78, Jan 1960 O: Mr. Mxyzptlk. 175.00
- ❑79, Mar 1960 .... 100.00
- ❑80, Apr 1960; Superboy meets Supergirl 150.00
- ❑81, Jun 1960 .... 90.00
- ❑82, Jul 1960 A: Bizarro Krypto. 90.00
- ❑83, Sep 1960 O: Kryptonite Kid. 1: Kryptonite Kid. 90.00
- ❑84, Oct 1960 V: Rainbow Raider. 90.00
- ❑85, Dec 1960 .... 90.00
- ❑86, Jan 1961 1: Pete Ross. A: Legion of Super-Heroes. 200.00
- ❑87, Mar 1961 .... 90.00
- ❑88, Apr 1961 .... 90.00
- ❑89, Jun 1961 O: Mon-El. 1: Mon-El. 275.00
- ❑90, Jul 1961 CS (a) 90.00
- ❑91, Sep 1961 .... 90.00
- ❑92, Oct 1961 .... 90.00
- ❑93, Dec 1961 A: Legion of Super-Heroes. 90.00
- ❑94, Jan 1962 .... 75.00
- ❑95, Mar 1962 .... 75.00
- ❑96, Apr 1962 .... 75.00
- ❑97, Jun 1962 .... 75.00
- ❑98, Jul 1962 CS (a); O: Ultra Boy. 1: Ultra Boy. A: Legion of Super-Heroes. 100.00
- ❑99, Sep 1962 .... 75.00
- ❑100, Oct 1962, 100th anniversary issue 1: Phantom Zone villains. A: Legion of Super-Heroes. 175.00

N-MINT

- ❑101, Dec 1962 .... 60.00
- ❑102, Jan 1963, Superbaby back-up 60.00
- ❑103, Mar 1963, Red K story 60.00
- ❑104, Apr 1963 O: Phantom Zone. 60.00
- ❑105, Jun 1963 .... 60.00
- ❑106, Jul 1963 .... 60.00
- ❑107, Sep 1963 .... 60.00
- ❑108, Oct 1963 .... 60.00
- ❑109, Dec 1963 .... 60.00
- ❑110, Jan 1964 .... 60.00
- ❑111, Mar 1964 .... 60.00
- ❑112, Apr 1964 .... 60.00
- ❑113, Jun 1964 .... 60.00
- ❑114, Jul 1964 .... 60.00
- ❑115, Sep 1964, Atomic Superboy 60.00
- ❑116, Oct 1964 .... 60.00
- ❑117, Dec 1964 A: Legion. 60.00
- ❑118, Jan 1965 .... 60.00
- ❑119, Mar 1965 .... 60.00
- ❑120, Apr 1965 .... 60.00
- ❑121, Jun 1965, Clark loses his super-powers; Jor-El back-up 50.00
- ❑122, Jul 1965 .... 50.00
- ❑123, Sep 1965 .... 50.00
- ❑124, Oct 1965 1: Insect Queen. 50.00
- ❑125, Dec 1965 O: Kid Psycho. 1: Kid Psycho. 50.00
- ❑126, Jan 1966 O: Krypto. 50.00
- ❑127, Mar 1966 .... 50.00
- ❑128, Apr 1966, A: Dev-Em. A: Kryptonite Kid. Imaginary Story 50.00
- ❑129, May 1966; Giant-size; aka 80 Page Giant #G-22 .... 75.00
- ❑130, Jun 1966, Superbaby 40.00
- ❑131, Jul 1966 .... 40.00
- ❑132, Sep 1966 .... 40.00
- ❑133, Oct 1966 A: Robin. 40.00
- ❑134, Dec 1966, Krypto back-up 40.00
- ❑135, Jan 1967 .... 40.00
- ❑136, Mar 1967, CS (a); A: White Kryptonite. reprints story from Adventure Comics #279 .... 40.00
- ❑137, Apr 1967 .... 40.00
- ❑138, Jun 1967; Giant-size; aka 80 Page Giant #G-35 .... 55.00
- ❑139, Jun 1967 .... 40.00
- ❑140, Jul 1967 .... 40.00
- ❑141, Sep 1967 .... 35.00
- ❑142, Oct 1967 A: Beppo. 35.00
- ❑143, Dec 1967 NA (c) 35.00
- ❑144, Jan 1968 CS (c) 35.00
- ❑145, Mar 1968 NA (c) 35.00
- ❑146, Apr 1968 NA (c) 35.00
- ❑147, Jun 1968; Giant-size; CS, JM (a); O: Saturn Girl. O: Cosmic Boy. aka 80 Page Giant #G-47; new story w/ reprints from Superboy #93 and #98, Action Comics #276, Adventure Comics #293, and Superman #147. .... 50.00
- ❑148, Jun 1968 NA (c); 25.00
- ❑149, Jul 1968 NA (c); 25.00
- ❑150, Sep 1968 NA (c); JAb (a); V: Mr. Cipher. 25.00
- ❑151, Oct 1968 NA (c); JAb (a) 25.00
- ❑152, Dec 1968 NA (c); WW (a) 25.00
- ❑153, Jan 1969 NA (c); FR (w); WW (a) 25.00

Other grades: Multiply price above by 5/6 for VF/NM • 2/3 for VERY FINE • 1/3 for FINE • 1/5 for VERY GOOD • 1/8 for GOOD

	N-MINT
❑154, Mar 1969 NA (c); WW (a)	25.00
❑155, Apr 1969 NA (c); WW (a)	25.00
❑156, Jun 1969; Giant-size; aka Giant #G-59	65.00
❑157, Jun 1969 WW (a)	25.00
❑158, Jul 1969 WW (a)	25.00
❑159, Sep 1969 WW (a)	25.00
❑160, Oct 1969 WW (a)	25.00
❑161, Dec 1969 FR (w); WW (a)	25.00
❑162, Jan 1970	25.00
❑163, Mar 1970 NA (c);	25.00
❑164, Apr 1970 NA (c);	25.00
❑165, Jun 1970; Giant-size; CS (c); CS (a); aka Giant #G-71; reprints Adventure #210 & #283, and Superman #161	50.00
❑166, Jun 1970 NA (c);	25.00
❑167, Jul 1970 NA (c);	25.00
❑168, Sep 1970 NA (c);	25.00
❑169, Oct 1970	20.00
❑170, Dec 1970	20.00
❑171, Jan 1971	20.00
❑172, Mar 1971 A: Legion of Super-Heroes.	20.00
❑173, Apr 1971 NA (c); GT, DG (a); O: Cosmic Boy.	20.00
❑174, Jun 1971; Giant-size; aka Giant #G-83; reprints Adventure #219, #225, and #262, Superboy #53 and #105	30.00
❑175, Jun 1971 NA (c); MA (a)	20.00
❑176, Jul 1971 NA (c); MA, GT, WW (a); A: Legion of Super-Heroes.	20.00
❑177, Sep 1971; Giant-size MA (a)	20.00
❑178, Oct 1971; Giant-size NA (c); MA (a)	20.00
❑179, Nov 1971; Giant-size	15.00
❑180, Dec 1971; Giant-size	15.00
❑181, Jan 1972; Giant-size; reprints Adventure #355	15.00
❑182, Feb 1972; Giant-size	20.00
❑183, Mar 1972; Giant-size	12.00
❑184, Apr 1972; Giant-size O: Dial "H" For Hero. O: Dial H for Hero.	12.00
❑185, May 1972, NC (c); CS (a); A: Legion of Super-Heroes. a.k.a. DC 100-Page Super Spectacular #185; Reprints from Adventure #208, #289 and 323, Brave and the Bold #60, Hit Comics #46, Sensation #1, and Star Spangled Comics #55; wraparound cover	12.00
❑186, May 1972	12.00
❑187, Jun 1972	12.00
❑188, Jul 1972 O: Karkan.	12.00
❑189, Aug 1972	12.00
❑190, Sep 1972	12.00
❑191, Oct 1972 O: Sunboy.	12.00
❑192, Dec 1972, Superbaby	12.00
❑193, Feb 1973	12.00
❑194, Apr 1973	12.00
❑195, Jun 1973, 1: Wildfire. A: Legion of Super-Heroes. Wildfire joins team	12.00
❑196, Jul 1973, last Superboy solo story	12.00
❑197, Sep 1973, MA (a); Legion of Super-Heroes stories begin	20.00
❑198, Oct 1973 V: Fatal Five.	12.00
❑199, Nov 1973	12.00
❑200, Feb 1974, Wedding of Bouncing Boy and Duo Damsel	15.00
❑201, Apr 1974	12.00
❑202, Jun 1974, 100-page giant; NC (c); MGr, DC, CS (a); New stories and reprints from Superboy #91 and Adventure #342, #344, and #345	30.00
❑203, Aug 1974 MGr (a); D: Invisible Kid I (Lyle org). V: Validus.	12.00
❑204, Oct 1974 MGr (a); 1: Anti Lad.	12.00
❑205, Dec 1974, MGr, DC, CS (a); reprints Superboy #88, Adventure #350 and #351	40.00
❑206, Jan 1975 MGr (a)	12.00
❑207, Feb 1975 MGr (a)	12.00
❑208, Apr 1975 MGr, CS (a)	15.00
❑209, Jun 1975 MGr (a)	10.00
❑210, Aug 1975 MGr (a); O: Karate Kid.	15.00
❑211, Sep 1975 MGr (a); A: Legion Subs.	10.00
❑212, Oct 1975; MGr (a); Matter-Eater Lad leaves team	10.00
❑213, Dec 1975 A: Miracle Machine.	7.00
❑214, Jan 1976	7.00
❑215, Mar 1976	7.00
❑216, Apr 1976 1: Tyroc.	7.00
❑217, Jun 1976 1: Laurel Kent.	7.00
❑218, Jul 1976, Tyroc joins team; Bicentennial #22	7.00
❑219, Sep 1976 V: Fatal Five.	7.00
❑220, Oct 1976	7.00
❑221, Nov 1976 O: Charma. O: Grimbor. 1: Charma. 1: Grimbor.	7.00
❑222, Dec 1976	5.00
❑223, Jan 1977 1: Pulsar Stargrave. V: Time Trapper.	5.00
❑224, Feb 1977 V: Stargrave.	5.00
❑225, Mar 1977 1: Dawnstar.	5.00
❑226, Apr 1977, Dawnstar joins team; Stargrave's identity revealed	5.00
❑227, May 1977	5.00
❑228, Jun 1977 D: Chemical King.	5.00
❑229, Jul 1977	5.00
❑230, Aug 1977, Bouncing Boy's powers restored; series continues as Superboy and the Legion of Super-Heroes	5.00
❑Annual 1, Sum 1964	175.00
❑SP 1, ca. 1980; Superboy Spectacular; giant; 1st direct-sale only DC title; reprints; pin-up back cover	4.00

SUPERBOY (2ND SERIES)
DC

	N-MINT
❑1, Jan 1990 JM (a)	2.00
❑2, Feb 1990	1.50
❑3, Mar 1990	1.50
❑4, Apr 1990	1.50
❑5, May 1990	1.50
❑6, Jun 1990	1.50
❑7, Jul 1990 JM (a)	1.50
❑8, Aug 1990; Bizarro	1.50
❑9, Sep 1990 CS (a)	1.50
❑10, Oct 1990 CS (a)	1.50
❑11, Nov 1990 CS (a)	1.50
❑12, Dec 1990 CS (a)	1.50
❑13, Jan 1991; Mxyzptlk	1.50
❑14, Feb 1991 V: Brimstone.	1.50
❑15, Mar 1991	1.50
❑16, Apr 1991 A: Superman.	1.50
❑17, May 1991	1.50
❑18, Jun 1991; Series continued in Adventures of Superboy #19	1.50
❑Special 1, ca. 1992; CS (a); One-shot associated with TV series	3.00

SUPERBOY (3RD SERIES)
DC

	N-MINT
❑0, Oct 1994; O: Superboy (clone). Comes between issues #8 and 9	2.00
❑1, Feb 1994	2.50
❑2, Mar 1994 1: Scavenger. 1: Knockout.	2.00
❑3, Apr 1994 V: Scavenger.	2.00
❑4, May 1994	2.00
❑5, Jun 1994	2.00
❑6, Jul 1994; Worlds Collide, Part 3; crossover with Milestone Media	2.00
❑7, Aug 1994; Worlds Collide, Part 8; crossover with Milestone Media	2.00
❑8, Sep 1994; Zero Hour; meets original Superboy	2.00
❑9, Nov 1994	2.00
❑10, Dec 1994	2.00
❑11, Jan 1995	2.00
❑12, Feb 1995	2.00
❑13, Mar 1995; Watery Grave, Part 1.	2.00
❑14, Apr 1995; Watery Grave, Part 2.	2.00
❑15, May 1995; Watery Grave, Part 3	2.00
❑16, Jun 1995 V: Loose Cannon.	2.00
❑17, Jul 1995	2.00
❑18, Aug 1995 V: Valor.	2.00
❑19, Sep 1995; Valor enters Phantom Zone	2.00
❑20, Oct 1995 A: Green Lantern.	2.00
❑21, Nov 1995; Future Tense, Part 1; continues in Legion of Super-Heroes #74	2.00
❑22, Dec 1995; A: Killer Frost. Underworld Unleashed	2.00
❑23, Jan 1996	2.00
❑24, Feb 1996; V: Silver Sword. Knockout's past revealed	2.00
❑25, Mar 1996; Giant-size; Losin' It, Part 1; pin-up pages	3.00
❑26, Apr 1996; Losin' It, Part 2	2.00
❑27, May 1996; Losin' It, Part 3	2.00
❑28, Jun 1996; A: Supergirl. Losin' It, Part 4	2.00
❑29, Jul 1996; Losin' It, Part 5	2.00
❑30, Aug 1996; Losin' It, Part 6; Knockout captured	2.00
❑31, Sep 1996	2.00
❑32, Oct 1996 O: Superboy.	2.00
❑33, Nov 1996; Final Night	2.00
❑34, Dec 1996; Dubbilex regains powers	2.00
❑35, Jan 1997 1: The Agenda.	2.00
❑36, Feb 1997 V: Match.	2.00
❑37, Mar 1997 SB (a)	2.00
❑38, Apr 1997 SB (a)	2.00
❑39, May 1997	2.00
❑40, Jun 1997; continues in Superboy & the Ravers #10	2.00
❑41, Jul 1997	2.00
❑42, Aug 1997	2.00
❑43, Sep 1997	2.00
❑44, Oct 1997; Superboy goes to timeless island	2.00
❑45, Nov 1997 A: Legion of Super-Heroes. V: Silver Sword.	2.00
❑46, Dec 1997; Face cover	2.00
❑47, Jan 1998; A: Green Lantern. Continued from Green Lantern #94	2.00
❑48, Feb 1998	2.00
❑49, Mar 1998	2.00
❑50, Apr 1998; Last Boy on Earth, Part 1	2.00
❑51, May 1998; Last Boy on Earth, Part 2	1.95
❑52, Jun 1998; Last Boy on Earth, Part 3; Superboy returns to Hawaii.	1.95
❑53, Jul 1998; Last Boy on Earth, Part 4	1.95
❑54, Aug 1998 A: Guardian.	1.95
❑55, Sep 1998 1: new Hex. V: Grokk.	1.95
❑56, Oct 1998; Mechanic takes over Cadmus	1.95
❑57, Dec 1998; Demolition Run, Part 1	1.99
❑58, Jan 1999; Demolition Run, Part 2	1.99
❑59, Feb 1999; A: Superman. A: Project: Cadmus. on Krypton	1.99
❑60, Mar 1999	1.99
❑61, Apr 1999; learns Superman's identity	1.99
❑62, May 1999 O: Black Zero.	1.99
❑63, Jun 1999 V: Doomsdays.	1.99
❑64, Jul 1999	1.99
❑65, Aug 1999 A: Metal Men. A: Steel. A: Inferno. A: Green Lantern. A: Impulse. A: Creeper. A: Robin. A: Hero Hotline. A: Damage.	1.99
❑66, Sep 1999; back to Wild Lands	1.99
❑67, Oct 1999 V: King Shark.	1.99
❑68, Nov 1999; Day of Judgment	1.99
❑69, Dec 1999	1.99
❑70, Jan 2000	1.99
❑71, Feb 2000	1.99
❑72, Mar 2000	1.99
❑73, Apr 2000	1.99
❑74, May 2000; Sins of Youth	1.99
❑75, Jun 2000	1.99
❑76, Jul 2000	1.99
❑77, Aug 2000	2.25
❑78, Sep 2000	2.25
❑79, Oct 2000	2.25
❑80, Nov 2000	2.25
❑81, Dec 2000	2.25
❑82, Jan 2001	2.25
❑83, Feb 2001	2.25
❑84, Mar 2001	2.25
❑85, Apr 2001	2.25
❑86, May 2001	2.25
❑87, Jun 2001	2.25
❑88, Jul 2001	2.25
❑89, Aug 2001	2.25
❑90, Sep 2001	2.25
❑91, Oct 2001	2.25
❑92, Nov 2001	2.25
❑93, Dec 2001; Joker: Last Laugh crossover	2.25
❑94, Jan 2002	2.25
❑95, Feb 2002	2.25
❑96, Mar 2002	2.25
❑97, Apr 2002	2.25

Other grades: Multiply price above by 5/6 for VF/NM • 2/3 for VERY FINE • 1/3 for FINE • 1/5 for VERY GOOD • 1/8 for GOOD

Superman (1st Series)

Silver Age silliness gave way to social concerns
©DC

Superman (2nd Series)

Revamped Man of Steel made for fresh start
©DC

Superman 3-D

Occasional 3-D only works from time to time
©DC

Superman Adventures

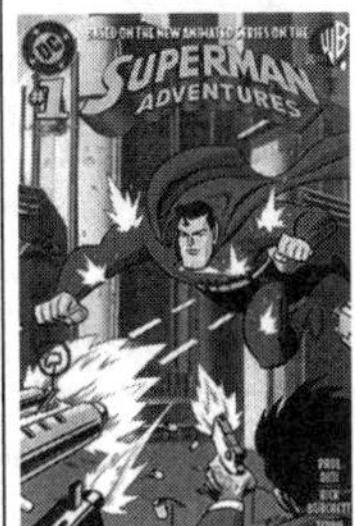

Animated tales provide fodder for spin-off
©DC

Superman: A Nation Divided

Civil War sees super-weapon from Kansas
©DC

	N-MINT
❑98, May 2002	2.25
❑99, Jun 2002	2.25
❑100, Jul 2002; Giant-size	3.00
❑1000000, Nov 1998; Comes between issues #56 and 57	4.00
❑Annual 1, ca. 1994; Elseworlds; concludes story from Adventures of Superman Annual #6	3.00
❑Annual 2, ca. 1995; Year One; Identity of being who Superboy was cloned from is revealed	4.00
❑Annual 3, ca. 1996; Legends of the Dead Earth	2.95
❑Annual 4, ca. 1997; Pulp Heroes	3.95

SUPERBOY AND THE LEGION OF SUPER-HEROES
DC

	N-MINT
❑231, Sep 1977, V: Fatal Five. Giant-Size	5.00
❑232, Oct 1977	5.00
❑233, Nov 1977 O: Infinite Man. 1: Infinite Man	5.00
❑234, Dec 1977	5.00
❑235, Jan 1978	5.00
❑236, Feb 1978	5.00
❑237, Mar 1978, Saturn Girl leaves team; Lightning Lad leaves team	5.00
❑238, Apr 1978, reprints Adventure Comics #359 and 360; wraparound cover	5.00
❑239, May 1978	5.00
❑240, Jun 1978 O: Dawnstar. V: Grimbor	5.00
❑241, Jul 1978	5.00
❑241/Whitman, Jul 1978, Whitman variant	8.00
❑242, Aug 1978	5.00
❑242/Whitman, Aug 1978, Whitman variant	8.00
❑243, Sep 1978 A: Legion Subs.	5.00
❑243/Whitman, Sep 1978, A: Legion Subs. Whitman variant	8.00
❑244, Oct 1978, Mordru returns	5.00
❑244/Whitman, Oct 1978, Mordru returns; Whitman variant	8.00
❑245, Nov 1978, Lightning Lad and Saturn Girl rejoin	5.00
❑245/Whitman, Nov 1978, Lightning Lad and Saturn Girl rejoin; Whitman variant	8.00
❑246, Dec 1978	5.00
❑246/Whitman, Dec 1978, Whitman variant	8.00
❑247, Jan 1979	5.00
❑247/Whitman, Jan 1979, Whitman variant	8.00
❑248, Feb 1979	5.00
❑248/Whitman, Feb 1979, Whitman variant	8.00
❑249, Mar 1979	5.00
❑250, Apr 1979	5.00
❑251, May 1979	4.00
❑251/Whitman, May 1979, Whitman variant	7.00
❑252, Jun 1979	4.00
❑252/Whitman, Jun 1979, Whitman variant	7.00
❑253, Jul 1979 1: Blok. V: League of Super-Assassins.	4.00
❑253/Whitman, Jul 1979, 1: Blok. V: League of Super-Assassins. Whitman variant	7.00
❑254, Aug 1979	4.00
❑254/Whitman, Aug 1979, Whitman variant	7.00
❑255, Sep 1979, Legion visits Krypton before it's destroyed	4.00
❑255/Whitman, Sep 1979, Legion visits Krypton before it's destroyed; Whitman variant	7.00
❑256, Oct 1979 O: Brainiac 5.	4.00
❑256/Whitman, Oct 1979, O: Brainiac 5. Whitman variant	7.00
❑257, Nov 1979, SD (a); Return of Bouncing Boy; Return of Duo Damsel	4.00
❑257/Whitman, Nov 1979, SD (a); Return of Bouncing Boy; Return of Duo Damsel; Whitman variant	7.00
❑258, Dec 1979, V: Psycho Warrior. series continues as Legion of Super-Heroes	4.00
❑258/Whitman, Dec 1979, V: Psycho Warrior. series continues as Legion of Super-Heroes; Whitman variant	7.00

SUPERBOY & THE RAVERS
DC

	N-MINT
❑1, Sep 1996	1.95
❑2, Oct 1996	1.95
❑3, Nov 1996	1.95
❑4, Dec 1996	1.95
❑5, Jan 1997	1.95
❑6, Feb 1997	1.95
❑7, Mar 1997	1.95
❑8, Apr 1997	1.95
❑9, May 1997	1.95
❑10, Jun 1997; continued from Superboy #40, continues in Superboy #41	1.95
❑11, Jul 1997	1.95
❑12, Aug 1997	1.95
❑13, Sep 1997	1.95
❑14, Oct 1997; Genesis	1.95
❑15, Nov 1997	1.95
❑16, Dec 1997	1.95
❑17, Jan 1998	1.95
❑18, Feb 1998	1.95
❑19, Mar 1998	1.95

SUPERBOY PLUS
DC

	N-MINT
❑1, Jan 1997	2.95
❑2, Fal 1997; continues in Catwoman Plus #1	2.95

SUPERBOY/RISK DOUBLE-SHOT
DC

	N-MINT
❑1, Feb 1998	1.95

SUPERBOY/ROBIN: WORLD'S FINEST THREE
DC

	N-MINT
❑1, ca. 1996; prestige format	4.95
❑2, ca. 1996; prestige format	4.95

SUPERBOY'S LEGION
DC

	N-MINT
❑1, Apr 2001	5.95
❑2, May 2001	5.95

SUPERCAR
GOLD KEY

	N-MINT
❑1, Nov 1962	250.00
❑2, Feb 1963	200.00
❑3, May 1963	200.00
❑4, Aug 1963	200.00

SUPERCOPS
NOW

	N-MINT
❑1, Sep 1990; double-sized	2.75
❑2, Oct 1990	1.75
❑3, Nov 1990	1.75
❑4, Feb 1991	1.75

SUPER COPS
RED CIRCLE

	N-MINT
❑1, Jul 1974; GM (c); GM (a); based on MGM movie	2.00

SUPER DC GIANT
DC

	N-MINT
❑13, Sep 1970; really S-13; Binky	75.00
❑14, Sep 1970; really S-14; Westerns	30.00
❑15, Sep 1970; really S-15; Westerns	30.00
❑16, Sep 1970; really S-16; Brave & the Bold	30.00
❑17, Sep 1970; really S-17; Romance	125.00
❑18, Oct 1970; really S-18; Three Mouseketeers	50.00
❑19, Oct 1970; really S-19; Jerry Lewis	50.00
❑20, Oct 1970; really S-20; House of Mystery	40.00
❑21, Jan 1971; really S-21; Romance	175.00
❑22, Mar 1971; really S-22; Westerns	25.00
❑23, Mar 1971; really S-23; Unexpected	40.00
❑24, May 1971; CS (c); JM (a); really S-24; reprints Supergirl stories from Action Comics #295-298	30.00
❑25, Aug 1971; really S-25; Challengers of the Unknown	25.00
❑26, Aug 1971; really S-26; Aquaman	25.00
❑27, Sum 1976; Flying Saucers	15.00

SUPERFAN
MARK 1

	N-MINT
❑1, b&w	1.95

SUPERFIST AYUMI
FANTAGRAPHICS / EROS

	N-MINT
❑1, Oct 1996	2.95
❑2, Nov 1996	2.95

SUPER FRIENDS
DC

	N-MINT
❑1, Nov 1976 ATh (a)	20.00
❑2, Dec 1976	9.00
❑3, Feb 1977	7.00
❑4, Apr 1977	7.00
❑5, Jun 1977	7.00
❑6, Aug 1977	6.00
❑7, Oct 1977 1: Wonder Twins. 1: Tasmanian Devil.	6.00
❑8, Nov 1977	6.00
❑9, Dec 1977 1: Iron Maiden.	6.00
❑10, Mar 1978	6.00
❑11, May 1978	4.00
❑12, Jul 1978 1: Doctor Mist.	4.00
❑13, Sep 1978	4.00
❑13/Whitman, Sep 1978, Whitman variant	8.00

Other grades: Multiply price above by 5/6 for VF/NM • 2/3 for VERY FINE • 1/3 for FINE • 1/5 for VERY GOOD • 1/8 for GOOD

	N-MINT
❑14, Nov 1978	6.00
❑14/Whitman, Nov 1978, Whitman variant	12.00
❑15, Dec 1978	4.00
❑15/Whitman, Dec 1978; Whitman variant	12.00
❑16, Jan 1979	6.00
❑16/Whitman, Jan 1979, Whitman variant	12.00
❑17, Feb 1979	4.00
❑18, Mar 1979	4.00
❑19, Apr 1979	4.00
❑20, May 1979	4.00
❑20/Whitman, May 1979; Whitman variant	12.00
❑21, Jun 1979	6.00
❑21/Whitman, Jun 1979; Whitman variant	12.00
❑22, Jul 1979	6.00
❑22/Whitman, Jul 1979; Whitman variant	12.00
❑23, Aug 1979	6.00
❑23/Whitman, Aug 1979; Whitman variant	12.00
❑24, Sep 1979	4.00
❑25, Oct 1979 1: Fire.	4.00
❑25/Whitman, Oct 1979, 1: Fire. Whitman variant	8.00
❑26, Nov 1979	4.00
❑27, Dec 1979	4.00
❑28, Jan 1980	4.00
❑29, Feb 1980	4.00
❑30, Mar 1980	4.00
❑31, Apr 1980 A: Black Orchid.	4.00
❑32, May 1980	5.00
❑32/Whitman, May 1980, Whitman variant	10.00
❑33, Jun 1980	4.00
❑34, Jul 1980	4.00
❑35, Aug 1980	4.00
❑36, Sep 1980	4.00
❑37, Oct 1980	4.00
❑38, Nov 1980	4.00
❑39, Dec 1980	4.00
❑40, Jan 1981	4.00
❑41, Feb 1981	4.00
❑42, Mar 1981 1: Green Flame.	4.00
❑43, Apr 1981	4.00
❑44, May 1981	4.00
❑45, Jun 1981	4.00
❑46, Jul 1981	4.00
❑47, Aug 1981	4.00
❑Special 1, ca. 1981; giveaway; says A TV Comic on cover	5.00

SUPERGIRL (1ST SERIES)
DC

	N-MINT
❑1, Nov 1972	15.00
❑2	10.00
❑3, Feb 1973	8.00
❑4, Apr 1973	8.00
❑5, Jun 1973, origin of Zatana	8.00
❑6, Aug 1973	8.00
❑7, Oct 1973	8.00
❑8, Nov 1973	8.00
❑9, Jan 1974	8.00
❑10, Sep 1974 A: Prez.	8.00

SUPERGIRL (2ND SERIES)
DC

	N-MINT
❑14, Dec 1983; Title changes to Supergirl; Series continued from "Daring New Adventures of Supergirl"	3.00
❑15, Jan 1984	3.00
❑16, Feb 1984 CI (a); A: Ambush Bug.	3.00
❑17, Mar 1984	3.00
❑18, Apr 1984	3.00
❑19, May 1984	3.00
❑20, Jun 1984 A: Teen Titans. A: Justice League of America.	3.00
❑21, Jul 1984 CI (a)	3.00
❑22, Aug 1984 CI (a)	3.00
❑23, Sep 1984 CI (a)	3.00
❑DOT 1, ca. 1984; Department of Transportation giveaway JO (w); AT (a)	4.00

SUPERGIRL (3RD SERIES)
DC

	N-MINT
❑1, Sep 1996; PD (w); Matrix merges with Linda Danvers	10.00
❑1/2nd, Sep 1996 PD (w)	3.00
❑2, Oct 1996; PD (w); Matrix learns more of Linda Danvers' past	4.00
❑3, Nov 1996; PD (w); V: Gorilla Grodd. Final Night	3.50
❑4, Dec 1996 PD (w); V: Gorilla Grodd.	3.00
❑5, Jan 1997 PD (w); V: Chemo.	3.00
❑6, Feb 1997 PD (w); A: Superman. V: Rampage.	2.50
❑7, Mar 1997 PD (w)	2.50
❑8, Apr 1997 PD (w)	2.00
❑9, May 1997 PD (w); V: Tempus.	2.00
❑10, Jun 1997 PD (w)	2.00
❑11, Jul 1997 PD (w); V: Silver Banshee.	2.00
❑12, Aug 1997 PD (w)	2.00
❑13, Sep 1997 PD (w)	2.00
❑14, Oct 1997; PD (w); Genesis	2.00
❑15, Nov 1997 PD (w); V: Extremists.	2.00
❑16, Dec 1997; PD (w); V: Extremists. Face cover	2.00
❑17, Jan 1998 PD (w); V: Despero.	2.00
❑18, Feb 1998 PD (w); V: Despero.	2.00
❑19, Mar 1998 PD (w); V: Blastoff.	2.00
❑20, Apr 1998; PD (w); Millennium Giants	2.00
❑21, May 1998 PD (w)	2.00
❑22, Jun 1998 PD (w)	2.00
❑23, Jul 1998 PD (w); A: Steel.	2.00
❑24, Aug 1998 PD (w); A: Resurrection Man.	2.00
❑25, Sep 1998 PD (w)	2.00
❑26, Oct 1998 PD (w); O: Comet.	2.00
❑27, Dec 1998 PD (w); V: Female Furies.	2.00
❑28, Jan 1999 PD (w); V: Female Furies.	2.00
❑29, Feb 1999 PD (w); A: Twilight. A: Female Furies. A: Granny Goodness.	2.00
❑30, Mar 1999 PD (w); A: Matrix. V: Matrix.	2.00
❑31, Apr 1999 PD (w); V: Matrix.	1.99
❑32, May 1999 PD (w)	1.99
❑33, Jun 1999 PD (w)	1.99
❑34, Jul 1999 PD (w); V: Parasite.	1.99
❑35, Aug 1999 PD (w); V: Parasite.	1.99
❑36, Sep 1999 PD (w); A: Young Justice.	1.99
❑37, Oct 1999 PD (w); A: Young Justice.	1.99
❑38, Nov 1999; PD (w); A: Zauriel. Day of Judgment	1.99
❑39, Dec 1999 PD (w)	1.99
❑40, Jan 2000 PD (w)	1.99
❑41, Feb 2000 PD (w)	1.99
❑42, Mar 2000 PD (w)	1.99
❑43, Apr 2000 PD (w)	1.99
❑44, May 2000 PD (w)	1.99
❑45, Jun 2000 PD (w)	1.99
❑46, Jul 2000 PD (w)	1.99
❑47, Aug 2000 PD (w)	2.25
❑48, Sep 2000 PD (w)	2.25
❑49, Oct 2000 PD (w)	2.25
❑50, Nov 2000; Giant-size PD (w)	3.95
❑51, Dec 2000 PD (w)	2.25
❑52, Jan 2001 PD (w)	2.25
❑53, Feb 2001 PD (w)	2.25
❑54, Mar 2001 PD (w)	2.25
❑55, Apr 2001 PD (w)	2.25
❑56, May 2001 PD (w)	2.25
❑57, Jun 2001	2.25
❑58, Jul 2001	2.25
❑59, Aug 2001	2.25
❑60, Sep 2001	2.25
❑61, Oct 2001	2.25
❑62, Nov 2001 A: Two-Face.	2.25
❑63, Dec 2001	2.25
❑64, Jan 2002	2.25
❑65, Feb 2002	2.25
❑66, Mar 2002 A: Demon.	2.25
❑67, Apr 2002 A: Demon.	2.25
❑68, May 2002	2.25
❑69, Jun 2002	2.25
❑70, Jul 2002	2.25
❑71, Aug 2002	2.25
❑72, Sep 2002	2.25
❑73, Oct 2002	2.50
❑74, Nov 2002	2.50
❑75, Dec 2002	2.50
❑75/Dynamic	19.95
❑76, Jan 2003	2.50
❑77, Feb 2003	2.50
❑78, Mar 2003	2.50
❑79, Apr 2003	2.50
❑80, May 2003	2.50
❑1000000, Nov 1998 PD (w); A: R'E'L.	4.00
❑Annual 1, ca. 1996; DG (a); Legends of the Dead Earth	2.95
❑Annual 2, ca. 1997; Pulp Heroes	3.95

SUPERGIRL (4TH SERIES)
DC

	N-MINT
❑0, Aug 2005	5.00
❑1, Sep 2005	6.00
❑1/Turner, Sep 2005	8.00
❑1/Sketch, Sep 2005	8.00
❑2 2005	2.99
❑3, Jan 2006	2.99
❑4, Apr 2006	2.99
❑5, May 2006	2.99
❑6, Jul 2006	2.99

SUPERGIRL AND THE LEGION OF SUPER-HEROES
DC

	N-MINT
❑17, Jul 2006	2.99
❑18, Aug 2006	2.99
❑19, Sep 2006	2.99

SUPERGIRL/LEX LUTHOR SPECIAL
DC

	N-MINT
❑1, ca. 1993; includes pin-up gallery; cover says Supergirl and Team Luthor	2.50

SUPERGIRL (MINI-SERIES)
DC

	N-MINT
❑1, Feb 1994	3.00
❑2, Mar 1994	2.50
❑3, Apr 1994	2.50
❑4, May 1994	2.50

SUPERGIRL MOVIE SPECIAL
DC

	N-MINT
❑1, Movie adaptation	1.25

SUPERGIRL PLUS
DC

	N-MINT
❑1, Feb 1997	2.95

SUPERGIRL/PRYSM DOUBLE SHOT
DC

	N-MINT
❑1, Feb 1998	1.95

SUPERGIRL: WINGS
DC

	N-MINT
❑1, Dec 2001	5.95

SUPER GOOF (WALT DISNEY...)
GOLD KEY

	N-MINT
❑1, ca. 1965	24.00
❑2, ca. 1967	12.00
❑3, May 1968	12.00
❑4, Sep 1968	10.00
❑5, Dec 1968	10.00
❑6, Mar 1969	10.00
❑7, Jun 1969	10.00
❑8, Sep 1969 V: The Beagle Boys.	10.00
❑9, Dec 1969	10.00
❑10, Mar 1970	10.00
❑11, Jun 1970	7.00
❑12, Feb 1970	7.00
❑13, May 1970	7.00
❑14, Aug 1970	7.00
❑15, Nov 1970	7.00
❑16, Feb 1971	7.00
❑17, May 1971	7.00
❑18, Aug 1971	7.00
❑19, Nov 1971 A: Uncle Scrooge.	7.00
❑20, Feb 1972	7.00
❑21, May 1972	5.00
❑22, Aug 1972	5.00
❑23, Nov 1972	5.00
❑24 1973	5.00
❑25 1973	5.00
❑26 1973	5.00
❑27, Oct 1973	5.00
❑28 1974	5.00
❑29 1974	5.00
❑30, Jun 1974	5.00
❑31, Aug 1974	3.00
❑32, Nov 1974	3.00

Superman & Batman: Generations

Doing the decades with aging heroes

©DC

Superman & Batman: Generations II

Originals' descendants carry on legacy

©DC

Superman & Batman: Generations III

Century-long issues didn't seem like it

©DC

Superman & Bugs Bunny

Looney Tunes get powers, mayhem ensues

©DC

Superman/Batman

Select parts of stories play into continuity

©DC

N-MINT

❑33 1975 .... 3.00
❑34 1975 .... 3.00
❑35, Sep 1975 .... 3.00
❑36, Dec 1975 .... 3.00
❑37, Feb 1976 .... 3.00
❑38, Jun 1976 .... 3.00
❑39, Sep 1976 .... 3.00
❑40, Nov 1976 .... 3.00
❑41, Feb 1977 .... 3.00
❑42, Jun 1977 .... 3.00
❑43, Sep 1977, Reprints stories from Super Goof #8 and #10 .... 3.00
❑44, Nov 1977 .... 3.00
❑45, Feb 1978 .... 3.00
❑46, Apr 1978 .... 3.00
❑47, Jun 1978 .... 3.00
❑48, Aug 1978, Has Tarzan parody 3.00
❑49, Oct 1978, V: Emil Eagle. Casper in Hostess ad ("A Real Oddball") 3.00
❑50, Dec 1978 .... 3.00
❑51, Feb 1979 .... 2.50
❑52, Apr 1979 .... 2.50
❑53, Jun 1979, A: Gus Goose. A: . V: Emil Eagle. Thor in Hostess ad ("Good Overcomes Evil") 2.50
❑54, Aug 1979 .... 2.50
❑55, Oct 1979 .... 2.50
❑56, Dec 1979 .... 2.50
❑57, Jan 1980 .... 2.50
❑58, Mar 1980, A: Uncle Scrooge. Reprints stories from Super Goof #19; Chip 'n' Dale on cover; Spider-Man in Hostess ad ("Puts Himself in the Picture") 4.00
❑59, May 1980 .... 4.00
❑60, Jul 1980 .... 15.00
❑61, Oct 1980 .... 70.00
❑62, Dec 1980 .... 15.00
❑63, Jan 1981 .... 2.50
❑64 1981 .... 5.00
❑65 1981 .... 5.00
❑66, Dec 1981 .... 5.00
❑67, Feb 1982 .... 8.00
❑68 1982 .... 8.00
❑69 1982 .... 8.00
❑70 1982 .... 15.00
❑71 1982 .... 15.00
❑72 1983 .... 15.00
❑73, Jul 1983 .... 15.00
❑74 1983 .... 15.00

SUPER GREEN BERET
MILSON

❑1, Apr 1967 .... 30.00
❑2 .... 24.00

SUPER HEROES BATTLE SUPER GORILLAS
DC

❑1, Win 1976 .... 10.00

SUPER HEROES PUZZLES AND GAMES
MARVEL

❑1, Apr 1980; giveaway O: Captain America. O: Spider-Man. O: The Hulk. O: Spider-Woman. 2.00

N-MINT

SUPER HEROES STAMP ALBUM
USPS / DC

❑1, 1900-1909 .... 3.00
❑2, 1910-1919 .... 3.00
❑3, 1920-1929 .... 3.00
❑4, 1930-1939; no Snow White coverage 3.00
❑5, 1940-1949 .... 3.00
❑6, 1950-1959; 3-D stamp 3.00
❑7, 1960-1969 .... 3.50
❑8, 1970-1979 .... 3.50
❑9, 1980-1989 .... 3.50
❑10, 1990-1999 .... 3.50

SUPER HEROES VERSUS SUPER VILLAINS
ARCHIE

❑1, ca. 1966 .... 50.00

SUPER HERO HAPPY HOUR
GEEKPUNK

❑1, ca. 2002, b&w 3.00
❑2, ca. 2003, b&w 3.00
❑3, ca. 2003, b&w 3.00
❑4, ca. 2003, b&w 3.00

SUPER INFORMATION HIJINKS: REALITY CHECK
TAVICAT

❑1, Oct 1995, b&w 2.95
❑2, Dec 1995, b&w 2.95
❑3, 1996 .... 2.95
❑4, 1996 .... 2.95
❑5, 1996 .... 2.95

SUPER INFORMATION HIJINKS: REALITY CHECK! (2ND SERIES)
SIRIUS

❑1, Sep 1996 .... 2.95
❑2, Oct 1996 .... 2.95
❑3, Nov 1996 .... 2.95
❑4, Dec 1996 .... 2.95
❑5, Jan 1997 .... 2.95
❑6, Feb 1997 .... 2.95
❑7, Mar 1997 .... 2.95
❑8, Jan 1998 .... 2.95
❑9, Mar 1998 .... 2.95
❑10, May 1998 .... 2.95
❑11, Jul 1998 .... 2.95
❑12, Oct 1998 .... 2.95

SUPERIOR SEVEN
IMAGINE THIS

❑1 .... 2.00
❑2 1992, b&w 2.00
❑3 1992, b&w 2.00
❑4 .... 2.00
❑5 .... 2.00

SUPERMAN (1ST SERIES)
DC

❑109, Nov 1956 .... 280.00
❑110, Jan 1957 .... 280.00
❑111, Feb 1957 .... 240.00
❑112, Mar 1957 .... 240.00
❑113, May 1957 .... 240.00
❑114, Jul 1957 .... 240.00
❑115, Aug 1957 .... 240.00
❑116, Sep 1957 .... 240.00

N-MINT

❑117, Nov 1957 .... 240.00
❑118, Jan 1958 CS (c); (w); (a) 240.00
❑119, Feb 1958 .... 240.00
❑120, Mar 1958 .... 240.00
❑121, May 1958 .... 195.00
❑122, Jul 1958 .... 195.00
❑123, Aug 1958; Supergirl prototype 195.00
❑124, Sep 1958 .... 195.00
❑125, Nov 1958 .... 195.00
❑126, Jan 1959 .... 195.00
❑127, Feb 1959 O: Titano. 1: Titano. 195.00
❑128, Apr 1959 .... 195.00
❑129, May 1959 O: Lori Lemaris. 1: Lori Lemaris. 195.00
❑130, Jul 1959 .... 195.00
❑131, Aug 1959 .... 155.00
❑132, Oct 1959 A: Batman & Robin. 155.00
❑133, Nov 1959 .... 155.00
❑134, Jan 1960 .... 155.00
❑135, Feb 1960 .... 155.00
❑136, Apr 1960 .... 155.00
❑137, May 1960 .... 155.00
❑138, Jul 1960 .... 155.00
❑139, Aug 1960 .... 155.00
❑140, Oct 1960 1: Bizarro Jr.. 1: Blue Kryptonite. 1: Bizarro Supergirl. A: Lex Luthor. 175.00
❑141, Nov 1960 .... 115.00
❑142, Jan 1961 .... 115.00
❑143, Feb 1961 .... 115.00
❑144, Apr 1961 A: Lex Luthor. 115.00
❑145, May 1961 .... 115.00
❑146, Jul 1961; O: Superman. Superman's life 160.00
❑147, Aug 1961 CS (a); 1: Legion of Super-Heroes (adult). 1: Legion of Super-Villains 135.00
❑148, Oct 1961 CS (a); V: Mxyzptlk. 115.00
❑149, Nov 1961 CS (a); A: Legion of Super-Heroes. 125.00
❑150, Jan 1962 .... 68.00
❑151, Feb 1962 .... 68.00
❑152, Apr 1962 A: Legion of Super-Heroes. 68.00
❑153, May 1962 .... 68.00
❑154, Jul 1962 CS (a) 68.00
❑155, Aug 1962 .... 68.00
❑156, Oct 1962 .... 68.00
❑157, Nov 1962 1: Gold Kryptonite. 68.00
❑158, Jan 1963 CS (a); 1: Nightwing. 1: Flamebird. 68.00
❑159, Feb 1963 .... 68.00
❑160, Apr 1963 .... 68.00
❑161, May 1963 D: Ma & Pa Kent. 68.00
❑162, Jul 1963 KS (c); CS, KS (a) 58.00
❑163, Aug 1963 .... 58.00
❑164, Oct 1963 CS (a) 58.00
❑165, Nov 1963 .... 58.00
❑166, Jan 1964 .... 58.00
❑167, Feb 1964 CS (a); O: Brainiac (new origin). O: Braniac 5 (new origin). 58.00
❑168, Apr 1964 .... 58.00
❑169, May 1964 .... 58.00
❑170, Jul 1964 A: John F. Kennedy. 58.00
❑171, Aug 1964 CS (a) 58.00
❑172, Oct 1964 .... 58.00

Other grades: Multiply price above by 5/6 for VF/NM • 2/3 for VERY FINE • 1/3 for FINE • 1/5 for VERY GOOD • 1/8 for GOOD

SUPERMAN

N-MINT

❑173, Nov 1964 ... 58.00
❑174, Jan 1965 ... 58.00
❑175, Feb 1965, Imaginary Story ... 58.00
❑176, Apr 1965 CS (a) ... 58.00
❑177, May 1965 ... 58.00
❑178, Jul 1965 ... 58.00
❑179, Aug 1965 ... 58.00
❑180, Oct 1965 ... 58.00
❑181, Nov 1965 CS (a) ... 55.00
❑182, Jan 1966 V: Toyman. ... 55.00
❑183, Jan 1966, Giant-size; aka 80 Page Giant #G-18; Golden Age reprints ... 55.00
❑184, Feb 1966 ... 55.00
❑185, Apr 1966 ... 55.00
❑186, May 1966 CS (a) ... 55.00
❑187, Jun 1966, Giant-size; CS, KS (a); aka 80 Page Giant #G-23; Fortress stories; reprints from Superman #17, Action Comics #164, #233, #244, and #261, and Jimmy Olsen #53 (incl. Action covers) ... 60.00
❑188, Jul 1966 CS (a) ... 55.00
❑189, Aug 1966 ... 55.00
❑190, Oct 1966 ... 55.00
❑191, Nov 1966 V: D.E.M.O.N. ... 55.00
❑192, Jan 1967, CS (a); Imaginary Story ... 55.00
❑193, Feb 1967, Giant-size; aka 80 Page Giant #G-31; reprints Action #223 and Superman #149 ... 60.00
❑194, Feb 1967, CS (a); Reprints Superman #133 ... 55.00
❑195, Apr 1967 CS (a) ... 55.00
❑196, May 1967 ... 55.00
❑197, Jul 1967, Giant-size; aka 80 Page Giant #G-36; All Clark Kent issue ... 55.00
❑198, Jul 1967 CS (a) ... 55.00
❑199, Aug 1967, 1st Superman/Flash race ... 180.00
❑200, Oct 1967 ... 60.00
❑201, Nov 1967 CS (a) ... 24.00
❑202, Dec 1967, Giant-size; aka 80 Page Giant #G-42; Bizarro issue ... 30.00
❑203, Jan 1968 CS (c); ... 24.00
❑204, Feb 1968 NA (c); 1: Q-energy. ... 24.00
❑205, Apr 1968 ... 24.00
❑206, May 1968 ... 24.00
❑207, Jun 1968, Giant-size; CS, KS (a); 30th Anniversary; aka 80 Page Giant #G-48; cover says July; reprints stories from Action Comics #265 and #266, Superman #135, and Superman's Girlfriend Lois Lane #15 ... 24.00
❑208, Jul 1968 CS, JAb (a) ... 24.00
❑209, Aug 1968 CS, JAb (a) ... 24.00
❑210, Oct 1968 CS (a) ... 24.00
❑211, Nov 1968 CS, JAb (a) ... 24.00
❑212, Jan 1969, Giant-size; CS (a); aka 80 Page Giant #G-54; Superbabies. ... 50.00
❑213, Jan 1969 CS, JAb (a); A: Lex Luthor. ... 24.00
❑214, Feb 1969 CS, JAb (a) ... 24.00
❑215, Apr 1969, CS, JAb (a); Imaginary Story; Superman as widower ... 24.00
❑216, May 1969, CS, JAb (a); in Vietnam ... 24.00
❑217, Jul 1969; Giant-size; CS (c); CS (a); aka Giant #G-60 ... 30.00
❑218, Jul 1969 CS, JAb (a) ... 20.00
❑219, Aug 1969 CS (a) ... 20.00
❑220, Oct 1969 CS (c); CS (a) ... 20.00
❑221, Nov 1969 CS (a) ... 20.00
❑222, Jan 1970; Giant-size; CS (c); CS (a); aka Giant #G-66 ... 30.00
❑223, Jan 1970 CS (a) ... 20.00
❑224, Feb 1970, CS (a); Imaginary Story ... 20.00
❑225, Apr 1970 CS (a) ... 20.00
❑226, May 1970 CS (a) ... 20.00
❑227, Jul 1970; Giant-size; CS (a); aka Giant #G-72 ... 30.00
❑228, Jul 1970 CS (c); CS, DA (a) ... 20.00
❑229, Aug 1970 CS, DA (a) ... 20.00
❑230, Oct 1970, CS, DA (a); Imaginary Story; ... 20.00
❑231, Nov 1970, NA, CS (c); NA, CS, DA (a); Imaginary Story; Luthor reprint ... 20.00
❑232, Jan 1971; Giant-size; CS (a); aka Giant #G-78; Title changes to "The Amazing New Adventures of Superman" ... 30.00

❑233, Jan 1971 CS (a) ... 40.00
❑234, Feb 1971, (c); MA, CS (a); A: Sand Superman. World of Krypton back-up ... 18.00
❑235, Mar 1971 MA, CS (a) ... 18.00
❑236, Apr 1971, MA, DG, CS (a); World of Krypton back-up ... 18.00
❑237, May 1971 MA, CS (a) ... 18.00
❑238, Jun 1971, MA, CI (c); MA, GM, CS (a); A: Sand Superman. World of Krypton back-up ... 18.00
❑239, Jul 1971, Giant-size; MA, GM, CS (a); aka Giant #G-84; reprints Action #267 and #268, Superman #127 and #164 ... 30.00
❑240, Jul 1971, DG, CS (a); A: I-Ching. World of Krypton back-up ... 18.00
❑241, Aug 1971, MA, CS (a); A: I-Ching. A: Sand Superman. Giant; Reprints Superman #112 and #176 ... 18.00
❑242, Sep 1971, CI, CS (a); A: final. Reprints Superman #96, and Strange Adventures #54 ... 18.00
❑243, Oct 1971 CS (a) ... 18.00
❑244, Nov 1971, CS (c); MA, CS (a); Reprints Superman #181 and Strange Adventures #34 ... 18.00
❑245, Jan 1972, CS (c); CS, MR (a); a.k.a. DC 100-Page Super-Spectacular #DC-7; back cover pin-up; reprints from All-Star Western #117, The Atom #3, Detective #66, Kid Eternity #3, Mystery in Space #89, and Superman #87, and #167 ... 22.00
❑246, Dec 1971 CS (c); CS (a) ... 18.00
❑247, Jan 1972, CS (c); MA, CS (a); A: Guardians of the Universe. 1st Private Life of Clark Kent; Superman of Tomorrow back-up; Reprints Action #338 ... 18.00
❑248, Feb 1972; CS (c); CS (a); Reprints Action #339 ... 18.00
❑249, Mar 1972 NA, CS (a); O: Terra-Man. 1: Terra-Man. ... 18.00
❑250, Apr 1972 CS (a) ... 18.00
❑251, May 1972 MA, CS (a) ... 18.00
❑252, Jun 1972, NA (c); MA, CS (a); a.k.a. DC 100-Page Super Spectacular #DC-13; wraparound cover ... 60.00
❑253, Jun 1972; MA, CS (a); Reprints ... 18.00
❑254, Jul 1972 NA, CS (a) ... 22.00
❑255, Aug 1972 CS (a) ... 9.00
❑256, Sep 1972 CS (a) ... 9.00
❑257, Oct 1972 CS (a) ... 9.00
❑258, Nov 1972, MA, DG, CS (a); Private Life of Clark Kent back-up ... 9.00
❑259, Dec 1972 CS (a) ... 9.00
❑260, Jan 1973, MA, DC, CS (a); World of Krypton back-up ... 9.00
❑261, Feb 1973 CS (a); A: Star Sapphire. ... 9.00
❑262, Mar 1973, MA, CS (a); Private Life of Clark Kent back-up ... 9.00
❑263, Apr 1973 CS (a) ... 9.00
❑264, Jun 1973 CS (a); 1: Steve Lombard. ... 9.00
❑265, Jul 1973 MA, CS (a) ... 8.00
❑266, Aug 1973 CS (a) ... 8.00
❑267, Sep 1973, BO, MA, CS (a); Private Life of Clark Kent back-up ... 8.00
❑268, Oct 1973 CS (a) ... 8.00
❑269, Nov 1973 CS (a) ... 8.00
❑270, Dec 1973 CS (a) ... 8.00
❑271, Jan 1974 CS (a) ... 8.00
❑272, Feb 1974, NC (c); BO, GK, CS (a); Reprints Action #97, and Green Lantern (2nd series) #42 ... 20.00
❑273, Mar 1974 BO, CS (a) ... 7.00
❑274, Apr 1974 BO, CS (a) ... 7.00
❑275, May 1974 BO, CS (a) ... 7.00
❑276, Jun 1974 BO, CS (a); 1: Captain Thunder. ... 7.00
❑277, Jul 1974, BO, CS (a); Private Life of Clark Kent back-up ... 7.00
❑278, Aug 1974, NC (c); BO, CS (a); Reprints Action #211 and #298, Superman #33 and #138, and World's Finest Comics #62 ... 17.00
❑279, Sep 1974, CS (a); A: Batgirl. World of Krypton back-up ... 5.00
❑280, Oct 1974, BO, CS (a); Private Life of Clark Kent back-up ... 5.00
❑281, Nov 1974 CS (a) ... 5.00

❑282, Dec 1974, CS, KS (a); World of Krypton back-up ... 5.00
❑283, Jan 1975 CS (a) ... 5.00
❑284, Feb 1975, NC (c); BO, CS (a); reprints Action #304, and Superman #25, #41, #42, and #148 ... 7.00
❑285, Mar 1975 CS (a); A: Roy Raymond. ... 5.00
❑286, Apr 1975 CS (a); V: Luthor. V: Parasite. ... 5.00
❑287, May 1975, BO, CS (a); Return of Krypto; Private Life of Clark Kent back-up ... 4.00
❑288, Jun 1975 CS (a) ... 4.00
❑289, Jul 1975 CS (a) ... 4.00
❑290, Aug 1975 CS (a) ... 4.00
❑291, Sep 1975 BO, CS (a) ... 4.00
❑292, Oct 1975, BO, AM, CS (a); O: Lex Luthor. Private Life of Clark Kent back-up ... 4.00
❑293, Nov 1975 BO, CS (a) ... 2.50
❑294, Dec 1975 CS (a) ... 2.50
❑295, Jan 1976 CS (a) ... 2.50
❑296, Feb 1976; CS (a); Superman loses powers when not in costume. ... 2.50
❑297, Mar 1976 CS (a) ... 2.50
❑298, Apr 1976 BO, CS (a) ... 2.50
❑299, May 1976 BO, CS (a) ... 2.50
❑300, Jun 1976, 300th anniversary issue BO, CS (a); O: Superman of 2001. ... 11.00
❑301, Jul 1976 CS (a) ... 2.50
❑302, Aug 1976 CS (a) ... 2.50
❑303, Sep 1976 CS (a) ... 2.50
❑304, Oct 1976 CS (a) ... 2.50
❑305, Nov 1976 CS (a) ... 2.50
❑306, Dec 1976 BO, CS (a); V: Bizarro. ... 2.50
❑307, Jan 1977 NA (c); CS, FS, JL (a) ... 2.50
❑308, Feb 1977 NA (c); CS, FS, JL (a) ... 2.50
❑309, Mar 1977 CS, FS, JL (a) ... 2.50
❑310, Apr 1977 CS (a) ... 2.50
❑311, May 1977 CS (a) ... 2.50
❑312, Jun 1977 CS (a) ... 2.50
❑313, Jul 1977 NA (c); CS, DA (a) ... 2.50
❑314, Aug 1977 CS (a) ... 2.50
❑315, Sep 1977 CS (a) ... 2.50
❑316, Oct 1977 CS (a) ... 2.50
❑317, Nov 1977, NA (c); CS, DA (a); Return of Lana Lang ... 2.50
❑318, Dec 1977 BO, RB (c); CS (a) ... 2.50
❑319, Jan 1978 CS (a) ... 2.50
❑320, Feb 1978 CS (a) ... 2.50
❑321, Mar 1978 DG (c); CS (a) ... 2.50
❑321/Whitman, Mar 1978, DG (c); CS (a); Whitman variant ... 5.00
❑322, Apr 1978 CS (a); V: Parasite ... 2.50
❑322/Whitman, Apr 1978, CS (a); V: Parasite. Whitman variant ... 5.00
❑323, May 1978 CS, DA (a); 1: Atomic Skull. V: Atomic Skull. ... 2.50
❑323/Whitman, May 1978, CS, DA (a); 1: Atomic Skull. V: Atomic Skull. Whitman variant ... 5.00
❑324, Jun 1978 RB, DG (c); CS (a); V: Titano. ... 2.50
❑324/Whitman, Jun 1978, RB, DG (c); CS (a); V: Titano. Whitman variant ... 5.00
❑325, Jul 1978 RB (c); CS (a) ... 2.50
❑325/Whitman, Jul 1978, RB (c); CS (a); Whitman variant ... 5.00
❑326, Aug 1978 CS (a) ... 2.50
❑326/Whitman, Aug 1978, CS (a); Whitman variant ... 5.00
❑327, Sep 1978 CS (a) ... 2.50
❑327/Whitman, Sep 1978, CS (a); Whitman variant ... 5.00
❑328, Oct 1978, DG (c); CS, KS (a); Private Life of Clark Kent back-up ... 2.50
❑328/Whitman, Oct 1978, DG (c); CS, KS (a); Private Life of Clark Kent back-up; Whitman variant ... 5.00
❑329, Nov 1978, DG, RA (c); CS, KS (a); Mr. and Mrs. Superman back-up ... 2.50
❑329/Whitman, Nov 1978, DG, RA (c); CS, KS (a); Mr. and Mrs. Superman back-up; Whitman variant ... 5.00
❑330, Dec 1978 CS (a) ... 2.50
❑330/Whitman, Dec 1978, CS (a); Whitman variant ... 5.00
❑331, Jan 1979 CS (a) ... 2.50
❑331/Whitman, Jan 1979, CS (a); Whitman variant ... 5.00

Other grades: Multiply price above by 5/6 for VF/NM • 2/3 for VERY FINE • 1/3 for FINE • 1/5 for VERY GOOD • 1/8 for GOOD

Superman: Birthright

Mark Waid rethinks John Byrne's revamp
©DC

Superman Family

Jimmy and Lois' solo series moved to anthology
©DC

Super Manga Blast!

Manga serials include crazy cat capers
©Dark Horse

Superman: Metropolis

The life of a city that comes alive
©DC

Superman Red/ Superman Blue

Two Supermen are better than one
©DC

	N-MINT
❑332, Feb 1979 CS (a)	2.50
❑332/Whitman, Feb 1979, CS (a); Whitman variant	5.00
❑333, Mar 1979 CS (a)	2.50
❑333/Whitman, Mar 1979, CS (a); Whitman variant	5.00
❑334, Apr 1979 CS (a)	2.50
❑334/Whitman, Apr 1979, CS (a); Whitman variant	5.00
❑335, May 1979 CS (a); V: Mxyzptlk.	2.50
❑335/Whitman, May 1979, CS (a); V: Mxyzptlk. Whitman variant	5.00
❑336, Jun 1979 CS (a)	2.50
❑336/Whitman, Jun 1979, CS (a); Whitman variant	5.00
❑337, Jul 1979 CS (a)	2.50
❑337/Whitman, Jul 1979, CS (a); Whitman variant	5.00
❑338, Aug 1979, DG, RA (c); CS (a); Kandor enlarged	2.50
❑338/Whitman, Aug 1979, DG, RA (c); CS (a); Kandor enlarged; Whitman variant	5.00
❑339, Sep 1979 CS (a)	2.50
❑339/Whitman, Sep 1979; CS (a); Whitman variant	5.00
❑340, Oct 1979 CS (a)	2.50
❑340/Whitman, Oct 1979; CS (a); Whitman variant	5.00
❑341, Nov 1979 DG, RA (c); CS (a); A: J. Wilbur Wolfingham.	2.50
❑341/Whitman, Nov 1979, DG, RA (c); CS (a); A: J. Wilbur Wolfingham. Whitman variant	5.00
❑342, Dec 1979 CS (a)	2.50
❑342/Whitman, Dec 1979, CS (a); Whitman variant	5.00
❑343, Jan 1980 CS (a)	2.50
❑343/Whitman, Jan 1980, CS (a); Whitman variant	5.00
❑344, Feb 1980 CS (a)	2.50
❑344/Whitman, Feb 1980, CS (a); Whitman variant	5.00
❑345, Mar 1980 CS (a)	2.50
❑345/Whitman, Mar 1980, CS (a); Whitman variant	5.00
❑346, Apr 1980 CS (a)	2.50
❑346/Whitman, Apr 1980, CS (a); Whitman variant	5.00
❑347, May 1980 CS (a)	2.50
❑347/Whitman, May 1980, CS (a); Whitman variant	5.00
❑348, Jun 1980 CS (a)	2.50
❑348/Whitman, Jun 1980, CS (a); Whitman variant	5.00
❑349, Jul 1980 CS (a)	2.50
❑349/Whitman, Jul 1980, CS (a); Whitman variant	5.00
❑350, Aug 1980 CS (a)	2.50
❑350/Whitman, Aug 1980, CS (a); Whitman variant	5.00
❑351, Sep 1980 CS (a)	2.00
❑352, Oct 1980 CS (a)	2.00
❑353, Nov 1980 CS (a)	2.00
❑354, Dec 1980 CS (a)	2.00
❑355, Jan 1981 JSn, CS (a)	2.00
❑356, Feb 1981 CS (a)	2.00
❑357, Mar 1981 CS (a)	2.00

	N-MINT
❑358, Apr 1981, DG, RA (c); CS (a); Imaginary story	2.00
❑359, May 1981 CS (a)	2.00
❑360, Jun 1981 CS (a)	2.00
❑361, Jul 1981 CS (a)	2.00
❑362, Aug 1981, DG, RA (c); CS, DA (a); Lana and Lois contract deadly virus that killed Kents; Superman The In-Between Years back-up	2.00
❑363, Sep 1981, RB, DG (c); CS (a); A: Lex Luthor. Imaginary Story	2.00
❑364, Oct 1981, GP, DG (c); CS (a); Superman 2020 back-up	2.00
❑365, Nov 1981, DG, RA (c); CS, KS (a); A: Supergirl. Superman the In-Between Years back-up	2.00
❑366, Dec 1981 CS (a)	2.00
❑367, Jan 1982 CS (a)	2.00
❑368, Feb 1982 CS (a)	2.00
❑369, Mar 1982 CS (a); V: Parasite	2.00
❑370, Apr 1982 CS (a)	2.00
❑371, May 1982 CS (a)	2.00
❑372, Jun 1982 CS (a)	2.00
❑373, Jul 1982 CS (a)	2.00
❑374, Aug 1982 CS (a)	2.00
❑375, Sep 1982 CS (a)	2.00
❑376, Oct 1982, RB (c); BO, CI, CS, DA (a); Supergirl back-up	2.00
❑377, Nov 1982 CS (a)	2.00
❑378, Dec 1982 CS (a)	2.00
❑379, Jan 1983 DG, RA (c); CS (a); A: Bizarro	2.00
❑380, Feb 1983 CS (a)	2.00
❑381, Mar 1983 CS (a)	2.00
❑382, Apr 1983 CS (a)	2.00
❑383, May 1983 CS (a)	2.00
❑384, Jun 1983 CS (a)	2.00
❑385, Jul 1983 CS (a)	2.00
❑386, Aug 1983 CS (a)	2.00
❑387, Sep 1983 CS (a)	2.00
❑388, Oct 1983 (c); CS (a)	2.00
❑389, Nov 1983 CS (a)	2.00
❑390, Dec 1983 CS (a)	2.00
❑391, Jan 1984 CS (a)	2.00
❑392, Feb 1984 CS (a)	2.00
❑393, Mar 1984 CS (a)	2.00
❑394, Apr 1984 CS (a)	2.00
❑395, May 1984 CS (a)	2.00
❑396, Jun 1984 CS (a)	2.00
❑397, Jul 1984 CS (a)	2.00
❑398, Aug 1984 CS (a)	2.00
❑399, Sep 1984 CS (a)	2.00
❑400, Oct 1984, Giant-size; HC (c); JSo (w); JD, WP, AW, SD, BSz, BWr, JO, JOy, WE, JBy, MGr, JK, BB, FM, CS, JSo, KJ, MR (a); multiple short stories	5.00
❑401, Nov 1984 CS (a)	2.00
❑402, Dec 1984 BO, CS (a)	2.00
❑403, Jan 1985 CS (a)	2.00
❑404, Feb 1985, BO, CI (a); imaginary story	2.00
❑405, Mar 1985 CS (a)	2.00
❑406, Apr 1985 CS (a)	2.00
❑407, May 1985, JOy (c); IN (a); powers passed along	2.00

	N-MINT
❑408, Jun 1985, AW (c); AW, CS (a); nuclear nightmare	2.00
❑409, Jul 1985 AW (c); AW, CS, KS (a)	2.00
❑410, Aug 1985 KJ (c); AW, CS (a)	2.00
❑411, Sep 1985, MA, CS (w); MA, CS (a); Julius Schwartz' birthday; MASK preview comic	2.00
❑412, Oct 1985 CS (a)	2.00
❑413, Nov 1985 KJ (c); AW, CS (a)	2.00
❑414, Dec 1985, AW, CS (a); Crisis on Infinite Earths cross-over	2.00
❑415, Jan 1986, AW, CS (a); Crisis on Infinite Earths cross-over	2.00
❑416, Feb 1986, AW, CS (a); Superman learns Luthor's connection to Einstein	2.00
❑417, Mar 1986, CS (a); imaginary story	2.00
❑418, Apr 1986 CS (a)	2.00
❑419, May 1986 CS (a)	2.00
❑420, Jun 1986 CS (a)	2.00
❑421, Jul 1986, (c); CS (a); MASK comic insert	2.00
❑422, Aug 1986 BB (c); TY, CS (a)	2.00
❑423, Sep 1986, AMo (w); GP, CS (a); series continues as Adventures of Superman; imaginary story	5.00
❑Annual 1, Oct 1960; O: Supergirl. 1: Supergirl. 1: Supergirl reprinted. Reprints Action Comics #252	600.00
❑Annual 1/2nd, Oct 1998, Replica edition; CS, KS (a); Cardstock cover; Replica Edition; reprints Giant Superman Annual #1	5.00
❑Annual 2, ca. 1960 O: Titano.	325.00
❑Annual 3, Sum 1961; Strange Lives of Superman	210.00
❑Annual 4, Win 1961 O: Legion of Super-Heroes. A: Legion of Super-Heroes.	180.00
❑Annual 5, Sum 1962, (c); (w); (a); Krypton related stories	105.00
❑Annual 6, Win 1962; 1: Legion of Super-Heroes. Reprints Adventure Comics #247	90.00
❑Annual 7, Jun 1963, 25th anniversary (c); (w); (a); O: Superman-Batman team.	62.00
❑Annual 8, Sum 1963, (c); (w); (a); Untold Stories and Secret Origins	46.00
❑Annual 9, ca. 1983	5.00
❑Annual 10, ca. 1984 MA, CS (a)	5.00
❑Annual 11, ca. 1985 DaG (c); AMo (w); DaG (a); A: Wonder Woman. A: Robin. A: Batman. V: Mongul.	4.00
❑Annual 12, ca. 1986 BB (c); V: Luthor's Warsuit.	3.00
❑Special 1, ca. 1983 (c); GK (w); GK (a)	4.00
❑Special 2, Apr 1984	4.00
❑Special 3, Apr 1985 IN (a); V: Amazo.	4.00

SUPERMAN (2ND SERIES)
DC

❑0, Oct 1994, ▲1994-38	3.00
❑1, Jan 1987 JBy (w); JBy (a); 1: Metallo (new)	4.00
❑2, Feb 1987 JBy (c); JBy (w); JBy (a)	3.50
❑3, Mar 1987, JBy (c); JBy (w); JBy (a); 1: Amazing Grace. cross-over Legends chapter 17	3.00

Other grades: Multiply price above by 5/6 for VF/NM • 2/3 for VERY FINE • 1/3 for FINE • 1/5 for VERY GOOD • 1/8 for GOOD

	N-MINT
❑4, Apr 1987 JBy (c); JBy (w); JBy (a); 1: Bloodsport.	2.50
❑5, May 1987 JBy (c); JBy (w); JBy (a)	2.50
❑6, Jun 1987 (c); JBy (w); JBy (a)	2.00
❑7, Jul 1987 JBy (c); JBy (w); JBy (a); O: Rampage (DC). 1: Rampage (DC).	2.00
❑8, Aug 1987 JBy (c); JBy (w); JBy (a); A: Superboy. A: Legion of Super-Heroes.	2.00
❑9, Sep 1987 JBy (c); JBy (w); JBy (a); A: Joker. V: Joker. V: Luthor.	3.50
❑10, Oct 1987 JBy (c); JBy (w); JBy (a)	2.00
❑11, Nov 1987 JBy (c); JBy (w); JBy (a); O: Mr. Mxyzptlk.	2.00
❑12, Dec 1987 (c); JBy (w); JBy (a); O: Lori Lemaris.	2.00
❑13, Jan 1988, JBy (c); JBy (w); JBy (a); Millennium Week 2	2.00
❑14, Feb 1988, JBy (c); JBy (w); JBy (a); A: Green Lantern. Millennium Week 6	2.00
❑15, Mar 1988 JBy (c); JBy (w); JBy (a)	2.00
❑16, Apr 1988 JBy (c); JBy (w); JBy (a); V: Prankster.	2.00
❑17, May 1988 JBy (c); JBy (w); JBy (a); V: Silver Banshee	2.00
❑18, Jun 1988 JBy (w)	2.00
❑19, Jul 1988 JBy (w); JBy (a); 1: Dreadnaught. 1: Psi-Phon.	2.00
❑20, Aug 1988 JBy (c); JBy (w); JBy (a); A: Doom Patrol.	2.00
❑21, Sep 1988, JBy (c); JBy (w); JBy (a); Supergirl	2.00
❑22, Oct 1988, (c); JBy (w); JBy (a); Supergirl	2.00
❑23, Nov 1988 CR (a); A: Batman.	2.00
❑24, Dec 1988 KGa (c); KGa (a)	2.00
❑25, Dec 1988 KGa (c); KGa (a)	2.00
❑26, Jan 1989, KGa (c); KGa (a); Invasion!	2.00
❑27, Jan 1989, KGa (c); KGa (a); Invasion!	2.00
❑28, Feb 1989, KGa (c); KGa (a); in space	2.00
❑29, Mar 1989, KGa (c); in space	2.00
❑30, Apr 1989, KGa (c); KGa (a); in space	2.00
❑31, May 1989, KGa (c); Mxyzptlk vs. Luthor	2.00
❑32, Jun 1989 KGa (c); KGa (a); V: Mongul.	2.00
❑33, Jul 1989 KGa (c); KGa (a)	2.00
❑34, Aug 1989 KGa (c); JOy (w); KGa (a); V: Skyhook.	2.00
❑35, Sep 1989, KGa (c); JOy (w); CS, KGa (a); A: Black Racer. simultaneous stories	2.00
❑36, Oct 1989 JOy (c); JOy (w); JOy (a); V: Prankster.	2.00
❑37, Nov 1989 JOy (w); JOy (a); A: Newsboys.	2.00
❑38, Dec 1989 JOy (c); JOy (w)	2.00
❑39, Jan 1990 JOy (c); JOy (w); KGa, BMc (a)	2.00
❑40, Feb 1990 JOy (c); JOy (w); JOy (a)	2.00
❑41, Mar 1990, JOy (c); JOy (w); JOy (a); A: Lobo. The Day of the Krypton Man part 1	2.00
❑42, Apr 1990, JOy (c); JOy (w); JOy (a); The Day of the Krypton Man part 4	2.00
❑43, May 1990 JOy (c); JOy (w); JOy (a); V: Kryptonite Man.	2.00
❑44, Jun 1990, JOy (c); JOy (w); JOy (a); A: Batman. Dark Knight over Metropolis	2.00
❑45, Jul 1990, JOy (c); JOy (w); JOy (a); Jimmy Olsen's Diary insert	2.00
❑46, Aug 1990 JOy (c); JOy (w); JOy (a); A: Jade. A: Obsidian. V: Terraman.	2.00
❑47, Sep 1990, (c); JOy (w); JOy (a); V: Blaze. Soul Search - Chapter 2	2.00
❑48, Oct 1990 KGa, BMc (c); CS (a); A: Sinbad.	2.00
❑49, Nov 1990 JOy (w); JOy (a)	2.00
❑50, Dec 1990, JOy (c); JOy (w); JOy, JBy, CS, KGa (a); Clark Kent proposes to Lois Lane	4.00
❑50/2nd, Dec 1990, JOy (w); JOy, JBy, CS, KGa (a); Clark Kent proposes to Lois Lane	1.75
❑51, Jan 1991, JOy (c); JOy (w); JOy (a); 1: Mister Z. V: Mr. Z. ▲1991-1.	2.00

	N-MINT
❑52, Feb 1991 JOy (c); JOy (w); KGa (a); V: Terraman	2.00
❑52/2nd, Feb 1991	1.50
❑53, Mar 1991, JOy (c); JOy (w); JOy (a); ▲1991-7; Lois reacts to Superman disclosing identity	2.50
❑53/2nd, Mar 1991, JOy (w); Lois reacts to Superman disclosing identity	1.50
❑54, Apr 1991, JOy (c); JOy (w); JOy (a); ▲1991-10; Time & Time Again, Part 3; Newsboy Legion back-up	1.75
❑55, May 1991, JOy (c); JOy (w); JOy (a); A: Demon. ▲1991-13; Time & Time Again, Part 6; Newboy Legion back-up	1.75
❑56, Jun 1991	1.75
❑57, Jul 1991, Double-size; BMc (a); Krypton Man	2.00
❑58, Aug 1991 V: Bloodhounds.	1.50
❑59, Sep 1991	1.50
❑60, Oct 1991 1: Agent Liberty. V: Intergang	2.00
❑61, Nov 1991 A: Linear Men. A: Waverider.	1.50
❑62, Dec 1991	1.50
❑63, Jan 1992 A: Aquaman.	1.50
❑64, Feb 1992, BG (a); Christmas issue	1.50
❑65, Mar 1992 A: Guy Gardner. A: Deathstroke. A: Captain Marvel. A: Batman. A: Aquaman.	1.50
❑66, Apr 1992 A: Guy Gardner. A: Deathstroke. A: Captain Marvel. A: Batman. A: Aquaman.	1.50
❑67, May 1992	1.50
❑68, Jun 1992, Deathstroke	1.50
❑69, Jul 1992	1.50
❑70, Aug 1992, Robin	1.50
❑71, Sep 1992	1.50
❑72, Oct 1992	1.50
❑73, Nov 1992 A: Doomsday. A: Waverider.	3.00
❑73/2nd, Nov 1992	1.75
❑74, Dec 1992, Doomsday; ▲1992-74	4.00
❑74/2nd, Dec 1992, ▲1992-74.	1.50
❑75, Jan 1993, D: Superman. newsstand; unbagged	5.00
❑75/CS, Jan 1993 D: Superman.	12.00
❑75/Platinum, Jan 1993, Platinum edition D: Superman.	40.00
❑75/2nd, Jan 1993 D: Superman.	2.00
❑75/3rd, Jan 1993 D: Superman.	1.50
❑75/4th, Jan 1993 D: Superman.	1.50
❑76, Feb 1993	2.50
❑77, Mar 1993	2.50
❑78, Jun 1993 1: Cyborg Superman.	2.00
❑78/CS, Jun 1993, 1: Cyborg Superman. Die-cut cover	2.50
❑79, Jul 1993	2.00
❑80, Aug 1993, V: Mongul. Coast City destroyed; Cyborg Superman revealed as evil	2.00
❑81, Sep 1993	2.00
❑82, Oct 1993, return of Superman; Reign of the Superman ends; True Superman revealed	2.00
❑82/Variant, Oct 1993, Chromium cover; with poster; Reign of the Superman ends; True Superman revealed	3.50
❑83, Nov 1993	2.00
❑84, Dec 1993 D: Adam Grant. V: Toyman.	2.00
❑85, Jan 1994	2.00
❑86, Feb 1994	2.00
❑87, Mar 1994, Bizarro	2.00
❑88, Apr 1994, Bizarro	2.00
❑89, May 1994	2.00
❑90, Jun 1994 BA (a)	2.00
❑91, Jul 1994 BA (a)	2.00
❑92, Aug 1994	2.00
❑93, Sep 1994, Zero Hour	2.00
❑94, Nov 1994	2.00
❑95, Dec 1994 A: Atom.	2.00
❑96, Jan 1995, ▲1995-2	2.00
❑97, Feb 1995 1: Shadowdragon.	2.00
❑98, Mar 1995	2.00
❑99, Apr 1995 A: Agent Liberty.	2.00
❑100, May 1995, 100th anniversary edition; ▲1995-18	3.00
❑100/Variant, May 1995, 100th anniversary edition; enhanced cover; ▲1995-18	4.00

	N-MINT
❑101, Jun 1995, ▲1995-22	2.00
❑102, Jul 1995 V: Captain Marvel.	2.00
❑103, Aug 1995 V: Arclight.	2.00
❑104, Sep 1995, Cyborg is released by Darkseid	2.00
❑105, Oct 1995 A: Green Lantern.	2.00
❑106, Nov 1995	2.00
❑107, Dec 1995	2.00
❑108, Jan 1996 D: Mope.	2.00
❑109, Feb 1996, Christmas story; return of Lori Lemaris; ▲1996-7	2.00
❑110, Mar 1996, A: Plastic Man. ▲1996-11	2.00
❑111, Apr 1996, ▲1996-16	2.00
❑112, Jun 1996	2.00
❑113, Jul 1996	2.00
❑114, Aug 1996 CS (a)	2.00
❑115, Sep 1996, Lois becomes foreign correspondent	2.00
❑116, Oct 1996, Teen Titans preview	2.00
❑117, Nov 1996, Final Night; ▲1996-42	2.00
❑118, Dec 1996, A: Wonder Woman. Lois decides to return to Metropolis; ▲1996-46	2.00
❑119, Jan 1997, A: Legion. ▲1997-1.	2.00
❑120, Feb 1997	2.00
❑121, Mar 1997, ▲1997-10	2.00
❑122, Apr 1997, energy powers begin to manifest	2.00
❑123, May 1997, New costume	3.00
❑123/Variant, May 1997, glow-in-the-dark cardstock cover; New costume	5.00
❑124, Jun 1997 A: Booster Gold.	2.00
❑125, Jul 1997, A: Atom. in Kandor	2.00
❑126, Aug 1997 A: Batman.	2.00
❑127, Sep 1997, Superman Revenge Squad leader's identity revealed	2.00
❑128, Oct 1997, V: Cyborg Superman. Genesis	2.00
❑129, Nov 1997, A: Scorn. ▲1997-44	2.00
❑130, Dec 1997, Face cover	2.00
❑131, Jan 1998, D: Mayor Berkowitz. birth of Lena Luthor	2.00
❑132, Feb 1998	2.00
❑133, Mar 1998	2.00
❑134, Apr 1998, Millennium Giants	2.00
❑135, May 1998, leads into Superman Forever #1; End of Superman Red/Blue	2.00
❑136, Jul 1998	2.00
❑137, Aug 1998 V: Muto.	2.00
❑138, Sep 1998 A: Kismet. V: Dominus.	2.00
❑139, Oct 1998 V: Dominus.	1.99
❑140, Dec 1998, in Kandor; Inventor's identity revealed	1.99
❑141, Jan 1999 1: Outburst.	1.99
❑142, Feb 1999 A: Outburst.	1.99
❑143, Mar 1999 A: Supermen of America. A: Superman Robots.	1.99
❑144, Apr 1999, Fortress destroyed	1.99
❑145, Jun 1999, ▲1999-23	1.99
❑146, Jul 1999 A: Toyman.	1.99
❑147, Aug 1999, Superman as Green Lantern	1.99
❑148, Sep 1999	1.99
❑149, Oct 1999, SB (a); ▲1999-40	1.99
❑150, Nov 1999	1.99
❑150/Variant, Nov 1999, Special cover	3.95
❑151, Dec 1999, Daily Planet reopens	1.99
❑152, Jan 2000, JPH (w); ▲2000-1	1.99
❑153, Feb 2000, JPH (w); ▲2000-5	1.99
❑154, Mar 2000	1.99
❑155, Apr 2000	1.99
❑156, May 2000, JPH (w); ▲2000-18	1.99
❑157, Jun 2000, JPH (w); ▲2000-22	1.99
❑158, Jul 2000	1.99
❑159, Aug 2000	1.99
❑160, Sep 2000	2.25
❑161, Oct 2000, JPH (w); ▲2000-39.	2.25
❑162, Nov 2000, JPH (w); ▲2000-43	2.25
❑163, Dec 2000, JPH (w); ▲2000-47	2.25
❑164, Jan 2001, JPH (w); ▲2001-1	2.25
❑165, Feb 2001, JPH (w); ▲2001-6	2.25
❑166, Mar 2001, JPH (w); ▲2001-10	2.25
❑167, Apr 2001, JPH (w); ▲2001-14.	2.25
❑168, May 2001, JPH (w); ▲2001-18	2.25
❑169, Jun 2001, ▲2001-22	2.25
❑170, Jul 2001 A: Krypto.	2.25

Other grades: Multiply price above by 5/6 for VF/NM • 2/3 for VERY FINE • 1/3 for FINE • 1/5 for VERY GOOD • 1/8 for GOOD

Superman's Girl Friend Lois Lane

Jimmy got his series first, but Lois wasn't far behind

©DC

Superman's Nemesis: Lex Luthor

A focal shift from good friends to bad enemies

©DC

Superman's Pal Jimmy Olsen

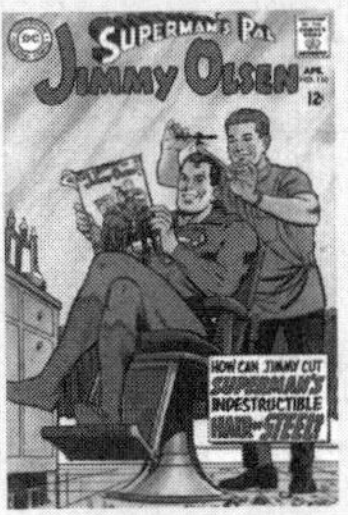

Cub reporter grows up, becomes Mr. Action

©DC

Superman: Speeding Bullets

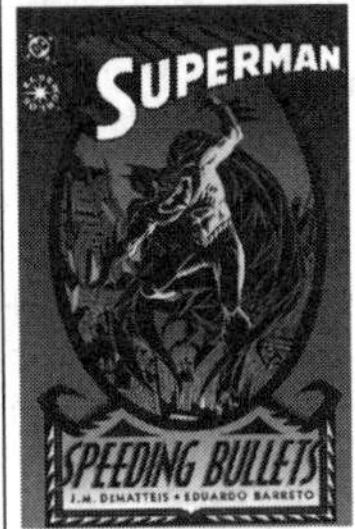

First Superman Elseworlds casts Kal as Batman

©DC

Superman: The Dark Side

Man of Steel seduced by Apokolips' ruler

©DC

	N-MINT
❑171, Aug 2001	4.00
❑172, Sep 2001 JPH (w)	2.25
❑173, Oct 2001	2.25
❑174, Nov 2001, ▲2001-42	2.25
❑175, Dec 2001, Giant-size; ▲2001-46; Joker: Last Laugh crossover	3.50
❑176, Jan 2002, ▲2002-1	2.25
❑177, Feb 2002	2.25
❑178, Mar 2002	2.25
❑179, Apr 2002	2.25
❑180, May 2002	2.25
❑181, Jun 2002	2.25
❑182, Jul 2002	2.25
❑183, Aug 2002	2.25
❑184, Sep 2002	2.25
❑185, Oct 2002 BA (a)	2.25
❑186, Nov 2002	2.25
❑187, Dec 2002	2.25
❑188, Jan 2003, Aquaman (6th series) #1 preview	2.25
❑189, Feb 2003	2.25
❑190, Apr 2003	2.25
❑190/A, Apr 2003	3.95
❑191, May 2003	2.25
❑192, Jun 2003	3.00
❑193, Jul 2003	2.25
❑194, Aug 2003	2.25
❑195, Sep 2003	2.25
❑196, Oct 2003	2.25
❑197, Nov 2003	2.25
❑198, Dec 2003	2.25
❑199, Jan 2004	2.25
❑200, Feb 2004	3.50
❑201, Mar 2004	8.00
❑202, Apr 2004	2.25
❑203, May 2004, Jim Lee sketchbook	6.00
❑204, Jun 2004 JLee (c); JLee (a)	4.00
❑204/Sketch, ca. 2004, JLee (c); JLee (a); Jim Lee Sketch Cover; Diamond Retailer Summit variant	250.00
❑204/DF Lee, Jun 2004; Dynamic Forces variant	30.00
❑204/DF Azzarell, Jun 2004; Dynamic Forces variant	25.00
❑205/Lee, Jul 2004 JLee (c); JLee (a)	4.00
❑205/Turner, Jul 2004, JLee (a); Variant cover	3.00
❑205/DF Lee, Jul 2004, JLee (c); JLee (a); Dynamic Forces variant	30.00
❑205/DF Turner, Jul 2004, JLee (a); Dynamic Forces variant	25.00
❑206, Aug 2004 JLee (c); JLee (a)	2.50
❑207, Sep 2004 JLee (c); JLee (a)	2.50
❑208, Oct 2004 JLee (c); JLee (a)	5.00
❑209, Nov 2004 JLee (c); JLee (a)	4.00
❑210, Dec 2004	2.50
❑211, Jan 2005	2.50
❑212, Feb 2005	2.50
❑213, Mar 2005	2.50
❑214, Apr 2005	2.50
❑215, May 2005	2.50
❑216, Jun 2005	5.00
❑217, Jul 2005	7.00
❑218, Aug 2005	5.00
❑219, Sep 2005	6.00

	N-MINT
❑219/Variant, Sep 2005	2.50
❑220, Oct 2005	2.50
❑221, Nov 2005	2.99
❑222, Dec 2005	2.99
❑223, Jan 2006	2.99
❑224, Jan 2006	2.99
❑225, Mar 2006	2.99
❑226, Apr 2006	2.99
❑650, May 2006, Resumes numbering from Superman (1st series).	2.99
❑651, Jun 2006	2.99
❑652, Jul 2006	2.99
❑653, Aug 2006	2.99
❑1000000, Nov 1998	4.00
❑1000000/Ltd., Nov 1998, Signed edition	14.99
❑Annual 1, ca. 1987 O: Titano.	4.00
❑Annual 2, ca. 1988, Private Lives	3.00
❑Annual 3, ca. 1991	2.50
❑Annual 3/2nd, ca. 1991	2.00
❑Annual 3/3rd, ca. 1991, silver	2.00
❑Annual 4, ca. 1992	2.50
❑Annual 5, ca. 1993 1: Myriad.	2.50
❑Annual 6, ca. 1994, Elseworlds	2.95
❑Annual 7, ca. 1995, A: Dr. Occult. A: Doctor Occult. Year One	3.95
❑Annual 8, ca. 1996, Legends of the Dead Earth; The League of Supermen	2.95
❑Annual 9, Jul 1997, A: Doc Savage. Pulp Heroes	2.95
❑Annual 10, Oct 1998, A: Phantom Zone villains. Ghosts	2.95
❑Annual 11, Oct 1999, JLApe	2.95
❑Annual 12, Aug 2000, 2000 Annual; Planet DC	3.50
❑Giant Size 1, Feb 1999, 80 page giant size	4.95
❑Giant Size 2, Jun 1999, 80 page giant size	4.95
❑Giant Size 3, Nov 2000, 80 page giant size	5.95
❑Special 1, ca. 1992, 1992 Special	4.00
❑3D 1	5.00

SUPERMAN 3-D
DC

❑1, Dec 1998	4.00

SUPERMAN ADVENTURES
DC

❑1, Nov 1996; based on animated series; follow-up to pilot episode	3.00
❑2, Dec 1996 V: Metallo.	2.50
❑3, Jan 1997 V: Brainiac.	2.50
❑4, Feb 1997	2.00
❑5, Mar 1997 V: Livewire.	2.00
❑6, Apr 1997	2.00
❑7, May 1997 V: Mala. V: Jax-ur.	2.00
❑8, Jun 1997 V: Mala. V: Jax-ur.	2.00
❑9, Jul 1997	2.00
❑10, Aug 1997 V: Toyman.	2.00
❑11, Sep 1997	2.00
❑12, Oct 1997	2.00
❑13, Nov 1997	2.00
❑14, Dec 1997; ME (w); Face cover	2.00
❑15, Jan 1998 ME (w); A: Bibbo.	2.00
❑16, Feb 1998	2.00
❑17, Mar 1998	2.00

	N-MINT
❑18, Apr 1998 DGry (w)	2.00
❑19, May 1998	2.00
❑20, Jun 1998	2.00
❑21, Jul 1998; double-sized; adapts Supergirl episode	3.95
❑22, Aug 1998	2.00
❑23, Sep 1998 A: Livewire. V: Brainiac.	2.00
❑24, Oct 1998 V: Parasite.	2.00
❑25, Nov 1998 A: Batgirl.	2.00
❑26, Dec 1998 V: Mxyzptlk.	2.00
❑27, Jan 1999 1: Superior-Man.	2.00
❑28, Feb 1999; A: Jimmy Olsen. Jimmy and Superman switch bodies	2.00
❑29, Mar 1999; A: Bizarro. A: Lobo. Lobo apperance	2.00
❑30, Apr 1999	2.00
❑31, May 1999	2.00
❑32, Jun 1999	2.00
❑33, Jul 1999	2.00
❑34, Aug 1999 A: Doctor Fate.	2.00
❑35, Sep 1999 V: Toyman.	2.00
❑36, Oct 1999	2.00
❑37, Nov 1999 V: Multi-Face.	2.00
❑38, Dec 1999	2.00
❑39, Jan 2000	2.00
❑40, Feb 2000	2.00
❑41, Mar 2000	1.99
❑42, Apr 2000	1.99
❑43, May 2000	1.99
❑44, Jun 2000	1.99
❑45, Jul 2000	1.99
❑46, Aug 2000	1.99
❑47, Sep 2000	1.99
❑48, Oct 2000	1.99
❑49, Nov 2000	1.99
❑50, Dec 2000	1.99
❑51, Jan 2001	1.99
❑52, Feb 2001	1.99
❑53, Mar 2001 ME (w)	1.99
❑54, Apr 2001	1.99
❑55, May 2001	1.99
❑56, Jun 2001	1.99
❑57, Jul 2001	1.99
❑58, Aug 2001	1.99
❑59, Sep 2001	1.99
❑60, Oct 2001	1.99
❑61, Nov 2001	1.99
❑62, Dec 2001	1.99
❑63, Jan 2002	1.99
❑64, Feb 2002	1.99
❑65, Mar 2002	1.99
❑66, Apr 2002	1.99
❑Annual 1, ca. 1997; JSa (a); ties in with Adventures in the DC Universe Annual #1 and Batman and Robin Adventures Annual #2	3.95
❑Special 1, Feb 1998 V: Lobo.	2.95

SUPERMAN/ALIENS 2: GOD WAR
DC

❑1, May 2002	2.99
❑2, Jun 2002	2.99
❑3, Jul 2002	2.99
❑4, Aug 2002	2.99

Other grades: Multiply price above by 5/6 for VF/NM • 2/3 for VERY FINE • 1/3 for FINE • 1/5 for VERY GOOD • 1/8 for GOOD

SUPERMAN: A NATION DIVIDED
DC

❑1, prestige format; Elseworlds; Superman in Civil War 4.95

SUPERMAN & BATMAN: GENERATIONS
DC

❑1, Jan 1999; Elseworlds story 4.95
❑2, Feb 1999; Elseworlds story 4.95
❑3, Mar 1999; Elseworlds story 4.95
❑4, Apr 1999; Elseworlds story 4.95

SUPERMAN & BATMAN: GENERATIONS II
DC

❑1, Oct 2001 5.95
❑2, Nov 2001 5.95
❑3, Dec 2001 5.95
❑4, Jan 2002 5.95

SUPERMAN & BATMAN: GENERATIONS III
DC

❑1, Mar 2003 2.95
❑2, Apr 2003 2.95
❑3, May 2003 2.95
❑4, Jun 2003 2.95
❑5, Jul 2003 2.95
❑6, Aug 2003 2.95
❑7, Sep 2003 2.95
❑8, Oct 2003 2.95
❑9, Nov 2003 2.95
❑10, Dec 2003 2.95
❑11, Jan 2004 2.95
❑12, Feb 2004 2.95

SUPERMAN & BATMAN MAGAZINE
WELSH

❑1, Sum 1993, bagged with poster 3.00
❑2, Fal 1993 2.00
❑3, Win 1993, trading cards 3.00
❑4, Spr 1994 2.00
❑5, Sum 1994, magazine 2.00
❑7, Win 1995, magazine 2.00
❑8, Spr 1995, magazine 2.00

SUPERMAN AND BATMAN: WORLD'S FUNNEST
DC

❑1, ca. 2000 6.95

SUPERMAN & BUGS BUNNY
DC

❑1, Jul 2000 2.50
❑2, Aug 2000 2.50
❑3, Sep 2000 2.50
❑4, Oct 2000 2.50

SUPERMAN & SAVAGE DRAGON: CHICAGO
DC

❑1, Dec 2002 5.95

SUPERMAN & SAVAGE DRAGON: METROPOLIS
DC

❑nn, Nov 1999; Prestige-format one-shot crossover with Image 4.95

SUPERMAN: AT EARTH'S END
DC

❑1, ca. 1995 4.95

SUPERMAN/BATMAN SECRET FILES
DC

❑1, Dec 2003 4.95

SUPERMAN/BATMAN
DC

❑1, Oct 2003 8.00
❑1/Retailer ed., Oct 2003; Retailer incentive edition (aka RRP edition); no cover price 125.00
❑1/2nd, Oct 2003 4.00
❑1/3rd, Oct 2003 4.00
❑2, Nov 2003 6.00
❑3, Dec 2003 5.00
❑3/2nd, Mar 2004 2.95
❑4, Jan 2004 4.00
❑5, Feb 2004 2.95
❑6, Mar 2004 JPH (w) 4.00
❑7, Apr 2004 JPH (w) 2.95
❑8, May 2004 10.00
❑8/2nd, May 2004, Turner sketch cover 7.00
❑8/3rd, May 2004, Wonder Woman cover by Michael Turner 6.00
❑8/4th, Aug 2004 2.95
❑9, Jun 2004 5.00
❑9/2nd, Jul 2004; reprint 4.00
❑9/3rd, Aug 2004 2.95
❑10, Jul 2004 5.00
❑10/2nd, Aug 2004 4.00
❑11, Sep 2004 5.00
❑12, Oct 2004 4.00
❑13, Dec 2004 5.00
❑13/Supergirl, Dec 2004 7.00
❑14, Jan 2005 5.00
❑15, Feb 2005 4.00
❑16, Mar 2005 5.00
❑17, Apr 2005 4.00
❑18, May 2005 2.95
❑19, Jun 2005 4.00
❑20, Jul 2005 2.99
❑21, Aug 2005 4.00
❑22 2005 2.99
❑23, Feb 2006 2.99
❑24, Jun 2006 2.99
❑26, Aug 2006 2.99
❑27, Sep 2006 2.99

SUPERMAN: BIRTHRIGHT
DC

❑1, Sep 2003 2.95
❑2, Oct 2003 2.95
❑3, Nov 2003 2.95
❑4, Jan 2004 2.95
❑5, Feb 2004 2.95
❑6, Mar 2004 2.95
❑7, Apr 2004 2.95
❑8, May 2004 2.95
❑9, May 2004 2.95
❑10, Jul 2004 2.95
❑11, Aug 2004 2.95
❑12, Sep 2004 2.95

SUPERMAN: BLOOD OF MY ANCESTORS
DC

❑1, Nov 2003 6.95

SUPERMAN: DAY OF DOOM
DC

❑1, ca. 2003 9.95

SUPERMAN: DISTANT FIRES
DC

❑1, Feb 1998; prestige format; Elseworlds 5.95

SUPERMAN/DOOMSDAY: HUNTER/PREY
DC

❑1, ca. 1994, prestige format 6.00
❑2, ca. 1994, prestige format O: Doomsday. 6.00
❑3, ca. 1994, prestige format D: Doomsday. 6.00

SUPERMAN: EMPEROR JOKER
DC

❑1, Oct 2000 3.50

SUPERMAN: END OF THE CENTURY
DC

❑Book 1/HC, Feb 2000 24.95
❑Book 1, ca. 2003 14.95

SUPERMAN FAMILY
DC

❑164, May 1974, NC (c); CS, JM, KS (a); Series continued from Superman's Pal Jimmy Olsen; reprints from Action #339, Adventure #272, Lois Lane #51, and Jimmy Olsen #76 35.00
❑165, Jul 1974, reprints from Action #296, Jimmy Olsen #59, Lois Lane #47, Superboy #111, #133, and Superman #186 13.00
❑166, Sep 1974, NC (c); Reprints w/ new Lois Lane story 13.00
❑167, Nov 1974, NC (c); KS (a); Reprints from Superboy (1st series) #100, and #124; Jimmy Olsen stories new 13.00
❑168, Jan 1975, Supergirl reprinted from Action #350; Bizarro Luthor reprinted from Adventure #293; Lois Lane story new 13.00
❑169, Mar 1975 NC (c); JM (a) 13.00
❑170, May 1975 11.00
❑171, Jul 1975 11.00
❑172, Sep 1975, KS (c); CS, KS (a); A: Green Lantern. Reprints from Action #364, and Jimmy Olsen #85 11.00
❑173, Nov 1975 11.00
❑174, Jan 1976 11.00
❑175, Mar 1976 11.00
❑176, May 1976 11.00
❑177, Jul 1976, reprints from Jimmy Olsen #74 and Lois Lane #53 11.00
❑178, Sep 1976 5.00
❑179, Oct 1976 5.00
❑180, Nov 1976 5.00
❑181, Jan 1977 3.50
❑182, Apr 1977 3.50
❑183, Jun 1977 3.50
❑184, Aug 1977 V: Prankster. 3.50
❑185, Oct 1977 3.50
❑186, Dec 1977 A: Earth-2 Superman. 3.50
❑187, Feb 1978 A: Earth-2 Superman. 3.50
❑188, Apr 1978; Red Kryptonite 3.50
❑189, Jun 1978 3.50
❑190, Aug 1978 3.50
❑191, Oct 1978 3.50
❑192, Dec 1978 3.50
❑193, Feb 1979 3.50
❑194, Apr 1979 MR (a); V: Jimmy clones. 3.50
❑195, Jun 1979 3.50
❑196, Aug 1979 3.50
❑197, Oct 1979 3.50
❑198, Dec 1979 3.50
❑199, Feb 1980 3.50
❑200, Apr 1980; Imaginary Story 3.50
❑201, Jun 1980 3.00
❑202, Aug 1980 3.00
❑203, Oct 1980 1: Lana Lang. 3.00
❑204, Dec 1980 V: Enchantress. 3.00
❑205, Feb 1981 1: H.I.V.E.. V: Enchantress. 3.00
❑206, Apr 1981 A: Lesla-Lar. 3.00
❑207, Jun 1981 A: Legion. V: Universo. 3.00
❑208, Jul 1981; Supergirl relocates to New York 3.00
❑209, Aug 1981 3.00
❑210, Sep 1981 3.00
❑211, Oct 1981 3.00
❑212, Nov 1981 3.00
❑213, Dec 1981 1: Insect Queen (Lana Lang). 3.00
❑214, Jan 1982 3.00
❑215, Feb 1982 3.00
❑216, Mar 1982 3.00
❑217, Apr 1982 3.00
❑218, May 1982 3.00
❑219, Jun 1982 V: Master Jailer. 3.00
❑220, Jul 1982 V: Master Jailer. 3.00
❑221, Aug 1982 V: Master Jailer. 3.00
❑222, Sep 1982 3.00

SUPERMAN/FANTASTIC FOUR
DC

❑1, ca. 1999; Tabloid-sized crossover byDC and Marvel 9.95

SUPERMAN FOR ALL SEASONS
DC

❑1, Sep 1998; prestige format 4.95
❑2, Oct 1998; prestige format 4.95
❑3, Nov 1998; prestige format 4.95
❑4, Dec 1998; prestige format 4.95

SUPERMAN FOR EARTH
DC

❑1, Apr 1991 4.95

SUPERMAN FOREVER
DC

❑1, Jun 1998; newsstand edition; JBy, DG (a); Superman returns to normal powers 5.50
❑1/Autographed, Jun 1998 JBy, DG (a) 30.00
❑1/Variant, Jun 1998; prestige format; lenticular animation cover; Superman returns to normal powers 7.00

SUPER MANGA BLAST!
DARK HORSE

❑1, Mar 2000, b&w 4.95
❑2, Apr 2000, b&w 4.95

Other grades: Multiply price above by 5/6 for VF/NM • 2/3 for VERY FINE • 1/3 for FINE • 1/5 for VERY GOOD • 1/8 for GOOD

Superman: The Man of Steel

When three monthly titles just aren't enough

©DC

Superman: The Man of Tomorrow

Fill-in for those pesky skip weeks

©DC

Superman: The Secret Years

Bridges the gap between Boy and Man

©DC

Super Mario Bros. (1st Series)

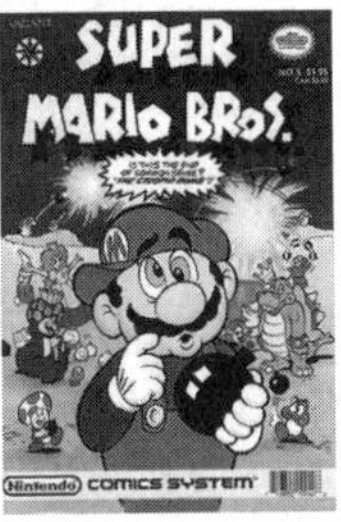

Pre-hero Valiant plumbed videogame depths

©Valiant

Supernaturals

Monster masks highlight of each issue

©Marvel

N-MINT

❑3, May 2000, b&w 4.95
❑4, Jun 2000, b&w 4.95
❑5, Jul 2000, b&w 4.95
❑6, Aug 2000, b&w 4.95
❑7, Sep 2000, b&w 4.95
❑8, Nov 2000, b&w 4.95
❑9, Jan 2001, b&w 4.95
❑10, Feb 2001, b&w 4.99
❑11, Mar 2001, b&w 4.99
❑12, May 2001, b&w 4.99
❑13, Jun 2001, b&w 4.99
❑14, Jul 2001, b&w 4.99
❑15, Aug 2001, b&w 4.99
❑16, Sep 2001, b&w 4.99
❑17, Oct 2001, b&w 4.99
❑18, Nov 2001, b&w 4.99
❑19, Feb 2002, b&w 5.99
❑20, Mar 2002, b&w 5.99
❑21, Apr 2002, b&w 5.99
❑22, May 2002, b&w 5.99
❑23, Jun 2002, b&w 5.99
❑24, Jul 2002, b&w 5.99
❑25, Sep 2002, b&w 5.99
❑26, Oct 2002, b&w 5.99
❑27, Nov 2002, b&w 5.99
❑28, Dec 2002, b&w 5.99
❑29, Jan 2003, b&w 5.99
❑30, Apr 2003, b&w 5.99
❑31, May 2003, b&w 5.99
❑32, Jun 2003, b&w 5.99
❑33, Jul 2003, b&w 5.99
❑34, Aug 2003, b&w 5.99
❑35, Oct 2003, b&w 5.99
❑36, Nov 2003, b&w 5.99
❑37, Jan 2004, b&w 5.99
❑38, Feb 2004, b&w 5.99
❑39, Feb 2004, b&w 5.99
❑40, Mar 2004, b&w 5.99
❑41, Mar 2004, b&w 5.99
❑42, May 2004, b&w 5.99
❑43, Jul 2004, b&w 5.99
❑44, Aug 2004, b&w 5.99
❑45, Sep 2004, b&w 5.99
❑46, Oct 2004, b&w 5.99
❑47, Nov 2004, b&w 5.99
❑48, Dec 2004, b&w 5.99
❑49, Jan 2005, b&w 5.99
❑50, Feb 2005 5.99
❑51, Jun 2005 5.99
❑52, Jul 2005 5.99
❑53, Aug 2005 5.99
❑54, Sep 2005 5.99
❑55, Oct 2005 5.99
❑56, Nov 2005 5.99
❑57, Nov 2005 5.99
❑58, Dec 2005 5.99
❑59, Mar 2006 5.99

SUPERMAN GALLERY
DC

❑1, ca. 1993 2.95

SUPERMAN/GEN13
WILDSTORM

❑1, Jun 2000 2.50
❑1/A, Jun 2000; Fairchild opening shirt to show Supergirl costume on cover 2.50
❑2, Jul 2000; Supergirl/Fairchild cover 2.50
❑2/A, Jul 2000; Large figures looking down on cover 2.50
❑3, Aug 2000 2.50

SUPERMAN (GIVEAWAYS)
DC

❑1; game giveaway 1.00
❑2; Pizza Hut 1.00
❑3, Jul 1980; Radio Shack 1.00
❑4; Radio Shack 1.00
❑5; Radio Shack 1.00

SUPERMAN, INC.
DC

❑1, Jan 2000 6.95

SUPERMAN IV MOVIE SPECIAL
DC

❑1, Oct 1987 2.00

SUPERMAN: KAL
DC

❑1; prestige format one-shot 5.95

SUPERMAN: KANSAS SIGHTING
DC

❑1, Jan 2004 6.95
❑2, Feb 2004 6.95

SUPERMAN: KING OF THE WORLD
DC

❑1, Jun 1999, ▲1999-22 3.95
❑1/Gold, Jun 1999, enhanced cardstock cover; ▲1999-22 4.95

SUPERMAN: LAST SON OF EARTH
DC

❑1, Sep 2000 5.95
❑2, Oct 2000 5.95

SUPERMAN: LAST STAND ON KRYPTON
DC

❑1, May 2003 6.95

SUPERMAN: LEX 2000
DC

❑1, Jan 2001 3.50

SUPERMAN: LOIS LANE
DC

❑1, Jun 1998; Girlfrenzy 1.95

SUPERMAN/MADMAN HULLABALOO
DARK HORSE / DC

❑1, Jun 1997; crossover with DC 2.95
❑2, Jul 1997; crossover with DC 2.95
❑3, Aug 1997; crossover with DC 2.95

SUPERMAN MEETS THE QUIK BUNNY
DC

❑1; promotional giveaway from Nestle CI, DG (a) 1.00

SUPERMAN: METROPOLIS
DC

❑1, Apr 2003 2.95
❑2, May 2003 2.95
❑3, Jun 2003 2.95
❑4, Jul 2003 2.95
❑5, Aug 2003 2.95
❑6, Sep 2003 2.95
❑7, Oct 2003 2.95
❑8, Nov 2003 2.95
❑9, Dec 2003 2.95
❑10, Jan 2004 2.95
❑11, Feb 2004 2.95
❑12, Mar 2004 2.95

SUPERMAN METROPOLIS SECRET FILES
DC

❑1, Jul 2000 4.95

SUPERMAN MONSTER
DC

❑1 5.95

SUPERMAN MOVIE SPECIAL
DC

❑1, Sep 1983; GM, CS (a); adapts Superman III 2.00

SUPERMAN: OUR WORLDS AT WAR
DC

❑1, Oct 2002 19.95
❑2, Oct 2002 19.95

SUPERMAN: OUR WORLDS AT WAR SECRET FILES
DC

❑1, Aug 2001 5.95

SUPERMAN: PEACE ON EARTH
DC

❑1/2nd 9.95
❑1, Jan 1999; Oversized 9.95
❑1/Autographed; Oversized 22.95

SUPERMAN PLUS
DC

❑1, Feb 1997 2.95

SUPERMAN: PRESIDENT LEX
DC

❑1, ca. 2003 17.95

SUPERMAN: RED SON
DC

❑1, Jun 2003 7.00
❑2, Jul 2003 5.95
❑3, Aug 2003 5.95

SUPERMAN RED/SUPERMAN BLUE
DC

❑1, Feb 1998 3.95
❑Deluxe 1, Feb 1998; one-shot with 3-D cover; Superman splits into two beings 4.95

SUPERMAN RETURNS: KRYPTON TO EARTH
DC

❑1, Aug 2006 3.99
❑2, Aug 2006 3.99
❑3, Sep 2006 3.99
❑4, Sep 2006 3.99

SUPERMAN: SAVE THE PLANET
DC

❑1, Oct 1998; Daily Planet sold to Lex Luthor 2.95
❑1/Variant, Oct 1998; acetate overlay 3.95

Other grades: Multiply price above by 5/6 for VF/NM • 2/3 for VERY FINE • 1/3 for FINE • 1/5 for VERY GOOD • 1/8 for GOOD

N-MINT

SUPERMAN: SECRET FILES
DC

❑1, Jan 1998; background material.... 4.95
❑2, May 1999; background material... 4.95

SUPERMAN: SECRET FILES 2004
DC

❑1, Aug 2004 ... 4.95

SUPERMAN SECRET FILES AND ORIGINS 2004
DC

❑0, Jul 2005 ... 6.00

SUPERMAN SECRET FILES 2005
DC

❑1, Jan 2006 ... 4.95

SUPERMAN: SECRET IDENTITY
DC

❑1, Mar 2004 ... 5.95
❑2, Apr 2004 ... 5.95
❑3, May 2004 ... 5.95
❑4, Jun 2004 ... 5.95

SUPERMAN'S GIRL FRIEND LOIS LANE
DC

❑1, Apr 1958 ... 2600.00
❑2, Jun 1958 ... 625.00
❑3, Aug 1958 ... 415.00
❑4, Oct 1958 ... 300.00
❑5, Nov 1958 ... 300.00
❑6, Jan 1959 ... 220.00
❑7, Feb 1959 ... 220.00
❑8, Apr 1959 CS (c); KS (a) ... 220.00
❑9, May 1959 A: Pat Boone. ... 220.00
❑10, Jul 1959 ... 220.00
❑11, Aug 1959 ... 125.00
❑12, Oct 1959 ... 125.00
❑13, Nov 1959, CS, KS (a); G-87; Reprints from issues #41, #43, #49, #54, and #57 ... 125.00
❑14, Jan 1960 ... 125.00
❑15, Feb 1960 KS (a) ... 125.00
❑16, Apr 1960 ... 125.00
❑17, May 1960 ... 125.00
❑18, Jul 1960 ... 125.00
❑19, Aug 1960 ... 215.00
❑20, Oct 1960 ... 125.00
❑21, Nov 1960 ... 86.00
❑22, Jan 1961 ... 86.00
❑23, Feb 1961 ... 86.00
❑24, Apr 1961 ... 86.00
❑25, May 1961 ... 86.00
❑26, Jul 1961 ... 86.00
❑27, Aug 1961 KS (a) ... 86.00
❑28, Oct 1961 ... 86.00
❑29, Nov 1961 ... 86.00
❑30, Jan 1962 KS (a) ... 48.00
❑31, Feb 1962 ... 48.00
❑32, Apr 1962 ... 48.00
❑33, May 1962 A: Phantom Zone. A: Mon-El. ... 48.00
❑34, Jul 1962 ... 48.00
❑35, Aug 1962 CS (a) ... 48.00
❑36, Oct 1962 KS (a) ... 48.00
❑37, Nov 1962 KS (a) ... 48.00
❑38, Jan 1963 ... 48.00
❑39, Feb 1963 CS (a) ... 48.00
❑40, Apr 1963 KS (a) ... 48.00
❑41, May 1963 CS, KS (a) ... 48.00
❑42, Jul 1963 ... 48.00
❑43, Aug 1963 KS (a) ... 48.00
❑44, Oct 1963 ... 48.00
❑45, Nov 1963 ... 48.00
❑46, Jan 1964 ... 48.00
❑47, Feb 1964 ... 48.00
❑48, Apr 1964 ... 48.00
❑49, May 1964 KS (a) ... 48.00
❑50, Jul 1964 ... 48.00
❑51, Aug 1964 KS (a) ... 34.00
❑52, Oct 1964 ... 34.00
❑53, Nov 1964, KS (a); How Lois fell in love with Superman ... 34.00
❑54, Jan 1965 KS (a) ... 34.00
❑55, Feb 1965 ... 34.00
❑56, Apr 1965 ... 34.00
❑57, May 1965 KS (a) ... 34.00
❑58, Jul 1965 ... 34.00
❑59, Aug 1965 ... 34.00
❑60, Oct 1965 ... 34.00
❑61, Nov 1965 KS (a) ... 34.00
❑62, Jan 1966 ... 34.00
❑63, Feb 1966, V: S.K.U.L.. Noel Neill interview ... 34.00
❑64, Apr 1966 ... 34.00
❑65, May 1966 ... 34.00
❑66, Jul 1966 ... 34.00
❑67, Aug 1966 ... 34.00
❑68, Sep 1966, Giant-size; aka 80 Page Giant #G-26 ... 44.00
❑69, Oct 1966 ... 34.00
❑70, Nov 1966, A: Catwoman. 1st Catwoman in Silver Age. ... 175.00
❑71, Jan 1967 A: Catwoman. ... 105.00
❑72, Feb 1967 ... 15.00
❑73, Apr 1967 ... 15.00
❑74, May 1967 1: Bizarro Flash. ... 34.00
❑75, Jul 1967 ... 15.00
❑76, Aug 1967 ... 15.00
❑77, Sep 1967, Giant-size; aka 80 Page Giant #G-39 ... 24.00
❑78, Oct 1967 ... 15.00
❑79, Nov 1967 ... 10.00
❑80, Jan 1968 ... 10.00
❑81, Feb 1968 ... 10.00
❑82, Apr 1968 IN (a) ... 10.00
❑83, May 1968 IN (a) ... 10.00
❑84, Jul 1968 IN (a) ... 10.00
❑85, Aug 1968 IN (a) ... 10.00
❑86, Sep 1968; Giant-size; NA, KS (a); aka 80 Page Giant #G-51; Reprints stories from Lois Lane #37 and #41 ... 16.00
❑87, Oct 1968 IN (a) ... 10.00
❑88, Nov 1968 IN (a) ... 10.00
❑89, Jan 1969, Imaginary Story; Lois marries Batman ... 10.00
❑90, Feb 1969 IN (a) ... 10.00
❑91, Apr 1969 CS (a) ... 10.00
❑92, May 1969 IN (a) ... 10.00
❑93, Jul 1969 IN (a); A: Wonder Woman. ... 10.00
❑94, Aug 1969 IN (a) ... 10.00
❑95, Sep 1969, b&w; Giant-size; KS (a); Giant-size; Reprints stories from Lois Lane #8, #27, #36, and #40 .... 25.00
❑96, Oct 1969 IN (a) ... 8.00
❑97, Nov 1969 IN (a) ... 8.00
❑98, Jan 1970, IN (a); aka Giant #G-63 8.00
❑99, Feb 1970 IN (a) ... 8.00
❑100, Apr 1970 IN (a) ... 8.00
❑101, May 1970 IN (a) ... 8.00
❑102, Jul 1970 IN (a) ... 8.00
❑103, Aug 1970 IN (a) ... 8.00
❑104, Sep 1970, Giant-size; aka Giant #G-75 ... 16.00
❑105, Oct 1970 O: Rose & Thorn II (Rose Forrest). 1: Rose & Thorn II (Rose Forrest). 1: The 1,000. ... 14.00
❑106, Nov 1970 ... 14.00
❑107, Dec 1970 ... 6.00
❑108, Feb 1971 ... 6.00
❑109, Apr 1971 ... 6.00
❑110, May 1971 ... 6.00
❑111, Jul 1971 ... 10.00
❑112, Aug 1971; KS (a); Reprints from Lois Lane #30 ... 6.00
❑113, Sep 1971, Giant-size; aka Giant #G-87 ... 14.00
❑114, Sep 1971; KS (a); Reprints from Lois Lane #61 ... 6.00
❑115, Oct 1971; BO (a); Reprints Lois Lane feature from Superman (1st series) #28, and Lady Danger feature from Sensation Comics #84 ... 6.00
❑116, Nov 1971 ... 6.00
❑117, Dec 1971 ... 6.00
❑118, Jan 1972 ... 6.00
❑119, Feb 1972 ... 6.00
❑120, Mar 1972; KS (a); Reprints from Lois Lane #43, and Superman (1st series) #29 ... 6.00
❑121, Apr 1972 ... 5.00
❑122, May 1972; CS (a); Reprints from Lois Lane #35, and Superman (1st series) #30 ... 8.00
❑123, Jun 1972 ... 8.00
❑124, Jul 1972 ... 5.00
❑125, Aug 1972 ... 5.00
❑126, Sep 1972 ... 5.00
❑127, Oct 1972 ... 5.00
❑128, Dec 1972 ... 5.00
❑129, Feb 1973 ... 5.00
❑130, Apr 1973 ... 5.00
❑131, Jun 1973, KS (a); Reprints from Lois Lane #8 ... 5.00
❑132, Jul 1973 ... 5.00
❑133, Sep 1973 ... 5.00
❑134, Oct 1973 ... 5.00
❑135, Nov 1973 ... 5.00
❑136, Jan 1974 A: Wonder Woman.... 5.00
❑137, ca. 1974 ... 5.00
❑Annual 1, Sum 1962 ... 75.00
❑Annual 2, Sum 1963 ... 50.00

SUPERMAN/SHAZAM: FIRST THUNDER
DC

❑1, Oct 2005 ... 2.99
❑2 2005 ... 2.99
❑3, Feb 2006 ... 2.99
❑4, May 2006 ... 2.99

SUPERMAN: SILVER BANSHEE
DC

❑1, Dec 1998 ... 2.25
❑2, Jan 1999 ... 2.25

SUPERMAN'S METROPOLIS
DC

❑1, Jan 1997; prestige format; Elseworlds ... 5.95

SUPERMAN'S NEMESIS: LEX LUTHOR
DC

❑1, Mar 1999 ... 2.50
❑2, Apr 1999 ... 2.50
❑3, May 1999 ... 2.50
❑4, Jun 1999 ... 2.50

SUPERMAN'S PAL JIMMY OLSEN
DC

❑1, Oct 1954 CS (a) ... 4000.00
❑2, Dec 1954 ... 1250.00
❑3, Feb 1955 ... 675.00
❑4, Apr 1955 ... 475.00
❑5, Jun 1955 ... 475.00
❑6, Aug 1955 ... 335.00
❑7, Sep 1955 ... 335.00
❑8, Nov 1955 ... 335.00
❑9, Dec 1955 ... 335.00
❑10, Feb 1956 ... 335.00
❑11, Mar 1956 ... 235.00
❑12, Apr 1956 ... 235.00
❑13, Jun 1956 CS (a) ... 235.00
❑14, Aug 1956 ... 235.00
❑15, Sep 1956 ... 235.00
❑16, Oct 1956 ... 235.00
❑17, Dec 1956 ... 235.00
❑18, Feb 1957 ... 235.00
❑19, Mar 1957 CS (c); ... 235.00
❑20, Apr 1957 ... 235.00
❑21, Jun 1957 ... 150.00
❑22, Aug 1957 CS (a) ... 150.00
❑23, Sep 1957 ... 150.00
❑24, Oct 1957 CS (a) ... 150.00
❑25, Dec 1957 ... 150.00
❑26, Feb 1958 ... 150.00
❑27, Mar 1958 CS (a) ... 150.00
❑28, Apr 1958 CS (a) ... 150.00
❑29, Jun 1958 ... 150.00
❑30, Aug 1958 ... 150.00
❑31, Sep 1958 1: Elastic Lad (Jimmy Olsen). ... 100.00
❑32, Oct 1958 ... 100.00
❑33, Dec 1958 ... 100.00
❑34, Jan 1959 ... 100.00
❑35, Mar 1959 ... 100.00
❑36, Apr 1959 1: Lucy Lane. ... 100.00
❑37, Jun 1959 ... 100.00
❑38, Jul 1959 ... 100.00
❑39, Sep 1959 ... 100.00
❑40, Oct 1959 CS (a); A: Supergirl. ... 100.00
❑41, Dec 1959 ... 75.00
❑42, Jan 1960 ... 75.00
❑43, Mar 1960 ... 75.00
❑44, Apr 1960 ... 75.00
❑45, Jun 1960 ... 75.00
❑46, Jul 1960 ... 75.00

Super-Villain Team-Up

Doom, Red Skull kept trying to make friends

©Marvel

Supreme

Image's answer to The Man of Steel

©Image

Supreme Power

Straczynski provides Squadron Supreme origins

©Marvel

Swamp Thing (1st Series)

Wrightson and Wolfman's shambling hero

©DC

Swamp Thing (2nd Series)

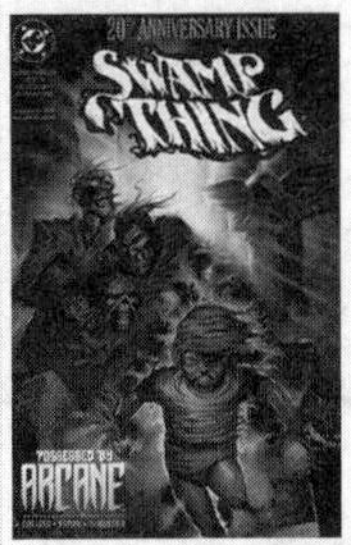

Elemental origins revealed in second series

©DC

	N-MINT
❑47, Sep 1960	75.00
❑48, Oct 1960 1: Superman Emergency Squad.	75.00
❑49, Dec 1960; Jimmy Olsen becomes Congorilla	75.00
❑50, Jan 1961	75.00
❑51, Mar 1961	50.00
❑52, Apr 1961	50.00
❑53, Jun 1961 CS (a)	50.00
❑54, Jul 1961	50.00
❑55, Sep 1961	50.00
❑56, Oct 1961	50.00
❑57, Dec 1961 CS (a); A: Supergirl.	30.00
❑58, Jan 1962	30.00
❑59, Mar 1962 CS (a)	30.00
❑60, Apr 1962	30.00
❑61, Jun 1962	30.00
❑62, Jul 1962, Elastic Lad in Phantom Zone	30.00
❑63, Sep 1962	30.00
❑64, Oct 1962	30.00
❑65, Dec 1962	30.00
❑66, Jan 1963	30.00
❑67, Mar 1963	30.00
❑68, Apr 1963	30.00
❑69, Jun 1963 CS (a)	30.00
❑70, Jul 1963, Silver Kryptonite	30.00
❑71, Sep 1963	25.00
❑72, Oct 1963 CS (a); A: Legion of Super-Heroes.	30.00
❑73, Dec 1963	30.00
❑74, Jan 1964 CS (a); A: Lex Luthor.	25.00
❑75, Mar 1964 A: Supergirl.	25.00
❑76, Apr 1964 A: Lightning Lass. A: Saturn Girl, Lightning Lass, Triplicate Girl. A: Triplicate Girl. A: Saturn Girl.	30.00
❑77, Jun 1964	25.00
❑78, Jul 1964	25.00
❑79, Sep 1964, Jimmy as Beatle	25.00
❑80, Oct 1964 1: Bizarro-Jimmy Olsen.	25.00
❑81, Dec 1964	25.00
❑82, Jan 1965	25.00
❑83, Mar 1965	25.00
❑84, Apr 1965, CS (a); Gorilla cover	25.00
❑85, Jun 1965 CS (a)	25.00
❑86, Jul 1965	25.00
❑87, Sep 1965 A: Legion of Super-Villains. A: Bizarro Jimmy.	25.00
❑88, Oct 1965	25.00
❑89, Dec 1965	20.00
❑90, Jan 1966	20.00
❑91, Mar 1966	16.00
❑92, Apr 1966 A: Batman.	16.00
❑93, Jun 1966	16.00
❑94, Jul 1966	16.00
❑95, Aug 1966, Giant-size; aka 80 Page Giant #G-25	25.00
❑96, Sep 1966	16.00
❑97, Oct 1966	16.00
❑98, Dec 1966	16.00
❑99, Jan 1967, Jimmy as one-man Legion	16.00
❑100, Mar 1967, Wedding of Jimmy and Lucy Lane	25.00
❑101, Apr 1967	12.00
❑102, Jun 1967	12.00
❑103, Jul 1967	12.00
❑104, Aug 1967; Giant-size; aka 80 Page Giant #G-38; Weird Adventures	35.00
❑105, Sep 1967	12.00
❑106, Oct 1967	12.00
❑107, Dec 1967 CS (a)	12.00
❑108, Jan 1968 CS (a)	12.00
❑109, Mar 1968 A: Luthor.	12.00
❑110, Apr 1968 CS (a)	12.00
❑111, Jun 1968	12.00
❑112, Jul 1968	12.00
❑113, Aug 1968; CS (a); aka 80 Page Giant #G-50; Anti-Superman issue; Reprints from Jimmy Olsen #22, #27, and #28	25.00
❑114, Sep 1968	12.00
❑115, Oct 1968 A: Aquaman.	12.00
❑116, Dec 1968, CS (a); Reprints from Jimmy Olsen #24	12.00
❑117, Jan 1969	12.00
❑118, Mar 1969	12.00
❑119, Apr 1969	12.00
❑120, Jun 1969	10.00
❑121, Jul 1969	10.00
❑122, Aug 1969; aka Giant #G-62	10.00
❑123, Sep 1969	10.00
❑124, Oct 1969	10.00
❑125, Dec 1969	10.00
❑126, Jan 1970 A: Kryptonite Plus.	10.00
❑127, Mar 1970	16.00
❑128, Apr 1970	10.00
❑129, Jun 1970	10.00
❑130, Jul 1970	10.00
❑131, Aug 1970, aka Giant #G-74	8.00
❑132, Sep 1970	8.00
❑133, Oct 1970 JK (a); 1: Newsboy Legion. 1: Habitat.	10.00
❑134, Dec 1970 1: Darkseid.	25.00
❑135, Jan 1971 1: Project Cadmus.	12.00
❑136, Mar 1971 O: Guardian (new).	12.00
❑137, Apr 1971	12.00
❑138, Jun 1971	12.00
❑139, Jul 1971 A: Don Rickles.	12.00
❑140, Aug 1971, aka Giant #G-86; reprints Jimmy Olsen #69, #72, and Superman #158	12.00
❑141, Sep 1971	10.00
❑142, Oct 1971	10.00
❑143, Nov 1971 JK (a)	10.00
❑144, Dec 1971 JK (a)	10.00
❑145, Jan 1972	10.00
❑146, Feb 1972	10.00
❑147, Mar 1972	10.00
❑148, Apr 1972	10.00
❑149, May 1972 BO (a)	10.00
❑150, Jun 1972	10.00
❑151, Jul 1972	8.00
❑152, Aug 1972	7.00
❑153, Oct 1972	7.00
❑154, Nov 1972	7.00
❑155, Jan 1973	7.00
❑156, Feb 1973	7.00
❑157, Mar 1973	7.00
❑158 1973	7.00
❑159, Aug 1973	7.00
❑160, Oct 1973	7.00
❑161, Nov 1973	7.00
❑162, Dec 1973	7.00
❑163, Feb 1974, Series continues as The Superman Family	7.00

SUPERMAN SPECTACULAR
DC

❑1 V: Luthor. V: Brainiac.	3.00

SUPERMAN: SPEEDING BULLETS
DC

❑1, ca. 1993; prestige format; Elseworlds	4.95

SUPERMAN: STRENGTH
DC

❑1, Mar 2005	5.95
❑2, Apr 2005	5.95
❑3, May 2005	5.95

SUPERMAN/TARZAN: SONS OF THE JUNGLE
DARK HORSE

❑1, Oct 2001	2.99
❑2, Nov 2001	2.99
❑3, May 2002	2.99

SUPERMAN: THE DARK SIDE
DC

❑1, Oct 1998	4.95
❑2, Nov 1998	4.95
❑3, Dec 1998	4.95

SUPERMAN: THE DOOMSDAY WARS
DC

❑1, ca. 1999	4.95
❑1/Ltd.; Signed edition	24.95
❑2, ca. 1999	4.95
❑3, ca. 1999	4.95

SUPERMAN: THE EARTH STEALERS
DC

❑1, May 1988	2.95

SUPERMAN: THE GREATEST STORIES EVER TOLD
DC

❑1, ca. 2004	19.95

SUPERMAN: THE LAST GOD OF KRYPTON
DC

❑1, Aug 1999; prestige format	4.95

SUPERMAN: THE LEGACY OF SUPERMAN
DC

❑1, Mar 1993; Follows up after Superman's demise	2.50

SUPERMAN: THE MAN OF STEEL
DC

❑0, Oct 1994; ▲1994-37	2.50
❑1, Jul 1991; 1: Cerberus. ▲1991-19	6.00
❑2, Aug 1991 V: Sgt. Belcher. V: Rorc.	2.50
❑3, Sep 1991; War of the Gods	2.50
❑4, Oct 1991 V: Angstrom.	2.00
❑5, Nov 1991 V: Atomic Skull	2.00
❑6, Dec 1991	2.00
❑7, Jan 1992 V: Blockhouse. V: Jolt.	2.00
❑8, Feb 1992 V: Blockhouse. V: Jolt.	2.00

Other grades: Multiply price above by 5/6 for VF/NM • 2/3 for VERY FINE • 1/3 for FINE • 1/5 for VERY GOOD • 1/8 for GOOD

N-MINT

❑9, Mar 1992 .... 2.00
❑10, Apr 1992 .... 2.00
❑11, May 1992 .... 1.50
❑12, Jun 1992 .... 1.50
❑13, Jul 1992 .... 1.50
❑14, Aug 1992 A: Robin. 1.50
❑15, Sep 1992 KG (a); A: Satanus. A: Blaze. 1.50
❑16, Oct 1992 .... 1.50
❑17, Nov 1992 1: Doomsday (cameo). 3.00
❑18, Dec 1992; 1: Doomsday (full appearance). ▲1992-18 .... 4.00
❑18/2nd, Dec 1992; A: Doomsday. ▲1992-18 .... 2.00
❑18/3rd, Dec 1992; A: Doomsday. ▲1992-18 .... 1.50
❑19, Jan 1993; V: Doomsday. ▲1993-1 3.00
❑20, Feb 1993 .... 2.50
❑21, Mar 1993; Pa Kent has heart attack 2.50
❑22, Jun 1993 1: Steel (John Henry Irons). 2.00
❑22/Variant, Jun 1993; Die-cut cover . 2.50
❑23, Jul 1993; Steel vs. Superboy 2.00
❑24, Aug 1993; Steel vs. Last Son of Krypton 2.00
❑25, Sep 1993 .... 2.00
❑26, Oct 1993 .... 2.00
❑27, Nov 1993 .... 2.00
❑28, Dec 1993 .... 2.00
❑29, Jan 1994 .... 2.00
❑30, Feb 1994; Lobo 2.00
❑30/Variant, Feb 1994; vinyl clings cover 3.00
❑31, Mar 1994 .... 2.00
❑32, Apr 1994; Bizarro 2.00
❑33, May 1994 .... 2.00
❑34, Jun 1994 .... 2.00
❑35, Jul 1994; crossover with Milestone Media 2.00
❑36, Aug 1994; A: Static. A: Icon. A: Hardware. ▲1994-29 .... 2.00
❑37, Sep 1994; Zero Hour 2.00
❑38, Nov 1994 .... 2.00
❑39, Dec 1994 .... 2.00
❑40, Jan 1995; ▲1995-1 .... 2.00
❑41, Feb 1995 .... 2.00
❑42, Mar 1995 .... 2.00
❑43, Apr 1995 A: Mr. Miracle. 2.00
❑44, May 1995 .... 2.00
❑45, Jun 1995 .... 2.00
❑46, Jul 1995 .... 2.00
❑47, Aug 1995 .... 2.00
❑48, Sep 1995 A: Aquaman. 2.00
❑49, Oct 1995 .... 2.00
❑50, Nov 1995; Giant-size 3.00
❑51, Dec 1995 V: Freelance. 2.00
❑52, Jan 1996 V: Cyborg. 2.00
❑53, Feb 1996 V: Brawl. 2.00
❑54, Mar 1996; A: Spectre. ▲1996-10 2.00
❑55, Apr 1996; D: Jeb Friedman. ▲1996-15 .... 2.00
❑56, May 1996 V: Mxyzptlk. 2.00
❑57, Jun 1996 A: Golden Age Flash 2.00
❑58, Jul 1996 .... 2.00
❑59, Aug 1996 V: Parasite. 2.00
❑60, Sep 1996 .... 2.00
❑61, Oct 1996; polybagged with On the Edge; ▲1996-41 .... 2.00
❑62, Oct 1996; O: Superman. Final Night; ▲1996-45 .... 2.00
❑63, Dec 1996; Lois rescues Clark from terrorists; ▲1996-50 .... 2.00
❑64, Jan 1997; ▲1997-4 .... 2.00
❑65, Mar 1997; SB (a); V: Superman Revenge Squad. ▲1997-9 .... 2.00
❑66, Apr 1997 .... 2.00
❑67, May 1997; A: Scorn. destruction of old costume 2.00
❑68, Jun 1997 V: Metallo. 2.00
❑69, Jul 1997; A: Atom. in Kandor 2.00
❑70, Aug 1997 A: Scorn. V: Saviour. .. 2.00
❑71, Sep 1997 1: Baud. 2.00
❑72, Oct 1997; V: Mainframe. Genesis 2.00
❑73, Nov 1997 V: Parademons. 2.00
❑74, Dec 1997; A: Sam Lane. V: Rajiv. Face cover; ▲1997-47 .... 2.00
❑75, Jan 1998; A: Mike Carlin. D: Mr. Mxyzptlk. ▲1998-1 .... 2.00

N-MINT

❑76, Feb 1998 A: Simyan. A: Morgan Edge. A: Mokkari. 2.00
❑77, Mar 1998; cover forms diptych with Action Comics #742 .... 2.00
❑78, Apr 1998; Millennium Giants 2.00
❑79, May 1998; Millennium Giants aftermath 2.00
❑80, Jun 1998; set in late '30s 2.00
❑81, Jul 1998; set in late '30s 2.00
❑82, Aug 1998 A: Kismet. V: Dominus. 2.00
❑83, Sep 1998 A: Waverider. 2.00
❑84, Dec 1998; 1: Inventor. in Kandor 2.00
❑85, Jan 1999 V: Simyan. V: Mokkari. 2.00
❑86, Feb 1999 .... 2.00
❑87, Mar 1999 A: Steel. A: Superboy. A: Supergirl. 2.00
❑88, May 1999 V: Robots. 2.00
❑89, Jun 1999; V: Dominus. ▲1999-21 2.00
❑90, Jul 1999; ▲1999-26 .... 2.00
❑91, Aug 1999; ▲1999-31 .... 1.99
❑92, Sep 1999; Superman as Martian Manhunter; ▲1999-35 .... 1.99
❑93, Oct 1999; ▲1999-39 .... 1.99
❑94, Nov 1999 A: Strange Visitor. V: Parasite. 1.99
❑95, Dec 1999; ▲1999-48 .... 1.99
❑96, Jan 2000; ▲2000-3 .... 1.99
❑97, Feb 2000 .... 1.99
❑98, Mar 2000 .... 1.99
❑99, Apr 2000; ▲2000-16 .... 1.99
❑100, May 2000; Giant-size; ▲2000-20 2.99
❑100/Variant, May 2000; Giant-size; Special fold-out cover; ▲2000-20.. 3.99
❑101, Jun 2000 .... 1.99
❑102, Jul 2000 .... 1.99
❑103, Aug 2000 .... 2.25
❑104, Sep 2000; ▲2000-36 .... 2.25
❑105, Oct 2000; ▲2000-41 .... 2.25
❑106, Nov 2000; ▲2000-45 .... 2.25
❑107, Dec 2000; ▲2000-49 .... 2.25
❑108, Jan 2001; ▲2001-4 .... 2.25
❑109, Feb 2001; ▲2001-8 .... 2.25
❑110, Mar 2001; A: Stars and S.T.R.I.P.E.. ▲2001-12 .... 2.25
❑111, Apr 2001; ▲2001-16 .... 2.25
❑112, May 2001; ▲2001-20 .... 2.25
❑113, Jun 2001 .... 2.25
❑114, Jul 2001 .... 2.25
❑115, Aug 2001 .... 2.25
❑116, Sep 2001 .... 2.25
❑117, Oct 2001; ▲2001-40 .... 2.25
❑118, Nov 2001 .... 2.25
❑119, Dec 2001; ▲2001-48 .... 2.25
❑120, Jan 2002; ▲2002-3 .... 2.25
❑121, Feb 2002 .... 2.25
❑122, Mar 2002 .... 2.25
❑123, Apr 2002 .... 2.25
❑124, May 2002 .... 2.25
❑125, Jun 2002 .... 2.25
❑126, Jul 2002 .... 2.25
❑127, Aug 2002 .... 2.25
❑128, Sep 2002 .... 2.25
❑129, Oct 2002 .... 2.25
❑130, Nov 2002 .... 2.25
❑131, Dec 2002 .... 2.25
❑132, Jan 2003 .... 2.25
❑133, Feb 2003 .... 2.25
❑134, Mar 2003 .... 2.25
❑1000000, Nov 1998 JOy (a) 3.00
❑Annual 1, ca. 1992 A: Eclipso. 3.00
❑Annual 2, ca. 1993 1: Edge. 3.00
❑Annual 3, ca. 1994; Elseworlds 3.00
❑Annual 4, ca. 1995; A: Justice League. Year One 3.00
❑Annual 5, Nov 1996; KB (w); 1: Kaleb. Legends of the Dead Earth 3.00
❑Annual 6, Aug 1997; Pulp Heroes 3.95

SUPERMAN: THE MAN OF STEEL GALLERY
DC

❑1, Dec 1995; pin-ups 3.50

SUPERMAN: THE MAN OF TOMORROW
DC

❑1, Sum 1995 .... 2.00
❑2, Fal 1995 A: Alpha Centurion. 2.00

N-MINT

❑3, Win 1995; A: how Luthor regained strength and. Underworld Unleashed 2.00
❑4, Spr 1996; A: Captain Marvel. ▲1996-13 .... 2.00
❑5, Sum 1996; Wedding of Lex Luthor and Contessa 2.00
❑6, Fal 1996; V: Jackal. ▲1996-38 .... 2.00
❑7, Win 1997 V: Maxima. 2.00
❑8, Sum 1997 V: Rock. 2.00
❑9, Fal 1997; Ma and Pa Kent remember Superman's career 2.00
❑10, Win 1998; Obsession vs. Maxima 2.00
❑11, Fal 1998 .... 2.00
❑12, Win 1998 .... 2.00
❑13, Spr 1999 .... 2.00
❑14, Sum 1999 V: Riot. 2.00
❑15, Fal 1999; V: Neron. Day of Judgment 3.00
❑1000000, Nov 1998 .... 2.00

SUPERMAN: THE ODYSSEY
DC

❑1, Jul 1999; prestige format 4.95

SUPERMAN: THE SECRET YEARS
DC

❑1, Feb 1985 FM (c); FM, CS (a) 1.50
❑2, Mar 1985; FM (c); FM, CS (a); A: Lori Lemaris. Clark reveals his secret to Billy Cramer 1.50
❑3, Apr 1985 FM (c); FM, CS (a); D: Billy Cramer. 1.50
❑4, May 1985; FM (c); FM, CS (a); Superboy becomes Superman; Clark Kent meets Perry White 1.50

SUPERMAN: THE WEDDING ALBUM
DC

❑1, Dec 1996; newsstand edition with gatefold back cover; JOy, GP, JBy, BG, GK, CS, KGa, JM, BMc (a); newsstand edition with gatefold back cover: Wedding of Clark Kent and Lois Lane; ▲1996-47 .... 6.00
❑1/Direct ed., Dec 1996; Wedding of Clark Kent and Lois Lane; white cardstock wraparound cover with gatefold back cover 4.95
❑1/Gold, Dec 1996; Gold Foil Edition; Retailer incentive; Limited to 250 copies 10.00

SUPERMAN/THUNDERCATS
DC

❑1, ca. 2004 .... 5.95

SUPERMAN/TOYMAN
DC

❑1, ca. 1996; promo for toy line 1.95

SUPERMAN: UNDER A YELLOW SUN
DC

❑1, ca. 1994; prestige format one-shot 5.95

SUPERMAN VS. ALIENS
DC / DARK HORSE

❑1, Jul 1995; prestige format; crossover with Dark Horse 4.95
❑2, Aug 1995; prestige format; crossover with Dark Horse 4.95
❑3, Sep 1995; prestige format; crossover with Dark Horse 4.95

SUPERMAN VS. PREDATOR
DC / DARK HORSE

❑1, Jul 2000 .... 4.95
❑2, Aug 2000 .... 4.95
❑3, Sep 2000 .... 4.95

SUPERMAN VS. THE AMAZING SPIDER-MAN
DC / MARVEL

❑1, treasury-sized; DG, RA (a); V: Lex Luthor. V: Doctor Octopus. first DC/ Marvel crossover 20.00

SUPERMAN VS. THE TERMINATOR: DEATH TO THE FUTURE
DARK HORSE

❑1, Dec 1999 .... 2.95
❑2, Jan 2000 .... 2.95
❑3, Feb 2000 .... 2.95
❑4, Mar 2000 .... 2.95

SUPERMAN VILLAINS SECRET FILES
DC

❑1, Jun 1998; biographical info on Superman's Rogues Gallery 4.95

Swamp Thing (4th series)

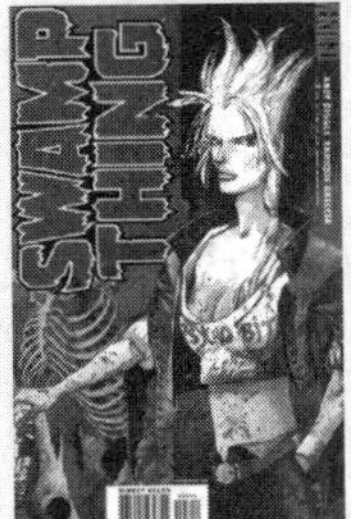

Swamp Thing intervenes with rebellious teen

©DC

Sword of Sorcery

Chaykin adapts Lieber's fantasy stories

©DC

Swords of Cerebus

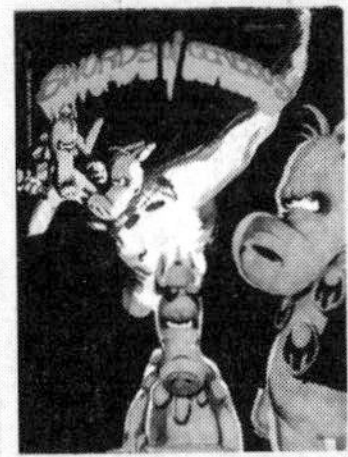

Reprint series skipped an issue with #6

©Aardvark-Vanaheim

Swords of the Swashbucklers

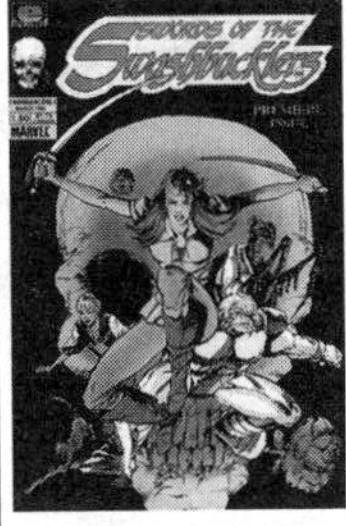

Intergalactic pirates seek treasure

©Marvel

Tales Calculated to Drive You Mad

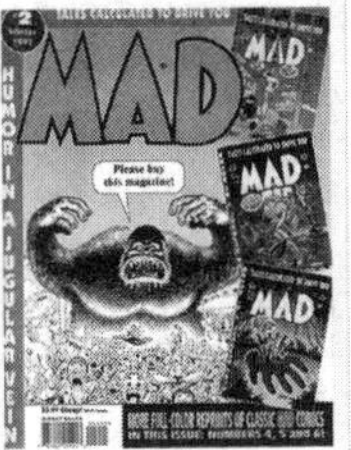

Takes the place of Mad Super Specials

©E.C.

N-MINT

SUPERMAN VS. DARKSEID: APOKOLIPS NOW
DC

❑1, Apr 2003 .... 2.95

SUPERMAN: WAR OF THE WORLDS
DC

❑1, Dec 1998; prestige format one-shot; Elseworlds 5.95
❑1/Ltd., ca. 1999; Signed edition 18.95

SUPERMAN: WHERE IS THY STING?
DC

❑1, Jul 2001 .... 6.95

SUPERMAN/WONDER WOMAN: WHOM GODS DESTROY
DC

❑1, Dec 1996; prestige format; Elseworlds 4.95
❑2, Jan 1997; prestige format; Elseworlds 4.95
❑3, Feb 1997; prestige format; Elseworlds 4.95
❑4, Mar 1997; prestige format; Elseworlds 4.95

SUPER MARIO BROS. (1ST SERIES)
VALIANT

❑1, ca. 1991 .... 2.00
❑2, ca. 1991 .... 2.00
❑3, ca. 1991 .... 2.00
❑4, ca. 1991 .... 2.00
❑5, ca. 1991 .... 2.00
❑6, ca. 1991 .... 2.00
❑Special 1, ca. 1990 .... 2.50

SUPER MARIO BROS. (2ND SERIES)
VALIANT

❑1, ca. 1991 .... 2.00
❑2, ca. 1991 .... 2.00
❑3, ca. 1991 .... 2.00
❑4, ca. 1991 .... 2.00
❑5, ca. 1991 .... 2.00

SUPERMARKET
IDEA & DESIGN WORKS

❑1, Feb 2006 .... 2.99
❑2, Apr 2006 .... 2.99
❑3, Jun 2006 .... 2.99

SUPERMEN OF AMERICA
DC

❑1, Mar 1999 .... 3.95
❑1/CS, Mar 1999; Collector's edition; Gatefold cardstock cover 4.95
❑2, Apr 1999 .... 2.50
❑3, May 1999 .... 2.50
❑4, Jun 1999 .... 2.50

SUPERMODELS IN THE RAINFOREST
SIRIUS

❑1, Dec 1998, b&w 2.95
❑2, Feb 1999, b&w 2.95
❑3, Apr 1999 .... 2.95

SUPERNATURAL FREAK MACHINE
IDEA & DESIGN WORKS

❑1, ca. 2005 .... 3.99
❑2, ca. 2005 .... 3.99

N-MINT

SUPERNATURAL LAW
EXHIBIT A

❑24, Oct 1999, b&w; was Wolff & Byrd, Counselors of the Macabre 2.50
❑25, Feb 2000, b&w 2.50
❑26, May 2000, b&w 2.50
❑27, Jul 2000, b&w 2.50
❑28, Oct 2000, b&w 2.50
❑29, Feb 2001, b&w 2.50
❑30, Apr 2001, b&w 2.50
❑31, Oct 2001, b&w 2.50
❑32, Nov 2001 .... 2.50
❑33, Mar 2002 .... 2.50
❑34, May 2002 .... 2.50
❑35, Jul 2002 .... 2.50
❑36, Sep 2002 .... 2.50
❑37, Apr 2003 .... 2.50
❑38, Jul 2003 .... 2.50

SUPERNATURALS
MARVEL

❑1/A, Dec 1998 .... 3.99
❑1/B, Dec 1998 .... 3.99
❑1/C, Dec 1998 .... 3.99
❑1/D, Dec 1998 .... 3.99
❑1/E, Dec 1998 .... 4.50
❑1/Ltd., Dec 1998 .... 29.99
❑2/A, Dec 1998 .... 3.99
❑2/B, Dec 1998 .... 3.99
❑2/C, Dec 1998 .... 3.99
❑2/D, Dec 1998 .... 3.99
❑2/E, Dec 1998 .... 3.99
❑3/A, Dec 1998 .... 3.99
❑3/B, Dec 1998 .... 3.99
❑3/C, Dec 1998 .... 3.99
❑3/D, Dec 1998 .... 3.99
❑3/E, Dec 1998 .... 3.99
❑4/A, Dec 1998 .... 3.99
❑4/B, Dec 1998 .... 3.99
❑4/C, Dec 1998 .... 3.99
❑4/D, Dec 1998 .... 3.99
❑4/E, Dec 1998 .... 3.99
❑Ashcan 1; Character bios, sketches, creator bios 2.99

SUPERNATURALS TOUR BOOK
MARVEL

❑1, Oct 1998; preview of series; cardstock cover 2.99

SUPERNATURAL THRILLERS
MARVEL

❑1, Dec 1972, It! (Theodore Sturgeon adaptation) 27.00
❑2, Feb 1973, Invisible Man 10.00
❑3, Apr 1973, GK (a); The Valley of the Worm 10.00
❑4, Jun 1973, Dr. Jekyll and Mr. Hyde 10.00
❑5, Aug 1973 O: Living Mummy. 1: Living Mummy 27.00
❑6 1974, The Headless Horseman 10.00
❑7 1974 A: Living Mummy. 10.00
❑8 1974; A: Living Mummy. Marvel Value Stamp #36: Ancient One 10.00
❑9 1974; A: Living Mummy. Marvel Value Stamp #29: Baron Mordo 10.00
❑10 1974 A: Living Mummy. 10.00
❑11, Feb 1975; A: Living Mummy. Marvel Value Stamp #86: Zemo 10.00
❑12, Apr 1975; A: Living Mummy. Marvel Value Stamp #49: Odin 10.00
❑13, Jun 1975 A: Living Mummy. 10.00
❑14, Aug 1975 A: Living Mummy. 10.00
❑15, Oct 1975 TS (a); A: Living Mummy. 10.00

N-MINT

SUPERPATRIOT
IMAGE

❑1, Jul 1993 KG, EL (w) 2.00
❑2, Sep 1993 .... 2.00
❑3, Oct 1993 .... 2.00
❑4, Nov 1993; cover says Dec, indicia says Nov 2.00

SUPERPATRIOT: AMERICA'S FIGHTING FORCE
IMAGE

❑1, Jul 2002 .... 2.95
❑2, Aug 2002 .... 2.95
❑3, Sep 2002; August cover date 2.95
❑4, Oct 2002 .... 2.95

SUPERPATRIOT: LIBERTY & JUSTICE
IMAGE

❑1, Jun 1995 .... 2.50
❑2, Aug 1995 .... 2.50
❑3, Sep 1995 .... 2.50
❑4, Oct 1995 .... 2.50

SUPERPATRIOT: WAR ON TERROR
IMAGE

❑1, Feb 2004 .... 4.00
❑2, Mar 2004 .... 2.95

SUPER POWERS (1ST SERIES)
DC

❑1, Jul 1984, JK (c) 2.00
❑2, Aug 1984, JK (c) 1.00
❑3, Sep 1984, JK (c) 1.00
❑4, Oct 1984, JK (c) 1.00
❑5, Nov 1984, JK (c); JK (w); JK (a) 1.00

SUPER POWERS (2ND SERIES)
DC

❑1, Sep 1985 JK (a) 1.00
❑2, Oct 1985 JK (a) 1.00
❑3, Nov 1985 JK (a) 1.00
❑4, Dec 1985 JK (a) 1.00
❑5, Jan 1986 JK (a) 1.00
❑6, Feb 1986 JK (a) 1.00

SUPER POWERS (3RD SERIES)
DC

❑1, Sep 1986 CI (a) 1.00
❑2, Oct 1986 CI (a) 1.00
❑3, Nov 1986 CI (a) 1.00
❑4, Dec 1986 CI (a) 1.00

SUPER SEXXX
FANTAGRAPHICS / EROS

❑1, b&w 3.25

SUPER SHARK HUMANOIDS
FISH TALES

❑1, Apr 1992 .... 2.75

SUPER SOLDIER
DC / AMALGAM

❑1, Apr 1996 .... 1.95

Other grades: Multiply price above by 5/6 for VF/NM • 2/3 for VERY FINE • 1/3 for FINE • 1/5 for VERY GOOD • 1/8 for GOOD

N-MINT N-MINT N-MINT

SUPER SOLDIER: MAN OF WAR
DC / AMALGAM
- ❑1, Jun 1997 ... 1.95

SUPER SOLDIERS
MARVEL
- ❑1, Apr 1993; foil cover ... 2.50
- ❑2, May 1993 ... 1.75
- ❑3, Jun 1993 ... 1.75
- ❑4, Jul 1993 ... 1.75
- ❑5, Aug 1993 ... 1.75
- ❑6, Sep 1993 ... 1.75
- ❑7, Oct 1993; X-Men cameo ... 1.75
- ❑8, Nov 1993 ... 1.75

SUPERSONIC SOUL PUDDIN COMICS & STORIES
FOUR CATS FUNNY BOOKS
- ❑1, Jun 1995 ... 3.50

SUPER SONIC VS. HYPER KNUCKLES
ARCHIE
- ❑1 ... 2.00

SUPERSTAR: AS SEEN ON TV
IMAGE
- ❑1, Jul 2001 ... 5.95

SUPER STREET FIGHTER II: CAMMY
VIZ
- ❑Book 1 ... 15.95

SUPERSWINE
CALIBER
- ❑1, b&w ... 2.50
- ❑2, b&w ... 2.50

SUPER TABOO
FANTAGRAPHICS / EROS
- ❑1, Dec 1995 ... 2.95
- ❑2, Jan 1996 ... 2.95

SUPER-TEAM FAMILY
DC
- ❑1, Nov 1975 ... 12.00
- ❑2, Jan 1976 A: Speedy. A: Wildcat. A: Deadman. A: Superman. A: Green Arrow. A: Creeper. A: Batman. ... 6.00
- ❑3, Mar 1976 ... 6.00
- ❑4, May 1976 A: Justice Society of America. A: Superman. A: Solomon Grundy. A: Robin. A: Batman. ... 6.00
- ❑5, Jul 1976 ... 4.00
- ❑6, Sep 1976 ... 4.00
- ❑7, Nov 1976, Teen Titans ... 4.00
- ❑8, Jan 1977, A: Challengers of the Unknown. New stories begin ... 4.00
- ❑9, Mar 1977 A: Challengers of the Unknown ... 4.00
- ❑10, May 1977 A: Challengers of the Unknown ... 4.00
- ❑11, Jul 1977, Flash, Atom, Supergirl ... 3.00
- ❑12, Sep 1977 ... 3.00
- ❑13, Nov 1977, Atom, Aquaman, Captain Comet ... 3.00
- ❑14, Jan 1978 ... 3.00
- ❑15, Apr 1978 ... 3.00

SUPER-VILLAIN CLASSICS
MARVEL
- ❑1, May 1983, O: Galactus. Reprints .. 3.00

SUPER-VILLAIN TEAM-UP
MARVEL
- ❑1, Aug 1975 GE, BEv, GT (a); A: Doctor Doom. A: Sub-Mariner. ... 7.00
- ❑2, Oct 1975 SB (a); A: Doctor Doom. A: Sub-Mariner. ... 5.00
- ❑3, Dec 1975 A: Doctor Doom. A: Sub-Mariner. ... 4.00
- ❑4, Feb 1976 A: Doctor Doom. A: Sub-Mariner. ... 4.00
- ❑5, Apr 1976 1: Shroud. A: Doctor Doom. A: Sub-Mariner. ... 4.00
- ❑5/30 cent, Apr 1976 ... 20.00
- ❑6, Jun 1976 A: Doctor Doom. A: Sub-Mariner. ... 3.00
- ❑6/30 cent, Jun 1976 ... 20.00
- ❑7, Aug 1976 O: Shroud. A: Doctor Doom. A: Sub-Mariner. ... 3.00
- ❑7/30 cent, Aug 1976 ... 20.00
- ❑8, Oct 1976 1: Rajah. A: Doctor Doom. A: Sub-Mariner. ... 3.00
- ❑9, Dec 1976 A: Doctor Doom. A: Sub-Mariner. ... 3.00
- ❑10, Feb 1977 BH (a); A: Doctor Doom. A: Sub-Mariner. ... 3.00
- ❑11, Apr 1977 BH (a) ... 3.00
- ❑12, Jun 1977, BH (a); Newsstand edition (distributed by Curtis); issue number in box ... 3.00
- ❑12/Whitman, Jun 1977, BH (a); Special markets edition (usually sold in Whitman bagged prepacks); price appears in a diamond; UPC barcode appears ... 3.00
- ❑12/35 cent, Jun 1977, BH (a); 35 cent regional price variant; newsstand edition (distributed by Curtis); issue number in box ... 15.00
- ❑13, Aug 1977 ... 3.00
- ❑13/35 cent, Aug 1977, 35 cent regional price variant ... 15.00
- ❑14, Oct 1977, BH (a); Newsstand edition (distributed by Curtis); issue number in box ... 3.00
- ❑14/Whitman, Oct 1977, BH (a); Special markets edition (usually sold in Whitman bagged prepacks); price appears in a diamond; no UPC barcode ... 3.00
- ❑14/35 cent, Oct 1977, BH (a); 35 cent regional price variant; newsstand edition (distributed by Curtis); issue number in box ... 15.00
- ❑15, Nov 1977 A: Red Skull. A: Doctor Doom. ... 3.00
- ❑16, May 1979 A: Red Skull. A: Doctor Doom. ... 3.00
- ❑17, Jun 1980 A: Red Skull. A: Doctor Doom. ... 3.00

SUPPRESSED!
TOME
- ❑1, b&w ... 2.95

SUPREME
IMAGE
- ❑0, Aug 1995 RL (c); RL (a) ... 2.50
- ❑1, Nov 1992 RL (w) ... 2.50
- ❑1/Gold, Nov 1992; Gold promotional edition; Embossed cover ... 2.50
- ❑2, Feb 1993; 1: Grizlock. covers says May, indicia says Feb ... 2.00
- ❑3, Jun 1993 RL (w); 1: Khrome ... 2.00
- ❑4, Jul 1993 ... 2.00
- ❑5, Aug 1993 1: Thor (Image) ... 2.00
- ❑6, Oct 1993 1: the Starguard ... 2.00
- ❑7, Nov 1993 ... 2.00
- ❑8, Dec 1993 ... 2.00
- ❑9, Jan 1994 ... 2.00
- ❑10, Feb 1994 ... 2.00
- ❑11, Mar 1994 ... 2.00
- ❑12, Apr 1994 ... 2.00
- ❑13, Jun 1994 ... 2.50
- ❑14, Jun 1994 ... 2.50
- ❑15, Jul 1994 ... 2.50
- ❑16, Jul 1994 ... 2.50
- ❑17, Aug 1994 V: Pitt ... 2.50
- ❑18, Aug 1994 ... 2.50
- ❑19, Sep 1994 ... 2.50
- ❑20, Oct 1994 A: Kid Supreme ... 2.50
- ❑21, Nov 1994 ... 2.50
- ❑22, Dec 1994 ... 2.50
- ❑23, Jan 1995; polybagged with trading card ... 2.50
- ❑24, Feb 1995 ... 2.50
- ❑25, May 1994; Images of Tomorrow; Shipped out of sequence after #12 to give preview of future ... 2.50
- ❑26, Mar 1995 V: Kid Supreme ... 2.50
- ❑27, Apr 1995 ... 2.50
- ❑28, May 1995 ... 2.50
- ❑28/A, May 1995 A: Glory ... 2.50
- ❑28/B, May 1995 A: Glory ... 2.50
- ❑29, Jun 1995; polybagged with Power Cardz ... 2.50
- ❑30, Jul 1995; polybagged with Power Cardz ... 2.50
- ❑31, Aug 1995 ... 2.50
- ❑32, Oct 1995 ... 2.50
- ❑33, Nov 1995; Babewatch ... 2.50
- ❑34, Dec 1995 ... 2.50
- ❑35, Jan 1996; polybagged with Lady Supreme card ... 2.50
- ❑36, Feb 1996 ... 2.50
- ❑37, Mar 1996 ... 2.50
- ❑37/A, Mar 1996; alternate cover ... 2.50
- ❑37/B, Mar 1996; alternate cover ... 2.50
- ❑38, Apr 1996 ... 2.50
- ❑39, May 1996 V: Loki ... 2.50
- ❑40, Jul 1996 ... 2.50
- ❑41, Aug 1996; Newmen Special Preview Edition back-up AMo (w) ... 3.50
- ❑41/Ltd., Aug 1996; limited edition; alternate cover (Superman homage) 15.00
- ❑41/American Ent, Aug 1996; alternate cover (American Entertainment exclusive) ... 9.00
- ❑41/2nd ... 2.50
- ❑42, Sep 1996; AMo (w); Superman homage; moves to Maximum Press 3.00
- ❑43, Oct 1996; AMo (w); Superman homage ... 3.00
- ❑44, Jan 1997 AMo (w) ... 3.00
- ❑45, Jan 1997 AMo (w) ... 2.50
- ❑46, Feb 1997 AMo (w); 1: Suprema. 2.50
- ❑47, Mar 1997 AMo (w); 1: Twilight... 2.50
- ❑48, Apr 1997 AMo (w) ... 2.50
- ❑49, May 1997; AMo (w); cover says Jun, indicia says May ... 2.50
- ❑50, Jun 1997; Giant-size AMo (w) ... 2.50
- ❑51, Jul 1997 AMo (w) ... 2.50
- ❑52/A, Sep 1997 AMo (w) ... 2.50
- ❑52/B, Sep 1997 AMo (w) ... 2.50
- ❑53, Sep 1997 AMo (w) ... 2.50
- ❑54, Nov 1997 AMo (w) ... 2.50
- ❑55, Nov 1997; AMo (w); GK (a); cover says Dec, indicia says Nov ... 2.50
- ❑56, Feb 1998 ... 2.50
- ❑Annual 1, May 1995 A: The Allies ... 4.00

SUPREME: GLORY DAYS
IMAGE
- ❑1, Oct 1994, RL (w) ... 3.00
- ❑2, Dec 1994, RL (w) ... 2.50

SUPREME POWER
MARVEL
- ❑1, Oct 2003 ... 4.00
- ❑1/Special, Oct 2003 ... 4.99
- ❑2, Nov 2003 ... 2.99
- ❑3, Dec 2003 ... 2.99
- ❑4, Jan 2003 ... 2.99
- ❑5, Feb 2004 ... 4.00
- ❑6, Mar 2004 (c) ... 2.99
- ❑7, Apr 2004 ... 2.99
- ❑8, May 2004 ... 2.99
- ❑9, Jun 2004 ... 2.99
- ❑10, Jul 2004 ... 2.99
- ❑11, Sep 2004 ... 2.99
- ❑12, Oct 2004 ... 2.99
- ❑13, Nov 2004 ... 2.99
- ❑14, Dec 2004 ... 2.99
- ❑15, Jan 2005 ... 2.99
- ❑16 2005 ... 2.99
- ❑17 2005 ... 2.99
- ❑18, Oct 2005 ... 2.99

SUPREME POWER: HYPERION
MARVEL / MAX
- ❑1 ... 2.99
- ❑2, Dec 2005 ... 2.99
- ❑3, Feb 2006 ... 2.99
- ❑5, Jun 2006 ... 2.99

SUPREME POWER: NIGHTHAWK
MARVEL
- ❑1, Oct 2005 ... 2.99
- ❑2, 2005 ... 2.99
- ❑3, Jan 2006 ... 2.99
- ❑4, Feb 2006 ... 2.99
- ❑5, Mar 2006 ... 2.99
- ❑6, Mar 2006 ... 2.99

SUPREME: THE RETURN
AWESOME
- ❑1, May 1999; continues story from Supreme #56 ... 2.99
- ❑2, Jun 1999; infinite Darius Daxes ... 2.99
- ❑3 ... 2.99
- ❑4, Mar 2000 ... 2.99
- ❑5, May 2000 ... 2.99
- ❑6, Jun 2000 ... 2.99

SUPREMIE
PARODY
- ❑1, b&w ... 2.50

SURFCRAZED COMICS
PACIFICA
- ❑1 ... 2.50
- ❑3; 3-D ... 3.95
- ❑4 ... 2.50

Other grades: Multiply price above by 5/6 for VF/NM • 2/3 for VERY FINE • 1/3 for FINE • 1/5 for VERY GOOD • 1/8 for GOOD

Tales from the Crypt (Gladstone)

Crypt Keeper's origin appears in first issue

©Gladstone

Tales from the Fridge

Cover homage to Tales from the Crypt #42

©Kitchen Sink

Tales of Asgard (Vol. 1)

Collects Journey into Mystery back-ups

©Marvel

Tales of G.I. Joe

Reprints joined recycled syndication

©Marvel

Tales of Suspense

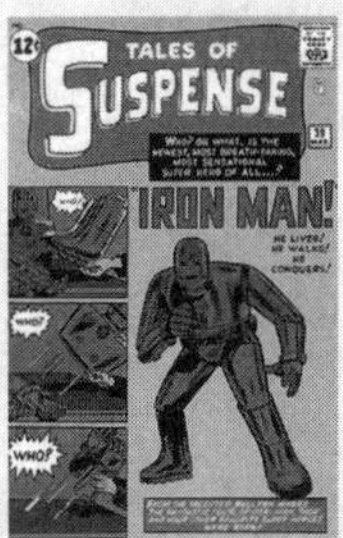

Iron Man repulsed horror stories

©Marvel

N-MINT

SURF 'N' WHEELS
CHARLTON

- ❑1, Nov 1969 ... 12.00
- ❑2, Jan 1970 ... 12.00
- ❑3, Mar 1970 ... 12.00
- ❑4, May 1970 ... 12.00
- ❑5, Jul 1970 ... 12.00
- ❑6, Sep 1970 ... 12.00

SURF SUMO
STAR TIGER

- ❑1 ... 2.95
- ❑1/2nd, Jun 1997; 2nd printing with insert noting rights had reverted to Mighty Graphics; June 1997 ... 2.95

SURGE
ECLIPSE

- ❑1, Jul 1984 ME (w) ... 1.75
- ❑2, Aug 1984 ME (w) ... 1.75
- ❑3, Oct 1984 ME (w) ... 1.75
- ❑4, Jan 1985 ME (w) ... 1.75

SURROGATES
TOP SHELF PRODUCTIONS

- ❑1, Jul 2005 ... 2.95

SURROGATE SAVIOUR
HOT BRAZEN COMICS

- ❑1, Sep 1995, b&w ... 2.50
- ❑2, Nov 1995, b&w ... 2.75
- ❑3, Jun 1996, b&w ... 2.95

SURVIVE!
APPLE

- ❑1, b&w ... 2.75

SURVIVORS (FANTAGRAPHICS)
FANTAGRAPHICS

- ❑1 ... 2.50
- ❑2 ... 2.50

SURVIVORS (PRELUDE)
PRELUDE

- ❑1, Oct 1986 ... 1.95
- ❑2 ... 1.95

SURVIVORS (BURNSIDE)
BURNSIDE

- ❑1 ... 1.95

SUSHI
SHUNGA

- ❑1, b&w ... 3.00
- ❑1/2nd ... 2.50
- ❑2, b&w ... 3.00
- ❑3, b&w ... 3.00
- ❑4, b&w ... 3.00
- ❑5, b&w ... 3.00
- ❑6, b&w ... 3.00
- ❑7 ... 2.50
- ❑8 ... 2.50

SUSPIRA: THE GREAT WORKING
CHAOS

- ❑1, Mar 1997 ... 2.95
- ❑2, Apr 1997 ... 2.95
- ❑3, May 1997 ... 2.95
- ❑4, Jun 1997 ... 2.95

SUSSEX VAMPIRE
CALIBER

- ❑1 ... 2.95

N-MINT

SUSTAH-GIRL: QUEEN OF THE BLACK AGE
ONLI

- ❑1, b&w ... 2.00

SWAMP FEVER
BIG MUDDY

- ❑1 ... 3.00

SWAMP THING (1ST SERIES)
DC

- ❑1, Nov 1972 BWr (a); O: Swamp Thing. ... 60.00
- ❑2, Jan 1973 BWr (a) ... 30.00
- ❑3, Mar 1973 BWr (a); 1: Patchwork Man. ... 20.00
- ❑4, May 1973 BWr (a) ... 20.00
- ❑5, Aug 1973 BWr (a) ... 15.00
- ❑6, Oct 1973 BWr (a) ... 15.00
- ❑7, Dec 1973, BWr (a); A: Batman. Batman ... 12.00
- ❑8, Feb 1974 BWr (a) ... 10.00
- ❑9, Apr 1974 BWr (a) ... 10.00
- ❑10, Jun 1974 BWr (a) ... 10.00
- ❑11, Aug 1974 NR (a) ... 5.00
- ❑12, Oct 1974 NR (a) ... 5.00
- ❑13, Dec 1974 NR (a) ... 5.00
- ❑14, Feb 1975 NR (a) ... 5.00
- ❑15, Apr 1975 NR (a) ... 5.00
- ❑16, May 1975 NR (a) ... 5.00
- ❑17, Jul 1975 NR (a) ... 5.00
- ❑18, Sep 1975 NR (a) ... 5.00
- ❑19, Oct 1975 NR (a) ... 5.00
- ❑20, Jan 1976 NR (a) ... 5.00
- ❑21, Mar 1976 NR (a) ... 5.00
- ❑22, May 1976 NR (a) ... 5.00
- ❑23, Jul 1976 NR (a) ... 5.00
- ❑24, Sep 1976 NR (a) ... 5.00

SWAMP THING (2ND SERIES)
DC

- ❑46, Mar 1986; AMo (w); A: John Constantine. Crisis; Series continued from "Saga of the Swamp Thing" ... 4.00
- ❑47, Apr 1986 AMo (w); 1: Parliament of Trees ... 3.00
- ❑48, May 1986 AMo (w) ... 3.00
- ❑49, Jun 1986 AMo (w); AA (a) ... 3.00
- ❑50, Jul 1986; Giant-size AMo (w); D: Sargon. ... 4.00
- ❑51, Aug 1986 AMo (w) ... 3.00
- ❑52, Sep 1986; AMo (w); A: Arkham Asylum. A: Joker. A: Joke. Joker ... 4.00
- ❑53, Oct 1986; AMo (w); A: Batman. Arkham Asylum story ... 4.50
- ❑54, Nov 1986 AMo (w) ... 3.00
- ❑55, Dec 1986 AMo (w) ... 3.00
- ❑56, Jan 1987 AMo (w); AA (a) ... 3.00
- ❑57, Feb 1987 AMo (w) ... 3.00
- ❑58, Mar 1987; AMo (w); Spectre preview ... 3.00
- ❑59, Apr 1987 AMo (w) ... 3.00
- ❑60, May 1987; AMo (w); new format ... 3.00
- ❑61, Jun 1987 AMo (w) ... 3.00
- ❑62, Jul 1987 ... 3.00
- ❑63, Aug 1987 AMo (w) ... 3.00
- ❑64, Sep 1987; AMo (w); last with Moore ... 3.00

N-MINT

- ❑65, Oct 1987; 1: Sprout. Arkham Asylum ... 3.00
- ❑66, Nov 1987; Arkham Asylum ... 2.50
- ❑67, Dec 1987 1: Hellblazer. ... 2.50
- ❑68, Jan 1988 ... 2.50
- ❑69, Feb 1988 ... 2.50
- ❑70, Mar 1988 ... 2.50
- ❑71, Apr 1988 ... 2.50
- ❑72, May 1988 ... 2.50
- ❑73, Jun 1988 ... 2.50
- ❑74, Jul 1988 ... 2.50
- ❑75, Aug 1988 ... 2.50
- ❑76, Sep 1988; Continues from Hellblazer #9; continues in Hellblazer #10 ... 2.50
- ❑77, Oct 1988 AA (a) ... 2.50
- ❑78, Nov 1988 AA (a) ... 2.50
- ❑79, Dec 1988 A: Superman. ... 2.50
- ❑80, Win 1988 ... 2.50
- ❑81, Hol 1989; Invasion! ... 2.50
- ❑82, Jan 1989; Sgt. Rock ... 2.25
- ❑83, Feb 1989; Enemy Ace ... 2.25
- ❑84, Mar 1989 A: Sandman. ... 5.00
- ❑85, Apr 1989; Jonah Hex, Bat Lash .. 2.25
- ❑86, May 1989; Tomahawk, Rip Hunter, Demon ... 2.25
- ❑87, Jun 1989; Shining Knight, Demon 2.25
- ❑88, Sep 1989 ... 2.25
- ❑89, Oct 1989 ... 2.25
- ❑90, Dec 1989; 1: Tefe Holland. Formerly known as Sprout ... 2.50
- ❑91, Jan 1990 A: Woodgod. ... 2.25
- ❑92, Feb 1990 ... 2.25
- ❑93, Mar 1990 ... 2.25
- ❑94, Apr 1990 ... 2.25
- ❑95, May 1990 ... 2.25
- ❑96, Jun 1990 ... 2.25
- ❑97, Jul 1990 ... 2.25
- ❑98, Aug 1990 ... 2.25
- ❑99, Sep 1990 ... 2.25
- ❑100, Oct 1990; Giant-size ... 3.00
- ❑101, Nov 1990 ... 2.25
- ❑102, Dec 1990 ... 2.25
- ❑103, Jan 1991 ... 2.25
- ❑104, Feb 1991 ... 2.25
- ❑105, Mar 1991 ... 2.25
- ❑106, Apr 1991 ... 2.25
- ❑107, May 1991 ... 2.25
- ❑108, Jun 1991 ... 2.25
- ❑109, Jul 1991 ... 2.25
- ❑110, Aug 1991 ... 2.25
- ❑111, Sep 1991 ... 2.25
- ❑112, Oct 1991 ... 2.25
- ❑113, Nov 1991 ... 2.25
- ❑114, Dec 1991 ... 2.25
- ❑115, Jan 1992 ... 2.25
- ❑116, Feb 1992 ... 2.25
- ❑117, Mar 1992 JDu (a) ... 2.25
- ❑118, Apr 1992 ... 2.25
- ❑119, May 1992 1: Lady Jane. ... 2.25
- ❑120, Jun 1992 ... 2.25
- ❑121, Jul 1992 ... 2.00
- ❑122, Aug 1992 ... 2.00
- ❑123, Sep 1992 ... 2.00
- ❑124, Oct 1992 ... 2.00

Other grades: Multiply price above by 5/6 for VF/NM • 2/3 for VERY FINE • 1/3 for FINE • 1/5 for VERY GOOD • 1/8 for GOOD

N-MINT

❑125, Nov 1992; 20th Anniversary Issue; Arcane 3.25
❑126, Dec 1992 ..... 2.00
❑127, Jan 1993 ..... 2.00
❑128, Feb 1993; Vertigo line begins 2.00
❑129, Mar 1993 ..... 2.00
❑130, Apr 1993 ..... 2.00
❑131, May 1993 ..... 2.00
❑132, Jun 1993 ..... 2.00
❑133, Jul 1993 ..... 2.00
❑134, Aug 1993 ..... 2.00
❑135, Sep 1993 ..... 2.00
❑136, Oct 1993 ..... 2.00
❑137, Nov 1993 ..... 2.00
❑138, Dec 1993 ..... 2.00
❑139, Jan 1994 ..... 2.00
❑140, Mar 1994 ..... 2.00
❑140/Platinum, Mar 1994 ..... 6.00
❑141, Apr 1994 ..... 2.00
❑142, May 1994 ..... 2.00
❑143, Jun 1994 ..... 2.00
❑144, Jul 1994 ..... 2.00
❑145, Aug 1994 ..... 2.00
❑146, Sep 1994 ..... 2.00
❑147, Oct 1994 ..... 2.00
❑148, Nov 1994 ..... 2.00
❑149, Dec 1994 ..... 2.00
❑150, Jan 1995; Giant-size 3.00
❑151, Feb 1995 ..... 2.00
❑152, Mar 1995 ..... 2.00
❑153, Apr 1995 ..... 2.00
❑154, May 1995 ..... 2.25
❑155, Jun 1995 ..... 2.25
❑156, Jul 1995 ..... 2.25
❑157, Aug 1995 ..... 2.25
❑158, Sep 1995 ..... 2.25
❑159, Oct 1995 ..... 2.50
❑160, Nov 1995 ..... 2.50
❑161, Dec 1995 ..... 2.50
❑162, Jan 1996 ..... 2.50
❑163, Feb 1996 ..... 2.50
❑164, Mar 1996 ..... 2.50
❑165, Apr 1996 CS (a) 2.50
❑166, May 1996 ..... 2.50
❑167, Jun 1996 ..... 2.50
❑168, Jul 1996 ..... 2.50
❑169, Aug 1996 A: John Constantine. 2.50
❑170, Sep 1996 ..... 2.50
❑171, Oct 1996 ..... 2.50
❑Annual 4 A: Batman. 3.50
❑Annual 5 A: Brother Power. 3.50
❑Annual 6 ..... 2.95
❑Annual 7; Children's Crusade 3.95

SWAMP THING (3RD SERIES)
DC / Vertigo

❑1, May 2000 ..... 4.00
❑2, Jun 2000 ..... 2.50
❑3, Jul 2000 ..... 2.50
❑4, Aug 2000 ..... 2.50
❑5, Sep 2000 ..... 2.50
❑6, Oct 2000 ..... 2.50
❑7, Nov 2000 ..... 2.50
❑8, Dec 2000 ..... 2.50
❑9, Jan 2001 ..... 2.50
❑10, Feb 2001 ..... 2.50
❑11, Mar 2001 ..... 2.50
❑12, Apr 2001 ..... 2.50
❑13, May 2001 ..... 2.50
❑14, Jun 2001 ..... 2.50
❑15, Jul 2001 ..... 2.50
❑16, Aug 2001 ..... 2.50
❑17, Sep 2001 ..... 2.50
❑18, Oct 2001 ..... 2.50
❑19, Nov 2001 ..... 2.50
❑20, Dec 2001 ..... 2.50

SWAMP THING (4TH SERIES)
DC / Vertigo

❑1, May 2004 ..... 4.00
❑2, Jun 2004 ..... 2.95
❑3, Jul 2004 ..... 2.95
❑4, Aug 2004 ..... 2.95
❑5, Sep 2004 ..... 2.95
❑6, Oct 2004 ..... 2.95
❑7, Nov 2004 ..... 2.95
❑8, Dec 2004 ..... 2.95
❑9, Jan 2005 ..... 2.95
❑10, Feb 2005 ..... 2.95
❑11, Mar 2005 ..... 2.95
❑12, Apr 2005 ..... 2.95
❑13, May 2005 ..... 2.95
❑14, Jun 2005 ..... 2.95
❑15, Jul 2005 ..... 2.99
❑16, Aug 2005 ..... 2.99
❑17, Sep 2005 ..... 2.99
❑18, Oct 2005 ..... 2.99
❑19, Nov 2005 ..... 2.99
❑20, Dec 2005 ..... 2.99
❑21, Jan 2006 ..... 2.99
❑22, Jan 2006 ..... 2.99
❑23, Mar 2006 ..... 2.99
❑24, Mar 2006 ..... 2.99
❑25, May 2006 ..... 2.99
❑26, Jun 2006 ..... 2.99
❑27, Jul 2006 ..... 2.99
❑28, Sep 2006 ..... 2.99

SWAMP THING: ROOTS
DC / Vertigo

❑1; prestige format one-shot 7.95

SWAN
Little Idylls

❑1, Jun 1995, b&w 2.95
❑2, Jun 1995, b&w 2.95
❑3 ..... 2.95
❑4 ..... 2.95

SWEATSHOP
DC

❑1, Jun 2003 ..... 2.95
❑2, Jul 2003 ..... 2.95
❑3, Aug 2003 ..... 2.95
❑4, Sep 2003 ..... 2.95
❑5, Oct 2003 ..... 2.95
❑6, Nov 2003 ..... 2.95

SWEET
Adept

❑1 ..... 3.95

SWEETCHILDE
New Moon

❑1, b&w 2.95

SWEET CHILDE: LOST CONFESSIONS
Anarchy Bridgeworks

❑1 ..... 2.95

SWEET LUCY
Brainstorm

❑1, Jun 1993, b&w 2.95
❑2, b&w 2.95

SWEET LUCY: BLONDE STEELE
Brainstorm

❑1 ..... 2.95

SWEET LUCY COMMEMORATIVE EDITION
Brainstorm

❑1 ..... 3.95

SWEETMEATS
Atomeka

❑1, b&w one-shot 3.95

SWEET XVI
Marvel

❑1, May 1991 ..... 1.00
❑2, Jun 1991 ..... 1.00
❑3, Jul 1991 ..... 1.00
❑4, Aug 1991 ..... 1.00
❑5, Sep 1991 ..... 1.00
❑6, Oct 1991 ..... 1.00
❑Special 1, Back to School Special 2.25

SWERVE
Slave Labor / Amaze Ink

❑1, Dec 1995 ..... 1.50
❑2, Mar 1996 ..... 1.50

SWIFTSURE
Harrier

❑1, May 1985 ..... 2.00
❑2 ..... 2.00
❑3, Aug 1985 ..... 2.00
❑4 ..... 2.00
❑5, Nov 1985 ..... 2.00
❑6, Jan 1986 ..... 2.00
❑7, Mar 1986 ..... 2.00
❑8, May 1986 ..... 2.00
❑9, Jul 1986; Redfox 2.00
❑10, Sep 1986 ..... 2.00
❑11, Nov 1986 ..... 2.00
❑12, Jan 1987 ..... 2.00
❑13, Mar 1987 ..... 2.00
❑14, May 1987 ..... 2.00
❑15, Jul 1987 ..... 2.00
❑16, Sep 1987 ..... 2.00
❑17, Nov 1987 ..... 2.00
❑18, Jan 1988 ..... 2.00

SWIFTSURE & CONQUEROR
Harrier

❑1 ..... 2.00
❑2 ..... 1.75
❑3 ..... 1.75
❑4 ..... 1.75
❑5 ..... 1.75
❑6 ..... 1.75
❑7 ..... 1.75
❑8 ..... 1.75
❑9 A: Redfox 2.50
❑10 ..... 1.50
❑11 ..... 1.50
❑12 ..... 1.50
❑13 ..... 1.95
❑14 ..... 1.95
❑15 ..... 1.95
❑16 ..... 1.95
❑17 ..... 1.95
❑18 ..... 1.95

SWING WITH SCOOTER
DC

❑1, Jul 1966 ..... 30.00
❑2, Sep 1966 ..... 18.00
❑3, Nov 1966 JO (a) 15.00
❑4, Jan 1967 ..... 12.00
❑5, Mar 1967 ..... 12.00
❑6, May 1967 ..... 10.00
❑7, Jul 1967 ..... 10.00
❑8, Sep 1967 ..... 10.00
❑9, Nov 1967 ..... 10.00
❑10, Jan 1968 ..... 10.00
❑11, Mar 1968 ..... 8.00
❑12, May 1968 ..... 8.00
❑13, Jul 1968 ..... 8.00
❑14, Sep 1968 ..... 8.00
❑15, Nov 1968 ..... 8.00
❑16, Jan 1969 ..... 8.00
❑17, Mar 1969 ..... 8.00
❑18, May 1969 ..... 8.00
❑19, Jul 1969 ..... 8.00
❑20, Aug 1969 ..... 8.00
❑21, Sep 1969 ..... 6.00
❑22, Oct 1969 ..... 6.00
❑23 1969 ..... 6.00
❑24 1970 ..... 6.00
❑25, Feb 1970 ..... 6.00
❑26 1970 ..... 6.00
❑27, May 1970 ..... 6.00
❑28 1970 ..... 6.00
❑29 1970 ..... 6.00
❑30, Oct 1970 ..... 6.00
❑31, Nov 1970 ..... 5.00
❑32, Mar 1971 ..... 5.00
❑33 1971 ..... 5.00
❑34 1971 ..... 5.00
❑35 1971 ..... 5.00
❑36, Aug 1971 ..... 5.00

SWITCHBLADE
Silverline

❑1, Dec 1997 ..... 2.95

SWORD IN THE STONE
Gold Key

❑1, Feb 1964 ..... 30.00

SWORD OF DAMOCLES
Image

❑1, Mar 1996 ..... 2.50
❑2, Jul 1996 ..... 2.50

SWORD OF DRACULA
Image

❑1, Oct 2003 ..... 2.95
❑2, Dec 2003 ..... 2.95
❑3, Apr 2004 ..... 2.99
❑4, Apr 2004 ..... 2.95
❑5 2004 ..... 2.95
❑6 2004 ..... 2.95

Other grades: Multiply price above by 5/6 for VF/NM • 2/3 for VERY FINE • 1/3 for FINE • 1/5 for VERY GOOD • 1/8 for GOOD

Tales of Terror

Horror tales eclipsed by other offerings

©Eclipse

Tales of the Beanworld

Simple, surreal, and high protein stories

©Eclipse

Tales of the Green Beret

No super-heroes here, just real heroes

©Dell

Tales of the Legion

First dozen issues fresh, rest reprints

©DC

Tales of the Teen Titans

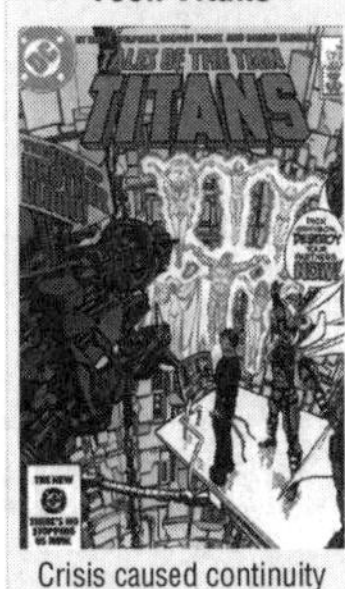

Crisis caused continuity problem with reprints

©DC

N-MINT

SWORD OF SORCERY
DC
❑1, Mar 1973, HC, NA (a); Fafhrd and The Gray Mouser ... 10.00
❑2, May 1973, HC (a); Fafhrd and The Gray Mouser ... 8.00
❑3, Aug 1973, HC (a); Fafhrd and The Gray Mouser ... 8.00
❑4, Oct 1973, HC (a); Fafhrd and The Gray Mouser ... 6.00
❑5, Dec 1973, JSe (a); Fafhrd and The Gray Mouser ... 6.00

SWORD OF THE ATOM
DC
❑1, Sep 1983 GK (a) ... 1.50
❑2, Oct 1983 GK (a) ... 1.50
❑3, Nov 1983 GK (a) ... 1.50
❑4, Dec 1983 GK (a) ... 1.50
❑Special 1, ca. 1984, GK (a) ... 1.50
❑Special 2, ca. 1985, GK (a) ... 1.50
❑Special 3, ca. 1988, PB (a) ... 1.50

SWORD OF THE SAMURAI
AVALON
❑1 1996, b&w; Reprints ... 2.50

SWORD OF VALOR
A+
❑1 ... 2.50
❑2 ... 2.50
❑3 ... 2.50
❑4 ... 2.50

SWORDSMEN AND SAURIANS
ECLIPSE
❑1, b&w ... 19.95

SWORDS OF CEREBUS
AARDVARK-VANAHEIM
❑1, b&w; Reprints Cerebus #1-4 ... 5.00
❑1/2nd, b&w; Reprints Cerebus #1-4 ... 5.00
❑1/3rd, b&w; Reprints Cerebus #1-4 ... 5.00
❑2, b&w; Reprints Cerebus #5-8 ... 5.00
❑2/2nd, b&w; Reprints Cerebus #5-8 ... 5.00
❑3, b&w; Reprints Cerebus #9-12 ... 6.00
❑3/2nd, b&w; Reprints Cerebus #9-12 ... 6.00
❑3/3rd, b&w; Reprints Cerebus #9-12 ... 6.00
❑4, b&w; Reprints Cerebus #13-16 ... 6.00
❑4/2nd, b&w; Reprints Cerebus #13-16 ... 6.00
❑5, b&w; Reprints Cerebus #17-20 ... 5.00
❑6, b&w; Reprints Cerebus #21-24; first printing omitted issue #25 ... 5.00

SWORDS OF CEREBUS SUPPLEMENT
AARDVARK-VANAHEIM
❑1, b&w; giveaway to buyers of Swords of Cerebus #6 first printing; Giveawawy to buyers of Swords of Cerebus #6 first printing; reprints Cerebus #25 ... 1.00

SWORDS OF SHAR-PEI
CALIBER
❑1, b&w ... 2.50
❑2, b&w ... 2.50

SWORDS OF TEXAS
ECLIPSE
❑1, Oct 1987 ... 1.75
❑2 ... 1.75
❑3, Jan 1988 ... 1.75
❑4, Mar 1988 ... 1.75

N-MINT

SWORDS OF THE SWASHBUCKLERS
MARVEL / EPIC
❑1, May 1985 BG (a) ... 2.00
❑2, Jul 1985 BG (a) ... 1.75
❑3, Sep 1985 BG (a) ... 1.75
❑4, Nov 1985 BG (a) ... 1.50
❑5, Jan 1986 BG (a) ... 1.50
❑6, Mar 1986 BG (a) ... 1.50
❑7, May 1986 BG (a) ... 1.50
❑8, Jul 1986 BG (a) ... 1.50
❑9, Sep 1986 BG (a) ... 1.50
❑10, Nov 1986 BG (a) ... 1.50
❑11, Jan 1987 BG (a) ... 1.50
❑12, Mar 1987 BG (a) ... 1.50

SWORDS OF VALOR
A-PLUS
❑1, b&w ... 2.50
❑2, b&w ... 2.50
❑3, b&w ... 2.50
❑4, b&w ... 2.50

SYLVIA FAUST
IMAGE
❑1 2004 ... 2.95
❑2 2004 ... 2.95

SYMBOLS OF JUSTICE
HIGH IMPACT
❑1, Jun 1995 ... 2.95

SYN
DARK HORSE
❑1, Aug 2003 ... 2.99
❑2, Oct 2003 ... 2.99
❑3, Nov 2003 ... 2.99
❑4, Jan 2004 ... 2.99
❑5, Mar 2004 ... 2.99

SYNN, THE GIRL FROM LSD
AC
❑1, Aug 1990, b&w ... 3.95

SYNTHETIC ASSASSIN
NIGHT REALM
❑1 ... 1.50

SYPHONS
NOW
❑1, Jul 1986, !1&O: Syphons ... 2.00
❑2, Sep 1986 ... 1.50
❑3, Nov 1986 ... 1.50
❑4, Jan 1987 ... 1.50
❑5, Mar 1987 ... 1.50
❑6, Jul 1987 ... 1.50
❑7, Aug 1987 ... 1.50

SYPHONS (VOL. 2)
NOW
❑0, Dec 1993; Preview edition ... 1.00
❑1, May 1994 ... 2.50
❑2, Jun 1994 ... 2.50
❑3, Jul 1994 ... 2.50

SYPHONS: THE SYGATE STRATAGEM
NOW
❑1, ca. 1994 ... 2.95
❑2, ca. 1994 ... 2.95
❑3, ca. 1994 ... 2.95

N-MINT

SYSTEM
DC / VERTIGO
❑1, May 1996 ... 2.95
❑2, Jun 1996 ... 2.95
❑3, Jul 1996 ... 2.95

SYSTEM SEVEN
ARROW
❑1, Dec 1987 ... 1.50
❑2 ... 1.50
❑3 ... 1.50

TABOO
SPIDERBABY / TUNDRA
❑1, b&w ... 9.95
❑2, b&w ... 9.95
❑3, b&w ... 9.95
❑4, b&w ... 14.95
❑5 ... 14.95
❑6; with booklet ... 14.95
❑7; with booklet ... 14.95
❑8, Jun 1995, b&w ... 14.95
❑9 ... 14.95

TABOUX
ANTARCTIC
❑1, Aug 1996 ... 3.95
❑2, Aug 1996 ... 3.95

TAILGUNNER JO
DC
❑1, Sep 1988 ... 1.25
❑2, Oct 1988 ... 1.25
❑3, Nov 1988 ... 1.25
❑4, Dec 1988 ... 1.25
❑5, Win 1988 ... 1.25
❑6, Jan 1989 ... 1.25

TAILS
ARCHIE
❑1, Dec 1995 ... 1.50
❑2, Jan 1996 ... 1.50
❑3, Feb 1996 ... 1.50

TAINTED
DC / VERTIGO
❑1, Feb 1995 ... 4.95

TAINTED BLOOD
WEIRDLING
❑1, Apr 1996 ... 2.95

TAKEN UNDER COMPENDIUM
CALIBER
❑1, b&w ... 2.95

TAKION
DC
❑1, Jun 1996 ... 1.75
❑2, Jul 1996 ... 1.75
❑3, Aug 1996 ... 1.75
❑4, Sep 1996 ... 1.75
❑5, Oct 1996 ... 1.75
❑6, Nov 1996 ... 1.75
❑7, Dec 1996; Lightray returns ... 1.75

TALE OF HALIMA
FANTAGRAPHICS / EROS
❑1, b&w ... 2.75
❑2, b&w ... 2.75

Other grades: Multiply price above by 5/6 for VF/NM • 2/3 for VERY FINE • 1/3 for FINE • 1/5 for VERY GOOD • 1/8 for GOOD

TALE OF MYA ROM
AIRCEL
❑1, b&w ... 1.70

TALE OF ONE BAD RAT
DARK HORSE
❑1, Oct 1994, BT, NG (w); BT (a); Introduction by Neil Gaiman ... 4.00
❑2, Nov 1994, BT (w); BT (a) ... 3.00
❑3, Dec 1994, BT (w); BT (a) ... 3.00
❑4, Jan 1995, BT (w); BT (a) ... 3.00
❑Book 1, Oct 1995, Trade Paperback; BT (w); BT (a); Collects The Tale of One Bad Rat #1-4 ... 14.95
❑Book 1/HC, ca. 1995, Hardcover edition; BT (w); BT (a); Hardcover; Collects The Tale of One Bad Rat #1-4; limited to 1,000 copies ... 69.95

TALE OF THE BODY THIEF (ANNE RICE'S...)
SICILIAN DRAGON
❑1, Sep 1999 ... 2.95
❑2, Oct 1999 ... 2.95
❑3, 1999 ... 2.95
❑4, 2000 ... 2.95
❑5, 2000 ... 2.95
❑6, 2000 ... 2.95
❑7, 2000 ... 2.95
❑8, 2000 ... 2.95
❑9, 2000 ... 2.95
❑10, 2000 ... 2.95
❑11, 2000 ... 2.95
❑12, 2000 ... 2.95

TALES CALCULATED TO DRIVE YOU MAD
E.C.
❑1, ca. 1997 ... 3.99
❑2, ca. 1997 ... 3.99
❑3, ca. 1997 ... 3.99
❑4, ca. 1998 ... 3.99
❑5, ca. 1998 ... 3.99
❑6, Mar 1999; Reprints Mad #16-18 ... 3.99
❑7, Nov 1999 ... 3.99
❑8, Jan 2000; Reprints Mad #22, 23 ... 3.99

TALES FROM GROUND ZERO
EXCEL
❑1, b&w ... 4.95

TALES FROM NECROPOLIS
BRAINSTORM
❑1, b&w ... 2.95

TALES FROM ... RIVERDALE DIGEST MAGAZINE
ARCHIE
❑1, Jun 2005 ... 2.79
❑2, Jul 2005 ... 2.79
❑3, Aug 2005 ... 2.79
❑4, Sep 2005 ... 2.79
❑5, Oct 2005 ... 2.79
❑6, Nov 2005 ... 2.79
❑7, Dec 2005 ... 2.79
❑8, Jan 2006 ... 2.79
❑9, Apr 2006 ... 2.79
❑10, May 2006 ... 2.79
❑12, Aug 2006 ... 2.79

TALES FROM SHOCK CITY
FANTAGRAPHICS
❑nn, Oct 2001, b&w; Printed in black, white, and red ... 3.95

TALES FROM SLEAZE CASTLE
GRATUITOUS BUNNY
❑1 ... 2.50
❑2 ... 2.50
❑3 ... 2.50

TALES FROM THE AGE OF APOCALYPSE
MARVEL
❑1, Dec 1996 ... 5.95

TALES FROM THE AGE OF APOCALYPSE: SINISTER BLOODLINES
MARVEL
❑1, Dec 1997 ... 5.99

TALES FROM THE ANIVERSE
MASSIVE
❑1, Jan 1992, b&w ... 2.25
❑2 1992 ... 2.25
❑3 1992 ... 2.25

TALES FROM THE ANIVERSE
ARROW
❑1 ... 2.00
❑2 ... 1.50
❑3 ... 1.50
❑4 ... 1.50
❑5 ... 1.50
❑6 ... 1.50

TALES FROM THE BOG
ABERRATION
❑1, Nov 1995, b&w ... 3.00
❑2, Feb 1996, b&w ... 3.00
❑3, Jun 1996, b&w ... 3.00
❑4, Sep 1996, b&w ... 3.00
❑5, Apr 1997, b&w ... 3.00
❑6, Jun 1997, b&w ... 3.00
❑7, Nov 1997, b&w ... 3.00
❑Ashcan 1, Sep 1995, b&w ... 2.95

TALES FROM THE BOG (DIRECTOR'S CUT)
ABERRATION
❑1 1998, b&w ... 2.95

TALES FROM THE BULLY PULPIT ONE SHOT
IMAGE
❑1 2004 ... 6.95

TALES FROM THE CLONEZONE
DARK HORSE
❑1 ... 1.75

TALES FROM THE CRYPT (GLADSTONE)
GLADSTONE
❑1, Jul 1990; GE, AW, FF, BE, GI (w); GE, AW, JCr, FF, BE, JKa, GI (a); O: Crypt-Keeper. Reprints Tales From the Crypt #33, Crime SuspenStories #17 ... 3.00
❑2, Sep 1990; JO, JCr, JKa, GI (w); JO, JCr, JKa, GI (a); Reprints Tales From the Crypt #35, Crime SuspenStories #18 ... 2.50
❑3, Nov 1990; HK, JO, WW, JKa, GI (w); HK, JO, JCr, WW, JKa, GI (a); Reprints Tales From the Crypt #39, Crime SuspenStories #1 ... 2.50
❑4, Jan 1991; AF, AW, HK, JO, JCr, JKa (a); Reprints Tales From the Crypt #18, Crime SuspenStories #16 ... 2.50
❑5, Mar 1991; JCr, BK, JKa, GI (a); Reprints Tales From the Crypt #45, Crime SuspenStories #5 ... 2.50
❑6, May 1991; JCr, BK, JKa, GI (a); Reprints Tales From the Crypt #42, Crime SuspenStories #27 ... 2.50

TALES FROM THE CRYPT (COCHRAN ONE-SHOT)
COCHRAN
❑1, Jul 1991; over-sized reprint of Tales #31 and Crime SuspenStories #12 ... 3.95

TALES FROM THE CRYPT (COCHRAN)
COCHRAN
❑1 ... 2.00
❑2, Oct 1991 ... 2.00
❑3, Dec 1991 ... 2.00
❑4, Feb 1992 ... 2.00
❑5, Mar 1992 ... 2.00
❑6, May 1992 ... 2.00
❑7, Jul 1992 ... 2.00

TALES FROM THE CRYPT (RCP)
GEMSTONE
❑1, Sep 1992; AF, JCr (a); Reprints Crypt of Terror (EC) #17 ... 2.00
❑2, Dec 1992; Reprints Crypt of Terror (EC) #18 ... 2.00
❑3, Mar 1993; Reprints Crypt of Terror (EC) #19 ... 2.00
❑4, Jun 1993; AF, JCr, JKa, GI (a); Reprints Tales From the Crypt (EC) #20 ... 2.00
❑5, Sep 1993; AF, HK, WW, GI (a); Reprints Tales From the Crypt (EC) #21 ... 2.00
❑6, Dec 1993; AF, JCr, GI (a); Reprints Tales From the Crypt (EC) #22 ... 2.00
❑7, Mar 1994; AF, JCr, GI (a); Reprints Tales From the Crypt (EC) #23 ... 2.00
❑8, Jun 1994; AF (c); JCr, WW, GI (a); Reprints Tales From the Crypt (EC) #24 ... 2.00
❑9, Sep 1994; Reprints Tales From the Crypt (EC) #25 ... 2.00
❑10, Dec 1994; Reprints Tales From the Crypt (EC) #26 ... 2.00
❑11, Mar 1995; JO, JKa, GI (w); JO, JKa, GI (a); Reprints Tales From the Crypt (EC) #27 ... 2.00
❑12, Jun 1995; JO, JKa, GI (w); JO, JKa, GI (a); Reprints Tales From the Crypt (EC) #28 ... 2.00
❑13, Sep 1995; JO, JKa, GI (w); JO, JKa, GI (a); Reprints Tales From the Crypt (EC) #29 ... 2.00
❑14, Dec 1995; JO, JKa, GI (w); JO, JKa, GI (a); Reprints Tales From the Crypt (EC) #30 ... 2.00
❑15, Mar 1996; AW, JKa, GI (w); AW, JKa, GI (a); Reprints Tales From the Crypt (EC) #31 ... 2.00
❑16, Jun 1996; GE, GI (w); GE, GI (a); Reprints Tales From the Crypt (EC) #32 ... 2.50
❑17, Sep 1996; GE, JKa, GI (w); GE, JKa, GI (a); O: the The Crypt Keeper. Reprints Tales From the Crypt (EC) #33 ... 2.50
❑18, Dec 1996; GE, JKa, GI (w); GE, JKa, GI (a); Reprints Tales From the Crypt (EC) #34 ... 2.50
❑19, Mar 1997; JO, JKa, GI (w); JO, JKa, GI (a); Reprints Tales From the Crypt (EC) #35 ... 2.50
❑20, Jun 1997; GE, JKa, GI (w); GE, JKa, GI (a); Reprints Tales From the Crypt (EC) #36 ... 2.50
❑21, Sep 1997; JO, BE, GI (w); JO, BE, GI (a); Reprints Tales From the Crypt (EC) #37 ... 2.50
❑22, Dec 1997; BE, GI (w); BE, GI (a); Reprints Tales From the Crypt (EC) #38 ... 2.50
❑23, Mar 1998; JO, JKa, GI (w); JO, JKa, GI (a); Reprints Tales From the Crypt (EC) #39 ... 2.50
❑24, Jun 1998; GE, BK, GI (w); GE, BK, GI (a); Reprints Tales From the Crypt (EC) #40 ... 2.50
❑25, Sep 1998; GE, JKa, GI (w); GE, JKa, GI (a); Reprints Tales From the Crypt (EC) #41 ... 2.50
❑26, Dec 1998; Reprints Tales From the Crypt (EC) #42 ... 2.50
❑27, Mar 1999; Reprints Tales From the Crypt (EC) #43 ... 2.50
❑28, Jun 1999; Reprints Tales From the Crypt (EC) #44 ... 2.50
❑29, Sep 1999; Reprints Tales From the Crypt (EC) #45 ... 2.50
❑30, Dec 1999; Reprints Tales From the Crypt (EC) #46; material originally prepared for Crypt of Terror #1 ... 2.50
❑Annual 1; Collects Tales From the Crypt #1-5 ... 8.95
❑Annual 2 ... 9.95
❑Annual 3 ... 10.95
❑Annual 4 ... 12.95
❑Annual 5; Collects Tales From the Crypt #37-41 ... 13.50

TALES FROM THE EDGE!
VANGUARD
❑1, Jun 1993, b&w; Flip-book WW (a) 3.50
❑2, Sep 1993, b&w ... 5.00
❑3, Dec 1993, b&w ... 3.00
❑4, Jul 1994, b&w ... 3.00
❑5, ca. 1994 ... 3.00
❑6, ca. 1995 ... 3.00
❑7, Jul 1995, b&w ... 3.00
❑8, b&w ... 4.00
❑9, b&w ... 5.00
❑10, b&w ... 4.00
❑11, Mar 1998 ... 5.00
❑12 ... 4.00
❑13 ... 3.00
❑14 ... 5.00
❑15; BSz (a); Bill Sienkiewicz Special. 5.55
❑Summer 1, Aug 1994, b&w; cardstock cover ... 3.50

TALES FROM THE FRIDGE
KITCHEN SINK
❑1, Jun 1973, b&w ... 3.00

Other grades: Multiply price above by 5/6 for VF/NM • 2/3 for VERY FINE • 1/3 for FINE • 1/5 for VERY GOOD • 1/8 for GOOD

Tales of the Unexpected

Science fiction turned to mystery, er, horror

©DC

Tales of the Witchblade

Stories of weapon-wielding police officer

©Image

Tales to Astonish (Vol. 1)

Ant-Man, Giant-Man, Hulk anthology

©Marvel

Tales Too Terrible to Tell

Obscure pre-Code horror tales reprinted

©NEC

Tangled Web

Spider-Man stories from all over his career

©Marvel

N-MINT

TALES FROM THE HEART
Entropy

- ❑1 1988; no cover date ... 4.00
- ❑2 1988 ... 3.25
- ❑3, Dec 1988, b&w ... 3.00
- ❑4, Jan 1989, b&w ... 3.00
- ❑5, May 1989, b&w ... 2.95
- ❑6, Oct 1989, b&w ... 2.95
- ❑7, Nov 1990 ... 2.95
- ❑8, Apr 1991 ... 2.95
- ❑9, Aug 1992 ... 2.95
- ❑10, Mar 1993, b&w ... 2.95
- ❑11, May 1994, b&w ... 2.95

TALES FROM THE HEART OF AFRICA: THE TEMPORARY NATIVES
Marvel / Epic

- ❑1, Aug 1990 ... 3.95

TALES FROM THE KIDS
David G. Brown

- ❑1, Apr 1996, b&w; No cover price; anthology by children; produced for L.A. Cultural Affairs Dept. ... 2.00

TALES FROM THE LEATHER NUN
Last Gasp

- ❑1 ... 14.00

TALES FROM THE OUTER BOROUGHS
Fantagraphics

- ❑1, b&w ... 2.25
- ❑2, b&w ... 2.25
- ❑3, b&w ... 2.25
- ❑4, b&w ... 2.50
- ❑5, b&w ... 2.50

TALES FROM THE PLAGUE
Eclipse

- ❑1 ... 3.95

TALES FROM THE RAVAGED LANDS
Magi

- ❑0; no indicia; b&w introduction to series ... 2.00
- ❑1, b&w; no indicia or cover date ... 2.50
- ❑2, b&w; no indicia or cover date ... 2.50
- ❑3, Jan 1996, b&w ... 2.50
- ❑4, ca. 1996, b&w; no indicia or cover date ... 2.50
- ❑5, May 1996, b&w ... 2.50
- ❑6, Aug 1996, b&w ... 2.50

TALES FROM THE STONE TROLL CAFÉ
Planet X

- ❑1, ca. 1986 ... 1.75

TALES FROM THE TOMB
Dell

- ❑1, Oct 1962 JS (w); FS (a) ... 125.00

TALES OF A CHECKERED MAN
D.W. Brubaker

- ❑1, b&w; no cover price ... 2.00

TALES OF ASGARD (VOL. 1)
Marvel

- ❑1, Oct 1968; SL (w); JK (a); reprints "Tales of Asgard" stories from Journey Into Mystery #98-106 ... 30.00

N-MINT

TALES OF ASGARD (VOL. 2)
Marvel

- ❑1, Feb 1984; SL (w); JK (a); reprints "Tales of Asgard" stories from Journey Into Mystery #129-136 ... 1.50

TALES OF BEATRIX FARMER
Mu

- ❑1, Feb 1996, b&w ... 2.95

TALES OF BLUE & GREY
Avalon

- ❑1, b&w ... 2.95

TALES OF EVIL
Atlas-Seaboard

- ❑1, Feb 1975 ... 9.00
- ❑2, Apr 1975 TS (a) ... 7.00
- ❑3, Jul 1975 RB (w); RB (a) ... 7.00

TALES OF GHOST CASTLE
DC

- ❑1, May 1975 NR (a) ... 10.00
- ❑2, Jul 1975 AN (a) ... 9.00
- ❑3, Sep 1975 ... 9.00

TALES OF G.I. JOE
Marvel

- ❑1, Jan 1988; Reprints G.I. Joe, A Real American Hero #1 ... 1.00
- ❑2, Feb 1988; Reprints G.I. Joe, A Real American Hero #2 ... 1.00
- ❑3, Mar 1988; Reprints G.I. Joe, A Real American Hero #3 ... 1.00
- ❑4, Apr 1988; Reprints G.I. Joe, A Real American Hero #4 ... 1.00
- ❑5, May 1988; Reprints G.I. Joe, A Real American Hero #5 ... 1.00
- ❑6, Jun 1988; Reprints G.I. Joe, A Real American Hero #6 ... 1.00
- ❑7, Jul 1988; Reprints G.I. Joe, A Real American Hero #7 ... 1.00
- ❑8, Aug 1988; Reprints G.I. Joe, A Real American Hero #8 ... 1.00
- ❑9, Sep 1988; Reprints G.I. Joe, A Real American Hero #9 ... 1.00
- ❑10, Oct 1988; Reprints G.I. Joe, A Real American Hero #10 ... 1.00
- ❑11, Nov 1988; Reprints G.I. Joe, A Real American Hero #11 ... 1.00
- ❑12, Dec 1988; Reprints G.I. Joe, A Real American Hero #12 ... 1.00
- ❑13, Jan 1989; Reprints G.I. Joe, A Real American Hero #13 ... 1.00
- ❑14, Feb 1989; Reprints G.I. Joe, A Real American Hero #14 ... 1.00
- ❑15, Mar 1989; Reprints G.I. Joe, A Real American Hero #15 ... 1.00

TALES OF JERRY
Hacienda

- ❑1, b&w ... 2.50
- ❑2 ... 2.50
- ❑3 ... 2.50
- ❑4 ... 2.50
- ❑5 ... 2.50
- ❑6 ... 2.50
- ❑7 ... 2.50
- ❑8 ... 2.50
- ❑9 ... 2.50
- ❑10 ... 2.50

N-MINT

TALES OF LETHARGY
Alpha

- ❑1, b&w ... 2.50
- ❑2, b&w ... 2.50
- ❑3, b&w ... 2.50

TALES OF ORDINARY MADNESS
Dark Horse

- ❑1, b&w ... 2.50
- ❑2, b&w ... 2.50
- ❑3, b&w ... 2.50
- ❑4, b&w ... 2.50

TALES OF SCREAMING HORROR
Fantaco

- ❑1, ca. 1992, b&w ... 3.50

TALES OF SEX AND DEATH
Print Mint

- ❑1, Apr 1971 ... 3.00
- ❑2 ... 3.00

TALES OF SHAUNDRA
Rip Off

- ❑1 ... 12.95

TALES OF SUSPENSE
Marvel

- ❑1, Jan 1959 ... 1400.00
- ❑2, Mar 1959 ... 540.00
- ❑3, May 1959 ... 475.00
- ❑4, Jul 1959 AW (a) ... 450.00
- ❑5, Sep 1959 ... 325.00
- ❑6, Nov 1959 ... 325.00
- ❑7, Jan 1960 1: Neptune. ... 325.00
- ❑8, Mar 1960 ... 325.00
- ❑9, May 1960 1: Chondu the Mystic ... 325.00
- ❑10, Jul 1960 ... 325.00
- ❑11, Sep 1960 ... 240.00
- ❑12, Nov 1960 ... 240.00
- ❑13, Jan 1961 ... 240.00
- ❑14, Feb 1961 1: It, the Living Colossus. ... 240.00
- ❑15, Mar 1961 ... 240.00
- ❑16, Apr 1961 JK (c); SL (w); JK (a); 1: Iron Man prototype. ... 240.00
- ❑17, May 1961 ... 240.00
- ❑18, Jun 1961 ... 240.00
- ❑19, Jul 1961 ... 240.00
- ❑20, Aug 1961 JK (c); SL (w); SD, DH, JK (a); A: It, the Living Colossus. ... 240.00
- ❑21, Sep 1961 ... 150.00
- ❑22, Oct 1961 ... 150.00
- ❑23, Nov 1961 ... 150.00
- ❑24, Dec 1961 ... 150.00
- ❑25, Jan 1962 ... 150.00
- ❑26, Feb 1962 ... 150.00
- ❑27, Mar 1962 ... 150.00
- ❑28, Apr 1962 ... 150.00
- ❑29, May 1962 ... 150.00
- ❑30, Jun 1962 ... 150.00
- ❑31, Jul 1962 1: Doctor Doom-prototype ("The Monster in the Iron Mask"). ... 150.00
- ❑32, Aug 1962 1: Doctor Strange-prototype ("Sazik the Sorcerer"). ... 150.00
- ❑33, Sep 1962 ... 135.00
- ❑34, Oct 1962 ... 135.00
- ❑35, Nov 1962 ... 135.00

❑36, Dec 1962 .... 135.00
❑37, Jan 1963 .... 135.00
❑38, Feb 1963 .... 135.00
❑39, Mar 1963, JK (a); O: Iron Man. 1: Iron Man. Grey armor 3500.00
❑40, Apr 1963 JK (a); 1: Iron Man gold armor. 2: Iron Man. 1100.00
❑41, May 1963 JK (a) 650.00
❑42, Jun 1963 SD, DH (a); 1: Mad Pharoah. 325.00
❑43, Jul 1963 O: Kala. 1: Kala. 325.00
❑44, Aug 1963 .... 325.00
❑45, Sep 1963 1: Pepper Potts. 1: Happy Hogan. 1: Jack Frost II (Gregor Shapanka). V: Jack Frost II (Gregor Shapanka) 325.00
❑46, Oct 1963 1: Crimson Dynamo. ... 210.00
❑47, Nov 1963 SL (w); SD, DH (a); O: Melter. 1: Melter 210.00
❑48, Dec 1963, SL (w); SD (a); New armor for Iron Man (red and gold).. 265.00
❑49, Jan 1964, SL (w); SD (a); A: Angel II. Watcher back-up 210.00
❑50, Feb 1964, SL (w); DH (a); 1: The Mandarin. Watcher back-up 155.00
❑51, Mar 1964, SL (w); DH (a); O: Scarecrow (Marvel). 1: Scarecrow (Marvel). Watcher back-up 105.00
❑52, Apr 1964, SL (w); DH (a); 1: Black Widow. Watcher back-up 140.00
❑53, May 1964, SL (w); DH (a); O: The Watcher. A: Black Widow. Watcher back-up 120.00
❑54, Jun 1964, SL (w); DH (a); 1: Black Knight II (Nathan Garrett). Watcher back-up 62.00
❑55, Jul 1964, SL (w); DH (a); A: The Mandarin. Watcher back-up 62.00
❑56, Aug 1964, SL (w); DH (a); 1: Unicorn I (Milos Masaryk). Watcher back-up 62.00
❑57, Sep 1964, DH (a); 1: Hawkeye. A: Black Widow. Watcher back-up .. 170.00
❑58, Oct 1964, DH, GT (a); A: Captain America. Watcher back-up 210.00
❑59, Nov 1964, DH, JK (a); 1: Jarvis. V: Black Knight. Captain America second feature begins 210.00
❑60, Dec 1964 JK (a) 120.00
❑61, Jan 1965 DH, JK (a) 82.00
❑62, Feb 1965, DH, JK (a); O: Mandarin. redesign of Iron Man's helmet 82.00
❑63, Mar 1965 O: Bucky. O: Captain America. A: Dr. Erskine. A: General Phillips. A: Sgt. Duffy. 180.00
❑64, Apr 1965 1: Agent 13 (Peggy Carter) 72.00
❑65, May 1965 A: Red Skull. 125.00
❑66, Jun 1965, O: Red Skull. Red Skull returns 125.00
❑67, Jul 1965 .... 52.00
❑68, Aug 1965 .... 52.00
❑69, Sep 1965 1: Titanium Man I (Boris Bullski). 52.00
❑70, Oct 1965 .... 52.00
❑71, Nov 1965 DH, WW (a) 42.00
❑72, Dec 1965 GT, JK (a) 42.00
❑73, Jan 1966 GC, GT, JK (a); D: Black Knight II (Nathan Garrett). 42.00
❑74, Feb 1966 GC, GT, JK (a) 42.00
❑75, Mar 1966 GC (a); 1: Second Agent 13 (Sharon Carter). 1: Batroc. 42.00
❑76, Apr 1966 JK (c); SL (w); GC, JR (a); 1: Ultimo (cameo). A: The Mandarin. A: Batroc. 42.00
❑77, May 1966 SL (w); GC (a); O: Ultimo. 1: Ultimo (full appearance). 1: Peggy Carter. 42.00
❑78, Jun 1966 JK (c); SL (w); GC, JK (a); A: Nick Fury. A: Ultimo. A: The Mandarin 42.00
❑79, Jul 1966 GC (c); SL (w); GC, JK, JAb (a); 1: Cosmic Cube (Kubik). A: Namor. A: Red Skull 42.00
❑80, Aug 1966, SL (w); GC, JK (a); A: Namor. A: Red Skull. Cosmic Cube; Sub-Mariner vs. Iron Man..... 42.00
❑81, Sep 1966 GC (c); SL (w); GC, JK (a); A: Titanium Man. A: Red Skull. . 32.00
❑82, Oct 1966 JK (c); SL (w); GC, JK (a); 1: Adaptoid. A: Titanium Man. A: Scarlet Witch. A: Quicksilver. 32.00
❑83, Nov 1966 GC (c); SL (w); GC, JK (a); A: Titanium Man. 32.00
❑84, Dec 1966 JK (c); SL (w); GC, JK (a); 1: Super-Adaptoid. A: Goliath. A: Hawkeye. A: The Mandarin. A: The Wasp. 32.00
❑85, Jan 1967, GC (c); SL (w); GC, JK (a); A: Batroc. V: Mandarin. Happy substitutes as Iron Man 32.00
❑86, Feb 1967 SL (w); GC, JK (a) 32.00
❑87, Mar 1967 .... 32.00
❑88, Apr 1967 GK (c); SL (w); GC, GK (a); A: Mole Man. A: Swordsman. A: Power Man I (Erik Josten) 32.00
❑89, May 1967 GC (c); SL (w); GC, GK (a); A: Red Skull. A: Melter. 32.00
❑90, Jun 1967 GC, GK (a); O: Byrrah. 32.00
❑91, Jul 1967 GC, GK (a) 32.00
❑92, Aug 1967 GC, GK (a) 32.00
❑93, Sep 1967 GC, GK (a) 32.00
❑94, Oct 1967 1: Modok. 32.00
❑95, Nov 1967, GC, GK (a); 1: Walter Newell (later becomes Stingray). Captain America's identity revealed 32.00
❑96, Dec 1967 GC, GK (a) 32.00
❑97, Jan 1968 SL (w); GC, JK, GK (a); 1: Whiplash. A: Black Panther. 32.00
❑98, Feb 1968 GC, GK (a); O: Whitney Frost. 1: Whitney Frost. 32.00
❑99, Mar 1968, GC, GK (a); V: Red Skull. Series continued in Captain America #100, Iron Man #1 .... 32.00

TALES OF SUSPENSE: CAPTAIN AMERICA/IRON MAN
MARVEL

❑1, Feb 2005 .... 5.99

TALES OF SUSPENSE (VOL. 2)
MARVEL

❑1, Jan 1995; prestige format one-shot; acetate outer cover 6.95

TALES OF TELLOS
IMAGE

❑1, Nov 2004 .... 3.50
❑2, Dec 2004 .... 3.50
❑3, Feb 2005 .... 3.50

TALES OF TERROR
ECLIPSE

❑1, Jul 1985 .... 2.00
❑2, Sep 1985 .... 2.00
❑3, Nov 1985 .... 2.00
❑4, Jan 1986 .... 2.00
❑5, Mar 1986 .... 2.00
❑6, May 1986 .... 2.00
❑7, Jul 1986 .... 2.00
❑8, Sep 1986 .... 2.00
❑9, Nov 1986 .... 2.00
❑10, Jan 1987 .... 2.00
❑11, Mar 1987 .... 2.00
❑12, May 1987 .... 2.00
❑13, Jul 1987 .... 2.00

TALES OF THE ARMORKINS
CO. & SONS

❑1 .... 3.00

TALES OF THE BEANWORLD
ECLIPSE

❑1, ca. 1985 .... 4.00
❑2, ca. 1985 .... 3.00
❑3, ca. 1986 .... 3.00
❑4, ca. 1986 .... 3.00
❑5, ca. 1986 .... 3.00
❑6, Apr 1987 .... 3.00
❑7, ca. 1987 .... 3.00
❑8, ca. 1987 .... 3.00
❑9, ca. 1988 .... 3.00
❑10, ca. 1988 .... 3.00
❑11, ca. 1988 .... 2.00
❑12, Feb 1989 .... 2.00
❑13, ca. 1989 .... 2.00
❑14, ca. 1989 .... 2.00
❑15, ca. 1990 .... 2.00
❑16, ca. 1990 .... 2.00
❑17, ca. 1990 .... 2.00
❑18, ca. 1991 .... 2.00
❑19, ca. 1991 .... 2.00
❑20, ca. 1993 .... 2.50
❑21, ca. 1993 .... 2.95

TALES OF THE CLOSET
HETRIC-MARTIN

❑1, Sum 1987, b&w 2.50
❑2, b&w 2.50
❑3, b&w 2.50
❑4, b&w 2.50
❑5, b&w 2.50
❑6, b&w 2.50
❑7, Spr 1992 .... 2.50
❑8, Win 1992 .... 2.50

TALES OF THE CRIMSON LION
GARY LANKFORD

❑1, Jul 1987 .... 1.95

TALES OF THE CYBORG GERBILS
HARRIER

❑1, Nov 1987 .... 1.95

TALES OF THE DARKNESS
IMAGE

❑½, Apr 1998, BSz (a); Female demon on cover 2.95
❑½/A, Apr 1998, BSz (a); Man atop demons on cover 4.00
❑1, Apr 1998 .... 2.95
❑2, Jun 1998 .... 2.95
❑3, Aug 1998 .... 2.95
❑4, Dec 1998 .... 2.95

TALES OF THE FEHNNIK
ANTARCTIC

❑1, Aug 1995, b&w 2.95

TALES OF THE FEHNNIK
RADIO

❑1, Jun 1998, b&w 2.95

TALES OF THE GREAT UNSPOKEN
TOP SHELF

❑1, b&w; no cover price 1.00

TALES OF THE GREEN BERET
DELL

❑1, Jan 1967 .... 25.00
❑2, Mar 1967 .... 18.00
❑3, Jun 1967 .... 18.00
❑4, Sep 1967 .... 18.00
❑5, ca. 1968 .... 18.00

TALES OF THE GREEN BERETS
AVALON

❑1, "The Green Berets" in the indicia.. 2.95
❑2, "The Green Berets" in the indicia.. 2.95
❑3, "The Green Berets" in the indicia.. 2.95
❑4 .... 2.95
❑5 .... 2.95
❑6 .... 2.95
❑7, "Green Berets" in the indicia 2.95

TALES OF THE GREEN HORNET (1ST SERIES)
NOW

❑1, Sep 1990 .... 2.00
❑2, Oct 1990 .... 2.00

TALES OF THE GREEN HORNET (2ND SERIES)
NOW

❑1, Jan 1992 .... 2.00
❑2, Feb 1992, O: The Green Hornet. ... 2.00
❑3, Mar 1992 .... 2.00
❑4, Apr 1992 .... 2.00

TALES OF THE GREEN HORNET (3RD SERIES)
NOW

❑1, Sep 1992; bagged with hologram card 2.75
❑2, Oct 1992 .... 2.50
❑3, Nov 1992 .... 2.50

TALES OF THE GREEN LANTERN CORPS
DC

❑1, May 1981 FMc, JSe (a); O: Green Lantern. 1.50
❑2, Jun 1981 FMc, JSe (a) 1.25
❑3, Jul 1981 FMc, JSa, JSe (a) 1.25
❑Annual 1 .... 1.50

TALES OF THE JACKALOPE
BLACKTHORNE

❑1, 1986 .... 2.00
❑2, 1986 .... 2.00
❑3, 1986 .... 2.00
❑4, 1986 .... 2.00
❑5, 1986 .... 2.00

Tank Girl

Jet Girl and Sub Girl forgot Jeep Girl
©Dark Horse

Tarzan (Gold Key)

Manning masterpieces in majority of issues
©Gold Key

Tarzan (DC)

Joe Kubert adapted Burroughs' books
©DC

Tarzan (Marvel)

John Buscema covers post-World War I tales
©Marvel

Tarzan (Disney's...)

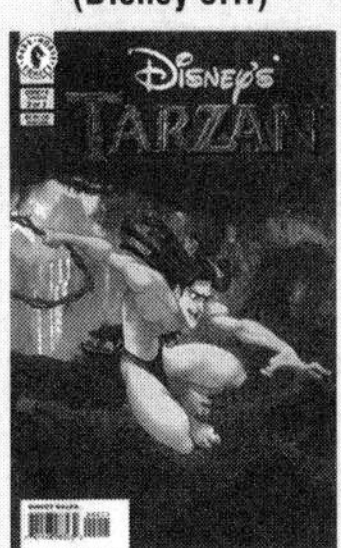

Disney animation returned to ape man's roots
©Dark Horse

N-MINT

❑6, 1986 ... 2.00
❑7, Feb 1987 ... 2.00

TALES OF THE KUNG FU WARRIORS
CFW

❑1 1: Ethereal Black; 1: Squamous. ... 2.00
❑2 ... 2.00
❑3 ... 2.00
❑4 ... 2.00
❑5 ... 2.00
❑6 ... 2.00
❑7 ... 2.00
❑8 ... 2.00
❑9 ... 2.00
❑10 ... 2.25
❑11 ... 2.25
❑12 ... 2.25
❑13 ... 2.25
❑14, Aug 1989 1: Sumo. ... 2.25

TALES OF THE LEGION
DC

❑314, Aug 1984 O: White Witch. ... 1.25
❑315, Sep 1984 KG (w); KG (a); V: Dark Circle. ... 1.25
❑316, Oct 1984 O: White Witch. ... 1.25
❑317, Nov 1984 ... 1.25
❑318, Dec 1984 V: Persuader. ... 1.25
❑319, Jan 1985 ... 1.25
❑320, Feb 1985 ... 1.25
❑321, Mar 1985 ... 1.25
❑322, Apr 1985 ... 1.25
❑323, May 1985 ... 1.25
❑324, Jun 1985 V: Dark Circle. ... 1.25
❑325, Jul 1985 ... 2.00
❑326, Aug 1985; V: Legion of Super-Villains. begins reprints of Legion of Super-Heroes (3rd series) ... 1.00
❑327, Sep 1985 V: Legion of Super-Villains. ... 1.00
❑328, Oct 1985 V: Legion of Super-Villains. ... 1.00
❑329, Nov 1985 D: Karate Kid. V: Legion of Super-Villains. ... 1.00
❑330, Dec 1985 V: Legion of Super-Villains. ... 1.00
❑331, Jan 1986 O: Lightning Lord. O: Lightning Lass. O: Lightning Lad. ... 1.00
❑332, Feb 1986 ... 1.00
❑333, Mar 1986 ... 1.00
❑334, Apr 1986 ... 1.00
❑335, May 1986 ... 1.00
❑336, Jun 1986 ... 1.00
❑337, Jul 1986 ... 1.00
❑338, Aug 1986 ... 1.00
❑339, Sep 1986; Magnetic Kid, Tellus, Polar Boy, Quislet, and Sensor Girl join team ... 1.00
❑340, Oct 1986 V: Doctor Regulus. ... 1.00
❑341, Nov 1986 ... 1.00
❑342, Dec 1986 ... 1.00
❑343, Jan 1987 O: Wildfire. ... 1.00
❑344, Feb 1987 ... 1.00
❑345, Mar 1987 ... 1.00
❑346, Apr 1987 ... 1.00
❑347, May 1987 V: Universo. ... 1.00
❑348, Jun 1987; in Phantom Zone ... 1.00

N-MINT

❑349, Jul 1987 ... 1.00
❑350, Aug 1987; Sensor Girl's identity revealed ... 1.00
❑351, Sep 1987 V: Fatal Five. ... 1.00
❑352, Oct 1987 ... 1.00
❑353, Nov 1987 ... 1.00
❑354, Dec 1987 ... 1.00
❑Annual 4 ... 1.50
❑Annual 5 O: Validus. ... 1.50

TALES OF THE MARVELS: BLOCKBUSTER
MARVEL

❑1, Apr 1995; prestige format; acetate overlay outer cover ... 5.95

TALES OF THE MARVELS: INNER DEMONS
MARVEL

❑1, ca. 1995, acetate overlay outer cover ... 5.95

TALES OF THE MARVELS: WONDER YEARS
MARVEL

❑1, Aug 1995; wraparound acetate outer cover ... 4.95
❑2, Sep 1995; wraparound acetate outer cover ... 4.95

TALES OF THE MARVEL UNIVERSE
MARVEL

❑1, Feb 1997; wraparound cover ... 2.99

TALES OF THE NEW TEEN TITANS
DC

❑1, Jun 1982 GP (a); O: Cyborg. ... 1.50
❑2, Jul 1982 GP (a); O: Raven. ... 1.00
❑3, Aug 1982 GP, GD (a); O: Changeling. ... 1.00
❑4, Sep 1982 GP (a); O: Starfire II (Koriand'r). 1: Ryand'r. ... 1.00

TALES OF THE NINJA WARRIORS
CFW

❑1, b&w ... 2.25
❑2, b&w ... 2.25
❑3, b&w ... 2.25
❑4, b&w ... 2.25
❑5, b&w ... 2.25
❑6, b&w ... 2.25
❑7, b&w ... 2.25
❑8, b&w ... 2.25
❑9, b&w ... 2.25
❑10, b&w ... 2.25
❑11, b&w ... 2.25
❑12, b&w ... 2.25
❑13, b&w ... 2.25
❑14, b&w ... 2.25
❑15, b&w ... 2.25
❑16, b&w ... 2.25

TALES OF THE SUN RUNNERS
SIRIUS

❑1, Jul 1986 ... 1.50
❑2 1986 ... 1.95
❑3 1986 ... 1.95

TALES OF THE TEENAGE MUTANT NINJA TURTLES
MIRAGE

❑1, May 1987 ... 3.00

N-MINT

❑2, Jul 1987 ... 2.00
❑3, Oct 1987 ... 2.00
❑4, Feb 1988; cover says Jan, indicia says Feb ... 2.00
❑5, May 1988 ... 2.00
❑6, Aug 1988 ... 2.00
❑7, Aug 1989; cover says Apr, indicia says Aug ... 2.00

TALES OF THE TEENAGE MUTANT NINJA TURTLES (VOL. 2)
MIRAGE

❑1 2004 ... 2.95
❑2 2004 ... 2.95
❑3 2004 ... 2.95
❑4 2004 ... 2.95
❑5 2004 ... 2.95

TALES OF THE TEEN TITANS
DC

❑41, Apr 1984; GP (a); A: Brother Blood. Series continued from New Teen Titans (1st Series) #40 ... 2.00
❑42, May 1984 GP (a); V: Deathstroke. ... 2.00
❑43, Jun 1984 GP (a); V: Deathstroke. V: H.I.V.E. ... 3.00
❑44, Jul 1984 GP (a); O: Jericho. 1: Nightwing. ... 6.00
❑45, Aug 1984 GP (a); A: Aquagirl. A: Aqualad. ... 1.50
❑46, Sep 1984 GP (a); V: H.I.V.E. ... 1.50
❑47, Oct 1984 GP (a); V: H.I.V.E. ... 1.50
❑48, Nov 1984 GP, SR (a); V: Recombatants. ... 1.50
❑49, Dec 1984 CI, GP (a); V: Doctor Light. ... 1.50
❑50, Feb 1985; Giant-size; GP (a); Wedding of Wonder Girl ... 2.00
❑51, Mar 1985 1: Azrael (cameo, not Batman character). V: Cheshire. ... 1.50
❑52, Apr 1985 RB (a); 1: Azrael (full appearance, not Batman character). V: Cheshire. ... 1.50
❑53, May 1985 A: Deathstroke. ... 1.50
❑54, Jun 1985; RB, DG (a); A: Deathstroke. Trial of Deathstroke ... 1.50
❑55, Jul 1985; Changeling vs. Deathstroke ... 1.50
❑56, Aug 1985 V: Fearsome Five. ... 1.50
❑57, Sep 1985; V: Fearsome Five. Cyborg transformed ... 1.50
❑58, Oct 1985 A: Monitor. A: Harbinger. V: Fearsome Five. ... 1.50
❑59, Nov 1985; reprints DC Comics Presents #26 ... 1.50
❑60, Dec 1985; V: Trigon. series begins reprinting New Teen Titans (second series) ... 1.00
❑61, Jan 1986 V: Trigon. ... 1.00
❑62, Feb 1986 V: Trigon. ... 1.00
❑63, Mar 1986 V: Trigon ... 1.00
❑64, Apr 1986 V: Trigon. ... 1.00
❑65, May 1986 ... 1.00
❑66, Jun 1986 O: Lilith. ... 1.00
❑67, Jul 1986 ... 1.00
❑68, Aug 1986 A: Kole. ... 1.00
❑69, Sep 1986 ... 1.00
❑70, Oct 1986 O: Kole. ... 1.00
❑71, Nov 1986 ... 1.00

N-MINT

❑72, Dec 1986 A: Outsiders. 1.00
❑73, Jan 1987 1.00
❑74, Feb 1987 1.00
❑75, Mar 1987 A: Omega Men. 1.00
❑76, Apr 1987; Wedding of Starfire 1.00
❑77, May 1987 1.00
❑78, Jun 1987; new team 1.00
❑79, Jul 1987 1.00
❑80, Aug 1987 A: Cheshire, Lian. 1.00
❑81, Sep 1987 1.00
❑82, Oct 1987 1.00
❑83, Nov 1987 1.00
❑84, Dec 1987 1.00
❑85, Jan 1988 1.00
❑86, Feb 1988 V: Twister. 1.00
❑87, Mar 1988 V: Brotherhood of Evil. 1.00
❑88, Apr 1988 V: Brother Blood. 1.00
❑89, May 1988 V: Brother Blood. 1.00
❑90, Jun 1988 1.00
❑91, Jul 1988 1.00
❑Annual 4; A: Superman. V: Vanguard. reprints New Teen Titans Annual #1 1.50

TALES OF THE UNEXPECTED
DC

❑1, Feb 1956 750.00
❑2, Apr 1956 385.00
❑3, Jul 1956 275.00
❑4, Aug 1956 225.00
❑5, Sep 1956 225.00
❑6, Oct 1956 165.00
❑7, Nov 1956 165.00
❑8, Dec 1956 165.00
❑9, Jan 1957 165.00
❑10, Feb 1957 165.00
❑11, Mar 1957 125.00
❑12, Apr 1957 125.00
❑13, May 1957 125.00
❑14, Jun 1957 125.00
❑15, Jul 1957 125.00
❑16, Aug 1957 JK (a) 125.00
❑17, Sep 1957 125.00
❑18, Oct 1957 125.00
❑19, Nov 1957 125.00
❑20, Dec 1957 125.00
❑21, Jan 1958 100.00
❑22, Feb 1958 100.00
❑23, Mar 1958 100.00
❑24, Apr 1958 100.00
❑25, May 1958 100.00
❑26, Jun 1958 100.00
❑27, Jul 1958 100.00
❑28, Aug 1958 100.00
❑29, Sep 1958 100.00
❑30, Oct 1958, Binky: Lost, A Free Education (PSA) 100.00
❑31, Nov 1958 85.00
❑32, Dec 1958 85.00
❑33, Jan 1959 85.00
❑34, Feb 1959 85.00
❑35, Mar 1959 85.00
❑36, Apr 1959 85.00
❑37, May 1959 85.00
❑38, Jun 1959 85.00
❑39, Jul 1959 85.00
❑40, Aug 1959; Space Ranger stories begin 650.00
❑41, Sep 1959 A: Space Ranger. 275.00
❑42, Oct 1959 A: Space Ranger. 275.00
❑43, Nov 1959; A: Space Ranger. Space Ranger cover 450.00
❑44, Dec 1959 A: Space Ranger. 200.00
❑45, Jan 1960 A: Space Ranger. 200.00
❑46, Feb 1960 A: Space Ranger. 150.00
❑47, Mar 1960 A: Space Ranger. 150.00
❑48, Apr 1960 A: Space Ranger. 150.00
❑49, May 1960 A: Space Ranger. 150.00
❑50, Jun 1960 A: Space Ranger. 150.00
❑51, Jul 1960 A: Space Ranger. 125.00
❑52, Aug 1960 A: Space Ranger. 125.00
❑53, Sep 1960 A: Space Ranger. 125.00
❑54, Oct 1960 A: Space Ranger. 125.00
❑55, Nov 1960 A: Space Ranger. 125.00
❑56, Dec 1960 A: Space Ranger. 100.00
❑57, Jan 1961 A: Space Ranger. 100.00
❑58, Feb 1961 A: Space Ranger. 100.00
❑59, Mar 1961 A: Space Ranger. 100.00
❑60, Apr 1961 A: Space Ranger. 100.00

N-MINT

❑61, May 1961 A: Space Ranger. 85.00
❑62, Jun 1961 A: Space Ranger. 85.00
❑63, Jul 1961 A: Space Ranger. 85.00
❑64, Aug 1961 A: Space Ranger. 85.00
❑65, Sep 1961 A: Space Ranger. 85.00
❑66, Oct 1961 A: Space Ranger. 85.00
❑67, Nov 1961 A: Space Ranger. 85.00
❑68, Dec 1961 A: Space Ranger. 85.00
❑69, Feb 1962 A: Space Ranger. 85.00
❑70, Apr 1962 A: Space Ranger. 85.00
❑71, Jun 1962 A: Space Ranger. 60.00
❑72, Aug 1962 A: Space Ranger. 60.00
❑73, Oct 1962 A: Space Ranger. 60.00
❑74, Jan 1963 A: Space Ranger. 60.00
❑75, Feb 1963 A: Space Ranger. 50.00
❑76, Apr 1963 A: Space Ranger. 50.00
❑77, Jun 1963 A: Space Ranger. 50.00
❑78, Aug 1963 A: Space Ranger. 50.00
❑79, Oct 1963 A: Space Ranger. 50.00
❑80, Dec 1963 A: Space Ranger. 50.00
❑81, Feb 1964 A: Space Ranger. 50.00
❑82, Apr 1964 A: Space Ranger. 50.00
❑83, Jun 1964 30.00
❑84, Aug 1964 30.00
❑85, Oct 1964 30.00
❑86, Dec 1964 30.00
❑87, Feb 1965 30.00
❑88, Apr 1965 30.00
❑89, Jun 1965 30.00
❑90, Aug 1965 30.00
❑91, Oct 1965 22.00
❑92, Dec 1965 22.00
❑93, Feb 1966 22.00
❑94, Apr 1966 22.00
❑95, Jun 1966 22.00
❑96, Aug 1966 22.00
❑97, Oct 1966 A: Automan. 22.00
❑98, Dec 1966 22.00
❑99, Feb 1967 22.00
❑100, Apr 1967 22.00
❑101, Jun 1967 20.00
❑102, Aug 1967 20.00
❑103, Oct 1967 20.00
❑104, Dec 1967, Series continues as The Unexpected 20.00

TALES OF THE VAMPIRES
DARK HORSE

❑1, Dec 2003 2.99
❑2, Jan 2004 2.99
❑3, Feb 2004 2.99
❑4, Mar 2004 2.99
❑5, Apr 2004 2.99

TALES OF THE WITCHBLADE
IMAGE

❑½, Jun 1997; Wizard promotional item 4.00
❑½/A, Jun 1997; Wizard "Certified Authentic" exclusive 8.00
❑½/Gold, Jun 1997; Wizard promotional item; gold logo 5.00
❑1, Nov 1996 2.95
❑1/A, Nov 1996; alternate cover; Green background with Witchblade front, arms behind back 2.95
❑1/B, Nov 1996; alternate cover (blue background with black panther) 2.95
❑1/Gold, Nov 1996; Gold edition 2.95
❑1/Platinum, Nov 1996; Platinum edition 5.00
❑2, Jun 1997 2.95
❑3, Oct 1997 2.95
❑4, Jan 1998 2.95
❑5, May 1998 2.95
❑6, Sep 1998 2.95
❑7/A, Jun 1999; Woman turning around, eyes in background on cover 2.95
❑7/B, Jun 1999; Alternate cover (woman standing before pyramid) 2.95
❑7/C 2.95
❑8, Oct 1999 2.95
❑9, Jan 2001 2.95

TALES OF THE ZOMBIE
MARVEL

❑1, Aug 1973, b&w; magazine O: Zombie 25.00
❑2, Oct 1973 18.00
❑3, Jan 1974 15.00
❑4, Mar 1974 15.00

N-MINT

❑5, May 1974 15.00
❑6, Jul 1974 10.00
❑7, Sep 1974 10.00
❑8, Nov 1974 10.00
❑9, Jan 1975 10.00
❑10, Mar 1975 10.00
❑Annual 1; Reprints 15.00

TALES OF TOAD
PRINT MINT

❑1, Apr 1970, b&w 0.00
❑2, Jan 1971, b&w 0.00
❑3, Dec 1973, b&w 0.00

TALES OF TORMENT
MIRAGE

❑1, Apr 2004 2.95

TALE SPIN
DISNEY

❑1, Jun 1991 1.50
❑2, Jul 1991 1.50
❑3, Aug 1991 1.50
❑4, Sep 1991 1.50
❑5, Oct 1991 1.50
❑6, Nov 1991 1.50
❑7, Jan 1992 1.50

TALE SPIN LIMITED SERIES
DISNEY

❑1, Jan 1991 1.50
❑2, Feb 1991 1.50
❑3, Mar 1991 1.50
❑4, Apr 1991 1.50

TALESPIN (ONE-SHOT)
DISNEY

❑1; Sky-Raker 3.50

TALES TO ASTONISH (VOL. 1)
MARVEL

❑1, Jan 1959 2000.00
❑2, Mar 1959 635.00
❑3, May 1959 440.00
❑4, Jul 1959 440.00
❑5, Sep 1959 440.00
❑6, Nov 1959 SD, JSt (a) 355.00
❑7, Jan 1960 355.00
❑8, Mar 1960 355.00
❑9, May 1960 355.00
❑10, Jul 1960 355.00
❑11, Sep 1960 265.00
❑12, Oct 1960 265.00
❑13, Nov 1960 265.00
❑14, Dec 1960 265.00
❑15, Jan 1961 265.00
❑16, Feb 1961 265.00
❑17, Mar 1961 265.00
❑18, Apr 1961 265.00
❑19, May 1961 265.00
❑20, Jun 1961 265.00
❑21, Jul 1961 JK (a) 200.00
❑22, Aug 1961 200.00
❑23, Sep 1961 200.00
❑24, Oct 1961 200.00
❑25, Nov 1961 200.00
❑26, Dec 1961 200.00
❑27, Jan 1962 SD, JK (a); 1: Ant-Man (out of costume). 1: Hijacker. 3600.00
❑28, Feb 1962 SD, JK (a) 175.00
❑29, Mar 1962 SD, JK (a) 175.00
❑30, Apr 1962 SD, JK (a) 175.00
❑31, May 1962 SD, JK (a) 175.00
❑32, Jun 1962 SD, JK (a) 175.00
❑33, Jul 1962 SD, JK (a) 175.00
❑34, Aug 1962 SD, JK (a) 175.00
❑35, Sep 1962 SD, JK (a); 1: Ant-Man (in costume). 1900.00
❑36, Oct 1962 SD, JK (a) 625.00
❑37, Nov 1962 SD, JK (a) 350.00
❑38, Dec 1962 DH (a); 1: Egghead. 350.00
❑39, Jan 1963 350.00
❑40, Feb 1963 350.00
❑41, Mar 1963 SD, DH (a) 230.00
❑42, Apr 1963 SD, DH (a); O: The Voice. 1: The Voice. 230.00
❑43, May 1963 SD, DH (a) 230.00
❑44, Jun 1963 SD, JK (a); O: Wasp. 1: Wasp. 500.00
❑45, Jul 1963 SD, DH (a) 150.00
❑46, Aug 1963 SD, DH (a) 150.00

Other grades: Multiply price above by 5/6 for VF/NM • 2/3 for VERY FINE • 1/3 for FINE • 1/5 for VERY GOOD • 1/8 for GOOD

Tarzan/ Carson of Venus

Jungle lord travels to planet of love
©Dark Horse

Tarzan: The Lost Adventure (Edgar Rice Burroughs'...)

Previously unpublished tale captures pulp feel
©Dark Horse

Team Titans

Time-traveling team meets present-day Titans
©DC

Tech Jacket

Kirkman creation not Invincible
©Image

Teenage Hotrodders

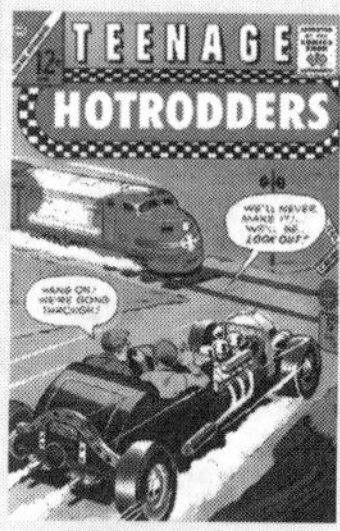

Thrill-seeking youngsters tightly tune heaps
©Charlton

	N-MINT
❑47, Sep 1963 SD, DH (a)	150.00
❑48, Oct 1963 SD, DH (a); O: Porcupine. 1: Porcupine.	150.00
❑49, Nov 1963, DH, JK (a); 1: Giant Man. Ant-Man becomes Giant Man.	250.00
❑50, Dec 1963 SD, JK (a); 1: Human Top (later becomes Whirlwind).	95.00
❑51, Jan 1964 JK (a)	95.00
❑52, Feb 1964 O: Black Knight II (Nathan Garrett). 1: Black Knight II (Nathan Garrett).	95.00
❑53, Mar 1964	95.00
❑54, Apr 1964	95.00
❑55, May 1964	95.00
❑56, Jun 1964 V: Magician.	95.00
❑57, Jul 1964 A: Spider-Man.	125.00
❑58, Aug 1964	95.00
❑59, Sep 1964, JK (c); SL (w); Giant-Man vs. Hulk	150.00
❑60, Oct 1964, JK (c); SL (w); SD (a); Giant Man/Hulk double feature begins	175.00
❑61, Nov 1964 JK (c); SL (w); SD (a).	75.00
❑62, Dec 1964 JK (c); SL (w); SD (a); 1: The Leader.	90.00
❑63, Jan 1965 JK (c); SL (w); SD (a); O: The Leader. 1: The Wrecker II.	75.00
❑64, Feb 1965 JK (c); SL (w); SD (a).	75.00
❑65, Mar 1965, JK (c); SL (w); SD (a); Giant-Man's new costume	75.00
❑66, Apr 1965 JK (c); SL (w); SD (a).	70.00
❑67, May 1965 JK (c); SL (w); SD (a)	70.00
❑68, Jun 1965 JK (c); SL (w); JK (a); V: Leader.	70.00
❑69, Jul 1965, JK (c); SL (w); JK (a); Giant Man feature ends	70.00
❑70, Aug 1965, JK (c); SL (w); JK (a); Sub-Mariner begins	100.00
❑71, Sep 1965 GC (c); SL (w); JK (a); 1: Vashti.	55.00
❑72, Oct 1965 JK (c); SL (w); JK (a).	55.00
❑73, Nov 1965 GC (c); SL (w); JK (a).	55.00
❑74, Dec 1965 GC (c); SL (w); JK (a).	55.00
❑75, Jan 1966 GC (c); SL (w); JK (a); 1: Behemoth.	55.00
❑76, Feb 1966 GC (c); SL (w); JK, GK (a)	55.00
❑77, Mar 1966, JK, JR (c); SL (w); JK, JR (a); Banner revealed as Hulk	55.00
❑78, Apr 1966 GC (c); SL (w); BEv, JK (a)	55.00
❑79, May 1966 JK (c); SL (w); BEv, JK (a)	55.00
❑80, Jun 1966 GC (c); SL (w); BEv, JK (a)	55.00
❑81, Jul 1966 BEv, JK (c); SL (w); BEv, JK (a); 1: Boomerang.	55.00
❑82, Aug 1966, GC (c); SL (w); BEv, JK (a); Iron Man vs. Sub-Mariner; Hulk	78.00
❑83, Sep 1966, BEv, JK (c); SL (w); BEv, JK (a); Sub-Mariner, Hulk	55.00
❑84, Oct 1966 GC (c); SL (w)	55.00
❑85, Nov 1966 BEv, JK (c); SL (w); JB (a)	55.00
❑86, Dec 1966 GC (c); SL (w); JB (a).	55.00
❑87, Jan 1967 GK (c); SL (w); JB (a).	55.00
❑88, Feb 1967 GC (c); SL (w); GK (a).	55.00
❑89, Mar 1967 GK (c); SL (w); GK (a)	55.00
❑90, Apr 1967 JK (c); SL (w); GK (a); 1: The Abomination. 1: Byrrah.	55.00
❑91, May 1967, GK (c); SL (w); GK (a); Sub-Mariner story continues in Avengers #40	52.00
❑92, Jun 1967, DA (c); SL (w); A: Silver Surfer. Sub-Mariner story continued from Avengers #40	75.00
❑93, Jul 1967 SL (w); A: Silver Surfer.	75.00
❑94, Aug 1967, DA (c); SL (w); BEv, HT (a); Hulk story continues from Thor #135	50.00
❑95, Sep 1967, JK (c); SL (w); HT (a); Sub-Mariner story continues from Daredevil #24	50.00
❑96, Oct 1967 DA (c); SL (w); HT (a).	50.00
❑97, Nov 1967 JK (c); SL (w); HT (a)	50.00
❑98, Dec 1967 DA (c); SL (w); HT (a); 1: Seth (Namor's advisor)	50.00
❑99, Jan 1968 SL (w)	50.00
❑100, Feb 1968, SL (w); DA (a); Hulk vs. Sub-Mariner	75.00
❑101, Mar 1968, JK (c); SL (w); Hulk feature continued in Incredible Hulk #102; Sub-Mariner feature continued in Iron Man & Sub-Mariner #1	85.00

TALES TO ASTONISH (VOL. 2)
MARVEL

	N-MINT
❑1, Dec 1979 JB (a)	2.00
❑2, Jan 1980 JB (a)	1.50
❑3, Feb 1980 JB (a)	1.50
❑4, Mar 1980 JB (a)	1.50
❑5, Apr 1980 JB (a)	1.50
❑6, May 1980 JB (a)	1.50
❑7, Jun 1980 JB (a)	1.50
❑8, Jul 1980 JB (a)	1.50
❑9, Aug 1980 JB (a)	1.50
❑10, Sep 1980 JB (a)	1.50
❑11, Oct 1980 JB (a)	1.50
❑12, Nov 1980 JB (a)	1.50
❑13, Dec 1980 JB (a)	1.50
❑14, Jan 1981 JB (a)	1.50

TALES TO ASTONISH (VOL. 3)
MARVEL

	N-MINT
❑1, Dec 1994; prestige format one-shot; acetate outer cover	6.95

TALES TO OFFEND
DARK HORSE

	N-MINT
❑1, Jul 1997; Lance Blastoff	2.95

TALES TOO TERRIBLE TO TELL
NEC

	N-MINT
❑1, b&w; Reprints from Mister Mystery #13, Weird Chills #1, Weird Chills #3, Mister Mystery #16, Purple Claw #1, Strange Mysteries #7, Mister Mystery #17	2.95
❑1/2nd, May 1993; 2nd printing with new cover; Reprints from Mister Mystery #13, Weird Chills #1, Weird Chills #3, Mister Mystery #16, Purple Claw #1, Strange Mysteries #7, Mister Mystery #17	3.50
❑2, Mar 1991, b&w; Reprints from Strange Mysteries #6, Weird Mysteries #11, Unseen #14, Black Cat Mystery #45, Journey into Fear #5, Ghoul Tales #3, Dark Mysteries #13	3.50
❑3, Jun 1991, b&w; Reprints from Weird Chills #3, Weird Mysteries #10, Weird Chills #1, Adventures into Darkness #13, Horrific #5	3.50
❑4, Dec 1991, b&w; Reprints from Mister Mystery #13, Fantastic Fears #8, Unseen #14, Journey into Fear #12, Fantastic Fears #6, Purple Claw #1, Fantastic Fears #4, Dark Mysteries #19	3.50
❑5 1992, b&w; Reprints	3.50
❑6 1992, b&w; Reprints	3.50
❑7 1992, b&w; Reprints	3.50

TALEWEAVER
WILDSTORM

	N-MINT
❑1, Nov 2001	3.50
❑2, Dec 2001	2.95
❑3, Jan 2002	2.95
❑4, Feb 2002	2.95
❑5, Mar 2002	2.95
❑6, Apr 2002	2.95

TALISMEN: SCSI VOODOO
BLINK

	N-MINT
❑1	2.75
❑2	2.75
❑3	2.75

TALK DIRTY
FANTAGRAPHICS / EROS

	N-MINT
❑1, b&w	2.50
❑2, b&w	2.50
❑3, b&w	2.95

TALKING ORANGUTANS IN BORNEO
GT-LABS

	N-MINT
❑1, ca. 1999, b&w; efforts to educate orangutans to communicate via sign language	3.50

TALL TAILS
GOLDEN REALM

	N-MINT
❑1, b&w	2.00
❑2, ca. 1993	2.00
❑3	2.95
❑4	2.95
❑5	2.95
❑6	2.95
❑7	2.95

TALONZ
STOP DRAGON

	N-MINT
❑1, Jan 1987, b&w	1.50

TALOS OF THE WILDERNESS SEA
DC

	N-MINT
❑1, ca. 1985	2.00

TAMMAS
PANDEMONIUM

	N-MINT
❑1, Dec 1986	1.50

TANGENT COMICS/DOOM PATROL
DC

	N-MINT
❑1, Dec 1997, alternate universe	2.95

TANGENT COMICS/GREEN LANTERN
DC

	N-MINT
❑1, Dec 1997, alternate universe	2.95

TANGENT COMICS/JLA
DC

	N-MINT
❑1, Sep 1998; alternate universe	1.95

TANGENT COMICS/METAL MEN
DC
❑1, Dec 1997, alternate universe 2.95

TANGENT COMICS/NIGHTWING
DC
❑1, Dec 1997, alternate universe 2.95

TANGENT COMICS/NIGHTWING: NIGHT FORCE
DC
❑1, Sep 1998; alternate universe 1.95

TANGENT COMICS/POWERGIRL
DC
❑1, Sep 1998; alternate universe 1.95

TANGENT COMICS/SEA DEVILS
DC
❑1, Dec 1997; alternate universe 2.95

TANGENT COMICS/SECRET SIX
DC
❑1, Dec 1997; alternate universe 2.95

TANGENT COMICS/ TALES OF THE GREEN LANTERN
DC
❑1, Sep 1998; alternate universe 1.95

TANGENT COMICS/THE ATOM
DC
❑1, Dec 1997, alternate universe 2.95

TANGENT COMICS/THE BATMAN
DC
❑1, Sep 1998; alternate universe 1.95

TANGENT COMICS/THE FLASH
DC
❑1, Dec 1997; alternate universe 2.95

TANGENT COMICS/THE JOKER
DC
❑1, Dec 1997, alternate universe 2.95

TANGENT COMICS/ THE JOKER'S WILD
DC
❑1, Sep 1998; alternate universe 1.95

TANGENT COMICS/THE SUPERMAN
DC
❑1, Sep 1998; alternate universe 1.95

TANGENT COMICS/ THE TRIALS OF THE FLASH
DC
❑1, Sep 1998; alternate universe 1.95

TANGENT COMICS/WONDER WOMAN
DC
❑1, Sep 1998; alternate universe 1.95

TANGLED WEB
MARVEL
❑1, Jun 2001 .... 2.99
❑2, Jul 2001 .... 2.99
❑3, Aug 2001 .... 2.99
❑4, Sep 2001 .... 2.99
❑5, Oct 2001 .... 2.99
❑6, Nov 2001 .... 2.99
❑7, Dec 2001 .... 2.99
❑8, Jan 2002 .... 2.99
❑9, Feb 2002 .... 2.99
❑10, Mar 2002 .... 2.99
❑11, Apr 2002 .... 2.99
❑12, May 2002 .... 2.99
❑13, Jun 2002 .... 2.99
❑14, Jul 2002 .... 2.99
❑15, Aug 2002 .... 2.99
❑16, Sep 2002 .... 2.99
❑17, Oct 2002 .... 2.99
❑18, Nov 2002 .... 2.99
❑19, Dec 2002 .... 2.99
❑20, Jan 2003 .... 2.99
❑21, Feb 2003 .... 2.99
❑22, Mar 2003 .... 2.99

TANK GIRL
DARK HORSE
❑1, May 1991, b&w; 1: Tank Girl (in American comics). trading cards; British 3.50
❑2, Jun 1991, b&w; British 3.00
❑3, Jul 1991, b&w; British 3.00
❑4, Aug 1991, b&w; British 3.00

TANK GIRL 2
DARK HORSE
❑1, Jun 1993 .... 3.00
❑2, Jul 1993 .... 3.00
❑3, Aug 1993 .... 3.00
❑4, Sep 1993 .... 3.00

TANK GIRL: APOCALYPSE
DC / VERTIGO
❑1, Nov 1995; Tank Girl becomes pregnant 2.25
❑2, Dec 1995 .... 2.25
❑3, Jan 1996 .... 2.25
❑4, Feb 1996; Tank Girl gives birth 2.25

TANK GIRL MOVIE ADAPTATION
DC / VERTIGO
❑1; prestige format one-shot 5.95

TANK GIRL: THE ODYSSEY
DC / VERTIGO
❑1, Jun 1995 .... 2.95
❑2, Jul 1995 .... 2.95
❑3, Aug 1995 .... 2.95
❑4, Oct 1995 .... 2.95

TANK VIXENS
ANTARCTIC
❑1, Jan 1994 .... 2.95
❑2, Mar 1994 .... 2.95
❑3, ca. 1995 .... 2.95
❑4, Mar 1996 .... 2.95

TANTALIZING STORIES
TUNDRA
❑1, Oct 1992 .... 2.25
❑2, Dec 1992 .... 2.25
❑3, Feb 1993 .... 2.25
❑4, Apr 1993 .... 2.25
❑6, Jun 1993 .... 2.50

TAOLAND
SUMITEK
❑1, Nov 1994, b&w; cardstock cover . 2.00
❑2, Aug 1995, b&w; cardstock cover . 5.95
❑3, Sep 1995, b&w; cardstock cover . 5.95
❑4, Feb 1996, b&w 5.95
❑5, Dec 1996; prestige format 5.95

TAOLAND ADVENTURES
ANTARCTIC
❑1, Mar 1999 .... 3.50
❑2, May 1999 .... 3.50

TAP
PROMETHEAN
❑1, Sep 1994 .... 2.95
❑2, Jan 1995 .... 2.95
❑3, Jan 1995; indicia is for issue #2 .. 2.95

TAPESTRY
SUPERIOR JUNK
❑1, b&w 1.50
❑1/2nd, Apr 1995 .... 1.50
❑2, Apr 1994, b&w 1.95
❑3, Jun 1994, b&w 1.95
❑4, Oct 1994, b&w 2.25
❑5, b&w 2.25

TAPESTRY ANTHOLOGY
CALIBER / TAPESTRY
❑1, Win 1997, b&w 2.95

TAPPING THE VEIN
ECLIPSE
❑1; prestige format; foil-embossed logo 7.50
❑2; prestige format; KJ (a); foil-embossed logo 7.00
❑3; prestige format; foil-embossed logo 7.00
❑4; prestige format; foil-embossed logo 7.95
❑5 .... 7.95

TARGET: AIRBOY
ECLIPSE
❑1, Mar 1988; A: Clint from A.R.B.B.H.. cardstock cover 2.00

TARGET: THE CORRUPTORS
DELL
❑2, Jun 1962, First issue published as Dell's Four Color #1306 .... 25.00
❑3, Dec 1962 .... 25.00

TARGITT
ATLAS-SEABOARD
❑1, Mar 1975 O: Targitt. 9.00
❑2, Apr 1975 .... 8.00
❑3, Jul 1975 .... 7.00

TAROT CAFE
TOKYOPOP
❑1, Mar 2005 .... 9.99
❑2, Jun 2005 .... 9.99
❑3, Sep 2005 .... 9.99
❑4, Dec 2005 .... 9.99

TAROT: WITCH OF THE BLACK ROSE
BROADSWORD
❑1, Mar 2000 .... 5.00
❑2, May 2000 .... 2.95
❑3, Jul 2000 .... 2.95
❑4, Sep 2000 .... 2.95
❑5, Nov 2000 .... 2.95
❑6, Jan 2001 .... 2.95
❑7, Mar 2001 .... 2.95
❑8, May 2001 .... 2.95
❑9, Jul 2001 .... 2.95
❑10, Sep 2001 .... 2.95
❑11, Nov 2001 .... 2.95
❑12, Jan 2002 .... 2.95
❑13, Mar 2002 .... 2.95
❑14, May 2002 .... 2.95
❑15, Jul 2002 .... 2.95
❑16, Sep 2002 .... 2.95
❑17, Nov 2002 .... 2.95
❑18, Jan 2003 .... 2.95
❑19, Mar 2003 .... 2.95
❑20, May 2003 .... 2.95
❑21 .... 2.95
❑22 .... 2.95
❑23 .... 2.95
❑24 .... 2.95
❑25 .... 2.95
❑26 .... 2.95
❑27 .... 2.95
❑28 .... 2.95
❑29 .... 2.95
❑29/Variant 4.00
❑30 2005 .... 2.95
❑30/Variant 2005 .... 20.00
❑31 2005 .... 2.95
❑31/Deluxe 2005 .... 19.99
❑31/Photo 2005 .... 15.00
❑32 2005 .... 2.95
❑32/Variant 2005 .... 5.00
❑33, Sep 2005 .... 2.95
❑33/Deluxe, Sep 2005 .... 19.99

TARZAN (DELL)
DELL
❑85, Oct 1956 RM (a) 30.00
❑86, Nov 1956 RM (a) 30.00
❑87, Dec 1956 RM (a) 30.00
❑88, Jan 1957 RM (a) 30.00
❑89, Feb 1957 RM (a) 30.00
❑90, Mar 1957 RM (a) 30.00
❑91, Apr 1957 RM (a) 30.00
❑92, May 1957 RM (a) 30.00
❑93, Jun 1957 RM (a) 30.00
❑94, Jul 1957 RM (a) 30.00
❑95, Aug 1957 RM (a) 30.00
❑96, Sep 1957 RM (a) 30.00
❑97, Oct 1957 RM (a) 30.00
❑98, Nov 1957 RM (a) 30.00
❑99, Dec 1957 RM (a) 30.00
❑100, Jan 1958 RM (a) 40.00
❑101, Feb 1958 RM (a) 28.00
❑102, Mar 1958 RM (a) 28.00
❑103, Apr 1958 RM (a) 28.00
❑104, May 1958 RM (a) 28.00
❑105, Jun 1958 RM (a) 28.00
❑106, Jul 1958 RM (a) 28.00
❑107, Aug 1958 RM (a) 28.00
❑108, Sep 1958 RM (a) 28.00
❑109, Nov 1958 RM (a) 28.00
❑110, Jan 1959 .... 28.00
❑111, Mar 1959 .... 25.00
❑112, May 1959 .... 25.00
❑113, Jul 1959 .... 25.00
❑114, Sep 1959 .... 25.00
❑115, Nov 1959 .... 25.00

Teenage Mutant Ninja Turtles (1st Series)

Irradiated amphibians trained by rodent master

©Mirage

Teenage Mutant Ninja Turtles (3rd Series)

Move to Image opens crossovers

©Image

Teenage Mutant Ninja Turtles Adventures (1st Series)

Lighter fare for Archie audience

©Archie

Teenage Mutant Ninja Turtles Movie II

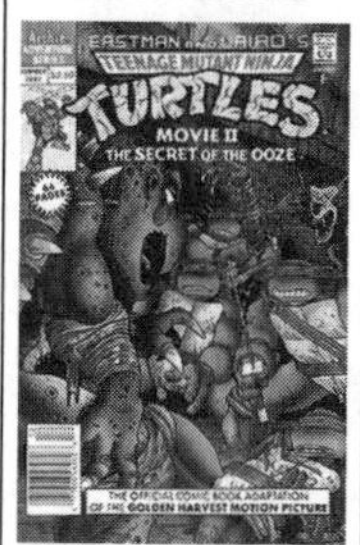

Turtles' true origins revealed

©Archie

Teen Comics

Unauthorized bios of youngsters' favorites

©Personality

N-MINT

❑116, Jan 1960 .... 25.00
❑117, Mar 1960 .... 25.00
❑118, May 1960 .... 25.00
❑119, Jul 1960 .... 25.00
❑120, Sep 1960 .... 25.00
❑121, Nov 1960 .... 20.00
❑122, Jan 1961 RM (a) 20.00
❑123, Mar 1961 RM (a) 20.00
❑124, May 1961 RM (a) 20.00
❑125, Jul 1961 RM (a) 20.00
❑126, Sep 1961 RM (a) 20.00
❑127, Nov 1961 .... 20.00
❑128, Jan 1962 RM (a) 20.00
❑129, Mar 1962 RM (a) 20.00
❑130, May 1962 RM (a) 20.00
❑131, Jul 1962, RM (a); Series continued in Tarzan (Gold Key) #132 20.00

TARZAN (GOLD KEY)

GOLD KEY

❑132, Nov 1962, RM (a); Continued from Tarzan (Dell) #131 .... 14.00
❑133, Jan 1963 RM (a) 14.00
❑134, Mar 1963 RM (a) 14.00
❑135, May 1963 RM (a) 14.00
❑136, Jul 1963 RM (a) 14.00
❑137, Aug 1963 RM (a) 14.00
❑138, Oct 1963 RM (a) 14.00
❑139, Dec 1963 RM (a) 14.00
❑140, Feb 1964 RM (a) 14.00
❑141, Apr 1964 RM (a) 14.00
❑142, Jun 1964 RM (a) 14.00
❑143, Jul 1964 RM (a) 14.00
❑144, Aug 1964 RM (a) 14.00
❑145, Sep 1964 RM (a) 14.00
❑146, Oct 1964 (w) 14.00
❑147, Dec 1964 RM (a) 14.00
❑148, Feb 1965 RM (a) 14.00
❑149, Apr 1965 RM (a) 14.00
❑150, Jun 1965 RM (a) 14.00
❑151, Aug 1965 RM (a) 14.00
❑152, Sep 1965 RM (a) 14.00
❑153, Oct 1965 RM (a) 14.00
❑154, Nov 1965 RM (a) 14.00
❑155, Dec 1965, RM (a); O: Tarzan. adapts Tarzan of the Apes 18.00
❑156, Feb 1966, RM (a); adapts Return of Tarzan 10.00
❑157, Apr 1966, RM (a); adapts Beasts of Tarzan 10.00
❑158, Jun 1966, RM (a); adapts Son of Tarzan 10.00
❑159, Aug 1966, RM (a); adapts Jewels of Opar 10.00
❑160, Sep 1966, RM (a); adapts Jewels of Opar 10.00
❑161, Oct 1966, RM (a); adapts Jewels of Opar 10.00
❑162, Dec 1966, (w); TV Adventures on cover 10.00
❑163, Jan 1967, RM (a); adapts Tarzan the Untamed 8.00
❑164, Feb 1967, RM (a); adapts Tarzan the Untamed 8.00
❑165, Mar 1967 (w); DS (a) 10.00
❑166, Apr 1967, RM (a); adapts Tarzan the Terrible 8.00

N-MINT

❑167, May 1967, RM (a); adapts Tarzan the Terrible 8.00
❑168, Jun 1967 (w) 10.00
❑169, Jul 1967, adapts Jungle Tales of Tarzan 8.00
❑170, Aug 1967, adapts Jungle Tales of Tarzan 8.00
❑171, Sep 1967, TV Adventures 10.00
❑172, Oct 1967, RM (a); adapts Tarzan and the Golden Lion 7.00
❑173, Dec 1967, RM (a); adapts Tarzan and the Golden Lion 7.00
❑174, Feb 1968, RM (a); adapts Tarzan and the Ant Men 7.00
❑175, Apr 1968, RM (a); adapts Tarzan and the Ant Men 7.00
❑176, Jun 1968, RM (a); adapts Tarzan; Lord of the Jungle 7.00
❑177, Jul 1968, RM (a); adapts Tarzan; Lord of the Jungle 7.00
❑178, Aug 1968, RM (a); reprints issue #155 .... 7.00
❑179, Sep 1968, adapts Tarzan at the Earth's Core 7.00
❑180, Oct 1968, adapts Tarzan at the Earth's Core 7.00
❑181, Dec 1968, adapts Tarzan at the Earth's Core 7.00
❑182, Feb 1969, adapts Tarzan the Invincible 7.00
❑183, Apr 1969, (c); adapts Tarzan the Invincible 7.00
❑184, Jun 1969, adapts Tarzan Triumphant 7.00
❑185, Jul 1969, adapts Tarzan Triumphant 7.00
❑186, Aug 1969, adapts Tarzan and the City of Gold 7.00
❑187, Sep 1969, adapts Tarzan and the City of Gold 7.00
❑188, Oct 1969, adapts Tarzan's Quest 7.00
❑189, Dec 1969, adapts Tarzan's Quest 7.00
❑190, Feb 1970, adapts Tarzan and the Forbidden City 7.00
❑191, Apr 1970, adapts Tarzan and the Forbidden City 7.00
❑192, Jun 1970, adapts Tarzan and the Foreign Legion 7.00
❑193, Jul 1970, adapts Tarzan and the Foreign Legion 7.00
❑194, Aug 1970, adapts Tarzan and the Lost Empire 7.00
❑195, Sep 1970, adapts Tarzan and the Lost Empire 7.00
❑196, Oct 1970, adapts Tarzan and the Tarzan Twins 7.00
❑197, Dec 1970 .... 7.00
❑198, Feb 1971 .... 7.00
❑199, Apr 1971 .... 7.00
❑200, Jun 1971 .... 7.00
❑201, Jul 1971 .... 6.00
❑202, Aug 1971, RM (a); astronauts land in jungle 6.00
❑203, Sep 1971 RM (a) 6.00
❑204, Oct 1971 .... 6.00
❑205, Dec 1971 .... 6.00
❑206, Feb 1972, moves to DC; Series continued in Tarzan (DC) #207 .... 6.00

N-MINT

TARZAN (DC)

DC

❑207, Apr 1972; Giant-size; JKu (c); JKu (w); MA, GM, JKu (a); O: Tarzan. John Carter of Mars back-up; Series continued from Tarzan (Dell) 17.00
❑208, May 1972; JKu (c); JKu (w); GM, JKu (a); O: Tarzan. John Carter of Mars back-up 10.00
❑209, Jun 1972; JKu (c); JKu (w); MA, JKu (a); O: Tarzan. John Carter of Mars back-up continues in Weird Worlds #1 .... 6.00
❑210, Jul 1972 JKu (c); JKu (w); JKu (a); O: Tarzan. 6.00
❑211, Aug 1972 JKu (c); JKu (w); JKu (a) 4.00
❑212, Sep 1972 JKu (c); JKu (w); JKu (a) 4.00
❑213, Oct 1972 JKu (c); JKu (w); DGr, JKu (a) 4.00
❑214, Nov 1972, JKu (c); JKu (w); DGr, JKu (a); Beyond the Farthest Star back-up 4.00
❑215, Dec 1972, JKu (c); JKu (w); JKu (a); Beyond the Farthest Star back-up 4.00
❑216, Jan 1973, JKu (c); JKu (w); HC, JKu (a); Beyond the Farthest Star back-up 4.00
❑217, Feb 1973, JKu (c); JKu (w); MA, JKu (a); Beyond the Farthest Star back-up 4.00
❑218, Mar 1973, JKu (c); JKu (w); MA, JKu (a); Beyond the Farthest Star back-up 4.00
❑219, May 1973 JKu (c); JKu (w); JKu (a) 4.00
❑220, Jun 1973 JKu (c); JKu (w); JKu (a) 4.00
❑221, Jul 1973 JKu (c); JKu (w); JKu (a) 4.00
❑222, Aug 1973 JKu (c); JKu (w); JKu (a) 4.00
❑223, Sep 1973 JKu (c); JKu (w); JKu (a) 4.00
❑224, Oct 1973 JKu (c); JKu (w); JKu (a) 4.00
❑225, Nov 1973 JKu (c); JKu (w); JKu (a) 4.00
❑226, Dec 1973 JKu (c); JKu (a) 4.00
❑227, Jan 1974 JKu (c); JKu (w); JKu (a) 4.00
❑228, Feb 1974 JKu (c); JKu (w); JKu (a) 4.00
❑229, Mar 1974 JKu (c); JKu (w); JKu (a) 4.00
❑230, May 1974, 100 Page giant JKu (c); JKu (w); CI, JKu, RM, RH (a) ... 8.00
❑231, Jul 1974, 100 Page giant JKu (c); JKu (w); CI, JKu, RM, AN (a) 8.00
❑232, Sep 1974, 100 Page giant JKu (c); JKu (w); NR, CI, JKu, GK, AA, RM, AN (a) 8.00
❑233, Nov 1974, 100 Page giant JKu (c); JKu (w); CI, JKu, GK, RM, AN (a) 8.00
❑234, Jan 1975, 100 Page giant JKu (c); JKu (w); CI, JKu, RM, AN, RMo (a) 8.00
❑235, Mar 1975, 100 Page giant JKu (c); JKu (w); CI, JKu, RM (a) 8.00

Other grades: Multiply price above by 5/6 for VF/NM • 2/3 for VERY FINE • 1/3 for FINE • 1/5 for VERY GOOD • 1/8 for GOOD

❑236, Apr 1975 JKu (c); (w) 3.00
❑237, May 1975 JKu (c); (w); JKu, RM (a) 3.00
❑238, Jun 1975 JKu (c); (w); RM (a) 3.00
❑239, Jul 1975 JKu (c); (w) 3.00
❑240, Aug 1975; JKu (c); (w); adapts The Castaways 3.00
❑241, Sep 1975 JKu (c); (w) 3.00
❑242, Oct 1975 JKu (c); (w) 3.00
❑243, Nov 1975 JKu (c); (w) 3.00
❑244, Dec 1975 JKu (c); (w) 3.00
❑245, Jan 1976 JKu (c); (w) 3.00
❑246, Feb 1976 JKu (c); (w) 3.00
❑247, Mar 1976 JKu (c); (w) 3.00
❑248, Apr 1976 JKu (c); (w) 3.00
❑249, May 1976 JKu (c); (w) 3.00
❑250, Jun 1976 JL (c); JL (a) 3.00
❑251, Jul 1976 JL (c); JL (a) 3.00
❑252, Aug 1976 JL (c); JKu (w); JKu, JL (a) 3.00
❑253, Sep 1976 JKu (c); JKu (w); JKu, JL (a) 3.00
❑254, Oct 1976 JL (c); FS, JL (a) 3.00
❑255, Nov 1976 FS, JL (a) 3.00
❑256, Dec 1976, adapts Tarzan the Untamed 3.00
❑257, Jan 1977 JKu (w); JKu (a) 3.00
❑258, Feb 1977 JKu (w); JKu (a) 3.00

TARZAN (MARVEL)
MARVEL

❑1, Jun 1977 JB (a) 3.00
❑1/35 cent, Jun 1977, JB (a); 35 cent regional price variant 15.00
❑2, Jul 1977, Newsstand edition (distributed by Curtis); issue number in box 2.00
❑2/Whitman, Jul 1977, Special markets edition (usually sold in Whitman bagged prepacks); price appears in a diamond; UPC barcode appears 2.00
❑2/35 cent, Jul 1977, 35 cent regional price variant; newsstand edition (distributed by Curtis); issue number in box 15.00
❑3, Aug 1977 2.00
❑3/35 cent, Aug 1977, 35 cent regional price variant 15.00
❑4, Sep 1977 2.00
❑4/35 cent, Sep 1977, 35 cent regional price variant 15.00
❑5, Oct 1977 2.00
❑5/35 cent, Oct 1977, 35 cent regional price variant 15.00
❑6, Nov 1977 1.50
❑7, Dec 1977 1.50
❑8, Jan 1978 1.50
❑9, Feb 1978 1.50
❑10, Mar 1978 1.50
❑11, Apr 1978, Newsstand edition (distributed by Curtis); issue number in box 1.50
❑11/Whitman, Apr 1978, Special markets edition (usually sold in Whitman bagged prepacks); price appears in a diamond; no UPC barcode 1.50
❑12, May 1978, Newsstand edition (distributed by Curtis); issue number in box 1.50
❑12/Whitman, May 1978, Special markets edition (usually sold in Whitman bagged prepacks); price appears in a diamond; no UPC barcode 1.50
❑13, Jun 1978, Newsstand edition (distributed by Curtis); issue number in box 1.50
❑13/Whitman, Jun 1978, Special markets edition (usually sold in Whitman bagged prepacks); price appears in a diamond; no UPC barcode 1.50
❑14, Jul 1978 1.50
❑15, Aug 1978 1.50
❑15/Whitman, Aug 1978, Special markets edition (usually sold in Whitman bagged prepacks); price appears in a diamond; no UPC barcode 1.50
❑16, Sep 1978, Newsstand edition (distributed by Curtis); issue number in box 1.50
❑16/Whitman, Sep 1978, Special markets edition (usually sold in Whitman bagged prepacks); price appears in a diamond; UPC barcode appears 1.50
❑17, Oct 1978, Newsstand edition (distributed by Curtis); issue number in box 1.50
❑17/Whitman, Oct 1978, Special markets edition (usually sold in Whitman bagged prepacks); price appears in a diamond; no UPC barcode 1.50
❑18, Nov 1978, Newsstand edition (distributed by Curtis); issue number in box 1.50
❑18/Whitman, Nov 1978, Special markets edition (usually sold in Whitman bagged prepacks); price appears in a diamond; no UPC barcode 1.50
❑19, Dec 1978, Newsstand edition (distributed by Curtis); issue number in box 1.50
❑19/Whitman, Dec 1978, Special markets edition (usually sold in Whitman bagged prepacks); price appears in a diamond; no UPC barcode 1.50
❑20, Jan 1979, BH (a); Newsstand edition (distributed by Curtis); issue number in box 1.50
❑20/Whitman, Jan 1979, BH (a); Special markets edition (usually sold in Whitman bagged prepacks); price appears in a diamond; no UPC barcode 1.50
❑21, Feb 1979, Newsstand edition (distributed by Curtis); issue number in box 1.50
❑21/Whitman, Feb 1979, Special markets edition (usually sold in Whitman bagged prepacks); price appears in a diamond; no UPC barcode 1.50
❑22, Mar 1979 1.50
❑23, Apr 1979 1.50
❑24, May 1979, BH (a); Newsstand edition (distributed by Curtis); issue number in box 1.50
❑24/Whitman, May 1979, BH (a); Special markets edition (usually sold in Whitman bagged prepacks); price appears in a diamond; no UPC barcode 1.50
❑25, Jun 1979 BH (a) 1.50
❑26, Jul 1979 BH (a) 1.50
❑27, Aug 1979 1.50
❑28, Sep 1979 1.50
❑29, Oct 1979 1.50
❑Annual 1, ca. 1977 3.00
❑Annual 2, ca. 1978 BH (c) 1.50
❑Annual 3, ca. 1979 1.50

TARZAN (DARK HORSE)
DARK HORSE

❑1, Jul 1996 3.00
❑2, Aug 1996 3.00
❑3, Aug 1996 3.00
❑4, Sep 1996 3.00
❑5, Nov 1996 3.00
❑6, Nov 1996 3.00
❑7, Jan 1997 3.00
❑8, Feb 1997 3.00
❑9, Mar 1997 3.00
❑10, Apr 1997 3.00
❑11, May 1997 3.00
❑12, Jun 1997 2.95
❑13, Aug 1997 2.95
❑14, Sep 1997 2.95
❑15, Sep 1997 2.95
❑16, Oct 1997 2.95
❑17, Dec 1997 TY (a) 2.95
❑18, Jan 1998 2.95
❑19, Feb 1998 2.95
❑20, Mar 1998 2.95

TARZAN (DISNEY'S...)
DARK HORSE

❑1, Jul 1999 2.95
❑2, Jul 1999 2.95

TARZAN AND THE JEWELS OF OPAR (EDGAR RICE BURROUGHS'...)
DARK HORSE

❑1, Jun 1999; digest; collects stories from Dell's Tarzan #159-161 plus pin-ups 10.95

TARZAN: A TALE OF MUGAMBI (EDGAR RICE BURROUGHS'...)
DARK HORSE

❑1, Jun 1995 2.95

TARZAN/CARSON OF VENUS
DARK HORSE

❑1, May 1998 2.95
❑2, Jun 1998 2.95
❑3, Jul 1998 2.95
❑4, Aug 1998 2.95

TARZAN DIGEST
DC

❑1, Aut 1972 3.00

TARZAN FAMILY
DC

❑60, Dec 1975 5.00
❑61, Feb 1976 5.00
❑62, Apr 1976 4.00
❑63, Jun 1976 4.00
❑64, Aug 1976 4.00
❑65, Sep 1976 4.00
❑66, Nov 1976 4.00

TARZAN IN THE LAND THAT TIME FORGOT AND THE POOL OF TIME (EDGAR RICE BURROUGHS'...)
DARK HORSE

❑Book 1, Jun 1996; collects two stories 12.95

TARZAN/JOHN CARTER: WARLORDS OF MARS
DARK HORSE

❑1, Jan 1996 2.50
❑2, Apr 1996, indicia says #3, cover says #2 2.50
❑3, May 1996 2.50
❑4, Jul 1996 2.50

TARZAN, LORD OF THE JUNGLE (GOLD KEY)
GOLD KEY

❑1, Sep 1965 40.00

TARZAN: LOVE, LIES AND THE LOST CITY
MALIBU

❑1, Aug 1992; Flip-book MW (w) 3.95
❑2, Sep 1992 3.95
❑3, Oct 1992 3.95

TARZAN OF THE APES
MARVEL

❑1, Jul 1984 ME (w); DS (a); O: Tarzan. 3.00
❑2, Aug 1984 ME (w); DS (a); O: Tarzan. 3.00

TARZAN OF THE APES (EDGAR RICE BURROUGHS'...)
DARK HORSE

❑1, May 1999; digest; collects stories from Dell's Tarzan #155-158 and spot illustrations from Tarzan #154-156 12.95

TARZAN: THE BECKONING
MALIBU

❑1, Nov 1992 2.50
❑2, Dec 1992 2.50
❑3, Jan 1993 2.50
❑4, Feb 1993 2.50
❑5, Mar 1993 2.50
❑6, Apr 1993 2.50
❑7, Jun 1993 2.50

TARZAN: THE LOST ADVENTURE (EDGAR RICE BURROUGHS'...)
DARK HORSE

❑1, Jan 1995, b&w; squarebound 2.95
❑2, Feb 1995, b&w; squarebound 2.95
❑3, Mar 1995, b&w; squarebound 2.95
❑4, Apr 1995, b&w; squarebound 2.95

TARZAN: THE RIVERS OF BLOOD (EDGAR RICE BURROUGHS'...)
DARK HORSE

❑1, Nov 1999 2.95
❑2, Dec 1999 2.95
❑3, Jan 2000 2.95
❑4, Feb 2000; final issue of planned eight-issue mini-series 2.95

TARZAN: THE SAVAGE HEART
DARK HORSE

❑1, Apr 1999 2.95
❑2, May 1999 2.95

Teen Confessions

Romantic revelations of youths

©Charlton

Teen Titans

Sidekicks form group to help non-powered peers

©DC

Teen Titans (2nd Series)

De-aged Atom leads adolescent adventurers

©DC

Teen Titans (3rd Series)

No longer Teens mentor new Teens

©DC

Tekworld

Shatner SF series features future cop

©Marvel

N-MINT

❑3, Jun 1999 ... 2.95
❑4, Jul 1999 ... 2.95

TARZAN THE WARRIOR
MALIBU

❑1, Mar 1992 ... 2.50
❑2, May 1992 ... 2.50
❑3, Jun 1992 ... 2.50
❑4, Aug 1992 ... 2.50
❑5, Sep 1992 ... 2.50

TARZAN VS. PREDATOR AT THE EARTH'S CORE
DARK HORSE

❑1, Jan 1996 ... 2.50
❑2, Feb 1996 ... 2.50
❑3, Mar 1996 ... 2.50
❑4, Jun 1996 ... 2.50

TARZAN WEEKLY
BYBLOS

❑1 ... 5.00

T.A.S.E.R.
COMICREATIONS

❑1, Sep 1992, b&w ... 2.00
❑2, Jun 1993, b&w ... 2.00

TASKMASTER
MARVEL

❑1, Apr 2002 ... 2.99
❑2, May 2002 ... 2.99
❑3, Jun 2002 ... 2.99
❑4, Jul 2002 ... 2.99

TASMANIAN DEVIL AND HIS TASTY FRIENDS
GOLD KEY

❑1, Nov 1962 ... 75.00

TASTY BITS
AVALON

❑1, Jul 1999 ... 2.95

TATTERED BANNERS
DC / VERTIGO

❑1, Nov 1998 ... 2.95
❑2, Dec 1998 ... 2.95
❑3, Jan 1999 ... 2.95
❑4, Feb 1999 ... 2.95

TATTOO
CALIBER

❑1 ... 2.95
❑2 ... 2.95

TATTOO MAN
FANTAGRAPHICS

❑1, b&w ... 2.75

TAXX
EXPRESS / PARODY

❑½ ... 1.50
❑1, b&w ... 2.75

T-BIRD CHRONICLES
ME COMIX

❑1, b&w ... 1.50
❑2, b&w ... 1.50

TEAM 7
IMAGE

❑1, Oct 1994 ... 3.00
❑1/A, Oct 1994 ... 3.00

N-MINT

❑2, Nov 1994 ... 2.50
❑3, Dec 1994 ... 2.50
❑4, Feb 1995 ... 2.50
❑Ashcan 1, Oct 1994, b&w; ashcan promo edition ... 1.00

TEAM 7: DEAD RECKONING
IMAGE

❑1, Jan 1996 ... 2.50
❑2, Feb 1996 ... 2.50
❑3, Mar 1996 ... 2.50
❑4, Apr 1996 ... 2.50

TEAM 7: OBJECTIVE: HELL
IMAGE

❑1, May 1995; with card ... 2.50
❑2, Jun 1995 ... 2.50
❑3, Jul 1995 ... 2.50

TEAM AMERICA
MARVEL

❑1, Jun 1982 O: Team America. ... 1.00
❑2, Jul 1982 LMc (a) ... 1.00
❑3, Aug 1982 LMc (a) ... 1.00
❑4, Sep 1982 LMc (a) ... 1.00
❑5, Oct 1982 ... 1.00
❑6, Nov 1982 ... 1.00
❑7, Dec 1982 ... 1.00
❑8, Jan 1983 ... 1.00
❑9, Feb 1983 A: Iron Man. ... 1.00
❑10, Mar 1983 ... 1.00
❑11, Apr 1983 A: Ghost Rider. ... 1.00
❑12, May 1983; Double-size; DP (a); Marauder unmasked ... 1.00

TEAM ANARCHY
DAGGER

❑1, Oct 1993 ... 2.75
❑2, Nov 1993 ... 2.50
❑3, Jan 1994 ... 2.50
❑4, Feb 1994 ... 2.50
❑5, Mar 1994 ... 2.50
❑6, Apr 1994 ... 2.50
❑7, May 1994 ... 2.50

TEAM NIPPON
AIRCEL

❑1, b&w ... 1.95
❑2, b&w ... 1.95
❑3, b&w ... 1.95
❑4, b&w ... 1.95
❑5, b&w ... 1.95
❑6, b&w ... 1.95
❑7, b&w ... 1.95

TEAM ONE: STORMWATCH
IMAGE

❑1, Jun 1995; cover says Jul, indicia says Jun ... 2.50
❑2, Aug 1995 ... 2.50

TEAM ONE: WILDC.A.T.S
IMAGE

❑1, Jul 1995 ... 2.50
❑2, Sep 1995 ... 2.50

TEAM SUPERMAN
DC

❑1, Jul 1999 ... 2.95

N-MINT

TEAM SUPERMAN SECRET FILES
DC

❑1, May 1998; biographical info on Superboy, Supergirl, Steel, and respective villains ... 4.95

TEAM TITANS
DC

❑1/A, Sep 1992; KGa (a); O: Killowat. Comes in five different covers ... 4.00
❑1/B, Sep 1992; KGa (a); O: Mirage. Comes in five different covers ... 3.00
❑1/C, Sep 1992; O: Nightrider. Comes in five different covers ... 3.00
❑1/D, Sep 1992; O: Redwing. Comes in five different covers ... 3.00
❑1/E, Sep 1992; O: Terra. Comes in five different covers ... 3.00
❑2, Oct 1992 1: Battalion. ... 1.75
❑3, Nov 1992 ... 1.75
❑4, Dec 1992 1: Judge & Jury. ... 1.75
❑5, Feb 1993 ... 1.75
❑6, Mar 1993 ... 1.75
❑7, Apr 1993 ... 1.75
❑8, May 1993 1: Deathwing. ... 1.75
❑9, Jun 1993 ... 1.75
❑10, Jul 1993 ... 1.75
❑11, Aug 1993 ... 1.75
❑12, Sep 1993 ... 1.75
❑13, Oct 1993 ... 1.75
❑14, Nov 1993 ... 1.75
❑15, Dec 1993 ... 1.75
❑16, Jan 1994 ... 1.75
❑17, Feb 1994 ... 1.75
❑18, Mar 1994 ... 1.75
❑19, Apr 1994 ... 1.75
❑20, May 1994 ... 1.75
❑21, Jun 1994 ... 1.75
❑22, Jul 1994 ... 1.75
❑23, Aug 1994 ... 1.95
❑24, Sep 1994; Zero Hour ... 1.95
❑Annual 1, 1: Chimera. ... 3.50
❑Annual 2, Elseworlds ... 2.95

TEAM X
MARVEL

❑2000, Feb 1999 ... 3.50

TEAM X/TEAM 7
MARVEL

❑1, Jan 1997, crossover with Image; squarebound ... 4.95

TEAM YANKEE
FIRST

❑1, Jan 1989 ... 1.95
❑2, Jan 1989 ... 1.95
❑3, Jan 1989 ... 1.95
❑4, Feb 1989 ... 1.95
❑5, Feb 1989 ... 1.95
❑6, Feb 1989 ... 1.95

TEAM YOUNGBLOOD
IMAGE

❑1, Sep 1993 ... 1.95
❑2, Oct 1993 ... 1.95
❑3, Nov 1993 ... 1.95
❑4, Dec 1993 ... 1.95
❑5, Jan 1994 ... 1.95

Other grades: Multiply price above by 5/6 for VF/NM • 2/3 for VERY FINE • 1/3 for FINE • 1/5 for VERY GOOD • 1/8 for GOOD

❑6, Feb 1994 1.95
❑7, Mar 1994 1.95
❑8, Apr 1994 1.95
❑9, May 1994 1.95
❑10, Jun 1994 2.50
❑11, Jul 1994 1.95
❑12, Aug 1994 2.50
❑13, Sep 1994 2.50
❑14, Oct 1994; Riptide poses nude 2.50
❑15, Nov 1994 2.50
❑16, Dec 1994; polybagged with trading card 2.50
❑17, Jan 1995; polybagged with trading card 2.50
❑18, May 1995 2.50
❑19, Jun 1995 2.50
❑20, Jul 1995 2.50
❑21, Mar 1996 2.50
❑22, Apr 1996 2.50

TEAM ZERO
DC / WILDSTORM

❑1, Jan 2006 2.99
❑2, Feb 2006 2.99
❑3, Mar 2006 2.99
❑4, May 2006 2.99
❑5, Jun 2006 2.99
❑6, Jul 2006 2.99

TEARS
BONEYARD

❑1, Oct 1992, b&w 2.95
❑2, Dec 1992, b&w 2.50

TEASER AND THE BLACKSMITH
FANTAGRAPHICS

❑1, b&w 3.50

TECH HIGH
VIRTUALLY REAL ENTERPRISES

❑1, Fal 1996, b&w 2.50
❑2, Win 1996, b&w 2.50
❑3, Spr 1997, b&w 2.50

TECH JACKET
IMAGE

❑1, Nov 2003 2.95
❑2, Dec 2003 2.95
❑3, Jan 2003 2.95
❑4, Feb 2003 2.95
❑5, Apr 2003 2.95
❑6, May 2003 2.95

TECHNO MANIACS
INDEPENDENT

❑1 1.95

TECHNOPOLIS
CALIBER

❑1 2.95
❑2 2.95
❑3 2.95
❑4 2.95

TECHNOPRIESTS
DC

❑1, ca. 2004 14.95

TEENAGE HOTRODDERS
CHARLTON

❑1, Apr 1963 35.00
❑2, Jun 1963 20.00
❑3, Aug 1963 20.00
❑4, Oct 1963 20.00
❑5, Dec 1963 20.00
❑6, Feb 1964 20.00
❑7, May 1964 20.00
❑8, Jul 1964 20.00
❑9, Oct 1964 20.00
❑10, Dec 1964 20.00
❑11, Feb 1965 15.00
❑12, May 1965 15.00
❑13, Jul 1965 15.00
❑14, Sep 1965 15.00
❑15, Nov 1965 15.00
❑16, Jan 1966 15.00
❑17, Apr 1966 15.00
❑18, Jun 1966 15.00
❑19, Aug 1966 15.00
❑20, Oct 1966 15.00
❑21, Dec 1966 15.00
❑22, Feb 1967 15.00
❑23, May 1967 15.00
❑24, Jul 1967, Becomes Top Eliminator #25 15.00

TEEN-AGE LOVE
CHARLTON

❑4 1958 30.00
❑5 1958 16.00
❑6 1958 14.00
❑7 1959 14.00
❑8 1959 14.00
❑9 1959 14.00
❑10, Sep 1959 14.00
❑11, Nov 1959 9.00
❑12, Jan 1960 9.00
❑13, Mar 1960 9.00
❑14, May 1960 9.00
❑15, Jul 1960 9.00
❑16, Sep 1960 9.00
❑17, Nov 1960 9.00
❑18, Jan 1961 9.00
❑19, Mar 1961 9.00
❑20, May 1961 9.00
❑21, Jul 1961 7.00
❑22, Sep 1961 7.00
❑23, Nov 1961 7.00
❑24 1962 7.00
❑25 1962 7.00
❑26 1962 7.00
❑27 1962 7.00
❑28 1962 7.00
❑29 1962 7.00
❑30 1963 7.00
❑31 1963 5.00
❑32 1963 5.00
❑33 1963 5.00
❑34, Oct 1963 5.00
❑35 1963 DG (c) 5.00
❑36 1964 5.00
❑37 1964 5.00
❑38, Jul 1964 5.00
❑39, Oct 1964 5.00
❑40 1964 5.00
❑41, ca. 1965 5.00
❑42, Jun 1965 5.00
❑43, Aug 1965 5.00
❑44, Oct 1965 5.00
❑45 1966 5.00
❑46, Mar 1966 5.00
❑47, May 1966 5.00
❑48, Jul 1966 5.00
❑49, Sep 1966 5.00
❑50, Nov 1966 5.00
❑51, Jan 1967 3.50
❑52, Mar 1967 3.50
❑53, May 1967 3.50
❑54, Jul 1967 3.50
❑55, Sep 1967 3.50
❑56, Nov 1967 3.50
❑57, Jan 1968 3.50
❑58, May 1968 3.50
❑59, Jul 1968 3.50
❑60, Sep 1968 3.50
❑61, Nov 1968 3.50
❑62, Jan 1969 3.50
❑63, Mar 1969 3.50
❑64, May 1969 3.50
❑65 1969 3.50
❑66 1969 3.50
❑67, Nov 1969 3.50
❑68, Jan 1970 3.50
❑69, Mar 1970 3.50
❑70, May 1970 3.50
❑71, Jul 1970 2.00
❑72, Sep 1970 2.00
❑73, Nov 1970 2.00
❑74, Jan 1971 2.00
❑75, Mar 1971 2.00
❑76, May 1971 2.00
❑77 1971 2.00
❑78 1971 2.00
❑79, Nov 1971 2.00
❑80, Dec 1971, David Cassidy pin-up 2.00
❑81, Jan 1972, Susan Dey pin-up 2.00
❑82, Feb 1972, Shirley Jones pin-up 2.00
❑83, Mar 1972 2.00
❑84, Jun 1972 2.00
❑85 1972 2.00
❑86 1972 2.00
❑87 1972 2.00
❑88, Nov 1972 2.00
❑89 1972 2.00
❑90 1973 2.00
❑91 1973 2.00
❑92, Apr 1973 2.00
❑93 1973 2.00
❑94 1973 2.00
❑95, Oct 1973 2.00
❑96, Dec 1973 2.00

TEENAGE MUTANT NINJA TURTLES (1ST SERIES)
MIRAGE

❑1, ca. 1984; 1: Teenage Mutant Ninja Turtles. 1st printing-Beware of counterfeits 300.00
❑1/Counterfeit; Counterfeit of first printing; Most counterfeit copies have streak or scratch marks across center of back cover, black part of cover is slightly bluish instead of black 1.50
❑1/2nd, ca. 1984 1: Teenage Mutant Ninja Turtles. 15.00
❑1/3rd, Feb 1985 1: Teenage Mutant Ninja Turtles. 8.00
❑1/4th 1985; 1: Teenage Mutant Ninja Turtles. says Reprinting the first issue on cover 4.00
❑1/5th, Aug 1988; 1: Teenage Mutant Ninja Turtles. fifth printing 3.00
❑2, ca. 1984; 1st printing-Beware of counterfeits 28.00
❑2/Counterfeit; Counterfeit: Uses glossy cover stock 1.50
❑2/2nd 1984 6.00
❑2/3rd 1986 3.00
❑2/4th 4.00
❑3 1985; first printing; correct 15.00
❑3/Misprint, ca. 1985; Giveaway, rare; first printing; misprints; Laird's photo appears in white instead of blue 15.00
❑3/2nd 3.00
❑4, ca. 1985 12.00
❑4/2nd, May 1987 2.00
❑5, ca. 1985 4.00
❑5/2nd 2.00
❑6, ca. 1986 3.00
❑6/2nd 2.00
❑7, ca. 1986; First color Teenage Mutant Ninja Turtles (color insert) 5.00
❑7/2nd; No color story 2.00
❑8, ca. 1986 A: Cerebus. 4.00
❑9, Sep 1986 3.00
❑10, Apr 1987, b&w 3.00
❑11, Jun 1987, b&w 4.00
❑12, Sep 1987 3.00
❑13, Feb 1988 3.00
❑14, May 1988; cover says Feb, indicia says May 3.00
❑15, Sum 1988 3.00
❑16, Sep 1988; cover says Jul, indicia says Sep 2.00
❑17, Jan 1989; cover says Nov, indicia says Jan 2.00
❑18, Feb 1989, b&w 2.00
❑18/2nd 2.00
❑19, Mar 1989; Return to NY 2.00
❑20, Apr 1989; Return to NY 2.00
❑21, May 1989; Return to NY 2.00
❑22, Jun 1989 2.00
❑23, Aug 1989; cover says Jul, indicia says Aug 2.00
❑24, Aug 1989 2.00
❑25, Sep 1989 2.00
❑26, Dec 1989; cover says Oct, indicia says Dec 2.00
❑27, Dec 1989; cover says Nov, indicia says Dec 2.00
❑28, Feb 1990 2.00
❑29, May 1990; cover says Mar, indicia says May 2.00
❑30, Jun 1990; cover says Apr, indicia says Jun 2.00
❑31, Jul 1990 2.00
❑32, Aug 1990 2.00
❑33 1990 2.00
❑34, Sep 1990 2.00
❑35, Mar 1991 2.00
❑36, Aug 1991 2.00
❑37, Jun 1991 2.00

Tellos

Fantasy series plagued by delays

©Image

Terminator (1st Series)

Back to the future for T-1000s, resistance

©Now

Terminator, The: The Burning Earth

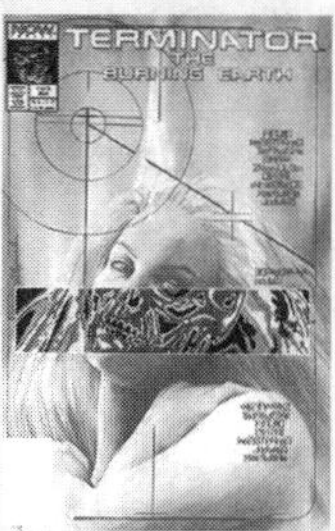

Alex Ross' early work already superb

©Now

Terra Obscura

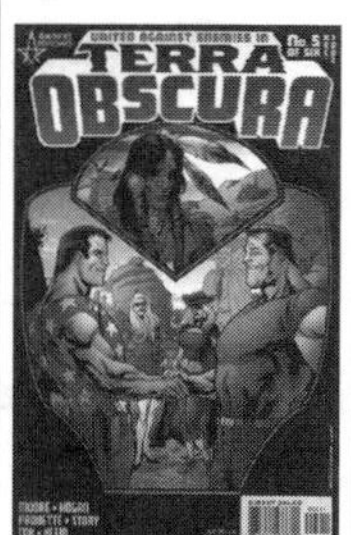

The nadir of Nedor characters form team

©DC

Terror Inc.

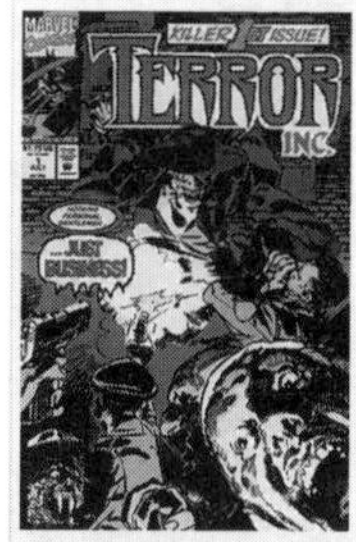

Mercenary acquires abilities with purloined parts

©Marvel

N-MINT

❑38, Jul 1991 .... 2.00
❑39, Sep 1991 .... 2.00
❑40, Oct 1991 .... 2.00
❑41, Nov 1991 .... 2.00
❑42, Dec 1991 .... 2.00
❑43, Jan 1992 .... 2.00
❑44, Feb 1992 .... 2.00
❑45, Mar 1992 .... 2.00
❑46, Apr 1992 .... 2.00
❑47, May 1992 .... 2.00
❑48, Jun 1992 .... 2.00
❑49, Jul 1992 .... 2.00
❑50, Aug 1992, b&w; City At War 2.00
❑51, Sep 1992, b&w 2.00
❑52, Oct 1992, b&w 2.25
❑53, Nov 1992, b&w 2.25
❑54, Dec 1992, b&w 2.25
❑55, Jan 1993, b&w 2.25
❑56, Feb 1993, b&w 2.25
❑57, Mar 1993, b&w 2.25
❑58, Apr 1993, b&w 2.25
❑59, May 1993, b&w 2.25
❑60, Jun 1993, b&w 2.25
❑61, Jul 1993, b&w 2.25
❑62, Aug 1993, b&w 2.25

TEENAGE MUTANT NINJA TURTLES (2ND SERIES)

MIRAGE

❑1, Oct 1993 .... 3.00
❑2, Dec 1993 .... 3.00
❑3, Feb 1994 .... 3.00
❑4, Apr 1994 .... 3.00
❑5, Jun 1994 .... 3.00
❑6, Aug 1994 .... 2.75
❑7, Oct 1994 .... 2.75
❑8, Nov 1994 .... 2.75
❑9, Aug 1995 .... 2.75
❑10, Aug 1995 .... 2.75
❑11, Sep 1995 .... 2.75
❑12, Sep 1995 .... 2.75
❑13, Oct 1995 .... 2.75
❑Special 1, Jan 1993 .... 4.00

TEENAGE MUTANT NINJA TURTLES (3RD SERIES)

IMAGE

❑1, Jun 1996 .... 3.50
❑2, Jul 1996 .... 3.25
❑3, Sep 1996 .... 3.25
❑4, Oct 1996 .... 3.00
❑5, Dec 1996 .... 3.00
❑6, Jan 1997 .... 3.00
❑7, Feb 1997 .... 3.00
❑8, Apr 1997 .... 3.00
❑9, May 1997 A: Knight Watchman. ... 3.00
❑10, Jul 1997 .... 3.00
❑11, Oct 1997 .... 2.95
❑12, Dec 1997 .... 2.95
❑13, Feb 1998 .... 2.95
❑14, Apr 1998 .... 2.95
❑15, May 1998 .... 2.95
❑16, Jul 1998 .... 2.95
❑17, Sep 1998 .... 2.95
❑18, Oct 1998 .... 2.95
❑19, Jan 1999 .... 2.95
❑20, Mar 1999 .... 2.95
❑21, May 1999 .... 2.95
❑22, Jul 1999 .... 2.95
❑23, Oct 1999 .... 2.95

TEENAGE MUTANT NINJA TURTLES ADVENTURES (1ST SERIES)

ARCHIE

❑1, Aug 1988 .... 3.00
❑2, Oct 1988 .... 2.50
❑3, Dec 1988 .... 2.50

TEENAGE MUTANT NINJA TURTLES ADVENTURES (2ND SERIES)

ARCHIE

❑1, Mar 1989 .... 3.00
❑2, May 1989 .... 2.50
❑3, Jul 1989 .... 2.50
❑4, Sep 1989 .... 2.00
❑5, Oct 1989 .... 2.00
❑6, Nov 1989 .... 2.00
❑7, Dec 1989 .... 2.00
❑8, Feb 1990 .... 2.00
❑9, Mar 1990 .... 2.00
❑10, May 1990 .... 2.00
❑11, Jun 1990 .... 1.50
❑12, Jul 1990 .... 1.50
❑13, Oct 1990 .... 1.50
❑14, Nov 1990 .... 1.50
❑15, Dec 1990 .... 1.50
❑16, Jan 1991 .... 1.50
❑17, Feb 1991 .... 1.50
❑18, Mar 1991 .... 1.50
❑19, Apr 1991, 1: Mighty Mutanimals. 1.50
❑20, May 1991 .... 1.50
❑21, Jun 1991 .... 1.50
❑22, Jul 1991 .... 1.50
❑23, Aug 1991 .... 1.50
❑24, Sep 1991 .... 1.50
❑25, Oct 1991 .... 1.50
❑26, Nov 1991 .... 1.50
❑27, Dec 1991 .... 1.50
❑28, Jan 1992 .... 1.50
❑29, Feb 1992 .... 1.50
❑30, Mar 1992 .... 1.50
❑31, Apr 1992 .... 1.50
❑32, May 1992 .... 1.50
❑33, Jun 1992 .... 1.50
❑34, Aug 1992 .... 1.50
❑35, Jul 1992 .... 1.50
❑36, Sep 1992 .... 1.50
❑37, Oct 1992 .... 1.50
❑38, Nov 1992 .... 1.50
❑39, Dec 1992 .... 1.50
❑40, Jan 1993 .... 1.50
❑41, Feb 1993 .... 1.50
❑42, Mar 1993 .... 1.50
❑43, Apr 1993 .... 1.50
❑44, May 1993 .... 1.50
❑45, Jun 1993 .... 1.50
❑46, Jul 1993 .... 1.50
❑47, Aug 1993 .... 1.50
❑48, Sep 1993 .... 1.50
❑49, Oct 1993 .... 1.50
❑50, Nov 1993 .... 1.50
❑51, Dec 1993 .... 1.50
❑52, Jan 1994 .... 1.50
❑53, Feb 1994 .... 1.50
❑54, Mar 1994 .... 1.50
❑55, Apr 1994 .... 1.50
❑56, May 1994 .... 1.50
❑57, Jun 1994 .... 1.50
❑58, Jul 1994 .... 1.50
❑59, Aug 1994 .... 1.50
❑60, Sep 1994 .... 1.50
❑61, Oct 1994 .... 1.50
❑62, Nov 1994 .... 1.50
❑63, Dec 1994 .... 1.50
❑64, Jan 1995 .... 1.50
❑65, Feb 1995 .... 1.50
❑66, Mar 1995 .... 1.50
❑67, Apr 1995 .... 1.50
❑68, May 1995 .... 1.50
❑69, Jun 1995 .... 1.50
❑70, Jul 1995 .... 1.50
❑71, Sep 1995 .... 1.50
❑72, Oct 1995 .... 1.50
❑Special 1, Sum 1992, Teenage Mutant Ninja Turtles Meet Archie 2.50
❑Special 2, Fal 1992 .... 2.50
❑Special 3, Win 1992 .... 2.50
❑Special 4, Spr 1993 .... 2.50
❑Special 5, Sum 1993 .... 2.50
❑Special 6, Fal 1993, Giant-Size Special #6 .... 2.00
❑Special 7, Win 1993 .... 2.00
❑Special 8, Spr 1994 .... 2.00
❑Special 9, Sum 1994 .... 2.00
❑Special 10, Fal 1994 .... 2.00
❑Special 11 .... 2.00

TEENAGE MUTANT NINJA TURTLES ADVENTURES (3RD SERIES)

ARCHIE

❑1, Jan 1996 .... 1.50
❑2, Feb 1996 .... 1.50
❑3, Mar 1996 .... 1.50

TEENAGE MUTANT NINJA TURTLES ANIMATED

DREAMWAVE

❑1, Jun 2003 .... 2.95
❑2, Jul 2003 .... 2.95
❑3, Aug 2003 .... 2.95
❑4, Sep 2003 .... 2.95
❑5, Oct 2003 .... 2.95
❑6, Nov 2003 .... 2.95
❑7, Dec 2003 .... 2.95

TEENAGE MUTANT NINJA TURTLES AUTHORIZED MARTIAL ARTS TRAINING MANUAL

SOLSON

❑1 1986 RB (w); RB (a) 2.50
❑2 1986 .... 2.50
❑3 1986 .... 2.50
❑4 .... 2.50

TEENAGE MUTANT NINJA TURTLES CLASSICS DIGEST

ARCHIE

❑1, ca. 1993 .... 2.00
❑2, ca. 1993 .... 1.75

❑3, ca. 1994 .... 1.75
❑4, ca. 1994 .... 1.75
❑5, ca. 1994 .... 1.75
❑6, ca. 1994 .... 1.75
❑7, Dec 1994; digest 1.75
❑8 .... 1.75

TEENAGE MUTANT NINJA TURTLES/ FLAMING CARROT CROSSOVER
Mirage

❑1, Nov 1993 .... 3.00
❑2, Dec 1993 .... 3.00
❑3, Jan 1994 .... 3.00
❑4, Feb 1994 .... 3.00

TEENAGE MUTANT NINJA TURTLES III THE MOVIE: THE TURTLES ARE BACK...IN TIME
Archie

❑1; newsstand 2.50
❑1/Prestige; Prestige edition 4.95

TEENAGE MUTANT NINJA TURTLES II: THE SECRET OF THE OOZE
Mirage

❑1 .... 5.95

TEENAGE MUTANT NINJA TURTLES MEET THE CONSERVATION CORPS
Archie

❑1 .... 2.50

TEENAGE MUTANT NINJA TURTLES MICHAELANGELO CHRISTMAS SPECIAL
Mirage

❑1 .... 1.75

TEENAGE MUTANT NINJA TURTLES MOVIE II
Archie

❑1, Jun 1991 .... 2.50

TEENAGE MUTANT NINJA TURTLES MUTANT UNIVERSE SOURCEBOOK
Archie

❑1 .... 2.00
❑2 .... 2.00
❑3 .... 2.00

TEENAGE MUTANT NINJA TURTLES PRESENT: APRIL O'NEIL
Archie

❑1, Apr 1993, Title for this issue only is Teenage Mutant Ninja Turtles Present (no 's') 1.25
❑2, May 1993 .... 1.25
❑3, Jun 1993 .... 1.25

TEENAGE MUTANT NINJA TURTLES PRESENTS: DONATELLO AND LEATHERHEAD
Archie

❑1, Jul 1993 .... 1.25
❑2, Aug 1993 .... 1.25
❑3, Sep 1993 .... 1.25

TEENAGE MUTANT NINJA TURTLES PRESENTS MERDUDE AND MICHAELANGELO
Archie

❑1, Oct 1993 .... 1.25
❑2, Nov 1993 .... 1.25
❑3, Dec 1993 .... 1.25

TEENAGE MUTANT NINJA TURTLES-SAVAGE DRAGON CROSSOVER
Mirage

❑1, Aug 1995 .... 3.00

TEENAGE MUTANT NINJA TURTLES: THE MOVIE (ARCHIE)
Archie

❑1, Sum 1990; newsstand 2.50
❑1/Direct ed., Sum 1990; prestige format 4.95
❑1/Prestige; Prestige edition 5.95

TEENAGE MUTANT NINJA TURTLES: THE MOVIE (MIRAGE)
Mirage

❑1, b&w 5.95

TEENAGENTS (JACK KIRBY'S...)
Topps

❑1, Aug 1993, three trading cards 2.95
❑2, Sep 1993, trading cards 2.95
❑3, Oct 1993, trading cards 2.95
❑4, Nov 1993, cards; Zorro preview 2.95

TEEN-AGE ROMANCE (ATLAS)
Atlas

❑77, Sep 1960 .... 15.00
❑78, Nov 1960 .... 15.00
❑79, Jan 1961 .... 15.00
❑80, Mar 1961 .... 15.00
❑81, May 1961 .... 15.00

TEEN-AGE ROMANCE (MARVEL)
Marvel

❑82, Jul 1961 .... 20.00
❑83, Sep 1961 .... 20.00
❑84, Nov 1961 .... 20.00
❑85, Jan 1962 .... 20.00
❑86, Mar 1962 .... 20.00

TEEN COMICS
Personality

❑1, ca. 1992; Beverly Hills 90210; Unauthorized biographies, text & pin-ups 2.50
❑2, ca. 1992 .... 2.50
❑3, ca. 1992; Luke Perry; Unauthorized biography, text & pin-ups 2.50
❑4; Melrose Place; Unauthorized biographies, text & pin-ups 2.50
❑5; Marky Mark; Unauthorized biography, text & pin-ups 2.50
❑6; Madonna; Prince; Unauthorized biographies, text & pin-ups 2.50

TEEN CONFESSIONS
Charlton

❑1, ca. 1959 .... 75.00
❑2 1959 .... 40.00
❑3, Jan 1960 .... 30.00
❑4, Mar 1960 .... 30.00
❑5, May 1960 .... 30.00
❑6, Jul 1960 .... 30.00
❑7, Sep 1960 .... 30.00
❑8, Nov 1960 .... 30.00
❑9, Jan 1961 .... 30.00
❑10, Mar 1961 .... 30.00
❑11, May 1961 .... 25.00
❑12, Jul 1961 .... 25.00
❑13, Sep 1961 .... 25.00
❑14, Nov 1961 .... 25.00
❑15, Jan 1962 .... 25.00
❑16, Mar 1962 .... 25.00
❑17, May 1962 .... 25.00
❑18, Jul 1962 .... 25.00
❑19, Sep 1962 .... 25.00
❑20, Nov 1962 .... 25.00
❑21, Feb 1963 .... 25.00
❑22, Apr 1963 .... 25.00
❑23, Jun 1963 .... 25.00
❑24, Aug 1963 .... 25.00
❑25, Oct 1963 .... 25.00
❑26, Dec 1963 .... 25.00
❑27, ca. 1964 .... 25.00
❑28, May 1964 .... 25.00
❑29, Jul 1964 .... 25.00
❑30, ca. 1964 .... 25.00
❑31, ca. 1965 .... 125.00
❑32, ca. 1965 .... 20.00
❑33, May 1965 .... 20.00
❑34, Jul 1965 .... 20.00
❑35, Sep 1965 .... 20.00
❑36, Nov 1965 .... 20.00
❑37, Jan 1966 .... 20.00
❑38, May 1966 .... 20.00
❑39, Jul 1966 .... 20.00
❑40, ca. 1966 .... 20.00
❑41, Nov 1966 .... 20.00
❑42, Jan 1967 .... 20.00
❑43, Mar 1967 .... 20.00
❑44, May 1967 .... 20.00
❑45, Jul 1967 .... 20.00
❑46, Sep 1967 .... 20.00
❑47, Nov 1967 .... 20.00
❑48, Jan 1968 .... 20.00
❑49, Mar 1968 .... 20.00
❑50, Jul 1968 .... 20.00
❑51, Sep 1968 .... 15.00
❑52, Nov 1968 .... 15.00
❑53, Jan 1968 .... 15.00
❑54, Mar 1969 .... 15.00
❑55, ca. 1969 .... 15.00
❑56, ca. 1969 .... 15.00
❑57, Aug 1969 .... 15.00
❑58, Nov 1969 .... 15.00
❑59, ca. 1970 .... 20.00
❑60, Feb 1970 .... 12.00
❑61, Apr 1970 .... 12.00
❑62, Jun 1970 .... 12.00
❑63, Aug 1970 .... 12.00
❑64, Oct 1970 .... 12.00
❑65, Dec 1970 .... 12.00
❑66, Feb 1971 .... 12.00
❑67, Apr 1971 .... 12.00
❑68, Jun 1971 .... 12.00
❑69, Aug 1971 .... 12.00
❑70, Oct 1971 .... 12.00
❑71, Dec 1971, David Cassidy pin-up. 12.00
❑72, Feb 1972 .... 12.00
❑73, Apr 1972, Shirley Jones pin-up .. 12.00
❑74, Jun 1972, Bobby Sherman pin-up 12.00
❑75, Aug 1972 .... 12.00
❑76, Oct 1972 .... 12.00
❑77, Dec 1972 .... 12.00
❑78, Feb 1973, Susan Dey pin-up 12.00
❑79, Apr 1973 .... 12.00
❑80, Jun 1973 .... 12.00
❑81, Jul 1973 .... 12.00
❑82, Sep 1973 .... 12.00
❑83, Nov 1973 .... 12.00
❑84, Jan 1974 .... 12.00
❑85, Sep 1974 .... 12.00
❑86, ca. 1974 .... 12.00
❑87, Feb 1975 .... 12.00
❑88, Apr 1975 .... 12.00
❑89, Jun 1975 .... 12.00
❑90, Aug 1975 .... 12.00
❑91, Oct 1975 .... 12.00
❑92, Dec 1975 .... 12.00
❑93, Feb 1976 .... 12.00
❑94, Apr 1976 .... 12.00
❑95, Jun 1976 .... 12.00
❑96, Aug 1976 .... 12.00
❑97, Oct 1976 .... 12.00

TEENS AT PLAY
Fantagraphics

❑1 2005 ....

TEEN TALES: THE LIBRARY COMIC
David G. Brown

❑1, Oct 1997; promotional comic book done for the L.A. Public Library 1.00

TEEN TITANS'
DC

❑1, Feb 1966, NC (c); NC (a); Peace Corps 260.00
❑2, Apr 1966 NC (c); NC (a) 100.00
❑3, Jun 1966 NC (c); NC (a) 40.00
❑4, Aug 1966 NC (c); NC (a) 40.00
❑5, Oct 1966 NC (c); NC (a) 40.00
❑6, Dec 1966 NC (c); 32.00
❑7, Feb 1967 NC (c); NC (a) 32.00
❑8, Apr 1967 NC (c); IN, JAb (a) 32.00
❑9, Jun 1967 NC (c); NC, IN (a) 32.00
❑10, Aug 1967 NC (c); NC, IN (a) 32.00
❑11, Oct 1967 NC (c); NC, IN (a) 28.00
❑12, Dec 1967 NC (c); NC, IN (a) 28.00
❑13, Feb 1968 NC (c); NC (a) 28.00
❑14, Apr 1968 NC (c); NC (a) 28.00
❑15, Jun 1968 NC (c); NC (a) 28.00
❑16, Aug 1968 NC (c); NC (a) 28.00
❑17, Oct 1968 NC (c); NC (a) 28.00
❑18, Dec 1968 NC (c); 1: Starfire. 33.00
❑19, Feb 1969 NC (c); GK, WW (a) 33.00
❑20, Apr 1969 NC (c); NA (w); NA, NC (a) 33.00
❑21, Jun 1969 NC (c); NA (w); NA, NC (a) 33.00
❑22, Aug 1969 NC (c); NA (w); NA, GK, NC (a); O: Wonder Girl. 33.00
❑23, Oct 1969 NC (c); GK, NC (a) 18.00
❑24, Dec 1969 NC (c); GK, NC (a) 18.00
❑25, Jan 1970 NC (c); DG (w); NC (a); 1: Lilith. 18.00
❑26, Mar 1970 NC (c); DG (w); NC (a) 12.00
❑27, May 1970, NC (c); DG (w); CI, GT, NC (a); in space 12.00
❑28, Jul 1970 NC (c); DG (w); NC (a). 12.00

THB

Paul Pope's perplexing pieces in large format
©Horse

Thing: Freakshow

Solo stories reveal rocky road
©Marvel

Thing from Another World

John Carpenter remake of classic 50s horror film
©Dark Horse

Thing

From Two-in-One team-ups to solo adventures
©Marvel

30 Days of Night

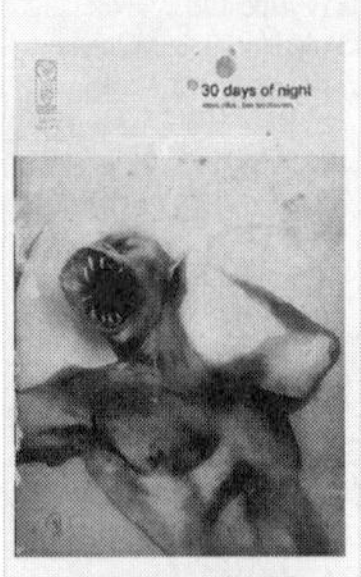

A vampire's paradise above the Arctic Circle
©Idea & Design Works

N-MINT

❑29, Sep 1970 NC (c); DG (w); NC (a); A: Hawk & Dove. 12.00
❑30, Nov 1970 NC (c); DG (w); CI, NC (a); A: Aquagirl 12.00
❑31, Jan 1971 NC (c); DG (w); GT, NC (a) 20.00
❑32, Mar 1971 NC (c); DG (w); NC (a) 18.00
❑33, May 1971, NC (c); DG (w); GT, NC (a); Robin returns 18.00
❑34, Jul 1971 NC (c); GT, NC (a) 18.00
❑35, Sep 1971, Giant-size NC (c); GT, NC (a); 1: Think Freak. 18.00
❑36, Nov 1971, Giant-size NC (c); GT, NC, JA (a) 18.00
❑37, Jan 1972, Giant-size NC (c); GT, NC (a) 18.00
❑38, Mar 1972, Giant-size NC (c); GT, NC (a) 18.00
❑39, May 1972, Giant-size NC (c); GT, GK, NC (a) 12.00
❑40, Jul 1972 NC (c); NC (a); 1: Black Moray. A: Aqualad. 12.00
❑41, Sep 1972 NC (c); DC, NC (a) 12.00
❑42, Nov 1972 NC (c); NC (a) 12.00
❑43, Jan 1973, NC (c); NC (a); series goes on hiatus 12.00
❑44, Nov 1976, 1: Guardian. V: Doctor Light. Series begins again (1976); New team: Kid Flash, Wonder Girl, Robin, Speedy, Mal 7.00
❑45, Dec 1976 IN (a) 7.00
❑46, Feb 1977 RB (c); IN (a); V: Fiddler. 7.00
❑47, Apr 1977 1: Darklight I. 1: Flamesplasher I. 1: Sizematic I. 1: Darklight II. 1: Flamesplasher II. 1: Sizematic II. 7.00
❑48, Jun 1977 RB, JAb (c); 1: Harlequin. 1: The Bumblebee. 12.00
❑49, Aug 1977 RB, JAb (c); 1: Bryan the Brain. 7.00
❑50, Oct 1977, RB, JAb (c); DH (a); Bat-Girl returns 20.00
❑51, Nov 1977 RB (c); DH (a); A: Titans West. 6.00
❑52, Dec 1977 RB, JAb (c); DH (a); A: Titans West. 6.00
❑53, Feb 1978 RB, JAb (c); O: Teen Titans. 1: The Antithesis. 6.00

TEEN TITANS (2ND SERIES)
DC

❑1, Oct 1996 GP (a); O: New team of four teen-agers led by Atom. 4.00
❑2, Nov 1996 GP (a) 3.00
❑3, Dec 1996; GP (a); A: Mr. Jupiter. A: Mad Mod. V: Jugular. team gets new costumes 3.00
❑4, Jan 1997 A: Captain Marvel Jr.. A: Nightwing. A: Robin. 2.50
❑5, Feb 1997 GP (a); A: Captain Marvel Jr.. A: Supergirl. A: Nightwing. A: Robin. 2.50
❑6, Mar 1997 GP (a) 2.50
❑7, Apr 1997 GP (a) 2.50
❑8, May 1997 ..... 2.50
❑9, Jun 1997 GP (a); A: Warlord. 2.50
❑10, Jul 1997; A: Warlord. in Skartaris 2.50
❑11, Aug 1997 GP (a); A: Warlord. 2.00
❑12, Sep 1997; GP, DG, GK (a); flashback with original Titans 2.95

N-MINT

❑13, Oct 1997; flashback with original Titans 2.00
❑14, Nov 1997; GP (a); identity of Omen revealed 2.00
❑15, Jan 1998; GP (a); D: Joto. real identity of Omen revealed 2.00
❑16, Feb 1998 ..... 2.00
❑17, Mar 1998; new members join 2.00
❑18, Apr 1998 ..... 2.00
❑19, Apr 1998; A: Superman. Millennium Giants 2.00
❑20, May 1998 ..... 2.00
❑21, Jun 1998 ..... 2.00
❑22, Jul 1998 A: Changeling. 2.00
❑23, Aug 1998 A: Superman. 1.95
❑24, Sep 1998 ..... 1.95
❑Annual 1, ca. 1997; Pulp Heroes 3.95
❑Annual 1999, ca. 1999; published in 1999 in style of '60s Annual; cardstock cover 4.95

TEEN TITANS (3RD SERIES)
DC

❑½, Aug 2004, Wizard 1/2 redemption premium 16.00
❑1, Oct 2003 ..... 12.00
❑1/2nd, Oct 2003 ..... 5.00
❑1/3rd, Oct 2003 ..... 4.00
❑1/4th, Oct 2003; sketch cover 8.00
❑2, Nov 2003 ..... 2.50
❑3, Dec 2003 ..... 2.50
❑4, Jan 2004 ..... 2.50
❑5, Feb 2004 ..... 2.50
❑6, Mar 2004 ..... 2.50
❑7, Apr 2004 ..... 2.50
❑8, May 2004 ..... 2.50
❑9, May 2004 ..... 2.50
❑10, Jun 2004 ..... 2.50
❑11, Jul 2004 ..... 2.50
❑12, Aug 2004 ..... 2.50
❑13, Sep 2004 ..... 2.50
❑14, Oct 2004 ..... 2.50
❑15, Nov 2004 ..... 2.50
❑16, Dec 2004 ..... 5.00
❑17, Jan 2005 ..... 4.00
❑18, Feb 2005 ..... 2.50
❑19, Mar 2005 ..... 2.50
❑20, Apr 2005 ..... 4.00
❑21, May 2005 ..... 2.50
❑22, Jun 2005 ..... 2.50
❑23, Jun 2005 ..... 2.50
❑24, Jul 2005 ..... 2.50
❑25, Aug 2005 ..... 2.50
❑26, Sep 2005 ..... 2.50
❑27, Oct 2005 ..... 2.50
❑28, Nov 2005 ..... 2.50
❑29, Jan 2006 ..... 2.50
❑30, Feb 2006 ..... 2.50
❑31, Mar 2006 ..... 2.50
❑32, Apr 2006 ..... 2.50
❑33, May 2006 ..... 2.50
❑34, Jun 2006 ..... 2.50
❑35, Jul 2006 ..... 2.50
❑36, Aug 2006 ..... 2.50
❑Annual 1, May 2006 ..... 2.50

N-MINT

TEEN TITANS GO!
DC

❑1, Jan 2004 ..... 2.25
❑2, Feb 2004 ..... 2.25
❑3, Mar 2004 ..... 2.25
❑4, Apr 2004 ..... 2.25
❑5, May 2004 ..... 2.25
❑6, Jun 2004 ..... 2.25
❑7, Jul 2004 ..... 2.25
❑8, Aug 2004 ..... 2.25
❑9, Sep 2004 ..... 2.25
❑10, Oct 2004 ..... 2.25
❑11, Nov 2004 ..... 2.25
❑12, Dec 2004 ..... 2.25
❑13, Jan 2005 ..... 2.95
❑14, Feb 2005 ..... 2.95
❑15, Mar 2005 ..... 2.25
❑16, Apr 2005 ..... 2.25
❑17, May 2005 ..... 2.25
❑18, Jun 2005 ..... 2.25
❑19, Jul 2005 ..... 2.25
❑20, Aug 2005 ..... 2.25
❑21, Sep 2005 ..... 2.25
❑22, Oct 2005 ..... 2.25
❑23, Nov 2005 ..... 2.25
❑24, Dec 2005 ..... 2.25
❑25, Jan 2006 ..... 2.25
❑26, Feb 2006 ..... 2.25
❑27, Mar 2006 ..... 2.25
❑28, May 2006 ..... 2.25
❑30, Jul 2006 ..... 2.25
❑31, Aug 2006 ..... 2.25
❑32, Sep 2006 ..... 2.25

TEEN TITANS/LEGION SPECIAL
DC

❑1 2004 ..... 4.00

TEEN TITANS/OUTSIDERS SECRET FILES
DC

❑1, Dec 2003 ..... 5.95

TEEN TITANS/OUTSIDERS SECRET FILES 2005
DC

❑1 2005 ..... 5.99

TEEN TITANS SPOTLIGHT
DC

❑1, Aug 1986; Starfire 1.25
❑2, Sep 1986; Starfire 1.25
❑3, Oct 1986; RA (a); Jericho 1.25
❑4, Nov 1986; RA (a); Jericho 1.25
❑5, Dec 1986; RA (a); Jericho 1.25
❑6, Jan 1987; RA (a); Jericho 1.00
❑7, Feb 1987 BG (a) 1.00
❑8, Mar 1987; BG (a); Hawk 1.00
❑9, Apr 1987; A: Robotman. Changeling 1.00
❑10, May 1987; EL (a); Aqualad 1.00
❑11, Jun 1987; JO (a); Brotherhood of Evil 1.00
❑12, Jul 1987; Wonder Girl 1.00
❑13, Aug 1987 A: Two-Face. 1.00
❑14, Sep 1987; Nightwing, Batman 1.00
❑15, Oct 1987; EL (a); A: Komand'r. A: Ryand'r. Omega Men 1.00

Other grades: Multiply price above by 5/6 for VF/NM • 2/3 for VERY FINE • 1/3 for FINE • 1/5 for VERY GOOD • 1/8 for GOOD

N-MINT

❑16, Nov 1987 .... 1.00
❑17, Dec 1987 DH (a) 1.00
❑18, Jan 1988; Millennium; Aqualad .. 1.00
❑19, Feb 1988; Millennium; Starfire ... 1.00
❑20, Mar 1988; Cyborg; Changeling ... 1.00
❑21, Apr 1988; DS (a); original Titans 1.00

TEKKEN FOREVER
IMAGE

❑1/A, Dec 2001 .... 2.95
❑1/B 2.95

TEK KNIGHTS
ARTLINE

❑1, b&w 2.95

TEKNO*COMIX HANDBOOK
TEKNO

❑1, May 1996, information on various Tekno characters 3.95

TEKNOPHAGE (NEIL GAIMAN'S...)
TEKNO

❑1, Aug 1995 .... 1.95
❑1/Variant, Jul 1995, Steel Edition; enhanced cover 3.00
❑2, Sep 1995 .... 1.95
❑3, Oct 1995 BT (a) 1.95
❑4, Nov 1995 .... 1.95
❑5, Dec 1995 .... 1.95
❑6, Dec 1995 .... 1.95
❑7, Jan 1996 .... 2.25
❑8, Feb 1996 .... 2.25
❑9, Feb 1996 .... 2.25
❑10, Mar 1996 .... 2.25

TEKNOPHAGE VERSUS ZEERUS
BIG

❑1, Jul 1996 .... 3.25

TEKQ
GAUNTLET

❑1, b&w 2.95
❑2, b&w 2.95
❑3, b&w 2.95
❑4, b&w 2.95

TEKWORLD
MARVEL / EPIC

❑1, Sep 1992 .... 2.50
❑2, Oct 1992 .... 2.00
❑3, Nov 1992 .... 2.00
❑4, Dec 1992 .... 2.00
❑5, Jan 1993 .... 2.00
❑6, Feb 1993 .... 2.00
❑7, Mar 1993 .... 2.00
❑8, Apr 1993 .... 2.00
❑9, May 1993 .... 2.00
❑10, Jun 1993 .... 2.00
❑11, Jul 1993 .... 1.75
❑12, Aug 1993 .... 1.75
❑13, Sep 1993 .... 1.75
❑14, Oct 1993; A: Jake Cardigan. Begins adaptation of TekLords 1.75
❑15, Nov 1993 .... 1.75
❑16, Dec 1993 .... 1.75
❑17, Jan 1994 .... 1.75
❑18, Feb 1994 .... 1.75
❑19, Mar 1994 .... 1.75
❑20, Apr 1994 .... 1.75
❑21, May 1994 .... 1.75
❑22, Jun 1994 .... 1.75
❑23, Jul 1994 .... 1.75
❑24, Aug 1994; Partial photo cover 1.75

TELEPATHIC WANDERERS
TOKYOPOP

❑1, Nov 2005 .... 9.99

TELLOS
IMAGE

❑1, May 1999 .... 2.50
❑2, Jun 1999 .... 2.50
❑3, Jul 1999 .... 2.50
❑4, Oct 1999 .... 2.50
❑4/A, Oct 1999; alternate cover w/moon in background 2.50
❑4/B, Oct 1999; alternate cover w/skeletons in bottom left 4.00
❑5, Dec 1999 .... 2.50
❑6, Feb 2000 .... 2.50
❑7, Apr 2000 .... 2.50
❑8, Aug 2000 .... 2.50
❑9, Sep 2000 .... 2.50

N-MINT

❑10, Nov 2000 .... 2.50
❑Ashcan 1; Dynamic Forces preview .. 2.00

TELLOS: MAIDEN VOYAGE
IMAGE

❑1, Mar 2001, Man atop demons on cover 5.95

TELLOS: SONS & MOONS
IMAGE

❑1, Dec 2002, Man atop demons on cover 5.95

TELLOS: THE LAST HEIST
IMAGE

❑1, Jun 2001, Man atop demons on cover 5.95

TELL TALE HEART AND OTHER STORIES
FANTAGRAPHICS

❑1, b&w 2.50

TELLURIA
ZUB

❑1 .... 2.50
❑2 .... 2.50
❑3 .... 2.50

TEMPEST
DC

❑1, Nov 1996, Tula returns 1.75
❑2, Dec 1996 .... 1.75
❑3, Jan 1997, Aqualad's true origin revealed 1.75
❑4, Feb 1997 .... 1.75

TEMPLATE
HEAD

❑0; flip-book with Max Damage #0 .... 2.95
❑1, Dec 1995, b&w 2.50
❑2, Feb 1996, b&w 2.50
❑3, Apr 1996, b&w 2.50
❑4, Jun 1996, b&w 2.50
❑5, Aug 1996, b&w 2.50
❑6, Nov 1996, b&w 2.50
❑7, Jul 1997, b&w 2.50
❑Special 1, Feb 1997, b&w 2.95
❑Spec 1/Ashcan, Feb 1997; Ashcan preview of special #1 .... 1.00
❑Special 1/Varia, Feb 1997; alternate cover 2.95

TEMPLE SNARE
MU

❑1, b&w 2.25

TEMPTRESS: THE BLOOD OF EVE
CALIBER

❑1 .... 2.95

TEMPUS FUGITIVE
DC

❑1, ca. 1990 .... 4.95
❑2, ca. 1990 .... 4.95
❑3, ca. 1990 .... 4.95
❑4, ca. 1990 .... 4.95

TENCHI MUYO!
PIONEER

❑1, Mar 1997 .... 2.95
❑2, Mar 1997 .... 2.95
❑3, May 1997 .... 2.95
❑4, Jul 1997 .... 2.95
❑5, Aug 1997 .... 2.95
❑6 .... 2.95

TENDER LOVE STORIES
SKYWALD

❑1, Feb 1971 .... 15.00
❑2, Apr 1971 .... 10.00
❑3 .... 10.00
❑4 .... 10.00

TENTH
IMAGE

❑0, Aug 1997; American Entertainment exclusive 3.00
❑½, Aug 1997; Wizard promotional edition with certificate of authenticity 5.00
❑1, Jan 1997; cover says Mar, indicia says Jan 3.00
❑1/A, Jan 1997; American Entertainment exclusive cover 4.00
❑2, Feb 1997; cover says Apr, indicia says Feb 2.50
❑3, May 1997 .... 2.50
❑4, Jun 1997 .... 2.50

N-MINT

TENTH (2ND SERIES)
IMAGE

❑0, Aug 1997 O: The Tenth 3.00
❑0/A, Aug 1997 O: The Tenth 8.00
❑0/American Ent, Aug 1997; O: The Tenth. American Entertainment exclusive 4.00
❑1, Sep 1997 .... 3.00
❑1/American Ent, Sep 1997; American Entertainment exclusive cover (logo at bottom right) 4.00
❑2, Oct 1997 .... 3.00
❑3, Nov 1997 .... 2.50
❑3/A, Nov 1997; Alternate "Adrenalyn" cover 3.00
❑3/B, Nov 1997; Wizard "Certified Authentic" limited edition 8.00
❑4, Dec 1997 .... 2.50
❑5, Jan 1998 .... 2.50
❑6, Feb 1998 .... 2.50
❑7, Mar 1998 .... 2.50
❑8, Apr 1998 .... 2.50
❑9, Jun 1998 .... 2.50
❑10, Jul 1998 .... 2.50
❑10/A, Jul 1998; alternate cover (logo on right) 2.50
❑11, Aug 1998 .... 2.50
❑11/A, Aug 1998; alternate cover (white background) 2.50
❑12, Oct 1998 .... 2.50
❑13, Nov 1998 .... 2.50
❑14, Jan 1999 .... 2.50
❑14/A, Jan 1999; alternate cover (solo face) 2.50

TENTH (3RD SERIES)
IMAGE

❑1, Feb 1999 .... 2.95
❑1/A, Feb 1999; alternate cover 2.95
❑1/B, Feb 1999; DFE chromium edition; alternate cover 10.00
❑2, Apr 1999 .... 2.50
❑3, May 1999 .... 2.50
❑4, Jun 1999 .... 2.50

TENTH (4TH SERIES)
IMAGE

❑1, Sep 1999 .... 2.50
❑1/A, Sep 1999, Girl wearing shirt and panties on cover 6.00
❑1/B, Sep 1999, Another Universe exclusive cover 3.00
❑2, Oct 1999 .... 2.50
❑3, Nov 1999 .... 2.50
❑4, Dec 1999 .... 2.50

TENTH CONFIGURATION
IMAGE

❑1, Aug 1998 .... 2.50

10TH MUSE
IMAGE

❑1, Nov 2000 .... 2.95
❑2/A, Jan 2001, Character leaping from right on cover 2.95
❑2/B, Jan 2001, Character leaping from left on cover 2.95
❑2/C, Jan 2001 .... 2.95
❑3/A, Mar 2001, Drawn cover with woman summoning lightning 2.95
❑3/B, Mar 2001, Cover with green border 2.95
❑3/C, Mar 2001, Drawn cover with woman leaping forward 2.95
❑3/D, Mar 2001, Wraparound Tower Records cover with red border 2.95
❑4, Mar 2001 .... 2.95
❑4/A, Mar 2001, Drawn cover 2.95
❑4/B, Mar 2001 .... 2.95
❑5, Jul 2001 .... 2.95
❑6, Sep 2001 .... 2.95
❑7, Oct 2001 .... 2.95
❑8/A, Nov 2001, Drawn cover 2.95
❑8/B, Nov 2001 .... 2.95
❑9/A, Dec 2001, Drawn cover 2.95
❑9/B, Dec 2001 .... 2.95

10TH MUSE (VOL. 2)
ALIAS

❑1, Feb 2005 .... 4.00
❑1/B cover, Feb 2005 .... 5.00
❑1/C cover, Feb 2005 .... 4.00
❑1/D cover, Feb 2005 .... 5.00

Other grades: Multiply price above by 5/6 for VF/NM • 2/3 for VERY FINE • 1/3 for FINE • 1/5 for VERY GOOD • 1/8 for GOOD

Thor	Thor (Vol. 2)	Thor Corps	Thor: Son of Asgard	Thor: Vikings

Thunder God journies to Marvel universe ©Marvel	He used to be Mighty, but now he's just Thor ©Marvel	Three different Thors team up ©Marvel	Teen-age version of the thunder god ©Marvel	Garth Ennis' adult version of Thor ©Marvel

	N-MINT
❑1/Photo foil, Feb 2005	6.00
❑2 2005	2.99
❑2/B cover 2005	4.00
❑2/Photo foil 2005	4.99
❑3, Jul 2005	2.99
❑3/B cover, Jul 2005	4.00
❑3/C cover, Jul 2005	2.99
❑4, Sep 2005	4.00
❑5, Nov 2005	2.99
❑5/Special, Nov 2005	2.99
❑6, Dec 2005	2.99
❑8, Jan 2006	2.99

TENTH, THE: RESURRECTED
DARK HORSE

❑1/A, Jul 2001; Lady standing in front of glowing skulls in background on cover	2.99
❑1/B, Jul 2001; Hulking figure on cover	2.99
❑2, Aug 2001	2.99
❑3, Nov 2001	2.99
❑4, Feb 2002	2.99

TEN YEARS OF LOVE & ROCKETS
FANTAGRAPHICS

❑1, Sep 1992, b&w	1.50

TERMINAL CITY
DC / VERTIGO

❑1, Jul 1996	2.50
❑1/Autographed, Jul 1996, Limited to 75 copies	5.00
❑2, Aug 1996	2.50
❑3, Sep 1996	2.50
❑4, Oct 1996	2.50
❑5, Nov 1996	2.50
❑6, Dec 1996	2.50
❑7, Jan 1997	2.50
❑8, Feb 1997	2.50
❑9, Mar 1997	2.50

TERMINAL CITY: AERIAL GRAFFITI
DC / VERTIGO

❑1, Nov 1997	2.50
❑2, Dec 1997	2.50
❑3, Jan 1998	2.50
❑4, Feb 1998	2.50
❑5, Mar 1998	2.50

TERMINAL POINT
DARK HORSE

❑1, Feb 1993, b&w	2.50
❑2, Mar 1993, b&w	2.50
❑3, Apr 1993, b&w	2.50

TERMINATOR, THE (1ST SERIES)
NOW

❑1, Sep 1988; movie tie-in	2.00
❑2, Oct 1988	1.75
❑3, Nov 1988	1.75
❑4, Jan 1989	1.75
❑5, Feb 1989	1.75
❑6, Mar 1989	1.75
❑7, Apr 1989	1.75
❑8, May 1989; Comics Code	1.75
❑9, Jun 1989; Comics Code	1.75
❑10, Jul 1989; PG (c); Comics Code	1.75
❑11, Aug 1989; Comics Code	1.75
❑12, Sep 1989; Comics Code	1.75
❑13, Oct 1989; Comics Code	1.75
❑14, Nov 1989; Comics Code	1.75
❑15, Dec 1989; Comics Code	1.75
❑16, Jan 1990; Comics Code	1.75
❑17, Feb 1990; Comics Code	1.75

TERMINATOR (2ND SERIES)
DARK HORSE

❑1, Aug 1990	3.00
❑2, Sep 1990	3.00
❑3, Oct 1990	3.00
❑4, Nov 1990	3.00

TERMINATOR (3RD SERIES)
DARK HORSE

❑1, ca. 1991; leads into 1998 series	2.95

TERMINATOR (4TH SERIES)
DARK HORSE

❑1, Sep 1998; no month of publication	2.95
❑2, Oct 1998	2.95
❑3, Nov 1998	2.95
❑4, Dec 1998	2.95

TERMINATOR (MAGAZINE)
TRIDENT

❑1	3.00
❑2	3.00
❑3	3.00
❑4	3.00

TERMINATOR 2: JUDGMENT DAY
MARVEL

❑1, Sep 1991, KJ (a)	2.00
❑2, Sep 1991, KJ (a)	2.00
❑3, Oct 1991, KJ (a)	2.00

TERMINATOR 2: JUDGMENT DAY (MAGAZINE)
MARVEL

❑1, Sep 1991, b&w; magazine	3.00

TERMINATOR 3
BECKETT

❑1, Jun 2003	5.95
❑2, Jul 2003	5.95
❑3, Aug 2003	5.95
❑4, Sep 2003	5.95
❑5, Nov 2003	5.95
❑6, Dec 2003	5.95

TERMINATOR, THE: ALL MY FUTURES PAST
NOW

❑1, Aug 1990	2.50
❑2, Sep 1990	2.50

TERMINATOR: ENDGAME
DARK HORSE

❑1, Sep 1992	2.50
❑2, Oct 1992	2.50
❑3, Oct 1992	2.50

TERMINATOR: HUNTERS AND KILLERS
DARK HORSE

❑1, Mar 1992	2.50
❑2, Apr 1992	2.50
❑3, May 1992	2.50

TERMINATOR, THE: ONE SHOT
DARK HORSE

❑1, Jul 1991; prestige format; pop-up	5.95

TERMINATOR: SECONDARY OBJECTIVES
DARK HORSE

❑1, Jul 1991	2.50
❑2, Aug 1991	2.50
❑3, Sep 1991	2.50
❑4, Oct 1991	2.50
❑Book 1	13.95

TERMINATOR, THE: THE BURNING EARTH
NOW

❑1, Mar 1990; ARo (a); 1st comics work by Alex Ross	7.50
❑2, Apr 1990; ARo (a)	5.00
❑3, May 1990; ARo (a)	5.00
❑4, Jun 1990; ARo (a)	6.00
❑5, Jul 1990; ARo (a)	6.00

TERMINATOR, THE: THE DARK YEARS
DARK HORSE

❑1, Sep 1999	2.95
❑2, Oct 1999	2.95
❑3, Nov 1999	2.95
❑4, Dec 1999	2.95

TERMINATOR, THE: THE ENEMY WITHIN
DARK HORSE

❑1, Nov 1991	2.50
❑2, Dec 1991	2.50
❑3, Jan 1992	2.50
❑4, Feb 1992	2.50

TERRAFORMERS
WONDER COLOR

❑1, Apr 1987	1.95
❑2 1987	1.95

TERRANAUTS
FANTASY GENERAL

❑1, ca. 1986	1.75

TERRA OBSCURA
DC / AMERICA'S BEST COMICS

❑1, Aug 2003	2.95
❑2, Sep 2003	2.95
❑3, Oct 2003	2.95
❑4, Dec 2003	2.95
❑5, Jan 2004	2.95
❑6, Feb 2004	3.95

TERRA OBSCURA (VOL. 2)
DC / AMERICA'S BEST COMICS

❑1, Oct 2004	2.95
❑2, Nov 2004	2.95
❑3, Dec 2004	2.95
❑4, Jan 2005	2.95
❑5, Feb 2005	2.95
❑6, Mar 2005	2.95

TERRARISTS
MARVEL / EPIC

❑1, Nov 1993	2.50
❑2, Dec 1993	2.50
❑3, Jan 1994	2.50
❑4, Feb 1994	2.50

TERRITORY
DARK HORSE
❑1, Jan 1999 .... 2.95
❑2, Feb 1999 .... 2.95
❑3, Mar 1999 .... 2.95
❑4, Apr 1999 .... 2.95

TERROR
LEADSLINGER
❑1, b&w 2.50

TERRORESS
HELPLESS ANGER
❑1, Dec 1990, b&w 2.50

TERROR, INC.
MARVEL
❑1, Jul 1992 1: Terror. 2.00
❑2, Aug 1992 1: Hellfire. 1.75
❑3, Sep 1992 .... 1.75
❑4, Oct 1992 .... 1.75
❑5, Nov 1992 .... 1.75
❑6, Dec 1992 A: Punisher. 1.75
❑7, Jan 1993 A: Punisher. 1.75
❑8, Feb 1993 .... 1.75
❑9, Mar 1993 A: Wolverine. 1.75
❑10, Apr 1993 A: Wolverine. 1.75
❑11, May 1993 A: Punisher. A: Silver Sable. 1.75
❑12, Jun 1993 .... 1.75
❑13, Jul 1993 A: Ghost Rider. 1.75

TERROR ON THE PLANET OF THE APES
ADVENTURE
❑1 1991, b&w 2.50
❑2 1991, b&w 2.50
❑3, Aug 1991, b&w; reprints Planet of the Apes (Marvel) #3 .... 2.50
❑4, Dec 1991, b&w; reprints Planet of the Apes (Marvel) #4 .... 2.50

TERROR TALES
ETERNITY
❑1, b&w 2.50

TERRY AND THE PIRATES (AVALON)
AVALON
❑1, b&w; strip reprints 2.95
❑2 .... 2.95

TERRY AND THE PIRATES (FEUCHTWANGER)
SIG. FEUCHTWANGER
❑1 .... 25.00

TESTAMENT
DC / VERTIGO
❑1, Feb 2006 .... 2.99
❑2, Mar 2006 .... 2.99
❑3, Apr 2006 .... 2.99
❑4, Jun 2006 .... 2.99
❑5, Jun 2006 .... 2.99
❑6, Aug 2006 .... 2.99
❑7, Sep 2006 .... 2.99

TEST DIRT
FANTAGRAPHICS
❑1, b&w 2.50

TEST DRIVE
M.A.I.N.
❑1, Flip Book Previews (Side A & B)... 3.00

TEX BENSON (3-D ZONE)
3-D ZONE
❑1, b&w (not 3-D) 2.50
❑2, b&w (not 3-D) 2.50

TEX BENSON (METRO)
METRO
❑1, b&w 2.00
❑2 .... 2.00
❑3 .... 2.00
❑4 .... 2.00

TEYKWA
GEMSTONE
❑1, Oct 1988, b&w 1.75

THACKER'S REVENGE
EXPLORER
❑1, b&w; Archie parody 2.95

THANE OF BAGARTH
AVALON
❑1 .... 2.95

THANOS
MARVEL
❑1, Dec 2003 JSn (c); JSn (w); AM, JSn (a) 4.00
❑2, Jan 2004 JSn (w); AM, JSn (a) 2.99
❑3, Feb 2004 (c); JSn (w); AM, JSn (a) 2.99
❑4, Mar 2004 JSn (w); AM, JSn (a) ... 2.99
❑5, Mar 2004 .... 2.99
❑6, Apr 2004 .... 2.99
❑7, May 2004 AM, JSn (c); KG (w); AM (a) 2.99
❑8, May 2004 KG (c); KG (w); AM (a) 2.99
❑9, Jun 2004 KG, KJ (c); KG (w); AM (a) 2.99
❑10, Jul 2004 KG, KJ (c); KG (w); AM (a) 2.99
❑11, Aug 2004 .... 2.99
❑12, Sep 2004 .... 2.99

THANOS QUEST
MARVEL
❑1, Sep 1990, acetate overlay outer cover 4.95
❑1/2nd, ca. 1991, acetate overlay outer cover 4.95
❑2, Oct 1990, acetate overlay outer cover 4.95
❑2/2nd, ca. 1991 .... 4.95
❑Special 1, ca. 1999; Collects issues #1 and #2 .... 3.99

THAT CHEMICAL REFLEX
CFD
❑1 .... 2.50
❑2 .... 2.50
❑3 .... 2.50

THB
HORSE
❑1, Oct 1994, b&w 12.00
❑1/2nd, b&w; reprints THB #1 with revised and additional material....... 5.50
❑2, ca. 1994, b&w 10.00
❑3, Jan 1995, b&w 8.00
❑4, Feb 1995, b&w 8.00
❑5, Mar 1995, b&w 6.00
❑6 1996 .... 6.00

T.H.E. CAT
GOLD KEY
❑1, Mar 1967 .... 12.00
❑2, Apr 1967 .... 10.00
❑3, Jun 1967 .... 10.00
❑4, Oct 1967 .... 10.00

THECOMICSTORE.COM PRESENTS
THECOMICSTORE.COM
❑1 .... 1.00

THERE'S A MADMAN IN MY MIRROR
BENCH
❑1, Mar 1999; cardstock cover 3.50

THESPIAN
DARK MOON
❑1, Apr 1995 .... 2.50

THEY CALL ME...THE SKUL
VIRTUAL
❑1, May 1996; digest; Only issue published 2.50
❑1/A, Oct 1996; digest 3.99
❑2, Nov 1996 .... 2.50

THEY CAME FROM THE 50S
ETERNITY
❑1, b&w; Reprints 9.95

THEY WERE 11
VIZ
❑1, b&w 2.75
❑2, b&w 2.75
❑3, b&w 2.75
❑4, b&w 2.75

THEY WERE CHOSEN TO BE THE SURVIVORS
SPECTRUM
❑1, Jun 1983 .... 2.00
❑2, Sep 1983 .... 2.00
❑3, Dec 1983 .... 2.00
❑4, Mar 1984 .... 2.00

THIEF
PENGUIN PALACE
❑1, Jul 1995, b&w 2.50

THIEF OF SHERWOOD
A-PLUS
❑1, b&w; Reprints 2.25

THIEVES
SILVERWOLF
❑1, Feb 1986, b&w 1.50

THIEVES & KINGS
I BOX
❑1, Sep 1994 .... 4.00
❑1/2nd 2.50
❑2, Nov 1994 .... 3.00
❑2/2nd 2.50
❑3, Jan 1995 .... 3.00
❑3/2nd 2.35
❑4, Mar 1995 .... 3.00
❑5, May 1995 .... 3.00
❑6, Jul 1995 .... 2.75
❑7, Sep 1995 .... 2.75
❑8, Nov 1995 .... 2.75
❑9, Jan 1996 .... 2.75
❑10, Mar 1996 .... 2.75
❑11, May 1996 .... 2.50
❑12, Jul 1996 .... 2.50
❑13, Sep 1996 .... 2.50
❑14, Nov 1996 .... 2.50
❑15, Jan 1997 .... 2.50
❑16, Mar 1997 .... 2.50
❑17, May 1997 .... 2.50
❑18, ca. 1997 .... 2.50
❑19, ca. 1997 .... 2.50
❑20 .... 2.50
❑21, ca. 1998 .... 2.35
❑22, May 1998 .... 2.35
❑23, Jul 1998 .... 2.35
❑24, Sep 1998 .... 2.35
❑25, Nov 1998 .... 2.50
❑26, Jan 1999 .... 2.50
❑27, Mar 1999 .... 2.50
❑28, Jul 1999 .... 2.50
❑29, Oct 1999 .... 2.50
❑30 .... 2.50
❑31, Mar 2000 .... 2.50
❑32, May 2000 .... 2.50
❑33, Aug 2000 .... 2.50
❑34, Nov 2000 .... 2.50
❑35, Feb 2001 .... 2.50
❑36, Jul 2001 .... 2.50

THING
MARVEL
❑1, Jul 1983 JBy (w); JBy (a); O: The Thing. 6.00
❑2, Aug 1983 JBy (w); JBy (a); O: The Thing. 1.50
❑3, Sep 1983 JBy (w); A: Inhumans... 1.50
❑4, Oct 1983 BA (c); JBy (w); BA (a); A: Inhumans. 1.50
❑5, Nov 1983 JBy (w); A: She-Hulk. A: Spider-Man. 1.50
❑6, Dec 1983, BA (c); JBy (w); BA (a); V: Puppet Master. all-black issue 1.50
❑7, Jan 1984, BA (c); BA (a); Asst. Editor Month 1.50
❑8, Feb 1984 JBy (w) 1.50
❑9, Mar 1984 JBy (w) 1.50
❑10, Apr 1984, JBy (w); Secret Wars. 1.50
❑11, May 1984, JBy (w); Secret Wars aftermath 1.25
❑12, Jun 1984 JBy (w) 1.25
❑13, Jul 1984 JBy (w) 1.25
❑14, Aug 1984 .... 2.00
❑15, Sep 1984 .... 1.25
❑16, Oct 1984 .... 1.25
❑17, Nov 1984 .... 1.25
❑18, Dec 1984 .... 1.25
❑19, Jan 1985 JBy (w) 1.25
❑20, Feb 1985 JBy (w) 1.25
❑21, Mar 1985 JBy (w) 1.25
❑22, Apr 1985, returns to Earth 1.25
❑23, May 1985, quits Fantastic Four .. 1.25
❑24, Jun 1985 D: Miracle Man (Marvel). V: Rhino. 1.25
❑25, Jul 1985 .... 1.25
❑26, Aug 1985 V: Taskmaster. 1.25
❑27, Sep 1985 .... 1.25
❑28, Oct 1985 1: Demolition Dunphy (later becomes D-Man). 1.25
❑29, Nov 1985 .... 1.25

Other grades: Multiply price above by 5/6 for VF/NM • 2/3 for VERY FINE • 1/3 for FINE • 1/5 for VERY GOOD • 1/8 for GOOD

Those Magnificent Men In Their Flying Machines

Adaptation of the movie by Gold Key

©Gold Key

3-D Substance

3-D comics from Jack Harris and Steve Ditko

©3-D Zone

3-D Zone

Get out your glasses for 3-D showcase

©3-D Zone

3 Geeks

Humor series about... well, three geeks

©3 Finger Prints

300

Ancient Greeks in action from Frank Miller

©Dark Horse

N-MINT

❑30, Dec 1985, Secret Wars II 1.25
❑31, Jan 1986 .... 1.25
❑32, Feb 1986 .... 1.25
❑33, Mar 1986 D: Titania. 1.25
❑34, Apr 1986 D: The Sphinx. 1.25
❑35, May 1986 .... 1.25
❑36, Jun 1986 .... 1.25

THING (2ND SERIES)
MARVEL

❑1, Jan 2006 .... 2.99
❑2, Feb 2006 .... 2.99
❑3, Mar 2006 .... 2.99
❑4, May 2006 .... 2.99
❑5, Jun 2006 .... 2.99
❑6, Jul 2006 .... 2.99
❑7, Aug 2006 .... 2.99

THING: FREAKSHOW
MARVEL

❑1, Aug 2002 .... 2.99
❑2, Sep 2002 .... 2.99
❑3, Oct 2002 .... 2.99
❑4, Nov 2002 .... 2.99

THING FROM ANOTHER WORLD
DARK HORSE

❑1, ca. 1993; cardstock cover 2.95
❑2, ca. 1993; cardstock cover 2.95
❑3 .... 2.99
❑4 .... 2.99

THING FROM ANOTHER WORLD: CLIMATE OF FEAR
DARK HORSE

❑1, ca. 1994 .... 2.50
❑2, ca. 1994 .... 2.50
❑3, ca. 1994 .... 2.50
❑4, ca. 1994 .... 2.50

THING FROM ANOTHER WORLD, THE: ETERNAL VOWS
DARK HORSE

❑1, Dec 1993 .... 2.50
❑2, Jan 1994 .... 2.50
❑3, Feb 1994 .... 2.50
❑4, Mar 1994 .... 2.50

THING/SHE-HULK: THE LONG NIGHT
MARVEL

❑1, May 2002, Man atop demons on cover 2.99

3RD DEGREE
NBM

❑1 .... 2.95

THIRD EYE (DARK ONE'S...)
SIRIUS

❑1 1998; prestige format; pin-ups 4.95
❑2, Dec 1998; pin-ups and stories; cardstock cover 4.95

THIRD WORLD WAR
FLEETWAY-QUALITY

❑1 .... 2.50
❑2 .... 2.50
❑3 .... 2.50
❑4 .... 2.50
❑5 .... 2.50
❑6 .... 2.50

N-MINT

13: ASSASSIN COMICS MODULE
TSR

❑1 .... 2.00
❑2 .... 2.00
❑3 .... 2.00
❑4 .... 2.00
❑5 .... 2.00
❑6 .... 2.00
❑7 .... 2.00
❑8 .... 2.00

13 DAYS OF CHRISTMAS, THE: A TALE OF THE LOST LUNAR BESTIARY
SIRIUS

❑1, b&w; wraparound cover 2.95

THIRTEEN O'CLOCK
DARK HORSE

❑1, b&w 2.95

THIRTEEN SOMETHING!
GLOBAL

❑1 .... 1.95

13TH SON: WORSE THING WAITING
DARK HORSE

❑1, Oct 2005 ....
❑2, Nov 2005 ....
❑3, Dec 2005 ....
❑4, Apr 2006 ....

30 DAYS OF NIGHT
IDEA & DESIGN WORKS

❑1, Jun 2002 .... 55.00
❑1/2nd, Aug 2002 .... 7.00
❑2, Aug 2002 .... 25.00
❑3, Oct 2002 .... 10.00
❑Annual 2004, Feb 2004 .... 4.99

30 DAYS OF NIGHT: BLOODSUCKER TALES
IDEA & DESIGN WORKS

❑1, ca. 2004 .... 3.99
❑2, ca. 2004 .... 3.99
❑3, ca. 2004 .... 3.99
❑4, ca. 2004 .... 3.99
❑5, ca. 2005 .... 3.99
❑6, ca. 2005 .... 3.99
❑7, ca. 2005 .... 3.99

30 DAYS OF NIGHT: DEAD SPACE
IDEA & DESIGN WORKS

❑1, Feb 2006 .... 3.99
❑2, Mar 2006 .... 3.99
❑3, Apr 2006 .... 3.99

30 DAYS OF NIGHT: RETURN TO BARROW
IDEA & DESIGN WORKS

❑1, ca. 2004 .... 12.00
❑1/2nd, Jun 2004 .... 3.99
❑2, ca. 2004 .... 8.00
❑3, ca. 2004 .... 5.00
❑4, Jun 2004 .... 3.99
❑5, Jul 2004 .... 3.99
❑6, Aug 2004 .... 3.99

39 SCREAMS
THUNDER BAAS

❑1, ca. 1986 .... 2.00
❑2, ca. 1986 .... 2.00

N-MINT

❑3, ca. 1986 .... 2.00
❑4, ca. 1986 .... 2.00
❑5, ca. 1987 .... 2.00
❑6, ca. 1987 .... 2.00

32 PAGES
SIRIUS

❑1, Jan 2001 .... 2.95

THIS IS HEAT
AEON

❑1, b&w 2.50

THIS IS NOT AN EXIT
DRACULINA

❑1 .... 2.95
❑2 .... 2.95

THIS IS SICK!
SILVER SKULL

❑1, b&w; Zen; foil cover 2.95
❑2 .... 2.95

THOR
MARVEL

❑126, Mar 1966, SL (w); JK (a); V: Hercules. Series continued from Journey into Mystery (Vol. 1) #125 125.00
❑127, Apr 1966 SL (w); JK (a); 1: Volla. 1: Midgard Serpent. 1: Pluto. 45.00
❑128, May 1966 SL (w); JK (a) 45.00
❑129, Jun 1966 SL (w); JK (a); 1: Ares. 1: Hela. 1: Tana Nile (disguised). 45.00
❑130, Jul 1966 SL (w); JK (a); 1: Tana Nile (in real form). 45.00
❑131, Aug 1966 SL (w); JK (a) 45.00
❑132, Sep 1966 SL (w); JK (a); 1: Recorder. 1: Ego. V: Ego, the Living Planet. 45.00
❑133, Oct 1966 SL (w); JK (a) 45.00
❑134, Nov 1966 SL (w); JK (a); O: Man-Beast. 1: Man-Beast. 1: High Evolutionary. 45.00
❑135, Dec 1966 SL (w); JK (a); O: High Evolutionary. 45.00
❑136, Jan 1967, SL (w); JK (a); 1: Sif. Jane Foster denied immortality 45.00
❑137, Feb 1967 SL (w); JK (a); 1: Ulik. 45.00
❑138, Mar 1967 SL (w); JK (a) 45.00
❑139, Apr 1967 SL (w); JK (a) 45.00
❑140, May 1967 SL (w); JK (a); 1: Growing Man. V: Growing Man. 45.00
❑141, Jun 1967 SL (w); JK (a) 32.00
❑142, Jul 1967 SL (w); JK (a) 32.00
❑143, Aug 1967 SL (w); BEv, JK (a) ... 32.00
❑144, Sep 1967 SL (w); JK (a) 32.00
❑145, Oct 1967, SL (w); JK (a); Tales of Asgard back-up story 32.00
❑146, Oct 1967, SL (w); JK (a); O: Inhumans. A: Ringmaster. A: Circus of Crime. Origins of the Inhumans backup story 32.00
❑147, Dec 1967, SL (w); JK (a); O: Inhumans. Origins of the Inhumans backup story 32.00
❑148, Jan 1968, SL (w); JK (a); O: The Wrecker III. O: Black Bolt. 1: The Wrecker III. Origins of the Inhumans backup story 32.00
❑149, Feb 1968, JK (c); SL (w); JK (a); O: Maximus. O: Medusa. O: Black Bolt. Origins of the Inhumans backup story 32.00

Other grades: Multiply price above by 5/6 for VF/NM • 2/3 for VERY FINE • 1/3 for FINE • 1/5 for VERY GOOD • 1/8 for GOOD

	N-MINT
❑150, Mar 1968, SL (w); JK (a); A: Inhumans. Origins of the Inhumans backup story	32.00
❑151, Apr 1968, SL (w); JK (a); A: Inhumans. Origins of the Inhumans backup story	32.00
❑152, May 1968, SL (w); JK (a); Origins of the Inhumans backup story	32.00
❑153, Jun 1968 SL (w); JK (a)	32.00
❑154, Jul 1968 SL (w); JK (a); V: Mangog.	32.00
❑155, Aug 1968 SL (w); JK (a)	32.00
❑156, Sep 1968 SL (w); JK (a)	32.00
❑157, Oct 1968 SL (w); JK (a)	32.00
❑158, Nov 1968 SL (w); JK (a); O: Don Blake. O: Thor.	32.00
❑159, Dec 1968 JK (a)	32.00
❑160, Jan 1969, JK (a); V: Galactus. Galactus	32.00
❑161, Feb 1969 JK (a); V: Galactus.	25.00
❑162, Mar 1969 JK (a); O: Galactus.	25.00
❑163, Apr 1969 JK (a)	25.00
❑164, May 1969 JK (a)	25.00
❑165, Jun 1969, JK (a); A: Him (Warlock). Warlock	40.00
❑166, Jul 1969 JK (a); A: Him (Warlock).	36.00
❑167, Aug 1969 JK (a); A: Sif.	24.00
❑168, Sep 1969 JK (a); O: Galactus.	36.00
❑169, Oct 1969, JK (a); O: Galactus. Origin of Galactus	36.00
❑170, Nov 1969 BEv, JK (a)	20.00
❑171, Dec 1969 BEv, JK (a)	20.00
❑172, Jan 1970 BEv, JK (a)	20.00
❑173, Feb 1970 BEv, JK (a)	20.00
❑174, Mar 1970 BEv, JK (a)	20.00
❑175, Apr 1970 BEv, JK (a)	20.00
❑176, May 1970 BEv (c); BEv, JK (a); V: Surtur the Fire Demon.	20.00
❑177, Jun 1970	20.00
❑178, Jul 1970	18.00
❑179, Aug 1970	18.00
❑180, Sep 1970 NA (a); V: Mephisto.	24.00
❑181, Oct 1970 NA (a); V: Mephisto. V: Loki.	23.00
❑182, Nov 1970	12.00
❑183, Dec 1970	12.00
❑184, Jan 1971 1: Infinity (as force).	12.00
❑185, Feb 1971	12.00
❑186, Mar 1971	12.00
❑187, Apr 1971	12.00
❑188, May 1971	12.00
❑189, Jun 1971	12.00
❑190, Jul 1971	12.00
❑191, Aug 1971	12.00
❑192, Sep 1971	12.00
❑193, Oct 1971 JB, SB (a); A: Silver Surfer.	55.00
❑194, Nov 1971	12.00
❑195, Dec 1971	12.00
❑196, Jan 1972	12.00
❑197, Feb 1972	12.00
❑198, Mar 1972	12.00
❑199, Apr 1972	12.00
❑200, Jun 1972, JB (a); Ragnarok	16.00
❑201, Jul 1972 JB (a)	9.00
❑202, Aug 1972 JB (a)	9.00
❑203, Sep 1972 JB (a)	9.00
❑204, Oct 1972 JB (a)	9.00
❑205, Nov 1972 JB (a)	9.00
❑206, Dec 1972 JB (a)	7.00
❑207, Jan 1973 JB (a)	7.00
❑208, Feb 1973 JB (a)	7.00
❑209, Mar 1973 JB (a); 1: Ultimus.	7.00
❑210, Apr 1973 JB (a)	7.00
❑211, May 1973 JB (a)	7.00
❑212, Jun 1973 JB (a)	7.00
❑213, Jul 1973 JB (a)	7.00
❑214, Aug 1973	7.00
❑215, Sep 1973	7.00
❑216, Oct 1973	7.00
❑217, Nov 1973	7.00
❑218, Dec 1973	7.00
❑219, Jan 1974	7.00
❑220, Feb 1974	7.00
❑221, Mar 1974, Marvel Value Stamp #1: Spider-Man	7.00
❑222, Apr 1974, Marvel Value Stamp #41: Gladiator	7.00

	N-MINT
❑223, May 1974, Marvel Value Stamp #12: Daredevil	7.00
❑224, Jun 1974, Marvel Value Stamp #87: J. Jonah Jameson	7.00
❑225, Jul 1974, 1: Firelord. Marvel Value Stamp #17: Black Bolt	14.00
❑226, Aug 1974, Marvel Value Stamp #58: Mandarin	7.00
❑227, Sep 1974, Marvel Value Stamp #76: Dormammu	5.00
❑228, Oct 1974, Marvel Value Stamp #40: Loki	5.00
❑229, Nov 1974, Marvel Value Stamp #80: Ghost Rider	5.00
❑230, Dec 1974	5.00
❑231, Jan 1975, Marvel Value Stamp #83: Dragon Man	5.00
❑232, Feb 1975, Marvel Value Stamp #85: Lilith	5.00
❑233, Mar 1975	5.00
❑234, Apr 1975	5.00
❑235, May 1975, 1: The Possessor. Marvel Value Stamp #23: Sgt. Fury	5.00
❑236, Jun 1975	5.00
❑237, Jul 1975, Marvel Value Stamp #18: Volstagg	5.00
❑238, Aug 1975, JB, JSt (a); Marvel Value Stamp #94: Electro	5.00
❑239, Sep 1975 1: Osiris. 1: Horus.	5.00
❑240, Oct 1975 1: Isis (Marvel). 1: Seth.	5.00
❑241, Nov 1975 JB (a)	5.00
❑242, Dec 1975 JB (a)	5.00
❑243, Jan 1976 JB (a)	5.00
❑244, Feb 1976 JB (a)	5.00
❑245, Mar 1976 JB (a)	5.00
❑246, Apr 1976 JB (a); A: Firelord.	5.00
❑246/30 cent, Apr 1976, 30 cent regional price variant	20.00
❑247, May 1976 JB (a); A: Firelord.	5.00
❑247/30 cent, May 1976, 30 cent regional price variant	20.00
❑248, Jun 1976 JB (a)	5.00
❑248/30 cent, Jun 1976, 30 cent regional price variant	20.00
❑249, Jul 1976, JB (a); Sif trades places with Jane	5.00
❑249/30 cent, Jul 1976, 30 cent regional price variant	5.00
❑250, Aug 1976 JB (a)	5.00
❑250/30 cent, Aug 1976, 30 cent regional price variant	5.00
❑251, Sep 1976	5.00
❑252, Oct 1976	5.00
❑253, Nov 1976	5.00
❑254, Dec 1976, Reprinted from Thor #159	5.00
❑255, Jan 1977	5.00
❑256, Feb 1977, Newsstand edition (distributed by Curtis); issue number in box	5.00
❑256/Whitman, Feb 1977, Special markets edition (usually sold in Whitman bagged prepacks); price appears in a diamond; UPC barcode appears	5.00
❑257, Mar 1977, Newsstand edition (distributed by Curtis); issue number in box	5.00
❑257/Whitman, Mar 1977, Special markets edition (usually sold in Whitman bagged prepacks); price appears in a diamond; UPC barcode appears	5.00
❑258, Apr 1977, Newsstand edition (distributed by Curtis); issue number in box	5.00
❑258/Whitman, Apr 1977, Special markets edition (usually sold in Whitman bagged prepacks); price appears in a diamond; UPC barcode appears	5.00
❑259, May 1977, Newsstand edition (distributed by Curtis); issue number in box	5.00
❑259/Whitman, May 1977, Special markets edition (usually sold in Whitman bagged prepacks); price appears in a diamond; UPC barcode appears	5.00
❑260, Jun 1977, Newsstand edition (distributed by Curtis); issue number in box	5.00

	N-MINT
❑260/Whitman, Jun 1977, Special markets edition (usually sold in Whitman bagged prepacks); price appears in a diamond; UPC barcode appears	5.00
❑260/35 cent, Jun 1977, 35 cent regional price variant newsstand edition (distributed by Curtis); issue number in box	15.00
❑261, Jul 1977, Newsstand edition (distributed by Curtis); issue number in box	5.00
❑261/Whitman, Jul 1977, Special markets edition (usually sold in Whitman bagged prepacks); price appears in a diamond; UPC barcode appears	5.00
❑261/35 cent, Jul 1977, 35 cent regional price variant newsstand edition (distributed by Curtis); issue number in box	15.00
❑262, Aug 1977, TD (a); Newsstand edition (distributed by Curtis); issue number in box	5.00
❑262/Whitman, Aug 1977, TD (a); Special markets edition (usually sold in Whitman bagged prepacks); price appears in a diamond; UPC barcode appears	5.00
❑262/35 cent, Aug 1977, TD (a); 35 cent regional price variant newsstand edition (distributed by Curtis); issue number in box	15.00
❑263, Sep 1977, Newsstand edition (distributed by Curtis); issue number in box	5.00
❑263/Whitman, Sep 1977, Special markets edition (usually sold in Whitman bagged prepacks); price appears in a diamond; UPC barcode appears	5.00
❑263/35 cent, Sep 1977, 35 cent regional price variant newsstand edition (distributed by Curtis); issue number in box	15.00
❑264, Oct 1977, Newsstand edition (distributed by Curtis); issue number in box	5.00
❑264/Whitman, Oct 1977, Special markets edition (usually sold in Whitman bagged prepacks); price appears in a diamond; no UPC barcode	5.00
❑264/35 cent, Oct 1977, 35 cent regional price variant newsstand edition (distributed by Curtis); issue number in box	15.00
❑265, Nov 1977, Newsstand edition (distributed by Curtis); issue number in box	2.50
❑265/Whitman, Nov 1977, Special markets edition (usually sold in Whitman bagged prepacks); price appears in a diamond; no UPC barcode	2.50
❑266, Dec 1977	2.50
❑267, Jan 1978	2.50
❑268, Feb 1978	2.50
❑269, Mar 1978	2.50
❑270, Apr 1978, Newsstand edition (distributed by Curtis); issue number in box	2.50
❑270/Whitman, Apr 1978, Special markets edition (usually sold in Whitman bagged prepacks); price appears in a diamond; no UPC barcode	2.50
❑271, May 1978, A: Iron Man. Newsstand edition (distributed by Curtis); issue number in box	2.50
❑271/Whitman, May 1978, A: Iron Man. Special markets edition (usually sold in Whitman bagged prepacks); price appears in a diamond; no UPC barcode	2.50
❑272, Jun 1978, JB (a); Newsstand edition (distributed by Curtis); issue number in box	2.50
❑272/Whitman, Jun 1978, JB (a); Special markets edition (usually sold in Whitman bagged prepacks); price appears in a diamond; no UPC barcode	2.50
❑273, Jul 1978 1: Red Norvell.	2.50
❑274, Aug 1978, 1: Sigyn. 1: Frigga. D: Balder. Newsstand edition (distributed by Curtis); issue number in box	2.50

Other grades: Multiply price above by 5/6 for VF/NM • 2/3 for VERY FINE • 1/3 for FINE • 1/5 for VERY GOOD • 1/8 for GOOD

Three Stooges

Decent adaptation of Stooges' hilarity

©Gold Key

THUNDER Agents

Classic art by Wood, Ditko, and Kane

©Tower

Thunderbolts

Supervillians hide out as super-heroes

©Marvel

Thunderbunny (2nd Series)

Don't investigate strange lights on mountains

©Warp

Thundercats

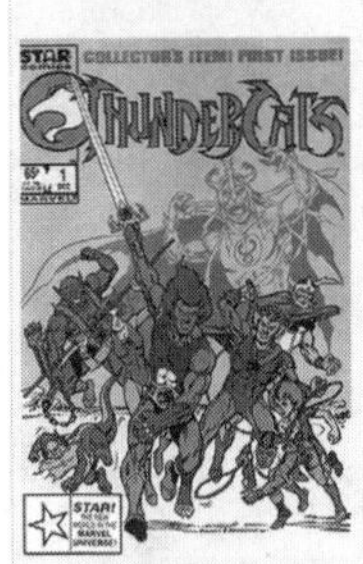

Mildy popular cartoon series had later revival

©Marvel

	N-MINT
❑274/Whitman, Aug 1978, 1: Sigyn. 1: Frigga. D: Balder. Special markets edition (usually sold in Whitman bagged prepacks); price appears in a diamond; no UPC barcode	2.50
❑275, Sep 1978, 1: Hermod. Newsstand edition (distributed by Curtis); issue number in box	2.50
❑275/Whitman, Sep 1978, 1: Hermod. Special markets edition (usually sold in Whitman bagged prepacks); price appears in a diamond; no UPC barcode	2.50
❑276, Oct 1978, Red Norvell named Thor; Newsstand edition (distributed by Curtis); issue number in box	2.50
❑276/Whitman, Oct 1978, Special markets edition (usually sold in Whitman bagged prepacks); price appears in a diamond; no UPC barcode	2.50
❑277, Nov 1978, Newsstand edition (distributed by Curtis); issue number in box	2.50
❑277/Whitman, Nov 1978, Special markets edition (usually sold in Whitman bagged prepacks); price appears in a diamond; no UPC barcode	2.50
❑278, Dec 1978, Newsstand edition (distributed by Curtis); issue number in box	2.50
❑278/Whitman, Dec 1978, Special markets edition (usually sold in Whitman bagged prepacks); price appears in a diamond; no UPC barcode	2.50
❑279, Jan 1979, Newsstand edition (distributed by Curtis); issue number in box	2.50
❑279/Whitman, Jan 1979, Special markets edition (usually sold in Whitman bagged prepacks); price appears in a diamond; no UPC barcode	2.50
❑280, Feb 1979, Newsstand edition (distributed by Curtis); issue number in box	2.50
❑280/Whitman, Feb 1979, Special markets edition (usually sold in Whitman bagged prepacks); price appears in a diamond; no UPC barcode	2.50
❑282, Apr 1979	3.00
❑281, Mar 1979 A: Immortus.	3.00
❑283, May 1979, A: Celestials. Newsstand edition (distributed by Curtis); issue number in box	3.00
❑283/Whitman, May 1979, A: Celestials. Special markets edition (usually sold in Whitman bagged prepacks); price appears in a diamond; no UPC barcode	3.00
❑284, Jun 1979 A: Externals.	3.00
❑285, Jul 1979	3.00
❑286, Aug 1979	3.00
❑287, Sep 1979	3.00
❑288, Oct 1979	3.00
❑289, Nov 1979	3.00
❑290, Dec 1979 V: El Toro Rojo.	3.00
❑291, Jan 1980	3.00
❑292, Feb 1980	3.00

	N-MINT
❑293, Mar 1980	3.00
❑294, Apr 1980 KP (a); O: Asgard. O: Odin. 1: Frey.	3.00
❑295, May 1980 KP (a)	3.00
❑296, Jun 1980 KP (a)	3.00
❑297, Jul 1980, KP (a); Thor as Siegfried	3.00
❑298, Aug 1980 KP (a)	3.00
❑299, Sep 1980 KP (a)	3.00
❑300, Oct 1980, KP (a); O: The Destroyer. O: Odin. D: Zuras (physical death). giant; Balder revived	8.00
❑301, Nov 1980, Thor meets other pantheons	2.00
❑302, Dec 1980	2.00
❑303, Jan 1981	2.00
❑304, Feb 1981 V: Wrecking Crew.	2.00
❑305, Mar 1981 KP (a)	2.00
❑306, Apr 1981 KP (a); O: Firelord. 1: Air-Walker (real form). D: Air-Walker (real form).	2.00
❑307, May 1981	2.00
❑308, Jun 1981 KP (a)	2.00
❑309, Jul 1981	2.00
❑310, Aug 1981 V: Mephisto.	2.00
❑311, Sep 1981	2.00
❑312, Oct 1981 KP (a); V: Tyr.	2.00
❑313, Nov 1981	2.00
❑314, Dec 1981 KP (a); 1: Shawna Lynde	2.00
❑315, Jan 1982 KP (a)	2.00
❑316, Feb 1982	2.00
❑317, Mar 1982 KP (a)	2.00
❑318, Apr 1982 GK (a)	2.00
❑319, May 1982 KP (a)	2.00
❑320, Jun 1982 KP (a)	2.00
❑321, Jul 1982	2.00
❑322, Aug 1982 D: Darkoth.	2.00
❑323, Sep 1982	2.00
❑324, Oct 1982	2.00
❑325, Nov 1982	2.00
❑326, Dec 1982 BA (c); BA (a)	2.00
❑327, Jan 1983	2.00
❑328, Feb 1983 1: Megatak.	2.00
❑329, Mar 1983	2.00
❑330, Apr 1983 BH (c); BH (w); BH (a); O: Crusader II (Arthur Blackwood). 1: Crusader II (Arthur Blackwood).	2.00
❑331, May 1983 BH (c); BH (w); BH (a)	2.00
❑332, Jun 1983	2.00
❑333, Jul 1983 V: Dracula.	2.00
❑334, Aug 1983	2.00
❑335, Sep 1983 1: The Possessor.	2.00
❑336, Oct 1983 HT (a)	2.00
❑337, Nov 1983, O: Beta Ray Bill. 1: Beta Ray Bill. 1st Simonson Thor	7.00
❑338, Dec 1983 A: Beta Ray Bill.	3.00
❑339, Jan 1984 1: Lorelei. A: Beta Ray Bill.	5.00
❑340, Feb 1984 A: Beta Ray Bill.	4.00
❑341, Mar 1984 1: Sigurd Jarlson.	3.00
❑342, Apr 1984	4.00
❑343, May 1984	2.00
❑344, Jun 1984 1: Malekith the Dark Elf.	2.00
❑345, Jul 1984	2.00

	N-MINT
❑346, Aug 1984	2.00
❑347, Sep 1984 1: Algrim.	2.00
❑348, Oct 1984	2.00
❑349, Nov 1984 O: Odin.	3.00
❑350, Dec 1984 A: Beta Ray Bill.	2.00
❑351, Jan 1985 A: Fantastic Four.	2.00
❑352, Feb 1985 A: Fantastic Four. A: Beta Ray Bill. A: Avengers.	2.00
❑353, Mar 1985	2.00
❑354, Apr 1985	2.00
❑355, May 1985	2.00
❑356, Jun 1985 BG (a)	2.00
❑357, Jul 1985	2.00
❑358, Aug 1985, Beta Ray Bill vs. Titanium Man	2.00
❑359, Sep 1985 A: Loki. D: Megatak.	2.00
❑360, Oct 1985	2.00
❑361, Nov 1985	2.00
❑362, Dec 1985	2.00
❑363, Jan 1986, Secret Wars II; Thor's face scarred	2.00
❑364, Feb 1986	2.00
❑365, Mar 1986, Thor turned into frog	2.00
❑366, Apr 1986	2.00
❑367, May 1986	2.00
❑368, Jun 1986	2.00
❑369, Jul 1986	2.00
❑370, Aug 1986	2.00
❑371, Sep 1986 A: Justice Peace.	2.00
❑372, Oct 1986	2.00
❑373, Nov 1986, Mutant Massacre	2.00
❑374, Dec 1986, A: X-Factor. Mutant Massacre	3.00
❑375, Jan 1987	2.00
❑376, Feb 1987	2.00
❑377, Mar 1987	2.00
❑378, Apr 1987	2.00
❑379, May 1987	2.00
❑380, Jun 1987	2.00
❑381, Jul 1987	1.50
❑382, Aug 1987, 300th Thor issue	2.00
❑383, Sep 1987, Secret Wars II	1.50
❑384, Oct 1987 1: Dargo (future Thor).	1.50
❑385, Nov 1987 A: Hulk.	1.50
❑386, Dec 1987 1: Leir.	1.50
❑387, Jan 1988	1.50
❑388, Feb 1988	1.50
❑389, Mar 1988	1.50
❑390, Apr 1988	1.50
❑391, May 1988 1: Eric Masterson. A: Spider-Man.	2.00
❑392, Jun 1988 1: Quicksand.	1.50
❑393, Jul 1988	1.50
❑394, Aug 1988 BH (a)	1.50
❑395, Sep 1988 O: Earth-Lord. O: Wind Warrior. 1: Earth-Lord. 1: Wind Warrior.	1.50
❑396, Oct 1988	1.50
❑397, Nov 1988	1.50
❑398, Dec 1988 1: Caber.	1.50
❑399, Jan 1989	1.50
❑400, Feb 1989, A: Avengers. V: Seth and Surtur. giant	2.00
❑401, Mar 1989	1.00
❑402, Apr 1989	1.00

Other grades: Multiply price above by 5/6 for VF/NM • 2/3 for VERY FINE • 1/3 for FINE • 1/5 for VERY GOOD • 1/8 for GOOD

	N-MINT
❑403, May 1989	1.00
❑404, Jun 1989	1.00
❑405, Jul 1989	1.00
❑406, Aug 1989	1.00
❑407, Sep 1989	1.00
❑408, Oct 1989, Eric Masterson absorbs Thor's essence; series continues as The Mighty Thor through #490	1.00
❑409, Nov 1989, Title changes to The Mighty Thor	1.00
❑410, Nov 1989	1.00
❑411, Dec 1989, 1: Night Thrasher. 1: New Warriors (cameo). 1: Chord. V: Juggernaut. Acts of Vengeance	3.00
❑412, Dec 1989, 1: New Warriors (full appearance). V: Juggernaut. Acts of Vengeance	2.00
❑413, Jan 1990	1.00
❑414, Feb 1990	1.00
❑415, Mar 1990 O: Thor.	1.00
❑416, Apr 1990	1.00
❑417, May 1990	1.00
❑418, Jun 1990	1.00
❑419, Jul 1990 O: Stellaris. 1: Stellaris. 1: Black Galaxy.	1.00
❑420, Aug 1990 O: Nobilus. 1: Nobilus (partial appearance).	1.00
❑421, Aug 1990	1.00
❑422, Sep 1990 O: Nobilus. 1: Analyzer.	1.00
❑423, Sep 1990 1: Nobilus (full appearance).	1.00
❑424, Oct 1990	1.00
❑425, Oct 1990	1.00
❑426, Nov 1990	1.00
❑427, Dec 1990 A: Excalibur.	1.00
❑428, Jan 1991 A: Excalibur.	1.00
❑429, Feb 1991 A: Ghost Rider.	1.00
❑430, Mar 1991 AM (a); A: Ghost Rider.	1.00
❑431, Apr 1991	1.00
❑432, May 1991, Giant size AM, JK (a); O: Thor. 1: Thor II (Eric Masterson). 1: Thor. A: 300th. D: Loki.	2.00
❑433, Jun 1991 AM (a)	2.00
❑434, Jul 1991 AM (a)	1.00
❑435, Aug 1991	1.00
❑436, Sep 1991	1.00
❑437, Oct 1991 AM (a)	1.00
❑438, Nov 1991 AM (a); V: Zarrko.	1.00
❑439, Nov 1991 AM (a)	1.00
❑440, Dec 1991 AM (a); 1: Thor Corps (Dargo, Beta Ray Bill, Eric Masterson)	1.00
❑441, Dec 1991 AM (a)	1.00
❑442, Jan 1992, AM (a); Return of Don Blake	1.00
❑443, Jan 1992 AM (a); A: Doctor Strange. A: Silver Surfer. V: Mephisto.	1.00
❑444, Feb 1992 AM (a)	1.25
❑445, Mar 1992, V: Gladiator. Galactic Storm	1.25
❑446, Apr 1992, A: Avengers. Galactic Storm	1.25
❑447, May 1992 AM (a); A: Spider-Man. A: Absorbing Man.	1.25
❑448, Jun 1992 AM (a); A: Spider-Man.	1.25
❑449, Jul 1992 AM (a); O: Bloodaxe. 1: Bloodaxe.	1.25
❑450, Aug 1992, Giant-size anniversary special AM (a); O: Loki.	2.50
❑451, Sep 1992 AM (a); V: Bloodaxe..	1.25
❑452, Oct 1992	1.25
❑453, Nov 1992 AM (a)	1.25
❑454, Nov 1992 AM (a)	1.25
❑455, Dec 1992 AM (a)	1.25
❑456, Dec 1992 AM (a)	1.25
❑457, Jan 1993, Original Thor returns	1.25
❑458, Jan 1993	1.25
❑459, Feb 1993 AM (a)	1.25
❑460, Mar 1993, JSn (w); Painted cover	1.25
❑461, Apr 1993	1.25
❑462, May 1993	1.25
❑463, Jun 1993, Infinity Crusade Crossover	1.25
❑464, Jul 1993	1.25
❑465, Aug 1993	1.25
❑466, Sep 1993	1.25
❑467, Oct 1993, A: Lady Sif. A: Valkyrie. A: Pluto. Infinity Crusade crossover	1.25
❑468, Nov 1993	1.25
❑469, Dec 1993	1.25
❑470, Jan 1994	1.25
❑471, Feb 1994	1.25
❑472, Mar 1994	1.25
❑473, Apr 1994	1.25
❑474, May 1994	1.50
❑475, Jun 1994, Giant-size O: Thor.	2.00
❑475/Variant, Jun 1994, Giant-size; O: Thor. foil cover	2.50
❑476, Jul 1994	1.50
❑477, Aug 1994	1.50
❑478, Sep 1994 A: Red Norvell.	1.50
❑479, Oct 1994	1.50
❑480, Nov 1994	1.50
❑481, Dec 1994 V: Grotesk.	1.50
❑482, Jan 1995, Giant-size	2.95
❑483, Feb 1995	1.50
❑484, Mar 1995 A: War Machine.	1.50
❑485, Apr 1995	1.50
❑486, May 1995	1.50
❑487, Jun 1995	1.50
❑488, Jul 1995	1.50
❑489, Aug 1995 V: Hulk.	1.50
❑490, Sep 1995 V: Absorbing Man.	1.50
❑491, Oct 1995, Title returns to Thor.	1.50
❑492, Nov 1995 A: Enchantress.	1.50
❑493, Dec 1995 A: Enchantress.	1.50
❑494, Jan 1996	1.50
❑495, Feb 1996	1.50
❑496, Mar 1996 A: Captain America. .	1.50
❑497, Apr 1996	1.50
❑498, May 1996	1.50
❑499, Jun 1996	1.50
❑500, Jul 1996, Giant-size; wraparound cover	2.50
❑501, Aug 1996 A: Red Norvell.	1.50
❑502, Sep 1996 O: Thor.	1.50
❑Annual 2, Sep 1966, Cover reads "King Size Special"; SL (w); JK, JSt (a); reprints from Journey into Mystery #96 and #103	65.00
❑Annual 2/2nd SL (w); JK, JSt (a)	2.50
❑Annual 3, Jan 1971, JK (a); A: Grey Gargoyle. A: Absorbing Man. reprints Thor stories from Journey into Mystery #113 and #114; reprints Tales of Asgard from Journey into Mystery #107-110	12.00
❑Annual 4, Cover reads "King Size Special"; JK (a); Cover reads King Size Special; reprints stories from Thor #131 and 132, and Journey Into Mystery #113	10.00
❑Annual 5, ca. 1976 JB, JK (a); 1: Apollo.	8.00
❑Annual 6, ca. 1977 JB, JK (a)	8.00
❑Annual 7, ca. 1978	7.00
❑Annual 8, ca. 1979	6.00
❑Annual 9, ca. 1981 LMc (a)	3.50
❑Annual 10, ca. 1982 BH (a); O: Chthon. 1: Ahpuch. 1: Erishkegal. 1: Yama..	3.50
❑Annual 11, ca. 1983 BH (a)	3.50
❑Annual 12, ca. 1984 1: Vidar.	3.50
❑Annual 13 V: Mephisto.	3.00
❑Annual 14, ca. 1989, Title changes to The Mighty Thor Annual	2.50
❑Annual 15, ca. 1990 O: Terminus.	2.50
❑Annual 16, ca. 1991, AM, HT (a); O: Thor. 1991 Annual	2.50
❑Annual 17, ca. 1992, Citizen Kang	2.50
❑Annual 18, ca. 1993, trading card	2.95
❑Annual 19, ca. 1994	2.95

THOR (VOL. 2)

MARVEL

	N-MINT
❑1, Jul 1998; Giant-size JR2 (a)	5.00
❑1/A, Jul 1998; gatefold summary; JR2 (a); sketch cover	20.00
❑1/B, Jul 1998; gatefold summary; JR2 (a); Sunburst cover	5.00
❑1/C, Jul 1998; JR2 (a); DFE alternate cover	5.00
❑1/D, Jul 1998; JR2 (a); DFE alternate cover	8.00
❑1/E, Jul 1998; Rough Cut cover	5.00
❑2, Aug 1998; gatefold summary; JR2 (a); Thor receives new mortal identity	2.50
❑2/A, Aug 1998; JR2 (a); variant cover	2.50
❑3, Sep 1998; gatefold summary JR2 (a); V: Sedna.	2.00
❑4, Oct 1998; gatefold summary JR2 (a); A: Namor.	2.00
❑5, Nov 1998; gatefold summary JR2 (a)	2.00
❑6, Dec 1998; gatefold summary JR2 (a); A: Hercules.	2.00
❑7, Jan 1999; gatefold summary JR2 (a); A: Hercules.	2.00
❑8, Feb 1999; gatefold summary; JR2 (a); A: Spider-Man. concludes in Peter Parker; Spider-Man #2	2.00
❑9, Mar 1999 JB (a)	2.00
❑10, Apr 1999 JR2 (a); V: Perrikus.	2.00
❑11, May 1999 A: Volstagg. V: Perrikus.	1.99
❑12, Jun 1999; A: Hercules. A: Destroyer. A: Warriors Three. A: Replicus. V: Perrikus. wraparound cover	2.99
❑12/DF, Jun 1999	15.00
❑13, Jul 1999 V: Marnot.	1.99
❑14, Aug 1999 A: Iron Man. V: Absorbing Man.	1.99
❑15, Sep 1999 A: Warriors Three.	1.99
❑16, Oct 1999	1.99
❑17, Nov 1999	1.99
❑18, Dec 1999	1.99
❑19, Jan 2000	1.99
❑20, Feb 2000	2.25
❑21, Mar 2000	2.25
❑22, Apr 2000	2.25
❑23, May 2000	2.25
❑24, Jun 2000	2.25
❑25, Jul 2000	2.25
❑25/Gold, Jul 2000	5.00
❑26, Aug 2000	2.25
❑27, Sep 2000	2.25
❑28, Oct 2000	2.25
❑29, Nov 2000 A: Wrecking Crew.	2.25
❑30, Dec 2000 A: Malekith. A: Beta Ray Bill.	2.25
❑31, Jan 2001	2.25
❑32, Feb 2001	3.50
❑33, Mar 2001 1: Thor Girl.	2.25
❑34, Apr 2001 A: Gladiator.	2.25
❑35, May 2001 A: Gladiator.	2.99
❑36, Jun 2001	2.25
❑37, Jul 2001	2.25
❑38, Aug 2001	2.25
❑39, Sep 2001	2.25
❑40, Oct 2001	2.25
❑41, Nov 2001	2.25
❑42, Dec 2001	2.25
❑43, Jan 2002	2.25
❑44, Feb 2002	2.25
❑45, Mar 2002	2.25
❑46, Apr 2002; wraparound cover	2.25
❑47, May 2002; wraparound cover	2.25
❑48, Jun 2002; wraparound cover	2.25
❑49, Jul 2002	2.25
❑50, Aug 2002	2.25
❑51, Sep 2002	2.25
❑52, Oct 2002	2.25
❑53, Oct 2002	2.25
❑54, Nov 2002	2.25
❑55, Dec 2002	2.25
❑56, Jan 2003	2.25
❑57, Feb 2003	2.25
❑58, Mar 2003	2.25
❑59, Apr 2003	2.25
❑60, May 2003	2.25
❑61, May 2003	2.25
❑62, Jun 2003	2.99
❑63, Jun 2003	2.99
❑64, Jul 2003	2.99
❑65, Aug 2003	2.99
❑66, Sep 2003	2.99
❑67, Oct 2003	2.99
❑68, Nov 2003	2.99
❑69, Nov 2003	2.99
❑70, Dec 2003	2.99
❑71, Jan 2004	2.99
❑72, Feb 2004	2.99
❑73, Mar 2004	2.99
❑74, Apr 2004	2.99
❑75, May 2004 (c);	2.99
❑76, May 2004 (c);	2.99
❑77, Jun 2004 (c);	2.99

Other grades: Multiply price above by 5/6 for VF/NM • 2/3 for VERY FINE • 1/3 for FINE • 1/5 for VERY GOOD • 1/8 for GOOD

Thunderstrike

When one Thor is never enough
©Marvel

Tick

the plot thicks...

Big hero with IQ of tomato paste
©NEC

Tilazeus Meets the Messiah

Jesus Christ deals with a demon
©Aiiie

Timber Wolf

Solo outing for the Legionnaire
©DC

Time Breakers

Housewife uses thought to alter reality
©DC

N-MINT

❑78, Jul 2004 .... 2.99
❑79, Jul 2004 .... 2.99
❑80, Aug 2004 .... 28.00
❑81, Aug 2004 .... 5.00
❑82, Sep 2004 .... 4.00
❑83, Oct 2004 .... 4.00
❑84, Nov 2004 .... 4.00
❑85, Dec 2004 .... 2.99
❑Annual 1999, Mar 1999; V: Doom. set between Heroes Reborn and Heroes Return; wraparound cover 4.00
❑Annual 2001, Mar 2001; A: Hercules. A: Beta Ray Bill. wraparound cover. 3.50

THOR: BLOOD OATH
MARVEL

❑1 .... 2.99
❑2 .... 2.99
❑3, Dec 2005 .... 2.99
❑4, Jan 2006 .... 2.99
❑5, Feb 2006 .... 2.99
❑6, Feb 2006 .... 2.99

THOR CORPS
MARVEL

❑1, Sep 1993 .... 1.75
❑2, Oct 1993 .... 1.75
❑3, Nov 1993 .... 1.75
❑4, Dec 1993 .... 1.75

THORION OF THE NEW ASGODS
MARVEL / AMALGAM

❑1, Jun 1997 .... 1.95

THORR-SVERD
VINCENT

❑1, b&w 1.00
❑2, b&w 1.00
❑3, b&w 1.00

THOR: SON OF ASGARD
MARVEL

❑1, May 2004 .... 2.99
❑2, May 2004 .... 2.99
❑3, Jun 2004 .... 2.99
❑4, Jul 2004 .... 2.99
❑5, Aug 2004 .... 2.99
❑6, Sep 2004 .... 2.99
❑7, Oct 2004 .... 2.99
❑8, Nov 2004 .... 2.99
❑9, Dec 2004 .... 2.99
❑10, Jan 2005 .... 2.99
❑11, Feb 2005 .... 2.99
❑12, Mar 2005 .... 2.99

THOR: THE LEGEND
MARVEL

❑1, Sep 1996; information on Thor's career and supporting cast; wraparound cover 3.95

THOR: VIKINGS
MARVEL

❑1, Sep 2003; cardstock cover 3.50
❑2, Oct 2003; cardstock cover 3.50
❑3, Nov 2003; cardstock cover 3.50
❑4, Dec 2003; cardstock cover 3.50
❑5, Jan 2004 .... 3.50
❑Book 1, ca. 2004 .... 13.99

N-MINT

THOSE ANNOYING POST BROS.
VORTEX

❑1 .... 3.00
❑2 .... 2.00
❑3 .... 2.00
❑4 .... 2.00
❑5 .... 2.00
❑6 .... 2.00
❑7 .... 2.00
❑8 .... 2.00
❑9 .... 2.00
❑10 .... 2.00
❑11 .... 2.00
❑12 .... 2.00
❑13 .... 2.00
❑14 .... 2.00
❑15 .... 2.00
❑16 .... 2.00
❑17 .... 2.00
❑18; Series continues as Post Brothers 2.00
❑39, Aug 1994, b&w; Series continued from "Post Brothers" #38 .... 2.50
❑40, Oct 1994, b&w 2.50
❑41, Dec 1994, b&w 2.50
❑42, Feb 1995, b&w 2.50
❑43, Jun 1995, b&w 2.50
❑44, Jul 1995, b&w 2.50
❑45, Aug 1995, b&w 2.50
❑46, Oct 1995, b&w 2.50
❑47, Nov 1995, b&w 2.50
❑48, Feb 1996, b&w 2.50
❑Annual 1, Aug 1995, b&w; cardstock cover 4.95

THOSE CRAZY PECKERS
U.S.COMICS

❑1, Feb 1987 .... 2.00

THOSE MAGNIFICENT MEN IN THEIR FLYING MACHINES
GOLD KEY

❑1, Oct 1965, movie adaptation 25.00

THOSE UNSTOPPABLE ROGUES
ORIGINAL SYNDICATE

❑1, Mar 1995 .... 3.95

THOSE WHO HUNT ELVES
ADV MANGA

❑1, ca. 2003 .... 9.99

THRAX
EVENT

❑1, Nov 1996 .... 2.95
❑2, Jan 1997 .... 2.95

THREAT!
FANTAGRAPHICS

❑1, Jun 1986, b&w 2.25
❑2, Jul 1986, b&w 2.25
❑3, Aug 1986, b&w 2.25
❑4, Sep 1986, b&w 2.25
❑5, Oct 1986, b&w 2.25
❑6, Nov 1986, b&w 2.25
❑7, Dec 1986, b&w 2.25
❑8, Jan 1987, b&w 2.25
❑9, May 1987, b&w 2.25
❑10, Sep 1987, b&w 2.25

N-MINT

THREE
INVINCIBLE

❑1 .... 2.00
❑2 .... 2.00
❑3 .... 2.00
❑4 .... 2.00

3-D ADVENTURE COMICS
STATS ETC.

❑1, Aug 1986 1: Statman 2.00

3-D ALIEN TERROR
ECLIPSE

❑1, Jun 1986 .... 2.50

3-D EXOTIC BEAUTIES
3-D ZONE

❑1, ca. 1990 .... 3.50

3-D HEROES
BLACKTHORNE

❑1, In 3-D, glasses not included 2.50

3-D HOLLYWOOD
3-D ZONE

❑1, paper dolls 2.95

THREE DIMENSIONAL ADVENTURES
DC

❑1 .... 900.00
❑1/2nd, b&w; Bundled with Superman Red/Superman Blue 1.00

3-D SPACE ZOMBIES
3-D ZONE

❑1 .... 3.95

3-D SUBSTANCE
3-D ZONE

❑1 .... 2.95
❑2 .... 3.95

3-D THREE STOOGES
ECLIPSE

❑1; Stuntgirl backup feature 2.50
❑2 .... 2.50
❑3 .... 2.50

3-D TRUE CRIME
3-D ZONE

❑1, ca. 1992 .... 3.95

3-D ZONE
3-D ZONE

❑1, ca. 1986 .... 2.50
❑2, ca. 1986 .... 2.50
❑3, ca. 1987 .... 2.50
❑4, ca. 1987; Electric Fear 2.50
❑5, ca. 1987; Krazy Kat 2.50
❑6, ca. 1987; Rat Fink 2.50
❑7, ca. 1987; Hollywood 2.50
❑8, Sep 1987; High Seas 2.50
❑9, ca. 1987; Red Mask 2.50
❑10, ca. 1987; Jet 2.50
❑11, ca. 1987; Matt Fox 2.50
❑12, ca. 1987; Presidents 2.50
❑13, ca. 1988; Flash Gordon 2.50
❑14, ca. 1988; Tyranostar 2.50
❑15, ca. 1988; humor 2.50
❑16, ca. 1988; space vixens 2.50
❑17, ca. 1988; Thrilling Love 2.50
❑18, ca. 1988; ca. 1988; Spacehawk 3-D 2.50

Other grades: Multiply price above by 5/6 for VF/NM • 2/3 for VERY FINE • 1/3 for FINE • 1/5 for VERY GOOD • 1/8 for GOOD

❑19, ca. 1989; Cracked 2.50
❑20, ca. 1989; Atomic Sub 2.50

.357!
Mu

❑1, Jul 1990, b&w 2.50

3 GEEKS
3 Finger Prints

❑1, Sep 1997, b&w 3.00
❑1/2nd, b&w 2.50
❑2, Oct 1997, b&w 2.50
❑3, Nov 1997, b&w; Brain Boy back-up 2.50
❑4, Jan 1998, b&w; Brain Boy back-up 2.50
❑5, ca. 1998, b&w 2.50
❑6, ca. 1998, b&w 2.50
❑7, ca. 1998, b&w 2.50
❑8, Sep 1998, b&w 3.50
❑9, Feb 1999, b&w; movie night 2.50
❑10, Apr 1999, b&w; Allen's birthday 2.50
❑11, Jun 1999, b&w; Allen's redemption 2.50

300
Dark Horse

❑1, May 1998 FM (w); FM (a) 3.50
❑2, Jun 1998 FM (w); FM (a) 3.50
❑3, Jul 1998 FM (w); FM (a) 3.25
❑4, Aug 1998 FM (w); FM (a) 3.25
❑5, Sep 1998 FM (w); FM (a) 3.95

3 LITTLE KITTENS: PURR-FECT WEAPONS (JIM BALENT'S...)
Broadsword

❑1, Aug 2002; 3 Kittens cover 2.95
❑1/A, Aug 2002; Catress cover 2.95
❑2, Oct 2002; 3 Kittens cover 2.95
❑2/A, Oct 2002; Jaguara cover 2.95
❑3, Dec 2002; 3 Kittens cover 2.95
❑3/A, Dec 2002; Baby Cat cover 2.95

THREE MOUSEKETEERS (2ND SERIES)
DC

❑1, May 1970 35.00
❑2, Jul 1970 18.00
❑3, Sep 1970 18.00
❑4, Nov 1970 18.00
❑5, Jan 1971 22.00
❑6, Mar 1971 22.00
❑7, May 1971 22.00

THREE MUSKETEERS (ETERNITY)
Eternity

❑1, Dec 1988, b&w 1.95
❑2, Feb 1989, b&w 1.95
❑3, Apr 1989, b&w 1.95

THREE MUSKETEERS (MARVEL)
Marvel

❑1, Dec 1993 1.50
❑2 1.50

3 NINJAS KICK BACK
Now

❑1, Jun 1994 1.95
❑2 1.95
❑3 1.95

303
Avatar

❑0, Jul 2004
❑1 2004 5.00
❑1/Wraparound 2004 10.00
❑2 2004 4.00
❑2/Platinum 2004 10.00
❑2/Wraparound 2004 4.00
❑3 2005 3.99
❑3/Wraparound 2005 5.00
❑4 2005 3.99
❑4/Wraparound 2005 5.00
❑5, Oct 2005 3.99
❑5/Incentive, Oct 2005 3.99
❑5/Wraparound, Oct 2005 3.99

THREE STOOGES
Gold Key

❑6, Nov 1961, Previous issues appeared as part of Dell Four Color. 65.00
❑7, Jan 1962 48.00
❑8, Mar 1962 40.00
❑9, Aug 1962 40.00
❑10, Oct 1962 40.00
❑11, Jan 1963 28.00
❑12, Apr 1963 28.00
❑13, Jul 1963 28.00
❑14, Oct 1963 28.00
❑15, Jan 1964 28.00
❑16, Mar 1964 28.00
❑17, May 1964 28.00
❑18, Jul 1964 28.00
❑19, Sep 1964, Three Musketeers parody 28.00
❑20, Nov 1964 28.00
❑21, Jan 1965 22.00
❑22, Mar 1965 22.00
❑23, May 1965 22.00
❑24, Jul 1965 22.00
❑25, Sep 1965 22.00
❑26, Nov 1965 22.00
❑27, Mar 1966 22.00
❑28, May 1966 22.00
❑29, Jul 1966 22.00
❑30, Sep 1966 22.00
❑31, Jan 1967 18.00
❑32, Mar 1967 18.00
❑33, May 1967 18.00
❑34, Jul 1967 18.00
❑35, Sep 1967 18.00
❑36, Nov 1967 18.00
❑37, Dec 1967, Golden Goose 18.00
❑38, Mar 1968 18.00
❑39, Jun 1968 18.00
❑40, Sep 1968 18.00
❑41, Dec 1968 15.00
❑42, Mar 1969 15.00
❑43, Jun 1969 15.00
❑44, Sep 1969 15.00
❑45, Dec 1969 15.00
❑46, Mar 1970, reprints #16 15.00
❑47, Jun 1970 15.00
❑48, Sep 1970, reprints #13; Baseball 15.00
❑49, Dec 1970 15.00
❑50, Mar 1971, as ape-men; Little Monsters back-up 15.00
❑51, Jun 1971 15.00
❑52, Sep 1971 15.00
❑53, Dec 1971 15.00
❑54, Mar 1972 15.00
❑55, Jun 1972, reprints #19; Three Musketeers parody 15.00

THREE STOOGES IN 3-D
Eternity

❑1 3.95

THREE STOOGES IN FULL COLOR
Eternity

❑1; Reprints 5.95

THREE STOOGES MEET HERCULES
Dell

❑1, Aug 1962 75.00

3X3 EYES
Innovation

❑1, Sep 1991, b&w; Japanese 2.50
❑2, Oct 1991, b&w; Japanese 2.25
❑3, Nov 1991, b&w; Japanese 2.25
❑4, Dec 1991, b&w; Japanese 2.25
❑5, Jan 1992, b&w; Japanese 2.25

3X3 EYES: CURSE OF THE GESU
Dark Horse / Manga

❑1, Oct 1995, b&w 2.95
❑2, Nov 1995, b&w 2.95
❑3, Dec 1995, b&w 2.95
❑4, Jan 1996, b&w 2.95
❑5, Feb 1996, b&w 2.95

3X3 EYES: DESCENT OF THE MYSTIC CITY
Dark Horse

❑1, ca. 2004 18.95

THRESHOLD (1ST SERIES)
Sleeping Giant

❑1, Oct 1996, b&w 2.50
❑2, Nov 1996, b&w 2.50

THRESHOLD (2ND SERIES)
Sleeping Giant

❑1, Dec 1997, b&w 2.50
❑2, Mar 1998, b&w 2.50
❑3 1998 2.50
❑3/Autographed 1998 2.50

THRESHOLD (3RD SERIES)
Avatar

❑1, Feb 1998 4.95
❑2, Mar 1998 4.95
❑3, Apr 1998 4.95
❑4, May 1998 4.95
❑5, Jun 1998 4.95
❑6, Jul 1998 4.95
❑7, Aug 1998 4.95
❑8, Sep 1998 4.95
❑9, Oct 1998 4.95
❑10, Nov 1998 4.95
❑11, Dec 1998 4.95
❑12, Jan 1999 4.95
❑13, Feb 1999 4.95
❑14, Mar 1999; Includes Kaos Moon story 4.95
❑15, Apr 1999 4.95
❑16, May 1999 4.95
❑17, Jun 1999 4.95
❑18, Jul 1999 4.95
❑19, Aug 1999 4.95
❑20, Sep 1999; Includes Kaos Moon story 4.95
❑21, Oct 1999 4.95
❑22, Nov 1999 4.95
❑23, Dec 1999 4.95
❑24, Jan 2000 4.95
❑25, Feb 2000 4.95
❑26, Mar 2000 4.95
❑27, Apr 2000 4.95
❑28, May 2000 4.95
❑29, Jun 2000 4.95
❑30, Jul 2000 4.95
❑31, Aug 2000 4.95
❑32, Sep 2000 4.95
❑33, Oct 2000 4.95
❑34, Nov 2000 4.95
❑35, Dec 2000 4.95
❑36, Jan 2001 4.95
❑37, Feb 2001 4.95
❑38, Mar 2001 4.95
❑39, Apr 2001 4.95
❑40, May 2001 4.95
❑41, Jun 2001 4.95
❑42, Jul 2001 4.95
❑43, Aug 2001 4.95
❑44, Sep 2001 4.95
❑45, Nov 2001 4.95
❑46, Jan 2002 4.95
❑47, Apr 2002 4.95
❑48 4.95
❑49 4.95
❑50, May 2003 4.95

THRESHOLD OF REALITY
Maintech

❑1, Sep 1986 1.00
❑2 1.00
❑3 1.00

THRESHOLD: THE STAMP COLLECTOR
Sleeping Giant

❑1, Mar 1997, b&w 2.50
❑2, May 1997, b&w 2.50

THRILLER
DC

❑1, Nov 1983 TVE (c); TVE (a) 2.00
❑2, Dec 1983 O: Thriller 1.75
❑3, Jan 1984 1.75
❑4, Feb 1984 1.50
❑5, Mar 1984; Elvis satire 1.50
❑6, Apr 1984; Elvis satire 1.50
❑7, May 1984 1.50
❑8, Jun 1984 1.50
❑9, Jul 1984 1.50
❑10, Aug 1984 1.50
❑11, Sep 1984 1.50
❑12, Oct 1984 1.50

THRILLING ADVENTURE STORIES
Atlas-Seaboard

❑1, Feb 1975, b&w; magazine RH (w); FT, EC, RH (a) 18.00
❑2, Aug 1975 25.00

THRILLING ADVENTURE STRIPS
Dragon Lady

❑5 1986; (formerly Best of Tribune Company) 2.95

Other grades: Multiply price above by 5/6 for VF/NM • 2/3 for VERY FINE • 1/3 for FINE • 1/5 for VERY GOOD • 1/8 for GOOD

Time Masters

Post-Crisis updating of Rip Hunter

©DC

Time Tunnel

Stargate's 1960s television ancestor

©Gold Key

Time Twisters

Reprinted short stories from 2000 A.D.

©Fleetway-Quality

Titans

Back to basics with 1999 post-Teen relaunch

©DC

To Be Announced

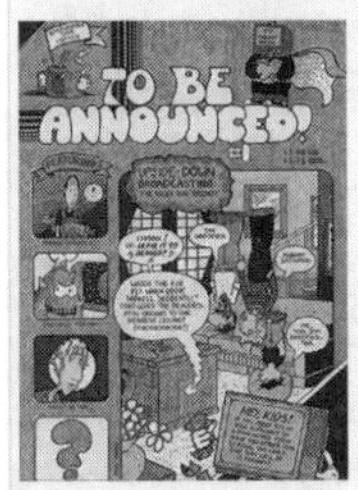

"It's a Municipal Holiday, Charlie Brown!"

©Strawberry Jam

N-MINT

❑6 1986 ... 2.95
❑7 1986 ... 2.95
❑8 1987 ... 2.95
❑9, Mar 1987 ... 2.95
❑10 1987 ... 2.95

THRILLING COMICS (2ND SERIES)
DC

❑1, May 1999; RH (a); A: Wildcat. A: Tigress. A: Hawkman. Manhunter apperance ... 2.00

THRILL KILL
CALIBER

❑1, b&w ... 2.50

THRILLKILLER
DC

❑1, Jan 1997; Elseworlds story ... 2.50
❑2, Feb 1997; Elseworlds story ... 2.50
❑3, Mar 1997; Elseworlds story ... 2.50

THRILLKILLER '62
DC

❑1 1998; prestige format; Elseworlds; sequel to Thrillkiller ... 4.95

THRILLOGY
PACIFIC

❑1 ... 1.50

THROUGH GATES OF SPLENDOR
SPIRE

❑1, ca. 1974, adapts book by Elisabeth Elliot ... 3.00

THUMB SCREW
CALIBER

❑1, b&w ... 3.50
❑2, b&w ... 3.50
❑3, b&w ... 3.50

THUMP'N GUTS
KITCHEN SINK

❑1, ca. 1993; Poly-bag reads Project X, includes poster and trading card ... 2.95

THUN'DA, KING OF THE CONGO
AC

❑1, b&w; Reprints ... 2.50

THUN'DA TALES (FRANK FRAZETTA'S...)
FANTAGRAPHICS

❑1, ca. 1986 ... 2.00

T.H.U.N.D.E.R.
SOLSON

❑1 ... 1.95

THUNDER AGENTS
TOWER

❑1, Nov 1965 WW (c); WW (a); O: Dynamo. O: The THUNDER Squad. O: Menthor. O: NoMan. 1: Dynamo. 1: Iron Maiden. 1: The THUNDER Squad. 1: Menthor. 1: NoMan. ... 140.00
❑2, Jan 1966 WW (c); WW (a); 1: Lightning. D: Egghead ... 75.00
❑3, Mar 1966 WW (c); WW (a) ... 55.00
❑4, Apr 1966 WW (a); O: Lightning. ... 55.00
❑5, Jun 1966 WW (a) ... 55.00
❑6, Jul 1966 WW (a) ... 42.00
❑7, Aug 1966 SD, WW (a); D: Menthor. 42.00

N-MINT

❑8, Sep 1966 WW (a); O: Raven. 1: Raven. ... 42.00
❑9, Oct 1966 ... 35.00
❑10, Nov 1966 ... 35.00
❑11, Mar 1967 WW (a) ... 38.00
❑12, Apr 1967 WW (a) ... 38.00
❑13, Jun 1967 WW (a); A: Undersea Agent. ... 38.00
❑14, Jul 1967 WW (a) ... 38.00
❑15, Sep 1967 WW (a) ... 38.00
❑16, Oct 1967 WW (a) ... 22.00
❑17, Dec 1967 WW (a) ... 22.00
❑18, Sep 1968 SD, WW (a) ... 22.00
❑19, Nov 1968 WW (a) ... 22.00
❑20, Jan 1969; WW (a); O: Dynamo. Reprints ... 15.00

T.H.U.N.D.E.R. AGENTS (VOL. 2)
J.C.

❑1, May 1983 ... 2.00
❑2, Jan 1984 ... 2.00

THUNDER AGENTS (WALLY WOOD'S)
DELUXE

❑1, Nov 1984 ... 2.00
❑2, Jan 1985 ... 2.00
❑3, Nov 1985 ... 2.00
❑4, Feb 1986 ... 2.00
❑5, Oct 1986 ... 2.00

THUNDERBOLT
CHARLTON

❑1, Jan 1966 O: Thunderbolt. 1: Thunderbolt. ... 16.00
❑51, Mar 1966, Series continues after hiatus (Son of Vulcan #50?) ... 10.00
❑52, Jun 1966 ... 9.00
❑53, Aug 1966 ... 9.00
❑54, Oct 1966 ... 9.00
❑55, Dec 1966 ... 9.00
❑56, Feb 1967 ... 9.00
❑57, May 1967 ... 9.00
❑58, Jul 1967 ... 9.00
❑59, Sep 1967 ... 9.00
❑60, Nov 1967 ... 9.00

THUNDERBOLT JAXON
DC / AMERICA'S BEST COMICS

❑1, Mar 2006 ... 2.99
❑2, May 2006 ... 2.99
❑3, Jun 2006 ... 2.99
❑4, Aug 2006 ... 2.99
❑5, Sep 2006 ... 2.99

THUNDERBOLTS
MARVEL

❑-1, Jul 1997; KB (w); A: Baron Zemo. A: Namor. Flashback ... 2.00
❑0, Jan 1997; KB (w); Free ... 1.00
❑1, Apr 1997; Giant-size; KB (w); Identities of Thunderbolts revealed ... 4.00
❑2, May 1997 KB (w); V: Mad Thinker. 3.00
❑2/A, May 1997; Alternate cover ... 3.00
❑3, Jun 1997 KB (w) ... 3.00
❑4, Jul 1997; KB (w); 1: Jolt. Jolt joins team ... 2.50
❑5, Aug 1997; gatefold summary; KB (w); Atlas vs. Growing Man ... 2.50
❑6, Sep 1997; gatefold summary KB (w) ... 2.00

N-MINT

❑7, Oct 1997; gatefold summary KB (w); V: Elements of Doom. ... 2.00
❑8, Nov 1997; gatefold summary KB (w); A: Spider-Man. ... 2.00
❑9, Dec 1997; gatefold summary KB (w); A: Black Widow. ... 2.00
❑10, Jan 1998; gatefold summary; KB (w); Thunderbolts revealed as Masters of Evil ... 2.00
❑11, Feb 1998; gatefold summary KB (w) ... 2.00
❑12, Mar 1998; gatefold summary KB (w); A: Fantastic Four. A: Avengers. 6.00
❑13, Apr 1998; gatefold summary KB (w) ... 2.00
❑14, May 1998; gatefold summary KB (w) ... 2.00
❑15, Jun 1998; gatefold summary KB (w) ... 2.00
❑16, Jul 1998; gatefold summary KB (w); V: Lightning Rods (formerly Great Lakes Avengers). ... 2.00
❑17, Aug 1998; gatefold summary KB (w); V: Graviton. ... 2.00
❑18, Sep 1998; gatefold summary KB (w) ... 2.00
❑19, Oct 1998; gatefold summary KB (w); 1: Charcoal. ... 2.00
❑20, Nov 1998; gatefold summary KB (w); V: new Masters of Evil. ... 2.00
❑21, Dec 1998; gatefold summary KB (w); A: Hawkeye. ... 2.00
❑22, Jan 1999; gatefold summary; KB (w); Hercules vs. Atlas ... 2.00
❑23, Feb 1999 KB (w); A: U.S. Agent.. 2.00
❑24, Mar 1999 KB (w); A: Citizen V. ... 2.00
❑25, Apr 1999; double-sized KB (w); A: Masters of Evil. V: Masters of Evil... 2.99
❑25/Autographed, Apr 1999 KB (w); A: Masters of Evil. ... 12.00
❑26, May 1999; Mach-1 in prison ... 1.99
❑27, Jun 1999 A: Archangel. ... 1.99
❑28, Jul 1999 A: Archangel. V: Graviton. ... 1.99
❑29, Aug 1999 A: Machine Man. V: Graviton. ... 1.99
❑30, Sep 1999; Hawkeye and Moonstone caught in clinch ... 1.99
❑31, Oct 1999 ... 1.99
❑32, Nov 1999 ... 1.99
❑33, Dec 1999 ... 1.99
❑34, Jan 2000 ... 1.99
❑35, Feb 2000 ... 2.25
❑36, Mar 2000 ... 2.25
❑37, Apr 2000 ... 2.25
❑38, May 2000 ... 2.25
❑39, Jun 2000 ... 2.25
❑40, Jul 2000 ... 2.25
❑41, Aug 2000 A: Sandman ... 2.25
❑42, Sep 2000 A: Wonder Man. ... 2.25
❑43, Oct 2000 A: Black Widow. ... 2.25
❑44, Nov 2000 A: Nefaria. A: Avengers. 2.25
❑45, Dec 2000 ... 2.25
❑46, Jan 2001; return of Jolt ... 2.25
❑47, Feb 2001 A: Captain Marvel ... 2.25
❑48, Mar 2001 ... 2.25
❑49, Apr 2001 ... 2.25
❑50, May 2001; double-sized A: Citizen V. 2.99

❑51, Jun 2001 .... 2.25
❑52, Jul 2001 .... 2.25
❑53, Aug 2001 .... 2.25
❑54, Sep 2001 .... 2.25
❑55, Oct 2001 .... 2.25
❑56, Nov 2001 .... 2.25
❑57, Dec 2001 .... 2.25
❑58, Jan 2002 .... 2.25
❑59, Feb 2002 .... 2.25
❑60, Mar 2002 .... 2.25
❑61, Apr 2002 .... 2.25
❑62, May 2002 .... 2.25
❑63, Jun 2002 .... 2.25
❑64, Jul 2002 .... 2.25
❑65, Aug 2002 .... 2.25
❑66, Aug 2002 .... 2.25
❑67, Sep 2002 .... 2.25
❑68, Sep 2002 .... 2.25
❑69, Oct 2002 .... 2.25
❑70, Oct 2002 .... 2.25
❑71, Nov 2002 .... 2.25
❑72, Nov 2002 .... 2.25
❑73, Dec 2002 .... 2.25
❑74, Jan 2003 .... 2.25
❑75, Feb 2003 .... 2.25
❑76, Mar 2003 .... 2.25
❑77, Apr 2003 .... 2.99
❑78, Jun 2003 .... 2.99
❑79, Jul 2003 .... 2.25
❑80, Aug 2003 .... 2.25
❑81, Sep 2003 .... 2.25
❑100, May 2006 .... 2.99
❑101, Jun 2006 .... 2.99
❑102, Jul 2006 .... 2.99
❑103, Aug 2006 .... 2.99
❑Annual 1997, Aug 1997; KB (w); GC, GP, BMc (a); O: Thunderbolts. 1997 Annual; wraparound cover 3.00
❑Ashcan 1; Ashcan preview; American Entertainment 2.50
❑Ashcan 1/Autogr; Ashcan preview 4.00

THUNDERBUNNY (1ST SERIES)
ARCHIE / RED CIRCLE

❑1, Jan 1984 .... 2.00

THUNDERBUNNY (2ND SERIES)
WARP

❑1, Jun 1985; O: retold. Warp publishes 2.00
❑2, Aug 1985 .... 2.00
❑3, Oct 1985 .... 2.00
❑4, Dec 1985 .... 2.00
❑5, Feb 1986 .... 2.00
❑6 1986, b&w; Apple begins publishing 2.00
❑7 1986, b&w 2.00
❑8 1987 .... 1.75
❑9 1987 .... 1.75
❑10, Jul 1987 .... 1.75
❑11, Sep 1987 A: THUNDER Agents 1.75
❑12, Nov 1987; last 1.75

THUNDERCATS
MARVEL / STAR

❑1, Dec 1985 .... 4.00
❑2, Feb 1986 .... 2.00
❑3, Apr 1986 .... 2.00
❑4, Jun 1986 .... 2.00
❑5, Aug 1986 .... 2.00
❑6, Oct 1986 .... 2.00
❑7, Dec 1986 .... 1.50
❑8, Feb 1987 .... 1.50
❑9, Mar 1987 .... 1.50
❑10, Apr 1987 .... 1.50
❑11, May 1987 .... 1.50
❑12, Jun 1987 .... 1.50
❑13, Jul 1987 .... 1.50
❑14, Aug 1987 .... 1.50
❑15, Sep 1987 .... 1.50
❑16, Oct 1987 .... 1.50
❑17, Nov 1987 .... 1.50
❑18, Dec 1987 .... 1.50
❑19, Jan 1988 .... 1.50
❑20, Feb 1988 .... 1.50
❑21, Mar 1988 .... 1.50
❑22, Apr 1988 .... 1.50
❑23, May 1988 .... 1.50
❑24, Jun 1988 .... 1.50

THUNDERCATS/ BATTLE OF THE PLANETS
DC / WILDSTORM

❑1, ca. 2003 .... 4.95

THUNDERCATS: DOGS OF WAR
DC

❑1, Aug 2003 .... 2.95
❑2, Sep 2003 .... 2.95
❑3, Oct 2003 .... 2.95
❑4, Nov 2003 .... 2.95
❑5, Dec 2003 .... 2.95

THUNDERCATS: ENEMY'S PRIDE
DC

❑1, Aug 2004 .... 2.95
❑2, Sep 2004 .... 2.95
❑3, Oct 2004 .... 2.95
❑4, Nov 2004 .... 2.95
❑5, Dec 2004 .... 2.95

THUNDERCATS: HAMMERHAND'S REVENGE
DC

❑1, Dec 2003 .... 2.95
❑2, Jan 2004 .... 2.95
❑3, Feb 2004 .... 2.95
❑4, Mar 2004 .... 2.95
❑5, Apr 2004 .... 2.95

THUNDERCATS ORIGINS: HEROES & VILLAINS
DC

❑1, Feb 2004 .... 3.50

THUNDERCATS ORIGINS: VILLAINS & HEROES
DC

❑1, Feb 2004 .... 3.50

THUNDERCATS: THE RETURN
DC / WILDSTORM

❑1, Apr 2003 .... 2.95
❑2, May 2003 .... 2.95
❑3, Jun 2003 .... 2.95
❑4, Jul 2003 .... 2.95
❑5, Aug 2003 .... 2.95

THUNDERCATS (DC/WILDSTORM)
DC / WILDSTORM

❑0, Oct 2002 .... 2.50
❑1, Oct 2002 .... 2.50
❑2, Nov 2002 .... 2.95
❑3, Dec 2002 .... 2.95
❑4, Jan 2003 .... 2.95
❑5, Feb 2003 .... 2.95

THUNDER GIRLS
PIN & INK

❑1, Sum 1997 .... 2.95
❑2, Sum 1999 .... 2.95
❑3, Fal 1999 .... 2.95

THUNDERGOD
CRUSADE

❑1/A, Aug 1996; Alternate cover (drawn cover, man and woman clasping) 2.95
❑1, Aug 1996, b&w; Painted cover 2.95
❑2, Oct 1996, b&w 2.95
❑3, Dec 1996, b&w 2.95

THUNDERMACE
RAK

❑1, Mar 1986, b&w 2.00
❑2 1986 .... 1.75
❑3, Apr 1987 .... 1.75
❑4 1987 .... 1.75
❑5 1987 .... 2.00
❑6 1987 .... 2.00
❑7 1987 .... 2.00

THUNDERSAURS: THE BODACIOUS ADVENTURES OF BIFF THUNDERSAUR
INNOVATION

❑1, b&w 2.25

THUNDERSKULL! (SIDNEY MELLON'S...)
SLAVE LABOR

❑1, Aug 1989, b&w 1.95

THUNDERSTRIKE
MARVEL

❑1, Jun 1993; Prism cover 2.95
❑2, Nov 1993 .... 1.25
❑3, Dec 1993 .... 1.25
❑4, Jan 1994 .... 1.25
❑5, Feb 1994 .... 1.25
❑6, Mar 1994 .... 1.25
❑7, Apr 1994 .... 1.25
❑8, May 1994 .... 1.25
❑9, Jun 1994 .... 1.50
❑10, Jul 1994 .... 1.50
❑11, Aug 1994 .... 1.50
❑12, Sep 1994 .... 1.50
❑13, Oct 1994 .... 1.50
❑13/A, Oct 1994; flip-book with Code Blue back-up; second indicia gives title as Marvel Double Feature ... Thunderstrike/Code Blue 2.50
❑14, Nov 1994 .... 1.50
❑14/A, Nov 1994; flip-book with Code Blue back-up; second indicia gives title as Marvel Double Feature ... Thunderstrike/Code Blue 2.50
❑15, Dec 1994 .... 1.50
❑15/A, Dec 1994; flip-book with Code Blue back-up; second indicia gives title as Marvel Double Feature ... Thunderstrike/Code Blue 2.50
❑16, Jan 1995 .... 1.50
❑16/A, Jan 1995; flip-book with Code Blue back-up; second indicia gives title as Marvel Double Feature ... Thunderstrike/Code Blue 2.50
❑17, Feb 1995 .... 1.50
❑18, Mar 1995 .... 1.50
❑19, Apr 1995 .... 1.50
❑20, May 1995 .... 1.50
❑21, Jun 1995; Avengers #1 homage cover 1.50
❑22, Jul 1995; Identity of Bloodaxe revealed 1.50
❑23, Aug 1995 .... 1.50
❑24, Sep 1995 .... 1.50

TICK
NEC

❑1, Jun 1988; Black background on cover 15.00
❑1/2nd 3.00
❑1/3rd 2.50
❑1/4th 2.25
❑1/5th 2.75
❑2, Sep 1988; Die-cut cover 8.00
❑2/Variant; Without die-cut cover 15.00
❑2/2nd 3.00
❑2/3rd 2.25
❑2/4th 2.25
❑2/5th 2.75
❑3, Dec 1988 .... 6.00
❑3/2nd, Nov 1989; Yellow stripe on cover saying "Encore Presentation" 3.00
❑3/3rd 2.75
❑3/4th 2.75
❑4, Apr 1989 1: Paul the Samurai. 8.00
❑4/2nd 1: Paul the Samurai. 2.25
❑4/3rd 1: Paul the Samurai 2.75
❑4/4th 1: Paul the Samurai 2.75
❑4/5th 1: Paul the Samurai 2.75
❑5, Aug 1989; Scarcer 8.00
❑5/2nd 2.75
❑6, Nov 1989 .... 5.00
❑6/2nd 2.75
❑6/3rd 2.75
❑7, Feb 1990 .... 5.00
❑7/2nd 2.75
❑7/3rd, Sep 1995 .... 2.75
❑8, Jul 1990; Has logo 8.00
❑8/Variant; No logo on cover 8.00
❑8/2nd 2.75
❑9, Mar 1991 1: The Chainsaw Vigilante. 3.00
❑10, Oct 1991 .... 3.00
❑11, Aug 1992 .... 3.00
❑12, May 1993 .... 3.00
❑12/Ltd.; Gold spider foil on front 20.00
❑13, Nov 2000; Pseudo-Tick edition 3.50
❑Special 1, Mar 1988; Special edition 1: The Tick. 50.00
❑Special 2, Jun 1988; Special edition 2: The Tick. 25.00

TICK & ARTHUR
NEC

❑1, Apr 1999 .... 3.50

Other grades: Multiply price above by 5/6 for VF/NM • 2/3 for VERY FINE • 1/3 for FINE • 1/5 for VERY GOOD • 1/8 for GOOD

Tomahawk

Revolutionary-era hero raised by Indians

©DC

Tom & Jerry Comics

Long-running title went from Dell to Gold Key

©Dell

Tomb of Darkness

Horro SF title had been called "Beware"

©Marvel

Tomb of Dracula

Cult 1970s series gave birth to Blade

©Marvel

Tomb of Dracula (Magazine)

Black-and-white magazine version

©Marvel

N-MINT

TICK & ARTIE
NEC

- ❑1/A 2002; Tick, Arthur on cover 3.50
- ❑1/B 2002; Bugs on cover 3.50

TICK BIG BLUE DESTINY
NEC

- ❑1, Oct 1997; Keen Edition; Arthur and Tick with #1 posing on cover 2.95
- ❑1/A, Oct 1997; Wicked Keen Edition; Die-cut cover 4.95
- ❑1/Ashcan, ca. 1997; ashcan edition; ashcan preview of mini-series 2.95
- ❑1/B, Oct 1997; Wicked Keen Edition without Die-Cut Cover; 500 printed. 19.00
- ❑2, Dec 1997 .... 2.95
- ❑2/Variant, Dec 1997; Tick-buster cover 2.95
- ❑3, Mar 1998 .... 3.50
- ❑4, Apr 1998; Justice Cover 3.50
- ❑4/A, Apr 1998; Ocean cover 3.50
- ❑5, Jul 1998 .... 3.50

TICK BIG RED-N-GREEN CHRISTMAS SPECTACLE
NEC

- ❑1, Dec 2001, Black background on cover 3.95

TICK BIG SUMMER ANNUAL
NEC

- ❑1, Jul 1999 .... 3.50

TICK, THE: CIRCUS MAXIMUS
NEC

- ❑1, Mar 2000 .... 3.50
- ❑2, Apr 2000 .... 3.50
- ❑3, May 2000 .... 3.50
- ❑4, Jun 2000 .... 3.50

TICK: DAYS OF DRAMA
NEW ENGLAND

- ❑1, Sep 2005 .... 4.95

TICK, THE: HEROES OF THE CITY
NEC

- ❑1, Feb 1999 .... 3.50

TICK INCREDIBLE INTERNET COMIC
NEC

- ❑1, Jul 2001, Black background on cover 3.95

TICK, THE: KARMA TORNADO
NEC

- ❑1, Oct 1993 .... 4.00
- ❑1/2nd, Jan 1997 .... 2.95
- ❑2, Jan 1994 .... 3.50
- ❑2/2nd, Feb 1997 .... 2.95
- ❑3, May 1994; Scarce 5.00
- ❑3/2nd, Mar 1997; flip book with The Tick's Back back-up 2.95
- ❑4, Jul 1994; Scarce 5.00
- ❑4/2nd, Apr 1997; flip book with The Tick's Back back-up 2.95
- ❑5, Aug 1994; Scarce 5.00
- ❑5/2nd 2.95
- ❑6, Oct 1994 .... 4.00
- ❑6/2nd 2.95
- ❑7 1994 .... 4.00
- ❑7/2nd 2.95

N-MINT

- ❑8 1995 .... 4.00
- ❑8/2nd 2.95
- ❑9 1995 .... 3.00
- ❑9/2nd 2.95

TICK: LUNY BIN TRILOGY
NEC

- ❑0, Jul 1998; A.k.a. The Tick: Big Blue Destiny #6; Preview 1.50
- ❑1, Oct 1998 .... 3.50
- ❑2, Sep 1998 .... 3.50
- ❑3, Oct 1998 .... 3.50

TICK'S BACK
NEC

- ❑0, Aug 1997; Red cover 2.95
- ❑0/A, Aug 1997; Green Cover 5.00
- ❑0/B, Aug 1997; Gold Tick Cover 7.50
- ❑0/C, Aug 1997, b&w; no logo; gold cover 10.00

TICK'S BIG BACK TO SCHOOL SPECIAL
NEC

- ❑1, ca. 1998 .... 3.50

TICK'S BIG CRUISE SHIP VACATION SPECIAL
NEC

- ❑1, Sep 2000 .... 3.50

TICK'S BIG FATHER'S DAY SPECIAL
NEC

- ❑1, Jun 2000 .... 3.50

TICK'S BIG HALLOWEEN SPECIAL
NEC

- ❑1, Oct 1999 .... 3.50

TICK'S BIG MOTHER'S DAY SPECIAL
NEC

- ❑1, Apr 2000 .... 3.50

TICK'S BIG ROMANTIC ADVENTURE
NEC

- ❑1, Feb 1998 .... 2.95

TICK'S BIG SUMMER FUN SPECIAL
NEC

- ❑1, Aug 1998 .... 3.50

TICK'S BIG TAX TIME TERROR
NEC

- ❑1, Apr 2000 .... 3.50

TICK'S BIG YEAR 2000 SPECIAL
NEC

- ❑1, Mar 2000 .... 3.50

TICK'S BIG YULE LOG SPECIAL
NEC

- ❑1/A, Dec 1997, b&w; Tick holding Arthur on cover 3.50
- ❑1, Dec 1997, b&w 3.50
- ❑1998, Feb 1998 .... 3.50
- ❑1999, Jan 1999 .... 3.50
- ❑2000, Nov 1999 .... 3.50
- ❑2000/Ltd., Nov 1999 .... 4.95
- ❑2001 .... 3.50

TICK'S GIANT CIRCUS OF THE MIGHTY
NEC

- ❑1, Sum 1992 .... 2.75
- ❑2, Sum 1992 .... 2.75

N-MINT

TICK'S GOLDEN AGE COMIC
NEC

- ❑1/A, May 2002; Red Timely-style cover 4.95
- ❑1/B, May 2002; Standing on top of world with Eagle cover 4.95
- ❑2/A, Aug 2002; Jungle cover 4.95
- ❑2/B, Aug 2002; EC spoof cover 4.95

TICK'S MASSIVE SUMMER DOUBLE SPECTACLE
NEC

- ❑1/B, Jul 2000 .... 3.50
- ❑1/A, Jul 2000 .... 3.50
- ❑1, Jul 2000 .... 3.50
- ❑2/B 2001 .... 3.50
- ❑2/A 2001 .... 3.50
- ❑2 2001 .... 3.50

TICK-TOCK FOLLIES
SLAVE LABOR

- ❑1, Dec 1996 .... 2.95

TIC TOC TOM
DETONATOR CANADA

- ❑1, Aut 1995, b&w 2.95
- ❑2, Win 1995, b&w 2.95
- ❑3, Spr 1996, b&w 2.95

TIGER 2021
ANUBIS

- ❑Ashcan 1, May 1994 .... 3.95

TIGER GIRL
GOLD KEY

- ❑1, Sep 1968 .... 35.00

TIGERMAN
ATLAS-SEABOARD

- ❑1, Sep 1975 1&O: Tigerman 9.00
- ❑2, Jun 1975 SD (a) 8.00
- ❑3, Sep 1975 SD (a) 8.00

TIGERS OF TERRA
MIND-VISIONS

- ❑1, ca. 1992 .... 3.00
- ❑2, ca. 1992 .... 3.00
- ❑3, ca. 1992 .... 3.00
- ❑4, ca. 1992 .... 3.00
- ❑5, ca. 1992 .... 3.00
- ❑6, ca. 1992 .... 3.00
- ❑7, ca. 1992 .... 3.00
- ❑8, ca. 1993 .... 3.00
- ❑9, ca. 1993; two covers: a and b 3.75
- ❑10, ca. 1993, b&w 3.75
- ❑11, ca. 1993, b&w 3.95
- ❑12, Jul 1993, b&w 3.95

TIGERS OF TERRA (VOL. 2)
ANTARCTIC

- ❑0, Aug 1993 .... 2.95
- ❑1, Oct 1993 .... 3.00
- ❑2, Dec 1993 .... 3.00
- ❑3, Feb 1994 .... 3.00
- ❑4, Apr 1994 .... 3.00
- ❑5, Jul 1994 .... 3.00
- ❑6, Sep 1994 .... 3.00
- ❑7, Dec 1994 .... 3.00
- ❑8, Jan 1995 .... 3.00
- ❑9, Mar 1995 .... 3.00

Other grades: Multiply price above by 5/6 for VF/NM • 2/3 for VERY FINE • 1/3 for FINE • 1/5 for VERY GOOD • 1/8 for GOOD

❑10, Apr 1995 .... 3.00
❑11, May 1995 .... 2.75
❑12, Jun 1995 .... 2.75
❑13, Jul 1995 .... 2.75
❑14, Aug 1995 .... 2.75
❑15, Sep 1995 .... 2.75
❑16, Oct 1995 .... 2.75
❑17, Nov 1995 .... 2.75
❑18, Dec 1996 .... 2.95
❑19, Jan 1996 .... 2.95
❑20, Mar 1996 .... 2.95
❑21, May 1996 .... 2.95
❑22, Jul 1996 .... 2.95
❑23, Sep 1996 .... 2.95
❑24, Nov 1996 .... 3.95
❑25, Jan 1997 .... 2.95

TIGERS OF TERRA (VOL. 3)
ANTARCTIC

❑1, Jul 2000 .... 2.95

TIGERS OF TERRA: TECHNICAL MANUAL
ANTARCTIC

❑1, Dec 1995, b&w 2.95
❑2, Jun 1996, b&w 2.95

TIGER WOMAN
MILLENNIUM

❑1, Sep 1994, no indicia 2.95
❑2, Apr 1995, no indicia; but title page says Tiger Woman #2, cover says Quest of the Tiger Woman #1 .... 2.95

TIGER-X
ETERNITY

❑1 1988, b&w; Story continued from Tiger-X Special #1 .... 2.00
❑2 1988, b&w 2.00
❑3 1988, b&w 2.00
❑Special 1 1988, b&w 2.25
❑Special 1/2nd, Dec 1988 .... 2.25

TIGER-X BOOK II
ETERNITY

❑1 1989, b&w 2.00
❑2 1989, b&w 2.00
❑3 1989, b&w 2.00
❑4 1989, b&w 2.00

TIGRA
MARVEL

❑1, May 2002 .... 2.99
❑2, Jun 2002 .... 2.99
❑3, Jul 2002 .... 2.99
❑4, Aug 2002 .... 2.99

TIGRESS
HERO

❑1, Aug 1992, b&w 2.95
❑2, Oct 1992, b&w 2.95
❑3, Dec 1992, b&w 2.95
❑4, Feb 1993, b&w 2.95
❑5, Apr 1993, b&w 2.95
❑6, Jun 1993 .... 3.95

TIGRESS (BASEMENT)
BASEMENT

❑1, Jul 1998 .... 2.95

TIJUANA BIBLE
STARHEAD

❑1, b&w 2.50
❑2, b&w 2.50
❑3, b&w 2.50
❑4, b&w; Bluesie Toons 2.50
❑5; World's Fair 2.50
❑6; Fuller Brush Man 2.50
❑7; Royalty issue 2.50
❑8; Hollywood women 2.50
❑9; An Artist's Affaire 2.50

TILAZEUS MEETS THE MESSIAH
AIIIE

❑1 .... 2.50

TIMBER WOLF
DC

❑1, Nov 1992 .... 1.50
❑2, Dec 1992 .... 1.50
❑3, Jan 1993 V: Creeper. 1.50
❑4, Feb 1993 .... 1.50
❑5, Mar 1993 .... 1.50

TIME BANDITS
MARVEL

❑1, Feb 1982 .... 1.50

TIME BREAKERS
DC / HELIX

❑1, Jan 1997 .... 2.25
❑2, Feb 1997 .... 2.25
❑3, Mar 1997 .... 2.25
❑4, Apr 1997 .... 2.25
❑5, May 1997 .... 2.25

TIME CITY
ROCKET

❑1, Mar 1992 .... 2.50

TIMECOP
DARK HORSE

❑1, Sep 1994 .... 2.50
❑2, Sep 1994 .... 2.50

TIMEDRIFTER (GERARD JONES'...)
INNOVATION

❑1, Dec 1990, b&w 2.25
❑2, b&w 2.25
❑3, b&w 2.25

TIME GATES
DOUBLE EDGE

❑1 .... 1.95
❑2 .... 1.95
❑3 .... 1.95

TIMEJUMP WAR
APPLE

❑1, Oct 1989, b&w 2.25
❑2, b&w 2.25
❑3, b&w 2.25

TIME KILLERS
FLEETWAY-QUALITY

❑1; Tales From Beyond Space: The Men In Red 2.95
❑2 .... 2.95
❑3 .... 2.95
❑4 .... 2.95
❑5 .... 2.95
❑6 .... 2.95
❑7 .... 2.95

TIMELESS TALES (BOB POWELL'S...)
ECLIPSE

❑1, Mar 1989, b&w 2.00

TIMELY PRESENTS: ALL-WINNERS
MARVEL

❑1, Dec 1999; Reprints All-Winners Comics #19 .... 3.99

TIMELY PRESENTS: HUMAN TORCH
MARVEL

❑1, Feb 1999; Painted cover; Contents reprinted from Human Torch Comics #5 .... 3.99

TIME MACHINE
ETERNITY

❑1, Apr 1990, b&w; Based on the story by H.G. Wells 2.50
❑2 1990, b&w 2.50
❑3 1990, b&w 2.50
❑Book 1 .... 9.95

TIME MASTERS
DC

❑1, Feb 1990 .... 2.00
❑2, Mar 1990 .... 1.75
❑3, Apr 1990 .... 1.75
❑4, May 1990 .... 1.75
❑5, Jun 1990 A: Viking Prince. 1.75
❑6, Jul 1990 A: Doctor Fate. 1.75
❑7, Aug 1990 A: Arion. 1.75
❑8, Sep 1990 .... 1.75

TIME OUT OF MIND
GRAPHIC SERIALS

❑1 .... 2.00
❑2 .... 1.75
❑3 .... 1.75

TIMESLIP COLLECTION
MARVEL

❑1, Nov 1998; collects short features from Marvel Vision; wraparound cover 2.99

TIMESLIP SPECIAL
MARVEL

❑1, Oct 1998; cardstock cover 5.99

TIMESPELL
CLUB 408 GRAPHICS

❑0, ca. 1997, b&w; cardstock cover 2.95
❑1, ca. 1998, b&w; cardstock cover 2.95
❑2, ca. 1998, b&w; cardstock cover 2.95
❑3, ca. 1998, b&w; cardstock cover 2.95
❑4, ca. 1998, b&w; cardstock cover 2.95
❑Ashcan 1, ca. 1997; no cover price; ashcan preview of upcoming series 1.00

TIMESPELL: THE DIRECTOR'S CUT
CLUB 408 GRAPHICS

❑1, ca. 1998, b&w; no price on cover; reprints #1 with revisions and additions 2.95

TIMESPIRITS
MARVEL / EPIC

❑1, Oct 1984 TY (a) 2.00
❑2, Dec 1984 .... 1.75
❑3, Feb 1985 .... 1.75
❑4, Apr 1985 AW (a) 1.75
❑5, Jul 1985 .... 1.75
❑6, Sep 1985 .... 1.75
❑7, Dec 1985 .... 1.75
❑8, Mar 1986 .... 1.75

TIME TRAVELER AI
CPM MANGA

❑1, Oct 1999, b&w 2.95
❑2, Nov 1999, b&w 2.95
❑3, Dec 1999, b&w 2.95
❑4, Jan 2000, b&w 2.95
❑5, Feb 2000, b&w 2.95
❑6, Mar 2000, b&w 2.95

TIME TRAVELER HERBIE
AVALON

❑1 .... 2.95

TIME TUNNEL
GOLD KEY

❑1, Feb 1967 .... 40.00
❑2, Jul 1967 .... 35.00

TIME TWISTED TALES
RIP OFF

❑1 .... 2.00

TIME TWISTERS
FLEETWAY-QUALITY

❑1 AMo (w); DaG (a) 1.50
❑2 AMo (w); DaG (a) 1.50
❑3 AMo (w); BT (a) 1.50
❑4 AMo (w); DaG (a) 1.50
❑5 .... 1.50
❑6 AMo (w) 1.50
❑7 AMo (w) 1.50
❑8 AMo (w); DaG (a) 1.50
❑9 AMo (w) 1.50
❑10 .... 1.50
❑11 .... 1.50
❑12 .... 1.50
❑13 .... 1.50
❑14 AMo (w); BB (a) 1.50
❑15 DaG (a) 1.50
❑16 .... 1.50
❑17 NG (w) 1.50
❑18 NG (w) 1.50
❑19 .... 1.50
❑20 .... 1.50
❑21 AMo (w); DaG (a) 1.50

TIMEWALKER
ACCLAIM / VALIANT

❑0, Mar 1996 BH (w); DP (a); O: Ivar. 5.00
❑1, Jan 1995; BH (w); DP (a); cover has Dec 94 coverdate 2.00
❑1/VVSS 75.00
❑2, Feb 1995; BH (w); DP (a); cover has Jan coverdate 1.00
❑3, Mar 1995; BH (w); cover has Feb coverdate 1.00
❑4, Apr 1995; BH (w); DP (a); cover has Mar coverdate 2.00
❑5, Apr 1995 BH (w) 2.00
❑6, May 1995 .... 2.00
❑7, Jun 1995 .... 2.00
❑8, Jul 1995; Birthquake 2.00
❑9, Jul 1995; BH (w); DP (a); Birthquake 2.00
❑10, Aug 1995 .... 2.00
❑11, Aug 1995 .... 2.00
❑12, Sep 1995 DP (a) 2.00

Tomb Raider: The Series

Extremely healthy woman from video game

©Image

Tom Mix Western

Reprinting tales of the old western hero

©AC

Tomoe

Series interacted with Crusade's Shi title

©Crusade

Tomorrow Stories

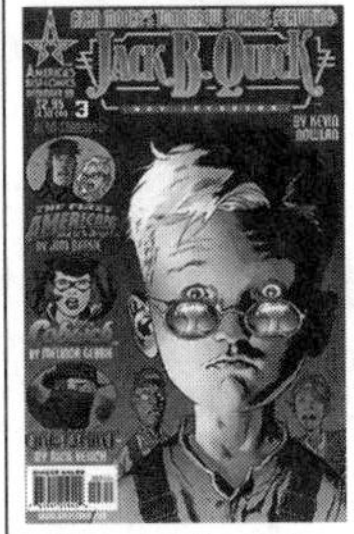

Showcases the stories of Alan Moore

©DC

Tom Strong

Doc Savage quality to Alan Moore title

©DC

N-MINT

❑13, Sep 1995 .... 2.00
❑14, Oct 1995 .... 2.00
❑15, Oct 1995 .... 2.00
❑Yearbook 1, May 1995; Yearbook A: H.A.R.D. Corps 3.00

TIME WANKERS
FANTAGRAPHICS / EROS

❑1, Sep 1996, b&w 2.25
❑2, b&w 2.25
❑3, b&w 2.25
❑4, b&w 2.25
❑5, b&w 2.25

TIME WARP
DC

❑1, Nov 1979 DN, TS, RB, SD, DG, JA, DA (a) 4.00
❑2, Jan 1980 .... 2.00
❑3, Mar 1980 .... 2.00
❑4, May 1980 .... 2.00
❑5, Jul 1980 .... 2.00

TIME WARRIOR
BLAZING

❑1 1993 .... 2.50

TIME WARRIORS: THE BEGINNING
FANTASY GENERAL

❑1 .... 1.50

TIM HOLT WESTERN ANNUAL
AC

❑1, b&w; Reprints 2.95

TIMMY THE TIMID GHOST (1ST SERIES)
CHARLTON

❑3, ca. 1956 .... 36.00
❑4, ca. 1956 .... 20.00
❑5, ca. 1956 .... 20.00
❑6, Mar 1957 .... 20.00
❑7, ca. 1957 .... 20.00
❑8, Sep 1957 .... 20.00
❑9, ca. 1957 .... 20.00
❑10, ca. 1957 .... 20.00
❑11, Apr 1958, Big book 18.00
❑12, Oct 1958, Bog Book 18.00
❑13, Feb 1959 .... 18.00
❑14, Apr 1959 .... 18.00
❑15, Jun 1959 .... 18.00
❑16, Aug 1959 .... 18.00
❑17, Oct 1959 .... 18.00
❑18, Dec 1959 .... 18.00
❑19, Feb 1960 .... 18.00
❑20, Apr 1960 .... 18.00
❑21, Jun 1960 .... 10.00
❑22, Aug 1960 .... 10.00
❑23, Oct 1960 .... 10.00
❑24, Dec 1960 .... 10.00
❑25, Feb 1961 .... 10.00
❑26, Apr 1961 .... 10.00
❑27, ca. 1961 .... 10.00
❑28, ca. 1961 .... 10.00
❑29, ca. 1962 .... 10.00
❑30, ca. 1962 .... 10.00
❑31, Sep 1962 .... 10.00
❑32, ca. 1963 .... 10.00
❑33, Jul 1963 .... 10.00

N-MINT

❑34, Sep 1963 .... 10.00
❑35, Nov 1963 .... 10.00
❑36, Jan 1964 .... 10.00
❑37, Mar 1964 .... 10.00
❑38, May 1964 .... 10.00
❑39, Jun 1964 .... 10.00
❑40, Jul 1964 .... 10.00
❑41, Aug 1964 .... 10.00
❑42, Sep 1964 .... 10.00
❑43, Oct 1964 .... 10.00
❑44, Nov 1964 .... 10.00
❑45, Sep 1966 .... 10.00

TIMMY THE TIMID GHOST (2ND SERIES)
CHARLTON

❑1, Oct 1967 .... 10.00
❑2, Feb 1968 .... 6.00
❑3, Apr 1968 .... 6.00
❑4, Jun 1968 .... 6.00
❑5, Aug 1968 .... 6.00
❑6, Oct 1968 .... 6.00
❑7, Dec 1968 .... 6.00
❑8, Feb 1969 .... 6.00
❑9, Apr 1969 .... 6.00
❑10, Jun 1969 .... 6.00
❑11, Aug 1969 .... 4.00
❑12, Oct 1969 .... 4.00
❑13, Dec 1969 .... 4.00
❑14, Jan 1970 .... 4.00
❑15, Mar 1970 .... 4.00
❑16, May 1970 .... 4.00
❑17, Jul 1970 .... 4.00
❑18, Sep 1970 .... 4.00
❑19, Nov 1970 .... 4.00
❑20, Jan 1971 .... 4.00
❑21, Mar 1971 .... 4.00
❑22, May 1971 .... 4.00
❑23, Jul 1971 .... 4.00
❑24, Sep 1985, reprints Timmy the Timid Ghost (1st series) #7 .... 4.00
❑25, Nov 1985, reprints Timmy the Timid Ghost (1st series) #6 (cover reversed & recolored) 4.00
❑26, Jan 1986, reprints Timmy the Timid Ghost (1st series) #9 .... 4.00

TINCAN MAN
IMAGE / VALIANT

❑1, Jan 2000 .... 2.95
❑2, Feb 2000 .... 2.95
❑Ashcan 1, Dec 1999; Preview issue 2.95

TINY DEATHS
YUGP

❑1 .... 1.75
❑2, Jan 1997 .... 1.75

TIPPER GORE'S COMICS AND STORIES
REVOLUTIONARY

❑1, Oct 1989, b&w 1.95
❑2, Jan 1990, b&w 1.95
❑3, Mar 1990, b&w 1.95
❑4, May 1990, b&w 1.95
❑5, Jul 1990, b&w 1.95

N-MINT

TITAN A.E.
DARK HORSE

❑1, May 2000 .... 2.95
❑2, Jun 2000 .... 2.95
❑3, Jul 2000 .... 2.95

TITANS
DC

❑1, Mar 1999; DGry (w); A: H.I.V.E.. new team 3.00
❑1/Autographed, Mar 1999 DGry (w); A: H.I.V.E. 15.95
❑2, Apr 1999 DGry (w); A: Superman. A: H.I.V.E. 2.50
❑3, May 1999 DGry (w); V: Goth. 2.50
❑4, Jun 1999 DGry (w); V: Goth. 2.50
❑5, Jul 1999 DGry (w) 2.50
❑6, Aug 1999 DGry (w); A: Green Lantern. V: Red Panzer. 2.50
❑7, Sep 1999 DGry (w) 2.50
❑8, Oct 1999 DGry (w) 2.50
❑9, Nov 1999 DGry (w) 2.50
❑10, Dec 1999 DGry (w) 2.50
❑11, Jan 2000 DGry (w) 2.50
❑12, Feb 2000 .... 2.50
❑13, Mar 2000 .... 2.50
❑14, Apr 2000 .... 2.50
❑15, May 2000 DGry (w) 2.50
❑16, Jun 2000 .... 2.50
❑17, Jul 2000 .... 2.50
❑18, Aug 2000 .... 2.50
❑19, Sep 2000 DGry (w) 2.50
❑20, Oct 2000 DGry (w) 2.50
❑21, Nov 2000 .... 2.50
❑22, Dec 2000 .... 2.50
❑23, Jan 2001 .... 2.50
❑24, Feb 2001 .... 2.50
❑25, Mar 2001; Giant-size GP, NC (a) 3.95
❑26, Apr 2001 .... 2.50
❑27, May 2001 .... 2.50
❑28, Jun 2001 .... 2.50
❑29, Jul 2001 .... 2.50
❑30, Aug 2001 .... 2.50
❑31, Sep 2001 .... 2.50
❑32, Oct 2001 .... 2.50
❑33, Nov 2001 .... 2.50
❑34, Dec 2001 .... 2.50
❑35, Jan 2002 .... 2.50
❑36, Feb 2002 .... 2.50
❑37, Mar 2002 .... 2.50
❑38, Apr 2002 .... 2.50
❑39, May 2002 .... 2.50
❑40, Jun 2002 .... 2.50
❑41, Jul 2002 .... 2.50
❑42, Aug 2002 .... 2.50
❑43, Sep 2002 .... 2.50
❑44, Oct 2002 .... 2.75
❑45, Nov 2002 .... 2.75
❑46, Dec 2002 .... 2.75
❑47, Jan 2003 .... 2.75
❑48, Feb 2003 .... 2.75
❑49, Mar 2003 .... 2.75
❑50, Apr 2003 .... 2.75
❑Annual 1, Sep 2000; Planet DC 3.50

Other grades: Multiply price above by 5/6 for VF/NM • 2/3 for VERY FINE • 1/3 for FINE • 1/5 for VERY GOOD • 1/8 for GOOD

N-MINT

TITANS/LEGION OF SUPER-HEROES: UNIVERSE ABLAZE
DC

❑1, ca. 2000 ... 4.95
❑2, ca. 2000 ... 4.95
❑3, ca. 2000 ... 4.95
❑4, 2000 ... 4.95

TITAN SPECIAL
DARK HORSE

❑1, Jun 1994 ... 3.95

TITANS: SCISSORS, PAPER, STONE
DC

❑1 1997; prestige format; manga-style; Elseworlds ... 4.95

TITANS SECRET FILES
DC

❑1, Mar 1999 ... 4.95
❑2, Oct 2000 ... 4.95

TITANS SELL-OUT! SPECIAL
DC

❑1, Nov 1992 ... 3.50

TITANS/YOUNG JUSTICE: GRADUATION DAY
DC

❑1, Jun 2003 ... 2.50
❑2, Jul 2003 ... 2.50
❑3, Aug 2003 ... 2.50
❑Book 1, ca. 2003 ... 6.95
❑Book 1/2nd, ca. 2004 ... 6.95

TIYU
EXPRESS / ENTITY

❑1, Oct 1996 ... 9.95

T-MINUS-1
RENEGADE

❑1, b&w ... 2.00

TMNT MUTANT UNIVERSE SOURCEBOOK
ARCHIE

❑1, A-M ... 2.00
❑2, N-Z ... 2.00

TMNT: TEENAGE MUTANT NINJA TURTLES
MIRAGE

❑1, Dec 2001, Man atop demons on cover ... 2.95
❑2, Feb 2002 ... 2.95
❑3, Apr 2002 ... 2.95
❑4, Jun 2002 ... 2.95
❑5, Aug 2002 ... 2.95
❑6, Oct 2002 ... 2.95
❑7, Dec 2002 ... 2.95
❑8, Feb 2003 ... 2.95
❑9, Apr 2003 ... 2.95
❑10, Jun 2003 ... 3.95
❑11, Aug 2003 ... 2.95
❑12, Oct 2003 ... 2.95
❑13, Dec 2003 ... 2.95
❑14, Feb 2004 ... 2.95
❑15, Apr 2004 ... 2.95
❑16, Nov 2004 ... 2.95
❑17, Nov 2004 ... 2.95
❑18, Nov 2004 ... 2.95

TO BE ANNOUNCED
STRAWBERRY JAM

❑1, ca. 1986, b&w ... 1.50
❑2, ca. 1986, b&w ... 1.50
❑3, ca. 1986, b&w ... 1.50
❑4, ca. 1986, b&w ... 1.50
❑5, ca. 1986, b&w ... 1.50
❑6, Feb 1987, b&w ... 1.50
❑7, ca. 1987, b&w ... 1.50

TODD MCFARLANE PRESENTS: KISS PSYCHO CIRCUS
IMAGE

❑1, Oct 1998; magazine; reprints #1-3 of comic book ... 6.95
❑2, Apr 1999 ... 4.95
❑3, Aug 1999 ... 4.95
❑4, Nov 1999 ... 4.95
❑5, Apr 2000 ... 4.95

TODD MCFARLANE PRESENTS: OZZY OSBOURNE
IMAGE

❑1, Jun 1999; magazine ... 4.95

N-MINT

TODD MCFARLANE PRESENTS: THE CROW MAGAZINE
IMAGE

❑1, Mar 2000 ... 4.95

TO DIE FOR
BLACKTHORNE

❑1, b&w ... 2.00
❑1/3D ... 2.50

TOE TAGS FEATURING GEORGE ROMERO
DC / WILDSTORM

❑1, Dec 2004 ... 2.95
❑2, Jan 2005 ... 2.95
❑3, Feb 2005 ... 2.95
❑4, Mar 2005 ... 2.95
❑5, Apr 2005 ... 2.95
❑6, May 2005 ... 2.95

TOKYO BABYLON
TOKYOPOP

❑1, May 2004 ... 9.99

TOKYO BOYS & GIRLS
VIZ

❑1, Jul 2005 ... 9.99
❑2, Oct 2005 ... 9.99

TOKYO MEW MEW
TOKYOPOP

❑1, Apr 2003, b&w; printed in Japanese format ... 9.99

TOKYOPOP (VOL. 3)
MIXX

❑1, Aug 1999 ... 4.99
❑2, Oct 1999 ... 4.99
❑3 ... 4.99
❑4, Dec 1999 ... 4.99
❑5, Jan 2000 ... 4.99
❑6 ... 4.99
❑7 ... 4.99

TOKYOPOP (VOL. 4)
MIXX

❑1 ... 4.99
❑2, Oct 2000 ... 4.99
❑3, Nov 2000 ... 4.99

TOKYO STORM WARNING
DC / CLIFFHANGER

❑1, Aug 2003 ... 2.95
❑2, Sep 2003 ... 2.95
❑3, Dec 2003 ... 2.95

TOKYO TRIBES
TOKYOPOP

❑1, Sep 2004 ... 9.99
❑2, Feb 2005 ... 9.99
❑3, Aug 2005 ... 9.99
❑4, Dec 2005 ... 9.99

TOMAHAWK
DC

❑44, Nov 1956 ... 56.00
❑45, Jan 1957 ... 56.00
❑46, Feb 1957 ... 56.00
❑47, Mar 1957 ... 56.00
❑48, May 1957 ... 56.00
❑49, Jul 1957 ... 56.00
❑50, Aug 1957 ... 56.00
❑51, Sep 1957 ... 45.00
❑52, Nov 1957 ... 45.00
❑53, Jan 1958 ... 45.00
❑54, Feb 1958 ... 45.00
❑55, Mar 1958 ... 45.00
❑56, May 1958 ... 45.00
❑57, Jul 1958 FF (a) ... 85.00
❑58, Sep 1958 ... 40.00
❑59, Nov 1958 ... 40.00
❑60, Jan 1959 ... 40.00
❑61, Mar 1959 ... 32.00
❑62, May 1959 ... 32.00
❑63, Jul 1959 ... 32.00
❑64, Sep 1959 ... 32.00
❑65, Nov 1959 ... 32.00
❑66, Jan 1960 ... 32.00
❑67, Mar 1960 ... 32.00
❑68, May 1960 ... 32.00
❑69, Jul 1960 ... 32.00
❑70, Sep 1960 ... 32.00
❑71, Nov 1960 ... 32.00
❑72, Jan 1961 ... 32.00

N-MINT

❑73, Mar 1961 ... 32.00
❑74, May 1961 ... 32.00
❑75, Jul 1961 ... 32.00
❑76, Sep 1961 ... 32.00
❑77, Nov 1961 ... 32.00
❑78, Jan 1962 ... 32.00
❑79, Mar 1962 ... 32.00
❑80, May 1962 ... 32.00
❑81, Jul 1962 1: Miss Liberty ... 25.00
❑82, Sep 1962 ... 25.00
❑83, Nov 1962 ... 25.00
❑84, Jan 1963 ... 25.00
❑85, Mar 1963 ... 25.00
❑86, May 1963 ... 25.00
❑87, Jul 1963 ... 25.00
❑88, Sep 1963 ... 25.00
❑89, Nov 1963 ... 25.00
❑90, Jan 1964 ... 25.00
❑91, Mar 1964 ... 15.00
❑92, May 1964 ... 15.00
❑93, Jul 1964 ... 15.00
❑94, Sep 1964 ... 15.00
❑95, Nov 1964 ... 15.00
❑96, Jan 1965 ... 15.00
❑97, Mar 1965 ... 15.00
❑98, May 1965 ... 15.00
❑99, Jul 1965 ... 15.00
❑100, Sep 1965 ... 15.00
❑101, Nov 1965 ... 10.00
❑102, Jan 1966 ... 10.00
❑103, Mar 1966 ... 10.00
❑104, May 1966 ... 10.00
❑105, Jul 1966 ... 10.00
❑106, Sep 1966 ... 10.00
❑107, Nov 1966 ... 10.00
❑108, Jan 1967 ... 10.00
❑109, Mar 1967 ... 10.00
❑110, May 1967 ... 10.00
❑111, Jul 1967 ... 8.00
❑112, Sep 1967 ... 8.00
❑113, Nov 1967 ... 8.00
❑114, Jan 1968 ... 8.00
❑115, Mar 1968 ... 8.00
❑116, May 1968 ... 8.00
❑117, Jul 1968 ... 8.00
❑118, Sep 1968 ... 8.00
❑119, Nov 1968 ... 8.00
❑120, Jan 1969 ... 8.00
❑121, Mar 1969 ... 6.00
❑122, May 1969 ... 6.00
❑123, Jul 1969 ... 6.00
❑124, Sep 1969 ... 6.00
❑125, Nov 1969 ... 6.00
❑126, Jan 1970 ... 6.00
❑127, Mar 1970 ... 6.00
❑128, May 1970 ... 6.00
❑129, Jul 1970 ... 6.00
❑130, Sep 1970 ... 6.00
❑131, Nov 1970, FF (a); Series becomes "Son of Tomahawk" ... 6.00
❑132, Jan 1971 ... 6.00
❑133, Mar 1971 FT (a) ... 4.50
❑134, May 1971 ... 4.50
❑135, Jul 1971 FT, JSe (a) ... 4.50
❑136, Sep 1971 ... 4.50
❑137, Nov 1971 ... 4.50
❑138, Jan 1972 ... 4.50
❑139, Mar 1972; FF (a); says Son of Tomahawk on cover ... 4.50
❑140, May 1972; says Son of Tomahawk on cover ... 4.50

TOM & JERRY 50TH ANNIVERSARY SPECIAL
HARVEY

❑1, Oct 1991; Reprints ... 2.50

TOM & JERRY ADVENTURES
HARVEY

❑1, May 1992; Reprints ... 1.25

TOM & JERRY AND FRIENDS
HARVEY

❑1, Dec 1991; Reprints ... 1.25
❑2, Feb 1992; Reprints ... 1.25
❑3, Apr 1992; Reprints ... 1.25
❑4, Jul 1992; Reprints ... 1.25

Too Much Coffee Man

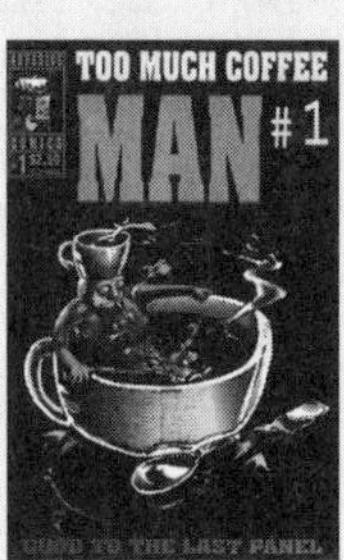

Cult favorite appeals to caffeine addicts

©Adhesive

Top Cat (Charlton)

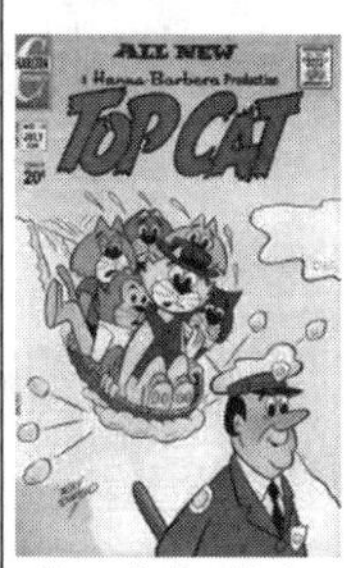

Hanna-Barbera hipster felines wreak havoc

©Charlton

Top Cow Classics in Black and White: The Darkness

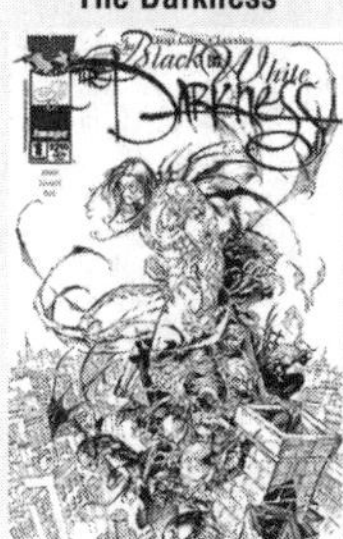

Top Cow gives readers a look at the inks

©Image

Top Dog

Talking canine becomes boy's best pal

©Marvel

Tor (DC)

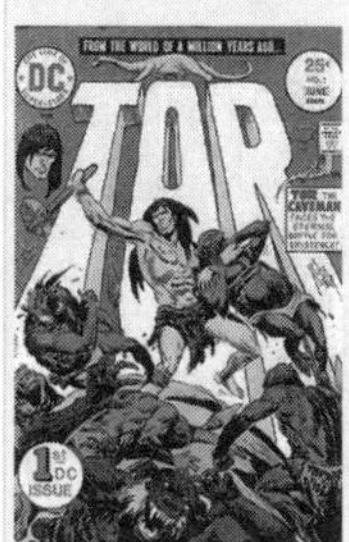

The savage world of a million years ago

©DC

TOM & JERRY BIG BOOK
Harvey

	N-MINT
❑1, Sep 1992	1.95
❑2	1.95

TOM & JERRY COMICS
Dell

	N-MINT
❑147, Oct 1956	7.00
❑148, Nov 1956	7.00
❑149, Dec 1956	7.00
❑150, Jan 1957	7.00
❑151, Feb 1957	6.00
❑152, Mar 1957	6.00
❑153, Apr 1957	6.00
❑154, May 1957	6.00
❑155, Jun 1957	6.00
❑156, Jul 1957	6.00
❑157, Aug 1957	6.00
❑158, Sep 1957	6.00
❑159, Oct 1957	6.00
❑160, Nov 1957	6.00
❑161, Dec 1957	6.00
❑162, Jan 1958	6.00
❑163, Feb 1958	6.00
❑164, Mar 1958	6.00
❑165, Apr 1958	6.00
❑166, May 1958	6.00
❑167, Jun 1958	6.00
❑168, Jul 1958	6.00
❑169, Aug 1958	6.00
❑170, Sep 1958	6.00
❑171, Oct 1958	5.00
❑172, Nov 1958	5.00
❑173, Dec 1958	5.00
❑174, Jan 1959	5.00
❑175, Feb 1959	5.00
❑176, Mar 1959	5.00
❑177, Apr 1959	5.00
❑178, May 1959	5.00
❑179, Jun 1959	5.00
❑180, Jul 1959	5.00
❑181, Aug 1959	5.00
❑182, Sep 1959	5.00
❑183, Oct 1959	5.00
❑184, Nov 1959	5.00
❑185, Dec 1959	5.00
❑186, Jan 1960	5.00
❑187, Feb 1960 A: Spike & Tyke.	5.00
❑188, Mar 1960	5.00
❑189, Apr 1960	5.00
❑190, May 1960	5.00
❑191, Jun 1960	4.00
❑192, Jul 1960	4.00
❑193, Aug 1960	4.00
❑194, Sep 1960	4.00
❑195, Oct 1960	4.00
❑196, Nov 1960	4.00
❑197, Dec 1960	4.00
❑198, Jan 1961	4.00
❑199, Feb 1961	4.00
❑200, Mar 1961	4.00
❑201, Apr 1961	3.00
❑202, May 1961	3.00
❑203, Jun 1961	3.00
❑204, Jul 1961	3.00
❑205, Aug 1961	3.00
❑206, Sep 1961	3.00
❑207, Oct 1961	3.00
❑208, Nov 1961	3.00
❑209, Jan 1962	3.00
❑210, Mar 1962	3.00
❑211, May 1962	3.00
❑212, Aug 1962	3.00
❑213, Nov 1962; Titled Tom and Jerry Funhouse	3.00
❑214, Feb 1963; Titled Tom and Jerry Funhouse	3.00
❑215, May 1963, Titled Tom and Jerry Funhouse	3.00
❑216, Aug 1963	3.00
❑217, Nov 1963	3.00
❑218, Feb 1964	3.00
❑219, May 1964	3.00
❑220, Aug 1964	3.00
❑221, Nov 1964	3.00
❑222, Feb 1965 A: Professor Putter.	3.00
❑223, Apr 1965	3.00
❑224, Jun 1965	3.00
❑225, Aug 1965 A: Professor Putter.	3.00
❑226, Oct 1965	3.00
❑227, Dec 1965 A: Professor Putter.	3.00
❑228, Feb 1966 A: Professor Putter.	3.00
❑229, Apr 1966 A: Professor Putter.	3.00
❑230, Jun 1966 A: Professor Putter.	3.00
❑231, Aug 1966	2.00
❑232, Oct 1966	2.00
❑233, Dec 1966	2.00
❑234, Feb 1967	2.00
❑235, Apr 1967	2.00
❑236, Jun 1967	2.00
❑237, Aug 1967	2.00
❑238, Nov 1967	2.00
❑239, Feb 1968	2.00
❑240, May 1968	2.00
❑241, Aug 1968	2.00
❑242, Nov 1968	2.00
❑243, Feb 1969	2.00
❑244, Apr 1969	2.00
❑245, Jun 1969	2.00
❑246, Aug 1969	2.00
❑247, Oct 1969	2.00
❑248, Dec 1969	2.00
❑249, Feb 1970	2.00
❑250, Apr 1970	2.00
❑251, Jun 1970	2.00
❑252, Aug 1970	2.00
❑253, Oct 1970	2.00
❑254, Dec 1970	2.00
❑255, Feb 1971	2.00
❑256, Apr 1971	2.00
❑257, Jun 1971	2.00
❑258, Aug 1971	2.00
❑259, Sep 1971	2.00
❑260, Dec 1971	2.00
❑261, Dec 1971	2.00
❑262, Feb 1972	2.00
❑263, Apr 1972	2.00
❑264, Jun 1972	2.00
❑265, Aug 1972	2.00
❑266, Sep 1972	2.00
❑267, Oct 1972	2.00
❑268, Dec 1972	2.00
❑269, Feb 1973	2.00
❑270, Apr 1973	2.00
❑271, Jun 1973	1.50
❑272, Jul 1973	1.50
❑273, Aug 1973	1.50
❑274, Sep 1973	1.50
❑275, Oct 1973	1.50
❑276, Nov 1973	1.50
❑277, Dec 1973	1.50
❑278, Jan 1974	1.50
❑279, Feb 1974	1.50
❑280, Mar 1974	1.50
❑281, Apr 1974	1.50
❑282, May 1974	1.50
❑283, Jun 1974	1.50
❑284, Jul 1974	1.50
❑285, Aug 1974	1.50
❑286, Sep 1974	1.50
❑287, Oct 1974	1.50
❑288, Nov 1974	1.50
❑289, Dec 1974	1.50
❑290, Jan 1975	1.50
❑291, Feb 1975	1.50
❑292, Mar 1977	1.50
❑293, Apr 1977	1.50
❑294, May 1977	1.50
❑295, Jun 1977	1.50
❑296, Jul 1977	1.50
❑297, Aug 1977	1.50
❑298, Sep 1977	1.50
❑299, Oct 1977	1.50
❑300, Nov 1977	1.50
❑301, Dec 1977	1.00
❑302, Jan 1978	1.00
❑303, Feb 1978	1.00
❑304, Mar 1978	1.00
❑305, Apr 1978	1.00
❑306, May 1978	1.00
❑307, Jun 1978	1.00
❑308, Jul 1978	1.00
❑309, Aug 1978	1.00
❑310, Sep 1978	1.00
❑311, Oct 1978	1.00
❑312, Nov 1978	1.00
❑313, Dec 1978	1.00
❑314, Jan 1979	1.00
❑315, Feb 1979	1.00
❑316, Mar 1979	1.00
❑317, Apr 1979	1.00
❑318, May 1979	1.00
❑319, Jun 1979	1.00
❑320, Jul 1979	1.00
❑321, Aug 1979	1.00
❑322, Sep 1979	1.00
❑323, Oct 1979	1.00
❑324, Nov 1979	1.00
❑325, Dec 1979	1.00
❑326, Jan 1980	1.00
❑327, Feb 1980	1.00
❑328, Apr 1980	5.00
❑329, Jun 1980	5.00

❑330, Aug 1980 ... 20.00
❑331, Oct 1980 ... 7.00
❑332, Dec 1980 ... 7.00
❑333, Feb 1981 ... 7.00
❑334, Apr 1981 ... 7.00
❑335, ca. 1981 ... 7.00
❑336, ca. 1981 ... 7.00
❑337, ca. 1981 ... 7.00
❑338, ca. 1982 ... 7.00
❑339, ca. 1982 ... 7.00
❑340, ca. 1982 ... 7.00
❑341, ca. 1982 ... 7.00
❑342, ca. 1982 ... 15.00
❑343, ca. 1983 ... 15.00
❑344, ca. 1983 ... 15.00

TOM & JERRY DIGEST
HARVEY

❑1, ca. 1992; Reprints ... 1.75

TOM & JERRY GIANT SIZE
HARVEY

❑1; Reprints ... 1.95
❑2 ... 2.25

TOM & JERRY SUMMER FUN (GOLD KEY)
GOLD KEY

❑1, Oct 1967, Droopy reprinted from Tom and Jerry Summer Fun (Dell) #1 ... 35.00

TOM & JERRY (VOL. 2)
HARVEY

❑1, Sep 1991; Reprints ... 1.50
❑2, Nov 1991; Reprints ... 1.25
❑3, Jan 1992; Reprints ... 1.25
❑4, Mar 1992; Reprints ... 1.25
❑5, Jun 1992; Reprints ... 1.25
❑6, Jan 1993; Reprints ... 1.25
❑7, ca. 1993; Reprints ... 1.25
❑8, ca. 1993; Reprints ... 1.25
❑9, ca. 1993 ... 1.50
❑10, Dec 1993 ... 1.50
❑11, Jan 1994 ... 1.50
❑12, Feb 1994 ... 1.50
❑13, Mar 1994 ... 1.50
❑14, Apr 1994 ... 1.50
❑15, May 1994 ... 1.50
❑16, Jun 1994 ... 1.50
❑17, Jul 1994 ... 1.50
❑18, Aug 1994 ... 1.50
❑Annual 1, Sep 1994 ... 2.25

TOMATO
STARHEAD

❑1, Apr 1994, b&w ... 2.75
❑2, Feb 1995, b&w ... 2.75

TOMB OF DARKNESS
MARVEL

❑9, Jul 1974, Series continued from Beware #8 ... 20.00
❑10, Sep 1974 ... 10.00
❑11, Nov 1974 ... 10.00
❑12, Jan 1975 ... 10.00
❑13, Mar 1975 ... 10.00
❑14, May 1975 ... 10.00
❑15, Jul 1975 ... 10.00
❑16, Sep 1975 ... 10.00
❑17, Nov 1975 ... 10.00
❑18, Jan 1976 ... 10.00
❑19, Mar 1976 ... 10.00
❑20, May 1976 ... 10.00
❑20/30 cent, May 1976, 30 cent regional price variant ... 20.00
❑21, Jul 1976 ... 10.00
❑21/30 cent, Jul 1976, 30 cent regional price variant ... 20.00
❑22, Sep 1976 ... 10.00
❑23, Nov 1976 ... 10.00

TOMB OF DRACULA
MARVEL

❑1, Apr 1972, NA (c); AW, GC (a); O: Frank Drake. 1: Frank Drake. 1: Dracula (Marvel). Dracula revived ... 100.00
❑2, May 1972 GC (a) ... 35.00
❑3, Jul 1972 GC (a); 1: Rachel Van Helsing ... 35.00
❑4, Sep 1972 GC (a) ... 30.00
❑5, Nov 1972 GC (a) ... 18.00
❑6, Jan 1973 GC (a) ... 18.00
❑7, Mar 1973 GC (a); 1: Edith Harker ... 15.00
❑8, May 1973 GC (a) ... 12.00
❑9, Jun 1973 GC (a); 1: Lucas Brand. ... 12.00
❑10, Jul 1973 GC (a); 1: Blade the Vampire Slayer. ... 100.00
❑11, Aug 1973 GC (a) ... 10.00
❑12, Sep 1973 GC (a); A: Blade the Vampire Slayer. ... 12.00
❑13, Oct 1973 GC (a); O: Blade the Vampire Slayer. 1: Deacon Frost. ... 35.00
❑14, Nov 1973 GC (a); A: Blade the Vampire Slayer. ... 12.00
❑15, Dec 1973 GC (a) ... 10.00
❑16, Jan 1974 GC (a) ... 10.00
❑17, Feb 1974 GC (a); A: Blade the Vampire Slayer. ... 12.00
❑18, Mar 1974, GC (a); V: Werewolf by Night. Marvel Value Stamp #7: Werewolf ... 10.00
❑19, Apr 1974, GC (a); A: Blade the Vampire Slayer. Marvel Value Stamp #26: Mephisto ... 12.00
❑20, May 1974, GC (a); 1: Doctor Sun. Marvel Value Stamp #88: Leader ... 10.00
❑21, Jun 1974, GC (a); O: Doctor Sun. A: Blade the Vampire Slayer. Marvel Value Stamp #96: Dr. Octopus ... 10.00
❑22, Jul 1974, GC (a); Marvel Value Stamp #27: Black Widow ... 8.00
❑23, Aug 1974, GC, TP (a); Marvel Value Stamp #50 : Black Panther ... 8.00
❑24, Sep 1974, GC (a); Marvel Value Stamp #57: Vulture ... 8.00
❑25, Oct 1974, GC (a); O: Hannibal King. 1: Hannibal King. Marvel Value Stamp #49: Odin ... 8.00
❑25/2nd, Oct 1974, GC (a); O: Hannibal King. 1: Hannibal King. (part of Marvel Value Pack) ... 1.50
❑26, Nov 1974, GC (a); Marvel Value Stamp #80: Ghost Rider ... 8.00
❑27, Dec 1974, GC, TP (a); Marvel Value Stamp #69: Marvel Girl ... 8.00
❑28, Jan 1975, GC, TP (a); 1: Adri Nitall. Marvel Value Stamp #57: Vulture ... 8.00
❑29, Feb 1975, GC, TP (a); Marvel Value Stamp #80: Ghost Rider ... 8.00
❑30, Mar 1975, GC (a); A: Blade the Vampire Slayer. Marvel Value Stamp #23: Sgt. Fury ... 10.00
❑31, Apr 1975, GC, TP (a); Marvel Value Stamp #45: Mantis ... 8.00
❑32, May 1975 GC (a) ... 8.00
❑33, Jun 1975 GC, TP (a) ... 7.00
❑34, Jul 1975, GC, TP (a); A: Brother Voodoo. Marvel Value Stamp #87: J. Jonah Jameson ... 7.00
❑35, Aug 1975, GC, TP (a); A: Brother Voodoo. Marvel Value Stamp #74: Stranger ... 7.00
❑36, Sep 1975 GC (a); A: Brother Voodoo. ... 7.00
❑37, Oct 1975, GC, TP (a); 1: Harold H. Harold. Marvel Value Stamp #12: Daredevil ... 7.00
❑38, Nov 1975 GC, TP (a); A: Doctor Sun. ... 7.00
❑39, Dec 1975, GC, TP (a); D: Dracula. Marvel Value Stamp #77: Swordsman ... 7.00
❑40, Jan 1976 GC, TP (a) ... 7.00
❑41, Feb 1976 GC (a); A: Blade the Vampire Slayer. ... 7.00
❑42, Mar 1976 GC (a); A: Blade the Vampire Slayer. V: Doctor Sun. ... 6.00
❑43, Apr 1976 GC (a) ... 6.00
❑43/30 cent, Apr 1976, 30 cent regional price variant ... 18.00
❑44, May 1976 GC (a); A: Hannibal King. A: Blade the Vampire Slayer. V: Doctor Strange. ... 6.00
❑44/30 cent, May 1976, GC (a); 30 cent regional price variant ... 18.00
❑45, Jun 1976, GC (a); A: Hannibal King. Blade vs. Hannibal King ... 6.00
❑45/30 cent, Jun 1976, GC (a); 30 cent regional price variant ... 18.00
❑46, Jul 1976, GC (a); A: Blade. A: Blade the Vampire Slayer. Wedding of Dracula ... 6.00
❑46/30 cent, Jul 1976, GC (a); 30 cent regional price variant ... 18.00
❑47, Aug 1976 GC (a); A: Blade the Vampire Slayer. ... 6.00
❑47/30 cent, Aug 1976, GC (a); 30 cent regional price variant ... 18.00
❑48, Sep 1976 GC (a); A: Hannibal King. A: Blade the Vampire Slayer. ... 6.00
❑49, Oct 1976 GC (a); A: Zorro. A: Tom Sawyer. A: D'Artagnan. A: Frankenstein. A: Blade the Vampire Slayer. ... 6.00
❑50, Nov 1976 GC (a); A: Blade the Vampire Slayer. A: Silver Surfer. ... 10.00
❑51, Dec 1976, GC, TP (a); 1: Janus. Blade vs. Hannibal King ... 6.00
❑52, Jan 1977 GC (a) ... 6.00
❑53, Feb 1977, GC (a); A: Son of Satan. Blade vs. Hannibal King and Deacon Frost ... 6.00
❑54, Mar 1977, GC, TP (a); O: Janus. A: Blade. birth of Dracula's son ... 6.00
❑55, Apr 1977 GC, TP (c); GC (a) ... 6.00
❑56, May 1977 GC (a) ... 6.00
❑57, Jun 1977 GC, TP (a) ... 6.00
❑57/35 cent, Jun 1977, GC, TP (a); 35 cent regional price variant ... 12.00
❑58, Jul 1977 GC (a) ... 6.00
❑58/35 cent, Jul 1977, 35 cent regional price variant ... 12.00
❑59, Aug 1977 GC (a) ... 6.00
❑59/35 cent, Aug 1977, GC (a); 35 cent regional price variant ... 12.00
❑60, Sep 1977 GC, TP (a) ... 6.00
❑60/35 cent, Sep 1977, GC, TP (a); 35 cent regional price variant ... 12.00
❑61, Nov 1977 GC (a); O: Janus. ... 5.00
❑62, Jan 1978 GC (a) ... 5.00
❑63, Mar 1978 GC (a) ... 5.00
❑64, May 1978 GC, TP (a) ... 5.00
❑65, Jul 1978 GC, TP (a) ... 5.00
❑66, Sep 1978 GC, TP (a) ... 5.00
❑67, Nov 1978 GC, TP (a); A: Lilith. ... 5.00
❑68, Feb 1979 GC (a) ... 5.00
❑69, Apr 1979 GC, TP (a) ... 5.00
❑70, Aug 1979, Double-size D: Dracula. ... 8.00

TOMB OF DRACULA (2ND SERIES)
MARVEL

❑1, 2004 ... 2.99
❑2, ... 2.99
❑3, ... 2.99
❑4, 2005 ... 2.99

TOMB OF DRACULA (MAGAZINE)
MARVEL

❑1, Oct 1979, b&w; magazine GC (a) ... 15.00
❑2, Dec 1979 SD (a) ... 6.00
❑3, Feb 1980 GC, FM, TP (a) ... 6.00
❑4, Apr 1980 GC, JB, TP (a) ... 6.00
❑5, Jun 1980 GC, JB, TP (a) ... 6.00
❑6, Aug 1980 GC (a) ... 6.00

TOMB OF DRACULA (LTD. SERIES)
MARVEL / EPIC

❑1, Nov 1991 AW, GC (a) ... 5.00
❑2, Dec 1991 AW, GC (a) ... 5.00
❑3, Jan 1992 AW, GC (a) ... 5.00
❑4, Feb 1992 AW, GC (a) ... 5.00

TOMB OF LIGEIA
DELL

❑1, Jun 1965, Adapts movie Tomb of the Cat ... 12.00

TOMB RAIDER: ARABIAN NIGHTS
IMAGE

❑1, Aug 2004 ... 5.99

TOMB RAIDER COVER GALLERY
IMAGE

❑1, Apr 2006 ...

TOMB RAIDER/DARKNESS SPECIAL
IMAGE

❑1, ca. 2001; Topcowstore.com exclusive ... 4.00
❑1/A, ca. 2001; Topcowstore.com exclusive; Gold foil logo on cover ... 6.00

TOMB RAIDER: EPIPHANY
IMAGE

❑1, Jul 2003 ... 4.99

TOMB RAIDER GALLERY
IMAGE

❑1, Dec 2000 ... 2.95

TOMB RAIDER: GREATEST TREASURE OF ALL ONE SHOT
IMAGE

❑1 ... 4.99

Other grades: Multiply price above by 5/6 for VF/NM • 2/3 for VERY FINE • 1/3 for FINE • 1/5 for VERY GOOD • 1/8 for GOOD

Torso

Eliot Ness' most horrifying case

©Image

Toxic Crusaders

Comics with the Troma touch

©Marvel

Transformers

Series got hot years after it was canceled

©Marvel

Transformers: Armada

Spinoff series with the evolving robots

©Dreamwave

Transformers: Generation 1

Dreamwave captures wave of nostalgia

©Dreamwave

N-MINT

TOMB RAIDER: JOURNEYS
IMAGE

❑1, Feb 2002 .... 2.95
❑2, Mar 2002 .... 2.95
❑3, May 2002 .... 2.95
❑4, Jun 2002 .... 2.95
❑5, Aug 2002 .... 2.95
❑6, Sep 2002 .... 2.95
❑7, Oct 2002 .... 2.99
❑8, Dec 2002 .... 2.99
❑9, Feb 2003 .... 2.99
❑10, Feb 2003 .... 2.99
❑11, Apr 2003 .... 2.99
❑12, May 2003 .... 2.99

TOMB RAIDER MAGAZINE
IMAGE

❑1 .... 4.95

TOMB RAIDER: TAKEOVER ONE SHOT
IMAGE

❑1, Dec 2003 .... 2.99

TOMB RAIDER: THE SERIES
IMAGE

❑0, Jun 2001 .... 2.50
❑0/Dynamic, Jun 2001; Painted cover; Dynamic Forces variant 5.00
❑½, Sep 2001 O: Lara Croft. 2.50
❑1, Dec 1999; Lara Croft crouching on rock with setting sun 2.50
❑1/C, Dec 1999; Lara climbing mountain 2.50
❑1/D, Dec 1999; Lara standing in front of ruins 2.50
❑1/Holofoil, Dec 1999; Holofoil cover: Lara on rock, no sun in background 7.00
❑1/Another Unive, Dec 1999; Another Universe Exclusive 5.00
❑1/Tower Gold, Dec 1999; Tower Records exclusive; Gold foil Tomb Raider logo; Lara on rock, no sun in background ... 6.00
❑1/Tower, Dec 1999; Tower records exclusive w/o gold logo 5.00
❑2, Jan 2000 .... 2.50
❑2/Tower, Jan 2000; Tower Records: Santa cover with blue background .. 5.00
❑2/Tower foil, Jan 2000; Tower Records: Santa cover with yellowish holo-foil background 6.50
❑3, Feb 2000 .... 2.50
❑3/Monster Mart, Feb 2000; Monster Mart Edition; Lara kneeling on ruins, Monster Mart logo in lower right 7.00
❑3/Gold Mart, Feb 2000; Gold Monster Mart edition; Lara kneeling on ruins, Monster Mart logo in lower right 6.00
❑4, Apr 2000; Lara sitting on root of tree, man standing, flames behind .. 2.50
❑4/Dynamic, Apr 2000; Lara in tree, DF logo at bottom left. 4.00
❑4/Dynamic with , Apr 2000; Similar cover to 4, with Certificate of Authenticity 8.00
❑5, May 2000; Lara standing, dinosaur skeleton in background 2.50
❑5/Dynamic, May 2000; Dynamic Forces variant, Tomb Raider logo in upper right, DF logo below, Lara standing on Triceratops skull 6.00
❑6, Jul 2000 .... 2.50
❑7, Jul 2000 .... 2.50
❑7/Museum, Jul 2000; Museum edition, limited to 25 copies.; Museum edition 125.00
❑8, Oct 2000 .... 2.50
❑9, Dec 2000; Lara sitting, faces in background 2.50
❑9/White, Dec 2000; White background, holding two guns 4.00
❑9/Dynamic, Dec 2000; Lara fighting crocodile, DF logo at top left 6.00
❑9/Dynamic blue, Dec 2000; Lara fighting crocodile, blue foil around DF logo at top left 7.00
❑9/Sketch, Dec 2000; Sketch cover, black and white 10.00
❑10, Jan 2001 .... 2.50
❑10/Gold foil, Jan 2001; Gold foil around Tomb Raider logo, includes Certificate of Authenticity 12.00
❑10/Red foil, Jan 2001; Red foil around Tomb Raider logo, includes Certificate of Authenticity 10.00
❑11, Mar 2001 .... 2.50
❑11/Graham, Mar 2001; Graham Crackers Blue Foil Edition; Limited to 1,000 copies; forms consecutive image with cover of exclusive Tomb Raider #12 Graham Crackers edition 7.00
❑12, Apr 2001 .... 2.50
❑12/Graham, Apr 2001; 2,500 produced; forms single image with #11 Graham Crackers exclusive 8.00
❑13, May 2001 .... 2.50
❑14, Jul 2001 .... 2.50
❑15, Sep 2001 .... 2.50
❑15/Dynamic, Sep 2001; DFE red foil cover 10.00
❑16, Oct 2001 .... 2.50
❑17, Nov 2001 .... 2.50
❑18, Dec 2001 .... 2.50
❑19, Jan 2002 .... 2.50
❑20, Feb 2002 .... 2.50
❑21, May 2002 .... 2.50
❑22, Jul 2002 .... 2.50
❑23, Aug 2002 .... 2.50
❑24, Oct 2002; Endgame Prelude 2.99
❑25, Nov 2002 .... 2.99
❑26, Feb 2003 .... 2.99
❑27, Feb 2003 .... 2.99
❑28, Apr 2003 .... 2.99
❑29, May 2003 .... 2.99
❑30, Jun 2003 .... 2.99
❑31, Jun 2003 .... 2.99
❑32, Aug 2003 .... 2.99
❑33, Sep 2003 .... 2.99
❑34, Oct 2003 .... 2.99
❑35, Nov 2003 .... 2.99
❑36, Jan 2004 .... 2.99
❑37, Feb 2004 .... 2.99
❑38, Apr 2004 .... 2.99
❑39, Apr 2004 .... 2.99
❑40, May 2004 .... 2.99
❑41, May 2004 .... 2.99
❑42, Aug 2004 .... 2.99
❑43, Aug 2004 .... 2.99
❑44 2004 .... 2.99
❑45 2004 .... 2.99
❑46 2004 .... 2.99
❑47, Hughes cover 4.00
❑47/Variant, Basaldua cover 2.99
❑48, Hughes cover 4.00
❑48/Variant, Basaldua cover 2.99
❑49, Feb 2005 .... 2.99
❑50, Mar 2005 .... 2.99
❑Ashcan 1; Convention edition; Preview cover, with second outer cover (black & white) with Lara Croft on front, logo with white space on back 5.00

TOMB RAIDER/WITCHBLADE
IMAGE

❑1, Dec 1997; Green Cover 6.00
❑1/A, Dec 1997; Brown cover 6.00
❑1/B, Dec 1997 .... 20.00
❑1/2nd, Dec 1998, titled "Tomb Raider/ Witchblade Revisited" 2.95

TOMB TALES
CRYPTIC

❑1, b&w; cardstock cover 3.00
❑2, Jun 1997, b&w; cardstock cover .. 3.00

TOM CORBETT
ETERNITY

❑1, Jan 1990, b&w; Original material . 2.25
❑2, Feb 1990, b&w; Original material . 2.25
❑3, Mar 1990, b&w; Space Academy photo inside front cover 2.25
❑4, May 1990, b&w; Interior photo of Tom (Frankie Thomas), Roger (Jan Merlin), Astro (Al Markin), Capt. Strong (Ed Bryce), and Dr. Joan Dale (Margaret Garland) [from Tom Corbett, Space Cadet (Dell) #10] 2.25

TOM CORBETT BOOK TWO
ETERNITY

❑1, Sep 1990, b&w 2.25
❑2, Oct 1990, b&w 2.25
❑3, Oct 1990, b&w 2.25
❑4, Nov 1990, b&w 2.25

TOM JUDGE: END OF DAYS
IMAGE

❑1, Sep 2003 .... 3.99

TOM LANDRY
SPIRE

❑1, ca. 1973 .... 3.00

TOMMI GUNN
LONDON NIGHT

❑1, May 1996 .... 3.00

TOMMI GUNN: KILLER'S LUST
LONDON NIGHT

❑1, Feb 1997 .... 3.00
❑1/Nude, Feb 1997; chromium cover . 3.00

TOM MIX WESTERN
AC

❑1; Reprints 2.95
❑2, b&w; Reprints 2.50

TOMMY AND THE MONSTERS
NEW COMICS

❑1, b&w 1.95

N-MINT N-MINT N-MINT

TOMOE
CRUSADE
❑0, Mar 1996 ... 3.00
❑0/Ltd., Mar 1996; Limited edition (5,000 printed) ... 4.00
❑0/Variant, Mar 1996; variant cover ... 3.00
❑1, Apr 1996 ... 3.00
❑1/Ltd., Apr 1996; Limited edition (5,000 printed) ... 4.00
❑1/2nd; Fan Appreciation Edition; contains preview of Manga Shi 2000 3.00
❑2, May 1996 ... 3.00
❑3, Jun 1996 ... 3.00

TOMOE: UNFORGETTABLE FIRE
CRUSADE
❑1, Jun 1997; prequel to Shi: The Series 2.95
❑1/Ltd., Jun 1997; American Entertainment Exclusive Edition; No cover price; prequel to Shi: The Series ... 3.50

TOMOE/WITCHBLADE: FIRE SERMON
CRUSADE
❑1, Sep 1996; one-shot crossover with Image ... 3.95
❑1/A, Sep 1996; Avalon edition; no cover price ... 3.95

TOMORROW KNIGHTS
MARVEL / EPIC
❑1, Jun 1990 ... 1.95
❑2, Jul 1990 ... 1.50
❑3, Sep 1990 ... 1.50
❑4, Nov 1990 ... 1.50
❑5, Jan 1991 ... 1.50
❑6, Mar 1991 ... 1.50

TOMORROW MAN
ANTARCTIC
❑1, Aug 1993, b&w; foil cover ... 2.95

TOMORROW MAN & KNIGHT HUNTER: LAST RITES
ANTARCTIC
❑1, Jul 1994, b&w ... 2.75
❑2, Oct 1994, b&w ... 2.75
❑3, Dec 1994, b&w ... 2.75
❑4, Feb 1995, b&w ... 2.75
❑5, Apr 1995, b&w ... 2.75
❑6, Jun 1995, b&w ... 2.75

TOMORROW STORIES
DC / AMERICA'S BEST COMICS
❑1, Oct 1999 AMo (w); KN (a) ... 4.00
❑1/Variant, Oct 1999 ... 6.00
❑2, Nov 1999 AMo (w) ... 3.00
❑3, Dec 1999 AMo (w); KN (a) ... 2.95
❑4, Jan 2000 AMo (w); KN (a) ... 2.95
❑5, Feb 2000 AMo (w) ... 2.95
❑6, Mar 2000 AMo (w) ... 2.95
❑7, Apr 2000 AMo (w) ... 2.95
❑8, Jan 2001 AMo (w) ... 2.95
❑9, Feb 2001 AMo (w); O: The First American ... 2.95
❑10, Jun 2001 KN (a) ... 2.95
❑11, Oct 2001 ... 2.95
❑12, Apr 2002 ... 2.95

TOMORROW STORIES SPECIAL
DC
❑1, Jan 2006 ... 4.99
❑2, May 2006 ... 4.99

TOM STRONG
DC / AMERICA'S BEST COMICS
❑1, Jun 1999 AMo (w); O: Tom Strong. 4.00
❑1/Variant, Jun 1999 ... 5.00
❑2, Jul 1999 AMo (w) ... 3.00
❑3, Aug 1999 AMo (w) ... 2.95
❑4, Oct 1999 AMo (w) ... 2.95
❑5, Dec 1999 AMo (w) ... 2.95
❑6, Feb 2000 AMo (w) ... 2.95
❑7, Mar 2000 AMo (w) ... 2.95
❑8, Jul 2000 AMo (w) ... 2.95
❑9, Sep 2000 AMo (w) ... 2.95
❑10, Nov 2000 AMo (w) ... 2.95
❑11, Jan 2001 AMo (w) ... 2.95
❑12, Jun 2001; AMo (w); JLA homage cover ... 2.95
❑13, Jul 2001; AMo (w); RH (a); Marvel Family homage cover ... 2.95
❑14, Oct 2001 AMo (w) ... 2.95
❑15, Mar 2002; AMo (w); Fantastic Four homage cover ... 2.95
❑16, Apr 2002 AMo (w) ... 2.95
❑17, Aug 2002 AMo (w) ... 2.95
❑18, Dec 2002 ... 2.95
❑19, Apr 2003 ... 2.95
❑20, Jun 2003 ... 2.95
❑21, Oct 2003 ... 2.95
❑22, Dec 2003 ... 2.95
❑23, Jan 2004 ... 2.95
❑24, Feb 2004 ... 2.95
❑25, May 2004 ... 2.95
❑26, Jul 2004 ... 2.95
❑27, Sep 2004 ... 2.95
❑28, Oct 2004 ... 2.95
❑29, Nov 2004 ... 2.95
❑30 2005 ... 2.95
❑31 2005 ... 2.95
❑32 2005 ... 2.95
❑33 2005 ... 2.99
❑34, Oct 2005 ... 2.99
❑35, Jan 2006 ... 2.99
❑36, May 2006 ... 2.99

TOM STRONG'S TERRIFIC TALES
DC / AMERICA'S BEST COMICS
❑1, Jan 2002 ... 3.50
❑2, Mar 2002 ... 2.95
❑3, Jun 2002 ... 2.95
❑4, Nov 2002 ... 2.95
❑5, Jan 2003 ... 2.95
❑6, Apr 2003 ... 2.95
❑7, Jul 2003 ... 2.95
❑8, Dec 2003 ... 2.95
❑9, Apr 2004 ... 2.95
❑10, Jun 2004 ... 2.95
❑11, Sep 2004 ... 2.95
❑12, Jan 2005 ... 2.95

TONGUE*LASH
DARK HORSE
❑1, Aug 1996 ... 2.95
❑2, Sep 1996 ... 2.95

TONGUE*LASH II
DARK HORSE
❑1, Feb 1999 ... 2.95
❑2, Mar 1999 ... 2.95

TONY BRAVADO, TROUBLE-SHOOTER
RENEGADE
❑1, b&w ... 2.00
❑2, b&w ... 2.00
❑3, b&w ... 2.50
❑4, b&w ... 2.50

TOOL & DIE
FLASHPOINT
❑1, Mar 1994 ... 2.50

TOO MUCH COFFEE MAN
ADHESIVE
❑1, ca. 1993, b&w ... 12.00
❑2, b&w ... 8.00
❑3, b&w ... 6.00
❑4, b&w ... 5.00
❑5, b&w ... 5.00
❑6 ... 3.00
❑7 ... 3.00
❑8, Feb 1998 ... 3.00
❑MC 1; Mini-comic ... 10.00
❑MC 1/2nd; Mini-comic ... 3.00
❑MC 2; Mini-comic ... 8.00
❑MC 2/2nd; Mini-comic ... 3.00
❑MC 3; Mini-comic ... 8.00
❑MC 3/2nd; Mini-comic ... 3.00
❑MC 4; Mini-comic ... 6.00
❑MC 4/2nd; Mini-comic ... 3.00
❑Special 1, Jul 1997, b&w ... 3.00
❑Special 2; Full-Color Special Edition. 3.00

TOO MUCH HOPELESS SAVAGES
ONI
❑1 2003, b&w ... 2.99
❑2 2003, b&w ... 2.99
❑3 2003, b&w ... 2.99
❑4 2003, b&w ... 2.99

TOON WARZ: THE FANDOM MENACE
SIRIUS
❑1/A, Jul 1999, Believe This Man cover 2.95
❑1/B, Jul 1999, Vain Affair cover ... 2.95
❑1/C, Jul 1999, Newspeak cover ... 2.95
❑1/D, Jul 1999, Primear cover ... 2.95

TOOTH AND CLAW
IMAGE
❑1, Aug 1999 ... 2.95
❑2, Sep 1999, Woman-cat holding skull on cover ... 2.95
❑2/A, Sep 1999, alternate cover ... 2.95
❑3, Oct 1999 ... 2.95
❑Ashcan 1 1999, DF Exclusive preview book ... 2.00

TOP 10
DC / AMERICA'S BEST COMICS
❑1, Sep 1999 AMo (w) ... 5.00
❑1/Variant, Sep 1999 ... 6.00
❑2, Oct 1999 AMo (w) ... 2.95
❑3, Nov 1999 AMo (w) ... 2.95
❑4, Dec 1999 AMo (w) ... 2.95
❑5, Jan 2000 AMo (w) ... 2.95
❑6, Feb 2000 AMo (w) ... 2.95
❑7, Apr 2000 AMo (w) ... 2.95
❑8, Jun 2000 AMo (w) ... 2.95
❑9, Oct 2000 AMo (w) ... 2.95
❑10, Jan 2001 AMo (w) ... 2.95
❑11, May 2001 AMo (w) ... 2.95
❑12, Oct 2001 ... 2.95

TOP CAT (DELL)
DELL
❑1, Dec 1961 ... 60.00
❑2, Mar 1962 ... 35.00
❑3, Jun 1962 ... 25.00
❑4, Oct 1962 ... 25.00
❑5, Jan 1963 ... 25.00
❑6, Apr 1963 ... 20.00
❑7, Jul 1963 ... 20.00
❑8, Oct 1963 ... 20.00
❑9, Jan 1964 ... 20.00
❑10, Apr 1964 ... 20.00
❑11, Jul 1964 ... 15.00
❑12, Oct 1964 ... 15.00
❑13, Jan 1965 ... 15.00
❑14, Apr 1965 ... 15.00
❑15, Jul 1965 ... 15.00
❑16, Oct 1965 ... 15.00
❑17, Jan 1966 ... 15.00
❑18, Apr 1966 ... 15.00
❑19 1966 ... 15.00
❑20 1967 ... 15.00
❑21, Dec 1967 ... 12.00
❑22, ca. 1968 ... 12.00
❑23, ca. 1968 ... 12.00
❑24, Dec 1968 ... 12.00
❑25, Mar 1969 ... 12.00
❑26, Jun 1969 ... 12.00
❑27, Sep 1969 ... 12.00
❑28, Dec 1969 ... 12.00
❑29, Mar 1970 ... 12.00
❑30, Jun 1970 ... 12.00
❑31, Sep 1970 ... 12.00

TOP CAT (CHARLTON)
CHARLTON
❑1, Nov 1970 ... 20.00
❑2, Jan 1971 ... 12.00
❑3, Mar 1971 ... 8.00
❑4, May 1971 ... 8.00
❑5, Jul 1971 ... 8.00
❑6, Sep 1971 ... 5.00
❑7, Nov 1971 ... 5.00
❑8, Dec 1971 ... 5.00
❑9, Feb 1972 ... 5.00
❑10, Apr 1972 ... 5.00
❑11, Jun 1972 ... 4.00
❑12, Aug 1972 ... 4.00
❑13, Oct 1972 ... 4.00
❑14, Nov 1972 ... 4.00
❑15, Feb 1973 ... 4.00
❑16, Mar 1973 ... 4.00
❑17, May 1973 ... 4.00
❑18, Jul 1973 ... 4.00
❑19, Sep 1973 ... 4.00
❑20, Nov 1973 ... 4.00

TOP COMICS: FLINTSTONES
GOLD KEY
❑1, ca. 1967 ... 10.00
❑2, ca. 1967 ... 10.00
❑3, ca. 1967 ... 15.00
❑4, ca. 1967 ... 15.00

Transmetropolitan	Treehouse of Horror (Bart Simpson's...)	Tribe	Trinity Angels	Triumph

Cyber-nightmare world of drugs and aliens ©DC	Annual comics tradition mirrors TV tradition ©Bongo	Second and third issue came from Axis Comics ©Image	Nicely written characters and stylish art ©Acclaim	Character's father drove a getaway car ©DC

N-MINT

TOP COMICS: FLIPPER
GOLD KEY
❑1, ca. 1967 .... 10.00

TOP COMICS: LASSIE
GOLD KEY
❑1, ca. 1967, Reprints Lassie #68; no cover price 10.00

TOP COMICS: MICKEY MOUSE
GOLD KEY
❑1, ca. 1967 .... 10.00
❑2, ca. 1967 .... 10.00
❑3, ca. 1967 .... 15.00
❑4, ca. 1967 .... 15.00

TOP COMICS: TWEETY & SYLVESTER
GOLD KEY
❑1, ca. 1967 .... 10.00
❑2, ca. 1967 .... 10.00

TOP COW 2003 COMPILATION SPECIAL
IMAGE
❑1, Mar 2003 .... 3.00

TOP COW: BOOK OF REVELATION 2003
IMAGE
❑1, Jun 2003 .... 3.99

TOP COW CLASSICS IN BLACK AND WHITE: APHRODITE IX
IMAGE
❑1, Sep 2000 .... 2.95
❑1/A, Sep 2000; Sketch cover (marked as such) ....

TOP COW CLASSICS IN BLACK AND WHITE: ASCENSCION
IMAGE
❑1/A, Apr 2000; Sketch cover (marked as such) 2.95
❑1, Apr 2000 .... 2.95

TOP COW CLASSICS IN BLACK AND WHITE: FATHOM
IMAGE
❑1, May 2000 .... 2.95

TOP COW CLASSICS IN BLACK AND WHITE: MAGDALENA
IMAGE
❑1, Oct 2002, Black background on cover 2.95

TOP COW CLASSICS IN BLACK AND WHITE: MIDNIGHT NATION
IMAGE
❑1, Mar 2001 .... 2.95

TOP COW CLASSICS IN BLACK AND WHITE: RISING STARS
IMAGE
❑1, Aug 2000 .... 2.95

TOP COW CLASSICS IN BLACK AND WHITE: THE DARKNESS
IMAGE
❑1, Mar 2000 .... 2.95

TOP COW CLASSICS IN BLACK AND WHITE: TOMB RAIDER
IMAGE
❑1, Dec 2000 .... 2.95

N-MINT

TOP COW CLASSICS IN BLACK AND WHITE: WITCHBLADE
IMAGE
❑1, Feb 2000 .... 2.95
❑1/A 5.00
❑25, Apr 2001 .... 2.95

TOP COW CON SKETCHBOOK 2004
IMAGE
❑1, Aug 2004 .... 3.00

TOP COW PRODUCTIONS INC./ BALLISTIC STUDIOS SWIMSUIT SPECIAL
IMAGE
❑1, May 1995 .... 2.95

TOP COW SECRETS
IMAGE
❑WS 1, Jan 1996; Special Winter Lingerie Edition; pin-ups 2.95

TOP COW SPECIAL
IMAGE
❑1, Spring/Summer 2001 .... 2.95

TOP DOG
MARVEL / STAR
❑1, Apr 1985 1: Top Dog. 1.00
❑2, Jun 1985 .... 1.00
❑3, Aug 1985 .... 1.00
❑4, Oct 1985 .... 1.00
❑5, Dec 1985 .... 1.00
❑6, Feb 1986 .... 1.00
❑7, Apr 1986 .... 1.00
❑8, Jun 1986 .... 1.00
❑9, Aug 1986 .... 1.00
❑10, Oct 1986 .... 1.00
❑11, Dec 1986 .... 1.00
❑12, Feb 1987 .... 1.00
❑13, Apr 1987 .... 1.00
❑14, Jun 1987 .... 1.00

TOP ELIMINATOR
CHARLTON
❑25, 1967, From Teenage Hotrodders #24 .... 10.00
❑26, Nov 1967 A: Scot Jackson and the Rod Masters. 10.00
❑27, 1968 .... 10.00
❑28, 1968 .... 10.00
❑29, Jul 1968, Becomes Drag 'n' Wheels with #30 .... 10.00

TOPPS COMICS PRESENTS
TOPPS
❑0, Jul 1993; Giveaway; Previewed Dracula vs. Zorro, Teenagents, Silver Star, Jack Kirby's Secret City Saga, Bill the Galactic Hero, etc. 1.50
❑1, Sep 1993; giveaway 1.00

TOP SHELF (PRIMAL GROOVE)
PRIMAL GROOVE
❑1, Win 1995, b&w 5.00

TOP SHELF (TOP SHELF)
TOP SHELF
❑1, ca. 1996 .... 6.95
❑2, ca. 1997 .... 6.95
❑3, ca. 1997 .... 6.95
❑4, ca. 1997 .... 6.95

N-MINT

❑5, ca. 1998 .... 6.95
❑6, ca. 1998 .... 6.95
❑7, ca. 1998 .... 6.95

TOP 10: BEYOND THE FARTHEST PRECINCT
DC / AMERICA'S BEST COMICS
❑1 .... 2.99
❑2 .... 2.99
❑3, Dec 2005 .... 2.99
❑4, Jan 2006 .... 2.99
❑5, Feb 2006 .... 2.99

TOR (DC)
DC
❑1, Jun 1975 JKu (w); JKu (a); O: Tor. 8.00
❑2, Aug 1975 JKu (w); JKu (a) 4.00
❑3, Oct 1975 JKu (w); JKu (a) 4.00
❑4, Dec 1975 JKu (w); JKu (a) 4.00
❑5, Feb 1976 JKu (w); JKu (a) 4.00
❑6, Apr 1976 JKu (w); JKu (a) 4.00

TOR (EPIC)
MARVEL / EPIC
❑1, Jun 1993, large size 5.95
❑2, Jul 1993, large size 5.95
❑3 1993, large size 5.95
❑4 1993, large size 5.95

TOR 3-D
ECLIPSE
❑1, Jul 1986 .... 2.50
❑2, Aug 1987 .... 2.50

TORCH OF LIBERTY SPECIAL
DARK HORSE
❑1, Jan 1995 .... 2.50

TORCHY (BELL)
BELL FEATURES
❑16, ca. 1964, Reprints #4 from Quality series 0.00

TORCHY (INNOVATION)
INNOVATION
❑1, b&w; Reprints 2.50
❑2, b&w; Reprints 2.50
❑3, b&w; Reprints 2.50
❑4, b&w; Reprints 2.50
❑5, b&w; Reprints 2.50
❑9, b&w; Reprints; 1st Olivia cover 2.50
❑Summer 1, b&w; Summer Fun Special 2.50

TORG
ADVENTURE
❑1, b&w 2.50
❑2, Mar 1992, b&w 2.50
❑3, Apr 1992, b&w 2.50
❑4, May 1992, b&w 2.50

TORI DO
PENGUIN PALACE
❑1, Aug 1994, b&w 2.25
❑1/2nd, Mar 1995 .... 2.25

TO RIVERDALE AND BACK AGAIN
ARCHIE
❑1, ca. 1990 .... 2.50

TOR JOHNSON: HOLLYWOOD STAR
MONSTER
❑1, b&w 2.50

TOR LOVE BETTY
FANTAGRAPHICS / EROS
- ❑1, b&w ... 2.75

TORMENT
AIRCEL
- ❑1, b&w ... 2.95
- ❑2, b&w ... 2.95
- ❑3, b&w ... 2.95

TORPEDO
HARD BOILED
- ❑1, b&w; Reprints ... 2.95
- ❑2, b&w; Reprints ... 2.95
- ❑3, b&w; Reprints ... 2.95
- ❑4, b&w; Reprints ... 2.95

TORRID AFFAIRS
ETERNITY
- ❑1 1988, b&w; Reprints ... 2.25
- ❑2/A, Feb 1989; tame cover ... 2.25
- ❑2/B, Feb 1989; sexy cover ... 2.25
- ❑3 1989 ... 2.95
- ❑4 1989 ... 2.95
- ❑5 1989 ... 2.95

TORSO
IMAGE
- ❑1 1999 BMB (w) ... 3.95
- ❑2 1999 BMB (w) ... 3.95
- ❑3 1999 BMB (w) ... 4.95
- ❑4 1999 BMB (w) ... 4.95
- ❑5, Jun 1999 BMB (w); BMB (a) ... 4.95
- ❑6 1999 BMB (w); BMB (a) ... 4.95

TORTOISE AND THE HARE
LAST GASP
- ❑1 ... 3.00

TO SEE THE STARS
NBM
- ❑1 ... 13.95

TOTAL ECLIPSE
ECLIPSE
- ❑1, May 1988 ... 3.95
- ❑2, Aug 1988 ... 3.95
- ❑3, Dec 1988 ... 3.95
- ❑4, Jan 1989 ... 3.95
- ❑5, Apr 1989 ... 3.95

TOTAL ECLIPSE: THE SERAPHIM OBJECTIVE
ECLIPSE
- ❑1, Nov 1988 ... 1.95

TOTAL JUSTICE
DC
- ❑1, Oct 1996; based on Kenner action figures ... 2.25
- ❑2, Nov 1996; based on Kenner action figures ... 2.25
- ❑3, Nov 1996; based on Kenner action figures ... 2.25

TOTALLY ALIEN
TRIGON
- ❑1, b&w ... 2.50
- ❑2, b&w ... 2.50
- ❑3, b&w ... 2.50
- ❑4, b&w ... 2.50
- ❑5, b&w ... 2.50

TOTALLY HORSES!
PAINTED PONY
- ❑1; magazine; horse stories ... 1.95
- ❑2, Spr 1997; magazine; horse stories ... 1.95
- ❑3; magazine; horse stories ... 1.95
- ❑4; magazine; horse stories ... 1.95
- ❑5, Sum 1998; magazine; horse stories ... 1.95

TOTAL RECALL
DC
- ❑1, ca. 1990 ... 2.95

TOTAL WAR
GOLD KEY
- ❑1, Jul 1965 ... 40.00
- ❑2, Oct 1965, Series continued in M.A.R.S. Patrol #3 ... 35.00

TOTEMS (VERTIGO)
DC / VERTIGO
- ❑1, Feb 2000 ... 5.95

TOTEMS (CARTOON FROLICS)
CARTOON FROLICS
- ❑1 ... 2.95
- ❑2 ... 2.95
- ❑3 ... 2.95

TOTEM: SIGN OF THE WARDOG (1ST SERIES)
ALPHA PRODUCTIONS
- ❑1, b&w ... 2.25
- ❑2, b&w ... 2.25

TOTEM: SIGN OF THE WARDOG (2ND SERIES)
ALPHA PRODUCTIONS
- ❑1, Apr 1992, b&w ... 2.50
- ❑2, b&w ... 2.50
- ❑Annual 1 ... 3.50

TOUCH
DC
- ❑1, Jun 2004 ... 2.50
- ❑2, Jul 2004 ... 2.50
- ❑3, Aug 2004 ... 2.50
- ❑4, Sep 2004 ... 2.50
- ❑5, Oct 2004 ... 2.50
- ❑6, Nov 2004 ... 2.50

TOUCH OF SILK, A TASTE OF LEATHER
BONEYARD
- ❑1, Mar 1994, b&w ... 2.95

TOUCH OF SILVER
IMAGE
- ❑1, Jan 1997, b&w; semi-autobiographical ... 2.95
- ❑2, Mar 1997, b&w; semi-autobiographical ... 2.95
- ❑3, May 1997, b&w; semi-autobiographical ... 2.95
- ❑4, Jul 1997, b&w; semi-autobiographical ... 2.95
- ❑5, Sep 1997; b&w with color section; semi-autobiographical ... 2.95
- ❑6, Nov 1997, b&w; semi-autobiographical ... 2.95

TOUGH
VIZ
- ❑1, Jan 2005 ... 9.99
- ❑2, Apr 2005 ... 9.99
- ❑3, Jul 2005 ... 9.99
- ❑4, Oct 2005 ... 9.99

TOUGH GUYS AND WILD WOMEN
ETERNITY
- ❑1, Mar 1989, b&w; Saint reprints ... 2.25
- ❑2, b&w; Saint reprints ... 2.25

TOWER OF SHADOWS
MARVEL
- ❑1, Sep 1969 JCr, JSo, SL (w); JB, JCr, JSo (a) ... 55.00
- ❑2, Nov 1969 NA (a) ... 25.00
- ❑3, Jan 1970 ... 25.00
- ❑4, Jan 1970 ... 25.00
- ❑5, May 1970 WW (a) ... 25.00
- ❑6, Jul 1970 TS, SL (w); TS, SD, GC, WW, DA (a) ... 15.00
- ❑7, Sep 1970 WW (a) ... 15.00
- ❑8, Nov 1970 SD, WW (a) ... 15.00
- ❑9, Nov 1970, Series continued in Creatures On the Loose #10 ... 8.00
- ❑Special 1, Dec 1971 ... 22.00

TOXIC!
APOCALYPSE
- ❑1, Marshal Law ... 2.50
- ❑2, Marshal Law ... 2.50
- ❑3, Marshal Law ... 2.50
- ❑4, Marshal Law ... 2.50
- ❑5, Marshal Law; Mutomatic; The Driver ... 2.50
- ❑6, Marshal Law ... 2.50
- ❑7, Marshal Law ... 2.50
- ❑8, Marshal Law ... 2.50
- ❑9, Marshal Law ... 2.50
- ❑10, Marshal Law ... 2.50
- ❑11, Marshal Law ... 2.50
- ❑12, Marshal Law ... 2.50
- ❑13, Marshal Law ... 2.50
- ❑14, Marshal Law ... 2.50
- ❑15, Marshal Law ... 2.50
- ❑16, Marshal Law ... 2.50
- ❑17, Marshal Law ... 2.50
- ❑18, Marshal Law ... 2.50
- ❑19, Marshal Law ... 2.50

TOXIC AVENGER
MARVEL
- ❑1, Apr 1991, O: Toxic Avenger. 1: Toxic Avenger ... 2.00
- ❑2, May 1991 ... 1.50
- ❑3, Jun 1991 ... 1.50
- ❑4, Jul 1991 ... 1.50
- ❑5, Aug 1991 ... 1.50
- ❑6, Sep 1991, VM (a) ... 1.50
- ❑7, Oct 1991, VM (a) ... 1.50
- ❑8, Nov 1991 ... 1.50
- ❑9, Dec 1991 ... 1.50
- ❑10, Jan 1992 ... 1.50
- ❑11, Feb 1992, VM (a) ... 1.50

TOXIC CRUSADERS
MARVEL
- ❑1, May 1992 ... 1.25
- ❑2, Jun 1992 ... 1.25
- ❑3, Jul 1992 ... 1.25
- ❑4, Aug 1992 ... 1.25
- ❑5, Sep 1992 ... 1.25
- ❑6, Oct 1992 ... 1.25
- ❑7, Nov 1992 ... 1.25
- ❑8, Dec 1992 ... 1.25

TOXIC GUMBO
DC / VERTIGO
- ❑1, May 1998; prestige format ... 5.95

TOXIC PARADISE
SLAVE LABOR
- ❑1, b&w; Love & Romance; cardstock cover ... 4.95

TOXIN
MARVEL
- ❑1, May 2005 ... 2.99
- ❑2, Jun 2005 ... 2.99
- ❑3, Jul 2005 ... 2.99
- ❑4, Aug 2005 ... 2.99
- ❑5, Sep 2005 ... 2.99
- ❑6, Oct 2005 ...

TOXINE
NOSE
- ❑1 ... 3.00

TOYBOY
CONTINUITY
- ❑1, Oct 1986 ... 2.00
- ❑2, Aug 1987 ... 2.00
- ❑3, Nov 1987 ... 2.00
- ❑4, Feb 1988 ... 2.00
- ❑5, Jun 1988 ... 2.00
- ❑6 1988 ... 2.00
- ❑7, Mar 1989 ... 2.00

TOY STORY (DISNEY'S...)
MARVEL
- ❑1, Dec 1995 ... 4.95

TRACI LORDS: THE OUTLAW YEARS
BONEYARD
- ❑1 ... 3.00

TRACKER
BLACKTHORNE
- ❑1, May 1988, b&w ... 2.00
- ❑2, b&w ... 2.00

TRAGG AND THE SKY GODS
WHITMAN
- ❑1, Jun 1975 DS (a) ... 5.00
- ❑2, Sep 1975 ... 3.00
- ❑3, Dec 1975 ... 2.50
- ❑4, Feb 1976 ... 2.50
- ❑5, Apr 1976 ... 2.50
- ❑6, Sep 1976 ... 2.50
- ❑7, Nov 1976 ... 2.50
- ❑8, Feb 1977 ... 2.50
- ❑9, May 1982 ... 2.50

TRAILER TRASH
TUNDRA
- ❑1, b&w ... 2.00
- ❑4, b&w ... 2.95
- ❑7, Jun 1996, b&w ... 2.95
- ❑8, Nov 1996, b&w ... 2.95

TRAKK: MONSTER HUNTER
IMAGE
- ❑1, Nov 2003 ... 2.95
- ❑2, Apr 2004 ... 2.95

Troublemakers

Characters more mellow than angst-ridden

©Acclaim

Trouble With Girls (Vol. 1)

Lots of tongue-in-cheek humor

©Malibu

Truth: Red, White & Black

Controversial storyline changed Cap's origin

©Marvel

TSR Worlds

DC special focused on role-playing universes

©DC

Turok, Dinosaur Hunter

Valiant revives Gold Key fighter

©Acclaim

N-MINT

TRAMPS LIKE US
Tokyopop

❑1, Aug 2004 ... 9.99
❑2, Oct 2004 ... 9.99
❑3, Dec 2004 ... 9.99
❑4, Feb 2005 ... 9.99
❑5, May 2005 ... 9.99
❑6, Aug 2005 ... 9.99
❑7, Nov 2005 ... 9.99

TRANCEPTOR
NBM

❑1 ... 11.95

TRANCERS
Eternity

❑1, Aug 1991 ... 2.50
❑2 ... 2.50

TRANQUILITY
Dreamsmith

❑1, Sep 1998, b&w ... 2.50
❑2, Oct 1998, b&w ... 2.50
❑3, Nov 1998, b&w ... 2.50

TRANQUILIZER
Luxurious

❑1 ... 2.95
❑2 ... 2.95

TRANSFORMERS
Marvel

❑1, Sep 1984; 1: Transformers. "Limited Series #1" ... 10.00
❑2, Nov 1984; "Limited Series #2" ... 5.00
❑3, Jan 1985; Spider-Man; "Limited Series #3" ... 5.00
❑4, Mar 1985; "Limited Series #4" ... 3.00
❑5, Jun 1985 ... 3.00
❑6, Jul 1985 ... 3.00
❑7, Aug 1985 ... 3.00
❑8, Sep 1985 A: Dinobots ... 3.00
❑9, Oct 1985 ... 3.00
❑10, Nov 1985 V: Devastator ... 3.00
❑11, Dec 1985 V: Jetfire ... 3.00
❑12, Jan 1986 ... 3.00
❑13, Feb 1986 ... 3.00
❑14, Mar 1986 ... 3.00
❑15, Apr 1986 ... 3.00
❑16, May 1986 ... 3.00
❑17, Jun 1986 ... 3.00
❑18, Jul 1986 ... 3.00
❑19, Aug 1986 ... 3.00
❑20, Sep 1986 ... 3.00
❑21, Oct 1986 1: Aerialbots ... 2.00
❑22, Nov 1986 ... 2.00
❑23, Dec 1986 ... 2.00
❑24, Jan 1987 ... 2.00
❑25, Feb 1987 ... 2.00
❑26, Mar 1987 ... 2.00
❑27, Apr 1987 ... 2.00
❑28, May 1987 ... 2.00
❑29, Jun 1987 ... 2.00
❑30, Jul 1987 ... 2.00
❑31, Aug 1987 ... 2.00
❑32, Sep 1987 ... 2.00
❑33, Oct 1987 ... 2.00
❑34, Nov 1987 ... 2.00

N-MINT

❑35, Dec 1987 ... 2.00
❑36, Jan 1988 ... 2.00
❑37, Feb 1988 ... 2.00
❑38, Mar 1988 ... 2.00
❑39, Apr 1988 ... 2.00
❑40, May 1988 ... 2.00
❑41, Jun 1988 ... 2.00
❑42, Jul 1988 ... 2.00
❑43, Aug 1988 ... 2.00
❑44, Sep 1988 ... 2.00
❑45, Oct 1988 ... 2.00
❑46, Nov 1988 ... 2.00
❑47, Dec 1988 ... 2.00
❑48, Jan 1989 ... 2.00
❑49, Feb 1989 ... 2.00
❑50, Mar 1989 ... 2.00
❑51, Apr 1989 ... 2.00
❑52, May 1989 ... 2.00
❑53, Jun 1989 ... 2.00
❑54, Jul 1989 ... 2.00
❑55, Aug 1989 ... 2.00
❑56, Sep 1989 ... 2.00
❑57, Oct 1989 ... 2.00
❑58, Nov 1989 ... 2.00
❑59, Nov 1989 ... 2.00
❑60, Dec 1989 ... 2.00
❑61, Dec 1989 ... 2.00
❑62, Jan 1990 ... 2.00
❑63, Feb 1990 ... 2.00
❑64, Mar 1990 ... 2.00
❑65, Apr 1990 ... 2.00
❑66, May 1990 ... 2.00
❑67, Jun 1990 ... 2.00
❑68, Jul 1990 ... 2.00
❑69, Aug 1990 ... 2.00
❑70, Sep 1990 ... 5.00
❑71, Oct 1990 ... 5.00
❑72, Nov 1990 ... 5.00
❑73, Dec 1990 ... 5.00
❑74, Jan 1991 ... 5.00
❑75, Feb 1991; Double-size ... 5.00
❑76, Mar 1991 ... 5.00
❑77, Apr 1991 ... 10.00
❑78, May 1991 ... 10.00
❑79, Jun 1991 ... 10.00
❑80, Jul 1991 ... 18.00

TRANSFORMERS: ARMADA
Dreamwave

❑1, Jul 2002 (w) ... 2.95
❑1/A, Jul 2002; (w); chromium cover ... 2.95
❑2, Aug 2002 ... 2.95
❑3, Oct 2002 ... 2.95
❑4, Nov 2002 ... 2.95
❑5, Dec 2002 ... 2.95
❑6, Dec 2002 ... 2.95
❑7, Jan 2003 ... 2.95
❑7/A, Jan 2003; White background on cover ... 3.50
❑8, Feb 2003 ... 2.95
❑9, Mar 2003 ... 2.95
❑10, Apr 2003 ... 2.95
❑11, May 2003 ... 2.95
❑12, Jun 2003 ... 2.95
❑13, Jul 2003 ... 2.95

N-MINT

❑14, Aug 2003 ... 2.95
❑15, Sep 2003 ... 2.95
❑16, Oct 2003 ... 2.95
❑17, Nov 2003 ... 2.95
❑18, Dec 2003 ... 2.95

TRANSFORMERS ARMADA: MORE THAN MEETS THE EYE
Dark Horse

❑1, Mar 2004 ... 4.95
❑2, Apr 2004 ... 4.95
❑3, May 2004 ... 4.95

TRANSFORMERS: BEAST WARS
Idea & Design Works

❑1, Feb 2006 ... 2.99
❑2, Mar 2006 ... 2.99
❑3, Apr 2006 ... 2.99
❑4, May 2006 ... 2.99

TRANSFORMERS COMICS MAGAZINE
Marvel

❑1, Jan 1987; digest ... 1.50
❑2, Mar 1987 ... 1.50
❑3, May 1987 ... 1.50
❑4, Jul 1987 ... 1.50
❑5, Sep 1987 ... 1.50
❑6, Nov 1987 ... 1.50
❑7, Jan 1988 ... 1.50
❑8, Mar 1988 ... 1.50
❑9, May 1988 ... 1.50
❑10, Jul 1988 ... 1.50

TRANSFORMERS: ENERGON
Dark Horse

❑19, Jan 2004 ... 2.95
❑20, Feb 2004 ... 2.95
❑21, Mar 2004 ... 2.95
❑22, Apr 2004 ... 2.95
❑23, May 2004 ... 2.95
❑24, Jun 2004 ... 2.95
❑25, Jul 2004 ... 2.95
❑26, Aug 2004 ... 2.95
❑27, Sep 2004 ... 2.95
❑28, Oct 2004 ... 2.95
❑29, Nov 2004 ... 2.95
❑30, Dec 2004 ... 2.95

TRANSFORMERS/GEN13
Marvel

❑Ashcan 1 ... 1.00

TRANSFORMERS: GENERATION 1
Dreamwave

❑1/Autobot, Apr 2002; (w); Autobot cover ... 4.00
❑1/Decepticon, Apr 2002; (w); Decepticon cover ... 4.00
❑1/Chromium, Apr 2002; (w); chromium cover ... 5.95
❑1/2nd, Apr 2002 (w) ... 2.95
❑1/3rd, Apr 2002 (w) ... 2.95
❑2/Autobot, May 2002; (w); Autobots cover ... 3.50
❑2/Decepticon, May 2002; (w); Decepticon cover ... 3.50
❑2/2nd, May 2002 (w) ... 2.95
❑3/Autobot, Jun 2002; (w); Autobots cover ... 2.95

Other grades: Multiply price above by 5/6 for VF/NM • 2/3 for VERY FINE • 1/3 for FINE • 1/5 for VERY GOOD • 1/8 for GOOD

❑3/Decepticon, Jun 2002; (w); Decepticon cover ... 2.95
❑4/Autobot, Jul 2002; (w); Autobots cover ... 2.95
❑4/Decepticon, Jul 2002; (w); Decepticon cover ... 2.95
❑5/Autobot, Aug 2002; Autobots cover 2.95
❑5/Decepticon, Aug 2002; Decepticon cover ... 2.95
❑5/2nd, Nov 2002 ... 2.95
❑6/Autobot, Oct 2002; Autobots cover 2.95
❑6/Decepticon, Oct 2002; Decepticon cover ... 2.95

TRANSFORMERS: GENERATION 1 (VOL. 2)
DREAMWAVE

❑1, Apr 2003 ... 2.95
❑1/Counterfeit, Apr 2003, Chrome Cover ... 5.95
❑2, May 2003 ... 2.95
❑3, Jun 2003 ... 2.95
❑4, Jul 2003 ... 2.95
❑5, Aug 2003 ... 2.95
❑6, Oct 2003 ... 2.95

TRANSFORMERS: GENERATION 1 (VOL. 3)
DREAMWAVE

❑0, Dec 2003 ... 2.95
❑1, Feb 2004 ... 4.00
❑1/SilvSnail ... 5.00
❑2, Feb 2004 ... 2.95
❑3, Mar 2004 ... 2.95
❑4, Apr 2004 ... 2.95
❑5, Jun 2004 ... 2.95
❑6, Jul 2004 ... 2.95
❑7, Aug 2004 ... 2.95
❑8, Sep 2004 ... 2.95
❑9, Nov 2004 ... 2.95
❑10, Dec 2005 ... 2.95

TRANSFORMERS: GENERATION 1 PREVIEW
DREAMWAVE

❑1/A, Apr 2002; Autobot cover ... 3.95
❑1/B, Apr 2002; Retailer Incentive Edition ... 3.95

TRANSFORMERS: GENERATION 2
MARVEL

❑1, Nov 1993 ... 1.75
❑1/Variant, Nov 1993; foil fold-out cover ... 2.95
❑2, Dec 1993 ... 1.75
❑3, Jan 1994 ... 1.75
❑4, Feb 1994 ... 1.75
❑5, Mar 1994 ... 1.75
❑6, Apr 1994 ... 1.75
❑7, May 1994 ... 1.75
❑8, Jun 1994 ... 1.75
❑9, Jul 1994 ... 1.75
❑10, Aug 1994 ... 1.75
❑11, Sep 1994 ... 1.75
❑12, Oct 1994; double-sized ... 2.25

TRANSFORMERS: GENERATIONS
IDEA & DESIGN WORKS

❑1, Apr 2006 ... 2.95
❑2, Apr 2006 ... 2.95
❑4, Jun 2006 ... 2.95

TRANSFORMERS/G.I.JOE
DREAMWAVE

❑1, Sep 2003 ... 2.95
❑1/Dynamic, Sep 2003 ... 1.48
❑1/H, Sep 2003; Holofoil cover ... 5.95
❑2, Oct 2003 ... 2.95
❑3, Nov 2003 ... 2.95
❑4, Dec 2003 ... 2.95
❑5, Jan 2004 ... 2.95
❑6, Mar 2004 ... 2.95

TRANSFORMERS, THE: HEADMASTERS
MARVEL

❑1, Jul 1987 ... 1.00
❑2, Sep 1987 FS (a) ... 1.00
❑3, Nov 1987 ... 1.00
❑4, Jan 1988 ... 1.00

TRANSFORMERS (IDW)
IDEA & DESIGN WORKS

❑0, Oct 2005 ... 2.99

TRANSFORMERS IN 3-D
BLACKTHORNE

❑1 ... 2.50
❑2, Dec 1987 ... 2.50
❑3, Apr 1988 ... 2.50

TRANSFORMERS: INFILTRATION
IDEA & DESIGN WORKS

❑1, Jan 2006 ... 2.99
❑2, Feb 2006 ... 2.99
❑3, Mar 2006 ... 2.99
❑4, Apr 2006 ... 2.99
❑5, Jun 2006 ... 2.99

TRANSFORMERS: MICROMASTERS
DREAMWAVE

❑1, Jun 2004 ... 2.95
❑2 2004 ... 2.95
❑3 2004 ... 2.95

TRANSFORMERS: MORE THAN MEETS THE EYE OFFICIAL GUIDE
DREAMWAVE

❑1, Apr 2003 ... 5.25
❑2, May 2003 ... 5.25
❑3, Jun 2003 ... 5.25
❑4, Jul 2003 ... 5.25
❑5, Sep 2003 ... 5.25
❑6, Sep 2003 ... 5.25
❑7, Oct 2003 ... 5.25
❑8, Nov 2003 ... 5.25

TRANSFORMERS MOVIE
MARVEL

❑1, Dec 1986 ... 1.00
❑2, Jan 1987 ... 1.00
❑3, Feb 1987 ... 1.00

TRANSFORMERS: THE WAR WITHIN
DREAMWAVE

❑Ashcan 1, Aug 2002; Preview issue ... 3.00
❑1, Oct 2002 ... 3.00
❑1/Variant, Oct 2002; lenticular animation cover ... 7.00
❑2, Nov 2002 ... 2.95
❑3, Dec 2002 ... 2.95
❑4, Jan 2003 ... 2.95
❑5, Feb 2003 ... 2.95
❑5/A, Feb 2003; Retailer Incentive edition; lenticular animation cover ... 5.00
❑6, Mar 2003 ... 2.95

TRANSFORMERS: THE WAR WITHIN (VOL. 2)
DREAMWAVE

❑1, Oct 2003 ... 2.95
❑2, Nov 2003 ... 2.95
❑3, Dec 2003 ... 2.95
❑4, Jan 2004 ... 2.95
❑5, Mar 2004 ... 2.95
❑6, Apr 2004 ... 2.95

TRANSFORMERS: THE WAR WITHIN (VOL. 3)
DREAMWAVE

❑1, Nov 2004 ... 2.95
❑2, Dec 2004 ... 2.95
❑3, Jan 2005 ... 2.95

TRANSFORMERS UNIVERSE
MARVEL

❑1, Dec 1986 ... 20.00
❑1/DirCut ... 10.00
❑2, Jan 1987 ... 10.00
❑2/OTFCC ... 20.00
❑2/FanClub ... 25.00
❑2/Conv ... 20.00
❑3, Feb 1987 ... 5.00
❑3/OTFCC ... 20.00
❑3/FanClub ... 20.00
❑3/Conv ... 20.00
❑4, Mar 1987 ... 2.00

TRANSIT
VORTEX

❑1, Mar 1987 ... 1.75
❑2, May 1987 ... 1.75
❑3, Jul 1987 ... 1.75
❑4, Sep 1987 ... 1.75
❑5, Nov 1987 ... 1.75

TRANSMETROPOLITAN
DC / HELIX

❑1, Sep 1997 ... 8.00
❑2, Oct 1997 ... 6.00
❑3, Nov 1997 ... 4.00
❑4, Dec 1997 ... 4.00
❑5, Jan 1998 ... 4.00
❑6, Feb 1998 ... 3.00
❑7, Mar 1998 ... 3.00
❑8, Apr 1998 ... 3.00
❑9, May 1998 ... 3.00
❑10, Jun 1998 ... 3.00
❑11, Jul 1998 ... 3.00
❑12, Aug 1998 ... 3.00
❑13, Sep 1998 ... 2.50
❑14, Oct 1998 ... 2.50
❑15, Nov 1998 ... 2.50
❑16, Dec 1998 ... 2.50
❑17, Jan 1999 ... 2.50
❑18, Feb 1999 ... 2.50
❑19, Mar 1999 ... 2.50
❑20, Apr 1999 ... 2.50
❑21, May 1999 ... 2.50
❑22, Jun 1999 ... 2.50
❑23, Jul 1999; 100 Bullets preview ... 2.50
❑24, Aug 1999 ... 2.50
❑25, Sep 1999 ... 2.50
❑26, Oct 1999 ... 2.50
❑27, Nov 1999 ... 2.50
❑28, Dec 1999 ... 2.50
❑29, Jan 2000 ... 2.50
❑30, Feb 2000 ... 2.50
❑31, Mar 2000 ... 2.50
❑32, Apr 2000 ... 2.50
❑33, May 2000 ... 2.50
❑34 2000 ... 2.50
❑35, Aug 2000 ... 2.50
❑36, Sep 2000 ... 2.50
❑37, Oct 2000 ... 2.50
❑38, Nov 2000 ... 2.50
❑39, Dec 2000 ... 2.50
❑40, Jan 2001 ... 2.50
❑41, Feb 2001 ... 2.50
❑42, Mar 2001 ... 2.50
❑43, Apr 2001 ... 2.50
❑44, May 2001 ... 2.50
❑45, Jun 2001 ... 2.50
❑46, Aug 2001 ... 2.50
❑47, Sep 2001 ... 2.50
❑48, Oct 2001 ... 2.50
❑49, Nov 2001 ... 2.50
❑50, Dec 2001 ... 2.50
❑51, Jan 2002 ... 2.50
❑52, Feb 2002 ... 2.50
❑53, Mar 2002 ... 2.50
❑54, Apr 2002 ... 2.50
❑55, Jun 2002 ... 2.50
❑56, Jul 2002 ... 2.50
❑57, Aug 2002 ... 2.50
❑58, Sep 2002 ... 2.50
❑59, Oct 2002 ... 2.50
❑60, Nov 2002 ... 2.50

TRANSMETROPOLITAN: FILTH OF THE CITY
DC / VERTIGO

❑1, Jul 2001, chromium cover ... 5.95

TRANSMETROPOLITAN: I HATE IT HERE
DC / VERTIGO

❑1, Jun 2000 ... 5.95

TRANSMUTATION OF IKE GARUDA
MARVEL / EPIC

❑1 ... 3.95
❑2 ... 3.95

TRANS NUBIANS
ADEOLA

❑1 ... 2.95

TRASH
FLEETWAY-QUALITY

❑1 ... 2.95
❑2 ... 2.95

TRAUMA CORPS
ANUBIS

❑1, Feb 1994 ... 2.75

TRAVELERS
SOUTH JERSEY REBELLION PROD.

❑1, b&w; no indicia ... 2.25

Turok, Son of Stone

Long-running adventure character

©Dell

TV Western

AC spotlighted old western reprints

©AC

Tweety and Sylvester (2nd Series)

Later issues had some clever pop culture gags

©Gold Key

22 Brides

Painkiller Jane plus twenty-one

©Event

Twilight Avenger (Eternity)

College football star avenges girlfriend

©Eternity

N-MINT

- ❑2 ... 2.25
- ❑3 ... 2.25

TRAVELLER'S TALE
Antarctic
- ❑1, b&w ... 2.50
- ❑2, Aug 1992, b&w ... 2.50
- ❑3, Oct 1992, b&w ... 2.50

TRAVELS OF JAIMIE MCPHEETERS
Gold Key
- ❑1, Dec 1963 ... 12.00

TREASURE CHESTS
Fantagraphics / Eros
- ❑1, Jun 1999 ... 2.95
- ❑2 1999 ... 2.95
- ❑3 ... 2.95
- ❑4, Feb 2000 ... 2.95
- ❑5, Jul 2000 ... 2.95

TREEHOUSE OF HORROR (BART SIMPSON'S...)
Bongo
- ❑1, 1995; JRo (w); Halloween stories. 3.50
- ❑2, 1996; infinity cover; Halloween stories ... 2.50
- ❑3, 1997; Halloween story ... 2.50
- ❑4, 1998; Halloween stories ... 2.50
- ❑5, 1999; SA (a); Halloween stories; Eisner award winner ... 3.50
- ❑6, 2000; Halloween stories ... 4.50
- ❑7, Oct 2001 ... 4.50
- ❑8, Oct 2002; Says #7 in indicia ... 3.50
- ❑9, Oct 2003 ... 4.99
- ❑10, Oct 2004 ... 4.99

TREKKER (DARK HORSE)
Dark Horse
- ❑1, May 1987, b&w ... 1.50
- ❑2, Jul 1987, b&w ... 1.50
- ❑3, Sep 1987 ... 1.75
- ❑4, Nov 1987 ... 1.50
- ❑5, Jan 1988 ... 1.50
- ❑6, Mar 1988 ... 1.50
- ❑7, May 1988 ... 1.50
- ❑8, Jul 1988 ... 1.50
- ❑9, Sep 1988 ... 1.50
- ❑Special 1 Special ... 2.95
- ❑Book 1, b&w ... 5.95

TREKKER (IMAGE)
Image
- ❑Special 1, Jun 1999 ... 2.95

TREK TEENS
Parody
- ❑1, Feb 1993, b&w ... 2.50
- ❑1/A, Feb 1993, b&w; alternate cover. 2.50

TRENCHCOAT BRIGADE
DC / Vertigo
- ❑1, Mar 1999 ... 2.50
- ❑2, Apr 1999 ... 2.50
- ❑3, May 1999 ... 2.50
- ❑4, Jun 1999 ... 2.50

TRENCHER
Image
- ❑1, May 1993 KG (w); KG (a) ... 2.00
- ❑2, Jun 1993 KG (a) ... 2.00
- ❑3, Jul 1993 KG (a) ... 2.00
- ❑4, Oct 1993 KG (a) ... 2.00

TRENCHER X-MAS BITES HOLIDAY BLOW-OUT
Blackball
- ❑1, Dec 1993 ... 2.50

TRESPASSERS
Amazing Montage
- ❑1 ... 2.50
- ❑2 ... 2.50
- ❑3 ... 2.50
- ❑4 ... 2.50
- ❑5 ... 2.50

TRIAD UNIVERSE
Triad
- ❑1, Jul 1994 ... 2.25
- ❑2, Aug 1994, b&w ... 2.25

TRIAL RUN
Miller
- ❑1, b&w ... 2.00
- ❑2, b&w ... 2.00
- ❑3, b&w ... 2.00
- ❑4, b&w ... 2.00
- ❑5, b&w ... 2.00
- ❑6, b&w ... 2.00
- ❑7, b&w ... 2.00
- ❑14 ... 2.50
- ❑15 ... 2.50

TRIARCH
Caliber
- ❑1, b&w ... 2.50
- ❑2, b&w ... 2.50

TRIBE
Image
- ❑1, Mar 1993; Embossed cover; Only issue published by Image; cover says April, indicia says March ... 2.50
- ❑1/Variant, Mar 1993; gold logo; White cover; cover says April, indicia says March ... 2.95
- ❑2, Sep 1993; Axis begins publishing 1.95
- ❑3, Apr 1994 ... 1.95

TRIBE (VOL. 2)
Good
- ❑0, Oct 1996 ... 2.95

TRICKSTER KING MONKEY
Eastern
- ❑1 ... 1.75

TRIDENT
Trident
- ❑1 1989, b&w ... 3.50
- ❑2 1989, b&w ... 3.50
- ❑3 1989, b&w ... 3.50
- ❑4 1990, b&w ... 3.50
- ❑5, Apr 1990, b&w ... 3.50
- ❑6 1990, b&w ... 3.50
- ❑7 1990, b&w ... 3.50
- ❑8 1990, b&w ... 3.50

TRIDENT SAMPLER
Trident
- ❑1 ... 1.00
- ❑2 ... 1.00

TRIGGER
DC
- ❑1, Jan 2005 ... 2.95
- ❑2, Mar 2005 ... 2.95
- ❑3, Apr 2005 ... 2.95
- ❑4, May 2005 ... 2.95
- ❑5, Jun 2005 ... 2.99
- ❑6, Jul 2005 ... 2.99
- ❑7, Aug 2005 ... 2.99
- ❑8, Sep 2005 ... 2.99

TRIGGERMAN
Caliber
- ❑1, ca. 1996, b&w ... 2.95
- ❑2, ca. 1997, b&w ... 2.95

TRIGGER TWINS
DC
- ❑1, Mar 1973, CI, RA (a); Reprints from All-Star Western #94, 81, 103 ... 18.00

TRIGUN
Dark Horse
- ❑1, ca. 2003 ... 14.95
- ❑2, ca. 2004 ... 14.95

TRIGUN MAXIMUM
Dark Horse
- ❑1, ca. 2004; Hero Returns ... 9.95

TRILOGY TOUR
Cartoon
- ❑1, Sum 1997, b&w; promotional comic for Summer 1997 tour ... 1.50

TRILOGY TOUR II
Cartoon
- ❑1, Jun 1998, promotional comic for Summer 1998 tour ... 4.95

TRINITY ANGELS
Acclaim / Valiant
- ❑1, Jul 1997 1: Rubberneck. 1: Teresa Angelina Barbella. 1: Trenchmouth. 1: Gianna Barbella. 1: Maria Barbella. 2.50
- ❑1/Variant, Jul 1997; alternate painted cover ... 2.50
- ❑2, Aug 1997 V: Prick ... 2.50
- ❑3, Sep 1997; Justice League America #1 homage cover ... 2.50
- ❑4, Oct 1997 ... 2.50
- ❑5, Nov 1997; new costumes ... 2.50
- ❑6, Dec 1997 1: The Lounge Lizard ... 2.50
- ❑7, Jan 1998; Showgirls tribute cover 2.50
- ❑8, Feb 1998 ... 2.50
- ❑9, Mar 1998 ... 2.50
- ❑10, Apr 1998 ... 2.50
- ❑11, Jan 1998; No cover date; indicia says Jan ... 2.50
- ❑12, Feb 1998; No cover date; indicia says Feb ... 2.50
- ❑Ashcan 1, Mar 1997, b&w; No cover price; preview of upcoming series .. 1.00

TRIPLE DARE
Alternative
- ❑1, May 1998, b&w ... 2.95

TRIPLE•X
Dark Horse
- ❑1, Dec 1994 ... 3.95
- ❑2, Jan 1995 ... 3.95

❑3, Feb 1995 .... 3.95
❑4, Mar 1995 .... 3.95
❑5, Apr 1995 .... 3.95
❑6, May 1995 .... 3.95
❑7, Jul 1995 .... 4.95

TRIPLE-X CINEMA: A CARTOON HISTORY
RE-VISIONARY

❑1, Mar 1997, b&w 3.50
❑2, Apr 1997, b&w 3.50
❑3, May 1997, b&w 3.50

TRIUMPH
DC

❑1, Jun 1995 .... 1.75
❑2, Jul 1995 .... 1.75
❑3, Aug 1995 .... 1.75
❑4, Sep 1995 .... 1.75

TRIUMPHANT UNLEASHED
TRIUMPHANT

❑0, ca. 1993; Unleashed Prologue 2.50
❑0/A, ca. 1993; free; Unleashed Prologue 1.00
❑0/Variant, ca. 1993; Mail-in special-cover edition. Given as promo from coupons in first 9 Triumphant books; No cover price; Unleashed Prologue; red logo; mail-away version 4.00
❑1, Nov 1993 .... 2.50

TRIUMVIRATE
CATACOMB

❑1, b&w; flipbook with Pinnacle #1 .... 2.50

TROLL
IMAGE

❑1, Dec 1993 .... 2.50

TROLL II
IMAGE

❑1, Jul 1994 .... 3.95

TROLL: HALLOWEEN SPECIAL
IMAGE

❑1, Oct 1994 .... 2.95

TROLL: ONCE A HERO
IMAGE

❑1, Aug 1994 .... 2.50

TROLLORDS: DEATH AND KISSES
APPLE

❑1, 1989, b&w 2.25
❑2, 1989, b&w 2.25
❑3, 1989, b&w 2.25
❑4, 1989, b&w 2.25
❑5, 1989, b&w 2.25
❑6, ... 2.50

TROLLORDS (VOL. 1)
TRU

❑1, Feb 1986, b&w 1: Trollords. 2.00
❑1/2nd, 1: Trollords. 1.50
❑2, ca. 1986 .... 1.50
❑3, ca. 1986 .... 1.50
❑4, ca. 1986 .... 1.50
❑5, ca. 1986 .... 1.50
❑6, ca. 1986 .... 1.50
❑7, ca. 1986 .... 1.50
❑8, ca. 1987 .... 1.50
❑9, ca. 1987 .... 1.50
❑10, ca. 1987 .... 1.50
❑11, ca. 1987 .... 1.50
❑12, ca. 1987 .... 1.50
❑13, ca. 1987 .... 1.50
❑14, ca. 1987 .... 1.50
❑15, Feb 1988 .... 1.50
❑Special 1, Feb 1987, Jerry's Big Fun Book 2.00

TROLLORDS (VOL. 2)
COMICO

❑1, ca. 1988 .... 2.00
❑2, ca. 1988 .... 2.00
❑3, ca. 1989 .... 2.00
❑4, ca. 1989 .... 2.50

TROLL PATROL
HARVEY

❑1, Jan 1993 .... 1.95

TROMBONE
KNOCKABOUT

❑1 .... 2.50

TROPO
BLACKBIRD

❑1, b&w 2.75
❑2, b&w 2.75
❑3, b&w 2.75
❑4, b&w 2.75
❑5, b&w 2.75

TROUBLE
MARVEL / EPIC

❑1, Sep 2003 .... 2.99
❑2, Oct 2003 .... 2.99
❑3, Nov 2003 .... 2.99
❑4, Dec 2003 .... 2.99
❑5, Jan 2004 .... 2.99

TROUBLE EXPRESS
RADIO

❑1, Nov 1998 .... 2.95
❑1/A, Nov 1998; Adam Warren cover. 2.95
❑2, Jan 1999 .... 2.95

TROUBLE MAGNET
DC

❑1, Feb 2000 .... 2.50
❑2, Mar 2000 .... 2.50
❑3, Apr 2000 .... 2.50
❑4, May 2000 .... 2.50

TROUBLEMAKERS
ACCLAIM / VALIANT

❑1, Apr 1997; 1: Troublemakers. 1: Calamity. 1: XL. 1: Rebound. 1: Blur. cover says Mar, indicia says Apr 2.50
❑1/Variant, Apr 1997; indicia and cover dates match 2.50
❑2, May 1997; cover says Apr, indicia says May 2.50
❑3, Jun 1997 .... 2.50
❑4, Jun 1997 .... 2.50
❑5, Aug 1997 .... 2.50
❑6, Sep 1997 .... 2.50
❑7, Oct 1997 .... 2.50
❑8, Nov 1997; Cover swipe from X-Men (1st Series) #100 .... 2.50
❑9, Dec 1997; teen sex issue 2.50
❑10, Jan 1998 .... 2.50
❑11, Feb 1998 .... 2.50
❑12, Mar 1998 .... 2.50
❑13, Apr 1998 .... 2.50
❑14, Jan 1998; no cover date; indicia says Jan 2.50
❑15, Feb 1998; no cover date; indicia says Feb 2.50
❑16, Mar 1998; month of publication repeated 2.50
❑17, Mar 1998; month of publication repeated 2.50
❑18, Mar 1998; month of publication repeated 2.50
❑19, Jun 1998 .... 2.50
❑Ashcan 1, Nov 1996, b&w; no cover price; preview of upcoming series 1.00

TROUBLEMAN
IMAGE / MOTOWN

❑1, Jun 1996 .... 2.25
❑2, Jul 1996 .... 2.25
❑3, Aug 1996 .... 2.25

TROUBLESHOOTERS INC.
NIGHTWOLF

❑1, Win 1995, b&w 2.50
❑2, Spr 1995, b&w 2.50

TROUBLE WITH GIRLS (VOL. 1)
MALIBU

❑1, Aug 1987, b&w 2.50
❑2, Sep 1987 .... 2.25
❑3, Oct 1987 .... 2.25
❑4, Nov 1987 .... 2.25
❑5, Dec 1987 .... 2.25
❑6, Jan 1988 .... 2.00
❑7, Feb 1988, b&w 2.00
❑8, Mar 1988, b&w 2.00
❑9, Apr 1988, b&w 2.00
❑10, May 1988, b&w 2.00
❑11, Jun 1988, b&w 2.00
❑12, Jul 1988, b&w 2.00
❑13, Aug 1988, b&w 2.00
❑14, Sep 1988, b&w 2.00
❑Annual 1, b&w 3.25
❑Holiday 1, b&w; Mail-in special-cover edition. Given as promo from coupons in first 9 Triumphant books; Mail-in special-cover edition. Given as promo from coupons in first nine Triumphant books 2.95

TROUBLE WITH GIRLS (VOL. 2)
COMICO

❑1, ca. 1989, Comico begins publishing 2.50
❑2, ca. 1989 .... 2.00
❑3, ca. 1989 .... 2.00
❑4, ca. 1989 .... 2.00
❑5, ca. 1989, b&w; Eternity begins publishing; Black & white format begins 1.95
❑6, ca. 1989, b&w 1.95
❑7, ca. 1989, b&w 1.95
❑8, ca. 1989, b&w 1.95
❑9, ca. 1990, b&w 1.95
❑10, ca. 1990, b&w 1.95
❑11, ca. 1990, b&w 1.95
❑12, ca. 1990, b&w 1.95
❑13, ca. 1990, b&w 1.95
❑14, ca. 1990, b&w 1.95
❑15, ca. 1990, b&w 2.25
❑16, ca. 1990 .... 2.25
❑17, ca. 1991 .... 2.25
❑18, ca. 1991 .... 2.25
❑19, ca. 1991 .... 2.25
❑20, ca. 1991 .... 2.25
❑21, ca. 1991 .... 2.25
❑22, ca. 1991 .... 2.25
❑23, ca. 1991 .... 2.25

TROUBLE WITH GIRLS, THE: THE NIGHT OF THE LIZARD
MARVEL / EPIC

❑1, Jun 1993; Embossed cover 2.50
❑2, Jul 1993 .... 2.25
❑3, Aug 1993 .... 2.25
❑4, Sep 1993 .... 2.25

TROUBLE WITH TIGERS
ANTARCTIC

❑1, Jan 1992, b&w 2.50
❑2, Feb 1992, b&w 2.50

TROUT FISSION
TALL TALE

❑1, Jul 1998, b&w 1.95
❑2, Oct 1998, b&w 1.95

TROY
TOME

❑1 .... 2.95

TRS-80 COMPUTER WHIZ KIDS
ARCHIE

❑1, giveaway 2.00

TRUE ADVENTURES OF ADAM AND BRYON
AMERICAN MULE

❑1, May 1998, b&w 2.50
❑2, 1998 .... 2.50
❑3, 1998 .... 2.50

TRUE CONFUSIONS
FANTAGRAPHICS

❑1, b&w 2.50

TRUE FAITH
DC

❑1; squarebound; reprints Garth Ennis' first story from 1990 .... 12.95

TRUE GEIN
BONEYARD

❑1, May 1993 .... 3.00

TRUE GLITZ
RIP OFF

❑1 .... 2.50

TRUE LOVE
ECLIPSE

❑1, DSt (c); ATh, NC (a); Reprints stories from New Romances #17, Thrilling Romances #22, #24, and Intimate Love #20 .... 2.00
❑2, ATh, NC (a); Reprints stories from Popular Romance #22, New Romances #13, #15, and Thrilling Romances #24 .... 2.00

Twilight Zone (Vol. 1)

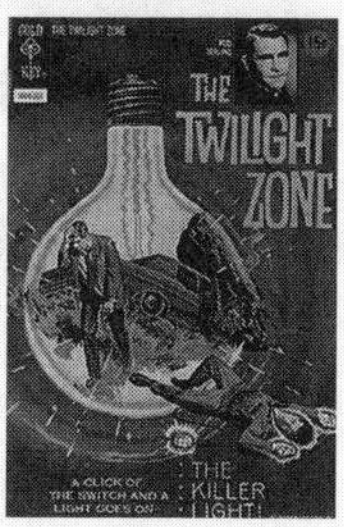

Rod Serling introduced these stories, too
©Gold Key

Twilight Zone (Vol. 2)

Second series based on famous TV show
©Now

Twilight Zone Premiere

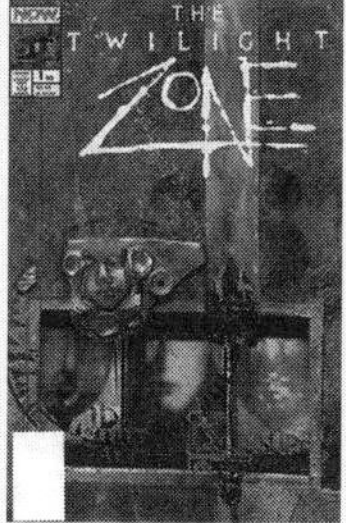

Many versions of this relaunch special
©Now

Two-Gun Kid

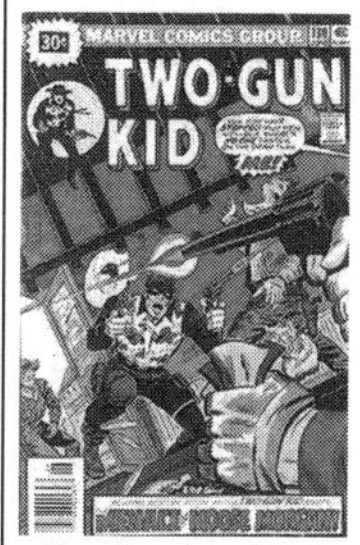

Marvel cowboy started back in the 1950s
©Marvel

2000 A.D. Presents

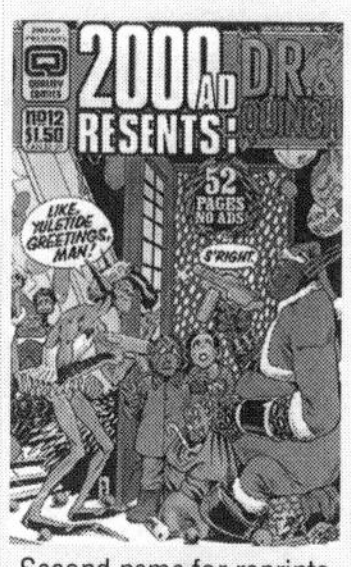

Second name for reprints of U.K. title
©Fleetway-Quality

N-MINT

TRUE NORTH
Comic Legends Defense Fund
❑1, ca. 1988, b&w; Cardstock cover; benefit comic 3.50

TRUE NORTH II
Comic Legends Defense Fund
❑1, ca. 1990; cardstock foldout cover 4.50

TRUE SIN
Boneyard
❑1 .... 2.95

TRUE SPY STORIES
Caliber / Tome
❑1, b&w; bios 2.95

TRUE SWAMP
Peristaltic
❑1, b&w 2.50
❑2, May 1994, b&w 2.50
❑3, ca. 1994 .... 2.50
❑4, Oct 1994, b&w 2.50
❑5, Feb 1995, b&w 2.95

TRUFAN ADVENTURES THEATRE
Paragraphics
❑1, ca. 1986, b&w 1.95
❑2, ca. 1986; 3-D 1.95

TRULY TASTELESS AND TACKY
Caliber
❑1, b&w 2.50

TRUTH
Dark Horse
❑0, Jul 1999, b&w; ashcan-sized preview of upcoming graphic novel given out at Comic-Con International: San Diego in 1999 .... 1.00
❑1, Aug 1999; prestige format; includes CD soundtrack 17.95

TRUTH, JUSTIN, AND THE AMERICAN WAY
Image
❑1, Apr 2006 .... 2.99
❑3, Jul 2006 .... 2.99

TRUTH: RED, WHITE & BLACK
Marvel
❑1, Jan 2003; cardstock cover 5.00
❑2, Feb 2003; cardstock cover 3.50
❑3, Mar 2003; cardstock cover 3.50
❑4, Apr 2003; cardstock cover 3.50
❑5, May 2003; cardstock cover 3.50
❑6, Jun 2003; cardstock cover 3.50
❑7, Jul 2003; cardstock cover 3.50

TRUTH SERUM
Slave Labor
❑1, Jan 2002, b&w; Smaller than comic-book size 2.95
❑2, Mar 2002, b&w; Smaller than comic-book size 2.95
❑3, May 2002, b&w; Smaller than comic-book size 2.95

TRYPTO THE ACID DOG
Renegade
❑1, b&w 2.00

TSC JAMS
TSC
❑0 .... 3.95
❑1 .... 3.95

N-MINT

TSR WORLDS
DC
❑Annual 1, ca. 1990 .... 2.00

TSUKUYOMI - MOON PHASE
Tokyopop
❑1, Dec 2005 .... 9.99

TSUNAMI GIRL
Image
❑1, Feb 1999, no month of publication 2.95
❑2, Apr 1999, no month of publication 2.95
❑3, Jun 1999 .... 2.95

TSUNAMI, THE IRRESISTIBLE FORCE
Epoch
❑1 .... 2.00

T2: CYBERNETIC DAWN
Malibu
❑0, Apr 1996; Flip-Book with T2 Nuclear Twilight #0 .... 3.00
❑1, Nov 1995; immediately follows events of T2 Judgment Day 2.50
❑2, Dec 1995 .... 2.50
❑3, Jan 1996 .... 2.50
❑4, Feb 1996 .... 2.50

T2: NUCLEAR TWILIGHT
Malibu
❑0, Apr 1996; Flip-book with T2 Cybernetic Dawn #0 .... 3.00
❑1, Nov 1995; prequel to first Terminator movie 2.50
❑2, Dec 1995 .... 2.50
❑3, Jan 1996 .... 2.50
❑4, Feb 1996 .... 2.50

TUBBY AND THE LITTLE MEN FROM MARS (MARGE'S...)
Gold Key
❑1, Oct 1964 .... 75.00

TUESDAY
Kim-Rehr
❑1, ca. 2003, b&w 2.95
❑2, ca. 2003, b&w 2.95
❑3, ca. 2004, b&w 2.95

TUFF GHOSTS, STARRING SPOOKY
Harvey
❑1, Jul 1962 .... 35.00
❑2, Sep 1962 .... 18.00
❑3, Nov 1962 .... 18.00
❑4, Jan 1963 .... 18.00
❑5, Mar 1963 .... 18.00
❑6, May 1963 .... 12.00
❑7, Jul 1963 .... 12.00
❑8, Sep 1963 .... 12.00
❑9, Nov 1963 .... 12.00
❑10, Jan 1964 .... 12.00
❑11, May 1964 .... 10.00
❑12, Jul 1964 .... 10.00
❑13, Nov 1964 .... 10.00
❑14, Jan 1965 .... 10.00
❑15, Mar 1965 .... 10.00
❑16, May 1965 .... 10.00
❑17, Jul 1965 .... 10.00
❑18, Sep 1965 .... 10.00
❑19, Nov 1965 .... 10.00
❑20, Jan 1966 .... 10.00

N-MINT

❑21, Mar 1966 .... 10.00
❑22, May 1966 .... 10.00
❑23, Jul 1966 .... 10.00
❑24, Sep 1966 .... 10.00
❑25, Nov 1966 .... 10.00
❑26, Jan 1967 .... 10.00
❑27, Mar 1967 .... 10.00
❑28, May 1967 .... 10.00
❑29, Jul 1967 .... 10.00
❑30, Sep 1967 .... 10.00
❑31, Nov 1967 .... 8.00
❑32, Jan 1968 .... 8.00
❑33, Jun 1968 .... 8.00
❑34, Aug 1968 .... 8.00
❑35, Oct 1968 .... 8.00
❑36, Nov 1968 .... 8.00
❑37, Apr 1969 .... 8.00
❑38, Sep 1969 .... 8.00
❑39, Nov 1969 .... 8.00
❑40, Sep 1971 .... 8.00
❑41, ca. 1972 .... 6.00
❑42, Jun 1972 .... 6.00
❑43, Oct 1972 .... 6.00

TUG & BUSTER (ART & SOUL)
Art & Soul
❑1, Nov 1995 .... 3.00
❑2, Jan 1996 .... 3.00
❑3, Mar 1996 .... 3.00
❑4, May 1996 .... 3.00
❑5, Aug 1996 .... 3.00
❑6 .... 3.00
❑7, Feb 1998 .... 3.00

TUG & BUSTER (IMAGE)
Image
❑1, Aug 1998, b&w 2.95

TUMBLING BOXES
Fantagraphics / Eros
❑1, Dec 1994, b&w 2.95

TUNDRA SKETCHBOOK SERIES
Tundra
❑1 .... 3.95
❑2 .... 3.95
❑3, Noodles 3.95
❑4, Rick Bryant 3.95
❑5 .... 3.95
❑6 .... 3.95
❑7 .... 3.95
❑8, Forg 3.95
❑9 .... 3.95
❑10, Skull Farmer 4.95
❑11 .... 3.95
❑12 .... 3.95

TUROK
Acclaim
❑1, Mar 1998 .... 2.50
❑2, Apr 1998 .... 2.50
❑3, May 1998 .... 2.50
❑4, Jun 1998 .... 2.50

TUROK ADON'S CURSE
Acclaim
❑1 .... 4.95

Other grades: Multiply price above by 5/6 for VF/NM • 2/3 for VERY FINE • 1/3 for FINE • 1/5 for VERY GOOD • 1/8 for GOOD

TUROK: CHILD OF BLOOD
Acclaim

❑1, Jan 1998 ... 3.95

TUROK, DINOSAUR HUNTER
Acclaim / Valiant

❑0, Nov 1995 O: Lost Land. O: Andar. O: Turok. ... 5.00
❑1, Jul 1993; (c); (a); chromium cover ... 2.00
❑1/Gold, Jul 1993; Gold edition; (c); (a); chromium cover ... 14.00
❑1/VVSS, Jul 1993 (c); (a) ... 20.00
❑2, Aug 1993 (c); (a) ... 1.00
❑3, Sep 1993 (c); (a) ... 1.00
❑4, Oct 1993 (a) ... 1.00
❑5, Nov 1993 (a) ... 1.00
❑6, Dec 1993 (a) ... 1.00
❑7, Jan 1994 ... 1.00
❑8, Feb 1994 ... 1.00
❑9, Mar 1994 ... 1.00
❑10, Apr 1994 (a) ... 1.00
❑11, May 1994; (a); trading card ... 2.00
❑12, Jun 1994 (a) ... 1.00
❑13, Aug 1994 (a); V: Captain Red. ... 1.00
❑14, Sep 1994 (a); V: Captain Red. ... 1.00
❑15, Oct 1994 (a); V: Captain Red. ... 1.00
❑16, Oct 1994 BL (c); (a) ... 1.00
❑17, Nov 1994 (c); ... 1.00
❑18, Dec 1994 ... 1.00
❑19, Jan 1995 A: X-O Manowar. ... 1.00
❑20, Feb 1995 ... 2.00
❑21, Mar 1995 ... 1.00
❑22, Apr 1995 ... 2.00
❑23, May 1995 MGr (c); ... 2.00
❑24, Jun 1995; back to the Lost Land ... 2.00
❑25, Jul 1995 ... 2.00
❑26, Jul 1995; A: Captain Red. Birthquake ... 2.00
❑27, Aug 1995 ... 2.00
❑28, Aug 1995 ... 2.00
❑29, Sep 1995 ... 2.00
❑30, Sep 1995 ... 2.00
❑31, Oct 1995 PG (c); PG, BMc (a) ... 2.00
❑32, Oct 1995 PG (c); PG, BMc (a) ... 2.00
❑33, Nov 1995 PG (c); PG (a) ... 2.00
❑34, Nov 1995 MGr (w) ... 2.00
❑35, Dec 1995; MGr (w); Painted cover ... 2.00
❑36, Dec 1995 ... 2.00
❑37, Jan 1996 ... 2.00
❑38, Jan 1996 ... 2.00
❑39, Feb 1996 PG (c); PG (a) ... 3.00
❑40, Mar 1996 PG (c); PG, (a) ... 4.00
❑41, Apr 1996 ... 4.00
❑42, Apr 1996 ... 4.00
❑43, May 1996 MGr (w) ... 3.00
❑44, May 1996 MGr (w) ... 3.00
❑45, Jun 1996 ... 6.00
❑46, Aug 1996 BG (a) ... 9.00
❑47, Aug 1996 ... 18.00
❑Yearbook 1; Yearbook 1 ... 3.95

TUROK: EVOLUTION
Acclaim

❑1, Aug 2002 ... 2.50

TUROK: REDPATH
Acclaim

❑1, Oct 1997 ... 3.95

TUROK: SEEDS OF EVIL
Acclaim

❑1; newsstand edition ... 4.99
❑1/Direct ed.; Direct cover ... 4.99

TUROK/SHADOWMAN
Acclaim / Valiant

❑1, Feb 1999 ... 3.95

TUROK: SHADOW OF OBLIVION
Acclaim

❑1, Sep 2000; Based on the video game ... 4.95

TUROK, SON OF STONE
Dell / Gold Key

❑3, May 1956; Earlier issues were Four Color #596 and #656 ... 155.00
❑4, Jun 1956 ... 125.00
❑5, Sep 1956 ... 125.00
❑6, Dec 1956 ... 110.00
❑7, Mar 1957 ... 110.00
❑7/15 cent, Mar 1957, Cover price variant ... 135.00
❑8, Jun 1957 ... 110.00
❑9, Sep 1957 ... 110.00
❑10, Dec 1957 ... 110.00
❑11, Mar 1958 ... 75.00
❑12, Jun 1958 ... 75.00
❑13, Sep 1958 ... 75.00
❑14, Dec 1958 ... 75.00
❑15, Mar 1959 ... 75.00
❑16, Jun 1959 ... 75.00
❑17, Sep 1959 ... 75.00
❑18, Dec 1959 ... 75.00
❑19, Mar 1960 ... 75.00
❑20, Jun 1960 ... 75.00
❑21, Sep 1960 ... 48.00
❑22, Dec 1960 ... 48.00
❑23, Mar 1961 ... 48.00
❑24, Jun 1961 ... 48.00
❑25, Sep 1961 ... 48.00
❑26, Dec 1961 ... 48.00
❑27, Mar 1962 ... 48.00
❑28, Jun 1962 ... 48.00
❑29, Sep 1962, Last Dell issue ... 48.00
❑30, Dec 1962, First Gold Key issue ... 48.00
❑31, Jan 1963 ... 38.00
❑32, Mar 1963 ... 38.00
❑33, May 1963 ... 38.00
❑34, Jul 1963, 10030-307 ... 38.00
❑35, Sep 1963 ... 38.00
❑36, Nov 1963, reprints two Dell Turok stories ... 38.00
❑37, Jan 1964 ... 38.00
❑38, Mar 1964 ... 38.00
❑39, May 1964 ... 38.00
❑40, Jul 1964 ... 38.00
❑41, Sep 1964 ... 28.00
❑42, Nov 1964 ... 28.00
❑43, Jan 1965 ... 28.00
❑44, Mar 1965 ... 28.00
❑45, May 1965 ... 28.00
❑46, Jul 1965, back cover pin-up ... 28.00
❑47, Sep 1965, 10030-509 ... 28.00
❑48, Nov 1965 ... 28.00
❑49, Jan 1966 ... 28.00
❑50, Mar 1966 ... 28.00
❑51, May 1966 ... 22.00
❑52, Jul 1966 ... 22.00
❑53, Sep 1966 ... 22.00
❑54, Nov 1966 ... 22.00
❑55, Jan 1967 ... 22.00
❑56, Mar 1967 ... 22.00
❑57, May 1967 ... 22.00
❑58, Jul 1967 ... 22.00
❑59, Oct 1967 ... 22.00
❑60, Jan 1968 ... 22.00
❑61, Apr 1968 ... 15.00
❑62, Jul 1968 ... 15.00
❑63, Oct 1968 ... 15.00
❑64, Jan 1969 ... 15.00
❑65, Apr 1969 ... 15.00
❑66, Jul 1969 ... 15.00
❑67, Oct 1969 ... 15.00
❑68, Jan 1970 ... 15.00
❑69, Apr 1970 ... 15.00
❑70, Jul 1970 ... 15.00
❑71, Oct 1970 ... 10.00
❑72, Jan 1971 ... 10.00
❑73, Apr 1971 ... 10.00
❑74, Jul 1971 ... 10.00
❑75, Oct 1971 ... 10.00
❑76, Jan 1972 ... 10.00
❑77, Mar 1972 ... 10.00
❑78, May 1972 ... 10.00
❑79, Jul 1972 ... 10.00
❑80, Sep 1972 ... 10.00
❑81, Nov 1972 ... 10.00
❑82, Jan 1973 ... 10.00
❑83, Mar 1973 ... 10.00
❑84, May 1973 ... 10.00
❑85, Jul 1973 ... 10.00
❑86, Sep 1973 ... 10.00
❑87, Nov 1973 ... 10.00
❑88, Jan 1974 ... 10.00
❑89, Mar 1974 ... 10.00
❑90, May 1974 ... 10.00
❑91, Jul 1974 ... 8.00
❑92, Sep 1974 ... 8.00
❑93, Nov 1974 ... 8.00
❑94, Jan 1975 ... 8.00
❑95, Mar 1975 ... 8.00
❑96, May 1975 ... 8.00
❑97, Jul 1975 ... 8.00
❑98, Aug 1975 ... 8.00
❑99, Sep 1975 ... 8.00
❑100, Nov 1975 ... 8.00
❑101, Jan 1976 ... 8.00
❑102, Mar 1976 ... 8.00
❑103, May 1976 ... 8.00
❑104, Jul 1976 ... 8.00
❑105, Sep 1976 ... 8.00
❑106, Nov 1976 ... 8.00
❑107, Jan 1977 ... 8.00
❑108, Mar 1977 ... 8.00
❑109, May 1977 ... 8.00
❑110, Jul 1977 ... 8.00
❑111, Sep 1977 ... 6.00
❑112, Nov 1977 ... 6.00
❑113, Jan 1978 ... 6.00
❑114, Mar 1978 ... 6.00
❑115, May 1978 ... 6.00
❑116, Jul 1978 ... 6.00
❑117, Sep 1978 ... 6.00
❑118, Nov 1978 ... 6.00
❑119, Jan 1979 ... 6.00
❑120, Mar 1979 ... 6.00
❑121, May 1979 ... 6.00
❑122, Jul 1979 ... 6.00
❑123, Sep 1979 ... 6.00
❑124, Nov 1979 ... 6.00
❑125, Jan 1980 ... 6.00
❑126, Mar 1981 ... 6.00
❑127, Oct 1981 ... 6.00
❑128, Dec 1981 ... 6.00
❑129, Feb 1982 ... 6.00
❑130, Apr 1982 ... 6.00
❑Giant Size 1, Nov 1966 ... 100.00

TUROK: SPRING BREAK IN THE LOST LAND
Acclaim / Valiant

❑1, Jul 1997 ... 3.95

TUROK: TALES OF THE LOST LAND
Acclaim

❑1, Apr 1998 ... 3.95

TUROK: THE EMPTY SOULS
Acclaim

❑1, Apr 1997 ... 3.95
❑1/Variant, Apr 1997; alternate painted cover ... 3.95
❑Ashcan 1, Nov 1996, b&w; No cover price; preview of upcoming series ... 1.00

TUROK THE HUNTED
Acclaim / Valiant

❑1, Mar 1996 MGr (w) ... 5.00
❑2, Mar 1996 MGr (w) ... 5.00

TUROK, TIMEWALKER: SEVENTH SABBATH
Acclaim / Valiant

❑1, Aug 1997; covers form diptych ... 2.50
❑2, Sep 1997; covers form diptych ... 2.50

TURTLE SOUP
Mirage

❑1, Sep 1987, b&w; b&w pin-ups, cardstock cover ... 5.00

TURTLE SOUP (2ND SERIES)
Mirage

❑1, Nov 1991 ... 2.50
❑2, Dec 1991 ... 2.50
❑3, Jan 1992 ... 2.50
❑4, Feb 1992 ... 2.50

TURTLE SOUP (ASTONISH)
Astonish

❑1, ca. 2003; Printed sideways with a cardstock cover ... 3.75

TUSK WORLD TOUR BOOK 2001
Tusk

❑nn, Apr 2001, b&w; Kaos Moon story ... 4.95

TUXEDO GIN
Viz

❑1, Aug 2003 ... 9.99
❑2, Oct 2003 ... 9.99
❑3, Dec 2005 ... 9.99

2000 A.D. Showcase (1st Series)

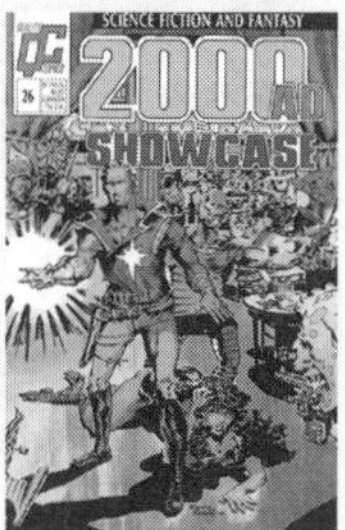

Title had changing name and double issues

©Fleetway-Quality

2001 Nights

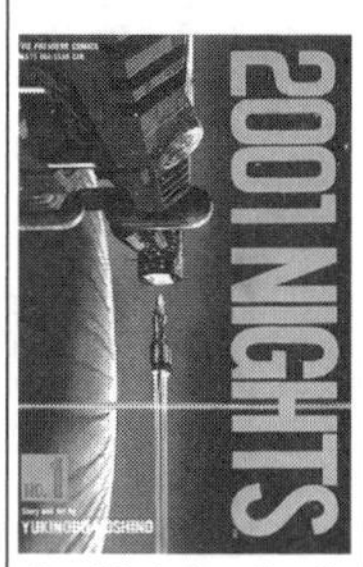

Possibly the best "hard" science-fiction comic

©Viz

2001, A Space Odyssey

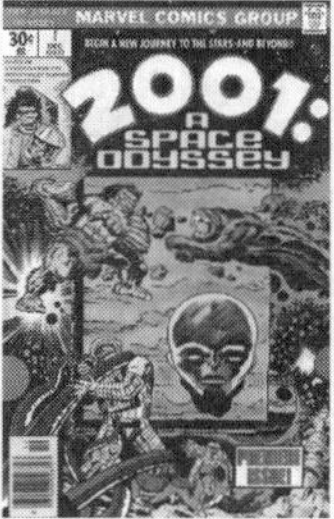

Kirby series had little to do with the movie

©Marvel

Ultimate Adventures

Quesada's entry in "U-Decide" promotion

©Marvel

Ultimate Elektra

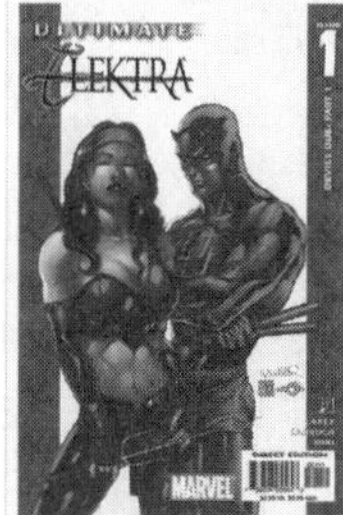

Series timed to help promote the movie

©Marvel

	N-MINT
❑4, Feb 2004	9.99
❑5, Apr 2004	9.99
❑6, Jun 2004	9.99
❑7, Aug 2004	9.99
❑8, Oct 2004	9.99
❑9, Dec 2004	9.99
❑10, Feb 2005	9.99
❑11, Apr 2005	9.99
❑12, Jun 2005	9.99
❑13, Aug 2005	9.99
❑14, Oct 2005	9.99

TV CASPER AND COMPANY
HARVEY

	N-MINT
❑1, Aug 1963, Harvey Giant	75.00
❑2, Oct 1963, Harvey Giant	30.00
❑3, Feb 1964, Harvey Giant	30.00
❑4 1964, Harvey Giant	30.00
❑5 1964, Harvey Giant	30.00
❑6 1964, Harvey Giant	20.00
❑7 1965, Harvey Giant	20.00
❑8 1965, Harvey Giant	20.00
❑9 1965, Harvey Giant	20.00
❑10 1965, Harvey Giant	20.00
❑11, Mar 1966, Harvey Giant	15.00
❑12 1966, Harvey Giant	15.00
❑13 1966, Harvey Giant	15.00
❑14 1967, Harvey Giant	15.00
❑15 1967, Harvey Giant	15.00
❑16, Nov 1967, Harvey Giant	15.00
❑17, Feb 1968, Harvey Giant	15.00
❑18, Apr 1968, Harvey Giant	15.00
❑19, Aug 1968, Harvey Giant	15.00
❑20, Nov 1968, Harvey Giant	15.00
❑21, Mar 1969, Harvey Giant	10.00
❑22 1969, Harvey Giant	10.00
❑23 1969, Harvey Giant	10.00
❑24 1969, Harvey Giant	10.00
❑25, Feb 1970, Harvey Giant	10.00
❑26, Apr 1970, Harvey Giant	10.00
❑27 1970, Harvey Giant	10.00
❑28 1970, Harvey Giant	10.00
❑29 1970, Harvey Giant	10.00
❑30 1971, Harvey Giant	10.00
❑31, Apr 1971, Harvey Giant	10.00
❑32, Aug 1971, Harvey Giant	8.00
❑33, Oct 1971, Harvey Giant	8.00
❑34 1971, Harvey Giant	8.00
❑35, Mar 1972, Harvey Giant	8.00
❑36, Aug 1972, Harvey Giant	8.00
❑37, Oct 1972, Harvey Giant	8.00
❑38, Dec 1972, Harvey Giant	8.00
❑39, Feb 1973, Harvey Giant	8.00
❑40, Apr 1973, Harvey Giant	8.00
❑41, Jun 1973, Harvey Giant	8.00
❑42, Aug 1973, Harvey Giant	8.00
❑43, Oct 1973, Harvey Giant	8.00
❑44, Dec 1973, Harvey Giant	8.00
❑45, Feb 1974, Harvey Giant	8.00
❑46, Apr 1974, Harvey Giant	8.00

TV STARS
MARVEL

	N-MINT
❑1, Aug 1978 1: Captain Caveman (in comics). 1: Grape Ape (in comics)	15.00
❑2, Oct 1978	7.00
❑3, Dec 1978	7.00
❑4, Feb 1979	7.00

TV WESTERN
AC

	N-MINT
❑1, ca. 2001, b&w; reprints stories from Range Rider #17, Roy Rogers, and Wild Bill Hickok	5.95

TWEETY AND SYLVESTER (2ND SERIES)
GOLD KEY / WHITMAN

	N-MINT
❑1, ca. 1964	35.00
❑2, Feb 1966	20.00
❑3, Aug 1966	20.00
❑4, Nov 1966	20.00
❑5, Feb 1967	20.00
❑6, May 1967	8.00
❑7, Aug 1967	8.00
❑8, Nov 1967	8.00
❑9, Oct 1968	8.00
❑10, Mar 1969	8.00
❑11, Aug 1969	5.00
❑12, Nov 1969	5.00
❑13, Feb 1970	5.00
❑14, May 1970	5.00
❑15, Sep 1970	5.00
❑16, Dec 1970	5.00
❑17, Mar 1971	5.00
❑18, Jun 1971	5.00
❑19, Aug 1971	5.00
❑20, Oct 1971	5.00
❑21, Dec 1971	4.00
❑22, Jan 1972	4.00
❑23, Mar 1972	4.00
❑24, May 1972	4.00
❑25, Jul 1972	4.00
❑26, Sep 1972	4.00
❑27, Nov 1972	4.00
❑28, Jan 1973	4.00
❑29, Mar 1973	4.00
❑30, May 1973	4.00
❑31, Jul 1973	4.00
❑32, Aug 1973	4.00
❑33, Sep 1973	4.00
❑34, Nov 1973	4.00
❑35, Jan 1974	4.00
❑36, Mar 1974	4.00
❑37, May 1974	4.00
❑38, Jul 1974	4.00
❑39, Aug 1974	4.00
❑40, Sep 1974	4.00
❑41, Nov 1974	3.00
❑42, Jan 1975	3.00
❑43, Mar 1975	3.00
❑44, Apr 1975	3.00
❑45, May 1975	3.00
❑46, Jun 1975	3.00
❑47, Jul 1975	3.00
❑48, Aug 1975	3.00
❑49, Sep 1975	3.00
❑50, Oct 1975	3.00
❑51, Nov 1975	3.00
❑52, Dec 1975	3.00
❑53, Jan 1976	3.00
❑54, Feb 1976	3.00
❑55, Mar 1976	3.00
❑56, Apr 1976	3.00
❑57, May 1976	3.00
❑58, Jun 1976	3.00
❑59, Jul 1976	3.00
❑60, Aug 1976	3.00
❑61, Sep 1976	3.00
❑62, Oct 1976	3.00
❑63, Nov 1976	3.00
❑64, Dec 1976	3.00
❑65, Jan 1977	3.00
❑66, Feb 1977	3.00
❑67, Mar 1977	3.00
❑68, Apr 1977	3.00
❑69, May 1977	3.00
❑70, Jun 1977	3.00
❑71, Jul 1977	3.00
❑72, Aug 1977	3.00
❑73, Sep 1977	3.00
❑74, Oct 1977	3.00
❑75, Nov 1977	3.00
❑76, Dec 1977	3.00
❑77, Jan 1978	3.00
❑78, Feb 1978	3.00
❑79, Mar 1978	3.00
❑80, Apr 1978	3.00
❑81, May 1978	2.50
❑82, Jun 1978	2.50
❑83, Jul 1978	2.50
❑84, Aug 1978	2.50
❑85, Sep 1978	2.50
❑86, Oct 1978	2.50
❑87, Nov 1978	2.50
❑88, Dec 1978	2.50
❑89, Jan 1979	2.50
❑90, Feb 1979	2.50
❑91, Mar 1979	2.50
❑92, Apr 1979	2.50
❑93, May 1979	2.50
❑94, Jun 1979	2.50
❑95, Jul 1979	2.50
❑96, Aug 1979	2.50
❑97, Sep 1979	2.50
❑98, Oct 1979	2.50
❑99, Nov 1979	2.50
❑100, Dec 1979	2.50
❑101, Jan 1980	2.00
❑102, Feb 1980	2.00
❑103, ca. 1980	5.00
❑104, ca. 1980	5.00
❑105, ca. 1980	12.00
❑106, ca. 1980	12.00
❑107, ca. 1981	17.00
❑108, ca. 1981	8.00
❑109, ca. 1981	8.00
❑110, Aug 1981	8.00
❑111, Sep 1981	8.00
❑112, ca. 1981	8.00
❑113, Feb 1982	8.00
❑114, Hol 1982	8.00
❑115, Mar 1982	8.00
❑116, Apr 1982	8.00
❑117, ca. 1982	10.00

Other grades: Multiply price above by 5/6 for VF/NM • 2/3 for VERY FINE • 1/3 for FINE • 1/5 for VERY GOOD • 1/8 for GOOD

❑118, ca. 1982 — 10.00
❑119, ca. 1982 — 10.00
❑120, Oct 1982 — 10.00
❑121 — 10.00

24 HOUR COMICS
About

❑1, ca. 2004 — 11.95

24: MIDNIGHT SUN
Idea & Design Works

❑0, Sep 2005 — 7.49

24 ONE-SHOT
Idea & Design Works

❑1, Jul 2004 — 6.99

20 NUDE DANCERS 20 YEAR ONE POSTER BOOK
Tundra

❑Book 1, ca. 1991, b&w — 9.95

20 NUDE DANCERS 20 YEAR TWO
Tundra

❑1, b&w — 3.50

21
Image

❑1, Feb 1996 — 2.50
❑1/A, Feb 1996 — 2.50
❑2, Mar 1996 — 2.50
❑3, Apr 1996 — 2.50

21 DOWN
DC / Wildstorm

❑1, Nov 2002 — 2.95
❑2, Dec 2002 — 2.95
❑3, Jan 2003 — 2.95
❑4, Feb 2003 — 2.95
❑5, Mar 2003 — 2.95
❑6, Apr 2003 — 2.95
❑7, May 2003 — 2.95
❑8, Jun 2003 — 2.95
❑9, Jul 2003 — 2.95
❑10, Jun 2003 — 2.95
❑11, Jul 2003 — 2.95
❑12, Sep 2003 — 2.95

22 BRIDES
Event

❑1, Mar 1996 — 2.95
❑1/Ltd., Mar 1996 — 3.50
❑2, Jun 1996 — 2.95
❑3, Sep 1996 — 2.95
❑4, Jan 1997 — 2.95
❑4/A, Jan 1997; O: Painkiller Jane. Painkiller Jane on Dinosaur cover — 3.50
❑CS 1, ca. 1997; Collector's Set. Includes #1-4, poster — 34.95

TWICE-TOLD TALES OF UNSUPERVISED EXISTENCE
Rip Off

❑1, Apr 1989, b&w — 2.00

TWILIGHT (DC)
DC

❑1, ca. 1991 — 4.95
❑2, ca. 1991 — 4.95
❑3, ca. 1991 — 4.95

TWILIGHT (AVATAR)
Avatar

❑1, Mar 1997 — 3.00
❑2 — 3.00

TWILIGHT AVENGER (ELITE)
Elite

❑1, Jul 1986 — 1.75
❑2, Oct 1986 — 1.75

TWILIGHT AVENGER (ETERNITY)
Eternity

❑1, Jul 1988, b&w — 1.95
❑2, Aug 1988, b&w — 1.95
❑3, Sep 1988, b&w — 1.95
❑4, Nov 1988, b&w — 1.95
❑5, Feb 1989, b&w — 1.95
❑6, May 1989, b&w — 1.95
❑7, Aug 1989, b&w — 1.95
❑8, Feb 1990, b&w — 1.95

TWILIGHT EXPERIMENT
DC

❑1, Apr 2005 — 2.95
❑2, May 2005 — 2.95
❑3, Jun 2005 — 2.95
❑4, Jun 2005 — 2.99
❑5, Jul 2005 — 2.99
❑6, Aug 2005 — 2.99

TWILIGHT GIRL
Cross Plains

❑1, Nov 2000 — 2.95
❑2, Dec 2000 — 2.95
❑3, Jan 2001 — 2.95

TWILIGHT MAN
First

❑1, Jun 1989 — 2.75
❑2, Jul 1989 — 2.75
❑3, Aug 1989 — 2.75
❑4, Sep 1989 — 2.75

TWILIGHT PEOPLE
Caliber

❑1, b&w — 2.95
❑2, b&w — 2.95

TWILIGHT X
Pork Chop

❑1, b&w — 2.00
❑2, b&w — 2.00
❑3, b&w — 2.00

TWILIGHT X (VOL. 2)
Antarctic

❑1, b&w — 2.50
❑2, b&w — 2.50
❑3, b&w — 2.50
❑4, Sep 1993, b&w — 2.50
❑5, Feb 1994, b&w — 2.75

TWILIGHT-X: INTERLUDE
Antarctic

❑1, Jul 1992, b&w — 2.50
❑2, Sep 1992, b&w — 2.50
❑3, Nov 1992, b&w — 2.50
❑4, Jan 1993, b&w — 2.50
❑5, Mar 1993, b&w — 2.50
❑6, May 1993, b&w — 2.50

TWILIGHT-X: INTERLUDE (VOL. 2)
Antarctic

❑1, Jun 1993, b&w — 2.50
❑2, Jul 1993, b&w — 2.50
❑3, Aug 1993, b&w — 2.50
❑4, Sep 1993, b&w — 2.50
❑5, Oct 1993, b&w — 2.75

TWILIGHT X QUARTERLY
Antarctic

❑1, Sep 1994, b&w — 2.95
❑2, Nov 1994, b&w — 2.95
❑3, Feb 1995, b&w — 2.95

TWILIGHT X: STORM
Antarctic

❑1 2003 — 3.50
❑2 2003 — 3.50
❑3, May 2003 — 3.50
❑4, Aug 2003 — 3.50
❑5, Sep 2003 — 3.50
❑6, Jan 2004 — 3.50

TWILIGHT ZONE (VOL. 1)
Gold Key

❑1, Nov 1962 — 90.00
❑2, Feb 1963 — 55.00
❑3, May 1963 — 42.00
❑4, Aug 1963 — 35.00
❑5, Nov 1963 — 35.00
❑6, Feb 1964 — 35.00
❑7, May 1964 — 35.00
❑8, Aug 1964 — 35.00
❑9, Nov 1964 — 35.00
❑10, Feb 1965 — 35.00
❑11, May 1965 — 30.00
❑12, Aug 1965 — 30.00
❑13, Nov 1965 — 30.00
❑14, Feb 1966, 10016-602 — 30.00
❑15, May 1966 — 30.00
❑16, Jul 1966 — 30.00
❑17, Sep 1966 — 30.00
❑18, Nov 1966 — 30.00
❑19, Jan 1966 — 30.00
❑20, Mar 1966 — 30.00
❑21, May 1967 — 16.00
❑22, Jul 1967 — 16.00
❑23, Oct 1967 — 16.00
❑24, Jan 1968 — 16.00
❑25, Apr 1968 — 16.00
❑26, Jul 1968, 10016-807 — 16.00
❑27, Dec 1968 — 16.00
❑28, Mar 1969 — 10.00
❑29, Jun 1969, 10016-906 — 10.00
❑30, Sep 1969 — 10.00
❑31, Dec 1969 — 8.00
❑32, Mar 1970 — 8.00
❑33, Jun 1970 — 8.00
❑34, Sep 1970 — 8.00
❑35, Dec 1970 — 8.00
❑36, Mar 1971 — 8.00
❑37, May 1971 — 8.00
❑38, Jul 1971 — 8.00
❑39, Sep 1971 — 8.00
❑40, Nov 1971 — 8.00
❑41, Jan 1972 — 6.00
❑42, Mar 1972, 90016-203 — 6.00
❑43, May 1972 — 6.00
❑44, Jul 1972 — 6.00
❑45, Sep 1972 — 6.00
❑46, Nov 1972 — 6.00
❑47, Jan 1973 — 6.00
❑48, Mar 1973 — 6.00
❑49, May 1973 — 6.00
❑50, Jul 1973 — 6.00
❑51, Aug 1973 — 6.00
❑52, Sep 1973 — 5.00
❑53, Nov 1973 — 5.00
❑54, Jan 1974 — 5.00
❑55, Mar 1974 — 5.00
❑56, May 1974 — 5.00
❑57, Jul 1974 — 5.00
❑58, Aug 1974 — 5.00
❑59, Sep 1974 — 5.00
❑60, Nov 1974 — 5.00
❑61, Jan 1975 — 5.00
❑62, Mar 1975 — 5.00
❑63, May 1975 — 5.00
❑64, Jul 1975 — 5.00
❑65, Aug 1975 — 5.00
❑66, Sep 1975 — 5.00
❑67, Nov 1975 — 5.00
❑68, Jan 1976 — 5.00
❑69, Mar 1976 — 5.00
❑70, May 1976 — 5.00
❑71, Jul 1976 — 4.00
❑72, Aug 1976 — 4.00
❑73, Sep 1976 — 4.00
❑74, Nov 1976 — 4.00
❑75, Jan 1977 — 4.00
❑76, Mar 1977 — 4.00
❑77, May 1977 — 4.00
❑78, Jul 1977 — 4.00
❑79, Aug 1977 — 4.00
❑80, Sep 1977 — 4.00
❑81, Nov 1977 — 4.00
❑82, Jan 1978 — 4.00
❑83, Apr 1978 — 4.00
❑84, Jun 1978 — 4.00
❑85, ca. 1978 — 4.00
❑86, ca. 1978 — 4.00
❑87, ca. 1978 — 4.00
❑88, ca. 1978 — 4.00
❑89, Feb 1979 — 4.00
❑90, Apr 1979 — 4.00
❑91, Jun 1979 — 4.00
❑92, ca. 1982 — 4.00

TWILIGHT ZONE (VOL. 2)
Now

❑1, Nov 1991; two covers — 2.50
❑1/Direct ed.; Direct Market edition — 2.50
❑2, Dec 1991 — 2.25
❑3, Jan 1992 — 2.25
❑4, Feb 1992 — 2.00
❑5, Mar 1992 — 2.00
❑6, Apr 1992 — 2.00
❑7, May 1992 — 2.00
❑8, Jun 1992 — 2.00
❑9, Jul 1992; 3-D; Holographic cover; bagged; hologram; Partial 3-D art — 2.95
❑9/Prestige, Jul 1992; 3-D; Holographic cover with glasses; hologram; Partial 3-D art; Extra stories — 4.95
❑10, Aug 1992 — 1.95
❑11, Sep 1992 — 1.95

Ultimate Fantastic Four

Bendis starts the title Fantastic

©Marvel

Ultimate Nightmare

X-Men vs. Ultimates in Tunguska

©Marvel

Ultimates

21st Century in-your-face Avengers

©Marvel

Ultimate Six

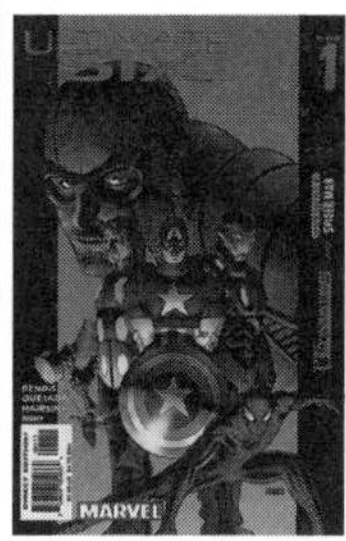

Ultimate Spidey joins the Sinister Six

©Marvel

Ultimate Spider-Man

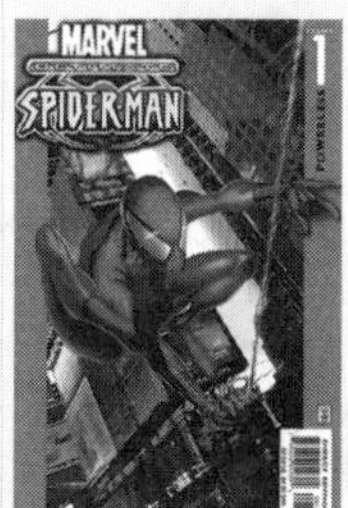

Bendis reboot ushered in a new age

©Marvel

N-MINT

❑12, Oct 1992 .... 1.95
❑13, Nov 1992 .... 1.95
❑14, Dec 1992 .... 1.95
❑15, Jan 1993 .... 1.95
❑16, Feb 1993 .... 1.95
❑SF 1, Mar 1993; hologram button; Science-Fiction Special 3.50

TWILIGHT ZONE (VOL. 3)
NOW

❑1, May 1993 .... 2.50
❑2, Jun 1993; two different covers; computer special 2.50
❑3, Jul 1993 .... 2.50
❑4, Aug 1993 .... 2.50
❑Annual 1993, Apr 1993 .... 2.50

TWILIGHT ZONE 3-D SPECIAL
NOW

❑1, Apr 1993; glasses 2.95

TWILIGHT ZONE PREMIERE
NOW

❑1, Oct 1991; Introduction by Harlan Ellison 2.50
❑1/CS; Collector's Set (polybagged, gold logo); Not code approved; Introduction by Harlan Ellison 2.95
❑1/Direct ed., Oct 1991; Introduction by Harlan Ellison 2.50
❑1/Prestige; Prestige edition; Introduction by Harlan Ellison 4.95
❑1/2nd; Introduction by Harlan Ellison 2.50
❑1/Direct ed./2n; Not code-approved; Introduction by Harlan Ellison 2.50

TWIN EARTHS
R. SUSOR

❑1, b&w; strip reprints 5.95
❑2, b&w; strip reprints 5.95

TWIST
KITCHEN SINK

❑1, b&w 2.00
❑2, May 1988 .... 2.00
❑3 .... 2.00

TWISTED
ALCHEMY

❑1, b&w 3.95

TWISTED 3-D TALES
BLACKTHORNE

❑1 .... 2.50

TWISTED SISTERS
KITCHEN SINK

❑1, b&w 3.50
❑2 .... 3.50
❑3 .... 3.50
❑4 .... 3.50

TWISTED TALES
PACIFIC

❑1, Nov 1982; AA (a); Pacific publishes 3.50
❑2, Apr 1983 VM, MP (a) 2.50
❑3, Jun 1983 .... 2.50
❑4, Aug 1983 .... 2.50
❑5 1983 VM (a) 2.50
❑6 1983 .... 2.50
❑7 1954 .... 2.50
❑8 1954; BG (a); Eclipse publishes 2.50

N-MINT

❑9 1954 VM (a) 2.50
❑10, Dec 1984 BWr, GM (a) 2.50
❑3D 1, Aug 1986 .... 2.50

TWISTED TALES OF BRUCE JONES
ECLIPSE

❑1, 1985 .... 2.00
❑2, Jul 1986 .... 2.00
❑3, Mar 1986 .... 2.00
❑4, 1986 .... 2.00

TWISTED TANTRUMS OF THE PURPLE SNIT
BLACKTHORNE

❑1 .... 1.75
❑2 .... 1.75

TWISTER
HARRIS

❑1; trading card 3.00

TWITCH (JUSTIN HAMPTON'S...)
AEON

❑1 .... 2.75

TWO-BITS
IMAGE

❑1, Feb 2005 .... 1.00

TWO FACES OF TOMORROW
DARK HORSE

❑1, Aug 1997, b&w 2.95
❑2, Sep 1997, b&w; wraparound cover 2.95
❑3, Oct 1997, b&w 2.95
❑4, Nov 1997, b&w 2.95
❑5, Dec 1997, b&w 2.95
❑6, Jan 1998, b&w 2.95
❑7, Feb 1998, b&w 2.95
❑8, Mar 1998, b&w 2.95
❑9, Apr 1998, b&w 2.95
❑10, May 1998, b&w 2.95
❑11, Jun 1998, b&w 2.95
❑12, Jul 1998, b&w 2.95
❑13, Aug 1998, b&w 2.95

TWO-FISTED SCIENCE
GENERAL TEKTRONICS LABS

❑1, b&w 2.50

TWO-FISTED TALES (RCP)
GEMSTONE

❑1, Oct 1992; AF, HK, JCr, WW (a); Reprints Two-Fisted Tales (EC) #18 .... 2.00
❑2, Jan 1993; HK, JCr, JSe, WW (a); Reprints Two-Fisted Tales (EC) #19 .... 2.00
❑3, Apr 1993; HK, JSe, WW (a); Reprints Two-Fisted Tales (EC) #20 .... 2.00
❑4, Jul 1993; HK, JSe, WW (a); Reprints Two-Fisted Tales (EC) #21 .... 2.00
❑5, Oct 1993; HK, JSe, WW, AT (a); Reprints Two-Fisted Tales (EC) #22 .... 2.00
❑6, Jan 1994; HK, JSe, WW (a); Reprints Two-Fisted Tales (EC) #23 .... 2.00
❑7, Apr 1994; HK, JSe, WW (a); Reprints Two-Fisted Tales (EC) #24 .... 2.00
❑8, Jul 1994; Reprints Two-Fisted Tales (EC) #25 .... 2.00
❑9, Oct 1994; Reprints Two-Fisted Tales (EC) #26 .... 2.00
❑10, Jan 1995; Reprints Two-Fisted Tales (EC) #27 .... 2.00

N-MINT

❑11, Apr 1995; Reprints Two-Fisted Tales (EC) #28 .... 2.00
❑12, Jul 1995; Reprints Two-Fisted Tales (EC) #29 .... 2.00
❑13, Oct 1995; Reprints Two-Fisted Tales (EC) #30 .... 2.00
❑14, Jan 1996; Reprints Two-Fisted Tales (EC) #31 .... 2.00
❑15, Apr 1996; Reprints Two-Fisted Tales (EC) #32 .... 2.00
❑16, Jul 1996; Reprints Two-Fisted Tales (EC) #33 .... 2.50
❑17, Oct 1996; Reprints Two-Fisted Tales (EC) #34 .... 2.50
❑18, Jan 1997; Reprints Two-Fisted Tales (EC) #35 .... 2.50
❑19, Apr 1997; Reprints Two-Fisted Tales (EC) #36 .... 2.50
❑20, Jul 1997; Reprints Two-Fisted Tales (EC) #37 .... 2.50
❑21, Oct 1997; JSe (w); JSe (a); Reprints Two-Fisted Tales (EC) #38 .... 2.50
❑22, Jan 1998; Reprints Two-Fisted Tales (EC) #39 .... 2.50
❑23, Apr 1998; Reprints Two-Fisted Tales (EC) #40 .... 2.50
❑24, Jul 1998; Reprints Two-Fisted Tales (EC) #41 .... 2.50
❑Annual 1; Collects Two-Fisted Tales #1-5 .... 8.95
❑Annual 2; Collects Two-Fisted Tales #6-10 .... 9.95
❑Annual 3 .... 10.95
❑Annual 4 .... 12.95
❑Annual 5 .... 13.50

TWO FOOLS
LAST GASP

❑1 .... 1.00

TWO-GUN KID
MARVEL

❑33, Oct 1956 .... 60.00
❑34, Dec 1956 .... 60.00
❑35, Feb 1957 .... 60.00
❑36, Apr 1957 .... 60.00
❑37, Jun 1957 .... 60.00
❑38, Aug 1957 .... 60.00
❑39, Dec 1957 .... 60.00
❑40, Feb 1958 .... 60.00
❑41, Apr 1958 .... 60.00
❑42, Jun 1958 .... 60.00
❑43, Aug 1958 .... 60.00
❑44, Oct 1958 .... 60.00
❑45, Dec 1958 .... 55.00
❑46, Feb 1959 .... 55.00
❑47, Apr 1959 .... 45.00
❑48, Jun 1959 .... 50.00
❑49, Aug 1959 .... 40.00
❑50, Oct 1959 .... 40.00
❑51, Dec 1959 .... 50.00
❑52, Feb 1960 .... 40.00
❑53, Apr 1960 .... 20.00
❑54, Jun 1960 .... 20.00
❑55, Aug 1960 .... 40.00
❑56, Oct 1960 .... 20.00
❑57, Dec 1960 .... 40.00
❑58, Feb 1961 O: Two-Gun Kid 20.00

Other grades: Multiply price above by 5/6 for VF/NM • 2/3 for VERY FINE • 1/3 for FINE • 1/5 for VERY GOOD • 1/8 for GOOD

N-MINT

❑59, Apr 1961 ... 20.00
❑60, Nov 1962 O: Two-Gun Kid. ... 30.00
❑61, Jan 1963 ... 12.00
❑62, Mar 1963 ... 12.00
❑63, May 1963 ... 12.00
❑64, Jul 1963 ... 12.00
❑65, Sep 1963 ... 12.00
❑66, Nov 1963 ... 12.00
❑67, Jan 1964 ... 12.00
❑68, Mar 1964 ... 12.00
❑69, May 1964 ... 12.00
❑70, Jul 1964 ... 12.00
❑71, Sep 1964 ... 12.00
❑72, Nov 1964 V: Geronimo. ... 12.00
❑73, Jan 1965 ... 12.00
❑74, Mar 1965 ... 12.00
❑75, May 1965 ... 12.00
❑76, Jul 1965 ... 12.00
❑77, Sep 1965 ... 12.00
❑78, Nov 1965 ... 12.00
❑79, Jan 1966 V: Joe Goliath. ... 12.00
❑80, Mar 1966 V: Billy the Kid. ... 12.00
❑81, May 1966 ... 8.00
❑82, Jul 1966 BEv (w); BEv (a) ... 8.00
❑83, Sep 1966 V: Durango. ... 8.00
❑84, Nov 1966 ... 8.00
❑85, Jan 1967 ... 8.00
❑86, Mar 1967 V: Cole Younger. ... 8.00
❑87, May 1967 ... 8.00
❑88, Jul 1967 V: Rattler. ... 8.00
❑89, Sep 1967 A: Rawhide Kid. A: Kid Colt. ... 8.00
❑90, Nov 1967 ... 8.00
❑91, Jan 1968 BEv (a); V: Silver Sidewinder. ... 8.00
❑92, Mar 1968, series goes on hiatus ... 8.00
❑93, Jul 1970, Reprints begin ... 4.00
❑94, Sep 1970 ... 4.00
❑95, Nov 1970 ... 4.00
❑96, Jan 1971 ... 4.00
❑97, Mar 1971 ... 4.00
❑98, May 1971 ... 4.00
❑99, Jul 1971 ... 4.00
❑100, Sep 1971 ... 4.00
❑101, Nov 1971 O: Two Gun Kid. ... 4.00
❑102, Jan 1972 ... 4.00
❑103, Mar 1972 ... 4.00
❑104, May 1972 ... 4.00
❑105, Jul 1972 ... 4.00
❑106, Sep 1972 ... 4.00
❑107, Nov 1972 ... 4.00
❑108, Jan 1973 ... 4.00
❑109, Mar 1973 SL (w) ... 4.00
❑110, May 1973 ... 4.00
❑111, Jul 1973 ... 4.00
❑112, Sep 1973 SL (w) ... 4.00
❑113, Oct 1973 ... 4.00
❑114, Nov 1973 ... 4.00
❑115, Dec 1973 ... 4.00
❑116, Feb 1974 ... 4.00
❑117, Apr 1974 ... 4.00
❑118, Jun 1974 ... 4.00
❑119, Aug 1974 ... 4.00
❑120, Oct 1974 ... 4.00
❑121, Dec 1974 ... 4.00
❑122, Feb 1975 ... 4.00
❑123, Apr 1975 ... 4.00
❑124, Jun 1975 ... 4.00
❑125, Aug 1975 ... 4.00
❑126, Oct 1975 ... 4.00
❑127, Dec 1975 ... 4.00
❑128, Feb 1976 ... 4.00
❑129, Apr 1976 ... 4.00
❑129/30 cent, Apr 1976, 30 cent regional price variant ... 20.00
❑130, Jun 1976 ... 4.00
❑130/30 cent, Jun 1976, 30 cent regional price variant ... 20.00
❑131, Aug 1976 ... 4.00
❑131/30 cent, Aug 1976, 30 cent regional price variant ... 20.00
❑132, Sep 1976 ... 4.00
❑133, Oct 1976 ... 4.00
❑134, Dec 1976 ... 4.00
❑135, Feb 1977 ... 4.00
❑136, Apr 1977 ... 4.00

TWO-GUN KID: SUNSET RIDERS
MARVEL

❑1, Nov 1995; Painted cover ... 6.95
❑2, Dec 1995; Painted cover ... 6.95

2-HEADED GIANT
A IS A

❑1, Oct 1995, b&w ... 2.95

2 HOT GIRLS ON A HOT SUMMER NIGHT
FANTAGRAPHICS / EROS

❑1, Apr 1991, b&w ... 3.00
❑2, May 1991, b&w ... 3.00
❑3, Jul 1991, b&w ... 3.00
❑4, Sep 1991, b&w ... 3.00

2 LIVE CREW COMICS
FANTAGRAPHICS / EROS

❑1, b&w ... 2.95

TWO STEP
DC

❑1, Dec 2003 ... 2.95
❑2, Mar 2004 ... 2.95
❑3, Jul 2004 ... 2.95

2000 A.D. MONTHLY (1ST SERIES)
EAGLE

❑1, Apr 1985 AMo (w) ... 2.00
❑2, May 1985 AMo (w) ... 2.00
❑3, Jun 1985 AMo (w) ... 2.00
❑4, Jul 1985 AMo (w) ... 2.00
❑5, Aug 1985 AMo (w) ... 2.00
❑6, Sep 1985 AMo (w) ... 2.00

2000 A.D. MONTHLY (2ND SERIES)
EAGLE

❑1, Apr 1986; Judge Anderson, D.R. & Quinch, Skizz ... 2.00
❑2, May 1986 ... 2.00
❑3, Jun 1986 ... 2.00

2000 A.D. PRESENTS
FLEETWAY-QUALITY

❑4, Jul 1986; Series continued from 2000 A.D. Monthly#3; Title changes to 2000 A.D. Presents; Quality begins publishing ... 1.50
❑5, Aug 1986 ... 1.50
❑6, Sep 1986 ... 1.50
❑7, Oct 1986 AMo (w); DaG (a) ... 1.50
❑8, Nov 1986 ... 1.50
❑9, Dec 1986 ... 1.50
❑10, Jan 1987 ... 1.50
❑11, Feb 1987 DaG (a) ... 1.50
❑12, Dec 1987 AMo (w); DaG (a) ... 1.50
❑13 ... 1.50
❑14, May 1988 ... 1.50
❑15 ... 1.50
❑16 ... 1.50
❑17 ... 1.50
❑18 ... 1.50
❑19 ... 1.50
❑20, DaG (a) ... 1.50
❑21 ... 1.50
❑22 ... 1.50
❑23 ... 1.50
❑24, Series continues as 2000 A.D. Showcase ... 1.50
❑25, Series continues as 2000 A.D. Showcase (1st Series) #25 ... 1.50

2000 A.D. SHOWCASE (1ST SERIES)
FLEETWAY-QUALITY

❑25, Series continued from 2000 A.D. Presents #24 ... 1.50
❑26 ... 1.50
❑27, DaG (a); double issue #27/28 ... 1.50
❑28, DaG (a); double issue #27/28 ... 1.50
❑29, double issue #29/30 ... 1.50
❑30, double issue #29/30 ... 1.50
❑31, Zenith ... 1.50
❑32, Zenith ... 1.50
❑33, Zenith ... 1.50
❑34, Zenith ... 1.50
❑35, Zenith ... 1.50
❑36, Zenith ... 1.50
❑37, Zenith ... 1.50
❑38, Zenith ... 1.50
❑39, Zenith ... 1.50
❑40, Zenith ... 1.50
❑41, Zenith ... 1.50
❑42, Zenith ... 1.50
❑43, Zenith ... 1.50
❑44, Zenith ... 1.50
❑45, Zenith ... 1.50
❑46 ... 1.50
❑47 ... 1.50
❑48 ... 1.75
❑49 ... 1.75
❑50 ... 1.75
❑51 ... 1.75
❑52 ... 1.75
❑53 ... 1.75
❑54 ... 1.75

2000 A.D. SHOWCASE (2ND SERIES)
FLEETWAY-QUALITY

❑1 ... 2.95
❑2 ... 2.95
❑3 ... 2.95
❑4, Axa ... 2.95
❑5, Axa ... 2.95
❑6, Strontium Dogs ... 2.95
❑7, Strontium Dogs ... 2.95
❑8 ... 2.95
❑9 ... 2.95
❑10 ... 2.95
❑11 ... 2.95

2002 TOKYOPOP MANGA SAMPLER
MIXX

❑1, ca. 2002 ... 1.00

TWO THOUSAND MANIACS
AIRCEL

❑1, b&w ... 2.50
❑2, b&w ... 2.50
❑3, b&w ... 2.50

2099 A.D.
MARVEL

❑1, May 1995, enhanced cover ... 3.95

2099 A.D. APOCALYPSE
MARVEL

❑1, Dec 1995, enhanced wraparound cover; continues in 2099 A.D. Genesis #1 ... 4.95

2099 A.D. GENESIS
MARVEL

❑1, Jan 1996, chromium cover ... 4.95

2099: MANIFEST DESTINY
MARVEL

❑1, Mar 1998 ... 5.99

2099 SPECIAL: THE WORLD OF DOOM
MARVEL

❑1, May 1995 ... 2.25

2099 UNLIMITED
MARVEL

❑1, Jul 1993 1: Hulk 2099. A: Spider-Man 2099. ... 3.95
❑2, Oct 1993, 1: R Gang 2099. Return of Hulk 2099 ... 3.95
❑3, Jan 1994 ... 3.95
❑4, Apr 1994 ... 3.95
❑5, Jul 1994 ... 3.95
❑6, Aug 1994 ... 3.95
❑7, Nov 1994 ... 3.95
❑8, Apr 1995 ... 3.95
❑9, Jul 1995 ... 3.95
❑10, Oct 1995 ... 3.95
❑Ashcan 1 1993, "2099 Limited" ashcan edition from Hero magazine; foil cover ... 0.75

2099: WORLD OF TOMORROW
MARVEL

❑1, Sep 1996, wraparound cover; 2099 anthology ... 2.50
❑2, Oct 1996 ... 2.50
❑3, Nov 1996 ... 2.50
❑4, Dec 1996 ... 2.50
❑5, Jan 1997 ... 2.50
❑6, Feb 1997 ... 2.50
❑7, Mar 1997 ... 2.50
❑8, Apr 1997 ... 2.50

2001 NIGHTS
VIZ

❑1, ca. 1990, b&w ... 4.00
❑2, ca. 1990, b&w ... 4.00
❑3, ca. 1990, b&w ... 4.00

Ultimate X-Men

Turn-of-the-millennium spin on the mutants
©Marvel

UltraForce (Vol. 1)

Malibu's version of the Justice League
©Malibu

Ultraverse Origins

99¢ one-shot covering Malibu characters
©Malibu

Uncanny Origins

Straightforward approach for new readers
©Marvel

Uncanny X-Men

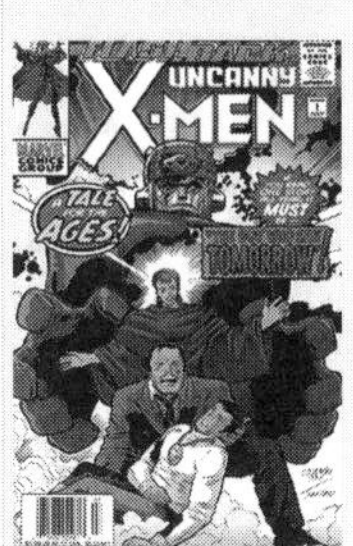

First 141 issues were "X-Men 1st Series"
©Marvel

	N-MINT
❑4, ca. 1991, b&w	4.00
❑5, ca. 1991, b&w	4.00
❑6, ca. 1991, b&w	4.25
❑7, ca. 1991, b&w	4.25
❑8, ca. 1991, b&w	4.25
❑9, ca. 1991, b&w	4.25
❑10, ca. 1991, b&w	4.25
❑Book 1, b&w	16.95
❑Book 1/HC, b&w	21.95

2001, A SPACE ODYSSEY
MARVEL

❑1, Dec 1976 JK (w); JK (a)	5.00
❑2, Jan 1977 JK (w); JK (a)	5.00
❑3, Feb 1977 JK (w); JK (a)	5.00
❑4, Mar 1977 JK (w); JK (a)	5.00
❑5, Apr 1977 JK (w); JK (a)	5.00
❑6, May 1977 JK (w); JK (a)	5.00
❑7, Jun 1977 JK (w); JK (a)	5.00
❑7/35 cent, Jun 1977, JK (w); JK (a); 35 cent price regional variant	20.00
❑8, Jul 1977 JK (w); JK (a); O: Machine Man (as Mister Machine). 1: Machine Man (as Mister Machine)	12.00
❑8/35 cent, Jul 1977, JK (w); JK (a); O: Machine Man (as Mister Machine). 1: Machine Man (as Mister Machine). 35 cent price regional variant	20.00
❑9, Aug 1977 JK (w); JK (a)	5.00
❑9/35 cent, Aug 1977, JK (w); JK (a); 35 cent price regional variant	20.00
❑10, Sep 1977 JK (w); JK (a); O: Machine Man	5.00
❑10/35 cent, Sep 1977, JK (w); JK (a); O: Machine Man. 35 cent price regional variant	20.00
❑Giant Size 1, ca. 1976, treasury-sized adaptation of movie JK (a)	12.00

2010
MARVEL

❑1, Apr 1984 TP (a)	1.50
❑2, May 1984 TP (a)	1.50

2112 (JOHN BYRNE'S...)
DARK HORSE

❑1, Nov 1991; prestige format	9.95
❑1/2nd	9.95
❑1/3rd	9.95

2024
NBM

❑1	16.95

2020 VISIONS
DC / VERTIGO

❑1, May 1997	2.50
❑2, Jun 1997	2.50
❑3, Jul 1997	2.50
❑4, Aug 1997	2.50
❑5, Sep 1997	2.50
❑6, Oct 1997	2.50
❑7, Nov 1997	2.50
❑8, Dec 1997	2.50
❑9, Jan 1998	2.50
❑10, Feb 1998	2.50
❑11, Mar 1998	2.50
❑12, Apr 1998	2.50

2 TO CHEST
DARK HORSE

	N-MINT
❑1, May 2004	3.00

TWO X JUSTICE
GRAPHIC SERIALS

❑1	2.00

TYKES
ALTERNATIVE

❑1, Nov 1997	2.95
❑Ashcan 1, Jul 1997; b&w and pink; smaller than normal comic book	2.95

TYPHOID
MARVEL

❑1, Nov 1995; wraparound cardstock cover	3.95
❑2, Dec 1995; wraparound cardstock cover	3.95
❑3, Jan 1996; wraparound cardstock cover	3.95
❑4, Feb 1996; wraparound cardstock cover	3.95

TYRANNOSAURUS TEX
MONSTER

❑1, Jul 1991, b&w	2.50
❑2, Sep 1991, b&w	2.50
❑3, Nov 1991	2.50

TYRANT (S.R. BISSETTE'S...)
SPIDER BABY

❑1, Sep 1994, b&w	3.00
❑2, Nov 1994, b&w	3.00
❑3, Feb 1995, b&w	3.00
❑3/Gold, Feb 1995, b&w	3.50
❑4, Win 1996, b&w	3.00
❑5, ca. 1996, b&w	3.00
❑6, Dec 1996, b&w	3.00

TZU THE REAPER
MURIM

❑1, Sep 1997	2.95
❑2, Oct 1997	2.95
❑3, Dec 1997	2.95

UBERDUB
CALIBER

❑1, Sep 1991	2.50
❑2, Sep 1991	2.50
❑3, Jan 1992	2.50

UFO & OUTER SPACE
WHITMAN

❑14, Jun 1978, Reprints UFO Flying Saucers #3	8.00
❑15, Jul 1978, Reprints UFO Flying Saucers #4	6.00
❑16 1978, Reprints	6.00
❑17 1978	6.00
❑18, Nov 1978	6.00
❑19 1979	6.00
❑20, Apr 1979	6.00
❑21, Jun 1979	5.00
❑22, Aug 1979	5.00
❑23, Oct 1979	5.00
❑24, Dec 1979	5.00
❑25, Feb 1980, Reprints UFO Flying Saucers #2	5.00

UFO ENCOUNTERS
GOLDEN PRESS

	N-MINT
❑1	1.95

UFO FLYING SAUCERS
GOLD KEY

❑1, Oct 1968, giant	25.00
❑2, Nov 1970	15.00
❑3, Nov 1972	15.00
❑4, Nov 1974	15.00
❑5, Feb 1975	10.00
❑6, May 1975	10.00
❑7, Aug 1975	10.00
❑8, Nov 1975	10.00
❑9, Jan 1976	10.00
❑10 1976	10.00
❑11 1976	10.00
❑12, Nov 1976	10.00
❑13, Jan 1977, series continues as UFO & Outer Space	10.00

ULTIMAN GIANT ANNUAL
IMAGE / BIG BANG

❑1, Nov 2001	4.95

ULTIMATE ADVENTURES
MARVEL

❑1, Nov 2002	2.25
❑2, Dec 2002	2.25
❑3, Mar 2003	2.25
❑4, May 2003	2.25
❑5, Jul 2003	2.99
❑6, Sep 2003	2.99

ULTIMATE DAREDEVIL & ELEKTRA
MARVEL

❑1, Jan 2003	3.00
❑2, Feb 2003	2.25
❑3, Feb 2003	2.25
❑4, Mar 2003	2.25

ULTIMATE ELEKTRA
MARVEL

❑1, Oct 2004	2.25
❑2, Nov 2004	2.25
❑3, Dec 2004	2.25
❑4, Jan 2005	2.25
❑5, Feb 2005	2.25

ULTIMATE EXTINCTION
MARVEL

❑1, Mar 2006	2.99
❑2, Apr 2006	2.99
❑3, May 2006	2.99
❑4, Jun 2006	2.99
❑5, Aug 2006	2.99

ULTIMATE FANTASTIC FOUR
MARVEL

❑1, Feb 2004 (c); BMB (w)	5.00
❑2, Mar 2004	4.00
❑3, Apr 2004 (c); BMB (w)	3.00
❑4, May 2004 (c); BMB (w)	2.25
❑5, Jun 2004 (c); BMB (w)	3.00
❑6, Jul 2004	2.25
❑7, Aug 2004	3.00
❑8, Sep 2004	4.00
❑9, Sep 2004	2.25
❑10, Oct 2004	2.25

N-MINT

❑11, Nov 2004 ... 2.25
❑12, Dec 2004 ... 2.25
❑13, Jan 2005 ... 2.25
❑13/Sketch, Jan 2005 ... 6.00
❑14, Feb 2005 ... 2.25
❑15, Mar 2005 ... 2.25
❑16, Apr 2005 ... 2.25
❑17, May 2005 ... 2.25
❑18, Jun 2005 ... 2.25
❑19, Jul 2005 ... 5.00
❑20, Aug 2005 ... 4.00
❑21, Sep 2005 ... 2.50
❑21/Variant, Sep 2005 ... 5.00
❑22, Oct 2005 ... 2.50
❑23, Nov 2005 ... 2.99
❑24, Dec 2005 ... 2.99
❑25, Jan 2006 ... 2.99
❑26, Feb 2006 ... 2.99
❑27, Apr 2006 ... 2.99
❑28, Jun 2006 ... 2.99
❑29, Jul 2006 ... 2.99
❑30, Aug 2006 ... 2.99
❑Annual 1 2005 ... 2.99

ULTIMATE FANTASTIC FOUR/ X-MEN SPECIAL
MARVEL

❑1, Mar 2006 ... 2.99

ULTIMATE IRON MAN
MARVEL

❑1/Kubert, Apr 2005 ... 5.00
❑1/Hitch, Apr 2005 ... 4.00
❑1/Sketch, Apr 2005 ... 6.00
❑2, Aug 2005 ... 2.99
❑3, Sep 2005 ... 2.99
❑4 2005 ... 2.99
❑5, Feb 2006 ... 2.99

ULTIMATE MARVEL FLIP MAGAZINE
MARVEL

❑1, Jul 2005 ... 3.99
❑2, Aug 2005 ... 3.99
❑3, Sep 2005 ... 3.99
❑4, Oct 2005 ... 3.99
❑5 2005 ... 3.99
❑6, Jan 2006 ... 3.99
❑7, Feb 2006 ... 3.99
❑8, Mar 2006 ... 3.99
❑9, Mar 2006 ... 3.99
❑10, May 2006 ... 3.99
❑11, Jun 20006 ... 3.99
❑12, Jul 2006 ... 3.99
❑13, Aug 2006 ... 3.99
❑14, Sep 2006 ... 3.99

ULTIMATE MARVEL MAGAZINE
MARVEL

❑1, Feb 2001, reprints Ultimate Spider-Man #1 and #2 ... 6.00
❑2, Mar 2001, reprints Ultimate Spider-Man #3 and Ultimate X-Men #1 ... 4.00
❑3, Apr 2001, reprints Ultimate Spider-Man #4 and Ultimate X-Men #2 ... 4.00
❑4, May 2001 ... 3.99
❑5, Jun 2001 ... 3.99
❑6, Jul 2001 ... 3.99
❑7, Aug 2001 ... 3.99
❑8, Sep 2001 ... 3.99
❑9, Oct 2001 ... 3.99
❑10, Nov 2001 ... 3.99
❑11, Dec 2001 ... 3.99

ULTIMATE MARVEL TEAM-UP
MARVEL

❑1, Apr 2001, BMB (w); MW (a); A: Wolverine. A: Sabretooth. A: Spider-Man. Cardstock cover; Listed in indicia as Ultimate Spider-Man and Wolverine ... 2.99
❑2, May 2001 BMB (w); A: Hulk. A: Spider-Man. ... 2.99
❑3, Jun 2001 ... 2.99
❑4, Jul 2001 ... 2.99
❑5, Aug 2001 ... 2.99
❑6, Sep 2001 ... 2.99
❑7, Oct 2001 ... 3.00
❑8, Nov 2001 ... 3.00
❑9, Dec 2001 ... 3.00
❑10, Jan 2002 ... 3.00
❑11, Feb 2002 ... 3.00
❑12, Mar 2002 ... 3.00

N-MINT

❑13, Apr 2002 ... 3.00
❑14, May 2002 ... 3.00
❑15, Jun 2002 ... 3.00
❑16, Jul 2002 ... 3.00

ULTIMATE NIGHTMARE
MARVEL

❑1, Oct 2004 ... 3.00
❑2, Nov 2004 ... 2.25
❑3, Dec 2004 ... 2.25
❑4, Jan 2005 ... 2.25
❑5, Feb 2005 ... 2.25

ULTIMATES
MARVEL

❑1, Mar 2002 ... 7.00
❑1/DF Millar, Mar 2002 ... 20.00
❑1/DF Quesada, Mar 2002; Dynamic Forces variant signed by Joe Quesada ... 25.00
❑2, Apr 2002 ... 9.00
❑3, May 2002 ... 6.00
❑4, Jun 2002 ... 10.00
❑5, Jul 2002 ... 8.00
❑6, Aug 2002 ... 7.00
❑7, Sep 2002 ... 6.00
❑8, Nov 2002 ... 5.00
❑9, Apr 2003 ... 6.00
❑10, Jul 2003 ... 4.00
❑11, Sep 2003 ... 3.00
❑12, Nov 2003 ... 2.25
❑13, Jun 2004 ... 3.50
❑13/DF Millar, Jun 2004; Dynamic Forces variant signed by Mark Millar ... 20.00

ULTIMATES 2
MARVEL

❑1, Feb 2005 ... 5.00
❑1/2nd, Feb 2005 ... 2.99
❑1/Sketch, Feb 2005 ... 35.00
❑2, Mar 2005 ... 2.99
❑3, Apr 2005 ... 2.99
❑4, May 2005 ... 2.99
❑5, Jun 2005 ... 2.99
❑6, Jul 2005 ... 2.99
❑7, Aug 2005 ... 2.99
❑8 2005 ... 2.99
❑9, Feb 2006 ... 2.99
❑10, May 2006 ... 2.99
❑11, Sep 2006 ... 2.99
❑Annual 1, Sep 2005 ... 3.99

ULTIMATE SECRET
MARVEL

❑1, May 2005 ... 2.99
❑2, Jun 2005 ... 2.99
❑3 2005 ... 2.99
❑4, Dec 2005 ... 2.99

ULTIMATE SIX
MARVEL

❑1, Nov 2003 BMB (w) ... 4.00
❑2, Nov 2003 BMB (w) ... 3.00
❑3, Dec 2003 BMB (w) ... 2.25
❑4, Jan 2004 BMB (w) ... 3.00
❑5, Feb 2004 BMB (w) ... 2.25
❑6, Mar 2004 ... 3.00
❑7, Jun 2004 BMB (w) ... 2.25

ULTIMATE SPIDER-MAN
MARVEL

❑½, ca. 2002, Wizard mail away incentive ... 8.00
❑½/A, ca. 2002, Wizard World East Con Edition ... 18.00
❑1, Oct 2000 BMB (w); O: Spider-Man. A: Mary Jane Watson. A: Norman Osborn. ... 65.00
❑1/White, Oct 2000, BMB (w); White background on cover-otherwise same as #1 ... 375.00
❑1/Dynamic, Oct 2000, BMB (w); Dynamic Forces cover ... 175.00
❑1/Kay-Bee, Jun 2001, BMB (w); K-B Toys Reprint ... 4.00
❑1/FCBD, May 2002, BMB (w); Free Comic Book Day Edition ... 3.00
❑1/Checkers 2000 ... 7.00
❑1/Payless ... 6.00
❑1/Target ... 175.00
❑2, Dec 2000, BMB (w); Cardstock cover; Spider-Man lifting car on cover ... 30.00

N-MINT

❑2/Swinging, Dec 2000, BMB (w); Cardstock cover; Spider-Man swinging on cover ... 25.00
❑3, Jan 2001, BMB (w); O: Green Goblin. Cardstock cover; Spider-Man gets his costume ... 16.00
❑4, Feb 2001, BMB (w); D: Uncle Ben (off-panel). cardstock cover ... 8.00
❑5, Mar 2001, BMB (w); D: Uncle Ben (revealed). cardstock cover ... 55.00
❑6, Apr 2001, BMB (w); 1: Green Goblin (full). cardstock cover ... 9.00
❑6/Niagara, Apr 2001; Available only at Marvel SuperHeroes Adventure City in Niagara Falls, Canada. Reads Niagara Falls, Canada at bottom of cover. ... 35.00
❑7, May 2001, BMB (w); A: Green Goblin. cardstock cover ... 9.00
❑8, Jun 2001 BMB (w) ... 8.00
❑8/Payless, Jun 2001; Spider-Man crawling up a wall; free with pair of shoes at Payless ... 6.00
❑8/Dynamic, Jun 2001, BMB (w); alternate cover with no cover price; Dynamic Forces signed and numbered edition ... 35.00
❑9, Jul 2001 BMB (w) ... 6.00
❑10, Aug 2001 BMB (w) ... 6.00
❑11, Sep 2001 BMB (w) ... 5.00
❑12, Oct 2001 BMB (w) ... 4.00
❑13, Nov 2001 BMB (w) ... 5.00
❑14, Jan 2002, BMB (w); "3-D" cover ... 4.00
❑15, Feb 2002 BMB (w) ... 5.00
❑16, Mar 2002 BMB (w) ... 3.00
❑17, Apr 2002 BMB (w) ... 3.00
❑18, May 2002 BMB (w) ... 3.00
❑19, May 2002 BMB (w) ... 3.00
❑20, Jun 2002 BMB (w) ... 3.00
❑21, Jun 2002 BMB (w) ... 3.00
❑22, Jul 2002 BMB (w) ... 3.50
❑23, Aug 2002 BMB (w) ... 3.00
❑24, Sep 2002 BMB (w) ... 3.00
❑25, Oct 2002 BMB (w) ... 3.00
❑26, Nov 2002 BMB (w) ... 3.00
❑27, Nov 2002 BMB (w) ... 4.00
❑28, Dec 2002 BMB (w) ... 3.00
❑29, Dec 2002 BMB (w) ... 4.00
❑30, Jan 2003 BMB (w) ... 3.00
❑31, Jan 2003 BMB (w); D: Captain Stacy. ... 4.00
❑32, Feb 2003 BMB (w) ... 3.00
❑33, Feb 2003 BMB (w) ... 4.00
❑34, Mar 2003 BMB (w) ... 3.00
❑35, Mar 2003 BMB (w); A: Venom. ... 3.00
❑36, Apr 2003 BMB (w); A: Venom. ... 3.00
❑37, May 2003 BMB (w); A: Venom. ... 3.00
❑38, May 2003 BMB (w); A: Venom. ... 3.00
❑39, Jun 2003 BMB (w) ... 3.00
❑40, Jul 2003 BMB (w) ... 3.00
❑41, Jul 2003 BMB (w) ... 3.00
❑42, Aug 2003 BMB (w) ... 3.00
❑43, Sep 2003 BMB (w) ... 3.00
❑44, Oct 2003 BMB (w) ... 3.00
❑45, Nov 2003 BMB (w) ... 3.00
❑46, Nov 2003 BMB (w) ... 3.00
❑47, Dec 2003 BMB (w) ... 4.00
❑48, Dec 2003 (c); BMB (w) ... 3.00
❑49, Jan 2004 (c); BMB (w) ... 3.00
❑50, Feb 2004 (c); BMB (w) ... 4.00
❑51, Feb 2004 (c); BMB (w) ... 2.25
❑52, Mar 2004 (c); BMB (w) ... 2.25
❑53, Apr 2004 ... 3.00
❑54, May 2004 BMB (w) ... 2.25
❑54/2nd, Sep 2004 ... 2.25
❑55, May 2004 BMB (w) ... 2.25
❑56, Jun 2004 BMB (w) ... 4.00
❑57, Jun 2004 BMB (w) ... 2.25
❑58, Jul 2004 BMB (w) ... 2.25
❑59, Jul 2004 BMB (w) ... 2.25
❑60, Aug 2004 ... 8.00
❑61, Sep 2004 ... 5.00
❑62, Sep 2004 ... 8.00
❑63, Oct 2004 ... 5.00
❑64, Oct 2004 ... 4.00
❑65, Nov 2004 ... 5.00
❑66, Dec 2004 ... 2.25
❑67, Dec 2004 ... 3.00
❑68, Jan 2005 ... 2.25

❑69, Jan 2005 .... 2.25
❑70, Feb 2005 .... 2.25
❑71, Mar 2005 .... 2.25
❑72, Apr 2005 .... 4.00
❑73, May 2005 .... 2.25
❑74, May 2005 .... 2.25
❑75, Jun 2005 .... 2.25
❑76, Jun 2005 .... 2.25
❑77, Jul 2005 .... 2.25
❑78, Aug 2005 .... 2.50
❑79, Sep 2005 .... 2.50
❑80, Oct 2005 .... 2.50
❑81, Oct 2005 .... 2.50
❑82, Nov 2005 .... 2.99
❑83, Nov 2005 .... 2.99
❑84, Dec 2005 .... 2.99
❑85, Jan 2006 .... 2.99
❑86, Jan 2006 .... 2.99
❑87, Feb 2006 .... 2.99
❑88, Feb 2006 .... 2.99
❑89, Mar 2006 .... 2.99
❑90, May 2006 .... 2.99
❑91, May 2006 .... 2.99
❑92, Jun 2006 .... 2.99
❑93, Jun 2006 .... 2.99
❑94, Jul 2006 .... 2.99
❑95, Aug 2006 .... 2.99
❑96, Sep 2006 .... 2.99
❑Annual 1, Oct 2005 .... 3.99
❑SP 1, Jul 2002 .... 3.50

ULTIMATE TALES FLIP MAGAZINE
MARVEL

❑1, Jul 2005 .... 3.99
❑2, Aug 2005 .... 3.99
❑3, Sep 2005 .... 3.99
❑4, Oct 2005 .... 3.99
❑5 2005 .... 3.99
❑6, Jan 2006 .... 3.99
❑7, Feb 2006 .... 3.99
❑9, Mar 2006 .... 3.99
❑10, May 2006 .... 3.99
❑11, Jun 2006 .... 3.99
❑12, Jul 2006 .... 3.99
❑13, Aug 2006 .... 3.99
❑14, Sep 2006 .... 3.99

ULTIMATE WAR
MARVEL

❑1, Feb 2003, chromium cover 2.50
❑2, Feb 2003 .... 3.00
❑3, Mar 2003 .... 3.00
❑4, Apr 2003 .... 3.00

ULTIMATE WOLVERINE VS. HULK
MARVEL

❑1, Feb 2006 .... 3.99
❑2, May 2006 .... 3.99

ULTIMATE X-MEN
MARVEL

❑½, ca. 2002 .... 5.00
❑1, Feb 2001, cardstock cover 14.00
❑1/Sketch, Feb 2001, sketch cover 20.00
❑1/Dynamic, Feb 2001, 7000 printed; DF alternate (color) cover 40.00
❑1/Checkers, Feb 2001, Checkers Reprint 30.00
❑1/NYPost, Feb 2001 .... 8.00
❑1/Universal, Dec 2000; Features Wolverine on the cover; this preview was distributed in December 2000 at Universal Studios, Orlando. Features an Islands of Adventure ad on the back promoting Marvel attractions. 60.00
❑2, Mar 2001, cardstock cover 7.00
❑3, Apr 2001, cardstock cover 6.00
❑4, May 2001 .... 5.00
❑5, Jun 2001 .... 5.00
❑6, Jul 2001 .... 4.00
❑7, Aug 2001 .... 4.00
❑8, Sep 2001 .... 4.00
❑9, Oct 2001 .... 4.00
❑10, Nov 2001 .... 4.00
❑11, Dec 2001 JKu (a) 3.00
❑12, Jan 2002 .... 3.00
❑13, Feb 2002 .... 4.00
❑14, Mar 2002 .... 3.00
❑15, Apr 2002 .... 4.00
❑16, May 2002 .... 3.00
❑17, Jun 2002 .... 3.00
❑18, Jul 2002 .... 5.00
❑19, Aug 2002 .... 4.00
❑20, Sep 2002 .... 3.00
❑21, Oct 2002 .... 2.50
❑22, Nov 2002 .... 2.50
❑23, Dec 2002 .... 2.50
❑24, Jan 2003 .... 2.50
❑25, Jan 2003 .... 2.50
❑26, Feb 2003 (c) 2.50
❑27, Mar 2003 .... 2.25
❑28, Apr 2003 .... 2.25
❑29, Apr 2003 .... 2.25
❑30, May 2003 .... 2.25
❑31, May 2003 .... 2.25
❑32, Jun 2003 .... 2.25
❑33, Jul 2003 .... 5.00
❑34, Jul 2003 BMB (w) 4.00
❑35, Sep 2003 BMB (w) 3.00
❑36, Oct 2003 BMB (w) 4.00
❑37, Nov 2003 BMB (w) 3.00
❑38, Dec 2003 BMB (w) 2.25
❑39, Jan 2004 BMB (w) 3.00
❑40, Feb 2004 .... 2.25
❑41, Mar 2004 .... 5.00
❑42, Apr 2004 BMB (w) 4.00
❑43, May 2004 BMB (w) 2.25
❑44, Jun 2004 BMB (w) 2.25
❑45, Jul 2004 (c); BMB (w) 2.25
❑46, Jul 2004 .... 2.25
❑47, Aug 2004 .... 2.25
❑48, Aug 2004 .... 2.25
❑49, Sep 2004 .... 2.25
❑50, Oct 2004 .... 5.00
❑50/Conv, Oct 2004 .... 15.00
❑51, Nov 2004 .... 2.25
❑52, Dec 2004 .... 2.25
❑53, Jan 2005 .... 2.25
❑54, Feb 2005 .... 2.25
❑55, Mar 2005 .... 2.25
❑56, Apr 2005 .... 2.25
❑57, May 2005 .... 2.25
❑58, Jun 2005 .... 2.25
❑59, Jul 2005 .... 2.25
❑60, Aug 2005 .... 2.50
❑61, Sep 2005 .... 2.50
❑61/Coipel, Sep 2005 .... 5.00
❑62, Oct 2005 .... 2.50
❑63, Nov 2005 .... 2.99
❑64, Dec 2005 .... 2.99
❑65, Jan 2006 .... 2.99
❑66, Mar 2006 .... 2.99
❑67, Apr 2006 .... 2.99
❑68, May 2006 .... 2.99
❑69, Jun 2006 .... 2.99
❑71, Aug 2006 .... 2.99
❑Annual 1, Oct 2005 .... 2.99

ULTIMATE X-MEN/ FANTASTIC FOUR SPECIAL
MARVEL

❑1, Feb 2006 .... 2.99

ULTRA
IMAGE

❑1 2004 .... 4.00
❑2 2004 .... 2.95
❑3 2004 .... 2.95
❑4 .... 2.95
❑5 .... 2.95
❑6, Mar 2005 .... 2.95
❑7, Apr 2005 .... 2.95
❑8, May 2005 .... 2.95

ULTRAFORCE (VOL. 1)
MALIBU / ULTRAVERSE

❑0, Sep 1994 GP (a) 2.50
❑0/Variant, Jul 1994; ashcan-sized; GP (a); no cover price 1.00
❑1, Aug 1994 GP (a); 1: Atalon. 2.50
❑1/Hologram, Aug 1994; GP (a); Hologram cover 5.00
❑2, Oct 1994 GP (c); GP (a) 1.95
❑3, Nov 1994 GP (a) 1.95
❑4, Jan 1995 GP (a) 1.95
❑5, Feb 1995 GP (a) 1.95
❑6, Mar 1995 GP (a) 2.50
❑7, Apr 1995 GP (a) 2.50
❑8, May 1995 GP (a) 2.50
❑9, Jun 1995 .... 2.50
❑10, Jul 1995 .... 2.50
❑Ashcan 1; Ashcan 0.75

ULTRAFORCE (VOL. 2)
MALIBU / ULTRAVERSE

❑0, Sep 1995; #Infinity 1.50
❑0/Variant, Sep 1995; #infinity on cover 1.50
❑1, Oct 1995 .... 1.50
❑2, Nov 1995; contains reprint of UltraForce #1 .... 1.50
❑3, Dec 1995 .... 1.50
❑4, Jan 1996 .... 1.50
❑5, Feb 1996 .... 1.50
❑6, Mar 1996 .... 1.50
❑7, Apr 1996 .... 1.50
❑8, May 1996 .... 1.50
❑9, Jun 1996 .... 1.50
❑10, Aug 1996 .... 1.50
❑11, Aug 1996 .... 1.50
❑12, Sep 1996 .... 1.50
❑13, Oct 1996 .... 1.50
❑14, Nov 1996 .... 1.50
❑15, Dec 1996 .... 1.50

ULTRAFORCE/AVENGERS
MALIBU / ULTRAVERSE

❑1, Fal 1995 .... 3.95

ULTRAFORCE/AVENGERS PRELUDE
MALIBU / ULTRAVERSE

❑1, Jul 1995; a.k.a. UltraForce #11 .... 2.50

ULTRAFORCE/SPIDER-MAN
MALIBU / ULTRAVERSE

❑1, Jan 1996; alternate cover 1A 3.95
❑1/Variant, Jan 1996; alternate cover 1B 3.95

ULTRAGIRL
MARVEL

❑1, Nov 1996 .... 1.50
❑2, Dec 1996 .... 1.50
❑3, Jan 1997; March 1997 on cover 1.50

ULTRAHAWK
D.M.S.

❑1 .... 1.50

ULTRA KLUTZ
ONWARD

❑1, Jun 1986 .... 2.00
❑2, Sep 1986 .... 2.00
❑3, Oct 1986 .... 2.00
❑4, Nov 1986 .... 2.00
❑5, Dec 1986 .... 2.00
❑6, Jan 1987 .... 2.00
❑7, Feb 1987 .... 2.00
❑8, Mar 1987 .... 2.00
❑9, Apr 1987 .... 2.00
❑10, May 1987 .... 2.00
❑11, Jun 1987 .... 2.00
❑12, Jul 1987 .... 2.00
❑13, Aug 1987 .... 2.00
❑14, Sep 1987 .... 2.00
❑15, Oct 1987 .... 2.00
❑16, Nov 1987 .... 1.50
❑17, Dec 1987 .... 1.50
❑18, Jan 1988 .... 1.75
❑19, Feb 1988 .... 1.75
❑20 1988 .... 1.75
❑21 1988 .... 1.75
❑22 1988 .... 1.75
❑23, Jul 1988 .... 2.00
❑24, Aug 1988 .... 2.00
❑25, Sep 1988 .... 2.00
❑26, Nov 1988 .... 2.00
❑27, Jan 1989 .... 2.00
❑28 1989 .... 2.00
❑29, Jun 1990 .... 2.00
❑30 1990 .... 2.00
❑31, May 1991 .... 2.00

ULTRA KLUTZ '81
ONWARD

❑1, Jun 1981 .... 2.00

ULTRAMAN (ULTRACOMICS)
HARVEY / ULTRACOMICS

❑1, Jul 1993; O: Ultraman. newsstand 2.00
❑1/CS, Jul 1993 .... 2.50
❑1/Direct ed., Jul 1993; trading card; no type on cover 3.50
❑2 1993; newsstand 1.75

N-MINT | N-MINT | N-MINT

❑2/CS 1993 .... 2.50
❑2/Direct ed. 1993; direct sale; trading card 2.50
❑3 1993; newsstand 1.75
❑3/CS 1993 .... 2.50
❑3/Direct ed. 1993; trading cards 2.50

ULTRAMAN (NEMESIS)
NEMESIS

❑-1, Mar 1994; negative image on cover 2.50
❑1, Apr 1994; Split cover 2.50
❑1/A, Apr 1994; alternate cover 2.25
❑2, May 1994 .... 1.95
❑3, Aug 1994 .... 1.95
❑4, Sep 1994 .... 1.95
❑5 1994 .... 1.95

ULTRAMAN CLASSIC: BATTLE OF THE ULTRA-BROTHERS
VIZ

❑1, b&w 4.95
❑2, b&w 4.95
❑3, b&w 4.95
❑4, b&w 4.95
❑5, b&w 4.95

ULTRAMAN TIGA
DARK HORSE

❑1, Sep 2003 .... 3.99
❑2, Oct 2003 .... 3.99
❑3, Nov 2003 .... 3.99
❑4, Dec 2003 .... 3.99
❑5, Jan 2004 .... 3.99
❑6, Mar 2004 .... 2.99
❑7, Apr 2004 .... 2.99
❑8, May 2004 .... 3.99
❑9, May 2004 .... 3.99
❑10, Aug 2004 .... 3.99

ULTRA MONTHLY
MALIBU

❑1, Jun 1993, actually giveaway 0.50
❑2, Jul 1993, actually giveaway 0.50
❑3, Aug 1993, actually giveaway; cover says Sep, indicia says Aug 0.50
❑4, Sep 1993 .... 0.50
❑5, Oct 1993 .... 0.50
❑6, Nov 1993 .... 0.50

ULTRAVERSE/AVENGERS PRELUDE
MALIBU / ULTRAVERSE

❑1, Jul 1995 .... 2.50

ULTRAVERSE DOUBLE FEATURE: PRIME AND SOLITAIRE
MALIBU / ULTRAVERSE

❑1, Jan 1995 .... 3.95

ULTRAVERSE: FUTURE SHOCK
MALIBU / ULTRAVERSE

❑1, Feb 1997; final Ultraverse adventure 2.50

ULTRAVERSE ORIGINS
MALIBU / ULTRAVERSE

❑1, Jan 1994; O: Prime. Origin 1.25

ULTRAVERSE PREMIERE
MALIBU / ULTRAVERSE

❑0, Nov 1993 .... 1.00

ULTRAVERSE UNLIMITED
MALIBU / ULTRAVERSE

❑1, Jun 1996 .... 2.50
❑2, Sep 1996, b&w 2.50

ULTRAVERSE YEAR ONE
MALIBU / ULTRAVERSE

❑1, Sep 1994 .... 4.95

ULTRAVERSE YEAR TWO
MALIBU / ULTRAVERSE

❑1, Aug 1995 .... 4.95

ULTRAVERSE YEAR ZERO: THE DEATH OF THE SQUAD
MALIBU / ULTRAVERSE

❑1, Apr 1995 .... 2.95
❑2, May 1995 .... 2.95
❑3, Jun 1995 .... 2.95
❑4, Jul 1995 .... 2.95

UMBRA
IMAGE

❑1, Jul 2006 .... 2.99

UNBOUND
IMAGE

❑1, Jan 1998, b&w 2.95

UNCANNY ORIGINS
MARVEL

❑1, Sep 1996 O: Cyclops. 1.25
❑1/A, Sep 1996; O: Cyclops. No price on cover; variant cover 1.25
❑2, Oct 1996 O: Quicksilver. 1.00
❑3, Nov 1996 O: Archangel. 1.00
❑4, Dec 1996 O: Firelord. 1.00
❑5, Jan 1997 O: Hulk. 1.00
❑6, Feb 1997 O: Beast. 1.00
❑7, Mar 1997; O: Venom. Flip book with Untold Tales of Spider-Man #19 .... 1.00
❑8, Apr 1997; O: Nightcrawler. Flip book with Untold Tales of Spider-Man #20 .... 1.00
❑9, May 1997 O: Storm. 1.00
❑10, Jun 1997 O: Black Cat. 1.00
❑11, Jul 1997 O: Black Knight. 1.00
❑12, Aug 1997 O: Doctor Strange. 1.00
❑13, Sep 1997 O: Daredevil. 1.00
❑14, Oct 1997 O: Iron Fist. 1.00

UNCANNY TALES (2ND SERIES)
MARVEL

❑1, Dec 1973 .... 20.00
❑2, Feb 1974 .... 12.00
❑3, Apr 1974 .... 12.00
❑4, Jun 1974 .... 12.00
❑5, Aug 1974 .... 12.00
❑6, Oct 1974 .... 12.00
❑7, Dec 1974 .... 12.00
❑8, Feb 1975 .... 12.00
❑9, Apr 1975 .... 12.00
❑10, Jun 1975 .... 12.00
❑11, Aug 1975 .... 12.00
❑12, Oct 1975 .... 12.00

UNCANNY X-MEN
MARVEL

❑-1, Jul 1997; Flashback 2.00
❑142, Feb 1981, JBy (a); A: Rachel Summers (Phoenix III). D: Colossus (future). D: Storm (future). D: Wolverine (future). Series continued from X-Men (1st Series) #141 .... 25.00
❑143, Mar 1981, JBy (a); Last Byrne art on X-Men 8.00
❑144, Apr 1981 BA (c); BA (a); A: Man-Thing 6.00
❑145, May 1981 DC (c); DC (a) 7.00
❑146, Jun 1981 DC (c); DC (a) 6.00
❑147, Jul 1981 DC (c); DC (a) 6.00
❑148, Aug 1981 DC (c); DC (a); 1: Caliban. A: Dazzler. A: Spider-Woman 6.00
❑149, Sep 1981 DC (c); DC (a) 5.00
❑150, Oct 1981; double-sized; DC (c); DC, BWi (a); V: Magneto. Cyclops rejoins the X-Men 5.00
❑151, Nov 1981 BMc (c); BMc (a) 5.00
❑152, Dec 1981 BMc (c); BMc (a) 5.00
❑153, Jan 1982 DC (c); DC (a) 5.00
❑154, Feb 1982 DC, BWi (c); DC, BWi (a) 5.00
❑155, Mar 1982 DC, BWi (c); DC, BWi (a) 5.00
❑156, Apr 1982 DC, BWi (c); DC, BWi (a) 5.00
❑157, May 1982 DC, BWi (c); DC, BWi (a); A: Phoenix. 5.00
❑158, Jun 1982 DC, BWi (c); DC, BWi (a); A: Rogue. 6.00
❑159, Jul 1982 BSz (c); BSz, BWi (a); A: Dracula. 5.00
❑160, Aug 1982 BA, BWi (c); BA, BWi (a); 1: Magik (Illyana Rasputin as teenager). 5.00
❑161, Sep 1982 DC, BWi (c); DC, BWi (a); O: Professor X. O: Magneto. 5.00
❑162, Oct 1982, DC, BWi (c); DC, BWi (a); Wolverine solo story 6.00
❑163, Nov 1982 DC, BWi (c); DC, BWi (a) 5.00
❑164, Dec 1982 DC, BWi (c); DC, BWi (a); 1: Binary. 5.00
❑165, Jan 1983 PS (c); PS, BWi (a) 5.00
❑166, Feb 1983; Double-size PS, BWi (c); PS, BWi (a); 1: Lockheed. 5.00
❑167, Mar 1983 PS, BWi (c); PS, BWi (a); A: New Mutants 4.00
❑168, Apr 1983 PS, BWi (c); PS, BWi (a); 1: Madelyne Pryor. 5.00
❑169, May 1983 PS, BWi (c); PS, BWi (a); 1: Morlocks. 1: Sunder. 5.00
❑170, Jun 1983 PS, BWi (c); PS, BWi (a) 5.00
❑171, Jul 1983, BWi (c); BWi (a); Rogue joins team 5.00
❑172, Aug 1983 PS (c); PS, BWi (a) 5.00
❑173, Sep 1983 BWi (c); PS (a); O: Silver Samurai. 5.00
❑174, Oct 1983 PS (c); PS, BWi (a) 5.00
❑175, Nov 1983; double-sized PS (c); PS, JR2, BWi (a) 5.00
❑176, Dec 1983 JR2 (c); JR2, BWi (a); 1: Valerie Cooper. 4.00
❑177, Jan 1984 JR2 (c); JR2 (a) 4.00
❑178, Feb 1984 DGr, JR2 (c); JR2, BWi (a) 5.00
❑179, Mar 1984 DGr, JR2 (c); DGr, JR2 (a) 4.00
❑180, Apr 1984 JR2 (c); DGr, JR2, BWi (a) 3.00
❑181, May 1984 JR2 (c); DGr, JR2 (a) 4.00
❑182, Jun 1984 JR2 (c); DGr, JR2 (a) 5.00
❑183, Jul 1984 JR2 (c); DGr, JR2 (a). 5.00
❑184, Aug 1984 DGr, JR2 (c); DGr, JR2 (a); 1: Forge. A: Rachel. A: Selene. 4.00
❑185, Sep 1984, DGr, JR2 (c); DGr, JR2 (a); Storm loses powers 4.00
❑186, Oct 1984; double-sized; Storm. 4.00
❑187, Nov 1984 DGr, JR2 (c); DGr, JR2 (a) 3.00
❑188, Dec 1984 JR2 (c); DGr, JR2 (a) 3.00
❑189, Jan 1985 JR2 (c); JR2 (a) 4.00
❑190, Feb 1985 DGr, JR2 (c); DGr, JR2 (a); A: Spider-Man. A: Avengers. 4.00
❑191, Mar 1985 DGr, JR2 (c); DGr, JR2 (a); A: Captain America. A: Spider-Man. A: Avengers. 5.00
❑192, Apr 1985, DGr, JR2 (c); DGr, JR2 (a); Magus 4.00
❑193, May 1985; double-sized; DGr, JR2 (c); DGr, JR2 (a); 20th anniv.; 100th New X-Men 5.00
❑194, Jun 1985 JR2 (c); DGr, JR2 (a); A: Juggernaut. V: Juggernaut. 3.00
❑195, Jul 1985 BSz, DGr (c); DGr, JR2 (a); A: Power Pack. 3.00
❑196, Aug 1985, JR2 (c); DGr, JR2 (a); Secret Wars II 3.00
❑197, Sep 1985 DGr, JR2 (c); DGr, JR2 (a) 3.00
❑198, Oct 1985. .... 3.00
❑199, Nov 1985 JR2 (c); DGr, JR2 (a); 1: Phoenix III (Rachel Summers). 3.00
❑200, Dec 1985; Double-size DGr, JR2 (c); DGr, JR2 (a) 6.00
❑201, Jan 1986, 1: Cable (as baby). 1st Whilce Portacio art in X-Men 5.00
❑202, Feb 1986; AW, JR2 (c); AW, JR2 (a); Secret Wars II 4.00
❑203, Mar 1986; AW, JR2 (c); AW, JR2 (a); Secret Wars II 4.00
❑204, Apr 1986; Nightcrawler solo story 4.00
❑205, May 1986; A: Power Pack. Wolverine solo story 4.00
❑206, Jun 1986 AW, JR2 (c); DGr, JR2 (a); V: Freedom Force. 4.00
❑207, Jul 1986; DGr, JR2 (c); DGr, JR2 (a); Wolverine vs. Phoenix 4.00
❑208, Aug 1986 DGr, JR2 (c); DGr, JR2 (a) 4.00
❑209, Sep 1986 DGr, JR2 (c); JR2, CR (a) 4.00
❑210, Oct 1986 JR2, BWi (c); DGr, JR2 (a); 1: Marauders. 5.00
❑211, Nov 1986 AW, JR2 (c); AW, JR2 (a) 5.00
❑212, Dec 1986; DGr (c); DGr (a); A: Sabretooth. Wolverine vs. Sabretooth 6.00
❑213, Jan 1987; Wolverine vs. Sabretooth 6.00
❑214, Feb 1987 BWi (a) 3.00
❑215, Mar 1987 DGr (c); DGr (a); 1: Crimson Commando. 3.00
❑216, Apr 1987 DGr, BG (a) 4.00
❑217, May 1987 BWi (c); BG (a); A: Juggernaut. 3.00
❑218, Jun 1987 BWi (c); DGr (a); V: Juggernaut. 3.00

Uncensored Mouse

Uncopyrighted Mickey reprints led to fight

©Eternity

Uncle Scrooge (Walt Disney...)

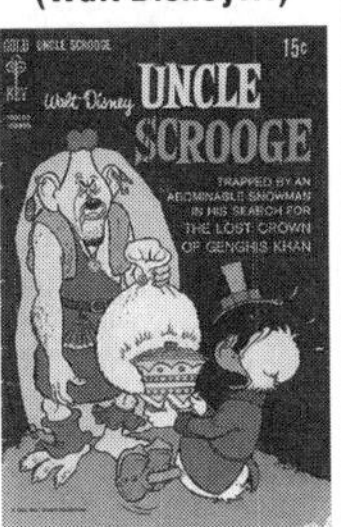

Carl Bark's most popular creation

©Dell

Uncle Scrooge and Donald Duck

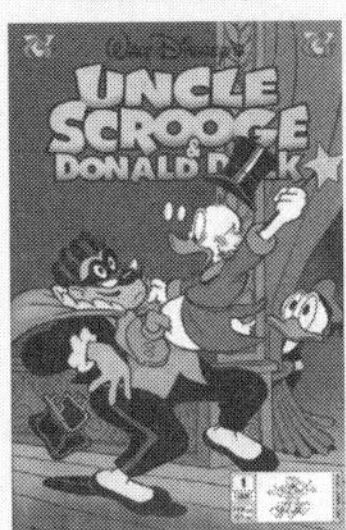

Gladstone spinoff ran two issues

©Gold Key

Uncle Slam & Fire Dog

Hero has a hole in his head

©Action Planet

Underdog (Charlton)

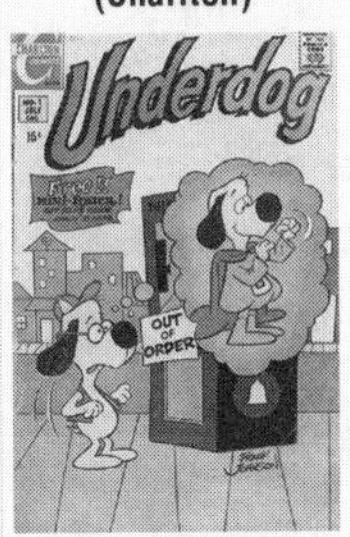

Have no fear, animated canine is here

©Charlton

N-MINT

❑219, Jul 1987; DGr (a); Havok joins X-Men 4.00
❑220, Aug 1987 DGr (c); DGr (a) 4.00
❑221, Sep 1987 DGr (c); DGr (a); 1: Mister Sinister. V: Mr. Sinister..... 7.00
❑222, Oct 1987 DGr (c); DGr (a); A: Sabretooth. V: Sabretooth. 5.00
❑223, Nov 1987 DGr, KGa (c); DGr, KGa (a) 4.00
❑224, Dec 1987; BWi (c); BWi (a); registration card 3.00
❑225, Jan 1988; DGr (c); DGr (a); Fall of Mutants 3.00
❑226, Feb 1988; Double-size; DGr (c); DGr (a); Fall of Mutants; Storm regains powers 3.00
❑227, Mar 1988; DGr (c); DGr (a); Fall of Mutants 3.00
❑228, Apr 1988 .... 3.00
❑229, May 1988 DGr (c); DGr (a); 1: The Reavers. 3.00
❑230, Jun 1988 .... 3.00
❑231, Jul 1988 DGr (c); DGr (a) 3.00
❑232, Aug 1988 DGr (c); DGr (a) 4.00
❑233, Sep 1988 DGr (c); DGr (a) 3.00
❑234, Sep 1988 DGr (c); 3.00
❑235, Oct 1988 CR (c); CR (a) 3.00
❑236, Oct 1988 DGr (c); DGr (a) 3.00
❑237, Nov 1988 .... 3.00
❑238, Nov 1988 DGr (c); DGr (a) 3.00
❑239, Dec 1988; DGr (c); DGr (a); Inferno 3.00
❑240, Jan 1989; DGr (c); DGr (a); A: Sabretooth. Inferno 3.00
❑241, Feb 1989; DGr (c); DGr (a); Inferno 3.00
❑242, Mar 1989; Double-size; DGr (c); DGr (a); Inferno 3.00
❑243, Apr 1989; DGr (c); Inferno 3.00
❑244, May 1989 DGr (c); DGr (a); 1: Jubilee. 5.00
❑245, Jun 1989 DGr, RL (c); DGr, RL (a) 3.00
❑246, Jul 1989 DGr (c); DGr (a) 3.00
❑247, Aug 1989 DGr (c); DGr (a) 3.00
❑248, Sep 1989; DGr, JLee (c); DGr, JLee (a); 1st Jim Lee art on X-Men. 5.00
❑248/2nd 1989; JLee (a); 1st Jim Lee art on X-Men 1.50
❑249, Oct 1989 DGr (c); DGr (a) 3.00
❑250, Oct 1989 DGr (c); 3.00
❑251, Nov 1989 DGr (c); DGr (a) 3.00
❑252, Nov 1989 BSz, JLee (c); 2.50
❑253, Nov 1989 DGr (c); 2.50
❑254, Dec 1989 DGr (c); DGr (a); D: Sunder. 2.50
❑255, Dec 1989 DGr (c); DGr (a) 2.50
❑256, Dec 1989; JLee (c); JLee (a); Acts of Vengeance 3.00
❑257, Jan 1990; JLee (c); JLee (a); Acts of Vengeance 3.00
❑258, Feb 1990; JLee (c); JLee (a); Acts of Vengeance 3.00
❑259, Mar 1990 DGr (c); DGr (a) 4.00
❑260, Apr 1990 JLee (c); DGr (a) 3.00
❑261, May 1990 JLee (c); DGr (a) 2.50
❑262, Jun 1990 .... 2.50
❑263, Jul 1990 .... 2.50

N-MINT

❑264, Jul 1990 JLee (c); 2.50
❑265, Aug 1990 .... 2.50
❑266, Aug 1990 1: Gambit (full appearance) 14.00
❑267, Sep 1990; JLee, BWi (c); JLee (a); Captain America, Wolverine, Black Widow team-up 6.00
❑268, Sep 1990 JLee (c); JLee (a) 6.00
❑269, Oct 1990 JLee (c); JLee (a) 3.00
❑270, Nov 1990 JLee (c); JLee (a) 4.00
❑270/2nd, Nov 1990; JLee (a); Gold cover 2.00
❑271, Dec 1990 JLee (c); JLee (a) 3.00
❑272, Jan 1991 JLee (c); JLee (a) 3.00
❑273, Feb 1991 JLee (c); MG, JBy, JLee, KJ (a) 3.00
❑274, Mar 1991 JLee (c); JLee (a); A: Ka-Zar. A: Magneto. A: Nick Fury. 3.00
❑275, Apr 1991; Double-size JLee (c); JLee (a) 3.00
❑275/2nd, Apr 1991; Double-size; JLee (a); gold logo 2.00
❑276, May 1991 JLee (c); JLee (w); JLee (a) 2.50
❑277, Jun 1991 JLee (c); JLee (w); JLee (a) 2.50
❑278, Jul 1991 PS (c); PS (a) 2.50
❑279, Aug 1991 .... 2.50
❑280, Sep 1991; JLee (c); X-Factor crossover 2.50
❑281, Oct 1991; JBy, JLee (w); 1: Fitzroy. wraparound cover; new team 2.00
❑281/2nd, Oct 1991; 1: Fitzroy. 2nd printing (red); New team begins; wraparound cover 1.50
❑282, Nov 1991 JBy (w); 1: Bishop (cameo). 3.00
❑282/2nd, Nov 1991; 1: Bishop (cameo). Gold cover 1.25
❑283, Dec 1991 JBy (w); 1: Bishop (full). 5.00
❑284, Jan 1992 JBy (w) 4.00
❑285, Feb 1992 JBy, JLee (w); AM (a); 1: Mikhail Rasputin 2.50
❑286, Mar 1992 JLee (c); JLee (w); JLee (a) 2.00
❑287, Apr 1992 JLee (w); BSz, JR2, BWi (a); O: Bishop 2.50
❑288, May 1992 JBy, JLee (w); BSz (a) 2.00
❑289, Jun 1992; Bishop joins X-Men. 2.00
❑290, Jul 1992 .... 2.00
❑291, Aug 1992 .... 2.00
❑292, Sep 1992 AM (a) 3.00
❑293, Oct 1992 .... 2.00
❑294/CS, Nov 1992 .... 3.00
❑295/CS, Dec 1992 .... 2.00
❑296/CS, Jan 1993 .... 3.00
❑297, Feb 1993 .... 1.50
❑298, Mar 1993 AM (c); AM (a) 2.00
❑299, Apr 1993 .... 1.50
❑300, May 1993; Double-size; DGr, JR2 (c); DGr, JR2 (a); holo-foil cover 3.00
❑301, Jun 1993 DGr, JR2 (c); DGr, JR2 (a) 1.50
❑302, Jul 1993 JR2 (c); DGr, JR2 (a). 1.50
❑303, Aug 1993 DGr (a); D: Illyana Rasputin. 3.00

N-MINT

❑304, Sep 1993; 30th Anniversary Issue; JR2 (c); DGr, PS, JR2, TP (a); hologram 1.50
❑305, Oct 1993 (c); JDu (a) 1.50
❑306, Nov 1993 JR2 (c); DGr, JR2 (a) 2.00
❑307, Dec 1993 DGr, JR2 (c); DGr, JR2 (a) 5.00
❑308, Jan 1994 DGr, JR2 (c); DGr, JR2 (a) 1.50
❑309, Feb 1994 DGr, JR2 (c); DGr, JR2 (a) 1.50
❑310, Mar 1994 DGr, JR2 (c); DGr, JR2 (a) 1.50
❑311, Apr 1994 JR2 (c); DGr, JR2 (a); A: Sabretooth. 1.50
❑312, May 1994 DGr (c); DGr (a) 1.50
❑313, Jun 1994 DGr (c); DGr (a) 1.50
❑314, Jul 1994 BSz (a) 1.50
❑315, Aug 1994 DGr (a) 1.50
❑316, Sep 1994 DGr (c); DGr (a) 1.50
❑316/Variant, Sep 1994; enhanced cover 1.50
❑317, Oct 1994 DGr (c); DGr (a) 1.50
❑317/Variant, Oct 1994; enhanced cover 1.50
❑318, Nov 1994 .... 2.00
❑318/Deluxe, Nov 1994; Deluxe edition 1.50
❑319, Dec 1994 DGr (a) 2.00
❑319/Deluxe, Dec 1994; Deluxe edition 1.50
❑320, Jan 1995 MWa (w) 2.00
❑320/Deluxe, Jan 1995; Deluxe edition 1.50
❑320/Gold, Jan 1995; Wizard edition; No cover price; gold logo 2.00
❑321, Feb 1995 (c); MWa (w); DGr (a) 1.50
❑321/Deluxe, Feb 1995; Deluxe edition 2.00
❑322, Jul 1995 AM, DGr (a); V: Onslaught. V: Juggernaut. 2.00
❑323, Aug 1995 1: Sack and Vessel. 1.50
❑324, Sep 1995 .... 2.00
❑325, Oct 1995; enhanced gatefold cardstock cover 2.00
❑326, Nov 1995 .... 2.00
❑327, Dec 1995; AM (a); A: Magneto. Magneto's fate revealed 2.00
❑328, Jan 1996; Psylocke vs. Sabretooth 2.00
❑329, Feb 1996 JPH (w) 4.00
❑330, Mar 1996 JPH (w) 2.00
❑331, Apr 1996; Iceman vs. White Queen 2.00
❑332, May 1996 V: Ozymandias. 2.00
❑333, Jun 1996 .... 2.00
❑334, Jul 1996 A: Juggernaut. 2.00
❑335, Aug 1996 A: Uatu. A: Apocalypse. 2.00
❑336, Sep 1996 .... 2.00
❑337, Oct 1996 .... 2.00
❑338, Nov 1996; Angel regains his wings 2.00
❑339, Dec 1996; A: Spider-Man. Cyclops vs. Havok 2.00
❑340, Jan 1997 .... 2.00
❑341, Feb 1997; Cannonball vs. Gladiator 2.00
❑342, Mar 1997 .... 2.00
❑342/A, Mar 1997; Variant cover (Rogue) 2.00
❑343, Apr 1997 .... 2.00

Other grades: Multiply price above by 5/6 for VF/NM • 2/3 for VERY FINE • 1/3 for FINE • 1/5 for VERY GOOD • 1/8 for GOOD

	N-MINT
❑344, May 1997	2.00
❑345, Jun 1997	2.00
❑346, Aug 1997; gatefold summary A: Spider-Man.	2.00
❑347, Sep 1997; gatefold summary AM (a)	2.00
❑348, Oct 1997; gatefold summary AM (a)	2.00
❑349, Nov 1997; gatefold summary V: Maggot.	2.00
❑350, Dec 1997; gatefold summary	2.00
❑350/Variant, Dec 1997; gatefold summary; enhanced cover	2.00
❑351, Jan 1998; gatefold summary; V: Pyro. Cecilia joins team	2.00
❑352, Feb 1998; gatefold summary	2.00
❑353, Mar 1998; gatefold summary; Rogue vs. Wolverine	3.00
❑354, Apr 1998; gatefold summary V: Sauron.	1.99
❑355, May 1998; gatefold summary A: Alpha Flight	1.99
❑356, Jun 1998; gatefold summary	1.99
❑357, Jul 1998; gatefold summary	1.99
❑358, Aug 1998; gatefold summary	1.99
❑359, Sep 1998; gatefold summary	1.99
❑360, Oct 1998; double-sized; Kitty Pryde, Colossus, Nightcrawler rejoin team	1.99
❑360/Variant, Oct 1998; Special cover	1.99
❑361, Nov 1998; gatefold summary; Return of Gambit	1.99
❑362, Dec 1998; gatefold summary	1.99
❑363, Jan 1999; gatefold summary	4.00
❑364, Jan 1999; gatefold summary; Leinil Francis Yu's first major comics work	2.99
❑365, Mar 1999; gatefold summary; cover says Feb, indicia says Mar	1.99
❑366, Apr 1999	1.99
❑367, Apr 1999 (c);	1.99
❑368, Jun 1999; Wolverine vs. Magneto; cover says May, indicia says Jun	1.99
❑369, Jun 1999 V: Juggernaut.	1.99
❑370, Jul 1999	1.99
❑371, Aug 1999 A: Warlock.	1.99
❑372, Sep 1999	1.99
❑373, Oct 1999	1.99
❑374, Nov 1999	1.99
❑375, Dec 1999; Giant-size	1.99
❑376, Jan 2000	1.99
❑377, Feb 2000	1.99
❑378, Mar 2000	1.99
❑379, Apr 2000	2.99
❑380, May 2000 (c);	1.99
❑381, Jun 2000	2.25
❑381/Dynamic, Jun 2000, Dynamic Forces chromium variant; no UPC box on cover	7.00
❑382, Jul 2000	2.25
❑383, Aug 2000; Giant-size	2.25
❑384, Sep 2000	2.25
❑385, Oct 2000	2.25
❑386, Nov 2000	2.25
❑387, Dec 2000	2.99
❑388, Jan 2001	2.25
❑389, Feb 2001	2.25
❑390, Feb 2001 D: Colossus.	2.25
❑391, Mar 2001 (c)	2.25
❑392, Apr 2001; Eve of Destruction	2.25
❑393, May 2001; Eve of Destruction	2.25
❑394, Jun 2001	2.25
❑395, Jul 2001	2.25
❑396, Aug 2001	2.25
❑397, Sep 2001	2.25
❑398, Oct 2001	2.25
❑399, Nov 2001	2.25
❑400, Dec 2001; Giant-size (c);	2.25
❑401, Jan 2002	2.25
❑402, Feb 2002	2.25
❑403, Mar 2002 (c);	2.25
❑404, Apr 2002	3.50
❑405, May 2002	2.25
❑406, Jun 2002	2.25
❑407, Jul 2002	2.25
❑408, Aug 2002	2.25
❑409, Sep 2002	2.25
❑410, Oct 2002	2.25
❑411, Oct 2002	2.25

	N-MINT
❑412, Nov 2002 (c);	2.25
❑413, Nov 2002	2.25
❑414, Dec 2002	2.25
❑415, Jan 2003	2.25
❑416, Feb 2003	3.00
❑417, Mar 2003	2.25
❑418, Mar 2003	2.25
❑419, Apr 2003	2.25
❑420, May 2003	2.25
❑421, Jun 2003	2.25
❑422, Jun 2003	2.25
❑423, Jul 2003	2.25
❑424, Jul 2003	2.25
❑425, Aug 2003	2.25
❑426, Aug 2003	2.25
❑427, Sep 2003	2.25
❑428, Oct 2003	2.25
❑429, Oct 2003	2.25
❑430, Oct 2003	2.99
❑431, Nov 2003	2.99
❑432, Dec 2003	2.99
❑433, Jan 2004	2.99
❑434, Feb 2004	2.99
❑435, Feb 2004	2.99
❑436, Feb 2004 DGr (a)	2.99
❑437, Mar 2004	2.99
❑438, Mar 2004	2.99
❑439, Apr 2004	2.25
❑440, Apr 2004	2.99
❑441, May 2004	2.99
❑442, May 2004	2.25
❑443, Jun 2004	2.99
❑444, Jul 2004 (c);	4.00
❑445, Aug 2004	2.25
❑446, Sep 2004	2.25
❑447, Oct 2004	2.25
❑448, Oct 2004	2.25
❑449, Nov 2004	2.25
❑450, Dec 2004, X-23 appearance	7.00
❑451, Jan 2005, X-23 appearance	6.00
❑452, Feb 2005	3.00
❑453, Feb 2005	2.25
❑454, Mar 2005	2.25
❑455, Apr 2005	4.00
❑456, May 2005	2.25
❑457, Jun 2005	2.25
❑458, Jul 2005	2.25
❑459, Aug 2005	2.25
❑460, Sep 2005	2.25
❑461, Sep 2005	2.25
❑461/Kubert, Sep 2005; Adam Kubert X-Babies incentive cover; available 1:15 copies	15.00
❑462, Oct 2005	2.50
❑463, Oct 2005	2.50
❑464, Nov 2005	2.99
❑465, Dec 2005	2.99
❑466, Jan 2006	2.99
❑467, Feb 2006	2.99
❑468, Mar 2006	2.99
❑469, Mar 2006	2.99
❑470, May 2006	2.99
❑471, Jun 2006	2.99
❑472, Jun 2006	2.99
❑473, Jul 2006	2.99
❑474, Sep 2006	2.99
❑Annual 1, Dec 1970; Cover reads "King Size Special"; JK (a); listed as X-Men in indicia, X-Men Special on cover; reprints X-Men #9 and 11	50.00
❑Annual 2, Nov 1971; Cover reads "King Size Special"; GK (c); Cover reads King Size Special; reprints X-Men #22 and 23	45.00
❑Annual 3, Jan 1980 FM (c); GP, FM (a); 1: Arkon.	14.00
❑Annual 4, Nov 1980; JR2 (a); A: Doctor Strange. series continues as Uncanny X-Men Annual	6.00
❑Annual 5, Nov 1981 BA, BMc (a); A: Fantastic Four.	5.00
❑Annual 6, Nov 1982 BSz (a); A: Dracula. D: Rachel Van Helsing.	7.00
❑Annual 7, ca. 1983 MG (a)	5.00
❑Annual 8, ca. 1984	4.00
❑Annual 9, ca. 1985	10.00
❑Annual 10, Jan 1986 1: Longshot. 1: X-babies.	8.00
❑Annual 11, ca. 1987	4.00

	N-MINT
❑Annual 12, ca. 1988	4.00
❑Annual 13, ca. 1989; Atlantis Attacks	3.00
❑Annual 14, ca. 1990 1: Gambit (cameo).	6.00
❑Annual 15, ca. 1991; 1991 annual; ca. 1991	4.00
❑Annual 16, ca. 1992; Shattershot	2.25
❑Annual 17, ca. 1993; trading card	2.95
❑Annual 18, ca. 1994 JR2 (a)	2.95
❑Annual 1995, Nov 1995; wraparound cover	3.95
❑Annual 1996, ca. 1996; wraparound cover	2.95
❑Annual 1997, Oct 1997; 1997 Annual; wraparound cover	2.99
❑Annual 1998, ca. 1998; Uncanny X-Men/Fantastic Four '98; wraparound cover	2.99
❑Annual 2000, Feb 2001	3.50
❑Annual 2001 2001	3.50

UNCENSORED MOUSE

ETERNITY

❑1, Apr 1989, b&w; Mickey Mouse	2.50
❑2, Apr 1989; Mickey Mouse	2.50

UNCLE JOE'S COMMIE BOOK FEATURING CUTEY BUNNY

RIP OFF

❑1 1995, b&w	2.95

UNCLE SAM

DC / VERTIGO

❑1, ca. 1997; prestige format ARo (a)	5.00
❑2, ca. 1997; prestige format ARo (a)	5.00

UNCLE SCROOGE (WALT DISNEY...)

DELL / GOLD KEY/WHITMAN

❑4, Dec 1953; CB (c); CB (w); CB (a); Takes place in Hawaii	310.00
❑5, Mar 1954 CB (c); CB (w); CB (a)	220.00
❑6, Jun 1954 CB (c); CB (w); CB (a)	185.00
❑7, Sep 1954 CB (c); CB (w); CB (a)	185.00
❑8, Dec 1954 CB (c); CB (w); CB (a)	140.00
❑9, Mar 1955 CB (c); CB (w); CB (a)	125.00
❑10, Jun 1955 CB (c); CB (w); CB (a).	125.00
❑11, Sep 1955 CB (c); CB (w); CB (a)	100.00
❑12, Dec 1955 CB (c); CB (w); CB (a)	100.00
❑13, Mar 1956; CB (c); CB (w); CB (a); Gyro Gearloose backup stories begin	100.00
❑14, Jun 1956 CB (c); CB (w); CB (a).	100.00
❑15, Sep 1956 CB (c); CB (w); CB (a)	100.00
❑16, Dec 1956 CB (c); CB (w); CB (a)	80.00
❑17, Mar 1957 CB (c); CB (w); CB (a)	80.00
❑18, Jun 1957 CB (c); CB (w); CB (a).	80.00
❑19, Sep 1957 CB (c); CB (w); CB (a)	80.00
❑20, Dec 1957 CB (c); CB (w); CB (a)	80.00
❑21, Mar 1958 CB (c); CB (w); CB (a)	65.00
❑22, Jun 1958 CB (c); CB (w); CB (a).	65.00
❑23, Sep 1958 CB (c); CB (w); CB (a)	65.00
❑24, Dec 1958 CB (c); CB (w); CB (a)	65.00
❑25, Mar 1959 CB (c); CB (w); CB (a)	65.00
❑26, Jun 1959 CB (c); CB (w); CB (a).	65.00
❑27, Sep 1959 CB (c); CB (w); CB (a)	65.00
❑28, Dec 1959 CB (c); CB (w); CB (a)	65.00
❑29, Mar 1960	65.00
❑30, Jun 1960 CB (w); CB (a)	65.00
❑31, Sep 1960 CB (w); CB (a)	55.00
❑32, Dec 1960	55.00
❑33, Mar 1961	55.00
❑34, Jun 1961	55.00
❑35, Sep 1961	55.00
❑36, Dec 1961; Old Number One Dime named as such	55.00
❑37, Mar 1962	55.00
❑38, Jun 1962	55.00
❑39, Sep 1962	55.00
❑40, Dec 1962; Gold Key begins as publisher	55.00
❑41, Mar 1963	45.00
❑42, May 1963 CB (w); CB (a)	45.00
❑43, Jul 1963	45.00
❑44, Aug 1963 CB (w); CB (a)	45.00
❑45, Oct 1963	45.00
❑46, Dec 1963	45.00
❑47, Feb 1964	45.00
❑48, Mar 1964 CB (w); CB (a)	45.00
❑49, May 1964	45.00
❑50, Jul 1964	45.00
❑51, Aug 1964	40.00
❑52, Sep 1964 CB (w); CB (a)	40.00

Underdog (Harvey)

Harvey reprints of older adventures

©Harvey

Undersea Agent

Sister title for T.H.U.N.D.E.R. Agents

©Tower

Undertaker

World Wrestling Federation gets graphic

©Chaos

Underworld (DC)

Series of little dramas tied together

©DC

Underworld Unleashed: Apokolips: Dark Uprising

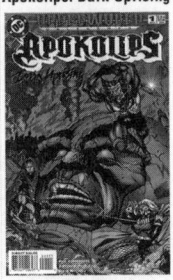

Villains sell souls for great power

©DC

	N-MINT
❑53, Oct 1964	40.00
❑54, Dec 1964	40.00
❑55, Feb 1965	40.00
❑56, Mar 1965	40.00
❑57, May 1965	40.00
❑58, Jul 1965	40.00
❑59, Sep 1965	40.00
❑60, Nov 1965	40.00
❑61, Jan 1966	40.00
❑62, Mar 1966	40.00
❑63, May 1966	40.00
❑64, Jul 1966	40.00
❑65, Sep 1966	40.00
❑66, Nov 1966; CB (c); CB (w); CB (a); Gyro reprinted from Uncle Scrooge (Walt Disney's...) #22	40.00
❑67, Jan 1967	40.00
❑68, Mar 1967	40.00
❑69, May 1967	40.00
❑70, Jul 1967 CB (c); CB (w); CB (a)	40.00
❑71, Oct 1967	38.00
❑72, Dec 1967; Gyro reprinted from Uncle Scrooge (Walt Disney's...) #19	32.00
❑73, Feb 1968; Reprints stories from Uncle Scrooge (Walt Disney's...) #33 and 36	32.00
❑74, Apr 1968	32.00
❑75, Jun 1968	32.00
❑76, Aug 1968	32.00
❑77, Oct 1968	32.00
❑78, Dec 1968	32.00
❑79, Feb 1969	32.00
❑80, Apr 1969	32.00
❑81, Jun 1969	32.00
❑82, Aug 1969; Reprints story from Uncle Scrooge (Walt Disney's...) #34	32.00
❑83, Oct 1969	32.00
❑84, Dec 1969; Reprints story from Uncle Scrooge (Walt Disney's...) #14	32.00
❑85, Feb 1970; Reprints story from Uncle Scrooge (Walt Disney's...) #52	32.00
❑86, Apr 1970; CB (w); CB (a); Reprints story from Uncle Scrooge (Walt Disney's...) #35	32.00
❑87, Jun 1970; Reprints story from Uncle Scrooge (Walt Disney's...) #25	32.00
❑88, Aug 1970; Reprints story from Uncle Scrooge (Walt Disney's...) #38	32.00
❑89, Oct 1970; Reprints story from Uncle Scrooge (Walt Disney's...) #15	32.00
❑90, Dec 1970; Reprints stories from Uncle Scrooge (Walt Disney's...) #37 and 35	32.00
❑91, Feb 1971; Reprints stories from Uncle Scrooge (Walt Disney's...) #11 and 26	32.00
❑92, Apr 1971; Reprints stories from Uncle Scrooge (Walt Disney's...) #24, 31 and 32	32.00
❑93, Jun 1971; Reprints stories from Uncle Scrooge (Walt Disney's...) #34 and 36	32.00
❑94, Aug 1971; Reprints stories from Uncle Scrooge (Walt Disney's...) #35 and 53	32.00
❑95, Oct 1971; Reprints stories from Uncle Scrooge (Walt Disney's...) #30 and 51	32.00
❑96, Dec 1971; Reprints story from Uncle Scrooge (Walt Disney's...) #47	32.00
❑97, Feb 1972; Reprints stories from Uncle Scrooge (Walt Disney's...) #32	32.00
❑98, Apr 1972; Reprints story from Uncle Scrooge (Walt Disney's...) #41	32.00
❑99, Jun 1972; Reprints story from Uncle Scrooge (Walt Disney's...) #42	32.00
❑100, Aug 1972; Reprints story from Uncle Scrooge (Walt Disney's...) #30	32.00
❑101, Sep 1972; Reprints stories from Walt Disney's Comics & Stories #157 and 159	20.00
❑102, Nov 1972; Reprints stories from Uncle Scrooge (Walt Disney's...) #39	20.00
❑103, Feb 1973; CB (w); CB (a); Reprints story from Uncle Scrooge (Walt Disney's...) #16	20.00
❑104, Apr 1973; Reprints stories from Uncle Scrooge (Walt Disney's...) #9 and 42	20.00
❑105, Jun 1973; Reprints stories from Four Color Comics #495 (Uncle Scrooge #3) and Uncle Scrooge (Walt Disney's...) #32	20.00
❑106, Aug 1973; Reprints stories from Uncle Scrooge (Walt Disney's...) #6	20.00
❑107, Sep 1973; Reprints story from Uncle Scrooge (Walt Disney's...) #21	20.00
❑108, Oct 1973; Reprints story from Uncle Scrooge (Walt Disney's...) #19	20.00
❑109, Dec 1973; Reprints story from Uncle Scrooge (Walt Disney's...) #13	20.00
❑110, Feb 1974; Reprints story from Uncle Scrooge (Walt Disney's...) #22	20.00
❑111, Jun 1974; Reprints story from Uncle Scrooge (Walt Disney's...) #8	20.00
❑112, Jun 1974; Reprints story from Uncle Scrooge (Walt Disney's...) #18	20.00
❑113, Aug 1974; CB (c); CB (w); CB (a); Reprints stories from Uncle Scrooge (Walt Disney's...) #24 and 44; cover reprinted from #20	20.00
❑114, Sep 1974; Reprints story from Uncle Scrooge (Walt Disney's...) #60	20.00
❑115, Oct 1974; Reprints story from Uncle Scrooge (Walt Disney's...) #58	20.00
❑116, Dec 1974; Reprints story from Uncle Scrooge (Walt Disney's...) #50	20.00
❑117, Feb 1975; Reprints stories from Uncle Scrooge (Walt Disney's...) #32 and 49	20.00
❑118, Apr 1975; Reprints stories from Uncle Scrooge (Walt Disney's...) #54	20.00
❑119, Jun 1975; Reprints stories from Uncle Scrooge (Walt Disney's...) #23 and 37	20.00
❑120, Jul 1975; Reprints stories from Uncle Scrooge (Walt Disney's...) #33 and 34	20.00
❑121, Aug 1975; Reprints story from Uncle Scrooge (Walt Disney's...) #55	18.00
❑122, Sep 1975; Reprints story from Uncle Scrooge (Walt Disney's...) #56	18.00
❑123, Oct 1975; Reprints story from Uncle Scrooge (Walt Disney's...) #57	18.00
❑124, Dec 1975; Reprints story from Uncle Scrooge (Walt Disney's...) #59	18.00
❑125, Jan 1976; Reprints story from Uncle Scrooge (Walt Disney's...) #68	18.00
❑126, Mar 1976; Reprints story from Uncle Scrooge (Walt Disney's...) #69	18.00
❑127, Apr 1976; Reprints story from Uncle Scrooge (Walt Disney's...) #61	18.00
❑128, May 1976; Reprints story from Uncle Scrooge (Walt Disney's...) #62	18.00
❑129, Jun 1976; Reprints story from Uncle Scrooge (Walt Disney's...) #63	18.00
❑130, Jul 1976; Reprints story from Uncle Scrooge (Walt Disney's...) #65	18.00
❑131, Aug 1976; CB (c); CB (w); CB (a); Reprints story from Uncle Scrooge (Walt Disney's...) #66	18.00
❑132, Sep 1976; CB (c); CB (w); CB (a); Reprints story from Uncle Scrooge (Walt Disney's...) #10; Hulk in Hostess ad ("vs. The Green Frog")	18.00
❑133, Oct 1976; CB (c); CB (w); CB (a); Reprints story from Uncle Scrooge (Walt Disney's...) #70; Casper in Hostess ad ("Spook-a-thon")	18.00
❑134, Nov 1976; Reprints story from Uncle Scrooge (Walt Disney's...) #64	18.00
❑135, Dec 1976; Reprints stories from Uncle Scrooge (Walt Disney's...) #23 and 24	18.00
❑136, Jan 1977; Reprints stories from Uncle Scrooge (Walt Disney's...) #37-39	18.00
❑137, Feb 1977; Reprints story from Uncle Scrooge (Walt Disney's...) #31	18.00
❑138, Mar 1977; CB (c); CB (w); CB (a); Reprints stories from Uncle Scrooge (Walt Disney's...) #28 and 48; Casper in Hostess ad ("The Boogy-Woogy Man")	18.00
❑139, Apr 1977; Reprints stories from Uncle Scrooge (Walt Disney's...) #45	18.00
❑140, May 1977; Reprints story from Uncle Scrooge (Walt Disney's...) #43	18.00
❑141, Jun 1977; CB (w); CB (a); Reprints story from Uncle Scrooge (Walt Disney's...) #42; Iron Man in Hostess ad ("A Dull Pain")	12.00
❑142, Jul 1977; Reprints story from Four Color Comics #456 (Uncle Scrooge #2)	12.00
❑143, Aug 1977; Reprints stories from Uncle Scrooge (Walt Disney's...) #26 and 29	12.00
❑144, Sep 1977; Reprints stories from Uncle Scrooge (Walt Disney's...) #28	12.00
❑145, Oct 1977; Reprints story from Uncle Scrooge (Walt Disney's...) #71	12.00
❑146, Nov 1977; Reprints story from Uncle Scrooge (Walt Disney's...) #30	12.00
❑147, Dec 1977; Reprints stories from Uncle Scrooge (Walt Disney's...) #34-36	12.00
❑148, Jan 1978; Reprints story from Uncle Scrooge (Walt Disney's...) #11	12.00
❑149, Feb 1978; Reprints story from Uncle Scrooge (Walt Disney's...) #46	12.00
❑150, Mar 1978; CB (c); CB (w); CB (a); Reprints stories from Uncle Scrooge (Walt Disney's...) #27; cover reprinted from #25; Spider-Man in Hostess ad ("vs. The Chairman")	12.00
❑151, Apr 1978; Reprints stories from Uncle Scrooge (Walt Disney's...) #25	12.00

Other grades: Multiply price above by 5/6 for VF/NM • 2/3 for VERY FINE • 1/3 for FINE • 1/5 for VERY GOOD • 1/8 for GOOD

N-MINT

❑152, May 1978; CB (w); CB (a); Reprints stories from Uncle Scrooge (Walt Disney's...) #48 and 52; Captain America in Hostess ad ("vs. the Aliens") ... 12.00
❑153, Jun 1978; Reprints story from Uncle Scrooge (Walt Disney's...) #44 ... 12.00
❑154, Jul 1978; Reprints stories from Uncle Scrooge (Walt Disney's...) #35 and 53 ... 12.00
❑155, Aug 1978; CB (w); CB (a); Reprints stories from Uncle Scrooge (Walt Disney's...) #11 and 30 ... 12.00
❑156, Sep 1978; Reprints stories from Four Color Comics #456 (Uncle Scrooge #2) and Uncle Scrooge (Walt Disney's...) #38; Captain America in Hostess ad ("vs. the Aliens") ... 12.00
❑157, Oct 1978; CB (w); CB (a); Reprints stories from Uncle Scrooge (Walt Disney's...) #31, #52 and #53; Casper in Hostess ad ("A Real Oddball") ... 12.00
❑158, Nov 1978 ... 12.00
❑159, Dec 1978; CB (w); CB (a); Reprints stories from Uncle Scrooge (Walt Disney's...) #35 and #42 ... 12.00
❑160, Jan 1979 ... 12.00
❑161, Feb 1979 ... 10.00
❑162, Mar 1979; (c); (w); (a); Reprints from #81; Spider-Man in Hostess ad (June Jitsui) ... 10.00
❑163, Apr 1979 ... 10.00
❑164, May 1979 ... 10.00
❑165, Jun 1979 ... 10.00
❑166, Jul 1979; (c); (w); (a); Reprints story from Uncle Scrooge (Walt Disney's...) #74 ... 10.00
❑167, Aug 1979 ... 10.00
❑168, Sep 1979; Reprints story from Uncle Scrooge (Walt Disney's...) #79; Casper in Hostess ad ("The Boo Keepers") ... 10.00
❑169, Oct 1979 ... 10.00
❑170, Nov 1979 ... 10.00
❑171, Dec 1979 ... 10.00
❑172, Jan 1980 ... 15.00
❑173, Feb 1980 ... 15.00
❑174, Mar 1980 ... 15.00
❑175, Apr 1980 ... 15.00
❑176, May 1980 ... 15.00
❑177, Jun 1980; CB (c); CB (w); CB (a); Reprints story from Uncle Scrooge (Walt Disney's...) #16 and #103; Hulk in Hostess ad ("Hulk Gets Even") ... 25.00
❑178, Jul 1980 ... 25.00
❑179, Sep 1980 ... 225.00
❑180, Nov 1980 ... 35.00
❑181, Dec 1980 ... 15.00
❑182, Jan 1981 (c); (w); (a); V: The Beagle Boys. ... 15.00
❑183, ca. 1981; CB (c); CB (w); CB (a); Cover reprinted from Uncle Scrooge (Walt Disney's...) #5; stories reprinted from #6 ... 15.00
❑184, ca. 1981; CB (c); CB (w); CB (a); Reprints stories from Uncle Scrooge (Walt Disney's...) #60 ... 15.00
❑185, Jun 1981 ... 15.00
❑186, Jul 1981 ... 10.00
❑187, Aug 1981 ... 10.00
❑188, Sep 1981 ... 10.00
❑189, Oct 1981 ... 10.00
❑190, Nov 1981 ... 10.00
❑191, Dec 1981 ... 10.00
❑192, Jan 1982 ... 10.00
❑193, Feb 1982 ... 10.00
❑194, Spr 1982 ... 10.00
❑195, Mar 1982 ... 10.00
❑196, Apr 1982 ... 10.00
❑197, May 1982 ... 10.00
❑198, ca. 1982 ... 15.00
❑199, May 1983 ... 10.00
❑200, ca. 1982 ... 10.00
❑201, ca. 1983 ... 6.00
❑202, ca. 1983 ... 6.00
❑203, Jul 1983 ... 6.00
❑204, Aug 1983 ... 6.00
❑205, Aug 1983 ... 6.00
❑206, ca. 1984 ... 6.00
❑207, May 1984 ... 6.00
❑208, Jun 1984 ... 6.00
❑209, Jul 1984 ... 6.00

N-MINT

❑210, Oct 1986 CB (w); CB (a) ... 6.00
❑211, Nov 1986 CB (w); CB (a) ... 6.00
❑212, Dec 1986 CB (w); CB (a) ... 6.00
❑213, Jan 1987 ... 6.00
❑214, Feb 1987 ... 6.00
❑215, Mar 1987 ... 6.00
❑216, Apr 1987 CB (w); CB (a) ... 6.00
❑217, May 1987 ... 6.00
❑218, Jun 1987 CB (w); CB (a) ... 6.00
❑219, Jul 1987; DR (a); 1st Rosa Disney story ... 6.00
❑220, Aug 1987 CB (w); CB, DR (a) ... 5.00
❑221, Sep 1987 CB (w); CB (a) ... 5.00
❑222, Oct 1987 CB (w); CB (a) ... 5.00
❑223, Nov 1987 CB (w); CB (a) ... 5.00
❑224, Dec 1987 CB (w); CB, DR (a) ... 5.00
❑225, Feb 1988 CB (w); CB (a) ... 5.00
❑226, May 1988 CB (w); CB, DR (a) .. 5.00
❑227, Jul 1988 CB (w); CB (a) ... 5.00
❑228, Aug 1988 CB (w); CB (a) ... 5.00
❑229, Sep 1988 CB (w); CB (a) ... 5.00
❑230, Oct 1988 CB (w); CB (a) ... 5.00
❑231, Nov 1988 DR (c); CB (w); CB (a) 5.00
❑232, Dec 1988 CB (w); CB (a) ... 5.00
❑233, Feb 1989 CB (w); CB (a) ... 5.00
❑234, May 1989 CB (w); CB (a) ... 5.00
❑235, Jul 1989 CB (w); DR (a) ... 5.00
❑236, Aug 1989 CB (w); CB (a) ... 5.00
❑237, Sep 1989 CB (w); CB (a) ... 5.00
❑238, Oct 1989 CB (w); CB (a) ... 5.00
❑239, Nov 1989 CB (w); CB (a) ... 5.00
❑240, Dec 1989 CB (w); CB (a) ... 5.00
❑241, Feb 1990 CB (w); CB, DR (a) ... 4.00
❑242, Apr 1990; double-sized CB (w); CB (a) ... 4.00
❑243, Jun 1990 ... 4.00
❑244, Jul 1990 ... 4.00
❑245, Aug 1990 ... 4.00
❑246, Sep 1990 ... 4.00
❑247, Oct 1990 ... 4.00
❑248, Nov 1990 ... 4.00
❑249, Dec 1990 ... 4.00
❑250, Jan 1991 CB (w); CB (a) ... 4.00
❑251, Feb 1991 CB (w); CB (a) ... 4.00
❑252, Mar 1991 ... 4.00
❑253, Apr 1991 CB (w); CB (a) ... 4.00
❑254, May 1991 CB (w); CB (a) ... 4.00
❑255, Jun 1991 CB (w); CB (a) ... 4.00
❑256, Jul 1991 CB (w); CB (a) ... 4.00
❑257, Aug 1991 ... 4.00
❑258, Sep 1991 CB (w); CB (a) ... 4.00
❑259, Oct 1991 ... 4.00
❑260, Nov 1991 ... 4.00
❑261, Dec 1991 DR (a) ... 2.50
❑262, Jan 1992 DR (a) ... 2.50
❑263, Feb 1992 DR (a) ... 2.50
❑264, Mar 1992 ... 2.50
❑265, Apr 1992 CB (w); CB (a) ... 2.50
❑266, May 1992 CB (w); CB (a) ... 2.50
❑267, Jun 1992; CB (w); CB (a); contains Duckburg map piece 3 of 9 2.50
❑268, Jul 1992; CB (w); CB (a); contains Duckburg map piece 6 of 9 2.50
❑269, Aug 1992; CB (w); CB (a); contains Duckburg map piece 9 of 9 2.50
❑270, Sep 1992; CB (w); CB (a); Olympics ... 2.50
❑271, Oct 1992 CB (w); CB (a) ... 2.50
❑272, Nov 1992 CB (w); CB (a) ... 2.50
❑273, Dec 1992 CB (w); CB (a) ... 2.50
❑274, Jan 1993 CB (w); CB (a) ... 2.50
❑275, Feb 1993 CB (w); CB (a) ... 2.50
❑276, Mar 1993 DR (a) ... 2.50
❑277, Apr 1993 CB (w); CB (a) ... 2.50
❑278, May 1993 CB (w); CB (a) ... 2.50
❑279, Jun 1993 CB (w); CB (a) ... 2.50
❑280, Jul 1993 ... 2.50
❑281, Aug 1993 DR (c); CB (w); CB (a) 2.50
❑282, Oct 1993 CB (w); CB (a) ... 2.50
❑283, Dec 1993 CB (w); CB (a) ... 2.50
❑284, Feb 1994 CB (w); CB (a) ... 2.50
❑285, Apr 1994 DR (a) ... 2.50
❑286, Jun 1994 DR (a) ... 2.50
❑287, Aug 1994 DR (a) ... 2.50
❑288, Oct 1994 DR (a) ... 2.50
❑289, Dec 1994 DR (a) ... 2.50
❑290, Feb 1995 DR (a) ... 2.50

N-MINT

❑291, Apr 1995 DR (a) ... 2.50
❑292, Jun 1995 DR (a) ... 2.50
❑293, Aug 1995 DR (a) ... 2.50
❑294, Oct 1995; DR (a); newsprint covers begin ... 2.50
❑295, Dec 1995 DR (a) ... 2.50
❑296, Feb 1996 DR (a) ... 2.50
❑297, Apr 1996 DR (a) ... 2.50
❑298, Jun 1996 ... 2.50
❑299, Aug 1996 ... 2.50
❑300, Oct 1996 ... 2.25
❑301, Dec 1996 ... 1.50
❑302, Feb 1997; CB (w); CB (a); reprints from WDC&S #297 ... 1.50
❑303, Apr 1997; newsprint covers end 1.50
❑304, Jun 1997; CB (w); CB (a); Reprints ... 1.50
❑305, Aug 1997; CB (w); CB (a); Reprints ... 1.50
❑306, Oct 1997 DR (c); DR (w); DR (a) 1.50
❑307, Dec 1997 ... 1.50
❑308, Feb 1998 ... 1.50
❑309, May 1998; prestige format begins ... 6.95
❑310, Jun 1998 ... 6.95
❑311, Jul 1998 ... 6.95
❑312, Aug 1998 ... 6.95
❑313, Sep 1998 ... 6.95
❑314, Oct 1998 ... 6.95
❑315, Nov 1998 ... 6.95
❑316, Dec 1998 ... 6.95
❑317, Jan 1999 ... 6.95
❑318, Feb 1999; series goes on hiatus; Gemstone resumes publishing in 2003 ... 6.95

UNCLE SCROOGE (GEMSTONE)

GEMSTONE

❑319, Jun 2003; prestige format ... 6.95
❑320, Jul 2003 ... 6.95
❑321, Aug 2003 ... 6.95
❑322, Sep 2003 ... 6.95
❑323, Oct 2003 ... 6.95
❑324, Nov 2003 ... 6.95
❑325, Dec 2003 ... 6.95
❑326, Jan 2004 ... 6.95
❑327, Feb 2004 ... 6.95
❑328, Mar 2004 ... 6.95
❑329, Apr 2004 ... 6.95
❑330, May 2004 ... 6.95
❑331, Jun 2004 ... 6.95
❑332, Jul 2004 ... 6.95
❑333, Aug 2004 ... 6.95
❑334, Sep 2004 ... 6.95
❑335, Oct 2004 ... 6.95
❑336, Nov 2004 ... 6.95
❑337, Dec 2004 ... 6.95
❑338, Jan 2005 ... 6.95
❑339, Feb 2005 ... 6.95
❑340, Mar 2005 ... 6.95
❑341, Apr 2005 ... 6.95
❑342, May 2005 ... 6.95
❑343, Jun 2005 ... 6.95
❑344, Jul 2005 ... 6.95
❑345, Aug 2005 ... 6.95
❑346, Sep 2005 ... 6.95
❑347, Oct 2005 ... 6.95
❑348, Nov 2005 ... 6.95
❑349, Dec 2005 ... 6.95

UNCLE SCROOGE ADVENTURES

GLADSTONE

❑1, Nov 1987 CB (a) ... 5.00
❑2, Dec 1987 CB (a) ... 3.00
❑3, Jan 1988 CB (a) ... 2.00
❑4, Apr 1988 CB (a) ... 2.00
❑5, Jun 1988 DR (a) ... 6.00
❑6, Aug 1988 CB (a) ... 2.00
❑7, Sep 1988 CB (a) ... 2.00
❑8, Oct 1988 CB (a) ... 2.00
❑9, Nov 1988 DR (a) ... 5.00
❑10, Dec 1988 CB (a) ... 2.00
❑11, Jan 1989 CB (a) ... 2.00
❑12, Mar 1989 CB (a) ... 2.00
❑13, Jun 1989 DR (c); CB (a) ... 2.00
❑14, Aug 1989 DR (a) ... 5.00
❑15, Sep 1989 CB (a) ... 2.00
❑16, Oct 1989 CB (a) ... 2.00
❑17, Nov 1989 CB (a) ... 2.00

Other grades: Multiply price above by 5/6 for VF/NM • 2/3 for VERY FINE • 1/3 for FINE • 1/5 for VERY GOOD • 1/8 for GOOD

Union (Mini-Series)

Strange soldier from another world's war

©Image

Union Jack

Fighting embodiment of the British spirit

©Marvel

Unity

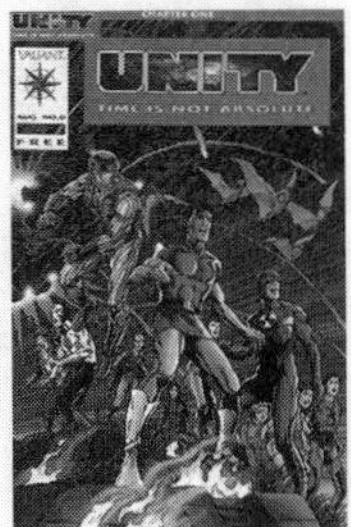

Very ambitious cross-over from Valiant

©Valiant

Universe X

Sequel limited series to Earth X

©Marvel

Unknown Soldier

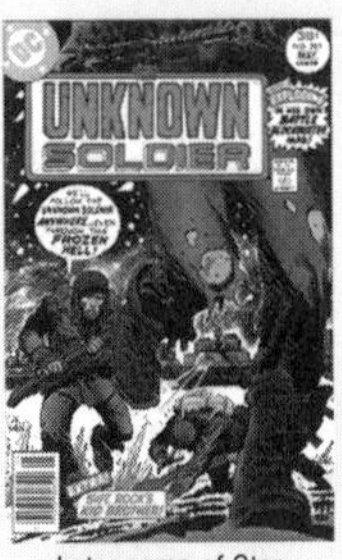

Later name of Star Spangled War Stories

©DC

N-MINT

- ❑18, Dec 1989 CB (a) 2.00
- ❑19, Jan 1990 DR (c); CB (a) 2.00
- ❑20, Mar 1990; double-sized CB, DR (a) 5.00
- ❑21, May 1990; double-sized CB, DR (a) 5.00
- ❑22, Sep 1993; CB (a); Reprints 1.50
- ❑23, Nov 1993; CB (a); Reprints 2.95
- ❑24, Jan 1994; CB (a); Reprints 1.50
- ❑25, Mar 1994; DR (c); CB (a); Reprints 1.50
- ❑26, May 1994; CB (a); Reprints 2.95
- ❑27, Jul 1994 DR (a); O: Junior Woodchucks Handbook. 1.50
- ❑28, Sep 1994; CB (a); A: Terries and Fermies. Reprints 2.95
- ❑29, Nov 1994 1.50
- ❑30, Jan 1995 2.95
- ❑31, Mar 1995 1.50
- ❑32, May 1995 1.50
- ❑33, Jul 1995; CB (w); CB (a); new story 2.95
- ❑34, Sep 1995 1.95
- ❑35, Nov 1995 1.95
- ❑36, Jan 1996 1.95
- ❑37, Mar 1996; newprint covers begin 1.50
- ❑38, May 1996 1.50
- ❑39, Aug 1996 1.50
- ❑40, Sep 1996 1.50
- ❑41, Nov 1996 1.95
- ❑42, Jan 1997 1.95
- ❑43, Feb 1997; CB (a); reprints The Queen of the Wild Dog Pack from US #62 1.50
- ❑44, Mar 1997 1.50
- ❑45, Apr 1997 1.50
- ❑46, May 1997; newprint covers end . 1.95
- ❑47, Jun 1997; CB (a); Reprints 1.95
- ❑48, Jul 1997 1.95
- ❑49, Aug 1997 1.95
- ❑50, Sep 1997; CB (a); Reprints 1.95
- ❑51, Oct 1997 DR (a) 1.95
- ❑52, Nov 1997 1.95
- ❑53, Dec 1997 1.95
- ❑54, Feb 1998 1.95

UNCLE SCROOGE AND DONALD DUCK
GOLD KEY

- ❑1, Jun 1965; Reprints stories from Four Color Comics #29 and 386 50.00

UNCLE SCROOGE & DONALD DUCK (WALT DISNEY'S...)
GLADSTONE

- ❑1, Jan 1998 2.00
- ❑2, Mar 1998 2.00

UNCLE SCROOGE AND MONEY
GOLD KEY

- ❑1, Mar 1967; CB (w); CB (a); Reprints story from Walt Disney's Comics #130; 10167-703 6.00

UNCLE SCROOGE COMICS DIGEST
GLADSTONE

- ❑1, Dec 1986; CB (a); reprints 3.00
- ❑2, Feb 1987; CB (a); reprints 2.00
- ❑3, Apr 1987; CB (a); reprints 2.00
- ❑4, Jun 1987; CB (a); reprints 2.00
- ❑5, Aug 1987; CB (a); reprints 2.00

UNCLE SCROOGE GOES TO DISNEYLAND (WALT DISNEY'S...)
GLADSTONE

- ❑1, Aug 1985; CB (a); Dell Giant 275.00
- ❑1/A, Aug 1985; digest 5.00
- ❑1/A/2nd; digest CB (a) 5.00
- ❑1/2nd CB (a) 6.00

UNCLE SCROOGE THE GOLDEN FLEECING (WALT DISNEY'S...)
WHITMAN

- ❑1; Reprints 8.00

UNCLE SLAM & FIRE DOG
ACTION PLANET

- ❑1, ca. 1997, b&w 2.95
- ❑2, b&w 2.95

UNCUT COMICS
UNCUT COMICS

- ❑1, Apr 1997, b&w; free handout; Origins 1.00
- ❑1/A, Feb 1997, b&w; non-slick cover 1.50
- ❑1/B, Feb 1997, b&w; non-slick alternate cover 1.50
- ❑2, May 1997, b&w; flip-book with alternate cover back-up 1.95

UNDERCOVER GENIE
DC

- ❑1, ca. 2003 14.95

UNDERDOG (CHARLTON)
CHARLTON

- ❑1, Jul 1970; poster 60.00
- ❑2, Sep 1970 38.00
- ❑3, Nov 1970 30.00
- ❑4, Jan 1971 30.00
- ❑5, Mar 1971 30.00
- ❑6, May 1971 25.00
- ❑7, Jul 1971 25.00
- ❑8, Sep 1971 25.00
- ❑9, Nov 1971 25.00
- ❑10, Jan 1972 25.00

UNDERDOG (GOLD KEY)
GOLD KEY

- ❑1 1975 35.00
- ❑2 1975 20.00
- ❑3 1975 12.00
- ❑4 1975 8.00
- ❑5 1976 8.00
- ❑6 1976 6.00
- ❑7, Jun 1976 6.00
- ❑8, Aug 1976 6.00
- ❑9, Oct 1976 6.00
- ❑10, Dec 1976 6.00
- ❑11, Feb 1976 5.00
- ❑12, Apr 1977 5.00
- ❑13, Jun 1977 5.00
- ❑14, Aug 1977 5.00
- ❑15, Oct 1977 5.00
- ❑16, Dec 1977 5.00
- ❑17, Feb 1978 5.00
- ❑18, Apr 1978 5.00
- ❑19, Jun 1978 5.00
- ❑20, Aug 1978 5.00
- ❑21, Oct 1978 4.00
- ❑22, Dec 1978 4.00
- ❑23, Feb 1979 4.00

UNDERDOG (SPOTLIGHT)
SPOTLIGHT

- ❑1, ca. 1987 2.50
- ❑2, ca. 1987 2.50

UNDERDOG (HARVEY)
HARVEY

- ❑1, Nov 1993; No creator credits listed 1.50
- ❑2, Jan 1993; No creator credits listed 1.50
- ❑3, Mar 1994; No creator credits listed 1.50
- ❑4, May 1994; No creator credits listed 1.50
- ❑5, Jul 1994; No creator credits listed 1.50
- ❑Summer 1, Oct 1993 2.25

UNDERDOG 3-D
BLACKTHORNE

- ❑1 2.50

UNDERGROUND
AIRCEL

- ❑1, b&w 1.70

UNDERGROUND (ANDREW VACHSS'...)
DARK HORSE

- ❑1, Nov 1993 3.95
- ❑2, Jan 1994 3.95
- ❑3, Mar 1994 3.95
- ❑4, May 1994 3.95

UNDERGROUND CLASSICS
RIP OFF

- ❑1, Dec 1985; Fabulous Furry Freak Brothers 6.00
- ❑2, Feb 1986; Dealer McDope 10.00
- ❑2/2nd 1986 2.00
- ❑2/3rd 1986 2.50
- ❑3, Mar 1986; Dealer McDope 8.00
- ❑3/2nd 2.00
- ❑4, Sep 1987 2.50
- ❑5, Nov 1987; Wonder Warthog 7.50
- ❑6, Feb 1988 5.00
- ❑7, Apr 1988 6.00
- ❑8, Jun 1988 5.00
- ❑9, Feb 1989; Art of Greg Irons 4.00
- ❑10; Jesus 4.00
- ❑11; Jesus 4.00
- ❑12, Jul 1990; Shelton 3-D 5.00
- ❑12/2nd 2.95
- ❑13; Jesus 4.00
- ❑14; Jesus 4.00
- ❑15 4.00

UNDERLORDS
EIDOLON ENTERTAINMENT

- ❑1 2005 2.95
- ❑2 2005 2.95
- ❑3 2005 2.95
- ❑4, Aug 2005 2.95

UNDERSEA AGENT
TOWER

- ❑1, Jan 1966 32.00
- ❑2, Apr 1966; Lt. Jones gains electrical powers 22.00

Other grades: Multiply price above by 5/6 for VF/NM • 2/3 for VERY FINE • 1/3 for FINE • 1/5 for VERY GOOD • 1/8 for GOOD

	N-MINT
❑3, Jun 1966	18.00
❑4, Aug 1966	18.00
❑5, Oct 1966	18.00
❑6, Mar 1967	18.00

UNDERSIDE
CALIBER

❑1	2.95

UNDERTAKER
CHAOS

❑0, Feb 1999; Collector's issue; Wizard	3.00
❑½, Mar 1999	4.00
❑1, Apr 1999; Drawn cover	4.00
❑1/A, Apr 1999; DFE red foil cover	6.00
❑1/B, Apr 1999; DFE red foil cover; Autographed	8.00
❑1/Variant, Apr 1999	4.00
❑2, May 1999	2.95
❑3, Jun 1999	2.95
❑4, Jul 1999	2.95
❑5, Aug 1999	2.95
❑6, Sep 1999	2.95
❑7, Oct 1999	2.95
❑8, Nov 1999	2.95
❑9, Dec 1999	2.95
❑10, Jan 2000	2.95
❑Holiday 1, Oct 1999; digest	2.95

UNDER TERRA
PREDAWN

❑2, b&w	2.45
❑3, b&w	2.45
❑4, b&w	2.45
❑5, b&w	2.45
❑6, b&w	1.75

UNDERWATER
DRAWN AND QUARTERLY

❑1, Aug 1994	2.95

UNDERWORLD
MARVEL

❑1, Mar 2006	2.99
❑2, May 2006	2.99
❑3, Jun 2006	2.99
❑4, Jul 2006	2.99
❑5, Aug 2006	2.99

UNDERWORLD (DC)
DC

❑1, Dec 1987	1.25
❑2, Jan 1988	1.25
❑3, Feb 1988	1.25
❑4, Mar 1988	1.25

UNDERWORLD (DEATH)
DEATH

❑1, b&w	2.00

UNDERWORLD: EVOLUTION
IDEA & DESIGN WORKS

❑1, Feb 2006	3.99

UNDERWORLD UNLEASHED
DC

❑1, Nov 1995 MWa (w); 1: Neron. D: Mongul. D: Boomerang. D: Weather Wizard. D: Mirror Master. D: Heat Wave. D: Captain Cold	3.50
❑2, Dec 1995 MWa (w)	3.25
❑3, Dec 1995 MWa (w)	3.25

UNDERWORLD UNLEASHED: ABYSS: HELL'S SENTINEL
DC

❑1, Dec 1995	2.95

UNDERWORLD UNLEASHED: APOKOLIPS: DARK UPRISING
DC

❑1, Nov 1995	1.95

UNDERWORLD UNLEASHED: BATMAN: DEVIL'S ASYLUM
DC

❑1 1995	2.95

UNDERWORLD UNLEASHED: PATTERNS OF FEAR
DC

❑1, Dec 1995	2.95

UNDIE DOG
HALLEY'S

❑1, b&w	1.50

UNEXPECTED
DC

	N-MINT
❑105, Feb 1968; Series continued from Tales of the Unexpected #104	30.00
❑106, Apr 1968	18.00
❑107, Jun 1968	18.00
❑108, Aug 1968	18.00
❑109, Oct 1968	18.00
❑110, Dec 1968	18.00
❑111, Feb 1969	18.00
❑112, Apr 1969	18.00
❑113, Jun 1969 CS (a)	18.00
❑114, Aug 1969	12.00
❑115, Oct 1969	12.00
❑116, Dec 1969	12.00
❑117, Feb 1970	12.00
❑118, Apr 1970 GT (a)	12.00
❑119, Jun 1970 BWr (a)	14.00
❑120, Aug 1970	12.00
❑121, Oct 1970 BWr (a)	16.00
❑122, Dec 1970	12.00
❑123, Feb 1971	12.00
❑124, Apr 1971	12.00
❑125, Jul 1971	12.00
❑126, Aug 1971	12.00
❑127, Sep 1971	12.00
❑128, Oct 1971 BWr (a)	14.00
❑129, Nov 1971	8.00
❑130, Dec 1971	8.00
❑131, Jan 1972 DD, NC (a)	8.00
❑132, Feb 1972	8.00
❑133, Mar 1972	8.00
❑134, Apr 1972	8.00
❑135, May 1972	8.00
❑136, Jun 1972	8.00
❑137, Jul 1972	8.00
❑138, Aug 1972	8.00
❑139, Sep 1972	8.00
❑140, Oct 1972 NC (c)	8.00
❑141, Nov 1972	8.00
❑142, Dec 1972	8.00
❑143, Jan 1973	8.00
❑144, Feb 1973	8.00
❑145, Mar 1973	8.00
❑146, Apr 1973	8.00
❑147, Jun 1973	8.00
❑148, Jul 1973	8.00
❑149, Aug 1973	8.00
❑150, Sep 1973	8.00
❑151, Oct 1973	8.00
❑152, Nov 1973	8.00
❑153, Dec 1973	8.00
❑154, Jan 1974	8.00
❑155, Feb 1974	8.00
❑156, Mar 1974	8.00
❑157, Jun 1974; 100 Page giant	14.00
❑158, Aug 1974; 100 Page giant	14.00
❑159, Oct 1974; 100 Page giant	14.00
❑160, Dec 1974; 100 Page giant MM (a)	14.00
❑161, Feb 1975; 100 Page giant	14.00
❑162, Mar 1975; 100 Page giant	14.00
❑163, Apr 1975	5.00
❑164, May 1975	5.00
❑165, Jun 1975	5.00
❑166, Jul 1975	5.00
❑167, Aug 1975	5.00
❑168, Sep 1975	5.00
❑169 1975	5.00
❑170, Dec 1975	5.00
❑171, Feb 1976	5.00
❑172, Apr 1976	5.00
❑173, Jun 1976	5.00
❑174, Aug 1976	5.00
❑175, Oct 1976	5.00
❑176, Dec 1976	5.00
❑177, Feb 1977	5.00
❑178, Apr 1977	5.00
❑179, Jun 1977	5.00
❑180, Aug 1977	5.00
❑181, Oct 1977	5.00
❑182, Dec 1977	5.00
❑183, Feb 1978	5.00
❑184, Apr 1978	5.00
❑185, Jun 1978	5.00
❑186, Aug 1978	5.00
❑187, Oct 1978	5.00
❑188, Dec 1978	5.00
❑189, Feb 1979	5.00
❑190, Apr 1979	5.00
❑191, Jun 1979 MR (a)	6.00
❑192, Aug 1979	4.00
❑193, Oct 1979	4.00
❑194, Dec 1979	4.00
❑195, Feb 1980	4.00
❑196, Mar 1980	4.00
❑197, Apr 1980	4.00
❑198, May 1980	4.00
❑199, Jun 1980	4.00
❑200, Jul 1980	4.00
❑201, Aug 1980	4.00
❑202, Sep 1980	4.00
❑203, Oct 1980	4.00
❑204, Nov 1980	4.00
❑205, Dec 1980	4.00
❑206, Jan 1981	4.00
❑207, Feb 1981	4.00
❑208, Mar 1981	4.00
❑209, Apr 1981	4.00
❑210, May 1981	4.00
❑211, Jun 1981	4.00
❑212, Jul 1981	4.00
❑213, Aug 1981	4.00
❑214, Sep 1981	4.00
❑215, Oct 1981	4.00
❑216, Nov 1981	4.00
❑217, Dec 1981	4.00
❑218, Jan 1982	4.00
❑219, Feb 1982	4.00
❑220, Mar 1982	4.00
❑221, Apr 1982	4.00
❑222, May 1982	4.00

UNFORGIVEN
MYTHIC

❑1	2.75

UNFUNNIES (MARK MILLAR'S)
AVATAR

❑1, Jan 2004	5.00
❑2, Mar 2004	3.50

UNFUNNY X-CONS
PARODY

❑1, Sep 1992; three variant covers (X, Y, Z)	2.50
❑1/2nd; 2nd Printing with trading card	2.50

UNHOLY (BRIAN PULIDO'S ...)
AVATAR

❑1 2005	3.99
❑1/Foil 2005	5.00
❑1/Platinum 2005	10.00
❑1/Haunted 2005	5.99
❑1/Premium 2005	8.00
❑1/Wraparound 2005	5.00
❑2 2005	3.50

UNICORN ISLE
APPLE

❑1, Oct 1986, b&w	2.00
❑2, Nov 1986, b&w	2.00
❑3, Dec 1986, b&w	2.00
❑4, Jan 1987	2.00
❑5, Feb 1987, b&w; While planned as a 12-issue series, #6-12 do not exist	2.00

UNICORN KING
KZ COMICS

❑1, Dec 1986, b&w	2.00

UNION (MINI-SERIES)
IMAGE

❑0, Jul 1994	2.50
❑0/A, Jul 1994; Variant edition cover; alternate cover	2.50
❑1, Jun 1993; Foil-embossed cover	2.50
❑2, Oct 1993	1.95
❑3, Dec 1993	1.95
❑4, Mar 1994	1.95

UNION
IMAGE

❑1, Feb 1995	2.50
❑2, Mar 1995	2.50
❑3, Apr 1995	2.50
❑4, May 1995; with cards	2.50
❑5, Jun 1995	2.50
❑6, Jul 1995	2.50
❑7, Aug 1995	2.50

Untold Tales of Spider-Man

Excellent title filled in the early blanks

©Marvel

Usagi Yojimbo (Vol. 1)

Stan Sakai's wonderful samurai rabbit tale

©Fantagraphics

U.S. War Machine 2.0

Chuck Austen mature-readers title

©Marvel

V

Based on the 1980s NBC TV series

©DC

Valiant Vision Starter Kit

Full-color variant on 3-D comics

©Valiant

	N-MINT
❑8, Oct 1995	2.50
❑9, Feb 1996; Story continued in Union: Final Vengeance; covers says Dec, indicia says Feb	2.50

UNION: FINAL VENGEANCE
IMAGE

❑1, Oct 1997; concludes story from Union #9	2.50

UNION JACK
MARVEL

❑1, Dec 1998; gatefold summary	2.99
❑2, Jan 1999; gatefold summary	2.99
❑3, Feb 1999	2.99

UNION JACKS
ANACOM

❑1, b&w	2.00

UNITY
VALIANT

❑0, Aug 1992; Blue cover (regular edition); BL (a); Blue cover (regular edition)	5.00
❑0/Red, Aug 1992	75.00
❑1, Oct 1992 BL (w); BL (a)	4.00
❑1/Gold, Oct 1992; Gold edition BL (w); BL (a)	10.00
❑1/Platinum, Oct 1992; Platinum edition BL (w); BL (a)	12.00
❑Yearbook 1; Yearbook 1; A: X-O Manowar. A: Solar. a.k.a. Unity: The Lost Chapter; cardstock cover	3.95

UNITY: THE LOST CHAPTER
VALIANT

❑1, Feb 1995	5.00

UNITY 2000
ACCLAIM

❑1, Nov 1999 JSn (a)	2.50
❑1/A, Nov 1999	5.00
❑2, Dec 1999 JSn (a)	2.50
❑3, Jan 2000; JSn (a); series canceled	2.50

UNIVERSAL MONSTERS: DRACULA
DARK HORSE

❑1 1993; Based on the classic Universal pictures film	4.95

UNIVERSAL MONSTERS: FRANKENSTEIN
DARK HORSE

❑1 1993; Based on the classic Universal pictures film	3.95

UNIVERSAL MONSTERS: THE CREATURE FROM THE BLACK LAGOON
DARK HORSE

❑1, Aug 1993	4.95

UNIVERSAL MONSTERS: THE MUMMY
DARK HORSE

❑1 1993; Based on the classic Universal pictures film	4.95

UNIVERSAL PICTURES PRESENTS DRACULA
DELL

❑1, Sep 1963	160.00

UNIVERSAL SOLDIER
NOW

	N-MINT
❑1, Sep 1992, newsstand	1.95
❑1/Direct ed., Sep 1992, Hologram cover; direct sale	2.50
❑1/Variant, Sep 1992, Waldenbooks; has UPC box and hologram	2.50
❑2, Oct 1992, newsstand	1.95
❑2/Direct ed., Oct 1992, direct-sale	2.50
❑3, Nov 1992, newsstand	1.95
❑3/Direct ed., Nov 1992, uncensored.	2.50

UNIVERSE
IMAGE

❑1, Aug 2001	2.50
❑2, Oct 2001	2.50
❑3, Nov 2001	2.50
❑4, Jan 2002	2.50
❑5, Mar 2002	2.50
❑6, Apr 2002	2.50
❑7, Apr 2002	2.50
❑8, Jul 2002	4.95

UNIVERSE X
MARVEL

❑0, Sep 2000; Cardstock cover; follows events of Earth X	3.99
❑1, Oct 2000; cardstock cover	3.50
❑2, Nov 2000; cardstock cover	3.50
❑3, Dec 2000; cardstock cover	3.50
❑4, Jan 2001; cardstock cover	3.50
❑5, Feb 2001; cardstock cover	3.50
❑6, Mar 2001; cardstock cover	3.50
❑7, Apr 2001; cardstock cover	3.50
❑8, May 2001; cardstock cover	3.50
❑9, Jun 2001	3.50
❑10, Jul 2001	3.50
❑11, Aug 2001	3.50
❑12, Sep 2001	3.50
❑X, Nov 2001	3.99

UNIVERSE X: BEASTS
MARVEL

❑1, Jun 2001	3.99

UNIVERSE X: CAP
MARVEL

❑1, Feb 2001 ARo (c); TY (a); D: Captain America.	5.00

UNIVERSE X: IRON MEN
MARVEL

❑1, Sep 2001	3.99

UNIVERSE X: OMNIBUS
MARVEL

❑1, Jun 2001	3.99

UNIVERSE X: SPIDEY
MARVEL

❑1, Jan 2001 ARo (c); BG (a)	10.00
❑1/A, Jan 2001; ARo (c); BG (a); Dynamic Forces variant	6.00
❑1/B, Jan 2001; ARo (c); BG (a); Dynamic Forces variant sketch cover	10.00
❑1/C, Jan 2001; recalled edition with potentially libelous statement in background of one panel ARo (c); BG (a)	90.00

UNKNOWN SOLDIER
DC

	N-MINT
❑205, May 1977	5.00
❑206, Jul 1977	5.00
❑207, Sep 1977 AM (c); AM, RE (a)	5.00
❑208, Oct 1977	5.00
❑209, Nov 1977 JKu (c); FT, JKu (a)	5.00
❑210, Dec 1977 JKu (c)	5.00
❑211, Jan 1978 JKu (c); JKu, RH (a)	4.00
❑212, Feb 1978 JKu (c)	4.00
❑213, Mar 1978	4.00
❑214, Apr 1978 JKu (c); RT (a); A: Mademoiselle Marie.	4.00
❑215, May 1978 JKu (c); JKu (a)	4.00
❑216, Jun 1978 RT (a)	4.00
❑217, Jul 1978 JKu (c); JKu (a)	4.00
❑218, Aug 1978	4.00
❑219, Sep 1978 JKu (c); JKu, FM, RT (a)	4.00
❑220, Oct 1978 JKu (c); JKu, RE (a)	4.00
❑221, Nov 1978 RT (a)	4.00
❑222, Dec 1978 JKu (c); JKu (a)	4.00
❑223, Jan 1979 RT (a)	4.00
❑224, Feb 1979 JKu (c); DA, RT (a)	4.00
❑225, Mar 1979	4.00
❑226, Apr 1979 JKu (c); JKu (a)	4.00
❑227, May 1979 JKu (c); JKu (a)	4.00
❑228, Jun 1979 JKu (c); JKu (a)	4.00
❑229, Jul 1979 JKu (c); JKu (a)	4.00
❑230, Aug 1979	3.00
❑231, Sep 1979 JKu (c); JKu (a)	3.00
❑232, Oct 1979 JKu (c); JKu (a)	3.00
❑233, Nov 1979 JKu (c); JKu (a)	3.00
❑234, Dec 1979	3.00
❑235, Jan 1980 RT (a)	3.00
❑236, Feb 1980	3.00
❑237, Mar 1980	3.00
❑238, Apr 1980	3.00
❑239, May 1980	3.00
❑240, Jun 1980	3.00
❑241, Jul 1980 JKu (c); JKu (a)	3.00
❑242, Aug 1980 JKu (c)	3.00
❑243, Sep 1980 RE (a)	3.00
❑244, Oct 1980 JKu (c); TY, RE (a); A: Captain Storm.	3.00
❑245, Nov 1980 RE (a)	3.00
❑246, Dec 1980	3.00
❑247, Jan 1981 JKu (c); JKu (a)	3.00
❑248, Feb 1981 O: Unknown Soldier.	5.00
❑249, Mar 1981 JKu (c); JKu (a); O: Unknown Soldier.	5.00
❑250, Apr 1981	3.00
❑251, May 1981 JSe (a)	3.00
❑252, Jun 1981 JSe (a)	3.00
❑253, Jul 1981 JKu (c); JSe (a)	3.00
❑254, Aug 1981	3.00
❑255, Sep 1981	3.00
❑256, Oct 1981	3.00
❑257, Nov 1981 JKu (c); JKu (a); O: Capt. Storm. A: John F. Kennedy.	3.00
❑258, Dec 1981 DS (a); A: John F. Kennedy.	3.00
❑259, Jan 1982 DS (a); A: John F. Kennedy.	3.00
❑260, Feb 1982 JKu (c); RE (a)	3.00

Other grades: Multiply price above by 5/6 for VF/NM • 2/3 for VERY FINE • 1/3 for FINE • 1/5 for VERY GOOD • 1/8 for GOOD

N-MINT

❑261, Mar 1982 RE (a) 3.00
❑262, Apr 1982 3.00
❑263, May 1982 3.00
❑264, Jun 1982 JKu (c); JKu, DS (a).. 3.00
❑265, Jul 1982 3.00
❑266, Aug 1982 3.00
❑267, Sep 1982 3.00
❑268, Oct 1982; JKu (c); JKu (a); D: Chat Noir. D: Hitler. D: The Unknown Soldier. Fall of Berlin 5.00

UNKNOWN SOLDIER (MINI-SERIES)
DC

❑1, Win 1988 O: Unknown Soldier 2.50
❑2, Hol 1988 2.50
❑3, Jan 1989 2.50
❑4, Mar 1989 2.50
❑5, Apr 1989 2.50
❑6, May 1989 2.50
❑7, Jul 1989 2.50
❑8, Aug 1989 2.50
❑9, Sep 1989 2.50
❑10, Oct 1989 2.50
❑11, Nov 1989 2.50
❑12, Dec 1989 2.50

UNKNOWN SOLDIER (MINI-SERIES)
DC / VERTIGO

❑1, Apr 1997 2.50
❑2, May 1997 2.50
❑3, Jun 1997 2.50
❑4, Jul 1997 2.50

UNKNOWN WORLDS
ACG

❑1, Aug 1960 90.00
❑2, Sep 1960 60.00
❑3, Oct 1960 45.00
❑4, Dec 1960 40.00
❑5, Feb 1961 40.00
❑6, Mar 1961 35.00
❑7, Apr 1961 35.00
❑8, Jun 1961 35.00
❑9, Aug 1961; Dinosaurs 50.00
❑10, Sep 1961 35.00
❑11, Oct 1961 28.00
❑12, Dec 1961 28.00
❑13, Feb 1962 28.00
❑14, Mar 1962 28.00
❑15, Apr 1962 28.00
❑16, Jun 1962 28.00
❑17, Aug 1962 28.00
❑18, Sep 1962 28.00
❑19, Oct 1962 28.00
❑20, Dec 1962 28.00
❑21, Feb 1963 20.00
❑22, Mar 1963 20.00
❑23, Apr 1963 20.00
❑24, Jun 1963 20.00
❑25, Aug 1963 20.00
❑26, Sep 1963 20.00
❑27, Oct 1963 20.00
❑28, Dec 1963 20.00
❑29, Feb 1964 20.00
❑30, Mar 1964 20.00
❑31, Apr 1964; avg sales of 143,258; cites 300,000 avg press run; Statement of Ownership for 1963 appears 16.00
❑32, Jun 1964 16.00
❑33, Aug 1964 16.00
❑34, Sep 1964 16.00
❑35, Oct 1964 16.00
❑36, Dec 1964 JCr (a) 16.00
❑37, Feb 1965 16.00
❑38, Mar 1965 16.00
❑39, Apr 1965 16.00
❑40, Jun 1965 16.00
❑41, Aug 1965 12.00
❑42, Sep 1965 12.00
❑43, Oct 1965 12.00
❑44, Dec 1965 12.00
❑45, Feb 1966 12.00
❑46, Mar 1966 12.00
❑47, Apr 1966 AW (a) 12.00
❑48, Jun 1966 12.00
❑49, Aug 1966 SD (a) 12.00
❑50, Nov 1966 SD (a) 12.00
❑51, Oct 1966 12.00
❑52, Dec 1966 12.00
❑53, Feb 1967 12.00
❑54, Mar 1967 12.00
❑55, Apr 1967 12.00
❑56, Jun 1967 12.00
❑57, Aug 1967 12.00

UNKNOWN WORLDS OF FRANK BRUNNER
ECLIPSE

❑1, Aug 1985 1.75
❑2, Aug 1985 1.75

UNKNOWN WORLDS OF SCIENCE FICTION
MARVEL

❑1, Jan 1975, b&w; magazine 12.00
❑2, Mar 1975, b&w; magazine 7.00
❑3, May 1975, b&w; magazine 7.00
❑4, Jul 1975, b&w; magazine 7.00
❑5, Sep 1975, b&w; magazine 7.00
❑6, Nov 1975, b&w; magazine 7.00
❑Special 1 1976, Reprints 10.00

UNLEASHED!
TRIUMPHANT

❑1 2.50

UNLIMITED ACCESS
MARVEL

❑1, Dec 1997, A: Wonder Woman. A: Spider-Man. A: Juggernaut. crossover with DC 2.50
❑2, Jan 1998, A: X-Men. A: Legion of Super-Heroes. crossover with DC... 2.00
❑3, Feb 1998, A: Justice League of America. A: Avengers. crossover with DC 2.00
❑4, Mar 1998, crossover with DC; new Amalgams 3.00

UNSUPERVISED EXISTENCE
FANTAGRAPHICS

❑1, b&w 2.00
❑2, b&w 2.00
❑3 2.00
❑4 2.00
❑5 2.00
❑6 2.00
❑7 2.00
❑7/2nd 2.00

UNTAMED
MARVEL / EPIC

❑1, Jun 1993; Embossed cover 2.50
❑2, Jul 1993 1.95
❑3, Aug 1993 1.95

UNTAMED LOVE (FRANK FRAZETTA'S...)
FANTAGRAPHICS

❑1, Nov 1987 2.00

UNTOLD LEGEND OF CAPTAIN MARVEL
MARVEL

❑1, Apr 1997 2.50
❑2, May 1997 2.50
❑3, Jun 1997 2.50

UNTOLD LEGEND OF THE BATMAN
DC

❑1, Jul 1980 JBy, JA (a); O: Batman. . 3.00
❑2, Aug 1980 JA (a) 2.00
❑3, Sep 1980 JA (a) 2.00

UNTOLD ORIGIN OF FEMFORCE
AC

❑1 1989 4.95

UNTOLD ORIGIN OF MS. VICTORY
AC

❑1, Dec 1989, b&w 2.50

UNTOLD TALES OF CHASTITY
CHAOS

❑1, Nov 2000 2.95

UNTOLD TALES OF LADY DEATH
CHAOS

❑1, Nov 2000 2.95

UNTOLD TALES OF PURGATORI
CHAOS

❑1, Nov 2000 2.95

UNTOLD TALES OF SPIDER-MAN
MARVEL

❑-1, Jul 1997; JR (a); Flashback 1.00
❑1, Sep 1995 KB (w); O: Spider-Man. 1.50
❑2, Oct 1995 KB (w) 1.25
❑3, Nov 1995 KB (w); V: Sandman 1.25
❑4, Dec 1995; KB (w); V: J. Jonah Jameson. Flip book with Avengers Unplugged #2 1.00
❑5, Jan 1996 KB (w); V: Vulture 1.00
❑6, Feb 1996 KB (w); A: Human Torch. 1.00
❑7, Mar 1996; KB (w); O: Electro. Flip book with Fantastic Four Unplugged #4 1.00
❑8, Apr 1996; KB (w); V: Enforcers. Flip book with Avengers Unplugged #4 . 1.00
❑9, May 1996 KB (w); V: Lizard 1.00
❑10, Jun 1996 KB (w) 1.00
❑11, Jul 1996 KB (w) 1.00
❑12, Aug 1996 KB (w); O: Betty Brant. 1.00
❑13, Sep 1996 KB (w); D: Bluebird. V: Black Knight 1.00
❑14, Oct 1996 KB (w) 1.00
❑15, Nov 1996 KB (w) 1.00
❑16, Dec 1996 KB (w); A: Mary Jane.. 1.00
❑17, Jan 1997 KB (w); AW (a); O: Hawkeye. A: Hawkeye. V: Hawkeye. 1.00
❑18, Feb 1997 KB (w); AW (a); A: Headsman. V: Headsman 1.00
❑19, Mar 1997; KB (w); AW (a); V: Doctor Octopus. Flip book with Uncanny Origins #7 1.00
❑20, Apr 1997; KB (w); AW (a); O: The Vulture. V: Vulture. Flip book with Uncanny Origins #8 1.00
❑21, May 1997 A: X-Men 1.00
❑22, Jun 1997 1.00
❑23, Aug 1997 V: Crime Master 1.00
❑24, Sep 1997 BMc (a) 1.00
❑25, Oct 1997; BMc (a); V: Green Goblin. cover says Sep, indicia says Oct 1.00
❑Annual 1996, ca. 1996; KB (w); GK, KJ (a); A: Namor. A: Fantastic Four. Untold Tales of Spider-Man '96 1.95
❑Annual 1997, ca. 1997; Untold Tales of Spider-Man '97 1.95

UNTOLD TALES OF THE NEW UNIVERSE: JUSTICE
MARVEL

❑1, May 2006 3.99

UNTOLD TALES OF THE NEW UNIVERSE: D.P. 7
MARVEL

❑1, Jun 2006 3.99

UNTOLD TALES OF THE NEW UNIVERSE: NIGHTMASK
MARVEL

❑1, May 2006 3.99

UNTOLD TALES OF THE NEW UNIVERSE: PSI-FORCE
MARVEL

❑1, Jun 2006 3.99

UNTOLD TALES OF THE NEW UNIVERSE: STAR BRAND
MARVEL

❑1, May 2006 3.99

UNTOUCHABLES (DELL)
DELL

❑3, Jul 1962 50.00
❑4, Aug 1962 50.00

UNTOUCHABLES
CALIBER

❑1, Aug 1997 2.95
❑2, Sep 1997 2.95
❑3, Oct 1997 2.95
❑4, Nov 1997 2.95

UNTOUCHABLES (EASTERN)
EASTERN

❑1 1.00
❑2 1.00

UP FROM BONDAGE
FANTAGRAPHICS / EROS

❑1, b&w 2.95

UP FROM THE DEEP
RIP OFF

❑1, ca. 1971 3.00

Other grades: Multiply price above by 5/6 for VF/NM • 2/3 for VERY FINE • 1/3 for FINE • 1/5 for VERY GOOD • 1/8 for GOOD

Valor (DC)

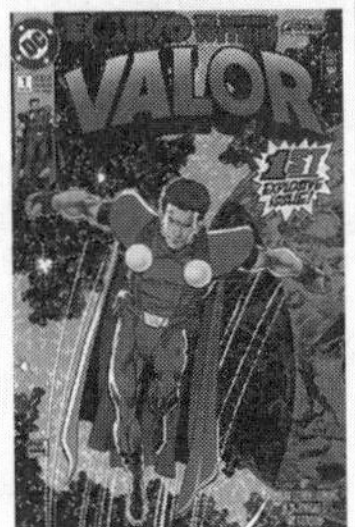

Interstellar teen-ager becomes super-hero
©DC

Vampirella (Magazine)

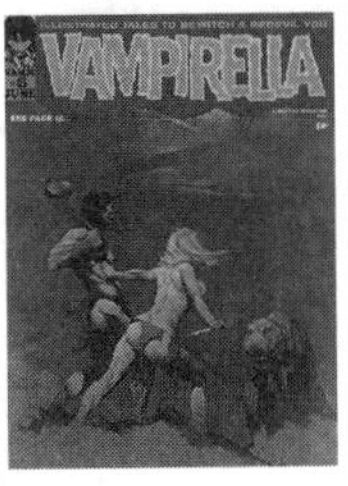

Magazine became cult phenomenon
©Warren

Vampirella Classic

Revisiting the stories of yesteryear
©Harris

Vampirella Monthly

One cover was never enough
©Harris

Vampirella's Summer Nights

Followed the events of Morning in America
©Harris

N-MINT

URBAN HIPSTER
ALTERNATIVE

❑1, Oct 1998, b&w ... 2.95

URBAN LEGENDS
DARK HORSE

❑1 1993, b&w ... 3.00

UROTSUKIDOJI: LEGEND OF THE OVERFIEND
CPM

❑1, Jul 1998 ... 2.95
❑2, Aug 1998 ... 2.95
❑3, Sep 1998 ... 2.95

URTH 4
CONTINUITY

❑1, May 1989 ... 2.00
❑2, Apr 1990 ... 2.00
❑3, Oct 1990 ... 2.00
❑4, Dec 1990 ... 2.00

URZA-MISHRA WAR ON THE WORLD OF MAGIC: THE GATHERING
ACCLAIM / ARMADA

❑1, Sep 1996; squarebound; polybagged with Soldevi Steam Beast card ... 5.95
❑2, Sep 1996; squarebound; polybagged with Soldevi Steam Beast and Phyrexian War Beast cards ... 5.95

U.S. 1
MARVEL

❑1, May 1983 HT (a); O: U.S. 1. ... 1.00
❑2, Jun 1983 HT (a) ... 1.00
❑3, Jul 1983 FS (a) ... 1.00
❑4, Aug 1983 FS (a) ... 1.00
❑5, Sep 1983 FS (a) ... 1.00
❑6, Oct 1983 FS (a) ... 1.00
❑7, Dec 1983 FS (a) ... 1.00
❑8, Feb 1984 FS (a) ... 1.00
❑9, Apr 1984 ... 1.00
❑10, Jun 1984 FS (a) ... 1.00
❑11, Aug 1984 FS (a) ... 1.00
❑12, Oct 1984 SD (a) ... 1.00

U.S.AGENT
MARVEL

❑1, Jun 1993 ... 2.00
❑2, Jul 1993 ... 2.00
❑3, Aug 1993 ... 2.00
❑4, Sep 1993 ... 2.00

USAGENT (2ND SERIES)
MARVEL

❑1, Aug 2001 ... 2.99
❑2, Sep 2001 ... 2.99
❑3, Oct 2001 ... 2.99

USAGI YOJIMBO (VOL. 1)
FANTAGRAPHICS

❑1, Jul 1987, b&w ... 8.00
❑1/2nd, Jul 1987 ... 2.50
❑2, Sep 1987, b&w ... 5.00
❑3, Oct 1987, b&w ... 5.00
❑4, Nov 1987, b&w ... 3.50
❑5, Jan 1988, b&w ... 3.50
❑6, Feb 1988, b&w ... 3.00
❑7, Mar 1988, b&w ... 3.00
❑8, May 1988, b&w ... 3.00

N-MINT

❑9, Jul 1988, b&w ... 3.00
❑10, Aug 1988, b&w A: Teenage Mutant Ninja Turtles. ... 3.00
❑10/2nd, Aug 1988 ... 2.00
❑11, Sep 1988, b&w SA (a) ... 2.50
❑12, Oct 1988, b&w ... 2.50
❑13, Jan 1989, b&w; indicia says Jan 88; a misprint ... 2.50
❑14, Jan 1989, b&w; indicia says Jan 89 ... 2.50
❑15, Mar 1989, b&w ... 2.50
❑16, May 1989, b&w ... 2.50
❑17, Jul 1989, b&w ... 2.50
❑18, Oct 1989, b&w ... 2.50
❑19, Dec 1989, b&w ... 2.50
❑20, Feb 1990, b&w ... 2.50
❑21, Apr 1990, b&w ... 2.50
❑22, May 1990, b&w ... 2.50
❑23, Jul 1990, b&w ... 2.50
❑24, Sep 1990, b&w; Lone Goat & Kid ... 2.50
❑25, Nov 1990, b&w ... 2.50
❑26, Jan 1991, b&w; indicia says Jan 90; another misprint ... 2.50
❑27, Mar 1991, b&w ... 2.50
❑28, May 1991, b&w ... 2.50
❑29, Jul 1991, b&w ... 2.50
❑30, Sep 1991, b&w; back cover reproduces front cover without logos ... 2.50
❑31, Nov 1991, b&w ... 2.50
❑32, Feb 1992, b&w ... 2.50
❑33, Apr 1992, b&w ... 2.50
❑34, Jun 1992, b&w ... 2.50
❑35, Aug 1992, b&w ... 2.50
❑36, Nov 1992, b&w ... 2.50
❑37, Feb 1993, b&w ... 2.50
❑38, Mar 1993, b&w ... 2.50
❑Special 1, Nov 1989; Color special #1 ... 3.50
❑Special 2, Oct 1991; Color special #2 ... 3.50
❑Special 3, Oct 1992; Color special #3 ... 3.50
❑Summer 1, Oct 1986, b&w; SA (a); introduction by Mark Evanier ... 5.00

USAGI YOJIMBO (VOL. 2)
MIRAGE

❑1, Mar 1993 A: Teenage Mutant Ninja Turtles. ... 4.50
❑2, May 1993 A: Teenage Mutant Ninja Turtles. ... 3.50
❑3, Jul 1993 A: Teenage Mutant Ninja Turtles. ... 3.50
❑4, Sep 1993 ... 3.50
❑5, Nov 1993 ... 3.50
❑6, Jan 1994 ... 3.00
❑7, Apr 1994 ... 3.00
❑8, Jun 1994 ... 3.00
❑9, Aug 1994 ... 3.00
❑10, Oct 1994 ... 3.00
❑11, Dec 1994 ... 2.75
❑12, Feb 1995 ... 2.75
❑13, Apr 1995 ... 2.75
❑14, Jun 1995 ... 2.75
❑15, Aug 1995 1: Lionheart (in color). ... 2.75
❑16, Oct 1995 ... 2.75

USAGI YOJIMBO (VOL. 3)
DARK HORSE

❑1, Apr 1996 ... 4.00

N-MINT

❑2, May 1996, Cover marked 2 of 3 ... 3.00
❑3, Jun 1996 ... 3.00
❑4, Jul 1996 ... 3.00
❑5, Aug 1996 ... 3.00
❑6, Oct 1996 ... 3.00
❑7, Nov 1996 ... 3.00
❑8, Dec 1996 ... 3.00
❑9, Jan 1997 ... 3.00
❑10, Feb 1997 ... 3.00
❑11, Mar 1997 ... 3.00
❑12, Apr 1997, b&w ... 3.00
❑13, Aug 1997, b&w ... 3.00
❑14, Sep 1997, b&w ... 2.95
❑15, Oct 1997, b&w ... 2.95
❑16, Nov 1997 ... 2.95
❑17, Jan 1998 ... 2.95
❑18, Feb 1998 ... 2.95
❑19, Mar 1998 ... 2.95
❑20 1998 ... 2.95
❑21, Jun 1998 ... 2.95
❑22, Jul 1998 ... 2.95
❑23, Sep 1998 ... 2.95
❑24, Oct 1998 ... 2.95
❑25, Nov 1998, Momo-Usagi-Taro ... 2.95
❑26, Jan 1999 ... 2.95
❑27, Feb 1999 ... 2.95
❑28, Apr 1999 ... 2.95
❑29, May 1999 ... 2.95
❑30, Jul 1999 ... 2.95
❑31, Sep 1999 ... 2.95
❑32, Oct 1999 ... 2.95
❑33, Nov 1999 ... 2.95
❑34, Dec 1999 ... 2.95
❑35, Jan 2000 ... 2.95
❑36, Feb 2000 ... 2.95
❑37, Apr 2000 ... 2.95
❑38, May 2000 ... 2.95
❑39, Jul 2000 ... 2.95
❑40, Aug 2000 ... 2.95
❑41, Sep 2000 ... 2.95
❑42, Oct 2000 ... 2.95
❑43, Nov 2000 ... 2.95
❑44, Dec 2000 ... 2.95
❑45, Jan 2001 ... 2.99
❑46, Mar 2001 ... 2.99
❑47, Apr 2001 ... 2.99
❑48, May 2001 ... 2.99
❑49, Jun 2001 ... 2.99
❑50, Jul 2001 ... 2.99
❑51, Aug 2001 ... 2.99
❑52, Oct 2001 ... 2.99
❑53, Dec 2001 ... 2.99
❑54, Jan 2002 ... 2.99
❑55, Feb 2002 ... 2.99
❑56, Mar 2002 ... 2.99
❑57, Apr 2002 ... 2.99
❑58, May 2002 ... 2.99
❑59, Jul 2002 ... 2.99
❑60, Aug 2002 ... 2.99
❑61, Oct 2002 ... 2.99
❑62, Nov 2002 ... 2.99
❑63, Jan 2003 ... 2.99
❑64, Feb 2003 ... 2.99
❑65, Mar 2003 ... 2.99

	N-MINT
❑66, Jun 2003	2.99
❑67, Jul 2003	2.99
❑68, Jul 2003	2.99
❑69, Oct 2003	2.99
❑70, Nov 2003	2.99
❑71, Nov 2003	2.99
❑72, Dec 2004	2.99
❑73, Feb 2004	2.99
❑74, Mar 2004	2.99
❑75, Apr 2004	2.99
❑76, May 2004	2.99
❑77, Aug 2004	2.99
❑78, Sep 2004	2.99
❑79, Oct 2004	2.99
❑80, Nov 2004, b&w	2.99
❑81, Dec 2004	2.99
❑82 2005	2.99
❑83, Jun 2005	2.99
❑84, Jul 2005	2.99
❑85, Aug 2005	2.99
❑86, Sep 2005	2.99
❑87 2005	2.99
❑88 2005	2.99
❑90, Feb 2006	2.99
❑91, Mar 2006	2.99
❑92, Apr 2006	2.99
❑93, May 2006	2.99
❑94, Jun 2006	2.99
❑Special 4, ca. 1997 Special	3.50

U.S. FIGHTING MEN
SUPER

❑10, ca. 1963 JSe (c)	15.00
❑11	15.00
❑12	12.00
❑13	12.00
❑14	12.00
❑15, ca. 1964 RH (a)	12.00
❑16, ca. 1964	12.00
❑17, ca. 1964	12.00
❑18	12.00

U.S. WAR MACHINE 2.0

❑1, Sep 2003	2.99
❑2, Sep 2003	2.99
❑3, Sep 2003	2.99

V
DC

❑1, Feb 1985; Cl (a); Based on TV series	1.50
❑2, Mar 1985 Cl (a)	1.00
❑3, Apr 1985 Cl (a)	1.00
❑4, May 1985 Cl (a)	1.00
❑5, Jun 1985	1.00
❑6, Jul 1985 Cl (a)	1.00
❑7, Aug 1985 Cl (a)	1.00
❑8, Sep 1985 Cl (a)	1.00
❑9, Oct 1985 Cl (a)	1.00
❑10, Nov 1985 Cl (a)	1.00
❑11, Dec 1985 Cl (a)	1.00
❑12, Jan 1986 Cl (a)	1.00
❑13, Feb 1986 Cl (a)	1.00
❑14, Mar 1986 Cl (a)	1.00
❑15, Apr 1986 Cl (a)	1.00
❑16, May 1986 Cl (a)	1.00
❑17, Jun 1986 DG (a)	1.00
❑18, Jul 1986 DG (a)	1.00

VAGABOND
IMAGE

❑1/A, Aug 2000; Pat Lee cover	2.95
❑1/B, Aug 2000	2.95

VAGABOND (VIZ)
VIZ

❑1, Dec 2001	4.95
❑2, Dec 2001	4.95
❑3, Jan 2002	4.95
❑4, Feb 2002	4.95
❑5, Mar 2002	4.95
❑6, Apr 2002	4.95
❑7, May 2002	4.95
❑8, Jun 2002	4.95
❑9, Jul 2002	4.95
❑10, Aug 2002	4.95
❑11, Sep 2002	4.95
❑12, Oct 2002	4.95
❑13, Nov 2002	4.95
❑14, Dec 2002	4.95
❑15, Jan 2003	4.95

VAISTRON
SLAVE LABOR

	N-MINT
❑1, 2005	2.99
❑2, Jan 2006	2.99

VALENTINE
REDEYE

❑1, Sep 1997, b&w	2.95

VALENTINO
RENEGADE

❑1, Apr 1985, b&w	2.00
❑2, Apr 1987, b&w; Valentino Too	2.00
❑3, Apr 1988, b&w; Valentino the 3rd	2.00

VALERIAN
FANTASY FLIGHT

❑1, Jul 1996, b&w; Heroes of the Equinox	2.95

VALERIA, THE SHE-BAT
CONTINUITY

❑1, May 1993; Promotional edition, never available for ordering; NA (w); NA (a); no cover price	3.00
❑2 1993; Promotional edition, never available for ordering	3.00
❑3 1993; Published out of sequence (after #5)	2.50
❑4 1993; Published out of sequence	2.50
❑5, Nov 1993; A: Knighthawk. Tyvek wraparound cover	2.00

VALERIA THE SHE-BAT
ACCLAIM / WINDJAMMER

❑1, Sep 1995	2.50
❑2, Sep 1995	2.50

VALHALLA
ANTARCTIC

❑1, Feb 1999	2.99

VALIANT EFFORTS (VOL. 2)
VALIANT COMICS

❑1, May 1991	1.95

VALIANT READER
VALIANT

❑1 1993; background	0.50

VALIANT VARMINTS
SHANDA FANTASY ARTS

❑1, b&w	4.50

VALIANT VISION STARTER KIT
VALIANT

❑1, Jan 1994; comic book, glasses, poster	2.95

VALKYR
IRONCAT

❑1, ca. 1999	2.95
❑2, ca. 1999	2.95
❑3, ca. 1999	2.95
❑4, ca. 1999	2.95
❑5, Aug 1999	2.95

VALKYRIE (1ST SERIES)
ECLIPSE

❑1, May 1987 PG (c); PG (a)	2.00
❑2, Jun 1987 PG (c); PG, BA (a)	2.00
❑3, Aug 1987 PG (c); PG, BA (a)	2.00

VALKYRIE (2ND SERIES)
ECLIPSE

❑1, Jul 1988 BA (a)	2.00
❑2, Aug 1988 BA (a)	2.00
❑3, Sep 1988 BA (a)	2.00

VALKYRIE (3RD SERIES)
MARVEL

❑1, Jan 1997	2.95

VALLEY OF THE DINOSAURS
HARVEY

❑1, Apr 1975	10.00
❑2, Jun 1975	6.00
❑3, Jul 1975	6.00
❑4, Oct 1975	6.00
❑5, Dec 1975	6.00
❑6, Feb 1976	4.00
❑7, Apr 1976	4.00
❑8, Jun 1976	4.00
❑9, Aug 1976	4.00
❑10, Oct 1976	4.00
❑11, Dec 1976	4.00

VALOR (DC)
DC

	N-MINT
❑1, Nov 1992	1.25
❑2, Dec 1992	1.25
❑3, Jan 1993	1.25
❑4, Feb 1993; Lobo	1.25
❑5, Mar 1993	1.25
❑6, Apr 1993	1.25
❑7, May 1993	1.25
❑8, Jun 1993	1.25
❑9, Jul 1993	1.25
❑10, Aug 1993	1.25
❑11, Sep 1993	1.25
❑12, Oct 1993	1.25
❑13, Nov 1993	1.50
❑14, Dec 1993	1.50
❑15, Jan 1994	1.50
❑16, Feb 1994	1.50
❑17, Mar 1994	1.50
❑18, Apr 1994	1.50
❑19, May 1994	1.50
❑20, Jun 1994	1.50
❑21, Jul 1994	1.50
❑22, Aug 1994	1.50
❑23, Sep 1994	1.50

VALOR (RCP)
GEMSTONE

❑1, Oct 1998	2.50
❑2, Nov 1998	2.50
❑3, Dec 1998	2.50
❑4, Jan 1999	2.50
❑5, Feb 1999	2.50

VALOR THUNDERSTAR AND HIS FIREFLIES
NOW

❑1, Dec 1986	1.50
❑2 1987	1.50
❑3 1987	1.50

VAMPEROTICA
BRAINSTORM

❑1, ca. 1994, b&w	8.00
❑1/Gold 1994; Gold edition	10.00
❑1/Platinum 1994; Platinum edition	10.00
❑1/2nd, Sep 1994	4.00
❑1/3rd, Dec 1994	3.00
❑2 1995, b&w	5.00
❑3 1995, b&w	3.00
❑4 1995, b&w	3.00
❑5 1995, b&w	3.00
❑6 1995, b&w	3.00
❑7 1995, b&w	3.00
❑8, Oct 1995, b&w	3.00
❑9, Nov 1995, b&w	3.00
❑10, Dec 1995, b&w	3.00
❑11, Jan 1996, b&w	3.00
❑12, Feb 1996, b&w	3.00
❑13, Mar 1996, b&w	3.00
❑14, Apr 1996, b&w	3.00
❑15, May 1996, b&w	3.00
❑16, Jun 1996	3.00
❑16/Nude, Jun 1996	5.00
❑17, Jul 1996	2.95
❑17/A, Jul 1996; chromium cover	4.95
❑18, Aug 1996	2.95
❑18/Nude, Aug 1996	5.00
❑19, Sep 1996	2.95
❑19/A, Sep 1996; variant cover	2.95
❑19/Nude, Sep 1996	5.00
❑20, Oct 1996	2.95
❑20/Nude, Oct 1996	5.00
❑21, Nov 1996	2.95
❑22, Dec 1996	2.95
❑22/Nude, Dec 1996	5.00
❑23, Jan 1997	3.00
❑24, Feb 1997	3.00
❑24/Nude, Feb 1997	5.00
❑25, Mar 1997	3.00
❑26, Apr 1997	3.00
❑27, May 1997	3.00
❑28, Jun 1997	3.00
❑29, Jul 1997	3.00
❑30, Aug 1997	3.00
❑31, Sep 1997	3.00
❑32, Oct 1997	3.00
❑33, Nov 1997	3.00
❑34, Dec 1997	3.00
❑35, Jan 1998	3.00
❑36, Feb 1998	3.00
❑37, Mar 1998	3.00

Vampire Tales

Comics, essays, and film commentary
©Marvel

Vamps

Five beautiful women with the same problem
©DC

Vanguard

Created in the 1980s for the series Megaton
©Image

Vanguard Illustrated

Daring science-fiction anthology series
©Pacific

Vanity Angel

Kaori Asamo's adult pleasureland
©Antarctic

N-MINT

❑38, Apr 1998 3.00
❑39, May 1998 3.00
❑40, Jun 1998 3.00
❑41, Jul 1998 3.00
❑42, Aug 1998 3.00
❑43, Sep 1998 3.00
❑44, Oct 1998 3.00
❑45, Nov 1998 3.00
❑45/Variant, Nov 1998 4.00
❑46, Dec 1998 3.00
❑47, Jan 1999 3.00
❑48, Feb 1999 3.00
❑49, Mar 1999 3.00
❑Annual 1 3.95
❑Annual 1/Gold; Annual #1-Gold Edition 8.00
❑SS 1; Blue cover (regular edition); Blue cover (regular edition) 4.00

VAMPEROTICA MAGAZINE
BRAINSTORM

❑1 4.95
❑1/Nude 6.00
❑1/Variant; Julie Strain Commemorative cover 10.00
❑2 4.95
❑2/Nude 6.00
❑2/Variant 5.95
❑3 4.95
❑3/Nude 6.00
❑3/Variant 6.00
❑4 5.95
❑4/Nude 6.00
❑4/Variant 5.95
❑5 5.95
❑5/Nude 6.00
❑6 5.95
❑6/Variant 5.95
❑7 5.95
❑7/Variant 5.95
❑8 5.95
❑8/Variant 5.95
❑9 5.95
❑9/Variant 5.95
❑10 5.95
❑10/Variant 5.95
❑11 2.50
❑11/Nude 3.00
❑12 2.50
❑12/Nude 3.00

VAMPEROTICA PRESENTS COUNTESS VLADIMIRA
BRAINSTORM

❑1, Dec 2001, b&w 2.95

VAMPFIRE
BRAINSTORM

❑1, Sep 1996, b&w 2.95

VAMPFIRE: EROTIC ECHO
BRAINSTORM

❑1 2.95
❑2, Feb 1997 2.95
❑2/Nude, Feb 1997 2.95

VAMPFIRE: NECROMANTIQUE
BRAINSTORM

❑1, Aug 1997 2.95
❑2 2.95

N-MINT

VAMPIRE COMPANION
INNOVATION

❑1, cardstock cover 2.50
❑2, cardstock cover 2.50
❑3 2.50

VAMPIRE GAME
TOKYOPOP

❑1, Jun 2003 9.99
❑2, Aug 2003 9.99
❑3, Oct 2003 9.99
❑4, Jan 2004 9.99
❑5, Mar 2004 9.99
❑6, May 2004 9.99
❑7, Jul 2004 9.99
❑8, Sep 2004 9.99
❑9, Nov 2004 9.99
❑10, Feb 2005 9.99
❑11, May 2005 9.99
❑12, Aug 2005 9.99
❑13, Nov 2005 9.99

VAMPIRE GIRLS: BUBBLE GUM & BLOOD
ANGEL

❑1 2.95
❑2 2.95

VAMPIRE GIRLS: CALIFORNIA 1969
ANGEL ENTERTAINMENT

❑0, May 1996, b&w 2.95
❑0/A, b&w; nude embossed foil cardstock cover; no indicia 5.00
❑0/Nude, May 1996, b&w; Nude cover 5.00
❑1, Aug 1996, b&w 2.95

VAMPIRE GIRLS, POETS OF BLOOD: SAN FRANCISCO
ANGEL

❑1 5.00
❑1/Nude 5.00
❑2; Flipbook Previews of Angel 5.00
❑2/Nude; Flipbook Previews of Angel. 5.00

VAMPIRE LESTAT (ANNE RICE'S...)
INNOVATION

❑1, Jan 1990 5.00
❑1/2nd 2.50
❑2, Feb 1990 3.00
❑2/2nd 2.50
❑2/3rd 2.50
❑3, May 1990 3.00
❑3/2nd 2.50
❑4, Jun 1990 2.50
❑5, Sep 1990 2.50
❑6, Nov 1990 2.50
❑7, Jan 1991 2.50
❑8, Mar 1991 2.50
❑9, May 1991 2.50
❑10 1991 2.50
❑11 1991 2.50
❑12 1991 2.50

VAMPIRELLA (MAGAZINE)
WARREN

❑1, Sep 1969, b&w FF (c); TS, NA (a); 1: Vampirella. 325.00
❑1/2nd, Oct 2001, b&w FF (c); TS, NA (a) 15.00

N-MINT

❑2, Nov 1969, b&w 125.00
❑3, Jan 1970, b&w; Scarce 200.00
❑4, Mar 1970, b&w 75.00
❑5, May 1970, b&w 75.00
❑6, Jul 1970, b&w 70.00
❑7, Sep 1970, b&w FF (c); FF (a) 70.00
❑8, Nov 1970, b&w; Horror format begins 70.00
❑9, Jan 1971, b&w 70.00
❑10, Mar 1971, b&w NA (a) 30.00
❑11, May 1971, b&w O: Pendragon. 1: Pendragon. 43.00
❑12, Jul 1971, b&w 43.00
❑13, Sep 1971, b&w 43.00
❑14, Nov 1971, b&w 43.00
❑15, Jan 1972, b&w 43.00
❑16, Apr 1972, b&w 30.00
❑17, Jun 1972, b&w 30.00
❑18, Aug 1972, b&w 30.00
❑19, Sep 1972, b&w; 1973 annual 30.00
❑20, Oct 1972, b&w 30.00
❑21, Dec 1972, b&w 30.00
❑22, Mar 1973, b&w 30.00
❑23, Apr 1973, b&w 30.00
❑24, May 1973, b&w 30.00
❑25, Jun 1973, b&w 30.00
❑26, Aug 1973, b&w 20.00
❑27, Sep 1973, b&w; 1974 annual 30.00
❑28, Nov 1973, b&w 25.00
❑29, Dec 1973, b&w 25.00
❑30, Jan 1974, b&w 25.00
❑31, Mar 1974, b&w FF (c); FF (a) 25.00
❑32, Apr 1974, b&w 25.00
❑33, May 1974, b&w 25.00
❑34, Jun 1974, b&w 25.00
❑35, Aug 1974, b&w 25.00
❑36, Sep 1974, b&w 25.00
❑37, Oct 1974, b&w; 1975 annual 20.00
❑38, Dec 1974, b&w 20.00
❑39, Feb 1974, b&w 20.00
❑40, Mar 1975, b&w 20.00
❑41, Apr 1975, b&w 20.00
❑42, May 1975, b&w 20.00
❑43, Jun 1975, b&w 20.00
❑44, Aug 1975, b&w 20.00
❑45, Sep 1975, b&w 20.00
❑46, Oct 1975, b&w O: Vampirella. 25.00
❑47, Dec 1975, b&w 20.00
❑48, Jan 1976, b&w 20.00
❑49, Mar 1976, b&w 20.00
❑50, Apr 1976, b&w 20.00
❑51, May 1976, b&w 17.00
❑52, Jul 1976, b&w 17.00
❑53, Aug 1976, b&w 17.00
❑54, Sep 1976, b&w 17.00
❑55, Oct 1976, b&w 17.00
❑56, Dec 1976, b&w 17.00
❑57, Jan 1977, b&w 17.00
❑58, Mar 1977, b&w RH (a) 17.00
❑59, Apr 1977, b&w 17.00
❑60, May 1977, b&w 17.00
❑61, Jul 1977, b&w 17.00
❑62, Aug 1977, b&w 17.00
❑63, Sep 1977, b&w 17.00

N-MINT

❑64 1977, b&w 17.00
❑65, Dec 1977, b&w 17.00
❑66, Jan 1978, b&w 17.00
❑67, Mar 1978, b&w 17.00
❑68, Apr 1978, b&w 17.00
❑69, May 1978, b&w 17.00
❑70, Jul 1978, b&w 17.00
❑71, Aug 1978, b&w 16.00
❑72, Sep 1978, b&w 16.00
❑73 1978, b&w 16.00
❑74, Dec 1978, b&w 16.00
❑75, Jan 1979, b&w 16.00
❑76, Mar 1979, b&w 16.00
❑77 1979, b&w RH (a) 16.00
❑78, May 1979, b&w 16.00
❑79 1979, b&w 16.00
❑80 1979, b&w 16.00
❑81 1979, b&w 16.00
❑82 1979, b&w 16.00
❑83, Dec 1979, b&w 16.00
❑84, Jan 1980, b&w 16.00
❑85, Mar 1980, b&w 16.00
❑86, Apr 1980, b&w 16.00
❑87 1980, b&w 16.00
❑88 1980, b&w 16.00
❑89 1980, b&w 16.00
❑90, Sep 1980, b&w 16.00
❑91, Oct 1980, b&w 16.00
❑92, Dec 1980, b&w 16.00
❑93, Jan 1981, b&w 16.00
❑94, Mar 1981, b&w 16.00
❑95, Apr 1981, b&w 16.00
❑96, May 1981, b&w 16.00
❑97, Jul 1981, b&w 16.00
❑98, Aug 1981, b&w 16.00
❑99, Sep 1981, b&w 16.00
❑100, Oct 1981, b&w 30.00
❑101, Dec 1981, b&w 16.00
❑102, Jan 1982, b&w 16.00
❑103, Mar 1982, b&w 16.00
❑104, Apr 1982, b&w 16.00
❑105, May 1982, b&w 16.00
❑106 1982, b&w 16.00
❑107 1982, b&w 16.00
❑108 1982, b&w 16.00
❑109 1982, b&w 16.00
❑110 1982, b&w 16.00
❑111 1983, b&w 16.00
❑112, Mar 1983, b&w 45.00
❑113 1983, b&w; 1st Harris comic; Scarce 195.00
❑Annual 1, b&w O: Vampirella 175.00
❑Special 1, b&w; Special edition 30.00

VAMPIRELLA
HARRIS

❑0, Dec 1994, contains Vampirella timeline; enhanced cover 5.00
❑0/A, Blue logo 5.00
❑0/Silver, Silver logo 5.00
❑0/Gold, Gold edition 15.00
❑1, Nov 1992 15.00
❑1/2nd 5.00
❑2, Feb 1993 A: Dracula. 12.00
❑3, Mar 1993 10.00
❑4, Jul 1993 8.00
❑5, Nov 1993 8.00

VAMPIRELLA & THE BLOOD RED QUEEN OF HEARTS
HARRIS

❑1, Sep 1996; Collects stories from Vampirella (Magazine) #49, 60, 61, 62, 65, 66, 101, and 102 9.95

VAMPIRELLA: ASCENDING EVIL
HARRIS

❑1 2.95
❑1/American Ent; American Entertainment variant cover 5.00
❑2 2.95
❑3 2.95
❑4 2.95

VAMPIRELLA: BLOOD LUST
HARRIS

❑1, Jul 1997; JRo (w); cardstock cover 5.00
❑2, Aug 1997; JRo (w); cardstock cover 5.00
❑Book 1; Crimson edition; JRo (w); hardcover 39.95

N-MINT

VAMPIRELLA CLASSIC
HARRIS

❑1, Feb 1995; Reprints Vampirella #12 in color 2.95
❑2, Apr 1995 2.95
❑3, Jun 1995 2.95
❑4, Aug 1995 2.95
❑5, Oct 1995 2.95

VAMPIRELLA COMMEMORATIVE EDITION
HARRIS

❑1, Nov 1996 2.95

VAMPIRELLA: CROSSOVER GALLERY
HARRIS

❑1, Sep 1997; wraparound cover; pin-ups; Crossover Pin-up of Hellshock, The Savage Dragon, Kabuki, Monkeyman and O'Brien, Rascals in Paradise, Madman, Pantha, Pain Killer Jane, Shi, Cyberfrog and Salamandroid, Body Bags 2.95

VAMPIRELLA: DEATH & DESTRUCTION
HARRIS

❑1, Jul 1996 2.95
❑1/A, Jul 1996; Vampirella sitting on cover 3.00
❑1/Ltd., Jul 1996; Vampirella logo only on cover 5.00
❑2, Aug 1996 2.95
❑3, Sep 1996 2.95
❑Ashcan 1 3.00

VAMPIRELLA/DRACULA & PANTHA SHOWCASE
HARRIS

❑1, Aug 1997; Vampirella on cover; flip-book with previews of Vampirella/ Dracula and Pantha 1.50
❑1/A, Aug 1997; Pantha on cover; flip-book with previews of Vampirella/ Dracula and Pantha 1.50

VAMPIRELLA/DRACULA: THE CENTENNIAL
HARRIS

❑1, Oct 1997 5.95
❑1/A, Oct 1997 5.95
❑1/B, Oct 1997 5.95
❑2, Oct 1997 5.95

VAMPIRELLA: JULIE STRAIN SPECIAL
HARRIS

❑1 3.95
❑1/A; Chrome version 14.95
❑1/B; Holo-chrome version; 500 copies printed 24.95

VAMPIRELLA/LADY DEATH
HARRIS

❑1, Feb 1999 3.50
❑1/A, Feb 1999; Valentine edition; Red foil 5.00
❑1/Ltd., Feb 1999 10.00

VAMPIRELLA LIVES
HARRIS

❑1, Dec 1996; white cardstock outer cover with cutout 3.50
❑1/A, Dec 1996; Cover depicts Vampirella leaning forward 4.00
❑1/B, Dec 1996; Cover depicts Vampirella side view 4.00
❑1/C, Dec 1996; Die-cut linen cover 10.00
❑2, Jan 1997; Vampirella bathing in blood 2.95
❑2/A, Jan 1997; Blue background 3.00
❑2/B, Jan 1997 4.00
❑3, Feb 1997; Drawn cover 2.95
❑3/A, Feb 1997 4.00

VAMPIRELLA MONTHLY
HARRIS

❑0; Vampirella standing, two figures in background 4.00
❑0/A; Vampirella bathing in blood 4.00
❑1, Nov 1997; Gold foil logo on cover 4.00
❑1/A, Nov 1997; Vampirella eating something bloody on cover 5.00
❑1/B, Nov 1997; Vampirella eating something bloody on cover; Gold marking 5.00

N-MINT

❑1/C, Nov 1997; Vampirella standing on cover, demon-eyed figures in background 5.00
❑1/D, Nov 1997; Vampirella standing on cover, black background, blue logo 5.00
❑1/E, Nov 1997; American Entertainment Edition; Vampirella reclining on skull 5.00
❑1/F, Nov 1997; Vampirella standing on cover, black background with foil logo 5.00
❑2, Dec 1997 3.00
❑2/A, Dec 1997; Man shooting gun at Vampirella 3.00
❑3, Jan 1998 3.00
❑3/A, Jan 1998; Vampirella on motorcycle (only figure on cover) 3.00
❑4, Feb 1998 3.00
❑4/A, Feb 1998; Crimson edition 4.00
❑4/B, Feb 1998; Vampirella holding gun 3.00
❑5, Mar 1998 3.00
❑6, Apr 1998 3.00
❑7, Jun 1998 A: Shi. 3.00
❑7/A, Jun 1998; Vampirella with finger to mouth 4.00
❑7/B, Jun 1998; Shi on cover in foreground, Vampirella in background 4.00
❑7/C, Jun 1998; Shi in background, Vampirella in foreground 4.00
❑7/D, Jun 1998; Vampirella and Shi on checkerboard floor, foil logo 6.00
❑7/E, Jun 1998; Vampirella and Shi on checkerboard floor 4.00
❑8, Jul 1998 A: Shi. 3.00
❑9, Aug 1998 A: Shi. 3.00
❑10, Sep 1998 3.00
❑10/A, Sep 1998; Black-and-white cover 6.00
❑10/B, Sep 1998; Color cover with no words 5.00
❑11, Oct 1998 3.00
❑12, Nov 1998 3.00
❑12/A, Nov 1998; Vampirella in spiky bodysuit 3.00
❑12/B, Nov 1998; Vampirella hurling woman 3.00
❑12/Variant, Nov 1998; Like B cover 6.00
❑13, Mar 1999 3.00
❑13/A, Mar 1999; Vampirella holding heart 3.00
❑14, Apr 1999 2.95
❑14/A, Apr 1999; Vampirella standing, figure in background 3.00
❑15, May 1999 2.95
❑15/A, May 1999 2.95
❑15/B, May 1999; alternate cover (facing away) 2.95
❑16, Jun 1999 2.95
❑16/A, Jun 1999; Vampirella - 4 other similarly clad women on cover 3.00
❑16/B, Jun 1999; Cover depicts Pantha standing, orange/red background 4.00
❑16/C, Jun 1999 5.00
❑16/D, Jun 1999; Pantha drawn cover 3.00
❑16/E, Jun 1999; Cover depicts Pantha crawling, white background 4.00
❑16/F, Jun 1999; Cover depicts Pantha standing, blue background 4.00
❑17, Jul 1999 2.95
❑17/A, Jul 1999; Vampirella bound on cover 3.00
❑17/B, Jul 1999; Cover depicts Pantha standiing, blue background 4.00
❑17/C, Jul 1999 4.00
❑17/D, Jul 1999; Two women with giant serpent in background on cover 3.00
❑17/E, Jul 1999; Cover depicts Pantha sitting with arm outstretched, blue background 4.00
❑18, Aug 1999 JPH (w) 2.95
❑18/A, Aug 1999; Vampirella with arms outstretched on cover 3.00
❑18/B, Aug 1999; "Chesty" close-up Vampirella cover 3.00
❑19, Sep 1999; Two Vampirellas on cover 2.95
❑19/A, Sep 1999; Vampirella holding skull on cover 3.00
❑20, Oct 1999; Vampirella with gun 2.95
❑20/A, Oct 1999; Vampirella standing with fangs present 3.00

Vault of Horror (Gladstone)

Reprints of classic E.C. comics

Veils

About the power of self-discovery

Vengeance of Vampirella

Led off the "bad girls" era of Vampirella

Venom

Most successful title of Marvel's Tsunami line

Venom: Lethal Protector

Some of #1's covers had a printing problem

N-MINT

❑21, Nov 1999; Cover has tinted background 2.95
❑21/A, Nov 1999; Drawn cover 3.00
❑21/B, Nov 1999 ..... 4.00
❑22, Dec 1999; Cover has red tinted background 4.00
❑22/A, Dec 1999; Drawn cover 3.00
❑22/B, Dec 1999 ..... 4.00
❑23, Jan 2000; Vampirella fighting Lady Death, cover has words 2.95
❑23/A, Jan 2000; Wordless cover with Vampirella on knees 7.00
❑23/B, Jan 2000; Red-logo cover with Vampirella on knees 5.00
❑23/C, Jan 2000; Silver logo cover with Vampirella on knees 3.00
❑23/D, Jan 2000; Wordless cover with Vampirella fighting Lady Death 6.00
❑24, Feb 2000; Vampirella with gun, fishnet stockings in foreground on cover 2.95
❑24/A, Feb 2000; Reflections in sunglasses on cover 3.00
❑24/B, Feb 2000; Vampirella on motorcycle, other female figure at top 3.00
❑25, Mar 2000; Vampirella in chains with male figure 2.95
❑25/A, Mar 2000; Two women on motorcycles 3.00
❑26, Apr 2000; Vampirella facing Lady Death on cover 2.95
❑26/A, Apr 2000; Vampirella in foreground, Lady Death in background 3.00
❑Ashcan 1, Aug 1997; "Ascending Evil" on cover 5.00
❑Ashcan 1/A; "Holy War" on cover 5.00
❑Ashcan 2 ..... 5.00
❑Ashcan 3 ..... 5.00
❑Ashcan 3/A; Leather cover; Convention exclusive limited to 1000 copies 15.00
❑Ashcan 4 ..... 3.00
❑Ashcan 5 ..... 3.00
❑Ashcan 6 ..... 3.00

VAMPIRELLA: MORNING IN AMERICA
HARRIS

❑1, b&w; distributed by Dark Horse; squarebound 3.95
❑2, Nov 1991, b&w; squarebound 3.95
❑3, Jan 1992, b&w; squarebound 3.95
❑4, Apr 1992, b&w; squarebound 3.95

VAMPIRELLA OF DRAKULON
HARRIS

❑0 ..... 2.95
❑1, Jan 1995 ..... 2.95
❑2, Mar 1995 ..... 2.95
❑3, May 1995; Poly-bagged 2.95

VAMPIRELLA/PAINKILLER JANE
HARRIS

❑1, May 1998; crossover with Event; foil-enhanced cover 2.95
❑1/A, May 1998; Variant cover, Vampirella and Painkiller Jane on rooftop 5.00
❑1/B, May 1998; Blue cover, Vampirella and Painkiller posing (in mid-air!) 24.95

N-MINT

❑1/Gold, May 1998; Gold edition 10.00
❑Ashcan 1, Jan 1998; no cover price 3.00

VAMPIRELLA PIN-UP SPECIAL
HARRIS

❑1, Oct 1995 ..... 2.95
❑1/A; White background and snake on cover 2.95

VAMPIRELLA: SAD WINGS OF DESTINY
HARRIS

❑1, Sep 1996; gold edition limited to 5000; cardstock cover 3.95
❑1/Gold, Sep 1996; Gold mark on cover 5.00

VAMPIRELLA/SHADOWHAWK: CREATURES OF THE NIGHT
HARRIS

❑1, Feb 1995; crossover with Image; concludes in Shadowhawk - Vampirella #2 ..... 4.95
❑2, "ShadowHawk/Vampirella" 4.95

VAMPIRELLA/SHI
HARRIS

❑1, crossover with Crusade; no cover price 2.95

VAMPIRELLA: SILVER ANNIVERSARY COLLECTION
HARRIS

❑1/A, Jan 1997; Good Girl cover 2.50
❑1/B, Jan 1997; Bad Girl cover 2.50
❑2/A, Feb 1997; Good Girl cover 2.50
❑2/B, Feb 1997; Bad Girl cover 2.50
❑3/A, Mar 1997; Good Girl cover 2.50
❑3/B, Mar 1997; Bad Girl cover 2.50
❑4/A, Apr 1997; Good Girl cover 2.50
❑4/B, Apr 1997; Bad Girl cover 2.50

VAMPIRELLA'S SUMMER NIGHTS
HARRIS

❑1, ca. 1992, b&w 3.95

VAMPIRELLA STRIKES
HARRIS

❑1, Oct 1995 ..... 3.00
❑1/A, Oct 1995; alternate cover; marble background 3.00
❑1/B, Oct 1995; Cover has Vampirella with moon in background 3.00
❑1/C, Oct 1995; Cover has Vampirella against blue background 3.00
❑1/Ltd., Oct 1995 ..... 10.00
❑2, Dec 1995 ..... 3.00
❑3, Feb 1996 ..... 3.00
❑4, Apr 1996 ..... 3.00
❑5, Jun 1996 A: Eudaemon 3.00
❑6, Aug 1996 ..... 3.00
❑7, Oct 1996 ..... 3.00
❑Annual 1, Dec 1996 ..... 3.00
❑Annual 1/A, Dec 1996 ..... 3.00
❑Annual 1/B, Dec 1996 ..... 3.00

VAMPIRELLA 25TH ANNIVERSARY SPECIAL
HARRIS

❑1, Oct 1996; prestige format 5.95
❑1/A, Oct 1996; Silver logo with no words on cover 6.00

N-MINT

VAMPIRELLA 30TH ANNIVERSARY CELEBRATION
HARRIS

❑1 ..... 3.00

VAMPIRELLA VS HEMORRHAGE
HARRIS

❑1, Apr 1997 ..... 3.50
❑1/A, Mar 1997; Vampirella with red hand on cover 3.50
❑1/Ashcan, Mar 1997; ashcan; no cover price 1.00
❑2, May 1997 ..... 3.50
❑3, Jun 1997 ..... 3.50

VAMPIRELLA VS PANTHA
HARRIS

❑1/A, Mar 1997; cardstock cover; Vampirella standing over body in street with police cars in background 3.50
❑1/B, Mar 1997; cardstock cover 3.50
❑1/C, Mar 1997; Pantha on cover with black background 3.50
❑Ashcan 1; "Special Showcase Edition" on cover; Special Showcase Edition on cover 3.50

VAMPIRELLA/WETWORKS
HARRIS

❑1, Jun 1997 ..... 3.00

VAMPIRE MIYU
ANTARCTIC

❑1, Oct 1995 ..... 3.50
❑2, Nov 1995 ..... 3.00
❑3, Dec 1995 ..... 3.00
❑4, Jan 1996 ..... 3.00
❑5, Feb 1996 ..... 3.00
❑6, Mar 1996 ..... 3.00
❑Ashcan 1; Ashcan promotional edition from 1995 San Diego Comic-Con 1: Vampire Miyu. 0.50

VAMPIRE'S CHRISTMAS
IMAGE

❑Book 1, ca. 2003 ..... 5.95

VAMPIRES LUST
CFD / BONEYARD

❑1, Sep 1996, b&w 2.95
❑1/Nude, Sep 1996; nude cover 3.95

VAMPIRE'S PRANK
ACID RAIN

❑1 ..... 2.95

VAMPIRE TALES
MARVEL

❑1, Aug 1973; ME (w); BEv (a); A: Morbius. 1st full Morbius story 35.00
❑2, Oct 1973 1: Satana. 18.00
❑3, Feb 1974 ..... 18.00
❑4, Apr 1974 ..... 18.00
❑5, Jun 1974 ..... 18.00
❑6, Aug 1974 A: Lilith. 18.00
❑7, Oct 1974 ..... 18.00
❑8, Dec 1974 A: Blade. 20.00
❑9, Feb 1975 A: Blade. 20.00
❑10, Apr 1975 A: Blade. 20.00
❑11, Jun 1975 ..... 25.00
❑Annual 1, Oct 1975; Reprints 30.00

Other grades: Multiply price above by 5/6 for VF/NM • 2/3 for VERY FINE • 1/3 for FINE • 1/5 for VERY GOOD • 1/8 for GOOD

N-MINT

VAMPIRE VERSES
CFD

❑1, Aug 1995, b&w 2.95
❑1/2nd, Dec 2001, b&w; 2nd printing from CFD 2.95
❑1/3rd, Dec 2001, b&w; 3rd printing from Asylum Press 2.95
❑1/Ltd., b&w; limited edition of 1000 copies; alternate nude cover 5.00
❑2, b&w 2.95
❑2/2nd, Jul 2002, b&w; 2nd printing from Asylum Press 2.95
❑2/3rd, b&w 2.95
❑2/Ltd., b&w; limited edition of 1000 copies; alternate cover 5.00
❑3, Jun 1996, b&w 2.95
❑3/2nd, Jun 1996, b&w; 2nd printing from Asylum Press
❑3/Ltd., Jun 1996, b&w; limited edition of 1000 copies; alternate nude cover 5.00
❑4, b&w 2.95
❑4/2nd, b&w 2.95
❑4/Ltd., b&w; limited edition of 1000 copies; alternate cover 5.00

VAMPIRE VIXENS
ACID RAIN

❑1 .... 2.75

VAMPIRE WORLD
ACID RAIN

❑1 .... 2.75

VAMPIRE YUI
IRONCAT

❑1, Jul 2000 .... 2.95

VAMPIRIC JIHAD
APPLE

❑1, b&w; cardstock cover; reprints material from Blood of Dracula #14-19 .... 4.95

VAMPORNELLA
ADAM POST

❑1 .... 2.95

VAMPRESS LUXURA
BRAINSTORM

❑1, Feb 1996; wraparound cover 2.95
❑1/Gold, Feb 1996 .... 8.00

VAMPS
DC / VERTIGO

❑1, Aug 1994 .... 2.50
❑2, Sep 1994 .... 2.50
❑3, Oct 1994 .... 2.50
❑4, Nov 1994 .... 2.50
❑5, Dec 1994 .... 2.50
❑6, Jan 1995 .... 2.50

VAMPS: HOLLYWOOD & VEIN
DC / VERTIGO

❑1, Feb 1996 .... 2.50
❑2, Mar 1996 .... 2.50
❑3, Apr 1996 .... 2.50
❑4, May 1996 .... 2.50
❑5, Jun 1996 .... 2.50
❑6, Jul 1996 .... 2.50

VAMPS: PUMPKIN TIME
DC / VERTIGO

❑1, Dec 1998 .... 2.50
❑2, Jan 1999 .... 2.50
❑3, Feb 1999 .... 2.50

VAMPURADA
TAVICAT

❑1, Jul 1995 .... 1.95

VAMPYRES
ETERNITY

❑1, b&w; Reprints 2.25
❑2, b&w; Reprints 2.25
❑3, Mar 1989, b&w; Reprints 2.25
❑4, b&w; Reprints 2.25

VAMPYRE'S KISS
AIRCEL

❑1, Jun 1990, b&w 2.50
❑2, Jul 1990, b&w 2.50
❑3, Aug 1990, b&w 2.50
❑4, Sep 1990, b&w 2.50

VAMPYRE'S KISS, BOOK II
AIRCEL

❑1, b&w 2.50
❑2, Dec 1990, b&w 2.50
❑3, Feb 1991, b&w 2.50
❑4, Mar 1991, b&w 2.50

VAMPYRE'S KISS, BOOK III
AIRCEL

❑1, Aug 1991, b&w 2.50
❑2, ca. 1991, b&w 2.50
❑3, ca. 1991, b&w 2.50
❑4, ca. 1991, b&w 2.50

VANDALA
CHAOS!

❑1, Aug 2000 .... 2.95

VANGUARD
IMAGE

❑1, Oct 1993 EL (w); EL (a) 2.00
❑2, Nov 1993 EL (w); EL (a) 2.00
❑3, Dec 1993 EL (w); EL (a); A: Savage Dragon. 2.00
❑4, Feb 1994 EL (w); EL (a) 2.00
❑5, Apr 1994 EL (w); EL (a) 2.00
❑6, May 1994 EL (w); EL (a) 2.00

VANGUARD (2ND SERIES)
IMAGE

❑1, Oct 1996, b&w 2.95
❑2, Oct 1996, b&w 2.95
❑3, Dec 1996, b&w 2.95
❑4, Jan 1997, b&w; cover says Feb, indicia says Jan 2.95

VANGUARD: ETHEREAL WARRIORS
IMAGE

❑1, Aug 2000 .... 5.95

VANGUARD ILLUSTRATED
PACIFIC

❑1, Nov 1983 SR, TY (a) 1.50
❑2, Jan 1984 DSt (a) 1.50
❑3, Mar 1984 SR, TY (a) 1.50
❑4, Apr 1984 .... 1.50
❑5, May 1984 .... 1.50
❑6, Jun 1984 GP (a) 1.50
❑7 1984 GE (a); 1: Mr. Monster. 4.00

VAN HELSING ONE-SHOT
DARK HORSE

❑1, May 2004 .... 2.99

VANITY
PACIFIC

❑1, Jun 1984 .... 1.50
❑2, Aug 1984 .... 1.50

VANITY ANGEL
ANTARCTIC

❑1, Sep 1994, b&w 3.50
❑1/2nd, May 1995 .... 3.50
❑2, Oct 1994, b&w 3.50
❑2/2nd, Jun 1995 .... 3.50
❑3, Nov 1994, b&w 3.50
❑4, Dec 1994, b&w 3.50
❑5, Jan 1995, b&w 3.50
❑6, Feb 1995, b&w 3.50

VARCEL'S VIXENS
CALIBER

❑1, Feb 1990, b&w 2.50
❑2, Mar 1990, b&w 2.50
❑3, Apr 1990, b&w 2.50

VARIATIONS ON THE THEME
SCARLET ROSE

❑1 .... 2.75
❑2 .... 2.75
❑3 .... 2.75
❑4 .... 2.75

VARICK: CHRONICLES OF THE DARK PRINCE
Q

❑1, Jul 1999 .... 1.95

VARIOGENESIS
DAGGER

❑0, Jun 1994 .... 3.50

VARLA VORTEX
BONEYARD

❑1 .... 2.95

VARMINTS
BLUE COMET

❑1 .... 2.00
❑Special 1; Panda Khan 2.50

VAST KNOWLEDGE OF GENERAL SUBJECTS
FANTAGRAPHICS

❑1, Sep 1994, b&w 4.95

VAULT OF DOOMNATION
B-MOVIE

❑1 1986, b&w 1.70

VAULT OF EVIL
MARVEL

❑1, Feb 1973 .... 60.00
❑2, Apr 1973 .... 25.00
❑3, Jun 1973 .... 25.00
❑4, Aug 1973 .... 25.00
❑5, Sep 1973 .... 15.00
❑6, Oct 1973 .... 15.00
❑7, Nov 1973 .... 15.00
❑8, Dec 1973 .... 15.00
❑9, Feb 1974 .... 15.00
❑10, Apr 1974 .... 15.00
❑11, Jun 1974 .... 12.00
❑12, Aug 1974 .... 12.00
❑13, Sep 1974 .... 12.00
❑14, Oct 1974 .... 12.00
❑15, Nov 1974 .... 12.00
❑16, Dec 1974 .... 12.00
❑17, Feb 1975 .... 12.00
❑18, Apr 1975 .... 12.00
❑19, Jun 1975 .... 12.00
❑20, Aug 1975 .... 12.00
❑21, Sep 1975 .... 12.00
❑22, Oct 1975 .... 12.00
❑23, Nov 1975 .... 12.00

VAULT OF HORROR (GLADSTONE)
GLADSTONE

❑1, Aug 1990; Reprints The Vault of Horror #34, The Haunt of Fear #1 ... 2.50
❑2, Oct 1990; Reprints The Vault of Horror #27, The Haunt of Fear #17. 2.50
❑3, Dec 1990; Reprints The Vault of Horror #13, The Haunt of Fear #22. 2.50
❑4, Feb 1991; Reprints The Vault of Horror #23, The Haunt of Fear #13. 2.50
❑5, Apr 1991; AF, JCr, WW, JKa, GI (a); Reprints The Vault of Horror #19, The Haunt of Fear #5 .... 2.50
❑6, Jun 1991; Reprints The Vault of Horror #32, Weird Fantasy #6 .... 2.50
❑7, Aug 1991; Reprints The Vault of Horror #26, Weird Fantasy #7 .... 2.50

VAULT OF HORROR (RCP)
COCHRAN

❑1, Sep 1991 .... 2.00
❑2, Nov 1991 .... 2.00
❑3, Jan 1992; Reprints Vault of Horror #26, Weird Science #7 .... 2.00
❑4, Mar 1992 .... 2.00
❑5, May 1992 .... 2.00

VAULT OF HORROR (RCP)
GEMSTONE

❑1, Oct 1992; Reprints The Vault of Horror #12 .... 2.00
❑2, Jan 1993; Reprints The Vault of Horror #13 .... 2.00
❑3, Apr 1993; Reprints The Vault of Horror #14 .... 2.00
❑4, Jul 1993; Reprints The Vault of Horror #15 .... 2.00
❑5, Oct 1993; Reprints The Vault of Horror #16 .... 2.00
❑6, Jan 1994; Reprints The Vault of Horror #17 .... 2.00
❑7, Apr 1994; Reprints The Vault of Horror #18 .... 2.00
❑8, Jul 1994; Reprints The Vault of Horror #19 .... 2.00
❑9, Oct 1994; Reprints The Vault of Horror #20 .... 2.00
❑10, Jan 1995; Reprints The Vault of Horror #21 .... 2.00
❑11, Apr 1995; Reprints The Vault of Horror #22 .... 2.00
❑12, Jul 1995; Reprints The Vault of Horror #23 .... 2.00
❑13, Oct 1995; Reprints The Vault of Horror #24 .... 2.00
❑14, Jan 1996; Reprints The Vault of Horror #25 .... 2.00
❑15, Apr 1996; Reprints The Vault of Horror #26 .... 2.00

Other grades: Multiply price above by 5/6 for VF/NM • 2/3 for VERY FINE • 1/3 for FINE • 1/5 for VERY GOOD • 1/8 for GOOD

Veronica

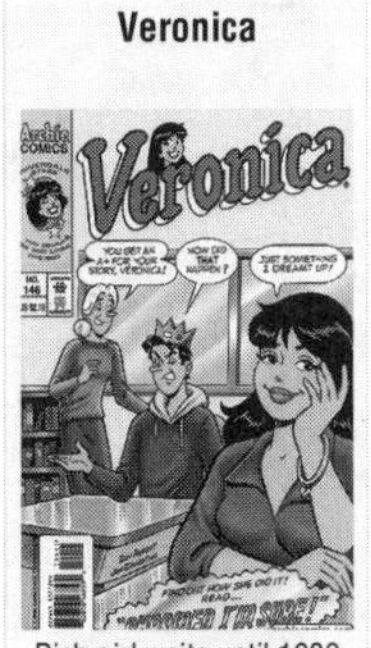

Rich girl waits until 1989 to get her solo series

©Archie

Vertigo Jam

Better than most compliation efforts

©DC

Vertigo Preview

An early look at the then-new Vertigo line

©DC

Vertigo Secret Files & Origins: Swamp Thing

One-shot examines all things Swampy

©DC

V for Vendetta

Life and death in totalitarian England

©DC

N-MINT

❑16, Jul 1996; Reprints The Vault of Horror #27 ..... 2.50
❑17, Oct 1996; Reprints The Vault of Horror #28 ..... 2.50
❑18, Jan 1997; Reprints The Vault of Horror #29 ..... 2.50
❑19, Apr 1997; Reprints The Vault of Horror #30 ..... 2.50
❑20, Jul 1997; Reprints The Vault of Horror #31 ..... 2.50
❑21, Oct 1997; Reprints The Vault of Horror #32 ..... 2.50
❑22, Jan 1998; Reprints The Vault of Horror #33 ..... 2.50
❑23, Apr 1998; Reprints The Vault of Horror #34 ..... 2.50
❑24, Jul 1998; Reprints The Vault of Horror #35 ..... 2.50
❑25, Oct 1998; Reprints The Vault of Horror #36 ..... 2.50
❑26, Jan 1999; Reprints The Vault of Horror #37 ..... 2.50
❑27, Apr 1999; Reprints The Vault of Horror #38 ..... 2.50
❑28, Jul 1999; Reprints The Vault of Horror #39 ..... 2.50
❑29, Oct 1999; Reprints The Vault of Horror #40 ..... 2.50
❑Annual 1; Collects The Vault of Horror #1-5 ..... 8.95
❑Annual 2; Collects The Vault of Horror #6-10 ..... 9.95
❑Annual 3; Collects The Vault of Horror #11-15 ..... 10.95
❑Annual 4 ..... 12.95
❑Annual 5 ..... 13.50

VAULT OF SCREAMING HORROR
FANTACO

❑1 ..... 3.50

VECTOR
NOW

❑1, Jul 1986 ..... 1.50
❑2, Sep 1986 ..... 1.50
❑3, Nov 1986 ..... 1.50
❑4, Jan 1987 ..... 1.50

VEGAS KNIGHTS
PIONEER

❑1 ..... 1.95

VEGETABLE LOVER
FANTAGRAPHICS / EROS

❑1, b&w 2.75

VEGMAN
CHECKER

❑1, Spr 1998, b&w 2.95
❑2, Sum 1998, b&w; indicia for #1 repeated inside 2.95

VEILS
DC / VERTIGO

❑1, Dec 1999; hardcover; art and photos 14.95
❑1/HC; hardcover; art and photos 19.95

VELOCITY (IMAGE)
IMAGE

❑1, Nov 1995 ..... 2.50
❑2, Dec 1995 ..... 2.50
❑3, Jan 1996 ..... 2.50

N-MINT

VELOCITY (ECLIPSE)
ECLIPSE

❑5, b&w 2.95

VELVET
ADVENTURE

❑1, Jan 1993, b&w 2.50
❑2, Feb 1993, b&w 2.50
❑3, Mar 1993, b&w 2.50
❑4, Apr 1993, b&w 2.50

VELVET ARTICHOKE THEATRE
VELVET ARTICHOKE

❑1, Sum 1998, b&w 2.00

VELVET TOUCH
ANTARCTIC

❑1, Oct 1993 ..... 4.00
❑1/Platinum, Oct 1993; platinum 4.00
❑1/2nd, Apr 1995 ..... 3.95
❑2, Jan 1994 ..... 3.95
❑3, Jul 1994 ..... 3.95
❑4, Aug 1994 ..... 3.95
❑5, Oct 1994 ..... 3.95
❑6, Jan 1995 ..... 3.95

VENDETTA: HOLY VINDICATOR
RED BULLET

❑1, b&w; first printing limited to 500 copies 2.50
❑2, b&w; first printing limited to 500 copies 2.50
❑3, b&w; first printing limited to 3000 copies 2.50
❑4, b&w 2.50

VENGEANCE OF THE AZTECS
CALIBER

❑1, b&w 2.95
❑2, b&w 2.95
❑3, b&w 2.95
❑4 ..... 2.95
❑5 ..... 2.95

VENGEANCE OF VAMPIRELLA
HARRIS

❑0, Nov 1995 ..... 2.95
❑½ 4.00
❑½/A 4.00
❑1, Apr 1994; red foil wraparound cover 3.50
❑1/A, Apr 1994; Blue foil 3.00
❑1/Gold, Apr 1994; Gold promotional edition 10.00
❑1/2nd, ca. 1994; blue foil wraparound cover 3.00
❑2, May 1994 ..... 3.00
❑3, Jun 1994 ..... 3.00
❑4, Jul 1994 ..... 3.00
❑5, Aug 1994 1: The Undead 3.00
❑6, Sep 1994 ..... 3.00
❑6/A, Sep 1994; Special Limited Edition on cover; Special Limited Edition on cover 4.00
❑7, Oct 1994 ..... 3.00
❑8, Nov 1994 ..... 3.00
❑9, Dec 1994 ..... 3.00
❑10, Jan 1995 ..... 3.00
❑11, Feb 1995; polybagged with trading card 3.00

N-MINT

❑12, Mar 1995; 1: Passion. cover date Feb 95 ..... 3.00
❑13, Apr 1995 ..... 3.00
❑14, May 1995 ..... 3.00
❑14/A, May 1995; Vampirella sitting, man at top 3.00
❑15, Jun 1995 ..... 3.00
❑15/A, Jun 1995; Back-to-back with man holding gun 3.00
❑16, Jul 1995 ..... 3.00
❑16/A, Jul 1995; Vampirella springing, fingernails outstretched 3.00
❑17, Aug 1995 ..... 3.00
❑17/A, Aug 1995; Woman with sword at right swinging at Vampirella 3.00
❑18, Sep 1995 ..... 3.00
❑18/A, Sep 1995; Vampirella against purple-red background 3.00
❑19, Oct 1995 ..... 3.00
❑19/A, Oct 1995; Vampirella holding heart 3.00
❑20, Nov 1995 ..... 3.00
❑21, Dec 1995 ..... 3.00
❑22, Jan 1996 ..... 3.00
❑23, Feb 1996 ..... 3.00
❑24, Mar 1996 ..... 3.00
❑25, Apr 1996; cardstock cover with red foil 3.00
❑25/A, ca. 1996; Vampirella with candles on cover 3.00
❑25/B, ca. 1996; Blue foil on cover 5.00
❑25/Gold, ca. 1996; Gold logo 5.00
❑25/Platinum, ca. 1996; Platinum logo 6.00
❑25/Ashcan, Mar 1995; Preview Ashcan 5.00

VENGEANCE SQUAD
CHARLTON

❑1, Jul 1975 ..... 9.00
❑2, Sep 1975 ..... 5.00
❑3, Nov 1975 PM (a) 5.00
❑4, Jan 1976 ..... 5.00
❑5, Mar 1976 ..... 5.00
❑6, May 1976 ..... 5.00

VENGEFUL SKYE
DAVDEZ

❑1, Sum 1998 ..... 2.95

VENGER ROBO
VIZ

❑1 ..... 2.75
❑2 ..... 2.75
❑3 ..... 2.75
❑4 ..... 2.75
❑5 ..... 2.75
❑6 ..... 2.75
❑7 ..... 2.75

VENOM
MARVEL

❑1, Jun 2003 ..... 10.00
❑2, Jul 2003 ..... 3.00
❑3, Aug 2003 ..... 2.25
❑4, Sep 2003 ..... 2.99
❑5, Oct 2003 ..... 2.99
❑6, Nov 2003 ..... 2.25
❑7, Dec 2003 ..... 2.99
❑8, Jan 2004 ..... 2.99

Other grades: Multiply price above by 5/6 for VF/NM • 2/3 for VERY FINE • 1/3 for FINE • 1/5 for VERY GOOD • 1/8 for GOOD

N-MINT

❑9, Feb 2004 .... 4.00
❑10, Mar 2004 .... 2.99
❑11, Apr 2004 .... 2.99
❑12, May 2004 .... 2.99
❑13, Jun 2004 .... 2.99
❑14, Jul 2004 .... 2.99
❑15, Jul 2004 .... 2.99
❑16, Aug 2004 .... 2.99
❑17, Sep 2004 .... 2.99
❑18, Oct 2004 .... 2.99

VENOM: ALONG CAME A SPIDER
MARVEL

❑1, Jan 1996 .... 2.95
❑2, Feb 1996 .... 2.95
❑3, Mar 1996 .... 2.95
❑4, Apr 1996 .... 2.95

VENOM: CARNAGE UNLEASHED
MARVEL

❑1, Apr 1995; cardstock cover 2.95
❑2, May 1995; cardstock cover 2.95
❑3, Jun 1995; cardstock cover 2.95
❑4, Jul 1995; cardstock cover 2.95

VENOM: DEATHTRAP: THE VAULT
MARVEL

❑1, one-shot (also published as Avengers: Deathtrap: The Vault) 6.95

VENOM: FINALE
MARVEL

❑1, Nov 1997; gatefold summary 2.00
❑2, Dec 1997; gatefold summary V: Spider-Man. 2.00
❑3, Jan 1998; gatefold summary V: Spider-Man. 2.00

VENOM: FUNERAL PYRE
MARVEL

❑1, Aug 1993; foil cover 2.95
❑2, Sep 1993 .... 2.95
❑3, Oct 1993 .... 2.95

VENOM: LETHAL PROTECTOR
MARVEL

❑1, Feb 1993; Metallic ink cover 3.00
❑1/Black, Feb 1993; Black Cover printing error 75.00
❑1/Gold, Feb 1993; Gold edition 5.00
❑2, Mar 1993 A: Spider-Man. 3.00
❑3, Apr 1993 AM (a) 3.00
❑4, May 1993 A: Spider-Man. 3.00
❑5, Jun 1993 A: Spider-Man. 3.00
❑6, Jul 1993 A: Spider-Man. 3.00

VENOM: LICENSE TO KILL
MARVEL

❑1, Jun 1997 .... 2.00
❑2, Jul 1997 .... 2.00
❑3, Aug 1997; gatefold summary 2.00

VENOM: NIGHTS OF VENGEANCE
MARVEL

❑1, Aug 1994, red foil cover 2.95
❑2, Sep 1994, cardstock cover 2.95
❑3, Oct 1994, cardstock cover 2.95
❑4, Nov 1994, cardstock cover 2.95

VENOM: ON TRIAL
MARVEL

❑1, Mar 1997 A: Daredevil. A: Spider-Man. 2.00
❑2, Apr 1997 A: Daredevil. A: Spider-Man. 2.00
❑3, May 1997 A: Daredevil. A: Carnage. A: Spider-Man. 2.00

VENOM: SEED OF DARKNESS
MARVEL

❑-1, Jul 1997; Flashback 2.00

VENOM: SEPARATION ANXIETY
MARVEL

❑1, Dec 1994; Embossed cover 2.95
❑2, Jan 1995 .... 2.95
❑3, Feb 1995 .... 2.95
❑4, Mar 1995 .... 2.95

VENOM: SIGN OF THE BOSS
MARVEL

❑1, Sep 1997; gatefold summary 2.00
❑2, Oct 1997; gatefold summary A: Ghost Rider. 2.00

VENOM: SINNER TAKES ALL
MARVEL

❑1, Aug 1995 .... 2.95
❑2, Sep 1995 .... 2.95
❑3, Oct 1995 .... 2.95
❑4, Nov 1995 .... 2.95
❑5, Dec 1995 .... 2.95

VENOM SUPER SPECIAL
MARVEL

❑1, Aug 1995; Flip-book; two of the stories continue in Spectacular Spider-Man Super Special #1 .... 3.95

VENOM: THE ENEMY WITHIN
MARVEL

❑1, Feb 1994; Glow-in-the-dark cover 2.95
❑2, Mar 1994 .... 2.95
❑3, Apr 1994 .... 2.95

VENOM: THE HUNGER
MARVEL

❑1, Aug 1996 .... 2.00
❑2, Sep 1996 .... 2.00
❑3, Oct 1996 .... 2.00
❑4, Nov 1996 .... 2.00

VENOM: THE HUNTED
MARVEL

❑1, May 1996 .... 2.95
❑2, Jun 1996 .... 2.95
❑3, Jul 1996 .... 2.95

VENOM: THE MACE
MARVEL

❑1, May 1994; Embossed cover 2.95
❑2, Jun 1994 .... 2.95
❑3, Jul 1994 .... 2.95

VENOM: THE MADNESS
MARVEL

❑1, Nov 1993; Embossed cover 2.95
❑2, Dec 1993 .... 2.95
❑3, Jan 1994 .... 2.95

VENOM: TOOTH AND CLAW
MARVEL

❑1, Nov 1996, A: Wolverine. V: Wolverine. 2.00
❑2, Dec 1996, V: Wolverine. 2.00
❑3, Jan 1997, V: Wolverine. 2.00

VENOM VS. CARNAGE
MARVEL

❑1, Sep 2004 .... 6.00
❑2, Oct 2004 .... 2.99
❑3, Nov 2004 .... 2.99
❑4, Dec 2004 .... 2.99

VENTURE
AC

❑1, Aug 1986 .... 1.75
❑2 1986 .... 1.75
❑3 1987 .... 1.75

VENTURE (IMAGE)
IMAGE

❑1, Jan 2003 .... 2.95
❑2, Feb 2003 .... 2.95
❑3, Apr 2003 .... 2.95
❑4, Sep 2003 .... 2.95

VENTURE SAN DIEGO COMIC-CON SPECIAL EDITION
VENTURE

❑1, Jul 1994, b&w 2.50

VENUMB
PARODY

❑1 1993, b&w 2.50
❑1/Deluxe 1993, b&w; enhanced cover 2.95

VENUS DOMINA
VEROTIK

❑1, ca. 1997 .... 4.95
❑2, ca. 1997 .... 4.95
❑3, Mar 1997 .... 4.95

VENUS INTERFACE (HEAVY METAL'S...)
HM COMMUNICATIONS

❑1 .... 6.00

VENUS WARS
DARK HORSE

❑1, Apr 1991, b&w; Japanese; trading cards 2.50
❑2, May 1991, b&w; Japanese; trading cards 2.25
❑3, Jun 1991, b&w; Japanese; trading cards 2.25
❑4, Jul 1991 .... 2.25
❑5, Aug 1991 .... 2.25
❑6, Sep 1991 .... 2.25
❑7, Oct 1991 .... 2.25
❑8, Nov 1991 .... 2.25
❑9, Dec 1991 .... 2.25
❑10, Jan 1992 .... 2.25
❑11, Feb 1992 .... 2.25
❑12, Mar 1992 .... 2.25
❑13, Apr 1992 .... 2.25
❑14, May 1992 .... 2.25

VENUS WARS II
DARK HORSE

❑1, Jun 1992 .... 2.50
❑2, Jul 1992 .... 2.50
❑3, Aug 1992 .... 2.50
❑4, Sep 1992 .... 2.50
❑5, Oct 1992, b&w 2.50
❑6, Nov 1992, b&w 2.50
❑7, Dec 1992, b&w 2.50
❑8, Jan 1993, b&w 2.50
❑9, Feb 1993, b&w 2.50
❑10, Mar 1993, b&w 2.50
❑11, Apr 1993, b&w 2.95
❑12, May 1993, b&w 2.95
❑13, Jun 1993 .... 2.95
❑14, Jul 1993 .... 2.95
❑15, Aug 1993 .... 2.95

VERBATIM
FANTAGRAPHICS

❑1, Apr 1993, b&w 2.75
❑2, ca. 1993, b&w 2.75

VERDICT
ETERNITY

❑1, ca. 1998 .... 1.95
❑2, ca. 1998 .... 1.95
❑3, Jun 1988 .... 1.95
❑4, ca. 1988 .... 1.95
❑Book 1, ca. 1998, b&w 12.95

VERMILLION
DC / HELIX

❑1, Oct 1996 .... 2.25
❑2, Nov 1996 .... 2.25
❑3, Dec 1996 .... 2.25
❑4, Jan 1997 .... 2.25
❑5, Feb 1997 .... 2.25
❑6, Mar 1997 .... 2.25
❑7, Apr 1997 .... 2.25
❑8, May 1997 .... 2.25
❑9, Jun 1997 .... 2.25
❑10, Jul 1997 .... 2.25
❑11, Aug 1997 .... 2.25
❑12, Sep 1997 .... 2.25

VERONICA
ARCHIE

❑1, Apr 1989 .... 2.00
❑2, Jul 1989 .... 1.50
❑3, Sep 1989 .... 1.50
❑4, Oct 1989 .... 1.50
❑5, Dec 1989 .... 1.50
❑6 1990 .... 1.50
❑7, Apr 1990 .... 1.50
❑8 1990 .... 1.50
❑9, Jul 1990 .... 1.50
❑10, Sep 1990 .... 1.50
❑11, Oct 1990 .... 1.50
❑12, Dec 1990 .... 1.50
❑13, Feb 1991 .... 1.50
❑14, Apr 1991 .... 1.50
❑15, Jun 1991 .... 1.50
❑16, Aug 1991 .... 1.50
❑17, Oct 1991 .... 1.50
❑18, Dec 1991 .... 1.50
❑19, Feb 1992 .... 1.50
❑20, Apr 1992 .... 1.50
❑21, Jun 1992 .... 1.25
❑22, Aug 1992 .... 1.25
❑23, Sep 1992 .... 1.25
❑24, Oct 1992 .... 1.25
❑25, Dec 1992 .... 1.25
❑26, Feb 1993 .... 1.25
❑27, Apr 1993 .... 1.25
❑28, Jun 1993 .... 1.25
❑29, Aug 1993 .... 1.25
❑30, Sep 1993 .... 1.25
❑31, Oct 1993 .... 1.25

Other grades: Multiply price above by 5/6 for VF/NM • 2/3 for VERY FINE • 1/3 for FINE • 1/5 for VERY GOOD • 1/8 for GOOD

Victorian

Strangeness on the streets of New Orleans
©Penny-Farthing

Vigilante

Adrian Chase chased bad guys
©DC

Vintage Magnus Robot Fighter

Reprints of the Gold Key Magnus comics
©Valiant

Violent Messiahs

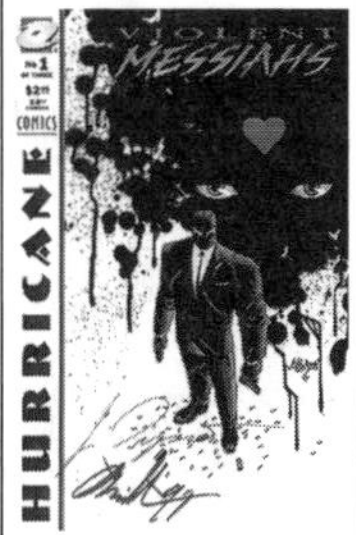

A gloomy black-and-white world
©Hurricane

Vision & Scarlet Witch (Vol. 1)

Part of Marvel's first wave of limited series
©Marvel

N-MINT

❑32, Dec 1993 .... 1.25
❑33, Feb 1994 .... 1.25
❑34, Apr 1994 .... 1.25
❑35, Jun 1994 .... 1.25
❑36, Aug 1994 .... 1.50
❑37, Sep 1994 .... 1.50
❑38, Oct 1994 .... 1.50
❑39, Dec 1994 .... 1.50
❑40, Jan 1995 .... 1.50
❑41, Mar 1995 .... 1.50
❑42, Apr 1995 .... 1.50
❑43, Jun 1995 .... 1.50
❑44, Jul 1995 .... 1.50
❑45, Aug 1995 .... 1.50
❑46, Sep 1995 .... 1.50
❑47, Oct 1995 .... 1.50
❑48, Nov 1995 .... 1.50
❑49, Jan 1996 .... 1.50
❑50, Feb 1996 .... 1.50
❑51, Apr 1996 .... 1.50
❑52, Jun 1996 .... 1.50
❑53, Jul 1996 .... 1.50
❑54, Aug 1996 .... 1.50
❑55, Sep 1996 .... 1.50
❑56, Oct 1996 .... 1.50
❑57, Nov 1996 .... 1.50
❑58, Dec 1996 .... 1.50
❑59, Jan 1997 .... 1.50
❑60, Feb 1997 .... 1.50
❑61, Mar 1997 .... 1.50
❑62, Apr 1997 .... 1.50
❑63, May 1997 .... 1.50
❑64, Jun 1997 .... 1.50
❑65, Jul 1997 .... 1.50
❑66, Aug 1997 .... 1.50
❑67, Sep 1997 .... 1.50
❑68, Oct 1997 .... 1.50
❑69, Nov 1997 .... 1.50
❑70, Dec 1997 .... 1.50
❑71, Jan 1998 .... 1.50
❑72, Feb 1998 .... 1.50
❑73, Mar 1998 .... 1.50
❑74, Apr 1998; Veronica markets Jughead's beanie 1.50
❑75, May 1998 .... 1.50
❑76, Jun 1998 .... 1.50
❑77, Jul 1998 .... 1.50
❑78, Aug 1998 .... 1.50
❑79, Sep 1998 .... 1.75
❑80, Oct 1998 .... 1.75
❑81, Nov 1998; Veronica in Oz 1.75
❑82, Dec 1998 .... 1.75
❑83, Jan 1999 .... 1.75
❑84, Feb 1999 .... 1.75
❑85, Mar 1999 .... 1.75
❑86, Apr 1999 .... 1.79
❑87, May 1999 .... 1.79
❑88, Jun 1999 .... 1.79
❑89, Jul 1999 .... 1.79
❑90, Aug 1999 .... 1.79
❑91, Aug 1999 .... 1.79
❑92, Oct 1999 .... 1.79
❑93, Nov 1999 .... 1.79
❑94, Dec 1999 .... 1.79

N-MINT

❑95, Jan 2000 .... 1.79
❑96, Feb 2000 .... 1.79
❑97, Mar 2000 .... 1.79
❑98, Apr 2000 .... 1.79
❑99, May 2000 .... 1.99
❑100, Jun 2000 .... 1.99
❑101, Jul 2000 .... 1.99
❑102, Aug 2000 .... 1.99
❑103, Sep 2000 .... 1.99
❑104, Oct 2000 .... 1.99
❑105, Nov 2000 .... 1.99
❑106, Dec 2000 .... 1.99
❑107, Jan 2001 .... 1.99
❑108, Feb 2001 .... 1.99
❑109, Mar 2001 .... 1.99
❑110, Apr 2001 .... 1.99
❑111, May 2001 .... 1.99
❑112, Jun 2001 .... 1.99
❑113, Jul 2001 .... 1.99
❑114, Jul 2001 .... 1.99
❑115, Aug 2001 .... 1.99
❑116, Sep 2001 .... 1.99
❑117, Oct 2001 .... 1.99
❑118, Nov 2001 .... 1.99
❑119, Dec 2001 .... 1.99
❑120, Jan 2002 .... 1.99
❑121, Feb 2002 .... 1.99
❑122, Mar 2002 .... 1.99
❑123, Apr 2002 .... 1.99
❑124, May 2002 .... 1.99
❑125, Jun 2002 .... 1.99
❑126, Jul 2002 .... 1.99
❑127, Jul 2002 .... 1.99
❑128, Aug 2002 .... 1.99
❑129, Sep 2002 .... 1.99
❑130, Oct 2002 .... 1.99
❑131, Nov 2002 .... 1.99
❑132, Dec 2002 .... 1.99
❑133, Jan 2003 .... 1.99
❑134, Feb 2003 .... 2.19
❑135, Mar 2003 .... 2.19
❑136, Apr 2003 .... 2.19
❑137, May 2003 .... 2.19
❑138, Jun 2003 .... 2.19
❑139, Jul 2003 .... 2.19
❑140, Jul 2003 .... 2.19
❑141, Aug 2003 .... 2.19
❑142, Sep 2003 .... 2.19
❑143, Oct 2003 .... 2.19
❑144, Nov 2003 .... 2.19
❑145, Dec 2003 .... 2.19
❑146, Jan 2004 .... 2.19
❑147, Feb 2004 .... 2.19
❑148, Mar 2004 .... 2.19
❑149, Apr 2004 .... 2.19
❑150, May 2004 .... 2.19
❑151, Jun 2004 .... 2.19
❑152, Jul 2004 .... 2.19
❑153, Aug 2004 .... 2.19
❑154, Sep 2004 .... 2.19
❑155, Oct 2004 .... 2.19
❑156, Jan 2004 .... 2.19
❑157, Feb 2005 .... 2.19
❑158, Mar 2005 .... 2.19

N-MINT

❑159, Apr 2005 .... 2.19
❑160, May 2005 .... 2.19
❑161, Jun 2005 .... 2.19
❑162, Jul 2005 .... 2.39
❑163, Aug 2005 .... 2.39
❑164, Sep 2005 .... 2.39
❑165, Oct 2005 .... 2.39
❑166, Dec 2005 .... 2.39
❑167, Jan 2006 .... 2.39
❑168, May 2006 .... 2.39
❑169, May 2006 .... 2.39
❑170, Jul 2006 .... 2.39
❑171, Aug 2006 .... 2.39

VERONICA'S DIGEST MAGAZINE
ARCHIE

❑1, ca. 1992 .... 2.00
❑2, ca. 1993 .... 1.75
❑3, ca. 1994 .... 1.75
❑4, Sep 1995 .... 1.75
❑5, Sep 1996 .... 1.75
❑6, Oct 1997 .... 1.79

VEROTIKA
VEROTIK

❑1 .... 4.00
❑2, Jan 1995 .... 3.00
❑3, May 1995 FF (c) 3.00
❑4 1995 .... 3.00
❑5 1995 .... 3.00
❑6 1995 .... 3.00
❑7 1995 .... 3.00
❑8, Feb 1996 .... 3.00
❑9 .... 3.00
❑10 .... 3.00
❑11 .... 3.00
❑12 .... 3.00
❑13 .... 3.00
❑14 .... 3.00
❑15 .... 3.95

VEROTIK ILLUSTRATED
VEROTIK

❑1, Aug 1997 .... 6.95
❑2, Dec 1997 .... 6.95
❑3, Apr 1998 .... 6.95

VEROTIK ROGUES GALLERY OF VILLAINS
VEROTIK

❑1, Nov 1997; pin-ups 3.95

VEROTIK WORLD
VEROTIK

❑1, Aug 2002; Regular edition 3.95
❑1/Variant, Aug 2002; Fan Club cover edition; no cover price; solicited with a $5 cost 5.00
❑2 .... 3.95
❑3 .... 3.95
❑3/Variant 10.00

VERSION
DARK HORSE

❑1.1, ca. 1993 .... 2.50
❑1.2, ca. 1993 .... 2.50
❑1.3, ca. 1993 .... 2.50
❑1.4, ca. 1993 .... 2.50
❑1.5, ca. 1993 .... 2.50

Other grades: Multiply price above by 5/6 for VF/NM • 2/3 for VERY FINE • 1/3 for FINE • 1/5 for VERY GOOD • 1/8 for GOOD

N-MINT

❑1.6, ca. 1993 .... 2.50
❑1.7, ca. 1993 .... 2.50
❑1.8, ca. 1993 .... 2.50
❑2.1, ca. 1993 .... 2.95
❑2.2, ca. 1993 .... 2.95
❑2.3, ca. 1993 .... 2.95
❑2.4, ca. 1993 .... 2.95
❑2.5, ca. 1993 .... 2.95
❑2.6, ca. 1993 .... 2.95
❑2.7, ca. 1993 .... 2.95

VERTICAL
DC

❑1, Feb 2004 .... 4.95

VERTIGO GALLERY: DREAMS AND NIGHTMARES
DC / VERTIGO

❑1, MW, BSz, ATh, CV (a); pin-ups 4.00

VERTIGO JAM
DC / VERTIGO

❑1, Aug 1993 .... 3.95

VERTIGO POP! BANGKOK
DC / VERTIGO

❑1, Jul 2003 .... 2.95
❑2, Aug 2003 .... 2.95
❑3, Sep 2003 .... 2.95
❑4, Oct 2003 .... 2.95

VERTIGO POP! LONDON
DC / VERTIGO

❑1, ca. 2002 .... 2.95
❑2, ca. 2002 .... 2.95
❑3, ca. 2002 .... 2.95
❑4, Feb 2003 .... 2.95

VERTIGO POP! TOKYO
DC / VERTIGO

❑1, Sep 2002 .... 2.95
❑2, Oct 2002 .... 2.95
❑3, Nov 2002 .... 2.95

VERTIGO PREVIEW
DC / VERTIGO

❑1, Previews DC Vertigo titles 1.50

VERTIGO RAVE
DC / VERTIGO

❑1, Aut 1994; Aut 1994 .... 1.50

VERTIGO SECRET FILES & ORIGINS: SWAMP THING
DC / VERTIGO

❑1, Nov 2000 .... 4.95

VERTIGO SECRET FILES: HELLBLAZER
DC / VERTIGO

❑1, Aug 2000 PG (a) 4.95

VERTIGO VERITÉ: THE UNSEEN HAND
DC / VERTIGO

❑1, Sep 1996 .... 2.50
❑2, Oct 1996 .... 2.50
❑3, Nov 1996 .... 2.50
❑4, Dec 1996 .... 2.50

VERTIGO VISIONS: DOCTOR OCCULT
DC / VERTIGO

❑1, Jul 1994 .... 3.95

VERTIGO VISIONS: DR. THIRTEEN
DC / VERTIGO

❑1, Sep 1998 .... 5.95

VERTIGO VISIONS: PREZ
DC / VERTIGO

❑1, Sep 1995 .... 3.95

VERTIGO VISIONS: THE GEEK
DC / VERTIGO

❑1 .... 3.95

VERTIGO VISIONS: THE PHANTOM STRANGER
DC / VERTIGO

❑1, Oct 1993 .... 3.50

VERTIGO VISIONS: TOMAHAWK
DC / VERTIGO

❑1, Jul 1998 .... 4.95

VERTIGO VOICES: THE EATERS
DC / VERTIGO

❑1 .... 4.95

VERTIGO: WINTER'S EDGE
DC / VERTIGO

❑1, Jan 1998; prestige format anthology; wraparound cover 7.95

N-MINT

❑2, Jan 1999; wraparound cover 6.95
❑3, Jan 2000 .... 6.95

VERTIGO X PREVIEW
DC / VERTIGO

❑1, Apr 2003 .... 0.99

VERY BEST OF DENNIS THE MENACE
MARVEL

❑1, Apr 1982; reprints 3.00
❑2, Jun 1982; reprints 2.00
❑3, Aug 1982; reprints 2.00

VERY MU CHRISTMAS
MU

❑1, Nov 1992 .... 2.95

VERY VICKY
ICONOGRAFIX

❑1, ca. 1993, b&w 2.95
❑1/2nd, ca. 1993 .... 2.50
❑2, ca. 1993, b&w 2.50
❑3, ca. 1993, b&w 2.50
❑4, ca. 1993, b&w 2.50
❑5, ca. 1993, b&w 2.50
❑6, ca. 1993, b&w 2.50
❑7, ca. 1993, b&w 2.50
❑8, ca. 1993, b&w 2.50

VESPERS
MARS MEDIA GROUP

❑1, Aug 1995 .... 2.50

VEXT
DC

❑1, Mar 1999 .... 2.50
❑2, Apr 1999 .... 2.50
❑3, May 1999 .... 2.50
❑4, Jun 1999 .... 2.50
❑5, Jul 1999 .... 2.50
❑6, Aug 1999 .... 2.50

V FOR VENDETTA
DC

❑1, Sep 1988 AMo (w) 3.00
❑2, Oct 1988 AMo (w) 2.50
❑3, Nov 1988 AMo (w) 2.50
❑4, Dec 1988 .... 2.50
❑5, Win 1988 AMo (w) 2.50
❑6, Hol 1988; AMo (w); Hol 1988 .... 2.50
❑7, Jan 1989 AMo (w) 2.50
❑8, Feb 1989 AMo (w) 2.50
❑9, Mar 1989 AMo (w) 2.50
❑10, May 1989 AMo (w) 2.50

VIBE
YOUNG GUN

❑1, Mar 1994 .... 1.95

VIC & BLOOD
MAD DOG

❑1, Oct 1987, b&w 2.00
❑2, Feb 1988, b&w 2.00

V.I.C.E.
IMAGE

❑1, Nov 2005 .... 2.95
❑1/Silvestri, Nov 2005 .... 2.95
❑1/Variant, Nov 2005 .... 2.95
❑2, Dec 2005 .... 2.95
❑3, Jan 2006 .... 2.95
❑4, Jan 2006 .... 2.95
❑5, Apr 2006 .... 2.95

VICIOUS
BRAINSTORM

❑1, b&w 2.95

VICKI
ATLAS-SEABOARD

❑1, Feb 1975; reprints Tippy Teen 28.00
❑2, Apr 1975; reprints Tippy Teen 18.00
❑3, Jun 1975; reprints Tippy Teen 12.00
❑4, Aug 1975; reprints Tippy Teen 12.00

VICKI VALENTINE
RENEGADE

❑1, Jul 1985, b&w 1.70
❑2, Nov 1985, b&w 1.70
❑3 1986, b&w 1.70
❑4 1986, b&w 1.70

VICTIM
SILVERWOLF

❑1, Feb 1987, b&w 1.50

VICTIMS
ETERNITY

❑1, Oct 1988, b&w; Reprints 2.00

N-MINT

❑2, Nov 1988, b&w; Reprints 2.00
❑3, Dec 1988, b&w; Reprints 2.00
❑4, Jan 1989, b&w; Reprints 2.00
❑5, Feb 1989, b&w; Reprints 2.00
❑6, Mar 1983 .... 2.00

VICTORIAN
PENNY-FARTHING

❑½, Aug 1998; preview of upcoming series; Sketches and notes for series 1.00
❑1, Mar 1999 .... 3.00
❑2, Apr 1999 .... 2.95
❑3, May 1999 .... 2.95
❑4, Jun 1999 .... 2.95
❑5, Jul 1999 .... 2.95
❑7 .... 2.95
❑6, Aug 1999 .... 2.95
❑8 .... 2.95
❑9 .... 2.95
❑10 .... 2.95
❑11 .... 2.95
❑12 .... 2.95
❑13 .... 2.95
❑14 .... 2.95
❑15 .... 2.95
❑16 .... 2.95
❑17 .... 2.95
❑18 .... 2.95
❑19 .... 2.95
❑20 .... 2.95
❑21 .... 2.95
❑22 .... 2.95
❑23 .... 2.95
❑24 .... 2.95
❑25 .... 2.95

VICTORIA'S SECRET SERVICE
ALIAS

❑0, Dec 2005 .... 2.99
❑1 .... 2.99

VIC TORRY
AVALON

❑1 .... 2.95

VICTOR VECTOR & YONDO
FRACTAL

❑1, Jul 1994 .... 1.95
❑2 1994 .... 1.95
❑3 1994 .... 1.95

VICTORY (TOPPS)
TOPPS

❑1, Jun 1994, First and final issue (series cancelled); Liefeld cover variant 2.50
❑1/Kirby, Jun 1994; First and final issue (series cancelled); Kirby cover variant 0.00

VICTORY (IMAGE)
IMAGE

❑1, Jun 2003 .... 2.95
❑1/A, Jul 2003 .... 2.95
❑1/B, Jul 2003 .... 2.95
❑2, Oct 2003 .... 2.95
❑2/A, Oct 2003 .... 2.95
❑3, Dec 2003 .... 2.95
❑3/A, Dec 2003 .... 2.95
❑4, May 2004 .... 2.95

VICTORY (IMAGE, VOL. 2)
IMAGE

❑1/A, ca. 2004 .... 2.95
❑1/B, ca. 2004 .... 2.95
❑2/A, ca. 2004 .... 2.95
❑2/B, ca. 2004 .... 2.95
❑3/A, ca. 2005 .... 2.95
❑3/B, ca. 2005 .... 2.95
❑4/A, ca. 2005 .... 2.95
❑4/B, ca. 2005 .... 2.95
❑4/C, ca. 2005 .... 2.95

VIDEO CLASSICS
ETERNITY

❑1, b&w; Mighty Mouse 3.50
❑2, b&w; Mighty Mouse 3.50

VIDEO GIRL AI
VIZ

❑1, Jun 2003 .... 9.99
❑2, Aug 2003 .... 9.99
❑3, Dec 2003 .... 9.99
❑4, Feb 2004 .... 9.99

Visitor

Visitor from another world isn't accepted
©Valiant

Void Indigo

Violent title was quickly canceled after protests
©Marvel

Voodoo (Image)

WildC.A.T.S member in web of dark magic
©Image

Wacky Adventures of Cracky

Starring Gold Key's own animal characters
©Gold Key

Wahoo Morris (Vol. 1)

Tales of an up-and-coming rock band
©Too Hip Gotta Go Graphics

N-MINT

❑5, Apr 2004 .... 9.99
❑6, Apr 2004 .... 9.99
❑7, Jun 2004 .... 9.99
❑8, Aug 2004 .... 9.99
❑9, Oct 2004 .... 9.99
❑10, Jan 2005 .... 9.99
❑11, Apr 2005 .... 9.99
❑12, Jul 2005 .... 9.99
❑13, Oct 2005 .... 9.99

VIDEO HIROSHIMA
AEON

❑1, Aug 1995, b&w 2.50

VIDEO JACK
MARVEL / EPIC

❑1, Sep 1987 .... 1.25
❑2, Nov 1987 .... 1.25
❑3, Mar 1988 .... 1.25
❑4, May 1988 .... 1.25
❑5, Jul 1988 .... 1.25
❑6, Sep 1988 .... 1.25

VIETNAM JOURNAL
APPLE

❑1, Nov 1987, b&w 2.00
❑1/2nd, ca. 1988 .... 2.00
❑2, Jan 1988 .... 2.00
❑3, Mar 1988 .... 2.00
❑4, May 1988 .... 2.00
❑5, Jul 1988 .... 2.00
❑6, Sep 1988 .... 2.00
❑7, Nov 1988 .... 2.00
❑8, Jan 1989 .... 2.00
❑9, Mar 1989 .... 2.00
❑10, May 1989 .... 2.00
❑11, Jul 1989 .... 2.25
❑12, Sep 1989 .... 2.25
❑13, Nov 1989 .... 2.25
❑14, Jan 1990 .... 2.25
❑15, Mar 1990 .... 2.25
❑16, May 1990 .... 2.25

VIETNAM JOURNAL: BLOODBATH AT KHE SANH
APPLE

❑1, b&w 2.75
❑2, b&w 2.75
❑3, b&w 2.75
❑4, b&w 2.75

VIETNAM JOURNAL: TET '68
APPLE

❑1, b&w 2.75
❑2, b&w 2.75
❑3, b&w 2.75
❑4, b&w 2.75
❑5, b&w 2.75
❑6, b&w 2.75

VIETNAM JOURNAL: VALLEY OF DEATH
APPLE

❑1, Jun 1994, b&w 2.75

VIGILANTE
DC

❑1, Nov 1983 .... 2.00
❑2, Jan 1984 .... 1.50
❑3, Feb 1984 .... 1.50
❑4, Mar 1984 .... 1.25
❑5, Apr 1984 .... 1.25
❑6, May 1984 .... 1.25
❑7, Jun 1984 .... 1.25
❑8, Jul 1984 .... 1.25
❑9, Aug 1984 .... 1.25
❑10, Sep 1984 .... 1.25
❑11, Oct 1984 .... 1.25
❑12, Nov 1984 .... 1.25
❑13, Dec 1984 .... 1.25
❑14, Feb 1985 .... 1.25
❑15, Mar 1985 .... 1.25
❑16, Apr 1985 .... 1.25
❑17, May 1985 .... 1.25
❑18, Jun 1985 .... 1.25
❑19, Jul 1985 .... 1.25
❑20, Aug 1985 .... 1.25
❑21, Sep 1985 .... 1.25
❑22, Oct 1985; Crisis 1.25
❑23, Nov 1985 .... 1.25
❑24, Dec 1985 .... 1.50
❑25, Jan 1986 .... 1.25
❑26, Feb 1986 .... 1.25
❑27, Mar 1986 .... 1.25
❑28, Apr 1986 .... 1.25
❑29, May 1986 .... 1.25
❑30, Jun 1986 .... 1.25
❑31, Jul 1986 .... 1.25
❑32, Aug 1986 .... 1.25
❑33, Sep 1986 .... 1.25
❑34, Oct 1986 .... 1.25
❑35, Nov 1986 .... 1.25
❑36, Dec 1986 .... 1.25
❑37, Jan 1987 .... 1.25
❑38, Feb 1987 .... 1.25
❑39, Mar 1987 .... 1.25
❑40, Apr 1987 .... 1.25
❑41, May 1987 .... 1.25
❑42, Jun 1987 .... 1.25
❑43, Jul 1987 .... 1.25
❑44, Aug 1987 .... 1.25
❑45, Sep 1987 .... 1.25
❑46, Oct 1987 .... 1.25
❑47, Nov 1987 .... 1.25
❑48, Dec 1987 .... 1.25
❑49, Jan 1988 .... 1.25
❑50, Feb 1988; Vigilante commits suicide 1.25
❑Annual 1, ca. 1985 .... 2.00
❑Annual 2, ca. 1986 .... 2.00

VIGILANTE 8: SECOND OFFENSE
CHAOS

❑1, Dec 1999 .... 2.95

VIGILANTE: CITY LIGHTS, PRAIRIE JUSTICE
DC

❑1, Nov 1995 .... 2.50
❑2, Dec 1995 .... 2.50
❑3, Jan 1996 .... 2.50
❑4, Feb 1996 .... 2.50

VIGILANTE (2ND SERIES)
DC

❑1 2005 .... 2.99
❑2, Jan 2006 .... 2.99
❑3, Jan 2006 .... 2.99
❑4, Feb 2006 .... 2.99
❑5, Mar 2006 .... 2.99
❑6, May 2006 .... 2.99

VIGIL: BLOODLINE
DUALITY

❑1, ca. 1998 .... 2.95
❑2, ca. 1998 .... 2.95
❑3, ca. 1998 .... 2.95
❑4, ca. 1998 .... 2.95
❑5, Nov 1998 .... 2.95
❑6, ca. 1999 .... 2.95
❑7, ca. 1999 .... 2.95
❑8, Jul 1999 .... 2.95

VIGIL: DESERT FOXES
MILLENNIUM

❑1, Jul 1995, b&w 3.95
❑2, Aug 1995, b&w 3.95

VIGIL: ERUPTION
MILLENNIUM

❑1, Aug 1996, b&w 2.95
❑2, ca. 1996 .... 2.95

VIGIL: FALL FROM GRACE
INNOVATION

❑1, Mar 1992, b&w 2.95
❑2, ca. 1992, b&w 2.95

VIGIL: KUKULKAN
INNOVATION

❑1 .... 2.95

VIGIL: REBIRTH
MILLENNIUM

❑1, Nov 1994, b&w 2.95
❑2, Dec 1994, b&w 2.95

VIGIL: SCATTERSHOTS
DUALITY

❑1, Jul 1997, b&w 3.95
❑2, ca. 1997 .... 3.95

VIGIL: THE GOLDEN PARTS
INNOVATION

❑1, b&w 2.95

VIGIL: VAMPORUM ANIMATURI
MILLENNIUM

❑1, May 1994, b&w 3.95

VIGNETTE COMICS
HARRIER

❑1, b&w 1.95

VILE
RAGING RHINO

❑1 .... 2.95

VILLAINS & VIGILANTES
ECLIPSE

❑1, Dec 1986 .... 1.50
❑2, Mar 1987 .... 1.50
❑3, Apr 1987 .... 1.50
❑4, Apr 1987 .... 1.50

VILLAINS UNITED
DC

❑1, Jun 2005 .... 12.00
❑1/2nd, Jun 2005 ....
❑1/3rd, Jun 2005 .... 3.00

Other grades: Multiply price above by 5/6 for VF/NM • 2/3 for VERY FINE • 1/3 for FINE • 1/5 for VERY GOOD • 1/8 for GOOD

❑2, Jul 2005 ... 5.00
❑3, Aug 2005 ... 2.50
❑4, Sep 2005 ... 2.50
❑5, Oct 2005 ... 2.50
❑6 2005 ... 2.50

VILLAINS UNITED: INFINITE CRISIS SPECIAL
DC

❑1, Jul 2006 ... 3.99

VILLA OF THE MYSTERIES
FANTAGRAPHICS

❑1, ca. 1998, b&w ... 3.95
❑2, ca. 1998, b&w ... 3.95
❑3, Jul 1998, b&w ... 3.95

VIMANARAMA!
DC

❑1, Apr 2005 ... 2.95
❑2, May 2005 ... 2.95
❑3, Jun 2005 ... 2.95

VINCENT J. MIELCAREK JR. MEMORIAL COMIC
COOPER UNION

❑1, b&w ... 3.00

VINTAGE COMIC CLASSICS
RECOLLECTIONS

❑1, Feb 1990; Red Demon reprint ... 2.00

VINTAGE MAGNUS ROBOT FIGHTER
VALIANT

❑1, Jan 1992; RM (w); RM (a); O: Magnus Robot Fighter. Reprints ... 5.00
❑2, Feb 1992; RM (w); RM (a); Reprints ... 5.00
❑3, Mar 1992; RM (w); RM (a); Reprints ... 5.00
❑4, Apr 1992; RM (w); RM (a); Reprints ... 5.00

VIOLATOR
IMAGE

❑1, May 1994, AMo (w); 1: The Admonisher ... 2.50
❑2, Jun 1994, AMo (w) ... 2.50
❑3, Jul 1994, AMo (w) ... 2.50

VIOLATOR VS. BADROCK
IMAGE

❑1, May 1995 ... 2.50
❑1/A, May 1995 ... 2.50
❑2, Jun 1995 ... 2.50
❑3, Jul 1995 ... 2.50
❑4, Aug 1995 ... 2.50
❑Book 1, Dec 1995 ... 9.95

VIOLENT CASES
TITAN

❑1 NG (w) ... 15.00
❑1/2nd; NG (w); In color, with new forward by Neil Gaiman ... 10.00
❑1/3rd; NG (w); Kitchen Sink publishes; New cover (red) by Dave McKean ... 12.95

VIOLENT MESSIAHS
HURRICANE

❑1, Jul 1997, b&w ... 2.95
❑2, ca. 1997 ... 2.95
❑3, ca. 1997 ... 2.95

VIOLENT MESSIAHS (2ND SERIES)
IMAGE

❑½/A, ca. 2000; Two pistols raised on cover ... 3.00
❑½/B, ca. 2000; One pistol up, one down on cover ... 3.00
❑1, Jun 2000 ... 2.95
❑2, Aug 2000 ... 2.95
❑3, Sep 2000 ... 2.95
❑4, Nov 2000 ... 2.95
❑5, Jan 2001 ... 2.95
❑6, Mar 2001 ... 2.95
❑7, Jun 2001 ... 2.95
❑8, Sep 2001 ... 2.95

VIOLENT MESSIAHS: GENESIS
IMAGE

❑1, Dec 2001, b&w; Collects Violent Messiahs 0.5, Hurricane #1-2, plus sketches ... 5.95

VIOLENT MESSIAHS: LAMENTING PAIN
IMAGE

❑1, Sep 2002 ... 2.95
❑3, Jan 2003 ... 2.95
❑4, Sep 2003 ... 2.95

VIOLENT TALES
DEATH

❑1, Nov 1997, b&w ... 2.95

VIPER
DC

❑1, Aug 1994 ... 1.95
❑2, Sep 1994 ... 1.95
❑3, Oct 1994 ... 1.95
❑4, Nov 1994 ... 1.95

VIPER FORCE
ACID RAM

❑1, Sep 1995 ... 2.50

VIRTEX
OKTOMICA

❑0, Oct 1998 ... 1.50
❑1, Dec 1998 ... 2.50
❑2, Jan 1999 ... 2.50
❑3 1999 ... 2.50
❑Ashcan 1 1999 ... 1.00

VIRTUA FIGHTER
MARVEL

❑1, Aug 1995 ... 2.95

VIRTUAL BANG
IRONCAT

❑1 ... 2.95
❑2 ... 2.95

VIRUS
DARK HORSE

❑1, ca. 1993 ... 2.50
❑2, ca. 1993 ... 2.50
❑3, ca. 1993 ... 2.50
❑4, ca. 1994 ... 2.50

VISAGE SPECIAL EDITION
ILLUSION

❑1, Aug 1996, b&w ... 2.00

VISION
MARVEL

❑1, Nov 1994 ... 1.75
❑2, Dec 1994 ... 1.75
❑3, Jan 1995 ... 1.75
❑4, Feb 1995 ... 1.75

VISION & SCARLET WITCH (VOL. 1)
MARVEL

❑1, Nov 1982 ... 1.50
❑2, Dec 1982 A: Whizzer ... 1.50
❑3, Jan 1983 A: Wonder Man ... 1.50
❑4, Feb 1983 A: Magneto ... 1.50

VISION & SCARLET WITCH (VOL. 2)
MARVEL

❑1, Oct 1985, RHo (a) ... 1.50
❑2, Nov 1985, RHo (a); D: Whizzer ... 1.25
❑3, Dec 1985, RHo (a) ... 1.25
❑4, Jan 1986, RHo (a) ... 1.25
❑5, Feb 1986, RHo (a) ... 1.25
❑6, Mar 1986, RHo (a) ... 1.25
❑7, Apr 1986, RHo (a) ... 1.25
❑8, May 1986, RHo (a) ... 1.25
❑9, Jun 1986, RHo (a) ... 1.25
❑10, Jul 1986, RHo (a) ... 1.25
❑11, Aug 1986, RHo (a); A: Spider-Man ... 1.25
❑12, Sep 1986, RHo (a) ... 1.25

VISIONARIES
MARVEL / STAR

❑1, Jan 1988; Giant sized ... 1.00
❑2, Feb 1988 ... 1.00
❑3, Mar 1988 ... 1.00
❑4, Apr 1988 ... 1.00
❑5, May 1988 ... 1.00
❑6, Jun 1988 ... 1.00

VISIONS
CALIBER

❑1 ... 4.95

VISIONS: DAVID MACK
CALIBER

❑1 ... 5.95

VISIONS OF CURVES
FANTAGRAPHICS / EROS

❑1, Apr 1994, b&w ... 4.95
❑2, ca. 1994 ... 4.95
❑3, May 1995; Sketchbook ... 4.95

VISIONS: R.G. TAYLOR
CALIBER

❑1, b&w ... 2.50

VISITATIONS
IMAGE

❑1, b&w; squarebound ... 6.95

VISITOR
VALIANT

❑1, Apr 1995 ... 2.00
❑2, May 1995 ... 2.00
❑3, Jun 1995; Acclaim begins publishing ... 2.00
❑4, Jul 1995 ... 2.00
❑5, Jul 1995 ... 2.00
❑6, Aug 1995 ... 2.00
❑7, Aug 1995 ... 2.00
❑8, Sep 1995; The Harbinger's identity is revealed ... 2.00
❑9, Sep 1995 ... 2.00
❑10, Oct 1995 ... 2.00
❑11, Oct 1995 ... 3.00
❑12, Nov 1995 ... 3.00
❑13, Nov 1995 ... 5.00

VISITOR VS. THE VALIANT UNIVERSE
VALIANT

❑1, Feb 1995; cardstock cover ... 3.00
❑1/$2.50, Feb 1995 ... 10.00
❑2, Mar 1995; cardstock cover ... 3.00
❑2/$2.50, Mar 1995 ... 10.00

VISUAL ASSAULT OMNIBUS
VISUAL ASSAULT

❑1, b&w ... 2.50
❑2, b&w ... 2.50
❑3, b&w; Flip-book ... 3.00

VIXEN 9
SAMSON

❑1, Flip-book; no indicia ... 2.50

VIXEN'S KEEP
MU

❑Book 1, Nov 1995; tpb b&w anthology ... 5.95

VIXEN WARRIOR DIARIES
RAGING RHINO

❑1, b&w ... 2.95

VIXEN WARS
RAGING RHINO

❑1, b&w ... 2.95
❑2, b&w ... 2.95
❑3, b&w ... 2.95
❑4, b&w ... 2.95
❑5, b&w ... 2.95
❑6 ... 2.95
❑7 ... 2.95
❑8 ... 2.95
❑9, Twisted Vixen stories begin ... 2.95
❑10, Title changes to Twisted Vixen ... 2.95

VOGUE
IMAGE

❑1, Oct 1995 ... 2.50
❑1/A, Oct 1995; alternate cover ... 2.50
❑2, Nov 1995 ... 2.50
❑3, Dec 1995 ... 2.50
❑4, Jan 1996 ... 2.50

VOID INDIGO
MARVEL / EPIC

❑1, Nov 1984; VM (a); Continued from Marvel Graphic Novel ... 2.00
❑2, Mar 1985 VM (a) ... 2.00

VOLCANIC NIGHTS
PALLIARD

❑1, b&w ... 2.95

VOLCANIC REVOLVER
ONI

❑1, Jan 1999, b&w ... 2.95
❑2, Jan 1999, b&w ... 2.95
❑3, Mar 1999, b&w ... 2.95

VOLTRON
SOLSON

❑1 ... 1.00
❑2 ... 1.00
❑3 ... 1.00

VOLTRON: DEFENDER OF THE UNIVERSE
IMAGE

❑0, May 2003 ... 2.50
❑1, May 2003 ... 2.95
❑2, Jun 2003 ... 2.95
❑3, Jul 2003 ... 2.95

Walt Disney's Comics and Stories

Timeless stories in landmark series

©Dell

Walt Disney's Comics and Stories Penny Pincher

Barks' reprints in bargain package

©Gladstone

Walt Disney's Holiday Parade

Classic Christmas fare meets new treats

©Disney

Walt Disney Showcase

Mostly movie adaptations

©Gold Key

Walt Disney's World of Adventure

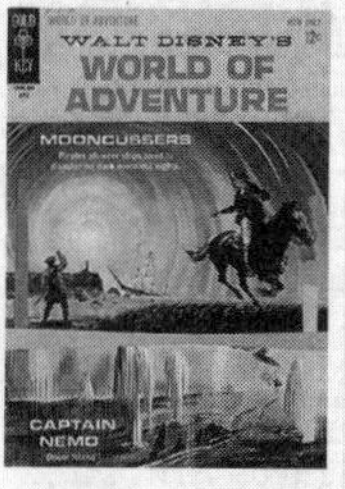

Action abounds in short-lived series

©Gold Key

N-MINT

- ❑4, Sep 2003 .... 2.95
- ❑5, Oct 2003 .... 2.95

VOLTRON: DEFENDER OF THE UNIVERSE (VOL. 2)
DEVIL'S DUE

- ❑1, Jan 2004 .... 2.95
- ❑2, Feb 2004 .... 2.95
- ❑3, Mar 2004 .... 2.95
- ❑4, Apr 2004 .... 2.95
- ❑5, May 2004 .... 2.95
- ❑6, Jun 2004 .... 2.95
- ❑7, Jul 2004 .... 2.95
- ❑8, Aug 2004 .... 2.95
- ❑9, Sep 2004 .... 2.95
- ❑10, Oct 2004 .... 2.95
- ❑11, Nov 2005 .... 2.95

VOLUNTEER COMICS SUMMER LINE-UP '96
VOLUNTEER

- ❑1, Sum 1996, b&w; previews 2.95

VOLUNTEER COMICS WINTER LINE-UP '96
VOLUNTEER

- ❑1, ca. 1996, b&w; previews 2.95

VOLUNTEERS QUEST FOR DREAMS LOST
LITERACY

- ❑1, b&w; Turtles; Trollords 2.00

VON FANGE BROTHERS: GREEN HAIR AND RED "S'S"
MIKEY-SIZED COMICS

- ❑1, Jul 1996, b&w 1.75

VON FANGE BROTHERS: THE UNCOMMONS
MIKEY-SIZED COMICS

- ❑1, Oct 1996, b&w 1.75

VONPYRE
EYEFUL

- ❑1 .... 2.95

VOODOO (IMAGE)
IMAGE

- ❑1, Nov 1997 .... 2.50
- ❑2, Dec 1997 .... 2.50
- ❑3, Jan 1998 .... 2.50
- ❑4, Mar 1998 .... 2.50

VOODOO INK
DEJA-VU

- ❑0, ca. 1989, b&w 1.95
- ❑1, ca. 1990, b&w 1.95
- ❑2, Sum 1990, b&w 1.95
- ❑3, Fal 1990, b&w 1.95
- ❑4, Win 1990, b&w 1.95
- ❑5, ca. 1991, b&w 1.95

VOODOOM
ONI

- ❑1, Jun 2000, b&w; smaller than regular comic book 4.95

VOODOO•ZEALOT: SKIN TRADE
IMAGE

- ❑1, Aug 1995 .... 4.95

N-MINT

VORTEX (VORTEX)
VORTEX

- ❑1, Nov 1982 .... 2.00
- ❑2, ca. 1983 .... 2.00
- ❑3, May 1983 .... 2.00
- ❑4, ca. 1983 .... 2.00
- ❑5, ca. 1983 .... 2.00
- ❑6, ca. 1983 .... 2.00
- ❑7, ca. 1984 .... 2.00
- ❑8, ca. 1984 .... 2.00
- ❑9, ca. 1984 .... 2.00
- ❑10, Sep 1984 GD (w); GD (a) 2.00
- ❑11, ca. 1984 .... 1.75
- ❑12, ca. 1985 .... 1.75
- ❑13, ca. 1985 .... 1.75
- ❑14, ca. 1985 .... 1.75
- ❑15, ca. 1985 .... 1.75

VORTEX (COMICO)
COMICO

- ❑1, Oct 1991 .... 2.50
- ❑2, ca. 1991 .... 2.50
- ❑3, ca. 1992, Exists? 2.50
- ❑4, ca. 1992, Exists? 2.50

VORTEX (HALL OF HEROES)
HALL OF HEROES

- ❑1, Aug 1993, b&w 2.50
- ❑2, Oct 1993 .... 2.50
- ❑3, Dec 1993 .... 2.50
- ❑4, Feb 1994 .... 2.50
- ❑5, Apr 1994 .... 2.50
- ❑6, Dec 1994 .... 2.50

VORTEX (ENTITY)
ENTITY

- ❑1, Jan 1996 .... 2.95

VORTEX THE WONDER MULE
CUTTING EDGE

- ❑1, b&w 2.95
- ❑2, b&w 2.95

VOX
APPLE

- ❑1, Jun 1989, b&w JBy (c); JBy (a) 2.00
- ❑2, ca. 1989 .... 2.25
- ❑3, ca. 1989 .... 2.25
- ❑4, ca. 1989 .... 2.25
- ❑5, ca. 1989 .... 2.25
- ❑6, ca. 1990 .... 2.25
- ❑7, ca. 1990 .... 2.25

VOYAGE TO THE BOTTOM OF THE SEA
GOLD KEY

- ❑1, Dec 1964 .... 60.00
- ❑2, ca. 1965 .... 45.00
- ❑3, Oct 1965 .... 35.00
- ❑4, May 1966 .... 35.00
- ❑5, Aug 1966 .... 35.00
- ❑6, Nov 1966 .... 25.00
- ❑7, Feb 1967 .... 25.00
- ❑8, May 1967 .... 25.00
- ❑9, Aug 1967 .... 25.00
- ❑10, Nov 1967 .... 25.00
- ❑11, Feb 1968 .... 18.00
- ❑12, May 1968 .... 18.00
- ❑13, Aug 1968 .... 18.00

N-MINT

- ❑14, Nov 1968 .... 18.00
- ❑15, Feb 1969 .... 12.00
- ❑16, May 1969 .... 12.00

VOYEUR
AIRCEL

- ❑1, b&w 2.50
- ❑2, b&w 2.50
- ❑3, b&w 2.50
- ❑4 .... 2.95

VROOM SOCKO
SLAVE LABOR

- ❑1, Nov 1993; reprints strips from Deadline U.K. 2.50

VULGAR VINCE
THROB

- ❑1 .... 1.75

VULTURES OF WHAPETON
CONQUEST

- ❑1, b&w 2.95

W
GOOD

- ❑1, Nov 1996 .... 2.95

WABBIT WAMPAGE
AMAZING

- ❑1 .... 1.95

WACKY ADVENTURES OF CRACKY
GOLD KEY

- ❑1, Dec 1972 .... 5.00
- ❑2, Mar 1973 .... 3.00
- ❑3, Jun 1973 .... 2.50
- ❑4, Sep 1973 .... 2.50
- ❑5, Dec 1973 .... 2.50
- ❑6, Mar 1974 .... 2.00
- ❑7, Jun 1974 .... 2.00
- ❑8, Sep 1974 .... 2.00
- ❑9, Dec 1974 .... 2.00
- ❑10, Mar 1975 .... 2.00
- ❑11, Jun 1975 .... 2.00
- ❑12, Sep 1975 .... 2.00

WACKY RACES
GOLD KEY

- ❑1, Aug 1969 .... 40.00
- ❑2, Feb 1971 .... 26.00
- ❑3, May 1971 .... 20.00
- ❑4, Aug 1971 .... 20.00
- ❑5, Nov 1971 .... 20.00
- ❑6, Feb 1972 .... 20.00
- ❑7, May 1972 .... 20.00

WACKY SQUIRREL
DARK HORSE

- ❑1 1987, b&w 2.00
- ❑2 1988 .... 2.00
- ❑3 1988 .... 2.00
- ❑4, Oct 1988 .... 2.00
- ❑Special 1, Oct 1987; Flip-book; A: Mr. Monster. Halloween Adventure Special 2.00
- ❑Summer 1, Jul 1987; Summer Fun Special 2.00

WACKY WITCH
GOLD KEY

- ❑1, Jan 1971 .... 12.00

❑2, Apr 1971 ... 7.00
❑3, Jul 1971 ... 5.00
❑4, Oct 1971 ... 5.00
❑5, Jan 1972 ... 5.00
❑6, Apr 1972 ... 4.00
❑7, Jul 1972 ... 4.00
❑8, Oct 1972 ... 4.00
❑9, Jan 1973 ... 4.00
❑10, Apr 1973 ... 4.00
❑11, Jul 1973 ... 3.00
❑12, Oct 1973 ... 3.00
❑13, Jan 1974 ... 3.00
❑14, Apr 1974 ... 3.00
❑15, Jul 1974 ... 3.00
❑16, Oct 1974 ... 3.00
❑17, Jan 1975 ... 3.00
❑18, Apr 1975 ... 3.00
❑19, Jul 1975 ... 3.00
❑20, Oct 1975 ... 3.00
❑21, Jan 1976 ... 3.00

WAGON TRAIN (DELL)
Dell

❑4, Jan 1960 ... 38.00
❑5, Apr 1960 ... 38.00
❑6, Jul 1960 ... 38.00
❑7, Oct 1960 ... 34.00
❑8, Jan 1961 ... 34.00
❑9, Apr 1961 ... 34.00
❑10, Jul 1961 ... 25.00
❑11, Oct 1961 ... 25.00
❑12, Jan 1962 ... 25.00
❑13, Apr 1962 ... 25.00

WAGON TRAIN (GOLD KEY)
Gold Key

❑1, Jan 1964 ... 38.00
❑2, Apr 1964 ... 25.00
❑3, Jul 1964 ... 25.00
❑4, Oct 1964 ... 25.00

WAHH
Frank & Hank

❑1, b&w; no indicia; cardstock cover.. 2.95
❑2, b&w; cardstock cover ... 2.95

WAHOO MORRIS (VOL. 2)
Too Hip Gott Go Graphics

❑1, Aug 2005 ... 2.75

WAHOO MORRIS (IMAGE)
Image

❑1, Mar 2000 ... 2.50

WAHOO MORRIS (VOL. 1)
Too Hip Gott Go Graphics

❑1, Jun 1998, b&w ... 2.75
❑2, Oct 1988, b&w ... 2.75
❑3, Mar 1999, b&w ... 2.75

WAITING FOR THE END OF THE WORLD
Rodent

❑1 ... 1.00
❑2 ... 1.00
❑3 ... 1.00

WAITING PLACE
Slave Labor

❑1, Apr 1997 ... 2.95
❑2, May 1997 ... 2.95
❑3, Jun 1997 ... 2.95
❑4, Jul 1997 ... 2.95
❑5, Aug 1997 ... 2.95
❑6, Sep 1997 ... 2.95

WAKE
NBM

❑1 ... 9.95
❑2 ... 8.95
❑3 ... 9.95

WALDO WORLD
Fantagraphics

❑1 ... 2.50
❑2 ... 2.50

WALKING DEAD (IMAGE)
Image

❑1, Oct 2003, b&w ... 35.00
❑2, Nov 2003, b&w ... 32.00
❑3, Dec 2003, b&w ... 15.00
❑4, Jan 2004, b&w ... 12.00
❑4/A, Jan 2004, b&w ... 6.00
❑5, Feb 2004, b&w ... 4.00
❑6, Mar 2004, b&w ... 2.95
❑7, Apr 2004, b&w ... 2.95
❑8, May 2004, b&w ... 2.95
❑9, Jun 2004, b&w ... 2.95
❑10, Jul 2004, b&w ... 2.95
❑11, Aug 2004, b&w ... 2.95
❑12, Sep 2004, b&w ... 2.95
❑13, Oct 2004, b&w ... 2.95
❑14, Nov 2004, b&w ... 2.95
❑15, Dec 2004 ... 2.95
❑16, Jan 2005 ... 2.95
❑17, Feb 2005 ... 2.95
❑18, ca. 2005 ... 2.95
❑19 2005 ... 2.95
❑20, Aug 2005 ... 2.99
❑21, Oct 2005 ... 2.99
❑22, Nov 2005 ... 2.99
❑23, Dec 2005 ... 2.99
❑24, Jan 2006 ... 2.99
❑25, Jan 2006 ... 2.99
❑26, Apr 2006 ... 2.99
❑27, May 2006 ... 2.99
❑28, Jul 2006 ... 2.99
❑Book 1, ca. 2004, b&w ... 9.95

WALKING DEAD
Aircel

❑1 1989 ... 5.00
❑2 1989 ... 3.00
❑3 1989 ... 3.00
❑4 1989 ... 3.00
❑Special 1 1989, b&w ... 4.00

WALK THROUGH OCTOBER
Caliber

❑1, ca. 1995, b&w ... 2.95

WALL OF FLESH
AC

❑1, b&w; Reprints ... 3.50

WALLY
Gold Key

❑1, Dec 1962 ... 30.00
❑2, Mar 1963 ... 22.00
❑3, Jun 1963 ... 22.00
❑4, Sep 1963 ... 22.00

WALLY THE WIZARD
Marvel / Star

❑1, Apr 1985 ... 1.00
❑2, May 1985 ... 1.00
❑3, Jun 1985 ... 1.00
❑4, Jul 1985 ... 1.00
❑5, Aug 1985 ... 1.00
❑6, Sep 1985 ... 1.00
❑7, Oct 1985 ... 1.00
❑8, Nov 1985 ... 1.00
❑9, Dec 1985 ... 1.00
❑10, Jan 1986 ... 1.00
❑11, Feb 1986 ... 1.00
❑12, Mar 1986 ... 1.00

WALT DISNEY COMICS DIGEST
Gold Key

❑1, Jun 1968 ... 60.00
❑2, Jul 1968 ... 40.00
❑3, Aug 1968 ... 40.00
❑4, Oct 1968 ... 40.00
❑5, Nov 1968 ... 40.00
❑6, Dec 1968 ... 25.00
❑7, Jan 1969 ... 25.00
❑8, Feb 1969 ... 25.00
❑9, Mar 1969 ... 25.00
❑10, Apr 1969 ... 25.00
❑11, May 1969 ... 25.00
❑12, Jun 1969 ... 25.00
❑13, Jul 1969 ... 25.00
❑14, Aug 1969 ... 20.00
❑15, Sep 1969 ... 20.00
❑16, Oct 1969 ... 20.00
❑17, Nov 1969 ... 20.00
❑18, Dec 1969 ... 20.00
❑19, Jan 1970 ... 20.00
❑20, Feb 1970 ... 20.00
❑21, Apr 1970 ... 15.00
❑22, Jun 1970 ... 15.00
❑23, Jul 1970 ... 15.00
❑24, Aug 1970 ... 15.00
❑25, Oct 1970 ... 15.00
❑26, Dec 1970 ... 15.00
❑27, Feb 1971 ... 15.00
❑28, Apr 1971 ... 15.00
❑29, Jun 1971 ... 15.00
❑30, Aug 1971 ... 15.00
❑31, Oct 1971 ... 15.00
❑32, Dec 1971 ... 15.00
❑33, Feb 1972 ... 15.00
❑34, Apr 1972 ... 15.00
❑35, Jun 1972; Feature on the 1972 film The Biscuit Eater ... 15.00
❑36, Aug 1972 ... 15.00
❑37, Oct 1972; Feature on the 1972 film Now You See Him, Now You Don't . 15.00
❑38, Dec 1972 ... 15.00
❑39, Feb 1973 ... 15.00
❑40, Apr 1973 ... 15.00
❑41, Jun 1973 ... 15.00
❑42, Aug 1973; Mary Poppins cover .. 15.00
❑43, Oct 1973 ... 15.00
❑44, Dec 1973 ... 40.00
❑45, Feb 1974 ... 15.00
❑46, Apr 1974 ... 15.00
❑47, Jun 1974 ... 15.00
❑48, Aug 1974 ... 15.00
❑49, Oct 1974 ... 15.00
❑50, Dec 1974 ... 15.00
❑51, Feb 1975 ... 10.00
❑52, Apr 1975 ... 10.00
❑53, Jun 1975 ... 10.00
❑54, Aug 1975 ... 10.00
❑55, Oct 1975 ... 10.00
❑56, Dec 1975 ... 10.00
❑57, Feb 1976 ... 10.00

WALT DISNEY GIANT
Gladstone

❑1, Sep 1995; newsprint cover ... 2.25
❑2, Nov 1995; newsprint cover ... 2.25
❑3, Jan 1996; newsprint cover ... 2.25
❑4, Mar 1996; Mickey Mouse; newsprint cover ... 2.25
❑5, May 1996; Mickey and Donald; newsprint cover ... 2.25
❑6, Jul 1996; Uncle Scrooge and the Junior Woodchucks; newsprint cover ... 2.25
❑7, Sep 1996; newsprint cover ... 2.25

WALT DISNEY'S AUTUMN ADVENTURES
Disney

❑1, Fal 1991 ... 2.95
❑2, Fal 1992 ... 2.95

WALT DISNEY'S CHRISTMAS PARADE (GOLD KEY)
Gold Key

❑1, May 1962 ... 75.00
❑2, Jan 1964 ... 50.00
❑3 1965 ... 50.00
❑4 1966 ... 50.00
❑5, Feb 1967 ... 50.00
❑6, Feb 1968 ... 50.00
❑7, Jan 1970 ... 50.00
❑8, Jan 1971 ... 50.00
❑9, Jan 1972 ... 20.00

WALT DISNEY'S CHRISTMAS PARADE (GLADSTONE)
Gladstone

❑1, Win 1988; cardstock cover; reprints ... 2.95
❑2, Win 1989; Reprints ... 2.95

WALT DISNEY'S CHRISTMAS PARADE (GEMSTONE)
Gemstone

❑1, Nov 2003 ... 8.95
❑3, Dec 2005

WALT DISNEY'S COMICS AND STORIES
Dell

❑193, Oct 1956 CB (w); CB (a) ... 80.00
❑194, Nov 1956 CB (w); CB (a) ... 80.00
❑195, Dec 1956 CB (w); CB (a) ... 80.00
❑196, Jan 1957 CB (w); CB (a) ... 80.00
❑197, Feb 1957 CB (w); CB (a) ... 80.00
❑198, Mar 1957 CB (w); CB (a) ... 80.00
❑199, Apr 1957 CB (w); CB (a) ... 80.00
❑200, May 1957 CB (w); CB (a) ... 80.00

Walter

Mask meanie gets solo shot
©Dark Horse

Wanderers

Legion spin-off features revived adventurers
©DC

Wandering Star

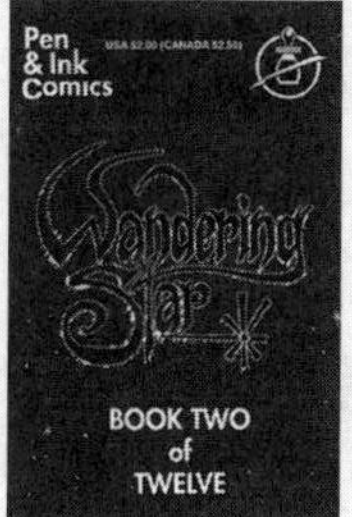

Academy attendees flashback on events
©Pen and Ink

Wanted

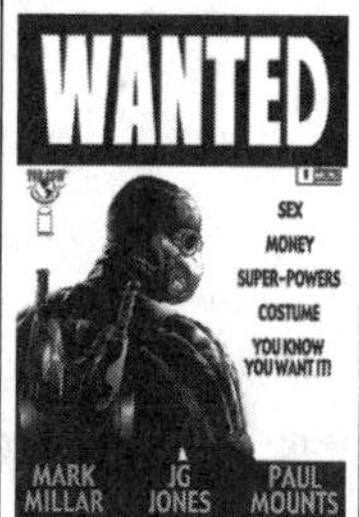

Super-villain son embraces destiny
©Image

Wanted, the World's Most Dangerous Villains

Secret origins for super-villains
©DC

	N-MINT
❑201, Jun 1957 CB (w); CB (a)	75.00
❑202, Jul 1957 CB (w); CB (a)	75.00
❑203, Aug 1957 CB (w); CB (a)	75.00
❑204, Sep 1957 CB (w); CB (a)	75.00
❑205, Oct 1957 CB (w); CB (a)	75.00
❑206, Nov 1957 CB (w); CB (a)	75.00
❑207, Dec 1957 CB (w); CB (a)	75.00
❑208, Jan 1958 CB (w); CB (a)	75.00
❑209, Feb 1958 CB (w); CB (a)	75.00
❑210, Mar 1958 CB (w); CB (a)	75.00
❑211, Apr 1958 CB (w); CB (a)	75.00
❑212, May 1958 CB (w); CB (a)	75.00
❑213, Jun 1958 CB (w); CB (a)	75.00
❑214, Jul 1958 CB (c); CB (w); CB (a)	75.00
❑215, Aug 1958 CB (w); CB (a)	75.00
❑216, Sep 1958 CB (w); CB (a)	75.00
❑217, Oct 1958 CB (w); CB (a)	75.00
❑218, Nov 1958 CB (w); CB (a)	75.00
❑219, Dec 1958 CB (w); CB (a)	75.00
❑220, Jan 1959 CB (w); CB (a)	75.00
❑221, Feb 1959 CB (w); CB (a)	75.00
❑222, Mar 1959 CB (w); CB (a)	75.00
❑223, Apr 1959 CB (w); CB (a)	75.00
❑224, May 1959 CB (w); CB (a)	75.00
❑225, Jun 1959 CB (w); CB (a)	75.00
❑226, Jul 1959 CB (w); CB (a)	75.00
❑227, Aug 1959 CB (w); CB (a)	75.00
❑228, Sep 1959 CB (w); CB (a)	75.00
❑229, Oct 1959 CB (w); CB (a)	75.00
❑230, Nov 1959 CB (w); CB (a)	75.00
❑231, Dec 1959 CB (w); CB (a)	75.00
❑232, Jan 1960 CB (w); CB (a)	75.00
❑233, Feb 1960 CB (w); CB (a)	75.00
❑234, Mar 1960 CB (w); CB (a)	75.00
❑235, Apr 1960 CB (w); CB (a)	75.00
❑236, May 1960 CB (w); CB (a)	75.00
❑237, Jun 1960 CB (w); CB (a)	75.00
❑238, Jul 1960 CB (w); CB (a)	75.00
❑239, Aug 1960 CB (w); CB (a)	75.00
❑240, Sep 1960 CB (w); CB (a)	75.00
❑241, Oct 1960 CB (w); CB (a)	60.00
❑242, Nov 1960 CB (w); CB (a)	60.00
❑243, Dec 1960 CB (w); CB (a)	60.00
❑244, Jan 1961 CB (w); CB (a)	60.00
❑245, Feb 1961 CB (w); CB (a)	60.00
❑246, Mar 1961 CB (w); CB (a)	60.00
❑247, Apr 1961 CB (w); CB (a)	60.00
❑248, May 1961 CB (w); CB (a)	60.00
❑249, Jun 1961 CB (w); CB (a)	60.00
❑250, Jul 1961 CB (w); CB (a)	60.00
❑251, Aug 1961 CB (w); CB (a)	60.00
❑252, Sep 1961 CB (w); CB (a)	60.00
❑253, Oct 1961 CB (w); CB (a)	60.00
❑254, Nov 1961 CB (w); CB (a)	60.00
❑255, Dec 1961 CB (w); CB (a)	60.00
❑256, Jan 1962 CB (w); CB (a)	60.00
❑257, Feb 1962 CB (w); CB (a)	60.00
❑258, Mar 1962 CB (w); CB (a)	60.00
❑259, Apr 1962 CB (w); CB (a)	60.00
❑260, May 1962 CB (w); CB (a)	60.00
❑261, Jun 1962 CB (w); CB (a)	50.00
❑262, Jul 1962 CB (w); CB (a)	50.00
❑263, Aug 1962 CB (w); CB (a)	50.00
❑264, Sep 1962 CB (w); CB (a)	50.00
❑265, Oct 1962 CB (w); CB (a)	50.00
❑266, Nov 1962 CB (w); CB (a)	50.00
❑267, Dec 1962 CB (w); CB (a)	50.00
❑268, Jan 1963 CB (w); CB (a)	50.00
❑269, Feb 1963 CB (w); CB (a)	50.00
❑270, Mar 1963 CB (w); CB (a)	50.00
❑271, Apr 1963 CB (w); CB (a)	50.00
❑272, May 1963 CB (w); CB (a)	50.00
❑273, Jun 1963 CB (w); CB (a)	50.00
❑274, Jul 1963 CB (w); CB (a)	50.00
❑275, Aug 1963 CB (w); CB (a)	50.00
❑276, Sep 1963 CB (w); CB (a)	50.00
❑277, Oct 1963 CB (w); CB (a)	50.00
❑278, Nov 1963 CB (w); CB (a)	50.00
❑279, Dec 1963 CB (w); CB (a)	50.00
❑280, Jan 1964 CB (w); CB (a)	50.00
❑281, Feb 1964 CB (w); CB (a)	50.00
❑282, Mar 1964 CB (w); CB (a)	50.00
❑283, Apr 1964 CB (w); CB (a)	50.00
❑284, May 1964	25.00
❑285, Jun 1964	25.00
❑286, Jul 1964 CB (w); CB (a)	28.00
❑287, Aug 1964	25.00
❑288, Sep 1964 CB (w); CB (a)	28.00
❑289, Oct 1964 CB (w); CB (a)	28.00
❑290, Nov 1964	25.00
❑291, Dec 1964 CB (w); CB (a)	28.00
❑292, Jan 1965 CB (w); CB (a)	28.00
❑293, Feb 1965 CB (w); CB (a)	28.00
❑294, Mar 1965	25.00
❑295, Apr 1965	25.00
❑296, May 1965	25.00
❑297, Jun 1965; CB (w); CB (a); Reprints story from Uncle Scrooge #20	28.00
❑298, Jul 1965; CB (w); CB (a); Reprints story from Four Color Comics #1055 (Daisy Duck's Diary)	28.00
❑299, Aug 1965; CB (w); CB (a); Reprints story from Walt Disney's Comics #117	28.00
❑300, Sep 1965; CB (w); CB (a); Reprints story from Walt Disney's Comics #43	28.00
❑301, Oct 1965; CB (w); CB (a); Reprints stories from Four Color Comics #1150 (Daisy Duck's Diary) and Walt Disney's Comics #44	28.00
❑302, Nov 1965; CB (w); CB (a); Reprints story from Walt Disney's Comics #47	28.00
❑303, Dec 1965; CB (w); CB (a); Reprints story from Walt Disney's Comics #49	28.00
❑304, Jan 1966; CB (w); CB (a); Reprints stories from Four Color Comics #1150 (Daisy Duck's Diary) and Walt Disney's Comics #63	28.00
❑305, Feb 1966; CB (w); CB (a); Reprints stories from Uncle Scrooge #25 andWalt Disney's Comics #70.	28.00
❑306, Mar 1966; CB (w); CB (a); Reprints story from Walt Disney's Comics #94	28.00
❑307, Apr 1966; CB (w); CB (a); Reprints story from Walt Disney's Comics #91	28.00
❑308, May 1966 CB (w); CB (a)	28.00
❑309, Jun 1966	25.00
❑310, Jul 1966	25.00
❑311, Aug 1966	25.00
❑312, Sep 1966 CB (w); CB (a)	28.00
❑313, Oct 1966	14.00
❑314, Nov 1966	14.00
❑315, Dec 1966	14.00
❑316, Jan 1967	14.00
❑317, Feb 1967	14.00
❑318, Mar 1967	14.00
❑319, Apr 1967	14.00
❑320, May 1967	14.00
❑321, Jun 1967	14.00
❑322, Jul 1967	14.00
❑323, Aug 1967	14.00
❑324, Sep 1967	14.00
❑325, Oct 1967	14.00
❑326, Nov 1967	14.00
❑327, Dec 1967	14.00
❑328, Jan 1968; CB (w); CB (a); Reprints story from Walt Disney's Comics #148	14.00
❑329, Feb 1968	14.00
❑330, Mar 1968	14.00
❑331, Apr 1968	14.00
❑332, May 1968	14.00
❑333, Jun 1968	14.00
❑334, Jul 1968	14.00
❑335, Aug 1968; CB (w); CB (a); Reprints story from Walt Disney's Comics #129	25.00
❑336, Sep 1968	14.00
❑337, Oct 1968	14.00
❑338, Nov 1968	14.00
❑339, Dec 1968	14.00
❑340, Jan 1969	14.00
❑341, Feb 1969	14.00
❑342, Mar 1969; CB (w); CB (a); Reprints story from Walt Disney's Comics #131	25.00
❑343, Apr 1969; CB (w); CB (a); Reprints story from Walt Disney's Comics #144	25.00
❑344, May 1969; CB (w); CB (a); Reprints story from Walt Disney's Comics #127	25.00
❑345, Jun 1969; CB (w); CB (a); Reprints story from Walt Disney's Comics #139	25.00
❑346, Jul 1969; CB (w); CB (a); Reprints story from Walt Disney's Comics #140	25.00
❑347, Aug 1969; CB (w); CB (a); Reprints story from Walt Disney's Comics #141	25.00
❑348, Sep 1969; CB (w); CB (a); Reprints story from Walt Disney's Comics #155	25.00
❑349, Oct 1969; CB (w); CB (a); Reprints story from Walt Disney's Comics #92	25.00
❑350, Nov 1969; CB (w); CB (a); Reprints story from Walt Disney's Comics #133	25.00
❑351, Dec 1969; CB (w); CB (a); Reprints story from Walt Disney's Comics #147	25.00

Other grades: Multiply price above by 5/6 for VF/NM • 2/3 for VERY FINE • 1/3 for FINE • 1/5 for VERY GOOD • 1/8 for GOOD

	N-MINT
❑351/Poster, Dec 1969; CB (w); CB (a); Reprints story from Walt Disney's Comics #147; with poster insert	30.00
❑351/No poster, Dec 1969; CB (w); CB (a); Reprints story from Walt Disney's Comics #147; poster insert removed	20.00
❑352, Jan 1970; CB (w); CB (a); Reprints story from Walt Disney's Comics #160	25.00
❑352/Poster, Jan 1970; CB (w); CB (a); Reprints story from Walt Disney's Comics #160; with poster insert	30.00
❑352/No poster, Jan 1970; CB (w); CB (a); Reprints story from Walt Disney's Comics #160; poster insert removed	20.00
❑353, Feb 1970; CB (w); CB (a); Reprints story from Walt Disney's Comics #173	25.00
❑353/Poster, Feb 1970; CB (w); CB (a); Reprints story from Walt Disney's Comics #173; with poster insert	30.00
❑353/No poster, Feb 1970; CB (w); CB (a); Reprints story from Walt Disney's Comics #173; poster insert removed	20.00
❑354, Mar 1970; CB (w); CB (a); Reprints story from Walt Disney's Comics #197	25.00
❑354/Poster, Mar 1970; CB (w); CB (a); Reprints story from Walt Disney's Comics #197; with poster insert	30.00
❑354/No poster, Mar 1970; CB (w); CB (a); Reprints story from Walt Disney's Comics #197; poster insert removed	20.00
❑355, Apr 1970; CB (w); CB (a); Reprints story from Walt Disney's Comics #206	25.00
❑355/Poster, Apr 1970; CB (w); CB (a); Reprints story from Walt Disney's Comics #206; with poster insert	30.00
❑355/No poster, Apr 1970; CB (w); CB (a); Reprints story from Walt Disney's Comics #206; poster insert removed	20.00
❑356, May 1970; CB (w); CB (a); Reprints story from Walt Disney's Comics #103	25.00
❑356/Poster, May 1970; CB (w); CB (a); Reprints story from Walt Disney's Comics #103; with poster insert	30.00
❑356/No poster, May 1970; CB (w); CB (a); Reprints story from Walt Disney's Comics #103; poster insert removed	20.00
❑357, Jun 1970; CB (w); CB (a); Reprints story from Walt Disney's Comics #145	25.00
❑357/Poster, Jun 1970; CB (w); CB (a); Reprints story from Walt Disney's Comics #145; with poster insert	30.00
❑357/No poster, Jun 1970; CB (w); CB (a); Reprints story from Walt Disney's Comics #145; poster insert removed	20.00
❑358, Jul 1970; CB (w); CB (a); Reprints story from Walt Disney's Comics #146	25.00
❑358/Poster, Jul 1970; CB (w); CB (a); Reprints story from Walt Disney's Comics #146; with poster insert	30.00
❑358/No poster, Jul 1970; CB (w); CB (a); Reprints story from Walt Disney's Comics #146; poster insert removed	20.00
❑359, Aug 1970; CB (w); CB (a); Reprints story from Walt Disney's Comics #154	25.00
❑359/Poster, Aug 1970; CB (w); CB (a); Reprints story from Walt Disney's Comics #154; with poster insert	30.00
❑359/No poster, Aug 1970; CB (w); CB (a); Reprints story from Walt Disney's Comics #154; poster insert removed	20.00
❑360, Sep 1970; CB (w); CB (a); Reprints story from Walt Disney's Comics #200	25.00
❑360/Poster, Sep 1970; CB (w); CB (a); Reprints story from Walt Disney's Comics #200; with poster insert	30.00
❑360/No poster, Sep 1970; CB (w); CB (a); Reprints story from Walt Disney's Comics #200; poster insert removed	20.00

	N-MINT
❑361, Oct 1970; CB (w); CB (a); Reprints story from Walt Disney's Comics #158	25.00
❑362, Nov 1970; CB (w); CB (a); Reprints story from Walt Disney's Comics #180	25.00
❑363, Dec 1970; CB (w); CB (a); Reprints story from Walt Disney's Comics #126	25.00
❑364, Jan 1971; CB (w); CB (a); Reprints story from Walt Disney's Comics #172	25.00
❑365, Feb 1971; CB (w); CB (a); Reprints story from Walt Disney's Comics #149	25.00
❑366, Mar 1971; CB (w); CB (a); Reprints story from Walt Disney's Comics #150	25.00
❑367, Apr 1971; CB (w); CB (a); Reprints story from Walt Disney's Comics #151	25.00
❑368, May 1971; CB (w); CB (a); Reprints story from Walt Disney's Comics #156	25.00
❑369, Jun 1971; CB (w); CB (a); Reprints story from Walt Disney's Comics #143	25.00
❑370, Jul 1971; CB (w); CB (a); Reprints story from Walt Disney's Comics #142	25.00
❑371, Aug 1971; CB (w); CB (a); Reprints story from Walt Disney's Comics #153	25.00
❑372, Sep 1971; CB (w); CB (a); Reprints story from Walt Disney's Comics #168	25.00
❑373, Oct 1971; CB (w); CB (a); Reprints story from Walt Disney's Comics #193	25.00
❑374, Nov 1971; CB (w); CB (a); Reprints story from Walt Disney's Comics #203	25.00
❑375, Dec 1971; CB (w); CB (a); Reprints story from Walt Disney's Comics #240	25.00
❑376, Jan 1972; CB (w); CB (a); Reprints story from Walt Disney's Comics #208	25.00
❑377, Feb 1972; CB (w); CB (a); Reprints story from Walt Disney's Comics #185	25.00
❑378, Mar 1972; CB (w); CB (a); Reprints story from Walt Disney's Comics #196	25.00
❑379, Apr 1972; CB (w); CB (a); Reprints story from Walt Disney's Comics #207	25.00
❑380, May 1972; CB (w); CB (a); Reprints story from Walt Disney's Comics #211	25.00
❑381, Jun 1972; CB (w); CB (a); Reprints story from Walt Disney's Comics #202	25.00
❑382, Jul 1972; CB (w); CB (a); Reprints story from Walt Disney's Comics #213	25.00
❑383, Aug 1972; CB (w); CB (a); Reprints story from Walt Disney's Comics #215	25.00
❑384, Sep 1972; CB (w); CB (a); Reprints story from Walt Disney's Comics #177	25.00
❑385, Oct 1972; CB (w); CB (a); Reprints story from Walt Disney's Comics #187	25.00
❑386, Nov 1972; CB (w); CB (a); Reprints story from Walt Disney's Comics #209	25.00
❑387, Dec 1972; CB (w); CB (a); Reprints story from Walt Disney's Comics #205	25.00
❑388, Jan 1973; CB (w); CB (a); Reprints story from Walt Disney's Comics #136	25.00
❑389, Feb 1973; CB (w); CB (a); Reprints story from Walt Disney's Comics #253	25.00
❑390, Mar 1973; CB (w); CB (a); Reprints story from Walt Disney's Comics #239	25.00
❑391, Apr 1973; CB (w); CB (a); Reprints story from Walt Disney's Comics #137	25.00
❑392, May 1973; CB (w); CB (a); Reprints story from Walt Disney's Comics #163	25.00

	N-MINT
❑393, Jun 1973; CB (w); CB (a); Reprints story from Walt Disney's Comics #167	25.00
❑394, Jul 1973; CB (w); CB (a); Reprints story from Walt Disney's Comics #176	25.00
❑395, Aug 1973; CB (w); CB (a); Reprints story from Walt Disney's Comics #214	25.00
❑396, Sep 1973; CB (w); CB (a); Reprints story from Walt Disney's Comics #210	25.00
❑397, Oct 1973; CB (w); CB (a); Reprints story from Walt Disney's Comics #218	25.00
❑398, Nov 1973; CB (w); CB (a); Reprints story from Walt Disney's Comics #217	25.00
❑399, Dec 1973; CB (w); CB (a); Reprints story from Walt Disney's Comics #183	25.00
❑400, Jan 1974; CB (w); CB (a); Reprints story from Walt Disney's Comics #171	25.00
❑401, Feb 1974; CB (w); CB (a); Reprints story from Walt Disney's Comics #219	14.00
❑402, Mar 1974; CB (w); CB (a); Reprints story from Walt Disney's Comics #258	14.00
❑403, Apr 1974; CB (w); CB (a); Reprints story from Walt Disney's Comics #255	14.00
❑404, May 1974; CB (w); CB (a); Reprints story from Walt Disney's Comics #223	14.00
❑405, Jun 1974; CB (w); CB (a); Reprints story from Walt Disney's Comics #259	14.00
❑406, Jul 1974; CB (w); CB (a); Reprints story from Walt Disney's Comics #191	14.00
❑407, Aug 1974; CB (w); CB (a); Reprints story from Walt Disney's Comics #221	14.00
❑408, Sep 1974; CB (w); CB (a); Reprints story from Walt Disney's Comics #229	14.00
❑409, Oct 1974; CB (w); CB (a); Reprints stories from Four Color Comics #1184 (Gyro Gearloose) and Walt Disney's Comics #249	14.00
❑410, Nov 1974; CB (w); CB (a); Reprints story from Walt Disney's Comics #216	14.00
❑411, Dec 1974; CB (w); CB (a); Reprints story from Walt Disney's Comics #254	14.00
❑412, Jan 1975; CB (w); CB (a); Reprints story from Walt Disney's Comics #220	14.00
❑413, Feb 1975; CB (w); CB (a); Reprints story from Walt Disney's Comics #294	14.00
❑414, Mar 1975; CB (w); CB (a); Reprints story from Walt Disney's Comics #269	14.00
❑415, Apr 1975; CB (w); CB (a); Reprints story from Walt Disney's Comics #265	14.00
❑416, May 1975; CB (w); CB (a); Reprints story from Walt Disney's Comics #222	14.00
❑417, Jun 1975; CB (w); CB (a); Reprints story from Walt Disney's Comics #225	14.00
❑418, Jul 1975; CB (w); CB (a); Reprints story from Walt Disney's Comics #236	14.00
❑419, Aug 1975; CB (w); CB (a); Reprints story from Walt Disney's Comics #138	14.00
❑420, Sep 1975; CB (w); CB (a); Reprints story from Walt Disney's Comics #65	14.00
❑421, Oct 1975; CB (w); CB (a); Reprints story from Walt Disney's Comics #152	14.00
❑422, Nov 1975; CB (w); CB (a); Reprints story from Walt Disney's Comics #169	14.00
❑423, Dec 1975; CB (w); CB (a); Reprints story from Walt Disney's Comics #231	14.00
❑424, Jan 1976; CB (w); CB (a); Reprints story from Walt Disney's Comics #256	14.00

Other grades: Multiply price above by 5/6 for VF/NM • 2/3 for VERY FINE • 1/3 for FINE • 1/5 for VERY GOOD • 1/8 for GOOD

War

Appropriately enough, followed The Draft
©Marvel

War Dancer

Mayan-like "god" comes to Earth
©Defiant

Warhammer Monthly

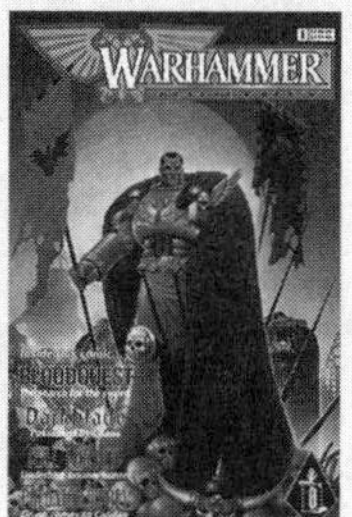

Ties in to Games Workshop's fantasy mini game
©Games Workshop

Warheads

Not the red-hot candy, but a Marvel UK comic
©Marvel

Warlock (1st Series)

Him got a series
©Marvel

	N-MINT
❑425, Feb 1976; CB (w); CB (a); Reprints story from Walt Disney's Comics #260	14.00
❑426, Mar 1976; CB (w); CB (a); Reprints story from Walt Disney's Comics #264	14.00
❑427, Apr 1976; CB (w); CB (a); Reprints story from Walt Disney's Comics #273	14.00
❑428, May 1976; CB (w); CB (a); Reprints story from Walt Disney's Comics #275	14.00
❑429, Jun 1976; CB (w); CB (a); Reprints story from Walt Disney's Comics #271	14.00
❑430, Jul 1976	10.00
❑431, Aug 1976; CB (w); CB (a); Reprints story from Walt Disney's Comics #288	12.00
❑432, Sep 1976; CB (w); CB (a); Reprints story from Walt Disney's Comics #291	12.00
❑433, Oct 1976	10.00
❑434, Nov 1976; CB (w); CB (a); Reprints story from Walt Disney's Comics #199	12.00
❑435, Dec 1976; CB (w); CB (a); Reprints story from Walt Disney's Comics #201	12.00
❑436, Jan 1977; CB (w); CB (a); Reprints story from Walt Disney's Comics #195	12.00
❑437, Feb 1977	10.00
❑438, Mar 1977	10.00
❑439, Apr 1977; CB (w); CB (a); Reprints story from Walt Disney's Comics #292	12.00
❑440, May 1977; CB (w); CB (a); Reprints story from Walt Disney's Comics #283	12.00
❑441, Jun 1977	10.00
❑442, Jul 1977; CB (w); CB (a); Reprints story from Walt Disney's Comics #312	10.00
❑443, Aug 1977; CB (w); CB (a); Reprints story from Walt Disney's Comics #297	10.00
❑444, Sep 1977	6.00
❑445, Oct 1977	6.00
❑446, Nov 1977; CB (w); CB (a); Reprints story from Walt Disney's Comics #277	10.00
❑447, Dec 1977; CB (w); CB (a); Reprints story from Walt Disney's Comics #212	10.00
❑448, Jan 1978; CB (w); CB (a); Reprints story from Walt Disney's Comics #266	10.00
❑449, Feb 1978; CB (w); CB (a); Reprints story from Walt Disney's Comics #280	10.00
❑450, Mar 1978; CB (w); CB (a); Reprints story from Walt Disney's Comics #270	10.00
❑451, Apr 1978; CB (w); CB (a); Reprints story from Walt Disney's Comics #272	10.00
❑452, May 1978; CB (w); CB (a); Reprints story from Walt Disney's Comics #274	10.00
❑453, Jun 1978; CB (w); CB (a); Reprints story from Walt Disney's Comics #206	10.00

	N-MINT
❑454, Jul 1978; CB (w); CB (a); Reprints story from Walt Disney's Comics #262	10.00
❑455, Aug 1978; CB (w); CB (a); Reprints story from Walt Disney's Comics #241	10.00
❑456, Sep 1978; CB (w); CB (a); Reprints story from Walt Disney's Comics #246	10.00
❑457, Oct 1978; CB (w); CB (a); Reprints stories from Walt Disney's Comics #247 and Mickey Mouse #91; has Casper in Hostess ad: "A Real Oddball"	10.00
❑458, Nov 1978; CB (w); CB (a); Reprints story from Walt Disney's Comics #263	10.00
❑459, Dec 1978; CB (w); CB (a); Reprints story from Walt Disney's Comics #242	10.00
❑460, Jan 1979 CB (w); CB (a)	10.00
❑461, Feb 1979 CB (w); CB (a)	10.00
❑462, Mar 1979 CB (w); CB (a)	10.00
❑463, Apr 1979 CB (w); CB (a)	10.00
❑464, May 1979 CB (w); CB (a)	10.00
❑465, Jun 1979 CB (w); CB (a)	10.00
❑466, Jul 1979	6.00
❑467, Aug 1979 CB (w); CB (a)	10.00
❑468, Sep 1979 CB (w); CB (a)	10.00
❑469, Oct 1979 CB (w); CB (a)	10.00
❑470, Nov 1979 CB (w); CB (a)	10.00
❑471, Dec 1979 CB (w); CB (a)	10.00
❑472, Jan 1980 CB (w); CB (a)	10.00
❑473, Feb 1980 CB (w); CB (a)	10.00
❑474, Mar 1980; CB (w); CB (a); Whitman begins publishing	10.00
❑475, Apr 1980 CB (w); CB (a)	10.00
❑476, May 1980 CB (w); CB (a)	10.00
❑477, Jun 1980 CB (w); CB (a)	10.00
❑478, Jul 1980 CB (w); CB (a)	10.00
❑479, Aug 1980 CB (w); CB (a)	30.00
❑480, Sep 1980 CB (w); CB (a)	125.00
❑481, Oct 1980 CB (w); CB (a)	30.00
❑482, Nov 1980 CB (w); CB (a)	30.00
❑483, Dec 1980 CB (w); CB (a)	30.00
❑484, Jan 1981 CB (w); CB (a)	30.00
❑485, Feb 1981 CB (w); CB (a)	10.00
❑486, Mar 1981 CB (w); CB (a)	10.00
❑487 1981 CB (w); CB (a)	10.00
❑488 1981 CB (w); CB (a)	10.00
❑489 1981 CB (w); CB (a)	10.00
❑490 1981 CB (w); CB (a)	10.00
❑491, Oct 1981 CB (w); CB (a)	10.00
❑492, Nov 1981 CB (w); CB (a)	10.00
❑493, Dec 1981; CB (w); CB (a); Reprints story from Walt Disney Comics and Stories #97	10.00
❑494, Jan 1981; CB (w); CB (a); Reprints story from Walt Disney Comics and Stories #98	10.00
❑495, Feb 1982 CB (w); CB (a)	10.00
❑496, Feb 1982 CB (w); CB (a)	10.00
❑497, Mar 1982 CB (w); CB (a)	10.00
❑498, Apr 1982 CB (w); CB (a)	10.00
❑499, May 1982 CB (w); CB (a)	10.00
❑500, ca. 1983 CB (w); CB (a)	10.00
❑501, ca. 1983 CB (w); CB (a)	10.00

	N-MINT
❑502, ca. 1983 CB (w); CB (a)	10.00
❑503, ca. 1983 CB (w); CB (a)	10.00
❑504, ca. 1983 CB (w); CB (a)	10.00
❑505, ca. 1983 CB (w); CB (a)	10.00
❑506, ca. 1983	10.00
❑507, ca. 1984 CB (w); CB (a)	10.00
❑508, ca. 1984 CB (w); CB (a)	10.00
❑509, ca. 1984 CB (w); CB (a)	10.00
❑510, ca. 1984 CB (w); CB (a)	10.00
❑511, ca. 1986; CB (w); CB (a); Gladstone begins publishing	15.00
❑512, Nov 1986	12.00
❑513, Dec 1986	12.00
❑514, Jan 1987	8.00
❑515, Feb 1987	8.00
❑516, Mar 1987 CB (w); CB (a)	8.00
❑517, Apr 1987	5.00
❑518, May 1987	5.00
❑519, Jun 1987 CB (w); CB (a)	14.00
❑520, Jul 1987 CB (w); CB (a)	10.00
❑521, Aug 1987 CB (w); CB, WK (a)	10.00
❑522, Sep 1987 CB (w); CB, WK (a); O: Huey, Dewey, Louie	10.00
❑523, Oct 1987; CB (w); CB, DR (a); 1st Rosa 10-page story	10.00
❑524, Nov 1987 CB (w); CB (a)	10.00
❑525, Dec 1987 CB (w); CB (a)	10.00
❑526, Jan 1988 CB (w); CB (a)	10.00
❑527, Mar 1988 CB (w); CB (a)	10.00
❑528, May 1988 CB (w); CB (a)	10.00
❑529, Jun 1988 CB (w); CB (a)	10.00
❑530, Jul 1988 CB (w); CB (a)	10.00
❑531, Aug 1988 WK (c); CB (w); CB, DR (a)	10.00
❑532, Sep 1988 CB (w); CB, DR (a)	10.00
❑533, Oct 1988 CB (w); CB (a)	10.00
❑534, Nov 1988 CB (w); CB (a)	10.00
❑535, Dec 1988 CB (w); CB (a)	10.00
❑536, Feb 1989 CB (w); CB (a)	10.00
❑537, Mar 1989; CB (w); CB (a); 1st Wm. Van Horn 10-page story	10.00
❑538, Apr 1989 WK (c); CB (w); CB (a)	10.00
❑539, Jun 1989 CB (w); CB (a)	10.00
❑540, Jul 1989 CB (w); CB (a)	10.00
❑541, Aug 1989; WK (c); CB (w); CB (a); 48 pgs.	10.00
❑542, Sep 1989 CB (w); CB (a)	10.00
❑543, Oct 1989 WK (c); CB (w); CB (a)	10.00
❑544, Nov 1989 WK (c); CB (w); CB (a)	10.00
❑545, Dec 1989 CB (w); CB (a)	10.00
❑546, Feb 1990 CB (w); CB, WK (a)	10.00
❑547, Apr 1990 CB (w); CB, DR (a)	10.00
❑548, Jun 1990; CB (w); CB (a); Disney begins publishing	10.00
❑549, Jul 1990 CB (w); CB (a)	10.00
❑550, Aug 1990; CB (w); CB (a); Milkman story	6.00
❑551, Sep 1990 CB (w); CB (a)	4.00
❑552, Oct 1990 CB (w); CB (a)	4.00
❑553, Nov 1990 CB (w); CB (a)	4.00
❑554, Dec 1990 CB (w); CB (a)	4.00
❑555, Jan 1991	3.00
❑556, Feb 1991	3.00
❑557, Mar 1991 CB (w); CB (a)	4.00
❑558, Apr 1991 CB (w); CB (a)	4.00

Other grades: Multiply price above by 5/6 for VF/NM • 2/3 for VERY FINE • 1/3 for FINE • 1/5 for VERY GOOD • 1/8 for GOOD

	N-MINT
❑559, May 1991 CB (w); CB (a)	4.00
❑560, Jun 1991 CB (w); CB (a)	4.00
❑561, Jul 1991 CB (w); CB (a)	4.00
❑562, Aug 1991 CB (w); CB (a)	4.00
❑563, Sep 1991 CB (w); CB (a)	4.00
❑564, Oct 1991 CB (w); CB (a)	4.00
❑565, Nov 1991 CB (w); CB (a)	4.00
❑566, Dec 1991 CB (w); CB (a)	4.00
❑567, Jan 1992 CB (w); CB (a)	4.00
❑568, Feb 1992 CB (w); CB (a)	4.00
❑569, Mar 1992 CB (w); CB (a)	4.00
❑570, Apr 1992; CB (w); CB (a); Valentine centerfold	4.00
❑571, May 1992 CB (w); CB (a)	4.00
❑572, Jun 1992; CB (w); CB (a); map piece	4.00
❑573, Jul 1992; CB (w); CB (a); map piece	4.00
❑574, Aug 1992; CB (w); CB (a); map piece	5.00
❑575, Sep 1992	5.00
❑576, Oct 1992 CB (w); CB (a)	5.00
❑577, Nov 1992; CB (w); CB (a); Reprints	5.00
❑578, Dec 1992; CB (w); CB (a); Reprints	3.00
❑579, Jan 1993 CB (w); CB (a)	3.00
❑580, Feb 1993; CB (w); CB (a); strip reprint	5.00
❑581, Mar 1993; CB (w); CB (a); Reprints	3.00
❑582, Apr 1993 FG, WK (a)	3.00
❑583, May 1993 FG, WK (a)	3.00
❑584, Jun 1993; CB (w); CB (a); Reprints	3.00
❑585, Jul 1993; CB, FG (a); Reprints	5.00
❑586, Aug 1993	3.00
❑587, Oct 1993	3.00
❑588, Dec 1993	3.00
❑589, Feb 1994	3.00
❑590, Apr 1994	3.00
❑591, Jun 1994	3.00
❑592, Aug 1994	3.00
❑593, Oct 1994	3.00
❑594, Dec 1994	3.00
❑595, Feb 1995	3.00
❑596, Apr 1995	3.00
❑597, Jun 1995	3.00
❑598, Aug 1995	4.00
❑599, Oct 1995	4.00
❑600, Dec 1995; Giant-size; CB (w); CB, DR (a); reprints first Donald Duck stories by trio	6.00
❑601, Feb 1996; upgrades to prestige format	5.95
❑602, Apr 1996	5.95
❑603, Jun 1996	5.95
❑604, Aug 1996	5.95
❑605, Oct 1996	5.95
❑606, Dec 1996	5.95
❑607, Jan 1996	5.95
❑608, Feb 1997	5.95
❑609, Mar 1997	5.95
❑610, Mar 1997	5.95
❑611, Apr 1997	5.95
❑612, May 1997	6.95
❑613, Jun 1997	6.95
❑614, Jul 1997	6.95
❑615, Aug 1997	6.95
❑616, Sep 1997	6.95
❑617, Oct 1997	6.95
❑618, Nov 1997	6.95
❑619, Dec 1997; Pinocchio features	6.95
❑620, Jan 1998	6.95
❑621, Feb 1998	6.95
❑622, Mar 1998	6.95
❑623, Apr 1998	6.95
❑624, May 1998	6.95
❑625, Jun 1998	6.95
❑626, Jul 1998	6.95
❑627, Aug 1998	6.95
❑628, Sep 1998	6.95
❑629, Oct 1998	6.95
❑630, Nov 1998	6.95
❑631, Dec 1998	6.95
❑632, Jan 1999	6.95
❑633, Feb 1999	6.95
❑634, Mar 1999	6.95
❑635, Apr 1999	6.95
❑636, May 1999	6.95
❑637, Jun 1999	6.95
❑638, Jul 1999	6.95
❑639, Aug 1999	6.95
❑640, Sep 1999	6.95
❑641, Oct 1999	6.95
❑642, Nov 1999	6.95
❑643, Dec 1999	6.95
❑644, Jan 2000	6.95
❑645, Feb 2000	6.95
❑646, Mar 2000	6.95
❑647, Apr 2000	6.95
❑648, May 2000	6.95

WALT DISNEY'S COMICS & STORIES (GEMSTONE)

GEMSTONE

	N-MINT
❑634, Jun 2003	6.95
❑635, Jul 2003	6.95
❑636, Aug 2003	6.95
❑637, Sep 2003	6.95
❑638, Oct 2003	6.95
❑639, Nov 2003	6.95
❑640, Dec 2003	6.95
❑641, Jan 2004	6.95
❑642, Feb 2004	6.95
❑643, Mar 2004	6.95
❑644, Apr 2004	6.95
❑645, May 2004	6.95
❑646, Jun 2004	6.95
❑647, Jul 2004	6.95
❑648, Aug 2004	6.95
❑649, Sep 2004	6.95
❑650, Oct 2004	6.95
❑651, Nov 2004	6.95
❑652, Dec 2004	6.95
❑653, Jan 2005	6.95
❑654, Feb 2005	6.95
❑655, Mar 2005	6.95
❑656, Apr 2005	6.95
❑657, May 2005	6.95
❑658, Jun 2005	6.95
❑659, Jul 2005	6.95
❑660, Aug 2005	6.95
❑661, Sep 2005	6.95

WALT DISNEY'S COMICS AND STORIES PENNY PINCHER

GLADSTONE

	N-MINT
❑1, May 1997; CB (a); Reprints	1.00
❑2, Jun 1997; CB (a); reprints Barks' Feud and Far Between	1.00
❑3, Jul 1997	1.00
❑4, Aug 1997	1.00

WALT DISNEY'S COMICS DIGEST

GLADSTONE

	N-MINT
❑1, Dec 1986; CB, WK (a); Reprints story from Uncle Scrooge #5	6.00
❑2 1987; CB (a); Reprints story from Uncle Scrooge #29	4.00
❑3, Mar 1987; CB (a); Reprints story from Uncle Scrooge #31	4.00
❑4, Apr 1987; CB (a); Reprints stories from Donald Duck #60 and Picnic Party #8	4.00
❑5, May 1987; CB (a); Reprints story from Uncle Scrooge #23	4.00
❑6, Jun 1987; CB (a); Reprints story from Uncle Scrooge #24	4.00
❑7, Jul 1987; CB (a); Reprints stories from Four Color Comics #1025 (Vacation in Disneyland)	4.00

WALT DISNEY'S HOLIDAY PARADE

DISNEY

	N-MINT
❑1, Win 1991	2.95
❑2, Win 1992	2.95

WALT DISNEY SHOWCASE

GOLD KEY

	N-MINT
❑1, Oct 1970; Boatniks	16.00
❑2, Jan 1971; Moby Duck	10.00
❑3, Apr 1971; Bongo & Lumpjaw	9.00
❑4, Jul 1971; Pluto	9.00
❑5, Oct 1971; $1,000,000 Duck	12.00
❑6, Jan 1972; Bedknobs & Broomsticks	12.00
❑7, Apr 1972; Pluto	9.00
❑8, Jun 1972; Daisy and Donald; Goofy and Clarabelle	9.00
❑9, Aug 1972; 101 Dalmatians	10.00
❑10, Sep 1972; DS (a); Napoleon and Samantha movie adaptation	12.00
❑11, Oct 1972; Moby Duck	8.00
❑12, Dec 1972; Dumbo	8.00
❑13, Feb 1973; Pluto	8.00
❑14, Apr 1973; The World's Greatest Athlete (movie adaptation)	12.00
❑15, Jun 1973; Three Little Pigs	8.00
❑16, Jul 1973; Aristocats movie adaptation reprint	12.00
❑17, Aug 1973; Mary Poppins movie adaptation reprint	12.00
❑18, Oct 1973; Gyro Gearloose; reprints stories from Four Color Comics #1047 and 1184 (Gyro Gearloose)	12.00
❑19, Dec 1973; That Darn Cat (move adaptation)	10.00
❑20, Feb 1974; Pluto	9.00
❑21, Apr 1974; Li'l Bad Wolf and the Three Little Pigs	8.00
❑22, Jun 1974; Alice in Wonderland	8.00
❑23, Jul 1974; Pluto	8.00
❑24, Aug 1974; Herbie Rides Again	7.00
❑25, Oct 1974; Old Yeller	7.00
❑26, Dec 1974; Lt. Robin Crusoe, USN	7.00
❑27, Feb 1975; Island at the Top of the World	7.00
❑28, Apr 1975; Brer Rabbit	7.00
❑29, Jun 1975; Escape to Witch Mountain	7.00
❑30, Jul 1975; Magica De Spell; reprints stories from Uncles Scrooge #36 and Walt Disney's Comics #258	15.00
❑31, Aug 1975; Bambi	9.00
❑32, Oct 1975; Spin and Marty	9.00
❑33, Jan 1976; Pluto	7.00
❑34, May 1976; Paul Revere's Ride	7.00
❑35, Aug 1976; Goofy	7.00
❑36, Sep 1976; Peter Pan	7.00
❑37, Nov 1976; Tinker Bell	7.00
❑38, Apr 1977; Mickey and The Sleuth	7.00
❑39, Jul 1977; Mickey and The Sleuth	7.00
❑40, Sep 1977; The Rescuers (movie adaptation)	8.00
❑41, Oct 1977; Herbie Goes to Monte Carlo (movie adaptation)	8.00
❑42, Jan 1978; Mickey and The Sleuth	7.00
❑43, Apr 1978; Pete's Dragon (movie adaptation)	9.00
❑44, May 1978; Return From Witch Mountain (movie adaptation); Castaways	10.00
❑45, Aug 1978; The Jungle Book	10.00
❑46, Oct 1978; The Cat From Outer Space	10.00
❑47, Nov 1978; Mickey Mouse Surprise Party	10.00
❑48, Jan 1979; The Wonderful Adventures of Pinocchio; The Small One	10.00
❑49, Mar 1979; The North Avenue Irregulars (Movie adaptation); Zorro double feature	7.00
❑50, May 1979; Bedknobs & Broomsticks reprint	7.00
❑51, Jul 1979; 101 Dalmatians	7.00
❑52, Sep 1979; Unidentified Flying Oddball	7.00
❑53, Nov 1979; The Scarecrow of Romney Marsh	7.00
❑54, Jan 1980; The Black Hole	7.00

WALT DISNEY'S SPRING FEVER

DISNEY

	N-MINT
❑1, Spr 1991	2.95

WALT DISNEY'S SUMMER FUN

DISNEY

	N-MINT
❑1	2.95

WALT DISNEY'S THREE MUSKETEERS

GEMSTONE

	N-MINT
❑1 2004	3.95

WALT DISNEY'S WORLD OF ADVENTURE

GOLD KEY

	N-MINT
❑1, Apr 1963	8.00
❑2	5.00
❑3	5.00

Warlock and the Infinity Watch

Infinity Gems divvied up to diverse group
©Marvel

Warlord

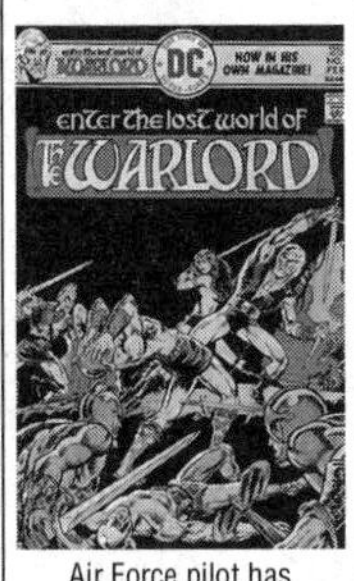

Air Force pilot has adventures in lost world
©DC

War Machine

Stark sidekick Rhodes gets own armor
©Marvel

War of the Gods

Circe manipulates pantheons into conflict
©DC

War of the Worlds (Caliber)

Wells' classic updated to mid-1990s
©Caliber

N-MINT

WALTER
DARK HORSE

❑1, Feb 1996 ... 2.50
❑2, Mar 1996 ... 2.50
❑3, Apr 1996 ... 2.50
❑4, May 1996 ... 2.50

WALTER KITTY IN... THE HOLLOW EARTH
VISION

❑1, Jul 1996 ... 1.95
❑2, Jul 1996 ... 1.95

WALT THE WILDCAT
MOTION COMICS

❑1, Sep 1995 ... 2.50

WANDA LUWAND & THE PIRATE GIRLS
FANTAGRAPHICS / EROS

❑1, b&w ... 2.50

WANDERERS
DC

❑1, Jun 1988 O: Aviax. O: The Wanderers. O: The Elvar. O: Re-Animage. 1: Aviax. 1: The Wanderers. 1: The Elvar. 1: Re-Animage. ... 1.50
❑2, Jul 1988 ... 1.50
❑3, Aug 1988 ... 1.50
❑4, Sep 1988 ... 1.50
❑5, Oct 1988 ... 1.50
❑6, Nov 1988 ... 1.50
❑7, Dec 1988 ... 1.50
❑8, Dec 1988 ... 1.50
❑9, Jan 1989 ... 1.50
❑10, Jan 1989 ... 1.50
❑11, Feb 1989 ... 1.50
❑12, Mar 1989 ... 1.50
❑13, Apr 1989 ... 1.50

WANDERING STAR
PEN AND INK

❑1, ca. 1993, b&w ... 8.00
❑1/2nd, Feb 1994 ... 4.00
❑1/3rd ... 3.00
❑2, ca. 1993, b&w ... 5.00
❑2/2nd, May 1994 ... 2.00
❑3, ca. 1993, b&w ... 4.00
❑3/2nd, May 1994 ... 2.00
❑4, ca. 1993, b&w ... 4.00
❑4/2nd, May 1994 ... 2.00
❑5, Jan 1994, b&w ... 4.00
❑5/2nd, May 1994 ... 2.00
❑6, Mar 1994, b&w ... 3.00
❑7, Jun 1994, b&w ... 3.00
❑8, Oct 1994, b&w D: Graikor. ... 3.00
❑9, Aug 1995, b&w ... 3.00
❑10, Oct 1995, b&w ... 3.00
❑11, Jan 1995, b&w ... 2.50
❑12 1996, b&w ... 2.50
❑13, Jun 1996, b&w ... 2.50
❑14 1996, b&w ... 2.50
❑15 1996, b&w ... 2.50
❑16 1996, b&w ... 2.50
❑17 1996, b&w ... 2.50
❑18 1996, b&w ... 2.50
❑19 1996, b&w ... 2.50

N-MINT

❑20 1997, b&w ... 2.50
❑21 1997, b&w ... 2.50

WANDERING STARS
FANTAGRAPHICS

❑1 ... 2.00

WANTED (CELEBRITY)
CELEBRITY

❑1, 1989 ... 0.75
❑2, 1989 ... 0.75
❑3, 1989 ... 0.75
❑4, 1989 ... 0.75
❑5, Dec 1989 ... 0.75

WANTED
IMAGE

❑1, Dec 2003 ... 12.00
❑1/A, Dec 2003 ... 9.00
❑1/B, Dec 2003 ... 8.00
❑1/C, Apr 2004 ... 2.99
❑1/D, Apr 2004; Wizard World ... 6.00
❑1/E, Apr 2004; Death Row Edition ... 5.00
❑2, Jan 2004 ... 2.99
❑2/B, Apr 2004 ... 4.00
❑2/C, May 2004; Death Row Edition ... 5.00
❑3, Apr 2004 ... 2.99
❑3/A, Apr 2004; Death Row Edition ... 4.00
❑4, Aug 2004 ... 2.99
❑4/Variant 2004; Death Row edition ... 2.99
❑5 2004 ... 2.99
❑6, Feb 2005 ... 2.99

WANTED: DOSSIER ONE-SHOT
IMAGE

❑1, Apr 2004 ... 2.99

WANTED DOSSIER ONE SHOT
IMAGE

❑1, May 2004 ... 2.99

WANTED, THE WORLD'S MOST DANGEROUS VILLAINS
DC

❑1, Aug 1972; reprints stories from Batman #112, World's Finest #111, and Green Lantern #1 ... 10.00
❑2, Oct 1972; reprints stories from Batman #25 and Flash #121 ... 8.00
❑3, Nov 1972; reprints stories from Action #69, More Fun #65, and Flash #100 ... 8.00
❑4, Dec 1972; 1: Solomon Grundy. reprints stories from All-American #61 and Kid Eternity #15 ... 6.00
❑5, Jan 1973; reprints stories from Green Lantern #33 and Doll Man #15 ... 6.00
❑6, Feb 1973; reprints stories from Adventure #77 and Sensation Comics #66 and 71 ... 6.00
❑7, Apr 1973; reprints stories from More Fun #76, Flash #90, and Adventure #72 ... 6.00
❑8, Jul 1973; reprints stories from Flash #114 and More Fun #73 ... 6.00
❑9, Sep 1973; CS (a); reprints stories from Action #57 and World's Finest Comics #6 ... 6.00

WAR
CHARLTON

❑1, Jul 1975, b&w; DP, WW (a); Reprints ... 8.00

N-MINT

❑2, Sep 1975 ... 5.00
❑3, Nov 1975 ... 5.00
❑4, Jan 1976 ... 5.00
❑5, Mar 1976 ... 5.00
❑6, May 1976 ... 5.00
❑7, Jul 1976 ... 5.00
❑8, Sep 1976 ... 5.00
❑9, Nov 1976 ... 5.00
❑10, Sep 1978 ... 5.00
❑11, Jan 1979 ... 3.00
❑12, Feb 1979 ... 3.00
❑13, Apr 1979 ... 3.00
❑14, Jun 1979 ... 3.00
❑15, Aug 1979 ... 3.00
❑16, Sep 1979 ... 3.00
❑17, Nov 1979 ... 3.00
❑18, Dec 1979 ... 3.00
❑19, Feb 1980 ... 3.00
❑20, Apr 1980 ... 3.00
❑21, Jun 1980 ... 3.00
❑22, Aug 1980 ... 3.00
❑23, Oct 1980 ... 2.00
❑24, Dec 1980 ... 2.00
❑25, Feb 1981 ... 2.00
❑26, Apr 1981 ... 2.00
❑27, Jun 1981 ... 2.00
❑28, Aug 1981 ... 2.00
❑29, Oct 1981 ... 2.00
❑30, Dec 1981 ... 2.00
❑31, Feb 1982 ... 2.00
❑32, Apr 1982 ... 2.00
❑33, Jun 1982 ... 2.00
❑34, Aug 1982 ... 2.00
❑35, Oct 1982 ... 2.00
❑36, Dec 1982 ... 2.00
❑37, Feb 1983 ... 2.00
❑38, Mar 1983 ... 2.00
❑39, ca. 1983 ... 2.00
❑40, ca. 1983 ... 2.00
❑41, Oct 1983 ... 2.00
❑42, Dec 1983 ... 2.00
❑43, Feb 1984 ... 2.00
❑44, Apr 1984 ... 2.00
❑45, Jun 1984 ... 2.00
❑46, Aug 1984 ... 2.00
❑47 1984 ... 2.00
❑48 1984 ... 2.00
❑49 1984 ... 2.00

WAR
MARVEL

❑1, Jun 1989; Series continued from story in "The Draft" ... 3.50
❑2, Jul 1989 ... 3.50
❑3, Aug 1989 ... 3.50
❑4, Feb 1990 ... 3.50

WAR AGAINST CRIME (GEMSTONE)
GEMSTONE

❑1, Apr 2000, Reprints War Against Crime #1 ... 2.50
❑2, May 2000, Reprints War Against Crime #2 ... 2.50
❑3, Jun 2000, Reprints War Against Crime #3 ... 2.50
❑4, Jul 2000, Reprints War Against Crime #4 ... 2.50

Other grades: Multiply price above by 5/6 for VF/NM • 2/3 for VERY FINE • 1/3 for FINE • 1/5 for VERY GOOD • 1/8 for GOOD

❑5, Aug 2000, Reprints War Against Crime #5 ... 2.50
❑Annual 1, ca. 2000, Collects issues #1-5 ... 13.50

WARBLADE: ENDANGERED SPECIES
IMAGE

❑1, Jan 1995; Tri-fold cover ... 2.50
❑2, Feb 1995 ... 2.50
❑3, Mar 1995 ... 2.50
❑4, Apr 1995 ... 2.50

WARCAT
COCONUT

❑Ashcan 1, Oct 1997, b&w; preview of issues #1 and 2; no indicia ... 2.95
❑Special 1 ... 2.95

WARCHILD
MAXIMUM

❑1/A, Dec 1994; Warchild charging on cover ... 2.50
❑1/B, Dec 1994; Variant cover with Warchild standing, red background ... 2.50
❑2/A, Jan 1995; Warchild and woman on cover ... 2.50
❑2/B, Jan 1995; Warchild alone on cover ... 2.50
❑3/A, Jun 1995; Warchild crouching on cover ... 2.50
❑3/B, Jun 1995; Warchild standing on cover, white background ... 2.50
❑3/C, Jun 1995; Warchild standing on cover, red background ... 2.50
❑4, Aug 1995 ... 2.50

WAR CRIMINALS
COMIC ZONE

❑1, b&w ... 2.95

WARCRY
IMAGE

❑1 ... 2.50

WAR DANCER
DEFIANT

❑1, Feb 1994 1: War Dancer. ... 2.50
❑2, Mar 1994 ... 2.50
❑3, Apr 1994 ... 2.50
❑4, May 1994; Giant-size O: War Dancer. A: Charlemagne. ... 3.25
❑5, Jun 1994 ... 2.50
❑6, Jul 1994 ... 2.50

WARGOD
SPEAKEASY COMICS

❑0, Jul 2005 ... 4.99

WARHAMMER MONTHLY
GAMES WORKSHOP

❑0, Feb 1998 ... 1.00
❑1, Mar 1998 ... 2.95
❑2, Apr 1998 ... 2.95
❑3, May 1998 ... 2.95
❑4, Jun 1998 ... 2.95
❑5, Jul 1998 ... 2.95
❑6, Aug 1998 ... 2.95
❑7, Sep 1998 ... 2.95
❑8, Oct 1998 ... 2.95
❑9, Nov 1998 ... 2.95
❑10, Dec 1998 ... 2.95
❑11, Jan 1999 ... 2.95
❑12, Feb 1999 ... 2.95
❑13, Mar 1999 ... 2.95
❑14, Apr 1999 ... 2.95
❑15, May 1999 ... 2.95
❑16, Jun 1999 ... 2.95
❑17, Jul 1999 ... 2.95
❑18, Aug 1999 ... 2.95
❑19, Sep 1999 ... 2.95
❑20, Oct 1999 ... 2.95
❑21, Nov 1999 ... 2.95
❑22, Dec 1999 ... 2.95
❑23, Jan 2000 ... 2.95
❑24, Feb 2000 ... 2.95
❑25, Mar 2000 ... 2.95
❑26, Apr 2000 ... 2.95
❑27, May 2000 ... 2.95
❑28, Jun 2000 ... 2.95
❑29, Jul 2000 ... 2.95
❑30, Aug 2000 ... 2.95
❑31, Sep 2000 ... 2.95
❑32, Oct 2000 ... 2.95
❑33, Nov 2000 ... 2.95
❑34, Dec 2000 ... 2.95
❑35, Jan 2001 ... 2.95
❑36, Feb 2001 ... 2.95
❑37, Mar 2001 ... 2.95
❑38, Apr 2001 ... 2.95
❑39, May 2001 ... 2.95
❑40, Jun 2001 ... 2.95
❑41, Jul 2001 ... 2.95
❑42, Aug 2001 ... 2.95
❑43, Sep 2001 ... 2.95
❑44, Oct 2001 ... 2.95
❑45, Nov 2001 ... 2.95
❑46, Dec 2001 ... 2.95
❑47, Jan 2002 ... 2.95
❑48, Feb 2002 ... 2.95
❑49, Mar 2002 ... 2.95
❑50, Apr 2002 ... 2.95
❑51, May 2002 ... 2.95
❑52, Jun 2002 ... 3.50
❑53, Jul 2002 ... 3.50
❑54, Aug 2002 ... 3.50
❑55, Sep 2002 ... 3.50
❑56, Oct 2002 ... 3.50
❑57, Nov 2002 ... 3.50
❑58, Dec 2002 ... 3.50
❑59, ca. 2003 ... 3.50
❑60, ca. 2003 ... 3.50
❑61, ca. 2003 ... 3.50
❑62, ca. 2003 ... 3.50
❑63, ca. 2003 ... 3.50
❑64, ca. 2003 ... 3.50
❑65, ca. 2003 ... 3.50
❑66, ca. 2003 ... 3.50
❑67, ca. 2003 ... 3.50
❑68, ca. 2003 ... 3.50
❑69, ca. 2003 ... 3.50
❑70, ca. 2003 ... 3.50
❑71, Aug 2003 ... 3.50
❑72, Sep 2003 ... 3.50
❑73, Oct 2003 ... 3.50
❑74, Nov 2003 ... 3.50
❑75, Nov 2003 ... 3.50
❑76, Hol 2004 ... 3.50
❑77, Feb 2004 ... 3.50
❑78 2004 ... 3.50
❑79 2004 ... 3.50
❑80 2004 ... 3.50
❑81 2004 ... 3.50
❑82 2004 ... 3.50
❑83 2004 ... 3.50
❑84 2004 ... 3.50
❑85 2004 ... 3.50

WARHAWKS COMICS MODULE
TSR

❑1, ca. 1990 ... 2.95
❑2, ca. 1990 ... 2.95
❑3, ca. 1990 ... 2.95
❑4, ca. 1990 ... 2.95
❑5, ca. 1990; Warhawks 2050 ... 2.95
❑6, ca. 1990; Warhawks 2050 ... 2.95
❑7, ca. 1990; Warhawks 2050 ... 2.95
❑8, ca. 1990; Warhawks 2050 ... 2.95
❑9, ca. 1990; Warhawks 2050 ... 2.95

WARHEADS
MARVEL

❑1, Jun 1992; Wolverine ... 1.75
❑2, Jul 1992 ... 1.75
❑3, Aug 1992 ... 1.75
❑4, Sep 1992 ... 1.75
❑5, Oct 1992 ... 1.75
❑6, Nov 1992; Death's Head II cameo ... 1.75
❑7, Dec 1992 ... 1.75
❑8, Jan 1993 ... 1.75
❑9, Feb 1993 ... 1.75
❑10, Apr 1993 ... 1.75
❑11, May 1993; MyS-TECH Wars Crossover ... 1.75
❑12, Jun 1993 ... 1.75
❑13, Jul 1993 ... 1.75
❑14, Aug 1993 ... 1.75

WARHEADS: BLACK DAWN
MARVEL

❑1, Jul 1993; foil cover ... 2.95
❑2 1993 ... 2.95

WAR HEROES CLASSICS
RECOLLECTIONS

❑1, b&w; Reprints ... 2.00

WAR IS HELL
MARVEL

❑1, Jan 1973; AW (a); Reprints ... 25.00
❑2, Mar 1973; Reprints ... 18.00
❑3, May 1973; Reprints ... 14.00
❑4, Jul 1973; Reprints ... 14.00
❑5, Sep 1973; Reprints ... 14.00
❑6, Nov 1973; Reprints ... 10.00
❑7, Jun 1974; SL (w); A: Sgt. Fury. Reprints Sgt. Fury #17 ... 10.00
❑8, Aug 1974; A: Sgt. Fury. Reprints .. 10.00
❑9, Oct 1974 ... 8.00
❑10, Dec 1974 ... 8.00
❑11, Feb 1975; Marvel Value Stamp #5: Dracula ... 8.00
❑12, Apr 1975 ... 8.00
❑13, Jun 1975; Marvel Value Stamp #23: Sgt. Fury ... 8.00
❑14, Aug 1975 ... 8.00
❑15, Oct 1975 ... 8.00

WARLANDS
IMAGE

❑1, Aug 1999 ... 3.00
❑1/A, Aug 1999; alternate cover ... 3.00
❑1/B, Aug 1999; alternate cover ... 3.00
❑2, Sep 1999 ... 2.50
❑2/A, Sep 1999; alternate cover ... 2.50
❑3, Nov 1999 ... 2.50
❑4 2000 ... 2.50
❑5, Mar 2000 ... 2.50
❑6 2000 ... 2.50
❑7, Jun 2000 ... 2.50
❑8, Jul 2000 ... 2.50
❑9, Aug 2000 ... 2.50
❑10, Oct 2000 ... 2.50
❑11, Nov 2000 ... 2.50
❑12, Feb 2001 ... 2.50
❑Deluxe 1, Darklyte ... 14.95

WARLANDS: DARK TIDE RISING
DREAMWAVE

❑1, Dec 2002 ... 2.95
❑2, Jan 2003 ... 2.95
❑3, Feb 2003 ... 2.95
❑4, Mar 2003 ... 2.95
❑5, Apr 2003 ... 2.95
❑6, May 2003 ... 2.95

WARLANDS EPILOGUE: THREE STORIES
IMAGE

❑1, Mar 2001 ... 5.95

WARLANDS: THE AGE OF ICE
DREAMWAVE

❑0, Feb 2002 ... 2.25
❑1, Jul 2001 ... 2.95
❑2/A, Sep 2001; Brown logo on cover; Flip-book with Warlands: Banished Knights preview ... 2.95
❑2/B, Sep 2001 ... 2.95
❑3, Oct 2001 ... 2.95

WARLASH
CFD

❑1, Apr 1995 ... 2.95

WARLOCK (1ST SERIES)
MARVEL

❑1, Aug 1972 GK (c); GK (a); O: Warlock. ... 32.00
❑2, Oct 1972 ... 15.00
❑3, Dec 1972 ... 15.00
❑4, Feb 1973 GK (a) ... 8.00
❑5, Apr 1973 ... 8.00
❑6, Jun 1973 ... 7.00
❑7, Aug 1973 ... 7.00
❑8, Oct 1973 ... 7.00
❑9, Oct 1975 JSn (a); A: Thanos. ... 10.00
❑10, Dec 1975; JSn (a); O: Thanos. Part 1 ... 10.00
❑11, Feb 1976; JSn (a); A: Thanos. Part 2 ... 10.00
❑12, Apr 1976 JSn (a) ... 8.00
❑12/30 cent, Apr 1976; 30 cent regional price variant ... 15.00
❑13, Jun 1976 JSn (a) ... 8.00
❑13/30 cent, Jun 1976; 30 cent regional price variant ... 15.00

Other grades: Multiply price above by 5/6 for VF/NM • 2/3 for VERY FINE • 1/3 for FINE • 1/5 for VERY GOOD • 1/8 for GOOD

Warrior Nun Areala (Vol. 1)

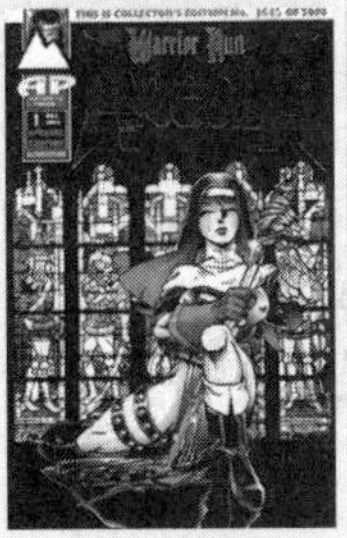

A gun-wielding convent tenant

©Antarctic

Warriors of Plasm

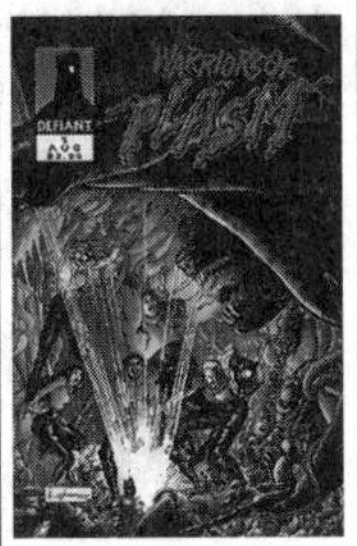

Trading cards contain true first appearances

©Defiant

Watchmen

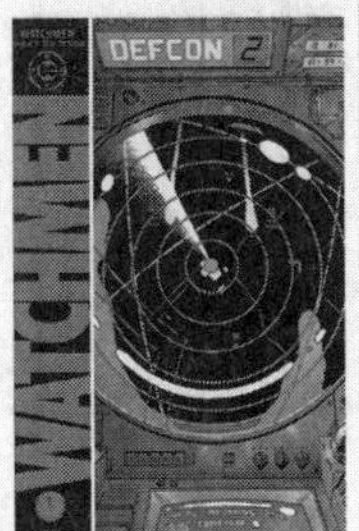

Thinly veiled Charlton copies regroup

©DC

Way of the Rat

Apprentice thief and monkey steal magic ring

©CrossGen

Weapon X (2nd Series)

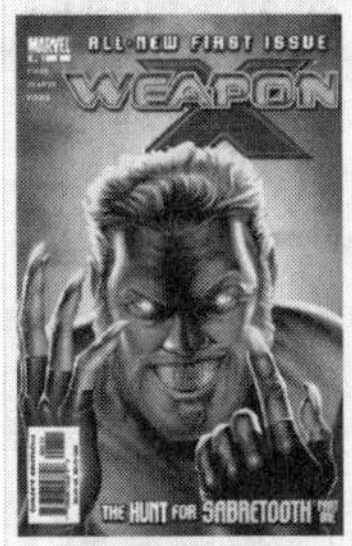

Wolverine's enemies unite against him

©Marvel

	N-MINT
❑14, Aug 1976 JSn (a)	8.00
❑14/30 cent, Aug 1976; 30 cent regional price variant	15.00
❑15, Nov 1976 JSn (a); A: Thanos	8.00

WARLOCK (2ND SERIES)
MARVEL

❑1, Dec 1982; JSn (a); Reprints	3.50
❑2, Jan 1983; JSn (a); Reprints Strange Tales #181, Warlock (1st Series) #9	3.00
❑3, Feb 1983; JSn (a); Reprints	3.00
❑4, Mar 1983; JSn (a); Reprints	3.00
❑5, Apr 1983; JSn, JBy (a); Reprints	3.00
❑6, May 1983; JSn (a); Reprints	3.00
❑Special 1, Dec 1982	2.00

WARLOCK (3RD SERIES)
MARVEL

❑1, May 1992; Reprints Warlock (2nd Series) #1	2.50
❑2, Jun 1992; Reprints Warlock (2nd Series) #2	2.50
❑3, Jul 1992; Reprints Warlock (2nd Series) #3	2.50
❑4, Aug 1992; Reprints Warlock (2nd Series) #4	2.50
❑5, Sep 1992; Reprints Warlock (2nd Series) #5	2.50
❑6, Oct 1992; Reprints Warlock (2nd Series) #6	2.50

WARLOCK (4TH SERIES)
MARVEL

❑1, Nov 1998; gatefold summary	3.00
❑2, Dec 1998; gatefold summary V: Captain Marvel	3.00
❑3, Jan 1999; gatefold summary V: Drax	3.00
❑4, Feb 1999 A: Syphonn. A: Blastaar. A: Annihilus	3.00

WARLOCK (5TH SERIES)
MARVEL

❑1, Oct 1999	2.00
❑2, Nov 1999	1.99
❑3, Nov 1999	1.99
❑4, Dec 1999	1.99

WARLOCK (6TH SERIES)
MARVEL

❑1 2004	2.99
❑2 2004	2.99
❑3 2004	2.99
❑4, Jan 2005	2.99

WARLOCK AND THE INFINITY WATCH
MARVEL

❑1, Feb 1992; JSn (w); follows events of The Infinity Gauntlet	2.50
❑2, Mar 1992 JSn (w)	2.00
❑3, Apr 1992 JSn (w); A: High Evolutionary	2.00
❑4, May 1992 JSn (w)	2.00
❑5, Jun 1992 JSn (w)	2.00
❑6, Jul 1992 JSn (w)	2.00
❑7, Aug 1992 JSn (w)	2.00
❑8, Sep 1992 JSn (w)	2.00
❑9, Oct 1992; JSn (w); O: Gamora. Infinity War	2.00
❑10, Nov 1992 JSn (w)	2.00
❑11, Dec 1992 JSn (w)	1.75
❑12, Jan 1993	1.75
❑13, Feb 1993	1.75
❑14, Mar 1993	1.75
❑15, Apr 1993	1.75
❑16, May 1993	1.75
❑17, Jun 1993	1.75
❑18, Jul 1993	1.75
❑19, Aug 1993	1.75
❑20, Sep 1993; A: Drax the Destroyer. A: Thor. A: Goddess. Infinity Crusade crossover	1.75
❑21, Oct 1993; JSn (w); A: Drax the Destroyer. A: Thor. A: Goddess. Infinity Crusade crossover	1.75
❑22, Nov 1993; A: Drax the Destroyer. A: Thor. A: Goddess. Infinity Crusade crossover	1.75
❑23, Dec 1993	1.75
❑24, Jan 1994	1.75
❑25, Feb 1994; diecut cover	2.95
❑26, Mar 1994	1.75
❑27, Apr 1994	1.75
❑28, May 1994	1.75
❑29, Jun 1994	1.95
❑30, Jul 1994	1.95
❑31, Aug 1994	1.95
❑32, Sep 1994	1.95
❑33, Oct 1994	1.95
❑34, Nov 1994	1.95
❑35, Dec 1994	1.95
❑36, Jan 1995	1.95
❑37, Feb 1995	1.95
❑38, Mar 1995	1.95
❑39, Apr 1995	1.95
❑40, May 1995	1.95
❑41, Jun 1995	1.95
❑42, Jul 1995	1.95

WARLOCK CHRONICLES
MARVEL

❑1, Jul 1993; Prism cover	2.95
❑2, Aug 1993; Infinity Crusade crossover	2.00
❑3, Sep 1993; Infinity Crusade crossover	2.00
❑4, Oct 1993; Infinity Crusade crossover	2.00
❑5, Nov 1993; Infinity Crusade crossover	2.00
❑6, Dec 1993	2.00
❑7, Jan 1994	2.00
❑8, Feb 1994	2.00

WARLOCK 5
AIRCEL

❑1 1986, b&w	2.00
❑2 1986, b&w	2.00
❑3, Jan 1987, b&w	2.00
❑4, Mar 1987, b&w	2.00
❑5, Apr 1987, b&w; robot skull cover	2.00
❑6, May 1987, b&w; woman's face on cover; misnumbered #5	2.00
❑7, Jun 1987, b&w	2.00
❑8 1987, b&w	2.00
❑9 1987, b&w	2.00
❑10 1987, b&w	2.00
❑11, Dec 1987, b&w	2.00
❑12, Jan 1988, b&w	2.00
❑13, Feb 1988, b&w	2.00
❑14, Mar 1988, b&w	2.00
❑15 1988, b&w	2.00
❑16, Nov 1988, b&w	2.00
❑17, Dec 1988, b&w	2.00
❑18, Jan 1989, b&w	2.00
❑19, Feb 1989, b&w	2.00
❑20, Mar 1989, b&w	2.00
❑21 1989, b&w	2.00
❑22 1989, b&w; final issue	2.00

WARLOCK 5 (SIRIUS)
SIRIUS

❑1, Jan 1998	2.50
❑2, Feb 1998	2.50
❑3, Mar 1998	2.50
❑4, Apr 1998	2.50

WARLOCK 5 BOOK II
AIRCEL

❑1, Jun 1989, b&w	2.00
❑2, Jul 1989, b&w	2.00
❑3, Aug 1989, b&w	2.00
❑4, Sep 1989, b&w	2.00
❑5, Nov 1989, b&w	2.00
❑6, Dec 1989, b&w	2.00
❑7, Jan 1990, b&w	2.00

WARLOCKS
AIRCEL

❑1 1988, b&w	2.00
❑2 1988, b&w	2.00
❑3 1988, b&w	2.00
❑4 1988, b&w	2.00
❑5 1989, b&w	2.00
❑6 1989, b&w	2.00
❑7 1989, b&w	2.00
❑8 1989, b&w	2.00
❑9 1989, b&w	2.00
❑10, Nov 1989, b&w	2.00
❑11, Mar 1990, b&w	2.00
❑12, Apr 1990, b&w	2.00
❑Special 1 1989, b&w	2.25

WARLORD
DC

❑1, Feb 1976 MGr (a); O: Warlord	10.00
❑2, Apr 1976 MGr (a); 1: Machiste	4.00
❑3, Nov 1976 MGr (a)	3.00
❑4, Jan 1977 MGr (a)	3.00
❑5, Mar 1977 MGr (a); 1: Dragonsword.	3.00
❑6, May 1977 MGr (a); 1: Mariah Romanola.	3.00
❑7, Jul 1977 MGr (a); O: Machiste.	2.00
❑8, Sep 1977 MGr (a)	2.00
❑9, Nov 1977 MGr (a)	2.00
❑10, Jan 1978; MGr (a); Deimos	2.00
❑11, Mar 1978; MGr (a); reprints 1st Issue Special	1.50
❑12, May 1978 MGr (a); 1: Aton	1.50
❑13, Jul 1978 MGr (a)	1.50
❑14, Sep 1978 MGr (a)	1.50
❑15, Nov 1978 MGr (a); 1: Joshua Morgan (Warlord's son)	1.50
❑16, Dec 1978 MGr (a)	1.50
❑17, Jan 1979 MGr (a)	1.50
❑18, Feb 1979 MGr (a)	1.50
❑19, Mar 1979 MGr (a)	1.50

	N-MINT
❑20, Apr 1979 MGr (a)	1.50
❑21, May 1979 MGr (a)	1.50
❑22, Jun 1979 MGr (a)	1.50
❑22/Whitman, Jun 1979; MGr (a); Whitman variant	8.00
❑23, Jul 1979 MGr (a)	1.50
❑24, Aug 1979 MGr (a)	1.50
❑25, Sep 1979 MGr (a)	1.50
❑26, Oct 1979 MGr (a)	1.50
❑27, Nov 1979 MGr (a)	1.50
❑28, Dec 1979 MGr (a); 1: Mongo Ironhand. 1: Wizard World.	1.50
❑29, Jan 1980 MGr (a)	1.50
❑30, Feb 1980 MGr (a)	1.00
❑31, Mar 1980 MGr (a)	1.00
❑32, Apr 1980 MGr (a); 1: Shakira.	1.00
❑33, May 1980 MGr (a)	1.00
❑34, Jun 1980 MGr (a)	1.00
❑35, Jul 1980 MGr (a)	1.00
❑36, Aug 1980 MGr (a)	1.00
❑37, Sep 1980; MGr (a); O: Omac (new origin). Omac back-up	1.00
❑38, Oct 1980; MGr (a); 1: Jennifer Morgan (Warlord's daughter). Omac back-up	1.00
❑39, Nov 1980; MGr (a); Omac back-up	1.00
❑40, Dec 1980 MGr (a)	1.00
❑41, Jan 1981 MGr (a)	1.00
❑42, Feb 1981 MGr (a); A: Omac.	1.00
❑43, Mar 1981 MGr (a); A: Omac.	1.00
❑44, Apr 1981 MGr (a)	1.00
❑45, May 1981 MGr (a)	1.00
❑46, Jun 1981 MGr (a)	1.00
❑47, Jul 1981; MGr (a); 1: Rostov. Omac back-up	1.00
❑48, Aug 1981; Giant-size MGr, EC (a); 1: Arak. 1: Claw the Unconquered.	1.50
❑49, Sep 1981; MGr (a); 1: The Evil One. Claw back-up	1.00
❑50, Oct 1981 MGr (a)	1.00
❑51, Nov 1981; MGr (a); reprints Warlord #1; Dragonsword back-up	1.00
❑52, Dec 1981; MGr (a); Dragonsword back-up	1.00
❑53, Jan 1982; Dragonsword back-up	1.00
❑54, Feb 1982	1.00
❑55, Mar 1982; MGr (c); 1: Lady Chian. 1: Arion. Arion back-up	1.00
❑56, Apr 1982; MGr (c); Arion back-up	1.00
❑57, May 1982; MGr (c); Arion back-up	1.00
❑58, Jun 1982; MGr (c); Arion back-up	1.00
❑59, Jul 1982; MGr (c); 1: Garn Daanuth. Arion back-up	1.00
❑60, Aug 1982; MGr (c); Arion back-up	1.00
❑61, Sep 1982; MGr (c); Arion back-up	1.00
❑62, Oct 1982; MGr (c); Arion back-up	1.00
❑63, Nov 1982; MGr (c); 1: Conqueror of the Barren Earth. Arion back-up	1.00
❑64, Dec 1982; Barren Earth back-up; Masters of the Universe preview	1.00
❑65, Jan 1983	1.00
❑66, Feb 1983	1.00
❑67, Mar 1983	1.00
❑68, Apr 1983	1.00
❑69, May 1983	1.00
❑70, Jun 1983	1.00
❑71, Jul 1983	1.00
❑72, Aug 1983	1.00
❑73, Sep 1983	1.00
❑74, Oct 1983	1.00
❑75, Nov 1983	1.00
❑76, Dec 1983	1.00
❑77, Jan 1984	1.00
❑78, Feb 1984	1.00
❑79, Mar 1984	1.00
❑80, Apr 1984	1.00
❑81, May 1984	1.00
❑82, Jun 1984	1.00
❑83, Jul 1984	1.00
❑84, Aug 1984	1.00
❑85, Sep 1984	1.00
❑86, Oct 1984	1.00
❑87, Nov 1984	1.00
❑88, Dec 1984	1.00
❑89, Jan 1985	1.00
❑90, Feb 1985	1.00
❑91, Mar 1985 O: Travis Morgan. O: Warlord.	1.00
❑92, Apr 1985	1.00
❑93, May 1985	1.00
❑94, Jun 1985	1.00
❑95, Jul 1985	1.00
❑96, Aug 1985	1.00
❑97, Sep 1985	1.00
❑98, Oct 1985	1.00
❑99, Nov 1985	1.00
❑100, Dec 1985; Giant-size MGr (c)	1.00
❑101, Jan 1986 MGr (c)	1.00
❑102, Feb 1986 MGr (c)	1.00
❑103, Mar 1986 MGr (c)	1.00
❑104, Apr 1986 MGr (c)	1.00
❑105, May 1986	1.00
❑106, Jun 1986	1.00
❑107, Jul 1986	1.00
❑108, Aug 1986	1.00
❑109, Sep 1986	1.00
❑110, Oct 1986	1.00
❑111, Nov 1986	1.00
❑112, Dec 1986 MGr (c)	1.00
❑113, Jan 1987	1.00
❑114, Feb 1987; Legends	1.00
❑115, Mar 1987; Legends	1.00
❑116, Apr 1987	1.00
❑117, May 1987 MGr (c)	1.00
❑118, Jun 1987	1.00
❑119, Jul 1987	1.00
❑120, Aug 1987	1.00
❑121, Sep 1987	1.00
❑122, Oct 1987	1.00
❑123, Nov 1987	1.00
❑124, Dec 1987	1.00
❑125, Jan 1988 D: Tara.	1.00
❑126, Feb 1988	1.00
❑127, Mar 1988	1.00
❑128, Apr 1988	1.00
❑129, May 1988	1.00
❑130, Jul 1988	1.00
❑131, Sep 1988; RL (a); Bonus Book #6; Rob Liefeld's first work at DC	2.00
❑132, Nov 1988	1.00
❑133, Dec 1988; Giant-size JDu (a)	1.50
❑Annual 1, ca. 1982 MGr (a)	3.00
❑Annual 2, ca. 1983	1.00
❑Annual 3, ca. 1984	1.00
❑Annual 4, ca. 1985	1.00
❑Annual 5, ca. 1986	1.00
❑Annual 6, ca. 1987	1.00

WARLORD (MINI-SERIES)
DC

	N-MINT
❑1, Jan 1992 MGr (c)	2.00
❑2, Feb 1992 MGr (c); MGr (w)	2.00
❑3, Mar 1992 MGr (c); MGr (w)	2.00
❑4, Apr 1992 MGr (c)	2.00
❑5, May 1992 MGr (c)	2.00
❑6, Jun 1992 MGr (c)	2.00

WARLORD (3RD SERIES)
DC

	N-MINT
❑1, May 2006	2.99
❑2, Jun 2006	2.99
❑3, Jul 2006	2.99
❑4, Aug 2006	2.99
❑5, Sep 2006	2.99

WAR MACHINE
MARVEL

	N-MINT
❑1, Apr 1994; Giant-size; newsstand.	2.00
❑1/Variant, Apr 1994; Giant-size; Embossed cover	2.95
❑2, May 1994	1.50
❑3, Jun 1994	1.50
❑4, Jul 1994	1.50
❑5, Aug 1994	1.50
❑6, Sep 1994	1.50
❑7, Oct 1994	1.50
❑8, Nov 1994	1.50
❑8/CS, Nov 1994; polybagged with 16-page Marvel Action Hour preview, acetate print, coupon, sweepstakes entry form	2.95
❑9, Dec 1994	1.50
❑10, Jan 1995	1.50
❑11, Feb 1995	1.50
❑12, Mar 1995	1.50
❑13, Apr 1995	1.50
❑14, May 1995	1.50
❑15, Jun 1995; flip book with War Machine: Brothers in Arms part 2	2.50
❑16, Jul 1995	1.50
❑17, Aug 1995	1.50
❑18, Sep 1995	1.50
❑19, Oct 1995	1.50
❑20, Nov 1995	1.50
❑21, Dec 1995	1.50
❑22, Jan 1996	1.50
❑23, Feb 1996	1.50
❑24, Mar 1996	1.50
❑25, Apr 1996	1.50
❑Ashcan 1, ca. 1994; ashcan edition	0.75

WAR MACHINE (VOL. 2)
MARVEL / MAX

	N-MINT
❑1, Nov 2001	1.50
❑2, Nov 2001	1.50
❑3, Nov 2001	1.50
❑4, Nov 2001	1.50
❑5, Dec 2001	1.50
❑6, Dec 2001	1.50
❑7, Dec 2001	1.50
❑8, Dec 2001	1.50
❑9, Dec 2001	1.50
❑10, Jan 2002	1.50
❑11, Jan 2002	1.50
❑12, Jan 2002	1.50

WAR MAN
MARVEL / EPIC

	N-MINT
❑1, Nov 1993	2.50
❑2, Dec 1993	2.50

WAR OF THE GODS
DC

	N-MINT
❑1, Sep 1991	1.75
❑2, Oct 1991; newsstand cover	1.75
❑2/Direct ed., Oct 1991; direct sale cover	1.75
❑3, Nov 1991; newsstand cover	1.75
❑3/Direct ed., Nov 1991; direct sale cover	1.75
❑4, Dec 1991; newsstand cover	1.75
❑4/Direct ed., Dec 1991; direct sale cover	1.75

WAR OF THE WORLDS (CALIBER)
CALIBER

	N-MINT
❑1, ca. 1996	2.95
❑2, ca. 1996	2.95
❑3, ca. 1996	2.95
❑4, ca. 1996	2.95
❑5, ca. 1997	2.95

WAR OF THE WORLDS (ETERNITY)
ETERNITY

	N-MINT
❑1, 1990	2.00
❑2, 1990	2.00
❑3, 1990	2.00
❑4, 1990	2.00
❑5, 1990	2.00
❑6, 1990	2.00

WAR OF THE WORLDS: THE MEMPHIS FRONT
ARROW

	N-MINT
❑1 1998, b&w; wrapraound cover	2.95
❑1/A 1998, b&w; expanded page count	2.95
❑2 1998	2.95
❑3 1998	2.95
❑4 1998	2.95
❑5 1998	2.95

WARP
FIRST

	N-MINT
❑1, Mar 1983, FB (a); 1: Lord Cumulus. 1: Chaos. This is the first comic published by First Comics	2.00
❑2, Apr 1983, FB (a)	1.50
❑3, May 1983, FB (a)	1.50
❑4, Jun 1983, FB (a)	1.50
❑5, Aug 1983, FB (a)	1.50
❑6, Sep 1983, FB (a)	1.50
❑7, Oct 1983, FB (a)	1.50
❑8, Nov 1983, Bill Willingham's first major comics work	1.25
❑9, Dec 1983	1.25
❑10, Feb 1984	1.25
❑11, Mar 1984	1.25
❑12, Apr 1984	1.25
❑13, May 1984	1.25
❑14, Jul 1984	1.25
❑15, Aug 1984	1.25
❑16, Sep 1984	1.25

Other grades: Multiply price above by 5/6 for VF/NM • 2/3 for VERY FINE • 1/3 for FINE • 1/5 for VERY GOOD • 1/8 for GOOD

Web

Government agents used tech for powers

©DC

Web of Spider-Man

A slender thread to hang a Spider-title from

©Marvel

Webspinners: Tales of Spider-Man

Updated early adventures for Spider-Man

©Marvel

Weird Melvin

CBG strip inspires ongoing comic book

©Marc Hansen Stuff!

Weird Science (RCP)

Final reprint series does E.C. stories in order

©Gemstone

	N-MINT
❑17, Oct 1984	1.25
❑18, Dec 1984	1.25
❑19, Feb 1985	1.25
❑Special 1, Jul 1983, O: Chaos.	1.00
❑Special 2, Jan 1984	1.00
❑Special 3, Jun 1984, Chaos	1.00

WARP-3
EQUINOX

❑1, Mar 1990, b&w	1.50

WAR PARTY
LIGHTNING

❑1, Oct 1994	2.95

WARP GRAPHICS ANNUAL
WARP

❑1; WP, PF (w); Elfquest, Panda Khan, Unicorn Isle, Captain Obese, Thunderbunny, MythAdventures	3.00

WARPWALKING
CALIBER

❑1, b&w	2.50
❑2, b&w	2.50
❑3, b&w	2.50
❑4, b&w	2.50

WARRIOR BUGS
ARTCODA

❑1, Mar 2002	2.95

WARRIOR NUN AREALA (VOL. 1)
ANTARCTIC

❑1, Dec 1994 1: Shotgun Mary. 1: Warrior Nun Areala.	5.00
❑1/Ltd., Dec 1994; Limited edition (5000 made); no cover price	5.00
❑1/2nd, Mar 1995	3.00
❑2, Feb 1995	4.00
❑3, Apr 1995	4.00
❑3/CS, Apr 1995	8.00
❑3/Ltd., Apr 1995; Limited edition (1000 made); no cover price	5.00

WARRIOR NUN AREALA (VOL. 2)
ANTARCTIC

❑1, Jun 1997	3.00
❑1/Variant, Jun 1997; Leather edition; Print run of 700	6.00
❑2, Sep 1997	3.00
❑3, Nov 1997	3.00
❑4, Jan 1998	3.00
❑5, Mar 1998	3.00
❑6, May 1998	3.00

WARRIOR NUN AREALA (VOL. 3)
ANTARCTIC

❑1, Jul 1999	2.50
❑2, Aug 1999	2.50

WARRIOR NUN AREALA AND AVENGELYNE
ANTARCTIC

❑1/A, Dec 1996; crossover with Maximum Press	2.95
❑1/B, Dec 1996; poster edition; logoless cover and poster insert	5.95

WARRIOR NUN AREALA AND GLORY
ANTARCTIC

	N-MINT
❑1, Sep 1997; crossover with Awesome	2.95
❑1/CS, Sep 1997; limited poster edition; crossover with Awesome	5.95

WARRIOR NUN AREALA/RAZOR: REVENGE
ANTARCTIC

❑1, Jan 1999	2.99
❑1/Deluxe, Jan 1999; Deluxe Edition with painted cover; Deluxe Edition with painted cover	5.99

WARRIOR NUN AREALA: RESURRECTION
ANTARCTIC

❑1, Nov 1998	3.00
❑1/Variant, Sum 1998, alternate logoless cover	3.00
❑2, Jan 1999	3.00
❑3, Mar 1999	3.00
❑4 1999	3.00
❑5 1999	3.00
❑6 1999	3.00
❑Ashcan 1, Nov 1998, b&w preview	1.00

WARRIOR NUN AREALA: RHEINTÖCHTER
ANTARCTIC

❑1, Dec 1997, b&w	2.95
❑2, Apr 1998, b&w	2.95

WARRIOR NUN AREALA: RITUALS
ANTARCTIC

❑1, Aug 1995	2.95
❑1/Variant, Aug 1995; no cover price.	4.00
❑2, Oct 1995	2.95
❑3, Dec 1995	2.95
❑4, Feb 1996	2.95
❑5, Apr 1996	2.95
❑6, Jun 1996	2.95

WARRIOR NUN: BLACK & WHITE
ANTARCTIC

❑1, Feb 1997	3.00
❑2, Apr 1997; cover says Jan, indicia says Apr	3.00
❑3, Jun 1997	3.00
❑4, Aug 1997	3.00
❑5, Oct 1997	3.00
❑6, Dec 1997	3.00
❑7, Feb 1998	3.00
❑8, Mar 1998	3.00
❑9, Apr 1998	3.00
❑10, May 1998	3.00
❑11, Jun 1998	3.00
❑12, Jul 1998	3.00
❑13, Sep 1998	3.00
❑14, Oct 1998	3.00
❑15, Nov 1998	2.95
❑16, Jan 1999	2.99
❑17, Feb 1999	2.99
❑18, Mar 1999	2.99
❑19, Apr 1999	2.99
❑20 1999	2.99
❑21, Jul 1999	2.50

WARRIOR NUN BRIGANTIA
ANTARCTIC

❑1, Jun 2000	2.99
❑2 2000	2.99
❑3 2000	2.99

WARRIOR NUN DEI
ANTARCTIC

	N-MINT
❑1, Comics Cavalcade Commemorative Edition	5.95

WARRIOR NUN DEI: AFTERTIME
ANTARCTIC

❑1, Jan 1997	3.00
❑2 1998	3.00
❑3, Mar 1999	3.00

WARRIOR NUN: FRENZY
ANTARCTIC

❑1, Jan 1998	2.95
❑2, Jun 1998	2.95

WARRIOR NUN: SCORPIO ROSE
ANTARCTIC

❑1, Sep 1996	2.95
❑2, Nov 1996	2.95
❑3, Jan 1997	2.95
❑4, Mar 1997	2.95

WARRIOR NUN VS RAZOR
ANTARCTIC

❑1, May 1996, crossover with London Night Studios	3.95

WARRIOR OF WAVERLY STREET
DARK HORSE

❑1, Nov 1996	2.95
❑2, Dec 1996	2.95

WARRIORS
ADVENTURE

❑1, ca. 1987, b&w	2.00
❑2, Dec 1987, b&w	2.00
❑3, ca. 1988, b&w	2.00
❑4, Jul 1988, b&w	2.00
❑5, Nov 1988, b&w	2.00

WARRIORS OF PLASM
DEFIANT

❑1, Aug 1993; O: Warriors of Plasm. 1: Lorca. 1: Warriors of Plasm. First Defiant Comic (not including Warriors of Plasm #0 promotion)	2.95
❑2, Sep 1993	2.95
❑3, Oct 1993	2.95
❑4, Nov 1993	2.95
❑5, Dec 1993	2.50
❑6, Jan 1994 1: Prudence.	2.50
❑7, Feb 1994	2.50
❑8, Mar 1994	2.75
❑9, Apr 1994	2.75
❑10, May 1994	2.50
❑11, Jun 1994	2.50
❑12, Jul 1994	2.50
❑13, Aug 1994; Final issue?	2.50

WARRIORS OF PLASM GRAPHIC NOVEL
DEFIANT

❑1 1993, Home for the Holidays	6.95

WARRIOR'S WAY
BENCH

❑1 1998	2.99
❑2, Aug 1998	2.99
❑2/A, Aug 1998; alternate cover	2.99
❑3 1998	2.99

Other grades: Multiply price above by 5/6 for VF/NM • 2/3 for VERY FINE • 1/3 for FINE • 1/5 for VERY GOOD • 1/8 for GOOD

WARRIOR (ULTIMATE CREATIONS)
ULTIMATE CREATIONS
- ❑1, May 1996 2.95
- ❑2 1996 2.95
- ❑3 1997 2.95
- ❑4 1997 2.95

WAR SIRENS AND LIBERTY BELLES
RECOLLECTIONS
- ❑1, b&w; cardstock cover 4.95

WAR SLUTS
PRETTY GRAPHIC
- ❑1, b&w 3.95
- ❑2, b&w; cardstock cover 3.95

WAR STORY: ARCHANGEL
DC / VERTIGO
- ❑1, ca. 2003 4.95

WAR STORY: D-DAY DODGERS
DC / VERTIGO
- ❑1, Dec 2001, b&w 4.95

WAR STORY: JOHANN'S TIGER
DC / VERTIGO
- ❑1, Nov 2001, b&w 4.95

WAR STORY: NIGHTINGALE
DC / VERTIGO
- ❑1, Feb 2002, b&w 4.95

WAR STORY: SCREAMING EAGLES
DC / VERTIGO
- ❑1, Jan 2002, b&w 4.95

WARSTRIKE
MALIBU / ULTRAVERSE
- ❑1, May 1994 1.95
- ❑2, Jun 1994 1.95
- ❑3, Jul 1994 1.95
- ❑4, Aug 1994 1.95
- ❑5, Sep 1994 1.95
- ❑6, Oct 1994 1.95
- ❑7, Nov 1994 1.95
- ❑Giant Size 1, Dec 1994, Giant-size; Lord Pumpkin reborn 2.50

WARWORLD!
DARK HORSE
- ❑1, Feb 1989, b&w 1.75

WARZONE
EXPRESS / ENTITY
- ❑1, ca. 1994, b&w; enhanced cardstock cover 2.95
- ❑2, ca. 1994, b&w; enhanced cardstock cover 2.95
- ❑3, ca. 1995, b&w; enhanced cardstock cover 2.95

WARZONE 3719
POCKET CHANGE
- ❑1 1.95

WASHMEN
NEW YORK
- ❑1 1.70

WASHOUTS
RENAISSANCE
- ❑1, Jul 2002, b&w 2.95

WASH TUBBS QUARTERLY
DRAGON LADY
- ❑1 4.95
- ❑2 5.95
- ❑3 5.95
- ❑4 5.95
- ❑5 5.95

WASTE L.A.: DESCENT
JOHN GAUSHELL
- ❑1, Jan 1996, b&w; fumetti 2.50
- ❑2, Mar 1996, b&w; fumetti 2.50
- ❑3, May 1996, b&w; fumetti 2.50

WASTELAND
DC
- ❑1, Dec 1987 2.00
- ❑2, Jan 1988 2.00
- ❑3, Feb 1988 2.00
- ❑4, Mar 1988 2.00
- ❑5, Apr 1988; correct cover 2.00
- ❑5/A, Apr 1988; cover of #6 2.00
- ❑6, May 1988; correct cover 2.00
- ❑6/A, May 1988; blank cover 2.00
- ❑7, Jun 1988 2.00
- ❑8, Jul 1988 2.00
- ❑9, Aug 1988 2.00
- ❑10, Sep 1988 2.00
- ❑11, Oct 1988 2.00
- ❑12, Nov 1988 JO (a) 2.00
- ❑13, Dec 1988 JO (a) 2.00
- ❑14, Win 1988 JO (a) 2.00
- ❑15, Hol 1988; JO (a); Hol 1988 2.00
- ❑16, Feb 1989 JO (a) 2.00
- ❑17, Apr 1989 JO (a) 2.00
- ❑18, May 1989 JO (a) 2.00

WATCHCATS
HARRIER
- ❑1 1.95

WATCHMEN
DC
- ❑1, Sep 1986 AMo (w); DaG (a); 1: Rorshach. 1: Doctor Manhattan. 1: Ozymandias. D: The Comedian 8.00
- ❑2, Oct 1986 AMo (w); DaG (a) 5.00
- ❑3, Nov 1986 AMo (w); DaG (a) 5.00
- ❑4, Dec 1986 AMo (w); DaG (a); O: Doctor Manhattan. 4.00
- ❑5, Jan 1987 AMo (w); DaG (a) 4.00
- ❑6, Feb 1987 AMo (w); DaG (a); O: Rorshach. 4.00
- ❑7, Mar 1987 AMo (w); DaG (a) 4.00
- ❑8, Apr 1987 AMo (w); DaG (a) 4.00
- ❑9, May 1987 AMo (w); DaG (a) 4.00
- ❑10, Jul 1987 AMo (w); DaG (a) 4.00
- ❑11, Aug 1987 AMo (w); DaG (a); O: Ozymandias. 4.00
- ❑12, Oct 1987 AMo (w); DaG (a); D: Rorshach. 4.00

WATERLOO SUNSET
IMAGE
- ❑1 2004 6.95
- ❑2 2004 6.95
- ❑3, Feb 2005 6.95
- ❑4, Jan 2006

WATERWORLD: CHILDREN OF LEVIATHAN
ACCLAIM
- ❑1, Aug 1997; no indicia 2.50
- ❑2, Sep 1997 2.50
- ❑3, Oct 1997 2.50
- ❑4, Nov 1997 2.50

WAVEMAKERS
BLIND BAT
- ❑1 3.00

WAVE WARRIORS
ASTROBOYS
- ❑1 2.00

WAXWORK
BLACKTHORNE
- ❑1, b&w 2.00
- ❑3D 1 2.50

WAY OF THE RAT
CROSSGEN
- ❑1, Jun 2002 2.95
- ❑2, Jul 2002 2.95
- ❑3, Aug 2002 2.95
- ❑4, Sep 2002 2.95
- ❑5, Oct 2002 2.95
- ❑6, Nov 2002 2.95
- ❑7, Dec 2002 2.95
- ❑8, Jan 2003 2.95
- ❑9, Feb 2003 2.95
- ❑10, Mar 2003 2.95
- ❑11, Apr 2003 2.95
- ❑12, May 2003 2.95
- ❑13, Jun 2003 2.95
- ❑14, May 2003 2.95
- ❑15, Jul 2003 2.95
- ❑16, Aug 2003 2.95
- ❑17, Nov 2003 2.95
- ❑18, Nov 2003 2.95
- ❑19, Dec 2003 2.95
- ❑20, Jan 2004 2.95
- ❑21, Feb 2004 2.95
- ❑22, Apr 2004 2.95
- ❑23, May 2004 2.95
- ❑23/2nd, Apr 2004 2.95
- ❑24, May 2004 2.95
- ❑Book 1, ca. 2003 15.95

WAY OUT STRIPS (FANTAGRAPHICS)
FANTAGRAPHICS
- ❑1 1994, b&w 2.50
- ❑2, May 1994, b&w 2.75
- ❑3, Aug 1994, b&w 2.75

WAY OUT STRIPS (TRAGEDY STRIKES)
TRAGEDY STRIKES
- ❑1 1992, b&w 2.95
- ❑2 1992, b&w 2.95
- ❑3 1992, b&w 2.95

WAYWARD WARRIOR
ALPHA PRODUCTIONS
- ❑1 1990, b&w 1.95
- ❑2 1990, b&w 1.95
- ❑3 1990, b&w 1.95

WCW WORLD CHAMPIONSHIP WRESTLING
MARVEL
- ❑1, Apr 1992 1.25
- ❑2, May 1992 1.25
- ❑3, Jun 1992 1.25
- ❑4, Jul 1992 1.25
- ❑5, Aug 1992 1.25
- ❑6, Sep 1992 1.25
- ❑7, Oct 1992 1.25
- ❑8, Nov 1992 1.25
- ❑9, Dec 1992 1.25
- ❑10, Jan 1993 1.25
- ❑11, Feb 1993 1.25
- ❑12, Mar 1993 1.25

WE 3
DC / VERTIGO
- ❑1, Oct 2004 2.95
- ❑2, Dec 2004 2.95
- ❑3, Mar 2005 2.95

WEAPONS FILE
ANTARCTIC
- ❑1, Jun 2005 4.95
- ❑2, Jul 2005 4.95

WEAPON X
MARVEL
- ❑1, Mar 1995; Age of Apocalypse 1.95
- ❑2, Apr 1995; Age of Apocalypse 1.95
- ❑3, May 1995; Age of Apocalypse 1.95
- ❑4, Jun 1995; Age of Apocalypse 1.95

WEAPON X (2ND SERIES)
MARVEL
- ❑1, Nov 2002 2.25
- ❑2, Dec 2002 2.25
- ❑3, Jan 2003 2.25
- ❑4, Feb 2003 2.25
- ❑5, Mar 2003 2.25
- ❑6, Apr 2003 2.25
- ❑7, May 2003 2.25
- ❑8, Jun 2003 2.25
- ❑9, Jul 2003 2.99
- ❑10, Aug 2003 2.99
- ❑11, Sep 2004 2.99
- ❑12, Oct 2003 2.99
- ❑13, Nov 2003 2.99
- ❑14, Dec 2003 2.99
- ❑15, Dec 2003 2.99
- ❑16, Jan 2004 2.99
- ❑17, Mar 2004 2.99
- ❑18, Apr 2004 2.99
- ❑19, May 2004 2.99
- ❑20, May 2004 2.99
- ❑21, Jun 2004 2.99
- ❑22, Jun 2004 2.99
- ❑23, Jul 2004 2.99
- ❑24, Jul 2004 2.99
- ❑25, Aug 2004 2.99
- ❑26, Sep 2004 2.99
- ❑27, Oct 2004 2.99
- ❑28, Nov 2004 2.99

WEAPON X: DAYS OF FUTURE NOW
MARVEL
- ❑1, Aug 2005 2.99
- ❑2, Sep 2005 2.99
- ❑3, Oct 2005 2.99
- ❑4, Dec 2005 2.99
- ❑5, Jan 2006 2.99

Other grades: Multiply price above by 5/6 for VF/NM • 2/3 for VERY FINE • 1/3 for FINE • 1/5 for VERY GOOD • 1/8 for GOOD

Weird Secret Origins 80-Page Giant

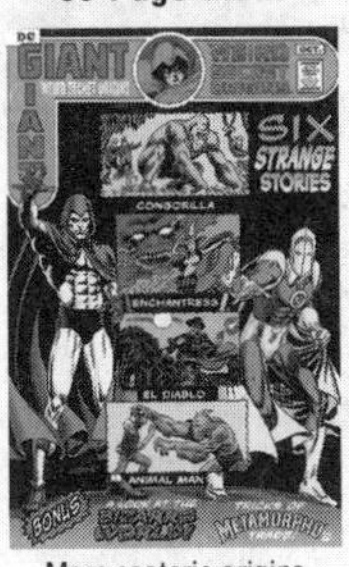

More esoteric origins collected

©DC

Weird War Tales

Horror comes to the battlefield

©DC

Weird Western Tales

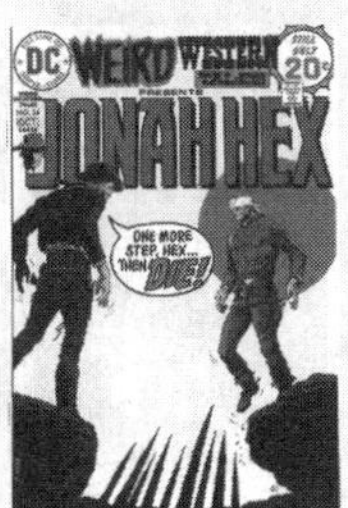

All-Star Western got Weird with Jonah Hex

©DC

Weird Worlds

Burroughs' other series found a home

©DC

Welcome Back, Kotter

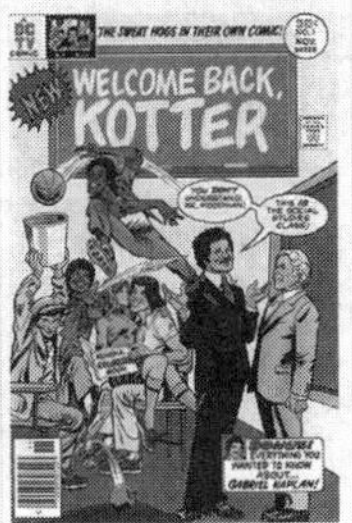

TV writer Mark Evanier also wrote comic

©DC

N-MINT

WEAPON X: THE DRAFT: KANE
MARVEL

❑1, Oct 2002 2.25

WEAPON XXX: ORIGIN OF THE IMPLANTS
FRIENDLY

❑1, Jul 1992 2.95
❑2 1992 2.95
❑3 1992 2.95

WEAPON ZERO
IMAGE

❑1, Jun 1995; 1: Weapon Zero. Issue #T-4 3.00
❑1/Gold, Jun 1995; Gold edition; Issue #T-4; 1000 copies produced for Chicago Comicon 2.50
❑2, Aug 1995; Issue #T-3 2.50
❑3, Sep 1995; Issue #T-2 2.50
❑4, Oct 1995; Issue #T-1 2.50
❑5, Dec 1995; Issue #T-0; Issue #T-0 2.50

WEAPON ZERO (VOL. 2)
IMAGE

❑1, Mar 1996; indicia gives year of publication as 1995 3.00
❑2, Apr 1996; indicia gives year of publication as 1995 3.00
❑3, May 1996 3.00
❑4, Jun 1996; indicia gives year of publication as 1995 3.00
❑5, Jul 1996; indicia gives year of publication as 1995 3.00
❑6, Aug 1996 2.50
❑7, Sep 1996 2.50
❑8, Nov 1996 2.50
❑9, Dec 1996 2.50
❑10, Feb 1997 2.50
❑11, Apr 1997 2.50
❑12, May 1997 2.50
❑13, Jun 1997 2.50
❑14, Sep 1997 2.50
❑15, Dec 1997 3.50

WEAPON ZERO/SILVER SURFER
TOP COW / IMAGE

❑1, Jan 1997; crossover with Marvel; continues in Cyblade/Ghost Rider 2.95
❑1/A, Jan 1997; alternate cover 2.95

WEASEL GUY: ROAD TRIP
IMAGE

❑1, Aug 1999 2.95
❑1/A, Aug 1999; alternate cover 2.95
❑2, Oct 1999 3.50

WEASEL PATROL
ECLIPSE

❑1, b&w 2.00

WEATHER WOMAN
CPM MANGA

❑1, Aug 2000, b&w 2.95
❑1/A, Aug 2000, b&w; alternate cover: Weather Woman smoking 2.95

WEAVEWORLD
MARVEL / EPIC

❑1, Dec 1991, prestige format 4.95
❑2, Jan 1992, prestige format 4.95
❑3, Feb 1992, prestige format 4.95

N-MINT

WEB
DC / IMPACT

❑1, Sep 1991 1: The Web (full appearance). 1: Bill Grady. 1: Templar. 1.25
❑2, Oct 1991 O: The Web. 1: Gunny. 1: The Sunshine Kid. 1: Brew. 1: Powell Jennings. 1: Jump. 1.00
❑3, Nov 1991 1: St. James. 1: Meridian. 1.00
❑4, Dec 1991 1: Silver. 1.00
❑5, Jan 1992 1.00
❑6, Feb 1992 1.00
❑7, Apr 1992 1.00
❑8, Apr 1992 1: Studs. 1.00
❑9, May 1992; trading card 1.00
❑10, Jun 1992 1.25
❑11, Jul 1992 1.25
❑12, Aug 1992 1.25
❑13, Sep 1992 1.25
❑14, Oct 1992 1.25
❑Annual 1, ca. 1992; trading card 2.50

WEBBER'S WORLD
ALLSTAR

❑1 4.95

WEB-MAN
ARGOSY

❑1, gatefold cover 2.50

WEB OF HORROR
MAJOR MAGAZINES

❑1, Dec 1969; Jeff Jones cover; Wrightson, Kaluta art 90.00
❑2, Feb 1970; Jeff Jones cover; Wrightson, Kaluta art 55.00
❑3, Apr 1970; 1st published Wrightson cover; Brunner, Kaluta, Bruce Jones art 65.00

WEB OF SCARLET SPIDER
MARVEL

❑1, Nov 1995, O: Scarlet Spider. 2.00
❑2, Dec 1995, A: Cyber-Slayers. 2.00
❑3, Jan 1996, A: Firestar. continues in New Warriors #67 2.00
❑4, Feb 1996 2.00

WEB OF SPIDER-MAN
MARVEL

❑1, Apr 1985 8.00
❑2, May 1985 6.00
❑3, Jun 1985 5.00
❑4, Jul 1985 V: Doctor Octopus. 4.00
❑5, Aug 1985 V: Doctor Octopus. 4.00
❑6, Sep 1985; Secret Wars II 4.00
❑7, Oct 1985 A: Hulk. V: Hulk. 4.00
❑8, Nov 1985 4.00
❑9, Dec 1985 4.00
❑10, Jan 1986 A: Dominic Fortune. 4.00
❑11, Feb 1986 3.00
❑12, Mar 1986 3.00
❑13, Apr 1986 3.00
❑14, May 1986 3.00
❑15, Jun 1986 1: The Foreigner. 1: Chance I (Nicholas Powell). 3.00
❑16, Jul 1986 3.00
❑17, Aug 1986; V: Magma. red suit destroyed 3.00
❑18, Sep 1986; Venom cameo 3.00

N-MINT

❑19, Oct 1986 1: Solo. 3.00
❑20, Nov 1986 3.00
❑21, Dec 1986 3.00
❑22, Jan 1987 3.00
❑23, Feb 1987 3.00
❑24, Mar 1987 3.00
❑25, Apr 1987 3.00
❑26, May 1987 3.00
❑27, Jun 1987 3.00
❑28, Jul 1987 3.00
❑29, Aug 1987 A: Wolverine. A: Hobgoblin II (Jason Macendale). 5.00
❑30, Sep 1987 O: The Rose 4.00
❑31, Oct 1987 V: Kraven. 5.00
❑32, Nov 1987 V: Kraven. 5.00
❑33, Dec 1987 BSz (c) 3.00
❑34, Jan 1988 3.00
❑35, Feb 1988 1: Tarantula II (Luis Alvarez). 3.00
❑36, Mar 1988 O: Tarantula II (Luis Alvarez). 4.00
❑37, Apr 1988 3.00
❑38, May 1988 A: Hobgoblin II (Jason Macendale). V: Hobgoblin. 5.00
❑39, Jun 1988 3.00
❑40, Jul 1988 3.00
❑41, Aug 1988 3.00
❑42, Sep 1988 3.00
❑43, Oct 1988 3.00
❑44, Nov 1988 A: Hulk. 2.50
❑45, Dec 1988 V: Vulture. 2.50
❑46, Jan 1989 2.50
❑47, Feb 1989; V: Hobgoblin. Inferno. 2.50
❑48, Mar 1989; O: Demogoblin. V: Hobgoblin. Inferno 8.00
❑49, Apr 1989 2.00
❑50, May 1989; Giant-sized 2.50
❑51, Jun 1989 2.00
❑52, Jul 1989 V: Chameleon 2.00
❑53, Aug 1989 2.00
❑54, Sep 1989 V: Chameleon. 2.00
❑55, Oct 1989 V: Chameleon. 2.00
❑56, Nov 1989 V: Rocket Racer. 2.00
❑57, Nov 1989 V: Skinhead. 2.00
❑58, Dec 1989; Acts of Vengeance 2.50
❑59, Dec 1989; Acts of Vengeance; Spider-Man with cosmic powers 8.00
❑60, Jan 1990; Acts of Vengeance 2.50
❑61, Feb 1990; Acts of Vengeance 2.50
❑62, Mar 1990 2.00
❑63, Apr 1990 2.00
❑64, May 1990; Acts of Vengeance 2.00
❑65, Jun 1990; Acts of Vengeance 2.00
❑66, Jul 1990 A: Green Goblin. 2.00
❑67, Aug 1990 A: Green Goblin. 2.00
❑68, Sep 1990 2.00
❑69, Oct 1990 2.00
❑70, Nov 1990; Spider-Hulk 2.00
❑71, Dec 1990 2.00
❑72, Jan 1991 2.00
❑73, Feb 1991 2.00
❑74, Mar 1991 2.00
❑75, Apr 1991 2.00
❑76, May 1991 A: Fantastic Four. 2.00
❑77, Jun 1991 2.00

Other grades: Multiply price above by 5/6 for VF/NM • 2/3 for VERY FINE • 1/3 for FINE • 1/5 for VERY GOOD • 1/8 for GOOD

	N-MINT
❑78, Jul 1991 A: Cloak & Dagger.	2.00
❑79, Aug 1991	2.00
❑80, Sep 1991 V: Silvermane.	2.00
❑81, Oct 1991 KB (w)	2.00
❑82, Nov 1991 KB (w)	2.00
❑83, Dec 1991 KB (w)	2.00
❑84, Jan 1992 A: Hobgoblin.	2.00
❑85, Feb 1992	2.00
❑86, Mar 1992	2.00
❑87, Apr 1992	2.00
❑88, May 1992	2.00
❑89, Jun 1992	2.00
❑90, Jul 1992; Double-size; hologram; Poster	5.00
❑90/2nd, Jul 1992; Double-size; hologram; Poster	2.95
❑91, Aug 1992	2.00
❑92, Sep 1992	2.00
❑93, Oct 1992	2.00
❑94, Nov 1992 V: Hobgoblin.	2.00
❑95, Dec 1992 A: Ghost Rider. A: Johnny Blaze. V: Venom.	2.00
❑96, Jan 1993 A: Ghost Rider. A: Johnny Blaze. V: Venom.	2.00
❑97, Feb 1993	2.00
❑98, Mar 1993	2.00
❑99, Apr 1993 V: New Enforcers.	2.00
❑100, May 1993; 1: Spider-Armor. foil cover	4.00
❑101, Jun 1993	2.00
❑102, Jul 1993	2.00
❑103, Aug 1993	2.00
❑104, Sep 1993	2.00
❑105, Oct 1993; A: Archangel. Infinity Crusade	2.00
❑106/CS, Nov 1993; Dirtbag special; Infinity Crusade; Polybagged with copy of Dirt Magazine, cassette tape	5.00
❑106, Nov 1993; Infinity Crusade	1.25
❑107, Dec 1993 A: Quicksand. A: Sandman.	2.00
❑108, Jan 1994 A: Quicksand. A: Sandman.	2.00
❑109, Feb 1994	2.00
❑110, Mar 1994	2.00
❑111, Apr 1994 V: Lizard	2.00
❑112, May 1994	2.00
❑113, Jun 1994 A: Gambit. A: Black Cat.	2.00
❑113/CS, Jun 1994; A: Gambit. A: Black Cat. TV preview; print	4.00
❑114, Jul 1994	2.00
❑115, Aug 1994	2.00
❑116, Sep 1994	2.00
❑117, Oct 1994; Flip-book A: Ben Reilly.	3.00
❑117/Variant, Oct 1994; Flip-book; O: Ben Reilly. A: Ben Reilly. foil cover	5.00
❑118, Nov 1994	3.00
❑118/2nd, Nov 1994; Has blank UPC code	1.50
❑119, Dec 1994; Scarlet Spider vs. Venom	2.00
❑119/CS, Dec 1994; polybagged with Marvel Milestone Edition: Amazing Spider-Man #150 and POP card for Amazing Spider-Ma; Scarlet Spider vs. Venom	6.45
❑120, Jan 1995; Giant-size A: Morbius.	4.00
❑121, Feb 1995 V: Kaine.	2.00
❑122, Mar 1995 A: Jackal.	2.00
❑123, Apr 1995 A: Jackal.	2.00
❑124, May 1995	2.00
❑125, Jun 1995; Giant-size	2.95
❑125/Variant, Jun 1995; Giant-size; Hologram on cover	3.95
❑126, Jul 1995	1.50
❑127, Aug 1995	1.50
❑128, Sep 1995	1.50
❑129, Oct 1995 A: New Warriors.	1.50
❑129/CS, Oct 1995	5.00
❑Annual 1, ca. 1985; A: 4th. Painted cover; 4th appearance Spider-Man's black costume; ca. 1985	7.00
❑Annual 2, ca. 1986 A: New Mutants..	6.00
❑Annual 3, ca. 1987; pin-ups	3.00
❑Annual 4, ca. 1988 1: Poison.	3.00
❑Annual 5, ca. 1989; O: Silver Sable. A: Fantastic Four. Atlantis Attacks	2.50
❑Annual 6, ca. 1990; V: Psycho-Man. Tiny Spidey	2.50
❑Annual 7, ca. 1991 O: Hobgoblin. O: Venom. O: Green Goblin. A: Iron Man. A: Black Panther. V: Ultron.	2.50
❑Annual 8, ca. 1992 A: New Warriors. A: Venom. V: Whiplash. V: Beetle. V: Constrictor. V: Rhino.	3.00
❑Annual 9, ca. 1993; 1: The Cadre. trading card	2.95
❑Annual 10, ca. 1994 V: Shriek.	2.95
❑SS 1, ca. 1995; Flip-book; Super Special	3.95

WEBSPINNERS: TALES OF SPIDER-MAN
MARVEL

	N-MINT
❑1, Jan 1999; gatefold summary	2.99
❑1/A, Jan 1999; variant cover: Spider-Man vs. Mysterio with statue against orange background	2.99
❑1/B, Jan 1999; gatefold summary; variant cover	2.99
❑1/Autographed, Jan 1999	10.00
❑1/Sunburst, Jan 1999	5.00
❑2/A, Feb 1999; Cover A	2.50
❑2/B, Feb 1999	2.50
❑3, Mar 1999	2.50
❑4, Apr 1999	2.50
❑5, May 1999	2.50
❑6, Jun 1999	2.50
❑7, Jul 1999	2.50
❑8, Aug 1999	2.50
❑9, Sep 1999	2.50
❑10, Oct 1999	2.50
❑11, Nov 1999	2.50
❑12, Dec 1999	2.50
❑13, Jan 2000	2.50
❑14, Feb 2000	2.50
❑15, Mar 2000	2.50
❑16, Apr 2000	2.50
❑17, May 2000	2.50
❑18, Jun 2000	2.50

WEDDING OF DRACULA
MARVEL

	N-MINT
❑1, Jan 1993; Reprints Tomb of Dracula #30, #45, and #46	2.00

WEDDING OF POPEYE AND OLIVE
OCEAN

	N-MINT
❑1, ca. 1998, b&w	2.75

WEEZUL
LIGHTNING

	N-MINT
❑1/A, Aug 1996	2.75
❑1/B, Aug 1996; alternate cover	3.00

WEIRD
DC

	N-MINT
❑1, Apr 1988	1.50
❑2, May 1988	1.50
❑3, Jun 1988	1.50
❑4, Jul 1988	1.50

WEIRD (MAGAZINE)
DC / PARADOX

	N-MINT
❑1, Sum 1997, b&w; magazine; reprints material from Big Book of Conspiracies; Summer 1997	2.99

WEIRD
AVALON

	N-MINT
❑1	2.99
❑2	2.99
❑3	2.99
❑4	2.99

WEIRDFALL
ANTARCTIC

	N-MINT
❑1, Jul 1995, b&w	2.75
❑2, Sep 1995, b&w	2.75
❑3, Nov 1995, b&w	2.75

WEIRD FANTASY (RCP)
GEMSTONE

	N-MINT
❑1, Oct 1992; AF, HK, WW, JKa (a); Reprints	2.50
❑2, Jan 1993; AF, HK, WW, JKa (a); Reprints Weird Fantasy #14	2.00
❑3, Apr 1993; AF, HK, WW, JKa (a); Reprints	2.00
❑4, Jul 1993; AF, HK, WW, JKa (a); Reprints	2.00
❑5, Oct 1993; AF, HK, WW, JKa (w); AF, HK, WW, JKa (a); Reprints	2.00
❑6, Jan 1994; AF, HK, WW, JKa (a); Reprints	2.00
❑7, Apr 1994; AF, WW, JKa (a); Reprints	2.00
❑8, Jul 1994; Reprints	2.00
❑9, Oct 1994; Reprints	2.00
❑10, Jan 1995; Reprints	2.00
❑11, Apr 1995; Reprints	2.50
❑12, Jul 1995; Reprints	2.50
❑13, Oct 1995; Reprints	2.50
❑14, Jan 1996; FF (a); Reprints	2.50
❑15, Apr 1996; AW (a); Reprints	2.50
❑16, Jul 1996; AW (a); Reprints	2.50
❑17, Oct 1996; AW (a); Reprints	2.50
❑18, Jan 1997; Reprints	2.50
❑19, Apr 1997; AW, JO, JSe, BE, JKa (w); AW, JO, JSe, BE, JKa (a); Reprints Weird Fantasy (EC) #19	2.50
❑20, Jul 1997; AW, JO, JSe, BE, JKa (w); AW, JO, JSe, BE, JKa (a); Reprints Weird Fantasy (EC) #20	2.50
❑21, Oct 1997; AW, JO, JSe, BE, JKa (w); AW, JO, JSe, BE, JKa (a); Reprints Weird Fantasy (EC) #21	2.50
❑22, Jan 1998; JO, BK, JKa (w); JO, BK, JKa (a); Reprints Weird Fantasy (EC) #22	2.50
❑Annual 1; Reprints Weird Fantasy #1-5	8.95
❑Annual 2; Reprints Weird Fantasy #6-10	9.95
❑Annual 3	8.95
❑Annual 4	9.95
❑Annual 5; Reprints Weird Fantasy #19-22	10.95

WEIRD MELVIN
MARC HANSEN STUFF!

	N-MINT
❑1, Feb 1995, b&w	2.95
❑2, Apr 1995, b&w	2.95
❑3, Jun 1995, b&w	2.95
❑4, Aug 1995, b&w	2.95
❑5, Oct 1995, b&w	2.95

WEIRD MYSTERY TALES
DC

	N-MINT
❑1, Jul 1972 JK (a)	30.00
❑2, Sep 1972	20.00
❑3, Nov 1972	15.00
❑4, Jan 1973	12.00
❑5, Apr 1973	12.00
❑6, Jul 1973	12.00
❑7, Sep 1973	12.00
❑8, Nov 1973	12.00
❑9, Dec 1973	12.00
❑10, Mar 1974	12.00
❑11, Apr 1974	10.00
❑12, Jul 1974	10.00
❑13, Aug 1974	10.00
❑14, Oct 1974	10.00
❑15, Jan 1975	10.00
❑16, Mar 1975	10.00
❑17, Apr 1975	10.00
❑18, May 1975	10.00
❑19, Jun 1975	10.00
❑20, Jul 1975	10.00
❑21, Aug 1975	15.00
❑22, Sep 1975	10.00
❑23, Oct 1975	10.00
❑24, Nov 1975	10.00

WEIRD ROMANCE
ECLIPSE

	N-MINT
❑1, ca. 1988, b&w	2.00

WEIRD SCIENCE (GLADSTONE)
GLADSTONE

	N-MINT
❑1, Sep 1990; AF, GE, AW, HK, JO, WW, JKa (w); AF, GE, AW, HK, JO, WW, JKa (a); Reprints Weird Science (EC) #22; Weird Fantasy (EC) #1	2.00
❑2, Nov 1990; AW, JO, WW, JKa (a); Reprints	2.00
❑3, Jan 1991; AF, HK, WW, JKa (a); Reprints Weird Science (EC) #9, Weird Fantasy (EC) #14	2.00
❑4, Mar 1991; AF, JO, WW, JKa (a); Reprints	2.00

WEIRD SCIENCE (RCP)
GEMSTONE

	N-MINT
❑1, Sep 1992; AF, HK, WW, JKa (w); AF, HK, WW, JKa (a); Reprints Weird Science (EC) #1	2.50
❑2, Dec 1992; Reprints Weird Science (EC) #2	2.00
❑3, Mar 1993; Reprints Weird Science (EC) #3	2.00
❑4, Jun 1993; AF, HK, JKa, GI (a); Reprints Weird Science (EC) #4	2.00

Other grades: Multiply price above by 5/6 for VF/NM • 2/3 for VERY FINE • 1/3 for FINE • 1/5 for VERY GOOD • 1/8 for GOOD

Wendy, the Good Little Witch (Vol. 1)

Precocious sorceress does white magic
©Harvey

Wendy Witch World

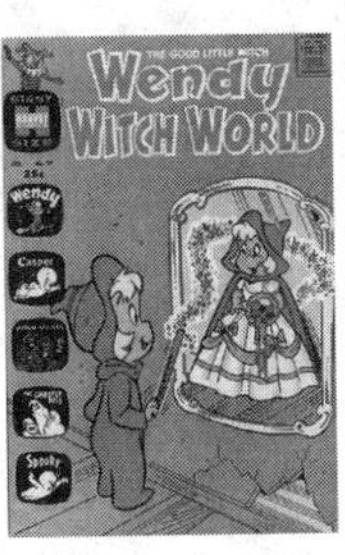

Lotta had Foodland, Richie had Money World ...
©Harvey

Werewolf By Night

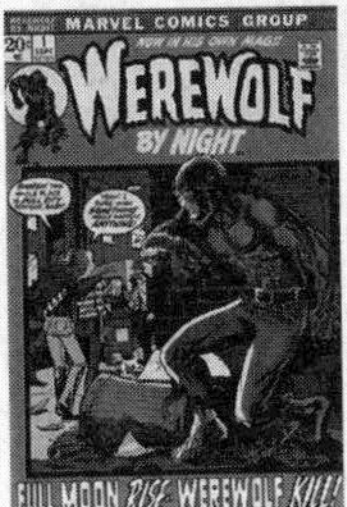

Main character was named after terrier
©Marvel

West Coast Avengers

Avengers branch out with B-characters
©Marvel

Western Gunfighters (2nd Series)

Reprints adventures of Old West's Kids
©Marvel

N-MINT

❑5, Sep 1993; AF, HK, WW, JKa (a); Reprints Weird Science (EC) #5 ...... 2.00
❑6, Dec 1993; AF, HK, WW, JKa (a); Reprints Weird Science (EC) #6 ...... 2.00
❑7, Mar 1994; AF (c); AF, HK, WW, JKa (a); Reprints Weird Science (EC) #7 ...... 2.00
❑8, Jun 1994; AF, WW, JKa (a); Reprints Weird Science (EC) #8 ...... 2.00
❑9, Sep 1994; Reprints Weird Science (EC) #9 ...... 2.00
❑10, Dec 1994; Reprints Weird Science (EC) #10 ...... 2.00
❑11, Mar 1995; Reprints Weird Science (EC) #11 ...... 2.00
❑12, Jun 1995; Reprints Weird Science (EC) #12 ...... 2.00
❑13, Sep 1995; Reprints Weird Science (EC) #13 ...... 2.00
❑14, Dec 1995; Reprints Weird Science (EC) #14 ...... 2.00
❑15, Mar 1996; Reprints Weird Science (EC) #15 ...... 2.50
❑16, Jun 1996; Reprints Weird Science (EC) #16 ...... 2.50
❑17, Sep 1996; Reprints Weird Science (EC) #17 ...... 2.50
❑18, Dec 1996; Reprints Weird Science (EC) #18 ...... 2.50
❑19, Mar 1997; AW, JO, BE, WW (w); AW, JO, BE, WW (a); Reprints Weird Science (EC) #19 ...... 2.50
❑20, Jun 1997; AW, JO, WW, JKa (w); AW, JO, WW, JKa (a); Reprints Weird Science (EC) #20 ...... 2.50
❑21, Sep 1997; AW, JO, WW, JKa (w); AW, JO, FF, WW, JKa (a); Reprints Weird Science (EC) #21; EC editors put themselves in story 2.50
❑22, Dec 1997; GE, AW, JO, WW (w); GE, AW, JO, WW (a); Reprints Weird Science (EC) #22; Wally Wood puts himself in story 2.50
❑Annual 1; Reprints Weird Science (EC) #1-5 ...... 8.95
❑Annual 2; Reprints Weird Science (EC) #6-10 ...... 9.95
❑Annual 3; Reprints Weird Science (EC) #11-14 ...... 10.95
❑Annual 4; Reprints Weird Science (EC) #15-18 ...... 9.95
❑Annual 5; Reprints Weird Science (EC) #19-22 ...... 10.50

WEIRD SCIENCE-FANTASY (RCP)
GEMSTONE

❑1, Nov 1992; Reprints Weird Science-Fantasy #23 ...... 2.00
❑2, Feb 1993; AF (c); AW, JO, WW, BK (w); AW, JO, WW, BK (a); Reprints Weird Science-Fantasy #24; "Upheaval" by Harlan Ellison (1st professional work by Harlan Ellison) 2.00
❑3, May 1993; AF (c); AW, JO, WW, BK (a); Reprints Weird Science-Fantasy #25 ...... 2.00
❑4, Aug 1993; UFO issue; Reprints Weird Science-Fantasy #26; Flying Saucer Report special issue 2.00
❑5, Nov 1993; JO, WW, JKa (a); Reprints Weird Science-Fantasy #27 ...... 2.00
❑6, Feb 1994; AF (c); AW, JO, WW, JKa (a); Reprints Weird Science-Fantasy #28 ...... 2.00
❑7, May 1994; FF (c); AW, JO, WW (a); Reprints Weird Science-Fantasy #29 ...... 2.00
❑8, Aug 1994; Reprints 2.00
❑9, Nov 1994; Reprints 2.00
❑10, Feb 1995; Reprints 2.00
❑11, May 1995; Reprints 2.00
❑Annual 1; Collects Weird Science-Fantasy (RCP) #1-5 ...... 8.95
❑Annual 2; Collects Weird Science-Fantasy (RCP) #? 12.95

WEIRD SECRET ORIGINS 80-PAGE GIANT
DC

❑1, Oct 2004 ...... 5.95

WEIRD SEX
FANTAGRAPHICS / EROS

❑1, Jan 1999 ...... 2.95

WEIRD SUSPENSE
ATLAS-SEABOARD

❑1, Feb 1975 O: The Tarantula. 1: The Tarantula 12.00
❑2, Apr 1975 ...... 8.00
❑3, Jul 1975 ...... 7.00

WEIRDSVILLE
BLINDWOLF

❑1, Feb 1997 ...... 2.95
❑2, Apr 1997 ...... 2.95
❑3, Jun 1997 ...... 2.95
❑4, Aug 1997 ...... 2.95
❑5, Sep 1997 ...... 2.95
❑6, Dec 1997 ...... 2.95
❑7 1998 ...... 2.95
❑8, Mar 1998 ...... 2.95
❑9, Jun 1998 ...... 2.95

WEIRD TALES ILLUSTRATED
MILLENNIUM

❑1 ...... 2.95
❑1/Deluxe; Deluxe edition with extra stories 4.95
❑2 ...... 2.95

WEIRD TALES OF THE MACABRE
ATLAS-SEABOARD

❑1, Apr 1975; 68 pps. Jeff Jones cover. Horror comic includes features on Hammer Films, Dark Shadows, Night Stalker/Dan Curtis. Comic stories feature werewolf, zombie, rats, and drag racing 20.00
❑2, Apr 1975; Scarce. Boris Vallejo cover 30.00

WEIRD TRIPS MAGAZINE
KITCHEN SINK

❑1 ...... 4.00

WEIRD WAR TALES
DC

❑1, Sep 1971 JKu (a) 125.00
❑2, Nov 1971 JKu (w); MD (a) 75.00
❑3, Jan 1972 ...... 45.00
❑4, Mar 1972 JKu (c) 30.00
❑5, May 1972 ...... 30.00
❑6, Jul 1972 JKu (c) 20.00
❑7, Sep 1972 ...... 20.00
❑8, Nov 1972 NA (c); NA, TD (a) 20.00
❑9, Dec 1972 AA (a) 20.00
❑10, Jan 1973 ATh (a) 20.00
❑11, Feb 1973 ...... 12.00
❑12, Mar 1973 DP (a) 12.00
❑13, Apr 1973 NR, TD (a) 12.00
❑14, Jun 1973 ...... 12.00
❑15, Jul 1973 DP (a) 12.00
❑16, Aug 1973 AA (a) 12.00
❑17, Sep 1973 GE (a) 12.00
❑18, Oct 1973 TD (a) 12.00
❑19, Nov 1973 ...... 12.00
❑20, Dec 1973 ...... 12.00
❑21, Jan 1974 FR (a) 8.00
❑22, Feb 1974 GE, TD (a) 8.00
❑23, Mar 1974 AA (a) 8.00
❑24, Apr 1974 ...... 8.00
❑25, May 1974 AA (a) 8.00
❑26, Jun 1974 ...... 8.00
❑27, Jul 1974 ...... 8.00
❑28, Aug 1974 AA (a) 8.00
❑29, Sep 1974 ...... 8.00
❑30, Oct 1974 ...... 8.00
❑31, Nov 1974 ...... 8.00
❑32, Dec 1974 ...... 6.00
❑33, Jan 1975 ...... 6.00
❑34, Feb 1975 ...... 6.00
❑35, Mar 1975 ...... 6.00
❑36, Apr 1975 ...... 6.00
❑37, May 1975 ...... 6.00
❑38, Jun 1975 ...... 6.00
❑39, Jul 1975 JKu (c) 6.00
❑40, Aug 1975 ...... 6.00
❑41, Sep 1975 ...... 6.00
❑42, Oct 1975 AA (a) 6.00
❑43, Nov 1975 ...... 6.00
❑44, Jan 1976 JKu (c) 6.00
❑45, Mar 1976 ...... 6.00
❑46, May 1976 ...... 6.00
❑47, Jul 1976 ...... 6.00
❑48, Sep 1976 ...... 6.00
❑49, Nov 1976 SD (a) 6.00
❑50, Jan 1977 ...... 6.00
❑51, Mar 1977 JKu (c) 5.00
❑52, Apr 1977 ...... 5.00
❑53, May 1977 ...... 5.00
❑54, Jul 1977 ...... 5.00
❑55, Sep 1977 ...... 5.00
❑56, Oct 1977 ...... 5.00
❑57, Nov 1977 ...... 5.00
❑58, Dec 1977 JKu (c); A: Hitler 5.00
❑59, Jan 1978 ...... 5.00
❑60, Feb 1978 ...... 5.00
❑61, Mar 1978 HC, AN (a) 5.00
❑62, Apr 1978 ...... 5.00
❑63, May 1978 ...... 5.00
❑64, Jun 1978 JKu (c); FM (a) 5.00
❑65, Jul 1978 ...... 5.00
❑66, Aug 1978 TS (a) 5.00
❑67, Sep 1978 JKu (c) 5.00
❑68, Oct 1978 FM (a) 5.00
❑69, Nov 1978 ...... 5.00
❑70, Dec 1978 ...... 5.00

Other grades: Multiply price above by 5/6 for VF/NM • 2/3 for VERY FINE • 1/3 for FINE • 1/5 for VERY GOOD • 1/8 for GOOD

	N-MINT
❑71, Jan 1979	5.00
❑72, Feb 1979	5.00
❑73, Mar 1979	5.00
❑74, Apr 1979	5.00
❑75, May 1979	5.00
❑76, Jun 1979 JKu (c)	5.00
❑77, Jul 1979	5.00
❑78, Aug 1979 JKu (c)	5.00
❑79, Sep 1979	5.00
❑80, Oct 1979 RE, RT (a)	5.00
❑81, Nov 1979	5.00
❑82, Dec 1979 DN, HC (a)	5.00
❑83, Jan 1980	5.00
❑84, Feb 1980	5.00
❑85, Mar 1980	5.00
❑86, Apr 1980	5.00
❑87, May 1980	5.00
❑88, Jun 1980	5.00
❑89, Jul 1980	5.00
❑90, Aug 1980	5.00
❑91, Sep 1980	5.00
❑92, Oct 1980 JKu (c)	5.00
❑93, Nov 1980 JKu (c); O: Creature Commandos. 1: Creature Commandos.	6.00
❑94, Dec 1980	5.00
❑95, Jan 1981	5.00
❑96, Feb 1981 JKu (c)	5.00
❑97, Mar 1981	5.00
❑98, Apr 1981	5.00
❑99, May 1981	5.00
❑100, Jun 1981; JKu (c); BH (a); Creature Commandos in War That Time Forgot.	5.00
❑101, Jul 1981 1: G.I. Robot I.	5.00
❑102, Aug 1981; A: Creature Commandos. Creature Commandos captured by Hitler.	3.50
❑103, Sep 1981 BH (a)	3.50
❑104, Oct 1981	3.50
❑105, Nov 1981 A: Creature Commandos.	3.50
❑106, Dec 1981	3.50
❑107, Jan 1982	3.50
❑108, Feb 1982 BH (a); A: G.I. Robot I. A: Creature Commandos.	3.50
❑109, Mar 1982 BH (a); A: Creature Commandos.	3.50
❑110, Apr 1982 1: Dr. Medusa. A: Creature Commandos.	3.50
❑111, May 1982; A: G.I. Robot I. A: Creature Commandos. G.I. Robot teams with Creature Commandos	3.50
❑112, Jun 1982 A: Creature Commandos.	3.50
❑113, Jul 1982 1: G.I. Robot II. V: Samurai Robot.	3.50
❑114, Aug 1982 A: Hitler. A: Creature Commandos.	3.50
❑115, Sep 1982 A: . A: G.I. Robot II. A: Creature Commandos.	3.50
❑116, Oct 1982 CI (a); A: . A: G.I. Robot II. A: Creature Commandos.	3.50
❑117, Nov 1982 A: . A: G.I. Robot II. A: Creature Commandos.	3.50
❑118, Dec 1982	3.50
❑119, Jan 1983 A: Creature Commandos.	3.50
❑120, Feb 1983	3.50
❑121, Mar 1983	3.50
❑122, Apr 1983; A: G.I. Robot II. V: Sumo Robot. V: . G.I. Robot vs. Sumo Robot	3.50
❑123, May 1983	3.50
❑124, Jun 1983	3.50

WEIRD WAR TALES (MINI-SERIES)
DC

❑1, Jun 1997	2.50
❑2, Jul 1997	2.50
❑3, Aug 1997	2.50
❑4, Sep 1997	2.50
❑Special 1, Apr 2000	4.95

WEIRD WEST
FANTACO

❑1 1992	2.95
❑2 1992	2.95
❑3 1992	2.95

WEIRD WESTERN TALES
DC

	N-MINT
❑12, Jun 1972; JKu (c); BWr, CI, NA (a); Series continued from All-Star Western (2nd series) #11	45.00
❑13, Aug 1972 (c); NA (a)	30.00
❑14, Oct 1972 (c); ATh (a)	20.00
❑15, Dec 1972; (c); NA, GK (a); No Jonah Hex	20.00
❑16, Feb 1973 (c); AA (a)	12.00
❑17, Apr 1973 (c); AA (a)	12.00
❑18, Jul 1973; (c); Jonah Hex issue	12.00
❑19, Sep 1973 AA (a)	12.00
❑20, Nov 1973 SA (w); GK (a)	12.00
❑21, Jan 1974	12.00
❑22, May 1974	12.00
❑23, Jul 1974; A: Ulysses S. Grant. Jonah Hex blinded	12.00
❑24, Sep 1974; Jonah Hex recovers sight	12.00
❑25, Nov 1974	12.00
❑26, Jan 1975	12.00
❑27, Mar 1975	12.00
❑28, May 1975	12.00
❑29, Jul 1975; O: Jonah Hex. Jonah Hex's Civil War flashback	16.00
❑30, Sep 1975	8.00
❑31, Nov 1975 (c)	8.00
❑32, Jan 1976 JL (c); JL (a)	8.00
❑33, Mar 1976 JKu (c); JL (a)	8.00
❑34, May 1976 (c)	8.00
❑35, Jul 1976; Bicentennial #3 on cover	8.00
❑36, Sep 1976	8.00
❑37, Nov 1976 RB, FS (a)	8.00
❑38, Jan 1977; JL (c); JL (a); Jonah Hex goes to his own series	8.00
❑39, Mar 1977 GE, JL (c); GE (a); O: . O: Scalphunter. 1: Scalphunter.	8.00
❑40, Jun 1977 GE (c); GE (a)	8.00
❑41, Aug 1977 GE (c); FS (a)	8.00
❑42, Oct 1977 GE (a)	8.00
❑43, Dec 1977 GE (c); GE (a)	6.00
❑44, Feb 1978 AM, JSn (c); GE (a)	6.00
❑45, Apr 1978 JSn (c); GE (a); A: Bat Lash.	6.00
❑46, Jun 1978 JL (c); GE (a); A: Bat Lash.	6.00
❑47, Aug 1978 (c); GE (a)	6.00
❑48, Oct 1978 DG (c); GE, JAb (a); 1: Cinnamon.	6.00
❑49, Nov 1978 HC (a)	6.00
❑50, Dec 1978 AM, RA (c)	6.00
❑51, Jan 1979	5.00
❑52, Feb 1979 A: Bat Lash.	5.00
❑53, Mar 1979 A: . A: Bat Lash. A: Abe Lincoln.	5.00
❑54, Apr 1979	5.00
❑55, May 1979 RT (a)	5.00
❑56, Jun 1979	5.00
❑57, Jul 1979	5.00
❑58, Aug 1979 RT (a)	5.00
❑59, Sep 1979 RT (a)	5.00
❑60, Oct 1979 RT (a)	5.00
❑61, Nov 1979 RT (a)	5.00
❑62, Dec 1979 RT (a)	5.00
❑63, Jan 1980 RT (a); A: Bat Lash.	5.00
❑64, Feb 1980 RT (a); A: Bat Lash.	5.00
❑65, Mar 1980 RT (a)	5.00
❑66, Apr 1980 RT (a)	5.00
❑67, May 1980 RT (a)	5.00
❑68, Jun 1980 RT (a)	5.00
❑69, Jul 1980 RT (a)	5.00
❑70, Aug 1980; RT (a); Scalphunter moves to back-ups in Jonah Hex	5.00

WEIRD WESTERN TALES (MINI-SERIES)
DC / VERTIGO

❑1, Apr 2001	2.50
❑2, May 2001	2.50
❑3, Jun 2001	2.50
❑4, Jul 2001	2.50

WEIRD WONDER TALES
MARVEL

	N-MINT
❑1, Dec 1973; (c); BW (a); Reprints Mystic #6 (Eye of Doom)	14.00
❑2, Feb 1974; (c); Reprints	7.00
❑3, Apr 1974; (c); BEv (a); Reprints	7.00
❑4, Jun 1974 (c); SL (w); SD (a)	5.00
❑5, Aug 1974; (c); SL (w); SD (a); Reprints	5.00
❑6, Oct 1974 (c); JK (a)	5.00
❑7, Dec 1974 (c)	5.00
❑8, Feb 1975 (c); SL (w)	4.00
❑9, Apr 1975 (c)	4.00
❑10, Jun 1975 (c); SD, JK (a)	4.00
❑11, Aug 1975 (c); SL (w); SD, JK (a)	4.00
❑12, Oct 1975 (c); SL (w); SD, MD (a)	4.00
❑13, Dec 1975 (c); SL (w); SD, JK, RH (a)	4.00
❑14, Feb 1976 (c); DH, JAb (a)	4.00
❑15, Apr 1976 TS (w); TS, DH (a)	4.00
❑15/30 cent, Apr 1976; 30 cent regional variant	20.00
❑16, Jun 1976 (c); BEv, JSt (a)	4.00
❑16/30 cent, Jun 1976; 30 cent regional variant	20.00
❑17, Aug 1976 (c); GC, BEv (a)	4.00
❑17/30 cent, Aug 1976; 30 cent regional variant	20.00
❑18, Oct 1976 BEv, JK (a)	4.00
❑19, Dec 1976; (c); SD, JK, BK (a); Doctor Druid; Reprints from Tales to Astonish #13, Astonishing Tales #47	4.00
❑20, Jan 1977; SL (w); SD, JK (a); Doctor Druid	4.00
❑21, Mar 1977; SL (w); SD (a); Doctor Druid	4.00
❑22, May 1977; SL (w); JK, JKu (a); Doctor Druid	4.00

WEIRD WORLDS
DC

❑1, Sep 1972; JKu (c); MA (a); continues John Carter of Mars from Tarzan #209 and Pellucidar from Korak	12.00
❑2, Nov 1972; JO, CI (c); MA (a); adapts Burroughs' Pellucidar and Martian novels	7.00
❑3, Jan 1973; JO (c); MA (a); adapts Burroughs' Pellucidar and Martian novels	7.00
❑4, Mar 1973; (c); adapts Burroughs' Pellucidar and Martian novels	7.00
❑5, May 1973; DGr (a); adapts Burroughs' Pellucidar and Martian novels	7.00
❑6, Aug 1973; (c); DGr (a); adapts Burroughs' Pellucidar and Martian novels	8.00
❑7, Oct 1973; HC (c); DGr (a); adapts Burroughs' Pellucidar and Martian novels; John Carter, Warlord of Mars ends	6.00
❑8, Dec 1973 HC (c); HC (w); HC (a); 1: Iron Wolf.	5.00
❑9, Feb 1974; (c); HC (w); HC (a); Iron Wolf	5.00
❑10, Nov 1974; HC (w); HC (a); Iron Wolf	5.00

WELCOME BACK, KOTTER
DC

❑1, Nov 1976; (c); BO (a); based on ABC TV series	10.00
❑2, Jan 1977; BO (c); based on ABC TV series	2.50
❑3, Mar 1977; (c); RE (a); based on ABC TV series	2.50
❑4, May 1977; BO (c); ME (w); BO, RE (a); based on ABC TV series	2.50
❑5, Jul 1977; (c); BO, RE (a); based on ABC TV series	2.50
❑6, Sep 1977; (c); BO, RE (a); based on ABC TV series	2.50
❑7, Nov 1977; RE (c); BO, RE (a); based on ABC TV series	2.50
❑8, Jan 1978; BO (c); BO, RE (a); based on ABC TV series	2.50
❑9, Feb 1978; BO (c); BO, RE (a); based on ABC TV series	2.50
❑10, Mar 1978; BO (c); BO, RE (a); based on ABC TV series	2.50

WELCOME BACK TO THE HOUSE OF MYSTERY
DC / VERTIGO

❑1, Jul 1998; collects stories from House of Mystery and Plop	5.95

WELCOME TO THE LITTLE SHOP OF HORRORS
ROGER CORMAN'S COSMIC COMICS

❑1, May 1995	2.50
❑2, Jun 1995	2.50
❑3, Jul 1995	2.50

WENDEL
KITCHEN SINK

❑1, b&w	2.95

Wetworks

Suicide mission squad acquires symbiotes
©Image

What If...? (Vol. 1)

Explores alternate possibilities
©Marvel

What If...? (Vol. 2)

Updated alternative choices at Marvel
©Marvel

What The-?!

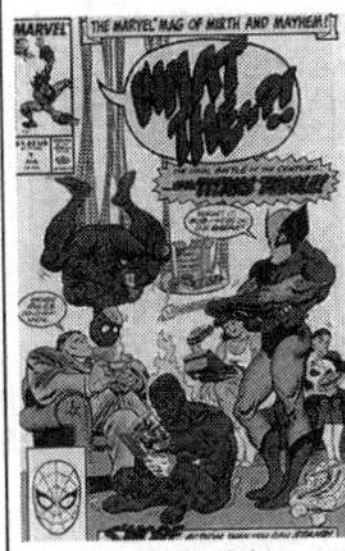

Longer-lived than Not Brand Ecch
©Marvel

Wheel of Worlds (Neil Gaiman's...)

Reversed title sounds like car show
©Tekno

N-MINT

WENDY, THE GOOD LITTLE WITCH (VOL. 1)
HARVEY

❑90, Oct 1975 (c); (w); (a) 2.00
❑91, Dec 1975 (c); (w); (a) 2.00
❑92, Feb 1976 (c); (w); (a) 2.00
❑93, Apr 1976; (c); (w); (a); Goes on hiatus 2.00
❑94, Sep 1990; (c); (w); (a); Series begins again (1990); cover erroneously says #194 .... 1.25
❑95, Oct 1990 (c); (w); (a) 1.25
❑96, Nov 1990 (c); (w); (a) 1.25
❑97, Dec 1990 (c); (w); (a) 1.25

WENDY THE GOOD LITTLE WITCH (VOL. 2)
HARVEY

❑1, Apr 1991 .... 2.00
❑2, Jun 1991 .... 1.50
❑3, Aug 1991 (w) 1.50
❑4, Oct 1991 (w) 1.50
❑5, Apr 1992 (w) 1.50
❑6, Jun 1992 .... 1.50
❑7, Aug 1992 .... 1.50
❑8, Oct 1992 .... 1.50
❑9, Jan 1993 .... 1.50
❑10, May 1993 .... 1.50
❑11, Aug 1993 (c); (w) 1.50
❑12, Dec 1993 (c); (w) 1.50
❑13, Mar 1994 (c); (w) 1.50
❑14, May 1994 .... 1.50
❑15, Aug 1994 .... 1.50

WENDY IN 3-D
BLACKTHORNE

❑1 .... 2.50

WENDY WHITEBREAD, UNDERCOVER SLUT
FANTAGRAPHICS / EROS

❑1, b&w 2.50
❑1/2nd, b&w 2.95
❑1/3rd, b&w 2.95
❑1/4th, b&w 2.95
❑1/5th, Nov 1990, b&w 3.95
❑2, b&w 2.50

WENDY WITCH WORLD
HARVEY

❑53, Sep 1974; (c); (w); (a); Casper cover 8.00

WEREWOLF
DELL

❑1, Dec 1966, TV show 8.00
❑2, Mar 1967, TV show 5.00
❑3, Apr 1967, O: Werewolf (Major Wiley Wolf). TV show 5.00

WEREWOLF (BLACKTHORNE)
BLACKTHORNE

❑1, Sep 1988, b&w 2.00
❑2 1988 .... 2.00
❑3 1988 .... 2.00
❑4, Jan 1989 .... 2.00

WEREWOLF AT LARGE
ETERNITY

❑1, Jun 1989, b&w 2.25

N-MINT

❑2, Aug 1989, b&w 2.25
❑3, Oct 1989, b&w 2.25

WEREWOLF BY NIGHT
MARVEL

❑1, Sep 1972 MP (c); MP (a) 80.00
❑2, Nov 1972 MP (c); MP (a) 30.00
❑3, Jan 1973 MP (c); MP (a) 15.00
❑4, Mar 1973 MP (c); MP (a) 18.00
❑5, May 1973 MP (c); MP (a) 15.00
❑6, Jun 1973 (c); MP (a) 15.00
❑7, Jul 1973 (c); MP, JM (a) 15.00
❑8, Aug 1973 MP (c) 15.00
❑9, Sep 1973 (c); TS (a) 15.00
❑10, Oct 1973 TS (c); TS (a) 15.00
❑11, Nov 1973 (c); TS, GK (a) 12.00
❑12, Dec 1973 (c); GK, DP (a) 12.00
❑13, Jan 1974 MP (c); MP (a) 12.00
❑14, Feb 1974 MP (c); MP (a) 12.00
❑15, Mar 1974; MP (c); MP (a); Marvel Value Stamp #75: Morbius 15.00
❑16, Apr 1974; (c); MP (a); Marvel Value Stamp #65: Iceman 12.00
❑17, May 1974; (c); DP (a); Marvel Value Stamp #99: Sandman 12.00
❑18, Jun 1974 (c); DP (a) 10.00
❑19, Jul 1974; (c); DP (a); Marvel Value Stamp #61: Red Ghost 10.00
❑20, Aug 1974; (c); DP (a); Marvel Value Stamp #97: Black Knight 10.00
❑21, Sep 1974; (c); DP (a); Marvel Value Stamp #72: Lizard 8.00
❑22, Oct 1974; (c); DP (a); Marvel Value Stamp #51: Bucky Barnes 8.00
❑23, Nov 1974; (c); DP (a); Marvel Value Stamp #93: Silver Surfer 8.00
❑24, Dec 1974; AM, GK (c); DP (a); Marvel Value Stamp #8: Captain America 8.00
❑25, Jan 1975; (c); DP (a); Marvel Value Stamp #63: Sub-Mariner 8.00
❑26, Feb 1975; (c); DP (a); Marvel Value Stamp #28: Hawkeye 8.00
❑27, Mar 1975; (c); DP (a); Marvel Value Stamp #9: Captain Marvel 8.00
❑28, Apr 1975 (c); DP (a) 8.00
❑29, May 1975 (c); DP (a) 8.00
❑30, Jun 1975 (c); DP (a) 8.00
❑31, Jul 1975 (c); DP (w); DP (a) 8.00
❑32, Aug 1975 (c); DP (a); O: Moon Knight. 1: Moon Knight 60.00
❑33, Sep 1975 (c); DP (a); 2: Moon Knight. 2: Moon Knight 30.00
❑34, Oct 1975 (c); DP (a) 8.00
❑35, Nov 1975 DP (a) 5.00
❑36, Jan 1976 DP (c); DP (a) 5.00
❑37, Mar 1976 DP (a); A: Moon Knight 10.00
❑38, May 1976 DP (c); DP (a) 5.00
❑38/30 cent, May 1976; 30 cent regional price variant 15.00
❑39, Jul 1976 RB (c); DP (a) 5.00
❑39/30 cent, Jul 1976; 30 cent regional price variant 15.00
❑40, Sep 1976 (c); DP (a) 5.00
❑41, Nov 1976 (c); DP (a) 5.00
❑42, Jan 1977 DC (c); DP (a) 12.00
❑43, Mar 1977 DP (a) 18.00

N-MINT

WEREWOLF BY NIGHT (VOL. 2)
MARVEL

❑1, Feb 1998 (c) 3.00
❑2, Mar 1998; gatefold summary MP (c) 3.00
❑3, Apr 1998; gatefold summary 3.00
❑4, May 1998; gatefold summary (c) 3.00
❑5, Jun 1998; gatefold summary (c) 3.00
❑6, Jul 1998; gatefold summary A: Ghost Rider 3.00

WEREWOLF IN 3-D
BLACKTHORNE

❑1, ca. 1988 .... 2.50

WEST COAST AVENGERS (LTD. SERIES)
MARVEL

❑1, Sep 1984 BH (c); BH (a); O: West Coast Avengers. 1: West Coast Avengers 2.50
❑2, Oct 1984 BH (c); BH (a) 2.00
❑3, Nov 1984 BH (c); BH (a) 2.00
❑4, Dec 1984 BH (c); BH (a) 2.00

WEST COAST AVENGERS
MARVEL

❑1, Oct 1985 AM, JSt (c); AM, JSt (a) 2.00
❑2, Nov 1985 AM, JSt (c); AM (a) 1.50
❑3, Dec 1985 AM, JSt (c); AM, JSt (a); V: Kraven 1.50
❑4, Jan 1986 AM, JSt (c); AM, JSt (a); 1: Master Pandemonium 3.00
❑5, Feb 1986 AM, JSt (c); AM, JSt (a) 1.00
❑6, Mar 1986 AM (c); AM (a) 1.00
❑7, Apr 1986 AM, JSt (c); AM, JSt (a); V: Ultron 1.00
❑8, May 1986 AM, JSt (c); AM, JSt (a); V: Rangers 1.00
❑9, Jun 1986 AM, JSt (c); AM, JSt (a); O: Master Pandemonium 1.00
❑10, Jul 1986 AM, JSt (c); AM, JSt (a) 1.00
❑11, Aug 1986 AM, JSt (c); AM, JSt (a) 1.00
❑12, Sep 1986 AM, JSt (c); AM, JSt (a); 1: Halflife. 1: Quantum. V: Zzzax 1.00
❑13, Oct 1986 AM, JSt (c); AM, JSt (a); O: Hellstorm. V: Graviton 1.00
❑14, Nov 1986 AM, JSt (c); AM, JSt (a); 1: Hellstorm 1.00
❑15, Dec 1986 (c); AM, JSt (a) 1.00
❑16, Jan 1987 AM, JSt (c); AM, JSt (a) 1.00
❑17, Feb 1987 (c); AM, JSt (a) 1.00
❑18, Mar 1987 AM, JSt (c); AM, JSt (a) 1.00
❑19, Apr 1987 (c); AM, JSt (a) 1.00
❑20, May 1987 AM, JSt (c); AM, JSt (a) 1.00
❑21, Jun 1987 AM, JSt (c); AM, JSt (a); A: Moon Knight 1.00
❑22, Jul 1987 AM, JSt (c); AM (a); A: Doctor Strange 1.00
❑23, Aug 1987 AM (c); AM, RT (a) 1.00
❑24, Sep 1987 AM (c); AM (a) 1.00
❑25, Oct 1987 AM (c); AM (a) 1.00
❑26, Nov 1987 AM (c); AM (a); V: Zodiac 1.00
❑27, Dec 1987 AM (c); AM (a); V: Zodiac 1.00
❑28, Jan 1988 AM (c); AM (a); V: Zodiac 1.00
❑29, Feb 1988 AM (c); AM (a) 1.00

Other grades: Multiply price above by 5/6 for VF/NM • 2/3 for VERY FINE • 1/3 for FINE • 1/5 for VERY GOOD • 1/8 for GOOD

N-MINT

❑30, Mar 1988 AM (c); AM (w); AM (a) 1.00
❑31, Apr 1988 AM (c); AM (a); V: Arkon. 1.00
❑32, May 1988 AM (c); AM, TD (a) 1.00
❑33, Jun 1988 AM (c); AM (a) 1.00
❑34, Jul 1988 AM (c); AM (a); V: Quicksilver. 1.00
❑35, Aug 1988 AM (c); AM (a); V: Doctor Doom. 1.00
❑36, Sep 1988 AM (c); AM (a) 1.00
❑37, Oct 1988 AM (c); AM (a) 1.00
❑38, Nov 1988 1.00
❑39, Dec 1988 (c); AM (a) 1.00
❑40, Jan 1989 AM (c); AM, MGu (a) 1.00
❑41, Feb 1989 1.00
❑42, Mar 1989 JBy (c); JBy (w); JBy (a) 1.00
❑43, Apr 1989 JBy (c); JBy (w); JBy (a) 1.00
❑44, May 1989 JBy (c); JBy (w); JBy (a); 1: U.S.Agent. 1.00
❑45, Jun 1989 JBy (c); JBy (w); JBy (a) 1.00
❑46, Jul 1989; JBy (c); JBy (w); JBy (a); 1: Great Lakes Avengers. 1: Big Bertha. Title changes to Avengers West Coast 1.00
❑Annual 1, ca. 1986; V: Quicksilver. ca. 1986; Concludes story begun in Avengers Annual #15 2.00
❑Annual 2, ca. 1987; AM (c); AM (a); Begins story concluded in Avengers Annual #16; ca. 1987 2.00
❑Annual 3, ca. 1988; AM (c); AM, TD (a); series continues as Avengers West Coast Annual 2.00

WESTERN TALES OF TERROR
HOARSE AND BUGGY

❑1 2004 3.50
❑2 3.50
❑3 3.50
❑4 3.50
❑5, Sep 2005 3.50

WESTERN ACTION
ATLAS-SEABOARD

❑1, Jun 1975 (c); AM, JAb (a) 9.00

WESTERN GUNFIGHTERS (2ND SERIES)
MARVEL

❑1, Aug 1970; giant 28.00
❑2, Oct 1970; O: Nightwind (The Apache Kid's horse). giant 15.00
❑3, Dec 1970; giant 15.00
❑4, Mar 1971; giant 18.00
❑5, Jun 1971; giant 15.00
❑6, Sep 1971; BEv (a); D: Ghost Rider. giant 15.00
❑7, Jan 1972; O: Night Rider (Ghost Rider). 1: Lincoln Slade as Ghost Rider. D: Phantom Rider I (Carter Slade). giant 15.00
❑8, Mar 1972 7.00
❑9, May 1972 7.00
❑10, Jul 1972 O: Black Rider. 7.00
❑11, Sep 1972 7.00
❑12, Nov 1972 O: Matt Slade. 7.00
❑13, Jan 1973 7.00
❑14, Mar 1973 7.00
❑15, May 1973 7.00
❑16, Jul 1973 7.00
❑17, Sep 1973 5.00
❑18, Oct 1973 5.00
❑19, Nov 1973 5.00
❑20, Jan 1974 SL (w); JR (a) 5.00
❑21, Mar 1974; JK (c); SL (w); JR (a); reprints stories from Kid Colt Outlaw #103, Western Kid #13, and Apache Kid #18 5.00
❑22, May 1974 5.00
❑23, Jul 1974 5.00
❑24, Sep 1974 5.00
❑25, Oct 1974 5.00
❑26, Nov 1974 5.00
❑27, Jan 1975 5.00
❑28, Mar 1975 5.00
❑29, May 1975 5.00
❑30, Jul 1975 5.00
❑31, Sep 1975 (c); SL (w); A: Gun-Slinger. A: Apache Kid. A: Kid Colt. 5.00
❑32, Nov 1975 5.00
❑33, Jan 1976 5.00

WESTERN KID (2ND SERIES)
MARVEL

❑1, Dec 1971 17.00
❑2, Feb 1972 8.00

N-MINT

❑3, Apr 1972 8.00
❑4, Jun 1972 8.00
❑5, Aug 1972 8.00

WESTERN TEAM-UP
MARVEL

❑1, Nov 1973 (c); 1: The Dakota Kid. 8.00

WEST OF THE DAKOTAS
COMIC BOOK STORIES

❑1, Dec 2002 4.99

WESTSIDE
ANTARCTIC

❑1, Mar 2000 2.50

WEST STREET STORIES
WEST STREET

❑0, Nov 1995, b&w 2.50
❑1, Jan 1997, b&w 2.50

WETWORKS
IMAGE

❑1, Jun 1994 1.95
❑1/3D, Jun 1994; 3-D edition 4.95
❑1/Ltd., Jun 1994; Special promotional edition distributed at the 1994 Chicago Comicon 1.95
❑2, Aug 1994; Standard cover: Beast attacking man 1.95
❑2/A, Aug 1994; Variant edition cover with whole team posing; alternate cover 1.95
❑3, Sep 1994 1.95
❑4, Nov 1994 2.50
❑5, Jan 1995 2.50
❑6, Mar 1995 2.50
❑7, Apr 1995 2.50
❑8, May 1995; bound-in trading cards 2.50
❑8/Variant, May 1995 2.50
❑9, Aug 1995 2.50
❑10, Aug 1995 2.50
❑11, Sep 1995 2.50
❑12, Nov 1995; indicia says Nov, cover says Dec 2.50
❑13, Jan 1996 2.50
❑14, Feb 1996 2.50
❑15, Mar 1996 2.50
❑16, Apr 1996 2.50
❑17, May 1996 2.50
❑18, Jul 1996 2.50
❑19, Aug 1996 2.50
❑20, Aug 1996 2.50
❑21, Sep 1996 2.50
❑22, Oct 1996 2.50
❑23, Nov 1996 2.50
❑24, Dec 1996 2.50
❑25, Jan 1997; Giant-size; wraparound cover 3.95
❑25/A, Jan 1997; alternate wraparound cover (previous covers in background) 3.95
❑26, Feb 1997 2.50
❑27, Mar 1997 2.50
❑28, Apr 1997 2.50
❑29, May 1997 2.50
❑30, Jun 1997 2.50
❑31, Jul 1997 2.50
❑32, Aug 1997 2.50
❑32/A, Aug 1997; Voyager pack; alternate cover (mostly b&w) 2.50
❑33, Sep 1997 2.50
❑34, Oct 1997 2.50
❑35, Nov 1997 2.50
❑36, Jan 1998 2.50
❑37, Feb 1998 2.50
❑38, Mar 1998 2.50
❑39, Apr 1998 2.50
❑40, May 1998 2.50
❑41, Jun 1998 2.50
❑42, Jul 1998 2.50
❑43, Aug 1998 2.50
❑3D 1, Feb 1998; with glasses; wraparound cover 4.95
❑Book 1, Oct 1996; Rebirth; collects issues #1-3 9.95

WETWORKS SOURCEBOOK
IMAGE

❑1, Oct 1994 2.50

WETWORKS/VAMPIRELLA
IMAGE

❑1, Jul 1997; crossover with Harris 2.95
❑1/A, Jul 1997; crossover with Harris; alternate cover 2.95

N-MINT

WHACKED!
RIVER GROUP

❑1, Mar 1994; Tonya Harding case parody; wraparound cover 2.50

WHA... HUH?
MARVEL

❑0, Oct 2005 4.99

WHAM-O GIANT COMICS
WHAM-O

❑1, Apr 1967; WW (w); WW (a); Wrap-around cover, oversized 14 X 21-inch book
❑ 100.00

WHAT IF...? (VOL. 1)
MARVEL

❑1, Feb 1977; (c); A: Spider-Man. Spider-Man 15.00
❑2, Apr 1977; GK (c); TS, HT (a); A: Hulk. Hulk 10.00
❑3, Jun 1977; GK, JSt (c); GK (w); GK, KJ (a); A: Avengers. Avengers 8.00
❑4, Aug 1977; GK (c); FR, FS (a); A: Invaders. Invaders 8.00
❑5, Oct 1977; (c); GT (a); O: Bucky II (Fred Davis). 1: Captain America II (William Nasland). 1: Captain America III (Jeffrey Mace). D: Captain America II (William Nasland). Captain America 8.00
❑6, Dec 1977; A: Fantastic 4. Fantastic Four 5.00
❑7, Feb 1978; GK, JSt (c); A: Spider-Man. Spider-Man 5.00
❑8, Apr 1978; GK, JR (c); JM (a); O: 'Mazing Man-Spider. Daredevil 5.00
❑9, Jun 1978; JK, GK, JSt (c); O: Marvel Boy. O: Human Robot. O: 3-D Man. O: Venus. O: Gorilla-Man. Avengers 5.00
❑10, Aug 1978; (c); A: Thor. Thor 5.00
❑11, Oct 1978; JK, JSt (c); JK (w); JK (a); Marvel Bullpen as Fantastic Four 3.50
❑12, Dec 1978; (c); SB (a); Rick Jones as Hulk 3.50
❑13, Feb 1979; JB (c); JB (a); A: Conan. Conan 5.00
❑14, Apr 1979; (c); HT (a); A: Sgt. Fury. Sgt. Fury 3.50
❑15, Jun 1979; JSt (c); JB, JSt (a); A: Nova. Nova 3.50
❑16, Aug 1979; A: Fu Manchu. Fu Manchu 3.00
❑17, Oct 1979; (c); CI (a); Ghost Rider, Captain Marvel, Spider-Woman 3.50
❑18, Dec 1979; (c); TS (a); Doctor Strange 3.00
❑19, Feb 1980; (c); PB (a); Spider-Man 3.00
❑20, Apr 1980; AM, JSt (c); Avengers 3.00
❑21, Jun 1980; (c); GC, BWi (a); Sub-Mariner 3.00
❑22, Aug 1980; RB, BMc (c); Doctor Doom 3.00
❑23, Oct 1980; AM (c); HT (a); Hulk 3.00
❑24, Dec 1980; JR2, BMc (c); RB, GK (a); Spider-Man 3.00
❑25, Feb 1981; (c); RB (a); O: Uni-Mind. Thor, Avengers 3.00
❑26, Apr 1981; JBy (c); HT (a); Captain America 3.00
❑27, Jul 1981; FM (c); FM (a); X-Men 5.00
❑28, Aug 1981; (c); FM (w); TS, FM, KJ (a); A: Ghost Rider. Daredevil 8.00
❑29, Oct 1981; MG (c); RB, BMc, JSt (a); Avengers 3.00
❑30, Dec 1981; BL (c); RB, JM, JSt (a); Spider-Man clone, Inhumans 8.00
❑31, Feb 1982; BWi (c); Wolverine 8.00
❑32, Apr 1982; BL (c); FM (a); Avengers 3.00
❑33, Jun 1982; (c); BL, DP (a); Dazzler 3.00
❑34, Aug 1982; BL (c); AM, BSz, FH, BL, JR2, FM, BA (w); AM, BSz, FH, JBy, BL, JR2, FM, BA, BH, JSt, FS, BWi, JAb (a); comedy issue 3.00
❑35, Oct 1982; FM (w); SD, FM (a); A: Yellowjacket. Elektra 5.00
❑36, Dec 1982; JBy (c); JBy (w); JBy (a); Fantastic Four; Nova 3.00
❑37, Feb 1983; JSt (c); Beast; Thing; Silver Surfer 3.00
❑38, Apr 1983; Daredevil, Captain America, Vision, Scarlet Witch 3.00
❑39, Jun 1983; Thor vs. Conan 3.00
❑40, Aug 1983; (c); BG (a); Doctor Strange 3.00

Where Monsters Dwell

Pre-hero tales from Marvel's past

©Marvel

Whiteout

GREG RUCKA • STEVE LIEBER

Criminal investigations in the Antarctic

©Oni

Who's Who in the DC Universe

Looseleaf bio pages added filing work

©DC

Wildcards

Based on super-hero prose anthologies

©Marvel

WildC.A.T.s

C.A.T.s are Covert Action Teams

©Image

	N-MINT
❑41, Oct 1983; (c); Sub-Mariner	3.00
❑42, Dec 1983; JSt (a); Fantastic Four	3.00
❑43, Feb 1984; BH, JAb (a); Conan	3.00
❑44, Apr 1984; SB (a); Captain America	3.00
❑45, Jun 1984; (c); Hulk	3.00
❑46, Aug 1984; BSz (c); Spider-Man	3.50
❑47, Oct 1984; BSz (c); Thor, Loki	3.00
❑Special 1, Jun 1988; (c); SD (a); Iron Man	4.00

WHAT IF...? (VOL. 2)

MARVEL

	N-MINT
❑-1, Jul 1997; Flashback; Bishop	2.00
❑1, Jul 1989; MGu (a); Avengers	4.00
❑2, Aug 1989; Daredevil	3.00
❑3, Sep 1989; AM (c); Captain America	3.00
❑4, Oct 1989; AM (c); Spider-Man	3.00
❑5, Nov 1989; Avengers	3.00
❑6, Nov 1989; X-Men	3.00
❑7, Dec 1989; RL (c); RL (a); Wolverine	3.00
❑8, Dec 1989; AM (c); Iron Man	2.50
❑9, Jan 1990; RB (c); RB (a); X-Men	2.50
❑10, Feb 1990; (c); BMc (a); Punisher	2.50
❑11, Mar 1990; TMc (c); Fantastic Four	2.50
❑12, Apr 1990; X-Men	2.50
❑13, May 1990; JLee (c); KB (w); X-Men	2.50
❑14, Jun 1990; Captain Marvel	2.50
❑15, Jul 1990; Fantastic Four, Galactus	2.50
❑16, Aug 1990; Wolverine; Conan	3.00
❑17, Sep 1990 JR2 (c); RHo (w); RHo (a); D: Spider-Man	2.50
❑18, Oct 1990; LMc (c); LMc (a); Fantastic Four, Doctor Doom	2.50
❑19, Nov 1990; Avengers	2.50
❑20, Dec 1990; BWi (c); Spider-Man	2.50
❑21, Jan 1991; BWi (c); D: Black Cat. Spider-Man	2.25
❑22, Feb 1991; Silver Surfer	2.25
❑23, Mar 1991; BMc (c); KB (w); X-Men	2.25
❑24, Apr 1991; vampire Wolverine	3.50
❑25, May 1991; Atlantis Attacks	3.25
❑26, Jun 1991; LMc (c); KB (w); LMc (a); Punisher	2.00
❑27, Jul 1991; Namor, Fantastic Four	2.00
❑28, Aug 1991; (c); Captain America	2.00
❑29, Sep 1991; (c); Captain America, Avengers	2.00
❑30, Oct 1991; Fantastic Four	2.00
❑31, Nov 1991; BMc (c); Spider-Man with cosmic powers	2.00
❑32, Dec 1991; Phoenix	2.00
❑33, Jan 1992; Phoenix	2.00
❑34, Feb 1992; JR (c); parody issue	2.00
❑35, Mar 1992; (c); Fantastic Four; Spider-Man; Doctor Doom	2.00
❑36, Apr 1992; Avengers vs. Guardians of the Galaxy	2.00
❑37, May 1992; Wolverine	2.00
❑38, Jun 1992; MR (a); Thor	2.00
❑39, Jul 1992; Watcher	2.00
❑40, Aug 1992; (c); X-Men	2.00
❑41, Sep 1992; Avengers vs. Galactus	2.00
❑42, Oct 1992; (c); Spider-Man	2.00
❑43, Nov 1992; Wolverine	2.00
❑44, Dec 1992; LMc (c); KB (w); LMc (a); Venom, Punisher	2.00
❑45, Jan 1993; (c); Ghost Rider	2.00
❑46, Feb 1993; KB (w); Cable	2.00
❑47, Mar 1993; KB (w); Magneto	2.00
❑48, Apr 1993; Daredevil	2.00
❑49, May 1993; (c); Silver Surfer	2.00
❑50, Jun 1993; silver sculpted cover; Hulk, Wolverine	2.95
❑51, Jul 1993; Punisher, Captain America	2.00
❑52, Aug 1993; Doctor Doom	2.00
❑53, Sep 1993; Spider-Man, Hulk, Iron Man 2020	2.00
❑54, Oct 1993; (c); A: Reed Richards. A: Fantastic Four. A: Cage. A: Death's Head II. A: War Machine. A: Captain America. A: Death's Head. A: Charnel. Death's Head	2.00
❑55, Nov 1993; Avengers	2.00
❑56, Dec 1993; Avengers	2.00
❑57, Jan 1994; (c); Punisher	2.00
❑58, Feb 1994; Punisher, Spider-Man	2.00
❑59, Mar 1994; (c); Wolverine/Alpha Flight	2.00
❑60, Apr 1994; KB (w); X-Men wedding	2.00
❑61, May 1994; KB (w); Spider-Man	2.00
❑62, Jun 1994; KB (w); Wolverine	2.00
❑63, Jul 1994; A: War Machine. War Machine	2.00
❑64, Aug 1994; (c); Iron Man	2.00
❑65, Sep 1994 (c); A: Archangel.	1.75
❑66, Oct 1994; (c); Rogue	1.75
❑67, Nov 1994; Captain America	1.75
❑68, Dec 1994; Captain America	1.75
❑69, Jan 1995; X-Men	1.75
❑70, Feb 1995; Silver Surfer	1.75
❑71, Mar 1995; Hulk	1.50
❑72, Apr 1995; (c); Spider-Man	1.50
❑73, May 1995; Daredevil	1.50
❑74, Jun 1995; (c); Mr. Sinister forms The X-Men	1.50
❑75, Jul 1995; Generation X	1.50
❑76, Aug 1995; Flash Thompson as Spider-Man; last Watcher	1.50
❑77, Sep 1995; (c); Legion	1.50
❑78, Oct 1995; New Fantastic Four remains a team	1.50
❑79, Nov 1995; Storm becomes Phoenix	1.50
❑80, Dec 1995; KGa (a); A: Maestro. Hulk becomes The Maestro	1.50
❑81, Jan 1996; (c); Age of Apocalypse didn't end	1.50
❑82, Feb 1996; J. Jonah Jameson adopts Peter Parker	1.50
❑83, Mar 1996	1.50
❑84, Apr 1996 A: Bishop and Shard	1.50
❑85, May 1996; Magneto ruled all mutants	1.50
❑86, Jun 1996; Scarlet Spider kills Spider-Man	1.50
❑87, Jul 1996; Sabretooth	1.50
❑88, Aug 1996; Spider-Man	1.50
❑89, Sep 1996; Fantastic Four	1.50
❑90, Oct 1996; Cyclops and Havok	1.50
❑91, Nov 1996; Hulk	1.50
❑92, Dec 1996; Joshua Guthrie and a Sentinel	1.50
❑93, Jan 1997; Wolverine	1.50
❑94, Feb 1997; Juggernaut	1.50
❑95, Mar 1997; (c); Ghost Rider	1.95
❑96, Apr 1997; Quicksilver	1.95
❑97, May 1997; A: Doctor Doom. Black Knight	1.95
❑98, Jun 1997; (c); Rogue, Nightcrawler	1.95
❑99, Aug 1997; gatefold summary; Spider-Man	1.99
❑100, Sep 1997; double-sized; (c); KJ (w); KJ (a); A: Fantastic 4. double-sized; gatefold summary; Gambit	1.99
❑101, Oct 1997; gatefold summary; (c); Archangel	1.99
❑102, Nov 1997; gatefold summary; (c); Daredevil	1.99
❑103, Dec 1997; gatefold summary (c)	1.99
❑104, Jan 1998; gatefold summary; Impossible Man with Infinity Gauntlet	1.99
❑105, Feb 1998; gatefold summary; (c); BSz (a); O: Spider-Girl. 1: Spider-Girl. leads into Marvel 2	12.00
❑106, Mar 1998; gatefold summary	1.99
❑107, Apr 1998; gatefold summary; BSz (c); BSz (a); V: Destroyer. Thor as ruler of Asgard	1.99
❑108, May 1998; gatefold summary; Avengers vs. Carnage	1.99
❑109, Jun 1998; gatefold summary; Thing in Liddleville	1.99
❑110, Jul 1998; gatefold summary; X-Men	1.99
❑111, Aug 1998; gatefold summary; Wolverine as War	1.99
❑112, Sep 1998; gatefold summary; (c); Ka-Zar	1.99
❑113, Oct 1998; gatefold summary; (c); Tony Stark as Sorcerer Supreme	1.99
❑114, Nov 1998; gatefold summary; Secret Wars 25 years later	2.50

WHAT IF ... AUNT MAY HAD DIED INSTEAD OF UNCLE BEN?

MARVEL

	N-MINT
❑1, Feb 2005	2.99

WHAT IF: CAPTAIN AMERICA

MARVEL

	N-MINT
❑1, Feb 2006	2.99

WHAT IF: DAREDEVIL

MARVEL

	N-MINT
❑1, Feb 2006	299

WHAT IF ... DR. DOOM HAD BECOME THE THING?

MARVEL

	N-MINT
❑1, Feb 2005	2.99

WHAT IF: FANTASTIC FOUR

MARVEL

	N-MINT
❑1, Feb 2006	2.99

WHAT IF ... GENERAL ROSS HAD BECOME THE HULK?

MARVEL

	N-MINT
❑1, Feb 2005	2.99

WHAT IF ... JESSICA JONES HAD JOINED THE AVENGERS?

MARVEL

	N-MINT
❑1, Feb 2005	2.99

Other grades: Multiply price above by 5/6 for VF/NM • 2/3 for VERY FINE • 1/3 for FINE • 1/5 for VERY GOOD • 1/8 for GOOD

WHAT IF ... KAREN PAGE HAD LIVED?
MARVEL

❑1, Feb 2005 ... 2.99

WHAT IF ... MAGNETO HAD FORMED THE X-MEN WITH PROFESSOR X?
MARVEL

❑1, Feb 2005 ... 2.99

WHAT IF: SUB-MARINER
MARVEL

❑1, Feb 2006 ... 2.99

WHAT IF: THOR
MARVEL

❑1, Feb 2006 ... 2.99

WHAT IF: WOLVERINE
MARVEL

❑1, Feb 2006 ... 2.99

WHAT IS...THE FACE?
ACE

❑1, Dec 1986 ... 1.75
❑2, May 1987 ... 1.75
❑3, Aug 1987 ... 1.75

WHAT THE-?!
MARVEL

❑1, Aug 1988 AM (c); AM, SD, JSe (a) ... 4.00
❑2, Sep 1988 JBy (c); AM, FH, JBy (w); AW, JBy, JSe, PF (a) ... 2.50
❑3, Oct 1988 (c); KB (w); TMc, BMc, KB (a) ... 3.00
❑4, Nov 1988 BWi (c); FH, KB, PD (w); FH (a) ... 2.50
❑5, Jul 1989 ... 2.50
❑6, Jan 1990; JBy (c); JBy (w); JBy (a); Acts of Vengeance parody ... 2.50
❑7, Apr 1990 JBy (c) ... 2.50
❑8, Jul 1990 JBy (c); KB (w) ... 2.50
❑9, Oct 1990; JBy (c); wraparound cover ... 1.75
❑10, Jan 1991; prestige format JBy (c); JBy (a) ... 1.75
❑11, Mar 1991 JBy (c); RL (a); O: Wolverina ... 1.50
❑12, May 1991 JBy (c) ... 1.50
❑13, Jul 1991 JBy (c) ... 1.50
❑14, Sep 1991 JBy (c) ... 1.50
❑15, Nov 1991 ... 1.50
❑16, Jan 1992; EC parody cover ... 1.50
❑17, Mar 1992 KB (w) ... 1.50
❑18, May 1992 ... 1.50
❑19, Jul 1992 ... 1.50
❑20, Aug 1992 ... 1.50
❑21, Sep 1992; JSa (a); Weapon X parody ... 1.50
❑22, Oct 1992 JSa (a) ... 1.50
❑23, Nov 1992 ... 1.50
❑24, Dec 1992 ... 1.50
❑25, Sum 1993; Summer Special ... 2.50
❑26, Fal 1993; Winter Special ... 2.50
❑27, Win 1993 ... 2.50

WHEELIE AND THE CHOPPER BUNCH
CHARLTON

❑1, May 1975 ... 20.00
❑2, Jul 1975 JBy (a) ... 12.00
❑3, Sep 1975 JBy (a) ... 10.00
❑4, Nov 1975 ... 10.00
❑5, Jan 1976 ... 10.00
❑6, Mar 1976 ... 10.00
❑7, May 1976 ... 10.00

WHEEL OF WORLDS (NEIL GAIMAN'S...)
TEKNO

❑0, Apr 1995; Direct Market edition; poster ... 2.95
❑0/CS, Apr 1995; poster ... 2.95
❑1, May 1996 ... 3.25

WHEN BEANIES ATTACK
BLATANT

❑1, Mar 1999 ... 2.95
❑1/Variant, Mar 1999; Violent cover ... 4.95

WHERE CREATURES ROAM
MARVEL

❑1, Jul 1970 JK (a) ... 25.00
❑2, Sep 1970 JK (a) ... 10.00
❑3, Nov 1970 JK (a) ... 10.00
❑4, Jan 1971 JK (a) ... 10.00
❑5, Mar 1971 JK (a) ... 10.00
❑6, May 1971 JK (a) ... 10.00
❑7, Jul 1971 JK (a) ... 10.00
❑8, Sep 1971 JK (a) ... 10.00

WHERE IN THE WORLD IS CARMEN SANDIEGO?
DC

❑1, Jun 1996, based on computer game series ... 1.75
❑2, Sep 1996 ... 1.75
❑3, Nov 1996 ... 1.75
❑4, Jan 1997, all-alien issue ... 1.75

WHERE MONSTERS DWELL
MARVEL

❑1, Jan 1970 ... 32.00
❑2, Mar 1970 ... 10.00
❑3, May 1970 JK (a) ... 10.00
❑4, Jul 1970 ... 10.00
❑5, Sep 1970 ... 10.00
❑6, Nov 1970 ... 8.00
❑7, Jan 1971 ... 8.00
❑8, Mar 1971 ... 8.00
❑9, May 1971 ... 8.00
❑10, Jul 1971 SD, SL (w); SD (a) ... 8.00
❑11, Sep 1971 ... 8.00
❑12, Nov 1971; Giant-size ... 10.00
❑13, Jan 1972 ... 8.00
❑14, Mar 1972 ... 8.00
❑15, May 1972 ... 8.00
❑16, Jul 1972 ... 8.00
❑17, Sep 1972 ... 8.00
❑18, Nov 1972 ... 8.00
❑19, Jan 1973 ... 8.00
❑20, Mar 1973 ... 8.00
❑21, May 1973 ... 8.00
❑22, Jul 1973 ... 8.00
❑23, Sep 1973 ... 8.00
❑24, Oct 1973 ... 8.00
❑25, Nov 1973 ... 8.00
❑26, Jan 1974 ... 8.00
❑27, Mar 1974 ... 8.00
❑28, May 1974 ... 8.00
❑29, Jul 1974 ... 8.00
❑30, Sep 1974 ... 8.00
❑31, Oct 1974 ... 8.00
❑32, Nov 1974 ... 7.00
❑33, Jan 1975 ... 7.00
❑34, Mar 1975 ... 7.00
❑35, May 1975 ... 7.00
❑36, Jul 1975 ... 7.00
❑37, Sep 1975 ... 7.00
❑38, Oct 1975 ... 7.00

WHILE FIFTY MILLION DIED
TOME

❑1, b&w; World War II ... 2.95

WHISPERS AND SHADOWS
OASIS

❑1 1984, b&w ... 1.50
❑2 1984, b&w ... 1.50
❑3 1984, b&w ... 1.50
❑4 1984, b&w ... 1.50
❑5 1985, b&w ... 1.50
❑6 1985, b&w ... 1.50
❑7 1985, b&w ... 1.50
❑8 1985, b&w ... 1.50

WHISPER (VOL. 1)
CAPITAL

❑1, Dec 1983, O: Whisper ... 2.50
❑2, Mar 1984 ... 2.00

WHISPER (VOL. 2)
FIRST

❑1, Jun 1986 ... 2.00
❑2, Aug 1986 ... 1.50
❑3, Oct 1986 ... 1.50
❑4, Dec 1986 ... 1.50
❑5, Feb 1987 ... 1.50
❑6, Apr 1987 ... 1.50
❑7, Jun 1987 ... 1.50
❑8, Aug 1987 ... 1.75
❑9, Oct 1987 ... 1.75
❑10, Dec 1987 ... 1.75
❑11, Feb 1988 ... 1.75
❑12, Apr 1988 ... 1.75
❑13, Jun 1988 ... 1.75
❑14, Jul 1988 ... 1.75
❑15, Aug 1988 ... 1.75
❑16, Sep 1988 ... 1.75
❑17, Oct 1988 ... 1.75
❑18, Nov 1988 ... 1.95
❑19, Dec 1988 ... 1.95
❑20, Jan 1989 ... 1.95
❑21, Feb 1989 ... 1.95
❑22, Mar 1989 ... 1.95
❑23, Apr 1989 ... 1.95
❑24, May 1989 ... 1.95
❑25, Jun 1989 ... 1.95
❑26, Jul 1989 ... 1.95
❑27, Aug 1989 ... 1.95
❑28, Sep 1989 ... 1.95
❑29, Oct 1989 ... 1.95
❑30, Nov 1989 ... 1.95
❑31, Dec 1989 ... 1.95
❑32, Jan 1990 ... 1.95
❑33, Feb 1990 ... 1.95
❑34, Mar 1990 ... 1.95
❑35, Apr 1990 ... 1.95
❑36, May 1990 ... 1.95
❑37, Jun 1990 ... 1.95
❑Special 1, Nov 1985; Giant-size ... 2.50

WHITE DEVIL
ETERNITY

❑1 1988, b&w ... 2.50
❑2 1988, b&w ... 2.50
❑3 1988, b&w ... 2.50
❑4 1988, b&w ... 2.50
❑5 1989, b&w ... 2.50
❑6 1989, b&w ... 2.50
❑7 1989, b&w ... 2.50
❑8 1989, b&w ... 2.50

WHITE FANG
DISNEY

❑1, ca. 1990; newsstand version ... 2.95
❑1/Direct ed., ca. 1990 ... 5.95

WHITE LIKE SHE
DARK HORSE

❑1, May 1994, b&w ... 2.95
❑2, Jun 1994, b&w ... 2.95
❑3, Jul 1994, b&w ... 2.95
❑4, Aug 1994, b&w ... 2.95

WHITE ORCHID
ATLANTIS

❑1 ... 2.95

WHITEOUT
ONI

❑1, Jul 1998 ... 2.95
❑2, Aug 1998 ... 2.95
❑3, Sep 1998 ... 2.95
❑4, Nov 1998 ... 2.95

WHITEOUT: MELT
ONI

❑1, Sep 1999 ... 2.95
❑2, Oct 1999 ... 2.95
❑3, Nov 1999 ... 2.95
❑4, Dec 1999 ... 2.95

WHITE RAVEN
VISIONARY

❑1, ca. 1995, b&w ... 2.95

WHITE TRASH
TUNDRA

❑1 ... 3.95
❑2 ... 3.95
❑3 ... 3.95
❑4 ... 3.95

WHIZ KIDS
IMAGE / BIG BANG

❑1, Apr 2003, b&w; one-shot ... 4.95

WHOA, NELLIE!
FANTAGRAPHICS

❑1, Jul 1996, b&w ... 2.95
❑2, Aug 1996, b&w ... 2.95
❑3, Sep 1996, b&w ... 2.95

WHODUNNIT?
ECLIPSE

❑1, Jun 1986 ... 2.00
❑2, Nov 1986 ... 2.00
❑3, Apr 1987 ... 2.00

WHO IS THE CROOKED MAN
CRUSADE

❑1, Sep 1996 ... 3.50

WildCats (2nd Series)

Move to DC lost acronym

©DC

Wild Dog

Small-town vigilante saves the day

©DC

Wild Person in the Woods

Orangutan researcher's life story

©G.T. Labs

Wildstar

A symbiote-sporting super-hero

©Image

WildStorm Rising

Windsor-Smith's turn at super-heroes

©Image

N-MINT

WHO REALLY KILLED JFK
REVOLUTIONARY

❑1, Oct 1993, b&w ... 2.50

WHO'S WHO IN STAR TREK
DC

❑1, Mar 1987 ... 1.50
❑2, Apr 1987; McGivers-Vulcans ... 1.50

WHO'S WHO IN THE DC UNIVERSE
DC

❑1, Aug 1990 ... 4.95
❑2, Sep 1990 ... 4.95
❑3, Oct 1990 ... 4.95
❑4, Nov 1990 ... 4.95
❑5, Dec 1990 ... 4.95
❑6, Jan 1991 ... 4.95
❑7, Feb 1991 ... 4.95
❑8, Apr 1991 ... 4.95
❑9, May 1991 ... 4.95
❑10, Jun 1991 ... 4.95
❑11, Jul 1991 ... 4.95
❑12, Aug 1991 ... 4.95
❑13, Oct 1991 ... 4.95
❑14, Nov 1991 ... 4.95
❑15, Jan 1992 ... 4.95
❑16, Feb 1992 ... 4.95

WHO'S WHO IN THE DC UNIVERSE UPDATE 1993
DC

❑1, Dec 1992 ... 5.95
❑2, Jan 1993 ... 5.95

WHO'S WHO IN THE IMPACT UNIVERSE
DC / IMPACT

❑1, Sep 1991 ... 4.95
❑2, Dec 1991 ... 4.95
❑3, May 1992 ... 4.95

WHO'S WHO IN THE LEGION OF SUPER-HEROES
DC

❑1, Apr 1988; GP, RL, DC, JSa, CS (a); Absorbancy Boy through Doctor Gym'll ... 1.50
❑2, Jun 1988; Doctor Mayavile through High Seer ... 1.50
❑3, Jul 1988; Heroes of Lallor through Legion of Super-Rejects; plus Planets of the 30th Century ... 1.50
❑4, Aug 1988 ... 1.50
❑5, Sep 1988; Mordru through Science Police Officer Quav; Plus Tour of Legion Headquarters ... 1.50
❑6, Oct 1988 ... 1.50
❑7, Nov 1988 ... 1.50

WHO'S WHO: THE DEFINITIVE DIRECTORY OF THE DC UNIVERSE
DC

❑1, Mar 1985; GP (c); JOy, GP, GK, MR (a); Abel through Auron ... 1.50
❑2, Apr 1985; JOy, GP, JK, GK, MR, JL (a); Automan through Blackhawk Plane ... 1.50
❑3, May 1985; DG (c); JOy, GP, JK, GK (a); Black Lightning through Byth ... 1.50
❑4, Jun 1985; DG (c); GP, JBy, JK, GK, DSt (a); The Cadre through Chril KL-99 ... 1.50
❑5, Jul 1985; DG (c); JOy, GP, JK, GK, MR (a); Chronos through Cyclotron ... 1.50
❑6, Aug 1985; DG (c); MW, JOy, JK, GK, MR, JL (a); Daily Planet through Doctor Polaris ... 1.50
❑7, Sep 1985; DG (c); BSz, JBy, GK, DSt (a); Doctor Psycho through Fastback ... 1.50
❑8, Oct 1985; DG (c); JOy, GP, JK, GK (a); Fatal Five through Garguax ... 1.50
❑9, Nov 1985; DG (c); BSz, GP, JK, GK (a); Garn Daanuth through Guardians of the Universe ... 1.50
❑10, Dec 1985; DG (c); JOy, GP, SR, JK, GK (a); Gunner & Sarge through Hyena ... 1.50
❑11, Jan 1986; DG (c); JOy, GP, JK, GK, MR (a); Icicle through Jonni Thunder ... 1.50
❑12, Feb 1986; DG (c); JOy, GP, JK, MR, JL (a); Johnny Double through Kong ... 1.50
❑13, Mar 1986; JSn, GP, JK, GK (a); Krona through Losers ... 1.50
❑14, Apr 1986; DG (c); JSn, BSz, GP, JBy, JK (a); Luther I through Masters of Disaster ... 1.50
❑15, May 1986; DG (c); BSz, GP, JK, MR (a); Matrix-Prime through Mister Tawky-Tawny ... 1.50
❑16, Jun 1986; DG (c); GP, JBy, JK, GK (a); Mr. Terrific through Nightmaster ... 1.50
❑17, Jul 1986; JOy, GP, JK, GK (a); Nightshade through Persuader ... 1.50
❑18, Aug 1986; DG (c); JOy, GP, JBy, SR, JK, DSt (a); Phantom Girl through Pursuer ... 1.50
❑19, Sep 1986; JBy, JK, GK, JL (a); Puzzler through Roy Raymond ... 1.50
❑20, Oct 1986; DG (c); JK, JL (a); Rubber Duck through Shining Knight ... 1.50
❑21, Nov 1986; GC, DG (c); SD, BSz, JOy, GK (a); Shrinking Violet through Starfinger ... 1.50
❑22, Dec 1986; JBy (c); SD, JOy, JBy, JK, GK, JL (a); Starfire I through Syonide ... 1.50
❑23, Jan 1987; JSa (c); MA, GK (a); Syrene through Time Trapper ... 1.50
❑24, Feb 1987; BSz, JBy, DG (a); Tim Trench through Universo ... 1.50
❑25, Mar 1987; DG (c); JKu, DS (a); Unknown Soldier through Witch Boy ... 1.50
❑26, Apr 1987; DG (c); MGr, RA, JL (a); Wizard through The 1000 ... 1.50

WHO'S WHO UPDATE '87
DC

❑1, Aug 1987; DG (c); KG, GP, JBy (a); All-Star Squadron through Calyst ... 1.50
❑2, Sep 1987; DG (c); TMc, GP, JSa (a); Catwoman II through Goldstar ... 1.50
❑3, Oct 1987; RHo, TMc, GP, JSa (a); Gray Man through Lionmane ... 1.50
❑4, Nov 1987; TMc (c); AM, PB, JBy (a); Lois Lane through Ame Starr ... 1.50
❑5, Dec 1987; DG, JSa (a); Reaper through Robert Campenella ... 1.50

WHO'S WHO UPDATE '88
DC

❑1, Aug 1988; Amazing Man through Harlequin II ... 1.50
❑2, Sep 1988; Icemaiden through Nightwing ... 1.50
❑3, Oct 1988; JOy, RL, AA, JM (a); Parliament of Trees through Trident ... 1.50
❑4, Nov 1988; DGr (a); Ultra-Humanite through Zuggernaut plus Supporting Characters (Abby Cable to Wade Eiling) ... 1.50

WHOTNOT
FANTAGRAPHICS

❑1, b&w ... 2.50
❑2, b&w ... 2.50
❑3, b&w ... 2.50

WICKED
MILLENNIUM

❑1 1994 ... 2.50
❑2 1995 ... 2.50
❑3, Apr 1995, b&w; cover dated Mar ... 2.50

WICKED
IMAGE

❑1, Dec 1999, Man, demon on cover ... 2.95
❑1/A, Dec 1999, Figure against red background on cover ... 2.95
❑1/B, Dec 1999, Girl with glowing book on cover ... 2.95
❑2, Feb 2000 ... 2.95
❑3, Mar 2000 ... 2.95
❑4 2000 ... 2.95
❑5, Jun 2000 ... 2.95
❑6, Jun 2000 ... 2.95
❑7, Aug 2000 ... 2.95
❑Ashcan 1, Jul 1999, Preview edition ... 5.00

WICKED: MEDUSA'S TALE
IMAGE

❑1, Nov 2000 ... 3.95

WIDOW
AVATAR

❑0 ... 3.95
❑0/Nude, Jun 2000, b&w ... 0.00

WIDOW: FLESH AND BLOOD
GROUND ZERO

❑1, Oct 1992 ... 2.50
❑2, Dec 1992 ... 2.50
❑3, Mar 1993 ... 2.50

WIDOW: METAL GYPSIES
LONDON NIGHT

❑1 ... 3.95

WIINDOWS
CULT

❑1, Mar 1993, b&w; Partial prism cover ... 3.50
❑2, Apr 1993, b&w ... 3.00
❑3, May 1993, b&w ... 3.00
❑4, Jun 1993, b&w ... 2.50
❑5, Jul 1993, b&w ... 2.50
❑6, Aug 1993, b&w ... 2.50
❑7, Sep 1993, b&w ... 2.50
❑8, Oct 1993, b&w ... 2.50
❑9, Nov 1993, b&w ... 2.50
❑10, Dec 1993, b&w ... 2.50
❑11, Jan 1994, b&w ... 2.50
❑12, Feb 1994, b&w ... 2.50
❑13, Mar 1994, b&w ... 2.50
❑14, Apr 1994, b&w ... 2.50
❑15, May 1994, b&w ... 2.50
❑16, Jun 1994, b&w ... 2.50
❑17, Jun 1994, b&w ... 2.50

WILD!
Mu

- ❑1 2003 .... 3.75
- ❑2 .... 3.75
- ❑3 .... 3.75
- ❑4 .... 3.75
- ❑5 .... 3.75
- ❑6 .... 3.75
- ❑7 .... 3.75
- ❑8 .... 3.75
- ❑9 .... 3.75
- ❑10 .... 3.75
- ❑11 .... 3.75
- ❑12 .... 3.75
- ❑13, Jul 2005 .... 3.75
- ❑14, Aug 2005 .... 3.75

WILD ANIMALS
Pacific

- ❑1, ca. 1982 .... 1.50

WILD BILL HICKOK
Super

- ❑10 .... 60.00
- ❑11, ca. 1963 (c) 60.00
- ❑12 .... 60.00

WILD BILL PECOS
AC

- ❑1, ca. 1989 .... 3.50

WILDB.R.A.T.S
Fantagraphics

- ❑1 .... 3.25

WILDCARDS
Marvel / Epic

- ❑1, Sep 1990; prestige format; based on prose anthology series 4.50
- ❑2, Oct 1990; prestige format; based on prose anthology series 4.50
- ❑3, Nov 1990; prestige format; based on prose anthology series 4.50
- ❑4, Dec 1990; prestige format; based on prose anthology series 4.50

WILDC.A.T.S
Image

- ❑0, Jun 1993 .... 3.00
- ❑1, Aug 1992 JLee (c); JLee (w); JLee (a); 1: Maul. 1: Grifter. 1: Spartan. 1: Gnome. 1: Tri-Ad. 1: Helspont. 1: Pike. 1: WildC.A.T.s. 1: Hightower. A: 1st. 4.00
- ❑1/3D, Aug 1997; 3-D edition JLee (w); JLee (a) 4.95
- ❑1/Gold, Aug 1992; Gold edition JLee (w); JLee (a) 10.00
- ❑1/Variant, Aug 1992; Wizard Ace edition JLee (w); JLee (a) 5.00
- ❑2, Sep 1992; JLee (c); JLee (w); JLee (a); 1: Black Razor. 1: Wetworks. Coupon for Image Comics #0 enclosed; Prism cover 4.00
- ❑3, Dec 1992 JLee (c); JLee (w); JLee (a); A: Youngblood. 3.00
- ❑4, Mar 1993 JLee (w); JLee (a) 3.00
- ❑4/A, Mar 1993; (c); JLee (w); JLee (a); bagged; red trading card 3.00
- ❑5, Nov 1993 JLee (c); JLee (w); JLee (a) 2.50
- ❑6, Dec 1993 JLee (c); JLee (w); JLee (a) 2.50
- ❑6/Gold, Dec 1993; Gold edition 3.00
- ❑7, Jan 1994 JLee (c); JLee (w); JLee (a) 2.50
- ❑7/Platinum, Jan 1994; Platinum edition 3.00
- ❑8, Feb 1994 JLee (c); JLee (w); JLee (a); A: Cyclops and Jean Grey. 2.50
- ❑9, Mar 1994 JLee (c); JLee (w); JLee (a) 2.50
- ❑10, Apr 1994; JLee (c); JLee (a); series becomes WildC.A.T.S. 2.50
- ❑11, Jun 1994; JLee (a); Title changes to WildC.A.T.S 15.00
- ❑11/Holofoil, Jun 1994; variant cover. 22.00
- ❑12, Aug 1994 1: Savant. 8.00
- ❑13, Sep 1994; Beavis and Butthead cameo 6.00
- ❑14, Sep 1994 .... 2.50
- ❑15, Nov 1994 .... 2.50
- ❑16, Dec 1994 .... 2.50
- ❑17, Jan 1995 A: StormWatch 2.50
- ❑18, Mar 1995 .... 2.50
- ❑19, Apr 1995 .... 2.50
- ❑20, May 1995; with cards 2.50
- ❑21, Jul 1995; JLee (c); AMo (w); JLee (a); 1st Moore-written issue 2.50
- ❑22, Aug 1995 AMo (w) 2.50
- ❑23, Sep 1995 AMo (w) 2.50
- ❑24, Nov 1995 AMo (w) 2.50
- ❑25, Dec 1995; AMo (w); enhanced wraparound cover 4.95
- ❑26, Feb 1996 AMo (w) 2.50
- ❑27, Mar 1996 AMo (w) 2.50
- ❑28, Apr 1996 AMo (w) 2.50
- ❑29, May 1996; AMo (w); cover says Apr, indicia says May 2.50
- ❑30, Jun 1996 AMo (w) 2.50
- ❑31, Sep 1996 AMo (w) 2.50
- ❑32, Jan 1997 AMo (w); JLee (a) 2.50
- ❑33, Feb 1997 AMo (w) 2.50
- ❑34, Feb 1997 AMo (w) 2.50
- ❑35, Mar 1997 .... 2.50
- ❑36, Mar 1997 .... 2.50
- ❑37, Apr 1997 .... 2.50
- ❑38, May 1997 .... 2.50
- ❑39, Jun 1997 .... 2.50
- ❑40, Jul 1997 .... 2.50
- ❑40/A, Jul 1997; alternate mostly b&w cover 2.50
- ❑40/B, Jul 1997; alternate mostly b&w cover 2.50
- ❑41, Aug 1997 .... 2.50
- ❑42, Sep 1997 .... 2.50
- ❑43, Oct 1997 .... 2.50
- ❑44, Nov 1997 .... 2.50
- ❑45, Jan 1998 .... 2.50
- ❑46, Feb 1998 .... 2.50
- ❑47, Mar 1998 .... 2.50
- ❑47/A, Mar 1998; alternate cover with Grifter 2.50
- ❑47/B, Mar 1998; alternate cover with Grifter 2.50
- ❑48, Apr 1998 .... 2.50
- ❑49, May 1998 .... 2.50
- ❑50, Jun 1998; Giant-size JRo, AMo (w); JLee (a) 4.00
- ❑50/Variant, Jun 1998; chromium cover 5.00
- ❑Annual 1, Feb 1998 JRo (w) 2.95
- ❑Special 1, Nov 1993 .... 3.50

WILDCATS (2ND SERIES)
DC / Wildstorm

- ❑1, Mar 1999, JLee (c) 2.50
- ❑1/B, Mar 1999 .... 2.50
- ❑1/C, Mar 1999 .... 2.50
- ❑1/D, Mar 1999 .... 2.50
- ❑1/E, Mar 1999 .... 2.50
- ❑1/F, Mar 1999 .... 2.50
- ❑1/Dynamic, Mar 1999, DFE alternate cover 6.95
- ❑1/Sketch, Mar 1999, Euro-Edition sketch cover; Euro-Edition sketch cover 10.00
- ❑2, May 1999 .... 2.50
- ❑3, Jul 1999 .... 2.50
- ❑4, Sep 1999 .... 2.50
- ❑5, Nov 1999 .... 2.50
- ❑6, Dec 1999 .... 2.50
- ❑7 2000 .... 2.50
- ❑8 2000 .... 2.50
- ❑9, May 2000 .... 2.50
- ❑10, Jun 2000 .... 2.50
- ❑11, Jul 2000 .... 2.50
- ❑12, Aug 2000 .... 2.50
- ❑13, Sep 2000 .... 2.50
- ❑14, Oct 2000 .... 2.50
- ❑15, Nov 2000 .... 2.50
- ❑16, Dec 2000 .... 2.50
- ❑17, Jan 2001 .... 2.50
- ❑18, Feb 2001 .... 2.50
- ❑19, Mar 2001 .... 2.50
- ❑20, Apr 2001 .... 2.50
- ❑21, May 2001 .... 2.50
- ❑22, Jun 2001 .... 2.50
- ❑23, Jul 2001 .... 2.50
- ❑24, Aug 2001 .... 2.50
- ❑25, Sep 2001 .... 2.50
- ❑26, Oct 2001 .... 2.50
- ❑27, Nov 2001 .... 2.50
- ❑28, Dec 2001 .... 2.50
- ❑Annual 2000, Dec 2000 .... 3.50

WILDC.A.T.S ADVENTURES
Image

- ❑1, Sep 1994 O: Warblade. O: WildC.A.T.s. 2.00
- ❑2, Nov 1994 .... 2.00
- ❑3, Nov 1994 .... 2.00
- ❑4, Dec 1994 .... 2.50
- ❑5, Jan 1995 .... 2.50
- ❑6, Feb 1995 .... 2.50
- ❑7, Mar 1995 .... 2.50
- ❑8, Apr 1995 .... 2.50
- ❑9, May 1995 .... 2.50
- ❑10, Jun 1995 .... 2.50

WILDC.A.T.S ADVENTURES SOURCEBOOK
Image

- ❑1, Jan 1995 .... 2.95

WILDC.A.T.S/ALIENS
Image

- ❑1, Aug 1998; crossover with Dark Horse; cardstock cover 4.95
- ❑1/A, Aug 1998; crossover with Dark Horse; alternate cardstock cover (Zealot vs. Alien) 4.95

WILDC.A.T.S (JIM LEE'S...)
Image

- ❑1, Apr 1995, no cover price; informational comic for San Diego Police Dept. 2.00

WILDCATS: LADYTRON
DC / Wildstorm

- ❑1, Oct 2000 .... 5.95

WILDCATS: MOSAIC
DC / Wildstorm

- ❑1, Feb 2000 .... 3.95

WILDCATS: NEMESIS
DC / Wildstorm

- ❑1, Oct 2005 .... 2.99
- ❑2 .... 2.99
- ❑3, Jan 2006 .... 2.99
- ❑4, Feb 2006 .... 2.99
- ❑5, Mar 2006 .... 2.99
- ❑6, Apr 2006 .... 2.99
- ❑7, May 2006 .... 2.99
- ❑8, Jun 2006 .... 2.99
- ❑9, Jul 2006 .... 2.99

WILDC.A.T.S SOURCEBOOK
Image

- ❑1, Sep 1993; (c); JLee (w); bio information on various WildC.A.T.S characters 2.50
- ❑1/Gold, Sep 1993; Gold edition; JLee (w); bio information on various WildC.A.T.S characters 3.00
- ❑2, Nov 1994; bio information on various WildC.A.T.S characters 2.50

WILDC.A.T.S TRILOGY
Image

- ❑1, Jun 1993; Foil cover 2.50
- ❑2, Sep 1993 .... 1.95
- ❑3, Nov 1993 .... 1.95

WILDCATS VERSION 3.0
DC / Wildstorm

- ❑1, Oct 2002 .... 2.95
- ❑2, Nov 2002 .... 2.95
- ❑3, Dec 2002 .... 2.95
- ❑4, Jan 2003 .... 2.95
- ❑5, Feb 2003 .... 2.95
- ❑6, Mar 2003 .... 2.95
- ❑7, Apr 2003 .... 2.95
- ❑8, May 2003 .... 2.95
- ❑9, Jun 2003 .... 2.95
- ❑10, Jul 2003 .... 2.95
- ❑11, Aug 2003 .... 2.95
- ❑12, Sep 2003 .... 2.95
- ❑13, Oct 2003 .... 2.95
- ❑14, Nov 2003 .... 2.95
- ❑15, Dec 2003 .... 2.95
- ❑16, Jan 2004 .... 2.95
- ❑17, Feb 2004 .... 2.95
- ❑18, Mar 2004 .... 2.95
- ❑19, May 2004 .... 2.95
- ❑20, Jun 2004 .... 2.95
- ❑21, Jul 2004 .... 2.95
- ❑22, Aug 2004 .... 2.95

Other grades: Multiply price above by 5/6 for VF/NM • 2/3 for VERY FINE • 1/3 for FINE • 1/5 for VERY GOOD • 1/8 for GOOD

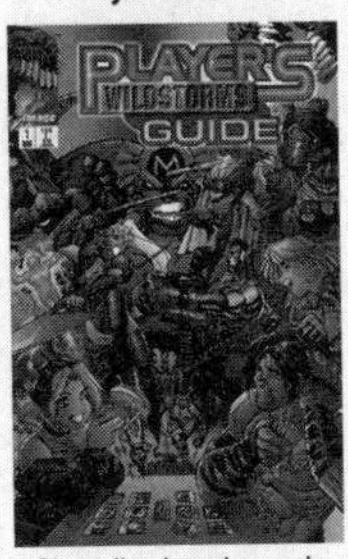
WildStorms Player's Guide
Short-lived card game's strategy guide
©Image

Wild Times: Deathblow
Time-traveling WildStorm adventures
©DC

Wild, Wild West (Gold Key)
Show stars featured on photo covers
©Gold Key

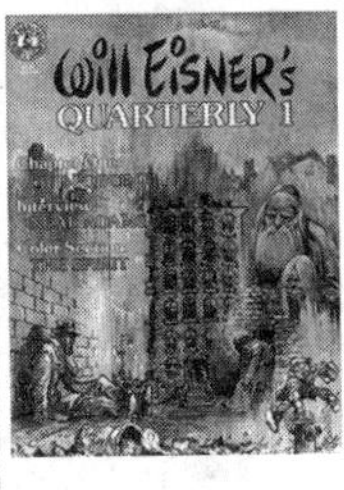
Will Eisner's Quarterly
Eisner's Spirit, other work profiled
©Kitchen Sink

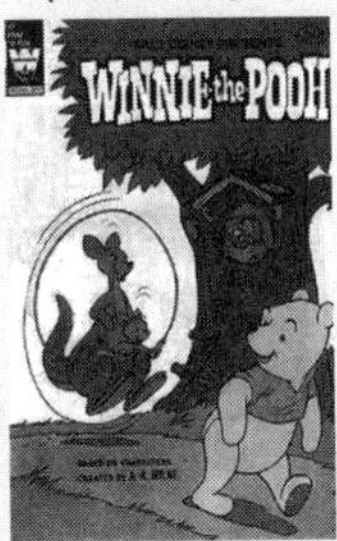
Winnie the Pooh (Walt Disney...)
Silly old adventures of silly old bear
©Gold Key

N-MINT

❑23, Sep 2004 .... 2.95
❑24, Oct 2004 .... 2.95

WILDC.A.T.S/X-MEN: THE GOLDEN AGE
IMAGE

❑1; crossover with Marvel 4.50
❑1/A, Feb 1997; JLee (c); crossover with Marvel; cardstock cover; Autographed by Travis Charest 5.00
❑1/Scroll, Feb 1997; crossover with Marvel; scroll cover; cardstock cover; Autographed by Jim Lee 8.00
❑1/C, Feb 1997; crossover with Marvel; cardstock cover 4.50
❑1/w. glasses, Sep 1997; crossover with Marvel; with glasses 6.50
❑1/Scroll w. gla, Sep 1997; crossover with Marvel; with glasses; scroll cover 9.00
❑1/F, Sep 1997; cardstock cover; crossover with Marvel; Autographed by Jim Lee 4.50

WILDC.A.T.S/X-MEN: THE MODERN AGE
IMAGE

❑1, Aug 1997; Cardstock cover with Wolverine 4.50
❑1/A, Aug 1997; crossover with Marvel; cardstock cover; Includes certificate of authenticity; Autographed by Adam Hughes 6.00
❑1/Nightcrawler, Aug 1997; crossover with Marvel; cardstock cover; Nightcrawler cover 8.00
❑1/w. glasses, Nov 1997; crossover with Marvel; 3-D glasses bound-in . 6.50
❑1/E, Nov 1997; cardstock cover; crossover with Marvel; Includes certificate of authenticity; Autographed by James Robinson ... 8.00
❑1/D, Nov 1997; crossover with Marvel; Nightcrawler cover; 3-D glasses bound-in 5.00

WILDC.A.T.S/X-MEN: THE SILVER AGE
IMAGE

❑1, Jun 1997; JLee (c); JLee (a); (Grifter standing center) 4.95
❑1/A, Jun 1997; NA (c); JLee (a); crossover with Marvel; cardstock cover; (Brood attacking) 4.95
❑1/B, Jun 1997; JLee (a); crossover with Marvel; cardstock cover 4.50
❑1/3D, Jun 1997; 3-D edition; JLee (a); 3-D edition 6.95
❑1/E, Oct 1997; JLee (c); JLee (a); cardstock cover; crossover with Marvel; (Grifter standing center); Autographed by Jim Lee 4.50
❑1/D, Oct 1997; JLee (a); crossover with Marvel; has indicia for WildC.A.T.S/X-Men: The Modern Age 3-D; 3-D glasses bound-in 6.50

WILDCORE
IMAGE

❑1, Nov 1997, Three figures fighting on cover 2.50
❑1/A, Nov 1997, white background 2.50
❑1/B, Nov 1997, alternate cover: white background 5.00
❑2, Dec 1997, Vigor standing on cover 2.50
❑2/A, Dec 1997, variant cover 3.00
❑3, Jan 1998 .... 2.50
❑4, Mar 1998 .... 2.50
❑5, Jun 1998 .... 2.50
❑6, Jul 1998 .... 2.50
❑7, Aug 1998 .... 2.50
❑8, Oct 1998 .... 2.50
❑9, Nov 1998 .... 2.50
❑10, Dec 1998 .... 2.50
❑Ashcan 1, Oct 1997, Preview edition 3.00

WILD DOG
DC

❑1, Sep 1987 DG (c); DG (a) 1.50
❑2, Oct 1987 DG (c); DG (a) 1.50
❑3, Nov 1987 DG (c); DG (a) 1.50
❑4, Dec 1987 DG (c); DG (a) 1.50
❑Special 1, Nov 1989 (c) 2.50

WILDFLOWER
SIRIUS

❑1, Feb 1998 .... 2.50
❑2, Apr 1998 .... 2.50
❑3, Jun 1998 .... 2.50
❑4, Aug 1998 .... 2.50
❑5, Oct 1998 .... 2.50

WILD FRONTIER (SHANDA)
SHANDA

❑1, Jan 2000, b&w 2.95
❑2 .... 2.95

WILD GIRL
DC / WILDSTORM

❑1, Jan 2005 .... 2.95
❑2, Feb 2005 .... 2.95
❑3, Mar 2005 .... 2.95
❑4, Apr 2005 .... 2.95
❑5, May 2005 .... 2.95
❑6, Jun 2005 .... 2.99

WILDGUARD: CASTING CALL
IMAGE

❑1, Sep 2003 .... 2.95
❑2, Oct 2003 .... 2.95
❑3, Nov 2003 .... 2.95
❑4, Dec 2003 .... 2.95
❑5, Jan 2004 .... 2.95
❑6, May 2004 .... 2.99

WILDGUARD: FIRE POWER
IMAGE

❑1/A 3.50
❑1/B 3.50

WILDGUARD: FOOL'S GOLD
IMAGE

❑1 2005 .... 3.50
❑2, Sep 2005 .... 3.50

WILD KINGDOM
MU

❑1, Oct 1991, b&w 2.50
❑2, May 1993, b&w 2.95
❑3, Jan 1995, b&w 2.95
❑4, Apr 1995, b&w; Mu Pub #249 .... 2.95
❑5, Aug 1995, b&w 2.95
❑6, Dec 1995, b&w 2.95
❑7 .... 0.00
❑8, Nov 1996, b&w; Mu Pub # 329 .... 3.50
❑9, May 1998, b&w; Mu Pub # 380 .... 0.00
❑10, Sep 1998, b&w; Mu Pub # 385 .. 0.00
❑11 .... 0.00
❑12 .... 0.00
❑13, Apr 2002, b&w; Mu Pub # 408 ... 0.00
❑14, Aug 2002, b&w; Mu Pub # 409 .. 0.00

WILD KNIGHTS
ETERNITY

❑1, Mar 1988, b&w 1.95
❑2, Apr 1988 .... 1.95
❑3 1988 .... 1.95
❑4 1988 .... 1.95
❑5 1988 .... 1.95
❑6 1988 .... 1.95
❑7 1988 .... 1.95
❑8, Apr 1989, b&w 1.95
❑9, Dec 1988 .... 1.95
❑10, Feb 1989 .... 1.95

WILD LIFE (ANTARCTIC)
ANTARCTIC

❑1, Feb 1993, b&w 2.50
❑2, May 1993, b&w 2.50
❑3, Jul 1993, b&w 2.50
❑4, Nov 1993, b&w 2.75
❑5, Feb 1994, b&w 2.75
❑6, Apr 1994, b&w 2.75
❑7, Jun 1994, b&w 2.75
❑8, Aug 1994, b&w 2.75
❑9, Oct 1994, b&w 2.75
❑10, Dec 1994, b&w 2.75
❑11, Feb 1995, b&w 2.75
❑12, Apr 1995, b&w 2.75

WILD LIFE (FANTAGRAPHICS)
FANTAGRAPHICS

❑1, Aug 1994, b&w 2.75
❑2, Aug 1994, b&w 2.75

WILDLIFERS
RADIO

❑1, Sep 1999, b&w 4.95

WILDMAN (GRASS GREEN'S...)
MEGATON

❑1 .... 1.50
❑2 .... 1.50

WILD PERSON IN THE WOODS
G.T. LABS

❑1 1999 .... 2.50

WILD SIDE
UNITED

❑1, Jan 1998, b&w 3.95
❑2 .... 0.00
❑3 .... 0.00
❑4, Oct 1998, b&w 3.95
❑5, Mar 1999, b&w 3.95
❑6, Jul 1999, b&w 3.95

WILDSIDERZ
DC

❑0, Jul 2005 .... 1.99
❑0/Variant, Jul 2005 .... 3.00
❑1/A cover, Sep 2005 .... 3.50
❑1/B cover, Sep 2005 .... 5.00
❑1/Lenticular, Sep 2005 .... 6.00
❑2, Jan 2006 .... 3.50

Other grades: Multiply price above by 5/6 for VF/NM • 2/3 for VERY FINE • 1/3 for FINE • 1/5 for VERY GOOD • 1/8 for GOOD

N-MINT | N-MINT | N-MINT

WILDSTAR
IMAGE
- ❑1, Sep 1995 ... 2.50
- ❑1/A, Sep 1995 ... 2.50
- ❑2, Nov 1995 ... 2.50
- ❑3, Jan 1996 ... 2.50
- ❑4, Mar 1996 ... 2.50

WILD STARS
COLLECTOR'S
- ❑1, Sum 1984, b&w ... 1.00

WILD STARS (VOL. 3)
LITTLE ROCKET
- ❑1, Jul 2001, b&w ... 2.95
- ❑2, Sep 2001, b&w ... 2.95
- ❑3, Nov 2001, b&w ... 2.95
- ❑4, Jan 2002, b&w ... 2.95
- ❑5, Mar 2002, b&w ... 2.95
- ❑6, May 2002, b&w ... 2.95
- ❑7, Jul 2002, b&w ... 2.95

WILDSTAR: SKY ZERO
IMAGE
- ❑1, Mar 1993; JOy (c); JOy (a); silver foil embossed cover ... 3.00
- ❑1/Gold, Mar 1993, JOy (a); gold embossed cover ... 4.00
- ❑2, May 1993 JOy (c); JOy (a) ... 2.00
- ❑3, Sep 1993 JOy (c); JOy (a); A: Savage Dragon. ... 2.50
- ❑4, Nov 1993 JOy (c); JOy (a); A: Savage Dragon. ... 2.50

WILDSTORM!
IMAGE
- ❑1, Aug 1995; Gen13, Grifter, Deathblow, Union, Spartan ... 2.50
- ❑2, Oct 1995; cover says Sep, indicia says Oct ... 2.50
- ❑3, Nov 1995 ... 2.50
- ❑4, Dec 1995; StormWatch Showcase 2.50

WILDSTORM ANNUAL
DC / WILDSTORM
- ❑2000, Dec 2000 ... 3.50

WILDSTORM CHAMBER OF HORRORS
IMAGE
- ❑1, Oct 1995 ... 3.50

WILDSTORM HALLOWEEN '97
IMAGE
- ❑1, Oct 1997 ... 2.50

WILDSTORM RARITIES
IMAGE
- ❑1, Dec 1994 ... 4.95

WILDSTORM RISING
IMAGE
- ❑1, May 1995; with cards ... 2.50
- ❑2, Jun 1995; bound-in trading cards 1.95

WILDSTORM SAMPLER
IMAGE
- ❑1; giveaway; no cover price ... 1.00

WILDSTORMS PLAYER'S GUIDE
IMAGE
- ❑1, Mar 1996; tips on WildStorms card game ... 1.95

WILDSTORM SPOTLIGHT
IMAGE
- ❑1, Feb 1997; Majestic ... 2.50
- ❑2, Mar 1997; Loner ... 2.50
- ❑3, Apr 1997; Loner ... 2.50
- ❑4, May 1997; StormWatch; no indicia 2.50

WILDSTORM SUMMER SPECIAL
DC / WILDSTORM
- ❑1, Oct 2001 ... 5.95

WILDSTORM SWIMSUIT SPECIAL
IMAGE
- ❑1, Dec 1994 ... 2.95
- ❑2, Aug 1995; pin-ups ... 2.50
- ❑1997, May 1997 ... 2.50

WILDSTORM THUNDERBOOK
DC / WILDSTORM
- ❑1, Oct 2000 ... 6.95

WILDSTORM ULTIMATE SPORTS OFFICIAL PROGRAM
IMAGE
- ❑1, Aug 1997; pin-ups ... 2.50

WILDSTORM UNIVERSE 97
IMAGE
- ❑1, Dec 1996; information on various Wildstorm characters ... 2.50
- ❑2, Jan 1997; information on various Wildstorm characters ... 2.50
- ❑3, Feb 1997; information on various Wildstorm characters ... 2.50

WILDSTORM UNIVERSE SOURCEBOOK
IMAGE
- ❑1, May 1995 ... 2.50
- ❑2 ... 2.50

WILDSTORM WINTER SPECIAL
DC / WILDSTORM
- ❑1, Jan 2005 ... 4.95

WILD THING
MARVEL
- ❑1, Apr 1993; Embossed cover ... 2.50
- ❑2, May 1993 ... 1.75
- ❑3, Jun 1993 ... 1.75
- ❑4, Jul 1993 ... 1.75
- ❑5, Aug 1993 ... 1.75
- ❑6, Sep 1993 ... 1.75
- ❑7, Oct 1993 ... 1.75

WILD THING (2ND SERIES)
MARVEL
- ❑1, Oct 1999 ... 1.99
- ❑2, Nov 1999 ... 1.99
- ❑3, Dec 1999 ... 1.99
- ❑4, Jan 1999 ... 1.99
- ❑5, Feb 2000 ... 1.99

WILD THINGS
METRO
- ❑1, ca. 1986, b&w ... 2.00
- ❑2, ca. 1987, b&w ... 2.00
- ❑3, ca. 1987, b&w ... 2.00

WILD THINGZ
ABC
- ❑0/A ... 3.00
- ❑0/B; swimsuit cover ... 5.95
- ❑0/Platinum; Virgin Special Preview; limited to 300 copies ... 3.00

WILD THINK
WILD THINK
- ❑1, Apr 1987 ... 2.00

WILD TIMES: DEATHBLOW
DC / WILDSTORM
- ❑1, Aug 1999; set in 1899 ... 2.50

WILD TIMES: DV8
DC / WILDSTORM
- ❑1, Aug 1999; set in 1944 ... 2.50

WILD TIMES: GEN13
DC / WILDSTORM
- ❑1, Aug 1999, b&w; set in 1969, 1972, and 1973 ... 2.50

WILD TIMES: GRIFTER
DC / WILDSTORM
- ❑1, Aug 1999; set in 1920s ... 2.50

WILD TIMES: WETWORKS
DC / WILDSTORM
- ❑1, Aug 1999 ... 2.50

WILD WEST (CHARLTON)
CHARLTON
- ❑58, Nov 1966; Series continued from Black Fury #57 ... 10.00

WILD WEST C.O.W.-BOYS OF MOO MESA
ARCHIE
- ❑1, Mar 1993 ... 1.25
- ❑2, May 1993 ... 1.25
- ❑3, Jul 1993 ... 1.25

WILD, WILD WEST (GOLD KEY)
GOLD KEY
- ❑1, Jun 1966; 10174-606 ... 70.00
- ❑2, Aug 1966 ... 45.00
- ❑3, Jun 1968 ... 35.00
- ❑4, Dec 1968 ... 35.00
- ❑5, Apr 1969 ... 35.00
- ❑6, Jul 1969 ... 35.00
- ❑7, Oct 1969 ... 35.00

WILD, WILD WEST (MILLENNIUM)
MILLENNIUM
- ❑1, ca. 1990; TV ... 2.95
- ❑2, ca. 1990; TV ... 2.95
- ❑3, ca. 1991; TV ... 2.95
- ❑4, ca. 1991; TV ... 2.95

WILD WOMEN
PARAGON
- ❑1 ... 4.95

WILD ZOO
RADIO
- ❑1, Jul 2000, b&w (c) ... 2.95
- ❑2 ... 2.95
- ❑3, Nov 2000, b&w (c) ... 2.95
- ❑4, Jan 2001, b&w (c) ... 2.95
- ❑5 ... 2.95
- ❑6, May 2001, b&w (c) ... 2.95
- ❑7, Jul 2001, b&w (c) ... 2.99
- ❑8, Sep 2001, b&w (c) ... 3.99

WILL EISNER PRESENTS
ECLIPSE
- ❑1, Dec 1990, b&w; Mr. Mystic ... 2.50
- ❑2; Mr. Mystic ... 2.50
- ❑3; Mr. Mystic ... 2.50

WILL EISNER'S 3-D CLASSICS: SPIRIT
KITCHEN SINK
- ❑1, Dec 1985 ... 2.00

WILL EISNER'S JOHN LAW: ANGELS AND ASHES, DEVILS AND DUST
IDEA & DESIGN WORKS
- ❑1, May 2006 ... 2.99

WILL EISNER'S QUARTERLY
KITCHEN SINK
- ❑1, Nov 1983 ... 2.95
- ❑2, Feb 1984 ... 3.50
- ❑3, Aug 1984 ... 2.00
- ❑4 1985 ... 2.00
- ❑5 1985 ... 2.00
- ❑6 1985 ... 2.00
- ❑7 1985 ... 2.00
- ❑8, Mar 1986 ... 2.00

WILLIAM SHATNER
CELEBRITY
- ❑1 ... 5.95

WILLOW (MARVEL)
MARVEL
- ❑1, Aug 1988 BH (c); BH (a) ... 1.50
- ❑2, Sep 1988 BH (c); BH (a) ... 1.50
- ❑3, Oct 1988 BH (c); BH (a) ... 1.50

WILLOW (ANGEL)
ANGEL
- ❑0, Jun 1996, b&w ... 2.95
- ❑0/Nude, Jun 1996; nude cardstock cover ... 10.00

WILL TO POWER
DARK HORSE
- ❑1, Jun 1994 ... 1.50
- ❑2, Jun 1994 ... 1.00
- ❑3, Jun 1994 ... 1.00
- ❑4, Jul 1994 1: Counterstrike. ... 1.00
- ❑5, Jul 1994 ... 1.00
- ❑6, Jul 1994 ... 1.00
- ❑7, Jul 1994 ... 1.00
- ❑8, Aug 1994 ... 1.00
- ❑9, Aug 1994 ... 1.00
- ❑10, Aug 1994 ... 1.00
- ❑11, Aug 1994 ... 1.00
- ❑12, Aug 1994 ... 1.00

WIMMEN'S COMIX
RENEGADE
- ❑1, ca. 1972; Published by Last Gasp 10.00
- ❑2, ca. 1973; Published by Last Gasp 8.00
- ❑3, ca. 1973; Published by Last Gasp 8.00
- ❑4, ca. 1974; Published by Last Gasp 8.00
- ❑5, ca. 1975; Published by Last Gasp 5.00
- ❑6; Published by Last Gasp ... 5.00
- ❑7, ca. 1976; Published by Last Gasp 5.00
- ❑8 ... 5.00
- ❑9 ... 4.00
- ❑10 ... 4.00
- ❑11, ca. 1987, b&w ... 3.00
- ❑12, Apr 1987; 3-D ... 3.00

Other grades: Multiply price above by 5/6 for VF/NM • 2/3 for VERY FINE • 1/3 for FINE • 1/5 for VERY GOOD • 1/8 for GOOD

Witchblade

Female cop acquires mystic armor

©Image

Witchfinder

Hunter becomes the hunted

©Image

Witching Hour

Fated to be lesser-known DC horror title

©DC

Wizard's Tale

Pre-Arrowsmith Busiek fantasy tale

©Image

Wolff & Byrd, Counselors of the Macabre

Barristers for beings from beyond

©Exhibit A

N-MINT

❑13; Occult issue 3.00
❑14, Feb 1989, b&w; Disastrous Relationships 2.50
❑15, Aug 1989, b&w 2.50
❑16, Nov 1990, b&w 2.50
❑17, Aug 1992, b&w 2.50
❑18 .... 2.50

WINDBURNT PLAINS OF WONDER
Lohman Hills

❑1, Fal 1996; b&w Emma Davenport one-shot 11.95

WIND IN THE WILLOWS
NBM

❑1 .... 15.95
❑2, Feb 1999 .... 15.95

WINDRAVEN
Heroic / Blue Comet

❑1, b&w 2.95

WINDRAVEN ADVENTURES
Blue Comet

❑1, Jan 1993, b&w 2.95

WINDSOR
Win-Mil

❑1 .... 1.95
❑2; Flip-cover format 1.95

WINGBIRD AKUMA-SHE
Verotik

❑1, Jan 1998; cardstock cover 3.95

WINGBIRD RETURNS
Verotik

❑1, Oct 1997; prestige format 9.95

WINGDING ORGY
Fantagraphics / Eros

❑1 .... 3.95
❑2 .... 3.95

WINGED TIGER
Cartoonists Across America

❑3, Sum 1999 .... 2.95

WINGING IT
Solo

❑1 .... 2.00

WINGS
Mu

❑1, Sep 1992 .... 2.50

WINGS COMICS (A-LIST)
A-List

❑1, Spr 1997, b&w; Golden Age reprint 2.50
❑2, Fal 1997, b&w; Golden Age reprint 2.50
❑3 .... 2.95
❑4 .... 2.95

WINGS OF ANASI
Image

❑0, Sep 2005 .... 6.95

WINNIE THE POOH (WALT DISNEY...)
Gold Key / Whitman

❑1, Jan 1977 .... 20.00
❑2, May 1977; (c); (w); (a); Cracky in Hostess ad ("Time on My Hands") 10.00
❑3, Sep 1977 .... 7.00
❑4 .... 7.00
❑5 .... 7.00

N-MINT

❑6 .... 7.00
❑7 .... 7.00
❑8 .... 7.00
❑9 .... 7.00
❑10 .... 7.00
❑11 .... 7.00
❑12 .... 7.00
❑13 .... 7.00
❑14 .... 7.00
❑15 .... 7.00
❑16 .... 7.00
❑17 .... 7.00
❑18 .... 10.00
❑19 .... 10.00
❑20, Aug 1980 .... 125.00
❑21, Oct 1980 .... 10.00
❑22, ca. 1980 .... 10.00
❑23, Jan 1981 .... 10.00
❑24, Feb 1981 .... 10.00
❑25 1981 .... 10.00
❑26, Nov 1981 .... 10.00
❑27, Feb 1982 .... 10.00
❑28, ca. 1982 .... 10.00
❑29, ca. 1982 .... 20.00
❑30, ca. 1982 .... 20.00
❑31, ca. 1983 .... 20.00
❑32, Apr 1984 .... 20.00
❑33, ca. 1984 .... 20.00

WINNING IN THE DESERT
Apple

❑1; booklet 2.95
❑2; booklet 2.95

WINTER MEN
DC / Wildstorm

❑1, Sep 2005 .... 2.99
❑2, Oct 2005 .... 2.99
❑3, Jan 2006 .... 2.99
❑4, Jun 2006 .... 2.99

WINTERSTAR
Echo

❑1, Dec 1996, b&w 2.95

WINTERWORLD
Eclipse

❑1, Sep 1987 .... 2.00
❑2, Dec 1987 .... 2.00
❑3, Mar 1988 .... 2.00

WISE SON: THE WHITE WOLF
DC / Milestone

❑1, Nov 1996 .... 2.50
❑2, Dec 1996 .... 2.50
❑3, Jan 1997 .... 2.50
❑4, Feb 1997 .... 2.50

WISH
Tokyopop

❑1, Aug 2002, b&w; printed in Japanese format 9.99

WISH UPON A STAR
Warp

❑1, May 1994; giveaway; no price 1.00

WISP
Oktomica

❑1, Feb 1999 .... 2.50

N-MINT

WITCH
Eternity

❑1, b&w; Reprints 1.95

WITCHBLADE
Image

❑0 .... 5.00
❑½, Nov 2002, Overstreet Fan promotional edition 30.00
❑1, Nov 1995 2: Witchblade. 25.00
❑1/B, Nov 1995; Wizard Ace edition 15.00
❑2, Jan 1996; Relatively scarce 18.00
❑2/A, Jan 1996; Wizard Ace edition 15.00
❑2/2nd; Encore edition 4.00
❑3, Mar 1996 .... 10.00
❑4, Apr 1996 .... 8.00
❑5, May 1996 .... 8.00
❑6, Jun 1996 1: Julie Pezzini. 6.00
❑7, Jul 1996 .... 6.00
❑8, Aug 1996; wraparound cover 5.00
❑9, Sep 1996 .... 5.00
❑9/A, Sep 1996 .... 5.00
❑10, Nov 1996 1: The Darkness. A: Darkness. 5.00
❑10/Dynamic, Nov 1996; 1: The Darkness. A: Darkness. Alternate cover sold through Dynamic Forces: Shows two characters back-to-back 20.00
❑10/American Ent, Nov 1996; A: Darkness. American Entertainment alternate cover 8.00
❑10/Autographed, Nov 1996; 1: The Darkness. Regular cover, signed by creators and sold through Dynamic Forces; limited to 2,500 copies 27.95
❑11, Dec 1996 .... 4.00
❑12, Mar 1997 .... 4.00
❑13, Apr 1997 .... 3.50
❑14, May 1997 .... 3.50
❑14/Gold, May 1997; Gold logo edition 6.00
❑15, Jul 1997 .... 3.50
❑16, Aug 1997 .... 3.00
❑17, Sep 1997 .... 3.00
❑18, Nov 1997; continues in The Darkness #9; Witchblade and Darkness face each other on cover 3.00
❑18/A, Nov 1997; variant cover 2.50
❑18/American Ent, Nov 1997; American Entertainment Edition; Green variant cover 5.00
❑19, Dec 1997 .... 3.00
❑20, Feb 1998 .... 3.00
❑21, Mar 1998 .... 2.50
❑22, May 1998 .... 2.50
❑23, Jun 1998 .... 2.50
❑24, Jul 1998 .... 2.50
❑24/Variant, Jul 1998; Variant cover .
❑25, Aug 1998; Yellow background cover 3.00
❑25/A, Aug 1998; With Fathom in pool cover 4.00
❑25/B, Aug 1998; Holofoil cover 8.00
❑25/C, Aug 1998; Printer Error; Holofoil cover 15.00
❑26, Oct 1998 .... 2.50
❑27, Nov 1998 .... 2.50
❑27/Variant, Nov 1998 ....
❑28, Feb 1999 .... 2.50

N-MINT

❑28/Variant, Feb 1999 .... 4.00
❑29, Mar 1999 .... 2.50
❑29/Variant, Mar 1999 .... 4.00
❑30, Apr 1999 .... 2.50
❑31, May 1999 .... 2.50
❑32, Jul 1999 .... 2.50
❑32/Variant, Jul 1999 .... 4.00
❑33, Aug 1999 .... 2.50
❑34, Sep 1999 .... 2.50
❑35, Oct 1999 .... 2.50
❑36, Dec 1999 .... 2.50
❑36/Variant, Dec 1999; wraparound variant cover 2.50
❑37, Feb 2000 .... 2.50
❑38, Mar 2000 .... 2.50
❑39, May 2000 .... 2.50
❑40, Jun 2000 .... 2.50
❑40/A, Jun 2000; alternate cover 2.50
❑40/Ashcan, Jun 2000; 5000 printed; Pittsburgh Convention Preview 2.50
❑41, Jul 2000 .... 2.50
❑41/A, Jul 2000; e-Wanted alternate cover (Pezzini sitting) 3.00
❑42, Sep 2000 .... 2.50
❑43, Nov 2000 .... 2.50
❑44, Jan 2001 .... 2.50
❑45, Mar 2001 .... 2.50
❑45/Variant, Mar 2001 .... 2.50
❑46, May 2001 .... 2.50
❑47, Jun 2001 .... 2.50
❑48, Jul 2001 .... 2.50
❑49, Aug 2001 .... 2.50
❑50, Sep 2001; Giant-size; wraparound cover 4.95
❑50/Dynamic, Sep 2001; DFE alternate cover 6.00
❑50/Autographed, Sep 2001; DFE Signed alternate cover 8.00
❑50/Silvestri, Sep 2001 .... 5.00
❑50/Keown, Sep 2001 .... 5.00
❑50/Turner, Sep 2001 .... 5.00
❑51, Oct 2001 .... 2.50
❑52, Nov 2001 .... 2.50
❑53, Dec 2001 .... 2.50
❑54, Jan 2002 .... 2.50
❑54/Dynamic, Jan 2002 .... 2.50
❑55, Feb 2002 .... 2.50
❑56, Jun 2002 .... 2.50
❑57, Aug 2002 .... 2.50
❑58, Sep 2002 .... 2.50
❑59, Oct 2002; Endgame Prelude 2.50
❑60, Nov 2002 .... 2.99
❑61, Feb 2002 .... 2.99
❑62, Mar 2003 .... 2.99
❑63, May 2003 .... 2.99
❑64, Jun 2003 .... 2.99
❑65, Jun 2003 .... 2.99
❑66, Jun 2003 .... 2.99
❑67, Aug 2003 .... 2.99
❑67/Manga, Aug 2003; Manga-style cover 2.99
❑68, Sep 2003 .... 2.99
❑69, Sep 2003 .... 2.99
❑70, Oct 2003 .... 2.99
❑71, Nov 2003 .... 2.99
❑72, Dec 2003 .... 2.99
❑73, Feb 2004 .... 2.99
❑73/Variant, Feb 2004 .... 4.00
❑74, May 2004 .... 2.99
❑75, Apr 2004 .... 4.99
❑75/Variant, Apr 2004 .... 6.00
❑76, Jul 2004 .... 2.99
❑77, Aug 2004 .... 2.99
❑78, Sep 2004 .... 2.99
❑78/Variant, Sep 2004 .... 4.00
❑79, Oct 2004 .... 2.99
❑80, Nov 2004 .... 2.99
❑80/Holiday, Nov 2004; Offered through Top Cow. Variant cover. A total of 1,000 copies made. 10.00
❑80/Cho, Nov 2004 .... 2.99
❑80/Land, Nov 2004 .... 2.99
❑80/Conv, Nov 2004 .... 2.99
❑81, Jan 2005 .... 2.99
❑82, Feb 2005 .... 2.99
❑83, Mar 2005 .... 2.99
❑84, Apr 2005 .... 2.99
❑85, ca. 2005 .... 2.99
❑86, Jul 2005 .... 2.99
❑87, Aug 2005 .... 2.99
❑87/Variant, Aug 2005 .... 2.99
❑88, Sep 2005 .... 2.99
❑89, Oct 2005 .... 2.99
❑90, Nov 2005 .... 2.99
❑91, Dec 2005 .... 2.99
❑92, Dec 2005 .... 2.99
❑93, Jan 2006 .... 2.99
❑94, Feb 2006 .... 2.99
❑95, Mar 2006 .... 2.99
❑96, Apr 2006 .... 2.99
❑97, May 2006 .... 2.99
❑98, Jun 2006 .... 2.99
❑99, Jul 2006 .... 2.99
❑500, ca. 1998; Limited edition foil cover; Limited edition foil cover; Given away as premium for subscription to Wizard 5.00

WITCHBLADE/DARK MINDS: RETURN OF PARADOX
IMAGE

❑1, ca. 2004 .... 9.99

WITCHBLADE/ALIENS/THE DARKNESS/PREDATOR
DARK HORSE

❑1, Nov 2000 .... 2.99
❑2, Dec 2000 .... 2.99
❑3, Jan 2001 .... 2.99

WITCHBLADE: ANIMATED ONE SHOT
IMAGE

❑1, Aug 2003 .... 2.99

WITCHBLADE: BLOOD OATH
IMAGE

❑1, Aug 2004 .... 4.99

WITCHBLADE/DARKCHYLDE
IMAGE

❑1, Sep 2000 .... 2.50

WITCHBLADE/DARKNESS SPECIAL
IMAGE

❑½/Platinum, Sep 2000; Promotional giveaway when applying for Wizard credit card 35.00
❑1, Dec 1999 .... 3.95

WITCHBLADE: DESTINY'S CHILD
IMAGE

❑1, May 2000 .... 2.95
❑2, Jul 2000 .... 2.95
❑3, Sep 2000 .... 2.95

WITCHBLADE/ELEKTRA
MARVEL

❑1, Mar 1997; crossover with Image; continues in Elektra/Cyblade #1 .... 2.95
❑1/American Ent, Mar 1997; American Entertainment Edition 5.00

WITCHBLADE GALLERY
IMAGE

❑1, Nov 2000 .... 2.95

WITCHBLADE INFINITY
IMAGE

❑1, May 1999 .... 3.50

WITCHBLADE/LADY DEATH
IMAGE

❑1, Nov 2001 .... 4.95

WITCHBLADE/LADY DEATH SPECIAL
IMAGE

❑1, Sep 2003 .... 0.00

WITCHBLADE: MOVIE EDITION
IMAGE

❑1, Aug 2000 .... 2.50
❑1/C, Aug 2000; Witchblade.com Exclusive cover (standing in alley) 2.50
❑1/B, Aug 2000; Witchblade.com Exclusive Holofoil cover (standing in alley, holofoil) 2.50
❑1/A, Aug 2000 .... 2.50

WITCHBLADE: NOTTINGHAM
IMAGE

❑1, Mar 2003 .... 4.99

WITCHBLADE: OBAKEMONO
IMAGE

❑1, Jul 2002 .... 9.95

WITCHBLADE ORIGIN
IMAGE

❑1/American Ent, Oct 1997; American Entertainment Edition 3.00

WITCHBLADE 10TH ANNIVERSARY COVER GALLERY
IMAGE

❑1, Dec 2005, b&w 4.99

WITCHBLADE/TOMB RAIDER
IMAGE

❑½, Jul 2000 .... 5.00
❑1/A, Dec 1998 .... 4.00
❑1/B, Dec 1998, alternate cover (white background) 5.00
❑1/C, Dec 1998, Croft standing on top of Pezzini with guns crossed on cover 7.00

WITCHBLADE & TOMB RAIDER
IMAGE

❑1 2005 .... 2.99

WITCHBLADE/WOLVERINE
IMAGE

❑1, Apr 2004 .... 2.99

WITCHCRAFT
DC / VERTIGO

❑1, Jun 1994, covers form triptych 2.95
❑2, Jul 1994, Sex, violence-recommended for mature readers. 2.95
❑3, Aug 1994 .... 2.95

WITCHCRAFT: LA TERREUR
DC / VERTIGO

❑1, Apr 1998; covers form triptych 2.50
❑2, May 1998; covers form triptych 2.50
❑3, Jun 1998; covers form triptych 2.50

WITCHES
MARVEL

❑1, Aug 2004 .... 2.99
❑2, Aug 2004 .... 2.99
❑3, Sep 2004 .... 2.99
❑4, Sep 2004 .... 2.99

WITCHES' CAULDRON: THE BATTLE OF THE CHERKASSY POCKET
HERITAGE COLLECTION

❑1, b&w 3.50

WITCHFINDER
IMAGE

❑1, Sep 1999; Man with torch on cover facing forward 2.95
❑1/A, Sep 1999 .... 2.95
❑1/B, Sep 1999; alternate cover 2.95
❑2, Nov 1999 .... 2.95

WITCH HUNTER
MALIBU / ULTRAVERSE

❑1, Apr 1996 .... 2.50

WITCHING
DC / VERTIGO

❑1, Aug 2004 .... 2.95
❑2, Sep 2004 .... 2.95
❑3, Oct 2004 .... 2.95
❑4, Nov 2004 .... 2.95
❑5, Dec 2004 .... 2.95
❑6, Jan 2005 .... 2.95
❑7, Feb 2005 .... 2.95
❑8, Mar 2005 .... 2.95
❑9, Apr 2005 .... 2.95
❑10, May 2005 .... 2.95

WITCHING HOUR
DC

❑1, Mar 1969 NC (c); ATh (a) 150.00
❑2, May 1969 NC (c) 70.00
❑3, Jul 1969 NC (c); BWr (a) 50.00
❑4, Sep 1969 NC (c); ATh (a) 25.00
❑5, Nov 1969 NC (c); BWr (a) 25.00
❑6, Jan 1970 NC (c) 25.00
❑7, Mar 1970 (c); ATh (a) 18.00
❑8, May 1970 (c); ATh, NC (a) 15.00
❑9, Jul 1970 (c); ATh (a) 15.00
❑10, Sep 1970 (c); GM (w); ATh, GM (a) 15.00
❑11, Nov 1970 NC (c); ATh (a) 15.00
❑12, Jan 1971 NC (c); ATh, GK (a) 15.00
❑13, Mar 1971 (c); GM (a); 1: Psions. 15.00
❑14, May 1971 (c); AW, JJ (a) 10.00
❑15, Jul 1971 NC (c); GM, WW (a) 10.00
❑16, Sep 1971 NC (c); GM (a) 10.00

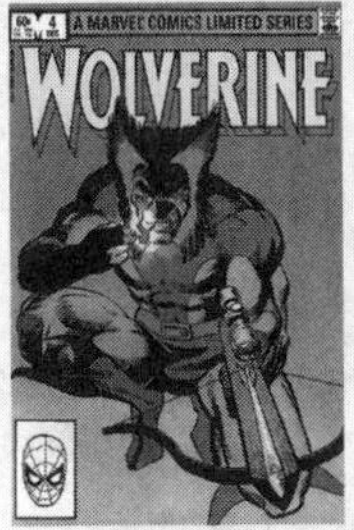
Wolverine (1st series)
Frank Miller sends Logan to Orient
©Marvel

Wolverine (2nd Series)
Ongoing series revealed more origin
©Marvel

Wolverine (3rd series)
Back to basics approach with solo stories
©Marvel

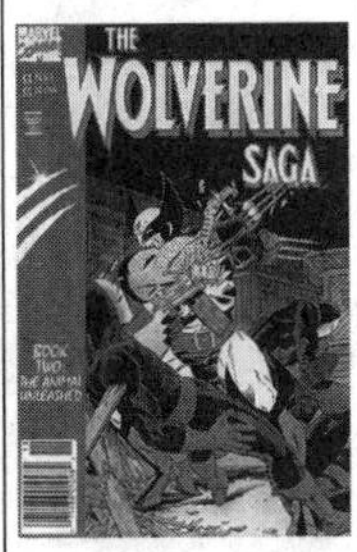
Wolverine Saga
Past stories assembled into timeline
©Marvel

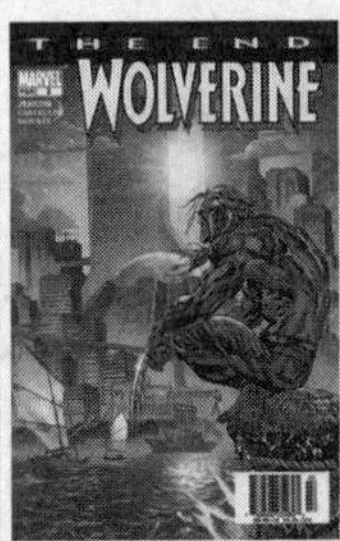
Wolverine: The End
Even nearly ageless mutants die
©Marvel

	N-MINT
❑17, Nov 1971 (c); DH (a)	10.00
❑18, Jan 1972 NC (c); JA (w); JK, NC, JA (a)	10.00
❑19, Mar 1972 NC (c); NC (a)	10.00
❑20, Apr 1972 NC (c); NR, DH (a)	10.00
❑21, Jun 1972 NC (c); NC (a)	10.00
❑22, Aug 1972 NC (c)	10.00
❑23, Sep 1972 NC (c); NR, TD (a)	10.00
❑24, Oct 1972 NC (c); AA (a)	10.00
❑25, Nov 1972 NC (c); JA (a)	10.00
❑26, Dec 1972 NC (c); DD, JAb (a)	10.00
❑27, Jan 1973 NC (c); AA (a)	10.00
❑28, Feb 1973 NC (c)	10.00
❑29, Mar 1973 NC (c)	10.00
❑30, Apr 1973 NC (c)	10.00
❑31, Jun 1973 NC (c); AN (a)	10.00
❑32, Jul 1973 NC (c)	10.00
❑33, Aug 1973 NC (c); AA (a)	10.00
❑34, Sep 1973 NC (c); NR (a)	10.00
❑35, Oct 1973 NC (c)	10.00
❑36, Nov 1973 NC (c)	10.00
❑37, Dec 1973 NC (c)	10.00
❑38, Jan 1974; NC (c); MA, ATh (a); Save The Last Dance For Me; Eternal Hour; The Perfect Surf; The Man With The Stolen Eyes; Brush With Death; Dream Girl; The Demon In The Mirror; The Phantom Ship; Round Trip To The Past; Trail of the Lucky Coin	10.00
❑39, Feb 1974 NC (c)	10.00
❑40, Mar 1974 NC (c); AN (a)	10.00
❑41, Apr 1974 NC (c); AA (a)	10.00
❑42, May 1974 NC (c)	10.00
❑43, Jun 1974 NC (c); AA (a)	10.00
❑44, Jul 1974 NC (c); DP (a)	10.00
❑45, Aug 1974 NC (c); DP, AN (a)	10.00
❑46, Sep 1974 NC (c)	10.00
❑47, Oct 1974 NC (c); AN (a)	10.00
❑48, Nov 1974 NC (c)	10.00
❑49, Dec 1974 NC (c)	10.00
❑50, Jan 1975 NC (c)	10.00
❑51, Feb 1975 NC (c)	10.00
❑52, Mar 1975 NC (c); DP (a)	8.00
❑53, Apr 1975	8.00
❑54, May 1975 (c)	8.00
❑55, Jun 1975	8.00
❑56, Jul 1975	8.00
❑57, Aug 1975	8.00
❑58, Sep 1975 (c)	8.00
❑59, Oct 1975	8.00
❑60, Nov 1975 NC (c)	8.00
❑61, Jan 1976	8.00
❑62, Mar 1976 (c)	8.00
❑63, May 1976	8.00
❑64, Jun 1976 (c)	8.00
❑65, Aug 1976 (c)	8.00
❑66, Nov 1976 (c)	8.00
❑67, Jan 1977	5.00
❑68, Feb 1977 RB (c)	5.00
❑69, Mar 1977 DP (a)	5.00
❑70, Apr 1977	5.00
❑71, May 1977 DP (a)	5.00
❑72, Jul 1977 (c)	5.00
❑73, Sep 1977	5.00
❑74, Oct 1977 (c)	5.00
❑75, Nov 1977	5.00
❑76, Jan 1978	5.00
❑77, Feb 1978	5.00
❑78, Mar 1978	5.00
❑79, Apr 1978	5.00
❑80, May 1978 AA, CS, JAb (a)	5.00
❑81, Jun 1978 PB (a)	5.00
❑82, Jul 1978	5.00
❑83, Aug 1978	5.00
❑84, Sep 1978	5.00
❑85, Oct 1978 (c)	5.00

WITCHING HOUR (VERTIGO)
DC / VERTIGO

❑1, Jan 2000	5.95
❑2, Feb 2000	5.95
❑3, Mar 2000	5.95

WITCHING HOUR (ANNE RICE'S...)
MILLENNIUM

❑1, ca. 1992	2.50
❑2, ca. 1993, bound-in Talamasca business card	2.50
❑3, ca. 1993	2.50
❑4, ca. 1993	2.50
❑5, Feb 1996	2.50
❑6	2.50
❑7	2.50
❑8	2.50
❑9	2.50
❑10	2.50
❑11	2.50
❑12	2.50
❑13	2.50

WITHIN OUR REACH
STAR*REACH

❑1; Spider-Man, Concrete, Gift of the Magi; Christmas benefit comic	7.95

WIZARD IN TRAINING
UPPER DECK

❑0, Jan 2002	2.95

WIZARD OF 4TH STREET (DARK HORSE)
DARK HORSE

❑1, ca. 1987, b&w	2.00
❑2, ca. 1987, b&w	2.00
❑3	2.00
❑4	2.00
❑5	2.00
❑6	2.00

WIZARD OF 4TH STREET (DAVID P. HOUSE)
DAVID P. HOUSE

❑1	1.50
❑2	1.50
❑3	1.50

WIZARD OF TIME
DPH

❑1	1.50
❑2, Oct 1986	1.50

WIZARDS OF THE LAST RESORT
BLACKTHORNE

	N-MINT
❑1, Feb 1987, b&w	1.75
❑2, Apr 1987	1.75
❑3, Jun 1987	1.75
❑4, Aug 1987	1.75

WIZARD'S TALE
IMAGE

❑1, ca. 1997	19.95
❑1/HC	29.95

WJHC
WILSON PLACE

❑1, Dec 1998	1.95

WOGGLEBUG
ARROW

❑1, ca. 1988; Dark Oz tie-in one shot	2.75

WOLF & RED
DARK HORSE

❑1, Apr 1995; based on Tex Avery cartoons; Droopy back-up	2.50
❑2, May 1995; based on Tex Avery cartoons; Screwball Squirrel back-up	2.50
❑3, Jun 1995; based on Tex Avery cartoons; Droopy back-up	2.50

WOLFF & BYRD, COUNSELORS OF THE MACABRE
EXHIBIT A

❑1, May 1994	4.00
❑2, Jul 1994	3.00
❑3, Sep 1994	3.00
❑4, Nov 1994	3.00
❑5, Feb 1995	3.00
❑6, Apr 1995	2.50
❑7, Jun 1995	2.50
❑8, Sep 1995	2.50
❑9, Nov 1995	2.50
❑10, Feb 1996	2.50
❑11, Apr 1996	2.50
❑12, Aug 1996	2.50
❑13, Oct 1996; cover purposely upside down and backwards	2.50
❑14, Jan 1997; Anne Rice parody	2.50
❑15, Mar 1997	2.50
❑16, Jul 1997	2.50
❑17, Oct 1997; Halloween issue; reprint strips	2.50
❑18, Mar 1998	2.50
❑19, Apr 1998	2.50
❑20, May 1998	2.50
❑21, Nov 1988	2.50
❑22, Feb 1999	2.50
❑23, Aug 1999, b&w; Title becomes Supernatural Law with #24	2.50

WOLFF & BYRD, COUNSELORS OF THE MACABRE'S SECRETARY MAVIS
EXHIBIT A

❑1, Aug 1998	2.95
❑2, Apr 1999	2.95
❑3, Jul 2001; Title changes to Supernatural Law Secretary Mavis	3.50
❑4, Jan 2003	3.50

WOLFPACK
MARVEL

❑1, Aug 1988, 0 & 1: Wolfpack	1.00
❑2, Sep 1988	1.00
❑3, Oct 1988	1.00
❑4, Nov 1988	1.00

Other grades: Multiply price above by 5/6 for VF/NM • 2/3 for VERY FINE • 1/3 for FINE • 1/5 for VERY GOOD • 1/8 for GOOD

N-MINT

❑5, Dec 1988 1.00
❑6, Jan 1989 1.00
❑7, Feb 1989 1.00
❑8, Mar 1989 1.00
❑9, Apr 1989 1.00
❑10, May 1989 1.00
❑11, Jun 1989 1.00
❑12, Jul 1989 1.00

WOLF RUN: A KNOWN ASSOCIATES MYSTERY

KNOWN ASSOCIATES

❑1, b&w 2.50

WOLPH

BLACKTHORNE

❑1 2.00

WOLVERBROAD VS. HOBO

SPOOF

❑1, b&w; parody 2.95

WOLVERINE (1ST SERIES)

MARVEL

❑1, Sep 1982 (c); FM (a); A: Mariko. 25.00
❑2, Oct 1982 (c); FM (a); 1: Yukio. 18.00
❑3, Nov 1982 (c); FM (a) 17.00
❑4, Dec 1982 (c); FM (a) 16.00

WOLVERINE (2ND SERIES)

MARVEL

❑-1, Jul 1997; A: Sabretooth. A: Carol Danvers. A: Nick Fury. Flashback; Flashback issue 2.00
❑½, ca. 1997; Wizard mail-away edition 3.00
❑½/Ltd., ca. 1997; Blue foil 8.00
❑1, Nov 1988 (c); AW, JB (a) 10.00
❑2, Dec 1988 JB, KJ (c); JB, KJ (a) 6.00
❑3, Jan 1989 AW, JB (c); AW, JB (a) 5.00
❑4, Feb 1989 AW, JB (c); AW, JB (a); A: Roughhouse. 5.00
❑5, Mar 1989 AW, JB (c); AW, JB (a); 1: Shotgun I. 1: Harriers. 1: Battleaxe II. 1: Hardcase 5.00
❑6, Apr 1989 AW, JB (c); AW, JB (a); A: Roughhouse. 4.00
❑7, May 1989 (c); JB (a); A: Hulk. 5.00
❑8, Jun 1989 (c); JB (a); A: Hulk. 5.00
❑9, Jul 1989 JB (c); PD (w); GC (a) 5.00
❑10, Aug 1989; BSz (c); BSz, JB (a); V: Sabretooth. vs. Sabretooth 8.00
❑11, Sep 1989; KN (c); PD (w); BSz, JB (a); New Costume 4.00
❑12, Sep 1989 KN (c); PD (w); BSz, JB (a) 4.00
❑13, Oct 1989 KN (c); PD (w); BSz, JB (a) 4.00
❑14, Oct 1989 KN (c); PD (w); BSz, JB (a) 4.00
❑15, Nov 1989 KN (c); PD (w); BSz, JB (a) 5.00
❑16, Nov 1989 KN (c); PD (w); BSz, JB (a) 4.00
❑17, Nov 1989 JBy (c); JBy, KJ (a); A: Roughhouse. 4.00
❑18, Dec 1989 JBy (c); JBy, KJ (a); A: Roughhouse. 4.00
❑19, Dec 1989; JBy (c); JBy, KJ (a); A: Tiger Shark. Acts of Vengeance. 4.00
❑20, Jan 1990; JBy (c); JBy, KJ (a); A: Tiger Shark. Acts of Vengeance. 5.00
❑21, Feb 1990 (c); JBy, KJ (a); A: Geist. 4.00
❑22, Mar 1990 JBy (c); JBy, KJ (a); A: Geist. 4.00
❑23, Apr 1990 JBy (c); JBy (a); A: Geist. 4.00
❑24, May 1990 JLee (c); PD (w); GC (a) 3.00
❑25, Jun 1990 JLee (c); JB (a) 3.00
❑26, Jul 1990 KJ (c); TP, KJ (a) 3.00
❑27, Jul 1990 JLee (c); JB, DGr (a) 3.00
❑28, Aug 1990 3.00
❑29, Aug 1990 KJ (c); AM (a) 3.00
❑30, Sep 1990 AM (c) 3.00
❑31, Sep 1990 DGr (c); DGr (a) 2.50
❑32, Oct 1990 DGr (c); DGr (a); A: Jean Grey. 2.50
❑33, Nov 1990 DGr (c); DGr (a) 2.50
❑34, Dec 1990 DGr (c); DGr (a) 2.50
❑35, Jan 1991 DGr (c); DGr (a); A: Lady Deathstrike. 2.50
❑36, Feb 1991 DGr (a); A: Lady Deathstrike. 2.50
❑37, Mar 1991 DGr (c); DGr (a); A: Lady Deathstrike. 2.50
❑38, Apr 1991 DGr (c); DGr (a); A: Storm. 2.50
❑39, May 1991 DGr (c); DGr (a); A: Storm. 2.50
❑40, Jun 1991 DGr (a) 2.50
❑41, Jul 1991 DGr (c); DGr (a); A: Sabretooth. A: Cable. V: Sabretooth. 4.00

N-MINT

❑41/2nd, Jul 1991; A: Sabretooth. Gold cover 1.75
❑42, Jul 1991 DGr (c); DGr (a); A: Sabretooth. A: Nick Fury. A: Cable. 2.00
❑42/2nd, Jul 1991; A: Sabretooth. A: Nick Fury. A: Cable. Gold cover 3.50
❑43, Aug 1991 DGr (a); A: Sabretooth. 3.00
❑44, Aug 1991 (c); PD (w); AM (a) 2.00
❑45, Sep 1991 DGr (c); DGr (a); A: Sabretooth. 2.50
❑46, Sep 1991 DGr (a); A: Sabretooth. 2.50
❑47, Oct 1991 2.50
❑48, Nov 1991; DGr (c); DGr (a); Weapons X sequel: Logan's past 2.50
❑49, Dec 1991; DGr (a); Weapons X sequel: Logan's past 2.50
❑50, Jan 1992; (c); DGr, TP (a); 1: Shiva. diecut cover 4.00
❑51, Feb 1992 DGr (a); A: Mystique 2.00
❑52, Mar 1992 DGr (c); DGr (a); A: Spiral. 2.00
❑53, Apr 1992 DGr (c); DGr, KJ (a); A: . A: Mojo 2.00
❑54, May 1992 A: Shatterstar. 2.00
❑55, Jun 1992 (c); DGr (a); A: Cylla. 2.00
❑56, Jul 1992 DGr (c); DGr (a); A: Cylla. 2.00
❑57, Jul 1992 DGr (c); AM, DGr (a); D: Mariko Yashida. 3.00
❑58, Aug 1992 A: Terror. 2.00
❑59, Aug 1992 A: Terror. 2.00
❑60, Sep 1992 DGr (c); A: Sabretooth. 2.00
❑61, Sep 1992 A: Sabretooth. 2.00
❑62, Oct 1992 A: Sabretooth. 2.00
❑63, Nov 1992 A: Sabretooth. 2.00
❑64, Dec 1992 A: Sabretooth. D: Silver Fox. 2.00
❑65, Jan 1993 2.00
❑66, Feb 1993 2.00
❑67, Mar 1993 2.00
❑68, Apr 1993 2.00
❑69, May 1993 (c) 2.00
❑70, Jun 1993 2.00
❑71, Jul 1993 KJ (c) 2.00
❑72, Aug 1993 A: Sentinel. 2.00
❑73, Sep 1993 A: Sentinel. 2.00
❑74, Oct 1993 A: Jubilee. A: Sentinel. 2.00
❑75, Nov 1993; DGr (a); hologram; Wolverine loses adamantium skeleton 4.00
❑76, Dec 1993 AM (a); A: Lady Deathstrike. 2.00
❑77, Jan 1994 A: Lady Deathstrike. 2.00
❑78, Feb 1994 D: Cylla. D: Bloodscream. 2.00
❑79, Mar 1994 2.00
❑80, Apr 1994 AM (c); AM (a) 8.00
❑81, May 1994 2.00
❑82, Jun 1994 JKu, BMc (a) 2.00
❑83, Jul 1994 2.00
❑84, Aug 1994 AM, TP (a) 2.00
❑85, Sep 1994 2.50
❑85/Variant, Sep 1994; enhanced cover 3.50
❑86, Oct 1994 (c) 2.00
❑87, Nov 1994 DGr (a) 1.50
❑87/Deluxe, Nov 1994; Deluxe edition 4.00
❑88, Dec 1994 1.50
❑88/Deluxe, Dec 1994; Deluxe edition 4.00
❑89, Jan 1995 1.50
❑89/Deluxe, Jan 1995; Deluxe edition 4.00
❑90, Feb 1995 DGr (a) 1.50
❑90/Deluxe, Feb 1995; Deluxe edition 4.00
❑91, Jul 1995 2.00
❑92, Aug 1995 DGr (a) 2.00
❑93, Sep 1995 DGr (a); V: Juggernaut. 2.00
❑94, Oct 1995 AM (a); A: Generation X. 2.00
❑95, Nov 1995 DGr (a); A: Vindicator. 2.00
❑96, Dec 1995 DGr (a); D: Cyber. 2.00
❑97, Jan 1996 DGr (a) 2.00
❑98, Feb 1996 (c); AM (a) 2.00
❑99, Mar 1996 DGr (a) 4.00
❑100, Apr 1996 DGr (a) 5.00
❑100/Variant, Apr 1996; enhanced cardstock cover with hologram 7.50
❑101, May 1996 DGr (c) 2.00
❑102, Jun 1996 DGr (c); DGr (a) 2.00
❑103, Jul 1996 A: Elektra. 2.00
❑104, Aug 1996 (c); A: Elektra. 2.00
❑105, Sep 1996 A: Stick. 2.00
❑106, Oct 1996 AM (a); A: Elektra. 2.00
❑107, Nov 1996 DGr (a) 2.00
❑108, Dec 1996 DGr (a) 2.00

N-MINT

❑109, Jan 1997 DGr (a) 2.00
❑110, Feb 1997 A: Shaman. 2.00
❑111, Mar 1997 DGr (a) 2.00
❑112, Apr 1997 DGr (a) 2.00
❑113, May 1997 2.00
❑114, Jun 1997 V: Deathstrike. 2.00
❑115, Aug 1997; gatefold summary; (c); Operation Zero Tolerance 2.00
❑116, Sep 1997; gatefold summary; (c); Operation Zero Tolerance 2.00
❑117, Oct 1997; gatefold summary; (c); A: Jubilee. Operation Zero Tolerance 2.00
❑118, Nov 1997; gatefold summary; (c); A: Jubilee. Operation Zero Tolerance Epilogue 2.00
❑119, Dec 1997; gatefold summary (c) 2.00
❑120, Jan 1998; gatefold summary (c) 2.00
❑121, Feb 1998 (c) 2.00
❑122, Mar 1998; gatefold summary (c) 2.00
❑123, Apr 1998; gatefold summary (c); BSz (a) 2.00
❑124, May 1998; gatefold summary BSz (a); A: Captain America. 2.00
❑125, Jun 1998; gatefold summary; A: Lady Hydra. wraparound cover 3.50
❑125/A, Jun 1998; DFE alternate cover 10.00
❑125/B, Jun 1998; DFE alternate cover 10.00
❑126, Jul 1998; gatefold summary V: Lady Hydra. V: Sabretooth. 1.99
❑127, Aug 1998; gatefold summary V: Sabretooth. 1.99
❑128, Sep 1998; gatefold summary A: Shadow Cat. A: Viper. V: Sabretooth. 1.99
❑129, Oct 1998; gatefold summary (c) 1.99
❑130, Nov 1998; gatefold summary (c) 1.99
❑131, Nov 1998; gatefold summary; (c); Letterer's error resulted in ethnic slur appearing (out of context, clearly unintentional) on page 6; issue recalled but copies did reach circulation 5.00
❑131/A, Nov 1998; Corrected edition; Corrected version 3.00
❑132, Dec 1998; gatefold summary 1.99
❑133, Jan 1999; gatefold summary A: Warbird. 1.99
❑133/Variant, Jan 1999 4.00
❑134, Feb 1999; gatefold summary EL (w); V: Everybody. 1.99
❑135, Feb 1999 EL (w); A: Starjammers. A: Aria. 1.99
❑136, Mar 1999 EL (w); V: Collector. 1.99
❑137, Apr 1999 EL (w); A: Starjammers. A: Collector. 1.99
❑138, May 1999 (c); EL (w); A: Galactus. 1.99
❑139, Jun 1999 EL (w); A: Cable. 1.99
❑140, Jul 1999 EL (w); A: Nightcrawler. V: Solo. V: Cardiac. 1.99
❑141, Aug 1999 EL (w) 1.99
❑142, Sep 1999 (c); EL (w) 1.99
❑143, Oct 1999; EL (w); wraparound cover 1.99
❑144, Nov 1999 EL (w); A: The Leader. 1.99
❑145, Dec 1999 EL (w); A: Hulk. 4.00
❑145/Gold foil, Dec 1999 25.00
❑145/DF, Dec 1999 50.00
❑145/Silver foil, Dec 1999 30.00
❑145/Nabisco, Dec 1999; Rare Nabisco variant; mail-in offer, fewer than 2,500 in circulation; cover reads "Limited Edition" 400.00
❑146, Jan 2000 EL (w) 5.00
❑147, Feb 2000 EL (w) 2.25
❑148, Mar 2000 EL (c); EL (w) 2.25
❑149, Apr 2000 2.25
❑150, May 2000; Giant-size A: Nova. 2.99
❑150/Dynamic, May 2000; Dynamic Forces chromium variant; no "Revolution" logo 14.00
❑151, Jun 2000 2.25
❑152, Jul 2000 2.25
❑153, Aug 2000 2.25
❑154, Sep 2000 RL (c); RL (w); RL (a) 2.25
❑155, Oct 2000 RL (c); RL (w); RL (a); A: Deadpool. 2.25
❑156, Nov 2000 RL (w); A: Spider-Man. 2.25
❑157, Dec 2000 RL (c); RL (w); A: Mole Man. 2.25
❑158, Jan 2001; polybagged with Marvel Online CD-ROM 2.25
❑159, Feb 2001 2.25
❑160, Mar 2001 2.25

Other grades: Multiply price above by 5/6 for VF/NM • 2/3 for VERY FINE • 1/3 for FINE • 1/5 for VERY GOOD • 1/8 for GOOD

Wolverine: The Origin

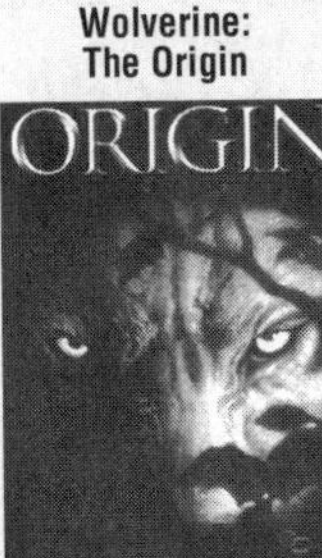

Logan's earliest days revealed
©Marvel

Wolverine vs. Spider-Man

Collects Marvel Comics Presents arc
©Marvel

Wonderland

Alice, Dorothy, and friends join forces
©Arrow

Wonder Man (2nd Series)

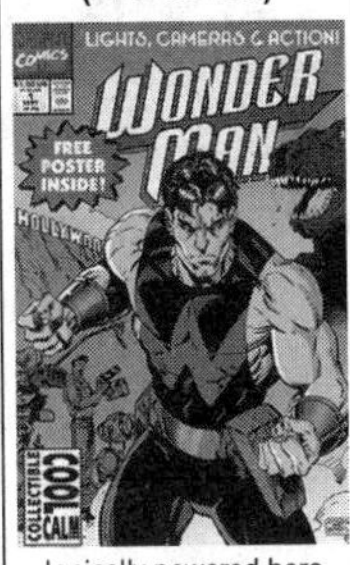

Ionically powered hero becomes icon
©Marvel

Wonder Wart-Hog, Hog of Steel

Philbert Desanex's dream becomes reality
©Rip Off

N-MINT

❑161, Apr 2001 ... 2.25
❑162, May 2001 ... 2.25
❑163, Jun 2001 ... 2.25
❑164, Jul 2001 ... 2.25
❑165, Aug 2001 (c) ... 2.25
❑166, Sep 2001 ... 3.00
❑166/A, Sep 2001; DFE Signed, limited edition ... 39.99
❑167, Oct 2001 ... 2.25
❑168, Nov 2001 ... 2.25
❑169, Dec 2001 ... 2.25
❑170, Jan 2002 ... 2.25
❑171, Feb 2002 ... 2.25
❑172, Mar 2002 A: Alpha Flight. ... 2.25
❑173, Apr 2002; A: Lady Deathstrike. wraparound cover ... 2.25
❑174, May 2002; wraparound cover ... 2.25
❑175, Jun 2002; A: Sabretooth. wraparound cover ... 2.25
❑176, Jul 2002; wraparound cover ... 2.25
❑177, Aug 2002; wraparound cover ... 2.25
❑178, Aug 2002; wraparound cover ... 2.25
❑179, Sep 2002; wraparound cover ... 2.25
❑180, Oct 2002; wraparound cover ... 2.25
❑181, Nov 2002; TP (a); wraparound cover ... 2.25
❑182, Dec 2002; TP (a); wraparound cover ... 2.25
❑183, Jan 2003; TP (a); A: Lady Deathstrike. wraparound cover ... 2.25
❑184, Feb 2003; TP (a); wraparound cover ... 2.25
❑185, Mar 2003; TP (a); wraparound cover ... 2.25
❑186, Apr 2003 A: The Punisher. ... 2.25
❑187, May 2003 ... 2.25
❑188, May 2003 ... 2.25
❑189, Jun 2003; wraparound cover ... 2.25
❑Annual 1995, Sep 1995 ... 3.95
❑Annual 1996, Oct 1996; (c); JPH (w); V: Red Ronin. wraparound cover ... 2.95
❑Annual 1997, ca. 1997; gatefold summary; wraparound cover ... 2.99
❑Annual 1999, ca. 1999 A: Deadpool. ... 3.50
❑Annual 2000, ca. 2000 ... 3.50
❑Annual 2001, ca. 2001 ... 2.99
❑Special 1, Win 1999; Blue Print edition ... 4.00

WOLVERINE (3RD SERIES)
MARVEL

❑1, Jul 2003 ... 7.00
❑2, Jul 2003 ... 5.00
❑3, Aug 2003 ... 4.00
❑4, Aug 2003 ... 3.00
❑5, Nov 2003 ... 3.00
❑6, Dec 2003 TP (a) ... 2.99
❑7, Jan 2004 ... 2.99
❑8, Jan 2004 ... 2.99
❑9, Feb 2004 ... 2.99
❑10, Mar 2004 ... 2.25
❑11, Apr 2004 ... 2.99
❑12, May 2004 TP (a) ... 2.99
❑13, Jun 2004 ... 2.99
❑14, Jun 2004 ... 2.99
❑15, Jul 2004 (c); TP (a) ... 2.99
❑16, Aug 2004 ... 2.25
❑17, Sep 2004 ... 2.99

N-MINT

❑18, Oct 2004 ... 2.25
❑19, Nov 2004 ... 2.25
❑20, Dec 2004 ... 2.25
❑20/Variant, Dec 2004; Retailer incentive ... 90.00
❑20/Texas 2004; Wizard World Texas giveaway ... 20.00
❑21, Jan 2005 ... 2.25
❑22, Jan 2005 ... 2.25
❑23, Feb 2005 ... 2.25
❑24, Mar 2005 ... 2.25
❑25 ... 2.25
❑26, Jan 2005; Greg Land cover ... 2.25
❑26/Silvestri, Jan 2005; Mark Silvestri cover; supplied to retailers at 1:15 regular copies of #26; Part 1 (of 6) ... 20.00
❑26/DF, Jan 2005; Signed by John Romita Sr., initially offered at $10, then priced at $49.99 ... 25.00
❑27 2005 ... 2.25
❑27/Quesada 2005 ... 30.00
❑28 2005 ... 2.25
❑29 2005 ... 2.25
❑30, Sep 2005 ... 2.50
❑31, Oct 2005 ... 2.99
❑32 2005 ... 2.99
❑33 2005 ... 2.99
❑34 ... 2.99
❑35, Dec 2005 ... 2.99
❑36, Jan 2006 ... 2.99
❑36/Quesada, Jan 2006 ... 2.99
❑37, Feb 2006 ... 2.99
❑38, Mar 2006 ... 2.99
❑39, May 2006 ... 2.99
❑40, Jun 2006 ... 2.99
❑41, Jul 2006 ... 2.99
❑42, Aug 2006 ... 2.99
❑43, Sep 2006 ... 2.99

WOLVERINE AND THE PUNISHER: DAMAGING EVIDENCE
MARVEL

❑1, Oct 1993 ... 2.00
❑2, Nov 1993 ... 2.00
❑3, Dec 1993 ... 2.00

WOLVERINE BATTLES THE INCREDIBLE HULK
MARVEL

❑1, ca. 1989; reprints Incredible Hulk #180 and #181 ... 4.95

WOLVERINE: BLACK RIO
MARVEL

❑1, Nov 1998 ... 5.99

WOLVERINE: BLOODLUST
MARVEL

❑1, Dec 1990 ... 4.95

WOLVERINE: BLOODY CHOICES
MARVEL

❑1, ca. 1993 ... 7.95

WOLVERINE/CAPTAIN AMERICA
MARVEL

❑1, Apr 2004 ... 4.00
❑2, Apr 2004 ... 2.99
❑3, Apr 2004 ... 2.99
❑4, Apr 2004 ... 2.99

N-MINT

WOLVERINE: DAYS OF FUTURE PAST
MARVEL

❑1, Dec 1997; gatefold summary; Wolverine in early 21st century ... 2.50
❑2, Jan 1998; gatefold summary; Wolverine in early 21st century ... 2.50
❑3, Feb 1998; gatefold summary; Wolverine in early 21st century ... 2.50

WOLVERINE: DOOMBRINGER
MARVEL

❑1, Nov 1997 ... 5.99
❑1/Variant; foil cover ... 14.95

WOLVERINE/DOOP
MARVEL

❑1, Jul 2003 ... 2.99
❑2, Jul 2003 ... 2.99

WOLVERINE: EVILUTION
MARVEL

❑1, Sep 1994; Direct Edition ... 5.95

WOLVERINE/GAMBIT: VICTIMS
MARVEL

❑1, Sep 1995; enhanced cardstock cover ... 2.95
❑2, Oct 1995; enhanced cardstock cover ... 2.95
❑3, Nov 1995; enhanced cardstock cover ... 2.95
❑4, Dec 1995; enhanced cardstock cover ... 2.95

WOLVERINE: GLOBAL JEOPARDY
MARVEL

❑1, Dec 1993; Embossed cover ... 2.95

WOLVERINE/HULK
MARVEL

❑1, Apr 2002 ... 3.50
❑2, May 2002 ... 3.50
❑3, Jun 2002 ... 3.50
❑4, Jul 2002 ... 3.50

WOLVERINE: INNER FURY
MARVEL

❑1, Nov 1992 ... 5.95

WOLVERINE: KILLING
MARVEL

❑1, Sep 1993 ... 5.95

WOLVERINE: KNIGHT OF TERRA
MARVEL

❑1, Aug 1995 ... 6.95

WOLVERINE: NETSUKE
MARVEL

❑1, Nov 2002 ... 3.99
❑2, Dec 2002 ... 3.99
❑3, Jan 2003 ... 3.99
❑4, Feb 2003 ... 3.99

WOLVERINE AND NICK FURY: SCORPIO RISING
MARVEL

❑1, Oct 1994, Sequel to Wolverine/Nick Fury: The Scorpio Connection; perfect bound ... 4.95

WOLVERINE: ORIGINS
MARVEL

❑1, Jun 2006 ... 10.00
❑3, Aug 2006 ... 8.00

Other grades: Multiply price above by 5/6 for VF/NM • 2/3 for VERY FINE • 1/3 for FINE • 1/5 for VERY GOOD • 1/8 for GOOD

WOLVERINE POSTER MAGAZINE
Marvel

❑1, pin-ups 4.95

WOLVERINE/PUNISHER
Marvel

❑1, May 2004 2.99
❑2, Jun 2004 2.99
❑3, Jul 2004 2.99
❑4, Aug 2004 2.99
❑5, Oct 2004 2.99

WOLVERINE/PUNISHER REVELATION
Marvel

❑1, Jun 1999 2.99
❑1/2nd, Apr 2001 2.99
❑2, Jul 1999 2.99
❑2/2nd, May 2001 2.99
❑3, Aug 1999 2.99
❑4, Sep 1999 2.99

WOLVERINE: RAHNE OF TERRA
Marvel

❑1, Aug 1991; prestige format 5.95

WOLVERINE SAGA
Marvel

❑1, Sep 1989 RL (c); O: Wolverine. 4.00
❑2, Nov 1989 BG (c) 4.00
❑3, Dec 1989 JR2, KJ (c) 4.00
❑4, Dec 1989 4.00

WOLVERINE: SAVE THE TIGER!
Marvel

❑1, May 1992 2.95

WOLVERINE: SNIKT!
Marvel

❑1, Jul 2003 2.99
❑2, Aug 2003 2.99
❑3, Sep 2003 2.99
❑4, Oct 2003 0.00
❑5, Nov 2003 2.99

WOLVERINE: SOULTAKER
Marvel

❑1 2005 2.99
❑2 2005 2.99
❑3 2005 2.99
❑4 2005 2.99
❑5 2005 2.99

WOLVERINE: THE END
Marvel

❑1, Jan 2004 7.00
❑1/Texas, Jan 2004 15.00
❑2, Mar 2004 6.00
❑3, May 2004 5.00
❑4, Aug 2004 4.00
❑5 2004 3.00
❑6 2004 2.99

WOLVERINE: THE JUNGLE ADVENTURE
Marvel

❑1, ca. 1990 4.50

WOLVERINE: THE ORIGIN
Marvel

❑1, Nov 2001 O: Wolverine. 25.00
❑1/Dynamic, Nov 2001; Dynamic Forces S&N w/ cert. 50.00
❑2, Dec 2001 O: Wolverine. 12.00
❑2/Dynamic, Dec 2001; Dynamic Forces S&N w/ cert. 24.00
❑3, Jan 2002 O: Wolverine. 8.00
❑3/Dynamic, Jan 2002; Dynamic Forces S&N w/ cert. 20.00
❑4, Feb 2002 O: Wolverine. 5.00
❑4/Dynamic, Feb 2002; Dynamic Forces S&N w/ cert. 20.00
❑5, May 2002 O: Wolverine. O: Sabretooth. 4.00
❑5/Dynamic, May 2002; Dynamic Forces S&N w/ cert. 20.00
❑6, Jul 2002 O: Wolverine. O: Sabretooth. 5.00
❑6/Dynamic, Jul 2002; Dynamic Forces S&N w/ cert. 20.00

WOLVERINE VS. NIGHT MAN
Marvel

❑0; limited edition 15.00

WOLVERINE VS. SPIDER-MAN
Marvel

❑1, Mar 1995; collects story arc from Marvel Comics Presents #48-50; cardstock cover 3.00

WOLVERINE/WITCHBLADE
Image

❑1, Mar 1997 4.50
❑1/A, Mar 1997; crossover with Marvel; continues in Witchblade/Elektra 2.95

WOLVERINE: XISLE
Marvel

❑1, Jun 2003 2.50
❑2, Jun 2003 2.50
❑3, Jun 2003 2.50
❑4, Jun 2003 2.50
❑5, Jun 2003 2.50

WOMEN IN FUR
Shanda Fantasy Arts

❑2, b&w 4.50

WOMEN IN ROCK SPECIAL
Revolutionary

❑1, Dec 1993, b&w 2.50

WOMEN ON TOP
Fantagraphics / Eros

❑1, b&w 2.25

WONDERLAND
Arrow

❑1, Sum 1985 2.95
❑2, Feb 1985 2.95
❑3, Apr 1986 2.95

WONDERLANDERS
Oktomica

❑1, Jan 1999 2.50

WONDER MAN (1ST SERIES)
Marvel

❑1, Mar 1986 1.50

WONDER MAN (2ND SERIES)
Marvel

❑1, Sep 1991; poster 1.50
❑2, Oct 1991 A: West Coast Avengers. 1.25
❑3, Nov 1991 1: Splice. 1.25
❑4, Dec 1991 1.25
❑5, Jan 1992 A: Beast. 1.25
❑6, Feb 1992 1.25
❑7, Mar 1992; A: Rick Jones. Operation Galactic Storm 1.25
❑8, Apr 1992; A: the Starjammers. Operation Galactic Storm 1.25
❑9, May 1992; (c); Operation Galactic Storm 1.25
❑10, Jun 1992 1.25
❑11, Jul 1992 1.25
❑12, Aug 1992 1.25
❑13, Sep 1992 1.25
❑14, Oct 1992; Infinity War 1.25
❑15, Nov 1992 1.25
❑16, Dec 1992 1.25
❑17, Jan 1993 1.25
❑18, Feb 1993 1.25
❑19, Mar 1993 1.25
❑20, Apr 1993 1.25
❑21, May 1993 A: Splice. 1.25
❑22, Jun 1993 1.25
❑23, Jul 1993; Covers to Wonder Man #21-24 form quadtych 1.25
❑24, Aug 1993 1.25
❑25, Sep 1993; Embossed cover 2.95
❑26, Oct 1993 A: Hulk. 1.25
❑27, Nov 1993 A: Hulk. 1.25
❑28, Dec 1993 A: Spider-Man. 1.25
❑29, Jan 1994 A: Spider-Man. 1.25
❑Annual 1, ca. 1992 KB (w) 2.25
❑Annual 2, ca. 1993; trading card 2.95

WONDERS AND ODDITIES (RICK GEARY'S...)
Dark Horse

❑1, Dec 1988, b&w 2.00

WONDER WART-HOG, HOG OF STEEL
Rip Off

❑1, b&w; Reprints 3.00
❑2, b&w; Reprints 2.50
❑3, b&w; Reprints 2.50

WONDER WOMAN (1ST SERIES)
DC

❑85, Oct 1956 155.00
❑86, Nov 1956 155.00
❑87, Jan 1957 155.00
❑88, Feb 1957 155.00
❑89, Apr 1957 155.00
❑90, May 1957 (c) 155.00
❑91, Jul 1957 120.00
❑92, Aug 1957 (c) 120.00
❑93, Oct 1957 (c) 120.00
❑94, Nov 1957 120.00
❑95, Jan 1958 120.00
❑96, Feb 1958 120.00
❑97, Apr 1958 120.00
❑98, May 1958 O: Wonder Woman (new origin). 120.00
❑99, Jul 1958 (c) 120.00
❑100, Aug 1958 120.00
❑101, Oct 1958 (c); RA (a) 90.00
❑102, Nov 1958 RA (a) 90.00
❑103, Jan 1959 90.00
❑104, Feb 1959 90.00
❑105, Apr 1959 (c); RA (a); O: 1st Wonder Girl. O: Wonder Woman ("secret origin"). 600.00
❑106, May 1959 (c); RA (a) 80.00
❑107, Jul 1959 (c) 80.00
❑108, Aug 1959 (c); RA (a) 80.00
❑109, Oct 1959 (c) 80.00
❑110, Nov 1959 (c) 80.00
❑111, Jan 1960 70.00
❑112, Feb 1960 (c); A: Wonder Girl. 70.00
❑113, Apr 1960; (c); A: Wonder Girl. Aloha, Hawaii (Public Service piece) 70.00
❑114, May 1960 70.00
❑115, Jul 1960 (c); A: Mer-Boy. 70.00
❑116, Aug 1960 (c); A: Wonder Girl. 70.00
❑117, Oct 1960 (c); A: The Holiday Girls. 70.00
❑118, Nov 1960 (c); A: Mer-Man. 70.00
❑119, Jan 1961 (c) 70.00
❑120, Feb 1961 (c); A: Wonder Girl. 70.00
❑121, Apr 1961 (c); (w); 1: Wonder Family. 70.00
❑122, May 1961 1: Wonder Tot. 70.00
❑123, Jul 1961 70.00
❑124, Aug 1961 1: Wonder Family. 70.00
❑125, Oct 1961 (a); A: Mer-Man 70.00
❑126, Nov 1961 (a); 1: Mister Genie. 70.00
❑127, Jan 1962 (c) 70.00
❑128, Feb 1962 (c); O: Wonder Woman's Invisible Jet. 70.00
❑129, Apr 1962 70.00
❑130, May 1962 (c) 70.00
❑131, Jul 1962 (c) 56.00
❑132, Aug 1962 (c); A: Mer-Man. 56.00
❑133, Oct 1962 (c); A: Wonder Family. 56.00
❑134, Nov 1962 (c); A: Wonder Girl. 56.00
❑135, Jan 1963 (c); A: Mer-Boy. 56.00
❑136, Feb 1963 (c) 56.00
❑137, Apr 1963 (c) 56.00
❑138, May 1963 (c); A: Wonder Family. 56.00
❑139, Jul 1963 (c) 56.00
❑140, Aug 1963 (c); A: Mer-Boy. 56.00
❑141, Oct 1963 (c) 56.00
❑142, Nov 1963 (c); A: Wonder Family. 56.00
❑143, Jan 1964 (c); RA (a) 56.00
❑144, Feb 1964 (c); RA (a) 56.00
❑145, Apr 1964 (c); (w); A: Wonder Family. 56.00
❑146, May 1964 (c) 56.00
❑147, Jul 1964 (c) 56.00
❑148, Aug 1964 (c) 56.00
❑149, Oct 1964 (c); A: Wonder Family. 56.00
❑150, Nov 1964 (c); A: Bird-Boy. 50.00
❑151, Jan 1965 (c); A: Mer-Boy. 50.00
❑152, Feb 1965 (c); A: Mer-Boy. 50.00
❑153, Apr 1965 (c); A: Mer-Boy. 50.00
❑154, May 1965 (c); A: Mer-Man. 50.00
❑155, Jul 1965 (c); A: Bird-Man. 50.00
❑156, Aug 1965 (c) 50.00
❑157, Oct 1965 (c); A: Egg Fu. 50.00
❑158, Nov 1965 (c); A: Egg Fu. 50.00
❑159, Jan 1966 O: Wonder Woman. 50.00
❑160, Feb 1966 (c); A: Cheetah I (Priscilla Rich). 30.00
❑161, Apr 1966 (c); A: Countess Draska Nishki. 30.00
❑162, May 1966 (c); O: Wonder Woman's Secret Identity. 40.00
❑163, Jul 1966 (c); A: Doctor Psycho. 30.00
❑164, Aug 1966 (c) 30.00
❑165, Oct 1966 RA (c); RA (a); A: Doctor Psycho. 30.00

Other grades: Multiply price above by 5/6 for VF/NM • 2/3 for VERY FINE • 1/3 for FINE • 1/5 for VERY GOOD • 1/8 for GOOD

Wonder Woman (1st Series)

Amazonian heroine had feet of clay
©DC

Wonder Woman (2nd Series)

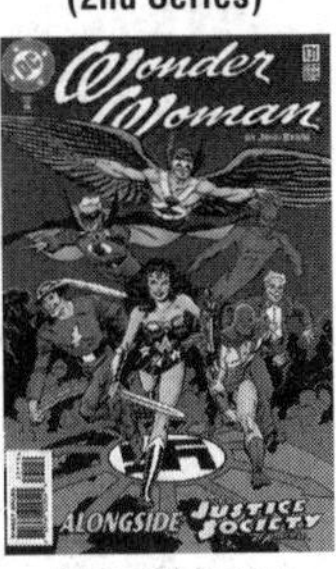

Revamped Amazon strives for peace
©DC

Wonder Woman Gallery

Pin-ups celebrate return of heroine
©DC

Wonder Woman: Our Worlds At War

Hippolyta's final fate revealed
©DC

Woodsy Owl

Conservation comic not on recycled paper
©Gold Key

N-MINT

❑166, Nov 1966 RA (c); RA (a); A: Egg Fu. 30.00
❑167, Jan 1967 RA (c); RA (a) 30.00
❑168, Feb 1967 RA (c); RA (a); A: Paula Von Gunta. 30.00
❑169, Apr 1967 RA (c); RA (a) 30.00
❑170, Jun 1967 (c); RA (a) 30.00
❑171, Aug 1967 RA (c); RA (a); A: Mouse Man. 25.00
❑172, Oct 1967 (c) 25.00
❑173, Dec 1967 (c) 25.00
❑174, Feb 1968 (c) 25.00
❑175, Apr 1968 (c) 25.00
❑176, Jun 1968 (c) 25.00
❑177, Aug 1968 IN (c); A: Supergirl. 25.00
❑178, Oct 1968 (c); 1: Mod Diana Prince. 25.00
❑179, Dec 1968 (c); 1: Doctor Cyber. 25.00
❑180, Feb 1969 (c); D: Steve Trevor (Wonder Woman's boyfriend). 25.00
❑181, Apr 1969 (c); A: Doctor Cyber. 33.00
❑182, Jun 1969 33.00
❑183, Aug 1969 (c) 33.00
❑184, Oct 1969 (c) 33.00
❑185, Dec 1969 (c) 33.00
❑186, Feb 1970 (c) 33.00
❑187, Apr 1970 (c); A: Doctor Cyber. 33.00
❑188, Jun 1970 (c); A: Doctor Cyber. 33.00
❑189, Aug 1970 (c) 33.00
❑190, Oct 1970 (c) 33.00
❑191, Dec 1970 (c) 40.00
❑192, Feb 1971 (c) 40.00
❑193, Apr 1971 (c) 40.00
❑194, Jun 1971 (c) 40.00
❑195, Aug 1971 40.00
❑196, Oct 1971 (c); DG (a); A: Cheetah. 40.00
❑197, Dec 1971 DG (c); DG (a) 40.00
❑198, Feb 1972 DG (c); DG (a) 40.00
❑199, Apr 1972 JJ (c); DH, DG (a); A: Jonny Double. 40.00
❑200, Jun 1972 JJ (c); DG (a); D: Doctor Cyber. 40.00
❑201, Aug 1972 DG (c); DG (a); A: Catwoman. 14.00
❑202, Oct 1972 DG (c); DG (a); A: Fafhrd and The Gray Mouser. 14.00
❑203, Dec 1972 DG (c); DG (a) 14.00
❑204, Feb 1973 (c); D: I-Ching. 14.00
❑205, Apr 1973; (c); BO, DH (a); Suggestive cover. 14.00
❑206, Jun 1973 (c); DH (a) 14.00
❑207, Aug 1973 (c) 14.00
❑208, Oct 1973 (c); RE (a); A: Steve Trevor. 14.00
❑209, Dec 1973 RE (c); RE (a) 14.00
❑210, Feb 1974 (c) 14.00
❑211, Apr 1974 NC (c); A: Mer-Boy. 25.00
❑212, Jun 1974 (c); CS (a); A: JLA. 11.00
❑213, Aug 1974 (c); IN (a); A: Flash. 11.00
❑214, Oct 1974 BO (c); CS, RA (a); A: Green Lantern. 30.00
❑215, Dec 1974 (c); A: Aquaman. 11.00
❑216, Feb 1975 NC (c); A: Black Canary. 11.00
❑217, Apr 1975 MGr (c); DD, RA (a); A: Green Arrow. 11.00
❑218, Jun 1975 (c); KS (a); A: Red Tornado. 11.00
❑219, Aug 1975 (c); CS (a); A: Elongated Man. 7.00
❑220, Oct 1975 DG (c); DG (a); A: Atom. 7.00
❑221, Dec 1975 CS (a); A: Hawkman. 7.00
❑222, Feb 1976 A: Batman. 7.00
❑223, Apr 1976; A: Steve Trevor. Return of Steve Trevor 7.00
❑224, Jun 1976 CS (a) 7.00
❑225, Aug 1976 7.00
❑226, Oct 1976 (c) 7.00
❑227, Dec 1976 7.00
❑228, Feb 1977 (c) 7.00
❑229, Mar 1977 JL (c) 7.00
❑230, Apr 1977 (c); A: Cheetah. 7.00
❑231, May 1977 MN (c) 7.00
❑232, Jun 1977 MN (c); MN (a) 7.00
❑233, Jul 1977 GM (c); DH (a) 7.00
❑234, Aug 1977 JL (c); DH (a) 7.00
❑235, Sep 1977 JL (c); A: Doctor Mid-Nite. 7.00
❑236, Oct 1977 RB (c) 7.00
❑237, Nov 1977 RB (c); O: Wonder Woman. 1: Kung. 6.00
❑238, Dec 1977 RB (c); A: Sandman. 6.00
❑239, Jan 1978 RB (c); A: Golden Age Flash. 6.00
❑240, Feb 1978 DG, JL (c); A: Golden Age Flash. 6.00
❑241, Mar 1978 DG, JSa (c); DG, JSa (a); A: new Spectre. 6.00
❑242, Apr 1978 RB (c) 6.00
❑243, May 1978 (c); A: Angle Man. 6.00
❑244, Jun 1978 RB (c) 6.00
❑245, Jul 1978 JSa (c) 6.00
❑246, Aug 1978 DG, JSa (c) 6.00
❑247, Sep 1978 RB, DG (c); A: Elongated Man. 6.00
❑248, Oct 1978 JL (c); D: Steve Trevor. 6.00
❑249, Nov 1978 RB, DG (c); A: Hawkgirl. 6.00
❑250, Dec 1978 RB, DG (c); 1: Orana (new Wonder Woman). 6.00
❑250/Whitman, Dec 1978; RB, DG (c); 1: Orana (new Wonder Woman). Whitman variant 12.00
❑251, Jan 1979 DG, RA (c) 6.00
❑251/Whitman, Jan 1979; DG, RA (c); Whitman variant 12.00
❑252, Feb 1979 DG, RA (c); 1: Stacy Macklin. 6.00
❑252/Whitman, Feb 1979; DG, RA (c); 1: Stacy Macklin. Whitman variant. 12.00
❑253, Mar 1979 DG (c) 6.00
❑254, Apr 1979 DG, RA (c); A: Angle Man. 6.00
❑255, May 1979 DG (c) 6.00
❑255/Whitman, May 1979; DG (c); Whitman variant 12.00
❑256, Jun 1979 (c) 6.00
❑256/Whitman, Jun 1979; (c); Whitman variant 12.00
❑257, Jul 1979 DG, RA (c); A: Multi-Man. 6.00
❑257/Whitman, Jul 1979; DG, RA (c); A: Multi-Man. Whitman variant 12.00
❑258, Aug 1979 DG (c) 6.00
❑258/Whitman, Aug 1979; DG (c); Whitman variant 12.00
❑259, Sep 1979 DG (c); A: Hercules. 6.00
❑259/Whitman, Sep 1979; DG (c); A: Hercules. Whitman variant 12.00
❑260, Oct 1979 A: Hercules. 6.00
❑260/Whitman, Oct 1979; A: Hercules. Whitman variant 12.00
❑261, Nov 1979 DG (c); A: Hercules. 5.00
❑261/Whitman, Nov 1979; DG (c); A: Hercules. Whitman variant 15.00
❑262, Dec 1979 DG (c); RE (a) 5.00
❑262/Whitman, Dec 1979; DG (c); RE (a); Whitman variant 10.00
❑263, Jan 1980 DG (c) 5.00
❑263/Whitman, Jan 1980; DG (c); Whitman variant 15.00
❑264, Feb 1980 DG, RA (c) 5.00
❑264/Whitman, Feb 1980; Whitman variant 10.00
❑265, Mar 1980 DG, RA (c); RE (a); A: Wonder Girl. 5.00
❑266, Apr 1980 (c); RE (a) 5.00
❑267, May 1980 DG, RA (c); A: Animal Man. 5.00
❑268, Jun 1980 DG, RA (c); A: Animal Man. 5.00
❑269, Jul 1980 DG, RA (c); WW (a) 4.00
❑270, Aug 1980 (c); A: Steve Trevor. 4.00
❑271, Sep 1980 DG, RA (c); JSa (a); A: Huntress. 4.00
❑272, Oct 1980 DG, DC (c); JSa (a); A: Huntress. 4.00
❑273, Nov 1980 DG, RA (c); JSa (a); A: Solomon Grundy. 4.00
❑274, Dec 1980 (c); JSa (a); 1: Cheetah II (Deborah Domaine). 4.00
❑275, Jan 1981 RB, DG (c); JSa (a); A: Power Girl. 4.00
❑276, Feb 1981 DG, RA (c); JSa (a); A: Kobra. 4.00
❑277, Mar 1981 DG, RA (c); JSa (a); A: Kobra. 4.00
❑278, Apr 1981 DG, RA (c); JSa (a); A: Kobra. 4.00
❑279, May 1981 DG, RA (c); JSa (a) 4.00
❑280, Jun 1981 DG, RA (c); JSa (a); A: Etrigan. 3.00
❑281, Jul 1981 DG, RA (c); JSa (a); A: Joker. 5.00
❑282, Aug 1981 RB, DG (c); JSa (a); A: Joker. 5.00
❑283, Sep 1981 DG (c); JSa (a); A: Joker. 5.00
❑284, Oct 1981 GP, DG (c); JSa (a); A: Earth-2 Robin. 2.50
❑285, Nov 1981 (c); JSa (a); A: Earth-2 Robin. 2.50
❑286, Dec 1981 DG, RA (c); JSa (a) 2.50
❑287, Jan 1982 (c); DH, JSa, RT (a); A: New Teen Titans. 2.50
❑288, Feb 1982 (c); GC, RT (a); 1: The Silver Swan. 2.50
❑289, Mar 1982 GC, DG (c); GC, JSa, RT (a); 1: Captain Wonder. 2.50
❑290, Apr 1982 (c); GC, JSa, RT (a); A: Captain Wonder. 2.50
❑291, May 1982 DG, RA (c); FMc, GC (a); A: Zatanna. 2.50
❑292, Jun 1982 DG, RA (c); FMc, GC (a); A: Supergirl. 2.50

Other grades: Multiply price above by 5/6 for VF/NM • 2/3 for VERY FINE • 1/3 for FINE • 1/5 for VERY GOOD • 1/8 for GOOD

❑293, Jul 1982 DG, RA (c); FMc, GC (a); A: Raven. A: Starfire. ... 2.50
❑294, Aug 1982 GK (c); FMc, GC, JOy, JSa (a); A: Blockbuster. ... 2.50
❑295, Sep 1982 RB (c); FMc, GC, JOy, JSa (a) ... 2.50
❑296, Oct 1982 FMc, GC, JOy, JSa (a) 2.50
❑297, Nov 1982 FMc, GC, JSa, CS (a); 1: Aegeus. ... 2.50
❑298, Dec 1982 DG, FM (c); FMc, GC, JSa (a) ... 2.50
❑299, Jan 1983 DG (c); FMc, GC, JSa (a) ... 2.50
❑300, Feb 1983; Giant-size DG (c); FMc, RB, GC, KG, JDu, KP, DG, RA (a); A: New Teen Titans. ... 6.00
❑301, Mar 1983 DG (c); FMc, GC, DH (a) ... 2.50
❑302, Apr 1983 DG (c); FMc, GC (a) .. 2.50
❑303, May 1983 GK (c); FMc, GC (a); A: Doctor Polaris. ... 2.50
❑304, Jun 1983 GK (c); FMc, GC (a); A: Green Lantern. ... 2.50
❑305, Jul 1983 GK (c); FMc, GC (a); 1: Circe (DC). ... 2.50
❑306, Aug 1983 DG, JL (c); DH (a); A: Aegeus. ... 2.50
❑307, Sep 1983 GK (c); DH (a); A: Aegeus. ... 2.50
❑308, Oct 1983 DG, RA (c); DH (a); A: Black Canary. ... 2.50
❑309, Nov 1983 (c); DH (a); 1: Earthworm. ... 2.50
❑310, Dec 1983 DG (c) ... 2.50
❑311, Jan 1984 DG, RA (c); DH (a) 2.50
❑312, Feb 1984 GK (c); DH, DS (a) 2.50
❑313, Mar 1984 DG (c); DH (a); A: Circe (DC). ... 2.50
❑314, Apr 1984 GK (c); DH (a); A: Circe (DC). ... 2.50
❑315, May 1984 DG (c); DH (a); A: Tezcatlipoca. ... 2.50
❑316, Jun 1984 DH (a); A: Tezcatlipoca. 2.50
❑317, Jul 1984 DH (a) ... 2.50
❑318, Aug 1984 KB (w); IN (a) ... 2.50
❑319, Sep 1984 DH (a); A: Doctor Cyber. ... 2.50
❑320, Oct 1984 DH (a); A: Doctor Cyber. ... 2.50
❑321, Nov 1984 DH (a); A: Doctor Cyber. ... 2.50
❑322, Dec 1984 DH (a); A: Eros. ... 2.50
❑323, Feb 1985 DH (a); A: The Monitor. 2.50
❑324, Apr 1985 RT (c); DH (a); A: Atomic Knight. ... 2.50
❑325, May 1985 DH (a); A: Atomic Knight. ... 2.50
❑326, Jul 1985 DH (a) ... 2.50
❑327, Sep 1985 DH (a); A: Tezcatlipoca. 2.50
❑328, Dec 1985; DG (c); DH (a); Crisis 2.50
❑329, Feb 1986; Giant-size; JL (c); DH (a); Crisis ... 2.50

WONDER WOMAN (2ND SERIES) DC

❑0, Oct 1994 BB (c); O: The Amazons. 6.00
❑1, Feb 1987 GP (c); GP (w); GP (a); O: Wonder Woman (new origin). 1: Ares (DC). ... 4.00
❑2, Mar 1987 GP (c); GP (w); GP (a); A: Steve Trevor. ... 3.00
❑3, Apr 1987 GP (c); GP (w); GP (a); 1: Vanessa Kapatelis. 1: Jack Kapatelis. 1: Decay. ... 3.00
❑4, May 1987 GP (c); GP (w); GP (a); 2: Decay. ... 3.00
❑5, Jun 1987 (c); GP (w); GP (a); V: Ares. 3.00
❑6, Jul 1987 GP (c); GP (w); GP (a); V: Ares. ... 2.50
❑7, Aug 1987 GP (c); GP (w); GP (a).. 2.50
❑8, Sep 1987 GP (c); GP (w); GP (a).. 2.50
❑9, Oct 1987 GP (c); GP (w); GP (a); 1: Cheetah. ... 2.50
❑10, Nov 1987; GP (c); GP (w); GP (a); gatefold ... 2.50
❑10/A, Nov 1987; no gatefold; gatefold 2.50
❑11, Dec 1987 GP (c); GP (w); GP (a) 2.00
❑12, Jan 1988; GP (c); GP (w); GP (a); Millennium ... 2.00
❑13, Feb 1988; GP (c); GP (w); GP (a); Millennium ... 2.00
❑14, Mar 1988 GP (c); GP (w); GP (a); A: Hercules. ... 2.00
❑15, Apr 1988 GP (c); GP (w); GP (a); 1: Silver Swan. 1: Ed Indelicato. ... 2.00
❑16, May 1988 GP (c); GP (w); GP (a); A: Silver Swan. ... 2.00
❑17, Jun 1988 GP (c); GP (w); GP, DG (a) 2.00
❑18, Jul 1988; GP (c); GP (w); GP, DG (a); A: Circe (DC). Bonus Book ... 2.00
❑19, Aug 1988 GP (c); GP (w); FMc, GP (a); A: Circe (DC). ... 2.00
❑20, Sep 1988 GP (c); GP (w); GP, BMc (a); A: Ed Indelicato. ... 2.00
❑21, Oct 1988 GP (c); GP (w); GP, BMc (a). ... 2.00
❑22, Nov 1988 GP (c); GP (w); GP, BMc (a). ... 2.00
❑23, Dec 1988 GP (c); GP (w); GP (a) 2.00
❑24, Hol 1988; GP (c); GP (w); GP (a); Hol 1988 ... 2.00
❑25, Jan 1989; GP (c); KG, GP (w); Invasion! ... 2.00
❑26, Jan 1989; GP (c); KG, GP (w); Invasion! ... 2.00
❑27, Feb 1989 GP (c); GP (w) ... 2.00
❑28, Mar 1989 GP (c); GP (w); A: Cheetah. ... 2.00
❑29, Apr 1989 GP (c); GP (w); O: Cheetah. ... 2.00
❑30, May 1989 GP (c); GP (w); A: Cheetah. ... 2.00
❑31, Jun 1989 GP (c); GP (w); A: Cheetah. ... 1.75
❑32, Jul 1989 GP (c); GP (w) ... 1.75
❑33, Aug 1989 GP (c); GP (w) ... 1.75
❑34, Sep 1989 GP (c); GP (w); A: Shim'Tar. ... 1.75
❑35, Oct 1989 GP (c); GP (w); A: Shim'Tar. ... 1.75
❑36, Nov 1989 GP (c); GP (w) ... 1.75
❑37, Dec 1989 GP (c); GP (w); A: Superman. ... 1.75
❑38, Jan 1990 GP (c); GP (w); A: Lois Lane. ... 1.75
❑39, Feb 1990 GP (c); GP (w); A: Lois Lane. ... 1.75
❑40, Mar 1990 GP (c); GP (w); A: Lois Lane. ... 1.75
❑41, Apr 1990 GP (c); GP (w); RT (a) 1.75
❑42, May 1990 GP (c); GP (w); RT (a); A: Silver Swan. ... 1.75
❑43, Jun 1990 GP (c); GP (w); RT (a); A: Silver Swan. ... 1.75
❑44, Jul 1990 GP (c); GP (w); RT (a); A: Silver Swan. ... 1.75
❑45, Aug 1990 GP (c); GP (w); RT (a) 1.75
❑46, Sep 1990 GP (c); GP (w); RT (a) 1.75
❑47, Oct 1990 GP (c); GP (w); RT (a); A: Troia. ... 1.75
❑48, Nov 1990 GP (c); GP (w); RT (a) 1.75
❑49, Dec 1990 GP (c); GP (w); A: Princess Diana ... 1.75
❑50, Jan 1991 GP (c); GP (w); MW, SA, BB, CR, KN, RT (a) ... 1.75
❑51, Feb 1991 GP (c); GP (w); RT (a); A: Lord Hermes. ... 1.50
❑52, Mar 1991 GP (c); GP (w); KN (a) 1.50
❑53, Apr 1991 GP (c); GP (w); RT (a); A: Pariah. ... 1.50
❑54, May 1991 GP (c); GP (w); RT (a); A: Doctor Psycho ... 1.50
❑55, Jun 1991 GP (c); GP (w); RT (a); A: Doctor Psycho ... 1.50
❑56, Jul 1991 GP (c); GP (w); RT (a). 1.50
❑57, Aug 1991 (c); GP (w); RT (a) 1.50
❑58, Sep 1991; GP (c); GP (w); RT (a); War of Gods ... 1.50
❑59, Oct 1991; GP (c); GP (w); RT (a); A: Batman. War of Gods ... 1.50
❑60, Nov 1991; GP (c); GP (w); A: Lobo. War of Gods ... 1.50
❑61, Jan 1992; GP (w); War of Gods . 1.50
❑62, Feb 1992 GP (w); RT (a) ... 1.50
❑63, Jun 1992 BB (c); RT (a); A: Deathstroke. ... 1.50
❑64, Jul 1992 BB (c); A: . A: Ed Indelicato. 1.50
❑65, Aug 1992 BB (c) ... 1.50
❑66, Sep 1992 BB (c); 1: Natasha Teranova. ... 1.50
❑67, Oct 1992 BB (c); A: Natasha Teranova. ... 1.50
❑68, Nov 1992 BB (c); FMc (a); A: Natasha Teranova. ... 1.50
❑69, Dec 1992 BB (c); A: Natasha Teranova. ... 1.50
❑70, Jan 1993 BB (c); RT (a); A: Natasha Teranova. ... 1.50
❑71, Feb 1993 BB (c); RT (a); A: Natasha Teranova. ... 1.50
❑72, Mar 1993 BB (c) ... 1.50
❑73, Apr 1993 BB (c) ... 1.50
❑74, May 1993 BB (c); A: White Magician. ... 1.50
❑75, Jun 1993 BB (c) ... 1.50
❑76, Jul 1993 BB (c); A: Doctor Fate.. 1.50
❑77, Aug 1993 BB (c); A: JLA. ... 1.50
❑78, Sep 1993 BB (c); A: Mayfly. ... 1.50
❑79, Oct 1993 BB (c); A: Flash. V: Mayfly. 1.50
❑80, Nov 1993 BB (c); A: Ares. ... 1.50
❑81, Dec 1993 BB (c) ... 1.50
❑82, Jan 1994 BB (c); V: Ares. ... 1.50
❑83, Feb 1994 BB (c) ... 1.50
❑84, Mar 1994 BB (c) ... 1.50
❑85, Apr 1994; BB (c); Mike Deodato Jr.'s first U.S. work ... 10.00
❑86, May 1994 BB (c) ... 4.00
❑87, Jun 1994 BB (c) ... 3.00
❑88, Jul 1994 BB (c); A: Superman.... 3.00
❑89, Aug 1994 BB (c); RT (a); A: Circe (DC). ... 3.00
❑90, Sep 1994 BB (c); A: Artemis ... 3.00
❑91, Nov 1994 BB (c); A: Artemis. ... 3.00
❑92, Dec 1994 BB (c); A: Artemis ... 3.00
❑93, Jan 1995 BB (c) ... 3.00
❑94, Feb 1995 BB (c); V: Cheshire. V: Poison Ivy. ... 2.00
❑95, Mar 1995 BB (c); V: Cheetah. V: Cheshire. V: Poison Ivy. ... 2.00
❑96, Apr 1995 BB (c); V: Joker. ... 2.00
❑97, May 1995 BB (c); V: Joker. ... 2.00
❑98, Jun 1995 BB (c) ... 2.00
❑99, Jul 1995 BB (c) ... 2.00
❑100, Jul 1995; Giant-size; D: Athena. Wonder Woman returns to old uniform 2.95
❑100/Variant, Jul 1995; Giant-size; (c); D: Athena. Wonder Woman returns to old uniform; enhanced cover ... 4.00
❑101, Sep 1995 JBy (c); JBy (w); JBy (a); A: Darkseid. ... 1.95
❑102, Oct 1995 JBy (c); JBy (w); JBy (a); A: Darkseid. ... 1.95
❑103, Nov 1995 JBy (c); JBy (w); JBy (a); A: Darkseid. ... 1.95
❑104, Dec 1995 JBy (c); JBy (w); JBy (a); A: Darkseid. ... 1.95
❑105, Jan 1996 JBy (c); JBy (w); JBy (a) 1.95
❑106, Feb 1996 JBy (c); JBy (w); JBy (a); A: Phantom Stranger. ... 1.95
❑107, Mar 1996 JBy (c); JBy (w); JBy (a); A: Demon. ... 1.95
❑108, Apr 1996 JBy (c); JBy (w); JBy (a); A: Phantom Stranger. ... 1.95
❑109, May 1996 JBy (c); JBy (w); JBy (a); V: Flash (fake). ... 1.95
❑110, Jun 1996 JBy (c); JBy (w); JBy (a); V: Sinestro (fake). ... 1.95
❑111, Jul 1996 JBy (c); JBy (w); JBy (a); V: Doomsday (fake). ... 1.95
❑112, Aug 1996 JBy (c); JBy (w); JBy (a); A: Decay. V: Doomsday (fake).. 1.95
❑113, Sep 1996 JBy (c); JBy (w); JBy (a); A: Wonder Girl. ... 1.95
❑114, Oct 1996 JBy (c); JBy (w); JBy (a); A: Doctor Psycho. ... 1.95
❑115, Nov 1996 JBy (c); JBy (w); JBy (a); A: Cave Carson. ... 1.95
❑116, Dec 1996 JBy (c); JBy (w); JBy (a); A: Cave Carson. ... 1.95
❑117, Jan 1997 (c); JBy (w); JBy (a); 1: Invisible Plane. ... 1.95
❑118, Feb 1997 JL (c); JBy (w); JBy (a); V: Cheetah. ... 1.95
❑119, Mar 1997 JL (c); JBy (w); JBy (a); V: Cheetah. ... 1.95
❑120, Apr 1997; 10th anniversary issue GP (c); JBy (w); JBy (a) ... 2.95
❑121, May 1997 JBy (c); JBy (w); JBy (a); A: Artemis. ... 1.95
❑122, Jun 1997 JBy (c); JBy (w); JBy (a); A: Jason Blood. ... 1.95
❑123, Jul 1997 JBy (w); JBy (a); V: Artemis. ... 1.95
❑124, Aug 1997 JL (c); JBy (w); JBy (a); V: Artemis. ... 1.95
❑125, Sep 1997; JL (c); JBy (w); JBy (a); O: Demon. A: Superman. A: Flash. A: Martian Manhunter. A: Green Lantern. A: Batman. Diana in intensive care.. 1.95

Other grades: Multiply price above by 5/6 for VF/NM • 2/3 for VERY FINE • 1/3 for FINE • 1/5 for VERY GOOD • 1/8 for GOOD

Woody Woodpecker (Walter Lantz...)

Birdbrain bashes head in silly situations

©Dell

World Below

Concrete's Chadwick goes spelunking

©Dark Horse

World of Archie

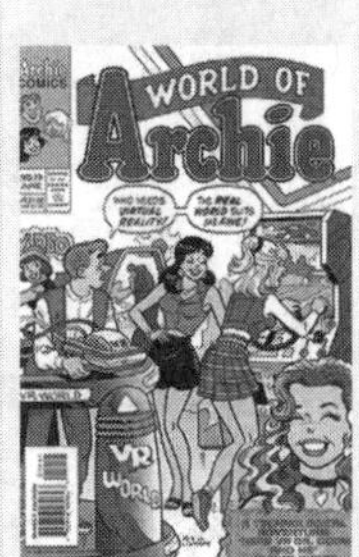

The Riverdale gang strikes again

©Archie

World of Wheels

Can't you just hear the echo effect?

©Charlton

World of Wood

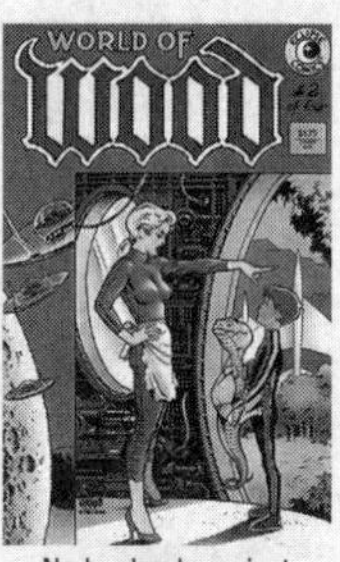

No lumber here, just Wally Wood work

©Eclipse

N-MINT

❑126, Oct 1997; JBy (c); JBy (w); JBy (a); Genesis 1.95
❑127, Nov 1997; JL (c); JBy (w); JBy (a); Diana is turned into a goddess and goes to Olympus 1.95
❑128, Dec 1997; JL (c); JBy (w); JBy (a); A: Egg Fu. Face cover 1.95
❑129, Jan 1998 JL (c); JBy (w); JBy (a); A: Demon. 1.95
❑130, Feb 1998 JBy (c); JBy (w); JBy (a); A: Justice Society of America. A: Jay Garrick. 1.95
❑131, Mar 1998 JBy (c); JBy (w); JBy (a); A: Justice Society of America. A: Jay Garrick. 1.95
❑132, Apr 1998 JBy (c); JBy (w); JBy (a); A: Justice Society of America. A: Jay Garrick. 1.95
❑133, May 1998 JBy (c); JBy (w); JBy (a); A: Justice Society of America. A: Jay Garrick. 1.95
❑134, Jun 1998 JBy (c); JBy (w); JBy (a); A: Dark Angel. 1.95
❑135, Jul 1998 JBy (c); JBy (w); JBy (a); O: Donna Troy. 1.95
❑136, Aug 1998; JBy (c); JBy (w); JBy (a); A: Donna Troy. Diana returns to Earth; Return of Donna Troy 1.99
❑137, Sep 1998 RT (a) 1.99
❑138, Oct 1998 RT (a) 1.99
❑139, Dec 1998; BMc (a); Diana becomes mortal again 1.99
❑139/Ltd., Dec 1998; Signed edition .. 14.95
❑140, Jan 1999 BMc (a); A: Superman. A: Batman. 1.99
❑141, Feb 1999 BMc (a); A: Superman. A: Batman. A: Oblivion. 1.99
❑142, Mar 1999 BMc (a) 1.99
❑143, Apr 1999 BMc (a); 1: Devastation. 1.99
❑144, May 1999 BMc (a); V: Devastation. 1.99
❑145, Jun 1999 BMc (a); V: Devastation. 1.99
❑146, Jul 1999 BMc (a); V: Devastation. 1.99
❑147, Aug 1999 BMc (a) 1.99
❑148, Sep 1999 BMc (a) 1.99
❑149, Oct 1999 BMc (a) 1.99
❑150, Nov 1999 .... 1.99
❑151, Dec 1999 .... 1.99
❑152, Jan 2000 .... 1.99
❑153, Feb 2000 .... 1.99
❑154, Mar 2000 .... 1.99
❑155, Apr 2000 .... 1.99
❑156, May 2000 .... 1.99
❑157, Jun 2000 .... 1.99
❑158, Jul 2000 .... 1.99
❑159, Aug 2000 .... 2.25
❑160, Sep 2000 .... 2.25
❑161, Oct 2000 .... 2.25
❑162, Nov 2000 .... 2.25
❑163, Dec 2000 .... 2.25
❑164, Jan 2001 .... 2.25
❑165, Feb 2001 .... 2.25
❑166, Mar 2001 A: Batman. 2.25
❑167, Apr 2001 .... 2.25
❑168, May 2001 GP (w) 2.25
❑169, Jun 2001 GP (w); GP (a) 2.25
❑170, Jul 2001 .... 2.25
❑171, Aug 2001 .... 2.25

N-MINT

❑172, Sep 2001 .... 2.25
❑173, Oct 2001 .... 2.25
❑174, Nov 2001 JLee (c) 2.25
❑175, Dec 2001; Joker: Last Laugh crossover 2.25
❑176, Jan 2002 .... 2.25
❑177, Feb 2002 .... 2.25
❑178, Mar 2002 .... 2.25
❑179, Apr 2002 .... 2.25
❑180, May 2002 .... 2.25
❑181, Jun 2002 .... 2.25
❑182, Aug 2002 .... 2.25
❑183, Sep 2002 (c) 2.25
❑184, Oct 2002 .... 2.25
❑185, Nov 2002 (c) 2.25
❑186, Dec 2002 .... 2.25
❑187, Feb 2003 .... 2.25
❑188, Mar 2003 .... 2.25
❑189, Apr 2003 JOy, CR (a) 2.25
❑190, May 2003 JOy, CR (a) 2.25
❑191, Jun 2003 JOy, CR (a) 2.25
❑192, Jul 2003 JOy, CR (a) 2.25
❑193, Aug 2003 JOy, CR (a) 2.25
❑194, Sep 2003 JOy, CR (a) 2.25
❑195, Oct 2003 .... 2.25
❑196, Nov 2003 .... 2.25
❑197, Dec 2003 .... 2.25
❑198, Jan 2004 .... 2.25
❑199, Feb 2004 .... 2.25
❑200, Mar 2004 .... 3.95
❑201, Apr 2004 .... 2.25
❑202, May 2004 .... 2.25
❑203, Jun 2004 .... 2.25
❑204, Jul 2004 .... 2.25
❑205, Aug 2004 .... 2.25
❑206, Sep 2004 .... 2.25
❑207, Oct 2004 .... 2.25
❑208, Nov 2004 .... 2.25
❑209, Jan 2005 .... 2.25
❑210, Feb 2005 .... 2.25
❑211, Mar 2005 .... 2.25
❑212, Apr 2005 .... 2.25
❑213, May 2005 .... 2.25
❑214, Jun 2005 .... 25.00
❑215, May 2005 .... 7.00
❑216, Jun 2005 .... 5.00
❑217, Jul 2005 .... 4.00
❑218, Aug 2005 .... 4.00
❑219, Sep 2005 .... 14.00
❑219/2nd, Sep 2005 .... 2.99
❑220, Oct 2005 .... 2.99
❑220/2nd, Oct 2005 .... 2.99
❑221, Nov 2005 .... 2.99
❑222, Dec 2005 .... 2.99
❑223, Jan 2006 .... 2.99
❑224, Feb 2006 .... 2.99
❑225, Mar 2006 .... 2.99
❑226, May 2006 .... 2.99
❑1000000, Nov 1998 .... 3.00
❑Annual 1, ca. 1988 GP (c); GP (w); GP, BB, CS, RA, BMc, JL (a) 2.00
❑Annual 2, Sep 1989 GP (c); GP (w); JDu, GP (a) 2.00
❑Annual 3, ca. 1992; KN (c); Eclipso .. 2.50

N-MINT

❑Annual 4, ca. 1995; (c); BA (a); Year One 3.50
❑Annual 5, ca. 1996; DC (c); JBy (w); DC (a); Legends of the Dead Earth; 1996 Annual 2.95
❑Annual 6, ca. 1997; JBy (w); TP (a); A: Artemis. Pulp Heroes 3.95
❑Annual 7, Sep 1998; (c); RT (a); Ghosts 2.95
❑Annual 8, Sep 1999; JLApe 2.95
❑Special 1, ca. 1992 JOy (c); A: Deathstroke. 1.75

WONDER WOMAN: AMAZONIA
DC

❑1; Oversized; Elseworlds 7.95

WONDER WOMAN: BLUE AMAZON
DC / VERTIGO

❑1, Nov 2003 .... 6.95

WONDER WOMAN: DONNA TROY
DC

❑1, Jun 1998; Girlfrenzy 1.95

WONDER WOMAN GALLERY
DC

❑1, ca. 1996; pin-ups 3.50

WONDER WOMAN: OUR WORLDS AT WAR
DC

❑1, Oct 2001; hardcover 2.95

WONDER WOMAN PLUS
DC

❑1, Jan 1997 .... 2.95

WONDER WOMAN SECRET FILES
DC

❑1, Mar 1998; background on Wonder Woman and supporting cast 4.95
❑2, Jul 1999; background on Wonder Woman and supporting cast 4.95
❑3, May 2002; nn; prestige format one-shot; domestic violence 4.95

WONDER WOMAN: SPIRIT OF TRUTH
DC

❑1/2nd 9.95
❑1, ca. 2000 .... 9.95

WONDER WOMAN: THE HIKETEIA
DC

❑1/HC, Aug 2002, hardcover 24.95
❑Book 1, ca. 2003 .... 17.95

WONDER WOMAN: THE ONCE AND FUTURE STORY
DC

❑1, ca. 1998; prestige format one-shot; domestic violence 4.95

WONDER WOMAN (3RD SERIES)
DC

❑1, Aug 2006 .... 2.99
❑1/Variant, Aug 2006 .... 2.99

WONDERWORLD EXPRESS
THAT OTHER COMIX CO.

❑1 1984, b&w 2.25

WONDERWORLDS
INNOVATION

❑1; Reprints 3.50

Other grades: Multiply price above by 5/6 for VF/NM • 2/3 for VERY FINE • 1/3 for FINE • 1/5 for VERY GOOD • 1/8 for GOOD

WOOD BOY (RAYMOND E. FEIST'S ...)
IMAGE

❑1, ca. 2005 ... 2.95

WOODSTOCK: THE COMIC
MARVEL

❑1 ... 5.95

WOODSY OWL
GOLD KEY

❑1, Nov 1973 ... 8.00
❑2, Feb 1974 ... 5.00
❑3, May 1974 ... 4.00
❑4, Aug 1974 ... 4.00
❑5, Nov 1974 ... 4.00
❑6, Feb 1975 ... 3.00
❑7, May 1975 ... 3.00
❑8, Aug 1975 ... 3.00
❑9, Nov 1975 ... 3.00
❑10, Feb 1976 ... 3.00

WOODY WOODPECKER (WALTER LANTZ...)
DELL

❑16, Dec 1952; Continued from Dell Four-Color issues ... 14.00
❑17, Feb 1953 ... 14.00
❑18, Apr 1953 ... 14.00
❑19, Jun 1953 ... 14.00
❑20, Aug 1953 ... 14.00
❑21, Oct 1953 ... 12.00
❑22, Dec 1953 ... 12.00
❑23, Feb 1954 ... 12.00
❑24, Apr 1954 ... 12.00
❑25, Jun 1954 ... 12.00
❑26, Aug 1954 ... 12.00
❑27, Oct 1954 ... 12.00
❑28, Dec 1954 ... 12.00
❑29, Feb 1955 ... 12.00
❑30, Apr 1955 ... 12.00
❑31, Jun 1955 ... 12.00
❑32, Aug 1955 ... 12.00
❑33, Oct 1955 ... 12.00
❑34, Dec 1955 ... 12.00
❑35, Feb 1956 ... 12.00
❑36, Apr 1956 ... 12.00
❑37, Jun 1956 ... 12.00
❑38, Aug 1956 ... 12.00
❑39, Oct 1956 ... 12.00
❑40, Dec 1956 ... 12.00
❑41, Feb 1957 ... 12.00
❑42, Apr 1957 ... 12.00
❑43, Jun 1957 ... 12.00
❑44, Aug 1957 ... 12.00
❑45, Oct 1957 ... 12.00
❑46, Dec 1957 ... 12.00
❑47, Feb 1958 ... 12.00
❑48, Apr 1958 ... 12.00
❑49, Jun 1958 ... 12.00
❑50, Aug 1958 ... 12.00
❑51, Oct 1958 ... 9.00
❑52, Dec 1958 ... 9.00
❑53, Feb 1959 ... 9.00
❑54, Apr 1959 ... 9.00
❑55, Jun 1959 ... 9.00
❑56, Aug 1959 ... 9.00
❑57, Oct 1959 ... 9.00
❑58, Dec 1959 ... 9.00
❑59, Feb 1960 ... 9.00
❑60, Apr 1960 ... 9.00
❑61, Jun 1960 ... 9.00
❑62, Aug 1960 ... 9.00
❑63, Oct 1960 ... 9.00
❑64, Dec 1960 ... 9.00
❑65, Mar 1961 ... 9.00
❑66, May 1961 ... 9.00
❑67, Jul 1961 ... 9.00
❑68, Sep 1961 ... 9.00
❑69, Nov 1961 ... 9.00
❑70, Jan 1962 ... 9.00
❑71, Mar 1962 ... 9.00
❑72, Jun 1962 ... 9.00
❑73, Oct 1962; Giant-size; Gold Key begins publishing ... 25.00
❑74, Dec 1962; Giant-size ... 25.00
❑75, Mar 1963; Giant-size ... 25.00
❑76, Jun 1963 ... 15.00
❑77, Sep 1963 ... 15.00
❑78, Dec 1963 ... 15.00
❑79, Mar 1964 ... 15.00
❑80, Jun 1964 ... 15.00
❑81, Sep 1964 ... 15.00
❑82, Dec 1964 ... 15.00
❑83, Mar 1965 ... 15.00
❑84, Apr 1965 ... 15.00
❑85, Jun 1965 ... 15.00
❑86, Aug 1965 ... 15.00
❑87, Oct 1965 ... 15.00
❑88, Dec 1965 ... 15.00
❑89, Feb 1966 ... 15.00
❑90, Apr 1966 ... 15.00
❑91, Jun 1966 ... 15.00
❑92, Aug 1966 ... 15.00
❑93, Oct 1966 ... 15.00
❑94, Dec 1966 ... 15.00
❑95, Feb 1967 ... 15.00
❑96, Apr 1967 ... 15.00
❑97, Jun 1967 ... 15.00
❑98, Aug 1967 ... 15.00
❑99, Nov 1967 ... 15.00
❑100, Feb 1968 ... 15.00
❑101, May 1968 ... 10.00
❑102, Aug 1968 ... 10.00
❑103, Nov 1968 ... 10.00
❑104, Feb 1969 ... 10.00
❑105, May 1969 ... 10.00
❑106, Aug 1969 ... 10.00
❑107, Sep 1969 ... 10.00
❑108, Nov 1969 ... 10.00
❑109, Jan 1970 ... 10.00
❑110, Mar 1970 ... 10.00
❑111, May 1970 ... 10.00
❑112, Jul 1970 ... 10.00
❑113, Sep 1970 ... 10.00
❑114, Nov 1970 ... 10.00
❑115, Jan 1971 ... 10.00
❑116, Mar 1971 ... 10.00
❑117, May 1971 ... 10.00
❑118, Jul 1971 ... 10.00
❑119, Sep 1971 ... 10.00
❑120, Nov 1971 ... 10.00
❑121, Jan 1972 ... 6.00
❑122, Mar 1972 ... 6.00
❑123, May 1972 ... 6.00
❑124, Jul 1972 ... 6.00
❑125, Sep 1972 ... 6.00
❑126, Nov 1972 ... 6.00
❑127, Jan 1973 ... 6.00
❑128, Mar 1973 ... 6.00
❑129, May 1973 ... 6.00
❑130, Jul 1973 ... 6.00
❑131, Sep 1973 ... 2.50
❑132, Oct 1973 ... 2.50
❑133, Nov 1973 ... 2.50
❑134, Jan 1974 ... 2.50
❑135, Mar 1974 ... 2.50
❑136, May 1974 ... 2.50
❑137, Jul 1974 ... 2.50
❑138, Sep 1974 ... 2.50
❑139, Oct 1974 ... 2.50
❑140, Nov 1974 ... 2.50
❑141, Jan 1975 ... 2.50
❑142, Mar 1975 ... 2.50
❑143, May 1975 ... 2.50
❑144, Jul 1975 ... 2.50
❑145, Sep 1975 ... 2.50
❑146, Oct 1975 ... 2.50
❑147, Nov 1975 ... 2.50
❑148, Jan 1976 ... 2.50
❑149, Mar 1976 ... 2.50
❑150, May 1976 ... 2.50
❑151, Jul 1976 ... 2.50
❑152, Aug 1976 ... 2.50
❑153, Sep 1976 ... 2.50
❑154, Oct 1976 ... 2.50
❑155, Dec 1976 ... 2.50
❑156, Feb 1977 ... 2.50
❑157, Apr 1977 ... 2.50
❑158, Jun 1977 ... 2.50
❑159, Aug 1977 ... 2.50
❑160, Oct 1977 ... 2.50
❑161, Dec 1977 ... 2.50
❑162, Jan 1978 ... 2.50
❑163, Feb 1978 ... 2.50
❑164, Mar 1978 ... 2.50
❑165, Apr 1978 ... 2.50
❑166, May 1978 ... 2.50
❑167, Jun 1978 ... 2.50
❑168, Jul 1978 ... 2.50
❑169, Aug 1978 ... 2.50
❑170, Sep 1978 ... 2.50
❑171, Oct 1978 ... 2.00
❑172, Nov 1978 ... 2.00
❑173, Dec 1978 ... 2.00
❑174, Jan 1979 ... 2.00
❑175, Feb 1979 ... 2.00
❑176, Mar 1979 ... 2.00
❑177, Apr 1979 ... 2.00
❑178, May 1979 ... 2.00
❑179, Jun 1979 ... 2.00
❑180, Jul 1979 ... 2.00
❑181, Aug 1979 ... 2.00
❑182, Sep 1979 ... 2.00
❑183, Oct 1979 ... 2.00
❑184, Nov 1979 ... 2.00
❑185, Dec 1979 ... 2.00
❑186, Jan 1980 ... 2.00
❑187, Feb 1980 ... 2.00
❑188, Mar 1980 ... 10.00
❑189 1980 ... 10.00
❑190 1980 ... 25.00
❑191 1980 ... 25.00
❑193 1981; #192 never printed ... 15.00
❑194, Oct 1981 ... 15.00
❑195, Dec 1982 ... 15.00
❑196, Feb 1982 ... 15.00
❑197, Apr 1982 ... 15.00
❑198, 1982 ... 15.00
❑199, 1983 ... 15.00
❑200, 1984 ... 15.00
❑201, 1984 ... 15.00

WOODY WOODPECKER (HARVEY)
HARVEY

❑1, Sep 1991 ... 1.50
❑2, Nov 1991 ... 1.25
❑3, Jan 1992 ... 1.25
❑4, Mar 1992 ... 1.25
❑5, Jun 1992 ... 1.25
❑6, Sep 1992 ... 1.25
❑7 ... 1.25
❑8, Jun 1993 ... 1.25
❑9 ... 1.50
❑10 ... 1.50
❑11 ... 1.50
❑12 ... 1.50

WOODY WOODPECKER 50TH ANNIVERSARY SPECIAL
HARVEY

❑1, Oct 1991; Reprints ... 2.50

WOODY WOODPECKER ADVENTURES
HARVEY

❑1, Reprints ... 1.25
❑2 ... 1.25
❑3 ... 1.25

WOODY WOODPECKER AND FRIENDS
HARVEY

❑1, Dec 1991; Reprints ... 1.25
❑2, Feb 1992; Reprints ... 1.25
❑3, Apr 1992; Reprints ... 1.25
❑4, Jun 1992; Reprints ... 1.25

WOODY WOODPECKER DIGEST
HARVEY

❑1; Reprints ... 1.75

WOODY WOODPECKER GIANT SIZE
HARVEY

❑1 ... 2.25

WOODY WOODPECKER'S CHRISTMAS PARADE
GOLD KEY

❑1, Nov 1968 ... 20.00

WOODY WOODPECKER SUMMER FUN
GOLD KEY

❑1, Sep 1966 ... 50.00

WOODY WOODPECKER SUMMER SPECIAL
HARVEY

❑1, Oct 1990 ... 1.95

Other grades: Multiply price above by 5/6 for VF/NM • 2/3 for VERY FINE • 1/3 for FINE • 1/5 for VERY GOOD • 1/8 for GOOD

World's Finest Comics

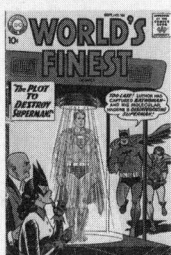

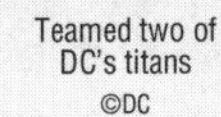

Teamed two of DC's titans
©DC

World's Worst Comics Awards

Golden Turkeys for the comics industry
©Kitchen Sink

Worst from Mad

Early annuals preceded Super Specials
©E.C.

Wrath

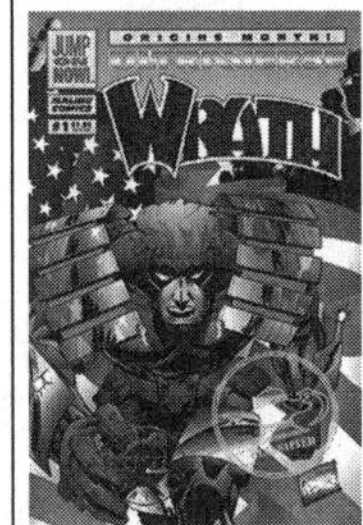

He worked for Aladdin, but was no genie
©Malibu

Wrath of the Spectre

Adventure reprints plus a new story
©DC

N-MINT

WOOFERS AND HOOTERS
FANTAGRAPHICS / EROS
❑1, b&w ... 2.50

WORDS & PICTURES
MAVERICK
❑1, Fal 1994, b&w ... 3.95
❑2, Spr 1995, b&w ... 3.95

WORDSMITH
RENEGADE
❑1, Aug 1985, b&w ... 1.70
❑2, Oct 1985, b&w ... 1.70
❑3, Dec 1985, b&w ... 1.70
❑4, Dec 1985, b&w ... 1.70
❑5, May 1986, b&w ... 1.70
❑6, Aug 1986 ... 1.70
❑7, Nov 1986 ... 2.00
❑8, Nov 1986 ... 2.00
❑9, May 1987 ... 2.00
❑10, Aug 1987 ... 2.00
❑11, Nov 1987 ... 2.00
❑12, Jan 1988 ... 2.00

WORDSMITH
CALIBER
❑1 1996 ... 2.95
❑2 1996 ... 2.95
❑3 1996 ... 2.95
❑4 1996 ... 2.95
❑5 1997 ... 2.95
❑6 1997 ... 2.95
❑Book 1, b&w; Reprints ... 14.95
❑Book 2, b&w; Reprints ... 14.95

WORD WARRIORS
LITERACY VOLUNTEERS
❑1, b&w; Ms. Tree, Jon Sable ... 1.50

WORGARD: VIKING BERSERKIR
STRONGHOLD
❑1, Oct 1997, b&w ... 2.95

WORKSHOP
BLUE COMET
❑1 ... 2.95

WORLD BANK
PUBLIC SERVICES INTERNATIONAL
❑1, educational comic; no indicia ... 2.95

WORLD BELOW
DARK HORSE
❑1, Mar 1999 ... 2.50
❑2, Apr 1999 ... 2.50
❑3, May 1999 ... 2.50
❑4, Jun 1999 ... 2.50

WORLD BELOW: DEEPER AND STRANGER
DARK HORSE
❑1, Dec 1999, b&w ... 2.95
❑2, Jan 2000, b&w ... 2.95
❑3, Feb 2000, b&w ... 2.95
❑4, Mar 2000, b&w ... 2.95

WORLD CLASS COMICS
IMAGE
❑1, Aug 2002, b&w; hardcover ... 4.95

WORLD EXISTS FOR ME
TOKYOPOP
❑1, Dec 2005 ... 9.99

N-MINT

WORLD HARDBALL LEAGUE
TITUS
❑1, Aug 1994, b&w ... 2.75
❑2, Jan 1995, b&w ... 2.75

WORLD OF ARCHIE
ARCHIE
❑1, Aug 1992 ... 2.00
❑2, Nov 1992 ... 1.50
❑3, Feb 1993 ... 1.50
❑4, May 1993 ... 1.50
❑5, Aug 1993 ... 1.50
❑6, Nov 1993 ... 1.50
❑7, Feb 1994 ... 1.50
❑8, Apr 1994 ... 1.50
❑9, Jun 1994 ... 1.50
❑10, Aug 1994 ... 1.50
❑11, Sep 1994 ... 1.50
❑12, Nov 1994 ... 1.50
❑13, Jan 1995 ... 1.50
❑14, Mar 1995 ... 1.50
❑15, Jun 1995 ... 1.50
❑16, Sep 1995 ... 1.50
❑17, Dec 1995 ... 1.50
❑18, Mar 1996 ... 1.50
❑19, Jun 1996 DDC (a) ... 1.50
❑20, Sep 1996 ... 1.50
❑21, Dec 1996; Archie and Veronica run for class president ... 1.50
❑22, Mar 1997 ... 1.50

WORLD OF GINGER FOX
COMICO
❑1 ... 6.95
❑1/HC ... 27.95

WORLD OF HARTZ
TOKYOPOP
❑1, May 2004 ... 9.99

WORLD OF KRYPTON (1ST SERIES)
DC
❑1, Jul 1979 MA, HC (a); O: Jor-El. ... 2.00
❑2, Aug 1979 HC (a) ... 2.00
❑3, Sep 1979 HC (a) ... 2.00

WORLD OF KRYPTON (2ND SERIES)
DC
❑1, Dec 1987 JBy (c); JBy (w) ... 2.00
❑2, Jan 1988 JBy (w) ... 2.00
❑3, Feb 1988 JBy (c); JBy (w) ... 2.00
❑4, Mar 1988 JBy (c); JBy (w) ... 2.00

WORLD OF METROPOLIS
DC
❑1, Aug 1988 (c); JBy (w); FMc, DG (a) ... 1.50
❑2, Sep 1988 (c); JBy (w); DG (a) ... 1.50
❑3, Oct 1988 (c); JBy (w); DG (a) ... 1.50
❑4, Nov 1988 (c); JBy (w); DG (a) ... 1.50

WORLD OF SMALLVILLE
DC
❑1, Apr 1988 (c); JBy (w); AA, KS (a) ... 1.50
❑2, May 1988 (c); JBy (w); AA, KS (a) ... 1.50
❑3, Jun 1988 (c); JBy (w); AA, KS (a) ... 1.50
❑4, Jul 1988 (c); JBy (w); AA, KS (a) 1.50

WORLD OF WHEELS
CHARLTON
❑17, Oct 1967; Previous issues published as Drag-Strip Hotrodders ... 12.00

N-MINT

❑18, Dec 1967 ... 12.00
❑19, Feb 1968 ... 12.00
❑20, Apr 1968 ... 12.00
❑21, Aug 1968 ... 8.00
❑22, Oct 1968 ... 8.00
❑23, Dec 1968 ... 8.00
❑24, Feb 1969 ... 8.00
❑25, Apr 1969 ... 8.00
❑26, Jun 1969 ... 8.00
❑27, Aug 1969 ... 8.00
❑28, Oct 1969 ... 8.00
❑29, Dec 1969 ... 8.00
❑30, Feb 1970 ... 8.00
❑31, Apr 1970 ... 8.00
❑32, Jun 1970 ... 8.00

WORLD OF WOOD
ECLIPSE
❑1, May 1986; DSt (c); WW (w); WW, DA (a); Indicia says #2 ... 2.00
❑2, May 1986; WW, DSt (c); WW (w); WW (a); Indicia for #1 corrected ... 2.00
❑3, Jun 1986; AW, WW (c); WW (w); WW (a); centaur ... 2.00
❑4, Jun 1986 WW (c); WW (w); WW (a) ... 2.00
❑5, Feb 1989, b&w; (c); AW, WW (a); reprints Flying Saucers #1; reprints Forbidden Worlds #3 ... 2.00

WORLD OF X-RAY
PYRAMID
❑1, b&w ... 1.80

WORLD OF YOUNG MASTER
NEW COMICS
❑1, Mar 1989, b&w; Demonblade ... 1.95

WORLD'S BEST COMICS: SILVER AGE DC ARCHIVE SAMPLER
DC
❑1, Aug 2004 ... 0.99

WORLDS COLLIDE
DC / MILESTONE
❑1, Jul 1994 1: Rift ... 2.50
❑1/CS, Jul 1994; 1: Rift. vinyl clings; Include press-apply stick-ons; enhanced cover ... 4.00
❑1/Platinum, Jul 1994; Platinum edition ... 4.00

WORLD'S FINEST
DC
❑1, ca. 1990 SR (c); DaG (w); SR (a) 5.00
❑2, ca. 1990 SR (c); DaG (w); SR (a) 4.50
❑3, ca. 1990 SR (c); DaG (w); SR (a) 4.50

WORLD'S FINEST COMICS
DC
❑84, Oct 1956 ... 235.00
❑85, Dec 1956 (c) ... 235.00
❑86, Feb 1957 (c) ... 235.00
❑87, Apr 1957 (c) ... 235.00
❑88, Jun 1957; (c); A: Lex Luthor. A: Joker. Lex Luthor & The Joker team-up for the first time ... 235.00
❑89, Aug 1957 (c) ... 235.00
❑90, Oct 1957 (c); A: Batwoman. ... 235.00
❑91, Dec 1957 (c) ... 175.00
❑92, Feb 1958 (c) ... 175.00
❑93, Apr 1958 (c) ... 175.00

❑94, Jun 1958 (c); O: Superman-Batman team. A: Lex Luthor. 525.00
❑95, Aug 1958 (c) 175.00
❑96, Sep 1958 (c); JK (a) 175.00
❑97, Oct 1958 (c); JK (a) 175.00
❑98, Dec 1959 (c); JK (a) 175.00
❑99, Feb 1959 (c); JK (a) 175.00
❑100, Mar 1959; (c); A: Lex Luthor. Luthor conquers Kandor 260.00
❑101, May 1959 (c) 105.00
❑102, Jun 1959 (c) 105.00
❑103, Aug 1959 (c) 105.00
❑104, Sep 1959 (c); A: Lex Luthor. A: Batwoman 105.00
❑105, Nov 1959 (c) 105.00
❑106, Dec 1959 (c) 105.00
❑107, Feb 1960 (c) 105.00
❑108, Mar 1960 (c) 105.00
❑109, May 1960 (c); CS (a) 105.00
❑110, Jun 1960 (c) 105.00
❑111, Aug 1960 (c); 1: Clock King 85.00
❑112, Sep 1960 (c) 85.00
❑113, Nov 1960 (c) 85.00
❑114, Dec 1960 (c) 85.00
❑115, Feb 1961 (c) 85.00
❑116, Mar 1961 (c) 85.00
❑117, May 1961 (c); A: Lex Luthor. A: Batwoman 85.00
❑118, Jun 1961 (c) 85.00
❑119, Aug 1961 (c) 85.00
❑120, Sep 1961 (c) 85.00
❑121, Nov 1961 (c); JM (a) 85.00
❑122, Dec 1961 (c) 75.00
❑123, Feb 1962 (c) 75.00
❑124, Mar 1962 (c) 75.00
❑125, May 1962 (c) 75.00
❑126, Jun 1962 (c); A: Lex Luthor. 75.00
❑127, Aug 1962 (c) 75.00
❑128, Sep 1962 (c) 75.00
❑129, Nov 1962 (c); A: Lex Luthor. A: Joker. 75.00
❑130, Dec 1962 (c); JM (a) 75.00
❑131, Feb 1963 (c) 75.00
❑132, Mar 1963 (c) 75.00
❑133, May 1963; (c); Aqua-Girl tryout 75.00
❑134, Jun 1963 (c); A: Miss Arrowette. 75.00
❑135, Aug 1963 (c) 75.00
❑136, Sep 1963 (c) 75.00
❑137, Nov 1963 (c); A: Lex Luthor. 75.00
❑138, Dec 1963 (c); JM (a) 75.00
❑139, Feb 1964 (c) 75.00
❑140, Mar 1964 (c); A: Clayface. 75.00
❑141, May 1964; (c); Back-up reprint stories begin 75.00
❑142, Jun 1964 (c); CS (a); 1: Composite Superman. A: Legion of Super-Heroes. 75.00
❑143, Aug 1964 (c); CS (a) 52.00
❑144, Sep 1964 (c); CS (a); A: Clayface. A: Brainiac 52.00
❑145, Nov 1964 (c); CS (a) 52.00
❑146, Dec 1964 (c); CS (a) 52.00
❑147, Feb 1965 (c); CS (a) 52.00
❑148, Mar 1965; (c); CS (a); A: Lex Luthor. A: Clayface. Congorilla back-ups begin 52.00
❑149, May 1965 (c); CS (a) 52.00
❑150, Jun 1965 (c); CS (a) 52.00
❑151, Aug 1965 (c) 50.00
❑152, Sep 1965 (c) 50.00
❑153, Nov 1965 (c); A: Lex Luthor. 45.00
❑154, Dec 1965 (c); A: Super-Sons. 45.00
❑155, Feb 1966 (c); RMo (a) 45.00
❑156, Mar 1966 (c); 1: Bizarro Batman. A: Joker. A: Bizarro Superman. 55.00
❑157, May 1966; (c); A: Super-Sons. Imaginary story 45.00
❑158, Jun 1966 (c); CS (a); A: Brainiac. 45.00
❑159, Aug 1966 (c); A: Joker. 45.00
❑160, Sep 1966 (c) 45.00
❑161, Nov 1966; Giant-size; (c); aka 80 Page Giant #G-28 45.00
❑162, Nov 1966 (c); CS (a) 38.00
❑163, Dec 1966 (c) 38.00
❑164, Feb 1967 (c); CS (a); A: Brainiac. 38.00
❑165, Mar 1967 (c) 38.00
❑166, May 1967 (c); RMo (a); A: Joker. 38.00
❑167, Jun 1967; (c); Imaginary story. 38.00
❑168, Aug 1967 (c); CS (a) 38.00
❑169, Sep 1967 (c); CS (a) 38.00
❑170, Nov 1967; Giant-size; (c); aka 80 Page Giant #G-40 38.00
❑171, Nov 1967 (c) 38.00
❑172, Dec 1967; (c); CS (a); A: Lex Luthor. Imaginary story; Clark and Bruce as brothers 38.00
❑173, Feb 1968; (c); CS (a); reprints from Action #241 38.00
❑174, Mar 1968 NA (c); JAb (a) 38.00
❑175, May 1968 (c); NA (a) 38.00
❑176, Jun 1968 (c); NA (a) 38.00
❑177, Aug 1968 (c); CS (a); A: Lex Luthor. A: Joker. 38.00
❑178, Sep 1968 (c); CS (a) 30.00
❑179, Nov 1968; (c); aka 80 Page Giant #G-52 30.00
❑180, Nov 1968 (c); RA (a) 30.00
❑181, Dec 1968 (c); RA (a) 25.00
❑182, Feb 1969 (c); RA (a) 25.00
❑183, Mar 1969; (c); RA (a); A: Lex Luthor. A: Brainiac. Reprints story from House of Mystery #80 25.00
❑184, May 1969 (c) 25.00
❑185, Jun 1969 (c); RA (a) 25.00
❑186, Aug 1969 (c); RA (a) 25.00
❑187, Sep 1969 CS (c); RA (a); O: Green Arrow 25.00
❑188, Oct 1969; Giant-size; (c); aka Giant #G-64 25.00
❑189, Nov 1969 (c); RA, RMo (a); A: Lex Luthor. 25.00
❑190, Dec 1969 (c); A: Lex Luthor. 25.00
❑191, Feb 1970 (c) 20.00
❑192, Mar 1970 (c) 20.00
❑193, May 1970 CS (c) 20.00
❑194, Jun 1970 (c); RA (a) 20.00
❑195, Aug 1970 (c); RA (a) 20.00
❑196, Sep 1970 (c); CS (a) 20.00
❑197, Nov 1970; Giant-size; (c); JK (a); aka Giant #G-76 20.00
❑198, Nov 1970; (c); DD (a); Superman/Flash race 80.00
❑199, Dec 1970; (c); DD (a); Superman/Flash race 80.00
❑200, Feb 1971 (c); DD (a); A: Robin. 16.00
❑201, Mar 1971 (c); DD (a); A: Doctor Fate. A: Green Lantern. 16.00
❑202, May 1971 (c); DD (a) 16.00
❑203, Jun 1971 (c); DD (a); A: Aquaman 16.00
❑204, Aug 1971 (c); MA, DD (a); A: Wonder Woman. 16.00
❑205, Sep 1971 (c); MA, FF, DD (a); A: Teen Titans. 16.00
❑206, Nov 1971; Giant-size; DG (c); JM (a); aka Giant #G-88 16.00
❑207, Nov 1971 (c); GC, DD (a) 16.00
❑208, Dec 1971 NA (c); DD (a); A: Doctor Fate 16.00
❑209, Feb 1972 (c); DD (a); A: Hawkman. 16.00
❑210, Mar 1972 (c); DD (a); A: Green Arrow 16.00
❑211, May 1972 (c); DD (a) 16.00
❑212, Jun 1972 (c); DD (a); A: Martian Manhunter. 16.00
❑213, Sep 1972 (c); DD (a); A: Atom. 14.00
❑214, Nov 1972 (c); DD (a); A: Vigilante. 14.00
❑215, Jan 1973 (c); DD (a); A: Super-Sons. 14.00
❑216, Mar 1973 (c); MA, DD (a); A: Super-Sons. 14.00
❑217, May 1973 (c); MA, DD (a); A: Metamorpho 14.00
❑218, Aug 1973 (c); DC, DD (a) 14.00
❑219, Oct 1973 (c); DD (a) 14.00
❑220, Dec 1973 (c); MA, DD (a) 14.00
❑221, Feb 1974 (c); MA, DD (a); A: Super-Sons. 14.00
❑222, Apr 1974 (c); DD (a); A: Super-Sons. 14.00
❑223, Jun 1974; Giant-size; NA, CS (a); O: Deadman. giant; Reprints from World's Finest Comics #77 and #142 14.00
❑224, Aug 1974; Giant-size; giant 14.00
❑225, Oct 1974; Giant-size; giant 14.00
❑226, Dec 1974; Giant-size; NA (a); A: Metamorpho. giant 14.00
❑227, Feb 1975; Giant-size; A: Deadman. giant 14.00
❑228, Mar 1975; Giant-size A: Super-Sons. 14.00
❑229, Apr 1975 6.00
❑230, May 1975; Giant-size; giant 6.00
❑231, Jul 1975 A: Super-Sons. 6.00
❑232, Sep 1975 6.00
❑233, Oct 1975 6.00
❑234, Dec 1975 6.00
❑235, Jan 1976 6.00
❑236, Mar 1976 6.00
❑237, Apr 1976 6.00
❑238, Jun 1976 6.00
❑239, Jul 1976 6.00
❑240, Sep 1976 6.00
❑241, Oct 1976 6.00
❑242, Dec 1976 A: Super-Sons. 6.00
❑243, Feb 1977 6.00
❑244, May 1977; Giant-size; NA (c); MN, MA, JL (a); Giant-size 6.00
❑245, Jul 1977; Giant-size; NA (c); MN, MA, GM, CS (a); A: Martian Manhunter. Giant-size 6.00
❑246, Sep 1977; NA (c); MN, MA, GM, DH, KS (a); 1: Baron Blitzkrieg. A: Justice League of America. Giant-size 6.00
❑247, Nov 1977; Giant-size; DG, JL (c); GM, KS (a); A: Justice League of America. Giant-size 6.00
❑248, Jan 1978; Giant-size; DG, JL (c); GM, DG, KS (a); Giant-size 6.00
❑249, Mar 1978; Giant-size; JA (c); SD (w); SD, KS (a); A: Phantom Stranger. Giant-size 6.00
❑250, May 1978; Giant-size; JA (c); SD (w); SD, GT (a); Giant-size 6.00
❑251, Jul 1978; Giant-size; JA (c); SD (w); SD, BL, GT, RE, JAb (a); 1: Count Vertigo. A: Speedy. Giant-size 6.00
❑252, Sep 1978; Giant-size; JA (c); SD (w); SD, GT, JAb (a); A: Poison Ivy. Giant-size 6.00
❑253, Nov 1978; Giant-size; JA (c); SD (w); DN, SD, KS (a); Giant-size; No ads begins; wraparound cover 6.00
❑254, Jan 1979; Giant-size; JA (c); SD (w); DN, SD, GT, KS (a); Giant-size. 6.00
❑255, Mar 1979; JA (c); SD (w); DN, SD, JL, KS, DA (a); A: Bulletman. A: Bulletgirl. Giant-size 6.00
❑256, May 1979; Giant-size; (c); DN, MA, DD, KS (a); Giant-size 6.00
❑257, Jul 1979; Giant-size; JA (c); DN, FMc, RB, GT, DD, KS, RT (a); Giant-size 6.00
❑258, Sep 1979; Giant-size; DG (c); DN, RB, DG, JL, KS, RT (a); Giant-size 6.00
❑259, Nov 1979; RB, DG (c); DN, MN, RB, DG, MR, KS (a); Giant-size; Ads begin again 6.00
❑260, Jan 1980; RB, DG (c); DN, MN, RB, DG (a); Giant-size 6.00
❑261, Mar 1980; DG, RA (c); RB, DG, RT (a); Giant-size 6.00
❑262, May 1980; DG, RA (c); DN, DG, JSa, DA, RT (a); Giant-size 6.00
❑263, Jul 1980; DG, RA (c); DN, RB, DG (a); A: Super-Sons. Giant-size 6.00
❑264, Sep 1980 DG (c); DN, RB, DG (a) 6.00
❑265, Nov 1980 JA (c); DN, DG, RE (a) 6.00
❑266, Jan 1981 JA (c); DN, RB (a); 1: Lady Lunar. 6.00
❑267, Mar 1981 RB, DG (c); DN, RB, DG (a); A: Challengers of the Unknown. 6.00
❑268, May 1981 DG (c); DN, RT (a) 6.00
❑269, Jul 1981 RB, DG (c); DN, FMc, RB, DA (a); 1: Doctor Jymbi Humm. 6.00
❑270, Aug 1981 (c); DN, RB, RT (a) 6.00
❑271, Sep 1981 (c); FMc, RB (a); O: Superman/Batman team in World's Finest. 4.00
❑272, Oct 1981 DG, RA (c); DN, RB (a) 4.00
❑273, Nov 1981 (c); DN, JSa, DA (a). 4.00
❑274, Dec 1981 DG, RA (c); DN, GC (a) 4.00
❑275, Jan 1982 (c); DN, FMc, RB, DS, DA (a) 4.00
❑276, Feb 1982 GP (c); DN, RB, CI, DS, DA (a) 4.00
❑277, Mar 1982 GP (c); DN, DH, DS, RT (a) 4.00
❑278, Apr 1982 (c); DN, RB, DS (a); A: Hawkman. 4.00

Wulf the Barbarian

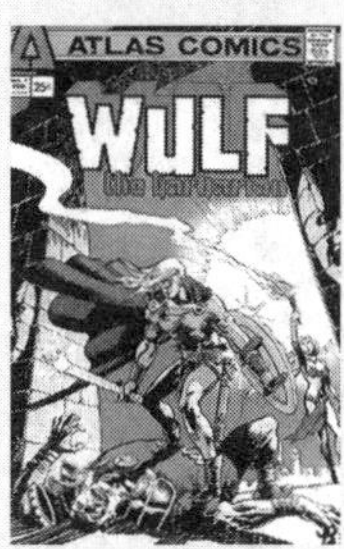

Conan copy at Atlas/ Seaboard

©Atlas-Seaboard

X

Dark Horse hero marks the spot

©Dark Horse

X-Calibre

Swashbuckling Nightcrawler seeks mutants

©Marvel

Xena: Warrior Princess (Vol. 1)

High-pitched screamer comes to comics

©Topps

Xenozoic Tales

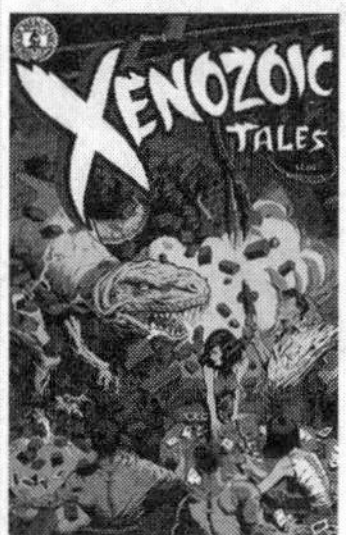

Dinosaurs return after disaster

©Kitchen Sink

	N-MINT
❑279, May 1982 (c); DN, KP (a); A: Kid Eternity.	4.00
❑280, Jun 1982 RB (c); DN, RB (a); A: Kid Eternity.	4.00
❑281, Jul 1982 GK (c); DN, IN (a); A: Kid Eternity.	4.00
❑282, Aug 1982 GK (c); FMc, CI, GK, IN (a); A: Kid Eternity.	4.00
❑283, Sep 1982 RB (c); FMc, GT, GK, IN (a); V: Composite Superman.	4.00
❑284, Oct 1982 KG (c); GT, DS (a); A: Legion. A: Composite Superman.	4.00
❑285, Nov 1982 DG, FM (c); RB (a); A: Zatanna.	4.00
❑286, Dec 1982 RB, DG (c); RB (a); A: Zatanna.	4.00
❑287, Jan 1983 RB, RT (c)	4.00
❑288, Feb 1983 DG (c)	4.00
❑289, Mar 1983 GK (c)	4.00
❑290, Apr 1983 KJ (c); TD (a)	4.00
❑291, May 1983 TD (a)	4.00
❑292, Jun 1983 KJ (c)	4.00
❑293, Jul 1983 KJ (c); TD (a); A: Null. A: Void.	4.00
❑294, Aug 1983 KJ (c)	4.00
❑295, Sep 1983 KJ (c); FMc (a)	4.00
❑296, Oct 1983 RA, KJ (c); RA (a)	4.00
❑297, Nov 1983 GC, KJ (c); GC (a)	4.00
❑298, Dec 1983 DG (c)	4.00
❑299, Jan 1984 KJ (c); GC (a)	4.00
❑300, Feb 1984; Giant-size; DG (c); GP, RA, KJ (a); A: Justice League of America. A: Titans. A: Outsiders. Giant-size	4.00
❑301, Mar 1984 KJ (c)	3.00
❑302, Apr 1984 KJ (c); DG, NA (a)	3.00
❑303, May 1984 KJ (c)	3.00
❑304, Jun 1984 KJ (c); O: Null. O: Void.	3.00
❑305, Jul 1984 KJ (c)	3.00
❑306, Aug 1984 KJ (c)	3.00
❑307, Sep 1984 KJ (c)	3.00
❑308, Oct 1984 KJ (c); KB (w); GT (a)	3.00
❑309, Nov 1984; KJ (c); KB (w); AA (a); Bonus Book	3.00
❑310, Dec 1984 KJ (c); A: Sonik.	3.00
❑311, Jan 1985 KJ (c); A: Monitor.	3.00
❑312, Feb 1985 (c); AA (a)	3.00
❑313, Mar 1985 KJ (c); AA (a)	3.00
❑314, Apr 1985 KJ (c); AA (a); A: Monitor.	3.00
❑315, May 1985	3.00
❑316, Jun 1985	3.00
❑317, Jul 1985	3.00
❑318, Aug 1985 RT (c); AA (a); A: Sonik.	3.00
❑319, Sep 1985 RT (c); AA (a)	3.00
❑320, Oct 1985	3.00
❑321, Nov 1985 RB (c); AA (a); V: Chronos.	3.00
❑322, Dec 1985 KG (c); KG (a)	3.00
❑323, Jan 1986 DG (c); AA (a)	3.00

WORLD'S FINEST: OUR WORLDS AT WAR
DC

❑1, Oct 2001; hardcover; Our Worlds At War; Casualties of War; Follows Action Comics #782	2.95

WORLD'S FUNNEST COMICS
MOORDAM

	N-MINT
❑1, Mar 1998, b&w; Cray-Baby Adventures, Mr. Beat	2.95

WORLDS OF H.P. LOVECRAFT: BEYOND THE WALL OF SLEEP
TOME

❑1	2.95

WORLDS OF H.P. LOVECRAFT: DAGON
CALIBER

❑1, b&w	2.95

WORLDS OF H.P. LOVECRAFT: THE ALCHEMIST
TOME

❑1	2.95

WORLDS OF H.P. LOVECRAFT: THE MUSIC OF ERICH ZANN
CALIBER

❑1, b&w	2.95

WORLDS OF H.P. LOVECRAFT: THE PICTURE IN THE HOUSE
CALIBER

❑1, b&w	2.95

WORLDS UNKNOWN
MARVEL

❑1, May 1973; (c); GK (w); GK, AT (a); adapted from Frederik Pohl story	17.00
❑2, Jul 1973; (c); VM, GK (a); adapted from L. Sprague de Camp story; adapted from Keith Laumer story	10.00
❑3, Sep 1973; WH (c); RA, WH (a); adapted from Harry Bates story	7.00
❑4, Nov 1973; (c); JB, DG (a); adapted from Frederic Brown story	5.00
❑5, Feb 1974; (c); JM, DA (a); adapted from A.E. Van Vogt story	5.00
❑6, Apr 1974; (c); adapted from Theodore Sturgeon story; Marvel Value Stamp #35: Killraven	5.00
❑7, Jun 1974; (c); GT (a); adapted from Brian Clemens screenplay; Marvel Value Stamp #32: Red Skull	5.00
❑8, Aug 1974; (c); GT (a); Final Issue; Marvel Value Stamp #75: Morbius	5.00

WORLD'S WORST COMICS AWARDS
KITCHEN SINK

❑1 1990, b&w	2.50
❑2, Jan 1991, b&w	2.50

WORLD WAR II: 1946
ANTARCTIC

❑1, Jul 1999; Families of Altered Wars #62	2.50
❑2, Aug 1999; Families of Altered Wars #63	2.50
❑3, Sep 1999; Families of Altered Wars #64	2.50
❑4, Oct 1999; Families of Altered Wars #65	2.50
❑5, Nov 1999; Families of Altered Wars #66	2.50
❑6, Dec 1999; Families of Altered Wars #67	2.50
❑7, Jan 2000; Families of Altered Wars #68	2.50

	N-MINT
❑8, Feb 2000; Families of Altered Wars #69	2.50
❑9, Mar 2000; Families of Altered Wars #70	2.50
❑10, Apr 2000; Families of Altered Wars #71	2.50
❑11, May 2000; Families of Altered Wars #72	2.50
❑12, Jun 2000; Families of Altered Wars #73	2.50

WORLD WAR II: 1946/FAMILIES OF ALTERED WARS
ANTARCTIC

❑1, Jul 1998, b&w; Compilation Edition	3.95
❑1/2nd, Oct 1998	3.95
❑2, Nov 1998, b&w; has indicia from #1	3.95
❑2/2nd, Aug 1998	3.95

WORLD WITHOUT END
DC

❑1, ca. 1990	2.50
❑2, ca. 1990	2.50
❑3, ca. 1990	2.50
❑4, ca. 1990	2.50
❑5, ca. 1990	2.50
❑6, ca. 1990	2.50

WORMWOOD GENTLEMAN CORPSE: THE TASTER
IDEA & DESIGN WORKS

❑1, May 2006	3.99

WORON'S WORLDS
ILLUSTRATION

❑1/A	2.95
❑1/B; Adults-only cover	2.95
❑1/A/2nd	3.25
❑1/B/2nd	3.25
❑2/A	2.95
❑2/B; Adults-only cover	2.95
❑3/A, Nov 1994	3.25
❑3/B, Nov 1994; Adults-only cover	3.25

WORST FROM MAD
E.C.

❑nn, ca. 1958; Magazine-sized; no number	400.00
❑2, ca. 1959; Magazine-sized	300.00
❑3, ca. 1960; Magazine-sized; has Alfred E. Neuman for president campaign poster	200.00
❑4, ca. 1961; Magazine-sized	175.00
❑5, ca. 1962; Magazine-sized; contains record	250.00
❑6, ca. 1963; Magazine-sized; contains record	250.00
❑7, ca. 1964; Magazine-sized	175.00
❑8, ca. 1965; Magazine-sized	175.00
❑9, ca. 1966; Magazine-sized; contains record	250.00
❑10, ca. 1967; Magazine-sized	175.00
❑11, ca. 1968; Magazine-sized; contains car-window stickers	175.00
❑12, ca. 1969, b&w; Magazine-sized	175.00

W.O.W. THE WORLD OF WARD
ALLIED AMERICAN ARTISTS

❑1, b&w; Reprints	3.95

Other grades: Multiply price above by 5/6 for VF/NM • 2/3 for VERY FINE • 1/3 for FINE • 1/5 for VERY GOOD • 1/8 for GOOD

N-MINT

WRAITHBORN
DC / WILDSTORM

- ❑1 .... 2.99
- ❑2 .... 2.99
- ❑3, Jan 2006 .... 2.99
- ❑4, Feb 2006 .... 2.99
- ❑5, May 2006 .... 2.99
- ❑6, Aug 2006 .... 2.99

WRAITH
OUTLANDER COMICS GROUP

- ❑1, Aug 1991, b&w 1.75
- ❑2, Oct 1991 .... 1.75

WRATH
MALIBU / ULTRAVERSE

- ❑1, Jan 1994 A: Mantra. 2.00
- ❑1/Ltd., Jan 1994; Ultra-limited edition A: Mantra. 3.00
- ❑2, Feb 1994 .... 2.00
- ❑3, Mar 1994 1: Slayer. 2.00
- ❑4, Apr 1994 A: Freex. 1.95
- ❑5, May 1994 A: Freex. 1.95
- ❑6, Jun 1994 .... 1.95
- ❑7, Jul 1994 1: Ogre. 1: Pierce. 1: Doc Virtual. 1.95
- ❑8, Oct 1994 1: Project Patriot. A: Warstrike. A: Mantra. 1.95
- ❑9, Dec 1994 D: Project Patriot. 2.25
- ❑Giant Size 1, Aug 1994; Giant-size Wrath #1 .... 2.50

WRATH OF THE SPECTRE
DC

- ❑1, May 1988; Reprints from Adventure Comics #431-433, 426 .. 2.50
- ❑2, Jun 1988; Reprints 2.50
- ❑3, Jul 1988; Reprints 2.50
- ❑4, Aug 1988; new stories 2.50

WRETCH
CALIBER

- ❑1, Jul 1997, b&w 2.95
- ❑2, Sep 1997, b&w 2.95
- ❑3, Nov 1997, b&w 2.95
- ❑4, 1998, b&w 2.95

WRETCH (VOL. 2)
SLAVE LABOR / AMAZE INK

- ❑1, Jul 1997, b&w; Dedicated to Alex Toth and Steve Ditko 2.95
- ❑2, Sep 1997, b&w; Dedicated to Alex Toth and Steve Ditko 2.95
- ❑3, Nov 1997, b&w; Dedicated to Frank Miller 2.95
- ❑4, May 1998, b&w; Dedicated to Jack Curtiss 2.95
- ❑5, May 1998, b&w; Dedicated to Will Eisner 2.95
- ❑6, Jul 1998, b&w; Dedicated to Stan, Jack, and Steve 2.95

WRITERS' BLOC ANTHOLOGY
WRITERS' BLOC

- ❑1 .... 3.00

WULF THE BARBARIAN
ATLAS-SEABOARD

- ❑1, Feb 1975; (c); O: Wulf. Larry Hama/ Klaus Janson 12.00
- ❑2, Apr 1975; (c); Hama/Janson; art assists by Neal Adams, Wally Wood and Ralph Reese 9.00
- ❑3, May 1975; (c); indicia says July ... 8.00
- ❑4, Sep 1975; (c); Jim Craig art 8.00

WU WEI
ANGUS

- ❑1 .... 2.50
- ❑2 .... 2.50
- ❑3 .... 2.50
- ❑4 .... 2.50
- ❑5 .... 2.50
- ❑6 .... 2.50

WW 2
NEC

- ❑1 .... 3.50
- ❑2, Nov 2000 .... 3.50

WW2 ROMMEL
NEW ENGLAND

- ❑1 2005 .... 3.95

WWF: WORLD WRESTLING FOUNDATION
VALIANT

- ❑1, 21841 .... 2.95
- ❑2, 21842 .... 2.95
- ❑3, 21843 .... 2.95
- ❑4, 21844 .... 2.95

WWW.
NBM

- ❑1 .... 10.95

WYATT EARP
MARVEL

- ❑1, Nov 1955 .... 120.00
- ❑2, Jan 1956 .... 70.00
- ❑3, Mar 1956 .... 50.00
- ❑4, May 1956 .... 50.00
- ❑5, Jul 1956 .... 50.00
- ❑6, Sep 1956 .... 50.00
- ❑7, Nov 1956 .... 50.00
- ❑8, Jan 1957 .... 50.00
- ❑9, Mar 1957 .... 50.00
- ❑10, Apr 1957 .... 50.00
- ❑11, May 1957 .... 42.00
- ❑12, Aug 1957 .... 42.00
- ❑13, Oct 1957 .... 42.00
- ❑14, Dec 1957 .... 42.00
- ❑15, Feb 1958 .... 42.00
- ❑16, Apr 1958 .... 42.00
- ❑17, Jun 1958 .... 42.00
- ❑18, Aug 1958 .... 42.00
- ❑19, Oct 1958 .... 42.00
- ❑20, Dec 1958 .... 42.00
- ❑21, Feb 1959 .... 30.00
- ❑22, Apr 1959 .... 30.00
- ❑23, Jun 1959 .... 30.00
- ❑24, Aug 1959 .... 30.00
- ❑25, Oct 1959 .... 30.00
- ❑26, Dec 1959 .... 30.00
- ❑27, Feb 1960 .... 30.00
- ❑28, Apr 1960 .... 30.00
- ❑29, Jun 1960; Final issue of original run 30.00
- ❑30, Oct 1972; Revival of old title; Series begins again 5.00
- ❑31, Dec 1972 SL (w) 5.00
- ❑32, Feb 1973 .... 5.00
- ❑33, Apr 1973 .... 5.00
- ❑34, Jun 1973 .... 5.00

WYATT EARP: DODGE CITY
MOONSTONE

- ❑1 2005 .... 2.95
- ❑2, Aug 2005 .... 2.95

WYNONNA EARP
IMAGE

- ❑1, Dec 1996 .... 2.50
- ❑2, Jan 1997 .... 2.50
- ❑3, Feb 1997; cover says Jan, indicia says Feb 2.50
- ❑4, Mar 1997 .... 2.50
- ❑5, Apr 1997; final issue 2.50

WYOMING TERRITORY
ARK

- ❑1, b&w 1.95

WYRD THE RELUCTANT WARRIOR
SLAVE LABOR

- ❑1, Jul 1999 .... 2.95
- ❑2, Aug 1999 .... 2.95
- ❑3, Sep 1999 .... 2.95
- ❑4, Oct 1999 .... 2.95
- ❑5, Nov 1999 .... 2.95
- ❑6, Dec 1999 .... 2.95

X
DARK HORSE

- ❑1, Feb 1994; embossed cardstock cover 2.50
- ❑2, Mar 1994 .... 2.50
- ❑3, Apr 1994 .... 2.50
- ❑4, May 1994 .... 2.00
- ❑5, Jun 1994 .... 2.00
- ❑6, Aug 1994 .... 2.00
- ❑7, Sep 1994 .... 2.00
- ❑8, Oct 1994 .... 2.50
- ❑9, Nov 1994 .... 2.50
- ❑10, Dec 1994 .... 2.50
- ❑11, Jan 1995 .... 2.50
- ❑12, Mar 1995 .... 2.50
- ❑13, Apr 1995 .... 2.50
- ❑14, May 1995 .... 2.50
- ❑15, Jun 1995 .... 2.50
- ❑16, Jul 1995 .... 2.50
- ❑17, Aug 1995 .... 2.50
- ❑18, Sep 1995 FM (c); FM (a); V: Predator. 2.50
- ❑19, Oct 1995 FM (c); FM (a) 2.50
- ❑20, Nov 1995 FM (c); FM (a) 2.50
- ❑21, Dec 1995 FM (c); FM (a) 2.50
- ❑22, Jan 1996 FM (c); FM (a) 2.50
- ❑23, Feb 1996 .... 2.50
- ❑24, Mar 1996 .... 2.50
- ❑25, Apr 1996 .... 2.50
- ❑Hero ed. 1, Jun 1994; Included with Hero Illustrated magazine 1.00

X-MEN: COLOSSUS: BLOODLINE
MARVEL

- ❑1, Oct 2005 .... 2.99
- ❑2, Dec 2005 .... 2.99
- ❑3, Jan 2006 .... 2.99
- ❑4, Feb 2006 .... 2.99
- ❑5, Mar 2006 .... 2.99

X-MEN: KITTY PRYDE: SHADOW & FLAME
MARVEL

- ❑1, Aug 2005 .... 2.99
- ❑2, Sep 2005 .... 2.99
- ❑3, Oct 2005 .... 2.99
- ❑4 2005 .... 2.99
- ❑5, Jan 2006 .... 2.99

X-MEN: THE 198
MARVEL

- ❑1, Mar 2006 .... 2.99
- ❑2, Apr 2006 .... 2.99
- ❑3, May 2006 .... 2.99
- ❑4, Jun 2006 .... 2.99
- ❑5, Jul 2006 .... 2.99

XANADU (THOUGHTS & IMAGES)
THOUGHTS & IMAGES

- ❑1, May 1988, b&w 2.00
- ❑2, Jun 1988, b&w; 1st appearance Firepetal; 1st appearance Gruht; 1st appearance Kajiko Firelake; 1st appearance Kinomon Firestar .. 2.00
- ❑3, Jul 1988, b&w 2.00
- ❑4, Aug 1988, b&w 2.00
- ❑5, Nov 1988, b&w; cover says Part Three of Five 2.00

XANADU (3-D ZONE)
3-D ZONE

- ❑1, 1986, b&w 2.00
- ❑2, 1986, b&w 2.00
- ❑3, 1986, b&w 2.00
- ❑4, 1986, b&w 2.00

XANADU: ACROSS DIAMOND SEAS
MU

- ❑1, Jan 1994, b&w 2.50
- ❑2, Feb 1994, b&w; MU PUB #205 .... 2.50
- ❑3, Mar 1994, b&w 2.95
- ❑4, Apr 1994, b&w 2.95
- ❑5, May 1994, b&w 2.95
- ❑Book 1, Jan 1994, b&w; Xanadu: Thief of Hearts 12.95

XANADU COLOR SPECIAL
ECLIPSE

- ❑1, Dec 1988 .... 2.00

XANDER IN LOST UNIVERSE (GENE RODDENBERRY'S...)
TEKNO

- ❑0, Nov 1995 .... 2.25
- ❑1, Dec 1995 .... 2.25
- ❑2, Dec 1995 .... 2.25
- ❑3, Jan 1996 .... 2.25
- ❑4, Jan 1996 .... 2.25
- ❑5, Feb 1996 .... 2.25
- ❑6, Mar 1996 .... 2.25
- ❑7, Apr 1996 .... 2.25
- ❑8, May 1996; The Big Crossover, Part 5: The Big Bang 2.25

XANTH GRAPHIC NOVEL
FATHER TREE

- ❑1 .... 9.95

X-BABIES: MURDERAMA
MARVEL

- ❑1, Aug 1998 .... 2.99

X-BABIES: REBORN
MARVEL

- ❑1, Jan 2000 .... 3.50

Other grades: Multiply price above by 5/6 for VF/NM • 2/3 for VERY FINE • 1/3 for FINE • 1/5 for VERY GOOD • 1/8 for GOOD

X-Factor

Original X-Men return to "hunt" mutants
©Marvel

X-Factor (Vol. 2)

Mutant hunting takes nasty turn
©Marvel

X-Farce

Forced parody of Liefeld book
©Eclipse

X-51

What makes Machine Man tick?
©Marvel

X-Files

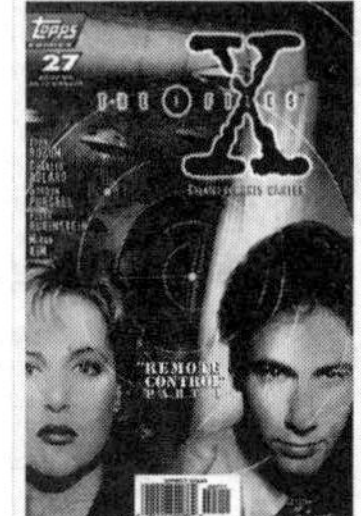

Mulder and Scully probe the paranormal
©Topps

N-MINT

X-CALIBRE
Marvel

- ❑1, Mar 1995; (c); The Age of Apocalypse 2.00
- ❑2, Apr 1995; cover says Jun; The Age of Apocalypse 2.00
- ❑3, May 1995; The Age of Apocalypse 2.00
- ❑4, Jun 1995; The Age of Apocalypse 2.00

XENA
Brainstorm

- ❑1, Jan 1995 .... 2.95

XENA: WARRIOR PRINCESS
Topps

- ❑0, Oct 1997 .... 2.95
- ❑1, Aug 1997; A: Hercules. back-up Tales of Salmoneus 2.95
- ❑1/A, Aug 1997 .... 4.00
- ❑1/American Ent, Aug 1997; American Entertainment 7.00
- ❑1/Variant, Aug 1997 .... 4.00
- ❑2, Sep 1997 .... 2.95
- ❑2/Variant, Sep 1997 .... 4.00

XENA: WARRIOR PRINCESS
Dark Horse

- ❑1, Sep 1999 .... 3.00
- ❑1/Variant, Sep 1999 .... 3.00
- ❑2, Oct 1999 .... 3.00
- ❑2/Variant, Oct 1999 .... 3.00
- ❑3, Nov 1999 .... 3.00
- ❑3/Variant, Nov 1999 .... 3.00
- ❑4, Dec 1999 .... 3.00
- ❑4/Variant, Dec 1999 .... 3.00
- ❑5, Jan 2000 .... 3.00
- ❑5/Variant, Jan 2000 .... 3.00
- ❑6, Feb 2000 .... 2.95
- ❑6/Variant, Feb 2000 .... 2.95
- ❑7, Mar 2000 .... 2.95
- ❑7/Variant, Mar 2000 .... 2.95
- ❑8, Apr 2000 .... 2.95
- ❑8/Variant, Apr 2000 .... 2.95
- ❑9, May 2000 .... 2.95
- ❑9/Variant, May 2000 .... 2.95
- ❑10, Jun 2000 .... 2.95
- ❑10/Variant, Jun 2000 .... 2.95
- ❑11, Jul 2000 .... 2.95
- ❑11/Variant, Jul 2000 .... 2.95
- ❑12, Aug 2000 .... 2.95
- ❑12/Variant, Aug 2000 .... 2.95
- ❑13, Sep 2000 .... 2.95
- ❑13/Variant, Sep 2000 .... 2.95
- ❑14, Oct 2000 .... 2.99
- ❑14/Variant, Oct 2000 .... 2.99

XENA: WARRIOR PRINCESS: AND THE ORIGINAL OLYMPICS
Topps

- ❑1, Jun 1998 .... 2.95
- ❑2, Jul 1998 .... 2.95
- ❑3, Aug 1998 .... 2.95

XENA: WARRIOR PRINCESS: BLOODLINES
Topps

- ❑1, May 1998 .... 2.95
- ❑2, Jun 1998 .... 2.95

N-MINT

XENA: WARRIOR PRINCESS/JOXER: WARRIOR PRINCE
Topps

- ❑1, Nov 1997 .... 2.95
- ❑1/Variant, Nov 1997 .... 2.95
- ❑2, Dec 1997 .... 2.95
- ❑2/Variant, Dec 1997 .... 2.95
- ❑3, Jan 1998 .... 2.95
- ❑3/Variant, Jan 1998 .... 2.95

XENA: WARRIOR PRINCESS: THE DRAGON'S TEETH
Topps

- ❑1, Dec 1997 .... 2.95
- ❑1/Variant, Dec 1997 .... 2.95
- ❑2, Jan 1998 .... 2.95
- ❑2/Variant, Jan 1998 .... 2.95
- ❑3, Feb 1998 .... 2.95
- ❑3/Variant, Feb 1998 .... 2.95

XENA: WARRIOR PRINCESS: THE ORPHEUS TRILOGY
Topps

- ❑1, Mar 1998 .... 2.95
- ❑1/Variant, Mar 1998 .... 2.95
- ❑2, Apr 1998 .... 2.95
- ❑2/Variant, Apr 1998 .... 2.95
- ❑3, May 1998 .... 2.95
- ❑3/Variant, May 1998 .... 2.95

XENA: WARRIOR PRINCESS: THE WARRIOR WAY OF DEATH
Dark Horse

- ❑1, Sep 1999 .... 2.95
- ❑1/Variant, Sep 1999 .... 2.95
- ❑2, Oct 1999 .... 2.95
- ❑2/Variant, Oct 1999 .... 2.95

XENA: WARRIOR PRINCESS VS. CALLISTO
Topps

- ❑1, Feb 1998 .... 2.95
- ❑1/A, Feb 1998; No cover price 5.00
- ❑1/Variant, Feb 1998 .... 2.95
- ❑2, Mar 1998 .... 2.95
- ❑2/Variant, Mar 1998 .... 2.95
- ❑3, Mar 1998 .... 2.95
- ❑3/Variant, Mar 1998 .... 2.95

XENA, WARRIOR PRINCESS: WRATH OF HERA
Topps

- ❑1 1998 .... 2.95
- ❑1/Variant 1998 .... 3.00
- ❑2 1998 .... 2.95
- ❑2/Variant 1998 .... 3.00

XENA: WARRIOR PRINCESS, YEAR ONE
Topps

- ❑1 1998 O: Xena. 5.00
- ❑1/Gold 1998; O: Xena. Gold logo cover 10.00

X-MEN: DAYS OF FUTURE PAST
Marvel

- ❑1, ca. 2004 .... 19.99

XENE
Eyeball Soup Designs

- ❑1, Jan 1996; cardstock cover 4.95
- ❑2, Mar 1996; cardstock cover 4.95
- ❑3, May 1996; cardstock cover 4.95
- ❑4, Jul 1996; cardstock cover 4.95

N-MINT

XENOBROOD
DC

- ❑0, Oct 1994 .... 1.50
- ❑1, Nov 1994 .... 1.50
- ❑2, Dec 1994 .... 1.50
- ❑3, Jan 1995 .... 1.50
- ❑4, Feb 1995 .... 1.50
- ❑5, Mar 1995 .... 1.50
- ❑6, Apr 1995; Final Issue 1.50

XENO-MEN
Blackthorne

- ❑1, Nov 1987, b&w 1.75

XENON
Eclipse / Viz

- ❑1, Dec 1987, b&w 2.00
- ❑2, Dec 1987, b&w 2.00
- ❑3, Jan 1988, b&w 2.00
- ❑4, Jan 1988, b&w 2.00
- ❑5, Feb 1988, b&w (c) 2.00
- ❑6, Feb 1988, b&w 2.00
- ❑7, Mar 1988, b&w 2.00
- ❑8, Mar 1988, b&w 2.00
- ❑9, Apr 1988, b&w 2.00
- ❑10, Apr 1988, b&w 2.00
- ❑11, May 1988, b&w 1.50
- ❑12, May 1988, b&w 1.50
- ❑13, Jun 1988, b&w 1.50
- ❑14, Jun 1988, b&w 1.50
- ❑15, Jul 1988, b&w 1.50
- ❑16, Jul 1988, b&w 1.50
- ❑17, Aug 1988, b&w 1.50
- ❑18, Aug 1988, b&w 1.50
- ❑19, Sep 1988, b&w 1.50
- ❑20, Sep 1988, b&w 1.50
- ❑21, Oct 1988, b&w 1.50
- ❑22, Oct 1988, b&w 1.50
- ❑23, Nov 1989, b&w; Final Issue 1.50

XENO'S ARROW
Cup O' Tea

- ❑1, Feb 1999, b&w 2.50
- ❑2, Apr 1999 .... 2.50
- ❑3, Jun 1999 .... 2.50
- ❑4, Aug 1999 .... 2.50

XENOTECH
Mirage / Next

- ❑1, Aug 1994; Includes trading cards. 2.75
- ❑1/A, Aug 1994; Variant cover with monster attacking; Includes trading cards 2.75
- ❑2, Oct 1994; Includes trading cards . 2.75
- ❑3, Dec 1994; Includes trading cards. 2.75

XENOZOIC TALES
Kitchen Sink

- ❑1, Feb 1987, b&w 8.00
- ❑1/2nd, Mar 1987, b&w; 2nd printing 3.00
- ❑2, Apr 1987, b&w 6.00
- ❑3, Jun 1987, b&w 6.00
- ❑4, Nov 1987, b&w 6.00
- ❑5, Feb 1988, b&w 6.00
- ❑6, May 1988, b&w; ca. 1988 .... 5.00

N-MINT

❑7, Oct 1988, b&w; ca. 1988 .... 5.00
❑8, Jan 1989, b&w; ca. 1988 .... 5.00
❑9, Sep 1989, b&w; ca. 1988 .... 5.00
❑10, Apr 1990, b&w; ca. 1989 .... 5.00
❑11, Apr 1991, b&w; ca. 1990 .... 4.00
❑12, Apr 1992, b&w; ca. 1991 .... 4.00
❑13, Dec 1994, b&w 4.00
❑14, Oct 1996, b&w; cardstock cover 4.00

XENYA
SANCTUARY

❑1, Jul 1994 .... 2.95
❑2, Sep 1994 .... 2.95
❑3, ca. 1995; no cover price 2.95

XERO
DC

❑1, May 1997 .... 2.00
❑2, Jun 1997 .... 1.75
❑3, Jul 1997 (c) 1.75
❑4, Aug 1997 (c) 1.75
❑5, Sep 1997 .... 1.75
❑6, Oct 1997; (c); V: Polaris. Genesis. 1.75
❑7, Nov 1997 .... 1.75
❑8, Dec 1997; (c); Face cover 1.95
❑9, Jan 1998 (c) 1.95
❑10, Feb 1998 (c) 1.95
❑11, Mar 1998 (c) 1.95
❑12, Apr 1998; Final Issue 1.95

X-FACTOR
MARVEL

❑-1, Jul 1997; (c); Flashback 2.00
❑1, Feb 1986; Giant-size; (c); BL (w); BG (a); O: X-Factor. 1: Rusty Collins. Giant-size 3.00
❑2, Mar 1986 MZ (c); BL (w); BG (a).. 2.00
❑3, Apr 1986 BL (w); BG (a) 2.00
❑4, May 1986 BL (w); KP (a); 1: Frenzy. 2.00
❑5, Jun 1986 BL (w); BG (a); 1: Apocalypse (in shadows). 3.00
❑6, Jul 1986 (c); BG (a); 1: Apocalypse (full appearance). 5.00
❑7, Aug 1986 (c); BG (a); 1: Skids. 3.00
❑8, Sep 1986 (c) 2.00
❑9, Oct 1989; Mutant Massacre 2.00
❑10, Nov 1989; Mutant Massacre 2.00
❑11, Dec 1989; Mutant Massacre 2.00
❑12, Jan 1987 O: Famine. 1: Famine. . 2.00
❑13, Feb 1987 A: Phoenix 2.00
❑14, Mar 1987 .... 2.00
❑15, Apr 1987 .... 2.00
❑16, May 1987 O: Skids. 2.00
❑17, Jun 1987 1: Rictor. 2.00
❑18, Jul 1987 (c) 2.00
❑19, Aug 1987 .... 2.00
❑20, Sep 1987 .... 2.00
❑21, Oct 1987 .... 2.00
❑22, Nov 1987 SB (a) 2.00
❑23, Dec 1987; 1: Archangel (cameo). registration card 5.00
❑24, Jan 1988 O: Apocalypse. 1: Archangel (full appearance). 8.00
❑25, Feb 1988 .... 2.00
❑26, Mar 1988 .... 2.00
❑27, Apr 1988 BWi (c) 2.00
❑28, May 1988 .... 2.00
❑29, Jun 1988 .... 2.00
❑30, Jul 1988 .... 2.00
❑31, Aug 1988 .... 2.00
❑32, Sep 1988 1: N'astirh. A: Avengers. 2.00
❑33, Oct 1988 .... 2.00
❑34, Nov 1988 .... 2.00
❑35, Dec 1988 .... 2.00
❑36, Jan 1989; Inferno 2.00
❑37, Feb 1989; Inferno 2.00
❑38, Mar 1989; Giant-size; D: Madelyn Pryor. Inferno; Giant-size 2.00
❑39, Apr 1989; Inferno 2.00
❑40, May 1989 AM, RL (c); RL (a) 2.00
❑41, Jun 1989 .... 2.00
❑42, Jul 1989 .... 2.00
❑43, Aug 1989 PS (c); PS (a) 2.00
❑44, Sep 1989 PS (c); PS (a) 2.00
❑45, Oct 1989 PS (c); PS (a) 2.00
❑46, Nov 1989 PS (c); PS (a) 2.00
❑47, Nov 1989; AM (c); Solo Archangel story 2.00
❑48, Dec 1989 PS (c); PS (a) 2.00
❑49, Dec 1989 AM (c); PS (a) 2.00

N-MINT

❑50, Jan 1990; Giant-size; TMc, RL (c); RB (a); Giant-size 2.50
❑51, Feb 1990 A: Sabretooth. 2.50
❑52, Mar 1990 AM, RL (c); A: Sabretooth. 2.50
❑53, Apr 1990 AM (c); A: Sabretooth. 2.50
❑54, May 1990 AM (c); 1: Crimson. ... 1.50
❑55, Jun 1990 PD (w) 1.50
❑56, Jul 1990 AM (c) 1.50
❑57, Aug 1990 .... 1.50
❑58, Sep 1990 AM (c) 1.50
❑59, Oct 1990 AM (c) 1.50
❑60, Nov 1990 AM (c) 2.50
❑60/2nd, Nov 1990; AM (c); Gold cover 1.50
❑61, Dec 1990 AM (c) 2.50
❑62, Jan 1991 JLee (c) 2.50
❑63, Feb 1991 .... 2.50
❑64, Mar 1991 .... 2.50
❑65, Apr 1991 JLee (w) 2.50
❑66, May 1991 JLee (w) 2.50
❑67, Jun 1991 JLee (w) 2.50
❑68, Jul 1991; JLee (w); Baby Nathan is sent into future 2.50
❑69, Aug 1991; Muir Island Saga 2.50
❑70, Sep 1991; PD (w); Muir Island Epilogue 2.00
❑71, Oct 1991; AM (c); PD (w); AM (a); new team; Havok, Madrox, Polaris & Wolfsbane 2.00
❑71/2nd, Oct 1991; AM (c); PD (w); Havok, Madrox, Polaris & Wolfsbane 1.50
❑72, Nov 1991 AM (c); PD (w) 1.50
❑73, Dec 1991 AM (c); PD (w) 1.50
❑74, Jan 1992 AM (c); PD (w) 1.50
❑75, Feb 1992; Giant-size; (c); PD (w); Giant-size 2.00
❑76, Mar 1992 AM (c); PD (w) 1.50
❑77, Apr 1992 AM (c); PD (w) 1.50
❑78, May 1992 PD (w) 1.50
❑79, Jun 1992 KN (c); PD (w); 1: Rhapsody. 1.50
❑80, Jul 1992 AM (c); PD (w) 1.50
❑81, Aug 1992 (c); PD (w) 1.50
❑82, Sep 1992 AM (c); PD (w) 1.50
❑83, Oct 1992 AM (c); PD (w) 1.50
❑84/CS, Nov 1992; AM (c); PD (w); Includes Caliban trading card 2.00
❑85/CS, Dec 1992; PD (w); Includes trading card 2.00
❑86/CS, Jan 1993; PD (w); Includes Dark Riders trading card 2.00
❑87, Feb 1993 AM (c); PD (w) 1.50
❑88, Mar 1993 AM (c); PD (w) 1.50
❑89, Apr 1993 AM (c); PD (w) 1.50
❑90, May 1993 .... 1.50
❑91, Jun 1993 AM (c) 1.50
❑92, Jul 1993; AM (c); Hologram cover; Fatal Attractions 4.00
❑93, Aug 1993 PS (c) 1.50
❑94, Sep 1993 (c) 1.50
❑95, Oct 1993 AM (c); A: Polaris. A: Random. 1.50
❑96, Nov 1993 AM (c) 1.50
❑97, Dec 1993; (c); JDu (a); Siege of Darkness preview 1.50
❑98, Jan 1994 AM (c) 1.50
❑99, Feb 1994 AM, JDu (c); JDu (a) .. 1.50
❑100, Mar 1994; Giant-size; (c); JDu (a); D: Multiple Man. Giant-size 2.00
❑100/Variant, Mar 1994; Giant-size; (c); JDu (a); D: Multiple Man. Giant-size; foil embossed cover 3.00
❑101, Apr 1994 AM, JDu (c); JDu (a) 1.50
❑102, May 1994; (c); JDu (a); Includes trading cards 1.50
❑103, Jun 1994 JDu (c); JDu (a) 1.50
❑104, Jul 1994 AM, JDu (c); JDu (a). 1.50
❑105, Aug 1994 (c) 1.50
❑106, Sep 1994; JDu (a); wraparound cover; Phalanx Covenant 2.00
❑106/Variant, Sep 1994; JDu (a); enhanced cover; Phalanx Covenant 2.95
❑107, Oct 1994 AM, KGa (c) 1.50
❑108, Nov 1994 JDu (a) 1.50
❑108/Deluxe, Nov 1994; Deluxe edition JDu (a) 2.00
❑109, Dec 1994 AM (c); JDu (a) 1.50
❑109/Deluxe, Dec 1994; Deluxe edition AM (c); JDu (a) 2.00
❑110, Jan 1995 AM (c); JDu (a); A: Lila Cheney 1.50

N-MINT

❑110/Deluxe, Jan 1995; Deluxe edition AM (c); JDu (a); A: Lila Cheney. 2.00
❑111, Feb 1995 AM (c); JDu (a) 1.50
❑111/Deluxe, Feb 1995; Deluxe edition AM (c); JDu (a) 2.00
❑112, Jul 1995 .... 1.95
❑113, Aug 1995 .... 1.95
❑114, Sep 1995 .... 1.95
❑115, Oct 1995; bound-in trading cards 1.95
❑116, Nov 1995 A: Alpha Flight. 1.95
❑117, Dec 1995 A: Cyclops. A: Wild Child. A: Havok. A: Mystique. A: Random. 1.95
❑118, Jan 1996 .... 1.95
❑119, Feb 1996 A: Shard 1.95
❑120, Mar 1996 (c) 1.95
❑121, Apr 1996 .... 1.95
❑122, May 1996 AM (c) 1.95
❑123, Jun 1996 .... 1.95
❑124, Jul 1996; Onslaught Update 1.95
❑125, Aug 1996 AM (c); AM (a) 2.95
❑126, Sep 1996; HT (a); A: real Beast. real Beast returns; Heroes Reborn Update 1.95
❑127, Oct 1996; AW (a); bound-in trading cards; Heroes Reborn Update 1.95
❑128, Nov 1996 AM (a) 1.95
❑129, Dec 1996 .... 1.95
❑130, Jan 1997 D: Graydon Creed. 2.50
❑131, Feb 1997 (c) 1.95
❑132, Mar 1997 .... 1.95
❑133, Apr 1997 .... 1.95
❑134, May 1997 .... 1.95
❑135, Jun 1997; A: Guido Carosella (Strong Guy). return of Strong Guy 1.95
❑136, Aug 1997; gatefold summary; A: Sabretooth. gatefold summary ... 1.99
❑137, Sep 1997; gatefold summary; gatefold summary 1.99
❑138, Oct 1997; gatefold summary; (c); A: Sabretooth. V: Omega Red. gatefold summary 1.99
❑139, Nov 1997; gatefold summary; (c); gatefold summary 1.99
❑140, Dec 1997; gatefold summary; A: Xavier's Underground Enforcers. gatefold summary 1.99
❑141, Jan 1998; gatefold summary; gatefold summary 1.99
❑142, Feb 1998; gatefold summary; gatefold summary 1.99
❑143, Mar 1998; gatefold summary; gatefold summary 1.99
❑144, Apr 1998; gatefold summary; (c); V: Random. gatefold summary 1.99
❑145, May 1998; gatefold summary; gatefold summary 1.99
❑146, Jun 1998; gatefold summary; A: Multiple Man. gatefold summary 1.99
❑147, Jul 1998; gatefold summary; (c); gatefold summary 1.99
❑148, Aug 1998; gatefold summary; (c); A: Polaris. V: Mandroids. gatefold summary 1.99
❑149, Sep 1998; gatefold summary; gatefold summary 1.99
❑Annual 1, ca. 1986 BL (c); BL (w); BL (a) 3.00
❑Annual 2, ca. 1987 .... 3.00
❑Annual 3, ca. 1988 O: High Evolutionary. 3.00
❑Annual 4, ca. 1989 JBy (c); JBy (w); JBy (a) 2.50
❑Annual 5, ca. 1990 PD (w); A: Fantastic Four. A: New Mutants 2.50
❑Annual 6, ca. 1991 PD (w); D: Proteus. 2.50
❑Annual 7, ca. 1992 PD (w) 2.25
❑Annual 8, ca. 1993; PD (w); A: Guido Carosella (Strong Guy). trading card 2.95
❑Annual 9, ca. 1994 KGa (a); V: Power. 2.95

X-FACTOR (VOL. 2)
MARVEL

❑1, Jun 2002; hardcover 2.50
❑2, Jul 2002; Spider-Man serial 2.50
❑3, Aug 2002 .... 2.50
❑4, Sep 2002 .... 2.50

X-FACTOR: PRISONER OF LOVE
MARVEL

❑1, Aug 1990 .... 4.95

X-FACTOR (VOL. 3)
MARVEL

❑1, Feb 2006 .... 2.99
❑2, Feb 2006 .... 2.99

X-Files Ground Zero

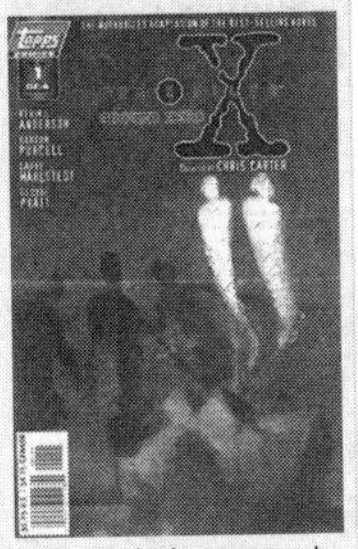

Adapts Anderson novel
©Topps

X-Force

Once-hot series faded after Liefeld left
©Marvel

X-Force (Vol. 2)

Less-heralded Liefeld return to title
©Marvel

X-Man

Holdover from "Age of Apocalypse"
©Marvel

X-Men (1st series)

Name for early issues of Uncanny X-Men
©Marvel

N-MINT

❑3, Mar 2006 ... 2.99
❑4, May 2006 ... 2.99
❑5, Jun 2006 ... 2.99
❑6, Jul 2006 ... 2.99
❑7, Aug 2006 ... 2.99
❑8, Sep 2006 ... 2.99

X-FARCE
ECLIPSE

❑1, Jan 1992, b&w; parody ... 2.50

X-FARCE VS. X-CONS: X-TINCTION
PARODY

❑1, 1993, b&w ... 2.75
❑1.5, 1993, b&w; w/ trading cards ... 2.75

X-51
MARVEL

❑0, ca. 1999; Wizard Promo ... 1.00
❑1, Sep 1999 ... 1.99
❑2, Sep 1999 ... 1.99
❑3, Oct 1999 ... 1.99
❑4, Nov 1999 ... 1.99
❑5, Dec 1999 ... 1.99
❑6, Jan 2000 ... 1.99
❑7, Feb 2000 ... 1.99
❑8, Mar 2000 ... 1.99
❑9, Apr 2000 ... 1.99
❑10, May 2000 ... 1.99
❑11, Jun 2000 ... 1.99
❑12, Jul 2000 ... 1.99

X-FILES
TOPPS

❑-2, Sep 1996; no cover price ... 10.00
❑-1, Sep 1996; no cover price ... 10.00
❑0/A; adapts pilot episode; forms diptych with Scully cover ... 4.00
❑0/B; adapts pilot episode; forms diptych with Mulder cover ... 4.00
❑0/C; adapts pilot episode ... 4.00
❑½; Wizard promotional edition ... 10.00
❑1, Jan 1995 ... 8.00
❑1/2nd, Jan 1995 ... 2.50
❑2, Feb 1995 ... 5.00
❑3, Mar 1995 ... 4.00
❑3/2nd, Mar 1995 ... 2.50
❑4, Apr 1995 ... 3.50
❑4/2nd, Apr 1995 ... 2.50
❑5, May 1995 ... 3.00
❑6, Jun 1995 ... 3.00
❑7, Jul 1995 ... 3.00
❑8, Aug 1995 ... 3.00
❑9, Sep 1995 ... 3.00
❑10, Oct 1995 ... 3.00
❑11, Nov 1995 ... 3.00
❑12, Dec 1995 ... 3.00
❑13, Feb 1996 ... 3.00
❑14, Apr 1996 ... 3.00
❑15, May 1996 ... 3.00
❑16, May 1996 ... 3.00
❑17, May 1996 ... 3.00
❑18, Jun 1996 ... 3.00
❑19, Jun 1996 ... 3.00
❑20, Jul 1996 ... 3.00
❑21, Aug 1996 ... 3.00
❑22, Sep 1996 ... 2.95

N-MINT

❑23, Nov 1996; Donor ... 2.95
❑24, Dec 1996 ... 2.95
❑25, Jan 1997 ... 2.95
❑26, Feb 1997 ... 2.95
❑27, Mar 1997 ... 2.95
❑28, Apr 1997 ... 2.95
❑29, May 1997 ... 2.95
❑30, Jun 1997 ... 2.95
❑31, Jul 1997 ... 2.95
❑32, Aug 1997 ... 2.95
❑33, Sep 1997 ... 2.95
❑33/Variant, Sep 1997 ... 5.00
❑34, Oct 1997 ... 2.95
❑35, Nov 1997 ... 2.95
❑36, Dec 1997 ... 2.95
❑37, Jan 1998 ... 2.95
❑38, Feb 1998 ... 2.95
❑39, Mar 1998 ... 2.95
❑40, Apr 1998 ... 2.95
❑41, May 1998 ... 2.95
❑41/Variant, Jun 1998 ... 2.95
❑Annual 1, Aug 1995 ... 3.95
❑Annual 2, ca. 1996; E.L.F.s ... 3.95
❑Ashcan 1, Jan 1995; no cover price; polybagged with Star Wars Galaxy #2 ... 4.00
❑Special 1, Jun 1995; reprints issues #1 and 2 ... 4.95
❑Special 2, ca. 1995; Reprints X-Files #4-6 ... 4.95
❑Special 3, ca. 1996; Reprints X-Files #7-9 ... 4.95
❑Special 4, Nov 1996; reprints Feelings of Unreality ... 4.95
❑Special 5, ca. 1997; Reprints X-Files #13, Annual #1 ... 4.95

X-FILES COMICS DIGEST
TOPPS

❑1, Dec 1995; Bradbury back-up stories ... 3.50
❑2, Apr 1996; Bradbury back-up stories ... 3.50
❑3, Sep 1996; Bradbury back-up stories ... 3.50

X-FILES GROUND ZERO
TOPPS

❑1, Dec 1997; adapts Kevin J. Anderson novel ... 2.95
❑2, Jan 1998; adapts Kevin J. Anderson novel ... 2.95
❑3, Feb 1998; adapts Kevin J. Anderson novel ... 2.95
❑4, Mar 1998; adapts Kevin J. Anderson novel ... 2.95

X-FILES: SEASON ONE
TOPPS

❑1, Jul 1997; prestige format; adapts pilot episode ... 4.95
❑2, ca. 1997; prestige format ... 4.95
❑2/A, ca. 1997; variant cover ... 4.95
❑3, Oct 1997 ... 4.95
❑3/A, Oct 1997; variant cover ... 4.95
❑4, Dec 1997 ... 4.95
❑5, Jan 1998 ... 4.95
❑6, Feb 1998 ... 4.95
❑7, Mar 1998 ... 4.95

N-MINT

❑8, Apr 1998 ... 4.95
❑9, Jul 1998 ... 4.95

X-FILES: AFTERFLIGHT
TOPPS

❑1 ... 5.95

X-FLIES BUG HUNT
TWIST AND SHOUT

❑1, Dec 1996 ... 2.95
❑2, Jan 1997 ... 2.95
❑3, Feb 1997 ... 2.95
❑4, Mar 1997 ... 2.95

X-FLIES CONSPIRACY
TWIST AND SHOUT

❑1, Mar 1996 ... 2.95

X-FLIES SPECIAL
TWIST AND SHOUT

❑1, Sep 1995 ... 2.95

X-FORCE
MARVEL

❑-1, Jul 1997; AM (a); Flashback; Proudstars team up ... 2.00
❑1/A, Aug 1991; RL (c); RL (w); RL (a); 1: G.W. Bridge. with Cable card ... 2.00
❑1/B, Aug 1991; RL (c); RL (w); RL (a); 1: G.W. Bridge. with Deadpool card ... 2.00
❑1/C, Aug 1991; RL (c); RL (w); RL (a); 1: G.W. Bridge. with Shatterstar card ... 2.00
❑1/D, Aug 1991; RL (c); RL (w); RL (a); 1: G.W. Bridge. with Sunspot & Gideon card ... 2.00
❑1/E, Aug 1991; RL (c); RL (w); RL (a); 1: G.W. Bridge. with X-Force group card ... 2.00
❑1/2nd, Aug 1991; RL (c); RL (w); RL (a); 1: G.W. Bridge. Gold cover ... 1.50
❑2, Sep 1991 RL (c); RL (w); RL (a); 1: Weapon X II (Garrison Kane). ... 2.50
❑3, Oct 1991 RL (c); RL (w); RL (a); V: Juggernaut. ... 2.00
❑4, Nov 1991; (c); RL (w); RL (a); A: Spider-Man. Sideways printing ... 2.00
❑5, Dec 1991 (c); RL (w); RL (a); A: Brotherhood of Evil Mutants. ... 2.00
❑6, Jan 1992 RL (c); RL (w); RL (a) ... 2.00
❑7, Feb 1992 RL (c); RL (w); RL (a) ... 2.00
❑8, Mar 1992 RL (c); RL (w); 1: Grizzly II. ... 2.00
❑9, Apr 1992 RL (c); RL (a) ... 2.00
❑10, May 1992 RL (w) ... 2.00
❑11, Jun 1992 RL (c); RL (w) ... 2.00
❑12, Jul 1992 RL (w) ... 2.00
❑13, Aug 1992 ... 2.00
❑14, Sep 1992 ... 2.00
❑15, Oct 1992 ... 2.00
❑16/CS, Nov 1992; Includes Cable card ... 2.00
❑17/CS, Dec 1992; O: Zero. O: Stryfe. Includes trading card ... 2.00
❑18/CS, Jan 1993; Includes trading card ... 2.00
❑19, Feb 1993 ... 1.50
❑20, Mar 1993 ... 1.50
❑21, Apr 1993 ... 1.50
❑22, May 1993 ... 1.50
❑23, Jun 1993 ... 1.50
❑24, Jul 1993 ... 1.50
❑25, Aug 1993; Hologram cover ... 3.00
❑26, Sep 1993 ... 1.50

❑27, Oct 1993 A: Mutant Liberation Front. 1.50
❑28, Nov 1993 (c) 1.50
❑29, Dec 1993 A: Arcade. 1.50
❑30, Jan 1994 1.50
❑31, Feb 1994 1.25
❑32, Mar 1994 1.25
❑33, Apr 1994 1.25
❑34, May 1994 (c) 1.50
❑35, Jun 1994 V: Nimrod. 1.50
❑36, Jul 1994 1.50
❑37, Aug 1994 AM (c) 1.50
❑38, Sep 1994; Phalanx Covenant 2.00
❑38/Variant, Sep 1994; enhanced cover; Phalanx Covenant 3.00
❑39, Oct 1994 1.50
❑40, Nov 1994 1.50
❑40/Deluxe, Nov 1994; Deluxe edition 1.95
❑41, Dec 1994 1.50
❑41/Deluxe, Dec 1994; Deluxe edition 1.95
❑42, Jan 1995 1.50
❑42/Deluxe, Jan 1995; Deluxe edition 1.95
❑43, Feb 1995 1.50
❑43/Deluxe, Feb 1995; Deluxe edition; bound-in trading cards 1.95
❑44, Jul 1995; (c); JPH (w); A: Cannonball. Cannonball leaves 1.95
❑45, Aug 1995 JPH (w) 1.95
❑46, Sep 1995 (c); JPH (w); V: Mimic. 1.95
❑47, Oct 1995; JPH (w); bound-in trading cards 1.95
❑48, Nov 1995 JPH (w) 1.95
❑49, Dec 1995 JPH (w); A: Holocaust. A: Sebastian Shaw. 1.50
❑49/Deluxe, Dec 1995; Direct Edition JPH (w) 1.90
❑50, Jan 1996; Giant-size; (c); JPH (w); Giant-size; wraparound fold-out cover 3.00
❑50/A, Jan 1996; Giant-size; RL (c); JPH (w); Giant-size 4.00
❑50/Variant, Jan 1996; Giant-size; (c); JPH (w); Giant-size; enhanced wraparound fold-out cardstock cover 1.95
❑51, Feb 1996 JPH (w); 1: Meltdown (formerly Boomer/Boom Boom). 1.95
❑52, Mar 1996 JPH (w); D: Gideon. V: Blob. 1.95
❑53, Apr 1996 JPH (w) 1.95
❑54, May 1996 (c); JPH (w) 1.95
❑55, Jun 1996 JPH (w); V: S.H.I.E.L.D. 1.95
❑56, Jul 1996 JPH (w) 1.95
❑57, Aug 1996 JPH (w) 1.95
❑58, Sep 1996 JPH (w) 1.95
❑59, Oct 1996; (c); JPH (w); bound-in trading cards 1.95
❑60, Nov 1996 (c); JPH (w); O: Shatterstar. 1.95
❑61, Dec 1996 JPH (w); O: Shatterstar. 1.95
❑62, Jan 1997 1.95
❑63, Feb 1997; team invades Doom's castle 1.95
❑64, Mar 1997 A: Baron Von Strucker. 1.95
❑65, Apr 1997 1.95
❑66, May 1997 1.95
❑67, Jun 1997 A: Dani Moonstar. 1.99
❑68, Aug 1997; gatefold summary; A: Vanisher. gatefold summary 1.99
❑69, Sep 1997; gatefold summary; gatefold summary 1.99
❑70, Oct 1997; gatefold summary; gatefold summary 1.99
❑71, Nov 1997; gatefold summary; gatefold summary 1.99
❑72, Dec 1997; gatefold summary; gatefold summary 1.99
❑73, Jan 1998; gatefold summary; (c); D: Warpath. gatefold summary 1.99
❑74, Feb 1998; gatefold summary; V: Stryfe. gatefold summary 1.99
❑75, Mar 1998; gatefold summary; A: Cannonball. gatefold summary 1.99
❑76, Apr 1998; gatefold summary; gatefold summary; Domino vs. Shatterstar 1.99
❑77, May 1998; gatefold summary; (c); gatefold summary 1.99
❑78, Jun 1998; gatefold summary; gatefold summary 1.99
❑79, Jul 1998; gatefold summary; O: Reignfire. gatefold summary 1.99
❑80, Aug 1998; gatefold summary; (c); gatefold summary 1.99

N-MINT

❑81, Sep 1998; gatefold summary; (c); gatefold summary; poster 1.99
❑82, Oct 1998; gatefold summary; gatefold summary 1.99
❑83, Nov 1998; gatefold summary; (c); gatefold summary 1.99
❑84, Dec 1998; gatefold summary; V: New Deviants. gatefold summary 1.99
❑85, Jan 1999; gatefold summary; (c); gatefold summary 1.99
❑86, Jan 1999; gatefold summary; (c); gatefold summary 1.99
❑87, Feb 1999 A: Hellions. 1.99
❑88, Mar 1999 A: Christopher Bedlam. A: Hellions. V: New Hellions. 1.99
❑89, Apr 1999 A: Armageddon Man. A: Hellions. 1.99
❑90, May 1999 (c) 1.99
❑91, Jun 1999; Siryn solo tale 1.99
❑92, Jul 1999; Domino vs. Halloween Jack 1.99
❑93, Aug 1999 1.99
❑94, Sep 1999 1.99
❑95, Oct 1999 1.99
❑96, Nov 1999 1.99
❑97, Dec 1999 2.25
❑98, Jan 2000 (c) 2.25
❑99, Feb 2000 BSz (c) 2.99
❑100, Mar 2000 (c) 2.25
❑101, Apr 2000 (c) 2.25
❑102, May 2000; Revolution 2.25
❑103, Jun 2000 2.25
❑104, Jul 2000 2.25
❑105, Aug 2000 2.25
❑106, Sep 2000 (c) 2.25
❑107, Oct 2000 2.25
❑108, Nov 2000 2.25
❑109, Dec 2000; indicia says Nov 2000 2.25
❑110, Jan 2001 2.25
❑111, Feb 2001 2.25
❑112, Mar 2001 2.25
❑113, Apr 2001 2.25
❑114, May 2001; indicia says March 01 2.25
❑115, Jun 2001 (c) 2.25
❑116, Jul 2001; indicia says May 01 2.25
❑117, Aug 2001; indicia says June 01 2.25
❑118, Sep 2001 2.25
❑119, Oct 2001 2.25
❑120, Nov 2001 A: Wolverine. 2.25
❑121, Dec 2001 2.25
❑122, Jan 2002 2.25
❑123, Feb 2002; 'Nuff Said (silent issue) 2.25
❑124, Mar 2002 2.25
❑125, Apr 2002 2.25
❑126, May 2002 2.25
❑127, Jun 2002 2.25
❑128, Jul 2002 2.25
❑129, Aug 2002 2.25
❑Annual 1, ca. 1992 (c); BSz (a) 2.50
❑Annual 2, ca. 1993; 1: Neurotap. 1: X-Treme. 1: Stronghold. Polybagged with trading card 2.95
❑Annual 3, ca. 1994; (c); BWi (a); 1994 Annual 2.95
❑Annual 1995, Dec 1995; JPH (w); wraparound cover; X-Force and Cable '95 3.95
❑Annual 1996, ca. 1996; wraparound cover; X-Force and Cable '96 2.99
❑Annual 1997, ca. 1997; (c); A: Asgard. wraparound cover; X-Force and Cable '97 2.99
❑Annual 1998, Dec 1998; gatefold summary; (c); wraparound cover; X-Force/Champions '98; gatefold summary 3.50
❑Annual 1999, ca. 1999 3.50

X-FORCE (VOL. 2)
MARVEL

❑1, Oct 2004 4.00
❑2, Nov 2004 2.99
❑3, Dec 2004 2.99
❑4, Jan 2005 2.99
❑5, Feb 2005 2.99
❑6, Mar 2005 2.99

X-FORCE: SHATTERSTAR
MARVEL

❑1 2005 2.99
❑2 2005 2.99

N-MINT

❑3, Jun 2005 2.99
❑4, Jul 2005 2.99

X-FORCE/YOUNGBLOOD
MARVEL

❑1, Aug 1996; crossover with Image; prestige format one-shot 4.95

XIII
ALIAS

❑1, Jul 2005 1.00
❑2, Oct 2005 2.99
❑3, Nov 2005 2.99
❑5, Jan 2006 2.99

XIMOS: VIOLENT PAST
TRIUMPHANT

❑1, Mar 1994 2.50
❑2, Mar 1994 2.50

XIOLA
XERO

❑0 1994, b&w 1.95
❑1, Oct 1994, b&w 1.95
❑2 1995, b&w 1.95
❑3, May 1995, b&w 1.95
❑Ashcan 1 1994, b&w; no cover price 1.00

XL
BLACKTHORNE

❑1, b&w 3.50

X-LAX
THWACK! POW!

❑1, Mini-Comic 1.25

X-MAN
MARVEL

❑-1, Jul 1997; Flashback 2.00
❑1, Mar 1995 JPH (w) 3.00
❑1/2nd, Mar 1995; 2nd printing 2.25
❑2, Apr 1995; (c); JPH (w); After Xavier: Age of Apocalypse 2.50
❑3, May 1995; (c); JPH (w); After Xavier: Age of Apocalypse 2.50
❑4, Jun 1995; JPH (w); After Xavier: Age of Apocalypse 2.50
❑5, Jul 1995 (c); JPH (w) 2.00
❑6, Aug 1995 (c); JPH (w) 2.00
❑7, Sep 1995 JPH (w) 2.00
❑8, Oct 1995; (c); JPH (w); OverPower cards bound in 2.00
❑9, Nov 1995 JPH (w) 2.00
❑10, Dec 1995 JDu (a); V: Xavier. 2.00
❑11, Jan 1996 A: Rogue. 1.95
❑12, Feb 1996 V: Excalibur. 1.95
❑13, Mar 1996 (c) 1.95
❑14, Apr 1996 (c) 1.95
❑15, May 1996 (c); A: Onslaught. 2.50
❑16, Jun 1996 V: Holocaust. 2.00
❑17, Jul 1996 V: Holocaust. 2.00
❑18, Aug 1996; Onslaught, Phase 1 1.95
❑19, Sep 1996 A: Mr. Sinister. 1.95
❑20, Oct 1996; V: Abomination. bound-in trading cards 1.95
❑21, Nov 1996 1.95
❑22, Dec 1996 1.95
❑23, Jan 1997 1.95
❑24, Feb 1997 A: Spider-Man. A: Morbius. V: Morbius. 1.95
❑25, Mar 1997; Giant-size; A: Madelyne Pryor. wraparound cover 2.99
❑26, Apr 1997 1.95
❑27, May 1997 1.95
❑28, Jun 1997 1.95
❑29, Aug 1997; gatefold summary; (c); gatefold summary 1.95
❑30, Sep 1997; gatefold summary; (c); gatefold summary 1.95
❑31, Oct 1997; gatefold summary; (c); gatefold summary 1.99
❑32, Nov 1997; gatefold summary; (c); gatefold summary 1.99
❑33, Dec 1997; gatefold summary; (c); gatefold summary 1.99
❑34, Jan 1998; gatefold summary; (c); gatefold summary 1.99
❑35, Feb 1998; gatefold summary; (c); gatefold summary 1.99
❑36, Mar 1998; gatefold summary; gatefold summary 1.99
❑37, Apr 1998; gatefold summary; A: Spider-Man. gatefold summary 1.99
❑38, May 1998; gatefold summary; A: Spider-Man. gatefold summary 1.99

X-Men (2nd Series)

First issue was all-time best-selling comic book

©Marvel

X-Men Adventures (Vol. 1)

Based on the TV series' first season

©Marvel

X-Men Adventures (Vol. 2)

Some copies of #4 included notorious catalog

©Marvel

X-Men Adventures (Vol. 3)

Third season of animated series adapted

©Marvel

X-Men Alpha

Kicked off the "Age of Apocalypse"

©Marvel

N-MINT

❑39, Jun 1998; gatefold summary; gatefold summary 1.99
❑40, Jul 1998; gatefold summary; (c); gatefold summary 1.99
❑41, Aug 1998; gatefold summary; A: Madelyne Pryor. gatefold summary 1.99
❑42, Sep 1998; gatefold summary; (c); A: Madelyne Pryor. gatefold summary 1.99
❑43, Oct 1998; gatefold summary; (c); gatefold summary 1.99
❑44, Nov 1998; gatefold summary; (c); V: Nemesis. gatefold summary 1.99
❑45, Dec 1998; gatefold summary; gatefold summary 1.99
❑46, Dec 1998; gatefold summary; gatefold summary 1.99
❑47, Jan 1999; gatefold summary; gatefold summary 1.99
❑48, Feb 1999; gatefold summary 1.99
❑49, Mar 1999 (c) 1.99
❑50, Apr 1999; A: Dark Beast. A: White Queen. Story continues from Generation X #50 ..... 1.99
❑51, May 1999 ..... 1.99
❑52, Jun 1999 ..... 1.99
❑53, Jul 1999 A: Cyclops. A: Jean Grey. 1.99
❑54, Aug 1999 (c) 1.99
❑55, Sep 1999 ..... 1.99
❑56, Oct 1999 A: Spider-Man. 1.99
❑57, Nov 1999 (c) 1.99
❑58, Dec 1999 ..... 1.99
❑59, Jan 2000 (c); A: Fantastic Four. .. 1.99
❑60, Feb 2000 ..... 1.99
❑61, Mar 2000 ..... 1.99
❑62, Apr 2000 ..... 1.99
❑63, May 2000; Revolution 1.99
❑64, Jun 2000 ..... 2.25
❑65, Jul 2000 ..... 2.25
❑66, Aug 2000 ..... 2.25
❑67, Sep 2000 (c) 2.25
❑68, Oct 2000 ..... 2.25
❑69, Nov 2000; polybagged with AOL CD-ROM 2.25
❑70, Dec 2000 (c) 2.25
❑71, Jan 2001 (c) 2.25
❑72, Feb 2001 ..... 2.25
❑73, Mar 2001 (c) 2.25
❑74, Apr 2001 (c) 2.25
❑75, May 2001; double-sized 2.99
❑Annual 1996, ca. 1996; (c); wraparound cover 3.50
❑Annual 1997, ca. 1997; (c); A: Sugar Man. A: Nemesis. A: Dark Beast. wraparound cover 3.50
❑Annual 1998, ca. 1998; (c); V: Thanos. wraparound cover; X-Man/Hulk '98 3.50

X-MAN: ALL SAINTS' DAY
MARVEL

❑1, Nov 1997 ..... 5.99

X-MEN (1ST SERIES)
MARVEL

❑1, Sep 1963 (c); SL (w); JK (a); O: X-Men. 1: X-Men. 1: Cyclops. 1: Professor X. 1: Angel II. 1: Marvel Girl. 1: Iceman. 1: Magneto. 1: Beast. 7000.00

N-MINT

❑2, Nov 1963 (c); SL (w); JK (a); 1: The Vanisher. 1: Vanisher. 1900.00
❑3, Jan 1964 (c); SL (w); JK (a); 1: The Blob. 1030.00
❑4, Mar 1964 (c); SL (w); JK (a); 1: Toad. 1: Mastermind. 1: Scarlet Witch. 1: Quicksilver. 1: Brotherhood of Evil Mutants. 900.00
❑5, May 1964 (c); SL (w); JK (a); A: Evil Mutants. 550.00
❑6, Jul 1964 (c); SL (w); JK (a); A: Evil Mutants. A: Sub-Mariner. 500.00
❑7, Sep 1964 (c); SL (w); JK (a); A: Blob. A: Evil Mutants. 475.00
❑8, Nov 1964 (c); SL (w); JK (a); O: Unus the Untouchable. 1: Unus the Untouchable. 360.00
❑9, Jan 1965 (c); SL (w); JK (a); 1: Lucifer. 360.00
❑10, Mar 1965 (c); SL (w); JK (a); 1: Ka-Zar. A: Ka-Zar. 360.00
❑11, May 1965 (c); SL (w); JK (a); 1: The Stranger. 1: Stranger. 300.00
❑12, Jul 1965 (c); SL (w); ATh, JK (a); O: Professor X. O: Juggernaut. 1: Juggernaut. 500.00
❑13, Sep 1965 (c); SL (w); JK, JSt (a); V: Juggernaut. 275.00
❑14, Nov 1965 (c); SL (w); JK (a); O: Sentinels. 1: Sentinels. 250.00
❑15, Dec 1965 (c); SL (w); JK (a); O: Beast. 190.00
❑16, Jan 1966 (c); SL (w); JK (a); A: Sentinels. A: Master Mold. 190.00
❑17, Feb 1966 (c); SL (w); JK (a); V: Magneto. 100.00
❑18, Mar 1966 SL (w); A: Stranger. V: Magneto. 100.00
❑19, Apr 1966 SL (w); O: Mimic. 1: Mimic. 100.00
❑20, May 1966 V: Unus. V: Lucifer. 100.00
❑21, Jun 1966 V: Lucifer. 90.00
❑22, Jul 1966 V: Count Nefaria. 90.00
❑23, Aug 1966 V: Count Nefaria. 90.00
❑24, Sep 1966 ..... 90.00
❑25, Oct 1966 A: El Tigre. 90.00
❑26, Nov 1966 (c) 90.00
❑27, Dec 1966; (c); V: Puppet Master. Mimic returns 90.00
❑28, Jan 1967 (c); 1: Banshee. 155.00
❑28/2nd, ca. 1993 (c); 1: Banshee. 2.00
❑29, Feb 1967 (c); V: Super-Adaptoid. 90.00
❑30, Mar 1967 (c); 1: Maha Yogi. 90.00
❑31, Apr 1967 (c); 1: Cobalt Man. 90.00
❑32, May 1967 (c); V: Juggernaut. 90.00
❑33, Jun 1967 (c); V: Juggernaut. 90.00
❑34, Jul 1967 (c); DA (a); V: Tyrannus. V: Mole Man. 90.00
❑35, Aug 1967 (c); DA (a); 1: Changeling. A: Spider-Man. A: Banshee. 150.00
❑36, Sep 1967 (c); RA (a); 1: Mekano. 65.00
❑37, Oct 1967 (c); DH, RA (a); V: Factor Three. 65.00
❑38, Nov 1967; DA (c); DH (a); V: Blob. V: Vanisher. The Origins of the X-Men back-ups begin 80.00
❑39, Dec 1967 GT (c); DH (a); D: Mutant-Master. 90.00

N-MINT

❑40, Jan 1968 GT (c); DH, GT (a); V: Frankenstein. 90.00
❑41, Feb 1968 GT (c); DH, GT (a); 1: Grotesk the Sub-Human. 65.00
❑42, Mar 1968 JB (c); HT, DH, GT (a); D: Changeling (disguised as Professor X). V: Grotesk. 65.00
❑43, Apr 1968 JB (c); GT (a); V: Brotherhood of Evil Mutants. 65.00
❑44, May 1968; DH (c); DH, GT (a); O: Red Raven. O: Iceman. 1: Red Raven (in modern age). A: Magneto. Return of Red Raven 65.00
❑45, Jun 1968 JB (c); DH, GT (a); O: Iceman. V: Evil Mutants. 65.00
❑46, Jul 1968 DH (c); DH, GT (a); O: Iceman. V: Juggernaut. 65.00
❑47, Aug 1968 DH (c); DH (a); V: Maha Yogi. 65.00
❑48, Sep 1968 JR (c); DH (a); V: Quasimodo. 65.00
❑49, Oct 1968 JSo (c); DH, JSo (a); 1: Mesmero. 1: Polaris. 75.00
❑50, Nov 1968 JSo (c); JSo (a); V: Mesmero. 75.00
❑51, Dec 1968 JSo (c); JSo (a); V: Mesmero. 75.00
❑52, Jan 1969 DH (a); O: Lorna Dane. 65.00
❑53, Feb 1969; V: Blastaar. Barry Windsor-Smith's 1st comic book art 72.00
❑54, Mar 1969 DH (a); O: Havok. 1: Alex Summers (Havok). 1: Living Pharaoh. 72.00
❑55, Apr 1969 DH (a); O: Havok. 72.00
❑56, May 1969; NA (c); NA, TP (a); 1: Living Monolith. V: Living Monolith. Living Pharaoh becomes Living Monolith 72.00
❑57, Jun 1969 NA (c); NA, TP (a); 1: Mark II Sentinels. 72.00
❑58, Jul 1969 NA (c); NA, TP (a); 1: Havok (in costume). 100.00
❑59, Aug 1969 NA (c); NA, TP (a); 1: Dr. Karl Lykos. 70.00
❑60, Sep 1969 NA (c); NA, TP (a); O: Sauron. 1: Sauron. 70.00
❑61, Oct 1969 NA (c); NA, TP (a); V: Sauron. 70.00
❑62, Nov 1969 NA (c); NA, TP (a); 1: Piper. 1: Lupo. 1: Barbarus. A: Ka-Zar. 70.00
❑62/2nd, ca. 1994 NA (a); 1: Piper. 1: Lupo. 1: Barbarus. A: Ka-Zar. 1.50
❑63, Dec 1969 NA (c); NA, TP (a); O: Piper. O: Lupo. A: Ka-Zar. V: Magneto. 70.00
❑63/2nd, ca. 1994 NA (a); O: Piper. O: Lupo. A: Ka-Zar. V: Magneto. 2.00
❑64, Jan 1970 SB (c); DH, TP (a); O: Sunfire. 1: Sunfire. 70.00
❑65, Feb 1970 TP (c); NA, TP (a); A: Havok, SHIELD, Fantastic Four. D: Changeling (revealed) 70.00
❑66, Mar 1970 SB (a); A: Havok. A: Hulk. 80.00
❑67, Dec 1970; (c); SL (w); ATh, JK, JSt (a); reprints stories from X-Men #12 and 13 ..... 35.00
❑68, Feb 1971; (c); SL (w); reprints stories from X-Men #14 and 15 ..... 35.00

Other grades: Multiply price above by 5/6 for VF/NM • 2/3 for VERY FINE • 1/3 for FINE • 1/5 for VERY GOOD • 1/8 for GOOD

❑69, Apr 1971; SB (c); SL (w); reprints stories from X-Men #16 and 19 ...... 35.00
❑70, Jun 1971; (c); SL (w); reprints stories from X-Men #17 and 18 ...... 35.00
❑71, Aug 1971; reprints X-Men #20 ... 35.00
❑72, Oct 1971; reprints stories from X-Men #21 and 24 ...... 35.00
❑73, Dec 1971; (c); reprints X-Men #25 35.00
❑74, Feb 1972; GK (c); reprints X-Men #26 ...... 35.00
❑75, Apr 1972; (c); reprints X-Men #27 35.00
❑76, Jun 1972; GK (c); reprints X-Men #28 ...... 35.00
❑77, Aug 1972; reprints X-Men #29 ... 35.00
❑78, Oct 1972; GK (c); reprints X-Men #30 ...... 35.00
❑79, Dec 1972; GK (c); reprints X-Men #31 ...... 35.00
❑80, Feb 1973; GK (c); reprints X-Men #32 ...... 35.00
❑81, Apr 1973; (c); reprints X-Men #33 40.00
❑82, Jun 1973; (c); DA (a); reprints X-Men #34 ...... 40.00
❑83, Aug 1973; (c); DA (a); reprints X-Men #35 ...... 40.00
❑84, Oct 1973; (c); RA (a); reprints X-Men #36 ...... 40.00
❑85, Dec 1973; (c); DH, RA (a); reprints X-Men #37 ...... 40.00
❑86, Feb 1974; DA (c); SL (w); SD, DH (a); reprints stories from X-Men #38 and Amazing Adult Fantasy #2 ...... 35.00
❑87, Apr 1974; GT (c); SL (w); SD, DH (a); reprints stories from X-Men #39 and Amazing Adult Fantasy #10 ...... 35.00
❑88, Jun 1974; GT (c); (w); DH, GT (a); reprints X-Men #40 ...... 35.00
❑89, Aug 1974; (c); SL (w); SD, DH, GT (a); reprints stories from X-Men #41 and Amazing Adult Fantasy #11 ...... 35.00
❑90, Oct 1974; JB (c); SL (w); SD, DH, GT (a); reprints stories from X-Men #42 and Amazing Adult Fantasy #7. 35.00
❑91, Dec 1974; JB (c); SL (w); SD, GT (a); reprints stories from X-Men #43 and Amazing Adult Fantasy #7 ...... 35.00
❑92, Feb 1975; (c); DH (a); reprints stories from X-Men #44 and Mystery Tales #30 ...... 35.00
❑93, Apr 1975; JB (c); SL (w); SD, DH (a); reprints stories from X-Men #45 and Journey Into Mystery #74 ...... 35.00
❑94, Aug 1975; New X-Men begin (from Giant-Size X-Men #1); GK, DC (c); DC, BMc (a); 1: New X-Men. Old X-Men leave 500.00
❑95, Oct 1975 DC (c); DC (a); D: Thunderbird 85.00
❑96, Dec 1975 DC (c); DC (a); 1: Moira MacTaggart 55.00
❑97, Feb 1976; RB, DC (c); DC (a); 1: Lilandra Neramani. Cyclops vs. Havok 48.00
❑98, Apr 1976 DC (c); DC (a); A: Nick Fury. A: Matt Murdock. V: Sentinels. 48.00
❑98/30 cent, Apr 1976; 30 cent regional variant 125.00
❑99, Jun 1976 DC (c); DC (a); 1: Black Tom Cassidy 48.00
❑99/30 cent, Jul 1976; 30 cent regional variant 125.00
❑100, Aug 1976; DC (c); DC (a); V: X-Men. Old X-Men vs. New X-Men 60.00
❑100/30 cent, Aug 1976; 30 cent regional variant; Old X-Men vs. New X-Men 135.00
❑101, Oct 1976 DC (c); DC (a); 1: Phoenix II (Jean Grey). A: Juggernaut. D: Jean Grey 55.00
❑102, Dec 1976 DC (c); DC (a); O: Storm. V: Juggernaut and Black Tom. 28.00
❑103, Feb 1977 DC (c); DC (a); V: Black Tom. V: Juggernaut 28.00
❑104, Apr 1977 DC (c); DC (a); 1: Starjammers (cameo). 1: Muir Island. V: Magneto 28.00
❑105, Jun 1977 DC (c); BL, DC (a); A: Firelord. 28.00
❑105/35 cent, Jun 1977; 35 cent regional variant 60.00
❑106, Aug 1977 DC (c); TS, DC (a); A: Firelord. 28.00
❑106/35 cent, Aug 1977; 35 cent regional variant 60.00
❑107, Oct 1977 DC (c); DGr, DC (a); 1: Starjammers. 28.00
❑107/35 cent, Oct 1977; 35 cent regional variant 60.00
❑108, Dec 1977; DC (c); JBy (a); O: Polaris. A: Fantastic Four. 1st Byrne art on X-Men 35.00
❑109, Feb 1978 DC (c); JBy (a); 1: Vindicator (Weapon Alpha) 30.00
❑110, Apr 1978 DC (c); DC, TD (a); A: Warhawk. 20.00
❑111, Jun 1978 DC (c); JBy (a); A: Beast, Magneto. V: Mesmero. 20.00
❑112, Aug 1978 GP, BL (c); JBy (a); V: Magneto. 20.00
❑113, Sep 1978 JBy, BL (c); JBy (w); JBy (a); V: Magneto 20.00
❑114, Oct 1978 JBy (c); JBy (w); JBy (a); V: Sauron. 20.00
❑115, Nov 1978 JBy (c); JBy (w); JBy (a); 1: Nereel. A: Ka-Zar. V: Sauron. 20.00
❑116, Dec 1978 JBy (c); JBy (w); JBy (a); A: Ka-Zar. 16.00
❑117, Jan 1979 DC (c); JBy (w); JBy (a); O: Professor X 16.00
❑118, Feb 1979; DC (c); JBy (w); JBy (a); 1: Mariko Yashida. Newsstand edition (distributed by Curtis); issue number in box 16.00
❑118/Whitman, Feb 1979; DC (c); JBy (w); JBy (a); 1: Mariko Yashida. Special markets edition (usually sold in Whitman bagged prepacks); price appears in a diamond; no UPC barcode 16.00
❑119, Mar 1979 DC (c); JBy (w); JBy (a); 1: Proteus (voice only) 16.00
❑120, Apr 1979 JBy (w); JBy (a); 1: Aurora. 1: Alpha Flight (cameo). 1: Snowbird. 1: Northstar. 1: Sasquatch. 1: Vindicator 28.00
❑121, May 1979 DC (c); JBy (w); JBy (a); 1: Alpha Flight (full). A: Mastermind 28.00
❑122, Jun 1979 DC (c); JBy (w); JBy (a); 1: Hellfire Club. V: Arcade. 12.00
❑123, Jul 1979 JBy (w); JBy (a); O: Colossus. V: Arcade. 12.00
❑124, Aug 1979 DC (c); JBy (w); JBy (a); O: Arcade. A: Arcade. 12.00
❑125, Sep 1979; DC (c); JBy (a); 1: Proteus (full appearance). Phoenix cover 12.00
❑126, Oct 1979 DC (c); JBy (a) 12.00
❑127, Nov 1979 JBy (c); JBy (w); JBy (a) 12.00
❑128, Dec 1979 GP (c); JBy (w); JBy (a); O: Proteus. D: Proteus. 12.00
❑129, Jan 1980; JBy (c); JBy (w); JBy (a); 1: Donald Pierce (the White Bishop). 1: White Queen (Emma Frost). 1: Kitty Pryde. 1: Sprite II (Kitty Pryde). Dark Phoenix Saga starts; Emma Front appearance 20.00
❑130, Feb 1980 JR2 (c); JBy (w); JBy (a); 1: Dazzler 12.00
❑131, Mar 1980 JBy (c); JBy (w); JBy (a); A: Angel, White Queen. A: Dazzler 12.00
❑132, Apr 1980 JBy (c); JBy (w); JBy (a); A: Hugh Hefner. A: Angel 12.00
❑133, May 1980 JBy (c); JBy (w); JBy (a); 1: Dark Phoenix. 1: Senator Edward Kelly. A: Angel. 12.00
❑134, Jun 1980 JBy (c); JBy (w); JBy (a); A: Dark Phoenix. 12.00
❑135, Jul 1980 JBy (c); JBy (w); JBy (a); A: Dark Phoenix. A: Spider-Man. 12.00
❑136, Aug 1980 JBy (c); JBy (w); JBy (a) 11.00
❑137, Sep 1980; Giant-size; JBy (c); JBy (w); JBy (a); 1: Hussar. A: Angel. D: Phoenix II (Jean Grey). Giant size 14.00
❑138, Oct 1980 JBy (c); JBy (w); JBy (a); A: Angel 8.00
❑139, Nov 1980; JBy (c); JBy (w); JBy (a); 1: Stevie Hunter. Kitty Pryde joins X-Men; New costume for Wolverine 11.00
❑140, Dec 1980 JBy (c); JBy (w); JBy (a); A: Alpha Flight. 11.00
❑141, Jan 1981; JBy (c); JBy (w); JBy (a); 1: Avalanche. 1: Rachel Summers (Phoenix III). 1: Pyro. series continues as Uncanny X-Men 11.00

X-MEN (2ND SERIES)

MARVEL

❑-1, Jul 1997; O: Magneto. Flashback 3.00
❑-1/A, Jul 1997; Variant cover: "Magneto's Rage, Xavier's Hope; I had a Dream!" 4.00
❑1/Beast, Oct 1991; JLee (c); JLee (w); JLee (a); Storm cover 5.00
❑1/Colossus, Oct 1991; JLee (c); JLee (w); JLee (a); Colossus cover 3.00
❑1/Cyclops, Oct 1991; JLee (c); JLee (w); JLee (a); Wolverine Cover 4.00
❑1/Magneto, Oct 1991; JLee (c); JLee (w); JLee (a); Magneto Cover 3.00
❑1/Collector's, Oct 1991; JLee (c); JLee (w); JLee (a); Double gatefold cover combining A-D images 5.00
❑2, Nov 1991 JLee (c); JLee (w); JLee (a) 4.00
❑3, Dec 1991 JLee (c); JLee (w); JLee (a) 3.00
❑4, Jan 1992 JLee (c); JBy, JLee (w); JLee (a); 1: Omega Red. 3.00
❑5, Feb 1992 JLee (c); JBy, JLee (w); JLee (a); 1: Maverick. 3.00
❑6, Mar 1992 JLee (w); JLee (a); A: Sabretooth. 3.00
❑7, Apr 1992 JLee (c); JLee (w); JLee (a) 3.00
❑8, May 1992 JLee (c); JLee (w); JLee (a); A: Ghost Rider. 3.00
❑9, Jun 1992 JLee (c); JLee (w); JLee (a); A: Ghost Rider. 3.00
❑10, Jul 1992 JLee (c); JLee (w); JLee, BWi (a); A: Longshot. 3.00
❑11, Aug 1992 JLee (c); JLee (w); JLee, BWi (a) 3.00
❑12, Sep 1992 ...... 3.00
❑13, Oct 1992 ...... 3.00
❑14/CS, Nov 1992; Apocalypse trading card 3.00
❑15/CS, Dec 1992; trading card 3.00
❑16/CS, Jan 1993; trading card 3.00
❑17, Feb 1993; indicia says February 1992 ...... 2.50
❑18, Mar 1993 ...... 2.50
❑19, Apr 1993 BWi (a) 2.50
❑20, May 1993 BWi (a) 2.50
❑21, Jun 1993 ...... 2.00
❑22, Jul 1993 ...... 2.00
❑23, Aug 1993 ...... 2.00
❑24, Sep 1993 ...... 2.00
❑25, Oct 1993; A: Magneto. Hologram cover; Wolverine loses adamantium skeleton 5.00
❑25/Gold, Oct 1993; Gold limited edition; A: Magneto. Hologram cover; limited Gold Edition 25.00
❑25/Ltd., Oct 1993; A: Magneto. Cover black and white w/ hologram 30.00
❑26, Nov 1993 ...... 2.00
❑27, Dec 1993 BWi (a) 2.00
❑28, Jan 1994 A: Sabretooth. 2.00
❑29, Feb 1994 A: Sabretooth. A: Sabretooth. 2.00
❑30, Mar 1994; Double-size; Double-sized; trading cards; wedding of Jean Grey and Scott Summers 3.00
❑31, Apr 1994 ...... 1.75
❑32, May 1994; Trading cards 1.75
❑33, Jun 1994 A: Sabretooth. 1.75
❑34, Jul 1994 ...... 1.75
❑35, Aug 1994 ...... 1.75
❑36, Sep 1994 ...... 1.50
❑36/Variant, Sep 1994; Foil cover 2.00
❑37, Oct 1994 ...... 1.50
❑37/Variant, Oct 1994; enhanced cover 2.00
❑38, Nov 1994 ...... 1.50
❑38/Deluxe, Nov 1994; Deluxe edition 2.00
❑39, Dec 1994 ...... 1.50
❑39/Deluxe, Dec 1994; Deluxe edition 2.00
❑40, Jan 1995 ...... 1.50
❑40/Deluxe, Jan 1995; Deluxe edition 2.00
❑41, Feb 1995 ...... 1.50
❑41/Deluxe, Feb 1995; Deluxe edition; trading cards 2.00
❑42, Jul 1995 PS (a) 2.00
❑43, Aug 1995 PS (a) 2.00
❑44, Sep 1995 ...... 2.00
❑45, Oct 1995; enhanced wraparound gatefold cardstock cover 2.00
❑46, Nov 1995 A: X-babies 2.00
❑47, Dec 1995 A: Dazzler. A: X-babies. 2.00
❑48, Jan 1996 A: Sugar Man. A: alternate Beast. 2.00

Other grades: Multiply price above by 5/6 for VF/NM • 2/3 for VERY FINE • 1/3 for FINE • 1/5 for VERY GOOD • 1/8 for GOOD

X-Men Classic

Renamed version of Classic X-Men
©Marvel

X-Men: Evolution

Adapts episodes from the animated series
©Marvel

X-Men Forever

Similar concept to Avengers Forever
©Marvel

X-Men Prime

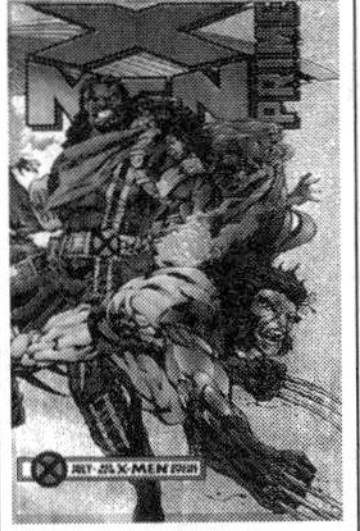

Final stages of "Age of Apocalypse"
©Marvel

X-Men: The Early Years

Reprints stories from the 1960s
©Marvel

	N-MINT
❑49, Feb 1996 MWa (w)	2.00
❑50, Mar 1996; Giant-size; wraparound cover; giant-size	3.00
❑50/Variant, Mar 1996; Giant-size; foil wraparound cardstock cover; giant-size	4.00
❑51, Apr 1996 MWa (w)	2.00
❑52, May 1996 MWa (w)	2.00
❑53, Jun 1996; MWa (w); Jean Grey vs. Onslaught	2.00
❑54, Jul 1996; MWa (w); Identity of Onslaught revealed	2.00
❑54/Silver, Jul 1996	25.00
❑55, Aug 1996 MWa (w)	2.00
❑56, Sep 1996 MWa (w)	2.00
❑57, Oct 1996	2.00
❑58, Nov 1996; Gambit vs. Magneto	2.00
❑59, Dec 1996 A: Hercules.	2.00
❑60, Jan 1997	2.00
❑61, Feb 1997	2.00
❑62, Mar 1997 A: Shang-Chi.	2.00
❑62/A, Mar 1997; A: Shang-Chi. alternate cover	3.00
❑63, Apr 1997 A: Kingpin. A: Sebastian Shaw.	2.00
❑64, May 1997	2.00
❑65, Jun 1997	2.00
❑66, Aug 1997; gatefold summary	2.00
❑67, Sep 1997; gatefold summary	2.00
❑68, Oct 1997; gatefold summary	2.00
❑69, Nov 1997; gatefold summary	2.00
❑70, Dec 1997; gatefold summary; giant-size	2.00
❑71, Jan 1998; gatefold summary; Cyclops and Phoenix leave	2.00
❑72, Feb 1998; gatefold summary	2.00
❑73, Mar 1998; gatefold summary	2.00
❑74, Apr 1998; gatefold summary A: Abomination.	2.00
❑75, May 1998; gatefold summary; wraparound cover; giant size	2.00
❑76, Jun 1998; gatefold summary O: Maggot.	2.00
❑77, Jul 1998; gatefold summary	2.00
❑78, Aug 1998; gatefold summary	2.00
❑79, Sep 1998; gatefold summary	2.00
❑80, Oct 1998; double-sized; double-sized	3.00
❑80/Holofoil, Oct 1998	10.00
❑80/DF, Oct 1998	7.00
❑81, Nov 1998; gatefold summary	2.00
❑82, Dec 1998; gatefold summary	2.00
❑83, Jan 1999; gatefold summary BWi (a)	2.00
❑84, Feb 1999; gatefold summary A: Nina.	2.00
❑85, Feb 1999 A: Magneto.	2.00
❑86, Mar 1999 O: Joseph. A: Astra. A: Joseph. A: Acolytes. A: Magneto.	1.99
❑87, Apr 1999; A: Joseph. A: Magneto. Cover says April, indicia says May	1.99
❑88, May 1999	1.99
❑89, Jun 1999	1.99
❑90, Jul 1999 A: Galactus.	1.99
❑91, Aug 1999	1.99
❑92, Sep 1999	1.99
❑93, Oct 1999	1.99

	N-MINT
❑94, Nov 1999; JBy (w); JBy, TP (a); double-sized	1.99
❑95, Dec 1999	1.99
❑96, Jan 2000	2.25
❑97, Feb 2000	2.25
❑98, Mar 2000	2.25
❑99, Apr 2000 PS (c)	2.99
❑100/A, May 2000; White background, team charging	2.99
❑100/B, May 2000; Nightcrawler vs. Villain cover	2.99
❑100/C, May 2000; Nightcrawler, Wolverine, Colossus, Jean Gray, Storm on cover	2.99
❑100/D, May 2000; Rogue vs. Villain on cover	2.99
❑100/E, May 2000; Team stacked cover	2.99
❑100/F, May 2000; Team in chains cover	2.99
❑100/G, May 2000; Rogue, Nightcrawler, Shadowcat, etc. charging	2.99
❑101, Jun 2000	2.25
❑102, Jul 2000	2.25
❑103, Aug 2000	2.25
❑104, Sep 2000	2.25
❑105, Oct 2000	2.99
❑106, Nov 2000; double-sized; double-sized	2.25
❑107, Dec 2000	2.25
❑108, Jan 2001	2.25
❑109, Feb 2001; JBy (w); JBy, DC (a); Monster sized; with reprints from X-Men (1st series) #98, 143, Uncanny X-Men #341	2.25
❑110, Mar 2001	2.25
❑111, Apr 2001 A: Magneto.	2.25
❑112, May 2001	2.25
❑113, Jun 2001; Title becomes New X-Men	2.25
❑114, Jul 2001	5.00
❑115, Aug 2001	2.25
❑116, Sep 2001	2.25
❑117, Oct 2001	2.25
❑118, Nov 2001	2.25
❑119, Dec 2001	2.25
❑120, Jan 2002	2.25
❑121, Feb 2002; 'Nuff Said month (silent issue)	2.25
❑122, Mar 2002	2.25
❑123, Apr 2002	2.25
❑124, May 2002	2.25
❑125, Jun 2002	2.25
❑126, Jul 2002	2.25
❑127, Aug 2002 BSz (a)	2.25
❑128, Aug 2002	2.25
❑129, Sep 2002	2.25
❑130, Oct 2002	2.25
❑131, Oct 2002 BSz (a)	2.25
❑132, Nov 2002	2.25
❑133, Dec 2002	2.25
❑134, Jan 2003	2.25
❑135, Feb 2003	2.25
❑136, Mar 2003	2.25
❑137, Apr 2003	2.25
❑138, May 2003	2.25

	N-MINT
❑139, Jun 2003	2.25
❑140, Jun 2003	2.25
❑141, Jul 2003; cardstock cover	2.25
❑142, Aug 2003; cardstock cover	2.25
❑143, Aug 2003	2.25
❑144, Sep 2003	2.25
❑145, Oct 2003	2.99
❑146, Nov 2003	2.99
❑147, Nov 2003	2.99
❑148, Dec 2003 (c)	2.25
❑149, Jan 2004	2.99
❑150, Feb 2004	3.50
❑151, Mar 2004	2.99
❑152, Mar 2004	2.25
❑153, Apr 2004	2.99
❑154, May 2004	2.99
❑155, Jun 2004	2.99
❑156, Jun 2004	2.99
❑157, Jul 2004; loses "New" from title, becomes X-Men again	2.99
❑158, Aug 2004	2.25
❑159, Sep 2004	2.99
❑160, Oct 2004	2.25
❑161, Nov 2004	2.25
❑162, Dec 2004	2.25
❑163, Jan 2005	2.25
❑164, Feb 2005	2.25
❑165, Mar 2005	2.99
❑166, Apr 2005	2.25
❑167, May 2005	2.25
❑168, Jun 2005	2.25
❑169, Jul 2005	2.25
❑170 2005	2.50
❑171 2005	2.50
❑172 2005	2.50
❑173, Sep 2005	2.50
❑174, Oct 2005	2.50
❑175, Nov 2005	2.50
❑176, Dec 2005	2.50
❑177, Jan 2006	2.50
❑178, Jan 2006	2.50
❑179, Feb 2006	2.50
❑180, Feb 2006	2.50
❑181, Mar 2006	2.50
❑182, Apr 2006	2.50
❑183, May 2006	2.50
❑184, Jun 2006	2.50
❑185, Jun 2006	2.50
❑187, Sep 2006	2.50
❑Annual 1, ca. 1992; JLee (c); CR, JLee (a); Rogue vs. Villain on cover	3.00
❑Annual 2, ca. 1993; (c); AM, BWi (a); 1: Empyrean. Polybagged w/ trading card; Rogue vs. Villain on cover	3.00
❑Annual 3, ca. 1994; TP, BWi (a); Rogue vs. Villain on cover	2.95
❑Annual 1995, Oct 1995; Rogue vs. Villain on cover	3.95
❑Annual 1996, Nov 1996; wraparound cover	2.99
❑Annual 1997, ca. 1997; wraparound cover	2.99
❑Annual 1998, ca. 1998; X-Men/Doctor Doom '98; wraparound cover	2.99
❑Annual 1999, Aug 1999 V: Red Skull.	3.50

Other grades: Multiply price above by 5/6 for VF/NM • 2/3 for VERY FINE • 1/3 for FINE • 1/5 for VERY GOOD • 1/8 for GOOD

	N-MINT
❑Annual 2001, Sep 2001; (c); Indicia says X-Men 2001	3.50
❑Ashcan 1, ca. 1995; ashcan edition	0.75

X-MEN ADVENTURES (VOL. 1)

MARVEL

❑1, Nov 1992	3.00
❑2, Dec 1992	2.00
❑3, Jan 1993	2.00
❑4, Feb 1993	2.00
❑5, Mar 1993	2.00
❑6, Apr 1993 A: Sabretooth.	2.00
❑7, May 1993; Slave Island, Part 1	2.00
❑8, Jun 1993; Slave Island, Part 2	2.00
❑9, Jul 1993	2.00
❑10, Aug 1993; The Muir Island Saga, Part 1	2.00
❑11, Sep 1993; The Muir Island Saga, Part 2	1.50
❑12, Oct 1993; A: Apocalypse. The Muir Island Saga, Part 3	1.50
❑13, Nov 1993; Days of Future Past, Part 1	1.50
❑14, Dec 1993; Days of Future Past, Part 2	1.50
❑15, Jan 1994; Giant-size	1.75

X-MEN ADVENTURES (VOL. 2)

MARVEL

❑1, Feb 1994	2.00
❑2, Mar 1994	1.25
❑3, Apr 1994	1.25
❑4, May 1994; Marvel Mart insert	1.25
❑5, Jun 1994	1.25
❑6, Jul 1994	1.25
❑7, Aug 1994; Time Fugitives, Part 1	1.25
❑8, Sep 1994; Time Fugitives, Part 2	1.25
❑9, Oct 1994; Includes comic insert promoting collecting football cards.	1.50
❑10, Nov 1994	1.50
❑11, Dec 1994	1.50
❑12, Jan 1995	1.50
❑13, Feb 1995; Reunion, Part 2	1.50

X-MEN ADVENTURES (VOL. 3)

MARVEL

❑1, Mar 1995 O: Lady Deathstrike.	2.00
❑2, Apr 1995	1.50
❑3, May 1995; The Phoenix Saga, Part 1	1.50
❑4, Jun 1995; The Phoenix Saga, Part 2	1.50
❑5, Jul 1995; The Phoenix Saga, Part 3	1.50
❑6, Aug 1995; The Phoenix Saga, Part 4	1.50
❑7, Sep 1995; The Phoenix Saga, Part 5	1.50
❑8, Oct 1995	1.50
❑9, Nov 1995	1.50
❑10, Dec 1995; A: Dazzler. A: Hellfire Club. A: Jason Wyngarde. The Dark Phoenix Saga, Part 1	1.50
❑11, Jan 1996; Dark Phoenix, Part 2	1.50
❑12, Feb 1996; Dark Phoenix, Part 3	1.50
❑13, Mar 1996	1.50

X-MEN: AGE OF APOCALYPSE (ONE-SHOT)

MARVEL

❑0 2005	3.99

X-MEN: AGE OF APOCALYPSE

MARVEL

❑1 2005	4.00
❑2 2005	2.99
❑3 2005	2.99
❑4 2005	2.99
❑5 2005	2.99
❑6 2005	2.99

X-MEN ALPHA

MARVEL

❑1, Feb 1995; MWa (w); 1: X-Men (Age of Apocalypse). enhanced cover; one-shot	3.00
❑1/Gold, Feb 1995; Gold edition; MWa (w); 1: X-Men (Age of Apocalypse). gold edition	20.00

X-MEN/ALPHA FLIGHT

MARVEL

❑1, Dec 1985 PS, BWi (c); PS, BWi (a); 1: The Berserkers	3.00
❑2, Feb 1986 PS, BWi (c); PS, BWi (a)	3.00

X-MEN/ALPHA FLIGHT (2ND SERIES)

MARVEL

	N-MINT
❑1, May 1998	2.99
❑2, Jun 1998	2.99

X-MEN/ALPHA FLIGHT: THE GIFT

MARVEL

❑1, May 1998	3.99

X-MEN AND POWER PACK

MARVEL

❑1, Dec 2005	2.99
❑2, Jan 2006	2.99
❑3, Feb 2006	2.99
❑4, Mar 2006	2.99

X-MEN & THE MICRONAUTS

MARVEL

❑1, Jan 1984; BG, BWi (c); BG, BWi (a); Limited Series	3.00
❑2, Feb 1984 BG, BWi (c); BG, BWi (a)	2.00
❑3, Mar 1984; BG (c); BG, BWi (a); centaur	2.00
❑4, Apr 1984 BG, BWi (c); BG, BWi (a)	1.00

X-MEN ANNIVERSARY MAGAZINE

MARVEL

❑1, Sep 1993; Celebrates 30th anniversary of the X-Men	3.95

X-MEN: APOCALYPSE VS. DRACULA

MARVEL

❑1, Apr 2006	2.99
❑2, May 2006	2.99
❑3, Jun 2006	2.99
❑4, Jul 2006	2.99

X-MEN ARCHIVES

MARVEL

❑1, Jan 1995; BSz (a); A: Legion. Reprints New Mutants #26; cardstock cover	2.50
❑2, Jan 1995; BSz (a); A: Legion. Reprints New Mutants #27; cardstock cover	2.50
❑3, Jan 1995; BSz (a); A: Legion. Reprints New Mutants #28; cardstock cover	2.50
❑4, Jan 1995; DC (a); A: Magneto. Reprints Uncanny X-Men #161; cardstock cover	2.50

X-MEN ARCHIVES FEATURING CAPTAIN BRITAIN

MARVEL

❑1, Jul 1995; wraparound cover; reprints Captain Britain stories from British Marvel Super Heroes #377-383	2.95
❑2, Aug 1995; reprints Captain Britain stories from British Marvel Super Heroes #384-88 and The Daredevils #1	2.95
❑3, Sep 1995; reprints stories from The Daredevils #2-5	2.95
❑4, Oct 1995; reprints stories from The Daredevils #6-8	2.95
❑5, Nov 1995; reprints stories from The Daredevils #9-11	2.95
❑6, Dec 1995; reprints stories from The Mighty World of Marvel #7-10	2.95
❑7, Jan 1996; reprints stories from The Mighty World of Marvel #11-13	2.95

X-MEN ARCHIVES SKETCHBOOK

MARVEL

❑1, Dec 2000; character sketches	2.99

X-MEN AT THE STATE FAIR

MARVEL

❑1; JR (c); KGa (a); 1: Eques. Dallas Times-Herald	2.00

X-MEN: BOOKS OF THE ASKANI

MARVEL

❑1, ca. 1995; wraparound cardstock cover; background info on Askani'son	2.95

X-MEN: CHILDREN OF THE ATOM

MARVEL

❑1, Nov 1999; SR (c); SR (a); prequel to X-Men (first series) #1; cardstock cover	3.00
❑2, Dec 1999; SR (c); SR (a); prequel to X-Men (first series) #1; cardstock cover	3.00
❑3, Jun 2000; SR (c); SR (a); prequel to X-Men (first series) #1; cardstock cover	3.00
❑4, Jul 2000; SR (c); PS (a); prequel to X-Men (first series) #1; cardstock cover	3.00
❑5, Aug 2000; prequel to X-Men (first series) #1; cardstock cover	2.99
❑6, Sep 2000; prequel to X-Men (first series) #1; cardstock cover	2.99

X-MEN CHRONICLES (FANTACO)

FANTACO

❑1, Jul 1981, b&w; magazine DC (c)	2.00

X-MEN CHRONICLES (MARVEL)

MARVEL

❑1, Mar 1995; Age of Apocalypse	3.95
❑2, Jun 1995; Age of Apocalypse	3.95

X-MEN: CLANDESTINE

MARVEL

❑1, Oct 1996, wraparound cover	2.95
❑2, Nov 1996, wraparound cover	2.95

X-MEN CLASSIC

MARVEL

❑46, Apr 1990, JBy (w); JBy (a); Series continued from Classic X-Men #45.	2.00
❑47, May 1990 JBy (w); JBy (a)	2.00
❑48, Jun 1990 BA (a)	2.00
❑49, Jul 1990 DC (a)	2.00
❑50, Aug 1990 DC (a)	2.00
❑51, Sep 1990; DC (a); Reprints Uncanny X-Men #147	2.00
❑52, Oct 1990; DC (a); Reprints Uncanny X-Men #148	2.00
❑53, Nov 1990 DC (a)	2.00
❑54, Dec 1990 DC, BWi (a)	2.00
❑55, Jan 1991; BMc (a); Reprints Uncanny X-Men #151	2.00
❑56, Feb 1991; BMc (a); Reprints Uncanny X-Men #152	2.00
❑57, Mar 1991 DC (a)	2.00
❑58, Apr 1991; DC, BWi (a); Reprints Uncanny X-Men #154	2.00
❑59, May 1991; DC, BWi (a); Reprints Uncanny X-Men #155	2.00
❑60, Jun 1991; DC, BWi (a); Reprints Uncanny X-Men #156	2.00
❑61, Jul 1991 DC, BWi (a)	2.00
❑62, Aug 1991; DC, BWi (a); Reprints Uncanny X-Men #158	1.75
❑63, Sep 1991; Reprints Uncanny X-Men #159	1.75
❑64, Oct 1991 BA (a)	1.75
❑65, Nov 1991; DC, BWi (a); Reprints Uncanny X-Men #161	1.75
❑66, Dec 1991; DC, BWi (a); Reprints Uncanny X-Men #162	1.75
❑67, Jan 1992 DC, BWi (a)	1.75
❑68, Feb 1992 DC (a)	1.75
❑69, Mar 1992; PS, BWi (a); Reprints Uncanny X-Men #165	1.75
❑70, Apr 1992; Giant-size PS, BWi (a)	1.75
❑71, May 1992 (c); PS (a)	1.50
❑72, Jun 1992; (c); PS (a); Reprints Uncanny X-Men #168	1.50
❑73, Jul 1992; (c); PS (a); Reprints Uncanny X-Men #169	1.50
❑74, Aug 1992 PS (a)	1.50
❑75, Sep 1992; Reprints Uncanny X-Men #171	1.50
❑76, Oct 1992; Reprints Uncanny X-Men #172	1.50
❑77, Nov 1992; Reprints Uncanny X-Men #173	1.50
❑78, Dec 1992	1.50
❑79, Jan 1993; Giant-size; Reprints Uncanny X-Men #175	1.75
❑80, Feb 1993; JR2 (a); 1: Valerie Cooper. Reprints Uncanny X-Men #176	1.50
❑81, Mar 1993; JR2 (a); Reprints Uncanny X-Men #177	1.50
❑82, Apr 1993; JR2 (a); Reprints Uncanny X-Men #178	1.50
❑83, May 1993; JR2 (a); Reprints Uncanny X-Men #179	1.50
❑84, Jun 1993; JR2 (a); Reprints Uncanny X-Men #180	1.50
❑85, Jul 1993; JR2 (a); Reprints Uncanny X-Men #181	1.50
❑86, Aug 1993; JR2 (a); Reprints Uncanny X-Men #182	1.50
❑87, Sep 1993; JR2 (a); Reprints Uncanny X-Men #183	1.50

Other grades: Multiply price above by 5/6 for VF/NM • 2/3 for VERY FINE • 1/3 for FINE • 1/5 for VERY GOOD • 1/8 for GOOD

X-Men: The Hidden Years

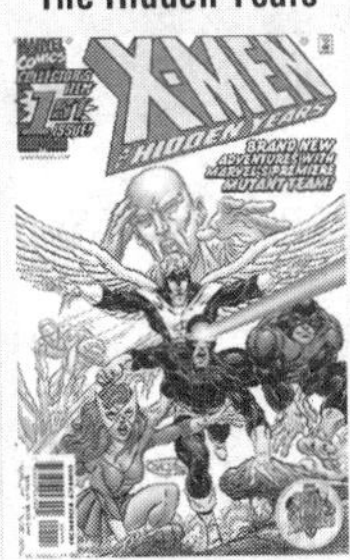

Covers the time that X-Men was in reprints
©Marvel

X-Men: The Search for Cyclops

Followed "The Twelve" storyline in X-Men titles
©Marvel

X-Men 2099

Enclave of outcasts, rebels, and mutants
©Marvel

X-Men Unlimited

Compilation of X-Men short stories
©Marvel

X-O Manowar

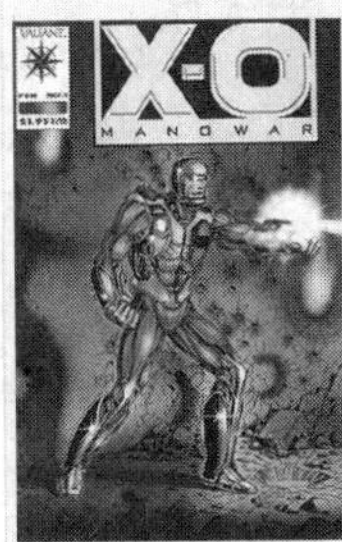

Name is most powerful of a line of alien armors
©Valiant

N-MINT

❑88, Oct 1993; JR2 (a); 1: Forge. A: Rachel. A: Selene. Reprints Uncanny X-Men #184 ..... 1.50
❑89, Nov 1993; JR2 (a); Reprints Uncanny X-Men #185; Storm loses powers 1.50
❑90, Dec 1993; double-sized; Reprints Uncanny X-Men #186 ..... 1.50
❑91, Jan 1994; JR2 (a); Reprints Uncanny X-Men #187 ..... 1.50
❑92, Feb 1994; JR2 (a); Reprints Uncanny X-Men #188 ..... 1.50
❑93, Mar 1994; JR2 (a); reprints Uncanny X-Men #189 ..... 1.50
❑94, Apr 1994; JR2 (a); A: Spider-Man. A: Avengers. Reprints Uncanny X-Men #190 ..... 1.50
❑95, May 1994; JR2 (a); A: Spider-Man. A: Avengers. Reprints Uncanny X-Men #191 ..... 1.50
❑96, Jun 1994; JR2 (a); Reprints Uncanny X-Men #192 ..... 1.50
❑97, Jul 1994; double-sized; JR2 (a); giant; Reprints Uncanny X-Men #193; 100th New X-Men 1.50
❑98, Aug 1994; JR2 (a); A: Juggernaut. Reprints Uncanny X-Men #194 ..... 1.50
❑99, Sep 1994; JR2 (a); A: Power-Pack. Reprints Uncanny X-Men #195 ..... 1.50
❑100, Oct 1994; JR2 (a); Reprints Uncanny X-Men #196 ..... 1.50
❑101, Nov 1994; JR2 (a); reprints Uncanny X-Men #197 ..... 1.50
❑102, Dec 1994; reprints Uncanny X-Men #198 ..... 1.50
❑103, Jan 1995; JR2 (a); 1: Phoenix III (Rachel Summers). reprints Uncanny X-Men #199 ..... 1.50
❑104, Feb 1995; Double-size; JR2 (a); reprints Uncanny X-Men #200 ..... 1.50
❑105, Mar 1995; 1: Cable (as baby). reprints Uncanny X-Men #201; 1st Portacio art in X-Men 1.50
❑106, Apr 1995; reprints Uncanny X-Men #202 ..... 1.50
❑107, May 1995; reprints Uncanny X-Men #203 ..... 1.50
❑108, Jun 1995; reprints Uncanny X-Men #204 ..... 1.50
❑109, Jul 1995; reprints Uncanny X-Men #205 ..... 1.50
❑110, Aug 1995; reprints Uncanny X-Men #206 ..... 1.50

X-MEN CLASSICS
MARVEL

❑1, Dec 1983; TP, MZ (c); NA (a); Reprints X-Men #56-58 ..... 3.50
❑2, Jan 1984; TP, MZ (c); NA (a); Reprints X-Men #59-61 ..... 3.50
❑3, Feb 1984; TP, MZ (c); NA (a); Reprints X-Men #62-63 ..... 3.50

X-MEN COLLECTOR'S EDITION
MARVEL

❑2; Pizza Hut giveaway in 1993; contains fold-out poster cover 1.00

X-MEN: DEADLY GENESIS
MARVEL

❑1, Jan 2006 ..... 3.99
❑1/Quesada, Jan 2006 ..... 3.99
❑1/Hairsine, Jan 2006 ..... 3.99
❑2, Feb 2006 ..... 3.99
❑3, Mar 2006 ..... 3.99
❑4, Apr 2006 ..... 3.99
❑5, Jun 2006 ..... 3.99
❑6, Jul 2006 ..... 3.99

X-MEN: DECLASSIFIED
MARVEL

❑1, Oct 2000 ..... 3.50

X-MEN: EARTHFALL
MARVEL

❑1, Sep 1996; wraparound cover; reprints The Brood saga 2.95

X-MEN: EVOLUTION
MARVEL

❑1, Feb 2002 DGry (w) 2.25
❑2, Mar 2002 DGry (w) 2.25
❑3, Apr 2002 DGry (w) 2.25
❑4, May 2002 DGry (w) 2.25
❑5, May 2002 DGry (w) 2.25
❑6, Jun 2002 DGry (w) 2.25
❑7, Jul 2002 DGry (w) 2.25
❑8, Aug 2002 DGry (w) 2.25
❑9, Sep 2002 ..... 2.25

X-MEN: FAIRY TALES
MARVEL

❑1, Aug 2006 ..... 2.99
❑2, Sep 2006 ..... 2.99

X-MEN/FANTASTIC FOUR
MARVEL

❑1, Jan 2005 ..... 3.50
❑2, Feb 2005 ..... 3.50
❑3, Mar 2005 ..... 3.50
❑4, Apr 2005 ..... 3.50
❑5, May 2005 ..... 3.50

X-MEN FIRSTS
MARVEL

❑1, Feb 1996; reprints Avengers Annual #10, Uncanny X-Men #221 and 266, and Incredible Hulk #181 ..... 4.95

X-MEN FOREVER
MARVEL

❑1, Jan 2001; cardstock cover 3.50
❑2, Feb 2001; cardstock cover 3.50
❑3, Mar 2001; cardstock cover 3.50
❑4, Apr 2001; cardstock cover 3.50
❑5, May 2001; cardstock cover 3.50
❑6, Jun 2001; cardstock cover .....

X-MEN: GOD LOVES, MAN KILLS -- SPECIAL EDITION
MARVEL

❑1, ca. 2003; wraparound cover; reprints Marvel Graphic Novel #5 ..... 4.99

X-MEN: HELLFIRE CLUB
MARVEL

❑1, Jan 2000 ..... 2.50
❑2, Feb 2000 ..... 2.50
❑3, Mar 2000 ..... 2.50
❑4, Apr 2000 ..... 2.50

X-MEN: LIBERATORS
MARVEL

❑1, Nov 1998 ..... 2.99
❑1/Ltd., Nov 1998; Signed edition 19.99
❑2, Dec 1998 ..... 2.99
❑3, Jan 1999 ..... 2.99
❑4, Feb 1999 ..... 2.99

X-MEN: LOST TALES
MARVEL

❑1, Apr 1997; reprints back-up stories from Classic X-Men #3-5 and 12 ..... 3.00
❑2, Apr 1997; reprints back-up stories from Classic X-Men #10, 17, 21, and 23 ..... 3.00

X-MEN: MILLENNIAL VISIONS
MARVEL

❑1, Jul 2000 JSn, BSz, KG (a) 3.99
❑1/A, Jul 2000; JSn, BSz, KG (a); Computer-generated cover 3.50

X-MEN MOVIE ADAPTATION
MARVEL

❑1, Sep 2000 ..... 5.95

X-MEN MOVIE PREMIERE PREQUEL EDITION
MARVEL

❑1, Jul 2000; Toys "R" Us giveaway 2.00

X-MEN MOVIE PREQUEL: MAGNETO
MARVEL

❑1, Aug 2000 ..... 5.95

X-MEN MOVIE PREQUEL: ROGUE
MARVEL

❑1, Aug 2000 ..... 5.95
❑1/Variant, Aug 2000 ..... 5.95

X-MEN MOVIE PREQUEL: WOLVERINE
MARVEL

❑1, Aug 2000 ..... 5.95
❑1/Variant, Aug 2000 ..... 5.95

X-MEN MUTANT SEARCH R.U. 1?
MARVEL

❑1, Aug 1998; no cover price; prototype for children's comic 2.00

X-MEN OMEGA
MARVEL

❑1, Jun 1995; JR2, KJ (c); MWa (w); AM (a); Age of Apocalypse finale; enhanced wraparound cover 6.00
❑1/Gold, Jun 1995; Gold edition; MWa (w); AM (a); Age of Apocalypse finale; gold cover 25.00

X-MEN: PHOENIX
MARVEL

❑1, Dec 1999 ..... 4.00
❑2, Jan 2000 ..... 2.50
❑3, Feb 2000 ..... 2.50

X-MEN: PHOENIX — ENDSONG
MARVEL

❑1, Jan 2005 ..... 8.00
❑1/Variant, Jan 2005 ..... 6.00
❑2, Feb 2005 ..... 6.00
❑2/Variant, Feb 2005 ..... 5.00
❑3, Mar 2005 ..... 4.00
❑4, Apr 2005 ..... 5.00
❑5, May 2005 ..... 5.00

N-MINT | N-MINT | N-MINT

X-MEN: PHOENIX — LEGACY OF FIRE
MARVEL

❑1, Jul 2003 ... 2.99
❑2, Aug 2003 ... 2.99
❑3, Sep 2003 ... 2.99

X-MEN POSTER MAGAZINE
MARVEL

❑1 1994 ... 4.95
❑2 1994 ... 4.95
❑3 1994 ... 4.95
❑4 1994; wraparound cover ... 4.95

X-MEN PRIME
MARVEL

❑1, Jul 1995; AM, TP, CR (a); enhanced wraparound cover with acetate overlay ... 5.00

X-MEN RARITIES
MARVEL

❑1, Jul 1995 ... 5.95

X-MEN: ROAD TO ONSLAUGHT
MARVEL

❑1, Oct 1996; background on Onslaught's origins ... 2.50

X-MEN: RONIN
MARVEL

❑1, May 2003 ... 4.00
❑2, May 2003 ... 2.99
❑3, Jun 2003 ... 2.99
❑4, Jun 2003 ... 2.99
❑5, Jul 2003 ... 2.99

X-MEN SPECIAL EDITION
MARVEL

❑1, Feb 1983; reprints Giant-Size X-Men #1; DC (a); O: Storm. O: Nightcrawler. 1: X-Men (new). 1: Thunderbird. 1: Colossus. 1: Storm. 1: Nightcrawler. 1: Illyana Rasputin. reprints Giant-Size X-Men #1 ... 4.50

X-MEN SPOTLIGHT ON... STARJAMMERS
MARVEL

❑1, May 1990 ... 4.50
❑2, Jun 1990 ... 4.50

X-MEN: THE EARLY YEARS
MARVEL

❑1, May 1994; SL (w); JK (a); O: X-Men. Reprints X-Men (1st Series) #1 ... 2.50
❑2, Jun 1994; SL (w); JK (a); Reprints X-Men (1st Series) #2 ... 2.00
❑3, Jul 1994; SL (w); JK (a); Reprints X-Men (1st Series) #3 ... 2.00
❑4, Aug 1994; SL (w); JK (a); Reprints X-Men (1st Series) #4 ... 2.00
❑5, Sep 1994; SL (w); JK (a); Reprints X-Men (1st Series) #5 ... 2.00
❑6, Oct 1994; SL (w); JK (a); Reprints X-Men (1st Series) #6 ... 2.00
❑7, Nov 1994; SL (w); JK (a); Reprints X-Men (1st Series) #7 ... 2.00
❑8, Dec 1994; SL (w); JK (a); Reprints X-Men (1st Series) #8 ... 2.00
❑9, Jan 1995; SL (w); JK (a); Reprints X-Men (1st Series) #9 ... 2.00
❑10, Feb 1995; SL (w); JK (a); Reprints X-Men (1st Series) #10 ... 2.00
❑11, Mar 1995; SL (w); JK (a); Reprints X-Men (1st Series) #11 ... 2.00
❑12, Apr 1995; SL (w); ATh, JK (a); Reprints X-Men (1st Series) #12 ... 2.00
❑13, May 1995; SL (w); JK (a); Reprints X-Men (1st Series) #13 ... 2.00
❑14, Jun 1995; SL (w); JK (a); Reprints X-Men (1st Series) #14 ... 2.00
❑15, Jul 1995; SL (w); JK (a); Reprints X-Men (1st Series) #15 ... 2.00
❑16, Aug 1995; SL (w); JK (a); Reprints X-Men (1st Series) #16 ... 2.00
❑17, Sep 1995; Double-size; SL (w); JK (a); Reprints X-Men (1st Series) #17 and #18 ... 2.50

X-MEN: THE END - DREAMERS AND DEMONS
MARVEL

❑1, Oct 2004 ... 4.00
❑2, Oct 2004 ... 2.99
❑3, Nov 2004 ... 2.99
❑4, Dec 2004 ... 2.99
❑5, Jan 2005 ... 2.99
❑6, Feb 2005 ... 2.99

X-MEN: THE END - HEROES & MARTYRS
MARVEL

❑1, Apr 2005 ... 2.99
❑2, May 2005 ... 2.99
❑3, Jun 2005 ... 2.99
❑4, Jul 2005 ... 2.99
❑5, Aug 2005 ... 2.99
❑6, Sep 2005 ... 2.99

X-MEN: THE END - MEN AND X-MEN
MARVEL

❑1, Mar 2006 ... 2.99
❑2, Mar 2006 ... 2.99
❑3, May 2006 ... 2.99
❑4, Jun 2006 ... 2.99
❑5, Jul 2006 ... 2.99
❑6, Aug 2006 ... 2.99

X-MEN: THE HIDDEN YEARS
MARVEL

❑1, Dec 1999 ... 3.50
❑2, Jan 2000 ... 2.50
❑3, Feb 2000 ... 2.50
❑4, Mar 2000 ... 2.50
❑5, Apr 2000 ... 2.75
❑6, May 2000 ... 2.50
❑7, Jun 2000 ... 2.50
❑8, Jul 2000 ... 2.50
❑9, Aug 2000 ... 2.50
❑10, Sep 2000 ... 2.50
❑11, Oct 2000 ... 2.50
❑12, Nov 2000 ... 2.50
❑13, Dec 2000 ... 2.50
❑14, Jan 2001 ... 2.50
❑15, Feb 2001 ... 2.50
❑16, Mar 2001 ... 2.50
❑17, Apr 2001 ... 2.50
❑18, May 2001 ... 2.50
❑19, Jun 2001 ... 2.50
❑20, Jul 2001 ... 2.50
❑21, Aug 2001 ... 2.50
❑22, Sep 2001 ... 2.50

X-MEN: THE MAGNETO WAR
MARVEL

❑1, Mar 1999 ... 2.99

X-MEN: THE MANGA
MARVEL

❑1, Mar 1998 ... 3.00
❑2, Apr 1998 ... 2.95
❑3, Apr 1998 ... 2.95
❑4, Apr 1998 ... 2.99
❑5, May 1998 ... 2.95
❑6, May 1998 ... 2.95
❑7, Jun 1998 ... 2.95
❑8, Jul 1998; cover says Jun, indicia says Jul ... 2.95
❑9, Jul 1998 ... 2.95
❑10, Aug 1998 ... 2.95
❑11, Aug 1998 ... 2.95
❑12, Sep 1998 ... 2.95
❑13, Sep 1998 ... 2.95
❑14, Oct 1998 ... 2.95
❑15, Oct 1998 ... 2.95
❑16, Nov 1998; Colossus vs. Juggernaut ... 3.99
❑17, Nov 1998 ... 3.99
❑18, Dec 1998 ... 3.99
❑19, Dec 1998 ... 3.99
❑20, Jan 1999 ... 3.99
❑21, Jan 1999 ... 3.99
❑22, Feb 1999 ... 3.99
❑23, Feb 1999 ... 3.99
❑24, Mar 1999 ... 3.99
❑25, Mar 1999 ... 3.99
❑26, Apr 1999; Mystique apperance ... 3.99

X-MEN: THE MOVIE SPECIAL
MARVEL

❑1, ca. 2000; Giveaway; wraparound cover ... 1.00

X-MEN: THE 198 FILES
MARVEL

❑1, Mar 2006 ... 3.99

X-MEN: THE SEARCH FOR CYCLOPS
MARVEL

❑1, Oct 2000; Single figure (red against black background) on cover ... 2.99
❑1/A, Oct 2000; Alternate cover: Blue/white split background, man with glowing eyes kneeling at right ... 2.99
❑2, Jan 2001 ... 2.99
❑2/A, Jan 2001 ... 2.99
❑3, Feb 2001 ... 2.99
❑4, Mar 2001 ... 2.99

X-MEN: THE ULTRA COLLECTION
MARVEL

❑1, Dec 1994; Pin-ups ... 2.95
❑2, Jan 1995; Pin-ups ... 2.95
❑3, Feb 1995; Pin-ups ... 2.95
❑4, Mar 1995; Pin-ups ... 2.95
❑5, Apr 1995; Pin-ups ... 2.95

X-MEN: THE WEDDING ALBUM
MARVEL

❑1 1994; BSz, (a); One-shot magazine 3.00

X-MEN: TRUE FRIENDS
MARVEL

❑1, Sep 1999 ... 2.99
❑2, Oct 1999 ... 2.99
❑3, Nov 1999 ... 2.99

X-MEN 2 MOVIE
MARVEL

❑1, Jun 2003; adapts X2: X-Men United 3.50

X-MEN 2 MOVIE PREQUEL: NIGHTCRAWLER
MARVEL

❑1, May 2003 ... 3.50

X-MEN 2 MOVIE PREQUEL: WOLVERINE
MARVEL

❑1, May 2003 ... 3.50

X-MEN 2099
MARVEL

❑1, Oct 1993; 1: X-Men 2099. foil cover 2.00
❑1/Gold, Oct 1993; Gold edition; 1: X-Men 2099. foil cover ... 3.00
❑1/2nd, Oct 1993; 1: X-Men 2099. foil cover ... 1.75
❑2, Nov 1993 ... 1.50
❑3, Dec 1993 D: Serpentina ... 1.50
❑4, Jan 1994 ... 1.50
❑5, Feb 1994 ... 1.50
❑6, Mar 1994 1: The Freakshow. ... 1.25
❑7, Apr 1994 (c) ... 1.25
❑8, May 1994 (c) ... 1.50
❑9, Jun 1994 ... 1.50
❑10, Jul 1994 ... 1.50
❑11, Aug 1994 ... 1.50
❑12, Sep 1994 ... 1.50
❑13, Oct 1994 ... 1.50
❑14, Nov 1994 ... 1.50
❑15, Dec 1994 ... 1.50
❑16, Jan 1995 ... 1.50
❑17, Feb 1995 ... 1.50
❑18, Mar 1995 ... 1.50
❑19, Apr 1995 (c) ... 1.50
❑20, May 1995 ... 1.95
❑21, Jun 1995 ... 1.95
❑22, Jul 1995 ... 1.95
❑23, Aug 1995 ... 1.95
❑24, Sep 1995 ... 1.95
❑25, Oct 1995 ... 2.50
❑25/Variant, Oct 1995; enhanced wraparound cardstock cover ... 3.95
❑26, Nov 1995 ... 1.95
❑27, Dec 1995; A: Herod. A: Doom. Story continued from 2099 Apocalypse and Doom 2099 #36 ... 1.95
❑28, Jan 1996 ... 1.95
❑29, Feb 1996 ... 1.95
❑30, Mar 1996; Story continued in X-Nation #1 ... 1.95
❑31, Apr 1996 ... 1.95
❑32, May 1996 JDu (a) ... 1.95
❑33, Jun 1996 JDu (c); JDu (a) ... 1.95
❑34, Jul 1996 JDu (c); JDu (a) ... 1.95
❑35, Aug 1996; (c); JDu (a); A: Nostromo. Final Issue ... 1.95
❑Special 1, Oct 1995 ... 3.95

X-MEN 2099: OASIS
MARVEL

❑1, Aug 1996 ... 5.95

Other grades: Multiply price above by 5/6 for VF/NM • 2/3 for VERY FINE • 1/3 for FINE • 1/5 for VERY GOOD • 1/8 for GOOD

X-O Manowar (Vol. 2)

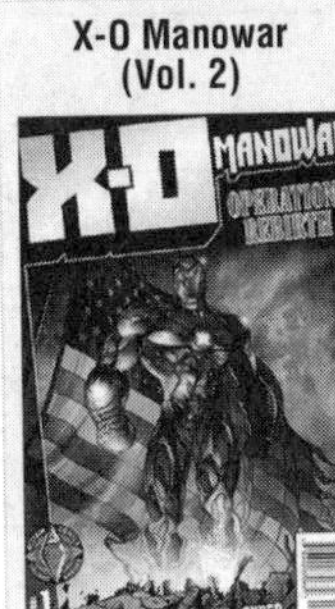

Series restarted under the Acclaim label

©Acclaim

Xombi

Your average man who can't die

©DC

X-Treme X-Men

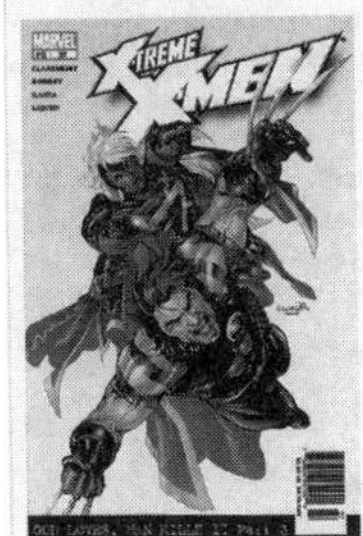

Claremont returns to writing X-Men

©Marvel

X-Universe

Filled in "Age of Apocalypse" background

©Marvel

Yeah!

Second issue pulped for adult language

©DC

N-MINT

X-MEN ULTRA III PREVIEW
MARVEL

❑1, Nov 1995; enhanced cardstock cover; previews Fleer card art 2.95

X-MEN UNIVERSE
MARVEL

❑1, Dec 1999; contains material originally published as Astonishing X-Men #1, Generation X #55, and Uncanny X-Men #373 .... 4.99
❑2, Jan 2000 .... 4.99
❑3, Feb 2000 .... 4.99
❑4, Mar 2000 .... 4.99
❑5, Apr 2000 .... 4.99
❑6, May 2000 .... 4.99
❑7, Jun 2000 .... 4.99
❑8, Jul 2000 .... 4.99
❑9, Aug 2000 .... 4.99
❑10, Sep 2000 .... 4.99
❑11, Oct 2000 .... 4.99
❑12, Nov 2000 .... 3.99
❑13, Dec 2000 .... 3.99
❑14, Jan 2001 .... 3.99
❑15, Feb 2001 .... 3.99
❑16, Mar 2001 .... 3.99
❑17, Apr 2001 .... 3.99

X-MEN UNIVERSE: PAST, PRESENT AND FUTURE
MARVEL

❑1, Feb 1999 .... 2.99

X-MEN UNLIMITED
MARVEL

❑1, Jun 1993 .... 3.00
❑2, Sep 1993 .... 3.00
❑3, Dec 1993 .... 3.00
❑4, Mar 1994 .... 3.00
❑5, Jun 1994 .... 3.00
❑6, Sep 1994 .... 3.00
❑7, Dec 1994 .... 3.00
❑8, Oct 1995 .... 3.00
❑9, Dec 1995 .... 3.00
❑10, Mar 1996; Age of Apocalypse Beast imprisons and replaces real Beast 3.00
❑11, Jun 1996; Magneto and Rogue .. 3.00
❑12, Sep 1996; Onslaught: Impact; Juggernaut imprisoned in Cyttorak Gem 2.95
❑13, Dec 1996 .... 2.95
❑14, Mar 1997 .... 2.99
❑15, Jun 1997; Wolverine vs. Maverick 2.99
❑16, Sep 1997 .... 2.99
❑17, Dec 1997 .... 2.99
❑18, Mar 1998 .... 2.99
❑19, Jun 1998 .... 2.99
❑20, Sep 1998 .... 2.99
❑21, Dec 1998 .... 2.99
❑22, Mar 1999 .... 2.99
❑23, Jun 1999 .... 2.99
❑24, Sep 1999 .... 2.99
❑25, Dec 1999 .... 2.99
❑26, Mar 2000; Age of Apocalypse..... 2.99
❑27, Jun 2000 .... 2.99
❑28, Sep 2000 .... 2.99
❑29, Dec 2000; Maximum Security 2.99
❑30, Mar 2001 .... 2.99
❑31, Jun 2001 .... 2.99
❑32, Sep 2001 .... 3.50
❑33, Dec 2001 .... 3.50
❑34, May 2002 .... 3.50
❑35, Jun 2002 .... 3.50
❑36, Jul 2002 .... 3.50
❑37, Sep 2002 .... 3.50
❑38, Nov 2002 .... 3.50
❑39, Jan 2003 .... 3.50
❑40, Feb 2003 .... 3.50
❑41, Mar 2003 .... 3.50
❑42, Apr 2003 .... 3.50
❑43, May 2003 .... 3.50
❑44, May 2003 .... 2.50
❑45, Jun 2003 .... 2.50
❑46, Jun 2003 .... 2.50
❑47, Jul 2003 .... 2.50
❑48, Jul 2003 .... 2.50
❑49, Aug 2003 .... 2.50
❑50, Sep 2003 .... 2.50

X-MEN UNLIMITED (2ND SERIES)
MARVEL

❑1, Apr 2004 .... 2.99
❑2, Jun 2004 .... 2.99
❑3, Aug 2004 .... 2.99
❑4, Oct 2004 .... 2.99
❑5, Dec 2005 .... 2.99
❑6, Feb 2005 .... 2.99
❑7, Apr 2005 .... 2.99
❑8, Jun 2005 .... 2.99
❑9, Jul 2005 .... 2.99
❑10, Aug 2005 .... 2.99
❑11 2005 .... 2.99
❑12, Feb 2006 .... 2.99
❑13, Apr 2006 .... 2.99
❑14, Jun 2006 .... 2.99

X-MEN VS. DRACULA
MARVEL

❑1, Dec 1993; BSz (a); Reprints Uncanny X-Men Annual #6............ 2.00

X-MEN VS. EXILES
MALIBU

❑0, Oct 1995; limited edition............ 3.00
❑0/Gold, Oct 1995; Limited edition with Certificate of Authenticity; Gold foil 5.00

X-MEN VS. THE AVENGERS
MARVEL

❑1, Apr 1987 1: Titanium Man II. A: Magneto. 4.00
❑2, May 1987 A: Magneto. 3.00
❑3, Jun 1987 A: Magneto. 3.00
❑4, Jul 1987 KP (c); KP (a); A: Magneto. 3.00

X-MEN VS. THE BROOD
MARVEL

❑1, Sep 1996; wraparound cover 2.95
❑2, Oct 1996; wraparound cover........ 2.95

X-MEN/WILDC.A.T.S: THE DARK AGE
MARVEL

❑1/A, May 1998; cardstock cover...... 4.50
❑1/B, May 1998; alternate cardstock cover 4.50

X-MEN: WRATH OF APOCALYPSE
MARVEL

❑1, Feb 1996; reprints X-Factor #65-68; Nathan Summers sent into future (becomes Cable) 4.95

X-MEN: YEAR OF THE MUTANTS COLLECTOR'S PREVIEW
MARVEL

❑1, Feb 1995 FH (w); FH (a) 2.00

X-NATION 2099
MARVEL

❑1, Mar 1996; foil cover 3.95
❑2, Apr 1996 .... 1.95
❑3, May 1996 .... 1.95
❑4, Jun 1996 .... 1.95
❑5, Jul 1996 .... 1.95
❑6, Aug 1996; Final Issue 1.95

X/1999
VIZ

❑1 1996, b&w 3.00
❑2 1996, b&w 2.75
❑3 1996, b&w 2.75
❑4 1996, b&w 2.75
❑5 1996, b&w 2.75
❑6 1996, b&w 2.75

X-O MANOWAR
VALIANT

❑0, Aug 1993; BL (w); O: X-O Manowar. chromium cover 2.00
❑0/Gold, Aug 1993; Gold logo edition; BL (w); O: X-O Manowar. chromium cover 35.00
❑½, Nov 1994; Mini-comic from Wizard Magazine.................... 8.00
❑½/Gold, Nov 1994 .... 55.00
❑1, Feb 1992 BL (c); BL (a); O: X-O Manowar. 1: X-O Manowar armor. 1: Aric Dacia. 7.00
❑2, Mar 1992 BL (c) 6.00
❑3, Apr 1992 BL (c); A: Solar............ 6.00
❑4, May 1992 (c); BL (w); 1: Shadowman (cameo, out of costume). A: Harbinger. 6.00
❑5, Jun 1992 .... 5.00
❑6, Jul 1992 BL (c); BL (w); SD (a).... 4.00
❑7, Aug 1992 FM (c); BL (w); FM (a) . 3.00
❑8, Sep 1992 BL (w) 3.00
❑9, Oct 1992 (c); BL (w).................... 2.00
❑10, Nov 1992 BL (w) 1.00
❑11, Dec 1992 BL (w) 1.00
❑12, Jan 1993 BL (w).................... 1.00
❑13, Feb 1993 BL (w); A: Solar........... 1.00
❑14, Mar 1993 BL (c); BL (w); (a); A: Turok. 1.00
❑15, Apr 1993 (c); BL (w); A: Turok. .. 1.00
❑15/Pink, Apr 1993 (c); BL (w) 8.00
❑16, May 1993 .... 1.00
❑17, Jun 1993 BL (c) 1.00
❑18, Jul 1993 .... 1.00
❑19, Aug 1993.................... 1.00
❑20, Sep 1993.................... 1.00
❑21, Oct 1993 BL (c) 1.00
❑22, Nov 1993 (c) 1.00
❑23, Dec 1993.................... 1.00
❑24, Jan 1994 .... 1.00

	N-MINT
❑25, Feb 1994; with Armorines #0	1.00
❑26, Mar 1994	1.00
❑27, Apr 1994 A: Turok.	1.00
❑28, May 1994; trading card	2.00
❑29, Jun 1994 A: Turok.	1.00
❑30, Aug 1994 A: Solar.	1.00
❑31, Sep 1994; (c); New armor	1.00
❑32, Oct 1994	1.00
❑33, Nov 1994; BL (c); Chaos Effect Delta 3	1.00
❑34, Dec 1994 (c)	1.00
❑35, Jan 1995	1.00
❑36, Feb 1995 (c)	2.00
❑37, Mar 1995	1.00
❑38, Mar 1995	1.00
❑39, Mar 1995	1.00
❑40, Mar 1995	1.00
❑41, Apr 1995	1.00
❑42, May 1995; V: Shadowman. contains Birthquake preview	2.00
❑43, Jun 1995	2.00
❑44, Jul 1995; Birthquake	2.00
❑45, Jul 1995; Birthquake	2.00
❑46, Aug 1995	2.00
❑47, Aug 1995 D: Ken Clarkson.	2.00
❑48, Sep 1995	2.00
❑49, Sep 1995	2.00
❑50, Oct 1995; cover forms diptych with X-O Manowar #50-O	2.00
❑50/A, Oct 1995; cover forms diptych with X-O Manowar #50-X.	2.00
❑51, Nov 1995	2.00
❑52, Nov 1995	2.00
❑53, Dec 1995	2.00
❑54, Dec 1995	2.00
❑55, Jan 1996 (c)	3.00
❑56, Jan 1996	3.00
❑57, Feb 1996	3.00
❑58, Feb 1996 KG (w)	3.00
❑59, Mar 1996 KG (w)	3.00
❑60, Mar 1996 KG, BL (w)	3.00
❑61, Apr 1996 KG (w)	3.00
❑62, Apr 1996 KG (w)	3.00
❑63, May 1996; KG (w); Master Darque acquires X-O armor	4.00
❑64, May 1996 (c); KG (w); PG (a); D: Master Darque.	4.00
❑65, Jun 1996; KG (w); X-O armor asserts control over itself	4.00
❑66, Jul 1996; (c); BL (w); D: Ax. D: Gamin. Aric's armor rebels	5.00
❑67, Aug 1996 BG (c); BL (w); BG (a)	7.00
❑68, Sep 1996 BG (c); BL (w); BG (a)	12.00
❑Yearbook 1, Apr 1995; 1995 Yearbook	3.50

X-O MANOWAR (VOL. 2)
ACCLAIM

❑1, Oct 1996; (c); MWa (w); D: Rand Banion. cover says Feb, indicia says Oct 96	2.50
❑1/Variant, Oct 1996; MWa (w); Painted cover	2.50
❑2, Mar 1997; (c); MWa (w); Donovan Wylie becomes X-O	2.50
❑3, Apr 1997 (c); MWa (w)	2.50
❑4, May 1997 MWa (w)	2.50
❑5, Jun 1997 MWa (w)	2.50
❑6, Jul 1997 MWa (w); V: Magnus.	2.50
❑7, Aug 1997 A: New Hard Corps.	2.50
❑8, Sep 1997	2.50
❑9, Oct 1997	2.50
❑10, Nov 1997; A: Bravado. Avengers #3 homage cover	2.50
❑11, Dec 1997	2.50
❑12, Jan 1998	2.50
❑13, Feb 1998	2.50
❑14, Mar 1998	2.50
❑15, Apr 1998	2.50
❑16, Jan 1998; V: Quantum & Woody. no cover date, indicia says Jan	2.50
❑17, Feb 1998	2.50
❑18, Mar 1998; return of Rand Banion	2.50
❑19, Apr 1998 1: Master Blaster.	2.50
❑20, May 1998	2.50
❑21, Jun 1998	2.50
❑Ashcan 1, Oct 1996, b&w; no cover price; preview of upcoming series	1.00

X-O DATABASE
VALIANT

	N-MINT
❑1, Jun 1993; BL (a); no cover price; polybagged with X-O TPB; armor schematics	4.00
❑1/VVSS, Jun 1993	30.00

X-O MANOWAR/IRON MAN: IN HEAVY METAL
ACCLAIM / VALIANT

❑1, Sep 1996; crossover with Marvel; concludes in Iron Man/X-O Manowar: In Heavy Metal	2.50

XOMBI
DC / MILESTONE

❑0, Jan 1994; 1: Xombi. Shadow War	2.50
❑1, Jun 1994 O: Xombi. 1: Catholic Girl. 1: Nun of the Above.	2.00
❑1/Platinum, Jun 1994; Platinum cover	3.00
❑2, Jul 1994 1: Knight of the Spoken Fire.	1.75
❑3, Aug 1994	1.75
❑4, Sep 1994	1.75
❑5, Oct 1994	1.75
❑6, Nov 1994	1.75
❑7, Dec 1994	1.75
❑8, Jan 1995	1.75
❑9, Feb 1995	1.75
❑10, Mar 1995	1.75
❑11, Apr 1995	1.75
❑12, May 1995	1.75
❑13, Jun 1995	1.75
❑14, Jul 1995	2.50
❑15, Aug 1995	2.50
❑16, Sep 1995	2.50
❑17, Oct 1995	0.99
❑18, Nov 1995	2.50
❑19, Dec 1995	2.50
❑20, Jan 1996	2.50
❑21, Feb 1996; Giant-size	3.50

X: ONE SHOT TO THE HEAD
DARK HORSE

❑1, Aug 1994, b&w	2.50

X-PATROL
MARVEL / AMALGAM

❑1, Apr 1996	1.95

X-PRESIDENTS
RANDOM HOUSE

❑1, Sep 2000	12.95

X-RAY COMICS
SLAVE LABOR / AMALGAM

❑1, Feb 1998	2.95
❑2, May 1998	2.95
❑3, Apr 1998	2.95

XSE
MARVEL

❑1, Nov 1996 (c); A: Bishop and Shard.	1.95
❑1/A, Nov 1996; A: Bishop and Shard. variant cover	2.50
❑2, Dec 1996 A: Bishop and Shard.	1.95
❑3, Jan 1997 A: Bishop and Shard.	1.95
❑4, Feb 1997; A: Bishop and Shard. final issue	1.95

XSTACY: THE FIRST LOOK EDITION
FRESCO

❑1, b&w; promotional comic book sold at convention; also collects cartoons that ran in CBG	2.95

XSTACY: THE LIBRETTO
FRESCO

❑1, b&w	2.95

X-STATIX
MARVEL

❑1, Sep 2002	2.99
❑2, Oct 2002	2.25
❑3, Nov 2002	2.25
❑4, Dec 2002	2.25
❑5, Jan 2003	2.25
❑6, Feb 2003	2.25
❑7, Mar 2003	2.25
❑8, Apr 2003	2.99
❑9, May 2003	2.99
❑10, Jun 2003	2.99
❑11, Aug 2003	2.99
❑12, Sep 2003	2.99
❑13, Oct 2003	2.99

	N-MINT
❑14, Nov 2003	2.99
❑15, Dec 2003	2.99
❑16, Jan 2004	2.99
❑17, Feb 2004	2.99
❑18, Mar 2004	2.99
❑19, Apr 2004	2.99
❑20, May 2004	2.99
❑21, Jun 2004; vs Avengers	2.99
❑22, Jun 2004; vs. Avengers	2.99
❑23, Jul 2004	2.99
❑24, Aug 2004	2.99
❑25, Sep 2004	2.99
❑26, Oct 2004	2.99

X-STATIX PRESENTS DEAD GIRL
MARVEL

❑1, Mar 2006	2.99
❑2, Apr 2006	2.99
❑3, Jun 2006	2.99
❑4, Jun 2006	2.99
❑5, Aug 2006	2.99

X-TERMINATORS
MARVEL

❑1, Oct 1988; 1: X-Terminators. Inferno	2.00
❑2, Nov 1988; Inferno	2.00
❑3, Dec 1988; Inferno	2.00
❑4, Jan 1989; Inferno	2.00

X MAN WITH X-RAY EYES
GOLD KEY

❑1, Sep 1963; Cover says "X, The Man With the X-Ray Eyes," indicia says "X, The Man With X-Ray Eyes"	50.00

X-TREME X-MEN
MARVEL

❑1, Jul 2001	2.99
❑2, Aug 2001	2.99
❑2/A, Aug 2001; Group Cover	2.99
❑2/B, Aug 2001; Psylocke Cover	2.99
❑3, Sep 2001	2.99
❑4, Oct 2001	2.99
❑5, Nov 2001	2.99
❑6, Dec 2001	2.99
❑7, Jan 2002	2.99
❑8, Feb 2002	2.99
❑9, Mar 2002	2.99
❑10, Apr 2002	2.99
❑11, May 2002	2.99
❑12, Jun 2002	2.99
❑13, Jul 2002	2.99
❑14, Aug 2002	2.99
❑15, Sep 2002	2.99
❑16, Sep 2002	2.99
❑17, Oct 2002	2.99
❑18, Nov 2002	2.99
❑19, Dec 2002	2.99
❑20, Mar 2003	2.99
❑21, Apr 2003	2.99
❑22, May 2003	2.99
❑23, May 2003	2.99
❑24, Jun 2003	2.99
❑25, Jul 2003	2.99
❑26, Jul 2003	2.99
❑27, Aug 2003	2.99
❑28, Sep 2003	2.99
❑29, Oct 2003	2.99
❑30, Oct 2003	2.99
❑31, Nov 2003	2.99
❑32, Dec 2003	2.99
❑33, Dec 2003	2.99
❑34, Jan 2004	2.99
❑35, Jan 2004	2.99
❑36, Feb 2004	3.50
❑37, Feb 2004	3.50
❑38, Feb 2004	3.50
❑39, Feb 2004	3.50
❑40, Mar 2004	2.99
❑41, Apr 2004	2.99
❑42, Apr 2004	2.99
❑43, May 2004	2.99
❑44, May 2004	2.99
❑45, Jun 2004	2.99
❑46, Jun 2004	2.99
❑Annual 2001, Dec 2001	4.95

X-TREME X-MEN: SAVAGE LAND
MARVEL

❑1, Nov 2001	2.99

Other grades: Multiply price above by 5/6 for VF/NM • 2/3 for VERY FINE • 1/3 for FINE • 1/5 for VERY GOOD • 1/8 for GOOD

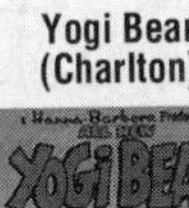

Yogi Bear (Charlton)

Smarter than your average Charlton title

©Charlton

Yosemite Sam

A few pop cultural gags snuck in

©Gold Key

Young All-Stars

Roy Thomas undoes parts of the Crisis

©DC

Youngblood

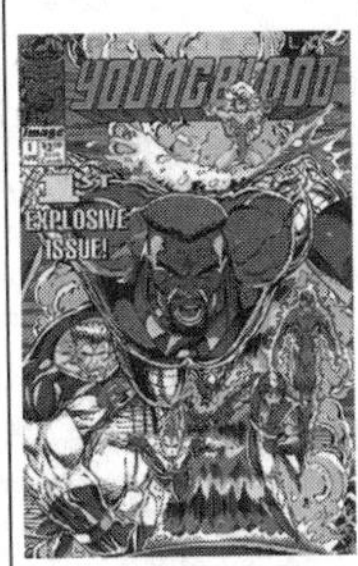

Rob Liefeld's leading title at Image

©Image

Young Heroes in Love

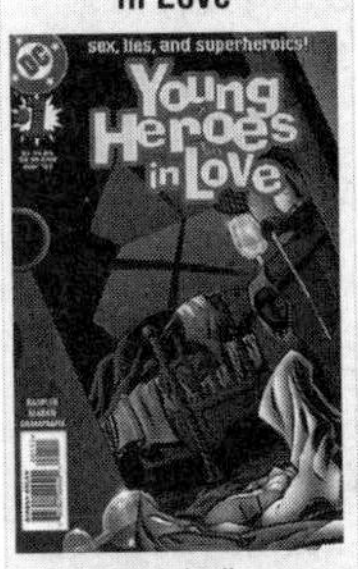

Goofy people discover super-powers

©DC

N-MINT

❑2, Dec 2001 ... 2.99
❑3, Jan 2001 ... 2.99
❑4, Feb 2001 ... 2.99

X-TREME X-MEN X-POSE
MARVEL

❑1, Jan 2003; hardcover; published between X-Treme X-Men #19-20 ... 2.99
❑2, Feb 2003 ... 2.99

X-TV
COMIC ZONE

❑1 1998, b&w ... 2.95
❑2 1998, b&w ... 2.95

X-23
MARVEL

❑1, Jan 2005 ... 7.00
❑1/Variant, Jan 2005 ... 3.00
❑2, Feb 2005 ... 4.00
❑2/Variant, Feb 2005 ... 6.00
❑3, Apr 2005 ... 5.00
❑4, May 2005 ... 4.00
❑5, Jun 2005 ... 2.99

X-UNIVERSE
MARVEL

❑1, May 1995; After Xavier: The Age of Apocalypse; foil cover ... 3.50
❑2, Jun 1995; After Xavier: The Age of Apocalypse; foil cover ... 3.50

XXXENOPHILE
PALLIARD

❑1, b&w; PF (w); PF (a); It's Not Cheap, But It Is Easy ... 8.00
❑1/2nd, Jun 1989, b&w; PF (c); PF (w); PF (a); It's Not Cheap, But It Is Easy ... 2.50
❑1/3rd, Dec 1989, It's Not Cheap, But It Is Easy ... 2.95
❑2, Dec 1989, b&w; PF (w); PF (a); Tales of One Fisted Adventure ... 5.00
❑2/2nd, Jun 1991, b&w; PF (c); PF (w); PF (a); Tales of One Fisted Adventure; 2nd Printing ... 2.50
❑3, Jul 1990, b&w; PF (w); PF (a); Just Plane Sex ... 4.00
❑3/2nd, Mar 1992, b&w; PF (w); PF (a); Just Plane Sex; 2nd Printing ... 2.50
❑4, Feb 1991, b&w; PF (w); PF (a); Practicing Safe Sex Until We Get It Right ... 4.00
❑4/2nd, Mar 1993, b&w; PF (w); PF (a); 2nd printing ... 2.95
❑5, Jul 1991, b&w; PF (c); PF (w); PF (a); Bringing Good Things To Life ... 2.95
❑6, Feb 1992, b&w; PF (c); PF (w); PF (a); Giving The Public What I Want ... 2.95
❑7, Jul 1992, b&w; PF (c); PF (w); PF (a); It's Okay, It's Art ... 2.95
❑8, Feb 1993, b&w; PF (c); PF (w); PF (a); The Comic in the Fancy Brown Paper Wrapper ... 2.95
❑9, Jan 1994, b&w; PF (w); PF (a); The Adventures of Le Petit Mort ... 2.95
❑10, Jan 1995, b&w; PF (c); PF (w); PF (a); trading-card game cover; led to Xxxenophile card game ... 2.95
❑11, Sep 1998, b&w; PF (c); PF (w); PF (a); New material from Books 1-5; published by Xxxenophile ... 3.50

N-MINT

XXXENOPHILE PRESENTS
PALLIARD

❑1, Apr 1992, b&w ... 2.95
❑2, Dec 1993, b&w ... 2.95
❑3, Aug 1994, b&w ... 2.95
❑4, Jul 1995, b&w ... 2.95

XXX WOMEN
FANTAGRAPHICS / EROS

❑1, b&w ... 2.95
❑2, b&w ... 2.95
❑3, b&w ... 2.95
❑4, b&w ... 2.95

XYZ COMICS
KITCHEN SINK

❑1, Jun 1972, b&w ... 25.00
❑1/2nd, b&w ... 12.00
❑1/3rd, b&w ... 8.00
❑1/4th, b&w ... 6.00
❑1/5th, b&w ... 6.00
❑1/6th, b&w; sixth printing ... 5.00
❑1/7th, Jan 1987, b&w; seventh printing ... 3.00

Y2K: THE COMIC
NEC

❑1, Oct 1999 ... 3.95

YAHOO
FANTAGRAPHICS

❑1, Oct 1988 ... 2.50
❑2, Oct 1989; In the Company of Longhair ... 2.25
❑3, Apr 1990 ... 2.00
❑4, Jan 1991; Airpower Through Victory ... 2.50
❑5, Dec 1991 ... 2.50
❑6, Aug 1992; Take It Off (Topless cover) ... 2.50

YAKUZA
ETERNITY

❑1, Sep 1987 ... 1.95
❑2, Nov 1987 ... 1.95
❑3, Jan 1988 ... 1.95
❑4, Apr 1988 ... 1.95

YAMARA
STEVE JACKSON GAMES

❑1, b&w; magazine-sized; collects strips from Dragon ... 9.95

YANG
CHARLTON

❑1, Nov 1973; 1: Yang. Series begins again (reprints) ... 9.00
❑2, May 1974; Indicia says Vol. 2 #2 . 5.00
❑3, Jul 1974 ... 5.00
❑4, Sep 1974 ... 5.00
❑5, Nov 1975 ... 5.00
❑6, Feb 1975; Indicia says Vol. 3 #6 .. 5.00
❑7, Apr 1975 ... 5.00
❑8, Jun 1975 ... 5.00
❑9, Sep 1975 ... 5.00
❑10, Nov 1975 ... 5.00
❑11, Jan 1976 ... 5.00
❑12, Mar 1976 ... 5.00
❑13, May 1976; Final issue of original run ... 5.00

N-MINT

❑15, Sep 1985; Series begins again (reprints); reprints #1 ... 3.00
❑16, Nov 1985; reprints #2 ... 3.00
❑17, Jan 1986; reprints #3 ... 3.00

YARN MAN
KITCHEN SINK

❑1, Oct 1989, b&w ... 2.00

YAWN
PARODY

❑1, b&w; Spawn parody ... 2.50
❑1/2nd, b&w ... 2.50

YEAH!
DC / HOMAGE

❑1, Oct 1999 ... 2.95
❑2, Nov 1999; all copies destroyed ... 2.95
❑3, Dec 1999 ... 2.95
❑4, Jan 2000 ... 2.95
❑5, Feb 2000 ... 2.95
❑6, Mar 2000 ... 2.95
❑7, Apr 2000 ... 2.95
❑8, May 2000 ... 2.95

YEAR IN REVIEW: SPIDER-MAN
MARVEL

❑1, Feb 2000 ... 2.99

YEAR OF THE MONKEY (AARON WARNER'S...)
IMAGE / HOMAGE

❑1, ca. 1997 ... 2.95
❑2, Oct 1997 ... 2.95

YEAR ONE: BATMAN/RA'S AL GHUL
DC

❑1, Jul 2005 ... 5.99
❑2, Sep 2005 ... 5.99

YEAR ONE: BATMAN-SCARECROW
DC

❑1, Jun 2005 ... 5.99
❑2, Jul 2005 ... 5.99

YELLOW JAR
NBM

❑1 ... 12.95

YELLOW SUBMARINE
GOLD KEY

❑1, Feb 1969; adapts movie; poster ... 110.00

YENNY
ALIAS

❑1, Dec 2005 ... 2.99
❑1/Variant, Dec 2005 ... 2.99

YIKES! (WEISSMAN)
WEISSMAN

❑1, ca. 1995, b&w ... 2.50
❑2, ca. 1995, b&w ... 2.50
❑3, ca. 1995, b&w ... 2.50
❑4, Win 1995, b&w ... 2.50
❑5, ca. 1996; b&w with spot color ... 2.50

YIKES! (ALTERNATIVE)
ALTERNATIVE

❑1, Nov 1997, b&w; green and white . 2.95
❑2, ca. 1998, b&w ... 2.95

YIN FEI THE CHINESE NINJA
DR. LEUNG'S

❑1, ca. 1988 ... 1.80

Other grades: Multiply price above by 5/6 for VF/NM • 2/3 for VERY FINE • 1/3 for FINE • 1/5 for VERY GOOD • 1/8 for GOOD

N-MINT

- ❑2, ca. 1988 .... 1.80
- ❑3, ca. 1988 .... 1.80
- ❑4, ca. 1988 .... 1.80
- ❑5, ca. 1988 .... 1.80
- ❑6, ca. 1988 .... 1.80
- ❑7, ca. 1988 .... 2.00
- ❑8, ca. 1988 .... 2.00

YOGI BEAR (DELL/GOLD KEY)
DELL / GOLD KEY

- ❑4, Sep 1961 .... 40.00
- ❑5, Nov 1961 .... 40.00
- ❑6, Jan 1962 .... 40.00
- ❑7, Mar 1962 .... 40.00
- ❑8, May 1962 .... 40.00
- ❑9, Jul 1962; Last Dell issue 40.00
- ❑10, Oct 1962; Jellystone Jollies 55.00
- ❑11, Jan 1963; Jellystone Jollies (Christmas issue) 55.00
- ❑12, Apr 1963; Jellystone Album 30.00
- ❑13, Jul 1963; Surprise Party 55.00
- ❑14, Oct 1963 .... 30.00
- ❑15, Jan 1964 .... 30.00
- ❑16, Apr 1964 .... 30.00
- ❑17, Jul 1964 .... 30.00
- ❑18, Oct 1964 .... 30.00
- ❑19, Jan 1965 .... 30.00
- ❑20, Apr 1965 .... 30.00
- ❑21, Jul 1965 .... 20.00
- ❑22, Oct 1965 .... 20.00
- ❑23, Jan 1966 .... 20.00
- ❑24, Apr 1966 .... 20.00
- ❑25, Jul 1966 .... 20.00
- ❑26, Oct 1966 .... 20.00
- ❑27, Jan 1967 .... 20.00
- ❑28, Apr 1967 .... 20.00
- ❑29, Jul 1967 .... 20.00
- ❑30, Oct 1967 .... 20.00
- ❑31, Jan 1968 .... 20.00
- ❑32, Apr 1968 .... 15.00
- ❑33, Jul 1968 .... 15.00
- ❑34, Oct 1968 .... 15.00
- ❑35, Jan 1969 .... 15.00
- ❑36, Apr 1969 .... 15.00
- ❑37, Jul 1969 .... 15.00
- ❑38, Oct 1969 .... 15.00
- ❑39, Jan 1970 .... 15.00
- ❑40, Apr 1970 .... 15.00
- ❑41, Jul 1970 .... 15.00
- ❑42, Oct 1970 .... 15.00

YOGI BEAR (CHARLTON)
CHARLTON

- ❑1, Nov 1970 .... 22.00
- ❑2, ca. 1971 .... 15.00
- ❑3, ca. 1971 .... 15.00
- ❑4, May 1971 .... 12.00
- ❑5, ca. 1971 .... 12.00
- ❑6, ca. 1971 .... 12.00
- ❑7, Sum 1971 .... 15.00
- ❑8, ca. 1971 .... 12.00
- ❑9, Feb 1972 .... 12.00
- ❑10, Mar 1972 .... 12.00
- ❑11, ca. 1972 .... 8.00
- ❑12, ca. 1972 .... 8.00
- ❑13, ca. 1972 .... 8.00
- ❑14, ca. 1972 .... 8.00
- ❑15, ca. 1972 .... 8.00
- ❑16, ca. 1973 .... 8.00
- ❑17, ca. 1973 .... 8.00
- ❑18, Jun 1973 .... 8.00
- ❑19, ca. 1973 .... 8.00
- ❑20, Oct 1973 .... 8.00
- ❑21, Dec 1973 .... 6.00
- ❑22, Sep 1974 .... 6.00
- ❑23, ca. 1974 .... 6.00
- ❑24, Feb 1975 .... 6.00
- ❑25, Apr 1975 .... 6.00
- ❑26, Jun 1975 .... 6.00
- ❑27, Aug 1975 .... 6.00
- ❑28, Oct 1975 .... 6.00
- ❑29, Dec 1975 .... 6.00
- ❑30, Feb 1976 .... 6.00
- ❑31, Apr 1976 .... 6.00
- ❑32, ca. 1976 .... 6.00
- ❑33, Sep 1976 .... 6.00
- ❑34, ca. 1976 .... 6.00
- ❑35, ca. 1977 .... 6.00

N-MINT

YOGI BEAR (MARVEL)
MARVEL

- ❑1, Nov 1977 .... 6.00
- ❑2, Jan 1978 .... 4.00
- ❑3, Mar 1978 .... 4.00
- ❑4, May 1978 .... 4.00
- ❑5, Jul 1978 .... 4.00
- ❑6, Sep 1978 .... 3.00
- ❑7, Nov 1978 .... 3.00
- ❑8, Jan 1979 .... 3.00
- ❑9, Mar 1979 .... 3.00

YOGI BEAR (HARVEY)
HARVEY

- ❑1, Sep 1992; No creator credits listed 1.50
- ❑2, Jan 1993; No creator credits listed 1.25
- ❑3, Jun 1993; No creator credits listed 1.25
- ❑4, Sep 1993; No creator credits listed 1.25
- ❑5, Dec 1993; No creator credits listed 1.25
- ❑6, Mar 1994; No creator credits listed 1.25

YOGI BEAR (ARCHIE)
ARCHIE

- ❑1, May 1997 .... 1.50

YOGI BEAR BIG BOOK
HARVEY

- ❑1, Nov 1992 .... 1.95
- ❑2, Mar 1993 .... 1.95

YOGI BEAR GIANT SIZE
HARVEY

- ❑1, Oct 1992 .... 2.25
- ❑2, Apr 1993 .... 2.25

YOSEMITE SAM
GOLD KEY / WHITMAN

- ❑1, Dec 1970 .... 35.00
- ❑2, Mar 1971 .... 20.00
- ❑3, Jun 1971 .... 20.00
- ❑4, Sep 1971 .... 20.00
- ❑5, Nov 1971 .... 20.00
- ❑6, Mar 1972 (c); (w); (a) 15.00
- ❑7, Apr 1972; (c); (w); (a); Cover code 90263-204 .... 15.00
- ❑8, Jun 1972 .... 15.00
- ❑9, Aug 1972 .... 15.00
- ❑10, Oct 1972 .... 15.00
- ❑11, Dec 1972 .... 10.00
- ❑12, Feb 1973 .... 10.00
- ❑13, Mar 1973 .... 10.00
- ❑14, ca. 1973 .... 10.00
- ❑15, ca. 1973 .... 10.00
- ❑16, ca. 1973 .... 10.00
- ❑17, Oct 1973 .... 10.00
- ❑18, Dec 1973 .... 10.00
- ❑19, Feb 1974 .... 10.00
- ❑20, Apr 1974 .... 10.00
- ❑21, ca. 1974 .... 4.00
- ❑22, ca. 1974 .... 4.00
- ❑23, ca. 1974 .... 4.00
- ❑24, ca. 1974 .... 4.00
- ❑25, Dec 1974 .... 4.00
- ❑26, Feb 1975 .... 4.00
- ❑27, Apr 1975 .... 4.00
- ❑28, Jun 1975 .... 4.00
- ❑29, Jul 1975 .... 4.00
- ❑30, Aug 1975 .... 4.00
- ❑31, Sep 1975 .... 4.00
- ❑32, Oct 1975 .... 4.00
- ❑33, Dec 1975 .... 4.00
- ❑34, Feb 1976 .... 4.00
- ❑35, Apr 1976 .... 4.00
- ❑36, Jun 1976 .... 4.00
- ❑37, Jul 1976 .... 4.00
- ❑38, Aug 1976 .... 4.00
- ❑39, Sep 1976 .... 4.00
- ❑40, Oct 1976 .... 4.00
- ❑41, Dec 1976 .... 4.00
- ❑42, Feb 1977 .... 4.00
- ❑43, Apr 1977 .... 4.00
- ❑44, Jun 1977 .... 4.00
- ❑45, Jul 1977 .... 4.00
- ❑46, Aug 1977 .... 4.00
- ❑47, Sep 1977 .... 4.00
- ❑48, Oct 1977 .... 4.00
- ❑49, Dec 1977 .... 4.00
- ❑50, Feb 1978 .... 4.00
- ❑51, Apr 1978 .... 2.50
- ❑52, Jun 1978 .... 2.50

N-MINT

- ❑53, Jul 1978 .... 2.50
- ❑54, Aug 1978 .... 2.50
- ❑55, Sep 1978 .... 2.50
- ❑56, Oct 1978 .... 2.50
- ❑57, Dec 1978 .... 2.50
- ❑58, Feb 1979 .... 2.50
- ❑59, Apr 1979 .... 2.50
- ❑60, Jun 1979 .... 2.50
- ❑61, Jul 1979 .... 2.50
- ❑62, Aug 1979 .... 2.50
- ❑63, Sep 1979 .... 2.50
- ❑64, Oct 1979 .... 2.50
- ❑65, Dec 1979 .... 2.50
- ❑66, ca. 1980 .... 8.00
- ❑67, ca. 1980 .... 8.00
- ❑68, ca. 1980 .... 20.00
- ❑69, ca. 1980 .... 17.00
- ❑70, ca. 1980 .... 17.00
- ❑71, Feb 1981 .... 10.00
- ❑72, ca. 1981 .... 10.00
- ❑73, Sep 1981 .... 10.00
- ❑74, Oct 1981 .... 10.00
- ❑75, Jan 1982 .... 10.00
- ❑76, Feb 1982 .... 10.00
- ❑77, Mar 1982 .... 10.00
- ❑78, Apr 1982 .... 10.00
- ❑79, Jul 1983 .... 17.00
- ❑80, Aug 1983 .... 17.00
- ❑81, Feb 1984 .... 17.00

YOTSUBA!
ADV MANGA

- ❑1, ca. 2005 .... 9.99
- ❑2, ca. 2005 .... 9.99
- ❑3, ca. 2005 .... 9.99

YOU AND YOUR BIG MOUTH
FANTAGRAPHICS

- ❑1, ca. 1993, b&w 2.50
- ❑2, ca. 1994, b&w 2.50
- ❑3, ca. 1994, b&w 2.50
- ❑4, Aug 1994, b&w 2.50

YOU CAN DRAW MANGA
ANTARCTIC

- ❑1, Feb 2004 .... 4.95
- ❑2, Mar 2004 .... 4.95
- ❑3, Apr 2004 .... 4.95
- ❑4, May 2004 .... 4.95
- ❑5, Jun 2004 .... 4.95
- ❑6, Jun 2004 .... 4.95
- ❑7, Jul 2004 .... 4.95
- ❑8, Aug 2004 .... 4.95
- ❑9, Sep 2004 .... 4.95
- ❑10, Oct 2004 .... 4.95
- ❑11, Nov 2004 .... 4.95
- ❑12 2005 .... 4.95

YOUNG ALL-STARS
DC

- ❑1, Jun 1987; 1: Iron Munroe. 1: . 1: . 1: Flying Fox. 1: Fury. Iron Munroe cover 3.00
- ❑2, Jul 1987; Tsunami cover 2.50
- ❑3, Aug 1987; Flying Fox cover 2.50
- ❑4, Sep 1987; Neptune Perkins cover 1.75
- ❑5, Oct 1987; Fury cover 1.75
- ❑6, Nov 1987; Dan the Dyna-Mite cover 1.75
- ❑7, Dec 1987 .... 1.50
- ❑8, Jan 1988; Millennium 1.50
- ❑9, Feb 1988; Millennium 1.50
- ❑10, Mar 1988 (c); O: Iron Munro 1.50
- ❑11, Apr 1988 (c); O: Iron Munro 1.50
- ❑12, May 1988 .... 1.50
- ❑13, Jun 1988 .... 1.50
- ❑14, Jul 1988 (c) 1.50
- ❑15, Aug 1988 (c) 1.50
- ❑16, Sep 1988 O: Neptune Perkins 1.50
- ❑17, Oct 1988 O: Neptune Perkins 1.50
- ❑18, Nov 1988 .... 1.50
- ❑19, Dec 1988 (c) 1.75
- ❑20, Dec 1988 TD (a); O: Flying Fox 1.75
- ❑21, Jan 1988 (c) 1.75
- ❑22, Jan 1989 (c) 1.75
- ❑23, Mar 1989 .... 1.75
- ❑24, Apr 1989 (c) 1.75
- ❑25, May 1989 .... 1.75
- ❑26, Jun 1989 (c) 1.75
- ❑27, Jul 1989 .... 1.75

Other grades: Multiply price above by 5/6 for VF/NM • 2/3 for VERY FINE • 1/3 for FINE • 1/5 for VERY GOOD • 1/8 for GOOD

Young Indiana Jones Chronicles

Based on series of television specials

©Dark Horse

Young Justice

Sort of a teen-age Justice League

©DC

Young Love (DC)

Romance series lasted far into the 1970s

©DC

Y: The Last Man

Last man alive in world full of women

©DC

Yummy Fur

Odd stories cheese off the establishment

©Vortex

N-MINT

❑28, Aug 1989 (c) ... 1.75
❑29, Sep 1989 ... 1.75
❑30, Oct 1989 (c) ... 1.75
❑31, Nov 1989 ... 1.75
❑Annual 1, ca. 1988; (c); MGu (a); A: Infinity Inc.. 1988; Private Lives . 3.00

YOUNG AVENGERS
MARVEL

❑1, Apr 2005 ... 10.00
❑1/DirCut, Apr 2005 ... 6.00
❑1/Conv, Apr 2005; Wizard World Los Angeles 2005 ... 15.00
❑2, May 2005 ... 7.00
❑3, Jun 2005 ... 2.99
❑4, Jul 2005 ... 2.99
❑5, Aug 2005 ... 2.99
❑6, Sep 2005 ... 2.99
❑8, Dec 2005 ... 2.99
❑9, Jan 2006 ... 2.99
❑10, Apr 2006 ... 2.99
❑11, Jun 2006 ... 2.99
❑12, Sep 2006 ... 2.99

YOUNG AVENGERS SPECIAL
MARVEL

❑1, Feb 2006 ... 3.99

YOUNGBLOOD
IMAGE

❑0, Dec 1992; RL (c); RL (w); RL (a); wraparound cover ... 2.00
❑0/Gold, Dec 1992; RL (c); RL (w); RL (a); gold ... 4.00
❑1, Apr 1992; Flip-book; RL (w); RL (a); 1: Chapel. 1: Youngblood. 1: The Four. trading card; First comic by Image Comics ... 2.50
❑1/2nd, May 1992; RL (w); RL (a); 1: Chapel. 1: Youngblood. 1: The Four. gold border; First comic by Image Comics ... 2.00
❑2, Jul 1992; RL (w); RL (a); 1: Kirby. 1: Shadowhawk. 1: Darkthorn. 1: Prophet. 1: Berserkers. red logo; cover says Jun, indicia says Jul ... 2.50
❑2/A, Jul 1992; RL (w); RL (a); 1: Kirby. 1: Shadowhawk. 1: Darkthorn. 1: Prophet. 1: Berserkers. green logo; cover says Jun, indicia says Jul ... 2.50
❑3, Aug 1992; Flip-book RL (w); RL (a); 1: Showdown. 1: Supreme ... 2.50
❑4, Feb 1993 RL (w); RL (a); 1: Pitt. .. 2.50
❑5, Jul 1993; backed with Brigade #4. 2.00
❑6, Jun 1994 ... 3.50
❑7, Jul 1994 ... 2.50
❑8, Sep 1994 ... 2.50
❑9, Sep 1994; Image X-Month ... 2.50
❑9/A, Sep 1994; Image X-Month ... 2.50
❑10, Dec 1994 A: Spawn. D: Chapel. .. 2.50
❑SS 1; Super Special ... 4.00
❑Yearbook 1, Jul 1993; 1: Kanan. 1: Tyrax. ... 3.00

YOUNGBLOOD (VOL. 2)
IMAGE

❑1, Sep 1995 ... 2.50
❑2, Oct 1995 ... 2.50
❑2/A, Oct 1995; alternate cover ... 2.50
❑3, Nov 1995; Babewatch ... 2.50

N-MINT

❑3/A, Nov 1995; Shaft cover ... 2.50
❑3/B, Nov 1995; Cougar cover ... 2.50
❑3/C, Nov 1995; Knightsabre cover ... 2.50
❑4, Jan 1996; polybagged with Riptide card ... 2.50
❑5, Feb 1996 ... 2.50
❑5/A, Feb 1996; alternate cover ... 2.50
❑6, Mar 1996 ... 2.50
❑7, Apr 1996; Shadowhunt ... 2.50
❑8, May 1996 ... 2.50
❑9, Jun 1996 ... 2.50
❑10, Jul 1996; flipbook with Blindside #1 preview ... 2.50
❑11, ca. 1996 ... 2.50
❑12, ca. 1996 ... 2.50
❑13, ca. 1996 ... 2.50
❑14, ca. 1997 ... 2.50
❑15, ca. 1997 ... 2.50

YOUNGBLOOD (VOL. 3)
AWESOME

❑1/A, Feb 1998; AMo (w); Blue Awesome logo, Orange Youngblood logo ... 2.50
❑1/B, Feb 1998; AMo (w); Purple Awesome and Youngblood logos ... 2.50
❑1/C, Feb 1998; AMo (w); Teal Awesome and Youngblood logos ... 2.50
❑1/D, Feb 1998; AMo (w); White Awesome logo, Yellow Youngblood logo; Shaft in foreground ... 2.50
❑1/E, Feb 1998; AMo (w); Blue Awesome logo, White Youngblood logo ... 2.50
❑1/F, Feb 1998; AMo (w); White Awesome and Youngblood logos ... 2.50
❑1/G, Feb 1998; AMo (w); White Awesome logo, Yellow Youngblood logo; Suprema in foreground ... 2.50
❑1/H, Feb 1998; AMo (w); Baby Shaft on cover; Blue Awesome logo ... 2.50
❑1/I, Feb 1998; AMo (w); Orange Awesome logo, Red Youngblood logo ... 2.50
❑1/J, Feb 1998; AMo (w); White Awesome logo, Teal Youngblood logo; Suprema in foreground ... 2.50
❑1/K, Feb 1998; AMo (w); 3 women on cover; White Awesome logo, Teal Youngblood logo ... 2.50
❑1/L, Feb 1998; AMo (w); Teal Awesome logo, Yellow Youngblood logo ... 2.50
❑1/M, Feb 1998; AMo (w); A! List exclusive; Foil logo; Three women posing on cover, leaning against wall 3.50
❑1/N, Feb 1998; AMo (w); 1+ issue.... 2.50
❑2, Aug 1998 AMo (w) ... 2.50

YOUNGBLOOD BATTLEZONE
IMAGE

❑1, Apr 1993; Diagrams and schematics of team headquarters, vehicles and equipment; Cover says May, indicia says April ... 1.95
❑2, Jul 1994 ... 2.95

YOUNGBLOOD: BLOODSPORT
ARCADE

❑1 2003 ... 3.00
❑1/Park 2003 ... 3.00

N-MINT

❑1/Dinner 2003 ... 3.00
❑1/Girl 2003 ... 3.00
❑1/Variant 2003 ... 3.00

YOUNGBLOOD: STRIKEFILE
IMAGE

❑1, Apr 1993 1: The Allies. 1: Giger. 1: Glory. ... 2.50
❑1/Gold, Apr 1993; Gold edition ... 2.50
❑2, Jul 1993 RL (a) ... 2.50
❑2/Gold, Jul 1993; Gold edition ... 2.50
❑3, Sep 1993 ... 2.50
❑4, Oct 1993 ... 2.50
❑5, Jul 1994 ... 2.50
❑6, Aug 1994 ... 2.50
❑7, Sep 1994 ... 2.50
❑8, Nov 1994; KB (w); Busiek short story; cover says Oct ... 2.50
❑9, Nov 1994 ... 2.50
❑10, Dec 1994 ... 2.50
❑11, Feb 1995; polybagged with card. 2.50

YOUNGBLOOD/X-FORCE
IMAGE

❑1/A, Jul 1996; prestige format; crossover with Marvel ... 4.95
❑1/B, Jul 1996; alternate cover (black background) ... 4.95
❑1/C, Jul 1996; alternate cover ... 4.95

YOUNGBROADS: STRIPFILE
PARODY

❑1, Jan 1994, foil cover ... 2.50

YOUNGBROTHER
MULTICULTURAL

❑1, Apr 1994 ... 2.25

YOUNG BUG
ZOO ARSONIST

❑1, ca. 1996 ... 2.95
❑2, ca. 1996 ... 2.95
❑3, ca. 1996 ... 2.95

YOUNG CYNICS CLUB
DARK HORSE

❑1, Mar 1993, b&w ... 2.50

YOUNG DEATH
FLEETWAY-QUALITY

❑1, ca. 1992 ... 2.95
❑2, ca. 1992 ... 2.95
❑3, ca. 1993 ... 2.95

YOUNG DRACULA
CALIBER

❑1, ca. 1993, b&w ... 3.50
❑2, ca. 1993, b&w ... 3.50
❑3, ca. 1993, b&w; indicia says #2 ... 3.50

YOUNG DRACULA: PRAYER OF THE VAMPIRE
BONEYARD

❑1, ca. 1997 ... 2.95
❑2, Feb 1998 ... 2.95
❑3, ca. 1998 ... 2.95
❑4, ca. 1998 ... 2.95

YOUNG GIRL ON GIRL: PASSION AND FASHION
ANGEL

❑1 ... 3.00
❑1/Nude; Nude edition ... 3.95

Other grades: Multiply price above by 5/6 for VF/NM • 2/3 for VERY FINE • 1/3 for FINE • 1/5 for VERY GOOD • 1/8 for GOOD

N-MINT

YOUNG GUN
AC

❑1, b&w; reprints Billy the Kid story... 2.95

YOUNG GUNS 2004 SKETCH BOOK
MARVEL

❑1, Jan 2005 ... 3.99

YOUNG HERO
AC

❑1, Dec 1989, b&w; reprints Daredevil #72 (1950)... 2.50
❑2, Aug 1990, b&w; reprints Little Wise Guys ... 2.75

YOUNG HEROES IN LOVE
DC

❑1, Jun 1997 1: Young Heroes. ... 1.75
❑1/Ltd., Jun 1997; Wizard "Certified Authentic" edition ... 6.00
❑2, Jul 1997 ... 1.75
❑3, Aug 1997 A: Superman. ... 1.75
❑4, Sep 1997 ... 1.75
❑5, Oct 1997; Genesis ... 1.75
❑6, Nov 1997 ... 1.75
❑7, Dec 1997; Face cover ... 1.95
❑8, Jan 1998 V: Scarecrow. ... 1.95
❑9, Feb 1998 ... 1.95
❑10, Mar 1998 ... 1.95
❑11, Apr 1998 ... 1.95
❑12, May 1998 ... 1.95
❑13, Jun 1998 ... 1.95
❑14, Jul 1998 ... 1.95
❑15, Aug 1998 ... 1.95
❑16, Sep 1998 ... 1.95
❑17, Oct 1998 ... 2.50
❑1000000, Nov 1998 ... 3.00

YOUNG INDIANA JONES CHRONICLES
DARK HORSE

❑1, Feb 1992 KB (w); A: T.E. Lawrence. 3.00
❑2, Mar 1992 KB (w); A: Pancho Villa. 2.50
❑3, Apr 1992 KB (w); GM (a); A: Teddy Roosevelt. ... 2.50
❑4, May 1992 KB (w); GM (a) ... 2.50
❑5, Jun 1992 KB (w) ... 2.50
❑6, Jul 1992 KB (w) ... 2.50
❑7, Aug 1992 KB (w) ... 2.50
❑8, Sep 1992 KB (w) ... 2.50
❑9, Oct 1992 KB (w) ... 2.50
❑10, Dec 1992 KB (w) ... 2.50
❑11, Jan 1993 KB (w) ... 2.50
❑12, Feb 1993 KB (w) ... 2.50

YOUNG INDIANA JONES CHRONICLES (2ND SERIES)
HOLLYWOOD

❑1, ca. 1992; reprints Dark Horse issues #1 and 2 for newsstand distribution ... 2.50
❑2, ca. 1992; reprints Dark Horse issues #3 and 4 for newsstand distribution ... 2.50
❑3, ca. 1992; Reprints ... 2.50

YOUNG JUSTICE
DC

❑1, Sep 1998 PD (w); 1: Supercycle. 1: Mighty Endowed. A: Superboy. A: Martian Manhunter. A: Impulse. A: Robin. ... 4.00
❑2, Oct 1998 PD (w); 1: Rip Roar. A: Ali Ben Styn. ... 3.00
❑3, Dec 1998 PD (w); A: Mr. Mxyzptlk. 3.00
❑4, Jan 1999 PD (w); 1: Harm. 1: Tora. A: Wonder Girl. A: Spirit. A: Arrowette. V: Harm. ... 3.00
❑5, Feb 1999 PD (w); V: Harm. ... 3.00
❑6, Mar 1999 PD (w); A: Wonder Woman. A: Superman. A: Justice League of America. A: Flash III (Wally West). A: Martian Manhunter. A: Green Lantern. A: Batman. A: Aquaman. A: Despero. ... 2.50
❑7, Apr 1999; PD (w); A: Nightwing. A: Max Mercury. Parent/Teacher conference ... 2.50
❑8, May 1999 A: Psyba-Rats. ... 2.50
❑9, Jun 1999 PD (w) ... 2.50
❑10, Jul 1999 PD (w) ... 2.50
❑11, Aug 1999 PD (w) ... 2.50
❑12, Sep 1999 PD (w) ... 2.50
❑13, Oct 1999 PD (w); A: Supergirl. ... 2.50
❑14, Nov 1999; PD (w); A: Harm. Day of Judgment ... 2.50
❑15, Dec 1999 PD (w) ... 2.50
❑16, Jan 2000 PD (w); 1: Old Justice. 2.50
❑17, Feb 2000 PD (w) ... 2.50
❑18, Mar 2000 PD (w) ... 2.50
❑19, Apr 2000 PD (w) ... 2.50
❑20, Jun 2000 PD (w); A: Li'l Lobo. A: JLA. ... 2.50
❑21, Jul 2000 (c); PD (w) ... 2.50
❑22, Aug 2000 PD (w) ... 2.50
❑23, Sep 2000; PD (w); at Olympic Games ... 2.50
❑24, Oct 2000; PD (w); Misprinted copies exist with duplicated ad ... 2.50
❑25, Nov 2000; PD (w); at Olympic Games ... 2.50
❑26, Dec 2000 PD (w) ... 2.50
❑27, Jan 2001 PD (w) ... 2.50
❑28, Feb 2001 PD (w); A: Forever People. ... 2.50
❑29, Mar 2001 PD (w); A: Forever People. A: Darkseid. ... 2.50
❑30, Apr 2001 PD (w) ... 2.50
❑31, May 2001 PD (w) ... 2.50
❑32, Jun 2001 PD (w) ... 2.50
❑33, Jul 2001 PD (w) ... 2.50
❑34, Aug 2001 PD (w) ... 2.50
❑35, Sep 2001; PD (w); Our Worlds At War; All-Out War ... 2.50
❑36, Oct 2001; PD (w); Our Worlds At War; Casualties of War ... 2.50
❑37, Nov 2001 PD (w); A: Darkseid. A: Granny Goodness. ... 2.50
❑38, Dec 2001; PD (w); Joker: Last Laugh crossover ... 2.50
❑39, Jan 2002 PD (w) ... 2.50
❑40, Feb 2002 PD (w) ... 2.50
❑41, Mar 2002; PD (w); A: The Ray. Lifesaver/Mad insert ... 2.50
❑42, Apr 2002 PD (w); A: Spectre. ... 2.50
❑43, May 2002 PD (w) ... 2.50
❑44, Jun 2002 PD (w) ... 2.50
❑45, Jul 2002 PD (w) ... 2.50
❑46, Aug 2002 PD (w) ... 2.50
❑47, Sep 2002 PD (w) ... 2.50
❑48, Oct 2002 PD (w) ... 2.50
❑49, Nov 2002 PD (w) ... 2.50
❑50, Dec 2002 PD (w) ... 3.95
❑51, Jan 2003 PD (w) ... 2.50
❑52, Feb 2003 PD (w) ... 2.50
❑53, Mar 2003 PD (w) ... 2.50
❑54, Apr 2003 ... 2.75
❑55, May 2003 ... 2.75
❑1000000, Nov 1998 PD (w); 1: Young Justice Legion S. ... 3.50
❑Giant Size 1, May 1999 PD (w) ... 4.95

YOUNG JUSTICE IN NO MAN'S LAND
DC

❑1, Jul 1999; in Gotham City ... 3.95

YOUNG JUSTICE: OUR WORLDS AT WAR
DC

❑1, Nov 2001; Our Worlds at War ... 2.95

YOUNG JUSTICE SECRET FILES
DC

❑1, Jan 1999; Includes profiles of Young Justice members; Includes timeline ... 4.95

YOUNG JUSTICE: SINS OF YOUTH
DC

❑1, May 2000 ... 2.50
❑2, May 2000 ... 2.50

YOUNG JUSTICE: THE SECRET
DC

❑1, Jun 1998; Girlfrenzy; leads into Young Justice: World Without Grown-Ups ... 1.95

YOUNG LAWYERS
DELL

❑1, Jan 1971 ... 10.00
❑2, Apr 1971 ... 10.00

YOUNG LOVE (DC)
DC

❑39, Oct 1963 ... 30.00
❑40, Dec 1963 ... 24.00
❑41, Feb 1964 ... 24.00
❑42, Apr 1964 ... 24.00
❑43, Jun 1964 ... 24.00
❑44, Aug 1964 ... 24.00
❑45, Oct 1964 ... 24.00
❑46, Dec 1964 ... 24.00
❑47, Feb 1965 ... 24.00
❑48, Apr 1965 ... 24.00
❑49, Jun 1965 ... 24.00
❑50, Aug 1965 ... 24.00
❑51, Oct 1965 ... 20.00
❑52, Dec 1965 ... 20.00
❑53, Feb 1966 ... 20.00
❑54, Apr 1966 ... 20.00
❑55, Jun 1966 ... 20.00
❑56, Aug 1966 ... 20.00
❑57, Oct 1966 ... 20.00
❑58, Dec 1966 ... 20.00
❑59, Feb 1967 ... 20.00
❑60, Apr 1967 ... 20.00
❑61, Jun 1967 ... 20.00
❑62, Aug 1967 ... 20.00
❑63, Oct 1967 ... 20.00
❑64, Dec 1967 ... 20.00
❑65, Feb 1968 ... 20.00
❑66, Apr 1968 ... 20.00
❑67, Jun 1968 ... 20.00
❑68, Aug 1968 ... 20.00
❑69, Sep 1968; Giant ... 20.00
❑70, Oct 1968 ... 20.00
❑71, Dec 1968 ... 14.00
❑72, Feb 1969 ... 14.00
❑73, Apr 1969 ... 14.00
❑74, Jun 1969 ... 14.00
❑75, Aug 1969 ... 14.00
❑76, Oct 1969 ... 14.00
❑77, Dec 1969 ... 14.00
❑78, Feb 1970 ... 14.00
❑79, Apr 1970 ... 14.00
❑80, Jun 1970 ... 14.00
❑81, Aug 1970 ... 14.00
❑82, Oct 1970 ... 14.00
❑83, Dec 1970 ... 14.00
❑84, Feb 1971 ... 14.00
❑85, Apr 1971 ... 14.00
❑86, Jun 1971 ... 14.00
❑87, Aug 1971 ... 14.00
❑88, Sep 1971 ... 14.00
❑89, Oct 1971 ... 14.00
❑90, Dec 1971 ... 14.00
❑91, Jan 1972 ... 10.00
❑92, Feb 1972 ... 10.00
❑93, Mar 1972 ... 10.00
❑94, Apr 1972 ... 10.00
❑95, May 1972 ... 10.00
❑96, Jun 1972 ... 10.00
❑97, Jul 1972 ... 10.00
❑98, Aug 1972 ... 10.00
❑99, Sep 1972 ... 10.00
❑100, Oct 1972 ... 10.00
❑101, Nov 1972 ... 7.00
❑102, Feb 1973 ... 7.00
❑103, Apr 1973 ... 7.00
❑104, Jun 1973 ... 7.00
❑105, Sep 1973 ... 7.00
❑106, Nov 1973 ... 7.00
❑107, Jan 1974 ... 25.00
❑108, Mar 1974 ... 20.00
❑109, May 1974 ... 20.00
❑110, Jul 1974 ... 20.00
❑111, Sep 1974 ... 20.00
❑112, Nov 1974 ... 20.00
❑113, Jan 1975 ... 20.00
❑114, Mar 1975 ... 20.00
❑115, May 1975 ... 12.00
❑116, Jul 1975 ... 12.00
❑117, Sep 1975 ... 12.00
❑118, Nov 1975 ... 12.00
❑119, Jan 1976 ... 12.00
❑120, Win 1976 ... 12.00
❑121 1976 ... 12.00
❑122 1976 ... 12.00
❑123 1977 ... 12.00
❑124 1977 ... 12.00
❑125 1977 ... 12.00
❑126, Jul 1977 ... 12.00

YOUNG LOVERS (AVALON)
AVALON

❑1, b&w; Indicia reads "Rock and Roll Romance" ... 2.95

Other grades: Multiply price above by 5/6 for VF/NM • 2/3 for VERY FINE • 1/3 for FINE • 1/5 for VERY GOOD • 1/8 for GOOD

Zatanna

Half-human, half-Atlantean sorceress

©DC

Zoo Funnies (3rd Series)

One-shot reprints strips from earlier runs

©Charlton

Zorro (Dell)

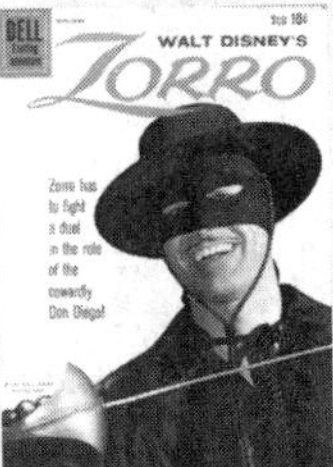

Dell issues were based on the Disney TV show

©Dell

Zot!

Hero crosses over to our world

©Eclipse

ZZZ

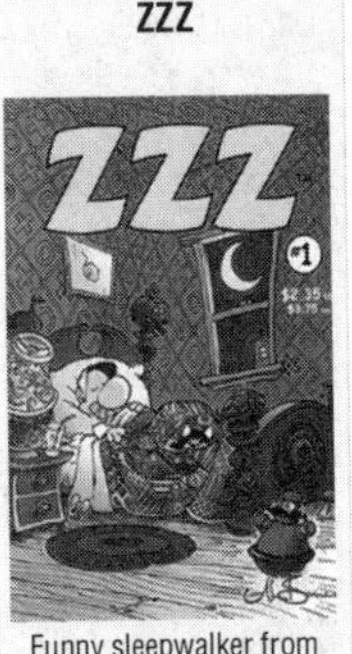

Funny sleepwalker from Alan Bunce

©Alan Bunce

N-MINT

YOUNG MASTER
NEW COMICS

❑1, Nov 1987, b&w 1.75
❑2, Dec 1987, b&w 1.75
❑3, Mar 1988, b&w 1.75
❑4, May 1988, b&w 1.75
❑5, Jul 1988, b&w 1.75
❑6, Oct 1988, b&w 1.75
❑7, Jan 1989, b&w 1.75
❑8, Mar 1989, b&w 1.95
❑9, May 1989, b&w 1.95

YOUNG REBELS
DELL

❑1, Jan 1971 .... 15.00

YOUNG ROMANCE (DC)
DC

❑125, Sep 1963; Series continued from Young Romance (Prize) #124 .... 42.00
❑126, Nov 1963 .... 18.00
❑127, Jan 1964 .... 18.00
❑128, Mar 1964 .... 18.00
❑129, May 1964 .... 18.00
❑130, Jul 1964 .... 18.00
❑131, Sep 1964 .... 18.00
❑132, Nov 1964 .... 18.00
❑133, Jan 1965 .... 18.00
❑134, Mar 1965 .... 18.00
❑135, May 1965 .... 18.00
❑136, Jul 1965 .... 18.00
❑137, Sep 1965 .... 18.00
❑138, Nov 1965 .... 18.00
❑139, Jan 1966 .... 18.00
❑140, Mar 1966 .... 18.00
❑141, May 1966 .... 15.00
❑142, Jul 1966 .... 15.00
❑143, Sep 1966 .... 15.00
❑144, Nov 1966 .... 15.00
❑145, Jan 1967 .... 15.00
❑146, Mar 1967 .... 15.00
❑147, May 1967 .... 15.00
❑148, Jul 1967 .... 15.00
❑149, Sep 1967 .... 15.00
❑150, Nov 1967 .... 15.00
❑151, Jan 1968 .... 12.00
❑152, Mar 1968 .... 12.00
❑153, May 1968 .... 12.00
❑154, Jul 1968 .... 12.00
❑155, Sep 1968 .... 12.00
❑156, Nov 1968 .... 12.00
❑157, Jan 1969 .... 12.00
❑158, Mar 1969 .... 12.00
❑159, May 1969 .... 12.00
❑160, Jul 1969 .... 10.00
❑161, Sep 1969 .... 10.00
❑162, Nov 1969 .... 10.00
❑163, Jan 1970 .... 10.00
❑164, Mar 1970 .... 10.00
❑165, May 1970 .... 10.00
❑166, Jul 1970 .... 10.00
❑167, Sep 1970 .... 10.00
❑168, Nov 1971 .... 10.00
❑169, Jan 1971 .... 10.00
❑170, Mar 1971 .... 10.00
❑171, May 1971 .... 9.00

N-MINT

❑172, Jul 1971 .... 9.00
❑173, Aug 1971 .... 9.00
❑174, Sep 1971 .... 9.00
❑175, Oct 1971 .... 9.00
❑176, Nov 1971 .... 9.00
❑177, Dec 1971 .... 9.00
❑178, Jan 1972 .... 9.00
❑179, Feb 1972 .... 9.00
❑180, Mar 1972 .... 9.00
❑181, Apr 1972 .... 9.00
❑182, May 1972 .... 9.00
❑183, Jun 1972 .... 9.00
❑184, Jul 1972 .... 9.00
❑185, Aug 1972 .... 9.00
❑186, Sep 1972 .... 9.00
❑187, Oct 1972 .... 9.00
❑188, Nov 1972 .... 9.00
❑189, Dec 1972 .... 9.00
❑190, Jan 1973 .... 9.00
❑191, Feb 1973 .... 9.00
❑192, Mar 1973 .... 9.00
❑193, May 1973 .... 9.00
❑194, Aug 1973 .... 9.00
❑195, Oct 1973 .... 9.00
❑196, Dec 1973 .... 9.00
❑197, Feb 1974 .... 9.00
❑198, Apr 1974 .... 20.00
❑199, Jun 1974 .... 20.00
❑200, Aug 1974 .... 20.00
❑201, Oct 1974 .... 20.00
❑202, Dec 1974 .... 8.00
❑203, Feb 1975 .... 8.00
❑204, Apr 1975 .... 8.00
❑205, Jun 1975 .... 8.00
❑206, Aug 1975 .... 8.00
❑207, Oct 1975 .... 8.00
❑208, Dec 1975 .... 8.00

YOUNGSPUD
SPOOF

❑1 .... 2.95

YOUNG WITCHES
FANTAGRAPHICS / EROS

❑1, May 1991, b&w 2.50
❑2, Jun 1991, b&w 2.50
❑3, Jul 1991, b&w (c) 2.50
❑4, Sep 1991, b&w 2.50

YOUNG WITCHES VI: WRATH OF AGATHA
FANTAGRAPHICS

❑1 .... 5.95
❑2 .... 5.95

YOUNG WITCHES: LONDON BABYLON
FANTAGRAPHICS / EROS

❑1, ca. 1992, b&w 3.50
❑2, ca. 1992, b&w 3.50
❑3, ca. 1992, b&w 3.50
❑4, ca. 1992, b&w 3.50
❑5, ca. 1992, b&w 3.50
❑6, ca. 1992, b&w 3.50

YOUNG ZEN: CITY OF DEATH
EXPRESS / ENTITY

❑1, b&w; cardstock cover 3.25

N-MINT

YOUNG ZEN INTERGALACTIC NINJA
EXPRESS / ENTITY

❑1, b&w; trading card 3.50
❑2, b&w 2.95

YOUR BIG BOOK OF BIG BANG COMICS
IMAGE

❑1, ca. 1998; reprints Big Bang Comics # 0, #1, #2 .... 11.00

YOU'RE UNDER ARREST!
DARK HORSE / MANGA

❑1, Dec 1995, b&w 2.95
❑2, Jan 1996, b&w 2.95
❑3, Feb 1996, b&w 2.95
❑4, Mar 1996, b&w 2.95
❑5, Apr 1996, b&w 2.95
❑6, May 1996, b&w 2.95
❑7, Jun 1996, b&w 2.95
❑8, Jul 1996, b&w 2.95
❑Book 1, b&w; Collects series 12.95

YOUR HYTONE COMIX
APEX NOVELTIES

❑1, Feb 1971, b&w; underground 8.00

Y'S GUYS
OCTOBER

❑1, Jul 1999 .... 2.95

Y: THE LAST MAN
DC / VERTIGO

❑1, Sep 2002 .... 30.00
❑2, Oct 2002 .... 15.00
❑3, Nov 2002 .... 5.00
❑4, Dec 2002 .... 4.00
❑5, Jan 2003 .... 4.00
❑6, Feb 2003 .... 2.95
❑7, Mar 2003 .... 2.95
❑8, Apr 2003 .... 2.95
❑9, May 2003 .... 2.95
❑10, Jun 2003 .... 2.95
❑11, Jul 2003 .... 2.95
❑12, Aug 2003 .... 2.95
❑13, Sep 2003 .... 2.95
❑14, Oct 2003 .... 2.95
❑15, Nov 2003 .... 2.95
❑16, Jan 2004 .... 2.95
❑17, Feb 2004 .... 2.95
❑18, Mar 2004 .... 2.95
❑19, Apr 2004 .... 2.95
❑20, May 2004 .... 2.95
❑21, Jun 2004 .... 2.95
❑22, Jul 2004 .... 2.95
❑23, Aug 2004 .... 2.95
❑24, Sep 2004 .... 2.95
❑25, Oct 2004 .... 2.95
❑26, Nov 2004 .... 2.95
❑27, Dec 2004 .... 2.95
❑28, Jan 2005 .... 2.95
❑29, Feb 2005 .... 2.95
❑30, Mar 2005 .... 2.95
❑31, Apr 2005 .... 2.95
❑32, May 2005 .... 2.95
❑33, Jun 2005 .... 2.99
❑34, Jul 2005 .... 2.99
❑35, Aug 2005 .... 2.99

Other grades: Multiply price above by 5/6 for VF/NM • 2/3 for VERY FINE • 1/3 for FINE • 1/5 for VERY GOOD • 1/8 for GOOD

N-MINT

❑36, Sep 2005 2.99
❑37, Oct 2005 2.99
❑38 2.99
❑39, Jan 2006 2.99
❑40, Jan 2006 2.99
❑41, Mar 2006 2.99
❑42, Mar 2006 2.99
❑43, May 2006 2.99
❑44, Jun 2006 2.99
❑45, Jul 2006 2.99
❑46, Aug 2006 2.99

YUGGOTH CULTURES (ALAN MOORE'S)
AVATAR

❑1, Oct 2003 3.95
❑2, Nov 2003 3.95
❑3, Dec 2003 3.95

YU-GI-OH!
VIZ

❑1 2003 7.95

YU-GI-OH!: DUELIST
VIZ

❑1, Feb 2005 9.99
❑2, Mar 2005 9.99
❑3, Apr 2005 9.99
❑4, May 2005 9.99
❑5, Jun 2005 9.99
❑6, Jul 2005 9.99
❑7, Aug 2005 9.99
❑8, Sep 2005 9.99
❑9, Oct 2005 9.99

YUMMY FUR
VORTEX

❑1, Dec 1986, b&w; reprint mini-comics #1-3 6.00
❑2 1986, b&w; reprint mini-comics #4-6; no date of publication; says #4 in indicia 5.00
❑3, Feb 1987, b&w; reprint mini-comic #7 4.00
❑4, Apr 1987, b&w 4.00
❑5, Jun 1987, b&w 4.00
❑6, Aug 1987, b&w 3.00
❑7 1987, b&w 3.00
❑8, Nov 1987, b&w 3.00
❑9 1988, b&w 3.00
❑10, May 1988, b&w 3.00
❑11, Jul 1988, b&w 2.50
❑12 1988, b&w; no date of publication 2.50
❑13, Nov 1988, b&w 2.50
❑14, Jan 1989, b&w 2.50
❑15, Mar 1989, b&w 2.50
❑16, Jun 1989, b&w 2.50
❑17, Aug 1989, b&w 2.50
❑18, Oct 1989, b&w 2.50
❑19, Jan 1990, b&w 2.50
❑20, Apr 1990, b&w 2.50
❑21, Jun 1990, b&w 2.50
❑22, Sep 1990, b&w 2.50
❑23, Dec 1990, b&w 2.50
❑24 1991, b&w 2.50
❑25, Jul 1991, b&w 2.50
❑26, Oct 1991, b&w 2.50
❑27 1992, b&w 2.50
❑28, May 1992, b&w 2.50
❑29, Aug 1992, b&w 2.50
❑30, Apr 1993, b&w 2.50
❑31 1993, b&w 2.50
❑32, Jan 1994, b&w; Drawn & Quarterly Publishes 2.95

YUPPIES FROM HELL
MARVEL

❑1, b&w 2.95

YUPPIES, REDNECKS AND LESBIAN BITCHES FROM MARS
FANTAGRAPHICS / EROS

❑1 1997, b&w 2.95
❑2 1997, b&w 2.95
❑3 1997, b&w 2.95
❑4 1997, b&w 2.95
❑5 1998, b&w 2.95
❑6 1998, b&w 2.95
❑7, May 1998, b&w 2.95

YUYU HAKUSHO
VIZ

❑1, Jun 2003 9.99
❑2, Oct 2003 9.99

❑3, Feb 2004 9.99
❑4, Jun 2004 9.99
❑5, Oct 2004 9.99
❑6, Feb 2005 9.99
❑7, Jun 2005 9.99
❑8, Oct 2005 9.99

Z
KEYSTONE GRAPHICS

❑1, Nov 1994, b&w 2.75
❑2, Jul 1995, b&w 2.75
❑3, Nov 1995, b&w 2.75

ZAIBATSU TEARS
LIMELIGHT

❑1, ca. 2000, b&w 2.95
❑2, ca. 2000 2.95
❑3, ca. 2000 2.95

ZATANNA
DC

❑1, Jul 1993 2.00
❑2, Aug 1993; Zatanna gets new costume 2.00
❑3, Sep 1993 2.00
❑4, Oct 1993 2.00

ZATANNA: EVERYDAY MAGIC
DC / VERTIGO

❑1, May 2003 5.95

ZATANNA SPECIAL
DC

❑1, ca. 1987 2.00

ZATCH BELL!
VIZ

❑1, Aug 2005 9.99
❑2, Sep 2005 9.99
❑3, Oct 2005 9.99

ZAZA THE MYSTIC (AVALON)
AVALON

❑1 2.95

ZEALOT
IMAGE

❑1, Aug 1995 2.50
❑2, Oct 1995 2.50
❑3, Nov 1995 2.50

ZELL SWORDDANCER (3-D ZONE)
3-D ZONE

❑1, b&w 2.00

ZELL, SWORDDANCER (THOUGHTS & IMAGES)
THOUGHTS & IMAGES

❑1, Jul 1986, b&w 2.00

ZENDRA
PENNY-FARTHING

❑1, Jan 2002 2.95
❑2, Feb 2002 2.95
❑3, Mar 2002 2.95
❑4, Apr 2002 2.95

ZEN ILLUSTRATED NOVELLA
ENTITY

❑1 2.95
❑2 2.95

ZEN, INTERGALACTIC NINJA (1ST SERIES)
ZEN

❑1, Nov 1987, b&w 3.00
❑1/2nd, ca. 1988 2.00
❑2, ca. 1988, b&w 2.00
❑3, ca. 1988, b&w 2.00
❑3/2nd, ca. 1988, b&w 2.00
❑4, ca. 1988, b&w 2.00
❑5, ca. 1988, b&w 2.00
❑6, ca. 1988, b&w 2.00

ZEN, INTERGALACTIC NINJA (2ND SERIES)
ZEN

❑1, ca. 1990, b&w 2.00
❑2, ca. 1990, b&w 2.00
❑3, ca. 1990, b&w 2.00
❑4, ca. 1990, b&w 2.00

ZEN, INTERGALACTIC NINJA (3RD SERIES)
ZEN

❑1, ca. 1992, b&w 2.25
❑2, ca. 1992, b&w 2.25
❑3, ca. 1992, b&w 2.25

❑4, ca. 1992, b&w 2.25
❑5, ca. 1992, b&w 2.25
❑Holiday 1, ca. 1992, b&w; Flip-book. 2.95

ZEN INTERGALACTIC NINJA (4TH SERIES)
ARCHIE

❑1, May 1992 1.25
❑2 1992 1.25
❑3 1992 1.25

ZEN INTERGALACTIC NINJA (5TH SERIES)
ARCHIE

❑1, Sep 1992 1.25
❑2, Oct 1992 1.25
❑3, Dec 1992 1.25
❑4, ca. 1993 1.25
❑5, ca. 1993 1.25
❑6, ca. 1993 1.25
❑7, ca. 1993 1.25

ZEN INTERGALACTIC NINJA (6TH SERIES)
EXPRESS / ENTITY

❑0, Jun 1993; 1: Nira X. Gray trim around outside cover 3.00
❑0/A, Jun 1993, b&w; 1: Nira X. foil cover 2.95
❑0/B, Jun 1993, b&w; 1: Nira X. chromium cover 3.50
❑0/Ltd., Jun 1993, b&w; 1: Nira X. Printing limited to 3,000 copies; All-gold trim 3.00
❑1, ca. 1993, b&w 3.00
❑1/Variant, ca. 1993, b&w; Chromium, die-cut cover 3.95
❑2, ca. 1994, b&w 3.00
❑3, ca. 1994, b&w 3.00
❑4, ca. 1994 3.00
❑Ashcan 1, ca. 1993, b&w; no cover price; contains previews of Zen: Hazardous Duty and Zen: Tour of the Universe 1.00
❑Spring 1, ca. 1994; Spring Spectacular 2.95

ZEN INTERGALACTIC NINJA ALL-NEW COLOR SPECIAL
EXPRESS / ENTITY

❑0, ca. 1994; Chronium Cover 3.50

ZEN INTERGALACTIC NINJA COLOR
EXPRESS / ENTITY

❑1, ca. 1994; diecut foil cover 3.95
❑2, ca. 1994 3.95
❑3, ca. 1994 3.95
❑4, ca. 1994 2.50
❑5, ca. 1994 2.50
❑6, ca. 1995 2.50
❑7, ca. 1995; says #6a on cover, #7 in indicia 2.95

ZEN INTERGALACTIC NINJA COLOR (2ND SERIES)
EXPRESS / ENTITY

❑1, ca. 1995 2.50
❑2, ca. 1995 2.50

ZEN, INTERGALACTIC NINJA EARTH DAY ANNUAL
ZEN

❑1, ca. 1993, b&w 2.95

ZEN INTERGALACTIC NINJA MILESTONE
EXPRESS / ENTITY

❑1, ca. 1994 2.95

ZEN INTERGALACTIC NINJA STARQUEST
EXPRESS

❑1, ca. 1994, b&w 2.95
❑2, ca. 1994, b&w 2.95
❑3, ca. 1994, b&w; enhanced cover 2.95
❑4, ca. 1994, b&w; cardstock cover 2.95
❑5, ca. 1994, b&w; enhanced cover 2.95
❑6, ca. 1995, b&w; enhanced cover 2.95
❑7, ca. 1995, b&w; enhanced cover 2.95

ZEN INTERGALACTIC NINJA SUMMER SPECIAL: VIDEO WARRIOR
EXPRESS

❑1, ca. 1994, b&w 2.95

Other grades: Multiply price above by 5/6 for VF/NM • 2/3 for VERY FINE • 1/3 for FINE • 1/5 for VERY GOOD • 1/8 for GOOD

ZEN INTERGALACTIC NINJA: TOUR OF THE UNIVERSE SPECIAL, THE AIRBRUSH ART OF DAN COTE
EXPRESS / ENTITY
❑1, ca. 1995; enhanced cardstock cover 3.95

ZENITH: PHASE I
FLEETWAY-QUALITY
❑1 .... 2.00
❑2 .... 2.00
❑3 .... 2.00

ZENITH: PHASE II
FLEETWAY-QUALITY
❑1 .... 1.95
❑2 .... 1.95

ZEN: THE NEW ADVENTURES
ZEN
❑1, ca. 1997 .... 2.50

ZERO
ZERO COMICS
❑1, Mar 1975, b&w 3.00
❑2, Mar 1975, b&w 3.00
❑3, May 1976, b&w 3.00

ZERO GIRL
HOMAGE
❑1, Feb 2001 .... 2.95
❑2, Mar 2001 .... 2.95
❑3, Apr 2001 .... 2.95
❑4, May 2001 .... 2.95
❑5, Jun 2001 (c) 2.95

ZERO GIRL: FULL CIRCLE
DC / HOMAGE
❑1, Jan 2004 .... 2.95
❑2, Feb 2004 .... 2.95
❑3, Mar 2004 .... 2.95
❑4, Apr 2004 .... 2.95
❑5, May 2004 .... 2.95

ZERO HOUR
DOG SOUP
❑1, Apr 1995, b&w; says Pat Leidy's Catfight on cover 2.95

ZERO HOUR: CRISIS IN TIME
DC
❑4, Sep 1994; JOy (a); (#1 in sequence) 2.00
❑3, Sep 1994; JOy (a); D: Atom. D: Hourman. remainder of Justice Society of America aged; (#2 in sequence).. 2.00
❑2, Sep 1994; JOy (a); (#3 in sequence) 2.00
❑1, Sep 1994; JOy (a); 1: Parallax. 1: David Knight. 1: Jack Knight. Silver Age Atom de-aged; (#4 in sequence)..... 3.00
❑0, Sep 1994; JOy (a); V: Extant. contains Zero Hour checklist and new DC timeline foldout; (#5 in sequence)... 2.00
❑Ashcan 1, ca. 1994; Ashcan Preview 1.00

ZERO PATROL (1ST SERIES)
CONTINUITY
❑1, Nov 1984 NA (c); NA (w); NA (a); O: The Zero Patrol. 1: The Zero Patrol. 2.00
❑2, Feb 1985 NA (c); NA (w); NA (a) .. 2.00

ZERO PATROL (2ND SERIES)
CONTINUITY
❑1, ca. 1987 .... 2.00
❑2, Nov 1987 .... 2.00
❑3, Apr 1988 .... 2.00
❑4, Mar 1989 .... 2.00
❑5, May 1989 .... 2.00

ZERO STREET
AMAZE INK
❑1, Sep 2000 .... 2.95

ZERO TOLERANCE
FIRST
❑1, Oct 1990 .... 2.25
❑2, Nov 1990 .... 2.25
❑3, Dec 1990; Vigil 2.25
❑4, Jan 1991 .... 2.25

ZERO ZERO
FANTAGRAPHICS
❑1, Mar 1995, b&w 4.00
❑2, May 1995, b&w 4.00
❑3, Jul 1995, b&w 4.00
❑4, Aug 1995, b&w; issue number determined by back cover cartoon.. 4.00
❑5, Sep 1995, b&w; issue number determined by back cover cartoon.. 4.00
❑6, Nov 1995, b&w 4.00
❑7, Jan 1996, b&w 4.00
❑8, Mar 1996, b&w; issue number determined by back cover cartoon . 5.95
❑9, May 1996, b&w; issue number determined by back cover cartoon . 3.95
❑10, Jul 1996, b&w; cover says Jul 96, indicia says May 3.95
❑11, Aug 1996, b&w 3.95
❑12, Sep 1996, b&w 3.95
❑13, Nov 1996, b&w 3.95
❑14, Jan 1997, b&w 3.95
❑15, Mar 1997, b&w; Bosnia prequel. 3.95
❑16, Apr 1997, b&w 3.95
❑17, Jun 1997, b&w 3.95
❑18, Jul 1997, b&w 3.95
❑19, Aug 1997, b&w 3.95
❑20, Sep 1997 .... 3.95
❑21, Nov 1997, b&w 3.95
❑22, Jan 1998, b&w 3.95
❑23, Mar 1998, b&w 3.95
❑24, Sum 1998, b&w 3.95
❑25, Fal 1998, b&w 3.95
❑26, ca. 1998, b&w 3.95

ZETRAMAN
ANTARCTIC
❑1, Sep 1991, b&w 1.95
❑2, Oct 1991, b&w 1.95
❑3, Feb 1992, b&w 1.95

ZETRAMAN: REVIVAL
ANTARCTIC
❑1, Oct 1993 .... 2.75
❑2, Dec 1993 .... 2.75
❑3, Aug 1995 .... 2.75

ZILLION
ETERNITY
❑1, Apr 1993, b&w 2.50
❑2, May 1993, b&w 2.50
❑3, Jun 1993, b&w 2.50
❑4, Jul 1993, b&w 2.50

ZIP COMICS (COZMIC)
COZMIC
❑1 .... 4.00

ZIPPY QUARTERLY
FANTAGRAPHICS
❑1, ca. 1993, b&w 4.95
❑2, ca. 1993, b&w 4.95
❑3, ca. 1993, b&w; strip reprint 3.50
❑4, ca. 1994, b&w; strip reprint 3.50
❑5, ca. 1994, b&w; strip reprint 3.50
❑7, Aug 1994, b&w; strip reprint 3.50
❑8, Nov 1994, b&w; strip reprint 3.50
❑12, Dec 1995, b&w; strip reprint...... 3.95
❑13, Aug 1996, b&w; cardstock cover; strip reprint 3.95

ZODIAC P.I.
TOKYOPOP
❑1, Jul 2003, b&w; printed in Japanese format 9.99

ZOIDS: CHAOTIC CENTURY
VIZ
❑1, ca. 2002 .... 6.99
❑2, ca. 2002 .... 6.99
❑3, ca. 2002 .... 6.99
❑4, ca. 2002 .... 6.99
❑5, ca. 2002 .... 6.99
❑6, ca. 2002 .... 6.99

ZÖLASTRÄYA AND THE BARD
TWILIGHT TWINS
❑1, Jan 1987, b&w 1.70
❑2, ca. 1987, b&w 1.70
❑3, ca. 1987, b&w 1.70
❑4, ca. 1987, b&w 1.70
❑5, ca. 1987, b&w 1.70

ZOMBIE 3-D
3-D ZONE
❑1 .... 3.95

ZOMBIE BOY (ANTARCTIC)
ANTARCTIC
❑1, Nov 1996, b&w; wraparound cover 2.95
❑2, ca. 1997, b&w 2.95
❑3, ca. 1997, b&w 2.95

ZOMBIE BOY RISES AGAIN
TIMBUKTU
❑1, Jan 1994, b&w; Collects Zombie Boy #1 and Zombie Boy's Hoodoo Tales #1; Beverly Hillbillies cameo.. 2.50

ZOMBIE BOY (TIMBUKTU)
TIMBUKTU
❑1, b&w 1.50

ZOMBIE KING
IMAGE
❑0, Aug 2005 .... 2.95

ZOMBIE LOVE
ZUZUPETAL
❑1 .... 2.50
❑2 .... 2.50
❑3 .... 2.50

ZOMBIES!
IDEA & DESIGN WORKS
❑1, Jun 2006 .... 3.99

ZOMBIE WAR (TUNDRA)
TUNDRA
❑1, ca. 1992 .... 3.50

ZOMBIE WAR (FANTACO)
FANTACO
❑1, ca. 1992, b&w 3.50
❑2, ca. 1992, b&w 3.50

ZOMBIE WAR: EARTH MUST BE DESTROYED
FANTACO
❑1, ca. 1993, b&w 2.95
❑1/CS, ca. 1993, b&w; trading card ... 2.95
❑2, ca. 1993, b&w 2.95
❑3, ca. 1993, b&w 2.95
❑4, ca. 1993, b&w 2.95

ZOMBIEWORLD: CHAMPION OF THE WORMS
DARK HORSE
❑1, Sep 1997, b&w 2.95
❑2, Oct 1997, b&w 2.95
❑3, Nov 1997, b&w 2.95

ZOMBIEWORLD: DEAD END
DARK HORSE
❑1, Jan 1998, b&w 2.95
❑2, Feb 1998, b&w 2.95

ZOMBIEWORLD: EAT YOUR HEART OUT
DARK HORSE
❑1, Apr 1998, b&w 2.95

ZOMBIEWORLD: HOME FOR THE HOLIDAYS
DARK HORSE
❑1, Dec 1997, b&w 2.95

ZOMBIEWORLD: TREE OF DEATH
DARK HORSE
❑1, Jun 1999, b&w 2.95
❑2, Aug 1999, b&w 2.95
❑3, Sep 1999, b&w 2.95
❑4, Oct 1999, b&w 2.95

ZOMBIEWORLD: WINTER'S DREGS
DARK HORSE
❑1, May 1998, b&w 2.95
❑2, Jun 1998, b&w 2.95
❑3, Jul 1998, b&w 2.95
❑4, Aug 1998, b&w 2.95

ZOMBOY
INFERNO
❑1, Aug 1996, b&w 2.95

ZOMOID ILLUSTORIES
3-D ZONE
❑1, b&w; not 3-D 2.50

ZONE
DARK HORSE
❑1, b&w 2.00

ZONE CONTINUUM
CALIBER
❑1, ca. 1994, b&w 2.95
❑1/A, ca. 1994, b&w; Orange background; no cover price 2.00
❑1/B, ca. 1994, b&w; Maroon background; no cover price 2.00
❑2, ca. 1994, b&w 2.95

ZONE CONTINUUM (VOL. 2)
CALIBER
❑1, b&w 2.95
❑2, b&w 2.95

ZONE ZERO
PLANET BOY
❑1, b&w 2.95

Other grades: Multiply price above by 5/6 for VF/NM • 2/3 for VERY FINE • 1/3 for FINE • 1/5 for VERY GOOD • 1/8 for GOOD

N-MINT

ZOO FUNNIES (3RD SERIES)
CHARLTON
❑1, Dec 1984 .... 2.00

ZOOM'S ACADEMY FOR THE SUPER GIFTED
ASTONISH
❑1, ca. 2000, b&w 3.50
❑2, ca. 2001, b&w 3.50
❑3, ca. 2002, b&w 3.50

ZOONIVERSE
ECLIPSE
❑1, Aug 1986 (c) 1.50
❑2, Oct 1986 .... 1.50
❑3, Dec 1986 .... 1.50
❑4, Feb 1987 .... 1.50
❑5, Apr 1987 .... 1.50
❑6, Jun 1987 .... 1.50

ZOOT!
FANTAGRAPHICS
❑1, Nov 1992, b&w 2.50
❑2, Mar 1993, b&w 2.50
❑3, May 1993, b&w 2.50
❑4, Jul 1993, b&w 2.50
❑5, Sep 1993, b&w 2.50
❑6, Nov 1993, b&w 2.50

ZORANN: STAR-WARRIOR!
BLUE COMET
❑0, May 1994, b&w 2.95
❑1, ca. 1994, b&w 2.00

ZORI J'S 3-D BUBBLE BATH
3-D ZONE
❑1, b&w 3.95

ZORI J'S SUPER-SWELL BUBBLE BATH ADVENTURE-OH BOY!
3-D ZONE
❑1, b&w 2.95

ZORRO (DELL)
DELL
❑8, Dec 1959 .... 70.00
❑9, Mar 1960 .... 70.00
❑10, Jun 1960 .... 68.00
❑11, Sep 1960 .... 68.00
❑12, Dec 1960 .... 68.00
❑13, Mar 1961 .... 65.00
❑14, Jun 1961 .... 65.00
❑15, Sep 1961 .... 65.00

ZORRO (GOLD KEY)
GOLD KEY
❑1, Jan 1966 .... 70.00
❑2, May 1966 .... 38.00
❑3, Sep 1966 .... 38.00
❑4, Dec 1966 .... 38.00
❑5, Mar 1967 .... 34.00
❑6, Jun 1967 .... 34.00
❑7, Sep 1967 .... 34.00
❑8, Dec 1967 .... 28.00
❑9, Mar 1968 .... 28.00

ZORRO (MARVEL)
MARVEL
❑1, Dec 1990 FM (c); FM (a); O: Zorro. 3.00
❑2, Jan 1991 .... 2.00
❑3, Feb 1991 .... 2.00
❑4, Mar 1991 .... 2.00
❑5, Apr 1991 .... 2.00
❑6, May 1991 .... 2.00
❑7, Jun 1991 .... 2.00
❑8, Jul 1991 .... 2.00
❑9, Aug 1991 .... 2.00
❑10, Sep 1991 ATh (c) 2.00
❑11, Oct 1991 ATh (c) 2.00
❑12, Nov 1991; ATh (c); Final Issue 2.00

ZORRO (TOPPS)
TOPPS
❑0, Nov 1993 1: Buck Wylde. 2.50
❑1, Jan 1994 FM (c); 1: Machete. 3.50
❑2, Feb 1994 1: Lady Rawhide (out of costume) 8.00
❑3, Mar 1994 1: Lady Rawhide (in costume) 3.00
❑4, Apr 1994 MGr (c); 1: Moonstalker. 3.00
❑5, May 1994 JSt (c); KG (a); A: Lady Rawhide. 3.00
❑6, Jun 1994 .... 3.00
❑7, Jul 1994 PG (c); A: Lady Rawhide. 2.50
❑8, Aug 1994 GP (c); GP (a); A: Lady Rawhide. 2.50
❑9, Sep 1994 .... 2.50
❑10, Oct 1994 A: Lady Rawhide. 2.95
❑11, Nov 1994 A: Lady Rawhide. 2.50

ZORRO: MATANZAS!
IMAGE
❑Ashcan 1 .... 1.00

ZORRO (NBM)
NBM
❑1 2005 .... 2.95
❑2 2005 .... 2.95
❑3, Sep 2005 .... 2.95
❑4, Oct 2005 .... 2.95
❑5 2005 .... 2.95
❑6, Nov 2005 .... 2.95

ZOT!
ECLIPSE
❑1, Apr 1984; (c); 1: Jenny Weaver. 1: Zot!. Color issues begin 5.00
❑2, May 1984 1: Dekko (cameo). 1: 9-Jack-9. .... 2.50
❑3, Jun 1984 1: Dekko (full). 2.50
❑4, Jul 1984 (c); O: Zot!. 2.50
❑5, Aug 1984; Wordless panels Inside front cover in B&W 2.50
❑6, Nov 1984 .... 2.50
❑7, Dec 1984; KB (w); DS (a); The Magic Shop back-up features begin 2.50
❑8, Mar 1985 (c) 2.50
❑9, May 1985 .... 2.50
❑10, Jul 1985 (c) 2.50
❑10½; Mini-comic 2.50
❑11, Jan 1987, b&w; Black & white issues begin 2.50
❑12, Mar 1987, b&w (c) 2.25
❑13, May 1987 .... 2.25
❑14, Jul 1987 .... 2.25
❑14.5; Adventures of Zot! in Dimension 10 1/2, The 2.25
❑15, Oct 1987 .... 2.25
❑16, Dec 1987 .... 2.25
❑17, Feb 1988 .... 2.25
❑18, Apr 1988 .... 2.25
❑19, Jun 1988 .... 2.25
❑20, Jun 1988 .... 2.25
❑21, Aug 1988 .... 2.25
❑22, Oct 1988 .... 2.25
❑23, Nov 1988 .... 2.25
❑24, Dec 1988 .... 2.25
❑25, Feb 1989 .... 2.25
❑26, Apr 1989 .... 2.25
❑27, Jun 1989 .... 2.25
❑28, Sep 1989 .... 2.25
❑29, Dec 1989 .... 2.25
❑30, Mar 1990 .... 2.25
❑31, May 1990 .... 2.25
❑32, Jul 1990 .... 2.25
❑33, Oct 1990 .... 2.25
❑34, Dec 1990 .... 2.25
❑35, Mar 1991 .... 2.25
❑36, Jul 1991 .... 2.95

ZU (ONE-SHOT)
MU
❑1, Feb 1992 .... 3.95

ZU
MU
❑1, Jan 1995, b&w 2.95
❑2, Mar 1995, b&w 2.95
❑3, May 1995, b&w 2.95
❑4, Jul 1995, b&w 2.95
❑5, Sep 1995, b&w 2.95
❑6, Nov 1995, b&w 2.95
❑7, Jan 1996, b&w 2.95
❑8, Mar 1996, b&w 2.95
❑9, May 1996, b&w 2.95
❑10, Jul 1996, b&w 2.95
❑11, Sep 1996, b&w 2.95
❑12, Nov 1996, b&w 2.95
❑13, Jan 1997, b&w 2.95
❑14, Mar 1997, b&w 2.95
❑15, May 1997, b&w 2.95
❑16, Jul 1997, b&w 2.95
❑17, Sep 1997, b&w 2.95
❑18, Nov 1997, b&w 2.95
❑19, Jan 1998, b&w 2.95

ZUGAL
BRYAN EVANS
❑1 .... 2.95

ZULUNATION
TOME
❑1, ca. 1995, b&w 2.95
❑2, ca. 1995, b&w 2.95
❑3, ca. 1995, b&w 2.95

ZWANNA, SON OF ZULU
DARK ZULU LIES
❑1 .... 2.00

ZZZ
ALAN BUNCE
❑1, Mar 2000, b&w 2.35

Other grades: Multiply price above by 5/6 for VF/NM • 2/3 for VERY FINE • 1/3 for FINE • 1/5 for VERY GOOD • 1/8 for GOOD

Suggested Reading

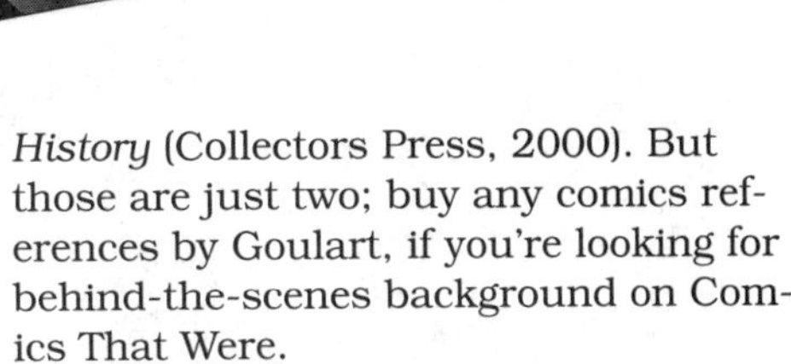

Even in a volume this big, there's only so much information we can cram in. Sooner or later, you're going to want to pursue a topic further than we've had room for here. So, as you expand your quest, consider these sources of information.

For starters, the third edition of our own ***Standard Catalog of Comic Books*** contains still more information on most of the comics contained in this book, including circulation data, distributor pre-orders, and CGC-grading data. And it covers older comics, too. Copies of the softcover edition are still available for $34.99.

The *ComicBase* CD-ROM contains all the comics found in this edition, as well as many foreign comics. There are summaries for thousands of titles in *ComicBase*, as well. That's *www.comicbase.com* or Human Computing, 4509 Thistle Dr., San Jose, CA 95136. The latest edition (in late 2005) is 10.0.

Then, there's the comics news magazine, *Comics Buyer's Guide*, 700 E. State St., Iola, WI 54945 (and *www.comic buyersguide.com*), which provides the latest news and updates on what's collectible, population reports, pricing reports, and the like — on comics old and new. And no magazine publishes more reviews of new comics each year!

A tireless researcher, one of the world's leading experts on comic books and strips, is Ron Goulart, and all his reference works on comics make informative *and* entertaining reading on the field. Among his most helpful works is *The Encyclopedia of American Comics from 1897 to the Present* (Facts on File, 1990), and, if you yearn for full-color tastes of Golden Age goodies, check out his *Comic Book Culture: An Illustrated History* (Collectors Press, 2000). But those are just two; buy any comics references by Goulart, if you're looking for behind-the-scenes background on Comics That Were.

The Overstreet Comic Book Price Guide, one of the leaders in the field of comics collecting, continues to publish an annual update with historical essays; the 2005 edition was its 35th. It also has information on many of the precursors of today's comic-book format. Check out *www.gem stonepub.com* or Gemstone Publishing, Inc., 1966 Greenspring Dr., Timonium, MD 21093.

The late Ernst Gerber put together incredible compendia of comic-book covers, including valuable information regarding publishing dates and the like. *The Photo Journal Guide to Comic Books*, for example, is a two-volume set of Golden Age covers and information, packed with beautiful photos. It's not cheap, but it's a major work and rewards the browser.

The entire CGC Census is available on the company's website, *www.cgc-comics.com*. The information appears at some delay from the company's actual grading, but it still provides valuable information on what's out there and being bought and sold for noticeable bucks.

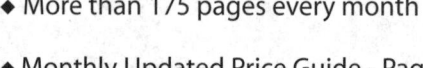

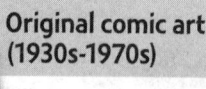